Larousse

GRAN DICCIONARIO

ESPAÑOL
INGLÉS

ENGLISH
SPANISH

Larousse

GRAN DICCIONARIO

ESPAÑOL-INGLÉS

dirigido y realizado por

Ramón GARCÍA-PELAYO Y GROSS

Profesor de la Universidad de París (Sorbona) y del Instituto de Estudios Políticos
Miembro c. de la Academia Argentina de Letras, de la Academia de San Dionisio de Ciencias,
Artes y Letras, de la Academia Boliviana de la Historia
y de la Real Academia de Bellas Artes de San Telmo

con la colaboración de

Micheline DURAND

Licenciada en Letras, Intérprete de Conferencia
Profesora de la Escuela Superior de Intérpretes y Traductores
de la Universidad de París y del Instituto de Ciencias Políticas

Barry TULETT
Alan Biggins, Carol Cockburn, Barbara Penick,
Della Roberts, Alan Taylor, Gary D. Wright
David E. WARHAM

y de

Fernando GARCÍA-PELAYO
Pilar Andrés Solana, Trinidad Fungairiño,
Elena Real Carbonell, Carmen Warren
José PAU ANDERSEN

EDICIONES Larousse

MARSELLA 53, MÉXICO 06600, D.F.

Paseo de Gracia 120
Barcelona 08008

17, rue du Montparnasse
75298 París Cedex 06

Valentín Gómez 3530
Buenos Aires R.13

FOREWORD

The growth of English, spoken by several hundred million men and women and used by many more in trade and as a second language, has received additional impetus from the technological, scientific, mercantile and political predominance of the Anglo-Saxon nations and, in particular, of the United States of America.

Over three hundred million people from some twenty countries on both sides of the Atlantic speak Spanish, a language destined to go from strength to strength. All International Organizations recognize Spanish as an official language. The vigour, versatility and flexibility of the language, as well as the originality of literary works in Spanish, make it one of the two greatest world languages, with English.

Moreover, several million U.S. inhabitants use Spanish for historical, sociological, economic or merely functional reasons. The discoverers, conquerors and settlers who first introduced Spanish left their mark on part of the Continent which was later taken over by the English. More than 1500 North American rivers, cities and mountains still bear their original Castilian names. Only Mexico, Spain, Argentina and Colombia can boast, in absolute figures, more Spanish-speaking inhabitants.

Clearly a dictionary providing equivalent terms in both languages, to assist professors, teachers, university students, school pupils, interpreters and translators in their work, was needed. We have drawn upon long experience in lexicography, translation, teaching and research whilst adopting an up-to-date approach.

The main aim of this dictionary constitutes a departure from conventional bilingual glossaries which cater for literal translation only. It is to gather together all the words, classic and MODERN, which go to make up the rich Anglo-Hispanic cultural heritage. Special care has been taken with the new technical and scientific terms progress brings, and which appear in our newspapers and periodicals and on radio and television every day. Equally, attention has been devoted to neologisms and foreign words in common use and to more recent colloquialisms. Following a practice long established in dictionary compilation at LAROUSSE, new words and phrases are assessed for inclusion on frequency of use and not on the whims of writers who misuse them.

Many *examples* are given to define the precise shades of meaning of terms in context. *Explanations*, in parentheses, are also given when they will guide the user in choosing the right translation and in avoiding pitfalls. Indications are also provided in the form of *footnotes* at the end of articles where further clarification of grammatical points is called for.

Due consideration has been given to vocabulary, spelling and phonetics peculiar to the Spanish- and English-speaking Americas so as to do justice to the countries that made these Old World languages universal. Despite the efforts deployed to maintain unity of language by English- and especially Spanish-speaking peoples, the facts are indisputable. Deep-rooted differences have grown up in many areas of language such as pronunciation, spelling and vocabulary. Each country has its own idioms and semantics, and they make for dissimilarities in both the written and spoken word. The languages treated, whilst basically the same in Europe and the New World, have perforce developed peculiarities due in part to the vast geographical area involved. These have been recorded to meet the range and scope the reader requires.

Finally, we would like to express our gratitude to Claude Bonne, Yvonne Bessière and Véronique de Macédo whose valuable assistance greatly facilitated the task. Since *errare humanum est*, we would also be grateful to readers for kindly bringing omissions and imperfections to our notice so that they may be corrected in future editions.

Ramón GARCÍA-PELAYO

PRIMERA EDICIÓN—Novena reimpresión

ISBN 2-03-451341-X (Librairie Larousse)
ISBN 968-6042-61-X (Ediciones Larousse)

Impreso en México — Printed in Mexico

PRÓLOGO

El idioma inglés, empleado por varios centenares de millones de seres humanos y utilizado por muchos otros más como vehículo comercial y a guisa de habla auxiliar, ha visto acrecentarse su expansión por la importancia técnica, científica, mercantil y política de las naciones anglosajonas, esencialmente de los Estados Unidos de América.

Más de trescientos millones de hombres, pertenecientes a unos veinte países situados a uno y otro lado del Atlántico, se expresan en castellano. Esta lengua, llamada a extenderse más y más, es reconocida de modo oficial como instrumento de trabajo por todos los organismos internacionales. El vigor, la constante transformación que se verifica en ella y la originalidad de la literatura hispánica hacen que ocupe en el presente, junto al inglés, uno de los dos primeros puestos de las que se hablan en el mundo.

Incluso varios millones de personas emplean también esta lengua neolatina, debido a razones históricas, sociológicas, económicas o puramente funcionales, en los Estados Unidos. El español, llevado al Nuevo Mundo por sus descubridores, conquistadores y colonizadores, dejó asimismo huellas en la parte del Continente ocupada más tarde por los ingleses. Más de mil quinientos ríos, ciudades y montañas de Norteamérica conservan aún el nombre castellano con el que fueron bautizados y el número de hispanohablantes en todo el país sólo es superado actualmente en cifras absolutas por México, España, Argentina y Colombia.

Era, por tanto, indispensable tratar de realizar un diccionario en el que se diesen las correspondencias entre ambos idiomas para ayudar en sus tareas a profesores, estudiantes universitarios, alumnos de enseñanza media, intérpretes y traductores. El alcance de la labor emprendida, a la que procuramos dar una acusada índole innovadora y actual, se nos ha hecho patente a través de una larga experiencia en el campo de la lexicografía, la traducción, el profesorado y la investigación.

El objetivo principal perseguido en esta obra, en la que no hemos querido seguir la tradición de los glosarios puramente bilingües, meras herramientas pasivas para efectuar una versión literal, ha sido la recopilación de todas aquellas palabras, tanto de sabor o cuño clásico como MODERNO, que forman parte del inmenso patrimonio cultural anglohispano. Se ha prestado atención minuciosa al vocabulario técnico y científico, nacido del ritmo impuesto por el progreso y hallado diariamente en la lectura de periódicos y revistas o en los programas de radio y televisión. No menos cuidado han merecido los incontables neologismos y extranjerismos de uso constante y las expresiones familiares más recientes. Siguiendo la práctica usual que nos guía cotidianamente en la redacción de otros diccionarios LAROUSSE en castellano, inglés y francés, las voces de creación moderna tienen carta de naturaleza en estas páginas según la frecuencia de su uso y no a causa de caprichos de escritores que se sirven desafortunadamente de estos términos.

Las equivalencias de los términos registrados, para distinguir con justeza los matices que poseen, están unas ilustradas con innumerables *ejemplos* que facilitan la comprensión en el contexto de una frase y otras con *explicaciones* entre paréntesis que permiten escoger la traducción adecuada y evitar que se cometan cuantiosos errores. Orientamos y aconsejamos también al lector por medio de *observaciones* al pie de algunos artículos para asistirle en caso de dudas o dificultades surgidas de ciertas peculiaridades gramaticales.

Huelga decir que analizamos con el mayor interés las variantes lexicológicas, ortográficas e incluso fonéticas propias de la América de habla castellana o inglesa para hacer justicia a los países cuya manera de expresarse, oriunda del Viejo Continente, ha adquirido gracias a ellos proyección universal. Aunque exista el anhelo de mantener la unidad lingüística entre los numerosos núcleos de hablantes que integran los mundos hispánico y anglosajón, singularmente en el primero, nos es forzoso aceptar la realidad indiscutible de que hay elementos diferenciadores de honda raigambre en distintos campos idiomáticos, como la pronunciación, la ortografía, el léxico, con vocablos y giros genuinos de cada país, y la semántica, que traen consigo algunas desemejanzas en el orden literario u oral. Los idiomas que estudiamos, aun cuando sean fundamentalmente los mismos en Europa y en el Nuevo Continente, tienen, no obstante, una serie de divergencias y particularismos favorecidos por la enorme expansión geográfica en que se desarrollan. No hemos vacilado, por tanto, en reseñar en nuestro repertorio las características de cada uno de ellos para darle así una dimensión que pueda satisfacer ampliamente las necesidades de nuestros lectores.

Pecaríamos de ingratitud si no mencionásemos por último los nombres de Claude Bonne, Yvonne Bessière y Véronique de Macédo, valiosas colaboradoras sin cuya ayuda la ejecución de nuestro empeño hubiese sido mucho más ardua, y de inmodestia si no rogásemos a nuestros lectores que tengan la amabilidad de indicarnos las omisiones e imperfecciones en que hubiéramos incurrido, *errare humanum est*, para enmendarlas en ediciones futuras.

Ramón GARCÍA-PELAYO

COMO USAR ESTE DICCIONARIO

ORDEN DE LAS PALABRAS

a) Las palabras siguen siempre un riguroso orden alfabético, pero, cuando dos voces tienen igual sentido y parecida ortografía, se reseñan en el mismo artículo (por ej., **estancación** o **estancamiento**).
b) Las palabras compuestas inglesas se registran también alfabéticamente. Así, **dress circle** figura a continuación de **dress** y no en el interior de este artículo. No obstante gran número de estos términos se pueden escribir de distintas maneras, con o sin guión e incluso en una sola palabra, y para su clasificación se ha escogido la ortografía del *Webster's Third New International Dictionary of The English Language*.
c) Se indican las ortografías existentes en Gran Bretaña y los Estados Unidos (véase BEHAVIOUR).
d) Los adverbios, diminutivos y aumentativos de formación regular, cuyos significados son fácilmente deducibles a partir de las palabras de las que se derivan, no se han estudiado (por ej. **fortunately**).
e) Se hace mención de los pretéritos y participios pasivos irregulares, lo mismo que de las contracciones, en el orden alfabético que les corresponde (véase **I'm**). En los dos primeros casos se remite al infinitivo del verbo (por ej. **got** pret. & p. p. See GET).

PRONUNCIACIÓN FIGURADA

La pronunciación figurada, colocada entre corchetes después del artículo, se indica solamente en la parte inglés-español y no en la otra, ya que las palabras se pronuncian en castellano tal y como se escriben, salvo contadas excepciones (V. PRONUNCIATION en *Summary of Spanish grammar*). Se ha utilizado el Alfabético Fonético Internacional (V. pág. VI, 2.ª parte). Cuando la pronunciación difiere entre Gran Bretaña y los Estados Unidos, se ha transcrito primero la inglesa y luego, tras U. S., la americana (por ej. **schedule**).

INDICACIONES GRAMATICALES

a) La naturaleza morfológica de cada palabra se señala con abreviaturas cuyas listas detalladas se encuentran en las pág. VIII (1.ª parte) y V (2.ª parte).
b) El género de los sustantivos españoles figura tanto en la primera como en la segunda parte y las palabras inglesas que son a la vez masculinas y femeninas están traducidas en las dos formas (por ej. **baker** equivale a **panadero, ra**). El número se precisa en la traducción únicamente si es diferente al de la palabra estudiada (por ej. **clothes** pl. n. Ropa, *f. sing.*).
Estas indicaciones existen igualmente en la traducción de las expresiones que vienen al final del artículo, por ej. *disturbance of the peace*, alteración (*f.*) del orden público, a menos que sea una palabra que ya figure en las acepciones o si el género y el número no ofrecen dudas gracias al contexto (por ej. *disturbance in the night*, escándalo nocturno).
c) Una observación al final del artículo señala el plural irregular de ciertos sustantivos. En la parte español-inglés se encuentran los plurales españoles y en la otra los ingleses.
d) Cuando un mismo vocablo tiene varias funciones en la oración (adjetivo, sustantivo, adverbio, etc.), éstas van reunidas en el mismo artículo, pero en distintos párrafos, excepto en el caso del verbo que se trata separadamente (por ej. en **right** se estudia en primer lugar el adjetivo, el sustantivo y el adverbio, en varios apartados, y el verbo tiene otra entrada aparte).
e) Los verbos irregulares llevan un asterisco que remite al compendio de gramática en el que se da la conjugación de los distintos modos y tiempos. En la parte inglés-español, las irregularidades de los verbos ingleses, que se limitan generalmente al pretérito y participio pasivo, se indican en una observación al final del artículo.
f) Si el régimen de los verbos, sustantivos o adjetivos varía de un idioma a otro se señala entre paréntesis o mediante un ejemplo (véase DESDECIR).

EXPLANATORY NOTES

ORDER OF MATERIAL

a) The material has been arranged in alphabetical order, except where two words are equivalent in meaning and spelt similarly. The latter are entered at the same entry (e.g. **estancación** o **estancamiento**).
b) English compound words also appear alphabetically. For instance, **dress circle** is listed as a separate entry following and not included under the headword **dress**. Many such terms can be hyphenated, written separately or simply run together. The orthography used in this dictionary is drawn from *Webster's Third New International Dictionary of The English Language*.
c) Variant British and American spellings are indicated (see BEHAVIOUR).
d) No provision is made for regular adverbs, diminutives and augmentatives whose meaning is obvious from the stem word (e. g. **fortunately**).
e) Preterites, past participles and contracted forms are also listed in their own alphabetical order (see **I'm**). In the two former instances the user is referred to the infinitive of the verb (e.g. **got** pret. & p. p. See GET).

PHONETIC TRANSCRIPTION

Phonetic transcription, in square brackets after the headword, appears only in the English-Spanish part as, with very few exceptions, the pronunciation of Spanish is well represented by normal orthography (see chapter on PRONUNCIATION in the *Summary of Spanish grammar*). The symbols used are those of the International Phonetic Alphabet (see table on page VI, part II). Where British and American pronunciation differ, British comes first followed, after U. S., by American (e.g. **schedule**).

GRAMMATICAL INFORMATION

a) The grammatical function of the headword is made clear using the abbreviations listed in full on pages VIII (part I) and V (part II).
b) Genders of Spanish nouns are printed in both parts of the dictionary and English nouns of common gender are translated into both masculine and feminine forms (e.g. **baker** n. Panadero, ra). Number is indicated only when it differs in translation (e.g. **clothes** pl. n. Ropa, *f. sing.*).
Number and gender are also recorded in the phrases at the end of entries (e.g. *disturbance of the peace*, alteración (*f.*) del orden público) except where the word treated has already been translated or where context suffices (e.g. *disturbance in the night*, escándalo nocturno).
c) English irregular noun plurals are indicated at the end of entries in the English-Spanish part and Spanish plurals in the other part.
d) Words which can assume various functions (adjective, noun, adverb, etc.) are contained in the same article. Verbs, however, are treated separately (e.g. under **right** the adjective followed by the noun and adverb come under subheadings while the verb is covered in a separate entry).
e) Irregular verbs bear asterisks referring the reader to the Grammar Section which discusses conjugation of modes and tenses. Irregular forms of English verbs, chiefly preterites and past participles, are indicated where necessary at the end of the entries in the English-Spanish part.
f) When verbs, nouns or adjectives take different prepositions in the two languages, an indication is given in parenthesis or in the form of an example (see DESDECIR).

DIFERENCIACIÓN DE LOS SENTIDOS

a) El signo || separa, en todos los artículos, las traducciones de cada acepción y existen a veces rúbricas para determinar las materias a las que pertenecen (V. lista de ABREVIATURAS, en la pág. VIII de la 1.ª parte, y la de ABBREVIATIONS en la pág. V de la 2.ª). Si un vocablo tiene varios sentidos correspondientes a una misma rúbrica, ésta figura solamente al principio y las acepciones sólo están separadas por el signo |. Las palabras que poseen numerosos significados van precedidas por un cuadro destinado a clasificar las diversas acepciones y facilitar así la tarea del lector. Si se intenta traducir *estar para*, basta consultar el párrafo 6 del artículo **estar** (que figura con el título "seguido de una preposición"), sin necesidad de recorrer todo lo que precede. Las acepciones más usuales aparecen al comienzo del artículo.
b) Las locuciones y expresiones, siguiendo el orden alfabético, se encuentran siempre después de las diferentes acepciones y tras el signo || —. Se prescinde del guión cuando sólo existe una locución o expresión.
c) Los verbos ingleses de uso corriente, que adquieren un sentido particular al ser acompañados por ciertas partículas, figuran en negritas al final del artículo separados entre sí por el signo ||. Las diferentes acepciones tienen entre ellas | y van seguidas de las locuciones o expresiones después de | — (V. TO GO).
d) Con objeto de orientar al lector y darle el nivel lingüístico de la palabra o expresión empleada se han distinguido dos grados de familiaridad: FAM., es decir "familiar, pero admitido", y POP., que corresponde a "popular" y "vulgar". Si estas rúbricas preceden a la traducción, se refieren a la palabra estudiada, mientras que si están a continuación se aplican al término dado como equivalente. Así el vocablo español *jeta* ha sido considerado familiar en la tercera acepción, al intercalarse la rúbrica FAM. En general, al escoger la traducción, se ha puesto el mismo grado de familiaridad, salvo cuando era completamente imposible.

DIFFERENTIATION OF MEANINGS

a) Translations of diverse meanings of headwords in all entries are separated by the symbol || and, in some cases, cross-references to relevant subject matter are provided (see lists of ABREVIATURAS on page VIII of part I and of ABBREVIATIONS on page V of part II). Where a word has several meanings pertaining to a single discipline, that discipline is indicated by an abbreviation only once at the beginning and the meanings are separated out using | symbol. Search lists are located before words with many meanings, to simplify use. To find the translation of *estar para* the user only need consult subheading 6 of the entry on **estar** (headed "followed by a preposition") without having to read through the preceding items. The more common meanings are listed at the beginning of the entry.
b) Phrases and expressions are placed, in alphabetical order, immediately after the various meanings and are preceded by the ||—symbol. The dash is omitted when there is only one phrase or expression.
c) Common English verbs that change their meaning when accompanied by some particles are printed in boldface at the end of entries and placed between ||. Meanings are marked off with | and followed by phrases and expressions after |—(see the verb TO GO).
d) By way of guidance to the user on social usage of words and phrases, we have drawn a distinction between colloquial or familiar but acceptable terms FAM. and vulgar or common parlance POP. These abbreviations are placed before the translation if they pertain to the word treated and after it if they apply to the equivalent word. For instance, the third application of the Spanish word *jeta* carries FAM. to denote its colloquial nature. As a general rule, wherever possible, care has been taken in translation to reflect social register.

DIFERENCIACIÓN DE LAS ACEPCIONES

Cuando una palabra tiene varias acepciones, cada una de ellas va seguida de una explicación. Ésta se coloca entre paréntesis, si está redactada en la lengua de la que se traduce, y entre corchetes, si está escrita en la otra (véase DESCUBRIMIENTO). Se procede del mismo modo con las expresiones que tienen diversos significados (por ej. *to get sick* quiere decir "ponerse enfermo" en el sentido más general y "marearse" al tratarse de un malestar producido por un viaje en coche, barco o avión). Las explicaciones, que no son más que meras orientaciones y no han de considerarse nunca como sinónimos, se sustituyen frecuentemente por ejemplos. Si diferentes ejemplos o expresiones tienen una primera parte común, ésta se indica sólo una vez y las variantes están unidas por *or* o por *o* (por ej. *edad de la razón* or *del juicio*, age of reason; *to get* o *to come to the point*, ir al grano). A veces se puede conservar u omitir una parte de la oración. Ésta se pone entre paréntesis, si se trata de la frase que se ha de traducir, o entre corchetes, si se refiere a la traducción (por ej. *hablando del rey de Roma por la puerta asoma*, talk of the devil [and he will appear]).

CLARIFICATION OF MEANINGS

Where words can assume several meanings each one is defined. Parentheses are used for definitions written in the language of the headword and square brackets for those which appear in the language of translations (see DESCUBRIMIENTO). The same procedure has been adopted when phrases have diverse meanings (e.g. *to get sick* would usually be the equivalent of "ponerse enfermo" but, when the reference is to travel sickness, the translation is "marearse"). As well as indications, which should be seen as such and not as synonyms, numerous examples are used. Where examples and phrases begin with the same words the latter are entered once only, the variant part following after the word *or* o *o* (e.g. *edad de la razón* or *del juicio*, age of reason; *to get* o *to come to the point*, ir al grano). Some expressions are not always used in full, in which case the words that can be omitted are placed in parentheses where they pertain to the item to be translated, and in square brackets where they pertain to the translation (e.g. *hablando del rey de Roma por la puerta asoma*, talk of the devil [and he will appear]).

OBSERVACIONES

Ciertos artículos tienen al final algunas observaciones, escritas en español o en inglés según el lector a quien van dirigidas, para precisar aún más el sentido de una palabra, el uso especial de la misma, su evolución, las irregularidades del plural o verbales o cualquier otra aclaración que se juzgue útil (véase MENOR).

ADDITIONAL NOTES

Additional explanatory notes are provided, in Spanish or in English as appropriate, to clarify the meaning of some words further, or peculiar usage, semantic evolution, irregular plurals, irregular verb forms or any other point requiring explanation (see MENOR).

AMERICANISMOS

Se ha procurado también, dada la importancia que siempre tuvieron y la pujanza que cobran en la actualidad las naciones de lengua castellana e inglesa en el Nuevo Mundo, incluir incontables americanismos en ambas partes del diccionario. Los empleados en Hispanoamérica van precedidos de la abreviatura *Amer.* y los utilizados en Norteamérica de las letras U. S.

AMERICANISMS

In the light of the importance and growing influence today of the English- and Spanish-speaking nations of the New World, numerous Americanisms have been included in both parts of the dictionary. The abbreviations used are *Amer.* before Latin American words or phrases and U.S. before North American ones.

ABREVIATURAS

abrev.	abreviatura	abbreviation	inv.	invariable	invariable
adj.	adjetivo	adjective	JUR.	Jurisprudencia	Jurisprudence
adv.	adverbio	adverb	loc. adv.	locución adverbial	adverbial phrase
AGR.	Agricultura, economía rural	Agriculture, rural economy	loc. lat.	locución latina	Latin phrase
			m.	masculino	masculine
Amer.	Americanismo	Americanism	MAR.	Marítimo	Maritime
ANAT.	Anatomía	Anatomy	MAT.	Matemáticas	Mathematics
(Ant.)	Anticuado	Antiquated, obsolete	MED.	Medicina	Medicine
ARQ.	Arquitectura, construcción	Architecture, building	MIL.	Militar	Military
			MIN.	Minas, mineralogía	Mining, mineralogy
art.	artículo	article	MIT.	Mitología	Mythology
ARTES.	Artes	Arts	MÚS.	Música	Music
ASTR.	Astronomía	Astronomy	n.	nombre	noun
AUT.	Automóvil	Automobile	n. pr.	nombre propio	proper noun
aux.	auxiliar	auxiliary	num.	numeral	numeral
AVIAC.	Aviación	Aviation	o.s.	se	oneself
BIOL.	Biología	Biology	pers.	personal	personal
BOT.	Botánica	Botany	pl.	plural	plural
CINEM.	Cinematografía	Cinematography	POÉT.	Poético	Poetry
COM.	Comercio, finanzas	Commerce, finance	POP.	Popular	Popular
comp.	comparativo	comparative	pos.	posesivo	possessive
compl.	complemento	complement	p.p.	participio pasivo	past participle
conj.	conjunción	conjunction	pr.	pronominal	pronominal
CULIN.	Culinario, cocina	Culinary, cooking	pref.	prefijo	prefix
def.	definido	definite	prep.	preposición	preposition
dem.	demostrativo	demonstrative	pret.	pretérito	preterite
DEP.	Deportes	Sports	pron.	pronombre	pronoun
dim.	diminutivo	diminutive	P. us.	Poco usado	Infrequent
ELECTR.	Electricidad	Electricity	QUÍM.	Química	Chemistry
exclamat.	exclamativo	exlamatory	RAD.	Radio, televisión	Radio, television
f.	femenino	feminine	rel.	relativo	relative
FAM.	Familiar	Familiar, colloquial	REL.	Religión	Religion
FIG.	Figurado	Figurative	s.	sustantivo	substantive
FIL.	Filosofía	Philosophy	s.o.	alguien, uno	someone
FÍS.	Física	Physics	sth.	algo	something
FOT.	Fotografía	Photography	superl.	superlativo	superlative
GEOGR.	Geografía	Geography	TAUR.	Tauromaquia	Tauromachy
GEOL.	Geología	Geology	TEATR.	Teatro	Theatre
GRAM.	Gramática	Grammar	TECN.	Tecnología, mecánica, industria	Technology, mechanical engineering, industry
HERÁLD.	Heráldica	Heraldry			
HIST.	Historia	History			
impers.	impersonal	impersonal	tr.	transitivo	transitive
IMPR.	Imprenta	Printing	U.S.	Estados Unidos	United States
indef.	indefinido	indefinite	v.	verbo	verb
interj.	interjección	interjection	V.	Véase	See
interr.	interrogativo	interrogative	VET.	Veterinaria	Veterinary science
intr.	intransitivo	intransitive	ZOOL.	Zoología	Zoology

Listas de vocabulario
que figuran en la primera parte

Automóvil
Bicicleta
Circulación de automóviles
Construcción
Deportes
Enseñanza
Fiestas religiosas
Geografía
Herramientas
Jurídico (vocabulario)
Medicina
Metalurgia
Música
Nombres de pila
Países
Química
Religión
Ropa
Telecomunicaciones
Trabajo
Viajes
Zoología

Word lists
included in the second part

Agriculture
Arts
Boats
Cinematography
Computer
Conferences
Economic and commercial terms
Entertainments
Food and meals
Games
Kinship
Maths and physics
Mining
Nuclear energy
Photography
Politics
Radio and television
Sailing
Town
Universe and weather
Vegetables and fruits

Láminas en color fuera de texto — Colour plates

Automóvil	Motorcar	*Transatlántico*	Liner
Avión	Aircraft	*Esqueleto*	Skeleton
Turborreactor	Turbojet engine	*Anatomía*	Anatomy
Motor	Motor	*Teatro*	Theatre
Motocicleta	Motorcycle	*Cinematografía*	Cinema
Ferrocarril	Railway	*Casa*	House
Locomotora	Locomotive	*Herramientas*	Tools
Velero	Sailing boat	*Iglesia*	Church

ESPAÑOL-INGLÉS

a f. A: *una a minúscula*, a small a. || *A por a y be por be*, in detail, point by point.

— OBSERV. The pronunciation of the Spanish *a* corresponds to the sound midway between the *a* in *at* and the *a* in *are*.

a prep.

> **1.** Complemento indirecto. — **2.** Entre dos verbos. — **3.** Verbos de exhortación, invitación, etc. — **4.** Tiempo. — **5.** Situación, lugar. — **6.** Precio: — **7.** Evaluación. — **8.** Modo. — **9.** Expresiones diversas.

1. COMPLEMENTO INDIRECTO. — To (destinación): *escribí a mi abuela*, I wrote to my grandmother; *dar el libro al maestro*, to give the book to the teacher. || From (procedencia): *se lo compré a Juan*, I bought it from John.
2. ENTRE DOS VERBOS. — To: *voy a escribir*, I'm going to write; *se sentó a comer*, he sat down to eat; *empezó a llover*, it began to rain; *le ayudaron a hacer la maleta*, they helped him to pack his suitcase.
3. VERBOS DE EXHORTACIÓN, INVITACIÓN, etc. — To: *los agitadores nos incitaron a la rebelión*, the agitators incited us to rebellion; *nos obligó a salir*, he obliged us to go out.
4. TIEMPO. — At (momento concreto): *a las dos de la tarde*, at two o'clock in the afternoon; *al principio*, at the beginning; *a los veinte años*, at twenty. || After (después): *a los seis meses de su llegada*, six months after his arrival. || Later, afterwards (más tarde): *a los diez minutos volvió*, ten minutes later he came back.
5. SITUACIÓN, LUGAR. — To: *ir a Inglaterra*, to go to England; *voy al peluquero*, I'm going to the hairdresser's. || At: *a la puerta*, at the door; *sentarse a la mesa*, to sit down at the table; *mi casa está al final de esta calle*, my house is at the end of this street. || On: *llevaba un cesto al brazo*, he carried a basket on his arm; *a orillas del Támesis*, on the banks of the Thames; *a la derecha, izquierda*, on the right, left; *a este lado*, on this side. || To: *el pueblo está al norte de Madrid*, the town is to the North of Madrid. || [Not translated]: *la fábrica está a dos kilómetros de su casa*, the factory is two kilometres from his house. || Into, in (dentro): *cayó al pozo*, he fell into the well; *échalo al fuego*, throw it in the fire. || In: *llegar a Inglaterra*, to arrive in England; *mirarse al espejo*, to look at o.s. in the mirror; *a lo lejos*, in the distance; *a los ojos de todos*, in everybody's eyes; *sentarse al sol*, to sit in the sun.
6. PRECIO. — At: *patatas a* or *de a cinco pesetas el kilo*, potatoes at five pesetas a kilogramme.
7. EVALUACIÓN. — To: *de tres a cinco años*, from three to five years. || In, by (distributivo): *a docenas*, in dozens, by the dozen; *a millares*, in thousands, by the thousand. || A, per: *gano veinte libras a la semana* I earn twenty pounds a week. || At: *a cien kilómetros por hora*, at a hundred kilometres an hour.
8. MODO. — By: *a mano*, by hand. || In: *escribir a lápiz*, to write in pencil; *a sangre fría*, in cold blood. || With: *a duras penas*, with great difficulty. || On: *a pie*, on foot; *a petición suya*, on his request; *acompañar al piano*, to accompany on the piano. || — *Escrito a máquina*, typewritten. || *Hecho a máquina*, machine-made.
9. EXPRESIONES DIVERSAS. — *A caballo*, on horseback. || *A casa*, home. || *A casa de Pérez*, to Pérez's house, to Pérez's. || *¡A comer!*, lunch [breakfast, dinner, etc.] is ready! || *¿A cuánto es esto? — A veinte pesetas*, how much is this? — Twenty pesetas (precio). || *¿A cuántos estamos? — A veinte de junio*, what is the date? *o* what date is it? — It's the twentieth of June (fecha). || *¡A dormir!, ¡a la cama!*, to bed!, bedtime! || *A eso de las dos*, [at] about two o'clock. || *A la francesa*, in the French way, in the French fashion, à la française. || *Al día siguiente*, the next day, the following day, the day after. || *A lo caballero*, like a gentleman. || *A lo grande*, in a big way. || *A los quince años*, at fifteen, at the age of fifteen (edad), fifteen years later (quince años más tarde), fifteen years after (quince años después de). || *Amor a la verdad*, love of the truth. || *A no ser por*, but for, if it were not for. || *A que*, I bet: *a que llego más pronto que tú*, I bet I get there before you. || *¿A qué viene Ud.?*, what do you want here? || *A su llegada*, on his arrival. || *A tiempo*, in time. || *A ver*, let's see, let's have a look. || *Cercano a*, near to, close to. || DEP. *Empatar a dos*, to draw two all. | *Ganar tres a dos*, to win three-two. || FAM. *Ir a por vino*, to go for some wine, to go and fetch some wine. || *Ir en fila de a dos*, to go in twos. || *Madrid, a 1º de febrero*, Madrid, 1st February. || *Matar a alguien a puñaladas*, to stab s.o. to death. || *Miedo al lobo*, fear of the wolf. || *Olor a rosas*, smell of roses. || *Subir al autobús*, to get on the bus. || *Torcer a la derecha*, to turn right, to turn to the right.

— OBSERV. I. The preposition *a* introduces the direct object of transitive verbs when the object is a person or, in certain cases, an animal, a town, a country or a personified noun. It can also be used to avoid possible ambiguity. It is not translated in English: *oigo a mi madre*, I can hear my mother; *este libro describe a Inglaterra*, this book describes England; *llama casa a este tugurio*, he calls this slum a house.
— II. The preposition *a* must introduce the emphatic pronoun in Spanish: *a éste le conozco bien*, I know him very well; *me dio el libro a mí*, he gave the book to me, he gave me the book.
— III. When the preposition *a* directly precedes the article *el*, *a el* is contracted to *al*.

abacá m. Abaca (árbol de Manila). || Manilla hemp (tejido).
abacería f. Grocer's, grocer's shop.
abacero, ra m. y f. Grocer.
abacial adj. Abbatial.
ábaco m. Abacus, counting frame. || ARQ. Abacus.
abad m. Abbot (de un monasterio).
abadejo m. Codfish, cod (bacalao). || Fire-crested wren (ave). || Spanish fly, cantharides (insecto).
abadengo, ga adj. Abbatial: *tierras abadengas*, abbatial lands.
abadesa f. Abbess.
abadía f. Abbey (convento). || Abbacy (dignidad). || Parsonage, rectory, vicarage (casa del cura).
abajeño, ña o **abajero, ra** o **abajino, na** adj. *Amer.* Lowland.
— M. y f. *Amer.* Lowlander.
abajero, ra adj. *Amer.* Bottom: *sábana abajera*, bottom sheet.
abajo adv. Below: *abajo hay gente esperando*, there are people waiting below. || Down here, down below: *estoy abajo*, I am down here *o* down below. || Down there, down here, down below, downstairs (en una casa): *el cartero está abajo*, the postman is down here *o* down below *o* downstairs (si el que habla está también abajo), the postman is down there *o* down below *o* downstairs (si el que habla está arriba). || Down, down below, downstairs: *vete abajo a abrir la puerta*, go down and open the door. || Down with: *¡abajo el tirano!* down with the tyrant! || — *Aquí abajo*, down here, here below. || *Calle abajo*, down the street. || *Cuesta abajo*, downhill. || *De arriba abajo*, from top to bottom. || *Desde abajo*, from below. || *Echar abajo*, V. ECHAR. || *El abajo firmante*, the undersigned. || *Escaleras abajo*, downstairs. || *Ir hacia abajo*, to go down. || *Los vecinos de abajo*, the neighbours below. || *Más abajo*, below: *el pasaje citado más abajo*, the passage quoted below; lower down (en un lugar inferior), further down: *cinco casas más abajo*, five houses further down. || *Por abajo*, underneath. || *Río* or *aguas abajo*, downstream. || *Tirar abajo*, V. TIRAR. || *Venirse abajo*, to fall down, to collapse (un edificio), to fall through, to collapse (un proyecto).
abalanzar v. tr. To balance (la balanza). || To throw (lanzar).
— V. pr. To rush: *abalanzarse sobre su adversario*, to rush [at] one's enemy; *abalanzarse hacia las lanchas de salvamento*, to rush towards the lifeboats. || To swoop: *el águila se abalanzó sobre el cordero*, the eagle swooped on the lamb. || To pounce: *los niños se abalanzaron sobre los pasteles*, the children pounced on the cakes. || *Amer.* To rear (el caballo).

abalaustrado, da adj. Balustered.
abalear v. tr. *Amer.* To shoot (fusilar).
abaleo m. Broom (escoba y planta).
abalizamiento m. MAR. Marking with buoys *o* beacons, buoying.
abalizar v. tr. MAR. To buoy, to mark with buoys *o* beacons.
abalorio m. Glass bead (cuenta). || Glass beads, *pl.* glass beadwork.
abaluartar v. tr. To fortify with bastions *o* with a bulwark.
abancaino, na o **abancayno, na** adj. [From *o* of] Abancay (Perú).
— M. y f. Native *o* inhabitant of Abancay.
abanderado m. MIL. Standard bearer. || FIG. Champion (defensor de una causa).
abanderamiento m. MAR. Registering (de un barco).
abanderar v. tr. MAR. To register. || FIG. To champion. || *Amer.* To draw up a programme for [politics, etc.]. || *Barco abanderado en España,* ship flying Spanish colours.
abanderizar v. tr. To divide, to cause discord in *o* between.
— V. pr. To join (un partido).
abandonado, na adj. Abandoned. || Neglected: *tener un jardín muy abandonado,* to have a very neglected garden. || FIG. Negligent, neglectful (desidioso). | Untidy: *una chica abandonada,* an untidy girl. || *Amer.* Depraved (depravado).
abandonamiento m. V. ABANDONO.
abandonar v. t. To leave (un lugar, algo): *abandonar la casa de sus padres,* to leave home *o* one's parents' house. || To abandon: *abandonar el barco,* to abandon ship. || To abandon, to desert: *abandonar a sus hijos,* to abandon one's children. || To desert, to forsake: *no me abandones,* don't desert me; *la suerte nunca nos abandona,* luck never forsakes us. || To give up: *abandonar la carrera,* to give up one's studies; *abandonar una idea,* to give up an idea. || FIG. To neglect: *abandonar sus deberes,* to neglect one's duties. || To renounce, to relinquish (un privilegio, etc.).
— V. intr. To give up, to withdraw (un deportista).
— V. pr. FIG. To give way, to give in, to succumb, to yield: *abandonarse a la tentación,* to give way to temptation. | To give o.s. over to (al alcohol, al vicio, etc.). | To let o.s. go, to become slovenly *o* careless (descuidarse). | To confide, to open one's heart: *abandonarse a su madre,* to confide in one's mother, to abandon one's heart to one's mother.
abandonismo m. Defeatism.
abandonista adj. / s. Defeatist: *política abandonista,* defeatist policy.
abandono m. Abandoning, abandonment: *el abandono de un niño,* the abandoning of a child. || Giving up: *el abandono de una idea, de una carrera,* the giving up of an idea, of one's studies. || Neglect, dereliction: *el abandono de sus deberes,* the neglect of one's duties. || Neglect (de uno mismo). || Abandon, derelict state (de un edificio). || Retirement: *el abandono de un ciclista,* the retirement of a cyclist. || FIG. Abandon (despreocupación). || — *Con abandono,* nonchalantly, casually. || *Ganar por abandono,* to win by default.
abanicar v. tr. To fan.
— V. pr. To fan o.s.
abanico m. Fan. || Tail [of a peacock] (del pavo real). || MAR. Derrick (cabria). || FIG. Range (de salarios). || — *En abanico,* fan-shaped. || *Poner los naipes en abanico,* to fan out one's cards.
abaniquear v. tr. To fan.
abaniqueo m. Fanning.
abaniquero m. Fan manufacturer (fabricante). || Fan dealer (vendedor).
abanto m. ZOOL. African vulture.
— Adj. Simple, stupid (necio). || Cowardly (toro).
abaratado, da adj. Cut-price, reduced in price: *géneros abaratados,* cut-price goods, goods reduced in price.
abaratamiento m. Reduction in price: *el abaratamiento de un producto,* the reduction in price of a product. || *El abaratamiento de la vida,* the fall in the cost of living.
abaratar v. tr. To reduce *o* to cut the price of, to make cheaper, to reduce: *abaratar las frutas,* to reduce the price of fruit. || To reduce, to cut, to lower: *abaratar los precios,* to lower prices.
— V. pr. To become cheaper, to come down in price (la vida). || To come down (precios).
abarca f. Sandal [worn by peasants].
abarcamiento m. Embracing.
abarcar v. tr. To get *o* to put one's arms round, to embrace: *no puedo abarcar esta columna,* I cannot get my arms round this column. || FIG. To embrace, to cover (comprender). || To be able to see *o* to take in: *desde la torre abarco todo el paisaje,* from the tower I can see all the countryside. || To undertake, to take on (varios trabajos). || *Amer.* To monopolize (acaparar). || *Quien mucho abarca poco aprieta,* do not bite off more than you can chew.
abaritonado, da adj. MÚS. Baritone.
abarloar v. tr. MAR. To bring alongside.
abarquillado, da adj. Warped (madera). || Curled up, wrinkled (papel, cartón). || Blistered (pintura). || Buckled (chapa).
abarquillamiento m. Warping (de madera). || Curling up, wrinkling (de papel, cartón). || Blistering (de pintura). || Buckling (de chapa).
abarquillar v. tr. To warp (madera). || To curl up, to wrinkle (papel, cartón). || To blister (pintura). || To buckle (chapa).
— V. pr. To warp (madera). || To curl up, to wrinkle (papel, cartón).
abarraganamiento m. Concubinage.
abarraganarse v. pr. To live together.
abarrajado, da adj. *Amer.* Shameless (desvergonzado). | Debauched (disoluto).
abarrancamiento m. Bogging down (enlodamiento).
abarrancar v. tr. To bog down.
— V. intr. MAR. To go *o* to run aground.
— V. pr. To get bogged down, to get stuck in the mud (atascarse). || FIG. To get bogged down, to get *o* to be stuck (en un asunto).
abarrotado, da adj. Packed, full, crammed (atestado): *un autobús abarrotado,* a packed bus; *una carta abarrotada de disparates,* a letter full of *o* packed with nonsense.
abarrotar v. tr. To put bars on (con barrotes). || MAR. To stow (la carga). || To cram, to pack, to overload (atestar). || *Amer.* To buy up (acaparar).
— V. pr. To fill up, to become packed. || *Amer.* To become cheaper, to go down in price (abaratarse). | To be over-plentiful (superabundar).
abarrote m. MAR. Bundle. || — Pl. *Amer.* Groceries (artículos). | Grocer's [shop], *sing.,* grocery, *sing.* (tienda). | Ironmonger's [shop], *sing.,* ironmongery, *sing.* (ferretería).
abarrotería f. *Amer.* V. ABARROTE, pl.
abarrotero, ra m. y f. *Amer.* Grocer.
Abasidas n. pr. pl. HIST. Abbasids.
abastardar v. intr. To degenerate, to become bastardized.
abastecedor, ra adj. Providing, supplying.
— M. y f. Supplier, purveyor. || *Amer.* Butcher (carnicero.
abastecer* v. tr. To supply, to provide: *abastecer un ejército de víveres,* to supply an army with provisions, to supply provisions to an army.
abastecido, da adj. Supplied, provisioned; *un ejército bien abastecido,* a well-supplied army. || Stocked: *una tienda bien abastecida,* a well-stocked shop.
abastecimiento m. Provisioning, supplying (avituallamiento). || Supply: *abastecimiento de aguas,* supply of water, water supply.
abastero m. *Amer.* Wholesale supplier, wholesaler.
abastionar v. tr. To bastion.
abasto m. Provisioning, supplying (abastecimiento). || Abundance, great amount. || *Amer.* Slaughterhouse, abattoir (matadero). || — Pl. Provisioning, *sing.* || — *Dar abasto a,* to supply. || *No poder dar abasto,* not to be able to keep up (sentido general): *tengo tantas cosas que hacer que no puedo dar abasto,* I have so many things to do that I cannot keep up; not to be able to satisfy (demanda).
abatanado, da adj. Fulled (el paño).
abatanador m. Fuller.
abatanar v. tr. To full (el paño). || FIG. To beat (golpear).
abatatar v. tr. *Amer.* FAM. To intimidate, to frighten (amedrentar).
— V. pr. FAM. To become lethargic (aplatanarse). || *Amer.* FAM. To become intimidated *o* frightened (acobardarse).
abate m. (P. us.). Father: *el abate Grégoire,* Father Grégoire.
abatí m. *Amer.* Maize [U.S., corn]. | Drink distilled from maize (bebida).
abatible adj. Folding (asiento, mesa).
abatido, da adj. Downcast, dejected, depressed, disheartened (desanimado): *estaba muy abatido por su desgracia,* he was very depressed by his misfortune. || Abject, despicable (despreciable). || Drooping: *párpados abatidos,* drooping eyelids.
abatimiento m. Dejection, low spirits, *pl.,* depression (desánimo). || Shame (cosa afrentosa). || MAR. *Abatimiento del rumbo,* leeway.
abatir v. tr. To knock *o* to pull down, to demolish (destruir): *abatir un edificio,* to knock down a building. || To fell, to cut down (árbol). || To take down (desmontar): *abatió la tienda de campaña,* he took down the tent. || To shoot down, to bring down (un pájaro, un avión). || FIG. To depress, to dishearten, to get down (deprimir): *la adversidad nos abate a todos,* adversity depresses us all *o* gets us all down. | To lay low (por una enfermedad, de dolor). | To humiliate, to humble (una persona). | To lower, to humble (orgullo, soberbia). || MAR. To strike, to lower: *abatir banderas, velas,* to strike the colours, the sails. || To lay on the table, to show (juegos de naipes). || MAT. *Abatir una perpendicular,* to drop *o* to draw a perpendicular.
— V. pr. To swoop, to sweep down (arrojarse): *el águila se abatió sobre su presa,* the eagle swooped on its prey. || FIG. To humble o.s., to lower o.s. (humillarse). | To fall: *la desgracia se abatió sobre su familia,* misfortune fell upon his family. | To become disheartened *o* depressed *o* dejected *o* downcast, to lose heart (desanimarse).
abayado, da adj. BOT. Bacciform, berry-shaped.
abazón m. Cheek pouch (de monos).

abdicación f. Abdication.
abdicar v. tr. To abdicate, to abdicate from: *abdicó el trono en su hijo,* he abdicated the throne *o* he abdicated from the throne in favour of his son. || To give up (la corona). || To give up, to surrender (derechos). || To give up (ideas, principios).
— V. intr. To abdicate (el rey).
abdomen m. ANAT. Abdomen.
abdominal adj. Abdominal: *músculos abdominales,* abdominal muscles.
abducción f. Abduction.
abductor adj. ANAT. Abducent.
— M. Abductor.
abecé m. ABC, alphabet (alfabeto). || FIG. Rudiments, *pl.*, basic steps, *pl.* || FIG. *Eso es el abecé,* that's child's play. | *No saber el abecé,* not to know A from B.
abecedario m. Alphabet (alfabeto). || Primer, spelling book (libro).
abedul m. Birch (árbol).
abeja f. Bee. || — *Abeja carpintera,* carpenter bee. || *Abeja maesa, maestra* or *reina,* queen bee. || *Abeja neutra* or *obrera,* worker, worker bee.
abejarrón m. Bumblebee, humble-bee.
abejaruco m. Bee-eater (pájaro).
abejera f. Apiary (colmenar). || BOT. Balm.
abejero, ra m. y f. Beekeeper, apiculturist, apiarist. ||
— M. Bee-eater (pájaro).
abejón m. Bumblebee, humble-bee (abejorro). || Drone (zángano).
abejorreo m. FAM. Buzzing, bumbling.
abejorro m. Bumblebee, humble-bee (insecto himenóptero). || Cockchafer (insecto coleóptero). || FIG. y FAM. *Ser un abejorro,* to be a nuisance.
Abel n. pr. m. Abel.
abellacado, da adj. Wicked, mean, villainous.
abellacar v. tr. To debase, to degrade.
— V. pr. To degrade o.s.
abellotado, da adj. Acorn-shaped.
abemolar *v.* tr. To soften (la voz) || MÚS. To flatten, to mark with a flat.
aberenjenado, da adj. Violet, egg-plant coloured (color). || Egg-plant shaped (forma).
aberración f. Aberration.
aberrante adj. Aberrant.
aberrar v. intr. To be mistaken.
abertura f. Opening, gap (boquete).|| Hole (agujero). || Cove, creek (ensenada). || Slit, crack (grieta). || Pass (entre dos montañas). || Aperture (del diafragma).|| Vent: *chaqueta con aberturas laterales,* jacket with side vents. || FIG. Openness, frankness (franqueza). || FIG. *Abertura de espíritu,* broad-mindedness.
abestiarse v. pr. To become an animal *o* a brute.
abetal o **abetar** m. Fir wood (pequeño), fir forest (grande).
abeto m. Fir (árbol). || — *Abeto blanco* or *albar,* silver fir. || *Abeto falso* or *rojo,* spruce.
abetunado, da adj. Very brown.
abetunar v. tr. To polish, to clean (zapatos).
abierto, ta adj. Open: *el niño dormía con la boca abierta,* the child was sleeping with his mouth open; *flor abierta,* open flower. || Open, clear (terreno). || GRAM. Open: *vocal abierta,* open vowel. || FIG. Open, frank, sincere: *una persona muy abierta,* a very open person. || — *Abierto de par en par,* wide-open, open wide. || *A cielo abierto,* open-cast (mina). || *A tumba abierta,* flat out, at top speed (conducir). || MIL. *Ciudad abierta,* open *o* unfortified city. || *Con las piernas abiertas,* with one's legs apart. || *Con los brazos abiertos,* with one's arms open wide. || *Dejar el grifo abierto,* to leave the tap running, to leave the tap on. || *Herida abierta,* open *o* gaping wound. || FIG. *Quedarse con la boca abierta,* to gape in amazement. | *Ver el cielo abierto,* to see a way out.
— M. *Amer.* Reclaimed land.
abigarrado, da adj. Multicoloured [U.S., multicolored]: *una tela abigarrada,* a multicoloured cloth. || FIG. Motley, mixed: *una multitud abigarrada,* a motley crowd.
abigarramiento m. Multicolouring [U.S., multicoloring]. || FIG. Motleyness, mixture.
abigarrar v. tr. To mottle, to variegate.
abigeato m. Rustling, rustle.
ab intestato loc. lat. Intestate.
abintestato m. JUR. Intestate estate.
abisagrar v. tr. To hinge.
abisal adj. Abyssal.
abiselar v. tr. To bevel.
Abisinia n. pr. f. GEOGR. Abyssinia.
abisinio, nia adj. s. Abyssinian.
abismal adj. Abysmal.
abismar v. tr. To throw into an abyss. || FIG. To humiliate, to humble (confundir).
— V. pr. To sink (en el mar). || FIG. To get absorbed (en los pensamientos, el trabajo). | To be plunged (en el dolor). || *Amer.* To be amazed *o* astonished (asombrarse).
abismático, ca adj. Abysmal.
abismo m. Abyss, gulf. || Hell (infierno). || FIG. Abyss: *un abismo de dolor,* an abyss of suffering. | World of difference: *hay un abismo entre tus ideas y las mías,* there is a world of difference between your ideas and mine. | Depth: *desde los abismos de la historia,* from the depths of history. | Gulf: *la guerra abrió un abismo entre las dos naciones,* the war opened a gulf between the two nations. || FIG. *Estar al borde del abismo,* to be on the brink of ruin.
abitar v. tr. MAR. To bitt.
abizcochado, da adj. Spongy.
abjuración f. Abjuration.
abjurar v. tr. e intr. To abjure, to forswear: *abjurar de su fe,* to abjure one's faith.
ablación f. MED. Ablation. || GEOL. Wearing away, ablation.
ablandabrevas m. y f. FIG. y FAM. Good-for-nothing.
ablandador, ra adj. Softening. || FIG. Soothing.
ablandadura f. o **ablandamiento** m. Softening. || FIG. Soothing (acción de calmar). | Dropping (del viento). | Softening: *el ablandamiento de una dictadura,* the softening of a dictatorship. | Moderation.
ablandar v. tr. To soften: *ablandar cera,* to soften wax. || To melt (nieve). || To make tender (la carne). || To loosen (con un laxante). || FIG. To soothe (calmar). | To move, to touch (conmover). | To soften up: *ablandó a sus padres,* he softened his parents up. | To moderate (harshness). || *Amer.* AUT. To run in.
— V. intr. To drop (el viento). || To get milder (el tiempo).
— V. pr. To soften, to go soft. || To get milder (el tiempo). || To drop (el viento). || To melt (nieve). || FIG. To become *o* to turn soft, to soften.
ablande m. *Amer.* AUT. Running-in.
ablandecer v. tr. To soften.
ablativo m. GRAM. Ablative: *ablativo absoluto,* ablative absolute.
ablución f. Ablution (lavatorio).
ablusado, da adj. Bloused.
abnegación f. Abnegation, self-denial.
abnegado, da adj. Self-sacrificing, unselfish.
abnegarse* v. pr. To sacrifice o.s., to deny o.s.
abobado, da adj. Silly, stupid (tonto).
abobamiento m. Stupefaction (asombro). || Silliness, stupidity (tontería).
abobar v. tr. To stupefy (asombrar). || To make stupid (atontar).
— V. pr. To become stupid.
abocado, da adj. Medium-dry (jerez). || *Estar abocado a la ruina,* to be heading for *o* destined for ruin.
abocar v. tr. To bring together the mouths [of two recipients]. || To seize in one's mouth (coger con la boca).
— V. intr. To arrive at, to come to: *abocar a una solución,* to arrive at a solution.
— V. pr. To meet, to confer (reunirse).
abocardado, da adj. Bell-shaped, funnel-shaped, wide-mouthed.
abocardar v. tr. To widen the mouth of, to widen the opening of.
abocardo m. Drill (barrena grande).
abocatero m. Avocado tree (aguacate).
abocelado, da adj. Torus-shaped.
abocetado, da adj. Rough (pintura). || Rough-hewn (escultura).
abocetar v. tr. To sketch: *abocetar un dibujo,* to sketch a drawing.
abocinado, da adj. Trumpet-shaped (como una trompeta). || ARQ. Splayed (arco).
abocinamiento m. Widening.
abocinar v. tr. To widen (un orificio).
abochornado, da adj. FIG. Ashamed: *estoy abochornado con tu conducta,* I am ashamed of your conduct.
abochornar v. tr. To suffocate: *el calor nos abochorna,* the heat is suffocating us. || FIG. To put to shame, to show up: *siempre intentas abochornarme delante de todos,* you always try to show me up in front of everyone.
— V. pr. FIG. To be ashamed (avergonzarse). || To blush (ruborizarse). || AGR. To parch, to become parched (las plantas).
abofeteamiento m. Slapping. || FIG. Insult.
abofetear v. tr. To slap (dar bofetadas). || FIG. To insult: *abofetear la moralidad,* to insult morality.
abogacía f. Legal profession.
abogada f. [Woman] lawyer. || FIG. Mediatrix, mediatress, patron saint (mediadora). | Advocate (defensora).
abogaderas f. pl. *Amer.* FAM. Irrational arguments.
abogadesco, ca o **abogadil** adj. FAM. Characteristic of lawyers. | Pettifogging (despectivo).
abogadete o **abogadillo** m. FAM. Pettifogger.
abogado m. JUR. Lawyer, solicitor (consejero). | Barrister [U.S., attorney *o* lawyer] (en el tribunal). || FIG. Advocate, defender (defensor). | Mediator, patron saint (intercesor). || — *Abogado consultor,* counsel. || *Abogado defensor,* counsel for the defence, defending counsel. || *Abogado del diablo,* Devil's advocate. || *Abogado del Estado,* public prosecutor [U.S., attorney general]. || FAM. *Abogado de secano,* quack lawyer, pettifogger. || *Abogado fiscal,* prosecuting counsel [U.S., district attorney]. || *Ejercer de abogado,* to be a lawyer, to practise law. || *Hacerse el abogado de,* to advocate, to defend. || *Pasante de abogado,* assistant lawyer.
abogar v. intr. To plead: *abogar por* or *en* or *a favor de uno,* to plead on s.o.'s behalf *o* for s.o. || FIG. To mediate (mediar). | To advocate, to champion (defender).
abolengo m. Lineage, ancestry. || *De abolengo,* of noble *o* proud lineage (ilustre).

abolición f. Abolition.
abolicionismo m. Abolitionism.
abolicionista adj. / s. Abolitionist.
abolir* v. tr. To abolish.
— OBSERV. *Abolir* is a defective verb used only in the forms whose endings begin with *i*: *abolí, aboliendo, abolido, aboliste, abolía, aboliera, aboliré*, etc.
abolsado, da adj. Baggy.
abolsarse v. pr. To pouch (la piel). || To be *o* to go baggy (tejido).
abollado, da adj. Dented: *una carrocería abollada*, dented bodywork. || FIG. Penniless.
abolladura f. Bump (hacia afuera), dent (hacia adentro).
abollar v. tr. To dent (chapa, etc.). || To emboss (como adorno).
abollonar v. tr. To emboss.
abombado, da adj. Convex: *cristal abombado*, convex pane of glass. || *Amer.* Stupefied, stunned (atontado). | Tipsy, fuddled (achispado).
abombar v. tr. To make convex, to convex. || FIG. y FAM. To stupefy, to stun (aturdir).
— V. pr. *Amer.* To get tipsy *o* fuddled (emborracharse). | To stagnate (el agua). | To curdle (la leche). | To rot (pudrirse).
abominable adj. Abominable: *el abominable hombre de las nieves*, the abominable snowman.
abominación f. Abomination.
abominar v. tr. To detest, to abominate, to loathe: *abomino la injusticia*, I detest injustice.
— V. intr. To curse: *abominar de su suerte*, to curse one's luck. || To detest, to loathe.
abonable adj. Payable (pagadero). || AGR. Improvable (tierras).
abonado, da adj. Paid (pagado). || Fertilized, manured. || *Abonado en cuenta* credited.
— M. y f. Subscriber (de teléfono, de revista). || Season ticket holder (para un espectáculo). || — M. AGR. Fertilizing, manuring, manure spreading (estercolado).
abonador, ra m. y f. Guarantor. || — M. Auger (de tonelero). || — F. AGR. Fertilizer spreading machine, manure spreader.
abonamiento m. V. ABONO.
abonanzar v. intr. MAR. To abate, to calm down (calmarse).
— V. pr. To calm down.
abonar v. tr. To pay: *abonar una gran cantidad*, to pay a large amount; *abonar sus deudas*, to pay one's debts. || To credit (*en*, to), to pay (*en*, into) [en una cuenta]. || To pay for (pagar una compra). || To take out a subscription for [s.o.] (a uno a un periódico, etc.). || To vouch for, to be guarantor of (salir fiador). || To vouch for, to guarantee (dar por cierto): *abono la certeza de lo que dijo*, I vouch for the truth of what he said. || To improve (mejorar). || AGR. To fertilize, to manure, to dress (la tierra). || — FIG. *Abonar el terreno*, to prepare the ground, to make the ground ready. || *Abonar en cuenta de*, to pay into the account of, to credit to [s.o.'s account].
— V. intr. To calm down (el mar).
— V. pr. To subscribe (a un periódico). || To buy a season ticket for (a un espectáculo).
abonaré m. COM. Promissory note, I. O. U. (pagaré).
abono m. Payment (pago). || AGR. Fertilizer (palabra general): *abonos nitrogenados*, nitrate fertilizers. | Manure, muck (estiércol). | Fertilizing, manuring, manure spreading (esparcimiento del abono). || Subscription (a un periódico). || Season ticket (para una temporada): *sacar un abono para las corridas*, to buy *o* to take out a season ticket for the bullfights. || Guarantee (fianza). || Improvement (mejora). || Credit (en una cuenta). || *En abono de*, in support of (una idea).
aboquillado, da adj. With a mouthpiece. || Wide-mouthed (abocardado). || Bevelled, chamfered (achaflanado).
aboquillar v. tr. To fit a mouthpiece to. || To widen the mouth *o* opening of (abocardar). || To bevel, to chamfer (achaflanar).
abordable adj. Within everyone's means, reasonable: *precio abordable*, price within everyone's means. || Which can be tackled (asunto). || Approachable (persona). || Accessible (lugar).
abordaje m. MAR. Boarding. || FIG. Approach. || MAR. *Saltar al abordaje*, to board a ship.
abordar v. tr. To tackle, to approach (un asunto, problema). || To undertake, to get down to (tarea). || To approach, to accost (una persona). || MAR. To come alongside (acercarse a). | To run foul of (chocar con). | To board (al enemigo).
— V. intr. MAR. To put in, to dock (llegar a puerto): *abordamos a Bilbao*, we put in at Bilbao. | To land (desembarcar): *abordar a* or *en una isla*, to land on an island. | To come alongside: *abordar al muelle*, to come alongside the quay.
— V. pr. MAR. To board (atacar). | To come alongside. | To run foul of (chocar con).
aborigen adj. / s. Native (indígena).
— OBSERV. Las palabras inglesas *aborigine* y *aboriginal*, a pesar de tener los mismos sentidos que la palabra española *aborigen*, se emplean principalmente con relación a los indígenas de Australia.
aborrajarse v. pr. To dry prematurely (mieses).
aborrascado, da adj. Stormy (tiempo).
aborrascarse v. pr. To turn *o* to become stormy (el tiempo).
aborrecedor, ra adj. Full of hate.
— M. y f. Hater.
aborrecer* v. tr. To hate, to abhor, to loathe, to detest: *aborrecer a su vecino*, to hate one's neighbour. || To abandon [nest or young] (los pájaros). || To annoy, to get on s.o.'s nerves (molestar).
aborrecible adj. Detestable, abhorrent, despicable, loathesome (detestable).
aborrecido, da adj. Detestable, loathed, hated. || FIG. Bored, fed up (aburrido).
aborrecimiento m. Hatred, hate, loathing, abhorrence (odio). || Disgust (repugnancia). || Boredom (aburrimiento).
aborregado, da adj. Mackerel, covered with fleecy clouds (cielo). || FIG. Like sheep.
aborregarse v. pr. To become covered with fleecy clouds (el cielo). || *Amer.* FIG. To get frightened (acobardarse).
aborricarse v. pr. To become coarse (embrutecerse).
abortar v. intr. MED. To miscarry, to have a miscarriage, to abort. || FIG. To fail, to abort, to miscarry: *la conspiración abortó*, the conspiracy failed. || *Hacerse abortar*, to have an abortion.
— V. tr. FIG. y FAM. To come up with (algo extraordinario).
abortivo, va adj. Abortive.
— M. Abortifacient.
aborto m. Miscarriage (involuntario), abortion (voluntario). || FIG. Failure, miscarriage (fracaso). || FIG. y FAM. Freak (persona). | Abortion (cosa).
abotagado, da o **abotargado, da** adj. Swollen (hinchado): *me levanté con la cara abotargada*, I got up with a swollen face.
abotagamiento o **abotargamiento** m. Swelling.
abotagarse o **abotargarse** v. pr. To swell, to swell up.
abotinado, da adj. High-fronted (zapatos).
abotonador m. Buttonhook.
abotonadura f. Buttoning, fastening.
abotonar v. tr. To button, to button up.
— V. intr. To bud (plantas).
— V. pr. To do one's buttons up, to fasten one's buttons (persona). || To button (ropa).
abovedado, da adj. Vaulted, arched.
— M. Vaulting.
abovedar v. tr. To arch, to vault.
aboyar v. tr. MAR. To buoy, to mark with buoys. || To put floats on (las redes).
abozalar v. tr. To muzzle, to put a muzzle on.
abra f. MAR. Cove, bay, creek (ensenada). || Dale (valle). || Fissure, cleft (en el suelo). || *Amer.* Leaf (de puerta o ventana). | Clearing (en un bosque).
abracadabra m. Abracadabra.
abracadabrante adj. Strange, unusual, extravagant.
— OBSERV. This word is a Gallicism and can be replaced by *extraordinario* or *extravagante*.
Abrahán n. pr. m. Abraham.
abrasado, da adj. Burnt.
abrasador, ra adj. Burning: *una pasión abrasadora*, a burning passion.
abrasar v. tr. To burn: *el sol abrasa*, the sun is burning; *las llamas lo abrasaron todo*, the flames burnt everything. || AGR. To scorch, to dry up (las plantas). || FIG. To squander, to waste (la fortuna). | To shame, to put to shame, to make ashamed (avergonzar). || — *Me abrasa la sed*, I'm parched, I'm dying of thirst. || *Morir abrasado*, to be burnt to death.
— V. pr. To burn: *el guisado se abrasó*, the stew burnt; *abrasarse de* or *en amor*, to burn with love. || To be scorched (plantas). || — *Abrasarse de calor*, to be sweltering. || *Abrasarse de sed*, to be dying of thirst.
abrasilado, da adj. Deep red.
abrasión f. Abrasion, graze. || Erosion (por el mar).
abrasivo, va adj. / s. m. Abrasive.
abrazadera f. Bracket, clasp.
abrazamiento m. Embrace, hug.
abrazar v. tr. To take in one's arms, to embrace. || To hug, to clasp in one's arms: *el padre abrazó al niño*, the father hugged the child, the father clasped the child in his arms. || To enclose (rodear). || FIG. To embrace, to comprise, to cover (comprender). | To embrace, to adopt (una causa, una religión).
— V. pr. To embrace.
abrazo m. Hug (con amistad), hug, embrace (con ternura). || — *Abrazos*, with love (en una carta). || *Dar un abrazo*, to hug, to embrace. || *Un (fuerte) abrazo de*, best wishes from, kind regards (entre amigos), with love from, love (entre un hombre y una mujer o entre mujeres), with all my love (entre íntimos).
abreboca m. y f. *Amer.* Daydreamer, absentminded person.
abrecartas m. inv. Letter opener, paper knife.
ábrego m. South wind (viento del Sur).
abrelatas m. inv. Tin opener [U. S., can opener].
abrevadero m. Drinking trough, water trough. || Watering place (natural). || *Amer.* Flooded mine.
abrevador, ra adj. Who waters, who gives water.
— M. Water trough, drinking trough (abrevadero).
abrevar v. tr. To water, to give water to. || TECN. To soak [skins]. || To water (regar).
— V. pr. To drink, to water (el ganado).

abreviación f. o **abreviamiento** m. Shortening, abridgement (acción). || Abridged text (texto abreviado).
abreviadamente adv. In short, briefly.
abreviado, da adj. Abridged, shortened (un texto). || Brief, short: *ésta es una explicación abreviada,* this is a brief explanation.
abreviar v. tr. To abridge, to shorten (un texto). || To shorten, to cut short (un plazo). || To cut short (una estancia). || To abbreviate (una palabra).
— V. intr. To take less time. || To be brief, to make it short (ser breve): *abrevia, que no tengo mucho tiempo,* be brief, I have not got much time.
abreviatura f. Abbreviation: *cuadro de abreviaturas,* table of abbreviations. || *En abreviatura,* abbreviated.
abribonarse v. pr. To become a rascal *o* a scoundrel.
abridor, ra adj. Who opens (persona). || Which opens (cosa).
— M. Opener. || Sleeper (arete de oro para las orejas). || Freestone peach (melocotón).
abrigada f. o **abrigadero** m. Shelter. || MAR. Natural harbour, sheltered cove. || *Amer.* Hideout (guarida).
abrigado, da adj. Sheltered, protected: *un lugar abrigado del viento,* a place sheltered from the wind. || Wrapped up (persona): *iba muy abrigado para no coger frío,* he was well wrapped up so as not to catch cold. || Cosy (confortable).
abrigaño m. Shelter. || AGR. Matt, matting.
abrigar v. tr. To shelter, to protect, to shield (proteger): *abrigar del viento,* to shelter from the wind. || FIG. To harbour, to cherish, to foster: *abrigar una esperanza,* to harbour a hope. | To have, to harbour (una sospecha, duda). || To be warm, to keep one warm: *este jersey abriga mucho,* this sweater is very warm *o* keeps one very warm. || To wrap up: *abrígalo bien que hace mucho frío,* wrap him up well because it is very cold. || MAR. To shelter.
— V. pr. To take shelter, to shelter: *abrigarse de la lluvia,* to take shelter from the rain. || To wrap o.s. up, to wrap up, to cover o.s. up (con prendas de vestir): *abrígate bien,* wrap up well.
abrigo m. Shelter (refugio). || Overcoat (prenda de hombre). || Coat (de mujer): *abrigo de pieles,* fur coat. || FIG. Protection, shield, shelter (protección). || MAR. Natural harbour. || — *Al abrigo de,* sheltered from, protected from (del viento, frío, etc.), safe from (del peligro), with *o* under the protection of (de la ley). || *De abrigo,* warm: *prendas de abrigo,* warm clothes; first-class, proper: *un tonto de abrigo,* a first-class fool; to be avoided (de cuidado). || *Fugarse al abrigo de la noche,* to flee under cover of darkness.
ábrigo m. South wind (viento sur).
abril m. April. || FIG. Springtime, youth. || — *En abril, aguas mil,* April showers bring May flowers. || *Muchacha de quince abriles,* a young girl of fifteen.
abrileño, ña adj. April, spring: *una mañana abrileña,* an April morning.
abrillantador m. Lapidary, polisher (persona). || Polishing tool, burnisher (instrumento). || Polish (producto).
abrillantar v. tr. To polish, to burnish (pulir). || To cut (piedras preciosas). || FIG. To enhance.
abrimiento m. Opening.
abrir v. tr. To open (la puerta, un libro, los ojos, una carta, una cuenta, una herida, una negociación, el fuego). || To make: *abrir un hueco,* to make a hole. || To build, to make: *abrir una carretera, un túnel,* to build a road, a tunnel. || To dig, to make: *abrir un surco,* to dig a trench. || To lance (un absceso). || To dig, to sink (un pozo). || To split open: *abrir la cabeza a alguien con la espada,* to split s.o.'s head open with one's sword. || To put up, to open (paraguas). || COM. To open: *abrir una cuenta,* to open an account. || To open (un establecimiento, un curso escolar, una suscripción). || To turn on (grifos). || FIG. To open (la frontera, la universidad). | To whet (el apetito). | To head, to lead: *abrir el desfile,* to head the procession. || — FIG. *Abrir el ojo,* to keep one's eyes open, to be careful. || *Abrir en canal un animal,* to slit an animal open. || FIG. *Abrir la mano,* to be more lenient. | *Abrir los ojos,* v. OJO. | *Abrir un abismo entre,* to open a gulf between. || *Abrir una puerta de par en par,* to open a door wide. || *Abrir un libro,* to cut the pages of a book (con cortapapel). || *A medio abrir,* half-open. || *En un abrir y cerrar de ojos,* in the twinkling of an eye, in a wink, in a jiffy.
— V. intr. To open up: *¡abre!,* open up!
— V. pr. To open (las flores, un paracaídas, las tiendas, la puerta). || To clear (el tiempo). || To burst (un absceso). || To sprain: *abrirse el tobillo,* to sprain one's ankle. || To split open: *abrirse la cabeza,* to split open one's head. || To look, to open (ventana). || To open (puerta): *puertas que se abren a la calle,* doors which open onto the street. || To confide (sincerarse): *abrirse con uno,* to confide in s.o. || To open up (la Tierra). || To spread out, to open out, to unfold (extenderse): *el paisaje se abría ante nosotros,* the countryside spread out before us. || *Amer.* To leave, to go away (largarse). | To back down, to give up (rajarse). || — *Abrirse camino,* v. CAMINO. || *Abrirse paso,* v. PASO.

— OBSERV. The past participle of *abrir* is irregular (abierto, ta).

abrochador m. Buttonhook.
abrochadura f. o **abrochamiento** m. Buttoning (con botones). || Fastening (con broches).
abrochar v. tr. To button, to button up, to do up (cerrar con botones). || To fasten (con broche). || To tie [up], to do up (los zapatos). || To lace up (un corsé). || *Amer.* To seize, to grasp (agarrar).
abrogación f. Abrogation, repeal.
abrogar v. tr. To abrogate, to repeal (anular).
abrojal m. Thistle patch.
abrojo m. BOT. Thistle. || MIL. Caltrop. || — Pl. MAR. Reef, *sing.* || FIG. Pains (dolores).
abroncar v. tr. FAM. To tear a strip off [U.S., to bawl out, to get mad at] (un superior a un inferior). | To boo, to whistle (abuchear). | To shame (avergonzar).
— V. pr. FAM. To be ashamed (avergonzarse). | To get annoyed, to loose one's temper (enfadarse).
abroquelado, da adj. Shield-shaped. || BOT. Peltate.
abroquelarse v. pr. To shield o.s. || FIG. To shield o.s., to defend o.s. (escudarse).
abrótano m. BOT. Southernwood.
abrumado, da adj. Overwhelmed: *abrumado por tantas atenciones,* overwhelmed by so much attention; *abrumado de trabajo,* overwhelmed with work.
abrumador, ra adj. Overwhelming, exhausting (trabajo, calor). || Overwhelming, crushing (derrota, mayoría). || Overwhelming, damning (testimonio).
abrumar v. tr. To overwhelm, to get on top of, to overcome (trabajo, preocupaciones, carga, años). || To overwhelm: *su noticia me abrumó,* his news overwhelmed me; *abrumar a preguntas,* to overwhelm with questions; *abrumar con atenciones,* to overwhelm with attention.
— V. pr. To become foggy *o* misty.
abrupto, ta adj. Craggy, rugged (roca). || Steep, sheer, abrupt (pendiente). || Abrupt: *tono abrupto,* abrupt tone.
abrutado, da adj. Brutish.
Abruzos n. pr. m. pl. GEOGR. Abruzzi.
absceso m. MED. Abscess: *el absceso se ha abierto,* the abscess has burst.
abscisa f. MAT. Abscissa.
abscisión f. MED. Abscission.
absentismo m. Absenteeism (de trabajadores). || Landlord absenteeism (de terratenientes).
absentista m. Absentee landlord (terrateniente). || Absentee (obrero).
ábsida f. o **ábside** m. y f. ARQ. Apse. || ASTR. Apsis.
absidal adj. Apsidal: *ornamentos absidales,* apsidal decorations.
absidiola f. o **absidiolo** m. ARQ. Apsidiole, absidiole.
absintio m. Absinthe, absinth.
absolución f. REL. Absolution (perdón): *el sacerdote me dio la absolución,* the priest granted me absolution. || JUR. Acquittal (de un reo).
absoluta f. Dogmatic statement *o* assertion. || MIL. Discharge (del servicio militar).
absolutamente adv. Absolutely, completely: *absolutamente absurdo,* absolutely absurd. || Not at all (de ninguna manera). || *Absolutamente nada,* nothing at all.
absolutismo m. Absolutism.
absolutista adj./s. Absolutist.
absoluto, ta adj. Absolute: *poder absoluto,* absolute power; *valor absoluto,* absolute value. || — *En absoluto,* absolutely (enteramente): *está prohibido en absoluto,* it is absolutely forbidden; not at all: *¿Le gusta esta película? — En absoluto,* Do you like this film? — Not at all. || *Nada en absoluto,* nothing at all, not anything. || *Obtener la mayoría absoluta,* to obtain an absolute majority.
absolutorio, ria adj. JUR. Of not guilty, of acquittal: *veredicto absolutorio,* verdict of acquittal.
absolvederas f. pl. FAM. Excessive leniency (*sing.*) of a confessor. || *Tener buenas* or *bravas absolvederas,* to be over-lenient.
absolver* v. tr. REL. To absolve (a un pecador). || JUR. To declare not guilty, to acquit (declarar no culpable).

— OBSERV. The past participle of *absolver* is *absuelto.*

absorbencia f. Absorbency.
absorbente adj. Absorbent. || FIG. Absorbing, engrossing (trabajo, conversación). | Demanding (que exige mucho tiempo).
— M. Absorbent.
absorber v. tr. To absorb, to soak up: *la esponja absorbe el agua,* sponge absorbs water. || To suck in (aspiradora). || To attract, to catch: *este tejido absorbe mucho polvo,* this material attracts a lot of dust. || FIG. To absorb, to take up (consumir): *la lectura absorbe todo mi tiempo,* reading absorbs all my time. || FIG. *Sus estudios le absorben tanto que nunca sale,* he becomes so absorbed *o* engrossed in his studies that he never goes out, he spends so much time studying that he never goes out.

— OBSERV. This verb has two past participles: *absorbido* and *absorto.* The first is used in compound tenses and the second as an adjective.

absorción f. Absorption. || FIG. Engrossment, absorption. || QUÍM. Absorption.
absorto, ta adj. Absorbed, engrossed: *absorto en su trabajo, en la lectura,* absorbed in one's work, in a book. || Astonished, astounded: *estoy absorto ante sus progresos,* I'm astonished at his progress. || *Absorto en sus pensamientos,* deep in thought.

abstemio, mia adj. Temperate, teetotal, abstemious (p.us.). || *Soy abstemio*, I am a teetotaller.
— M. y f. Teetotaller, abstainer.
abstención f. Abstention.
abstencionismo m. Abstentionism.
abstencionista adj./s. Abstentionist.
abstenerse* v. pr. To refrain: *abstenerse de intervenir*, to refrain from intervening. || To abstain: *abstenerse del vino, del tabaco*, to abstain from wine, from smoking. || To abstain (en una votación). || To give up, to stop: *abstente de decir tonterías*, stop talking nonsense. || *En la duda abstente*, when in doubt, don't.
abstinencia f. Abstinence. || REL. Fasting.
abstinente adj. Abstinent.
abstracción f. Abstraction. || Concentration, engrossment (concentración mental). || *Hacer abstracción de*, to leave aside.
abstracto, ta adj. Abstract: *pintura abstracta*, abstract painting. || GRAM. Abstract. || — *En abstracto*, in the abstract. || *Lo abstracto*, the abstract.
abstraer* v. tr. To abstract, to consider apart.
— V. intr. *Abstraer de*, to leave aside.
— V. pr. To absorb o.s., to engross o.s.
— OBSERV. This verb has two past participles: *abstraído* and *abstracto*. Only the first is used in compound tenses.
abstraído, da adj. Absorbed, engrossed: *estar abstraído por la lectura*, to be engrossed in a book. || FIG. Absentminded (distraído). || Isolated (aislado).
abstruso, sa adj. Abstruse.
absuelto, ta adj. REL. Absolved: *absuelto de todo pecado*, absolved from all sin. || JUR. Acquitted (un reo): *salir absuelto*, to be acquitted.
absurdidad f. Absurdity.
absurdo, da adj. Absurd. || — *Lo absurdo*, absurdity: *el colmo de lo absurdo*, the height of absurdity; the realm of the absurd: *caer en lo absurdo*, to fall into the realm of the absurd. || *Lo absurdo sería perder esta oportunidad*, it would be absurd to waste this opportunity.
— M. Absurd thing, absurdity (disparate): *decir absurdos*, to say absurd things.
abubilla f. Hoopoe (pájaro).
abuchear v. tr. To boo, to jeer at: *los actores fueron abucheados*, the actors were booed.
abucheo m. FAM. Booing, jeering: *salió bajo un abucheo*, he left amidst booing.
abuela f. Grandmother. || FIG. Old woman (mujer vieja). || FIG. y FAM. *¡Cuéntaselo a tu abuela!*, pull the other leg, it's got bells on [U.S., tell it to the marines]. | *¡Éramos pocos y parió la abuela!*, that's all we needed! | *No tener* or *no necesitar abuela*, not to be afraid of blowing one's own trumpet.
abuelastro, tra m. y f. Father *o* mother of one's father-in-law *o* mother-in-law. || Step-grandfather *o* step-grandmother.
abuelita f. Granny, grandma, nanny. || *Amer.* Baby's bonnet.
abuelito m. Grandpa, grandad.
abuelo m. Grandfather: *sólo me queda un abuelo*, I only have one grandfather left. || FIG. Old man (anciano). || — Pl. Grandparents. || Ancestors (antepasados): *nuestros abuelos eran muy valientes*, our ancestors were very brave. || FAM. Short hairs on the back of the neck (pelo).
abuhardillado, da adj. With an attic *o* garret.
abulense adj. [Of *o* from] Ávila.
— M. y f. Native *o* inhabitant of Ávila.
abulia f. Lack of willpower, abulia.
abúlico, ca adj. Lacking in willpower, abulic, weak-willed.
abultado, da adj. Bulky, big: *este paquete es muy abultado*, this parcel is very bulky. || Thick: *labios abultados*, thick lips. || Swollen: *tengo los labios abultados porque me ha picado una avispa*, my lips are swollen because a wasp stung me. || FIG. Exaggerated (exagerado). | Overwhelming (abrumador).
abultamiento m. Bulkiness (bulto). || Swelling (hinchazón). || Enlargement (crecimiento). || FIG. Exaggeration.
abultar v. tr. To enlarge (aumentar). || To swell (hinchar). || FIG. To exaggerate: *abultar una historia*, to exaggerate a story.
— V. intr. To be bulky: *este ropero abulta mucho*, this wardrobe is very bulky.
abundamiento m. Abundance. || *A mayor abundamiento*, furthermore (además), with all the more reason, with greater justification (con mayor razón).
abundancia f. Abundance, plenty. || — *Cuerno de la abundancia*, horn of plenty. || *De la abundancia del corazón habla la boca*, what the heart feels the mind speaks. || *En abundancia*, in abundance, in plenty. || FIG. *Nadar en la abundancia*, to be rolling in money.
abundante adj. Abundant, in abundance, plentiful. || *Abundante en*, abounding in.
abundar v. intr. To be plentiful, to abound: *la plata abunda en México*, silver is plentiful in Mexico. || To be rich in: *México abunda en plata*, Mexico is rich in silver. || — *Abundar en la opinión de*, to share the opinion of, to agree completely with, to be in complete agreement with. || *Lo que abunda no daña*, store is no sore.
abundoso, sa adj. Abundant, plentiful.
abuñolar* o **abuñuelar** v. tr. To make fritter-shaped. || To deep-fry (huevos, buñuelos).
¡abur! interj. FAM. Cheerio!, bye-bye!
aburguesamiento m. Adoption of a bourgeois way of life.
aburguesarse v. pr. To become bourgeois.
aburrarse v. pr. To become rough *o* brutish.
aburrido, da adj. Bored, weary: *estoy aburrido*, I am bored. || Boring, tiresome, tedious (que aburre): *es una película aburrida*, it is a boring film. || Tired, sick, fed up (fam.): *aburrido de la vida*, tired of *o* sick of *o* fed up with life.
aburrimiento m. Boredom, weariness (estado de aburrido): *cara de aburrimiento*, look of boredom. || Bore (cosa, persona). || — *¡Qué aburrimiento!*, what a bore! || *Ser un aburrimiento*, to be a bore, to be boring: *esta conferencia es un aburrimiento*, this lecture is boring.
aburrir v. tr. To bore, to weary: *aburrir con un largo discurso*, to bore with a long speech.
— V. pr. To be *o* to get bored, to be *o* to get weary. || FIG. y FAM. *Aburrirse como una ostra*, to be *o* to get bored to death, to be *o* to get bored stiff.
abusar v. intr. To go too far. || — *Abusar de*, to take advantage of: *abusar de un empleado*, to take advantage of an employee; to abuse, to misuse (la autoridad), to abuse, to make unfair demands on, to impose upon (la amabilidad, la hospitalidad), to betray (la confianza de alguien), to waste (el tiempo), to go beyond the limits of (los derechos). || *Abusar de la bebida, del tabaco, etc.*, to drink, to smoke, etc., too much.
abusivo, va adj. Excessive, exorbitant, extortionate: *precio abusivo*, excessive price. || Wrong, improper (impropio).
abuso m. Abuse, misuse (de autoridad). || Betrayal (de confianza). || Misuse, improper use (de palabra). || — *Abuso de la amabilidad de alguien*, unfair demand on *o* imposition on s.o's kindness. || *Es un abuso cobrar tanto dinero*, it is disgraceful to charge so much money.
abusón, ona adj. FAM. Selfish (aprovechado). || Barefaced, shameless (descarado).
— M. y f. Selfish person, person who takes unfair advantage of others (aprovechado). || Barefaced *o* shameless person (descarado).
abyección f. Abjection, wretchedness.
abyecto, ta adj. Abject, wretched: *condición abyecta*, abject condition.
acá adv. Here, over here: *ven acá*, come here; *vente para acá*, come over here. || — *Acá y allá* or *acullá*, here and there: *poner unas citas acá y allá*, to put a few quotations in here and there. || *¿De cuándo acá?*, since when?, how long? || *De acá para allá*, to and fro, up and down: *anduve de acá para allá*, I walked up and down. || *De ayer acá*, since yesterday (desde ayer), recently, lately (recientemente). || *De ... para acá*, from here to ...: *de Londres para acá hay veinte millas*, it is twenty miles from here to London. || *Desde entonces acá* or *de cuando acá*, since then, from then on. || *Más acá*, nearer (v. OBSERV.): *ven más acá*, come nearer. || *Más acá de*, on this side of. || *Muy acá*, very near. || *No tan acá*, not so near.
— OBSERV. *Acá* is less precise than *aquí*; thus *acá* has degrees of comparison not possible with *aquí*. — In certain Latin American countries (Argentina, for example) *acá* is almost always used to translate *here*.
acabable adj. Finishable, which can be finished.
acabado, da adj. Finished, completed (concluido): *tenemos que devolver el trabajo acabado lo más pronto posible*, we must give back the finished work as soon as possible. || Finished: *producto acabado*, finished product. || Perfect (perfecto). || Accomplished (persona): *un historiador acabado*, an accomplished historian. || Spent, worn-out (viejo, agotado). || Ruined (salud). || *Yo, acabado de llegar, dije...*, no sooner had I arrived than I said...
— M. Finish: *el acabado de un coche, de un cuadro*, the finish of a car, of a picture.
acabador, ra m. y f. Finisher.
acaballadero m. Stud farm.
acaballado, da adj. Horselike, horsy: *cara acaballada*, horselike face.
acaballar v. tr. To cover (el caballo).
acaballonador m. AGR. Ridger.
acaballonar v. tr. AGR. To ridge (un campo).
acabamiento m. Finishing, completion (acción de acabar). || End, finish (término). || TECN. Finish.
acabañar v. intr. To build a hut (los pastores).
acabar v. tr. To finish, to complete (terminar): *he acabado el libro*, I've finished the book. || To finish off (rematar). || To put the finishing touches to (perfilar). || To finish: *no ha acabado de tomarse la leche*, he has not finished drinking his milk. || To complete: *acabar su ruina*, to complete one's ruin. || *Amer.* To speak badly of, to gossip about (murmurar de). || *Acabar sus días*, to end one's days, to die.
— V. intr. To finish, to end: *acabar en punta*, to end *o* to finish in a point. || To finish: *ven cuando acabes*, come when you finish. || To end up, to finish up: *acabar agotado*, to end up exhausted. || — FAM. *¡Acaba de parir!*, let's have it!, spit it out! | *¡Acabáramos!*, at last!, finally! || *Acabar con*, to end with, to finish with (terminar con), to put paid to, to finish off: *por fin he acabado con este trabajo*, I've finally put paid

to this work; to finish with, to break with: *acabar con su novia*, to finish with one's fiancée; to get rid of, to finish with, to put an end to: *acabar con la influencia extranjera*, to get rid of foreign influence; to be the end of, to finish, to kill: *este clima va a acabar conmigo*, this climate will be the end of me. || *Acabar de*, to have just: *acaba de morir*, he has just died; *acababa de terminar su trabajo cuando...*, he had just finished his work when...; to finish: *cuando acabe de hacer esto*, when I finish doing this. || *Acabar de una vez*, to finish once and for all. || *Acabar diciendo*, to finish by saying (al final), to end up saying (en fin). || *Acabar en*, to end in. || *Acabar mal*, to come to a nasty end. || *Acabar por* (seguido de infinitivo), in the end, finally, eventually: *acabó por reconocerlo*, in the end he recognized him. || *Cuenta y no acaba*, he never stops talking about it. || *Es cosa* or *es el cuento de nunca acabar*, v. CUENTO. || *No acabo de comprender*, I don't quite *o* fully understand.

— V. pr. To finish, to end, to come to an end (terminarse): *se acabó el programa a las ocho*, the programme finished at eight o'clock. || To run out (gastarse): *se acabó el carbón*, the coal has run out. || To die (morirse). || — *Se acabó*, that's it, that's all. || *Se le acabó el dinero*, his money ran out, he ran out of money. || *Se me acabó la paciencia*, my patience has run out, I've lost my patience. || *Y san se acabó*, and that's all there is to it, and that's the end of it.

acabestrar v. tr. To accustom to a halter.

acabildar v. tr. To rally together.

acabóse m. FAM. End, limit (el colmo): *esto fue el acabóse*, this was the end.

acacalote m. *Amer.* Cormorant (ave).

acacia f. Acacia. || *Acacia blanca* or *falsa*, locust tree.

acacóyotl m. *Amer.* BOT. Job's tears.

acachetar v. tr. TAUR. To finish off [with a dagger].

acachetear v. tr. To slap.

academia f. Academy: *academia militar, naval*, military, naval academy. || Academy, school: *academia de baile, de idiomas*, dancing, language school. || ARTES. Nude study. || — *Academia de música*, conservatoire. || *La Real Academia Española*, the Spanish Academy.

academicismo m. Academicism.

académico, ca adj. Academic, academical. || University: *título académico*, university degree.

— M. y f. Academician, member of an academy: *académico correspondiente*, corresponding academician.

academismo m. Academism.

academista m. Academician, member of an academy.

acaecedero, ra adj. Possible.

acaecer* v. intr. To happen, to occur, to take place (ocurrir).

— OBSERV. This verb is defective and exists only in the third person.

acaecimiento m. Event, happening, occurrence.

acalabazado, da adj. Pumpkin-shaped.

acalabrotar v. tr. MAR. To braid, to twist [into a cable].

acalefo m. ZOOL. Acaleph. || — Pl. Acalepha.

acalenturarse v. pr. To become feverish.

acalia f. BOT. Marshmallow (malvavisco).

acaloradamente adv. FIG. Heatedly, fiercely: *discutir acaloradamente*, to argue heatedly. || Eagerly, keenly, enthusiastically: *defender acaloradamente un proyecto*, to defend a plan keenly.

acalorado, da adj. Hot: *estoy acalorado por tanto esfuerzo*, all this exertion has made me hot. || FIG. Excited, worked up: *acalorado por la disputa* worked up by the argument. | Heated: *una discusión acalorada*, a heated argument. | Eager, keen, enthusiastic: *es un defensor acalorado de mis ideas*, he is a keen supporter of my ideas.

acaloramiento m. Heat (del tiempo, por el esfuerzo). || FIG. Enthusiasm, eagerness, keenness: *defender una causa con mucho acaloramiento*, to defend a cause with great enthusiasm. | Heat: *en el acaloramiento de la pelea*, in the heat of the battle.

acalorar v. tr. To warm up, to make warm: *el correr me acalora*, running makes me warm. || FIG. To excite, to arouse, to inflame: *acalorar a las masas*, to excite the masses.

— V. pr. To get warm *o* hot. || FIG. To get excited, to get worked up (airarse). | To become enthusiastic, to become eager (entusiasmarse). | To become heated (una discusión).

acallar v. tr. To quieten, to silence: *el orador no consiguió acallar a la multitud*, the speaker was unable to quieten the crowd. || FIG. To ease (el dolor, la conciencia). | To appease (el hambre). | To silence (la crítica). | To pacify (a alguien que está enfadado).

acamar v. tr. To flatten (las plantas).

acamastronarse v. pr. *Amer.* To become sly *o* crafty.

acamellado, da adj. Camel-like.

acamellonar v. tr. *Amer.* AGR. To ridge.

acampanado, da adj. Bell-shaped. || Wide-mouthed (vasija). || Flared (ropa): *falda acampanada*, flared skirt; *pantalones acampanados*, flared trousers.

acampanar v. tr. To shape like a bell. || To flare (costura).

— V. pr. To become bell-shaped.

acampar v. tr. To encamp, to camp: *acampar tropas en el valle*, to encamp troops in the valley.

— V. intr. To camp, to encamp: *acampar en la playa*, to camp on the beach.

— V. pr. To camp, to encamp.

acanalado, da adj. Grooved (con estrías). || ARQ. Fluted: *columna acanalada*, fluted column. || Ribbed: *calcetines acanalados*, ribbed sòcks.

— M. V. ACANALADURA.

acanalador m. TECN. Grooving plane (de carpintero).

acanaladura f. Groove (ranura). || ARQ. Fluting, flute.

acanalar v. tr. To groove. || ARQ. To flute.

acanallado, da adj. Base, low, disreputable.

acanallar v. tr. To debase, to drag down (fam.).

— V. pr. To become debased, to go to the dogs (fam.).

acanelado, da adj. Cinnamon-coloured (color). || Cinnamon-flavoured (sabor).

acantilado, da adj. Steep, sheer, precipitous (abrupto). || Shelving (fondo del mar). || Rocky (rocoso).

— M. Cliff: *los acantilados de Dover*, the cliffs of Dover. || Steep slope (pendiente).

acanto m. ARQ. y BOT. Acanthus.

acantonamiento m. MIL. Cantonment, quarters, *pl.* (sitio). | Quartering (acción).

acantonar v. tr. MIL. To quarter.

acantopterigios m. pl. ZOOL. Acanthopterygii.

acaobado, da adj. Mahogany (color).

acaparador, ra adj. Monopolistic. || FIG. Acquisitive (instinto).

— M. y f. Monopolist, monopolizer. || Hoarder (de géneros).

aca aramiento m. Monopolizing. || Monopolizing, cornering (mercado, ventas). || Hoarding (existencias). || Monopolizing, commanding (de la atención).

acaparar v. tr. To monopolize. || To monopolize, to corner (el mercado, las ventas). || To hoard (las existencias). || To monopolize, to command (la atención).

acaparrosado, da adj. Copper-coloured, coppery.

acápite m. *Amer.* Paragraph. || *Amer. Punto acápite*, v. PUNTO.

acaponado, da adj. Effeminate: *voz acaponada*, effeminate voice. || Castrated (capado).

acaracolado, da adj. Spiral.

acaramelado, da adj. Caramelled, caramel-covered. || Caramel-coloured (color). || FIG. Overpolite (obsequioso). | Syrupy, sugary, sickly: *una voz acaramelada*, a syrupy voice. || FIG. *Estar acaramelados*, to be starry-eyed (novios).

acaramelar v. tr. To caramel, to coat with caramel.

— V. pr. FIG. y FAM. To be sugar-sweet (ser muy obsequioso). | To gaze lovingly at each other (mirar con cariño).

acardenalado, da adj. Covered with bruises, black and blue.

acardenalar v. tr. To beat black and blue, to cover with bruises, to bruise.

— V. pr. To become covered with bruises, to turn black and blue, to get bruised.

acardenillarse v. pr. To become covered with verdigris.

acariciador, ra adj. Caressing.

acariciante adj. Caressing.

acariciar v. tr. To caress, to fondle (personas). || To stroke (animales). || To brush (rozar). || FIG. To cherish, to harbour: *acariciar grandes ambiciones*, to cherish great ambitions. | To have in mind (proyectos, ideas).

acáridos m. pl. ZOOL. Acaridae.

acarminado, da adj. Crimson, carmine.

acarnerado, da adj. With a sheep-like head (caballo).

ácaro m. ZOOL. Acarus (arácnido).

acarralar v. tr. To catch (un hilo, una tela). || To ladder (una media).

acarreador, ra adj. Transporting, conveying.

— M. y f. Transporter, conveyor. || — M. Haulage contractor, haulier.

acarreamiento m. V. ACARREO.

acarrear v. tr. To transport, to convey, to carry, to haul (llevar). || To carry (arrastrar). || To carry along (un río). || FIG. To cause, to bring about, to bring: *el terremoto acarreó la ruina del país*, the earthquake brought about the country's ruin.

acarreo m. Transporting, conveying, carrying (transporte). || Haulage *o* transport costs, *pl.* (precio de transporte). || AGR. Bringing-in (cosechas). || GEOL. Alluvium (arrastre). || *Tierras de acarreo*, alluvium.

acarroñarse v. pr. (Ant.). To decay. || FAM. *Amer.* To get scared, to turn chicken (acobardarse).

acartonado, da adj. Cardboard-like. || FIG. y FAM. Wizened: *una cara acartonada*, a wizened face.

acartonarse v. pr. To go stiff *o* hard. || FIG. y FAM. To become wizened.

acasamatado, da adj. Casamated.

acaso m. Chance.

— Adv. Perhaps, maybe: *acaso venga*, perhaps he will come. || (Ant.). By chance (por casualidad). || — *¿Acaso...?*, by any chance...?: *¿acaso ha sido él?*, was it he by any chance? || *Al acaso*, to chance: *esta decisión no hay que dejarla al acaso*, this decision must not be left to chance. || *Por si acaso*, in case, just in case: *me llevo el paraguas por si acaso*, I am taking my umbrella just in case. || *Probablemente no podré ir de veraneo, si acaso en septiembre*, I shall probably not be able to take any summer holidays, but if I do, it will be in September. || *Si acaso*, if: *si acaso llueve espérame dentro*, if it rains *o* if it should rain, wait for me inside.

acatable adj. Worthy of respect.

acatadamente adv. With respect.

acatador, ra adj. Respectful.

acatamiento m. Respect (a una persona). || Observance, respect: *acatamiento de las leyes*, observance of the law.

acatar v. tr. To respect, to heed: *acatar los consejos de los mayores*, to respect the advice of one's elders. || To observe, to respect: *acatar la ley*, to observe the law. || *Amer.* To notice (notar).

acatarrarse v. pr. To catch a cold. || *Amer.* FAM. To get drunk.

acaudalado, da adj. Rich, wealthy (rico).

acaudalar v. tr. To accumulate, to amass.

acaudillador, ra adj. (P. us.). Commanding.
— M. y f. Leader, commander.

acaudillamiento m. Leadership, command.

acaudillar v. tr. To lead, to command.

acaule adj. BOT. Acaulescent, acauline.

acayú m. *Amer.* Mahogany (caoba).

acceder v. intr. To agree, to accede, to consent: *accedió a recibirnos*, he agreed to receive us. || To accede (al trono, a los honores).

accesibilidad f. Accessibility.

accesible adj. Accessible: *montaña accesible*, accessible mountain. || Approachable: *un jefe muy accesible*, a very approachable boss.

accesión f. Agreement, consent (consentimiento). || Accession (al poder). || JUR. Accession. || MED. Attack (de fiebre).

accésit m. Honourable mention, accessit.
— OBSERV. According to the Spanish Academy the plural of this word is *accésit*, but *accésits* is often found.

acceso m. Access: *tener acceso al jardín*, to have access to the garden. || Accession (al poder). || Access, approach (camino). || Approach (de un avión). || Sexual intercourse. || MED. Access (de fiebre). || Fit, attack (de tos, de locura, de ira). || FIG. Fit, moment (de generosidad). | Outburst, fit, outbreak: *acceso de fanatismo*, outburst of fanaticism.

accesoria f. Outbuilding, annexe.

accesorio, ria adj. Accessory. || *Gastos accesorios*, incidental expenses, contingencies.
— M. Accessory: *accesorios de automóvil*, car accessories. || — Pl. TEATR. Props, properties.

accesorista m. y f. TEATR. Property man *o* woman.

accidentado, da adj. Uneven (terreno). || FIG. Troubled, agitated: *una vida accidentada*, a troubled life. | Eventful (complicado). || Injured (persona). || Damaged (coche).
— M. y f. Accident victim.

accidental adj. Accidental, unintentional (involuntario). || Chance, fortuitous, unexpected (casual).
— M. MÚS. Accidental.

accidentarse v. pr. To have an accident, to be involved in an accident.

accidente m. Accident: *accidente de carretera*, road accident; *sufrir un accidente*, to have an accident. || GEOGR. Unevenness, irregularity (del terreno). || MED. Faint (desmayo). || GRAM. Accidence. || MÚS. Accidental. || Accident (cosa no esencial). || — *Accidente de trabajo*, industrial accident. || *Por accidente*, by accident, accidentally.

acción f. Action (en general): *la acción del ácido sobre los metales*, the action of acid on metals. || Deed, act: *ejecutar una buena acción*, to do a good deed. || COM. Share: *acción nominal, al portador*, registered, bearer share. || JUR. Action. || TEATR. Acting (de un actor). | Action (de una obra). || MIL. Action, fighting (combate). || — Pl. COM. Shares, stock, *sing.*, stocks: *tengo acciones en una compañía*, I hold stock in a company. || — *Acción de gracias*, thanksgiving. || *De acción retardada*, delayed-action (mecanismo). || JUR. *Ejercitar una acción*, to bring an action. || *Esfera de acción*, field of action. || *Ganar a uno la acción*, to beat s.o. to it. || *Hombre de acción*, man of action. || *Radio de acción*, range of action, operating range. || *Unir la acción a la palabra*, to suit the action to the word.
— Interj. CINEM. Action!

accionamiento m. Working.

accionar v. tr. To work, to actuate (una palanca). || To drive, to work (una máquina). || *Amer.* JUR. To bring an action against.
— V. intr. To gesticulate.

accionariado m. Shareholders, *pl.*, stockholders, *pl.*

accionista m. y f. COM. Shareholder, stockholder.

acebal m. o **acebada** f. o **acebado** m. Holly thicket.

acebo m. BOT. Holly, holly tree.

acebollado, da adj. Affected with ring shake (madera).

acebolladura f. Ring shake, cup shake.

acebrado, da adj. Striped.

acebuchal m. Grove of wild olive trees.

acebuche m. Wild olive tree.

acebuchina f. Wild olive.

acecinar v. tr. To cure (la carne).
— V. pr. FIG. To become wizened.
— OBSERV. Do not confuse with *asesinar*, to assasinate.

acechadera f. Hiding place.

acechanza f. V. ACECHO.
— OBSERV. Do not confuse with *asechanza*, ambush.

acechar v. tr. To watch (observar). || To lie in wait for (esperar). || To stalk (un animal).

acecho m. Watching, observation. || — *Cazar al acecho*, to stalk. || *Estar al acecho*, to be on the watch *o* on the lookout.

acedar v. tr. To turn sour, to sour (agriar). || FIG. To sour, to embitter.
— V. pr. To turn sour, to become sour (ponerse agrio). || To wither (ajarse).
— OBSERV. Do not confuse with *asedar*, to soften.

acedera f. BOT. Sorrel.

acederaque m. Cinnamon tree (árbol).

acederón m. Type of sorrel (planta).

acedía f. Sourness. || Acidity (en el estómago). || FIG. Sourness, harshness, unpleasantness (desabrimiento). || Withered state (de las plantas). || ZOOL. Plaice (pez).

acedo, da adj. Sour (ácido). || FIG. Sour, harsh, unpleasant (carácter).

acefalía f. o **acefalismo** m. Acephalia (ausencia de cabeza).

acéfalo, la adj. Acephalous (sin cabeza). || FIG. Leaderless.

aceitada f. Olive oil cake (torta de aceite).

aceitado m. Oiling.

aceitar v. tr. To oil. || CULIN. To add oil to.

aceitazo m. Thick oil.

aceite m. Oil: *aceite de oliva, de cacahuete*, olive, groundnut oil; *aceite de motor*, engine oil. || — *Aceite alcanforado*, camphorated oil. || *Aceite bruto*, crude oil (petróleo). || *Aceite de hígado de bacalao*, cod-liver oil. || *Aceite de linaza*, linseed oil. || *Aceite de ricino*, castor oil. || *Aceite de vitriolo*, oil of vitriol. || *Aceite lampante*, paraffin oil [U.S., kerosene]. || *Aceite pesado*, heavy oil: || *Aceite secante*, siccative oil. || *Aceite vegetal*, vegetable oil. || FIG. *Balsa de aceite*, millpond. | *Echar aceite al fuego*, to add fuel to the fire, to pour oil on the flames. | *Extenderse como mancha de aceite*, to spread like wildfire.

aceitera f. Oil bottle (vasija para el aceite). || Oilcan (alcuza).

aceitería f. Oilshop.

aceitero, ra adj. Oil: *producción aceitera*, oil production.
— M. Oil seller.

aceitón m. Thick oil. || Oil sediment, dregs, *pl.* (impurezas).

aceitoso, sa adj. Oily. || *Lo aceitoso*, oiliness.

aceituna f. Olive: *aceituna rellena*, stuffed olive. || — *Aceituna gordal*, queen olive. || *Aceituna picudilla*, crescent olive.

aceitunada f. Olive harvest.

aceitunado, da adj. Olive: *tiene una tez aceitunada*, he has an olive complexion.

aceitunero, ra m. y f. Olive seller (que las vende). || Olive harvester (que coge aceitunas). || — M. Olive store.

aceitunil adj. Olive.

aceituno, na adj. *Amer.* Olive, olive-coloured.
— M. Olive tree (árbol). || *Aceituno silvestre*, wild olive tree.

aceleración f. Acceleration. || FIG. Speeding up. || AUT. *Poder de aceleración*, acceleration.

aceleradamente adv. Quickly, rapidly, speedily.

acelerado, da adj. Quick, rapid, fast: *paso acelerado*, fast pace. || FÍS. Accelerated: *movimiento acelerado*, accelerated movement.
— F. Acceleration. || — M. CINEM. Quick motion.

acelerador, ra adj. Accelerating.
— M. Accelerator.

aceleramiento m. Acceleration.

acelerar v. tr. e intr. To accelerate. || FIG. To speed up. || *Acelerar el paso*, to quicken one's pace.
— V. pr. To hurry, to hasten.

aceleratriz adj. f. Accelerating: *fuerza aceleratriz*, accelerating force.

acelerón m. Sudden acceleration. || — *Dar acelerones al motor*, to rev the engine. || *Dar un acelerón*, to put one's foot down.

acelga f. Beet (planta). || FAM. *Cara de acelga*, dismal face, face a mile long (mal humor), washed-out face (por falta de salud).

acémila f. Mule, pack animal. || FAM. Ass (persona ruda).

acemilero m. Mule driver, muleteer.

acemita f. Bran bread

acemite m. Bran mixed with flour.

acendrado, da adj. Pure, untarnished: *amor acendrado*, pure love.

acendramiento m. Refining, purifying.

acendrar v. tr. To refine (metales). || FIG. To purify (purificar).

acensuar v. tr. To tax.

acento m. Accent: "*ático*" *lleva acento ortográfico*, "ático" has a written accent. || Accent, stress, emphasis: *el acento cae en la última sílaba*, the stress is on the last syllable. || Accent (manera de pronunciar): *acento andaluz*, Andalusian accent. || MÚS. Accent. || *Acento tónico*, tonic accent, stress.

acentuación f. Accentuation, stress.

acentuadamente adv. Markedly, clearly: *tendencia*

acentuadamente conservadora, clearly conservative tendency.
acentuado, da adj. Accentuated, with an accent (con acento gráfico): *letra acentuada*, accentuated letter, letter with an accent. || Stressed, accentuated (con acento tónico): *sílaba acentuada*, stressed syllable. || Marked, strong, notable, emphasized: *una tendencia social muy acentuada*, a very marked social tendency.
acentuar v. tr. To accent, to put an accent on (con acento gráfico). || To stress, to accentuate, to accent (con acento tónico). || FIG. To accentuate, to accent, to emphasize: *acentuar el carácter español de algo*, to emphasize the Spanish character of sth.
— V. pr. To have the accent, to be stressed *o* accentuated. || FIG. To become noticeable, to increase (aumentar). || To be heightened (*con*, by).
aceña f. Watermill.
aceñero m. Miller.
acepar v. intr. To take root (arraigar).
acepción f. Meaning, sense, acceptation (significado): *una palabra con muchas acepciones*, a word with many meanings. || Preference (de personas). || *Sin acepción de personas*, V. PERSONA.
acepilladora f. TECN. Planing machine, planer (máquina).
acepilladura f. V. CEPILLADO.
acepillar v. tr. V. CEPILLAR.
aceptabilidad f. Acceptability.
aceptable adj. Acceptable: *una proposición aceptable*, an acceptable suggestion. || Passable, acceptable: *un producto aceptable*, a passable product.
aceptación f. Acceptance (acción de aceptar). || Approval (aprobación). || Success: *tener poca aceptación*, to have little success.
aceptador, ra o **aceptante** adj. Who accepts, accepting.
— M. y f. COM. Acceptor.
aceptar v. tr. To accept: *aceptar una invitación*, to accept an invitation; *aceptar una letra de cambio*, to accept a bill of exchange. || *Aceptar hacer algo*, to agree to do sth., to undertake to do sth.
aceptor m. COM. Acceptor.
acequia f. Irrigation ditch, irrigation channel (para el riego). || *Amer.* Stream (arroyo).
acera f. Pavement [U.S., sidewalk]. || Side of the street: *la acera derecha*, the right-hand side of the street. || ARQ. Face (paramento). || FAM. *Ser de la acera de enfrente*, to be queer, to be gay (ser homosexual).
acerado, da adj. Steel (de acero). || Steely (parecido al acero). || Cutting (cortante). || FIG. Biting, cutting, caustic (mordaz): *una frase acerada*, a biting phrase.
— M. TECN. Steeling.
acerar v. tr. To steel (cubrir de acero). || To turn into steel: *acerar el hierro*, to turn iron into steel. || FIG. To strengthen (fortalecer). | To put an edge on, to make biting (hacer mordaz). || To build a pavement on (poner acera). || ARQ. To face.
acerbidad f. Harshness, acerbity.
acerbo, ba adj. Sour (sabor). || Bitter, scathing, harsh (mordaz): *tono acerbo*, harsh tone.
acerca de adv. About: *ha escrito un libro acerca de Cervantes*, he has written a book about Cervantes.
acercamiento m. Approach. || Bringing together, reconciling (de dos personas). || Coming together. || Nearness, closeness (de dos cosas). || Rapprochement (entre estados).
acercar v. tr. To draw up, to bring near, to bring up : *acerca tu silla a la mesa*, bring your chair near to the table. || To bring nearer (poner más cerca): *acerca tu silla a la mía*, bring your chair nearer to mine. || To bring over: *acerca aquella silla*, bring that chair over. || FIG. To draw *o* to bring together: *las medidas acercarán a los pueblos*, the measures will bring the nations together. | To bring nearer: *esto nos acerca a la solución*, this brings us nearer to the solution. || FAM. To pass, to give: *acércame ese libro*, pass me that book. | To drop: *¿puedes acercarme a mi casa?*, can you drop me at my house?
— V. pr. To approach, to draw near: *el ejército se acercó a la ciudad*, the army approached the city; *acercarse a la edad del retiro*, to approach retirement age. || To go up, to go over: *me acerqué a él*, I went up to him. || To come over, to come up, to approach: *se acercó a mí en la calle*, he came up to me in the street. || To lean towards (aproximarse mucho). || FIG. To approach, to border on: *una doctrina que se acerca al existencialismo*, a doctrine which approaches existentialism. || FAM. To drop in: *acércate a mi casa esta tarde*, drop in at my house this evening.
acería f. Steelworks, *pl.*, steel mill.
acerico o **acerillo** m. Pincushion (almohadilla para alfileres).
acerino, na adj. POÉT. Steellike, steely.
acero m. Steel: *acero inoxidable*, stainless steel; *acero colado*, cast steel. || FIG. Sword, steel (espada). || — *Acero dulce, duro*, soft, hard steel. || FIG. *Cruzar el acero*, to cross swords.
acerola f. BOT. Haw (fruto).
acerolo m. BOT. Hawthorn.
acérrimo, ma adj. FIG. Staunch, out-and-out: *un acérrimo partidario*, a staunch supporter.

— OBSERV. This adjective is the superlative form of *acre*, and is used only in its figurative sense.

acerrojar v. tr. To bolt.
acertado, da adj. Right, correct (opinión). || Wise, fitting: *no sería muy acertado que fueses a verle ahora*, it wouldn't be very wise for you to go and see him now. || Fitting, apt (comentario). || Skilful, clever (hábil): *decisión acertada*, clever decision. || Good: *una idea muy acertada*, a very good idea. || Well-chosen (color). || Well done: *es muy acertada la disposición de este libro*, the layout of this book is very well done. || *Lo acertado es marcharse ahora*, it is best to leave now.
acertante adj. Winning: *quiniela acertante*, winning coupon.
— M. y f. Winner: *ha habido cuatro acertantes*, there were four winners.
acertar* v. tr. To hit (el blanco). || To guess, to get right (adivinar): *a que no lo aciertas*, I bet you don't get it right. || To find (encontrar).
— V. intr. To guess right, to get right: *no acierto con la solución*, I can't get the answer right. || To be right, to hit the nail on the head, to guess right: *has acertado*, you are right. || To succeed, to manage: *acertó a abrir la puerta*, he succeeded in opening the door, he managed to open the door. || To find, to hit on: *has acertado con el color que quería*, you've hit on the colour I wanted. || To do right, to do the right thing: *acertaste en marcharte*, you did right in leaving. || To happen: *acertó a pasar un soldado*, a soldier happened to pass.
acertijo m. Riddle.
aceruelo m. Pincushion (acerico). || Small saddle (silla de montar).
acervo m. Pile, heap (montón). || Common property: *el acervo familiar*, the common property of the family. || FIG. Wealth, riches, *pl.*, patrimony: *el acervo cultural*, cultural wealth.
acetato m. QUÍM. Acetate.
acético, ca adj. QUÍM. Acetic: *ácido acético*, acetic acid.
acetificar v. tr. QUÍM. To acetify.
acetileno m. QUÍM. Acetylene.
acetilo m. QUÍM. Acetyl.
acetona f. QUÍM. Acetone.
acetosa f. BOT. Sorrel.
acetre m. (P. us.). Small bucket. || REL. Portable stoup (para agua bendita).
acetrinar v. tr. To make sallow.
aciago, ga adj. Unlucky, fateful, black: *aquél fue un día aciago para mí*, that was a black day for me. || Ill-fated, unlucky: *una persona aciaga*, an ill-fated person.
acial m. Barnacle (para caballos). || *Amer.* Whip.
aciano m. BOT. Cornflower.
acíbar m. BOT. Aloe. || Aloes, *pl.* (jugo). || FIG. Bitterness. | FIG. *Amargo como el acíbar*, as bitter as gall.
acibarar v. tr. To add aloes to. || FIG. To embitter, to make bitter (a una persona). | To make bitter, to make unpleasant, to make a misery: *acibararle a uno la vida*, to make s.o.'s life a misery.
acicalado, da adj. Polished (armas). || Dressed up, smart, dressed to kill (fam.), dressed up to the nines (fam.) [muy vestido]: *siempre va muy acicalado*, he's always dressed up. || Well groomed (pelo, etc.) || Done up: *el burro está acicalado para la feria*, the donkey is done up for the fair.
— M. Polishing.
acicaladura f. o **acicalamiento** m. Polishing (armas). || Dressing up (vestido). || Grooming (del pelo).
acicalar v. tr. To polish (armas). || FIG. To dress up, to deck out (en el vestido). | To groom (el pelo). | To do up (animales y cosas). | To sharpen (el espíritu).
— V. pr. To get dressed up, to deck o.s. out (vestirse). || To groom o.s. (el pelo).
acicate m. Spur. || FIG. Stimulus, incentive, spur: *el premio le sirve de acicate*, the prize is an incentive to him.
acicatear v. tr. To stimulate, to spur on (animar).
acíclico, ca adj. Acyclic.
acidez f. Sourness, tartness. || MED. Acidity (del estómago). || QUÍM. Acidity.
acidificación f. Acidification.
acidificar v. tr. To acidify.
— V. pr. To acidify.
acidímetro m. Acidimeter.
ácido, da adj. Sour, tart: *sabor ácido*, sour flavour. || FIG. Bitter, harsh: *hablar en un tono ácido*, to speak in a harsh tone.
— M. QUÍM. Acid: *ácido sulfúrico*, sulphuric acid; *ácido clorhídrico*, hydrochloric acid; *ácido nítrico*, nitric acid.
acidosis f. MED. Acidosis.
acidulado, da adj. Acidulated.
acidular v. tr. To acidulate.
acierto m. Success: *esta idea ha sido un acierto*, this idea has been a success. || Good choice: *el título de este libro fue un acierto*, the title of this book was a good choice. || Right answer (en un cuestionario). || Good idea: *ha sido un acierto el haber venido hoy*, it was a good idea to come today. || Coincidence (casualidad). || Wisdom (cordura). || Skill (habilidad): *el delantero remató con mucho acierto*, the forward shot with great skill. || *Obrar con acierto*, to do well.
ácigos adj./s.f. ANAT. Azygous.
acije m. QUÍM. Vitriol, copperas.
ácimo adj. Unleavened: *pan ácimo*, unleavened bread.

acimut m. Astr. Azimuth.
ación m. Stirrup strap.
acionera f. *Amer.* Stirrup strap ring.
acirate m. Ridge of earth (caballón entre dos campos).
aclamación f. Acclamation, acclaim.
aclamar v. tr. To acclaim, to applaud: *aclamar al rey*, to acclaim the king. || To acclaim, to name (nombrar): *le aclamaron jefe*, they acclaimed him leader.
aclaración f. Explanation: *al día siguiente, el autor publicó una aclaración a su artículo*, the next day the author published an explanation of his article. || Note, explanation: *una aclaración al margen*, a note in the margin.
aclarado m. Rinsing, rinse.
aclarar v. tr. To make lighter to lighten (un color, un líquido). || To thin out (un bosque, las filas). || To rinse (la ropa). || To clear (la voz). || To thin down (una salsa). || Fig. To throw light on, to clarify, to make clear: *un ejemplo aclarará el problema*, an example will throw light on the problem *o* will make the problem clear. | To resolve, to remove (dudas). | To explain, to make clear: *voy a aclarar lo dicho anteriormente*, I am going to explain what was said before. | To make it clear: *te aclaro que ya no debes salir*, I'm making it clear that you must not go out.
— V. intr. To clear (el tiempo). || To break (el día). || *Amer.* To clear (un líquido).
— V. pr. To clear (la voz, el tiempo, líquidos). || To become clear (ideas, dudas, problemas, etc.). || Fig. To explain o. s.: *aclárate*, explain yourself. | To understand each other: *estas dos personas no se aclaran*, these two people do not understand each other. | To recover, to come round: *después del puñetazo que había recibido tardó mucho en aclararse*, after the punch he had received he took a long time to come round. | To make out, to understand: *no consigo aclararme en este asunto*, I can't make this matter out. || *Amer.* To be broke (no tener dinero).
aclaratorio, ria adj. Explanatory: *nota aclaratoria*, explanatory note.
aclavelado, da adj. Carnation-like.
aclimatable adj. Able to be acclimatized [U.S., able to be acclimated].
aclimatación f. Acclimatization [U.S., acclimation].
aclimatar v. tr. To acclimatize [U.S., to acclimate].
— V. pr. To become acclimatized [U.S., to become acclimated].
acné f. Med. Acne.
acobardamiento m. Loss of nerve.
acobardar v. tr. To intimidate, to frighten, to unnerve. || To discourage, to dishearten (abatir).
— V. pr. To lose one's nerve, to become frightened *o* intimidated.
acobijar v. tr. Agr. To mulch, to earth up.
acobrado, da adj. Copper-coloured, coppery (color).
acocil o **acocili** m. *Amer.* Freshwater shrimp. || *Amer.* Fig. *Estar como un acocili*, to be as red as a lobster.
acocote m. *Amer.* Gourd used for collecting maguey juice.
acochambrar v. tr. *Amer.* To dirty, to soil.
acochinar v. tr. Fam. To murder, to kill, to bump off (fam.) [s.o. unable to defend himself].
acodado, da adj. Elbowed (doblado): *un tubo acodado*, an elbowed pipe. || Leaning (on one's elbows): *acodado en la barra*, leaning on the bar. || Agr. Layered.
acodadura f. Leaning on one's elbows. || Agr. Layering (de una planta). || Elbow (incurvación).
acodalamiento m. Arq. Propping, shoring.
acodalar v. tr. Arq. To prop up, to shore up.
acodamiento m. Leaning on one's elbows.
acodar v. tr. Arq. To prop up, to shore up (apuntalar). || To bend (doblar). || Agr. To layer.
— V. pr. To lean: *acodarse en la barra*, to lean on the bar.
acoderar v. tr. Mar. To turn [a ship] broadside on.
acodillar v. tr. To bend.
acodo m. Agr. Layer (esqueje). | Layering (acodadura).
acogedor, ra adj. Welcoming, hospitable (persona): *un pueblo muy acogedor*, a very hospitable people. || Welcoming, inviting: *un saloncito muy acogedor*, a very inviting little sitting room. || Warm, friendly: *un ambiente muy acogedor*, a very warm atmosphere.
acoger v. tr. To welcome, to make welcome: *acoger a los amigos*, to make one's friends welcome. || To take in (a un huérfano, etc.). || To shelter, to protect (proteger). || Fig. To receive, to take: *acoger las peticiones*, to receive requests. | To receive: *el actor fue acogido con una ovación*, the actor was received with great applause; *la proposición fue acogida con cierta frialdad*, the proposal was rather coolly received.
— V. pr. To take refuge: *se acogió a la corte del rey*, he took refuge in the king's court. || To resort to (recurrir a). || To have recourse to (la ley). || To base o.s.: *acogerse al artículo 13 de la ley*, to base o.s. on article 13 of the law. || To avail o.s. of (una promesa). || *Acogerse a* or *bajo sagrado*, to take holy sanctuary. || *Acogerse a uno*, to seek s.o.'s help (pedir auxilio), to seek s.o.'s protection (pedir protección).
acogida f. Welcome, greeting: *una acogida triunfal*, a triumphal welcome. || Fig. Refuge, shelter (refugio). || Reception: *la proposición tuvo una acogida favorable*, the proposal had a favourable reception.
acogido, da adj. Welcomed. || *Acogido a la ley*, protected by the law.
— M. y f. Inmate (de un hospicio).
acogimiento m. Welcome, greeting. || Refuge, shelter (refugio).
acogollar v. intr. Agr. To bud.
— V. tr. Agr. To cover up.
acogotar v. tr. To kill [with a rabbit punch] (matar). || To knock down (derribar). || Fig. To oppress (oprimir a alguien). | To intimidate (asustar). || *Amer.* To have at one's mercy (vencer).
acojinamiento m. Tecn. Cushioning.
acojinar v. tr. To pad (acolchar).
acojonamiento m. Pop. Jitters, *pl.*
acojonar v. tr. Pop. To put the wind up.
— V. pr. Pop. To get the wind up.
acolada f. Accolade (al armar caballero). || Hug, embrace (abrazo).
acolar v. tr. Heráld. To join, to unite [two coats of arms].
acolchado, da adj. Padded: *pared acolchada*, padded wall. || Quilted: *bata acolchada*, quilted dressing-gown. || Upholstered (muebles).
— M. Padding (relleno). || *Amer.* Mattress (colcha).
acolchar v. tr. To pad. || To upholster (muebles). || To quilt: *acolchar un tejido*, to quilt material. || Fig. To muffle, to deaden: *la nieve acolcha el ruido*, the snow deadens noise.
acolchonar v. tr. *Amer.* To quilt.
acolitado m. Acolyteship.
acolitar v. intr. *Amer.* To serve as acolyte. | Fig. y Fam. To share s.o's meal.
acolitazgo m. Acolyteship.
acólito m. Rel. Acolyte (ministro). | Altar boy, server (monaguillo). || Fig. Acolyte.
acollador m. Mar. Lanyard (cuerda).
acolladura f. Earthing up, covering up.
acollar* v. tr. Agr. To earth up, to cover up. || Mar. To caulk (calafatear). | To haul (cuerdas).
acollarado, da adj. Zool. Ring-necked: *mirlo acollarado*, ring-necked blackbird.
acollarar v. tr. To put a collar on (un animal). || To yoke (bueyes). || *Amer.* To couple (unir).
— V. pr. *Amer.* Pop. To live together (amancebarse), to get hitched (casarse).
acomedirse v. pr. *Amer.* To volunteer, to offer o.s.
acometedor, ra adj. Enterprising (atrevido). || Aggressive: *un delantero acometedor*, an aggressive forward.
acometer v. tr. To attack: *acometer al enemigo*, to attack the enemy. || To undertake: *acometer una reforma*, to undertake a reform. || To come over, to overcome: *me acometieron ganas de llorar*, a desire to cry came over me. || To fill: *estaba acometido por el miedo*, he was filled with fear. || To occur to, to come to: *le acometió la idea de irse*, the idea of going away came to him. || To connect with, to join (galería, cañería, etc.). || Fam. To attack, to get down to: *acometer un trabajo*, to attack a job. || *Me acometieron dudas*, I was filled with doubts, I began to have doubts.
acometida f. Attack. || Connection (de una cañería, de tubos).
acometimiento m. Attack. || Undertaking: *el acometimiento de un trabajo*, the undertaking of a job. || Connection (de cañería).
acometividad f. Aggression, aggressiveness (agresividad). || Enterprise (de un vendedor).
acomodable adj. V. ACOMODADIZO.
acomodación f. Arrangement (arreglo). || Accommodation (del ojo, de un anteojo). || Preparation (de un piso).
acomodadamente adv. Conveniently, suitably (convenientemente). || Easily, with ease (fácilmente). || *Vivir acomodadamente*, to live comfortably.
acomodadizo, za adj. Adaptable (que se aviene a todo). || Obliging, accommodating (complaciente).
acomodado, da adj. Suitable, convenient (conveniente). || Arranged, prepared: *un piso bien acomodado*, a well arranged flat. || Well-to-do, well off, comfortable: *una familia acomodada*, a well-to-do family. || Comfort-loving (comodón). || Moderate: *un precio acomodado*, a moderate price.
acomodador, ra m. y f. Usher (hombre), usherette (mujer) [en un espectáculo].
acomodamiento m. Convenience, suitability (comodidad). || Arrangement (convenio). || Preparation (de un sitio).
acomodar v. tr. To place, to arrange (ordenar). || To settle, to make comfortable: *acomodar al niño en un sillón*, to settle the child in an armchair, to make the child comfortable in an armchair. || To accommodate (en casa). || To adjust (ajustar). || To provide, to supply (proveer). || To adapt, to suit: *acomodar su conducta con*, to adapt one's conduct to. || To prepare, to get ready (preparar). || To accommodate (el ojo, una lente). || To show to one's seat (en el teatro, cine). || Fig. To reconcile, to bring together again (conciliar). || To apply: *acomodar una norma a un caso*, to apply a rule to a particular case. || *Amer.* To offer work to, to take on (ofrecer trabajo). | To repair, to mend (reparar). || *Haga usted lo que le acomode*, do as you please, please yourself, do whatever suits you.
— V. intr. To be suitable (convenir).
— V. pr. To sit down, to take one's seat (en un

espectáculo). || To settle down, to make o.s. comfortable (cómodamente): *acomodarse en un sillón*, to settle down in an armchair. || To stay (alojarse). || To accommodate (el ojo). || To go into service, to take a job: *acomodarse de criada*, to go into service as a maid. || To find work (lograr empleo). || To adapt o.s., to conform: *acomodarse con todo*, to adapt o.s. to *o* to conform with everything. || To comply, to conform: *acomodarse a una norma*, to comply with a rule. || *Amer.* To dress up (componerse). | To look after o.s., to fend for o.s. (amañarse).

acomodaticio, cia adj. Adaptable (que se adapta a todo). || Obliging, accommodating (complaciente).

acomodo m. Room (sitio). || Accommodation, lodgings, *pl.* (habitación). || Job, position (empleo). || Convenience (conveniencia). || *Amer.* Toilet, dress (compostura).

acompañado, da adj. Accompanied: *ir acompañado*, to be accompanied. || FAM. Busy, frequented (concurrido). || — *Estar bien, mal acompañado*, to be in good, in bad company. || *Más vale estar solo que mal acompañado*, better alone than in bad company.
— Adj./s. Assistant. || — M. *Amer.* Sewage pipe.

acompañador, ra adj. Accompanying.
— M. y f. Companion.

acompañamiento m. Accompaniment. || Retinue, escort (comitiva). || Funeral procession (cortejo). || TEATR. Supporting cast. || MÚS. Accompaniment. || FIG. Trail, sequel: *la guerra y su acompañamiento de horrores*, war and its trail of horrors. || *Sin acompañamiento*, unaccompanied.

acompañanta f. Companion.

acompañante adj. Accompanying.
— M. Companion. || MÚS. Accompanist. || — Pl. Retinue, *sing.*, escort, *sing.*: *el ministro y sus acompañantes*, the minister and his retinue.

acompañar v. tr. To go with, to accompany: *acompañar a su hijo al cine*, to go to the pictures with one's son. || To attend: *la Reina iba acompañada por dos damas de honor*, the Queen was accompanied by two ladies-in-waiting. || To escort (a una señorita). || To keep company: *acompañar a un enfermo*, to keep a sick person company. || To take, to see: *le acompañaré a su casa porque es tarde*, I'll take you home because it's late. || To see: *le acompañé hasta la puerta*, I saw him to the door. || To follow: *acompañar un entierro*, to follow a funeral. || To enclose (adjuntar). || To eat with, to accompany: *yo acompaño el jamón con piña*, I accompany ham with pineapple. || To go with, to accompany: *el vino tinto acompaña bien el queso*, red wine goes well with cheese. || MÚS. To accompany: *acompañar con el piano*, to accompany on the piano. || To join: *mañana organizamos un bridge en casa ¿quiere usted acompañarnos?*, tomorrow we're having a game of bridge at home, would you like to join us? || To share: *le acompaño en sus ideas*, I share your views. || *Le acompaño en su sentimiento*, my condolences. || *No quiero que me acompañen*, I would rather go alone.
— V. pr. To accompany o.s.: *acompañarse con el piano*, to accompany o.s. on the piano.

acompasadamente adv. Rhythmically. || Calmly, regularly, steadily, slowly: *hablar acompasadamente*, to speak slowly.

acompasado, da adj. Rhythmic: *el ruido acompasado de las olas*, the rhythmic sound of the waves. || Measured: *paso acompasado*, measured step. || FIG. Calm, steady.

acompasar v. tr. To keep in time: *el jinete debe acompasar su movimiento al del caballo*, the rider must keep his movement in time with the horse's. || MÚS. To mark the rhythm of, to mark the time of. || FIG. To adjust: *hay que acompasar las exportaciones con las importaciones*, exports must be adjusted according to imports.

acomplejado, da adj. With a complex. || *Está acomplejado por su estatura*, he has a complex about his size.

acomplejar v. tr. To make feel inferior, to give a complex: *me acomplejas con todos tus éxitos*, you make me feel inferior with all your successes.
— V. pr. To get a complex.

aconcagüino, na adj. From Aconcagua (Chile).

aconchabamiento m. Ganging together.

aconchabarse v. pr. FAM. To gang up, to gang together: *aconchabarse con malhechores*, to gang up with ruffians.

aconchar v. tr. To shelter, to protect. || MAR. To run aground, to beach.
— V. pr. MAR. To run aground.

acondicionado, da adj. Equipped, fitted-out, *un hospital bien acondicionado*, a well-equipped hospital. || — *Aire acondicionado*, air conditioning. || *Hotel con aire acondicionado*, air-conditioned hotel, hotel with air conditioning. || *Poner aire acondicionado*, to air-condition.

acondicionador m. Conditioner (de aire). || *Acondicionador de escaparates*, window dresser.

acondicionamiento m. Fitting out, fitting up: *el acondicionamiento de un palacio en museo*, the fitting out of a palace as a museum. || Preparation: *acondicionamiento de alimentos para la venta*, preparation of foodstuffs for sale. || Conditioning (del aire). || Improvement: *acondicionamiento de la red de carreteras*, improvement of the road network.

acondicionar v. tr. To fit out, to fit up, to set up: *acondicionar un sótano para tienda*, to fit out a basement as a shop. || To prepare: *acondicionar mercancías*, to prepare merchandise. || To improve: *acondicionar las carreteras*, to improve the roads. || To condition (el aire).

acongojar v. tr. To distress, to make anxious (angustiar).
— V. pr. To become anxious, to become distressed.

aconitina f. QUÍM. Aconitine.

acónito m. BOT. Aconite.

aconsejable adj. Advisable: *poco aconsejable*, not very advisable.

aconsejado, da adj. Advised. || — *Bien aconsejado*, well-advised. || *Mal aconsejado*, ill-advised.

aconsejador, ra adj. Advisory, advising, who advises.
— M. y f. Adviser, counsellor.

aconsejar v. tr. To advise, to counsel: *le aconsejo viajar* or *que viaje*, I advise you to travel. || To advise, to recommend (la moderación, etc.).
— V. pr. To seek advice, to consult: *aconsejarse con* or *de su médico*, to seek advice from *o* to consult one's doctor.

aconsonantar v. tr. To rhyme, to make rhyme.
— V. intr. To rhyme.

acontecedero, ra adj. Possible.

acontecer* v. intr. To happen, to occur, to take place: *todo aconteció conforme a lo previsto*, everything happened as planned.
— M. *El acontecer cotidiano*, everyday life, the normal course of events.

acontecimiento m. Event, happening (suceso).

acopiamiento m. Store, stock.

acopiar v. tr. To store, to collect (amontonar). || To collect (reunir).

acopio m. Store, stock (provisión). || Storing (acción de acopiar). || Abundance. || *Hacer acopio de*, to store up, to stock up.

acoplado, da adj. Matched: *un matrimonio bien acoplado*, a well-matched couple. || Coordinated: *un equipo bien acoplado*, a well-coordinated team. || Adjusted: *un horario mal acoplado*, a badly adjusted timetable.
— M. *Amer.* Trailer (vehículo).

acopladura f. Assembly.

acoplamiento m. Connecting, coupling, joining (acción de acoplar). || Connection, joint (unión de piezas). || Engaging (de engranajes). || Assembly (ensambladura). || Coordination (de un equipo). || Docking (de naves espaciales). || — ELECTR. *Acoplamiento en serie*, connection in series. || TECN. *Acoplamiento universal*, universal joint. | *Manguito de acoplamiento*, sleeve coupling.

acoplar v. tr. To fit: *acoplar una rueda al eje*, to fit a wheel to the axle. || ELECTR. To connect. || To fit together, to join: *acoplar dos vigas*, to fit two beams together. || To fit, to adapt: *acoplar un motor de coche a una lancha*, to fit a car engine to a launch. || To couple: *acoplar otro vagón al tren*, to couple another carriage to the train. || To coordinate: *acoplar un equipo*, to coordinate a team. || To fit in, to coordinate: *tengo que acoplar el horario de clases con mis días de trabajo*, I have to fit my timetable in with my working days. || To yoke (bueyes). || To make, to pair (parear animales).
— V. pr. To mate, to pair (animales). || To dock (naves espaciales).

acoquinamiento m. Fear, intimidation (miedo). || Loss of heart (desánimo).

acoquinar v. tr. FAM. To scare, to frighten, to intimidate (asustar).
— V. pr. To become scared *o* frightened *o* intimidated: *acoquinarse ante el enemigo*, to become scared in the face of the enemy. || To lose heart, to lose courage, to become disheartened (desanimarse).

acorazado, da adj. Armoured, armour-plated: *buque acorazado*, armoured ship. || FIG. Hardened: *persona acorazada contra el dolor*, person hardened to pain. || — *Cámara acorazada*, strongroom, safe. || MIL. *División acorazada*, armoured division.
— M. MAR. Battleship.

acorazamiento m. Armouring, armour-plating.

acorazar v. tr. To armour, to armour-plate.
— V. pr. FIG. To harden o.s.

acorazonado, da adj. Heart-shaped.

acorchado, da adj. Cork-like (como el corcho). || Spongy (correoso). || Numb (los miembros). || *Boca acorchada*, numb mouth (insensibilizada), furry mouth, mouth like sandpaper (por el alcohol).

acorchamiento m. Sponginess. || FIG. Numbness (de los miembros).

acorchar v. tr. To cover with cork.
— V. pr. To become corky *o* cork-like. || To become spongy (fruta). || FIG. To go numb: *se me acorcharon as piernas*, my legs went numb.

acordada f. Decree, order (de un tribunal).

acordadamente adv. Unanimously, by common consent (de común acuerdo). || With much thought (con reflexión).

acordado, da adj. Sensible, wise (prudente). || Agreed upon *o* agreed to. || *Lo acordado*, that which has been agreed upon.

acordar* v. tr. To agree, to resolve: *ambos estadistas han acordado estrechar la cooperación*, both statesmen have agreed to increase cooperation. || To decide (decidir). || To agree upon: *acordar un precio*, to agree upon a price. || To remind (recordar a uno). || ARTES. To match, to harmonize (colores). || MÚS. To tune (afinar). || *Amer*. To grant (otorgar).
— V. pr. To remember: *no me acuerdo de la guerra*, I don't remember the war. || To agree, to come to an agreement. || — *No se acuerda ni del santo de su nombre*, he can hardly remember his own name. || *Si mal no me acuerdo*, if I remember rightly. || FAM. *¡Te acordarás de mí!*, you haven't seen the last of me, you'll be hearing from me.
acorde adj. In agreement: *las diversas informaciones están acordes*, the different reports are in agreement. || According (*con, a*, to), in agreement (*con, a*, with): *construir un edificio acorde con las tendencias actuales*, to construct a building according to present trends. || Identical, same: *sentimientos acordes*, the same feelings, identical feelings. || MÚS. In tune.
— M. MÚS. Chord: *acorde perfecto*, common chord. | Tune: *cantar algo a los acordes de*, to sing sth. to the tune of. | Strain: *hacer algo a los acordes de*, to do sth. to the strains of.
acordelado, da adj. Perfectly straight.
acordelar v. tr. To measure with a string. || To mark out in straight lines (tirar a cordel). || To mark the boundary of [with string].
acordeón m. MÚS. Accordion. || *Plisado de acordeón*, accordion pleating.
acordeonista m. y f. Accordionist.
acordonado, da adj. Corded, ribbed (en figura de cordón). || Cordoned off, surrounded: *el barrio estaba acordonado por la policía*, the district was cordoned off by the police. || Milled (monedas). || *Amer*. Thin (animales).
acordonamiento m. Lacing, lacing up (lazada). || Cordon (de policía). || Milling (de las monedas).
acordonar v. tr. To lace, to lace up, to tie up (los zapatos). || To pipe (poner un cordón). || To mill (las monedas). || To cordon off, to surround: *la policía acordona la universidad*, the police surround the university. || *Amer*. To prepare [the ground] (para la siembra).
acornar o **acornear** v. tr. V. CORNEAR.
acorralado, da adj. Cornered (sin salida). || At bay: *un ciervo acorralado*, a stag at bay.
acorralamiento m. Cornering. || Enclosing, penning (de vacunos), folding (de ovinos).
acorralar v. tr. To enclose, to pen (vacunos), to fold (ovinos). || To put at bay (ciervos). || To corner: *acorralar al enemigo*, to corner the enemy.
acorrer v. tr. To help.
— V. intr. To run up.
acortamiento m. Shortening: *acortamiento de una falda*, shortening of a skirt. || Reduction.
acortar v. tr. To shorten. || FIG. To reduce: *acortar el racionamiento*, to reduce rationing. | To cut down, to reduce (distancia). | To abridge, to shorten (un cuento).
— V. pr. To become shorter, to shorten: *en agosto los días empiezan a acortarse*, in August the days start to become shorter. || To be shy (intimidarse).
acosador, ra adj. Pursuing.
— M. y f. Pursuer.
acosamiento m. Pursuit.
acosar v. tr. To pursue, to hound: *acosado por los perros*, hounded by the dogs. || To run to earth, to put at bay (acorralar). || FIG. To hound, to pursue: *acosar a un deudor*, to hound a debtor. | To pester, to hound, to harass: *acosar con preguntas*, to pester with questions. || To urge on (un caballo).
acoso m. Pursuit (acosamiento). || Hunting down (caza). || FIG. Hounding.
acostar* v. tr. To put to bed (en la cama). || To lay down, to lay (poner en posición horizontal). || MAR. To bring alongside.
— V. intr. MAR. To touch land, to reach land.
— V. pr. To go to bed: *voy a acostarme porque es muy tarde*, I'm going to bed because it is very late. || To lie down (tumbarse). || To sleep: *por falta de sitio, los niños se acostaron juntos*, because of the lack of room the children slept together. || To lean over, to bend over: *el trigo se acostó por el viento*, the wheat leant over in the wind. || MAR. To come alongside (arrimarse). || — FAM. *Acostarse con las gallinas*, to go to bed very early. || *La hora de acostarse*, bedtime.
acostumbrado, da adj. Usual, customary (que se hace por costumbre). || Used, accustomed: *una persona acostumbrada al trabajo*, a person used to work.
acostumbrar v. tr. To accustom, to get used: *me han acostumbrado al trabajo*, they've got me used to working. || To be used to, to be accustomed to, to be in the habit of, to usually: *acostumbro levantarme temprano*, I am used to getting up early, I usually get up early.
— V. pr. To become accustomed, to get used: *acostumbrarse al clima de un país*, to get used to the climate of a country. || To get into the habit: *se acostumbró a fumar después de comer*, he got into the habit of smoking after a meal. || To be usual, to be customary: *ahora no se acostumbra llevar miriñaque*, it is no longer usual to wear a crinoline.
acotación f. Demarcation (acción de limitar). || Boundary mark (señal). || Note (nota). || GEOGR. Elevation mark (en topografía). || TEATR. Stage direction.
acotado, da adj. Enclosed (terreno). || Annotated (texto).
acotamiento m. Demarcation (acción de limitar). || Boundary mark (señal). || Note, annotation (en un texto). || GEOGR. Elevation mark (topografía). || FIG. Outline.
acotar v. tr. To mark the boundary of, to demarcate, to delimit, to enclose (un terreno). || To reserve, to fence in, to preserve (para la caza). || FIG. To delimit, to outline, to define (limitar). | To accept (aceptar). | To vouch for (atestiguar). || To add notes to, to annotate (anotar). || GEOGR. To mark with elevations (poner cotas).
acotejar v. tr. *Amer*. To arrange (acomodar).
acotiledón, ona o **acotiledóneo, a** adj. BOT. Acotyledonous.
— M. y f. Acotyledon.
acotillo m. Blacksmith's hammer.
acoyundar v. tr. To yoke (bueyes).
acoyuntar v. tr. To yoke together [beasts of different owners].
acracia f. Anarchy.
ácrata adj./s. Anarchist.
acrático, ca adj. Anarchic, anarchical.
acre m. Acre (medida).
acre adj. Pungent, acrid (olor). || Sharp, tart, bitter (sabor). || FIG. Biting, caustic, bitter (mordaz): *palabras acres*, biting words. | Bitter, crabby (desabrido).
acrecencia f. Increase. || JUR. Accretion.
acrecentador, ra adj. Increasing.
acrecentamiento m. Increase.
acrecentar* v. tr. To increase, to augment.
— V. pr. To increase, to augment.
acrecer* v. tr. To increase.
— V. intr. To increase, to grow. || JUR. *Derecho de acrecer*, right of accretion.
acrecimiento m. JUR. Accretion.
acreción f. BIOL. y GEOL. Accretion.
acreditado, da adj. COM. Credited. || Reputable: *una marca acreditada*, a reputable make. || Accredited (embajador).
acreditar v. tr. To accredit: *el gobierno le ha acreditado embajador en España*, the government has accredited him as ambassador to Spain. || To prove, to support, to give proof of: *esto acredita lo que le decía*, this proves what I was saying to you. || To vouch for, to guarantee: *acreditar una firma*, to vouch for a signature. || To authorize, to sanction: *este documento me acredita para entrar*, this paper authorizes me to enter. || To be a credit to, to give credit to, to add to the reputation of: *un producto que acredita al fabricante*, a product which adds to the manufacturer's reputation. || COM. To credit. || *Acreditar como*, to prove to be, to prove that: *la carta me acredita como propietario*, the letter proves me to be the owner, the letter proves that I am the owner; *esta medida le acredita de loco*, this measure proves him to be mad *o* proves that he is mad.
— V. pr. To present one's credentials (un embajador). || To gain a reputation, to make one's name: *antes de que este bar se acredite habrá que esperar mucho tiempo*, we shall have to wait a long time before this bar gains a reputation *o* makes its name.
acreditativo, va adj. Which proves, which gives proof.
acreedor, ra adj. Deserving, worthy: *acreedor a mi cariño*, worthy of *o* deserving my affection.
— M. y f. Creditor: *tiene muchos acreedores*, he has many creditors. || *Acreedor hipotecario*, mortgagee.
acreencia f. *Amer*. Credit.
acribadura f. Sifting, riddling, sieving (acción). || — Pl. Siftings, riddlings, sievings (desperdicios).
acribar v. tr. To sift, to riddle, to sieve. || FIG. To riddle.
acribillar v. tr. To riddle, to pepper: *acribillar a balazos*, to riddle with bullet holes. || To cover: *acribillar de picaduras*, to cover with stings. || FIG. To pester, to harass: *me acribillaron a preguntas*, they pestered me with questions.
acrílico, ca adj. QUÍM. Acrylic.
acriminar v. tr. To charge, to accuse, to incriminate.
acrimonia f. Pungency, acridity (olor). || Sharpness, tartness, bitterness (sabor). || FIG. Acrimony, bitterness.
acrimonioso, sa adj. Acrimonious.
acriollarse v. pr. *Amer*. To go native.
acrisolado, da adj. Purified (metales). || Proven, tested (la verdad, el amor).
acrisolar v. tr. To purify (los metales). || To prove, to test (la verdad, el amor).
acritud f. V. ACRIMONIA.
acrobacia f. Feat of acrobatics. || — Pl. Acrobatics. || *Acrobacias aéreas*, aerobatics.
acróbata m. y f. Acrobat.
acrobático, ca adj. Acrobatic.
acrobatismo m. Acrobatics.
acrocéfalo, la adj. MED. Acrocephalic, acrocephalous.

acromático, ca adj. Achromatic: *lente acromática*, achromatic lense.
acromatismo m. Achromatism.
acromegalia f. MED. Acromegaly, acromegalia.
Acrópolis n. pr. f. Acropolis.
acróstico, ca adj./s. m. Acrostic.
acrotera o **acrótera** f. ARQ. Acroter.
acta f. Minutes, *pl.*, record (de una reunión). || Certificate of election (en elecciones). || Official document, deed. || *Amer.* Act, law. || — Pl. REL. Life, *sing.*, acts (de los santos). || Minutes, record, *sing.* || Register, *sing.* (para las notas de un examen). || — *Acta de acusación*, bill of indictment. || *Acta de bautismo*, certificate of baptism. || *Acta de nacimiento, de matrimonio*, birth, marriage certificate. || *Acta notarial*, notarial deed. || *Actas taquigráficas* or *literales*, verbatim record, *sing.* || *Levantar acta*, to draw up the minutes, to take the minutes (de una reunión). || *Tomar acta*, to take note.
actinia f. ZOOL. Actinia, sea anemone (anémona de mar).
actínico, ca adj. FÍS. y QUÍM. Actinic.
actinio m. QUÍM. Actinium (metal).
actinomorfo, fa adj. ZOOL. Actinomorphic.
actitud f. Posture, pose, position, attitude (postura del cuerpo): *adoptar una actitud pensativa*, to strike a pensive pose. || FIG. Attitude, position: *ha adoptado una actitud rebelde*, he has adopted *o* has taken up a rebellious attitude.
activación f. Speeding-up, quickening. || QUÍM. Activation.
activador m. QUÍM. Activator.
activamente adv. Actively, energetically. || GRAM. Actively, with an active meaning.
activar v. tr. To speed up, to quicken: *activar el trabajo*, to speed up the work. || To activate, to stimulate: *activar el mercado*, to stimulate the market. || QUÍM. To activate: *carbón activado* activated carbon. || To stir up (el fuego).
— V. pr. To hurry, to hurry up.
actividad f. Activity: *la actividad de un volcán, de un ácido*, the activity of a volcano, of an acid; *esfera de actividad*, field of activity. || Bustle, activity (en la calle). || Activity (ocupación): *cada uno tiene una actividad distinta*, each one has a different activity. || — *Tiene una actividad enorme*, he is very active *o* energetic. || *Volcán en actividad*, active volcano.
activismo m. Activism.
activista adj./s. Activist.
activo, va adj. Active. || Energetic, active: *una persona muy activa*, a very energetic person. || GRAM. Active: *verbo activo*, active verb. || GEOL. Active (volcán). || — *Dividendo activo*, dividend. || *En activo*, on active service: *militar en activo*, soldier on active service. || GRAM. *Participio activo*, present participle.
— M. COM. Assets, *pl.* (haber): *activo y pasivo*, assets and liabilities.
acto m. Act, action, deed (hecho): *se conoce un hombre por sus actos*, a man is known by his acts. || Act: *acto de fe, de contrición*, act of faith, of contrition. || Ceremony: *mañana se celebrará el acto de clausura*, the closing ceremony will take place tomorrow. || TEATR. Act: *comedia en dos actos*, two-act play, play in two acts. || — *Acto carnal*, sexual intercourse, carnal act. || *Acto continuo* or *seguido*, immediately, immediately afterwards, straight away, at once. || *Acto reflejo*, reflex action. || *Actos de los Apóstoles*, Acts of the Apostles. || JUR. *Actos de violencia*, assault and battery. || *En el acto*, immediately, on the spot. || *En el acto de*, in the act of. || *Hacer acto de presencia*, to be present, to put in an appearance. || *Muerto en acto de servicio*, killed in active service, killed in action. || *Salón de actos*, assembly hall.
actor, ra adj. f. JUR. *Parte actora*, prosecution.
— M. y f. JUR. Plaintiff, claimant.
actor, triz m. y f. Actor, actress. || — *Primer actor*, leading actor, star. || *Primera actriz*, leading lady *o* actress, star.
actuación f. Behaviour, conduct (conducta). || Action, intervention: *la actuación de la policía fue muy dura*, the police's action was very severe. || Performance: *la actuación de un artista*, an artist's performance. || — *Actuación pericial*, expert valuation. || — Pl. JUR. Proceedings.
actual adj. Present, present-day, modern: *la técnica actual*, present-day technology. || Topical: *un problema muy actual*, a very topical problem.
— M. This month: *el 12 del actual*, the 12th of this month.
actualidad f. Present, present time. || Topicality, current importance: *la actualidad de un problema*, a problem's topicality. || — Pl. Current events. || CINEM. Newsreel, *sing.* || — *En la actualidad*, at the present time, nowadays, at the moment. || *Un tema de gran actualidad*, a very topical subject, a subject of great importance today.
actualización f. Bringing up to date, modernization. || FIL. Actualization.
actualizador, ra adj. Modernizing.
actualizar v. tr To bring up to date, to modernize: *actualizar un texto*, to bring a text up to date. || FIL. To actualize.
actualmente adv. At present, at the moment, at the present time (en este momento). || Nowadays (hoy día).
actuante adj. Acting.
— M. y f. Performer. || Defender [of a thesis]. || Candidate [in an examination].
actuar v. intr. To act: *una medicina que actúa como calmante*, a medicine which acts as a sedative; *actuar de secretario*, to act as secretary. || CINEM. y TEATR. To act, to play, to perform. || To perform (un cantante, músico). || To behave: *ha actuado muy mal en este asunto*, he has behaved very badly in this matter. || To defend a thesis (en la universidad). || To take: *actuar en un ejercicio oral*, to take an oral examination. || JUR. To take proceedings. || TAUR. To fight.
— V. tr. To operate, to work (un mecanismo).
actuariado m. Position of actuary *o* of clerk of the court.
actuarial adj. Actuarian, actuarial.
actuario m. JUR. Clerk of the court, actuary. || Actuary (de seguros).
acuache m. *Amer.* Mate, pal, chum (amigo).
acuadrillar v. tr. To band together, to form into a band. || To lead [a band].
acuafortista m. ARTES. Aquafortist.
acuaplano m. Aquaplane.
acuarela f. ARTES. Watercolour [U.S., watercolor].
acuarelista m. Watercolourist [U.S., watercolorist].
acuario m. Aquarium (de peces). || ASTR. Aquarius.
acuartelado adj. HERÁLD. Quartered.
acuartelamiento m. MIL. Billeting, quartering. | Confinement to barracks (en previsión de disturbios).
acuartelar v. tr. MIL. To quarter, to billet. | To confine to barracks (en previsión de disturbios). || To divide into quarters.
— V. pr. MIL. To withdraw to barracks.
acuartillar v. intr. To bend its knees (caballo).
acuático, ca adj. Aquatic: *ave acuática*, aquatic bird. || *Esquí acuático*, water-skiing.
acuátil adj. Aquatic.
acuatinta f. ARTES. Aquatint.
acuatizar v. intr. To land on the water (un hidroavión).
acucia f. Haste (prisa). || Longing, desire (anhelo). || Diligence (diligencia).
acuciador, ra adj. Pressing, urgent (urgente). || Desirous (ansioso). || Stimulating (estimulante).
acuciamiento m. Stimulation, urging on (estímulo). || Desire (deseo, ansia). || Diligence (diligencia).
acuciante adj. Pressing, urgent.
acuciar v. tr. To urge on (estimular): *estar acuciado por la necesidad*, to be urged on by necessity. || To hound, to pester, to harass: *acuciar a alguien con preguntas*, to hound s.o. with questions. || To desire, to long for (anhelar). || *No me acucia marcharme*, there is no hurry for me to leave.
acucioso, sa adj. Diligent, keen. || Urgent, pressing (urgente). || Desirous (ansioso).
acuclillarse v. pr. To crouch down, to squat down.
acucharado, da adj. Spoon-shaped.
acuchillado, da adj. Knifed, slashed, stabbed. || FIG. Experienced. || Slashed: *mangas acuchilladas*, slashed sleeves.
— M. Surfacing (de madera).
acuchillador, ra adj. Quarrelsome (pendenciero).
— M. y f. Quarrelsome person. || Slasher, knifer, stabber. || Floor dresser (de suelos). || — M. Bully (espadachín).
acuchillamiento m. Surfacing (de madera).
acuchillar v. tr. To knife, to stab, to slash (apuñalar). || To slash (vestidos). || To slash, to cleave (el aire). || To surface (la madera).
— V. pr. To fight with knives, to hack at one another.
acudir v. intr. To come (venir): *ayer no acudió a la oficina*, yesterday he didn't come to the office; *el perro acude cuando le llaman*, the dog comes when they call him; *acudir a la mente*, to come to one's mind. || To go (ir): *mucha gente acudío al espectáculo*, a lot of people went to the show; *acudir a la puerta*, to go to the door. || To keep: *acudir a una cita*, to keep an appointment. || To take: *acudir a un examen*, to take an examination. || To answer: *¿quién acudió al teléfono?*, who answered the telephone? || To happen (sobrevenir): *siempre le acuden desdichas*, misfortunes always happen to him. || To carry out, to obey (una orden). || To see, to attend: *no pudo acudir a todo lo que tenía que hacer*, he couldn't see to everything he had to do. || To come forward: *pidió ayuda y muchos acudieron*, he asked for help and many came forward. || To help, to give aid *o* help: *acudir a alguien*, to give help to *o* to help s.o. || To come up: *acudieron a tiempo con la solución*, they came up with the solution in time. || To resort (recurrir): *sin acudir a las armas*, without resorting to weapons. || To consult (al médico). || To call, to turn (recurrir a una persona): *si es necesario, acudiré al ministro*, if it's necessary I'll turn to *o* call on the minister. || To obey (el caballo). || — *Acudir a la huida*, to take flight. || *Acudir en ayuda de alguien*, to come to s.o.'s aid *o* rescue. || *No saber a quién acudir*, not to know where to turn, to be at one's wits' end.
acueducto m. Aquaduct.
ácueo, a adj. Aqueous: *humor ácueo*, aqueous humour.
acuerdo m. Agreement, understanding: *tienen un acuerdo entre ellos*, they have an agreement between themselves; *llegar a un acuerdo*, to come to an agreement. || Agreement: *acuerdo general sobre tarifas arancelarias y comercio*, general agreement on tariffs and trade; *concertar un acuerdo*, to conclude an

agreement. || Harmony: *el acuerdo de dos colores,* the harmony of two colours. || Resolution (en el parlamento). || Sense, wisdom (cordura). || Advice, opinion (consejo). || Memory (recuerdo). || — *Acuerdo verbal,* verbal agreement, gentleman's agreement. || *¡De acuerdo!,* right!, O.K.!, all right!, alright! || *De acuerdo con,* in accordance with; as laid down in, in accordance with (una ley). || *De común acuerdo,* by common consent. || *Estar de acuerdo con una persona,* to agree with a person, to be in agreement with a person. || *Estar de acuerdo en,* to agree with, to be in agreement about: *estoy de acuerdo en el aumento del capital,* I agree with the increase in capital; *estoy de acuerdo en aumentar el capital,* I agree with increasing the capital. || *Estar en su acuerdo,* to have one's wits about one, to be in one's right mind. || *Llegar a un acuerdo,* to come to an agreement, to reach [an] agreement || *Poner de acuerdo,* to make agree, to bring to an agreement: *nos puso de acuerdo,* he made us agree, he brought us to an agreement. || *Ponerse de acuerdo,* to come to an agreement, to agree. || *Volver a su acuerdo,* to come back to one's senses.

acuidad f. Sharpness, acuity.

acuífero, ra adj. Aquiferous, water-bearing: *capa acuífera,* aquiferous layer.

acuitadamente adv. Sorrowfully, with grief.

acuitar v. tr. To grieve.

— V. pr. To grieve: *acuitarse por algo,* to grieve at sth., to grieve sth.

aculado, da adj. HERÁLD. Sejant.

acular v. tr. To back up, to drive back (arrimar). || FAM. To corner (acosar, arrinconar).

— V. pr. MAR. To run aground.

aculebrinado, da adj. Culverin.

acullá adv. There, over there. || *Acá y acullá,* here and there.

acumulación f. o **acumulamiento** m. Accumulation (acción). || Store, accumulation: *acumulación de recuerdos,* store of memories. || Plurality (de empleos). || JUR. Non-concurrence (de penas).

acumulador, ra adj. Accumulative.

— M. TECN. Storage battery, accumulator.

acumular v. tr. To accumulate, to store up, to amass (amontonar): *acumular riquezas,* to accumulate riches. || To store up, to collect: *acumular recuerdos,* to store up memories. || To accumulate: *acumular intereses al capital,* to accumulate interest on capital. || To pile, to heap, to load: *acumular preocupaciones sobre alguien,* to pile worries onto s.o. || *Acumular vapor,* to get up steam.

— V. pr. To accumulate, to build up (cosas). || To gather, to collect: *la gente se acumuló delante del escaparate,* the people gathered in front of the window.

acumulativamente adv. JUR. Non-concurrently, cumulatively.

acumulativo, va adj. Accumulative, which accumulates. || JUR. Non-concurrent, cumulative.

acunar v. tr. To rock: *acunar a un niño,* to rock a child.

acuñación f. Minting, striking, coining (de monedas).

acuñador m. Minter.

acuñar v. tr. To strike, to mint, to coin (monedas). || To strike (medallas). || To wedge (poner cuñas). || *Expresión acuñada,* set phrase.

— V. intr. To mint *o* to strike *o* to coin money.

acuosidad f. Wateriness (de fruta). || Aqueousness (de humor).

acuoso, sa adj. Aqueous: *humor acuoso,* aqueous humour. || Watery: *fruta acuosa,* watery fruit.

acuotubular adj. TECN. Watertube: *caldera acuotubular,* watertube boiler.

acupuntura f. MED. Acupuncture.

acure m. ZOOL. Agouti.

acurrucarse v. pr. To curl up, to nestle, to snuggle up: *se acurrucó en el sillón,* he curled up in the armchair. || To huddle (por el frío).

acurrullar v. tr. MAR. To lower [sails].

acusación f. Accusation: *lo que ha dicho es una acusación contra mi primo,* what he said is an accusation against my cousin. || — JUR. *Acta de acusación,* indictment. | *Cargo de acusación,* count of indictment.

acusado, da adj. Accused (inculpado). || Marked, clear, outstanding, pronounced (saliente).

— M. y f. Accused, defendant.

acusador, ra adj. Accusing: *en tono acusador,* in an accusing tone.

— M. y f. Accuser. || *Acusador público,* public prosecutor.

acusar v. tr. To accuse, to charge: *acusar de robo,* to accuse of robbery, to charge with robbery. || To point to: *todas las pruebas le acusan,* all the evidence points to him. || To blame: *le acuso de todas nuestras desdichas,* I blame him for all our misfortunes. || To show, to indicate: *el termómetro acusa un cambio de temperatura,* the thermometer shows a change in temperature. || To show, to reveal, to register, to reflect: *su cara acusa gran dolor,* his face reflects great pain. || To declare, to announce (naipes). || To denounce, to give away, to inform on: *su antiguo amigo le acusó,* his old friend gave him away. || To tell tales about: *es una mala costumbre acusar a los demás,* it is a bad habit to tell tales about others. || — *Acusar alegría, cansancio,* to look happy, tired. || *Acusar el golpe,* to feel the blow. || FIG. *Acusar las cuarenta a uno,* to tell s.o. a few home truths. || COM. *Acusar recibo de una cosa,* to acknowledge receipt of sth.

— V. pr. To confess (confesar): *acusarse de un crimen,* to confess to a crime; *acusarse de un pecado,* to confess a sin. || To become clear *o* pronounced *o* marked.

acusativo, va adj./m. GRAM. Accusative.

acusatorio, ria adj. Accusatory.

acuse m. Acknowledgement: *acuse de recibo,* acknowledgement of receipt. || Winning card (naipes).

acusetas o **acusete** m. *Amer.* FAM. Telltale, tattletale (niño). || Sneak (adulto).

acusica m. y f. FAM. Telltale, tattletale (niño). | Sneak (adulto).

acusón, ona adj. FAM. Fond of telling tales (niño). || Sneaky (adulto).

— M. y f. FAM. Telltale, tattletale (niño). || Sneak (adulto).

acústico, ca adj. Acoustic. || *Trompetilla acústica,* ear trumpet.

— F. Acoustics: *la acústica es la ciencia del sonido,* acoustics is the science of sound.

acutángulo, la adj. Acute-angled.

acutí m. *Amer.* ZOOL. Agouti (roedor).

achabacanar v. tr. To make vulgar *o* crude.

— V. pr. To become vulgar *o* crude.

achacable adj. Attributable.

achacar v. tr. To attribute: *me achacan unas frases que nunca he dicho,* they attribute statements to me that I have never made; *achacarle a uno una falta,* to attribute a fault to s.o. || To put on, to lay on: *me achacaron la culpa,* they laid the blame on me. || *Achacar a uno la responsabilidad de,* to hold s.o. responsible for.

achacosamente adv. Weakly, in a sickly fashion. || With difficulty: *andar achacosamente,* to walk with difficulty.

achacoso, sa adj. Sickly, ailing (enfermizo). || Ill, unwell, indisposed (ligeramente enfermo). || Faulty, defective (una cosa).

achaflanar v. tr. To chamfer, to bevel.

¡achalay! interj. *Amer.* How lovely!, how nice!

achampanado, da o **achampañado, da** adj. Champagne-type: *vino achampanado,* champagne-type wine. || Sparkling (espumoso). || *Sidra achampanada,* champagne cider.

achantar v. tr. FAM. To frighten (asustar). | To shut up (dejar desarmado). || POP. *¡Achanta la mui!,* shut your face!, shut up!

— V. pr. FAM. To hide [during danger]. | To climb down: *cuando saqué mi pistola se achantó,* when I got my gun out he climbed down.

achaparrado, da adj. Small and thick (árbol). || FIG. Stocky, squat, stumpy: *un viejo achaparrado,* a stocky old man. | Crushed, flattened (aplastado).

achaparrarse v. pr. To grow thick [without getting taller] (los árboles). || FIG. To get chubby (personas).

achapinarse v. pr. *Amer.* To adopt the way of life of Guatemala.

achaque m. Ailment, complaint (enfermedad ligera). || FIG. Excuse, pretext: *con el achaque de,* on the pretext of, with the excuse of. || *Achaques de la vejez,* old age complaints.

achaquiento, ta adj. Sickly, ailing (enfermizo). || Ill, indisposed, unwell (ligeramente enfermo).

achares m. pl. Jealousy, *sing.* || *Dar achares a,* to make jealous.

acharolar v. tr. To patent (la piel).

acharramarse v. pr. FAM. To become crude *o* vulgar.

achatamiento m. Flattening.

achatar v. tr. To flatten, to squash.

— V. pr. *Amer.* To become frightened, to lose heart.

achicado, da adj. Childish (aniñado).

achicador m. MAR. Baler.

achicamiento m. Reduction. || MAR. Baling. || Draining (en una mina). || FIG. Humiliation (humillación). | Feeling of inferiority.

achicar v. tr. To reduce: *achicar sus pretensiones,* to reduce one's claims. || To make smaller: *han achicado los jardines,* they have made the gardens smaller. || To take in (la ropa). || MAR. To bale out. || To drain (en una mina). || FIG. To humiliate, to belittle (humillar). | To bring down, to kill (matar).

— V. pr. FIG. To back down, to lose heart (amilanarse): *no te achiques ante el enemigo,* don't lose heart in the face of the enemy. | To humble o.s. (humillarse).

achicoria f. BOT. Chicory.

achicharradero m. Furnace, inferno (sitio caluroso).

achicharrante adj. Burning.

achicharrar v. tr. To burn (asar demasiado). || FIG. To roast, to burn (calentar con exceso). | To pester, to annoy (molestar). | To bombard, to plague: *le achicharraron a preguntas,* they bombarded him with questions. || *Amer.* To flatten, to crush (estrujar).

— V. pr. To burn (un guiso). || To roast, to burn (con el sol).

achicharronar v. tr. *Amer.* V. ACHICHARRAR.

achichinque m. *Amer.* Miner, mine worker (obrero). | Flatterer (adulador). | Minion (servidor).

achiguarse v. pr. *Amer.* To bulge (pared, tabla, etc.). | To put on weight (una persona).

achinado, da adj. Slanting (los ojos). || Oriental, eastern: *tiene una cara achinada,* he has an oriental face. || *Amer.* Half-caste (mestizo). | Vulgar, low.

achinar v. tr. FAM. To intimidate, to scare, to frighten (acoquinar).
achinelado, da adj. Slipper-shaped.
achique m. MAR. Baling. || Draining (en una mina).
achiquillado, da adj. Childish.
achiquitar v. tr. *Amer.* FAM. To make smaller.
— V. pr. *Amer.* FAM. To back down, to lose heart (amilanarse).
achira f. *Amer.* BOT. Canna (cañacoro).
achispado, da adj. Tipsy, tight, merry (medio ebrio).
achispar v. tr. To make tipsy *o* tight *o* merry (embriagar).
— V. pr. To get tipsy *o* merry *o* tight.
achocar v. tr. To throw *o* to dash against the wall (contra la pared). || To throw to the floor (contra el suelo).
achocolatado, da adj. Chocolate-brown.
achocharse v. pr. FAM. To become senile, to begin to dote, to become doddery.
acholado, da adj. *Amer.* Half-caste, half-breed (cobrizo). | Ashamed (avergonzado). | Scared (con miedo).
acholar v. tr. *Amer.* To shame, to make ashamed (avergonzar).
— V. pr. *Amer.* To be ashamed (avergonzarse). | To get scared (amedrentarse). | To get sunstroke (insolarse). | To adopt half-breed ways (volverse mestizo).
achubascarse v. pr. To become threatening *o* overcast (cielo).
achucutar o **achucuyar** v. tr. *Amer.* To shame, to make ashamed.
achuchado, da adj. FAM. Hard, difficult: *la vida está muy achuchada*, life is very hard.
achuchar v. tr. FAM. To squash, to flatten (aplastar). | To push, to jostle (empujar): *me achucharon por todos lados*, I was pushed from all sides. | To press [down] on (apretar). || To excite, to rouse (un perro).
— V. pr. FAM. To jostle, to push (empujarse).
achucharrar v. tr. *Amer.* To flatten.
— V. pr. *Amer.* To back down, to lose heart (amilanarse).
achuchón m. FAM. Push, shove: *me tiró al agua de un achuchón*, with a push he threw me into the water. || Flattening, squashing (aplastamiento). || — Pl. Pushing, *sing.*: *no voy al desfile porque detesto los achuchones*, I'm not going to the parade because I hate pushing. || *Dar un achuchón*, to push, to shove, to give a push *o* a shove.
achulado, da o **achulapado, da** adj. Vulgar, crude, coarse (grosero). || Funny, comical (gracioso). || Hard-faced, shameless (descarado). || Cocky (presumido).
achura f. *Amer.* Offal.
achurar o **achurear** v. tr. *Amer.* To gut, to eviscerate. | To knife *o* to stab to death.
achurruscar v. tr. *Amer.* To squash, to flatten.
— V. pr. To curl up (ensortijarse).
ādagio m. Proverb, adage. || MÚS. Adagio.
— Adj./adv. MÚS. Adagio.
adala f. MAR. Scupper.
adalid m. Leader. || Champion: *adalid de la democracia*, champion of democracy.
adamado, da adj. Effeminate (afeminado). || Refined, fine, delicate (fino). || Pretentious (pretencioso).
adamantino, na adj. Diamond-like, adamantine: *brillo adamantino*, diamond-like glitter.
adamarse v. pr. To become effeminate (afeminarse).
adamascado, da adj. Damask.
adamascar v. tr. To damask (tejidos).
adán m. FIG. y FAM. Sloven (descuidado). || Lazy bones, idler (haragán). || *Ir hecho un adán*, to be dressed in rags, to be slovenly dressed.
Adán n. pr. m. Adam. || — *Ir en el traje de Adán*, to be in one's birthday suit. || ANAT. *Manzana* or *nuez de Adán*, Adam's apple.
adaptable adj. Adaptable.
adaptación f. Adaptation: *la adaptación de una novela al teatro*, the adaptation of a novel for the theatre. || Fitting: *la adaptación de un segundo carburador a un motor*, the fitting of a second carburettor to an engine.
adaptador, ra adj. Adapting, fitting.
— M. y f. Adapter.
adaptar v. tr. To adapt: *adaptar una novela al teatro*, to adapt a novel for the theatre. || To adjust, to fit: *adaptar un sombrero a la cabeza de alguien*, to adjust a hat to s.o.'s head. || To adapt, to make suitable: *adaptar algo para otro uso*, to adapt sth. for a different use. || To model: *adaptar su conducta a la de su hermano*, to model one's conduct on one's brother's.
— V. pr. To adapt o.s.: *adaptarse a la vida del campo*, to adapt o.s. to country life.
adaraja f. ARQ. Toothing stone.
adarga f. Shield, targe (escudo).
adarme m. (Ant.). Dram [measurement of weight]. || FIG. Trace, grain: *no tiene un adarme de bondad*, there isn't a grain of goodness in him. || FIG. *No me importa ni un adarme*, I couldn't care less, I don't give a hang.
adarve m. Parapet walk (fortificación).
addenda m. inv. Addenda, *pl.*
adecentamiento m. Tidying-up.
adecentar v. tr. To tidy up, to clean up (ordenar): *adecentar una ciudad*, to tidy up a city.
— V. pr. To make o.s. decent, to tidy o.s. up.
adecuación f. Fitting, adjusting.
adecuadamente adv. Appropriately, suitably (convenientemente). || Sufficiently, adequately (suficientemente).
adecuado, da adj. Appropriate, suitable (conveniente): *vehículo adecuado para este tipo de terreno*, vehicle appropriate for this kind of land. || Adequate, sufficient (suficiente).
adecuar v. tr. To make appropriate *o* suitable, to adapt.
adefesio m. FAM. Ridiculously-dressed person, gaudily-dressed person. || Ridiculous *o* gaudy outfit (traje). || Absurdity, piece of nonsense (disparate). || — FAM. *Estar hecho un adefesio*, to look a sight, to be dressed like a clown, to be outrageously dressed. | *Poner como un adefesio*, to dress up like a clown.
adehala f. Tip, gratuity (propina). || Bonus (suplemento de sueldo).
adehesamiento m. Converting [of land] into pasture.
adehesar v. tr. To convert into pasture.
adelantadamente adv. Beforehand, in advance.
adelantado, da adj. Advanced, precocious (niño). || Early: *la vendimia está adelantada*, the grape harvest is early. || In advance: *pago adelantado*, payment in advance. || Developed, advanced: *un país adelantado*, a developed country. || Excellent, first-class (excelente). || Forward, bold (atrevido). || — *Eso tenemos* or *llevamos adelantado*, that's one thing we've got done. || *Pase adelantado*, long forward pass (en fútbol). || *Por adelantado*, in advance. || *Tengo el reloj adelantado*, my watch is fast.
— M. HIST. "Adelantado", governor (of a province). || FIG. Pioneer (precursor). || *Adelantado de mar*, captain of an expedition.
— OBSERV. The *adelantado* was the person with highest political, military and judicial powers in America at the time of the Spanish conquest and colonization.
adelantamiento m. Advance (adelanto). || Overtaking (de un coche). || HIST. Office of "adelantado". | District under an "adelantado" (territorio).
adelantar v. tr. To advance, to move forward, to go forward: *adelantar cuatro pasos*, to advance four steps. || To put on, to put forward: *adelantar el reloj*, to put one's watch forward. || To go up, to advance: *adelantar cuatro puestos en la clase*, to go up four places in the class. || To speed up, to hurry along: *adelantar un trabajo*, to speed up a job. || To overtake: *adelantar un vehículo, a un atleta*, to overtake a car, an athlete. || DEP. To pass forward (el balón). || To advance: *adelantar dinero*, to advance money. || To get, to win, to gain: *no adelantas nada gritando*, you don't get anywhere by shouting, you don't win *o* gain anything by shouting. || FIG. To further, to promote (una idea).
— V. intr. To go forward, to advance: *el ejército adelanta rápidamente*, the army is advancing quickly. || To progress, to make headway, to make progress: *ha adelantado mucho en matemáticas*, he has progressed a lot in mathematics, he has made a lot of progress in mathematics. || To be fast, to gain: *tu reloj adelanta mucho*, your watch is very fast *o* your watch gains a lot. || — *Adelantar en edad*, to be getting on. || AUT. *Prohibido adelantar*, no overtaking.
— V. pr. To go forward, to advance: *adelantarse al encuentro de alguien*, to go forward to meet s.o. || To be early: *el verano se ha adelantado este año*, summer was early this year. || To be first: *yo me adelanté a recibirle*, I was first to meet him. || To go ahead: *me adelanto un momento a comprar tabaco*, I'm going ahead a moment to buy some cigarettes. || To go earlier: *él se adelantó un día para buscar alojamiento*, he went a day earlier to look for lodgings. || To anticipate: *me adelanté a sus deseos*, I anticipated his wishes. || To be ahead: *adelantarse a su época*, to be ahead of one's time. || To gain (un reloj). || To overtake (un coche). || — *Adelantarse a la acción*, to be one step ahead. || *Adelantarse a uno*, to steal a march on s.o., to beat s.o. to it.
adelante adv. Further, ahead, forward: *marchemos adelante*, let us go forward. || — *Camino adelante*, further on. || *De aquí en adelante* or *de hoy en adelante* or *en adelante*, from now on, henceforth, in future. || *De diez libras en adelante*, from ten pounds up *o* upwards. || *Ir adelante*, to make progress, to progress. || *Llevar adelante*, to go ahead with, to carry out: *el general insiste en llevar adelante la ofensiva*, the general insists on going ahead with the attack; to keep going, to maintain (una familia), to carry on (un negocio). || *Más adelante*, later, later on, afterwards (luego), further on, later on (en textos). || *Para más adelante*, for later, for afterwards. || *Sacar adelante*, to give a good education to, to bring up well: *el padre sacó adelante a sus diez hijos*, the father gave a good education to his ten children; to make prosper (un negocio). || *Salir adelante*, to get on *o* by, to make out, to manage. || *Seguir adelante*, to go on, to carry on (en un trabajo), to go straight on (en un camino).
— Interj. Come in! (voz para que alguien entre), go on, carry on (siga). || FAM. *¡Adelante con los faroles!*, v. FAROL.

adelanto m. Advance, step forward: *el descubrimiento de la luz eléctrica fue un gran adelanto*, the discovery of electric light was a great step forward. || Improvement, advance, innovation: *el aparato lleva incorporados los últimos adelantos técnicos*, the machine incorporates the latest technical advances. || Lead: *este ciclista tiene veinte minutos de adelanto sobre los otros*, this cyclist has twenty minutes' lead over the others. || Advancement, progress: *el adelanto de las obras*, the advancement of the work. || Advance (de dinero): *pedir un adelanto*, to ask for an advance. || — *El reloj tiene un adelanto de cinco minutos*, the clock is five minutes fast. || *Los adelantos de la ciencia*, the progress of science. || *Llegar con un adelanto de media hora*, to arrive half an hour early. || *Tener un adelanto en su trabajo*, to be ahead with one's work.
adelfa f. BOT. Rosebay, common oleander.
adelfal m. Oleander grove.
adelgazador, ra adj. Slimming: *un régimen adelgazador*, a slimming diet.
adelgazamiento m. Slimming (pérdida de peso): *cura, régimen de adelgazamiento*, slimming cure, diet. || Thinning (de una cosa). || Tapering (de una punta).
adelgazar v. tr. To make thin, to thin (la madera, etc.). || To taper (una punta). || To lose: *he adelgazado tres kilos*, I have lost three kilogrammes. || To slim, to make slim (quitar peso a una persona): *esta medicina te adelgazará*, this medicine will make you slim. || To make thin (poner flaco). || To make look slim: *ese vestido la adelgaza mucho*, that dress makes her look very slim. || To scrimp (escatimar).
— V. intr. To get thin, to lose weight (ponerse flaco). || To slim, to lose weight (ponerse delgado): *he adelgazado mucho*, I've lost a lot of weight, I have slimmed a lot.
— V. pr. To slim, to lose weight.
ademán m. Expression, look: *ademán severo*, severe look. || Gesture, movement (de las manos): *con un ademán amenazador*, with a threatening gesture. || Position, posture (del cuerpo). || — Pl. Manners, ways (modales): *tiene ademanes muy groseros*, he has very crude manners. || Signs (manifestaciones). || — *En ademán de*, as if to, with the intention of (con intención de), as a sign of, as a token of: *en ademán de respeto*, as a sign of respect. || *Hacer ademán de*, to make a move to, to look as if one is going to *o* about to: *hizo ademán de marcharse*, he made a move to go, he looked as if he was about to go; to signal to, to motion to (mandar): *me hizo ademán de que me callase*, he signalled me to be quiet.
además adv. Besides, in addition, also, as well (formas corrientes), moreover, furthermore (formas cultas). || *Además de esto*, besides this, on top of this, in addition to this, as well as this, furthermore.
adenoideo, a adj. ANAT. Adenoid.
adentellar v. tr. To bite. || ARQ. To leave toothing stones in [a wall].
adentrarse v. pr. To penetrate *o* to go *o* to enter deep *o* deeply: *adentrarse en un bosque*, to penetrate deep into a wood. || To go deeply, to study thoroughly: *adentrarse en un asunto*, to go deeply into a subject, to study a subject thoroughly. || *Adentrarse en uno mismo*, to become absorbed in thought, to become deep in thought.
adentro adv. Inside: *vamos adentro*, let's go inside. || Far in: *la espina estaba tan adentro que no pude sacarla*, the thorn was so far in that I couldn't get it out. || — *Mar adentro*, out to sea, towards the open sea. || *Tierra adentro*, inland.
— M. pl. Heart, *sing.* || — *Decir para sus adentros*, to say to o.s. || *En* or *para sus adentros no quiere venir*, in his heart he does not want to come, deep down he does not want to come. || *Hablar para sus adentros*, to talk to o.s.
— Interj. Come in!
— OBSERV. In Latin America the interjection *¡adentro!* is often used in singing and dancing to encourage the singers to begin singing again and the dancers to begin dancing.
adepto, ta adj. Who supports, in favour, supporting.
— M. y f. Supporter, adept, follower: *adepto del gobierno*, government supporter. || Member, adept (afiliado).
aderezamiento m. V. ADEREZO.
aderezar v. tr. To adorn, to decorate (adornar). || To beautify (hermosear). || To deck out, to dress up (ataviar). || CULIN. To cook, to prepare, to get ready. | To dress (la ensalada). | To season (aliñar): *limón para aderezar*, lemon juice for seasoning. | To flavour (bebidas). || To prepare, to get ready (disponer). || To dress, to give a finish to (dar apresto a las telas). || To guide (guiar). || FIG. To season.
— V. pr. To get ready (prepararse). || To deck o.s. out, to dress up (ataviarse).
aderezo m. Dressing, toilet (acción de embellecerse). || Ornament, adornment, decoration (adorno). || Set of jewellery (joyas). || CULIN. Cooking, preparation (de la comida). | Dressing (de ensalada). | Seasoning (con especias, etc.). | Flavouring (de bebidas). || Finishing, dressing (de las telas).
adeudado, da adj. Owing (cantidad que se debe). || In debt (persona que debe dinero).
adeudar v. tr. To owe, to have a debt of: *adeudar un millón de pesetas*, to owe *o* to have a debt of a million pesetas. || COM. To charge, to debit (en una cuenta).
— V. pr. To get *o* to run into debt.
adeudo m. COM. Debit, charge (de una cuenta). || Duty (en las aduanas). || Debt (deuda).
adherencia f. Sticking, adhesion (acción de pegar). || Adherence (acción de adherir). || Roadholding (de un coche). || MED. Adhesion. || *Tener buena adherencia*, to have good roadholding, to hold the road well (un coche).
adherente adj. Adherent.
— M. y f. Adherent, follower. || — Pl. Accessories.
adherir* v. tr. To stick on: *adherir un sello*, to stick a stamp on.
— V. intr. To stick: *este parche no adhiere*, this patch will not stick.
— V. intr. y pr. To adhere, to follow (una doctrina, un partido): *no se adhiere a ningún partido*, he does not adhere to any party, he does not follow any party. || To join (afiliarse).
adhesión f. Adhesion, adherence (de algo pegado). || Adherence (a una doctrina, etc.). || Membership (afiliación). || Support (apoyo): *espero poder contar con su adhesión*, I hope to be able to count on your support.
adhesivo, va adj./s. m. Adhesive.
adiabático, ca adj. FÍS. Adiabatic.
adiamantado, da adj. Diamond-like.
adiar v. tr. To fix, to appoint.
adición f. Addition: *hacer adiciones a un texto*, to make additions to a text. || MAT. Addition. || JUR. Acceptance: *adición de una herencia*, acceptance of an inheritance. || *Amer.* Bill [U.S., check] (cuenta).
adicional adj. Additional, supplementary: *poner una cláusula adicional en un contrato*, to put an additional clause in a contract.
adicionar v. tr. To add: *adicionar un párrafo a un artículo*, to add a paragraph to an article. || MAT. To add [up].
adicto, ta adj. Devoted, faithful: *un amigo adicto*, a devoted friend. || *Ser muy adicto a una causa*, to be very devoted to a cause.
— M. y f. Follower, supporter.
adiestrado, da adj. Trained, instructed. || HERÁLD. Dexterwise.
adiestrador, ra adj. Who trains *o* instructs.
— M. y f. Trainer, instructor.
adiestramiento m. Training (de un animal). || Training, instruction: *adiestramiento de las tropas*, troop training.
adiestrar v. tr. To train (un animal). || To train, to instruct (una persona). || To guide, to lead (guiar).
— V. pr. To train o.s., to practise, to instruct o.s.: *adiestrarse en el uso de la espada*, to train o.s. to use a sword, to practise using a sword, to instruct o.s. in the use of the sword.
adietar v. tr. To put on a diet.
Adigio n. pr. m. GEOGR. Adige.
adinerado, da adj. Rich, wealthy, well-off, well-to-do.
— M. y f. Rich *o* wealthy person.
adinerarse v. pr. FAM. To get rich *o* wealthy, to make one's fortune.
adintelado, da adj. ARQ. Flat (arco).
¡adiós! interj. Good-bye, farewell, adieu (V. OBSERV.). || Hello (al cruzarse con alguien). || — FAM. *¡Adiós mi dinero!*, that's good-bye to my money!, there went my money! | *Decir adiós a sus pretensiones*, to give up one's ambitions, to say good-bye to one's ambitions.
— M. Good-bye, farewell.
— OBSERV. En inglés las interjecciones *farewell* y *adieu* son antiguas y sólo se emplean para una despedida definitiva.
¡adiosito! interj. *Amer.* Cheerio!
adiposidad f. MED. Adiposity, obesity.
adiposo, sa adj. ANAT. Fatty, adipose: *tejido adiposo*, fatty tissue. || Obese, fat (persona).
adir v. tr. JUR. To accept [an inheritance].
aditamento m. Addition (añadido). || Accessory (accesorio).
adivinable adj. Forseeable (previsible). || Guessable (por conjeturas).
adivinación f. o **adivinamiento** m. Divination (de los adivinos). || Solution (de un enigma o acertijo). || Guessing (descubrimiento por conjeturas). || *Adivinación del pensamiento*, thought reading, mind reading.
adivinador, ra m. y f. Fortune-teller (adivino).
adivinanza f. Riddle, puzzle, conundrum.
adivinar v. tr. To divine, to prophesy, to foretell (el porvenir, etc.). || To guess (acertar por conjeturas). || To read: *adivinar el pensamiento de alguien*, to read s.o.'s mind. || To solve: *adivinar un acertijo*, to solve a riddle. || — *¡Adivina quién soy!*, guess who! || *Adivina quién te dio*, blindman's buff (juego infantil). || *¡A que no lo adivina!*, I bet you can't guess. || *Dejar adivinar*, to hint at (con sustantivo), to hint that (con locución verbal): *dejó adivinar su descontento*, he hinted at his unhappiness, he hinted that he was unhappy.
adivinatorio, ria adj. Divinatory.
adivino, na m. y f. Fortune-teller.
adjetivación f. Adjectival use, use as an adjective.
adjetivamente adv. Adjectivally.
adjetival adj. Adjectival.

adjetivar v. tr. To use as an adjective, to use adjectivally. || To describe: *lo adjetivaron de inmenso*, they described it as immense.
adjetivo, va adj. Adjectival, adjective: *expresión adjetiva*, adjectival expression.
— M. Adjective.
adjudicación f. Award, awarding. || Sale (subasta).
adjudicador, ra adj. Awarding.
— M. y f. Awarder.
adjudicar v. tr. To award (conceder): *le adjudicaron el primer premio*, they awarded him first prize. || To sell, to knock down (algo en una subasta). || *¡Adjudicado!*, sold! (en una subasta).
— V. pr. To appropriate (apropiarse).
adjudicatario, ria m. y f. Awardee. || Successful bidder (en una subasta).
adjuntar v. tr. To attach, to append (a un documento). || To enclose: *le adjunto un sobre con un sello*, I enclose a stamped addressed envelope. || To give: *le van a adjuntar un auxiliar*, they are going to give him an assistant.
adjunto, ta adj. Attached (a un texto, documento, etc.). || Enclosed, attached (en una carta): *la tarifa adjunta*, the enclosed price list. || Assistant: *profesor adjunto*, assistant teacher. || *Remitir algo adjunto*, to enclose sth.
— M. y f. Assistant.
adjuración f. Adjuration.
adjurar v. tr. To adjure.
adjutor, ra adj. / s. Assistant.
adlátere m. Inseparable companion, lapdog.
adminículo m. Thing, gadget: *la patilla de las gafas tenía un adminículo para mejorar la audición*, the spectacles had a thing on the arm to improve one's hearing.
administración f. Administration: *administración pública*, public administration. || Management, running, administration (gestión). || Management (los gerentes). || Administrative centre, headquarters, *pl.* (oficina). || — *Administración de Correos*, Post Office. || *Consejo de administración*, board of directors.
administrado, da adj. Under administration.
— M. y f. Person under administration.
administrador, ra adj. Administrating.
— M. y f. Administrator. || Manager, administrator (de una finca). || — *Administrador de aduanas*, customs officer. || *Administrador de Correos*, Postmaster. || *Es buena administradora*, she is a good housewife.
administrar v. tr. To administer, to run, to manage, to administrate (regir). || To administer (sacramentos, medicamentos). || FAM. To hand out, to dish out (dar): *administrar una paliza*, to hand out a beating. || *Administrar (la) justicia*, to administer *o* to dispense justice.
administrativo, va adj. Administrative.
— M. Office worker, white-collar worker.
admirable adj. Admirable.
admiración f. Admiration: *causar admiración*, to inspire admiration. || Surprise, wonder, astonishment: *su llegada puntual me llenó de admiración*, his punctual arrival filled me with wonder. || GRAM. Exclamation mark. || — *Ser la admiración de alguien*, to be the object of s.o.'s admiration, to be admired by s.o. || *Tener* or *sentir admiración por alguien*, to feel admiration for s.o., to admire s.o.
admirador, ra adj. Admiring.
— M. y f. Admirer.
admirar v. tr. To admire: *admiro su valor*, I admire his courage. || To surprise, to astonish, to amaze (sorprender): *tanta generosidad me admira*, such generosity amazes me. || *Quedarse admirado*, to be astonished *o* astounded (maravillarse).
— V. pr. To be amazed *o* surprised *o* astonished: *me admiro de su insolencia*, I am amazed at his insolence. || To admire, to have great admiration for, to marvel at: *me admiro de los progresos científicos*, I have great admiration for scientific progress.
admirativamente adv. Admiringly, with admiration, in admiration. || Amazedly, in wonderment (con asombro).
admirativo, va adj. Admiring (que admira): *hablar en tono admirativo*, to speak in an admiring tone. || Amazed (asombrado).
admisibilidad f. Admissibility.
admisible adj. Admissible, acceptable, permissible: *tal conducta no es admisible*, such behaviour is not permissible. || Acceptable (excusa).
admisión f. Admission. || Acceptance (aceptación). || TECN. Induction, intake (en un motor de explosión). || — *Examen de admisión*, entrance examination. || *Reservado el derecho de admisión*, the management reserves the right to refuse admission. || TECN. *Válvula de admisión*, inlet valve.
admitancia f. ELECTR. Admittance.
admitir v. tr. To admit: *admitir a uno en una sociedad*, to admit s.o. to a society. || To accept, to admit: *en correos no admiten paquetes voluminosos*, bulky parcels are not accepted by the Post Office. || To accept for, to allow to sit (un examen). || To allow, to permit: *yo no puedo admitir esto*, I can't allow this. || To acknowledge, to admit, to recognize, to agree: *admito que estaba equivocado*, I admit I was wrong. || To suppose: *admitamos que tenga razón...*, supposing he is right..., let us suppose he is right... || To hold: *el estadio admite quinientos espectadores*, the stadium holds five hundred spectators. || To allow (explicación). || To lend o.s. to, to be open to: *esta frase admite varias interpretaciones*, this sentence lends itself to several interpretations. || — *Este asunto no admite dilación*, this matter must be dealt with immediately. || *Esto no admite duda*, there is no doubt about this, this leaves no room for doubt. || *No se admiten propinas*, no tipping.
admonición f. Rebuke, admonition, reprimand.
admonitor m. Admonisher.
admonitorio, ria adj. Admonitory, reprimanding.
adobado, da adj. CULIN. Marinated.
— M. CULIN. Marinated meat.
A.D.N. m. D.N.A. (ácido desoxirribonucléico).
adobador, ra m. y f. Pickler (de carnes). || Tanner (de pieles).
adobadura f. o **adobamiento** m. CULIN. Pickling, marinating (de la carne). | Dressing, seasoning (de ciertos platos). || Tanning (de las pieles).
adobar v. tr. CULIN. To pickle, to marinate (la carne, el pescado). | To season, to dress (sazonar). | To cook (guisar). || To tan (las pieles). || FIG. To twist, to turn round: *adobar un relato*, to twist a story.
adobe m. Sun-dried brick, adobe (ladrillo secado al sol). || *Amer.* Big foot (pie).
adobera f. Brick mould. || Adobe yard, brickyard (adobería). || *Amer.* Cheese mould. | Rectangular cheese (queso).
adobería f. Adobe yard, brickyard. || Tannery (curtiduría).
adobo m. CULIN. Seasoning, dressing (aderezamiento). | Cooking (acción de guisar). | Pickling sauce, marinade (para carne y pescado). || Tanning (de pieles). || Tanning mixture (mezcla para las pieles). || (P.us.). Makeup (afeite). || *Carne, pescado en adobo*, marinated meat, fish.
adocenado, da adj. Commonplace, ordinary, common or garden (fam.).
adocenar v. tr. To divide into dozens.
— V. pr. To become commonplace *o* ordinary.
adoctrinamiento m. Indoctrination. || Teaching (enseñanza).
adoctrinar v. tr. To indoctrinate (condicionar). || To teach (enseñar).
adolecer* v. intr. To fall ill (caer enfermo). || To suffer, to have: *adolecer de reúma*, to suffer from *o* to have rheumatism. || FIG. To have, to suffer: *adolecer de ciertos defectos*, to suffer from certain faults. || — FIG. *Adolece de ser apático*, his fault *o* failing is that he is apathetic, his fault *o* failing is his apathy. | *El libro adolece de monotonía*, the book's fault *o* failing is its monotony.
adolescencia f. Adolescence.
adolescente adj. / s. Adolescent.
Adolfo n. pr. m. Adolph.
adonde adv. Where, whither (ant.). || *El lugar adonde voy*, the place where I am going, the place I am going to.
— OBSERV. *Where* without the idea of movement is usually translated by *donde*: *la casa donde vivo*, the house where I live. *Adonde* is also sometimes seen where no movement is involved, but this usage is now obsolete. In an interrogative sentence, *adonde* has a written accent: *¿adónde va?*, where is he going?
adondequiera adv. Wherever, wheresoever (movimiento): *adondequiera que vayamos*, wherever we [may] go.
Adonis n. pr. m. Adonis.
adonizarse v. pr. To beautify o.s., to tittivate o.s.
adopción f. Adoption: *país de adopción*, country of adoption.
adoptar v. tr. To adopt (un hijo, una costumbre, una actitud, una resolución). || To assume, to adopt: *adoptar la nacionalidad británica*, to assume British nationality.
adoptivo, va adj. Adopted, adoptive (hijo). || Adoptive (padres). || — FIG. *Hijo adoptivo*, Honorary citizen (de una ciudad). || *Patria adoptiva*, country of adoption.
adoquín m. Paving stone (piedra). || FIG. y FAM. Numbskull, dunce, dimwit (necio): *eres un adoquín*, you're a numbskull. || *Amer.* Wooden paving block (tarugo). || FAM. y FIG. *Me comería hasta adoquines*, I could eat a horse.
adoquinado, da adj. Paved.
— M. Paving.
adoquinador m. Paver.
adoquinar v. tr. To pave.
adorable adj. Adorable.
adoración f. Worship, adoration (de Dios). || Adoration, idolization, worshipping (de una persona). || *Adoración de los Reyes*, Epiphany.
adorador, ra adj. Worshipping, adoring (que adora a Dios). || Adoring, idolizing (que adora a otra persona).
— M. y f. Worshipper, adorer (de Dios). || Adorer, idolizer (de una persona).
adorar v. tr. To worship, to adore (a Dios). || To adore, to worship, to idolize (a una persona).
— V. intr. To pray (orar).
adoratorio m. Portable retable. || *Amer.* Indian Temple.
adormecedor, ra adj. Soporific, sleep-inducing. || FIG. Sedative (sedante).

adormecer* v. tr. To make sleepy, to send to sleep: *esta música me adormece*, this music is sending me to sleep. || FIG. To calm, to soothe: *el opio adormece los dolores*, opium soothes pain.
— V. pr. To fall asleep (dormirse). || To grow drowsy, to drowse, to doze (amodorrarse). || FIG. To go to sleep, to turn numb (un miembro). || To give o.s. up to: *adormecerse en un vicio*. to give o.s. up to a vice.
adormecido, da adj. Sleepy, drowsy. || Numb, asleep (un miembro).
adormecimiento m. Drowsiness, sleepiness. || Numbness (de un miembro). || FIG. Calmness.
adormidera f. BOT. Poppy. || Narcotic, drug (estupefaciente).
adormilarse o **adormitarse** v. pr. To become drowsy, to drowse, to doze.
adornamiento m. Decoration, adornment. || Finery (atavío).
adornar v. tr. To decorate, to adorn: *adornar con* or *de flores*, to decorate with flowers. || To trim (trajes, etc.). || FIG. To elaborate on, to embellish: *adornar una historia*, to embellish a story. || To garnish (la comida). || FIG. *Las virtudes que le adornan*, the virtues with which he is endowed *o* blessed.
— V. pr. To be decorated *o* adorned. || To dress up (ataviarse).
adorno m. Decoration, adornment. || Trimming (de trajes). || CULIN. Garnishing. || TAUR. "Adorno" (V. OBSERV.). || — Pl. BOT. Balsamine, *sing.* || *De adorno*, decorative.

— OBSERV. The *adorno* is a gesture made by the bullfighter (turning his back on the bull, stroking the bull's head, touching its horns, etc.) which "adorns" his performance and is intended to show his domination of the bull.

adosamiento m. Leaning.
adosar v. tr. To lean: *adosar una silla a la pared*, to lean a chair against the wall. || ARQ. *Columna adosada*, embedded column.
adovelado, da adj. ARQ. Voussoir.
adquirente adj./s. V. ADQUISIDOR.
adquirido, da adj. Acquired: *velocidad adquirida*, acquired speed; *hábito adquirido*, acquired habit. || Purchased, bought, acquired (comprado).
adquiridor, ra adj./s. V. ADQUISIDOR.
adquirir* v. tr. To acquire: *adquirir un hábito*, to acquire a habit || To purchase, to buy, to acquire: *he adquirido una bicicleta*, I have purchased a bicyle.
adquisición f. Acquisition. || Acquisition, purchase (compra).
adquisidor, ra adj. Acquiring. || Purchasing, buying, acquiring.
— M. y f. Purchaser, buyer (comprador).
adquisitivo, va adj. Acquisitive. || — *Poder adquisitivo*, purchasing power. || JUR. *Prescripción adquisitiva*, positive prescription.
adragante o **adraganto** m. Tragacanth (goma). || BOT. Tragacanth.
adral m. Rail, rave, rack (de un carro).
adrede adv. On purpose, deliberately, purposely.
adrenalina f. BIOL. Adrenalin.
Adrián n. pr. m. Adrian.
Adriano n. pr. m. Hadrian.
Adriático n. pr. m. GEOGR. Adriatic.
adrizamiento m. MAR. Righting.
adrizar v. tr. MAR. To right.
adscribir v. tr. To attribute, to ascribe (atribuir). || To assign, to appoint (destinar): *le adscribieron al servicio de ventas*, they assigned him to the sales department.

— OBSERV. The past participle of *adscribir* is irregular (*adscrito, ta*, or the less common *adscripto, ta*).

adscripción f. Attribution (atribución). || Appointment, assignment (destino).
adscripto, ta o **adscrito, ta** adj. Attributed, ascribed. || Appointed, assigned (destinado).
adsorbente adj./s. m. QUÍM. Adsorbent.
adsorber v. tr. QUÍM. To adsorb.
adsorción f. QUÍM. Adsorption.
aduana f. Customs *pl.*: *derechos de aduana*, customs duty; *pasar por la aduana*, to go through customs. || Customhouse, customs building (oficina). || — *Oficial de aduana(s)*, customs officer. || *Sin aduana*, duty-free.
aduanar v. tr. To pay customs duty on.
aduanero, ra adj. Customs: *tarifa aduanera*, customs tariff.
— M. Customs officer.
aduar m. Douar, dowar (de beduinos). || Encampment, camp (de gitanos).
aducción f. Adduction.
aducir* v. tr. To allege, to plead (razones). || To adduce, to produce (pruebas). || To advance, to bring forward (disculpas). || To cite, to quote (un texto).
aductor adj. ANAT. Adductive.
— M. ANAT. Adductor.
adueñarse v. pr. To take possession of, to appropriate: *se adueñó de mi coche*, he appropriated my car.
aduja f. Coil (de un cable).
adujar v. tr. MAR. To coil.
— V. pr. To curl up.
adulación f. Flattery, adulation (lisonja).
adulador, ra adj. Flattering, adulating.
— M. y f. Flatterer, adulator.
adular v. tr. To flatter, to adulate.
adulatorio, ria adj. Flattering, adulating.
adulón, ona adj. Grovelling, fawning.
— M. y f. Crawler, toady.
adulonería f. V. ADULACIÓN.
adulteración f. Adulteration.
adulterado, da adj. Adulterated, adulterate.
adulterador, ra adj. Adulterating.
— M. y f. Adulterator.
adulterar v. tr. To adulterate: *adulterar la verdad*, to adulterate the truth; *adulterar la leche con agua*, to adulterate milk with water.
— V. intr. To commit adultery.
adulterinamente adv. Adulterously.
adulterino, na adj. Adulterine: *hijo adulterino*, adulterine child.
adulterio m. Adultery (acto).
adúltero, ra adj. Adulterous.
— M. y f. Adulterer, adulteress.
adulto, ta adj./s. Adult, grown-up. || *Una nación adulta*, a mature nation.
adulzar v. tr. TECN. To soften.
adustez f. Severity, austerity, harshness.
adusto, ta adj. (P.us.). Scorching hot (muy caliente). || FIG. Severe, austere, harsh: *rostro adusto*, harsh expression.
advenedizo, za adj./s. Upstart, parvenu: *en aquella época pululaban los advenedizos*, at that time there were swarms of upstarts.
advenimiento m. Coming (llegada). || Advent (del Mesías). || Arrival, coming, advent (de una época). || Accession (de un soberano). || FIG. y FAM. *Parece que estás esperando el santo Advenimiento*, you look as if you're waiting for Christmas.
advenir* v. intr. To come, to arrive.

— OBSERV. This verb is used only in the third person of the past historic.

adventicio, cia adj. Accidental, adventitious (ocasional). || BOT. Adventitious.
adventista adj./s. Adventist.
adverado, da adj. Certified, legalized (certificado).
adverar v. tr. To certify, to legalize.
adverbial adj. Adverbial: *locución adverbial*, adverbial phrase.
adverbializar v. tr. To use as an adverb.
adverbio m. GRAM. Adverb.
adversamente adv. Adversely.
adversario, ria adj. Opposing: *el equipo adversario*, the opposing team.
— M. y f. Opponent, adversary: *derribar al adversario*, to knock down one's opponent.
adversativo, va adj. GRAM. Adversative.
adversidad f. Adversity, misfortune, setback: *sufrió muchas adversidades*, he suffered many setbacks. || *Se conoce a los amigos en la adversidad*, a friend in need is a friend indeed.
adverso, sa adj. Adverse, unfavourable: *situación adversa*, unfavourable situation. || Bad: *suerte adversa*, bad luck. || Opposing (adversario): *el equipo adverso*, the opposing team. || Opposite (opuesto materialmente).
advertencia f. Warning: *después de repetidas advertencias se negaron a dispersarse*, after repeated warnings they refused to disperse. || Piece of advice (consejo). || Explanation (explicación). || Note, explanation, observation (nota). || Foreword (prólogo). || MAR. Call. || — JUR. *Advertencia conminatoria*, summons. || *Hacer una advertencia a un niño*, to correct a child, to tell a child off.
advertidamente adv. Knowingly.
advertido, da adj. Informed, warned (avisado). || Experienced: *una secretaria muy advertida*, a very experienced secretary.
advertidor adj. Warning.
advertimiento m. Warning (advertencia).
advertir* v. tr. To warn, to inform: *te advierto que mañana no vendré*, I warn you that I'm not coming tomorrow. || To warn of, to give warning of: *una señal de tráfico advertía el peligro*, a road sign gave warning of the danger. || To tell, to recommend, to advise: *adviértele que no llegue tarde a la reunión*, advise him not to arrive late at the meeting. || To warn: *te advierto que es la última vez que lo tolero*, I warn you that it's the last time I'll stand for it. || To point out (señalar): *le advierto algunos errores*, I will point out a few mistakes to you. || To notice, to observe, to see, to realize: *he advertido que había muchas faltas*, I noticed that there were many mistakes. || To tell: *te advierto que soy el menos interesado en esta reforma*, I tell you I am the least interested in this reform.
— V. intr. To realize, to understand (comprender).
Adviento m. Advent: *el cuarto domingo de Adviento*, the fourth Sunday of Advent.
advocación f. REL. Invocation. || — REL. *Bajo la advocación de la Virgen*, dedicated to the Virgin. | *Poner bajo la advocación de*, to dedicate to.
adyacente adj. Adjacent.
aedo m. Bard (poeta).
aeración f. QUÍM. Aeration. || Ventilation (ventilación).

aéreo, a adj. Aerial: *fotografía aérea*, aerial photography. || Air: *tráfico aéreo*, air traffic. || Flimsy, light (ligero). || — *Compañía aérea*, airline company. || *Ferrocarril aéreo*, overhead *o* elevated railway. || *Línea aérea*, airline. || *Toma aérea*, aerial. || *Transportador aéreo*, cableway.
aerífero, ra adj. Air.
aeriforme adj. Aeriform.
aerobio, bia adj. BIOL. Aerobic.
— M. BIOL. Aerobe.
aerobús m. Airbus.
aeroclub m. Flying club.
aerodeslizador m. Hovercraft.
aerodinámico, ca adj. Aerodynamic. || Streamlined: *la forma aerodinámica de un avión*, the streamlined shape of a plane. || — *Freno aerodinámico*, air brake. || *Túnel aerodinámico*, wind tunnel.
— F. Aerodynamics.
aerodino m. Aerodyne.
aeródromo m. Aerodrome [U.S., airdrome], airfield.
aerofagia f. Aerophagia.
aerofaro m. Runway beacon, aerial beacon.
aerofotografía f. Aerial photography (arte). || Aerial photograph (foto).
aerógrafo m. ARTES. Airbrush.
aerograma m. Aerogram.
aerolito m. ASTR. Aerolite, meteorite.
aeromancia f. Aeromancy.
aeromarítimo, ma adj. Aeromarine.
aerometría f. Aerometry.
aerómetro m. Aerometer.
aeromodelismo m. Aeromodelling, aeroplane modelling [U.S., airplane modeling].
aeromodelista adj. Aeroplane modelling, aeromodelling [U. S., airplane modeling].
— M. y f. Aeroplane modeller [U. S., airplane modeler].
aeromodelo m. Model aeroplane [U.S., model airplane].
aeromotor m. Aeromotor.
aeromoza f. *Amer.* Air hostess, stewardess (azafata).
aeromozo m. *Amer.* Steward.
aeronato, ta adj. Born in an aeroplane.
— M. y f. Person born in an aeroplane.
aeronauta m. y f. Aeronaut.
aeronáutico, ca adj. Aeronautical, aeronautic.
— F. Aeronautics.
aeronaval adj. Sea and air, aeromarine: *batalla aeronaval*, sea and air battle.
aeronave f. Airship. || *Aeronave espacial*, spaceship.
aeroplano m. Aeroplane [U.S., airplane] (avión).
aeropostal adj. Airmail.
aeropuerto m. Airport.
aerosol m. Aerosol.
aerostación f. Balloon-flying, aerostation.
aerostático, ca adj. Aerostatic.
— F. Aerostatics.
aeróstato m. Aerostat (globo).
aerostero m. Aeronaut. || Balloonist (de un globo).
aerotecnia o **aerotécnica** f. Aeronautics.
aerotécnico, ca adj. Aerotechnical.
aeroterapia f. Aerotherapy, aerotherapeutics.
aerotermodinámica f. Aerothermodynamics.
aeroterrestre adj. Land and air: *batalla aeroterrestre*, land and air battle.
aerotransportado, da adj. Airborne: *tropas aerotransportadas*, airborne troops.
aerovía f. Airway.
afabilidad f. Affability, geniality, pleasantness (amabilidad).
afabilísimo, ma adj. Very affable, very pleasant.
afable adj. Affable, pleasant, genial: *afable con* or *para con todos*, affable with everyone.
afabulación f. Moral of a fable.
afacetado, da adj. In facets.
afamado, da adj. Famous, renowned (famoso).
afamar v. tr. To make famous, to bring renown to.
— V. pr. To win fame, to become famous.
afán m. Toil, labour (trabajo penoso): *los afanes cotidianos*, the daily toils. || Enthusiasm, zeal, eagerness, fervour: *trabajar con afán*, to work with enthusiasm. || Desire, urge (deseo). || Anxiety (preocupación). || — *Afán de lucro*, profit motive. || *Cada día trae su afán*, sufficient unto the day is the evil thereof. || *Con afán*, enthusiastically, zealously, keenly. || *Poner todo su afán en*, to put all one's efforts into, to put everything one has into.
afanadamente adv. Enthusiastically, zealously, fervently. || Laboriously (con mucho trabajo). || *Desear afanadamente*, to want desperately *o* urgently.
afanador, ra adj. Enthusiastic, zealous, fervent.
— M. y f. Enthusiastic *o* zealous *o* eager *o* fervent person. || POP. Thief. || *Amer.* Labourer.
afanar v. intr. To toil (en trabajos penosos).
— V. tr. To work hard, to press hard (cansar con mucho trabajo). || FAM. To pinch, to swipe, to steal (robar). || *Amer.* To make, to earn [money].
— V. pr. To toil, to labour. || To do one's utmost, to strive: *afanarse por* or *en conseguir un buen puesto*, to do one's utmost to get a good job, to strive to get a good job.
afanosamente adv. Enthusiastically, zealously, fervently. || Laboriously (con mucho trabajo). || *Desear afanosamente*, to want desperately *o* urgently.
afanoso, sa adj. Laborious, hard, wearying, heavy (trabajoso). || Enthusiastic, industrious, hard-working, keen (concienzudo). || Worried, anxious (preocupado). || Hectic, feverish (la búsqueda).
afantasmado, da adj. FAM. Big-headed, conceited, vain (presumido).
afarolado, da adj. *Amer.* Worked up, excited (emocionado). | Angry (enfadado). || TAUR. *Pase afarolado*, "afarolado" pass [when the bullfighter swings his cape above his head].
— M. "Afarolado" pass.
afarolarse v. pr. *Amer.* To get excited *o* worked up (conturbarse). | To get angry (enfadarse).
afasia f. MED. Aphasia.
afásico, ca adj./s. MED. Aphasic.
afeador, ra adj. Disfiguring, which makes ugly. || Reproachful, condemning, censuring (que censura).
afeamiento m. Disfigurement. || Censure, condemnation.
afear v. tr. To make ugly, to disfigure: *este maquillaje le afea*, this makeup makes her ugly. || To reproach, to censure: *afear mucho a uno su conducta*, to reproach s.o. severely for his behaviour.
afección f. Affection (cariño). || MED. Affection, complaint, disease: *una afección del corazón*, a heart complaint.
afeccionarse v. pr. To become attached, to grow fond: *afeccionarse por uno*, to become attached to s.o., to grow fond of s.o.
afectación f. Affectation.
afectado, da adj. Affected, unnatural (amanerado). || Damaged, spoiled: *finca afectada por la inundación*, farm damaged by the flood. || Upset: *está muy afectado por la muerte de su madre*, he is very upset over the death of his mother. || — *Estar afectado del corazón*, to have a heart complaint. || *Estar afectado de un ataque gripal*, to be suffering from an attack of influenza.
afectar v. tr. To affect, to put on a show of: *afectar suma elegancia*, to affect great elegance, to put on a show of great elegance. || To pretend, to feign: *afectó un dolor de cabeza para salir de la conferencia*, he pretended to have a headache *o* he feigned a headache as an excuse to leave the lecture. || To adopt, to take on: *afectar la forma de estrella*, to adopt the shape of a star. || To concern, to affect (atañer): *esta ley afecta a todos los ciudadanos*, this law concerns all citizens. || To damage (dañar): *las tormentas han afectado las cosechas*, the storms have damaged the crops. || To upset, to make sad, to trouble: *la enfermedad de su madre le afecta mucho*, his mother's illness upsets him a lot. || To affect, to have an effect on: *su pulmonía le ha afectado mucho*, his pneumonia has affected him seriously.
— V. intr. To affect, to concern: *un problema que afecta a la economía*, a problem which affects the economy.
afectísimo, ma adj. My dear: *afectísimo amigo*, my dear friend. || COM. Sincerely, faithfully (al final de cartas): *suyo afectísimo*, yours sincerely, sincerely yours. || *Su afectísimo servidor*, your devoted servant.
afectividad f. Affectivity. || Sensitivity, sensitiveness (sensibilidad).
afectivo, va adj. Affective (referente a las emociones). || Sensitive (sensible). || Affectionate (cariñoso).
afecto, ta adj. Dear: *un amigo afecto*, a dear friend. || — *Afecto a*, fond of, attached to (alguien), subject to, liable to (los impuestos). || MED. *Afecto de*, suffering from, afflicted with.
— M. Affection, fondness (cariño). || *Tomar afecto a alguien*, to become attached to *o* fond of s.o.
afectuosidad f. Affection, fondness.
afectuoso, sa adj. Affectionate.
afeitado m. Shave. || TAUR. Blunting of the horns, shaving.
afeitadora f. Razor, shaver.
afeitar v. tr. To shave. || (Ant.). To make up, to put makeup on (poner afeites). || To trim (los animales). || To cut, to trim (césped, plantas). || TAUR. To blunt the horns of, to shave. || FIG. y FAM. To graze, to brush (rozar).
— V. pr. To shave, to have a shave (la barba, etc.). || To make up, to make o.s. up (ponerse afeites).
afeite m. (Ant.). Makeup, cosmetics, *pl.* (cosmético).
afelio m. ASTR. Aphelion.
afelpado, da adj. Plush, velvety.
afelpar v. tr. To make velvety *o* plush.
afeminación f. Effeminacy.
afeminadamente adv. In an effeminate way, effeminately.
afeminado, da adj. Effeminate.
— M. Effeminate person, sissy, cissy (fam.).
afeminamiento m. Effeminacy.
afeminar v. tr. To make effeminate.
— V. pr. To become effeminate.
aferente adj. ANAT. Afferent.
aféresis f. GRAM. Aphaeresis.
aferradamente adv. Obstinately, stubbornly.
aferrado, da adj. Obstinate, stubborn (obstinado). || FIG. Established: *una idea bien aferrada*, a well established idea. || *Seguir aferrado a*, to stand by, to stick to.
aferrador, ra adj. Grasping, seizing.

aferramiento m. Seizing, grasping (acción de agarrar). || MAR. Mooring, anchoring (acción de anclar). || FIG. Obstinacy, stubbornness.
aferrar* v. tr. To seize, to grasp, to clutch (agarrar). || MAR. To anchor, to moor (anclar). | To take in, to furl (las velas). | To hook, to grapple (con un garfio).
— V. intr. MAR. To bite, to grip (el ancla). | To anchor (el barco).
— V. pr. To cling. || MAR. To anchor. || FIG. To stick, to cling (obstinarse): *aferrarse a* or *en una idea, una opinión*, to cling to an idea, an opinion.
afestonado, da adj. Festooned (festonado). || Scalloped (labrado en forma de festón).
affaire m. Case, affair (caso).
Afganistán n. pr. m. GEOGR. Afghanistan.
afgano, na adj./s. Afghan.
afianzador, ra adj. Guaranteeing.
afianzamiento m. Guarantee (garantía). || Surety, bond (fianza). || Strengthening, reinforcement: *el afianzamiento de las estructuras*, the reinforcement of structures. || Establishment, consolidation: *el afianzamiento de un régimen*, the establishment of a régime. || Building up, restoring: *el afianzamiento de su salud*, the building up of one's health.
afianzar v. tr. To guarantee (garantizar). || To strengthen, to reinforce: *afianzar las patas de una silla*, to strengthen the legs of a chair. || To establish, to make secure: *su éxito le ha afianzado en su puesto*, his success has established him in his job. || To build up, to restore: *tienes que afianzar tu salud*, you must build up your health. || To make sure of, to fix in one's mind: *estudio un poco para afianzar lo que he oído en la conferencia*, I am studying a little to fix in my mind what I heard in the lecture, I'm studying a little to make sure of what I heard in the lecture. || To support, to back (sostener). || To grasp, to seize (agarrar).
— V. pr. To seize, to grasp (agarrar). || To cling (agarrarse). || FIG. To establish o.s., to secure o.s.: *afianzarse en un puesto*, to secure o.s. in a job. | To steady o.s. (afirmarse). | To become established (establecerse). | To set in (reacción, etc.).
afición f. Liking, love: *afición a la lectura*, liking for reading, love of reading. || Taste: *su empleo está de acuerdo con sus aficiones*, his job suits his tastes. || Fans, *pl.*, public: *la afición está satisfecha con el programa de corridas*, the fans are satisfied with the programme of bullfights. || Hobby, interest (interés). || Affection, fondness (cariño). || — *Cobrar* or *tomar afición a*, to acquire a taste for, to take a liking to. || *Por afición*, as a hobby: *pintar por afición*, to paint as a hobby; amateur: *pintor por afición*, amateur painter. || *Tener afición a*, to have a liking for, to like, to be fond of (cosas): *tengo afición al estudio*, I like studying; to be fond of, to be attached to: *tener afición a una persona*, to be fond of a person.
aficionado, da adj. Enthusiastic, keen (entusiasta). || Fond, keen: *aficionado a la pintura*, fond of *o* keen on painting. || Amateur (no profesional): *un ciclista aficionado*, an amateur cyclist.
— M. y f. Fan, enthusiast (a los deportes, al cine, etc.). || Amateur (no profesional): *los Juegos Olímpicos están reservados a los aficionados*, the Olympic Games are reserved for amateurs. || Lover (de las artes). || *Partido de aficionados*, amateur game.
— OBSERV. When used by itself *aficionados* usually applies to fans of bullfighting, and it can be used with this meaning in English.
aficionar v. tr. To make fond (inducir a amar). || To give a liking, to interest, to make fond: *me ha aficionado a la pintura*, he has interested me in painting, he has given me a liking for painting.
— V. pr. To become fond *o* attached: *aficionarse a una persona*, to become fond of a person, to become attached to a person. || To take a liking, to become fond: *aficionarse a la pintura*, to take a liking to painting, to become fond of painting.
afiche m. *Amer.* Poster, bill.
afidávit m. Sworn statement.
áfido m. Aphid (insect).
afiebrado, da adj. Feverish.
afiebrarse v. pr. *Amer.* To have a fever.
afijo, ja adj. GRAM. Affixed.
— M. GRAM. Affix.
afiladera adj. f. *Piedra afiladera*, hone, whetstone.
— F. Hone, whetstone.
afilado, da adj. Sharp: *cuchillo afilado*, sharp knife. || Sharpened, sharp: *lápiz afilado*, sharpened pencil. || Sharp, pointed: *diente afilado*, pointed tooth. || Slender, slim: *dedos afilados*, slender fingers. || Sharp, high-pitched, piercing: *voz afilada*, high-pitched voice. || — *Cara afilada*, long, thin face. || FIG. *Tener las uñas afiladas*, to be light-fingered.
— M. Sharpening (de un cuchillo, un lápiz).
afilador, ra adj. Sharpening.
— M. Knifegrinder (hombre). || Strop (correa). || *Amer.* Don Juan, Casanova. || — F. AGR. Grinding machine, sharpening machine.
afiladura f. Sharpening (acción de afilar).
afilalápices m. inv. Pencil sharpener (sacapuntas).
afilamiento m. Slenderness (de los dedos). || Sharpness, pointedness (de la nariz, la cara).
afilar v. tr. To sharpen, to grind: *afilar un cuchillo en una piedra*, to sharpen a knife on a stone. || To sharpen, to put an edge on (la hoja de algo). || To sharpen, to put a point on, to taper (sacar punta). || To sharpen (un lápiz). || To strop (la navaja). || To sharpen (la voz). || *Amer.* FAM. To court (cortejar). | To flatter (adular). || *Piedra de afilar*, whetstone, hone.
— V. pr. FIG. To become peaked *o* drawn, to sharpen (la cara). || To grow pointed *o* sharp *o* thin: *su nariz se ha afilado*, his nose has become pointed. || To be slender, to taper (los dedos). || *Amer.* To get ready (prepararse).
afiliación f. Affiliation.
afiliado, da adj. Affiliated. || Member: *los países afiliados*, the member countries. || Subsidiary (una empresa).
— M. y f. Member, affiliate: *afiliado a un partido*, member of a party.
afiliar v. tr. To affiliate.
— V. pr. To become affiliated to, to join, to become a member of: *afiliarse a un partido*, to join a party.
afiligranado, da adj. Filigreed, filagreed. || FIG Delicate, fine (cosas). | Delicate, dainty (personas).
afiligranar v. tr. To filigree, to filagree. || FIG. To polish (pulir). | To adorn, to decorate (hermosear).
afilosofado, da adj. Pseudo-philosophical.
afín adj. Adjacent: *campos afines*, adjacent fields. || Similar: *temperamentos, gustos, tendencias afines*, similar temperaments, tastes, tendencies. || Related: *palabras afines*, related words. || Similar, kindred: *ideas afines*, kindred ideas. || *La economía y los problemas afines*, economics and the problems related to it, economics and the problems connected with it, economics and its related problems.
— M. pl. Relatives, relations (parientes).
afinación f. TECN. Refining (afinado). || FIG. Refining, polishing (de una persona). || MÚS. Tuning (de un instrumento). | Intonation (en el canto). || Completion, perfection (acción de acabar).
afinadamente adv. In tune (cantar). || Delicately (delicadamente).
afinado, da adj. In tune, tuned: *piano afinado*, tuned piano, piano in tune. || Purified, refined (metales). || Finished, polished (acabado).
— M. Refining (depuración). || Tuning (de un piano).
afinador, ra m. y f. MÚS. Tuner (persona que afina). || — M. Tuning key (para afinar).
afinadura f. o **afinamiento** m. TECN. Refining (depuración). || Tuning (de un piano). || Intonation (en el canto). || FIG. Refinement, polish (de una persona).
afinar v. tr. TECN. To refine: *afinar el oro*, to refine gold. || FIG. To refine, to polish: *su estancia en la ciudad le ha afinado mucho*, his stay in the city has refined him a great deal. || MÚS. To tune: *afinar un piano*, to tune a piano. | To sing in tune (cantar). | To play in tune (tocar). || To complete, to finish, to perfect (acabar). || To sharpen, to improve: *afinar la puntería*, to sharpen one's aim.
— V. intr. To be exact: *no hemos afinado en la definición*, we have not been exact in the definition. || MÚS. To sing in tune (cantar). | To play in tune (tocar).
— V. pr. To become slimmer *o* thinner (adelgazar). || FIG. To become refined *o* polished (pulirse).
afincar v. intr. To come into property.
— V. pr. To settle down, to establish o.s.: *afincarse en Madrid*, to settle down in Madrid.
afine adj. V. AFÍN.
afinidad f. Similarity, likeness, affinity, resemblance (semejanza): *hay cierta afinidad entre estas dos personas*, there is a certain likeness between these two people. || BOT. y QUÍM. Affinity. || — *Las afinidades electivas*, elective affinities. || *Parentesco por afinidad*, relationship by marriage.
afino m. TECN. Refining (de metales).
afirmación f. Statement, affirmation, assertion: *afirmación atrevida*, daring statement. || Securing, strengthening (acción de sostener).
afirmado m. Road surface [U.S., roadbed] (firme de la carretera).
afirmante adj. Asserting, who affirms *o* asserts (que declara).
afirmar v. tr. To secure, to strengthen, to make firm: *poner unos clavos para afirmar un estante*, to put in a few nails to secure a shelf. || To assure: *le afirmo que es verdad*, I assure you that it is true. || To state, to say (decir): *un portavoz del gobierno ha afirmado que habrá elecciones*, a spokesman for the government has stated that there will be elections. || To declare (la lealtad).
— V. pr. To steady o.s. (apoyarse). || *Afirmarse en lo dicho*, to confirm one's statement.
afirmativo, va adj. Affirmative, positive: *respuesta afirmativa*, affirmative reply. || *En caso afirmativo*, if that is the case.
— F. Affirmative answer. || *Contestar con la afirmativa*, to answer in the affirmative, to give an affirmative answer.
afistolarse o **afistularse** v. pr. MED. To fistulate.
aflamencado, da adj. Flamenco-like.
aflatarse v. pr. *Amer.* To be sad *o* gloomy *o* downhearted.
aflautado, da adj. Flute-like. || High-pitched, piercing, fluty: *voz aflautada*, high-pitched voice.
aflautar v. tr. *Amer.* To make high-pitched *o* piercing (la voz, un sonido).

aflicción f. Affliction, grief, sorrow, sadness (pesar): *esta noticia me ha dado mucha aflicción*, this news has caused me great affliction.
aflictivo, va adj. JUR Corporal: *pena aflictiva*, corporal punishment. || Distressing, troubling (que causa aflicción): *una noticia aflictiva*, a distressing piece of news.
afligente adj. Distressing, troubling.
afligidamente adv. Sadly, sorrowfully (con tristeza). || *Llorar afligidamente*, to weep bitterly.
afligido, da adj. Distressed, troubled, grieved: *afligido con la noticia*, distressed by the news. || Suffering, afflicted: *afligido de sordera*, suffering from *o* afflicted by deafness. || Bereaved (por una muerte).
— M. Afflicted: *los afligidos*, the afflicted. || Bereaved (por una muerte).
afligimiento m. Affliction.
afligir v. tr. To afflict, to grieve, to distress (entristecer). || To afflict, to make suffer (causar molestia física). || To afflict, to trouble, to beset: *la desgracia que nos aflige*, the misfortune which afflicts us. || *Amer.* To beat, to thrash (apalear).
— V. pr. To be distressed, to be grieved, to grieve: *afligirse con* or *de algo*, to be distressed about sth., to be grieved by sth., to grieve over sth.
aflojamiento m. Loosening, slackening (de una cuerda). || Relaxing, relaxation (de la disciplina). || Loosening (de vínculos). || Abatement (de tormenta).
aflojar v. tr. To loosen, to slacken: *aflojar un nudo, la corbata, una tuerca*, to loosen a knot, one's tie, a nut. || To release (un muelle). || To relax, to ease (la severidad). || To moderate, to reduce (pretensiones). || To release, to take off (el freno). || FAM. To fork out, to cough up: *aflojar dinero*, to fork money out. || — *Aflojar el paso*, to slow down. || POP. *Aflojar la bolsa* or *la mosca*, to fork out, to cough up.
— V. intr. To let up, to die down: *el calor, la tormenta ha aflojado*, the heat, the storm has let up. || To slacken, to grow slack (cuerda). || To weaken, to give in, to relent (ceder). || To grow lax, to slack: *alumno que afloja en el estudio*, pupil who is slacking in his studies. || To grow weak, to fail: *fe que afloja*, faith which is failing. || To flag: *la conversación afloja*, conversation is flagging. || To abate (fiebre). || POP. To fork out, to cough up (pagar).
— V. pr. To grow slack, to slacken (cuerda). || To loosen, to come loose, to grow slack (la corbata, el cinturón, una tuerca). || To grow lax, to slack (en la aplicación). || To ease (un dolor). || To flag (interés, conversación). || To go down (los precios). || To let up, to die down (el calor, la fiebre).
afloramiento m. MIN. Outcrop.
aflorar v. intr. To outcrop, to crop out (minerales). || To spring (agua). || FIG. To appear, to arise (surgir).
— V. tr. To sift, to sieve (cerner).
afluencia f. Crowd, flow: *afluencia de espectadores*, flow of spectators. || Rush (tropel). || Inflow, influx: *la afluencia de refugiados al país*, the influx of refugees into the country. || Afflux, flow (de sangre). || Abundance (abundancia). || Eloquence (facundia).
afluente adj. Flowing, inflowing (que afluye). || Eloquent (facundo).
— M. Tributary: *el Segre es afluente del Ebro*, the Segre is a tributary of the Ebro.
afluir* v. intr. To flow: *la sangre afluye al cerebro*, the blood flows to the brain. || FIG. To flow, to flock: *los turistas afluyen a Madrid*, the tourists flock to *o* flow into Madrid. || To be a tributary, to flow: *este río afluye al Támesis*, this river is a tributary of the Thames, this river flows into the Thames. || To flow: *afluir al mar*, to flow into the sea. || To open, to lead: *esta calle afluye a la que buscas*, this street leads into *o* opens onto the one you are looking for.
aflujo m. MED. Afflux, flow.
afluxionarse v. pr. *Amer.* To catch a cold (resfriarse). | To swell (abotargarse).
afofado, da adj. Soft.
afofarse v. pr. To turn soft (ponerse fofo).
afogarar v. tr. (P.us.). To burn [food]. || To scorch, to burn [plant].
afollar* v. tr. (P.us.). To blow [with bellows]. || To pleat (plegar): *un cuello afollado*, a pleated collar.
— V. pr. To blister (avejigarse). || To hollow out (ahuecarse).
afonía f. MED. Aphony, aphonia, loss of voice.
afónico, ca o **áfono, na** adj. Aphonic (término médico). || Hoarse, voiceless (término común). || — *Estar afónico*, to have lost one's voice, to be hoarse. || *Volverse afónico*, to lose one's voice, to become hoarse.
aforado, da adj. Privileged, which has a "fuero" [a royal privilege granted to city or province in the Middle Ages].
aforador m. Gauge (instrumento). || Gauger (obrero).
aforamiento m. Gauging, measuring (de un barco, de un tonel). || Valuation (evaluación). || Appraisal, assessment (en las aduanas). || Privilege, exemption (fuero).
aforar* v. tr. To gauge, to measure the capacity of (un tonel). || To gauge, to measure the tonnage of (un barco). || To gauge, to measure: *aforar una corriente de agua*, to gauge a stream of water. || To appraise, to value, to assess (valorar). || To grant a privilege *o* a "fuero" to (una ciudad).
— V. pr. FAM. To cough up, to fork out (pagar). | To beat it, to make tracks (irse).
aforismo m. Aphorism (máxima).
aforístico, ca adj. Aphoristic.
aforo m. Gauging measuring, measurement: *el aforo de un barco*, the gauging of a boat. || Appraisal, assessment, valuation (evaluación). || Flow: *el aforo de un río*, the flow of a river. || *Este teatro tiene un aforo de dos mil personas*, this theatre holds two thousand people, this theatre has a seating capacity of two thousand.
afortunado, da adj. Fortunate, lucky: *una coincidencia afortunada*, a fortunate coincidence; *¡qué afortunado eres!*, how lucky you are! || Happy: *fue una época afortunada*, those were happy times. || Fortunate (que tiene buena fortuna): *un pueblo afortunado*, a fortunate nation. || MAR. Stormy (tiempo). || — *Hombre afortunado en amores*, a man who is lucky in love. || *Los afortunados por la lotería*, the winners of the lottery. || *Poco afortunado*, unsuccessful: *una reforma poco afortunada*, an unsuccessful reform; unpleasant: *una cara poco afortunada*, an unpleasant face; not very successful, not very good: *la decoración de este piso es poco afortunada*, the décor of this flat is not very successful. || *Un estilo afortunado en imágenes*, a style with good imagery.
afoscarse v. pr. MAR. To become misty (la atmósfera).
afrailado, da adj. Parsonic, parsonical. || IMPR. With a friar, with a defect [page].
afrailar v. tr. AGR. To trim, to cut off the branches of.
afrancesado, da adj. Francophile (francófilo). || FAM. Gallicized, Frenchified. || Supporting the French, pro-French.
— M. Person with French tastes and culture, francophile [especially in the eighteenth century]. || HIST. Supporter of Napoleon in the Peninsular War, French sympathizer.
afrancesamiento m. Frenchification, Gallicization.
afrancesar v. tr. To Frenchify, to Gallicize, to make French.
— V. pr. To become Gallicized (cosas). || To adopt French tastes *o* ways, to become Gallicized (personas). || HIST. To become a supporter of the French.
afrecho m. Bran.
afrenillar v. tr. MAR. To tie up.
afrenta f. Affront, insult: *aguantar una afrenta*, to suffer an insult. || Disgrace, shame: *es la afrenta de la familia*, he is the disgrace of the family. || *Hacer afrenta a alguien*, to insult s.o., to affront s.o.
afrentador, ra adj. Insulting, affronting (insultante). || Offensive, offending (que ofende).
— M. Insulter, affronter (que insulta). || Offender (que ofende).
afrentar v. tr. To insult, to affront (ultrajar). || To offend (ofender). || To disgrace, to dishonour, to shame (ser la vergüenza de). || To humiliate (humillar).
— V. pr. To be ashamed, to be embarrassed: *afrentarse de* or *por su pobreza*, to be ashamed of *o* embarrassed by one's poverty.
afrentoso, sa adj. Insulting (insultante). || Offensive, offending (que ofende). || Humiliating (humillador). || Disgraceful, shameful, outrageous, dishonourable (deshonroso): *una acción afrentosa*, a shameful action.
afretar v. tr. MAR. To scrub, to clean (limpiar el casco).
África n. pr. f. GEOGR. Africa: *África del Sur*, South Africa.
africado, da adj. GRAM. Affricative.
— F. Affricate (consonante).
africanista adj./s. Africanist.
africanización m. Africanization.
africanizar v. tr. To Africanize.
africano, na adj./s. African.
áfrico m. South wind.
afrikaans m. Afrikaans.
afrikánder m. Afrikaner, Afrikander.
afroamericano, na adj./s. Afro-American.
afroasiático, ca adj./s. Afro-Asian.
afrodisiaco, ca adj./s. m. Aphrodisiac.
Afrodita n. pr. f. Aphrodite.
afrontamiento m. Facing (acción de arrostrar). || Confrontation, confronting: *el afrontamiento de los manifestantes con la policía*, the confrontation of the demonstrators with the police; *el afrontamiento de dos ideologías*, the confrontation of two ideologies.
afrontar v. tr. To face, to confront, to face up to: *afrontar al enemigo*, to face the enemy. || To confront, to bring face to face (dos cosas o dos personas): *afrontar dos testigos*, to confront two witnesses. || To place opposite each other: *afrontar dos cuadros*, to place two paintings opposite each other.
afta f. MED. Aphtha.
aftoso, sa adj. Aphthous. || *Fiebre aftosa*, foot-and-mouth disease.
afuera adv. Out, outside: *váyase afuera*, get out; *afuera hace más frío*, it is colder outside. || Outside: *vengo de afuera*, I have been outside, I have come from outside. || — *De puertas afuera*, on the outside. || *La parte de afuera*, the outside. || *Más afuera*, further out. || *Por afuera*, outside, on the outside.
— F. pl. Outskirts: *las afueras de Madrid*, the outskirts of Madrid.

— Interj. Get out! (¡salga de aquí!). || Off! (abucheando).
afuereño, ña o **afuerino, na** adj. *Amer.* Strange, foreign (forastero).
afusión f. MED. Affusion (ducha).
afuste m. MIL. Gun carriage (de cañón).
agabachar v. tr. FAM. To Frenchify, to Gallicize.
— V. pr. To become Frenchified.
agachada f. FAM. Trick, dodge (astucia). || Bending over (acción de agacharse). || — Pl. Excuses, pretexts (pretextos).
agachadiza f. Snipe (ave). || FAM. *Hacer la agachadiza*, to duck, to try to hide.
agachado, da adj. *Amer.* Low (servil). || Sly, underhand (disimulado).
agachaparse v. pr. To bend over, to lean over (inclinarse). || To crouch (ponerse en cuclillas). || FIG. y FAM. To hide (ocultarse).
agachar v. tr. To lower, to bow, to bend: *agachar la cabeza*, to lower one's head.
— V. pr. To lean over, to bend over, to bend down: *agáchate para que te pueda peinar*, lean over so that I can comb your hair. || To crouch, to squat (ponerse en cuclillas). || To duck (para evitar algo). || FIG. To grin and bear it: *más vale agacharse*, it's better to grin and bear it. | To lie low, to hide away (retirarse). || *Amer.* To give in, to yield (someterse). | To get ready (prepararse).
agalbanado, da adj. FAM. Lazy, idle (perezoso).
agalerar v. tr. MAR. To tilt (las velas).
agalla f. BOT. Gall, gallnut. || ANAT. Tonsil. || Gill (de los peces). || Temple, side of head (de las aves). || *Amer.* Pole with hooked end (gancho). || — Pl. Sore throat, *sing.* (angina). || FIG. y FAM. Pluck, *sing.*, guts: *hay que tener muchas agallas para hacer frente a ciertas personas*, it takes a lot of pluck to face some people. || BOT. *Agalla de roble*, oak apple, oak gall.
agallegado, da adj. Like a Galician. || *Amer.* Spanish-sounding.
agallón m. Hollow silver bead (de collar). || Large bead (de rosario). || ARQ. Gadroon, godroon. || *Amer.* Gall, gallnut (agalla). || — Pl. *Amer.* Ganglions (cuerpos glandulosos). | Mumps (paperas).
agalludo, da adj. *Amer.* FAM. Plucky, daring (valiente). | Stingy, miserly (roñoso). | Cheeky, bold (desvergonzado).
agamí m. *Amer.* Trumpeter (ave).
ágamo, ma adj. BOT. Agamic, agamous
agamuzado, da adj. Chamois-coloured.
agamuzar v. tr. To chamois.
agangrenarse v. pr. To become gangrenous, to gangrene (una herida).
ágape m. Agape, love feast (convite entre los primeros cristianos). || Banquet (banquete).
agar agar m. Agar-agar, agar.
agarbanzado, da adj. Beige (color).
agarbillar v. tr. AGR. To sheave, to sheaf.
agareno, na adj./s. Mohammedan, Muslim, Moslem [especially in Spain].
agárico m. BOT. Agaric. || *Agárico mineral*, agaric mineral.
agarrada f. FAM. Quarrel, row (pelea): *tuvieron una agarrada*, they had a quarrel.
agarradera f. *Amer.* Handle (mango). || FAM. *Tener buenas agarraderas*, to have friends in the right places, to have connections.
agarradero m. Handle (asa). || Curtain hook (de las cortinas). || FIG. y FAM. Excuse (excusa). || FIG. y FAM. *Tener agarraderos*, to have friends in the right places, to have connections.
agarrado, da adj. FAM. Stingy, miserly, mean: *es un hombre muy agarrado*, he is a very stingy man. || — *Agarrados del brazo*, arm in arm. || FAM. *Baile agarrado*, dance in couples. || FIG. y FAM. *Ser más agarrado que un chotis* or *que el pasamanos de una escalera*, to be a tightfisted so-and-so.
agarrador, ra adj. *Amer.* Strong (bebida).
— M. Handle (de la plancha). || FAM. Cop, copper (guardia).
agarrar v. tr. To grasp, to seize, to grab, to clutch: *agarrar a una persona de* or *por la manga*, to grasp s.o. by the sleeve; *agarrar un palo*, to seize a stick. || FAM. To get, to land o.s. (obtener): *agarrar una buena colocación*, to get a good job. | To get, to hook: *agarrar un marido*, to get a husband. | To get, to win: *agarró dos puntos en el partido*, he got two points in the game. | To grasp, to get (comprender). | To get, to cop: *agarrar un bofetón*, to get a good hiding. | To catch: *agarrar un resfriado*, to catch a cold. | To catch, to get hold of: *si lo agarro lo mato*, if I catch him I'll kill him. | To take (tomar): *no se sabe por donde agarrarlo*, you don't know how to take him. || — *Agarrar del brazo*, to take by the arm. || FIG. *Agarrar el sueño*, to fall asleep, to be overcome by sleep. || FAM. *Agarrar un buen susto*, to have a fright. | *Agarrar una rabieta*, to go into a tantrum. || *Agarrar un autobús*, to catch a bus.
— V. intr. To take (vacuna, tinte, planta). || To stick: *el arroz ha agarrado en la sartén*, the rice has stuck to the frying pan. || *Amer.* To take (dirección): *agarró por esta calle*, he took this street. || — FAM. *Como no venga, agarro y me voy*, if he doesn't come, then I'm going. || FIG. *Estar siempre agarrado a las faldas de su madre*, to be tied to one's mother's apron strings.
— V. pr. To grasp, to hold on, to cling: *agarrarse a las ramas de un árbol*, to cling to *o* to hold on to the branches of a tree. || To cling: *la hiedra se agarra a las paredes*, ivy clings to walls. || To stick: *el arroz se ha agarrado a la sartén*, the rice has stuck to the frying pan. || To stick: *el humo se me agarra a la garganta*, smoke sticks in my throat. || To hold on: *agárrate a la barra*, hold on to the bar. || FIG. To use: *se agarra a cualquier pretexto para no hacer lo que le mando*, he uses any excuse not to do as I tell him. || FAM. To quarrel, to row, to argue (pelearse). || — AUT. *Agarrarse al camino*, to hold the road. || FIG. *Agarrarse a un clavo ardiendo*, to clutch at a straw *o* at straws. | *Agarrarse a* or *de un palo*, to use the least excuse. || *Agarrarse del brazo*, to link arms. || FIG. *Agarrarse del moño*, to pull each other's hair, to tear each other's hair out. || *Agarrarse una fiebre*, to catch a fever. || *Amer. Se agarraron a tiros*, they fought it out with pistols.
agarrochar v. tr. To goad (el picador). || MAR. To brace.
agarrón m. FAM. Quarrel, row, argument (agarrada). | Jerk, tug, pull (tirón).
agarrotado, da adj. Tightly bound (fardo). || Stiff (tieso). || Seized up (un motor). || FIG. Tied down (atado, restringido). || *Tener los músculos agarrotados*, to be stiff.
agarrotamiento m. Binding, tying up (acción de atar). || Seizing up, seizing (de un motor). || Stiffening, tightening (de un músculo). || Garotting, garrotting, garroting (de un reo).
agarrotar v. tr. To bind tightly, to tie up tightly (atar). || To stiffen, to tighten: *el agua muy fría agarrota los músculos*, very cold water stiffens one's muscles. || To garrote, to garrotte, to garotte (a un reo). || FIG. To tie down (poniendo restricciones).
— V. pr. To seize [up] (un motor). || To stiffen, to go numb (un músculo), to get *o* to have [a] cramp (una persona).
agasajado, da m. y f. Guest of honour.
agasajador, ra adj. Welcoming, cordial, warm.
agasajar v. tr. To receive warmly (acoger): *he sido muy agasajado durante mi estancia en Madrid*, I was very warmly received during my stay in Madrid. || To shower attentions on, to overwhelm with attentions (tener muchas atenciones con): *agasajar a sus convidados*, to overwhelm one's guests with attentions. || To wine and dine (dar muy bien de comer a).
agasajo m. Warm reception, royal *o* warm welcome (acogida calurosa). || Present, gift (regalo). || — Pl. Hospitality, *sing.* (hospitalidad). || *Me paso la vida en agasajos*, my life is one long round of parties and receptions.
ágata f. Agate.
agatizarse v. pr. To shine.
agauchado, da adj. *Amer.* Like the gauchos.
agaucharse v. pr. To assume a gaucho's way of life.
agavanza f. o **agavanzo** m. Wild rose, dogrose.
agave f. BOT. Agave (pita).
agavillador, ra m. y f. Binder, person who binds. || — F. AGR. Binder (machine).
agavillar v. tr. To bind, to sheave, to sheaf: *agavillar la mies*, to sheave the harvest.
— V. pr. To band together, to get together (personas).
agazapar v. tr. To catch, to get hold of.
— V. pr. FIG. To crouch, to duck (agacharse): *el niño se agazapó detrás de la puerta*, the child crouched behind the door.
agencia f. Agency: *agencia de viajes*, travel agency; *agencia inmobiliaria*, estate agency, real estate agency. || Bureau, agency: *agencia de colocaciones*, employment bureau. || Agency [which carries out official business for its clients] (gestoría). || FIG. Step (trámite). || *Amer.* Pawnshop. || — *Agencia de patentes*, patents office. || *Agencia de prensa*, news agency. || *Agencia de publicidad*, advertising agency. || *Agencia de transportes*, haulage contracting company. || *Agencia funeraria*, undertaker's.
agenciar v. tr. To get, to find: *te voy a agenciar una colocación muy buena*, I'll get you a very good job. || To engineer (conseguir que suceda algo). || FAM. To wangle (conseguir).
— V. pr. FAM. To look after o.s., to manage, to send for o.s.: *sabe agenciárselas*, he knows how to *o* he can look after himself. || To get o.s.: *agenciarse una buena colocación*, to get o.s. a good job; *se ha agenciado un piso magnífico*, he has got himself a marvellous flat. || *No te preocupes, yo me las agenciaré*, don't worry, I'll think of sth. *o* I'll manage.
agenciero m. *Amer.* Agent. | Pawnbroker.
agencioso, sa adj. Industrious, diligent.
agenda f. Diary. || *Agenda de entrevistas*, appointment book.
agente m. Agent: *agente químico*, chemical agent. || Agent (persona): *agente de seguros*, insurance agent; *agente secreto*, secret agent. || Policeman (policía). || GRAM. Agent. || — *Agente de bolsa* or *de cambio* or *de cambio y bolsa*, stockbroker. || *Agente de colocaciones*, manager of an employment agency. || *Agente de negocios*, business agent. || *Agente de policía*, policeman. || *Agente de transportes*, carrier. || *Agente ejecutivo*, bailiff. || *Agente inmobiliario*, estate agent [U.S.,

…ate broker *o* manager]. || *Agente provocador*, agent provocateur.

agermanado, da adj. Germanized.

agibílibus m. FAM. Know-how, knack (habilidad).

agible adj. Feasible (factible).

agigantado, da adj. Huge, gigantic. || *A pasos agigantados*, V. PASO.

agigantar v. tr. To exaggerate: *no hay que agigantar lo que pasó*, you should not exaggerate what happened. || To enlarge *o* to increase considerably, to make much greater: *este acontecimiento agiganta el problema*, this event makes the problem much greater, this event enlarges the problem considerably.
— V. pr. To take on huge proportions.

ágil adj. Agile, nimble: *está todavía muy ágil a pesar de su edad*, he is still very agile in spite of his age. || FIG. Agile, nimble, alert: *es muy ágil de pensamiento*, he has a very agile mind. | Flexible, nimble (estilo).

agílibus m. FAM. Know-how, knack (habilidad).

agilidad f. Agility: *para dar este salto hace falta mucha agilidad*, you need a great deal of agility to manage this jump. || FIG. Head: *tener mucha agilidad en los negocios*, to have a good head for business.

agilitar v. tr. To make agile (persona). || To facilitate (cosa). || *Amer*. To activate.

agilizar v. tr. V. AGILITAR.

agio m. COM. Agio (beneficio). | Agiotage, speculation, stockjobbing (especulación).

agiotador m. COM. Speculator, stockjobber.

agiotaje m. COM. Agiotage, speculation, stockjobbing. | Agio (beneficio).

agiotar v. intr. COM. To speculate, to gamble.

agiotista m. COM. Speculator, stockjobber.

agitación f. Shaking, agitation (de un líquido, etc.). || Bustle, jostle: *la agitación de la muchedumbre*, the bustle of the crowd. || Roughness (de las olas). || Movement, roll (de un barco). || Sway, swaying (de un árbol). || Waving, flapping (de una bandera). || Agitation, restlessness (nervios). || Excitement (emoción). || Agitation (política). || FIG. *Sembrar la agitación en el ánimo de alguien*, to cause s.o. unrest, to trouble s.o.

agitado, da p.p. V. AGITAR.
— Adj. Rough, choppy (el agua). || Turbulent (el aire). || FIG. Upset, worried (preocupado). | Hectic (la vida).

agitador, ra m. y f. Agitator.
— M. QUÍM. Stirring rod. || Shaker (máquina).

agitanado, da adj. Gypsy-like.

agitar v. tr. To shake: *agitar una botella antes de abrirla*, to shake a bottle before opening it. || To wave (un pañuelo, una bandera, los brazos, etc.). || To flap (el ala). || FIG. To upset, to disturb: *agitar el ánimo de uno*, to upset s.o., to disturb s.o. | To stir up, to excite, to agitate (excitar). || To brandish (un arma). || To stir, to stir up: *agitar un líquido con una cuchara*, to stir a liquid with a spoon.
— V. pr. To sway: *los árboles se agitan con el viento*, the trees sway in the wind. || To fidget: *el niño se agita en su silla*, the baby is fidgeting in its chair. || To flutter, to flap (una bandera). || To get rough, to get choppy (el mar). || To roll, to toss (un barco). || FIG. To become agitated (personas).

aglomeración f. Agglomeration, mass. || — *Aglomeración de tráfico*, traffic jam. || *Aglomeraciones de gente*, crowds of people.

aglomerado m. Briquette, briquet (combustible). || Agglomerate (conglomerado).

aglomerante m. Binding material.

aglomerar v. tr. To amass (amontonar).
— V. pr. To amass, to pile up, to agglomerate (amontonarse). || To form a crowd, to crowd round: *curiosos que se aglomeran*, inquisitive people who crowd round. || To crowd: *la gente se aglomera en las ciudades*, people are crowding the towns.

aglutinación f. Agglutination.

aglutinante adj. Agglutinant, adhesive, binding. || *Lengua aglutinante*, agglutinative language.
— M. Agglutinant.

aglutinar v. tr. To agglutinate, to bind.
— V. pr. To agglutinate.

aglutinativo, va adj. MED. Agglutinative.

agnación f. Agnation.

agnado m. JUR. Agnate.

agnosia f. Ignorance.

agnosticismo m. Agnosticism.

agnóstico, ca adj./s. Agnostic.

agobiado, da adj. Bent, bent over, bowed, weighed down: *agobiado por* or *con el peso de una carga, de los años*, bowed under the weight of a burden, of the years. || Overwhelmed, overburdened: *agobiado de trabajo*, overwhelmed with work. || Exhausted (cansado). || Round-shouldered (cargado de espaldas).

agobiador, ra adj. Exhausting, backbreaking (trabajo). || Crushing, backbreaking (carga). || Oppressive (calor). || Overwhelming (dolor, responsabilidad).

agobiante adj. Exhausting, backbreaking: *una tarea agobiante*, an exhausting job. || Oppressive: *calor agobiante*, oppressive heat. || Overwhelming (dolor, responsabilidad). || Tiresome: *es un niño agobiante*, he is a tiresome child. || *Es agobiante ir ahora allí*, it is a nuisance *o* it is annoying to have to go there now.

agobiar v. tr. To burden, to weigh down (recargar). || FIG. To overwhelm, to burden: *le agobian las penas*, he is overwhelmed by worry. | To overwhelm: *tanta bondad me agobia*, such kindness overwhelms me. | To get down, to tire: *me agobias con tus preguntas*, you get me down with your questions. | To depress, to dishearten (desanimar). | To humiliate (rebajar).

agobio m. Burden, weight (carga, peso). || Exhaustion (cansancio). || Anguish, worry (angustia). || Oppression (sofocación). || Boredom (aburrimiento). || *Soportar el agobio de tanta responsabilidad*, to bear the burden of so much responsibility.

agolpamiento m. Accumulation, pile (de cosas). || Crowd, throng, rush, flood (de gente).

agolparse v. pr. To crowd, to rush, to throng: *la gente se agolpó en el lugar del accidente*, people crowded to the scene of the accident. || FIG. To accumulate, to amass, to pile up (cosas). | To come all together, to come in one fell swoop (problemas). || *Se agolparon las lágrimas en sus ojos*, tears welled up *o* gathered in his eyes.

agonía f. Death *o* last throes, *pl.*, last agony, death agony (de un moribundo). || Knell (de las campanas por un moribundo). || FIG. Death *o* last throes, *pl.* (de una civilización, una sociedad). | Desire, yearning (deseo). | Agony, anguish (angustia). || — Pl. FAM. Misery, *sing.* (persona). || *Acortar la agonía a un animal*, to put an animal out of its misery.

agónico, ca adj. Death: *estertores agónicos*, death rattle. || Moribund, dying: *está agónico*, he is dying.

agonioso, sa adj. FAM. Selfish (egoísta). | Worrisome, anxious (angustiado). || FAM. *¡No seas tan agonioso!*, don't be such a nuisance *o* a pest!

agonizante adj. Moribund, dying (moribundo). || FIG. Failing, dying: *luz agonizante*, failing light.
— M. y f. Moribund, dying person. || — M. Monk who helps the dying.

agonizar v. intr. To be dying, to be moribund. || FIG. To fail, to falter: *luz que agoniza*, failing light. | To annoy, to pester, to bother (molestar). | To be dying: *agonizo por salir*, I'm dying to go out. | To be in agony (sufrir mucho).

ágora f. Agora.

agorafobia f. MED. Agoraphobia.

agorar* v. tr. To auger, to predict, to forecast.

agorero, ra m. y f. Soothsayer, fortune-teller.
— Adj. Of ill omen: *ave agorera*, bird of ill omen. || Ominous (que predice la desdicha). || Prophetic (profético).

agorgojado, da adj. Weevilled, weevilly, weevil-eaten.

agorgojarse v. pr. To be weevilled *o* weevilly *o* weevil-eaten.

agostadero m. Summer pasture (sitio). || Summer-pasture season (temporada).

agostamiento m. AGR. Withering.

agostar v. tr. To wither, to fade: *el sol agosta las flores*, the sun withers the flowers. || To plough in August (arar). || To hoe in August (desherbar).
— V. intr. To graze [in the dry season] (los animales). || To wither, to fade (secarse).

agosteño, ña adj. August, of August: *el calor agosteño*, the August heat, the heat of August.

agostero, ra adj. August. || Grazing (animales).

agostizo, za adj. August. || Weak (débil).

agosto m. August (mes): *el 15 de agosto*, the 15th of August, August the fifteenth. || Harvest (cosecha). || FIG. y FAM. *Hacer su agosto*, to make a fortune *o* a packet, to feather one's nest.

agotable adj. Exhaustible.

agotador, ra adj. Exhausting.

agotamiento m. Exhaustion.

agotar v. tr. To empty *o* to drain [completely]: *agotar una cisterna*, to drain a tank. || To exhaust, to deplete: *agotar las existencias, los recursos*, to exhaust the stocks, one's resources. || To exhaust (la tierra, un tema). || To exhaust, to tire out (cansar). || — *Agotar la paciencia de uno*, to try *o* to exhaust s.o.'s patience. | *Edición agotada*, edition out of print. || *Estar agotado*, to be exhausted.
— V. pr. To run out, to become exhausted (existencias). || To exhaust o.s., to wear o.s. out (persona). || To go out of print (un libro). || *Se me ha agotado la paciencia*, my patience has run out, I'm at the end of my tether.

agracejo m. Barberry, berberry. || Unripe grape (uva).

agraciado, da adj. Pretty, attractive: *un rostro agraciado*, a pretty face. || Graceful (gracioso). || Favoured: *agraciado por la suerte*, favoured by luck. || Winning: *el billete agraciado*, the winning ticket. || — *No agraciado*, losing (billete). || *Poco agraciado*, unattractive, plain: *una cara poco agraciada*, a plain face. || *Salir agraciado*, to be lucky
— M. y f. Lucky winner: *los agraciados recibirán su premio*, the lucky winners will receive their prize.

agraciar v. tr. To enhance s.o.'s looks (a una persor… *este vestido la agracia*, that dress enhances her… || To enhance (un vestido, etc.). || To award … with: *agraciar a uno con un premio, una* … to award s.o. a prize, a decoration. || … condenado).

agradable adj. Pleasant, agr… *agradable al tacto*, pleasan… *de sabor*, pleasant tastin… *agradable a la vista*… sight. || *Es difícil*… hard to please … *agradable*, it h…

evening. || *Unir lo útil con lo agradable*, to combine *o* to mix business and pleasure.

agradar v. intr. To please: *agradar a todos*, to please everyone; *un regalo que siempre agrada*, a present which is sure to please. || — *A mí este espectáculo me agrada mucho*, I like this show very much. || *Si le agrada*, if you wish, if you feel like it, if you want.
— V. pr. To like each other (dos personas).

— OBSERV. En inglés se suele emplear el verbo *to like*. En este caso el sujeto del verbo español viene a ser el complemento del verbo inglés: *esto me agrada*, I like this.

agradecer* v. tr. To thank: *le agradezco su oferta*, I thank you for your offer. || To be grateful, to be obliged: *si pudiera usted venir, se lo agradecería mucho*, if you could come, I should be very grateful. || *Se lo agradezco mucho*, I am very grateful to you, thank you very much.
— V. pr. To be welcome: *una copa de vino siempre se agradece*, a glass of wine is always welcome. || *Se agradece*, thank you very much, much obliged.

agradecido, da adj. Grateful: *agradecido a su bienhechor*, grateful to one's benefactor; *agradecido por un favor*, grateful for a favour. || — *Le estaría muy agradecido si me dejara el coche*, I should be very grateful *o* I should be much obliged if you would lend me your car. || *Me miró agradecido*, he looked at me gratefully. || *¡Muy agradecido!*, much obliged.

agradecimiento m. Gratitude, appreciation, gratefulness.

agrado m. Pleasure: *hallar agrado en hacer algo*, to take pleasure in doing sth. || Liking, taste: *no es de mi agrado*, it is not to my liking. || Affability, friendliness (afabilidad). || — *Con agrado*, with pleasure, willingly. || *Recibí con agrado sus noticias*, I was pleased to receive your news.

agrafe m. MED. Agraffe, clip (grapa).

— OBSERV. This word is a Gallicism widely used in medicine.

agramadera f. Brake.

agramado m. Braking.

agramador, ra adj. Braking.
— M. y f. Braker. || — M. Brake.

agramaduras f. pl. Boon, *sing.*, stalk, *sing.*

agramar v. tr. To brake (el cáñamo).

agramilar v. tr. To even out (ladrillos, etc.). || To face [a wall] in imitation brickwork (simular hileras de ladrillos).

agramiza f. Boon, stalk.

agrandamiento m. Enlargement, enlarging.

agrandar v. tr. To enlarge, to make larger: *agrandar una casa*, to enlarge a house; *agrandar un boquete*, to enlarge a hole. || To exaggerate, to magnify: *agrandar los defectos de alguien*, to exaggerate s.o.'s faults. || To increase: *esto agranda la diferencia de opinión que existe entre nosotros*, this increases the difference of opinion that exists between us.
— V. pr. To increase (una diferencia). || To grow larger, to expand (un boquete, etc.).

agranujado, da adj. Grained, rough. || Pimply, spotty: *una cara agranujada*, a spotty face. || FAM. Coarse (grosero). | Roguish (pícaro).

agranujarse v. pr. To become a rogue.

agrario, ria adj. Agrarian, land: *ley, reforma agraria*, land law, reform. || Agrarian, agricultural (política). || *La clase agraria*, the agricultural community.

agrarismo m. Agrarianism.

agravación f. o **agravamiento** m. Aggravation, worsening (empeoramiento).

agravante adj. Aggravating. || — JUR. *Circunstancias agravantes*, aggravating circumstances. || *Robo con agravante*, aggravated theft.
— F. JUR. Aggravating circumstance. || Further difficulty, added difficulty.

agravar v. tr. To aggravate, to worsen (hacer más grave). || To increase (una pena, un impuesto).
— V. pr. To worsen, to get worse.

agraviador, ra adj. Offensive, insulting.
— M. y f. Insulter, offender.

agraviamiento m. Insult.

agraviante m. Offender.
— Adj. Offensive, insulting.

agraviar v. tr. To offend (ofender). || To insult (insultar). || To wrong, to do wrong (perjudicar). || JUR. To appeal (apelar). || *Agraviar de palabra*, to insult.
— V. pr. To take offence, to be offended.

agravio m. Insult, offence (injuria). || Affront (afrenta). || Wrong, harm, damage (perjuicio). || JUR. Injustice || *Deshacer agravios*, to right wrongs (defender a los otros), to avenge o.s. (vengarse).

agravioso, sa adj. Insulting, offensive.

agraz m. Verjuice grape, sour grape (uva sin madurar). || Verjuice (zumo de uva en agraz). || BOT. Barberry, [illegible]erberry (agracejo). || FIG. y FAM. Bitterness (amar[illegible]). || *En agraz*, prematurely.

[illegible]n m. Verjuice grape (uva). || Gooseberry bush [illegible]). || FIG. Annoyance.

[illegible]r. To attack. || *Agredir de palabra*, to insult.

[illegible] Aggregable, which may be added.

[illegible]gregation.

[illegible]gregate (conjunto). || Addition [illegible]t (adjunto). || Attaché: *agregado* [illegible] commercial, cultural, naval attaché. || *Amer.* Métayer, farmer who pays [illegible] kind.

agregaduría f. Office of attaché.

agregar v. tr. To incorporate, to aggregate, to admit. || To join (unir). || To aggregate, to amass (reunir). || To add: *agregar cinco a diez*, to add five to ten. || To appoint: *ha sido agregado a la dirección*, he has been appointed to the managerial staff.
— V. pr. To be added: *agregarse a* or *con*, to be added to. || To be incorporated.

agremán m. Insertion.

agremiación f. Forming into a guild.

agremiar v. tr. To form into a guild.
— V. pr. To form a guild.

agresión f. Aggression. || Attack, assault (ataque).

agresividad f. Aggressiveness.

agresivo, va adj. Aggressive: *tono agresivo*, aggressive tone.

agresor, ra adj. Attacking: *el ejército agresor*, the attacking army.
— M. y f. Aggressor.

agreste adj. Country, rustic, rural (campestre). || Wild, uncultivated (inculto). || FIG. Uncouth (tosco).

agrete adj. Sour: *vino agrete*, sour wine.

agriado, da adj. Sour: *vino agriado*, sour wine. || FIG. Embittered, made bitter: *persona agriada por las injusticias*, person embittered by injustice.

agriamente adv. FIG. Sharply, sourly (con aspereza): *me contestó muy agriamente*, he answered me very sharply. || Bitterly (amargamente).

agriar v. tr. To sour, to turn sour. || FIG. To embitter, to make bitter (amargar). | To annoy (enfadar).
— V. pr. To turn sour: *el vino se ha agriado* the wine has turned sour. || To go sour, to go off (la leche). || FIG. To become embittered *o* bitter, to turn sour: *desde su última enfermedad se ha agriado mucho*, since his last illness he has become very bitter.

agrícola adj. Agricultural, farming.

agricultor, ra adj. Farming, agricultural.
— M. y f. Farmer.

agricultura f. Agriculture, farming.

agridulce adj. Bittersweet. || CULIN. *Cerdo agridulce*, sweet and sour pork.

agriera f. o **agrieras** f. pl. *Amer.* Heartburn, acidity of the stomach.

agrietamiento m. Cracking (en el suelo, una pared, un plato, etc.). || Chapping (en la piel).

agrietar v. tr. To crack, to make cracks in. || To chap (la piel, los labios, etc.).
— V. pr. To crack. || To get chapped (la piel, los labios).

Agrigento n. pr. GEOGR. Agrigento.

agrilla f. Sorrel (acedera).

agrimensor m. Surveyor.

agrimensura f. Surveying.

agrimonia o **agrimoña** f. Agrimony (planta).

agringarse v. pr. *Amer.* To behave like a gringo *o* foreigner.

agrio, gria adj. Sour, tart: *esta naranja está agria*, this orange is sour; *agrio de gusto*, sour-tasting. || FIG. Sour, bitter (carácter). || Short, brittle (metal).
— M. Acidity, sourness (sabor). || Sour juice (zumo). || — Pl. Citrus fruits.

agrior m. *Amer.* Heartburn, acidity of the stomach.

agripalma f. BOT. Motherwort.

Agripina n. pr. f. Agrippina.

agrisado, da adj. Grey, greyish.

agrisar v. tr. To grey, to gray.
— V. pr. To grey, to go *o* to become grey, to gray, to become gray.

agro m. Agriculture. || *Los problemas del agro*, agricultural problems.

agronomía f. Agronomy, agriculture.

agronómico, ca adj. Agronomic, agronomical.

agrónomo adj. m. Agricultural: *ingeniero agrónomo*, agricultural expert.
— M. Agronomist.

agropecuario, ria adj. Agricultural, farming. || — *Ingeniero agropecuario*, veterinarian, veterinary surgeon. || *Productos agropecuarios*, agricultural products.

agrupable adj. Which can be grouped.

agrupación f. o **agrupamiento** m. Grouping (acción). || Group (grupo). || Association, society: *agrupación de jóvenes*, association of young people. || *Agrupación coral*, choral society, choral group.

agrupar v. tr. To group, to assemble.
— V. pr. To form a group, to crowd together, to group together.

agrura f. Tartness, sourness.

agua f. Water (líquido): *dame agua*, give me some water. || Rain (lluvia). || Slope: *tejado de dos aguas*, roof with two slopes. || Tears, *pl.* (lágrimas). || MAR. Leak (agujero). | Tide, water (flujo o reflujo). || — Pl. FIG. Water, *sing.* (de una piedra preciosa). | Water, *sing.*, moiré, *sing.* (en las telas). || MAR. Waters: *aguas jurisdiccionales*, territorial waters. || Wake, *sing.* (estela). || Waters, watercures: *tomar las aguas*, to take the waters. || — *Agua* or *aguas abajo*, downstream, downriver. || *Agua* or *aguas arriba*, upstream, upriver. || *Agua bendita*, holy water. || *Agua calcárea*, hard water. || *Agua cibera*, irrigation water. || *Agua corriente*, running water. || *Agua cruda*, hard water. || *Agua de azahar*, orange-flower water. || *Agua de cal*, lime

water. || FAM. *Agua de cepas*, wine. || *Agua de colonia*, cologne. || *Agua de espliego*, lavender water. || *Agua de fregar*, dishwater. || *Agua de lejía*, bleach. || *Agua delgada*, soft water. || *Agua de limón*, lemonade. || *Agua de mar*, seawater. || *Agua de lluvia* or *llovediza*, rainwater. || *Agua de manantial*, spring water. || *Agua de olor*, toilet water. || *Agua de pie*, spring water. || *Agua de Seltz*, soda water, Seltzer water. || *Agua de sifón*, soda water, Seltzer water. || *Agua de socorro*, emergency baptism (bautismo). || *Agua de soda*, soda water, Seltzer water. || *Agua dulce*, fresh water. || *Agua dura*, hard water. || *Agua estancada*, stagnant water. || *Agua fuerte*, nitric acid, aqua fortis (ácido nítrico). || *Agua gorda*, hard water. || *Agua natural*, tapwater. || *Agua oxigenada*, hydrogen peroxide, oxygenated water. || FIG. *Agua pasada no mueve molino*, it's no use crying over spilt milk. || *Agua pesada*, heavy water. || *Agua potable*, drinking water. || FIG. *Agua que no has de beber...*, it's none of your business... || *Agua regia*, aqua regia. || *Agua salada*, salt water. || *Agua salobre*, brackish *o* briny water. || *Aguas de creciente*, flow, rising tide. || *Aguas de menguante*, ebb, ebbing tide. || *Aguas llenas*, high tide. || *Aguas madres*, mother water, mother liquor. || *Aguas mayores*, motion of the bowels, stool. || *Aguas menores*, urine. || *Aguas muertas*, neap tide. || *Aguas sucias* or *residuales*, sewage, *sing.* || *Aguas termales*, thermal spring, hot spring (caldas). || *Aguas vivas*, spring tide (marea). || *Agua viento*, squall. || *Agua viva*, springwater. || FIG. *Ahogarse en un vaso de agua*, to make a mountain out of a molehill. | *Algo tendrá el agua cuando la bendicen*, there must be sth. in it [in him, in her, etc.]. || FIG. y FAM. *Bailarle a uno el agua*, to lick s.o.'s boots. | *Bañarse en agua de rosas*, to see the world through rose-coloured glasses. || *Amer. Capa de agua*, raincoat. || *Como pez en el agua*, in one's element. || *Cubrir aguas*, to put the roof on a building (poner el techo). || *Dar agua a la ropa*, to wet the washing. || *Amer. Dar agua a uno*, to kill s.o. || *Del agua mansa me libre Dios, que de la brava me guardaré yo* or *me libro yo*, still waters run deep. || FIG. *Echar agua en el mar*, to carry coals to Newcastle. || *Echar el agua a*, to baptize (bautizar). || FIG. *Echarse al agua*, to take the plunge. || *Es agua sucia*, it's like dishwater (café). || *Amer. Estar como agua para chocolate*, to be hopping mad. || FIG. *Estar con el agua al cuello*, to have the noose round one's neck, to be in deep water, to be up to one's neck in it. | *Estar entre dos aguas*, to be in two minds, to be undecided. | *Estar hecho un agua*, to be dripping with sweat. | *Gastar dinero como agua*, to spend money like water. || MAR. *Hacer agua*, to leak, to have sprung a leak. || *Hacer aguas*, to urinate, to pass water. || *Amer. Hay agua puesta*, it is going to rain, it looks like rain. || FIG. *Irse al agua*, to fall through, to fail (fracasar). | *Llevar el agua a su molino*, to look after number one. | *Nadar entre dos aguas*, V. NADAR. | *Nadie diga de este agua no beberé*, we never know what the future has in store, don't be too sure! || *Parecerse como dos gotas de agua*, to be as like as two peas in a pod. || *Pescar en agua turbia*, to fish in troubled waters. || *Amer. Ponerse al agua*, to turn rainy, to turn to rain (el tiempo). || *Quedar en agua de borrajas*, to fizzle out, to peter out. || *Romper aguas*, to break one's water bag (una parturienta). || FIG. y FAM. *Sacar agua de las piedras*, to get blood out of stone. || *Se me hace la boca agua al ver ese pastel*, the sight of that cake makes my mouth water. || *Se mete en agua el tiempo*, it looks like rain. || *Ser como el agua por San Juan*, to be harmful, to be unwelcome. || FIG. *Ser más claro que el agua*, to be as clear as crystal *o* as a bell, to be crystal clear. || FIG. y FAM. *Sin decir agua va*, without warning. || *Tomar las aguas*, to take the waters (enfermo), to roof (arquitectura). || FAM. *Venir como agua de mayo*, to be a godsend, to come *o* to happen just at the right moment.
— Interj. Man overboard! (¡hombre al agua!). || *¡Agua va!*, look out below!

aguacatal m. Avocado plantation.
aguacate m. BOT. Avocado (árbol). || Avocado, avocado pear (fruto). || *Amer.* FAM. Drip, fool (tonto).
aguacero m. Downpour, shower: *cayó un aguacero*, there was a shower. || *Amer.* Glowworm (luciérnaga).
aguacibera f. AGR. Irrigation water.
aguacil m. V. ALGUACIL.
aguacha f. Stagnant water.
aguachar m. Puddle (charco).
aguachar v. tr. To flood. || *Amer.* To tame (amansar).
— V. pr. *Amer.* To get fat (un caballo). | To get attached (*de*, to) [encariñarse].
aguachento, ta adj. *Amer.* Watery, full of water.
aguachirle m. Dishwater (bebida o sopa sosa): *este café es aguachirle*, this coffee is like dishwater.
aguada f. MAR. Fresh water supply. | Water: *hacer aguada*, to take on water. || Watering place (sitio). || Flooding, flood (inundación en las minas). || Gouache (pintura). || *Amer.* Drinking trough (abrevadero).
aguaderas f. pl. Packsaddle, *sing.* [for carrying jars].
aguadero m. Drinking trough.
aguado, da adj. Watered-down: *vino aguado*, watered-down wine. || FIG. Troubled (trastornado).
— M. Watering (del vino).
aguador m. Water bearer, water carrier.
aguaducho m. Refreshment stand (puesto de agua). || Noria, Persian wheel (noria). || Aqueduct.
aguadura f. VET. Founder, laminitis.
aguafiestas m. y f. Wet blanket, killjoy, spoilsport.
aguafuerte f. Etching (grabado). || Nitric acid (ácido). || *Grabar al aguafuerte*, to etch.

— OBSERV. *Aguafuerte* meaning *etching* is often used as a masculine noun.

aguafuertista m. y f. Etcher.
aguaje m. MAR. Sea current. | Unusually high tide, spring tide (marea). | Wake (estela). | Fresh water supply (aguada). || Watering place (abrevadero). || *Amer.* Heavy shower, downpour (aguacero). | Dressing down, telling off, talking-to (reprimenda).
aguamala f. ZOOL. Jellyfish.
aguamanil m. Water jug (jarro). || Washbasin, washbowl (palangana). || Ewer (lavamanos).
aguamanos m. inv. Water jug.
aguamar m. Jellyfish.
aguamarina f. MIN. Aquamarine.
aguamiel f. Mead. || *Amer.* Agave juice [from which *pulque* is made].
aguanieve f. Sleet.
aguanieves f. inv. Wagtail (ave).
aguanoso, sa adj. Waterlogged, sodden: *terreno aguanoso*, sodden ground. || Watery (fruto, etc.). || *Amer.* FAM. Wet (persona).
aguantable adj. Bearable, tolerable.
aguantaderas f. pl. Patience, *sing.*: *para no enfadarse conmigo hace falta que tenga muchas aguantaderas*, he has to have a lot of patience not to get angry with me. || Endurance, *sing.*, stamina, *sing.*
aguantar v. tr. To put up with, to bear, to stand, to tolerate (soportar): *aguantar el dolor*, to stand the pain. || To stand, to tolerate, to bear: *no aguanto las impertinencias*, I will not tolerate insolence; *no poder aguantar a alguien*, not to be able to stand s.o. || To weather, to ride out, to withstand (una tempestad, un huracán). || To keep back, to hold back (contener): *aguantar la risa*, to keep back laughter. || To hold: *aguantar la respiración*, to hold one's breath. || To wait (esperar): *aguanté tres horas y luego me fui*, I waited three hours and then I went. || To hold: *aguanta el cuadro mientras yo lo cuelgo*, hold the picture while I hang it. || To hold up, to support (sostener). || To be good for, to last (durar): *este abrigo aguantará otro invierno*, this overcoat is good for *o* will last another winter. || TAUR. To take [the bull's attack at the kill] without moving. || — *Aguantar mucho bebiendo*, to be able to take *o* to hold one's drink. || *No aguanto más*, I've had enough. || *Sabe aguantar bromas*, he can take a joke. || *Su marido aguanta mucho*, her husband is very patient. || *Yo no lo aguanto*, I can't bear it, I can't stand it.
— V. intr. To hold out: *el enemigo aguantó tres horas*, the enemy held out for three hours. || To resist (resistir).
— V. pr. To keep quiet: *él se aguanta, no dice ni pío*, he keeps quiet, he doesn't say a word. || To put up with, to hold o.s. back: *hace tiempo que me aguanto pero ya no puedo más*, I have put up with this for some time, but now I've had enough. || To resign o.s.: *aguantarse con una cosa*, to resign o.s. to sth. || FIG. y FAM. *¡Pues, aguántate!*, well, you'll just have to put up with it! | *¡Que se aguante!*, that's his hard luck!
aguante m. Endurance, stamina (resistencia). || Patience (paciencia). || *Tener mucho aguante*, to be very patient, to have a lot of patience (paciencia), to have a lot of stamina (resistencia).
aguapié m. Weak *o* watery wine (vino malo).
aguar v. tr. To dilute *o* to water down, to water, to add water to (un líquido): *aguar el vino*, to water down the wine. || FIG. To spoil, to ruin: *la discusión le aguó la noche*, the argument ruined her evening; *aguó la fiesta al armar una bronca*, he ruined the party by kicking up a fuss. || *Amer.* To water. || FIG. *Aguar la fiesta a uno*, to spoil s.o.'s enjoyment *o* fun.
— V. pr. To be flooded (una casa, etc.). || FIG. To be ruined, to be spoilt *o* spoiled: *se aguó la fiesta*, the party was ruined. || To be exhausted, to founder (un caballo).
aguaraibá m. *Amer.* Terebinth, turpentine tree (árbol).
aguardada f. Wait, waiting (en la caza).
aguardar v. tr. To wait for, to await (esperar): *aguardar a alguien, otro día*, to wait for s.o., until another day. || *No sabes lo que te aguarda*, you don't know what is in store for you *o* what awaits you.
— V. intr. To wait, to hold on: *aguarda, ya voy*, hold on, I'm coming.
aguardentería f. *Amer.* Liquor store.
aguardentoso, sa adj. Alcoholic, which contains spirits. || — *Bebidas aguardentosas*, spirits. || *Voz aguardentosa*, husky *o* rough voice.
aguardiente m. Liquor, eau-de-vie (licor). || *Aguardiente de caña*, tafia, rum.
aguaribay m. *Amer.* Terebinth, turpentine tree (árbol).
aguarrás m. Turpentine.
— OBSERV. Pl. *aguarrases.*
aguasal f. Pickling brine.
aguasarse v. pr. *Amer.* To become coarse *o* rough (volverse rústico).
aguate m. *Amer.* Thorn, prickle.

aguatero m. *Amer.* Water bearer, water carrier (aguador).
aguaturma f. Bot. Jerusalem artichoke.
aguaverde f. Zool. Jellyfish.
aguaviento m. Squall.
aguavientos m. Bot. Phlomis.
aguazal m. Mire.
aguazar v. tr. To flood (encharcar).
agudamente adv. Shrewdly. || Subtly. || Wittily (ingeniosamente).
agudeza f. Sharpness, keenness (de un instrumento, de los sentidos). || Sharpness, acuteness (del dolor). || Fig. Insight, shrewdness (de ingenio). | Wit, wittiness (ingenio). | Bite, sting (de la sátira). | Wittiness (de un chiste). | Flash of wit (rasgo de ingenio). | Witticism (palabra chistosa). || *Es una persona muy graciosa, tiene mucha agudeza*, he's a very funny person, he is very witty.
agudizamiento m. Aggravation, worsening: *agudizamiento de la situación social*, aggravation of the social situation. || Increase (aumento): *agudizamiento de la tensión internacional*, increase in international tension.
agudizar v. tr. To sharpen. || To worsen, to make worse *o* more acute: *esto no hará más que agudizar la crisis*, that will only make the crisis worse.
— V. pr. To worsen, to become *o* to get worse (una enfermedad). || Fig. To intensify, to become more intense, to become more acute: *el conflicto político se ha agudizado*, the political conflict has become more intense. | To get worse, to worsen, to become more pronounced: *con la edad sus manías se agudizan*, his idiosyncracies get worse as he gets older.
agudo, da adj. Sharp (afilado). || Acute (ángulo y acento). || Fig. Sharp, shrewd (listo). | Witty, clever (gracioso): *una persona aguda*, a witty person. || Sharp, acute (dolor). || Acute (enfermedad, crisis). || Sharp (crítica). || High-pitched, shrill, piercing (voz). || Searching (pregunta). || Keen, sharp (vista). || Mús High (nota). | Treble (tono en el magnetófono, etc.). || Gram. Oxytone, with the accent on the last syllable. || — *Dicho agudo*, witticism. || *Ser agudo de ingenio*, to be witty.
— M. pl. Treble, *sing.* (botón del magnetófono, etc.).
Águeda n. pr. f. Agatha.
agüero m. Augury, omen, presage. || — *De buen agüero*, lucky, propitious. || *Pájaro de mal agüero*, bird of ill omen.
aguerrido, da adj. Hardened, veteran, trained. || Fig. Experienced.
aguerrir* v. tr. To harden, to season, to train.
— Observ. This is a defective verb used only in the forms whose endings begin with *i*.
aguijada f. Goad (de boyero). || Ploughstaff [U.S., plowstaff] (de labrador).
aguijadura f. Goading.
aguijar v. tr. To goad. || Fig. To goad, to spur on, to urge on.
— V. intr. To hurry along.
aguijón m. Spike of a goad. || Sting (del escorpión, de la avispa, etc.). || Prickle, thorn, sting (de las plantas). || Fig. Prick, sting: *el aguijón de los celos*, the prick of jealousy. | Stimulus, spur: *la gloria es un poderoso aguijón*, glory is a powerful stimulus. || *Cocear contra el aguijón*, to struggle *o* to kick in vain.
aguijonada f. o **aguijonazo** m. Jab, prick. || Sting (de un insecto).
aguijoneador, ra adj. Goading.
— M. y f. Goader.
aguijonear v. tr. To goad (a los animales). || Fig. To goad, to spur on. || — *Aguijonear la curiosidad de uno*, to arouse *o* to prick one's curiosity. || *Me aguijoneaba el deseo de decirle algo*, I was dying *o* itching to tell him sth.
águila f. Eagle (ave). || Eagle (condecoración): *el águila negra de Prusia*, the Black Eagle of Prussia. || Eagle, standard (estandarte). || Astr. Aquila, eagle (constelación). || Eagle (moneda). || Fig. Crack, ace: *ser un águila para los negocios*, to be a crack *o* an ace businessman. || Fam. *Amer.* Cheat, swindler (petardista). | Kite (cometa). || — Heráld. *Águila agrifada*, griffin, griffon, gryphon. || *Águila barbuda*, lammergeyer, bearded vulture. || *Águila blanca*, kind of osprey *o* sea eagle. || *Águila caudal* or *real*, royal *o* golden eagle. || *Águila de mar*, eagle ray (pez). || *Águila imperial*, Imperial Eagle. || Heráld. *Águila pasmada*, eagle with wings folded. || *Águila pescadora*, sea eagle, osprey, erne. || *Águila ratonera*, buzzard. || Fig. *Mirada de águila*, penetrating glance.
aguileña f. Columbine (planta).
aguileño, ña adj. Aquiline (nariz). || Sharp-featured (rostro).
aguilera f. Eyrie (nido del águila).
aguilón m. Jib, arm (de una grúa). || Arq. Draintile, chimney-flue tile (caño). | Gable (parte superior del muro).
aguilucho m. Eaglet, young eagle.
agüilla f. Water, fluid, watery liquid.
aguinaldo m. Christmas box, tip: *dar el aguinaldo al cartero*, to give the postman his Christmas box. || *Amer.* Christmas carol (canción).
agüista m. y f. Person taking water cures.
aguja f. Needle (de coser, etc.). || Needle, stylus (de gramófono). || Hand (del reloj). || Pointer, needle (de un indicador). || Needle (de la brújula). || Needle beam (de un puente). || Arq. Spire, steeple (de un campanario). || Zool. Pipefish, needlefish (pez). || Firing pin (de arma de fuego). || Agr. Graft (púa). || Bot. Needle (de pino). || Med. Needle (de inyección). || Artes. Etcher's needle (de grabador). || — Pl. Points [U.S., switches] (de ferrocarril): *entrar en agujas*, to approach the points; *dar agujas*, to change the points. || Ribs (de un animal). || — *Aguja colchonera*, v. colchonero. || *Aguja de gancho*, crochet hook, crochet needle. || *Aguja de hacer punto* or *de hacer media*, knitting needle. || Aut. *Aguja de la cuba del carburador*, float needle, float spindle. || *Aguja de marear*, compass (brújula). || *Aguja de pastor* or *de Venus*, scandix, Venus's comb, shepherd's needle (planta). || *Aguja de zurcir*, darning needle. || *Aguja imantada* o *magnética*, magnetic needle. || *Aguja mechera*, larding needle, larding pin. || *Aguja paladar*, garfish, hornfish (pez). || Fig. *Buscar una aguja en un pajar*, to look for a needle in a haystack. || *Carne de agujas*, clod, shoulder. || Fig. *Conocer la aguja de marear*, to be able to look after o.s. | *Meter aguja por sacar reja*, to throw out a sprat to catch a mackerel.
agujazo m. Prick *o* jab [with a needle].
agujereado, da adj. *Está agujereado*, it has a hole in it (con un solo agujero), it has holes in it, it is full of holes (con varios).
agujerar o **agujerear** v. tr. To make holes in: *agujerear una pared*, to make holes in a wall. || To perforate.
agujero m. Hole (abertura): *tapar un agujero*, to plug a hole. || Needle maker (fabricante) *o* seller (vendedor). || Pincushion (alfiletero). || *Tiene más agujeros que un colador*, it is like a sieve, it is riddled with holes.
agujeta f. *Amer.* Large needle. || — Pl. Stiffness, *sing.* (dolor). || *Estar lleno de agujetas*, to be stiff all over.
agujón m. Hairpin (pasador). || Large needle.
aguosidad f. Water, fluid, watery liquid.
aguoso, sa adj. Watery.
¡agur! interj. Cheerio!, bye-bye!
agusanado, da adj. Maggoty, wormy (fruto). || Worm-eaten (madera).
agusanarse v. pr. To become maggoty *o* wormy (frutos). || To become worm-eaten *o* rotten (madera).
Agustín n. pr. m. Augustine.
agustinianismo m. Augustinianism, Augustinism.
agustiniano, na adj. Augustinian.
agustino, na adj./s. Augustinian.
agutí m. Zool. Agouti, agouty.
aguzadero, ra adj. Sharpening. || *Piedra aguzadera*, whetstone.
aguzado, da adj. Sharpened. || Sharp (puntiagudo).
aguzador, ra adj. Sharpening.
— F. Whetstone (piedra).
aguzadura f. o **aguzamiento** m. Sharpening.
aguzanieves f. inv. Wagtail (ave).
aguzar v. tr. To sharpen: *aguzar un cuchillo, un lápiz*, to sharpen a knife, a pencil. || Fig. To goad, to spur on (estimular). | To whet (el apetito). | To sharpen (la inteligencia, etc.). || — *Aguzar el ingenio, el entendimiento*, to sharpen one's wits (mostrarse ingenioso), to concentrate very hard (concentrarse). || *Aguzar el oído*, to prick up one's ears. || *Aguzar las orejas*, to prick up its *o* his ears (un perro, etc.). || *Aguzar la vista*, to look closely *o* attentively.
¡ah! interj. Oh! || *Amer.* Eh?, what? || *¡Ah del barco!*, ship ahoy!
ahebrado, da adj. Fibrous.
ahechador, ra adj. Sifting, winnowing.
— M. y f. Sifter, winnower.
ahechaduras f. pl. Siftings, chaff, *sing.*
ahechar v. tr. To sift, to sieve, to winnow.
ahecho m. Sifting, winnowing.
aherrojamiento m. Chaining.
aherrojar v. tr. To chain, to shackle, to put in irons (cargar de cadenas). || Fig. To oppress (oprimir).
aherrumbrar v. tr. To turn rusty red (color). || To give a rusty taste to (sabor).
— V. pr. To rust, go rusty (oxidarse). || To become rusty red (color). || To taste of rust (sabor).
ahí adv. There: *ahí está el hombre que buscamos*, there's the man we are looking for. || — *Ahí está*, there he [it, etc.] is, here he [it, etc.] is. || *Ahí está la dificultad*, that's the problem, that is where the difficulty lies. || *Ahí fue ello* or *ella*, that was where it all started, that's when the trouble started. || Fam. *Ahí me las den todas*, that's the least of my worries, I couldn't care less. | *¡Ahí es nada!*, fancy that!, just fancy! || *Amer. Ahí no más*, right here. || Fam. *Ahí será ello*, there will be trouble. || *Ahí tienes lo que querías*, there's what you wanted. || *¡Ahí va!*, there it is!, there he is! (allí está), goodness me! (sorpresa). || *Ahí viene*, here he comes. || *¿De ahí?*, so what?, well? || *De ahí que*, so that, with the result that. || *De ahí se deduce que*, from that we can deduce that. || *¡Hasta ahí podíamos llegar!*, not so likely! || *He ahí*, there is, there's: *he ahí lo que buscaba*, there's what I was looking for. || *Por ahí*, there, that way: *ha pasado por ahí*, he went that way; for a walk: *me voy un rato por ahí*, I'm going for a little walk. || *Por ahí, por ahí* o *por ahí va la cosa*, something like that, more or less, thereabouts.

|| FAM. *Vete por ahí*, get away with you, go on, tell us another one.
ahidalgado, da adj. Noble.
ahijado, da m. y f. Godson (chico), goddaughter (chica), godchild. || Adopted child. || FIG. Protégé (protegido).
ahijamiento m. Adoption.
ahijar v. tr. To adopt. || FIG. To attribute, to impute.
¡ahijuna! interj. *Amer.* POP. Well, I'll be!, stone me!
ahilado, da adj. Light, soft (viento). || Thin, weak (voz).
ahilamiento m. Faint (desmayo).
ahilar v. intr. To go in single file.
— V. pr. To faint (desmayarse). || To go off, to go bad (vino, etc.). || FIG. To lose weight (adelgazar). || To droop, to wilt (ajarse). || To grow tall and thin (los árboles).
ahilo m. Faint.
ahincadamente adv. Insistently (con insistencia). || Tenaciously, earnestly, religiously.
ahincado, da adj. Insistent. || Eager, enthusiastic.
ahincar v. tr. To urge.
— V. pr. To hurry (darse prisa).
ahínco m. Insistence: *pedir con ahínco*, to ask with insistence. || Enthusiasm, eagerness. || *Trabajar con ahínco*, to work eagerly *o* hard.
ahitar v. tr. To give indigestion. || To stake *o* to mark out: *ahitar un terreno*, to mark out a piece of ground.
— V. pr. To gorge o.s., to stuff o.s. (fam.): *ahitarse de caramelos*, to stuff o.s. with sweets. || To have *o* to get indigestion.
ahíto, ta adj. Who has indigestion (malucho). || Full, satiated: *quedarse ahíto después de una buena comida*, to be full after a good meal. || FIG. Fed up (*de*, with) [harto de una cosa]. || FAM. *Estar ahíto*, to have had enough, to have had one's fill.
ahocicar v. tr. FIG. y FAM. To shut [s.o.] up, to show [s.o.] (en una discusión).
— V. intr. FIG. y FAM. To give in, to yield, to admit defeat: *al final no tuvo más remedio que ahocicar*, he had to admit defeat in the end. || To fall flat on one's face (caer de bruces). || To dip the bows (barco).
ahogadero m. Turkish bath, hothouse: *esta sala es un ahogadero*, this room is like a Turkish bath. || Hangman's rope (del ahorcado) || Throatlash, throatlatch (arreo del caballo).
ahogadilla f. Ducking. || *Darle a uno una ahogadilla*, to duck s.o., to give s.o. a ducking.
ahogadizo, za adj. Bitter, sharp, tarty (fruta). || Which does not float (madera).
ahogado, da adj. Drowned (en el agua): *en ese naufragio hubo diez personas ahogadas*, in that shipwreck ten people were drowned. || Asphyxiated, gassed (por el gas). || Strangled (estrangulado). || Suffocated (por falta de aire, en general). || Restricted: *respiración ahogada*, restricted breathing. || Pent-up (emoción). || Muffled, smothered (grito). || Stuffy, close (sin ventilación). || Stalemated (en ajedrez). || Overcrowded (atestado). || Harassed, at the end of one's tether (apurado). || *Amer.* Stewed (rehogado). || — FIG. *Ahogado de deudas*, up to one's neck in debt. | *Estar* or *verse ahogado*, to have the noose round one's neck, to be in a tight spot. || *Morir* or *perecer ahogado*, to drown (en agua), to suffocate (por falta de aire).
ahogador, ra adj. Suffocating.
— M. Choker (collar).
ahogamiento m. Suffocation (asfixia). || Drowning (en agua).
ahogar v. tr. To drown: *ahogar a un gato*, to drown a cat. || To suffocate (impedir la respiración). || To asphyxiate, to gas (por el gas). || To strangle: *ahogar a uno con una cuerda*, to strangle s.o. with a rope. || To flood (encharcar, inundar). || To drown (regar con exceso). || To smother, to put out: *ahogar la lumbre con ceniza*, to smother the fire with ashes. || To choke (las plantas, sembrándolas muy apretadas). || FIG. To stifle, to quell, to suppress, to put down: *ahogar una rebelión*, to suppress a rebellion. | To kill (un proyecto, etc.). | To overwhelm: *la pena le ahogaba*, he was overwhelmed by grief. | To stifle (los sollozos). | To keep back, to hold back: *ahogar el llanto*, to hold back one's tears. || To stalemate (en ajedrez). || — FIG. *Ahogar en germen*, to nip in the bud, to strangle at birth. || *Ahogar los remordimientos*, to clear *o* to ease one's conscience. || *Ahogar su pena embriagándose*, to drown one's sorrows.
— V. pr. To drown, to be drowned: *se ahogó en el río*, he drowned in the river. || To drown o.s. (suicidarse). || To suffocate, to be smothered (asfixiarse): *el niño se ahogó bajo la almohada*, the child suffocated under the pillow. || To go out (incendio). || To strangle o.s. (ahorcándose por accidente). || To suffocate: *ahogarse de calor*, to suffocate with heat. || — FIG. *Ahogarse en poca agua* or *en un vaso de agua*, to make a mountain out of a molehill. | *Uno se ahoga aquí*, it is stifling in here.
ahogo m. MED. Breathing trouble, breathlessness (dificultad para respirar). || FIG. Distress (angustia). | Financial difficulties, *pl.*: *pasar un ahogo*, to experience *o* to be in financial difficulties. || — *Me dio un ahogo*, I could not breathe. || *Perecer por ahogo*, to drown (en agua), to suffocate (por falta de aire).
ahoguío m. MED. Breathing trouble, breathlessness.
ahombrado, da adj. FAM. Masculine (hombruno).
ahondamiento m. Deepening, digging, excavation. || FIG. Investigation.
ahondar v. tr. To deepen: *ahondar un pozo*, to deepen a well. || To drive (una cosa en otra). || FIG. To go deeply into, to investigate thoroughly.
— V. intr. To go deep: *las raíces ahondan en la tierra*, the roots go deep in the ground. || FIG. To investigate thoroughly, to examine in depth, to go deeply into: *ahondar en una cuestión*, to examine a question in depth.
— V. pr. To get deeper.
ahonde m. Deepening.
ahora adv. Now, right now: *ahora no puedo ir*, I can't go now. || FIG. In a moment (dentro de un momento). | Right away, right now (en seguida). || — *Ahora me lo han dicho*, they've just told me. || *Ahora (que)*, mind you: *ahora (que) tampoco me disgustaría hacer ese trabajo*, mind you, I wouldn't mind doing that job. || *Ahora mismo*, right away, right now: *lo haré ahora mismo*, I'll do it right away; just: *ha salido ahora mismo*, he has just gone out. || *Ahora o nunca*, it's now or never. || *Ahora sí que me voy*, this time I really am going. || *¡Ahora vengo!*, coming! || *De ahora en adelante* or *desde ahora*, from now on, in future, in the future. || *Hasta ahora*, see you later, see you soon (hasta luego), up till now, until now, to date (hasta la fecha). || *Por ahora*, for the moment, at the moment, for the time being.
— Conj. Now, now then: *lo hemos discutido, ahora, ¿qué hacemos?*, we have talked about it, now, what shall we do? || But: *es perezoso, ahora, si le haces trabajar...*, he is lazy, but if you make him work... || — *Ahora... ahora*, either... or: *ahora vengas, ahora no vengas*, either you come or you don't come; one minute... the next minute, now ... now: *ahora corre, ahora anda*, one minute he's running, the next minute he's walking. || *Ahora* or *ahora bien*, now: *ahora bien, su padre ha vuelto*, now, his father has come back; but, however: *no me gusta; ahora bien, si lo quieres absolutamente*, I don't like it, but if you really insist; come now: *ahora bien, ¡qué te crees!*, come now, do you really think so? || *Ahora que*, but: *es inteligente, ahora que es perezoso*, he is intelligent, but [he is] lazy.
ahorca f. *Amer.* Present, gift.
ahorcado, da m. y f. Hanged person, dead man.
ahorcadura f. Hanging.
ahorcajarse v. pr. To sit astride, to straddle: *ahorcajarse en una silla*, to sit astride a chair.
ahorcar v. tr. To hang. || — *Ahorcar los hábitos*, to give up the cloth. || FIG. *A la fuerza ahorcan*, I [you, he, etc.] have no choice *o* alternative. | *¡Que me ahorquen si lo cuento!*, cross my heart and hope to die! | *¡Que me ahorquen si lo sé!*, I'm hanged if I know.
— V. pr. To hang o.s.: *ahorcarse de* or *en una rama de árbol*, to hang o.s. from the branch of a tree.
ahorita adv. FAM. Right now, this very minute.
ahormar v. tr. To form (los zapatos, los sombreros). || To fit (un vestido). || To break in (los zapatos al andar). || To wear in (un vestido, un traje, al llevarlo). || FIG. To mould (el carácter). || TAUR. To manoeuvre [the bull] into a good position for the kill.
— V. pr. FIG. To conform, to yield. | To mould o.s. to, to get used to: *ahormarse a una nueva vida*, to mould o.s. to a new life, to get used to a new life.
ahornagamiento m. Parching (tierra).
ahornagarse v. pr. To become parched (tierra). || To dry up (tierra, frutos, etc.).
ahornar v. tr. To put in an oven.
— V. pr. To bake on the outside only.
ahorquillado, da adj. Forked.
ahorquillar v. tr. To prop up [with forks]. || To shape like a fork (dar forma de horquilla).
— V. pr. To fork.
ahorrador, ra adj. Thrifty.
— M. y f. Thrifty person: *sus padres son unos ahorradores*, his parents are thrifty people. || Saver: *el Estado estimula a los ahorradores*, the government encourages savers.
ahorramiento m. Saving.
ahorrar v. tr. To save, to put aside: *la sociedad ahorró dinero*, the society saved money; *he ahorrado unos cuartos para irme de vacaciones*, I've put aside some money to go on holiday. || FIG. To save: *esto me ahorra hacerlo*, that saves me doing it; *ahorrar sus fuerzas*, to save one's strength; *ahorrar saliva*, to save one's breath. || To free (un esclavo). || *No ahorraremos sacrificios para mantener la paz*, there is no sacrifice we would not make to keep the peace.
— V. intr. To save, to save up.
— V. pr. To save *o* to spare o.s.: *ahorrarse un trabajo penoso*, to spare o.s. a difficult job. || To save: *ahorrarse trabajo, tiempo*, to save work, time. || To save, to save o.s.: *fue andando para ahorrarse el billete*, he went on foot to save himself the fare. || To avoid, to save: *así se ahorra usted discusiones*, that way you avoid arguments.
ahorrativo, va adj. Thrifty.
ahorro m. Saving: *tener algunos ahorros*, to have a few savings. || Saving, thrift: *hay que fomentar el ahorro*, saving must be encouraged. || FIG. Saving: *es un ahorro de tiempo*, it's a saving of time. || — *Esos son ahorros de chicha y nabo*, this is cheeseparing

economy. || *Hacer ahorros de chicha y nabo*, to count every penny, to over-economize. || *Caja postal de ahorros*, Post Office savings bank.
ahuate m. *Amer.* Thorn.
ahuecado, da adj. Deep (voz). || Hollow (hueco). || Bouffant (vestido).
ahuecador m. Bustle, crinoline (miriñaque).
ahuecamiento m. Hollowing-out, scooping-out (acción de dejar hueco). || Loosening: *ahuecamiento del suelo*, loosening of the soil. || Fluffing-up (de un colchón, etc.). || Inflation (inflado). || Fig. Vanity.
ahuecar v. tr. To hollow *o* to scoop out: *ahuecar un tronco de árbol*, to hollow out a tree trunk. || To loosen (la tierra). || To fluff up (lana, etc.). || To expand (un vestido). || — Fam. *¡Ahueca!*, beat it!, clear off! | *Ahuecar* or *ahuecar el ala*, to take off, to make o.s. scarce (largarse). || *Ahuecar la voz*, to deepen one's voice, to put on a solemn *o* sanctimonious voice.
— V. pr. To become hollow. || To fluff up (hacerse menos compacto). || To bubble, to blister (el enlucido, etc.). || Fig. y fam. To puff o.s. up, to put on airs.
ahuehué o **ahuehuete** m. Mexican coniferous tree.
ahuesado, da adj. Bone-coloured, bone, yellowish (amarillento). || Bone-hard (duro).
ahuesarse v. pr. *Amer.* To be spoilt (cosas). | To lose weight (personas).
ahuizote m. *Amer.* Nuisance, bore (pesado). | Witchcraft (brujería).
ahulado m. *Amer.* Oilcloth, oilskin.
ahumado, da adj. Smoke-filled, smoky (lleno de humo). || Smoked: *salmón ahumado*, smoked salmon; *gafas ahumadas*, smoked glasses. || Smoky: *cuarzo ahumado*, smóky quartz. || Fig. Tipsy, merry: *cuando salió del casino estaba algo ahumado*, when he left the casino he was a bit tipsy. || *Arenque ahumado*, smoked herring, kipper.
— M. Smoking: *el ahumado de la carne*, the smoking of meat. || Smoking-out (de las abejas, etc.).
ahumar v. tr. To smoke: *ahumar el jamón*, to smoke ham. || To cure (acecinar). || To smoke (una superficie). || To fill with smoke (llenar de humo). || To smoke out (las abejas, etc.).
— V. intr. To smoke. || To intoxicate, to be intoxicating: *los licores ahuman*, drink intoxicates.
— V. pr. To acquire a smoky taste. || To blacken, to get black (ennegrecerse). || Fam. To get sozzled *o* tipsy (emborracharse). || Fam. *Ahumársele a uno el pescado*, to get all steamed up, to get annoyed: *se le ahumó el pescado*, he got all steamed up.
ahusado, da adj. Streamlined. || Fine, thin, tapered (dedos).
ahusar v. tr. To taper.
— V. pr. To taper.
ahuyentador, ra adj. Which drives *o* scares away.
ahuyentar v. tr. To scare away, to drive away: *el perro ahuyentó a los ladrones*, the dog scared the thieves away. || To drive out *o* away: *el fuego ahuyentó las fieras de la selva*, the fire drove the animals out of the forest. || To keep at bay, to keep off (mantener a distancia). || Fig. To dismiss, to dispel, to banish: *ahuyentar un pensamiento*, to dismiss a thought. || Fig. *Ahuyentar las penas con vino*, to drown one's sorrows in wine.
— V. pr. To run away, to flee (huir).
aijada f. Goad.
ailanto m. Bot. Ailanthus (árbol).
aíllo m. *Amer.* Line, race (entre los quechuas). | Agricultural community.
aimara o **aimará** adj. Aymaran.
— M. y f. Aymara (raza andina). || — M. Aymara, Aymaran (lengua).
aindiado, da adj. Indian-like, Indian.
airado, da adj. Angry, annoyed: *con gesto airado*, with an angry look on his face; *respondió con un tono airado*, he replied in an angry voice. || In a temper *o* rage, seething: *salió airado*, he left in a temper. || Immoral, loose (la vida). || *Mujer de vida airada*, loose woman.
airamiento m. Anger, annoyance.
airampo m. Cactus found in Peru and northern Argentina.
airar v. tr. To annoy, to anger.
— V. pr. To get annoyed, to get angry.
aire m. Zool. Solenodon (animal de Cuba).
aire m. Air (fluido): *bocanada de aire*, breath of air. || Air: *el avión vuela por los aires*, the aeroplane flies through the air. || Draught (corriente): *¿de dónde viene este aire?* where is this draught coming from? || Fig. Likeness (parecido): *aire de familia*, family likeness. | Look, appearance (aspecto): *con un aire triste*, with a sad look; *tiene un aire severo*, he has a severe appearance, he has a severe look about him. | Allure, bearing (porte): *aire marcial*, soldierly bearing. || Mús. Movement. | Tune, air (música): *aire bailable*, dance tune. | Tune, song (canción): *un aire popular*, a folk song. || Aut. Choke (estrangulador). || Gait (del caballo). || Fam. Attack: *le dio un aire que le dejó paralizado*, he had an attack which left him paralyzed. || — *Aire acondicionado*, air conditioning. || *Aire colado*, draught. || *Aire comprimido*, compressed air. || *Aire de suficiencia*, conceited air. || Min. *Aire detonante*, firedamp. || *Aire líquido*, liquid air. || *Al aire*, into the air: *disparar al aire*, to shoot into the air. || *Al aire libre*, in the open air: *dormir al aire libre*, to sleep in the open air; open-air: *la vida al aire libre*, open-air life. || Fig. *Beber el aire por*, to be madly in love with. || *Cambia el aire*, the wind is changing. || Fig. y fam. *Cogerlas* or *matarlas en el aire*, to be quick on the uptake. || *Con aire acondicionado*, air-conditioned. || *Corriente de aire*, draught. || *Dar aire a uno*, to fan s.o. (airear). || *Dar buen aire al dinero*, to spend money freely, to spend money like mad. || *Darse aires*, to put on airs and graces, to put on airs. || *Darse aires de intelectual*, to put on intellectual airs, to play the intellectual. || Fam. *Darse aires de suficiencia*, to get on one's high horse. || *Darse un aire a*, to look rather like, to resemble. || Fig. *De buen aire*, willingly. | *Dejar en el aire*, to leave pending *o* in the air. | *De mal aire*, reluctantly, unwillingly. || *Echar al aire*, to uncover (desnudar), to throw into the air. || Fig. *Estar de buen aire*, to be in a good mood. | *Estar en el aire*, to be in the air (un negocio), to be on the air (un programa de la radio). | *Hablar al aire*, to talk idle rubbish. || *Hace aire*, it's windy. || *Hacer aire con un abanico*, to fan o.s. || Fig. *Herir el aire*, to rend the air. | *Levantar castillos en el aire*, to build castles in the air *o* in Spain. || Fig. *Mudar a cualquier aire*, to be fickle, to change with the wind. || *Mudar* or *cambiar de aires*, to have a change of air (enfermo). || *Nivel de aire*, spirit level. || Fig. *Promesas en el aire*, worthless *o* idle promises. | *¿Qué aires le traen por aquí?* what brings you here?, to what do we owe your visit?, to what do wc owc the honour? | *Seguir el aire a alguien*, to do s.o.'s every wish. | *Ser aire*, to be worthless. | *Sustentarse del aire*, to live on next to nothing, to live on fresh air (vivir con poco). || *Tener aires de gran señor*, to have the air of *o* to look like a gentleman. || Fig. *Tiene la cabeza llena de aire*, he is empty-headed. || *Tomar el aire*, to go out for a breath of air (pasearse). || Fig. *¡Vete a tomar el aire!*, clear off!, get out!
— Interj. Fam. Clear off!
aireación f. Ventilation.
aireado, da adj. Ventilated (ventilado). || Sour, bitter: *vino aireado*, bitter wine.
airear v. tr. To air. || To ventilate (ventilar). || Fig. To air (discutir). | To make public, to air. || *Airear la atmósfera*, to clear the air.
— V. pr. To catch a cold (coger un resfriado). || *Ha salido para airearse*, he has gone out for a breath of fresh air.
airón m. Heron (ave). || Crest, tuft, aigrette (penacho). || Panache, crest (de cascos). || *Pozo airón*, very deep well.
airosamente adv. Gracefully, elegantly (con elegancia): *andar airosamente*, to walk gracefully. || *Salir airosamente de algo*, to come out of sth. with flying colours.
airosidad f. Gracefulness, grace, elegance.
airoso, sa adj. Ventilated (ventilado). || Windy (ventoso). || Fig. Graceful, elegant (garboso): *una postura airosa*, a graceful pose. | Neat: *una respuesta airosa*, a neat reply. || *Quedar* or *salir airoso de algo*, to come out of sth. with flying colours.
aislable adj. Isolable. || Electr. Insulatable.
aislacionismo m. Isolationism.
aislacionista adj./s. Isolationist.
aisladamente adv. On one's own, alone, by o.s.
aislado, da adj. Alone, by o.s., on one's own (solo): *vivir aislado*, to live alone. || Remote, isolated (casa, aldea, sitio). || Isolated (apartado). || Electr. Insulated. || — *Con inodoro aislado*, with separate W.C. || *Se les estropeó la radio dejándoles aislados de la civilización*, their radio broke down cutting them off from civilization.
aislador, ra adj. Insulating: *cinta aisladora*, insulating tape.
— M. Insulator: *el vidrio es un buen aislador*, glass is a good insulator. || Electr. Insulator (aparato).
aislamiento m. Isolation: *vivir en el aislamiento*, to live in isolation. || Electr. Insulation. || *Aislamiento de sonido*, soundproofing.
aislante adj. Insulating: *cinta aislante*, insulating tape.
— M. Insulator.
aislar v. tr. To isolate: *aislar un edificio*, to isolate a building. || Electr. To insulate. || Fig. To isolate (dejar solo).
— V. pr. To isolate o.s., to go into seclusion.
¡ajá! interj. Fam. Fine! good! (aprobación). | Aha! (sorpresa).
ajado, da adj. Shabby, crumpled, creased (vestido, etc.). || Withered (flor). || Aged, drawn (persona). || Wrinkled (piel).
¡ajajá! o **¡ajajay!** interj. V. ¡ajá!
ajamiento m. Shabbiness: *el ajamiento de una tela*, the shabbiness of a piece of material. || Wrinkling (de la piel).
ajamonado, da adj. Fam. Plump, stout: *una mujer ajamonada*, a plump woman.
ajamonarse v. pr. Fam. To get plump (una mujer).
ajar m. Garlic field, garlic patch.
ajar v. tr. To crumple, to mess up (telas, etc.): *ajar un vestido*, to crumple a dress. || To fade: *flores ajadas*, faded flowers. || To make fade: *el sol aja las cortinas*, sunlight makes the curtains fade. || To wrinkle: *tez*

ajada, wrinkled complexion. || Fig. To age: *los sufrimientos la han ajado prematuramente*, her suffering has aged her prematurely. | To hurt: *ajar el amor propio de alguien*, to hurt s.o.'s pride. | To abuse, to disparage (rebajar).
— V. pr. To fade, to wither (flores). || To get crumpled *o* creased *o* shabby (un vestido). || To wrinkle (la piel).

ajardinado, da adj. Laid out with gardens, landscaped (arreglado como un jardín).

aje m. *Amer.* Yam (planta). | Kind of cochineal.

ajebe m. Alum (alumbre).

ajedrecista m. y f. Chess player.

ajedrez m. Chess (juego). || Chess set (piezas y tablero). || Mar. Grating (enjaretado).

ajedrezado, da adj. Check (tejido). || Chequered: *escudo ajedrezado*, chequered coat of arms.

ajengibre m. Ginger.

ajenjo m. Wormwood, absinth, absinthe (planta). || Absinthe, absinth (bebida).

ajeno, na adj. Other people's, other's, of other people, of others (de otros, de los demás): *las desgracias ajenas*, other people's misfortunes, the misfortunes of others; *los bienes ajenos*, other people's property. || Someone else's (de otro): *vive con un corazón ajeno*, he is living with someone else's heart. || Unaware of, out of: *yo era completamente ajeno a* or *de lo que ocurría*, I was completely unaware of what was happening. || Irrelevant: *pregunta ajena al tema*, question irrelevant to the subject. || Detached: *vivía completamente ajeno a las cosas de este mundo*, he lived completely detached from the things of this world. || Free (libre): *ajeno de prejuicios*, free from prejudice. || Different: *mis preocupaciones son muy ajenas a las tuyas*, my worries are very different from yours. || Not in keeping with, inconsistent with: *ajeno de su estado, a su carácter*, not in keeping with his position, his character. || Outside: *eso es ajeno a su especialidad*, that is outside his speciality *o* field. || Strange, alien: *este asunto me es completamente ajeno*, this matter is completely strange to me. || Without, devoid of: *ajeno de sentido común*, devoid of common sense. || — *Estar ajeno de sí*, to be beside o.s. || Dep. *Este equipo va a jugar en campo ajeno*, this team is going to play away [from home]. || *Lo ajeno, el bien ajeno*, other people's property. || *Persona ajena a un asunto*, person who has nothing to do with a matter, outsider to a matter. || *Por razones ajenas a nuestra voluntad*, for reasons beyond our control. || *Prohibida la entrada a las personas ajenas al servicio*, staff only. || *Ser ajeno a un crimen*, to have no part in a crime. || *Vivir a costa ajena*, to live off other people, to live at other people's expense.

ajerezado, da adj. Sherry-like.

ajete m. Young garlic. || Garlic sauce (salsa).

ajetreado, da adj. Busy: *una persona, una vida muy ajetreada*, a very busy person, life.

ajetrearse v. pr. To be busy (atarearse). || To wear o.s. out, to exhaust o.s.: *me he ajetreado mucho para nada*, I've worn myself out for nothing. || To rush, to hurry (darse prisa).

ajetreo m. Activity (actividad). || Rush: *¡qué ajetreo!, no paré ni un momento*, what a rush! I didn't stop for a second. || Rushing about, hard work: *la preparación de un viaje acarrea mucho ajetreo*, preparing for a journey involves a lot of rushing about. || Bustle, life, movement: *hay mucho ajetreo en la calle*, there's a lot of bustle in the street. || Hustle and bustle, bustle: *el ajetreo de la vida en la ciudad*, the hustle and bustle of town life. || Exhaustion, weariness (cansancio).

ají m. Red pepper, chili. || Chili sauce (salsa). || — *Amer.* Fam. *Ponerse como un ají*, to go as red as a beetroot (sonrojarse), to go up the wall, to lose one's temper (enfadarse). | *Ser más bravo que el ají*, to have a nasty character.

ajiaceite m. Garlic sauce (salsa).

ajiaco m. Chili sauce (salsa). || *Amer.* Chili stew.

ajilimoje o **ajilimójili** m. Piquant sauce. || — Pl. Fig. y fam. Bits and pieces. || Fig. y fam. *Y con todos sus ajilimójilis*, and the whole bag of tricks, and the whole caboodle.

ajipuerro m. Wild leek.

ajo m. Garlic: *ristra de ajos*, string of garlics. || Clove of garlic (diente de ajo). || Garlic sauce (salsa). || — *Ajo blanco*, garlic soup. || *Ajo cañete* or *castañete*, garlic with reddish skin. || *Ajo cebollino*, chive, chives. || *Ajo chalote*, shallot. || *Ajo porro* or *puerro*, leek. || Fig. *Bueno anda el ajo*, things are really looking bad, things are really in a state. || *Diente de ajo*, clove of garlic. || Fig. y fam. *Estar en el ajo*, to be in on it (saber lo que sucede), to be involved, to be mixed up in it. | *Estar harto de ajos*, to be ill-bred, to be uncouth. | *Quien se pica, ajos come*, if the cap fits, wear it. | *Revolver el ajo*, to stir up trouble, to add fuel to the fire. | *Soltar ajos*, to swear, to curse.

¡ajo! o **¡ajó!** interj. Coo coo!, goo goo! [talking to a baby].

ajoarriero m. Dish prepared with cod, eggs and garlic.

ajobar v. tr. To carry on one's back.

ajofaina f. Washbowl, washbasin (palangana).

ajolín m. Kind of bedbug.

ajolote m. Axolotl (animal anfibio).

ajomate m. Conferva (alga).

ajonjolí m. Bot. Sesame (alegría).

ajorca f. Bracelet (pulsera).

ajornalar tr. To employ by the day.

ajuanetado, da adj. Deformed by a bunion (pie). || With prominent cheekbones (rostro).

ajuar m. Furnishings, *pl.* (de una casa). || Trousseau (de novia). || *Ajuar de niño*, layette.

ajuglarado, da adj. Minstrel-like.

ajuiciado, da adj. Wise, sensible (juicioso).

ajuiciar v. tr. To bring to one's senses (volver juicioso). || To judge (juzgar).

ajumado, da adj. Fam. Canned, tight, sozzled.
— M. Fam. Drunk.

ajumarse v. pr. Fam. To get sozzled *o* drunk *o* canned.

ajustado, da adj. Adjusted. || Correct, right: *una solución ajustada*, a correct answer. || Tight, clinging: *un vestido muy ajustado*, a very tight dress. || Close: *resultados ajustados*, close results. || *Bien ajustado, mal ajustado*, well-fitting, badly-fitting.
— M. Fitting: *el ajustado de las piezas del motor*, the fitting of engine parts.

ajustador m. (Ant.). Jerkin (prenda de vestir). || Corselet (ropa interior). || Fitter (obrero). || Impr. Compositor, maker-up.

ajustamiento m. V. ajuste.

ajustar v. tr. To fit: *ajustar un vestido*, to fit a dress. || To make fit: *ajustar una tapa a una caja*, to make a lid fit a box. || To arrange: *ajustar un matrimonio*, to arrange a marriage. || To work out, to arrange: *ajustar un horario*, to work out a timetable. || To reconcile (enemigos). || To take on, to employ (un criado, un empleado). || To settle, to pay (una cuenta). || To draw up (un tratado). || To fix: *hemos ajustado el alquiler en 2 000 pesetas*, we have fixed the rent at 2,000 pesetas. || To give (un golpe). || To adapt: *ajustar su conducta a*, to adapt one's conduct to. || Impr. To make up. || Tecn. To fit: *ajustar dos piezas*, to fit two parts. | To adjust, to regulate (una máquina). || *Amer.* To catch (una enfermedad). || — Fig. *Ajustar el paso al de aguien*, to keep pace with s.o. || Com. *Ajustar las cuentas*, to balance the accounts. || Fig. *Ajustar las cuentas a uno*, to settle accounts with s.o. | *Ajustarle las clavijas a uno*, to put the pressure on s.o., to tighten up on s.o., to put the screws on s.o.
— V. intr. To fit: *esta tapadera no ajusta*, this lid doesn't fit. || To cling, to be tight (un vestido). || Fig. To fit in: *esto ajusta con lo que te dije*, that fits in with what I said.
— V. pr. To adjust *o* to adapt o.s.: *me ajusto a todo*, I adapt myself to everything. || To conform: *ajústate exactamente a mis instrucciones*, conform exactly with my instructions. || To be consistent, to fit in: *lo que me dices se ajusta a la verdad*, what you say is consistent with the truth. || To cling, to be tight (un vestido). || To tighten: *ajustarse el cinturón*, to tighten one's belt. || To come to an agreement (llegar a un acuerdo). || To agree: *se ajustaron en que iban a venir*, they agreed to come. || — *Ajustarse a razones*, to yield to reason. || *Ajustarse en sus costumbres*, to settle down.

ajuste m. Fitting (acción de ajustar un vestido, etc.). || Adjustment (encaje, adaptación). || Agreement, compromise (acuerdo): *llegar a un ajuste*, to come to an agreement. || Engagement, hiring, employment (de un criado, obrero). || Fixing (del precio). || Tecn. Fitting, assembly (ensamblaje). | Adjustment (arreglo). || Impr. Composition, makeup. || Com. Settlement, payment (de una cuenta). || Cinem. Splicing. || Fot. Framing, centring. || Bonus (sobre el sueldo). || — Fig. *Ajuste de cuentas*, settling of accounts. || *Ajuste de la paz*, peace talks. || *Anillo de ajuste*, bush. || *Carta de ajuste*, test card (en la televisión). || *Más vale mal ajuste que buen pleito*, a poor agreement is better than a good court case. || *Tornillo de ajuste*, adjusting screw.

ajusticiado, da m. y f. Executed person.

ajusticiamiento m. Execution (de un reo).

ajusticiar v. tr. To execute.

al contraction of the preposition *a* and the masculine definite article *el*.
1. *Seguido de un sustantivo.* — Véase a (preposición). || Into: *traducir al italiano*, to translate into Italian. || — *Al mediodía*, at midday, at noon. || *Al menos*, at least. || *Dar la vuelta al mundo*, to go round the world.
2. *Seguido del infinitivo.* — When, on: *al llegar se cayó*, when he arrived, he fell over; on arriving, he fell over; *al entrar vio a su tío*, when he came in *o* on entering he saw his uncle. || — *Al dar las cinco*, on the stroke of five, when the clock struck five. || *Al anochecer*, at nightfall. || *Al salir el sol*, at sunrise.

ala f. Wing (de ave, insecto, avión, edificio, ejército, partido político). || Brim: *sombrero de ala ancha*, wide-brimmed hat. || Lobe (del hígado). || Wing, ala (de nariz). || Eave (del techo). || Leaf, flap (de mesa). || Blade (de hélice). || Sail (de molino). || Dep. Wing (parte del campo). | Winger (jugador). || — Fig. y fam. *Ahuecar el ala*, to take off, to make o.s. scarce (marcharse). || *Ala del corazón*, auricle. || Fig. *Caérsele a uno las alas del corazón*, to lose heart. || *Con alas en delta*, delta-winged. || *Con alas en flecha*, swept-wing. || Fig. *Cortarle las alas a uno*, to clip s.o.'s wings (estorbar), to take the wind out of s.o.'s sails (desanimar). | *Dar alas a alguien*, to encourage s.o. || Fam. *Del ala*, peseta: *veinte del ala*, twenty pesetas. || *Ser como ala de mosca*,

to be paper-thin. || FIG. *Volar con sus propias alas*, to stand on one's own two feet.
¡ala! interj. Come on! (para incitar). || Hey! (para llamar).
Alá n. pr. m. Allah.
alabado, da adj. Praised. || *¡Alabado sea Dios!*, God be praised!, praise be to God!
— M. Eulogy (motete). || *Amer.* Dawn call [of night watchman]. || *Amer. Al alabado*, at dawn.
alabador, ra adj. Laudatory, praiseful, adulatory (que adula). || Approving, praiseful (de aprobación).
— M. y f. Praiser, lauder, adulator.
alabamiento m. Praise. || Boasting (jactancia).
alabancioso, sa adj. FAM. Boastful.
alabanza f. Praise [*a*, *de*, of]: *cantar las alabanzas de*, to sing the praises of. || Boasting, boastfulness (jactancia). || *En alabanza de*, in praise of.
alabar v. tr. To praise, to laud (celebrar). || *Alabar a uno de discreto* or *por su discreción*, to praise s.o. for his discretion, to praise s.o.'s discretion.
— V. intr. *Amer.* To call dawn.
— V. pr. To boast (jactarse). || To be glad *o* pleased: *me alabo de tu triunfo*, I am pleased about your triumph.
alabarda f. Halberd.
alabardado, da adj. Halberd-shaped.
alabardazo m. Blow with a halberd.
alabardero m. Halberdier. || — Pl. Claque, *sing.*, hired applauders (en el teatro).
alabastrado, da adj. Alabastrine, alabaster.
alabastrino, na adj. Alabastrine, alabaster.
— F. Thin sheet of alabaster.
alabastrita o **alabastrites** f. Translucent gypsum.
alabastro m. Alabaster. || *Alabastro yesoso*, translucent gypsum.
álabe m. TECN. Paddle, blade (de rueda hidráulica). | Tooth [of a cog]. || Drooping branch (de un árbol).
alabeado, da adj. Warped: *una tabla alabeada*, a warped plank.
alabear v. tr. To warp.
— V. pr. To warp.
alabeo m. Warp, warping (torcedura).
alacena f. Cupboard [U.S., closet].
alacrán m. Scorpion (arácnido). || S-shaped hook (de un corchete). || Cheek (del bocado). || *Amer.* Scandalmonger, gossip (maldiciente). || — *Alacrán cebollero*, mole cricket. || *Alacrán marinero*, angler (pez).
alacranado, da adj. Stung by a scorpion. || FIG. Rotten, corrupt (viciado).
alacranera f. Scorpiurus (planta).
alacridad f. Alacrity, readiness. || Briskness (vivacidad). || *Con alacridad*, with alacrity, readily.
alacha f. o **alache** m. ZOOL. [Fresh] anchovy.
alada f. Flap *o* stroke of the wing.
aladares m. pl. Hair (*sing.*) on the temples, hair (*sing.*) that falls over the temples.
aladierna f. o **aladierno** m. Buckthorn (arbusto).
Aladino n. pr. m. Aladdin.
alado, da adj. Winged, flying: *hormiga alada*, winged ant. || BOT. Wing-shaped. || FIG. Swift, rapid, quick (ligero).
alagartado, da adj. Motley.
alajú m. Kind of gingerbread.
alalia f. MED. Aphasia.
alalimón m. A children's game. || V. ALIMÓN.
alamar m. Decorative clasp (presilla). || Frog (adorno de casaca). || Fringe (fleco). || Tassel (en el traje del torero).
alambicadamente adv. Subtly, obscurely.
alambicado, da adj. FIG. Elaborate, subtle, intricate: *una teoría alambicada*, an elaborate theory. | Restricted, minimal, reduced to the bare minimum (escaso). | Precious, subtle (estilo). | Affected (afectado). || FIG. *Precios alambicados*, rock-bottom prices, cheapest possible prices.
alambicamiento m. Distillation. || FIG. Excessive subtlety: *el alambicamiento de un razonamiento*, the exessive subtlety of an argument. | Affectation (afectación). | Preciosity (del lenguaje, etc.).
alambicar v. tr. To distil, to distill (destilar). || FIG. To subtilize (sutilizar). | To overrefine (pulir excesivamente). | To complicate, to make over-intricate (complicar). | To elaborate (precisar). | To minimize, to keep to a minimum, to bring down to the lowest possible level (precio, etc.).
alambique m. Still. || — FIG. *Pasar algo por el alambique*, to scrutinize sth., to go through sth. with a fine toothcomb.
alambrada f. Barbed-wire barrier *o* entanglement (en la guerra). || Wire netting (reja). || Wire fence (valla).
alambrado m. Wire netting (alambrera). || Wire fence *o* fencing (valla). || ELECTR. Wiring, wiring system.
alambrar v. tr. To enclose with wire netting (una ventana). || To fence, to enclose with wire fencing (un terreno).
alambre m. Wire (de metal). || Bells, *pl.* (del ganado). || — *Alambre de púas* or *de espino* or *espinoso*, barbed wire. || FIG. y FAM. *Piernas de alambre*, matchstick legs, skinny legs. || FAM. *Ser un alambre*, to be as thin as a rake.
alambrera f. Wire netting (red de alambre). || Wire gauze (red muy fina). || Wire cover. || Food safe (alacena). || Fireguard (en el brasero o chimenea).
alambrista m. y f. Tightrope walker.
alameda f. Tree-lined avenue, boulevard (avenida). || Poplar grove (plantío de álamos).
alamín m. (Ant.). Inspector of weights and measures. | Surveyor of buildings (de obras arquitectónicas). | Irrigation superintendant (de los riegos).
álamo m. BOT. Poplar: *álamo blanco, negro*, white, black poplar. || *Álamo temblón*, aspen.
alampar v. intr. To long, to be longing *o* dying: *alampar por ir al cine, por un coche*, to be longing to go to the cinema, for a car.
alanceado, da adj. BOT. Lanceolate.
alancear v. tr. To lance, to spear.
alano adj. m. *Perro alano*, mastiff.
— M. pl. Alans, Alani.
Alano n. pr. m. Alan, Allen, Allan.
alantoides f. ANAT. Allantois.
alar m. Eaves, *pl.* (alero).
alarde m. MIL. Review, parade, march past. || FIG. Show, display: *un alarde de buen gusto*, a display of good taste. || *Hacer alarde de*, to display, to show off, to boast of: *hacer alarde de su riqueza*, to show off one's wealth; to put on a show of, to display: *hacer alarde de indiferencia*, to put on a show of indifference, to display indifference.
alardear v. intr. To boast, to brag, to show off: *alardear de sus conocimientos*, to boast *o* to brag about one's knowledge, to show off one's knowledge. || To boast, to brag: *alardea de tener influencia con el ministro*, he boasts that he has influence with the Minister. || *Alardea de buen mozo*, he thinks he is good-looking.
alardeo m. Show, display (alarde). || Boasting, bragging (jactancia).
alargadera f. Extension piece, extension (de un compás, de un goniómetro). || Adapter (retorta).
alargado, da adj. Elongated, lengthened, long: *forma alargada*, elongated shape.
alargador, ra adj. Lengthening, extending.
alargamiento m. Lengthening. || Extension: *el alargamiento de una calle*, the extension of a street. || Prolongation (en el tiempo). || TECN. Elongation. || Stretch, stretching: *el alargamiento de un elástico*, the stretch of an elastic band.
alargar v. tr. To lengthen, to let down: *alargar un vestido*, to lengthen a dress. || To lengthen (en longitud). || To prolong (en el tiempo): *alargar su estancia, un discurso*, to prolong one's stay, a speech. || To spin out (un cuento). || To put off, to defer (diferir). || To raise (un sueldo). || To extend, to lengthen: *alargar un plazo*, to extend a time limit. || To pass, to reach, to hand (dar): *alárgame ese libro*, pass me that book. || To hold out, to stretch out (la mano). || To crane, to stretch (el cuello). || FIG. To make stretch, to stretch out: *no puede alargar más su paga*, he cannot make his wages stretch any further. || To let out, to pay out: *alarga un poco de cuerda*, pay some rope out. || FIG. y FAM. To make drag on, to draw out: *la indecisión del general alargó la guerra*, the general's indecision made the war drag on *o* drew the war out. || To increase (aumentar). || — *Alargarle el camino a uno*, to take s.o. out of one's way. || *Alargar el paso*, to lengthen one's stride, to step out, to stride out.
— V. pr. To lengthen, to grow *o* to get longer. || To grow longer, to draw out: *en marzo los días se alargan*, in March the days get longer. || To get longer, to stretch: *este traje se alarga al lavarse*, this dress gets longer when it is washed. || To drag on *o* out (un discurso). || FIG. To get carried away, to be long-winded, to go on: *me he alargado mucho en mi carta*, I went on a lot in my letter. || FIG. y FAM. To carry on: *alargarse a* or *hasta la ciudad*, to carry on to the town. | To nip round, to pop over *o* round: *alárgate a casa de tu hermano*, nip round to your brother's. || MAR. To change (el viento). || To enlarge: *alargarse en un tema*, to enlarge upon a theme.
Alarico n. pr. m. Alaric.
alarido m. (Ant.). War cry of the Moors. || Howl, yell, shriek (grito fuerte). || *Dar alaridos*, to howl, to yell, to shriek.
alarifazgo m. Position of master builder.
alarife m. Master builder (maestro albañil). || Bricklayer (albañil). || *Amer.* Clever one, crafty one.
alarije m. Variety of grape.
alarma f. Alarm: *dar la alarma*, to raise *o* to give the alarm. || Emergency: *proclamar* or *declarar el estado de alarma*, to declare a state of emergency. || Anxiety: *vivir en alarma*, to live in anxiety. || — *Alarma aérea*, air-raid siren, air-raid warning. || *Con creciente alarma*, with increasing concern, with increasing alarm. || *Dar un toque de alarma*, to sound the alarm. || *Falsa alarma*, false alarm. || *Señal de alarma*, alarm, alarm signal. || *Voz de alarma*, alarm, alarm call.
alarmado, da adj. Alarmed.
alarmante adj. Alarming.
alarmar v. tr. To alarm, to frighten: *me alarma la gravedad de la situación*, the seriousness of the situation alarms me. || To alert, to rouse (dar la alarma a). || To call to arms (incitar a tomar las armas).
— V. pr. To be *o* to get alarmed, to be frightened. || *No alarmarse por nada*, not to be alarmed by anything.

alarmista m. y f. Alarmist (que hace cundir noticias alarmantes). || Nervous *o* jumpy *o* easily-frightened person (persona inclinada a alarmarse).
a latere m. FIG. y FAM. Lapdog, inseparable companion (compañero).
alaterno m. BOT. Buckthorn (aladierna).
Álava n. pr. GEOGR. Alava [one of the Basque provinces in Spain].
alavense o **alavés, esa** adj. [Of *o* from] Alava.
— M. y f. Native *o* inhabitant of Alava.
alazán, ana o **alazano, na** adj./s. Chestnut. || *Alazan dorado, tostado*, golden, burnt chestnut (caballo).
alba f. Dawn, daybreak: *me levanté al alba*, I got up at dawn. || Alb (de los sacerdotes). || — *Al rayar el alba*, at dawn, at daybreak: *levantarse al rayar el alba*, to get up *o* to rise at daybreak. || *Clarea* or *raya* or *rompe el alba*, dawn is breaking. || *Misa del alba*, early morning mass.
albacea m. y f. Executor (hombre), executrix (mujer).
albaceazgo m. Executorship.
albaceteño, ña o **albacetense** adj. [Of *o* from] Albacete [Spanish town].
— M. y f. Inhabitant of Albacete.
albacora f. Early fig (breva). || ZOOL. Tunny, tunny fish [U.S., tuna, tuna fish] (bonito).
albahaca f. Basil (planta).
albalá m. or f. Letters patent, *pl.* || Document (documento).
— OBSERV. Pl. *albalaes*.
albanegra f. Hairnet (para el pelo). || Net (para cazar).
albanés, esa adj./s. Albanian.
Albania n. pr. f. GEOGR. Albania.
albañal o **albañar** m. Sewer, drain (alcantarilla).
albañil m. Bricklayer. || — *Oficial de albañil*, master bricklayer. || *Peón de albañil*, hodman, bricklayer's labourer.
albañila adj. f. *Abeja albañila*, mason-bee.
albañilería f. Bricklaying (arte). || Masonry, brickwork. || *Pared de albañilería*, brick wall.
albar adj. White: *conejo albar*, white rabbit.
— M. Dry, white land (terreno).
albarán m. "To let" sign. || Letters patent, *pl.* (albalá). || Delivery note, invoice (lista de mercancías entregadas).
albarazado, da adj. Leprous (gafo). || Whitish (blanquecino). || Motley (abigarrado). || *Amer.* Chinese and Indian half-breed.
albarda f. Packsaddle (de una caballería). || *Amer.* Saddle (silla de montar). || Slice of bacon fat (albardilla de tocino).
albardado, da adj. With the back of a different colour from the rest of the body (animal).
albardar v. tr. To put a packsaddle on, to saddle.
albardería f. Saddler's shop, saddlery (talabartería).
albardero m. Saddler and harness maker.
albardilla f. Saddle for breaking horses (silla de montar). || ARCH. Coping (tejadillo). || Small cushion (almohadilla). || Mound of earth (en un huerto). || Slice of bacon fat, lard (de tocino).
albardón m. Large saddle. || *Amer.* Mound of earth (de tierra).
albareque m. Sardine net (red).
albaricoque m. Apricot (fruta). || Apricot, apricot tree (árbol).
albaricoquero m. Apricot, apricot tree (árbol).
albarillo m. White apricot (fruto y árbol). || Lively guitar tune.
albariza f. Lagoon (laguna). || Dry, white land (terreno).
albarizo, za adj. Whitish (blanquecino).
— M. Dishcloth (paño).
albarrada f. Dry-stone wall (muro). || Terrace (en una pendiente). || Mud wall (tapia). || Defensive wall (defensa). || Clay jar (alcarraza).
albarrana adj. f. Flanking (torre). || *Cebolla albarrana*, scilla (planta).
albatros m. Albatross.
albayaldado, da adj. Covered in white lead.
albayalde m. White lead.
albazano, na adj. Bay (caballo).
albazo m. *Amer.* Dawn attack (acción de guerra). | Dawn music, aubade (música). | Early riser (madrugón).
albeador m. *Amer.* Early riser.
albear m. Clay track.
albear v. intr. To turn white, to whiten. || *Amer.* To get up early (madrugar).
albedrío m. Will: *libre albedrío*, free will. || Whim, fancy (capricho). || Custom (costumbre). || *Hazlo a tu albedrío*, do it as you like *o* as the fancy takes you, do it at your pleasure.
albéitar m. Veterinary surgeon, vet [U.S., veterinarian].
albeitería f. Veterinary surgery.
alberca f. Tank, [small] reservoir (estanque). || Retting pit, rettery (poza para cáñamo). || *Amer.* Swimming pool (piscina). || *En alberca*, roofless.
albérchigo m. Clingstone peach (melocotón). || Clingstone apricot (albaricoque). || Clingstone-peach tree (melocotonero). || Clingstone-apricot tree (albaricoquero).
alberchiguero m. Clingstone-peach tree (melocotonero). || Clingstone-apricot tree (albaricoquero).
albergador, ra adj. (P.us.). Accommodating.
— M. Host (anfitrión). || Landlord (ventero). || — F. Hostess (anfitriona). || Landlady (ventera).
albergar v. tr. To give shelter to (servir de albergue). || To accommodate, to house, to lodge: *el bloque de viviendas albergará a doscientas familias*, the block of flats will house two hundred families; *la compañía alberga a los trabajadores extranjeros*, the company houses its foreign workers. || To accommodate, to house: *el viejo edificio no albergaba todos los ministerios*, the old building did not house all the ministries. || To accommodate, to take in, to put up: *una familia me alberga cuando voy a España*, a family puts me up when I go to Spain. || FIG. To cherish, to harbour, to foster: *alberga la esperanza de ir a México*, he cherishes hopes of going to Mexico. | To harbour (odio). | To experience: *albergar cierta inquietud*, to experience a certain anxiety.
— V. intr. y pr. To stay: *nos albergamos en el mismo hotel*, we are staying at the same hotel. || To shelter (refugiarse).
albergue m. Accommodation, lodgings, *pl.* (alojamiento): *tengo un albergue en un barrio central*, I have got accommodation in the town centre. || Hostel (posada): *albergue de juventud*, youth hostel. || Lair, den (de animales). || Shelter, refuge (refugio): *encontrar albergue en casa de un amigo*, to find shelter in a friend's house. || — *Albergue de carretera*, [roadside] inn, roadhouse. || *Dar albergue a alguien*, to give s.o. lodgings, to take s.o. in.
albero, ra adj. (P.us.). White (albar).
— M. Dishcloth (paño). || Dry, white land (terreno).
Alberto n. pr. m. Albert.
albigense adj. [Of *o* from] Albi. || Albigensian (de los albigenses).
— M. y f. Native *o* inhabitant of Albi. || — HIST. *La cruzada de los albigenses*, the Albigensian Crusade. | *Los albigenses*, the Albigenses.
albillo, lla adj./s. f. *Uva albilla*, white grape.
albina f. Salt lake *o* marsh.
albinismo m. Albinism.
albino, na adj./s. Albino: *una niña albina*, an albino girl. || *Amer.* Half-caste.
Albión n. pr. f. GEOGR. Albion.
albis (in) adv. FAM. *Quedarse in albis*, not to have a clue, not to understand a thing, to be completely flummoxed, to be left in the dark.
albita f. MIN. Albite.
albitana f. Fence to protect plants (para las plantas). || — M. MAR. Apron (en la proa). | Inner sternpost (en la popa).
albo, ba adj. POÉT. White.
albóndiga o **albondiguilla** f. Meatball, rissole (de carne).
albor m. Whiteness (blancura). || Dawn, daybreak (alba). || FIG. Beginning (principio). || — *Albores de la vida*, springtime of life. || *A los albores*, at dawn.
alborada f. Dawn, daybreak (alba). || MÚS. Aubade, dawn song. || MIL. Reveille.
alborear v. impers. To break, to dawn [the day] (amanecer): *ya alborea*, day is dawning *o* breaking, dawn is breaking.
alborno m. BOT. Alburnum, sapwood.
albornoz m. Burnous (de los árabes). || Bathrobe (para el baño).
alboronía f. Stew (guiso).
alboroque m. Gratuity, tip (agasajo).
alborotadamente adv. Noisily, boisterously.
alborotadizo, za adj. Irritable, excitable.
alborotado, da adj. Agitated, excited, worked up: *los ánimos están alborotados*, people are excited. || FIG. Eventful, full, busy: *hoy ha sido un día alborotado*, today has been an eventful day. || Rough, choppy (el mar). || Mutinous (amotinado). || Hasty, rash, reckless (aturdido).
alborotador, ra adj. Rowdy, noisy, boisterous: *alumnos alborotadores*, rowdy schoolchildren. || Rebellious (rebelde). || Seditious: *ideas alborotadoras*, seditious ideas.
— M. y f. Agitator, troublemaker: *siempre hay alborotadores en las manifestaciones*, there are agitators in every demonstration. || Subversive element (sedicioso). || Unruly *o* noisy child (en un colegio).
alborotamiento m. V. ALBOROTO.
alborotapueblos m. inv. Agitator, troublemaker.
alborotar v. intr. To make a din *o* racket, to kick up a row (hacer ruido). || To create *o* to cause disorder (causar desorden). || To move about (agitarse). || — *Él no deja de alborotar*, he won't keep still. || *¡No alborotéis más, niños!*, children, behave yourselves!
— V. tr. To upset, to cause a stir in *o* among, to agitate: *un acontecimiento que ha alborotado a toda la familia*, an event which has upset the whole family. || To stir up: *alborotar el barrio*, to stir up the district. || To upset, to turn upside down: *lo has alborotado todo*, you've upset everything. || To ruffle: *el viento alborota el pelo*, the wind ruffles one's hair. || To arouse the curiosity of (excitar la curiosidad de). || FIG. y FAM. *Alborotar el gallinero* or *el cotarro*, to cause trouble, to cause a stir.
— V. pr. To get upset, to get agitated (perturbarse). || To get excited (excitarse). || To riot (una multitud). || To lose one's temper, to get angry (encolerizarse).

|| To get worked up, to lose one's head: *no te alborotes por tan poca cosa,* don't get worked up over such a little thing. || To get rough *o* choppy (el mar).

alborotero, ra o **alborotista** adj. *Amer.* Noisy, rowdy (que mete jaleo). | Troublesome, rebellious (rebelde).

alboroto m. Uproar, disturbance (jaleo). || Din, racket, row (ruido): *hubo tal alboroto que la gente salió a ver lo que ocurría,* there was such a din that people came out to see what was happening. || Disturbance, riot (disturbio). || Scare, fright (susto). || — Pl. *Amer.* Roasted grains of maize. || — *Alboroto nocturno,* disturbance of the peace at night. || *Alborotos públicos,* public disturbances.

alborotoso, sa adj. *Amer.* Troublesome, rebellious (rebelde). | Rowdy, noisy (que mete jaleo). || — *Amer. Ideas alborotosas,* seditious ideas. | *Persona alborotosa,* agitator (dispuesta a promover disturbios).

alborozadamente adv. Joyfully, merrily.

alborozado, da adj. Joyful, overjoyed.

alborozador, ra adj. Cheering, heartening.

alborozar v. tr. To make laugh: *los payasos alborozan a la chiquillería,* clowns make children laugh. || To delight, to gladden, to make happy, to fill with joy (llenar de alegría): *la noticia me alborozó,* the news delighted me.

— V. pr. To be overjoyed, to rejoice.

alborozo m. Joy, gaiety, merriment.

albricias f. pl. Reward, *sing.*, gift, *sing.* (regalo). || *Amer.* Air holes (en metalurgia). || *Dar albricias,* to congratulate.

— Interj. Great!, good!, smashing!

albufera f. Lagoon, pool, "albufera" [especially in Valencia].

álbum m. Album: *álbum de fotografías,* photograph album. || *Álbum de recortes,* scrapbook.

— OBSERV. The plural of *álbum* is *álbumes.*

albumen m. BOT. Albumen, endosperm.

albúmina f. BIOL. Albumin, albumen.

albuminado, da adj. Albuminous.

albuminoide m. QUÍM. Albuminoid.

albuminoideo, a adj. QUÍM. Albuminoid.

albuminoso, sa adj. Albuminous.

albuminuria f. MED. Albuminuria.

albur m. Bleak (pez). || First draw in the game of monte (en el juego). || FIG. Hazard, risk: *los albures de la vida,* the hazards of life. || — Pl. Card game. || *Jugar* or *correr un albur,* to run a risk.

albura f. Whiteness (blancura). || White [of an egg] (de huevo). || BOT. Alburnum, sapwood.

alburno m. BOT. Alburnum, sapwood (albura).

alca f. ZOOL. Razorbill (ave).

alcabala f. (Ant.). Sales tax.

alcabalero m. Tax collector (recaudador).

alcacel o **alcacer** m. BOT. Green barley. || Barley field (terreno).

alcací o **alcacil** m. [Wild] artichoke.

alcachofa f. Artichoke (planta). || Head of thistle (del cardo). || Rose (de regadera). || Sprinkling nozzle, sprinkler (de la ducha). || Strainer, rose (de un tubo).

alcachofado, da adj. Artichoke-shaped.

— M. Dish of artichokes.

alcachofero, ra adj. Producing artichokes.

— F. Artichoke (planta).

alcade m. V. ALCALDE.

alcahueta f. Procuress, bawd, go-between (celestina). || FIG. y FAM. Scandalmonger, gossip (chismosa).

alcahuete m. Procurer, pimp (proxeneta). || FIG. y FAM. Scandalmonger, gossip (chismoso). | Receiver (de cosas robadas). || TEATR. Draw curtain. || *Amer.* Informer (soplón).

alcahuetear v. intr. To procure, to pimp (el proxeneta). || To gossip (chismorrear). || To be a receiver (de cosas robadas).

alcahuetería f. Procuring, pimping. || FIG. y FAM. Complicity. | Trap (artimaña).

alcaicería f. (Ant.). Customs house for silk (aduana). || Silk merchant's district (sitio con tiendas de seda).

alcaico, ca adj./m. POÉT. Alcaic.

alcaide m. (Ant.). Governor (de una fortaleza). || Prison governor (de una prisión).

alcaidesa f. Governor's wife, governess.

alcaidía f. Governorship (cargo del alcaide). || Governor's house (casa del alcaide).

alcalaíno, na adj. [Of *o* from] Alcalá [especially Alcalá de Henares].

— M. y f. Native *o* inhabitant of Alcalá.

alcaldada f. Abuse of authority.

alcalde m. Mayor: *el alcalde de Madrid,* the mayor of Madrid. || Card game (juego de cartas). || Justice of the peace (juez). || — *Alcalde de barrio* or *teniente de alcalde,* deputy mayor. || FAM. *Alcalde de monterilla,* village mayor. || *Alcalde mayor,* magistrate.

alcaldesa f. Mayoress.

alcaldía f. Mayorship, mayoralty (dignidad de alcalde). || Mayor's office (oficina).

alcalescencia f. QUÍM. Alkalescence.

alcalescente adj. QUÍM. Alkalescent.

álcali m. QUÍM Alkali. || *Álcali volátil,* ammonia.

alcalímetro m. QUÍM. Alkalimeter.

alcalinidad f. QUÍM. Alkalinity.

alcalinización f. QUÍM. Alkalinization.

alcalino, na adj. QUÍM. Alkaline.

alcalinotérreo, a adj. QUÍM. Alkaline-earth.

— M. QUÍM. Alkaline earth.

alcalizar v. tr. QUÍM. To alkalize, to alkalify, to alkalinize.

alcaloide adj./s. m. QUÍM. Alkaloid.

alcaloideo, a adj. QUÍM. Alkaloid.

alcalosis f. MED. Alkalosis.

alcance m. Reach: *libro que está a mi alcance,* book which is within my reach; *póngalo fuera del alcance de los niños,* put it out of the children's reach *o* out of reach of the children. || Range (de telescopio, arma de fuego, emisora de radio, etc.): *cañón de largo alcance,* long-range gun; *estar al alcance,* to be within range. || FIG. Importance, significance: *noticia de mucho alcance,* news of great importance. | Scope: *un proyecto de mucho alcance,* a plan with great scope. || Deficit (en las cuentas). || Stop press (en los periódicos). || Pastern tumour (del caballo). || — *Afirmación de mucho alcance,* far-reaching statement. || *Al alcance de la mano,* within reach, handy. || *Al alcance de la vista,* in sight. || *Al alcance de la voz,* within call. || *Al alcance del oído,* within earshot. || *Buzón de alcance,* late collection box. || FIG. *Dar alcance a uno,* to catch up with s.o. | *Estar fuera del alcance de uno,* to go over s.o.'s head (demasiado complicado), to be inaccessible (demasiado caro). | *Ir al alcance de uno,* to chase s.o., to pursue s.o. (perseguir), to shadow s.o. (espiar). | *Persona de pocos* or *cortos alcances,* unintelligent person. | *Política de largo alcance,* far-reaching policy. | *Poner algo al alcance de todos,* to put sth. within everybody's reach. | *Ser corto de alcances* or *tener pocos* or *cortos alcances,* to be unintelligent, not to be very bright.

alcancía f. Money box (hucha).

alcándara f. Perch (cetrería). || Clothes rack (para la ropa).

alcandía f. BOT. Indian millet.

alcanfor m. Camphor.

alcanforar v. tr. To camphorate.

— V. pr. *Amer.* To disappear, to vanish.

alcanforero m. Camphor tree (árbol).

alcantarilla f. Sewer (cloaca): *las alcantarillas de una ciudad,* a town's sewers. || Culvert (paso dejado por debajo de los caminos). || Drain (boca de alcantarilla). || Small bridge (puentecillo). || *Amer.* Fountain.

alcantarillado m. Sewers, *pl.*, drains, *pl.*

alcantarillar v. tr. To lay sewers in: *alcantarillar una calle,* to lay sewers in a street.

alcantarillero m. Sewerman.

alcantarino, na adj. [Of *o* from] Alcántara.

— M. y f. Native *o* inhabitant of Alcántara. || — M. Knight of the order of Alcántara. || Reformed Franciscan.

alcanzable o **alcanzadizo, za** adj. Attainable, accessible, within reach.

alcanzado, da adj. Reached: *el nivel alcanzado,* the level reached. || — *Ir alcanzado,* to be short [of money], to be broke. || *Salir alcanzado,* to make a loss.

alcanzadura f. Pastern tumour (del caballo).

alcanzar v. tr. To reach: *alcanzar con la mano el techo,* to reach the ceiling with one's hand. || To catch up, to catch up with: *alcanzar a los que van en cabeza,* to catch up with the leaders. || To understand, to grasp: *no alcanzo lo que me dices,* I can't grasp what you're saying. || To reach, to come to, to join: *allí alcanzas la carretera,* there you come to the road. || FIG. To live through (una guerra, etc.). | To live in the time of (a una persona). || To hit: *la bala le alcanzó en la frente,* the bullet hit him in the forehead. || To reach, to attain: *alcanzar su objetivo,* to reach one's goal. || To reach, to amount to: *la producción alcanza tanto,* production reaches so much. || To affect: *ley que alcanza a todos los damnificados,* law which affects all the victims. || To see: *desde la ventana se alcanzaba la torre de la iglesia,* from the window you could see the church tower. || To make out, to perceive (con los sentidos). || To run to: *este libro ha alcanzado tres ediciones,* this book has run to three editions. || To get, to obtain: *siempre alcanza lo que quiere,* he always gets what he wants. || To rise to (la montaña). || To catch up with: *le he alcanzado en sus estudios,* I've caught up with him in his studies. || To have, to enjoy: *la película alcanzó gran éxito,* the film enjoyed great success. || To be able to get *o* to catch: *todavía alcanzas el tren de las siete,* you can still catch the seven o'clock train. || To pass: *alcánzame el pan,* pass me the bread. || To knock down: *el coche alcanzó al peatón,* the car knocked the pedestrian down.

— V. intr. To succeed, to manage: *por fin alcanzó a comprenderlo,* he finally succeeded in understanding *o* managed to understand. || To fall, to be left: *a mí me alcanzó una finca inmensa,* a huge estate was left *o* fell to me. || To be enough *o* sufficient: *la gasolina alcanza para el camino,* the petrol will be sufficient for the journey; *el sueldo no me alcanza para todo el mes,* my wage is not sufficient for the whole month. || To last (durar). || To have a range, to carry: *los cañones modernos alcanzan muy lejos,* modern guns have a very long range *o* carry a long way. || — *No alcanzo a comprenderle,* I just can't understand him. || *No creo que una sola tortilla alcance para todos,* I

don't think one omelette will be enough to go round.
— V. pr. To catch one another up, to meet. || To overreach (caballos).
alcaparra f. Caper bush (arbusto). || Caper (flor y condimento).
alcaparrado, da adj. Dressed with capers.
alcaparral m. Caper plantation.
alcaparrera f. o **alcaparrero** m. Caper bush.
alcaparrón m. Caper.
alcaraván m. Stone curlew (ave).
alcaravea f. Caraway.
alcarraza f. Clay jar.
alcarria f. Barren plateau.
alcatifa f. Carpet (alfombra).
alcatraz m. Gannet (ave). || Arum (planta).
alcaucí o **alcaucil** m. BOT. Wild artichoke (silvestre). | Artichoke (comestible).
alcaudón m. Shrike, butcher-bird (ave).
alcayata f. Hook (escarpia).
alcazaba f. Citadel, fortress, castle. || Casbah (en África del Norte).
alcázar m. Palace (palacio). || Citadel, fortress (fortaleza). || MAR. Quarterdeck.
alce m. ZOOL. Elk, moose. || Cut (naipes). || *Amer.* Rest, respite (tregua). | Gathering [of sugar cane].
alcedo m. Maple tree grove.
Alcestes n. pr. m. Alcestis.
Alcibíades n. pr. m. Alcibiades.
alcino m. Wild basil.
alción m. Kingfisher (ave). || Halcyon (ave fabulosa). || Alcyonium (pólipo).
— F. Alcyone.
alciónico adj. m. *Días alciónicos*, halcyon days.
alcista m. y f. Bull (en la Bolsa).
— Adj. Rising, upward: *tendencia alcista*, upward tendency. || *Mercado alcista*, bull market (en la Bolsa).
alcoba f. Bedroom (dormitorio). || Bedroom suite (muebles). || FIG. *Secretos de alcoba*, intimacies [of married life].
alcohol m. Alcohol: *alcohol absoluto*, pure alcohol. || Spirit, spirits, *pl.*: *alcohol de quemar* or *desnaturalizado* or *metílico*, methylated spirits. || Alcohol, spirits, *pl.* (bebida). || Galena (mineral). || Kohl (afeite). || — *Alcohol etílico*, ethyl alcohol. || *Lámpara de alcohol*, spirit lamp.
alcoholar v. tr. To alcoholize. || To make up with kohl (pintarse). || To clean with alcohol. || MAR. To tar.
alcoholato m. Spirit, alcoholate.
alcoholero, ra adj. Alcohol, of alcohol.
— F. Distillery.
alcohólico, ca adj./s. Alcoholic. || *Bebida no alcohólica*, non-alcoholic drink, soft drink.
alcoholificación f. Alcoholic fermentation.
alcoholímetro m. Alcoholometer.
alcoholismo m. Alcoholism.
alcoholización f. Alcoholization.
alcoholizado, da adj. Poisoned by alcohol. || *Está alcoholizado*, he has alcohol poisoning.
— M. y f. Alcoholic.
alcoholizar v. tr. To alcoholize.
— V. pr. To become an alcoholic.
alcohómetro m. Breathalyser.
alcor m. Hill (colina).
Alcorán n. pr. m. Koran.
alcoránico, ca adj. Koranic.
alcornocal m. Cork oak grove.
alcornoque m. Cork oak. || FIG. Dimwit, dope: *¡qué alcornoque es!*, what a dope he is!
alcornoqueño, ña adj. Cork oak.
alcorza f. Icing.
alcotán m. ZOOL. Lanner.
alcotana f. Pickaxe. || Ice axe (de alpinista).
alcubilla f. Tank, reservoir.
alcurnia f. Ancestry, lineage (estirpe). || — *Familia de alcurnia*, old family, family with long history. || *Ser de alta alcurnia*, to come from a good *o* noble family, to have noble ancestry, to be of noble birth (ser noble).
alcuza f. Oil bottle, cruet (aceitera).
alcuzcuz m. Couscous (plato árabe).
aldaba f. Doorknocker (llamador). || Latch, bolt, bar (de puerta o ventana). || FAM. *Tener buenas aldabas*, to have friends in the right places, to have contacts.
aldabada f. Knock. || *Dar aldabadas en*, to knock at.
aldabazo m. Loud knock.
aldabear v. intr. To knock at *o* on the door.
aldabeo m. Knocking at *o* on the door.
aldabilla f. Hook, catch, latch (de cerradura).
aldabón m. Large doorknocker (aldaba). || Handle (asa).
aldabonazo m. Loud knock, bang. || FIG. Shock, warning (advertencia).
aldea f. Village, hamlet.
aldeaniego, ga adj. V. ALDEANO.
aldeano, na adj. Village (de aldea). || Rustic, country (campesino). || FIG. Peasant.
— M. y f. Villager (que vive en una aldea). || Peasant, rustic.
aldehído m. QUÍM. Aldehyde.
aldehuela f. Small village, hamlet.
aldeorrio o **aldehorro** m. Backwater (poblacho).
alderredor adv. (Ant.). Round, around (V. ALREDEDOR.) || *Alderredor mío, tuyo, suyo, etc.*, round me, you, him, etc.
ale m. Ale (cerveza).
¡ale! interj. Come on!
álea m. Risk (riesgo).
aleación f. Alloy.
alear v. intr. To flap its wings (aletear). || To convalesce, to recover (convalecer).
— V. tr. To alloy: *alear el cobre con el oro*, to alloy copper with gold.
aleatorio, ria adj. Aleatory, contingent.
alebrarse o **alebrestarse** o **alebronarse** v. pr. To lie down flat (agazaparse). || FIG. To cower, to lose heart.
aleccionador, ra adj. Instructive, enlightening: *una historia muy aleccionadora*, a very instructive story. || Exemplary, which serves as an example, which teaches one a lesson: *un castigo aleccionador*, an exemplary punishment, a punishment which serves as an example.
aleccionamiento m. Instruction.
aleccionar v. tr. To instruct, to teach: *aleccionar a un aprendiz en el uso de un torno*, to instruct an apprentice in the use of a lathe, to teach an apprentice to use a lathe. || To lecture: *su madre le aleccionó para que no volviera a hacer lo mismo*, his mother lectured him so that he would not do it again. || To train: *aleccionar a un criado*, to train a servant. || To teach: *esto te aleccionará para no volver a caer en los mismos errores*, that will teach you not to make the same mistakes again. || *Estar aleccionado*, to have learnt one's lesson.
aleche m. [Fresh] anchovy (boquerón).
alechugar v. tr. To goffer, to crimp, to pleat, to flute. || *Cuello alechugado*, ruff.
aledaño, ña adj. Bordering, adjacent: *región aledaña del* or *al Támesis*, region bordering on *o* adjacent to the Thames.
— M. pl. Outskirts, surrounding district, *sing.*, surroundings.
alegación f. Assertion. || JUR. Allegation. || *Alegación de falsedad*, plea of forgery.
alegar v. tr. To allege (menos usado en inglés que en español), to say, to claim: *para disculparse de no haber venido alegó que había estado enfermo*, as an excuse for not having come, he claimed that he had been ill. || To point out, to emphasize, to stress (méritos, etc.). || To quote (una autoridad, un dicho). || To put forward: *alegar razones*, to put forward reasons. || JUR. To allege, to plead, to claim. || *Amer.* To dispute.
— V. intr. *Amer.* To argue.
alegato m. JUR. Allegation, plea: *el alegato del abogado defensor*, the allegation of the counsel for the defence. || FIG. Statement, declaration: *pronunció un alegato en defensa de su postura*, he made a declaration in defence of his position.
alegoría f. Allegory.
alegórico, ca adj. Allegorical, allegoric.
alegorizar v. tr. To allegorize.
alegrar v. tr. To make happy, to cheer up, to gladden: *la noticia me alegra*, the news makes me happy. || FIG. To brighten up, to liven up: *unos cuadros alegran las paredes*, a few pictures brighten up the walls; *para alegrar la fiesta vamos a cantar*, let's sing to liven up the party. || To make merry *o* tipsy: *este vinillo me ha alegrado*, this wine has made me merry. || FIG. To be pleasing to: *ramillete de flores que alegra la vista*, bouquet of flowers which is pleasing to the eye. | To poke, to stir (la lumbre). | To make brighter, to brighten up: *alegrar los colores*, to brighten up the colours. || TAUR. To rouse *o* to excite [the bull] into attacking. || MAR. To slack [a rope] (aflojar). || — *Me alegra verte*, I'm glad *o* happy to see you. || *Tu venida me alegra*, I am glad *o* happy that you have come.
— V. pr. To be happy, to be glad: *me alegro por* or *de* or *con la noticia*, I am happy to hear the news, I am happy about the news. || To cheer up: *alégrate, no pongas esta cara de duelo*, cheer up, don't pull such a long face. || To light up (los ojos, la cara). || FAM. To get merry, to get tipsy (achisparse). || — *¡Aquí está!* — *Me alegro*, here he is! — I'm glad *o* Good. || *Me alegro de verle*, I am glad *o* happy to see you.
alegre adj. Happy, joyful, cheerful: *un niño alegre*, a happy child; *una cara alegre*, a cheerful face. || Happy, glad: *alegre con la noticia*, happy with *o* about *o* glad about the news. || Good, happy: *una noticia alegre*, good news. || Pleasant, bright (tiempo). || Gay, lively: *música alegre*, lively music. || Bright, gay (color). || Tipsy, merry (achispado). || Spicy, naughty (chiste). || Daring, rash (atrevido). || Loose, loose-living (mujer). || Fast, immoral (vida). || — *Alegre como unas pascuas* or *como unas castañuelas*, as happy as a lark, as chirpy as a cricket. || *Alegre como un niño con zapatos nuevos*, as happy as a dog with two tails, as pleased as Punch. || *Alegre de cascos*, scatterbrained, harebrained. || *Alegre de corazón*, lighthearted.
alegremente adv. Gaily, merrily, happily.
alegreto adv./s.m. MÚS. Allegretto.
alegría f. Joy: *la alegría de vivir*, the joy of living. || Gaiety, cheerfulness, joy, happiness (buen humor).

|| Merriment, gaiety (regocijo). || Happiness, joyfulness (de una ocasión). || Brightness (de colores, etc.). || BOT. Sesame (ajonjolí). || — Pl. "Alegrías", song and dance from Cádiz. || Public festivities (fiestas). || — *¡Qué alegría!*, that's marvellous!, that's great! || *Saltar de alegría*, to jump for joy. || *Tener mucha alegría*, to be very happy *o* glad: *tengo mucha alegría en anunciarte esta noticia*, I am very happy to give you this news.
alegro adv./s. m. MÚS. Allegro.
alegrón m. FAM. Great joy *o* happiness. || FIG. Flare-up, blaze (llamarada breve). || *Me dio un alegrón con su éxito*, his success gave me a great thrill, I was thrilled to bits about his success.
— Adj. *Amer.* Flirtatious, gallant (enamoradizo). | Tipsy, merry (medio ebrio).
alejado, da adj. Far away, faraway, remote: *un lugar alejado de todo*, a place far away from everything, a faraway *o* remote place. || A long way from: *su casa está muy alejada de la mía*, his house is a very long way from mine. || Aloof, apart: *alejado de los intereses del mundo*, aloof from worldly interests. || *Está alejado de la política*, he takes no part in politics.
alejamiento m. Absence (ausencia). || Estrangement (enfriamiento entre novios, amigos, etc.) || Withdrawal (acción de alejarse). || Removal (acción de alejar).
Alejandría n. pr. GEOGR. Alexandria.
alejandrino, na adj./m. Alexandrine (verso).

— OBSERV. The Spanish *alejandrino* has 14 syllables, divided into two hemistiches.
— El *alexandrine* inglés tiene 12 sílabas y dos hemistiquios.

alejandrita f. Alexandrite.
Alejandro n. pr. m. Alexander: *Alejandro Magno*, Alexander the Great.
alejar v. tr. To move away, to remove: *si no lo alejas del fuego se quemará*, if you don't move it away from the fire it will burn. || To keep away: *hay que alejarle de las malas compañías*, he must be kept away from bad company. || To remove (una cosa, persona, peligro). || To avert: *alejar las sospechas*, to avert suspicion. || To get rid of: *aleja de ti esa idea*, get rid of that idea. || To remove: *alejar a alguien del poder*, to remove s.o. from power. || To separate (separar).
— V. pr. To go away (marcharse). || To move away *o* off: *el tren se alejó*, the train moved off. || To move *o* to go off into the distance (en la distancia). || To keep away: *alejarse de las malas compañías*, to keep away from bad company. || To go off, to leave: *alejarse del buen camino*, to go off the right road. || To give up, to relinquish: *alejarse del poder*, to relinquish one's power. || *Alejarse cada vez más*, to grow more and more distant.
alelado, da adj. Bewildered, stupefied (atontado). || Stupid (lelo).
alelamiento m. Bewilderment, stupefaction.
alelar v. tr. To stupefy, to bewilder.
— V. pr. To be stupefied *o* bewildered.
alelí m. BOT. Wallflower (amarillo). || BOT. *Alelí de Mahón*, Virginian stock.

— OBSERV. Pl. *alelíes*.

aleluya m. y f. Hallelujah, alleluia (canto religioso). || — M. Easter (Pascuas). || — F. Small religious print (estampita). || Small print depicting a story explained by rhyming couplets. || Rhyming couplet (pareado). || Wood sorrel (planta). || FAM. Bad painting (cuadro malo). || — Pl. FIG. y FAM. Doggerel (versos malos). | Joy (alegría). || *Estar de aleluya*, to rejoice.
alemán, ana adj./s. German. || *Plata alemana*, German silver, nickel silver.
alemanesco, ca adj. Germanic.
Alemania n. pr. f. GEOGR. Germany.
alemánico, ca adj. Germanic.
alemanisco, ca adj. Germanic. || Damask (mantel).
alentada f. Breath: *de una alentada*, in one breath.
alentado, da adj. Encouraged: *alentado por sus éxitos*, encouraged by his success. || Brave (valiente). || Haughty, proud (orgulloso).
alentador, ra adj. Encouraging: *palabras alentadoras*, encouraging words; *noticia alentadora*, encouraging news.
alentar* v. intr. To breathe. || FIG. To burn, to glow: *en su pecho alienta el amor a la patria*, his love for his country glows in his heart.
— V. tr. To encourage (animar): *alentar a uno para que siga adelante*, to encourage s.o. to continue; *alentar la rebelión*, to encourage rebellion. || To raise (las esperanzas, los ánimos). || *Amer.* To clap, to applaud (palmotear). | To give birth to (dar a luz).
— V. pr. To pluck up courage (envalentonarse). || To cheer up, to take heart (alegrarse). || MED. To get better, to recover (reponerse). || *Amer.* To give birth.
aleonado, da adj. Tawny.
alerce m. Larch (árbol).
alergia f. Allergy.
alérgico, ca adj. Allergic: *alérgico a los gatos*, allergic to cats.
— M. y f. Person suffering from an allergy.
alero m. ARQ. Eaves, *pl.* (tejado). || AUT. Mudguard [U.S., fender]. || FIG. *Estar en el alero*, to be in the balance, to be uncertain.
alerón m. Aileron.
alerta adv. Alertly. || On the alert, alert. || — *Estar alerta* or *ojo alerta*, to be on the alert *o* on one's guard, to watch out, to be alert. || *Ponerse alerta*, to become alert.
— Adj. Alert. || Agile (estilo).
— F. Alert: *dar la alerta*, to give the alert. || *Dar la voz de alerta*, to give the alert, to raise the alarm.
— Interj. Look out!, watch out!
alertamente adv. Alertly.
alertar v. tr. To alert, to put on one's guard, to give the alert to (poner en guardia). || To alert, to warn (avisar).
— V. intr. To keep one's eyes open, to keep a lookout, to keep watch.
alerto, ta adj. (P.us.). V. ALERTA.
aleta f. ZOOL. Fin (de los peces). | Flipper (de la foca). || Wing (de la nariz, de un coche). || Ala (de la nariz). || Fin, rib, gill (de radiador). || Vane (de una bomba). || Blade (de hélice). || Aileron (alerón). || Flipper (para nadar). || MAR. Fashion piece (de la popa).
aletada f. Flap of the wing.
aletargado, da adj. Lethargic. || Numb (pierna, etc.). || FIG. Drowsing, dozing: *aletargado en un rincón*, dozing in a corner.
aletargamiento m. Lethargy (letargo). || Drowsiness (adormecimiento). || Numbness (de una pierna, etc.).
aletargar v. tr. To make drowsy *o* sleepy (una persona). || To numb, to send to sleep (una pierna, etc.).
— V. pr. To become sleepy, to grow drowsy.
aletazo m. Flap of the wing, wingbeat (de un ave). || Flick of the fin (del pez). || *Amer.* FAM. Slap (bofetada).
aletear v. intr. To flap its wings, to flutter (las aves). || To wave *o* to flap one's arms (un niño).
aleteo m. Flapping *o* beating of the wings, fluttering. || FIG. Beating (del corazón).
aleto m. Osprey (ave).
aleudar v. tr. To leaven.
— V. pr. To rise.
aleurona f. BOT. Aleurone.
aleve adj. Treacherous, perfidious.
alevín o **alevino** m. Fry, young fish (pez).
alevosa f. Ranula (del ganado).
alevosamente adv. Treacherously. || In cold blood (fríamente).
alevosía f. Treachery (traición). || Premeditation (premeditación). || Caution [before committing crime] (cautela). || *Con* or *por alevosía*, treacherously (a traición), in cold blood (fríamente).
alevoso, sa adj. Treacherous, perfidious.
— M. Traitor. || — F. Traitress.
alexia f. MED. Alexia.
alexifármaco m. Alexipharmic.
alezo m. MED. Abdominal belt.
alfa f. Alpha (letra griega). || *Rayos alfa*, alpha rays.
alfabéticamente adv. Alphabetically.
alfabético, ca adj. Alphabetical, alphabetic: *por orden alfabético*, in alphabetical order.
alfabetización f. Teaching to read and write, education. || *Campaña de alfabetización*, literacy campaign.
alfabetizado, da adj. Literate.
alfabetizar v. tr. To make literate, to teach to read and write (a una persona). || To alphabetize, to arrange in alphabetical order (poner en orden alfabético).
alfabeto m. Alphabet. || *Alfabeto Morse*, Morse code.
alfaguara f. Abundant spring (manantial).
alfajía f. V. ALFARJÍA.
alfajor m. Kind of gingerbread (alajú). || *Amer.* Macaroon (dulce redondo).
alfalfa f. BOT. Lucerne, alfalfa [U.S., alfalfa].
alfalfal o **alfalfar** m. Alfalfa field, lucerne field [U.S., alfalfa field].
alfandoque m. *Amer.* A paste made from treacle and cheese with aniseed or ginger. | Nougat. | Maraca (instrumento).
alfaneque m. ZOOL. Kestrel.
alfanje m. Scimitar (sable). || Swordfish (pez).
alfanumérico, ca adj. Alphanumeric.
alfañique m. *Amer.* Stick of barley sugar (alfeñique).
alfaque m. MAR. Bar, sand bank (banco de arena).
alfaquí m. Ulema, ulama.
alfar m. Potter's workshop, pottery (el taller). || Clay (arcilla).
alfaraz m. Charger (caballo).
alfarda f. ARQ. Rafter. || Tax [formerly paid by Moors and Jews].
alfardilla f. Gold *o* silver braid.
alfarería f. Pottery (arte). || Potter's workshop, pottery (taller).
alfarero m. Potter.
alfarje m. Oil-mill stone. || ARQ. Panelled ceiling.
alfarjía f. Timber [for door or window frame] (madero).
alfayate m. (Ant.). Tailor.
alfeiza o **alféizar** m. ARQ. Embrasure (de puerta o ventana). | Windowsill (en la parte inferior).
alfénido m. Britannia metal (metal blanco).
alfeñicarse v. pr. FIG. y FAM. To lose weight, to get thin. | To make a fuss, to stand on ceremony (remilgarse).
alfeñique m. Stick of barley sugar. || Almond paste (de almendra). || FIG. y FAM. Weakling: *su hijo es un*

alfeñique, his son is a weakling. | Affectation, fuss (remilgo).

alferazgo m. Rank of standard-bearer (oficio de abanderado). || Rank of second lieutenant.

alferecía f. MED. Epilepsy. | Epileptic fit: *darle a uno una alferecía*, to have an epileptic fit.

alférez m. Second lieutenant (oficial). || Standard-bearer (abanderado). || *Amer.* Person responsible for the expenses of a party. || — MAR. *Alférez de fragata*, commissioned officer [U.S., ensign]. | *Alférez de navío*, sub-lieutenant [U.S., lieutenant Junior Grade].

alfil m. Bishop (en el ajedrez).

alfiler m. Pin (en costura). || Pin, brooch (joya). || — *Alfiler de corbata*, tiepin. || *Alfiler de la ropa*, clothes-peg [U.S., clothespin]. || *Amer. Alfiler de nodriza* or *de criandera*, safety pin. || *Alfiler de sombrero*, hatpin. || FIG. y FAM. *Aquí no cabe un alfiler*, it's packed tight *o* out, it's crammed full. | *El alumno lleva la lección prendida con alfileres*, the pupil has learnt the lesson very sketchily. | *Estar de veinticinco alfileres*, to be dressed up to the nines, to be dressed to kill. || *Estar prendido con alfileres*, to be pinned [up] (vestido, etc.), to be rather shaky (poco seguro). || *Amer. No caberle un alfiler de gusto*, to be beside o.s. with joy. || FIG. y FAM. *Para alfileres*, as a tip (propina), for pocket money (a un niño), for pin money (a una mujer). || *Sujetar con un alfiler*, to pin [up].

alfilerar v. tr. To pin: *alfilerar un vestido*, to pin a dress.

alfilerazo m. Pinprick. || FIG. y FAM. Dig: *siempre me está tirando alfilerazos*, he's always having digs at me.

alfilerillo m. *Amer.* Fodder plant, erodium. | Cactus (pita). | Parasitic insect [found on tobacco].

alfiletero o **alfilerero** m. Pin box, pin case.

alfolí m. Public granary (granero). || Salt warehouse.

alfombra f. Carpet (grande): *alfombra persa*, Persian carpet. || Rug, mat (más pequeña). || FIG. Carpet: *alfombra de flores*, carpet of flowers. || *Alfombra de baño*, bathmat. || *Alfombra voladora*, flying carpet.

alfombrado, da adj. Carpeted: *salón alfombrado*, carpeted drawing room.
— M. Carpeting, carpets, *pl.* (conjunto de alfombras). || Carpeting, laying carpets (acción). || *El alfombrado de la escalera*, the stair carpet.

alfombrar v. tr. To carpet. || FIG. To carpet: *calles alfombradas de flores*, streets carpeted with flowers.

alfombrero, ra m. y f. Carpet maker (fabricante). || Carpet dealer (vendedor).

alfombrilla f. Rug (alfombra pequeña). || Doormat (esterilla en las puertas). || MED. German measles. || *Alfombrilla de cama*, bedside rug.

alfombrista m. Carpet dealer (vendedor). || Carpet fitter (que instala alfombras).

alfóncigo m. Pistachio (árbol). || Pistachio nut (fruto).

alfonsí o **alfonsino, na** adj. Alphonsine [concerning one of the Spanish kings called Alfonso]. || *Tablas alfonsinas*, Alphonsine tables [of Alfonso X].

alfónsigo m. Pistachio (árbol).

alfonsismo m. Alphonsism.

Alfonso n. pr. m. Alfonso (King).

alforfón m. Buckwheat.

alforjas f. pl. Saddlebags (sobre las caballerías). || Knapsack, *sing.* (colgadas al hombro). || Provisions, supplies (provisión). || — FIG. y FAM. *Para este viaje no se necesitan alforjas*, a fat lot of good that is. || *Amer.* FIG. y FAM. *Pasarse a la otra alforja*, to go too far (excederse). | *Sacar los pies de las alforjas*, to go off on a different track.

alforza f. Tuck (en costura). || Scar (cicatriz).

alforzar v. tr. To tuck, to put tucks in: *alforzar la manga de una camisa*, to put tucks in *o* to tuck a shirt sleeve.

Alfredo n. pr. m. Alfred.

alga f. BOT. Alga. || *Había algas en la playa*, there was seaweed on the beach.

— OBSERV. En inglés el plural de *alga* es *algae* o *algas.*

algaida f. Thicket, bush. || Dune, sand hill (duna).

algalia f. Civet (perfume). || Abelmosk (planta). || MED. Catheter. || *Gato de algalia*, civet cat (animal).

algara f. MIL. Raid. | Raiding party (tropa). || Skin (de la cebolla).

algarabía f. (Ant.). Arabic (lengua). || FIG. Greek: *para mí esto es algarabía*, this is Greek to me. | Double Dutch, gibberish: *hablar en algarabía*, to speak double Dutch. | Racket, row: *los niños armaban una algarabía tremenda*, the children were kicking up a terrible row. || BOT. Broom.

algarada m. MIL. Raid (ataque). | Raiding party (tropa). || FIG. BOT. Racket, din, row (jaleo).

algarroba f. BOT. Vetch (planta forrajera). | Vetch, vetch seed (semilla). | Carob bean (fruto del algarrobo).

algarrobal m. Vetch plantation (de algarroba). || Carob tree plantation (de algarrobo).

algarrobera f. o **algarrobero** m. Carob tree (árbol).

algarrobilla f. Vetch (algarroba). || Alga, seaweed (fam.) (alga).

algarrobillo m. *Amer.* Carob bean (fruto).

algarrobo m. Carob tree (árbol). || *Algarrobo loco*, Judas tree.

algazara f. Arab war cry. || Racket, din, row, uproar (jaleo).

algazul m. Carpetweed (planta).

álgebra f. MAT. Algebra. || MED. Bonesetting.

algebraico, ca o **algébrico, ca** adj. Algebraic, algebraical.

algebrista m. y f. MAT. Algebraist. || MED. Bonesetter.

algecireño, ña adj. [Of *o* from] Algeciras.
— M. y f. Native *o* inhabitant of Algeciras.

algidez f. MED. Algidity.

álgido, da adj. MED. Algid: *fiebre álgida*, algid fever. || FIG. Decisive, critical (decisivo). || FIG. *Punto álgido*, height.

— OBSERV. The figurative use of this word, though frequent, is considered incorrect.

algo pron. indef. Something: *aquí hay algo que no entiendo*, there is something here which I don't understand; *quiero algo original*, I want something original. || Anything (cualquier cosa): *yo daría algo por tenerlo*, I'd give anything to have it. || Anything, something (v. OBSERV.) [en interrogación]: *¿ha pasado algo?*, has something happened?, has anything happened? || — *Algo así*, something like that. || *Algo así como*, a sort of, a kind of, a type of (una especie de), something like, about: *vive a algo así como a tres kilómetros de aquí*, he lives something like three kilometres from here. || *Algo de*, some (v. OBSERV.): *algo de vino*, some wine. || *Algo es algo* or *ya es algo*, it is better than nothing, it's a start. || FAM. *Creerse algo*, to think one is something *o* somebody. || *De hacer algo me iría de vacaciones*, if anything I'd go on holiday. || *Más vale algo que nada*, something is better than nothing. || *Por algo lo hice*, I had my reason for doing it, I didn't do it for nothing. || *Por algo será*, there's bound to be *o* there must be a reason for it. || FAM. *Si no se callan me va a dar algo*, I'll go mad if they don't shut up. || *Tener algo que ver con*, to have something to do with. || *Tomar algo*, to have a drink (de beber), to have a bite to eat, to have something to eat (de comer).
— Adv. Rather, quite, somewhat: *algo lejos*, quite far, quite a long way; *algo tímido*, rather shy. || A little, slightly, a bit, somewhat: *el enfermo está algo mejor*, the patient is a little better; *anda algo escaso de dinero*, he's somewhat short of money. || At all, any (en preguntas): *¿te ha dolido algo?*, did it hurt you at all?; *¿estás algo mejor?*, are you any better?
— M. Snack, something to eat: *tomé un algo antes de salir*, I had a snack before I left. || Something: *tiene un algo de su madre*, there is something of his mother in him. || — *Tiene un algo*, he has that certain something, there is something about him (encanto). || *Tiene un algo de egoísmo*, he is rather selfish.

— OBSERV. En las oraciones interrogativas, *something* se convierte generalmente en *anything* (*¿encontraste algo nuevo?*, did you find anything new?) y *some* en *any* (*¿tiene algo de vino?*, have you any wine?).

algodón m. BOT. Cotton plant (planta). || Cotton: *algodón hidrófilo, en rama*, cotton wool, raw cotton. || Cotton (tejido): *vestido de algodón*, cotton dress. || Cotton wool (hidrófilo). || Candy floss [U.S., cotton candy] (golosina de azúcar). || MED. Swab. || — *Algodón pólvora*, guncotton. || FIG. y FAM. *Criado entre algodones*, mollycoddled, pampered.

algodonal m. Cotton plantation.

algodonar v. tr. To pad *o* to pack with cotton wool.

algodoncillo m. BOT. Milkweed.

algodonero, ra adj. Cotton: *industria algodonera*, cotton industry.
— M. y f. Cotton worker (obrero). || Cotton dealer (comerciante). || — M. Cotton plant (planta). || — F. Cotton mill (fábrica).

algodonoso, sa adj. Cottony. || Downy (fruta).
— F. Cottonweed (planta).

algorín m. Olive bin.

algoso, sa adj. Full of seaweed.

alguacil m. Alguazil (en España). || Sheriff, constable. || Governor (gobernador). || TAUR. Alguazil. || ZOOL. Jumping spider. || *Amer.* Dragonfly (insecto).

alguacilazgo m. Position of alguazil.

alguacilesco, ca adj. Alguazil's, of the alguazil.

alguacilillo m. Alguazil (en las corridas de toros).

alguien pron. indef. Somebody, someone: *alguien llama a la puerta*, someone is knocking at the door. || Anybody, anyone (interrogación): *¿hay alguien en casa?*, is there anybody at home? || — *Creerse alguien*, to think one is somebody. || *Para alguien que haya hecho esto*, for anybody *o* anyone who has done this. || *Ser alguien*, to be somebody. || *Si llama alguien*, if anyone *o* anybody calls, if someone *o* somebody calls.

algún adj. Some, any (v. ALGUNO [*Observ.*]): *algún pobre niño*, some poor child. || Some or other, some, a, a certain: *algún hombre*, some man or other, a man. || — *Algún que otro*, one or two, the odd, a few, some: *algún que otro libro*, one or two books, the odd book. || *Algún tanto*, a little, a bit. || *Algún tiempo*, some time. || *En algún sitio*, somewhere.

alguno, na adj. A, some, some or other, a certain: *vino alguna mujer*, a woman came, some woman or other came. || Some: *alguna pobre niña*, some poor child; *quiere algunos libros*, he wants some books. || Any: *si viene alguna carta para mí, avísame*, if any letters come for me, let me know: *¿necesitas alguna* *ayuda?*, do you need any help? || Any, a (interrogación): *¿hay alguna traducción para esto?*, is there a translation for this? || — *Alguna cosa*, something. || *Alguna que otra vez*, from time to time, now and again. || *Algunas veces*, sometimes. || *Alguna vez*, occasionally, sometimes: *alguna vez voy al teatro*, I sometimes go to the theatre; ever (interrogación): *¿vas alguna vez al teatro?*, do you ever go to the theatre? || *No... alguno*, not... any, not... any at all, no... at all: *no tengo dinero alguno*, I haven't any money, I have no money at all. || *No he visto cosa alguna*, I haven't seen anything at all. || *Por alguna razón que otra*, for some reason or other. || *Sin prisa alguna*, without hurrying.

— Pron. One (*sing.*), some (*pl.*): *alguno de ellos me lo preguntó*, one of them asked me. || Someone, somebody (alguien) [v. OBSERV.]. || — *Alguno que otro*, one or two, some, a few. || *Algunos piensan*, some [people] think, certain people think. || *Hacer alguna*, to be up to one's tricks: *el niño habrá hecho alguna* (*de las suyas*), the child will have been up to his tricks again.

— OBSERV. En las oraciones interrogativas, *some* suele ser sustituido por *any* (*¿quieres algunos libros?*, do you want any books?) y *somebody* o *someone* por *anybody* o *anyone* (*¿ha quedado alguno sin entrada?*, is anyone without a ticket?).

— The adjective *alguno* is apocopated to *algún* before masculine singular nouns: *algún pobre niño*, some poor child.

alhaja f. Jewel, gem, piece of jewellery: *una alhaja de oro*, a piece of gold jewellery. || Jewel: *las alhajas de la corona*, the crown jewels. || FIG. Jewel, treasure, gem: *nuestra criada es una alhaja*, our maid is a jewel; *la catedral es una verdadera alhaja del arte gótico*, the cathedral is a real gem of Gothic art. | Darling, gem, jewel: *este niño es una alhaja*, this child is a darling. || — Pl. Jewels, gems, jewellery, *sing.* [U.S, jewelry, *sing.*]. || FIG. *¡Buena alhaja!*, he's [she's, etc.] a fine one *o* a right one!

alhajar v. tr. To deck with jewels: *alhajar a una chica*, to deck a girl with jewels. || To furnish (amueblar).

alhajera f. o **alhajero** m. *Amer.* Jewel box, jewel case.

alharaca f. Fuss, fuss and bother. || *A pesar de sus alharacas*, despite all the fuss he makes.

alharma f. BOT. Harmal, harmala, harmel.

alhelí m. Wallflower (amarillo). || BOT. *Alhelí de Mahón*, Virginian stock.

— OBSERV. Pl. *alhelíes.*

alheña f. Privet (arbusto). || Henna (polvo y arbusto). || Privet blossom (flor). || Blight, mildew, rust (de las mieses). || *Estar hecho una alheña* or *molido como una alheña*, to be exhausted (agotado).

alheñar v. tr. To dye with henna (teñir).

— V. pr. To wither, to dry up (secarse). || To become mildewed (tener añublo).

alhóndiga f. Corn exchange.

alhucema f. Lavender (espliego).

aliabierto, ta adj. With its wings spread *o* open.

aliacán m. Jaundice.

aliado, da adj. Allied.

— M. y f. Ally. || *Los Aliados*, the Allies.

aliadófilo, a adj. Allied.

aliaga f. BOT. Furze, gorse (aulaga).

alianza f. Alliance (unión): *pacto de alianza*, alliance treaty. || Wedding ring (anillo). || Covenant (en la Biblia). || *La Santa Alianza*, The Holy Alliance.

aliar v. tr. To combine, to ally: *aliar el valor a* or *con la inteligencia*, to combine courage with intelligence. || To ally (un país).

— V. pr. To be combined. || To become allies, to form an alliance (dos países).

alias adv. Alias, otherwise known as: *Antonio López alias el Cojo*, Antonio López alias Hopalong.

— M. Alias.

alibi m. Alibi (coartada).

alicaído, da adj. With drooping wings. || FIG. y FAM. Weak, frail: *el enfermo anda alicaído*, the patient is a bit weak. | Depressed, crestfallen, dejected: *desde que ha recibido la noticia anda muy alicaído*, ever since he received the news he has been very depressed. || *Tener la moral alicaída*, to be depressed *o* crestfallen.

alicante m. Cerastes, horned viper (víbora). || Nougat (dulce).

Alicante n. pr. GEOGR. Alicante.

alicantino, na adj. [Of *o* from] Alicante.

— M. y f. Native *o* inhabitant of Alicante.

alicatado, da adj. Tiled, decorated with glazed tiles.

— M. Glazed tiling.

alicatar v. tr. To tile, to decorate with glazed tiles. || To shape, to cut, to work (los azulejos).

alicates m. pl. Pliers, pincers: *alicates universales*, multipurpose pliers. || *Alicates de uñas*, nail clippers.

Alicia n. pr. f. Alice. || — *Alicia en el país de las maravillas*, Alice in Wonderland. || *Alicia en el país del espejo*, Alice through the looking glass.

aliciente m. Attraction, lure: *los alicientes del campo*, the attractions of the countryside. || Interest: *este viaje no tiene aliciente para mí*, this journey has no interest for me. || Encouragement, incentive, inducement (incentivo): *las primas son un aliciente para el trabajador*, bonuses are an incentive for the worker. || *Un aliciente para que trabajen más*, an inducement *o* an incentive for them to work harder.

alicortar v. tr. To clip the wings of (cortar). || To wing, to wound in the wing (herir). || FIG. To clip s.o.'s wings (a uno).

alicuanta adj.f./s.f. Aliquant: *parte alicuanta*, aliquant part.

alícuota adj. Aliquot: *parte alícuota*, aliquot part.

alidada f. Alidade, alidad (regla).

alienable adj. Alienable.

alienación f. JUR. Alienation. || MED. *Alienación mental*, alienation, mental derangement.

alienado, da adj. Mentally ill, insane.

— M. y f. Lunatic. || *Los alienados*, the mentally ill, the insane.

alienar v. tr. To alienate (enajenar).

— OBSERV. *Alienar* is used less frequently than *enajenar*.

alienista m. y f. Psychiatrist, alienist.

aliento m. Breath: *perder el aliento*, to get out of breath. || FIG. Encouragement: *su apoyo es un aliento para mí*, his support is an encouragement for me. | Enthusiasm, vitality: *ya no tiene los alientos de su juventud*, he no longer has the enthusiasm of his youth. || — *Aguantar el aliento, contener el aliento*, to hold one's breath. || *Cobrar aliento*, to catch one's breath, to get one's breath back. || *Dejar sin aliento*, to leave breathless, to wind. || *De un aliento*, in one breath. || *Estar sin aliento*, to be out of breath (jadeante), to be depressed, to be dejected (desanimado). || *Exhalar el postrer aliento*, to breath one's last, to draw one's last breath. || *Tener mal aliento*, to have bad breath. || *Tomar aliento*, to catch one's breath, to get one's breath back.

alifafe m. Windgall (de las caballerías). || FAM. Ailment, complaint: *mi abuelo tiene muchos alifafes*, my grandfather has always got some ailment or other.

aliforme adj. Aliform, wing-shaped.

aligación f. Bond, tie. || MAT. Alligation.

aligátor m. Alligator.

aligeramiento m. Lightening (de una carga, etc.). || Cutting-down, reduction (de un programa, etc.). || Lessening, reduction (de una obligación). || Alleviation, relief, easing (alivio).

aligerar v. tr. To lighten, to make lighter: *aligerar una carga*, to lighten a burden. || To cut down, to reduce: *aligerar un programa*, to cut down a programme. || To shorten (abreviar): *aligerar un discurso*, to shorten a speech. || FIG. To relieve, to alleviate: *la morfina aligera el dolor*, morphine relieves pain. | To alleviate, to lessen, to relieve: *su presencia aligeraba mi tristeza*, his presence lessened my sadness. || To quicken: *aligerar el paso*, to quicken one's pace.

— V. intr. y pr. To hurry, to get a move on (fam.): *aligera* or *aligérate que hay que irse*, get a move on, we've got to go. || To lighten, to get lighter (la carga). || *Aligerarse de ropa*, to put lighter clothes on (cuando hace calor), to take a garment *o* an article of clothing off (quitar).

alígero, ra adj. POÉT. Winged: *Mercurio alígero*, winged Mercury. | Swift, rapid.

aligustre m. Privet (alheña).

alijador m. MAR. Barge, lighter (barcaza). | Docker, stevedore (descargador). || Smuggler (matutero).

alijar m. Waste land (terreno). || Tile (azulejo). || — Pl. Common land, *sing.*

alijar v. tr. To lighten (aligerar). || To smuggle (contrabando). || To unload (descargar un barco). || To gin (el algodón). || To sandpaper (pulir con lija).

alijarar v. tr. To share out (waste land for cultivation).

alijo m. Unloading (de un barco). || Smuggling (contrabando). || Contraband (géneros de contrabando). || *Un alijo de whisky*, a consignment *o* a load of smuggled whisky.

alimaña f. Vermin, pest, noxious animal.

alimañero m. Gamekeeper, pest controller.

alimentación f. Food: *la higiene de la alimentación*, food hygiene; *una región donde la alimentación es excelente*, a region where the food is excellent. || Feeding, nourishment (acción de alimentar). || TECN. Feed: *la alimentación de un alto horno*, the feed of a blast furnace. || — *Alimentación equilibrada*, balanced diet. || *Alimentación por gravedad*, gravity feed. || *Ramo de la alimentación*, food trade. || *Tubo de alimentación*, feed pipe.

alimentador, ra adj. Feeding.

— M. TECN. Feeder.

alimentar v. tr. To feed: *alimentar a su familia*, to feed one's family. || To be nourishing: *las patatas alimentan poco*, potatoes are not very nourishing. || TECN. To feed: *alimentar una computadora con datos*, to feed data into a computer, to feed a computer with data. || To supply: *mineral que alimenta la industria siderúrgica*, mineral which supplies the iron and steel industry. || FIG. To feed: *la lectura alimenta el espíritu*, reading feeds the mind. | To foster, to encourage: *hay libertades que alimentan toda clase de disturbios*, certain kinds of freedom foster all sorts of disturbances. | To feed (las pasiones). | To cherish, to feed (esperanzas). | To put fuel on (un fuego).

— V. pr. To feed, to live: *alimentarse con* or *de arroz*, to feed *o* to live on rice. || TECN. To be fed (una máquina, etc.). || To be supplied (una industria, etc.). || FIG. *Alimentarse de quimeras*, to live in a dream world.

alimenticio, cia adj. Food: *la industria alimenticia*, the food industry. || Nourishing: *los huevos son muy alimenticios*, eggs are very nourishing. || — *Pastas alimenticias*, pasta. || *Pensión alimenticia*, alimony, allowance. || *Productos alimenticios*, foodtuffs, food products. || *Valor alimenticio*, food value, nutritional value.
alimentista m. y f. Person receiving alimony *o* an allowance.
alimento m. Food: *el pan es un alimento*, bread is a food. || FIG. Food: *la lectura es un alimento del espíritu*, reading is food for the mind. | Fuel (para las pasiones). || — Pl. JUR. Alimony, *sing.*, maintenance allowance, *sing.* || *De mucho alimento*, very nourishing.
alimentoso adj. Nourishing, nutritive.
alimoche m. ZOOL. Egyptian vulture.
alimón (al) loc. adv. Together: *lo han hecho al alimón*, they did it together. || — *Hacer un trabajo al alimón*, to share a piece of work. || TAUR. *Torear al alimón*, to fight a bull together [two toreros holding the cape].
alimonarse v. pr. To yellow, to turn yellow (las hojas de un árbol).
alindado, da adj. Dandified (afectadamente pulcro). || Conceited (presumido).
alindamiento m. Marking out [of boundaries].
alindar v. tr. To mark out the boundaries of: *alindar dos fincas*, to mark out the boundaries of two estates. || To embellish, to beautify, to make beautiful, to make pretty (embellecer).
— V. intr. To border on, to be adjacent *o* next to: *tu campo alinda con el mío*, your field borders on mine *o* is adjacent to mine. || To be next to one another, to be adjacent: *nuestras casas alindan*, our houses are next to one another.
alinderar v. tr. *Amer.* To mark out the boundaries of (deslindar).
alineación f. Alignment, lining up. || Line-up (deportes): *la alineación de un equipo*, the line-up of a team. || — *Fuera de alineación*, out of alignment, out of true. || *Política de no alineación*, nonalignment policy.
alineado, da adj. Aligned, lined-up. || *País no alineado*, nonaligned country.
alineamiento m. Alignment, lining up. || *Política de no alineamiento*, nonalignment policy.
alinear v. tr. To align, to line up, to put in line. || MIL. To form up (tropas). || FIG. To bring into line.
— V. pr. To join: *me he alineado en el equipo de España*, I have joined the Spanish team. || To line up: *se alinearon contra la pared*, they lined up against the wall. || MIL. To fall in, to form up.
aliñado, da adj. Neat (aseado).
aliñador, ra adj. Decorative. || CULIN. Seasoning.
— M. y f. *Amer.* Bonesetter.
aliñar v. tr. CULIN. To season, to flavour (condimentar). | To dress: *aliñar la ensalada*, to dress the salad. || To set [a bone] (arreglar los huesos dislocados). || To adorn (adornar). || To prepare (preparar). || TAUR. To prepare [the bull] for a quick kill.
aliño m. CULIN. Seasoning (con condimentos). | Dressing (para la ensalada). || Preparation (preparación). || Neatness (aseo). || Adornment (adorno). || TAUR. *Faena de aliño*, short "faena" performed in order to kill the bull quickly.
alioli m. Garlic and oliveoil sauce.
alionín m. ZOOL. Blue tit.
alípede o **alípedo** adj. m. POÉT. With winged feet.
aliquebrado, da adj. Broken-winged, with a broken wing. || FIG. y FAM. Depressed, dejected, crestfallen (desanimado). | Weak, weakened (débil).
alisado m. Smoothing.
alisador, ra adj. Smoothing.
— M. Smoother (instrumento). || Polisher (persona). || *Amer.* Toothcomb.
alisadura f. Smoothing, polishing (acción de alisar). || — Pl. Shavings (de madera).
alisar m. Alder grove.
alisar v. tr. To smooth, to polish (pulir). || To flatten, to level (allanar). || To smooth (el pelo).
— V. pr. To smooth. || *Alisarse el pelo*, to smooth one's hair (arreglarse el pelo).
aliseda f. Alder grove.
alisios adj. m. pl. MAR. Trade: *los vientos alisios*, the Trade Winds.
— M. pl. Trade Winds.
aliso m. Alder (árbol). || *Aliso negro*, black alder.
alistado, da adj. Enlisted, enrolled: *alistado en el ejército*, enlisted in the army. || Striped (listado).
— M. Volunteer.
alistador m. Recruiting officer.
alistamiento m. MIL. Enlistment, recruitment. | Enlistment: *alistamiento voluntario*, voluntary enlistment. || Joining, enrolment [U.S., enrollment] (en un partido político, etc.). || Annual contingent (quinta).
alistar v. tr. To enlist, to recruit (reclutar). || To list, to put on a list (registrar). || To prepare, to make ready (preparar).
— V. pr. To enroll, to enrol. || To enlist, to enroll, to enrol (en el ejército). || To prepare, to make ready (prepararse). || FIG. To rally: *alistarse en las filas monárquicas*, to rally to the royalist flag.
aliteración f. Alliteration.
aliterado, da adj. Alliterative.
alitierno m. Buckthorn (aladierna).
alitranca f. *Amer.* Brake (retranca).
aliviadero m. Overflow channel, spillway (desaguadero).
aliviador, ra adj. Comforting, consoling.
— M. Lever for raising or lowering a millstone.
alivianar v. tr. *Amer.* V. ALIVIAR.
aliviar v. tr. To lighten, to make lighter: *aliviar una carga*, to make a burden lighter. || To help [out] (ayudar): *aliviarle a uno en el trabajo*, to help s.o. out with his work. || To give relief: *esta medicina le aliviará*, this medicine will give you relief. || To relieve, to alleviate, to soothe: *aliviar el dolor*, to relieve the pain. || To comfort, to console, to soothe (consolar). || To lessen, to relieve (una pena). || To quicken (el paso). || — *Aliviar el luto*, to go into half mourning. || FIG. y FAM. *Aliviar la cartera a uno*, to relieve s.o. of his wallet (robar).
— V. pr. To be better, to feel better, to recover (un enfermo). || To diminish, to ease up (un dolor). || *¡Que se alivie!*, get better soon!, get well soon!
alivio m. Lightening (de una carga). || Relief: *con estas inyecciones sentirá pronto un alivio*, with these injections you will soon feel relief. || Relief: *su marcha fue un alivio para mí*, his departure was a relief for me. || Comfort, consolation: *tus palabras son un alivio*, your words are a comfort to me. || Relief, mitigation, alleviation (pena, sufrimiento). || — *Alivio de luto*, half mourning. || FAM. *De alivio*, a hell of a: *un catarro de alivio*, a hell of a cold; *un susto, un pesado de alivio*, a hell of a fright, of a bore; horrible: *él es muy simpático, pero su mujer es de alivio*, he is very nice, but his wife is horrible.
aljaba f. Quiver (para las flechas). || *Amer.* Fuchsia (planta).
aljama f. Synagogue (sinagoga). || Mosque (mezquita). || Assembly of Moslems *o* Jews. || Arab quarter (barrio de moros). || Jewish quarter (barrio judío).
aljamía f. Spanish [Name given to Spanish by the Arabs]. || Spanish text written in Arabic characters.
aljamiado, da adj. Written in Spanish with Arabic characters. || Spanish-speaking (que habla español).
aljez m. Gypsum.
aljibe m. Tank, cistern (de agua). || MAR. Tanker. || *Amer.* Spring (manantial). | Well (pozo). || Dungeon (cárcel). || *Barco aljibe*, tanker.
aljofaina f. Washbowl, washbasin (jofaina).
aljófar m. [Small] pearl (perla). || Dewdrop (gota de rocío).
aljofarar v. tr. To moisten, to pearl (el rocío).
aljofifa f. Floorcloth.
aljofifado m. Wash, washing.
aljofifar v. tr. To clean with a floorcloth, to mop.
aljuba f. (Ant.). Jubbah.
alma f. Soul. || Spirit, heart: *alma noble*, noble spirit; *tener el alma destrozada*, to have a broken heart. || Soul: *es un alma inocente*, he is an innocent soul. || FIG. Soul, living soul: *no hay ni un alma*, there is not a soul. | Soul, person: *ciudad de cien mil almas*, town with a hundred thousand people *o* persons. | Lifeblood, moving spirit, heart and soul: *es el alma de la rebelión*, he is the lifeblood of the rebellion. | Life and soul: *es el alma de la fiesta*, he is the life and soul of the party. || Scaffold pole (de un andamio). || Bore (de cañón). || Core (de cable, de estatua). || BOT. Pith. || MÚS. Sound post (de un violín). || — *Alma de Caín* or *de Judas*, devil, fiend. || FIG. y FAM. *Alma de cántaro*, fathead, drip. || *Alma de Dios*, good soul, good-hearted person. || *Alma en pena*, soul in Purgatory; lost *o* poor soul (fig.). || *Alma gemela*, kindred spirit. || *Alma mía*, my dear, my darling (querido), for heaven's sake! (por Dios). || *Alma viviente*, living soul. || *Arrancarle el alma a alguien*, to shock s.o. deeply. || *Con el alma* or *con toda el alma*, out of the goodness of one's heart: *me lo ofreció con el alma*, he offered it to me out of the goodness of his heart; with all one's heart: *siente con toda su alma no poder hacerlo*, he regrets with all his heart that he cannot do it. || *Con el alma y la vida*, with heart and soul, with all one's heart. || *Dar el alma*, to pass away, to give up the ghost. || *De mi alma*, dear, darling: *hijo de mi alma*, my dear *o* my darling son. || *Dolerle a uno en el alma*, to break one's heart, to hurt one: *me duele en el alma que no me haya escrito*, it hurts me to think that she hasn't written. || FAM. *Echarse el alma a las espaldas*, to do just as one pleases (no preocuparse nada). || *Encomendar el alma a Dios*, to commend one's soul to God. || *En cuerpo y alma*, body and soul. || *En lo más hondo de mi alma*, deep down, in my heart of hearts, in the depth of my heart. || *Entregar* or *rendir uno el alma (a Dios)*, to pass away, to give up the ghost. || *Estar como el alma de Caribay*, not to be able to make up one's mind. || *Estar como un alma perdida*, to be undecided, to be lost. || *Estar con el alma en la boca*, to be at death's door, to have one foot in the grave. || *Estar con el alma en un hilo*, to be worried stiff, to be on tenterhooks (estar inquieto), to be scared stiff, to have one's heart in one's mouth (de miedo). || *Hablar al alma*, to speak in earnest. || FAM. *Ir como alma que lleva el diablo*, to run hell for leather, to run like hell. || *Llegarle al alma a uno*, to move s.o., to touch s.o. || *Llevar la música en el alma*, to have music in one's blood. || *Me da en el alma que no volverá*, I have a

feeling that he will not come back. || FIG. *No tener alma*, to have a heart of stone, to have no heart (ser duro). || *Partir* or *romper el alma a uno*, to break s.o.'s heart. || FAM. *Romperse el alma*, to break one's neck. || *Se le cayó el alma a los pies*, his heart sank. || *Sentir en el alma*, to be deeply sorry. || *Tener su alma en el almario*, to have a heart (ser sensible), to have a lot of pluck. || *Tocar en el alma a uno*, to touch s.o.'s heart. || *Vender el alma al diablo*, to sell one's soul to the devil. || *Volverle a uno el alma al cuerpo*, to calm down (tranquilizarse).

almacén m. Warehouse (depósito). || Department store: *los grandes almacenes*, the big department stores. || Magazine (de un arma). || IMPR. Magazine. || *Amer*. Grocer's shop (tienda de comestibles). || *Almacén de depósito*, bonded warehouse (de la aduana).

almacenaje m. Warehouse dues, *pl.*, storage charges, *pl.* (gastos). || Storage, warehousing. || *Almacenaje frigorífico*, cold storage.

almacenamiento m. Storage, warehousing: *estar encargado del almacenamiento de las mercancías*, to be in charge of the storage of the goods. || Stock, supply: *hay almacenamientos de víveres aquí*, there are stocks of food here.

almacenar v. tr. To store, to warehouse. || To store, to store up: *almacenar recuerdos*, to store memories. || To keep, to hoard: *¿por qué almacenas tantas porquerías?*, why do you keep so much rubbish?

almacenero m. Storekeeper, warehouseman. || *Amer*. Grocer, shopkeeper.

almacenista m. Warehouseman (dueño de un almacén). || Shopkeeper (comerciante).

almáciga f. Mastic (resina). || AGR. Seedbed, nursery (semillero).

almácigo m. BOT. Mastic tree, lentiscus. || AGR. Plantation, nursery (semillero).

almádana o **almádena** f. Sledgehammer, large hammer (de cantero).

almadraba f. Mandrague, tunny net (red). || Tunny fishing (pesca). || Tunny-fishing ground (lugar de pesca).

almadrabero m. Tunny fisherman.

almadreña f. Clog, sabot (zueco).

almagesto m. Almagest.

almagra f. Red ochre.

almagradura f. Red ochre colouring.

almagral m. Ochre deposit.

almagrar v. tr. To dye with red ochre.

almagre m. Red ochre.

almagrero, ra adj. Red-ochre bearing (terreno).

almajal m. V. ALMARJAL.

almajaneque m. HIST. Mangonel, catapult (máquina de guerra).

almalafa f. Haik, haick.

alma máter f. Alma mater.

almanaque f. Almanac. || Diary (agenda). || Calendar: *almanaque de taco*, tear-off calendar.

almandina f. Almandite, almandine.

almarjal m. Field of barilla *o* saltwort. || Marsh.

almarjo m. Barilla, saltwort (planta).

almazara f. Oil mill.

almea f. BOT. Water plantain (azúmbar). || Storax bark (corteza).

almecina f. Hackberry, fruit of the nettle tree.

almecino m. BOT. Nettle tree.

almeja f. Clam (molusco).

almejar m. Clam bed.

almena f. Merlon (de piedra). || Crenel (hueco). || — Pl. Battlements.

almenado, da adj. Battlemented, crenellated.

almenaje m. Battlements, *pl.*

almenar v. tr. To build battlements on, to crenellate.

almenara f. Beacon, signal fire. || Candelabrum, candelabra (candelero).

almendra f. Almond: *almendra amarga*, bitter almond. || FIG. y FAM. Pebble (guijarro). || — Pl. Pendants, drops, crystals (de araña). || — *Almendras garapiñadas*, pralines. || *Almendras tostadas*, burnt almonds.

almendrada f. Almond milk (bebida). || Almond paste (salsa).

almendrado m. Almond paste.

almendral m. Almond grove.

almendrera f. Almond tree.

almendrilla f. Gravel (grava). || TECN. Round-ended file (lima).

almendro m. Almond tree (árbol).

almenilla f. Scalloping (en la ropa).

almeriense adj. [From *o* of] Almería [Spain].
— M. y f. Native *o* inhabitant of Almería.

almete m. Helmet (casco).

almez m. Nettle tree, hackberry (árbol).

almeza f. Hackberry, fruit of the nettle tree.

almezo m. Nettle tree, hackberry (árbol).

almiar m. AGR. Haystack, hayrick (pajar).

almíbar m. Syrup: *melocotones en almíbar*, peaches in syrup. || FAM. *Estar hecho un almíbar*, to be as sweet as can be, to be as sweet as sugar pie.

almibarado, da adj. Syrupy (muy dulce). || FIG. y FAM. Sugary, syrupy (meloso).

almibarar v. tr. To preserve [in syrup] (confitar). || To cover in syrup. || FIG. To sweeten [one's words].

almidón m. Starch. || *Dar almidón a una camisa*, to starch a shirt.

almidonado, da adj. Starched: *un cuello almidonado*, a starched collar. || FIG. y FAM. Dressed up to the nines, dressed to kill (muy compuesto).
— M. Starching.

almidonar v. tr. To starch.

almidonería f. Starch factory *o* works.

almijar m. Place for drying olives or grapes.

almilla f. Jerkin, [tight-fitting] jacket. || TECN. Tenon (espiga). || Breast of pork (carne).

almimbar m. Mimbar, minbar, almemor, almemar (de mezquita).

alminar m. Minaret.

almiranta f. Viceadmiral's ship (barco). || Admiral's wife.

almirantazgo m. Admiralty. || Admiralty court (tribunal). || Admiral's jurisdiction.

almirante m. Admiral.

almirez m. Mortar (mortero).

almizcate m. Space between two houses.

almizcle m. Musk.

almizcleña f. BOT. Grape hyacinth.

almizcleño, ña adj. Musky, scented with musk.

almizclero, ra adj. Musky, scented with musk. || — *Lirón almizclero*, dormouse. || *Ratón almizclero*, muskrat.
— M. Musk deer (rumiante). || — F. Desman (roedor).

almo, ma adj. POÉT. Nourishing (que alimenta). | Venerable.

almocadén m. (Ant.). Commander.

almocafre m. Spud, weeding hoe.

almocárabes o **almocarbes** m. pl. Interlaced design, *sing.*

almocela f. Hood.

almocrí m. Reader of the Koran [in a mosque].

almogávar m. Raiding soldier, raider.

almogavaría f. Raiding party, body of raiding troops.

almohada f. Pillow (de la cama). || Cushion (para sentarse). || Pillowslip, pillowcase (funda). || ARQ. Boss, bossage (almohadilla). || FIG. y FAM. *Hay que consultar con la almohada*, I'll [you'll, etc.] have to sleep on it.

almohadado, da adj. ARQ. Bossed, with a bossage.

almohadazo m. Blow with a pillow.

almohadilla f. Small cushion (cojincillo). || Harness pad (en los arreos). || Inkpad (para sellar). || ARQ. Boss (piedra). | Coussinet, cushion (de la voluta jónica). || *Amer*. Pincushion (acerico). | Holder (de la plancha).

almohadillado, da adj. Padded (acolchado). || ARQ. Bossed, with a bossage.
— M. ARQ. Boss, bossage. || Padding (relleno).

almohadillar v. tr. ARQ. To boss, to decorate with bosses *o* bossage. || To pad (acolchar).

almohadón m. Cushion: *almohadones de pluma*, feather cushions. || ARQ. Coussinet, cushion (de un arco). || REL. Hassock (cojín).

almohaza f. Currycomb (para los caballos).

almohazar v. tr. To curry, to brush down.

almojarifazgo m. (Ant.). Former duty on imports and exports.

almojarife m. (Ant.). King's tax collector (recaudador). | Customs officer (aduanero).

almóndiga f. Meatball, rissole.

almoneda f. Auction (subasta). || [Clearance] sale (a bajo precio). || *Vender en almoneda*, to auction (el subastador), to put up for auction (el vendedor), to sell off (a bajo precio).

almonedear v. tr. To auction (el subastador). || To put up for auction (el vendedor). || To sell off (a bajo precio).

almorávide adj./s. Almoravid, Almoravide.

almorranas f. pl. MED. Haemorrhoids, piles.

almorta f. Vetchling, vetch (planta).

almorzada f. Cupped handful, handful.

almorzado, da adj. *Viene almorzado*, he has already eaten.

almorzar* v. intr. To lunch, to have lunch (al mediodía). || To have breakfast, to breakfast (desayunar).
— V. tr. To have for lunch, to lunch on (al mediodía). || To have for breakfast, to breakfast on (desayuno).

almotacén m. Inspector of weights and measures.

almotacenazgo m. Office of the inspector of weights and measures (cargo u oficina).

almozárabe adj./s. V. MOZÁRABE.

almud m. Almud, almude (medida).

almudí o **almudín** m. Corn exchange (alhóndiga).

almuecín o **almuédano** m. Muezzin.

almuerzo m. Lunch (al mediodía). || Breakfast (por la mañana).

¡alo! o **¡aló!** interj. Hello?, hullo? (teléfono).

alocación f. Allocation: *alocación de créditos*, allocation of credits.

alocadamente adv. Foolishly, hastily, thoughtlessly.

alocado, da adj. Scatterbrained (distraído): *es un niño alocado, lo olvida todo*, he's a scatterbrained child, he forgets everything. || Irresponsible: *es una persona demasiado alocada para que le confíes algo importante*, he is too irresponsible a person to be trusted with anything important. || Mad, crazy (loco). || Thoughtless, hasty: *un gesto alocado*, a hasty gesture. || Strange (extraño).
— M. y f. Madcap.

alocar v. tr. To drive mad.
— V. pr. To go *o* to become mad (volverse loco). || FIG. To lose one's head: *no hay que alocarse por tan poca cosa*, you shouldn't lose your head over such a trivial matter.
alocución f. Allocution, speech, address.
alodial adj. JUR. Alodial, allodial.
alodio m. JUR. Alodium, allodium.
áloe o **aloe** m. Aloe (planta). || MED. Aloes.
aloja f. A sort of mead. || *Amer.* A refreshing drink made from fermented carob beans.
alojado, da adj. Housed, lodged.
— M. Soldier billeted in a private house. || — M. y f. *Amer.* Guest, lodger (persona hospedada).
alojamiento m. Accommodation, lodging (acción). || Accommodation, lodgings, *pl.* (sitio): *buscar alojamiento*, to look for lodgings. || MIL. Quartering, billeting (acción). | Billet, quarters, *pl.* (sitio). | Camp (campamento). || — MIL. *Boleta de alojamiento*, billeting order. || *Dar alojamiento a*, to accommodate, to take in, to put up.
alojar v. tr. To accommodate, to house, to lodge (hospedar). || To house, to accommodate (albergar): *el nuevo edificio alojará a doscientas familias*, the new block of flats will house two hundred families. || MIL. To billet, to quarter. || FIG. To fit in: *no puedo alojar tantos libros aquí*, I can't fit so many books in here. || *Tiene una bala alojada en el brazo*, he has a bullet lodged in his arm.
— V. pr. To put up, to stay, to lodge: *alojarse en un hotel*, to put up at a hotel, to stay *o* to lodge in a hotel. || To lodge: *la bala se le alojó en el brazo*, the bullet lodged in his arm. || MIL. To take up position (situarse). | To be billeted (vivir).
alomado, da adj. High-backed (caballo, mulo). || AGR. Ridged.
alomar v. tr. AGR. To ridge.
alón m. Wing (de ave).
— Adj. m. *Amer.* Large-winged.
alondra f. Lark (pájaro).
Alonso n. pr. m. Alphonse.
alópata adj. Allopathic.
— M. Allopath, allopathist (médico).
alopatía f. MED. Allopathy.
alopático, ca adj. Allopathic.
alopecia f. MED. Alopecia.
aloque adj. Light-red. || Rosé (vino).
— M. Rosé wine.
alotropía f. Allotropy.
alotrópico, ca adj. Allotropic.
alpaca f. Alpaca (animal, tejido): *un traje de alpaca*, a suit made of alpaca. || German *o* nickel silver (metal).
alpargata f. Canvas shoe, rope-soled shoe.
alpargatazo m. *Como sigas así te doy un alpargatazo*, if you carry on like that you'll get a taste of my slipper *o* you'll get a slippering.
alpargate m. Canvas shoe, rope-soled shoe.
alpargatería f. Canvas shoe factory (fábrica). || Shoe shop (tienda).
alpargatero, ra m. y f. Manufacturer of canvas shoes (fabricante). || Canvas shoe dealer (vendedor).
alpargatilla m. y f. FIG. Schemer, crafty person.
alpechín m. Foul-smelling liquid which runs from piled-up olives.
alpechinera f. Pit in which olive juice is collected.
alpenstock m. Alpenstock (bastón de alpinista).
Alpes n. pr. m. pl. GEOGR. Alps.
alpestre adj. Alpine (de los Alpes). || FIG. Mountainous.
alpinismo m. Mountaineering, climbing (montañismo).
alpinista m. y f. Mountaineer, climber.
alpino, na adj. Alpine: *raza alpina*, alpine race. || *Cordillera alpina*, Alpine range.
alpiste m. BOT. Alpist, canary grass. || FAM. Drink, booze (la bebida). | Dough, brass (dinero). || FAM. *Gustarle a uno mucho el alpiste*, to be a boozer.
alpistelado, da adj. FAM. Sozzled, sloshed (borracho).
alpistelarse v. pr. FAM. To get sozzled, to get drunk.
alpistera f. Small cake [made from flour, eggs and sesame].
alpujarreño, ña adj. From the Alpujarras [South Andalusian mountains].
alquequenje m. Winter cherry, strawberry tomato, husk tomato (planta).
alquería f. Farmstead, farm (granja). || Hamlet (aldea).
alquilable adj. Rentable, which can be rented (piso, televisor, etc.). || Which can be hired, for hire (coche, barca, etc.).
alquiladizo, za adj. To let, for rent (piso). || For hire (coche, barca, televisor, etc.). || Hireling (persona).
— M. y f. Hireling.
alquilador, ra m. y f. Landlord, proprietor (el que da de alquiler un piso, etc.). || Tenant, occupier (el que toma en alquiler el piso, etc.). || Owner (el que da de alquiler un coche, televisor, etc.). || Renter (el que toma en alquiler el televisor). || Hirer (el que toma en alquiler un coche, una barca, etc.).
alquilamiento m. V. ALQUILER.
alquilar v. tr. To rent (piso, etc.): *alquilar un piso en 1000 pesetas*, to rent a flat for 1,000 pesetas. || To hire, to hire out (dar en alquiler un coche, una barca, etc.): *alquilar por horas, por meses*, to hire by the hour, by the month. || To hire (tomar en alquiler un coche, una barca, etc.). || To charter (avión). || — *Es cosa de alquilar balcones*, it's sth. worth seeing, it's a must. || *Piso por alquilar*, flat to let.
— V. pr. To be let (casa). || To be for hire (coche, taxi). || To hire o.s. out (persona). || *Se alquila*, to let (casa), for hire (taxi, coche).
alquiler m. Renting, letting (acción de alquilar un piso, un televisor). || Hiring (acción de alquilar otra cosa). || Rent: *hay que pagar el alquiler del piso*, we must pay the rent for the flat. || Hire charge, rental (de un coche, barca, etc.). || — Pl. Rent. || — *Alquiler con opción a compra*, hire with option of purchase. || *Alquiler trimestral*, quarterly rent (de una casa). || *Casa de alquiler*, block of flats. || *Control de alquileres*, rent control. || *De alquiler*, to let (pisos), for rent (televisor), for hire (coches, animales, etc.). || *Exento de alquiler*, rent-free.
alquimia f. Alchemy.
alquimista m. Alchemist.
alquitara f. Still (alambique).
alquitarar v. tr. To distil (destilar). || FIG. *Estilo alquitarado*, over-refined *o* precious style.
alquitrán m. Tar: *alquitrán de hulla*, coal tar.
alquitranado, da adj. Tarred, tarry.
— M. MAR. Tarpaulin (lienzo). || Tarring (acción de alquitranar): *el alquitranado de las carreteras*, the tarring of the roads. || Tarmac, tar (revestimiento).
alquitranador, ra adj. Tarring.
— M. y f. Tar spreader. || — F. Tar-spreading machine (máquina).
alquitranar v. tr. To tar. || *Máquina de alquitranar*, tar-spreading machine.
alrededor adv. Round, around: *girar alrededor de la mesa*, to go round the table. || FAM. About, around, round about: *alrededor de mil pesetas*, about a thousand pesetas; *llegó alrededor de las nueve*, he arrived around nine o'clock. || — *Alrededor suyo*, around him. || *Todo alrededor*, all around.
— M. pl. Surrounding districts, outskirts: *los alrededores de París*, the outskirts of Paris. || Surroundings (ambiente). || *Mirar a su alrededor*, to look around one, to look all around.
Alsacia n. pr. f. GEOGR. Alsace.
alsaciano, na adj./s. Alsatian.
alta f. Discharge: *ya tengo el alta del hospital*, my hospital discharge has come through. || Enrollment (ingreso). || Army enlistment form (documento). || — *Dar de alta*, to pass as fit (un militar enfermo), to enrol (incorporar los militares a sus unidades), to discharge (a un enfermo). || — *Darse de alta*, to enrol. | MIL. *Ser alta*, to enrol into active service.
altaico, ca adj. Altaic (raza).
altamente adv. Highly, extremely.
altanería f. High flight (de pájaros). || Falconry (forma de caza). | Pride, haughtiness, arrogance (orgullo).
altanero, ra adj. Proud, haughty, arrogant (orgulloso). || High-flying (pájaro).
altar m. Altar. || MIN. Furnace bridge, fire bridge (de horno). || — *Altar mayor*, high altar. || FIG. *Llevar a una mujer al altar*, to lead a woman to the altar. | *Poner en un altar*, to put on a pedestal, to praise to the skies. | *Quedarse para adornar altares*, to be left on the shelf.
altaverapacense adj. [Of *o* from] Alta Verapaz (Guatemala).
— M. y f. Native *o* inhabitant of Alta Verapaz.
altavoz m. Loudspeaker: *altavoces potentes*, powerful loudspeakers.
alterabilidad f. Changeability.
alterable adj. Changeable (que cambia o puede ser cambiado). || Perishable, prone to deterioration (que se pudre rápidamente).
alteración f. Alteration: *alteración del horario*, alteration of the timetable. || Change for the worse, deterioration. *alteración de la salud*, deterioration in health. || Irregularity (del pulso). || Argument, quarrel, upset (altercado). || *Alteración del orden público*, breach of the peace, disturbance of the peace.
alteradizo, za adj. Changeable, fickle (carácter). || Changeable (cara).
alterado, da adj. Altered. || Disturbed (orden, etc.). || FIG. Changed (voz, cara). | Agitated, upset, disturbed (una persona). | Upset (estómago, etc.). | Angry (enfadado).
alterador, ra o **alterante** adj. Changing, which changes. || Disturbing, which disturbs.
alterar v. tr. To alter, to change: *el acontecimiento alteró mis proyectos*, the event changed my plans. || To change for the worse (empeorar). || FIG. To disturb: *alterar el orden público*, to disturb the peace. | To upset, to disturb: *mis palabras le alteraron*, my words upset him. | To annoy, to anger (enfadar). | To frighten (asustar). || To spoil, to make go bad, to cause to go bad: *el calor altera los alimentos*, heat makes food go bad. || *Alterar la verdad*, to distort the truth.
— V. pr. To change, to alter (cambiar). || To go bad, to go off (la comida). || To go sour, to go off (la leche). || To be disturbed, to be upset: *no alterarse por nada*, not to be upset by anything. || To falter (la voz). || To get angry, to lose one's temper (enojarse). || To get excited (emocionarse). || — *¡No te alteres!*, there's no need to lose your temper! || *Se altera con la humedad*, store in a dry place (medicina, etc.).

altercación f. o **altercado** m. Argument, quarrel, altercation.
altercador, ra adj. Quarrelsome, argumentative.
— M. y f. Quarrelsome *o* argumentative person.
altercante adj. Quarrelsome, argumentative.
altercar v. intr. To quarrel, to argue.
alternación f. Alternation.
alternado, da adj. Alternate.
alternador m. ELECTR. Alternator.
alternancia f. Alternation.
alternante adj. Alternating.
alternar v. tr. To alternate: *alternar trabajos*, to alternate jobs. || AGR. *Alternar cultivos*, to rotate the crops.
— V. intr. To alternate. || To relieve one another, to take turns, to work in relays: *alternar en un trabajo*, to take turns on a job. || To mix, to associate, to go around: *alternar con poetas*, to mix with poets. || To go out, to mix with people: *a María le gusta mucho alternar*, Mary loves to go out. || MAT. To interchange [the terms of two fractions].
— V. pr. To take turns: *nos alternamos en el volante*, we took turns at the wheel.
alternativa f. Alternation (sucesión). || Alternative, option, choice: *no dejar una alternativa*, to leave no option. || Shift work (trabajo en turnos). || AGR. Rotation (de las cosechas). || TAUR. Ceremony in which the senior matador confers professional status on the novice (novillero) thus accepting him as a professional equal capable of dispatching any bull in the proper manner. || — TAUR. *Tomar la alternativa*, to become a qualified bullfighter. || *Tomar una alternativa*, to make a decision *o* a choice.
alternativamente adv. Alternately.
alternativo, va adj. Alternating: *el movimiento alternativo del péndulo*, the alternating swing of the pendulum. || *Huelga alternativa*, staggered strike.
alterno, na adj. Alternating: *corriente alterna*, alternating current. || Alternate: *hojas alternas*, alternate leaves; *ángulos alternos*, alternate angles. || *Clases alternas*, lessons on alternate days.
alteza f. Highness (tratamiento): *Su Alteza Real*, His *o* Her Royal Highness; *en seguida, Alteza*, at once, your Highness. || Height (altura). || Sublimity, grandeur (de sentimientos). || *Alteza de miras*, high-mindedness.
altibajo m. Downward thrust (esgrima). || — Pl. Bumps, roughness, *sing.* (de un terreno). || FIG. y FAM. Ups and downs, vicissitudes: *los altibajos de la política*, the ups and downs of politics.
altilocuencia f. Grandiloquence.
altilocuente o **altilocuo, cua** adj. Grandiloquent.
altillano m. o **altillanura** f. *Amer.* Plateau (meseta).
altillo m. Hill, hillock (cerrillo). || Attic (desván).
altimetría f. Altimetry.
altímetro m. Altimeter.
altiplanicie f. High plateau (meseta).
altiplano m. *Amer.* High plateau (altiplanicie).
altísimo, ma adj. Very high: *una torre altísima*, a very high tower. || Very tall: *un hombre altísimo*, a very tall man.
— M. *El Altísimo*, the Almighty.
altisonancia f. Grandiloquence.
altisonante o **altísono, na** adj. Grandiloquent, pompous, bombastic (estilo, discurso, etc.). || High-sounding, pompous (apellido).
altitonante adj. Thundering: *Júpiter altitonante*, thundering Jove.
altitud f. AVIAC. Altitude, height. || GEOGR. Height, elevation.
altivarse o **altivecerse** v. pr. To be haughty, to put on airs.
altivez o **altiveza** f. Arrogance, haughtiness.
altivo, va adj. Arrogant, haughty.
alto, ta adj. Tall: *una mujer alta, un árbol alto*, a tall woman, a tall tree. || High (edificio, puesto, frecuencia, cuello, precio, río, porcentaje, mando). || Upper: *el Alto Rin*, the Upper Rhine; *el Alto Egipto*, Upper Egypt. || Upper: *los pisos altos*, the upper floors. || Loud (fuerte): *voz alta*, loud voice. || MÚS. Alto (instrumento). || High (de sonido agudo). || Rough (mar). || GRAM. High: *alto alemán*, High German. || Advanced: *altos estudios de matemáticas*, advanced studies in mathematics. || FIG. High, lofty: *tener alta idea de sus méritos*, to have a high opinion of one's merits. || Highly-placed (personaje). || Noble, lofty: *altos sentimientos*, noble sentiments. || Fine: *el más alto ejemplo de patriotismo*, the finest example of patriotism. || *Amer.* Short (vestido). || — *A altas horas de la noche*, late at night. || *Alta presión*, high pressure. || *Alta sociedad*, high society. || *Alta traición*, high treason. || *Alto horno*, blast furnace. || *Alto personal*, high officials. || *Cámara alta*, upper chamber. || *Clase alta*, upper class. || *Desde lo alto de*, from the top of. || *En alta mar*, on the high seas. || *En las altas esferas*, in high places *o* circles. || *En lo alto del árbol*, at the top of the tree. || *En voz alta*, in a loud voice. || *Estar en lo alto*, to be high up. || *Hacer algo por (todo) lo alto*, to do sth. in style. || *Lo alto*, the top: *en lo alto de*, on the top of. || *Pasar por lo alto*, to pass overhead. || *Tener tantos metros de alto*, to be so many metres high *o* in height.
— M. Height (altura). || Hill (elevación de terreno). || High floor: *vivir en un alto*, to live on a high floor. || MÚS. Viola (instrumento). || Contralto (voz). || MIL. Halt. || Stop (parada). || *Amer.* Pile (montón). || — MIL. *Dar el alto a uno*, to challenge s.o., to order s.o. to halt. || *Hacer alto*, to halt. || *Los altos y bajos*, the ups and downs. || *Un alto el fuego*, a cease-fire.
— Adv. High, high up: *poner un libro muy alto*, to put a book very high up. || Out loud: *gritar alto*, to shout out loud. || Loudly, loud: *hablar alto*, to speak loudly. || — *De alto abajo*, from top to bottom. || *Mantener en alto*, to hold up high. || *Pasar por alto*, to pass over, to ignore. || FIG. *Picar alto*, to aim high. || *Poner la radio más alto*, to turn the radio up. || *Poner muy alto*, to praise to the skies, to put on a pedestal (alabar). || *Se me pasó por alto*, it completely slipped my mind. || *Tirando por lo alto*, at the outside, at the most. || *Tirar por alto*, to throw away (tirar). || *Ver las cosas de alto*, to look at things on a lofty plane.
— Interj. Halt! || — *¡Alto ahí!*, halt! || *¡Alto el fuego!*, cease fire!, cease firing!
altoparlante m. *Amer.* Loudspeaker (altavoz).
altozano m. Hill, hillock (cerro). || *Amer.* Parvis (de iglesia).
altramuz m. Lupin (planta).
altruismo m. Altruism.
altruista adj. Altruistic.
— M. y f. Altruist.
altura f. Height, altitude: *las nubes circulan a gran altura*, the clouds go by at a very great height. || Height: *la altura de un peldaño, de una persona*, the height of a step, of a person. || Depth (del agua). || MAT. Height: *altura de un triángulo*, height of a triangle. || GEOGR. Latitude: *a la altura de*, on the same latitude as. || Level (nivel): *estar a la misma altura*, to be on the same level. || FIG. Merit, worth. || Nobleness, loftiness (de sentimiento). || MÚS. Pitch. || ASTR. Elevation. || — Pl. Heights (cumbres): *hay nieve en las alturas*, there is snow on the heights. || REL. Heaven, *sing.* || — *A estas alturas*, at this hour, at this stage, as late as this. || *A la altura del corazón*, in the region of the heart. || *A la altura de la tarea*, equal to the task, up to the task. || *Altura de caída*, fall (de catarata). || *Altura de la vegetación*, timber line. || *Altura del barómetro*, barometer reading. || *Altura de miras*, high-mindedness. || *Barco de altura*, oceangoing *o* seagoing ship. || *Estar a la altura de las circunstancias*, to rise to the occasion. || *Estar a la altura del tiempo*, to be abreast of the times. || *Gloria a Dios en las alturas*, Glory to God in the highest. || *Navegación de altura*, ocean navigation. || *No llega a la altura de su padre*, he does not measure up to his father. || *Pesca de altura*, deep-sea fishing. || FIG. *Poner a alguien a la altura del betún* or *de una zapatilla*, to make s.o. feel very small. || *Quedar a la altura del betún* or *de una zapatilla*, to give a poor show, to do very badly. || *Rayar a gran altura*, to shine. || *Salto de altura*, high jump. || *Tomar altura*, to climb (avión). || *Un poste de cinco metros de altura*, a post five metres high *o* in height. || FIG. *Un programa de altura*, a first-rate programme.
alúa f. *Amer.* Pyrophorus, firefly (insecto).
aluato m. ZOOL. Howler monkey.
alubia f. Bean (judía).
alucinación f. Hallucination.
alucinador, ra adj. Delusive, deceptive (engañoso). || Hallucinatory (impresionante).
alucinamiento m. Hallucination (alucinación). || Delusion (error). || Deceit (engaño).
alucinante adj. Hallucinating, hallucinatory.
alucinar v. tr. To hallucinate. || To delude, to deceive (engañar). || To fascinate (fascinar).
— V. pr. To delude o.s.
alucinógeno, na adj. Hallucinogenic.
— M. Hallucinogen.
alud m. Avalanche.
aluda f. ZOOL. Winged ant, flying ant.
aludido, da adj. In question, above-mentioned, being talked about: *la persona aludida*, the person in question. || FIG. *Darse por aludido*, to take the hint (cuando es una indirecta), to feel as though one is being got at (fam.), to take it personally. || *No darse por aludido*, to turn a deaf ear.
aludir v. intr. To allude to, to mention (hablar de): *no ha aludido a este negocio*, he has not mentioned this deal. || To allude to (referirse indirectamente). || To refer (referirse en un texto).
alumbrado, da adj. Lighted, lit: *alumbrado con gas*, lighted by gas, gas-lit. || Illuminated (calle, parque, etc.). || FAM. Tipsy, merry (achispado).
— M. y f. Alumbrado, perfectibilist (de la secta española), illuminist. || — M. Lighting: *alumbrado público de gas*, gas street lighting. || Lights, *pl.* (de un coche).
alumbramiento m. Lighting, lighting-up (acción de alumbrar). || Illumination (de una calle). || Childbirth, confinement (parto).
alumbrante adj. Lighting, illuminating. || FIG. Enlightening, illuminating.
alumbrar v. tr. To light: *cuando la sala estaba alumbrada con gas*, when the room was lit by *o* with gas. || To illuminate, to light up (en gran escala): *aquella noche la luna alumbraba los campos*, that night the moon lit up the fields. || To give light: *el Sol nos alumbra*, the Sun gives us light. || To light the way: *voy a alumbrarte para ir a la bodega*, I'll light your way down to the cellar. || To restore the sight of (a un ciego). || FIG. To strike, to find, to discover [under-

ground streams]. || To shed light on (un asunto). || To enlighten (enseñar). || FIG. y FAM. To beat (golpear). || TECN. To treat with alum, to aluminate.
— V. intr. To give birth (parir). || To give light, to give off a light: *la lámpara alumbra bien*, the lamp gives off a good light. || To give light: *alumbra aquí para que vea bien*, give me some light here so that I can see properly. || To shine (brillar).
— V. pr. FAM. To get tipsy *o* merry.
alumbre m. Alum.
alúmina f. QUÍM. Alumina.
aluminar v. tr. TECN. To treat with alumina, to aluminate.
aluminio m. Aluminium [U.S., aluminum].
aluminoso, sa adj. Aluminous.
aluminotermia f. Aluminothermy.
alumnado m. Pupils, *pl.* (de colegio). || Student body (de universidad).
alumno, na m. y f. Pupil: *un alumno modelo*, a model pupil. || Student (en la universidad). || — *Alumno externo*, day pupil. || *Alumno interno*, boarder. || *Antiguo alumno*, old boy (chico), old girl (chica), former pupil.
alunado, da adj. Whimsical, capricious (lunático). || Mad, insane (loco).
alunarado, da adj. Spotted, mottled (res).
alunarse v. pr. To spoil, to go off (la carne). || To fester (las heridas).
alunita f. Alunite (mineral).
alunizaje m. Landing on the moon, moon landing.
alunizar v. intr. To land on the moon.
alusión f. Allusion (referencia). || Mention, reference.
alusivo, va adj. Allusive (*a*, to).
aluvial adj. Alluvial.
aluvión m. Flood (inundación). || Alluvium, alluvion (depósito). || FIG. Flood (gran cantidad). || — *Terrenos de aluvión*, alluvial land, alluvium. || FAM. *Un aluvión de improperios*, a shower of insults, a torrent of abuse.
alveario m. External auditory duct.
álveo m. Bed (madre de un río).
alveolado, da adj. Honeycombed, alveolate.
alveolar adj. Alveolar.
alveolo o **alvéolo** m. ANAT. Alveolus. || Cell (de panal). || *Alveolos pulmonares*, alveoli, air cells of the lungs.
alverja o **alverjana** f. V. ARVEJA.
alverjilla o **alverjita** f. *Amer.* Sweet pea (guisante de olor).
alza f. Rise: *el alza de los precios*, the rise in prices. || Back sight, sight (de un arma de fuego). || IMPR. Underlay. || Sluice gate (de presa). || Extension (para suplir falta de altura). || — COM. *En alza*, rising (precios). || FAM. *Estar en alza*, to be coming up, to be rising [in popularity, etc.]. || COM. *Jugar al alza*, to speculate on a rising market, to bull the market (en la Bolsa). || FAM. *Un joven autor en alza*, an up-and-coming writer.
alzacuello m. Bands, *pl.*, collar (corbatín de eclesiástico).
alzada f. Height at the withers (de los caballos). || Summer pasture (pasto). || JUR. Appeal (apelación). || *Caballo de mucha, de poca alzada*, horse long in the leg, short in the leg.
alzado, da adj. Fraudulently bankrupt. || Fixed (precio). || *Amer.* Wild, runaway (montaraz). || In rut, on heat (en celo). || Insolent (insolente). || Rebellious (rebelde). || — *A tanto alzado*, by the job (trabajar), in a lump sum (pagar). || *Precio a tanto alzado*, fixed price.
— M. ARQ. Elevation (proyección). || IMPR. Gathering. || *Máquina de alzado*, gatherer.
alzador m. IMPR. Gathering room (taller). || Gatherer (obrero).
alzamiento m. Raising, lifting (levantamiento). || Uprising: *un alzamiento popular*, a popular uprising. || Increase, rise (de precios). || Higher bid (puja). || IMPR. Gathering. || COM. *Alzamiento de bienes*, fraudulent bankruptcy.
alzapaño m. Curtain holder (para cortinas).
alzaprima f. Crowbar, lever (palanca). || Wedge (calce). || *Amer.* Timber cart (para transportar árboles). || MÚS. Bridge.
alzaprimar v. tr. To lever up (con una palanca).
alzar v. tr. To raise, to lift [up]: *alzar la mano*, to raise one's hand. || To raise (la voz, los precios). || To make higher (pared, etc.). || To turn up (el cuello de un abrigo). || To remove, to take off (quitar). || To draw up, to make out: *alzar un plano*, to draw up a plan. || To raise, to put up (la caza). || FIG. To lift (un castigo, el embargo, etc.). || AGR. To gather, to bring in: *alzar la cosecha*, to bring in the harvest. || To plough for the first time (arar). || REL. To elevate (la hostia). || IMPR. To gather. || To cut (una baraja). || — *¡Alza!*, bravo! || *Alzar con una cosa*, to carry off *o* to lift sth. || *Alzar el vuelo*, to take off (empezar a volar), to clear off, to beat it (fam.) [irse]. || *Alzar los ojos* to look up. || *Alzar velas*, to hoist sail.
— V. pr. To get up, to rise (levantarse). || To stand out (sobresalir). || To run off with, to carry off, to lift (fam.): *alzarse con los fondos*, to run off with the funds. || FIG. To rise: *el ejército se ha alzado contra el gobierno*, the army has risen against the government. || To rebel: *alzarse contra el orden establecido*, to rebel against the established order. || To leave the table when one is in pocket (en el juego). || COM. To go bankrupt fraudulently (quebrar). || JUR. To lodge an appeal. || *Amer.* To go back to the wild, to run away (un animal). || — *Alzarse con la victoria*, to carry off the victory. || *Se alzó con el santo y la limosna*, he cleared off with everything.
allá adv. Over there, there (lugar). || Long ago, back (tiempo): *allá en mis mocedades*, long ago in my youth. || — *Allá abajo*, down there. || *Allá arriba*, up there (arriba), in Heaven, above (en el Cielo). || *Allá cada uno*, that is for each one to decide. || *Allá él*, it's his business, it's his affair, that's his funeral. || *Allá en esos tiempos*, back in those days. || *Allá en mis tiempos*, in my day. || *Allá por el año 1980*, around about 1980. || *Allá se las componga*, let him get on with it. || *Allá se va*, there's not much difference, it's more or less the same thing. || *Allá usted*, that's your lookout, it's up to you. || *Allá voy*, I'm coming. || *De Madrid para allá*, from Madrid onwards *o* on. || *El más allá*, the beyond. || *Más allá*, further on. || *No más allá de*, not any more than, not beyond. || *No ser muy allá*, not to be up to much, not to be very good (no ser muy bueno). || *No tan allá*, not so far [away]. || *Vamos allá*, let's go.

— OBSERV. *Allá* (which is less precise than *allí*) can be modified to express certain degrees of comparison: *tan allá*, so far: *no tan allá*, not so far: *más allá*, further away *o* on: *muy allá*, a long way away. When *allá* is followed by an adverbial phrase of time or place, it is, in many cases, not translated: *allá en América*, in America.

allanador, ra adj. Which levels, levelling.
— M. y f. Leveller. || JUR. Burglar, housebreaker (de morada).
allanamiento m. Levelling, smoothing, flattening (acción de poner llano). || FIG. Smoothing-out: *el allanamiento de las dificultades*, the smoothing-out of difficulties. || JUR. Submission [to a legal decision]. || JUR. *Allanamiento de morada*, housebreaking, breaking and entering.
allanar v. tr. To level [out], to flatten [out], to smooth [out]: *allanar el suelo*, to level the ground. || FIG. To smooth out, to overcome, to iron out (una dificultad). || JUR. To break into, to burgle (una casa). || FIG. *Allanar el terreno*, to clear the way.
— V. pr. To collapse (derrumbarse). || To level out (nivelarse). || To submit, to give in (darse por vencido). || To agree, to comply, to submit (conformarse): *éste se allana a todo*, he agrees to *o* he complies with everything.
allegado, da adj. Close: *la gente allegada al Presidente*, those close to the President. || Supporting (partidario).
— M. y f. [Close] relation, relative (pariente). || Supporter, follower (partidario). || Close friend (a una casa, etc.).
— M. pl. Entourage, *sing.*, suite, *sing.*: *los allegados al rey*, the king's entourage. || *Los allegados al Ministro*, those closest to the Minister.
allegador, ra adj. Gathering, collecting.
— M. Rake (rastro). || Poker (hurgón).
allegamiento m. Collection, gathering together, raising (de fondos).
allegar v. tr. To collect, to raise (recoger): *allegar fondos*, to raise money *o* funds. || To bring closer, to bring near (acercar). || AGR. To pile up (la parva trillada). || To add (añadir).
— V. intr. To arrive (llegar).
— V. pr. To approach, to come near (acercarse). || To conform (conformarse).
allegretto adv./s. m. MÚS. Allegretto.
allegro adv./s. m. MÚS. Allegro.
allende adv. Beyond: *allende el estrecho de Gibraltar está África*, beyond the straits of Gibraltar lies Africa. || Besides (además). || *Allende los mares*, overseas, beyond the seas.
allí adv. There: *voy allí todos los días*, I go there every day; *allí arriba*, up there. || Then (entonces). || — *Allí dentro*, in there. || *Allí donde*, wherever. || *Allí están*, there they are. || FAM. *Allí fue ello* or *ella*, v. ELLO o ELLA. || *Aquí y allí*, here and there. || *Hasta allí*, as far as that. || *Por allí*, over there, that way.
ama f. Lady of the house (señora de la casa). || Owner (dueña). || Mistress (para los criados). || Housekeeper (de un soltero, de un clérigo). || Wet nurse (ama de leche). || — *Amer. Ama de brazos*, nursemaid. || *Ama de casa*, housewife. || *Ama de cría* or *de leche*, wet nurse. || *Ama de gobierno* or *ama de llaves*, housekeeper. || *Ama seca*, dry nurse.
amabilidad f. Kindness: *le estoy agradecido por su amabilidad*, I am grateful for your kindness. || Amiability, affability. || — *Es de una gran amabilidad*, he is an extremely nice person. || *Tenga la amabilidad de pasar*, would you be so kind as to come in. || *Tuvo la amabilidad de traerme un regalo*, he was kind enough to bring me a present.
amabilísimo, ma adj. Very kind (servicial). || Very nice *o* friendly (afable).
amable adj. Kind, nice, pleasant, amiable (afable): *es un profesor muy amable*, he is a very nice teacher; *el ministro ha sido muy amable conmigo*, the minister has been very kind to me. || — *Amable con* or *para con todos*, kind to everybody. || *Es amable de carácter*, he

has a pleasant character. || *Ha sido usted muy amable viniendo,* it was very kind *o* good of you to come. || *¿Sería usted tan amable de ...?,* would you be so kind as to...?
amachetar o **amachetear** v. tr. To hack with a machete.
amadamado, da adj. Effeminate (amanerado).
Amadeo n. pr. m. Amadeus.
amado, da adj. Dear, beloved.
— M. y f. Dear one, sweetheart.
amador, ra adj. Loving.
— M. y f. Lover.
amadrigarse v. pr. To go to ground (en la madriguera).
amadrinamiento m. Yoking in pairs (de caballos). || FIG. Sponsorship (apadrinamiento).
amadrinar v. tr. To yoke together (dos caballos). || FIG. To sponsor (apadrinar).
amaestrado, da adj. Trained (animal). || Performing: *pulga amaestrada,* performing flea.
amaestrador, ra adj. Who trains, training.
— M. y f. Trainer.
amaestramiento m. Training.
amaestrar v. tr. To train.
amagar v. intr. To promise to be: *amaga un día hermoso,* it promises to be a fine day. || To threaten: *amaga una tempestad,* a storm is threatening; *está amagando con golpearle,* he is threatening to hit him. || To appear the first signs: *amagó una epidemia de cólera en la ciudad,* the first signs of a cholera epidemic appeared in the town. || DEP. To feint (boxeo, esgrima). || — *Amaga (con) llover,* it looks like rain. || *Amagar una sonrisa,* to smile weakly. || *Amagar y no dar,* to make a threat and not carry it out.
— V. pr. FAM. To hide (esconderse).
amago m. Threat (amenaza). || Sign (señal). || MED. Symptom, sign (de una enfermedad). || DEP. Feint (finta). || Beginning (comienzo). || Attempt: *sólo hemos oído hablar de amagos de industrialización,* we have only heard talk about attempts at industrialization. || *Hizo un amago de sacar su pistola,* he made a move to draw his revolver.
amainar v. tr. MAR. To lower, to take in (las velas). || FIG. To moderate, to calm.
— V. intr. y pr. To die down: *amaina el temporal,* the storm is dying down. || To drop, to die down: *el viento amaina,* the wind is dropping. || FIG. To moderate: *amainar en sus pretensiones,* to moderate one's claims. | To calm down (los ánimos).
amaine m. MAR. Lowering, taking in [of the sails]. || Dying-down (del viento, etc.). || FIG. Moderation. | Calming down (de la furia, etc.).
amajadar v. tr. AGR. To pen, to put in the fold (rebaños).
— V. intr. To return to the fold.
amalgama f. QUÍM. Amalgam. || FIG. Amalgam, combination.
amalgamación f. o **amalgamiento** m. QUÍM. Amalgamation. || FIG. Amalgamation, amalgam, combination.
amalgamar v. tr. QUÍM. To amalgamate. || FIG. To amalgamate, to combine.
— V. pr. QUÍM. To amalgamate. || FIG. To amalgamate, to combine.
amamantador, ra adj. Suckling.
amamantamiento m. Suckling, breast-feeding.
amamantar v. tr. To suckle, to breast-feed.
amán m. Pardon (amnistía).
amancebamiento m. Living together, cohabitation, living in sin (ant.).
amancebarse v. pr. To live together, to cohabit, to live in sin (ant.).
amanecer* v. impers. To dawn, to break [day *o* dawn]: *amanece tarde en invierno,* day breaks late in winter, it dawns late in winter. || *Amaneciendo,* at dawn, at daybreak.
— V. intr. To be at dawn *o* daybreak: *amanecimos en París,* we were in Paris at dawn; *el jardín amaneció cubierto de nieve,* at dawn the garden was covered in snow. || To arrive at dawn *o* at daybreak (llegar). || To wake up [in the morning]: *ayer amanecí con mucha fiebre,* yesterday I woke up with a high temperature. || FIG. To appear, to begin to show. || *El día amaneció nublado,* the sky was cloudy at dawn.
amanecer m. o **amanecida** f. Dawn, daybreak: *al amanecer,* at daybreak, at dawn.
amaneradamente adv. Affectedly.
amanerado, da adj. Affected, mannered: *una persona amanerada,* an affected person.
amaneramiento m. Affectation.
amanerarse v. pr. To become affected *o* mannered, to adopt an affected style.
amanita f. BOT. Amanita (hongo).
amanojar v. tr. To gather into bundles.
amansador, ra m. y f. Horsebreaker (de caballos). || Tamer (de fieras).
amansamiento m. Breaking (de caballos). || Taming (de fieras).
amansar v. tr. To break in: *amansar un caballo,* to break in a horse. || To tame: *amansar una fiera,* to tame a wild animal. || FIG. To ease (dolor, pena). | To calm (tranquilizar). | To tame (el carácter).
— V. pr. To tame o.s. || To calm down (los ánimos).
amante adj. Fond: *amante de la buena mesa,* fond of good food; *amante de la belleza,* fond of beauty.
— M. y f. Lover: *un amante de la gloria,* a lover of glory; *Romeo y Julieta eran amantes,* Romeo and Juliette were lovers. || — M. Lover (querido). || MAR. Runner. || — F. Mistress, lover (querida).
amantillo m. MAR. Topping lift.
amanuense m. Scribe, clerk (escribiente). || Copyist (copista).
amanzanar v. tr. *Amer.* To parcel out [a piece of ground].
amañado, da adj. Skilful [U.S., skillful] (hábil). || Fake (falso). || Rigged, fixed (elecciones).
amañar v. tr. To fix, to arrange. || To fix, to rig (las elecciones). || To alter (falsificar). || To fake (una foto, un documento). || To cook (cuentas).
— V. pr. To arrange things, to fix things: *siempre te las amañas para conseguir lo que quieres,* you always arrange things to get what you want. || To be skilful (ser habilidoso).
amaño m. Skill, cleverness (maña). || Scheme, trick, ruse (ardid, arreglo). || — Pl. Tools (herramientas, aperos).
amapola f. BOT. Poppy. || *Ponerse rojo como una amapola,* to turn as red as a beetroot.
amar v. tr. To love: *amar al prójimo,* to love one's neighbour; *amar con locura,* to love madly.

— OBSERV. *To love* is usually expressed in Spanish by *querer*. *Amar* is more poetic and tends to define more abstract or lofty sentiments (*to love one's country,* etc.). It never means "to find pleasing": *I love apples,* me encantan las manzanas.

amaraje m. Landing [on the sea] (de un hidroavión). || Splashdown (de astronave).
amaranto m. BOT. Amaranth.
amarar v. intr. To land [on the sea] (un hidroavión). || To splash down (astronave).
amargado, da adj. FIG. Embittered, bitter: *amargado por su fracaso,* embittered by his failure, bitter from his failure.
— M. y f. Bitter *o* embittered person, person with a grudge.
amargar v. intr. To be bitter, to taste bitter: *esta fruta amarga,* this fruit is bitter.
— V. tr. To make bitter (dar sabor amargo). || FIG. To grieve (afligir). | To make bitter, to embitter: *los reveses de la fortuna le han amargado,* reverses of fortune have made him bitter. | To get down: *me amarga la vida,* life is getting me down. || — *Amargarle la vida a alguien,* to make s.o.'s life a misery. || *A nadie le amarga un dulce,* a gift is always welcome.
— V. pr. To become bitter (una cosa). || FIG. To become bitter, to become embittered (una persona).
amargo, ga adj. Bitter: *almendra amarga,* bitter almond. || FIG. Bitter: *un recuerdo amargo,* a bitter memory. | Bitter, embittered (persona, carácter).
— M. Bitterness (sabor amargo). || Bitters, *pl.* (licor). || *Amer.* Bitter maté.
amargón m. BOT. Dandelion.
amargor m. Bitterness.
amargura f. Bitterness (sabor). || FIG. Bitterness: *sus fracasos le han llenado de amargura,* his failures have filled him with bitterness. | Grief (pena). || — *¡Qué amargura!,* what a pity! || FIG. *Traer* or *llevar a uno por la calle de la amargura,* to give s.o. a hard time.
amaricado, da o **amariconado, da** adj. FAM. Queer, effeminate.
amarilis f. BOT. Amaryllis.
amarillar o **amarillear** o **amarillecer*** v. intr. To go yellow, to yellow: *en otoño las hojas amarillean,* the leaves go yellow in autumn. || To be yellowish (tirar a amarillo).
amarillento, ta adj. Yellowish. || Sallow, yellowish: *tener la tez amarillenta,* to have a sallow complexion.
amarilleo m. Yellowing.
amarillez f. Yellow (amarillo) || Sallowness (de la piel).
amarillo, lla adj. Yellow: *raza amarilla,* yellow race. || — *Amarillo como la cera,* as yellow as a guinea. || MED. *Fiebre amarilla,* yellow fever. || *Ponerse amarillo,* to turn yellow.
— M. Yellow (color): *amarillo claro,* light yellow.
Amarillo adj. m. GEOGR. *Mar Amarillo, Río Amarillo,* Yellow Sea, Yellow River.
amariposado, da adj. BOT. Papilionaceous, butterfly-like.
amaro m. BOT. Clary, clary sage (planta).
amaromar v. tr. To moor, to tie up (atar).
amarra f. MAR. Mooring rope *o* line (cabo). || Martingale (de un arnés). || — Pl. FIG. y FAM. Connections: *tener buenas amarras,* to have good connections. || *Soltar las amarras,* to let go, to cast off (un barco), to break loose (quedar libre).
amarradero m. MAR. Bollard (poste). | Mooring ring (argolla). | Mooring, berth (sitio donde se amarran los barcos).
amarrado, da adj. FIG. Tied down (sujeto).
amarradura f. Mooring.
amarraje m. MAR. Mooring charge (impuesto).
amarrar v. tr. MAR. To make fast, to tie up, to moor (un barco). || To tie, to fasten: *amarra tus zapatos,* fasten your shoes. || To tie up: *amarrar un paquete,* to tie up a parcel. || To tie, to bind: *le amarraron a una silla,* they tied him to a chair. || To stack (las cartas

al barajarlas). || — FIG. *Jugar muy amarrado*, to play safe (en el póker). | *Lo lleva bien amarrado*, he knows it back to front (un alumno).
— V. intr. FAM. To study hard, to swot (empollar).
— V. pr. To fasten, to tie (los zapatos). || *Amer.* POP. *Amarrársela*, to get sozzled *o* sloshed, to get drunk.
amarre m. Stacking (al barajar las cartas). || MAR. Mooring.
amartelado, da adj. In love, infatuated: *están muy amartelados*, they are very much in love, they are completely infatuated with each other.
amarteladamente adv. Madly, passionately.
amartelamiento m. Infatuation, passionate love. || *Ya no está en edad de amartelamientos*, he is past it, a man of his age doesn't go falling head over heels in love.
amartelar v. tr. To make jealous (dar celos). || To make fall in love (enamorar).
— V. pr. To fall madly in love (enamorarse).
amartillar v. tr. To hammer (golpear). || To cock (un arma de fuego).
amasadera f. Kneading trough.
amasadero m. Kneading room.
amasador, ra adj. Kneading. || MED. Massaging (masajista).
— M. y f. Kneader. || — M. MED. Masseur. || — F. MED. Masseuse. || Kneading machine (máquina).
amasadura f. V. AMASAMIENTO.
amasamiento m. Kneading (del pan). || MED. Massage (masaje). || Mixing (de yeso, mortero, etc.).
amasar v. tr. To knead (el pan). || TECN. To mix (yeso, mortero). || MED. To massage (dar masajes). || FIG. To amass: *amasar una fortuna*, to amass a fortune. || FIG. y FAM. To cook up (tramar): *están amasando algo*, they're cooking sth. up.
amasijo m. Dough (masa de harina). || Kneading (amasamiento). || Mixture (de yeso, cal, etc.). || FIG. y FAM. Jumble, hotchpotch, mixture (mezcolanza): *este libro es un amasijo de tópicos*, this book is a jumble of clichés.
amateur adj./s. Amateur.
amatista adj./s.f. MIN. Amethyst.
amatorio, ria adj. Love: *cartas amatorias*, love letters.
amaurosis f. MED. Amaurosis (ceguera).
amauta m. *Amer.* Indian sage (sabio).
amazacotado, da adj. Hard (un colchón, etc.). || FIG. Clumsy, heavy, stodgy (estilo): *autor con un estilo amazacotado*, author with a heavy style. | Stodgy: *un arroz con leche amazacotado*, stodgy rice pudding. | Crammed: *libro amazacotado de fechas*, book crammed with dates. | Over-ornate: *una fachada amazacotada*, an over-ornate façade.
amazona f. Amazon (mujer guerrera). || FIG. Amazon, mannish woman (mujer varonil). || Horsewoman (mujer que monta a caballo). || FIG. Lady's riding habit (traje). || *Montar en amazona* or *a la amazona*, to ride sidesaddle.
Amazonas n. pr. m. GEOGR. Amazon.
amazónico, ca adj. Amazonian, Amazon.
ambages m. pl. FIG. Circumlocution, *sing.*, ambages. || — *Andarse con ambages*, to beat around the bush. || *Hablar sin ambages*, to speak frankly, to get straight to the point, to speak in plain language.
ámbar m. Amber. || — *Ámbar gris o pardillo*, ambergris. || *Ámbar negro*, jet (azabache). || *De ámbar*, perfumed with ambergris (perfumado).
ambarino, na adj. Amber.
Amberes n. pr. GEOGR. Antwerp.
amberino, na adj. [Of *o* from] Antwerp.
— M. y f. Inhabitant *o* native of Antwerp.
ambición f. Ambition.
ambicionar v. tr. To strive after, to seek, to want: *ambiciona el poder*, he is striving after power. || To want: *ambiciona que su hijo se haga profesor de inglés*, he wants his son to become an English teacher. || *Ambicionar hacer algo*, to have an ambition to do sth.
ambicioso, sa adj. Ambitious. || Self-seeking (egoísta).
— M. y f. Ambitious person.
ambidextro, tra adj. Ambidextrous.
— M. y f. Ambidextrous person.
ambientación f. Atmosphere (ambiente). || Setting (marco). || RAD. Sound effects, *pl.* || *Ruido de ambientación*, background noises, *pl.*
ambiental adj. Environmental.
ambientar v. tr. To give atmosphere to: *ambientar una exposición*, to give atmosphere to an exhibition. || To bring to life (dar vida). || To set: *la obra está ambientada en una cárcel*, the play is set in prison. || *Un cuadro bien ambientado*, a painting with a lot of atmosphere.
— V. pr. To adapt o.s.: *se ambienta rápidamente en todos los países*, he adapts himself quickly to every country.
ambiente adj. Ambient: *la temperatura ambiente*, the ambient temperature. || *Medio ambiente*, environment.
— M. Atmosphere: *ambiente cargado de humo*, smoky atmosphere. || Environment (medio ambiente): *contaminación del ambiente*, pollution of the environment. || FIG. Environment, milieu (medio): *un ambiente intelectual*, an intellectual environment. | Atmosphere: *un ambiente optimista*, an optimistic atmosphere; *no hay ambiente para trabajar*, the atmosphere is not conducive to work; *no entres en esa sala de fiestas, que no hay ambiente*, don't go into that nightclub, there is no atmosphere. || *Amer.* Room (habitación). || — *Ambiente rural*, country atmosphere. || *Cambiar de ambiente*, to change one's surroundings. || *Dar ambiente a*, to give atmosphere to.
ambigú m. Buffet (comida, lugar donde se sirve).
ambiguamente adv. Ambiguously.
ambigüedad f. Ambiguity.
ambiguo, gua adj. Ambiguous: *una contestación ambigua*, an ambiguous answer. || Effeminate (afeminado). || GRAM. Of either gender.
ámbito m. Environment, atmosphere (ambiente). || Scope, compass: *en el ámbito de la ley*, within the scope of the law. || Field, world, sphere: *en el ámbito artístico*, in the field of art. || Enclosure (recinto). || Expanse (extensión). || MÚS. Compass. || — *Empresa constructora de ámbito nacional*, nationwide building firm. || *En el ámbito nacional*, throughout the whole country.
ambivalencia f. Ambivalence.
ambivalente adj. Ambivalent.
amblador, ra adj. Pacing, ambling (caballo).
ambladura f. Amble (modo de andar los cuadrúpedos).
amblar v. intr. To amble, to pace.
ambliopía f. MED. Amblyopia.
ambón m. Ambo (púlpito).
ambos, as adj. Both: *llegaron ambos hermanos*, both brothers came. || — *De ambas partes*, on both sides. || *Por ambos lados*, from both sides.
— Pron. pl. Both. || *Ambos vinieron*, they both came, both of them came.

— OBSERV. This word is used when referring to people or things which usually go in pairs: *con ambas manos*, with both hands.

ambrosía f. Ambrosia.
ambrosiaco, ca adj. Ambrosial: *perfume ambrosiaco*, ambrosial perfume.
ambrosiano, na adj. Ambrosian: *rito, canto ambrosiano*, Ambrosian rite, chant.
Ambrosio n. pr. m. Ambrose.
ambulancia f. Ambulance. || Field ambulance, field hospital (hospital móvil). || *Ambulancia de correos*, travelling post office.
ambulanciero, ra m. y f. Ambulance man, ambulance woman.
ambulante adj. Travelling: *circo ambulante*, travelling circus. || Strolling, itinerant: *actor ambulante*, strolling player; *trovador ambulante*, strolling troubador. || Walking (que anda). || — *Biblioteca ambulante*, mobile library. || *Vendedor ambulante* pedlar, street salesman, hawker (en la calle), travelling salesman (representante).
— M. *Ambulante de correos*, travelling post office worker (en los trenes).
ambulatorio, ria adj. Ambulatory.
— M. National health clinic.
ameba f. ZOOL. Amoeba, ameba.
amedrentador, ra adj. Terrifying, frightening.
amedrentamiento m. Fright, terror.
amedrentar v. tr. To scare, to frighten, to terrify, to intimidate: *no amedrento a nadie*, I don't frighten anyone. || To terrify, to frighten: *los gritos amedrentaron a los vecinos*, the shouting terrified the neighbours.
— V. pr. To be frightened, to be scared, to be terrified: *se amedrenta por cualquier cosa*, he is frightened by the slightest thing. || To become nervous *o* intimidated: *se amedrentaba ante el profesor*, he became nervous in front of the teacher.
amelar v. intr. To make honey (las abejas).
amelcochar v. tr. *Amer.* To thicken (un dulce).
amelga f. AGR. Land (sembrado).
amelgado, da adj. Unevenly sown (el trigo).
amelgar v. tr. AGR. To furrow (surcar).
amelocotonado, da adj. Peachlike.
amelonado, da adj. Melon-shaped.
amén m. inv. Amen. || — FAM. *Decir amén a todo*, to agree with everything, to be a yes-man. | *En un decir amén* or *en un amén*, in the twinkling of an eye, before you can say Jack Robinson.
— Interj. Amen: *líbranos del mal, amén*, deliver us from evil, amen.
— Prep. FAM. *Amén de*, except for (excepto), besides: *amén de lo dicho*, besides what has been said.
amenaza f. Threat, menace: *amenazas vanas*, vain threats.
amenazador, ra o **amenazante** adj. Threatening, menacing: *mirada amenazadora*, menacing look.
amenazar v. tr. To threaten, to menace: *amenazar a uno con una pistola*, to threaten s.o. with a revolver; *nos amenaza una gran catástrofe*, we are menaced by a terrible catastrophe. || To threaten: *la casa amenaza derribarse* or *amenaza ruina*, the house is threatening to fall down *o* into ruins. || FIG. To threaten, to be imminent (estar inminente): *amenaza nieve*, it is threatening to snow, snow is imminent. || *Amenazar a alguien de muerte*, to threaten to kill s.o.
amenguamiento m. Lessening.
amenguar v. tr. To lessen. || FIG. To defame, to denigrate (deshonrar).

amenidad f. Pleasantness, agreeableness, amenity.
amenizar v. tr. To brighten up, to liven up: *amenizar la conversación*, to brighten up the conversation; *amenizar la fiesta*, to liven up the party. || To make more interesting *o* more entertaining: *amenizar un discurso con citas*, to make a speech more interesting by adding quotations. || To make pleasanter, to make more agreeable: *un poco de música de fondo para amenizar la comida*, a little background music to make the meal pleasanter.
ameno, na adj. Pleasant, nice, agreeable (agradable). || Charming: *es un hombre muy ameno, siempre tiene algo gracioso que contar*, he is a very charming man, he always has sth. amusing to say.
amenorrea f. MED. Amenorrhoea.
amentáceo, a o **amentífero, ta** adj. BOT. Amentaceous, amentiferous.
amento m. BOT. Ament, catkin.
amerengado, da adj. Meringue-like. || FIG. Sugary (remilgado).
América n. pr. f. GEOGR. America: *América del Norte, Central, del Sur*, North, Central, South America. Latin America (Iberoamérica).

— OBSERV. On its own, the Spanish word *América* often refers solely to Latin America, although it can also mean the United States.
— En inglés, la palabra *America*, empleada a solas, se refiere normalmente a los Estados Unidos.

americana f. Jacket, coat: *una americana cruzada*, a double-breasted jacket; *su americana no es del mismo color que su pantalón*, his coat isn't the same colour as his trousers. || American phaeton (faetón).
americanismo m. Americanism.
americanista m. y f. Americanist.
americanización f. Americanization.
americanizar v. tr. To Americanize.
— V. pr. To become Americanized.
americano, na adj./s. American (del continente). || Latin American (de Iberoamérica). || American (de los EE.UU.).

— OBSERV. I. Traditionally the adjective *americano* refers to a person or a thing from Latin America, but owing to the modern influence of the United States of America it is often the equivalent of *estadounidense* or *norteamericano*.
— II. En inglés *American*, sin otra indicación, significa normalmente *estadounidense*.

americio m. QUÍM. Americium (metal).
amerindio, dia adj. Amerindian.
— M. y f. Amerind.
amerizaje m. Landing [on the sea]. || Splashdown (de astronave).
amerizar v. intr. To land [on the sea] (amarar). || To splash down (un astronave).
amestizado, da adj. Like a half-breed.
ametrallador, ra adj. *Fusil ametrallador*, automatic rifle.
— M. Machine gunner. || — F. Machine gun.
ametrallar v. tr. To machine-gun.
ametropía f. MED. Ametropia.
amianto m. MIN. Amianthus, asbestos.
amiba f. ZOOL. Amoeba, ameba.
amida f. QUÍM. Amide.
amidol m. QUÍM. Amidol.
amiga f. Friend. || Mistress (amante). || Girlfriend, sweetheart (de un joven). || Schoolmistress (maestra). || Girls' school (escuela).
amigable adj. Friendly, amicable: *contrato amigable*, friendly contract. || *Amigable componedor*, arbitrator.
amigablemente adv. Amicably, in a friendly way.
amigacho, cha m. y f. FAM. Pal, mate.
amigar v. tr. To make friends (hacer amigos).
— V. pr. To live together. || To make friends.
amígdala f. ANAT. Tonsil, amygdala. || *Ser operado de amígdalas*, to have one's tonsils out.
amigdaláceo, a adj. BOT. Amygdalaceous.
— F. pl. BOT. Amygdalaceae.
amigdalino, na adj. ANAT. Amygdaline, tonsillar.
— F. QUÍM. Amygdalin.
amigdalitis f. MED. Tonsillitis.
amigo, ga adj. Friendly: *una voz amiga*, a friendly voice. || Fond, given: *es más amigo de salir que de quedarse en casa*, he is more fond of *o* given to going out than staying in. || Fond: *ser amigo de las cosas buenas*, to be fond of good things.
— M. y f. Friend: *amigo de siempre* or *de toda la vida*, lifelong friend; *es un amigo mío*, he is a friend of mine; *amigo íntimo*, close friend. || Supporter (partidario). || Lover (amante). || — M. Boyfriend, sweetheart (novio). || — F. Véase AMIGA. || — FAM. *Amigo del asa*, close *o* intimate friend. || *Amigo de la casa*, friend of the family. || *Amigo de lo ajeno*, thief. || *Bueno es tener amigos hasta en el infierno*, it's worth having friends anywhere. || *Como amigos*, like friends, as friends. || *En el peligro se conoce al amigo*, a friend in need is a friend indeed. || *Es muy amigo mío*, he is a very good friend of mine. || *Ganar amigos*, to make friends. || *Hacerse amigo de*, to make friends with. || *Hacerse amigos*, to become friends. || *Poner cara de pocos amigos*, to pull a long face. || *Seguir siendo amigo de*, to keep friends with. || *Son muy amigos*, they are very good friends. || *Soy amigo de decir las cosas claramente*, I'm one for *o* I'm all for *o* I'm in favour of saying things frankly. || *Tener cara de pocos amigos*, to look unfriendly, to have an unfriendly face.
— Interj. *¡Amigo, qué alegre vienes hoy!*, I say, you're happy today! || *¡Pero no es lo mismo, amigo!*, but it's not the same thing, old boy! || *Vaya en paz, amigo*, go in peace, my friend.
amigote m. FAM. Mate, chum, friend [U.S , buddy].
amiláceo, a adj. QUÍM. Starchy, amylaceous.
amilanamiento m. Fear (miedo). || Discouragement (desánimo).
amilanar v. tr. To frighten, to terrify, to intimidate (asustar). || FIG. To discourage (desanimar).
— V. pr. To be frightened, to get frightened (acobardarse). || To be discouraged (desanimarse).
amilasa f. BIOL. Amylase.
amileno m. QUÍM. Amylene.
amílico, ca adj. QUÍM. Amyl, amylic: *alcohol amílico*, amyl alcohol.
amilo m. QUÍM. Amyl.
amiloide adj. BIOL. Amyloid.
amilosis f. MED. Amyloidosis.
amillaramiento m. Cadastre, tax assessment.
amillarar v. tr. To register in the cadastre.
amina f. QUÍM. Amine.
aminado, da adj. QUÍM. Amino.
aminoácido m. QUÍM. Amino acid.
aminoración f. Lessening, decrease: *una aminoración de los intercambios comerciales*, a decrease in trade. || Reduction, cut: *la aminoración de los precios*, the reduction of prices, the cut in prices. || Slackening: *la aminoración del ritmo de los negocios*, the slackening of business. || *Aminoración de la velocidad*, decrease in speed, slowing down.
aminorar v. tr. To reduce, to decrease, to cut, to lessen. || — *Aminorar el paso*, to slow down, to walk more slowly. || *Aminorar la velocidad*, to slow down.
amistad f. Friendship: *granjearse la amistad de alguien*, to win s.o.'s friendship. || — Pl. Friends: *tener amistades poco recomendables*, to have rather undesirable friends. || — *Contraer* or *trabar amistad con alguien*, to make friends with s.o. || *Estar en buenas amistades*, to be on friendly terms. || *Hacer las amistades*, to make it up. || *Romper las amistades*, to fall out, to break up.
amistar v. tr. To make friends, to bring together. || To make it up between, to reconcile (reconciliar).
— V. pr. To become friends. || To make it up (reconciliarse).
amistosamente adv. Amicably, in a friendly way.
amistoso, sa adj. Friendly, amicable: *un consejo amistoso*, a friendly piece of advice.
amito m. Amice (paño sacerdotal).
amnesia f. MED. Amnesia.
amnésico, ca adj. Amnesic.
— M. y f. Amnesiac.
amnios f. ANAT. Amnion.
amniótico, ca adj. ANAT. Amniotic.
amnistía f. Amnesty.
amnistiado, da adj. Amnestied.
— M. y f. Amnestied person.
amnistiar v. tr. To amnesty, to grant an amnesty to.
amo m. Master: *el amo del perro*, the dog's master. || Master, head of the family (cabeza de familia). || Landlord (propietario de una casa). || Owner (de una finca, coche, etc.). || Employer, boss (de un taller). || — *El ojo del amo engorda al caballo*, it is the master's eye that makes the mill go. || *Amer. Nuestro Amo*, the Blessed Sacrament. || FIG. *Perro de muchos amos*, Jack of all trades. || FIG. y FAM. *Ser el amo del cotarro*, to be the boss, to rule the roost.
amodita f. ZOOL. Cerastes, horned viper (víbora). || Ammodyte (pez).
amodorrado, da adj. Drowsy, sleepy, dozy.
amodorramiento m. Drowsiness, sleepiness, doziness.
amodorrarse v. pr. To get drowsy *o* sleepy, to doze.
amohinar v. tr. To annoy, to irritate, to vex.
— V. pr. To get annoyed, to sulk.
amojamado, da adj. Wizened, dried up (flaco).
amojamamiento m. Wizening, drying up.
amojamar v. tr. To dry and salt [tuna].
— V. pr. To become wizened (apergaminarse).
amojonamiento m. Marking out.
amojonar v. tr. To mark out, to mark the boundaries of: *amojonar un campo*, to mark out a field.
amoladera adj. f. *Piedra amoladera*, whetstone, grindstone.
— F. Grindstone (rueda). || Grindstone, whetstone (piedra).
amolador m. Grinder. || FIG. y FAM. Nuisance (latoso).
amoladura f. Grinding, sharpening. || — Pl. Grinding dust, *sing.* (arenilla).
amolar* v. tr. To sharpen, to grind, (un cuchillo, etc.). || FIG. y FAM. To annoy, to pester, to get on s.o.'s nerves (fastidiar).
amoldamiento m. Fitting, adapting, adjusting (ajuste). || FIG. Adaptation: *amoldamiento a*, adaptation to.
amoldar v. tr. To mould. || To fit: *amoldar un zapato a la forma del pie*, to fit a shoe to the shape of the foot. || FIG. To mould, to shape: *amoldar su conducta a los principios cristianos*, to mould one's conduct according to Christian principles.
— V. pr. To adapt [o.s.], to adjust [o.s.]: *amoldarse*

a las costumbres locales, to adapt o.s. to the local customs; *amoldarse a las circunstancias*, to adapt o.s. to the circumstances.

amondongado, da adj. Flabby (rechoncho).

amonedar v. tr. To coin, to mint.

amonestación f. Reprimand, admonition, rebuke (reprensión). || Warning (advertencia). || Bann (anuncio de bodas): *correr las amonestaciones*, to publish the banns.

amonestador, ra adj. Reprimanding (reprensivo). || Warning: *en tono amonestador*, in a warning tone.

amonestar v. tr. To reprimand, to admonish (reprender). || To warn (advertir). || To publish the banns of (anunciar la boda).

amoniacado, da adj. Ammoniated.

amoniacal adj. QUÍM. Ammoniacal.

amoniaco, ca o **amoníaco, ca** adj. QUÍM. Ammoniac: *sal amoniaca*, sal ammoniac.
— M. QUÍM. Ammonia. || Gum ammoniac (goma).

amonio m. QUÍM. Ammonium.

amonita f. ZOOL. Ammonite (fósil).

amontillado, da adj. "Amontillado".
— M. "Amontillado", pale dry sherry.

amontonadamente adv. In a pile, in a heap.

amontonador, ra adj. Heaping.
— F. Heaper, heaping machine.

amontonamiento m. Piling, heaping (acción de apilar). || Hoarding (de riquezas). || Gathering, collection (de datos). || Crowding (de gente). || Pile, heap (montón).

amontonar v. tr. To pile up, to heap up, to put in a pile (poner en montón): *amontonaron todos los libros*, they piled up all the books, they put all the books in a pile. || FIG. To accumulate, to hoard (riquezas). | To collect, to gather: *amontonó datos, pruebas*, he collected data, proof. | To accumulate: *amontonar conocimientos*, to accumulate knowledge.
— V. pr. To crowd together: *se amontonaba la gente en la plaza*, the people crowded together in the square. || To pile up, to heap up: *las pruebas contra él se amontonaban*, proof against him was piling up. || To gather (nubes). || FIG. y FAM. To get angry, to fly into a temper (enfadarse). | To live together (amancebarse).

amor m. Love: *el amor de un padre a su hijo*, a father's love for his son; *amor a la música*, love of music; *amor materno*, motherly love. || Devotion: *trabajo con amor*, he worked with devotion. || Loving care: *limpió con amor los vasos*, he cleaned the glasses with loving care. || Love (persona o cosa amada): *eres mi amor*, you are my love; *su gran amor es la pintura*, painting is his great love. || Lover (amante). || — Pl. Loves, love affairs: *los amores de Luis XV*, the love affairs of Louis XV. || — *Al amor de la lumbre*, by the fireside, by the fire. || *Amor con amor se paga*, one good turn deserves another (en buen sentido), an eye for an eye and a tooth for a tooth (irónicamente). || *Amor correspondido*, requited love. || BOT. *Amor de hortelano*, cleavers. || *Amor interesado*, love for money. || *Amor pasajero*, passing fancy. || *Amor propio*, self-respect, self-esteem, amour propre. || *Con* or *de mil amores*, with pleasure, with the greatest pleasure. || *En amor y compañía*, peacefully. || *Hacer el amor*, to court (cortejar), to make love (tener relaciones sexuales). || *Por amor al arte*, for the love of it. || *Por el amor de*, for the love of, for the sake of. || *Por (el) amor de Dios*, for the love of God. || *Requerir de amores*, to court. || *Tener amores con*, to have a love affair with.

amoral adj. Amoral.

amoralidad f. Amorality.

amoralismo m. Amoralism.

amoratado, da adj. Purple, blue: *tengo las manos amoratadas de frío*, my hands are blue with cold. || Black and blue, badly bruised: *un rostro amoratado de golpes*, a badly bruised face.

amoratar v. tr. To make blue *o* purple (el frío). || To make black and blue, to bruise (golpes).
— V. pr. To turn blue *o* purple (por el frío). || To turn black and blue, to bruise (por golpes).

amorcillo n. Cupid (figura). || FIG. Affair, flirtation.

amordazamiento m. Gagging (de personas). || Muzzling (de perros). || FIG. Gagging, silencing (de la prensa).

amordazar v. tr. To gag: *los ladrones le amordazaron*, the thieves gagged him. || To muzzle: *amordazar un perro*, to muzzle a dog. || FIG. To gag, to silence: *amordazar la prensa*, to gag the press.

amorecer* v. tr. To mate with [the ewe] (el morueco).

amorfismo m. Amorphism.

amorfo, fa adj. Amorphous.

amoricones m. pl. FAM. Caresses.

amorío m. FAM. Flirtation, affair.

amoriscado, da adj. Moorish. || ARQ. Moresque, mauresque.

amoroso, sa adj. Affectionate, loving: *un padre amoroso*, a loving father. || Amorous: *miradas amorosas*, amorous glances. || Love: *cartas amorosas*, love letters. || AGR. Workable (tierra). || FIG. Mild (tiempo).

amortajador, ra m. y f. Shrouder, person who puts on the shroud.

amortajamiento m. Shrouding.

amortajar v. tr. To shroud, to wrap in a shroud. || TECN. To join [tenon and mortise]. | To box [the tenon in the mortise].

amortecer* v. tr. To muffle, to deaden (ruido). || To subdue, to soften, to dim (la luz). || To absorb (golpe).
— V. pr. To faint.

amortiguación f. o **amortiguamiento** m. Muffling, deadening (del ruido). || Subduing, softening, dimming (de la luz). || Damping, cushioning (de un golpe). || Damping (del fuego). || FIG. Lessening, reduction. | Toning down (de colores).

amortiguador, ra adj. Muffling, deadening (del sonido). || Subduing, softening (de la luz). || Absorbing, cushioning (de un golpe).
— M. TECN. Shock absorber, damper.

amortiguar v. tr. To muffle, to deaden (el ruido). || To subdue, to soften, to dim (la luz). || To absorb, to cushion (un golpe). || To damp [down] (el fuego). || FIG. To alleviate, to mitigate (mitigar). | To tone down (colores).
— V. pr. To die down (el ruido). || To grow dim, to soften (la luz).

amortizable adj. COM. Redeemable: *renta amortizable*, redeemable annuity.

amortización f. COM. Paying-off, amortization: *la amortización de una deuda*, the paying-off of a debt. | Depreciation (de máquina, etc.). | Writing off (de capital). || JUR. Amortization. || Abolition (de un empleo). || COM. *Fondo de amortización*, sinking fund.

amortizar v. tr. COM. To pay off, to repay, to amortize: *amortizar una deuda*, to pay off a debt. | To depreciate (una máquina, etc.). | To write off (capital). || JUR. To amortize. || To abolish (un empleo).

amoscamiento m. Anger, temper.

amoscarse v. pr. FAM. To get cross, to get into a huff.

amostazar v. tr. FAM. To make cross.
— V. pr. FAM. To get into a huff, to get cross (enfadarse). || *Amer.* To get embarrassed (avergonzarse).

amotinado, da adj. Insurgent, riotous (insurrecto). || Rebellious (rebelde). || Mutinous (soldado, marinero).
— M. y f. Insurgent, rioter (insurrecto). || Rebel (rebelde). || Mutineer (soldado, marinero).

amotinador m. V. AMOTINADO.

amotinamiento m. Riot (motín). || Uprising, insurrection (rebelión). || Mutiny (motín de soldados o marineros).

amotinar v. tr. To stir to rebellion, to incite to revolt (incitar a la rebelión). || To incite to riot (incitar a motín): *el aumento de impuestos amotinó a los habitantes*, the increase in taxes incited the inhabitants to riot. || To incite to mutiny (soldados, marineros). || FIG. To upset, to disturb.
— V. pr. To rise up, to revolt, to rebel (rebelarse). || To riot (promover un motín): *los estudiantes se amotinaron porque la policía entró en la universidad*, the students rioted because the police entered the university. || To mutiny: *los marineros se amotinaron*, the sailors mutinied. || FIG. To become upset *o* disturbed.

amovible adj. Removable, detachable. || Revocable (empleo).

amovilidad f. Detachability, removability. || Revocability (de un empleo).

amparador, ra adj. Protecting, defending.
— M. y f. Protector, defender.

amparar v. tr. To aid, to help (ayudar). || To protect, to harbour, to shelter: *amparar a un criminal*, to protect a criminal. || To protect: *esta ley ampara nuestros derechos*, this law protects our rights. || *¡Dios le ampare!*, God help you!
— V. pr. To seek help (buscar ayuda). || To shelter, to take shelter: *ampararse de la lluvia*, to shelter from the rain. || To seek protection: *ampararse en la ley*, to seek protection in the law; *ampararse en una persona*, to seek s.o.'s protection.

amparo m. Protection: *al amparo de alguien, de la ley*, under s.o.'s protection, under the protection of the law. || Shelter: *ponerse al amparo de la lluvia*, to take shelter from the rain. || Help, assistance, protection: *puedo contar con su amparo*, I can count on his help. || Refuge: *la Iglesia ha sido siempre el amparo de los desdichados*, the Church has always been a refuge for the unfortunate.

amperaje m. TECN. Amperage.

amperímetro m. TECN. Ammeter.

amperio m. ELECTR. Ampere, amp. || ELECTR. *Amperio hora*, ampere-hour. | *Amperio segundo*, ampere-second. | *Amperio vuelta*, ampere-turn.

ampliable adj. Which can be enlarged, enlargeable.

ampliación f. Extension, enlargement: *la ampliación de una tienda*, the extension of a shop. || Extension: *la ampliación de las actividades, de un acuerdo, de un plazo*, the extension of activities, of an agreement, of a time limit. || FOT. Enlargement. || Amplification, development (de una explicación). || Widening (de una calle). || — COM. *Ampliación de capital*, increase of capital. || *Ampliación de estudios*, furthering of studies.

ampliado, da adj. Enlarged, extended. || Extended: *un programa ampliado de asistencia técnica*, an extended programme of technical aid.

ampliador, ra adj. Enlarging, extending.
— F. Enlarger (de fotos).
ampliar v. tr. To enlarge, to extend: *ampliar un almacén, un acuerdo,* to extend a store, an agreement. || To lengthen, to elaborate on, to amplify on: *ampliar una explicación,* to lengthen an explanation. || To develop: *ampliar su argumento,* to develop one's argument. || To extend, to increase: *ampliar los poderes del gerente,* to extend the manager's powers. || To expand (el comercio, un negocio). || To increase: *ampliar el número de accionistas, el capital,* to increase the number of shareholders, the capital. || To widen: *ampliar una carretera,* to widen a road. || Fot. To enlarge.
ampliativo, va adj. Enlarging.
amplificación f. Amplification: *la amplificación del sonido,* sound amplification. || Amplification (de una idea).
amplificador, ra adj. Amplifying.
— M. Amplifier, amp (fam.).
amplificar v. tr. To amplify: *amplificar un sonido,* to amplify a sound. || To amplify (una idea). || To magnify: *el microscopio amplifica los pequeños cuerpos,* the microscope magnifies small bodies.
amplificativo, va adj. Amplifying.
amplio, plia adj. Wide, full: *una falda amplia,* a wide skirt. || Wide, big: *este pantalón te está un poco amplio,* these trousers are rather big for you. || Wide, extensive: *tener amplios poderes,* to have extensive powers; *tener un conocimiento amplio de la historia,* to have an extensive knowledge of history; *un amplio cambio de impresiones,* a wide exchange of views. || Vast, extensive: *una finca muy amplia,* a very vast estate. || Considerable, extensive, great: *el amplio desarrollo de la economía,* the considerable development of the economy. || Roomy, spacious: *un comedor muy amplio,* a very spacious dining room. || *El sentido amplio de una palabra,* the broad sense of a word.
amplísimo, ma adj. Very extensive, very wide.
amplitud f. Width, fullness: *la amplitud de una falda,* the width of a skirt. || Extent: *la amplitud de sus poderes, de sus conocimientos, de un desastre,* the extent of one's powers, of one's knowledge, of a disaster. || Expanse, size, extent: *la amplitud de una finca,* the expanse of an estate. || Spaciousness (de una habitación, etc.). || Room, space (espacio): *quitamos la mesa para dar más amplitud,* we removed the table to make more room. || Fís. Amplitude (de una oscilación). || — *Amplitud de ideas, de miras,* broad-mindedness, broad outlook. || *Con amplitud,* easily: *aquí caben con amplitud veinte personas,* twenty people fit in here easily, there is easily room for twenty people here. || *De gran amplitud,* far-reaching, with a large scope: *un proyecto de gran amplitud,* a far-reaching plan, a plan with a large scope.
ampo m. Brilliant whiteness: *el ampo de la nieve,* the brilliant whiteness of the snow. || Snowflake (copo de nieve).
ampolla f. Med. Blister: *tengo ampollas en las manos,* I have blisters on my hands. || Phial, ampoule (de medicamento). || Flask, bottle (frasco).
ampollar v. tr. To blister.
— V. pr. To blister: *se me ampollaron los pies,* my feet blistered.
ampolleta f. Hourglass (reloj). || Bulb [of an hourglass]. || Time taken by sand to pour through an hourglass (tiempo).
ampón, ona adj. Wide, baggy.
ampulosidad f. Fig. Bombast, pomposity (estilo).
ampuloso, sa adj. Fig. Bombastic, pompous (estilo). || *Tener un nombre muy ampuloso,* to have a high-sounding name.
ampurdanés, esa adj. [From *o* of] Ampurdán (Cataluña).
— M. y f. Native *o* inhabitant of Ampurdán.
amputación f. Amputation: *amputación de un miembro,* amputation of a limb. || Fig. Cutting-out, deletion (en un texto). | Curtailment, curtailing (de créditos).
amputar v. tr. To amputate: *amputar un miembro,* to amputate a limb. || Fig. To cut out, to delete (un párrafo, etc.). | To curtail (créditos).
Amsterdam n. pr. Geogr. Amsterdam.
amueblar v. tr. To furnish. || *Piso amueblado,* furnished flat.
amuelar v. tr. To collect into a pile [grain].
amugronar v. tr. Agr. To provine, to layer.
amujerado, da adj. Effeminate (afeminado).
amulatado, da adj. Like a mulatto, mulatto-like.
amuleto m. Amulet.
amunicionar v. tr. To supply with munitions.
amuñecado, da adj. Doll-like: *rostro amuñecado,* doll-like face.
amura f. Mar. Tack (cabo). | Bow (proa).
amurada f. Mar. Ceiling.
amurallar v. tr. To wall, to fortify.
amurar v. tr. Mar. To haul in (velas).
amurrarse o **amurriarse** v. pr. *Amer.* To become sad, to get depressed.
amusgar v. tr. To put back, to throw back (las orejas). || To screw up (los ojos).
— V. intr. To put *o* to throw back its ears (toro, caballo).
— V. pr. *Amer.* To give way, to back down.
amustiar v. tr. To wither.
ana f. Ell [measurement of length approximately equivalent to a metre].
Ana n. pr. f. Ann, Anne.
anabaptismo m. Rel. Anabaptism.
anabaptista adj./s. Rel. Anabaptist.
anábasis f. Med. Anabasis.
anabolismo m. Biol. Anabolism.
anacarado, da adj. Pearly, mother-of-pearl.
anacardo m. Cashew tree (árbol). || Cashew nut (fruto).
anacoluto m. Gram. Anacoluthon.
anaconda f. Zool. Anaconda (serpiente).
anacora f. Horn (clarín).
anacoreta m. y f. Anchoret, anchorite.
Anacreonte n. pr. m. Anacreon.
anacreóntico, ca adj. Anacreontic.
anacreontismo m. Imitation of Anacreon.
anacrónico, ca adj. Anachronic, anachronistic.
anacronismo m. Anachronism.
anacrusis f. Anacrusis (métrica).
ánade m. y f. Duck (pato).
anadear v. intr. To waddle.
anadeo m. Waddle.
anadino, na m. y f. o **anadón** m. Duckling (patito).
anaerobio, bia adj. Biol. Anaerobic.
— M. Biol. Anaerobe.
anafase f. Biol. Anaphase.
anafe m. Portable stove (hornillo).
anafiláctico, ca adj. Med. Anaphylactic.
anafilaxia o **anafilaxis** f. Med. Anaphylaxis.
anáfora f. Anaphora (repetición).
anafre m. Portable stove (hornillo).
anafrodisia f. Anaphrodisia.
anafrodisiaco, ca adj./s.m. Anaphrodisiac.
anáglifo m. Arts. Phot. Anaglyph.
anagoge m. o **anagogía** f. Rel. Anagoge, anagogy.
anagrama m. Anagram.
anagramático, ca adj. Anagrammatic, anagrammatical.
anal adj. Anat. Anal.
analectas f. pl. Analects, analecta, florilegium, *sing.*
analéptico, ca adj./s.m. Med. Analeptic.
anales m. pl. Annals.
analfabetismo m. Illiteracy.
analfabeto, ta adj./s. Illiterate.
analgesia f. Med. Analgesia.
analgésico, ca adj./s.m. Med. Analgesic.
análisis m. Analysis: *análisis cuantitativo,* quantitative analysis. || Med. Test: *análisis de sangre,* blood test. | Analysis: *análisis de orina,* urine analysis.
analista m. y f. Analyst (el que hace análisis). || Annalist (escritor de anales).
analítico, ca adj. Analytic, analytical.
— F. Analytics.
analizable adj. Analysable, analyzable.
analizador, ra adj. Analysing, analyzing, who analyses.
— M. Fís. Analyser, analyzer.
analizar v. tr. To analyse, to analyze.
análogamente adv. Similarly, analogously, in a similar way, likewise.
analogía f. Similarity, analogy (semejanza). || Analogy (relación): *establecer una analogía entre dos cosas,* to draw an analogy between two things. || Gram. Analogy.
analógico, ca adj. Gram. Analogical, analogic.
analogismo m. Analogism.
análogo, ga adj. Similar, analogous.
Anam n. pr. m. Geogr. Annam.
anamita adj./s. Annamite (de Anam).
ananá o **ananás** m. Bot. Pineapple (planta y fruto).
— Observ. The plural is either *ananaes* or *ananases.*

anapelo m. Bot. Monkshood (acónito).
anapéstico, ca adj. Anapaestic [U.S., anapestic].
anapesto m. Anapaest [U.S., anapest].
anaquel m. Shelf (estante).
anaquelería f. Shelves, *pl.*, shelving.
anaranjado, da adj./s.m. Orange (color).
anarquía f. Anarchy.
anárquico, ca adj. Anarchic, anarchical.
anarquismo m. Anarchism.
anarquista adj./s. Anarchist.
anarquizante adj. Anarchic.
Anastasio, sia n. pr. m. y f. Anastasius, Anastasia. || Fig. y fam. *Doña Anastasia,* the censorship of the press.
anastigmático, ca adj. Anastigmatic: *objetivo anastigmático,* anastigmatic lens.
anastomosarse v. pr. Biol. To anastomose.
anastomosis f. Biol. Anastomosis.
anatema m. Rel. Anathema. || Fig. *Lanzar* or *fulminar un anatema contra alguien,* to put a curse on s.o., to curse s.o.
anatematización f. Rel. Anathematization. || Fig. Cursing.
anatematizar v. tr. Rel. To anathematize. || To curse.
anatife m. Zool. Barnacle (percebe).
Anatolia n. pr. f. Geogr. Anatolia.
anatomía f. Anatomy (ciencia). || Anatomy (cuerpo): *varias partes de su anatomía,* various parts of his

anatomy. || Dissection: *hacer la anatomía de un cadáver*, to do a dissection on a body.
anatómico, ca adj. Anatomic, anatomical.
anatomista m. y f. Anatomist.
anatomizar v. tr. e intr. To anatomize, to dissect.
anatoxina f. MED. Toxoid, anatoxin.
anátropo, pa adj. BOT. Anatropous, anatropal.
Anaxágoras n. pr. m. Anaxagoras.
anca f. Haunch (parte posterior lateral del caballo). || Crupper, rump (parte posterior superior). || — Pl. FAM. Bottom, *sing.*, behind, *sing.* (nalgas). || — *A ancas*, behind another person: *montar a ancas*, to ride behind another person. || *Ancas de rana*, frogs' legs.
ancestral adj. Ancestral.
ancianidad f. Old age.
anciano, na adj. Old, elderly, aged (de edad).
— M. Old *o* elderly man. || REL. Elder. || — F. Old *o* elderly lady. || — Pl. Old men, old ladies, old people.

— OBSERV. *Anciano* is the polite term for *old man*, whilst *viejo* is usually derogatory.

ancla f. MAR. Anchor. || — FIG. *Ancla de salvación*, last hope, sheet anchor. || MAR. *Echar anclas*, to cast anchor, to anchor. | *Levar anclas*, to weigh anchor.
ancladero m. MAR. Anchorage (fondeadero).
anclaje m. MAR. Anchorage (acción de anclar, fondeadero, derechos que se pagan).
anclar v. tr. e intr. To anchor.
anclote m. MAR. Grapnel, small anchor.
ancolía f. BOT. Columbine.
ancón m. o **anconada** f. MAR. Cove, inlet, small bay (bahía pequeña). || *Amer.* Corner (rincón).
áncora f. MAR. TECN. ARQ. Anchor. || FIG. *Áncora de salvación*, sheet anchor, last hope.
ancoraje m. MAR. Anchorage (acción de anclar, fondeadero, derechos).
ancorar v. intr. MAR. To anchor, to cast anchor.
anchar v. tr. e intr. To widen.
ancho, cha adj. Broad, wide: *una carretera ancha*, a broad road. || Wide, full: *falda ancha*, wide skirt. || Thick (espeso): *una pared ancha*, a thick wall. || Too wide (demasiado grande): *esta mesa es ancha para la habitación*, this table is too wide for the room. || Big, large: *el abrigo te está ancho*, the overcoat is big for you; *el piso nos viene ancho*, the flat is big for us. || FIG. Relieved: *se quedó ancho después de acabar el trabajo*, he was relieved after finishing the work. | Satisfied with o.s., smug, self-satisfied (satisfecho). || — *A lo largo y a lo ancho*, lengthwise and breadthwise. || FIG. *A mis, a tus, a sus anchas*, at ease, comfortable. | FIG. *Ancha es Castilla*, everything is yours, the future is yours. | *La independencia viene un poco ancha al país*, the country is not yet ready for independance. | *Le viene un poco ancho su cargo*, his job is too much for him. | *Ponerse a sus anchas*, to make o.s. comfortable, to make o.s. at home. | *Quedarse tan ancho*, to behave as if nothing had happened. || *Ser ancho de espaldas*, to be broad-shouldered, to have broad shoulders. || FIG. *Tener la conciencia ancha*, not to be overscrupulous. | *Tener miras anchas* or *tener la manga ancha*, to be broad-minded.
— M. Width, breadth (anchura): *el ancho de la acera*, the width of the pavement; *estos dos objetos tienen lo mismo de ancho*, these two objects are the same width. || Width: *una falda plegada necesita tres anchos*, a pleated skirt takes three widths. || Gauge (ferrocarril): *el ancho de vía*, the gauge of the rails. || — *Tener menos ancho que*, to be narrower than. || *Tener un metro de ancho*, to be one metre wide.
anchoa f. Anchovy (pescado).
— OBSERV. "Anchovy" can be translated two ways: *boquerón* is used for the live or fresh fish an *anchoa* for the salted fish packed in tins.
anchova o **anchoveta** f. Anchovy (pez).
anchura f. Width, breadth (dimensión): *la anchura de un libro*, the width of a book; *la anchura de un río*, the width of a river. || Measurement (medida): *anchura de pecho, de cintura*, chest, waist measurement. || Fullness: *la anchura de una falda*, the fullness of a skirt. || FIG. Cheek (frescura). || IMPR. Justification. || — *A mis anchuras*, at ease, comfortable. || FIG. *Anchura de miras*, broad-mindedness.
anchuroso, sa adj. Wide, large: *un campo anchuroso*, a large field. || Spacious: *una habitación anchurosa*, a spacious room.
anda f. *Amer.* Stretcher (para enfermos). | Bier (féretro). | Portable platform (para una imagen).
andada f. *Amer.* Long walk (caminata). || — Pl. Tracks (huellas). || — FIG. *Cuéntame tus andadas por Londres*, tell me what you've been up to in London. | *Volver a las andadas*, to fall back into one's old ways *o* habits, to revert to one's old habits *o* ways (reincidir en un vicio).
andaderas f. pl. Baby walker, *sing.* (para niños).
andadero, ra adj. Passable (camino, terreno). || Wandering (andador).
andado, da adj. Busy: *calle andada*, busy street. || Ordinary, everyday, common (corriente). || Worn, threadbare (vestidos).
andador, ra adj. Good at walking (capaz de andar mucho). || Who walks quickly, quick, fast-walking (veloz). || Fond of wandering about, wandering (andariego).
— M. y F. Good walker (que anda mucho). || Quick *o* fast walker (veloz). || Wanderer (andariego). || — M. Baby walker (andaderas). || (P.us.). Messenger (recadero). | Path (senda). || — Pl. Reins, harness, *sing.* (de niño). || FIG. *Ese chico no necesita andadores*, that boy can look after himself.
andadura f. Walking (acción). || Walk, gait (manera de andar). || Pace, gait (del caballo). || *Paso de andadura*, amble.
Andalucía n. pr. f. Andalusia.
andalucismo m. Andalusian word *o* expression (expresión). || Andalusian way of speaking (modo de hablar). || Love of things typical of Andalusia (amor a lo andaluz).
andaluz, za adj./s. Andalusian.
andaluzada f. FAM. Tall story: *decir andaluzadas*, to tell tall stories.
andaluzarse v. pr. To become Andalusian.
andamiaje m. TECN. Scaffolding.
andamio m. TECN. Scaffold. || Stage, platform (tablado). || — Pl. Scaffolding, *sing*: *andamios suspendidos* or *colgantes*, hanging scaffolding. || FAM. *Flor de andamio*, old rope, bad tobacco, third-rate tobacco.
andana f. Row, line (hilera). || FAM. *Llamarse andana*, to go back on one's word, to break a promise (no cumplir su promesa), to wash one's hands of the matter (hacerse el desentendido).
andanada f. Broadside (descarga): *soltar una andanada*, to fire a broadside. || FAM. Scolding, telling off (reprimenda). | Shower: *una andanada de injurias*, a shower of insults. || Covered stand (gradería). || FAM. *Soltarle a uno una andanada*, to give s.o. a rocket *o* a tongue-lashing (echar una bronca).
andancia f. o **andancio** m. *Amer.* Mild epidemic (epidemia). || — Pl. *Amer.* Adventures (andanzas).
¡andandito! o **¡andando!** interj. FAM. Come on!, let's go!, let's get a move on!
andante adv./s. m. MÚS. Andante. || Errant: *caballero andante*, knight-errant.
andantino adv./s. m. MÚS. Andantino.
andanza f. Adventure: *a su regreso de América me contó todas sus andanzas*, on his return from America he told me all about his adventures. || Event, occurrence (suceso). || Luck, fortune: *buena, mala andanza*, good, bad luck. || *Amer.* *Volver a las andanzas*, v. ANDADA.
andar* v. intr. To walk: *andar de prisa*, to walk quickly: *andar a gatas, con las manos*, to walk on all fours, on one's hands. || To move: *los planetas andan*, the planets move; *los peces andan por el mar*, fish move about the sea. || To go, to work, to function: *mi reloj anda bien*, my watch works well. || To go: *el negocio anda mal estos días*, business is going badly these days. || To be: *anda alguien por el jardín*, there is s.o. in the garden; *anda un poco malo estos días*, he is not very well these days; *anda tras un empleo*, he's after a job; *¿dónde andan mis guantes? — Por ahí andarán*, where are my gloves? — They will be over there somewhere; *¿estás leyendo mi libro?, ¿por dónde andas?*, are you reading my book?, where are you up to?; *ando muy ocupado*, I am very busy; *ando escaso de dinero*, I am short of money. || To be (con el gerundio): *andaba escribiendo*, he was writing. || To pass (el tiempo). || — *¡Anda!*, come on! (para animar), go on!, get away with you! (desconfianza), my word! (admiración), come on now (para rechazar): *¡anda, déjame en paz!*, come on now, leave me alone!; so there! (triunfo): *me han puesto mejor nota que a ti, ¡anda!*, they've given me a better mark than you, so there!; what! (sorpresa): *¡anda!, si estás tú aquí!*, what, you're here! || *¡Anda, anda!*, don't be silly! || *Andar a*, to go on, to ride: *andar a caballo*, to go on horseback, to ride a horse. || *Andar a golpes*, to fight, to come to blows. || *Andar a gusto*, to be comfortable. || *Andar a la greña*, to tear each other's hair out. || *Andar a la que salta*, to live from day to day. || *Andar bien de salud*, to be in good health. || *Andar como alma en pena*, to wander about like a lost soul. || *Andar con*, to be (con adjetivo en inglés): *andar con miedo*, to be afraid; *andar con cuidado* or *con ojo*, to be careful; to mess about with, to play about with: *andar con pólvora*, to mess about with gunpowder; to wear, to have on: *andar con traje nuevo*, to have a new suit on; to have: *andar con ojos enrojecidos*, to have red eyes. || FIG. *Andar con cumplidos*, to stand on ceremony. | *Andar con pies de plomo*, to tread carefully. | *Andar con rodeos*, to beat about the bush. | *Andar con secreteos*, to be secretive. || *Andar de acá para allá*, to wander about *o* from place to place. || FIG. *Andar de cabeza*, to be in a flurry *o* a fluster *o* a tizzy. | *Andar de Herodes a Pilato*, to fall out of the frying pan into the fire. || *Andar de puntillas*, to tiptoe, to walk on tiptoe. || *Andar en*, to rummage in: *andar en un cajón*, to rummage in a drawer; to be mixed up in: *andar en negocios raros*, to be mixed up in strange business; to be almost *o* nearly: *andar en los treinta años*, to be almost thirty. || FIG. *Andar en dimes y diretes*, to bicker. | *Andar en boca de todos* or *en lenguas*, to be on everyone's lips, to be the talk of the town. | *Andar en tratos*, to be negotiating, to be in negotiations. | *Andar mal de la cabeza*, not to be right in the head. | *Andar por*, to be about: *andar por los siete años*, to be about seven. | *Andar por las nubes*, to have one's

head in the clouds. || *Andar tras*, to be after (desear *o* perseguir). | Fig. *Ande yo caliente, ríase la gente*, I'm all right Jack. | *A todo* or *a más andar*, at full speed. | *¿Cómo anda eso?*, how are things going? | *¿Cómo andamos de dinero, de tiempo?*, how are we [off] for money, for time? | *Dime con quién andas y te diré quién eres*, a man is known by the company he keeps. || *Ir andando*, to go on foot, to walk || Fig. *Más viejo que andar a pie* or *para adelante*, as old as the hills. | *No andar por las nubes*, to have one's feet firmly planted on the ground. | *Quien mal anda, mal acaba*, those who fall into bad ways will come to a bad end. | *¡Vamos, anda!*, come on, hurry up! (date prisa), come on, do something! (haz algo) come now!, go on!, come off it! (incredulidad).

— V. tr. To walk (a pie): *andar diez millas en un día*, to walk ten miles in a day. || To cover, to travel, to go (recorrer): *andar tres kilómetros*, to cover three kilometres. || To travel, to go along (un camino).

— V. pr. To leave, to go away (marcharse). || — Fig. *Andarse con* or *en*, to be mixed up in: *siempre te andas en negocios raros*, you are always mixed up in strange business; to use: *siempre se anda con los mismos cuentos*, he always uses the same stories; *andarse con paños calientes*, to use half measures. | *Andarse con bromas*, to joke, to make jokes. | *Andarse por las ramas* or *por las márgenes*, to beat about the bush. | *Dejar los años que se anduvo a gatas*, to leave one's childhood behind. | *No andarse con chiquitas*, v. CHIQUITO. | *No andarse con rodeos*, not to beat about the bush, to get straight to the point. | *Todo se andará*, all in good time, everything comes to him who waits.

andar m. Walk, gait (acción). || — Pl. Walk, *sing.*, gait, *sing.*: *con sus andares femeninos*, with her feminine walk.

andariego, ga adj. Fond of walking, good at walking (que anda mucho). || Fond of gadding about, fond of wandering (callejero). || Wandering, roving, roaming (errante).

— M. y f. Good walker (de mucho andar). || Gadabout (callejero). || Wanderer, rover, roamer (errante).

andarín, ina adj. Good at walking.

— M. y f. Good walker. || — F. Zool. Swallow (golondrina).

andarivel m. Cable ferry (en un río). || Mar. Lifeline (pasamanos). || *Amer.* Ferryboat (barco).

andas f. pl. Stretcher, *sing.* (para enfermos). || Bier, *sing.* (féretro). || Portable platform, *sing.* (para una imagen).

andén m. Platform (de estación). || Side, side of the road (de carretera). || Hard shoulder (de autopista). || Shelf (anaquel). || Quayside (muelle). || *Amer.* Footpath, pavement [U.S., sidewalk] (acera).

Andes n. pr. m. pl. Geogr. Andes.

andesita f. Andesite.

andinismo m. *Amer.* Mountaineering [in the Andes].

andinista m. y f. *Amer.* Mountaineer [in the Andes].

andino, na adj. Andean.

andolina f. Zool. Swallow (golondrina).

andorga f. Fam. Belly (barriga).

andorina f. Zool. Swallow (golondrina).

Andorra n. pr. f. Geogr. Andorra.

andorrano, na adj./s. Andorran.

andrajo m. Rag, tatter: *ir vestido de andrajos*, to be dressed in rags. || Fig. Rag (cosa de poco valor). || — *Estar hecho un andrajo*, to be in rags (cosa), to be in rags and tatters (persona). || Fig. *Ser un andrajo humano*, to be a [physical] wreck.

andrajoso, sa adj. Ragged, tattered.

Andrés n. pr. m. Andrew.

Andrinópolis n. pr. Geogr. Adrianople.

androceo m. Bot. Androecium.

andrógeno m. Biol. Androgen.

andrógino, na adj. Biol. Androgynous, androgyne.

— M. y f. Biol. Androgyne.

androide m. Android.

Andrómaca n. pr. f. Andromache.

Andrómeda n. pr. f. Astr. Andromeda.

andrómina f. Fam. Tall story, tale, fib (embuste).

andullo m. Rolled tobacco-leaf (hoja de tabaco). || Plug (para masticar). || Mar. Fender.

andurriales m. pl. Fam. Out-of-the-way place, *sing.*, parts: *¿qué haces por estos andurriales?*, what are you doing in this out-of-the-way place?

anea f. Bot. Cat's-tail, reed mace, bulrush. || *Silla de anea*, rush-bottomed chair.

anécdota f. Anecdote.

anecdotario m. Collection of anecdotes.

anecdótico, ca adj. Anecdotal, anecdotic, anecdotical.

anecdotista m. y f. Anecdotist.

anegable adj. Subject to flooding.

anegación f. Flooding.

anegadizo, za adj. Subject to flooding: *terreno anegadizo*, land subject to flooding.

anegamiento m. Flooding.

anegar v. tr. To flood: *anegar un campo*, to flood a field. || To drown (ahogar). || *Anegado en sangre*, bathed in blood.

— V. pr. To drown. || To flood (inundarse). || Mar. To sink (un navío). || — *Anegarse en llanto*, to fill with tears (los ojos), to be bathed in tears (el rostro), to dissolve into tears (una persona).

anejar v. tr. To annex (un territorio). || To annex, to append (un documento).

anejo, ja adj. Dependent, attached. || — *Anejo a*, joined to, attached to: *edificio anejo a la fábrica*, building attached to the factory. || *Edificios anejos*, outbuildings. || *Escuela aneja*, school annex.

— M. Annex, annexe (edificio). || Dependency (parroquia dependiente de otra). || Annex, annexe, appendix (de un texto).

anélido m. Zool. Annelid, annelide.

anemia f. Med. Anaemia, anemia.

anemiante adj. Debilitating: *un clima anemiante*, a debilitating climate.

anémico, ca adj. Anaemic, anemic.

— M. y f. Anaemia sufferer.

anemófilo, la adj. Bot. Anemophilous.

anemógrafo m. Fís. Anemograph.

anemometría f. Fís. Anemometry.

anemómetro m. Fís. Anemometer.

anémona o **anemone** f. Bot. Anemone (planta). || *Anémona de mar*, sea anemone (actinia).

aneroide adj. Fís. Aneroid (barómetro).

anestesia f. Med. Anaesthesia [U.S., anesthesia]: *anestesia local*, local anaesthesia.

anestesiar v. tr. Med. To anaesthetize [U.S., to anesthetize], to give an anaesthetic to.

anestésico, ca adj./s. m. Med. Anaesthetic [U.S., anesthetic].

anestesista m. y f. Anaesthetist [U.S., anesthetist].

aneurisma m. Med. Aneurysm, aneurism.

anexar v. tr. To annex (un territorio). || To annex, to append (un documento).

anexidades f. pl. Jur. Annexes, appurtenances.

anexión f. Annexation.

anexionar v. tr. To annex.

anexionismo m. Annexationism, annexionism.

anexionista adj./s. Annexationist, annexionist.

anexo, xa adj. Dependent, annexed, attached (edificio). || Attached (documento). || *Anexo a*, joined to, attached to.

— M. Annex, annexe: *el anexo de un hotel*, a hotel annex. || Annex, annexe, appendix (documento). || — Pl. Anat. Adnexa.

anfibio, bia adj. Amphibious (que vive dentro y fuera del agua). || Amphibian (vehículo).

— M. Amphibian. || — Pl. Zool. Amphibia.

anfíbol m. Min. Amphibole.

anfibolita f. Min. Amphibolite.

anfibología f. Amphibology (ambigüedad).

anfibológico, ca adj. Amphibological.

anfictión m. Hist. Amphictyon (diputado griego).

anfictionía f. Hist. Amphictyony.

anfioxo m. Zool. Amphioxus.

anfisbena f. Zool. Amphisbaena.

anfiscios m. pl. Amphiscians.

anfiteatro m. Amphitheatre [U.S., amphitheater]. || Lecture theatre (de una universidad). || Teatr. Gallery. || *Anfiteatro anatómico*, dissecting room.

Anfitrión n. pr. m. Amphitryon.

anfitrión, ona m. y f. Host, hostess.

Anfitrite n. pr. f. Mit. Amphitrite.

ánfora f. Amphora (cántaro).

anfractuosidad f. Roughness, cragginess (desigualdad). || Twisting, turning, winding (cualidad de torcido). || Anat. Anfractuosity, convolution, fold. || — Pl. Roughness, *sing.*, cragginess, *sing.*: *las anfractuosidades de las montañas*, the roughness of the mountains. || Twisting, *sing.*, turning, *sing.*, winding, *sing.*: *las anfractuosidades de la carretera*, the twisting of the road.

anfractuoso, sa adj. Rough, craggy (desigual). || Twisting, winding, anfractuous (torcido).

angaria f. Angaria.

angarillas f. pl. Stretcher, *sing.* (para enfermos). || Portable platform, *sing.* (para llevar imágenes). || Handbarrow, *sing.* (para piedras). || Panniers (de las caballerías). || Cruet set, *sing.* (vinagreras).

ángel m. Angel: *ángel de la guarda* or *ángel custodio*, guardian angel. || Fig. Charm (encanto). || — *Angel caído*, fallen angel. || *Angel malo* or *de las tinieblas*, Devil. || *Bueno como un ángel*, as good as gold, like a little angel. || *Cantar como los ángeles*, to sing like an angel. || *No tener ángel* or *tener mal ángel*, to be dull, to have no charm. || *Salto del ángel*, swallow dive. || *Ser como un ángel*, to be extemely good-looking (hermoso), to be as good as gold, to be a little angel (bueno). || *Tener ángel*, to have charm, to be charming.

angélica f. Bot. Angelica.

angelical adj. Angelic, angelical: *mirada angelical*, angelic look.

angélico, ca adj. Angelic, angelical. || Rel. *La salutación angélica*, the Hail Mary.

— M. Little angel, cherub.

angelito m. Little angel, cherub. || Fig. y Fam. *Estar con los angelitos*, to be miles away, to be asleep (estar distraído).

angelote m. Angel (estatua). || Fig. y Fam. Chubby child (niño gordinflón). | Good type, good sort, decent sort (persona sencilla). || Zool. Angelfish (pez). || Bot. Type of clover.

Angelus m. Angelus.

angevino, na adj./s. Angevin, Angevine.

angina f. MED. Angina. || — *Angina de pecho*, angina pectoris. || *Angina diftérica*, diptheria.
anginoso, sa adj. MED. Anginous.
angiografía f. MED. Angiography.
angiología f. MED. Angiology.
angioma m. MED. Angioma.
angiospermas f. pl. BOT. Angiospermae.
angiospermo, ma adj. BOT. Angiospermous.
anglesita f. MIN. Anglesite.
anglicanismo m. REL. Anglicanism.
anglicanizar v. tr. To anglicize.
anglicano, na adj./s. REL. Anglican. || *La Iglesia Anglicana*, the Anglican Church, the Church of England.
anglicismo m. Anglicism (giro inglés).
anglicista m. y f. Anglicist.
anglo, gla adj. Anglian.
— M. y f. Angle, Anglian.
angloamericano, na adj./s. Anglo-American. || American (de los Estados Unidos).
angloárabe adj. Anglo-Arabian.
— M. y f. Anglo-Arab.
anglofilia f. Anglophilia.
anglófilo, la adj./s. Anglophile, Anglophil.
anglofobia f. Anglophobia.
anglófobo, ba adj./s. Anglophobe.
anglomanía f. Anglomania.
anglómano, na adj. Anglomaniacal.
— M. y f. Anglomaniac.
anglonormando, da adj./s. Anglo-Norman. || *Las Islas Anglonormandas*, the Channel Islands.
anglosajón, ona adj./s. Anglo-Saxon.
angolés, esa adj./s. Angolese.
Angora n. pr. HIST. Angora (Ankara). || *Gato, cabra de Angora*, Angora cat, goat.
angostar v. tr. To narrow.
— V. pr. To narrow: *allí el camino se angosta*, the road narrows there.
angosto, ta adj. Narrow.
angostura f. Narrowness (estrechez). || Narrow part (parte estrecha). || GEOGR. Narrow pass (entre montañas). | Narrows, *pl.* (de un río). || BOT. Angostura.
angra f. MAR. Creek, cove (ensenada).
angrelado, da adj. HERÁLD. Engrailed.
angström m. FÍS. Angstrom (unidad de longitud de onda).
anguila f. ZOOL. Eel (pez). || — Pl. MAR. Slipway, *sing.* (maderos). || — *Anguila de cabo*, whip (rebenque). || ZOOL. *Anguila de mar*, conger eel (pez).
anguilazo m. Whiplash, lash of a whip (latigazo).
anguílula f. ZOOL. Anguillule, vinegar eel.
anguina f. ZOOL. Inguinal vein.
angula f. Elver (cría de anguila).
angulado, da adj. Angular.
angular adj. Angular. || — FOT. *Objetivo gran angular*, wide-angle lens. || *Piedra angular*, cornerstone.
— M. TECN. Angle iron.
angularidad f. Angularity.
ángulo m. Angle: *ángulo recto, agudo*, right, acute angle; *ángulo interno, externo*, internal, external angle. || Corner (rincón, esquina). || Bend (curva). || TECN. Angle iron (angular). || — ANAT. *Ángulo facial*, facial angle. || FIG. *Desde este ángulo*, from this angle. || *En* or *de ángulo recto*, right-angled. || *Estar en ángulo*, to be at an angle. || *Formar ángulo con*, to be at an angle to. || *Formar un ángulo de 10°*, to be at 10°.
anguloso, sa adj. Angular: *cara angulosa*, angular face. || Twisting, winding: *camino anguloso*, winding road.
angurria f. MED. y FAM. Strangury. || *Amer.* FAM. Starvation, hunger (hambre). | Miserliness, stinginess (avaricia).
angurriento, ta adj. *Amer.* FAM. Gluttonish, gluttonous, greedy (glotón). | Miserly, stingy (avaro).
angustia f. Anguish, distress: *vivir en la angustia*, to live in anguish. || FIL. Anguish. || Anguish (malestar físico). || — Pl. Throes, pangs, agonies: *angustias de la muerte*, death throes. || — *Angustia vital*, anxiety. || *Dar angustia a*, to trouble, to distress, to worry, to grieve: *me da angustia verlo tan enfermo*, it troubles me to see him so ill; to make ill: *me da angustia presenciar una operación*, it makes me ill to see an operation.
angustiadamente adv. Distressedly, with anguish.
angustiado, da adj. Anguished, distressed: *están angustiados con la desaparición de su hijo*, they are distressed by the disappearance of their son. || Narrow (estrecho). || Miserable, wretched (apocado). || Worried, anxious (preocupado): *a finales de mes está siempre angustiado porque no le queda dinero*, he's always worried at the end of the month because he has no money left.
angustiar v. tr. To distress, to anguish. || To worry (inquietar).
— V. pr. To become distressed. || To worry, to get anxious (inquietarse).
Angustias n. pr. f. Angustias.
— OBSERV. This name is derived from *María de las Angustias*, and has no English equivalent.
angustiosamente adv. With anguish, in an anguished way (con angustia). || In a distressing way, distressingly (causando angustia). || Anxiously (con preocupación).
angustioso, sa adj. Distressing: *una situación angustiosa*, a distressing situation. || Agonizing: *es angustioso esperar el resultado de los exámenes*, it is agonizing waiting for exam results. || Anguished, distressed (angustiado): *con voz angustiosa*, in a distressed voice. || *Un momento angustioso*, a moment of anguish, a moment's anguish.
angustura f. BOT. Angostura.
anhelante adj. Panting, out of breath, gasping: *estar anhelante*, to be out of breath. || Longing, eager, yearning (deseoso). || *Esperar anhelante una cosa*, to long for *o* to yearn for sth.
anhelar v. intr. To pant, to gasp. || FIG. *Anhelar por algo*, to long for sth.
— V. tr. FIG. To long for, to yearn for: *anhelo su regreso*, I am longing for his return. || To long, to yearn (con infinitivo): *anhela vivir en el campo*, he longs to live in the country. || To aspire to, to crave: *anhelar la gloria, dignidades*, to aspire to glory, honours.
anhelo m. (P.us.). Panting, gasping. || FIG. Yearning, longing, craving (deseo). || — Pl. Aspirations: *sus anhelos de gloria*, his aspirations to glory. || Yearning, *sing.*, craving, *sing.*, longing, *sing.* (deseos).
anheloso, sa adj. Panting, gasping (persona). || Laboured (respiración). || FIG. Longing, eager, yearning (deseoso).
anhídrido m. QUÍM. Anhydride.
anhidrita f. MIN. Anhydrite.
anhidro, dra adj. QUÍM. Anhydrous.
Aníbal n. pr. m. Hannibal.
anidar v. intr. To nest, to make one's nest: *el águila anida en los altos peñascos*, the eagle nests on high rocks, the eagle makes its nest on high rocks. || FIG. *El odio anida en su alma*, his soul is filled with hate.
— V. tr. FIG. To take in, to shelter (acoger).
— V. pr. To nest, to make one's nest (las aves). || FIG. *No dejes que la avaricia se anide en tu alma*, harbour *o* nurture no avarice in your bosom, drive all avarice from your soul.
anilina f. QUÍM. Aniline, anilin.
anilla f. Ring. || Curtain ring (de cortinas). || Ring (de un ave). || — Pl. Rings (de gimnasia).
anillado, da adj. ZOOL. Annelid (gusano). || Ringed (ave). || Ring-like, annular (en forma de anillo). || Curly (pelo).
— M. y f. ZOOL. Annelid.
anillar v. tr. To ring, to put rings on (poner anillas). || To fasten with a ring, to ring (sujetar). || To make into a ring (dar forma de anillo). || To ring (poner anillas a las aves).
anillo m. Ring: *anillo de boda*, wedding ring; *los anillos de Saturno*, the rings of Saturn; *anillo de pedida* or *de compromiso* or *de comprometida*, engagement ring. || ARQ. Annulet (de una columna). | Circular base (de cúpula). || ZOOL. Annulus: *los anillos de un gusano*, the annuli of a worm. | Coil: *los anillos de la culebra*, the coils of a snake. || HERÁLD. Annulet. || TAUR. Bullring, ring (redondel). || BOT. Ring (de los árboles). || — *Anillo pastoral*, bishop's ring. || *Sentar como anillo al dedo*, v. SENTAR. || *Viene como anillo al dedo*, it's just what the doctor ordered (adecuado), it's come just at the right time (oportuno).
ánima f. Soul [in Purgatory]. || Bore (de un cañón). || — Pl. Evening bell (campana). || *Ánima bendita*, soul in Purgatory.
animación f. Animation (acción y efecto de animar). || Life, vivacity (de una persona): *tener mucha animación*, to be full of life. || Liveliness: *la animación de una discusión*, the liveliness of an argument. || Life (de un cuadro). || Movement, bustle, life, activity: *había mucha animación en la calle*, there was a lot of activity in the street. || Activity: *ha habido mucha animación en la Bolsa*, there has been a lot of activity on the Stock Exchange. || CINEM. Animation. || Starting (de un mecanismo). || *Dar animación a*, to put life into, to enliven, to liven up.
animadamente adv. In a lively way.
animado, da adj. Prompted, moved, animated: *animado de buenas intenciones*, prompted by good intentions. || Busy, lively, bustling: *una calle muy animada*, a very busy street. || Lively, full of life, animated: *la fiesta estuvo muy animada*, the party was very lively; *una persona muy animada*, a very lively person, a person full of life. || Encouraged, inspired: *animado por sus primeros éxitos, siguió cantando*, encouraged by his first successes, he continued to sing. || On form, in high spirits: *hoy no estoy nada animado*, I'm not at all on form today. || Animate: *seres animados*, animate beings. || *Dibujos animados*, [animated] cartoons.
animador, ra adj. Encouraging, inspiring: *noticia animadora*, encouraging news.
— M. y f. Entertainer [in bar, café, etc.]. || Compère (presentador), hostess (presentadora).
animadversión f. Ill will: *tener animadversión hacia alguien*, to bear s.o. ill will.
animal adj. Animal: *el reino animal*, the animal kingdom. || FIG. y FAM. Rough, brutish: *es tan animal que lo rompe todo*, he is so rough that he breaks everything. || Stupid, daft (estúpido).
— M. Animal: *animales domésticos*, domestic animals; *animal de asta* or *cornudo*, horned animal. || FIG. Blockhead, fool, dunce (persona estúpida). | Brute, lout, animal, beast (persona tosca en sus maneras). || — *Animal de bellota*, pig (cerdo), blockhead, fool,

dunce (persona estúpida). || *Animal de carga*, pack animal, beast of burden. || *Animales vivos*, animals on the hoof. || *Animal salvaje*, wild animal. || FIG. *Comer como un animal*, to eat like a horse. | *Es un animal*, he's as strong as an ox (persona robusta).

animalada f. FAM. Stupid thing, piece of nonsense (burrada). | Piece of coarse language (grosería). | Disgrace (conducta): *el bombardeo fue una animalada*, the bombing was a disgrace. | Piece of gluttonous behaviour (gula). || — FAM. *Decir animaladas*, to speak *o* to talk nonsense, to speak *o* to talk rubbish (tonterías), to be crude, to be vulgar (groserías). | *¡Qué animalada comerse dos pollos enteros!*, what a pig, eating two whole chickens! | *¡Qué animalada haber venido andando desde tan lejos!*, fancy walking all that way!

animálculo m. ZOOL. Animalcule.

animalejo m. Nasty animal, creepy-crawly.

animalidad f. Animality.

animalismo m. Animalism.

animalista adj./s. Animalist (pintor o escultor de animales).

animalizar v. tr. To animalize.
— V. pr. To become animalized. || FIG. To become brutish.

animalucho m. Nasty beast (repugnante). || Creepy-crawly (pequeño).

animar v. tr. To animate, to give life to: *el alma anima al cuerpo*, the soul animates the body. || To encourage: *animar a los soldados al combate*, to encourage the soldiers to fight; *no animo a nadie a seguir mi ejemplo*, I encourage no one to follow my example. || To liven up, to put life into, to enliven (la conversación, la reunión, etc.). || To brighten up, to liven up: *para animar las calles han puesto guirnaldas*, they've put up garlands to brighten up the streets. || To cheer up, to buck up (fam.): *estaba muy decaído pero conseguí animarle*, he was very depressed but I managed to cheer him up. || To give new life to: *una mano de pintura animará este cuarto*, a coat of paint will give new life to this room. || To move, to prompt, to activate, to inspire (mover): *no le anima ningún deseo de riqueza*, he is not prompted by any desire for riches. || To intensify (dar intensidad).
— V. pr. To pluck up courage, to regain courage, to take heart (cobrar ánimo). || To brighten up, to light up: *sus ojos se animan cuando habla*, his eyes brighten up when he speaks. || To liven up, to get livelier (conversación, reunión, etc.). || To cheer up, to liven up: *cuando ha tomado unas copas siempre se anima*, when he's had a few drinks he always cheers up. || To make up one's mind, to decide (decidirse): *al final me animé y me fui de excursión*, in the end I made up my mind and went on a trip. || — *¡Anímate!*, cheer up! (para dar ánimo), make up your mind! (¡decídete!). || *¿Te animas?*, are you game? || *¿Te animas a dar un paseo?*, do you fancy going out for a stroll?

anímico, ca adj. Psychic.

animismo m. Animism.

animista adj. Animistic.
— M. y f. Animist.

ánimo m. Soul (alma). || Spirit (espíritu). || Spirit, heart: *hombre de ánimo valiente*, man with a brave heart. || Mind: *quiero grabar esto en el ánimo de todos*, I want to fix this in everyone's mind. || Intention: *mi ánimo no es hacerte daño*, it is not my intention to hurt you. || FIG. Courage (valor): *cobrar ánimo*, to pluck up courage; *recobrar ánimo*, to pluck up courage again. || — *¡Ánimo!*, come on! || *Con ánimo de*, in *o* with the intention of. || *Dar ánimos a*, to encourage, to give encouragement to. || *Está en mi ánimo vender el coche* o *tengo el ánimo de vender el coche* o *mi ánimo es vender el coche*, I intend to sell the car, it is my intention to sell the car. || *Estado de ánimo*, state of mind, mood, spirits, *pl.*: *estoy en buen estado de ánimo*, I'm in a good mood, I'm in good spirits. || *Estar sin ánimo*, to be in low spirits. || *Hacerse el ánimo*, to get used to the idea: *tengo que hacerme el ánimo de que se ha ido*, I must get used to the idea that he has left. || *Levantar el ánimo*, to cheer up, to buck up. || *Presencia de ánimo*, presence of mind. || *Tener ánimos de* o *estar con ánimos de* o *sentirse con ánimos de hacer algo*, to feel like doing sth., to be in the mood for doing sth. || *Tener muchos ánimos*, to have a lot of spirit: *a pesar de sus años tiene muchos ánimos*, in spite of his age he has a lot of spirit.

animosidad f. Animosity, enmity (antipatía).

animoso, sa adj. Brave, daring, spirited: *animoso en la lucha*, brave in battle. || Determined (decidido).

aniñadamente adv. Childishly.

aniñado, da adj. Childlike: *una cara aniñada*, a childlike face. || Childish: *comportamiento aniñado*, childish behaviour.

aniñarse v. pr. To become childish.

anión m. FÍS. Anion.

aniquilable adj. Annihilable, destroyable.

aniquilación f. Annihilation, destruction.

aniquilador, ra adj. Annihilating, destructive.

aniquilamiento m. Annihilation, destruction.

aniquilar v. tr. To annihilate, to destroy, to wipe out: *el ejército enemigo fue aniquilado*, the enemy army was wiped out. || To destroy, to ruin (acabar con): *esto aniquila todas mis esperanzas*, this destroys all my hopes; *este trabajo aniquilará tu salud*, this work will ruin your health. || To crush, to defeat (en una discusión). || To overwhelm, to overcome (anonadar).
— V. pr. To deteriorate (la salud). || To vanish, to disappear (la fortuna).

anís m. BOT. Anise (planta): *anís estrellado*, star anise. | Aniseed (grano). || Aniseed balls, *pl.* (confite). || Aniseed oil (esencia). || Anisette (licor). || FIG. y FAM. *No ser grano de anís*, to be no small matter, to be no trifle.

anisado, da adj. Flavoured with aniseed.
— M. Anisette (licor).

anisar v. tr. To flavour with aniseed.

anisete m. Anisette.

anisófilo, la adj. BOT. Anisophyllous.

anisopétalo, la adj. BOT. Anisopetalous.

anisotropía f. Anisotropy.

anisótropo, pa adj. Anisotropic.

Anita n. pr. f. Annie.

aniversario, ria adj./s. m. Anniversary: *el primer aniversario del final de la guerra*, the first anniversary of the end of the war. || Anniversary of [s.o.'s] death: *hoy es el décimo aniversario de su padre*, today is the tenth anniversary of his father's death. || *Aniversario de boda*, wedding anniversary.

Ankara n. pr. f. GEOGR. Ankara.

ano m. ANAT. Anus.

anoche adv. Last night, yesterday evening: *anoche fui al teatro*, yesterday evening I went to the theatre. || Last night: *anoche no pude dormir*, I couldn't sleep last night. || *Antes de anoche*, the night before last.

anochecedor, ra adj. Fond of *o* in the habit of going to bed late.
— M. y f. Late bird, night owl.

anochecer* v. impers. To get dark: *anochece*, it's getting dark. || — *Anocheció despejado*, the sky was clear at nightfall *o* at dusk, the sky was clear when it got dark. || *Cuando anochezca*, at nightfall, at dusk. || *Me anocheció mientras estaba buscando su casa*, night fell while I was looking for his house.
— V. intr. To be at nightfall, to be at dusk (estar): *anocheció en París*, he was in Paris at nightfall. || To arrive at nightfall *o* at dusk (llegar): *anochecí en Londres*, I arrived in London at dusk.

anochecer m. o **anochecida** f. Nightfall, dusk: *al anocheoer*, at nightfall.

anochecido adv. Night, dark: *era ya anochecido y no pudo distinguir el número de la casa*, it was already dark and he couldn't make out the number of the house.

anódico, ca adj. FÍS. Anodic.

anodinia f. MED. Anodynia.

anodino, na adj. MED. Anodyne. || Insignificant, insubstantial (insubstancial). || Uninteresting, anodyne (sin interés): *una película anodina*, an anodyne film.
— M. Anodyne (medicina).

ánodo m. FÍS. Anode.

anodonte m. ZOOL. Anodont, anodon.

anodontia f. MED. Anodontia.

anofeles m. ZOOL. Anopheles (mosquito).

anomalía f. Anomaly.

anómalo, la adj. Anomalous.

anona f. BOT. Anona, annona, soursop (arbusto y fruto).

anonadación f. o **anonadamiento** m. Annihilation, destruction (aniquilación).

anonadar v. tr. To annihilate, to destroy (aniquilar). || To overcome, to overwhelm (apocar): *me anonadó esa noticia*, that news overwhelmed me. || To crush, to defeat (en una discusión, en una lucha). || To astound, to dumbfound, to flabbergast (pasmar).

anonimato m. Anonimity.

anónimo, ma adj. Anonymous: *carta anónima*, anonymous letter; *un admirador anónimo*, an anonymous admirer. || *Sociedad anónima*, limited company [U.S., incorporated company].
— M. Anonimity (anonimato). || Anonymous person (persona). || Anonymous letter (carta). || Anonymous work (obra). || *Conservar* or *guardar el anónimo*, to remain anonymous, to remain nameless.

anorak m. Anorak (chaqueta impermeable).

anorexia f. MED. Anorexy.

anormal adj. Abnormal, irregular (no normal): *una situación anormal*, an irregular situation. || MED. Subnormal (deficiente mentalmente).
— M. y f. Abnormal person. || Subnormal *o* mentally deficient person.

anormalidad f. Abnormality.

anosmia f. Anosmia.

anotación f. Noting, jotting down (acción de apuntar). || Annotation (acción de poner notas). || Note (nota).

anotador, ra adj. Who takes note (que apunta). || Who annotates (que pone anotaciones).
— M. y f. Note taker (que toma apuntes). || Annotator (que pone anotaciones). || — F. CINEM. Continuity girl.

anotar v. tr. To make a note of, to jot down (fam.), to note down (apuntar): *voy a anotar su dirección*, I'm going to make a note of your address. || To put down, to put down the name of, to register: *me han anotado en la lista de candidatos*, they have put me down on the list of candidates, they have put down my name on the list of candidates. || To annotate, to add notes to (poner notas): *anotar un texto*, to annotate a text.

anoxemia f. Anoxemia.
anquilosamiento m. MED. Anchylosis, ankylosis. || FIG. Paralysing, paralysis: *el anquilosamiento de la economía*, the paralysing of the economy.
anquilosar v. tr. To anchylose, to ankylose.
— V. pr. To anchylose. || FIG. To be paralysed: *se está anquilosando la economía*, the economy is being paralysed.
anquilosis f. MED. Anchylosis, ankylosis.
anquilostoma m. ZOOL. Hookworm.
anquilostomiasis f. MED. Anchylostomiasis, ankylostomiasis.
ansa f. HIST. Hanse (confederación).
ánsar m. ZOOL. Goose (oca).
ansarino, na adj. Anserine.
ansarino o **ansarón** m. Gosling (pollo del ánsar).
anseático, ca adj. HIST. Hanseatic: *Liga anseática*, Hanseatic League.
ansí adv. (Ant.). Thus, in this way.
ansia f. Anxiety (ansiedad). || Anguish (angustia). || Longing, yearning: *satisfacer el ansia de libertad*, to satisfy one's longing for freedom. || — Pl. Pangs, throes: *las ansias de la muerte*, death pangs. || Nausea, sing. || — *Con ansia*, longingly. | *Desear con ansia*, to long for, to yearn for. || *Tener ansias*, to feel sick.
ansiar v. tr. To long for, to yearn for: *ansiar la tranquilidad*, to yearn for peace. || — *Ansiar hacer algo*, to long to do sth., to yearn to do sth. || *El día tan ansiado*, the much longed-for day.
ansiedad f. Anxiety, worry (estado de agitación). || Longing, yearning (deseo). || MED. Anxiety.
ansiosamente adv. Longingly, yearningly (anhelosamente). || Anxiously (con inquietud).
ansioso, sa adj. Anxious, worried, uneasy (inquieto). || Eager (deseoso): *ansioso de gloria*, eager for glory. || Greedy (avaricioso): *es muy ansioso y lo quiere todo para él*, he's very greedy and wants everything for himself. || *Estamos ansiosos por saber donde está*, we are anxious *o* eager to know where he is.
anta f. ZOOL. Elk, moose (rumiante). || Menhir (menhir). || ARQ. Anta (pilastra). || *Amer.* ZOOL. Tapir.
antagónico, ca adj. Antagonistic.
antagonismo m. Antagonism.
antagonista adj. Antagonistic, antagonist.
— M. y f. Antagonist.
antaño adv. Last year (el año pasado). || Formerly, in days gone by, in the past (antiguamente). || *Un libro de antaño*, an ancient book (muy antiguo).
antañón, ona adj. Ancient, very old.
antártico, ca o **antárctico, ca** adj./s. m. Antarctic.
Antártida f. GEOGR. Antarctica.
ante m. ZOOL. Elk, moose (ciervo). || Suède [U.S., suede]: *un abrigo de ante*, a suède overcoat. || Bubal, bubale (antílope). || Buff (color). || (Ant.) First course (primer plato). || *Amer.* Cold fruit drink (bebida). | Almond cake (pastel). | Broth made from cereals and honey.
ante prep. In front of, before: *comparecer ante un tribunal*, to appear before the court; *ante él se extendía un paisaje hermoso*, a beautiful landscape stretched out before him. || With regard to: *ante este asunto*, with regard to this question. || Before, in the presence of: *se prosternó ante la reina*, he prostrated himself before the queen. || In the face of (el peligro, el enemigo). || To, in the face of: *se rindió ante mis razones*, he gave way to my reasoning. || Next to, compared with: *ante ella yo soy fea*, I'm ugly compared with her. || — *Ante el juez*, before the judge, in the presence of the judge. || *Ante el temor de que*, for fear that. || *Ante las circunstancias*, under the circumstances. || *Ante los ojos*, before one's eyes. || *Ante notario*, in the presence of the notary. || *Ante tantas posibilidades*, faced with all these possibilities. || *Ante todo*, above all, first of all.
— OBSERV. *Ante* usually indicates an abstract relationship (in the presence of, compared with) as opposed to *delante de*, which indicates a position in space, and to *antes de* which indicates time.
antealtar m. Chancel, choir.
anteanoche adv. The night before last, two nights ago.
anteayer adv. The day before yesterday, two days ago. *le vi anteayer*, I saw him two days ago.
antebrazo m. Forearm.
anteburro m. *Amer.* Tapir.
antecama f. Bedside mat, bedside rug (alfombra).
antecámara f. Antechamber, anteroom, lobby (vestíbulo).
antecambriano, na adj./s. m. GEOL. Precambrian.
antecapilla f. Antechapel.
antecedencia f. Antecedence.
antecedente adj. Antecedent, previous, preceding.
— M. Antecedent: *los antecedentes y las consecuencias*, the antecedents and the consequences. || Cause, antecedent (causa): *los antecedentes del accidente*, the causes of the accident. || Antecedent (matemáticas, gramática, música). || — Pl. History, *sing.*, background, *sing.*: *¿cuáles son sus antecedentes?*, what is his background? || — JUR. *Antecedentes penales*, criminal record: *persona con antecedentes penales*, person with a criminal record. || *Estar en antecedentes*, to be in the picture. || *No tener antecedentes penales*, to have a clean record. || *Poner una persona en antecedentes*, to put s.o. in the picture. || *Tener malos antecedentes*, to have a bad record.
antecedentemente adv. Previously, before, formerly.
anteceder v. tr. e intr. To precede, to go before.
antecesor, ra m. y f. Predecessor: *he sido tu antecesor en este despacho*, I was your predecessor in this office. || Ancestor, forebear, forefather (antepasado).
antecocina f. Scullery, pantry.
antecoro m. ARQ. Antechoir.
antecristo m. Antichrist.
antedata f. JUR. Antedate. || *Poner antedata en una carta*, to put an antedate on a letter, to antedate a letter.
antedatar v. tr. To antedate.
antedecir* v. tr. To predict, to foretell.
antedía adv. Before the appointed day (antes del día previsto). || The day before (la víspera).
antedicho, cha adj. Aforementioned, aforesaid.
antediluviano, na adj. Antediluvian, before the flood. || FIG. Antiquated, antediluvian (muy antiguo).
antefijo m. ARQ. Antefix.
antefirma f. Title of the signatory (título). || Formal ending to a letter (fórmula).
anteiglesia f. Porch.
antelación f. Time in advance, advance. || — *Con antelación*, in advance, beforehand. || *Con antelación a*, before. || *Con cinco días de antelación*, five days in advance *o* beforehand. || *Con la debida antelación*, in due time.
antelina f. Suède [U.S., suede], suède cloth.
antemano (de) loc. adv. In advance, beforehand: *lo preparó de antemano*, he prepared it beforehand.
antemeridiano, na adj. Antemeridian.
ante meridiem loc. lat. Ante meridiem, before noon.
antena f. RAD. Aerial, antenna. || MAR. Lateen yard. || ZOOL. Antenna, feeler. || — *Antena emisora, receptora*, transmitting, receiving aerial. || *Antena interior*, indoor aerial.
antenatal adj. Antenatal, prenatal.
antenombre m. Title [used before the Christian name] (e.g. *san, don*, etc.).
anteojera f. Blinker [U.S., blinder] (de caballo). || Spectacle case (estuche).
anteojero m. Telescope maker (fabricante de telescopios). || Telescope dealer (vendedor). || Spectacle maker, optician (de gafas).
anteojo m. Telescope (telescopio). || — Pl. Opera glasses (gemelos). || Binoculars, field glasses (prismáticos). || Blinkers [U.S., blinders] (de caballo). || Spectacles, glasses (gafas). || — *Anteojo de larga vista*, telescope. || *Serpiente de anteojo*, cobra.
antepalco m. Vestibule of a box [in the theatre].
antepasado, da adj. Before last, previous.
— M. Ancestor, forefather, forebear (ascendiente).
antepatio m. Forecourt.
antepecho m. Handrail, guardrail, parapet (de escalera, de puente, de balcón). || Sill (de ventana). || Narrow balcony, ledge (balcón). || Breast collar (de las caballerías). || MIN. Stratum, layer (banco).
antepenúltimo, ma adj./s. Antepenultimate, last but two.
anteponer* v. tr. To place in front, to put in front. || FIG. To put before: *el chico antepone el deber al interés personal*, the boy puts duty before personal interest.
anteportada f. IMPR. Half title, bastard title.
anteportal m. Porch.
anteposición f. Placing in front, anteposition. || Preference (preferencia).
anteproyecto m. Preliminary plan, draft. || FIG. Blueprint.
antepuerto m. MAR. Outer harbour.
antepuesto, ta adj. Placed in front *o* before. || Put before, preferred (preferido).
Antequera n. pr. GEOGR. Antequera. || *Que salga el sol por Antequera*, come what may.
antequerano, na adj. [From *o* of] Antequera.
— M. y f. Native *o* inhabitant of Antequera.
antera f. BOT. Anther.
anteridia f. BOT. Antheridium.
anterior adj. Front, anterior, fore (pierna, parte). || Previous, before: *el año anterior*, the previous year, the year before; *la página anterior*, the previous page, the page before. || Earlier: *ese éxito fue anterior al que digo*, that success was earlier than the one I'm talking about. || — *Anterior a*, previous to, before, prior to: *el hombre anterior a mí en la lista*, the man before me on the list. || *El nuevo es mejor que el anterior*, the new one is better than the last *o* the previous one.
anterioridad f. Anteriority (de tiempo). || Priority (prioridad). || — *Con anterioridad*, before, formerly, previously (antes), in advance, beforehand (con antelación). || *Con anterioridad a*, prior to.
anteriormente adv. Before, previously (antes): *esto no había ocurrido nunca anteriormente*, this had never happened before. || Beforehand, in advance (con antelación): *su secretaria había ido anteriormente para preparar el despacho*, his secretary had gone beforehand to get the office ready. || *Véase anteriormente*, see above.
antes adv. Before: *cuatro días antes*, four days before; *antes que llegue*, before I arrive; *antes todo era distinto*, before, everything was different. || First: *yo lo vi antes*, I saw it first. || Earlier: *no quise hacerlo antes*, I didn't want to do it earlier. || Rather, better: *antes morir que faltar a su deber*, rather die than fail in one's duty.

|| — *Antes de*, before: *la última calle antes de los semáforos*, the last street before the traffic lights. || *Antes de anoche*, the night before last. || *Antes de ayer*, the day before yesterday. || *Antes de Jesucristo*, before Christ. || *Antes de que me vaya*, before I leave. || *Antes hoy que mañana*, the sooner the better. || *Antes que*, before: *lo he visto antes que tú*, I saw it before you. || *Antes que nada*, above all, more than anything else. || *Cuanto antes* or *lo antes posible*, as soon as possible. || *Cuanto antes mejor*, the sooner the better. || *De antes de la guerra*, pre-war (sentido literal), something else, first-rate (muy bueno). || *Mucho antes*, a long time before, long before. || *Poco antes*, a short time before, not long before, shortly before.
— Conj. On the contrary (más bien): *no teme la muerte, antes la desea*, he does not fear death, on the contrary, he longs for it. || *Antes bien* or *antes al contrario*, on the contrary.
— Adj. Before, previous: *el día antes*, the previous day, the day before.
antesala f. Anteroom, antechamber. || — FIG. *Estar en la antesala de*, to be on the verge of. | *Hacer antesala*, to wait to be received, to cool one's heels (fam.).
antevíspera f. Two days before.
anti pref. Anti [indicating "against" or "opposite"]. (The following list of words constructed with this prefix is by no means complete).
antiácido, da adj.s./ m. Antacid.
antiaéreo, a adj. Antiaircraft (cañón, etc.).
antialcohólico, ca adj. Teetotal.
— M. y f. Teetotaller.
antialcoholismo m. Antialcoholism.
antiamericano, na adj. Anti-American.
antiatómico, ca adj. *Refugio antiatómico*, fallout shelter.
antibiótico, ca adj./s. m. MED. Antibiotic.
anticanceroso, sa adj. Anticancerous.
anticátodo m. Fís. Anticathode.
anticiclón m. Anticyclone.
anticiclonal adj. Anticyclonic.
anticipación f. Bringing forward (de una fecha etc.). || COM. Advance (de dinero). || Prediction, anticipation (predicción). || — *Con anticipación*, in advance: *pagar con anticipación*, to pay in advance; early: *la nieve ha venido este año con anticipación*, the snow has come early this year. || *Con bastante anticipación*, in good time, well in advance. || *Con cinco minutos de anticipación*, five minutes early. || *Llegar con anticipación*, to arrive early, to arrive in good time.
anticipadamente adv. In advance.
anticipado, da adj. Advance, in advance: *pago anticipado*, payment in advance, advance payment. || — *Gracias anticipadas*, thanks in advance *o* in anticipation. || *Por anticipado*, in advance.
anticipamiento m. Bringing forward (de una fecha, etc.). || Advancing, advance (de dinero). || Prediction, anticipation (predicción). || Time in advance, anticipation (tiempo).
anticipante adj. Bringing forward, advancing.
anticipar v. tr. To bring forward, to advance: *anticipar su viaje, la fecha de los exámenes*, to bring forward one's journey, the date of the examinations. || To advance, to lend (dinero). || To predict, to foretell (predecir). || To pay in advance: *anticipar el alquiler*, to pay the rent in advance. || FIG. To anticipate (prever). || *Anticipar las gracias*, to thank in advance.
— V. pr. To be early: *se anticipa la primavera*, spring is early. || To arrive before: *se anticipó a la carta en que anunciaba su llegada*, he arrived before the letter in which he announced his arrival. || To get there before, to beat [s.o.] to it: *fui a coger un trabajo pero se me anticiparon*, I went for a job but s.o. got there before me *o* s.o. beat me to it. || To anticipate, to be one step ahead of: *anticiparse a un rival*, to be one step ahead of a rival. || To be premature, to be born prematurely: *el niño se anticipó*, the child was born prematurely. || FIG. To see sth. coming, to foresee: *me anticipé a la lluvia y cogí el paraguas*, I saw the rain coming and took my umbrella. | To predict, to foretell (precedir). | To anticipate (adivinar). || — *Anticiparse a* (con infinitivo), to ... before: *anticiparse a pagar*, to pay before; *se me anticipó a decir el final del chiste*, he told the end of the joke before me. || *Anticiparse a su época*, to be ahead of one's time.
anticipo m. Advance (sobre un sueldo). || Advance payment, payment on account (sobre una deuda). || FIG. Foretaste: *esto es sólo un anticipo de lo que te podría pasar*, this is merely a foretaste of what could happen to you. || JUR. Retainer, retaining fee: *el anticipo de un abogado*, a lawyer's retainer. || *Llegar con anticipo*, to arrive early *o* in advance.
anticlerical adj./s. Anticlerical.
anticlericalismo m. Anticlericalism.
anticlinal adj. GEOL. Anticlinal.
— M. Anticline.
anticoagulante adj./s. m. Anticoagulant.
anticolonialismo m. Anticolonialism.
anticolonialista adj./s. Anticolonialist.
anticomunista adj./s. Anticommunist.
anticoncepcional o **anticonceptivo, va** adj. Contraceptive, birh-control.
— M. Contraceptive.
anticonformismo m. Non-conformism.
anticonformista adj./s. Non-conformist.
anticongelante m. AUT. Antifreeze (de radiador). || De-icer (de parabrisas).
anticonstitucional adj. Unconstitutional, contrary to the constitution.
anticresis f. JUR. Antichresis (contrato).
anticristiano, na adj. Antichristian, unchristian.
anticristo m. Antichrist.
anticuado, da adj. Antiquated, obsolete, out-of-date (máquina, palabra, uso). || Outdated, out-of-date, old-fashioned (fuera de moda). || Antiquated, old-fashioned (persona). || Old, ancient, out-of-date (película). || *Quedarse anticuado*, to go out of fashion, to date: *este vestido se ha quedado anticuado*, this dress has gone out of fashion *o* has dated.
anticuar v. tr. To declare obsolete *o* out-of-date.
— V. pr. To date, to go out of fashion (vestido). || To become obsolete, to go out of use (máquina, uso). || To go out of use, to become obsolete *o* antiquated (palabra).
anticuario m. Antique dealer (vendedor de antigüedades). || Anticuary, anticuarian (aficionado). || Antique shop (tienda).
anticuerpo m. BIOL. Antibody.
antidemócrata m. y f. Antidemocrat.
antidemocrático, ca adj. Antidemocratic, undemocratic.
antideportivo, va adj. Unsportsmanlike, unsporting.
antideslizante adj. Nonskid, antiskid (neumático).
— M. Antiskid device.
antideslumbrante adj. Antiglare, antidazzle.
antidetonante adj./s. m. Antiknock.
antídoto m. Antidote (*contra*, to, for, against).
antidumping adj. *Medidas antidumping*, antidumping measures, measures against dumping.
antieconómico, ca adj. Uneconomical.
antiemético, ca adj./s. m. Antiemetic, antemetic.
antier adv. FAM. The day before yesterday.
antiesclavista adj. Antislavery.
— M. Abolitionist.
antiescorbútico, ca adj./s. m. MED. Antiscorbutic.
antiespasmódico, ca adj./s. m. MED. Antispasmodic.
antiestético, ca adj. Unsightly, ugly.
antifascismo s. Antifascism.
antifascista adj./s. Antifascist.
antifaz m. Mask.
antifebril o **antifebrífugo, ga** adj. MED. Antifebrile.
antifederalista m. y f. Antifederalist.
antifeminismo m. Antifeminism.
antifeminista adj./s. Antifeminist.
antifermento m. Antiferment.
antifilosófico, ca adj. Anti-philosophic, anti-philosophical.
antiflogistico, ca adj./s. m. MED. Antiphlogistic.
antífona f. REL. Antiphon.
antifonario m. Antiphonary.
antifonero m. Precentor.
antífrasis f. Antiphrasis.
antifricción f. Antifriction.
antigás adj. inv. Gas: *careta antigás*, gas mask.
antígeno m. MED. Antigen.
Antígona n. pr. f. Antigone.
antigualla f. Old relic: *su coche es una antigualla*, his car is an old relic. || Has-been, relic (persona). || Old story (cuento). || Old news, stale news, old hat (noticia). || *Vestirse de antiguallas*, to dress in old rags.
antiguamente adv. Before, formerly (antes). || In former times, in olden days (en la Antigüedad).
antiguar v. tr. To declare out of use *o* obsolete (una palabra).
— V. intr. y pr. To gain seniority (en un empleo). || — V. pr. To go out of fashion, to date, to become old-fashioned (anticuarse).
antigubernamental adj. Anti-government.
antigüedad f. Antiquity (época antigua). || Seniority: *ascenso por antigüedad*, promotion by seniority. || Antiquity, age (cualidad de antiguo). || — Pl. Antiques (objetos antiguos). || Antiquities (monumentos, etc.): *las antigüedades de Roma*, the antiquities of Rome. || — *De toda antigüedad*, from time immemorial. || *Tener mucha antigüedad*, to have great seniority, to have held a post for a long time. || *Tienda de antigüedades*, antique shop.
antiguo, gua adj. Antique, ancient (de la Antigüedad). || Old (viejo): *tradición antigua*, old tradition; *porcelana antigua*, old porcelain. || Old (ya pasado): *una herida antigua*, an old wound. || Former, old: *es el antiguo presidente*, he is the former president; *antiguos alumnos*, old pupils. || Old-fashioned, out-of-date, out-dated (pasado de moda): *un traje antiguo*, an old-fashioned suit. || — *A la antigua* or *a lo antiguo*, in an old-fashioned way. || *Antiguo testamento*, Old Testament. || *De antiguo*, for a long time. || *Desde muy antiguo*, from time immemorial. || *En lo antiguo*, formerly, in olden times. || *Estar chapado a la antigua*, to be old-fashioned [in one's ways]. || *Más antiguo*, senior: *es más antiguo que yo*, he is senior to me, he is my senior. || *Venir de antiguo*, to be ancient.
— M. Antiquity. || — Pl. Ancients: *los antiguos eran supersticiosos*, the Ancients were superstitious.
antihalo adj./s.m. Non-helation (fotografía).
antihelmíntico, ca adj./s.m. MED. Anthelmintic.
antihigiénico, ca adj. Unsanitary, unhygienic, unhealthy.

antihistamínico, ca adj./s.m. MED. Antihistamine.
antihistérico, ca adj. Antihysteric.
antiimperialista adj./s. Anti-imperialist.
antiinflacionista adj. Anti-inflationary.
antilogaritmo m. MAT. Antilogarithm.
antilogía f. Antilogy (contradicción).
antilógico, ca adj. Illogical.
antílope m. ZOOL. Antelope.
antillano, na adj./s. West Indian, Antillean.
Antillas n. pr. f. pl. GEOGR. West Indies, Antilles.
antimacasar m. Antimacassar (cubierta de una butaca).
antimagnético, ca adj. Antimagnetic.
antimasónico, ca adj. Antimasonic.
antimateria f. Antimatter.
antimilitarismo m. Antimilitarism.
antimilitarista adj./s. Antimilitarist.
antimonárquico, ca adj. Antimonarchical.
antimoniado, da adj. QUÍM. Antimoniated.
antimonial adj. QUÍM. Antimonial.
antimoniato m. QUÍM. Antimoniate.
antimonio m. QUÍM. Antimony (metal).
antimonopolista adj. Antitrust: *ley antimonopolista*, antitrust law.
antinacional adj. Antinational.
antinatural adj. Unnatural, contrary to nature.
antineurálgico, ca adj. MED. Antineuralgic.
antiniebla adj. *Faro antiniebla*, fog light *o* lamp. || *Sirena antiniebla*, foghorn.
antinodo m. Antinode (en acústica).
antinomia f. Antinomy.
antinómico, ca adj. Antinomic, antinomical.
Antíoco n. pr. m. Antiochus.
antioqueno, na adj. [From *o* of] Antioch [in Syria].
— M. y f. Native *o* inhabitant of Antioch.
antioqueño, ña adj. [From *o* of] Antioquia [in Colombia].
— M. y f. Native *o* inhabitant of Antioquia.
Antioquía n. pr. f. GEOGR. Antioch.
antioxidante adj. Antirust, rustproof.
antipalúdico, ca adj. Antimalarial.
antipapa m. Antipope.
antipara f. Screen (biombo). || Gaiter (polaina).
antiparásito, ta o **antiparasitario, ria** adj./s.m. Suppressor (radio).
antiparlamentario, ria adj. Antiparliamentary.
antiparlamentarismo m. Antiparliamentarianism.
antiparras f. pl. FAM. Glasses, specs (gafas).
antipartícula f. FÍS. Antiparticle.
antipatía f. Dislike: *los niños han cogido antipatía al nuevo profesor*, the children have taken a dislike to the new teacher. || Unpleasantness, antipathy (cualidad de antipático). || Antipathy, opposition (entre dos cosas). || *Le tengo antipatía a tu primo*, I dislike your cousin, I do not like your cousin.
antipático, ca adj. Disagreeable, unpleasant: *es un chico muy antipático*, he's a very unpleasant boy. || Unfriendly, uncongenial (ambiente). || *Su hermana me cae antipática*, I don't like his sister, I find his sister unpleasant.
— M. y f. Unpleasant *o* disagreeable person.
antipatriota adj. Unpatriotic (sin patriotismo). || Antipatriotic (perjudicial a la patria).
— M. y f. Unpatriotic person. || Antipatriotic person.
antipatriótico, ca adj. Unpatriotic (sin patriotismo). || Antipatriotic (perjudicial a la patria).
antipatriotismo m. Lack of patriotism (falta de patriotismo). || Antipatriotism.
antiperistáltico, ca adj. Antiperistaltic.
antipersonal adj. MIL. Antipersonnel.
antipirético, ca adj./s. m. MED. Antipyretic.
antipirina f. MED. Antipyrine.
antípoda adj. Antipodal.
— M. Antipode.
antipoético, ca adj. Unpoetical.
antiprogresista adj./s. Antiprogressive.
antiprohibicionista adj./s. Antiprohibitionist.
antiproteccionista adj./s. Antiprotectionist.
antiprotón m. FÍS. Antiproton.
antipútrido, da adj./s.m. BIOL. Antiputrefactive.
antiquísimo, ma adj. Very old, ancient.
antirrábico, ca adj. MED. Antirabic: *vacuna antirrábica*, antirabic vaccine.
antirradar adj. Anti-radar.
antirraquítico, ca adj. MED. Antirachitic.
antirreglamentario, ria adj. Against the rules, unlawful.
antirreligioso, sa adj. Antireligious.
antirrepublicano, na adj./s. Antirepublican.
antirrevolucionario, ria adj./s. Antirevolutionary.
antirrobo m. Antitheft device (para vehículos, etc.). || Burglar alarm (para casas, etc.).
antiscios m. pl. Antiscians.
antisemita adj. Anti-Semitic.
— M. y f. Anti-Semite.
antisemítico, ca adj. Anti-Semitic.
antisemitismo m. Anti-Semitism.
antisepsia f. MED. Antisepsis.
antiséptico, ca adj./s.m. MED. Antiseptic.
antisociable adj. Unsociable.
antisocial adj. Antisocial.
antistrofa f. POÉT. Antistrophe.
antisubmarino, na adj. Antisubmarine.
antitanque adj. Antitank.
antítesis f. Antithesis.
antitetánico, ca adj. MED. Antitetanic.
antitético, ca adj. Antithetic, antithetical.
antitipo m. Antitype.
antitóxico, ca adj. Antitoxic.
antitoxina f. MED. Antitoxin.
antituberculoso, sa adj. MED. Antitubercular.
antivenenoso, sa adj. Antitoxic.
antivenéreo, a adj. MED. Antivenereal.
antojadizo, za adj. Whimsical, capricious, fanciful (caprichoso). || Unpredictable, fickle (cambiadizo).
antojado, da adj. Longing, eager, desirous.
antojarse v. pr. To fancy, to feel like: *no hace más que lo que se le antoja*, he does just as he fancies; *se le antojó un pastel*, he fancied a cake. || To take it into one's head, to have the idea: *se le antojó dar la vuelta al mundo*, he took it into his head to go round the world, he had the idea of going round the world. || To have a feeling, to fancy: *se me antoja que va a llover*, I have a feeling it is going to rain.

— OBSERV. The subject of the verb in English becomes the indirect object in Spanish: *se me antoja un helado*, I feel like an ice cream.

antojo m. Whim, [passing] fancy, caprice, fad: *no es más que un antojo*, it is only a whim. || Sudden craving: *los antojos son un síntoma del embarazo*, sudden cravings are a symptom of pregnancy. || Birthmark (mancha en la piel). || — *Cada uno a su antojo*, each to his own. || *Manejar a uno a su antojo*, to twist s.o. round one's little finger. || *No obrar sino a su antojo*, to like to have one's own way, to do exactly as one pleases. || *Seguir sus antojos*, to do as one's fancy takes one. || *Vivir a su antojo*, to live as one pleases, to live one's own life.
antología f. Anthology. || FAM. *De antología*, fantastic, terrific, great: *Rodríguez marcó un gol de antología*, Rodríguez scored a fantastic goal.
antológico, ca adj. Anthological.
antónimo m. Antonym (contrario).
Antonino n. pr. m. Antoninus.
Antonia n. pr. f. Antoinette.
Antonio n. pr. m. Anthony.
antonomasia f. Antonomasia.
antorcha f. Torch. || FIG. Guiding light (persona).
antozoarios m. pl. ZOOL. Anthozoans.
antraceno m. Anthracene.
antracita f. Anthracite.
— Adj. Black (color).
ántrax m. inv. MED. Anthrax.
antreno m. ZOOL. Anthrenus (insecto).
antro m. Cavern, cave (cueva). || ANAT. Antrum. || FIG. y FAM. Hole, dump: *no me gusta trabajar en ese antro*, I don't like working in that hole. || FIG. *Antro de corrupción* or *de perdición*, den of iniquity, den of vice.
antropocéntrico, ca adj. Anthropocentric.
antropocentrismo m. Anthropocentrism.
antropofagia f. Anthropophagy, cannibalism.
antropófago, ga adj. Anthropophagous.
— M. y f. Anthropohagite, anthropophagus, cannibal.
antropoide o **antropoideo, a** adj./s.m. Anthropoid.
antropología f. Anthropology.
antropológico, ca adj. Anthropological, anthropologic.
antropologista o **antropólogo, ga** m. y f. Anthropologist.
antropometría f. Anthropometry.
antropométrico, ca adj. Anthropometric, anthropometrical.
antropomorfismo m. Anthropomorphism.
antropomorfita m. y f. Anthropomorphist, anthropomorphite.
antropomorfo, fa adj. Anthromorphous.
— M. y f. Anthropomorph.
antroponimia f. Anthroponymy.
antropopiteco m. Anthropopithecus.
antruejo m. Carnival.
antucá m. Parasol, sunshade (sombrilla).
antuerpiense o **antuerpino, na** adj. [Of *o* from] Antwerp (de Amberes).
— M. y f. Native *o* inhabitant of Antwerp.
anual adj. Annual: *planta anual*, annual plant. || *Trescientas mil pesetas anuales*, three hundred thousand pesetas per annum *o* a year.
anualidad f. Annuity, annual payment: *pagar las anualidades*, to pay the annuities. || Annual occurrence *o* event (acontecimiento).
anualmente adv. Annually, yearly.
anuario m. Yearbook, annual. || *Anuario telefónico*, telephone directory.
anubarrado, da adj. Cloudy, overcast: *cielo anubarrado*, cloudy sky.
anublar v. tr. To cloud (el cielo). || To cover, to hide, to cloud over (los astros). || FIG. To tarnish (la fama). | To cloud over (la alegría). || AGR. To wither (las plantas).
— V. pr. To cloud over, to become overcast: *el cielo se va anublando*, the sky is clouding over. || To wither (plantas). || FIG. To fade away (desvanecerse).
anublo m. Blight (añublo).

anudadura f. o **anudamiento** m. Knotting. || Fastening, tying (de zapatos). || Tying (de corbata). || Knot (nudo).

anudar v. tr. To knot, to tie [in a knot] (hilo, cinta). || To tie (la corbata). || To tie, to fasten (los zapatos). || FIG. To join, to unite (unir). | To begin (empezar). || *Anudamos nuestra amistad en Londres*, our friendship began *o* we became friends in London.
— V. pr. To get tied up, to get into knots. || AGR. To remain stunted (las plantas). || To remain underdeveloped (las personas, los animales). || FIG. *Se le anudó la voz*, he got a lump in his throat.

anuencia f. Consent.

anuente adj. Consenting, who gives consent.

anulable adj. Revocable, that can be annulled *o* repealed (ley). || That can be annulled *o* nullified *o* cancelled (contrato).

anulación f. Repeal, revocation, annulment (de ley). || Cancellation, annulment, invalidation (de contrato). || Cancellation (de cheque, encargo, etc.). || Annulment (de testamento). || Repeal, rescission (de fallo).

anulador, ra adj. Who annuls *o* repeals.
— M. y f. Person who annuls *o* repeals.

anular adj. Annular, ring-shaped.
— M. Ring finger.

anular v. tr. To repeal, to revoke (ley). || To invalidate, to cancel, to annul (un contrato). || To cancel (un cheque). || To cancel out (un efecto). || To disallow (un gol). || To annul, to declare void (un testamento). || To cancel: *anular un encargo*, to cancel an order. || To repeal (fallo). || FIG. To overshadow, to dominate (hacer perder personalidad). || MAT. To cancel out.
— V. pr. FIG. To give up everything: *vivir en ese pueblo equivale a anularse*, living in that town is like giving up everything. || To be overshadowed, to be diminished (perder autoridad). || MAT. y FÍS. To cancel out.

anulativo, va adj. Annulling, cancelling.

anunciación f. Announcement (anuncio).

Anunciación n. pr. f. Annunciation (de la Virgen).

anunciador, ra adj. Who announces. || Who advertises. || Advertising: *empresa anunciadora*, advertising company.
— M. y f. Advertiser (en un periódico). || Announcer.

anunciante m. y f. Advertiser.

anunciar v. tr. To announce: *anunciar una noticia*, to announce a piece of news; *anunciar al presidente*, to announce the president. || To forebode (augurar). || To tell, to announce: *me ha anunciado que se va a Inglaterra*, he told me that he is going to England. || To announce, to advertise: *anunciar una subasta*, to announce an auction. || To advertise: *es un producto que han anunciado mucho*, it's a product that has been advertised a lot. || To be a sign of: *las golondrinas anuncian la primavera*, swallows are a sign of Spring. || *El tiempo anuncia lluvia*, it looks like rain.
— V. pr. To promise to be, to look like being: *la cosecha se anuncia buena*, the harvest promises to be a good one.

anuncio m. Announcement: *hacer un anuncio*, to make an announcement. || Sign, omen (presagio). || Advertisement: *los anuncios de un diario*, the advertisements in a daily paper. || Notice, bill, poster (cartel). || Hoarding, billboard: *había un gran anuncio de madera al borde de la carretera*, there was a large wooden hoarding at the side of the road. || — *Anuncios por palabras*, classified advertisements (en un periódico). || *Hombre anuncio*, sandwichman. || *Prohibido fijar anuncios*, stick no bills. || *Tablón* or *tablilla de anuncios*, notice board.

anuo, nua adj. Annual: *planta anua*, annual plant.

anuria f. MED. Anury.

anuro, ra adj. ZOOL. Anurous, anuran.
— M. ZOOL. Anuran.

anverso m. Obverse, head (de moneda). || Recto (de una página).

anzuelo m. Fishhook, hook. || FIG. Lure (aliciente). || FIG. *Tragar el anzuelo* or *picar en el anzuelo*, to take *o* to swallow the bait; to be taken in; to be taken in hook, line and sinker; to fall for it.

añada f. Year: *una añada de lluvias*, a year of rain. || AGR. Break, strip of land.

añadido, da adj. Added. || *Lo añadido*, what is added, the additions, *pl.*
— M. False piece, switch, hairpiece (de cabello). || Addition: *hacer un añadido a un texto*, to make an addition to a text. || Extra leaf (de una mesa). || Piece added on: *llevaba un añadido en la manga*, he had a piece added on to his sleeve.

añadidura f. Addition (en un texto). || Extra weight *o* measure (suplemento). || Piece added on (de un vestido). || *Por añadidura*, besides, in addition, into the bargain (además).

añadir v. tr. To add: *añadir agua al vino*, to add water to the wine. || To increase (aumentar). || To add, to lend (interés, etc.).
— V. intr. To make additions (a un texto).

añafea f. Rough brown paper.

añagaza f. Decoy, stool pigeon, lure (pájaro que atrae a los demás). || FIG. Trick, ruse, scheme (ardid).

añal adj. Annual (anual). || Year-old (las reses).
— M. Year-old lamb, yearling (cordero). || Year-old kid, yearling (cabrito). || Offering made on the first anniversary of a death.

añalejo m. REL. Liturgical calendar, ordo.

añejamiento m. Maturing (de vino). || Curing (de jamón).

añejar v. tr. To mature, to age.
— V. pr. To mature, to age (el vino).

añejo, ja m. Mature: *vino añejo*, mature wine. || Cured: *jamón añejo*, cured ham. || Old: *colonia añeja*, old cologne. || FIG. y FAM. Stale, old (noticia).

añicos m. pl. Bits, fragments, pieces. || — FIG. *Estar hecho añicos*, to be worn out (una persona). || *Hacer añicos*, to smash to smithereens (jarrón, objeto), to tear to shreds (papel).

añil m. BOT. Indigo plant, indigo (arbusto). || Indigo (color). || Blue (para el lavado).

añinos m. pl. Lambskin, *sing.* (piel). || Lamb's wool, *sing.* (lana).

año m. Year: *tener veinte años*, to be twenty years old; *durante todo el año*, all the year round; *el año que viene*, next year; *año bisiesto, civil, académico, escolar*, leap, civil, academic,school year; *cada año* or *todos los años*, every year. || — Pl. Days: *en aquellos años felices de nuestra juventud*, in those happy days of our youth. || — *Al año de casado*, within a year of getting married, after a year of marriage. || *Año de gracia*, year of grace. || *Año del Señor*, year of our Lord. || ASTR. *Año de luz, año luz*, light year. || *Año económico*, financial year. || *Año entrante*, coming year. || *Año Nuevo*, New Year. || *Año tras año*, year after year; year in, year out. || *¡Buen año!* or *¡Feliz Año Nuevo!*, Happy New Year! || *Cada dos años*, every other year. || *Con los años que tiene*, at his age. || *El año antepasado*, the year before last. || *En los años cuarenta*, in the forties. || *En los años que corren*, at the present time, nowadays. || *En mis últimos años*, in my later years. || *En sus años mozos*, in his youth, in his younger days. || *Entrado en años*, elderly. || *Estar de buen año*, to be in good health. || *Felicitar el día de Año Nuevo, felicitar por Año Nuevo*, to wish a Happy New Year. || *Hace años*, years ago, ages ago: *le conocí hace años*, I met him years ago; for years, for ages: *hace años que está así*, he has been like that for years. || *No hay quince años feos*, youth is beauty in itself. || *No pasan los años por él*, he doesn't seem to get any older. || *¡Qué años aquellos!*, those were the days! || *¿Qué* or *cuántos años tienes?*, how old are you? || FIG. *Ser del año de la nana* or *del rey que rabió*, to be as old as the hills, to be ancient. || *Tardará años y años*, it will take years. || *Tener muchos años*, to be very old. || *Un año con otro*, taking one year with another. || *Un año sí y otro no*, every other year. || *Una vez al año* or *por año*, once a year.

añojal m. AGR. Break, strip of land.

añojo m. Yearling (becerro).

añoranza f. Longing, yearning, nostalgia (nostalgia). || Grief, sense of loss (dolor). || *Tener añoranza de su país*, to be homesick.

añorar v. tr. To miss, to long for, to yearn for (el pasado). || To grieve, to mourn (una persona muerta).
— V. intr. To pine, to grieve.

añoso, sa adj. Old, aged (viejo).

añublo m. AGR. Blight (enfermedad). | Rust (tizón).

añusgar v. intr. To choke.

aojador, ra adj. Who casts the evil eye.
— M. y f. Hexer.

aojadura f. o **aojamiento** m. Evil eye, curse, jinx (mal de ojo).

aojar v. tr. To cast the evil eye on, to put a curse on, to jinx.

aojo m. Evil eye, curse, jinx.

aoristo m. GRAM. Aorist.

aorta f. ANAT. Aorta.

aórtico, ca adj. Aortic.

aortitis f. MED. Aortitis.

aovado, da adj. Oval, egg-shaped.

aovar v. intr. To lay eggs.

apabullar v. tr. FAM. To squash, to flatten (aplastar). || FIG. y FAM. To crush, to silence (callar): *lo apabulló con sus argumentos*, he silenced him with his arguments.

apacentadero m. AGR. Pasture.

apacentador, ra m. y f. Shepherd (hombre), shepherdess (mujer).

apacentamiento m. AGR. Pasturing, grazing (acción). || Pasture (pasto).

apacentar* v. tr. AGR. To pasture, to graze, to put to graze *o* to pasture (los rebaños). || FIG. To feed (el intelecto). | To minister to, to teach (discípulos). | To gratify, to satisfy (deseos, pasiones).
— V. pr. To pasture, to graze (comer). || FIG. To feed (*con*, on), to be nourished (*con*, with).

apacibilidad f. Gentleness, mildness, even temper, placidity (de persona). || Calmness, peacefulness (de vida). || Calmness (del tiempo, del mar).

apacible adj. Gentle, mild, even-tempered, placid (persona). || Calm, peaceful (vida). || Calm (tiempo, mar).

apaciguador, ra adj. Calming, pacifying.
— M. y f. Pacifier.

apaciguamiento m. Appeasement, calming, pacifying.

apaciguar v. tr. To calm, to pacify, to appease, to calm down, to quieten down (a personas). || To relieve, to soothe (un dolor).
— V. pr. To calm down, to become calm (el mar). || To

die down, to abate: *la tempestad se apaciguó*, the storm died down. || To calm down, to quieten down (personas).

apache m. Apache (piel roja). || FIG. Apache, tough, thug (malhechor).

apacheta f. *Amer.* Barrow, shrine (túmulo funerario en los Andes).

apadrinado m. Sponsored person, protégé (protegido).

apadrinador, ra adj. Sponsoring, who sponsors.
— M. y f. Sponsor (protector). || — M. Second (en un desafío).

apadrinamiento m. Function of best man (en una boda). || Function of godfather (en un bautizo). || Function of second (en un desafío). || Sponsorship, sponsoring, patronage (de un escritor, etc.).

apadrinar v. tr. To be *o* to stand godfather to: *apadrinar a un niño en un bautizo*, to be godfather to a child at a baptism. || To be best man for (en una boda). || To act as second for (en un desafío). || To sponsor: *apadrinar a un escritor joven*, to sponsor a young writer. || To support, to defend: *apadrina todas las ideas humanitarias*, he supports all humanitarian ideas.

apagable adj. Extinguishable, which can be put out.

apagadizo, za adj. Fire-resistant, flame-resistant (ignífugo). || Hard to light (difícil de encender). || Slow to burn (que arde mal).

apagado, da adj. Extinguished, that has been put out, that is out: *fuego apagado*, extinguished fire, fire that has been put out. || Out: *el fuego está apagado*, the fire is out. || Dull, lifeless (color). || Weak (voz). || Muffled, muted (sonido). || Lifeless, listless (mirada, persona). || FIG. Dull: *una mujer muy apagada*, a very dull woman. || — *Cal apagada*, slaked lime. || *Volcán apagado*, extinct volcano.

apagador, ra adj. Which extinguishes, extinguishing.
— M. y f. Extinguisher. || — M. Extinguisher (útil para apagar). || Fire extinguisher (de incendio). || Candle snuffer (apagavelas). || MÚS. Damper (del piano).

apagamiento m. Extinction, extinguishing, putting-out (del fuego). || Switching-off, turning-off, putting-out (de la luz). || Muffling, deadening (de un sonido).

apagar v. tr. To put out, to extinguish (un fuego, un incendio). || To turn *o* to switch off, to put out (luz). || To switch off, to turn off (la radio, etc.). || To muffle, to deaden (sonido). || To fade: *el sol apaga los colores*, the sun fades colours. || To quench (la sed). || To slake (cal). || To soften (color). || FIG. To calm, to soothe: *apagar su ira*, to calm one's anger. | To deaden, to kill, to soothe (el dolor). | To calm down, to quieten (disturbios). || MÚS. To mute, to damp (sonido). || MIL. To silence (la artillería enemiga). || FAM. *Apaga y vámonos*, that's enough, let's leave it at that.
— V. pr. To go out (fuego). || To go out *o* off (la luz). || To fade *o* to die away (sonido). || FIG. To pass away (morir). | To subside (la ira).

apagavelas m. inv. Candle snuffer.

apagón m. Blackout.

apainelado, da adj. ARQ. Basket-handle (arco).

apaisado, da adj. Oblong: *formato apaisado*, oblong format.

apajarado, da adj. *Amer.* Silly, stupid.

apalabrar v. tr. To make a verbal agreement on, to agree to: *apalabrar una compra con un amigo*, to make a verbal agreement with a friend on a purchase. || To engage, to take on: *apalabrar una criada*, to engage a maid.
— V. pr. To make *o* to come to a verbal agreement.

Apalaches n. pr. m. pl. GEOGR. Appalachian Mountains.

apalancamiento m. Leverage.

apalancar v. tr. To lever up, to lift with a lever (levantar). || To lever open, to pry open [with a lever] (abrir). || To lever, to move with a lever (mover). || FIG. To support (apoyar).

apaleado, da adj. Beaten.

apaleador, ra adj. Who beats, which beats, beating.
— M. y f. Winnower, thresher. || Beater, thrasher (de frutos).

apaleamiento m. Winnowing, threshing (del grano). || Beating (de alfombras, etc.). || Beating, thrashing (de los frutos). || Beating, thrashing, striking (de personas).

apalear v. tr. To winnow, to thresh (el grano). || To beat (alfombras). || To beat, to thrash (los frutos). || To beat, to thrash (maltratar). || FIG. To be rolling in: *apalear dinero*, to be rolling in money.

apaleo m. Beating, thrashing. || AGR. Threshing, winnowing (del trigo). | Thrashing, beating (de los frutos).

apamparse v. pr. To become confused.

apanalado, da adj. Faveolate, alveolate, honeycombed.

apanojado, da adj. BOT. Panicled.

apantanar v. tr. To flood (un terreno).

apañado, da adj. FIG. y FAM. Handy, clever, skilful: *es muy apañado para toda clase de cosas*, he's very handy at all kinds of things. | Handy, practical: *me he comprado un vestido muy apañado*, I've bought myself a very practical dress. | Dolled up: *esta chica va siempre bien apañada*, this girl is always well dolled up. || — FIG. y FAM. *¡Estamos apañados!*, that's all we needed!, we're really in it now! | *¡Vas apañado si crees que te van a hacer caso!*, if you think they are going to take any notice of you you've got another think coming!

apañamiento n. Repairing, mending (arreglo).

apañar v. tr. FAM. To get ready (preparar). | To patch up, to mend, to repair: *apañar unos pantalones*, to mend a pair of trousers. | To suit, to be all right for: *¿te apaña coger el avión de la noche?*, does it suit you *o* is it all right for you to catch the night plane? | To dress up (ataviar). | To wrap up (abrigar, arropar). | To pick up, to grab (coger). | To swipe, to lift (robar). || *Amer.* To cover up for (un criminal). | To excuse, to forgive (disculpar). || FAM. *Ya le apañaré*, I'll fix him, I'll sort him out (amenaza).
— V. pr. FAM. To fix things, to arrange things, to contrive: *yo me apaño siempre para conseguir lo que quiero*, I always fix things to get what I want. | To get o.s.: *me apañé un coche muy bonito para irme de vacaciones*, I got myself a very nice car to go on holiday. || *Apañárselas*, to manage, to get by: *me las apañaré*, I'll manage, I'll get by.

apaño m. FAM. Repair, mend (arreglo). | Skill, knack (habilidad). | Mistress (concubina). || — FAM. *Esta maleta es de mucho* or *de gran apaño*, this case is very handy *o* useful. | *No tiene apaño*, there's no way out, there's nothing I [we, etc.] can do about it.

apañuscar v. tr. FAM. To pinch, to swipe (robar). | To crumple (apretujar y ajar).

aparador m. Sideboard (mueble). || Workshop (taller). || Shopwindow, window (escaparate).

aparato m. Pomp, show, fuss: *la corte está rodeada de mucho aparato*, the court is surrounded by a great deal of pomp. || Set: *aparato de radio, de televisión*, radio, television set. || Instrument (brújula, reloj, velocímetro). || Device (dispositivo). || FAM. Telephone, phone (teléfono). | Plane (avión). || ANAT. System, apparatus: *aparato digestivo, circulatorio*, digestive, circulatory system. || MED. Brace (para los dientes). | Bandage (vendaje). || QUÍM. FÍS. Apparatus. || *Amer.* Ghost. || — *Aparato auditivo* or *del oído*, hearing aid. || *Aparato electrodoméstico*, domestic appliance. || *Aparato escénico*, staging. || *Aparatos de gimnasia*, gymnastic apparatus. || *Aparatos de mando*, controls (en un avión). || *Aparatos sanitarios*, bathroom fittings. || *Ponerse al aparato*, to come to the phone. || *¿Quién está en el aparato?*, who's speaking? (teléfono).

aparatosamente adv. Ostentatiously, pretentiously (con ostentación). || Spectacularly (espectacularmente).

aparatosidad f. Ostentation, show (ostentación).

aparatoso, sa adj. Pompous (pomposo). || Spectacular: *accidente aparatoso*, spectacular accident. || Showy, flashy, ostentatious (vistoso): *un traje aparatoso*, a showy dress.

aparcamiento m. Parking (acción de aparcar). || Car park [U.S., parking lot] (sitio reservado). || Lay-by (en la carretera).

aparcar v. tr. To park: *aparcar su coche*, to park one's car.
— V. intr. To park: *en esta calle nunca puede uno aparcar*, you can never park in this street. || — *Aparcar en batería*, to park obliquely, to park at a slant to the kerb. || *Prohibido aparcar*, no parking.

aparcería f. AGR. Partnership, métayage. | Contract of métayage, partnership contract (contrato).

aparcero, ra m. y f. AGR. Métayer, tenant farmer. || Part owner (copropietario). || *Amer.* Companion.

apareamiento m. Pairing off, matching up (de cosas). || Mating (de animales).

aparear v. tr. To match up, to pair off (cosas). || To mate (animales). || To make equal (hacer igual).
— V. pr. To mate (animales). || To match, to go together (cosas).

aparecer* v. intr. To appear: *apareció un barco en el horizonte*, a boat appeared on the horizon. || To come out, to be published (un libro). || To be, to appear (en una lista). || FAM. To show up, to turn up: *no suele aparecer por la oficina*, he doesn't usually turn up at the office; *el mechero perdido no ha aparecido*, the lost lighter has not turned up. || — *Aparecer como*, to look like: *el río Amazonas aparece como un mar immenso*, the Amazon river looks like an immense sea. || *Aparecer en escena*, to appear on the stage.
— V. pr. To appear: *Dios se apareció a Moisés*, God appeared to Moses.

aparecido m. Ghost.

aparejado, da adj. Ready, fit (preparado). || Convenient, suitable, fitting, apt (adecuado). || — *Ir aparejado con*, to go hand in hand with: *su ignorancia va aparejada con una irresponsabilidad absoluta*, his ignorance goes hand in hand with complete irresponsibility. || *Traer aparejado*, to entail, to lead to, to involve, to mean: *la no asistencia a clase trae aparejada la expulsión*, absence from school leads to *o* involves *o* means *o* entails expulsion.

aparejador m. Quantity surveyor (ayudante de arquitecto). || MAR. Rigger.

aparejar v. tr. To get ready, to prepare (preparar). || To harness, to saddle (los caballos). || MAR. To rig out. || To prime (un cuadro).
— V. pr. To get ready, to get o.s. ready.

aparejo m. Preparation (preparativo). || Equipment, gear, tackle (conjunto de cosas). || Harness (arreo). || ARQ. Bond. || MAR. Rigging (jarcia). || TECN. Block and tackle (poleas). || Priming (de un cuadro). || — Pl. Equipment, *sing.*, materials, gear, *sing.* || Tools (herramientas). || *Aparejo de pescar*, fishing tackle.

aparentador, ra adj. Who pretends.
— M. y f. Pretender.

aparentar v. tr. To feign, to affect (simular). || To pretend: *aparentó desvanecerse*, she pretended to faint. || — *Aparentar* (con sustantivo), to pretend to be (con adjetivo) [simular]: *aparentar alegría*, to pretend to be happy; to look *o* to seem (con adjetivo) [parecer]: *aparentar tristeza*, to seem sad. || *Aparentar trabajar* or *que se trabaja*, to pretend to be working. || *Aparentar treinta años*, to look thirty years old. || *No aparentar la edad que se tiene*, not to look one's age.
— V. intr. To show off: *a esta mujer le gusta aparentar*, this woman likes to show off.

aparente adj. Apparent: *un éxito aparente*, an apparent success. || Suitable (adecuado). || Visible, apparent (visible). || Evident (patente). || *Un vestido muy aparente*, a very showy dress.

aparición f. Appearance (acción de aparecer). || Apparition (visión). || Publication, appearance, issue (publicación). || *De próxima aparición*, forthcoming (libro).

apariencia f. Appearance, outward appearance: *fiarse de las apariencias*, to trust outward appearances. || FIG. y FAM. Show: *un vestido con mucha apariencia*, a dress with a lot of show. || — Pl. Appearances: *según todas las apariencias ganará las elecciones*, to all appearances he will win the election; *a juzgar por las apariencias*, judging by appearances. || — *Apariencia falsa*, false appearance. || *Cubrir* or *guardar* or *salvar las apariencias*, to save *o* to keep up appearances, to save face. || *En apariencia*, apparently, seemingly. || *Las apariencias engañan*, appearances are deceptive. || *Tener apariencia de*, to look like, to have the appearance of: *tiene apariencia de gran señor*, he looks like an important gentleman.

aparroquiar v. tr. (P.us.) COM. To provide with customers.
— V. pr. To become a customer.

apartadamente adv. Apart.

apartadero m. Siding (vía muerta). || Lay-by (en el camino). || TAUR. Yard where bulls are selected [for bullfights].

apartado, da adj. Remote, isolated: *un pueblo apartado*, a remote town. || Aloof, solitary (persona). || — *Mantenerse apartado*, to keep to o.s., to remain in the background. || FIG. *Vivir apartado*, to live in a world apart.
— M. Paragraph, section (párrafo). || MIN. Refining (del oro). || TAUR. Penning [of bulls before the bullfight]. || TEATR. Aside (aparte). || Spare room (habitación). || — *Apartado de correos*, post-office box. || *Apartado de localidades*, ticket agency.

apartador, ra adj. Who separates, which separates, separating (que aparta).
— M. y f. Sorter (que selecciona). || *Amer.* Goad, stick (para el ganado).

apartamento m. Flat [U.S., apartment].
— OBSERV. The word *apartamento* is applied to a small flat.

apartamiento m. Separation, putting aside (acción de apartar). || Extraction (del mineral). || Flat [U.S., apartment] (piso). || Remoteness, seclusion, isolation (lejanía). || Remote *o* secluded *o* isolated place (lugar apartado). || JUR. Withdrawal.

apartar v. tr. To remove, to move away: *apartar el armario de la pared*, to move the wardrobe away from the wall. || To put aside: *he apartado todo lo que tengo que llevar*, I've put aside everything that I have to take. || To separate, to part: *apartar a dos personas que riñen*, to separate two people who are arguing. || To take aside: *apartar a alguien para hablar con él*, to take s.o. aside to talk to him. || To turn away: *apartar la atención de un tema*, to turn one's attention away from a subject. || FAM. To begin, to start: *apartó a correr*, he began to run. | To keep, to save: *apártame la cena*, keep my dinner for me. || To extract (el mineral). || To separate (separar). || To put off, to dissuade (disuadir). || To shunt (vagones de ferrocarril). || To push aside, to knock aside: *apartó el perro con el pie*, he pushed the dog aside with his foot. || — *Apartar a alguien de un tema*, to turn s.o. off a subject, to change the subject. || *Apartar de sí una idea*, to put an idea out of one's mind. || *Apartar la vista* or *la mirada (de)*, to look away [from]. || *No apartar la mirada de*, not to take one's eyes off, to keep one's eyes glued to.
— V. pr. To go away, to leave (irse). || To part, to separate (separarse). || To move over *o* up (correrse). || To move aside *o* away, to stand aside (quitarse de en medio). || To stray, to move away: *apartarse del cristianismo*, to stray from Christianity. || To withdraw, to cut o.s. off, to retire: *apartarse del mundo*, to withdraw from the world. || To fail in: *apartarse de su deber*, to fail in one's duty. || To wander off, to go off, to stray from: *apartarse del tema*, to wander off the subject. || To turn off, to stray from (de un camino). || JUR. To withdraw an action. || — *Apartarse de los peligros de*, to flee *o* to avoid the dangers of. || *¡Apártate!*, get out of the way!, move out of the way! || *¡Apártate de mi vista!*, get out of my sight!

aparte adv. Separated: *las pesetas y los chelines están aparte*, the pesetas and the shillings are separated. || Aside, apart: *poner aparte*, to put aside; *bromas aparte*, joking aside. || Apart: *es una niña aparte*, she's a child apart. || Besides (además): *aparte recibe ayuda del exterior*, besides he receives help from outside. || Separately (por separado). || Separately, on one's own: *me habló aparte*, he spoke to me on my own. || TEATR. Aside. || — *Aparte de*, apart from: *aparte del estilo la obra no vale nada*, apart from the style the work is of no value; as well as (además de): *aparte del estilo, el tema de esta obra vale mucho*, as well as the style, the subject-matter of this work is of great value. || *Conversación aparte*, private conversation. || *Dejando aparte*, leaving aside, not to mention. || *Eso aparte*, apart from that; besides that (además). || *Eso es capítulo aparte*, that's another story, that's beside the point. || *Hacer párrafo aparte*, to begin a new paragraph. || *Hacer rancho aparte*, to keep to o.s. || *Llamar aparte*, to call aside. || *Poner aparte*, to separate (separar): *poner aparte las patatas y el arroz*, to separate the potatoes and the rice; to put aside (poner de lado). || *Tener aparte*, to exclude, to leave out: *sus amigos siempre le tienen aparte*, his friends always leave him out; to keep apart *o* separate (separar).
— M. TEATR. Aside. || New paragraph (párrafo). || *Punto y aparte*, full stop, new paragraph [U.S., period, new paragraph].

apartijo m. Small share *o* portion.

aparvadera f. Wooden rake (rastrillo).

aparvar v. tr. To spread out on the threshing floor (el trigo).

apasionado, da adj. Extremely *o* passionately fond, very keen: *apasionado por la caza*, extremely fond of *o* very keen on hunting. || Impassioned, intense, fervent (discusión, etc.). || Madly in love: *estar apasionado por una chica*, to be madly in love with a girl. || Passionate: *amor apasionado*, passionate love. || Partial, biassed, prejudiced: *un juicio muy apasionado*, a very partial judgement. || Passionate, keen, fervent, enthusiastic: *es un defensor apasionado de*, he is a keen defender of.
— M. y f. Admirer, enthusiast, devotee (de un autor). || Enthusiast, lover (de la música, etc.).

apasionamiento m. Passion (amor intenso). || Great fondness, passion, enthusiasm: *mostrar apasionamiento por el arte*, to show great fondness for art. || Rousing, stirring, excitement (acción de apasionar): *el apasionamiento de los ánimos*, the rousing of one's spirits. || *Con apasionamiento*, passionately (con amor), enthusiastically, keenly (con entusiasmo).

apasionante adj. Exciting, thrilling.

apasionar v. tr. To rouse, to stir, to excite, to work up: *la discusión apasionó los ánimos*, the discussion stirred people's spirits. || — *Es un tema que apasiona*, it is a thrilling *o* an enthralling *o* an exciting subject. || *Le apasiona el fútbol, la música*, he's very keen on *o* he's mad on *o* he's very fond of football, of music. || *Me apasiona esa mujer*, I'm mad about *o* crazy about her.
— V. pr. To get excited, to get worked up (excitarse). || To get very keen, to become very interested: *apasionarse por cualquier cosa*, to get very keen on anything, to become very interested in anything. || To fall madly in love (*por*, with) [enamorarse].

apaste o **apastle** m. *Amer.* Bowl.

apatía f. Apathy, indifference. || Listlessness (pereza).

apático, ca adj. Apathetic, indifferent (*a*, *en*, towards). || Listless (perezoso).

apatito m. MIN. Apatite.

apátrida adj. Stateless.
— M. y f. Stateless person.

apeadero m. Halt (ferrocarriles): *la línea cuenta con cuarenta estaciones y once apeaderos*, the line has forty stations and eleven halts. || Halt, stopping place (en el camino). || Horse block (poyo). || Small flat, pied-à-terre (casa).

apeador m. Surveyor (agrimensor).

apealar v. tr. *Amer.* To hobble (trabar).

apeamiento m. Dismounting (de un caballo). || Alighting, getting off (de un autobús, tren). || Getting out (de un coche).

apear v. tr. To help down (de un carruaje, un caballo, un vagón). || To help out (de un coche). || To tie the legs of, to hobble (trabar un caballo). || To chock (un vehículo). || To take down (un objeto): *apear una estatua*, to take down a statue. || To fell (un árbol). || ARQ. To prop up (apuntalar). || To survey (medir). || FIG. y FAM. To dissuade, to make back down: *no pude apearlo*, I couldn't dissuade him *o* make him back down. || *Apear el tratamiento a uno*, to drop s.o.'s formal title, to address s.o. informally.
— V. pr. To dismount, to get off *o* down (bajarse de un caballo). || To get off, to alight: *apearse de un autobús*, to get off a bus, to alight from a bus. || To get out (de un coche). || FIG. y FAM. To back down: *no quiere apearse*, he won't back down. || *Amer.* To put up (en un hotel). || — FAM. *Apearse por las orejas*, to be thrown over the horse's head. | *No apearse del burro*, not to back down, not to climb down, to refuse to back down, to refuse to recognize one's mistake.

apechugar v. intr. To push with one's chest (empujar). || FIG. y FAM. *Apechugar con*, to shoulder, to take on: *siempre tengo que apechugar con todo el trabajo*, I always have to take on *o* to shoulder all the work; to face, to put up with: *hay que apechugar con las consecuencias de su acción*, you have to face the consequences of your action.

apedreado, da adj. Stoned. || Variegated, mottled (abigarrado). || Pock-marked (de viruelas). || *San Esteban murió apedreado*, Saint Stephen was stoned to death.

apedreador, ra adj. Who throws stones, who stones.
— M. y f. Stone thrower.

apedreamiento m. Stoning.

apedrear v. tr. To throw stones at (lanzar piedras contra). || To stone to death, to stone (ejecutar).
— V. impers. To hail (granizar).
— V. pr. To be damaged by hail (cosechas).

apedreo m. Stoning. || Damage by hail (de las cosechas).

apegadamente adv. Devotedly.

apegado adj. Attached, devoted: *está muy apegado a las costumbres*, he is very attached to *o* very devoted to tradition.

apegarse v. pr. To become attached *o* devoted, to grow fond: *apegarse a una persona*, to become attached to *o* devoted to a person, to grow fond of a person. || *Amer.* To approach (acercarse).

apego m. Affection, attachment: *apego a una persona, a la patria*, affection for a person, for one's country, attachment to a person, to one's country. || Interest: *el chico demuestra poco apego a los estudios*, the boy shows little interest in his studies. || — *Tener apego a*, to be fond of *o* attached to: *tengo mucho apego a este vestido*, I'm very fond of *o* I'm very attached to this dress; to value: *tiene apego a su reputación*, he values his reputation. || *Tomar* or *cobrar apego a*, to become attached to *o* fond of.

apegualar v. tr. *Amer.* To hobble, to tie the legs of.

apelable adj. JUR. Appealable.

apelación f. JUR. Appeal: *presentar* or *interponer una apelación*, to make an appeal. || Consultation (entre médicos). || — JUR. *Juicio sin apelación*, judgment without appeal, final judgment. || *Médico de apelación*, consultant doctor. || *Recurso de apelación*, appeal. || FIG. *Sin apelación*, irremediable, hopeless (sin arreglo). || *Tribunal de apelación*, court of appeal.

apelambrar v. tr. To remove the hair from [skins by soaking].

apelante adj./s. JUR. Appellant.

apelar v. intr. JUR. To appeal: *apelar de una sentencia*, to appeal against a sentence. || FIG. To appeal: *apelo a su buena voluntad*, I appeal to your good will. | To resort to, to have recourse to: *apelar a la violencia*, to resort to violence.

apelativo, va adj./s.m. Appellative.

apelmazado, da adj. Soggy, stodgy: *arroz apelmazado*, soggy rice. || Compact, solid, compressed (compacto). || Matted (pelo). || FIG. Clumsy, heavy, stodgy (estilo).

apelmazamiento m. Sogginess, stodginess (de la comida). || Flattening, compressing (de la tierra).

apelmazar v. tr. To make soggy *o* stodgy. || To compress (la tierra).
— V. pr. To go soggy *o* stodgy.

apelotonar v. tr. To roll into a ball.
— V. pr. To go lumpy: *el colchón se ha apelotonado*, the mattress has gone lumpy. || To form balls (la lana). || To crowd together, to gather together (personas).

apellidar v. tr. To call by one's surname (llamar por su apellido). || To call: *a este indio le apellidan Toro Sentado*, they call this Indian Sitting Bull. || FIG. To call: *yo a esto lo apellido una broma pesada*, I call this a bad joke.
— V. pr. To be called. || *Se apellida López*, his surname is López, he is called López.

apellido m. Surname, last name: *me acuerdo de su nombre pero no de su apellido*, I can remember his Christian name but not his surname. || Nickname (apodo): *le han dado un apellido muy feo*, they've given him a horrible nickname. || Shout, call (llamamiento). || *Apellido de soltera*, maiden name.

apenar v. tr. To grieve, to pain: *su conducta ha apenado mucho a su madre*, his behaviour has greatly grieved his mother.
— V. pr. To be grieved *o* pained, to grieve, to distress o.s.

apenas adv. Hardly, scarcely: *apenas se mueve*, he is hardly moving. || With difficulty (penosamente). || As soon as: *apenas llegó se puso a trabajar*, as soon as he arrived he began to work. || — *Apenas ... cuando*, no sooner... than: *apenas había llegado Juan cuando entró la policía*, sooner had John arrived than the police came in; only just ... when: *apenas había llegado Juan cuando lo vi*, John had only just arrived when I saw him. || *Apenas si*, hardly scarcely: *apenas si me tenía de pie*, I could hardly stand up.

apencar v. intr. FAM. To take on, to shoulder: *apenca con el trabajo más pesado*, he takes on the hardest work. | To face, to put up with: *apencar con las consecuencias*, to face the consequences.

apendectomía f. MED. Appendicectomy, appendectomy.

apéndice m. ANAT. Appendix (del intestino grueso). | Appendage (protuberancia). || Appendix (de un libro). || FIG. Lapdog (persona que acompaña).

apendicitis f. MED. Appendicitis.

apendicular adj. Appendicular.

Apeninos n. pr. m. pl. GEOGR. Apennines.

apeñuscar v. tr. To press together, to pack, to cram together.

apeo m. Surveying (de tierras). || Felling (de árboles). || ARQ. Propping up (con puntales). | Prop, support (puntal). | Scaffolding (andamiaje).

apeonar v. intr. To run (las aves).

apepsia f. MED. Apepsy.

aperar v. tr. To make (hacer). || To provide, to equip (*de*, with) [proveer].

apercibimiento m. Warning (aviso). || Preparation.

apercibir v. tr. To prepare, to get ready (preparar). || To provide, to equip (proveer): *apercibir de ropa*, to provide with clothing. || To warn (advertir): *nos apercibieron de la presencia de lobos en el bosque*, they warned us about the presence of wolves in the woods. || To threaten: *le han apercibido con una sanción si sigue llegando tarde*, they have threatened him with punishment if he continues to arrive late. || JUR. To warn.
— V. pr. To get ready: *apercibirse para un viaje*, to get ready for a journey. || *Apercibirse de*, to provide o.s. with, to equip o.s. with.

apercollar* v. tr. To grab by the neck (agarrar). || FAM. To kill with a rabbit punch *o* with a blow on the back of the neck (matar). || FIG. y FAM. To swipe, to snatch (coger).

apergaminado, da adj. Parchment-like. || FIG. Wizened: *rostro apergaminado*, wizened face. | Wrinkled, dried (la piel). || *Papel apergaminado*, parchment paper.

apergaminarse v. pr. FIG. y FAM. To become wizened, to wrinkle, to dry up.

aperiódico, ca adj. Aperiodic.

aperitivo, va adj. MED. Aperitive, aperient.
— M. "Apéritif", appetizer (bebida). || MED. Aperitive, aperient.

apero m. AGR. Agricultural implements *pl.*, farm equipment. || Draught animals, *pl.* (animales). || Tools, *pl.*, equipment, gear (utensilios). || *Amer.* Fancy harness, trappings, *pl.* (guarniciones). || — Pl. Implements, equipment, *sing.* (herramientas): *aperos de labranza*, farm equipment, farming implements.

aperreado, da adj. FAM. Lousy, wretched. || *Una vida aperreada*, a dog's life.

aperreador, ra adj. Tiresome (cargante).

aperrear v. tr. To set the dog's on. || FIG. y FAM. To tire out, to wear out (cansar). | To plague, to pester (molestar).
— V. pr. FAM. To wear o.s. out, to tire o.s. out (trabajar demasiado). | To insist: *¿por qué te aperreas en ir tan lejos?*, why do you insist on going so far?

aperreo m. FAM. Nuisance (molestia): *¡qué aperreo tener que ir a trabajar!*, what a nuisance it is having to go to work! | Exhaustion (cansancio). | Rage, anger (ira). || — FAM. *El niño cogió un aperreo*, the child flew into a rage. | *¡Qué aperreo de vida!*, it's a dog's life!

apersogar v. tr. To tether, to tie.

apersonado, da adj. *Bien apersonado*, presentable. || *Mal apersonado*, not presentable, scruffy.

apersonamiento m. JUR. Appearance.

apersonarse v. pr. To appear, to appear in person.

apertura f. Opening: *apertura de la pesca, del congreso, de la sesión*, opening of the fishing season, of the congress, of the session. || Reading: *la apertura de un testamento*, the reading of a will. || Opening (de una calle). || Beginning: *apertura de hostilidades*, beginning of hostilities. || Opening move, gambit (ajedrez). || — *Apertura de crédito*, opening of credit. || *Apertura de curso*, beginning of term. || *Medio de apertura*, standoff half, fly-half (rugby).
— OBSERV. Unlike its paronym *abertura*, *apertura* often has an abstract meaning: *apertura de las hostilidades*.

apesadumbrar o **apesarar** v. tr. To grieve, to trouble, to upset.
— V. pr. To be grieved, to be troubled, to be upset: *apesadumbrarse con, de* or *por una noticia*, to be grieved by a piece of news.

apestado, da adj. Pestilential, foul (olor). || Plague-stricken, suffering from the plague (que tiene peste). || FIG. Infested: *la ciudad está apestada de pordioseros*, the city is infested with beggars.
— M. y f. Plague-stricken person, person suffering from the plague. || *Hospital para apestados*, pesthouse.

apestar v. tr. To infect with the plague. || FIG. y FAM. To plague: *me apesta con sus quejas*, he plagues me with his complaints. | To stink out: *apestas el cuarto con esa pipa*, you're stinking the room out with that pipe.
— V. intr. To smell, to stink: *apestar a ajo*, to smell of garlic; *aquí apesta*, it smells here.
— V. pr. To catch the plague. || *Amer.* To catch a cold.

apestoso, sa adj. Stinking, foul-smelling (hediondo). || Foul, awful: *un olor apestoso*, a foul smell. || FIG. Annoying, sickening (enojoso). || *Bolas apestosas*, stink bombs.

apétalo, la adj. BOT. Apetalous.

apetecedor, ra adj. Tempting: *lo que me propones es muy apetecedor*, your proposition is very tempting. || Desirable.

apetecer* v. tr. To long for, to crave for, to yearn for: *apetezco la llegada de la primavera*, I am longing for Spring to arrive.
— V. intr. To be welcome: *una taza de té siempre apetece*, a cup of tea is always welcome. || To tempt, to fancy: *esta tarta con nata me apetece*, this cream cake tempts me, I fancy this cream cake. || — *Esto no me apetece nada*, I don't feel like it at all, I don't fancy it at all. || *Hoy no me apetece salir*, I don't feel like going out today. || *Me apetece un helado*, I feel like an ice cream, I fancy an ice cream. || *Si le apetece, podemos ir al cine*, if you feel like it *o* if you like, we can go to the cinema.
apetecible adj. Tempting, attractive.
apetecido, da adj. Desired: *puede que la búsqueda de petróleo no dé el resultado apetecido*, it is possible that the search for oil will not give the desired result.
apetencia f. Longing, yearning, desire, craving, hunger: *apetencia de riquezas*, longing for riches. || Appetite (ganas de comer).
apetitivo, va adj. Appetitive. || Tempting, appetizing (gustoso).
apetito m. Appetite: *tener apetito*, to have an appetite; *tener mucho apetito*, to have a good *o* a big appetite. || FIG. Yearning, desire, hunger: *el apetito de riquezas*, the desire for riches. || — *Abrir* or *dar* or *despertar el apetito*, to whet one's appetite. || *Apetito carnal*, sexual appetite *o* desire. || *Comer con mucho apetito*, to eat heartily.
apetitoso, sa adj. Appetizing, tempting: *este pastel parece muy apetitoso*, this cake looks appetizing. || Tasty: *hemos comido un plato apetitoso*, we ate a tasty dish. || FIG. y FAM. Tempting, attractive.
ápex m. ASTR. Apex.
apezonado, da adj. Mamillated.
Apia (Vía) n. pr. f. Appian Way.
apiadar v. tr. To move to pity: *su desgracia apiada a sus amigos*, his misfortune moves his friends to pity.
— V. pr. To take pity, to pity: *apiadarse de uno*, to take pity on s.o., to pity s.o.
apical adj. Apical.
apicararse v. pr. To take up bad ways.
ápice m. Apex, tip, point (extremo). || End, tip (de la lengua). || Accent (signo gráfico). || FIG. Height (apogeo). | Crux (de un problema). | Iota (cosa muy pequeña). || — FIG. *No ha cedido ni un ápice*, he hasn't given an inch. | *No ha perdido ni un ápice de su prestigio*, he hasn't lost an ounce of his prestige.
apícola adj. Apicultural (de las abejas).
apicultor, ra m. y f. Beekeeper, apiarist, apiculturist.
apicultura f. Beekeeping, apiculture.
apilador, ra adj. Piling.
— M. y f. Piler.
apilamiento o **apilado** m. Piling up, heaping up.
apilar, apilarse v. tr. y pr. To pile up, to heap up.
apimplarse v. pr. FAM. To get tipsy, to get merry (emborracharse).
apimpollarse v. pr. AGR. To bud.
apiñado, da adj. Packed, crammed, jammed (apretado). || Cone-shaped, conical (de figura de piña).
apiñamiento m. Packing, cramming, jamming.
apiñar v. tr. To pile up, to heap up (amontonar). || To pack, to cram, to jam (apretar).
— V. pr. To pack together, to cram together, to crowd together, to jam together: *la gente se apiñaba ante los escaparates*, the people packed together in front of the windows. || To press: *la gente se apiñaba alrededor del orador*, the people pressed round the speaker.
apiñonado, da adj. *Amer.* Brown-skinned, with a brown complexion (moreno).
apio m. BOT. Celery.
apiolar v. tr. FIG. y FAM. To do in, to bump off (matar). | To nab, to catch (prender).
apiparse o **apiporrarse** v. pr. To guzzle, to stuff o.s. (atracarse).
apirético, ca adj. MED. Apyretic.
apirexia f. MED. Apyrexy.
apisonadora f. Steamroller, road roller.
apisonamiento m. Rolling (con la apisonadora). || Ramming (con el pisón).
apisonar v. tr. To roll (la apisonadora). || To ram (el pisón).
apitonar v. intr. To begin to grow (los cuernos). || To begin to grow horns (los animales). || BOT. To sprout (los brotes).
— V. tr. To pierce, to crack (el huevo).
— V. pr. FIG. y FAM. To get into a huff (amostazarse).
apizarrado, da adj. Slate-coloured.
aplacamiento m. Appeasement, placation, calming.
aplacar v. tr. To appease, to placate, to calm: *aplacar la ira*, to placate one's anger. || To quench: *aplacar la sed*, to quench one's thirst. || To satisfy (el hambre).
— V. pr. To calm down, to die down: *la tempestad se aplacó*, the storm calmed down.
aplanacalles m. inv. Idler, loafer, loiterer (paseante).
aplanadera f. TECN. Rammer (para apisonar).
aplanador, ra adj. Levelling, flattening, smoothing.
— F. AGR. Leveller.
aplanamiento m. Smoothing. || Levelling: *el aplanamiento del suelo*, the levelling of the ground. || Collapse (derrumbamiento).
aplanar v. tr. To smooth, to flatten (allanar). || To level off, to make level (suelo). || FIG. y FAM. To knock out, to bowl over: *la noticia le aplanó*, the news bowled him over *o* knocked him out. | To overcome, to knock out: *estar aplanado por el calor*, to be overcome *o* to be knocked out by the heat. || *Amer. Aplanar las calles*, to loiter about the streets, to hang about the streets, to loaf about.
— V. pr. To fall down, to collapse (edificio). || FIG. To grow weak, to lose one's strength (perder el vigor).
aplanético, ca adj. FÍS. Aplanatic.
aplastador, ra o **aplastante** adj. Overwhelming, crushing: *un triunfo aplastante*, an overwhelming triumph.
aplastamiento m. Squashing, flattening, crushing. || Squashing: *aplastamiento de un tomate*, squashing of a tomato. || FIG. Crushing (de argumentos, críticas, etc.). | Dumbfounding (confusión). | Crushing, flattening, defeat (en una discusión, una lucha): *el aplastamiento de las tropas*, the crushing of the troops.
aplastar v. tr. To squash, to flatten, to crush: *aplastar un sombrero*, to flatten a hat. || To squash: *aplastar un tomate*, to squash a tomato. || FIG. To crush, to destroy: *sus argumentos aplastan las críticas*, his arguments destroy any criticism. | To leave speechless, to floor, to dumbfound (dejar confuso). | To crush, to flatten, to overwhelm (en una discusión, una lucha): *aplastar al ejército enemigo*, to crush the enemy army. || *Amer.* To overwork (una caballería).
— V. pr. To be crushed *o* flattened *o* squashed: *el sombrero se aplastó*, the hat was crushed. || To crash, to smash: *el coche se aplastó contra el árbol*, the car crashed against the tree. || FIG. To flatten o.s.: *se aplastó contra el suelo para no ser alcanzado por las balas*, he flattened himself against the ground so that he wouldn't be hit by the bullets. || *Amer.* To collapse (en un sillón). | To lose heart (desanimarse).
aplatanado, da adj. FAM. Lethargic, listless.
aplatanarse v. pr. FAM. To get listless, to become lethargic. || *Uno se aplatana con este clima*, this climate makes one very listless.
aplaudidor, ra m. y f. Applauder.
aplaudir v. tr. e intr. To applaud, to clap: *aplaudir a un artista*, to applaud an artist. || FIG. To applaud (aprobar): *aplaudo tu decisión*, I applaud your decision.
aplauso m. Applause (ovación). || Applause, praise, acclaim: *su obra merece el mayor aplauso*, his work is worthy of the greatest praise. || — Pl. Applause, *sing.*: *una salva de aplausos*, thunderous applause. || *Con el aplauso de*, to the applause of.
aplazamiento m. Postponement, adjournment: *el aplazamiento de una reunión*, the postponement of a meeting. || Deferment (de un pago).
aplazar v. tr. To postpone, to adjourn: *aplazar una reunión*, to postpone a meeting. || To defer: *aplazar un pago*, to defer a payment. || To call, to summon (convocar).
aplebeyamiento m. Degradation: *el aplebeyamiento de las costumbres*, the degradation of customs.
aplebeyar v. tr. To demean, to degrade.
— V. pr. To lower o.s., to degrade o.s.
aplicabilidad f. Applicability.
aplicable adj. Applicable (*a*, to).
aplicación f. Application: *la aplicación de una teoría*, the application of a theory; *la aplicación de una pomada*, the application of an ointment. || Fixing, attaching (de una cosa sobre otra). || Putting into practice, application: *la aplicación del plan de desarrollo*, the putting into practice of the development plan. || Use, application: *el acero tiene muchas aplicaciones*, steel has many applications. || Application, diligence, industry (esmero). || Appliqué: *mueble con aplicaciones de marfil*, piece of furniture with ivory appliqués. || MIL. *Escuela de aplicación*, school of instruction.
aplicado, da adj. Diligent, industrious, painstaking: *un trabajador muy aplicado*, a very industrious worker. || Studious: *un alumno aplicado*, a studious pupil.
aplicar v. tr. To apply: *aplicar una capa de pintura*, to apply a coat of paint; *aplicar un criterio a un problema*, to apply a criterion to a problem. || To put into effect, to apply (ley). || To attach, to fix: *aplicar algo a la pared*, to attach sth. to *o* to fix sth. on the wall. || To put into practice, to use, to apply: *aplicar un método empírico*, to use an empirical method. || To put on: *aplicar un ribete a una chaqueta*, to put an edging on a jacket. || To assign (dinero, hombres, recursos). || *Aplicar el oído*, to put one's ear (sentido propio), to listen carefully *o* attentively (escuchar).
— V. pr. To work hard, to be devoted: *aplicarse en el estudio*, to work hard at one's studies, to be devoted in one's studies. || To devote o.s.: *aplicarse en hacer algo*, to devote o.s. to doing sth. || To be used for: *el agua se aplica al riego*, the water is used for irrigation. || To apply, to be applicable to: *la ley se aplica a todos*, the law applies to everyone. || To come into effect, to take effect (entrar en vigor). || *Aplíquese el cuento*, you might take a lesson from it yourself.

— OBSERV. En inglés, *to apply* significa frecuentemente *solicitar*: *to apply for a job*, solicitar un puesto.

aplique m. Wall lamp, wall light (lámpara).
aplomado, da adj. Leaden, lead-coloured (plomizo). || Vertical: *un muro bien aplomado*, a completely vertical

wall. || FIG. Cool, level-headed, self-assured: *una persona muy aplomada*, a very cool person. || TAUR. Which refuses to move (toro).
aplomar v. tr. To test with a plumb line, to plumb (comprobar la verticalidad). || To plumb, to make vertical (poner vertical).
— V. pr. To gain self-assurance (cobrar aplomo). || To collapse, to fall down (desplomarse). || *Amer.* To be ashamed, to be embarrassed.
aplomo m. Verticality. || Sense, aplomb (sensatez). || Aplomb, assurance, self-assurance, level-headedness (serenidad). || Set of the legs (del caballo). || *Hacer que alguien pierda el aplomo*, to rattle *o* to rile s.o.
apnea f. MED. Apnoea, apnea.
apocado, da adj. Diffident, timid (tímido, sin ánimo). || Lowly (bajo).
apocalipsis m. Apocalypse. || *El Libro del Apocalipsis*, the Book of Revelation, the Apocalypse.
apocalíptico, ca adj. Apocalyptic, apocalyptical.
apocamiento m. Diffidence, timidity (timidez). || Lowliness (bajeza).
apocar v. tr. To make smaller, to diminish, to reduce (disminuir). || FIG. To belittle, to humiliate (humillar). | To intimidate (intimidar).
— V. pr. FIG. To humble o.s. (humillarse). | To feel small (sentirse humillado). | To be frightened *o* scared: *no me apoco por nada*, I'm not scared of anything.
apócopa f. GRAM. Apocopation, apocope.
apocopar v. tr. GRAM. To apocopate.
apócope f. GRAM. Apocopation, apocope.
apócrifo, fa adj. Apocryphal (supuesto).
apodar v. tr. To nickname (dar un apodo a).
apoderado m. Agent, representative (que tiene poder). || Manager (de deportista). || JUR. Proxy (poderhabiente).
apoderamiento m. Empowering, granting of powers (acción de apoderar). || Seizure, seizing (acción de apoderarse).
apoderar v. tr. To empower, to authorize. || JUR. To grant power of attorney to.
— V. pr. To seize: *apoderarse del poder*, to seize power. || To take possession, to seize: *se apoderaron de la casa*, they took possession of *o* they seized the house. || FIG. To take hold of, to grip: *el miedo se apoderó de ellos*, fear took hold of them.
apodíctico, ca adj. Apodictic (indiscutible).
apodo m. Nickname (mote).
ápodo, da adj. ZOOL. Apodal.
— M. ZOOL. Apod.
apódosis f. Apodosis.
apófisis f. ANAT. Apophysis.
apofonía f. Ablaut.
apogeo m. ASTR. Apogee. || FIG. Height, summit, acme: *el apogeo de la gloria*, the acme of glory. || *Estar en todo su apogeo*, to be on one's best form: *este artista está ahora en todo su apogeo*, this artist is now on his best form; at one's height: *la temporada turística está en todo su apogeo en el mes de agosto*, the tourist season is at its height in August.
apolillado, da adj. Moth-eaten (ropa). || Worm-eaten (madera).
apolilladura f. Moth hole (en la ropa). || Woodworm hole (en la madera).
apolillamiento m. Damage done by moths (en las telas). || Woodworm (en la madera).
apolillar v. tr. To eat, to make holes in (la polilla). || *Amer.* POP. *Estarla apolillando*, to be snoozing (dormir).
— V. pr. To get worm-eaten (la madera). || To get moth-eaten (la ropa).
apolíneo, a adj. Apollonian (relativo a Apolo). || FAM. Apollonian (esbelto).
apolítico, ca adj. Apolitical.
apolitismo m. Apoliticism.
Apolo n. pr. m. MIT. Apollo.
apologético, ca adj. Apologetic.
— F. Apologetics (en teología).
apología f. Vindication, defence, apology, justification. || *Hacer la apología de uno, de algo*, to defend *o* to justify *o* to vindicate s.o., sth.
apológico, ca adj. Apological.
apologista m. y f. Apologist.
apólogo m. Apologue.
apoltronado, da adj. Lazy, idle.
apoltronarse v. pr. To get lazy *o* idle, to let o.s. go (hacerse poltrón).
apomazar v. tr. To smooth with a pumice stone.
aponeurosis f. Aponeurosis.
aponeurótico, ca adj. Aponeurotic.
apoplejía f. MED. Apoplexy. || *Ataque de apoplejía*, stroke.
apoplético, ca adj./s. Apoplectic.
apoquinar v. tr. e intr. POP. To fork out, to cough up (pagar).
aporca o **aporcadura** f. AGR. Earthing-up.
aporcar v. tr. AGR. To earth up.
aporco m. *Amer.* Earthing-up.
aporía f. FIL. Aporia.
aporrar v. intr. To get stuck for words, to dry up.
— V. pr. To become a bore.
aporreado, da adj. Beaten (golpeado). || Miserable, wretched: *llevar una vida aporreada*, to lead a miserable life. || Rascally (pícaro).
aporreadura f. o **aporreamiento** m. Beating, thumping.
aporrear v. tr. To hit, to thump, to give a beating to: *aporrear a uno*, to hit s.o., to give s.o. a beating. || To bang on, to hammer on: *aporrear la puerta*, to bang on the door. || To thump, to pound, to hammer away on: *aporrear el piano*, to thump the piano. || FIG. *Apporrearle a uno los oídos*, to go right through one, to get on one's nerves (un ruido).
— V. pr. To fight, to hit each other (pelearse). || FIG. To slave, to slog, to wear o.s. out (trabajar).
aporreo m. Beating, thumping (golpeo).
aportación f. Contribution: *la aportación de este país ha sido considerable*, the contribution of this country has been considerable; *la aportación de fondos*, the contribution of funds.
aportar v. intr. MAR. To reach port (tocar tierra). || FIG. To arrive (llegar). | To be: *hace mucho tiempo que no aporta por aquí*, it's a long time since he was here, he hasn't been here for a long time.
— V. tr. To contribute (contribuir). || To bring forward, to provide: *aportar pruebas*, to bring forward evidence.
aporte m. *Amer.* Contribution.
aportillar v. tr. To breach, to break open, to make a breach in (un muro).
— V. pr. To collapse.
aportuguesado, da adj. Who seems Portuguese.
aposentador, ra m. Landlord, person who gives lodgings. || MIL. Quartermaster.
— F. Landlady, person who gives lodgings.
— Adj. Lodging. || MIL. *Partida aposentadora*, quartering party.
aposentamiento m. Lodging, putting-up (acción).
aposentar v. tr. To lodge, to put up, to give lodgings to.
— V. pr. To put up, to lodge, to stay: *aposentarse en un hotel*, to put up at a hotel, to lodge *o* to stay in *o* at a hotel.
aposento m. Room (habitación). || Lodgings, *pl.* (hospedaje). || *Tomar aposento*, to put up, to stay: *tomar aposento en una fonda*, to put up at an inn, to stay at *o* in an inn.
aposición f. GRAM. Apposition: *en aposición*, in apposition.
apositivo, va adj. GRAM. Appositive.
apósito m. MED. Dressing: *poner un apósito*, to put on a dressing.
aposta o **apostas** adv. On purpose, deliberately, purposely: *lo hizo aposta para molestarme*, he did it on purpose to annoy me.
apostadero m. MIL. Post, station. || MAR. Military port, naval station.
apostador, ora o **apostante** adj. Betting.
— M. y f. Better.
apostar* v. tr. To bet, to stake, to lay: *apostar mil pesetas a un caballo*, to bet a thousand pesetas on a horse. || To post, to station (colocar a gente en un sitio): *apostar a un centinela*, to post a sentry.
— V. intr. To bet: *apostar en las carreras de caballos*, to bet on horse races; *apuesto a que no lo haces*, I bet you don't.
— V. pr. To bet: *me he apostado mil pesetas con él*, I have bet him a thousand pesetas. || To take up one's post *o* one's station (en un lugar). || — FIG. *Apostarse la cabeza a que*, to bet anything that. || *¿Qué te apuestas a que se rompe?*, what do you bet that it breaks?, I bet you it breaks, what's the betting it breaks? (fam.).

— OBSERV. This verb is irregular in the sense *to bet*, and is conjugated like *contar*. It is regular when it means *to post*.

apostasía f. Apostasy.
apóstata adj./s. Apostate.
apostatar v. intr. To apostatize. || FIG. To change sides.
apostema f. MED. Aposteme.
apostemar v. tr. MED. To apostemate.
apostilla f. Note.
apostillar v. tr. To add notes to (anotar).
— V. pr. MED. To scab over: *la herida se ha apostillado*, the wound has scabbed over.
apóstol m. Apostle: *los Hechos de los Apóstoles*, the Acts of the Apostles. || FIG. Champion, apostle: *apóstol de la paz*, champion of peace.
apostolado m. Apostolate.
apostólico, ca adj. Apostolic. || Papal, apostolical (del Papa). || *Nuncio apostólico*, papal nuncio.
apostrofar v. tr. To apostrophize.
apóstrofe m. Apostrophe.
apóstrofo m. Apostrophe (signo ortográfico).
apostura f. Bearing (aspecto): *de buena apostura*, of good bearing; *una noble apostura*, noble bearing. || Elegance, grace (elegancia).
apotegma m. Apothegm, apophtegm.
apotema f. MAT. Apothem.
apoteósico, ca adj. Tremendous: *un triunfo apoteósico*, a tremendous triumph.
apoteosis f. Apotheosis. || TEATR. *Apoteosis final*, grand finale.
apotrerar v. tr. *Amer.* To divide [land] into pastures.
apoyar v. tr. To lean: *apoyar el armario en la pared*, to lean the wardrobe against the wall. || To rest: *apoyar*

la cabeza en las manos, to rest one's head in one's hands. || To put, to rest: *apoyar los codos en la mesa*, to rest one's elbows on the table; *apoyar el pie en un escalón*, to put one's foot on a step. || Fig. To support, to back up: *sus discursos apoyan su decisión*, his speeches support his decision; *apoyar a un candidato*, to support a candidate. | To base, to found: *apoya su teoría en hechos concretos*, he bases his theory on concrete facts. | To second (una moción). | To confirm (confirmar). || Mil. To support. || Arq. y Tecn. To support, to hold up.
— V. intr. To rest: *la viga apoya en una columna*, the beam rests on a column.
— V. pr. To lean: *apoyarse en un bastón*, to lean on a walking stick. || To rest, to be supported: *la viga se apoya en una columna*, the beam rests on *o* is supported by a column. || Fig. To be based on, to rest on: *un argumento que se apoya en la realidad*, an argument which is based on reality. | To base o.s. on: *me apoyo en las estadísticas oficiales*, I am basing myself on official statistics. | To rely: *puedo apoyarme en Rodríguez para esta empresa*, I can rely on Rodriguez for this job. || *Apoyarse demasiado en sus padres*, to be overdependent on one's parents.

apoyatura f. Mús. Appoggiatura.

apoyo m. Support: *una columna que sirve de apoyo*, a column which acts as a support. || Fig. Support, backing (protección, ayuda). | Approval (aprobación). || Mil. Support. || — Tecn. *Cigueñal de cinco apoyos*, five main bearing crankshaft. || *Punto de apoyo*, fulcrum (física), base: *establecer un punto de apoyo para una red comercial*, to set up a base for a commercial network.

apreciable adj. Appreciable: *una diferencia apreciable*, an appreciable difference. || Audible, sensible (ruido). || Fig. Worthy, estimable: *una persona apreciable*, a worthy person.

apreciación f. Appreciation. || Appraisal (valoración).

apreciador adj. Who appreciates.
— M. y f. Person who appreciates.

apreciar v. tr. To appraise, to value (valorar). || To price, to value (poner precio a). || To register: *este cronómetro aprecia centésimas de segundos*, this cronometer registers hundredths of a second. || To make out: *desde lejos no puedo apreciar los detalles*, from afar I can't make out the details. || To see, to notice (percibir). || Fig. To appreciate: *apreciar la cocina francesa*, to appreciate French cooking. | To have esteem for, to hold in esteem: *apreciar mucho a un muchacho*, to have great esteem for a boy, to hold a boy in high esteem. || — *Apreciar algo en su justo valor*, to appreciate sth. for its true value. || *El médico le apreció una doble fractura*, the doctor observed that he was suffering from a double fracture.
— V. pr. To be observed, to be registered, to be noted: *se aprecia un alza en el costo de la vida*, a rise in the cost of living is observed.

apreciativo, va adj. Appreciative.

aprecio m. Appraisal, valuation (evaluación). || Fig. Esteem, regard, appreciation: *tener gran aprecio a uno*, to have great esteem for s.o. || *Es una persona de mi mayor aprecio*, he is a person that I hold in the highest esteem *o* regard.

aprehender v. tr. To seize: *aprehender contrabando*, to seize contraband. || To apprehend, to arrest (apresar). || To conceive of, to imagine (concebir). || To understand (comprender).

aprehensible adj. Conceivable, understandable.

aprehensión f. Apprehension, capture, arrest: *la aprehensión de un ladrón*, the apprehension of a thief. || Seizure (de contrabando). || Comprehension, understanding (comprensión). || Conception.

aprehensivo, va adj. Perceptive (perspicaz).

apremiable adj. Jur. Coercible.

apremiador, ra o **apremiante** adj. Urgent, pressing: *trabajo apremiante*, urgent work.

apremiantemente adv. Urgently.

apremiar v. tr. To urge, to press: *apremialo para que termine*, urge him to finish. || To compel, to oblige, to force (obligar). || To hurry [up] (dar prisa).
— V. intr. To be urgent (ser urgente): *apremia dar salida a la mercancía*, it is urgent that we sell the merchandise. || *El tiempo apremia*, time is pressing *o* short.

apremio m. Hurry, haste, urgency (prisa). || Obligation, compulsion (obligación). || Jur. Writ: *comisionado de apremios*, writ server. || — *Por apremio de tiempo*, because time is [*o* was] pressing. || Jur. *Por vía de apremio*, under duress.

aprender v. tr. To learn: *aprender de memoria*, to learn by heart. || — Fig. *Aprender en cabeza ajena*, to learn from other people's mistakes. | *Para que aprenda*, that will teach him [her, you], he [she, you] asked for that.
— V. pr. To learn: *aprenderse la lección*, to learn one's lesson.

aprendiz, za m. y f. Beginner, novice, learner (principiante). || Apprentice, trainee: *aprendiz de pastelero*, confectioner's apprentice, apprentice confectioner. || Learner: *aprendiz de conductor*, learner driver. || — *Colocar de aprendiz*, to apprentice, to find an apprenticeship for. || Fig. *Ser aprendiz de todo y oficial de nada*, to be a Jack of all trades and master of none.

aprendizaje m. Apprenticeship, traineeship. || *Hacer su aprendizaje*, to serve one's apprenticeship.

aprensión f. Apprehension, fear (miedo): *aunque está sano tiene la aprensión de que se va a morir*, although he is healthy he has the apprenhension that he is going to die. || Good manners, *pl.*, courtesy (delicadeza). || — Pl. Strange ideas, strange notions. || — *Me da aprensión aceptar este trabajo porque se lo quito a otro*, I don't like *o* I hesitate to accept this job because I'm taking it from s.o. else. || *Me da aprensión beber en su vaso porque está acatarrado*, I'm afraid to drink *o* I hesitate to drink *o* I'm apprehensive about drinking from his glass because he has a cold.

aprensivo, va adj. Fearful, apprehensive, squeamish: *es tan aprensivo que nunca va a ver a los enfermos*, he is so apprehensive that he never goes to see sick people. || Worried, anxious: *está muy aprensivo con su tos*, he is very worried about his cough. || Fig. *Ser aprensivo*, to be a hypochondriac.

apresador, ra adj. Capturing, who captures.
— M. y f. Captor.

apresamiento m. Capture, seizure.

apresar v. tr. To catch, to seize [with teeth or claws]: *el lobo apresó el cordero*, the wolf seized the lamb. || Mar. To capture, to seize: *apresar un barco enemigo*, to capture an enemy ship. || (Ant.). To imprison, to put in prison (aprisionar).

aprestador, ra m. y f. Sizer (de tela).

aprestar v. tr. To prepare, to get ready (preparar). || Tecn. To size (telas). || — *Aprestar el oído*, to lend an ear, to listen. || *Aprestar la atención*, to pay attention, to give one's attention.
— V. pr. To make *o* to get ready, to prepare: *aprestarse para salir*, to get ready to go out.

apresto m. Preparation (preparación). || Tecn. Size (substancia). | Sizing (acción).

apresuradamente adv. Hurriedly, in a hurry (con prisa). || Fig. Hastily.

apresurado, da adj. In a hurry: *que las personas apresuradas pasen primero*, let those who are in a hurry go first. || Hurried, hasty (hecho con prisa): *un viaje apresurado*, a hurried journey. || Fig. Hasty: *conclusión apresurada*, hasty conclusion.

apresuramiento m. Hurry, haste (prisa). || Fig. Haste.

apresurar v. tr. To quicken up, to speed up, to hurry up, to accelerate: *apresurar el trabajo*, to quicken up the work. || To hurry, to rush: *si me apresuras no lo haré bien*, if you hurry me I shan't do it well. || *Apresurar el paso*, to walk more quickly, to go faster, to quicken one's pace.
— V. pr. To hurry, to make haste, to hurry up: *hay que apresurarse, ya es muy tarde*, we'll have to hurry, it's late. || — *Apresurarse a hacer algo*, to hurry *o* to hasten to do sth., to do sth. at once *o* straight away. || *Apresurarse en contestar*, to waste no time in replying, to reply as quickly as possible. || *Apresurémonos por llegar*, let's hurry up and get there, let's get there as soon as we can. || *No apresurarse*, to take one's time: *no se apresure*, take your time.

apretadamente adv. Tightly. || [Only] just: *ganó apretadamente*, he [only] just won. || — *Con su sueldo vive muy apretadamente*, his wage gives him just enough to live on. || *Llegar muy apretadamente al final del mes*, to just manage to the end of the month.

apretadera f. Strap (correa).

apretado, da adj. Tight: *el corcho de la botella está muy apretado*, the cork of the bottle is very tight; *un lío muy apretado*, a very tight bundle; *un vestido apretado*, a tight dress; *un nudo apretado*, a tight knot. || Close: *los codos apretados al cuerpo*, with one's elbows close to one's body; *un tejido apretado*, a close weave. || Hard: *un colchón apretado*, a hard mattress. || Crowded together, squashed together, tightly packed (la gente). || Cluttered: *con tantos muebles el cuarto está muy apretado*, with so much furniture the room is very cluttered. || Compact, dense (compacto). || Fig. Difficult, tricky: *asunto, lance apretado*, difficult matter, moment. | Cramped (escritura). | Tight (los labios). | Tightfisted, miserly, stingy (tacaño). || — Fig. y Fam. *Estar muy apretado*, to be very hard up, to be very short of money (de dinero), to have problems (tener problemas). || *La gente iba muy apretada en el tren*, the train was packed *o* very crowded. || *Vivir muy apretado en un piso*, not to have much room in a flat, to be cramped in a flat.

apretador, ra adj. Which tightens.
— M. Corset (corsé). || Jerkin (almilla). || Body bandage (faja de niños). || Clamp (grapa).

apretamiento m. Squeezing. || Tightening (de un tornillo, de un cinturón, etc.). || Crowding (de la gente). || Difficult situation, tight spot (situación).

apretar* v. tr. To squeeze, to hug: *apretar entre los brazos*, to squeeze in one's arms. || To grip, to grasp: *me apretó el brazo*, he gripped my arm. || To tighten: *apretar un tornillo, un cinturón*, to tighten a screw, a belt. || To press: *apretar el botón*, to press the button. || To pinch, to be too tight for: *me aprietan los zapatos*, my shoes pinch, my shoes are too tight for me. || To pull (el gatillo). || To press down (comprimir). || To shake: *apretar la mano a alguien*, to shake s.o.'s hand. || To quicken up, to quicken, to speed up (acelerar):

apretar el paso, to quicken up one's pace. || To pack, to squeeze: *apretar cosas en una caja*, to pack *o* to squeeze things into a box. || To put pressure on: *le están apretando para que dimita*, they are putting pressure on him to resign. || — FIG. *Apretar la mano* or *las clavijas a alguien*, to clamp down on s.o., to tighten up on s.o. || *Apretar los dientes*, to grit *o* to clench one's teeth. || *Apretarse el cinturón*, to tighten one's belt. || *Me aprieta el tiempo*, time is running out, I'm short of time.
— V. intr. To get worse (frío, dolor). || To get heavier (lluvia). || To get stronger *o* worse (calor). || To be too tight (un vestido). || To hurt, to pinch (zapatos). || To make an effort, to pull one's socks up: *tienes que apretar, si quieres sacar buenas notas*, you've got to make an effort if you want to get good marks. || To hurry up: *¡apriete!*, hurry up! || To be strict (ser exigente). || *Apretar a correr*, to break into a run.
— V. pr. To crowd, to crowd together (apiñarse). || To huddle together (para entrar en calor, etc.).

apretón m. Squeeze (presión fuerte y rápida). || FAM. Call of nature, urgent need (necesidad natural). || FIG. y FAM. Difficult *o* awkward situation, fix, tight spot (aprieto). || FAM. Dash (carrera). || Dash of dark colour (pintura). || — *Apretón de manos*, handshake. || *Me dio un apretón de manos*, he shook my hand, we shook hands. || *Odio los apretones de los transportes públicos*, I hate the crush of public transport. || *Reciba un apretón de manos*, best wishes (en una carta).

apretujar v. tr. FAM. To squeeze hard.
— V. pr. FAM. To squash up together, to squeeze together, to cram together (las personas por falta de espacio).

apretujón m. FAM. Crush, crowding (de las personas). | Hard squeeze (apretón).

apretura f. Scarcity (escasez). || Hurrying (prisa). || FIG. Difficult *o* awkward situation, tight spot, fix, jam (apuro). || — Pl. Crowds, crush, *sing.*: *no me gustan las apreturas del autobús*, I don't like the crush on the bus.

aprieto m. Difficult *o* awkward situation, tight spot, tight corner, fix, jam: *estar* or *hallarse* or *verse en un aprieto, pasar un aprieto*, to be in a tight spot. || — *Poner en un aprieto*, to put into a difficult situation *o* in a tight corner *o* in a tight spot. || *Salir del aprieto*, to get out of trouble.

a priori adj./adv. A priori.

apriorismo m. Apriority.

aprisa adv. Quickly: *se fue muy aprisa*, he left very quickly. || *¡Aprisa!*, quick!, quickly!, be quick!

apriscar v. tr. To fold, to put in a fold [sheep].
— V. pr. To go into a fold (el ganado).

aprisco m. Fold.

aprisionar v. tr. To imprison, to put into prison (encarcelar). || To trap: *la carrocería le aprisionó una pierna*, the bodywork trapped one of his legs. || FIG. To clasp, to grasp: *aprisionar a alguien en los brazos*, to clasp s.o. in one's arms. | To tie down: *estoy aprisionado en el engranaje administrativo*, I am tied down by red tape.

aproar v. intr. MAR. To head, to steer.

aprobación f. Approval, approbation: *dar su aprobación*, to give one's approval. || Passing (de una ley).

aprobado, da adj. Approved: *aprobado por el Ministerio de Educación Nacional*, approved by the Ministry of Education. || Passed (una ley). || *Salir aprobado*, to pass (en un examen).
— M. Pass, passing grade: *tuvo tres aprobados*, he got three passes.

aprobador, ra adj. Approving.

aprobar* v. tr. To approve: *aprobar un proyecto*, to approve a plan. || To approve of: *su padre no aprueba sus amistades*, his father doesn't approve of his friends. || To pass: *he aprobado el examen de matemáticas*, I have passed the mathematics examination. || To pass (una ley). || *Aprobar por unanimidad*, to approve unanimously.
— V. intr. To pass: *ha aprobado en español*, he has passed in Spanish.

aprobativo, va o **aprobatorio, ria** adj. Approving, approbative, approbatory.

aproches m. pl. MIL. Approaches. || *Amer.* Surrounding districts, environs (cercanías). | Neighbourhood (vecindad).

apropiado, da adj. Appropriate, suitable.

apropiar v. tr. To adapt, to fit: *apropiar las leyes a las costumbres*, to adapt laws to customs.
— V. pr. To appropriate, to take: *siempre se apropia de lo que no le pertenece*, he always takes what doesn't belong to him.

apropincuarse v. pr. To approach: *apropincuarse a algo*, to approach sth.

apropósito m. TEATR. Skit.

aprovechable adj. Usable, serviceable. || Wearable: *tu vestido es aún aprovechable*, your dress is still wearable. || *Estos restos son todavía aprovechables*, these leftovers can still be used.

aprovechadamente adv. Profitably.

aprovechado, da adj. Thrifty, economical: *una ama de casa muy aprovechada*, a very thrifty housewife. || Resourceful (apañado). || Diligent, studious (estudioso). || Industrious (trabajador). || Planned: *casa bien aprovechada*, well-planned house. || Selfish (egoísta). || Spent: *dinero, tiempo bien aprovechado*, money, time well spent. || FAM. *Es un tipo muy aprovechado*, he's a real sponger. || — Adj./s. Opportunist.

aprovechador, ra adj./s. Opportunist.

aprovechamiento m. Advantage: *sacaron el máximo aprovechamiento de ello*, they used it to the greatest advantage, they took the greatest advantage of it. || Exploitation, tapping, use: *el aprovechamiento de los recursos naturales*, the exploitation of natural resources. || Use: *aprovechamiento en común de un bosque*, joint use of a wood. || Development, improvement: *el aprovechamiento de las tierras*, land development. || Harnessing: *el aprovechamiento de un río*, the harnessing of a river.
— Pl. Products.

aprovechar v. intr. To be helpful, to be useful, to be a help: *les aprovechará mucho a tus hermanos*, it will be a great help to *o* it will be very helpful to your brothers. || To take advantage of it, to make the most of it, to seize the opportunity: *como hacía buen tiempo, aprovecharon y se fueron al campo*, as the weather was fine, they took advantage of it and went into the country. || FIG. To make progress, to progress: *no hemos aprovechado en esa clase*, we have made no progress *o* we haven't progressed in that class. || MAR. To haul as close as possible. || — *No aprovechar para nada*, to be of no use at all. || *¡Que aproveche!*, [I hope you] enjoy your meal, bon appétit. (V. OBSERV.)
— V. tr. To take advantage of, to make the most of: *aprovechar el tiempo, la situación*, to take advantage of the weather, of the situation. || To make good use of, to put to good use: *un cocinero que sabe aprovechar toda clase de alimentos*, a cook who can make good use of any kind of food, a cook who can put any kind of food to good use. || To use: *no aprovecho nunca los restos*, I never use the leftovers. || To take [unfair] advantage of (de una manera egoísta). || To exploit (los recursos naturales). || To develop, to improve (tierras). || To harness (curso de agua). || To take advantage of, to take up (una oferta). || *Aprovechar la ocasión*, to take *o* to seize the opportunity, to make the most of the opportunity.
— V. pr. To take advantage, to use to one's advantage (sacar provecho). || To make the most of it, to take advantage: *aprovéchate ahora, luego será demasiado tarde*, make the most of it now, before it is too late. || To take advantage of: *aprovecharse de uno, de un momento de descuido*, to take advantage of s.o., of a moment's negligence.
— OBSERV. *¡Que aproveche!* is a polite expression used by one person to others who are already eating. As no fixed expression is used in these circumstances in English, only an approximate translation can be given.

aprovechón, ona adj. Selfish, opportunist (que saca provecho de todo).
— M. y f. Advantage-taker, selfish person, opportunist.

aprovisionamiento m. Supply, supplying, provision (acción de abastecer). || Supply, provision (vituallas).

aprovisionar v. tr. To supply, to give supplies to, to give provisions to.

aproximación f. Approximation: *cálculo con aproximación*, calculation by approximation. || Prize for runners-up, consolation prize (en la lotería). || Proximity, closeness, nearness (proximidad). || Bringing together (de dos personas). || Rapprochement (de dos países). || Approximation (acercamiento). || — *Con una aproximación del uno por ciento*, to the nearest one per cent. || *Sólo es una aproximación*, it is only a rough estimate *o* an approximation.

aproximadamente adv. Approximately.

aproximado, da adj. Approximate, rough: *valor, cálculo aproximado*, approximate value, calculation.

aproximar v. tr. To bring nearer: *aproxima tu silla a la mía*, bring your chair nearer to mine. || To draw up: *aproximar una silla a la mesa*, to draw a chair up to the table. || To put nearer: *aproxima la mesa a esa pared*, put the table nearer to that wall. || To pass: *aproxímame el libro*, pass me the book. || To bring together (dos personas).
— V. pr. To move nearer: *aproximarse al fuego*, to move nearer to the fire. || To draw near, to approach: *se aproxima su cumpleaños*, his birthday is drawing near. || To be nearly: *se aproxima a los veinte*, he is nearly twenty. || To be near *o* close: *me aproximé bastante a la solución*, I was quite near to the answer. || To approach, to near: *aproximarse a su destino*, to approach *o* to near one's destination. || FIG. To approach. || *¡Ni se le aproxima!*, it's nothing like it! (es completamente distinto).

aproximativo, va adj. Approximate, rough (aproximado).

ápside m. ASTR. Apsis: *los ápsides*, the apsides.

aptamente adv. Conveniently.

ápterix m. ZOOL. Apteryx.

áptero, ra adj. ZOOL. Apterous (sin alas).

aptitud f. Suitability, aptness, aptitude (de una cosa). || Capacity, ability (capacidad). || — Pl. Gift, *sing.*, aptitude, *sing*: *tiene aptitudes para la pintura*, he has a gift for painting. || — *Aptitudes físicas*, physical capacities. || *Aptitud para los negocios*, business sense. || *Prueba de aptitud*, aptitude test.

apto, ta adj. Capable: *un obrero muy apto*, a very capable worker. || Suitable, fitted: *apto para ocupar este cargo*, suitable for this post. || Fit [*para*, to] (en con-

diciones de). || — MIL. *Apto para el servicio*, fit for service. || *Película apta para todos los públicos*, U-certificate film. || *Película no apta para menores*, X-certificate film, film unsuitable for children.
apuesta f. Bet, wager. || *Apuestas mutuas*, pari-mutuel.
apuesto, ta adj. Spruce, neat, smart (elegante).
Apuleyo n. pr. m. Apuleius.
apulgarar v. tr. To press with one's thumb, to thumb.
— V. pr. To get mildewed, to become spotted with mildew (la ropa blanca).
apunarse v. pr. *Amer.* To have mountain sickness.
apuntación f. Note (nota). || Aiming (de armas). || MÚS. Notation.
apuntado, da adj. Pointed, sharp (puntiagudo). || ARQ. Gothic, pointed (arco).
apuntador, ra adj. Who makes notes (que apunta). || Aiming, who aims (artillería).
— M. Aimer (artillería). || TEATR. Prompter: *concha del apuntador*, prompter's box. || FIG. *En esta película muere hasta el apuntador*, there's not a soul left alive at the end of the film.
apuntalamiento m. Propping-up, shoring-up. || Spragging, propping-up, shoring-up (de minas).
apuntalar v. tr. To prop up, to shore up. || To sprag, to prop up, to shore up (una mina).
apuntamiento m. Aiming (de un arma). || Note (nota). || JUR. Records (*pl.*) of the proceedings.
apuntar v. tr. To aim, to point (un arma). || To point at (señalar): *apuntar a uno con el dedo*, to point at s.o. with one's finger. || To point out (sugerir): *el ministro apuntó la necesidad de una reforma*, the minister pointed out the need for a reform. || To show: *este principiante apunta excelentes cualidades*, this beginner shows excellent qualities. || To take *o* to note down, to make a note of (anotar): *apunta sus señas*, take down his address. || To put down, to put: *apúntelo en mi cuenta*, put it on my account; *me apuntó en la lista*, he put me on the list. || To put a mark on (señalar un escrito). || To sharpen (sacar punta): *apuntar un lápiz*, to sharpen a pencil. || To bet, to stake (jugar): *apuntar mil pesetas*, to bet a thousand pesetas. || To score (en deportes, juegos). || To tack (en costura). || To fasten *o* to fix temporarily (fijar provisionalmente). || FAM. To darn, to mend (zurcir). || To sketch out (bosquejar). || TEATR. To prompt. || To prompt with, to whisper: *le apuntaron la solución*, they prompted him with the answer, they whispered the answer to him. || — FAM. *Apúntalo en la barra de hielo*, you can forget it, you can give it up as lost. || *Apuntar presente*, to mark present.
— V. intr. To aim: *apuntar a uno a la cabeza*, to aim at s.o.'s head; *apuntar a un blanco con un arma*, to aim a weapon at a target; *objetivos que apuntan a la supresión de los privilegios*, objectives which aim at the suppression of privileges. || To dawn, to break (el día). || To sprout, to begin to grow (la barba). || To sprout, to come through: *la hierba apunta*, the grass is sprouting. || TEATR. To prompt. || To point: *la proa de la nave apuntaba al sur*, the bow of the ship pointed towards the south. || MIL. *¡Apunten!*, take aim!
— V. pr. To begin to turn sour (el vino). || To put one's name: *me apunté en la lista*, I put my name on the list. || FAM. To enrol, to enroll: *me apunté en el colegio*, I enrolled in the school. | To get tipsy (embriagarse). || — FIG. *Apuntarse un tanto, un triunfo*, to chalk up *o* to score a point, a victory. | *Yo me apunto*, I'm with you, I'm game, count me in.
apunte m. Note (nota). || Sketch (dibujo). || TEATR. Prompter (apuntador). | Prompt (voz de apuntador). | Prompter's script, promptbook (texto). || Staker (jugador). || Stake, bet (puesta en el juego). || COM. Entry. || *Amer. Llevar el apunte a uno*, to respond to s.o. (corresponder).
— Pl. Notes: *tomar apuntes*, to take notes. || ARTES. *Sacar apuntes*, to do some sketches.
apuntillar v. tr. TAUR. To deal the coup de grâce [to the bull] with a dagger.
apuñalar v. tr. To stab: *lo apuñaló por la espalda*, he stabbed him in the back. || FIG. *Apuñalar con la mirada*, to look daggers at.
apuñar v. tr. To take in one's fist.
apuracabos m. inv. Save-all (palmatoria).
apuradamente adv. With difficulty. || In want, in need: *vivir apuradamente*, to live in want. || FAM. Exactly. || *Vino a decírmelo muy apuradamente*, he was very embarrassed when he came to tell me.
apurado, da adj. Hard up: *estar apurado de dinero*, to be hard up for money. || Difficult, awkward: *estoy en una situación apurada*, I'm in an awkward situation. || Worn-out, tired-out, exhausted (agotado). || Embarrassed (avergonzado): *me vi apurado cuando tuve que pedirle dinero*, I was embarrassed when I had to ask him for money. || Exact (preciso). || *Amer.* In a hurry (apresurado). || — *Estar apurado de tiempo*, to be short of time, not to have much time. || *Estar apurado por uno*, to be annoyed by s.o. || *Verse apurado*, to be in a jam *o* a fix (estar en un apuro).
apurador, ra adj. Tiring, exhausting (que agota).
apuramiento m. Purification (acción de purificar). || Exhaustion (agotamiento). || FIG. Clarification (aclaración).
apurar v. tr. To purify (purificar). || To exhaust: *apurar todos los medios para conseguir algo*, to exhaust every means of obtaining sth. || To drain: *apurar una copa*, to drain a glass. || To use up, to finish off: *apurar la pintura*, to use up the paint. || To exhaust, to wear out, to tire out (abrumar): *los padres apuraron al niño*, the parents exhausted the child. || To examine thoroughly *o* in detail (examinar a fondo). || To embarrass (causar vergüenza): *me apura pedirle dinero*, it embarrasses me to ask him for money. || To exhaust the patience of, to make lose one's patience: *si me apuras, sufrirás las consecuencias*, if you make me lose my patience *o* if you exhaust my patience, you will suffer the consequences. || To rush, to hurry (dar prisa): *no me apures tanto*, don't rush me so. || — *Apurándolo mucho*, at the most (como mucho): *apurándolo mucho esta casa le ha costado tres mil libras*, this house cost him three thousand pounds at the most. || *Apurar el cáliz hasta las heces*, to drain the cup to the dregs. || *Me apura tener que decirle esto*, I don't like having to tell you this, I hate to have to tell you this. || *Si me apura mucho, se lo vendería por mil libras*, at a push I would sell it to him for a thousand pounds.
— V. intr. To be unbearable: *el calor apuraba*, the heat was unbearable.
— V. pr. To worry, to get worried: *no se apure por eso*, don't worry about that. || To hurry, to hurry up (apresurarse): *apúrate o llegaremos tarde*, hurry up or we'll be late. || *Apurarse la barba*, to have a close shave.
apuro m. Difficult situation, tight spot, trouble, mess, jam, fix: *estar en un apuro*, to be in a fix *o* in trouble; *sacar a alguien de un apuro*, to get s.o. out of a mess. || Difficulty, hardship: *al principio pasé muchos apuros en este país*, at first I had a lot of difficulties in this country. || Embarrassment (vergüenza). || *Amer.* Hurry (prisa). || — *Estar en apuros* or *estar en un apuro de dinero* or *tener apuros de dinero*, to be short of money, to be hard up. || *Me da apuro hacer eso*, I'm afraid of doing that, I don't like to do that. || *Pasar un apuro*, to be embarrassed. || *Salir de apuro*, to get out of trouble *o* out of a tight spot *o* out of a difficult situation.
aquejado, da adj. Suffering (de una enfermedad).
aquejar v. tr. To trouble. || — FIG. *Estar* or *encontrarse aquejado de*, to be suffering from: *la economía se encuentra aquejada de falta de mano de obra*, the economy is suffering from a lack of manpower. || *Le aqueja una grave enfermedad*, he is suffering from a serious illness.
aquel m. FAM. Certain something, special something: *no es guapa pero tiene un aquel*, she is not pretty but she has a certain something.
aquel, aquella adj. dem. That (*pl.*, those): *aquel sombrero*, that hat; *aquella casa*, that house; *aquellos años de mi juventud*, those years of my youth; *las mujeres aquellas*, those women. || The former: *Juana y Diana son hermanas, aquella hermana tiene veinte años y ésta treinta*, Joan and Diana are sisters, the former [sister] is twenty and the latter thirty. (V. AQUÉL [OBSERV.].)
— Pron. The one, that one: *aquel que ves allí*, the one you can see there; *aquellos de quienes te hablo*, the ones *o* those I am talking about. || *Todo aquel que*, anyone who.
aquél, aquélla pron. dem. That one (*pl.* those): *éste es más barato que aquél, que aquéllos*, this one is cheaper than that one, than those. || The former: *Juan y Pedro se han casado, aquél con una chica inglesa y éste con una española*, John and Peter got married, the former to an English girl and the latter to a Spaniard.
— OBSERV. *Aquel* and *aquél* denote remoteness from both the speaker and the person spoken to, and remoteness in time either in the past or in the future. They are often opposed to *este* and *éste*. The pronouns *aquél* and *aquélla* have accents to distinguish them from the adjectives when they are not followed by a relative pronoun.
aquelarre m. [Nocturnal] Witches' sabbath. || FIG. Uproar, din (ruido).
aquella adj. dem. V. AQUEL.
aquélla pron. dem. V. AQUÉL.
aquello pron. dem. That: *esto no es tan bueno como aquello*, this is not as good as that. || The former (anterior). || That affair, that business, that matter: *aquello del ministro y la empresa*, that affair about the minister and the firm. || — *¡Aquello fue para morirse de risa!*, it was hilarious! || *Por aquello del orgullo*, because of pride, out of pride. || *Por aquello de no quedar mal*, so as not to look bad.
aquende adv. On this side of: *aquende los Pirineos*, on this side of the Pyrenees.
aquenio m. BOT. Achene.
aqueo, a adj./s. Achæan.
aquerenciarse v. pr. To become fond of *o* attached to.
aquese, sa, so adj. dem. POÉT. V. ESE, ESA, ESO.
aqueste, ta, to adj. dem. POÉT. V. ESTE, ESTA, ESTO.
aquí adv. Here: *aquí abajo*, down here; *aquí dentro*, in here; *ven aquí*, come here. || Then, at that moment, here (entonces): *aquí no pudo contenerse*, then he could not restrain himself. || Now, here: *aquí viene lo mejor del caso*, now comes the good part. || POP. He, she. || — *Andar de aquí para allá*, to come and go, to walk up and down, to walk to and fro. || *Aquí está*, here it is, here he is, here she is (como interjección), here is: *aquí está tu libro*, here is your book. || *¡Aquí fue Troya!*, then the trouble began, that was when it started. || *Aquí*

presente, present. || *Aquí y allí* or *aquí y allá*, here and there. || *Aquí yace*, here lies. || *De aquí*, hence: *de aquí los males que venimos padeciendo*, hence the evils which plague us; from here: *de aquí arranca la evolución de la economía española*, from here stems the development of the Spanish economy. || *De aquí a* or *en ocho días*, in eight days, within eight days, in *o* within a week (plazo), a week today (fecha). || *De aquí a poco*, in a short time, soon. || *De aquí en adelante*, from now on, henceforth. || *De aquí hasta entonces*, until then. || *De aquí que*, hence: *es muy tímido, de aquí que no le guste ir a la escuela*, he is very shy, hence he does not like going to school. || *Hasta aquí*, this far, as far as here (lugar), so far, until now (tiempo). || *He aquí*, here is. || *Heme aquí*, here I am. || *Por aquí*, round here: *no ha pasado por aquí*, he hasn't been round here; this way: *por aquí por favor*, this way please; somewhere round here, near here: *vive por aquí*, he lives somewhere round here; through here: *la autopista va a pasar por aquí*, the motorway is going to pass through here. || *Por aquí y por allá*, here and there.

aquiescencia f. Acquiescence, assent.

aquietador, ra adj. Soothing, calming (que calma). || Soothing, which eases (que alivia).

aquietar v. tr. To calm down, to calm: *aquietar a un caballo*, to calm a horse down. || To ease, to soothe (el dolor). || To calm (el temor).

— V. pr. To calm down (calmarse). || To ease (el dolor).

aquilatado, da adj. Proven, tested: *hombre de aquilatada virtud*, man of proven virtue. || *Precio aquilatado*, rock-bottom price, lowest possible price.

aquilatamiento m. Assay.

aquilatar v. tr. To assay (el oro). || To value (piedras preciosas). || FIG. To purify (purificar). | To make as cheap as possible, to reduce as much as possible (precio).

Aquiles n. pr. m. Achilles. || — *Talón de Aquiles*, Achilles heel. || *Tendón de Aquiles*, Achilles tendon.

aquilino, na adj. Aquiline (aguileño): *nariz aquilina*, aquiline nose.

aquilón m. North wind.

aquillado, da adj. Keel-shaped.

Aquisgrán n. pr. GEOGR. Aachen. || HIST. Aix-la-Chapelle.

Aquitania n. pr. f. GEOGR. Aquitaine. || HIST. Aquitania.

ara f. Altar (altar). || Altar stone (piedra). || *En aras de*, for the sake of, for, in honour of: *en aras de nuestra amistad*, for the sake of our friendship.

— M. ZOOL. Ara, macaw (guacamayo). || ASTR. Altar, Ara (constelación).

árabe adj. Arab, Arabic, Arabian.

— M. y f. Arab, Arabian. || — M. Arabic (lengua). || FAM. *Eso es árabe para mí*, that's Greek *o* double Dutch to me.

arabesco, ca adj. Arabesque.

— M. Arabesque.

arabia f. *Amer.* Blue and white checked cotton material.

Arabia n. pr. f. GEOGR. Arabia: *Arabia Saudí* o *Arabia Saudita*, Saudi Arabia.

arábico, ca o **arábigo, ga** adj. Arabic: *número arábigo*, Arabic numeral; *goma arábiga*, gum arabic. || *Golfo Arábico*, Arabian Gulf.

— M. Arabic (lengua).

arabismo m. Arabicism, Arabic expression [used in another language].

arabista m. y f. Arabist, student of Arabic.

arabización f. Arabicization.

arabizar v. tr. To Arabicize.

arable adj. Arable.

arácnido, da adj./s. m. ZOOL. Arachnid, arachnidan.

aracnoideo, a adj. Arachnoid.

aracnoides f. ANAT. Arachnoid.

arada f. AGR. Ploughing [U.S., plowing, ploughing] (acción de arar). | Farming (labranza). | Ploughed land [U.S., plowed *o* ploughed land] (tierra arada). | Day's ploughing (jornal).

arado m. AGR. Plough [U.S., plow, plough]: *arado bisurco*, double-furrow plough. || *Amer.* Farming (labranza). || AGR. *Arado de balancín*, balance plough.

arador, ra adj. Who ploughs, ploughing.

— M. Ploughman [U.S., plowman, ploughman] (labrador). || ZOOL. Itch mite.

aradura f. Ploughing [U.S., plowing, ploughing].

Aragón n. pr. m. GEOGR. Aragon.

aragonés, esa adj./s. Aragonese. || FIG. *Testarudo* or *terco como un aragonés*, as stubborn as a mule.

aragonito m. MIN. Aragonite.

araguato m. Ursine howler (mono).

arambel m. Hangings, *pl.* (colgadura). || FIG. Rag, tatter (andrajo).

arameo, a adj./s. Aramaean. || — M. Aramaean, Aramaic (lengua).

arana f. Trick, swindle.

arancel m. Customs tariff *o* duty (tarifa).

arancelario, ria adj. Tariff: *barreras arancelarias*, tariff barriers. || — *Derechos arancelarios*, customs duties. || *Leyes arancelarias*, customs laws.

arándano m. BOT. Bilberry, whortleberry.

arandela f. Washer (para tornillos). || Candle ring (de bujía). || Frill, flounce (chorrera). || Guard (de lanza). || Candlestick (candelabro).

arandillo m. ZOOL. Marsh warbler (pájaro).

araña f. ZOOL. Spider. || BOT. Love-in-a-mist (arañuela). || Chandelier (lámpara de techo). || Bird net (red). || MAR. Clew (de hamaca). || FIG. y FAM. Resourceful *o* thrifty person. | Whore (prostituta). || — *Araña de mar*, sea spider, spider crab. || *Red* or *tela de araña*, spider's web.

arañadura f. Scratch.

arañar v. tr. To scratch: *el gato me ha arañado*, the cat has scratched me. || To scratch, to scrape: *arañar la pared con algo*, to scratch the wall with sth. || FIG. To scrape together (recoger). | To scrape (un instrumento de cuerda).

— V. intr. To scratch: *este cepillo araña*, this brush scratches.

— V. pr. To scratch o.s.

arañazo m. Scratch (rasguño). || Scratch, scrape (en la pared, en un metal).

arañero m. ZOOL. Creeper (pájaro).

arañuela f. ZOOL. Small spider. | Insect's larva (larva). || BOT. Love-in-a-mist, nigella.

arañuelo m. ZOOL. Insect's larva. | Tick (garrapata).

arapaima m. ZOOL. Arapaima (pez de Amazonia).

arar m. BOT. Juniper (enebro). | Larch (alerce).

arar v. tr. AGR. To plough [U.S., to plow, to plough]. || FIG. To plough through (surcar). | To furrow, to wrinkle: *rostro arado por el sufrimiento*, face furrowed by suffering. || FIG. *Arar en el mar*, to plough the sands.

araucano, na adj./s. Araucanian.

araucaria f. BOT. Araucaria.

aravico m. *Amer.* Bard [amongst the Indians of Peru].

arbitrable adj. Submissible to arbitration.

arbitraje m. Arbitration. || DEP. Refereeing (en fútbol, boxeo, etc.). | Umpirage (en críquet, tenis, béisbol).

arbitral adj. JUR. By arbitration: *sentencia arbitral*, judgement by arbitration. || DEP. Of the referee (del árbitro).

arbitrar v. tr. e intr. JUR. To arbitrate [*en*, in; *entre*, between]. || DEP. To referee: *arbitrar un partido de fútbol*, to referee a football match. | To umpire (en tenis, críquet, béisbol). || To find, to work out: *arbitrar los medios para lograr algo*, to work out the means of achieving sth. || To raise, to get together (fondos, recursos).

— V. pr. To manage (arreglárselas).

arbitrariedad f. Arbitrariness (cualidad de arbitrario). || Outrage, abuse, arbitrary action: *la sanción que me impusieron fue una arbitrariedad*, the sanction that they imposed on me was an outrage.

arbitrario, ria adj. Arbitrary: *una orden arbitraria*, an arbitrary order.

arbitrio m. Will, wishes, *pl.* (voluntad): *seguir el arbitrio de sus padres*, to obey the will of one's parents. || Free will (albedrío). || Fancy (capricho). || Means, expedient (recurso). || JUR. Judgement, judgment. || — Pl. Taxes (impuestos). || *Dejar al arbitrio de alguien*, to leave to s.o.'s discretion.

arbitrista m. y f. Armchair politician, political dreamer, soapbox politician. || Idealist (idealista).

árbitro m. JUR. Arbitrator, arbiter. || DEP. Umpire (en tenis, críquet, béisbol). | Referee (en fútbol, boxeo, etc.). || *Petronio, árbitro de la elegancia*, Petronious, arbiter of elegance.

árbol m. Tree: *árbol frutal*, fruit tree. || Body (de la camisa). || Newel (de escalera). || IMPR. Shank (del tipo). || MAR. Mast (palo). || TECN. Shaft: *árbol motor*, drive *o* driving shaft. || — BOT. *Árbol de la cera*, wax myrtle, candleberry. || MAR. *Árbol de la hélice*, propeller shaft. || BOT. *Árbol del diablo*, sandbox tree. || AUT. *Árbol de levas*, camshaft. || BOT. *Árbol del pan*, breadfruit tree. || *Árbol de Navidad*, Christmas tree. || BOT. *Árbol desmochado*, pollard. || *Árbol genealógico*, v. GENEALÓGICO. || ANAT. *Árbol respiratorio*, respiratory system. || FIG. *Del árbol caído todos hacen leña*, a fallen man is everybody's prey. | *Por el fruto se conoce el árbol*, a tree is known by its fruit.

arbolado, da adj. Wooded: *región arbolada*, wooded area.

— M. Trees, *pl.*, woodland (conjunto de árboles).

arboladura f. MAR. Masts and spars, *pl.*

arbolar v. tr. MAR. To mast (poner mástiles). || To hoist: *arbolar bandera española*, to hoist the Spanish flag. || To brandish (un arma).

— V. pr. To rear up (encabritarse).

arboleda f. Wood, copse, spinney.

arborecer* v. intr. To grow [into a tree].

arbóreo, a adj. Arboreal, sylvan (de árboles). || Arboreal (animal). || Arborescent, treelike (de forma de árbol). || *Vegetación arbórea*, woodland, trees, *pl.*

arborescencia f. BOT. Arborescence.

arborescente adj. BOT. Arborescent.

arborícola adj. ZOOL. Tree-dwelling, arboreal.

arboricultor m. Arboriculturist, nurseryman.

arboricultura f. Arboriculture, cultivation of trees.

arborización f. MIN. Arborization.

arbotante m. ARQ. Flying buttress. || MAR. Outrigger.

arbustivo, va adj. BOT. Shrublike, bushlike.

arbusto m. BOT. Shrub, bush.

arca f. Chest (cofre). || Safe, strongbox (caja de caudales). || Ark: *Arca de Noé*, Noah's Ark. || TECN. Tempering oven [for blown glass]. || — Pl. Vaults (en tesorerías). || ANAT. Flanks, sides (debajo de las costillas).

|| — *Arca de agua*, water tower. || *Arca de la Alianza*, Ark of the Covenant. || *Arca del cuerpo*, [human] trunk. || *Arcas públicas*, Treasury, *sing.*, public coffers.

arcabucear v. tr. To shoot at *o* to fire at with an arquebus (disparar contra). || To kill with an arquebus (matar).

arcabucería f. Arquebus factory (fábrica). || Arquebuses, *pl.* (conjunto de arcabuses). || Arquebusiers, *pl.* (tropa).

arcabucero m. Arquebusier, harquebusier.

arcabuz m. Arquebus, harquebus. || Arquebusier, harquebusier (arcabucero).

arcada f. Arcade (arcos). || Arches, *pl.* (de un puente). || — Pl. Retching (náuseas). || *Puente de una sola arcada*, single-span bridge.

Arcadia n. pr. f. GEOGR. Arcadia.

arcadio, dia adj./s. Arcadian.

arcaduz m. Pipe, conduit (caño). || Scoop, bucket (de noria).

arcaico, ca adj. Archaic (primitivo).

arcaísmo m. Archaism.

arcaísta m. y f. Archaist.

arcaizante adj. Archaistic.

arcaizar v. intr. To archaize, to imitate the archaic.
— V. tr. To archaize, to make archaistic.

arcángel m. Archangel.

arcangélico, ca adj. Archangelic.

arcano, na adj. Arcane.
— M. Mystery, secret: *los arcanos del universo*, the secrets of the universe.

arce m. BOT. Maple.

arcedianato m. Archdeaconship (cargo). || Archdeaconry (jurisdicción).

arcediano m. Archdeacon.

arcén m. Hard shoulder (de autopista). || Verge, side of the road (de una carretera). || Curb, kerb (de la acera).

arcilla f. Clay (greda). || Matter, substance (materia). || — *Arcilla cocida*, baked clay. || *Arcilla figulina*, potter's clay.

arcillar v. tr. AGR. To clay, to dress with clay.

arcilloso, sa adj. Clayey, argillaceous.

arciprestal adj. Of an archpriest, archpriest's.

arciprestazgo m. Archpriesthood, archpriestship.

arcipreste m. Archpriest.

arco m. MAT. Arc: *arco de círculo*, arc of a circle. || Bow (arma). || MÚS. Bow (de violín). || Hoop (de tonel). || ANAT. Arch: *arco alveolar*, dental arch. || ARQ. Arch. || ELECTR. Arc. || — ARQ. *Arco abocinado*, splayed arch. | *Arco adintelado* or *a nivel*, flat arch. | *Arco apuntado*, pointed arch. | *Arco capialzado*, splayed arch. | *Arco carpanel* or *arco apainelado* or *rebajado*, basket-handle arch. | *Arco conopial*, ogee arch. | *Arco de cortina*, inflected arch. | *Arco de herradura* or *morisco* or *arábigo*, horseshoe *o* Moorish arch. | *Arco de medio punto*, semicircular arch. | *Arco de todo punto* or *ojival*, Gothic arch, ogive. | *Arco de triunfo* or *triunfal*, triumphal arch. | *Arco escarzano*, segmental arch. || *Arco iris*, rainbow. || ARQ. *Arco lanceolado*, lancet arch. | *Arco peraltado*, stilted arch. | *Arco por tranquil*, flying arch. | *Arco tercelete*, tierceron. | *Arco trebolado* or *trilobulado*, trefoil arch. || ELECTR. *Arco voltaico*, electric arc. || *Tirar con arco*, to shoot with bow and arrow. || DEP. *Tiro con arco* or *de arco*, archery.

arcón m. Large chest.

arcontado m. Archonship, archontate.

arconte m. Archon (magistrado griego).

archi pref. FAM. This prefix is often added to an adjective in Spanish to intensify it (*architonto*, extremely stupid).

archicofradía f. Archconfraternity.

archiconocido, da adj. FAM. Known by everyone, extremely well-known.

archidiácono m. Archdeacon.

archidiocesano, na adj. Archdiocesan.

archidiócesis f. Archbishopric, archdiocese.

archiducado m. Archduchy.

archiducal adj. Archducal.

archiduque, quesa m. y f. Archduke (hombre), archduchess (mujer).

archifamoso, sa adj. FAM. World famous.

archilaúd m. MÚS. Archlute.

archimandrita m. Archimandrite (sacerdote griego).

archimillonario, ria m. y f. Multimillionaire (hombre), multimillionairess (mujer).

archipámpano m. FAM. *Se cree el archipámpano de las Indias* or *de Sevilla*, he thinks he's a big shot *o* the Great Panjandrum.

archipiélago m. Archipelago.

archisabido, da adj. FAM. Very well-known. || *Eso es una cosa archisabida*, that's common knowledge.

archivador, ra m. y f. Archivist, keeper of records (persona). || — M. Filing cabinet (mueble).

archivar v. tr. To file, to file away (clasificar). || To put into the archives, to archive. || FIG. To shelve: *han archivado los mayores problemas*, they have shelved the main problems. || FIG. *Archivar algo en su cabeza*, to make a mental note of sth.

archivero, ra o **archivista** m. y f. Archivist.

archivo m. File: *buscaré su dirección en su archivo personal*, I shall look for his address in his personal file. || Archives, *pl.*, files, *pl.* (conjunto de documentos custodiados): *el archivo de una casa editorial*, the archives of a publishing company. || Filing cabinet (mueble). || FIG. Soul of discretion. | Example, model, paragon (dechado). || — Pl. Archives: *los archivos de la biblioteca municipal*, the town library's archives. || *Archivo Nacional*, Public Records Office [U.S., National Archives].

archivolta f. ARQ. Archivolt.

ardentía f. Heat (ardor). || Phosphorescence (en el mar). || MED. *Sentir ardentía* or *ardentías*, to have heartburn.

arder v. intr. To burn: *la leña seca arde bien*, dry wood burns well. || FIG. To seethe, to boil, to burn: *arder de* or *en ira*, to seethe with anger. | To burn: *arder en deseos de*, to burn with desire to. | To burn, to be consumed: *arder en celos*, to be consumed by jealousy, to burn with jealousy. || AGR. To decompose (el estiércol). || — *Arder sin llama*, to smoulder. || FIG. *El país entero arde en guerra*, war is raging throughout the country. | *La ciudad arde en fiestas*, celebrations in the town are in full swing. | *La cosa está que arde*, the situation is very tense, things are getting very hot. | *Me arde la boca*, my mouth is on fire. | *Toma un duro, y vas que ardes*, take five pesetas, and that's more than enough.
— V. tr. To burn (quemar).
— V. pr. To burn, to burn up. || AGR. To scorch, to parch (quemarse).

ardid m. Ruse, scheme, trick. || *Valiéndose de ardides*, by trickery.

ardido, da adj. (Ant.). Bold, brave.

ardiente adj. Hot, scalding. || FIG. Ardent, passionate, fervent: *ardiente partidario*, fervent supporter. | Burning, keen: *deseo ardiente*, burning desire. | Ardent, passionate (muy amoroso). | Blazing, flaming (color). || *Capilla ardiente*, mortuary chapel [lit with tapers].

ardientemente adv. Ardently, passionately, fervently.

ardilla f. ZOOL. Squirrel. || — ZOOL. *Ardilla rayada*, chipmunk. | *Ardilla terrestre*, gopher.

ardimiento m. Burning (ardor). || FIG. Fervour, [U.S., fervor], keenness (fervor). | Bravery, boldness (valor).

ardite m. (Ant.). "Ardite" [old Spanish coin of very little value]. || — FAM. *Me importa un ardite*, I don't give a damn *o* two hoots *o* a hang. | *No vale un ardite*, it's not worth a brass farthing.

ardor m. Heat: *el ardor del Sol*, the heat of the sun; *en el ardor de la batalla*, in the heat of the battle. || Burn (quemazón), burning (sensación de quemarse). || FIG. Ardour [U.S., ardor], keenness, enthusiasm, fervour [U.S., fervor]: *ardor en el trabajo*, keenness in one's work. || *Ardor de estómago*, heartburn.

ardorosamente adv. Ardently.

ardoroso, sa adj. Hot, burning (ardiente). || Feverish, fevered (febril). || Passionate, fervent.

arduo, dua adj. Arduous, difficult.

área f. Area (superficie): *el área de un triángulo*, the area of a triangle. || ARQ. Plot area, area (de un edificio). || Are [100 square metres] (medida agraria). || AGR. Bed (de flores). | Patch (de hortalizas). || — DEP. *Área de castigo*, penalty area. | *Área de gol*, goal area (fútbol), in-goal (rugby). || *Área metropolitana* or *urbana*, Metropolitan area. || *Área metropolitana de Londres, de Nueva York*, Greater London, metropolitan New York.

areca f. BOT. Areca palm, betel palm (palmera). | Areca nut, betel nut (fruto).

arena f. Sand: *la arena de la playa está mojada*, the sand on the beach is wet; *las arenas del desierto*, the sands of the desert. || Arena (en el circo romano). || TAUR. Bullring (ruedo). || — Pl. MED. Stones, gravel, *sing.* (en el riñón). || Dust, *sing.*: *arenas de oro*, gold dust. || — *Arena movediza*, quicksand. || FIG. *Edificar sobre arena* or *sembrar en arena*, to build on sand. || *Reloj de arena*, hourglass, sandglass; egg-timer (en la cocina). || *Una playa de arena*, a sandy beach.

arenáceo, a adj. Arenaceous.

arenal m. Large expanse of sand. || Quicksand (arena movediza).

arenar v. tr. To sand, to sprinkle with sand (enarenar). || To sand, to abrade with sand (frotar con arena).

arenero m. Sand dealer, sand merchant (vendedor). || Sandbox (de locomotora). || TAUR. Sand boy [who keeps the surface smooth in the bullring].

arenga f. Harangue, sermon: *dirigir una arenga*, to give a harangue.

arengar v. tr. To harangue.

arenícola adj. Arenicolous, sand-dwelling.
— F. Lugworm.

arenilla f. Blotting powder (para la tinta). || — Pl. MED. Stones, gravel, *sing.* (en el riñón). || Granulated saltpetre, *sing.* (salitre).

arenillero m. Powder sprinkler [for drying ink].

arenisco, ca adj. Sandy (arenoso). || Stoneware: *vaso arenisco*, stoneware vase. || *Piedra arenisca*, sandstone.
— F. Sandstone (piedra).

arenoso, sa adj. Sandy: *playa arenosa*, sandy beach.

arenque m. ZOOL. Herring. || — *Arenque ahumado*, kippered herring, kipper. || FIG. y FAM. *Seco como un arenque*, as dry as a bone.

arenquera f. Herring net (red). || FIG. y FAM. Fishwife (vendedora de pescado).

areola o **aréola** f. MED. y ANAT. Areola, areole.

areometría f. Areometry.
areómetro m. Areometer, hydrometer.
areopagita m. Areopagite.
areópago m. Areopagus.
arepa f. *Amer.* Round maize loaf. || FAM. *Ganar la arepa*, to earn one's bread and butter.
arepero, ra adj. *Amer.* Loutish.
arepita f. *Amer.* Fried maize cake.
arestín m. BOT. Eryngium. || VET. Thrush (enfermedad de los caballos).
arete m. Small ring (anillo). || *Amer.* Earring (pendiente).
arfada f. MAR. Pitch, pitching.
arfar v. intr. MAR. To pitch.
argadijo o **argadillo** m. Winding frame (devanadera).
argallera f. Croze.
argamasa f. Mortar.
argamasar v. tr. To mortar (trabar con argamasa).
— V. intr. To make *o* to mix mortar (hacer argamasa).
argamasón m. Large piece of dried mortar (pedazo). || Rubble (conjunto de pedazos).
árgana f. Crane (grúa).
árganas f. pl. Baskets, panniers [used on pack animals].
arganeo m. MAR. Anchor ring.
árgano m. Crane (grúa).
Argel n. pr. GEOGR. Algiers.
Argelia n. pr. f. GEOGR. Algeria.
argelino, na adj./s. Algerian.
argén m. HERÁLD. Argent.
argentado, da adj. Silver-plated, silvered (bañado de plata). || Silvery, silver (de color de plata).
argentar v. tr. To silver-plate, to silver (platear). || To adorn with silver (guarnecer). || To give a silvery shine to (hacer brillar).
argénteo, a adj. Silver (de plata). || Silver-plated (bañado de plata). || Silvery (semejante a la plata). || HERÁLD. Argent.
argentería f. Gold embroidery, orphrey (bordado de oro). || Silver embroidery, orphrey (bordado de plata). || Silversmith's shop (tienda). || Silversmithing (oficio de platero).
argentero m. Silversmith (platero).
argentífero, ra adj. Argentiferous.
argentina f. BOT. Silverweed.
Argentina n. pr. f. GEOGR. Argentina, the Argentine.
argentinismo m. Argentine expression *o* word.
argentinizarse v. pr. To adapt to Argentine life.
argentino, na adj. Silvery, argentine (de aspecto de plata). || Crystal-clear, silvery: *voz argentina*, crystal-clear voice. || Argentinean, Argentine (de la República Argentina).
— M. y f. Argentinean, Argentine.
argento m. POÉT. Silver, argent.
argentoso, sa adj. Argentiferous.
argivo, va adj./s. Argive (de Argos).
argólico, ca adj. Argive (argivo).
argolla f. Ring (aro de metal). || [Type of] croquet (juego). || Carcan, iron collar (castigo público). || Collar (adorno de mujer). || Bracelet (pulsera). || FIG. Shackles, *pl.* (sujeción). || *Amer.* Wedding *o* engagement ring (de matrimonio).
árgoma f. BOT. Furze, gorse, whin (aulaga).
argón m. QUÍM. Argon (gas).
argonauta m. MIT. Argonaut. || ZOOL. Argonaut, paper nautilus (molusco).
argos m. FIG. Argus, watchful person (persona muy vigilante). || ZOOL. Argus.
Argos n. pr. MIT. Argus.
argot n. Jargon: *argot médico*, medical jargon. || Slang (lenguaje familiar).
argucia f. Sophism, fallacy (argumento falso).
árguenas o **árgueñas** f. pl. Handbarrow, *sing.* (angarillas). || Saddlebags (alforjas).
argüir* v. tr. To argue (alegar). || To deduce, to infer, to conclude: *de esto arguyo que vendrá*, from this I deduce that he will come. || To indicate (indicar). || To demonstrate (demostrar). || To prove, to show (probar). || To reproach, to accuse (echar en cara).
— V. intr. To argue.
argumentación f. Argumentation, arguing (acción de argumentar). || Argument (argumento).
argumentador, ra adj. Argumentative (aficionado a discutir).
— M. y f. Arguer, debater (el que argumenta). || Arguer (el que discute).
argumentar v. intr. To argue, to dispute.
— V. tr. To conclude, to deduce (concluir). || To indicate (indicar). || To demonstrate (demonstrar). || To prove, to show (probar). || To argue, to claim, to say: *argumenta que las mujeres tienen que trabajar en casa*, she argues that women have to work at home. || To say, to put forward an argument: *no tiene nada que argumentar para su defensa*, he has nothing to say in his defence, he has no argument to put forward in his defence.
argumentista m. y f. Scenarist.
argumento m. Argument, reasoning: *no sigo tu argumento*, I cannot follow your reasoning. || Plot (de una obra literaria). || Story, plot (de una película). || Scenario, summary, synopsis (resumen). || *Argumento cornuto*, dilemma.
arguyente adj. Arguing.
aria f. MÚS. Aria.
Ariana n. pr. f. MIT. Ariadne.
aricar v. tr. To plough roughly (arar).
aridecer* v. tr. To make arid, to dry up.
— V. intr. To become arid, to dry up.
aridez f. Aridity. || FIG. Aridity, dryness.
árido, da adj. Arid: *terreno árido*, arid land. || FIG. Dull, arid, dry: *asunto árido*, dull subject.
— M. pl. COM. Dry commodities. || TECN. Aggregate, *sing.* || *Medida de áridos*, dry measure.
Aries n. pr. m. ASTR. Aries, the Ram (constelación).
ariete m. MIL. Battering ram (máquina de guerra). || Centre forward (en fútbol). || *Ariete hidráulico*, hydraulic ram.
arije adj. *Uva arije*, black grape.
arijo, ja adj. Light, loose (tierra).
arilo m. BOT. Aril, seed coat (tegumento).
arillo m. Wooden hoop [used to stiffen priest's bands]. || Earring (pendiente).
arimez m. ARQ. Projection, ledge.
ario, a adj./s. Aryan.
arisco, ca adj. Unfriendly, surly, unsociable (huraño). || Unfriendly, vicious (animales). || Shy (tímido). || *Amer.* Frightened, fearful (miedoso).
arista f. BOT. Beard (del trigo). || MAT. Edge: *arista de un cubo*, edge of a cube. || ARQ. Arris, edge (de una viga). | Groin (de una bóveda). || Boon (parte leñosa del cáñamo). || Arête (de montaña).
aristado, da adj. With prominent edges. || Bearded (trigo).
aristarco m. FIG. Aristarch, severe critic (crítico severo).
Arístides n. pr. m. Aristides.
aristocracia f. Aristocracy. || Nobility, distinction (en las maneras).
aristócrata adj. Aristocratic.
— M. y f. Aristocrat.
aristocrático, ca adj. Aristocratic. || Aristocratic, distinguished, noble (maneras, aspecto).
aristocratizar v. tr. To make aristocratic.
Aristófanes n. pr. m. Aristophanes.
aristoloquia f. BOT. Aristolochia.
Aristóteles n. pr. m. Aristotle.
aristotélico, ca adj./s. Aristotelian.
aritmética f. Arithmetic.
aritmético, ca adj. Arithmetic, arithmetical: *progresión aritmética*, arithmetical progression; *media aritmética*, arithmetic mean.
— M. y f. Arithmetician.
arlequín m. TEATR. Harlequin. || Harlequin's mask (máscara). || Clown, fool, buffoon (persona ridícula y despreciable). || FIG. y FAM. Neapolitan ice cream (helado).
arlequinada f. FAM. Clowning, buffoonery, fooling.
arlequinesco, ca adj. Harlequin. || FIG. y FAM. Ridiculous, buffoonish, foolish.
arma f. Weapon, arm: *el arcabuz es un arma antigua*, the arquebus is an ancient weapon. || Arm: *armas portátiles*, small arms. || MIL. Arm: *arma de caballería*, cavalry arm. || Means of defence, weapon (de los animales). || FIG. Weapon, arm: *su pluma es su única arma*, his pen is his only weapon. || — Pl. MIL. Forces: *las armas aliadas*, the allied forces. | Army, *sing.* (carrera militar): *mi hijo ha elegido la carrera de las armas*, my son has chosen the army as his career. | Weapons: *armas nucleares*, nuclear weapons. || HERÁLD. Coat (*sing.*) of arms, arms (escudo). | Arms (blasones). || — *¡A las armas!* or *¡a formar con armas!* or *¡arma, arma!*, to arms! || *Alzarse* or *levantarse en armas*, to rise up in arms. || *Arma arrojadiza*, missile, projectile [weapon which is thrown]. || *Arma blanca*, steel, cold steel. || *Arma de depósito*, magazine-loading weapon. || *Arma de fuego*, firearm. || FIG. *Arma de dos filos* or *de doble filo*, argument which cuts both ways (argumento), double-edged sword. || *Arma de repetición*, repeater, repeating firearm. || *Arma de retrocarga*, breech-loading firearm. || *Arma homicida*, murder weapon. || *Con las armas en la mano*, weapon in hand, armed. || MIL. *¡Cuelguen armas!*, sling arms! || FIG. *Dar armas contra sí mismo*, to make a rod for one's own back. | *De armas tomar*, formidable (temible). || MIL. *Descansar las armas*, to order arms. | *¡Descansen armas!*, order arms! || HERÁLD. *Escudo de armas*, coat of arms. || *Estar en arma* or *en armas*, to be up in arms. || FIG. *Hacer sus primeras armas*, to make one's début, to take one's first steps: *hizo sus primeras armas en el foro*, he made his début at the bar. || *Hecho de armas*, feat of arms. || HERÁLD. *Libro de armas*, armorial, book of heraldry. || *Licencia de armas*, firearm licence (autorización legal). || *Llegar a las armas*, to take up arms. || *Medir las armas*, to cross swords, to fight. || MIL. *Pasar por las armas*, to shoot, to execute. || *Poner en armas*, to arm (armar), to rouse up (sublevar). || MIL. *Presentar las armas*, to present arms. | *¡Presenten armas!*, present arms! || *Rendir el arma*, to present arms to the Holy Sacrament. || *Rendir las armas*, to surrender one's arms, to lay down one's arms (entregar las armas), to give in, to surrender (rendirse). || MIL. *¡Sobre el hombro, arma!*, slope arms! || *Sobre las armas*, under arms. || *Tocar el arma*, to sound the call to arms. || *Tomar (las) armas*, to take up arms (armarse), to present arms (hacer los honores militares). || *Velar las armas*, to carry out the vigil of arms. || FIG. *Volver el*

arma contra alguien, to give s.o. a taste of his own medecine, to turn the tables on s.o.

armada f. Navy, fleet, naval forces, *pl.* (conjunto de fuerzas navales). || Fleet, squadron (escuadra). || *Amer.* Preparation of a lasso [for throwing]. || *La Armada Invencible*, the Spanish Armada.

armadía f. Raft.

armadijo m. Trap (trampa).

armadillo m. ZOOL. Armadillo.

armado, da adj. Armed (en armas). || Loaded: *una pistola armada*, a loaded gun. || Reinforced: *hormigón armado*, reinforced concrete. || Provided (provisto). || Assembled (montado). || *Amer.* Stubborn (terco).
— M. Man dressed as a Roman soldier [in processions]. || *Amer.* Hand-rolled cigarette.

armador m. MAR. Shipowner (naviero). || Jerkin (jubón). || Fitter (de máquinas, coches, etc.). || *Amer.* Waistcoat (chaleco). | Hanger (percha).

armadura f. Armour [U.S., armor]. || Suit of armour (para proteger el cuerpo). || Frame: *armadura de las gafas*, spectacle frame. || Skeleton, framework (del tejado). || Skeleton (esqueleto). || Assembly, fitting (montaje). || Fitting together (en costura). || Casing (de neumático). || FÍS. Armature (de imán). | Plate (de condensador). || Reinforcement (del hormigón). || MÚS. Key signature. || *Armadura de la cama*, bedstead.

armajo m. Saltwort (almarjo).

armamentista adj. Arms, armaments: *carrera armamentista*, arms race.

armamento m. Arms, *pl.*, armaments, *pl.* (de un país). || Armament (de un barco, un cuerpo militar). || Arms, *pl.* (de un soldado). || *Carrera de armamentos*, arms race.

Armando n. pr. m. Herman.

armar v. tr. To arm: *armado con un fusil*, armed with a rifle; *armar a cien mil hombres*, to arm a hundred thousand men. || To prepare for war, to arm: *armar a un país*, to prepare a country for war. || To load (un arma de fuego). || To fix (una bayoneta). || To brace (un arco). || MAR. To fit out, to equip (un navío). || To assemble, to fit together, to mount (una máquina). || To pitch (una tienda de campaña). || To put up (una cama). || To set (una trampa). || To fit together (en costura). || To reinforce (reforzar). || FIG. To provide: *le han armado de una buena educación*, they have provided him with a good education. | To arrange, to prepare, to get ready (preparar). || FIG. y FAM. To arrange, to organize (organizar). | To make, to kick up: *armar jaleo, ruido*, to kick up a fuss, a noise. | To cause, to create: *armar dificultades a uno*, to cause s.o. difficulties. || *Amer.* To roll [a cigarette]. || — *Armar caballero*, to knight. || FIG. y FAM. *Armarla* or *armar una* or *armarla buena* or *armar un escándalo*, to kick up a rumpus *o* a fuss *o* a stink. || *Armar una intriga* or *una cábala*, to hatch a plot, to scheme, to intrigue. || *Armar un lío*, to make a fuss, to kick up a rumpus. || *Armar pendencia*, to look for fight *o* for trouble. || FIG. y FAM. *¡Buena la has armado!*, you've really done it now!
— V. pr. To arm o.s. (un soldado). || To arm, to prepare for war (un país). || FIG. To arm o.s., to provide o.s.: *armarse de una escoba*, to provide o.s. with a broom. | To break out: *se armó una riña*, an argument broke out. || *Amer.* To stop dead (plantarse). | To balk, to shy (un caballo, etc.). | To be obstinate *o* stubborn (obstinarse). || — *Armarse de paciencia*, to muster one's patience. || *Armarse de valor*, to pluck up courage, to summon one's courage. || FIG. y FAM. *¡Qué lío se armó!*, what a fuss there was!, what a rumpus there was! || FIG. *Se está armando una tempestad*, a storm is brewing, a storm is imminent. || FIG. y FAM. *Se va a armar la de Dios es Cristo* or *la gorda* or *la de San Quintín*, there's going to be a tidy row *o* a hell of a row, there's going to be real trouble.

armario m. Cupboard (para cosas). || Wardrobe (para ropa): *armario de luna*, wardrobe with a mirror. || — *Armario botiquín*, first-aid cabinet. || *Armario empotrado*, built-in wardrobe, fitted wardrobe. || *Armario frigorífico*, refrigerator. || *Armario para libros*, bookcase.

armatoste m. Monstrosity (cosa grande y fea). || FIG. y FAM. Big oaf, great brute (persona corpulenta).

armazón f. Frame, framework: *armazón de una pantalla*, frame of a lampshade. || Timberwork (maderamen). || FIG. Framework, outline (de una obra). || Chassis (bastidor). || Rib (de un violín). || — M. Skeleton (esqueleto). || *Amer.* Set of shelves (estantería). | Bookcase (para libros).

armella f. Eyebolt (tornillo). || Staple, socket (de cerrojo).

Armenia n. pr. f. GEOGR. Armenia.

arménico, ca adj. Armenian: *bol arménico*, Armenian bole.

armenio, nia adj./s. Armenian.

armería f. Gunsmith's shop (tienda del armero). || Museum of arms, military *o* war museum (museo). || Gunsmith's craft (oficio de armero). || Heraldry (heráldica).

armero m. Gunsmith (fabricante de armas de fuego). || Armourer [U.S., armorer] (fabricante de armas). || Weapon rack (para colocar las armas).

armilar adj. ASTR. Armillary (esfera).

armilla f. ARQ. Astragal (de columna). || ASTR. Armillary sphere.

arminiano, na adj./s. Arminian.

armiñado, da adj. Ermine-trimmed, trimmed with ermine. || HERÁLD. Ermine.

armiño m. ZOOL. Ermine (animal).

armisticio m. Armistice.

armón m. Limber (del cañón).

armonía f. MAT. y MÚS. Harmony. || FIG. Harmony: *vivir en armonía*, to live in harmony.

armónicamente adv. Harmoniously, in harmony.

armónico, ca adj. Harmonic.
— M. Harmonic (sonido). || — F. Harmonica, mouth organ (instrumento de música).

armonio m. MÚS. Harmonium.

armonioso, sa adj. Harmonious, tuneful.

armonista m. MÚS. Harmonist.

armonización f. MÚS. Harmonizing. || Harmonizing, reconciliation (de personas). || Matching, harmonizing (de colores).

armonizar v. tr. MÚS. To harmonize. || To reconcile (reconciliar). || To match, to harmonize (colores).
— V. intr. To harmonize (al cantar). || To be in harmony, to harmonize (sonidos). || To match, to harmonize (colores). || To be in harmony (personas).

armorial m. Armorial, book of heraldry (libro de armas).

armuelle m. BOT. Orach (planta).

arnés m. Armour, harness (armadura). || — Pl. Harness, *sing.*, trappings (de las caballerías). || FIG. y FAM. Things, gear, *sing.*, equipment, *sing.*

árnica f. BOT. Arnica. || *Tintura de árnica*, arnica tincture, arnica.

aro m. Hoop (de tonel). || Hoop: *los niños ya no juegan al aro*, children do not play hoop any more. || Iron ring (argolla). || BOT. Cuckoopint, lords-and-ladies. || *Amer.* Ring (sortija). | Earring (pendiente). || — *Aro para las servilletas*, napkin *o* serviette ring. || FIG. y FAM. *Tener que pasar* or *tener que entrar por el aro*, to knuckle under.

aroma m. Aroma, perfume, fragrance. || Aroma: *el aroma del café*, the aroma of coffee. || Bouquet (del vino).

aromático, ca adj. Fragrant, sweet-smelling, aromatic (oloroso). || Aromatic: *bebida aromática*, aromatic drink.

aromatización f. Perfuming. || CULIN. Flavouring [U.S., flavoring].

aromatizador m. *Amer.* Spray.

aromatizante adj. Perfuming. || CULIN. Flavouring [U.S., flavoring].

aromatizar v. tr. To perfume, to scent (dar aroma). || CULIN. To flavour [U.S., to flavor], to aromatize

aron m. BOT. Cuckoopint, lords-and-ladies.

arpa f. MÚS. Harp: *arpa eolia*, Aeolian harp; *tocar* or *tañer el arpa*, to play the harp.

arpado, da adj. Serrated, saw-edged. || POÉT. Sweet-sounding, melodious (pájaros).

arpar v. tr. To scratch (rasguñar). || To rip up, to tear up (desgarrar).

arpegiar v. intr. MÚS. To arpeggio.

arpegio m. MÚS. Arpeggio.

arpeo m. MAR. Grapnel.

arpía f. MIT. Harpy (ave). || FIG. Hussy, old witch, harpy (mujer mala). | Hag (mujer fea).

arpillar v. tr. *Amer.* To wrap in sackloth *o* sacking.

arpillera f. Sackcloth, sacking (tela).

arpista m. y f. Harpist.

arpón m. Harpoon, gaff (para pescar). || ARQ. Cramp, cramp iron (grapa).

arponado, da adj. Harpoon-like.

arponar o **arponear** v. tr. To harpoon.

arponeo m. Harpooning.

arponero m. Harpooner.

arqueado, da adj. Bow-shaped, curved, arched. || *Piernas arqueadas*, bow legs, bandy legs.

arqueador m. Ship gauger (de las embarcaciones). || Beater (de la lana).

arqueaje o **arqueamiento** m. Gauging (acción de arquear). || Tonnage (cabida).

arquear v. tr. To arch, to curve (curvar). || TECN. To beat (la lana). || MAR. To gauge, to measure the tonnage of (un navío). || COM. To check (los caudales). || *Arquear el lomo*, to arch one's back.
— V. intr. FAM. To retch.
— V. pr. To curve, to arch. || To arch one's back (persona).

arquegonio m. BOT. Archegonium.

arqueo m. Arching, curving (acción de arquear). || Arching (del cuerpo). || MAR. Gauging (acción de medir la capacidad). | Tonnage (tonelaje): *arqueo neto, de registro, bruto*, net, registered, gross tonnage. || Beating (de la lana). || COM. Checking, cashing up. || COM. *Hacer el arqueo*, to cash up.

arqueolítico, ca adj. Stone-age.

arqueología f. Archaeology.

arqueológico, ca adj. Archaeological.

arqueólogo m. Archaeologist.

arqueoptérix m. Archaeopteryx (ave fósil).

arquería f. Arcade, series of arches.

arquero m. Archer, bowman (soldado). || (P.us.). COM. Cashier (cajero). || Hoopmaker (para toneles). || *Amer.* Goalkeeper (en fútbol).

arqueta f. Small chest.
arquetipo m. Archetype, prototype (prototipo). || Archetype, perfect example: *este chico es el arquetipo del estudiante moderno*, this boy is the archetype of the modern student.
arquidiócesis f. Archbishopric, archdiocese.
arquiepiscopal adj. Archiepiscopal.
arquillo m. Mús. Bow.
Arquímedes n. pr. m. Archimedes.
arquípteros m. pl. ZOOL. Archips.
arquita f. Small chest.
arquitecto m. Architect. || *Arquitecto paisajista*, landscape architect.
arquitectónico, ca adj. Architectonic, architectural.
— F. Architectonics.
arquitectura f. Architecture.
arquitectural adj. Architectural.
arquitrabe m. ARQ. Architrave.
arquivolta f. ARQ. Archivolt.
arrabal m. Suburb. || — Pl. Outskirts, suburbs (afueras). || Slums (tugurios).
arrabalero, ra o **arrabalesco, ca** adj. Suburban. || Common, coarse, rough (de modales groseros).
— M. y f. Suburbanite (que vive en las afueras). || Coarse person (persona tosca).
arrabio m. Cast iron (hierro colado). || *Lingote de arrabio*, pig iron.
arracacha f. *Amer.* Arracacha, Peruvian carrot. || *Amer.* FIG. y FAM. Stupid thing (tontería).
arracada f. Pendant earring.
arracimado, da adj. In a bunch (en forma de racimo). || Clustered together, bunched together (apiñado).
arracimarse v. pr. To form a bunch, to bunch together, to cluster together.
arraclán m. BOT. Buckthorn (árbol). || ZOOL. Scorpion (alacrán).
arraigamiento m. V. ARRAIGO.
arraigadamente adv. Staunchly: *arraigadamente protestante*, staunchly protestant. || Firmly, securely (fijamente).
arraigado, da adj. Deeply rooted, deep-rooted: *costumbres, ideas arraigadas*, deeply rooted customs, ideas. || Influential, respected (persona).
— M. MAR. Mooring. || Landowner (propietario).
arraigar v. intr. To take root (plantas). || FIG. To take root (costumbres, vicios, etc.). | To settle down (establecerse).
— V. pr. BOT. To take root. || FIG. To settle down: *se arraigó en París*, he settled down in Paris. | To take root, to take hold, to become fixed (costumbres, etc.).
arraigo m. Rootedness (situación de arraigado). || Rooting (acción de arraigar). || FIG. Roots, *pl.*: *tener arraigo en una ciudad*, to have roots in a city. | Property (bienes raíces). | Influence (influencia). || FIG. *Tener mucho arraigo*, to be very respected *o* influential, to have great influence (ser estimado).
arramblar v. tr. To cover with sand (cubrir de arena).
— V. intr. FIG. y FAM. To make off with, to pinch, to carry off (robar, coger): *arrambló con todos mis lápices*, he made off with *o* he carried off all my pencils.
— V. pr. To be covered with sand, to become covered with sand.
arramplar v. tr. V. ARRAMBLAR.
arrancaclavos m. inv. Nail puller, nail claw.
arrancada f. Sudden start (de un coche). || Dart forward, dash forward (de una persona o cosa que se mueve). || Start (de una carrera, de un corredor). || Sudden acceleration (aceleración repentina). || Jerk, jolt (sacudida). || Track (de la res). || Snatch (halterofilia). || MAR. Starting, setting off.
arrancado, da adj. Uprooted (árboles, plantas). || FIG. y FAM. Penniless, broke (arruinado). || HERÁLD. Erased. || FAM. *Es más malo que arrancado*, he's a little devil (un niño).
arrancador m. Grubber (herramienta). || AUT. Starter (de un motor).
arrancadora f. AGR. Lifter, picker: *arrancadora de patatas*, potato lifter.
arrancadura f. o **arrancamiento** m. Pulling up, uprooting (de plantas). || Uprooting (de árboles). || Extraction, pulling out (de un diente). || Snatching, grabbing (acción de coger). || Picking (de patatas).
arrancar v. tr. To pull up, to uproot: *arrancar una planta*, to pull up a plant. || To uproot: *la tormenta arrancó el árbol*, the storm uprooted the tree. || To extract, to pull out (un diente). || To pull, to tear: *arrancar una rama del árbol*, to pull a branch off a tree. || To tear off (una página, un botón). || To pull out, to tear out (el pelo). || To cough up, to hawk (las flemas). || To heave (un suspiro). || To snatch, to grab (coger): *arrancó al niño de los brazos de su madre*, he snatched the child from his mother's arms. || To wrest (con dificultad): *lograron arrancarle la pistola*, they managed to wrest the pistol from him. || FIG. To drive out: *han arrancado a los extranjeros que vivían allí*, they have driven out the foreigners who lived there. | To drag away: *es imposible arrancarle de una fiesta*, it is impossible to drag him away from a party. | To wipe out, to put an end to, to eradicate (suprimir). | To wean, to stop: *no hay quien le arranque del tabaco*, no one can wean him away from smoking, no one can stop him smoking. | To get, to force, to wangle: *le arrancaron la verdad, una promesa*, they got the truth out of him, a promise out of him. | To draw: *arrancar aplausos*, to draw applause. | To snatch: *el equipo arrancó un punto, la victoria*, the team snatched a point, victory. || AUT. To start: *a ver si podemos arrancar este motor*, let's see if we can start this engine. || AGR. To lift, to pick (patatas). || — *Arrancar de raíz* or *de cuajo*, v. RAÍZ y CUAJO. || *Es una película que arranca lágrimas*, the film is a tearjerker.
— V. intr. To start (un coche). || To set off, to start out: *el tren arrancó en seguida*, the train set off at once. || To set sail (un barco). || To make a move, to leave (marcharse): *no arrancan aunque hace horas que están aquí*, they're not making a move although they've been here ages. || To begin: *la carretera arranca de San Sebastián*, the road begins in San Sebastián. || FIG. To stem, to arise, to originate: *dificultades que arrancan de su mala gestión*, difficulties which stem from his bad management. | To date back to (remontar a). || To begin (empezar): *arrancó a hablar*, he began speaking. || To set off at a run, to start running, to break into a run (echar a correr). || *Arrancar contra*, to charge at: *el toro arrancó contra el matador*, the bull charged at the matador.
— V. pr. To begin (empezar). || To start to charge: *el toro se arrancó en dirección del hombre*, the bull started to charge at the man. || To tear o.s. away (tener que irse). || — *Arrancarse a cantar, a llorar*, to burst into song, into tears. || FAM. *Se arrancó con mil pesetas* or *dándome mil pesetas*, he suddenly gave me a thousand pesetas.
arranchar v. tr. MAR. To hug, to sail close to (la costa, etc.). | To brace (las velas).
— V. pr. To get together (reunirse, juntarse).
arranque m. Starting (de un coche, una máquina). || Start (de un atleta, de una carrera). || Beginning (de una carretera). || Dash forward, sudden spurt (de una persona que echa a correr). || Jump, start, jerk (arrebato). || FIG. Beginning: *el arranque de la película es bueno*, the beginning of the film is good. | Outburst, fit, attack: *arranque de ira, de locura*, fit of anger, of madness. | Burst: *arranque de energía*, burst of energy. | Origin, root: *el arranque de las dificultades*, the origin of the difficulties. | Impulse: *en un arranque decidió comprar un coche*, on an impulse he decided to buy a car. | Thrust, drive, go (ímpetu, pujanza). | Flash of wit (ocurrencia). || ANAT. Start, beginning. || ARQ. Foot: *el arranque de una escalera*, the foot of a staircase. | Spring (de bóveda o arco). || BOT. Base. || TECN. Starter (de un motor). || MIN. Ragging. || — *Esperando el arranque del tren*, waiting for the train to start *o* to move *o* to leave. || *Motor de arranque*, starting motor.
arrapiezo m. Rag, tatter (harapo). || FIG. y FAM. Scallywag (niño).
arras f. pl. Security, *sing.*, earnest, *sing.*, pledge, *sing.* (prenda). || Thirteen coins given by bridegroom to bride (monedas).
arrasadura f. Smoothing, levelling (allanamiento). || Striking (de los granos).
arrasamiento m. Smoothing, levelling (allanamiento). || Devastation, ravaging (de un terreno). || Demolition, razing, destruction (de un edificio).
arrasar v. tr. To smooth, to level (allanar). || To fill to the brim (llenar hasta el borde). || To demolish, to raze to the ground (un edificio). || To devastate, to ravage: *el ciclón ha arrasado la región*, the cyclone has devastated the area. || To strike (los granos). || *Ojos arrasados en lágrimas*, eyes brimming with tears.
— V. intr. y pr. To clear (el cielo). || *Arrasarse en lágrimas*, to fill with tears (los ojos).
arrastradamente adv. FIG. y FAM. Miserably, wretchedly: *vivir arrastradamente*, to live miserably. | With difficulty (con dificultad).
arrastradero m. TECN. Timber slide (camino). || TAUR. Place where dead bulls are left when dragged from the ring. || *Amer.* Gambling den (garito).
arrastradizo, za adj. That can be pulled *o* dragged (que se puede arrastrar). || Dragging, trailing (que se arrastra).
arrastrado, da adj. FIG. y FAM. Miserable, wretched: *llevar una vida arrastrada*, to lead a miserable life. | Rascally, roguish (bribón). | Hard-up (mal de dinero). || In which one must follow suit (juegos).
— M. y f. FIG. y FAM. Rogue, rascal (bribón). || — F. FIG. y FAM. Whore, prostitute (mujer pública).
arrastramiento m. Dragging, trailing.
arrastrar v. tr. To pull, to haul: *el caballo arrastraba el carruaje*, the horse was pulling the carriage. || To drag, to trail: *arrastrar los pies*, to drag one's feet. || To haul, to transport (una mercancía). || To drag along, to trail, to drag: *la niña arrastraba la muñeca detrás de ella*, the child was dragging the doll along behind her. || To sweep away *o* along, to carry away *o* along: *la corriente arrastró el barco*, the current swept the boat away. || To blow away, to carry off: *el viento arrastró las hojas*, the wind blew the leaves away. || FIG. To lead: *su éxito como ladrón arrastró a sus hermanos a cometer crímenes*, his success as a criminal lead his brothers to commit crimes. | To lead to, to give rise to: *eso arrastró muchas dificultades*, it gave rise to many difficulties. | To win over: *su discurso arrastró a la*

multitud, his speech won over the crowd. | To lead: *arrastra una vida miserable*, he leads a miserable life. || — FIG. *Dejarse arrastrar*, to get carried away (por el juego, etc.). | *Un déficit que arrastramos desde hace mucho tiempo*, a deficit which has been hanging over us for a long time.
— V. intr. To trail, to trail on the ground (una cortina, un vestido). || To lead (juegos).
— V. pr. To crawl, to creep (reptar). || To drag o.s.: *el herido se arrastró hasta la puerta*, the injured man dragged himself to the door. || To drag, to trail (una cosa). || FIG. To grovel (humillarse).
arrastre m. Dragging. || Haulage, transportation, transport (de una mercancía). || Lead (juegos). || AVIAC. Drag (fricción). || *Amer.* Ore crusher. || — FIG. y FAM. *Estar para el arrastre*, to have had it, to be worn out (persona), to have had it (cosa). | *Ser de mucho arrastre*, to be very influential, to have a lot of influence.
arrayán m. Myrtle.
arrayanal m. Myrtle patch.
¡arre! interj. Gee up!, giddy up! (a los caballos). || FAM. Come on then!
arrea f. *Amer.* Packtrain (recua).
¡arrea! interj. Come on!, hurry up! (para meter prisa), get away! (para manifestar sorpresa).
arreador m. *Amer.* Whip (látigo).
arrear v. tr. To spur on, to urge on (a las caballerías). || To harness (poner los arreos). || To decorate, to adorn (adornar). || To hurry, to rush (dar prisa). || FAM. To deal, to fetch: *arrear un golpe*, to deal a blow.
— V. intr. To hurry, to go quickly (ir de prisa). || *Irse arreando*, to rush off, to hurry away.
arrebañaduras f. pl. Leftovers, remains.
arrebañar v. tr. FAM. To scrape together (juntar). | To make off with (arramblar). || To eat up, to finish off (comida). || To clean up, to clean (un plato).
arrebatadamente adv. In a hurry, hurriedly (con prisa). || Impulsively (irreflexivamente).
arrebatadizo, za adj. FIG. Irritable, short-tempered, quick-tempered (carácter).
arrebatado, da adj. Enraged, carried away (de ira). || Impulsive, impetuous, rash (irreflexivo). || Violent, sudden, hasty, rash (con prisa). || Very red, flushed (rostro).
arrebatador, ra adj. Which snatches. || FIG. Captivating: *una sonrisa arrebatadora*, a captivating smile. | Catchy (ritmo). | Devouring (pasión).
arrebatamiento m. Snatch, seizure, snatching (acción de quitar). || Ecstasy (éxtasis). || Rage, fury (furor).
arrebatar v. tr. To snatch, to wrench: *arrebatar algo de las manos de alguien*, to snatch sth. from s.o.'s hands; *arrebatarle la victoria a alguien*, to snatch victory from s.o. || To blow away, to carry off, to snatch up: *el viento le arrebató el sombrero*, the wind blew his hat away. || To sweep away, to carry away: *la corriente arrebató a los nadadores*, the current swept the swimmers away. || To take: *arrebatar la vida a alguien*, to take s.o.'s life. || To tear *o* to rip off (una página, un botón). || To win, to win over: *arrebataba los corazones con su elocuencia*, he won people's hearts with his eloquence. || To sweep off one's feet, to captivate: *arrebata a las chicas con su manera de hablar*, he sweeps girls off their feet with the way he speaks. || To force (las plantas). || To cook too quickly (en cocina). || To enrage, to make furious (de ira). || *Amer.* To knock down (atropellar).
— V. pr. To get carried away (de emoción). || To burn (en cocina). || *Arrebatarse en cólera* or *de ira*, to lose one's temper, to fly into a rage.
arrebato m. Rage, fury (furor): *hablar con arrebato*, to speak with rage. || Fit, attack, outburst: *lo hizo en un arrebato de cólera*, he did it in a fit of anger. || Flurry, sudden fit (de entusiasmo). || Ecstasy (éxtasis). || JUR. Alienation. || JUR. *Con arrebato y obcecación*, without malice aforethought.
arrebol m. Red glow: *el sol poniente tiene arreboles magníficos*, the sun gives off a magnificent red glow at sunset. || Rouge (colorete). || Rosiness, ruddiness (en las mejillas).
arrebolada f. Red clouds, *pl.* [at sunrise or at sunset].
arrebolar v. tr. To redden, to give a red glow to: *la aurora arrebolaba el cielo*, the dawn gave a red glow to the sky. || *Tener el rostro arrebolado*, to have a red face.
— V. pr. To go red, to flush. || To glow red (el cielo). || To put on rouge (con colorete).
arrebolera f. Rouge jar. || BOT. Marvel of Peru [U.S., pretty-by-night] (dondiego de noche).
arrebozar v. tr. To coat, to roll (con harina, etc.).
— V. pr. To wrap o.s. up, to muffle o.s.: *arrebozarse en la capa*, to wrap o.s. up in one's cape. || To swarm (las abejas).
arrebozo m. V. REBOZO.
arrebujadamente adv. FIG. In confusion.
arrebujar v. tr. To crumple up, to crease (arrugar). || To wrap up (envolver). || To muddle up, to jumble (enredar).
— V. pr. To wrap o.s. up: *arrebujarse en una capa*, to wrap o.s. up in a cape. || To muffle o.s. up: *arrebujarse en una manta*, to muffle o.s. up in a blanket.
arreciar v. intr. To get worse, to get heavier: *arrecia la lluvia*, the rain is getting heavier. || To get stronger (el viento).
arrecife m. MAR. Reef: *arrecife de coral*, coral reef.
arrecirse* v. pr. To be frozen stiff, to be frozen to the bone.
arrechucho m. FAM. Fit, outburst, attack: *arrechucho de cólera*, fit of anger. | Turn, bad turn (indisposición): *le dió un arrechucho*, he had a bad turn.
arredramiento m. Fear, fright (miedo).
arredrar v. tr. To move away (apartar). || FIG. To frighten away (hacer retroceder). || To frighten (asustar).
— V. pr. To move away (apartarse). || To be frightened, to be afraid: *no se arredra por nada*, he's not afraid of anything.
arredro adv. Backwards, back (hacia atrás).
arregazado, da adj. Tucked up (faldas). || Turned-up (nariz).
arregazar v. tr. To tuck up.
arreglable adj. Repairable, reparable (reparable). || Which can be settled *o* sorted out (que se puede resolver).
arreglado, da adj. Regulated (sujeto a regla). || Settled, fixed (un asunto). || FIG. Moderate (moderado). | Neat, tidy (limpio y ordenado). | Reasonable, sensible (razonable). | Smart, well-dressed (bien vestido). | Arranged, set out: *una casa que está bien arreglada*, a house that is nicely set out. | Well-ordered (ordenado). | Orderly: *vida arreglada*, orderly life. | Good (conducta). | Reasonable: *me ha hecho un precio muy arreglado*, he sold it to me for a very reasonable price. || — *Arreglado a la ley*, in accordance with the law. || FAM. *¡Estamos arreglados!*, that's all we needed!, a fine mess we're in! | *Estar arreglado con alguien*, to be in a fine mess *o* pickle with s.o.: *¡arreglados estamos con estos invitados!*, we're in a fine mess with these guests! | *¡Pues estaría yo arreglado si lo tuviera que pagar!*, I'd be in a fine spot if I had to pay it, it would be a fine thing if I had to pay it. | *Va arreglado si cree que...*, he's got another think coming if he thinks that....
arreglar v. tr. To regulate, to organize (someter a una regla). || To arrange, to lay *o* to set out (disponer): *no sé cómo arreglar este cuarto*, I can't think how to arrange this room. || To tidy up, to put straight, to put in order (poner en orden): *arreglar la casa*, to tidy up the house. || To repair, to mend: *arreglar un mueble roto*, to repair a damaged piece of furniture. || To settle, to sort out, to fix: *arreglaré este asunto*, I will settle this matter. || To get ready, to fix up: *arreglar todo para una fiesta*, to get everything ready for a party. || To arrange, to fix up (una entrevista, una cita). || To get in order: *arreglar los papeles para un viaje*, to get one's papers in order for a journey. || To get ready (preparar): *tenemos que arreglar a los niños para salir*, we'll have to get the children ready to go out. || To put right, to right (rectificar). || To settle: *esta taza de caldo te arreglará el estómago*, this cup of broth will settle your stomach. || To dress (los escaparates). || To prepare, to dress (una comida). || To pack (una maleta). || *Amer.* To castrate. || — *Arreglar el cuello*, to trim one's hair. || *Le han arreglado el pelo muy bien*, they've done your hair very well *o* very nicely. || FAM. *Lo han arreglado de lo lindo*, they've made a fine mess of him, they've fixed him up good and proper. | *No te preocupes, yo te lo arreglo*, don't worry, I'll fix it *o* I'll arrange it for you *o* I'll see to it. | *¡Ya te arreglaré!*, I'll fix you!, I'll show you!, I'll teach you!
— V. pr. To make do, to be content *o* satisfied: *me tendré que arreglar con lo que me han dado*, I'll have to make do with what they've given me. || To get ready: *me voy a arreglar para salir*, I'm going to get ready to go out. || To dress: *esa mujer se arregla muy bien*, that woman dresses very well. || To arrange things, to come to an agreement: *arréglate con tu madre para salir esta tarde*, arrange things with your mother so that you can come out this afternoon. || To work sth. out, to manage: *ya nos arreglaremos*, we'll work sth. out. || To improve, to clear up (el tiempo). || To work out right: *si se arreglan mis asuntos...*, if things work out right... || To improve, to get better: *espero que se arreglará tu situación*, I hope your situation will improve. || To get by, to manage: *no sabe arreglarse sin teléfono*, he can't get by without a telephone. || To manage: *no sé cómo se arregla para llegar siempre tarde*, I don't know how he always manages to be late. || To agree, to come to an agreement (ponerse de acuerdo). || To agree, to come to terms: *arreglarse en el precio*, to come to terms on the price. || — *Arreglarse el pelo*, to have one's hair done (por otro), to do one's hair (uno mismo). || FAM. *Arreglárselas*, to manage, to get by: *¡que se las arregle como pueda!*, let him get by as best he can! | *Arreglárselas para*, to manage to. || *Arreglarse muy bien con alguien*, to get on very well with s.o. || *Arreglarse por las buenas*, to come to a friendly agreement. || *Espero que se arreglarán tus problemas*, I hope your problems will sort themselves out. || FAM. *Saber arreglárselas*, to be able to look after o.s., to know what one is doing.
arreglo m. Agreement, arrangement (acuerdo): *llegar a un arreglo*, to come to an arrangement, to reach an agreement. || Settlement arrangement (acción y efecto):

el arreglo de un asunto, the settlement of a matter. || Repair, reparation, repairing: *el arreglo de algo roto*, the repairing of sth. broken. || Order (orden). || Mús. Arrangement. || FAM. Relationship, affair (amancebamiento). || — *Arreglo personal*, personal appearance. || *Con arreglo a*, in accordance with, according to: *con arreglo a la ley*, in accordance with the law; in comparison with, compared with (en comparación). || *El asunto no tiene arreglo*, there's no way out, there's no solution, there's nothing we can do about it. || *Este coche no tiene arreglo*, this car is beyond repair. || FAM. *Este hombre ya no tiene arreglo*, he is a hopeless case.

arrellanarse v. pr. To sit back, to lounge, to make o.s. comfortable: *arrellanarse en un sillón*, to sit back in an armchair.

arremangar v. tr. To tuck *o* to hitch up (falda), to roll up (mangas, pantalones). || FIG. *Nariz arremangada*, turned-up *o* snub nose.
— V. pr. To roll up one's shirt sleeves.

arremetedor, ra adj. Attacking.
— M. y f. Attacker.

arremeter v. intr. To attack, to charge, to rush: *arremeter al* or *contra el enemigo*, to attack the enemy, to rush at the enemy. || FIG. To attack: *arremeter contra la Constitución*, to attack the Constitution. | To offend (a la vista).
— V. tr. To attack (atacar). || To spur on (un caballo).

arremetida f. Attack, assault (acción de atacar). || Rush, crush (empujón). || FIG. Attack.

arremolinadamente adv. In confusion. || *Las cabras entraron arremolinadamente en el redil*, the goats scrambled into the pen.

arremolinarse v. pr. To whirl [about], to swirl: *las hojas se arremolinan en el suelo*, the leaves whirl about on the ground. || To swirl, to eddy (el agua). || FIG. To mill, to rush, to scramble (la gente).

arrendable adj. Rentable (alquilable). || JUR. Leasable (contrato legal).

arrendadero m. Ring for tethering horses.

arrendado, da adj. Obedient [to the reins]. || Rented (alquilado). || JUR. Leased (por contrato legal).

arrendador, ra m. y f. JUR. Lessor (que da en arriendo), lessee (que toma en arriendo). || Landlord (hombre), landlady (mujer) [que da en alquiler], tenant, renter (que toma en alquiler). || Tenant farmer (de finca rústica). || — M. Ring for tethering horses (anillo).

arrendajo m. ZOOL. Jay (pájaro europeo). | American oriole. || FIG. y FAM. Mimic, ape (persona que remeda a otra).

arrendamiento m. JUR. Leasing (cuando hay contrato legal). || Renting (acción de alquilar). || JUR. Lease (contrato legal). || Rent (cantidad que se paga). || *Tomar en arrendamiento*, to lease, to rent.

arrendar* v. tr. JUR. To lease (ceder y tomar en arriendo): *arrendar tierras*, to lease land. || To rent (alquilar). || To tether, to tie up (un caballo). || FIG. *No le arriendo la ganancia*, V. GANANCIA.

arrendatario, ria adj. Leasing. || *Compañía Arrendataria de Tabacos*, State-owned tobacco company.
— M. y f. JUR. Lessee (con contrato legal). || Tenant (que alquila). || JUR. Tenant farmer (de una finca rústica).

arrendaticio, cia adj. Lease, of a lease.

arrenquín m. *Amer.* Muleteer's horse (caballo). | Assistant, helper (ayudante).

arreo m. Adornment, ornament (adorno). || *Amer.* Drove, herd (recua). || — Pl. Harness, *sing.*, trappings (para los caballos). || FIG. y FAM. Trappings, stuff, *sing.*, gear, *sing.*: *llegó a casa con todos sus arreos*, he arrived at our house with all his gear.

arrepanchigarse o **arrepanchingarse** v. pr. To sit back, to loll, to lounge (arrellanarse).

arrepentido, da adj. Repentant, regretful, sorry. || *Estar arrepentido de algo*, to regret sth., to be sorry about *o* for sth.
— M. y f. Penitent. || — F. Magdalen, reformed prostitute.

arrepentimiento m. Repentance (contrición), regret (pesar). || ARTES. Alteration. || *Tener arrepentimiento por haber hecho algo*, to repent of having done sth.

arrepentirse* v. pr. To repent: *arrepentirse de sus pecados*, to repent one's sins; *se arrepintió de haberlo robado*, he repented of having stolen it. || To be sorry, to regret: *me arrepiento de haber venido*, I'm sorry I came, I regret having come. || *¡Ya se arrepentirá usted!*, you'll be sorry!, you'll regret it!

arrequesonarse v. pr. To curdle (la leche).

arrequives m. pl. FAM. Sunday best, *sing.*, best clothes, finery, *sing.*: *Juana iba con todos sus arrequives*, Joan was decked out in all her finery. || Requirements (requisitos).

arrestado, da adj. Imprisoned (preso). || Bold, daring (audaz).

arrestar v. tr. To put under arrest, to detain, to arrest.
— V. pr. To rush boldly: *arrestarse a hacer algo*, to rush boldly into sth.

arresto m. MIL. Arrest: *arresto mayor, menor* or *simple*, close arrest, open arrest. || Arrest (civil): *bajo arresto domiciliario*, under house arrest. || Detention under remand (provisional). || Imprisonment (reclusión). || — Pl. Boldness, *sing.*, daring, *sing.* (arrojo). || *Tener arrestos para hacer algo*, to be bold enough to do sth.

arretranca f. *Amer.* Brake.

arrezagar v. tr. To lift up (falda). || To roll up (mangas, pantalón). || To lift up, to raise (el brazo).

arriada f. Overflowing, flood (riada). || MAR. Lowering of the sails.

arrianismo m. Arianism (herejía).

arriano, na adj./s. Arian (hereje).

— OBSERV. No hay que confundir la palabra inglesa *Arian* con *Aryan*, que significa *ario*, de la raza aria.

arriar v. tr. MAR. To strike, to lower: *arriar bandera*, to strike the flag. | To lower (vela). | To slacken (un cable).
— V. pr. To be flooded (inundarse).

arriata f. o **arriate** m. Flower bed, border. || Road (camino).

arriba adv. Upstairs (en casa): *Pepe está arriba*, Pepe is upstairs; *vete arriba*, go upstairs. || Up there: *¿dónde está? — Arriba, en el árbol*, where is he? — Up there, in the tree. || Above (encima). || Above: *lo arriba mencionado*, the above mentioned. || Up, upwards (dirección): *ir arriba*, to go up. || — *Aguas* or *río arriba*, upstream, upriver. || *Allá arriba*, up there. || *Arriba del todo*, right on the top, on the very top. || *Arriba mencionado*, aforesaid. || *Calle arriba*, up the street. || *Cuesta arriba*, uphill. || *De arriba*, from above, from up there; from above, from on high, from God (del cielo), free, for nothing (gratuito). || *De arriba abajo*, from top to bottom; up and down, from head to foot (personas): *mirar a uno de arriba abajo*, to look s.o. up and down, to eye s.o. from head to foot. || *De la cintura para arriba*, from the waist up. || *Hacia arriba*, upwards. || *Lo de arriba*, what is on top, the top part. || *¡Manos arriba!*, hands up! || *Más arriba*, above (en una carta), higher up, further up (más alto). || *Más arriba de*, more than: *más arriba de cincuenta años*, more than fifty years. || *Para arriba*, upwards: *gana de veinte libras para arriba*, he earns upwards of twenty pounds; *hay artículos que cuestan de mil pesetas para arriba*, there are items which cost from a thousand pesetas upwards. || *Patas arriba*, on one's back: *caerse patas arriba*, to fall flat on one's back; back to front, upside down, muddled: *ponerlo todo patas arriba*, to get everything muddled. || *Peñas arriba*, towards the summit. || FAM. *Que si arriba que si abajo*, this that and the other, and so on and so forth. || *Véase más arriba*, see above.
— Interj. Get up!, stand up!, up you get! (levántate). || Come on! (ánimo). || — *¡Arriba España!*, long live Spain! || *¡Arriba los corazones!*, don't lose heart!, chin up!

arribada f. MAR. Arrival (llegada de un barco). | Tack (bordada). || Arrival: *arribada de mercancías*, arrival of goods. || *Arribada forzosa*, unscheduled stop.

arribaje m. MAR. Arrival.

arribano, na m. y f. *Amer.* Inhabitant of the northern coast of Peru. | Inhabitant of the southern provinces of Chile.

arribar v. intr. MAR. To arrive (llegar). | To put into port (hacer escala). | To drift with the wind (derivar). || To arrive (por tierra). || *Arribar a buen puerto*, to arrive safely.

arribazón m. Large shoals (*pl.*) of fish.

arribeño, ña adj. *Amer.* Highland.
— M. y f. *Amer.* Highlander.

arribismo m. Arrivism.

arribista adj. Self-seeking.
— M. y f. Arriviste, arrivist.

arribo m. MAR. Arrival (de un barco, de mercancías).

arricés m. Stirrup strap buckle.

arriendo m. JUR. Leasing (cuando hay contrato legal). || Renting (acción de alquilar). || Rent (cantidad que se paga). || JUR. Lease (contrato legal). || *Tomar en arriendo*, to lease.

arriero m. Muleteer, mule driver.

arriesgadamente adv. Riskily, hazardously (con riesgo). || Dangerously: *vivir arriesgadamente*, to live dangerously. || Boldly, bravely (con valor).

arriesgado, da adj. Risky, hazardous, dangerous (peligroso). || Risky, rash: *una empresa arriesgada*, a risky venture. || Daring, bold, brave (audaz).

arriesgar v. tr. To risk, to endanger: *arriesgar la vida*, to risk one's life. || To risk, to stake: *arriesgar dinero, su buena fama*, to risk money, one's good name. || To venture: *arriesgar una nueva hipótesis*, to venture a new theory. || FAM. *Arriesgar el pellejo*, to risk one's neck *o* skin.
— V. pr. To take a risk (correr un riesgo). || To risk: *arriesgarse a perderlo todo*, to risk losing everything; *arriesgarse a salir*, to risk going out. || *Quien no se arriesga no pasa el río* or *la mar*, nothing ventured, nothing gained.

arrimadero m. Support (apoyo). || Horse block (para montar a caballo).

arrimador m. Log (leña).

arrimadura f. Approach (acción de acercarse). || Leaning (acción de apoyarse).

arrimar v. tr. To bring closer, to draw up: *arrima tu silla a la mía*, bring your chair closer to mine. || To bring together (juntar). || To put: *arrima tu silla a la pared*, put your chair against the wall. || To lean (*a*, against) [apoyar]. || To put away (arrinconar). || To ignore (a una persona). || — POP. *Arrimar candela a*

uno, to thrash s.o., to give s.o. a good thrashing *o* beating. || FIG. *Arrimar el hombro*, to put one's shoulder to the wheel (trabajar mucho), to lend a hand (ayudar). | *Arrimarle un golpe a uno*, to hit s.o. | *Arrimarle a uno un palo*, to hit s.o. with a stick. || *Estar arrimado a alguien*, to live off s.o. (parásito). || *Vivir arrimado con una mujer*, to live with a woman (sin estar casados).
— V. pr. To come *o* to go *o* to get close *o* near, to draw up, to approach: *arrimarse al fuego*, to draw up to the fire. || To gather: *se arrimó mucha gente*, many people gathered. || To lean (apoyarse): *arrimarse a la pared*, to lean against the wall. || FIG. To join together (juntarse). | To seek the protection (*a*, of), to lean (*a*, on) [buscar apoyo]. | To live together (amancebarse). || FIG. *Arrimarse al sol que más calienta*, to get on the winning side.

arrimo m. FIG. Support, protection, help (apoyo). | Attachment (inclinación). || Dividing wall (pared). || Living together (amancebamiento). || — FIG. *Hacer algo al arrimo de alguien*, to do sth. with s.o.'s support *o* help. | *Tener buen arrimo*, to have good support (gozar de apoyo).

arrinconado, da adj. Forgotten, neglected, laid aside: *un objeto arrinconado*, a forgotten object. || Forsaken, deserted, abandoned: *un hombre arrinconado y solitario*, a lonely and forsaken man.

arrinconamiento m. Discarding, laying aside.

arrinconar v. tr. To put in a corner. || To corner (perseguir y acorralar): *arrinconé al ladrón*, I cornered the thief. || To discard, to put aside *o* away: *arrinconar un mueble desvencijado*, to discard a rickety piece of furniture. || To ignore, to leave out (apartar a alguien).
— V. pr. FIG. y FAM. To withdraw from the world, to live in isolation (vivir solo).

arriñonado, da adj. Kidney-shaped, reniform.

arriostrar v. tr. ARQ. To shore up, to prop up, to stay.

arriscadamente adv. Boldly, daringly.

arriscado, da adj. Rough, uneven, craggy (terreno). || Bold, daring (audaz). || Reckless (temerario). || *Amer. Nariz arriscada*, turned-up nose, snub nose (nariz respingona).

arriscador, ra m. y f. Olive picker, olive gleaner.

arriscamiento m. Boldness, daring.

arriscar v. tr. To risk. || *Amer.* To lift up, to turn up (levantar).
— V. intr. *Amer.* To come (*a*, to) [ascender]. || *No arrisca a cien pesos*, it is less than a hundred pesos, it does not come to a hundred pesos.
— V. pr. To fall headlong (las reses). || *Amer.* To dress elegantly (vestirse con esmero). | To get angry (enfurecerse).

arritmia f. MED. Arrhythmia.

arrítmico, ca adj. MED. Arrhythmic.

arritranca f. Breeching (correa).

arrivismo m. V. ARRIBISMO.

arrivista adj./s. V. ARRIBISTA.

— OBSERV. *Arrivismo* and *arrivista* are barbarisms better replaced by *arribismo* and *arribista*.

arrizar v. tr. MAR. To reef, to take in a reef (tomar rizos). | To lash, to tie down (atar).

arroba f. "Arroba", 25 pounds [11.5 kg.]. || "Arroba", about 28.5 pints [16.1 litres of wine]. || "Arroba", about 22 pints [12.6 litres of oil]. || — FIG. *Por arrobas*, in abundance, galore. || *Tiene gracia por arrobas*, he's extremely witty, he's full of wit.

arrobado, da adj. In ecstasy, in transports, in raptures (sumo placer). || In a trance (fuera de sí).

arrobador, ra adj. Entrancing, bewitching.

arrobamiento m. Ecstasy, rapture, transports, *pl.* (sumo placer). || Trance (de un místico).

arrobar v. tr. To entrance, to send into raptures.
— V. pr. To go into raptures, to go into transports, to go into ecstasies. || To go into a trance (los místicos).

arrobo m. Ecstasy, rapture (sumo placer). || Trance (de un místico).

arrocero, ra adj. Rice: *industria arrocera*, rice industry. || *Molino arrocero*, rice mill.
— M. y f. Rice grower.

arrodillamiento m. Kneeling.

arrodillar v. tr. To make kneel down. || *Estar arrodillado*, to be kneeling, to be on one's knees.
— V. intr. y pr. To kneel, to kneel down, to go down on one's knees.

arrodrigar o **arrodrigonar** v. tr. AGR. To prop, to stake (la vid).

arrogación f. Arrogation.

arrogancia f. Arrogance, arrogancy (soberbia). || Bravery, boldness (valor). || Pride (orgullo).

arrogante adj. Arrogant (altanero). || Proud (airoso). || Bold, brave (valiente).

arrogantemente adv. Arrogantly. || Bravely (con valor). || Proudly, with bearing (airosamente).

arrogarse v. pr. To arrogate to o.s., to assume: *se arrogó el derecho de castigar a los presos*, he assumed the right to punish the prisoners.

arrojadamente adv. Bravely, boldly, daringly.

arrojadizo, za adj. Throwable. || *Arma arrojadiza*, projectile, missile.

arrojado, da adj. FIG. Brave, bold (valiente). || Rash, daring (temerario).

arrojador, ra adj. Throwing, projectile.

arrojar v. tr. To throw: *arrojar una piedra, una pelota*, to throw a stone, a ball; *arrojar algo por la borda*, to throw sth. overboard. || To fling, to hurl (con fuerza). || To throw out, to belch out *o* forth: *volcán que arroja lava*, volcano belching out lava. || To belch, to send out (humo). || To drop: *arrojar bombas*, to drop bombs. || To give out *o* off, to emit: *arrojar rayos*, to give out rays. || To cast (el sedal). || To indicate, to show: *el balance arroja un beneficio*, the balance shows a profit. || FAM. To throw up, to vomit (vomitar). || BOT. To sprout (flores, brotes). | To put out (raíces). || To throw out: *le arrojaron del bar*, they threw him out of the bar. || — *Los tres diamantes arrojan un valor de 1000 dólares*, the three diamonds are worth a total of 1000 dollars. || *Prohibido arrojar basuras*, no tipping. || *Según lo que arrojan las estadísticas*, according to statistics.
— V. intr. FAM. To be sick, to vomit (vomitar).
— V. pr. To throw o.s., to fling o.s., to hurl o.s., to rush, to plunge: *arrojarse al agua*, to throw o.s. into the water; *arrojarse al combate*, to hurl o.s. into the fray. || To jump: *el perro se arrojó sobre el hombre*, the dog jumped at *o* on the man. || — *Arrojarse a los pies de uno*, to throw o.s. at s.o.'s feet. || *Arrojarse de cabeza*, to throw o.s. headlong *o* headfirst. || *Arrojarse por la ventana*, to throw o.s. out of the window.

arrojo m. Courage, daring, boldness: *hace falta mucho arrojo para obrar de esta manera*, you need a lot of courage to do that.

arrollable adj. Rollable.

arrollado m. *Amer.* Dressed pork.

arrollador, ra adj. Rolling (que enrolla). || FIG. Sweeping, devastating: *un viento arrollador*, a devastating wind. | Irresistible: *argumentos arrolladores*, irresistible arguments. | Resounding, overwhelming: *éxito arrollador*, overwhelming success; *una mayoría arrolladora*, a resounding majority.
— M. Windlass (cilindro).

arrollamiento m. Rolling, rolling-up (acción de arrollar). || ELECTR. Winding.

arrollar v. tr. To roll, to roll up, to coil (enrollar). || To sweep away, to carry off: *el agua de la crecida lo arrolló*, the floodwater swept it away. || To run over, to knock down: *el coche arrolló a un peatón*, the car ran over a pedestrian. || FIG. To rout, to crush: *arrollar los batallones enemigos*, to rout the enemy battalions. | To squash, to leave speechless, to silence: *en la discusión le arrolló en seguida*, he immediately squashed him in the discussion. | To have no respect for, to trample over: *arrollar los derechos ajenos*, to trample over other people's rights.

arromanzar v. tr. To translate into Castilian Spanish.

arropamiento m. Wrapping up, covering up.

arropar v. tr. To wrap up: *en invierno hay que arropar mucho a los niños*, in winter you must wrap the children up well. || To tuck up (a alguien en una cama). || To add grape syrup [to wine]. || FIG. To shelter: *dos montañas arropan la bahía*, two mountains shelter the bay. || *Estar muy arropado en la cama*, to be well tucked up in bed.
— V. pr. To wrap o.s. up: *arrópate bien que hace mucho frío*, wrap yourself up well, it's very cold. || To tuck o.s. up (en la cama).

arrope m. Boiled must. || Syrup (jarabe).

arropía f. Taffy (melcocha).

arrorró m. Lullaby (canción de cuna). || *Arrorró mi nene*, hushaby baby.

arrostrar v. tr. To face, to face up to, to brave: *arrostrar el frío, un peligro*, to brave the cold, a danger. || To face, to face up to: *arrostrar la muerte*, to face up to death; *arrostrar las consecuencias de una acción*, to face the consequences of an action.
— V. pr. To stand up, to face up: *arrostrarse con uno*, to stand up to s.o.

arroyar v. tr. To channel, to hollow out. || To form channels in (la lluvia).
— V. pr. To be channelled, to be hollowed out. || AGR. To mildew.

arroyo m. Stream, brook (riachuelo). || Gutter (en una calle). || FIG. Street, gutter (calle): *tirar al arroyo* or *plantar* or *poner en el arroyo*, to throw into the street. | Stream, flood: *arroyos de lágrimas*, streams *o* floods of tears. || *Amer.* River (río). || FIG. *Sacar del arroyo*, to drag from the gutter.

arroyuelo m. Streamlet, rivulet, rill, brooklet.

arroz m. Rice: *arroz descascarillado*, husked rice. || — *Arroz a la italiana*, risotto. || *Arroz blanco* or *en blanco*, boiled rice. || *Arroz con leche*, rice pudding, creamed rice. || *Amer. Arroz de leche*, rice pudding, creamed rice. || *Arroz picón* or *quebrantado*, broken rice. || *Más pesado que el arroz con leche*, as heavy as lead (comida), as dull as dishwater, as boring as can be (aburrido). || *Polvos de arroz*, face powder. || FIG. y FAM. *Tener arroz y gallo muerto*, to have a meal fit for a king, to have a slap-up meal.

arrozal m. Rice field, rice plantation. || Rice paddy, paddy (en China).

arrufadura f. MAR. Sheer (curvatura del puente del navío).

arrufar v. tr. MAR. To build with a sheer.
— V. pr. FAM. To fly off the handle, to lose one's temper.

arrufianado, da adj. Rascally, vulgar, coarse.

arrufo m. MAR. Sheer (curvatura del puente del navío).
arruga f. Wrinkle, line: *una cara surcada de arrugas*, a face furrowed with wrinkles. || Crease (en la ropa). || *Amer.* Fraud, swindle (estafa). || *Mi vestido tiene muchas arrugas*, my dress is very creased.
arrugamiento m. Wrinkling (de la piel). || Creasing (de la ropa).
arrugar v. tr. To wrinkle, to line (hacer arrugas). || To crumple up, to screw up: *con rabia arrugó la carta que tenía en la mano*, he furiously crumpled up the letter that he held in his hand. || To crease (la ropa). || *Amer.* To annoy, to bother. || — *Arrugar el ceño* or *el entrecejo*, to frown. || *Arrugar la cara*, to screw one's face up.
— V. pr. To shrink (encogerse). || To wrinkle (la cara). || To crease (la ropa).
arruinamiento m. Ruin, ruination. || *Provocar el arruinamiento de algo*, to bring about the ruin of sth.
arruinar v. tr. To ruin: *la guerra arruinó a mucha gente*, the war ruined many people. || To destroy, to lay waste (destruir). || FIG. To ruin, to wreck: *arruinar la salud*, to ruin one's health. | To ruin: *arruinar la reputación*, to ruin one's reputation.
— V. pr. To be ruined (perder la fortuna). || To fall into ruins, to fall down (un edificio). || To go to rack and ruin (estropearse).
arrullador, ra adj. Cooing (de las palomas). || Lulling (voz, canto). || FIG. Cajoling, coaxing.
arrullar v. tr. To coo at (una paloma). || FIG. To lull, to sing to sleep (dormir a un niño cantándole). || FIG. y FAM. To say sweet nothings to, to bill and coo to (enamorar).
— V. pr. FIG. y FAM. To bill and coo (los enamorados).
arrullo m. Cooing: *el arrullo de las palomas*, the cooing of the doves. || FIG. Billing and cooing (de los enamorados). | Lullaby (canción de cuna).
arrumaco m. FAM. Cajolery, flattery (zalamería). || Fondling, caressing. || Trinket, frill (adorno ridículo). || — *Andar con arrumacos*, to flatter. || *No me vengas con arrumacos*, don't try and get round me.
arrumaje m. MAR. Stowing, stowage.
arrumar v. tr. MAR. To stow.
— V. pr. MAR. To cloud over.
arrumazón f. MAR. Stowing. | Clouds, *pl.* (nublado).
arrumbador m. Wine-cellar worker.
arrumbamiento m. MAR. Course, direction (rumbo).
arrumbar v. tr. To discard, to lay aside, to put away (arrinconar). || FIG. To ignore, to exclude (a una persona).
— V. intr. MAR. To head, to set course (*hacia*, for).
— V. pr. MAR. To take one's bearings (determinar la situación del barco).
arrurruz m. Arrowroot (fécula).
arsenal m. Shipyard (astillero). || Naval dockyard (para buques de guerra). || Arsenal (de armas). || FIG. Store, storehouse, arsenal.
arseniato m. QUÍM. Arsenate, arseniate.
arsenical adj. QUÍM. Arsenical.
arsénico, ca adj./s.m. QUÍM. Arsenic.
arsenioso, sa adj. QUÍM. Arsenious, arsenous.
arseniuro m. QUÍM. Arsenide.
arsina f. QUÍM. Arsine.
arsis m. Arsis (métrica).
— OBSERV. El plural de la palabra inglesa *arsis* es *arses*.
arsonvalización f. MED. Treatment by diathermy.
arta f. BOT. Plantain (llantén).
Artajerjes n. pr. m. Artaxerxes.
artanica o **artanita** f. BOT. Cyclamen.
arte m. o f. Art: *una obra de arte*, a work of art; *no comprendo el arte abstracto*, I do not understand abstract art; *el arte culinario*, [the art of] cooking. || Skill (habilidad). || Artistry, workmanship: *mira con qué arte está hecho*, just look at the workmanship. || Cunning (astucia). || Rules, *pl.* (reglas). || Arts, *pl.*: *dedicarse al arte*, to dedicate o.s. to the arts. || — *Arte cisoria*, art of carving [meat]. || *Arte plumaria*, embroidery with feathers. || *Arte poética*, art of poetry. || *Artes de pesca*, fishing tackle, *sing.* || *Artes domésticas*, domestic science, *sing.* || *Artes liberales*, liberal arts. || *Bellas artes*, fine arts. || *Con arte*, skilfully. || *Con todas las reglas del arte*, according to the book *o* to the rules. || *El arte por el arte*, art for art's sake. || *Escuela de artes y oficios*, school of arts and crafts. || *No tener arte ni parte en una cosa*, to have nothing to do with sth. || *Por amor al arte*, for the love of it. || *Por arte de birlibirloque* or *por arte de magia*, as if by magic. || *Por buenas o malas artes*, by fair means or foul. || *Sin arte*, clumsily.
— OBSERV. The word *arte* is always feminine in the plural (*las artes gráficas*, the graphic arts) and usually masculine in the singular except when it is followed by certain adjectives (*arte cisoria, poética, plumaria*, etc.)
artefacto m. Device, contrivance, appliance: *un extraño artefacto*, a strange device. || *Artefacto nuclear*, nuclear device.
artejo m. ANAT. Knuckle. || ZOOL. Article (de los insectos).
arteramente adv. Cunningly, slyly, craftily.
arteria f. ANAT. Artery. || FIG. Artery (vía de comunicación).
artería f. Cunning, slyness, craftiness.
arterial adj. Arterial.
arteriola f. ANAT. Arteriole.
arteriosclerosis f. MED. Arteriosclerosis.
arteritis f. MED. Arteritis.
artero, ra adj. Cunning, sly, crafty.
artesa f. Trough.
artesanado m. Craftsmen, *pl.*
artesanía f. Handicrafts, *pl.*, crafts, *pl.*: *artesanía mexicana*, Mexican crafts. || Craftsmanship (habilidad): *está realizado con gran artesanía*, it is made with great craftsmanship. || *Objeto de artesanía*, handmade article.
artesano, na m. y f. Artisan, craftsman (hombre), artisan, craftswoman (mujer).
artesiano, na adj. Artesian: *pozo artesiano*, artesian well.
artesilla f. Small trough.
artesón m. Tub (cubo). || ARQ. Coffer (de un techo). | Coffered ceiling (techo).
artesonado, da adj. ARQ. Coffered.
— M. Coffered ceiling (techo).
artesonar v. tr. ARQ. To coffer.
ártico, ca adj. Arctic. || — *Círculo Polar Ártico*, Arctic Circle. || *Océano Ártico*, Arctic Ocean.
— M. Arctic.
articulación f. ANAT. Articulation, joint. || Articulation (pronunciación). || TECN. Joint: *articulación universal*, universal joint.
articuladamente adv. Articulately, distinctly.
articulado, da adj. Articulate: *lenguaje articulado*, articulate speech. || Articulated: *camión articulado*, articulated lorry. || ANAT. Jointed, articulated.
— M. Articles, *pl.* (de una ley).
articular adj. Articular: *reúma articular*, articular rheumatism.
articular v. tr. To articulate, to join together, to joint: *articular dos piezas de una máquina*, to articulate two parts of a machine. || To articulate (las sílabas). || JUR. To write in separate articles.
articulista m. Contributor, writer of articles (periodista).
artículo m. Article: *un artículo de periódico*, a newspaper article. || Entry (de un diccionario). || JUR. Article. || Article, item (mercancía): *artículo de primera calidad*, top-quality article. || ZOOL. Article (de los insectos). || GRAM. Article: *artículo definido, indefinido, partitivo*, definite, indefinite, partitive article. || — Pl. Goods: *artículos de consumo*, consumer goods. || — *Artículo de fe*, article of faith (afirmación religiosa), gospel truth (verdad). || *Artículo de fondo*, leader, leading article, editorial. || *Artículos alimenticios*, foodstuffs, food products. || *Artículos de caballero*, men's accessories. || *Artículos de escritorio*, stationery. || *Artículos de fantasía*, fancy goods. || *Artículos de primera necesidad*, basic commodities *o* necessities. || *Artículos de tocador*, cosmetics. || *Como artículo de fe*, as though it were gospel truth. || *En el artículo de la muerte*, in the article of *o* at the point of death. || *Hacer el artículo a*, to boost, to plug (fam.).
artífice m. y f. FIG. Author: *Dios es el artífice de la Creación*, God is the author of Creation. || Maker, artificer (hacedor). || Craftsman, artificer (artesano). || — *El Artífice Supremo*, the Maker (Dios). || *Ha sido el artífice de su fortuna*, he is a self-made man.
artificial adj. Artificial: *inseminación artificial*, artificial insemination; *pierna artificial*, artificial leg; *una sonrisa artificial*, an artificial smile. || *Fuegos artificiales*, fireworks.
artificiero m. Firework maker, pyrotechnist (de fuegos artificiales). || MIL. Artificer.
artificio m. Skill, ingenuity (habilidad). || Device (aparato). || FIG. Trick, artifice: *emplea muchos artificios para disimular su edad*, he uses lots of tricks to hide his age. || Firework (pirotecnia). || *Fuegos de artificio*, fireworks.
artificioso, sa adj. Crafty, cunning: *conducta artificiosa*, crafty behaviour. || Skilful, clever (hecho con habilidad).
artilugio m. FAM. Device, contraption, gadget (cosa). || FIG. Scheme, trick (trampa).
artillar v. tr. To arm with artillery.
artillería f. MIL. Artillery: *artillería pesada*, heavy artillery. || Armament (de un buque). || MIL. *Artillería antiaérea*, antiaircraft guns, *pl.*
artillero m. MIL. Artilleryman. || Gunner (en barcos, aviones).
artimaña f. Trick, scheme (astucia). || Trap (trampa).
artimón m. MAR. Mizzen, mizen (vela). | Mizzenmast, mizenmast (palo).
artista m. y f. Artist (escultor, pintor, etc.). || Artist, artiste (espectáculos). || TEATR. Actor (actor), actress (actriz). || — *Artista de cine*, film actor (actor), film actress (actriz). || FIG. *Es un artista conduciendo*, he makes driving an art.
artísticamente adv. Artistically.
artístico, ca adj. Artistic.
artralgia f. MED. Arthralgia.
artrítico, ca adj./s. MED. Arthritic.
artritis f. MED. Arthritis.
artritismo m. MED. Arthritism.
artrópodo, da adj. ZOOL. Arthropod, arthropodous.
— M. Arthropod. || — Pl. Arthropoda.
artuña f. Ewe which has lost its lamb.
arturiano, na o **artúrico, ca** adj. Arthurian.
Arturo n. pr. m. Arthur.

Artús n. pr. m. Arthur (rey).
aruco m. *Amer.* ZOOL. Horned screamer (ave).
arúspice m. HIST. Haruspex.
— OBSERV. El plural de *haruspex* es *haruspices.*
arveja f. BOT. Vetch, tare. || *Amer.* Pea (guisante). || *Arveja silvestre*, everlasting pea.
arvejal m. Vetch field, tare field. || *Amer.* Pea field.
arvejana f. BOT. V. ARVEJA.
arvejera f. BOT. Vetch, tare.
arvejo m. BOT. Pea (guisante).
arvejona f. BOT. Vetch, tare.
arzobispado m. Archbishopric (dignidad, territorio). || Archiepiscopate (dignidad, duración).
arzobispal adj. Archiepiscopal. || *Palacio arzobispal*, archbishop's palace.
arzobispo m. Archbishop.
arzolla f. BOT. Centaury.
arzón m. Saddletree (de la silla de montar). || *Potro con arzón*, v. POTRO.
as m. Ace (carta y dado): *pareja de ases*, pair of aces; *un as de diamantes*, an ace of diamonds. || As (moneda romana). || FIG. Ace, star: *un as del volante*, an ace driver.
asa f. Handle (de una vasija, cesta, etc.). || Bend (del intestino). || BOT. Juice (jugo). || — *Asa dulce*, benzoin, asa dulcis. || *Asa fétida*, asafetida, asafoetida. || *Los brazos en asa*, hands on hips.
asá adv. FAM. *Así que asá*, either way: *a mí se me da así que asá*, I don't mind either way.
asadero, ra adj. Roasting, for roasting.
— M. Spit roaster.
asado, da adj. Roast, roasted: *carne asada*, roast meat.
— M. Roast. || *Amer.* Barbecued beef. || *Amer. Asado con cuero*, joint roasted in its skin.
asador m. Spit (varilla para asar). || Spit roaster (aparato para asar).
asadura f. Liver (hígado). || FAM. Sluggishness, slowness (pachorra). || — Pl. Offal, *sing.*, innards. || FIG. y FAM. *Echar las asaduras*, to slog one's heart out.
— M. Sluggish person, big lump (fam.).
asaetear v. tr. To shoot *o* to wound with arrows (herir o matar con flechas). || To fire *o* to shoot arrows at (disparar contra). || FIG. To pester, to badger: *asaetear a* or *con preguntas*, to pester with questions.
asalariado, da adj. Salaried.
— M. y f. Salary earner.
asalariar v. tr. To pay a salary to.
asalmonado, da adj. Salmon-like (salmonado). || Salmon pink (color). || *Trucha asalmonada*, salmon trout.
asaltador, ra o **asaltante** adj. Attacking, assaulting.
— M. y f. Attacker, assailant (de una persona, de un sitio). || Robber, raider (de un banco).
asaltar v. tr. To storm, to attack, to assault (soldados). || To assault, to attack: *el ladrón le asaltó*, the thief assaulted him. || To raid, to rob (un banco). || To assail: *los mendigos le asaltaron*, the beggars assailed him. || FIG. To cross one's mind, to come to one: *una idea me asaltó*, an idea crossed my mind. | To afflict, to assail (las dudas).
asalto m. Assault, attack, raid: *dar asalto a*, to make an assault on. || DEP. Round (boxeo). | Bout (esgrima). || FAM. Party (fiesta). || *Tomar por asalto*, to take by storm.
asamblea f. Assembly (reunión). || Congress, conference (congreso). || MIL. Assembly (toque).
asambleísta m. y f. Member of an assembly. || Member of a congress, congressist (congresista).
asao adv. FAM. *Lo mismo me da así que asao*, I don't mind either way, it's all the same to me, I'm easy.
asar v. tr. To roast. || FIG. To annoy, to pester, to plague: *me asaron a preguntas*, they pestered me with questions. || — *Asar a la plancha*, to griddle. || *Asar en* or *a la parrilla*, to grill. || *Eso no se le ocurre ni al que asó la manteca*, only a fool would think of doing that.
— V. pr. To be roasted *o* roasting, to be boiling hot: *me aso en este abrigo*, I'm roasting in this overcoat. || FIG. *Asarse vivo*, to be roasted alive.
asargado, da adj. Twilled, serge-like.
asaz adv. Rather, quite (bastante). || Very, exceedingly (muy).
asbesto m. MIN. Asbestos.
asca f. BOT. Ascus.
ascalonia f. BOT. Shallot (chalote).
ascáride f. ZOOL. Threadworm.
ascendencia f. Descent, ancestry, origin: *es de ascendencia americana*, he is of American descent. || Ascendancy, ascendency, influence (predominio).
ascendente adj. Ascending, upward, rising. || *Marea ascendente*, incoming *o* rising tide.
ascender* v. intr. To go up, to rise, to ascend: *ascender por los aires*, to rise into the air; *la temperatura ha ascendido durante la mañana*, the temperature has risen during the morning. || To come to, to amount to, to add up to: *la cuenta asciende a tres libras*, the bill amounts to three pounds. || To climb (montaña). || To reach: *la producción de acero asciende a cinco mil toneladas*, steel production reaches five thousand tons. || FIG. To be promoted, to be raised, to rise: *ascender a capitán*, to rise to the rank of captain. || — *Ascender a la primera división*, to be promoted to the first division. || *Ascender al trono*, to ascend [to] the throne.
— V. tr. To promote, to raise: *ser ascendido a jefe por antigüedad*, to be promoted to boss by seniority.
ascendido, da adj. Promoted.
ascendiente adj. Ascending, upward, rising.
— M. Influence, ascendancy, ascendency. || — Pl. Ancestors, ancestry, *sing.* (parientes).
ascensión f. Ascent, climbing: *la ascensión del Everest*, the ascent of Everest. || Promotion (de grado, de división). || Ascension: *día de la Ascensión*, Ascension Day. || Accession (al pontificado, al trono).
ascensional adj. Upward, ascendant, ascendent.
ascensionista m. y f. Mountaineer (alpinista). || Balloonist.
ascenso m. Ascent, climbing, climb (subida). || FIG. Promotion (en un empleo): *conseguir un ascenso*, to obtain promotion; *el ascenso a capitán*, promotion to captain. || — *Ascenso por antigüedad, por méritos*, promotion by seniority, on merit. || *Lista de ascenso*, promotion list.
ascensor m. Lift [U.S., elevator]: *el hueco del ascensor*, the lift shaft. || *Ascensor de subida y bajada*, two-way lift.
ascensorista m. y f. Lift attendant [U.S., elevator operator].
ascesis f. Ascesis.
asceta m. y f. Ascetic.
ascético, ca adj. Ascetic.
— F. Asceticism.
ascetismo m. Asceticism.
asco m. Disgust, repulsion (repugnancia). || — FIG. *Canta que da asco*, he's an awful singer. || *Coger, cobrar* or *tomar asco a algo*, to take a dislike to sth. || *¡Da asco!*, it's revolting *o* horrible *o* disgusting! || *Da asco que no se pueda salir por la noche*, it makes you sick not being able to go out at night. || *Dar asco*, to make sick, to disgust: *le da asco*, it makes him sick. || FAM. *Está hecho un ascò*, he's disgusting, he's disgustingly filthy, it makes you feel sick to look at him. | *Hacer asco* (*a todo*), to turn one's nose up [at everything], to pull a face [at everything]. | *Le da asco la carne*, he can't stand meat, he loathes meat. | *Le tengo asco*, I can't stand the sight of him (le odio), he makes me sick (me da asco). | *Le tiene asco al agua*, he can't bear water, he can't stand the sight of water. | *Me da asco verlo*, it makes me feel sick to see it. || *Poner cara de asco*, to look disgusted. || *¡Qué asco!*, how revolting! || FIG. y FAM. *Ser un asco*, to be worthless (no tener valor), to be filthy, to be disgusting (estar sucio). || *Tener asco a la vida*, to be disgusted with life.
ascomiceto m. BOT. Ascomycete (hongo).
ascua f. Ember, live coal. || — FIG. *Arrimar uno el ascua a su sardina*, to look after number one. | *Estar echando ascuas*, to be furious *o* livid. | *Estar en* or *sobre ascuas*, to be on tenterhooks. || *Hierro hecho ascua*, red-hot iron. || FIG. *Pasar como sobre ascuas por un asunto*, to touch lightly on *o* to skim over a subject. | *Ser un ascua de oro*, to glitter like a diamond. | *Tener ojos como ascuas*, to have eyes which sparkle like diamonds.
aseadamente adv. Cleanly (limpiamente). || Neatly, tidily (arregladamente).
aseado, da adj. Clean (limpio). || Neat, tidy (arreglado).
asear v. tr. To wash (lavar). || To clean (limpiar). || To tidy up (arreglar). || To decorate (adornar).
— V. pr. To have a wash [and brush up], to wash o.s. (lavarse). || To tidy o.s. up, to get ready (componerse).
asechamiento m. o **asechanza** f. Trap (trampa).
asechar v. tr. To set a trap for.
asecho m. Trap (trampa).
asedar v. tr. To make as soft as silk (suavizar). || To hackle (el cáñamo).
asediador, ra adj. Besieging. || FIG. Annoying (importuno).
— M. y f. Besieger.
asediar v. tr. To besiege, to lay siege to (sitiar). || FIG. To snow under, to besiege, to bombard: *estaba asediado de solicitudes*, he was snowed under with requests; *los periodistas le asediaron a preguntas*, the reporters bombarded him with questions.
asedio m. Siege (cerco). || FIG. Nuisance, annoyance.
asegurado, da adj. Insured, assured: *casa asegurada de incendio*, house insured against fire; *asegurado en un millón de pesetas*, insured for one million pesetas.
— M. y f. Insured, policyholder.
asegurador, ra adj. Insurance, assurance: *compañía aseguradora*, insurance company.
— M. Insurer, underwriter.
aseguramiento m. Securing, fastening (acción de fijar). || Assurance (afirmación). || Insurance, assurance (seguro).
asegurar v. tr. To secure, to fix, to make safe (sujetar). || To put in a safe place (poner en sitio seguro). || To safeguard, to keep secure (preservar). || To strengthen, to make secure (consolidar). || To reassure (tranquilizar). || To insure, to assure: *asegurar contra incendio* or *de incendio*, to assure against fire. || To assure: *le aseguro que...*, I assure you that...
— V. pr. To make sure: *asegúrate de que esté bien cerrada la puerta*, make sure that the door is properly closed. || To insure *o* to assure o.s., to take out an insurance [policy].
asemejar v. tr. To make alike *o* like *o* similar (hacer parecido). || To liken, to compare (comparar).

— V. pr. To resemble each other, to be alike (parecerse). || *Asemejarse a*, to resemble, to be like.
asendereado, da adj. FIG. Overworked, overwhelmed (agobiado). || Beaten, well-trodden (camino). || FIG. Experienced (experto).
asenderear v. tr. To open paths through: *asenderear un bosque*, to open paths through a forest. || To bother, to annoy (acosar). || To chase, to pursue (perseguir).
asenso m. Consent, approbation, assent.
asentada f. Session, sitting: *de una asentada*, at one sitting.
asentaderas f. pl. FAM. Buttocks, behind, *sing.*, bottom, *sing.*
asentado, da adj. Situated: *San Sebastián está asentada a orillas del Urumea*, San Sebastián is situated on the banks of the Urumea. || FIG. Settled, stable (estable). | Established: *reputación muy asentada*, well-established reputation.
asentador m. Wholesale merchant (de un mercado al por mayor). || TECN. Chisel (de herrero). || Strop (suavizador). || *Amer.* Planer (en la imprenta). || *Asentador de vías*, tracklayer.
asentamiento m. Sitting [down] (acción de sentarse). || Establishment, settling (de personas). || Emplacement (emplazamiento). || COM. Entry, registration. || FIG. Wisdom, common sense (juicio).
asentar* v. tr. To seat, to sit [down] (sentar). || To place (colocar). || To settle: *la lluvia ha asentado el polvo*, the rain has settled the dust. || To lay: *asentar los cimientos*, to lay the foundations. || To found: *asentar una ciudad*, to found a city. || To pitch, to set up: *asentar un campamento*, to pitch camp. || To hone, to sharpen (afilar). || To level, to flatten down (la tierra). || TECN. To seat (una válvula). || To note, to enter (anotar). || To affirm, to assure, to assert (afirmar). || To establish (establecer). || FAM. To land, to give, to fetch (una bofetada, etc.). || To agree: *se asentó que*, it was agreed that. || To draw up (un contrato, un convenio). || To steady, to calm down: *asentar a una persona inestable*, to calm an unstable person down. || To set down (principio, argumento). || JUR. To award. || *Asentar el juicio*, v. JUICIO.
— V. intr. To be suitable (ir o sentar bien). || To be steady (una mesa, etc.).
— V. pr. To sit down, to seat o.s. || To alight, to land (los pájaros). || To settle (los líquidos, el polvo, el tiempo, un edificio). || To sink, to subside (la tierra). || To rub (arreos). || To be situated (estar situado). || FIG. To establish o.s. (en un empleo). | To settle down (establecerse). | To develop, to settle down (el carácter). || *Asentarse en el estómago*, to lie [heavily] on one's stomach (los alimentos).
asentimiento m. Consent, assent (aprobación).
asentir* v. intr. To agree, to assent, to approve (aprobar). || — *Asentir a*, to agree to, to approve. || *Asentir con la cabeza*, to nod [one's approval]. || *Asentir con un gesto*, to signal one's approval.
asentista m. Supplier (suministrador). || Contractor (contratista).
aseñorado, da adj. Haughty, pompous, stuck-up (fam.), toffee-nosed (fam.).
aseo m. Cleanliness (limpieza). || Tidiness, neatness (pulcritud). || Washing and dressing, toilet. || [Small] bathroom, toilet (cuarto). || — Pl. Toilets [U.S., rest room, *sing.*] (en un restaurante, etc.). || — *Aseo personal*, personal toilet (acción), personal cleanliness (efecto). || *Cuarto de aseo*, [small] bathroom, toilet.
asépalo, la adj. BOT. Having no sepals.
asepsia f. Asepsis (saneamiento).
aséptico, ca adj. Aseptic.
aseptizar v. tr. To asepticize.
asequible adj. Reasonable: *precio asequible*, reasonable price. || Obtainable, accessible (alcanzable). || Practicable, feasile (proyecto). || Easy to get on with, affable, easily-approached, approachable: *una persona asequible*, an affable *o* approachable person, a person easy to get on with. || Comprehensible, understandable (entendible). || *Libros asequibles a todos*, books within everybody's reach.
aserción f. Assertion, affirmation.
aserradero m. Sawmill.
aserradizo, za adj. Easily sawn (madera).
aserrado, da adj. Serrated.
— M. Sawing.
aserrador, ra adj. Sawing.
— M. Sawyer, sawer. || — F. Power saw.
aserradura f. Sawing (acción). || Saw cut (corte que hace la sierra). || — Pl. Sawdust, *sing.* (serrín).
aserrar* v. tr. To saw.
aserruchar v. tr. *Amer.* To saw.
asertivo, va adj. Assertive, affirmative.
aserto m. Assertion, affirmation (aserción).
asertor, ra m. y f. Assertor, affirmer.
asertorio, ria adj. Assertory, affirmatory (juicio).
asesinar v. tr. To murder. || To assassinate. || FIG. To murder (una obra, etc.).
— OBSERV. Cuando *asesinar* significa matar por motivos políticos, y especialmente a una persona destacada, se suele traducir por *to assassinate.*
asesinato m. Murder, assassination. (V. ASESINAR, Observ.)
asesino, na adj. Murderous: *mano asesina*, murderous hand.
— M. Murderer, killer, assassin. || *Asesino pagado*, hired assassin. || — F. Murderess, killer, assassin.
— OBSERV. V. ASESINAR (Observ.).
asesor, ra adj. Advisory.
— M. Consultant, adviser, advisor: *asesor jurídico*, legal adviser. || *Asesor agrónomo*, agricultural advisor, farming expert.
asesoramiento m. Advising (acción de asesorar). || Opinion (de asesor jurídico). || Advice (consejo): *con el asesoramiento técnico de*, with the technical advice of.
asesorar v. tr. To advise, to counsel.
— V. pr. To consult, to take advice: *asesorarse con* or *de un letrado*, to consult a lawyer, to take legal advice.
asesoría f. Consultantship (cargo del asesor). || Consultant's office (oficina). || Consultant's fee (estipendio).
asestadura f. Aiming, levelling, pointing.
asestar v. tr. To aim, to level, to point (un arma). || To give, to deliver, to fetch, to land (un golpe). || To fire: *asestar un tiro*, to fire a shot. || — *Asestar una puñalada*, to stab. || *Asestar un puñetazo*, to land a punch, to punch.
aseveración f. Assertion, contention, asseveration, affirmation.
aseverar v. tr. To assert, to affirm, to asseverate.
asexual o **asexuado, da** adj. Asexual.
asfaltado, da adj. Asphalted, asphalt, covered with asphalt.
— M. Asphalting (acción de asfaltar). || Asphalt (pavimento de asfalto).
asfaltar v. tr. To asphalt, to cover with asphalt.
asfalto m. Asphalt.
asfixia f. Asphyxia, suffocation.
asfixiado, da adj. Asphyxiated, suffocated.
asfixiante o **asfixiador, ra** adj. Asphyxiating, suffocating: *gas asfixiante*, asphyxiating gas. || FIG. Suffocating, stifling: *calor asfixiante*, suffocating heat.
asfixiar v. tr. To asphyxiate, to suffocate. || FIG. To stifle: *la miseria asfixia muchos talentos*, a great deal of talent is stifled by poverty.
— V. pr. To suffocate, to asphyxiate.
asfódelo m. BOT. Asphodel.
así adv. Thus, so, in this way, in that way, like this, like that: *yo lo hago así*, I do it like this. || Like that, such: *un amigo así no se encuentra todos los días*, you don't find a friend like that *o* such a friend every day. || Like that: *quiero un coche así*, I want a car like that. || So, then: *¿así me dejas?*, so you're leaving me?, you're leaving me, then? || Thereabouts: *cuesta 200 pesetas o así*, it costs 200 pesetas or thereabouts. || In such a way: *así lo dijo que toda la gente se lo creyó*, he said it in such a way that everybody believed it. || Therefore, consequently, so: *se resfrió, así no pudo venir*, he caught a cold, so he couldn't come. || — *Así* (con el subjuntivo), even if: *iremos así llueva a cántaros*, we'll go even if it pours with rain; I hope (ojalá): *¡así llegue pronto!*, I hope it comes soon! || *Así, así* or *así como así*, so-so, middling. || *Así como*, as well as: *estaban sus padres así como sus hermanas*, his parents were there as well as his sisters; as soon as: *así como llegue, le hablaré*, as soon as he arrives I shall speak to him; [just] like: *así como lo hiciste, lo hice yo*, I did it just like you. || *Así... como*, both... and, as well as, alike: *así los buenos como los malos*, both the good and the bad, the good as well as the bad, the good and the bad alike. || *Así como así*, just like that: *me pidieron así como así que les prestara un millón de pesetas*, they asked me to lend them a million pesetas just like that; anyhow, anyway (de todos modos). || *Así como... así*, in the same way that... [so], as... so: *así como los sordos no oyen, así los ciegos no ven*, in the same way that the deaf cannot hear, [so] the blind cannot see. || FAM. *Así de*, so, as... as that, that: *así de grande*, so big, as big as that, that big. || *Así Dios te ayude*, [may] God help you. || *Así es*, that's how it is, that's how it goes. || *Así es* or *fue como*, that is *o* was how: *así fue como se nos escapó*, that was how he escaped from us. || *Así es la vida*, that's life, such is life, life's like that. || *¡Así me gusta!*, well done!, bravo!, that's the way I like it! || *Así mismo*, likewise, in the same way. || *Amer. Así no más*, so-so. || *Así o asá*, either way. || *Así pues*, so, then: *nos están esperando, así pues date prisa*, they're waiting for us, so hurry up. || *Así que*, as soon as: *así que amanezca, me levantaré*, as soon as it's dawn, I shall get up; so, consequently, therefore: *llovía, así que no salimos*, it was raining, so we didn't go out. || *Así... que*, so much... that: *así había trabajado que estaba agotado*, he had worked so much that he was exhausted. || FAM. *Así que asá* or *así que asao lo mismo me da*, either way, it's all the same to me. || *Así sea*, so be it, let it be so. || *Así te mueras*, on your own head be it (allá tú). || *Así y todo*, even so, in spite of everything, just the same. || *¿Cómo así?*, how's that?, what was that? || *Es hombre bueno y así honrado*, he's a good man and honest as well. || *¿No es así?*, isn't it so?, isn't that so?, isn't that the case? || *No es así como hay que hacerlo*, that's not the way to do it, that's not how it should be done. || *Por decirlo así*, so to speak, as it were. || *Puesto que así es*, since that is so, since that is the case. || *Si así como*, instead of: *si así como lo hicieron ellos lo hubiéramos hecho nosotros*, if we had done it instead of them. || *Y así*, so, and so, so that: *¡y así ya*

puedes devolvérmelo!, so you can just give it back to me! || *Y así [sucesivamente]*, and so on.

Asia n. pr. f. GEOGR. Asia. || *Asia Menor*, Asia Minor.

asiático, ca adj./s. Asiatic, Asian.

asidera f. *Amer.* Saddle horn.

asidero m. Handle (agarradero). || FIG. Excuse, pretext (pretexto). || FIG. *Tengo un buen asidero en el ministerio*, I've got a good connection in the ministry.

asido, da adj. Grasped. || *Asidos del brazo*, arm in arm.

asidonense adj. From Medina Sidonia [Andalusian town, formerly called *Asido*].

asiduamente adv. Assiduously. || Regularly, frequently (frecuentemente).

asiduidad f. Assiduity. || Regularity, frequency (frecuencia).

asiduo, dua adj. Assiduous, industrious, hard-working (porfiado). || Regular, frequent (frecuente).
— M. y f. Regular, habitué: *un asiduo del café*, a regular of the café. || *Un asiduo del cine*, a regular cinemagoer [U.S., a regular moviegoer].

asiento m. Seat, chair: *estos asientos no son muy confortables*, these seats are not very comfortable. || Seat (de un coche, un tren, etc.): *asiento delantero, trasero*, front, rear seat. || Place, seat: *déjame tu asiento*, let me have your place. || Seat (localidad en un espectáculo): *reservar un asiento*, to book a seat. || Site (sitio en que está un pueblo o edificio). || Hold: *ese partido político no tiene asiento en este país*, that political party does not have a hold in this country. || Bottom, base (de botellas, vasijas, etc.). || Sediment (poso). || ARQ. Settling (de un edificio). || Trading contract (contrato para aprovisionamiento). || Treaty (tratado). || COM. Entry, registry (en un libro). | Item (de un presupuesto, en una cuenta, etc.). || Establishment (del impuesto, hipotecas). || Note (anotación). || Mouthpiece (del freno del caballo). || Bars, *pl.* (de la boca del caballo). || TECN. Seating: *asiento de válvula*, valve seating. | Layer (de argamasa). || FIG. Permanence (estabilidad). | Common sense: *persona de asiento*, person with common sense. || *Amer.* Mining area. | Farm buildings, *pl.*, centre of a farm (centro de hacienda). || — Pl. Seat, *sing.*, bottom, *sing.* (asentaderas). || — *Asiento de colmenas*, apiary. || *Asiento de estómago*, attack of indigestion. || BOT. *Asiento de pastos*, kind of broom (Erinacea pungens). || *Asiento de rejilla*, wickerwork *o* cane seat. || COM. *Asiento duplicado*, duplication. || *Asiento giratorio*, revolving *o* swivel chair. || AVIAC. *Asiento proyectable*, ejector seat. | *Avión de un solo asiento*, single-seater plane. || *Baño de asiento*, hip bath. || *Estar de asiento*, to reside. || *Tomar asiento*, to sit down, to take a seat: *tome usted asiento*, sit down, take a seat.

asignación f. Appointment, rendezvous (cita). || Assigning, allocation, assignment (atribución): *la asignación de fondos*, the allocation of funds. || Allowance, grant (subsidio). || Pension (pensión). || Salary, wages, *pl.*, remuneration (sueldo).

asignar v. tr. To assign (valor, trabajo, papel, cualidad, plazo, misión): *le han asignado una tarea difícil*, they have assigned him a difficult task. || To ascribe, to attribute, to assign (valor, papel, nombre, cualidad). || To allot, to give, to allocate (trabajo, número, pensión, tiempo): *me han asignado una semana para terminar el trabajo*, they have allotted me a week to finish off the work. || To grant, to award (pensión, salario, derecho). || To allocate (fondos).

asignatario, ria m. y f. *Amer.* Legatee, heir.

asignatura f. Subject (disciplina): *me aprobaron en seis asignaturas y me suspendieron en una*, I passed six subjects and failed one.

asilado, da m. y f. Inmate.

asilar v. tr. To put in a home (a un anciano, a un pobre, etc.). || To take in, to give shelter (albergar). || *Asilar a un extranjero*, to grant asylum to a foreigner.
— V. pr. To take refuge.

asilo m. Home: *asilo de ancianos*, old people's home. || Sanctuary, asylum: *derecho de asilo*, right of asylum. || FIG. Refuge, shelter: *nos dieron asilo por la noche*, they gave us shelter for the night. | Haven: *asilo de la paz*, haven of peace. || ZOOL. Asilus, hornet fly (insecto). || — *Buscar* or *pedir* or *solicitar asilo (político)*, to seek [political] asylum. || *Dar* or *conceder asilo (político)*, to grant [political] asylum.

asimetría f. Asymmetry.

asimétrico, ca adj. Asymmetrical, asymmetric.

asimiento m. Grasping, holding (acción de asir). || FIG. Attachment (afecto).

asimilable adj. Assimilable. || Comparable (equiparable).

asimilación f. Assimilation. || Comparison (equiparación).

asimilar v. tr. To assimilate. || To compare (equiparar). || To put on the same footing: *a este efecto los residentes extranjeros están asimilados a los nacidos en territorio nacional*, for this purpose foreign residents are put on the same footing as those born in the country.
— V. intr. To assimilate.
— V. pr. To be assimilated, to assimilate. || To resemble, to be like (asemejarse): *esto se asimila a mi trabajo*, this resembles my work. || To be alike (dos cosas).

asimilativo, va adj. Assimilative, assimilatory.

asimismo adv. In like manner, in the same way, likewise (del mismo modo). || Also, too (también).

asimplado, da adj. Simple, foolish.

asincrónico, ca adj. Asynchronous.

asindeton m. Asyndeton (supresión de conjunciones).

asíntota f. MAT. Asymptote.

asintótico, ca adj. Asymptotic, asymptotical.

asir* v. tr. To get hold of, to grasp, to take, to seize: *asir del brazo*, to get hold of by the arm. || To grip: *asió el puñal con los dientes*, he gripped the dagger between his teeth. || — *Asidos del brazo*, arm in arm. || *Asir la ocasión por los cabellos*, to seize the opportunity by the scruff of the neck.
— V. intr. To take root (las plantas).
— V. pr. To take hold, to get hold, to grab hold: *asirse a* or *de algo*, to take hold of sth. || FIG. To seize, to avail o.s.: *se asió del primer pretexto*, he seized [upon] the first pretext, he availed himself of the first pretext. || FIG. y FAM. To fight, to quarrel (reñir).

Asiria n. pr. f. GEOGR. Assyria.

asirio, ria adj./s. Assyrian.

asiriología f. Assyriology.

asistencia f. Audience (en el teatro, etc.). || Crowd: *la asistencia al estadio fue numerosa*, there was a large crowd in the stadium. || Attendance: *la asistencia es obligatoria*, attendance is compulsory; *la reunión se celebró con mediana asistencia*, there was a moderate attendance at the meeting. || Assistance, help: *prestar asistencia a uno*, to give s.o. assistance *o* help. || Care, aid: *asistencia médica*, medical care *o* aid. || Presence: *con asistencia de*, in the presence of. || TAUR. Staff [of bullring]. || *Amer.* Private drawing room (saloncito). || — Pl. Allowance, *sing.*, maintenance, *sing.* (pensión alimenticia). || — *Asistencia facultativa*, medical treatment (tratamiento), medical staff (médicos). || *Asistencia social*, social welfare. || *Amer. Casa de asistencia*, boardinghouse.

asistenta f. Charwoman, charlady, daily help (criada no permanente). || Assistant (en un convento). || Chambermaid (en un palacio). || *Asistenta social*, welfare worker.

asistente adj. Assistant, assisting, helping.
— M. Assistant (de obispo, etc.). || MIL. Orderly. || Person present, member of the audience (que está presente). || — Pl. Audience, *sing.* (en el teatro, etc.), crowd, *sing.* (en un estadio, etc.): *había numerosos asistentes*, there was a large audience. | Those present: *entre los asistentes se encontraban varios artistas*, among those present were several artists.

asistido, da adj. Assisted (socorrido). || — *Dirección asistida*, power steering. || *Frenos asistidos*, power brakes.

asistir v. tr. To assist, to help: *le asiste en su trabajo*, he assists him in his work. || To treat, to attend: *le asiste un buen médico*, he is being treated by a good doctor. || To serve, to attend (servir). || To help out: *como estoy sin criada me asiste Pepe*, I have no maid at the moment so Joe is helping me out. || *Me asiste el derecho*, the law is on my side, I have the law on my side.
— V. intr. To attend, to be present, to come, to go: *no asiste nunca a esta clase*, he never attends *o* comes to *o* goes to this lesson, he is never present at this lesson. || To be [present]: *asistía una multitud impresionante*, there was an impressive crowd [present]. || To witness, to be present at the time of: *asistir a un accidente*, to witness an accident. || To follow suit (en los naipes).

asma f. MED. Asthma.

asmático, ca adj. MED. Asthmatic, asthmatical.

asna f. She-ass (hembra del asno). || — Pl. Rafters (vigas).

asnada f. FIG. y FAM. Stupid thing, silly thing.

asnal adj. Donkey, ass, of a donkey, of an ass, asinine. || FIG. y FAM. Stupid, silly. || *Especie asnal*, asinine species.

asnería f. FAM. Herd of asses *o* donkeys. || FIG. y FAM. Stupid thing, silly thing (tontería). || *Decir asnerías*, to talk nonsense.

asno m. Donkey, ass (animal). || FIG. y FAM. Ass, fool, dunce, dimwit, twit (torpe). | Boor, pig, lout (grosero). || — FIG. *Al asno muerto, la cebada al rabo*, it's no good closing the stable door after the horse has bolted. || FIG. y FAM. *Apearse* or *caer uno de su asno*, to back down, to climb down, to give in. | *No ver tres en un asno*, to be as blind as a bat. | *Parecerse al asno de Buridán*, to be in two minds, to be like Buridan's ass. || FIG. *Puente de los asnos*, v. PUENTE.

asociable adj. Associable.

asociación f. Association: *Asociación Europea de Libre Cambio*, European Free Trade Association. || COM. Partnership. || *Asociación de ideas*, association of ideas.

asociacionismo m. Associationism.

asociado, da adj. Associate, associated: *miembro asociado*, associate member.
— M. Associate, member. || COM. Associate, partner.

asociamiento m. Association, partnership.

asociar v. tr. To associate. || COM. To take into partnership: *asoció a su hijo al negocio*, he took his son into partnership in the business. || To pool, to put together (esfuerzos). || To bracket (en categoría, etc.).
— V. pr. To associate, to join forces, to team up. || COM. To enter into partnership, to become partners. || FIG. To share: *asociarse a la alegría de uno*, to share s.o.'s joy. || — *El granizo y las heladas se han asociado*

para destruir la cosecha, between them the hail and ice have ruined the harvest. || *Su recuerdo se asocia con mi estancia en Inglaterra,* he reminds me of when I was in England, I associate him with the time I was in England.
asocio m. *Amer.* Association. || *En asocio de,* in collaboration with, in association with.
asolador, ra adj. Devastating, destructive.
asolamiento m. Devastation, destruction.
asolar* v. tr. To devastate, to destroy (destruir): *el granizo ha asolado las viñas,* the hail has devastated the vines. || To raze, to flatten (arrasar): *el terremoto asoló la ciudad,* the earthquake flattened the city. || AGR. To scorch, to dry up, to parch (el sol, el calor). || To ravage (una epidemia).
— V. pr. To be devastated, to be destroyed. || To settle (los líquidos).
asoleada f. *Amer.* Sunstroke (insolación).
asolear v. tr. To put in the sun, to insolate, to expose to the sun.
— V. pr. To sunbathe (tomar el sol). || To tan, to become tanned, to get a tan (tostarse al sol). || VET. To suffocate (los animales).
asomada f. Brief appearance.
asomar v. intr. To show, to appear: *la torre de la iglesia asomaba en el horizonte,* the church tower showed on the horizon. || To loom up: *asomó una figura en la niebla,* a figure loomed up in the fog. || To come out: *hoy el sol no asoma,* the sun is not coming out today. || To break: *asoma el día,* day is breaking. || To show: *su vestido asomaba debajo del abrigo,* her dress was showing below her coat. || To hang out: *un pañuelo asomaba fuera de su bolsillo,* a handkerchief was hanging out of his pocket.
— V. tr. To put out, to stick out: *asomar la cabeza a* or *por la ventana,* to put one's head out of the window. || To show, to reveal: *asomar la punta de la oreja,* to reveal one's real self *o* one's true colours.
— V. pr. To lean out: *prohibido asomarse al exterior,* do not lean out of the window. || FAM. To become tipsy (achisparse). || To take a brief look: *si nos asomamos al panorama de la situación económica española,* if we take a brief look at the Spanish economic panorama. || To glance, to look: *usted no se ha asomado siquiera a la lección,* you haven't even glanced at the lesson. || To show one's face (negativo): *no me asomé a la reunión,* I didn't show my face at the meeting. || To look in, to pop in (positivo): *no hice más que asomarme a la reunión,* I only popped in to the meeting.
asombradizo, za adj. Easily astonished (asombro). || Easily scared (espanto).
asombrado, da adj. Surprised. || Astonished, amazed (pasmado).
asombrador, ra adj. Surprising. || Astonishing, amazing (pasmoso).
asombramiento m. Surprise. || Astonishment, amazement (pasmo).
asombrar v. tr. To shade (dar sombra). || To deepen, to darken (color). || To surprise (sorprender). || To astonish, to amaze (pasmar). || To frighten, to scare (asustar).
— V. pr. FIG. To be frightened *o* scared (asustarse). | To be surprised: *no se asombra de* or *por* or *con nada,* he is not surprised at *o* by anything; *me asombro de verte aquí,* I'm surprised to find you here. | To be amazed *o* astonished (quedarse pasmado): *asombrarse de algo,* to be amazed at sth., to be astonished by sth.
asombro m. Fright, fear (susto). || Surprise, astonishment, amazement (sorpresa): *con gran asombro de mi madre,* to my mother's great amazement. || Amazement, wonder (estupefacción). || FAM. Ghost, phantom, apparition (aparecido). || — *De asombro,* astonishing, surprising. || *¡No salgo de mi asombro!,* I can't get over it!, it's amazing!
asombrosamente adv. Wonderfully, amazingly.
asombroso, sa adj. Amazing, astonishing (sorprendente). || Bewildering, stupefying (estupefaciente).
asomo m. Appearance (apariencia). || Shadow: *sin el menor asomo de duda,* without the shadow of a doubt. || Hint, sign, trace, indication (indicio): *sin un asomo de cansancio,* without a trace of tiredness. || Suspicion, supposition (sospecha). || — *Ni por asomo,* by no means, not in the least. || *No le conozco ni por asomo,* I don't know him from Adam, I don't know him at all.
asonada f. Riot, disturbance (motín).
asonancia f. Assonance (poesía, retórica). || Consonance, harmony (entre sonidos). || Relation, connection (entre dos cosas).
asonantado, da adj. Assonated.
asonantar v. intr. To assonate.
— V. tr. To make assonant.
asonante adj./s. Assonant.
asonar* v. intr. To assonate.
asorocharse v. pr. *Amer.* To get mountain sickness. || FAM. To blush, to go red (ruborizarse).
aspa f. St-Andrew's cross, an X-shaped cross. || MAT. Multiplication sign. || Reel, winding frame (devanadera). || Arms, *pl.* (armazón de molino). || Arm (ala de molino). || — HERÁLD. Saltire. || *Amer.* Horn (asta). || *Colocado en aspa, en forma de aspa,* X-shaped, cross-shaped.
aspadera f. Reel, winding frame (devanadera).
aspado, da adj. With the arms extended like a cross (los penitentes de una procesión). || FIG. y FAM. Awkward, stiff (llevando ropa estrecha). || X-shaped, cross-shaped.
aspar v. tr. To reel, to wind (hilo). || To crucify (crucificar). || FIG. y FAM. To mortify (mortificar). | To vex, to annoy (vejar). || *¡Que me aspen si....!,* I'll be hanged if...!
— V. pr. FIG. *Asparse a gritos,* to shout o.s. hoarse (desgañitarse).
asparagus m. BOT. Asparagus (planta ornamental).
aspaventero, ra adj. Theatrical, given to making extravagant gestures.
aspaviento m. Fuss, extravagant behaviour, theatricality.
aspecto m. Look, appearance: *no me gusta el aspecto de la herida,* I don't like the look of the wound; *la casa tenía un aspecto austero,* the house had an austere appearance; *este hombre tiene un aspecto elegante,* this man has a smart appearance. || ASTR. Aspect. || Aspect, side: *el problema tiene varios aspectos,* the problem has several aspects, there are several sides to the problem. || — *Al* or *a primer aspecto,* at first sight. || *Bajo este aspecto,* from this point of view, viewed from this angle, in this respect. || *En ciertos aspectos,* in some respects. || *En todos los aspectos,* in every respect, in all respects, on every account, in every way. || *Persona de aspecto salubre, perverso,* a healthy-looking, evil-looking person. || *Tener buen aspecto,* to look nice (cosas), to look well (personas).
aspereza f. Roughness, asperity (al tacto). || Tartness, sourness (al gusto). || Harshness, roughness, gruffness (de la voz). || Roughness, ruggedness, unevenness (del terreno). || Rudeness, brusqueness, gruffness, harshness (del carácter, de una respuesta). || — FIG. *Limar asperezas,* to smooth things over. || *Un terreno lleno de asperezas,* a very uneven piece of ground.
asperges m. REL. Asperges, sprinkling.
aspergilo m. BOT. Aspergillus (hongo).
asperidad f. V. ASPEREZA.
asperilla f. BOT. Woodruff.
asperillo m. Sour *o* bitter taste (de fruta no madura, etc.).
asperjar v. tr. To sprinkle (rociar). || REL. To sprinkle with holy water.
áspero, ra adj. Rough, asperous (p.us.) [al tacto]. || Tart, sour (al gusto). || Harsh, gruff, brusque, rude (carácter, respuesta). || Harsh, rough, gruff (voz). || Rough, rugged, uneven (terreno). || Harsh, hard (clima). || *Ser áspero de condición* or *de genio,* to be bad-tempered.
asperón m. Sandstone (piedra).
aspersión f. Aspersion, sprinkling. || AGR. Spraying.
aspersorio m. REL. Aspergillum.
aspérula f. BOT. Woodruff.
áspid o **áspide** m. ZOOL. Asp, aspic.
aspidistra f. BOT. Aspidistra.
aspillera f. Loophole.
aspiración f. Inhalation, breathing in (respiración). || GRAM. Aspiration. || TECN. Intake: *aspiración de aire,* intake of air. || FIG. Aspiration, desire (deseo). || MÚS. Pause.
aspirado, da adj. Aspirate: *hache aspirada,* aspirate aitch.
aspirador, ra adj. Suction: *bomba aspiradora,* suction pump.
— M. y f. Vacuum cleaner (aparato doméstico).
aspirante adj. Suction: *bomba aspirante,* suction pump. || FIG. Aspiring.
— M. y f. Candidate, applicant, aspirant (p.us.).
aspirar v. tr. To inhale, to breathe in (respirar). || To suck, to suck up (máquina). || GRAM. To aspirate.
— V. intr. To inhale, to breathe in. || To suck (máquina). || FIG. To aspire: *aspirar a altos cargos,* to aspire to high positions.
aspiratorio, ria adj. Aspiratory.
aspirina f. Aspirin.
asquear v. tr. To sicken, to nauseate, to turn [s.o.'s] stomach: *las ostras me asquean,* oysters turn my stomach. || To disgust, to nauseate, to sicken: *su conducta me asquea,* his behaviour disgusts me. || *Esta vida me asquea* or *estoy asqueado de la vida,* I'm sick of this life.
— V. intr. To be sickening *o* nauseating *o* disgusting.
— V. pr. To be disgusted *o* nauseated *o* sickened. || *Asquearse de la vida,* to become sick of life.
asquerosamente adv. Dirtily, filthily, disgustingly.
asquerosidad f. Dirtiness, filthiness, filth. || Obscenity. || Dirty trick (mala jugada). || Mess: *este niño siempre hace asquerosidades en la mesa,* this child always makes a mess at the table.
asqueroso, sa adj. Revolting, foul, sickening, nauseating, nasty, awful, vile: *una comida asquerosa,* a revolting meal; *un olor asqueroso,* a foul smell. || Dirty, filthy: *tiene las manos asquerosas,* his hands are filthy. || Dirty, squalid: *vive en una habitación asquerosa,* he lives in a squalid room. || Disgusting (conducta). || Dirty, filthy (obsceno). || Vile, loathsome (muy malo). || Repulsive, disgusting (aspecto). || Squeamish (que siente asco).
— M. y f. Vile *o* disgusting person (obsceno). || Vile *o* loathsome person (muy malo).
asta f. Lance, spear, pike (arma). || Shaft (palo de la lanza). || Staff, pole (de la bandera). || Handle, haft,

helve (mango). || Handle (del pincel). || Horn (cuerno). || Antler (del ciervo). || Horn (materia): *gafas con montura de asta*, horn-rimmed spectacles. || — *A media asta*, at half-mast (bandera). || FIG. y FAM. *Dejar a uno en las astas del toro*, to leave s.o. in the lurch, to leave s.o. high and dry, to leave s.o. stranded.

astado, da adj. BOT. Hastate. || Horned (animal).
— M. Bull (toro). || Pike bearer (soldado).

astático, ca adj. FÍS. Astatic.

astenia f. MED. Asthenia.

asténico, ca adj./s. Asthenic.

aster m. BOT. Aster.

asterisco m. Asterisk. || *Poner asterisco a*, to asterisk.

asterismo m. ASTR. y MIN. Asterism.

astero m. Pike bearer (soldado romano).

asteroide adj./s.m. ASTR. Asteroid.

astifino, na adj. Narrow-horned (toro).

astigitano, na adj. y s. Ecijan [from Ecija, town in Andalusia, formerly *Astigi*].

astigmático, ca adj. Astigmatic.
— M. y f. Astigmat.

astigmatismo m. MED. Astigmatism.

astil m. Handle, helve, haft (mango de instrumento). || Shaft (de la flecha). || Arm, beam (de la balanza). || Quill (de la pluma).

astilla f. Splinter, chip (de madera, leña, hueso, piedra, etc.). || — Pl. Chips, firewood, *sing.* (leña menuda). || — *De tal palo, tal astilla*, like father, like son. || *Hacer astillas*, to smash into fragments, to splinter, to smash to smithereens (fam.). || *No hay peor astilla que la del mismo palo*, former friends can be dangerous enemies.

astillar v. tr. To splinter, to smash, to break (hacer pedazos). || To splinter [wood].
— V. pr. To splinter, to split [wood].

Astillejos n. pr. m. pl. ASTR. Gemini, *sing.*, the Twins (estrellas).

astillero m. MAR. Shipyard, dockyard (taller). || Rack (de armas).

astilloso, sa adj. Splintery, easily splintered.

astracán m. Astrakhan, astrachan.

astracanada f. FAM. Farce.

astrágalo m. BOT. Astragalus. || ARQ. Astragal. || ANAT. Astragalus, astragal.

astral adj. Astral: *influencia astral*, astral influence; *cuerpos astrales*, astral bodies.

astreñir* v. tr. To astringe (los tejidos orgánicos). || FIG. To bind (sujetar).

astricción f. MED. Astriction.

astricto, ta adj. Obliged, compelled, bound, forced: *astricto a un servicio*, obliged *o* forced to do a duty, duty bound. || Astricted, bound: *astricto al respeto de la ley*, bound to observe the law.

astringencia f. Astringency.

astringente adj./s. m. Astringent.

astringir o **astriñir*** v. tr. To astringe, to contract (los tejidos). || FIG. To bind (sujetar).

astro m. ASTR. Heavenly body, star (estrella). || FIG. Star (de cine, etc.). || *El astro rey* or *del día*, the sun (el sol).

astrobiología f. Astrobiology.

astrocompás m. TECN. Astrocompass.

astrofísico, ca m. y f. Astrophysicist. || — F. Astrophysics.

astrolabio m. ASTR. Astrolabe.

astrología f. Astrology.

astrológico, ca adj. Astrological, astrologic.

astrólogo m. Astrologer.

astronauta m. y f. Astronaut.

astronáutica f. Astronautics.

astronave f. Spaceship, spacecraft.

astronomía f. Astronomy.

astronómico, ca adj. Astronomical, astronomic. || FIG. y FAM. Astronomical (cifra): *un precio astronómico*, an astronomical price.

astrónomo m. Astronomer.

astrosamente adv. Shabbily, untidily.

astroso, sa adj. Dirty, unclean (sucio). || Shabby, slovenly, untidy (desaseado). || Unfortunate, wretched, unhappy (desgraciado). || Despicable, contemptible, vile (despreciable).

astucia f. Cleverness, astuteness (habilidad). || Cunning, craftiness, artfulness (peyorativo). || Trick, ruse, artifice: *las astucias del ratero*, the tricks of the pickpocket. || *Obrar con astucia*, to act cunningly *o* astutely *o* with cunning, to be cunning.

astucioso, sa adj. V. ASTUTO.

astur o **asturiano, na** adj./s. Asturian.

asturianismo m. Asturianism.

Asturias n. pr. f. pl. GEOGR. Asturias. || *El príncipe de Asturias*, the prince of Asturias [crown prince of Spain].

astuto, ta adj. Astute, clever (hábil): *un abogado astuto*, an astute lawyer. || Cunning, crafty, artful, foxy, sly: *un ladrón astuto*, a crafty thief. || *Astuto como un zorro*, as sly as a fox.

asueto m. Short vacation, time off, holiday (vacación corta): *un día de asueto*, a day off, a day's holiday. || School holiday.

asumir v. tr. To assume, to take on, to take upon o.s.: *asumir una responsabilidad*, to assume a responsibility. || To adopt (una actitud). || *Asumir la dirección*, to take control.

asunceno, na adj. [Of *o* from] Asunción.
— M. y f. Native *o* inhabitant of Asunción.

asunción f. Assumption, taking-on (acción de asumir). || FIG. Accession, ascension (al trono). || Rising, promotion (a un cargo). || Elevation (a una dignidad).

Asunción n. pr. f. REL. Assumption. || GEOGR. Asunción (capital del Paraguay).

asunto m. Theme, subject, subject matter (tema). || Question, matter, issue: *asuntos de orden económico*, economic questions. || Affair, business: *esto es asunto mío*, that's my business; *un asunto peliagudo*, a tricky business; *un asunto sucio*, a dirty business. || Matter, affair: *trataré el asunto*, I shall deal with the matter. || Fact (caso): *el asunto es que*, the fact is that. || Affair (sentimental, etc.): *tuvo un asunto con María*, he had an affair with Mary. || — *Asunto concluido*, closed affair *o* matter: *es asunto concluido*, the matter is closed; let that be the end of the matter: *toma esto y asunto concluido*, take this and let that be the end of the matter. || *Asuntos exteriores* or *extranjeros*, foreign affairs. || *Asuntos pendientes*, unsolved matters, matters in hand *o* not yet settled (sin resolver), outstanding matters, matters in abeyance (sin estudiar). || *Conocer el asunto*, to know what's what. || *Eso es otro asunto*, that's another matter, that's another story. || *Ir al asunto*, to get down to the heart of the matter. || *Ministerio de Asuntos Exteriores*, v. MINISTERIO || *No me gusta el asunto*, I don't like the look of it. || *Amer. Poner el asunto*, to watch one's step, to take care. || *Suspendiendo todos los demás asuntos*, to the exclusion of all other matters. || *Volvamos a nuestro asunto*, let's get back to the subject in hand.

asustadizo, za adj. Easily frightened *o* scared, timid, timorous, fearful. || Shy, skittish (caballo). || FAM. *Más asustadizo que una mona*, as timid as a mouse.

asustar v. tr. To frighten, to alarm, to scare: *le asusta el trueno*, thunder frightens him. || To scare away (ahuyentar). || FIG. To horrify: *me asusta su conducta*, I'm horrified at his behaviour, his behaviour horrifies me.
— V. pr. To be frightened *o* scared: *se asusta por* or *de* or *con nada*, he is frightened *o* scared by *o* of the slightest thing. || FIG. To be horrified. || *Nada le asusta*, nothing can scare *o* frighten him.

atabacado, da adj. Tobacco-coloured.

atabal m. MÚS. Kettledrum.

atabalear v. intr. To stamp (el caballo). || To drum, to tap [the fingers] (tamborilear).

atabalero m. Kettledrummer (timbalero).

atabanado, da adj. Spotted white (caballo).

atabe m. Vent (para la ventilación de una cañería). || Peephole (para la inspección de una cañería).

atacable adj. Attackable, assailable.

atacador, ra adj. Attacking, assailing (que ataca).
— M. y f. Attacker, assailant. || — M. Ramrod (de cañón).

atacante adj. Attacking, assailing (que ataca).
— M. Attacker, assailant.

atacar v. tr. To attack, to assail: *atacar a un adversario*, to attack an adversary. || To attack: *las langostas han atacado las cosechas*, the locusts have attacked the crops. || To attack, to seize, to affect (una enfermedad). || To overcome (el sueño). || MÚS. To attack (un instrumento, una pieza). | To strike (una nota). | To strike up: *la banda atacó una marcha*, the band struck up a march. || To pack, to cram, to stuff (recalcar). || To ram home, to ram (carga de arma de fuego). || To fasten, to button, to do up (una prenda de vestir). || QUÍM. To attack, to corrode, to eat away *o* into, to erode (corroer): *el ácido ataca el metal*, acid attacks metal. || FIG. To begin, to start upon: *atacar la ascensión del Aconcagua*, to begin the ascent of Aconcagua. | To grapple with, to tackle (una dificultad, un problema, etc.). || — JUR. *Atacar de falsedad*, to deny, to contradict. || *Atacar los nervios*, to get on the nerves: *este ruido me ataca los nervios*, this noise gets on my nerves.

atacola f. Tail strap (arreo).

ataderas f. pl. FAM. Garters (ligas).

atadero m. Tether, rope, cord (cuerda). || Hitching ring *o* hook (sitio donde se ata). || FIG. Tie, bond (vínculo).

atadijo m. FAM. Bundle.

atado, da adj. FIG. Timid, bashful, shy, diffident (apocado).
— M. Bundle (paquete): *un atado de ropa*, a bundle of clothing. || *Amer. Atado de cigarrillos*, packet [U.S., pack] of cigarettes.

atador, ra adj. Binding, bundling.
— M. y f. Binder, bundler. || — F. AGR. Binding machine, [sheaf] binder. || — M. *Amer.* Halter, tether, headrope, lunge.

atadura f. Tying, binding, attaching, fastening (acción de atar). || String, rope, cord (para atar). || Binding (de esquís). || FIG. Tie, bond (vínculo). | Tie (traba): *ataduras matrimoniales*, marriage ties.

atafagar v. tr. To stifle, to suffocate (olor). || To pester (molestar).

atafetanado, da adj. Resembling taffeta.

atagallar v. intr. MAR. To crowd sail.

ataguía f. Cofferdam.

ataharre m. Crupper (para sujetar la silla).

ataire m. Moulding.

atajadero m. Stemming ridge [for irrigation].
atajador, ra adj. Barring, checking, damming, stemming, stopping.
— M. y f. Interceptor. || — M. *Amer.* Muleteer, mule driver (arriero).
atajar v. intr. To take a shortcut: *atajar por los campos,* to take a shortcut across the fields.
— V. tr. To cut off, to head off, to intercept: *atajaron al fugitivo,* they intercepted the fugitive. || To bar, to block, to obstruct: *atajar un camino,* to block a road. || To divide (dividir). || To partition [off] (separar). || FIG. To cut (suprimir). | To stop from spreading, to check: *atajar un incendio, una enfermedad,* to stop a fire, a disease from spreading. | To stop, to check, to put an end to, to stem: *hay que atajar el aumento de la delincuencia juvenil,* the rise in juvenile delinquency must be checked. | To cut short: *atajar los comentarios,* to cut short criticism. | To interrupt, to cut short: *atajar al orador,* to interrupt the speaker. | To cross out, to strike out (tachar).
— V. pr. FIG. To stop short (turbarse, cortarse). || FAM. To get drunk (emborracharse).
atajea o **atajía** f. Drain, sewer.
atajo m. Shortcut (camino): *tirar por un atajo,* to take a shortcut. || Division (separación). || Cut (en un escrito). || — FIG. *No hay atajo sin trabajo,* no gains without pains. | *Tirar* or *tomar por el atajo,* to take the easiest way out.
— OBSERV. Do not confuse *atajo* with *hatajo,* meaning *heap, bunch, lot.*
atalaya f. Watchtower, observation tower (torre). || Vantage point (lugar elevado). || — M. Lookout (el que vigila).
atalayar v. tr. To watch, to observe (vigilar). || FIG. To spy on (espiar).
atalayero m. Scout, lookout.
atanasia f. BOT. Sisymbrium. || IMPR. English type [14 points].
atañer* v. intr. To concern, to have to do with: *este asunto no te atañe,* this matter has nothing to do with you. || To be incumbent on (incumbir). || *En* or *por lo que atañe a,* with respect to, with regard to, as far as... is concerned: *en lo que atañe a mi viaje, todavía no he decidido nada,* as far as my trip is concerned, I still haven't decided anything.
ataque m. Attack: *ataque por sorpresa,* surprise attack; *ataque al corazón,* heart attack. || Fit: *ataque epiléptico, de apoplejía,* epileptic, apoplectic fit. || Fit, attack: *ataque de nervios, de risa, de tos,* fit of hysterics, of laughter, of coughing. || — *Ataque aéreo,* air raid. || MIL. *Iniciar un ataque,* to launch an attack.
atar v. tr. To tie, to bind: *atar a un árbol,* to tie to a tree. || To tie, to do up, to fasten, to knot (los cordones del zapato, etc.). || To tether, to tie up (un animal). || CULIN. To truss (un ave). || FIG. To bind: *estas obligaciones me atan,* I am bound by these obligations. | To tie down: *este trabajo me ata mucho,* this work ties me down a lot. || — FIG. y FAM. *Átame esta mosca por el rabo,* you will have your work cut out. || FIG. *Atar cabos,* to put two and two together. || *Atar corto a un perro,* to keep a dog on a short lead. || FIG. y FAM. *Atar corto a uno,* to keep a tight rein over s.o. | *Atar de pies y manos,* to bind hand and foot. | *Atar la lengua a uno,* to silence s.o. || *El poder de atar y desatar,* the power to bind and to loose. || *No atar ni desatar,* to lead nowhere, to settle *o* to decide nothing (no decidir nada). || *Ser un loco de atar,* to be as mad as a hatter.
— V. pr. FIG. To get tied up (crearse trabas). | To become involved (en un asunto). | To stick to (a una opinión). | To limit o.s. (limitarse). || *Es hombre que no se ata por tan poco,* he doesn't let such things hinder him.
atarantado, da adj. Bitten by a tarantula. || FIG. y FAM. Restless (bullicioso). | Stunned, dazed, stupefied (aturdido). | Terrified, frightened (espantado).
atarantamiento m. Dizziness, giddiness.
atarantar v. tr. To daze, to stun (aturdir). || FIG. To stun, to bewilder, to dumbfound.
ataraxia f. Ataraxia, ataraxy (impasibilidad).
atarazana f. Shipyard (astillero). || Ropemaker's workshop (taller del cordelero). || Wine store. || *Amer.* Pointed roof.
atardecer* v. impers. To get late, to get *o* to grow dark.
atardecer m. Late afternoon, evening, dusk. || *Al atardecer,* at dusk.
atareado, da adj. Busy: *un hombre muy atareado,* a very busy man.
atarear v. tr. To assign work *o* a job to.
— V. pr. To busy o.s.: *atarearse en hacer algo,* to busy o.s. doing sth.
atarjea f. Culvert (bóveda). || Sewer, drain (alcantarilla). || *Amer.* Water conduit (conducto de agua).
atarquinar v. tr. To cover with mud *o* with slime.
— V. pr. To cover o.s. with mud *o* with slime.
atarugamiento m. Pegging, pinning (acción de poner cuñas). || Plugging (acción de tapar con tarugos). || FIG. y FAM. Confusion. | Stuffing, gorging, guzzling (acción de atracarse). | Stuffing, packing, cramming (atestamiento).
atarugar v. tr. To peg, to pin (fijar con tarugos). || To plug (tapar con tarugos). || FIG. y FAM. To silence, to shut up (hacer callar). | To stuff, to pack, to cram (llenar). To stuff, to cram [with food] (atracar).
— V. pr. FIG. y FAM. To stop short (quedar sin saber qué responder). | To become confused (turbarse). | To stuff o.s., to gorge o.s., to guzzle (atracarse).
atascadero m. Bog, mire, mudhole. || FIG. Stumbling block (estorbo).
atascamiento m. V. ATASCO.
atascar v. tr. To obstruct, to block [up], to choke [up], to clog [up] (una cañería). || To plug, to stop up (un agujero). || To jam, to make stick (un mecanismo). || FIG. To hinder, to impede (a una persona).
— V. pr. To get *o* to become stuck, to get bogged down (un coche). || To become obstructed *o* blocked [up] *o* choked [up] *o* clogged [up] (atorarse una cañería). || To jam, to stick, to become *o* to get jammed *o* stuck (un mecanismo). || FIG. To get into a muddle *o* into a tangle, to get all mixed up *o* tangled up (embrollarse). | To get bogged down (en un asunto).
atasco m. Obstruction, blockage (cosa que atasca). || Obstruction, blocking, choking, clogging (acción de atascar). || Bogging down (de un coche). || Traffic jam: *siempre hay atascos en las horas punta,* there are always traffic jams in the rush hour. || Jamming, sticking (de un mecanismo). || FIG. Stumbling block (obstáculo). | Muddle, tangle (en un discurso, etc.).
ataúd m. Coffin [U.S., casket].
ataujía f. Inlaid work, damascene work.
ataviar v. tr. To dress [up], to array, to adorn, to deck [out] (adornar).
— V. pr. *Ataviarse con* or *de,* to dress o.s. up in, to array o.s. in, to adorn o.s. with, to deck o.s. out in.
atávico, ca adj. Atavistic, atavic.
atavío m. Dressing, adornment (acción de ataviar). || Dress, attire (vestidos). || Garb, getup, rig (peyorativo).
atavismo m. Atavism.
ataxia f. MED. Ataxia, ataxy.
ateísmo m. Atheism.
ateísta adj. Atheistic (ateo).
— M. y f. Atheist (ateo).
atelaje m. Team (caballos). || Harness (arreos).
atelanas f. pl. Atellans (comedia latina).
ateles m. ZOOL. Ateles (mono).
atemorizar v. tr. To frighten, to scare (asustar).
— V. pr. *Atemorizarse de* or *por algo,* to be frightened of *o* at sth.
atemperación f. Moderation, restraint.
atemperar v. tr. To moderate, to restrain (moderar). || To adjust, to accomodate (*a,* to).
— V. pr. To restrain o.s. || To adjust o.s., to accomodate o.s.: *la formación professional debe atemperarse al ritmo de la industria,* vocational training should adjust itself to the pace of industry.
atenacear o **atenazar** v. tr. To tear [the flesh] with red-hot pincers (suplicio). || FIG. To torture, to torment (un pensamiento, los remordimientos). || FIG. *Estar atenazado,* to be held in a vice-like grip.
Atenas n. pr. GEOGR. Athens.
atención f. Attention: *prestar atención a,* to pay attention to. || Courtesy, politeness (cortesía). || Care, attention: *hacer un trabajo con mucha atención,* to do a job with great care. || Interest: *su atención por estos problemas ha sido muy grande,* he has taken a great interest in these problems. || — Pl. Respect, *sing.,* consideration, *sing.: tener atenciones con las personas de edad,* to have *o* to show respect for old people, to show consideration towards old people. || Affairs, duties, obligations (ocupaciones). || — *A la atención de,* for the attention of. || *Deshacerse en atenciones* or *tener atenciones delicadas* or *tener mil atenciones con* or *para uno,* to be very nice to s.o., to shower attention on s.o., to make a great fuss over s.o. || *En atención a,* in view of, considering, taking into consideration: *en atención a sus méritos,* in view of his merits, taking his merits into consideration. || *Llamar la atención,* to be conspicuous, to attract attention. || *Llamar la atención a alguien,* to attract s.o.'s attention (llamar), to tell s.o. off, to tick s.o. off (reprender), to catch s.o.'s eye, to attract s.o.'s attention (despertar la curiosidad). || *Llamar la atención de alguien sobre algo,* to draw s.o.'s attention to sth. || *No me llamó la atención,* I didn't notice. || *Poner atención,* to pay attention.
— Interj. Look out! (¡cuidado!). || Your attention, please! (para que la gente escuche). || Beware! (en letreros).
atendedor, ra m. y f. IMPR. Copyholder.
atender* v. tr. To attend to: *atiendo mis negocios,* I attend to my business. || To serve, to see to, to attend to (en una tienda): *¿le atienden?,* are you being served? || To look after, to tend: *el médico atiende al enfermo,* the doctor looks after *o* tends the patient. || To take care of, to attend to: *el propio director atendió al visitante,* the manager himself attended to the visitor. || To service (una máquina). || To take charge of (un servicio). || To heed, to listen to (un aviso, un consejo). || To meet, to satisfy: *atender una petición,* to meet a request. || (Ant.). To wait (esperar).
— V. intr. To pay attention, to mind, to be careful: *atiende a lo que haces,* pay attention to *o* mind *o* be careful what you're doing. || To pay attention, to be attentive: *atender a una lección,* to pay attention to a lesson, to be attentive to a lesson. || IMPR. To follow a galley proof as the proofreader reads aloud. || — *Atender al nombre de* or *atender por,* to answer to the name

of. || *Atender a lo más urgente*, to attend to what is most urgent *o* pressing. || *Atender al teléfono*, to answer the telephone. || *Atender a sus necesidades*, to meet *o* to satisfy one's needs. || *Atendiendo a las circunstancias*, in view of the circumstances. || *El servicio postal, este hotel, está mal atendido*, the postal service, this hotel, is badly run *o* organized. || *Este almacén está muy bien atendido*, this store is very well staffed, customers are very well attended to in this store. || *Iglesia bien atendida*, well-administered church. || *No atender a razones*, not to listen to reason.

atendible adj. Worthy of consideration.

ateneísta m. y f. Member of an athenaeum.

ateneo, a adj./s. POÉT. Athenian.

— M. Athenaeum (sociedad científica o literaria).

atenerse* v. pr. To abide, to adhere, to hold, to stick: *me atengo a lo que él me dijo*, I am abiding by what he told me, I am sticking to what he told me; *atenerse a las reglas*, to abide by the rules. || To rely on (a una persona). || — *Atenerse a su promesa*, to stand by one's promise, to keep one's word. || *Aténgase a las consecuencias*, be prepared to meet *o* to face the consequences. || *No saber a qué atenerse*, not to know what to think *o* to believe, not to know where *o* how one stands. || *Querer saber a qué atenerse*, to want to know where *o* how one stands; to want to know how matters stand, to want to know what is going on.

ateniense adj./s. Athenian.

atentado, da adj. Moderate, prudent (prudente). || Discreet, cautious (hecho sin ruido).

— M. Attempted murder, attempt upon s.o.'s life (contra personas). || Attack (ataque): *atentado con bomba*, bomb attack. || Offence [U.S., offense], transgression (contra la ley). || — *Atentado contra las buenas costumbres*, indecent behaviour, immoral offence. || *Atentado contra la seguridad del Estado*, treason.

atentamente adv. Attentively (con atención). || Courteously, politely. || *Le saluda atentamente*, I remain, yours faithfully; Yours faithfully (en una carta).

atentar v. intr. To make an attempt, to attempt: *atentar contra* or *a la vida de su hermano*, to make an attempt on one's brother's life, to attempt one's brother's life. || To offend: *atentar contra la moralidad pública*, to offend public decency. || To commit an offence *o* a crime. || *Atentar contra la honra de alguien*, to indecently assault s.o. (atacar), to cast a slur on s.o.'s honour (difamar).

atentatorio, ria adj. Which constitutes an attempt: *medida atentatoria a la libertad*, measure which constitutes an attempt on liberty.

atento, ta adj. Attentive, heedful: *atento al menor ruido*, attentive to *o* heedful of the slightest sound. || Attentive: *un alumno muy atento*, a very attentive pupil. || Thoughtful, considerate, attentive: *este hombre es atento con todos*, this man is thoughtful *o* considerate towards everyone. || Mindful, aware: *atento a los peligros*, mindful of *o* aware of the danger. || Kind, nice: *es usted muy atento*, you're very kind. || Careful, mindful: *atento a hablar bien*, careful to speak well. || Special: *su atenta atención a los problemas árabes*, his special attention to Arab problems. || — *Contesto a su atenta del 13 de febrero*, in reply to your letter of the 13th February (v. OBSERV.). || *Su atento y seguro servidor* [abbreviated to s.a.s.s.], yours truly, yours faithfully (fórmula de correspondencia).

— Adv. Considering, in view of, taking into consideration (en atención a).

— OBSERV. *Su atenta* is a commercial term widely used in Spanish with the meaning *your letter*; it is often abbreviated to *su atta.*

atenuación f. Attenuation, diminishing (disminución). || Litotes (retórica). || JUR. Extenuation.

atenuante adj. Extenuating, extenuatory, palliative. || JUR. Extenuating: *circunstancia atenuante*, extenuating circumstance.

— M. Extenuating circumstance.

atenuar v. tr. To attenuate (poner tenue). || JUR. To extenuate, to mitigate (el suplicio, la sentencia). || To diminish, to lessen, to reduce (disminuir). || To dim, to subdue (la luz). || To tone down (los colores).

— V. pr. To attenuate.

ateo, a adj. Atheistic, atheistical.

— M. y f. Atheist.

aterciopelado, da adj. Velvety, velvet-like: *cutis, papel aterciopelado*, velvety skin, paper.

aterido, da adj. Frozen [stiff], perished [with cold].

aterimiento m. Stiffness (de frío).

aterirse* v. pr. To be frozen, to be perished [with cold].

— OBSERV. This verb is used only in the infinitive and past participle forms.

atérmano, na adj. FÍS. Athermanous.

aterrador, ra adj. Terrifying, terrible, frightening, frightful, fearful, dreadful.

aterrajado m. Threading (de un tornillo). || Tapping (de una tuerca).

aterrajar v. tr. To thread (tornillo). || To tap (tuerca).

aterrar* v. tr. To knock down (echar por tierra). || To demolish, to pull down (abatir). || MIN. To dump. || To terrify, to frighten, to scare: *me aterra pensar que...*, it terrifies me to think that... || *Amer.* To fill with earth (llenar). || *Quedó aterrado por la noticia*, he was horror-stricken at the news.

— V. intr. MAR. To keep *o* to stand inshore. || AVIAC. To land, to touch down (aterrizar).

— V. pr. To be horror-stricken *o* terrified *o* frightened.

aterrizaje m. AVIAC. Landing, touchdown. || — *Aterrizaje forzoso, de emergencia*, forced, emergency landing. || *Aterrizaje sin visibilidad* or *a ciegas*, blind landing. || *Tren de aterrizaje plegable*, retractable undercarriage.

aterrizar v. intr. AVIAC. To land, to touch down.

aterrorizador, ra adj. Terrifying, frightening, fearful, frightful.

aterrorizar v. tr. To terrify, to frighten, to scare. || To terrorize: *los bandidos aterrorizaron a la población*, the bandits terrorized the population.

— V. pr. To be *o* to become terrified *o* frightened.

atesoramiento m. Hoarding, amassing, accumulation (acción de atesorar).

atesorar v. tr. To hoard, to accumulate, to amass (acumular). || FIG. To possess: *Juan atesora muchas cualidades*, John possesses many qualities.

atestación f. Attestation (escrita). || Testimony, evidence, statement, deposition (más bien oral).

atestado m. JUR. Attestation, constat (documento). || Report (relato): *hacer un atestado*, to make a report.

atestado, da adj. Full up, crammed, stuffed (lleno). || Crammed, crowded, packed, full up (lugar público). || Obstinate, stubborn, pigheaded (fam.) [testarudo].

atestadura o **atestamiento** m. Cramming, stuffing, packing (acción de atestar). || Must [for filling up casks] (mosto). || Ullage (de una cuba).

atestar* v. tr. To fill up, to cram, to stuff, to pack (llenar). || To fill up, to cram, to crowd, to pack: *un tren atestado*, a crowded train. || To clutter up: *atestar un piso con muebles*, to clutter up a flat with furniture. || To fill up (las cubas de vino). || JUR. To attest, to testify, to bear witness (atestiguar).

— V. pr. FIG. y FAM. To stuff o.s., to cram o.s., to gorge o.s.: *atestarse de pasteles*, to stuff *o* to cram o.s. with cakes, to gorge o.s. on cakes.

atestiguar v. tr. To attest, to testify, to give evidence of, to bear witness to. || FIG. To prove, to bear witness to, to give a clear indication of: *esto atestigua el valor de estas medidas*, this proves the worth of these measures.

atezado, da adj. Brown, bronzed, tanned (piel). || Black, blackened (negro). || Polished, smooth (pulido).

atezar v. tr. To brown, to bronze, to tan (la piel). || To blacken. || To polish, to smooth (pulir).

— V. pr. To become brown *o* tanned, to tan.

atiborrar v. tr. To cram, to stuff, to pack (llenar).

— V. pr. To stuff *o* to cram o.s. (*de*, with), to gorge o.s. (*de*, on).

Ática n. pr. f. GEOGR. Attica.

aticismo m. Atticism (delicadeza).

ático, ca adj./s. Attic. || Athenian.

— M. ARQ. Attic (buhardilla). || Top flat (piso último). || Penthouse (lujoso).

atigrado, da adj. Striped, marked like a tiger's skin. || Skewbald (caballo).

Atila n. pr. m. Attila.

atildado, da adj. Elegant, neat, smart. || FIG. Elegant: *prosa atildada*, elegant prose. | Affected, recherché: *estilo atildado*, affected style.

atildamiento m. Criticism, censure. || Elegance, neatness, smartness, tidiness (del vestido). || Punctuation (puntuación). || *Vestido con atildamiento*, elegantly dressed.

atildar v. tr. (P. us.). To put a tilde *o* an accent on *o* over [a letter]. || FIG. To criticize, to censure.

— V. pr. FIG. To smarten o.s. [up], to spruce o.s. [up], to titivate o.s. [up].

atinadamente adv. Wisely, cleverly, sensibly (con sagacidad). || Correctly, accurately, precisely (acertadamente).

atinado, da adj. Sensible, wise, sound: *una observación atinada*, a sensible remark. || Apt, fitting, relevant, felicitous: *una contestación atinada*, an apt reply. || Opportune, timely, appropriate: *una medida atinada*, an opportune measure. || Wise, sensible (una persona). || Correct, accurate (acertado).

atinar v. intr. To find, to discover, to hit upon: *atinar con la solución*, to hit upon the solution. || To guess right (acertar). || To be right: *has atinado en coger el paraguas*, you were right in bringing your umbrella. || To succeed: *atinó a encontrar la solución*, he succeeded in finding the solution. || To hit the mark (dar en el blanco).

atiplado, da adj. High-pitched, shrill: *una voz atiplada*, a high-pitched voice.

atiplar v. tr. To raise the pitch of.

— V. pr. To become sharp, to rise in pitch.

atirantar v. tr. To tighten, to tauten. || ARQ. To stay, to brace with ties.

atisbadero m. Lookout post.

atisbadura f. Watch, watching, lookout.

atisbar v. tr. To watch for, to be on the lookout for (acechar). || To spy on, to watch, to observe (mirar). || To distinguish, to make out, to see faintly *o* indistinctly (vislumbrar).

atisbo m. Spying, watching (acecho). || FIG. Hint, sign, trace, indication (asomo). | Flash, spark: *no es muy*

astuto pero a veces tiene atisbos de inteligencia, he is not very smart, but at times he has flashes of intelligence.
¡atiza! interj. Goodness me!, oh, my word!, good Lord! (¡arrea!).
atizador, ra adj. Stirring, inciting, rousing (que atiza).
— M. Poker (instrumento).
tizar v. tr. To poke [up], to stir (el fuego). || FIG. To stir up: *atizar la discordia*, to stir up discord. | To excite, to rouse, to fan (las pasiones). || FIG. y FAM. To give, to land: *atizar un puntapié a uno*, to give s.o. a kick.
— V. pr. FAM. To swig, to knock back: *se atizó el vaso de un trago*, he knocked the glassful back in one gulp.
atizonar v. tr. To embed *o* to set [in a wall] (una viga).
— V. pr. To blight (el trigo).
atlante m. ARQ. Atlas, telamon.
Atlántico n. pr. m. GEOGR. Atlantic.
atlántico, ca adj. GEOGR. Atlantic.
Atlántida n. pr. f. Atlantis.
atlas m. Atlas.
atleta m. y f. Athlete. || — M. FIG. Muscleman (hombre fuerte).
atlético, ca adj. Athletic.
atletismo m. Athletics: *practicar el atletismo*, to do *o* to practise athletics.
atmósfera o **atmosfera** f. Atmosphere: *atmósfera cargada de humo*, smoke-laden atmosphere. || FIG. Atmosphere: *en la reunión la atmósfera estaba muy cargada*, the atmosphere was electric at the meeting.
atmosférico, ca adj. Atmospheric.
atoaje m. MAR. Towing, warping.
atoar v. tr. To tow, to warp.
atocinado, da adj. FIG. y FAM. Fat, fleshy.
atocinar v. tr. To cut up [a pig] (partir un cerdo). || To cure (preparar el tocino). || FIG. y FAM. To do in, to knock off, to bump off (matar).
— V. pr. FAM. To get mad (amostazarse). | To fall madly in love (enamorarse).
atocha f. Esparto [grass].
atochar v. tr. To fill with esparto. || To stuff, to pack (rellenar). || MAR. To jam (una vela).
atol o **atole** m. *Amer.* Drink made from cornflour.
atolón m. Atoll (arrecife).
atolondradamente adv. Thoughtlessly, recklessly, foolishly. || Bewilderedly, confusedly.
atolondrado, da adj. Thoughtless, reckless, scatterbrained. || Bewildered, confused.
atolondramiento m. Thoughtlessness, recklessness, foolishness (irreflexión). || Bewilderment, confusion (aturdimiento). || *Obrar con atolondramiento*, to act thoughtlessly.
atolondrar v. tr. To stun, to daze, to make [s.o.] dizzy *o* giddy. || To bewilder, to confuse.
— V. pr. FIG. To lose one's head, to become *o* to get bewildered *o* confused (turbarse).
atolladero m. Bog, mire, slough, mudhole (atascadero). || FIG. Impasse, deadlock: *las negociaciones están ahora en un atolladero*, the negotiations are now in an impasse, the negotiations have now reached a deadlock. || — FIG. *Cada sendero tiene su atolladero*, every path has a puddle. | *Estar en un atolladero*, to be in a tight corner *o* in a fix *o* in a jam (fam.) *o* in the soup (fam.). | *Sacar del atolladero*, to get [s.o.] out of trouble *o* out of a scrape. | *Salir del atolladero*, to get out of difficulty *o* out of trouble *o* out of a jam (fam.).
atollar, atollarse v. intr. y pr. To get bogged down, to stick *o* to get stuck in the mud.
atomicidad f. QUÍM. Atomicity.
atómico, ca adj. Atomic: ***bomba, cabeza, energía, pila atómica***, atomic bomb, warhead, energy, pile; *número, peso atómico*, atomic number, weight; *masa atómica*, atomic mass.
atomismo m. Atomism.
atomista m. y f. Atomist.
atomístico, ca adj. Atomistic.
— F. FÍS. Atomics.
atomización f. Atomization, spraying.
atomizador m. Atomizer, spray.
atomizar v. tr. To atomize, to spray.
átomo m. Atom. || — *Átomo-gramo*, gram atom. || FIG. y FAM. *Ni un átomo de*, not an ounce of, not a grain of, not an atom of.
atonal adj. MÚS. Atonal, toneless.
atonalidad f. MÚS. Atonality, tonelessness.
atonía f. MED. Atony.
atónico, ca adj. Atonic.
atónito, ta adj. Astonished, amazed, astounded (estupefacto). || Aghast, dumbfounded, flabbergasted (boquiabierto): *quedarse atónito*, to be aghast.
átono, na adj. Atonic, unstressed.
atontado, da adj. Stupid, dimwitted (tonto). || Stunned, dazed (por el asombro, un golpe, un ruido). || Dumbfounded, flabbergasted (boquiabierto). || Dulled, stupefied (embrutecido): *atontado por un trabajo monótono*, dulled by monotonous work. || Dopey, stupefied (por una medicina, por las drogas). || *Atontado por el alcohol*, sodden with drink, groggy.
atontamiento m. Dazed *o* stunned state (por el asombro, un golpe, un ruido). || Astoundment, dumbfoundedness (por la sorpresa). || Dullness, stupefaction (embrutecimiento). || Dopiness (por una medicina, las drogas). || Grogginess, stupor (por las bebidas).
atontar v. tr. To stun, to daze (un ruido, un golpe, el asombro). || To dumbfound, to flabbergast (la sorpresa). || To dull, to deaden, to stupefy (embrutecer). || To make [s.o.] giddy *o* dizzy, to go to s.o.'s head (un perfume, una bebida). || To make stupid *o* dopey (una medicina, las drogas). || To drive [s.o.] mad *o* insane (volver loco).
— V. pr. To become stunned *o* dazed. || To become dull *o* stupid.
atontolinamiento m. FAM. Stunned state, stupor, daze (atontamiento). | Dullness, stupidity (embrutecimiento).
atontolinar v. tr. FAM. To stun, to daze, to stupefy (atontar). || *Estar atontolinado*, to be all at sea (aturdido), to be groggy (por un golpe, las bebidas).
atoramiento m. Blockage, obstruction, clogging, choking (atascamiento).
atorar v. tr. To block [up], to obstruct, to clog [up], to choke [up] (una cañería, etc.).
— V. intr. y pr. To get blocked [up] *o* obstructed *o* clogged [up] *o* choked [up]. || FAM. To choke [o.s.] (atragantarse).
atormentadamente adv. Painfully. || Sorrowfully, grievously.
atormentador, ra adj. Tormenting, distressing, troubling, worrying (una persona, una cosa).
— M. y f. Torturer.
atormentar v. tr. To torture (al reo). || To torment, to trouble, to distress (causar dolor físico). || FIG. To torment, to torture: *¿por qué me atormentas con estos recuerdos?*, why do you torment me with these memories?
— V. pr. To torment o.s., to worry. || *No atormentarse por nada*, not to worry about anything.
atornillar v. tr. To screw in (introducir un tornillo). || To screw down (sujetar). || To screw on (fijar con tornillos): *atornillar algo a la pared*, to screw sth. onto the wall.
atoro m. *Amer.* Obstruction, blockage (atascamiento). || FIG. Difficulty, jam, fix.
atorrante m. *Amer.* Tramp, vagabond, vagrant [U.S., bum, hobo].
atorrantismo m. *Amer.* Vagrancy.
atorrar v. intr. *Amer.* To live as a vagabond *o* as a tramp.
atortolar v. tr. FAM. To rattle, to disquiet (turbar). || FIG. *Estar muy atortolados*, to be like two turtledoves.
atosigador, ra adj. Poisonous (envenenador). || Harassing, harrying, pestering, pressing (que apremia).
— M. y f. Poisoner (envenenador). || Harasser, tormentor (que apremia).
atosigamiento m. Poisoning (envenenamiento). || Harassing, harrying, pestering.
atosigar v. tr. To poison (envenenar). || FIG. To harass, to harry, to pester, to press (dar prisa). || FAM. To badger, to pester, to annoy, to bother (molestar).
— V. pr. To toil away (atarearse).
atrabiliario, ria o **atrabilioso, sa** adj. Irritable, irascible, atrabilious.
atrabilis f. MED. Black bile. || FIG. Ill humour, irascibility.
atracada f. MAR. Coming alongside (al lado de otra embarcación). | Docking (en el muelle). || *Amer.* Gorging, stuffing (atracón). | Brawl, scuffle, fight (pelea).
atracadero m. MAR. Landing stage, quay.
atracador m. Bandit, robber, raider (ladrón).
atracar v. tr. MAR. To bring alongside. || FAM. To stuff, to gorge (hartar). || To hold up, to rob, to raid (robar).
— V. intr. MAR. To come alongside. || *Atracar en el muelle*, to dock, to berth.
— V. pr. FAM. To stuff o.s., to gorge o.s. (hartarse): *atracarse de melocotones*, to stuff o.s. with *o* to gorge o.s. on peaches. || *Amer.* To adhere, to follow: *atracarse a una teoría*, to adhere to *o* to follow a theory. | To fight, to brawl (reñir).
atracción f. Attraction: *atracción molecular*, molecular attraction. || Attraction (espectáculo): *la atracción principal de la feria*, the main attraction at the fair. || — Pl. Entertainment, *sing.*, floor show, *sing.*, cabaret, *sing.* (en una sala de fiestas). || — *Atracción universal*, gravity. || *Parque de atracciones*, fairground. || *Sentir atracción por una persona*, to be attracted to a person.
atraco m. Holdup, robbery, raid. || *Ser víctima de un atraco*, to be held up.
atracón m. FAM. Gorging, stuffing. || *Amer.* Fight, brawl (riña). || *Darse un atracón de caramelos*, to gorge [o.s.] on sweets, to stuff o.s. with sweets.
atractivo, va adj. Attractive, of attraction (fuerza). || Gravitational (de la gravitación). || Attractive (persona, cosa): *es una idea atractiva*, it is an attractive idea.
— M. Attractiveness, attraction, charm, appeal (encanto). || Lure, attraction: *el atractivo de la ganancia*, the lure of profit.
atractriz adj. FÍS. Attractive (fuerza).
atraer* v. tr. To attract: *el imán atrae el hierro*, a magnet attracts iron. || FIG. To attract, to draw: *atraer las miradas*, to attract attention. | To attract, to

lure: *el clima atrae a los turistas*, the climate attracts the tourists.

atragantamiento m. Choking (ahogo).

atragantarse v. pr. To choke [o.s.]: *come tan de prisa que se atraganta*, he eats so quickly that he chokes. || To stick in s.o.'s throat: *se me ha atragantado una espina*, a bone has stuck in my throat, I have a bone stuck in my throat. || FIG. y FAM. To get mixed up (turbarse). | To stop short, to become tongue-tied (cortarse). || — FIG. y FAM. *Atragantársele (algo* or *alguien) a uno*, to sicken s.o., to make s.o. sick. | *Se me atraganta este tío*, I can't stomach this fellow, this fellow makes me sick.

atraillar v. tr. To leash (perros).

atramojar v. tr. *Amer.* To leash.

atramparse v. pr. To become blocked [up] *o* choked *o* clogged [up] (cegarse un conducto). || To become jammed, to stick (un pestillo).

atrancar v. tr. To bar: *atrancó la puerta por miedo a los bandidos*, he barred the door through fear of the bandits. || To block [up], to choke, to clog [up] (obstruir).
— V. pr. To become blocked [up] *o* choked *o* clogged [up] (obstruirse). || To become jammed, to jam, to stick (un mecanismo). || To get *o* to become stuck (atascarse). || To get muddled *o* mixed up *o* confused (al hablar). || *Amer.* To be obstinate *o* stubborn (empeñarse).

atranco o **atranque** m. Bog, mire, slough, mudhole (atasco). || FIG. Difficulty, fix, jam (apuro). || FIG. *No hay barranco sin atranco*, no gains without pains.

atrapamoscas m. inv. BOT. Venus's-flytrap.

atrapar v. tr. FAM. To catch, to trap. | To land: *atrapar un empleo*, to land a job. | To catch (un constipado).

atrás adv. Behind: *quedar atrás*, to stay behind. || Behind, in the rear, at the back: *ir atrás*, to walk in the rear. || Rear, back (de un coche): *los asientos de atrás*, the rear seats. || Backwards, back: *dar un paso atrás*, to step backwards. || Back, at the back: *en las filas de atrás*, in the back rows, in the rows at the back. || Ago, back: *algunos días atrás*, a few days back (hace algunos días). || Earlier, previously: *dos semanas atrás*, two weeks earlier (hacía dos semanas). || — *Cuenta (hacia) atrás*, countdown. || *Dejar atrás*, to leave behind. || *Echado para atrás*, thrown *o* flung back: *la cabeza echada para atrás*, [with] one's head thrown back. || *El de atrás*, the one behind. || *El pelo echado para atrás*, [with] one's hair brushed back. || *Estos problemas vienen de muy atrás*, these problems date back a long time. || *Hacia atrás* or *para atrás*, backwards: *mirar hacia atrás* or *para atrás*, to look backwards. || AUT. *Marcha atrás*, reverse. || *Quedarse atrás*, to fall *o* to lag behind. || *Volverse atrás*, to go back. || FIG. *Volverse* or *echarse para atrás*, to go back on *o* to break one's word, to change one's mind.
— Interj. Back!, get back!, go back!, back up!

atrasado, da adj. Late: *llegué atrasado*, I arrived late. || Behind: *está atrasado en los estudios*, he is behind in his studies; *estar atrasado en el pago del alquiler*, to be behind with one's rent; *este país está mucho más atrasado que sus vecinos*, this country is far behind its neighbours. || In arrears, outstanding, overdue: *pago atrasado*, payment in arrears, outstanding *o* overdue payment. || Backward: *pueblo atrasado*, backward nation. || FIG. In debt, in the red (entrampado). || Slow (reloj). || — *¡Andas atrasado de noticias!*, you're behind the times! || *Lo atrasado*, arrears, back payments: *saldar lo atrasado*, to make up arrears *o* back payments. || *Número atrasado*, back number (de una revista). || *Tener trabajo atrasado*, to be behind with one's work. || *Un atrasado mental*, a mentally retarded person, a mental defective.

atrasar v. tr. To put back, to set back: *atrasar un reloj*, to put a clock back. || To retard, to slow down *o* up (algo que adelanta). || To postpone, to delay (diferir).
— V. intr. To lose: *mi reloj atrasa*, my watch loses. || To be slow: *atrasar cinco minutos*, to be five minutes slow.
— V. pr. To stay *o* to remain behind, to lag [behind] (quedarse atrás). || To be late (llevar atraso). || To be retarded (mentalmente). || To be slow (reloj). || *Atrasarse en el pago del alquiler*, to get into arrears with the rent.

atraso m. Slowness (de un reloj). || Backwardness (mental, cultural). || Lateness, delay (retraso de tiempo). || — Pl. Arrears: *tener atrasos*, to be in arrears. || — *Con atraso*, late: *con cinco minutos de atraso*, five minutes late. || *Mi reloj tiene un atraso de diez minutos*, my watch is ten minutes slow. || *Su hija tiene mucho atraso en los estudios*, his daughter is a long way behind in her studies.

atravesado, da adj. Lying across: *había un árbol atravesado en la carretera*, there was a tree lying across the road. || Pierced, transfixed: *atravesado por flechas*, pierced with arrows. || Cross-eyed (bizco). || Crossbred, mongrel (animales). || FIG. Wicked, evil: *una persona atravesada*, a wicked person. || — *Poner atravesado*, to place *o* to lay across. || FIG. *Tener a alguien atravesado*, not to be able to stand *o* to bear *o* to abide s.o.: *le tengo atravesado*, I can't stand him. || *Tener el genio atravesado*, to be bad-humoured *o* bad-tempered. || *Tener la cara atravesada*, to be grim-faced *o* glum-faced *o* surly.

atravesar* v. tr. To place *o* to put *o* to lay across (poner). || To pass *o* to go through, to penetrate: *el agua atraviesa este impermeable*, water goes through this mackintosh. || To pierce (traspasar): *un balazo le atravesó el pecho*, a bullet pierced his chest; *atravesar de parte a parte*, to pierce right through. || To run through (con una espada, lanza). || To cross, to go across (cruzar): *atravesar los Alpes, la calle*, to cross the Alps, the road. || To cross, to span: *el puente atraviesa el río*, the bridge spans the river. || FIG. To go *o* to pass through: *la economía atraviesa un periodo difícil*, the economy is going through a difficult period. | To cross: *atravesar el pensamiento*, to cross one's mind. || To bet, to wager, to stake (apostar). || MAR. To heave to. || FIG. *Atravesar el Rubicón*, to cross the Rubicon.
— V. pr. To lie across (una cosa). || To stand across, to bar: *se atravesó en mi camino*, he stood across *o* barred my path. || To stick, to get stuck: *se le atravesó una espina en la garganta*, a bone [got] stuck in his throat. || FIG. To interfere, to butt in, to meddle (entrometerse). | To quarrel, to argue, to dispute (tener pendencia). || FAM. *Atravesársele a uno una persona*, not to be able to stand *o* to bear *o* to abide s.o.: *se me atraviesa*, I cannot bear him.

atrayente adj. Attractive.

atreverse v. pr. To dare: *hazlo, si te atreves*, do it, if you dare; *no me atrevería a salir sola*, I wouldn't dare to go out alone. || To venture, to dare: *atreverse a hablar*, to venture to speak. || To be insolent *o* disrespectful: *atreverse con un superior*, to be disrespectful towards one's superior. || FIG. To manage: *¿te atreves con un pastel?*, could you manage a cake? || — *Atreverse con un adversario*, to take on an opponent. || *¡Atrévete!*, just you dare!

atrevidamente adv. Boldly, daringly. || Insolently, disrespectfully (con insolencia).

atrevido, da adj. Daring, bold, adventurous: *una política atrevida*, an adventurous policy. || Insolent, disrespectful, impertinent, cheeky (descarado). || Daring, bold: *una película atrevida*, a daring film. || Forward, bold: *atrevido con las mujeres*, forward with women.
— M. y f. Audacious *o* bold *o* daring person, daredevil. || Insolent *o* disrespectful *o* impertinent *o* cheeky person.

atrevimiento m. Boldness, daring (osadía). || Audacity, effrontery: *tiene el atrevimiento de interrumpirme*, he has the audacity to interrupt me. || Insolence, disrespectfulness, impertinence, cheekiness (insolencia).

atribución f. Attribution: *la atribución de una obra a Bacon*, the attribution of a work to Bacon. || Duty, function (función). || — Pl. Authority, *sing.*, jurisdiction, *sing.*: *esto sale de mis atribuciones*, this does not come within my authority.

atribuir* v. tr. To attribute, to credit: *le atribuyen palabras que nunca ha dicho*, they attribute him with words he has never uttered. || To attribute, to put down: *atribuye su fracaso a una falta de experiencia*, he puts his failure down to inexperience. || To confer: *atribuir una función a alguien*, to confer authority on s.o.
— V. pr. To [lay] claim, to take the credit: *se atribuyó el éxito de la producción*, he laid claim to *o* he took the credit for the success of the production. || *Se atribuye la culpa*, he blames himself.

atribulado, da adj. Full of tribulation: *una vida atribulada*, a life full of tribulation.

atribular v. tr. To afflict, to grieve, to distress.
— V. pr. To be afflicted *o* grieved *o* distressed: *se atribuló con la noticia de su muerte*, he was grieved at the news of his death.

atributivo, va adj. Attributive.

atributo m. Attribute: *uno de sus muchos atributos es la generosidad*, generosity is one of his many attributes. || GRAM. Attribute (predicado). || Symbol (símbolo).

atrición f. Attrition.

atril m. Bookrest. || Lectern (facistol). || MÚS. Music stand (con pie), music rest (sin pie).

atrincheramiento m. MIL. Entrenchment.

atrincherar v. tr. To entrench (fortificar).
— V. pr. To entrench [o.s.], to dig in. || FIG. To entrench o.s.: *atrincherarse en su silencio*, to entrench o.s. in one's silence.

atrio m. ARQ. Atrium (de la casa romana). | Portico (de un templo, un palacio). | Cloister (claustro). | Vestibule, entrance (zaguán).

atrito, ta adj. Attrite (arrepentido).

atrocidad f. Atrocity, outrage: *los invasores hicieron atrocidades por todo el país*, the invaders committed atrocities throughout the country. || FIG. y FAM. V. BARBARIDAD.

atrochar v. intr. To take a shortcut.

atrofia f. MED. Atrophy.

atrofiar v. tr. To atrophy.
— V. pr. To atrophy, to become atrophied.

atrompetado, da adj. Funnel-shaped, trumpet-shaped, bell-mouthed. || *Nariz atrompetada*, turned-up nose, snub nose.

atronado, da adj. Thoughtless, reckless (irreflexivo).

atronador, ra adj. Deafening, thundering, thunderous: *un ruido atronador*, a deafening noise; *una voz atronadora*, a thundering voice. || *Unos aplausos*

atronadores or *una atronadora ovación*, thunderous applause, a thunder of applause.
atronar* v. tr. To deafen, to stun, to daze (con el ruido). || To stun, to daze (con un golpe). || TAUR. To kill [a bull] by a stab in the back of the neck.
atropar v. tr. To gather [together], to assemble.
atropelladamente adv. Hurriedly, hastily (con descuido). || Helter-skelter, pell-mell (en desorden). || *Hablar atropelladamente*, to gabble.
atropellado, da adj. Hasty, precipitate.
— F. *Amer.* Hustle, scuffle, scurry (atropello).
atropellador, ra adj. Brusque, impetuous, hasty, precipitate.
— M. y f. Hothead, tearaway.
atropellamiento m. V. ATROPELLO.
atropellaplatos adj. inv. FAM. Clumsy, careless.
— M. y f. inv. FAM. Clumsy *o* careless person, butterfingers.
atropellar v. tr. To knock *o* to run down *o* over: *fue atropellado por un coche*, he was knocked down by a car. || To trample on (pisotear): *fue atropellado por la muchedumbre*, he was trampled on by the crowd. || To hustle, to jostle (empujar con violencia). || To push past, to push aside (para abrirse paso). || To knock down *o* over, to push over (derribar). || FIG. To ignore, to disregard, to brush aside: *atropellar todo principio moral*, to disregard all moral principles. | To outrage, to offend (ultrajar). | To oppress, to bully (agraviar). | To rush, to hurry, to scamp (un trabajo). | To crush, to overwhelm (las desgracias).
— V. intr. *Atropellar por*, to ignore, to disregard.
— V. pr. To rush, to hurry (empujarse). || To splutter, to gabble (al hablar).
atropello m. Pushing, hustling, jostling (acción de empujar). || Push (empujón). || Accident, running over, knocking down (por un vehículo). || FIG. Violation, infraction (de las leyes). | Violation, breach (de los principios). | Outrage, offence [U.S., offense] (insulto). | Abuse, outrage, high-handed behaviour (agravio). || FIG. *Hablar con atropello*, to gabble.
atropina f. QUÍM. Atropine.
atroz adj. Atrocious, cruel, inhuman (cruel). || FAM. Enormous, huge (enorme). | Atrocious, dreadful, awful: *tiempo atroz*, atrocious weather.
atrozmente adv. Atrociously. || FIG. Awfully, dreadfully, terrible: *me duele atrozmente*, it hurts terribly.
atruchado adj. m. Mottled (hierro).
attrezzista m. TEATR. Property man.
attrezzo o **atrezo** m. TEATR. Properties, *pl.*, props, *pl.*
atuendo m. Dress, attire (vestidos). || Getup, rig (extravagante). || (P.us.). Pomp, ostentation.
atufado, da adj. Irritated, angry (irritado). || Offended, bothered (por el tufo). || Overcome, choked (ahogado). || *Amer.* Reckless, scatterbrained (atolondrado).
atufamiento m. Anger, irritation.
atufar v. tr. FIG. To anger, to irritate (enfadar). || To overcome, to choke (un olor).
— V. intr. To smell bad, to stink (fam.) [oler mal].
— V. pr. FIG. To become angry *o* irritated: *se atufa por* or *con* or *de nada*, he becomes angry *o* irritated over the slightest thing. || To be offended *o* bothered (por un olor). || To be overcome *o* choked (por el tufo). || To turn sour *o* acid (vino).
atufo m. Anger, irritation.
atún m. Tunny, tunnyfish, tuna, tuna fish. || FIG. y FAM. *Pedazo de atún*, fool, nitwit, idiot, nincompoop.
atunara f. Madrague, tunny net (red). || Tunny fishery, tunny-fishing ground (lugar).
atunero, ra m. y f. Tunny seller, tuna seller (que vende atún). || — M. Tunny fisher, tuna fisher (pescador). || Tunny boat (barco). || — F. Tuna hook (anzuelo).
— Adj. Tunny, tuna: *industria atunera*, tuna industry; *barco atunero*, tunny boat.
aturdido, da adj. Reckless, scatterbrained, thoughtless (imprudente). || Dazed, bewildered (confuso).
aturdidor, ra adj. Deafening: *un ruido aturdidor*, a deafening noise.
aturdimiento m. Daze, stunned state (por un golpe). || Dizziness, giddiness (mareo). || Amazement, bewilderment (sorpresa). || FIG. Carelessness, thoughtlessness, recklessness: *a causa de su aturdimiento no se puede uno fiar de él*, because of his carelessness he cannot be trusted. | Clumsiness, awkwardness (torpeza).
aturdir v. tr. To daze, to stun, to make dizzy *o* giddy (el ruido, un golpe, etc.). || To make dizzy o giddy (un movimiento, el vino). || FIG. To amaze, to bewilder, to stun: *su éxito me aturde*, his success amazes *o* stuns me, I'm amazed at *o* stunned by his success.
— V. pr. FIG. To try to forget.
aturquesado, da adj. Turquoise (color).
aturrullamiento o **aturullamiento** m. FAM. Confusion, bewilderment.
aturrullar o **aturullar** v. tr. FAM. To confound, to bewilder, to fluster.
— V. pr. FAM. To become *o* to get confused *o* flustered (turbarse). | To become frantic, to panic: *aturrullarse por el tráfico*, to panic over the traffic.
atusar v. tr. To trim (cortar el pelo). || To smooth (el pelo, el bigote). || To stroke: *atusarle el cuello a un caballo*, to stroke a horse's neck. || *Amer.* To cut *o* to trim the mane and tail [of an animal] (de un animal).
— V. pr. FIG. To titivate o.s., to smarten *o* to spruce o.s. up (componerse mucho). || *Amer.* To become angry (enfadarse).
atutía f. Tutty (óxido de zinc).
audacia f. Audacity, boldness, daring (valentía): *demostrar audacia*, to show *o* to display audacity. || Audacity, cheek, impudence (desfachatez).
audaz adj. Audacious, bold, daring (valiente). || Audacious, cheeky, impudent (descarado).
— M. y f. Audacious *o* bold *o* daring person, daredevil. || Audacious *o* cheeky *o* impudent person. || *La fortuna es de los audaces*, fortune favours the brave.
audibilidad f. Audibility.
audible adj. Audible.
audición f. Audition, hearing (acción de oír). || Audition (prueba). || Concert (concierto).
audiencia f. Audience: *conceder audiencia*, to grant an audience. || Hearing (audición): *audiencia pública*, public hearing. || Court (tribunal de justicia): *audiencia territorial*, regional court. || Lawcourt, court of law (palacio de justicia). || (Ant.). Audiencia [in Spain and South America].
audífonos m. pl. *Amer.* Earphones.
audiofrecuencia f. Audio frequency.
audiograma m. Audiogram.
audiómetro m. FÍS. Audiometer.
auditivo, va adj. Auditory.
audiovisual adj. Audio-visual: *enseñanza audiovisual*, audio-visual teaching; *medios audiovisuales*, audio-visual aids.
auditor m. Judge advocate. || Auditor (interventor de cuentas).
auditoría f. Office of judge advocate (cargo del auditor). || Judge advocate's court (tribunal). || Judge advocate's office (despacho). || Auditorship (empleo de interventor de cuentas).
auditorio m. Audience (público). || FIG. Public: *persona que tiene mucho auditorio*, person with a large public. || Auditorium (sala).
auditorium m. Auditorium.
auge m. Peak, climax (punto máximo). || Prosperity, development, progress, expansion (progreso). || ASTR. Apogee. || — *Auge económico*, economic boom *o* expansion. || *En periodo de* or *en pleno auge*, progressing *o* developing *o* expanding rapidly.
augita f. MIN. Augite.
augur m. Augur (adivino).
augurador, ra adj. Who predicts, who foretells.
augural adj. Augural.
augurar v. tr. To predict, to foresee, to foretell, to prophesy: *le auguro a la chica un futuro feliz*, I foresee a happy future for the girl. || To augur: *las nubes auguran lluvia*, the clouds augur rain; *augurar bien, mal*, to augur well, ill.
augurio m. Augury, omen, sign.
augusto m. Auguste (payaso).
Augusto n. pr. m. Augustus.
augusto, ta adj. August, illustrious.
aula f. Lecture hall (grande), lecture room (pequeña). || Classroom (de una escuela). || POÉT. Palace (palacio). || *Aula magna*, main lecture theatre *o* amphitheatre.
aulaga f. BOT. Gorse, furze.
áulico, ca adj. Palace, court.
— M. Courtier.
aullador, ra adj. Howling.
— M. Howler monkey, howler (mono).
aullar v. intr. To howl.
aullido o **aúllo** m. Howl.
aumentación f. Increase (aumento). || Progression (en retórica).
aumentador, ra adj. Increasing, which increases.
aumentar v. tr. To increase: *aumentar la velocidad*, to increase speed; *aumentar el tamaño de algo*, to increase the size of sth. || To raise, to increase (el sueldo). || To put up, to raise (el precio). || To augment, to add to: *trabaja para aumentar los ingresos familiares*, she works to augment the family income. || To magnify: *el microscopio aumenta los objetos*, the microscope magnifies objects. || *Aumentar la producción, el voltaje*, to step up production, the voltage.
— V. intr. To increase, to rise: *los precios han aumentado en un diez por ciento*, prices have risen by ten per cent; *el ruido aumenta*, the noise is increasing. || To get worse (empeorar): *el frío va aumentando*, the cold is getting worse. || To get better (mejorar). || — *Aumentar de peso*, to put on weight. || *Aumentar de velocidad*, to increase one's speed.
— V. pr. To increase, to augment.
aumentativo, va adj./s. m. Augmentative.
aumento m. Increase, rise: *aumento de precio*, price increase. || Addition (acción de añadir, cosa añadida). || Magnification (de microscopio). || *Amer.* Postscript (posdata). || — *Aumento de sueldo*, wage increase, rise (fam.). || *Ir en aumento*, to be on the increase.
aun adv. Even: *te daría mil libras y aun dos mil*, I would give you a thousand pounds or even two thousand; *aun en verano, siempre lleva un abrigo*, he always wears an overcoat, even in summer. || — *Aun* (con gerundio), although, even though [with indicative]: *aun siendo viejo, trabaja mucho*, although he is old he works a lot. || *Aun así, ni aun así*, even so, all the same: *aun así no llegaré a tiempo*, all the same I shan't arrive in time; *ni aun así tendré el tiempo de verte*, even so, I'm not going to have time to see you.

‖ *Aun cuando, aun si*, even if: *aun cuando quisiera ir, no podría*, even if I wanted to go, I could not. ‖ *Ni aun* (con gerundio), not even if [with indicative], not even by [with gerund]: *ni aun amenazándole le harás confesar*, not even if you threaten him will you make him confess, not even by threatening him will you make him confess.
aún adv. Still, yet: *no ha llegado aún*, he still hasn't arrived, he has not yet arrived: *yo tengo más aún*, I have still more. ‖ Still: *aún está aquí*, he is still here. ‖ *Aún no*, not yet.

— OBSERV. *Aún* is written with an accent when it means *todavía*.

aunar v. tr. To join, to unite: *aunar esfuerzos*, to join forces.
— V. pr. To unite, to join together.
aunche o **aunchi** m. *Amer.* Remains, *pl.*
aunque conj. Although, though, even though: *aunque estoy malo, no faltaré a la cita*, although I am ill I shall keep the appointment. ‖ Even if, even though: *aunque no venga nadie, debes quedarte aquí*, even if no one comes *o* even though no one may come you must stay here; *iré aunque llueva*, I will go even if it rains.

— OBSERV. *Aunque* is followed by the subjunctive when the clause it introduces expresses a hypothesis. It is used with the indicative when the clause expresses a fact.
— En inglés se puede utilizar el subjuntivo después de *though* o *although* pero se emplea más frecuentemente el indicativo.

¡aúpa! interj. Hup!, hup la! ‖ — FAM. *De aúpa*, fantastic, great, terrific (magnífico), terrible (malo). ‖ *Los de aúpa*, the picadors.

— OBSERV. The expression *de aúpa* is used to intensify the meaning of the word it qualifies (*una bofetada de aupa*, a tremendous wallop).

aupar v. tr. FAM. To lift up (levantar). | To help up (ayudar). ‖ FIG. To praise, to praise to the skies (ensalzar).
aura f. ZOOL. Urubu (buitre de América). ‖ POÉT. Zephyr, breeze (viento apacible). ‖ FIG. General approval (aceptación). ‖ Aura, atmosphere (atmósfera inmaterial). ‖ MED. Aura: *aura epiléptica*, epileptic aura.
áureo, a adj. Gold (de oro). ‖ Golden, aureate (parecido al oro). ‖ Golden: *edad áurea*, golden age. ‖ *Número áureo*, golden number.
aureola f. REL. Aureole (gloria). ‖ Halo, aureole, nimbus (en la cabeza de imágenes sagradas). ‖ ASTR. Aureole. ‖ FIG. Reputation, aureole (fama).
aureolar v. tr. To aureole, to halo.
aureomicina f. MED. Aureomycin.
áurico, ca adj. Auric, gold.
— Adj. f. MAR. Fore-and-aft (vela).
aurícula f. ANAT. Auricle (del corazón). | Pinna, auricle (de la oreja). ‖ BOT. Auricle, auricula.
auriculado, da adj. Auriculate.
auricular adj. Auricular.
— M. Little finger (dedo meñique). ‖ Earpiece, receiver (de teléfono). ‖ — Pl. Earphones, headphones, headset, *sing.*
aurífero, ra adj. Auriferous, gold-bearing.
auriga m. POÉT. Coachman (cochero). ‖ ASTR. Wagoner, Auriga (constelación).
auroch m. Aurochs, urus.
aurora f. Dawn, daybreak (amanecer). ‖ FIG. Dawn, beginning (principio). ‖ — *Aurora austral*, aurora australis. ‖ *Aurora boreal*, aurora borealis, northern lights. ‖ *Despunta* or *rompe la aurora*, day *o* dawn is breaking.
auscultación f. MED. Auscultation, sounding.
auscultar v. tr. MED. To auscultate, to sound.
ausencia f. Absence (de una persona, de una cosa). ‖ — FAM. *Brillar por su ausencia*, to be conspicuous by one's absence. ‖ *En ausencia de*, in the absence of.
ausentarse v. pr. To leave, to absent o.s., to take one's leave (irse). ‖ To be absent, to stay away (no volver).
ausente adj. Absent (alumno). ‖ Away, out: *está ausente de la capital*, he is away from *o* he is out of the capital. ‖ JUR. Missing. ‖ — FIG. *Estar ausente*, to be in a dream, to be distracted *o* inattentive, to be woolgathering. ‖ *Estar ausente de su domicilio*, to be away from home.
— M. y f. Absentee, person absent. ‖ JUR. Missing person. ‖ *Ni ausente sin culpa, ni presente sin disculpa*, the absent are always in the wrong.
ausentismo m. Absenteeism (absentismo).
auspiciar v. tr. *Amer.* To patronize, to favour [U.S., to favor].
auspicio m. Omen, auspice: *con buenos auspicios*, with good omens. ‖ *Bajo los auspicios de*, under the auspices of, under the patronage of, sponsored by.
auspicioso, sa adj. *Amer.* Auspicious, favourable [U.S., favorable].
austeridad f. Austerity. ‖ Severity (severidad).
austero, ra adj. Austere: *lleva una vida austera*, he leads an austere life.
austral adj. Southern, austral.
Australasia n. pr. f. GEOGR. Australasia.
Australia n. pr. f. GEOGR. Australia.
australiano, na adj./s. Australian.
Austrasia n. pr. f. GEOGR. Austrasia.
Austria n. pr. f. GEOGR. Austria.
austriaco, ca adj./s. Austrian.
austro m. South wind (viento del sur).
autarquía f. National self-sufficiency, autarky (económica). ‖ Autarchy (gobierno).
autárquico, ca adj. Autarkic, autarkical (economía). ‖ Autarchic, autarchical (gobierno).
auténtica f. Certificate, attestation (certificado). ‖ Legal *o* certified copy (copia).
autenticación f. Certification, authentication, legalization.
autenticar v. tr. JUR. To authenticate, to legalize.
autenticidad f. Authenticity, genuineness.
auténtico, ca adj. Genuine, authentic, real: *joya auténtica*, genuine jewel; *un gitano auténtico*, a real gipsy. ‖ MÚS. Authentic (modo). ‖ JUR. Authentic. ‖ *Una auténtica tormenta*, a real storm.
autentificar o **autentizar** v. tr. JUR. To authenticate, to legalize.
autillo m. ZOOL. Tawny owl. ‖ Judgement of the Inquisition (auto particular del tribunal de la Inquisición).
auto m. JUR. Judgement, sentence (sentencia). | Judgement (de un pleito). ‖ "Auto", mystery play [mainly in the 16th and 17th centuries.]. ‖ — Pl. Proceedings. ‖ — *Auto de comparecencia*, summons. ‖ *Auto de fe*, auto-da-fé. ‖ *Auto de prisión*, warrant for arrest. ‖ *Auto de procesamiento*, indictment. ‖ *Auto sacramental*, "auto sacramental," mystery play. ‖ *El día de autos*, the day of the crime.
auto m. FAM. Car (coche). ‖ *Autos de choque*, dodgems, bumper cars.
autoacusación f. Self-accusation.
autoacusarse v. pr. To accuse o.s.
autoadhesivo, va adj. Self-adhesive.
autoametralladora f. Light armoured car.
autobiografía f. Autobiography.
autobiográfico, ca adj. Autobiographical, autobiographic.
autobiógrafo m. Autobiographer.
autobombo m. FAM. Self-praise. ‖ FAM. *Hacerse el autobombo*, to blow one's own trumpet, to praise o.s.
autobús m. Bus. ‖ — *Autobús de dos pisos*, double-decker bus. ‖ *Autobús de línea*, long-distance bus.
autocamión m. Lorry [U.S., truck].
autocar m. Coach, motor coach [U.S., bus]: *viaje en autocar*, coach trip.
autocarril m. *Amer.* Railcar.
autoclave f. Autoclave (cámara hermética). ‖ Sterilizer (para esterilizar).
autocracia f. Autocracy.
autócrata m. y f. Autocrat.
autocrático, ca adj. Autocratic, autocratical.
autocrítica f. Self-criticism. ‖ Criticism by the author (de una obra).
autóctono, na adj. Autochthonous, autochthonic.
— M. y f. Autochthon.
autodefensa f. Self-defence [U.S., self-defense].
autodegradación f. Self-abasement.
autodeterminación f. Self-determination.
autodeterminado, da adj. Self-determining.
autodidáctico, ca o **autodidacto, ta** adj. Self-taught, autodidactic.
— M. y f. Self-taught person, autodidact.

— OBSERV. According to the Real Academia de la Lengua, *autodidacto, ta* exists in both masculine and feminine forms. In practice, however, the form *autodidacta* is applied to both masculine and feminine nouns.

autodirigido, da adj. Self-directing.
autodisciplina f. Self-discipline.
autódromo m. Motor-racing track, racing circuit.
autoencendido m. AUT. Self-ignition.
autoescuela f. Driving school.
autoexcitación f. ELECTR. Self-excitation.
autofecundación f. Self-fertilization.
autofinanciación f. o **autofinanciamiento** m. Self-financing.
autogamia f. BOT. Autogamy.
autogénesis f. BIOL. Autogenesis, autogeny.
autógeno, na adj. Autogenous. ‖ *Soldadura autógena*, autogenous welding, fusion welding.
autogiro m. Autogiro, autogyro.
autografía f. Autography.
autográfico, ca adj. Autographic, autographical.
autógrafo, fa adj. Autographic, autographical.
— M. Autograph.
autoinducción f. Self-induction.
autoinfección f. MED. Autoinfection.
autoinoculación f. MED. Autoinoculation.
autointoxicación f. Autointoxication.
autólisis f. Autolysis.
automación f. Automation.

— OBSERV. *Automación* is an Anglicism which it is usually considered preferable to replace by *automatización*.

autómata m. Automaton, robot.
automaticidad f. Automaticity, automatic working.
automático, ca adj. Automatic.
— M. Press stud [U.S., snap fastener].
automatismo m. Automatism.
automatización f. Automation.
automatizar v. tr. To automate.

AUTOMÓVIL *m.* — AUTOMOBILE

I. Términos (*m.*) generales. — General terms.

primera, segunda velocidad *f.*	first, second gear
marcha (*f.*) atrás	reverse
motor (*m.*) de dos tiempos	two-stroke engine
diesel *m.*	diesel
limusina *f.*	limousine
coche (*m.*) descapotable	convertible
coche (*m.*) de carrera	racing car
sedán *m.*	saloon [U.S., sedan]
propulsión (*f.*) total, doble tracción *f.*	four-wheel drive
tracción (*f.*) delantera	front-wheel drive
remolque *m.*	trailer

II. Partes (*f.*) exteriores. — External parts.

rueda (*f.*) delantera, trasera	front, rear wheel
[ranuras (*f. pl.*) de la] banda de rodadura	tread, *sing.*
bastidor *m.*	chassis
carrocería *f.*	bodywork, body
cristal (*m.*) trasero	rear window
parabrisas *m. inv.*	windscreen [U.S., windshield]
limpiaparabrisas *m. inv.*	windscreen wiper [U.S., windshield wiper]
guardabarros *m. inv.*	mudguard
rejilla (*f.*) del radiador, calandra *f.*	radiator grille
retrovisor *m.* (exterior)	wing mirror
capó *m.*	bonnet [U.S., hood]
cofre *m.*	boot [U.S., trunk]
baca *f.*	roof rack, luggage rack
placa (*f.*) de matrícula	number plate
aleta *f.*	wing
tapacubos *m. inv.*	hubcap
parachoques *m. inv.*	bumper
tope (*m.*) del parachoques	bumper guard, overrider

III. Partes (*f.*) interiores. — Internal parts.

volante *m.*	steering wheel, wheel
asiento (*m.*) del conductor	driver's seat, driving seat
asiento (*m.*) del pasajero	passenger seat
asiento (*m.*) trasero	back *o* rear seat
retrovisor *m.*	rear-view *o* driving mirror
palanca (*f.*) de cambio de velocidades	gear stick, gear change [U.S., gearshift]
caja (*f.*) de velocidades *or* de cambios	gearbox
velocímetro *m.*	speedometer, clock
cuentakilómetros *m. inv.*	milometer
estrangulador *m.*, stárter *m.*	choke
arranque *m.*	starter, self-starter
señal (*f.*) acústica	horn, hooter
pedal (*m.*) de freno, de embrague	brake, clutch pedal
salpicadero *m.*	dashboard
freno (*m.*) de mano, de pie	hand, foot brake
transmisión *f.*	transmission
pistón *m.*, émbolo *m.*	piston
radiador *m.*	radiator
correa (*f.*) del ventilador	fan belt
eje *m.*, árbol *m.*	shaft
cámara (*f.*) de aire	inner tube
grifo (*m.*) de vaciado	drain tap
silencioso *m.*	silencer [U.S., muffler]
depósito *m.*	tank
tubo (*m.*) de desagüe	overflow
válvula *f.*	valve
tubo (*m.*) de escape	exhaust pipe
rueda (*f.*) de recambio *or* de repuesto	spare wheel
carburador *m.*	carburettor [U.S., carburetor]

IV. Electricidad, *f.* — Electricity.

instalación (*f.*) eléctrica	electrical system, wiring
luces *f. pl.*	lights
faro *m.*	headlight
luz (*f.*) de cruce	dipped headlight
pilotos *m. pl.*	rear lights
luces (*f. pl.*) de posición	sidelights, parking lights
indicador (*m.*) de dirección	direction indicator
intermitente *m.*	indicator, blinker
batería *f.* (de recambio)	[spare] battery
bujía *f.*	sparking plug [U.S., spark plug]

V. Reparaciones *f.* — Repairs and maintenance.

cinta (*f.*) aislante	insulating tape
gato *m.*	jack
bidón *m.*	can, jerrican
carburante *m.*	fuel
gasolina *f.* [*Amer.*, nafta *f.*]	petrol [U.S., gas]
agua (*f.*) de refrigeración	cooling water
aceite *m.*	oil
engrase *m.*	lubrication, oiling
anticongelante *m.*	antifreeze
antideslizante	antiskid
cadena (*f.*) antideslizante	tyre chain [U.S., tire chain]
caja (*f.*) de herramientas	toolbox, tool kit
manivela *f.*	crank
coche (*m.*) de auxilio en carretera, grúa (*f.*) remolque	breakdown lorry *o* van [U.S., tow car *o* truck]
piezas (*f. pl.*) de recambio *or* de repuesto	spare parts, spares
nivel (*m.*) del aceite	oil level
indicador (*m.*) de nivel de aceite	dipstick
vaciado *m.*, cambio (*m.*) de aceite	oil change
vulcanizar	to vulcanize
inflar, hinchar	to inflate
presión (*f.*) de los neumáticos	tyre pressure [U.S., tire pressure]
llenar el depósito de gasolina	to fill the tank
encargado (*m.*) del surtidor de gasolina	[petrol] pump attendant
surtidor (*m.*) de gasolina	petrol pump [U.S., gasoline pump]
gasolina (*f.*) super	super
bomba (*f.*) de aire	pump, air pump
ajustar	to adjust
cargar una batería	to charge *o* to recharge a battery
descarburar	to decoke [U.S., to decarbonize]
avería *f.*	breakdown
avería (*f.*) mecánica	mechanical failure
taller (*m.*) de reparación	repair shop
agarrotarse	to seize up
accidente *m.*	accident
pinchazo *m.*	puncture, blowout
parche *m.*	patch
patinar	to skid
golpear (el motor)	to knock
remolcar	to tow, to take in tow
seguro (*m.*) contra accidentes	accident insurance
seguro (*m.*) contra robo	insurance against theft
seguro (*m.*) a todo riesgo	fully comprehensive insurance
seguro (*m.*) de daños a tercero	third-party insurance

VI. Conducción, *f.* — Driving.

código (*m.*) de la circulación	highway code
carnet (*m.*) de conducir *or* permiso (*m.*) de conducción	driving licence [U.S., driver's license]
señal (*f.*) de tráfico	traffic *o* road sign
acelerar	to accelerate
frenar	to brake
embragar	to engage the clutch
desembragar	to declutch
calar, calarse	to stall
cambiar de velocidad	to change gear
arrancar	to start up
adelantar, pasar	to overtake
pisar el acelerador	to put one's foot down [U.S., to step on the gas]
soltar el acelerador	to decelerate
velocidad (*f.*) máxima	top speed
límite (*m.*) de velocidad	speed limit
aparcar, estacionar	to park
aparcamiento *m.*	car park [U.S., parking lot]
cortar el encendido	to switch off the motor
autopista *f.*	motorway [U.S., freeway, superhighway].
carretera (*f.*) de peaje	toll road [U.S., turnpike]
atasco *m.*, embotellamiento *m.*	traffic jam

automotor, ra adj. Self-propelled, self-driven, automotive.
— M. Railcar.

automotriz adj. f. Self-propelled, self-driven, automotive.

automóvil adj. Self-propelled, self-driven, automotive. || Motor: *vehículo automóvil*, motor vehicle.
— M. Car, motorcar [U.S., automobile] (coche). || *Ir en automóvil*, to go by car.

automovilismo m. Motoring, driving.

automovilista m. y f. Motorist, driver.

automovilístico, ca adj. Motoring. || — *Accidente automovilístico*, road accident, car crash. || *Carrera automovilística*, motor race.

autonomía f. Autonomy, self-government. || MIL. y AVIAT. Range.

autonómico, ca adj. Autonomous, self-governing.

autonomista adj. Autonomous.
— M. y f. Autonomist.

autónomo, ma adj. Autonomous. || Autonomous, self-governing (país).

autopista f. Motorway [U.S., freeway, superhighway]. || *Autopista de peaje*, toll-paying motorway [U.S., turnpike].

autoplastia f. MED. Autoplasty.

autopropulsado, da adj. Self-propelled: *cohete autopropulsado*, self-propelled rocket.

autopropulsión f. Self-propulsion.

autopropulsor adj. Self-propelling.

autopsia f. MED. Autopsy, postmortem

autopsiar v. tr. MED. To autopsy, to carry out an autopsy on *o* a postmortem on.

autopullman m. Pullman.

autor, ra m. y f. Author (hombre o mujer). || Authoress (mujer). || Author, perpetrator (de un crimen). || Author, originator, creator (de una idea). || TEATR. Treasurer.

autoría f. TEATR. Treasurership.

autoridad f. Authority: *tener autoridad sobre sus empleados*, to have authority over one's employees. || Official: *las autoridades que acompañan al jefe del Estado*, the officials who accompany the Head of

State. || Authority, expert: *es una autoridad en literatura griega*, he is an authority on Greek literature. || Authorities, *pl.*: *entregarse a la autoridad*, to give o.s. up to the authorities. || — *Con plena autoridad*, with complete authority. || *Por su propia autoridad*, on one's own authority, on one's own account. || *Tener autoridad para*, to have the authority to (con verbo).

autoritoriamente adv. In an authoritarian way.

autoritario, ria adj. Authoritarian.

autoritarismo m. Authoritarianism.

autorización f. Authorization, permission (permiso): *pedir autorización para salir*, to ask permission to go out.

autorizadamente adv. With authority (con autoridad). || With authorization *o* permission (con permiso).

autorizado, da adj. Legal, authorized, official: *precio autorizado*, official price. || Authoritative reliable: *opinión autorizada*, authoritative opinion; *fuente autorizada*, reliable source.

autorizamiento m. Authorization, permission.

autorizar v. tr. To authorize, to give permission to: *autorizar a uno para salir*, to authorize s.o. to go out, to give s.o. permission to go out. || To authorize, to give permission for: *autorizar una manifestación*, to authorize *o* to give permission for a demonstration. || To give [the] authority to, to give [the] power to, to authorize, to empower: *el ser capitán no le autoriza a insultar a sus soldados*, the fact that he is captain does not give him the authority *o* does not authorize him to insult his soldiers. || To authorize, to legalize (un documento). || To accept: *palabra autorizada por su uso constante*, word accepted through its constant use.

autorregulación f. Self-regulation.

autorregulador, ra adj. Self-regulating.

autorretrato m. Self-portrait.

autorriel m. *Amer.* Railcar.

autorzuelo m. Hack, poor writer.

autoservicio m. Self-service store, supermarket (tienda). || Self-service [restaurant] (restaurante).

autostop m. Hitchhiking, hitching. || *Hacer autostop*, to hitchhike, to hitch.

autostopista m. y f. Hitchhiker.

autosuficiencia f. Self-sufficiency.

autosuficiente adj. Self-sufficient.

autosugestión f. Autosuggestion.

autotomía f. Autotomy.

autovacuna f. Autovaccine, autogenous vaccine.

autovía f. Railcar.

autrigones m. pl. Former inhabitants of the western Basque provinces.

autumnal adj. Autumnal, autumn.

Auvernia n. pr. f. GEOGR. Auvergne.

auxiliador, ra adj. Helping, assisting.
— M. y f. Helper.

auxiliar adj. Assistant: *catedrático auxiliar*, assistant lecturer. || Auxiliary: *servicios auxiliares*, auxiliary services. || GRAM. Auxiliary.
— M. y f. Assistant, auxiliary. || — M. Assistant teacher (de instituto, etc.). || Assistant lecturer (de universidad). || GRAM. Auxiliary, auxiliary verb. || — *Auxiliar de contabilidad*, assistant accountant. || *Auxiliar de farmacia*, assistant chemist *o* pharmacist. || *Auxiliar de laboratorio*, laboratory assistant. || *Auxiliar de vuelo*, steward (avión).

auxiliar v. tr. To help, to assist, to give help *o* aid to: *auxiliar a uno con donativos*, to help s.o. *o* to give help to s.o. with donations. || To attend [a dying person].

auxiliaría f. Assistant professorship.

auxilio m. Help, aid, assistance: *con el auxilio de*, with the help of. || — *Auxilio en carretera*, breakdown service. || *Auxilios espirituales*, last rites. || *Darle* or *prestarle auxilio a una persona*, to give aid *o* help *o* assistance to a person, to help *o* to aid *o* to assist a person. || *En auxilio de*, in aid of. || *Pedir auxilio*, to cry for help. || *Primeros auxilios*, first aid.
— Interj. Help!

aval m. Guarantor's signature (firma). || Guarantee (garantía). || — *Dar su aval a*, to act as guarantor to (persona), to guarantee (cosa). || *Por aval*, as a guarantee.

avalancha f. Avalanche.

avalar v. tr. COM. To guarantee (un documento). || To be the guarantor of, to answer for (a una persona).

avalentonado, da adj. Boastful, arrogant (valentón).

avalorar v. tr. To enhance (realzar). || FIG. To encourage, to inspire.

avaluación f. Evaluation, appraisal, valuation.

avaluar v. tr. To evaluate, to appraise, to value (valuar).

avalúo m. Evaluation, appraisal, valuation.

avance m. Advance (acción de avanzar). || Advance (espacio avanzado). || FIG. Step forward, advance: *un avance en el campo de la ciencia*, a step forward in the field of science. | Advance, progress (progreso). || Advance (de dinero). || Budget (presupuesto de un Estado). || COM. Balance (balance). || MIL. Advance. || TECN. Feed. || ELECTR. Lead. || CINEM. Trailer. || *Avance al encendido*, ignition advance.

avant m. DEP. Knock-on (al caerse la pelota). | Forward pass (pase).

avante adv. MAR. Forward, ahead.

avantrén m. MIL. Limber.

avanzada f. MIL. Advance guard *o* party, outpost.

avanzadilla f. MIL. Advance guard *o* party, outpost (avanzada). || Pier (muelle).

avanzado, da adj. Advanced, progressive: *ideas avanzadas*, advanced ideas. || Advanced: *fase avanzada de desarrollo*, advanced stage of development. || Prominent (saliente). || — *Avanzado de* or *en edad*, advanced *o* well on in years. || *Una hora muy avanzada*, a very late hour.

avanzar v. tr. To move forward: *hay que avanzar su silla*, you must move your chair forward. || To put forward: *avanzar un pie*, to put one foot forward. || To advance: *avanzar una pieza de ajedrez*, to advance a chessman.
— V. intr. To advance: *el ejército avanzó rápidamente*, the army advanced swiftly. || To progress, to advance (progresar). || To draw on: *avanzaba el verano*, summer was drawing on. || *Avanzar en edad*, to be getting on in years.

avanzo m. COM. Balance sheet, balance (balance). | Estimate (presupuesto).

avaricia f. Avarice, miserliness (tacañería). || Avarice, greed, greediness (codicia). || *La avaricia rompe el saco*, a rich man and his money are soon parted.

avaricioso, sa o **avariento, ta** adj. Miserly, avaricious, mean (tacaño). || Greedy, avaricious (codicioso). || REL. *La parábola del rico avariento*, the parable of Lazarus and the rich man.
— M. y f. Miser (tacaño). || Greedy *o* avaricious person (codicioso).

avariosis f. MED. Syphilis.

avaro, ra adj. Miserly, avaricious, mean (tacaño). || Greedy, avaricious (codicioso). || — *Hombre avaro de palabras*, a man of few words. || *Ser avaro de alabanzas*, to be sparing *o* mean with one's praise.
— M. y f. Miser (tacaño). || Greedy *o* avaricious person (codicioso).

avasallador, ra adj. Domineering. || FIG. Overpowering, overwhelming: *la fuerza avasalladora de su discurso*, the overpowering force of his speech.
— M. y f. Enslaver.

avasallamiento m. Enslavement.

avasallar v. tr. To enslave, to subjugate. || To dominate (dominar).
— V. intr. FAM. To throw one's weight about: *¡sin avasallar!*, there's no need to throw your weight about!
— V. pr. To become a slave. || To submit, to yield (someterse).

avatar m. Avatar (de Visnú). || Reincarnation (reincarnación). || Change, transformation (cambio). || — Pl. Ups and downs: *los avatares de su vida*, the ups and downs of his life.

ave f. ZOOL. Bird. || — *Ave canora* o *cantora*, songbird. || *Ave de corral*, fowl. || *Ave del Paraíso*, bird of paradise. || FIG. *Ave de mal agüero*, bird of ill omen. || *Ave de presa* o *de rapiña*, bird of prey. || *Ave lira*, lyre bird. || *Ave nocturna*, night bird (animal), night bird, night rake (persona). || *Ave pasajera* or *de paso*, migratory bird, bird of passage (sentido propio), rolling stone, bird of passage (sentido figurado). || *Ave zancuda*, wader.

— OBSERV. *Ave* is used mainly for large birds, whereas *pájaro* indicates smaller birds.

avecasina f. *Amer.* Woodcock.

avecilla f. Small bird. || *Avecilla de las nieves*, wagtail.

avecinarse v. pr. To approach, to get nearer: *se avecina la tormenta*, the storm is approaching. || To take up residence, to settle (establecerse).

avecindamiento m. Settling (en un lugar). || Residence, domicile (lugar).

avecindar v. tr. To domicile, to give residence to.
— V. pr. To take up residence, to settle.

avechucho m. Ugly bird (pájaro). || FIG. Ragamuffin, pest (persona despreciable).

avefría f. ZOOL. Lapwing. || FIG. y FAM. Wet blanket, drip (persona).

avejentar v. tr. To age.
— V. intr. y pr. To age, to get old: *Felipe se ha avejentado mucho*, Philip has aged a lot.

avejigar v. tr. To blister.
— V. pr. To blister.

avellana f. Hazelnut. || — *Color de avellana* or *color avellana*, hazel, hazel-coloured: *ojos color de avellana*, hazel eyes. || *Más seco que una avellana*, parched, wizened, shrivelled (rostro).

avellanado, da adj. Wizened, shrivelled, parched (seco y arrugado). || Hazel, hazel-coloured (color).
— M. TECN. Countersinking.

avellanador m. TECN. Countersink.

avellanal o **avellanar** m. Hazel grove.

avellanar v. tr. TECN. To countersink.
— V. pr. To become wizened, to shrivel up, to wrinkle (envejecer).

avellaneda f. o **avellanedo** m. Hazel grove.

avellanera f. BOT. Hazel tree (avellano). || Hazelnut seller (vendedora).

avellano m. Hazel tree.

avemaría f. Ave Maria, Hail Mary (oración). || Ave Maria, small rosary bead (cuenta del rosario). || Ave Maria, Angelus. || — FIG. *Al avemaría*, in a wink, in the twinkling of an eye. | *Saber algo como el avemaría*, to know sth. by heart, to know sth. backwards.

¡ave María! interj. Goodness gracious!, good Lord!

|| *¡Ave María!* or *¡ave María Purísima!*, God bless this house [said on entering a house].
avena f. BOT. Oats, *pl.*: *la avena sirve para la alimentación de los animales*, oats are used for feeding animals. || POÉT. Pipe (zampoña). || *Avena loca*, wild oats, *pl.*
avenado, da adj. Touched (algo loco). || Drained: *terreno avenado*, drained land.
avenal m. Oat field.
avenamiento m. Drainage. || *Tubos de avenamiento*, drainage pipes.
avenar v. tr. To drain.
avenate m. Oatmeal drink (bebida). || Fit of madness (ataque de locura).
avenencia f. Agreement (acuerdo). || Compromise (arreglo). || COM. Deal (transacción). || *Más vale mala avenencia que buena sentencia*, a poor agreement is better than a good court case.
avenida f. Swell, swelling, freshet (crecida). || Flood (desbordamiento). || Avenue (calle).
avenido, da adj. *Estar bien, mal avenido con*, to be on good, bad terms with.
avenimiento m. Agreement (acuerdo).
avenir* v. tr. To bring to an agreement, to bring into agreement, to reconcile, to bring together.
— V. intr. To happen (suceder).
— V. pr. To agree, to come to an agreement: *avenirse en el precio*, to agree about *o* on the price. || To get on, to agree: *no puede avenirse con su hermano*, he cannot agree with *o* get on with his brother. || To adapt *o* to adjust o.s.: *una persona que se aviene a* or *con todo*, a person who adjusts himself to everything. || To correspond to, to be in agreement with (corresponder). || — FAM. *Allá se las avenga*, that's his look-out, let him get on with it. || *Avenirse a razones*, to listen to reason.
aventador, ra adj. Winnowing.
— M. y f. Winnower (persona). || — M. Fan (para el fuego). || Winnowing fork (bieldo). || Leather valve (de tubo de aspiración). || — F. Winnowing machine (máquina).
aventadura f. Windgall (de los caballos).
aventajado, da adj. Outstanding (notable). || Advantageous, favourable (ventajoso).
aventajamiento m. Advantage (ventaja).
aventajar v. tr. To come *o* to finish ahead of *o* in front of: *le aventajó en la carrera*, he came ahead of him in the race. || To lead, to be ahead of: *el piloto inglés aventaja al francés*, the English driver leads the French one. || To surpass, to excel, to outstrip, to be superior to: *aventaja a todos en los deportes*, he surpasses everyone in sports. || To give an advantage to, to be to the advantage of (dar ventaja). || To better, to improve (mejorar). || To prefer, to put before (preferir). || *Aventaja a todos en simpatía*, he beats everyone for friendliness.
aventamiento m. AGR. Winnowing.
aventar* v. tr. To blow away (el viento). || To expose to the wind (exponer al viento). || To fan, to blow (el fuego). || AGR. To winnow. || To throw *o* to cast to the winds (las cenizas). || *Amer.* To expose [sugar] to the sun and air. || FIG. y FAM. To throw out (expulsar).
— V. pr. To swell in the wind (llenarse de aire). || FIG. y FAM. To dash off, to rush off, to beat it (marcharse).
aventura f. Adventure: *novela de aventuras*, adventure novel. || Risk (riesgo). || Chance (casualidad). || Affair (de amor). || — FIG. *A la aventura*, at random. || *Nos contaba las aventuras de su juventud*, he would tell us about his youthful adventures *o* exploits *o* escapades.
aventurado, da adj. Risky, hazardous, dangerous (peligroso): *empresa aventurada*, risky undertaking. || Venturesome, risky: *proyecto aventurado*, risky plan. || *No es aventurado decir que*, one can say that, it can be said that, it is safe to say that.
aventurar v. tr. To risk, to venture, to chance: *aventurar su vida*, to risk one's life. || FIG. To venture, to hazard: *aventurar una teoría*, to hazard a theory.
— V. pr. To venture, to dare. || *El que no se aventura no pasa la mar*, nothing ventured, nothing gained.
aventurero, ra adj. Adventurous, venturesome (que busca aventura). || *Amer.* Produced out of season (maíz, arroz).
— M. Adventurer. || *Amer.* Hired mule driver (arriero). || — F. Adventuress.
avergonzado, da adj. Ashamed. || Embarrassed (confuso).
avergonzar* v. tr. To shame, to put to shame (escarnecer): *el orador avergonzó públicamente a su rival*, the speaker shamed his rival publicly. || To embarrass (poner en un apuro).
— V. pr. To be ashamed: *me avergüenzo de tu conducta*, I am ashamed of your conduct. || To be embarrassed (pasar un apuro).
avería f. Breakdown (en un coche): *tuvimos una avería*, we had a breakdown. || Damage (daño). || — MAR. *Avería gruesa*, general average. || AUT. *El coche tiene una avería*, there is sth. wrong with the car.
averiado, da adj. AUT. Broken down (un automóvil, un motor). || Damaged (estropeado). || Spoilt, spoiled (echado a perder). || *Está averiado*, it has broken down, there is sth. wrong with it.
averiar v. tr. To damage (estropear). || To spoil (echar a perder).
— V. pr. To break down (un coche). || To fail (los frenos, etc.). || To be *o* to get damaged (estropearse). || To spoil (echarse a perder). || To be *o* to get damaged (un buque).
averiguable adj. Verifiable. || Ascertainable.
averiguación f. Verification (examen). || Ascertainment. || Investigation, inquiry (investigación).
averiguador, ra adj. Inquiring, investigating.
— M. y f. Investigator, inquirer (el que investiga).
averiguamiento m. V. AVERIGUACIÓN.
averiguar v. tr. To check, to verify (examinar). || To ascertain, to find out (enterarse de): *voy a averiguar lo que ha sucedido*, I am going to ascertain what has happened. || To investigate, to ascertain, to inquire into (investigar): *hay que averiguar las causas del accidente*, we must investigate the causes of the accident. || To guess (adivinar). || To look up, to check: *averígualo en el diccionario*, look it up *o* check it in the dictionary. || *¡Averigüelo Vargas!*, find out for yourself!, make your own inquiries!
— V. intr. *Amer.* To quarrel, to argue (andarse en disputas).
averno m. POÉT. Hades, the nether regions, *pl.*, the underworld.
Averroes n. pr. Averroes, Averrhoes.
averrugado, da adj. Warty.
aversión f. Aversion, loathing, abhorrence: *aversión al trabajo*, aversion for work. || — *Cobrarle* or *cogerle aversión a uno*, to develop an aversion *o* a loathing for s.o., to take an extreme dislike to s.o. || *Tenerle aversión a uno*, to have an aversion *o* a loathing for s.o., to loathe *o* to hate s.o.
avestruceras f. pl. "Bolas" [weapon consisting of several ropes tied together, each with a metal ball at the end, and used by Argentinian "gauchos" for catching ostriches].
avestruz m. Ostrich (ave). || — *Avestruz de América*, rhea, nandu, nandow. || FIG. *Política del avestruz*, ostrich policy.
avetado, da adj. Veined.
avetoro m. ZOOL. Bittern.
avezado, da adj. Used, accustomed (acostumbrado). || Hardened, inured: *avezado a la lucha*, hardened against *o* to strife. || Experienced, inured: *avezado en los negocios*, experienced in business.
avezar v. tr. To accustom, to get used, to inure: *avezar a una persona al trabajo*, to get a person used to work. || To harden, to inure: *avezar a un soldado al frío*, to harden a soldier against the cold.
— V. pr. To get used, to become accustomed: *avezarse a todo*, to get used to everything. || To become *o* to be hardened (al frío, a las desgracias, etc.).
aviación f. Aviation: *aviación civil*, civil aviation. || MIL. Air force: *capitán de aviación*, air force captain.
aviado, da adj. Ready: *aviado para salir*, ready to go out. || *¡Aviado estoy* or *voy!*, I'm in a real mess!, I'm done for!
aviador, ra m. y f. Aviator, flyer, flier (que tripula un avión). || Pilot (piloto). || MIL. *Mi padre era aviador*, my father was in the air force.
aviar adj. Avian. || *Peste aviar*, fowl pest.
aviar v. tr. To prepare, to get ready: *aviar una comida*, to get a meal ready. || To tidy: *aviar una habitación*, to tidy a room. || To mend, to repair (reparar). || To equip, to supply, to provide (equipar). || To fit out, to equip: *aviarle a uno de ropa*, to fit s.o. out with clothes. || FAM. To help out: *¿me puedes prestar mil pesetas para aviarme?*, can you lend me a thousand pesetas to help me out? | To help: *¿te avía si te llevo en coche?*, will it help you if I take you by car? || — *Dejar a alguien aviado*, to leave s.o. stranded. || FAM. *Ir aviando*, to get a move on, to hurry up: *vamos aviando*, let's get a move on.
— V. pr. To get ready: *aviarse para ir a cenar*, to get ready to go to dinner. || FAM. To manage: *se avía con muy poca cosa*, he manages with very little. | To hurry up, to get a move on (darse prisa): *¡avíate!*, hurry up!, get a move on!
aviario, ria adj. V. AVIAR.
avícola adj. Poultry.
avicultor, ra m. y f. Poultry keeper.
avicultura f. Poultry keeping (aves de corral). || Aviculture (de otras aves).
avidez f. Avidity, greed, greediness (ansia). || Eagerness (ganas).
ávido, da adj. Avid, greedy (*de*, for) [ansioso]. || Eager, avid (*de*, for) [con ganas]. || *Ávido de sangre*, bloodthirsty.
aviejar v. tr. V. ENVEJECER.
aviesamente adv. Perversely.
avieso, sa adj. Perverse, wicked, depraved: *espíritu avieso*, perverse character.
avilés, esa adj. [Of *o* from] Avila [in Spain].
— M. y f. Native *o* inhabitant of Avila.
avilesino, na adj. [Of *o* from] Avilés [in Asturias].
— M. y f. Native *o* inhabitant of Avilés.
avillanado, da adj. Common (no noble).
avillanamiento m. Lowering, debasing.
avillanar v. tr. To lower, to debase.
avinado, da adj. Drunken.

— OBSERV. This word is a Gallicism.

avinagrado, da adj. Sour, vinegary. || FIG. Sour, bitter: *carácter avinagrado*, sour character.

avinagrar v. tr. To turn to vinegar, to turn sour, to sour. || FIG. To sour, to embitter, to make sour.
— V. pr. To turn sour, to turn to vinegar (el vino). || FIG. To turn bitter *o* sour, to become bitter *o* sour.
Aviñón n. pr. GEOGR. Avignon.
avío m. Preparation. || Provisions, *pl.* (de un pastor). || *Amer.* Loan [made to farmer or miner]. || — Pl. FAM. Things (cosas). || Equipment, *sing.*, materials: *avíos de coser, de escribir*, sewing, writing equipment. || Tackle, *sing.*: *avíos de pesca*, fishing tackle. || Gear, *sing.*: *avíos de afeitar*, shaving gear. || Ingredients (de cocina). || — *¡Al avío!*, let's get cracking!, down to work!, let's get down to it! || *Hacer avío*, to be a help: *esta bicicleta me hace un avío imponente*, this bicyle is a great help to me; *hace mi avío*, it is a help to me. || FAM. *Ir a su avío*, to think only of o.s., to be selfish. || TAUR. *Tomar los avíos de matar*, to take the muleta and the sword.
avión m. Aeroplane [U.S., airplane], plane, aircraft: *avión de reacción, de carga, de reconocimiento, sin piloto, supersónico*, jet, cargo, reconnaissance, remote-controlled, supersonic plane. || — Pl. Aircraft, planes: *la compañía tiene veinte aviones*, the company has twenty aircraft. || — *Avión de bombardeo*, bomber. || *Avión de caza*, fighter [plane]. || *Avión de distancias medias* or *continental*, medium-haul aircraft. || *Avión de larga distancia* or *transcontinental*, long-range *o* long-haul aircraft. || *Avión de pasajeros* or *de línea*, airliner, passenger aircraft. || *Avión sin motor*, glider. || *Ir* or *viajar en avión*, to fly, to go by air *o* by plane. || *Por avión*, [by] air mail (una carta), by air (viaje).
avión m. ZOOL. Martin (pájaro).
avioneta f. Light aircraft *o* plane.
avisadamente adv. Wisely, prudently, sensibly.
avisado, da adj. Wise, circumspect, prudent. || TAUR. Experienced [bull]. || *Mal avisado*, rash, thoughtless.
avisador, ra adj. Warning.
— M. TECN. Warning device (alarma). | Fire alarm (contra incendios). || Errand boy (chico de los recados).
avisar v. tr. To warn: *me avisó que me llevara el paraguas*, he warned me to take my umbrella. || To let know, to tell, to notify, to warn: *le han avisado que llegarán tarde*, they have warned him that they will arrive late; *me acaba de avisar que se tiene que ir*, he has just told me that he has to go. || To send for, to call: *avisar al médico*, to send for the doctor. || To notify, to warn: *avisar a la policía*, to notify the police. || *Hacer algo sin avisar*, to do sth. without warning.
aviso m. Warning: *darle un aviso a uno por sus retrasos repetidos*, to give s.o. a warning about repeatedly being late; *el ataque del país es un aviso*, the attack on the country is a warning. || Announcement (anuncio): *dar un aviso al público*, to make an announcement to the public. || Note (nota). || MAR. Dispatch boat, aviso. || TAUR. Warning [given by the president of the bullfight to the bullfighter when the bull has not been killed within the time laid down by the rules]. || — *Andar* or *estar sobre aviso*, to be on one's guard, to be on the alert. || *Aviso por escrito*, written notice. || *Aviso telefónico*, call from the operator. || *Carta de aviso*, advice note. || *Conferencia telefónica con aviso*, person-to-person call. || *Dar previo aviso de un mes*, to give a month's notice. || *Hasta nuevo aviso*, until further notice. || *Poner a uno sobre aviso*, to alert s.o., to put s.o. on his guard. || *Salvo aviso en contrario*, unless otherwise informed. || *Sin el menor aviso*, without the slightest *o* least warning: *le han echado sin el menor aviso*, they have thrown him out without the slightest warning. || *Sin previo aviso*, without previous warning, without notice.
avispa f. Wasp (insecto). || *Cintura de avispa*, wasp waist.
avispado, da adj. FIG. y FAM. Sharp, quick, bright, clever (despabilado). | Sly, crafty (astuto).
avispar v. tr. To spur on (a los caballos). || FIG. y FAM. To liven up, to quicken up, to prod (espabilar).
— V. pr. FIG. y FAM. To brighten up, to liven up, to quicken up (espabilarse). | FIG. To get worried, to worry (preocuparse).
avispero m. Wasps' nest (nido de avispas). || Comb (panal). || FIG. y FAM. Mess, tight spot, jam: *meterse en un avispero*, to get o.s. into a mess. || MED. Carbuncle.
avispón m. Hornet (insecto).
avistar v. tr. To sight, to glimpse: *por la tarde avistamos la costa*, in the afternoon we sighted the coast.
— V. pr. To meet [to discuss business], to have a business interview.
avitaminosis f. Avitaminosis, vitamin deficiency.
avituallamiento m. Provisioning. || MAR. Victualling.
avituallar v. tr. To provision, to supply with food. || MAR. To victual.
avivado, da adj. FIG. Quicker, livelier, brighter (espíritu). | Brighter, livelier (color). | Quicker, livelier (paso). | Excited, roused (ira).
avivador, ra adj. Livening, quickening, enlivening. || Exciting, rousing (que excita).
— M. ARQ. Quirk (espacio entre dos molduras). || TECN. Rabbet plane (cepillo).
avivamiento m. Livening, quickening, enlivening (del espíritu). || Brightening, livening (de un color). || Quickening, livening (del paso). || Rousing, excitement (de la ira).
avivar v. tr. To revive, to arouse, to stimulate (estimular). || To stoke, to stoke up (el fuego). || FIG. To enliven, to liven up, to quicken (el espíritu). || To brighten [up], to liven up, to enliven (los colores). || To quicken, to liven up, to enliven (el paso). || To excite, to stir, to arouse (una pasión, una cólera). || To intensify (el dolor). || To stir up: *avivar el fuego de la insurrección*, to stir up the flames of insurrection.
— V. intr. y pr. To come back to life, to revive. || To hatch (gusanos de seda). || — FAM. *¡Avívate!*, get a move on!, look lively! (date prisa), snap out of it!, cheer up! (anímate).
avizor adj. *Estar ojo avizor*, to be on one's guard, to keep one's eyes open, to keep a sharp lookout. || *¡Ojo avizor!*, look out!, be careful!
avizorar v. tr. To spy on, to watch, to keep watch on (acechar). || To foresee (ver).
avo, va MAT. Suffix added to cardinal numbers to indicate fractions whose denominators are greater than ten: *un onzavo*, an eleventh; *un quinzavo*, a fifteenth; *tres dieciseisavos*, three sixteenths; *una treintava parte*, a thirtieth.
— OBSERV. *Octavo* [eighth] is an exception to this rule, its denominator being smaller than ten.
avoceta f. ZOOL. Avocet, avoset.
avulsión f. MED. Extraction.
avutarda f. ZOOL. Bustard (ave zancuda).
axial o **axil** adj. Axial: *líneas axiales*, axial lines.
axila f. BOT. Axil. || ANAT. Axilla, armpit (sobaco).
axilar adj. Axillary, axillar.
axiología f. Axiology.
axioma m. Axiom.
axiomático, ca adj. Axiomatic.
axiómetro m. MAR. Telltale, helm indicator.
axis m. ANAT. Axis (vértebra).
axolotl m. ZOOL. Axolotl.
ay m. ZOOL. Ai, three-toed sloth (perezoso).
¡ay! interj. Ouch! (dolor físico). || Oh!, oh dear! (aflicción). || Followed by *de* and a noun or pronoun *¡ay!* expresses pain, threat, fear or pity: *¡ay de mí!*, poor me!, why me?, woe is me! (dolor); *¡ay de él!*, poor thing! (compasión); *¡ay de Pedro!*, woe betide Peter! (amenaza). || — *¡Ay de los vencidos!*, woe unto the vanquished. || *¡Ay del que...!* woe betide the man who...!, beware he who...! (amenaza), pity on him who...! (compasión). || *¡Ay, Dios mío!*, my goodness!, goodness me!
— M. Moan, lament: *se oían tristes ayes*, sad moans could be heard. || *Dar ayes*, to moan, to lament.
aya f. Governess.
ayacuá f. *Amer.* Little invisible devil [in South American Indian mythology].
ayahasca o **ayahuasa** f. *Amer.* Narcotic plant.
ayer adv. Yesterday: *ayer por la tarde*, yesterday afternoon; *ayer hizo un año que nos encontramos*, it was a year ago yesterday that we met. || FIG. Yesterday (poco tiempo ha): *parece que fue ayer*, it seems like yesterday. | Before, formerly (en tiempo pasado): *ella ya no es lo que era ayer*, she is not what she was before, she is not like she was before. || — *Antes de ayer*, the day before yesterday. || *Ayer noche*, last night. || FIG. *De ayer acá* or *de ayer a hoy*, lately: *de ayer a hoy la aviación se ha desarrollado mucho*, aviation has developed a great deal lately. || *El Madrid de ayer*, the Madrid of yesteryear. || *Lo que va de ayer a hoy*, things aren't what they used to be, things have changed a lot. || *No es cosa de ayer*, it is nothing new. || *No ha nacido ayer*, he was not born yesterday.
— M. Past (pasado).
ayllu m. V. AÍLLO.
ayo m. [Private] tutor.
ayocote m. *Amer.* Kidney bean.
ayote m. *Amer.* Gourd, pumpkin (fruto).
ayotera f. *Amer.* Gourd, pumpkin (planta).
ayuda f. Help, aid, assistance: *hacer el trabajo con ayuda de alguien*, to do the work with s.o.'s help; *acudir en ayuda de uno*, to come to s.o.'s assistance. || Aid, assistance (económica): *ayuda estatal*, state aid. || MED. Enema (lavativa). || — Pl. Aids. || — *Ayuda mutua*, mutual aid *o* assistance. || FAM. *No necesitar ayuda del vecino*, not to need anyone's help, to need no one's help. || *Prestar ayuda*, to give help *o* aid, to help, to aid.
— M. Valet, manservant. || — *Ayuda de cámara*, valet. || *No hay hombre grande para su ayuda de cámara*, no man is great in the eyes of his manservant.
ayudado m. TAUR. Pass holding the cape in both hands.
ayudante m. Assistant. || MIL. Adjutant. || — *Ayudante de campo*, aide-de-camp. || *Ayudante de laboratorio*, laboratory assistant *o* technician. || *Ayudante de obras públicas*, assistant civil engineer. || CINEM. *Ayudante de operador*, assistant cameraman. || *Ayudante de peluquería*, apprentice hairdresser.
ayudantía f. Assistantship. || MIL. Adjutancy, adjutant's rank.
ayudar v. tr. To help, to aid, to assist: *ayudar a uno con consejos*, to help s.o. with some advice; *ayudar a los pobres*, to help the poor. || To help, to assist: *ayudar a uno a llevar una maleta*, to help s.o. to carry a suitcase. || — *Ayudar a misa*, to serve at Mass. || *Ayudar a uno a bajar*, to help s.o. down.
— V. pr. To help *o* to aid *o* to assist each other: *en la vida hay que ayudarse*, we have to help each other in life. || To use, to make use of (valerse): *ayudándose con los dientes, desató la cuerda*, using his teeth he undid

the string. || *Ayúdate y ayudarte he* or *ayúdate y el cielo te ayudará* or *ayúdate y Dios te ayudará,* God helps those who help themselves.
ayunador, ra o **ayunante** m. y f. Faster.
ayunar v. intr. To fast: *ayunar en cuaresma,* to fast during Lent. || FIG. To go without.
ayunas (en) loc. adv. Fasting (abstinencia). || Without breakfast (sin desayunar). || — *Estar en ayunas,* not to have eaten breakfast (sin desayunar), to be in the dark, to have no idea (no saber). || *Quedarse en ayunas,* not to understand a thing.
ayuno, na adj. FIG. Deprived, completely lacking: *estar ayuno en educación moral,* to be deprived of *o* completely lacking in moral education. || FIG. *Estar ayuno de un asunto,* to know nothing about a matter, to have no idea about a matter (no saber), not to understand a matter (no entender).
— M. Fasting, fast. || *Guardar ayuno,* to fast.
ayuntamiento m. Town council, city council (institución). || Town hall, city hall (edificio). || Meeting (reunión). || Copulation (cópula). || *Ayuntamiento carnal,* sexual intercourse.
ayuntar v. tr. MAR. To splice.
azabachado, da adj. Jet black.
azabache m. Jet (variedad de lignito). || Coal tit (pájaro).
azacán, ana adj. Hard-working.
— M. Slave, drudge. || Water carrier (aguador). || FIG. y FAM. *Estar hecho un azacán,* to work like a slave, to be overworked.
azacanear v. intr. FAM. To slave away, to toil.
azache m. Rough silk (seda basta).
azada f. AGR. Hoe.
azadada f. o **azadado** m. Stroke of *o* blow with a hoe.
azadilla f. Small hoe, gardener's hoe (escardillo).
azadón m. Hoe (instrumento agrícola). || *Azadón de peto* or *de pico,* mattock.
azadonada f. Stroke of *o* blow with a hoe.
azadonar v. tr. To hoe.
azadonazo m. Stroke of *o* blow with a hoe.
azafata f. Lady-in-waiting (en palacio). || Air hostess, stewardess (en avión).
azafrán m. Saffron.
azafranado, da adj. Saffron-flavoured, saffroned (guiso). || Saffron, saffron-coloured (color).
azafranal m. Saffron plantation.
azafranar v. tr. To add saffron to, to saffron. || To colour saffron.
azafranero, ra m. y f. Saffron grower (cultivador).
azagaya f. Assegai, assagai, light javelin.
azahar m. Orange blossom, lemon blossom. || — *Agua de azahar,* orange-flower water. || *Corona de azahar,* orange-blossom wreath.
azalea f. BOT. Azalea.
azar m. Chance (casualidad): *por puro azar encontré a mi amigo,* by pure chance I met my friend. || Accident, misfortune (desgracia). || — *Al azar,* at random. || *Juego de azar,* game of chance. || *Los azares de la vida,* the ups and downs of life.
azarado, da adj. Embarrassed, flustered.
azaramiento m. Frightening (acción de dar miedo). || Fright (susto). || Fear (miedo). || Embarrassment, fluster (confusión).
azarar v. tr. To embarrass, to fluster (avergonzar).
— V. pr. To be embarrassed (turbarse): *se azara fácilmente,* she is easily embarrassed. || To get flustered (perder la serenidad). || To go wrong, to turn out badly (malograrse).
azarosamente adv. With difficulty.
azaroso, sa adj. Risky, dangerous, hazardous (arriesgado). || Difficult: *una vida azarosa,* a difficult life.
ázimo adj. m. Unleavened. || *Pan ázimo,* unleavened bread, azyme, azym.
azimut m. ASTR. Azimuth (acimut).
azoado, da adj. QUÍM. (P.us.). Nitrogenous.
azoar v. tr. QUÍM. (P.us.). To nitrogenate.
azoato, ta adj. QUÍM. (P.us.). Nitrate.
ázoe m. QUÍM. (P.us.). Nitrogen, azote (nitrógeno).
azofaifo m. Jujube (fruto).
azófar m. Brass (latón).
azogadamente adv. Restlessly.
azogado, da adj. Quicksilvered, silvered (espejos). || MED. Suffering from mercurialism, mercurial. || FIG. Restless, fidgety (agitado).
— M. y f. MED. Person with mercurialism. || FIG. Restless *o* fidgety person. || — M. Silvering, quicksilvering (de un espejo). || FIG. *Temblar como un azogado,* to shake like a leaf.
azogador m. Silverer.
azogamiento m. Quicksilvering, silvering (de los espejos). || FIG. Restlessness, fidgetiness (agitación). || MED. Mercurialism, mercury poisoning.
azogar v. tr. To quicksilver, to silver (los espejos). || To slake (la cal viva).
— V. pr. MED. To contract mercurialism *o* mercury poisoning. || FIG. y FAM. To be restless *o* fidgety (agitarse mucho).
azogue m. Quicksilver, mercury (metal). || — FIG. *Ser un azogue* or *tener azogue en las venas,* to be always on the move, to never keep still for a minute. | *Temblar como el azogue,* to shake like a leaf.
azoico, ca adj. QUÍM. Nitric. || GEOL. Azoic.
azolar* v. tr. To adze, to adz, to dress with an adze *o* adz (la madera).
azor m. Goshawk (ave).
azorado, da adj. V. AZARADO.
azoramiento m. V. AZARAMIENTO.
azorar v. tr. V. AZARAR.
Azores n. pr. f. pl. GEOGR. *Islas Azores,* Azores.
azorrarse v. pr. To get drowsy.
azotacalles m. y f. inv. FAM. Idler, loafer.
azotado, da adj. Beaten. || Whipped, lashed, flogged (con un látigo). || Whipped (por el viento). || Lashed (por la lluvia). || Variegated (flor). || *Amer.* Striped (acebrado).
— M. Criminal condemned to be whipped (reo). || Penitent (disciplinante).
azotador, ra adj. Lashing (lluvia, viento).
azotaina f. Spanking, smacking (a los niños). || Beating (paliza): *dar una azotaina,* to give a beating. || Whipping, lashing, flogging (con un látigo).
azotamiento m. Whipping, lashing, flogging.
azotar v. tr. To whip, to lash, to flog (con un látigo). || To spank, to smack (a los niños). || To beat (pegar). || To whip (el viento). || To beat against, to lash: *el mar azotaba las rocas,* the sea beat against the rocks. || To beat down on, to lash: *la tormenta azotó la isla,* the storm lashed the island. || FIG. To scourge (la peste, una calamidad). || — *Azotar las calles,* to loaf about *o* to roam about *o* to idle about the streets. || FIG. *Azotar el aire,* to waste one's efforts, to flog a dead horse.
— V. pr. *Amer.* To idle, to loaf.
azotazo m. Smack (a un niño). || Lash (con un látigo).
azote m. Whip (látigo). || Cat-o'-nine tails (con nueve cuerdas). || Stroke [of the whip], lash [of the whip] (latigazo): *veinte azotes,* twenty lashes. || Spanking, smacking (golpes en las nalgas). || FIG. Lash, beating (del viento, del mar). | Scourge: *la peste es un azote,* the plague is a scourge; *Atila, el Azote de Dios,* Attila, the scourge of God. || — Pl. Public whipping *o* flogging (suplicio antiguo). || *Dar azotes* or *de azotes,* to whip, to flog, to lash.
azotea f. Flat roof (terraza). || *Amer.* Flat-roofed house. || FIG. y FAM. *Estar mal de la azotea,* to have bats in the belfry.
azotina f. FAM. Spanking, smacking.
azteca adj./s. Aztec.
azúcar m. o f. Sugar: *un terrón de azúcar,* a lump of sugar. || — *Azúcar blanco* or *de flor* or *floreta* or *refinado,* refined sugar. || *Azúcar cande* or *candi,* sugar candy. || *Azúcar de caña,* cane sugar. || *Azúcar de cortadillo* or *en terrones,* lump sugar. || *Azúcar de pilón,* loaf sugar. || *Azúcar de quebrados,* rough lump sugar. || *Azúcar en polvo,* powdered sugar. || *Azúcar extra fina,* castor sugar. || *Azúcar mascabada,* inferior cane sugar. || *Azúcar morena* or *negra,* brown *o* Demerara sugar. || *Azúcar terciada,* brown *o* Demerara sugar. || *Echar azúcar a,* to put sugar in, to sugar (el café, el té). || *¿Le pongo dos azúcares?,* would you like two lumps *o* two sugars?
— OBSERV. In the singular *azúcar* is more usually feminine than masculine, but in the plural it is always masculine: *los azúcares finos,* fine sugars.
azucarado, da adj. Sugared, sweetened: *café azucarado,* sugared coffee. || Sweet (dulce): *sabor azucarado,* sweet taste. || FIG. Sugary, sweet (almibarado).
azucarar v. tr. To sugar, to put sugar in, to sweeten: *azucarar el té,* to put sugar in one's tea. || FIG. To sweeten.
azucarera f. Sugar bowl (vasija para el azúcar). || Sugar factory (fábrica).
azucarería f. Sugar refinery *o* factory (fábrica). || *Amer.* Sugar shop (tienda).
azucarero, ra adj. Sugar: *industria azucarera,* sugar industry.
— M. Sugar bowl (recipiente). || Tree creeper (ave).
azucarillo m. Lemon candy used to flavour drinks.
azucena f. BOT. White *o* Madonna lily. || *Azucena de agua,* water lily.
azud m. o **azuda** f. Waterwheel (rueda). || Dam (presa).
azuela f. Adz, adze.
azufaifa f. Jujube (fruto).
azufaifo m. Jujube tree (árbol).
azufrado, da adj. Sulphured (plantas, toneles). || Sulphurated (impregnado de azufre). || Sulphur-coloured.
— M. Sulphuring.
azuframiento m. Sulphuring.
azufrar v. tr. To sulphur (toneles, plantas). || To sulphurate (impregnar de azufre).
azufre m. Sulphur. || *Flor de azufre,* flower of sulphur.
azufrera f. Sulphur mine (mina).
azufroso, sa adj. Sulphurous.
azul adj. Blue. || *Amer.* Indigo (añil). || — *Azul celeste, claro, oscuro, de cobalto, marino, de Prusia, de ultramar, verdoso,* sky, light *o* pale, dark *o* deep, cobalt, navy, Prussian, ultramarine, petrol blue. || *Azul turquí,* indigo. || *El príncipe azul,* Prince Charming. || *Enfermedad azul,* blue disease, cyanosis. || GEOGR. *La Costa Azul,* the Riviera. || *Sangre azul,* blue blood.
— M. Blue (color). || Blue, blueness (del cielo, del mar).
azulado, da adj. Bluish, blue.
— M. Blueing.
azulaque m. Lute.

azular v. tr. To colour blue, to blue.
— V. pr. To turn blue.
azulear v. intr. To look blue (mostrarse azul). || To be bluish, to have a bluish cast (tirar a azul).
— V. pr. To turn blue.
azulejar v. tr. To tile.
azulejería f. Tiling, tiles, *pl.* (revestimiento). || Tile manufacturing (fabricación). || Tile works, *pl.*, tile factory (fábrica).
azulejo m. Tile. || Glazed tile (con dibujos). || BOT. Bluebottle, cornflower (aciano). || ZOOL. Bee-eater (abejaruco). | Bluebird (pájaro).
— Adj. Bluish (azulado).
azulenco, ca adj. Bluish.
azuleo m. Blueing.
azulete m. Blue (para la ropa blanca). || *Dar azulete a*, to blue, to colour blue.
azulgrana adj. inv. Blue and scarlet.
azulillo m. Indigo dye.
azulino, na adj. Bluish.
azuloso, sa adj. Bluish.
azumar v. tr. To dye, to tint (los cabellos).
azúmbar m. BOT. Water plantain.
azumbrado, da adj. FIG. Tipsy (borracho).
azumbre f. "Azumbre" [liquid measure approximately equal to half a gallon].
azuquita m. Sugar.
azur adj./s. HERÁLD. Azure.
azurita f. MIN. Azurite.
azurronarse v. pr. To remain in the husk [grain of wheat].
azuzador, ra adj. Teasing, who teases. || FIG. Troublesome (molesto).
— M. y f. Troublemaker.
azuzar v. tr. To set [a dog] on s.o. (a los perros). || FIG. To incite, to urge (incitar).
— V. intr. To cause trouble, to stir things up.

B

b f. B: *una b mayúscula, minúscula*, a capital, small b. || *Probar por a más b*, to prove conclusively, to demonstrate clearly.

— OBSERV. When the Spanish *b* comes at the beginning of a word or after the letters *m* or *n* it is pronounced rather like the English *b*. In all other cases the pronunciation is less explosive than that of the English *b*.

baalita adj./s. Baalite.
baba f. Dribble (de niños), spittle, slobber (de adultos). || Froth, foam (de animales). || Sap (de plantas). || Slime (de caracoles). || — FIG. *Caérsele a uno la baba*, to be charmed, to be delighted (estar embelesado), to be an idiot. | *Se le cae la baba con su niño*, she dotes on her child.
babada f. Stifle.
babadero o **babador** m. *Amer.* Bib.
babaza f. Slime (de caracoles).
babear v. intr. To dribble (niños), to slobber (adultos). || To foam *o* to froth at the mouth (animales). || FIG. To drool [over a woman].
babel m. o f. Bedlam: *la casa es una babel*, it is bedlam in the house.
Babel n. pr. HIST. Babel: *Torre de Babel*, Tower of Babel.
babeo m. Dribbling (de niños), slobbering (de adultos). || Foaming, frothing (de animales). || Slime (de caracoles). || FIG. Drooling.
babera f. Beaver (de la armadura). || Bib (de niño).
babero m. Bib: *los niños llevan un babero para comer*, children wear a bib for eating. || Overall [U.S., frock] (bata). || Smock (para el colegio).
Babia n. pr. FIG. y FAM. *Estar en Babia*, to have one's head in the clouds.
babieca adj. FAM. Simple, silly.
— M. y f. Simpleton, fool.
Babieca n. pr. Babieca [El Cid's horse].
babilonia f. FIG. y FAM. Bedlam, mess.
Babilonia n. pr. f. GEOGR. Babylon (ciudad). | Babylonia (reino).
babilónico, ca adj. Babylonian.
babilonio, nia adj./s. Babylonian.
babilla f. Stifle.
babirusa f. ZOOL. Babiroussa, babirusa, wild hog (cerdo salvaje).
bable m. Asturian dialect.
babor m. MAR. Port, port side, larboard || — *A babor*, to port, on the port side. || *De babor a estribor*, athwartships. || *¡Tierra a babor!*, land to port!
babosa f. ZOOL. Slug.
babosear v. tr. To dribble over (niños), to slobber over (adultos).
— V. intr. FIG. To drool.
baboseo m. V. BABEO.
baboso, sa adj. Slimy (caracoles). || Dribbly (niños), slobbery (adultos). || FIG. Runny, lightly done (tortilla). || FIG. y FAM. Sloppy, maudlin (sentimental).
— M. FAM. Bore (empalagoso). | Drip (mocoso): *este chico es un baboso*, this boy is a drip. || FAM. *Viejo baboso*, dirty old man.
babucha f. Babouche, baboush, slipper, mule (zapatilla).
babuino m. ZOOL. Baboon (mono).
baby m. FAM. Overall [U.S., frock] (bata). | Smock (de niños). || *Amer.* Baby.
baca f. Top, roof (de la diligencia). || AUT. Roof *o* luggage rack. || Tarpaulin, rainproof cover (lona).
bacalada f. Cured cod, stockfish.
bacaladero, ra o **bacalaero, ra** adj. Cod-fishing. || *Industria bacaladera*, cod industry.
— M. Cod-fishing boat (barco). || Codfisherman (pescador).
bacalao m. Cod, codfish: *bacalao seco*, cured cod. || — FIG. y FAM. *Cortar* or *partir el bacalao*, to be the boss. | *Te conozco bacalao aunque vienes* or *vengas disfrazado*, I can see straight through you, you can't fool me.
bacanal f. Orgy (orgía). || — Pl. Bacchanalia.
bacante f. Bacchanal, bacchante.
bacarrá o **bacará** m. Baccarat (juego).
Baccarat n. pr. GEOGR. Baccarat. || *Cristal de Baccarat*, baccarat glass.
bacía f. Barber's bowl (de barbero). || Basin (recipiente).
bacilar adj. MED. Bacillary, bacillar.
baciliforme adj. Bacilliform, rod-shaped.
bacilo m. MED. Bacillus.
bacilosis f. MED. Bacillus infection (tuberculosis).
bacín m. Chamber pot (orinal). || Alms plate (para pedir limosna). || FIG. Cur (persona despreciable).
bacineta f. Alms plate (para limosna). || Small chamber pot (orinal).
bacinete m. Basinet (de armadura). || ANAT. Pelvis.
bacinica o **bacinilla** f. Alms plate (para limosna). || Small chamber pot (orinal).
Baco n. pr. m. Bacchus.
baconiano, na adj./s. Baconian (de Francis Bacon).
bacteria f. Bacterium.

— OBSERV. En inglés el plural de *bacterium* es *bacteria*.

bacteriano, na adj. Bacterial.
bactericida adj. Bactericidal, germ-killing.
— M. Bactericide, germicide.
bacteriología f. Bacteriology.
bacteriológico, ca adj. Bacteriological: *guerra bacteriológica*, bacteriological warfare.
bacteriólogo m. Bacteriologist.
báculo m. Walking stick, staff (bastón). || Crosier, crozier, staff (de obispo). || Staff (de peregrino). || FIG. Staff, support (apoyo). || FIG. *Báculo de la vejez*, comfort *o* help in one's old age.
bache m. Hole, pothole (en una carretera). || Air pocket (en avión). || FIG. Bad patch: *los baches de la vida*, the bad patches in life. | Slump (depresión).
bachicha o **bachiche** m. *Amer.* FAM. Eyetie [italiano].
bachiller m. y f. Holder of the General Certificate of Education [U.S., holder of a high school diploma]. || HIST. Bachelor (de una universidad).
bachiller, ra m. y f. FIG. y FAM. Chatterbox (hablador). || — F. FIG. y FAM. Bluestocking.
bachillerato m. General Certificate of Education, G.C.E. [U.S., high school diploma]. || HIST. Bachelor's degree. || — *Bachillerato elemental*, lower certificate ["O" level]. || *Bachillerato superior*, higher certificate ["A" level].

— OBSERV. The term *bachillerato* is more general than G.C.E. or high school diploma, as it denotes the whole period of one's secondary education (*estoy en quinto de bachillerato*, I am in the fifth form). The *bachillerato* ends with a final examination called the *reválida*, and is followed by a year's preparatory study for those wishing to go on to university.

bachillerear intr. FAM. To prattle away (charlar).
bachillería f. FAM. Prattle (charla).
badajada f. o **badajazo** m. Stroke of a bell (de campana). || FIG. y FAM. Rubbish, sth. stupid: *soltar una badajada*, to talk rubbish, to come out with sth. stupid.
badajear v. intr. To prattle away.
badajo m. Clapper (de campana). || FIG. y FAM. Chatterbox (charlatán).
badajocense o **badajoceño, ña** adj. [Of a from] Badajoz.
— M. y f. Native *o* inhabitant of Badajoz.
badana f. Sheepskin, basan, bazan (piel). || FIG. y FAM. *Zurrarle a uno la badana*, to tan s.o.'s hide (pegar), to give s.o. a dressing down (reprender).
badén m. Furrow drain (para las aguas de lluvia). || Pothole, hole (en una carretera). || Uneven road surface (señal de tráfico).
baderna f. MAR. Nipper.
badián m. Anise (árbol).
badiana f. Aniseed (fruto).
badil m. o **badila** f. Fire shovel. || FIG. y FAM. *Darle a uno con la badila en los nudillos*, to rap s.o.'s knuckles.
bádminton m. Badminton (juego del volante).
badulacada f. FAM. Silly *o* stupid thing.
badulaque m. y f. Fool, nincompoop (idiota). || *Amer.* Rogue (pillo).
baffle m. RAD. Baffle (caja de resonancia).
baga f. Flaxseed head, boll.
bagaje m. MIL. Baggage. || *Amer.* Luggage [U.S., baggage] (equipaje). || Beast of burden (acémila). || FIG. Stock of knowledge (intelectual).

— OBSERV. This word is a Gallicism in the sense of luggage.

bagar v. intr. To go to seed (lino).
bagatela f. Knick-knack (objeto pequeño). || Trifle: *no hay por qué enfadarse por bagatelas*, it is not worth getting angry over such trifles. || Triviality: *no gastemos el tiempo en bagatelas*, let us not waste time with trivialities.
bagazo m. Waste pulp (de la caña de azúcar). || Husk (del lino). || Marc (de aceitunas, uvas, etc.). || *Amer.* Cur (persona despreciable).
bagre m. Catfish (pez). || *Amer.* FIG. y FAM. Crafty one, sly one (persona lista). | Hag (mujer fea). | Unfriendly person (persona antipática).
bagual adj. *Amer.* Wild (animal). | Rough (persona).
— M. *Amer.* Wild horse (caballo). | FIG. Bumpkin, yokel [U.S., hick].
bagualada f. *Amer.* Herd of wild horses. | — FAM. *Decir bagualadas*, to talk rubbish. | *Decir una bagualada*, to come out with a stupid remark.
bagualón m. Half-tamed horse.
baguarí m. *Amer.* Type of white stork.
baguío m. Hurricane [in the Philippines].
¡bah! interj. Bah!
bahareque m. *Amer.* V. BAJAREQUE.
baharí m. Hobby (halcón).
bahía f. GEOGR. Bay: *la bahía de Málaga*, the bay of Malaga.
bailable adj. For dancing, dance: *música bailable*, music for dancing, dance music. || — *Esta música no es bailable*, you can't dance to this music. || *Amer. Té bailable*, tea dance.
— M. Ballet (ballet).
bailador, ra m. y f. Dancer.

— OBSERV. This word applies to Spanish folk dancers, especially Flamenco dancers. It is usually written *bailaor*. In the more general sense, dancer is translated by *bailarín*.

bailaor, ra m. y f. Flamenco dancer.
bailar v. intr. To dance. || To spin (el trompo). || FIG. To dance. || FIG. y FAM. To swim: *mis pies bailan en los zapatos*, my feet swim in these shoes. || — *Bailar agarrado*, to dance close together. || FIG. *Bailar al son que tocan*, V. SON. || *Bailar como una peonza* or *un trompo*, to spin like a top. || FIG. y FAM. *Bailar con la más fea*, to get the short end of the stick. || *Bailar de puntas*, to dance on points. || FIG. *Bailar en la cuerda floja*, to walk the tightrope. || FIG. y FAM. *Le bailaban los ojos de alegría*, his eyes sparkled with joy. | *Otro que tal baila*, they are two of a kind. | *¡Que me quiten lo bailado!*, nothing can take away the good times I've had. || *Sacar a bailar a una chica*, to ask a girl to dance.
— V. tr. To dance: *bailar un vals*, to dance a waltz. || To spin (el trompo).
bailarín, ina adj. Dancing.
— M. y f. Dancer. || Ballet dancer (de baile clásico). || — F. Ballerina (de baile clásico).
baile m. Dance: *música de baile*, dance music. || Dancing (acción): *me gusta el baile*, I like dancing. || Dance, ball (v. OBSERV.): *voy al baile*, I am going to the dance. || Ballroom, dance hall (lugar). || TEATR. Ballet. || — *Baile clásico*, ballet. || FAM. *Baile de candil* or *de botón gordo*, local hop, public dance. || *Baile de etiqueta*, ball, formal dance. || *Baile de gala*, gala ball. || *Baile de máscaras* or *de disfraces*, masked ball, fancy dress ball. || *Baile de piñata*, carnival ball. || *Baile de San Vito*, Saint Vitus's dance. || *Baile de trajes*, fancy dress ball. || *Baile folklórico*, folk dancing. || FIG. *Dirigir el baile*, to rule the roost, to run the show.

— OBSERV. La palabra inglesa *ball* se refiere sobre todo a los bailes de etiqueta.

baile m. Bailiff (magistrado).
bailete m. TEATR. Ballet.
bailía f. Bailiwick.
bailiaje m. Bailiwick.
bailiazgo m. Bailiwick.
bailío m. Knight commander of Malta. || Bailiff (magistrado).
bailón, ona m. y f. FAM. Dancing enthusiast, keen dancer.
bailongo m. *Amer.* Public dance.
bailotear v. intr. To jig about, to dance about.
bailoteo m. Jigging about, dancing about: *le gusta mucho el bailoteo*, he loves dancing about.
baivel m. Bevel (escuadra falsa).
baja f. Fall, drop, decrease (de los precios, de la temperatura). || Drop (en la Bolsa). || Ebb (de la marea). || MIL. Loss, casualty: *el ejército tuvo muchas bajas en el combate*, the army suffered many losses in the battle. || — *Baja por enfermedad*, sick leave. || *Dar de baja*, to report missing (a un soldado muerto, un desertor), to discharge as unfit (en el servicio militar), to lay off (a un obrero, un empleado), to give notice to (despedir), to strike off the list (echar de una sociedad). || *Darse de baja*, to resign, to drop out (dejar de pertenecer, dimitir), to take sick leave (declararse enfermo). || *Darse de baja en una suscripción*, to withdraw one's subscription. || *Estar dado de baja*, to be on sick leave, to be off sick (por enfermedad). || *Estar de* or *en baja*, to be dropping *o* falling *o* going down (perder valor). || *Jugar a la baja*, to bear (en la Bolsa). || *Ser baja*, to be reported missing (un soldado), to be struck off the list (en una sociedad, etc.).
bajá m. Pasha (dignatario turco).
bajada f. Ebb (de las aguas). || Slope (pendiente). || Descent, going down (descendimiento). || Way down: *la bajada hacia el río*, the way down to the river. || Drop (caída). || — *Bajada de aguas*, down pipe, down spout. || *Bajada de bandera*, minimum fare (en un taxi). || *Bajada del telón*, fall *o* lowering of the curtain (teatro).
bajamar m. Low tide, low water.
bajante f. *Amer.* Low tide, low water.
bajapieles m. inv. Orange stick (de manicura).
bajar v. intr. To go down, to descend, to sink: *el Sol bajaba detrás de las colinas*, the sun went down behind the hills. || To come down: *bajaré a verte ahora mismo*, I'll come down and see you right away. || To go down: *no bajaré a verle*, I will not go down and see him. || To get off (de una bicicleta, un caballo, un autobús): *bajar del autobús*, to get off the bus. || To get out (de un coche). || To ebb, to go out *o* down (la marea). || To go down, to drop, to fall (los precios, la temperatura). || To fall (ventas, compras): *nuestros pedidos no han bajado de quinientos*, our orders have not fallen below five hundred. || To fail (la vista). || FIG. To go down: *Miguel ha bajado en mi estima*, Michael has gone down in my esteem. || — *Bajar de tono*, to lower one's tone. || *No bajará de dos horas*, it will take at least two hours.
— V. tr. To get *o* to bring *o* to take down: *bájame este libro de la repisa*, get that book down from the shelf for me; *baja esta botella a la bodega*, take this bottle down to the cellar; *bájame la maleta del desván*, bring me the suitcase down from the attic. || To lower [down]: *bajar el cubo al pozo*, to lower the bucket [down] into the well. || To go down, to come down: *para ir a la cocina hay que bajar la escalera*, to get to the kitchen you have to go down the stairs; *baja la escalera para que te hable*, come down the stairs so that I can speak to you. || To bow, to bend: *bajar la cabeza en signo de deferencia*, to bow one's head in deference. || To lower, to bend: *bajó la cabeza para pasar por la puerta*, he lowered his head to go through the door. || To put down: *baja el brazo*, put your arm down. || To turn down: *bajar las alas de un sombrero*, to turn down the brim of a hat. || To lower (cortina, párpados, voz, precios). || To give *o* to make a reduction: *me ha bajado la cuenta*, he has given me a reduction on the bill. || To turn down (radio, etc.). || To lessen (reducir). || — FIG. *Bajar el orgullo a uno*, to take s.o. down a peg or two. || *Bajar el tono*, to lower one's tone. || FIG. *Bajarle los humos a uno*, to put s.o. in his place, to take s.o. down a peg or two. || *Bajar sus pretensiones*, to lower one's aspirations.
— V. pr. To stoop, to bend over *o* down (inclinarse). || To get off (de una bicicleta, un autobús, un caballo). || To get out (de un coche).

— OBSERV. The verb *bajar* in the reflexive from can mean "to go or to come down with a certain effort": *me bajo la escalera veinte veces al día*, I go up and down the stairs twenty times a day.

bajareque m. *Amer.* Wattle and daub wall (pared). | Hut, hovel (choza).

bajel m. Vessel, ship.
bajero, ra adj. Bottom, lower: *sábana bajera*, bottom sheet.
bajete m. Mús. Baritone.
bajeza f. Baseness, lowness (del carácter, de los sentimientos). || Vile deed *o* action (acción). || Vulgarity (de una expresión).
bajines (por) o **bajini (por lo)** adv. Fam. On the sly, on the quiet, in an underhand way: *hacer algo por bajines*, to do sth. in an underhand way. | In a whisper: *hablar por bajines*, to speak in a whisper. || Fam. *Reírse por lo bajini*, to laugh up one's sleeve.
bajío m. Sandbank, shoal. || *Amer.* Lowland.
bajista m. Bear.
bajito adv. Quietly, softly: *le gusta hablar bajito*, he likes to speak quietly.
bajo, ja adj. Low: *una silla baja*, a low chair. || Small, short (estatura): *una mujer muy baja*, a very small woman. || Downcast, lowered, on the ground: *con los ojos bajos*, with downcast eyes, with one's eyes on the ground. || Bowed, lowered: *con la cabeza baja*, with bowed head. || Low (cifra, precios). || Pale, pallid (color): *azul bajo*, pale blue. || Base (metal). || Low: *Bajo Latín*, Low Latin. || Lower (en comparación con algo más alto): *el Bajo Rin*, the lower Rhine: *en la parte baja de la casa*, in the lower part of the house. || Soft (sonido). || Low (voz): *en voz baja*, in a low voice. || Humble, low (nacimiento). || Menial (tarea). || Mús. Deep (sonido, voz). || Fig. Degrading (degradante). | Vile, low (acción). | Disgraceful, base (conducta). | Lowly (de condición). | Lower: *clase baja*, lower class. | Base, contemptible (motivo). | Overcast, low (cielo). || — *Baja temporada*, off season, slack season. || *Bajo relieve*, low relief, bas-relief. || Fig. *Bajos fondos*, scum, dregs, depths (de la sociedad), low district, *sing.* (de una ciudad). || Impr. *Caja baja*, lower case. || *De baja ralea*, low-class. || *En este bajo mundo*, here below. || *Golpe bajo*, low punch, blow below the belt. || *Los barrios bajos*, the lower-class districts. || *Monte bajo*, bush. || *Tierras bajas*, lowlands.
— Adv. Low: *este avión vuela bajo*, this aeroplane flies low. || In a low voice, softly: *hablar bajo*, to speak in a low voice. || Quietly, softly: *cantar bajo*, to sing quietly. || *¡Más bajo!*, not so loud!
— Prep. Under: *bajo la dominación romana*, under Roman rule. || Under, underneath, beneath: *bajo el árbol*, under the tree. || On: *bajo palabra*, on one's word. || In: *bajo la lluvia*, in the rain. || Below: *dos grados bajo cero*, two degrees below zero. || — *Bajo el reinado de*, in the reign of, under the reign of. || *Bajo juramento*, under oath, on oath || *Bajo mano*, secretly, sneakily. || *Bajo pena de muerte*, under penalty of death. || *Bajo tutela*, under guardianship (un menor de edad), under trusteeship (un país). || *Echando por bajo*, at the very least, at the lowest estimate. || *Por lo bajo*, in secret, on the quiet (fam.) [en secreto], in a whisper, under one's breath (en voz baja), at the very least (por lo menos). || *Tirando por bajo*, at the very least, at the lowest estimate.
— M. Lowland (terreno). || Mar. Shoal, sandbank. || Hollow (hondonada). || Ground floor [U.S., first floor] (piso). || Mús. Cellist (artista). | Cello (instrumento). | Bass (cantante, voz). || — Pl. Underclothes (ropa interior). || Bottoms (de pantalones). || Hem, *sing.* (de una falda). || Ground floor, *sing.* [U.S., first floor, *sing.*] (piso).
bajón m. Mús. Bassoon (instrumento). | Bassoonist (músico). || Com. Slump. || Fig. y fam. Great drop, fall (bajada brusca). | Turn for the worse (salud, situación): *dar un bajón*, to take a turn for the worse. | Fall, slump (de la moral).
bajonazo m. Taur. V. golletazo.
bajonista m. Mús. Bassoonist.
bajorrelieve m. Low relief, bas-relief.
bajuno, na adj. Base, vile, mean.
bajura f. *Navegación de bajura*, coasting. || *Pesca de bajura*, inshore fishing, coastal fishing.
bakelita f. Bakelite.
bala f. Bullet (de escopeta, pistola): *a prueba de balas*, bullet-proof. || Cannonball (de cañón). || Bale (de algodón). || Bale, pack (de lana). || — *Bala fría*, spent bullet. || *Bala perdida*, stray bullet. || *Bala trazadora*, tracer bullet. || Fig. *Como una bala*, like a shot. || *¿Cuántas balas te quedan?*, how many shots have you left? || *Amer. Ni a bala*, by no means. || Fam. *Salir como una bala*, to shoot out.
— M. Fam. Hooligan (golfo). || — Fig. y fam. *Bala perdida*, scatterbrain. | *Bala rasa*, hothead, daredevil.
balada f. Ballad (canción). || Ballade, ballad (poema).
baladí adj. Trivial, trifling: *asuntos baladíes*, trivial matters.
baladrón, ona adj. Boastful, bragging.
— M. y f. Braggart.
baladronada f. Brag, boast (bravuconería). || Bravado, piece of bravado (acción). || *Decir* or *soltar baladronadas*, to brag, to boast.
baladronear v. intr. To brag, to boast.
balagar m. Haystack, hayrick.
bálago m. Grain stalk, straw (paja).
balaj o **balaje** m. Balas (rubí).
balalaica m. Mús. Balalaika.
balance m. Com. Balance sheet (declaración): *hacer el balance*, to draw up the balance sheet. | Stocktaking (inventario). | Balance (de una cuenta). || Fig. Result. || *Hacer el balance (de)*, to take stock [of], to make an inventory [of] (en una empresa), to weigh up, to take stock [of] (la situación).
balancé m. Balancing (paso de baile).
balancear v. tr. To balance.
— V. intr. Fig. To hesitate (vacilar). || To roll (un barco).
— V. pr. To rock (en una mecedora). || To swing (en un columpio, etc.). || To roll (un barco). || To oscillate, to swing to and fro (un péndulo).
balanceo m. Swinging (de un columpio). || Rocking (de una mecedora). || Rolling, roll (barco). || To-and-fro motion, oscillation (de un péndulo).
balancín m. Swingletree (de vehículo). || Rudder bar (de avión). || Beam (de máquina). || Rocker, rocker arm (de motor). || Balance pole (de volatinero). || Seesaw [U.S., seesaw, teeter-totter] (columpio). || Rocking chair (mecedora). || Outrigger (para dar estabilidad a una barca). || Coining press (para acuñar monedas).
balandra f. Mar. Sloop (barco).
balandrista m. y f. Mar. Yachtsman (hombre), yachtswoman (mujer).
balandro m. Mar. Yacht (de vela).
bálano o **balano** m. Anat. Glans penis. || Acorn barnacle, balanus (molusco).
balanza f. Scales, *pl.*, balance (para pesar). || Com. Balance: *balanza comercial, de cuentas, de pagos*, balance of trade, of accounts, of payments. || Comparison (confrontación). || *Amer.* Balance pole (de volatinero). || — *Balanza romana*, steelyard. || Fig. *Estar en la balanza*, to be in the balance. | *Inclinar el fiel de la balanza*, to tip the balance *o* the scales. | *Poner en balanza*, to weigh up, to compare (comparar), to put in the balance (poner en juego).
Balanza n. pr. f. Astr. The Scales, Libra.
balar v. intr. To bleat, to baa (las ovejas).
balarrasa m. Fig. Hothead, daredevil.
balastar v. intr. To ballast.
balasto o **balastro** m. Ballast (grava).
balata f. Ballade, ballad (poesía).
balaustrada f. Balustrade, railing.
balaustrar v. tr. To build a balustrade on.
balaustre o **balaústre** m. Banister, baluster (columnita).
balay m. *Amer.* Wicker basket.
balazo m. Shot (tiro). || Bullet wound (herida): *murió de un balazo*, he died of a bullet wound. || *Le dieron un balazo en el pecho*, he was shot in the chest.
balboa m. Balboa [Panamanian currency].
balbucear v. tr. e intr. To stammer, to stutter. || To babble (un niño).
balbuceo m. Stammering, stuttering. || Babble, babbling (de un niño).
balbuciente adj. Stammering, stuttering. || Babbling (niño).
balbucir* v. tr. e intr. V. balbucear.
Balcanes n. pr. m. pl. Geogr. Balkans.
balcánico, ca adj. Balkan.
balcón m. Balcony: *asomarse al balcón*, to look over the balcony. || Fig. y fam. *Es cosa de alquilar balcones*, it is sth. not to be missed, it is sth. worth seeing.
balconada f. o **balconaje** m. Row of balconies.
balconcillo m. Enclosure over the bullpen (en la plaza de toros). || Teatr. Dress circle.
balconear v. tr. *Amer.* To watch out of the window.
— V. intr. *Amer.* To talk at the window.
balda f. Shelf (de un armario).
baldada f. *Amer.* Bucket.
baldado, da adj. Crippled, disabled. || Fig. y fam. Shattered (cansado).
— M. y f. Cripple (inválido).
baldadura f. o **baldamiento** m. Disability, infirmity.
baldaquín o **baldaquino** m. Baldachin, canopy.
baldar v. tr. To cripple, to maim, to disable. || To trump (en los naipes). || Fam. To beat up (dar una paliza). | To inconvenience (molestar). | To cripple: *este impuesto le ha baldado*, this tax has crippled him. || Fam *Estar* or *quedarse baldado*, to be shattered [U.S., to be bushed] (estar cansado).
— V. pr. Fig. y fam. To wear o.s. out, to break one's back.
balde m. Mar. Pail (cubo de madera) || Bucket (de metal). || — Fig. y fam. *Caerle a uno como un balde de agua fría*, to hit s.o. like a ton of bricks. || Fig. *De balde*, free of charge, free: *viajar de balde*, to travel free of charge. || *En balde*, in vain, for nothing: *tanto esfuerzo en balde*, so much effort in vain.
baldear v. tr. To swill down, to wash down (lavar). || To bale out (achicar).
baldeo m. Swilling.
baldíamente adv. In vain, fruitlessly, for nothing.
baldío, a adj. Waste, uncultivated (sin cultivo): *terreno baldío*, waste land. || Agr. Uncultivated. || Fig. Useless, fruitless, vain: *esfuerzos baldíos*, vain efforts.
— M. Waste *o* uncultivated land.
baldón m. Insult (afrenta): *esto es un baldón para nosotros*, this is an insult to us. || Shame, disgrace: *este hijo es el baldón de la familia*, this son is the shame of the family.
baldonar v. tr. To insult. || To disgrace, to shame.
baldosa f. Tile. || Flagstone (de mayor tamaño).

baldosado m. Tiling, flagging (acción). || Tiled floor, flagging (suelo).
baldosador m. Tiler.
baldosar v. tr. To tile (con baldosas pequeñas). || To flag (con baldosas grandes).
baldosín m. Tile.
baldragas adj. FAM. Spineless, meek.
— M. inv. FAM. Mouse.
balduque m. Tape (cinta). || FIG. Red tape (papeleo).
balear v. tr. *Amer.* To shoot.
balear adj Balearic: *Islas Baleares*, Balearic Islands.
— M. y f. Native *o* inhabitant of the Balearic Islands. || — F. pl. GEOGR. Balearics.
baleárico, ca adj. Balearic.
balénidos m. pl. ZOOL. Whales.
baleo m. Mat (estera). || *Amer.* Exchange of shots (tiroteo).
balido m. Bleat (grito de las ovejas). || Bleating (varios gritos). || *Dar balidos*, to bleat, to baa.
balín m. Small bullet (pequeña bala). || Shot (perdigón).
balista m. MIL. Ballista.
balístico, ca adj. Ballistic: *proyectiles balísticos*, ballistic missiles.
— F. Ballistics.
balita f. *Amer.* Marble (canica).
balitar v. intr. To bleat continually.
baliza f. MAR. Buoy, beacon. || AVIAC. Beacon.
balizar v. tr. MAR. To mark out with buoys, to beacon. || AVIAC. To mark out with beacons, to beacon.
balneario, ria adj. *Estación balnearia*, spa, watering place (medicinal), seaside resort (con playa).
— M. Spa, watering place (medicinal), seaside resort (con playa).
balneoterapia f. Balneotherapy.
balompédico, ca adj. Of football, football [U.S., of soccer, soccer].
balompié m. Football [U.S., soccer].
balón m. Ball, football (pelota). || QUÍM. Bag. || Bale (fardo). || — *Balón alto*, lob [U.S., fly ball] (fútbol), up-and-under (rugby). || *Balón de fútbol*, football. || *Balón de oxígeno*, oxigen cylinder. || *Balón muerto*, dead ball.
balonazo m. Blow [from a ball].
baloncesto m Basketball: *jugador de baloncesto*, basketball player
balonmano m. Handball (juego).
balonvolea m. Volleyball (juego).
balota f. Ballot (para votar).
balotada f. Ballotade (salto del caballo).
balotaje m. *Amer.* Voting (votación). | Tie (empate en una elección).
balotar v. intr. *Amer.* To ballot, to vote by ballot papers.
balsa f. Raft (embarcación): *balsa insuflable*, inflatable raft. || Pond, pool (charca). || BOT. Balsa (árbol y madera). || *Amer.* Ferry. || — FIG. *Como una balsa (de aceite)*, as calm as a millpond (mar). | *Este lugar es una balsa de aceite*, this is a very quiet place.
balsadera f. o **balsadero** m. Ferry crossing.
balsamera f. Flask for balsam.
balsamero m. Balsam fir (árbol).
balsámico, ca adj. Balsamic, balmy, soothing. || BOT. *Álamo balsámico*, balsam poplar.
balsamina f. Balsam apple (planta).
bálsamo m. Balm, balsam. || BOT. Balsam. || FIG. Balm.
balsar m. *Amer.* Overgrown marshland.
balsero m. Ferryman.
Baltasar n. pr. m. Balthasar. || Belshazzar (de Babilonia).
báltico, ca adj. Baltic: *el mar Báltico*, the Baltic Sea.
— M. Baltic language (lengua).
Báltico n. pr. m. GEOGR. Baltic Sea.
balto, ta adj./s. Baltic.
baluarte m. Bastion, bulwark || FIG. Bastion, bulwark, stronghold: *esta provincia es un baluarte del Cristianismo*, this province is a bulwark of Christianity.
baluma o **balumba** f. Bulk (bulto). || Pile (montón). || Racket, din (barullo). || Mess (desorden).
ballena f. Whale (mamífero). || Stay, bone (de corsé). || Bone (de cuello). || ASTR. Whale.
ballenato m. Whale calf, young whale.
ballenero, ra adj. Whaling.
— M. Whaler (pescador). || Whaler, whaling ship (barco). || — F. Whaler, whaling ship (barco).
ballesta f. Crossbow (arma antigua). || Ballista (máquina de guerra). || Spring (de coche).
ballestero m. Crossbowman. || Maker of crossbows.
ballestilla f. Swingletree (balancín pequeño). || Fleam (navajilla de veterinario).
ballet m. Ballet (baile y música): *los ballets rusos*, the Russian ballets.
ballico m. BOT. Rye grass.
ballueca f. Wild oats, *pl.* (gramínea).
bamba f. Fluke (en el billar). || *Amer.* Name of several currencies. | Knar (en un árbol). | "Bamba" [popular Mexican dance] (baile).
bambalear v. intr. V. BAMBOLEAR.
bambalina f. TEATR. Border. || — FIG. *Actor nacido entre bambalinas*, actor born into the profession, actor born on the stage. | *Detrás de las bambalinas*, behind the scenes.
bambalinón m. TEATR. Valance.
bambarria m. y f. FAM. Dumb (tonto). || — F. Fluke (en el billar).
bambino, na m. y f. *Amer.* Child.
bamboche m. FAM. Plump person.
bambolear, bambolearse v. intr. y pr. To swing. || To sway, to reel (titubear al andar, etc.). || To sway: *el árbol se bambolea*, the tree sways. || To wobble: *la mesa se bambolea*, the table wobbles. || To rock, to roll: *el barco se bambolea*, the ship is rolling. || To sway, to rock (vehículo). || *Hacer bambolear*, to rock.
bamboleo m. Swinging. || Rocking, rolling (de un barco). || Swaying, rocking (de un coche). || Wobble: *el bamboleo de la mesa me impide escribir*, the wobble of the table prevents me from writing. || Swaying, reeling (de una persona). || Swaying (de un árbol, etc.).
bambolla f. FAM. Sham, show (fachada). | Show, fuss: *una fiesta con mucha bambolla*, a party with lots of show. || *Amer.* Chatter (charla). | Bragging (fanfarronería).
bambollero, ra adj. FAM. Bragging (fanfarrón). | Showy (aparatoso).
bambú m. BOT. Bamboo.

— OBSERV. The plural form of *bambú* is *bambúes*.

banal adj. Banal, commonplace.
banalidad f. Banality. || Triviality (palabra).
banana f. Banana (fruto). || Banana tree (árbol).

— OBSERV. In Spain the usual word for *banana* or *banana tree* is *plátano*. *Banana* or *banano* is usually employed in Latin America.

bananal o **bananar** m. *Amer.* Banana plantation.
bananero, ra adj. Banana: *producción bananera*, banana production.
— M. Banana tree (árbol). || Banana boat (barco).
banano m. Banana (fruto). || Banana tree (árbol).
banasta f. Hamper, large basket (cesto).
banastero, ra m. y f. Basket maker (fabricante). || Basket dealer (vendedor).
banasto m. Large round basket (cesto).
banca f. Bench (asiento). || Bank (juegos): *hacer saltar la banca*, to break the bank. || COM. Banking: *el sector de la banca*, the banking sector. | Bank (establecimiento de crédito). || Stand (de lavandera). || Type of Philippine canoe. || *Amer.* Bench (asiento, escaño en el Parlamento). || — *Copar la banca*, to hold the bank (bacarrá). || *Amer. Tener banca*, to have connections (tener influencias). || *Tener la banca*, to be banker.

— OBSERV. At present the word *banca* or *casa de banca* is rarely used to mean a banking establishment, the usual term being *banco*, but, when referring to the banking profession or to all the banks as a whole, *banca* is commonly employed: *la nacionalización de la banca*, *la banca hace jornada intensiva*.

bancada f. Stone bench (banco). || Large table (mesa). || Thwart (de un bote de remos). || TECN. Bed (soporte). || MIN. Step. || — Pl. Litter, *sing.* (en una cuadra).
bancal m. Patch, bed (de verduras): *bancal de lechugas*, lettuce patch. || Terrace (en una montaña). || Bench cover (tapete). || *Campo de bancales*, terraced field.
bancario, ria adj. Bank: *descuento bancario*, bank discount; *cheque bancario*, bank check. || Banking: *sistema bancario*, banking system.
bancarrota f. Bankruptcy. || FIG. Bankruptcy, complete failure. || *Hacer bancarrota*, to go bankrupt.
banco m. Bench (de piedra, de madera, de carpintero). ||Settee (en un salón, una antesala). || Pew (en una iglesia). || Form, desk (en el colegio). || COM. Bank (establecimiento de crédito). [V. BANCA, *Observ.*] || Bank, shoal (de arena). || Thwart (de una barca). || Shoal, school (de peces). || JUR. Box [U.S., seat] (de los testigos). || ARQ. Attic, garret (sotabanco). || GEOL. Layer (estrato). || *Amer.* Dock (de los acusados). | Bank (juego). || — *Banco agrícola*, farmer's bank. || *Banco azul*, front bench (en las Cortes). || *Banco de ahorros*, savings bank. || *Banco de arena*, sandbank. || MAR. *Banco de coral*, coral reef. || *Banco de emisión*, issuing bank. || *Banco de hielo*, ice floe. || *Banco de liquidación*, clearing house. || *Banco de préstamos*, lending bank [U.S., loans bank]. || *Banco de pruebas*, testing bench. || *Banco de sangre*, blood bank. || *Banco hipotecario*, mortgage bank. || *Banco Mundial*, World Bank. || *Banco por acciones*, joint-stock bank. || *Billete de banco*, bank note. || *Empleado de banco*, bank clerk.
banda f. Sash, band (faja). || Ribbon (cinta, condecoración). || Strip (de una momia). || Party, group (grupo de personas). || Throng (multitud de personas). || Gang, pack (de ladrones, de gente desordenada). || Group (de animales en general). || Flock (de pájaros). || Covey (de perdices). || Side (lado): *de la banda de acá de la montaña*, on this side of the mountain. || Bank (orilla): *de la banda de allá del río*, on the opposite bank of the river. || Lane (de una carretera). || Strip (de tierra). || Wing (de un partido político). || Cushion (billar): *jugar por la banda*, to play off the cushion. || MÚS. Band. || RAD. Band: *banda de frecuencia*, frequency band. || MAR. Side: *de banda a banda*, from side to side. || HERÁLD. Bend. || REL. Humerus. || *Amer.* Leaf (de puerta). | Flap (de ventana). || — MAR. *Arriar en banda*, to cast off. || MAR. *Banda de estribor*, starboard side. || *Banda de rodadura*, tread (de una rueda). || *Banda de tambores*, drum corps. || CINEM. *Banda sonora*, sound track. || *Banda transportadora*, conveyor belt. || FIG. y FAM. *Cerrarse en*

banda, to stick to one's guns. || MAR. *Dar a la banda*, to lie alongside ship. || DEP. *Fuera de banda*, in touch. || MAR. *Irse a la banda*, to list. || DEP. *Juez de banda*, linesman (fútbol, tenis), touch judge (rugby). | *Línea de banda*, sideline, touchline. | *Quedarse en la banda*, to stay on the sideline. | *Saque de banda*, throw-in (fútbol), line-out (rugby).

bandada f. Flock (de pájaros). || Covey (de perdices). || Shoal, school (de peces). || Party (de personas)

bandazo m. MAR. Violent roll. || FAM. Stroll (paseo). || *Dar bandazos*, to swerve, to lurch (coche).

bandear v. tr. *Amer.* To cross (cruzar). | To shoot through (traspasar de un balazo). | To pursue (perseguir). | To wound (herir). | To court (a una mujer).
— V. pr. To manage, to look after o.s., to get by: *sabe bandearse*, he knows how to manage, he can look after himself.

bandeja f. Tray. || *Amer.* Dish (fuente). || — *Bandeja para los cubiletes de hielo*, ice tray. || FIG. *En bandeja de plata*, on a silver platter *o* plate. | *Poner* or *traer algo en bandeja a alguien*, to hand sth. to s.o. on a plate.

bandera f. Flag: *la bandera española*, the Spanish flag; *bandera blanca*, white flag. || Flag, colours, *pl.* [U.S., colors]: *izar la bandera*, to hoist the flag *o* the colours; *la bandera del regimiento*, the regimental colours. || Banner (estandarte): *la bandera de una cofradía*, the banner of a guild. || (Ant.). MIL. Company (compañía). || — FIG. *A banderas desplegadas*, in the open, openly. || MAR. *Afianzar*, *afirmar* or *asegurar la bandera*, to enforce the colours by a shot. || MIL. *Alzar* or *levantar (la) bandera*, to raise men. || MAR. *Arriar (la) bandera*, to haul down the flag, to strike one's colours. || *Bajada de bandera*, minimum fare (taxi). || MAR. *Bandera amarilla*, quarantine flag. || *Bandera de Gran Bretaña*, Union Jack, British flag. || MAR. *Bandera de inteligencia*, answering flag. || *Bandera de los Estados Unidos de América*, Stars and Stripes, American flag. || *Bandera de parlamento* or *de paz*, flag of truce. || MAR. *Bandera de popa*, ensign. | *Bandera de práctico*, pilot flag. | *Bandera de proa*, jack. || *Bandera a media asta*, flag at half-mast. || MIL. *Batir banderas*, to salute with the colours. || FIG. y FAM. *De bandera*, terrific. || *Jurar la bandera*, to take the pledge of allegiance to the flag. || FIG. y FAM. *Lleno hasta la bandera*, full to the brim, packed full. || *Militar bajo* or *seguir la bandera de uno*, to follow s.o.'s flag. || MAR. *Rendir la bandera*, to salute with the colours. || MIL. *Salir con banderas desplegadas*, to come out with flying colours.

bandería f. Faction, party (partido).

banderilla f. TAUR. "Banderilla". || IMPR. Sticker indicating a correction. || Cocktail snack on a stick (tapa). || *Amer.* FIG. y FAM. Tapping, touching (sablazo). || — TAUR. *Banderilla de fuego*, banderilla with fireworks attached. || FIG. y FAM. *Clavar* or *plantar* or *poner banderillas a uno*, to taunt s.o., to goad s.o.

banderillazo m. *Amer.* FAM. Tapping, touching (sablazo).

banderillear v. tr. TAUR. To stick the "banderillas" in [a bull].

banderillero m. TAUR. "Banderillero".

banderín m. MIL. Pennant (bandera). | Pennant bearer (soldado). || Signal flag (ferrocarriles). || DEP. Flag (de un juez de línea). || *Banderín de enganche*, recruiting office.

banderita f. Little flag. || *Fiesta de la banderita*, flag day.

banderizo, za adj. Factious, seditious. || FIG. Turbulent, fiery.

banderola f. Banderole. || MIL. Pennant (con dos o varias puntas). || *Amer.* Transom (de una puerta).

bandidaje m. Banditry, brigandage.

bandido m. Bandit, outlaw, brigand. || FIG. Crook, bandit: *este comerciante es un bandido*, this shopkeeper is a crook.

bando m. Edict, proclamation: *echar un bando*, to proclaim an edict, to make a proclamation. || Decree: *bando de policía, de la alcaldía*, police decree, mayor's decree. || Party, faction (facción). || Flock (de pájaros). || Shoal, school (de peces). || — Pl. Marriage banns (amonestaciones). || FIG. *Pasarse al otro bando*, to go over to the other side.

bandola f. MÚS. Mandolin, mandoline. || MAR. Jurymast.

bandolera f. [Woman] bandit (mujer). || Bandoleer, bandolier (correa). || — *A la* or *en bandolera*, over one's shoulder. || *A la bandolera*, in a sling (brazo).

bandolerismo m. Banditry, brigandage.

bandolero m. Brigand, bandit, highwayman (bandido).

bandolina f. MÚS. Mandolin, mandoline (bandola).

bandolinista m. y f. Mandoline player.

bandoneón m. MÚS. Concertina.

bandullo m. FAM. Paunch, belly (vientre).

bandurria f. MÚS. Mandola, mandora.

baniano m. Banian (miembro de una secta brahmánica).

banjo m. MÚS. Banjo.

banquear v. tr. *Amer.* To level.

banquero, ra m. y f. Banker.

banqueta f. Bench, long seat, form (banco corrido). || Wall seat (de restaurante, etc.). || Stool (taburete). || Footstool (para los pies). || Banquette, bank (terraplén). || MIL. Berm, banquette. || Pavement [U.S., sidewalk] (acera).

banquetazo m. Slap-up meal, huge feast.

banquete m. Banquet, feast (festín).

banquetear v. tr. e intr. To banquet.

banquillo m. JUR. Dock. || Stool, footstool (taburete). || Bench (de zapatero). || FIG. *Colocar* or *sentar a uno en el banquillo de los acusados*, to have s.o. on the carpet.

banquisa f. Ice floe, ice field.

bántam m. DEP. Bantamweight. || *Gallina bántam*, bantam.

banzo m. Frame, edge (del bastidor para bordar). || Upright (de una escalera de mano, de una silla).

baña f. V. BAÑADERO.

bañadera f. *Amer.* Bath, bathtub (bañera).

bañadero m. Lair (de un jabalí).

bañado m. *Amer.* Marsh, bog, swamp (pantano).

bañador, ra m. y f. Bather, swimmer (que se baña). || — M. Bathing costume, swimsuit, bathing suit (traje de baño de mujer y de hombre), bathing trunks, *pl.* (de hombre). || *Bañador de dos piezas*, two-piece swimsuit, two-piece bathing costume.

bañar v. tr. To bath, to bathe (a un niño). || To dip, to bathe, to immerse (un cuerpo). || To wash (el mar): *costas bañadas por el mar*, coasts washed by the sea. || To water, to wash (un río): *el arroyo bañaba hermosas huertas*, the brook watered some beautiful gardens. || To coat, to cover: *un pastel bañado en chocolate*, a cake coated in chocolate. || To bathe, to flood (luz, sol, etc.): *el sol baña la habitación de una luz cruda*, the sun floods the room with *o* bathes the room in a harsh light. || FIG. *Bañado en llanto* or *en lágrimas*, *en sangre*, *en sudor*, bathed in tears, in blood, in sweat.
— V. pr. To bathe, to have a swim, to go swimming (en el mar). || To take *o* to have a bath (en la bañera).

bañera f. Bath, bathtub (baño).

bañero m. Lifesaver, lifeguard.

bañil m. Lair (de un jabalí).

bañista m. y f. Bather, swimmer (en el mar). || Patient at a spa (en un balneario).

baño m. Bath. || Swim, dip (de mar, de río). || Bath, bathtub (bañera). || Coat (capa): *un baño de pintura*, a coat of paint. || Coating, covering (de chocolate, etc.). || FIG. Smattering: *allí reciben un baño de formación militar*, there they receive a smattering of military training. | Touch: *tiene un cierto baño de distinción*, he has a touch of class. || QUÍM. Bath. || — Pl. Baths. || — *Baño de asiento, de vapor*, hip bath, steam bath. || *Baño (de) maría*, bain-marie. || *Baños de mar*, sea bathing, *sing.* || FIG. *Baño de sangre*, bloodbath. || *Baño de sol*, sunbath. || *Baño turco*, Turkish bath: *esta habitación es un baño turco*, it is like a Turkish bath in here. || *Casa de baños*, public baths. || *Darse un baño*, to take a bath. || FIG. *Darse un baño de francés, de matemáticas, etc*, to brush up one's French, mathematics, etc. || FAM. *Dar un baño a uno*, to outshine s.o. (superar), to beat s.o. hollow: *el equipo rojo ha dado un baño al equipo verde*, the red team beat the green team hollow. || *Ir a los baños*, to take the waters, to go for a water cure. || *Tomar un baño*, to take a bath. || *Tomar un baño de mar*, to go for a swim, to take a dip, to bathe in the sea. || *Tomar un baño de sol*, to sunbathe.

bao m. MAR. Beam.

baobab m. BOT. Baobab.

baptista m. y f. Baptist.

baptisterio m. Baptistry, baptistery (edificio). || Font (pila).

baque m. Bang, bump (golpe). || Fall (caída).

baqueano, na adj./s. V. BAQUIANO.

baquear v. intr. MAR. To drift with the current.

baquelita Bakelite.

baqueta f. Cleaning rod, ramrod (de fusil). || ARQ. Beading. || — Pl. Drumsticks (de tambor). || FIG. y FAM. *Llevar or mandar* or *tratar a la baqueta*, to rule with an iron hand, to treat harshly.

baqueteado, da adj. Hardened (avezado). || Experienced (experimentado).

baquetear v. tr. FIG. To treat harshly (tratar mal). | To train, to harden, to season (ejercitar). | To bother, to put out (incomodar).

baqueteo m. Bother (molestia). || Hardening, seasoning, training (ejercitación). || Jolting, shaking (traqueteo).

baquía f. Local knowledge, local expertise (conocimiento de una región). || *Amer.* Skill, expertise (habilidad).

baquiano, na adj. *Amer.* Experienced, expert (experto): *ser baquiano en el comercio*, to be experienced in commerce.
— M. y f. Guide (guía). || *Amer.* Local expert.

báquico, ca adj. Bacchic, bacchanalian.

báquira o **baquira** m. *Amer.* ZOOL. Peccary.

bar m. Bar, café, snack bar. || Bar (unidad de presión atmosférica).

baraca f. Luck (suerte).

baracuda f. Barracuda (pez).

barahúnda f. Uproar, row, din (alboroto). || Confusion, chaos, uproar (confusión): *meterse en la barahúnda*, to get mixed up in the confusion.

baraja f. Pack [of cards], deck [of cards] (de naipes).

|| FIG. Quarrel, argument (disputa). || FIG. y FAM. *Jugar con dos barajas*, to double-deal.

— OBSERV. The Spanish pack is composed of 48 cards. — La baraja inglesa consta de 52 cartas.

barajar v. intr. To fall out (*con*, with) [enemistarse]. — V. tr. To shuffle (naipes). || FIG. To mix up, to shuffle around (mezclar, revolver). | To juggle with, to play with (cifras, nombres). | To be in the balance: *barajaron varios nombres para esta colocación*, several names were in the balance for this job. || *Amer.* FIG. To catch (agarrar al vuelo). | To hinder, to obstruct, to get in the way of (estorbar). || FIG. *Barajar ideas*, to toy with ideas.

baranda f. Handrail, banister (de escalera). || Balustrade, handrail, railing (de un balcón). || Cushion (de billar).

barandado o **barandaje** m. Railing, balustrade, handrail.

barandal m. Base (larguero inferior de una balustrada). || Rail, handrail (larguero superior). || Banister (barandilla).

barandilla f. Handrail, banister (de una escalera). || Balustrade (balaustrada). || Handrail, balustrade, railing (de un balcón). || Bar (de un tribunal). || *Amer.* Rail (de un carro).

baratear v. tr. To sell off cheap, to sell at a loss (saldar).

baratería f. JUR. Barratry. || Fraud, fraudulence (fraude). || MAR. Barratry.

baratía f. *Amer.* Cheapness, low price.

baratija f. Trinket, bauble (frusleria). || — Pl. Rubbish, *sing.*, junk, *sing.* (cosas sin valor).

baratillero m. Secondhand dealer, junk dealer.

baratillo m. Secondhand shop, junk shop (tienda). || Secondhand sale, jumble sale (subasta). || Secondhand goods, *pl.*, jumble, junk (conjunto de cosas).

barato, ta adj. Cheap, inexpensive (no caro): *una falda barata*, a cheap skirt. || — *Lo barato es* or *sale caro*, cheap things are dear in the long run. || *Salir barato*, to turn out cheap.

— M. Sale, bargain sale, clearance sale (venta).

— Adv. Cheap, cheaply: *vender barato*, to sell cheap *o* cheaply.

báratro m. POÉT. Kingdom of the dead, Hades (infierno).

baratura f. Cheapness, low price.

baraúnda f. V. BARAHÚNDA.

barba f. Beard (pelo): *barba cerrada* or *bien poblada*, thick beard (v. OBSERV.). || Beard (de cabra, etc.). || Wattle (de ave). || Chin (parte de la cara). || Whalebone (de ballena). || AGR. Swarm (enjambre). | Upper part of beehive (de la colmena). || — Pl. Barbs (de pluma, flecha, planta, papel). || Beard, *sing.*: *barbas enmarañadas*, bushy beard. || — *Barba corrida*, full beard. || *Barbas de chivo*, goatee. || FAM. *Con toda la barba*, for good. || FIG. *Cuando las barbas del vecino veas pelar, echa las tuyas a remojar*, when the next house is on fire, it's high time to look to your own. || FAM. *Echar a las barbas de uno*, to throw in s.o.'s face. | *En las barbas de uno*, to *o* in s.o.'s face: *reírse en las barbas de uno*, to laugh to *o* in s.o.'s face. || *Hacer la barba*, to shave (afeitar), to butter up (adular). || FIG. *Hazme la barba, hacerte he el copete*, you scratch my back and I will scratch yours. || *Llevar o gastar barba*, to have a beard. || FIG. y FAM. *Nos salió a tanto por barba*, it cost us so much per head. | *Subirse a las barbas de*, to treat disrespectfully. | *Tener pelos en la barba*, to be old enough to look after o.s. | *Tener pocas barbas*, to be wet behind the ears. || *Tirarse de las barbas*, to tear one's hair out.

— OBSERV. *Barba* is also expressed in the plural form in Spanish, usually to indicate a thick or bushy beard.

barba m. TEATR. Old man's part (comediante).

Barba Azul n. pr. m. Bluebeard.

barbacana f. Barbican (fortificación, tronera).

barbacoa f. Barbecue (parrilla). || Barbecued *o* grilled meat (carne asada). || *Amer.* Litter, rough bed [made from a mat of rushes fastened to four stakes]. | Hut [built on stilts or in a tree] (choza). | Loft (para guardar los granos).

barbada f. Lower jaw (de un caballo). || Curb (cadenilla del freno). || Brill (pez). || *Amer.* V. BARBOQUEJO.

barbado, da adj. Bearded.

— M. Shoot (sarmiento). || Cutting (esqueje). || Shoot, sucker (rama que brota al pie de un árbol).

Barbados n. pr. GEOGR. Barbados.

Bárbara n. pr. f Barbara

bárbaramente adv. Barbarously, savagely. || FIG. Terribly well, awfully well.

barbaridad f. Barbarity, cruelty (crueldad). || Outrage, atrocity: *durante la guerra se cometieron barbaridades*, during the war outrages were committed. || FIG. Nonsense (palabra): *decir barbaridades*, to talk *o* to speak nonsense. | Terrible thing (acción). || — FAM. *Comer una barbaridad*, to eat an awful lot *o* like a horse. | *Costar una barbaridad*, to cost a fortune. | *Habla una barbaridad*, she goes on and on, she never stops talking. || FIG. y FAM. *Hacer barbaridades*, to act the fool. | *Me divertí una barbaridad*, I had a marvellous time. | *¡Qué barbaridad!*, how awful!, how terrible! (¡qué vergüenza!), good grief!, fancy that! (de asombro), it's amazing *o* incredible: *¡qué barbaridad, hay que ver cómo las ciencias adelantan!*, it's incredible the way science progresses. | *Se ve una barbaridad*, it is terribly obvious (es evidente), you see them everywhere (se ven mucho). | *Una barbaridad*, an awful lot, a lot, lots: *bebe una barbaridad*, he drinks an awful lot; *una barbaridad de libros*, lots of books, an awful lot of books.

barbarie f. FIG. Barbarism, barbarity.

barbarismo m. GRAM. Barbarism. || FIG. Barbarity (crueldad).

barbarizar v. intr. To talk *o* to speak nonsense.

bárbaro, ra adj. HIST. Barbarian. || FIG. Barbaric, barbarous (cruel, grosero): *un soldado bárbaro*, a barbarous *o* barbaric soldier. | Daring, bold, reckless (temerario). | Rough, uncouth (bruto). || FAM. Fantastic, terrific, fabulous, marvellous (muy bueno): *esta película es bárbara*, this film is fantastic. | Massive (muy grande). || — FAM. *Hace un calor bárbaro*, it is terribly hot. | *Hacer un efecto bárbaro*, to have a tremendous effect. | *Lo he pasado bárbaro*, I had a great *o* a fantastic time. | *¡Qué bárbaro!*, fantastic!, great!

— M. y f. Barbarian. || FIG. Lout, brute.

— Interj. FAM. Great!, fantastic!

barbarote, ta adj. FAM. Brutish, savage.

— M. y f. FAM. Brute.

barbear v. tr. *Amer.* To shave (afeitar). | To butter up (adular). | To throw (un animal).

barbechar v. tr. AGR. To leave fallow (dejar descansar la tierra). | To fallow, to plough (arar).

barbechera f. o **barbecho** m. AGR. Fallow land, fallow. || *Estar en barbecho*, to be left fallow, to be in fallow.

barbería f. Barber's shop, barber's.

barberil adj. FAM. Barber's.

barbero, ra adj. *Navaja barbera*, cutthroat razor [U.S., straight razor].

— M. Barber.

barbeta f. Barbette (fortificación).

barbián m. FAM. Gay dog.

barbicano adj. m. With a white *o* grey beard, white-bearded, grey-bearded: *un hombre barbicano*, a white-bearded man, a man with a white beard.

barbicastaño adj. m. With a brown beard, brown-bearded.

barbiespeso adj. m. With a bushy beard, thick-bearded.

barbijo m. *Amer.* V. BARBOQUEJO.

barbilampiño adj. m. Smoothfaced, beardless (sin barba). || With a scanty beard (con poca barba).

— M. FIG. Greenhorn, novice (novicio).

barbilindo o **barbilucio** m. Dandy.

barbilla f. ANAT. Chin. || Barb, barbel (de pez). || TECN. Tenon. || VET. Ranula.

barbillas m. *Amer.* Scantily bearded man.

barbillera f. Chin strap

barbinegro adj. m. Black-bearded.

barbiquejo m. Chin strap (barboquejo). || *Amer.* Halter (cabestro). || MAR. *Barbiquejo de bauprés*, bobstay.

barbirrojo adj. m. Red-bearded, ginger-bearded.

barbirrubio adj. m. Fair-bearded, blond-bearded.

barbirrucio adj. m. Grey-bearded.

barbitúrico adj./s.m. QUÍM. Barbiturate.

barbo m. Barbel (pez). || *Barbo de mar*, red mullet (salmonete).

barbón m. Bearded man. || He-goat, billy goat (macho cabrío).

barboquejo m. Chin strap.

barbotar o **barbotear** v. tr. e intr. To mumble, to mutter.

barboteo m. Mumbling, muttering.

barbotina f. TECN. Barbotine, slip (cerámica).

Barbuda n. pr. f. GEOGR. Barbuda.

barbudo, da adj. Bearded.

— M. *Amer.* Shoot, sucker (de árbol).

barbulla f. FAM. Din, row.

barbullador, ra m. y f. Stammerer.

barbullar v. intr. To stammer.

barbullón, ona m. y f. Stammerer.

barbuquejo m. Chin strap (barboquejo).

barca f. Boat: *barca de pesca*, fishing boat. || *Barca de pasaje*, ferryboat.

barcada f. Boatload (carga de una barca). || Crossing (viaje).

barcaje m. Ferrying, transport (transporte). || Fare (lo que se paga).

barcarola f. MÚS. Barcarolle, barcarole.

barcaza f. Lighter, barge (embarcación). || Ferryboat, ferry (transbordador). || MIL. *Barcaza de desembarco*, landing craft.

Barcelona n. pr. GEOGR. Barcelona.

barcelonés, esa adj. [Of *o* from] Barcelona.

— M. y f. Native *o* inhabitant of Barcelona.

barceo m. BOT. Esparto, esparto grass.

barcia f. Chaff (del trigo).

barcino, na adj. Reddish, rust-coloured (color).

— M. y f. *Amer.* FIG. y FAM. Turncoat (que muda de partido).

barco m. Boat: *ir en barco*, to go by boat. || Ship, vessel (grande). || Car, nacelle (de un globo). || Cockpit, capsule (de nave espacial). || Gully, shallow ravine (barranco). ‖ — *Barco aljibe* or *cisterna*, tanker. ‖ *Barco bomba*, fireboat. ‖ *Barco de guerra*, warship. ‖ *Barco del práctico*, pilot boat. ‖ *Barco de pasajeros*, liner, passenger liner. ‖ *Barco de recreo*, pleasure boat. ‖ *Barco de vapor*, steamer, steam boat (pequeño), steam ship, steamer (grande). ‖ *Barco de velas*, sailing boat (pequeño), sailing ship (grande), yacht (yate). ‖ *Barco faro*, lightship. ‖ *Barco mercante* or *de carga*, merchant boat, cargo boat (pequeño), merchant ship, cargo ship (grande). ‖ *Barco náufrago*, wreck, wrecked ship. ‖ *Barco ómnibus*, pleasure boat, pleasure steamer. ‖ *Barco patrullero*, patrol boat.

— OBSERV. *Barco* is a very general term; *buque* and *navío* are only used for vessels of large tonnage; *nave* is a poetic or archaic word (*las naves de Cristóbal Colón*).

barchilón, ona m. y f. *Amer.* Nurse (de un hospital). | Quack (curandero).

barda f. Bard (armadura de caballo). ‖ Protective covering of brambles [on a wall] (de una tapia). ‖ MAR. Low black cloud (nubarrón oscuro).

bardado, da adj. Barded (caballo).

bardal m. Bramble-topped wall (tapia). ‖ Fence (vallado).

bardana f. BOT. Burdock (lampazo).

bardar v. tr. To top with brambles (una tapia). ‖ To bard (con una armadura).

bardo m. Bard (poeta).

baremo m. Scale, schedule (de impuestos, precios). ‖ Ready reckoner (libro para hacer cálculos).

bargueño m. Decorated Spanish cabinet.

— OBSERV. The *bargueño*, a typically Spanish piece of furniture, is a richly decorated cabinet which stands on legs and has a large number of small drawers.

baria f. Barye (unidad de presión).

baricentro m. Barycentre.

barín m. Lord, nobleman.

bario m. Barium (metal).

barisfera f. Barysphere.

barita f. QUÍM. Baryta.

baritina f. MIN. Barytes.

barítono m. MÚS. Baritone.

barloa f. MAR. Mooring rope.

barloar v. tr. MAR. To moor (a un muelle). | To moor alongside (un barco con otro).

barloventear v. intr. MAR. To tack to windward. ‖ FIG. y FAM. To wander about (vagabundear).

barlovento m. MAR. Windward: *banda de barlovento*, windward side; *estar a barlovento*, to be to windward. ‖ GEOGR. *Islas de Barlovento*, Windward Isles.

barman m. Barman.

— OBSERV. In Spanish the plural of *barman* is *barmans*.

barn m. FÍS. Barn (unidad de superficie).

barnabita adj./s. Barnabite.

barnacla m. Barnacle goose (pato marino).

barnio m. FÍS. Barn.

barniz m. Varnish (muebles). ‖ Glaze (cerámica). ‖ Makeup (afeite). ‖ Nail varnish (para las uñas). ‖ FIG. Veneer: *sólo tiene un barniz de cultura*, he only has a veneer of culture. | Smattering (conocimiento superficial). ‖ BOT. *Barniz del Japón*, laquer tree, varnish tree.

barnizado m. Varnishing, varnish (madera). ‖ Glazing, glaze (cerámica).

barnizador m. Varnisher (madera). ‖ Glazer (cerámica).

barnizar v. tr. To varnish (madera). ‖ To glaze (cerámica).

barógrafo m. Barograph.

barométrico, ca adj. Barometric, barometrical.

barómetro m. Barometer: *barómetro aneroide, registrador, de mercurio, de cubeta*, aneroid, recording, mercury, cistern barometer.

barón m. Baron (título).

baronesa f. Baroness (título).

baronet m. Baronet (título).

baronía f. Barony (dignidad, territorio).

baroscopio m. FÍS. Baroscope.

barquear v. tr. To cross in a boat, to sail across. ‖ To row across (remando).

barquero, ra m. y f. Boatman (hombre), boatwoman (mujer) ‖ FIG. *Decirle* or *cantarle a uno las verdades del barquero*, V. VERDAD.

barqueta f. o **barquete** m. o **barquichuelo** m. Small boat (barco pequeño).

barquilla f. MAR. Log chip, log ship. ‖ Basket, nacelle, car (de un globo). ‖ Nacelle (de un motor de avión).

barquillero, ra m. y f. Wafer seller.

barquillo m. Rolled wafer.

barquín m. Large bellows (fuelle).

barquinazo m. Jolt (tumbo). ‖ Overturning, roll (vuelco). ‖ *Dar barquinazos*, to jolt (dar tumbos), to overturn, to turn over (volcar).

barquito m. Soldier, finger (de pan).

barra f. Bar (de madera, metal, chocolate, jabón de lavar). ‖ Rod (vara delgada y redonda). ‖ Rod (de cortinas). ‖ Ingot, bar (de plata, oro). ‖ Lever, crowbar (palanca). ‖ Stick (de lacre, de jabón de afeitar). ‖ Crossbar (de bicicleta). ‖ Pin (joya). ‖ French loaf (pan de forma alargada). ‖ Block (de hielo). ‖ Bar (banco de arena). ‖ Bar (mostrador): *tomar una cerveza en la barra*, to have a beer at the bar. ‖ HERÁLD. Bar. ‖ JUR. Witness box (de los testigos). | Dock (de los acusados). | Bar (que separa el público del tribunal). ‖ MAR. Tiller, bar (de barca), helm (de barco grande). ‖ MÚS. Bar. ‖ DEP. Kind of javelin. ‖ *Amer.* Audience (público). ‖ — Pl. Bars (de la quijada del caballo). ‖ — AUT. *Barra de acoplamiento*, track rod. ‖ *Barra de labios* or *de carmín*, lipstick. ‖ DEP. *Barra fija*, horizontal bar. ‖ *Barra para cortinas*, curtain rod. ‖ *Barras paralelas*, parallel bars. ‖ *Ejercicios en la barra*, bar exercises. ‖ JUR. *Llevar a la barra*, to impeach, to bring to court. ‖ FIG. *No pararse en barras*, not to stop at anything, to stop at nothing.

barrabás m. FIG. y FAM. Rascal, little scamp (niño). | Scamp, rogue, villain (tunante).

Barrabás n. pr. m. Barabbas.

barrabasada f. FAM. Dirty *o* low trick (mala jugada). ‖ — FAM. *Decir barrabasadas*, to talk nonsense. | *Hacer barrabasadas*, to get up to mischief, to play up (ser malo), to play the fool (hacer tonterías).

barraca f. Hut, cabin. ‖ Stand, stall (en las ferias). ‖ Thatched house [in the Valencian and Murcian *huertas*]. ‖ *Amer.* Shed. | Stall (en un mercado). | Barracks, *pl.* (militar).

barracón m. Large hut *o* cabin. ‖ Large stand *o* stall. ‖ *Barracón de tiro al blanco*, shooting gallery, rifle range.

barracuda f. Barracuda.

barrado, da adj. Striped, streaked: *tela barrada*, striped material. ‖ HERÁLD. Barred.

barragana f. Concubine.

barraganería f. Concubinage.

barraganete m. MAR. Stanchion, futtock

barranca f. Ravine, gully (barranco).

barrancal m. Ravinated land.

barranco m. Ravine, gully. ‖ Precipice, cliff (precipicio). ‖ FIG. Obstacle, difficulty. ‖ FIG. *Salir del barranco*, to get out of trouble.

barrancoso, sa adj. Ravinated.

barranquera f. Ravine, gully (barranco).

barredero, ra adj. Sweeping. ‖ MAR. *Red barredera*, trawl.

— F. Sweeper (máquina): *barredera de alfombras*, carpet sweeper. ‖ Road sweeper (de calles).

barredor, ra adj. Sweeping.

— F. Road sweeper (municipal). ‖ *Barredora-regadora*, road cleaner.

barredura f. Sweeping. ‖ — Pl. Sweepings (basura).

barreminas m. inv. Minesweeper.

barrena f. Drill, bit (sin mango). ‖ Auger, gimlet, drill (con mango). ‖ Jumper, jumper bar (de minero). ‖ — *Barrena de mano*, gimlet. ‖ *Entrar en barrena* or *hacer la barrena*, to go into a spin (un avión).

barrenado, da adj. FAM. Barmy, daft, dotty (loco).

barrenador m. Person who lays explosive charges, blaster.

barrenadora f. Drill, boring machine.

barrenar v. tr. To drill, to bore (abrir agujeros). ‖ To mine (una roca, etc.). ‖ MAR. To scuttle (un barco). ‖ FIG. To undermine, to frustrate (un proyecto, una empresa). | To infringe, to break, to violate (las leyes, los reglamentos). ‖ TAUR. To twist the pikehead in the bull's wound.

barrendero, ra m. y f. Sweeper.

barrenero m. Driller, borer (minero).

barrenillo m. ZOOL. Borer.

barreno m. Large mechanical drill *o* borer (barrena grande). ‖ Bore, borehole, drill hole (agujero). ‖ MIN. Charge (de pólvora). ‖ Blasthole (taladro). ‖ FIG. Constant worry (preocupación). | Vanity, presumptuousness (vanidad). ‖ *Amer.* Idiosyncrasy, mania (manía). ‖ MAR. *Dar barreno a un barco*, to scuttle a ship.

barreño m. Earthenware bowl (de barro). ‖ Bowl (metálico, de plástico).

barrer v. tr. To sweep (limpiar). | To sweep, to rake (con un arma). ‖ FIG. To sweep, to trail on: *su abrigo era tan largo que barría el suelo*, his overcoat was so long that it swept the floor. | To sweep away: *el viento barre las hojas secas*, the wind sweeps the dead leaves away. | To sweep aside (un adversario). ‖ — FIG. *Barrer con todo*, to make a clean sweep, to take everything away. | *Barrer para adentro*, to look after number one.

barrera f. Barrier, gate (cierre de un camino). ‖ Gate (de paso a nivel). ‖ FIG. Barrier: *los Pirineos sirven de barrera natural entre España y Francia*, the Pyrenees act as a natural barrier between Spain and France. | Obstacle, barrier (obstáculo). ‖ Claypit (de arcilla). ‖ MIL. Barricade (barricada). | Barrage (de tiros). ‖ TAUR. Barrier, fence (para saltar el torero). | Ringside seat, seat in the first row (localidad). ‖ Defensive wall (fútbol): *formar barrera*, to form a defensive wall. ‖ — *Barrera coralina*, coral reef. ‖ *Barrera de contención*, retaining wall. ‖ *Barrera del sonido*, sound barrier. ‖ *Barrera racial*, colour bar. ‖ *Barreras arancelarias*, customs barriers. ‖ FIG. *Poner barreras a*, to obstruct, to hinder.

barrero m. Potter (alfarero). ‖ Claypit (de arcilla). ‖ Mire, bog (barrizal). ‖ *Amer.* Saltpetrous land (terreno salitroso).

barreta f. Small bar (barra pequeña). ‖ Jumper bar (de minero, albañiles). ‖ Bar (de turrón, etc.). ‖ *Amer.* Pickaxe (pico).

barretear v. tr. To bar, to fasten with bars. || *Amer.* To jump, to drill (abrir agujeros con la barrena).
barretero m. MIN. Miner, drill runner.
barretina f. Catalan cap (gorro).

— OBSERV. The *barretina* resembles the Phrygian cap.

barretón m. Pickaxe.
barriada f. Quarter, district [in the suburbs].
barrial m. Claypit (gredal). || Mire, quagmire (barrizal).
barrica f. Barrel, cask (tonel).
barricada f. Barricade (obstáculo): *levantar una barricada*, to put up *o* to erect a barricade.
barrida f. o **barrido** m. Sweeping. || Swoop, raid (de la policía). || — Pl. Sweepings, swept-up rubbish (barreduras). || — *Dar un barrido ligero*, to run the broom round. || FIG. *Lo mismo sirve para un barrido que para un fregado*, he is a jack-of-all-trades.
barriga f. Belly (vientre). || FAM. Paunch, potbelly, corporation: *tiene mucha barriga*, he has quite a paunch. | Belly, bulge (de una vasija). || Bulge (de una pared). || — *Dolor de barriga*, bellyache. || *Echar barriga*, to get a paunch, to get fat. || POP. *Hacer una barriga a una chica*, to get a girl pregnant. || FIG. *Llenar el ojo antes que la barriga*, to have eyes bigger than one's belly. || FAM. *Llenarse la barriga*, to fill one's belly. | *Rascarse la barriga*, to lounge about, to twiddle one's thumbs.
barrigón, ona o **barrigudo, da** adj. FAM. Potbellied.
— M. y f. FAM. Tiny tot, kiddy, little child (niño).
barriguera f. Bellyband, girth (arreo).
barril m. Barrel, cask (tonel): *un barril de vino*, a barrel of wine. || Keg (de pólvora). || Keg, herring barrel (para pescado salado). || Small earthenware jug (de barro). || — *Cerveza de barril*, draught beer. || FIG. *Este país es un barril de pólvora*, this country is a powder keg.
barrilaje m. o **barrilamen** m. o **barrilería** f. *Amer.* Stock of barrels *o* casks.
barrilero m. Cooper.
barrilete m. Small barrel. || Clamp, dog (de carpintero). || Fiddler crab (crustáceo). || Chamber (de un revólver). || Barrel (de un clarinete). || *Amer.* Kite (cometa). | Tubby person (persona gorda). | Junior barrister (pasante de abogado).
barrilla f. BOT. Saltwort, barilla.
barrillar m. Place covered with saltwort.
barrillo m. Blackhead (en la piel).
barrio m. District, area: *una ciudad se divide en varios barrios*, a city is divided in several districts; *un barrio residencial*, a residential district. || Quarter (v. OBSERV.) || Suburb (arrabal). || — *Barrio de las latas*, shantytown, slums, *pl.*, slum area. || FIG. y FAM. *El otro barrio*, the other world. | *Irse al otro barrio*, to kick the bucket. || *Los barrios bajos*, the lower-class districts. || FAM. *Mandar a uno al otro barrio*, to do s.o. in. | *Ser el hazmerreír de todo el barrio*, to be the laughingstock of the whole neighbourhood.

— OBSERV. En inglés, la palabra *quarter* se emplea hoy día sobre todo para designar un barrio donde viven extranjeros (*the Chinese quarter*, el barrio chino).

barriobajero, ra adj. Vulgar, low-class, common: *acento barriobajero*, vulgar *o* low-class accent.
barrista m. Gymnast who works on the horizontal bar.
barritar v. intr. To trumpet, to bellow (el elefante).
barrito m. Bellowing, trumpeting (del elefante).
barrizal m. Mire, quagmire (lodazal).
barro m. Mud (lodo): *después de un aguacero los caminos están llenos de barro*, after a shower the paths are covered with mud. || Clay (arcilla). || Earthenware, clay: *jarro de barro*, earthenware jar. || Earthenware (objetos de barro). || FIG. Trifle, mere nothing (cosa sin importancia). || MED. Blackhead (granillo). | Pustule (pústula). || *Amer.* Blunder, clanger (metedura de pata). || — *Barro cocido*, baked earth. || *Barro de alfareros*, modelling clay, potters' clay. || *Barro esmaltado*, glazed terra-cotta. || *Barro refractario*, fireclay. || *Dios hizo al hombre de barro*, God made man from dust. || FIG. y FAM. *Estar comiendo* or *mascando barro*, to be pushing up daisies (estar enterrado). | *Estar de barro hasta los ojos*, to be up to one's eyes in mud. || *Mancharse de barro*, to spatter o.s. with mud, to get mud on o.s.
barroco, ca adj. Baroque. || FIG. Ornate, extravagant (con adornos superfluos).
— M. Baroque period (período). || Baroque style (estilo).
barroquismo m. Baroque style. || FIG. Extravagance.
barroso, sa adj. Clayish (con arcilla). || Muddy (lleno de barro). || Earth-coloured, brownish (de color rojizo). || Pimply, spotty: *rostro barroso*, pimply face.
barrote m. Bar: *barrotes de hierro*, iron bars. || Crosspiece (entre las patas de un mueble). || Rung (peldaño).
barruntador, ra adj. Prophetic: *signos barruntadores*, prophetic signs.
barruntamiento m. Presentiment.
barruntar v. tr. To have a feeling: *barrunto que me va a dar un sablazo*, I have a feeling that he is going to touch me for a loan. || To suppose, to guess (suponer).
barrunte o **barrunto** m. Sign, indication (indicio). || Feeling, presentiment (presentimiento). || Suspicion (sospecha). || Guess (suposición). || *Tener barruntos de que*, to have a feeling that.
bartola (a la) loc. adv. FIG. y FAM. Carelessly, nonchalantly. || — FAM. *Echarse* or *tenderse* or *tumbarse a la bartola*, to put one's feet up, to idle away one's time: *este alumno se ha tumbado a la bartola durante el segundo semestre*, this student idled his time away during the second term.
bartolillo m. Type of small meat pie.
Bartolomé n. pr. m. Bartholomew.
bártulos m. pl. Things, odds and ends, bits and pieces: *preparar todos los bártulos para un viaje*, to get all the things ready for a trip; *llévate tus bártulos de aquí*, take your odds and ends away from here; *compró todos los bártulos para pintar*, he bought all the bits and pieces he needs for painting. || FIG. y FAM. *Liar los bártulos*, to pack one's bags.
barullero, ra adj./s. Riotous.
barullo m. FAM. Confusion, hubbub, din, racket. | Hell (alboroto): *armar barullo*, to raise hell. | Confusion: *tengo tal barullo en la cabeza que no comprendo nada*, there is so much confusion in my head that I cannot understand a thing. || — FAM. *A barullo*, galore: *había pasteles a barullo*, there were cakes galore. | *Armarse* or *hacerse un barullo*, to get into a muddle.
barzón m. Walk, stroll (paseo). || *Dar barzones*, to wander *o* to walk about aimlessly.
barzonear v. intr. To wander *o* to walk about aimlessly.
basa f. Base (de una columna). || FIG. Basis.
basada f. Cradle (de un barco).
basal adj. Basal: *metabolismo basal*, basal metabolism.
basáltico, ca adj. Basaltic.
basalto m. Basalt.
basamento m. Plinth, base (de una columna). || FIG. Basis, foundation.
basar v. tr. To base: *basar una opinión en*, to base an opinion on.
— V. pr. To base o.s. || To be based on.
basca f. Sick feeling, nausea. || *Este olor da bascas*, this smell is nauseating, this smell makes you feel sick.
bascosidad f. Repugnance (asco). || Nausea. || Filth (suciedad). || Obscenity (grosería). || *Dar bascosidad a uno*, to make one feel sick.
bascoso adj. Queasy (que tiene bascas). || Filthy, disgusting (repugnante). || Obscene (grosero).
báscula f. Scales, *pl.* (peso). || TECN. Weighbridge (para camiones).
basculador m. Tilter.
basculante adj. Bascule: *puente basculante*, bascule bridge.
bascular v. intr. To tilt.
base f. Base, basis. || Base: *una inscripción en la base de una estatua*, an inscription on the base of a statue. || QUÍM. y MAT. Base. || Main ingredient (de una receta de cocina). || MIL. Base: *base aérea, naval*, air, naval base. || DEP. Base (en béisbol). || FIG. Foundation, basis: *este argumento carece de base*, this argument has no foundation. | Basis, grounds, *pl.*: *base de comparación*, basis for comparison. | Cornerstone: *Juan es la base del grupo*, John is the cornerstone of the group. | Foundation: *sentar las bases de*, to lay the foundations for. || — *A base de*, by: *a base de no hacer nada*, by doing nothing; with the help of, by means of: *traducir a base de diccionarios*, to translate with the help of a dictionary; thanks to: *a base de muchos esfuerzos*, thanks to all his efforts. || FAM. *A base de bien*, extremely well. || *Alimento base*, staple food. || *Base imponible*, taxable income. || *Bebida a base de ron*, rum-based drink. || *De base*, basic. || *Pelota base*, baseball. || *Salario* or *sueldo base*, minimum wage, basic wage. || *Teniendo como base* or *si tomamos como base*, taking as a basis. || *Una comida a base de productos españoles*, a meal based on Spanish products. || *Un jarrón de poca base se cae fácilmente*, a narrow-based vase falls over easily.
basicidad f. QUÍM. Basicity.
básico, ca adj. Basic, essential: *un hecho básico*, a basic fact. || QUÍM. Basic, basal. || *Industrias básicas*, basic industries.
basidio m. Basidium (hongo).
basidiomiceto adj. Basidiomycetous.
— M. Basidiomycete.
basilar adj. ANAT. Basilary, basilar.
Basilea n. pr. GEOGR. Basle, Bale, Basel.
basileense o **basilense** adj. [Of *o* from] Basle.
— M. y f. Native *o* inhabitant of Basle.
basílica f. Basilica.
basílico, ca adj. ANAT. Basilic: *vena basílica*, basilic vein.
basiliense adj./s. V. BASILEENSE.
Basilio n. pr. m. Basil.
basilisco m. Basilisk (animal fabuloso, reptil). || FIG. y FAM. *Estar hecho un basilisco, ponerse como un basilisco*, to be, to become furious.
basquear v. intr. To feel sick.
— V. tr. To nauseate, to make sick.
basquilla f. A disease of sheep.
basquiña f. Outer skirt, skirt (falda).
basta f. Coarse stitching, tacking, basting (hilvanado). || Quilting (en los colchones).
bastante adv. Quite, rather, fairly: *es bastante viejo*, he is quite old; *habla bastante bien francés*, she

speaks fairly good French. || Enough: *no hemos comido bastante*, we have not eaten enough; *bastante grande, rápido*, large, fast enough. || Long enough (mucho tiempo): *ya ha trabajado bastante*, he has worked long enough. || *Lo bastante para*, enough to, sufficiently to (con verbo): *es lo bastante rico para comprar un coche*, he is rich enough to buy a car, he is sufficiently rich to buy a car; enough for, sufficiently for (con sustantivo o pronombre): *lo bastante salado para mí*, salty enough for me.
— Adj. Enough (suficiente): *no tengo bastante tiempo*, I have not got enough time; *no tengo bastantes textos para todos*, I have not got enough texts for everyone. || Quite a lot of, enough (mucho): *parece tener bastante dinero*, he seems to have quite a lot of money. || Quite a lot of, quite a few, quite a number of, enough (muchos): *tiene bastantes amigos*, he has quite a few friends. || Quite a lot (mucho, muchos): *¿había mucha gente? — Sí, bastante*, were there many people there? — Yes, quite a lot.

bastanteo m. JUR. Recognition, validation (de un documento).

bastar v. intr. To be sufficient, to be enough, to suffice: *basta pulsar el botón para que el motor arranque*, it suffices to push the button for the motor to start. || — *¡Basta!* or *¡basta ya!*, that's enough! || *Basta con decir*, suffice it to say. || *Basta con escribirlo*, you need only write it down. || *¡Basta de bromas!*, that's enough joking, joking aside. || *¡Basta de tonterías!*, enough of your nonsense! || *Basta y sobra*, that's more than enough. || *Con eso basta*, that will do, that's enough. || *Eso te basta*, that's enough for you. || *Hasta decir basta*, until one has had enough. || *Me basta con tu palabra*, your word is good enough for me. || *Me basta y me sobra*, I have more than enough.
— V. pr. To be self-sufficient (a sí mismo). || To do sth. by o.s., to rely only on o.s. (valerse por sí mismo).

bastarda f. Bastard file (lima). || Slanting hand (letra). || MAR. Lateen mainsail.

bastardear v. intr. To degenerate, to decline. || FIG. To degenerate.
— V. tr. To bastardize, to degrade. || FIG. To bastardize, to distort: *bastardear una doctrina política*, to bastardize a political doctrine.

bastardeo m. Bastardization, degeneration.

bastardía f. Bastardy. || FIG. Meanness, baseness (bajeza). | Villainous *o* infamous deed *o* action: *cometer una bastardía*, to commit a villainous deed.

bastardillo, lla adj. Italic.
— F. Italics, *pl.*, italic type: *escrito en bastardilla*, written in italics. || Type of flute (flauta). || *Poner en bastardilla*, to italicize.

bastardo, da adj. Bastard. || Crossbred, mongrel (perro). || Hybrid (plant). || FIG. Hybrid, mixed (híbrido). | Mean, base (bajuno). || *Letra bastarda*, slanting hand.
— M. y f. Bastard (persona). || Mongrel (perro). || Hybrid (planta).

baste m. Coarse stitch, tacking, basting (hilván). || Saddle pad (de la silla de montar).

bastear v. tr. To tack, to baste (hilvanar).

bastedad f. Coarseness, rudeness.

basteza f. Coarseness, rudeness (de una persona). || Coarseness (de una cosa).

bastida f. MIL. Small moving fortress.

bastidor m. Frame: *bastidor de una puerta*, door frame. || Stretcher, frame (de lienzo para pintar). || Sash: *bastidor de una ventana*, window sash. || Embroidery frame (para bordar). || Chassis (de vagón, de coche). || Frame (de una máquina). || MAR. Frame of a screw propeller (de la hélice). || *Amer.* Latticework (celosía). | Box-spring mattress (colchón de muelles). || — Pl. TEATR. Flats (decorado). | Wings (partes laterales del escenario). || — *Entre bastidores*, behind the scenes. || *Estar entre bastidores*, to be offstage (un actor).

bastilla f. Hem (dobladillo).

bastillado, da adj. HERÁLD. Embattled.

bastimentar v. tr. To supply, to provision.

bastimento m. Vessel (barco). || Supply (abastecimiento). || Supplies, *pl.*, provisions, *pl.* (provisiones).

bastión m. Bastion.

basto m. Packsaddle (arnés). || Saddle pad (de la silla de montar). || Ace of clubs (as de bastos). || — Pl. Clubs (naipes).

basto, ta adj. Coarse, rough: *una tela basta*, a coarse material. || FIG. Rude, coarse: *un hombre basto*, a rude man.

bastón m. Stick, cane, walking stick (para apoyarse): *un bastón con contera de plata*, a cane with a silver knob. || Baton (insignia): *bastón de mariscal*, field marshall's baton. || HERÁLD. Baton. || — *Bastón alpino*, alpenstock. || *Bastón de mando*, staff of command. || *Bastón de montañero*, ice axe. || FIG. *Empuñar el bastón*, to take command. | *No hay razón como la del bastón*, might makes right.

bastonada f. o **bastonazo** m. Blow *o* hit with a cane (golpe). || *Dar un bastonazo a alguien*, to hit s.o. with a stick *o* a cane.

bastoncillo m. Small cane. || ANAT. Rod (de la retina). || BIOL. Rod bacterium (bacteria).

bastonera f. Umbrella stand.

bastonero m. Cane manufacturer *o* merchant. || Maitre de ballet. || Caller (en ciertas danzas). || Master of ceremonies.

basura f. Rubbish, refuse [U.S., trash, garbage]: *tirar la basura*, to throw out the rubbish. || Litter (en la calle). || FIG. Rubbish, trash: *esa película es una basura*, that film is rubbish. || — *Cubo de la basura*, rubbish bin [U.S., trash can] (en la casa), dustbin [U.S., trash can, garbage can] (en la calle). || *Prohibido arrojar basuras*, no tipping. || *Vertedero* or *colector de basuras*, rubbish chute [U.S., garbage disposal].

basurero m. Dustman [U.S., garbage collector] (el que recoge la basura). || Rubbish dump [U.S., garbage dump] (sitio donde se amontona la basura). || Rubbish bin [U.S., trash can] (cubo de la basura).

bata f. Dressing gown (salto de cama). || Housecoat (traje de casa). || Overall [U.S., frock] (de un alumno). || White coat (de farmacéutico, médico, etc.).
— M. Young native of the Philippines.

batacazo m. Crash, bump, bang (ruido). || Fall (caída). || *Amer.* Unexpected win of a horse. || FAM. *Darse un batacazo*, to come a cropper.

batahola f. FAM. Row, din, rumpus: *armar una batahola infernal*, to make *o* to kick up an infernal row.

batalla f. Battle: *batalla campal*, pitched battle. || Battle order, battle formation: *formar en batalla*, to line up in battle order. || FIG. Inner struggle, agitation (en el espíritu). || Seat (de la silla de montar). || Wheelbase (de un coche, etc.). || Bout (esgrima). || ARTES. Battle scene. || Groove (de la ballesta). || — *Dar batalla*, to give battle. || FIG. *De batalla*, everyday: *traje de batalla*, everyday suit. | *Estos niños dan mucha batalla*, these children are a real handful *o* cause a lot of trouble *o* get up to all kinds of mischief. || *Librar* or *trabar batalla*, to do *o* to join battle. || *Presentar batalla*, to draw up in battle array. || FIG. *Quedar sobre el campo de batalla*, to pass away.

batallador, ra adj. Fighting, battling: *un equipo batallador*, a fighting team.
— M. y f. Fighter, battler (persona animosa). || Fencer (esgrimidor).

batallar v. intr. To battle, to make war (guerrear). || FIG. To fight, to quarrel (disputar): *batallar por pequeñeces*, to fight over trifles. | To battle, to struggle, to fight (esforzarse): *he tenido que batallar mucho para sacar adelante a mi familia*, I've had to battle a lot to get my family ahead. || To fence (en esgrima).

batallola f. MAR. Rail, rails, *pl.*

batallón, ona adj. FAM. Quarrelsome (una persona). || Boisterous, unruly, wild (un niño). || — *Cuestión batallona*, v. CUESTIÓN. || FAM. *Traje batallón*, everyday suit.
— M. MIL. Battalion.

batán m. Fulling mill (máquina para el paño). || — Pl. Children's game. || *Tierra de batán*, fuller's earth.

batanadura f. Fulling (del paño).

batanar v. tr. To full, to beat.

batanear v. tr. FIG. y FAM. To give [s.o.] a thrashing, to beat.

batanero m. Fuller.

batanga f. Outrigger (de algunas embarcaciones filipinas).

bataola f. V. BATAHOLA.

batata f. BOT. Sweet potato, "batata". || *Amer.* Bashfulness (timidez). || — M. Spineless person, mouse (apocado).

batatar o **batatal** m. Sweet potato plantation.

batatazo (dar un) loc. *Amer.* To win the race (un caballo). | To play a fluky *o* lucky shot (billar).

bátavo, va adj./s. Batavian (holandés).

batayola f. MAR. Rail, rails, *pl.*

bate m. Bat (béisbol, cricket).

batea f. Tray (bandeja). || Wicker tray (de mimbre). || Flat-bottomed boat (barco). || Flatcar (vagón descubierto). || MIN. Washing trough. || *Amer.* Washtub (para lavar), pail (cubeta).

bateador m. DEP. Batsman (cricket). | Batter (béisbol).

batear v. tr. *Amer.* To bat, to hit.
— V. intr. To bat.

batel m. Small boat, dinghy, dingey.

batelero, ra m. y f. Boatman (hombre), boatwoman (mujer): *los bateleros del Volga*, the Volga boatmen.

batería f. MIL. Battery: *batería antiaérea*, antiaircraft battery. | Artillery: *batería contracarro*, antitank artillery. | Breach (brecha). || MAR. Gundeck (entrepuente). || ELECTR. Battery: *batería de acumuladores*, storage battery. || MÚS. Percussion (en una orquesta). | Drums, *pl.* (en un conjunto). || TEATR. Footlights, *pl.* || — *Aparcar en batería*, to park obliquely *o* at an angle to the kerb (automóviles). || *Batería de cocina*, kitchen utensils. || TEATR. *Batería de luces*, footlights. || MIL. *Entrar en batería*, to prepare for action.
— M. Drummer (músico).

batey m. *Amer.* Sugar refinery (fábrica de azúcar). | Machinery in a refinery (maquinaria).

batiborrillo o **batiburrillo** m. FAM. Mess, jumble: *había un batiburrillo terrible en sus papeles*, his papers were in a terrible mess; *esta novela es un batiborrillo de ideas inconexas*, this novel is a jumble of incoherent ideas.

baticola f. Crupper (arnés).

batida f. Beat, battue (cacería). || Searching, combing (acción de registrar). || MIL. Reconnaissance. || *Batida de la policía*, police raid.
batidera f. Larry, mortar hoe (de albañil). || Honeycomb cutter (de apicultor).
batidero m. Banging (golpes seguidos). || Stony ground (terreno).
batido, da adj. Beaten (camino, tierra). || Shot (tejido). || Whipped: *nata batida*, whipped cream.
— M. Beaten egg (de huevos). || White of egg beaten stiff (clara de huevos a punto de nieve). || Milk shake (de leche): *batido de fresa*, strawberry milk shake. || Beating (acción de batir). || Churning (de la mantequilla). || Batter (para hacer un dulce). || Battu (danza).
batidor, ra adj. Which beats, beating.
— M. MIL. Scout (explorador). || Large-toothed comb (peine). || Beater (cacería). || Plunger, dasher (para la mantequilla). || Beater: *batidor de oro, de plata*, gold, silver beater. || *Amer.* Chocolate pot (chocolatera). | Informer (soplón). || — F. Mixer (aparato de cocina).
batiente adj. Banging. || FIG. *Reírse a mandíbula batiente*, V. MANDÍBULA.
— M. Leaf (hoja de la puerta). || Jamb (marco de puerta o ventana). || MAR. Place where waves break. || MÚS. Damper.
batifondo m. *Amer.* Rumpus, uproar.
batiesfera f. Bathysphere.
batihoja m. Gold *o* silver beater (batidor).
batimento m. ARTES. Shading.
batimetría f. Bathymetry.
batimiento m. Beating.
batín m. Short dressing gown.
batintín m. Gong.
batiporte m. MAR. Sill.
batir v. tr. To beat (los huevos, el metal). || To hammer (el metal). || To beat against: *las olas baten el acantilado*, the waves beat against the cliff. || To beat down on (el sol). || To break down, to knock down: *la artillería batió las murallas enemigas*, the artillery broke down the enemy walls. || To take down (desmontar). || To flap (los pájaros pequeños): *el ruiseñor bate las alas*, the nightingale flaps its wings. || To beat (ave grande): *el águila bate las alas*, the eagle beats its wings. || To clap (las manos). || To mix, to beat, (la leche). || To cream (la mantequilla). || To whip (la nata). || DEP. To beat (la caza). || To coin, to mint (monedas), to strike (medalla). || To beat, to defeat (vencer). || To backcomb (el pelo). || MIL. To reconnoitre (registrar una región). || To sweep: *el viento batió la región durante tres días*, the wind swept the region for three days. || To beat (tambor). || *Amer.* To rinse (la ropa). || — FIG. *Al hierro candente batir de repente*, strike while the iron is hot. || *Batir en brecha*, to batter (sentido militar), to attack (sentido figurado). || *Batir palmas*, to clap one's hands. || *Batir una mayonesa*, to beat a mayonnaise. || *Batir un récord*, to break a record.
— V. pr. To fight: *batirse en duelo*, to fight a duel. || — FIG. y FAM. *Batirse el cobre por hacer algo*, V. COBRE. || *Batirse en retirada*, to beat a retreat.
batiscafo m. Bathyscaphe.
batisfera f. Bathysphere.
batista f. Cambric, batiste (tela).
batitú m. *Amer.* Snipe.
bato m. Peasant, country bumpkin (rústico). || Simpleton (tonto). || POP. Old man (padre): *mi bato me dijo que*, my old man told me that.
batojar v. tr. To beat, to thrash (varear).
batología f. Battology (repetición).
batómetro m. Bathometer.
batracio, cia adj./m. ZOOL. Batrachian.
Batuecas n. pr. f. pl. FIG. y FAM. *Estar en las Batuecas*, to be daydreaming, to be woolgathering.
batueco, ca adj. [Of *o* from] Batuecas.
— M. y f. Inhabitant *o* native of Batuecas.
batuque m. *Amer.* Row, uproar, racket (ruido). | FAM. Mess, shambles, jumble (confusión).
baturrada f. Act *o* saying of Aragonese peasants.
baturrillo m. FIG. y FAM. Jumble, hotchpotch, mess (mezcla). || Gibberish, double Dutch (galimatías).
baturro, rra m. y f. Aragonese peasant.
batuta f. MÚS. Baton (de un director de orquesta). || *Llevar la batuta*, to direct *o* to conduct the orchestra (una orquesta), to be the boss, to rule the roost (dirigir un asunto).
baúl m. Trunk (maleta grande). || Boot (de un automóvil). || FIG. y FAM. Paunch, potbelly (barriga). || *Baúl mundo*, Saratoga trunk.
baumé m. Baumé (grado).
bauprés m. MAR. Bowsprit.
bausa f. *Amer.* FAM. Laziness, idleness (pereza).
bautismal adj. Baptismal: *pila bautismal*, baptismal font.
bautismo m. Baptism, christening. || — *Bautismo de fuego*, baptism of fire (de soldado). || *Bautismo del aire*, first flight. || *Fe de bautismo*, baptismal certificate, certificate of baptism. || *Pila del bautismo*, baptismal font. || FIG. y FAM. *Romper el bautismo a uno*, to smash s.o.'s head in.
bautista m. Baptist (miembro de una secta protestante). || *San Juan Bautista*, Saint John the Baptist.
bautisterio m. Baptistry, baptistery.
bautizar v. tr. To baptize, to christen. || FIG. To name: *bautizar una calle*, to name a street. || FAM. To water down (aguar el vino, la leche). | To drench, to soak (mojar).
bautizo m. Baptism, christening (ceremonia). || Christening party (fiesta).
bauxita f. Bauxite.
bauza f. Log, billet (madero).
bávaro, ra adj./s. Bavarian.
Baviera n. pr. f. GEOGR. Bavaria.
baya f. BOT. Berry (fruto). | Type of hyacinth (planta). || *Amer.* Fermented grape drink (bebida).
bayadera f. Bayadere.
Bayardo n. pr. m. Bayard.
bayeta f. Flannel (tejido de lana). || Floorcloth (para fregar el suelo). || *Amer.* FAM. *Este chico es una bayeta*, this boy is a weakling, this boy has no backbone.
bayetón m. Duffle, duffel, thick woollen cloth (tejido).
bayo, ya adj. Bay (caballo).
— M. Silkworm moth (mariposa). || Bay (caballo). || *Amer.* Coffin (féretro).
Bayona n. pr. GEOGR. Bayonne.
bayonés, esa adj. [Of *o* from] Bayonne.
— M. y f. Inhabitant *o* native of Bayonne.
bayonesa f. Mayonnaise (mayonesa).
— OBSERV. This word is a barbarism used instead of *mayonesa*.
bayoneta f. MIL. Bayonet: *ataque a la bayoneta*, bayonet charge. || — *Armar* or *calar la bayoneta*, to fix the bayonet. || *Con bayonetas caladas*, with fixed bayonets. || *Hacer frente con la bayoneta*, to resist with fixed bayonet.
bayonetazo m. Bayonet thrust (golpe). || Bayonet wound (herida).
bayú m. *Amer.* Brothel.
baza f. Trick (en el juego): *una baza de menos*, one trick less. || FIG. Asset: *tiene muchas bazas para conseguir lo que quiere*, he has many assets to help him get what he wants. || — FIG. *Jugar otra baza*, to try a new tack. | *Meter baza en*, to poke one's nose into, to interfere in (un asunto), to butt into, to intervene in, to interrupt (la conversación). | *No me dejó meter baza*, he did not let me get a word in edgeways. | *Sentada esta baza*, having established this point. | *Tiene todas las bazas en su mano*, he's holding all the trumps.
bazar m. Bazar, bazaar.
bazo, za adj. Brown, wholemeal (pan). || Brownish, fawn (tela).
— M. ANAT. Spleen.
bazofia f. Leftovers, *pl.* (de comida). || FIG. Filth, rubbish (cosa sucia). | Pigswill, slop (mala comida).
bazooka o **bazuca** m. MIL. Bazooka.
be f. B [name of the letter *b*]. || — FIG. *Be por be* or *be por be y ce por ce*, in detail, down to the last detail. || FAM. *Tener (una cosa) las tres bes*, to have everything [to have three advantages *bonita*, pretty, *barata*, cheap, *buena*, good]: *esta casa tiene las tres bes*, this house has everything.
be m. Bleat, bleating (balido).
beata f. Very devout woman. || Lay sister, Beguine sister (mujer que vive en comunidad). || FAM. Sanctimonious woman, bigot (mojigata). || POP. Peseta.
beatería f. Religious bigotry.
beaterio m. Beguine convent.
beatificación f. Beatification.
beatíficamente adj. Blissfully.
beatificar v. tr. To beatify.
beatífico, ca adj. Beatific: *visión beatífica*, beatific vision. || Blissful: *una sonrisa beatífica*, a blissful smile.
beatísimo, ma adj. *Beatísimo Padre*, Holy Father (el Papa).
beatitud f. REL. Beatitude. || Bliss (placidez).
beatnik m. y f. Beatnik.
beato, ta adj. REL. Blessed (beatificado). || Devout (piadoso). || FAM. Sanctimonious (exageradamente devoto). || Blessed, happy (feliz).
— M. y f. REL. Blessed person. || Devout person (piadoso). || FAM. [Religious] bigot, sanctimonious person. || — M. Lay brother (religioso). || Devout man.
beatón, ona o **beatuco, ca** adj./s. FAM. V. BEATO.
Beatriz n. pr. f. Beatrice, Beatrix.
bebé m. Baby.
— OBSERV. In Argentina the forms *bebe* (niño) and *beba* (niña) also exist.
bebedero, ra adj. Drinkable (que se puede beber). || Tasty (sabroso).
— M. Water trough, drinking trough (de animales). || Watering place (donde beben los animales y los pájaros). || Lip, spout (de algunas vasijas).
bebedizo, za adj. Drinkable (bebedero).
— M. MED. Potion. || Philtre, love potion (filtro mágico). || Poisonous drink (veneno).
bebedor, ra adj. Drinking, hard-drinking.
— M. y f. Drinker: *es buen bebedor*, he is a good drinker.
beber m. Drinking: *el beber en exceso puede tener malas consecuencias*, excessive drinking can have bad consequences.
beber v. intr. y tr. To drink: *beber agua*, to drink water, *beber de la botella*, to drink from the bottle: *beber en un vaso*, to drink out of *o* from a glass. || To drink (bebida alcohólica): *este hombre bebe demasiado*, this man drinks too much. || To drink (brindar): *beber por*

or *a la salud de alguien*, to drink to s.o.'s health, to drink to s.o. || FIG. To drink in: *estaba bebiendo tus palabras mientras hablabas*, he was drinking in your words as you spoke. || — *Beber a chorro*, to pour drink into one's mouth (de bota, etc.). || *Beber a sorbos*, to sip. || *Beber a tragos*, to gulp. || FIG. y FAM. *Beber como una esponja* or *como un cosaco*, to drink like a fish. || *Beber de un trago*, to down in one, to drink down in one. || FIG. *Beber en buenas fuentes*, to have reliable sources of information. | *Beber en las fuentes*, to draw upon the sources: *beber en las fuentes latinas*, to draw upon Latin sources. | *Beber los sesos a*, V. SESO. | *Beber los vientos por*, V. VIENTO. || *Dar de beber*, to give a drink (a personas, a animales), to water (animales). || *Echar de beber*, to pour a drink (a personas), to give water (a animales). || FIG. *Esto es como quien se bebe un vaso de agua*, this is as easy as A B C *o* as pie. | *Sin comerlo ni beberlo*, without asking for it, for no apparent reason, through no fault of one's own.
— V. pr. To drink. || FIG. To drink: *beberse todo lo que se gana*, to drink one's wages. || *Bébete eso, que nos vamos*, drink up, we're leaving.
beberrón, ona m. y f. FAM. Soak, drunkard.
bebestible adj. FAM. Drinkable.
— M. Beverage, drink.
bebezón m. *Amer.* Drunkenness (borrachera). | Drink (bebida).
bebible adj. FAM. Drinkable.
bebida f. Drink: *sirven bebidas en el avión*, they serve drinks on the plane. || Drink, beverage: *bebida alcohólica*, alcoholic beverage. || Drinking, drink: *no se puede vivir sin bebida ni comida*, one cannot live without drinking and eating, one cannot live without food and drink. || *Amer.* Potion (potingue). || — *Dado a la bebida*, given to drink. || *Darse a la bebida*, to take to drinking, to take to drink, to indulge in drinking. || *Tener mala bebida*, to turn nasty with drink, to be quarrelsome in one's cups.
bebido, da adj. Tipsy, merry.
bebistrajo m. Concoction, nasty drink, foul drink (bebida desagradable). || Strange concoction, strange mixture (mezcla extraña de bebidas).
be-bop m. MÚS. Be-bop.
beborrotear v. intr. FAM. To tipple.
beca f. Grant, scholarship.
becacina f. Snipe (agachadiza).
becada f. Woodcock (pájaro).
becado, da m. y f. *Amer.* Scholarship holder. || *Los alumnos becados*, the scholarship holders.
becafigo m. ZOOL. Beccafico (pájaro).
becardón m. Snipe (agachadiza).
becario, ria m. y f. Scholarship holder.
becasina f. Snipe (agachadiza).
becerra f. Yearling calf (animal). || Snapdragon (planta).
becerrada f. Fight with yearling bulls.
becerril adj. Of a calf, calf.
becerrillo m. Calfskin, calf (cuero).
becerrista m. Bullfighter who fights very young bulls.
becerro m. Yearling calf. || Calfskin (cuero): *botas de becerro*, calfskin boots. || Cartulary (libro para la Iglesia). || Register of landed property (para la nobleza). || — *Becerro de oro*, golden calf. || *Becerro marino*, sea calf, seal (foca). || FAM. *No seas becerro*, don't be stupid. | *Sangrar como un becerro*, to bleed freely.
becuadro m. MÚS. Natural sign.
bechamel o **bechamela** f. White sauce, béchamel sauce (salsa).
bedano m. Chisel (cincel).
bedel m. Beadle, porter (en la Universidad).
bedelía f. Beadleship.
beduino, na adj./s. Bedouin, Beduin (árabe nómada). || — M. FIG. Brute (hombre brutal).
befa f. Jeering, scoffing, mockery (acción y efecto). || *Hacer befa de*, to jeer at, to mock, to scoff at.
befar v. intr. To move the lips [horses] (los caballos).
— V. tr. To mock, to jeer at, to scoff at.
befo, fa adj. Thick-lipped, blubber-lipped (de labio grueso). || Knock-kneed (zambo).
— M. Pendulous lips (de mono, perro, gato), chops (de rumiantes). || Thick lower lip (labio inferior grueso). || Ape (mico).
begonia f. BOT. Begonia.
begoniáceas f. pl. BOT. Begoniaceae.
beguina f. Beguine (religiosa).
begum f. Begum.
behaviorismo m. Behaviourism [U.S., behaviorism].
behetría f. HIST. Free town whose inhabitants had the right to elect their own master. || FIG. Confusion, bedlam.
beige adj./s.m. Beige (color).
Beirut n. pr. GEOGR. Beirut, Beyrouth.
béisbol m. Baseball: *jugador de béisbol*, baseball player.
bejucal m. Rattan field.
bejuco m. Liana, rattan, reed.
bejuquear v. tr. *Amer.* To thrash (un árbol). | To hit with a cane (una persona).
bel m. Bel (unidad de intensidad sonora).
Belcebú n. pr. m. Beelzebub.
belcho m. BOT. Ephedra, horsetail.
beldad f. Beauty. || Beauty (mujer bella): *ella es unà beldad*, she is a beauty.
beldar* v. tr. AGR. To winnow [grain] with a fork.
belemnita f. Belemnite, finger stone (fósil).
belén m. Nativity scene, crib (del niño Jesús). || FIG. y FAM. Bedlam, mess (confusión). | Madhouse, bedlam (lugar donde hay desorden). || FIG. y FAM. *Meterse en belenes*, to stir up a hornet's nest.
Belén n. pr. GEOGR. Bethlehem. || FIG. *Estar en Belén*, to daydream.
beleño m. BOT. Henbane.
belérico m. BOT. Myrobalan.
belesa f. BOT. Leadwort.
belfo, fa adj. Thick-lipped, blubber-lipped (de labio grueso).
— M. Pendulous lips (de mono, perro, gato), chops (de rumiantes). || Thick lower lip (labio inferior grueso).
belga adj./s. Belgian.
Bélgica n. pr. f. GEOGR. Belgium.
Belgrado n. pr. GEOGR. Belgrade.
Belice n. pr. m. GEOGR. Belize.
belicismo m. Warmongering, militarism.
belicista adj. Warmongering, bellicist.
— M. y f. Warmonger, militarist.
bélico, ca adj. Warlike, bellicose: *espíritu bélico*, warlike spirit. || *Preparativos bélicos*, preparations for war.
belicosidad f. Bellicosity, aggressiveness.
belicoso, sa adj. Bellicose, warlike (nación). || Aggressive (persona).
beligerancia f. Belligerency. || — FIG. *No dar beligerancia a uno*, to pay no attention to s.o., to take no notice of s.o. || *Política de no beligerancia*, policy of non-aggression.
beligerante adj./s. Belligerent.
belígero, ra adj. POÉT. Bellicose.
belinograma m. Belinogram.
belio m. FÍS. Bel (unidad de intensidad sonora).
Belisario n. pr. m. Belisarius.
belísono, na adj. POÉT. With warlike sound, with martial sound.
belitre adj. Foolish (bobo). || Vile (vil).
— M. y f. Fool (bobo). || Knave, scoundrel (granuja).
Beltrán n. pr. m. Bertrand.
beluario m. Animal tamer.
beluza f. ZOOL. Beluza (esturión, cetáceo).
belvedere m. Belvedere.
bellacada f. V. BELLAQUERÍA.
bellacamente adv. Knavishly, roguishly.
bellaco, ca adj. Sly, cunning (astuto). || Roguish, wicked, evil (malo). || *Amer.* Restive, vicious (caballo).
— M. y f. Sly dog (astuto). || Rogue, villain (malo). || *Mentir como un bellaco*, to lie one's head off.
belladona f. BOT. Belladona, deadly nightshade.
bellaquear v. intr. To do evil. || To cheat, to play a sly trick (obrar con astucia). || *Amer.* To buck, to rear (los caballos).
bellaquería f. Fiendish trick (acción). || Knavery, roguery (carácter). || Cunning (astucia).
belleza f. Beauty. || — *Concurso de belleza*, beauty contest. || *Crema de belleza*, beauty cream. || *Diplomada en belleza*, qualified beautician. || *Es una belleza*, it's beautiful (cosa). || *Tratamiento de belleza*, beauty treatment. || *Una belleza*, a beauty (mujer).
bellido, da adj. V. BELLO.
bellísimo, ma adj. Ravishing, gorgeous, very beautiful. || *Una bellísima persona*, an extremely nice person, a wonderful person.
bello, lla adj. Beautiful (mujer), handsome (hombre), fair (termino poético). || Noble, fine (sentimiento). || — *Bello como un sol*, fine-looking, extremely handsome (adolescente), as pretty as a picture, divine (niño, chica). || *El bello sexo*, the fair sex. || *La bella durmiente del bosque*, Sleeping Beauty. || *La bella y la bestia*, Beauty and the Beast. || *Las bellas artes*, the fine arts. || FIG. y FAM. *Por su bella cara*, for love, for s.o.'s pretty face.
bellota f. BOT. Acorn (de la encina). || ANAT. Glans penis (bálano). || Tassel (adorno). || Carnation bud (del clavel). || *Animal de bellota*, pig (cerdo), blockhead, fool, dunce (persona estúpida).
bellotero, ra m. y f. Gatherer *o* seller of acorns. || — F. Crop of acorns, mast (cosecha).
bembo, ba adj. *Amer.* FAM. Thick-lipped (de labios gruesos). | Foolish, silly, simple (bobo).
— M. y f. *Amer.* FAM. Thick lower lip (labio grueso). | Snout (hocico).
bembón, ona o **bembudo, da** adj. *Amer.* FAM. Thick-lipped.
— M. y f. *Amer.* FAM. Thick-lipped person.
bemol adj./s.m. MÚS. Flat: *si bemol*, B flat. || — FIG. *Esto tiene bemoles* or *muchos bemoles* or *tres bemoles*, this is not an easy job at all, this is a tough one. || MÚS. *Hacer bemol*, to flatten.
bemolado, da adj. Flat.
bemolar v. tr. MÚS. To flatten
ben m. Ben (hijo de). || BOT. Horseradish.
bencedrina f. MED. Benzedrine.
benceno m. QUÍM. Benzene.
bencílico, ca adj. Benzilic.
bencina f. QUÍM. Benzine.

bendecidor, ra adj. Benedictory.
— M. y f. Person who blesses.
bendecir* v. tr. To bless: *estar bendecido por los dioses*, to be blessed by the gods. || — *Bendecir la mesa*, to say grace. || *¡Dios le bendiga!*, God bless you!
— OBSERV. The Spanish verb *bendecir* has two past participles: *bendecido* and *bendito*. The former is the regular form and is used to denote an action or its result (*esta iglesia fue bendecida por*, this church was blessed by). The latter, which is irregular, is used as an adjective. *Bendito* is currently used in prayers and invocations (*bendita eres entre todas las mujeres, bendito sea tu nombre*, blessed art Thou amongst women, blessed be Thy name).
bendición f. Blessing: *el padre dio su bendición a su hijo*, the father gave his blessing to his son. || REL. Benediction: *la bendición papal* or *del Papa*, the Pope's benediction. || — *Bendición de la mesa*, grace. || *Bendición nupcial*, blessing [in marriage ceremony]. || FAM. *Echar la bendición a uno*, to give one's blessing to s.o. | *Es una bendición de Dios*, it is a blessing, it is a Godsend. | *La cosecha este año es una bendición*, the harvest is magnificent this year. | *Toca que es una bendición*, he plays extremely well *o* divinely *o* marvellously. | *Ya nos echaron las bendiciones*, the knot has been tied (matrimonio). | *Y llovió que era una bendición*, and it really rained, and you should have seen it rain.
bendito, ta adj. Blessed. || Holy: *agua bendita*, holy water; *la bendita Virgen María*, the holy Virgin Mary. || Joyful (dichoso). || Lucky (que tiene suerte). || Simple, silly (de poco alcance). || — FAM. *¡Bendita la madre que te hizo!*, what a child for a mother to have! || *¡Bendito sea Dios!*, good God! (de disgusto), thank goodness!, thank heavens! (de alivio).
— M. Saint (santo). || Simpleton (bobo). || Good sort *o* soul (bonachón). || Prayer which begins with the words "bendito y alabado, etc.". || *Amer.* Niche for a statue (hornacina). | Type of tent (tienda de campaña). || — FIG. y FAM. *Dormir como un bendito*, to sleep like a baby. | *Reír como un bendito*, to laugh one's head off.
— OBSERV. Cuando *blessed* expresa una acción o su resultado, p.ej. en la frase *the church was blessed by*, se pronuncia "blest". Cuando se utiliza como adjetivo (*the blessed martyrs, blessed be Thy name*) se pronuncia "blesid".
benedícite m. Benedicite, grace (oración).
benedictino, na adj./s. Benedictine. || FIG. *Obra de benedictinos*, task requiring a great deal of patience. || — M. Benedictine (licor).
Benedicto n. pr. m. Benedict (solamente los papas).
benefactor, ra adj. Beneficent.
— M. y f. Benefactor (hombre), benefactress (mujer).
beneficencia f. Beneficence, benevolence, charity. || Welfare, public welfare (organización pública). || — *Sección de beneficencia*, charity board. || *Vivir de la beneficencia*, to be on relief, to live on public welfare.
beneficiación f. Exploitation, benefitting.
beneficiado, da m. y f. Beneficiary. || — M. Beneficiary (eclesiástico).
beneficiador, ra m. y f. Beneficiary.
beneficial adj. Of ecclesiastical benefices.
beneficiar v. tr. To benefit (hacer bien): *beneficiar al género humano*, to benefit humanity. || To exploit (una cosa, un terreno, una mina). || To cultivate (la tierra). || To reduce (un mineral). || To favour [U.S., to favor] (favorecer). || *Amer.* To slaughter (matar una res). | To quarter, to cut into pieces (descuartizar).
— V. intr. To benefit: *beneficiar de una ley*, to benefit from *o* by a law; *beneficiar de la ayuda de*, to benefit from the help of. || To profit (*de*, from) [sacar provecho].
— V. pr. To benefit. || To profit (sacar provecho).
beneficiario, ria m. y f. Beneficiary. || — *Beneficiario del cheque*, payee. || *Beneficiario de patente*, patentee.
beneficio m. Profit (ganancia): *los beneficios anuales*, yearly profits. || Advantage: *los beneficios del empleo*, the advantages of the job. || Benefit: *beneficios sociales*, social benefits. || FIG. Favour (bien): *colmar a uno de beneficios*, to heap favours on s.o. | Benefit, behalf (provecho): *trabajar para el* or *a* or *en beneficio de la humanidad*, to labour for the benefit of *o* on behalf of humanity. || REL. Benefice. || Exploitation (explotación). || AGR. Cultivation (cultivo). || MIN. Reduction (de un mineral). || Benefit (en el teatro). || *Amer.* Slaughter (matanza). | Quartering (descuartizamiento). | Rural development (hacienda). | Manure (abono). || — *A beneficio de*, for the benefit of. || *A beneficio de inventario*, under beneficium inventarii, under the benefit of inventory (sentido jurídico), with reservations (con reservas). || *Beneficio bruto*, gross profit. || *Beneficio neto*, net profit. || *Beneficios adicionales*, fringe benefits. || *En beneficio propio*, to one's own advantage, in one's own interest. || *Margen de beneficio*, profit margin. || FIG. *No tener oficio ni beneficio*, to have no job, to be out of a job. || *Vender con beneficio*, to sell at a profit *o* at a premium.
beneficioso, sa adj. Beneficial, advantageous. || Profitable (provechoso).
benéfico, ca adj. Beneficent, charitable: *obras benéficas*, charitable works. || Beneficial: *lluvia benéfica*, beneficial rain. || Favourable: *influencia benéfica de los planetas*, favourable influence of the planets. || — *Función benéfica*, charity performance. || *Obra benéfica*, charity. || *Una cena benéfica*, a charity dinner.
benemérito, ta adj. Meritorious, worthy (muy bueno). || Distinguished: *el benemérito profesor*, the distinguished professor. || *Los hijos beneméritos de la patria*, the glorious sons of the motherland.
— F. *La Benemérita*, the Spanish Civil Guard.
beneplácito m. Blessing, approval, consent: *negar el beneplácito*, to refuse to give one's blessing; *di mi beneplácito*, I gave my consent.
benévolamente adv. Benevolently, kindly.
benevolencia f. Benevolence, kindness.
benevolente o **benévolo, la** adj. Benevolent, kind.
bengala f. BOT. Rattan. || Bengal light, flare.
Bengala n. pr. m. GEOGR. Bengal. || *Luz de Bengala*, Bengal light, flare.
bengali adj./s. Bengali, Bengalese.
— M. Waxbill (pájaro). || Bengali (lengua).
bengalina f. Bengaline (tejido).
benignamente adv. Benignly, kindly. || Mildly (sin gravedad).
benignidad f. Benignancy, benignity, kindness. || Mildness (falta de gravedad).
benigno, na adj. Benign, kindly (amable). || Mild (sin gravedad, templado): *enfermedad benigna*, mild illness; *invierno benigno*, mild winter. || Benign, nonmalignant: *tumor benigno*, benign tumour, nonmalignant tumour.
Benito n. pr. m. Benedict.
benjamín m. Youngest son (hijo menor).
Benjamín n. pr. m. Benjamin.
benjamita adj./s. Benjamite, Benjaminite.
benjuí m. Benjamin, benzoin (bálsamo).
bentonita f. GEOL. Bentonite (arcilla).
benzamida f. QUÍM. Benzamide.
benzoato m. QUÍM. Benzoate.
benzoico, ca adj. QUÍM. Benzoic.
benzoína f. QUÍM. Benzoin.
benzol m. QUÍM. Benzol.
Beocia n. pr. f. GEOGR. Boetia.
beocio, cia adj./s. Boeotian.
beodez f. Drunkenness.
beodo, da adj. Drunk, drunken (borracho).
— M. y f. Drunk, drunkard.
berberecho m. Cockle (molusco).
berberí adj./s. V BERÉBER.
Berbería n. pr. f. GEOGR. Barbary.
berberidáceas f. pl. BOT. Berberidaceae.
berberisco, ca adj. Barbaresque, Berber.
— M. Berber.
berbiquí m. Brace, carpenter's brace.
beréber o **berebere** adj./s. Berber.
berenjena f. BOT. Aubergine, eggplant: *berenjenas rellenas*, stuffed aubergines.
berenjenal m. Field of aubergines *o* eggplants. || FIG. y FAM. Mess, confusion: *armar un berenjenal*, to make a mess. || FIG. y FAM. *Meterse en un berenjenal*, to get into a fine mess *o* a fine pickle *o* a fine predicament.
bergamota f. BOT. Bergamot.
bergamoto m. BOT. Bergamot.
bergante m. FAM. Scoundrel, rascal, knave.
bergantín m. MAR. Brig, brigantine.
berginización f. Berginization.
bergsonismo m. FIL. Bergsonism (de Bergson).
beri m. FAM. *Con las del beri*, maliciously.
beriberi m. MED. Beriberi.
berilio m. QUÍM. Beryllium.
berilo m. MIN. Beryl.
berkelio m. Berkelium.
berlanga f. Three of a kind (trío de cartas).
Berlín n. pr. GEOGR. Berlin: *Berlín Occidental*, West Berlin. || *El muro de Berlín*, the Berlin wall.
berlina f. Saloon (vehículo). || Berlin, berline (coche cerrado de dos asientos).
berlinés, esa adj. [Of *o* from] Berlin.
— M. y f. Berliner, inhabitant *o* native of Berlin.
berma f. Berm, foreland (fortificación).
bermejear v. intr. To be reddish.
bermejizo, za adj. Reddish.
bermejo, ja adj. Red, vermilion (rojo). || Red, ginger (cabellos).
bermellón m. Vermilion.
bermudas m. pl. Bermuda shorts.
Bermudas n. pr. f. pl. GEOGR. Bermuda, *sing.*
Berna n. pr. GEOGR. Bern, Berne.
Bernabé n. pr. m. Barnabas, Barnaby.
bernabita m. Barnabite (monje).
bernardo, da adj./s. Bernardine (religiosos).
Bernardo, da n. pr. m. y f. Bernard, Bernadette.
bernés, esa adj./s. Bernese (de Berna).
berra o **berraza** f. Cress.
berraco m. FIG. y FAM. Noisy brat, squalling brat (niño).
berrear v. intr. To low (los becerros). || FIG. y FAM. To bawl, to howl (gritar, cantar o llorar). | To lose one's temper, to fly off the handle (enfadarse).
berrenchín m. Foul-smelling breath of the wild boar. || FIG. y FAM. V. BERRINCHE.
berrendo, da adj. Mottled, speckled: *berrendo en negro*, mottled with black (toro).

— M. *Amer.* Type of cereal with a blue stalk (trigo). | Type of antelope.
berrido m. Lowing (del becerro). || FIG. Shout, bellow, howl (grito).
berrinche m. FAM. Temper, rage (rabieta): *mi padre ha cogido un berrinche*, my father flew into a temper. | Tantrum (disgusto de los niños): *el niño cogió un berrinche*, the child threw a tantrum. || *Como sigas así me vas a dar un berrinche*, if you carry on like that you are going to make me cross.
berrinchudo, da adj. *Amer.* Quick-tempered, irascible, choleric.
berrizal m. Watercress bed *o* pond.
berro m. BOT. Cress, watercress.
berrocal m. Rocky ground, craggy place.
berroqueña adj. f. *Piedra berroqueña*, granite.
berrueco m. Granite rock (roca). || Baroque, baroque pearl (perla). || MED. Tumour of the eye.
Berta n. pr. f. Bertha.
berza f. Cabbage (col).
berzal m. Cabbage field (grande), cabbage patch (pequeño).
berzas o **berzotas** m. y f. inv. FAM. Twerp, drip.
besalamano m. Card, unsigned note with the abbreviation B.L.M. [*besa la mano*, kisses your hand].
besamanos m. inv. Royal audience (recepción de los reyes). || Hand kissing (modo de saludar).
besamela o **besamel** f. White sauce, béchamel sauce (salsa).
besana f. AGR. Ploughed field (surcos paralelos). | First furrow (primer surco). | Catalan agricultural measure [21.87 ares].
besante m. Besant, bezant (moneda). || HERÁLD. Besant, bezant.
besar v. tr. To kiss (dar un beso): *le besé en las mejillas*, I kissed him on the cheeks. || FIG. To touch, to graze, to brush against (rozar). || — FAM. *Aquello fue llegar y besar el santo*, V. SANTO. | *Besa la tierra que pisa su amada*, he worships the ground his loved one walks on. | *Hacer besar la lona*, V. LONA.
— V. pr. To kiss, to kiss each other: *se besaron al verse*, they kissed each other when they met. || To brush, to touch *o* to graze *o* to brush against each other (rozarse).
besico o **besito** m. Little kiss, peck: *dar un besito*, to give a little kiss *o* a peck. || BOT. *Besico de monja*, campanula.
beso m. Kiss: *beso de paz*, kiss of peace. || FIG. Clash, bump, blow (golpe). || — FIG. y FAM. *Comerse a besos*, to kiss each other passionately, to eat each other (dos personas), to smother in kisses (a uno). || *Tirar un beso*, to blow a kiss.
besotear v. tr. FAM. To kiss, to cover with kisses.
bestezuela f. Creepy-crawly, beastie.
bestia f. Beast, animal. || — M. y f. FIG. Beast, brute, animal (persona ruda): *¡vaya bestia!*, what a brute!, what an animal! | Ignoramus, dunce, idiot (ignorante). || — *Bestia de albarda*, pack animal. || *Bestia de carga*, beast of burden. || *Gran bestia*, elk (anta), tapir. || FIG. y FAM. *Mala bestia*, nasty piece of work, brute (persona muy mala), dunce (ignorante).
bestial adj. Animal, bestial, beastly (irracional): *instintos bestiales*, animal instincts. || FIG. y FAM. Terrific, great, fabulous, smashing (magnífico). | Huge, big, enormous (enorme): *tiene un apetito bestial*, he has a huge appetite.
bestialidad f. Bestiality, beastliness || FAM. Stupidity (estupidez). | Horrible thing (acción mala). || — FAM. *Decir bestialidades*, to say horrible things (cosas malas), to speak *o* to talk nonsense (tonterías). | *¡Qué bestialidad!*, how awful!, how terrible! (disgusto), good grief! (asombro). | *Una bestialidad de*, piles *o* stacks of, a great number of, lots and lots of.
bestiario m. Bestiary.
best seller m. Best seller.
besucar v. tr. FAM. To kiss, to cover with kisses.
besucón, ona adj. FAM. Fond of kissing.
— M. y f. Person fond of kissing.
besugo m. Sea bream (pez). || FIG. y FAM. Idiot, drip, twerp. || FAM. *Ojos de besugo*, bulging eyes.
besuguera f. Sea bream seller. || Fish pan (recipiente para el pescado).
besuguete m. Sea bream (pez).
besuquear v. tr. FAM. To kiss, to cover with kisses.
— V. pr. FAM. To smooch, to kiss and cuddle.
besuqueo m. FAM. Smooching, kissing and cuddling.
beta f. Beta (letra griega). || Piece of rope *o* string (cuerda). || MAR. Rope, cable (cable). || *Rayos beta*, beta rays.
betarraga o **betarrata** f. Beetroot [U.S., beet] (remolacha).
betatrón m. FÍS. Betatron.
betel m. BOT. Betel.
Bética n. pr. f. Andalusia.
bético, ca adj. Andalusian.
betún m. Asphalt, bitumen. || Shoe polish, polish (para el calzado). || — *Betún de Judea*, asphalt. || FIG. *Negro como el betún*, as black as coal. || FAM. *Quedar a la altura del betún*, to be the lowest of the low (ser el peor de todos), to do badly *o* poorly (en una competición).
betunero m. Bootblack, shoeblack, shoeshine boy (limpiabotas).
bevatrón m. FÍS. Bevatron.
bey m. Bey (soberano musulmán).
bezaar m. Bezoar.
bezante m. HERÁLD. Besant, bezant.
bezar m. Bezoar.
bezo m. Thick lip (labio grueso). || Lip (de una herida).
bezoar m. Bezoar.
bezoácico m. Antidote (contraveneno).
bezote m. Indian lip ring.
bezudo, da adj. Thick-lipped.
biaba f. *Amer.* FAM. Slap, smack (bofetada). | Spanking, thrashing, beating (zurra).
biácido, da adj. QUÍM. Biacid, diacid.
bianual adj. Biennial.
biatómico, ca adj. QUÍM. Diatomic.
biaxial adj. Biaxial.
bíbaro m. Beaver (castor).
bibásico, ca adj. QUÍM. Bibasic, dibasic.
bibelot m. Bibelot, curio, trinket.
biberón m. Baby's bottle, feeding bottle. || *Dar el biberón al niño*, to give the baby his bottle, to feed the baby.
bibijagua f. *Amer.* Type of large ant found in Cuba (hormiga). | FIG. Busy bee.
bibijaguera f. *Amer.* Anthill.
biblia f. Bible: *la Santa Biblia*, the Holy Bible. || — *Papel biblia*, Bible paper. || FIG. *Saber más que la Biblia*, to know everything.
bíblico, ca adj. Biblical.
bibliofilia f. Bibliophilism.
bibliófilo, la m. Bibliophile, booklover.
bibliografía f. Bibliography.
bibliográfico, ca adj. Bibliographical, bibliographic.
bibliógrafo, fa m. y f. Bibliographer.
bibliomanía f. Bibliomania.
bibliómano, na m. y f. Bibliomaniac.
biblioteca f. Library: *biblioteca de consulta, de préstamo*, reference, lending library; *biblioteca circulante*, mobile library. || Bookcase, bookshelves, *pl.* (mueble). || FIG. *Es una biblioteca viviente*, he is a walking encyclopedia.
bibliotecario, ria m. y f. Librarian.
bicameral adj. Bicameral, two-chamber.
bicameralismo m. Bicameralism, bicameral system, two-chamber system.
bicarbonato m. QUÍM. Bicarbonate: *bicarbonato de sosa* or *sódico*, bicarbonate of soda (nombre corriente), sodium bicarbonate (nombre científico).
bicarburo m. QUÍM. Bicarbide.
bicéfalo, la adj. Bicephalous, two-headed: *águila bicéfala*, two-headed eagle.
bicentenario m. Bicentennial, bicentenary.
bíceps m. inv. ANAT. Biceps.
bici f. FAM. Bike (bicicleta).
bicicleta f. Bicycle: *ir en bicicleta*, to go by bicycle; *no sabe montar en bicicleta*, he doesn't know how to ride a bicycle.
biciclo m. Velocipede.
bicipital adj. Bicipital (de los bíceps).
bicípite adj. Bicephalous, two-headed.
bicloruro m. QUÍM. Dichloride, bichloride.
bicoca f. FIG. y FAM. Trinket, knick-knack (fruslería). | Bargain (ganga). || Trifle (casi nada). | Cushy job (puesto ventajoso). || Small fort (fortificación). || *Amer.* Calotte, skullcap (de los clérigos). | Flick (capirotazo). || FIG. y FAM. *Por una bicoca*, for a song (muy barato).
bicolor adj. Two-tone, two-colour, bicolour [U.S., bicolor]. || *Un coche bicolor*, a two-tone car.
bicóncavo, va adj. Biconcave.
biconvexo, xa adj. Biconvex.
bicorne adj. Two-cornered (sombrero).
bicornio m. Two-cornered hat (sombrero).
bicromato m. QUÍM. Dichromate, bichromate.
bicromía f. Two-colour print.
bicuadrado, da adj. MAT. Biquadratic (ecuación).
bicúspide adj./s. m. Bicuspid.
bicha f. (Ant.). Little animal, tiny creature *o* beast (bicho). || Snake (culebra). || ARQ. Mask, mascaron.
bichear v. tr. *Amer.* To spy on, to keep watch on.
bichero m. MAR. Boathook (para barco).
bicho m. Little animal, tiny beast (animal pequeño). || Bug, creepy-crawly (insecto). || FAM. Bull (toro de lidia). || FIG. Queer specimen, queer card (persona extraña). | Ugly person, freak (persona fea). || — *Amer. Bicho colorado*, harvest bug, harvest louse. || FIG. y FAM. *Bicho malo* or *mal bicho*, swine, nasty piece of work (hombre), bitch (mujer). | *Bicho malo nunca muere*, bad pennies always turn up. | *No hay bicho viviente que no lo sepa*, it is common knowledge. | *Todo bicho viviente*, every Tom, Dick and Harry, every living soul.
bichoco, ca adj. *Amer.* Old, no longer fit for work (caballo). | Old, decrepit (persona).
bidé m. Bidet (mueble).
bidentado, da adj. Bidentate, double-toothed.
— M. AGR. Pitchfork.
bidón m. Can: *bidón de gasolina*, petrol can, can of petrol.
biela f. AUT. Connecting rod (biela de conexión). || — *Biela de acoplamiento*, drag link. || AUT. *Cabeza de biela*, big end. | *Pie de biela*, small end. | *Una biela se ha fundido*, a big end has gone.

BICICLETA, *f.* — BICYCLE

I. Generalidades, f. — Generalities.

ciclista *m.* y *f.*	cyclist
bicileta *f.*; bici *f.*	bicycle, cycle; bike
pista (*f.*) para cilistas	cycle track
cilismo *m.*	cycling
montar en bicicleta	to ride a bicycle
señales *f. pl.* (con el brazo)	hand signals
rueda (*f.*) libre	freewheel
tándem *m.*	tandem
bicicleta (*f.*) de carrera	racing cycle
velódromo *m.*	velodrome, cycling stadium
draisina *f.*	penny farthing

II. Partes (f.) principales. — Main parts.

manillar *m.*, guía *m.*	handlebars *pl.*
manillar (*m.*) de carrera	racing *o* drop handlebars *pl.*
puños (*m. pl.*) del manillar	handlebar grips
timbre *m.*	bell
bocina *f.*	hooter
freno (*m.*) delantero, trasero	front, back brake
palanca (*f.*) del freno	brake handle
cable (*m.*) del freno	brake cable
zapata (*f.*) del freno	brake shoe *o* rubber
sillín *m.*	saddle
muelles (*m. pl.*) del sillín	saddle springs
cartera *f.*	saddlebag
portaequipajes *m. inv.*	carrier
cuadro (*m.*) ligero	lightweight frame
barra *f.*	crossbar
palanca (*f.*) de cambio de velocidades	gear lever *o* change [U.S., gearshift]
horquilla (*f.*) delantera	front fork
dinamo *m.*	dynamo
soporte (*m.*) del faro	lamp bracket
faro *m.*	lamp, front light
piloto *m.*	rear light
catafaro *m.*	reflector
cojinete (*m.*) de bolas	ball bearing
rueda (*f.*) delantera	front wheel
radio *m.*	spoke
palometa *f.*	wing *o* butterfly nut
llanta *f.*	rim
neumático *m.*	tyre
cámara (*f.*) de aire	inner tube
válvula *f.*	valve
guardabarros *m. inv.*	mudguard [U.S., fender]
pedal *m.*	pedal
pedalear	to pedal
plato *m.*	chain *o* sprocket wheel
piñón *m.*	rear sprocket wheel
piñón (*m.*) fijo	fixed wheel
cárter *m.*	chain guard
cadena *f.*	chain
piñón (*m.*) de tres velocidades	three-speed gear
cambio (*m.*) de velocidades	gear change mechanism

III. Averías (f.) y reparaciones, f. — Breakdowns and repairs.

rueda (*f.*) alabeada	buckled wheel
bloquearse (la rueda)	to lock [the wheel]
pinchazo *m.*	puncture
arreglar, reparar	to mend, to fix
bolsa (*f.*) de herramientas	tool bag, saddlebag
herramientas *f. pl.*	tool kit, repair kit, *sing.*
llave (*f.*) inglesa	spanner
desmontable *m.*	tyre lever
parche *m.*	patch
disolución *f.*	glue

bielda f. AGR. Winnowing fork. | Winnowing (acción de bieldar).

bieldar v. tr. To winnow (los cereales).

bieldo m. AGR. Winnowing fork. | Pitchfork (con dos dientes).

bien m. Good: *lo hice por tu bien* or *en bien tuvo*, I did it for your good; *el bien de la patria*, the good of the country; *el bien público*, the common good. || Interest, benefit, good (provecho): *hacer algo por el bien común*, to do sth. in the common interest *o* for the common good. || Property: *bienes comunes*, public property. || Right, good: *discernir el bien del mal*, to tell right from wrong *o* good from evil. || — Pl. Goods: *bienes de consumo*, consumer goods. || — *Bienes de equipo*, capital goods. || *Bienes gananciales*, acquest, property acquired in married life. || *Bienes inmuebles*, real estate. || *Bienes mal adquiridos a nadie han enriquecido*, ill-gotten gains seldom prosper. || *Bienes mostrencos*, ownerless property. || *Bienes muebles*, personal property, movables. || *Bienes públicos*, public property. || *Bienes raíces* or *bienes sedientes*, real estate, *sing.* || *Bienes semovientes*, livestock, *sing.* || *Bienes terrestres*, worldly goods. || *Bienes y personas*, all hands and goods (en un naufragio). || *Comunidad de bienes gananciales*, joint estate, community of property acquired during marriage. || FAM. *Decir mil bienes de*, to speak highly of. || *Devolver bien por mal*, to repay evil with good. || *En bien de*, for the good of, for the benefit of. || *Hacer bien* or *el bien*, to do good. || *Haz bien y no mires a quien*, do well and dread no shame. || *Hombre de bien*, upright *o* honest man. || *Mi bien*, my darling. || *No hay mal que por bien no venga*, every cloud has a silver lining. || *Para* or *por el bien de*, for the good of, in the interest of.

bien adv. Well: *hablar bien un idioma*, to speak a language well; *bien criado*, well brought-up; *el negocio marcha bien*, the business is going well. || Properly (de acuerdo con los principios): *obrar bien*, to act properly. || Properly, right, well (según las reglas): *lo has hecho bien*, you did it right. || Correctly, right (exactamente): *respondió bien*, he answered correctly. || Soundly: *razonar bien*, to reason soundly. || Comfortably, well: *vivo bien*, I live comfortably. || Good: *oler bien*, to smell good. || Willingly, gladly, with pleasure: *bien le ayudaría si*, I would help you with pleasure if. || Quite, pretty, very: *está bien cansado*, he is quite tired; *es bien cruel*, he is very cruel; *es bien tarde*, it is quite late. || A lot: *hemos caminado bien*, we have walked a lot. || All right, okay (de acuerdo). || — *Ahora bien*, now, now then. || *¡Bien!*, good!, great! || *Bien es verdad que*, it is quite *o* very true that. || *Bien... o bien* or *bien sea... o bien*, either... or: *bien en coche o bien andando*, either by car or on foot. || *Bien se ve que*, it is quite plain that, it is easy to see that. || *Bien te lo dije*, I told you so. || *Como bien le parezca*, as you wish, as you want. || *De bien en mejor*, better and better. || *¡Está bien!*, fine!, all right (de acuerdo), that's enough! (¡basta!). || *Está bien que lo haga*, is it all right for me [*o* him, etc.] to do it. || *Estar bien con*, to be well in with. || *Estar bien de dinero*, to be well off. || *Estar bien de salud*, to be well. || *Estar bien en un sitio*, to feel comfortable *o* happy in a place. || *Gente bien*, v. GENTE. || *Hacer bien en*, to do well to, to be right to. || *Lo bien fundado*, the grounds. || *Mal que bien*, as best as one can (lo mejor posible), one way or another (de cualquier manera). || *Más bien*, rather. || *Más o menos bien*, quite well. || *¡Muy bien!*, hear, hear! (asentimiento). || *No bien*, as soon as, no sooner... than; *no bien vio el relámpago, echó a correr*, as soon as he saw the lightning he started to run, no sooner did he see the lightning than he started to run. || *No sentar bien a*, v. SENTAR. || *O bien*, or, or else. || *¡Pues bien!*, well, well then. || FAM. *¡Qué bien!*, oh, good!, great! || *Quien bien te quiere te hará llorar*, you have to be cruel to be kind, spare the rod and spoil the child. || *Sentar bien*, v. SENTAR. || *Si bien*, while, although. || *Tener a bien*, to be so kind *o* so good as to: *tenga usted a bien decirme*, be so kind as to tell me; to think it better, to see fit: *tuve a bien quedarme más tiempo*, I thought it better to stay longer. || *Tomar a bien*, to take well: *tomar a bien una broma*, to take a joke well. || *¡Ya está bien!*, that's enough! || *Y bien*, now then.

bienal adj./s. f. Biennial.

bienandante adj. Happy (feliz). || Prosperous.

bienandanza f. Happiness (felicidad). || Success (éxito). || Prosperity (prosperidad).

bienaventurado, da adj. Happy, fortunate. || REL. Blessed. || FIG. Simple, naïve.
— My f. FIG. Simpleton, naïve person (inocente). || Fortunate person (feliz).

bienaventuranza f. Well-being (bienestar). || Happiness (felicidad). || Bliss (suma felicidad). || REL. Blessedness. || — Pl. REL. Beatitudes.

bienestar m. Well-being, welfare.

bienhablado, da adj. Well-spoken.

bienhadado, da adj. Fortunate, lucky.

bienhechor, ra adj. Beneficent, beneficial.
— M. y f. Benefactor (hombre), benefactress (mujer).

bienintencionado, da adj. Well-meaning.

bienio m. Biennium, two-year period.

bienmandado, da adj. Obedient.

bienoliente adj. Fragrant, sweet-smelling.

bienquerencia f. o **bienquerer** m. Affection. || Goodwill (buena voluntad).

bienquerer* v. tr. To appreciate, to like.

bienquistar v. tr. To reconcile, to bring together.
— V. pr. To make it up, to become reconciled.

bienquisto, ta adj. Well-liked.

— OBSERV. This word is the irregular past participle of *bienquerer*.

bienteveo m. Lookout post [hut built on piles for watching vineyards]. || Observation post, lookout post (mirador).

bienvenida f. Welcome. || *Dar la bienvenida a*, to welcome, to bid welcome to.

bienvenido, da adj. Welcome. || *¡Que sea usted bienvenido!*, welcome!

bienvivir v. intr. To live well *o* comfortably (con holgura). || To live honestly *o* decently (decentemente).

bies m. Bias binding, band cut on the cross (trozo de tela). || *Al bies*, on the bias, on the cross.

bifásico, ca adj. Two-phase (corriente).

bife m. *Amer.* Steak: *bife a caballo*, steak with two fried eggs. | Slap (bofetada).

bífido, da adj. BOT. Bifid.

bifocal adj. Bifocal. || *Lentes bifocales*, bifocal glasses, bifocals.
biftec m. Steak.
bifurcación f. Bifurcation. || Fork (de la carretera, etc.). || Junction (en ferrocarriles).
bifurcarse v. pr. To fork, to bifurcate (dividirse en dos): *la carretera se bifurca en Soria*, the road forks at Soria. || To branch off (separarse).
bigamia f. Bigamy.
bígamo, ma adj. Bigamous.
— M. y f. Bigamist.
bigardear v. intr. FAM. To roam idly (vagar).
bigardo, da o **bigardón, ona** adj. Idle, lazy (vago). || Licentious.
— M. y f. Idler, lazybones (vago). || Libertine.
bígaro m. Winkle (molusco).
bigarrado, da adj. Variegated, mottled.
bigarro m. Winkle (molusco).
bignoniáceas f. pl. BOT. Bignoniaceae.
bigorneta f. Small anvil, small beakiron, small bickiron.
bigornia f. Beakiron, bickiron, two-beaked anvil.
bigote m. Moustache [U.S., mustache]: *bigote retorcido*, handlebar moustache; *bigote con guías*, curled-up moustache. || Whiskers, *pl.* (de gato). || IMPR. Rule. || Tap *o* tapping hole (en un horno). || — FAM. *De bigote*, great, terrific (bien): *estar de bigote*, to be terrific. | *Tener bigotes* or *ser un hombre de bigotes*, to be a man of energy.
bigotera f. Moustache support (para el bigote). || Flap seat, folding seat (en los coches). || Bow compass (compás). || Toe-cup (del zapato). || Slag tap (en un horno). || — Pl. Moustache, *sing.* [U.S., mustache] (bocera en los labios).
bigotudo, da adj. Moustached [U.S., mustached].
bigudí m. Curler.
bikini m. Bikini (bañador).
bilabarquín m. *Amer.* Brace and bit.
bilabiado, da adj. BOT. Bilabiate.
bilabial adj./s. f. Bilabial.
bilarciasis f. MED. Bilharziasis, bilharziosis, bilharzia.
bilateral adj. Bilateral: *acuerdo bilateral*, bilateral agreement.
bilbaína f. Beret (boina).
bilbaíno, na adj. [Of *o* from] Bilbao.
— M. y f. Native *o* inhabitant of Bilbao.
bilbilitano, na adj. [Of *o* from] Calatayud [city in Aragon formerly *Bilbilis*].
— M. y F. Native *o* inhabitant of Calatayud.
bilharciasis f. MED. V. BILARCIASIS.
biliar o **biliario, ria** adj. Biliary. || — MED. *Cálculo biliar*, bile stone. || ANAT. *Conducto biliar*, bile duct.
bilingüe adj. Bilingual.
bilingüismo m. Bilingualism.
bilioso, sa adj. Bilious.
bilis f. Bile (humor). || FIG. Bile, bad temper. || — FIG. *Descargar la bilis contra uno*, to rail at s.o. | *Exaltar la bilis a uno*, to rile s.o.
bilobulado, da adj. Bilobed, bilobate.
bilocular adj. BOT. Bilocular.
bilongo *Amer.* Evil eye: *echar bilongo a*, to cast the evil eye on.
billa f. Billiard ball.
billar m. Billiards: *jugar al billar*, to play billiards. || — *Billar ruso*, snooker. || *Bola, mesa, taco de billar*, billiard ball, table, cue.
billarista m. Billiard player.
billetaje m. Tickets, *pl.* (de un espectáculo).
billete m. Note (carta). || Note [U.S., bill] (de banco). || Ticket (de tren, de lotería, de espectáculo, etc.): *sacar un billete*, to buy *o* to get a ticket; *billete circular*, round-trip ticket. || Note: *billete al portador*, note payable to bearer. || HERÁLD. Billet. || — *Billete a mitad de precio*, half-price ticket. || *Billete amoroso*, love letter. || *Billete de banco*, banknote. || *Billete de ida*, single ticket. || *Billete de ida y vuelta*, return ticket [U.S., round-trip ticket]. || *Billete postal*, lettercard. || *Billete semanal*, weekly ticket. || *Billete tarifa completa*, full fare ticket. || *Dar una función con el cartel de "no hay billetes"*, to give a sell-out performance. || *Medio billete*, half, half-price ticket, half fare. || *No hay billetes*, sold out, house full.
billetera f. o **billetero** m. Wallet [U.S., pocketbook, billfold].
billón m. Billion [U.S., trillion] (millón de millones).

— OBSERV. En los Estados Unidos la palabra *billion* equivale a mil millones.

billonésimo, na adj./s. Billionth [U.S., trillionth].
bimano, na adj. Bimanous, bimanal, two-handed.
— M. Bimane.
bimba f. FAM. Topper (chistera). | Punch (puñetazo). || *Amer.* FAM. Beanpole (persona alta). | Drunkenness (borrachera).
bimbalete m. *Amer.* Seesaw (columpio). | Shadoof, shaduf (para extraer agua).
bimensual adj. Twice-monthly, fortnightly, bimonthly.
bimestral adj. Bimonthly, bimestrial.
bimestre m. Two months.
bimetálico, ca adj. Bimetallic.
bimetalismo m. Bimetallism.
bimetalista adj./s. Bimetallist.
bimotor, ra adj. Twin-engine, twin-engined.
— M. Twin-engine plane, twin-engined plane.
bina f. AGR. Second ploughing.
binadera f. AGR. Hoe.
binador m. AGR. Hoer. | Hoe (herramienta).
binadora m. AGR. Mechanical hoe.
binadura f. AGR. Second ploughing.
binar v. tr. AGR. To plough for the second time (arar). | To hoe for the second time (cavar).
binario, ria adj. Binary. || MÚS. Two-four (compás). || MAT. *Sistema binario*, binary system.
binazón f. AGR. Second ploughing.
bincha f. *Amer.* Hairband.
bingarrote m. *Amer.* Agave liquor.
binocular adj. Binocular.
binóculo m. Pince-nez.
binomio, mia adj./s.m. MAT. Binomial.
binza f. Membrane (telilla). || Skin (de cebolla).
biobibliografía f. Biobibliography.
biodegradable adj. Biodegradable.
biofísica f. Biophysics.
biogénesis f. Biogenesis.
biogenético, ca adj. Biogenetic, biogenetical.
biogeografía f. Biogeography.
biografía f. Biography.
biografiar v. tr. To write [s.o.'s] biography.
biográfico, ca adj. Biographic, biographical.
biógrafo, fa m. y f. Biographer.
biología f. Biology.
biológico, ca adj. Biological: *guerra biológica*, biological warfare.
biólogo m. Biologist.
biombo m. Folding screen.
biomecánica f. Biomechanics.
biometría f. Biometry.
biopsia f. MED. Biopsy.
bioquímico, ca adj. Biochemical.
— M. y f. Biochemist. || — F. Biochemistry.
bioscopio m. Bioscope.
biosfera f. Biosphere.
biosíntesis f. Biosynthesis.
biotecnia f. Biotechnics.
bioterapia f. MED. Biotherapy.
biótico, ca adj. Biotic.
biotita f. MIN. Biotite.
biotropismo m. Biotropism.
bióxido m. QUÍM. Dioxide.
bipartición f. Bipartition.
bipartido, da adj. Bipartite.
bipartito, ta adj. Bipartite: *acuerdo bipartito*, bipartite agreement.
bípedo, da adj./s. m. Biped.
biplano m. Biplane (avión).
biplaza adj./s.m. Two-seater.
bipolar adj. Bipolar, two-pole.
bipolaridad f. Bipolarity.
biricú m. Sword belt.
birimbao m. MÚS. Jew's-harp.
birla f. Skittle, ninepin (bolo).
birlar v. tr. To bowl a second time (en el juego de los bolos). || FIG. y FAM. To pinch (robar, quitar). | To bump off (matar).
birlibirloque (por arte de) loc. adv. As if by magic.
birlocha f. Kite (cometa).
birlocho m. Open carriage.
birlonga f. Brelan (juego).
Birmania n. pr. f. GEOGR. Burma.
birmano, na adj./s. Burmese.
birreactor adj. Twin-jet.
— M. Twin-jet plane.
birrefringencia f. FÍS. Birefringence.
birrefringente adj. FÍS. Birefringent.
birreme f. MAR. Bireme.
birreta f. Biretta.
birrete m. Biretta (birreta). || Cap (de un magistrado). || Bonnet (gorro). || Mortarboard (de catedrático).
birretina f. MIL. Hussar's cap.
birria f. FAM. Horror (cosa o persona fea). | Piece of junk *o* trash *o* rubbish (cosa mala o sin valor). || *Amer.* Mania (capricho). || *Ser una birria*, to be horrible.
bis adv. A (número): *vivo en el 22 bis*, I live at 22 A. || MÚS. Bis. || Twice, bis (dos veces).
— M. Encore.
— Interj. Encore!
bisabuelo, la m. y f. Great-grandfather, great-grandmother. || — M. pl. Great-grandparents.
bisagra f. Hinge (de puerta, etc.).
bisanual o **bisanuo, nua** adj. Biennial.
bisar v. tr. To encore [an actor], to call [an actor] to give an encore. || To repeat (una canción).
bisbisar o **bisbisear** v. tr. FAM. To mutter, to mumble (decir entre dientes). | To whisper (al oído).
bisbiseo m. Whisper, whispering (susurro). || Muttering, mumbling (murmullo).
biscuit m. Biscuit (porcelana).

— OBSERV. The Spanish translation of *biscuit* (pastry) is *galleta*.

bisecar v. tr. MAT. To bisect.
bisección f. MAT. Bisection.
bisector, triz adj. MAT. Bisecting.
— F. MAT. Bisector, bisectrix.
bisegmentar v. tr. MAT. To bisect.

bisel m. Bevel, bevel edge. || — *El espejo tiene el borde en bisel*, the mirror has a bevelled edge. || *Tallar en bisel*, to bevel.
biselado m. Bevelling.
biselar v. tr. To bevel.
bisemanal adj. Twice-weekly, biweekly: *una revista bisemanal*, a biweekly magazine.
bisemanario m. *Amer.* Twice-weekly o biweekly magazine.
bisexual adj. Bisexual.
bisiesto adj. Bissextile. || *Año bisiesto*, leap year.
bisilábico, ca o **bisílabo, ba** adj. Two-syllabled.
bismuto m. Bismuth.
bisnieto, ta m. y f. Great-grandchild (chico o chica), great-grandson (chico), great-granddaughter (chica). || — M. pl. Great-grandchildren.
bisojo, ja adj. Cross-eyed, squinting (bizco). || *Un chico bisojo*, a cross-eyed boy, a boy with a squint.
bisonte m. ZOOL. Bison.
bisoñada o **bisoñería** f. FIG. y FAM. Beginner's mistake, blunder.
bisoñé m. Toupee.
bisoño, ña adj. Green, inexperienced (principiante). || MIL. Raw (recluta).
— M. y f. Greenhorn, novice. || — M. MIL. Raw recruit, rookie (fam.).
bistec o **bisté** m. Steak.
bistorta f. BOT. Bistort.
bistre m. Bistre [U.S., bister] (color).
bisturí m. MED. Bistoury, scalpel.
bisulco, ca adj. ZOOL. Bisulcate, cloven-hoofed.
bisulfato m. Bisulphate.
bisulfito m. QUÍM. Bisulphite.
bisurco adj. m. *Arado bisurco*, double-furrow plough.
bisutería f. Imitation jewellery, paste. || *Una joya de bisutería*, a piece of imitation jewellery.
bita f. MAR. Bitt, bollard.
bitácora f. MAR. Binnacle. || *Cuaderno de bitácora*, logbook.
Bitinia n. pr. f. Bithynia.
bitongo adj. m. FAM. *Niño bitongo*, young upstart.
bitoque m. Spigot, spile (de barril). || *Amer.* Tap (grifo). | Cannula (de una jeringa). | Sewer, drain (sumidero).
bitter m. Bitters, *pl.* (aperitivo)
bituminoso, sa adj. Bituminous: *carbón bituminoso*, bituminous coal.
bivalencia f. QUÍM. Bivalence.
bivalente adj. QUÍM. Bivalent, divalent.
bivalvo, va adj./s. m. Bivalve.
Bizancio n. pr. GEOGR. Byzantium.
bizantinismo m. Byzantinism.
bizantino, na adj./s. Byzantine. || *Discusiones bizantinas*, hairsplitting.
bizarrear v. intr. To show courage (valor). || To show generosity (generosidad).
bizarría f. Bravery, gallantry (valor). || Generosity (generosidad). || Dash (gallardía).
bizarro, rra adj. Brave, gallant: *un bizarro coronel*, a brave colonel. || Generous. || Dashing (gallardo).
bizaza f. o **bizazas** f. pl. Double bag, *sing.*
bizcar v. intr. To squint, to be cross-eyed.
bizco, ca adj. Cross-eyed, squinting. || — FIG. y FAM. *Dejar bizco*, to dumbfound, to flabbergast. || *Ponerse bizco*, to squint (ojos), to be dumbfounded, to be flabbergasted (pasmado).
— M. y f. Cross-eyed person, person with a squint.
bizcochar v. tr. To warm up: *pan bizcochado*, warmed-up bread. || To bake (porcelana).
bizcochería f. *Amer.* Confectioner's shop, confectioner's.
bizcocho m. CULIN. Sponge (masa). | Sponge cake (pastel). || TECN. Biscuit (de porcelana). || *Bizcocho borracho*, rum baba.
bizcotela f. Iced cake.
biznaga f. BOT. Bishop's weed. || Small bouquet of jasmine (ramillete).
biznieto, ta m. y f. Great-grandchild (chico o chica), great-grandson (chico), great-granddaughter (chica).
bizquear v. intr. FAM. To squint, to be cross-eyed.
bizquera f. Squint (estrabismo).
black-rot m. Black rot (enfermedad de la vid).
blanca f. Ancient coin (antigua moneda). || MÚS. Minim. || ZOOL. Magpie (urraca). || — *Blanca doble*, double blank (dominós). || FIG. y FAM. *No tener blanca* or *estar sin blanca*, to be stony broke, not to have two halfpennies to rub together.
Blancanieves n. pr. f. Snow White.
blanco, ca adj. White: *pan, vino blanco*, white bread, wine. || White, light (piel). || White (raza). || Fair (tez). || FIG. y FAM. Yellow, cowardly (cobarde). || — *Arma blanca*, knife. || *Bandera blanca*, white flag. || *Blanco como el papel*, as white as a sheet, as white as a ghost. || *Darle carta blanca a uno*, to give s.o. a free hand. || *Manjar blanco*, blancmange (natilla). || *Más blanco que la nieve*, as white as snow. || *Ropa blanca*, V. ROPA.
— M. y f. White man, white woman, white person, white (de raza blanca). || — M. White (color). || Interval, interlude (intervalo). || Gap (en una fila). || Blank (espacio). || Target (de tiro). || White patch (mancha de un animal). || FIG. Goal, aim, target (objetivo). || — *Blanco de ballena*, spermaceti. || *Blanco de cinc*, zinc white. || *Blanco de España*, whiting. || *Blanco de la uña*, half-moon. || *Blanco del ojo*, white of the eye. || *Blanco de plomo*, white lead. || *Calentar al blanco*, to bring to white heat, to make white-hot (metal). || *Caseta de tiro al blanco*, shooting gallery. || *Como de lo blanco a lo negro*, as different as chalk and cheese. || *Dar en el blanco* or *hacer blanco*, to hit the mark, to hit the bull's eye. || *Dejar algo en blanco*, to leave sth. blank. || *En blanco*, blank (papel), useless: *ha sido un día en blanco*, it has been a useless day; disappointed: *quedarse en blanco*, to be disappointed. || *Mirarle a uno en el blanco de los ojos*, to look s.o. in the face. || *No distinguir lo blanco de lo negro*, not to distinguish black from white. || *Pasar una noche en blanco*, to spend a sleepless night. || *Ser el blanco de las burlas*, to be a laughingstock, to be the object of ridicule. || *Ser el blanco de las miradas*, to be the centre of attention. || *Tirar al blanco*, to shoot at a target. || *Tiro al blanco*, target shooting. || *Votar en blanco*, to vote blank.
blancor m. Whiteness (blancura).
blancote, ta adj. Sickly white. || FAM. Yellow (cobarde).
blancura f. Whiteness. || FIG. Purity (del alma).
blancuzco, ca adj. Whitish.
blandear v. intr. To weaken, to yield.
— V. tr. To convince. || To brandish (blandir).
— V. pr. To weaken, to yield.
blandengue adj. FAM. Weak, feeble, soft.
— M. y f. Softy, weakling (débil). || — M. Soldier who protected the frontiers of Argentina.
blandenguería f. Weakness, feebleness, softness.
blandicia f. Softness (molicie). || Flattery (lisonja).
blandir* v. tr. To brandish (un arma).
blando, da adj. Soft: *este colchón es blando*, this mattress is soft. || Tender (carne, etc.). || FIG. Gentle (mirada, palabras, etc.). | Weak: *carácter blando*, weak character. | Soft: *un profesor blando con sus alumnos*, a teacher who is soft with his pupils. | Easy, cushy (fam.): *una vida blanda*, an easy life. | Soft, gentle: *blando murmullo de las olas*, soft murmuring of the waves. | Mild (clima). | Cowardly (cobarde). || — *Blando de carnes*, flabby. || *Blando de corazón*, tender-hearted, soft-hearted. || FIG. y FAM. *Ojos blandos*, watery eyes (llorosos).
— Adv. Softly, gently.
blandón m. Torch (hachón). || Candlestick (candelero).
blanducho, cha o **blandujo, ja** adj. FAM. Softish. | Flabby (carne, cuerpo).
blandura f. Softness (cualidad). || Tenderness (de los alimentos). || FIG. Gentleness (de la mirada, las palabras, etc.). | Weakness (de carácter). | Ease, easiness (de vida). | Flabbiness (de carne). | Mildness (del tiempo). | Blandishment (lisonja). | Endearment (amabilidad).
blanduzco, ca adj. FAM. Softish.
blanqueado m. V. BLANQUEO.
blanqueador, ra m. y f. Whitewasher.
blanqueadura f. o **blanqueamiento** m. V. BLANQUEO.
blanquear v. tr. To whiten (volver blanco). || To whitewash (encalar las paredes). || To bleach (tejidos, etc.). || To blanch (almendras, metales). || To wax [the honeycomb after winter] (las abejas). || IMPR. To space out. || To refine (azúcar). || *Sepulcro blanqueado*, whited sepulchre.
— V. intr. To turn white, to whiten. || To show white, to appear white: *blanquean algunas manchas de nieve en la ladera*, a few patches of snow show white on the hillside. || To be whitish (tirar a blanco).
blanquecedor m. Metal blancher (de moneda).
blanquecer* v. tr. To whiten. || To blanch (metales).
blanquecimiento m. Blanching (metales).
blanquecino, na adj. Whitish.
blanqueo m. Whitening. || Whitewashing (encalado). || Bleaching (con lejía). || TECN. Blanching. | Refining (del azúcar).
blanquete m. Whiting (sustancia para blanquear). || White cosmetic (afeite).
blanquición f. Blanching (metales).
blanquillo, lla adj. *Trigo blanquillo*, white wheat.
— M. *Amer.* White-skinned peach (durazno). | Whitefish (pez). | Egg (huevo).
blanquinegro, gra adj. Black and white.
blanquinoso, sa adj. Whitish.
blanquizco, ca adj. Whitish.
Blas n. pr. m. Blase. || *Díjolo* or *lo dijo Blas, punto redondo*, you're always right, whatever you say [said ironically].
blasfemador, ra adj. Blasphemous.
— M. y f. Blasphemer.
blasfemar v. intr. To blaspheme. || FIG. To curse.
blasfematorio, ria adj. Blasphemous.
blasfemia f. Blasphemy. || FIG. Curse.
blasfemo, ma adj. Blasphemous.
— M. y f. Blasphemer.
blasón m. Heraldry (heráldica). || Coat of arms, armorial bearings, *pl.*, blazon (escudo de armas). || Bearing, device (divisa). || FIG. Honour, glory. || — Pl. Noble ancestry, *sing.*: *está orgulloso de sus blasones*, he is proud of his noble ancestry. || *Hacer blasón de*, to boast of o about, to brag of o about.
blasonador, ra adj. Boasting, bragging.
— M. y f. Boaster, braggart.

blasonar v. tr. To emblazon.
— V. intr. Fig. To boast of *o* about, to brag of *o* about: *blasonar de rico*, to boast of being rich.
blasonería f. Boasting, bragging.
blastema m. Biol. Blastema.
blastodermo m. Biol. Blastoderm.
blastómero m. Biol. Blastomere.
blastomicetos m. pl. Blastomycetes (hongos).
blastomicosis f. Med. Blastomycosis.
blástula f. Biol. Blastula.
bledo m. Blite (planta). || Fig. y fam. *Me importa un bledo* or *no se me da un bledo*, I don't care two hoots, I don't give a damn.
blenda f. Min. Blende.
blenorragia f. Med. Blennorrhagia.
blenorrea f. Med. Blennorrhoea.
blinda f. Mil. Blind.
blindado, da adj. Mil. Armoured, armour-plated. || Tecn. Shielded.
blindaje m. Mil. Blindage (fortificación). | Armour plate, armour (revestimiento de tanques, etc.). | Armour plating (operación). || Tecn. Shield.
blindar v. tr. To armour, to armour-plate. || Tecn. To shield.
bloc m. Pad (para apuntes). || Writing pad (para cartas).
blocao m. Blockhouse.
block-system m. Tecn. Block system.
blonda f. Spanish lace, blond lace.
blondo, da adj. Blond, fair (rubio).
bloom m. Bloom (lingote bruto).
bloque m. Block: *un bloque de mármol*, a block of marble. || Bloc (política): *el bloque atlántico*, the Atlantic Bloc. || Block, brick (de helado). || — Tecn. *Bloque de cilindros*, cylinder block. | *Bloque del motor*, engine block. | *Bloque de matrizar*, female die. || *Bloque de viviendas*, block of flats. || *Bloque diagrama*, block diagram. || *De un solo bloque*, in one piece. || Fig. *En bloque*, en bloc. | *Formar bloque con*, to form a block with.
bloqueador, ra adj. Blocking, which blocks. || Blockading: *armada bloqueadora*, blockading fleet. || Besieging (sitiador).
— M. y f. Besieger.
bloquear v. tr. Mil. y Mar. To blockade. || Com. To freeze, to block. || Dep. To block: *bloquear una pelota*, to block a ball. || To block, to jam (un mecanismo, etc.). || To obstruct, to block (obstruir). || Fig. To block (un proyecto de ley, etc.). || *Estar bloqueado por la tormenta*, to be cut off by the storm.
bloqueo m. Mil. y Mar. Blockade: *levantar un bloqueo*, to raise a blockade; *romper un bloqueo*, to run a blockade. || Com. Freezing, blocking.
blue-jean m. Jeans, *pl.* (pantalón vaquero).
blues m. Mús. Blues.
bluff m. Bluff.
blusa f. Blouse (de mujer). || Overall [U.S., frock] (guardapolvo).
blusón m. Long *o* loose shirt (blusa larga). || Sailor blouse (de mujer).
boa f. Boa (reptil). || Boa (adorno de pieles *o* de plumas).
boardilla f. Attic, garret (buhardilla).
boato m. Show, ostentation (ostentación). || Pomp (pompa).
bobada f. Stupid *o* silly thing: *decir, hacer una bobada*, to say, to do sth. stupid. || — *Déjate de bobadas*, that's enough of your nonsense. || *¡Qué bobadas dices!*, you're talking nonsense.
bobalicón, ona adj. Fam. Simple, stupid, idiotic.
— M. y f. Fam. Simpleton, idiot, nincompoop.
bobear v. intr. To talk nonsense, to be silly (decir tonterías). || To be stupid *o* silly, to play the fool (hacer el tonto).
bobería f. V. bobada. || Silliness, stupidity.
bobeta adj./s. *Amer.* V. bobalicón.
bóbilis bóbilis (de) adv. Fam. Without lifting a finger (sin esfuerzo). | For nothing (de balde).
bobina f. Reel: *las bobinas de una máquina de escribir*, the reels on a typewriter. || Bobbin, reel, spool (de hilo). || Spool, reel (de fotos). || Electr. Coil: *bobina de sintonía, de encendido*, tuning, ignition coil.
bobinado m. Winding.
bobinador, ra m. y f. Winder (operario). || — F. Winding machine (máquina).
bobinar v. tr. To wind.
bobito m. Zool. Cuban flycatcher.
bobo, ba adj. Stupid, silly, foolish (tonto). || Naïve, simple (candoroso).
— M. y f. Dunce, fool.
— M. Teatr. Buffoon. || Central American fresh water fish. || — Fig. *A los bobos se les aparece la Madre de Dios*, fortune favours fools. | *El bobo de Coria*, the village idiot. | *Entre bobos anda el juego*, they are as thick as thieves.
bobsleigh m. Bobsleigh (trineo).
boca f. Anat. Mouth. || Pincers, *pl.*, nippers, *pl.* (de crustáceo). || Lip, mouth (de vasija). || Muzzle (de cañón). || Entrance, mouth (de puerto, metro, túnel). || Tecn. Opening (de un horno). | Mouth, throat (de alto horno). | Cutting edge (de una herramienta cortante). | Jaws, *pl.* (de las pinzas). | Peen (de un martillo). || Entry, entrance (de una calle). || Aroma, bouquet (del vino). || Opening (en el teatro). || Fig. Mouth: *tener seis bocas que alimentar*, to have six mouths to feed. || — Pl. Mouth, *sing.*: *las bocas del Nilo*, the mouth of the Nile. || — *A boca de cañón*, point-blank (desde muy cerca), suddenly (repentinamente). || Fig. *A boca de jarro*, point-blank (a quemarropa). | *A boca de noche*, at dusk, at twilight. | *A boca llena*, without mincing one's words, straight out. | *Abrir boca*, to give an appetite. || Fam. *¡A callarse la boca!*, shut up!, shut your mouth! || *Ancho de boca*, wide-mouthed (vasija). || Fig. *Andar de boca en boca*, to be on everyone's lips. | *Andar en boca de las gentes*, to be the main talking point. | *A pedir de boca*, to one's heart's content, for the asking. || *Blando de boca*, soft-mouthed, tender-mouthed (un caballo). || *Boca abajo*, face down, on one's stomach. || *Boca a boca*, mouth-to-mouth respiration, kiss of life. || *Boca arriba*, face up, on one's back (una persona): *le volvieron boca arriba*, they turned him onto his back; face up (una cosa). || Fig. *Boca de escorpión*, evil tongue (maldiciente). | *Boca de espuerta*, big mouth. || Mil. *Boca de fuego*, piece of artillery, gun. || *Boca de incendio*, fire hydrant. || *Boca del estómago*, pit of the stomach. || *Boca de metro*, underground station entrance, tube station entrance [U.S., subway entrance]. || Fig. *Boca de oro*, silver tongue. || *Boca de riego*, hydrant. || Fig. *Buscarle a uno la boca*, to try to pick a quarrel with s.o. | *Calentársele a uno la boca*, to get carried away (hablar con extensión), to get heated, to lose one's temper (enfadarse). | *Callar la boca*, to keep quiet, to keep one's mouth shut. | *Cerrarle a uno la boca*, to shut s.o. up. || *Con la boca abierta*, gaping, agape, open-mouthed: *quedarse con la boca abierta*, to stand gaping. || *Con toda la boca*, in one mouthful. || Fam. *Darle a uno en la boca*, to smash s.o.'s face in (romper las narices), to leave s.o. speechless (dejar asombrado). || Fig. *Decir algo con la boca chica* o *chiquita*, to say one thing and mean another. || *Decir uno lo que le viene a la boca*, to say whatever comes into one's head. || *De la mano a la boca se pierde la sopa*, there's many a slip 'twixt the cup and the lip. || *Despegar la boca*, to open one's mouth. || *Duro de boca*, hard-mouthed (caballo). || Fig. *Echar por aquella boca*, to spit out (insultos). | *El que tiene boca se equivoca*, anyone can make a mistake. | *En boca cerrada no entran moscas*, silence is golden. | *Estar colgado de la boca de uno*, to hang on to s.o.'s every word. | *Estar oscuro como boca de lobo*, to be pitch dark, to be pitch black (túnel, noche, etc.). | *Estar uno a qué quieres boca*, to be well off, to be comfortable. | *Estar uno con la boca a la pared*, to be down and out. | *Hablar uno por boca de ganso*, to speak from hearsay. | *Hablar por boca de uno*, to have s.o. as spokesman. | *Hacer boca*, to give an appetite. | *Hacer una promesa de boca para fuera*, to make a half-hearted promise. | *Írsele la boca a uno*, to let the cat out of the bag, not to be able to keep one's mouth shut. | *Meterse en la boca del lobo*, to put one's head into the lion's mouth. | *No abrir* or *descoser la boca*, not to open one's mouth. | *No caérsele a uno algo de la boca*, to always have sth. on one's lips. | *No decir esta boca es mía*, not to say a word. | *¡No me busques la boca!*, you're asking for it! | *No tener nada que llevarse a la boca*, not to have a bite to eat. | *Poner boca de corazoncito*, to pout. | *Poner en boca de*, to put into the mouth of. || *Poner* or *volver las cartas boca arriba*, to lay one's cards face up (sentido propio), to put one's cards on the table (descubrir sus intenciones). | Fig. *Por la boca muere el pez*, the least said the better, silence is golden, least said is soonest mended. | *Por una boca*, in one voice, in unison. | *¡Punto en boca!*, mum's the word!, don't say a word! | *Quitarle a uno las palabras de la boca*, to take the words right out of s.o.'s mouth. | *Quitarse algo de la boca por otra persona*, to deprive o.s. of sth. for the sake of s.o. else. | *Respira este chico por boca de su padre*, in this boy's eyes his father cannot do a thing wrong. | *Salir a pedir de boca*, to turn out perfectly. | *Se me hace la boca agua al ver este pastel*, that cake makes my mouth water. || Fam. *Taparle la boca a uno*, to shut s.o. up (hacer callar), to shut s.o. up, to keep s.o. quiet (sobornar). || *Telón de boca*, drop curtain. || Fig. *Torcer la boca*, to grimace. | *Venir a pedir de boca*, to come at the right moment, to come at an opportune moment.
bocacalle f. Intersection. || *Tuerza a la tercera bocacalle a la izquierda*, take the third turning *o* street on your left.
bocacaz f. Outlet to irrigation ditch.
bocacha f. Big mouth. || Mil. Blunderbuss (trabuco).
bocadear v. tr. To divide into pieces.
bocadillo m. Sandwich (emparedado): *un bocadillo de queso*, a cheese sandwich. || Snack, bite to eat (comida ligera): *tomar un bocadillo*, to have a snack. || Fancy ribbon (cinta). || *Amer.* Guava or coconut sweet.
bocado m. Mouthful: *un bocado de pan*, a mouthful of bread. || Snack, bite to eat: *comer* or *tomar un bocado*, to have a snack *o* a bite to eat. || Beakful, billful (lo que coge el ave de una vez con el pico). || Bite (mordisco): *el niño me dio un bocado*, the child gave me a bite. || Bit (freno del caballo). || — *Bocado de Adán*, Adam's apple. || Fam. *Bocado de cardenal*, choice morsel. | *Comer algo en un bocado*, to eat sth.

in one mouthful. | *Con el bocado en la boca*, having scarcely finished eating. | *Me la comería a bocados*, I could eat her. | *No hay para un bocado*, there's not enough to feed a sparrow. || *No pruebo bocado desde ayer*, I haven't had a bite to eat since yesterday.
bocajarro (a) adv. Point-blank.
bocal m. Jar, pitcher.
bocamanga f. Cuff, wristband.
bocamina f. Pithead, mine entrance.
bocana f. *Amer*. Mouth (de un río).
bocanada f. Puff, whiff (de humo). || Blast, whiff (de olor desagradable). || Mouthful, swallow: *una bocanada de vino*, a swallow of wine. || — FIG. *Bocanada de aire*, some air: *abrió la ventana para que entrara una bocanada de aire*, he opened the window to let some air in; rush of air: *al abrir la ventana entró una bocanada de aire*, when he opened the window there was a rush of air into the room. | *Bocanada de gente*, crowd *o* throng of people. | *Bocanada de viento*, gust of wind.
bocarte m. MIN. Ore crusher, stamp mill.
bocateja f. Front tile [of a roof].
bocatijera f. Futchel, futchell (de carruaje).
bocaza f. FAM. Big mouth.
bocazas m. inv. FAM. Big mouth (que habla demasiado).
bocazo m. Fizzle, dud explosion (de mina, de cohete).
bocel m. ARQ. Torus. || *Cuarto bocel*, quarter round, ovolo.
bocelar v. tr. ARQ. To make mouldings on.
bocelete m. V. BOCEL.
bocera f. Moustache [U.S., mustache] (smear left on lips after eating or drinking): *boceras de chocolate*, moustache of chocolate. || MED. Lip sore [in the corners of the mouth].
boceras m. inv. Big mouth (que habla demasiado).
boceto m. Sketch (dibujo). || Rough study (escultura). || Rough draught, outline (escrito).
bocina f. MÚS. Horn. || Megaphone (para hablar desde lejos). || AUT. Horn: *tocar la bocina*, to sound one's horn. || Horn (de los gramófonos). || ASTR. Ursa Minor, the Little Bear. || ZOOL. Whelk. || *Amer*. Hubcap (de rueda). | Ear trumpet (aparato para los sordos).
bocinar v. intr. MÚS. To play the horn. || To sound one's horn (un automóvil).
bocinazo m. Hoot, toot, honk. || FAM. Telling off, scolding.
bocinero m. Horn player.
bocio m. MED. Goitre [U.S., goiter].
bock m. Tankard, beer mug (de cerveza).
bocón, ona adj. FAM. Big-mouthed. || FIG. y FAM. Big-mouthed (fanfarrón).
— M. FIG. y FAM. Braggart (fanfarrón). || ZOOL. Species of Antillian sardine. || *Amer*. MIL. Blunderbuss.
bocoy m. Hogshead, cask (tonel).

— OBSERV. Pl. *bocoyes*.

bocudo, da adj. Big-mouthed.
bocha f. Bowl. || — Pl. Bowls (juego).
bochar v. tr. To displace, to send flying (en el juego de bochas). || FIG. y FAM. To snub (desairar). | To fail (en un examen). | To reject (rechazar).
bochazo m. Blow of one bowl against another.
boche m. Small hole (agujero). || *Amer*. Blow of one bowl against another. | Quarrel (pendencia). | Din, uproar, row (jaleo). | Executioner (verdugo). || *Amer*. *Dar boche a uno*, to snub s.o.
bochinche m. FAM. Row, din, uproar (alboroto): *armar un bochinche*, to kick up a row, to cause uproar: | Dive (taberna, cafetucho).
bochinchero, ra adj./s. FAM. Rowdy.
bochista m. Bowls player.
bochorno m. Sultry *o* heavy weather (tiempo). || Stifling atmosphere (atmósfera). || Warm breeze (viento). || FIG. Shame (vergüenza). | Blushing (rubor). | Dizziness, giddiness (mareo corto). || MED. Flush. || — FIG. *¡Qué bochorno!*, how embarrassing! | *Sufrir un bochorno*, to feel so embarrassed *o* ashamed (estar avergonzado).
bochornoso, sa adj. Sultry, heavy: *un día bochornoso*, a sultry day. || Stifling (atmósfera). || FIG. Shameful (vergonzoso): *una acción bochornosa*, a shameful action. | Embarrassing (molesto).
boda f. Wedding, marriage. || — FIG. *Boda de negros*, rowdy party. | *Bodas de Camacho*, banquet. || *Bodas de plata, de oro, de diamante*, silver, golden, diamond wedding.
bodega f. Wine cellar (para guardar y criar el vino). || Cellar (en una casa). || Wine shop (tienda). || Hold (de un barco). || Warehouse (almacén en un puerto). || *Amer*. Grocery store, grocer's (tienda de abarrotes). | Restaurant.
bodegaje m. *Amer*. Storage.
bodegón m. Cheap restaurant (restaurante malo). || Dive (tabernucho). || Still life (pintura). || FIG. *¿En qué bodegón hemos comido juntos?*, please remember whom you are talking to.
bodeguero, ra m. y f. Owner of a wine cellar.
bodijo m. Unequal marriage, misalliance (boda desigual). || Quiet wedding (sin aparato).
bodoque m. Pellet (de ballesta). || FIG. y FAM. Dunce, blockhead (persona tonta). || *Amer*. Lump (chichón).
bodoquera f. Pellet mould (molde). || Blowpipe (cerbatana).
bodorrio m. FAM. V. BODIJO.
bodrio m. Hotchpotch (comida). || Muddle, mess (de cosas).
bóer adj./s. Boer.
bofe m. o **bofes** m. pl. Lights, *pl.*, lungs, *pl.* (de ternera, etc.). || — M. sing. *Amer*. Child's play (cosa muy fácil). || FIG. y FAM. *Echar el bofe* or *los bofes*, to slog away, to go at it hammer and tongs (trabajar), to pant heavily, to blow like a grampus (jadear).
bofetada f. o **bofetón** m. Slap (guantazo). || FIG. Blow: *fue una bofetada para su orgullo*, it was a blow to his pride. || — FIG. *Darse de bofetadas por una cosa*, to come to blows over sth. || *Dar una bofetada a alguien*, to slap s.o. [in the face], to slap s.o.'s face. || FIG. *Esos dos colores se dan de bofetadas*, these two colours clash horribly.
boga f. MAR. Rowing. || FIG. Fashion, vogue: *estar en boga*, to be in fashion. || — M. y f. MAR. Rower.
bogada f. Stroke of the oar.
bogador, ra m. y f. Rower.
bogar v. intr. To row (remar). || To sail (navegar). || TECN. To skim (metal fundido).
bogavante m. ZOOL. Lobster. || MAR. Stroke (primer remero).
bogie o **boggie** m. Bogie, bogy, bogey (carretón).
bogotano, na adj. [Of *o* from] Bogotá.
— M. y f. Native *o* inhabitant of Bogotá.
Bohemia n. pr. f. GEOGR. Bohemia.
bohémico, ca adj. Bohemian.
bohemio, mia adj. Bohemian: *vida bohemia*, Bohemian life. || — Adj./s. Bohemian. || Gipsy (gitano). || — F. Bohemianism, Bohemian life.
bohemo, ma adj./s. Bohemian.
bohío m. *Amer*. Cabin, hut.
bohordo m. Scape, stem (tallo).
boicot m. Boycott.
boicotear v. tr. To boycott.
boicoteo m. Boycott, boycotting.
boíl m. Cowshed.
boina f. Beret (vasca).
boite f. Nightclub.
boj m. BOT. Box (árbol). | Boxwood (madera).
bojar o **bojear** v. tr. MAR. To measure the perimeter of [an island].
— V. intr. MAR. To have a perimeter of [an island]. | To coast (costear).
boje m. V. BOJ.
bojedal m. Box shrubbery.
bojeo m. MAR. Measurement of the perimeter of an island (acción de medir). | Perimeter (medida). | Coasting (acción de costear).
bol m. Bowl. || Dragnet (red). || *Bol arménico*, Armenian bole (barro rojo).
bola f. Ball (cuerpo esférico): *bola de billar*, billiard ball. || Marble (canica). || Slam (bridge): *media bola*, little slam. || Shoe polish (betún). || FIG. y FAM. Ball (fútbol). | Lie, fib (cuento): *contar* or *meter bolas*, to tell fibs. | Globe (del mundo). || *Amer*. Round kite (cometa). | Rowdy party (reunión ruidosa). || — Pl. V. BOLEADORAS. || — *Bola de cristal*, crystal ball. || *Bola de naftalina*, mothball. || *Bola de nieve*, snowball. || *Bola negra*, blackball (en una votación). || *Carbón de bola*, ovoid. || *Cojinete de bolas*, ball bearing. || FAM. *¡Dale bola!*, what, again?, come off it! || *Dar bola*, to polish, to clean [U.S., to shine]. || *Amer*. *Dar en bola*, to hit the bull's-eye. || FIG. *Dejar que ruede la bola*, to let things take their course. | *Echar bola negra*, to blackball, to turn down. || *El Niño de la Bola*, Baby Jesus. || FIG. y FAM. *No da pie con bola*, he can't do a thing right. | *¡Ruede la bola!*, let us chance it!, here goes!
bolada f. Throw (lanzamiento). || Stroke (en el billar). || *Amer*. Opportunity, chance (oportunidad). | Sweet [U.S., candy] (golosina). | Dirty trick (jugarreta). | Witticism, witty remark [U.S., wisecrack]. || *Amer*. *Estar de bolada*, to be in luck.
bolardo m. MAR. Bollard (noray)
bolazo m. Blow (golpe). || *Amer*. Silly remark (tontería). | Fib, lie (mentira).
bolchevique adj./s. Bolshevik.
bolcheviquismo o **bolchevismo** m. Bolshevism.
bolchevista adj./s. Bolshevist.
boleada f. *Amer*. Hunting with "boleadoras".
boleadoras f. pl. Bolas [weapon used by Argentine gauchos which consists of several ropes tied together with metal balls at the ends].
bolear v. intr. To knock the balls about (al billar). || FIG. To lie, to fib (mentir).
— V. tr. FAM. To throw (arrojar). || *Amer*. To throw the bolas at. | To blackball (en una votación). | To fail (en un examen). | To mix up, to confuse (enredar). | To polish, to clean [U.S., to shine] (el calzado). | To play a dirty trick on (hacer una jugarreta).
— V. pr. *Amer*. To be wrong, to be mistaken (equivocarse). | To get mixed up, to get confused (enredarse). | To rear (un potro).
bolera f. Skittles (juego de bolos). || Bowling alley (local). || Skittle alley (en un bar, etc.). || *Bolera americana*, bowling alley.
bolero, ra adj. Lying, fibbing (mentiroso). || Who

plays truant [U.S., who plays hookey] (estudiante). || *Escarabajo bolero*, dung beetle.
— M. y f. FIG. y FAM. Fibber (embustero). || — M. Bolero (baile y chaquetilla). || *Amer.* Top hat (sombrero de copa). | Bootblack, shoeblack [U.S., shoeshine boy] (limpiabotas).

boleta f. Ticket (billete). || MIL. Billet. || Pass (permiso). || Voucher (vale). || Ballot paper, voting paper (de votación). || *Amer.* Bulletin, report: *boleta de sanidad*, health bulletin.

boletería f. *Amer.* Ticket office, box office (en un teatro). | Ticket office, booking office (en una estación, un estadio, etc.).

boletero, ra m. y f. *Amer.* Ticket seller.

boletín m. Bulletin. || Report (de los alumnos). || Journal (publicación de una sociedad). || Form (para suscribirse a algo). || Ticket (billete). || MIL. Billet. || — *Boletín meteorológico*, weather forecast, weather report. || *Boletín Oficial del Estado*, Official Gazette.

boleto m. BOT. Boletus (hongo). || Ticket (de lotería). || *Amer.* Ticket (billete de ferrocarril, teatro, etc.). | Coupon (de quinielas). | Slip (de apuestas). | FAM. Fib (embuste).

bolichada f. FIG. y FAM. Lucky break.

boliche m. Jack (en la petanca). || Skittles (juego de bolos). || Bowling alley (bolera americana). || Cup-and-ball (juego de niños). || Small dragnet (red). || Small fry (morralla). || Small furnace (horno). || *Amer.* Small grocery store (tenducho). | Dive (taberna).

bolichear v. intr. *Amer.* To potter about, to tinker about [U.S., to putter].

bolichero, ra m. y f. Bowling alley manager. || Fishmonger (pescadero). || *Amer.* Grocer.

bólido m. ASTR. Bolide, meteorite. || Racing car (coche de carreras).

bolígrafo m. Ball-point pen.

bolilla f. Small ball. || *Bolilla pestosa*, stink bomb.

bolillo m. Bobbin: *encaje de bolillos*, bobbin lace. || Fetlock (de las caballerías). || *Amer.* Bread roll. || — Pl. Lollipops (caramelos). || *Amer.* Drumsticks.

bolina f. MAR. Sounding line (sonda). | Bowline (cuerda). || FIG. y FAM. Din, row (alboroto). || MAR. *Ir* or *navegar de bolina*, to sail close-hauled *o* close to the wind.

bolinear v. intr. MAR. To sail close-hauled *o* close to the wind.

bolista adj. FAM. Lying, fibbing.
— M. y f. FAM. Fibber (mentiroso).

bolívar m. Bolivar [monetary unit of Venezuela].

Bolivia n. pr. f. GEOGR. Bolivia.

boliviano, na adj./s. Bolivian. || — M. Boliviano (currency of Bolivia).

bolo m. Skittle, ninepin (juego). || Newel (de una escalera). || Slam (en los naipes). || Capot (el que no hace baza en el juego). || Bolus (píldora). || FAM. Clod, dimwit (persona torpe). || — Pl. Skittles, *sing.* || Bowling alley, *sing.* (bolera). || — *Bolo alimenticio*, alimentary bolus. || *Bolo arménico*, Armenian bole. || *Jugador de bolos*, skittles player.

bolo, la adj. *Amer.* Drunk (ebrio). | Tailless (sin cola).

bolómetro m. Bolometer.

bolón m. ARQ. Quarry stone.

Bolonia n. pr. GEOGR. Bologna (Italia). | Boulogne (Francia).

bolonio, nia m. y f. FIG. y FAM. Dunce, ignoramus.

boloñés, esa adj./s. Bolognan, Bolognian, Bolognese.

bolsa f. Purse (para el dinero): *tener la bolsa repleta*, to have a well-lined purse; *tener la bolsa vacía*, to have a light *o* empty purse. || Bag (para objetos en general): *bolsa del cartero, de papel*, postman's bag, paper bag. || Pouch (para el tabaco). || Foot muff (para los pies). || Pucker, bag (de un vestido). || COM. Exchange: *Bolsa de Comercio*, Commodity Exchange; *Bolsa de Valores*, Stock Exchange; *operaciones de Bolsa*, exchange transactions. || ANAT. Bursa: *bolsas sinoviales*, synovial bursae. | Sac (lagrimal). || Bag (bajo los ojos). || Bag (de abeja, serpiente), pouch (de canguro, calamares). || MED. Ice bag (de hielo). | Hot-water bottle (de agua caliente). || MIN. Pocket (de mineral, de gas). || DEP. Purse (de un boxeador). || *Amer.* Pocket (bolsillo). || — Pl. ANAT. Scrotum, *sing.* (escroto). || — AVIAT. *Bolsa de aire*, air pocket. || *Bolsa de herramientas*, toolbag. || *Bolsa de labores*, workbag. || *Bolsa de la compra*, shopping bag. || MED. *Bolsa de las aguas*, bag of waters. || *Bolsa del automóvil, de la propiedad inmobiliaria*, vehicles for sale, property for sale. || BOT. *Bolsa de pastor*, shepherd's purse. || *Bolsa de Trabajo*, Labour Exchange, Employment Exchange [U.S., Employment Bureau]. || *Bolsa de viaje*, travelling bag. || *Bolsa negra*, black market. || FIG. *Bolsa rota*, spendthrift. || *Jugar a la Bolsa*, to speculate, to play the market. || COM. *La Bolsa*, the Stock Exchange. || *La Bolsa baja*, there is a drop on the Stock Exchange. || *¡La bolsa o la vida!*, your money or your life! || *Se me han hecho bolsas en el pantalón*, my trousers have gone baggy at the knees. || FIG. *Sin aflojar la bolsa*, without spending a penny.

bolsear v. intr. To bag, to pucker (los vestidos).
— V. tr. *Amer.* FAM. To send packing (echar). | To tap s.o. for (pedir). | To pick *o* to steal [sth.] from the pocket of (robar).

bolsero, ra m. y f. Maker (fabricante) *o* seller (vendedor) of purses.
— M. *Amer.* Sponger, parasite (gorrón). | Pickpocket (ratero).

bolsico m. *Amer.* Pocket.

bolsicón m. *Amer.* Thick petticoat.

bolsillo m. Pocket (de un vestido): *bolsillo de parche, con cartera*, patch pocket, flap pocket. || Fob (para el reloj). || Purse [U.S., pocketbook] (monedero). || — *Bolsillo de pecho*, breastpocket. || *Consultar con el bolsillo*, to see whether one has enough money. || *De bolsillo*, pocket: *edición de bolsillo*, pocket edition. || FIG. y FAM. *Meterse a alguien en el bolsillo*, to win s.o. over to one's side. | *Pagar a alguien de su bolsillo*, to pay s.o. out of one's own pocket. | *Poner de su bolsillo*, to dip into one's own pocket. | *Rascarse el bolsillo*, to dig deep. | *Sin echarse la mano al bolsillo*, without spending a penny. | *Tener a uno en el bolsillo*, to have s.o. in one's pocket.

bolsín m. COM. Outside market.

bolsiquear v. tr. *Amer.* To pick [sth.] from the pocket of.

bolsista m. COM. Stockbroker. || *Amer.* Pickpocket (ladrón).

bolsita f. Small bag.

bolso m. Handbag, bag [U.S., purse, pocketbook] (de mujer). || Purse [U.S., pocketbook] (portamonedas). || Pocket (bolsillo). || *Bolso de mano*, handbag [U.S., purse, pocketbook].

bolsón m. Handbag [U.S., purse, pocketbook] (bolso). || *Amer.* School satchel (de colegial) | Ore pocket (mineral). | Hollow [ground] (en una zona desértica). | Lagoon (lago). || *Amer.* FAM. Dunce (alumno malo).

bolladura f. Dent (hacia dentro). || Bump (hacia fuera).

bollar v. tr. To dent (hacia dentro). || To bump (hacia fuera).

bollería f. Bakery, baker's shop.

bollero, ra m. y f. Baker.

bollo m. Bun, roll (panecillo). || Dent (abolladura). || Bump, swelling (bulto, chichón). || Puff (en una tela). || *Amer.* Punch (puñetazo). || — FIG. y FAM. *No está el horno para bollos*, the time is not right, this is not the right time. || FIG. *Perdonar el bollo por el coscorrón*, to realize that it is not worth the effort. || FIG. y FAM. *¡Se va a armar un bollo!*, there is going to be trouble *o* a rumpus!

bollón m. Stud (tachuela). || Button earring (pendiente). || BOT. Bud (de la vid).

bollonado, da adj. Studded.

bomba f. TECN. Pump: *bomba aspirante*, suction pump; *bomba impelente*, force pump; *bomba aspirante impelente*, suction and force pump; *bomba de bicicleta*, bicycle pump; *bomba de aire*, air pump. || MIL. Bomb: *bomba atómica, de efecto retardado*, atomic bomb, time bomb. || Globe (de lámpara). || MÚS. Slide. || FIG. Bombshell (noticia inesperada). || Improvised poem (poema). || *Amer.* Round kite (cometa). | Soap bubble (burbuja). | Ladle (cucharón). | Top hat (chistera). | Lie (mentira). | Hoax (noticia falsa). | Aerostatic balloon (globe). | Drunkenness (borrachera). || — *Amer.* FIG. y FAM. *Agarrar una bomba*, to get plastered *o* canned *o* drunk (emborracharse). || *A prueba de bombas*, bombproof, shellproof. || MED. *Bomba de cobalto*, cobalt bomb. || *Bomba de hidrógeno*, hydrogen bomb. || *Bomba de humo* or *fumígena*, smoke bomb. || *Bomba de incendios*, fire engine. || *Bomba de inyección*, injection pump. || MIL. *Bomba de mano*, hand grenade, grenade. || *Bomba fétida*, stink bomb. || MED. *Bomba gástrica*, stomach pump. || *Bomba lacrimógena*, tear-gas bomb. || *Bomba volcánica* or *de lava*, volcanic bomb. || FIG. *Caer como una bomba*, to drop *o* to burst like a bomb *o* a bombshell. || *Dar a la bomba*, to pump. || FIG. y FAM. *Estar echando bombas*, to be boiling hot. | *Éxito bomba*, fantastic success. | *Pasarlo bomba*, to have a great time *o* a ball *o* a whale of a time.

bombacha f. *Amer.* Baggy trousers, *pl.* || Knickers, *pl.* (de niño, de mujer).

— OBSERV. The word *bombacha* is usually used in the plural form *bombachas*.

bombacho adj. m./s. m. *Pantalón bombacho*, knickerbockers, *pl.* (de hombre), knickers, *pl.* (de niño), plus fours, *pl.* (de jugador de golf, etc.), baggy trousers, *pl.* (de zuavo, etc.).

bombarda f. MIL. Bombard. || MÚS. Bombardon.

bombardear v. tr. MIL. To bomb, to bombard, to shell. || FÍS. To bombard.

bombardeo m. MIL. Bombing, bombardment: *bombardeo de una ciudad*, bombing of a city. || FÍS. Bombardment. || *Bombardeo en picado*, dive bombing.

bombardero, ra adj. Bombing, bomber. || *Lancha bombardera*, gunboat.
— M. Bombardier (soldado). || Bomber (avión).

bombardino m. MÚS. Saxhorn.

bombardón m. MÚS. Bombardon.

bombasí m. Bombazine, bombasine (tela).

bombástico, ca adj. Bombastic.

bombazo m. Explosion [of a bomb].

bombeador m. *Amer.* Fireman (bombero). | Spy (espía).

bombear v. tr. To pump, to pump up (recoger): *bombear agua*, to pump water. || To pump out (sacar

el agua). || To bend (arquear). || To warp (alabear). || FIG. y FAM. To puff up (dar bombo). || *Amer.* To spy on (espiar). | To scout, to spy out, to reconnoitre (explorar). | To fire (despedir). || DEP. To lob (la pelota). || *Un balón bombeado*, a lob.
— V. pr. To warp (alabearse).
bombeo m. Bulge, convexity (convexidad). || Warp (alabeo). || Camber (de la calzada). || *Estación de bombeo*, pumping station.
bombero m. Fireman (de incendios). || MIL. Mortar (cañón). || *Amer.* Scout (explorador). | Spy (espía). || *Cuerpo de bomberos*, fire brigade.
bómbice o **bómbix** m. Bombix, silkworm.
bombilla f. ELECTR. Bulb: *el casquillo de una bombilla*, the socket of a bulb; *se ha fundido la bombilla*, the bulb has gone. || MAR. Lantern (farol). || *Amer.* Small pipe for drinking maté. | Ladle (cucharón).
bombillo m. U-bend, trap (sifón). || Pipette (para sacar líquidos). || MAR. Small pump. || *Amer.* Bulb (bombilla).
bombín m. FAM. Bowler [U.S., derby] (sombrero). || Pump (de bicicleta).
bombo, ba adj. Dumbfounded, stunned (atolondrado). || — FAM. *Ponerle la cabeza bomba a uno*, to make s.o.'s head split. | *Tengo la cabeza bomba*, my head is splitting.
— M. Bass drum (tambor). || Bass-drum player (músico). || Barge, lighter (barco). || Lottery drum (de lotería). || FIG. Song and dance (publicidad): *dar mucho bombo a una novela*, to make a great song and dance about a novel. || — FAM. *Anunciar a bombo y platillos* or *a todo bombo*, to announce with a lot of ballyhoo. | *Darse bombo*, to boast, to blow one's own trumpet. | *Amer. Irse al bombo*, to fail. || *Publicidad a bombo y platillos*, noisy *o* loud publicity. || *Sin bombo ni platillos*, quietly, without fuss.
bombón m. Chocolate: *una caja de bombones*, a box of chocolates. || Philippine bamboo container (recipiente). || *Amer.* Type of ladle (cucharón). || FIG. y FAM. *Ser un bombón*, to be gorgeous (una mujer), to be cute enough to eat (un niño).
bombona f. Carboy. || Gas cylinder (de butano).
bombonera f. Chocolate box (caja). || FIG. Cosy little place (casita, teatro).
bombonería f. Confectioner's shop, sweetshop.
Bona n. pr. GEOGR. Bonn.
bonachón, ona adj. FAM. Easy going (acomodadizo). | Good-natured (bueno). | Naïve (cándido).
— M. y f. Good soul.
bonachonería f. Good nature (bondad). | Naïveté (candidez).
bonaerense adj. [From *o* of] Buenos Aires.
— M. y f. Inhabitant *o* native of Buenos Aires.
bonancible adj. Calm (mar). || Fair (tiempo).
bonanza f. MAR. Fair weather, calm at sea. || FIG. Prosperity, bonanza (prosperidad). | Peacefulness (tranquilidad). || *Amer.* MIN. Bonanza (en una mina).
bonapartismo m. Bonapartism.
bonapartista adj./s. Bonapartist.
bondad f. Goodness (benevolencia): *la bondad es una virtud rara*, goodness is a rare virtue. || Kindness, kindliness (generosidad): *se le conoce por su extrema bondad*, he is known for his extreme kindliness. || *Tenga la bondad de*, be kind enough to, be good enough to: *tenga la bondad de ayudarme*, be kind enough to help me; please: *tenga la bondad de no escupir en el suelo*, please do not spit on the floor.
bondadosamente adv. Kindly.
bondadoso, sa adj. Kind, good, goodnatured.
bonderización f. Bonderizing (protección contra la herrumbre).
boneta f. MAR. Bonnet.
bonete m. Cap (de eclesiástico, colegiales, graduados, etc.). || Biretta (de cardenal). || FIG. Secular priest (clérigo). || Fruit dish (tarro). || Bonnet (fortificación). || ZOOL. Bonnet (de un rumiante). || — FIG. y FAM. *A tente bonete*, doggedly. | *Tirarse los bonetes*, to bicker, to quarrel, to squabble.
bonetería f. Hat factory (fábrica). || *Amer.* Haberdashery.
bonetero, ra m. y f. Hatter. || *Amer.* Haberdasher. || — M. Spindle tree (arbusto).
bongo m. *Amer.* Barge (barco). | Canoe (canoa).
bongó m. Bongo drum, bongo.
boniato m. Sweet potato (buniato).
bonico, ca adj. FAM. Cute, sweet.
Bonifacio n. pr. m. Boniface.
bonificación f. Improvement (mejora). || COM. Allowance, discount (descuento).
bonificar v. tr. To improve: *bonificar la tierra*, to improve the land. || COM. To allow, to discount (descontar).
bonísimo, ma adj. Very good.
bonitamente adv. Nicely. || Artfully, craftily (con habilidad). || Slowly, little by little (despacio).
bonito, ta adj. Pretty (persona). || Nice, pretty (sitio). || Pretty, nice (cantidad). || *¡Muy bonito!*, that's nice!, very nice!
— M. Tuna [fish] (atún): *bonito en aceite*, tuna fish in oil.
bono m. Voucher (papeleta). || Bond: *Bonos del Tesoro*, Treasury bonds.
bonzo m. Bonze (monje budista).
boñiga f. o **boñigo** m. Cow dung.
bookmaker m. Bookie, bookmaker (corredor de apuestas).
boom m. Boom.
boomerang m. Boomerang.
Bootes n. pr. m. ASTR. Bootes.
bootlegger m. Bootlegger (contrabandista de licores).
boqueada f. Last breath. || *Dar las últimas boqueadas*, to be at one's last gasp, to be on one's last legs (persona), to be on its last legs (cosa).
boquear v. tr. To say, to utter, to mouth (palabras).
— V. intr. To gape, to gasp. || To be at one's last gasp (persona). || FIG. y FAM. To be on one's last legs (cosa y persona).
boquera f. MED. Lip sore. || Sluice [in an irrigation channel] (para regar). || Window in a hayloft (del pajar). || Sore mouth (de animal).
boquerón m. Anchovy (pez). || Wide opening, large breach (abertura).
— OBSERV. *Boquerón* is used only to denote fresh anchovy. Canned anchovy is called *anchoa*.
boquete m. Narrow opening (paso angosto). || Hole (agujero). || Breach (brecha).
boquiabierto, ta adj. Agape, gaping, open-mouthed: *me quedé boquiabierto cuando la vi*, I stood agape *o* gaping when I saw her.
boquiancho, cha adj. Wide-mouthed.
boquiangosto, ta adj. Narrow-mouthed.
boquiblando, da adj. Soft-mouthed, tender-mouthed (caballo).
boquiduro, ra adj. Hard-mouthed (caballo).
boquifresco, ca adj. Tender-mouthed (caballo). || FIG. y FAM. Cheeky, shameless, impudent (descarado).
boquilla f. Cigarette holder (para fumar cigarrillos). || Cigar holder (para fumar cigarros puros). || Tip: *boquilla con filtro*, filter tip. || Mouthpiece (de pipa). || Sluice in irrigation channel (para regar). || MÚS. Mouthpiece (de varios instrumentos). || Mortise, mortice (escopleadura). || Opening (orificio). || Clasp (de un bolso). || Teat [U.S., nipple] (de biberón). || Metal mouth (de la funda de la espada). || Burner (de lámpara). || Nozzle (de tobera). || Coupling, joint (de dos tubos). || *Decir algo de boquilla*, to say one thing and mean another.
boquirroto, ta adj. FAM. Loose-tongued, talkative (parlanchín).
— M. y f. FAM. Chatterbox.
boquirrubio, bia adj. Loose-tongued, talkative (parlanchín). || Naïve, innocent (candoroso).
— M. y f. Chatterbox (parlanchín). || — M. FAM. Dandy.
boquiseco, ca adj. Dry-mouthed (caballo).
boquituerto, ta adj. Wry-mouthed.
boracita f. MIN. Boracite.
borato m. QUÍM. Borate.
bórax m. QUÍM. Borax.
borbollar o **borbollear** v. intr. To bubble. || FIG. To stammer, to stutter (hablar mal).
borbolleo m. V. BORBOTEO.
borbollón m. V. BORBOTÓN.
borbollonear v. intr. To bubble (borbollar).
Borbón n. pr. Bourbon.
borbónico, ca adj. Bourbon. || *Nariz borbónica*, Bourbon nose.
borbor m. Bubbling.
borborigmo m. MED. Rumblings, *pl.* [in the bowels].
borboritar o **borbotar** o **borbotear** v. intr. To bubble.
borboteo m. Bubbling.
borbotón m. Bubbling. || — *El agua hierve a borbotones*, the water is boiling furiously. || *Hablar a borbotones*, to gabble. || *La sangre corre a borbotones*, the blood gushes out. || *Salir a borbotones*, to gush forth.
borceguí m. Half boot (calzado).
borda f. MAR. Gunwale, rail | Mainsail (de una galera). || Hut, cabin (choza). || — FIG. y FAM. *Arrojar* or *echar* or *tirar por la borda*, to throw overboard. || *Motor de fuera borda*, outboard motor.
bordada f. MAR. Tack, board. || *Dar una bordada*, to tack, to make a board.
bordado, da adj. Embroidered. || FIG. *Salir bordado*, to turn out perfectly.
— M. Embroidery: *bordado de realce*, raised embroidery.
bordador, ra m. y f. Embroiderer, embroideress.
bordadura f. Embroidery.
bordar v. tr. To embroider. || FIG. To perform perfectly: *este actor bordó su papel*, this actor performed his role perfectly. | To do perfectly (un trabajo). || *Bordar en calado*, to do drawnwork.
borde m. Edge: *al borde del abismo, de la mesa*, on the edge of the abyss, of the table. || Hem, edge (de un vestido). || Border (banda). || Brim (de un sombrero). || Brim, rim (de una vasija). || Side (de una carretera). || Lip (de una herida). || — *Al borde de*, on the edge of (en la linde de), on the brink of, on the verge of: *estar al borde de la ruina*, to be on the brink of ruin. || *Al borde del mar*, at the seaside. || AVIAC. *Borde de ataque, de salida*, leading, trailing edge. || *Borde de la acera*, kerb [U.S., curb]. || FIG. *Estar al borde de la tumba*, to be at death's door, to have one foot in the grave.

bordear v. intr. MAR. To tack. || *El agua del vaso bordeaba*, the glass was full to overflowing.
— V. tr. To border: *bordear una foto con una lista blanca*, to border a photo with a white band. || To border on: *mi campo bordea el tuyo*, my field borders on yours. || FIG. To border on, to verge on: *esto bordea el ridículo*, this borders on the ridiculous. | MAR. To skirt: *bordear una isla*, to skirt an island.
bordelés, esa adj. [Of *o* from] Bordeaux: *un vino bordelés*, a Bordeaux wine.
— M. y f. Inhabitant *o* native of Bordeaux.
bordillo m. Kerb [U.S., curb] (de la acera).
bordo m. MAR. Board: *subir a bordo*, to go on board. | Side (lado). | Tack (bordada). || — MAR. *A bordo del barco*, on board [the] ship. | *Barco de alto bordo*, seagoing vessel. | *Diario de a bordo*, ship's log, logbook. || COM. *Franco a bordo*, free on board. || MAR. *Los hombres de a bordo*, the ship's company, the crew. | *Segundo de a bordo*, first mate. | *Virar de bordo*, to put round.
bordón m. Pilgrim's staff (de peregrino). || Refrain (estribillo). || FIG. Pet phrase (repetición). | Helping hand (ayuda). || IMPR. Omission, out. || MÚS. Bass string (cuerda). | Bourdon (de un órgano).
bordoncillo m. Pet phrase.
bordonear v. intr. To buzz, to hum (zumbar).
— V. tr. MÚS. To strum (la guitarra).
bordoneo m. Buzz, buzzing, hum, humming.
bordura f. HERÁLD. Bordure.
boreal adj. Northern, boreal. || *Aurora boreal*, aurora borealis, northern lights.
bóreas m. Boreas, the north wind.
borgoña m. Burgundy (vino).
Borgoña n. pr. f. GEOGR. Burgundy.
borgoñón, ona adj./s. Burgundian.
bórico, ca adj. Boric, boracic.
borinqueño, na adj./s. Puerto Rican (puertorriqueño).
borla f. Tassel (adorno). || Tassel, pompon (del gorro militar). || Puff: *borla para polvos*, powder puff. || Tassel [on doctor's cap] (insignia). || FIG. *Tomar la borla*, to graduate as a doctor.
borlarse o **borlearse** v. pr. *Amer.* To graduate as a doctor.
borne m. ELECTR. Terminal.
bornear v. tr. To look along with one eye (para comprobar la rectitud de algo). || To bend (doblar). || ARQ. To put in place.
— V. intr. MAR. To swing at anchor.
— V. pr. To warp (madera).
boro m. QUÍM. Boron.
borona f. Millet (mijo). || Maize [U.S., corn] (maíz). || Maize bread [U.S., corn bread] (pan de maíz). || *Amer.* Crumb (migaja).
borra f. Flock (para rellenar colchones, etc.). || Floss (de seda). || Fluff (pelusa de suciedad). || Sediment, lees, *pl.* (de la tinta, etc.). || FIG. Padding. || FIG. *Meter borra*, to pad [out].
borrachera f. Drunkenness (ebriedad). || FIG. Rapture, ecstasy: *la borrachera de los triunfos*, the rapture of victories. || — *Agarrar* or *coger una borrachera*, to get drunk. || *Ir de borrachera*, to go on a binge, to go on a drinking spree [U.S., to go on a drunk].
borrachín m. FAM. Drunkard, soak.
borracho, cha adj. Drunk: *está borracho*, he is drunk. || Hard-drinking (aficionado a beber). || FIG. Drunk: *borracho de ira*, drunk with rage. || Violet (morado). || — *Bizcocho borracho*, rum baba. || FAM. *Borracho como una cuba*, drunk as a lord. | *Estar borracho perdido*, to be paralytic, to be blind drunk.
— M. y f. Drunkard, drunk. || *Ser un borracho perdido*, to be an inveterate drunkard.
borrador m. Rough copy [U.S., first draft] (texto). || Rough notebook [U.S., scratch pad] (cuaderno). || Rough paper [U.S., scratch paper] (papel). || COM. Daybook. || Eraser, rubber (goma de borrar). || Board rubber, rubber (de la pizarra).
borradura f. Erasure, crossing-out.
borraja f. BOT. Borage. || FIG. *Quedar en agua de borrajas*, to fizzle out, to come to nothing, to peter out.
borrajear v. tr. To scribble (palabras). || To scribble on (papel).
borrar v. tr. To cross out (tachar). || To cross (*de*, off) [suprimir]. || To clean (la pizarra). || To rub off: *borrar algo de la pizarra*, to rub sth. off the board. || To rub out, to erase (con una goma). || To blurr (dejar borroso). || FIG. To erase, to wipe away: *el tiempo todo lo borra*, time erases everything. || *Goma de borrar*, eraser, rubber.
— V. pr. FIG. To fade, to disappear, to be erased: *esta historia se borró de mi memoria*, this story faded from my memory. | To resign: *me he borrado del club*, I have resigned from the club.
borrasca f. Storm (tormenta). || Squall (chubasco). || Flurry (de nieve). || FIG. Peril, hazard (riesgo): *las borrascas de la vida*, the perils of life. | Orgy, spree (orgía).
borrascoso, sa adj. Stormy (lugar, mar, etc.). || Gusty, squally (viento). || FIG. y FAM. Stormy, tumultuous (vida, conducta, reunión).
borregada f. Flock of lambs.
borrego, ga m. y f. Lamb [one or two years old]. || FIG. y FAM. Simpleton, dope (tonto). || *Amer.* Hoax (noticia falsa).
borreguil adj. *Tener un espíritu borreguil*, to follow the crowd.
borrica f. Donkey, she-ass (asna). || FIG. y FAM. Dunce, dimwit, ass (mujer ignorante).
borricada f. Drove of asses. || Donkey ride: *dar una borricada*, to go for a donkey ride. || FIG. y FAM. Nonsense, stupid thing: *soltar borricadas*, to talk nonsense, to say stupid things. || *Hacer borricadas*, to act the goat, to do stupid things.
borrical adj. Of an ass, of a donkey.
borrico m. Donkey, ass (asno). || Sawhorse, trestle (de carpintero). || FIG. y FAM. Ass, dimwit, dunce (necio). || — FIG. *Apearse de su borrico, caerse de su borrico*, to climb down, to back down. | *Ser muy borrico*, to be a real ass *o* dunce.
borricón o **borricote** adj. FIG. y FAM. Dense, stupid, dim (necio). || — FIG. y FAM. *Ser borricón*, to be as strong as an ox (fuerte). | *Ser muy borricote para las matemáticas*, to be hopeless at mathematics.
— M. FAM. Dunce, ass, dimwit.
borrilla f. Fur, fuzz (de las frutas).
borriquero adj. m. *Cardo borriquero*, cotton thistle.
— M. Donkey driver.
borriquete m. Sawhorse, trestle (caballete).
borriquillo o **borriquito** m. Donkey. || *El borriquito por delante, para que no se espante*, it is impolite to put one's own name first.
borro m. Lamb [one or two years old].
Borromeas n. pr. f. pl. GEOGR. *Islas Borromeas*, Borromean Islands.
borrón m. Blot, blotch, smudge (de tinta). || Rough copy (texto). || Scribbling pad [U.S., scratch pad] (cuaderno). || Rough sketch (de una pintura). || FIG. Blemish (defecto). | Blot, blemish (deshonor): *este acto es un borrón en su vida*, this deed is a blemish on his life. | Scrawl, scribble (escrito). || FIG. y FAM. *Borrón y cuenta nueva*, let's forget about it, let's wipe the slate clean, let's start afresh.
borronear v. tr. To scribble (palabras). || To scribble on: *borronear el papel*, to scribble on the paper.
borroso, sa adj. Muddy (líquido). || Confused (escritura). || Blurred, fuzzy (fotografía, pintura). || Indistinct (contornos). || Hazy, vague (ideas). || IMPR. Blurred, mackled.
borujo m. Marc (orujo). || Lump (bulto). || Cattle cake made of olives or grapes (para el ganado).
borujón m. Large lump (bulto).
boscaje m. Grove, thicket, copse (bosque pequeño). || Woodland scene (pintura).
boscoso, sa adj. Wooded.
Bósforo n. pr. m. GEOGR. Bosporus.
Bosnia n. pr. f. GEOGR. Bosnia.
bosniaco, ca o **bosnio, nia** adj./s. Bosnian.
bosorola f. Sediment, dregs, *pl.* (poso).
bosque m. Wood (pequeño), forest (más grande): *un bosque de pinos*, pine wood; *bosque comunal*, communal wood; *bosque del Estado*, State wood; *bosque maderable*, timber-yielding wood.

— OBSERV. En inglés *wood* y *forest* difieren sólo por la extensión. La primera palabra se aplica a un sitio poblado de árboles generalmente menos extenso que *forest*. *Forest* no corresponde al español *selva* sino cuando se trata de superficies arboladas muy extensas y de carácter salvaje: *the Black Forest*, la Selva Negra.

bosquecillo m. Grove, small wood, copse.
bosquejar v. tr. To sketch: *bosquejar un retrato*, to sketch a portrait. || To roughhew (una escultura). || FIG. To draft (proyecto). || FIG. *Bosquejar un cuadro de*, to outline, to give an outline of: *bosquejar un cuadro de la situación*, to give an outline of the situation.
bosquejo m. Sketch (de una pintura). || Study, rough shape (de una escultura). || FIG. Outline, draft (de un proyecto).
bosquete m. Grove, thicket, copse.
bosquimano, na adj./s. Bushman.
bosta f. Dung (de los bovinos, de los caballos).
bostezar v. intr. To yawn.
bostezo m. Yawn.
bostón m. Boston (juego, baile).
bota f. Wineskin (para el vino). || Barrel (cuba). || Boot: *botas de campaña*, top boots; *botas altas* or *de montar*, riding boots. || — *El Gato con botas*, Puss-in-Boots. || FIG. *Estar con las botas puestas*, to be ready to go out. | *Morir con las botas puestas*, to die with one's boots on. || FIG. y FAM. *Ponerse las botas* to feather one's nest (ganar mucho dinero), to have one's fill (beber o comer mucho).
botada f. Launching (botadura).
botadero m. *Amer.* Ford (vado). | Tip, rubbish dump (vertedero).
botado, da adj. *Amer.* Foundling (expósito). | Cheeky, saucy, bold (descarado). | Dirt cheap (barato). | Spendthrift (derrochador). | Blind drunk (borracho).
— M. y f. *Amer.* Foundling (expósito). | Cheeky person (descarado). | Cheap thing (barato). | Spendthrift (derrochador). | Drunk, drunkard (borracho).
botador m. MAR. Pole (palo para impulsar un barco). || Nail puller, claw hammer (para sacar clavos). || Forceps (de un dentista). || IMPR. Shooting stick.
— Adj m./s. m. *Amer.* Spendthrift (derrochador).

botadura f. Launching [of a ship].
botafuego m. MIL. Linstock. || FIG. Firebrand (persona que provoca alborotos). | Quick-tempered person (persona irritable).
botafumeiro m. Censer, incense burner (en Santiago de Compostela).
botalón m. MAR. Boom. || Stake, post (estaca).
botana f. Patch [of a wineskin]. || Cork, stopper (tapón), bung (de un tonel). || FIG. y FAM. Plaster (con que se cubre una herida). | Scar (cicatriz). || *Amer.* Leather hood [used in cockfighting]. | Cocktail snack (tapa).
botánico, ca adj. Botanical, botanic. || *Jardín botánico*, botanical garden.
— M. y f. Botanist. || — F. Botany (ciencia).
botanista m. y f. (P. us.). Botanist.
botar v. tr. To throw out (arrojar). || MAR. To launch (barco). | To turn the helm: *botar a babor*, to turn the helm to port. || FAM. To chuck out (echar): *lo botaron del colegio*, they chucked him out of school. || To take (fútbol): *botar un córner*, to take a corner. || *Amer.* To throw away (tirar). | To squander (malgastar).
— V. intr. To bounce, to rebound (una pelota, una piedra). || To jolt, to bounce (pegar botes). || To jump: *botar de alegría*, to jump for joy. || To buck (un caballo). || FIG. *Está que bota*, he is hopping mad.
— V. pr. *Amer.* To become (volverse).
botaratada f. FAM. Stupid thing, foolish thing, piece of nonsense. || — *Decir botaratadas*, to talk nonsense. || *Hacer botaratadas*, to act the fool.
botarate m. FAM. Fool, idiot: *no seas botarate*, don't be a fool. || *Amer.* Spendthrift (manirroto).
botarel m. ARQ. Flying buttress.
botarete adj. ARQ. *Arco botarete*, flying buttress.
botarga f. Motley, jester's outfit.
botasillas f. pl. MIL. Boots and saddles (toque de clarín).
botavara f. MAR. Spanker boom.
bote m. Jump, leap, bound (salto). || Bounce, rebound (de una pelota). || Bump, jolt (sacudida). || Tin, can: *bote de leche condensada*, tin of condensed milk. || Jar (de farmacia, etc.): *bote de tabaco*, tobacco jar. || MAR. Boat: *bote de remos*, rowing boat. || Thrust, lunge (de pico o lanza). || Hole (boche). || Jump, prance (caballo). || FAM. Pocket (bolsillo). || Box for tips (en un bar). || Jackpot (en el juego). || — *Bote de carnero*, buck (de caballo). || DEP. *Bote neutro*, bounce-up. || MAR. *Bote salvavidas*, lifeboat. || *Dar botes de alegría*, to jump for joy, to jump with happiness. || FIG. y FAM. *Dar el bote*, to chuck out (echar). | *Darse el bote*, to beat it. | *De bote en bote*, packed, full to overflowing: *el cuarto está de bote en bote*, the room is packed. | *Estar en el bote*, to be in the bag. || *Pegar un bote*, to jump. || FIG. y FAM. *Tener a uno metido en el bote*, to have won s.o. over, to have s.o. in one's pocket: *tenemos a mi padre metido en el bote*, we have won my father over.
botella f. Bottle: *beber de la botella*, to drink from the bottle. || — FÍS. *Botella de Leiden*, Leyden jar. || *Botella termo*, thermos flask, thermos, thermos bottle. || *En botella*, bottled.
botellazo m. Blow with a bottle.
botellero m. Bottle rack (estante). || Bottle basket (cesta). || Bottle maker (fabricante). || Bottle seller (comerciante).
botellín m. Small bottle.
botellón m. Large bottle. || *Amer.* Demijohn (damajuana).
botepronto m. Dropkick (rugby). || Half volley (fútbol).
botería f. MAR. Casks, *pl.* || Wineskin workshop (taller del botero). || *Amer.* Cobbler's shop, shoemaker's shop (zapatería).
botero m. Wineskin maker. || Skipper, master (de un bote). || Cobbler, shoemaker (zapatero). || FAM. *Pedro Botero*, Satan, the Fiend.
botica f. Chemist's shop, pharmacy [U.S., drugstore] (farmacia). || FIG. Medicine cabinet (botiquín). | Medicines, *pl.* (medicamentos). || (P. us.). Shop (tienda). || — *Hay de todo como en botica*, there is everything under the sun. || FAM. *Oler a botica*, to smell like a chemist's shop.
boticaria f. Chemist's *o* pharmacist's wife (esposa). || Chemist, pharmacist [U.S., druggist].
boticario m. Chemist, pharmacist, apothecary (ant.) [U.S., druggist]. || FIG. *Venir como pedrada en ojo de boticario*, to come in the nick of time, to come just right.
botija f. Earthenware pitcher. || *Amer.* Buried treasure.
botijero, ra m. y f. Pitcher maker (el que hace botijos). || Pitcher seller (vendedor).
botijo m. Earthenware pitcher [with spout and handle]. || — FAM. *Cara de botijo*, face like a full moon. || *Tren botijo*, excursion train.
botilla f. Ankle boot, bootee (de señora). || Half boot (borceguí).
botillería f. Refreshment bar.
botín m. Spat, legging (polaina). || Bootee, ankle boot (calzado). || MIL. Booty, loot. || *Amer.* Sock (calcetín).
botina f. Bootee, ankle boot.
botinería f. Cobbler's shop, shoemaker's shop (zapatería).
botinero m. Cobbler, shoemaker (zapatero).
botiquín m. Medicine chest (maletín). || First-aid kit (estuche). || Medicine cabinet (mueble). || Sick room, sick bay (enfermería). || *Amer.* Wine shop.
botivoleo m. Striking a ball on the bounce *o* rebound [in ball games].
boto m. Boot (calzado). || Wineskin (odre).
boto, ta adj. Blunt. || FIG. Dull, dense (torpe).
botón m. Button (en los vestidos). || BOT. Bud (de una planta). || Button [U.S., bell push] (de timbre): *pulsar el botón*, to press the button. || Handle, knob (de puerta, etc.). || DEP. Button (del florete). || MÚS. Key (de instrumento de viento). || RAD. Knob: *botón de sintonización*, tuning knob. || Buttons, bellboy (muchacho en un hotel). || *Amer.* FAM. Copper [U.S., cop] (poli). || — *Amer. Al botón*, in vain (en vano), at random (al buen tuntún). || *Botón automático*, press stud [U.S., snap fastener]. || *Botón de fuego*, ignipuncture. || FIG. *Botón de muestra*, sample: *como botón de muestra*, as a sample. || *Botón de oro*, buttercup (planta). || *Dar al botón*, to turn the knob; to press the button. || FAM. *De botones adentro*, deep down, in one's heart of hearts.
botonadura f. Buttons, *pl.*, set of buttons.
botonazo m. Touché (en la esgrima).
botonería f. Button maker's shop.
botonero, ra m. y f. Button maker (fabricante), button seller (vendedor).
botones m. inv. Buttons, bellboy (de un hotel). || Messenger, errand boy (recadero).
bototo m. *Amer.* Calabash (calabaza). || — Pl. *Amer.* Heavy shoes *o* boots (zapatos).
botulismo m. MED. Botulism.
botuto m. War trumpet of the Orinoco Indians (trompeta). || BOT. Stalk of pawpaw.
bou m. Seine fishing (pesca). || Seiner (barco).
bóveda f. ARQ. Vault. | Crypt (cripta). || — *Bóveda celeste*, vault of heaven, celestial vault. || *Bóveda craneana* or *craneal*, cranial cavity. || *Bóveda de cañón*, barrel vault. || *Bóveda de crucería*, V. CRUCERÍA. || *Bóveda de medio punto*, semicircular arch. || *Bóveda palatina*, palate, roof of the mouth. || *Bóveda por arista* or *claustral* or *esquifada*, groined *o* cloister vault. || *Clave de bóveda*, keystone.
bovedilla f. ARQ. Small vault (bóveda pequeña). | Space between girders (parte del techo entre vigas). || MAR. Curved part of the stern.
bóvidos m. pl. ZOOL. Bovidae, bovines.
bovino, na adj. Bovine.
— M. pl. Bovines, bovidae.
boxcalf m. Box calf (cuero).
boxeador m. Boxer (deportista).
boxear v. intr. To box.
boxeo m. Boxing.
bóxer m. Boxer (perro).
boy m. Boy (criado indígena).
boya f. MAR. Buoy: *boya luminosa*, light buoy. || Float (de una red). || *Boya de salvamento* or *salvavidas*, lifebuoy.
boyada f. Drove of oxen.
boyante adj. TAUR. Easy to fight (toro) || Prosperous, successful (próspero). || Happy, buoyant (feliz). || MAR. Buoyant.
boyar v. intr. To float (flotar).
boyardo m. Boyar.
boycot, boycotear, boycoteo V. BOICOT, BOICOTEAR, BOICOTEO.
boyera o **boyeriza** f. Cowshed.
boyerizo m. Cowherd.
boyero m. Cowherd. || ASTR. Bootes, the Wagoner, the Waggoner.
boyezuelo m. Young bullock [U.S., steer].
boy-scout m. Boy scout (explorador).
boyuno, na adj. Bovine.
boza m. MAR. Stopper (cable).
bozal adj. (Ant.) Pure (negro). || FIG. y FAM. Green, raw (novicio). | Daft, stupid, silly (tonto). || Wild, untamed: *caballo bozal*, wild horse. || *Amer.* Who speaks bad *o* broken Spanish.
— M. y f. Pure negro (negro). || FIG. y FAM. Greenhorn, novice (novato). | Fool, idiot, clod (tonto). || *Amer.* Foreigner who speaks bad *o* broken Spanish. || — M. Muzzle (para los animales). || *Amer.* Halter (cabestro).
bozo m. Down, fuzz (vello). || Mouth (parte exterior de la boca). || Halter (cabestro). || *A este niño ya le apunta el bozo*, the boy is already starting to get fuzz on his upper lip.
Brabante n. pr. m. GEOGR. Brabant.
braceada f. Violent waving of the arms.
braceador, ra adj. High-stepping (caballo).
braceaje m. Minting (de las monedas). || MAR. Depth (profundidad en brazas).
bracear v. intr. To wave *o* to swing one's arms (agitar los brazos). || To swim (nadar). || FIG. To strive, to struggle (luchar). || To step high (un caballo). || MAR. To brace (las velas).
braceo m. Waving of the arms. || Stroke (natación).
bracero m. Labourer.
bracmán m. Brahman, Brahmin.
bráctea f. BOT. Bract.
bradipepsia f. Bradypepsia (digestión difícil).
braga f. Panties, *pl.*, knickers, *pl.* (de mujer). || Napkin, nappy [U.S., diaper] (de niño de pecho). || Guy

(cuerda). || — Pl. Breeches (calzón ancho). || Panties, knickers (de mujer). || FIG. *No se pescan truchas a bragas enjutas*, nothing ventured, nothing gained (no se consigue nada sin correr riesgos).
bragado, da adj. FIG. y FAM. Resolute, tough (decidido). | Wicked (malintencionado). || FIG. y FAM. *Hay que ser muy bragado para hacer algo tan peligroso*, it takes a lot of guts to do such a dangerous thing.
bragadura f. Crutch, crotch (entrepierna).
bragazas m. inv. FAM. Henpecked man.
braguerista m. Truss maker.
braguero m. Truss (ortopédico).
bragueta f. Flies, *pl.*, fly (de pantalón). || — *Casamiento de bragueta*, marriage of convenience. || *Hidalgo de bragueta*, one who becomes a nobleman by siring seven successive sons.
braguetazo m. FIG. y FAM. Marriage of convenience. || FIG. y FAM. *Dar un braguetazo*, to marry money.
braguetón m. *Amer.* Tierceron (de bóveda).
Brahma n. pr. m. Brahma.
brahmán m. Brahmin, Brahman.
brahmánico, ca adj. Brahminic, Brahminical, Brahmanic, Brahmanical.
brahmanismo m. Brahminism, Brahmanism.
brahmín m. Brahmin, Brahman.
braille m. Braille (sistema de escritura para ciegos).
brama f. Rut, rutting (de los ciervos, etc.). || Rutting season, rut (época).
bramadero m. Rutting place (de los ciervos, etc.). || Tethering post (poste).
bramador, ra adj. Lowing (vacas). || Bellowing, roaring (toros).
bramante m. String, cord (cuerda). || Twine (especialmente de cáñamo).
bramar v. intr. To low (vacas). || To roar, to bellow (toros). || To bell, to troat (el venado). || To trumpet (el elefante). || FIG. To howl, to roar (el viento). | To roar, to thunder (el mar). | To rumble, to roll (el trueno). | To roar, to bellow, to thunder (de ira). || FAM. To bawl, to bellow, to howl (gritar).
bramido m. Lowing (de la vaca). || Bellowing, bellow, roar (del toro). || Bell, troat (del venado). || Trumpeting (del elefante). || FIG. Howling, roaring (del viento). | Roaring, thundering (del mar). | Rumbling, rolling (del trueno). | Roaring, bellowing, thundering (de ira). || FAM. Howl (grito). | Bawling, howling, bellowing (gritos). || FAM. *Dar bramidos de dolor*, to bellow *o* to howl with pain.
brancada f. Trammel net, trammel (red).
brancal m. Side members, *pl.* (de un carro).
brandal m. MAR. Backstay.
Brandeburgo o **Brandenburgo** n. pr. m. GEOGR. Brandenburg.
brandy m. Brandy (coñac).
branquia f. Branchia, gill (del pez).
— OBSERV. El plural de la palabra inglesa *branchia* es *branchiae*.
branquial adj. Branchial.
branquiópodos n. pl. ZOOL. Branchiopodes.
braquial adj. ANAT. Brachial.
braquicefalia f. Brachycephaly.
braquicefalismo m. Brachycephalism.
braquicéfalo, la adj. Brachycephalic.
braquiópodos m. pl. Brachiopodes (gusanos).
braquiuro m. Brachyuran (crustáceos).
brasa f. Ember (ascua). || — *Carne a la brasa*, braised meat. || FIG. *Estar como en brasas* or *en brasas*, to be on tenterhooks. | *Pasar como sobre brasas por un asunto*, to touch lightly on *o* to skim over a subject.
brasca f. Lute.
braseado, da adj. Braised.
braserillo m. Small brazier.
brasero m. Brazier. || Stake (hoguera). || *Amer.* Hearth (hogar).
— OBSERV. In Spain a *brasero* is a kind of brazier used for heating the house. It is frequently placed under a table which is called a *camilla*.
brasil m. Brazilwood, brazil (palo brasil).
Brasil n. pr. m. GEOGR. Brazil. || — BOT. *Nuez del Brasil*, Brazil nut. || *Palo del Brasil*, brazilwood, brazil.
brasileño, na adj./s. Brazilian.
brasilero, ra adj./s. *Amer.* Brazilian.
brasilete m. BOT. Brazilette.
bravata f. Swanking, boasting, bragging (jactancia). || Boast, brag (fanfarronada). || Piece of bravado (acción descarada). || *Decir bravatas*, to swank, to boast, to brag.
bravear v. intr. To swank, to boast, to brag. || To cheer (aplaudir).
bravera f. Vent (de un horno).
braveza f. Bravery, valour (bravura). || Fury (de los elementos).
bravío, a adj. Wild, untamed (salvaje). || Wild (silvestre). || FIG. Uncouth, coarse (rústico).
— M. Wildness, ferocity, fierceness.
¡bravísimo! interj. Well done!, wonderful!
bravo, va adj. Brave, courageous, valiant (valeroso). || Fierce, ferocious (feroz). || TAUR. Brave (toro). || Wild (salvaje): *un paisaje muy bravo*, a very wild countryside. || Rugged (accidentado). || Uncivilized: *indio bravo*, uncivilized Indian. || Wild, furious (los elementos). || Rough (mar). || Good, excellent (excelente). || FAM. Boastful, swaggering (valentón). || FIG. y FAM. Rough, churlish, rude (de mal carácter). | Magnificent, superb, marvellous (magnífico). | Wild, angry (enfadado). | Hot (picante). || *Toros bravos*, fighting bulls.
— M. Cheer (aplauso).
— Interj. Well done!, bravo!
bravucón, ona adj. Boastful, swaggering, swaggering.
— M. Boaster, braggart, swaggerer.
bravuconada o **bravuconería** f. Bragging, boasting (jactancia). || Brag, boast, swagger (fanfarronada).
bravura f. Ferocity, fierceness (de los animales). || Fighting spirit, bravery (de un toro). || Bravery, courage, valour (valor). || Boasting, bragging (jactancia).
braza f. MAR. Fathom (medida). | Brace (cuerda). || Breaststroke (modo de nadar): *nadar a la braza*, to swim breaststroke. || — *Braza de espalda*, backstroke. || *Braza mariposa*, butterfly.
— OBSERV. The Spanish *braza* equals 1.671 metres, and the English *fathom* 6 feet (1.83 metres).
brazada f. Stroke (del nadador, de un remo). || Armful (lo que abarcan los brazos). || *Amer.* Fathom (medida).
brazado Armful.
brazal m. Brassard (de la armadura). || Armband (en la manga). || Irrigation ditch (de un río).
brazalete m. Armband (en la manga). || Bracelet (pulsera).
brazo m. ANAT. Arm. || Foreleg (de un caballo, etc.). || Arm (de palanca, balanza, ancla, sillón, tocadiscos). || Boom (del micrófono). || Branch (de candelabro, de río). || Arm (de mar). || Jib, arm (de grúa). || Limb (de la cruz). || Limb, branch (de árbol). || Handle (de herramienta). || Sail arm (pala de molino). || Leg (de tijera para podar). || FIG. Arm (fuerza). || Estate (en las Cortes). || — Pl. Hands: *aquí hacen falta brazos*, more hands are needed here. | Protectors (ayudas). || — *A brazo*, by hand. || *A brazo partido*, hand to hand (sin armas), tooth and nail (con violencia), for all one is worth, with all one's might (con empeño). || *A fuerza de brazos*, by hard work. || FIG. *Brazo de gitano*, Swiss roll, roly-poly (pastel). | *Brazo derecho*, right hand, right arm. || *Con los brazos abiertos*, with open arms. || *Con los brazos cruzados*, with one's arms folded (con los brazos en el pecho), twiddling one's thumbs (sin hacer nada). || *Cruzarse de brazos*, to fold one's arms; to sit back and do nothing, to twiddle one's thumbs (no obrar). || *Dar el brazo a uno*, to give s.o. one's arm. || FIG. *Dar su brazo a torcer*, to give in. || *Del brazo*, arm in arm. || *Echar los brazos al cuello de alguien*, to throw one's arms around s.o.'s neck. || FIG. *Echarse* or *entregarse en brazos de uno*, to put o.s. into s.o.'s hands. || *En brazos*, in one's arms. || *Entregar al brazo secular*, to hand over to the secular arm. || FIG. *Estar atado de brazos*, to be bound hand and foot. | *Estar hecho un brazo de mar*, to be dressed up to the nines, to be dressed to kill. || *Huelga de brazos caídos*, down tools, sit-down strike. || *Ir del brazo* or *dándose el brazo* or *cogidos del brazo*, to walk arm in arm. || FIG. *Levantar los brazos al cielo*, to throw one's arms in the air.
brazola f. MAR. Coaming [of the hatches].
brazolargo m. *Amer.* Spider monkey.
brazuelo m. Forearm (de caballo). || Shoulder (de carnero). || Knuckle (del cerdo).
brea f. Pitch, tar: *brea mineral*, mineral pitch. || Tarpaulin (tela embreada).
break m. Brake, shooting brake, estate car [U.S., station wagon] (coche).
brear v. tr. FIG. y FAM. To thrash, to beat (pegar). | To ill-treat (maltratar). || — FIG. y FAM. *Le brearon a palos*, they showered him with blows. | *Le brearon a preguntas*, they bombarded him with questions.
— V. pr. FAM. *Brearse de trabajar*, to wear one's fingers to the bone.
brebaje m. Concoction, brew.
brebajo m. Drink of bran, salt and water for animals.
breca f. ZOOL. Bleak (albur). | Sea bream (pagel).
brecol m. o **brecolera** f. BOT. Broccoli, brocoli.
brecha f. MIL. Breach: *abrir una brecha en la muralla*, to make a breach in the wall. || Opening, gap, break (en muro, vallado, etc.). || FIG. Breach. || — *Batir en brecha*, to batter (una muralla), to attack (atacar). || FIG. *Estar siempre en la brecha*, to be always at it. | *Hacer brecha en*, to make an impression on. || *Hacerse una brecha en la frente*, to open a gash in one's forehead. || FIG. *Morir en la brecha*, to die in harness.
brega f. Struggle, fight (pelea): *la brega de la vida*, the struggle for life. || Quarrel, row (pendencia). || Hard task, arduous work (trabajo). || Practical joke, trick (burla). || — FIG. *Andar a la brega*, to slog away. || TAUR. *Capote de brega*, cape used by the matador for his passes with the bull before taking the cape used for the kill. || *En brega con*, struggling with, fighting against.
bregar v. intr. To struggle, to fight: *bregar con*, to struggle with *o* against, to fight with *o* against. || To quarrel (reñir). || FIG. To slog away, to toil away, to slave away (trabajar). | To wear o.s. out (cansarse).
— V. tr. To knead (amasar). || TAUR. To make passes with [the bull].
brema f. Bream (pez).
Brema o **Bremen** n. pr. GEOGR. Bremen.
breña f. Scrub.

breñal m. Scrub.
breñoso, sa adj. Scrubby, bushy.
breque m. Sea bream (pez). || *Amer.* Handbrake (freno). | Luggage van (vagón de equipajes). | Brake (coche).
Bretaña n. pr. f. GEOGR. Britain: *Gran Bretaña*, Great Britain. | Brittany (provincia francesa).
brete m. Shackles, *pl.*, fetters, *pl.* [of prisoners]. || — FIG. *Estar en un brete*, to be in a tight spot. | *Poner a uno en un brete*, to put s.o. in a tight spot.
bretón, ona adj./s. Breton. || — M. Breton (lengua). || BOT. Tree cabbage (col).
breva f. Early fig (higo). || FIG. y FAM. Stroke of luck: *cogió* or *le cayó una buena breva*, he had a real stroke of luck. | Cushy *o* soft job (buena colocación). || Flat cigar (puro). || *Amer.* Chewing tobacco (tabaco). || — FIG. y FAM. *De higos a brevas*, once in a blue moon. | *¡No caerá esa breva!*, no such luck!
breve adj. Brief, short (corto). || A few: *me lo dijo en breves palabras*, he told me so in a few words. || GRAM. Short. || *En breve*, shortly, soon (pronto).
— M. Papal brief (bula apostólica). || — F. MÚS. Breve (nota). || GRAM. Breve (sílaba, vocal).
brevedad f. Briefness, brevity, shortness. || — *Con brevedad*, concisely, briefly. || *Con la mayor brevedad*, as soon as possible. || *Para mayor brevedad*, to be brief.
brevete m. Heading (membrete).
breviario m. Breviary (libro de rezos). || Compendium (compendio). || IMPR. Brevier.
brezal m. Moor, moorland, heath.
brezo m. Heather, heath.
briba f. Vagabond's *o* tramp's life. || *Andar* or *vivir a la briba*, to loaf around, to idle around.
bribón, ona adj. Roguish, rascally (pícaro).
— M. y f. Rascal, rogue (pícaro). || Beggar, vagabond, tramp (mendigo).
bribonada f. Roguishness (cualidad de bribón). || Rascally trick (acción).
bribonear v. intr. To lead a rascally *o* roguish life. || To play roguish *o* rascally tricks (hacer bribonadas).
bribonería f. V. BRIBONADA.
bricbarca f. MAR. Bark, barque.
brida f. Bridle (freno, correaje y riendas). || Rein (rienda). || Clamp, clip (para apretar). || Flange (de un tubo). || MED. Bride [U.S., adhesion]. || FIG. *A toda brida*, at full gallop.
bridge m. Bridge (naipes): *jugar al bridge*, to play bridge.
bridón m. Snaffle. || MIL. Bridoon. || POÉT. Steed (caballo).
brigada f. MIL. Brigade. || Squad (de policías): *brigada móvil*, flying squad. || Gang (de obreros). || MIL. *General de brigada*, brigadier [U.S., brigadier general].
— M. MIL. Warrant officer.
brigadier m. (Ant.). Brigadier.
Bright (mal de) m. MED. Bright's disease (nefritis).
Brígida n. pr. f. Bridget.
Briján n. pr. FIG. y FAM. *Saber más que Briján* or *ser más listo que Briján*, to have all one's wits about one.
brillante adj. Brilliant. || Sparkling, glittering, bright (luz, piedra preciosa). || Brilliant, bright (color). || Sparkling, scintillating (conversación, estilo, ojos). || Bright (acero). || Bright, brilliant: *es el alumno más brillante*, he is the brightest pupil. || Shining (ejemplo). || Radiant: *estaba brillante de juventud*, she was radiant with youth. || Glittering, brilliant (reunión). || Brilliant (grupo). || Lustrous, shimmering (seda).
— M. Brilliant, diamond (diamante). || *Un collar de brillantes*, a diamond necklace.
brillantez f. Brightness, brillance (de un metal, del sol, etc.). || Splendour (de una ceremonia). || Brilliance (del estilo). || *Terminó sus estudios con gran brillantez*, he finished his studies brilliantly.
brillantina f. Brilliantine.
brillar v. intr. To shine (en general). || To glisten, to glint (el acero). || To glitter, to glisten (el oro, etc.). || To sparkle (los ojos). || To glimmer (una vela, el agua). || To glitter, to sparkle, to twinkle, to shine (las joyas, las estrellas). || To shine (la luna). || To blaze (las llamas). || To shimmer (la seda). || To glare (los faros de un coche). || To glow (las ascuas). || FIG. To stand out (sobresalir por su inteligencia, etc.). | To shine (en la conversación). || FIG. *Brillar por su ausencia*, to be conspicuous by one's absence.
brillazón f. *Amer.* Mirage (en la pampa).
brillo m. Sheen (del cabello, del agua, de una tela). || Lustre, sheen (de la seda). || Shine, polish (del betún, del barniz). || Brilliance (de un color, de la inteligencia, del estilo). || Sparkle (de un diamante, de los ojos). || Sparkling, shimmer (de las estrellas). || Light, brightness, shimmer (de la luna). || Brightness (del Sol). || Gloss, shine (del papel, de una fotografía). || Gloss, sheen, shine (de una superficie). || Shine, glint (de un metal). || Glow (de las ascuas). || FIG. Brilliance, splendour: *le gusta el brillo de la vida pública*, he likes the brilliance of public life. || *Dar* or *sacar brillo a*, to polish, to shine.
brin m. Coarse linen cloth.
brincar v. intr. To jump, to hop (saltar). || To jump up and down, to jump about, to leap about (saltar repetidamente). || To gambol (las ovejas, etc.). || FIG. To explode, to flare up (enfadarse). | To jump: *brincaron de alegría*, they jumped for joy. || FIG. y FAM. *Está que brinca*, he's hopping mad.
brinco m. Jump, hop, leap (salto). || Bound, jump (de un caballo, cabra, etc.). || — *Dar* or *pegar un brinco*, to jump, to hop. || FIG. *En un brinco* or *en dos brincos*, before you can say Jack Robinson, in no time at all.
brindar v. intr. To drink, to drink a toast, to toast: *brindemos por nuestra amistad*, let us drink to our friendship, let us toast our friendship. || To touch *o* to clink glasses (chocar las copas).
— V. tr. To offer: *le brindo la opotunidad de*, I am offering you the opportunity to. || — TAUR. *Brindar el toro*, to dedicate the bull. || *Esto nos brinda la ocasión de hablar*, this affords us the opportunity to talk.
— V. pr. To offer: *se brindó a pagar*, he offered to pay.
brindis m. Toast. || TAUR. « Brindis » [the matador's dedication of the bull he is about to kill]. || *Echar un brindis*, to toast, to drink a toast.
brío m. Energy (energía). || Determination (decisión). || Spirit: *hablar con brío*, to speak with spirit. || Dash, go, fire (empuje): *lleno de brío*, full of go. || Elegance (gracia). || — FIG. *Cortar a uno los bríos*, to clip s.o.'s wings. || *Hombre de bríos*, man of spirit.
briofita f. BOT. Bryophyte.
briol m. MAR. Buntline (cabo).
briología f. BOT. Bryology.
brionia f. BOT. Bryony.
bríos! (¡voto a) interj. fam. Damn!
briosamente adv. Courageously, bravely (con valor). || Resolutely (con determinación). || Vigorously, energetically (con ardor). || With spirit (con brío).
brioso, sa adj. Energetic, vigorous (enérgico). || Resolute, determined (determinado). || Fiery, spirited (caballo). || Elegant (garboso).
briozoario o **briozoo** m. BOT. Bryozoan bryozoon.
briqueta f. Briquette, briquet (carbón).
brisa f. Breeze: *brisa marina*, sea breeze.
brisca f. Card game (juego de naipes). || Brisque (as).
briscar v. tr. To brocade.
brístol m. Bristol board.
británico, ca adj. British: *Las Islas Británicas*, the British Isles. || *Su Majestad Británica*, Her Britannic Majesty (reina), His Britannic Majesty (rey).
— M. y f. Britisher. || *Los británicos*, the British.
britano, na adj. British.
M y f. HIST. Briton.
brizna f. Blade (de hierba). || String (de judía). || Bit, piece (trozo).
broca f. Drill, bit (taladro). || Tack (clavo). || Bobbin (de bordadora).
brocado, da adj. Brocaded.
— M. Brocade (tela).
brocal m. Curb (de un pozo).
brocamantón m. Large jewelled brooch.
brocatel m. Brocatelle (tela). || Brocatello (mármol).
bróculi m. Brocoli, broccoli.
brocha f. Paintbrush (pincel grande). || Powder puff (para polvos). || Shaving brush (de afeitar). || — *Pintor de brocha gorda*, painter and decorator (de casa), dauber (mal pintor). || *Versos de brocha gorda*, doggerel.
brochada f. o **brochazo** m. Brushstroke, stroke of the brush.
broche m. Brooch [U.S., breastpin] (joya). || Fastener, clip, clasp (de un vestido). || *Amer.* Paper clip (para sujetar papeles). || — Pl. *Amer.* Cuff links (gemelos). || FIG. *El broche final* o *de oro*, grand finale, finishing flourish.
brocheta f. CULIN. Skewer.
brocho adj. m. TAUR. With horns close together.
brodequín m. V. BORCEGUÍ.
broma f. Joke: *¡no es ninguna broma!*, it is no joke! | Joke, prank, trick, practical joke: *gastar bromas a*, to play jokes on. || ZOOL. Shipworm (gusano). || — *¡Basta de bromas!* or *dejémonos de bromas*, that's enough joking, joking aside. || *Broma aparte*, joking apart, seriously. || *Broma de mal gusto*, joke in bad taste. || *Broma pesada*, practical joke. || *Dar una broma a*, to play a joke on. || *En broma*, in fun, jokingly, as a joke. || *Entre bromas y veras*, half jokingly, half in earnest. || *Es pura broma*, it's a big *o* a huge joke. || *Estar de broma*, to be in a joking mood. || *Fuera de broma*, joking apart, seriously. || *Lo decía en broma*, I was only joking. || *Medio en broma, medio en serio*, half jokingly. || *Ni en broma*, not on any account. || *No estar para bromas*, not to be in the mood for joking, to be in no mood for joking. || *Saber (cómo) tomar una broma*, to be able to take a joke. || FIG. *Salir por la broma de*, to cost a mere, to cost the huge amount of. || *Ser amigo de bromas*, to like a joke, to like joking. || *Sin broma*, joking apart, seriously. || *Tienda de bromas y engaños*, joke shop. || *Tomar a broma*, to make fun of, to deride (ridiculizar), to take as a joke (tomar a guasa).
bromar v. tr. To gnaw (roer).
bromato m. QUÍM. Bromate.
bromazo m. Stupid joke, stupid trick: *dar un bromazo a*, to play a stupid trick on.

bromear v. intr. To JOKE: *no estoy bromeando*, I am not joking.
bromhídrico, ca adj. QUÍM. Hydrobromic.
brómico, ca adj. QUÍM. Bromic.
bromista adj. Fond of joking.
— M. y f. Practical joker (que gasta bromas). || Joker (que cuenta chistes). || Funny person, laugh (persona graciosa).
bromo m. QUÍM. Bromine.
bromuro m. QUÍM. Bromide. || FOT. *Papel de bromuro*, bromide paper.
bronca f. Quarrel, row, fight (riña). || Telling off, ticking off (reprensión). || Scuffle, brawl, fight (pelea). || Jeering, jeers, *pl.*, boos, *pl.* (gritos de desagrado). || — *Armarle una bronca a uno*, to boo *o* to jeer s.o. (abuchearle), to give s.o. hell (reprenderle). || *Armar una bronca*, to kick up a rumpus. || *Buscar bronca*, to look for a fight. || *Echar una bronca*, to tell off, to tick off, to haul over the coals. || *Ganarse una bronca*, to be booed, to be jeered (ser abucheado). || *Llevarse una bronca*, to be told off *o* ticked off, to be hauled over the coals. || *Se armó una bronca*, there was a tremendous quarrel *o* row.
bronce m. Bronze (metal y objeto de arte). || Copper coin (moneda de cobre). || FIG. *Ser de bronce*, to have a heart of stone.
bronceado, da adj. Bronze, bronze coloured (color). || Tanned, brown, sunburnt (tostado por el sol).
— M. Bronzing: *el bronceado de las medallas*, the bronzing of medals. || Suntanning (acción de broncearse). || Tan, suntan (piel tostada).
bronceador m. Suntan oil.
bronceadura f. Bronzing.
broncear v. tr. To bronze (un metal, una estatua). || To tan, to bronze (la piel).
— V. pr. To tan, to get brown, to get a suntan (la piel). || TECN. To bronze.
broncíneo, a adj. Bronze (del color del bronce). || Bronze, bronzed (de bronce).
broncista m. Bronzesmith.
bronco, ca adj. Rough, coarse (tosco). || Brittle (metales). || Raucous, harsh, rough (voz, sonido). || FIG. Surly (carácter).
bronconeumonía f. MED. Bronchopneumonia.
broncoscopio m. Bronchoscope.
bronquedad o **bronquera** f. Roughness, coarseness (tosquedad). || Brittleness (metales). || Harshness, roughness (voz, sonido). || FIG. Surliness (carácter).
bronquial adj. ANAT. Bronchial.
bronquio m. ANAT. Bronchus. || — Pl. ANAT. Bronchi, bronchia.
bronquiolos m. pl. ANAT. Bronchioles.
bronquítico, ca adj. MED. Bronchitic.
bronquitis f. MED. Bronchitis.
broquel m. Shield.
broquelarse v. pr. To shield o.s. || FIG. To defend o.s., to protect o.s.
broqueta f. Skewer. || *Riñones en broqueta*, kidney kebab.
brotadura f. Budding, shooting (de una planta). || Gushing (de una fuente).
brotar v. intr. To sprout, to come up, to spring up: *ya ha brotado el trigo*, the wheat has come up. || To bud, to shoot (echar renuevos): *el árbol empieza a brotar*, the tree is starting to bud. || To sprout, to come out: *los renuevos han brotado*, the buds have sprouted. || To gush forth, to spring up (las fuentes). || To rise (los ríos). || To shoot out: *brotaron chispas*, sparks shot out. || To well up: *brotaron las lágrimas de sus ojos*, tears welled up in his eyes. || To appear, to break out (erupción cutánea). || FIG. To spring up: *brotó una llamarada*, a flame sprang up. | To appear: *en mi mente brotó una duda*, a doubt appeared in my mind. || *Hacer brotar chispas*, to make sparks fly.
— V. tr. To produce.
brote m. BOT. Bud, shoot (renuevo). | Budding (brotadura). || Gushing (del agua). || Welling-up (de lágrimas). || MED. Rise (de fiebre). | Appearance (de erupción cutánea). || FIG. Outbreak: *los primeros brotes de una epidemia*, the first outbreaks of an epidemic.
browniano adj. m. FÍG. Brownian (movimiento).
browning m. Browning (pistola).
broza f. Dead leaves, *pl.* (hojas muertas). || Dead wood (ramas). || Rubbish (desechos). || Thicket, undergrowth, brushwood (matorrales). || FIG. Rubbish: *en su libro había mucha broza*, there was a lot of rubbish in his book. || IMPR. Printer's brush (bruza).
brozno, na adj. V. BRONCO.
bruces (de) loc. adv. Face downwards. || *Caer de bruces*, to fall flat on one's face, to fall headlong.
bruja f. Witch (hechicera). || Barn owl (lechuza). || FIG. Old witch, hag (mujer fea). | Witch (mujer mala). || *Amer. Estar bruja*, to be poverty-stricken, to be penniless.
Brujas n. pr. GEOGR. Bruges.
brujear v. intr. To practise witchcraft.
brujería f. Witchcraft, sorcery.
brujidor m. Glass cutter (herramienta).
brujir v. tr. To trim [glass].
brujo m. Sorcerer, wizard. || Witch doctor (en las tribus primitivas). || *Amer.* Medicine man. || *El aprendiz de brujo*, the Sorcerer's Apprentice.
brújula f. Compass: *brújula marina*, mariner's compass. || (P. us). Sight (mira). || FIG. *Perder la brújula*, to lose one's bearings.
brujulear v. tr. FIG. y FAM. To guess (adivinar). | To plot, to scheme (tramar). || To uncover (las cartas).
— V. intr. FIG. y FAM. To loaf about (vagar).
brujuleo m. FIG. y FAM. Guessing.
brulote m. MAR. Fire ship. || *Amer.* Insult (insulto). | Scorching article (escrito incendiario).
bruma f. Mist (niebla). || Haze (de calor). || — Pl. FIG. Confusion, *sing.*, fog, *sing.*, haze, *sing.*
brumazón f. Fog.
brumoso, sa adj. Misty, hazy (ligeramente neblinoso), foggy (muy neblinoso).
bruno, na adj. Dark brown.
— M. BOT. Black plum (ciruela, ciruelo).
bruñido m. Polishing, burnishing (acción). || Polish, burnish (resultado).
bruñidor, ra m. y f. Polisher, burnisher. || — M. Polisher, burnisher (herramienta).
bruñir* v. tr. To polish, to burnish. || *Amer.* To pester (fastidiar).
— V. pr. FIG. y FAM. To make up (maquillarse).
brusco, ca adj. Brusque, abrupt: *una persona brusca*, a brusque person. || Sudden, abrupt (repentino): *un cambio brusco*, a sudden change. || Sharp (curva). || Sharp (cambio de temperatura).
— M. Butcher's broom (arbusto).
brusela f. Periwinkle (flor).
bruselas f. pl. Jeweller's tweezers.
Bruselas n. pr. GEOGR. Brussels. || *Coles de Bruselas*, Brussels sprouts.
bruselense adj. [Of *o* from] Brussels.
— M. y f. Native o inhabitant of Brussels.
brusquedad f. Brusqueness, abruptness (de una persona). || Suddenness, abruptness (de cosas).
brutal adj. Brutal, rough: *hombres brutales*, brutal men. || FIG. Sudden, abrupt (repentino). || FAM. Terrific (formidable). | Colossal, huge, gigantic (enorme).
brutalidad f. Brutality, savagery (crueldad). || Brutality, brutishness (de una persona). || Brutal *o* savage act (salvajada). || FAM. Foolish act (acción estúpida). | Foolishness (estupidez).
brutalizar v. tr. To brutalize.
bruteza f. V. BRUTALIDAD.
bruto, ta adj. Stupid, dense (estúpido): *este chico es muy bruto*, this boy is very dense. || Ignorant (sin cultura). || Uncouth, coarse, rough (tosco). || Brutal, brutish (brutal). || Crude: *petróleo bruto*, crude oil. || Rough, uncut (piedra, diamante). || Unworked (madera). || — *Amer. A la bruta* or *a lo bruto*, crudely. || *En bruto*, gross: *peso en bruto*, gross weight; rough, uncut: *diamante en bruto*, uncut diamond; unworked (madera). || FIG. y FAM. *¡Pedazo de bruto!*, stupid brute! || *Producto nacional bruto*, gross national product.
— M. y f. Brute (estúpido, cruel). || Lout, country bumpkin (rústico). || — M. Brute, beast (animal). || *El noble bruto*, the noble beast (el caballo).
bruza f. Scrubbing brush (para restregar). || Brush (para caballos). || IMPR. Printer's brush.
bruzar v. tr. To clean with a brush, to brush.
bu m. Bogeyman.
búa f. V. BUBA.
buarillo o **buaro** m. Scops owl.
buba f. MED. Bubo.
bubi m. Bubi (de Fernando Poo).
bubón m. MED. Bubo.
bubónico, ca adj. MED. Bubonic: *peste bubónica*, bubonic plague.
bucal adj. ANAT. Buccal: *órganos bucales*, buccal organs. || Oral.
bucanero m. Buccaneer.
bucarán m. Buckram (tela).
Bucarest n. pr. Bucharest.
búcaro m. Odoriferous clay (arcilla). || Jar made of [odoriferous] clay (vasija). || Vase (florero).
buccinador m. ANAT. Buccinator.
buccino m. Whelk (molusco).
buceador m. Diver (buzo). || Pearl diver (de perlas).
bucear v. intr. To dive (el buzo). || To swim under water (nadar). || FIG. To investigate, to explore, to sound (un asunto).
bucéfalo m. FIG. y FAM. Blockhead, jackass (tonto).
Bucéfalo n. pr. m. Bucephalus.
buceo m. Diving (de buzo, de nadador). || Skin diving (natación submarina). || Dive (zambullida). || FIG. Investigation.
bucero m. Griffon (perro).
bucle m. Ringlet, curl (de cabellos).
bucólica f. Bucolic (composición poética). || FAM. Grub, chow (comida).
bucólico, ca adj. Bucolic.
buchaca f. *Amer.* Bag.
buchada f. Mouthful [of liquid].
buche m. Crop, craw (de aves), maw (de animales). || Pucker, bag (que hace la ropa). || Mouthful (de líquido). || FIG. y FAM. Belly, stomach (estómago): *llenarse el buche*, to fill one's belly. | Bosom (fuero interno). || Newly-born donkey (borrico). || *Amer.* Top hat (chistera). | Goitre [U.S., goiter] (bocio). || FAM. *No le cupo en el buche esta broma*, he couldn't stomach *o* take the joke.
buchinche m. V. BOCHINCHE.

buchón, ona adj. Potbellied (barrigón). || *Paloma buchona*, pouter [pigeon].
Buda n. pr. m. Buddha.
Budapest n. pr. GEOGR. Budapest.
budare m. *Amer*. Dish for baking corn bread.
budín m. CULIN. Pudding.
budinadora f. TECN. Extruder.
budinera f. Pudding bowl, pudding basin.
budión m. ZOOL. Wrasse (pez).
budismo m. Buddhism.
budista adj./s. Buddhist.
buen adj. Apocopated form of *bueno*. (V. BUENO).

— OBSERV. The adjective *bueno* is apocopated to *buen* when it *precedes* the word it qualifies, whether it is a masculine noun (*un buen libro*, a good book; *un buen hombre*, a good man, etc.) or a verb in the infinitive used as a noun (*un buen andar*, a good pace, etc.).

buenamente adv. Simply (sencillamente). || Easily, effortlessly (fácilmente). || Readily, happily, unthinkingly: *cree buenamente cualquier cosa que se le diga*, he readily believes everything he is told. || Willingly (de buen grado).
buenandanza f. V. BIENANDANZA.
buenaventura f. Good fortune, good luck (suerte). || Fortune: *echar* or *decir la buenaventura a uno*, to tell s.o.'s fortune.
Buenaventura n. pr. m. Bonaventura.
buenazo, za adj. Good-natured.
— M. y f. Good-natured person, good soul.
bueno, na adj. Good: *es un hombre muy bueno*, he is a very good man; *¡qué niño más bueno!*, there's a good boy!; *buena conducta*, good behaviour; *ser de buena familia*, to be from a good family; *un buen obrero*, a good worker; *dele una buena paliza*, give him a good beating; *una buena ocasión*, a good opportunity. || Good, fine, fair (tiempo). || Bad, nasty: *un buen constipado*, a bad cold. || Strong, sound (constitución física). || Nice, pleasant (agradable): *es bueno pasearse en el jardín*, it is nice to walk in the garden. || Good (deseable, útil): *sería bueno que acabaras esto muy pronto*, it would be good if you finished it as soon as possible; *este barco es bueno para pescar*, this boat is good for fishing; *este jarabe es bueno para la tos*, this syrup is good for coughs. || Sound (doctrina, argumento). || Nice, kind, good (amable): *una buena chica*, a nice girl; *eres muy bueno conmigo*, you are very kind to me. || Good, fine, beautiful: *tiene buena voz*, he has a fine voice. || Polite, good (sociedad). || FAM. Considerable: *una buena cantidad*, a considerable amount. || Real, proper: *¡buen sinvergüenza estás hecho!*, you are a real good-for-nothing! | Fine: *en buen lío nos hemos metido!*, a fine mess we have got ourselves into. || — *¿Adónde* or *a dónde bueno?*, where are you going? || *A la buena de Dios*, in a slapdash way, any old how (a lo que salga). || FAM. *¡Buena es ésa!*, that's a good one! || *Buena jugada*, V. JUGADA. || FAM. *¡Buena la has hecho!* or *¡buena la has armado!*, that's done it!, you've done it now! | *¡Buenas!*, hello! || *Buenas noches*, good evening (al atardecer), good night (al acostarse). || *Buenas tardes*, good afternoon (después del mediodía), good evening (al atardecer). || *Bueno de comer*, good to eat. || *¡Bueno está!*, that's enough!, that will do! (¡basta!). || *¡Bueno está lo bueno!*, enough is enough. || *Buenos días*, good morning. || *Dar por bueno*, to approve, to accept. || *Darse buena vida*, V. VIDA. || *De buena gana*, willingly, gladly. || *De buenas a primeras*, all at once, without warning (de repente), at first sight, from the very start, right from the start (a primera vista), straight away (en seguida). || *¿De dónde bueno?*, where did you spring from? || *De las buenas*, first-rate. || *De verdad de la buena*, really and truly. || *El buen camino*, the straight and narrow. || *En el buen momento*, at the proper time, at the right time. || *Es bueno saberlo*, it is nice *o* good to know. || FAM. *¡Estamos buenos!*, we're in a fine mess! || *Estar a buenas con uno*, to be on good terms with s.o. || FAM. *Estar buena*, to be hot stuff, to be gorgeous (mujer). || *Estar bueno*, to be well, to be in good health. || FAM. *Estar de buenas*, to be in a good mood (de buen humor), to be in luck (tener suerte). || FIG. *Estaría bueno (que)*, it would be just fine [if], it would be the last straw [if]. || *Hace buen tiempo*, the weather is good. || *Ir por buen camino*, to be on the right road. || FAM. *Librarse de una buena*, to have a narrow escape *o* a close call. || *Los buenos tiempos*, the good old days, the good times. || *Por las buenas*, willingly. || *Por las buenas o por las malas*, willy-nilly (de buen grado o por fuerza), by fair means or foul (de cualquier modo). || *¡Qué buena!* or *¡muy buena!*, that's a good one! (historia). || *¡Qué bueno!* or *¡muy bueno!*, bravo!, very good! (excelente). || *¿Qué dice de bueno?*, what's new? || *Ser bueno como un ángel*, to be as good as gold. || *Ser más bueno que el pan*, to be kindness *o* goodness itself. || *Ser muy buena persona*, to be very nice *o* kind. || FAM. *Tirarse una buena vida*, to lead a soft life. || *Verás lo que es bueno*, you will see sth. really good (sentido propio), just you wait (sentido irónico).
— M. Good one (persona). || Quality: *preferir lo bueno a lo bello*, to put quality before looks. || — Pl. The good [ones]: *los buenos y los malos*, the good [ones] and the bad [ones]. || — FAM. *Lo bueno es que*, the good part about it is that, the strange thing is that. || *Lo bueno, si breve, dos veces bueno*, brevity is the soul of wit, the shorter the better.
— Interj. Well! || Very well!, all right!, O.K.! (de acuerdo). || That's enough!, that'll do! (¡basta!). || Come on!, come off it! (con incredulidad).
Buenos Aires n. pr. GEOGR. Buenos Aires.
buey m. ZOOL. Bullock, ox (toro castrado). || Ox (animal de tiro). || — *Buey marino*, manatee, sea cow. || FIG. *El buey suelto bien se lame*, there is nothing like freedom. | *Habló el buey y dijo mu*, what can you expect from a pig but a grunt?
bueyada f. Drove of oxen (boyada).
bueyecillo o **bueyezuelo** m. Little bullock, steer.
bueyuno, na adj. Bovine, of oxen.
bufa f. Joke (broma). || Jest, piece of bufoonery (bufonada). || *Amer*. Drunkenness (borrachera).
bufado, da adj. Blown (vidrio).
búfalo, la m. y f. ZOOL. Buffalo.
bufanda f. Scarf, muffler.
bufar v. intr. To snort (el toro, etc.). || To spit (el gato). || To neigh (el caballo). || FIG. To snort [with rage] (persona). || FIG. y FAM. *Está que bufa*, he is hopping mad.
bufete m. Writing table, writing desk (mesa). || Lawyer's office (despacho). || Practice (clientela).
buffet m. Buffet.
bufido m. Snort (del toro). || Roar (del león, etc.). || Hiss (del gato). || Neigh (del caballo). || FIG. y FAM. Outburst (de ira). | Telling off, bawling out (reprimenda): *recibir un bufido*, to get a telling off. | Yell (grito). || FIG. y FAM. *Dar bufidos de rabia*, to bellow with rage.
bufo, fa adj. Comic: *actor bufo*, comic actor. || *Ópera bufa*, opera bouffe, comic opera.
— M. Buffoon.
bufón, ona adj. Farcical, comical.
— M. Buffoon, fool. || HIST. Jester.
bufonada f. Piece of buffoonery, jest.
bufonearse v. pr. To play the fool (hacer bufonadas). || To laugh at, to make fun of (burlarse de).
bufonesco, ca adj. Farcical, comical.
buganvilla f. BOT. Bougainvillea.
buggy m. Buggy (coche).
bugle m. MÚS. Bugle.
buglosa f. Bugloss (planta).
buharda o **buhardilla** f. Attic, garret. || Dormer [window] (ventana).
buharro m. Scops owl.
búho m. Owl. || FIG. Recluse, unsociable person. || *Búho real*, eagle owl.
buhonería f. Pedlar's wares, hawker's wares (objetos). || Peddling, hawking (oficio).
buhonero m. Pedlar [U.S., peddler], hawker.
buido, da adj. Sharp (afilado). || Grooved (acanalado). || *Estilo buido*, easy *o* fluent style.
buitre m. ZOOL. Vulture (ave). || FIG. Vulture (persona).
buitrear v. tr. *Amer*. To hunt [vultures]. | To vomit (vomitar).
buitrón m. Fish trap (para pescar).
buje m. Axle box, bushing (de un eje).
bujería f. Knick-knack (fruslería).
bujía f. Candle (vela). || Candlepower (unidad de intensidad luminosa). || Sparking plug [U.S., spark plug] (del encendido).
bula f. Bull (del papa). || Bulla (adorno romano). || — *Bula de oro*, Golden Bull. || FIG. *No poder con la bula*, to be finished, to have had it.
bulbo m. BOT. Bulb. || ANAT. y ARQ. Bulb.
bulboso, sa adj. Bulbous.
buldog o **bulldog** m. Bulldog (perro).
buldozer o **bulldozer** m. Bulldozer (excavadora).
bulerías f. pl. Bulerias [Andalusian song and dance].
buleto m. Papal brief.
bulevar m. Boulevard (alameda).
Bulgaria n. pr. f. GEOGR. Bulgaria.
búlgaro, ra adj./s. Bulgarian.
bulo m. FAM. Hoax, false report, false piece of news.
bulto m. Volume, size, bulk (volumen). || Shape, form (objeto o persona de aspecto confuso): *he visto dos bultos cerca de la casa*, I saw two shapes near the house. || Bump (chichón). || Lump, swelling (protuberancia). || Parcel, package (paquete). || Piece of luggage (equipaje). || Bundle: *un bulto de ropa*, a bundle of clothes. || Body: *el toro busca el bulto*, the bull goes for the body. || *Amer*. Satchel (cartapacio). || — *A bulto*, roughly, approximately. || FIG. y FAM. *Buscar a uno el bulto*, to hound s.o., to try to rile s.o. || *Cuanto menos bulto, más claridad*, good riddance to bad rubbish. || *De bulto*, obvious, striking, glaring. || *De mucho bulto*, bulky. || *De poco bulto*, small. || *Escoger a bulto*, to choose at random. || FAM. *Escurrir el bulto*, to get out of it, to dodge it. || *Hacer (de) bulto*, to help to make up a crowd, to swell the numbers. || *Hacer mucho bulto*, to be very bulky, to be cumbersome, to take up a lot of space.
bulla f. Uproar, noise, racket, row: *armar* or *meter bulla*, to make a racket. || Crowd, mob (muchedumbre). || Bustling, jostling: *hay mucha bulla en las tiendas*, there is a lot of bustling in the shops. || Confusion. || — *Meter bulla*, to hurry (meter prisa). || *Tener bulla*, to be in a hurry.
bullabesa f. Bouillabaisse.
bullanga f. Tumult, disturbance, racket, riot (tumulto).

bullanguero, ra adj. Riotous, noisy, uproarious.
— M. y f. Noisy person (persona ruidosa). || Rioter, troublemaker (persona alborotadora).
bullaranga f. *Amer.* V. BULLANGA.
bullebulle m. y f. Busybody.
bullicio m. Hubbub, noise, din (ruido). || Bustle, hustle and bustle: *retirarse al campo para huir del bullicio de la ciudad*, to retire to the country to escape from the hustle and bustle of the city. || Crush (muchedumbre): *ser cogido en el bullicio*, to be caught in the crush. || Confusion.
bullicioso, sa adj. Busy, bustling: *una calle bulliciosa*, a busy street. || Boisterous, restless (turbulento): *un niño bullicioso*, a boisterous child. || Noisy (ruidoso). || Riotous (alborotador).
bullidor, ra adj. Restless, bustling (que se mueve mucho). || Active (que tiene muchas actividades).
bullir* v. intr. To boil (hervir). || To bubble, to bubble up (a borbotones). || To swarm, to teem (pulular). || FIG. To boil (la sangre, de enfado). | To seethe: *bullía de ira*, he was seething with rage. | To bustle about (agitarse). | To bustle: *bullir de actividad*, to bustle with activity. || — FIG. *Le bullen los pies al ver bailar a los demás*, he is itching to dance as he watches the others. | *Me bulle la lengua*, I am dying to talk.
— V. tr. To stir, to move: *no bullía pie ni mano*, he did not stir hand or foot.
— V. pr. To move (moverse).
bullón m. Stud (adorno de metal). || Puff (en un vestido).
bulterrier m. Bull terrier (perro).
bumerang m. Boomerang.
bungalow m. Bungalow.
buniato m. BOT. Sweet potato (boniato).
bunker m. Bunker.
buñolada f. Fair.
buñolería f. Doughnut shop.
buñolero, ra m. y f. Doughnut seller.
buñuelo m. Doughnut. || FIG. y FAM. Mess, botch: *esa película es un buñuelo*, that film is a botch. || — *Buñuelo de viento*, fritter. || FIG. y FAM. *Hacer un buñuelo*, to make a botch, to make a mess.
buque m. Ship, boat, vessel. || *Buque aljibe*, tanker. || *Buque carguero* or *mercante*, cargo boat, freighter, merchant ship. || *Buque costanero* or *de cabotaje*, coasting vessel, coaster. || *Buque de desembarco*, landing craft. || *Buque de guerra*, warship. || *Buque de pasajeros*, passenger ship. || *Buque de ruedas*, paddle steamer. || *Buque de vapor*, steamship, steamer. || *Buque de vela*, sailing ship. || *Buque escuela*, training ship. || *Buque insignia*, flagship. || *Buque nodriza*, mother ship.
buqué m. Bouquet (del vino).
burbuja f. Bubble. || *Hacer burbujas*, to bubble, to make bubbles.
burbujear v. intr. To bubble. || To sparkle, to fizz (champán, agua mineral).
burbujeo m. Bubbling. || Fizz, sparkle (de champán, agua mineral).
burda f. MAR. Backstay.
burdégano m. ZOOL. Hinny.
burdel m. Brothel.
burdeos adj./s.m. Bordeaux (vino).
Burdeos n. pr. GEOGR. Bordeaux.
burdo, da adj. Clumsy (torpe): *una excusa burda*, a clumsy excuse. || Coarse, rough (tosco): *paño burdo*, coarse cloth; *modales burdos*, rough manners.
bureo m. FAM. Pastime, amusement (diversión). || FAM. *Estar* or *irse de bureo*, to go on a spree *o* on a binge.
bureta f. QUÍM. Burette.
burgalés, esa adj. [Of *o* from] Burgos.
— M. y f. Native *o* inhabitant of Burgos.
burgo m. (Ant.). Hamlet, borough (población pequeña). || *Burgo podrido*, rotten borough.
burgomaestre m. Burgomaster.
burgrave m. Burgrave.
burgués, esa adj. Bourgeois, middle-class.
— M. y f. Bourgeois, middle-class man *o* woman.
burguesía f. Bourgeoisie, middle-class.
burí m. BOT. Sago palm.
buril m. Burin.
burilada o **buriladura** f. Burin stroke.
burilado m. Engraving.
burilar v. tr. To engrave [with a burin].
burjaca f. [Pilgrim's] scrip.
burla f. Gibe, jeer, taunt (mofa). || Joke (broma). || — *Burla burlando*, without noticing it, merrily (sin darse cuenta), jokingly (bromeando), on the quiet, craftily (disimuladamente). || *De burlas* or *en son de burlas*, in fun. || *Entre burlas y veras*, half jokingly. || *Gastar burlas*, to play tricks. || *Hacer burla de uno*, to mock s.o., to make fun of s.o. (mofarse). || *Hacer burla de uno con la mano*, to thumb one's nose at s.o. (un palmo de narices).
burladero m. TAUR. Refuge [in a bullring].
burlador, ra adj. Mocking.
— M. y f. Mocker. || — M. Seducer, Don Juan.
burlar v. tr. To deceive, to trick, to take in (engañar). || To outwit (chasquear). || To deceive (a una mujer). || FIG. To flout: *burlar las leyes*, to flout the law. | To frustrate (una esperanza, etc.). | To evade (la vigilancia).
— V. pr. To mock, to ridicule, to make fun of.
burlería f. Mockery (mofa). || Deceit (engaño). || Tall story (cuento fabuloso).
burlesco, ca adj. Burlesque: *el género burlesco*, the burlesque style. || FIG. Funny, comic: *una situación muy burlesca*, a very funny situation.
burlete m. Draught excluder.
burlón, ona adj. Mocking: *un aire burlón*, a mocking air.
— M. y f. Joker.
buró m. Bureau, writing desk (mesa de escribir). || Executive committee (junta directiva). || *Amer.* Bedside table.
burocracia f. Bureaucracy.
burócrata m. y f. Bureaucrat.
burocrático, ca adj. Bureaucratic.
burra f. She-ass (hembra del burro). || FIG. y FAM. Dunce, ass (ignorante). | Hard worker (mujer trabajadora).
burrada f. Drove of donkeys. || FIG. y FAM. Stupid *o* foolish remark (necedad): *dijo una burrada*, he made a stupid remark. | Stupid *o* foolish thing (acción estúpida): *hizo una burrada*, he did a stupid thing. | Vulgar *o* rude remark, vulgarity (grosería). | Atrocity (atrocidad). || — FIG. y FAM. *Decir burradas*, to talk nonsense. | *Una burrada*, a lot, an awful lot: *una burrada de gente*, a lot of people; *me gusta una burrada*, I like it a lot.
burrero m. Donkey driver.
burriciego, ga adj. FAM. As blind as a bat.
burrillo m. FAM. Liturgical calendar, ordo.
burrito m. Young donkey, foal. || *Amer.* Fringe (flequillo).
burro m. ZOOL. Donkey, ass. || Sawhorse (para serrar). || FIG. y FAM. Ass, dunce, fool: *este chico es muy burro*, this boy is a real dunce. | Lout, brute (tosco). || *Amer.* Stepladder, folding ladder (escalera de tijera). || — FIG. *A burro muerto cebada al rabo*, it is no good shutting the stable door after the horse has bolted. | *Apearse* or *caerse del burro*, to back down, to climb down. | *Burro cargado de letras*, pompous ass. | *Burro de carga*, hard worker (que trabaja mucho), dogsbody, person who does the donkey work, drudge (que carga con todo el trabajo). || *Ir en burro*, to ride on a donkey. || FIG. y FAM. *No ver tres en un burro*, to be as blind as a bat.
bursátil adj. Stock-exchange: *información bursátil*, stock-exchange news.
burujo m. Lump (en una masa). || Knot, tangle (en la lana, etc.). || Cattle cake made of olives or grapes (para el ganado).
burujón m. Bump, lump (chichón).
busca f. Search: *ir en* or *a la busca de*, to go in search of. || Party of hunters (cacería). || — Pl. *Amer.* Perks (fam.).
buscador, ra adj. Seeking, searching. || *Cabeza buscadora*, homing device (de un cohete).
— M. y f. Seeker, searcher. || Prospector. || — M. TECN. Finder (de telescopio).
buscaniguas m. inv. *Amer.* Jumping jack, firecracker (petardo).
buscapié m. Feeler [in conversation].
buscapiés m. inv. Jumping jack, firecracker (petardo).
buscapleitos m. inv. Troublemaker.
buscar v. tr. To search for, to look for: *lo busqué en toda la casa sin encontrarlo*, I looked for it all over the house without finding it; *buscar una solución a un problema*, to search for a solution to a problem. || To seek: *buscar ayuda, un consejo, la amistad*, to seek help, advice, friendship. || To be after, to be out for (perseguir): *sólo busca su propio beneficio*, he is only after what he can gain. || To look for: *buscar un trabajo*, to look for work. || To look up (en un libro). || To fumble for (con dificultad): *buscar sus palabras, el ojo de la cerradura*, to fumble for words, for the keyhole. || FIG. y FAM. To ask for, to look for (provocar). || — FIG. y FAM. *Buscarle las cosquillas a uno*, v. COSQUILLA. | *Buscarle tres pies al gato*, v. PIE. | *Buscar una aguja en un pajar*, to look for a needle in a haystack. || *Ir a buscar*, to fetch, to go and get, to bring. || *Pasaré a buscarte a las tres*, I'll pick you up at three o'clock.
— V. intr. To look, to search. || *Quien busca halla*, seek and ye shall find.
— V. pr. FIG. *Buscarse la vida*, to try to earn one's living. || FIG. y FAM. *Buscársela*, to ask for it. || *Buscarse la ruina*, to be on the road to ruin.
buscarruidos m. y f. inv. FIG. y FAM. Troublemaker, quarrelsome person (pendenciero).
buscavidas m. y f. inv. Hustler (persona muy activa). || Go-getter (ambicioso). || Busybody (entrometido).
buscón, ona m. y f. (P. us.). Searcher (que busca). || — M. Pickpocket (ratero). || Petty thief (ladrón). || Crook, swindler (estafador). || — F. POP. Streetwalker, prostitute.
busilis m. Snag, hitch (dificultad). || Core (parte central). || *Allí está el busilis*, that's the rub, that's the catch.
búsqueda f. Search.
busto m. Bust.
butaca f. Seat (en un teatro). || Easy chair, armchair (en una casa). || — Pl. Stalls (en un teatro). || — *Butaca*

de patio, seat in the stalls [U.S., seat in the orchestra]. || *Patio de butacas*, stalls [U.S., orchestra].
butadieno m. QUÍM. Butadiene.
butano m. QUÍM. Butane: *bombona de butano*, butane cylinder; *gas butano*, butane gas.
buten (de) loc. adv. FAM. First-rate, fabulous, terrific.
butifarra f. Catalan sausage.
butileno m. QUÍM. Butylene.
butilo m. QUÍM. Butyl.
butírico, ca adj. QUÍM. Buryric: *ácido butírico*, butyric acid.
buyo m. Betel.
buzamiento m. MIN. Dip (del filón).
buzar v. intr. MIN. To dip.
buzo m. Diver. || — *Campana de buzo*, diving bell. || *Enfermedad de los buzos*, the bends, caisson disease, diver's paralysis.
buzón m. Letter box [U.S., mailbox] (en general). || Sluice (de un estanque). || Stopper, plug, bung (tapón). || *Echar una carta a* or *en el buzón*, to post a letter
buzonero m. *Amer.* Postman.
byroniano, na adj. Byronic.
byronismo m. Byronism.

C

c f. C: *una c mayúscula*, a capital c.

— OBSERV. Before *e* or *i* the *c* has the same sound as the Spanish *z* (an interdental fricative) and it is pronounced with the tip of the tongue between the teeth, as in the English *th* sound [θ]. In other cases the *c* is a voiceless velar occlusive like the *k*. The first of these sounds is often confused with the *s* sound in Latin American and Andalusian pronunciation.

¡ca! interj. FAM. Not at all!, never! [indicates negation].
cabal adj. Exact, right, accurate: *una cuenta cabal*, an exact sum; *una definición cabal*, an exact definition. || Perfect (sin defecto): *un hombre cabal*, a perfect man. || Whole, full: *el peso cabal*, the full weight. || Complete, total: *un cabal fracaso*, a total defeat. || Exactly: *duró tres horas cabales*, it lasted exactly three hours. || — *Es hermosa a carta cabal*, she is beauty itself. || *Estar en sus cabales*, to be in one's right mind. || *No estar en sus cabales*, not to be in one's right mind, to be out of one's mind: *cuando hiciste eso, no estabas en tus cabales*, you must have been out of your mind to do that. || *Por sus cabales*, properly (perfectamente), at a fair price (precio).
cábala f. Cabala, cabbala (doctrina). || FIG. Intrigue, cabal: *andar metido en una cábala*, to be mixed up in an intrigue. || FIG. *Hacer cábalas sobre algo*, to speculate *o* to make guesses about sth.
cabalgada f. Troop of cavalry (tropa de jinetes). || Cavalry raid (correría).
cabalgador, ra m. y f. Rider, horseman, horsewoman.
cabalgadura f. Mount (bestia de silla). || Pack animal, beast of burden (bestia de carga).
cabalgar v. intr. To ride: *cabalgar en un burro*, to ride an ass, to ride on an ass. || To straddle (sentarse a horcajadas): *el niño cabalgaba sobre la tapia*, the child straddled the wall.
— V. tr. To ride. || To cover, to mount (cubrir una hembra).
cabalgata f. Cavalcade, procession (desfile). || Ride (correría a caballo). || *La cabalgata de los Reyes Magos*, the procession of the Three Wise Men.
cabalista adj./s. Cabalist, cabbalist. || Intriguer (intrigante).
cabalístico, ca adj. Cabalistic, cabbalistic. || FIG. Occult.
cabalmente adv. Exactly (exactamente, precisamente). || At a fair price (a su precio). || Completely, entirely (completamente). || Properly (perfectamente).
caballa f. Mackerel (pescado).
caballada f. Herd of horses. || *Amer.* Blunder (acción desacertada): *hacer una caballada*, to make a blunder. | Stupid thing (necedad). || *Amer. Hacer caballadas*, to make an ass of o.s., to act the goat.
caballar adj. Equine: *raza caballar*, equine race. || — *Cara* or *perfil caballar*, horseface. || *Cría caballar*, horse breeding. || *Ganado caballar*, horses, *pl.*
caballejo m. FAM. Nag.
caballeresco, ca adj. Chivalrous, knightly (propio de un caballero andante). || FIG. Chivalrous, gentlemanly: *conducta caballeresca*, chivalrous conduct. | Chivalrous, noble: *sentimientos caballerescos*, chivalrous feelings. || *Literatura caballeresca*, books of chivalry.
caballerete m. FAM. Young dandy.
caballería f. Mount, steed (bestia de silla). || Cavalry (cuerpo militar): *una carga de caballería*, a cavalry charge. || Chivalry (orden). || *Amer.* Name of different types of land measurements [1,343 ares in Cuba, 7,858 ares in Puerto Rico and 4,279 ares in Mexico and Guatemala]. || — FIG. y FAM. *Andarse en caballerías*, to overdo the compliments. || *Caballería andante*, knight-errantry. || MIL. *Caballería ligera*, light cavalry, light horse.
caballeriza f. Stable (cuadra). || Stud (para la cría de caballos). || Grooms, *pl.*, stable hands, *pl.* (personal).
caballerizo m. Groom, stableman (de caballeriza). || *Caballerizo mayor del rey*, Master of the King's Horse.
caballero, ra adj. Mounted, riding: *caballero en un asno*, mounted on an ass. || FIG. Firm (porfiado).
— M. Sir [sólo en el singular]: *caballero, por favor*, please, sir. || Gentleman: *traje de caballero*, gentleman's suit. || FIG. Gentleman: *es un verdadero caballero*, he is a real gentleman. || Noble, nobleman (noble). || Knight (de una orden): *el Caballero de la Triste Figura*, the Knight of the Sorrowful Countenance. || MIL. Cavalry man. || — Pl. Gentlemen: *¡entren, señoras y caballeros!*, come in ladies and gentlemen! || — *Armar caballero a uno*, to knight s.o., to dub s.o. knight. || *Caballero andante*, knight-errant. || *Caballero de industria*, swindler. || TAUR. *Caballero en plaza*, bullfighter on horseback. || *Poderoso caballero es don Dinero*, money talks.
caballerosamente adv. Chivalrously.
caballerosidad f. Chivalry.
caballeroso, sa adj. Noble, chivalrous (noble): *una acción caballerosa*, a noble action. || Chivalrous, gentlemanly (galante, cortés): *un hombre caballeroso*, a chivalrous man.
caballete m. Ridge (del tejado). || Rack (de tortura). || Trestle (soporte). || Cowl (de una chimenea). || Bridge (de la nariz). || AGR. Ridge (caballón). || ARTES. Easel (de pintor). || *Caballete de aserrar*, sawhorse.
caballista m. y f. Rider, horseman, horsewoman.
caballito m. Small horse. || *Amer.* Bridge (de la nariz). | Nappy [U.S., diaper] (metedor de niños). | Raft (balsa). || Toy horse (caballo de juguete). || Hobbyhorse (juguete en el cual se monta el niño). || — Pl. Roundabout, merry-go-round [U.S., carrousel] (en las ferias). || Type of roulette (juego). || — *Caballito de balancín*, rocking horse. || ZOOL. *Caballito del diablo*, dragonfly. | *Caballito de mar* or *marino*, sea horse. || *Amer. Caballito de totora*, small reed raft.
caballo m. ZOOL. Horse: *montar a caballo*, to ride a horse. || Knight (juego de ajedrez). || "Caballo" (en la baraja) [the "caballo" in the Spanish pack of cards corresponds to the queen in the English pack]. || Sawhorse (burro de serrar). || MIN. Mass of rock. || MIL. Horse soldier, cavalryman (soldado de a caballo). || — *A caballo*, on horseback. || FIG. *A caballo regalado no le mires el diente*, don't look a gift horse in the mouth. | *A uña de caballo*, at full gallop *o* speed. || *Caballo blanco*, backer. || *Caballo castrado*, gelding. || FIG. *Caballo de batalla*, hobbyhorse. | *Caballo de buena boca*, obliging person. || *Caballo de carga*, pack-horse. || *Caballo de carrera*, racehorse. || MIL. *Caballo de frisa*, cheval-de-frise (defensa). || *Caballo del diablo*, V. CABALLITO. || *Caballo de mar*, V. CABALLITO. || *Caballo de montar* or *de silla*, saddle horse. || *Caballo de tiro*, cart horse. || *Caballo de Troya*, Trojan horse, wooden horse [of Troy]. || FIG. *Caballo de vapor*, horsepower. || *Caballo entero*, stallion. || FIG. *Caballo fiscal*, Treasury horsepower. || *Caballo padre* or *semental*, stallion. || FIG. *Como caballo desbocado*, hastily. | *Fuerte como un caballo*, strong as an ox. || *Soldado de a caballo*, horse soldier, cavalryman. || *Subir* or *montar a caballo*, to get on *o* to mount a horse. || *Tropas de a caballo*, mounted troops. || *Un coche de diez caballos*, a ten horsepower car.

— OBSERV. El *horsepower* (H.P.) difiere ligeramente del *caballo de vapor* (C.V.). Un H.P. equivale a 1,0138 C.V.

caballón m. AGR. Ridge.
caballuno, na adj. Horsy, horse-like: *una cara caballuna*, an horse-like face.
cabaña f. Cabin, hut, shack (choza de ramas). || Livestock (conjunto del ganado): *la cabaña nacional*, the national livestock. || *Cabaña alpina*, Alpine chalet.
cabañal adj. Animal: *camino cabañal*, animal track *o* path.
— M. Hamlet.
cabañero, ra o **cabañil** adj. Livestock (del ganado). || *Perro cabañero*, sheep dog.
— M. Shepherd (pastor). || Mule driver, muleteer (arriero).
cabañuela f. Small cabin *o* hut. || — Pl. Weather forecast [according to observations made during the first 24 days of August, September or January, depending on the region]. || *Amer.* First summer rains (lluvias de verano), first winter rains (lluvias de invierno).
cabaret m. Night club, cabaret.
cabaretera f. Cabaret entertainer.
cabe prep. (Ant.). POÉT. Next to: *cabe la casa*, next to the house.
cabeceada f. *Amer.* Butt (golpe dado con la cabeza). | Nod (al dormitar). || *Dar cabeceadas*, to nod (el que duerme sentado).
cabeceamiento m. V. CABECEO.
cabecear v. intr. To shake *o* to nod one's head (balancear). || To shake one's head (negar). || To nod (durmiéndose). || To head the ball (fútbol). || To toss its head (caballo). || MAR. To pitch (los barcos). || To lurch, to jolt (carruajes). || To slip (moverse una carga, etc.).
— V. tr. To blend (vino). || To bind (los tapices). || To put a headband on (un libro). || To foot, to put a new foot in (las medias viejas). || To head (el balón). || AGR. To plough [U.S., to plow]. || *Amer.* To bind together by the stalks [tobacco leaves].
cabeceo m. Nodding, nod, shaking (de la cabeza). || Nodding (oscilación ligera). || Lurch, jolt (de un carruaje). || Toss of the head (de un caballo). || MAR. Pitching. || Slipping (de una carga, etc.).
cabecera f. Top (parte principal). || Head, bedhead (de la cama). || Headboard (pieza que limita la cama). || Bedside: *estar a la cabecera del enfermo*, to be at the invalid's bedside; *libro de cabecera*, bedside book. || Place of honour, head (plaza de honor en la mesa). || Source, headwaters, *pl.* (fuente de un río). || County town [U.S., county seat] (capital de distrito o territorio). || Head (persona principal): *la cabecera del partido*, the head of the party. || IMPR. Frontispiece, headband (de un libro). | Headline (en un periódico). || (P.us.). Pillow (almohada). || Headland (extremo de un campo). || Sanctuary (de una iglesia). || — *Cabecera del reparto*, top of the bill. || *Cabecera de puente*, bridgehead. || *Estar a la cabecera de la mesa*, to be at the head of the table. || *Médico de cabecera*, family doctor.
cabecero m. Headrest.
cabecilla m. Leader (jefe).
cabellera f. Hair, head of hair: *una hermosa cabellera negra*, beautiful black hair, a beautiful head of black hair. || Tail (de cometa). || — *Cabellera de Berenice*, Coma Berenices. || *Cabellera postiza*, wig.
cabello m. Hair (pelo): *cabellos postizos*, false hair; *tenía el cabello rubio*, she had blond hair. || — Pl. Corn silk, *sing.*, beard, *sing.* (del maíz). || — FIG. *Agarrar la ocasión por los cabellos*, to seize the oppotunity by the scruff of the neck. | *Asirse de un cabello*, to clutch at a straw. || *Cabello de ángel*, vermicelli (fideos). || *Cabello lacio*, straight hair. || BOT. *Cabello de Venus*, maidenhair. || FIG. *Cortar* or *partir un cabello en el aire*, to split hairs. | *Estar pendiente de un cabello*, to be hanging by a thread. | *Llevar por los cabellos*, to twist round one's little finger. || *Mesarse los cabellos*, to tear one's hair. || FIG. *Se le pusieron los cabellos de punta*, his hair stood on end. | *Traído por los cabellos*, far-fetched: *explicación traída por los cabellos*, far-fetched explanation.
cabelludo, da adj. Hairy (persona). || Shaggy (animal). || BOT. Downy. || *Cuero cabelludo*, scalp.
caber* v. intr. To fit, to go: *mi chaqueta no cabe en la maleta*, my jacket does not fit *o* will not go in the suitcase. || There is room for, to hold: *caben seis personas en el coche*, there is room for six people in the car, the car holds six people; *en este local no caben tantas personas*, there is not room for so many people in this place. || To go, to fit: *el armario no cabe por la puerta*, the wardrobe will not go through the door. || To be possible: *cabía que viniese más tarde, pero no tanto*, it was possible that he would come late, but not this late; *cabe decir que*, it is possible to say that. || To have: *me cabe la satisfacción de anunciarle esta noticia*, I have the pleasure of announcing this news to you. || To go: *veinte entre tres caben a seis y sobran dos*, three into twenty goes six and two over. || To be for: *no me cabe decirlo*, it is not for me to say. || — *¿Cabe mayor disparate que...?*, can you imagine anything more stupid than...? || *Cabe pensar que*, one might think that. || *Caber a uno*, to fall to s.o.: *me cupo ir a decírselo*, it fell to me to go and tell him. || *Dentro de* or *en lo que cabe*, as far as possible. || *¡Esto no me cabe en la cabeza!*, it is beyond me! || *No cabe duda*, there is no doubt. || *No cabe más*, it is full, there is no more room (lleno), that is the last straw, that's the lot, that beats all (el colmo). || *No cabe más holgazán*, they don't come any lazier. || *No cabe perdón*, it is inexcusable. || *No caber en el pellejo*, to be bursting. || *No caber en sí*, to be swollen-headed. || *No caber en sí de gozo, de júbilo* or *de contento*, to be beside o.s. with enjoyment *o* joy *o* happiness. || *No caberle a uno el corazón en el pecho*, v. CORAZÓN. || *No cabe un alfiler*, it is full to overflowing, it is packed. || *No me cabe en la cabeza* (*la idea*) *que...*, I cannot believe *o* get it into my head that... || *¿Quepo yo?*, is there room for me? || *Si cabe*, if one might say so. || FAM. *Todo cabe en él*, he is capable of anything. || *Todo cabe en lo humano*, everything is possible, nothing is impossible.
— OBSERV. When *caber* is translated by *to hold, to have*, the subject of the Spanish verb becomes the object of the English verb and vice versa.
cabestrante m. Capstan (cabrestante).
cabestrar v. tr. To halter.
cabestrillo m. Sling: *brazo en cabestrillo*, arm in a sling.
cabestro m. Halter (rienda). || Leading ox (buey guía).
cabeza f. ANAT. Head. || Head (individuo): *pagar tanto por cabeza*, to pay so much per head, to pay so much a head. || Head (res): *rebaño de cien cabezas*, a hundred head of sheep. || FIG. Good judgment (juicio): *un hombre de cabeza*, a man with good judgment. | Head (mente): *tener algo metido en la cabeza*, to have sth. in one's head. | Head, life (vida): *pedir la cabeza del reo*, to ask for the head of the accused. | Head: *estar en cabeza de una cola*, to be at the head of a queue. | Front: *el ciclista que está en cabeza en la carrera*, the cyclist who is at the front of the race. | Top: *estar a la cabeza de la clase*, to be at the top of the class. || GEOGR. Summit, top (de una montaña). || Head (de un alfiler, de un clavo, de ajo, de procesión, de un rotor, etc.). || MAR. Head. || End (de una viga). || Head (de magnetófono): *cabeza sonora, auditiva, supresora*, recording, playback, erasing head. || *Amer.* Source (de un río).
— M. Head: *cabeza de familia*, head of a family.
— *Agachar la cabeza*, to lower one's head (bajar), to give in, to back down (humillarse). || *Alzar* or *levantar cabeza*, to raise one's head (sentido propio), to pick up (recuperarse). || FIG. *Andar* or *ir de cabeza*, to be in a flurry *o* in a fluster *o* in a tizzy (estar muy ocupado). | *Andar mal de la cabeza*, to be weak in the head, to have a screw loose. | *Apostar* or *apostarse la cabeza*, to bet one's life *o* shirt, to stake one's life *o* shirt. || *Asentir con la cabeza*, to nod. || TECN. *Cabeza atómica*, atomic warhead. | *Cabeza buscadora*, homing device (de un cohete). || FIG. *Cabeza caliente*, hothead. || TECN. *Cabeza de biela*, big end. || FIG. *Cabeza de cordada*, leader (alpinismo). | *Cabeza de chorlito*, scatterbrain. || *Cabeza de espárrago*, asparagus tip. || FIG. *Cabeza de hierro*, stubborn person. || *Cabeza de línea*, terminus. || IMPR. *Cabeza de muerto*, turning. || *Cabeza de partido*, county town. || *Cabeza de playa*, beachhead. || MIL. *Cabeza de puente*, bridgehead. || *Cabeza de serie*, seeded player, seed (tenis). || FIG. *Cabeza de turco*, scapegoat. | *Cabeza dura*, stubborn person (testarudo). | *Cabeza hueca* or *sin seso*, idiot, blockhead. | *Cabeza loca*, scatterbrain. | *Cabeza redonda*, Roundhead. || FIG. *Calentarle a uno la cabeza con*, to pester s.o. with. | *Calentarse la cabeza*, to get worked up (perder la calma), to rack one's brains (estudiar). || *Con la cabeza alta*, with one's head held high. || *Con la cabeza baja*, head down. || *Darle a uno dolores de cabeza*, to make s.o.'s head ache (dolor físico), to get headaches: *cuando me dan estos dolores de cabeza me tengo que acostar*, when I get these headaches I have to lie down; to be a pain in the neck (dar la lata). || FIG. *Dar en la cabeza*, to rub up the wrong way (contrariar). || *Darle a uno vueltas la cabeza*, one's head to be swimming, to feel dizzy: *la cabeza me da vueltas*, my head is swimming, I feel dizzy. | *Darse de cabeza en la pared*, to beat one's head against a brick wall. || FIG. y FAM. *Dar un buen lavado de cabeza*, to haul s.o. over the coals. || *De cabeza*, by heart (de memoria), like a flash (con rapidez), headfirst: *caerse de cabeza*, to fall headfirst. || *De pies a cabeza*, from head to foot, from top to toe. || FIG. *De mi* (*tu*, etc.) *cabeza*, out of my (your, etc.) own head. || *Dolor de cabeza*, headache. || FIG. *Estar de cabeza*, to have a lot on (muy ocupado). || FIG. y FAM. *Estar mal de la cabeza*, to be weak in the head, to be dotty *o* daft. | *Estar tocado de la cabeza*, to be off one's rocker, to be touched [U.S., to be nuts *o* goofy]. || *Ganar por una cabeza*, to win by a head. || FIG. *Hinchar la cabeza a uno*, v. HINCHAR. || *Ir en cabeza*, to be in the lead. || FIG. y FAM. *Írsele a uno la cabeza*, to lose one's head (perder la cabeza), to feel giddy (marearse). || FIG. *Írsele a uno de la cabeza*, to slip s.o.'s mind: *se me fue de la cabeza*, it slipped my mind. | *Jugarse la cabeza*, to bet one's life *o* shirt, to stake one's life *o* shirt. || *Lavarse la cabeza*, to wash one's hair. || *Llevarle a uno la cabeza*, to be taller than s.o. by a head. || FIG. *Llevarse las manos a la cabeza*, to throw one's hands to one's head. | *Más vale ser cabeza de ratón que cola de león*, it is better to reign in Hell than to serve in Heaven. | *Meter la cabeza en alguna parte*, to get a look in somewhere. | *Meterle a uno en la cabeza*, to put into s.o.'s head. | *Meterse de cabeza en algo*, to plunge headfirst into sth. | *Metérsele a uno en la cabeza hacer algo*,

to take it into one's head to do sth. (ocurrírsele): *se le metío en la cabeza ir solo*, he took it into his head to go alone; to set one's mind on doing sth. (empeñarse). | *Nadie escarmienta en cabeza ajena*, one only learns by one's own mistakes. || *Negar con la cabeza*, to shake one's head. || FIG. *No levantar cabeza*, not to lift one's head (trabajar), not to pick up (no recuperarse). | *No se me va* or *no se me puede ir de la cabeza la muerte de mi amigo*, I can't get my friend's death off my mind. | *No tener cabeza*, to be forgetful, to be absentminded. | *No tener ni pies ni cabeza*, V. PIE. | *Pasarle a alguien por la cabeza*, to occur to s.o., to cross s.o.'s mind. | *Perder la cabeza*, to lose one's head, to panic. | *Poner la cabeza bomba* or *tarumba a alguien*, to drive s.o. mad. || *Poner la cabeza de uno a precio*, to put a price on s.o.'s head. || *Por una cabeza*, by a head (ganar o perder una carrera). | FIG. *Quebradero de cabeza*, headache. | *Quebrarse* or *romperse la cabeza*, to rack one's brains. | *¡Quítate eso de la cabeza!*, get that out of your head! || *Sacar la cabeza*, to put one's head out. || *Sacarle la cabeza a uno*, to be taller by a head than s.o. || FIG. *Se le subieron los humos a la cabeza*, he got on his high horse, he became conceited. | *Sentar cabeza*, to calm down, to settle down. | *Ser duro de cabeza*, to be slow on the uptake, to be thick-headed. | *Subirse a la cabeza*, to go to one's head. | *Tener algo metido en la cabeza*, to have sth. on the brain. | *Tener la cabeza a las once*, to be brainless (tonto), to be miles away (distraído). | *Tener la cabeza en su sitio*, to have one's head screwed on. | *Tener la cabeza loca*, to be in a whirl. | *Tener la cabeza llena de pájaros* or *tener pájaros en la cabeza*, V. PÁJARO. | *Tener mala cabeza*, to be absentminded. | *Tengo la cabeza como un bombo*, my head is splitting. || *Tirarse de cabeza*, to dive (de un trampolín, etc.). || FIG. *Traer a uno de cabeza*, V. TRAER. | *Venir a la cabeza*, to come to mind. || *Volver la cabeza*, to turn one's head.

cabezada f. Butt (golpe dado con la cabeza). || Blow *o* bump on the head (golpe recibido en la cabeza). || Nod (al dormirse, saludo). || Vamp (de bota). || Headband (encuadernación). || MAR. Pitching, pitch. || Cavesson (del caballo). || *Amer.* Saddlebow (arzón). || — FIG. y FAM. *Dar cabezadas*, to nod (persona), to pitch (barco). | *Darse de cabezadas*, to rack one's brains. | *Echar una cabezada*, to have a nap *o* a snooze.

cabezal m. Pillow (almohada). || Bolster (almohada larga). || Headrest (de un sillón). || MED. Compress. || TECN. Front carriage (de coche). | Poppet, lathehead (de torno).

cabezazo m. Butt (golpe dado con la cabeza). || Blow on the head (golpe recibido en la cabeza). || Header (fútbol). || *Dar un cabezazo*, to head the ball.

cabezón, ona adj. FAM. Bigheaded, with a big head. || FIG. y FAM. Stubborn, pigheaded, obstinate: *ser cabezón como un aragonés*, to be as stubborn as a mule. — M. y f. FAM. Big head. || FIG. y FAM. Stubborn person, pigheaded person, obstinate person, mule.

cabezonada f. FIG. y FAM. Obstinacy, stubbornness, pigheadedness. || Obstinate *o* stubborn *o* pigheaded action (capricho).

cabezonería f. FIG. y FAM. Obstinacy, stubbornness, pigheadedness.

cabezota f. FAM. Big head. || — M. y f. Obstinate *o* stubborn *o* pigheaded person.

cabezudo, da adj. Bigheaded, with a big head. || FIG. y FAM. Stubborn, obstinate, pigheaded (terco). || Heady (bebidas).

— M. ZOOL. Mullet (mújol). || Carnival figure with a huge head (en algunas fiestas).

cabezuela f. Small head. || Third flour (harina). || Fungoid growth (del vino). || BOT. Capitulum, flower head (inflorescencia). | Rose bud (de rosa). | Tip (de espárrago). || FIG. Scatterbrain, birdbrain (alocado).

cabiai m. ZOOL. Capybara.

cabida f. Capacity: *esta sala tiene cabida para cien personas*, this hall has a capacity of a hundred people. || Place: *estas ideas no tienen cabida en una mente equilibrada*, these ideas have no place in a balanced mind. || — *Dar cabida a*, to leave room for, to leave space for. || FIG. *Dar cabida a circunstancias imprevistas*, to leave room for unforeseen circumstances.

cabila adj./s. Kabyle.

cabildada f. FAM. Abuse of authority.

cabildante m. *Amer.* Town councillor.

cabildear v. intr. To scheme (intrigar). || To lobby (influir en las autoridades).

cabildeo m. Scheming (intriga). || Speculation, surmise (suposiciones). || Lobbying (para ejercer presión). || *Andar de cabildeos*, to scheme.

cabildero m. Schemer (intrigante). || Lobbyist (que ejerce presión sobre las autoridades).

cabildo m. Chapter (de iglesia). || Chapter house (sala). || Chapter (reunión de canónigos). || Town council (ayuntamiento). || Town hall (sala del ayuntamiento). || Council meeting (reunión del ayuntamiento). || Organization formed in the Canary Islands of representatives from all the towns of the Islands.

cabilla f. MAR. Treenail (clavo grueso). | Belaying pin (de los cabos).

cabillo m. BOT. Stalk of a peduncle. || End (extremo).

cabina f. Kiosk, box [U.S., booth] (telefónica). || Cabin (en un barco). || Cab (de camión, grúa). || AVIAC. Cabin, cockpit. || Room, booth (en un cine): *cabina de proyección*, projection room *o* booth. || Booth (de intérpretes). || Car (de ascensor). || Bathing hut (caseta de baños). || — *Cabina de cambio de agujas*, signal box. || *Cabina electoral*, polling booth, voting booth.

cabio m. ARQ. Joist, beam (viga). | Lintel (de ventana o puerta). || *Cabio bajo*, lower transom (de ventana).

cabizbajo, ja adj. Crestfallen: *iba cabizbajo y meditabundo*, he was crestfallen and pensive.

cable m. Cable (maroma, de electricidad). || Cable (cablegrama). || MAR. Cable length (medida de 185,19 metros). || — *Cable de remolque*, towline, towrope. || FIG. y FAM. *Echar un cable*, to give a hand.

cablear v. tr. To twist (alambres).

cablegrafiar v. tr. e intr. To send a cable, to cable.

cablegrama m. Cablegram, cable.

cablero m. MAR. Cable ship (barco).

cabo m. End (extremidad). || End, stub, stump (pedazo que queda): *cabo de vela*, stub of a candle. || Handle (de herramienta). || Bit, piece (trozo): *un cabo de hilo*, a piece of thread. || GEOGR. Cape. || Parcel (paquete). || MAR. Rope, line (cuerda). || MIL. Corporal (de escuadra, de caballería). || Sergeant (de policía). || — Pl. Accessories [of clothing]. || ANAT. Ankle, *sing.* (tobillo). | Wrist, *sing.* (muñeca). || Tail and mane, *sing.* (del caballo). || — *Al cabo*, in the end. || *Al cabo de*, after, in: *al cabo de un año*, after a year, in a year. || *Al fin y al cabo*, after all, when all is said and done (no obstante). || FIG. *Atar* or *juntar cabos*, to put two and two together. || *Cabo de fila*, leading man in a line (soldado), leading ship (barco). || MAR. *Cabo de la Marina*, leading seaman. || *Cabo de vara*, prison guard. || FIG. *Cabo suelto*, loose end: *en la novela quedan muchos cabos sueltos*, there are a lot of loose ends in the novel. || *Dar cabo a una cosa*, to finish sth. off. || *Dar cabo de*, to put an end to. || *De cabo a cabo* or *de cabo a rabo*, from beginning to end. || *En mi, en tu, en su solo cabo*, by myself, by yourself, by himself (a solas). || FIG. *Estoy al cabo (de la calle)*, I'm well up on this, I'm well acquainted with this. || *Llevar a cabo*, to carry out (ejecutar, efectuar), to conclude (concluir). || FIG. *No dejar cabo suelto*, not to leave any loose ends. || *Por ningún cabo*, by no means, in no way.

Cabo n. pr. m. GEOGR. *Cabo de Buena Esperanza*, Cape of Good Hope. | *Cabo de Hornos*, Cape Horn. | *El Cabo*, Cape Town, Capetown. | *Islas de Cabo Verde*, Cape Verde Islands.

cabotaje m. MAR. Coastal traffic, cabotage. || *Barco de cabotaje*, coaster, coasting vessel.

cabra f. ZOOL. Goat. || *Amer.* Loaded dice (dado cargado). | Type of sulky (carruaje). || — *Cabra de almizcle*, muskdeer. || *Cabra de los Alpes*, ibex. || *Cabra montés*, chamois, wild goat. || FAM. *Estar como una cabra*, to be daft *o* dotty *o* stupid. || FIG. *La cabra siempre tira al monte*, what's bred in the bone will come out in the flesh.

cabrahigadura f. AGR. Caprification.

cabrahigal o **cabrahigar** m. Plantation of wild fig trees.

cabrahigo m. BOT. Wild fig tree, caprifig (árbol). | Wild fig (fruto).

cabrajo m. Lobster (bogavante).

cabreado, da adj. FAM. In a foul *o* a filthy mood (de muy mal humor). | Livid (enfadado).

cabrear v. tr. FAM. To get one's goat, to get worked up (enojar).

— V. intr. *Amer.* To leap *o* to prance about (jugar).

— V. pr. FAM. To get worked up, to see red (irritarse). | To get furious, to fly off the handle (ponerse furioso).

cabreo m. FAM. *Coger* or *pillar* or *agarrar un cabreo*, to fly off the handle. | *Dar un cabreo a uno*, to get one's goat, to get s.o. worked up. | *Tener un cabreo*, to be really annoyed *o* worked up.

cabreriza f. Goatherd (pastora). || Goatherd's hut (choza del cabrero). || Goat shed (para las cabras).

cabrerizo, za adj. Goatish, caprine.

— M. Goatherd (cabrero).

cabrero, ra m. y f. Goatherd (pastor).

cabrestante m. MAR. Capstan.

cabria f. TECN. Gin.

cabrilla f. TECN. Sawyer's trestle, sawhorse. || — Pl. ASTR. The Pleiades. || White horses, foam-crested waves (olas en el mar). || Scorches on the legs (producidas por el brasero). || Ducks and drakes (juego). || *Jugar al juego de cabrillas*, to play ducks and drakes.

cabrillear v. intr. To form white crests, to break into white horses (las olas). || To glisten, to sparkle, to shimmer (rielar).

cabrilleo m. Breaking, foaming, white horses (en el mar). || Shimmer (centelleo).

cabrio m. ARQ. Joist. || HERÁLD. Chevron.

cabrío, a adj. Caprine: *raza cabría*, caprine race. || *Macho cabrío*, he-goat, billy goat.

— M. Herd of goats.

cabriola f. Jump, skip, leap (salto). || Capriole (de caballo). || FIG. Trick, device, dodge. || *Hacer cabriolas*, to romp, to scamper about, to gambol, to frisk, to caper about (los niños), to capriole (el caballo).

cabriolar v. intr. To romp, to scamper about, to gambol, to frisk, to caper about (los niños). || To capriole (un caballo).

cabriolé o **cabriolet** m. Cabriolet.

cabriolear v. intr. V. CABRIOLAR.

cabrita f. Small goat, kid (cabra pequeña).

cabritilla f. Kid: *guantes de cabritilla*, kid gloves.
cabrito m. Kid. || POP. Bastard, swine, bugger (canalla). || — Pl. *Amer.* Popcorn (rosetas de maíz).
cabrón m. He-goat, billy goat. || POP. Bastard, swine, bugger (canalla). | Deceived husband, cuckold (cornudo). || *Amer.* Pimp (rufián).
cabronada f. FAM. Dirty trick: *hacerle a uno una cabronada*, to play a dirty trick on s.o.
cabruno, na adj. Caprine.
cabuchón o **cabujón** m. Cabochon (piedra).
cabuya f. BOT. Agave. || Aloe fibre, Mexican hemp (fibra). || MAR. Rope. || — *Amer. Dar cabuya*, to moor. | *Ponerse en la cabuya*, to cotton on.
cabuyera f. Crowfoot, clew (de la hamaca).
caca f. FAM. Duty, business: *hacer caca:* to do one's business. | Muck, cack (excremento, suciedad). || — FAM. *Eso es una caca*, this is rubbish. | *Tira eso, es una caca*, throw that away, it's dirty *o* nasty.
cacahual m. AGR. Cacao plantation.
cacahuate m. V. CACAHUETE.
cacahué o **cacahuey** m. Peanut, monkey nut.
cacahuete m. Monkey nut, peanut. || *Aceite de cacahuete*, groundnut oil [U.S., peanut oil].
cacahuetero m. Peanut seller.
cacalote m. *Amer.* Crow (cuervo). | Popcorn (rosetas).
cacao m. Cacao (árbol y grano). | Cocoa (en el comercio). || *Amer.* Chocolate. || *Manteca de cacao*, cocoa butter, cacao butter.
cacaotal m. AGR. Cacao plantation.
cacaraña f. Pockmark.
cacarañado, da adj. Pockmarked (picado de viruelas).
cacarañar v. tr. To pockmark (la viruela). || *Amer.* To pinch (pellizcar).
cacareado, da adj. Hackneyed, trite: *un éxito muy cacareado*, a very hackneyed success.
cacareador, ra adj. Clucking (que cacarea). || Boastful, bragging, crowing (que presume).
cacarear v. intr. To cluck (las gallinas).
— V. tr. FIG. y FAM. To make a big noise about, to boast about (presumir): *¡cómo cacarea las pocas cosas buenas que ha hecho!*, what a big noise he is making about the few good things he has done!
cacareo m. Clucking (de la gallina). || FIG. Shower of praises (alabanzas). | Bragging, boasting, crowing (presunción).
cacatúa f. ZOOL. Cockatoo (ave).
cacera f. Irrigation ditch.
cacería f. Hunting: *ir de cacería*, to go hunting. || Hunt (partida de caza): *cacería de leones*, lion hunt.
cacerola f. Casserole.
cacicazgo o **cacicato** m. Chieftainship.
cacillo m. Ladle (cucharón). || Small saucepan (cacerola).
cacique m. Cacique, Indian chief (jefe indio). || FIG. y FAM. Local political boss, cacique. | Despot, tyrant.
caciquismo m. Caciquism. || FIG. Caciquism, despotism.
cacle m. *Amer.* Leather sandal.
caco m. Thief, crook (ladrón).
cacodilato m. QUÍM. Cacodylate.
cacofonía f. Cacophony.
cacofónico, ca adj. Cacophonous.
cacoquimia f. Cacochymy.
cactáceo, a o **cácteo, a** adj. BOT. Cactaceous.
— F. pl. Cactaceae.
cacto o **cactus** m. BOT. Cactus.
cacumen m. FIG. y FAM. Acumen, brains, *pl.*
cacha f. Handle (mango). || Butt (de una pistola). || FAM. Cheek (nalga). || *Amer.* Horn (cuerno). | Money (dinero). | Leg (anca). || — *Amer. Hacer la cacha*, to joke. || FIG. y FAM. *Hasta las cachas*, up to the hilt: *se ha metido en el asunto hasta las cachas*, he's got himself up to the hilt in the affair.

— OBSERV. The word *cacha* is usually used in the plural.

cachaciento, ta adj. *Amer.* Calm, phlegmatic (cachazudo). | Lazy, idle, loafing (perezoso).
cachada f. *Amer.* Gore, butt (cornada). | Joke (burla).
cachafaz m. *Amer.* Rogue, scoundrel (pillo).
cachalote m. ZOOL. Sperm whale, cachalot.
cachar v. tr. To break, to smash (romper). || To split (la madera). || AGR. To plough up, to break up. || *Amer.* FAM. To get, to obtain (obtener). | To seize (asir). | To surprise, to catch (sorprender). | To ridicule (ridiculizar). | To catch (el autobús, tranvía, etc.). | To butt, to gore (con los cuernos).
cacharpari m. *Amer.* Farewell celebration.
cacharpas f. pl. *Amer.* Things, bits and pieces (cosas).
cacharrazo m. FAM. Blow (porrazo). | Fall (caída). || *Amer.* FAM. Drink (trago).
cacharrería f. Pottery shop.
cacharrero, ra m. y f. Pottery dealer.
cacharro m. Earthenware vessel (recipiente tosco). || Vase (vasija). || Piece of broken pottery, potsherd (tiesto). || FAM. Thing (chisme). | Boneshaker (bicicleta). | Old tub (barco). | Wreck (máquina). | Joanna (piano). | Old crock, jaloppy (coche). || *Amer.* Prison (cárcel). || — Pl. Things: *llegó con todos sus cacharros*, he came with all his things. || Utensils: *los cacharros de la cocina*, the kitchen utensils. || *Lavar los cacharros*, to do the washing up, to wash the dishes (fregar los platos).
cachava f. Shinny (juego y bastón).
cachavazo m. Blow with a shinny.
cachaza f. Sluggishness, slowness (lentitud). || Phlegm, forbearance (flema): *hombre que tiene mucha cachaza*, man who has a lot of phlegm. || Tafia, rum (aguardiente). || *Amer.* Froth from cane [when making sugar] (impurezas).
cachazo m. *Amer.* Butt, gore (cornada).
cachazudo, da adj. Phlegmatic, calm (flemático). || Slow, sluggish (lento).
— M. y f. Slow coach (lento). || Phlegmatic person (flemático).
cachear v. tr. To search, to frisk (registrar). || *Amer.* To gore (cornear).
cachemir m. o **cachemira** f. Cashmere (tela).
Cachemira n. pr. f. GEOGR. Kashmir.
cacheo m. Search, searching, frisking (registro).
cachería f. *Amer.* FAM. Small shop (cambalache). | Lack of dress sense, bad taste (falta de gusto en el vestir).
cachetada f. o **cachetazo** m. Slap, whack: *dar una cachetada a uno*, to give s.o. a slap.
cachete m. FAM. Cheek (carrillo). | Cheek (nalga). | Swollen cheek (mejilla abultada). || Punch, blow (golpe). | Slap, whack (bofetada). || Dagger (puñal). || FAM. *Pegar un cachete a uno*, to slap *o* to whack *o* to wallop s.o.
cachetear v. tr. To whack, to slap.
cachetero m. Dagger. || TAUR. Bullfighter who finishes off the bull with a dagger.
cachetudo, da o **cachetón, ona** adj. FAM. Chubby-faced, chubby-cheeked (mofletudo).
cachicamo m. *Amer.* Armadillo (animal).
cachicuerno, na adj. With a horn handle, horn-handled (cuchillo).
cachifollar v. tr. FAM. To foil (un plan). | To squash, to flatten (apabullar). | To spoil, to ruin (estropear).
cachimba f. o **cachimbo** m. Pipe: *fumar en cachimba*, to smoke a pipe. || *Amer. Chupar cachimbo*, to smoke a pipe (fumar en pipa), to suck one's thumb (un niño).
cachipolla f. Mayfly, ephemera (insecto).
cachiporra f. Club, truncheon.
cachiporrazo m. Blow with a club.
cachirulo m. Flask [for spirits]. || Earthenware jar (botijo). || Small ship with three masts (embarcación). || FAM. Lid, hat (sombrero). || Reinforcement on jodhpurs (de pantalón de montar). || — Pl. Things.
cachito m. Small piece, little bit (trocito). || *A cachitos*, in bits.
cachivache m. Utensil (utensilio). || Pot, pan (recipiente). || Thing (chisme). || Bauble, knick-knack (fruslería).
cacho, cha adj. Bent (encorvado).
— M. Piece, bit: *un cacho de pan*, a piece of bread. || Brelan (juego de cartas). || *Amer.* Horn (cuerno). || — FIG. y FAM. *¡Cacho bestia!*, you beast! | *Ella es un cacho de pan*, she is a darling *o* an angel.
cachondearse v. pr. FIG. y FAM. To take the mickey out of: *cachondearse de alguien*, to take the mickey out of s.o. | To treat as a joke: *se cachondea de todo*, he treats everything as a joke.
cachondeo m. FAM. Ragging, jeering, leg-pulling (burla), skylarking, messing about (jarana), joking (guasa). || — FAM. *Armar cachondeo*, to lark about. | *La fiesta fue un cachondeo*, the party was a scream. | *Te lo digo sin cachondeo*, I mean it, no messing about. | *Tomar a cachondeo*, to treat as a joke.
cachondez f. Heat (de perra), rut (de perro). || Lust, randiness, sensuality (de persona).
cachondo, da adj. On heat (perra), in rut, rutting (perro). || POP. Randy (sensual). | Hilarious (gracioso).
cachopín m. *Amer.* V. CACHUPÍN.
cachorrillo m. Small pistol (arma).
cachorro, ra m. y f. Pup, puppy (del perro). || Cub (del león, tigre, oso, lobo). || Kitten (de gato). || Young (de otros mamíferos).
— Adj. *Amer.* Ill-mannered, uncouth (malcriado).
cachú m. Catechu (extracto vegetal). || Cachou (pastilla).
cachucha f. MAR. Small rowing boat (bote). || Cap (gorra).
cachuchear v. tr. To fondle, to caress (acariciar).
cachucho m. Pin box, pin case (alfiletero). || Jar (vasija tosca). || Pitcher (botijo). || MAR. Small rowing boat (bote).
cachudo, da adj. *Amer.* Horned, long-horned.
cachuela f. Stew (guiso).
cachumbo m. *Amer.* Husk, shell.
cachunde m. Catechu (pasta aromática).
cachupín, ina m. y f. *Amer.* FAM. Spanish immigrant.
cachureco, ca adj. *Amer.* Conservative (en política). | Deformed (deformado).
cada adj. inv. Every, each: *cada día*, every day. || Every (con un sustantivo en plural): *cada tres días*, every three days, every third day. || Each (cuando se trata de dos cosas): *cada uno de los dos chicos tiene su coche*, each one of the two boys has his car. || — *A cada paso*, at every step *o* turn. || *Cada cierta distancia*, every so often, at intervals. || *Cada cierto tiempo*, every so often. || *Cada cual* or *cada uno, cada una*, each one, everyone. || *¿Cada cuánto?*, how often? || *Cada día más, cada día menos*, v. DÍA. || *Cada dos días*, every other day, every two days. || *Cada dos por tres*, every five minutes. || FAM. *Cada hijo de vecino* or *cada quisque*, everyone. || FIG. *Cada oveja con su pareja*, every Jack

has his Jill. | *Cada uno en su casa y Dios en la de todos*, every man for himself and God for us all. | *Cada uno es rey en su casa*, every man's home is his castle. || *Cada vez*, every time, each time. || *Cada vez más, cada vez menos*, v. VEZ. || *Cada vez peor*, from bad to worse, worse and worse. || *El pan nuestro de cada día*, our daily bread. || FAM. *¡Le dio cada bofetada!*, he gave him such a slap! || *¡Se veían señoras con cada sombrero!*, you should have seen the hats the women were wearing! || *Uno de cada diez*, one in ten, one out of ten.
cadalso m. Scaffold, scaffolding (patíbulo).
cadáver m. Corpse, body, dead body: *hacer la autopsia de un cadáver*, to do an autopsy on a corpse. || Body, carcass (de un animal). || — *Ingresó cadáver*, he was dead on arrival. || *Rígido como un cadáver*, as stiff as a corpse.
cadavérico, ca adj. Cadaverous (relativo al cadáver). || Cadaverous, deathly pale (muy pálido). || *Rigidez cadavérica*, rigor mortis.
caddy m. Caddie (en el juego de golf).
cadena f. Chain (de hierro, de bicicleta, etc.). || MAR. Cablechain. || Chain (de presidiarios). || Chain gang (cuerda de presos). || JUR. Imprisonment: *cadena perpetua*, life imprisonment. || FIG. Chains, *pl.*, bondage: *la cadena de la esclavitud*, the chains of slavery. | Chain, sequence (sucesión de hechos). || ARQ. Shoring. || Chain (de periódicos, de cines, etc.). || Channel (de televisión). || QUÍM. Chain. || — Pl. Chains. || — *Cadena antirrobo*, anti-theft chain, chain-lock. || *Cadena de agrimensor*, surveyor's chain, land chain, measuring chain. || *Cadena de enganche*, chain coupling. || *Cadena de fabricación*, production line. || *Cadena de montaje*, assembly line. || GEOGR. *Cadena de montañas*, mountain chain *o* range. || *Cadena de seguridad*, safety chain (de pulsera). || *Cadena de transmisión*, driving chain. || *Hacer cadena*, to form *o* to make a chain. || *Reacción en cadena*, chain reaction. || *Tirar de la cadena*, to pull the chain, to flush. || *Trabajar en cadena*, to work on the production line. || *Trabajo en cadena*, assembly line work [U.S., serial production].
cadencia f. Rhythm, cadence (ritmo). || MÚS. Cadence.
cadencioso, sa adj. Rhythmic, rhythmical (verso). || Measured (pasos). || Melodious (voz).
cadeneta f. Headband (encuadernación). || Paper chain (adorno de papel). || *Punto de cadeneta*, chain stitch.
cadenilla o **cadenita** f. Small chain.
cadera f. ANAT. Hip: *con las manos en las caderas*, with one's hands on one's hips.
cadete m. MIL. Cadet.
cadí m. Cadi (juez musulmán).
Cádiz n. pr. GEOGR. Cádiz.
cádmico, ca adj. QUÍM. Cadmic.
cadmio m. QUÍM. Cadmium.
caducar v. intr. To expire, to become invalid, to lapse (perder su validez): *su pasaporte ha caducado*, his passport has expired. || To become senile, to be in one's dotage (una persona).
caduceo m. Caduceus, Mercury's wand (emblema).
caducidad f. JUR. Expiration, expiry, lapse. || Senility, dotage, decrepitude (de un anciano).
caduco, ca adj. Decrepit, senile (viejo). || FIG. Expired, invalid. | Gone by: *tiempos caducos*, times gone by. || BOT. Deciduous (hojas). || JUR. Null and void: *testamento caduco*, null and void will. || Transitory (bienes). || Fleeting (placer).
caedizo, za adj. Deciduous (hojas).
caer* v. intr. To fall, to fall down *o* over (las personas): *el niño ha caído a tierra* or *por tierra*, the child has fallen on the ground *o* to the ground: *caer de cabeza*, to fall head first *o* on one's head; *caer de espaldas, de rodillas*, to fall on one's back, on one's knees; *cayó muerto*, he fell dead. || To fall (las cosas): *las hojas de los árboles caían lentamente*, the leaves fell slowly from the trees; *la nieve cae*, the snow falls. || To crash, to come down (un avión). || FIG. To fall: *caer en la trampa*, to fall into the trap; *caer en desgracia*, to fall into disgrace; *caer en desuso*, to fall into disuse. | To make: *caer en un error*, to make a mistake. | To fall (imperio, ministerio, precio, temperatura, etc.). | To fall (la noche). | To set (el sol). | To drop, to die down (el viento). | To draw in: *al caer el día*, when day draws in. | To fall (morir): *el capitán cayó al frente de sus tropas*, the captain fell at the head of his troops. | To fall: *nuestras ilusiones caen una tras otra*, our illusions fall one after another; *su cumpleaños cae en domingo*, his birthday falls on a Sunday. | To find, to hit upon: *he caído en la solución*, I have found the solution. | To be: *la puerta cae a la derecha*, the door is on the right; *este detalle cae en el capítulo 10*, this point is in chapter 10; *ese pueblo cae dentro de esta provincia*, that village is in this province. | To look onto: *una ventana que cae a la calle*, a window which looks onto the street. | To come: *al final de esta calle cae usted en el parque*, at the end of this street you come to the park. | To come, to fall: *esto no cae dentro de la jurisdicción del gobierno*, this does not come within the jurisdiction of the government. | To fall: *me cayó en suerte hacerlo*, it fell on me *o* to my lot *o* to me to do it. | To lapse (costumbre). | To fall: *caer entre* or *en las manos de alguien*, to fall into s.o.'s hands. | To end (la conversación). | To lapse: *relato que cae a veces en lo vulgar*, story which at times lapses into vulgarity. || To fall, to hang: *los pelos le caen en la espalda*, her hair falls down her back. || To strike: *un rayo cayó en su casa*, lightning struck his house. || To dip: *la falda te cae por un lado*, your skirt dips at one side. || FIG. To fall, to be taken: *caer enfermo*, to fall ill; *cayó la ciudad en la batalla*, the town was taken in the battle. | To drop: *cayó por mi casa cuando menos lo esperaba*, he dropped by my house when I was least expecting him. | To win: *le cayó el premio gordo en la lotería*, he won first prize in the lottery. | To give in: *caer en la tentación*, to give in to temptation. | To fail: *caí en matemáticas*, I failed in mathematics. | To be due: *el pago cae al final del mes*, payment is due at the end of the month. | To get (entender): *ahora caigo en lo que dices*, now I get what you mean. | To think, to imagine: *no caigo en la persona de quien me hablas*, I can't think who [it is] you are talking about. | To be able to remember: *no caigo en cuál es su nombre*, I can't remember what his name is. | To pounce, to descend: *cayeron sobre él como lobos*, they pounced on him like wolves.
— *Al caer la noche*, at nightfall. || FIG. *Caer a mano*, to be near at hand. | *Caer a tiempo*, to be well-timed. | *Caer como chinches* or *moscas*, to fall *o* to drop like flies. | *Caer como un jarro de agua fría*, to fall like a ton of bricks. | *Caer como un muerto*, to fall in a heap, to fall like a log. | *Caer de bruces*, to fall flat on one's face. | *Caer de las nubes*, to come down to earth. | *Caer de perlas*, to be perfect. | *Caer de pie*, to fall on one's feet. | *Caer de su peso* or *de suyo*, to go without saying. | *Caer encima de* or *sobre uno*, to fall on s.o.'s head (cosa, falta), to fall on s.o.'s shoulders (responsabilidad). | *Caer en el garlito* or *en el lazo*, to fall into the trap. | *Caer en la cuenta*, to realize (darse cuenta), to remember (acordarse). | *Caer en saco roto*, v. SACO. | *Caer en suerte*, to fall to one's lot. || *Caer en un grupo simpático*, to fall in with a friendly group of people. || FIG. *Caer gordo* or *pesado a uno*, to get on s.o.'s nerves. || *Caer hecho jirones*, to fall in rags. || FIG. *Caerle a uno seis meses de cárcel*, to get six months in prison. || *Caer(le) bien, mal a alguien*, to suit, not to suit s.o.: *no le cae bien esta chaqueta*, this jacket does not suit him; to like, not to like: *lo que Juan dijo me cayó mal*, I did not like what John said. || *Caerle bien, mal uno a alguien*, to get on well, badly with s.o.: *me cae bien Miguel*, I get on well with Michael. || *Caer patas arriba*, to fall with one's feet in the air. || *Cayó cuan largo era* or *de plano*, he fell full length, he fell flat. || *Dejar caer*, to drop. || *Dejarse caer*, to let o.s. go. || FIG. *Dejarse caer con*, to come out with (decir, pedir), to come up with (dar). || *Dejarse caer en la cama*, to lie down on *o* to drop onto the bed. || *Dejarse caer en un sillón*, to drop into an armchair. || FIG. *Estar al caer*, to be about to happen, to be due. || *Hacer caer*, to knock over. || *Hacer caer el gobierno*, to bring about the fall of the government, to bring down the government. || FIG. *Hacerle caer a uno la venda de los ojos*, to open s.o.'s eyes. | *Juan me cae simpático* or *en gracia*, I like John, I think John is nice. | *Tomar las cosas cuando caen*, to take things as they come. | *¡Ya caigo (en la cuenta)!*, I've got it!, the penny has dropped!
— V. pr. To fall, to fall down, to fall over: *caerse de espaldas*, to fall on one's back. || To drop, to fall: *el dinero se me cayó del bolsillo*, the money dropped out of my pocket. || To fall out: *se me cae el pelo*, my hair is falling out. || To fall: *caerse del caballo*, to fall off one's horse. || To fall down, to collapse (hundirse): *la casa se cayó*, the house fell down. || To fall out: *se le cayó un diente*, one of his teeth fell out. || To come off: *se cayó un botón*, a button came off. || To drop: *se caía de cansancio*, he was dropping with tiredness. || To fall in (paredes). || To crash, to come down (avión). || — *Caerse al agua*, to fall into the water. || *Caerse a pedazos*, to fall to pieces. || FIG. *Caerse de debilidad*, to fall with weakness. | *Caerse de risa, de miedo*, to be helpless with laughter, with fear. | *Caerse de sueño*, to be falling asleep [on one's feet]. | *Caerse de tonto*, to be a complete fool. | *Caerse de viejo*, to be falling apart with age. | *Caérsele a uno la cara de vergüenza*, to die of shame. | *Caerse redondo* or *en redondo*, v. REDONDO. | *No se cayó de la cuna*, he wasn't born yesterday. | *No tener dónde caerse muerto*, not to have a penny to one's name.
Cafarnaum pr. n. HIST. Capernaum.
café m. Coffee (planta, grano y bebida): *café solo, con leche*, black, white coffee; *café torrefacto*, roasted coffee. || Café, coffee bar, coffee shop, coffeehouse (establecimiento). || *Amer.* FAM. Scolding, telling off (regañina). || — *Café cantante*, bar with cabaret. || *Café teatro*, café where plays are put on. || FAM. *Estar de mal café*, to be in a foul mood. || *Grano de café*, coffee bean. || FIG. *Los estrategas de café*, the armchair strategists. || FAM. *Tener mal café*, to be a nasty piece of work.
— Adj. *Color café*, coffee-coloured: *un vestido de color café*, a coffee-coloured dress.
cafeína f. QUÍM. Caffeine, caffein.
cafetal f. AGR. Coffee plantation.
cafetalero, ra adj. Coffee: *producción cafetalera*, coffee production.
— M. Coffee planter *o* grower.
cafetera f. Coffeepot. || FAM. Old crock, heap, jaloppy (coche). | Piece of junk, wreck (aparato que funciona mal). || — *Cafetera exprés*, expresso-coffee machine. || FIG. y FAM. *Estar como una cafetera*, to be daft *o* batty *o* nuts.

cafetería f. Snack bar, coffee house.
— OBSERV. The *cafetería* is a café which serves food and drink. The *cafetería* in England is essentially a self-service restaurant.
cafetero, ra adj. Coffee. || FAM. *Juan es muy cafetero*, John loves a cup of coffee.
— M. y f. Café proprietor, café owner (dueño de un café). || Coffee grower (cafetalero). || Coffee merchant (comerciante).
cafetín o **cafetucho** m. FAM. Third-rate café (establecimiento). || *Cafetucho cantante*, third-rate concert hall.
cafeto m. BOT. Coffee.
cáfila m. FAM. Crowd (de personas). | Line (de coches, etc.). || FIG. y FAM. String: *soltar una cáfila de mentiras*, to tell a string of lies.
cafre adj. Kaffir. || FIG. Barbarous, brutal (cruel y bárbaro). | Wild (zafio).
— M. y f. Kaffir. || FIG. Savage, beast (bruto).
caftán m. Caftan, kaftan.
cagaaceite m. Missel thrush (ave).
cagachín m. Small red fly (mosquito). || Finch (pájaro).
cagada f. Flyspeck (de mosca). || Droppings, *pl.* (de ave). || POP. Shit (de persona). || FIG. y POP. A load of crap: *su última película es una cagada*, his latest film is a load of crap.
cagadero m. POP. Bog, loo [U.S., head, john].
cagado, da adj. POP. Yellow, cowardly. || POP. *Estar cagado*, to be shit-scared.
— M. y f. POP. Chicken.
cagafierro m. Slag (escoria).
cagajón m. Dung.
cagalaolla m. y f. FAM. Masquerader, harlequin (mamarracho).
cagalera o **cagaleta** f. POP. Diarrhoea, the runs, *pl.* || FIG. y POP. *Tener cagalera*, to be scared stiff *o* shit-scared (tener miedo).
cagar v. intr. POP. To shit.
— V. tr. FIG. y FAM. To bungle (chapucear).
— V. pr. POP. To shit. || FIG. y POP. To be scared stiff, to be shit-scared. || FIG. y POP. *¡Me cago en la mar!*, stone me!, shit!, goddamn!
cagarria f. Morel (seta).
cagarruta f. Pellet, dropping (bolita de excremento).
cagatinta o **cagatintas** m. FAM. Penpusher (chupatintas, oficinista).
cagatorio m. POP. Bog, loo [U.S., head, john].
cagón, ona o **cagueta** adj. POP. Yellow (cobarde). | Diarrhoeic (que hace de vientre).
— M. y f. POP. Chicken (cobarde). | Diarrhoeic child.
caid m. Kaid (gobernador musulmán).
caída f. Falling, fall (acción de caer): *la caída de las hojas, de la nieve*, the falling of the leaves, of the snow. || Fall: *después de su caída, le dolía la pierna*, after his fall he had a sore leg. || Tumble, spill (de una motocicleta, etc.). || Crash, crashing (de un avión). || Loss (de pelo, dientes). || Slope, drop (declive): *aquí hay una caída muy brusca del terreno*, there is a very steep slope here. || Slope, tilt (inclinación): *la mesa de billar tiene mucha caída*, the billiard table has a lot of slope. || Setting (del sol). || Drawing-in, close, closing (del día). || Hangings, *pl.* (tapicería colgante). || Body (peso): *esta tela tiene mucha caída*, this material has a lot of body. || Hang (manera de caer un vestido, etc.). || Width (ancho): *la falda lleva tres caídas*, the skirt has three widths. || Length (longitud de tela): *una caída de mangas*, a sleeve length. || GEOL. Dip. || ELECTR. Drop (de potencia, de voltaje, etc.). || DEP. Landing (de un salto). || FIG. Sin (pecado). | Fall, drop (de precio, de temperatura). | Mistake, slip (equivocación). | Fall, downfall: *la caída del gobierno*, the fall of the government. | Witticism, flash of wit (ocurrencia). || MAR. Rake (de una vela). || — *A la caída de la tarde*, at nightfall, at the close of day. || *A la caída de la hoja*, in autumn [U.S., in the fall]. || *A la caída del sol*, at sunset. || TEATR. *Caída del telón*, curtain. || *Caída en desuso*, disappearance, falling into disuse (de una cosa). || *Caída libre*, free fall (paracaidista). || *Caída vertical de los precios*, sudden drop in prices. || *Hacerle a uno una caída de ojos*, to make goo-goo eyes at s.o. || *Ir de caída*, to ease off, to let up (fiebre, calor), to be on the decline (una persona). || *La caída del primer hombre*, the Fall of Man.
caído, da adj. Fallen: *un árbol caído*, a fallen tree. || FIG. Faint, weak (desfallecido). | Downcast, dejected, low-spirited (abatido). || Turned-down (cuello de vestido). || Drooping: *tener los hombros caídos*, to have drooping shoulders. || FIG. *Caído del cielo*, out of the blue (inesperado), heaven-sent (oportuno).
— M. pl. Dead, fallen (en la guerra). || Oblique lines (de un cuaderno). || *Monumento a los Caídos*, war memorial.
Caifás n. pr. m. Caiaphas. || FIG. Bully, brute.
caimacán n. FAM. Big shot (pez gordo).
caimán m. Cayman, caiman (reptil). || FIG. Sly old fox.
caimiento m. Fall (caída).
Caín n. pr. m. Cain. || — FIG. y FAM. *Ir con* or *tener las de Caín*, to have evil intentions, to be up to no good. | *Pasar las de Caín*, to go through murder.
Cairo (El) n. pr. m. GEOGR. Cairo.
cairel m. Wig (peluca). || Fringe (pasamanería).
cairelar v. tr. To trim with a fringe.
caja f. Box (pequeña o de cartón): *una caja de bombones*, a box of chocolates. || Case, crate (de gran tamaño y de madera): *una caja de uva*, a case of grapes. || Box, case, crate, boxful (contenido). || Till: *ayer robaron la caja*, they robbed the till yesterday. || Cashdesk, cashbox (donde se efectúan los pagos). || Cash, funds, *pl.*: *ocuparse de la caja*, to take charge of the cash. || Coffin [U.S., casket] (ataúd). || Cabinet (de radio). || TECN. Housing, casing. | Watch case (de reloj). || MÚS. Drum (tambor). | Case (estuche). | Body (de violín). | Case (de piano). || AUT. Body (carrocería). | Interior (interior). || ARQ. Well (de escalera). | Well, shaft (de ascensor). || Stock (de un arma de fuego). || IMPR. Case: *caja alta*, upper case; *caja baja*, lower case. || BOT. Capsule (fruto). || *Amer.* Bed (de un río). || — ANAT. *Caja craneana*, skull, cranium. || *Caja de ahorros*, savings bank. || TECN. *Caja de cambios* o *de velocidades*, gearbox. || *Caja de caudales* or *fuerte*, safe, strongbox. || *Caja de colores*, paintbox. || *Caja de Depósitos y Consignaciones*, V. CONSIGNACIÓN. || TECN. *Caja de empalmes*, junction box. | *Caja de engrase*, journal box, axle box. | *Caja de fusibles*, fuse box. | *Caja de herramientas*, toolbox. | *Caja de humos*, smokebox. || *Caja de jubilaciones*, pension fund. || *Caja de la cama*, bedstead. || FAM. *Caja de las muelas*, mouth, gob. || TECN. *Caja del cigüeñal*, crankcase. || ANAT. *Caja del cuerpo*, rib cage. || *Caja del tímpano*, eardrum. || *Caja de música*, musical box. || MIL. *Caja de recluta*, recruiting office. || *Caja de registro*, manhole. || MÚS. *Caja de resonancia*, sounding board, soundbox. || MIL. *Caja de respetos*, spares kit. || *Caja de sorpresa*, jack-in-the box. || *Caja postal de ahorros*, post office savings bank. || *Caja registradora*, cash register. || ANAT. *Caja torácica*, thoracic cage. || FAM. *Echar* or *despedir a uno con cajas destempladas*, to throw s.o. out by the scruff of the neck, to send s.o. packing. || *Entrar en caja*, to be called up (militar), to settle down (una persona). || *Hacer caja*, to cash up. || *Ingresar en caja*, to take (un almacén, etc.), to deposit (en un banco). || *Libro de caja*, cash book. || *Valores en caja*, cash in hand.
cajel adj. *Naranja cajel*, Seville orange.
cajero, ra m. y f. Cashier (encargado de la caja). || — M. Box *o* case maker (fabricante de cajas). || — F. MAR. Sheave channel (de polea).
cajetilla f. Packet [U.S., pack] (de cigarrillos, de tabaco). || Box: *una cajetilla de cerillas*, a box of matches.
— M. *Amer.* FAM. Dandy, dude.
cajetín m. Small box (cajita). || Hole (en el marco de la puerta). || ELECTR. Rod. || IMPR. Box.
cajiga f. Gall oak.
cajigal m. Gall oak grove.
cajista m. y f. IMPR. Compositor, typesetter.
cajón m. Chest, case, crate (caja grande). || Drawer (de mueble). || Shelf space (en los estantes). || Stall (puesto en el mercado). || Shop (tienda). || IMPR. Half-case. || Caisson (obras públicas). || *Amer.* Gorge, gulley (cañada). | Coffin [U.S., casket] (ataúd). || — *Cajón de herramientas*, toolbox, toolchest. || FIG. *Cajón de sastre* or *de turco*, muddle, jumble, mess (objetos en desorden). || FIG. y FAM. *Ser de cajón*, to be obvious, to go without saying (ser evidente). | *Un reloj de cajón*, an ordinary watch.
cake m. Fruit cake.
cal f. Lime: *cal apagada* or *muerta, hidráulica*, slaked, hydraulic lime. || — FIG. y FAM. *A* or *de cal y canto*, solidly built *o* made (cosa), very strong (person). || *Cal viva*, quicklime. || FIG. *Cerrar a cal y canto*, to shut tight, to shut firmly. || *Lechada de cal*, milk of lime. || FIG. *Una de cal y otra de arena*, six of one and half a dozen of the other.
cala f. Sample slice (primer trozo) [to taste a fruit]. || MED. Suppository (supositorio). | Probe (sonda). || MAR. Hold (de un barco). | Fishing ground (sitio para pescar). || GEOGR. Creek, cove, bight. || Test boring (agujero para explorar). || BOT. Arum. || FIG. Opinion poll (sondeo de opinión). || *Vender a cala y cata*, to allow the customer to taste the merchandise.
calabacear v. tr. FAM. To fail, to plough (en un examen). | To send packing, to jilt (a un pretendiente).
calabacín m. Marrow (fruto). || FIG. y FAM. Fathead, dope.
calabacino m. Gourd, calabash (recipiente).
calabaza f. BOT. Gourd. | Pumpkin (de gran tamaño). || Gourd, calabash (recipiente). || FIG. y FAM. Fathead, dolt (persona tonta). | Big tub (buque pesado). || — FIG. y FAM. *Dar calabazas a uno*, to fail s.o., to plough s.o. (en un examen), to jilt, to send s.o. packing, to reject (a un pretendiente). | *Recibir* o *llevarse calabazas*, to get the brush-off, to be jilted (un pretendiente), to fail (en un examen).
calabazada f. FAM. Butt (golpe dado con la cabeza). | Bump *o* blow on the head (golpe en la cabeza).
calabazar m. AGR. Gourd field, pumpkin field.
calabazazo m. Blow with a gourd *o* pumpkin. || FAM. Bump, blow on the head.
calabazo m. Pumpkin, gourd.
calabobos m. inv. FAM. Drizzle (lluvia).
calabocero m. Gaoler, jailer (carcelero).
calabozo m. Gaol, jail, prison (prisión): *meter en el calabozo*, to put in prison. || MIL. FAM. Glasshouse [U.S., calaboose]. || Cell (celda de cárcel).
calabrés, esa adj./s. Calabrian.
calabrote m. MAR. Hawser, warp.

calada f. Soaking (en o con un líquido). || Puff (de cigarrillo). || Swoop, dive (vuelo de ave hacia abajo), soar (hacia arriba).
calado m. Openwork embroidery (bordado). || Perforation, openwork (perforado de papel, tejidos, etc.). || MAR. Depth (de agua). | Draught (del barco). || TECN. Stalling (de un motor).
calador m. MED. Probe. || *Amer.* Borer, probe [for taking samples].
calafate m. MAR. Caulker.
calafateado m. o **calafateadura** f. MAR. Caulking.
calafatear v. tr. MAR. To caulk (barcos). || To fill in *o* up (cualquier juntura).
calafateo m. o **calafatería** f. Caulking.
calamar m. Squid, calamary (molusco).
calambre m. Cramp: *calambre de estómago,* stomach cramp; *me ha dado un calambre en la pierna,* I got cramp in my leg. || Electric shock, shock: *si tocas ese enchufe te dará calambre,* if you touch that socket you'll get a shock. || — *Calambre del escribiente,* writer's cramp. || *Ese hilo da calambre,* that wire is live.
calamidad f. Calamity, disaster (desastre). || Upset, problem (desgracia): *ha pasado muchas calamidades,* he has had a lot of upsets. || — FIG. y FAM. *Estar hecho una calamidad,* to look a sight. | *Ser una calamidad,* to be useless, to be a dead loss (un incapaz), to be jinxed (desgraciado).
calamina f. Calamine (carbonato de cinc).
calamita f. MIN. Lodestone (piedra imán).
calamitoso, sa adj. Calamitous, disastrous.
cálamo m. MÚS. Reed, reed pipe. || POÉT. Reed, stalk (planta). | Pen (para escribir). || *Cálamo currente,* hastily.
calamocano, na adj. FAM. Tipsy, merry (borracho).
calamoco m. Icicle (carámbano).
calamón m. Sultana bird, purple gallinule (ave). || Stud (clavo).
calamorra f. FAM. Head, nut.
calandrado m. TECN. Calendering (de telas, de papel).
calandrajo m. FAM. Rag (jirón). | Rag, tatter (harapo). || FIG. y FAM. Drip, dope (persona despreciable).
calandrar v. tr. To calender (tela, papel).
calandrero m. Calenderer (de tela, papel).
calandria f. Calandra lark (ave). || TECN. Calender (para lustrar). | Treadmill (torno). || AUT. Radiator grille. || FIG. y FAM. Malingerer (enfermo fingido).
calaña f. Sample, pattern (muestra). || FIG. Nature, disposition (personas), quality (cosas). || Stamp, kind (sentido despectivo): *estos dos chicos son de la misma calaña,* these two boys are of the same stamp. || Cheap fan (abanico). || *Gente de mala calaña,* undesirable people.
calañés adj. m. *Sombrero calañés,* Andalusian hat with an upturned brim.
calar adj. Calcareous, lime.
— M. Limestone quarry (cantera).
calar v. tr. To soak through, to soak, to drench (un líquido): *la lluvia ha calado el abrigo,* the rain has soaked through the coat. || To penetrate, to pierce: *calar una tabla con la barrena,* to pierce a board with the drill. || To do openwork embroidery on (bordar). || To pierce, to perforate (agujerear). || To sample, to plug (la fruta). || To jam on (un sombrero). || FIG. To rumble, to find out: *me han calado,* they've found me out; *te caló las intenciones,* he found out your intentions. | To probe: *calar hondamente en un asunto,* to probe deeply into a matter. || MAR. To strike (una vela). | To lower (las redes). || MIL. To fix (la bayoneta). || *Amer.* To humiliate (humillar). | To take a sample. || FIG. *Te tengo calado,* I am wise to you, I've got your number.
— V. intr. MAR. To draw. || To swoop (el ave).
— V. pr. To get soaked *o* drenched: *se caló hasta los huesos,* he got soaked to the skin. || To soak in (un líquido). || To leak, to let in water (zapatos). || To jam on: *calarse el sombrero,* to jam on one's hat. || To come through: *la lluvia se cala por el tejado,* the rain comes through the roof. || To swoop (el ave). || FAM. To push one's way into (introducirse). || TECN. To stall: *se me caló el motor,* my engine stalled. || *Calarse las gafas,* to put on one's spectacles.
calato, ta adj. *Amer.* Naked (desnudo). | Broke (sin dinero).
calatravo, va adj. Of Calatrava.
— M. Knight of the order of Calatrava.
calavera f. Skull (cráneo). || ZOOL. Death's-head hawk moth (mariposa).
— M. FIG. Gay dog (juerguista). | Madcap (cabeza loca).
calaverada f. Revel, spree, binge (juerga). || Foolish stunt *o* trick (acción insensata).
calaverear v. intr. To act recklessly (obrar con poco juicio). || To live it up, to have a ball (andar de juerga).
calcado m. Tracing.
calcador, ra m. y f. Tracer.
calcáneo m. Calcaneus (hueso).
calcañal o **calcañar** o **calcaño** m. Heel.
calcar v. tr. To trace (un dibujo, etc.) || FIG. To copy (imitar). || To tread on (pisar). || FIG. *Calcar una cosa en otra,* to model one thing on another.
calcáreo, a adj. Calcareous.
Calcas n. pr. m. Calchas.
calce m. Rim (de rueda). || Metal cutting edge (de instrumentos cortantes). || Wedge (cuña, alza): *poner un calce a una mesa coja,* to put a wedge under a wobbly table. || *Amer.* Foot (de un documento).
calcedonia f. MIN. Chalcedony.
calceolado, da adj. BOT. Calceolate.
calceolaria f. Calceolaria (planta).
calcés m. MAR. Masthead.
calceta f. Stocking (media). || Fetters, *pl.*, shackles, *pl.* (de preso). || *Hacer calceta,* to knit.
calcetería f. Hosier's, hosiery shop (tienda). || Hosiery (oficio).
calcetero, ra m. y f. Hosier (comerciante). || Knitter (que hace punto).
calcetín m. Sock. || FIG. *Volverle a uno como a un calcetín,* to change s.o.'s mind.
calcetón m. Long heavy sock (polaina).
cálcico, ca adj. QUÍM. Calcic. || *Óxido cálcico,* calcium oxide.
calcífero, ra adj. Calciferous.
calciferol m. QUÍM. Calciferol.
calcificación f. Calcification.
calcificar v. tr. To calcify.
calcina f. Concrete (hormigón).
calcinación f. Calcination.
calcinar v. tr. To calcine. || To roast, to burn: *piedras calcinadas por el sol,* stones roasted by the sun. || FIG. y FAM. *Este hombre me calcina,* this fellow gets on my nerves (fastidiar).
— V. pr. To calcine.
calcio m. Calcium (metal).
calcita f. MIN. Calcite, calcspar.
calco m. Tracing (acción de calcar). || Tracing (dibujo calcado). || FIG. Copy (copia). || *Papel de calco,* tracing paper.
calcografía f. Chalcography.
calcógrafo m. Chalcographer (grabador).
calcomanía f. Transfer.
calcopirita MIN. Chalcopyrite.
calculable adj. Calculable.
calculador, ra adj. Calculating.
— M. y f. Calculator, calculating machine (máquina). || FIG. Calculator (interesado). || *Calculadora electrónica,* [electronic] computer.
calcular v. tr. To calculate, to work out: *calcular una raíz cuadrada,* to calculate a square root. || To do the calculations for: *calcular un puente,* to do the calculations for a bridge. || To compute (una calculadora). || FIG. To calculate: *calcular los gastos del viaje,* to calculate the cost of the journey. | To think, to reckon: *calculo que lo terminaré mañana,* I think I shall finish it tomorrow. || — *Calculando por bajo* or *por lo bajo,* at the lowest estimate. || *Le calculo siete años,* I should say he is seven years old. || *Máquina de calcular,* calculating machine.
calculista adj. Calculating.
— M. y f. Calculator, planner (proyectista).
cálculo m. Calculation: *el cálculo de una raíz cuadrada,* the calculation of a square root. || Estimation, calculation (acción): *cálculo de gastos,* estimation of costs. || Estimate (resultado): *hizo un cálculo de gastos,* he made an estimate of costs. || MAT. Calculus: *cálculo diferencial, integral,* differential, integral calculus. || FIG. Reckoning (conjetura, reflexión): *según tus cálculos,* by your reckoning. | Caution, care: *obrar con cálculo,* to act with caution. || MED. Calculus, stone (piedra). || — Pl. MED. Gallstones. || — *Cálculo de costo,* costing. || *Cálculo mental,* mental arithmetic. || *Regla de cálculo,* slide rule.
calculoso, sa adj. MED. Calculous.
calcha f. *Amer.* Fetlock (del caballo), leg feather (de ciertas aves). | Clothes, *pl.*, clothing (prendas de vestir).
calda f. Heating (acción de calentar). || Stoking (introducción del combustible). || TECN. Heat (metal). || — Pl. Thermal springs (baños).
caldaico, ca adj. Chaldaic.
Caldea n. pr. f. GEOGR. Chaldea.
caldeamiento m. Heating, warming.
caldear v. tr. To heat, to warm (calentar). || To bring to red heat (los metales). || FIG. To heat up *o* to warm up (el ambiente, etc.).
— V. pr. To become warm *o* hot: *en cinco minutos se caldeó la habitación,* the room became warm in five minutes. || To be heated *o* warmed: *la habitación se caldea con el sol,* the room is heated by the sun. || To become red-hot (metales). || FIG. To warm up (el ambiente).
caldeo m. Heating, warming (caldeamiento): *el caldeo de una habitación,* the heating of a room.
caldeo, a adj./s. Chaldean (de Caldea).
caldera f. Boiler: *caldera de vapor,* steam boiler. || Cauldron, caldron (caldero). || Boilerful, cauldronful (calderada). || MIN. Sump (pozo). || *Amer.* Coffee-pot (para café), teapot (para té). | Crater. || FIG. y FAM. *Las calderas de Pedro Botero,* Hell.
calderada f. Boilerful, cauldronful.
calderería f. Boilermaking (oficio). || Boilermaker's shop (taller).
calderero m. Boilermaker.
caldereta f. Small boiler, small cauldron (caldera). || REL. Holy-water vessel (de agua bendita). || CULIN. Fish soup (sopa de pescado). | Lamb stew (guiso).

calderilla f. Coppers, *pl.*, small change (moneda fraccionaria). || REL. Holy-water vessel (de agua bendita).
caldero m. Cauldron, boiler (recipiente). || Cauldronful (contenido). || TECN. Ladle (para la colada).
calderón m. Large cauldron *o* boiler (recipiente). || IMPR. Paragraph mark (signo). || MÚS. Pause (signo).
calderoniano, na adj. Calderonian [of the playwright Calderón].
caldibache m. FAM. Dishwater (caldo malo).
caldillo m. Thin sauce *o* gravy (salsa).
caldo m. Stock, broth: *caldo de gallina, de pescado*, chicken, fish stock. || Soup (sopa). || Dressing [of salad]. || *Amer.* Sugar-cane juice (jugo de caña). || — Pl. Liquid foodstuffs (vinagre, aceite, etc.). || Wines: *los caldos de Jerez*, the wines of Jerez. || — FIG. *Al que no quiere caldo, la taza llena* or *taza y media* or *tres tazas*, things have a way of turning out just the way you don't want them to. || *Caldo bordelés*, Bordeaux mixture. || *Caldo corto*, stock of wine and spice [for cooking fish]. || *Caldo de carne*, beef tea. || QUÍM. *Caldo de cultivo*, culture medium. || FIG. *Gallina vieja da* or *hace buen caldo*, there's many a good tune played on an old fiddle. || FIG. y FAM. *Hacerle a uno el caldo gordo*, to make it easy for s.o.
caldoso, sa adj. With a lot of stock *o* dressing.
calducho m. FAM. Dishwater (caldo malo).
calé m. Gypsy (gitano). || Copper coin (moneda).
Caledonia n. pr. f. GEOGR. Caledonia. || *Nueva Caledonia*, New Caledonia.
calefacción f. Heating: *calefacción central*, central heating; *calefacción por fuel-oil*, oil heating. || Calefaction (acción de calentarse). || TECN. *Superficie de calefacción*, heating surface.
calefactor m. Heating engineer (encargado de la calefacción).
caleidoscópico, ca adj. Kaleidoscopic.
caleidoscopio m. Kaleidoscope.
calendario m. Calendar: *calendario gregoriano, juliano*, Gregorian, Julian calendar. || Almanac (con varios datos). || — *Calendario americano* or *exfoliador* or *de taco*, tear-off calendar, day calendar. || FIG. *Hacer calendarios*, to make hasty forecasts (pronósticos), to be woolgathering (estar pensativo).
calendas f. pl. Calends (día del mes).
caléndula f. BOT. Calendula, marigold.
calentador, ra adj. Heating, warming.
— M. Heater (aparato). || Water heater (para calentar agua). || Geyser (de baño). || Warming pan, bed warmer (de cama). || TECN. Superheater (de locomotora). || FIG. y FAM. Large clumsy pocket watch (reloj muy grueso).
calentamiento m. Heating. || DEP. *Ejercicios de calentamiento*, warming-up exercises.
calentar* v. tr. To heat [up], to warm [up]: *calentar un horno*, to heat an oven; *caliéntame un poco de agua*, heat me a drop of water. || To warm [up] (habitación, cuerpo, comida). || To heat (metales): *calentar al rojo blanco*, to heat until white hot. || FIG. To tone up, to warm up: *calentar los músculos*, to tone up one's muscles. || FIG. y FAM. To warm: *calentar el asiento*, to warm the seat. | To liven up (animar): *el vino nos calentó los ánimos*, the wine livened up our spirits. || FAM. To tan, to warm (azotar). | To inflame, to excite (pasiones). || — FIG. *Calentar a alguien la cabeza* or *los cascos con*, to pester s.o. with. | *Calentar las orejas a alguien*, to get on s.o.'s nerves (fastidiar), to box s.o.'s ears (pegar), to send s.o. away with a flea in his ear (reprender). | *Calentarle la sangre a alguien*, to rub s.o. up the wrong way, to irritate s.o.
— V. pr. To warm o.s. (el que tiene frío): *nos calentamos alrededor de la chimenea*, we warmed ourselves round the fire. || To get hot *o* warm (una cosa). || To be on heat (animales hembras), to be in rut (animales machos). || POP. To get randy (personas). || FIG. y FAM. To become inflamed *o* excited (pasiones). | To pick up (excitarse): *se nos calentaron los ánimos*, our spirits picked up. | To get annoyed *o* irritated (irritarse). | To get heated, to get excited (en una discusión). || — FIG. *Las manos se le calientan*, his fingers are itching. | *No calentarse los cascos*, not to worry.
calentón, ona adj. POP. Randy.
— M. *Darse un calentón*, to overheat (un motor). || — M. y f. POP. Randy person.
calentura f. MED. Fever, temperature: *tener calentura*, to have a fever. || *Amer.* Type of asclepias (planta). | Phthisis, consumption, tuberculosis (tisis). | Anger (ira).
calenturiento, ta adj. MED. Feverish. || *Amer.* Consumptive, tuberculous. || FIG. Feverish, restless: *tener la mente calenturienta*, to have a feverish mind.
calenturón m. MED. Very high fever *o* temperature.
calero, ra adj. Limestone.
— M. Lime burner. || — F. Limestone quarry (cantera). || Lime kiln (horno).
calesa f. Calèche, calash (carruaje).
calesera f. Bolero jacket [worn by carriage driver] (chaqueta). || Andalusian folk song (cante).
calesero m. Caleche driver (cochero).
caleta f. Creek, cove (ensenada). || *Amer.* Small coaster (barco).
caletero m. *Amer.* Stevedore, docker (descargador de barcos). | Coaster (barco).
caletre m. FAM. Common sense, gumption (seso): *tener poco caletre*, to have little common sense. || — FAM. *De su propio caletre*, out of one's own little head. | *No le cabe en el caletre*, it's too much for him.
calibración f. Calibration.
calibrado m. TECN. Boring (de un tubo o un cilindro). || Gauging (medición).
calibrador m. Gauge, gage: *calibrador de mordazas*, calliper gauge; *calibrador de profundidades*, depth gauge. || Borer (de un tubo). || *Calibrador micrométrico*, vernier calliper.
calibrar v. tr. To gauge, to gage, to measure (medir). || To bore (mandrilar). || To calibrate (un termómetro). || FIG. To size up, to judge (juzgar). || *Máquina de calibrar*, boring machine.
calibre m. MIL. Calibre [U.S., caliber], bore: *de grueso calibre*, large calibre. || TECN. Bore (diámetro interior). | Gauge (de alambre). || FIG. Importance: *un asunto de mucho calibre*, a matter of great importance.
calicata f. MIN. Bore.
calicó m. Calico (tejido de algodón).
caliche m. *Amer.* Saltpetre [U.S., saltpeter] (nitrato). | Bruise (maca). | Flake [of paint, etc.] (de pintura, de cal). | Crack (en una vasija).
calidad f. Quality: *tela de buena calidad*, good quality material. || Capacity (condición): *por su calidad de ciudadano*, in his capacity as a citizen. || Class (categoría): *naranjas de primera, de segunda calidad*, first-class, second-class oranges. || Class, nobility, quality (nobleza): *una persona de calidad*, a person of class. || FIG. Importance: *asunto de calidad*, a matter of importance. || Condition (cláusula de contrato). || — Pl. Qualities. || Conditions, rules (de juego). || — *Control de calidad*, quality control. || *En calidad de*, as: *en calidad de amigo*, as a friend. || FIG. *De dinero y calidad la mitad de la mitad;* v. DINERO. || *Voto de calidad*, casting vote.
cálido, da adj. Warm: *colorido cálido*, warm tone. || Hot, warm: *clima cálido*, hot climate.
calidoscópico, ca adj. Kaleidoscopic.
calidoscopio m. Kaleidoscope.
calientapiés m. inv. Foot warmer.
calientaplatos m. inv. Chafing dish, hot plate.
caliente adj. Warm, hot (v. OBSERV.): *agua caliente*, hot water; *la sopa está caliente*, the soup is hot. || Warm: *colorido caliente*, warm tone. || FIG. Angry (enfadado). | Heated: *discusión caliente*, heated argument. | Fiery, spirited (apasionado). | Hot, randy (ardiente sexualmente). || — FIG. *Caliente, caliente*, now you're hot (en juegos de niños). | *En caliente*, there and then, straight away, on the spot (en el acto). || *Estar caliente*, to be on heat (los animales), to be in the mood (personas). || *Mantener caliente*, to keep warm (un guiso). || FIG. *Ser caliente de cascos*, to be hotheaded.

— OBSERV. El primer significado de *caliente* se traduce por dos palabras en inglés según la intensidad sea mayor (*hot*) o menor (*warm*).

califa f. Caliph.
califato m. Caliphate.
calificable adj. Qualifiable.
calificación f. Qualification. || Assessment (evaluación). || Mark (de un ejercicio).
calificado, da adj. Qualified. || Skilled (obrero). || Eminent (científico). || Necessary (pruebas). || Proven (theft).
calificador, ra adj. Examining: *el jurado calificador*, the examining jury.
— M. Examiner, marker (de exámenes, de ejercicios). || REL. Qualificator.
calificar v. tr. To describe, to qualify: *la crítica califica la obra de atrevida*, the critics describe the work as daring. || To assess (evaluar). || To mark (un examen, un ejercicio). || GRAM. To qualify. || To label: *esas palabras le califican de orgulloso*, those words label him as proud. || To call (tratar): *le calificó de mentiroso*, he called him a liar. || FIG. To make famous (ilustrar). || *Yo le calificaría de estafador*, I think *o* say hes' a swindler.
— V. pr. To give proof of nobility.
calificativo, va adj. Qualifying: *adjetivo calificativo*, qualifying adjective.
— M. Epithet: *un calificativo injurioso*, an insulting epithet. || GRAM. Qualifier.
California n. pr. f. GEGR. California.
californiano, na o **californio, nia** adj./s. Californian (de California).
califórnico, ca adj. Californian.
californio m. QUÍM. Californium.
calígine f. POÉT. Darkness, gloom.
caliginoso, sa adj. Dark, gloomy, caliginous (oscuro). || Misty, caliginous (brumoso).
caligrafía f. Calligraphy.
caligrafiar v. tr. To write ornamentally, to calligraph.
caligráfico, ca adj. Calligraphic.
calígrafo, fa m. y f. Calligrapher, calligraphist.
calilla f. Small suppository (supositorio). || *Amer.* FAM. Pest, bore (cargante). | Nuisance (molestia).
calina f. Haze, mist (niebla). || Heat (calor).
calinoso, sa adj. Hazy, misty (brumoso). || Hot, warm (caluroso).
Calíope n. pr. f. MIT. Calliope.

calipso m. Calypso (baile).
Calipso n. pr. f. MIT. Calypso.
calistenia f. Callisthenics.
Calixto n. pr. m. Calixtus.
cáliz m. REL. Chalice (copa). || BOT. Calyx. || POÉT. Cup, chalice, goblet. || ANAT. Calyx (del riñón). || FIG. *Apurar el cáliz hasta las heces*, to drain the cup to the dregs, to drain the bitter cup.
caliza f. Limestone (roca sedimentaria). || *Caliza litográfica*, lithographic stone.
calizo, za adj. Calcareous, lime.
calma f. Calm, calmness, tranquility (tranquilidad). || FIG. Calm: *la calma de la noche*, the calm of the night. | Lull (de una tormenta). | Lull, slack period: *el negocio está en calma*, business is going through a slack period. | Abatement, lull (de dolor). | Composure (serenidad de una persona): *perder la calma*, to lose one's composure. | Calm, phlegm (flema): *lo hace todo con una calma increíble*, he does everything with incredible calm. || — MAR. *Calma chicha*, dead calm. || *Con calma*, calmly, with composure. || *Después de la tempestad viene la calma*, it's the calm after the storm. || COM. *El mercado está en calma*, the market is steady *o* calm. || *En calma*, calm: *todo está en calma*, all is calm.
calmante adj. MED. Sedative, tranquillizing, calmative.
— M. MED. Sedative, tranquillizer.
calmar v. tr. To calm, to calm down (tranquilizar). || To soothe, to relieve: *esta medicina calma el dolor*, this medicine soothes pain. || To soothe, to steady (los nervios).
— V. intr. y pr. To calm down. || To drop, to abate (el viento). || To let up, to die down (el calor). || *¡Cálmate!*, calm down!
calmazo m. MAR. Dead calm. || Lull, short period of calm (calma momentánea).
calmo, ma adj. AGR. Uncultivated (erial). | Fallow (en barbecho).
calmoso, sa adj. Calm, quiet, tranquil (tranquilo). || FAM. Nonchalant, phlegmatic (indolente). | Sluggish (lento).
calmuco, ca adj./s. Kalmuck.
caló m. Gypsy dialect.
— OBSERV. Since certain words or expressions of this dialect are now used in everyday speech, the word *caló* often means *slang*.
calofrío m. Shiver (escalofrío).
calomel m. o **calomelanos** m. pl. Calomel, *sing* (cloruro de mercurio).
calor m. FÍS. Heat: *calor específico, latente*, specific, latent heat. || Heat, warmth (V. OBSERV.): *el calor del verano*, the heat of summer; *el calor del fuego*, the warmth of the fire. || FIG. Heat: *en el calor de la batalla, de la discusión*, in the heat of the battle, of the argument. | Ardour (de sentimientos). | Warmth: *acoger con calor*, to welcome with warmth. | Enthusiasm: *tomar las cosas con demasiado calor*, to take things with too much enthusiasm. | Passion (pasión). || — FIG. y FAM. *Asarse* or *morirse de calor*, to be boiling [hot] *o* roasting. || *Calor blanco*, white heat. || *Calor rojo*, red heat. || *Dar calor*, to encourage (animar), to keep warm. || *Darse calor*, to keep warm. || *Entrar en calor*, to get warm (cuando se tiene frío), to warm up (los deportistas). || *Hace calor*, it is warm *o* hot. || *Hacer entrar en calor*, to warm up. || *¡Qué calor!*, isn't it hot! || *Tener calor*, to be hot.
— OBSERV. Ciertos significados de *calor* se traducen por dos palabras en inglés según la intensidad sea mayor (*hot, heat*) o menor (*warm, warmth*).
caloría f. FÍS. Calorie, calory: *caloría grande*, large calorie; *caloría pequeña*, small calorie; *caloría gramo*, gramme calorie.
calórico, ca adj. Caloric.
calorífero, ra adj. Heat-producing.
— M. Radiator, heater.
calorífico, ca adj. Calorific: *potencia calorífica*, calorific value *o* power.
calorífugo, ga adj. Heat-resistant (mal conductor del calor). || Uninflammable.
calorimetría f. Calorimetry.
calorimétrico, ca adj. Calorimetric, calorimetrical.
calorímetro m. Calorimeter.
calostro m. Colostrum (primera leche).
calote m. *Amer.* Fraud, swindle (estafa). || *Amer. Dar calote*, to cheat, to swindle.
calotear v. tr. *Amer.* To cheat, to swindle (estafar).
calpense adj./s. Gibraltarian (de Gibraltar).
calta f. BOT. Marsh marigold.
caluma f. *Amer.* Pass (entre los Andes).
calumet m. Calumet, peace pipe (pipa de la paz).
calumnia f. Calumny, false accusation (acusación falsa). || Calumniation (acción). || JUR. Slander (oral). | Libel (*de*, on) [escrita].
calumniador, ra adj. Calumniatory, slanderous.
— M. y f. Calumniator, slanderer.
calumniar v. tr. To calumniate, to slander. || To libel (por escrito).
calumnioso, sa adj. Calumnious, calumniatory, slanderous.
calurosamente adv. Warmly: *el Presidente fue recibido calurosamente*, the President was warmly received; *felicitar calurosamente*, to congratulate warmly.
caluroso, sa adj. Warm, hot: *un día caluroso*, a warm day. (V. CALIENTE [Observ.]). || FIG. Warm: *un recibimiento caluroso*, a warm reception.
calva f. Bald patch *o* pate (calvicie). || Bald *o* bare patch (de una piel). || Clearing (en un bosque).
calvario m. REL. Calvary. | Stations (*pl.*) of the Cross (vía crucis). || FIG. y FAM. Cross, tribulations, *pl.*, ordeal, suffering (adversidades). || *Tener un calvario de deudas*, to be head over heels in debt, to be crippled with debt.
calvero m. Clearing (en un bosque). || Claypit (yacimiento de arcilla).
calvicie f. Baldness.
calvinismo m. Calvinism.
calvinista adj. Calvinist, calvinistic.
— M. y f. Calvinist.
Calvino n. pr. HIST. Calvin.
calvo, va adj. Bald (cabeza, persona): *quedarse calvo*, to go bald. || Barren, desert (terreno). || Bald, threadbare (tejido). || — FIG. *A la ocasión la pintan calva*, V. OCASIÓN. | *Ni tanto ni tan calvo*, neither one extreme nor the other.
— M. y f. Bald *o* bald-headed person (persona). || — F. V. CALVA.
calza f. Wedge, scotch (cuña). || FAM. Stocking (media). || Ring (señal que se pone a ciertos animales). || — Pl. Breeches (vestido antiguo). || — *Medias calzas*, knee socks. || FAM. *Verse en calzas prietas*, to be in a fix *o* in a tight spot.
calzada f. Road, roadway.
calzado, da adj. Wearing shoes, with shoes on (que lleva zapatos): *un niño calzado*, a child with shoes on. || Wearing [on one's feet]: *calzado con zapatos rojos*, wearing red shoes. || Shod: *los pies calzados con sandalias*, feet shod in sandals; *calzado por el mejor zapatero del pueblo*, shod by the best shoemaker in the town. || Calced (religioso). || With feet of a different colour (animales). || *Caballo calzado de blanco*, horse with white stockings.
— M. Footwear, shoe: *industria del calzado*, footwear industry. || Shoe: *una tienda de calzado*, a shoe shop.
calzador m. Shoehorn. || *Amer.* Penholder (portaplumas). | Pencil (lápiz).
calzadura f. Wedging (con calce). || Wooden tyre *o* rim (llanta).
calzapiés m. inv. Toe clip (de pedal).
calzar v. tr. To put on shoes for: *hay que calzar a los niños porque no pueden hacerlo solos*, you have to put children's shoes on for them because they cannot do it themselves. || To wear: *calzar nuevos zapatos*, to wear new shoes. || To take, to wear: *calzo un 43*, I take size 43. || To make the shoes of: *le calza un zapatero inglés*, an English shoemaker makes his shoes. || To wedge, to scotch (poner un calce). || To wear [gloves, spurs] (guantes, espuelas). || To take (armas de fuego). || To put on tyres (poner neumáticos).
— V. intr. To wear shoes: *calza bien*, he wears good shoes.
— V. pr. To put one's shoes on. || To put on (ponerse): *calzarse las sandalias*, to put on one's sandals.
calzo m. Wedge, scotch (calce). || Dangerous kicking (en fútbol). || TECN. Brake shoe (del freno). || MAR. Skid.
calzón m. Trousers, *pl.* (prenda): *calzón bombacho*, baggy trousers. || TECN. Safety belt (para sujetarse). || *Amer.* Panties, *pl.*, knickers, *pl.* (de mujer), underpants, *pl.* [U.S., shorts, *pl.*] (de hombre). | Pork stew (guiso). | Disease affecting sugarcane. || — Pl. Trousers. || — FIG. y FAM. *Hablar a calzón quitado*, to speak frankly, to speak one's mind. | *Llevar los calzones* or *tener los calzones bien puestos*, to wear the trousers (en un matrimonio).
calzonazos m. inv. FAM. Henpecked husband.
calzoncillos m. pl. Underpants, pants [U.S., shorts].
calzoneras f. pl. *Amer.* Trousers buttoned up the sides.
calzonudo adj. m. *Amer.* FAM. Henpecked [husband].
calzorras m. inv. FAM. Henpecked husband.
calla f. *Amer.* Dibble.
callada f. Silence (silencio). || — *A la callada* or *de callada*, on the quiet, on the sly. || *Dar la callada por respuesta*, to say nothing in reply, not to deign to answer.
calladamente adv. Silently, without saying a word.
callado, da adj. Silent, quiet: *esos niños están demasiado callados*, those children are too quiet. || Reserved, quiet: *un chico muy callado*, a very reserved boy. || Secret (secreto). || — *De callado*, quietly, discreetly. || FIG. *Más callado que un muerto*, as close as a clam, as quiet as a mouse. || *No se queda nunca callado*, he always has an answer, he has an answer to everything. || *Tener a alguien callado*, to keep s.o. quiet. || *Tener algo callado*, to keep sth. quiet.
callampa f. *Amer.* Mushroom (hongo). | FAM. Felt hat (sombrero). | Umbrella (paraguas).
callana f. *Amer.* Dish [used by Indians for roasting maize].
callandico o **callandito** adv. FAM. On the quiet, on the sly (en secreto). | Quietly, silently (en silencio).
callar v. intr. y pr. To be quiet, to keep quiet: *los niños deben callar cuando hablan las personas mayores*, children should be quiet when adults are speaking. || To remain silent, to shut up (fam.): *dicho esto, calló*,

having said this, he remained silent. || To stop (ruido). || To stop, to fall silent (un motor). || To be stilled (el mar, el viento). || — FIG. *Al buen callar llaman Sancho*, discretion is the better part of valour. || *A la chita callando*, on the quiet, on the sly. || FIG. *¡Calla! o ¡calle!*, never!, go on!, no! (de asombro). | *Calla callando*, discreetly, quietly. || *¡Cállate!*, keep quiet!, be quiet! || FAM. *Cállate la boca*, shut up!, shut your mouth! || *¡Cállense!*, keep quiet!, be quiet! || *Hacer callar a uno*, to silence s.o., to shut s.o. up (fam.). || *Quien calla otorga*, silence gives consent. || *Sería mejor callarse*, it would be best to say nothing.
— V. tr. To silence, to shut up (fam.) [a una persona]. || To keep (un secreto). || Not to mention, to say nothing about, to keep to o.s.: *he callado su nombre*, I have not mentioned his name. || To hush up, to keep quiet about (un asunto vergonzoso).

calle f. Street, road: *calle mayor*, main *o* high street; *en la calle*, in the street. || Lane (de autopista, piscina, atletismo). || IMPR. River. || — FIG. y FAM. *Abrir calle*, to clear the way, to make way. | *Azotar calles*, to roam the streets. || *Calle abajo*, down the street. || *Calle arriba*, up the street. || *Calle de dirección única*, one-way street. || FAM. *Coger la calle*, to clear off. | *Dejar en la calle*, to throw out, to turn [s.o.] out onto the street (despedir), to leave destitute (arruinar). || *Doblar la calle*, to turn the corner. || FIG. *Echar* or *tirar por la calle de en medio*, to forge ahead *o* to go ahead regardless. | *Echarse a la calle*, to go out into the street (salir), to riot (sublevarse). | *El hombre de la calle*, the man in the street. | *Estar en la calle*, to be out (haber salido), to be destitute (ser pobre). | *Hacer calle*, to line the streets. | *Llevarse de calle a uno*, to win s.o. over (despertar simpatía, etc.), to defeat (en una discusión). | *Pasear* or *rondar la calle*, to court. || FIG. y FAM. *Plantar en la calle* or *echar a la calle*, to throw *o* to turf out. | *Poner de patitas en la calle*, to throw *o* to turf out. | *Quedarse en la calle*, to be homeless, to be in the street (sin casa), to be left jobless (sin empleo).

calleja f. Alley, narrow street (calle pequeña).

callejear v. intr. To wander *o* to stroll about the streets (deambular). || To loiter about (vagar).

callejeo m. Strolling *o* wandering about (paseo). || Loitering (vagabundeo).

callejero, ra adj. Fond of wandering about (amigo de callejear). || In the street: *la animación callejera*, animation in the street. || Street: *festejo callejero*, street festivity; *venta callejera*, street sale. || Popular: *obra callejera*, popular work. || Stray: *perro callejero*, stray dog.
— M. Street guide *o* map (guía de calles). || Directory classified by streets (guía telefónica).

callejón m. Alley, narrow street. || TAUR. Barricaded passage around the edge of bullring. || — *Callejón sin salida*, cul-de-sac, blind alley (calle). || FIG. *En un callejón sin salida*, at an impasse, deadlocked, at a stalemate.

callejuela f. Back street, back alley (calle). || FIG. Way out, loophole (evasiva).

callicida m. MED. Corn remover, corn plaster, corn cure.

callista m. y f. Chiropodist.

callo m. MED. Corn (en los pies), callus, callous (en los pies o en las manos). | Callus (de una fractura). || Caulk, calk (de herradura). || FIG. y FAM. Horror, sight (persona fea). || — Pl. Tripe, *sing.* (plato). || *Callos a la madrileña*, tripe speciality of Madrid.

callosidad f. Callosity, callus.

calloso, sa adj. Callous, hard: *manos callosas*, callous hands. || ANAT. *Cuerpo calloso*, corpus callosum.

cama f. Bed: *cama de campaña*, camp bed; *cama de matrimonio*, double bed; *camas separadas* or *gemelas*, twin beds; *destapar la cama*, to throw the covers off the bed; *ir a la cama*, to go to bed. || Bedstead (armadura del lecho). || Bed: *hospital de cien camas*, hundred-bed hospital. || Form (de la liebre). || Harbour [U.S., harbor] (del ciervo). || Lair (de otros animales salvajes). || Litter (camada de perros, de gatos, etc.). || Brood (camada de aves). || Floor (suelo de la carreta). || Part of melon which touches the ground. || FIG. Layer: *una cama de tierra*, a layer of earth. || AGR. Beam (del arado). || MAR. Bed (hoyo del casco en la arena). || — FIG. *Caer en (la) cama*, to fall ill. || *Cama de paja*, litter. || DEP. *Cama elástica*, trampolin. || *Cama individual*, single bed. || *Cama turca*, couch, divan. || *Echarse en la cama*, to lie down on the bed. || *Estar en cama*, *guardar cama* or *hacer cama*, to be confined to bed, to stay in bed. || *Hacer la cama a la inglesa*, to straighten the bed. || *Hacer las camas*, to make the beds. || FIG. y FAM. *Hacerle a uno la cama*, to put the skids under s.o. (causar perjuicio). || *Meterse en la cama*, to go to bed (acostarse), to get into bed (entre las sábanas).

camada f. Litter (de animales). || Brood (de pájaros). || Layer: *caja con dos camadas de huevos*, box with two layers of eggs. || FIG. y FAM. Band, gang (de ladrones). || FAM. *Son lobos de la misma camada*, v. LOBO.

camafeo m. Cameo (piedra grabada, pintura).

camagua f. *Amer.* Ripening maize, ripening corn (maíz).

camal m. Halter (cabestro). || *Amer.* Slaughterhouse, abattoir.

camaleón m. Chameleon (reptil). || FIG. Chameleon (persona).

camamila f. Camomile.

camándula f. Rosary. || FAM. Cunning, slyness (astucia). | Trick (treta). | Hypocrisy (hipocresía).

camandulero, ra adj. FAM. Sly, cunning (astuto). | Hypocritical (hipócrita).
— M. y f. FAM. Sly *o* cunning dog (persona astuta). | Hypocrite (hipócrita). | Trickster (tramposo). || Sanctimonious person (beato). || — M. Bigot, hypocrite (mojigato).

cámara f. Room (habitación). || (Ant.). Royal chamber (dormitorio). || Council, board, chamber (consejo). || House, chamber: *cámara alta, baja*, upper, lower house. || Inner tube (neumático). || Loft (desván). || ANAT. Cavity (de la boca). | Socket (del ojo). || CINEM. Camera. || AGR. Granary. || MAR. Wardroom (de los oficiales). | Saloon (de los pasajeros). || MIL. Breech, chamber (de las armas de fuego). || TECN. Chamber (de un horno, de un motor, de una esclusa). || — Pl. Faeces (excremento), diarrhoea, *sing.* (diarrea). || — CINEM. *A cámara lenta*, v. LENTO. || *Ayuda de cámara*, valet. || *Cámara acorazada*, strongroom, vault. || *Cámara de cine*, cinecamera. || *Cámara de comercio*, chamber of commerce. || *Cámara de compensación*, clearinghouse. || *Cámara de compresión*, compression chamber. || *Cámara de Diputados*, Chamber of Deputies. || *Cámara de gas*, gas chamber. || *Cámara de los Comunes, de los Lores*, House of Commons, of Lords. || *Cámara de Representantes*, House of Representatives (en los Estados Unidos). || *Cámara de resonancia*, echo chamber. || *Cámara de televisión*, television camera. || *Cámara fotográfica*, camera, still camera. || *Cámara frigorífica*, cold-storage room. || *Cámara mortuoria*, funeral chamber, chapelle ardente. || *Cámara nupcial*, bridal suite. || *Cámara oscura*, camera obscura. || *De cámara*, royal, court: *médico de cámara*, royal doctor. || *Gentilhombre de cámara*, gentleman-in-waiting. || *Música de cámara*, chamber music.
— M. CINEM. Cameraman.

camarada m. Colleague: *mi camarada el Doctor Blanco*, my colleague, Doctor Blanco. || Comrade (en política). || — *Camarada de colegio*, classmate, fellow pupil, schoolfellow: *somos camaradas de colegio*, we are classmates. || *Camarada de trabajo*, workmate, fellow worker, workfellow.

camaradería f. Comradeship, friendship, companionship, camaraderie (relación entre camaradas). || Team spirit (de un equipo).

camarera f. Waitress (en un café, restaurante). || Stewardess (en un barco, avión). || Chambermaid (que arregla las habitaciones en un hotel). || Servant, maid (sirvienta). || Headmaid (en casa principal). || Lady-in-waiting (de una reina). || — *Camarera de teatro*, wardrobe mistress. || *Camarera mayor de la Reina*, the Queen's first lady-in-waiting.

camarería f. Position of head maid.

camarero m. Waiter (en un café, restaurante). || Steward (en un barco, avión). || Valet (de un rey). || Wardrobe master (en el teatro). || (Ant.). Chamberlain (del papa). || *Camarero de piso*, boots (en un hotel).
— Interj. Waiter!

camareta f. MAR. Deck cabin. || *Amer.* Type of gun for shooting fireworks.

camarilla f. Clique, camarilla, cabal, pressure group (grupo). || Lobby (en el Parlamento).

camarín m. Dressing room (de los actores, tocador). || Alcove, niche (para las estatuas). || Room (donde se guarda una colección). || Study (despacho).

camarista f. Lady-in-waiting.

camarlengado m. Office of camerlengo *o* camerlingo.

camarlengo m. Camerlingo, camerlengo (dignidad eclesiástica).

camarón m. Shrimp (de mar). || Camaron (de agua dulce). || *Amer.* Tip (propina).

camaronero, ra m. y f. Shrimp fisher, shrimp catcher (pescador). || Shrimp seller (vendedor).

camarote m. MAR. Cabin.

camarotero m. *Amer.* Steward.

camastro m. Rough old bed, makeshift bed (cama mala).

camastrón, ona m. y f. FAM. Sly *o* cunning dog, crafty person, sly old fox (astuto).

cambalache m. FAM. Swap, exchange. || *Amer.* Secondhand shop.

cambalachear v. tr. FAM. To swap, to exchange.

cámbaro m. Crayfish, crawfish (cangrejo de mar).

cambiable adj. Changeable (susceptible de ser alterado). || Exchangeable (susceptible de ser cambiado por otra cosa).

cambiadiscos m. inv. Record changer.

cambiadizo, za adj. Changeable, inconsistent: *persona cambiadiza*, changeable person.

cambiador, ra m. y f. Moneychanger. || — M. Control, control switch (mando). || *Amer.* Pointsman [U.S., switchman] (guardagujas). || TECN. *Cambiador de calor*, heat exchanger.

cambiante adj. Changing (que altera). || Exchanging. || Changeable, inconsistent (carácter).
— M. Watered effect, iridescence (de tela). || Lustre, glitter, gleam (visos) [used mainly in the plural]. || Money changer (de monedas).

cambiar v. tr. To change: *cambiar una rueda*, to change a wheel; *han cambiado el horario*, they have changed the timetable. || To exchange: *cambiar sellos con un filatelista*, to exchange stamps with a stamp collector; *cambiar impresiones*, to exchange views; *he cambiado mi pluma por otra*, I've exchanged my pen for another; *nos cambiamos los libros*, we exchanged books. || To move: *lo cambié a otro sitio*, I moved it to another place. || To change: *cambiar pesetas en libras*, to change pesetas into pounds; *la noticia cambió la tristeza en alegría*, the news changed sadness into joy. || To change, to give change for: *¿me puede cambiar un billete de mil pesetas?*, can you change a thousand peseta note for me?, can you give me change for a thousand peseta note? || To change (devolver a una tienda). || To alter (un vestido). || To reverse: *cambiar los papeles*, to reverse the roles. || — FIG. *Cambiar el disco*, to change the record. | *Cambiar la chaqueta*, to turn one's coat, to change sides.
— V. intr. To change: *no has cambiado nada*, you haven't changed a bit; *ha cambiado el tiempo*, the weather has changed; *cambiar de libros, de costumbres*, to change books, one's habits. || To veer, to change round (el viento). || To give change (dar cambio). || To get some change (pedir cambio). || AUT. To change gear, to change (de velocidad). || — *Cambiar de casa*, to move. || *Cambiar de dueño*, to change hands (una cosa). || *Cambiar de idea*, to change one's mind. || *Cambiar de manos* or *de mano*, to change hands. || MAR. *Cambiar de rumbo*, to come about. || *Cambiar de sitio*, to move, to change places. || FIG. *Cambiar más que una veleta*, to change with the wind. || *Amer.* FAM. *Mandarse cambiar*, to get out.
— V. pr. To change (de ropa). || To change: *se cambió de zapatos*, he changed his shoes. || To change, to change round (el viento). || — *Cambiarse de ropa*, to change one's clothes, to get changed. || FIG. *Cambiarse la chaqueta*, to turn one's coat, to change sides.
cambiazo m. Switch. || FAM. *Dar el cambiazo a uno*, to do a switch on s.o. || *Dar un cambiazo*, to do a switch.
cambio m. Changing: *el cambio de una rueda*, the changing of a wheel; *cambio de guardia*, changing of the guard. || Exchanging: *el cambio de una cosa por otra*, the exchanging of one thing for another. || Reversal: *el cambio de papeles*, the reversal of roles. || Turn (de la marea). || Shift, move (de sitios). || Change (modificación): *cambio de tiempo*, change in the weather; *cambio de plan*, change of plan; *cambio de política*, change of policy. || COM. Rate of exchange: *¿a cuánto está el cambio de la peseta hoy?*, what is the rate of exchange of the peseta today? || Changeover: *el cambio al sistema decimal*, the changeover to the decimal system. || Price, quotation: *el cambio de acciones*, the price of shares. || Change (moneda fraccionaria): *¿tiene usted cambio?*, have you any change? || Exchange (trueque): *perder con el cambio*, to lose in the exchange. || Gear change [U.S., gearshift] (de velocidad). || FIG. Change, reversal (en su opinión). || — *A cambio de*, in exchange for. || COM. *Agente de Cambio y Bolsa*, stockbroker. || FIG. *A las primeras de cambio*, v. PRIMERA. || AUT. *Caja de cambios*, gearbox. | *Cambio automático*, automatic transmission. || *Cambio de impresiones*, exchange of views. || AUT. *Cambio de marcha* or *de velocidades*, gear change [U.S., gearshift] || *Cambio de vía*, points. || *Cambio escénico*, scene change (teatro). || *Casa de cambio*, foreign exchange office. || *Caseta* or *cabina de cambio de agujas*, signal box. || *En cambio*, on the other hand, however (al contrario), in return: *hazme este favor y en cambio te haré otro*, do me this favour and in return I'll do you one. || *En cambio de*, instead of, in the place of in place of. || *Letra de cambio*, bill of exchange. || *Libre cambio*, free trade. || *Zona de libre cambio*, free-trade area.
cambista m. Cambist (de letras de cambio). || Money changer (de moneda).
Camboya n. pr. f. GEOGR. Cambodia.
camboyano, na adj./s. Cambodian.
cambray m. Cambric (tela).
cambriano, na o **cámbrico, ca** adj. GEOL. Cambrian.
cambrón m. BOT. Buckthorn (espino cerval). | Bramble (zarza). | Christ's thorn (espina santa).
cambronal m. Bramble patch.
cambullón m. *Amer.* Trick (trampa). | Swap, exchange (cambalache). | Intrigue (intriga).
camelador, ra adj. Flattering (halagador).
— M. y f. Flatterer.
camelar v. tr. FAM. To flatter, to butter up, to get round (halagar): *hace lo que puede para camelar al jefe*, he does what he can to flatter the boss. || To woo, to court (enamorar). || *Amer.* To watch, to look at (mirar).
— V. pr. To flatter, to butter up, to get round.
cameleo m. FAM. Flattery.
camelia f. BOT. Camellia (planta).
camélidos m. pl. ZOOL. Camelidae.
camelista m. y f. FAM. Joker (cuentista). | Flatterer (el que halaga).
— Adj. FAM. Would-be, sham: *un pintor camelista*, a would-be artist.
camelo m. FAM. Flattery, flirting (galanteo). | Cock-and-bull story (cuento). | Joke, hoax: *es puro camelo*, it's a big hoax. | Con (timo). || — FAM. *Dar el camelo a uno*, to take s.o. in, to pull a fast one on s.o., to diddle s.o. | *De camelo*, would-be, sham: *un escritor de camelo*, a would-be writer. | *Me huele a camelo*, it smells fishy to me.
camella f. She-camel (rumiante). || AGR. Ridge (caballón). || Trough (artesa).
camellero Cameleer.
camello m. Camel (rumiante). || MAR. Camel (pontón).
camellón m. AGR. Ridge (caballón). || Trough (artesa, bebedero).
cameraman m. Cameraman.
— OBSERV. Pl. *cameramen* en ambos idiomas.
— *Cameraman* is an Anglicism which can be replaced by the Spanish word *cámara, m.*
camerino m. TEATR. Dressing room.
camero, ra adj. Double-bed, double: *manta camera*, double-bed blanket. || *Cama camera*, double bed.
Camerún n. pr. m. GEOGR. Cameroons, *pl.* (antiguo protectorado). | Cameroun (estado actual).
Camila n. pr. f. Camilla, Camille.
Camilo n. pr. m. Camillus.
camilla f. Small bed (cama para descansar). || Stretcher (para enfermos). || Round table under which a brazier is placed. || — *Camilla de ruedas*, hospital trolley. || *Mesa camilla*, round table under which a brazier is placed.
camillero Stretcher-bearer.
caminante m. y f. Traveller.
caminar v. intr. To travel (viajar): *caminar de noche*, to travel by night. || To walk (andar). || To move (desplazarse). || FIG. To make its way, to move (un río, un astro). | To head: *caminar a su perdición*, to be heading for ruin. || FIG. *Caminar derecho*, to keep to the straight and narrow.
— V. tr. To travel, to go, to cover (recorrer): *hemos caminado tres kilómetros*, we have covered three kilometres.
caminata f. FAM. Long walk (paseo largo): *darse una caminata*, to go for *o* to take a long walk. | Trek, hike (largo y fatigoso). || Distance, stretch (distancia).
caminero, ra adj. Road. || *Peón caminero*, navvy, roadman.
camino m. Path, track (vía): *camino de cabaña*, animal path. || Road (carretera): *camino vecinal*, local road. || Route, itinerary (itinerario). || Way: *te vi en el camino de casa al colegio*, I saw you on the way to school. || Journey: *hizo dos veces el camino al despacho*, he made the journey to the office twice. || FIG. Path, road [*de*, to] (del honor, de la gloria, de la virtud, etc.). | Way (medio): *el camino para hacerse rico*, the way to make o.s. rich. || — *Abrir camino*, to make *o* to clear a way. || *Abrirse camino*, to make one's way, to force one's way (al andar), to go places, to get on well (en la vida). || *A camino largo, paso corto*, slow and steady wins the race. || *Allanar el camino*, to smooth the way. || *A medio camino* or *a la mitad del camino*, halfway. || *Camino adelante*, straight on. || *Camino carretero* or *de ruedas*, road. || *Camino de*, towards: *vamos camino de España*, we are going towards Spain; on the way to: *camino del colegio le encontramos*, we met him on the way to school. || *Camino de entrada*, approach road. || *Camino de herradura*, bridle path. || *Camino de hierro*, railway. || *Camino de ronda*, parapet walk, rampart walk. || FIG. y FAM. *Camino de rosas*, bed of roses. || ASTR. *Camino de Santiago*, the Milky Way. || *Camino de sirga*, towpath. || *Camino forestal*, forest track. || *Camino real*, main road (carretera), the shortest way (lo más corto). || *Caminos, canales y puertos*, civil engineering (carrera). || FIG. *Camino trillado* or *trivial*, the beaten track. || *¿Cuánto camino hay de aquí a Madrid?*, how far is it from here to Madrid? || *De camino*, on the way, on one's way: *su casa nos coge de camino*, his house is on the way *o* on our way; travelling: *traje de camino*, travelling clothes; at the same time (al mismo tiempo). || FIG. *Dejar en el camino*, to leave unfinished. || *Después de un día de camino*, after a day's travelling. || FIG. *Echar camino adelante*, to strike out. | *En camino de desaparecer*, on its way out. | *Errar el camino*, to go the wrong way, to mistake the way. | *Escoger el buen camino*, to make the right choice. || *Hacerse su camino*, to go places, to get on well. || *Ir de camino por un sitio*, to pass through *o* to travel through a place. || *Ir fuera de camino*, to go the wrong way. || *Ir por buen camino*, to be on the right road, to be going the right way (seguir la buena dirección), to follow the straight and narrow (obrar como es debido). || *Ir por mal camino*, to be going the wrong way (dirección), to go astray (conducta). || FIG. *Ir por su camino*, to go one's own sweet way. | *Llevar a alguien por mal camino*, to lead s.o. astray. | *Llevar buen camino*, to be on the right track, to be going the right way, to be doing well *o* getting along well. | *Llevar camino de*, to be on the way to, to look as if: *lleva camino de ganar*, he is on the way to victory *o* to winning, he looks as if he will win; to look as if: *el trabajo lleva camino de no acabarse nunca*, it looks as if this job will never be finished. || *Pillarle de camino a uno*, to be on the way. || *Ponerse en camino*, to set off. || *Por buen camino*, along the right road. || *Salirle a uno al camino*, to go to meet s.o. || *¡Siga usted su camino!*, on your way!, pass along! || *Si te quieres*

matar vas por buen camino, if you want to kill yourself you're going the right way about it. || FIG. *Todos los caminos van a Roma*, all roads lead to Rome. || *Tomar el camino más largo*, to go the long way round. || FIG. *Traer a uno al buen camino*, to put s.o. right, to put s.o. on the right track.

camión m. Lorry [U.S., truck] (vehículo). || — *Camión cisterna*, tanker. || *Camión de bomberos*, fire engine. || *Camión de carga pesada*, heavy lorry, heavy goods vehicle. || *Camión de la basura*, dustcart, refuse lorry. || *Camión de mudanzas*, removal van. || *Camión de riego*, water cart, water wagon. || FIG. y FAM. *Está como un camión*, she's a bit of all right, she's gorgeous. || *Transportar en camión*, to ship *o* to haul by lorry.

camionaje m. Haulage, cartage (transporte y precio pagado).

camionero m. Lorry driver [U.S., truck driver, teamster].

camioneta f. Van.

camisa f. Shirt (ropa). || Skin (de ciertas semillas). || Slough (de las serpientes). || Folder (envoltura de papel). || Jacket, dust jacket (de un libro). || TECN. Lining (de horno). | Sleeve (de cilindro). | Gas mantle (manguito). | Facing (enlucido de cemento y yeso). | Jacket: *camisa de agua*, water jacket. || — FAM. *Cambiar de camisa*, to turn one's coat, to change sides (chaquetear). || *Camisa de dormir*, nightdress, nightgown, nightie (fam.) [de mujer], nightshirt (de hombre). || *Camisa de fuerza*, straightjacket, straitjacket. || FAM. *Dejarle a uno sin camisa*, to ruin s.o., to leave s.o. penniless. || *Estar en mangas de camisa*, to be in one's shirt-sleeves. || FAM. *Jugarse uno hasta la camisa*, to stake one's shirt. | *Meterse en camisa de once varas*, to poke one's nose in other people's business (entrometerse), to bite off more than one can chew (abarcar demasiado). | *No llegar a uno la camisa al cuerpo*, to be scared stiff. | *¡No te metas en camisa de once varas!*, mind your own business! | *Perder hasta la camisa*, to lose one's shirt.

camisería f. Shirt shop, outfitter's (tienda). || Shirt industry (industria).

camisero, ra m. y f. Shirt maker, outfitter (persona).
— Adj. *Blusa camisera*, shirt blouse, shirtwaist. || *Vestido camisero*, shirtwaist dress.

camiseta f. T-shirt (camisa corta). || Vest [U.S., undershirt] (de ropa interior). || Shirt (de rugby, fútbol). || Singlet, vest (para el atletismo). || *Camiseta de punto*, vest [U.S., undershirt].

camisola f. Camisole (blusa, camisa). || Shirt (camisa, camiseta).

camisolín m. Dicky, dickey.

camisón m. Nightgown, nightdress, nightie (fam.) [de mujer]. || Nightshirt (de hombre). || *Amer.* Lady's shirt.

camoatí m. *Amer.* Wasp (avispa).

camomila f. BOT. Camomile (manzanilla).

camorra f. FAM. Quarrel, fight, trouble: *buscar camorra*, to be asking for trouble, to be looking for a fight *o* a quarrel. | Row: *armar camorra*, to kick up a row.

camorrero, ra o **camorrista** adj. Quarrelsome, rowdy.
— M. y f. Troublemaker, rowdy.

camote m. *Amer.* Sweet potato (batata). | Bulb (bulbo). | Love, infatuation (enamoramiento). | Lover, mistress (querida). | Fool, simpleton (tonto). || *Amer.* FIG. y FAM. *Tragar camote*, to stammer, to stutter.

campal adj. f. *Batalla campal*, pitched battle.

campamento m. Encampment, camping (acción de acampar). || Camp, encampment (lugar). || Camp (tropa acampada): *campamento volante*, temporary camp. || — *Campamento de trabajo*, workcamp. || *Campamento de verano*, summer camp.

campana f. Bell: *las campanas de la iglesia*, the church bells. || Mantelpiece (parte exterior de la chimenea), hood (parte interior). || TECN. Caisson (obras públicas). || Bell (objeto de forma de campana). || Parish (parroquia). || Parish church (iglesia). || Curfew (queda). || — *Campana de buzo* or *de inmersión*, diving bell. || *Campana de cristal*, bell jar, bell glass. || *Campana mayor*, great bell. || *Dar la vuelta de campana*, to overturn (un coche). || *Echar las campanas a vuelo*, to set all the bells ringing, to ring all the bells full peal (sentido propio), to shout from the rooftops (cacarear), to be overcome with joy, to rejoice (alegrarse). || *Por quién doblan las campanas*, for whom the bell tolls (obra). || *Tañer las campanas* or *tocar las campanas*, to peal the bells, to ring the bells. || *Un toque de campana*, a peal *o* a stroke of the bell. || FIG. *Usted ha oído campanas y no sabe dónde*, you don't really know what you are talking about.

campanada f. Peal *o* stroke *o* ring of a bell (toque). || FIG. Scandal, sensation (escándalo): *dar una* or *la campanada*, to cause a scandal, to cause a sensation.

campanario m. Belfry, bell tower (de iglesia).

campanear v. intr. To ring the bells (tañer). || *Amer.* To spy (espiar). || FAM. *Allá se las campanee*, let him look after himself.

campaneo m. Peal *o* chime of bells (de campana). || FIG. y FAM. Swagger (contoneo).

campanero m. Bell founder (fundidor). || Bellringer (el que tañe).

campaniforme adj. Campanulate.

campanil adj. Bell: *metal campanil*, bell metal.
— M. Belfry, bell tower (campanario), campanile (campanilo).

campanilo m. Bell tower, campanile (en Italia).

campanilla f. Small bell (campana). || Electric bell (eléctrica). || Handbell (para llamar). || Bubble (burbuja). || Tassel (adorno de pasamanería). || ANAT. Uvula (úvula). || BOT. Bellflower (flor). || FIG. *De muchas campanillas*, of great importance.

campanillazo m. Ring *o* tinkle of a bell. || Clang (ruido fuerte).

campanillear v. intr. To tinkle, to ring (campanillas).

campanilleo m. Tinkling, ringing (tintineo).

campanillero m. Bellringer.

campanología f. Campanology.

campante adj. FAM. Unruffled, relaxed, cool (tranquilo): *había perdido todo su dinero, pero se quedó tan campante*, he had lost all his money, but he remained quite cool *o* but he was completely unruffled. || Proud, pleased: *va tan campante con sus nuevos zapatos*, he is so proud of *o* pleased with his new shoes.

campanudo, da adj. Bell-shaped. || FIG. High-sounding, bombastic, pompous (lenguaje), pompous, grandiloquent (orador).

campánula f. BOT. Campanula (farolillo). || *Campánula azul*, bluebell.

campanuláceas f. pl. BOT. Campanulaceae.

campaña f. Plain: *campaña fértil*, fertile plain. || MIL. Campaign. || FIG. Campaign: *campaña publicitaria*, *parlamentaria*, *electoral*, advertising, parliamentary, electoral campaign. || *Amer.* Countryside. || — *Cama de campaña*, camp bed. || MAR. *Campaña de pesca*, fishing trip. || MIL. *De campaña*, field. || *Misa de campaña*, open-air mass. || *Tienda de campaña*, tent.

campañol m. Vole (animal).

campar v. intr. To stand out, to excel (sobresalir). || To camp (acampar). || FIG. *Campar por sus respetos*, to do as one pleases.

campeador adj. m. Valiant, extremely brave.
— M. Warrior.

campear v. intr. AGR. To graze in the fields (los animales). || FIG. To abound: *en su prosa campea la ironía*, irony abounds in his prose. || To turn *o* to show green (los sembrados). || *Amer.* To search *o* to scour the countryside.

campechanía f. FAM. Good nature, geniality (bondad). || Openness, straightforwardness.

campechano, na adj. FAM. Good-natured, genial (bonachón). | Straightforward, open (sin cumplidos).
— F. *Amer.* Whore (prostituta).

campeche m. BOT. *Palo (de) campeche*, logwood, campeachy wood.

campeón, ona adj. Champion.
— M. y f. Champion: *un campeón ciclista*, a champion cyclist. || FIG. *Hacerse el campeón de una causa*, to champion a cause.

campeonato m. Championship. || FIG. y FAM. *De campeonato*, terrific, fantastic, great: *una paliza de campeonato*, a terrific beating; absolute, out-and-out: *un tonto de campeonato*, an absolute idiot.

campero, ra adj. Country, rural (relativo al campo). || Open-air (al aire libre). || Not brought in at night (ganado). || *Amer.* With experience of the country. || *Traje campero*, outfit worn by Andalusian herdsman.
— M. Jeep (coche).

campesinado m. Peasants, *pl.*, peasantry.

campesino, na adj. Country, rural, rustic (del campo): *costumbres campesinas*, rural customs. || *Ratón campesino*, field mouse.
— M. y f. Peasant, countryman, countrywoman.

campestre adj. Rural, country, rustic.

camping m. Camping (actividad). || Camping ground, camping site (terreno). || *Hacer camping*, to camp, to go camping.
— OBSERV. The plural of the Spanish word *camping* is *campings*.

campiña f. Stretch of cultivated land. || Countryside: *la campiña española*, the Spanish countryside.

campista m. Camper. || *Amer.* Herdsman (ganadero).

campo m. Field: *un campo de trigo*, a field of wheat. || Open country (en contraposición a montaña): *desde mi ventana se ve un trozo de campo*, from my window you can see a stretch of open country. || Country: *pasar las vacaciones en el campo*, to spend one's holidays in the country. || Countryside (paisaje): *el campo está hermoso después de la lluvia*, the countryside is beautiful after the rain. || FIG. Field: *campo de actividad*, *de la medicina*, field of activity, of medicine. | Camp (facción): *el campo carlista*, the Carlist camp. || DEP. Pitch (terreno de juego, en fútbol), ground (conjunto de terreno y tribunas). | Course (de golf). | Court (de tenis). | Side (lado del terreno). || HERÁLD. Field. || Background (fondo). || MIL. Field. | Camp: *campo atrincherado*, entrenched camp. | Army (ejército). || — *A campo raso*, open to the sky (sin techo), in the open air, under the stars: *dormir a campo raso*, to sleep in the open air. || *A campo traviesa*, across country. || *Batir* or *descubrir* or *reconocer el campo*, to scour the countryside. || *Campo aurífero*, goldfield. || *Campo de aterrizaje*, landing field. || *Campo de aviación*, airfield. || MIL. *Campo de batalla*, battlefield. || *Campo de concentración*, concentration camp. || *Campo deportivo* or *de deportes*, sports ground, playing field. || MIL. *Campo de minas*, minefield. || *Campo de trabajo*, work camp. || ELECTR. y FÍS. *Campo de un microscopio,* field of a microscope. | *Campo eléctrico, magnético, óptico,* electric, magnetic, optic field. || MED. *Campo operatorio,* operative field. || *Campo petrolífero,* oilfield. || *Campo raso,* open country. || *Campo santo,* cemetery. || MIT. *Campos Elíseos,* Elysian Fields. || *Campo visual,* field of vision. || *Carrera a campo través* or *traviesa,* cross-country [race]. || *Casa de campo,* country house. || *Conejo de campo,* wild rabbit. || FIG. *Creer que todo el campo es orégano,* to think that life is just a bowl of cherries. || *Dejar el campo libre,* to leave the field open. || *En campo raso,* in the open country. || *Feria del campo,* agricultural show. || *Hacer campo,* to clear a space. || *Levantar el campo,* to strike *o* to break camp (sentido propio), to leave (largarse), to give up (abandonar el campo). || *Montar el campo,* to pitch camp. || FOT. *Profundidad de campo,* depth of field. || *Retirarse al campo,* to retire to the country. || FIG. *Tener campo libre,* to have a clear field, to have an open hand. || *Trabajo de campo,* fieldwork.

camposanto m. Cemetery.

campus m. Campus (recinto universitario).

camuesa f. Pippin (manzana).

camueso m. Apple tree. || FIG. Fool, idiot.

camuflaje m. MIL. Camouflage.

camuflar v. tr. MIL. To camouflage. || FIG. To hide, to cover up.

can m. Dog (perro). || ARQ. Corbel. | Modillion (modillón). || MIL. Trigger (gatillo). || — ASTR. *Can* or *Can Mayor,* Greater Dog. | *Can Menor,* Lesser Dog.

— OBSERV. The word *can* is used especially in poetry. *Perro* is the usual word for dog.

cana f. White *o* grey hair. || — FIG. y FAM. *Echar una cana al aire,* to have a fling, to cut loose, to let one's hair down. | *Peinar canas,* to be getting old, to be going grey.

canaca m. *Amer.* Chinese, Chinaman (chino). | Brothel keeper (dueño de un burdel).

canaco, ca adj. Kanaka (de Nueva Caledonia). || *Amer.* Yellowish.

Canadá n. pr. m. GEOGR. Canada.

canadiense adj./s. Canadian. || — F. Fur-lined lumber jacket (pelliza).

canal m. Canal: *canal navegable,* navigable canal; *canal de Panamá,* Panama canal. || Channel, ditch: *canal de riego,* irrigation channel. || Channel: *el canal del puerto,* the channel of the port; *el canal de la Mancha,* the English Channel. || Channel (de televisión). || FIG. Channel (vía): *canales comerciales,* commercial channels. || Pipe: *el agua pasa por canales de plomo,* the water flows through lead pipes. || ANAT. Canal. || ARQ. Gutter tile (del tejado). || — *Canal de desagüe,* sewer. || MAR. *Canal de experiencia,* experimental tank. || — F. Carcass, carcase, dressed body (de un animal). || Fluting, canal (de una columna). || Front edge (de un libro). || — *Abrir en canal,* to slit from top to bottom. || *Canal maestra,* gutter. || FAM. *Mojar la canal maestra,* to wet one's whistle.

— Adj. FÍS. *Rayos canales,* canal rays.

canalado, da adj. Fluted, grooved.

canaladura f. ARQ. Flute.

canalera f. ARQ. Guttering.

canaleta f. *Amer.* Gutter.

canalete m. Paddle (remo).

canalizable adj. Canalizable (río).

canalización f. Canalization. || TECN. Piping (tubería). || *Amer.* Sewage system, sewers, *pl.*

canalizar v. tr. To canalize (un río). || To channel (agua). || To pipe (por tuberías). || FIG. To channel: *canalizar ideas,* to channel ideas.

canalizo m. MAR. Fairway, navigable channel.

canalón m. Fallpipe, drainpipe (conducto vertical). || Gutter (conducto en el borde del tejado). || Shovel hat.

canalones m. pl. Cannelons, canneloni (pasta alimenticia).

canalla f. Mob, rabble, riffraff.

— M. FAM. Swine, rotter: *¡qué canalla!,* the swine!

canallada f. Vile trick, dirty trick.

canallesco, ca adj. Vile, dirty, rotten: *acción canallesca,* vile deed. || Rascally, roguish: *risa canallesca,* roguish laughter.

canana f. Cartridge belt. || *Amer.* Goitre (bocio).

cananeo, a adj./s. Canaanite.

canapé m. Sofa, couch, settee. || CULIN. Aperitive snack, canapé.

Canarias n. pr. f. pl. GEOGR. *Islas Canarias,* Canary Islands.

canario, ria adj./s. Canarian (de las islas Canarias). || — M. ZOOL. Canary.

canasta f. Basket (cesta): *canasta para la ropa,* clothes basket. || Hamper (cesta muy grande). || Canasta (juego de cartas). || Basket (en el baloncesto).

canastero m. Basket maker (fabricante). || Basket dealer (vendedor). || *Amer.* Barrow boy.

canastilla f. Basket: *la canastilla de la costura,* the sewing basket. || Layette (ropa para recién nacido).

canastillo m. Small basket (canasto pequeño). || Basket: *un canastillo de flores,* a basket of flowers.

canasto m. Basket (canasta). || Hamper (cesta muy grande).

— Interj. *¡Canastos!,* dash! (disgusto, enfado), good grief!, my goodness! (sorpresa).

cáncamo m. Eyebolt (armella).

cancamurria f. FAM. Misery, blues, gloom. || *Amer.* FAM. *Tener cancamurria,* to be fed up, to be down in the dumps.

cancamusa f. FAM. Trick, fraud.

cancán m. Cancan (baile). || Frilly petticoat (ropa interior).

cáncana f. Large brown spider (araña).

cancanear v. intr. FAM. To lounge about, to loaf about, to laze about (vagar). || *Amer.* To stutter, to stammer (tartamudear).

cancaneo m. *Amer.* Stuttering, stammering (tartamudeo).

cáncano m. FAM. Louse (piojo).

cancel m. Storm door (puerta). || Screen partition (mámpara). || *Amer.* Folding screen (biombo).

cancela f. Iron gate.

— OBSERV. In Andalusian houses, the *cancela* separates the porch from the yard.

cancelación f. Cancellation.

cancelar v. tr. To cancel (anular): *cancelaron el contrato,* they cancelled the contract. || To settle, to pay (una deuda).

cancelaría f. Papal chancery.

cáncer m. MED. Cancer. || FIG. Cancer (de la sociedad, etc.).

Cáncer m. ASTR. Cancer.

cancerado, da adj. Cancerous. || FIG. Corrupt.

cancerarse v. pr. MED. To become cancerous (un tumor). | To get cancer (persona). || FIG. To become corrupt (corromperse).

cancerbero m. FIG. Ogre (portero antipático). | Goalkeeper (guardameta).

Cancerbero n. pr. m. MIT. Cerberus.

cancerígeno, na adj. MED. Cancerigenic, cancerogenic.

cancerólogo m. MED. Cancerologist.

canceroso, sa adj. MED. Cancerous: *tumor canceroso,* cancerous tumour.

cancilla f. Gate (puerta).

canciller m. Chancellor (alto funcionario). || *Amer.* Minister of Foreign Affairs (ministro de Asuntos Exteriores).

cancilleresco, ca adj. Diplomatic: *lenguaje cancilleresco,* diplomatic language. || Of chancellors (propio del canciller).

cancillería f. Chancellory, chancellery. || *Amer.* Ministry of Foreign Affairs (ministerio de Asuntos Exteriores).

canción f. Song. || — *Canción báquica,* drinking song. || *Canción cuartelera,* barrack-room song. || *Canción de cuna,* lullaby. || *Canción de gesta,* chanson de geste, epic poem. || *Canción infantil,* nursery rhyme. || FIG. *Volver siempre a* or *estar siempre con la misma canción,* to harp on the same old story.

cancionero m. Collection of lyrical poems. || Songwriter (cancionista). || Song book (libro de canciones).

cancioneta f. Short song.

cancionista m. y f. Songwriter (compositor).

canco m. Earthenware pot (olla). || FAM. Buttocks, *pl.* (nalgas). | Queer (marica).

cancro m. MED. Cancer. || BOT. y VET. Canker.

cancroide m. MED. Cancroid.

cancroideo, a adj. Cancroid.

cancha f. DEP. Ground (de fútbol). | Court (de tenis, de pelota vasca). | Cockpit (de peleas de gallos). | Racecourse (hipódromo). || *Amer.* Open space (terreno libre). | Yard: *cancha de maderas,* timber yard. | Wide part (en un río). || Roasted maize *o* beans (maíz, habas). || — *Amer.* FIG. *Abrir cancha,* to make way, to clear a path. | *Dar cancha a uno,* to give s.o. an advantage. | *Estar en su cancha,* to be in one's element. | *Tener cancha,* to be experienced.

— Interj. *Amer.* Make way!, gangway!

canchal m. Rocky place (peñascal).

canchar v. intr. *Amer.* To spar, to pretend to fight. | To fight with bare fists. | To do business (negociar). | To earn a lot of money (ganar).

canchear v. intr. *Amer.* To mess about.

canchero, ra adj. *Amer.* Expert, skilled.

— M. Groundsman (dueño de una cancha). || Expert (experto). || Grasping priest (párroco).

cancho m. Boulder, rock. || *Amer.* Fees, *pl.* (emolumentos). | Tip (propina).

candado m. Padlock. || *Amer.* Goatee beard (perilla).

candaliza f. MAR. Brail.

candanga f. *Amer.* Devil.

cande adj. Candied, crystalized. || *Azúcar cande,* candy, sugar candy.

candeal adj. *Pan, trigo candeal,* white bread, wheat.

— M. *Amer.* Egg flip.

candela f. Candle (vela de sebo). || Fire (fuego). || Blossom (de encina, de castaño). || FÍS. Candle, candela (unidad de intensidad). || FAM. Light: *pedir, dar candela para un cigarrillo,* to ask for, to give a light for a cigarette. || — FIG. y FAM. *Acabarse la candela,* to kick the bucket, to snuff it. | *Arrimar candela a uno,* to give s.o. a beating. || MAR. *En candela,* on end.

candelabro m. Candelabrum, candelabra. || BOT. Type of cactus.

candelada f. Bonfire (hoguera).
Candelaria f. Candlemas (fiesta).
candelecho m. Vineyard guard's hut.
candelero m. Candlestick (utensilio). || Oil lamp (velón). || Fishing torch (para la pesca). || MAR. Stanchion. || — FIG. *Estar en el candelero,* to be at the top, to be high up (en un lugar destacado), to be very popular (ser popular). | *Poner en el candelero,* to put at the top (en lugar destacado), to make popular (hacer popular).
candelilla f. Small candle (candela pequeña). || MED. Bougie (sonda). || BOT. Catkin (inflorescencia). || *Amer.* Will-o'-the-wisp (fuego fatuo). | Glowworm (luciérnaga). | Type of euphorbia (planta). || — BOT. *Echar candelillas,* to sprout catkins. || FIG. y FAM. *Se le hacen candelillas los ojos,* he's tipsy *o* merry.
candente adj. Candescent, white-hot (blanco). || Incandescent, red-hot (rojo). || FIG. Burning: *problema, cuestión candente,* burning problem, question. | Electric (atmósfera).
candi adj. Crystalized, candied. || *Azúcar candi,* candy, sugar candy.
candidato, ta m. Candidate: *candidato a* or *para un puesto,* candidate for a post.
candidatura f. Candidature, candidacy: *presentar su candidatura,* to put forward one's candidature. || List of candidates (conjunto de candidatos).
candidez f. Frankness, candour. || FIG. Naïvety, ingenuousness (ingenuidad). | Silly remark, stupidity (tontería).
cándido, da adj. POÉT. White, snowy (blanco). | Innocent, pure. || FIG. Naïve, ingenuous, gullible (ingenuo). | Frank, candid (franco).
candil m. Oil lamp (lámpara). || Tine (cuerno). || FIG. y FAM. Point [of cocked hat] (de sombrero). || *Amer.* Chandelier (araña). || — *Baile de candil,* local hop. || FIG. *Ni buscado con candil,* it couldn't be better, it's just what the doctor ordered. || *Pescar al candil,* to fish by torchlight.
candileja f. Small lamp. || BOT. Nigella (neguilla). || — Pl. TEATR. Footlights.
candiota adj./s. Candiote, Candiot. || — F. Barrel (barril). || Earthenware jar (recipiente de barro).
candombe m. *Amer.* South American negro dance. | Drum (tambor).
candombear v. intr. *Amer.* To engage in underhand dealings [in politics].
candonga f. FAM. Blarney (zalamería). | Joking, teasing (burla). | Draught mule (mula). || *Amer.* Stomach band (de recién nacido). || — Pl. *Amer.* Earrings.
candongo, ga adj. FAM. Wheedling, coaxing (zalamero). | Sly, crafty (astuto). | Lazy, idle (holgazán).
— M. y f. FAM. Wheedler, coaxer (zalamero). | Crafty devil, sly one (astuto). | Shirker, layabout, lazybones (holgazán).
candonguear v. tr. FAM. To tease (burlarse de).
— V. intr. FAM. To shirk (ser holgazán).
candonguero, ra adj. FAM. V. CANDONGO.
candor m. Innocence: *el candor de un niño,* the innocence of a child. || Naïvety, ingenuousness, gullibility, credulity (ingenuidad). || Frankness, candidness (candidez). || POÉT. Whiteness.
candoroso, sa adj. Innocent: *un niño candoroso,* an innocent child. || Naïve, gullible, ingenuous, credulous (ingenuo). || Frank, candid (franco).
caneca f. Earthenware bottle (vasija de barro). || *Amer.* Wooden bucket (cubo).
canecillo m. ARQ. Corbel. | Modillion (modillón).
caneco, ca adj. *Amer.* Tipsy, merry (ebrio).
canela f. Cinnamon (especia). || FIG. *Ser canela fina,* to be exquisite (cosa), to be wonderful (persona).
canelé m. Rib (de los calcetines).
canelero m. BOT. Cinnamon [tree] (árbol).
canelo, la adj. Cinnamon, cinnamon-coloured (color).
— M. BOT. Cinnamon (árbol). || FAM. *Hacer el canelo,* to be a mug.
canelón m. Drainpipe, fallpipe (canalón). || Icicle (carámbano). || Curl (de pelo). || Cord (pasamanería). || — Pl. Cannelons, canneloni (pastas alimenticias).
canesú m. Bodice (de vestido de mujer). || Yoke (de camisa).
canevá m. *Amer.* Canvas (cañamazo).
caney m. *Amer.* Hut, cabin (bohío). | Bend (de un río).
cangalla m. y f. *Amer.* Coward (cobarde).
cangilón m. Bucket (de rueda hidráulica). || Scoop, bucket (de una draga). || Earthenware jug *o* jar (vasija). || Goffering, gauffering (pliegue). || *Amer.* Rut (carril). | Pothole (hoyo).
cangreja f. MAR. Brig sail, fore-and-aft sail (vela).
cangrejero, ra m. y f. Crab seller, crayfish seller (vendedor). || — F. Nest of crabs (nido).
cangrejo m. ZOOL. Crab (de mar). | Crayfish (de río). || MAR. Gaff (verga). || Truck (ferrocarril). || ASTR. Cancer. || — FIG. y FAM. *Andar* or *ir para atrás como los cangrejos,* to be slipping. | *Rojo como un cangrejo,* as red as a lobster, as red as a beetroot.
canguelo m. FAM. Funk. || FAM. *Tener canguelo,* to have the wind up.
canguro m. ZOOL. Kangaroo.
caníbal adj. Cannibal, cannibalistic (antropófago). || FIG. Savage, fierce (cruel).
— M. y f. Cannibal.
canibalismo m. Cannibalism.
canica f. Marble: *jugar a las canicas,* to play marbles.
canicie f. Whiteness, greyness (de los cabellos).
canícula f. Dog days, *pl.*
canicular adj. Canicular. || *Calor canicular,* midsummer heat.
— M. pl. Dog days.
caniche m. Poodle (perro).
cánidos m. pl. ZOOL. Canidae.
canijo, ja adj. FAM. Weak, puny (enclenque).
canilla f. ANAT. Long bone, slender bone (hueso). || Wing bone (de ave). || TECN. Bobbin, reel, spool (para el hilo). | Tap, spout, faucet (caño). || *Amer.* Tap (grifo). | Strength (fuerza). || Rib (defecto de tela). || — *Canilla de la pierna,* shinbone. || FIG. y FAM. *Irse de canilla,* to have diarrhoea (padecer diarrea), to spout, to babble (hablar sin ton ni son).
canillera f. Shin guard (para deportes). || Greave (de armadura).
canillero m. Tap hole (piquera).
canillita m. *Amer.* News boy, newspaper boy.
canillón, ona o **canilludo, da** adj. *Amer.* Long-legged.
canino, na adj. Canine: *raza canina,* canine race. || — MED. *Hambre canina,* ravenous hunger. || FIG. *Tener hambre canina,* to be starving.
— M. Canine [tooth].
canje m. Exchange: *canje de prisioneros, de notas diplomáticas,* exchange of prisoners, of diplomatic notes.
canjeable adj. Exchangeable.
canjear v. tr. To exchange: *canjear los bonos por premios,* to exchange the vouchers for prizes.
cano, na adj. White, grey (el cabello): *un anciano de pelo cano,* an old man with white hair. || White-haired, grey-haired: *un viejo cano,* a white-haired old man. || FIG. Old (viejo). || POÉT. Snowy, snow-white (blanco). || *Ponerse cano,* to go grey.
canoa f. Canoe (piragua). || Boat (bote de remo o con motor). || Motor boat (con motor). || Launch (lancha).
canódromo m. Greyhound track, dog track.
canoero o **canoísta** m. Canoeist.
canon m. REL. y MÚS. Canon. || Canon, norm (regla, precepto). || Model, perfect example (tipo perfecto). || Canon (pago). || COM. Rent (renta). | Tax, levy (tributo). || — Pl. REL. Canon law. || — *Como mandan los cánones,* according to the rules. || IMPR. *Doble canon,* canon. || *No estar de acuerdo con los cánones,* to be unorthodox, not to be in accordance with the rules.
canonesa f. Canoness.
canonical adj. Canonical.
canonicato m. Canonry.
canónico, ca adj. Canon: *derecho canónico,* canon law. || — *Horas canónicas,* canonical hours. || *Matrimonio canónico,* canonical marriage.
canóniga f. Nap before a meal.
canónigo m. Canon. || FIG. y FAM. *Vivir como un canónigo* or *llevar una vida de canónigo,* to live like a lord.
canonista m. Canonist, canon lawyer.
canonización f. Canonization.
canonizar v. tr. To canonize. || FIG. To sing the praises of (alabar).
canonjía f. Canonry (beneficio de canónigo). || FIG. y FAM. Sinecure, cushy job (fam.) [sinecura].
canoro, ra adj. Musical, melodious (melodioso). || *Ave canora,* songbird.
canoso, sa adj. White-haired, grey-haired: *anciano canoso,* white-haired old man; *estar canoso,* to be grey-haired. || — *Barba canosa,* white *o* grey beard. || *Pelo canoso,* grey *o* white hair. || *Sienes canosas,* greying *o* grey temples.
canotié o **canotier** m. Straw hat, boater (sombrero).
canquén m. *Amer.* Wild duck found in Chili.
cansadamente adv. Wearily (con cansancio). || Boringly, tiresomely (con pesadez).
cansado, da adj. Tired, weary: *cansado por un largo viaje,* tired by a long journey; *con voz cansada,* in a weary voice. || Tired, strained (los ojos). || FIG. Tiring (fatigoso): *un viaje muy cansado,* a very tiring journey. | Tiresome, tedious (fastidioso): *es cansado oír todos los días la misma canción,* it's tiresome to hear the same song every day. || AGR. Exhausted. || — *Marfil cansado,* old ivory. || *Nacer cansado,* to be permanently tired. || *Tener la cara cansada,* to look drawn, to look peaked.
cansancio m. Tiredness, weariness. || MED. Exhaustion. || FIG. *Estar muerto de cansancio,* to be dead tired.
cansar v. tr. To tire, to make tired, to weary (causar cansancio): *este trabajo nos cansa muchísimo,* this work tires us a lot, this work makes us very tired. || MED. To exhaust. || To tire, to strain (los ojos). || FIG. To bore, to make bored: *el discurso me cansó,* the speech bored me. || AGR. To exhaust. || — FIG. *Estar cansado,* to be tired, to be fed up (fam.): *estoy cansado de verlo,* I'm tired of seeing him. | *Me cansa ir al cine todos los días,* I get tired of going to the cinema every day, I get fed up going to the pictures every day (fam.).
— V. intr. To be tiring: *este trabajo cansa mucho,* this work is very tiring. || FIG. To be *o* to get boring *o* tedious *o* tiresome (fastidiar): *la misma comida todos*

los días acaba por cansar, the same meal day after day gets boring in the end.
— V. pr. To get tired, to tire: *se cansa fácilmente*, he gets tired easily, he tires easily. || FIG. To get tired, to get fed up (fam.): *me canso de repetir tantas veces la misma cosa*, I get tired of saying the same thing over and again.
cansera f. FAM. Nuisance, bother (molestia). || Tiredness (cansancio).
cansino, na adj. Tired (animales). || Weary, tired, lifeless: *paso cansino*, weary pace; *voz cansina*, lifeless voice.
cantábile adj. Cantabile.
cantable adj. Which can be sung, singable: *un trozo cantable*, a piece which can be sung, a singable piece.
— M. MÚS. Cantabile (trozo lento y fácil de cantar). | Singing part (de zarzuela).
cantábrico, ca adj. Cantabrian. || — GEOGR. *Cordillera Cantábrica*, Cantabrian Mountains. | *Mar Cantábrico*, Bay of Biscay.
cántabro, bra adj./s. Cantabrian.
cantador, ra m. y f. Singer: *cantador de baladas*, ballad singer.
cantaletear v. tr. *Amer*. To harp on, to repeat (repetir).
cantalupo m. BOT. Cantaloup, cantaloupe (melón).
cantante adj. Singing, who sings (que canta). || *Café cantante*, bar with cabaret.
— M. y f. Singer. || Opera singer (en la ópera).
cantaor, ra m. y f. Flamenco singer.
cantar m. Ballad, song. || Song (canto). || — *Cantar de gesta*, chanson de geste. || *Cantar de Mio Cid*, Poem of the Cid. || REL. *El Cantar de los Cantares*, the Canticles, Song of Songs. || FIG. *¡Ese es otro cantar!*, that's a different kettle of fish!, that's different!
cantar v. tr. To sing: *cantar una canción muy corta*, to sing a very short song. || To sing, to sing of: *cantar la gloria de una nación*, to sing the glory of a nation. || *Cantar misa*, to sing *o* to say one's first mass (después de la ordenación), to say *o* to sing mass.
— V. intr. To sing: *canta muy bien*, he sings very well; *cantar a dos voces*, to sing a duet. || To sing, to chirp (los pájaros). || To chirp (el grillo). || To call (naipes). || FIG. y FAM. To creak (rechinar). | To talk, to squeal, to sing (confesar). || MÚS. To play a solo. || — *Al cantar el gallo*, at cockcrow, at daybreak. || FIG. y FAM. *Cantar de plano*, to talk, to spill the beans, to sing (confesar). || *Cantar entonado*, to sing in tune. || FAM. *Cantarlas claras a uno*, to give s.o. a piece of one's mind. | *Cantarle a uno las cuarenta* v. CUARENTA. | *En menos que canta un gallo*, in a flash, before you can say Jack Robinson. | *Eso es coser y cantar*, v. COSER.
cántara f. Pitcher. || Churn (metálica). || Liquid measure [16.13 litres, approximately 3.5 gallons].
cantarela f. MÚS. First *o* highest string of a violin.
cantarera f. Shelf for pitchers.
cantarería f. Pottery shop.
cantarero, ra m. y f. Potter (alfarero).
cantárida f. ZOOL. Spanish fly, cantharis. || MED. Cantharides, *pl.*
cantarín, ina adj. Singsong: *voz cantarina*, singsong voice. || Singing (cantador).
— M. y f. Singer.
cántaro m. Pitcher. || Pitcherful (contenido). || — FIG. y FAM. *Alma de cántaro*, dimwit, blockhead. || FIG. *Llover a cántaros*, to rain cats and dogs, to pour down. | *Tanto va el cántaro a la fuente que al fin se rompe*, the pitcher goes so often to the well that in the end it breaks.
cantata f. Cantata.
cantatriz f. Opera singer.
cantazo m. Blow with a stone.
cante m. Folk song.

— OBSERV. One must not confuse *cante* with *canto*. The former applies only to *cante hondo* or *jondo* and *cante flamenco* which are types of Andalusian folk music.

cantera f. Quarry (de piedra). || FIG. Breeding ground, nursery: *Sevilla es una cantera de toreros*, Seville is a nursery for bullfighters. || *Amer*. Freestone, ashlar, hewn stone (cantería).
cantería f. Hewing of stones (labra de piedras). || ARQ. Building made of hewn stone (obra). | Freestone, ashlar, hewn stone (sillar).
cantero m. Stonemason (que labra las piedras). || Plot *o* strip of land (haza). || Crust (de pan).
cántico m. MÚS. Canticle. || Song (canción).
cantidad f. Quantity: *una gran cantidad*, a large quantity. || Sum: *abonar una cantidad de mil pesetas*, to pay a sum of a thousand pesetas. || A lot (mucho). || — *Adjetivo, adverbio de cantidad*, quantitative *o* quantitive adjective, adverb. || *Cantidad alzada*, inclusive price (tanto alzado). || *Cantidad de electricidad*, amperage. || *¡Había una cantidad* or *cantidad de gente!*, there were loads of people!
cántiga o **cantiga** f. (Ant.) Song, poem, ballad.
cantil m. Cliff (acantilado). || Shelf (en el fondo del mar). || *Amer*. Cliff edge (borde de un despeñadero).
cantilena f. Cantilena, ballad (composición poética). || FIG. y FAM. *Siempre la misma cantilena*, always the same old story.
cantiléver adj./s. m. TECN. Cantilever.
cantillo m. Small stone, pebble (piedra pequeña). || — Pl. Jacks (juego de las tabas).
cantimpla adj. Simple, stupid.
— M. y f. Simpleton, stupid person.
cantimplora f. Canteen (para llevar líquidos). || *Amer*. Goitre (bocio).
cantina f. Buffet (en una estación). || Wine cellar (sótano). || Canteen (comedor). || Picnic basket (fiambrera). || *Amer*. Bar (taberna). || — Pl. *Amer*. Saddlebags (en un caballo).
cantinela f. V. CANTILENA.
cantinera f. Barmaid (en un bar). || Camp follower (en la guerra).
cantinero m. Bar attendant, barman.
canto m. Song: *canto de victoria*, victory song. || Canto (de un poema). || Singing: *me gusta el canto*, I like singing. || — *Al canto del gallo*, at cockcrow, at daybreak. || *Canto gregoriano* or *llano*, Gregorian chant, plain song. || FIG. *El canto del cisne*, the swan song.
canto m. Edge (de moneda, etc.). || Blunt edge, back (de cuchillo). || Corner (ángulo). || Crust (pedazo de pan). || Pebble, stone (guijarro). || — FAM. *Al canto*, in support: *pruebas al canto*, evidence in support; for sure: *si se entera tu padre, disgusto al canto*, if your father finds out, there will be trouble for sure; *cada vez que voy a Bilbao, lluvia al canto*, every time I go to Bilbao, it rains for sure. || *Canto rodado*, boulder (grande), pebble (pequeño). || FIG. y FAM. *Darse con un canto en los dientes*, to be thankful for small mercies. || *De canto*, on edge. || FIG. y FAM. *Le faltó el canto de un duro*, he had a narrow escape, he escaped by the skin of his teeth. || *Libro de canto dorado*, gilt-edged book. || *Tiene dos centímetros de canto*, it is two centimetres thick.
cantón m. Corner (esquina). || HERÁLD. Canton. || Canton: *Suiza se divide en cantones*, Switzerland is divided into cantons. || MIL. Cantonment. || *Cantón redondo* rasp (lima de grano grueso).
cantonal adj. Cantonal.
cantonera f. Corner piece (encuadernación). || Butt plate (de arma). || Corner cabinet *o* table (rinconera).
cantonero, ra adj. Idling, loafing.
— M. y f. Idler, loafer.
cantor, ra adj. Singing. || *Ave cantora*, songbird.
— M. y f. Singer: *cantor callejero*, street singer. || FIG. Bard, songster (poeta).
cantoral m. Choir book.
Cantorbery n. pr. GEOGR. Canterbury.
cantueso m. Type of red lavender (espliego).
canturrear o **canturriar** v. intr. To hum, to sing softly.
canturreo m. Humming, soft singing.
cánula f. MED. Cannula.
canutero m. Pin case, pin box (alfiletero). || *Amer*. Pen holder. | Fountain pen.
canutillo m. Golden *o* silver purl (hilo de oro o plata). || *Pana de canutillo*, corduroy.
canuto m. BOT. Internode. || Pin case, pin box (canutero). || Tube (tubo). || Blowpipe (cerbatana). || FAM. Demobbing (licencia del soldado).
canzonetista f. Singer.
caña f. BOT. Cane, stem (tallo). | Reed: *caña común*, common reed. | Rattan (caña de Indias). || ANAT. Shinbone (hueso de la pierna), arm bone (hueso del brazo). | Cannon bone (del caballo). | Marrow (tuétano). || Leg (de la bota). || Glass: *una caña de cerveza*, a glass of beer. || Rod: *pescar con caña*, to fish with a rod. || Stock (de un fusil). || MIN. Gallery. || ARQ. Shaft (de una columna). || Shank (del ancla). || MAR. Helm (del timón). || MÚS. Andalusian folk song. || *Amer*. Sugar cane. | Tafia (aguardiente de caña). | Boasting (bravata). || — Pl. Jousting, *sing.* (torneo). || — *Caña de azúcar*, sugar cane. || ARQ. *Media caña*, gorge (moldura semicircular).
cañacoro m. BOT. Canna.
cañada f. Gorge, ravine (entre dos montañas). || Cattle track (camino). || *Amer*. Stream (arroyo).
cañaduz f. Sugar cane.
cañafístola o **cañafístula** f. BOT. Cassia (árbol, fruto).
cañamazo m. Tow (estopa). || Tow cloth, burlap (tela). || Canvas (para bordar). || Sketch (de pintura): *sólo está hecho el cañamazo del cuadro*, only the sketch of the painting is done. || FIG. Rough draft *o* outline (de una novela, etc.).
cáñamo m. Hemp (planta y fibra): *cáñamo de Manila*, Manila hemp. || *Cáñamo indio, índico* or *de Indias*, Indian hemp, cannabis.
cañamón m. BOT. Hempseed.
cañaveral m. Cane plantation (plantación de cañas). || Sugar-cane plantation (de caña de azúcar). || Reedbed (sitio poblado de cañas).
cañazo m. Blow with a cane (golpe). || *Amer*. Tafia (aguardiente de caña).
cañería m. Piping (tubería). || Pipe, length of pipe (tubo).
cañí adj./s. Gipsy.

— OBSERV. Pl. *cañís*.

cañizal o **cañizar** m. Cane plantation (plantación de cañas). || Sugar-cane plantation (cañaveral).
cañizo m. Wattle screen.
caño m. Pipe (tubo). || Jet (de una fuente). || Sewer (albañal). || Gallery (de una mina). || Cellar (sótano). || MAR. Navigable channel.

cañón m. Pipe (de órgano). || Flue (de chimenea). || Flute (pliegue de la ropa). || Tube, pipe (tubo). || Shaft (de una pluma de ave). || Whisker (de la barba). || Mil. Gun, cannon (ant.): *cañón antiaéreo*, anti-aircraft gun. | Barrel (de fusil). || Trunk (tronco de árbol). || Geogr. Canyon (desfiladero). || — *Bóveda de cañón*, barrel vault. || Fís. *Cañón de electrones* or *electrónico*, electron gun. || Mil. *Cañón rayado*, rifled barrel. || *Escopeta de dos cañones*, double-barrelled rifle. || Fig. *Estar siempre al pie del cañón*, to be always on the job. | *Morir al pie del cañón*, v. pie.
— Adj. Fam. Terrific, great.
— Adv. *Lo pasé cañón*, I had a marvellous time.
cañonazo m. Gunshot (tiros y ruido). || Shot (fútbol). || — Pl. Gunfire, shellfire. || *Salva de 21 cañonazos*, 21-gun salute.
cañonear v. tr. To shell: *el acorazado cañoneó la costa*, the battleship shelled the coast.
cañoneo m. Gunfire, shellfire.
cañonera f. Mil. Embrasure (tronera). || Mar. Gun port (porta). || Gunboat (lancha). || *Amer.* Holster (funda para pistola).
— Adj. Mar. *Lancha cañonera*, gunboat.
cañonería f. Artillery (conjunto de cañones). || Pipes, *pl.* (de un órgano).
cañonero m. Mar. Gunboat.
cañuto m. V. canuto.

— Observ. The term *cañuto* is rarely used; *canuto* is preferred. This preference also applies to the derivatives of the two words.

caoba f. Mahogany (árbol y madera).
caolín m. Kaolin.
caos m. Chaos.
caótico, ca adj. Chaotic.
cap m. Cup (bebida).
capa f. Cape, cloak (vestido sin mangas). || Cape (de torero). || Coat (de pintura). || Layer (de aire, de tierra). || Geol. Stratum, layer (de roca, etc.). || Pall (de humo). || Outer leaf (de cigarro). || Film, layer (de polvo). || Fig. Stratum, layer, sector (social). | Cloak, sheet, layer (de nieve, etc.). | Mask: *bajo una capa de humildad*, behind a mask of humility. || Coat (color del pelaje). || Culin. Coating, coat. || Quím. Shell (de átomo). || Wealth (bienes). || — Fig. *Andar de capa caída*, to be in a bad way (estar mal), to have come down in the world, to have seen better days (decaer). || *Capa del cielo*, celestial vault. || *Capa freática*, water table. || Rel. *Capa pluvial*, pluvial, cope. || *De capa y espada*, cloak-and-dagger. || Fig. *Echar una capa a alguien*, to cover up for s.o. | *Hacer de su capa un sayo*, to do as one pleases. || *Madera de cuatro capas*, 4-ply wood. || *Primera capa*, undercoat (de pintura). || Fig. *So capa de*, on *o* under the pretext of. | *Una buena capa todo lo tapa*, you cannot judge a book by its cover.
capacidad f. Capacity: *capacidad de trabajo*, work capacity; *la capacidad de un tonel*, the capacity of a barrel. || Jur. Capacity. || Fig. Capacity, ability (mental). || Electr. Capacity. || — *Capacidad adquisitiva*, purchasing power. || *Capacidad de arrastre*, pulling power. || *Capacidad financiera*, financial status. || *Tener capacidad para*, to be capable of (ser capaz de), to have talent for (tener talento para). || *Un avión con capacidad para 300 pasajeros*, a plane which seats 300 passengers, a plane with room for 300 passengers.
capacitación f. Training (formación). || Qualification (capacidad de un obrero). || *Escuela de capacitación profesional*, technical school.
capacitado, da adj. Qualified (obrero, persona). || Jur. Qualified, competent: *capacitado para suceder*, qualified to succeed. || *Capacitado para*, capable of.
capacitancia f. Electr. Capacitance.
capacitar v. tr. To train (instruir). || To qualify, to entitle: *este título me capacita para ejercer*, this diploma entitles me to practise. || Jur. To capacitate, to entitle.
capacha f. Shopping basket, basket.
capacho m. Shopping basket, basket. || Hemp pressing bag (para la aceituna). || *Amer.* Old hat (sombrero). || Tecn. Dipper (de pala mecánica).
capador m. Castrator, gelder.
capadura f. Castration (castradura).
capar v. tr. To castrate (castrar). || Fig. To curtail.
caparazón m. Shell (de tortuga, de crustáceo). || Hist. Caparison. || Fig. Cover (cubierta). || Nosebag (para el pienso del caballo). || *Quitar el caparazón*, to shell (un cangrejo).
caparrosa f. Vitriol: *caparrosa azul*, blue vitriol.
capataz m. Foreman (en una empresa). || *Capataz de campo*, overseer.
capaz adj. Capable, able, competent: *un gobernante capaz*, a capable ruler. || Qualified (para un trabajo). || Capable: *este hombre es capaz de todo*, this man is capable of anything. || Which holds: *estadio capaz para cien mil personas*, stadium which holds a hundred thousand people. || Spacious, roomy: *una sala muy capaz*, a very spacious hall. || Enough: *este frío es capaz de matarme*, this cold is enough to kill me. || Jur. Qualified, competent. || *¿Serías capaz?*, you wouldn't dare!
capazo m. Shopping basket. || Carrycot (para un niño).
capcioso, sa adj. Captious, insidious, artful. || *Pregunta capciosa*, catch question, captious question.
capciosidad f. Captiousness, insidiousness, artfulness.
capea f. Taur. Amateur bullfight using young bulls (lidia con novillos). | Cape work, passes (*pl.*) with the cape (toreo con la capa).
capeador m. Taur. Amateur *o* novice bullfighter (de novillos). | Cape man (torero con capa).
capear v. tr. Taur. To make passes with a cape. || Fig. y fam. To stall, to put off (entretener con promesas, etc.). | To take in, to fool (engañar): *a mí no me capea nadie*, you can't fool me. | To get round [s.o.] (embaucar). || Mar. To ride out: *capear el temporal*, to ride out the storm. || Fig. To brave, to ride out: *ha capeado las consecuencias del accidente*, he has braved the consequences of the accident. | To shirk, to dodge (una dificultad). | To avoid, to dodge (evitar).
capelina f. Med. Capeline (vendaje).
capelo m. Cardinal's hat (sombrero). || Cardinalship (dignidad de cardenal). || *Amer.* Bell glass (fanal).
capellán m. Rel. Chaplain: *capellán castrense*, army chaplain.
capellanía f. Rel. Chaplaincy.
capellina f. Capeline (sombrero). || Med. Capeline (vendaje).
capeo m. Taur. Passes with the cape, cape work. | Amateur bullfight using young bulls.
caperucita f. Small hood. || *Caperucita Roja*, Little Red Riding Hood.
caperuza f. Pointed hood *o* cap (gorro terminado en punta). || Hood, cowl (de chimenea, etc.). || Cap: *la caperuza de una pluma*, the cap of a pen.
Capeto n. pr. m. Hist. Capetian.
capialzado m. Arq. Splay.
capialzar v. tr. Arq. To splay.
capibara f. Zool. Capybara.
capicúa m. Palindrome, reversible word *o* number: *el número 1991 es capicúa*, the number 1991 is a palindrome.
capilar adj. Hair: *loción capilar*, hair lotion. || Anat. Capillary (vaso). || Fís. Capillary (tubo).
— M. Anat. Capillary.
capilaridad f. Capillarity.
capilla f. Chapel (pequeña iglesia): *capilla ardiente*, funeral chapel. || Mús. Chapel, choir: *maestro de capilla*, chapel *o* choir master. || Hood, cowl (capucha). || Fig. y fam. Clan (camarilla). || Impr. Proof, proof sheet. || *Estar en capilla*, to be awaiting execution (condenado a muerte), to be like a cat on hot bricks, to be on tenterhooks (esperar con ansia).
capillita f. Clan (camarilla).
capillo m. Hood (capucha). || Bonnet (de niño). || Christening *o* baptism cape (para bautizo). || Toe lining (del calzado). || Coffee strainer (para colar el café).
capirotazo m. Flip, fillip.
capirote adj. With the head of a different colour from the rest of the body (res).
— M. Hennin (para mujeres). || Hood (gorro puntiagudo). || Hood (de doctores). || Penitent's hood (de penitente). || Flip, fillip (con los dedos). || Fig. y fam. *Tonto de capirote*, dunce, nitwit, nincompoop, ass.
capirucho m. Fam. Hood (capuchón).
capisayo m. Hooded cape. || Mantelletta (episcopal).
capitación f. Capitation, poll tax (impuesto).
capital adj. Capital, chief, principal (principal): *error capital*, capital mistake. || Main (rasgo). || Capital: *ciudad capital*, capital city. || — Impr. *Letra capital*, capital letter. || *Pecado capital*, deadly sin. || *Pena* or *sentencia capital*, death sentence, capital punishment.
— M. Capital (dinero): *capital activo, social, suscrito*, working, share, subscribed capital. || *Capital circulante*, working *o* operational capital. || — F. Capital (sede del gobierno). || Impr. Capital (letra). || — *Capital de condado*, county town (en Inglaterra). || *Capital de provincia*, county town [U.S., county seat].
capitalino, na adj. Of the capital.
— M. y f. Inhabitant of the capital.
capitalismo m. Capitalism.
capitalista adj. Capitalist, capitalistic.
— M. y f. Capitalist.
capitalizable adj. Capitalizable.
capitalización f. Capitalization.
capitalizar v. tr. To capitalize.
capitán m. Mar. y Mil. Captain (oficial). || Shipmaster (mercante). || Captain, skipper (de un equipo). || Fig. Chief, leader, commander (jefe). || — Mar. *Capitán de corbeta*, lieutenant commander. | *Capitán de fragata*, commander. | *Capitán de navío*, captain. || Mil. *Capitán general*, field marshal.
capitana f. Flagship (buque principal de la escuadra).
capitanear v. tr. To lead, to command (mandar): *capitanear una banda de ladrones*, to lead a band of robbers. || To captain (un equipo deportivo). || To command, to captain (un barco).
capitanía f. Captaincy, captainship (empleo). || Harbour dues, *pl.* (derechos que se pagan para fondear). || *Capitanía General*, military headquarters (oficina), Captaincy General (dependencia de un virreinato): *la Capitanía General de Guatemala*, the Captaincy General of Guatemala.
capitel m. Arq. Capital.
capitolio n. Capitol. || Imposing building (edificio majestuoso).

capitoné m. Removal van, furniture van (para mudanzas).
— Adj. Upholstered (acolchado).

— OBSERV. The word *capitoné* is a Gallicism.

capitoste m. FAM. Big wheel, big boss.
capitulación f. Capitulation, surrender (rendición): *capitulación sin condiciones*, unconditional surrender. || Agreement, pact (convenio). || — Pl. Marriage settlement *o* contract, *sing*.
capitular adj. Capitular, capitulary. || REL. Chapter: *sala capitular*, chapter house.
— M. Capitular, capitulary (miembro de un cabildo). || — F. pl. HIST. Capitulars, capitularies (ordenanzas de los francos).
capitular v. intr. To capitulate, to surrender (rendirse). || To make *o* to reach an agreement (pactar).
— V. tr. To charge.
capítulo m. Chapter (de un libro). || REL. Reproof, reprimand (reprensión). || Subject, matter (tema). || Chapter (de una orden militar, de una congregación). || ANAT. BOT. Capitulum. || — *Capítulos matrimoniales*, marriage settlement *o* contract, *sing*. || FIG. *Eso es otro capítulo*, that is another story. | *Llamar a alguien a capítulo*, to call s.o. to account.
capitulum m. ANAT. Capitulum.
capó m. AUT. Bonnet [U.S., hood].
capoc m. o **capoca** f. Kapok (fibra).
capón m. Capon (pollo). || Rap with the knuckles (golpe). || *Amer*. Sheep (carnero).
— Adj. Castrated, gelded (capado).
caponada f. *Amer*. Flock of sheep.
caponera f. Coop (jaula para cebar capones). | Caponier (fortificación). || Open house (lugar donde se recibe buen trato). || FAM. Nick, clink (cárcel).
caporal m. Farm manager (capataz). || MIL. Corporal (cabo). || FIG. Chief, leader.
capot m. AUT. Bonnet [U.S., hood].
capota f. Bonnet (de mujer). || Hood (de automóvil y de coche de niños). || AUT. *Capota plegable*, folding hood *o* top.
capotar v. intr. To overturn (automóvil). || To nose-dive (avión).
capotazo m. TAUR. Pass with a cape.
capote m. Capote, cape (prenda de abrigo). || MIL. Greatcoat. || TAUR. Cape: *lucirse con el capote*, to be brilliant with the cape; *capote de paseo*, ceremonial cape. || Slam (en el juego de naipes). || *Amer*. Hiding, beating, thrashing (paliza). || — *Amer*. *Capote de monte*, poncho. || *Dar capote*, to win all the tricks (naipes). || FIG. y FAM. *Echar un capote a uno*, v. ECHAR. || *Para mi, tu, su capote*, to myself, yourself, himself.
capotear v. tr. TAUR. To make passes using the cape. || FIG. y FAM. To stall, to put off (entretener con promesas, etc.). | To get out of, to dodge (dificultades).
capoteo m. TAUR. Cape work, passes with the cape. || FIG. y FAM. Trickery (engaño). | Shirking (escamoteo).
capotera f. *Amer*. Coat hanger.
capotillo m. Short cape. || TAUR. *Capotillo de paseo*, ceremonial cape.
Capricornio n. pr. m. ASTR. Capricorn.
capricho m. Whim, fancy, caprice: *los caprichos de la moda*, the whims of fashion. || Fancy (deseo). || Frill (adorno). || MÚS. Caprice, capriccio. || — *Hacer algo a capricho*, to do sth. as the fancy takes one. || *Le dio el capricho de tomar fresas*, she suddenly fancied some strawberries.
caprichoso, sa o **caprichudo, da** adj. Whimsical, fanciful, capricious: *un niño muy caprichoso*, a very whimsical child.
cápsico m. BOT. Capsicum (planta).
cápsula f. Capsule (de un cohete, de las plantas, de medicamentos). || Top, cap (de botella, de envase). || MIL. Cap (de proyectil). || QUÍM. Dish. || ANAT. Capsule: *cápsulas suprarrenales*, suprarenal capsules. || *Poner cápsulas a*, to cap.
capsulado m. Capping.
capsuladora f. Capping machine.
capsular adj. ANAT. y BOT. Capsular.
capsular v. tr. To cap.
captación f. Harnessing (de aguas). || Reception (de ondas). || Grasping, comprehension (comprensión). || *Captación de partidarios*, winning *o* convincing of supporters.
captar v. tr. To harness (aguas). || RAD. To pick up, to receive (ondas). || To grasp: *captar el sentido de una palabra*, to grasp the meaning of a word. || To hold: *captar la atención del oyente*, to hold the attention of the listener. || To win, to get (la confianza, etc.). || To win over (partidarios, etc.).
— V. pr. To win, to gain, to capture: *captarse la amistad de todos*, to win everyone's friendship.
captura f. Capture: *la captura de un criminal*, the capture of a criminal.
capturar v. tr. To capture, to seize.
capucha f. Hood. || IMPR. Circumflex accent. || Pouch (de pulpo).
capuchino, na adj. Capuchin.
— M. Capuchin monk. || Capuchin monkey (mono). || — F. Capuchin nun (monja). || BOT. Nasturtium. || Small lamp.
capuchón m. Hood (de abrigo). || Capuchin (capa). || Cap (de pluma estilográfica). || TECN. Valve cap (válvula)
capullo m. Cocoon (de insecto). || BOT. Bud (de flor). | Cup (de bellota). || Coarse spun silk (tela de seda). || ANAT. Prepuce.
capuz m. Hood (capuchón). || Type of cloak *o* cape (capa).
caquéctico, ca adj. MED. Cachectic.
caquexia f. MED. Cachexy, cachexia.
caqui m. BOT. Persimmon (árbol y fruto). || Khaki (color). || FIG. y FAM. *Ponerse el caqui*, to dress in khaki (soldado).
— Adj. inv. Khaki: *una camisa caqui*, a khaki shirt.
cara f. Face: *la cara de un niño*, a child's face; *asomar la cara*, to show one's face. || Expression, face: *juzgar por la cara*, to judge by one's expression; *me recibió con buena cara*, he received me with a friendly face. || Head (de una moneda): *si sale cara ganas tú*, if it's heads you win. || Side: *las dos caras de una hoja, de un disco*, the two sides of a sheet, of a record. || Face, surface (superficie). || FIG. Side: *las dos caras de un asunto*, the two sides of a matter. || Right side (anverso). || MAT. y ARQ. Face. || FIG. y FAM. Nerve, cheek: *ese tío tiene mucha cara*, that fellow has got a lot of cheek. || FIG. Look (cariz): *no me gusta la cara de este asunto*, I do not like the look of this affair. || — FIG. *A cara descubierta*, openly. | *Caérsele a uno la cara de vergüenza*, to die of shame, to blush with shame. || *Cara a*, facing (hacia): *cara a la pared, al sol*, facing the wall, the sun; into, towards: *andar cara al viento*, to walk into the wind. || *Cara a cara*, face to face: *a la vuelta de la esquina se encontraron cara a cara*, round the corner they met face to face; in private: *tener una conversación cara a cara*, to hold a conversation in private; to one's face: *decir algo a alguien cara a cara*, to say sth. to s.o.'s face. || *Cara adelante, atrás*, forwards, backwards. || FIG. *Cara de circunstancias*, serious look. | *Cara de Cuaresma* or *de viernes*, sad *o* dismal face. | *Cara de perro*, scowling face. | *Cara de pascua* or *de risa*, cheerful *o* smiling face. | *Cara de pocos amigos* or *de vinagre*, sour *o* grim *o* unfriendly face. | *Cara dura*, nerve, cheek (descaro). | *Cara larga*, long face. || FAM. *Cruzar la cara a uno*, v. CRUZAR. || *Dar con la puerta en la cara a uno*, to shut the door in s.o.'s face. || FIG. *Dar la cara*, to face up to things (afrontar). | *Dar la cara por uno*, to stand up for s.o., to defend s.o. (defender), to answer for s.o., to vouch for s.o. (salir fiador). || *Decir algo a uno en su cara*, to say sth. to s.o.'s face. || FIG. *Echar algo en cara a uno*, to throw sth. in s.o.'s face. || *Echar* or *jugarse algo a cara o cruz*, to toss [up] for sth. || *En la cara se le conoce*, one can see it in his face. || *Hacer cara a*, to face (afrontar). || FAM. *No lo hice por tu bella* or *linda cara*, I didn't do it because I like your face *o* for your pretty face. || FIG. *No mirar la cara a alguien*, not to be on speaking terms with s.o. || *No saber qué cara poner*, not to know what to do with o.s. *o* where to put o.s. || FAM. *Nos veremos las caras*, I'll see you later (amenaza). || FIG. *No tener cara para hacer algo*, not to dare to do sth., not to have the nerve to do sth. || *No volver la cara atrás*, not to look back. || FIG. *Plantar cara a alguien*, to face up to s.o. | *Poner a mal tiempo buena cara*, to keep a stiff upper lip, to keep one's chin up, to look on the bright side. || *Poner buena cara*, to look happy *o* pleased. || FIG. *Poner buena cara a algo*, to take sth. well. | *Poner buena cara a alguien*, to be nice to s.o. || *Poner cara de*, to look like (con sustantivo), to look as if (con verbo). || *Poner cara de asco*, to look disgusted. || FIG. *Poner mala cara* or *cara larga*, to pull a face *o* a long face. || *Reírse en la cara de alguien*, to laugh in s.o.'s face. || FAM. *Romper la cara*, to smash s.o.'s face [in]. || FIG. *Sacar la cara por alguien*, to stick up for s.o. || *Tener cara de*, to look: *tener cara de tristeza*, to look sad. || *Tener cara de alma en pena* or *de duelo*, to have a face as long as a fiddle. || FIG. *Tener dos caras*, to be two-faced. || *Tener el sol de cara*, to be facing the sun. || *Tener el viento de cara*, to be facing into the wind. || *Tener mala cara*, to look bad. || FIG. y FAM. *Tener más cara que un buey con paperas*, to have a lot of cheek, to be a cheeky devil. || *Terciar la cara a uno*, to slash s.o.'s face. || *Tiene cara de no haber dormido*, he looks as if he hasn't slept. || *Volver la cara*, to turn away, to look the other way.
caraba f. FAM. *Éste es la caraba*, he's the limit. | *Esto es la caraba*, this is the end *o* the limit *o* the last straw.
carabao m. Carabao (buffalo).
cárabe m. Amber (ámbar).
carabela f. MAR. Caravel, carvel.
carabina f. Carbine, rifle (arma). || FIG. Chaperon, chaperone (que acompaña). || — FAM. *Eso es la carabina de Ambrosio*, that's as much good as a poultice on a wooden leg. || FIG. y FAM. *Ir* or *hacer de carabina*, to be chaperon (vigilar a una pareja), to play gooseberry (llevar la cesta).
carabinero m. Customs officer. || Large prawn (crustáceo).

— OBSERV. In Spain the name *carabineros* was given to the body of armed policemen whose main function is the suppression of smuggling.

cárabo m. Carabus, carabid beetle (coleóptero). || Tawny owl (autillo).
caracará f. *Amer*. Caracara (bird of prey).

Caracas n. pr. f. GEOGR. Caracas.

caracol m. ZOOL. Snail (molusco terrestre). | Winkle (de mar). || Sea shell, conch (concha). || CULIN. Snail: *purgar los caracoles*, to purge the snails. || Kiss-curl (rizo). || Snail wheel (de reloj). || ANAT. Cochlea. || — Pl. Andalusian folk song. || — *Escalera de caracol*, spiral staircase. || *Hacer caracoles*, to caracol, to caracole (el caballo).

— Interj. *¡Caracoles!*, goodness me! (asombro, sorpresa), damn it! (enfado).

caracola f. ZOOL. Conch.

caracolada f. Dish made from snails.

caracolear v. intr. To caracole, to prance (hacer caracoles un caballo).

caracoleo m. Caracole.

caracolillo m. BOT. Snail-flowered kidney bean (judía). || Pea-bean coffee (café). || Densely grained mahogany (caoba).

carácter m. Character (genio, personalidad): *una pintura, un hombre de mucho carácter*, a painting, a man with a lot of character. || Kind, nature (índole). || Characteristic (característica). || IMPR. Character. || Handwriting (letra manuscrita). || Character (personaje de un libro). || — *Caracteres de imprenta*, type, typeface. || *Con carácter de*, as: *con carácter de embajador*, as an ambassador. || *Escribir en caracteres de imprenta*, to write in block letters. || *Persona de poco carácter*, person with a weak character. || *Tener buen carácter*, to be good-natured. || *Tener mal carácter*, to be bad-tempered.

— OBSERV. Pl. *caracteres*. (Note the transferring of the stress in the plural).

característico, ca adj. Characteristic, typical: *una cualidad característica*, a characteristic quality.

— M. y f. TEATR. Character actor (actor, actriz). || — F. Characteristic, feature (particularidad): *la cortesía es una característica de los japoneses*, politeness is a characteristic of the Japanese; *las características de un avión*, the characteristics of a plane. || MAT. Characteristic (del logaritmo).

caracterización f. Characterization.

caracterizado, da adj. Characterized. || Special, peculiar (especial). || Distinguished (notable): *un científico caracterizado*, a distinguished scientist.

caracterizar v. tr. To characterize (distinguir). || To portray, to capture, to characterize: *el escritor ha caracterizado brillantemente el ambiente*, the writer portrays the atmosphere brilliantly. || TEATR. To play well.

— V. pr. To be characterized. || To make up (un actor).

caracterología f. Characterology.

caracú m. *Amer.* Marrow (tuétano).

caracul m. Caracul, karakul (piel y carnero).

caradura m. y f. FAM. Cheeky devil (fresco). || — F. FAM. Nerve, cheek: *tener mucha caradura*, to have a lot of cheek. || *¡Qué caradura es!*, he's got a nerve!, of all the nerve!

— Adj. FAM. Cheeky, shameless. || *¡Qué tío más caradura!*, what a nerve!, he's got a nerve!

carajo m. POP. Prick. || — POP. *Carajo!*, bloody hell! | *¡Vete al carajo!* go to hell!, get stuffed!

caramanchel m. MAR. Hatch cover (escotillón). || Slum, hovel (tugurio). || *Amer.* Snack bar, cheap restaurant, eating house (figón).

¡caramba! interj. Goodness me! (asombro, sorpresa), damn it! (enfado). || *¡Caramba con él!*, to hell with him!

carámbano m. Icicle.

carambola f. Cannon [U.S., carom] (billar). || FIG. y FAM. Fluke: *he aprobado por carambola*, I passed by a fluke. | Trick (faena hecha a alguien).

carambolear v. tr. To cannon [U.S., to carom] (billar).

caramelizar v. tr. To caramel, to caramelize.

caramelo m. Sweet [U.S., candy] (golosina). || Caramel (azúcar fundida y pasta de azúcar). || — *A punto de caramelo*, syrupy (el azúcar), tasty (sabroso). || *Caramelo blando*, caramel, toffee. || FAM. *De caramelo*, excellent.

caramillo m. MÚS. Pipe, shawm (ant.). || Pile, heap (montón). || FIG. Piece of gossip, tale (chisme). | Fuss (enredo).

carancho m. *Amer.* Owl (búho). | Caracara (caracará).

carángano m. *Amer.* Louse (piojo).

carantoña f. FIG. y FAM. Mutton dressed as lamb (mujer vieja y presumida). || — Pl. Flattery, *sing.*, soft soap, *sing.* (fam.), coaxing, *sing.* (zalamerías). || Caresses (caricias). || *Hacerle carantoñas a alguien*, to caress s.o. (acariciar), to butter s.o. up, to soft-soap s.o. (para conseguir algo).

carantoñero, ra m. y f. Coaxer, flatterer.

carapacho m. Carapace (de tortuga, cangrejo etc.).

¡carape! interj. Goodness me! (asombro, sorpresa), damn it! (enfado).

caraqueño, ña adj. [From *o* of] Caracas (Venezuela).

— M. y f. Inhabitant *o* native of Caracas.

carátula f. Mask (careta). || FAM. Theatre, stage (teatro): *dejó la espada por la carátula*, he left the army for the theatre. || *Amer.* Title page (de un libro). | Dial, face (de reloj).

caravana f. Caravan (de camellos, de peregrinos). || Long line *o* queue (de coches, etc.). || Caravan [U.S., trailer] (remolque). || — Pl. *Amer.* Earrings (pendientes). | Courtesies, compliments. || *En caravana*, in Indian file, in single file.

caravanero m. Caravaneer (de camellos).

caravaning m. Caravanning.

caravanseray o **caravasar** o **caravanserrallo** m. Caravanserai, caravansary.

¡caray! interj. Goodness me!, good Lord! (asombro, sorpresa), damn it! (enfado).

carbohidrato m. Carbohydrate (hidrato de carbono).

carbón m. Coal (combustible). || Carbon paper (para reproducir). || Charcoal (para dibujar). || ELECTR. Carbon. || — *Carbón de bola*, ovoid. || *Carbón de gas*, gas coal. || *Carbón de leña* or *vegetal*, charcoal. || *Carbón de piedra* or *mineral*, coal. || *Carbón en polvo*, coal dust. || *Carbón vegetal*, charcoal. || *Copia al carbón*, carbon copy. || *Cubo del carbón*, coal scuttle. || *Negro como el carbón*, black as coal. || *Papel carbón*, carbon paper. || FAM. *Se acabó el carbón*, that's that, that's it.

carbonada f. Load of coal (paletada de carbón). || Dish made of stewed meat which is then grilled (plato de carne). || *Amer.* Stew [made from meat, potatoes, maize, rice and marrow] (guisado).

carbonado m. MIN. Black diamond, carbonado (diamante negro).

carbonar v. tr. To turn into charcoal.

carbonario m. HIST. Carbonaro.

carbonatación f. Carbonation, carbonatation.

carbonatado, da adj. QUÍM. Carbonated.

carbonatar v. tr. QUÍM. To carbonate.

carbonato m. QUÍM. Carbonate.

carboncillo m. Charcoal: *dibujo al carboncillo*, charcoal drawing. || AUT. Carbon.

carbonear v. tr. To turn into charcoal.

carboneo m. Charcoal making.

carbonera f. Charcoal stack *o* pile (para hacer carbón). || Coal cellar *o* bunker (para guardar carbón). || MAR. Coal bunker, bunker. || Coalmine (mina). || *Amer.* Coal tender (de locomotora).

carbonería f. Coal merchant's yard, coalyard.

carbonero, ra adj. Coal: *industria carbonera*, coal industry. || Charcoal. || *Barco carbonero*, collier.

— M. Coal merchant, coalman, coalheaver. || Collier (barco). || FIG. *La fe del carbonero*, simple faith.

carbónico, ca adj. QUÍM. Carbonic: *gas, ácido carbónico*, carbonic gas, acid. || *Anhídrido carbónico*, carbon dioxide, carbonic acid gas.

carbonífero, ra adj. Carboniferous. || GEOL. *El período carbonífero*, the Carboniferous, the Carboniferous Period.

carbonilla f. Coaldust (polvo de carbón). || Soot (de la locomotora). || *Amer.* Charcoal (carboncillo).

carbonización f. Carbonization. || Charring, burning (acción de quemar).

carbonizar v. tr. To carbonize (transformar en carbón). || To burn, to char (quemar). || *Quedar carbonizado*, to be burnt to a cinder (una cosa), to be electrocuted (electrocutarse), to be burnt down (un edificio).

— V. pr. To carbonize.

carbono m. QUÍM. Carbon: *ciclo del carbono*, carbon cycle. || *Bióxido* or *dióxido de carbono*, carbon dioxide.

carbonoso, sa adj. Carbonaceous.

carbunclo o **carbunco** m. MED. Carbuncle (tumor). | Anthrax (enfermedad).

carbunclo o **carbúnculo** m. Carbuncle (piedra preciosa).

carburación f. Carburation [U.S., carburetion] (de un motor). || Carburization (en metalurgia). || QUÍM. Carburetting.

carburador m. Carburettor, carburetter [U.S., carburetor, carbureter].

carburante m. Fuel.

carburar v. tr. To carburate, to carburet (un motor). || FIG. y FAM. To go strong, to go well.

carburo m. QUÍM. Carbide: *carburo de calcio*, calcium carbide.

carca adj./s. FAM. Carlist. || FIG. y FAM. Reactionary (reaccionario). | Square (chapado a la antigua).

carcaj m. Quiver (caja de las flechas). || Standard holder (de la bandera). || *Amer.* Holster (de arma de fuego).

carcajada f. Burst of laughter, guffaw. || — *Reír a carcajadas*, to split one's sides laughing. || *Soltar la carcajada*, to burst out laughing.

carcajear v. intr. To laugh heartily, to roar with laughter.

— V. pr. To laugh heartily, to roar with laughter. || FIG. *Me carcajeo de tus principios*, I laugh at your principles, your principles make me laugh, principles be damned.

carcamal m. FAM. Old fogy, old fogey (persona vieja).

cárcel f. Prison, gaol, jail: *salir de la cárcel*, to come out of prison. || TECN. Clamp (herramienta). | Groove (ranura).

carcelario, ria adj. Prison, gaol, jail: *la vida carcelaria es dura*, prison life is hard.

carcelero, ra adj. Prison, gaol, jail (carcelario).

— M. y f. Gaoler, jailer, warder. || — F. Andalusian folk song.

carcinógeno, na adj. MED. Carcinogen.

carcinoma m. MED. Carcinoma, cancer.

carcinomatoso, sa adj. Carcinomatous.

cárcola f. Pedal (del telar).

carcoma f. ZOOL. Woodworm. || Wood dust (polvo de la madera). || FIG. y FAM. Anxiety, grief (preocupación). | Spendthrift (persona gastosa).

carcomer v. tr. To eat away, to eat into (la madera). || FIG. To gnaw [at], to eat up, to consume: *le carcomía la envidia*, he was gnawed *o* eaten up by envy. | To undermine (la salud).
— V. pr. To become eaten away, to become worm-eaten. || FIG. To waste away, to decay.

carcomido, da adj. Eaten away, worm-eaten (madera). || FIG. Eaten away, rotten (podrido). | Undermined (salud).

carda f. Carding (acción). || Teasel (cabeza de la cardencha). || Card, teasel (instrumento). || FIG. y FAM. Telling off, dressing down, scolding (reprimenda).

cardado m. TECN. Carding. || Back-combing (del pelo).

cardador, ra m. y f. TECN. Carder (persona). || — M. ZOOL. Millepede. || — F. TECN. Carder, carding machine (máquina).

cardadura f. Carding.

cardamomo m. Cardamom (planta).

cardán f. TECN. Cardan, cardan joint (articulación).

cardar v. tr. To card (la lana). || To back-comb (el pelo). || FIG. *Unos cobran la fama y otros cardan la lana*, some people do all the work while others get the credit.

cardenal m. Cardinal (prelado, pájaro). || Bruise (equimosis). || *Amer.* Geranium.

cardenalato m. Cardinalate, cardinalship.

cardenalicio, cia adj. Of a cardinal, cardinal's: *la púrpura cardenalicia*, cardinal's purple. || *Colegio cardenalicio*, college of cardinals.

cardencha f. BOT. Card thistle. || TECN. Card, teasel (carda).

cardenillo m. Verdigris. || *Criar cardenillo*, to become covered with verdigris.

cárdeno, na adj. Cardinal red (color). || Black and white (color de reses). || Opaline blue (líquidos). || Livid (lívido).

cardiaco, ca o **cardíaco, ca** adj. Cardiac, heart: *enfermedad cardiaca*, cardiac illness. || — *Ataque cardiaco*, heart attack. || *Tónico cardiaco*, heart tonic.
— M. y f. Heart sufferer, sufferer of a heart disease.

cardias m. ANAT. Cardia (del estómago).

cardillo m. BOT. Golden thistle

cardinal adj. Cardinal: *los puntos cardinales*, the cardinal points; *las virtudes cardinales*, the cardinal virtues; *número cardinal*, cardinal number.

cardiografía f. MED. Cardiography.

cardiográfico, ca adj. MED. Cardiographic.

cardiógrafo m. MED. Cardiograph (instrumento).

cardiograma m. MED. Cardiogram.

cardiología f. MED. Cardiology.

cardiológico, ca adj. Cardiological.

cardiólogo, ga m. y f. Cardiologist.

cardiotónico m. MED. Heart tonic.

carditis f. MED. Carditis.

cardizal m. Land covered with thistles.

cardo m. Cardoon (planta comestible). || Thistle (planta espinosa). || — *Cardo borriquero*, cotton thistle. || FIG. *Ser un cardo (borriquero)*, to be a prickly customer.

cardón m. Card, teasel (instrumento para cardar). || Carding (acción de cardar). || *Amer.* Type of giant cactus.

Cardona n. pr. *Más listo que Cardona*, as sharp as a needle.

cardoncillo m. BOT. Milk thistle.

cardume o **cardumen** m. Shoal of fish (banco de peces). || *Amer.* Abundance, great quantity.

carear v. tr. JUR. To confront, to bring face to face: *carear a dos personas*, to bring two people face to face. || FIG. To compare (cosas).
— V. pr. To come face to face (entrevistarse).

carecer* v. intr. To lack: *carecer de los recursos necesarios*, to lack the necessary resources. || — *Carecer de sentido*, to make no sense, not to make sense, to lack meaning. || *No podemos empezar careciendo de tantas cosas*, we can't start with so many things lacking *o* missing.

carena o **carenadura** f. MAR. Careening. || AUT. y AVIAC. Streamlining.

carenar v. tr. MAR. To careen. || AUT. y AVIAC. To streamline.

carencia f. Lack, shortage: *carencia de datos*, lack of data. || Deficiency: *enfermedad por carencia*, deficiency disease.

carenero m. MAR. Careenage (lugar).

carente adj. Lacking: *carente de datos*, lacking [in] data.

careo m. JUR. Confrontation (de personas). | Comparison (de cosas).

carero, ra adj. Expensive, dear: *este carnicero es muy carero*, this butcher is very expensive.
— M. y f. Expensive *o* dear shopkeeper.

carestía f. Shortage, scarcity (escasez). || High price, high cost (precio subido): *la carestía de la vida*, the high cost of living.

careta f. Mask. || — *Careta antigás* or *contra gases*, gasmask. || FIG. *Quitarle la careta a uno*, to unmask s.o.

carey m. Sea turtle (tortuga). || Turtleshell (caparazón). || Tortoiseshell: *un peine de carey*, a tortoiseshell comb.

carga f. Load (peso y cosas llevadas). || Loading (acción): *la carga de un camión*, the loading of a lorry. || Refill (de bolígrafo, de estilográfica). || MAR. Cargo (lo contenido). || Charge (de pólvora). || ELECTR. Charge (de un condensador). | Load (en un circuito). || FOT. Magazine. || DEP. Charge (en fútbol). || MIL. Charge: *carga de caballería*, cavalry charge. || FIG. Burden: *la carga de los años*, the burden of the years. | Liability, obligation (obligación). | Responsibility: *las cargas de un ministro*, the responsibilities of a minister. | Tax, duty, charge (impuesto): *propiedad libre de cargas*, property free from taxes. | Contribution, payment: *cargas sociales*, social contributions. || — *Andén de carga*, loading platform. || MIL. *A paso de carga*, at the double. || MAR. *Barco de carga*, cargo boat, freighter. || *Bestia de carga*, beast of burden. || *Carga de familia*, dependent relative. || *Carga de pólvora*, blasting powder. || *Carga de profundidad*, depth charge. || *Carga máxima*, maximum load, peak load. || *Carga útil de un vehículo*, carrying capacity *o* payload of a vehicle. || FIG. *Llevar la carga de algo*, to be responsible for sth., to be in charge of sth. || *Permitido carga y descarga*, loading and unloading. || MIL. *Tocar paso de carga*, to sound the charge. || *Tomar carga*, to load up (un camión, etc.). || *Volver a la carga*, to renew the attack *o* the assault, to charge again (las tropas), to keep at it (insistir).

cargadero m. Loading base. || Loading platform (de estación). || ARQ. Lintel (dintel).

cargado, da adj. Loaded. || FIG. Burdened, weighed down (de penas, problemas, etc.). || Heavy (tiempo). || MIL. Live (bala). || ELECTR. Charged (pila), live (hilo). || Heavy, dense: *ambiente cargado*, heavy atmosphere. || Stuffy: *tener la cabeza cargada*, to have a stuffy head. || Strong: *un whisky muy cargado*, a very strong whisky. || — *Cargado de años*, burdened by the years. || *Cargado de espaldas*, round-shouldered. || FIG. y FAM. *Estar un poco cargado*, to be tipsy (borracho). | *Tener los ojos cargados*, to have heavy eyes. || *Un árbol cargado de fruto*, a tree laden with fruit.

cargador, ra adj. *Pala cargadora*, mechanical digger.
— M. Loader (sentido general). || Docker, stevedore (de los muelles). || Stoker (de alto horno). || MIL. Chamber. | Ramrod (de cañones). || TECN. Charger (de acumuladores, etc.). || Filler (de bolígrafo, pluma). || *Amer.* Porter. || FOT. Cartridge. || — F. Mechanical digger.

cargamento m. MAR. Cargo. || Load, shipment (de camión).

cargante adj. FIG. y FAM. Annoying, tiresome.

cargar v. tr. To load (una acémila, un barco, un arma de fuego, una máquina de foto). || To fill (una pluma estilográfica). || To hold: *este depósito carga mil litros*, this reservoir holds a thousand litres. || To stoke (un horno). || FIG. To charge (un precio). || JUR. To charge, to accuse. || ELECTR. To charge (batería). || FIG. To burden, to weigh down (con penas, impuestos, deudas). | To fill (la imaginación, etc.). | To levy, to impose (un impuesto). || FIG. y FAM. To annoy, to get on one's nerves (molestar): *este niño me carga*, this child annoys me. | To load with: *me han cargado este trabajo*, they've loaded me with this work. | To place (la responsabilidad). | To put, to lay: *le cargaron la culpa*, they put the blame on him. || To trump (naipes). || To load (dados). || MAR. To take in (las velas). || MIL. To charge: *cargar al enemigo*, to charge the enemy. || *Amer.* To wear (ropa). | To carry (llevar consigo). || — COM. *Cargar algo en cuenta a uno*, to debit s.o.'s account with sth.: *le hemos cargado esta cantidad en cuenta*, we have debited your account with this amount; to charge sth. to s.o.'s account (en un almacén, etc.). || FAM. *Cargar la cuenta*, to overcharge. to add to the bill. | *Cargar la mano*, V. MANO. | *Cargar las tintas*, to lay it on. || FIG. *Cargar una salsa de especias*, to put too much spice in a sauce, to overdo the spice in a sauce. | *Me cargaron de menos*, they undercharged me
— V. intr. To load [up] (un camión, etc.). || To rest: *el peso del arco carga sobre el contrafuerte*, the weight of the arch rests on the buttress. || To come down on, to sweep down on (tempestad, ejército). || To take charge (encargarse). || To take, to pick up: *yo he cargado con el paquete*, I have taken the parcel. || FIG. To take, to shoulder: *cargar con la responsabilidad, con la culpa*, to take the responsibility, the blame. | To rest, to fall: *los impuestos cargan sobre el pueblo*, the taxes rest on the people. | To bear [the burden of]: *el pueblo carga con los impuestos*, the people bear the burden of the taxes. | To be annoying, to be a nuisance: *este niño carga*, this child is annoying. || GRAM. To fall (el acento). || — FAM. *Cargar con las consecuencias*, to suffer the consequences. | *Cargar con uno*, to take charge of s.o. | *Cargar sobre alguien*, to press s.o., to pester s.o.
— V. pr. To become overcast (el cielo, el tiempo). || To become oppressive (la atmósfera). || To fill: *se le cargaron los ojos de lágrimas*, his eyes filled with tears. || To load o.s., to burden o.s.: *cargarse de preocupaciones*, to load o.s. with worries. || To overburden o.s.: *me cargué de deudas*, I overburdened myself with debts. || ELECTR. To become charged (pila), to become live (cable). || FAM. To smash: *me he cargado este reloj*, I have smashed this watch. | To get o.s.: *se cargó seis meses de cárcel*, he got himself six months in prison. | To bump off, to knock off (matar). | To bring [about]

the downfall of, to topple (derribar): *cargarse a un gobierno*, to bring about the downfall of a government. | To fail, to plough (suspender): *cargarse a un alumno*, to fail a pupil. | To get bored (fastidiarse). || — *Cargarse de años*, to get very old. || *Cargarse de paciencia*, to summon up *o* to muster up one's patience. || FAM. *Cargársela*, to get into trouble.

cargazón f. MAR. Cargo (cargamento). || Heavy feeling (del estómago, de la cabeza). || Overcast sky (de nubes). || *Amer.* Good harvest (de frutos). || *Cargazón de espaldas*, stoop.

cargo m. Post: *desempeñar un cargo de profesor*, to have a teacher's post. || Charge, accusation: *formular graves cargos*, to make serious charges. || Charge (responsabilidad): *tener alguien a su cargo*, to have s.o. in one's charge. || COM. Charge, debit. || MAR. Cargo boat, freighter (buque de carga). || — *A cargo de uno*, in one's charge. || *Con cargo a*, charged to: *gastos con cargo a mi cuenta*, expenses charged to my account. || *Correr a cargo de*, V. CORRER. || *Cuenta a cargo*, charge account. || *Es un cargo de conciencia*, it is a weight on one's conscience. || *Girar* or *librar a cargo de*, to draw on. || *Hacerse cargo de*, to take charge of. || *Hacerse cargo de la gravedad de la situación*, to realize the gravity of the situation. || *Hacerse cargo de la situación*, to understand the situation. || *Jurar un cargo*, to take an oath. || *Las tropas se hicieron cargo del poder*, the troops took over power, the troops seized power. || JUR. *Testigo de cargo*, V. TESTIGO.

cargoso, sa adj. *Amer.* Annoying, tiresome (cargante).

carguero m. *Amer.* Beast of burden (acémila). | Cargo boat, freighter (barco). | Transport plane (avión).

cari adj. *Amer.* Lead grey (gris plomo).
— M. Curry (especia).

cariacontecido, da adj. Down in the mouth, dejected, crestfallen.

cariado, da adj. Decayed, carious (dientes).

cariancho, cha adj. Broad-faced, with a broad face.

cariar v. tr. To cause to decay (dientes).
— V. pr. To decay.

cariátide f. ARQ. Caryatid.

Caríbdis n. pr. V. ESCILA.

caribe adj. Caribbean. || *Mar Caribe*, Caribbean Sea.
— M. y f. Carib. || — M. Carib (lengua).

caribú m. ZOOL. Caribou.

caricato m. Comedian (actor cómico).

caricatura f. Caricature.

caricatural o **caricaturesco, ca** adj. Caricatural.

caricaturista m. y f. Caricaturist.

caricaturizar v. tr. To caricature.

caricia f. Stroke: *hacer una caricia al gato*, to give the cat a stroke. || Caress (muestra de cariño). || *Hacer caricias a*, to stroke, to caress.

caridad f. Charity (virtud, limosna): *vivir de la caridad*, to live on charity. || REL. — *Hermana de la Caridad*, sister of charity. || FIG. *La caridad bien entendida comienza por uno mismo*, charity begins at home. || *¡Por caridad!*, for pity's sake!

caries f. inv. Decay, caries.

carilampiño, na adj. Beardless, smoothfaced.

carilargo, ga adj. FAM. Long-faced, with a long face.

carilla f. Side, page (de una hoja de papel). || Mask (de colmenero).

carillón m. MÚS. Carillon (campanas y sonido).

carimba f. o **carimbo** m. Brand (marca con hierro candente). || Branding iron (hierro candente).

cariñito m. FAM. Caress (caricia). | Little darling (apelativo cariñoso).

cariño m. Affection: *tener mucho cariño a alguien*, to have a lot of affection for s.o. || Loving care (esmero): *hacer una cosa con cariño*, to do sth. with loving care. || FIG. Caress (caricia). || — Pl. Love (en una carta). || — *¡Cariño mío!*, my darling! || *Sentir cariño por alguien* or *tener cariño a alguien*, to be fond of s.o. || *Tener cariño a una cosa*, to be attached to sth., to cherish sth. || *Tomar cariño a*, to get attached to, to take a liking to (a uno, a una cosa).

cariñoso, sa adj. Affectionate, loving (afectuoso): *una carta muy cariñosa*, a very affectionate letter. || Nice: *estuvieron muy cariñosos conmigo*, they were very nice to me. || *Recibir a alguien con un cariñoso saludo*, to greet s.o. warmly *o* fondly.

carioca adj. From Rio de Janeiro, of Rio de Janeiro.
— M. y f. Person from *o* inhabitant of Rio de Janeiro.

carioplasma m. Karyoplasm.

cariópside f. BOT. Caryopsis.

carisma m. Charisma, charism.

carismático, ca adj. Charismatic.

caritativo, va adj. Charitable: *caritativo con los pobres*, charitable towards the poor.

carite m. *Amer.* Edible fish from Venezuela.

cariz m. Look: *no me gusta el cariz de este asunto*, I don't like the look of this business. || Look of the weather (del tiempo). || *La situación presenta mal cariz*, the situation looks bad.

carlanca f. Mastiff's collar (collar con púas para el perro).

carlinga f. MAR. y AVIAC. Cockpit (del piloto). | Cabin (de los pasajeros).

carlismo m. Carlism.

carlista adj./s. Carlist: *guerras carlistas*, Carlist Wars.

Carlomagno n. pr. m. Charlemagne.

Carlos n. pr. m. Charles.

Carlota n. pr. f. Charlotte.

carlovingio, gia adj./s. Carlovingian, Carolingian.

carmañola f. Carmagnole.

carmelita adj./s. REL. Carmelite: *la orden carmelita*, the Carmelite order. || *Un carmelita, una carmelita*, a Carmelite monk, nun. || — Adj./s. f. Light brown (color). || — F. Flower of a type of cress.

carmelitano, na adj. REL. Carmelite.

Carmelo n. pr. m. Carmel (monte de Palestina).

carmen m. Villa [in Granada]. || POÉT. Verse (verso).

Carmen n. pr. m. REL. Carmelite order (orden). || — F. Carmen [girl's name].

carmenador m. Large-toothed comb (peine). || Carder (para la lana).

carmenadura f. Combing, disentangling (el pelo). || Carding (la lana).

carmenar v. tr. To comb, to disentangle (el pelo). || To card (la lana). || FIG. y FAM. To fleece, to rob (robar).

carmesí adj./s. m. Crimson (color). || — M. Cochineal powder.

carmín adj. inv. Carmine, crimson (color).
— M. Carmine, crimson (color). || BOT. Wild rose. || *Carmín de labios*, lipstick.

carminativo, va adj./s. m. Carminative.

carmíneo, a adj. Carmine, crimson.

carnación f. Flesh colour.

carnada f. Bait [meat] (cebo).

carnadura f. Robustness (de una persona). || Healing capacity (disposición para cicatrizar).

carnal adj. Carnal. || Sensual (sensual). || Full, blood: *hermano carnal*, full brother. || FIG. Material.

carnauba f. BOT. Carnauba.

carnaval m. Carnival. || REL. Shrovetide. || *Martes de Carnaval*, Shrove Tuesday.

carnavalada f. Carnival (fiesta o broma). || FIG. Farce.

carnavalesco, ca adj. Carnivalesque. || FIG. Ludicrous, absurd, farcical (grotesco).

carnaza f. (P.us.). Derma (cara interior de las pieles). || Meat (carne). || *Amer.* Bait [meat] (cebo). | Scapegoat (cabeza de turco).

carne f. ANAT. Flesh (tejidos). || FIG. Flesh (cuerpo): *la carne es flaca*, the flesh is weak. || Meat (comestible): *carne poco hecha, congelada*, rare, frozen meat. || Flesh (de los frutos). || Heart (de un árbol). || — FIG. *Abrírsele las carnes a uno*, to be frightened to death. || *Carne de cañón*, cannon fodder (soldados). || FIG. *Carne de gallina*, gooseflesh, goose pimples, *pl.*: *me pone la carne de gallina*, it gives me goose pimples. | *Carne de horca*, gallows bird. || *Carne de membrillo*, quince preserve *o* jelly. || FIG. *Carne de mi carne*, flesh of my flesh. || *Carne de pelo*, ground game. || *Carne de pluma*, winged game. || *Carne de ternera*, veal. || *Carne de vaca*, beef. || *Carne magra* or *mollar*, lean meat. || *Carne picada*, mince, minced meat. || *Carne sin hueso*, boned meat. || *Carne viva*, raw flesh. || *Color carne*, flesh colour. || *Criar* or *echar carnes*, to put on weight. || *De abundantes* or *muchas carnes*, fat. || *De pocas carnes*, thin. || FIG. *Echar* or *poner toda la carne en el asador*, to put everything into it, to give it everything one has. || *En carnes* or *en carne viva*, naked, in the raw (fam.). || *En carne y hueso*, in the flesh. || *En carne viva*, red raw (la espalda, la piel etc.), like an unhealed wound: *el recuerdo de la guerra está todavía en carne viva*, the memory of the war is still like an unhealed wound. || FIG. *Herir en carne viva*, to touch *o* to cut to the quick (ofender), to rub salt in a wound (volver a herir). || FAM. *Metido* or *metidito en carnes*, plump, chubby. || FIG. *No ser ni carne ni pescado*, to be neither fish nor fowl. | *Ser de carne y hueso*, to be only human, to be flesh and blood. | *Ser uña y carne*, to be inseparable, to be hand in glove. | *Temblarle a uno las carnes*, to tremble with fright.

carné o **carnet** m. Card: *carné de identidad*, identity card. || Pocket notebook (librito). || *Carné de conducir*, driving licence.

— OBSERV. Pl. *carnés.*

carneada f. *Amer.* Slaughtering.

carnear v. tr. *Amer.* To slaughter (matar reses). | To cheat, to trick (engañar). | To butcher, to slaughter (matar).

carnecería f. Butcher's shop, butcher's.

— OBSERV. This word is sometimes used in Castile and Aragon instead of *carnicería.*

carnerada f. Flock of sheep.

carnero m. Sheep (animal vivo). || Ram (macho de la oveja). || Mutton (carne del animal). || Sheepskin (piel). || Cemetery (cementerio). || Charnel house, ossuary (osario). || *Amer.* Llama. | FIG. Sheep (sin voluntad). || — *Carnero marino*, seal (foca). || *Carnero padre* or *morueco*, ram. || FIG. *No hay tales carneros*, it can't be true, there's no such thing.

carneruno, na adj. Sheep-like.

Carnestolendas f. pl. Carnival (época). || REL. Shrovetide.

carnet m. V. CARNÉ.

carnicería f. Butcher's shop, butcher's (tienda). || FIG. Massacre, slaughter, carnage (matanza): *la batalla de Stalingrado fue una carnicería*, the battle of Stalingrad was a massacre. || *Amer.* Slaughterhouse, abattoir (matadero).

carnicero, ra adj. Carnivorous (que mata para alimentarse): *el lobo es carnicero*, the wolf is carnivorous.

|| FAM. Fond of meat (person). || FIG. y FAM. Bloodthirsty (cruel).
— M. Butcher. || FIG. Butcher (hombre sanguinario). || Carnivore (animal).
cárnico, ca adj. Meat: *industrias cárnicas*, meat industries.
carnicol m. Hoof (pezuña).
carnívoro, ra adj. Carnivorous: *el hombre y el gato son carnívoros*, man and the cat are carnivorous.
— M. Carnivore.
carnosidad f. MED. Outgrowth (excrecencia). | Proud flesh (en una herida). || Fatness, plumpness (gordura).
carnoso, sa o **carnudo, da** adj. Fleshy: *fruto carnoso*, fleshy fruit; *parte carnosa del brazo*, fleshy part of the arm.
caro, ra adj. Expensive, dear: *hotel caro*, expensive hotel; *la langosta es cara*, lobster is expensive. || Dear: *caro amigo*, dear friend.
— Adv. *Pagar caro*, to pay a high price, to pay a lot. || *Salir caro*, to work out *o* to turn out dear *o* expensive. || FIG. *Su error le costó caro*, his mistake cost him dearly. || *Vender caro*, to sell at a high price.
— OBSERV. When used as an adverb, *caro* may or may not agree with the subject, whereas with the verbs *resultar, quedar, permanecer, seguir*, there must be agreement: *la casa me resultó cara*, the house worked out expensive for me.
carocha f. Eggs, *pl.* (de algunos insectos).
Carolina n. pr. f. Caroline (nombre de mujer). || GEOGR. Carolina: *Carolina del Norte*, North Carolina.
carolingio, gia adj./s. Carlovingian, Carolingian (de Carlomagno).
carolino, na adj. Caroline. || GEOGR. *Islas Carolinas*, Caroline Islands.
carota m. y f. FAM. Cheeky devil (caradura).
caroteno m. QUÍM. Carotene, carrotene, carotin, carrotin.
carotenoide adj./s. m. QUÍM Carotenoid, carotinoid.
carótida f. ANAT. Carotid.
carotídeo, a adj. ANAT. Carotid.
carozo m. Cob (de la mazorca de maíz). || Stone (de aceituna, melocotón, etc.).
carpa f. Carp (pez). || Part of a bunch of grapes, small bunch of grapes (racimillo). || *Amer.* Tent (de camping). | Big top (de circo). | Awning (toldo). | Stall (en la feria). || — DEP. *En carpa*, pike (salto). | *Salto de la carpa*, jackknife.
carpanel adj. MAT. y ARQ. Basket-handle.
carpanta f. FAM. Ravenous hunger (hambre). || *Amer.* Band *o* gang of rowdies (pandilla). || FAM. *Tener carpanta*, to be ravenous *o* famished.
Cárpatos n. pr. m. pl. Carpathian Mountains.
carpelo m. BOT. Carpel (del pistilo).
carpeta f. Portfolio (cartones con cintas). || Folder, file (cartón doblado): *ordenar los documentos en una carpeta*, to arrange documents in a folder. || Briefcase (cartera). || Table cover (de mesa). || Blotting pad (para escribir). || *Cerrar la carpeta*, to close the file (de una investigación).
carpetazo (dar) loc. FIG. To shelve: *dar carpetazo a un asunto*, to shelve a matter.
carpetovetónico, ca adj. FIG. y FAM. Spanish to the core
carpiano, na adj. ANAT. Carpal.
carpincho m. ZOOL. Capybara (capibara).
carpintear v. intr. To do carpenter's *o* joiner's work, to carpenter.
carpintería f. Carpentry, joinery (oficio y elementos de madera en una construcción). || Carpenter's *o* joiner's shop (taller). || *Carpintería metálica*, metal structural work.
carpintero, ra adj. Carpenter: *abeja, hormiga, polilla carpintera*, carpenter bee, ant, moth. || *Pájaro carpintero*, woodpecker.
— M. Carpenter, joiner.
carpo m. ANAT. Carpus.
carpología f. BOT. Carpology (estudio de las frutas).
carpológico, ca adj. BOT. Carpological.
carpólogo m. BOT. Carpologist.
carraca f. MAR. Carack, carrack (navío). || FIG. Old tub (barco viejo). | Old crock (coche viejo). | Decrepit old person (persona vieja). || (Ant.). Shipyard. || TECN. Ratchet brace (trinquete). || MÚS. Rattle (instrumento). || *Amer.* Jaw (quijada).
carraco, ca adj. FAM. Decrepit.
Carracuca n. pr. *Estar más perdido que Carracuca*, to have no way out, to be doomed, to be hopelessly lost.
carrada f. Cartload (carga de un carro). || FAM. Heaps, *pl.*, loads, *pl.* (cantidad grande). || *Ganar dinero a carradas*, to rake in money.
carraleja f. ZOOL. Black beetle with yellow stripes.
carrasca f. BOT. Holm oak (encina pequeña).
carrascal m. Holm-oak forest. || *Amer.* Stony ground (pedregal).
carraspear v. intr. To clear one's throat (aclararse la voz). || To speak with a hoarse voice (hablar con voz ronca).
carraspeo m. o **carraspera** f. Clearing of the throat. || Hoarseness (aspereza en la garganta). || *Tener carraspera*, to have a hoarse voice, to have a frog in one's throat (fam.).
carrasposo, sa adj. Very hoarse (ronco). || *Amer.* Rough (áspero).
carrasqueño, ña adj. Rough (áspero).
carrera f. Race (deportes): *carrera ciclista, de caballos, de sacos, de fondo*, cycling, horse, sack, long-distance race; *carrera pedestre*, footrace. || Run (béisbol, cricket). || Run (acción). || Route: *la carrera de una procesión*, the route of a procession. || Ride (de taxi). || TECN. Stroke (de émbolo). || FIG. Row, line: *carrera de árboles*, row of trees. | Ladder (en la media). | Life: *una carrera bien aprovechada*, a life well spent. || Career: *la carrera diplomática, militar*, the diplomatic, military career. || Profession (profesión). || Course (de estudios). || ARQ. Girder, beam (viga). || Avenue, boulevard (calle). || Parting (raya del pelo). || ASTR. Course. || — Pl. DEP. Races. || — *Abrir carrera*, to set the pace. || *A carrera tendida*, at full speed. || *A la carrera*, at full speed. || *Carrera a campo traviesa* or *a campo través*, cross-country running (deporte), cross-country race (una competición). || *Carrera contra el reloj*, race against the clock, race against time (en deporte), race against time (prisa). || *Carrera de armamentos*, arms race. || *Carrera de obstáculos*, v. OBSTÁCULO. || *Carrera de relevos*, relay race. || *Carrera de vallas*, hurdle race (atletas, caballos). || *Cubrir la carrera*, to line the route. || *Dar carrera a uno*, to pay for s.o.'s studies, to send s.o. to university. || *Dar carrera libre a*, to give free rein to. || *Darse una carrera*, to hurry, to rush. || FIG. *De carrera*, parrot-fashion: *recitar de carrera*, to recite parrot-fashion. || *Exámenes de fin de carrera*, finals, final examinations. || FIG. *Hacer carrera*, to get on: *este hombre ha hecho carrera en Australia*, this man has got on in Australia. || FAM. *Hacer la carrera*, to solicit, to streetwalk (prostituta). || *Hacer la carrera de derecho*, to study law. || *Hacer una cosa a la carrera*, to race through sth. || FAM. *No puedo hacer carrera con* or *de mi hijo*, I can't get anywhere with this son of mine, I am getting nowhere with this son of mine. || *Tener la carrera de derecho*, to have a degree in law. || *Tomar carrera*, to take a run (para saltar).
carrerilla f. MÚS. Run. || Ladder (en una media): *coger una carrerilla*, to mend a ladder. || — *Saber de carrerilla*, v. SABER. || *Tomar carrerilla*, to take a run (para saltar).
carrerista m. Racegoer (aficionado a las carreras). || Rider (ciclista). || Runner (a pie). || Punter (persona que apuesta). || — F. FAM. Street prostitute, streetwalker (ramera).
carrero m. Cart driver, carter (carretero).
carreta f. Cart. || — FIG. *Andar como una carreta*, to go at a snail's pace. || *Carreta de bueyes*, oxcart. || *Carreta de mano*, barrow, handcart. || FAM. *Tren carreta*, slow train.
carretada f. Cartload (carga de una carreta). | FIG. y FAM. Load, heap (gran cantidad). || FIG. y FAM. *Naranjas a carretadas*, loads of oranges.
carrete m. Bobbin, reel (de hilo). || Spool (de película). || Reel (de caña de pescar). || ELECTR. Coil: *carrete de inducción*, induction coil. || — *Dar carrete*, to pay out the line (pesca). || FIG. *Dar carrete a uno*, to keep s.o. on a string.
carretear v. tr. To cart (transportar en carro).
carretel m. Reel (de caña de pescar). || MAR. Winch (de la corredera). || *Amer.* Bobbin, reel (carrete).
carretera f. Road: *carretera secundaria* or *comarcal*, B road [U.S., secondary road]; *carretera de acceso*, approach road. || — *Albergue de carretera*, roadside hotel. || *Carretera de circunvalación*, bypass, ring road. || *Carretera general* or *nacional*, A *o* arterial road [U.S., arterial highway]. || *Carretera radial*, radial road. || *Estrechamiento de carretera*, road narrows (señal de tráfico). || *Mapa de carreteras*, road map. || *Por carretera*, by road. || *Red de carreteras*, road network.
carretería f. Cartwright's work (oficio). || Cartwright's shop (taller).
carretero adj. For vehicles. || *Camino carretero*, cart track.
— M. Cartwright (constructor). || Cart driver, carter (conductor). || FIG. *Blasfemar* or *jurar como un carretero*, to swear like a trooper.
carretilla f. Wheelbarrow, barrow (de jardinero, etc.). || Trolley [U.S., pushcart] (en tiendas, estaciones, etc.). || Baby walker (para los niños). || Banger, cracker, squib (cohete). || *Amer.* Jaw (quijada). || — *Carretilla eléctrica*, electric truck *o* trolley. || *Carretilla elevadora*, forklift truck. || *De carretilla*, by heart.
carretón m. Small cart (carro). || Handcart (tirado a mano). || Cart (del afilador). || Bogie, bogy, bogey (ferrocarril). || *Amer.* Bobbin, reel (de hilo).
carricoche m. FAM. Old crock, jalopy (coche malo). || Caravan (de gitanos).
carricuba f. Water cart.
carril m. Rut (huella). || Furrow (surco). || Track (camino). || Lane (de una autopista). || Rail (de vía férrea). || *Amer.* Railway (ferrocarril), train (tren).
carrilano o **carrilero** m. *Amer.* Railwayman (que trabaja en los ferrocarriles). | Robber (ladrón).
carrilera f. Rut (huella). || *Amer.* Siding (apartadero).
carrillada f. Chop, cheek (de un cerdo).
carrillera f. Jaw (quijada). || Chin strap (barboquejo).
carrillo m. Cheek (parte de la cara). || Trolley (mesa para servir). || Trolley [U.S., pushcart] (en las tiendas, estaciones, etc.). || Pulley (garrucha). || Carrier tricycle (triciclo de reparto). || FIG. *Comer a dos carrillos*, to guzzle, to gobble (comer con gula).

carrilludo, da adj. Fat-cheeked, chubby-cheeked.
carrito m. Trolley (para servir la mesa). || Trolley [U.S., pushcart] (en tiendas, estaciones, etc.). || Shoe (en juegos de cartas).
carrizal m. Reedbed.
carrizo m. Reed (caña).
carro m. Cart (vehículo de dos ruedas). || Cartload (carga). || IMPR. Press carriage. || Carriage (de máquina de escribir). || MIL. Tank (carro de combate). || *Amer.* Car (automóvil). | Tram [U.S., streetcar] (tranvía). | Carriage (vagón). || — FAM. *Aguantar* or *tragar carros y carretas*, to put up with murder. || MIL. *Carro blindado*, armoured car [U.S., armored car]. || *Carro cuba*, water cart. || MIL. *Carro de combate*, tank. || ASTR. *Carro Mayor* or *de David*, Great Bear. | *Carro Menor*, Little Bear. || FIG. *Empujar el carro*, to put one's shoulder to the wheel. | *Parar el carro a alguien*, to calm s.o. down (calmar), to put s.o. in his place (hacer callar). | *Poner el carro delante de las mulas*, to put the cart before the horse. | *Tirar del carro*, to pull all the weight, to do all the donkey work. | *Untar el carro a uno*, to bribe s.o., to grease s.o.'s palm.
carrocería f. Body, bodywork (de automóvil). || *Taller de carrocería*, bodywork *o* coachwork *o* coach-building shop.
carrocero m. Coachbuilder, body-builder (constructor de carrocería). || Panel beater (chapista).
carrocha f. Eggs, *pl.* (de insectos).
carrochar v. intr. To lay eggs (los insectos).
carromato m. Covered wagon *o* cart (carro). || Caravan (de gente de circo, gitanos).
carroña f. Decaying carcass, carrion. || FIG. Trash (gente despreciable).
carroño, ña adj. Decayed (podrido).
carroza f. Coach, carriage (coche antiguo de lujo). || Float (en carnaval). || MAR. Awning. || *Carroza fúnebre*, hearse.
carruaje m. Carriage.
carrusel m. Horse tattoo (ejercicio hípico). || Roundabout, merry-go-round [U.S., carrousel].
carta f. Letter (misiva): *carta certificada*, registered letter; *echar una carta*, to post a letter. || Card (naipe): *baraja de cartas*, pack of cards. || JUR. Deed. || Menu (lista de platos) [V. OBSERV.]. || List (de vinos). || Charter (ley): *carta del Atlántico*, Atlantic charter. || MAR. Chart: *carta de marear* or *marina*, maritime chart. || — *A carta cabal*, completely, totally, perfectly, one hundred per cent: *un hombre honrado a carta cabal*, a perfectly honest man; perfect (con sustantivo): *un caballero a carta cabal*, a perfect gentleman. || *A cartas vistas*, with the cards on the table: *jugar a cartas vistas*, to play with the cards on the table. || *A la carta*, à la carte (en un restaurante). || *Carta abierta*, open letter. || *Carta adjunta*, covering letter. || *Carta aérea*, air-mail letter. || *Carta blanca*, carte blanche, free hand: *dar carta blanca a alguien*, to give s.o. a free hand. || *Carta de ajuste*, test card (televisión). || *Carta de crédito*, letter of credit. || *Carta de despido*, letter of dismissal. || *Carta de hidalguía*, letters patent of nobility. || *Carta de llamada*, letter of sponsorship (para un emigrante). || *Carta de naturaleza* or *de ciudadanía*, naturalization papers. || *Carta de origen*, pedigree (de un animal). || COM. *Carta de pago*, receipt. | *Carta de pedido*, order. || *Carta de pésame*, letter of condolence. || *Carta de porte*, consignment paper [U.S., waybill]. || *Carta de presentación* or *de recomendación*, letter of introduction. || *Carta de solicitud*, application. || *Carta de vecindad*, certificate of residence. || *Carta Magna*, Magna Carta. || *Carta pastoral*, pastoral letter. || *Cartas al director*, letters to the editor (en un periódico). || *Cartas credenciales*, letter (*sing.*) of credence, letters credential, credential letters. || *Carta urgente*, express letter, special delivery letter. || *Echar las cartas*, to read the cards. || FIG. *Jugar bien sus cartas*, to play one's cards right *o* well. | *Jugarse la última carta*, to play one's last card. | *Jugárselo todo a una carta*, to put all one's eggs in one basket. | *Mostrar* or *enseñar las cartas*, to show one's hand, to put one's cards on the table. | *No saber a qué carta quedarse*, to be all at sea, to be in a dilemma. | *Poner las cartas sobre la mesa* or *boca arriba*, to put *o* to lay one's cards on the table *o* face upwards. | *Tener* or *tomar cartas en un asunto*, to intervene in an affair.

— OBSERV. En inglés *menu* significa tanto el menú fijo como la carta. Sin embargo la expresión *comer a la carta* se traduce por *to eat à la carte*.

cartabón m. Set square, triangle (de dibujante, de agrimensor). || Foot gauge (de zapatero). || *Amer.* Measuring apparatus, measure (talla).
cartaginense o **cartaginés, esa** adj./s. Carthaginian.
Cartago n. pr. GEOGR. Carthage.
cartapacio m. Portfolio (para libros, dibujos, etc.). || Writing pad (para escribir). || Notebook (cuaderno).
cartearse v. pr. To correspond, to write to each other.
cartel m. Poster, bill (anuncio). || Wall chart (en la escuela). || (Ant.). Cartel (de desafío). || Pasquinade (pasquín). || — *Colgar el cartel de "no hay billetes"*, to put up the "house full" sign *o* the "sold out" sign. || *De cartel*, celebrated: *un equipo, un torero de cartel*, a celebrated team, bullfighter. || *Obra que continúa en cartel*, a work which is still on *o* still running. || *Pegar* or *fijar carteles*, to put up *o* to stick up *o* to post bills. || *Se prohibe* or *prohibido fijar carteles*, post *o* stick no bills. || FIG. *Tener buen* or *mucho cartel*, to be very successful, to be a hit, to be good box office.
cártel m. Cartel, trust: *cártel industrial*, industrial cartel. || Coalition: *el cártel de las izquierdas*, the coalition of the left.

— OBSERV. Pl. *cárteles*.

cartelera f. Billboard, hoarding (para carteles). || Entertainments. *pl.* (en el periódico). || *Llevar mucho tiempo en cartelera*, to run *o* to be on for a long time.
cartelero m. Billposter.
cartelista m. y f. Poster designer (dibujante).
cartelización f. Grouping into cartels.
cartelón m. Large poster, large bill.
carteo m. Exchange of letters, correspondence.
cárter m. TECN. Housing (en general). | Crankcase (de automóvil). | Chain guard (de bicicleta).
cartera f. Wallet (de bolsillo). || Purse [U.S., pocketbook] (monedero). || Briefcase, document case (portadocumentos). || Satchel (de colegial). || Bag (de cobrador). || Saddlebag, pannierbag (de bicicleta). || Flap (pieza que cubre el bolsillo). || FIG. Portfolio: *ministro sin cartera*, minister without portfolio. || COM. Portfolio (de valores). || — *Cartera de pedidos*, order book. || FAM. *Echar mano a la cartera*, to dip into one's pocket (para pagar). || FIG. *En cartera*, planned (un proyecto). | *Tener en cartera*, to have plans for, to be planning. || *Valores en cartera*, holdings, stocks.
cartería f. Postman's job *o* work. || Sorting office (en correos).
carterilla f. Flap (de un bolsillo).
carterista m. Pickpocket.
carterita f. Book (de cerillas).
cartero m. Postman [U.S., mailman].
cartesianismo m. Cartesianism.
cartesiano, na adj./s. Cartesian.
cartilagíneo, a o **cartilaginoso, sa** adj. ANAT. Cartilaginous, cartilaginoid: *tejido cartilaginoso*, cartilaginous tissue.
cartílago m. ANAT. Cartilage.
cartilla f. First reader, first reading book (libro). || FIG. Primer (tratado elemental). || Book: *cartilla de ahorros, de racionamiento*, savings, ration book. || MIL. Record: *cartilla militar*, military record. || REL. Ordo, liturgical calendar (añalejo). || Certificate of ordination (de un sacerdote). || — FIG. y FAM. *Leerle a uno la cartilla*, to give s.o. a lecture. | *No saber ni la cartilla*, not to have the faintest *o* the slightest idea.
cartografía f. Cartography.
cartográfico, ca adj. Cartographic, cartographical.
cartógrafo, fa m. y f. Cartographer.
cartograma m. Cartogram.
cartomancia o **cartomancía** f. Cartomancy, fortune telling.
cartomántico, ca adj. Fortune telling.
— M. y f. Fortune teller.
cartón m. Cardboard: *caja de cartón*, cardboard box. || ARTES. Cartoon, sketch. || Board (de un libro). || Carton (de cigarrillos). || — *Cartón ondulado*, corrugated cardboard. || *Cartón piedra*, papier mâché.
cartonaje m. Cardboard box industry *o* trade.
cartoné (en) adj. In boards. || *Un libro en cartoné*, a book bound in boards.
cartonería f. Cardboard box industry *o* trade.
cartonero, ra adj. Cardboard: *industria cartonera*, cardboard industry.
— M. y f. Cardboard maker.
cartuchera f. MIL. Cartridge holder (en general), cartridge belt (cinturón).
cartuchería f. Cartridge factory.
cartucho m. MIL. Cartridge: *cartucho de fogueo* or *de salvas*, blank cartridge. | Cartridge bag (saquete de pólvora). || Paper cone (de papel grueso). || Roll (de moneda). || — FIG. *Luchar hasta quemar el último cartucho*, to fight to the bitter end. | *Quemar el último cartucho*, to play one's last card.
cartuja f. REL. Carthusian order (orden). | Charterhouse, chartreuse (monasterio).
cartujano, na adj./s. Carthusian. || *Caballo cartujano*, breed of horse found in Jerez [Andalusia].
cartujo adj. m./s.m. Carthusian. || FIG. y FAM. *Vivir como un cartujo*, to live like a hermit.
cartulario m. Cartulary.
cartulina f. Bristol board.
carúncula f. ANAT. y ZOOL. Caruncle: *carúncula lagrimal*, lachrymal caruncle.
carvallar o **carvalledo** m. (P.us.). Oak grove *o* wood.
casa f. House: *casa de campo*, country house; *casa de juego*, gambling house. || Flat [U.S., apartment] (piso). || Building (edificio). || Home (hogar): *quedarse en casa*, to stay at home; *me gusta mi casa*, I like my home. || House (familia): *la casa de los Estuardos*, the house of Stuart. || Household, family (habitantes de una casa). || Firm, company (empresa). || Branch (sucursal). || Square (casilla): *el tablero de ajedrez tiene 64 casas*, the chessboard has 64 squares. || ASTR. House. || — *A casa*, home (de uno mismo): *irse a casa*, to go home. || *A casa de Pedro*, to Peter's house, to Peter's. || *Aquí está usted en su casa*, make yourself at home. || *Aquí tiene usted su casa*, you are always welcome here. || *Buscar casa*, to look for somewhere to

live. || FIG. *Cada uno en su casa y Dios en la de todos*, every man for himself and God for us all. | *Cada uno es rey en su casa*, a man's home is his castle. || *Casa central*, head office, main branch. || *Casa civil*, household (del rey o del jefe de Estado). || *Casa comercial*, business firm. || *Casa consistorial*, town hall. || *Casa cuna*, nursery. || *Casa de banca*, bank. || *Casa de baños*, public baths, bathhouse. || *Casa de bebidas*, bar. || *Casa de beneficencia*, poorhouse. || *Casa de cambio*, exchange office. || *Casa de citas*, house of call. || *Casa de comidas*, eating house. || *Casa de correos*, general post office. || *Casa de Dios*, House of God. || *Casa de empeños* or *de préstamos*, pawnbroker's [shop], pawnshop. || *Casa de fieras*, zoo, menagerie. || *Casa de huéspedes*, boarding house. || *Casa de labor* or *de labranza*, farmhouse. || *Casa de la Villa*, Town Hall. || *Casa de lenocinio*, brothel. || *Casa de locos*, lunatic asylum (manicomio). || *Casa de maternidad*, maternity hospital *o* home. || *Casa de la Moneda*, mint, Royal Mint. || *Casa de modas*, fashion house. || *Casa de pisos*, block of flats [U.S., apartment building]. || *Casa de recreo*, country house. || *Casa de reposo*, rest home. || *Casa de socorro*, emergency *o* casualty hospital, first-aid post. || *Casa de trato*, licensed brothel. || *Casa de vecindad* or *de vecinos*, block of flats [U.S., apartment building]. || *Casa editorial*, publishing house. || REL. *Casa matriz*, mother house. || *Casa militar*, Royal Guard. || *Casa mortuoria*, house of the deceased. || *Casa paterna*, parents' house. || *Casa pública*, brothel. || *Casa real*, Royal Family. || *Casa religiosa*, convent (de monjas), monastery (de frailes). || *Casa remolque*, caravan [U.S., trailer]. || *Casa solariega*, ancestral home, family seat, country seat. || *Casa y comida*, board and lodging. || FIG. y FAM. *Como Pedro por su casa*, as if he owned the place. || FIG. *De* or *para andar por casa*, ordinary, everyday (insignificante). | *Echar* or *tirar la casa por la ventana*, to spare no expense, to go overboard, to lash out (fam.). | *Empezar la casa por el tejado*, to put the cart before the horse. | *En casa del herrero cuchillo de palo*, the shoemaker's wife is always worst shod. | *Es mi segunda casa*, it is my home from home. || *Estar de casa*, to be dressed casually. || *Estar en casa*, to be at home, to be in. || *Estar fuera de casa*, to be out, not to be in. || *Hacer la casa*, to do the housework. || *Inaugurar la casa*, to have a house-warming. || DEP. *Jugar en casa*, to play at home. || FAM. *La casa de Tócame Roque*, bear garden, bedlam. || *Levantar casa*, to move house. || *Llevar la casa*, to run the house. || *Marcharse de casa*, to leave home. || *Mujer de su casa*, good housekeeper. || *No parar en casa*, to be never at home, to be always out. || *No salir de casa*, not to go out. || *No tener ni casa ni hogar*, to have neither house nor home. || *Ofrecer la casa*, to offer one's house. || *Pasar por casa de alguien*, to call on s.o. || *Poner casa*, to settle down, to set up house (instalarse). || FIG. y FAM. *Se me cae la casa encima*, I can't stand being in the house, the house is getting me down. || *Sentirse como en casa*, to feel at home. || *Tener casa abierta*, to keep open house. || *Un amigo de (la) casa*, a friend of the family.

casabe m. Cassava flour (harina). || Cassava bread (pan).

Casablanca n. pr. GEOGR. Casablanca.

Casa Blanca n. pr. f. White House.

casaca f. Dress coat (vestido). || FIG. *Volver casaca* or *la casaca*, to turn one's coat, to change sides.

casación f. JUR. Cassation, annulment.

casacón m. Greatcoat.

casadero, ra adj. Old enough to marry, marriageable, of marrying age: *una muchacha casadera*, a marriageable girl, a girl old enough to marry.

casado, da adj. Married: *hombre casado*, married man; *una mujer recién casada*, a newly-married woman. || — *Estar casado*, to be married (*con*, to). || *Mal casado*, unhappily married.
— M. y f. Married man *o* woman. || — *El casado casa quiere*, everyone wants his own home. || *Los recién casados*, the newlyweds. || — M. IMPR. Imposition.

casamata f. MIL. Casemate.

casamentero, ra adj. Matchmaking: *una mujer casamentera*, a matchmaking woman.
— M. y f. Matchmaker.

casamiento m. Marriage: *un casamiento ventajoso*, a marriage for money. || — *Casamiento desigual*, misalliance, unequal marriage. || *Casamiento por amor*, love match.

Casandra n. pr. f. Cassandra.

casapuerta f. Porch, entrance (zaguán).

casaquilla f. Short cassock.

casar v. tr. To marry (unir en matrimonio). || To marry off: *ha casado muy bien a sus hijas*, she has married off her daughters quite well. || FIG. To match (poner en armonía). | To join (unir). || IMPR. To impose. || JUR. To annul, to quash.
— V. intr. To marry, to get married: *Fernando II de Aragón casó con Isabel I de Castilla*, Fernando II of Aragon married Isabel I of Castile *o* got married to Isabel I of Castile. || To match, to go together (armonizar): *estos colores no casan bien*, these colours do not match. || To balance, to tally: *las cuentas no casan*, the accounts do not tally. || To fit together: *estas dos piezas no casan*, these parts do not fit together. || To tally: *esas dos versiones no casan*, those two versions do not tally.
— V. pr. To marry, to get married: *casarse con una hermosa mujer*, to get married to *o* to marry a beautiful woman. || — FIG. *Antes que te cases mira lo que haces*, look before you leap. || *Casarse en segundas nupcias*, to remarry, to marry again. || *Casarse por detrás de la iglesia*, to live together [as a married couple]. || *Casarse por interés*, to marry [for] money. || *Casarse por lo civil*, to get married in a registry office. || *Casarse por poderes*, to get married by proxy. || FAM. *¡Cásate y verás!*, live and learn! || FIG. *No casarse con nadie*, to keep o.s. to o.s.

casca f. Skin of pressed grapes (piel de la uva). || Marc (orujo). || Bark, tan, tanning bark (para curtir). || — Pl. Rind, *sing.*, peel, *sing.* (fruta confitada).

cascabel m. Bell (campanilla). || — FIG. y FAM. *De cascabel gordo*, cheap (obra). | *Poner el cascabel al gato*, to stick one's neck out, to bell the cat. || *Serpiente de cascabel*, rattlesnake.

cascabelada f. FIG. y FAM. Stupid thing, stupidity.

cascabelear v. tr. FIG. y FAM. To lure, to take in.
— V. intr. To tinkle, to jingle (hacer ruidos como cascabeles). || FIG. y FAM. To act recklessly. || *Amer.* To grumble (refunfuñar).

cascabeleo m. Jingling, tinkling.

cascabelero, ra adj. Tinkling, jingling.

cascada f. Waterfall, cascade. || FIG. Cascade.

cascado, da adj. Broken-down, broken, worn-out: *un anciano muy cascado*, a very broken-down old man. || Harsh, cracked: *tener la voz cascada*, to have a harsh voice. || Broken-down (desvencijado). || Cracked: *el jarrón, el vaso está cascado*, the vase, the glass is cracked.

cascadura f. Crack.

cascajal o **cascajar** m. Pebbly ground.

cascajo m. Gravel (guijo), grit (guijarrillo). || Screenings, *pl.* (escombros). || Broken pieces, *pl.*, fragments, *pl.* (de vasijas, etc.). || Nut (fruto). || FIG. y FAM. Decrepit old man (viejo). | Old crock (coche). | Old scrap, junk (trastos viejos). || FAM. *Estar hecho un cascajo*, to be a wreck.

cascajoso, sa adj. Gravelly, covered with gravel.

cascanueces m. inv. Nutcrackers, *pl.*, nutcracker: *¿dónde está el cascanueces?*, where are the nutcrackers? || ZOOL. Nutcracker (pájaro). || *Un cascanueces*, a pair of nutcrackers.

cascapiñones m. inv. Nutcrackers, *pl.*, nutcracker.

cascar v. tr. To crack (una vasija, un huevo, una nuez). || FAM. To beat up, to give a beating to: *le han cascado en el mitin*, they beat him up at the meeting. | To blow: *hoy casqué mil pesetas en el juego*, today I blew a thousand pesetas gambling. | To cough up (pagar). | To give (poner): *le han cascado un cero en matemáticas*, they've given him a goose egg in mathematics.
— V. intr. FAM. To chatter: *esta mujer está siempre cascando*, this woman is always chattering. | To swot up: *cascarle fuerte al latín*, to swot up Latin hard. | To kick the bucket (morir).
— V. pr. To crack, to become harsh (la voz). || To crack, to split (romperse).

cáscara f. Shell (del huevo, de los frutos secos). || Bark (de los troncos). || Husk (de cereales). || Skin, peel (de las frutas). || Peel (de naranja o limón). || Rind (del queso). || — *¡Cáscaras!*, damn!, dash! || FAM. *Ser de la cáscara amarga*, to be a queer (ser homosexual).

cascarilla f. Husk (corteza). || Metal covering (de un botón). || Flake (fragmento desprendido del enlucido). || Cocoa (del cacao). || FAM. *El hermanito jugó de cascarilla*, their little brother played but they didn't count him.

cascarillo m. Cascarilla (árbol).

cascarón m. Shell, eggshell (de huevo). || — FIG. y FAM. *Aún no ha salido del cascarón*, he is still a baby. || *Cascarón de nuez*, nutshell (barco).

cascarrabias m. y f. inv. Grouse, irritable *o* crabby *o* grumpy person.

casco m. Helmet (de soldado, bombero, aviador). || Crown (del sombrero). || Headband (del auricular). || Skull, cranium (cráneo). || FAM. Nut, head (cabeza). || Broken piece, fragment (de botella, de vidrio). || Piece of shrapnel (de metralla, de obús). || BOT. Coat, skin (de la cebolla). | Segment (de naranja). || Barrel (tonel). || Empty (botella vacía). || Central area (de población). || MAR. Hull (del barco). || ZOOL. Hoof (de las caballerías). || — Pl. Head (*sing.*) of sheep *o* calf [without brain and tongue] (cabeza de res). || — FIG. y FAM. *Alegre* or *ligero de cascos*, scatterbrained. | *Calentarle a alguien los cascos con*, to pester s.o. with. || *Casco protector*, crash helmet. || *El casco antiguo de una ciudad*, the old part of a city. || FIG. y FAM. *Estar mal de los cascos*, to be dotty, to be off one's rocker. | *Romperse* or *calentarse los cascos*, to rack one's brains. | *Sentar los cascos*, to settle down.

cascotes m. pl. Rubble, *sing.*

caseína f. QUÍM. Casein.

cáseo adj. Caseous, cheesy.
— M. Curd (requesón).

caseoso, sa adj. Caseous, cheesy.

caserío m. Hamlet, small village (pueblecito). || Country house and its outbuildings (de un cortijo).

casero, ra adj. Domestic (animal): *conejo casero*, domestic rabbit. || Home-made: *tarta casera*, home-

made tart. || Family: *una reunión casera*, a family gathering. || Indoor, everyday (ropa). || Home-loving, stay-at-home (amante del hogar). || Household (medicina). || *Cocina casera*, home cooking.
— M. y f. Proprietor, owner, landlord (hombre), landlady (mujer) [de casa alquilada]. || Keeper (de finca rústica). || Stay-at-home, home-lover (amante del hogar). || House agent (administrador de casa).

caserón m. Big rambling house.

caseta f. Small house, cottage (casita). || Booth, stall (de feria). || Bathing cabin, bathing hut [U.S., bathhouse] (de bañista). || Stand, stall (de exposición). || Cubicle (en la piscina). || Pavilion (en otros deportes). || — *Caseta de cambios de agujas*, signal box (ferrocarriles). || MAR. *Caseta del timón*, wheelhouse. || *Caseta de perro*, kennel, doghouse.

casi adv. Almost, nearly: *tiene casi cien años*, he is almost a hundred years old. || — *Casi, casi*, very nearly: *eran casi, casi las doce*, it was very nearly twelve o'clock. || *Casi nada*, hardly any: *¿cuánto queda de azúcar? — Casi nada*, how much sugar is there left? — Hardly any; hardly anything: *no dijo casi nada*, he hardly said anything; hardly at all: *la vacuna no me ha dolido casi nada*, the vaccination hardly hurt me at all. || *¡Casi nada!* (irónicamente), is that all!: *le ha tocado el gordo en la lotería. — ¡Casi nada!*, he has won first prize in the lottery. — Is that all! || *Casi no*, hardly: *casi no me duele ya*, it hardly hurts now; hardly any: *casi no tiene amigos*, he has hardly any friends. || *Casi nunca*, hardly ever: *casi nunca pasa por casa*, he hardly ever comes round. || *Casi prefiero el otro modelo*, I think I prefer the other model. || *Casi sin*, without hardly: *se fue casi sin decir adiós*, he left without hardly saying goodbye. || *Es casi tonto. — Sin casi*, he's almost stupid. — More than almost.

casia f. BOT. Cassia (arbusto).

casicontrato m. JUR. Quasi-contract, implied contract.

casilla f. Small house, cottage (casita). || Lodge, hut (de guarda). || Cabin, hut (de madera). || Stall, booth (puesto de venta). || Ticket office, box office (taquilla). || Square (de papel rayado, de crucigrama, de ajedrez). || Pigeonhole (de estante). || FAM. Clink (prisión). || *Amer.* Toilet, lavatory (excusado). | Bird trap, snare (trampa). || — *Amer. Casilla postal*, post-office box (apartado). || FIG. *Sacar a uno de sus casillas*, to shake s.o. up, to bring s.o. out of his shell (trastornar), to make s.o. mad, to infuriate s.o. (enfurecer). | *Salir de sus casillas*, to come out of one's shell (cambiar de costumbres), to lose one's temper, to fly off the handle (enfurecerse).

casillero m. Set of pigeonholes, pigeonholes, *pl.*

casimir m. o **casimira** f. Cashmere (tela).

Casimiro n. pr. m. Casimir.

casino m. Casino (casa de recreo). || Club, circle (asociación y lugar donde se reúne).

Casio n. pr. m. Cassius.

casiopea f. ASTR. Cassiopeia.

casis m. Blackcurrant liqueur (licor).

casita f. Small house, little house. || *Vámonos a casita*, let's go home.

casiterita f. MIN. Cassiterite, tinstone.

caso m. Case (circunstancia). || Event, happening (suceso). || Case, instance: *fue un caso de falta de cuidado*, it was an instance of carelessness. || Affair: *el caso Dreyfus*, the Dreyfus affair. || MED. Case: *un caso de meningitis*, a case of meningitis. || GRAM. Case. || Case, subject (de un experimento, etc.). || — *Caso de conciencia*, case of conscience. || *Caso de fuerza mayor*, case of dire necessity (necesidad), force majeure (término jurídico). || *Caso fortuito*, v. FORTUITO. || *Caso perdido*, hopeless case. || *Caso que* or *en caso de que ganemos*, in case we win, if we should win. || *Dado el caso de que*, supposing [that]. || *El caso es que*, the fact is that. || *En caso de incendio*, in the event of *o* in case of fire. || *En caso de necesidad*, should the need arise, if need be. || *En el mejor de los casos*, at best. || *En el peor de los casos*, if the worst comes to the worst, at worst. || *En este* or *en tal caso*, in this case, in such a case. || *En todo caso*, in any case, anyway, at all events. || *En último caso*, as a last resort. || *¡Es un caso!*, he is a case, he's a right one. || *Eso no viene* or *no hace al caso*, that is beside the point, that has nothing to do with it, that is irrelevant. || *Hacer caso a*, to take notice of. || *Hacer caso de algo*, to take notice of sth., to take sth. into account. || *Hacer caso de alguien*, to look after s.o., to pay attention to s.o.: *haz caso del niño*, look after the child. || *Hacer caso omiso de*, to take no notice of, to pay no attention to, to ignore. || *Lo mejor del caso*, the best part. || *Llegado* or *si llega el caso*, if the case arises, if need be. || *Maldito el caso que me hace*, a fat lot of attention he pays to me. || *No hacerle caso a uno*, to pay no attention to s.o., not to look after s.o. (no ocuparse), to take no notice of s.o., not to listen to s.o. (desobedecer). || *No hizo caso*, he didn't pay attention, he wasn't careful. || *No sea caso que*, in case. || *Para el caso es igual*, it's all the same, it makes no difference. || *Poner por caso*, to suppose, to assume. || *Según el caso*, as the case may be. || *Según lo requiera el caso*, as the case may be *o* require. || *Servir para el caso*, to serve one's purpose. || *Vamos al caso*, let's come *o* get to the point. || *Venir* or *hacer al caso*, to be relevant. || *Verse en el caso de*, to be compelled to. || *Y en el caso contrario*, and if not, otherwise.

casón m. o **casona** f. Big rambling house.

casorio m. FAM. Wedding.

caspa f. Dandruff (del pelo). || Scurf (de la piel).

caspera f. Toothcomb.

caspio, pia adj./s. Caspian (pueblo). || *Mar Caspio*, Caspian Sea.

¡cáspita! interj. My goodness! (sorpresa, asombro), damn it! (enfado).

casposo, sa adj. Full of *o* covered in dandruff.

casquería f. Tripe shop.

casquero m. Tripe seller (tripicallero).

casquete m. Skullcap, toque (sombrero). || Toupée (peluca). || MED. Cataplasm (de tiñoso). || MIL. Helmet. || — *Casquete esférico*, segment of a sphere. || *Casquete glaciar*, ice cap.

casquillo m. TECN. Collar, ferrule, tip (anillo). || Cap: *casquillo de bayoneta, de rosca*, bayonet cap, screw cap. || Case (de cartucho). || Metal base (parte metálica de un cartucho). || Head (de saeta). || *Amer.* Horseshoe (herradura). | Penholder (portaplumas).

casquivano, na adj. FAM. Scatterbrained, dizzy (atolondrado).

cassette f. Cassette (de cinta magnetofónica).

casta f. Breed (de animales). || Lineage, descent (de personas). || Caste (en la India). || FIG. Clan, circle (mundo cerrado). | Class (clase). || IMPR. Fount (fundición). || — *De casta*, thoroughbred (animal), of breeding (persona), real (torero, bailarín, etc.). || *De casta le viene al galgo* (*el ser rabilargo*), like father, like son. || *Le viene de casta*, it runs in the family.

castaña f. Chestnut (fruto). || Demijohn (botella). || Bun (peinado de mujer). || FIG. y FAM. Punch, thump: *arrear una castaña*, to land a punch. | Booze-up [U.S., drunk] (borrachera). || — *Castaña apilada, maya* or *pilonga*, dried chestnut. || *Castaña confitada*, glacé chestnut. || *Castaña de Indias*, horse chestnut. || *¡Castañas calentitas!*, hot chestnuts! (pregón). || FIG. y FAM. *Parecerse como un huevo a una castaña*, to be as different as chalk and cheese. | *Sacar las castañas del fuego a uno*, to pull s.o.'s chestnuts out of the fire for him.

castañal o **castañar** m. o **castañeda** f. Chestnut grove.

castañazo m. FAM. Punch, thump (puñetazo). || FAM. *Pegarse un castañazo contra*, to crash into.

castañero, ra m. y f. Chestnut seller.

castañeta f. Snap *o* click of the fingers (chasquido). || MÚS. Castanet (castañuela).

castañetazo m. Cracking *o* crackling of chestnuts (de la castaña en el fuego). || Snap *o* click of the fingers. || Crack (de los huesos). || FAM. Punch, thump (golpe). || FAM. *Pegarse un castañetazo contra*, to crash into.

castañetear v. tr. To play [castanets] (con castañuelas). || To snap (los dedos).
— V. intr. To chatter (los dientes). || To snap (los dedos). || To crack (los huesos). || To cry (las perdices). || To play the castanets (con las castañuelas).

castañeteo m. Clacking *o* clicking of castanets. || Chattering (de los dientes). || Cracking (de los huesos). || Snapping (de los dedos).

castaño, ña adj. Chestnut-brown, chestnut (color): *una cabellera castaña*, chestnut-brown hair.
— M. Chestnut tree, chestnut (árbol). || Chestnut (madera, color). || — *Castaño de Indias*, horse chestnut [tree]. || FIG. y FAM. *Pasar de castaño oscuro*, to be going too far, to be a bit much.

castañuela f. MÚS. Castanet. || Type of cyperus (planta). || FIG. y FAM. *Alegre como unas castañuelas*, as happy as a lark, as chirpy as a cricket.

castellanía f. Castellany.

castellanismo m. Word *o* expression common to Castile.

castellanizar v. tr. To make Spanish, to hispanicize, to castilianise.

castellano, na adj./s. Castilian (de Castilla). || *A la castellana*, in the Castilian way.
— M. y f. Castilian, Spaniard.
— M. Spanish, Castilian (lengua).

castellonense adj. [From *o* of] Castellón de la Plana.
— M. y f. Native *o* inhabitant of Castellón de la Plana.

casticidad f. o **casticismo** m. Correction, purity (en el lenguaje). || Traditionalism (de las costumbres). || Genuineness, authenticity (de personas).

casticista adj./s. Purist.

castidad f. Chastity.

castigable adj. Punishable.

castigador, ra adj. Castigatory (que castiga).
— M. y f. Punisher, chastiser, castigator. || — M. FIG. y FAM. Lady-killer, Don Juan.

castigar v. tr. To punish, to chastise, to castigate: *castigado por su temeridad*, punished for his rashness. || DEP. To penalize (a un jugador). || FIG. To make suffer (hacer sufrir). | To mortify (mortificar). | To afflict (por una enfermedad). | To correct (un escrito). | To reduce, to cut (los gastos). | To cause damage to *o* in: *las inundaciones castigaron mucho la región*, the floods caused a lot of damage in the area. | To ride hard (un caballo). || FIG. y FAM. To lead on (a las mujeres). || TAUR. To wound [the bull in order to excite it]. || FIG. *La vida le ha castigado mucho*, life has been very hard on him, he has suffered a lot.

castigo m. Punishment, chastisement, castigation: *infligir un duro castigo*, to inflict a harsh punishment. || Punishing, punishment, chastising, chastisement (acción de castigar). || Penalty: *la pena capital es el castigo para los traidores*, the death sentence is the penalty for traitors. || Correction (de un escrito). || MIL. Punishment. || TAUR. Wound [in order to excite the bull]. || — DEP. *Área de castigo*, penalty area. | *Castigo máximo*, penalty (fútbol), penalty kick (rugby). || *Levantar el castigo*, to withdraw the punishment.
Castilla n. pr. f. GEOGR. Castile: *Castilla la Vieja*, Old Castile. || FIG. *¡Ancha es Castilla!*, come on, we've got nothing to lose!
castillejo m. Baby walker (para enseñar a andar a los niños). || Scaffold, scaffolding (andamio).
castillete m. Small castle (pequeño castillo). || MIN. Headgear, derrick. || MIN. *Castillete de extracción*, headframe, gallows.
castillo m. Castle (edificio): *en Segovia hay un castillo*, there is a castle in Segovia. || — *Castillo de fuego*, firework display (pirotecnia). || FIG. *Castillo de naipes*, house of cards. || MAR. *Castillo de popa*, quarterdeck. | *Castillo de proa*, forecastle, fo'c'sle. || *Castillo en la arena*, sandcastle. || FIG. *Levantar* or *hacer castillos en el aire*, to build *o* to make castles in the air *o* in Spain.
castina f. Limestone flux (fundente).
castizo, za adj. True, through and through, pure-blooded, genuine (puro): *un madrileño castizo*, a true Madrilenian, a Madrilenian through and through. || Pure (lenguaje): *estilo castizo*, pure style. || Typical, traditional (típico).
casto, ta adj. Chaste, pure.
castor m. Beaver, castor (p.us.) [animal y su piel].
Cástor m. ASTR. Castor: *Cástor y Pólux*, Castor and Pollux.
castoreño m. Beaver hat. || Felt hat. || TAUR. Picador's hat. | Picador.
castóreo m. Castor, castoreum.
castorina f. Castor, beaver (tejido).
castra o **castración** f. Castration. || Gelding (de caballos). || Pruning (poda de árboles). || Uncapping (de la colmena).
castradera f. Uncapping knife (de apicultor).
castrado, da adj. Castrated. || Gelded (caballo).
— M. Eunuch (eunuco).
castrador m. Castrator. || Gelder (de caballos).
castradura f. Castration. || Gelding (de caballos). || Pruning (de los árboles). || Uncapping (de la colmena).
castrar v. tr. To castrate (capar). || To doctor (un gato). || To geld (los caballos). || To uncap (las colmenas). || FIG. To weaken (debilitar). || AGR. To prune (podar).
castrazón f. Uncapping (de las colmenas).
castrense adj. Military: *vida, costumbre, capellán castrense*, military life, custom, chaplain.
casual adj. Accidental, fortuitous, casual, chance: *un encuentro casual*, an accidental meeting.
casualidad f. Chance, accident: *por* or *de casualidad*, by chance. || Coincidence (coincidencia): *una verdadera casualidad*, a real coincidence. || — *Dar la casualidad*, to [just] happen: *dio la casualidad que*, it [just] happened that. || *El otro día entré por casualidad*, the other day I just happened to drop in. || *¿Tiene por casualidad un peine?*, have you a comb by any chance?
casualismo m. Casualism.
casualmente adv. By chance, by accident.
casuario m. Cassowary (ave).
casuca o **casucha** f. o **casucho** m. Hovel, shabby little house.
casuista m. Casuist.
casuístico, ca adj. Casuistical, casuistic.
— F. Casuistry.
casulla f. REL. Chasuble.
casullero m. Chasuble maker.
cata f. Tasting (acción de catar). || Sample (porción para probar). || *Amer.* Parakeet (cotorra).
catabólico, ca adj. BIOL. Katabolic, catabolic.
catabolismo m. BIOL. Katabolism, catabolism.
catacaldos m. inv. FIG. y FAM. Dabbler (persona inconstante). | Busybody, nosey parker (persona entrometida).
cataclismo m. Cataclysm.
catacresis f. inv. Catachresis (extensión del sentido de una palabra).
catacumba f. Catacomb (cementerio).
catador m. Taster, sampler (que prueba alimentos). || FIG. Connoisseur. || *Catador de vinos*, wine taster (persona).
catadura f. Tasting, sampling. || FIG. y FAM. *Un individuo de mala catadura*, a nasty-looking type.
catafalco m. Cataphalque, catafalque.
catafaro o **catafoto** m. Reflector (de automóviles).
catalán, ana adj./s. Catalan, Catalonian. || — M. Catalan (lengua).
catalanismo m. Catalan expression used in Spanish, Catalanism. || Quality of being Catalan. || Catalan separatist sympathies, *pl.*
catalanista adj. In favour of regional autonomy for Catalonia.
— M. y f. Catalanist.
Cataláunicos n. pr. m. pl. HIST. *Campos Cataláunicos*, Catalaunian Fields.
catalejo m. Telescope (anteojo).
catalepsia f. MED. Catalepsy.
cataléptico, ca adj./s. Cataleptic.
catalicores m. inv. Wine taster. || Sampling tube (pipeta).
catalina f. FAM. Dirt, droppings, *pl.* (excremento). || *Rueda catalina*, balance wheel (de un reloj).
Catalina n. pr. f. Catherine, Catharine, Katherine, Kathleen.
catálisis f. QUÍM. Catalysis.
catalítico, ca adj. Catalytic.
catalizador, ra adj. QUÍM. Catalytic.
— M. Catalyst.
catalizar v. tr. To catalyse. || FIG. To act as a catalyst for.
catalogación f. Cataloguing.
catalogar v. tr. To catalogue. || FIG. To classify, to class: *catalogar a uno de conservador*, to classify s.o. as conservative.
catálogo m. Catalogue [U.S., catalog].
Cataluña n. pr. f. GEOGR. Catalonia.
catamarán m. MAR. Catamaran.
catanga f. *Amer.* Dung beetle, dor (escarabajo).
cataplasma f. Cataplasm, poultice (pasta medicinal). || FIG. y FAM. Bore, drag.
¡cataplum! o **¡cataplún!** interj. Crash!, bang!
catapulta f. Catapult.
catapultar v. tr. To catapult.
catapún (el año) loc. FAM. The year dot. || *Ser del año catapún*, to be as old as the hills, to be ages old.
catar v. tr. To sample, to taste (probar). || (Ant.). To look at (mirar). | To inspect, to examine (examinar). || To uncap (colmenas).
catarata f. Waterfall (de agua), cataract (muy grande). || MED. Cataract (del ojo): *tener una catarata*, to have a cataract. || — *Las cataratas del Niágara*, Niagara Falls. || *Operar de catarata*, to remove a cataract from s.o.'s eye. || FIG. *Se abrieron las cataratas del cielo*, the heavens opened, it poured down.
cátaro, ra adj. Catharian (hereje).
catarral adj. MED. Catarrhal: *afección catarral*, catarrhal infection.
catarro m. Cold (palabra usual), catarrh (p.us.): *coger un catarro*, to catch a cold. || *Catarro pradial*, hay fever.
catarroso, sa adj. With a cold, having a cold, catarrhous (p.us.). || Prone to colds (propenso a acatarrarse).
catarsis f. FIL. Catharsis, catharses, katharsis, katharses.
catártico, ca adj. Cathartic, kathartic.
catastral adj. Cadastral: *levantamiento catastral*, cadastral survey.
catastro m. Official land register, cadastre.
catástrofe f. Catastrophe, disaster (desastre).
catastrófico, ca adj. Catastrophic, disastrous.
cataviento m. MAR. Dogvane (grímpola).
catavino m. Wine taster (copa).
catavinos m. inv. Wine taster (persona). || FIG. y FAM. Drunkard, boozer (borracho).
catch m. DEP. Wrestling. || *Luchador de catch*, wrestler.
cate m. FAM. Punch (puñetazo). | Thump, blow (golpe). | Slap, smack (bofetada). || FAM. *Le han dado un cate en física*, they failed him in physics (en un examen).
cateador m. *Amer.* Prospector.
catear v. tr. To look for, to search for (buscar). || FAM. To fail (suspender): *me han cateado*, they failed me. || *Amer.* To prospect (minas).
catecismo m. Catechism.
catecú m. Catechu.
catecúmeno, na m. y f. Catechumen.
cátedra f. Chair (puesto de catedrático). || Senior teaching post (en un colegio). || Lecture room (aula). || FIG. Chair. || — *Cátedra del Espíritu Santo*, pulpit. || *Cátedra de San Pedro*, Holy See. || *Hablar ex cátedra*, to speak ex cathedra. || *Hacer oposiciones a cátedra* or *opositar a una cátedra*, to compete for a chair. || FIG. *Poner* or *sentar cátedra de algo*, to give a lesson in sth., to show how to do sth.
catedral adj./s.f. Cathedral. || FIG. y FAM. *Como una catedral*, massive, huge, enormous.
catedralicio, cia adj. Cathedral: *iglesia catedralicia*, cathedral church.
catedrático, ca m. y f. Professor (de universidad), teacher, head of department (de instituto).
categoría f. Category. || Class: *hotel de primera categoría*, first-class hotel. || Class, type, category (clase): *de la misma categoría*, of the same type. || Rank (graduación). || Class: *categoría social*, social class; *un equipo de gran categoría*, a first-class team. || FIL. Category. || — *Dar categoría*, to give prestige: *una sortija de brillantes da categoría*, a diamond ring gives prestige. || FAM. *De categoría*, important (notable), luxury (de lujo): *un coche de categoría*, a luxury car; standing: *persona de cierta categoría*, person of some standing; serious: *un sarampión de categoría*, a serious bout of measles; real good: *le han dado una paliza de categoría*, they gave him a real good beating. || *De segunda categoría*, second-rate.
categórico, ca adj. Categoric, categorical. || Strict, express (orden). || *Negativa categórica*, flat refusal.
catenario, ria adj./s.f. TECN. Catenary.
catequesis f. o **catequismo** m. Catechesis, catechizing. || Catechism (catecismo).

catequista m. y f. Catechist.
catequístico, ca adj. Catechetic, catechetical.
catequización f. Catechization, catechizing.
catequizar v. tr. To catechize. || FIG. To preach to (predicar). | FIG. To talk round, to convince (convencer).
caterva f. Host, crowd, band: *caterva de pillos*, crowd of rascals. || Load, heap: *una caterva de cosas viejas*, a load of old things.
catéter m. MED. Catheter (sonda).
cateterismo m..MED. Catheterism (sondaje).
cateto, ta adj./s. FAM. Peasant, yokel (palurdo).
— M. MAT. Side of right-angled triangle [adjacent to the right angle].
catetómetro m. Cathetometer.
catgut m. MED. Catgut.
catilinaria f. Outburst of criticism (sátira).
catinga f. *Amer.* Bad smell (mal olor). | Forest (bosque). | Soldier (soldado).
catión f. FÍS. Cation.
catire o **catiro, ra** adj. Redheaded, red-haired, ginger-haired.
— M. y f. Redhead.
catite m. Loaf of best refined sugar (azúcar). || Slap (golpe o bofetada). || — FAM. *Dar catite a uno*, to slap s.o. (golpear). || *Sombrero de catite*, sugar-loaf hat.
cato m. Catechu (pasta aromática).
catódico, ca adj. Cathodic, cathode.
cátodo m. Cathode.
catolicidad f. Catholicity (universalidad y cualidad de católico). || Catholicism (mundo católico).
catolicismo m. Catholicism, Roman Catholicism.
católico, ca adj./s. Roman Catholic, Catholic. || — FIG. y FAM. *No estar muy católico*, to feel under the weather (pachucho), to be a bit off (alimento). | *No ser muy católico*, to sound fishy (asunto).
catolizar v. tr. To catholicize.
catón m. FIG. Severe critic. || First reading book (libro).
Catón n. pr. m. Cato.
catóptrica f. FÍS. Catoptrics.
catorce adj. Fourteen: *catorce lápices*, fourteen pencils. || Fourteenth (decimocuarto): *Luis XIV* (*catorce*), Louis XIV [the fourteenth]; *el siglo XIV* (*catorce*), the fourteenth century.
— M. Fourteen (número). || Fourteenth (fecha): *el 14* (*catorce*) *de febrero*, 14 February, February 14th [the fourteenth] (encabezamiento de una carta), February the fourteenth, the fourteenth of February (en la conversación). || *El catorce*, fourteen, number fourteen.
catorceno, na adj. Fourteenth.
catorzavo, va adj./s. Fourteenth.
catre m. FAM. Bed (cama). || *Catre de tijera* or *de viento*, camp bed.
catrecillo m. Folding chair (asiento).
catrera f. *Amer.* FAM. Bed (cama).
catrín m. *Amer.* Beau, toff [U.S., dude].
Cátulo n. pr. m. Catullus.
caucasiano, na o **caucásico, ca** adj./s. Caucasian.
Cáucaso n. pr. m. GEOGR. Caucasus.
cauce m. Bed [of a river]. || Ditch, trench (acequia). || FIG. Way, channel: *los cauces constitucionales*, constitutional channels *o* ways. | Course: *las cosas han vuelto a su cauce*, things have resumed their course.
caución f. Guarantee, security (fianza). || Cover (en Bolsa). || Caution (precaución). || JUR. Bail.
caucionar v. tr. To guarantee. || To stand bail for (alguien en la cárcel).
cauchero, ra adj. Rubber: *industria cauchera*, rubber industry.
— M. Rubber collector (el que busca el caucho). || — F. Rubber tree (planta).
caucho m. Rubber: *caucho vulcanizado*, vulcanized rubber. || *Industria del caucho*, rubber industry.
cauchutado m. Rubberizing, treating with rubber.
cauchutar v. tr. To rubberize, to treat with rubber.
caudado, da adj. ZOOL. Caudate.
caudal adj. Caudal: *plumas caudales*, caudal feathers.
— M. Fortune, wealth (riqueza). || Flow (de un río). || FIG. Wealth, great amount, abundance (abundancia). || COM. Assets, *pl.*
caudaloso, sa adj. Mighty, swift, large (río). || Rich, wealthy (rico). || Copious, abundant (abundante).
caudatario m. Train bearer.
caudillaje o **caudillismo** m. Government by a caudillo. || *Amer.* Bossism, tyranny. || *Bajo el caudillaje de*, under the leadership of.
caudillo m. Leader. || Caudillo [in Spain]. || *Amer.* FIG. Boss.
caudinas adj. f. pl. HIST. *Las Horcas Caudinas*, The Caudine Forks.
caulescente adj. BOT. Caulescent.
cauri m. Cowrie, cowry.
causa f. Cause: *causa y efecto*, cause and effect; *causa primera*, prime cause. || Reason, cause, motive: *hablar sin causa*, to speak without reason. || Cause, side, sake: *luchar por la causa de la libertad*, to fight for the cause of liberty. || JUR. Case, suit, cause, lawsuit (pleito). | Trial (proceso). || *Amer.* Snack (comida ligera). || — *A causa de* or *por causa de*, because of, on account of. || JUR. *Entender* or *conocer una causa*, to hear a case. || *Fuera de causa*, irrelevant. || *Hacer causa común con*, to make common cause with, to side with. || JUR. *Instruir causa*, to take legal proceedings. || FIG. *No hay efecto sin causa*, there's no smoke without fire. || *Por causa tuya*, for your sake, because of you. || *Por cuya causa*, on account of which, because of which. || *Por esta causa*, on this account, because of this. || *¿Por qué causa?*, for what reason?, why? || *Sin causa*, for no reason, without reason (adverbio), caseless, groundless (adjetivo).
causahabiente m. JUR. Assignee, executor, trustee.
causal adj. GRAM. Causal.
— F. Reason, cause.
causalidad f. Causality, causation: *el principio de causalidad*, the principle of causality. || Origin (origen).
causante adj. Causing, which caused: *la acción causante del alboroto*, the action which caused the disturbance.
— M. y f. Person who caused, cause: *el causante del accidente*, the person who caused the accident.
causar v. tr. To cause, to be the cause of (ser causa): *causar perjuicio*, to cause damage. || To make (una impresión). || To provoke (ira, etc.). || — *Causar placer*, to give pleasure. || *Causar risa a uno*, to make s.o. laugh.
causticidad f. Causticity. || FIG. Causticity.
cáustico, ca adj. Caustic. || *Sosa cáustica*, caustic soda.
— M. FIG. Caustic.
cautela f. Caution, cautiousness: *obrar con cautela*, to act with caution. || *Tener la cautela de hacer algo*, to take the precaution of doing sth.
cautelarse v. pr. To guard (*de*, against), to take precautions (*de*, against).
cautelosamente adv. Cautiously, warily.
cauteloso, sa adj. Cautious, wary: *un hombre muy cauteloso*, a very cautious man.
cauterio m. Cautery (instrumento). || FIG. Drastic measure.
cauterización f. Cauterization.
cauterizador, ra adj. Cauterizing, cauterant.
— M. Person who cauterizes. || Cautery (cosa).
cauterizar v. tr. To cauterize. || FIG. To apply drastic measures to.
cautivador, ra o **cautivante** adj. Captivating: *una sonrisa cautivadora*, a captivating smile.
cautivar v. tr. To take prisoner, to capture (a un enemigo). || FIG. To hold, to capture (la atención, a un auditorio). | To captivate, to charm (fascinar).
cautiverio m. o **cautividad** f. Captivity: *vivir en cautividad*, to live in captivity.
cautivo, va adj./s. Captive. || *Globos cautivos*, barrage balloons, captive balloons.
cauto, ta adj. Cautious, wary.
cava adj. f. ANAT. *Vena cava*, vena cava.
— F. Digging. || Dressing of vines (de las viñas). || TECN. Banking up.
cavador m. Digger.
cavadura f. Digging. || AGR. Dressing.
cavar v. tr. To dig (excavar). || To dig, to sink (un pozo). || AGR. To dress. || TECN. To bank up. || FIG. *Cavar su* (*propia*) *fosa* or *sepultura*, to dig one's own grave.
— V. intr. To dig. || FIG. To examine closely, to go thoroughly into (ahondar). | To meditate on, to ponder on: *cavar en los misterios de la fe*, to meditate on the mysteries of faith.
cavatina f. MÚS. Cavatina.
cavazón m. Digging. || AGR. Dressing.
caverna f. Cave, cavern. || Cavity (en el pulmón).
cavernario, ria adj. Cave, cavern.
cavernícola adj. Cave-dwelling (personas, animales). || FIG. Reactionary (en política). || *Hombre cavernícola*, caveman, troglodyte.
— M. y f. Cave dweller, caveman, troglodyte. || FIG. Reactionary (en política).
cavernoso, sa adj. Cavernous. || FIG. Deep, hollow: *voz cavernosa*, deep voice.
caveto m. ARQ. Cavetto (moldura).
caviar m. Caviar, caviare (hueva de esturión).
cavidad f. Cavity.
cavilación f. Pondering, meditation, deep thought.
cavilar v. intr. To ponder, to meditate, to think deeply (pensar mucho).
caviloso, sa adj. Pensive (pensativo). || Worried, troubled (preocupado).
cavitación f. MAR. y AVIAC. Cavitation.
cayado m. Shepherd's crook (de pastor). || Crozier (de obispo). || ANAT. *Cayado de la aorta*, arch of the aorta.
cayo m. Key: *Cayo Hueso*, Key West.
cayuco m. *Amer.* Small Indian boat.
caz m. Millrace (de molino). || Irrigation canal (acequia).
caza f. Hunting: *ir de caza*, to go hunting. || Shooting (con arma de fuego). || Trapping (con trampas). || Game (animales que se cazan): *caza mayor*, *menor*, big, small game. || Hunt (partida de caza). || Shoot (partida con arma de fuego). || Trapping (con trampas). || Open season, hunting season (temporada). || MAR. Chase. || — FIG. *Andar a la caza de*, to be in search of, to be hunting for. || *Caza a la espera* or *al aguardo* or *en puesto*, still hunt, stalking. || *Caza con hurón*, ferreting. || *Caza de cabezas*, headhunting. || *Caza del tesoro*, treasure hunt. || *Caza furtiva*, poaching. || *Caza submarina*, underwater fishing. || *Dar caza*, to give chase, to pursue. || FIG. *Ir a la caza del hombre*, to go

on a manhunt. || *Levantar la caza,* to put up the game (los cazadores), to let the cat out of the bag (figurado). || *Partida de caza,* hunting party (gente), hunt (actividad). || *Permiso de caza,* hunting licence. || *Vedado de caza,* game preserve.
— M. AVIAC. Fighter, pursuit plane, fighter plane. || *Piloto de caza,* fighter pilot.
cazabe m. Cassava flour (harina). || Cassava bread (pan).
cazabombardero m. Fighter bomber.
cazador, ra adj. Hunting (que caza). || *Diana Cazadora,* Diana the Huntress.
— M. y f. Hunter (en general), huntsman (cazador de zorros). || — *Cazador de cabezas,* headhunter. || FIG. *Cazador de dotes,* fortune hunter. || *Cazador furtivo,* poacher. || *Cazador de pieles,* trapper. || — F. Jerkin (chaqueta).
cazadotes m. inv. Fortune hunter.
cazalla f. Aniseed spirit [made in Cazalla (Sevilla)].
cazar v. tr. To hunt (los animales): *han ido a cazar conejos,* they are out hunting rabbits. || To catch, to bag: *hemos cazado diez conejos,* we have bagged ten rabbits. || FIG. To hunt down, to track down (a una persona). || FIG. y FAM. To get, to land: *cazar un buen destino,* to land a good job. | To pick out (una falta). | To catch, to surprise (sorprender). | To catch, to trap, to land (un marido). || MAR. To haul taut (una vela). || — *Cazar furtivamente,* to poach. || FIG. y FAM. *Cazar una cosa al vuelo,* V. VUELO.
cazasubmarinos m. inv. MAR. Submarine chaser.
cazatorpedero m. MAR. Destroyer, torpedo-boat destroyer.
cazcarria f. Splash *o* spatter of mud. || *Amer.* Sheep dung.
cazo m. Ladle (cucharón). || Saucepan (para calentar el agua). || Glue pot (de carpintero). || — TECN. *Cazo de colada,* casting ladle. || *Cazo eléctrico,* electric kettle.
cazolada f. Panful.
cazolero o **cazoletero** adj./s. Sissy (hombre entrometido en cosas de mujeres).
cazoleta f. Small saucepan. || Bowl (de pipa). || Hand guard (de la espada). || Boss (del escudo). || Pan (de arma de chispa). || TECN. Housing.
cazoletear v. intr. To meddle, to interfere.
cazón m. Dogfish (pez).
cazuela f. Casserole (de arcilla). || Stewpan (metálico). || Casserole, stew (guiso). || TEATR. Gods, *pl.* (gallinero). || Cup (de un sostén).
cazumbre m. Hemp cord.
cazurro, rra adj. Taciturn, sullen (huraño). || Obstinate, stubborn (obstinado). || Stupid (bruto).
ce f. C (letra). || Psst (llamando a alguien). || *Por ce o por be,* for one reason or another.
ceba f. Fattening [of animals]. || Stoking (de un horno). || *Amer.* Primer (de un arma).
cebada f. Barley (planta, semilla): *cebada perlada,* pearl barley. || FIG. *A burro muerto cebada al rabo,* V. BURRO.
cebadal m. Barley field.
cebadera f. Nosebag. || Barley hopper (cajón para la cebada). || TECN. Hopper (de un horno).
cebadero m. Barley dealer (el que vende). || TECN. Mouth [of a furnace]. || Lead mule (mula que va delante).
cebadilla f. Wild barley.
cebado, da adj. Fattened (un animal). || FIG. y FAM. Very fat. || (Ant.) Fatted (becerro en la Biblia).
cebadura f. Fattening (de un animal). || Stoking (de un horno). || Priming (de un arma). || *Amer.* Quantity of maté leaves [used at one time].
cebar v. tr. To fatten (engordar un animal). || To bait (con un anzuelo, una trampa). || FIG. To feed: *cebar el fuego,* to feed the fire. || MIL. To prime (armas). || TECN. To stoke (un horno). | To prime (una bomba, un sifón). || *Amer. Cebar mate,* to prepare maté.
— V. intr. To go in, to grip (un tornillo). || To grip, to bite (un tuerco). || To go in (un clavo).
— V. pr. To set upon: *se cebó en su víctima, conmigo,* he set upon his victim, upon me. || To rage (incendio, plaga).
cebellina adj. f./s. f. Sable.
cebiche m. *Amer.* Dish of marinated raw fish.
cebo m. Feed, food (para los animales). || Bait (para atraer los peces, etc.). || Primer (de un arma). || Charge, fuel (horno). || FIG. Bait, lure, incentive (señuelo). | Food, fuel (pábulo). || — *Cebo artificial,* artificial bait. || *Cebo artificial de cuchara,* spoon bait (para la pesca).
cebo m. Sajou, sapajou (mono).
cebolla f. Onion (planta y bulbo): *una ristra de cebollas,* a string of onions. || Bulb (de tulipán). || Rose, nozzle (de ducha). || *Amer.* FAM. Power (mando): *agarrar la cebolla,* to seize power. || — BOT. *Cebolla albarrana,* squill. | *Cebolla escalonia,* shallot.
cebollar m. Onion patch.
cebollero, ra adj. *Alacrán cebollero,* mole cricket.
— M. Onion seller.
cebolleta f. BOT. Chive. || Tender onion.
cebollino m. Small onion. || FIG. y FAM. *Mandar a alguien a escardar cebollinos,* to tell s.o. to jump in the lake, to send s.o. packing.
cebollón m. Large sweet onion. || *Amer.* FAM. Confirmed bachelor.
cebollona f. *Amer.* FAM. Old maid, confirmed spinster (solterona).
cebolludo, da adj. Bulbaceous (plantas). || Coarse (personas).
cebón, ona adj. Fattened.
— M. Fattened pig (puerco). || Fattened animal (otro animal).
cebra f. Zebra (animal). || *Paso de cebra,* zebra crossing.
cebrado, da adj. Striped.
cebú m. Zebu (animal).
ceca f. (Ant.). Royal Mint (casa de la Moneda). || FIG. y FAM. *Ir de la Ceca a la Meca,* to chase about, to dash all over the place, to go from place to place.
cecal adj. ANAT. Caecal, cecal.
cecear v. intr. To lisp (tener frenillo). || To pronounce the Spanish *s* as a Spanish *z* (característica regional).
— V. tr. To call, to call [s.o.] over (llamar).
ceceo m. Lisp (frenillo). || V. OBSERV.

— OBSERV. *Ceceo* is a linguistic feature whereby the Spanish *s* is pronounced as the Spanish *z* [θ]. It is common in southern Andalusia, especially in Seville and Cadiz, and also in certain parts of Latin America.

cecidia f. BOT. Cecidium, gall.
Cecilia n. pr. f. Cecily.
Cecilio n. pr. m. Cecil.
cecina f. Cured meat. || *Amer.* Jerked meat (tasajo).
cecinar v. tr. To jerk, to cure.
ceda f. Z (letra).
cedacear v. intr. To fail (la vista).
cedacero m. Sieve maker *o* seller.
cedacillo m. Quaking grass.
cedazo m. Sieve.
cedente adj. Assigning, transferring, granting.
— M. y f. Assignor, grantor.
ceder v. tr. To transfer, to make over: *ceder un comercio,* to transfer a business. || To give up, to hand over (entregar). || To give: *ceder el paso,* to give way; *ceder el sitio a una señora,* to give one's seat to a lady. || To cede (un territorio). || To pass (el balón). || — *Ceda el paso,* give way (señal de tráfico). || *Ceder terreno,* to give way, to yield ground.
— V. intr. To yield, to give in (no poder resistir). || To collapse, to give way: *el puente ha cedido,* the bridge has given way. || To drop, to ease off, to let up (el viento). || To let up, to lull (la tormenta). || To let up (el frío). || To abate, to ease off (el dolor). || To slacken (aflojarse). || MED. To yield. || — *Ceder a,* to yield to, to give way to, to submit to (alguien), to yield to (una solicitud, al miedo), to succumb to (el sueño), to yield to, to bow to (voluntad). || *Ceder en un derecho,* give up a right. || *La puerta cedió,* the door gave way. || *No cederle a alguien en algo,* to match s.o. at *o* for sth., to hold one's own to s.o. in sth. || *Obligar a ceder,* to bring to terms.
cedilla f. Cedilla.

— OBSERV. The *cedilla* is no longer used in Spanish.

cedrino, na adj. Cedrine.
cedro m. Cedar (árbol, madera).
cédula f. Document. || I.O.U. (de reconocimiento de deuda). || Index card (ficha de catálogo). || COM. Warrant (catálogo). || — (Ant.). *Cédula personal,* identity card. | *Cédula real,* royal warrant.
cefalalgia f. MED. Cephalalgia, headache.
cefalea f. MED. Migraine.
cefálico, ca adj. Cephalic.
cefalópodo, da adj./s.m. Cephalopod.
cefalotórax m. ZOOL. Cephalothorax.
céfiro m. Zephyr (viento).
cefo m. Sajou, sapajou (mono).
cegado, da adj. Blinded. || Blocked (cerrado).
cegador, ra adj. Blinding.
cegar* v. intr. To go blind (perder la vista).
— V. tr. To blind (quitar la vista). || FIG. To blind, to dazzle (deslumbrar). | To block up: *cegar un pozo,* to block up a well. | To wall up (puerta, ventana). | To blind: *le ciega la ira,* anger blinds him.
— V. pr. To be blinded.
cegarra o **cegarrita** adj. Short-sighted. || *A cegarritas,* blindly.
— M. y f. Short-sighted person.
cegato, ta o **cegatón, ona** adj. Short-sighted
— M. y f. Short-sighted person
cegesimal adj. C.G.S.: *sistema cegesimal,* C.G.S. system.
cegetista adj. C.G.T. (de la Confederación General del Trabajo).
— M. y f. Member of the C.G.T.
ceguedad o **ceguera** f. Blindness. || FIG. Short-sightedness, blindness.
ceiba f. Ceiba, silk-cotton tree, bombax (árbol).
ceibo m. BOT. Ceibo.
Ceilán n. pr. GEOGR. Ceylon.
ceilanés, esa adj./s. Ceylonese.
ceja f. Eyebrow (del ojo). || Projecting edge (borde saliente de un objeto). || Piping, edging (en la ropa). || Joint (de un libro). || Summit, top (cumbre de una sierra). || Cap of clouds [on a hill]. || TECN. Rim, flange. || MÚS. Nut (de la guitarra). | Capotasto (abrazadera). || *Amer.* Track, path (vereda). || — *Arquear* or *enarcar las cejas,* to raise one's eyebrows (gesto de sorpresa o asombro). || FIG. y FAM. *Estar hasta las cejas de,* to be fed up to the teeth of, to have had

enough of. || *Fruncir las cejas*, to frown. || FIG. y FAM. *Quemarse las cejas*, to burn the midnight oil. | *Tener a uno entre ceja y ceja* or *entre cejas*, not to be able to stand s.o. | *Tener* or *meterse una cosa entre ceja y ceja*, to get sth. into one's head. || *Tener la ceja abierta*, to have a cut above the eye (en boxeo).

cejar v. intr. To go *o* to move backwards, to back up (andar hacia atrás). || FIG. To slack, to let up, to relax: *no cejes en tu esfuerzo*, don't slack in your effort. | To back down, to climb down (ceder en un argumento).

cejijunto, ta adj. Bushy-browed, with thick eyebrows. || FIG. Frowning (ceñudo).

cejilla f. MÚS. Nut (en la guitarra). | Capotasto (abrazadera).

cejudo, da adj. Bushy-browed, with thick eyebrows.

celacanto m. ZOOL. Coelacanth.

celada f. Sallet, helmet (de la armadura). || FIG. Ambush: *caer en una celada*, to fall into an ambush. | Trap (trampa). || *Celada borgoñota*, burgonet.

celador, ra m. y f. Monitor (en un colegio). || Guard, warden (en una cárcel). || Attendant, curator (de museo). || Attendant (de biblioteca). || Maintenance man (que arregla máquinas).

celaje m. Coloured cloud effect (en pintura). || Coloured clouds, *pl.* (en el cielo). || Skylight (claraboya). || FIG. Presage, indication, foreboding (presagio).

celar v. tr. To supervise (en un colegio). || To guard, to keep watch over (en una cárcel). || To observe closely (las leyes). || To hide, to conceal (ocultar).
— V. intr. *Celar por* or *sobre*, to watch over.

celda f. Cell.

celdilla f. Cell (de una colmena). || Niche (hornacina).

cele adj. *Amer.* Unripe, green (no maduro).

celebérrimo, ma adj. Most famous, renowned, illustrious.

celebración f. Celebration (de un acto solemne). || Holding (de una reunión).

celebrado, da adj. Popular.

celebrante adj. REL. Celebrant.
— M. Celebrant priest (oficiante).

celebrar v. tr. To praise, to extol: *celebrar su belleza*, to praise her beauty. || To sing (las hazañas). || To celebrate (una fiesta, una ceremonia). || To perform, to celebrate (una boda). || To say, to celebrate (la misa). || To hold (reunión, conversaciones). || To be glad *o* happy (alegrarse): *celebro que no sea grave*, I am glad that it is not serious. || To laugh at: *celebrar las gracias del niño*, to laugh at the child's remarks. || To welcome: *celebraron la mejoría del enfermo*, they welcomed the patient's recovery. || To reach (un acuerdo).
— V. intr. To say mass (misa).
— V. pr. To take place: *ayer se celebró la ceremonia de clausura*, the closing ceremony took place yesterday. || To fall on, to be celebrated on: *mi cumpleaños se celebra el dos de marzo*, my birthday falls on the second of March. || *Se celebró ayer un consejo de administración*, there was a meeting of the board of directors yesterday, a meeting of the board of directors was held yesterday.

célebre adj. Famous, renowned, noted, celebrated. || FAM. Funny (gracioso).

celebridad f. Fame, renown, celebrity: *ganar celebridad*, to win fame. || Celebrity (persona célebre).

celemín m. Dry measure of about a half-peck (para áridos). || Castilian land measure of about an eighth of an acre (medida agraria).

celentéreo m. ZOOL. Coelenterate.

celeridad f. Speed, swiftness, quickness, celerity, rapidity (velocidad). || *Con toda celeridad*, as quickly as possible, in all haste, at full speed.

celeste adj. Celestial, heavenly (del cielo): *los espacios celestes*, the celestial spaces. || — *Bóveda celeste*, vault of heaven. || *Cuerpo celeste*, heavenly body. || *El Celeste Imperio*, The Celestial Empire. || — Adj./s.m. Sky blue (color).

celestial adj. Celestial, heavenly (del cielo): *música celestial*, celestial music. || FIG. Divine (don). | Delightful, heavenly (delicioso). || FIG. y FAM. Stupid, daft (bobo).

celestina f. FIG. Procuress, bawd (alcahueta).

Celestina n. pr. f. Celestine.

celestino m. Celestine (monje).

celiaco, ca o **celíaco, ca** adj. Coeliac, celiac (intestinal).
— F. MED. Coeliac disease, celiac disease.

celibato m. Celibacy: *el celibato eclesiástico*, ecclesiastical celibacy.

célibe adj. Celibate, unmarried, single.
— M. y f. Celibate, single person (hombre o mujer), bachelor (hombre), spinster (mujer).

celidonia f. BOT. Celandine.

celinda f. Syringa (planta).

celo m. Zeal, fervour [U.S., fervor] (cuidado). || REL. Religious fervour, piety. || ZOOL. Oestrus, heat (de la hembra). | Rut (del macho). || — Pl. Jealousy, *sing.* || — *Dar celos*, to make jealous. || *Entrar en celos*, to come on heat (animal hembra), to come into rut (animal macho). || *Estar en celo*, to be on heat (animal hembra), to be in rut (animal macho). || *Tener celos*, to be jealous.

celofán m. o **celófana** f. Cellophane.

celosamente adv. Enthusiastically, zealously. || Fervently. || Jealously (con envidia).

celosía f. Lattice window (ventana). || Lattice (enrejado).

celoso, sa adj. Enthusiastic, zealous (esmerado). || Jealous (que tiene celos): *un hombre celoso*, a jealous man. || Jealous (que mantiene algo con rigor): *es muy celoso de sus derechos*, he is very jealous of his rights. || MAR. Light and unsteady (embarcación).

celsitud f. Sublimity, grandeur (elevación).

celta m. y f. Celt, Kelt (persona). || — M. Celtic, Keltic (lengua).
— Adj. Celtic, keltic.

Celtiberia n. pr. f. Celtiberia.

celtibérico, ca o **celtiberio, ria** adj./s. Celtiberian.

celtíbero, ra o **celtibero, ra** adj./s. Celtiberian.

céltico, ca adj./s.m. Celtic, Keltic.

celtismo m. Celticism, Kelticism.

celtista m. y f. Celtologist, Keltologist.

celtohispánico, ca o **celtohispano, na** adj. Celtic-Spanish, Keltic-Spanish, Celto-Spanish, Kelto-Spanish.

celtolatino, na adj. Celto-Latin, Kelto-Latin.

célula f. Cell (celda). || BIOL. y ZOOL. Cell: *célula nerviosa*, nerve cell. || FIG. Cell (política). || *Célula fotoeléctrica*, photoelectric cell.

celulado, da adj. Celled, cellated.

celular adj. ANAT. Cellular: *tejido celular*, cellular tissue. || *Coche celular*, police van, Black Maria (fam.).

celulita o **celulitis** f. MED. Cellulitis.

celuloide m. Celluloid. || — FIG. *Celuloide rancio*, old film. | *Llevar al celuloide*, to make a film of (obra de teatro, novela, etc.).

celulosa f. QUÍM. Cellulose.

celulósico, ca adj. Cellulose.

cella f. ARQ. Cella, body [of temple].

cellisca f. Sleetstorm, sleet.

cellisquear v. impers. To sleet.

cello m. Hoop (de tonel).

cementación f. TECN. Case hardening, cementation (de metales).

cementador m. Cement maker *o* mixer (obrero).

cementar v. tr. TECN. To case harden, to cement, to face-harden.

cementerio m. Cemetery, graveyard. || *Cementerio de coches*, wrecked-car dump, wrecker's yard, breaker's yard.

cementista m. Cement manufacturer (fabricante). || Cement worker (obrero).

cemento m. Cement. || Concrete (hormigón): *cemento armado*, reinforced concrete. || Cement (de los dientes). || FAM. *Tener una cara de cemento armado* or *tener la cara como cemento*, to have a lot of cheek (ser muy descarado).

cementoso, sa adj. Cement-like.

cena f. Dinner, supper (v. OBSERV.): *cena con baile*, dinner dance,dinner and dance. || *La Última* or *la Santa Cena*, The Last Supper.

— OBSERV. *Supper* suele ser una comida más ligera que *dinner*.

cenáculo m. Cenacle (de la Última Cena). || FIG. Cenacle, coterie (reunión literaria).

cenacho m. Basket (de esparto): *un cenacho de legumbres*, a basket of vegetables.

cenado, da adj. Who has eaten dinner *o* supper. || *Estar cenado*, to have dined, to have eaten dinner *o* supper.

cenador, ra m. y f. Diner, person eating dinner *o* supper. || — M. Bower, arbour [U.S., arbor] (en un jardín). || Loggia (galería).

cenagal m. Bog, marsh, swamp (sitio pantanoso). || FIG. y FAM. Mess, jam, tight spot: *estar metido en un cenagal*, to be in a mess.

cenagoso, sa adj. Muddy: *camino cenagoso*, muddy road.

cenar v. intr. To dine, to have dinner *o* supper. (V. CENA [Observ.].) || — *Invitar a uno a cenar*, to invite s.o. to dinner. || *Quedarse sin cenar*, to go without dinner *o* supper.
— V. tr. To have for dinner *o* supper, to dine on: *cenó una tortilla*, he had an omelette for supper.

cenceño, ña adj. Thin, slim.

cencerrada f. Din, racket, row (alboroto): *dar una cencerrada*, to make a row. || Noisy serenade [given to a widow who remarries].

cencerrear v. intr. To ring bells continually (agitar una campanilla). || To jingle, to jangle, to clang (campanillas, etc.). || FIG. y FAM. To scrape a violin (violín). | To strum, to twang away (con guitarra, laúd). | To rattle (puerta, ventana).

cencerreo m. Jingling *o* ringing *o* clanging of bells (de campanillas). || Row, din (ruido). || Rattle (de puerta, ventana). || Twang (de guitarra).

cencerro m. Cowbell (campanilla de los animales). || — FIG. *A cencerros tapados*, on the quiet, on the sly. | *Estar más loco que un cencerro*, to be completely mad.

cencuate m. Poisonous snake [from Mexico].

cendal m. Veil (velo). || Sendal (tela). || REL. Humeral veil. || — Pl. Barbs (de la pluma).

cenefa f. Border, edging (de alfombra, de toalla, de jardín, etc.). || Frieze, ornamental border (en una pared). || Skirting board [U.S., baseboard] (zócalo).

cenicero m. Ashtray.

Cenicienta n. pr. f. Cinderella.

ceniciento, ta adj. Ash, ashen, ashy (color).
cenit m. ASTR. Zenith.
cenital adj. Zenithal.
ceniza f. Ash: *reducir a cenizas*, to reduce to ashes. || — Pl. Ashes, mortal remains (restos mortales). || Dust, *sing.: cenizas radiactivas*, radioactive dust. || — *Miércoles de Ceniza*, Ash Wednesday. || FIG. *Reducir a cenizas*, to burn to ashes, to reduce to ashes. || *Remover las cenizas*, to rake up the past.
cenizo, za adj. Ash-grey, ashen, ashy (ceniciento).
— M. FAM. Wet blanket, spoilsport, killjoy (aguafiestas). | Jinx (mala suerte): *tiene el cenizo*, he has a jinx on him. || FIG. y FAM. *Ser un cenizo*, to be a jinx (ser gafe).
cenobial adj. Cenobitic, coenobitic, cenobitical, coenobitical.
cenobio m. Monastery (monasterio).
cenobita m. y f. Cenobite, coenobite.
cenobítico, ca adj. Cenobitic, coenobitic, cenobitical, coenobitical.
cenobitismo m. Cenobitism, coenobitism.
cenotafio m. Cenotaph.
cenote m. *Amer.* Natural well.
cenozoico, ca adj. GEOL. Cenozoic, Caenozoic.
censar v. tr. To take a census of.
censo m. Census (empadronamiento): *hicieron el censo de*, they took a census of. || JUR. Tax (tributo). | Annuity, pension, allowance (renta): *censo muerto*, perpetual annuity. | Ground rent (sobre una casa). | Lease, agreement (arrendamiento): *constituir un censo*, to draw up a lease *o* an agreement. || FIG. Burden (carga): *la educación de su hijo es un censo*, his son's education is a burden. || — *Censo electoral*, electorate (número de electores), electoral roll *o* register (lista de electores). || *Censo enfitéutico*, long lease. || FIG. y FAM. *Ser un censo para uno*, to be a constant drain on s.o.'s money (costarle dinero), to be a burden on s.o. (pesarle).
censor m. Censor. || Auditor (de cuentas). || FIG. Critic.
censual adj. Census, censual (del empadronamiento). || Pertaining to an annuity.
censualista m. y f. Annuitant (que percibe una renta). || Lessor (arrendador).
censura f. Censure (acción): *moción de censura*, motion of censure. || Censorship (de prensa, espectáculos). || Censure, criticism, disapproval (reproche). || — *Digno de censura*, censurable. || *Pasar por la censura*, to go through the censor, to undergo censorship.
censurable adj. Censurable, blameworthy.
censurador, ra adj. Censorious.
censurar v. tr. To censor: *censurar una película*, to censor a film. || To censure, to condemn, to criticize, to disapprove of: *censurar a* or *en uno su conducta*, to disapprove of s.o.'s conduct.
centaura o **centaurea** f. BOT. Centaury.
centauro m. Centaur.
centavo, va adj. Hundredth (centésimo).
— M. Hundredth, hundredth part. || *Amer.* Cent, "centavo" [one hundredth part of peso, etc.]. || FAM. *Estar sin un centavo*, not to have two halfpennies to rub together, to be broke.
centella f. Flash (rayo). || Lightning, flash of lightning (relámpago): *cayó una centella sobre la torre*, the tower was struck by lightning. || Spark (chispa). || FIG. Spark. || FIG. *Raudo como la centella*, as quick as lightning *o* as a flash.
centellar v. intr. V. CENTELLEAR.
centelleador, ra o **centellante** o **centelleante** adj. Sparkling, flashing. || Twinkling (las estrellas). || Flickering (fuego, llamas).
centellear v. intr. To sparkle, to flash. || To twinkle (las estrellas). || To flicker (un fuego).
centelleo m. Sparkling, flashing. || Twinkling (de las estrellas).
centena f. Hundred.
centenada f. Hundred. || *A centenadas*, by the hundred, in hundreds.
centenal o **centenar** m. Rye field.
centenar m. Hundred (centena): *centenares de hombres*, hundreds of men. || Centenary, centennial (centenario). || *A* or *por centenares*, by the hundred, in hundreds.
centenario, ria adj. Hundred-year-old, centenarian (persona). || Centennial, centenary (fecha). || — M. y f. Centenarian (persona). || — M. Centenary, centennial (aniversario).
centenaza adj. f. *Paja centenaza*, rye straw.
centeno m. BOT. Rye.
centesimal adj. Centesimal.
centésimo, ma adj. Hundredth. || *La centésima parte*, a hundredth, one hundredth part.
— M. Hundredth, hundredth part. || "Centésimo", cent (centavo en Uruguay y Panamá).
centiárea m. Square metre, centiare.
centigrado, da adj. Centigrade: *escala centígrada*, centigrade scale.
centigramo m. Centigramme [U.S., centigram].
centilitro m. Centilitre [U.S., centiliter].
centimetro m. Centimetre [U.S., centimeter]: *centímetro cuadrado, cúbico*, square, cubic centimetre.
céntimo, ma adj. Hundredth (centésimo).
— M. Cent, centime [one hundredth part of peseta, peso, etc.]. || — *No tener un céntimo*, not to have a penny. || FIG. *No valer un céntimo*, not to be worth a brass farthing.
centinela m. MIL. Sentry, guard. || Look-out, look-out man (persona que vigila). || FIG. Watch, look-out: *hacer centinela*, to keep watch, to keep a look-out. || MIL. *Estar de centinela* or *hacer centinela*, to mount guard, to be on guard, to stand sentry.

— OBSERV. The word *centinela* is used both as a masculine and a feminine noun. Common usage gives preference to the masculine form.

centinodia f. Knotgrass (planta).
centolla f. o **centollo** m. Spider crab.
centón m. Cento (poesía). || Patchwork quilt (colcha).
centrado, da adj. Centred [U.S., centered]. || FIG. Balanced: *una persona bien centrada*, a well-balanced person.
— M. Centring [U.S., centering].
centrador m. TECN. Centring device *o* tool [U.S., centering device *o* tool].
central adj. Central, centric: *punto central*, central point. || *Casa central*, head office.
— F. Power station: *central hidroeléctrica, nuclear, térmica*, hydroelectric, nuclear, thermal power station. || Switchboard (teléfono interior). || Head office (casa matriz). || Plant, station (industrial). || — *Central azucarera*, sugar mill, sugar refinery. || *Central de correos*, central post office. || *Central telefónica*, telephone exchange (de una ciudad).
centralismo m. Centralism.
centralista adj./s. Centralist.
centralita f. Switchboard (teléfono).
centralización f. Centralization, centralizing.
centralizador, ra adj. Centralizing.
— M. y f. Centralizer.
centralizar v. tr. To centralize.
— V. pr. To be centralized.
centrar v. tr. To centre [U.S., to center] (colocar bien). || To aim, to point (arma de fuego). || To focus (rayos de luz). || FIG. To centre [U.S., to center] (*en*, on, around), to focus (*en*, on) [la atención, la discusión, etc.]. | To base, to centre [U.S., to center] (basar): *centra su vida en la política*, he centres his life around politics; *centrar una novela sobre las cuestiones sociales*, to base a novel on social questions.
— V. tr. e intr. To centre [U.S., to center] (en deportes).
— V. pr. To centre [U.S., to center] (*en*, on, around): *la discusión se centró en la política*, the discussion centred on politics. || To be based (*en*, on) [basarse]. || To find one's feet (orientarse una persona).
céntrico, ca adj. Central: *barrios céntricos*, central districts.
centrifugador, ra adj. Centrifugal.
— F. Centrifugal machine, centrifuge (máquina).
centrifugar v. tr. To centrifuge.
centrífugo, ga adj. Centrifugal: *bomba centrífuga*, centrifugal pump.
centrípeto, ta adj. Centripetal: *aceleración centrípeta*, centripetal acceleration.
centrista m. y f. Centrist [U.S., middle-of-the-roader] (en política).
— Adj. Centre [U.S., Center], of the Centre: *partido político centrista*, Centre political party.
centro m. Centre [U.S., center] (medio): *el centro del círculo*, the centre of the circle. || Town centre, city centre: *comprar algo en el centro*, to buy sth. in the town centre. || FIG. Aim, goal, objective (objeto principal). || Middle: *en el centro de la calle*, in the middle of the street. || Circle: *en los centros diplomáticos*, in diplomatic circles. || FIG. Heart, centre: *el centro de la rebelión*, the heart of the rebellion. || Centre (club). || Centre (en el fútbol). || ANAT. y MAT. Centre. || MED. Root, origin (de una enfermedad). || — *Centro comercial*, shopping centre. || DEP. *Centro chut*, centre. || *Centro de atracción, de gravedad*, centre of attraction, of gravity. || *Centro de interés*, centre of interest. || *Centro de masa*, centre of mass. || *Centro de mesa*, centrepiece (en la mesa). || *Centro docente*, educational institution. || *Centro nervioso* or *neurálgico*, nerve centre. || *Delantero centro*, centre forward. || *En el mismísimo centro*, right in the centre, in the very centre. || FIG. *Estar en su centro*, to feel at home, to be in one's element. || *Medio centro*, centre half. || *Partido del centro*, Centre party.
Centroamérica n. pr. f. GEOGR. Central America.
centroamericano, na adj./s. Central American.
Centroeuropa n. pr. f. GEOGR. Central Europe.
centroeuropeo, a adj./s. Central European.
centrosfera f. BIOL. Centrosphere.
centrosoma m. BIOL. Centrosome.
centuplicar v. tr. To increase a hundredfold, to centuple, to centuplicate, to multiply by one hundred.
céntuplo, a adj. Hundredfold, centuple.
— M. Hundredfold, centuple, centuplicate.
centuria f. Century.
centurión m. HIST. Centurion.
cénzalo m. Mosquito.
ceñido, da adj. Tight-fitting, close-fitting, figure-hugging, clinging: *un vestido muy ceñido*, a very tight-fitting dress. || Tight (una curva). || Close (cerca). || Pediculate, pedicellate (los insectos).
ceñidor m. Belt (cinturón), girdle (cordón).

ceñir* v. tr. To be tight for: *ese vestido te ciñe demasiado*, that dress is too tight for you. || To wreath, to crown (con flores). || To gird, to circle, to encircle, to surround: *el mar ciñe la isla*, the sea circles the island; *las murallas ciñen la ciudad*, the walls encircle the city. || To frame: *cabellos negros que ciñen un rostro*, black hair which frames a face. || To cling to, to be tight on: *el jersey la ciñe mucho*, the pullover is very tight on her. || To get hold of *o* to grip round the waist (abrazar): *ceñir a un adversario*, to get hold of an opponent round the waist. || To gird (la espada). || To shorten, to cut down (una narración). || To take in (estrechar un vestido). || *Ceñir la cabeza con una corona*, to crown s.o., to put a crown on s.o.'s head.
— V. pr. To limit o.s., to cut down: *tenemos que ceñirnos en los gastos*, we have to cut down on spending *o* limit our spending. || To stick, to keep: *ceñirse al tema*, to stick to the subject. || To keep to: *ceñirse a la derecha*, to keep to the right. || To adapt o.s., to conform (amoldarse): *hay que ceñirse al reglamento de la universidad*, you have to conform to the university rules. || To cling: *este traje se ciñe al cuerpo*, this dress clings to the body. || TAUR. To get very close [to the bull]. || — *Ceñirse a la curva*, to take the bend tightly (un coche). || *Ceñirse a un sueldo modesto*, to live with a modest salary. || *Ceñirse la espada*, to gird one's sword, to put on one's sword.
ceño m. Scowl, frown. || *Fruncir el ceño*, to scowl, to frown, to knit one's brow.
ceñudo, da adj. Frowning, scowling.
cepa f. Stock, vine (vid). || Stump (tronco de árbol). || FIG. Stock, origin (origen de una persona): *de pura* or *de vieja cepa*, of pure stock. || Pillar (de un puente). || — *De buena cepa*, of good stock. || FIG. *De pura cepa*, real, genuine, authentic (de verdad).
cepillado m. o **cepilladura** f. Planing (carpintería). || Brushing, brush (de un vestido). || — Pl. Shavings.
cepillar v. tr. To brush (los trajes, etc.). || To plane (carpintería).
— V. pr. FAM. To fail (en un examen): *cepillarse a uno en física*, to fail s.o. in physics. | To kill, to polish off (matar). | To polish off, to brush off (comiendo). || POP. To lay (acostarse con).
cepillo m. Brush: *cepillo para el suelo, las uñas, los zapatos*, scrubbing brush, nail brush, shoe brush. || Collecting box, poor box, alms box (en las iglesias). || Plane (carpintería). || — *Cepillo bocel*, moulding plane (herramienta). || *Cepillo de dientes*, toothbrush. || *Cepillo para el pelo*, hairbrush. || *Tener el pelo al cepillo*, to have a crew cut.
cepo m. Branch, bough (rama). || Block, stock (para el yunque). || Stocks, *pl.*, pillory (instrumento de tortura). || Trap (trampa). || Collecting box, poor box, alms box (en las iglesias). || Fetters, *pl.*, shackles, *pl.* (grilletes). || TECN. Clamp (objeto para sujetar). || ZOOL. Sajou, sapajou (mono). || — FIG. *Caer en el cepo*, to fall into the trap. || MAR. *Cepo del ancla* anchor stock.
cepón m. Large vine.
ceporro m. Old vine used for fuel. || FIG. y FAM. Fat lump, fatty (persona muy gruesa). | Thickhead, blockhead (estúpido). || FIG. *Dormir como un ceporro*, to sleep like a log.
cequí m. Sequin (moneda antigua).
cequia f. Irrigation ditch *o* channel (acequia).
cera f. Wax: *cera amarilla, mineral*, yellow, mineral wax. || *Amer.* Candle (vela). || — Pl. Honeycomb, *sing.* (alvéolos). || — FIG. *Amarillo como la cera*, as yellow as a guinea. || *Cera de abejas*, beeswax. || MED. *Cera de los oídos*, earwax, cerumen. || *Cera para suelos*, floor polish. || FIG. *Estar pálido como la cera*, to be as white as a sheet. | *No hay más cera que la que arde*, that is all there is, there is nothing more than what you see.
cerámica f. Ceramics (arte). || Pottery (cosas).
cerámico, ca adj. Ceramic. || *Gres cerámico*, stoneware.
ceramista m. y f. Ceramist, potter.
cerapez f. V. CEROTE.
cerasta f. o **cerastes** m. Cerastes, horned viper (víbora).
cerato m. Cerate, ointment (ungüento).
cerbatana f. Blowpipe. || Peashooter (de niños). || Ear trumpet (para los sordos).
Cerbero n. pr. m. MIT. Cerberus.
cerca f. Fence (valla). || Hedge (seto).
cerca adv. Near, nearby, close: *vivimos muy cerca*, we live very nearby. || Near, close: *no te pongas tan cerca*, do not get so near. || — *Aquí cerca*, near here, nearby. || *Cerca de*, about: *cerca de mil muertos*, about a thousand dead; nearly, almost (casi): *son cerca de las diez*, it is nearly ten o'clock; with: *medié cerca del director para que no le expulsasen*, I had a word with the boss so that they would not sack him. || *Cerca de mí, de ti, etc.*, near me, you, etc. || *De cerca*, closely, from close up. || *Embajador cerca de la Santa Sede*, Ambassador to the Holy See. || *Estar cerca de hacer algo*, to be near to doing sth., to be on the point of doing sth. || *Mirar de cerca*, to look closely, to take a close look. || *Muy de cerca*, very closely, from very close quarters. || *Por aquí cerca*, nearby, somewhere round here. || *Ya están cerca las Navidades*, Christmas is nearly *o* almost here, it will soon be Christmas, Christmas will soon be here.
— M. pl. ARTES. Foreground, *sing.*
cercado m. Enclosed garden, fenced-in garden (huerto). || Enclosure (terreno cercado). || Enclosure, fence (valla). || Enclosure (terreno). || *Amer.* Territorial division, district (distrito).
cercanamente adv. Nearby, close by (a poca distancia). || Soon, shortly (dentro de poco).
cercanía f. Proximity, nearness. || — Pl. Outskirts (alrededores): *vive en las cercanías de Leeds*, he lives in the outskirts of Leeds. || Suburbs (afueras). || — *Trabaja en la cercanía de su casa*, he works near his house, he works in his neighbourhood. || *Tren de cercanías*, suburban train.
cercano, na adj. Near, close (próximo, inmediato). || Close: *un pariente cercano*, a close relative. || Nearby, neighbouring: *ir a un pueblo cercano*, to go to a neighbouring village. || FIG. Impending (muerte). || — *Cercano a su fin*, nearing *o* near one's end. || *Cercano Oriente*, Near East.
cercar v. tr. To enclose, to fence, to wall in (rodear con una cerca). || MIL. To besiege, to surround, to encircle (sitiar). | To surround, to hem in (al enemigo). || To surround, to crowd round, to encircle: *la muchedumbre cercaba al rey*, the crowd surrounded the King.
cercén (a) loc. adv. Close, flush, right down to the roots: *cortar a cercén*, to cut close.
cercenador, ra adj. Cutting, trimming.
— M. y f. Trimmer, cutter.
cercenadura f. o **cercenamiento** m. Cutting, trimming, clipping (parte cortada, acción de cercenar). || Abridgement, shortening (de un texto, discurso). || Reduction, curtailment (de gastos).
cercenar v. tr. To cut, to trim (cortar el borde). || To cut down, to reduce, to curtail (disminuir, suprimir una parte de): *cercenar los gastos*, to cut down expenditure. || To shorten, to abridge, to cut down (un texto). || To cut off, to amputate (amputar). || To cut off (quitar algo cortando).
cerceta f. Garganey (ave). || — Pl. First antlers (del ciervo).
cerciorar v. tr. To assure (asegurar). || To convince (convencer).
— V. pr. To make sure: *cerciorarse de un hecho*, to make sure of a fact.
cerco m. Circle, ring (lo que rodea). || Hoop (aro de tonel). || Group (corrillo). || Magic circle (figura mágica). || Ring, circle (de una mancha). || ASTR. Halo (corona, halo). || TECN. Rim (de una rueda). || Frame (marco de puerta, etc.). || MIL. Siege (asedio): *alzar* or *levantar el cerco*, to raise the siege. || *Amer.* Enclosure (cercado). | Fence (cerca). | Quickset hedge (seto vivo). || — *Cerco policíaco*, police cordon. || MIL. *Poner cerco a*, to besiege, to lay siege to.
cercopiteco m. ZOOL. Cercopithecus (mono).
cerchar v. tr. AGR. To layer (la vid).
cerchearse v. pr. To warp (alabearse).
cerchón m. ARQ. Truss (cimbra).
cerda f. Bristle (del cerdo). || Horsehair (del caballo). || Sow (hembra del cerdo). || Noose, snare (lazo para cazar). || [Harvested] corn (mies segada). || — *Cepillo de cerda*, bristle brush. || *Ganado de cerda*, pigs.
cerdada f. FAM. Foul *o* lousy trick (acción que perjudica a uno). | Mess: *el niño está haciendo cerdadas en la mesa*, the child is making a mess on the table.
cerdamen m. Tuft of bristle *o* horsehair.
Cerdaña n. pr. f. GEOGR. Cerdagne Valley.
cerdear v. intr. To be lame *o* weak in the forelegs (los animales). || MÚS. To be out of tune (un instrumento). || FIG. y FAM. To play a foul *o* a lousy trick (jugar una mala pasada). | To back out *o* down (esquivar). | To play up, to give trouble: *este coche empieza a cerdear*, this car is starting to play up. | To put things off, to hedge (aplazar). || *Amer.* To cut the hair of a horse (cortar la cerda a un caballo).
Cerdeña n. pr. f. GEOGR. Sardinia.
cerdo m. Pig (puerco). || FIG. y FAM. Pig (persona sucia, etc.). || — FIG. *A cada cerdo le llega su San Martín*, every dog has his day. || *Carne de cerdo*, pork. || *Cerdo marino*, porpoise. || *Cerdo salvaje*, wild boar.
cerdoso, sa adj. Bristly: *barba cerdosa*, bristly beard.
cereal m. Cereal. || — Pl. Celebration (*sing.*) in honour of Ceres. || Cereals, grain, *sing.* || *Mercado de cereales*, corn exchange.
cerealista adj. Cereal (de los cereales). || Cereal-producing: *región cerealista*, cereal-producing district.
— M. Cereal farmer (productor) *o* dealer (comerciante).
cerebelo m. ANAT. Cerebellum.
cerebral adj. Cerebral.
cerebro m. ANAT. Cerebrum (parte del encéfalo). | Brain (encéfalo). || FIG. Brains, *pl.* (inteligencia). || — *Cerebro electrónico*, electronic brain. || FIG. *Torturar su cerebro*, to rack one's brains.
cerebroespinal adj. Cerebrospinal.
cereceda f. Cherry orchard (cerezal).
ceremonia f. Ceremony. || Fuss, ceremony (cumplidos): *andarse con* or *hacer ceremonias*, to stand on ceremony, to make a fuss. || REL. Ceremony, service. || — *Con gran ceremonia*, with great ceremony, ceremoniously, with a lot of fuss *o* of to-do (fam.). || *Hablar sin ceremonia*, to speak informally. || *Maestro de ceremonias*, master of ceremonies. || *Traje de ceremonia*, formal dress.
ceremonial adj./s. m. Ceremonial.

ceremonioso, sa adj. Ceremonious, formal.
céreo, a adj. Wax, waxen.
cerería f. Chandler's shop, chandlery
cerero, ra m. y f. Chandler.
cereza f. Cherry (fruta). || *Amer.* Husk of coffee bean (de café). | Coffee cherry *o* berry (fruto del café). || — *Cereza gordal* or *garrafal*, white-heart cherry, bigarreau. || *Cereza pasa*, dried cherry. || *Cereza silvestre*, wild cherry, gean, merry. || *Rojo cereza*, cherry-red.
cerezal m. Cherry orchard (plantío de cerezos).
cerezo m. Cherry tree (árbol). || *Cerezo silvestre*, wild cherry tree, gean tree, merry tree.
cerífero, ra adj. Ceriferous.
cerilla f. Match (fósforo): *una caja de cerillas*, a box of matches. || Small wax taper (vela). || Earwax (cera de los oídos).
cerillera f. o **cerillero** m. Matchbox (caja). || Match vendor (vendedor). || Match pocket (bolsillo).
cerillo m. V. CERILLA.
cerina f. Cerin (del alcornoque). || MIN. Cerium silicate. || QUÍM. Cerin, cerotic acid (ácido cerótico).
cerio m. QUÍM. Cerium (metal raro).
cerita f. MIN. Cerite.
cermeño m. Boor, lout, uncouth chap (tosco).
cernada f. Leached ashes, *pl.* (de lejía). || ARTES. Primer (para imprimar los lienzos).
cerne adj. Hard, strong.
— M. Heart of the tree (parte más dura).
cernedera f. Bolter, bolting machine (tamiz).
cernedero m. Bolting cloth, sifter's apron (tela). || Bolting mill (sitio).
cernedor m. Sieve, bolter (cedazo). || Sifter (persona).
cerneja f. Fetlock (del caballo).
cerner* v. tr. To bolt, to sieve, to sift (la harina). || To sieve, to sift (cualquier materia). || FIG. To scan: *cerner el horizonte*, to scan the horizon. | To sift, to clear, to purge (los pensamientos).
— V. intr. To bloom (florecer). || To drizzle (llover muy fino).
— V. pr. To hover (los pájaros). || To circle (los aviones). || FIG. To hang, to loom: *se cernía sobre Europa la amenaza de la guerra*, the threat of war hung over Europe. || To swing *o* to sway one's hips, to wiggle (al andar).
cernícalo m. Kestrel (pájaro). || FIG. y FAM. Lout, brute (bruto). || FAM. *Coger, pillar un cernícalo*, to get sozzled, drunk.
cernidillo m. Drizzle (lluvia fina). || FIG. Swing of one's hips, wiggle (al andar).
cernido m. Sifting, sieving (acción de cerner). || Sifted flour (harina).
cernidor m. Sieve.
cernidura f. Sifting, sieving (cernido). || — Pl. Siftings, sievings, residue, *sing.* (residuos del cernido).
cernir* v. tr. V. CERNER.
cero m. MAT. y FÍS. Zero: *cero absoluto*, absolute zero; *seis grados bajo cero*, six degrees below zero. || Nil (fútbol, rugby, etc.): *tres a cero*, three nil. || Love (tenis): *cuarenta a cero*, forty-love. || Nought, nothing (la cifra O). || — *Me pusieron un cero en inglés*, I got a nought in *o* for English. || FIG. *Partir de cero*, to start from scratch. || FIG. y FAM. *Ser un cero* or *un cero a la izquierda*, to be a nobody.
cerón m. Wax residue.
ceroplástica f. Ceroplastics.
ceroso, sa adj. Waxen, waxy, ceraceous. || *Tez cerosa*, waxy *o* sallow complexion.
cerote m. Cobbler's wax. || FIG. y FAM. Funk, fear (miedo).
cerotear v. tr. To wax (los hilos).
cerquillo m. Fringe (de monje). || Welt (del calzado). || *Amer.* Fringe (flequillo).
cerquita adv. Very near.
cerrado, da adj. Shut, closed: *la puerta está cerrada*, the door is shut. || Shut in, enclosed: *un lugar cerrado de árboles*, a place shut in by trees. || FIG. Hidden (oculto): *el sentido cerrado de una carta*, the hidden meaning of a letter. || Clenched, closed (puño). || Dark, black (la noche). || Overcast, dark (cielo). || Heavy (lluvia). || Sharp, tight (curva). || Obstinate (obstinado). || Thick, bushy: *una barba cerrada*, a thick beard. || FIG. y FAM. Reticent, uncommunicative, secretive (poco expansivo). | Thick, dense, dim (muy torpe). | Typical: *es un alemán cerrado*, he's a typical German. || GRAM. Close: *vocales cerradas*, close vowels. || Broad, with a marked accent: *hablar un andaluz cerrado*, to speak broad Andalusian, to speak with a marked Andalusian accent. || — *A ojos cerrados*, with one's eyes closed, blindfold. || *A puerta cerrada*, in camera (jurisprudencia), behind closed doors. || FAM. *Cerrado de mollera*, thick, dim, dense. || *Descarga cerrada*, v. DESCARGA. || FAM. *Oler a cerrado*, to smell stuffy. || *Ovación cerrada*, thunderous ovation. || *Pliego* or *sobre cerrado*, sealed letter. || *Tomar una curva muy cerrada*, to take a bend very tightly.
— M. Enclosure (cercado). || FIG. y FAM. Blockhead, dunce, dimwit (poco inteligente).
cerrador m. Catch, fastener.
cerradura f. Lock (para cerrar): *cerradura de seguridad*, safety lock. || Closing, shutting (acción de cerrar). || — *Cerradura antirrobo*, antitheft lock. || *Cerradura de combinación*, combination lock.
cerraja f. Lock (cerradura). || BOT. Sow thistle. || FIG. *Volverse* or *quedar en agua de cerrajas*, to fizzle out, to come to nothing, to peter out.
cerrajería f. Locksmith's trade (oficio). || Locksmith's [shop] (taller).
cerrajero m. Locksmith.
cerramiento m. Closing, shutting (cierre). || Enclosure (cercado). || Partition (tabique).
cerrar* v. tr. To shut, to close (caja, puerta, etc.): *cierra la ventana*, close the window. || To close the entrance to: *la puerta cierra el jardín*, the gate closes the entrance to the garden. || To bolt (con cerrojo). | To enclose (cercar). || To close (los ojos, las piernas, etc.). || To clench, to close (el puño). || To seal (una carta). || To close (abanico). || To close, to shut, to put down (paraguas). || ELECTR. To close, to complete (el circuito). || FIG. To rule out: *este fracaso cierra otra posibilidad*, this failure rules out any other possibility. || To close (puerto, universidad, frontera). || To block, to close: *cerrar el camino*, to block the road. || FIG. To bar: *me cerraron el paso*, they barred my way. || To block up, to stop, to plug (abertura, conducto). || To fasten (cinturón). || To turn off: *cerrar un grifo*, to turn off a tap. || To turn out *o* off (el gas). || To close (unir estrechamente): *cerrar las filas*, to close the ranks. || To stitch up (un ojal, etc.). || To block (en dominó). || To end, to finish (discusión). || To clinch: *cerrar un trato*, to clinch a deal. || To conclude (contrato, negocio). || To close (cuenta, etc.). || To shut, to close (una tienda). || To close down (cerrar definitivamente). || — *Cerrar con dos vueltas*, to double-lock. || *Cerrar con llave*, to lock. || FIG. y FAM. *Cerrar con siete llaves*, to lock and double-lock. || FAM. *Cerrar el pico*, to belt up, to shut one's trap, to shut one's mouth. | *Cerrarle el pico a uno*, to shut s.o. up. || *Cerrar la marcha*, to bring up the rear. || *Cerrar la puerta en las narices de alguien*, to shut the door in s.o.'s face. || *Cerrar los puños*, to clench one's fists.
— V. intr. To close, to shut: *ventana que cierra mal*, window which closes badly. || To close with (con el enemigo). || To cast off (géneros de punto). || To come down (la noche). || To close, to heal (una herida). || — *Dejar una ventana sin cerrar*, to leave a window open. || *La noche está cerrada*, it is a dark night.
— V. pr. To close, to shut (puerta, flor, etc.). || To close up, to heal (una herida). || To cut in on: *el camión se me ha cerrado*, the lorry cut in on me. || MIL. To close ranks. || FIG. To persist: *se cierra en callar*, he persists in keeping quiet. | To become overcast, to cloud over (el cielo, el horizonte). || FIG. y FAM. *Cerrarse a la* or *por* or *en banda*, to stick to one's guns.
cerrazón f. Dark *o* overcast sky, storm clouds, *pl.* (cielo nublado). || FIG. Denseness, slowness (torpeza). | Obstinacy (obstinación). || GRAM. Closeness (de vocales). || *Amer.* Spur (de montañas).
cerrejón m. Hillock, small hill.
cerrero, ra adj. Wild, roaming (salvaje, vagabundo). || Wild, untamed (caballo, mula). || FIG. Loutish, uncouth, rough, coarse (bruto). || *Amer.* Bitter: *café cerrero*, bitter coffee.
cerril adj. Hilly, uneven, rough (terreno). || Wild (animal), wild, untamed (caballo, mula). || FIG. y FAM. Uncouth, rough, coarse, loutish (bruto). | Dense, dim, slow (torpe).
cerrillo m. Hillock (colina). || BOT. Couch grass (grama).
cerro m. Hill (colina). || — FIG. y FAM. *Echar* or *irse por los cerros de Úbeda*, to wander from the subject, to go off at a tangent (salirse del tema). || *Montar en cerro*, to ride bareback.
cerrojazo m. FIG. *Dar cerrojazo*, to shut up shop (una tienda, empresa), to drop everything (dejar lo que se hacía). || *Dar un cerrojazo*, to shoot a bolt roughly.
cerrojillo m. Coal titmouse (pájaro).
cerrojo m. Bolt (de puerta, etc.). || Bolt (del fusil). || Blanket defence (en fútbol). || — *Cerrar con cerrojo*, *echar* or *correr el cerrojo*, to bolt [the door, etc.], to shoot the bolt. || *Descorrer el cerrojo*, to unbolt [the door].
certamen m. Contest (desafío). || Tournament, contest, competition (torneo). || [Literary] competition: *participar en un certamen*, to take part in a competition.
certero, ra adj. Good, accurate: *tiro certero*, good shot. || Good, crack (tirador): *un tirador certero*, a crack shot. || Good, skilful: *un cazador certero*, a skilful hunter. || Well-founded, sound: *juicio certero*, well-founded judgment.
certeza o **certidumbre** f. Certainty, certitude (cualidad de cierto).. || Accuracy (exactitud): *la certeza de la noticia*, the accuracy of the news. || — *Saber algo con certeza*, to be certain of sth. || *Tener la certeza (de) que*, to be quite sure that, to be certain that, to know for certain that.
certificable adj. Certifiable. || Registrable, which can be registered (carta, paquete).
certificación f. Certification (acción de certificar). || Registration, registering (de carta o paquete). || Certificate (certificado).

certificado, da adj. Registered (carta, paquete). || Certified.
— M. Certificate. || Registered letter *o* package. || — *Certificado de favor*, certificate delivered as a favour. || *Certificado de penales*, copy of one's police record. || *Certificado de vacuna*, vaccination certificate. || *Certificado médico*, medical certificate.
certificador m. Certifier.
certificar v. tr. To certify, to guarantee (asegurar). || To register (carta, paquete).
certificativo, va o **certificatorio, ria** adj. Which certifies, certifying.
certísimo, ma adj. Very certain (segurísimo). || Very true (muy verdadero).
certitud f. V. CERTEZA.
cerúleo, a adj. Cerulean, azure, deep-blue.
cerumen m. Cerumen, earwax (cerilla de los oídos).
cerusa f. Ceruse.
cerusita f. MIN. Cerussite.
cerval adj Cervine, deer. || — *Gato cerval*, lynx. || *Lobo cerval*, v. LOBO. || FIG. *Tener un miedo cerval*, to be scared stiff.
cervantesco, ca o **cervántico, ca** o **cervantino, na** adj. Cervantic, Cervantine, of Cervantes.
cervantismo m. Study of Cervantes' works.
cervantista adj. Cervantist.
— M. y f. Cervantist, expert on Cervantes.
cervantófilo, la adj. Of a person who admires *o* collects Cervantes' works.
— M. y f. Person who admires *o* collects Cervantes' works.
cervatillo m. ZOOL. Musk deer.
cervato m. Fawn (ciervo).
cerveceo m. Beer fermentation.
cervecería f. Brewery (fábrica). || Public house, bar.
cervecero m. Brewer (fabricante).
cerveza f. Beer, ale: *cerveza dorada*, light *o* pale ale, light beer. || — *Cerveza de barril*, draught beer. || *Cerveza de botella*, bottled beer. || *Cerveza negra*, stout; brown ale.
cervical adj. Cervical.
cérvido m. ZOOL. Cervid.
cervigón m. Thick *o* fat neck.
cerviguillo m. Thick *o* fat neck.
cervino, na adj. Cervine.
cerviz f. Nape of the neck, cervix (nuca). || — FIG. *Bajar* or *doblar* or *humillar la cerviz*, to bow one's head, to humble o.s. | *Levantar la cerviz*, to lift one's head high. | *Ser de dura cerviz*, to be pigheaded, to be stubborn.
cervuno, na adj. Cervine.
cesación f. o **cesamiento** m. Cessation, discontinuation, suspension: *cesación de pagos*, suspension of payments. || *Cesación a divinis*, interdict.
cesante adj. Dismissed, removed from office, suspended (funcionario), recalled (embajador), jobless (empleado). || MIL. Unattached, on half-pay. || — *Dejar a uno cesante*, to relieve s.o. of his office, to dismiss s.o. || *Lucro cesante*, lucrum cessans.
— M. y f. Suspended official.
cesantía f. Suspension (sin trabajo). || Pension [of suspended official]. || Leave of absence (descanso).
cesar v. intr. To stop, to cease (parar): *no cesó de reír*, he never stopped laughing. || To leave, to quit, to give up (en el trabajo). || — *Cesar en el cargo*, to cease one's functions. || *Cesar en sus quejas*, to stop complaining, to cease one's complaints. || *Sin cesar*, unceasingly, ceaselessly, nonstop.
— V. tr. To stop, to suspend (los pagos).
César m. Caesar (emperador). || FIG. *Hay que dar a Dios lo que es de Dios y al César lo que es del César*, render therefore unto Caesar the things which are Caesar's and unto God the things that are God's.
cesaraugustano, na adj. Of *o* from Cesaraugusta [now called Saragossa].
— M. y f. Inhabitant *or* native of Cesaraugusta.
cesáreo, a adj. Caesarean, Caesarian. || — Adj. f. Caesarean (operación).
— F. Caesarean section *o* operation.
cesariano, na adj. Caesarean, Caesarian (relativo a Julio César).
— M. Follower of Julius Caesar.
cesarismo m. Caesarism.
cese m. Cessation, ceasing, discontinuation (suspensión). || Order for the suspension of payments. || Dismissal (revocación de un oficial). || *Dar el cese a alguien*, to dismiss s.o.
cesibilidad f. JUR. Transferability, assignability.
cesible adj. JUR. Transferable, assignable.
cesio m. Caesium, cesium (metal).
cesión f. Cession (acción de ceder): *cesión de territorios*, cession of territories. || JUR. Transfer, assignment: *cesión de tierras, de bienes*, assignment of land, of property.
cesionario, ria m. y f. JUR. Cessionary, transferee, assignee.
cesionista m. y f. Grantor, transferor, transferer, assignor (que hace cesión de bienes).
césped m. Lawn, grass: *cortar el césped*, to mow the lawn, to cut the grass. || Pitch (para juegos). || Green (en las bochas). || Turf, sod (trozo de tierra con hierba).
cesta f. Basket (recipiente de mimbre, etc.): *cesta de la compra*, shopping basket; *cesta de costura*, sewing basket; *cesta de los papeles*, wastepaper basket. || Cesta, chistera, jai-alai basket [used in the Basque game of jai-alai]. || Basket (en el juego del baloncesto). || — *Cesta de labores*, workbasket, sewing basket. || *Cesta de Navidad*, Christmas hamper. || FIG. y FAM. *Llevar la cesta a uno*, to play gooseberry [to s.o.] (acompañar a dos enamorados).
cestada f. Basketful.
cestería f. Basketwork, wickerwork, basketmaking (trabajo). || Basketworks, *pl.* (fábrica). || Basketwork shop (tienda).
cestero, ra m. y f. Basketmaker.
cestillo m. Small basket. || Basket (de globo).
cesto m. Basket (grande o pequeño): *cesto de los papeles*, wastepaper basket. || Hamper (con asas y tapa). || Cestus (guante de atletas romanos). || — FIG. *Echar una carta al cesto de los papeles*, to discard a letter. | *Quien hace un cesto, hará ciento*, once a thief, always a thief.
cestodo m. ZOOL. Cestode.
cestón m. MIL. Gabion.
cestonada f. MIL. Gabionade, line of gabions.
cesura f. POÉT. Caesura, cesura (pausa).
ceta f. V. ZETA.
cetáceo m. ZOOL. Cetacean.
cetonia f. ZOOL. Cetonia.
cetona f. QUÍM. Ketone.
cetrería f. Falconry, hawking.
cetrero m. Falconer. || REL. Verger.
cetrino, na adj. Sallow. || FIG. Melancholy, despondent.
cetro m. Sceptre [U.S., scepter] (insignia de mando). || Perch (para los halcones). || FIG. Power, dominion (poder). || FIG. Sceptre (reinado). || — *Cetro de bufón*, fool's sceptre, jester's bauble. || *Empuñar el cetro*, to ascend the throne.
ceugma f. GRAM. Zeugma.
ceutí adj. [Of *o* from] Ceuta.
— M. y f. Inhabitant *or* native of Ceuta.
cía f. ANAT. Hipbone.
ciaboga f. MAR. Turn.
cianhídrico, ca adj. QUÍM. Hydrocyanic.
cianita f. MIN. Cyanite.
cianógeno m. QUÍM. Cyanogen.
cianosis f. MED. Cyanosis.
cianotipo m. Blueprint, cyanotype.
cianuración f. Cyanidation, cyaniding.
cianuro m. QUÍM. Cyanide.
ciar v. intr. To back up, to walk backwards (retroceder). || MAR. To backwater, to back the oars. || FIG. To give up, to drop: *ciar en sus pretensiones*, to give up *o* to drop one's claims. | To back down (rajarse). || To reverse (el vapor).
ciático, ca adj. MED. Sciatic.
— F. MED. Sciatica.
Cibeles n. pr. f. MIT. Cybele.
cibelina f. ZOOL. Sable.
cibera adj. f. Feeding.
— F. Food, feed (pienso). || Load, primer (de un molino). || Marc (residuos).
cibernética f. Cybernetics.
ciborio m. ARQ. Ciborium (baldaquino). || Goblet (copa).
cicatear v. intr. FAM. To be stingy, to be tightfisted, to be closefisted, to be mean.
cicatería f. Stinginess, meanness.
cicatero, ra adj. Stingy, mean, tightfisted, closefisted.
— M. y f. Miser, skinflint, stingy *o* tightfisted person.
cicatrícula f. Cicatricle, tread (de huevo).
cicatriz f. Scar, cicatrice, cicatrix. || FIG. Scar.
cicatrizable adj. Likely to heal.
cicatrización f. Healing, cicatrization.
cicatrizante adj. MED. Healing, cicatrizing.
— M. MED. Cicatrizant.
cicatrizar v. tr. e intr. To heal, to cicatrize.
— V. pr. To heal, to cicatrize.
cícero m. IMPR. Pica, twelve-point type.
Cicerón n. pr. m. Cicero.
cicerone m. Guide, cicerone (guía).
ciceroniano, na adj. Ciceronian.
cicindela f. Cicindela, tiger beetle.
ciclamen o **ciclamino** m. BOT. Cyclamen.
ciclamor m. BOT. Judas tree.
cíclico, ca adj. Cyclic, cyclical.
ciclismo m. Cycling. || Cycle racing (carrera).
ciclista adj. Cycle, cycling: *carrera ciclista*, cycling race, cycle race.
— M. y f. Cyclist.
ciclo m. Cycle (lunar, vital, etc.). || Course, series (de conferencias).
ciclocrós m. DEP. Cyclo-cross.
cicloidal o **cicloideo, a** adj. MAT. Cycloidal.
cicloide f. MAT. Cycloid.
ciclomotor m. Autocycle, moped.
ciclón m. Cyclone (huracán). || — FIG. *Entrar como un ciclón*, to burst in. | *Llegar como un ciclón*, to arrive like a whirlwind.
ciclonal o **ciclónico, ca** adj. Cyclonal.
cíclope m. Cyclops.
ciclópeo, a o **ciclópico, ca** adj. Cyclopean, gigantic.
ciclorama m. Cyclorama.
ciclostilo m. Cyclostyle, mimeograph.

ciclóstomos m. pl. Cyclostomes, cyclostomi (peces).
ciclotimia f. MED. Cyclothymia.
ciclotrón m. FÍS. Cyclotron.
cicloturismo m. Touring by bicycle.
cicuta f. Conium, cicuta, hemlock (planta). || *Cicuta menor*, fool's parsley.
Cid n. pr. m. The Cid. || FIG. Brave man. || FAM. *Se cree descendiente de la pata del Cid*, he thinks he's the cat's whiskers, he thinks he's the Lord God Almighty.
cidra f. BOT. Citron (fruta).

— OBSERV. Not to be confused with *sidra*, cider [drink].

cidracayote m. *Amer.* Gourd, calabash.
cidrada f. Citron preserve *o* jam.
cidro m. BOT. Citron.
cidronela f. BOT. Melissa.
ciegamente adv. Blindly. || Fearlessly: *los soldados atacaron ciegamente*, the soldiers attacked fearlessly. || *Confiar ciegamente en*, to have blind faith in, to trust implicitly.
ciego, ga adj. Blind (que no ve): *quedarse ciego*, to go blind; *ciego de nacimiento*, blind from birth. || FIG. Blinded, blind (cegado): *ciego de ira*, blinded by anger, blind with anger. || Blocked up, plugged, stopped (cañería). || Closely baked (pan). || With no holes (pan, queso). || — FIG. y FAM. *Está ciego con los naipes*, he is mad about cards. | *Estar ciego*, to be blind drunk, to be sozzled, to be paralytic (borracho). || FIG. *Fe ciega*, blind faith. || FIG. y FAM. *Más ciego que un topo*, blind as a bat. | *Para los defectos de su marido está ciega*, she is blind to her husband's faults. || ANAT. *Punto ciego del ojo*, blind spot. || FIG. *Tan ciego el uno como el otro*, it's like the blind leading the blind.
— M. y f. Blind man, blind woman. || — M. ANAT. Caecum (intestino). || — *A ciegas*, blindly. || *Andar a ciegas*, to go blindly on (en la vida), to grope one's way along (en la oscuridad). || *Comprar a ciegas*, to buy haphazardly *o* blindly *o* at random. || *Coplas de ciego*, trashy verse. || FIG. *Dar palos de ciego*, V. PALO. | *En tierra* or *en país de ciegos el tuerto es rey*, in the land of the blind the one-eyed man is king. || *Jugar a la ciega*, to play blindfold (ajedrez). || *Los ciegos*, the blind. || FIG. *Un ciego lo ve*, it's staring you in the face, it stands out a mile.
cielito m. *Amer.* Popular Argentinian song and dance.
cielo m. Sky: *cielo azul, sereno, encapotado*, blue, calm, overcast sky. || REL. Heaven. | God (Dios). || Prosperity (bienaventuranza). || Roof (de la boca). || Canopy (de la cama). || ARQ. Ceiling (techo). || — *A cielo abierto*, opencast [U.S., opencut] (minas). || *A cielo descubierto*, in the open [air]. || *A cielo raso*, in the open [air], under the stars (al aire libre). || FIG. *Bajado del cielo*, heaven-sent (muy opotuno), out of the blue (inesperado). || *Cerrarse* or *entoldarse el cielo*, to become overcast, to cloud over [the sky]. || *Cielo aborregado*, mackerel sky. || ARQ. *Cielo raso*, ceiling. || *¡Cielos!, ¡cielo santo!*, good heavens! || *Clamar al cielo*, to cry out to heaven. || *Con paciencia se gana el cielo*, all things come to him who waits. || *Desencapotarse el cielo*, to brighten up [the weather], to clear [the sky]. || *El reino de los cielos*, the kingdom of heaven. || FIG. *Estar en el séptimo cielo*, to be in the seventh heaven. | *Estar hecho un cielo*, to be an angel. | *Esto va al cielo*, his word is law, what he says goes. || *Ganar el cielo*, to go to Heaven. || *Ir al cielo*, to go to heaven. || FAM. *Juntársele a uno el cielo con la tierra*, to be in a fix, to be in a tight spot. || FIG. *Llovido del cielo*, heaven-sent (oportuno), out of the blue (inesperado). | *¡Mi cielo!, ¡cielo mío!*, my darling!, my dear! | *Mover* or *revolver cielo y tierra*, to move heaven and earth. | *Poner a uno por los cielos*, to praise s.o. to the skies. | *Poner el grito en el cielo*, V. GRITO. || FIG. y FAM. *Se me ha ido el santo al cielo*, I clean *o* completely forgot. | *Ser un cielo*, to be an angel. || FIG. *Se vino el cielo abajo*, the heavens opened (llovió mucho). || FIG. *Si escupes al cielo, en la cara te caerá*, V. ESCUPIR. || *Subir al cielo*, to ascend to heaven (Cristo), to go to heaven (los hombres). || *Un aviso del cielo*, a warning from heaven. || FIG. *Ver el cielo abierto*, to see a way out, to see one's chance (para salir de un apuro).
ciempiés m. inv. Centipede.
cien adj. A hundred. || — *Cien por cien*, one hundred per cent, completely. || *De cien en cien*, in hundreds, by the hundred.

— OBSERV. *Ciento* is apocopated to *cien* before nouns (*cien años, cien pesetas*, a hundred years, a hundred pesetas), and before numbers which it multiplies (*cien mil pesetas*, a hundred thousand pesetas).

ciénaga f. Marsh, bog, swamp (zona pantanosa).
ciencia f. Science: *los adelantos de la ciencia*, the progress of science. || FIG. Learning, knowledge: *un pozo de ciencia*, a well of knowledge. || — *Ciencia ficción*, science fiction. || *Ciencia infusa*, intuition, mystical vision (comunicada directamente por Dios), intuitive *o* innate knowledge (saber intuitivo). || *Ciencias naturales, exactas*, natural, exact *o* pure sciences. || *Ciencias ocultas*, occult sciences. || *Creer algo a ciencia cierta*, to firmly believe sth. || *Hombre de ciencia*, scientist. || FIG. *No tener ciencia* or *tener poca ciencia*, to be as easy as pie *o* as ABC. || *Saber a* or *de ciencia cierta*, to know for certain *o* for a fact.
cienmilésimo, ma adj./s. Hundred thousandth. || *La cienmilésima parte*, one hundred thousandth, the hundred thousandth part.
cienmilímetro m. Hundredth of a millimetre.
cienmillonésimo, ma adj./s. Hundred millionth. || *La cienmillonésima parte*, one hundred millionth.
cieno m. Mud, mire, muck (fango).
científico, ca adj. Scientific.
— M. y f. Scientist.
cientifismo m. Scientism.
ciento adj./s. m. A hundred, one hundred: *ciento veinticuatro*, one hundred and twenty-four. || Hundredth (centésimo). || — M. Hundred: *un ciento de ostras*, a hundred oysters. || About a hundred, a hundred-odd: *un ciento de huevos*, about a hundred eggs. || — Pl. Piquet, *sing.* (juego de naipes). || — *Ciento diez*, a hundred and ten. || FIG. *Darle ciento y raya a uno*, to run rings round s.o., to knock spots off s.o. || *Devolver ciento por uno*, to repay a hundredfold. || FIG. y FAM. *El ciento y la madre*, a crowd, a whole string of people. || *Por cientos*, in hundreds, by the hundred. || *Veinte por ciento*, twenty per cent.

— OBSERV. V. HUNDRED.

cierne m. Blossoming, blooming. || *En cierne* or *en ciernes*, in flower, in blossom, in bloom (la vid), green, unripe, in the blade (el trigo), budding, in the making (persona, cosa), in embryo, in its infancy (una cosa).
cierre m. Closing, shutting. || Shutdown, shutting-down: *el cierre temporal de la fábrica*, the temporary shutdown of the factory. || Closedown (de una emisión de radio, etc.). || Closing (de la Bolsa, de una sesión). || Closure (de un debate). || End (de inventario). || End, close: *cierre de ejercicio*, end of the financial year. || Fastener (de un vestido). || Clasp, fastener (de un bolso). || Buckle, clasp (de un cinturón). || Shutter, blind (de una tienda, escaparate, etc.). || Catch (de puerta). || Choke (de un automóvil). || Binding (de los esquís). || — *Cierre de cremallera*, zip, zip fastener [U.S., zipper]. || *Cierre patronal*, lockout.
cierro m. Closing, shutting (cierre). || *Amer.* Enclosure, fence (vallado). | Envelope (sobre). || *Cierro de cristales*, bay window.
cierto, ta adj. Certain, some (algún, algunos): *ciertos escritores*, certain writers; *cierto tiempo*, a certain time, some time. || Sure, certain (seguro): *estar cierto de tener razón*, to be sure of being right. || True (verdad): *eso es cierto*, that's true. || Correct (exacto). || Definite, sure: *hay indicios ciertos de mejoría*, there are definite signs of improvement. || — Pl. Some, certain: *en ciertos casos*, in some cases. || — *Estar en lo cierto*, to be right. || *Lo cierto es que...*, the fact is that.... || *Persona de cierta edad*, elderly person.
— Adv. Of course, certainly. || — *De cierto*, for certain. || *Lo que hay de cierto es que...*, the truth *o* the fact is that... || *No por cierto*, of course not, certainly not. || *Por cierto*, of course, indeed, certainly. || *Por cierto...*, by the way...: *por cierto ayer fui a verte y no te encontré*, by the way I went to see you yesterday and you weren't in. || *Por cierto que*, of course. || *Saber por cierto*, to know for sure *o* for certain. || *Si es cierto que*, if it is true that. || *Tan cierto como dos y dos son cuatro*, as sure as eggs are eggs.

— OBSERV. In Spanish, the indefinite article is omitted when *cierto* is placed before a noun (*cierto día*, a certain day), but is used in cases such as *un dato cierto*, a definite fact.

cierva f. Hind (rumiante).
ciervo m. ZOOL. Deer (macho y hembra), stag, hart (macho). || — *Ciervo común*, red deer. || *Ciervo volante*, stag beetle (coleóptero).
cierzo m. North wind.
cifosis f. Cyphosis.
cifra f. Figure: *un número de tres cifras*, a three-figure number. || Figure, number, numeral: *en nuestro sistema empleamos diez cifras*, in our system we use ten numbers. || Code (escritura secreta): *en cifra*, in code. || Monogram (monograma). || Quantity, amount (cantidad). || Number: *la cifra de muertos*, the number of dead. || — *Cifra global*, lump sum. || *Cifra de mortalidad*, mortality rate. || *Cifra romana*, Roman numeral. || FIG. *En cifra*, obscurely (ininteligiblemente), briefly, in brief (abreviadamente).
cifrado, da adj. In code, coded: *carta cifrada*, letter in code. || MÚS. *Bajo cifrado*, figured bass.
— M. Putting into code.
cifrar v. tr. To write in code, to code, to put into code (un mensaje). || To summarize, to resume (resumir). || COM. To evaluate. || — *Cifrar la felicidad en el dinero*, for him money is happiness. || *Cifrar en*, to place in, to put in: *cifrar la esperanza en Dios*, to place one's hope in God. || *Cifro mi placer en la lectura*, my only pleasure is reading.
— V. pr. To amount, to come: *cifrarse en*, to come to.
cigala f. Norway lobster.
cigarra f. Cicada (insecto).
cigarral m. Country house [on the outskirts of Toledo].
cigarrera f. Cigarette manufacturer (que fabrica cigarros). || Cigarette seller (que vende cigarrillos). || Tobacconist (que tiene un estanco). || Cigar case (para puros). || Tobacco pouch (petaca).
cigarrería f. *Amer.* Tobacconist's, tobacconist's shop.

cigarrillo m. Cigarette: *liar un cigarrillo*, to roll a cigarette; *una cajetilla* or *un paquete de cigarrillos*, a packet of cigarettes. || *Cigarrillo con filtro*, filter cigarette, filter-tip cigarette, tipped cigarette.
cigarro m. Cigar (puro). || Cigarette (cigarrillo). || *Amer.* Dragonfly. || — *Cigarro de papel*, cigarette. || *Cigarro puro* or *habano*, cigar.
cigarrón m. Grasshopper (saltamontes)
cigomático, ca adj. ANAT. Zygomatic.
cigoñal m. Shadoof, shaduf (para sacar agua).
cigoñino m. Young stork (cría de la cigueña).
cigoto m. BIOL. Zygote.
ciguatarse v. pr. To get food poisoning from eating fish.
cigüeña f. Stork (ave). || TECN. Crank, winch. || *Amer.* Barrel organ (órgano de manubrio). || FIG. *Lo trajo la cigüeña*, the stork brought him (un niño).
cigüeñal m. Crank (manubrio). || TECN. Crankshaft (de motor).
cilantro m. BOT. Coriander.
ciliado, da adj. Ciliated, ciliate.
— M. BOT. Ciliate.
ciliar adj. ANAT. Ciliary.
cilicio m. Cilice, hair shirt.
cilindrada f. Cylinder capacity: *gran cilindrada*, large cylinder capacity.
cilindrado m. TECN. Rolling (de acero, etc.). | Mangling, calendering (de tejido).
cilindrar v. tr. To roll (acero, etc.). || To mangle, to calender (tejido).
cilíndrico, ca adj. Cylindrical, cylindric.
cilindro m. MAT. Cylinder. || TECN. Cylinder: *cilindro maestro*, master cylinder. || Roller (de máquina de escribir). || IMPR. Cylinder, drum (para los tipos). | Roller (para la tinta). || *Amer.* Top hat (sombrero). | Barrel organ (organillo). || *Cilindro compresor*, steamroller, road roller (rodillo).
cilindroeje m. ANAT. Axis cylinder.
cilio m. BIOL. Cilium: *cilio vibrátil*, vibratile cilium.
cillerero m. Cellarer (de un monasterio).
cillero m. Granary keeper.
cima f. Summit, top (de una montaña). || Top (de un árbol). || BOT. Cyme. | Stalk (tallo). || Crest (de una ola). || FIG. Summit, height, peak (apogeo). | End (fin). || — FIG. *Dar cima a*, to finish off, to crown, to complete. || *Por cima*, on top, at the top.

— OBSERV. Do not confuse with *sima*, precipice.

cimacio m. ARQ. Cyma, ogee moulding, dado (moldura).
cimarra (hacer la) loc. *Amer.* To play truant [U.S., to play hookey].
cimarrón, ona adj. *Amer.* Runaway, fugitive, wild [formerly "slave" in America, but now an animal which has run wild]. | Wild (animal, planta). | Lazy, idle (vago).
— M. *Amer.* Fugitive slave (esclavo). | Unsweetened maté *o* Paraguay tea (mate).
cimarronada f. *Amer.* Herd of wild animals.
cimarronear v. intr. *Amer.* To take maté *o* Paraguay tea without sugar. || To run away, to escape, to flee (huir).
cimbalero o **cimbalista** m. MÚS. Cymbalist.
cimbalillo m. Small bell.
címbalo m. Small bell (campanita). || MÚS. Cymbal.
cimbel m. Rope for tying decoy pigeons. || Decoy bird (pájaro que sirve de señuelo). || FIG. Lure, enticement (añagaza). || FIG. y FAM. Telltale (soplón).
cimborio o **cimborrio** m. ARQ. Dome, cupola (en el crucero).
cimbra f. ARQ. Centering (armazón). | Soffit (curvatura interior). || MAR. Curvature, sweep. || *Amer.* Trap (trampa).
cimbrado, da adj. Centred.
— M. Bend from the waist (en el baile).
cimbrar v. tr. To waggle, to shake, to make quiver [a flexible object]. || FIG. y FAM. To bash, to hit (golpear): *cimbrar de un bastonazo*, to bash with a stick. || ARQ. To erect the centering for (una bóveda).
cimbreante adj. Supple, flexible. || Waving (ondulante). || Swaying (al andar). || Quivering (vara, etc.).
cimbrear v. tr. To waggle, to shake, to make quiver (un objeto flexible). || To bend (curvar).
— V. pr. To sway (con el viento). || To move gracefully (al andar). || To bend (doblarse).
cimbreño, ña adj. Supple, flexible.
cimbreo m. Bending. || Quivering (de vara o junco). || Swaying (al andar).
címbrico, ca adj. HIST. Cimbric, Cimbrian.
cimentación f. Laying of foundations (acción de cimentar). || Foundation, foundations, *pl.* (resultado).
cimentar* v. tr. ARQ. To lay the foundations of (un edificio). || To cement (fijar con cemento). || To case harden, to face-harden (hacer la cementación). || To refine [gold]. || FIG. To strengthen, to consolidate (la amistad, las relaciones, la paz). | To found, to lay the foundations of (una sociedad, etc.).
cimera f. Crest (del casco).
cimero, ra adj. Highest, uppermost, top, topmost. || FIG. Dominant, dominating.
cimiento m. ARQ. Foundations, *pl.*, foundation: *abrir, echar los cimientos*, to dig, to lay the foundations. || FIG. Origin, source (origen). | Foundation: *su autoridad tiene sólidos cimientos*, his authority has solid foundations *o* a solid foundation. || — FIG. *Desde los cimientos*, from the very start. | *Echar los cimientos de un acuerdo*, to lay the foundations for an agreement. | *Echar los cimientos de una sociedad*, to found a company.
cimitarra f. Scimitar (arma).
cinabrio m. MIN. Cinnabar. || ARTES. Vermilion.
cinámico, ca adj. QUÍM. Cinnamic.
cinamomo m. BOT. Cinnamon.
cinc m. Zinc.

— OBSERV. Pl. *cincs*.
— In Spanish, the spelling *zinc* is also correct.

cincel m. Chisel.
cincelado, da adj. Chiselled.
— M. Chiselling.
cincelador m. Chiseller. || Engraver (grabador).
cinceladura f. Chiselling, carving.
cincelar v. tr. To chisel, to carve with a chisel.
cincelete m. TECN. Graver, small chisel.
cinco adj. Five: *los cinco dedos*, the five fingers. || Fifth, five: *el capítulo V (cinco)*, chapter five, the fifth chapter. || Fifth (la fecha).
— M. Five (cifra). || Fifth: *el 5 (cinco) de septiembre*, September the fifth, the fifth of September (en la conversación), 5 September, September 5th (encabezamiento de una carta). || *Amer.* Five-stringed guitar (guitarrilla). || — FIG. y FAM. *Decir a uno cuántas son cinco*, to tell s.o. a few home truths. | *Esos cinco*, that paw *o* mitt *o* fist *o* hand. | *Estar sin cinco*, to be broke. | *No tener los cinco sentidos*, to be off one's rocker, not to be all there. | *Saber cuántas son cinco*, to know what's what. || *Son las cinco*, it is five o'clock. || FIG. y FAM. *Vengan* or *choca esos cinco*, done!, let's shake on it (para concluir un acuerdo), shake!, let's shake (para reconciliarse). || *Vivo en el cinco*, I live at number five.
cincoenrama f. BOT. Cinquefoil, cinqfoil.
cincograbado m. Zincograph.
cincografía m. Zincography.
cincuenta adj./s. m. Fifty. || Fiftieth (quincuagésimo). || *Los cincuenta*, fifty: *andar por los cincuenta*, to be getting on for fifty, to be pushing fifty (fam.).
cincuentavo, va adj./s. Fiftieth.
cincuentenario m. Quinquagenary, fiftieth anniversary.
cincuenteno, na adj. Fiftieth.
— F. Fifty.
cincuentón, ona adj. Fifty-year-old, in one's fifties.
— M. y f. Fifty-year-old, person in his [*o* her, etc.] fifties.
cincha f. Girth, cinch. || FIG. *A revienta cinchas*, at full speed, at full tilt, hell for leather.
cinchada f. *Amer.* V. CINCHADURA.
cinchadura f. Girthing, cinching.
cinchar v. tr. To girth (la cincha). || To hoop (un tonel).
cinchazo m. *Amer.* Blow with the flat of the sword.
cinchera f. Belly (de caballo). || Girth gall (desolladura).
cincho m. Belt (cinturón). || Hoop (para los toneles). *Amer.* Girth (cincha).
cine m. Cinema, pictures [U.S., movies]: *ir al cine*, to go to the pictures. Cinema (arte). || Cinema, picture house [U.S., movie theater] (edificio). || — *Cine de estreno*, first-run cinema. || *Cine de sesión continua*, continous performance cinema. || *Cine en colores*, films in colour. || *Cine mudo*, silent cinema *o* films. || *Cine sonoro*, talking cinema, talkies. || *Hacer cine*, to make films.
cineasta m. [Film] actor. || — M. y f. Person who works in the film industry (en general). || Film director (director).
cineclub m. Film society [U.S., film club].
cinegético, ca adj. Cynegetic.
— F. Cynegetics, hunting.
Cinemascope m. (nombre registrado). Cinemascope.
cinemateca f. Film library.
cinemática f. FÍS. Kinematics, cinematics.
cinematografía f. Cinematography, films, *pl.*, film-making.
cinematografiar v. tr. To film.
cinematográfico, ca adj. Cinematographic, film.
cinematógrafo m. Cinematograph (arte y actividad). || Cinema (espectáculo). || Film projector, projector (máquina).
cinerama m. Cinerama.
cinerario, ria adj. Cinerary: *urna cineraria*, cinerary urn.
— F. BOT. Cineraria.
cinéreo, a o **cinericio, cia** adj. Cinereous, ash-grey, ashen, ashy.
cinestesia f. Kinaesthesis, kinesthesis.
cinético, ca adj. Kinetic.
— F. Kinetics.
cingalés, esa adj. Singhalese, Cingalese, Cinghalese.
cíngaro, ra adj. Tzigane, Hungarian gypsy.
— M. y f. Tzigane, Hungarian gypsy. || — M. Gypsy.
cingiberáceas f. pl. BOT. Zingiberaceae.
cinglar v. intr. MAR. To scull.
— V. tr. TECN. To puddle (el hierro).
cíngulo m. REL. Cord (para ceñir el alba).
cínico, ca adj. FIL. Cynical. || Hard-faced, brazen, shameless.

— M. y f. FIG. Cynic. || Hard-faced *o* brazen *o* shameless person.
cinife m. Mosquito (insecto).
cinismo m. FIL. Cynicism. || Shamelessness, brazenness. || *¡Qué cinismo!*, what a nerve!
cinocéfalo m. Cynocephalus, dog-faced baboon.
cinódromo m. Greyhound track (canódromo).
cinoglosa f. BOT. Cynoglossum, hound's tongue.
cinquero m. Zinc worker.
cinta f. Band (en general). || Ribbon (para adornar, envolver, etc., para el pelo). || Braid, edging (para adornar una prenda de vestir). || Film (película). || Tape (magnética). || Ribbon (de máquina de escribir). || Shoelace (cordón del zapato). || ARQ. Fillet. || MAR. Bend, wale. || Kerb, curb [U.S., curb] (de la acera). || Coronet (del casco de las caballerías). || Skirting board [U.S., baseboard] (que rodea una habitación). || TECN. Belt: *cinta transportadora*, conveyor belt. || MIL. Loading belt (de ametralladora). || — *Cinta adhesiva*, adhesive tape. || *Cinta aisladora*, insulating tape. || *Cinta cinematográfica*, film. || *Cinta de freno*, brake lining. || *Cinta de llegada*, finishing tape (en una carrera). || *Cinta magnetofónica*, magnetic tape, recording tape. || *Cinta métrica*, tape measure. || *Cinta para el pelo*, hairband, ribbon.

—OBSERV. *En cinta* when used to mean *encinta* (pregnant) is a barbarism.

cintarazo m. Blow with the flat of the sword.
cinteado, da adj. Decorated with ribbons, ribboned, beribboned (guarnecido de cintas).
cintería f. Ribbons, *pl.* (cintas). || Ribbon industry (industria). || Ribbon shop, haberdasher's (tienda).
cintilar v. intr. To scintillate, to twinkle, to sparkle.
cinto, ta adj. Encircled.
— M. Swordbelt (para el sable). || Belt (cinturón). || Waist (cintura).

— OBSERV. The adjective *cinto* is the irregular past participle of *ceñir*.

cintra f. ARQ. Arch, curvature.
cintrado, da adj. ARQ. Arched.
cintura f. ANAT. Waist (talle): *coger por la cintura*, to get hold of [s.o.] round the waist. || Waist, waistline (medida): *tiene poca cintura*, she has a slim waist. || Belt (ceñidor). || Throat (de chimenea). || — ANAT. *Cintura pelviana*, pelvic girdle *o* arch. || FIG. *Doblarse por la cintura*, to be in stitches. || FIG. y FAM. *Meter a uno en cintura*, to make s.o. behave. || *Tener una cintura de avispa*, to have a wasp waist.
cinturón m. Belt (de cuero, etc.): *un cinturón de lagarto*, a lizard-skin belt. || Swordbelt (para el sable). || FIG. Circle, belt, cordon (de murallas, etc.). || Belt, zone: *cinturón industrial*, industrial belt. || Belt (de montañas). || Belt (en judo): *cinturón negro*, black belt. || — FIG. *Apretarse el cinturón*, to tighten one's belt. || *Cinturón de castidad*, chastity belt. || *Cinturón de seguridad*, safety belt, seat belt. || *Cinturón salvavidas*, life belt
cipayo m. Sepoy.
cipo m. ARQ. Cippus, memorial stone. || Milestone (en los caminos).
cipolino m. Cipolin, onion marble (mármol).
cipote m. y f. *Amer.* Kid, nipper, youngster (chiquillo). || — M. POP. Tool (miembro viril).
ciprés m. Cypress (tree).
cipresal m. BOT. Cypress grove *o* plantation.
ciprino m. Cyprinid (pez). || — Pl. Cyprinidae.
ciprino, na o **ciprio, pria** *o* **cipriota** adj./s. Cypriot.
circense adj. Circus.
circo m. Circus (espectáculo). || Amphitheatre, circus. || GEOL. Cirque (entre montañas).
circón m. Zircon (piedra preciosa).
circona f. QUÍM. Zirconia (óxido).
circonio m. Zirconium (metal).
circonita f. QUÍM. Zirconite.
circuito m. ELECTR. Circuit. || DEP. Circuit, track, course (sitio). || Circumference (contorno). || Tour (viaje): *circuito organizado*, organized tour. || Circuit (con vuelta al punto de partida). || — ELECTR. *Circuito cerrado*, closed circuit. || *Circuito cerrado de televisión* or *televisión por circuito cerrado*, closed-circuit television. || *Circuito impreso*, printed circuit. || TECN. *Circuito precintado*, sealed system. || ELECTR. *Circuito primario, secundario*, primary, secundary coil.
circulación f. Circulation (de savia, sangre, ideas, vehículos, artículos de comercio, etc.). || Traffic (conjunto de vehículos). || — *Billetes en circulación*, notes in circulation. || *Calle de mucha circulación*, busy street. || *Cerrado a la circulación rodada*, closed to traffic. || BIOL. *Circulación de la sangre* or *sanguínea*, circulation of the blood, blood circulation. || COM. *Circulación fiduciaria*, banknotes in circulation, paper currency. || *Circulación rodada*, traffic, vehicular traffic. || *Código de la circulación*, highway code. || *La circulación es por la izquierda*, they drive on the left. || *Poner en circulación*, to put into circulation. || *Retirar de la circulación*, to withdraw from circulation.
circulante adj. Circulating. || Working (capital). || *Biblioteca circulante*, mobile library.
circular adj. Circular: *movimiento circular*, circular motion. || Circular (carta). || *Viaje circular*, round trip, circular tour.
circular v. intr. To flow, to circulate (corriente eléctrica, sangre, agua): *la corriente circula por el circuito*, the current flows through the circuit; *el agua circula por la cañería*, water flows through the pipes. || To drive (automóviles): *circular por la derecha*, to drive on the right. || To use: *muchos coches circulan por esta calle*, many cars use this street. || To walk about: *circulaba mucha gente por la calle*, there were a lot of people walking about in the street. || To run (trenes y autobuses): *por esta vía ya no circulan trenes*, trains no longer run on this line. || To keep (ceñirse): *circulen por la derecha*, keep to the right. || FIG. To go around, to spread: *el rumor circuló rápidamente*, the rumour spread quickly. || To circulate (cartas). || To circulate: *el dinero circula*, money circulates. || — *Al abrir esta ventana circula mucho aire*, if you open this window there is a big draught. || *¡Circulen, por favor!*, move along, please! || *Hacer circular*, to keep moving (coches), to move along (gente), to circulate (una cosa): *hicieron circular un documento*, they circulated a document.
— V. tr. To circulate: *circular una orden*, to circulate an order.
circularmente adv. Circularly.
circulatorio, ria adj. Circulatory.
círculo m. MAT. Circle. || FIG. Circle, club: *círculo de juego*, gambling club. || Circle, clique (cenáculo). || Clubhouse (sitio de reunión de un club). || Circle (extensión). || GEOGR. Circle: *círculo polar*, polar circle. || FIG. Environment (medio). | Scope, extent. || — Pl. Circles (medios): *en los círculos bien informados*, in well-informed circles. | Suite, *sing.*: *en los círculos allegados al rey*, in the king's suite. || — MAR. *Círculo acimutal*, azimuth circle. || *Círculo familiar*, family circle. || MAT. *Círculo máximo, menor*, great, small circle. || *Círculo polar antártico, ártico*, Antarctic, Arctic Circle. || FIG. *Círculo vicioso*, vicious circle. || *En círculo*, in a circle. || *Formar un círculo alrededor de alguien*, to form a circle around s.o.
circumpolar adj. Circumpolar.
circuncidar v. tr. To circumcise.
circuncisión f. Circumcision.
circunciso, sa adj. Circumcised.
— M. Circumcised man.
circundante adj. Surrounding.
circundar v. tr. To surround.
circunferencia f. Circumference.
circunferente adj. Surrounding, limiting, circumscribing.
circunferir* v. tr. To circumscribe, to surround (rodear). || To limit (limitar).
circunflejo adj./s. m. Circumflex.
circunlocución f. o **circunloquio** m. Circumlocution.
circunnavegación f. Circumnavigation.
circunnavegar v. tr. To circumnavigate, to sail round.
circunscribir v. tr. To circumscribe. || FIG. To confine, to limit, to circumscribe.
— V. pr. To confine o.s., to limit o.s., to restrict o.s.: *circunscribirse a algo*, to confine o.s. to sth.
circunscripción f. Circumscription, circumscribing. || District, area (distrito). || *Circunscripción electoral*, electoral constituency, electoral district.
circunscrito, ta o **circunscripto, ta** adj. Circumscribed. || FIG. Limited (limitado).
circunspección f. Circumspection.
circunspecto, ta adj. Circumspect. || Carefully chosen (palabras).
circunstancia f. Circumstance: *adaptarse a las circunstancias*, to adapt o.s. to the circumstances. || — JUR. *Circunstancia agravante, atenuante*, aggravating, extenuating circumstance. || *De circunstancias*, out of necessity, for a reason: *estaba en un viaje de circunstancias*, he was making a journey for a reason *o* out of necessity; improvised: *una silla de circunstancias*, an improvised chair. || *En estas circunstancias* or *en las circunstancias presentes*, under *o* in the circumstances. || *Estar a la altura de las circunstancias*, to rise to the occasion.
circunstanciadamente adv. In detail, circumstantially.
circunstanciado, da adj. Detailed, circumstantial.
circunstancial adj. Incidental, circumstantial. || GRAM. Adverbial: *complemento circunstancial*, adverbial complement.
circunstancialmente adv. Temporarily.
circunstante m. y f. Person present, bystander.
circunvalación f. Circumvallation. || — *Carretera de circunvalación*, ring road, bypass (en una ciudad). || *Línea de circunvalación*, circular line (de ferrocarril), circular route (de autobús). || *Tren, ferrocarril de circunvalación*, circular train, railway line.
circunvalar v. tr. To surround, to circumvallate.
circunvecino, na adj. Surrounding, neighbouring, adjacent.
circunvolar v. tr. To fly around.
circonvolución f. Circumvolution. || *Circunvoluciones cerebrales*, cerebral convolutions.
circunyacente adj. Circumjacent.
Cirenaica n. pr. f. GEOGR. Cyrenaica.
cirial m. Church candlestick (candelero). || Processional candlestick (en las procesiones).
cirílico, ca adj. Cyrillic (alfabeto).

CIRCULACIÓN (*f.*) DE AUTOMÓVILES — MOTORING

I. Términos (*m.*) generales. — General terms.

tráfico *m.*	traffic
hora (*f.*) punta *or* de mayor afluencia	rush hour
atasco *m.*, embotellamiento *m.*	traffic jam
policía (*f.*) de tráfico	traffic police *pl.*
guardia (*m.*) de tráfico	traffic policeman
usuario (*m.*) de la carretera	road user
código (*m.*) de la circulación	highway code
peatón *m.*	pedestrian
coche (*m.*) de turismo	private car
coche (*m.*) utilitario	utility car
vehículo (*m.*) comercial	commercial vehicle
camión *m.*	lorry [U.S., truck]
furgoneta *f.*	van

II. Carreteras, *f.* — Roads.

autopista *f.*	motorway [U.S., freeway, superhighway]
carretera (*f.*) nacional	A road, arterial road [U.S., arterial highway]
carretera (*f.*) secundaria *or* comarcal	B road, secondary road
empalme *m.*	slip road (de autopista)
bifurcación *f.*	fork
cruce *m.*; intersección *f.*	crossroads; intersection, junction
andén *m.*, arcén *m.*	side of the road, verge; hard shoulder (de autopista)
vía (*f.*) de dirección única	one-way street
dirección (*f.*) prohibida	no entry
prohibido aparcar	no parking
glorieta *f.*	roundabout
trébol *m.*	cloverleaf junction
refugio *m.*, isleta *f.*	traffic island refuge
aparcamiento *m.*	car park [U.S., parking lot]
circulación (*f.*) rodada	traffic, vehicular traffic

III. Obstáculos, *m.* — Obstructions.

descenso (*m.*) peligroso	steep hill
paso (*m.*) superior	flyover
paso (*m.*) subterráneo	subway (para peatones), underpass (para coches)
paso (*m.*) a nivel (con guarda, sin guarda)	[manned, unmanned] level crossing
paso (*m.*) de peatones	pedestrian crossing
bache *m.*, badén *m.*	pothole, hole
gravilla *f.*	gravel
curva (*f.*) a la derecha, a la izquierda	right-hand, left-hand bend
curva (*f.*) sin visibilidad	blind bend
doble curva *f.*	Z bend, double bend
curva (*f.*) peligrosa *or* muy cerrada	dangerous *o* hairpin bend
estrechamiento (*m.*) de carretera	road narrows
cambio (*m.*) de rasante	brow of a hill
obras *f. pl.*	road works
desviación *f.* desvío *m.*	diversion
firme (*m.*) *or* piso (*m.*) deslizante	slippery road surface

IV. Seguridad (*f.*) en carretera. — Road safety.

señalización *f.*	traffic *o* road signs *pl.*
prohibido girar a la derecha	no right turn
prohibido dar la vuelta	no U-turns
semáforos *m. pl.*	traffic lights
disco (*m.*) rojo	red light
señal (*f.*) intermitente	flashing amber (semáforo)
stop *m.*: parada *f.*	stop
prioridad *f.*, preferencia (*f.*) de paso	right of way
ceder el paso	to give way
señal (*f.*) acústica	horn
señales (*f.*) ópticas	hand signals (con la mano), signals (en general)
luces *f. pl.*	lights
luz (*f.*) de carretera	headlights on full beam
luces (*f. pl.*) de cruce	dipped headlights
faros *m. pl.*	headlights
apagar los faros, poner las luces de cruce	to dip one's headlights
luces (*f. pl.*) de población	sidelights
indicador (*m.*) de dirección	direction indicator, indicator
cinturón (*m.*) de seguridad	safety belt, seat belt

V. Accidentes (*m.*) e infracciones, *f.* — Accidents and offences.

perder el dominio del vehículo	to lose control of one's vehicle
patinar, resbalar	to skid
dar una vuelta de campana	to turn over
chocar entrar en colisión	to crash, to collide
chocar con, entrar en colisión con	to hit, to crash into, to run into
no respetar la prioridad	not to give way
adelantamiento (*m.*) por la derecha	overtaking on the inside
conducción (*f.*) en estado de embriaguez	drunken driving
delito (*m.*) de fuga	hit-and-run accident
toma (*f.*) de sangre	blood test
alcohómetro *m.*	breathalyser
índice (*m.*) de alcohol	alcohol level
daños *m. pl.*	damage *sing.*
retirada (*f.*) del premiso de conducción	withdrawal of one's driving licence.

VI. Seguro, *m.* — Insurance.

seguro (*m.*) contra terceros	third-party insurance
seguro (*m.*) de vida	life insurance
seguro (*m.*) a todo riesgo	fully comprehensive insurance
seguro (*m.*) contra accidentes	accident insurance
seguro (*m.*) contra robo	insurance against theft
descuento (*m.*) por no declaración de siniestro	no-claims bonus

Cirilo n. pr. m. Cyril.

cirineo, a adj./s. Cyrenian.

cirio m. Wax candle. || BOT. Cereus. || *Cirio pascual,* paschal candle.

Ciro n. pr. m. Cyrus.

cirrípedo m. ZOOL. Cirriped.

cirro m. Cirrus (nube). || MED. Scirrhus (tumor). || BOT. y ZOOL. Cirrus.

cirrocúmulo m. Cirrocumulus.

cirroestrato m. Cirrostratus.

cirrópodo m. ZOOL. Cirriped.

cirrosis f. MED. Cirrhosis.

cirroso, sa adj. MED. Cirrhotic. || BOT. y ZOOL. Cirrous.

ciruela f. BOT. Plum (fruta). | — *Ciruela amarilla,* mirabelle plum. || *Ciruela claudia,* greengage. || *Ciruela damascena,* damson. || *Ciruela pasa,* prune.

ciruelo m. BOT. Plum tree (árbol).

cirugía f. Surgery. || *Cirugía estética* or *plástica,* plastic surgery.

cirujano m. Surgeon. || *Cirujano dentista,* dental surgeon.

cisalpino, na adj. Cisalpine.

cisca f. BOT. Sedge.

ciscar v. tr. FAM. To dirty, to soil (ensuciar).
— V. pr. FAM. To soil o.s.

cisco m. Slack (carbón muy menudo). || FIG. y FAM. Row, din: *meter* or *armar cisco,* to kick up a row. | Chaos (jaleo). || — FIG. y FAM. *Estar hecho cisco,* to be in a sorry state, to be all in. | *Hacer cisco,* to smash, to smash to pieces. | FIG. *Hacer cisco a uno,* to knock s.o. out, to exhaust s.o. (agotarle).

ciscón m. Clinker, ashes, *pl.*

cisión f. Incision.

cisma m. Schism. || FIG. Disagreement, discord (desacuerdo). | Split (en política).

cismático, ca adj./s. Schismatic, schismatical, dissident.

cisne m. Swan (ave). || ASTR. Swan, the northern constellation, cygnus. || FIG. Swan, bard (poeta, músico). || *Amer.* Powder puff (para polvos).

cisoide f. MAT. Cissoid.

cisoria adj. f. *Arte cisoria,* art of carving.

cisquero m. Pounce bag (para el dibujo).

cista f. Cist.

Cistel o **Cister** n. pr. m. Cistercian Order (orden religiosa).

cisterciense adj./s. Cistercian (de la orden del Cister).

cisterna f. Cistern, tank, reservoir. || Cistern (de retrete). || *Vagón, buque cisterna,* tanker.

cisternilla f. Cistern.

cisticerco m. Cysticercus (larva de la tenia).

cístico, ca adj. Cystic.

cistitis f. MED. Cystitis.

cisto m. BOT. Cistus.

cistotomía f. Cystotomy.

cisura f. Incision (incisión).

cita f. Appointment: *arreglar una cita con el médico,* to make an appointment with the doctor; *el médico me ha dado cita a las seis,* I have an appointment with the doctor at six o'clock. || Date (entre chico y chica): *tengo una cita con Juan,* I've got a date with John. || Meeting (de amantes). || Quotation, quote (nota sacada de una obra). | — *Casa de citas,* house of call. || *Cita espacial,* space link-up. || *Con motivo de la Exposición se han dado cita unos mil científicos,* on the occasion of the Exhibition some thousand scientists have come together. || *Darle cita a un amigo,* to arrange to meet a friend. || *Darse cita,* to arrange to meet [one another] (sentido general), to make a date (chica y chico). || *Tengo cita con un amigo,* I've got to go and see a friend.

citación f. JUR. Writ of summons, citation. || Quotation, quote (de un escritor).

citado, da adj. Aforementioned: *el citado libro,* the aforementioned book.

citador, ra m. y f. Quoter.
citar v. tr. To arrange to meet, to make an appointment with: *citar a uno en un café*, to arrange to meet s.o. in a café; *le cité para* or *a las cinco*, I arranged to meet him at five o'clock. || To quote, to cite (hacer una cita literaria). || JUR. To summon (llamar el juez a una persona). | To call: *citar a juicio*, to call to witness. | To subpoena (a un testigo). | To summon: *citar ante un consejo de guerra*, to summon before a court martial. || TAUR. To attract the attention of [the bull], to call [the bull]. || To mention (mencionar). || — JUR. *Citar ante la justicia*, to sue, to prosecute, to indict, to arraign. || *Para no citar otros*, to mention but a few, to mention only a few.
— V. pr. To arrange to meet [one another] (sentido general), to make a date (chica y chico).
citara f. Brick partition (tabique de ladrillos).
cítara f. MÚS. Zither.
citarista m. y f. Zither player, zitherist.
citerior adj. Hithermost, hither.
citiso m. BOT. Cytisus.
cítola f. Millclapper.
citología f. BIOL. Cytology.
citoplasma m. ANAT. Cytoplasm.
citrato m. QUÍM. Citrate.
cítrico, ca adj. QUÍM. Citric. || *Productos cítricos*, citric produce.
— M. pl. Citrus fruits (agrios): *exportación de cítricos*, export of citrus fruits.
citrón m. (P.us.). Lemon (limón).
citronela f. BOT. Citronella.
ciudad f. Town, city (v. OBSERV.) || — *Ciudad del Cabo*, Cape Town. || *Ciudad de lona*, canvas town. || *Ciudad del Vaticano*, Vatican City. || *Ciudad hermana*, twin town. || *Ciudad hongo*, boom town. || *Ciudad Imperial*, Toledo [in Spain]. || *Ciudad jardín*, garden city. || *Ciudad obrera*, workers' housing estate. || *Ciudad satélite*, satellite town. || *Ciudad universitaria*, university campus. || *Ir a la ciudad*, to go to town *o* into town. || *La Ciudad Eterna*, the Eternal City, Rome. || *Sr. don Juan Ruiz, Ciudad* (en cartas), Mr. Juan Ruiz, local [on an envelope].
— OBSERV. *Ciudad* se traduce por dos palabras en inglés según que el tamaño sea más grande (city) o menos grande (town).
ciudadanía f. Citizenship. || — *Cuidadanía de honor*, freedom of the city. || *Derechos de ciudadanía*, citizen's rights.
ciudadano, na m. y f. Citizen, townsman, townswoman (de una ciudad). || Citizen (de un Estado). || — *Ciudadano de honor*, freeman of the city. || *Los ciudadanos*, [the] townspeople, [the] city dwellers.
— Adj. Civic, city.
ciudadela f. Citadel, fortress.
civeta f. (P.us.). ZOOL. Civet.
civeto m. Civet.
cívico, ca adj. Civic. || FIG. Public-spirited: *un acto cívico*, a public-spirited act.
— M. *Amer.* Policeman. | Tankard (de cerveza).
civil adj. Civil: *guerra, matrimonio civil*, civil war, marriage. || Lay, secular (no eclesiástico). || Civilian, civil (no militar): *población civil*, civilian population. || Civil (sociable). || — *Administración civil*, civil service. || *Casarse por lo civil*, to get married in a registry office *o* in a register office (en Inglaterra), to get married by a civil ceremony, to have a civil marriage *o* wedding (en los demás países). || JUR. *Derecho civil*, civil law. || *Derechos civiles*, civil rights. || *Incorporado a la vida civil*, reinstated in civilian life. || *Ingeniería civil*, civil engineering. || *Muerte civil*, civil death. || *Por lo civil*, in a civil court.
— M. FAM. Civil guard, guardia civil [type of policeman] (guardia civil). || Civilian (paisano).
civilidad f. Civility (cortesía).
civilista m. Person versed in civil law (jurisconsulto).
civilizable adj. Civilizable.
civilización f. Civilization.
civilizado, da adj. Civilized.
— M. y f. Civilized person.
civilizador, ra adj. Civilizing.
— M. y f. Civilizer.
civilizar v. tr. To civilize.
— V. pr. To become civilized.
civilmente adv. Civilly. || *Casarse civilmente*, to get married in a registry office *o* in a register office (en Inglaterra), to get married by a civil ceremony (en los demás países).
civismo m. Civism, good citizenship, community spirit (cualidad de buen ciudadano). || Civility (cualidad de cortés).
cizalla f. o **cizallas** f. pl. Shears, *pl.*, metal clippers, *pl.* (tijeras). || Shearing machine, *sing.* (máquina). || Metal parings, *pl.*, metal clippings, *pl.*, metal cuttings, *pl.* (cortaduras de metal).
cizalladura f. o **cizallamiento** m. Shearing, cutting.
cizallar v. tr. To shear, to cut.
cizaña f. BOT. Bearded darnel. || FIG. Discord, trouble (enemistad): *meter* or *sembrar cizaña*, to sow discord, to cause *o* to make trouble. || *Separar la cizaña del buen grano*, to separate the chaff from the grain.
cizañar o **cizañear** v. intr. To sow discord, to cause *o* to make trouble.
cizañero, ra m. y f. Troublemaker.
clac m. Opera hat, crush hat (sombrero de copa plegable). || Cocked hat (sombrero de tres picos).
— Interj. Crack!, bang!
clachique m. *Amer.* Unfermented pulque.
clamar v. tr. To cry out, to clamour [U.S., to clamor]: *clamar su inocencia, su indignación*, to cry out one's innocence, one's indignation. || To beseech (implorar): *clamar a Dios*, to beseech God. || *Clamar venganza*, to cry out for revenge, to clamour for vengeance.
— V. intr. To cry out, to clamour [U.S., to clamor]: *clamar por la paz*, to cry out for peace; *clamar contra una injusticia*, to cry out against an injustice. || FIG. To cry out: *la tierra clama por agua*, the land is crying out for water. || FIG. *Esto clama al cielo* or *a Dios*, this cries out to heaven.
clámide f. Chlamys (abrigo griego).
clamor m. Shout, cry, scream (grito). || Clamour [U.S., clamor], noise (ruido). || Groan, moan (voz lastimosa). || Cheer (vítores). || Knell, toll (toque de campana fúnebre). || FIG. Outcry, protest (protesta).
clamorear v. tr. To appeal for, to cry out for, to clamour for (con instancia). || To beseech (suplicar). || To complain (quejarse). || To cry out for (clamar).
— V. intr. To toll (las campanas).
clamoreo m. Shouting, clamour [U.S., clamor] (clamor). || FAM. Pestering (ruego).
clamoroso, sa adj. Resounding: *éxito clamoroso*, resounding success. || Loud, clamorous (ruidoso). || Complaining (quejoso).
clan m. Clan.
clandestinidad f. Secrecy. || *En la clandestinidad*, in secret, in secrecy.
clandestino, na adj. Secret, clandestine: *reunión clandestina*, secret meeting. || Clandestine, underground (actividades políticas). || Secret (casamiento, policía).
claque f. FIG. y FAM. Claque, paid applauders, *pl.*
claqueta f. Clapper boards, *pl.* (de cine). || — Pl. Clapper, *sing.* (tablillas).
clara f. White of the egg (del huevo). || Clearness (claridad). || Bright interval (del tiempo). || Threadbare *o* thin *o* bald patch (en una tela). || Bald patch (en el cráneo). || *Amer.* Nun of the order of Saint Clare (monja). || *Levantarse con las claras del día*, to get up with the larks, to get up at daybreak.
Clara n. pr. f. Clara, Clare.
claraboya f. Skylight (tragaluz). || Hinged skylight (en un tejado). || Clerestory (en una iglesia).
clarear v. tr. To light up, to illuminate (dar claridad). || To brighten, to make lighter (aclarar): *clarear un color*, to brighten a colour, to make a colour lighter. || *Amer.* To go through (una bala).
— V. intr. To dawn, to break (el día). || To clear up, to brighten up: *el cielo va clareando*, the sky is clearing up. || *Al clarear el día*, at dawn, at daybreak.
— V. pr. To wear thin *o* threadbare: *el codo de la chaqueta se clarea*, the elbow of the jacket is wearing thin. || To be transparent, to let the light through (ser transparente). || FIG. y FAM. To give o.s. away: *este chico se ha clareado sin querer*, that boy has give himself away unintentionally. || — *Sus intenciones se clarean*, his intentions are clear *o* evident, his intentions are plain to see. || *Tu vestido es tan fino que se clarea*, your dress is so thin you can see through it.
clarecer* v. intr. To dawn.
clareo m. Clearing (de un bosque).
clarete adj./s. m. Claret (vino).
claridad f. Light, brightness: *la claridad del día*, the light of day. || Clearness, clarity, lucidity (lucidez). || Fame (fama). || FIG. Home truth (verdad desagradable): *decir claridades a uno*, to tell s.o. a few home truths. || — *Claridad de vista*, clear-sightedness, perspicacity. || *Con claridad*, clearly: *me lo explicó con mucha claridad*, he explained it to me very clearly. || FIG. *Cuanto menos bulto, más claridad*, good riddance, good riddance to bad rubbish. || *De una claridad meridiana*, v. MERIDIANO. || *Todavía hay claridad*, it is still light.
clarificación f. Clarification, clearing (de un líquido). || Illumination, lighting (acción de iluminar). || FIG. Explanation, clarification (explicación).
clarificador m. Clarifier (para el vino).
clarificadora f. Clarifier (de azúcar).
clarificar v. tr. To clarify, to clear: *clarificar vino*, to clarify wine. || To light up, to illuminate (iluminar). || FIG. To clarify, to explain.
clarín m. MÚS. Bugle (instrumento): *toque de clarín*, bugle call. || Bugler (músico). || Clarion stop, clarion (del órgano). || Kind of batiste *o* cambric (tela). || FIG. Clarion. || *Amer.* ZOOL. *Clarín de la selva*, solitaire (Myadestes unicolor), mockingbird (sinsonte).
clarinazo m. Bugle call (toque). || FIG. Warning signal: *el resultado de las elecciones fue un clarinazo*, the result of the elections was a warning signal.
clarinete m. MÚS. Clarinet (instrumento). || Clarinettist [U.S., clarinetist] (instrumentista).
clarinetista m. MÚS. Clarinettist [U.S., clarinetist].
clarión m. Chalk.

clarisa f. Nun of the order of St. Clare, Poor Clare, Clare (monja).
clarividencia f. Clairvoyance. || FIG. Farsightedness.
clarividente adj. Clairvoyant. || FIG. Farsighted.
claro, ra adj. Bright, well-lit (con mucha luz): *una habitación clara*, a bright room. || Bright (ojos, día, luz, etc.). || Clear: *agua, voz clara*, clear water, voice; *letra clara*, clear handwriting. || Clear (prueba, explicación, lenguaje): *que quede esto bien claro*, let this be quite clear. || Thin, sparse (poco abundante): *pelo claro*, thin hair. || Illustrious, famous (ilustre): *claros varones de Castilla*, famous men of Castile. || Light: *azul claro*, light blue; *una tela azul claro*, a light blue cloth. || Threadbare (tela). || Light (cerveza). || Weak (café, chocolate, té, etc.). || Thin (puré, líquido, etc.). || Straight (que obra sin disimulo). || TAUR. Predictable (toro). || — *Claro que*, of course. || *Claro que no*, of course not, certainly not. || *Claro que sí*, of course, certainly. || *¿Está claro?*, is that clear? || *Está claro que...*, it is plain that..., evidently..., of course... || FIG. *¡Las cosas claras y el chocolate espeso!*, let's get things clear. || *Más claro que el agua*, as clear as crystal. || *Más claro que el Sol*, as clear as daylight. || *Tan claro como la luz del día*, as clear as daylight, as plain as a pikestaff.
— M. Opening, crack (agujero). || Space, gap (entre dos palabras escritas, en una multitud). || Light (porción luminosa en una pintura o fotografía). || Bald patch (en el pelo). || Opening (entre las nubes). || Clearing (en un bosque, etc.). || ARQ. Space (entre columnas). || Pause (en un discurso, en la caída de la nieve). || Bright interval, break in the rain (en la lluvia). || Opening (entre las nubes). || — *Claro de luna*, moonlight. || *Llenar un claro*, to fill in *o* to stop a gap.
— Adv. Clearly: *hablar claro*, to speak clearly. || — *A las claras*, openly. || *De claro en claro*, from dusk till dawn. || *Pasar en claro una noche*, to spend a sleepless night. || *Poner en claro*, to clear up, to clarify, to get *o* to make clear. || *Por lo claro*, clearly. || *Sacar en claro*, v. SACAR. || *Ver poco claro*, not to be able to see very clearly *o* very well.
— Interj. Of course!, obviously! || — *¡Claro está!*, of course. || *¡Pues claro!*, of course!
claroscuro m. Light and shade, chiaroscuro.
clarucho, cha adj. Very thin (tela). || Watery, thin (con mucha agua): *sopa clarucha*, watery soup. || Weak (café, té, etc.).
clascal m. *Amer.* Maize omelette.
clase f. Class: *la clase media*, the middle class. || Class (escuela): *está en la clase de los párvulos*, he is in the infant's class. || Classroom (aula). || Lecture room (en la universidad). || Class: *clase nocturna*, evening class. || Lesson: *dar clases particulares*, to give private lessons; *clase de conducir*, driving lesson. || Class (en un tren, barco, avión): *primera clase*, first class. || Sort, kind: *¿qué clase de cosas me traes ahí?*, what sort of things are you bringing me?; *cosas de toda clase*, all sorts of things; *de una misma clase*, of the same kind. || Quality, class (calidad): *lana de buena clase*, good quality wool. || Class: *esta persona tiene mucha clase*, this person has a lot of class. || BOT. y ZOOL. Class. || — Pl. MIL. N.C.O.'s, non-commissioned officers. || — *Clase alta, baja, dirigente, obrera* or *trabajadora*, upper, lower, governing, working class. || *Clases pasivas*, pensioners. || *Dar clase*, to teach (el profesor), to lecture (en la universidad). || *Dar clase a alguien*, to teach s.o., to give a lesson *o* lessons to s.o. (en general), to lecture s.o., to give lectures to s.o. (en la universidad). || *Dar clase con alguien*, to take lessons from s.o. (solo), to attend s.o.'s lessons (en general), to attend s.o.'s lectures (en la universidad). || *Es un modelo en su clase*, he is a perfect example of his class. || *Faltar a clase*, to miss school. || FAM. *Fumarse una clase*, to skip a class (escuela), to skip a lecture (universidad). || *Gente de toda clase*, all sorts of people. || *La clase agraria*, the agricultural community. || *La lucha de clases*, the class struggle, class warfare. || *Sin ninguna clase de dudas*, without a shadow of doubt, without any doubt whatsoever. || *Te deseo toda clase de felicidades*, I wish you every kind of happiness.
clasicismo m. Classicism..
clasicista adj. Classicistic.
— M. y f. Classicist.
clásico, ca adj. Classical, classic: *obras, lenguas clásicas*, classical works, languages. || FIG. Classic, typical (típico). || *El remedio clásico*, the time-honoured remedy.
— M. Classic (escritor, obra literaria).
clasificable adj. Classifiable.
clasificación f. Classification, classing (acción de asignar a una clase). || Sorting (del correo, de carbones, etc.). || Order (alfabética, etc.). || DEP. League, table. || *Clasificación nacional del disco*, top twenty, hit parade.
clasificado, da adj. Classified.
clasificador, ra m. y f. Classifier. || — M. Filing cabinet (mueble). || MIN. Classifier.
clasificar v. tr. To class, to classify (asignar a una clase). || To sort (seleccionar). || To grade, to class (según la calidad).
— V. pr. To come: *él se clasificó después de mi hermano*, he came after my brother. || To qualify: *el equipo se clasificó para la final*, the team qualified for the final.
clástico, ca adj. GEOL. Clastic.
claudia adj. f. *Ciruela* or *reina claudia*, greengage.
Claudia n. pr. f. Claudia, Claudette.
claudicación f. Shirking [of duty, responsibility, etc.] (incumplimiento de los deberes). || Submission (acción de ceder). || Giving up (acción de abandonar un esfuerzo). || Limp, lameness (cojera).
claudicante adj. Who shirks one's duty (que deja de cumplir deberes). || Yielding, who gives in (que cede). || Who gives up easily (que abandona un esfuerzo). || Limping, lame (que cojea). || Failing, faltering: *sus fuerzas claudicantes*, his failing strength.
claudicar v. intr. (P.us.). To limp (cojear). || FIG. To shirk [one's duty, responsibility, etc.] (dejar de cumplir deberes). | To abandon one's principles (no seguir sus principios). | To give in, to yield (ceder). | To give up (abandonar un esfuerzo). || To falter, to fail (disminuir).
Claudio n. pr. m. Claud, Claude.
claustral adj. Claustral, cloistral, monastic.
claustrar v. tr. To enclose, to shut in.
claustro m. Cloister (de un convento). || FIG. Monastic life, cloister. | Staff (conjunto de profesores en la universidad), senate (junta de profesores). || ANAT. *Claustro materno*, womb.
claustrofobia f. Claustrophobia.
cláusula f. Clause (de un contrato). || GRAM. Clause. || — *Cláusula absoluta*, ablative absolute (en latín), absolute construction (en inglés). || *Cláusula adicional*, additional clause. || *Cláusula de escape*, escape clause. || *Cláusula del país más favorecido*, most-favoured-nation clause.
clausura f. Enclosure (religiosa). || Closure (de debates). || Closing, closure (cierre). || — *Monja de clausura*, enclosed nun. || *Sesión de clausura*, closing session.
clausurar v. tr. To conclude, to close, to bring to a close (una sesión, un debate). || To adjourn (el parlamento). || To shut, to close (cerrar).
clava f. Club (porra).
clavadizo, za adj. Nail-studded, studded.
clavado, da adj. Nail-studded, studded (guarnecido con clavos). || Pinned, fixed: *quedó clavado en la pared*, it remained fixed to the wall. || — FIG. *Clavado en la cama*, tied to one's bed, bedridden, confined to one's bed. | *Con la mirada clavada en el cielo*, staring up at the sky. | *Dejar clavado a uno*, to leave s.o. dumbfounded. | *Es clavado el retrato de su padre* or *es su padre clavado*, he is the spitting image of his father. | *Es la traducción clavada*, it's the exact translation. | *Este traje le está clavado*, this suit fits him like a glove *o* fits him perfectly. | *Llegó a las siete clavadas*, he arrived dead on *o* bang on seven o'clock, he arrived at seven o'clock on the dot.
— M. Nailing.
clavadura f. Prick (en el casco de un caballo).
clavar v. tr. To nail (poner con clavos): *clavar algo a* or *en la pared*, to nail sth. to the wall. || To knock in, to bang in (un clavo). || To nail together (dos cosas). || To drive, to stick (introducir una cosa con punta): *clavar un palo en el suelo*, to drive a stake into the ground. || To spike (un cañón). || To pierce, to prick (el casco del caballo). || FIG. To fix: *clavar la atención en*, to fix one's attention on. || To set (piedras preciosas). || FIG. y FAM. To cheat (engañar). | To get right (acertar exactamente). || — FIG. *Clavar los ojos en*, to stare at, to rivet one's eyes on. || FIG. y FAM. *En ese restaurante te clavan*, they sting *o* they fleece you in that restaurant.
— V. pr. To get (pincharse): *me clavé una astilla en el pie*, I got a splinter in my foot. || — *Clavarse un pincho*, to prick o.s. on a thorn. || *Se clavó un puñal en el corazón*, he plunged *o* thrust a dagger into his heart.
clave f. Key, clew, clue (explicación). || Key, cipher, code (de un texto cifrado). || ARQ. Keystone: *clave de arco*, keystone of an arch. || MÚS. Clef: *clave de sol*, treble clef; *clave de fa*, bass clef; *clave de do*, tenor *o* alto clef. || FIG. Key: *la clave de su actitud*, the key to his attitude. || — Pl. Claves (instrumento de música). || — *Escribir en clave*, to write in code. || *La clave del enigma*, the key *o* the clue to the riddle.
— M. MÚS. Harpsichord.
— Adj. Key: *una posición clave*, a key position; *la palabra clave*, the key word.
clavecín m. MÚS. Clavecin, harpsichord.
clavel m. Carnation (flor).
clavelito m. Pink (flor).
clavelón m. African marigold.
clavellina f. Carnation (clavel). || *Clavellina de pluma*, cottage pink.
clavero m. Clove tree, clove (árbol). || Keeper of the keys (persona).
clavete m. Small nail, tack (clavo pequeño). || MÚS. Plectrum. || Stud (adorno).
claveteado m. Studding.
clavetear v. tr. To stud [with nails].
clavicémbalo m. MÚS. Clavicymbal, harpsichord (instrumento).
clavicordio m. MÚS. Clavichord (instrumento).
clavícula f. ANAT. Clavicle (voz culta), collar bone (palabra usual).

el compás, to keep time (música), to keep a sense of proportion (ser comedido). || *Llevar el compás*, V. LLEVAR. || *Perder el compás*, to lose the beat. || *Salió a los compases de un himno bien conocido*, he went out to the strains of a well-known hymn.
compasado, da adj. Measured, moderate (mesurado).
compasar v. tr. To measure with compasses. || MÚS. To divide into bars.
compasillo m. MÚS. Common *o* four-four time.
compasión f. Compassion, pity. || — *Llamar* or *mover a uno a compasión*, to move s.o. to pity. || *¡Por compasión!*, for pity's sake! || *Sin compasión*, merciless (adj.), mercilessly (adv.). || *Tener compasión de*, to take pity on, to feel sorry for.
compasivamente adv. Compassionately, sympathetically.
compasivo, va adj. Compassionate, sympathetic, understanding: *compasivo con los demás*, understanding towards other people. || Merciful (clemente).
compatibilidad f. Compatibility.
compatible adj. Compatible.
compatiblemente adv. Compatibly.
compatriota m. y f. Compatriot, fellow countryman (hombre), fellow countrywoman (mujer).
compeler v. tr. To force, to compel: *le compelieron a hablar*, they forced him to speak.
compendiadamente adv. V. COMPENDIOSAMENTE.
compendiar v. tr. To summarize, to abridge.
compendio m. Résumé, précis, summary, synopsis, outline: *compendio de gramática francesa*, summary of French grammar. || Compendium (breve tratado). || — *Compendio de historia*, short history. || *Compendio de química*, synopsis of chemistry. || *En compendio*, in brief, in short.
compendiosamente adv. Summarily, concisely, in brief.
compendioso, sa adj. Concise, compendious.
compenetración f. Compenetration, interpenetration. || FIG. [Mutual] understanding (entre personas).
compenetrarse v. pr. QUÍM. To compenetrate, to interpenetrate. || FIG. To share each other's feelings, to understand each other (dos personas). || *Compenetrarse con su papel*, to identify o.s. with one's role (actor).
compensación f. Compensation. || Compensation, damages, *pl.* (pago). || — COM. *Cámara de compensación*, clearing house. | *Compensación bancaria*, clearing. || *En compensación*, in payment, in compensation: *reciben cinco libras en compensación a su asistencia*, they receive five pounds in payment for their attendance; in return, in exchange: *tú me enseñas español y en compensación yo te enseñaré inglés*, you teach me Spanish and in return I'll teach you English.
compensador, ra adj. Compensating: *péndulo compensador*, compensating pendulum.
— M. Compensator.
compensar v. tr. To compensate, to make up for: *compensar las pérdidas con las ganancias*, to compensate *o* to make up for the losses with the gains. || To make amends for, to make up for (un error). || To indemnify, to compensate: *compensar a uno de algo*, to compensate s.o. for sth. || TECN. To balance, to compensate. || To be worthwhile: *trabajo que compensa*, work which is worthwhile. — *Me compensó con cien francos por el tiempo perdido*, he gave me a hundred francs compensation for lost time. || *No me compensa hacer esto*, it's not worth my while doing it. || *Resultados que compensan*, worthwhile results.
compensativo, va o **compensatorio, ria** adj. Compensatory, in compensation.
competencia f. Scope field, province (incumbencia): *esto no es de mi competencia* or *no cae dentro de mi competencia*, this is outside my scope, this is not in my field, this is not my province. || Competence, ability (capacidad). || Competition (rivalidad): *la competencia frena la subida de los precios*, competition checks rising prices; *competencia desleal*, unfair competition. || JUR. Competence. || — *En competencia con*, in competition with. || *Hacer la competencia a*, to compete with *o* against.
competente adj. Competent: *tribunal competente*, competent court; *persona muy competente*, very competent person. || Appropriate: *el departamento competente*, the appropriate department.
competer v. intr. To be in the field of, to come under the jurisdiction of, to be the business of: *eso compete al ayuntamiento*, that comes under the town council's jurisdiction, that is in the town council's field. || To be up to: *a él no le compete castigar a los empleados*, it is not up to him to punish the employees. || To concern, to have to do with: *no me compete*, it has nothing to do with me, it doesn't concern me.
competición f. Competition (deportes, comercio).
competido, da adj. Hard-fought, tough (partido, campeonato, etc.).
competidor, ra adj. Competing (que compete). || Rival (oponente). || Competitive: *espíritu competidor*, competitive spirit.
— M. y f. Competitor (en el comercio, los deportes). || Contestant (participante). || Candidate (en los exámenes). || Rival (rival).
competir* v. intr. To compete: *muchas personas compiten para esta colocación*, many people are competing for this job. || To compete, to contend, to vie: *competir para el título*, to vie for the title. || To compete: *este almacén compite con aquél*, this shop competes with that one.
competitivo, va adj. Competitive.
compilación f. Compiling (acción de compilar). || Compilation, collection (obra).
compilador, ra m. y f. Compiler.
compilar v. tr. To compile.
compinche m. y f. FAM. Pal, chum (amigote). | Accomplice (cómplice).
complacencia f. Pleasure, satisfaction: *tener complacencia en ayudar a los demás*, to find pleasure in helping others. || Indulgence (indulgencia). || *Tener excesivas complacencias hacia alguien*, to be over-indulgent towards s.o.
complacer* v. tr. To please, to be pleasant to: *los cortesanos procuran complacer al rey*, the courtiers try to please the king. || To gratify (un deseo, etc.). || To oblige, to please: *le gusta complacer a sus amigos*, he likes to oblige his friends. || — *¿En qué puedo complacerle?*, can I help you?, what can I do for you? || *Me complace su éxito*, I am happy about his success. || *Nos complace que haya usted venido*, we are pleased *o* glad that you have come.
— V. pr. To take pleasure, to delight: *complacerse en su desdicha*, to take pleasure in one's misfortune; *complacerse en criticar*, to delight in criticizing. || To have [the] pleasure, to be pleased: *me complazco en saludar al señor X*, I have the pleasure to greet Mr. X., I have pleasure in greeting Mr. X.
complacido, da adj. Satisfied, content, happy, pleased: *complacido con su suerte*, satisfied with one's lot.
complaciente adj. Obliging, accommodating, helpful (que ayuda). || Complaisant (marido).
complejidad f. Complexity.
complejo, ja adj. Complex, complicated, involved. || GRAM. Complex. || MAT. Compound (número).
— M. Complex: *complejo industrial*, industrial complex; *complejo de inferioridad*, inferiority complex; *complejo de Edipo*, Oedipus complex.
complementar v. tr. To complement, to complete.
— V. pr. To be complementary [to each other], to complement each other. || *Caracteres que se complementan*, complementary characters.
complementario, ria adj. Complementary: *ángulos complementarios*, complementary angles.
complemento m. Complement. || GRAM. Object, complement: *el complemento del verbo*, the object of the verb; *complemento directo, indirecto*, direct, indirect object. || MAT. Complement. || — MIL. *Oficial de complemento*, reserve officer. || *Sería el complemento de su felicidad*, it would make his happiness complete.
completar v. tr. To complete: *completar una suma*, to complete an amount.
completas f. pl. REL. Compline, *sing.*
completivo, va adj. GRAM. Object: *oración completiva*, object clause.
completo, ta adj. Full: *el autobús está completo*, the bus is full. || Complete: *un estudio completo*, a complete study. || Completed, finished (acabado). || — *Pensión completa*, full board. || *Por completo*, completely. || *Registrar una casa por completo*, to search a house from top to bottom. || *Terminar algo por completo*, to finish sth. off, to completely finish sth.
complexidad f. V. COMPLEJIDAD.
complexión f. Constitution, disposition, nature.
complexo, xa adj. V. COMPLEJO.
complicación f. Complication.
complicado, da adj. Complicated, complex, intricate (intrincado): *sistema complicado*, complicated system. || Complicated (carácter). || Implicated, involved: *persona complicada en una conspiración*, person involved in a conspiracy. | MED. Compound (fractura). || Elaborate (decorado, etc.).
complicar v. tr. To complicate, to make complicated: *complicar una cosa sencilla*, to make a simple thing complicated; *esto vino a complicar las cosas*, this just complicated matters. || *Complicar en*, to involve in: *complicado en un robo*, involved in a theft.
— V. pr. To get complicated (volverse complicado). || To make difficult *o* to complicate for o.s., to make complicated for o.s. (hacer más difícil): *complicarse la vida*, to make life difficult for o.s. || To get involved *o* mixed up: *complicarse en un negocio ilegal*, to get involved in an illegal business. || *¡Esto se complica!*, it's getting serious!
cómplice m. y f. Accomplice. || *Cómplice de un crimen*, accomplice in a crime, party to a crime.
complicidad f. Complicity: *está demostrada su complicidad en el robo*, his complicity in the theft has been proved.
complot m. FAM. Plot, conspiracy.
complotar v. intr. To plot, to conspire.
complutense adj. Of *o* from Alcalá de Henares. || *Biblia Políglota Complutense*, Bible written in Hebrew, Chaldean, Greek and Latin and published in Alcalá de Henares in the 16th century.
— M. y f. Inhabitant *o* native of Alcalá de Henares.
componedor, ra m. y f. *Amer.* Bonesetter (algebrista). || IMPR. Compositor (obrero). || JUR. *Amigable*

componedor, arbitrator. || — M. IMPR. Setting stick, composing stick.
componenda f. Compromise, arrangement, settlement, agreement (expediente de conciliación). || FAM. Trick (combinación). || *Componendas electorales*, electoral scheming.
componente adj. Component.
— M. Component, part, constituent (de un todo). || Ingredient (de un plato de cocina, bebida). || Member (miembro). || *Viento de componente sur*, south *o* southerly wind.
componer* v. tr. To form, to make up, to compose (formar): *componer un ramillete con diversas flores*, to make up a bouquet with different flowers; *los once jugadores componen el equipo*, the eleven players make up the team. || To repair, to mend (arreglar lo que está roto). || To compose (música, versos). || To write (novelas, etc.). || To settle (resolver): *componer un asunto*, to settle a matter. || To prepare, to decorate, to arrange: *están componiendo la casa para la fiesta*, they are preparing the house for the celebration. || To settle (desacuerdo). || To reconcile: *componer a dos enemigos*, to reconcile two enemies. || To adjust (ajedrez). || FAM. To settle: *una buena taza de té te compondrá el estómago*, a nice cup of tea will settle your stomach. || IMPR. To set. || MED. To set (hueso). || *Amer*. To castrate (castrar).
— V. pr. To be made up, to consist, to be composed: *el equipo se compone de once jugadores*, the team is made up of eleven players. || To get ready, to smarten o.s. up (una mujer). || To agree, to come to an agreement (ponerse de acuerdo). || — FAM. *Componérselas*, to manage: *compóntelas como puedas*, manage as best you can. | *No sabía cómo componérselas*, he didn't know what to do, he didn't know how to get out of it.
comportamiento m. Behaviour [U.S., behavior], conduct.
comportar v. tr. To involve, to entail (contener). || To bear, to put up with (aguantar).
— V. pr. To behave [o.s.] (conducirse): *compórtate como es debido*, behave properly. || To behave, to act: *se comporta como un niño mimado*, he acts like a spoilt child. || *Comportarse mal*, to misbehave, to behave badly.
composición f. Composition: *la composición del agua*, the composition of water. || Composition (obra). || Composition (ejercicio de redacción). || Mixture (medicamento). || Agreement (acuerdo). || Arrangement, settlement (arreglo). || IMPR. Setting, composition. || GRAM. y MÚS. Composition. || — JUR. *Composición amigable*, arbitration. || *Hacer composición de lugar*, to size up the situation (considerar una situación), to decide on one's plan of action (determinar lo que uno va a hacer).
compositivo, va adj. Which can be used to form compound words.
compositor, ra m. y f. MÚS. Composer.
— M. *Amer*. Horse trainer.
compostelano, na adj. Of *o* from Santiago de Compostela.
— M. y f. Inhabitant *o* native of Santiago de Compostela.
compostura f. Composition, structure (disposición de las partes de una cosa). || Repair, repairing, mending (arreglo): *la compostura de un reloj*, the repair of a watch. || Bearing, demeanour, comportment (manera de comportarse). || Moderation, restraint (moderación). || Composure (dignidad). || Arrangement, agreement (convenio): *hacer una compostura con sus acreedores*, to come to an arrangement with *o* to make an agreement with one's creditors. || CULIN. Seasoning (condimento). || *¡Juan, las composturas!*, John, behave yourself!
compota f. Compote: *una compota de manzanas*, an apple compote. || FAM. *Un ojo en compota*, a black eye.
compotera f. Compote dish.
compound m. TECN. Compound.
compra f. Buy, purchase: *una compra ventajosa*, an advantageous buy. || — *Compra al contado*, cash purchase. || *Compra a plazos*, hire-purchase, buying on credit [U.S., installment plan]. || *Hacer compras*, to shop, to go shopping. || *Hacer la compra, ir a la compra*, to do the shopping, to go shopping. || *Ir de compras*, to go shopping. || *Jefe de compras*, chief buyer. || *Precio de compra*, purchase price.
comprable o **compradero, ra** adj. Buyable, purchasable.
comprador, ra m. y f. Buyer, purchaser. || Shopper, customer (en una tienda).
comprar v. tr. To buy, to purchase: *lo volví a comprar*, I bought it back. || FIG. To bribe, to buy (sobornar): *comprar a uno*, to bribe s.o. || — *Comprar al contado*, to pay cash. || *Comprar algo al contado*, to pay cash for sth., to buy sth. for cash, to purchase sth. for cash. || *Comprar al por mayor, al por menor*, to buy wholesale, retail. || *Comprar con pérdida, en firme*, to buy at a loss, firm. || *Comprar fiado*, to buy on credit.
compraventa f. Buying and selling. || *Contrato de compraventa*, contract of sale and purchase.
comprender v. tr. To understand (entender): *no comprendo el alemán*, I don't understand German. || To comprise, to include (componerse de): *esta obra comprende cuatro tomos*, this work comprises four volumes. || To include (incluir): *servicio no comprendido*, service not included. || To realize (darse cuenta). || To see (ver). || — *Compréndame*, try to understand me. || *Comprender mal*, to misunderstand: *has comprendido mal lo que he dicho*, you have misunderstood what I said. || *¿Comprendes?*, you see? || *Comprendida la suma de*, including the sum of. || *Hacerse comprender*, to make o.s. understood. || *Todo comprendido*, all-in, inclusive: *viaje todo comprendido*, all-in trip. || *¡Ya comprendo!*, I see!, I get it!
— V. pr. To understand one another. || *Se comprende*, it is understandable.
comprensibilidad f. Comprehensibility.
comprensible adj. Comprehensible, understandable.
comprensión f. Comprehension, understanding (entendimiento). || Understanding (tolerancia). || Intension (en lógica). || *Ser tardo de comprensión*, to be slow in understanding *o* in picking things up.
comprensivo, va adj. Understanding: *hombre comprensivo*, understanding man.
compresa f. MED. Compress (debajo de un vendaje). | Sanitary towel (de mujer).
compresibilidad f. Compressibility.
compresible adj. Compressible.
compresión f. Compression. || GRAM. Synaeresis [U.S., syneresis].
compresivo, va adj. Compressive.
compreso, sa adj. Compressed.

— OBSERV. The adjective *compreso* is the irregular past participle of *comprimir*.

compresor m. Compressor. || *Cilindro compresor*, steamroller.
comprimible adj. Compressible.
comprimido, da adj. Compressed. || *Escopeta de aire comprimido*, air rifle.
— M. MED. Tablet (tableta).
comprimir v. tr. To compress. || FIG. To keep back (lágrimas, una sonrisa). | To stifle (la risa). | To cram together, to pack: *viven comprimidos en una sola habitación*, they live crammed together in a single room.
— V. pr. To be compressed. || To restrict o.s. (en los gastos). || To restrain o.s. (refrenarse). || *Me comprimí la risa*, I stifled a laugh, I managed not to laugh.
comprobable adj. Provable, verifiable (que se puede verificar).
comprobación f. Verification, check, checking, proof (acción de comprobar). || Proof (prueba). || *De fácil comprobación*, easy to prove *o* to ascertain.
comprobante adj. In proof.
— M. Proof (justificación). || JUR. Document in proof. || Guarantee, warrant, voucher (lo que garantiza). || Receipt (recibo). || *Comprobante de compra* or *de caja*, receipt.
comprobar* v. tr. To check (averiguar): *hay que comprobar la marca antes de comprar*, you must check the make before buying. || To see, to observe (observar): *pudiste comprobar tú mismo que había dicho la verdad*, you could see for yourself that he had told the truth. || To prove (demostrar). || To confirm (confirmar).
comprobatorio, ria adj. In proof.
comprometedor, ra adj. Compromising: *situación comprometedora*, compromising situation.
comprometer v. tr. To endanger, to jeopardize, to put in jeopardy: *comprometer sus intereses*, to jeopardize one's interests. || To compromise (a una persona). || To commit: *esto no te compromete a nada*, this does not commit you to anything. || To implicate, to mix up, to involve: *comprometer a uno en un robo*, to involve s.o. in a theft. || To impair (la salud).
— V. pr. To compromise o.s. || To commit o.s.: *comprometerse a defender una causa*, to commit o.s. to the defence of a cause. || To get involved (meterse). || *Amer*. To get engaged. || — *Comprometerse a hacer algo*, to engage to do sth., to undertake to do sth. || *Se compromete a todo*, he will agree to anything.
comprometido, da adj. Involved, implicated, mixed up (en un mal negocio). || Embarrassing, compromising (situación). || Committed (escritor). || — *Estar comprometido para hacer algo*, to be obliged to do sth., to have an obligation to do sth. || *Política no comprometida*, non-committal policy.
comprometimiento m. Implication, involvement (en un mal negocio).
compromisario m. Representative, delegate.
compromiso m. Obligation, commitment: *hacer honor a sus compromisos* or *cumplir sus compromisos*, to meet one's obligations. || Commitment: *hoy tengo muchos compromisos*, I have many commitments today. || Engagement, date (cita). || Agreement (acuerdo). || Compromising *o* difficult situation: *poner en un compromiso*, to put in a difficult situation. || JUR. Arbitration, compromise. || — *Compromiso matrimonial*, engagement. || *Compromiso verbal*, verbal agreement. || *Libre de compromiso*, without obligation. || *Política sin compromisos*, non-committal policy. || *Poner en el compromiso de tener que hacer algo*, to put in the position of having to do sth. || *Por compromiso*, out of a sense of duty. || *¡Qué compromiso!*, what a nuisance! || *Sin compromiso por su parte*, without obligation, without committing

himself. || *Soltero y sin compromiso*, single and fancy-free.
comprovinciano, na m. y f. Person from the same province as another.
compuerta f. Sluice, floodgate (de presa o esclusa). || *Compuerta de esclusa*, sluice gate, lock gate.
compuesto, ta adj. Compound (cuerpo químico, tiempo, nombre, etc.). || Mended, repaired (arreglado). || Dressed up, smart, elegant (muy bien vestido). || BOT. Composite. || ARQ. Composite: *orden compuesto*, composite order.
— M. QUÍM. Compound. || — F. pl. BOT. Compositae.
compulsa f. JUR. Certified true copy (de un documento). || Collation, comparison (cotejo).
compulsación f. Collation, comparison (cotejo).
compulsar v. tr. JUR. To compare, to collate. || To make a certified true copy of (sacar una compulsa). || To oblige, to compel (compeler).
compulsión f. Constraint, compulsion (apremio).
compulsivo, na adj. Compulsive, compelling (que compele). || Compulsory (obligatorio).
compunción f. Compunction, remorse (remordimiento). || Sorrow, sadness (tristeza).
compungido, da adj. Sad, sorrowful (dolorido): *voz compungida*, sad voice. || Remorseful, regretful.
compungir v. tr. To make remorseful.
— V. pr. To be sad, to feel remorseful, to be grieved (entristecerse): *compungirse por*, to be grieved about.
computable adj. Computable.
computación f. V. CÓMPUTO.
computador m. Computer.
computadora f. Computer: *computadora electrónica*, electronic computer.
computar v. tr. To compute, to calculate.
cómputo m. Computation, calculation (cálculo). || REL. Computation.
comulgante adj./s. Communicant.
comulgar v. tr. To administer Holy Communion to.
— V. intr. To receive Holy Communion. || FIG. To share. || *Comulgar por Pascua Florida*, to take the Sacrament at Easter, to do one's Easter duty.
comulgatorio m. Communion rail.
común adj. Common (corriente): *una flor muy común*, a very common flower; *sentido común*, common sense. || Common, commonplace: *expresión común*, common expression. || Common, widespread (opinión, costumbre). || Common, vulgar (vulgar): *modales comunes*, common manners. || Communal, shared, common: *cuarto de baño común*, communal bathroom. || Mutual: *amigos comunes*, mutual friends. || GRAM. Common: *nombre común*, common noun. || MAT. Common: *denominador común*, common denominator. || — *Bien común*, public interest, common interest *o* good. || *De común acuerdo* or *por acuerdo común*, by common consent *o* agreement. || *En común*, in common. || *Fuera de lo común*, out of the ordinary. || *Gastos comunes*, shared expenses. || *Hacer algo en común*, to do sth. jointly *o* together. || *La voz común*, rumour, hearsay. || *Lugar común*, cliché, commonplace, hackneyed expression. || *Mercado Común*, Common Market. || *Poco común*, unusual. || *Por lo común*, generally, normally. || *Tener en común*, to have in common (semejante), to have together, to share (compartir).
— M. REL. *Común de mártires*, common of martyrs. || *El común*, the community, the public. || *El común de la gente* or *de los mortales*, most people, the majority of people. || *La Cámara de los Comunes*, the House of Commons. || *Los Comunes*, the Commons.
comuna f. *Amer.* Commune [smallest territorial division].
comunal adj. Municipal, community, communal.
comunalista m. y f. Communalist.
comunalmente adv. Generally, usually (generalmente). || Communally. || Together (juntos).
comunero, ra adj. HIST. Of the "comuneros" (relativo a las antiguas comunidades de Castilla, etc.).
— M. Joint owner (copropietario). || HIST. "Comunero" [supporter of the "comunidades" in Castile, of independence in Colombia and Paraguay].
comunicabilidad f. Communicability.
comunicable adj. Communicable. || Sociable, communicative (persona)
comunicación f. Communication (acción de comunicar). || Communication, message (aviso, informe). || Communiqué (oficial). || Transmission (de un movimiento). || Connection (por teléfono). || — Pl. Communications: *las comunicaciones entre las dos ciudades son muy malas*, communications between the two towns are very poor. || — *Estar, ponerse en comunicación con*, to be, to get in touch with, to be, to get in contact with (tener relaciones), to be, to get through to (por teléfono). || *Palacio de Comunicaciones (en Madrid)*, [equivalent of] General Post Office (en Londres). || *Poner en comunicación con*, to connect with, to link with (carretera), to put in touch with (poner en relación), to connect with, to put through to (por teléfono). || *Puerta de comunicación*, communicating door. || *Vía de comunicación*, thoroughfare.
comunicado, da adj. Served: *barrio bien comunicado*, well-served district.
— M. Communiqué, communication (aviso). || *Comunicado a la prensa*, press release, official statement to the press.
comunicador, ra adj. Transmitting (que transmite). || Communicating (puerta, etc.).
comunicante adj. Communicating: *vasos comunicantes*, communicating vessels.
— M. y. f. Communicant.
comunicar v. tr. To communicate, to convey: *nos comunicó a todos su alegría*, he conveyed his joy to us all. || To pass on, to give, to communicate, to convey (información). || To communicate, to inform of, to make known, to convey, to tell: *me comunicó sus ideas, un secreto*, he communicated his ideas to me, he told me a secret. || To transmit, to communicate, to pass on, to give (enfermedad). || To transmit, to communicate, to impart (movimiento). || To transmit (calor). || To pass on (miedo). || To join, to connect (dos habitaciones).
— V. intr. To communicate: *comunicamos por medio de gestos*, we communicated by sign language. || To correspond (por carta): *comunicar con alguien*, to correspond with s.o. || To call (por teléfono): *comunicar con alguien*, to call s.o. || To communicate: *cuartos que comunican*, rooms which communicate. || To be engaged (el teléfono): *está comunicando*, it's engaged. || To report: *comunican de Madrid que*, it is reported from Madrid that.
— V. pr. To communicate. || To spread (propagarse): *enfermedad que se comunica*, disease which spreads. || To keep in touch with one another (por carta, por teléfono, etc.), to correspond, to communicate (por carta). || To pass, to be transmitted (el temor, etc.). || To communicate (dos casas, habitaciones, lagos, etc.). || To exchange: *nos comunicamos nuestras ideas*, we exchanged ideas.
comunicativo, va adj. Communicative, talkative (una persona). || Infectious, catching: *risa comunicativa*, infectious laugh. || *Poco comunicativo*, not very talkative, reticent.
comunicatoria adj. f. *Letra comunicatoria*, testimonial.
comunidad f. COM. Community (de intereses, ideas, etc.): *Comunidad Económica Europea*, European Economic Community. || REL. Community (de religiosos). || (Ant.). Parish (vecinos de un municipio). || — Pl. HIST. "Comunidades" [popular uprising in the time of Charles V]. || — *Comunidad Británica de Naciones*, British Commonwealth of Nations. || *Comunidad de bienes*, co-ownership (entre esposos). || *Comunidad de propietarios*, owners' association. || *En comunidad*, together.
comunión f. Fellowship, communion: *comunión de ideas*, fellowship of ideas. || Holy Communion, Communion, sacrament of the Lord's Supper (sacramento).
comunismo m. Communism.
comunista adj./s. Communist.
comunistoide adj. FAM. Communistic.
— M. y f. FAM. Communist sympathizer.
comunitario, ria adj. Of the community. || *Centro comunitario*, community center.
comunizar v. tr. To communize.
comúnmente adv. Normally, generally, usually (generalmente). || Commonly, frequently (frecuentemente).
comuña f. AGR. Mixture of wheat and rye (trigo mezclado con cebada).
con prep.

1. With. — **2.** In. — **3.** To. — **4.** Con el infinitivo. — **5.** Locuciones.

1. WITH. — *Comer con una cuchara*, to eat with a spoon; *un anciano con gafas de oro*, an old man with gold spectacles; *contento con las noticias*; happy with the news; *estar disgustado con uno*, to be annoyed with s.o.; *hacer una cosa con la idea de*, to do sth. with the idea of; *con las manos juntas*, with one's hands together.
2. IN. — *Hablar con voz ronca*, to speak in a raucous voice; *con buena salud*, in good health; *con toda franqueza*, in all frankness; *estás muy bien con ese sombrero*, you look nice in that hat; *no puedo salir con este frío*, I can't go out in this cold; *con ira, con enojo*, in anger.
3. TO. — *Amable con todos*, nice to everybody; *disculparse con*, to apologize to; *escribirse con alguien*, to write to s.o.; *antipático con todos*, unfriendly to everyone.
4. CON EL INFINITIVO. — By (con el gerundio), if: *con pulsar este botón se enciende la luz*, by pressing this switch you put the light on, if you press this switch the light goes on. || As, since: *con llegar muy tarde, se quedó sin comer*, as he arrived very late, he had no lunch. || Even though, in spite of the fact that, in spite of: *con ser tan inteligente no ha conseguido triunfar*, even though *o* in spite of the fact that he is very intelligent, he has not been able to succeed. || Provided that, as long as: *con escribirme mañana*, as long as you write to me tomorrow.
5. LOCUCIONES. — *Con arreglo a la ley*, in accordance with *o* according to the law. || *Con ello*, for that. || *Con el título de*, under the title of. || *Con esto y con todo*, however, nevertheless. || *Con mucho gusto*, with [great]

pleasure. || *Con objeto de*, in order to, to, with the aim of. || *Con que*, so, then. || *Con tal que* or *con que* or *con sólo que*, so long as, provided that. || *Con todo* or *con todo y con eso*, in spite of everything, nevertheless, even so. || *Con todos los requisitos*, in due form. || *Están todos con gripe*, they have all got the flu. || *Salvó al niño con gran admiración de los que le rodeaban*, he rescued the child to the great admiration of those around him. || FAM. *¡Vaya con el niño!*, that child!

conato m. (P. us.). Effort, endeavour (empeño). | Intention, purpose (propósito). || Beginnings, *pl.* (principio): *conato de incendio*, beginnings of a fire. || Attempt: *hizo un conato de*, he made an attempt to. || *Conato de revolución*, attempted revolution.

conca f. Shell.

concadenar v. tr. V. CONCATENAR.

contatenación f. Concatenation, chain, linking: *concatenación de ideas*, chain of ideas.

concatenado, da adj. Concatenate, linked up.

concatenar v. tr. To link, to link up, to concatenate.

concausa f. Cause, factor (causa).

concavidad f. Concavity. || Hollow, cavity (hoyo).

cóncavo, va adj. Concave: *espejo cóncavo*, concave mirror.

cóncavoconvexo, xa adj. Fís. Concavo-convex.

concebible adj. Conceivable, thinkable, imaginable.

concebir* v. tr. To conceive (una mujer). || To understand, to conceive: *eso se concibe fácilmente*, that is easily understood. || To imagine (imaginar). || To conceive (idea, amistad, amor, proyecto, esperanzas). || To view (un asunto). || To form (un proyecto). || To take: *concibió antipatía hacia su vecino*, he took a dislike to his neighbour. || *Hacer concebir esperanzas a uno*, to give s.o. hope, to raise s.o.'s hopes.
— V. intr. To conceive, to become pregnant (quedar encinta). || To conceive, to imagine (imaginar).

conceder v. tr. To grant, to concede (otorgar): *conceder una gracia, un privilegio*, to grant a favour, a privilege. || To allow, to give, to grant (crédito, plazo, etc.). || To pay (atención). || To spare, to give: *no puedo concederle sino algunos minutos*, I can only spare you a few minutes. || To award: *conceder una indemnización, un premio*, to award damages, a prize. || To admit, to agree (reconocer): *concedo que tiene usted razón*, I admit that you are right. || To confer (*a*, on) [honores]. || *Conceder importancia, valor*, to give *o* to attach importance, value.

concejal m. Town councillor, councillor.

concejala f. Town councillor's wife. || [Female] councillor, councilwoman.

concejero m. *Amer.* Town councillor.

concejil adj. Municipal.

concejo m. Town council (ayuntamiento).

— OBSERV. This word must not be confused with *consejo*.

conceller m. Town councillor in Catalonia.

concentrable adj. Concentrative.

concentración f. Concentration: *la concentración de un producto químico*, the concentration of a chemical; *campo de concentración*, concentration camp. || — *Concentración parcelaria*, [land] consolidation. || *Llevar a cabo la concentración parcelaria*, to consolidate land.

concentrado, da adj. Concentrated. || FIG. Absorbed (absorto).
— M. Concentrate: *concentrado de tomates*, tomato concentrate. || *Concentrado de carne*, meat extract.

concentrar v. tr. To concentrate (tropas, rayos, etc.). || To focus (la observación, los sonidos, etc.). || FIG. To concentrate: *concentrar la atención en*, to concentrate one's attention on. | To concentrate, to centre (los esfuerzos).
— V. pr. FIG. To concentrate (abstraerse). || To concentre [U.S., to concenter] (rayos). || To concentrate, to be concentrated (tropas, rayos, etc.).

concéntrico, ca adj. Concentric.

concentricidad f. Concentricity.

concepción f. Conception (de un niño). || FIG. Conception, idea: *tener una curiosa concepción de la vida*, to have a strange conception of life. || *Inmaculada Concepción*, Immaculate Conception.

Concepción n. pr. f. Girl's name derived from María de la Concepción [there is no equivalent in English].

concepcional adj. Conceptional.

conceptible adj. Conceivable, thinkable, imaginable.

conceptismo m. Conceptism (estilo literario).

conceptista adj. Devoted to conceptism.
— M. y f. Devotee of conceptism.

conceptivo, va adj. Conceptive.

concepto m. Concept: *el concepto del tiempo*, the concept of time. || Idea, notion, conception: *no tengo un concepto claro de lo que es esta doctrina*, I haven't got a clear idea of what this doctrine is. || Opinion (juicio). || Witticism, pun (agudeza). || Reason (razón). || (Ant.). Conceit. || Heading, section (de una cuenta). || — *En concepto de*, as, by way of. || *En mi concepto*, in my opinion. || *En ningún concepto*, on no account, under no circumstances. || *En su amplio concepto*, in its broad *o* broadest sense. || *Formarse un concepto de*, to form *o* to get an idea of, to see (la forma de algo), to form an opinion of (hacerse una opinión). || *Perdí el concepto que tenía de él*, I have changed my opinion of him. || *Por* or *bajo todos los conceptos*, from every point of view, in every respect. || *Por ningún concepto*, by no means, in no way. || *Tener buen concepto de* or *tener en buen concepto a alguien*, to have a high opinion of s.o., to think well *o* highly of s.o. (tener buena opinión).

conceptual adj. Conceptual.

conceptualismo m. Conceptualism.

conceptualista adj. Conceptualistic.
— M. y f. Conceptualist.

conceptuar v. tr. To consider, to deem, to think: *conceptuar a uno de* or *por* or *como inteligente*, to consider s.o. intelligent. || *Bien, mal conceptuado*, well, badly thought of.

conceptuoso, sa adj. Affected, forced, laboured (estilo). || Affected (escritor). || Witty (agudo).

concerniente adj. Concerning, regarding, about, dealing with: *los reglamentos concernientes a los transportes*, the regulations concerning transport. || *En lo concerniente a*, with regard to.

concernir* v. intr. To concern, to regard (afectar). || To be up to (corresponder): *no me concierne decidir*, it's not up to me to decide. || — *En lo que a mí concierne*, as for me, for my part, as far as I am concerned. || *En lo que concierne a*, as for, with regard to, with respect to, concerning.

— OBSERV. This is a defective verb; it is only used in the third persons singular and plural of the present and imperfect indicative and subjunctive.

concertadamente adv. Of a common accord, together (puestos de acuerdo). || Systematically, methodically (con orden).

concertado, da adj. Concerted (acción).

concertador, ra adj. Conciliatory, conciliating (conciliador). || Coordinating.
— M. y f. Peacemaker, appeaser. || *Concertador de privilegios*, issuer of royal privileges.

concertante adj. MÚS. Concerted.

concertar* v. tr. To concert, to plan (proyectar en común). || To coordinate (coordinar). || To arrange: *concertar una venta*, to arrange a sale. || To agree on, *o* upon, to fix: *concertar un precio*, to agree on *o* upon a price. || To settle, to conclude, to clinch: *concertar un negocio*, to clinch a deal. || To agree, to arrange: *hemos concertado reunirnos el sábado*, we have agreed to meet on Saturday. || To arrive at, to come to, to conclude, to reach: *concertar un acuerdo*, to reach an agreement. || To conclude (un tratado). || To tune (instrumentos de música). || To harmonize (voces). || To concert, to coordinate: *concertar los esfuerzos*, to concert one's efforts. || To reconcile (reconciliar).
— V. intr. To agree, to tally: *dos pasajes que no conciertan*, two passages which do not tally. || GRAM. To agree (las palabras). || MÚS. To harmonize, to be in tune.
— V. pr. To plot (conchabarse). || To come to *o* to arrive at an agreement, to agree (llegar a un acuerdo).

concertina f. MÚS. Concertina.

concertino m. MÚS. First violin [U.S., concertmaster].

concertista m. y f. Concert performer, soloist.

concesión f. Granting, concession (acción de conceder). || Grant (cosa concedida): *concesión perpetua*, grant in perpetuity. || Awarding: *la concesión de un premio*, the awarding of a prize. || FIG. Concession: *hacer concesiones*, to make concessions.

concesionario, ria adj. Concessionary.
— M. Licence holder, licensee (de bebidas). || Concessionaire, concessionnaire (obras, etc.).

conciencia f. Consciousness, awareness (conocimiento). || Conscience (moralidad): *tener la conciencia limpia* or *tranquila*, to have a clear conscience; *caso de conciencia*, matter of conscience. || Mind: *tener la conciencia deformada*, to have a twisted *o* warped mind. || — *A conciencia*, conscientiously: *trabajo hecho a conciencia*, work done conscientiously. || *Acusar a uno la conciencia*, to have a guilty conscience, to have pangs of conscience. || *Cargar la conciencia*, to burden *o* to prick one's conscience. || *Conciencia de clase*, class-consciousness. || *Conciencia sucia*, guilty conscience. || *En conciencia*, in all conscience. || FAM. *Gusanillo de la conciencia*, remorse (remordimiento). || *Libertad de conciencia*, freedom of worship. || *Objetor de conciencia*, conscientious objector. || *Para descargar la conciencia*, to ease one's conscience. || *Remorderle a uno la conciencia*, to have a guilty conscience. || *Ser ancho, estrecho de conciencia*, to be unscrupulous, scrupulous. || *Tener conciencia de*, to be aware *o* conscious of. || *Tener un peso en la conciencia*, to have sth. *o* a burden on one's conscience. || *Tomar conciencia de*, to become aware of.

concienzudo, da adj. Conscientious.

concierto m. Agreement (acuerdo). || MÚS. Concert (función): *concierto al aire libre*, open-air concert. | Concerto (obra): *concierto de piano*, piano concerto. || FIG. Concord, harmony, concert (armonía). | Chorus (de alabanzas): *concierto de elogios*, chorus of praise. || — *Concierto económico*, flat rate (impuesto). || *De concierto*, in concert, together, in unison. || *Sin orden ni concierto*, v. ORDEN.

conciliable adj. Reconcilable, conciliable.

conciliábulo m. Secret meeting (reunión). || Confabulation (entrevista). || REL. Conciliabule.

conciliación f. Conciliation, reconciliation, reconcilement. || — *Espíritu de conciliación*, conciliatory spirit. || *Tribunal de conciliación*, conciliation court. || *Tribunal de conciliación laboral*, conciliation board.
conciliador, ra adj. Conciliatory, conciliating.
— M. y f. Conciliator.
conciliar adj. Conciliar.
— M. Councillor.
conciliar v. tr. To reconcile, to conciliate: *conciliar a dos enemigos*, to reconcile two enemies. || To reconcile, to harmonize (textos, ideas, etc.). || *Conciliar el sueño*, to get to sleep.
— V. pr. To win, to gain: *conciliarse la amistad de todo el mundo*, to gain everybody's friendship.
conciliativo, va o **conciliatorio, ria** adj. Conciliatory, conciliative.
concilio m. Council. || *El Concilio Vaticano Segundo*, the Second Vatican Council.
concisamente adv. Concisely, tersely, briefly.
concisión f. Concision, conciseness, succinctness.
conciso, sa adj. Concise, terse, brief.
concitar v. tr. To stir up: *concitó contra su amigo la ira de su padre*, he stirred up his father's anger against his friend.
conciudadano, na m. y f. Fellow citizen (en general). || Fellow townsman (hombre de la misma ciudad). || Fellow townswoman (mujer). || Fellow countryman (hombre del mismo país). || Fellow countrywoman (mujer).
cónclave o **conclave** m. Conclave.
conclavista m. Conclavist.
concluir* v. tr. To finish (acabar). || To close (un trato). || To conclude, to deduce, to infer (deducir). || To settle, to solve (solucionar). || To convince (convencer). || To put the finishing touches to (una obra de arte).
— V. intr. To finish, to end: *es tiempo de concluir*, it is time to finish. || — *Concluir con un trabajo*, to finish *o* to finish with a piece of work. || *Concluir haciendo algo* or *por hacer algo*, to finish by *o* to end up [by] doing sth. || *Concluyeron por pedir un armisticio*, they decided to seek an armistice, they eventually requested an armistice.
— V. pr. To come to an end, to finish, to end.
conclusión f. Concluding, settlement (de un negocio). || Conclusion (de un razonamiento). || Conclusion, close (fin). || — *En conclusión*, in conclusion. || *Llegar a la conclusión de que*, to come to the conclusion that.
conclusivo, na adj. Conclusive.
concluso, sa adj. JUR. Closed pending sentence.

— OBSERV. This adjective is the irregular past participle of the verb *concluir*.

concluyente adj. Conclusive, decisive: *una prueba concluyente*, conclusive evidence. || Categorical.
concoide adj. Conchoidal (en forma de concha).
— F. MAT. Conchoid (curva).
concoideo, a adj. Conchoidal (en forma de concha).
concomer v. tr. FIG. To gnaw at, to corrode.
— V. pr. To wriggle one's back, to squirm. || — FIG. y FAM. *Concomerse de envidia*, to be green with envy, to squirm with envy. | *Concomerse de impaciencia*, to itch with impatience. | *Concomerse de rabia*, to be hopping mad, to be seething.
concomitancia f. Concomitance, concomitancy.
concomitante adj. Concomitant.
concordancia f. Concordance, agreement. || GRAM. Agreement (entre sustantivo y adjetivo, etc.), sequence (de los tiempos). || MÚS. Harmony.
concordante adj. Concordant.
concordar* v. tr. To reconcile, to bring into agreement: *concordar a dos enemigos*, to reconcile two enemies. || GRAM. To make agree.
— V. intr. To agree: *los médicos concuerdan en que*, the doctors agree that. || To agree, to tally: *mi versión no concuerda con la tuya*, my version does not tally with yours. || GRAM. To agree: *el verbo concuerda con el sujeto*, the verb agrees with the subject. || — *Las opiniones concuerdan en que*, there is a consensus of opinion that. || *Los indicios concuerdan en que*, the signs all point to the fact that.
concordata f. V. CONCORDATO.
concordato m. Concordat.
concordatorio, ria adj. Of a concordat, concordat.
concorde adj. In agreement. || — *Estamos concordes en la necesidad de marcharnos*, we all agree that we must leave, we all recognize the need for us to leave. || *Estar concorde en hacer algo*, to be for doing sth., to agree to doing sth. || *Poner concordes a dos personas*, to make two people agree *o* see eye to eye.
concordemente adv. Together, of a common accord.
concordia f. Harmony, concord, concordance (armonía). || Double ring (sortija). || *De concordia*, together, of a common accord.
concreción f. Concretion. || MED. Stone.
concretamente adv. Concretely. || In particular, specifically: *referirse concretamente a alguien*, to refer to s.o. in particular. || Specifically: *me dijo concretamente que lo hiciera*, he specifically told me to do it. || Exactly: *no sé concretamente lo que significa esto*, I don't know exactly what this means. || *Se lo dije a uno de vosotros, concretamente a Juan*, I said it to one of you, to John to be exact *o* to John in fact.
concretar v. tr. To state explicitly: *concretar una idea*, to state an idea explicitly. || To limit (limitar). || To specify (precisar). || *Concretemos*, let us sum up (al final), let us be more specific (precisemos). || *Concretó sus esperanzas en*, he set his hopes on.
— V. pr. To confine o.s. to: *me concretaré a hablar de*, I shall confine myself to speaking about. || To become definite, to come out, to be established: *su desacuerdo se concretó durante la última asamblea*, their disagreement came out during the last meeting. || To take shape: *el proyecto parece concretarse*, the project seems to be taking shape. || To keep: *concrétese usted al tema*, keep to the subject.
concreto, ta adj. Concrete. || Actual, particular, specific (caso). || — *Algo concreto*, something concrete. || *En concreto*, definite (seguro), in short, in brief (en resumen). || *En el caso concreto de*, in the particular case of, in the specific case of. || *Lo concreto*, the concrete aspect. || *Nada se ha dicho hasta ahora en concreto* or *nada concreto se ha dicho hasta ahora*, up to now nothing definite has been said.
— M. Concretion. || *Amer.* Concrete (hormigón).
concubina f. Concubine.
concubinato m. Concubinage.
conculcación f. Infringement, violation.
conculcar v. tr. To infringe, to violate, to break (infringir): *conculcar la ley*, to break the law.
concuñada f. Sister of one's brother-in-law or sister-in-law.
concuñado m. Brother of one's brother-in-law or sister-in-law.
concupiscencia f. Concupiscence, lustfulness, lust of the flesh. || Greed (avaricia).
concupiscente adj. Concupiscent, lustful (sensual). || Greedy (avaro).
concurrencia f. Audience (en un espectáculo): *una concurrencia numerosa*, a large audience. || Crowd, gathering (muchedumbre). || Concurrence, conjunction (simultaneidad): *la concurrencia de dos muertes*, the conjunction of two deaths. || — *Divertir a la concurrencia*, to keep the audience amused. || *Hasta concurrencia de*, up to, to the amount of, not exceeding.
concurrente adj. Concurrent (que coincide). || Competing, contending (participante en un concurso).
— M. y f. Competitor (competidor, participante en un concurso). || Candidate (en un examen). || Member of the audience (en el teatro, etc.). || Spectator (en espectáculos deportivos). || *Los concurrentes*, those present, the audience.
concurrido, da adj. Popular, well-attended (exposición, museo, etc.). || Busy, crowded (calle). || Much frequented (muy frecuentado).
concurrir v. intr. To go (a un lugar). || To converge, to meet (converger). || To attend (presenciar). || To coincide, to concur (en el tiempo). || To contribute: *concurrir al éxito de*, to contribute to the success of. || To concur (en un dictamen). || To compete, to take part (*a*, in) [tomar parte en un concurso o una competición]. || To be a candidate (examen). || *Concurren en él todas las cualidades*, he combines *o* has all the qualities.
concursante m. y f. Competitor, participant (en un concurso). || Candidate (para un empleo). || DEP. Contestant.
concursar v. intr. To compete (en un concurso). || To be a candidate (en un examen, para un empleo).
concurso m. Concourse (concurrencia). || Gathering, crowd (muchedumbre). || Help, aid, assistance (ayuda): *prestar su concurso*, to lend assistance, to give one's help. || Cooperation. || Competition: *un concurso literario*, a literary competition. || Contest: *concurso de tiro con arco, de belleza, de pesca*, archery, beauty, fishing contest. || Show: *concurso hípico*, horse show. || Meeting: *concurso de atletismo*, athletics meeting. || Tender (de una obra, servicio). || Competitive examination, competition (examen). || Coincidence, concurrence (de hechos). || FIG. Combination: *concurso de circunstancias*, combination of circumstances. || — JUR. *Concurso de acreedores*, meeting of creditors. || *Concurso radiofónico*, radio quiz programme. || *Fuera de concurso*, out of the running. || *Se ha anunciado concurso para proveer una plaza de médico en el hospital*, applications are invited to fill a post of doctor at the hospital.
concusión f. MED. Concussion. || Peculation, extortion (de un funcionario).
concusionario, ria m. y f. Extortioner, extortionist, peculator.
concha f. Shell (de molusco, tortuga). || Tortoiseshell (carey): *peine de concha*, tortoiseshell comb. || Bay, cove (pequeña bahía). || Chip (de porcelana). || Nether millstone (de molino). || ANAT. Concha, conch (de la oreja). || *Amer.* POP. Cunt. || — TEATR. *Concha del apuntador*, prompt box. || *Concha de peregrino*, scallop, scallop shell. || *Concha de perla*, pearl oyster (madreperla). || FIG. *Meterse en su concha*, to withdraw into one's shell. || FIG. y FAM. *Tener muchas conchas* or *más conchas que un galápago*, to be reserved (reservado), to be a sly one (taimado).
conchabamiento m. o **conchabanza** f. Plot, conspiracy.

conchabar v. tr. To gather together (unir). || To mix (mezclar). || *Amer.* To take on, to hire [mainly servants].
— V. pr. To join *o* to band together. || To gang up, to join up: *conchabarse con malhechores*, to join up with evildoers. || *Estar conchabado con*, to be in league with, to be hand in glove with.
conchífero, ra adj. GEOL. Conchiferous.
concho m. *Amer.* Corn husk (del maíz). | Sediment, dregs, *pl.*, deposit (poso). | End (final). || — Pl. *Amer.* Leftovers (sobras).
— Interj. *Amer.* FAM. Damn!
condado m. County, shire (territorio). || Countship, earldom (dignidad).
condal adj. Of a count, count's. || *La Ciudad Condal*, Barcelona.
conde m. Count, earl (título). || *El señor conde*, his lordship.
condecoración f. Decoration, medal (insignia). || Decoration (acción de condecorar). || *Imponer una condecoración a uno*, to decorate s.o.
condecorado, da adj. Decorated.
— M. y f. Holder of a decoration *o* of decorations.
condecorar v. tr. To decorate: *condecorar con una cruz*, to decorate with a cross.
condena f. JUR. Conviction, sentence (sentencia). | Condemnation (a muerte). || Condemnation (acción de reprochar, censurar). || Sentence: *el penado cumplió* or *sufrió su condena*, the prisoner served his sentence. || — *Condena a perpetuidad*, life sentence. || *Condena condicional*, suspended sentence.
condenable adj. Condemnable, reprehensible, blameworthy (que merece ser condenado). || Damnable, heinous (digno de condenación divina).
condenación f. JUR. Conviction, sentence (acción de condenar). | Condemnation (a muerte). || REL. Damnation (al infierno). || Condemnation (censura).
condenadamente adv. FAM. Darned, damned (muy).
condenado, da adj. Condemned, convicted (por un tribunal). || Condemned, damned (al infierno). || Condemned (puerta, etc.). || Hopeless, beyond help (enfermo). || Doomed: *una raza condenada*, a doomed race. || FIG. Damned, wretched: *este condenado Pablo siempre nos está dando la lata*, that damned Paul is always annoying us; *este condenado trabajo*, this damned job. || *Condenado a muerte*, condemned to death.
— M. y f. Condemned person (a muerte). || Convicted person, prisoner (a otra pena). || Reprobate, damned person (al infierno). || Wretch: *¡como vuelva a ver a ese condenado...!*, if I see the wretch again...! || — FIG. y FAM. *Correr como un condenado*, to run like a hare, to run for dear life. | *Forcejear como un condenado*, to struggle for dear life. | *Sufrir como un condenado*, to go through hell. | *Trabajar como un condenado*, to work like a horse, to slave away.
condenar v. tr. To convict, to find guilty: *condenar por ladrón*, to find guilty of theft. || To condemn, to sentence: *condenar a cinco años, a muerte*, to condemn to five years' imprisonment, to death. || To condemn, to censure, to blame (una doctrina, una conducta). || To condemn, to doom (obligar). || To condemn, to damn (al infierno). || MED. To give up (a un enfermo). || *Amer.* To annoy, to irritate. || — *Condenar a una multa*, to fine. || *Condenar en costas*, to order to pay costs. || *Condenar en rebeldía*, to judge by default. || *Condenar una puerta*, to condemn a door, to brick up *o* to board up *o* to wall up a door (tabicarla).
— V. pr. To condemn o.s., to be damned, to doom o.s. (al infierno). || To condemn o.s. || To get annoyed (irritarse).
condenatorio, ria adj. JUR. Condemnatory.
condensabilidad f. Condensability.
condensable adj. Condensable.
condensación f. Condensation (acción y resultado). || Condensing (acción).
condensado, da adj. Condensed: *leche condensada*, condensed milk.
condensador m. ELECTR. Condenser, capacitor. || Condenser (de gases, máquinas de vapor).
condensar v. tr. To condense.
— V. pr. To condense, to become condensed.
condesa f. Countess (título). || *La señora condesa*, her ladyship.
condescendencia f. Condescension, condescendence (deferencia). | Complaisance, indulgence (amabilidad).
condescender* v. intr. To yield, to comply (avenirse a, ceder): *condescender a los deseos de uno*, to yield to s.o.'s wishes. || To condescend (dignarse): *condescender en ir a verle*, to condescend to go and see him.
condescendiente adj. Condescending. || Obliging, complaisant, indulgent (amable).
condestable m. High Constable.
condición f. Nature, condition (naturaleza de las cosas): *la condición humana*, the human condition. || Quality: *mercancía de mala condición*, poor quality goods. || Condition, state (estado): *en buenas condiciones*, in a good condition. || Character, nature, disposition: *ser áspero de condición*, to have a surly character *o* nature, to be of a surly disposition. || Rank, status, position, condition (situación social): *de humilde condición*, of modest status. || Sort, kind (clase). || Capacity: *en mi condición de ministro*, in my capacity as minister. || Condition, circumstance (circunstancia): *en estas condiciones*, under these circumstances, in these conditions. || Condition: *condiciones de pago*, conditions of payment. || Condition: *condiciones de trabajo*, working conditions. || Condition (en una promesa): *imponer condiciones*, to lay down *o* to impose conditions. || JUR. Condition: *condición casual, tácita*, contingent, implicit *o* tacit condition. || — Pl. Aptitude, *sing.*, talent, *sing.*, capacity, *sing.*: *tener condiciones para el dibujo*, to have an aptitude for drawing. || Conditions, terms (de un contrato). || State, *sing.*: *condiciones de salud*, state of health. || — *A condición de tener tiempo, lo haré*, I shall do it, provided that *o* as long as I have time. || *A condición (de) que* or *con la condición de que no llueva*, on condition that *o* provided that *o* as long as it does not rain. || *Condiciones requeridas*, requirements, requisites. || *Condición sine qua non*, V. SINE QUA NON. || *Con esta condición*, on this condition. || *De buena, mala condición*, good-tempered, ill-tempered *o* bad-tempered. || *En condiciones de marcha*, in working order. || *En iguales condiciones*, in the same conditions. || *Estar en condiciones de hacer algo*, to be in a fit state to do sth. (físicamente), to be in a position to do sth. (legalmente, moralmente, etc.). || *Estar en malas condiciones*, to be off. || *Persona de condición*, person of rank *o* importance, high-class person. || *Poner en condiciones*, to prepare, to get ready. || *Rendición sin condiciones*, unconditional surrender. || *Rendirse sin condiciones*, to surrender unconditionally. || *Tener condición*, to have character, to have a backbone. || *Tener mala condición*, to be evil-minded.
condicionado, da adj. Conditioned (acondicionado): *reflejo condicionado*, conditioned reflex. || Conditional (condicional). || *La oferta está condicionada a* or *por la demanda*, supply is conditioned by demand.
condicional adj. Conditional.
condicionamiento m. Conditioning.
condicionar v. intr. To fit, to agree.
— V. tr. To suit, to adapt [*a*, to], to make depend [*a*, on]: *ha condicionado su decisión a la opinión de los demás*, he suited his decision to the opinion of the others. || To condition (temperature, etc.). || To condition (poner condiciones). || To test (las fibras). || *Su aceptación condiciona la mía*, his acceptance determines mine, my acceptance depends on his.
cóndilo m. ANAT. Condyle.
condiloideo, a adj. BOT. Condyloid.
condiloma m. MED. Condyloma.
condimentación f. Seasoning.
condimentar v. tr. To season, to flavour (sazonar). || FIG. To spice, to flavour.
condimento m. Condiment, seasoning (aliño). || Dressing (de ensalada).
condiscípulo, la m. y f. Fellow student, schoolmate, classmate.
condolencia f. Condolence, sympathy.
condolerse* v. pr. To feel pity [*de*, for], to pity, to sympathize [*de*, with], to feel sorry [*de*, for] (compadecerse): *condolerse de los miserables*, to feel sorry for the unfortunate.
condominio m. Condominium (de un territorio). || Joint ownership (de una cosa).
condón m. POP. French letter.
condonación f. Remission, condonation (de una pena, de una deuda). || Remission (de contribuciones).
condonar v. tr. To condone, to pardon. || To cancel (una deuda).
cóndor m. Condor (ave, moneda).
conducción f. Driving: *la conducción de un coche*, the driving of a car. || FÍS. Conduction. || Leading (guía). || Transportation (transporte). || Pipe (tubería). || Piping (por tubos). || Wiring (cables). || — *Conducción por la izquierda*, driving on the left. || *Permiso de conducción*, driving licence.
conducente adj. Conducive, leading.
conducir* v. tr. To drive: *conducir un coche*, to drive a car. || To lead: *conducir un ejército*, to lead an army. || To convey (un líquido). || To carry (electricidad). || To lead (a una persona). || To manage (un negocio). || To conduct (una encuesta, etc.). || To accompany (acompañar). || To transport, to carry (transportar). || *Conducir a la ruina a alguien*, to bring s.o. to his ruin, to bring about s.o.'s ruin.
— V. intr. To drive: *no sabe conducir*, he cannot drive. || To lead (llevar): *eso no conduce a nada*, that leads nowhere *o* to nothing.
— V. pr. To behave, to conduct o.s. (portarse).
conducta f. Conduct, behaviour [U.S., behavior] (manera de comportarse): *tiene siempre malas notas de conducta*, he always has bad marks for conduct. || Management (dirección). || Convoy (de mulas, etc.). || — *Cambiar de conducta*, to change one's ways. || *Mala conducta*, misconduct, misbehaviour.
conductancia f. ELECTR. Conductance.
conductibilidad f. FÍS. Conductivity.
conductible adj. FÍS. Conductive.
conductividad f. ELECTR. Conductivity.
conductivo, va adj. Conductive.
conducto m. Pipe, conduit (cañería). || ELECTR. Cable, lead, culvert. || ANAT. Duct: *conducto auditivo, lagrimal*, auditory, tear duct. || — ANAT. *Conducto*

alimenticio, alimentary canal. || *Conducto de desagüe*, drain. || *Conducto de humos*, flue. || *Por conducto de*, through, via. || *Por conducto oficial* or *regular* or *reglamentario*, through official channels.
conductor, ra adj. Who drives (de automóvil, etc.). || ELECTR. Conductive. || FIG. Leading, guiding.
— M. y f. Driver (de coche, autobús, etc.). || FIG. Leader (jefe). || — M. ELECTR. Conductor. || IMPR. Machine minder [U.S., pressman]. || Inspector (coche cama). || *Amer.* Conductor (cobrador).
condueño, ña m. y f. Joint owner.
condumio m. FAM. Grub, food (comida).
conectado, da adj. Connected.
conectador m. TECN. Connector, connecter.
conectar v. tr. e intr. TECN. To connect [up]. | To plug in (enchufar). | To switch on (poner). || TECN. To couple (acoplar). || — *Conectar a alguien*, to put s.o. in touch. || ELECTR. *Conectar a tierra*, to earth. || RAD. *Conectar con*, to tune in with (dar), to tune in to (coger). | *Conectamos con Madrid*, over to you, Madrid. || ELECTR. *Conectar con la red*, to connect to the mains. || *Conectar un golpe en la mandíbula*, to land a punch on the jaw (boxeo). || *Estar conectado con*, to be in touch with. || FAM. *Estar mal conectados*, not to be on the same wavelength.
coneja f. Doe (hembra del conejo). || FAM. *Esa mujer es una coneja*, she breeds like a rabbit.
conejal o **conejar** m. Rabbit hutch.
conejera f. Rabbit warren, rabbit burrow (de los conejos en libertad). || Rabbit hutch (conejal). || FIG. Cave (cueva). | Den, dive (de gente de mal vivir). | Rabbit hutch *o* warren (lugar donde viven muchos).
conejero, ra adj. Rabbit-hunting.
— M. y f. Rabbit breeder.
conejillo m. Young rabbit. || Bunny (en lenguaje infantil). || *Conejillo de Indias*, guinea pig.
conejo m. Rabbit (mamífero): *conejo casero*, tame rabbit. || — *Conejo de Angora*, Angora rabbit. || *Conejo de campo* or *de monte*, wild rabbit.

— OBSERV. In South America, the word *conejo* is applied to several rodents. One of the most common is the *tapetí* or *tapití* of Brazil.

conejuno, na adj. Of a rabbit, rabbit.
conexión f. Connection, connexion. || — *Estar en conexión con*, to be connected to. || *Vuelo de conexión*, liaison flight.
conexionarse v. pr. To make connections.
conexo, xa adj. Connected, related.
confabulación f. Conspiracy, plot, collusion.
confabular v. intr. To converse.
— V. pr. To conspire, to plot (conspirar).
confalón m. Gonfalon, banner, standard (estandarte).
confalonier o **confaloniero** m. Gonfalonier, standard bearer.
confección f. Tailoring, making-up, confection (de traje). || Ready-made *o* ready-to-wear *o* off-the-peg clothes, *pl.* || Clothing: *ramo de la confección*, clothing industry. || Making, making-up (realización). || Mixing (de un cóctel). || Drawing up (de una lista). || IMPR. Makeup. || *Tienda, traje de confección*, ready-made *o* off-the-peg shop, suit.
confeccionado, da adj. Ready-made, ready-to-wear, off-the-peg (ropa). || *Confeccionado a la medida*, made to measure.
confeccionador, ra m. y f. Ready-made outfitter. || Maker-up (en la redacción).
confeccionar v. tr. To make up (traje, lista, etc.). || CULIN. To make (pasteles). || IMPR. To make up.
confederación f. Confederacy, alliance, confederation.
confederado, da adj./s. Confederate.
confederal adj. Confederal.
confederar v. tr. To confederate.
— V. pr. To confederate.
confederativo, va adj. Confederative.
confer (abrev.: *cf.*, *conf.* *cof.*). Confer [abbrev.: *cf.*].
conferencia f. Conference, meeting (política). || Lecture, talk: *dar una conferencia*, to give a talk. || Call: *conferencia interurbana*, long-distance call, trunk call. || — *Conferencia a cobro revertido*, reverse-charge call [U.S., collect telephone call]. || *Conferencia de prensa*, press conference. || *Conferencia en la cumbre* or *de alto nivel*, summit conference. || *Poner una conferencia a Madrid*, to make a call to Madrid.
conferenciante m. y f. Lecturer, speaker.
conferenciar v. intr. To hold a conversation, to converse, to talk, to discuss.
conferencista m. y f. *Amer.* Lecturer.
conferir* v. tr. To confer, to bestow (conceder una dignidad, etc.). || To give: *conferir a uno nuevas responsabilidades*, to give s.o. new responsibilities. || To award (premio).
— V. intr. To confer, to consult.
confesante adj. JUR. Who confesses.
confesar* v. tr. To admit, to confess: *confesar su ignorancia*, to confess one's ignorance. || To own to, to acknowledge (un error). || To own up to (un crimen). || To confess (proclamar): *confesar la fe*, to confess one's faith. || REL. To confess, to hear in confession (oír en confesión). | To confess (los pecados). || *Confesar de plano*, to own up, to admit everything.
— V. pr. To go to confession, to confess. || — *Confesarse con el párroco*, to confess to the parish priest. || *Confesarse culpable, vencido*, to admit one's guilt, to admit defeat. || *Confesarse de un pecado*, to confess a sin. || *Ir a confesarse*, to go to confession.

— OBSERV. *Confesar* has two past participles: *confesado* is regular and *confeso* irregular, the latter being used as an adjective.

confesión f. Confession, admission (admisión). || REL. Confession (acto de confesarse). | Confession, faith, avowal (credo religioso). || *Oír en confesión*, to confess, to hear in confession.
confesional adj. Confessional. || Denominational (disputas, escuela, etc.), doctrinal (disputas, etc.).
confesionario m. Confessional [box].
confeso, sa adj. Self-confessed. || Converted (judío).
— M. Lay brother (lego). || Converted Jew (judío convertido).
confesonario m. Confessional [box].
confesor m. Confessor.
confesorio m. Confessional [box].
confeti m. pl. Confetti, *sing.* (papelillos).
confiadamente adv. Confidently (con confianza). || Conceitedly (con presunción).
confiado, da adj. Trusting (que se fía). || Gullible, unsuspecting (crédulo). || Confident, self-confident (seguro de sí mismo). || Conceited (presumido). || *Estamos muy confiados en el resultado*, we are very confident about the result.
confianza f. Confidence: *tener confianza en el porvenir*, to have confidence in the future; *hacerlo con confianza*, to do it with confidence. || Trust, confidence (en alguien). || Intimacy, familiarity (intimidad). || Conceit (presunción). || — *Amigo de confianza*, close friend. || *Con toda confianza*, in all confidence. || *Creía que teníamos bastante confianza para que te dijese la verdad*, I thought we were sufficiently good friends for me to tell you the truth, I thought we were close enough for me to tell you the truth. || *De confianza*, trustworthy, reliable: *él es de confianza*, he is reliable; of trust, confidential (puesto, empleo). || *Defraudar la confianza de alguien*, to betray s.o.'s confidence. || *En confianza*, confidentially, in confidence. || *Estar en confianza*, to be among friends. || *Plantear la cuestión de confianza*, to ask for a vote of confidence. || *Poner toda su confianza en una persona*, to trust s.o. implicitly. || *Tener confianza en sí mismo*, to be self-confident. || *Tener mucha confianza con alguien*, to be on very close *o* intimate terms with s.o. || *Tomarse demasiadas confianzas*, to take liberties. || *Tratar a uno con confianza*, to treat s.o. informally *o* like a friend.
confiar v. tr. To entrust (encargar): *confiar un trabajo a alguien*, to entrust s.o. with a job. || To commit: *confiar algo a la memoria*, to commit sth. to memory. || To confide, to tell in confidence (decir en confianza). || *Confiar a uno sus problemas*, to tell s.o. about one's problems.
— V. intr. To put one's trust *o* one's faith in, to have trust *o* faith in: *confiar en Dios*, to put one's trust in God. || To trust: *confío en mi amigo*, I trust my friend, I trust in my friend. || To count, to rely: *confío en su discreción*, I am counting on your discretion; *confiar en sus fuerzas*, to count on one's strength. || To be *o* to feel confident: *confío en que esta obra será un éxito*, I am confident that this work will be a success. || To hope (esperar): *confío en que no le pasará nada*, I hope nothing will happen to him.
— V. pr. To put o.s.: *me confié en sus manos*, I put myself in his hands. || To put one's trust (*en*, in). || To confide (hacer confidencias): *confiarse a un amigo*, to confide in a friend.
confidencia f. Secret, confidence. || *Hacer confidencias a uno*, to confide in s.o. (confiarse a), to reveal secrets to s.o. (revelar secretos a).
confidencial adj. Confidential. || *De modo confidencial*, confidentially, in confidence.
confidencialmente adv. Confidentially.
confidenta f. TEATR. Confidante.
confidente adj. Faithful (fiel).
— M. y f. Confidant (hombre), confidante (mujer). || Informer (de policía). || — M. Sociable (canapé).
confidentemente adv. Confidentially.
configuración f. Shape, form, configuration. || *Configuración del terreno*, lie of the land.
configurar v. tr. To shape, to form.
confín adj. Bordering.
— M. pl. Border, *sing.*: *los confines de España y Francia*, the border between Spain and France, the border of Spain with France. || Boundaries, limits, confines (límites). || — *En los confines del horizonte*, as far as the eye can see. || *Por todos los confines del mundo*, to the four corners of the earth.
confinación f. o **confinamiento** m. Exile, banishment (destierro). || Confinement (encarcelamiento).
confinado m. Exile (exilado). || Prisoner (preso).
confinar v. intr. To border, to be contiguous (*con*, to): *Francia confina con España*, France borders on Spain. || FIG. To border: *su estado confina con la locura*, his condition borders on madness.
— V. tr. To confine: *confinar a uno en un monasterio*, to confine s.o. in a monastery. || To banish, to exile (desterrar).
— V. pr. To shut o.s. away, to shut o.s. up.

confinidad f. Adjacency, nearness (proximidad).
confirmación f. Confirmation, corroboration: *la confirmación de una noticia*, the confirmation of a piece of news. || REL. Confirmation.
confirmado, da adj. Confirmed.
— M. y f. Confirmed man *o* woman.
confirmador, ra adj. Confirming, confirmative.
— M. y f. Confirmer.
confirmamiento m. V. CONFIRMACIÓN.
confirmando, da m. y f. REL. Confirmand.
confirmante adj./s. V. CONFIRMADOR.
confirmar v. tr. To confirm: *confirmar una noticia*, to confirm a piece of news; *su actitud confirma mis sospechas*, his attitude confirms my suspicions. || To uphold (una decisión, un veredicto). || To bear out, to corroborate (un testimonio). || To establish, to confirm: *esta nueva novela le confirma como uno de nuestros mejores novelistas*, this new novel confirms him as one of our best novelists. || REL. To confirm. || *La excepción confirma la regla*, the exception proves the rule.
— V. pr. To be confirmed.
confirmativo, va o **confirmatorio, ria** adj. Confirmative, confirmatory.
confiscable adj. Confiscable, liable to be confiscated.
confiscación f. Confiscation.
confiscador, ra m. y f. Confiscator.
confiscar v. tr. To confiscate.
confitado, da adj. Glacé, candied, crystallized: *peras confitadas*, glacé pears. || — *Castañas confitadas*, iced chestnuts. || *Frutas confitadas*, comfits.
confitar v. tr. To preserve in syrup (conservar). || To coat with sugar, to candy.
confite m. Sweet [U.S., candy].
confíteor m. Confiteor (oración). || FIG. Full confession.
confitera f. Sweet box [U.S., candy box] (caja de confites).
confitería f. Sweetshop, confectionery, confectioner's [U S., candy shop] (tienda). || *Amer*. Tea room, tea shop (salón de té).
confitero, ra m. y f. Confectioner.
confitura f. Jam, preserve (mermelada). || Crystallized fruit (fruta escarchada).
conflagración f. Blaze, conflagration. || FIG. War (guerra). | Flare-up (estallido de la guerra).
conflictivo, va adj. Of conflict (tiempos, etc.). || Conflicting (que están en conflicto).
conflicto m. Conflict, struggle: *conflicto entre dos naciones*, conflict between two nations. || Conflict, clash: *conflicto de ideas, opiniones*, clash of ideas, opinions. || FIG. Quandary, dilemma (apuro). || *Conflicto laboral*, industrial dispute, trade dispute.
confluencia f. MED. Confluence. || Confluence, concourse (de los ríos). || FIG. *Punto de confluencia*, common ground, meeting point.
confluente adj. Confluent.
— M. Confluence (de dos ríos).
confluir* v. intr. To converge, to meet, to come together (ríos, caminos, etc.). || To converge, to gather, to flock together (personas).
conformación f. Conformation, shape, structure. || *Vicio de conformación*, malformation, defect in shape.
conformar v. tr. To shape (dar forma a). || To adapt, to adjust, to conform: *conformar los gastos con los ingresos*, to adjust spending to income. || To reconcile (enemigos).
— V. intr. To agree, to be of the same opinion (estar conformes). || *Ser de buen conformar*, to be easy going, to be easy to get on with (una persona).
— V. pr. To conform, to comply: *conformarse con la voluntad de Dios*, to conform to *o* to comply with God's will. || To agree: *sus ideas se conforman con las mías*, his ideas agree with mine. || To resign o.s. to the fact, to get used to the idea: *no iremos de vacaciones, hay que conformarse*, we shan't go on holiday, we'll have to get used to the idea. || To resign o.s.: *conformarse con su suerte*, to resign o.s. to one's fate. || To make do: *como no había carne se conformó con las verduras*, as there was no meat he made do with vegetables. || *Conformarse con el parecer de uno*, to agree with s.o.
conforme adj. In keeping with: *el resultado está conforme con nuestras esperanzas*, the result is in keeping with our hopes. || In accordance with: *es conforme a la ley*, it is in accordance with the law. || Satisfied: *se mostró conforme con la propuesta*, he was satisfied with the suggestion. || According: *conforme con la razón*, according to reason. || In agreement with: *declararse conforme con*, to declare o.s. in agreement with. || Resigned: *conforme con su suerte*, resigned to one's fate. || Seen and approved (un documento). || *Estar* or *quedar conforme*, to agree. || *Estar conformes con el precio*, to be agreed on the price (las dos partes).
— Conj. As: *te describo la escena conforme la vi*, I am describing the scene as I saw it. || As soon as: *conforme amanezca, iré*, as soon as day breaks, I shall go. || As: *colocar a la gente conforme llegue*, to seat the people as they arrive. || — *Conforme a*, in accordance with, according to: *pagar a uno conforme a su trabajo*, to pay s.o. according to his work; *conforme a lo establecido en la ley*, according to what is laid down in the law. || *Según y conforme*, it [all] depends (depende).
— Interj. Okay, all right.
— M. Approval, endorsement.
conformemente adv. In accordance, according: *conformemente con*, in accordance with, according to.
conformidad f. Conformity, similarity (parecido). || Consent, approval: *me ha dado su conformidad*, he has given me his consent. || Agreement (acuerdo). || Resignation, patience (tolerancia): *aceptar con conformidad las pruebas de la vida*, to accept life's trials with resignation. || — *Conformidad en*, conformity of. || *Cuente usted con mi conformidad*, you can count on my agreement *o* approval. || *De* or *en conformidad con*, according to, in accordance *o* agreement with. || *En esta* or *en tal conformidad*, in that case. || *No conformidad*, nonconformity.
conformismo m. Conformism, orthodoxy, conventionalism. || REL. Conformism.
conformista adj. Conformist, orthodox. || REL. Conformist.
— M. y f. Conformist.
confort m. Comfort: *esta casa tiene gran confort*, this house has every comfort. || *Todo confort*, All Mod. Cons. (en anuncios).
confortable adj. Comfortable (cómodo): *un sillón muy confortable*, a very comfortable armchair.
confortablemente adv. Comfortably.
confortador, ra adj. Strengthening (que fortalece). || FIG. Comforting, cheering.
confortante adj. Strengthening (que fortalece). || FIG. Comforting, cheering.
confortar v. tr. To strengthen, to give strength to (fortalecer). || To comfort, to console (consolar): *confortar a un desgraciado*, to console an unhappy person. || To cheer, to encourage (animar).
confortativo, va adj. Comforting, consoling. || Strengthening.
confraternal adj. Fraternal, brotherly.
confraternidad f. Brotherhood, confraternity, fellowship, fraternity (unión). || Brotherliness, fellowship (amistad)
confraternizar v. intr. To fraternize.
confrontación f. Confrontation, confronting. || Comparison, collation (de textos, etc.).
confrontar v. tr. To confront (dos personas). || To face, to confront (afrentar). || To compare, to collate (comparar).
— V. intr. *Confrontar con*, to be next to, to border on.
— V. pr. To confront, to face. || *Nos confrontamos con una gran dificultad*, we are faced with a great difficulty.
confundible adj. Confusing, easily confused. || *Fácilmente confundible*, easily confused.
confundido, da adj. Embarrassed (confuso). || Mistaken, confused (equivocado).
confundir v. tr. To blur (borrar los perfiles). || To confuse, to mistake (equivocarse): *confundir una calle con otra*, to confuse one street with another, to mistake a street for another. || To confuse, to confound (no distinguir). || To confuse: *me confundió con sus teorías*, he confused me with his theories. || To mix up, to jumble, to confound (mezclar). || To confound, to crush, to floor (dejar sin argumentos). || To humble, to humiliate (humillar). || To embarrass, to confuse, to confound (avergonzar). || To disconcert, to confuse, to perplex, to bewilder (turbar). || *Hemos confundido la carretera*, we took the wrong road.
— V. pr. To be embarrassed (avergonzarse). || To be perplexed *o* disconcerted *o* bewildered (turbarse). || To be mistaken, to make a mistake (equivocarse): *me he confundido*, I have made a mistake. || To be blurred (ponerse borroso). || To disappear: *se confundió con la muchedumbre*, he disappeared into the crowd. || To blend: *su ropa se confundía con los árboles*, his clothes blended with the trees. || To mingle (mezclarse): *los actores se confundían con el público*, the actors mingled with the audience. || To get mixed up: *los papeles se han confundido*, the papers have got mixed up. || *Confundirse de número*, to dial the wrong number (teléfono).
confusión f. Confusion, chaos, disorder (desorden): *en esta casa reina la mayor confusión*, this house is in great confusion. || Embarrassment, shame (vergüenza). || Confusion, perplexity, bewilderment (turbación). || Mistake (equivocación). || JUR. *Confusión de penas*, concurrency of sentences.
confusionismo m. Confusion.
confuso, sa adj. Mixed up, jumbled up (mezclado). || Indistinct (ruido). || Obscure (discurso, estilo, etc.). || Blurred (recuerdo). || Confused: *ideas confusas*, confused ideas. || Embarrassed, confused (avergonzado). || Perplexed, confused, disconcerted, bewildered (turbado). || Blurred (imagen).
confutar v. tr. To refute, to confute (impugnar).
congelable adj. Congealable.
congelación f. Freezing, congelation. || Deep freezing (a temperatura muy baja). || COM. Freeze (en el sector económico): *congelación de salarios*, wage freeze. || MED. Frostbite.
congelado, da adj. Frozen. || MED. Frostbitten.
congelador m. Freezer.
congelamiento m. V. CONGELACIÓN.

congelar v. tr. To freeze: *carne congelada*, frozen meat. || To deep freeze (a temperatura muy baja). || To congeal (la sangre). || COM. To freeze: *créditos, fondos congelados*, frozen credits, funds. || MED. To affect with frostbite.
— V. pr. To freeze (agua, etc.). || To congeal (aceite, grasas, sangre, etc.). || MED. To become frostbitten.
congénere adj. Congenerous (músculo). || Congeneric, of the same species (planta). || Cognate (palabra).
— M. y f. pl. Sort, kind: *el ladrón y sus congéneres*, the thief and his kind.
congeniar v. intr. To get on: *congeniar con*, to get on with.
congénitamente adv. Fundamentally.
congénito, ta adj. Congenital: *defecto congénito*, congenital defect. || FIG. Deep-seated, innate: *una mala fe congénita*, innate dishonesty.
congestión f. MED. Congestion. || FIG. Congestion (de tráfico). || — *Congestión cerebral*, stroke, apoplexy. || *Congestión pulmonar*, pneumonia.
congestionado, da adj. Congested. || Flushed (la cara).
congestionar v. tr. To congest, to produce congestion in. || *Congestionar a uno*, to make s.o. flush, to make s.o. go red [in the face.].
— V. pr. MED. To become congested. || To turn purple *o* red in the face (una persona). || To flush, to go red (la cara). || To become congested (las calles).
congestivo, va adj. Congestive.
conglobar v. tr. To conglobate.
conglomeración f. Conglomeration.
conglomerado, da adj. Conglomerate.
— M. Conglomerate. || TECN. Cemented gravel. || FIG. Collection, conglomeration.
conglomerar v. tr. To conglomerate.
— V. pr. To conglomerate.
conglutinación f. Conglutination.
conglutinar v. tr. To conglutinate.
— V. pr. To conglutinate.
Congo n. pr. m. GEOGR. Congo.
congoja f. Anguish, distress (angustia). || Grief, sorrow, affliction (tristeza).
congojoso, sa adj. Distressed (angustiado). || Sad (triste). || Distressing, afflicting (que causa congoja).
congoleño, ña o **congolés, esa** adj./s. Congolese (del Congo).
congraciar v. tr. To win over.
— V. pr. To ingratiate o.s. (*con*, with).
congratulación f. Congratulation.
congratular v. tr. To congratulate (felicitar): *congratular por un éxito*, to congratulate on a success.
— V. pr. To be pleased, to congratulate o.s.: *congratularse de* or *por algo*, to be pleased about *o* with sth., to congratulate o.s. on sth.
congratulatorio, ria adj. Congratulatory.
congregación f. REL. Congregation. || Congregation, gathering, assembly (reunión). || *La congregación de los fieles*, the Catholic Church, Christendom.
congregacionalismo m. REL. Congregationalism.
congregacionalista adj. REL. Congregationalist. || *La Iglesia Congregacionalista*, the Congregational Church.
congregado, da adj. Congregate.
congregante, ta m. y f. Member of a congregation.
congregar, congregarse v. tr. y pr. To congregate, to assemble.
congresal m. y f. *Amer.* Congress member.
congresista m. y f. Delegate, congress member.
congreso m. Congress (conferencia, etc.). || Congress (del gobierno estadounidense).
congrio m. Conger eel, conger (pez).
congrua f. Extra emolument (para funcionarios). || Adequate emolument (para eclesiásticos).
congruamente adv. Congruously, appropriately, fittingly.
congruencia f. Congruity. || Congruity, appropriateness, suitability. || MAT. Congruence.
congruente adj. Suitable, fitting, appropriate (apropiado). || Pertinent (pertinente). || MAT. Congruent.
congruentemente adv. Pertinently, appropriately, adequately.
congruo, grua adj. Congruous, fitting, suitable, appropriate. || MAT. Congruent. || *Porción congrua*, adequate emolument.
cónico, ca adj. Conical (de forma de cono). || Conic (proyección, sección).
— F. Conic section, conic.
conidio m. BOT. Conidium.
conífero, ra adj. BOT. Coniferous.
— F. Conifer.
coniforme adj. Coniform, cone-shaped.
conjetura f. Conjecture, surmise: *hacer conjeturas sobre el futuro*, to make conjectures about the future.
conjeturable adj. Supposable, presumable.
conjetural adj. Conjectural.
conjeturar v. tr. To conjecture, to surmise.
conjugable adj. GRAM. That can be conjugated, conjugable.
conjugación f. GRAM. y BIOL. Conjugation.
conjugado, da adj. Conjugated. || FIG. Combined.
conjugar v. tr. GRAM. To conjugate. || FIG. To combine.
— V. pr. GRAM. To be conjugated, to conjugate. || FIG. To fit together.
conjunción f. Conjunction.
conjuntado, da adj. Coordinated: *un equipo bien conjuntado*, a well-coordinated team.
conjuntamente adv. Jointly, together.
conjuntar v. tr. To coordinate: *conjuntar un equipo*, to coordinate a team.
conjuntiva f. ANAT. Conjunctiva.
conjuntivitis f. MED. Conjunctivitis.
conjuntivo, va adj. GRAM. MED. Conjunctive.
conjunto, ta adj. Combined, joint, conjoint: *esfuerzos conjuntos*, combined efforts. || Joint: *la base aérea conjunta de Torrejón*, the joint air force base at Torrejón.
— M. Collection: *un conjunto de casas*, a collection of houses. || Whole: *el conjunto de sus obras*, the whole of his works; *un conjunto decorativo*, a decorative whole. || Suit, outfit, ensemble (vestido). || Twinset (de jerseys). || MÚS. Ensemble: *conjunto vocal*, vocal ensemble. | Group (de música pop). || Set (de cosas diversas). || Suite (de muebles). || — *Conjunto urbanístico* or *residencial*, housing estate. || *De conjunto*, overall. || *En conjunto*, on the whole, altogether. || *En su conjunto*, as a whole. || *Formar un conjunto*, to form a whole.
conjura o **conjuración** f. Conspiracy, plot.
conjurado, da m. y f. Conspirator, plotter.
conjurador m. Exorcist.
conjurar v. intr. To plot, to conspire.
— V. tr. To exorcise (exorcizar). || To beg: *os conjuro que vengáis*, I beg you to come. || To stave off, to avert, to ward off (un peligro). || To get rid of (pensamientos).
— V. pr. To conspire, to plot: *conjurarse contra la República*, to conspire against the Republic.
conjuro m. Exorcism (exorcismo). || Plea, entreaty, supplication (ruego). || Incantation, spell (encantamiento).
conllevar v. tr. To put up with, to bear, to endure: *conllevar una enfermedad, una persona*, to put up with an illness, with s.o. || To bear (una pena). || To assist, to help (ayudar).
conmemorable adj. Memorable, noteworthy.
conmemoración f. Commemoration, remembrance. || *Conmemoración de los difuntos*, All Souls' Day.
conmemorar v. tr. To commemorate.
conmemorativo, va o **conmemoratorio, ria** adj. Commemorative. || Memorial (monumento).
conmensurabilidad f. Commensurability.
conmensurable adj. Commensurable.
conmigo pron. pers. With me: *ven conmigo*, come with me. || To me: *es muy amable conmigo*, he is very kind to me. || — *No tengo dinero conmigo*, I haven't got any money on me. || *Tendrá que habérselas conmigo*, he'll have me to deal with.
conminación f. Commination, threat.
conminador, ra adj. Threatening, menacing.
conminar v. tr. To threaten, to menace (amenazar). || To warn (avisar).
conminativo, va o **conminatorio, ria** adj. Threatening, menacing, comminatory. || Coercive (sentencia).
conmiseración f. Commiseration, pity, sympathy.
conmoción f. Shock. || Tremor, earthquake (terremoto). || FIG. Shock: *la noticia de su muerte me produjo una gran conmoción*, the news of his death was a great shock to me. | Upheaval: *una conmoción política*, a political upheaval. | Commotion, disturbance (trastorno). || MED. *Conmoción cerebral*, concussion.
conmocionar v. tr. MED. To concuss. | To shock. || FIG. To upset, to disturb, to trouble.
conmovedor, ra adj. Moving, touching, poignant: *un discurso, un espectáculo conmovedor*, a moving speech, scene.
conmover* v. tr. To move, to touch (enternecer, emocionar, impresionar, etc.): *su desgracia me conmovió mucho*, his misfortune touched me deeply. || To shake: *un terremoto conmovió la ciudad*, an earthquake shook the town. || FIG. To shake: *conmover la fe de uno*, to shake s.o.'s faith. || *Me conmovió mucho ver cómo se ocupaba de mí*, I was really touched by the way he took care of me.
— V. pr. To be touched, to be moved, to be affected: *no se conmovió*, he was not moved. || To be shaken (un edificio, etc.).
conmutabilidad f. Commutability.
conmutable adj. Commutable.
conmutación f. Commutation: *conmutación de pena*, commutation of sentence. || Pun, play on words (figura retórica).
conmutador m. ELECTR. Switch, commutator.
conmutar v. tr. JUR. To commute: *conmutar la pena de muerte por la de cadena perpetua*, to commute the death sentence to life imprisonment. || To exchange: *conmutar una cosa por otra*, to exchange one thing for another. || ELECTR. To commutate, to commute.
conmutativo, va adj. Commutative.
connatural adj. Connatural, innate, inherent, inborn.
connaturalización f. Adaptation, adjustment.
connaturalizarse v. pr. To adjust o.s., to adapt o.s. (*con*, to) [adaptarse]. || To become accustomed (*con*, to) [acostumbrarse].

connivencia f. Connivance, complicity. || *Estar en connivencia con*, to be in league *o* in collusion with.
connotación f. Connotation. || Distant relationship (connotado).
connotado m. Distant relationship.
connotar v. tr. To connote.
connubial adj. POÉT. Connubial, conjugal.
connubio m. POÉT. Matrimony, marriage.
cono m. BOT. y ANAT. Cone. || MAT. Cone: *cono circular* circular cone; *cono recto*, right cone; *cono truncado*, truncated cone. || ASTR. *Cono de sombra*, umbra.
conocedor, ra adj. Expert, skilled. || *Ser conocedor de las últimas noticias*, to be well up on the latest news.
— M. y f. Expert, connoisseur: *ser conocedor de caballos*, to be an expert on horses, to be a connoisseur of horses. || — M. Head herdsman.
conocer* v. tr. To know: *le conozco sólo de vista*, I only know him by sight. || To know: *conocer el latín*, to know Latin; *no conoce nada de pintura*, he knows nothing about painting. || To know, to recognize (distinguir): *conocer a uno por la voz*, to recognize s.o. by his voice. || To meet, to make the acquaintance of, to get to know: *le conocí en Londres el año pasado*, I met him last year in London. || To be (estar): *cuando conocí Londres por primera vez*, the first time I was in London. || To get to know: *ir a conocer un país*, to go to get to know a country. || To know (en el sentido bíblico). || *Dar algo a conocer a uno*, to make sth. known to s.o., to inform s.o. of sth., to tell s.o. sth., to let s.o. know sth. || — *Darse a conocer*, to make o.s. known. || *No conocer a uno ni por asomo*, not to know s.o. from Adam.
— V. intr. *Conocer de*, to know about (saber). || JUR. *Conocer de* or *en*, to try, to hear (una causa).
— V. pr. To know o.s.: *conócete a ti mismo*, know yourself. || To know each other (dos personas). || To meet, to get to know each other: *se conocieron en un bar*, they met in a bar. || — *Se conoce a la legua*, it stands out a mile. || *Se conoce que*, apparently: *se conoce que no puede venir*, he can't come apparently; you can tell: *se conoce que el motor está estropeado por el ruido que hace*, you can tell that there is sth. wrong with the motor by the noise it makes.
conocible adj. Knowable.
conocidamente adv. Evidently, clearly, obviously.
conocido, da adj. Known. || Well-known: *un abogado conocido*, a well-known lawyer. || *El tema no me es conocido*, I am not familiar with the subject.
— M. y f. Acquaintance: *un conocido mío*, an acquaintance of mine.
conocimiento m. Knowledge: *tener un conocimiento profundo del inglés*, to have a thorough knowledge of English. || Consciousness (sentido): *perder, recobrar el conocimiento*, to lose, to regain consciousness. || Good sense, sensibleness (sensatez). || Acquaintance (conocido). || COM. Bill of lading (de la carga de un buque). | Proof of identity (del portador de una letra de cambio, etc.). || — Pl. Knowledge, *sing.* || — *Con conocimiento de causa*, with full knowledge of the facts. || *Dar conocimiento de algo a uno*, to make sth. known to s.o., to inform s.o. of sth. || *Habla con conocimiento de causa*, he knows perfectly what he is talking about. || *Ha perdido el conocimiento*, he is unconscious, he has lost consciousness. || *Lo hizo con conocimiento de causa*, he was perfectly aware of what he was doing. || *Poner algo en conocimiento de uno*, to make sth. known to s.o., to inform s.o. of sth. || *Venir en conocimiento* or *llegar al conocimiento de uno*, to come to s.o.'s knowledge *o* notice *o* attention.
conoidal adj. MAT. Conoid.
conoide m. MAT. Conoid.
conoideo, a adj. MAT. Conoid.
conopeo m. Canopy (del sagrario).
conopial adj. m. *Arco conopial*, ogee arch.
conque conj. FAM. So: *tú eres un ignorante, conque cállate*, you don't know anything, so be quiet; *¿conque sigue convencido?*, so you're still convinced [then]?; *¿conque te mudas de casa?*, so you're moving house [then]? || So, whereupon: *conque fuimos a la cama*, so we went to bed.
conquense adj. [Of *o* from] Cuenca.
— M. y f. Inhabitant *o* native of Cuenca.
conquista f. Conquest. || FIG. *Hacer una conquista*, to make a conquest, to win s.o.'s heart (enamorar a alguien).
conquistable adj. Which can be taken.
conquistador, ra adj. Conquering. || FIG. *Tiene un aire conquistador*, he looks a real lady-killer.
— M. y f. Conqueror. || — M. Conqueror: *Guillermo el Conquistador*, William the Conqueror. || Conquistador (de América). || FIG. y FAM. Don Juan, lady-killer, Casanova.
conquistar v. tr. To conquer: *conquistar un reino*, to conquer a kingdom. || To win (un puesto, el mercado). || FIG. To win over: *por su simpatía nos ha conquistado a todos*, he won us all over by his kindness. | To win the heart of, to win (a una mujer). || *Conquistar laureles*, to win glory.
Conrado n. pr. m. Conrad.
consabido, da adj. Usual, traditional: *el consabido discurso inaugural*, the usual opening speech. || Well-known (muy conocido). || Abovementioned (anteriormente citado).
consagración f. Consecration (del pan y del vino, de un obispo). || Consecration, dedication (dedicación). || FIG. Establishment: *la consagración de una costumbre*, the establishment of a custom. || Recognition (de un escritor, artista, etc.). || *La consagración de la Primavera*, the Rite of Spring (de Stravinsky).
consagrado, da adj. Consecrated. || Dedicated, consecrated (dedicado). || Recognized (artista, escritor). || Time-honoured, stock, household (frase, etc.). || Time-honoured (costumbre).
consagrante adj. m. Consecrating.
— M. Consecrating priest, consecrator.
consagrar v. tr. REL. To consecrate (una iglesia, un obispo, el pan y el vino). || FIG. To dedicate, to devote: *consagrar su vida a*, to dedicate one's life to. | To accept, to recognize: *consagrar una nueva palabra*, to accept a new word. | To confirm as (un escritor, un artista). || *Vino de consagrar*, Communion wine.
— V. pr. To dedicate o.s., to devote o.s.: *consagrarse al estudio*, to dedicate o.s. to studying. || To establish o.s., to prove o.s. (como artista, etc.).
consanguíneo, a adj. Consanguineous. || — *Hermano consanguíneo, hermana consanguínea*, half brother, half sister. || *Matrimonio consanguíneo*, intermarriage.
— M. y f. Blood relation.
consanguinidad f. Consanguinity, blood relationship.
consciencia f. V. CONCIENCIA.
consciente adj. Conscious, aware: *consciente de sus derechos*, aware of one's rights. || Of sound mind (sano de juicio). || MED. Conscious. || Reliable, responsible (responsable).
conscientemente adv. Knowingly, consciously.
conscripción f. *Amer.* Conscription (reclutamiento).
conscripto adj. m. Conscript: *padre conscripto*, conscript father (en la antigua Roma).
— M. *Amer.* Conscript (quinto).
consecución f. Obtaining: *la consecución de un premio literario*, the obtaining of a literary prize. || Realization: *la consecución de un deseo*, the realization of a wish. || Success (de un proyecto). || Attainment (de un objetivo). || Consecution (encadenamiento). || *De difícil consecución*, hard to obtain, difficult to obtain.
consecuencia f. Consequence. || Result, outcome (resultado). || Consistency (firmeza). || — *A* or *como consecuencia de*, as a result of, as a consequence of. || *Atenerse a* or *aceptar las consecuencias*, to suffer the consequences. || *En consecuencia*, consequently, therefore. || *Por consecuencia*, consequently, therefore. || *Sacar en consecuencia*, to conclude, to come to the conclusion. || *Ser de consecuencia*, to be of importance *o* of consequence. || *Sufrir las consecuencias*, to suffer the consequences. || *Tener* or *traer buenas consecuencias*, to do good, to be beneficial. || *Tener* or *traer malas consecuencias*, to have unfortunate consequences, to do harm. || *Traer como consecuencia*, to result in.
consecuente adj. Consistent. || FIL. Consequent.
— M. Consequent.
consecuentemente adv. Consistently. || Consequently, therefore (por consiguiente).
consecutivo, va adj. Consecutive.
conseguimiento m. V. CONSECUCIÓN.
conseguir* v. tr. To obtain, to come by: *consiguió un permiso*, he obtained a licence. || To get, to get hold of: *conseguir billetes para el partido de fútbol*, to get hold of tickets for the football match. || To obtain, to find, to get: *le consiguió una buena colocación*, he found a good job for him. || To win (una victoria, fama). || To manage: *conseguí ver al ministro*, I managed to see the minister. || To attain, to reach, to achieve (un objetivo). || — *Conseguir la mayoría*, to gain *o* to secure *o* to win a majority (en una votación). || *Dar por conseguido*, to take for granted. || *Una cosa muy conseguida*, a very successful thing.
conseja f. Legend, tale, fable.
consejero, ra m. y f. Adviser, counsellor (persona que aconseja). || Adviser, consultant: *consejero técnico*, technical adviser. || Member (de un consejo de administración, etc.). || Councillor (miembro de un consejo): *consejero en Corte*, Court councillor. || — *Consejero delegado*, managing director. || FIG. y FAM. *Ser buen consejero*, to give sound advice.
consejo m. Advice, counsel: *me pidió consejo*, he asked me for advice, he sought my advice; *tomar consejo de uno*, to take s.o.'s advice. || Piece of advice: *me dio un consejo*, he gave me a piece of advice. || Hint, tip: *le di un consejo muy útil para preparar un buen té*, I gave her a very useful hint for making a good cup of tea. || Council: *Consejo de Estado*, Council of State. || — Pl. Advice, *sing.*: *hay que seguir los consejos del médico*, you must follow the doctor's advice. || — *Celebrar consejo*, to hold council. || *Consejo de administración*, board of directors (cuerpo), board meeting, meeting of the board of directors (reunión). || *Consejo de Ciento*, [formerly] the town council of Barcelona. || *Consejo de disciplina*, disciplinary council. || JUR. *Consejo de familia*, board of guardians. || *Consejo de guerra*, court-martial. || *Consejo de la Inquisición*, the Inquisition. || *Consejo de ministros*, council of ministers, cabinet (cuerpo), cabinet meeting (reunión).
— OBSERV. V. CONCEJO.

consenso m. Consent (consentimiento): *de mutuo consenso*, by common consent. || Consensus (opinión general).
consensual adj. JUR. Consensual (contrato).
consentido, da adj. Spoilt, spoiled, pampered (mimado): *niño consentido*, spoilt child. || Easy going, indulgent (demasiado tolerante). || Complaisant (marido).
consentidor, ra adj. Tolerant, acquiescent (tolerante). || Complaisant (marido). || Indulgent (madre).
consentimiento m. Consent.
consentir* v. intr. To consent: *consentir en algo*, to consent to sth.; *consentir en hacer algo*, to consent to do sth.
— V. tr. To allow, to tolerate (tolerar): *no consiento que le ridiculicen*, I cannot tolerate their ridiculing him *o* his being ridiculed, I won't allow them to ridicule him. || To let, to allow: *no tienes por qué consentirle que traiga a todos sus amigos a tu casa*, there's no reason why you should let him bring all his friends to your house. || To spoil, to pamper (mimar). || To stand, to bear (soportar): *el estante no consiente más peso*, the shelf won't stand any more weight.
— V. pr. To break, to give way.
conserje m. Porter (en una empresa, un ministerio). || Hall porter (de un hotel).
conserjería f. Porter's lodge. || Reception desk (de un hotel).
conserva f. Preserve, preserves, *pl.*: *conserva de fresas*, strawberry preserve. || Preserving (acción). || — Pl. Tinned *o* canned food, *sing.* || — *Carne en conserva*, canned *o* pickled meat. || MAR. *Navegar en conserva*, to sail in convoy.
conservación f. Preservation (de alimentos, etc.). || Conservation (del calor, de la energía). || Upkeep, maintenance (de un edificio). || *Instinto de conservación*, instinct of self-preservation.
conservador, ra adj. Conservative: *partido conservador*, conservative party.
— M. y f. Conservative (en política). || Curator (de museo).
conservaduría f. Curatorship (cargo). || Curator's office (oficina).
conservadurismo m. Conservatism.
conservar v. tr. To keep (un secreto, sus amigos, etc.). || To preserve (la salud, un edificio, etc.). || To preserve: *el frío conserva los alimentos*, cold preserves food. || To keep in, to retain: *la lana conserva el calor*, wool keeps in the warmth. || To tin, to can (en lata), to bottle (en bocal): *conservar los tomates*, to tin tomatoes. || To retain, to have: *conserva un buen recuerdo de su viaje*, he retains a pleasant memory of his journey. || — *Bien conservado*, well-preserved. || *Conserva la costumbre de levantarse muy temprano*, he still gets up very early. || *Conserva una cicatriz de la guerra*, he still has a scar from the war. || *Conserve su derecha*, keep to the right. || *El ejercicio conserva la salud*, exercise keeps one fit.
— V. pr. To keep: *conservarse con* or *en salud*, to keep fit. || To save *o* to conserve one's strength: *me conservo para mañana*, I am conserving my strength for tomorrow. || To remain (ruinas, etc.). || To keep (alimentos).
conservatismo m. *Amer.* Conservatism.
conservativo, va adj. Preservative, preserving (que sirve para conservar).
conservatorio, ria adj. Conservatory.
— M. Conservatory, conservatoire, academy, school (de música, etc.). || *Amer.* Greenhouse (invernadero).
conservería f. Canning industry, tinned-food industry (industria). || Cannery (fábrica).
conservero, ra adj. Canning, tinned-food: *industria conservera*, canning industry, tinned-food industry.
— M. y f. Tinned-food manufacturer, canner (fabricante).
considerable adj. Considerable.
consideración f. Consideration, regard, esteem: *un hombre que merece nuestra mayor consideración*, a man worthy of our highest consideration. || Attention: *un asunto digno de la mayor consideración*, a matter that deserves the greatest attention. || Reason, consideration, motive (motivo). || Consideration, respect: *tratarle a uno sin consideración*, to treat s.o. without consideration. || Consideration, deliberation (deliberación). || — *De consideración*, considerable, great: *daños de consideración*, considerable damage; serious: *quemaduras de consideración*, serious burns. || *Amer. De mi consideración, de nuestra consideración*, Dear Sir, Dear Sirs [beginning of a letter]. || *En consideración a*, considering, in consideration of. || *Falta de consideración*, lack of consideration. || *Por consideración a*, out of consideration for, out of respect for, out of regard for: *no le echan por consideración a su padre*, they do not sack him out of consideration for his father. || *Ser de consideración*, to be worthy of consideration. || *Sin consideración a*, irrespective of, regardless of. || *Tener consideraciones con*, to be considerate *o* thoughtful towards. || *Tomar* or *tener en consideración*, to take into consideration, to take into account. || *Tratar una cosa con consideración*, to treat sth. with care.
considerado, da adj. Respected (respetado). || Considerate, thoughtful (atento). || Considered: *los puntos considerados*, the items considered. || *Bien considerado*, all things considered.
considerando m. Whereas (de una resolución).
considerar v. tr. To consider, to ponder, to weigh up: *considerar un asunto en* or *bajo todos sus aspectos*, to consider every aspect of a matter. || To give consideration: *le pido que considere mi propósito con la debida atención*, I ask you to give my proposal all due consideration. || To think about, to consider: *estoy considerando las ventajas y desventajas de su oferta*, I am thinking about the advantages and disadvantages of your offer. || To bear in mind, to remember: *tienes que considerar que aún es un niño*, you have to bear in mind that he is still a child. || To consider, to think: *no le considero capaz de tal acción*, I do not consider him capable *o* think he is capable of doing such a thing. || To consider, to esteem, to regard, to respect: *se le considera mucho en los círculos literarios*, he is highly considered in literary circles. || — *Considerando que*, bearing in mind that, considering that. || *Considerar a alguien con desprecio*, to look down on s.o. || *Considerar a alguien responsable*, to hold s.o. responsible.
— V. pr. To consider o.s. (uno mismo). || To be considered: *se considera grosero*, it is considered rude.
consigna f. Orders, *pl.*, instructions, *pl.* || Watchword, slogan (slogan). || Left-luggage office [U.S., checkroom] (en las estaciones). || *Violar la consigna*, to disobey orders.
consignación f. Allocation: *consignación de créditos*, allocation of credits. || COM. Consignment (de mercancías). || Deposit (de dinero). || Noting down, recording (citación). || — *Caja de depósitos y consignaciones*, Deposit and Consignment Office. || *Mercancías en consignación*, goods on consignment.
consignador m. COM. Consignor, consigner.
consignar v. tr. To allocate, to assign, to earmark: *consignar créditos*, to allocate credits. || To consign (mercancías). || To deposit (dinero). || To send (enviar). || To note down, to record (citar). || To write in (escribir).
consignatario m. COM. Consignee. || JUR. Depositary, trustee. || MAR. *Consignatario de buques*, ship broker, shipping agent.
consigo pron. pers. With him, with her: *se lo llevó consigo*, he took it with him. || With you [only used with *usted* and *ustedes*]: *¿ha traído usted dinero consigo?*, have you brought any money with you? || With them: *se llevaron a sus hijos consigo*, they took their children with them. || — *Consigo mismo*, with himself, with herself, with o.s.: *está rabioso consigo mismo*, he is furious with himself; with yourself, with yourselves [only used with *usted* and *ustedes*]: *tienen que entrar en cuentas consigo mismos*, you have to reckon with yourselves; with themselves: *están muy contentos consigo mismos*, they are very pleased with themselves. || FAM. *No tenerlas todas consigo*, not to rate one's chances, to have one's doubts (no estar muy seguro de algo), to have the wind up (tener miedo). || FIG. *Traer consigo*, to entail, to involve, to bring about: *esta medida traerá consigo numerosas dificultades*, this measure will entail many difficulties.
consiguiente adj. Resulting, arising: *los gastos consiguientes a mi viaje*, the expenses resulting from my trip. || Consequent: *mi viaje y los gastos consiguientes*, my trip and its consequent expenses. || *Por consiguiente*, consequently, therefore.
consiguientemente adv. Consequently, accordingly, therefore.
consistencia f. Consistency, consistence. || — *Sin consistencia*, insubstantial: *argumento sin consistencia*, insubstantial argument; without body, thin: *una salsa sin consistencia*, a sauce without body, a thin sauce. || *Tomar consistencia*, to materialize, to take form (una idea), to thicken (crema, mayonesa).
consistente adj. Firm, solid (firme). || Thick (salsa, crema, etc.). || Sound, solid (argumento). || Consisting: *una cena consistente en platos exóticos*, a dinner consisting of exotic dishes.
consistir v. intr. To lie in: *la felicidad consiste en la virtud*, happiness lies in virtue. || To consist of, to be composed of: *su fortuna consiste en acciones*, his fortune consists of stocks. || To be up to: *en ti consiste el hacerlo*, it is up to you to do it. || *El truco consiste en hacerlo rápido*, the trick is to do it quickly.
consistorial adj. REL. Consistorial. || *Casa consistorial*, town hall.
consistorio m. Consistory (de cardenales). || Town council (concejo). || Town hall (casa consistorial).
consocio, cia m. y f. Fellow member. || COM. Copartner, joint partner.
consola f. Console table (mueble). || Console (de órgano, de ordenador).
consolable adj. Consolable.
consolación f. Consolation.
consolador, ra adj. Consoling, comforting.
— M. y f. Consoler, comforter.
consolar* v. tr. To console, to comfort: *consolar a los desgraciados*, to console the unfortunate. || To console: *consolar a uno por la pérdida de su padre*, to console s.o. for the loss of his father.
— V. pr. To console o.s., to comfort o.s. || To get over

(reponerse): *consolarse de una pérdida*, to get over a loss.
consolidación f. Bracing, strengthening, consolidation (de una construcción). || FIG. Consolidation, strengthening (fortalecimiento). || Consolidation (unificación). || Consolidation (de una deuda). || MIL. Strengthening.
consolidar v. tr. To brace, to strengthen, to consolidate: *consolidar una pared*, to brace a wall. || FIG. To consolidate, to strengthen: *consolidar los poderes presidenciales*, to consolidate presidential powers. || To consolidate (unificar): *consolidar las posesiones del rey*, to consolidate the king's possessions. || COM. To consolidate (una deuda flotante). || MIL. To strengthen, to consolidate: *consolidar el frente oriental*, to consolidate the eastern front.
— V. pr. To consolidate.
consomé m. Consommé (caldo).
consonancia f. MÚS. Consonance. || Consonance (rima). || FIG. Agreement, harmony (similitud). || *En consonancia con*, in harmony with.
consonante adj. Consonant (que consuena). || GRAM. Consonantal.
— F. Consonant (letra).
consonántico, ca adj. Consonantal.
consonantismo m. Consonantism.
consonar* v. intr. To rhyme (rimar). || MÚS. To be harmonious. || FIG. To agree, to harmonize.
consorcio m. Association (asociación). || Consortium (comercial). || Conjunction (de circunstancias). || Fellowship, harmony (unión). || *Vivir en buen consorcio*, to live *o* to get on well together.
consorte m. y f. Spouse, consort (cónyuge). || Companion (persona que comparte la existencia de otra). || — Pl. JUR. Joint litigants (que litigan juntos). | Accomplices. || *Príncipe consorte*, prince consort.
conspicuo, cua adj. Illustrious, prominent, eminent.
conspiración f. Conspiracy, plot: *conspiración contra el Estado*, conspiracy against the State.
conspirador, ra m. y f. Conspirator, plotter.
conspirar v. intr. To conspire, to plot: *conspirar contra el Estado*, to conspire against the State. || FIG. To conspire (*a*, to).
constancia f. Constancy. || Perseverance: *trabajar con constancia*, to work with perseverance. || Certainty (certeza). || Proof, evidence (prueba): *no hay constancia de ello*, there is no proof of that. || *Dejar constancia de*, to put on record (en un acta), to demonstrate, to prove (atestiguar).
constante adj. Constant (que no cambia). || Steadfast (friend, love).
— F. MAT. Constant.
constantemente adv. Constantly.
Constantino n. pr. m. Constantine.
Constantinopla n. pr. GEOGR. Constantinople.
Constanza n. pr. GEOGR. Constance.
constar v. intr. To consist, to be composed: *este informe consta de tres partes*, this report consists of three parts. || To be established *o* stated: *consta por este documento que*, it is established by this document that. || To be included, to be stated: *esto consta en el contrato*, this is stated in the contract. || To be listed: *no consta en los archivos*, it is not listed in the archives. || To appear, to figure: *palabra que no consta en un diccionario*, word which does not appear in a dictionary. || — *Hacer constar*, to point out: *el periodista hace constar el incremento de la producción*, the journalist points out the increase in production; to mention, to state, to include (en un informe). || *Hacer constar por escrito*, to register, to write down (en general), to put on record (en un acta). || *Me consta que*, I am certain *o* sure that, I feel certain *o* sure that. || *Que conste que*, let be clearly understood that. || *Y para que así conste*, and for the record.
constatación f. Verification (verificación). || Recording (consignación).
constatar v. tr. To verify (averiguar). || To note, to find (encontrar). || To record (consignar).

— OBSERV. *Constatar* and *constatación* are Gallicisms.

constelación f. ASTR. Constellation.
constelado, da adj. Star-spangled, starry (estrellado): *cielo constelado*, star-spangled sky. || FIG. Strewn, bespangled, studded (sembrado): *manto constelado de pedrerías*, mantle strewn with precious stones.
constelar v. tr. To constellate, to spangle: *las estrellas que constelan la bóveda celeste*, the stars that spangle the canopy of heaven.

— OBSERV. *Constelado* and *constelar* are Gallicisms.

consternación f. Consternation, dismay (desolación): *producir consternación*, to cause dismay.
consternar v. tr. To dismay.
— V. pr. To be dismayed: *se consternó con la muerte de*, he was dismayed by the death of.
constipación f. Cold (resfriado). || Constipation (estreñimiento).
constipado, da adj. *Estar constipado*, to have a cold.
— M. Cold (catarro): *tengo un constipado muy fuerte*, I have a bad cold.
constipar v. tr. To give a cold to.
— V. pr. To catch a cold (acatarrarse).
constitución f. Constitution (acción). || Setting up, constitution (p. us.) [establecimiento]. || ANAT. y JUR. Constitution.
constitucional adj. Constitutional: *ley constitucional*, constitutional law.
constitucionalidad f. Constitutionality.
constitucionalismo m. Constitutionalism.
constitucionalizar v. tr. To constitutionalize.
constituir* v. tr. To constitute, to form: *esta molécula está constituida por tres átomos*, this molecule is constituted by three atoms. || To constitute: *las autoridades oficialmente constituidas*, the duly constituted authorities; *la discreción constituye su encanto*, discretion constitutes her charm. || To set up, to establish, to create (crear). || To make: *Kubitschek constituyó Brasilia en capital del Brasil*, Kubitschek made Brasilia the capital of Brazil. || To be: *esto no constituye obstáculo*, this is no obstacle. || *Lo constituyen cinco partes*, it consists of *o* it is composed of *o* it is made up of five parts.
— V. pr. To constitute o.s., to set o.s. up as: *me constituyo en juez*, I constitute myself judge. || To be established (establecerse). || — JUR. *Constituirse parte civil*, to bring a civil action. || *Constituirse por* or *en fiador de*, to answer for. || *Constituirse prisionero*, to give o.s. up.
constitutivo, va adj. Constitutive (*de*, of). || Constituent, component (constituyente).
constituyente adj. Constituent: *asamblea constituyente*, constituent assembly. || Constituent, component (componente).
— M. Constituent: *el hidrógeno es un constituyente del agua*, hydrogen is one of the constituents of water.
contreñimiento m. Constraint, compulsion. || Restriction (restricción).
constreñir* v. tr. To constrain, to compel, to force (obligar): *constreñir a uno a que salga*, to constrain s.o. to leave. || MED. To constrict (apretar). || To restrict (restringir).
constricción f. Constriction.
constrictivo, va adj. Constrictive.
constrictor, ra adj. Constricting, constrictive. || ZOOL. *Boa constrictor*, boa constrictor.
— M. Constrictor (músculo).
constringente adj. Constringent.
construcción f. Construction, building: *la construcción de un puente*, the construction of a bridge. || Construction, building industry: *trabaja en la construcción*, he works in construction. || Building: *una construcción elevada*, a tall building. || GRAM. Construction. || — *Construcción de buques* or *naval*, shipbuilding. || *En* or *en vías de construcción*, under construction. || *Solar para construcción*, building site.
constructivo, va adj. Constructive: *crítica constructiva*, constructive criticism.
constructor, ra adj. Building, construction: *empresa constructora*, building firm, construction company.
— M. y f. Manufacturer (de automóviles), builder (de edificios), constructor (de maquinaria). || *Constructor de buques* or *naval*, shipbuilder.
construir* v. tr. To manufacture (automóviles), to build, to construct (edificios, barcos). || MAT. To construct. || GRAM. To construe.
consubstanciación f. Consubstantiation.
consubstancial adj. Consubstantial.
consubstancialidad f. Consubstantiality.
consuegro, gra m. y f. Father-in-law or mother-in-law of one's child.
consuelo m. Solace, consolation, comfort: *la lectura es su único consuelo*, reading is his only solace. || Relief (alivio): *su marcha ha sido un consuelo para mí*, his departure has been a relief for me.
consuetudinario, ria adj. Consuetudinary, customary (habitual). || *Derecho consuetudinario*, Common Law (en Inglaterra), Consuetudinary Law (en otros países).
cónsul m. Consul.
cónsula f. FAM. Consul (mujer cónsul).
consulado m. Consulate (oficina). || Consulship (cargo).
consular adj. Consular.
consulta f. Consultation (acción). || Opinion, advice (dictamen). || Consultation, conference (de varios médicos). || Consulting room, surgery (consultorio de un médico). || — *Consulta a domicilio*, home visit. || *Consulta previa petición de hora*, consultation by appointment. || *Horas de consulta*, consulting hours, surgery hours. || *Obra de consulta*, reference book. || *Pasar la consulta* or *tener la consulta*, to hold surgery (un médico), to have consultation (un especialista). || REL. *Sacra consulta*, judiciary court.
consultación f. Consultation (entre abogados o médicos).
consultante adj. Consulting, consultant.
consultar v. tr. e intr. To consult: *tengo que consultar con mis amigos*, I must consult with my friends. || To consult: *consultar el diccionario*, to consult the dictionary. || To look up, to check: *consultar una palabra en el diccionario*, to look up a word in the dictionary. || — *Consultar con un abogado*, to consult a lawyer, to take legal advice. || *Consultar con un médico*, to consult a doctor, to take medical advice. || FIG. *Consultarlo con la almohada*, to sleep on it.
consultivo, va adj. Advisory, consultative.
consultor, ra adj. Consultant, consulting (médico).
— M. Advisor (dignatario de la Corte de Roma): *consultor del Santo Oficio*, advisor of the Holy

CONSTRUCCIÓN, *f.* — CONSTRUCTION

I. Términos (*m.*) generales. — General terms.

construir, edificar	to build, to construct
edificio *m.*	building
rascacielos *m. inv.*	skyscraper
bloque (*m.*) de oficinas de diez pisos	ten-storey office block
bloque de viviendas	block of flats [U.S., apartment block]
casa *f.*	house
monumento *m.*	monument
palacio *m.*	palace
templo *m.*	temple
basílica *f.*	basilica
catedral *f.*	cathedral
iglesia *f.*	church
torre *f.*	tower
arquitectura *f.*	architecture
orden (*m.*) dórico	Doric order
columna *f.*	column
columnata *f.*	colonnade
arco *m.*	arch
urbanismo *m.*	town planning [U.S., city planning]
permiso (*m.*) de construir	building permission
zona (*f.*) verde	greenbelt
elevación *f.*	elevation
plano *m.*	plan
escala *f.*	scale
prefabricar	to prefabricate
excavación *f.*	excavation
cimientos *m. pl.*	foundations
echar los cimientos	to lay the foundations
hilada (*f.*) de ladrillos	course of bricks
andamio *m.*	scaffold
andamios *m. pl.*, andamiaje *m.*	scaffolding

II. Personas, *f.* — People.

promotor *m.*	promoter
arquitecto *m.*	architect
aparejador *m.*	quantity surveyor
dibujante *m.*, delineante *m.*	draftsman
ingeniero (*m.*) de caminos	civil engineer
constructor *m.*	builder
maestro (*m.*) de obras	master builder
capataz *m.*	foreman
(oficial de) albañil *m.*	[master] bricklayer
peón (*m.*) de albañil	hodman, hod carrier
yesero *m.*	plasterer
soldador *m.*	welder
carpintero *m.*	joiner
electricista *m.*	electrician
vidriero *m.*, cristalero *m.*	glazier
fontanero *m.*	plumber
ayudante (*m.*) de fontanero	plumber's mate
pintor *m.*, decorador *m.*	painter, decorator
gruísta *m.*	crane driver

III. Materiales (*m.*) de construcción. — Building materials.

arena *f.*	sand
cemento *m.*	cement
mortero *m.*, argamasa *f.*	mortar
yeso *m.*	plaster
hormigón *m.* (*Amer.*, concreto *m.*)	concrete
hormigón (*m.*) armado, pretensado	reinforced, prestressed concrete
gravilla *f.*	gravel
ladrillo *m.*	brick
pizarra *f.*	slate
mármol *m.*	marble
viga *f.*	beam (de madera), girder (metal)
hierro (*m.*) ondulado	corrugated iron
madera (*f.*) de construcción	timber
cañerías *m. pl.*	pipes
instalación (*f.*) eléctrica	wiring

IV. Herramientas, *f.* — Tools.

carretilla *f.*	wheelbarrow
cubo *m.*	bucket, pail
escalera (*f.*) de mano	ladder
pala *f.*	shovel
laya *f.*	spade
piqueta *f.*, zapapico *m.*	pickaxe, pickax
paleta *f.*, palustre *m.*	trowel
llana *f.*	float
plomada *f.*	plumb line
nivel (*m.*) de burbuja	spirit level
polea *f.*	pulley
martillo *m.*	hammer
almádana *f.*, almádena *f.*	sledgehammer
cincel *m.*	chisel
cortafrío *m.*	cold chisel
cizalla *f.*	wire cutter *o* cutters *pl.*
alicates *m. pl.*	pliers
tenazas *f. pl.*	pincers
llave *f.*	spanner [U.S., wrench]
llave (*f.*) inglesa	[monkey] wrench, adjustable spanner
destornillador *m.*	screwdriver
sierra (*f.*) circular	circular saw
cepillo *m.*	plane
mazo *m.*	mallet

V. Máquinas, *f.* — Machines.

apisonadora *f.*	steamroller
bulldozer *m.*	bulldozer
excavadora *f.*	mechanical digger, excavator
grúa *f.*	crane
generador *m.*	generator
soplete (*m.*) oxiacetilénico	oxyacetylene torch
soplete *m.*	blowtorch
perforadora eléctrica	power drill
volquete *m.*	tip lorry [U.S., dump truck]
hormigonera *f.*	cement *o* concrete mixer

VI. Casa, *f.* — House.

sótano *m.*	basement
planta *f.*	ground plan (plano), floor, storey (nivel)
planta baja	ground floor [U.S., first floor]
piso *m.*	flat [U.S., apartment] (vivienda), floor, storey (nivel)
caja (*f.*) de la escalera	stair well
caja (*f.*) *or* hueco (*m.*) del ascensor	lift shaft [U.S., elevator shaft]
escalera (*f.*) de incendios	fire escape
calefacción (*f.*) central	central heating
pozo (*m.*) de ventilación	ventilation shaft
aire acondicionado	air conditioning
con aire acondicionado	air-conditioned
ventana *f.*	window
escalera *f.*	staircase
ascensor *m.*	lift [U.S., elevator]
montacargas *m. inv.*	goods lift [U.S., freight elevator]
ático *m.*	penthouse (piso lujoso)
desván *m.*, buhardilla *f.*	attic, garret
tejado *m.*	roof
techo *m.*	ceiling
teja *f.*	tile, roof tile
azotea *f.*	flat roof, roof garden
revestimiento (*m.*) del suelo	flooring
tabla (*f.*) del suelo	floorboard
entarimado *m.*	parquet
entarimado (*m.*) en espinapez	herringbone parquet
baldosa *f.*	tile
terrazo *m.*	terrazzo
muro *m.*, pared *f.*	wall
pared (*f.*) maestra	main wall
pared (*f.*) divisoria	partition wall
enyesado *m.*	plastering
zócalo *m.*, cenefa *f.*	skirting board
enlucir	to whitewash
fachada *f.*	façade
cocina *f.*	kitchen
comedor *m.*	dining room
sala (*f.*) de estar	living room
salón *m.*	lounge
cuarto (*m.*) de baño	bathroom
retrete *m.*	toilet
chimenea *f.*	chimney (exterior), fireplace (interior)
canalón *m.*	gutter
bajada (*f.*) de aguas	drainpipe

Office. || Consultant (asesor). || *Ingeniero consultor*, engineering consultant, consulting engineer.

consultorio m. Consulting room, surgery (de un médico), surgery (de un dentista), office (de un abogado). || Outpatients' department (dispensario). || Technical advice bureau (consejos técnicos). || Information bureau (de información). || *Consultorio sentimental*, problem page *o* column, advice page *o* column (en una revista).

consumación f. Consummation, completion: *la consumación de su obra*, the consummation of his work. || Perpetration (de un crimen). || Consummation (del matrimonio). || *Hasta la consumación de los siglos*, to the end of time.

consumado, da adj. Consummated. || FIG. Consummate, perfect: *sabiduría consumada*, consummate wisdom. | Accomplished: *bailarín consumado*, accomplished dancer. || FAM. Absolute, perfect: *un bribón, un imbécil consumado*, a perfect scoundrel, an absolute fool. || *Hecho consumado*, accomplished fact.

consumar v. tr. To complete (terminar). || To carry out (hacer). || To perpetrate (un crimen). || To consummate (el matrimonio, un sacrificio). || To carry out (sentencia).

consumible adj. Consumable.

consumición f. Drink (bebida). || Consumption (acción). || *Consumición mínima*, cover charge (en un club).

consumido, da adj. FIG. Emaciated, wasting away (flaco). | Exhausted (agotado). | Consumed (atormentado): *consumido por los celos*, consumed with jealousy. | Undermined: *su salud consumida por la fiebre*, his health undermined by fever.

consumidor, ra m. y f. Consumer.

consumir v. tr. To consume, to destroy (destruir): *el fuego consumió todos los edificios*, the blaze consumed all the buildings. || To dry up, to evaporate (un líquido). || To consume, to eat (comestibles, bebidas). || To consume (gastar): *consumir gasolina*, to consume petrol. || To use (utilizar). || FIG. To take up: *esta tarea consumía todo su tiempo*, this task took up all his time. | To wear away: *las preocupaciones le consumían*, worry was wearing him away. | To wear out (agotar): *tanto viajar le consume*, all that travelling wears him out. | To undermine, to sap, to consume: *su pasión le consumía las fuerzas*, his passion undermined his strength. | To gnaw at (carcomer). | To wear down, to try (la paciencia). | To get on one's nerves (poner nervioso). || — FIG. *El tiempo lo consume todo*, time is all-consuming. | *Estar consumido por*, to be eaten up *o* consumed with (celos, envidia), to be consumed with, to be tormented with (una pasión), to be tormented by (el dolor).
— V. pr. To waste away, to pine [away]: *consumirse de pena*, to waste away with grief. || To wear o.s. out: *se consumió en esfuerzos inútiles*, he wore himself out in useless efforts. || To boil away (líquido). || To waste away: *este anciano se está consumiendo*, this old man is wasting away. || To burn itself out: *la vela se ha consumido*, the candle has burnt itself out. || — *Consumirse con la fiebre*, to waste away with fever. || *Consumirse de envidia*, to be eaten up with jealousy. || *Consumirse de fastidio*, to be bored to death. || *Consumirse de impaciencia*, to be burning with impatience.
consumo m. Consumption (de víveres, etc.). || — Pl. Toll, *sing.* || — *Bienes de consumo*, consumer goods. || *Sociedad de consumo*, consumer society.
consunción f. MED. Consumption.
consuno (de) adv. With one accord, by common consent (decidir), in concert (actuar).
consuntivo, va adj. Consuming.
contabilidad f. Bookkeeping, accounting (tiendas y firmas): *contabilidad por partida doble, simple*, double-entry bookkeeping, single-entry bookkeeping. || Accountancy (profesión): *contabilidad mecanizada*, machine accountancy. || *Contabilidad de costos*, cost accounting.
contabilizar v. tr. COM. To enter [in the books].
contable adj. Countable (calculable). || Relatable (decible).
— M. Bookkeeper (en una empresa). || Accountant (de varias empresas).
contacto m. Contact: *ciertas enfermedades se transmiten por simple contacto*, certain diseases are transmitted by simple contact. || AUT. Contact. || FIG. Contact, touch: *poner en contacto a dos personas*, to put two people in touch with each other. | Contact: *establecer contactos radiofónicos*, to establish radio contact. || — *Contacto sexual*, sexual contact, sexual intercourse. || *Entrar* or *ponerse en contacto con* or *establecer contacto con*, to get in *o* into contact with, to get in touch with, to contact. || *Lentes de contacto*, contact lenses. || *Mantenerse en contacto con*, to keep in contact with, to keep in touch with.
contadero, ra adj. Countable. || Beginning, starting (empezando). || *Dentro de un plazo de diez días contaderos desde esta fecha*, within ten days [beginning] from this date.
contado, da adj. Counted. || Told, said, related (dicho). || Scarce (escaso). || Few and far between: *son contados los que saben el griego*, people who know Greek are few and far between. || — *En contadas ocasiones*, seldom, rarely. || *Tiene contados los días* or *sus días están contados*, his days are numbered.
— M. *Amer.* Instalment [U.S., installment]: *pagar una deuda en tres contados*, to pay off a debt in three instalments. || *Al contado*, cash: *pagar al contado*, to pay cash; *pago al contado*, cash payment.
contador, ra adj. Counting (para contar).
— M. Counter, checker (que cuenta). || Bookkeeper, accountant (contable). || Meter (instrumento): *contador de agua, de gas*, water meter, gas meter. || — *Contador de aparcamiento*, parking meter. || *Contador Geiger*, Geiger counter. || — M. y f. *Amer.* Moneylender (prestamista).
contaduría f. Bookkeeping, accounting (contabilidad) || Accountant's office (oficina). || Accountancy (oficio). || Box office, booking office (teatro). || *Contaduría general*, Audit Office.
contagiar v. tr. To contaminate: *contagiar a un país*, to contaminate a country. || To infect, to give: *me ha contagiado su enfermedad*, he has infected me with his disease. || FIG. To infect, to contaminate.
— V. pr. To be communicable, to be infectious, to be contagious, to be catching: *enfermedad que no se contagia*, disease that is not communicable. || To be infected (*de*, with). || FIG. To be contagious *o* infectious *o* catching: *el bostezar se contagia fácilmente*, yawning is very contagious.
contagio m. MED. Contagion. || FIG. Contagion.
contagiosidad f. Contagiousness.
contagioso, sa adj. Contagious, infectious, communicable, catching: *una enfermedad contagiosa*, an infectious disease. || Infectious (persona). || FIG. Contagious, infectious: *risa muy contagiosa*, very infectious laugh.

contaminación f. Contamination. || Pollution (del agua, del aire, etc.). || Corruption (corrupción).
contaminador, ra adj. Contaminating. || Polluting: *agente contaminador*, polluting agent.
contaminante adj. Polluting.
— M. Polluting agent.
contaminar v. tr. To contaminate. || To pollute, to contaminate (el agua, el aire, etc.). || FIG. To contaminate, to infect. | To corrupt (corromper).
— V. pr. FIG. To be contaminated, to be corrupted, to be infected: *contaminarse con el mal ejemplo*, to be corrupted by a bad example.
contante adj. m. Cash (dinero). || *Dinero contante y sonante*, hard cash.
contar* v. tr. To count (numerar): *contar dinero*, to count money. || To count, to consider: *te cuento entre mis amigos*, I count you among my friends, I consider you one of my friends. || To talk *o* to tell about: *cuando ha bebido, siempre me cuenta su vida*, when he is drunk, he always tells me about his life. || To tell, to recount (un cuento). || To include, to count (incluir). || To take into account, to bear in mind (tener en cuenta). || — *Contar una cosa por hecha*, to consider sth. as good as done. || *Cuenta ochenta años de edad*, he is eighty years old. || *¡Cuéntamelo a mí!*, you're telling me!, you can say that again! || FAM. *¡Cuénteselo a su abuela!*, tell that to the marines! | *Me lo contó un pajarito*, a little bird told me. || *¿Qué cuentas?*, how is it going?, what's new?, how are things? (saludo) || *¿Qué cuentas de nuevo?*, what's new? || *Se dejó contar la otra versión del suceso por su amigo*, he let his friend tell him the other side of the story. || *Se pueden contar con los dedos*, you can count them on your fingers. || *Si me lo cuentan no lo creo*, I can hardly believe my own eyes. || *Sin contar*, not counting, not to mention, excluding: *éramos siete sin contar los niños*, there were seven of us, not to mention the children. || *Tener mucho que contar*, to have a lot *o* a great deal to say.
— V. intr. To count: *contar hasta diez*, to count up to ten; *contar con los dedos*, to count on one's fingers. || To count: *estos puntos no cuentan*, these points don't count. || To be fitted with, to be equipped with: *el barco cuenta con un motor eléctrico*, the boat is equipped with an electric motor. || To command, to have at one's disposal *o* at one's command: *cuento con un capital considerable*, I have a substantial capital at my disposal. || To have (tener). || — *Contar con uno*, to count on s.o., to rely on s.o. || *¡Cuenta con ello!*, you can count on it! || *Cuenta conmigo*, you can rely on me. || *Es largo de contar*, it is a long story. || *Hay que contar con que siempre pueden ocurrir desgracias*, one must always allow for mishaps. || *No contaba con encontrar tantos problemas*, he didn't bargain for so many problems. || *No contaba con que podía llover*, I did not think it was going to rain, I did not foresee the possibility of rain.
— V. pr. To be said: *se cuenta que lo mataron*, it is said that he was killed; *¡se cuentan tantas cosas de su vida!*, so many things are said about his life! || To rank (*entre*, among): *se cuenta entre los partidarios del proyecto*, he ranks among the plan's supporters. || FAM. *¿Qué te cuentas?*, how's it going?, how's things?
contemplación f. Contemplation. || Meditation (meditación). || — Pl. Indulgence, *sing.* || Ceremony, *sing.*: *no andar con contemplaciones*, not to stand on ceremony. || *Tener demasiadas contemplaciones con alguien*, to be overindulgent with s.o.
contemplador, ra adj. Contemplative.
— M. y f. Contemplator.
contemplar v. tr. To contemplate (mirar, meditar). || To be pleasant to, to be considerate towards (complacer).
— V. intr. To contemplate, to meditate.
contemplativo, va adj. Contemplative: *vida contemplativa*, contemplative life. || Obliging, indulgent (amable).
— M. y f. Contemplative person. || REL. Contemplative.
contemporaneidad f. Contemporaneity. || *Obra literaria de constante contemporaneidad*, literary work of timeless significance.
contemporáneo, a adj. Contemporary: *historia contemporánea*, contemporary history. || Contemporaneous (*de*, with).
— M. y f. Contemporary.
contemporización f. Temporization, compliance.
contemporizador, ra adj. Temporizing, compliant.
— M. y f. Temporizer.
contemporizar v. intr. To temporize, to comply: *contemporizar con alguien*, to temporize with s.o.
contención f. Contention (contienda). || JUR. Suit. || *Muro de contención*, retaining wall.
contencioso, sa adj. Contentious. || JUR. Litigious. || *Lo contencioso*, contentious business, matters in dispute.
contender* v. intr. To contend, to fight, to struggle (batallar). || FIG. To quarrel (disputar). | To compete (competir).
contendiente adj. Contending, opposing.
— M. y f. Contender, contestant (contrincante).
contenedor, ra adj. Containing.
— M. Container.

contener* v. tr. To contain: *este libro contiene muchos ejemplos*, this book contains many examples. || To hold: *le contuvo por el brazo*, he held him by the arm. || To restrain, to control: *contuvo su cólera*, he restrained his anger. || To hold (la respiración). || To hold back (lágrimas). || To suppress (risa). || To check, to curb (una tendencia). || To keep in check: *un cordón de policía contuvo a la muchedumbre*, a line of policemen kept the crowd in check. || MIL. To contain, to keep in check. || To stop: *contener la sangre de una herida*, to stop the flow of blood from a wound. || — *El decalitro contiene diez litros*, there are ten litres in one decalitre. || *No pude contener la risa*, I couldn't refrain from laughing, I couldn't help laughing.
— V. pr. To control o.s., to restrain o.s., to check o.s.
contenido, da adj. Contained, restrained, pent-up (reprimido). || Contained, suppressed: *risa contenida*, contained laughter. || Reserved (circunspecto).
— M. Contents, *pl.* || Contents, *pl.*, subject matter, content (de una carta, de un informe). || Content (proporción): *contenido en carbono*, carbon content.
contentadizo, za adj. Easily pleased *o* satisfied. || *Mal contentadizo*, hard to please.
contentamiento m. Contentment.
contentar v. tr. To content, to satisfy, to please. || COM. To endorse. || *Amer.* To reconcile. || FAM. *Ser de buen contentar*, to be easily pleased *o* satisfied. | *Ser de mal contentar*, to be hard to please *o* to satisfy.
— V. pr. To be content, to be satisfied: *conténtate con lo que tienes*, be content with what you have. || To content o.s., to make do: *se contentó con un bocadillo*, he contented himself *o* he made do with a sandwich.
contento, ta adj. Happy, pleased: *estaban muy contentos con sus regalos*, they were very happy with their presents. || Glad, pleased: *¡estoy tan contento de verte!*, I am so glad to see you! || Satisfied, pleased: *estoy muy contento con mi nuevo coche*, I am very satisfied with my new car. || Content (en estilo literario): *estoy contento con mi suerte*, I am content with my lot. || || — FIG. *Darse por contento*, to consider o.s. lucky. | *Más contento que unas Pascuas*, as happy as a lark, as pleased as Punch. | *Para dejarlo contento*, in order to please him. || *Vivir contento*, to live happily.
— M. Contentment, happiness, joy. || — FIG. *No caber en sí de contento*, to be beside o.s. with joy. || *Sentir gran contento*, to be extremely happy.
contera f. Ferrule, tip (de bastón, de paraguas), chape (de la vaina de una espada). || Cap (de lápiz). || FIG. *Por contera*, to top it all, to cap it all.
contertuliano, na o **contertulio, lia** m. y f. Participant in a social gathering. || *Uno de los contertulianos*, one of the people present.
contesta f. *Amer.* Talk (conversación). | Answer (contestación).
contestable adj. Contestable, questionable, debatable (impugnable). || Answerable (una carta).
contestación f. Answer, reply (respuesta). || Dispute, argument (debate). || JUR. Plea (del demandado). || — JUR. *Contestación a la demanda*, defendant's plea. || *Dejar sin contestación*, to leave unanswered. || *En contestación a su carta del 13 del corriente*, in reply to your letter of the 13th inst. || *Escribir cuatro letras de contestación*, to drop s.o. a line in reply. || *Mala contestación*, wrong answer (equivocada), retort (irrespetuosa).
contestador m. *Contestador automático*, answerphone [U.S., answering service].
contestar v. tr. e intr. To answer, to reply to: *contestar una carta, una pregunta*, to answer a letter, a question; *no contestó*, he did not reply *o* answer. || To answer (el teléfono). || To return (saludo). || To answer back: *¡no contestes a tu madre!*, do not answer your mother back! || To contest, to impugn (impugnar). || JUR. To corroborate. || *Amer.* To talk (conversar).
contexto m. Context.
contextura f. Contexture, texture (de tejidos, etc.). || Build, physique (constitución del cuerpo).
contienda f. War, conflict (guerra). || FIG. Dispute, altercation (disputa). | Struggle, fight, battle (lucha).
contigo pron. pers. With you: *¿tienes dinero contigo?*, have you any money with you? || With Thee (refiriéndose a Dios).
— OBSERV. *Contigo* is only used in conjunction with *tu*.
contigüidad f. Contiguity.
contiguo, gua adj. Contiguous (*a*, to), adjoining, adjacent (adyacente). || — *La casa contigua*, the house next door. || *La habitación contigua*, the adjoining room.
continencia f. Continence.
continental adj. Continental.
— M. (P. us.). Letter sent by messenger (carta).
continente adj. Containing (que contiene). || Continent (moderado).
— M. GEOGR. Continent. || Container (lo que contiene): *el continente y el contenido*, the container and the contents. || Countenance, bearing (actitud).
continentemente adv. Moderately, with moderation.
contingencia f. FIL. Contingency. || Possibility, eventuality, contingency: *prever cualquier contingencia*, to provide for all eventualities.
contingente adj. FIL. Contingent.
— M. Quota (cupo). || MIL. Contingent.
contingentemente adv. Fortuitously, by chance.
continuación f. Continuation. || Prolongation (prolongación). || — *A continuación*, next, immediately after (seguidamente), below (en un escrito). || *A continuación de*, after, following.
continuadamente adv. V. CONTINUAMENTE.
continuador, ra m. y f. Continuator.
continuamente adv. Continuously, continually, unceasingly.
continuar v. tr. To continue, to carry on, to go on, to keep on: *continuar hablando*, to continue talking. || To continue on, to go on, to proceed on: *continuó su camino*, he continued on his way. || To extend (carretera).
— V. intr. To continue, to go on: *la lucha continúa*, the struggle continues; *el coche continuó hasta Soria*, the car continued on to Soria. || To continue, to go on, to keep on, to carry on: *continuar con su trabajo*, to continue with one's work; *continuaron en sus pesquisas*, they continued with their enquiries. || — *Continuará*, to be continued (revista). || *Continuar con buena salud*, to keep in good health, to be still in good health. || TEATR. *Continuar en cartel*, to be still running. || *Continuar en el mismo sitio*, to be still in the same place. || *Continuar en vigor*, to remain in force.
continuativo, na adj. Continuative.
continuidad f. Continuity. || *Solución de continuidad*, interruption, solution of continuity (interrupción).
continuo, nua adj. Continuous, unbroken (no dividido en el espacio): *línea continua*, continuous line. || Continual, continuous, constant, never-ending: *un temor continuo*, a continual fear. || — ELECTR. *Corriente continua*, direct current. || *Movimiento continuo*, perpetual motion. || *Ondas continuas*, undampened *o* continuous waves.
— Adv. Continuously, continually. || *De continuo* or *a la continua*, continually, ceaselessly, unceasingly, constantly.
contonearse v. pr. To sway one's hips, to wiggle (una mujer). || To swagger (un hombre).
contoneo m. Swaying of the hips, wiggle (de mujer). || Swagger (de hombre).
contornar o **contornear** v. tr. To sketch *o* to trace the outline of (perfilar). || To skirt, to pass round: *contornear una montaña*, to skirt a hill. || TECN. To saw round a curved outline.
contorno m. Outline, contour (línea que perfila). || Periphery (perímetro). || Edge (de una moneda). || Girth (medida). || — Pl. Outskirts, environs, surroundings (de una ciudad). || *Contorno de cintura*, waist measurement.
contorsión f. Contortion. || *Hacer contorsiones*, to contort one's body, to writhe.
contorsionista m. y f. Contortionist.
contra prep. Against: *lucha contra el enemigo*, fight against the enemy. || For: *remedio contra la tos*, remedy for coughs. || Over: *alcanzar una victoria contra el enemigo*, to win a victory over the enemy. || Opposite, facing (enfrente): *su casa está contra la iglesia*, his house is opposite the church. || — *Contra todos*, despite everyone (a pesar de todos). || *Diez contra uno*, ten to one. || *En contra*, against: *en contra suya*, against him. || *En contra de*, against: *hablar en contra de uno*, to speak against s.o. || *En contra de lo que pensaban*, contrary to what they thought. || *Ir en contra de la opinión pública*, to run counter to *o* against public opinion. || *Opinar en contra*, to disagree. || *Salvo prueba en contra*, unless otherwise proved. || *Tengo a todo el mundo en contra*, everyone is against me. || *Viento en contra*, head wind.
— M. Cons, *pl.*: *el pro y el contra*, the pros and the cons. || MÚS. Organ pedal. || — F. FAM. Rub, catch, hitch: *ahí está la contra*, there's the rub. || Counter (esgrima). || *Amer.* Free gift [given to a customer with every purchase] (adehala). || — Pl. Lowest bass stops of an organ. || — FAM. *Hacerle* or *llevarle la contra a uno*, to contradict s.o. || *Jugar a la contra*, to play [a game] on the defensive.
contraalmirante m. Rear admiral.
contraamura f. MAR. Preventer tack.
contraatacar v. tr. MIL. To counterattack.
contraataque m. MIL. Counterattack.
contraaviso m. Countermand (contraorden).
contrabajo m. MÚS. Contrabass, double bass (instrumento). | Contrabass player, double bass player, contrabassist (músico). | Bass (voz y cantante).
contrabalancear v. tr. To counterbalance, to counterpoise. || FIG. To counterbalance, to compensate: *sus buenas cualidades contrabalancean sus defectos*, his good qualities counterbalance his defects.
contrabandear v. intr. To smuggle.
contrabandista m. y f. Contrabandist, smuggler. || *Contrabandista de armas*, gunrunner.
contrabando m. Smuggling (actividad): *vivir del contrabando*, to live by smuggling. || Contraband, smuggled goods, *pl.* (mercancías). || — *De contrabando*, contraband. || *Pasar algo de contrabando*, to smuggle sth. in.
contrabarrera f. TAUR. Second row of seats [in the bullring].
contracaja f. IMPR. Right upper case.
contracarril m. Check rail, guard rail (ferrocarriles).

contracción f. Contraction.
contracepción f. MED. Contraception.
contraceptivo, va adj./s. m. Contraceptive.
contracifra f. Key (clave de signos).
contraclave f. ARQ. Voussoir next to the keystone.
contracorriente f. Countercurrent, crosscurrent. || *Ir a contracorriente*, to go against the current.
contractabilidad f. Contractility.
contráctil adj. Contractile.
contractilidad f. Contractility.
contractivo, va adj. Contractive.
contracto, ta adj. GRAM. Contracted: *artículo contracto*, contracted article.
contractual adj. Contractual.
contrachapado o **contrachapeado** m. Plywood.
contradanza f. Contra dance, contredanse.
contradecir* v. tr. To contradict: *siempre me estás contradiciendo*, you are always contradicting me. || || FIG. To be inconsistent with, to be at variance with: *su conducta contradice sus palabras*, his behaviour is inconsistent with his words.
— V. pr. To contradict o.s., to be inconsistent.
contradeclaración f. Counterstatement.
contradenuncia f. JUR. Counterclaim.
contradicción f. Contradiction: *lleno de contradicciones*, full of contradictions. || Inconsistency, contradiction: *las contradicciones de la mente humana*, the inconsistencies of the human mind. || Contradiction, discrepancy: *existe una contradicción entre las dos versiones del asunto*, there is a discrepancy between the two accounts of the affair. || — *Espíritu de contradicción*, contrariness. || *Estar en contradicción con*, to be contradictory to *o* inconsistent with, to be at variance with. || *Pruebas que no admiten contradicción*, incontrovertible proofs.
contradictoriamente adv. Contradictorily.
contradictorio, ria adj. Contradictory, conflicting.
— F. Contradictory proposition (lógica).
contradique m. Strengthening dike.
contradriza f. MAR. Auxiliary halyard.
contraenvite m. Bluff call (cartas).
contraer* v. tr. To contract: *el frío contrae los metales*, cold contracts metals. || FIG. To contract, to catch (una enfermedad). | To acquire, to develop (un hábito). || GRAM. To contract. || — *Contraer amistad*, to make friends. || *Contraer deudas*, to incur *o* to contract debts. || *Contraer matrimonio*, to contract marriage. || *Contraer matrimonio con*, to marry. || *Contraer obligaciones*, to enter into obligations.
— V. pr. To contract: *su cara se contrajo en una mueca de dolor*, his features contracted into a pained grimace. || *Amer*. To apply o.s. (al estudio, al trabajo).
contraescarpa f. Counterscarp.
contraespionaje m. Counterespionage.
contraestay m. MAR. Preventer stay.
contrafagot m. MÚS. Double bassoon, contrabassoon.
contrafallar v. tr. To overtrump (en los naipes).
contrafallo m. Overtrumping.
contrafilo m. Sharpened back (de una espada).
contrafirma f. Countersignature.
contrafirmar v. tr. To countersign.
contrafoque m. MAR. Fore staysail.
contrafoso m. TEATR. Below-stage.
contrafuego m. Backfire.
contrafuero m. Violation of a privilege.
contrafuerte m. ARQ. Buttress. || Spur (de una montaña): || Stiffener, reinforcement (del calzado).
contrafuga f. MÚS. Counterfugue.
contragolpe m. MED. Counterstroke. || TECN. Kickback. || FIG. Counterblow.
contraguerrilla f. Anti-guerrilla warfare (sistema). || Anti-guerrilla force (tropas).
contrahacer* v. tr. To fake (en general), to counterfeit (la moneda), to forge (un documento, una escritura). || To plagiarize (plagiar). || To imitate: *contrahacer el canto del gallo*, to imitate the crowing of the cock.
contrahecho, cha adj. Fake (falso). || Counterfeit (moneda). || Forged (documento, escritura). || Hunchbacked (jorobado).
— M. y f. Hunchback.
contrahechura f. Fake (en general), counterfeit (de moneda), forgery (de documentos).
contrahílo (a) adv. Against the grain.
contrahuella f. Riser (de un escalón).
contraindicación f. MED. Contraindication.
contraindicante adj. MED. Contraindicative.
contraindicar v. tr. MED. To contraindicate: *tratamiento contraindicado*, contraindicated treatment.
contralmirante m. Rear admiral.
contralto m. y f. MÚS. Contralto.
contraluz m. Back lighting (en fotografía, pintura). || *Fotografiar a contraluz*, to take pictures against the light.
contramaestre m. Foreman. || MAR. Boatswain. || *Contramaestre de segunda*, chief petty officer.
contramandar v. tr. To countermand.
contramandato m. Countermand.
contramanifestación f. Counter-demonstration.
contramanifestar* v. intr. To counter-demonstrate.
contramano (a) adv. The wrong way [in a one-way street, etc.]: *circulación a contramano*, traffic going the wrong way.
contramarca f. COM. Countermark. || Customs duty (impuesto).
contramarcha f. MIL. Countermarch. || AUT. Reverse.
contramarchar v. intr. To countermarch.
contramina f. MIL. Countermine.
contraminar v. tr. MIL. To countermine. || FIG. To frustrate, to thwart, to countermine (frustrar).
contramuralla f. o **contramuro** m. ARQ. Countermure, outer wall.
contraofensiva f. MIL. Counteroffensive.
contraorden f. Countermand.
contrapartida f. Compensation (compensación). || *La contrapartida de la gloria*, the price of glory.
contrapaso m. Back step. || MÚS. Counterpart.
contrapelo (a) adv. The wrong way: *acariciar un perro a contrapelo*, to stroke a dog the wrong way. || Against the nap *o* pile, the wrong way (un tejido). || FIG. Counter to the general trend (contra la tendencia general), against one's will, unwillingly (contra la inclinación personal).
contrapesar v. tr. To counterbalance, to counterpoise. || FIG. To compensate, to offset, to counterbalance (equilibrar).
contrapeso m. Counterpoise, counterweight, counterbalance. || Balancing pole (balancín de equilibrista). || FIG. Counterbalance.
contraponer* v. tr. To oppose: *contraponer su voluntad a la de alguien*, to oppose one's will to s.o. else's. || To compare, to contrast (cotejar).
— V. pr. To oppose, to be opposed (oponerse). || To contrast (*a*, with) [contrastar].
contraposición f. Opposition. || Comparison (cotejo). || Conflict: *contraposición de intereses*, conflict of interests. || Contrast (contraste).
contraproducente adj. Self-defeating, counterproductive: *esta medida es contraproducente*, this measure is self-defeating. || Contraindicative: *medicina contraproducente*, contraindicative medicine.
contraproposición f. Counterproposal.
contraproyecto m. Counterplan, alternative project.
contraprueba f. Second proof (imprenta). || Counterproof (grabado).
contrapuerta f. Storm door. || Second gate, inner door (fortaleza).
contrapuesto, ta p. p. V. CONTRAPONER.
contrapunta f. TECN. Tailstock (de un torno).
contrapuntista m. MÚS. Contrapuntist.
contrapunto m. MÚS. Counterpoint. || *Amer*. Poetry contest (concurso de poesía).
contrariamente adv. Contrarily. || *Contrariamente a lo que puedas creer*, contrary to what you may think.
contrariar v. tr. To vex, to annoy, to upset: *esto me contraría mucho*, this upsets me a great deal. || To contradict (contradecir). || To hinder, to hamper, to interfere with (obstaculizar): *contrariar un proyecto*, to interfere with a plan.
contrariedad f. Annoyance, vexation (disgusto). || Disappointment (desengaño). || Obstacle: *tropezar con una contrariedad*, to encounter an obstacle. || Setback (contratiempo). || Mishap (desgracia): *he tenido una contrariedad, he pinchado al cabo de algunos kilómetros*, I had a mishap: after a few miles I got a puncture.
contrario, ria adj. Opposite, contrary (opuesto): *correr en sentido contrario*, to run in the opposite direction; *sostener opiniones contrarias*, to hold contrary opinions. || Opposed: *es contrario a todo cambio*, he is opposed to any change. || Opposing (gustos). || FIG. Harmful: *el tabaco es contrario a la salud*, tobacco is harmful to the health. || Adverse, bad: *suerte contraria*, adverse fortune. || *La parte contraria*, the opposing party (en un pleito), the opposing team (en deportes).
— M. y f. Opponent, rival (adversario). || — *Al contrario*, on the contrary. || *Al contrario de lo que pensaban*, contrary to what they thought. || *De lo contrario*, otherwise. || *Eso es lo contrario de lo que me dijo ayer*, that is the opposite of what you told me yesterday. || *Llevar la contraria a uno*, to oppose s.o., to get in s.o.'s way (poner obstáculo), to contradict s.o. (contradecir). || *Llevar siempre la contraria*, to always contradict s.o., to be contrariness personified. || *Por el contrario*, on the contrary. || *Salvo prueba en contrario*, unless otherwise proved, unless proved to the contrary, unless the contrary be proved. || *Todo lo contrario*, quite the opposite *o* the contrary.
Contrarreforma f. Counter Reformation.
contrarregistro m. Second examination.
contrarreguera f. AGR. Transversal irrigation ditch.
contrarréplica f. Rejoinder.
contrarrestar v. tr. To counteract, to check, to block, to oppose (oponerse). || To resist (resistir). || To counteract (un efecto). || To return [the ball].
contrarresto m. Counteraction, opposition (oposición). || Resistance (resistencia). || Return (en el frontón de pelota). || Player who returns the ball (jugador).
contrarrevolución f. Counterrevolution.
contrarrevolucionario, ria adj./s. Counterrevolutionary.
contrarriel m. Guard rail, check rail (contracarril).
contrarroda m. MAR. Apron.
contraseguro m. Counterinsurance.

contrasellar v. tr. To counterseal.
contrasello m. Counterseal.
contrasentido m. Mistranslation (en una traducción). || Misinterpretation (interpretación mala). || Contradiction (contradicción). || Nonsense (disparate): *lo que has dicho es un contrasentido*, what you said is nonsense.
contraseña f. Countersign (seña). || Countermark (contramarca). || MIL. Countersign, watchword, password. || Pass out (en un teatro).
contrastable adj. Contrastable. || Comparable (para pesas y medidas).
contrastante adj. Contrasting.
contrastar v. tr. To resist, to repel (oponerse a): *contrastar el ataque*, to resist the attack. || To assay and hallmark (metales preciosos). || To check, to verify (averiguar).
— V. intr. To contrast (formar contraste): *colores que contrastan*, contrasting colours; *su conducta actual contrasta con su moderación habitual*, his present behaviour contrasts with his usual restraint. || To be different: *dos personas que contrastan mucho entre sí*, two persons who are very different. || *Hacer contrastar*, to contrast.
contraste m. Resistance, opposition. || Contrast: *formar contraste*, to form a contrast. || Hallmark (en metales preciosos). || Verification, inspection (de pesos y medidas). || Assay (acción de controlar). || Assay officer (el que controla). || Inspector of weights and measures (que comprueba la exactitud de pesas y medidas). || Hallmarker (de metales preciosos). || MAR. Sudden change of the wind. || — *En contraste con*, in contrast to. || *Por contraste*, in contrast.
contrata f. [Written] contract (obligación por escrito): *firmar una contrata*, to sign a contract. || Hiring (obreros), taking-on, engagement (empleados y artistas). || Lump sum contract (contrato a tanto alzado).
contratación f. Contract (contrato). || Hiring: *la contratación del personal temporero*, the hiring of seasonal workers. || Engagement, taking-on (de un maestro, etc.). || (Ant.). Trade (comercio). || HIST. *Casa de contratación*, chamber of commerce set up by Isabella I and Ferdinand V in Seville.
contratante adj. Contracting: *las partes contratantes*, the contracting parties.
— M. (Ant.). Trader. || Contracting party.
contratar v. tr. To sign a contract for (firmar un contrato por). || To engage (empleados), to hire (obreros), to sign up (deportistas), to engage, to book (artistas): *contratado al mes*, engaged by the month.
contratiempo m. Setback, difficulty: *los contratiempos que sufrió le obligaron a vender sus propiedades*, as a result of the setbacks he suffered, he had to sell his possessions. || Mishap: *tuve un pequeño contratiempo en el camino*, I had a slight mishap on the way. || MÚS. Syncopation. || *A contratiempo*, on the offbeat (en música), untimely, inopportunely (inoportunamente).
contratista m. y f. Contractor: *contratista de obras*, building contractor; *contratista de obras públicas*, public works contractor.
contrato m. Contract: *contrato gratuito, oneroso*, gratuitous, onerous contract. || Contract (en bridge). || — *Contrato de trabajo*, work contract. || *Contrato enfitéutico*, long lease.
contratorpedero m. Destroyer.
contratuerca f. TECN. Locknut.
contravapor m. Reversed steam. || *Dar contravapor*, to reverse the steam.
contravención f. JUR. Infringement, contravention (infracción).
contraveneno m. Antidote.
contravenir* v. intr. JUR. To infringe, to contravene: *contravenir a la ley*, to infringe the law.
contraventana f. Shutter.
contraventor, ra adj. JUR. Contravening, infringing.
— M. y f. Contravener, infringer.
contraviento m. ARQ. Windbrace.
contravisita f. MED. Consultation for a second opinion.
contrayente adj. Contracting (person).
— M. y f. Contracting party [in a marriage].
contribución f. Contribution: *la contribución de la tecnología al progreso*, technology's contribution to progress. || Tax: *contribuciones directas, indirectas*, direct, indirect taxes. || — *Contribución territorial*, land tax. || *Recaudador de contribuciones*, tax collector.
contribuidor, ra adj. Contributing, contributory.
— M. y f. Contributor.
contribuir* v. tr. e intr. To pay taxes (pagar). || To contribute: *contribuyó con una suma considerable a la construcción del hospital*, he contributed a substantial amount to the construction of the hospital; *contribuir en* or *por una tercera parte*, to contribute one third.
contributivo, va adj. Contributive.
contribuyente adj. Taxpaying (que paga impuestos). || Contributing.
— M. y f. Taxpayer (de impuestos). || Contributor.
contrición f. Contrition: *acto de contrición*, act of contrition.
contrincante m. Rival, opponent, competitor.
contristar v. tr. To sadden, to grieve.
— V. pr. To become sad *o* unhappy, to be saddened *o* grieved.
contrito, ta adj. Contrite, repentant.
control m. Check, checking (comprobación). || Examination (inspección). || Control: *pasar por el control de pasaportes*, to go through passport control. || Control: *botón de control*, control knob; *punto de control*, control point; *sala de control*, control room: *control automático*, automatic control; *torre de control*, control tower; *control de la natalidad*, birth control. || Checkpoint (de un rally). || — *Bajo control*, under control. || *Control de frontera*, frontier checkpoint. || *Control de sí mismo*, self-control. || *Fuera de control*, out of control, beyond control. || *Perder el control*, to lose control.
controlable adj. Controlable (regulable). || Verifiable (comprobable).
controlador m. *Controlador del tráfico aéreo*, air traffic controller.
controlar v. tr. To control (dominar, regular). || To check, to verify (comprobar). || To inspect, to examine (examinar).
controversia f. Controversy, dispute (discusión). || *Mantener una controversia*, to dispute.
controversista m. y f. Controversialist, disputant.
controvertible adj. Controversial (que provoca controversias). || Questionable, debatable (discutible).
controvertir* v. tr. To controvert, to debate, to discuss, to dispute (discutir). || *Es un punto controvertido*, it is a controversial point.
— V. intr. To argue.
contubernio m. (P. us.) Concubinage, cohabitation. || FIG. Base alliance, collusion.
contumacia f. JUR. Contumacy. || *Juzgar en contumacia*, to sentence [a prisoner] in his absence *o* in default.
contumaz adj. Contumacious, insubordinate (insubordinado). || Stubborn, obstinate (obstinado). || JUR. Guilty of default, contumacious.
— M. y f. JUR. Defaulter.
contumelia f. Contumely, insult.
contumelioso, sa adj. Contumelious, insulting.
contundencia f. Contusive properties, *pl.* [of a blunt weapon] || FIG. Weight (de un argumento).
contundente adj. Blunt, offensive: *un arma contundente*, a blunt weapon. || Blunt (instrumento). || FIG. Impressive, forceful, convincing: *argumento contundente*, forceful argument. | Overwhelming, conclusive: *prueba contundente*, overwhelming proof.
contundir v. tr. To bruise, to contuse.
conturbación f. Restlessness, uneasiness, anxiety.
conturbado, da adj. Restless, uneasy, perturbed.
conturbador, ra adj. Perturbing, disturbing.
conturbar v. tr. To trouble, to perturb, to disturb.
— V. pr. To be perturbed *o* disturbed, to become uneasy.
contusión f. Bruise, contusion. || *Estar lleno de contusiones*, to be bruised all over.
contusionar v. tr. To bruise, to contuse.

— OBSERV. This verb is a barbarism used instead of *contundir*.

contuso, sa adj. MED. Bruised, contused.
conurbación f. Conurbation.
convalecencia f. Convalescence. || *Casa de convalecencia*, convalescent home, sanatorium.
convalecer* v. intr. To convalesce, to recover: *convalecer de una enfermedad*, to recover from an illness.
convaleciente adj./s. Convalescent.
convalidación f. Ratification. || Authentication (de un documento).
convalidar v. tr. To ratify (ratificar). || To authenticate (dar por válido).
convección f. FÍS. Convection.
convecino, na adj. Neighbouring [U.S., neighboring].
— M. y f. Neighbour [U.S., neighbor].
convencedor, ra adj. Convincing, persuasive.
convencer v. tr. To convince: *intenté convencerle para que viniera*, I tried to convince him to come. || FIG. *Ese hombre no me convence*, I don't like that man.
— V. pr. To be *o* to become convinced: *convencerse de la verdad de la afirmación*, to become convinced of the truth of the assertion.
convencido, da adj. Convinced.
convencimiento m. Convincing (acción). || Conviction (seguridad). || — *Llegar al convencimiento de*, to become convinced of. || *Tener el convencimiento de que*, to be convinced that.
convención f. Convention.
convencional adj. Conventional: *signos convencionales*, conventional signs.
convencionalismo m. Conventionality, conventionalism.
convencionalista m. y f. Conventionalist.
convenible adj. Fair (precio). || Accommodating (persona). || V. CONVENIENTE.
convenido adv. Agreed, settled.
conveniencia f. Conformity, agreement (de gustos, de opinión, etc.), compatibility (de caracteres). || Suitability (lo apropiado). || Advisability, desirability: *la conveniencia de esa gestión*, the advisability of that move. || Convenience: *a su conveniencia*, at your convenience. || Agreement (acuerdo). || Place,

position (acomodo de un criado): *buscar conveniencia*, to look for a place [as a servant]. || — Pl. A servant's perquisites. || Property, *sing.*, income, *sing.* || — *Matrimonio de conveniencia*, marriage of convenience. || *Según sus conveniencias*, at your convenience. || *Ser de la conveniencia de uno*, to be convenient to s.o., to suit s.o.
conveniente adj. Convenient. || Suitable (adecuado). || Advisable (aconsejable). || Desirable (deseable). || Proper: *una conducta conveniente*, proper behaviour; *no es la respuesta conveniente*, that is not the proper answer. || — *Creer* or *juzgar conveniente*, to think fit, to see fit. || *Es conveniente hacer esto*, it is advisable to do this. || *Ser conveniente*, to suit: *este trabajo es conveniente para mí*, this job suits me.
convenio m. Agreement: *convenios colectivos, comerciales*, collective, trade agreements; *llegar a un convenio*, to reach an agreement. || Covenant (pacto). || Convention: *convenio postal internacional*, international postal convention. || *Vinculado por un convenio*, bound by an agreement.
convenir* v. tr. e intr. To arrange, to agree (estar de acuerdo): *hemos convenido (en) irnos mañana*, we have agreed to leave tomorrow; *convino con su amigo que vendría a la fiesta*, he arranged with his friend to come to the party. || To agree, to come to an agreement: *convenir en una cuestión, en el precio*, to come to an agreement about a question, about the price. || To be worth one's while (ser rentable). || To be convenient for, to suit: *hágalo cuando le convenga*, do it whenever it is convenient for you *o* whenever it suits you. || To suit (ser adecuado): *me convendría mucho esta casa*, this house would suit me well *o* fine. || To be advisable (ser aconsejable): *no nos conviene actuar ahora*, it is not advisable for us to act now. || — *Convengo en ello*, I agree to that. || *Cuando más le convenga*, at your convenience. || *El día convenido*, [on] the appointed day. || *Eso me convendrá mucho*, that will suit me well *o* fine, that will be just right for me. || *No te conviene tomar este trabajo*, that job is not right for you, you should not take that job. || *Según le convenga*, as you see fit. || *Sueldo a convenir*, salary to be arranged *o* to be agreed. || *Te convendría más olvidarlo*, you would do better to forget it, it is best that you forget it.
— V. impers. To be fitting, to be advisable: *conviene que vayas*, it is advisable for you to go. || *Conviene olvidar que*, it is as well to forget that.
— V. pr. To agree (*en*, on).
conventícula f. o **conventículo** m. Conventicle (asamblea clandestina).
conventillo m. *Amer.* Tenement house.
convento m. Convent (de monjas o monjes), nunnery (de monjas), monastery (de monjes).
conventual adj./s.m. Conventual: *vida conventual*, conventual life.
convergencia f. Convergence, convergency.
convergente adj. Convergent, converging: *sistema de lentes convergentes*, system of converging lenses. || MIL. *Tiro convergente*, cross fire.
converger o **convergir** v. intr. To converge. || FIG. To unite (unirse).
conversación f. Conversation (plática). || Talk: *el ministro ha tenido conversaciones con el presidente*, the minister has had talks with the President. || Colloquy (coloquio). || — *Conversación a solas*, private talk *o* conversation. || *Dar conversación a uno*, to chat with s.o., to entertain s.o. || *Sacar la conversación de*, to turn the talk to, to bring the conversation round to [a subject]. || *Tener mucha conversación*, to have always plenty to say. || *Tener poca conversación*, not to be very talkative. || *Trabar conversación con*, to strike up a conversation with.
conversador, ra adj. Talkative.
— M. y f. Conversationalist, talker.
conversante m. y f. Interlocutor.
conversar v. intr. To converse, to chat, to talk: *siguió conversando con nosotros*, he went on conversing with us. || To talk: *conversar sobre varios asuntos*, to talk about several matters.
conversión f. Conversion. || MIL. Wheel. || Conversion (de monedas).
converso, sa adj. Converted.
— M. y f. Convert (persona convertida a una religión). || Lay brother, lay sister (lego, lega).
conversor m. Fís. Converter.
convertibilidad f. Convertibility.
convertible adj. Convertible, transformable. || Convertible: *moneda convertible*, convertible currency. || *Amer.* Convertible (coche).
— M. Convertible (coche).
convertidor m. TECN. Converter. || *Convertidor de frecuencia*, frequency changer.
convertir* v. tr. To turn, to change, to transform, to convert (p. us. en este sentido): *convertir el agua en vino*, to turn water into wine. || To exchange, to change, to convert: *convertir dólares en oro*, to exchange dollars for gold, to convert *o* to change dollars into gold. || To convert: *San Pablo convirtió a los gentiles al cristianismo*, St Paul converted the gentiles to Christianity.
— V. pr. To convert, to be converted (al catolicismo, etc.). || To turn, to change: *el vino se convirtió en vinagre*, the wine turned into vinegar. || FIG. To become (llegar a ser): *con el tiempo, se convirtió en mi mejor amigo*, as time went by, he became my best friend.
convexidad f. Convexity.
convexo, xa adj. Convex.
convicción f. Conviction.
convicto, ta adj. JUR. Convicted. || *Convicto y confeso*, guilty in fact and in law.
— M. Convict (en los países anglosajones).
convidada f. FAM. Round of drinks: *dar, pagar una convidada*, to stand *o* to pay for a round of drinks.
convidado, da m. y f. Dinner guest (que asiste a un convite). || Guest (invitado). || *Estar como el convidado de piedra*, to be as silent as the grave.
convidar v. tr. To invite: *me ha convidado a cenar*, he has invited me to dinner. || To offer: *convidar a uno con algo*, to offer sth. to s.o., to offer s.o. sth. || FIG. To cause: *los alimentos salados convidan a beber*, salty food causes one to drink. | To be conducive to: *un ambiente que convida al estudio*, an atmosphere which is conducive to study. || *Convidar a tomar una copa*, to treat s.o. to a drink, to offer s.o. a drink.
convincente adj. Convincing. || *Testimonios convincentes*, conclusive evidence.
convite m. Invitation (acción de invitar): *rehusar un convite*, to turn down an invitation. || Feast, party, banquet [in which one is a guest].
convivencia f. Cohabitation, living together. || Coexistence.
convivir v. intr. To live together, to cohabit. || To coexist.
convocación f. Convocation, convening, calling together, summoning (de una asamblea, etc.).
convocar v. tr. To summon, to call together, to convoke, to convene (una reunión). || To acclaim, to hail (aclamar). || To call (una huelga).
convocatoria f. V. CONVOCACIÓN. || Convocation notice for an examination (escrito con que se convoca a un examen). || Examination session: *convocatoria de septiembre*, autumn examination session [U.S., fall examination session]. || Notice (anuncio).
convocatorio, ria adj. Summoning, convoking.
convolvuláceo, a adj. BOT. Convolvulaceous.
— F. pl. BOT. Convolvulaceae.
convoy m. Convoy (de buques y escolta). || Escort (escolta). || Train (tren). || FIG. y FAM. Retinue (acompañamiento). || Cruet (vinagrera). || FAM. Cowboy.
convoyar v. tr. To convoy. || To escort (escoltar).
convulsión f. Convulsion, spasm (de los músculos). || Tremor (de la tierra). || FIG. Upheaval: *convulsiones políticas*, political upheavals.
convulsionar v. tr. To convulse. || To throw into confusion: *las actividades subversivas que han convulsionado el país*, the subversive activities that have thrown the country into confusion.
convulsionario, ria adj. Convulsionary.
convulsivo, va adj. Convulsive.
convulso, sa adj. Convulsed: *rostro convulso de terror*, face convulsed by *o* with terror.
conyugal adj. Conjugal. || Married: *vida conyugal*, married life.
cónyuge m. y f. Spouse. || — Pl. [Married] couple, *sing.*
coña f. POP. Joke: *tomar a coña*, to take it as a joke. || POP. *Estar siempre de coña*, to be always joking.
coñac m. Brandy, cognac.
coño m. POP. Cunt.
— Interj. POP. Shit! (enfado). | Christ! (asombro).
coolí m. Coolie (trabajador chino o indio).
cooperación f. Cooperation.
cooperador, ra adj. Collaborating. || Cooperative.
— M. y f. Collaborator, cooperator.
cooperante adj. Contributory. || Cooperating.
cooperar v. intr. To cooperate. || To collaborate (colaborar). || — *Cooperar al buen éxito de*, to contribute to the success of. || *Cooperar a un mismo fin*, to work for a common purpose *o* cause.
cooperativo, va adj./s.f. Cooperative.
coopositor, ra m. y f. Rival, competitor (rival). || Candidate (candidato).
cooptación f. Co-optation, co-option.
cooptar v. tr. To co-opt.
coordenada f. MAT. Coordinate.
coordinación f. Coordination.
coordinado, da adj. Coordinated.
coordinador, ra adj. Coordinating.
— M. y f. Coordinator.
coordinamiento m. Coordination.
coordinar v. tr. To coordinate: *coordinar (los) esfuerzos*, to coordinate efforts. || To classify (ordenar).
coordinativo, va adj. Coordinative, coordinating.
copa f. Glass (V. OBSERV.): *copa de champaña*, champagne glass. || (Ant). Goblet. || Glass, glassful: *tomar una copa de jerez*, to have a glass of sherry. || Drink: *convidar a una copa*, to treat to a drink. || Cup (trofeo). || Top, crown (de un árbol). || Crown (del sombrero). || Cup (del sostén). || Brazier (brasero). || Measure of volume (1/8 of a litre). || — Pl. "Copas" [a suit in Spanish playing cards]. || Bit bosses (del bocado del caballo). || — FIG. *Apurar la copa del dolor*, to drain the cup of sorrow. || *Copa del horno*, dome *o* crown of a furnace. || *Copa graduada*, measuring cup. || FAM. *Estar de copas*, to be out drinking. || *Llevar una copa*

de más, to have had one over the eight. || *Sombrero de copa* or *de copa alta*, top hat [U.S., derby hat]. || *Tomar una copa*, to have a drink.
— OBSERV. *Copa* applies only to glasses having stems.
copaiba f. Copaiba (árbol).
copal m. Copal (resina y barniz).
copante m. *Amer*. Stepping stones, *pl*.
copaquira f. *Amer*. Blue copperas.
copar v. tr. To win: *copar todos los puestos en una elección*, to win all the posts in an election. || MIL. To corner, to cut off the retreat of (un ejército). || — *Copar la banca*, to go banco (naipes). || *Copar los primeros puestos*, to win the first places, to sweep the board (en deportes). || FAM. *Estar copado*, to be up a gum tree.
coparticipación f. Joint partnership, copartnership.
copartícipe m. y f. Co-participant, fellow participant (que participa). || Copartner (que comparte).
copayero m. Copaiba (árbol).
copear v. intr. To have a few drinks. || FAM. To tipple, to booze (beber mucho).
copec m. Kopeck (moneda rusa).
copela f. Cupel (crisol).
copelación f. TECN. Cupellation.
copelar v. tr. To cupel (un metal).
Copenhague n. pr. GEOGR. Copenhagen.
copeo m. Pub crawl. || *Estar, irse de copeo*, to be, to go out drinking *o* on a pub crawl.
Copérnico n. pr. m. Copernicus.
copero m. Cupbearer: *copero mayor*, chief cupbearer. || Cabinet for glasses (armario).
copete m. Tuft [of hair]. || Topknot (peinado). || Crest (de un pájaro). || Forelock (del caballo). || Top (de un helado). || Top, summit (de una montaña). || Ornamental top (de un mueble). || Haughtiness, arrogance (altanería). || — FIG. *De alto copete*, high-class, upper-crust (fam.): *una familia de alto copete*, a high-class family. | *Estar hasta el copete*, to be completely fed up.
copetín m. Small glass. || *Amer*. Cocktail.
copetón adj. *Amer*. Crested.
— M. Crested sparrow (gorrión).
copetuda f. Lark, skylark (alondra).
copetudo, da adj. Crested (que tiene copete). || High-class, high-ranking (encumbrado). || Haughty, disdainful, arrogant (presumido).
copia f. Profusion, abundance, plethora (gran cantidad). || Duplicate, copy (de una carta). || Copy (de una obra de arte). || Copy: *cien copias de este libro*, one hundred copies of this book; *copia legalizada*, certified true copy. || Imitation, copy (imitación). || Print: *hacer una copia de una fotografía*, to make a print of a photograph; *copia por contacto*, contact print. || FIG. Image: *es una copia de su madre*, she is the image of her mother. || — *Copia al carbón*, carbon copy. || *Copia en limpio*, fair copy. || *Copia intermedia*, lavender print (cine). || *Máquina para sacar copias*, printer, copying machine. || *Sacar una copia*, to make a copy.
copiador, ra adj. Copying (máquina). || *Libro copiador*, letter book.
copiante m. y f. Copyist.
copiar v. tr. To copy: *copiar del natural*, to copy from nature. || To copy down (escribir) || To imitate (imitar). || *Copiar al pie de la letra*, to copy word for word.
copiloto m. Copilot (de avión). || Co-driver (de un coche).
copinar v. tr. To skin (un animal).
copión, ona m. y f. FAM. Copycat.
copiosidad f. Abundance.
copioso, sa adj. Copious, plentiful: *una comida copiosa*, a copious meal. || Heavy: *lluvias copiosas*, heavy rains. || Large: *copioso botín*, large booty. || *Copiosa cabellera*, long *o* flowing hair.
copista m. Copyist.
copla f. Verse, stanza (combinación métrica). || Song (canción). || Ballad (balada). || — Pl. FAM. Poetry, *sing*. || — FAM. *Andar en coplas*, to be on everyone's lips, to be the talk of the town. || *Coplas de ciego*, doggerel, *sing*. || FAM. *Echar coplas a uno*, to speak ill of s.o.
coplanarias adj. f. pl. MAT. Coplanar: *fuerzas coplanarias*, coplanar forces.
coplear v. intr. To compose *o* to write verse *o* songs. || To recite verse. || To sing.
coplero o **coplista** m. FIG. Poetaster.
copo m. Flake (de nieve, maíz, etc.). || Small bundle (cáñamo, lino, seda, etc.). || Ball (de algodón). || Flock, tuft (de lana). || Clot, curd (coágulo). || Lump (de harina). || MIL. Cornering, trapping (del enemigo). || Bottom of a seine (de una red). || *Amer*. Cloud, raincloud (nube). || MAR. *Sacar el copo*, to haul the seine.
copón m. Large cup. || REL. Ciborium, pyx.
coposesión f. Joint ownership.
coposesor, ra m. y f. Joint owner, co-owner.
coposo, sa adj. Thick-topped, bushy (árbol).
copra f. Copra [dried kernel of the coconut].
coproducción f. CINEM. Coproduction, joint production.
coprolito m. GEOL. Coprolite.
copropiedad f. Joint ownership.
copropietario, ria m. y f. Joint owner, co-owner, coproprietor.
copto, ta adj. Coptic.
— M. y f. Copt (persona). || Coptic (lengua).
copudo, da adj. Thick-topped, bushy (árbol).
cópula f. Copulation, sexual intercourse. || ANAT. Copula. || Copula (en la lógica).
copular v. tr. (Ant.). To link.
— V. pr. To copulate (aparearse).
copulativo, va adj. Copulative.
coque m. Coke (carbón).
coquear v. intr. *Amer*. To chew coca.
coquefacción f. Coking.
coqueluche m. MED. Whooping cough.
coquera f. Head of a spinning top (del trompo). || Coal scuttle (para el coque). || Hollow in a stone (en una piedra). || *Amer*. Coca store (lugar). | Coca bag (bolsa).
coquería f. TECN. Coking plant.
coquero, ra m. y f. Coca addict (aficionado a la coca).
coqueta adj. f. Coquettish, flirtatious.
— F. Coquette, flirt. || Dressing table (tocador).
coquetear v. intr. To flirt.
coqueteo m. Flirtation, flirting.
coquetería f. Coquetry, flirtatiousness (de una persona). || Flirtation (flirteo).
coqueto adj./s.m. V. COQUETÓN.
coquetón, ona adj. FAM. Cute, charming: *un apartamento coquetón*, a charming apartment. | Coquettish (persona).
— M. FAM. Philanderer. || — F. FAM. Coquette.
coquificación f. Coking.
coquificar v. tr. To coke.
coquina f. Small cockle (molusco comestible).
coquito m. Face [to amuse children]. || Ringlet, small curl (rizo). || *Amer*. Type of small coconut (coco). | Turtle dove (tórtola mejicana).
coquización f. Coking.
coquizar v. tr. To coke.
coracero m. Cuirassier (soldado). || FIG. y FAM. Bad cigar.
coracha f. Leather bag.
coraje m. Anger, rage (ira). || Courage, valour, bravery (valor). || — FAM. *Dar coraje*, to make livid (poner furioso). | *Echarle coraje a algo*, to put some life *o* spirit into sth. | *¡Qué coraje!*, how annoying!
corajina f. FAM. Fit of anger.
corajinoso, sa o **corajoso, sa** adj. Angry, irate.
corajudo, da adj. Quick-tempered (que tiene mal genio). || *Amer*. Courageous: *un hombre corajudo*, a courageous man.
coral adj. Choral: *música coral*, choral music.
— M. ZOOL. Coral. || MÚS. Chorale, choral (composición). || — Pl. Coral beads (collar). || Wattle and comb (del pavo). || FIG. *Fino como un coral* or *más fino que un coral*, as sharp as a needle.
— F. Coral snake (serpiente). || MÚS. Choir, choral society.
coralero m. Worker *o* dealer in coral.
coralífero, ra adj. Coralliferous.
coraliforme adj. Coralliform.
coralillo m. Coral snake (serpiente).
coralino, na adj. Coralline, coral-red (color). || Coralline.
— F. Coralline (alga).
corambre f. Hides, *pl*., skins, *pl*., (curtidos). || Wineskin (odre).
corán m. Koran (alcorán).
coránico, ca adj. Koranic.
coraza f. Cuirass. || MAR. Armour plate [U.S., armor plate]. || ZOOL. Shell, carapace (de la tortuga). || FIG. Armour, protection.
corazón m. Heart (víscera). || FIG. Core, heart (centro). || FIG. Heart, courage (valor). | Heart (afecto): *te amo de todo corazón*, I love you with all my heart. || Heart (naipe). || HERÁLD. Heart. || — Pl. ARQ. Hearts. || — FIG. *Blando de corazón*, soft-hearted. | *Con el corazón en un puño*, with one's heart in one's mouth. | *Con todo mi corazón*, wholeheartedly, with all my heart. || *Corazón* or *corazón mío*, my love, my heart. || *Corazón de alcachofa*, artichoke heart. || *De corazón*, in all honesty, in all sincerity. || *Dedo del corazón*, middle finger. || *Duro de corazón*, hardhearted. || *Hablar al corazón*, to appeal to s.o.'s heart. || *Hablar con el corazón en la mano*, to speak from the heart, to speak sincerely. || *Llegar al corazón de alguien*, to touch s.o.'s heart. || *Llevar el corazón en la mano*, to wear one's heart on one's sleeve. || *Me da* or *me dice el corazón que*, something tells me that, I have a hunch that. || *Morir con el corazón destrozado*, to die of a broken heart. || *No caberle a uno el corazón en el pecho*, to have a heart of gold (ser bueno), to be beside o.s. with joy (estar muy contento). || *No tener corazón*, to have no heart. || *No tener corazón para hacer algo*, not to have the heart to do sth. || *Ojos que no ven, corazón que no siente*, out of sight, out of mind. || FIG. *Partir* or *traspasar el corazón*, to break s.o.'s heart, to rend s.o.'s heart. | *Poner el corazón en algo*, to set one's heart on sth. | *Salir* or *brotar del corazón*, to come from the bottom of one's heart. | *Ser uno todo corazón*, to be the soul of kindness. | *Sin corazón*, heartless. | *Tener buen corazón*, to be kind-hearted *o* good-hearted. || FIG.

Tener el corazón que se sale del pecho, to have a heart of gold. | *Tener mal corazón*, to have no heart.
corazonada f. Hunch, feeling: *tengo la corazonada de que vendrá*, I have a hunch he will come. || Impulse.
corazoncillo m. BOT. St.-John's-wort.
corbata f. Tie [U.S., necktie] (prenda de vestir): *ponerse la corbata*, to put one's tie on. || Cravat (banda de tela). || Bow and tassels (de la bandera). || Insignia. || — *Con corbata*, with a tie on, wearing a tie. || *Corbata de lazo*, bow tie.
corbatería f. Tie shop [U.S., necktie shop].
corbatero, ra m. y f. Tie maker, tie dealer [U.S., necktie maker *o* dealer].
corbatín m. Bow tie. || Bow and tassels (de la bandera).
corbeta f. Corvette (embarcación).
Córcega n. pr. f. GEOGR. Corsica.
corcel m. Steed, charger, courser.
corcino m. Fawn (corzo pequeño).
corcova f. Hump, hunch (joroba, jiba).
corcovado, da adj. Humpbacked, hunchbacked.
— M. y f. Hunchback.
corcovar v. tr. To bend, to crook, to curve (encorvar).
corcovear v. intr. To buck, to curvet (caballería).
corcoveta m. y f. FAM. Hunchback.
corcovo m. Caper, prance (salto). || Buck, curvet (de caballo). || FIG. Crookedness.
corchea f. MÚS. Quaver.
corchera f. Line of cork floats (en una piscina). || Wine cooler (recipiente de corcho).
corchero, ra adj. Cork.
corcheta f. Eye [of a clasp].
corchete m. Clasp (para sujetar). || Hook [of the hook and eye of a clasp] (que se engancha en la hembra). || Bench hook (de carpintería). || Square bracket (signo tipográfico). || (Ant.). FIG. Constable (alguacil).
corcho m. Cork, cork bark (corteza de alcornoque). || Cork (tapón). || Float [of a fishing line] (para pescar). || Wine cooler (corchera). || Beehive (colmena). || Fire-guard made of cork. || — Pl. Floats (para nadar).
¡córcholis! interj. Heavens!, good heavens!, gosh!, goodness! [U.S., holy smoke!, gee!, geewhizz!].
corchoso, sa adj. Corklike.
corchotaponero, ra adj. Cork, cork stopper.
cordado, da adj. HERÁLD. With strings in a different coloured enamel. || ZOOL. Chordate.
— M. ZOOL. Chordate. || — F. Rope (alpinismo). || *Primero* or *cabeza* or *jefe de cordada*, leader, first on the rope, head of the rope.
cordaje m. Ropes, *pl.*, cordage (conjunto de cuerdas). || MAR. Rigging, cordage (jarcia).
cordal adj. *Muela cordal*, wisdom tooth.
— M. Tailpiece (del violín).
cordel m. Thin rope, cord, line (cuerda). || Length of five paces (distancia). || Cattle path (cañada). || *A cordel*, in a straight line.
cordelería f. Rope manufacturing (oficio). || Rope trade (comercio). || Ropes, *pl.* (cuerdas). || MAR. Rigging, cordage.
cordelero, ra m. y f. Ropemaker (fabricante). || Rope dealer (comerciante).
cordera f. Ewe lamb (ovejita). || FIG. Meek and gentle woman, lamb.
cordería f. Ropes, *pl.*, cordage.
corderillo m. Little lamb. || Dressed lambskin (piel).
cordero m. Lamb (cría de la oveja). || Lamb (carne de cordero menor), mutton (carne de cordero mayor). || Lambskin (piel). || FIG. Lamb: *manso como un cordero*, as gentle as a lamb. || — FIG. *Ahí está* or *ésa es la madre del cordero*, that is the crux of the matter (lo esencial), there's the rub (dificultad), that is the key to it (causa). || *Cordero lechal*, sucking lamb. || *Cordero pascual*, paschal lamb. || FIG. *El Divino Cordero* or *Cordero de Dios*, the Lamb of God.
cordial adj. Stimulating, tonic (reconfortante): *remedio cordial*, stimulating medicine. || FIG. Cordial, hearty, warm: *una cordial bienvenida*, a warm welcome. || — *Dedo cordial*, middle finger. || *Saludos cordiales*, cordially yours (en una carta).
— M. Tonic (bebida reconfortante). || MED Cordial.
cordialidad f. Cordiality, warmth: *la cordialidad con que recibió a sus amigos*, the cordiality with which he received his friends.
cordialmente adv. Cordially, warmly, heartily. || Sincerely (al final de una carta).
cordillera f. Mountain range, cordillera, chain. || *Amer. Por cordillera*, through a third party.
cordillerano, na adj. *Amer.* From the Andes.
córdoba m. Córdoba [the basic monetary unit of Nicaragua].
Córdoba n. pr. GEOGR. Cordova (en España), Córdoba (en Argentina).
cordobán m. Cordovan leather (cuero de Córdoba).
cordobés, esa adj./s. Cordovan (de Córdoba).
cordón m. String (cuerda pequeña). || Braid, cord, cordon (de carácter ornamental). || Ribbon (cinta). || Cord (de algunos religiosos). || ELECTR. Flex, wire. || Lace, string (para los zapatos). || ANAT. Cord (umbilical). || ARQ. Cable moulding, twisted fillet, cordon (bocel). || MAR. Strand (de cable). || FIG. Cordon: *cordón sanitario*, sanitary cordon; *cordón de policía, de tropas*, cordon of police, of troops. || *Amer.* Curb, kerb (de la acera). || — Pl. Aglets, shoulder braids (de uniforme militar).
cordonazo m. Lash with a cord (golpe).
cordoncillo m. Small cord. || Rib, cord (de tela). | Milling (de una moneda). || Piping, braid (costura). || IMPR. Ornamental border of a page.
cordura f. Good sense, wisdom, sensibleness (sensatez). || Sanity (estado de cuerdo).
corea f. MED. Chorea, St. Vitus's dance.
Corea n. pr. f. GEOGR. Korea: *Corea del Norte*, North Korea; *Corea del Sur*, South Korea.
coreano, na adj./s. Korean.
corear v. tr. MÚS. To chorus. || FIG. To chorus.
— V. intr. To sing in chorus.
coreo m. Trochee (poesía griega). || MÚS. Chorus.
coreografía f. Choreography.
coreográfico, ca adj. Choreographic.
coreógrafo m. Choreographer.
coriáceo, a adj. Coriaceous.
coriambo m. Choriamb (poesía).
coriana f. *Amer.* Blanket, rug (cobertor).
corifeo m. Coryphaeus. || FIG. Leader.
corimbo m. BOT. Corymb.
corindón m. Corundum (piedra fina).
corintio, tia adj./s. Corinthian.
Corinto n. pr. GEOGR. Corinth.
corion m. Chorion (membrana del huevo).
corista m. Chorister (en una iglesia). || — M. y f. Chorus singer (ópera). || — F. Chorus girl (revista, music-hall).
coriza f. MED. Coryza (resfriado).
cormorán m. Cormorant (cuervo marino).
cornac o **cornaca** m. Elephant keeper, mahout.
cornada f. Goring (herida). || Butt (golpe). || — *Dar cornadas* a, to gore, to butt. || FAM. *Más cornadas da el hambre*, I'd rather have this than starve, it's better than nothing.
cornadura f. Horns, *pl.* (de toro, etc.). || Antlers, *pl.* (de ciervo).
cornalina f. Cornelian, carnelian (piedra).
cornalón adj. m. Long-horned [bull].
— M. Serious goring.
cornamenta f. Horns, *pl.* (de toro). || Antlers, *pl.* (de ciervo).
cornamusa f. MÚS. Bagpipe.
córnea f. ANAT. Cornea (del ojo). || — *Córnea opaca*, sclera (esclerótica). || *Córnea transparente*, cornea. || *De la córnea*, corneal.
cornear v. tr. To butt, to gore (dar cornadas).
corneja f. ZOOL. Crow (cuervo). | Scops owl (búho).
cornejal m. Dogwood field.
cornejo m. Dogwood (arbusto).
córneo, a adj. Corneous, horny (sustancia), hornlike (hoja, etc.).
— F. pl. BOT. Cornaceae.
córner m. Corner, corner kick (saque de esquina): *tirar un córner*, to take a corner.
cornerina f. Carnelian, cornelian.
corneta f. MÚS. Bugle (militar). || Pennant (bandera de un regimiento). || Coif, cornet (de monjas). || — *A toque de corneta*, under the bugle call. || *Corneta acústica*, ear trumpet. || *Corneta de llaves*, cornet. || *Corneta de monte*, hunting horn (trompa). || *Toque de corneta*, bugle call.
— M. MIL. Bugler (persona que toca la corneta).
cornete m. Turbinate, turbinate bone (de la nariz).
cornetilla f. Hot pepper.
cornetín m. Cornet (instrumento). | Cornet player, cornetist, cornettist (instrumentista). || MIL. Bugler (soldado).
corneto, ta adj. *Amer.* Bow-legged. | With down-turned horns (res).
cornezuelo m. Ergot (del centeno). || Crescent-shaped olive (aceituna). || VET. Horn.
corniabierto, ta adj. Wide-horned.
corniapretado, da adj. Having *o* with close-set horns.
cornigacho, cha adj. With downturned horns.
cornijal m. Corner.
cornijón m. Entablature (cornisamiento). || Corner (esquina).
cornisa f. ARQ. y GEOGR. Cornice.
cornisamento o **cornisamiento** m. Entablature.
corniveleto, ta adj. Having *o* with straight and upturned horns.
corno m. BOT. Dogwood (cornejo). || MÚS. *Corno inglés*, English horn, tenor oboe, cor anglais.
Cornualles n. pr. GEOGR. Cornwall.
cornucopia f. Cornucopia, horn of plenty (emblema decorativo). || Small mirror (espejo).
cornudo, da adj. Horned (con cuernos). || FIG. y FAM. Deceived (marido).
— M. FIG. y FAM. Deceived husband, cuckold (p. us.) [marido]. || *Tras cornudo apaleado*, adding insult to injury, insult on top of injury.
cornúpeta o **cornúpeto** m. Bull (toro).
coro m. MÚS. Chorus, choir: *cantar a* or *en coro*, to sing in chorus. || Choir, chancel (en las iglesias). || TEATR. Chorus. || — *Hablar a coro*, to speak all at the same time *o* all together *o* all at once. || *Hacer coro* or *repetir a coro*, to chorus. || *Hacer coro a alguien*, to back s.o. up. || *Niño de coro*, choirboy.
corografía f. Chorography.
coroideo, a adj. Choroid, chorioid.

coroides f. inv. Anat. Choroid, chorioid (del ojo).
corojo m. Bot. Corozo, corojo.
corola f. Corolla (de flor).
corolario m. Corollary.
corona f. Crown (de rey, de gloria, de martirio, etc.): *corona de espinas*, crown of thorns. || Halo (halo). || Wreath, crown, garland (de flores, de laurel). || Coronet (de duque, de marqués, de conde, de vizconde). || Crown [of the head] (coronilla). || Tonsure (de clérigos). || Crown (moneda). || Wreath: *corona mortuoria*, funeral wreath. || Fig. Crown (reino, soberanía): *ceñirse la corona*, to take over the crown. || Zool. Coronet (del casco). || Anat. Crown (de un diente). || Astr. Corona: *corona solar*, solar corona. || Mat. Annulus, ring. || Arq. Corona, crown. || Bot. Corona. || Tecn. Washer (arandela). | Rim (de una polea, de una rueda). | Winder (del reloj). || — *Media corona*, half crown, half-a-crown (moneda). || *Muela con una corona*, crowned tooth. || *Poner una corona a una muela*, to crown a tooth. || *Rey sin corona*, uncrowned king.
coronación f. Coronation, crowning (de un soberano). || Fig. Crowning, culmination. || Arq. Crown.
coronado, da adj. Crowned.
— M. Cleric.
coronador, ra adj. Crowning.
coronamiento m. Crowning, completion (término). || Arq. Crown (adorno superior).
coronar v. tr. To crown (poner una corona). || To crown (en el juego de damas). || Fig. To crown, to top (acabar, rematar): *una estatua corona el edificio*, a statue crowns the building. | To crown (colmar).
— V. pr. To crown (el niño en el parto).
coronario, ria adj. Coronary: *la arteria coronaria*, the coronary artery.
corondel m. Impr. Reglet. | Vertical watermark lines, *pl.* (rayas).
coronel m. Mil. Colonel. || Aviac. Group captain [U.S., colonel].
coronela f. Fam. Colonel's wife.
coronilla f. Crown of the head. || Tonsure (de los sacerdotes). || Bot. Coronilla. || — Fig. y fam. *Andar* or *ir de coronilla*, to bend over backwards [to please s.o.]. | *Estar uno hasta la coronilla*, to be fed up, to be sick and tired.
corosol f. Bot. Custard apple (fruto). | Custard-apple tree (árbol).
corotos m. pl. *Amer.* Odds and ends, stuff, *sing.*, things (trastos).
coroza f. Cone-shaped hat [formerly worn by convicts].
corozo m. Bot. Corojo, corozo.
corpachón o **corpanchón** o **corpazo** m. Fam. Big body, carcass. || Carcass of a fowl (del ave).
corpiño m. Sleeveless bodice. || *Amer.* Bra, brassière (sostén).
corporación f. Corporation.
corporal adj. Corporal, bodily. || *Pena corporal*, corporal punishment.
— M. Rel. Corporal, corporale.
corporalidad f. Corporality.
corporativismo m. Corporativism.
corporativista adj./s. Corporativist.
corporativo, va adj. Corporate, corporative.
corporeidad f. Corporeity.
corpóreo, a adj. Corporeal.
corps m. *Guardia de corps*, royal guard. || *Sumiller de corps*, Lord chamberlain of the royal guard.
corpulencia f. Corpulence, stoutness.
corpulento, ta adj. Corpulent, stout.
Corpus n. pr. m. Rel. Corpus Christi.
corpuscular adj. Corpuscular.
corpúsculo m. Corpuscle, corpuscule: *los microbios son corpúsculos*, microbes are corpuscles.
corral m. Poultry yard (para aves). || Pen, run (para otros animales). || Yard, courtyard (junto a una casa). || Weir, corral (de pesca). || Playpen (para niños). || (Ant.) Playhouse (teatro). || *Amer.* Corral (redil). || — *Aves de corral*, poultry. || Fig. y fam. *Corral de vacas*, pigsty.
corralera f. Andalusian song.
corralero, ra m. y f. Poulterer (de aves de corral). || Manure dealer (de estiércol).
corraliza f. Poultry yard (para aves).
corralón m. Yard. || Inner yard (de una casa de vecindad). || *Amer.* Warehouse (almacén).
correa f. Leather strip, thong, strap (tira de cuero). || Leash, lead (del perro). || Tecn. Belt: *correa de transmisión*, drive belt, driving belt; *correa conductora* or *transportadora*, conveyor belt; *correa sin fin*, continuous *o* endless belt. || Belt (cinturón). || Watchband, watchstrap (de un reloj). || Fig. Pliability, give, elasticity (flexibilidad). || Arq. Purlin. || — *Correa de ventilación*, fan belt. || *Correa extensible*, expanding bracelet (de reloj). || Fig. y fam. *Tener correa*, to have a lot of patience.
correaje m. Leather equipment (de un soldado). || Harness (arnés).
correazo m. Blow *o* lash with a belt.
correcalles m. inv. Fam. Loiterer, loafer (holgazán).
corrección f. Correction (enmienda). || Rebuke, reprimand (represión). || Propriety, politeness, good manners, *pl.* (buenos modales). || Correctness (del lenguaje, etc.). || Impr. Proofreading. || — *Corrección de pruebas*, proofreading. || *Corrección modelo*, answers, *pl.*, solutions, *pl.*
correccional adj. Correctional: *establecimiento correccional*, correctional institution.
— M. Reformatory.
correctivo, va adj./s.m. Corrective.
correcto, ta adj. Correct: *su conducta correcta*, his correct behaviour; *la contestación correcta*, the correct answer. || Polite, courteous, well-mannered: *no estuviste muy correcto conmigo*, you were not very polite to me.
corrector, ra m. y f. Corrector. || Impr. Proofreader.
corredero, ra adj. Sliding: *puerta corredera*, sliding door.
— F. Runner, groove (de puerta o ventana). || Runner (muela superior de un molino). || Zool. Cockroach (cochinilla). || Dep. Racetrack. || Road, street (calle). || Mar. Log. || Tecn. Slide, slide valve (de la máquina de vapor). || Fig. y fam. Procuress (alcahueta). || Fam. Diarrhoea, the runs. || *De corredera*, sliding: *puerta de corredera*, sliding door.
corredizo, za adj. Running, slip: *nudo corredizo*, slip knot. || — *Puerta corrediza*, sliding door. || *Techo corredizo*, sunshine roof, sliding roof (de los coches).
corredor, ra adj. Running. || Racing, race (de carreras). || Zool. Ratite (ave que no puede volar).
— M. y f. Runner (que corre): *corredor de fondo*, long-distance runner. || — M. Com. Broker, agent. || Mil. Scout (soldado). || Corridor, gallery, hall (pasillo). || Covered way (fortificación). || — *Corredor de Bolsa* or *de cambio*, stockbroker. || *Corredor de coches*, racing driver. || *Corredor de fincas*, land agent.
— F. Ratite [pl. ratitae] (ave).
corredura f. Overflow [of liquid].
correduría f. Brokerage.
corregible adj. Corrigible, rectifiable.
corregidor m. Corregidor (antiguo magistrado español). || Mayor (antiguo alcalde).
corregidora f. Corregidor's wife.
corregir* v. tr. To correct (una falta, un defecto físico, un vicio). || To correct, to rectify (la conducta de alguien). || To correct, to adjust (un instrumento). || To admonish, to scold, (reprender): *hay que corregir a los niños para que se porten bien*, children have to be admonished so that they behave. || To chastise, to punish (castigar). || Impr. To read (pruebas). || — *Corregir a alguien*, to set s.o. straight. || Mil. *Corregir el tiro*, to correct the range.
— V. pr. To correct o.s. (de una equivocación). || To reform, to mend one's ways (manera de comportarse). || *Corregirse de una mala costumbre*, to break o.s. of a bad habit.
correinado m. Joint reign *o* rule.
correinante adj. Jointly reigning.
correlación f. Correlation.
correlacionar v. tr. To correlate.
— V. pr. To be correlated *o* correlative.
correlativo, va adj./s.m. Correlative.
correligionario, ria m. y f. Coreligionist.
correntada f. *Amer.* Strong current.
correntío adj. Flowing, running (corriente).
correntón, ona adj. Gadabout (trotacalles). || Lively, jolly, sociable (festivo).
— M. y f. Gadabout. || Joker (bromista).
correntoso, sa adj. *Amer.* Rapid, swift, having *o* with a strong current (río).
correo m. Courier (mensajero). || Post, post office, mail, mail services, *pl.* (servicio postal). || Mil. Dispatch rider. || Post office (oficina): *voy a correo*, I'm going to the post office. || Mail, post (cartas): *hoy no hay mucho correo*, there isn't much mail today. || Mail train (tren correo). || Postman [U.S., mailman] (cartero). || Jur. Accomplice (cómplice). || — Pl. Post office, *sing.*: *voy a correos*, I'm going to the post office. || — *Apartado de correos*, post-office box. || *A vuelta de correo*, by return of post. || *Casa de correos*, post office. || *Central de Correos*, central post office. || *Correo aéreo*, air mail, airmail. || *Correo certificado*, resgistered post *o* mail. || *Correo urgente*, special delivery. || *Director general de Correos*, Postmaster General. || *Echar una carta al correo*, to post a letter [U.S., to mail a letter]. || *Estafeta de Correos*, sub-post office [U.S., branch post office]. || *La Administración de Correos*, the General Post Office [U.S., the Post Office Administration]. || *Lista de Correos*, "poste restante" [U.S., General Delivery]: *escribir a lista de Correos*, to write care of "poste restante". || *Por correo*, by post. || *Sello de correo*, postage stamp.
correón m. Large leather strap.
correosidad f. Flexibility (flexibilidad). || Toughness, leatheriness (de la carne).
correoso, sa adj. Flexible. || Doughy (el pan). || Tough, leathery (la carne).
correr v. intr. To run: *correr tras uno*, to run after s.o.; *correr en busca de uno*, to run in search of s.o. || To rush, to hurry (apresurarse). || Fig. To run: *la senda corre entre las viñas*, the path runs through the vineyards; *la sangre corrió en la batalla*, blood ran in the fray. | To flow (agua, electricidad): *el río corre entre los árboles*, the river flows through the trees. | To blow (el viento). | To play (una fuente). | To fly, to pass (el tiempo): *¡cómo corre el tiempo!*, how time flies!

|| To go fast, to be fast: *este coche corre mucho*, this car goes really fast. || FIG. To be legal tender: *esta moneda corre*, this coin is legal tender; *esta moneda no corre*, this coin is not legal tender. | To be payable, to run (interés, sueldo, renta, etc.): *correrá tu sueldo desde el primero de marzo*, your wages will run from the 1st of March. | To circulate (noticia, rumor). | To slide (puerta corrediza). | To run: *los cajones corren gracias a un sistema de rodamiento de bolas*, the drawers run on ball bearings. | To run (extenderse). || — *Al correr de la pluma*, as one writes. || *A todo* or *a más correr*, at full *o* top speed. || *¡Corre!, ¡corre!*, hurry up!, hurry, hurry!, be quick! || *Corre a cargo de*, it is the responsibility of (incumbir a), it is to be paid by (estar pagado por), it is in the hands of (depender de). || *Corre a su perdición*, he is heading for his downfall. || *Corre la voz que*, rumour has it that. || *Corre el peligro de que*, there is a risk *o* a danger that. || *Correr como un gamo*, to run like a hare. || *Correr con alguna cosa*, to be in charge of sth., to be responsible for sth., to take care of sth. || *Correr con los gastos*, to foot the bill, to meet the expenses. || *Correr en una carrera*, to run in a race, to run a race. || *Correr prisa*, to be urgent. || FAM. *Correr uno que se las pela*, to run like mad. || *Dejar correr las cosas*, to let things take their course. || *De prisa y corriendo*, in a hurry, with utmost speed, at full speed. || *El mes que corre*, this month, the present month, the current month. || *En las cunetas corría agua*, the gutters were running with water. || *En lo que corre del año*, so far this year. || *En los tiempos que corren*, nowadays. || *Eso corre de* or *por mi cuenta*, V. CUENTA. || FIG. *Este hombre ha corrido mucho*, this man has been around. || *Ir corriendo*, to run along. || *Por debajo de la puerta corre mucho aire*, there is a considerable draught under the door.

— V. tr. To race, to run: *correr un caballo*, to race a horse. || To hunt, to run: *correr un jabalí*, to run a wild boar. || To fight (los toros). || To cover, to travel (una distancia). || To make run (un color). || To run: *correr la milla*, to run the mile. || To visit, to travel through (recorrer). || To move: *correr los botones de un vestido*, to move the buttons on a dress. || To overrun (en una guerra). || To pull up, to move: *correr una silla*, to move a chair. || To draw: *correr las cortinas*, to draw the curtains. || To untie, to undo (desatar). || To tip (la balanza). || To have (una aventura). || To put to confusion, to make blush (avergonzar). || — *Correr el cerrojo*, to bolt the door, to shoot the bolt. || FAM. *Correrla*, to go on a spree, to paint the town red (ir de juerga), to live it up, to have one's fling (llevar una vida airada). || *Correr las amonestaciones*, to publish the banns. || FIG. *Correr las mozas*, to be a one for the girls. || *Correr mundo*, V. MUNDO. || *Correr parejas*, to be on an equal footing. || *Correr peligro*, to be in danger. || *Correr peligro de*, to run the risk of. || *Correr un peligro*, to run *o* to take a risk. || FIG. *Correr un tupido velo sobre*, V. VELO. | *Estar corrido*, to be ashamed.

— V. pr. FIG. To move over, to move up: *córrase un poco*, move over a bit. || To slide (un objeto). || To shift (una carga). || FAM. To blush: *correrse de vergüenza*, to blush with shame. | To get embarrassed (estar confuso). || To melt (hielo). || To gutter (vela). || To run (tinta, color, maquillaje). || POP. To come, to have an orgasm (tener orgasmo). || — FAM. *Correrse una juerga*, to go on a binge. || *Se le ha corrido la media*, her stocking has a ladder, there is a run in her stocking.

correría f. Incursion, raid (en país enemigo). || Trip (viaje).

correspondencia f. Correspondence (relación). || Correspondence (por escrito). || Letters, *pl.* (cartas). || Mail, post: *llevar* or *encargarse de la correspondencia*, to be in charge of the mail. || Communication (comunicación). || Interchange, connection (en el metro). || — *Curso por correspondencia*, correspondence course. || *Mantener correspondencia con alguien*, to correspond with s.o., to be in correspondence with s.o.

corresponder v. intr. To return (un favor, el amor, etc.). || To repay (amabilidad). || To tally: *esta cifra no corresponde con esa*, this figure doesn't tally with that one. || To belong: *este mueble no corresponde a esta habitación*, this piece of furniture does not belong in this room. || To correspond, to match: *estos botones no corresponden*, these buttons don't match. || To become, to befit (ser propio de): *esa conducta no corresponde a una persona bien educada*, that behaviour does not become an educated person. || To fit: *el lugar correspondía a la descripción*, the place fitted the description; *la llave no correspondía a la cerradura*, the key didn't fit the keyhole. || To be the job *o* the responsibility of, to fall to (incumbir): *corresponde al Estado velar por la salud pública*, it falls to the State *o* it is the responsibility of the State to look after public health. || To be the job of (ser el trabajo de). || To come up to, to meet: *el éxito no correspondió a mis esperanzas*, the success did not come up to my expectations. || ARQ. To communicate. || — *Ahora te corresponde a ti saltar*, now it is your turn to jump. || *Amor no correspondido*, unrequited love. || *A quien corresponda*, to whom it may concern. || *Correspondió a sus atenciones*, she responded to his attentions. || *Le correspondió con un bolso nuevo*, he gave her a new handbag in return. || *Le contesté como correspondía*, I gave him a suitable reply. || *Les correspondió una libra a cada uno*, each one got a pound. || *Te corresponde a ti hacer ese trabajo*, that is your job, it is for you to do that job. || *Toma la parte que te corresponde y vete*, take your share and go.

— V. pr. To love one another (amarse). || To go together: *las cortinas y los muebles no se corresponden*, the curtains and the furniture don't go together. || To correspond (cartearse).

correspondiente adj. Corresponding: *ángulos correspondientes*, corresponding angles. || *Miembro correspondiente*, corresponding member (Academia).

corresponsal m. Correspondent: *corresponsal de periódico*, newspaper correspondent. || Correspondent, agent (de un banco, etc.). || News correspondent (en radio y televisión).

corresponsalía f. Post of a newspaper correspondent (cargo). || Correspondents' office (oficina). || *Jefe de corresponsalía*, chief correspondent.

corretaje m. COM. Brokerage.

corretear v. intr. To loiter about the streets (vagar). | To run about (ir de un sitio para otro).

— V. tr. *Amer.* To pursue, to chase (perseguir).

correteo m. Loitering about the streets (del vago). || Running about, games, *pl.*, frolic (de los niños). || Running about (acción de ir de un sitio para otro).

corretón, ona adj. Fidgety (inquieto). || FIG. Gadabout.

correvedile o **correveidile** m. y f. FIG. y FAM. Gossip (chismoso). | Go-between, pimp (alcahuete).

corrida f. Race, run (carrera). || Bullfight, corrida (de toros). || *Amer.* Outcrop (minas). | Spree (juerga). || — Pl. Popular Andalusian song, *sing.* (playera). || — *De corrida*, hastily (apresuradamente), fluently (hablar), at sight (traducción). || *Voy en una corrida a la tienda*, I'll run straight round to the shop.

corrido m. *Amer.* Fugitive (fugitivo). | Mexican ballad.

corrido, da adj. Good: *una libra corrida*, a good pound. || Cursive (escritura). || FIG. Abashed, ashamed, embarrassed (avergonzado). | Experienced, sharp (experimentado). || — *Balcón corrido*, continous balcony. || *Barba corrida*, bushy beard. || *De corrido*, fluently: *leer de corrido*, to read fluently; *hablar un idioma de corrido*, to speak a language fluently; at sight: *traducir de corrido*, to translate at sight. || FAM. *Mujer corrida*, woman who has been around. || *Pesar corrido*, to give good weight. || *Saber de corrido*, to have sth. at one's fingertips. || *Trece días corridos*, thirteen days running.

corriente adj. Running (que corre). || Common, usual (común). || Current, valid (dinero, etc.). || Current, present (año). || Ordinary: *un hombre corriente*, an ordinary man. || Fluent, flowing (estilo). || Average: *el inglés corriente*, the average Englishman. || — *Agua corriente*, running water. || *Corriente y moliente*, ordinary, run-of-the-mill, common or garden: *una cena corriente y moliente*, an ordinary dinner. || *Cuenta corriente*, current account [U.S., checking account]. || FIG. *Es cosa corriente* or *es moneda corriente*, it's everyday stuff, it's run-of-the-mill stuff. || *Lo corriente*, the usual thing, the normal thing. || *Salirse de lo corriente*, to be out of the ordinary, to be unusual.

— F. Current (movimiento de un fluido): *corriente marina, submarina, de aire*, ocean, underwater, air current. || Stream, current (curso): *seguir la corriente de un río*, to follow the stream, to sail with the current; *navegar contra la corriente*, to go against the stream, to sail against the current. || Stream, flow (de lava). || Draught [U.S., draft] (en una habitación). || FIG. Trend: *las últimas corrientes de la moda*, the latest fashion trends. || ELECTR. Current: *corriente alterna, continua, trifásica*, alternating, direct, three-phase current. || — FIG. *Abandonarse a la corriente*, to drift with the tide *o* the current. || *Corriente sanguínea*, bloodstream. || FIG. *Dejarse llevar de* or *por la corriente*, to follow the herd. | *La corriente de la opinión*, the current of opinion. || GEOGR. *La corriente del Golfo, la corriente de Humboldt*, the Gulf Stream, the Humboldt Current. || FIG. *Llevarle* or *seguirle la corriente a uno*, to humour s.o. [U.S., to humor s.o.]. | *Seguir la corriente*, to swim with the stream, to follow the tide *o* the crowd (ser conformista).

— M. Current month. || — *Al corriente*, aware (al tanto), up-to-date (sin atraso). || *El diez del corriente*, the tenth inst., the tenth of the current month. || *Estar al corriente de*, to be aware of, to know about. || *Mantenerse al corriente*, to keep up-to-date. || *Poner al corriente*, to inform. || *Tener al corriente*, to keep informed *o* posted.

corrientemente adv. Usually (normalmente). || Fluently (con soltura).

corrillo m. Small group *o* knot of people talking (grupo). || Round enclosure (en la Bolsa). || FIG. Clique (círculo de gente).

corrimiento m. GEOL. Landslide. || Slipping, sliding. || AGR. Failure of a vine crop (de la uva). || MED. Discharge. || FIG. Embarrassment (vergüenza). || *Amer.* Rheumatism (reumatismo).

corro m. Circle, ring (de personas). || Circle (espacio circular). || Ring-a-ring-a-roses (baile de niños). || FIG. Round enclosure (en la Bolsa). | Stocks, *pl.*: *el corro bancario*, bank stocks. || — *Bailar en corro*,

to dance in a ring. || *Entrar en el corro*, to join in the circle. || *Hacer corro*, to stand in a ring *o* circle. || *Hacer corro aparte*, to keep to o.s. || *Hacerle corro a alguien*, to stand *o* to gather round s.o.
corroboración f. Corroboration.
corroborante adj. Corroborating.
— M. (Ant.). MED. Tonic.
corroborar v. tr. (Ant.). To strengthen, to fortify (fortificar). || To corroborate: *corroborar con hechos*, to corroborate with facts.
corroborativo, va adj. Corroborating, corroborative.
corroer* v. tr. To corrode, to eat away, to wear away (carcomer). || GEOL. To erode. || FIG. To consume, to eat away. || FIG. *Las preocupaciones le corroen*, he is beset by worries.
— V. pr. To become corroded, to corrode.
corromper v. tr. To corrupt, to pervert (gente, lenguaje, costumbres, etc.). || To bribe (sobornar). || To rot (madera). || To turn bad (alimentos).
— V. pr. To become corrupted (personas, etc.). || To rot (madera). || To go bad (alimentos).
corrompido, da adj. Rotten (cosas). || Corrupt (personas).
corrosible adj. Corrodible.
corrosión f. Corrosion.
corrosivo, va adj./s.m. Corrosive.
corroyente adj. Corrosive.
corrupción f. Corruption. || Rot (de la madera). || FIG. Corruption, vitiation (de voces, de costumbres). || Bribery (soborno). || *Corrupción de menores*, corruption of minors.
corruptela f. Corruptness, corruption.
corruptibilidad f. Corruptibility. || Perishability (de productos).
corruptible adj. Corruptible (personas). || Perishable (productos).
corruptivo, va adj. Corruptive.
corrupto, ta adj. Corrupt.
— OBSERV. This adjective is the irregular past participle of *corromper*.
corruptor, ra adj. Corruptive, corrupting.
— M. y f. Corrupter.
corrusco m. FAM. Stale bread crust.
corsario, ria adj. *Buque corsario, nave corsaria*, privateer. || *Capitán corsario*, privateer.
— M. Corsair, privateer (pirata).
corsé m. Stays, *pl.*, corset. || *Corsé ortopédico*, corset.
corsetería f. Corset factory *o* corset shop.
corsetero, ra m. y f. Corsetier, corsetière.
corso, sa adj. Corsican.
— M. MAR. Privateering. || *Amer.* Parade (desfile). || — M. y f. Corsican (de Córcega).
corta f. Felling [of trees] (tala).
cortaalambres m. inv. Wire cutters, *pl.*
cortable adj. That can be cut.
cortabolsas m. inv. FAM. Pickpocket (ratero).
cortacallos m. inv. Corn cutter *o* parer.
cortacésped m. Lawnmower.
cortacigarros m. inv. Cigar cutter.
cortacircuitos m. inv. ELECTR. Circuit breaker.
cortacorriente m. ELECTR. Switch, current breaker.
cortada f. *Amer.* Cut (herida).
cortadillo m. Tumbler (vaso). || *Azúcar de cortadillo*, lump sugar.
cortado, da adj. Cut. || FIG. Embarrassed (confuso): *se quedó cortado*, he became embarrassed. | Ashamed (avergonzado). | Tongue-tied (sin poder hablar). | Sour: *leche cortada*, sour milk. | Jerky (estilo). || HERÁLD. Parted in the middle. || — *Amer. Andar cortado*, to be broke. || *Cortado a pico*, sheer, steep. || *Dejar cortado*, to cut short: *eso lo dejó cortado*, that cut him short. || FIG. *Tener el cuerpo cortado*, to feel queer.
— M. Coffee with cream, coffee with only a little milk (café con muy poca leche). || Caper, leap (paso de baile).
cortador, ra adj. Cutting (que corta).
— M. y f. Cutter (que corta). || Cutter (sastre). || — F. TECN. Cutting machine [for trimming velvet]. || *Cortadora de césped*, lawnmower.
cortadura f. Cut (incisión). || Slit (corte largo). || Gorge, pass (entre montañas). || Clipping, cutting (de un periódico). || — Pl. Clippings, cuttings (de periódico). || Trimmings (recortes). || *Hacerse una cortadura en la cara con la cuchilla de afeitar*, to cut *o* to nick one's face with the razor.
cortafierro m. *Amer.* Cold chisel.
cortafrío m. TECN. Cold chisel.
cortafuego m. AGR. Firebreak. || ARQ. Fire wall.
cortahierro m. TECN. Cold chisel.
cortalápices m. inv. Pencil sharpener.
cortalegumbres m. inv. Vegetable cutter.
cortante adj. Cutting, sharp (utensilio), cutting, keen (filo). || Bitter (frío). || Biting (viento).
— M. Chopper, cleaver.
cortapapel m. o **cortapapeles** m. inv. Paper knife. || Letter opener (para abrir cartas).
cortapicos m. inv. ZOOL. Earwig.
cortapiés m. inv. FAM. Slash at the legs.
cortapisa f. Condition, restriction: *poner cortapisas a*, to impose conditions on, to make restrictions on. || Obstacle, impediment (traba). || Trimming, border, edging (guarnición). || FIG. Charm, spice (gracia). || — *Hablar sin cortapisas*, to talk freely. || *Sin cortapisas*, with no strings attached.
cortaplumas m. inv. Penknife.
cortapuros m. inv. Cigar cutter.
cortar v. tr. To cut: *cortar un papel con las tijeras*, to cut a paper with scissors; *cortarle el pelo a alguien*, to cut s.o.'s hair; *cortar una película*, to cut a film. || To cut out, to cut: *cortar un vestido*, to cut a dress out. || To cut out (suprimir): *cortar un capítulo de un libro*, to cut out a chapter of a book. || To crack, to chap, to split: *el frío corta la piel*, the cold cracks the skin. || To cut *o* to chop down, to fell: *cortar un árbol*, to cut a tree down. || To cut off: *cortarle la cabeza a alguien*, to cut s.o.'s head off. || MAT. To cut. || To carve, to cut up (carne). || To cut off (teléfono, gas, etc.). || FIG. To cleave, to cut: *la flecha cortó el aire*, the arrow clove the air. | To cut through, to slice through: *el navío cortaba las olas*, the ship cut through the waves. | To cut (el vino, un líquido). | To cut off, to divide (separar). | To cut (los naipes). | To seal off, to bar (una calle). | To cut short (una discusión). | To cut off, to interrupt (una comunicación, la inspiración). | To settle once and for all (decidir). | To curdle (la leche, etc.). || DEP. To cut, to slice (una pelota). || — FAM. *¡Corta!* or *¡corta el rollo!*, give over!, knock it off! || FIG. *Cortar algo de raíz*, to nip sth. in the bud. | *Cortar bien una poesía*, to recite a poem well. | *Cortar el apetito*, to ruin *o* to take away one's appetite. | *Cortar el bacalao*, to be the boss. | *Cortar el camino a alguien*, to bar s.o.'s way, to cut s.o. off. | *Cortar el hilo del discurso*, to cut the thread of the argument. || *Cortar el pelo al cepillo*, to give a crew cut. || FIG. *Cortar en seco*, to cut short. || *Cortar la digestión*, to upset one's digestion. || *Cortar la fiebre*, to bring down the fever. || *Cortar la palabra*, to interrupt. || MIL. *Cortar la retirada*, to cut off the retreat. || FAM. *Cortarle a uno un vestido*, to slate s.o., to pull s.o. to pieces, to run s.o. down. | *Cortar vestidos*, to gossip, to criticize people, to tittle-tattle, to backbite.
— V. intr. To cut: *un cuchillo que corta bien*, a knife that cuts well. || To bite (el viento). || To cut off (teléfono). || To cut (en los naipes). || — *Cortar con el pasado*, to break with the past. || FIG. *Cortar por lo sano*, to take drastic action, to settle things once and for all.
— V. pr. To cut o.s.: *me corté con un cuchillo*, I cut myself with a knife. || To cut: *esta madera se corta fácilmente*, this wood cuts easily. || To be embarrassed (estar confuso). | To become tongue-tied (no poder hablar). || To curdle, to turn sour: *la leche se ha cortado*, the milk has turned sour. || To get chapped *o* cracked (la piel). || To have cut: *me corto el pelo en la peluquería*, I have my hair cut at the hairdresser's. || *Amer.* FAM. To peg out (morir). || *Cortarse las uñas, la mano*, to cut one's nails, one's hand.
cortarraíces m. inv. Root slicer.
cortatubos m. inv. Pipe cutter.
cortaúñas m. inv. Nail clipper.
cortavidrios m. inv. Glass cutter.
cortaviento m. Windbreak, windshield.
corte m. Cutting (acción de cortar). || Felling (de árboles). || Cut (de corriente eléctrica). || Cutting edge (filo): *el corte de una espada*, the cutting edge of a sword. || Cut (en un periódico, película, etc.). || Cut, haircut (del pelo): *corte con navaja*, razor cut. || Cut (de un traje). || Length (tela de vestido). || Cutting (del heno). || Cut (herida). || Cut (de la cara). || Wafer [U.S., ice-cream sandwich] (helado). || Cut (en los naipes). || Edge (de un libro). || Cross section (dibujo de una sección). || Cut (trozo de carne). || Cut (en el tenis). || FIG. Squelch (réplica). || *Amer.* Harvest, harvesting (siega). || — *Corte y confección*, dressmaking. || FIG. *Darle un corte a uno*, to cut s.o. short. || FAM. *Darse corte*, to put on airs (darse tono). | *¡Qué corte le di!*, he didn't know what to say.
— F. Court (residencia de los reyes). || Court (familia real y gentes de palacio). || Retinue, suite (acompañamiento). || *Amer.* Court: *corte suprema*, supreme court. || — *Hacer la corte a*, to court, to woo. || *La corte celestial*, the Heavenly Host.
cortedad f. Smallness (poca extensión), brevity, shortness (brevedad). || FIG. Lack, dearth [of means, education, courage]: *cortedad de ánimo*, lack of courage. | Shyness, bashfulness, timidity (timidez). || *Cortedad de genio*, faintheartedness.
cortejar v. tr. To court, to woo (galantear). || To court, to curry favour with (halagar).
cortejo m. Courting, wooing (acción de cortejar). || Train, retinue, suite, cortège (séquito). || — *Cortejo fúnebre*, funeral procession, funeral cortège. || *Cortejo nupcial*, wedding party.
Cortes n. pr. f. pl. HIST. States General of Spain. || Cortes [Spanish parliament]. || *Cortes Constituyentes*, constituent assembly.
cortés adj. Courteous, polite. || FAM. *Lo cortés no quita lo valiente*, courtesy and valour are not mutually exclusive.
cortesanesco, ca adj. Of courtiers.
cortesanía f. Courtesy, politeness.
cortesano, na adj. Of the court, court (de la corte). || Courteous, courtly, polite (cortés). || *Literatura cortesana*, court literature.

— M. y f. Courtier. || — F. Courtezan, courtesan (mujer de mala vida).

cortesía f. Courtesy, politeness: *rivalizar en cortesía*, to vie with each other *o* to outdo each other in courtesy. || Formal ending (en las cartas). || Bow, curtsy (reverencia). || Present (regalo). || COM. Grace [for redeeming a debt]. || Grace (merced). || Title (tratamiento). || IMPR. Blank. || — *Cortesía de la Dirección General de Turismo*, courtesy of the General Office of Tourism. || *Visita de cortesía*, courtesy call.

cortésmente adv. Courteously, politely.

corteza f. Bark (del árbol). || Rind, peel (de naranja o limón). || Crust (del pan). || Rind (del queso, del tocino). || ZOOL. Sandgrouse (ave). || BOT. Cortex. || FIG. Appearance, façade (apariencia). | Rudeness, uncouthness (rusticidad). || *La corteza terrestre*, the Earth's crust.

cortical adj. ANAT. Cortical.

cortijada f. Farm, farmhouse (finca). || Farm buildings, *pl.*, farmhouses, *pl.* (edificios).

cortijero, ra m. y f. Farmer (granjero). || Foreman (capataz).

cortijo m. Farm [especially in Andalusia] (finca). || Country home (casa de campo).

cortina f. Curtain: *correr la cortina*, to draw the curtain. || Canopy (dosel). || FIG. Curtain, screen (lo que oculta): *cortina de humo*, smoke curtain. || Curtain (fortificación). || Retaining wall of a pier (muelle). || MIL. *Cortina de fuego*, barrage.

cortinado o **cortinaje** m. Drapery, set of curtains, hangings, *pl.*

cortinilla f. Small lace curtain (visillo).

cortisona f. MED. Cortisone.

corto, ta adj. Short: *una falda muy corta*, a very short skirt. || Scant, lacking (escaso). || Short, brief: *un discurso corto*, a short speech. || FIG. Shy, bashful, timid (apocado). || — *A corta distancia*, a short distance away. || *A la corta o a la larga*, sooner or later. || *Caldo corto*, sauce prepared from wine and spices for cooking fish. || *Corto de alcances*, dull-witted. || *Corto de estatura*, very small. || *Corto de medios*, of scant means. || *Corto de oído*, hard of hearing. || *Corto de vista*, shortsighted. || *El abrigo se me ha quedado corto*, my coat has become too short for me, I have grown out of my coat. || *El chico va de corto*, the boy is in short trousers. || *Ni corto ni perezoso*, without thinking twice. || *Novela corta*, short story. || *Onda corta*, short wave. || *Quedarse corto*, to fall short (un tiro), to be *o* to go short (de dinero), to underestimate, to miscalculate (calcular mal), not to say all one could, to be unable to say enough (en un relato). || *Ser corto de genio*, to be fainthearted. || *Tonelada corta*, short ton. || *Y me quedo corto*, and that's only half of it (en un relato), and that's a conservative estimate *o* an underestimation (en cifras).

cortocircuito m. ELECTR. Short circuit. || *Poner en cortocircuito*, to short-circuit.

cortometraje m. CINEM. Short film.

Coruña (La) n. pr. f. GEOGR. Corunna.

coruñés, esa adj. [Of or from] Corunna.
— M. y f. Native *o* inhabitant of Corunna.

coruscante adj. (P. us) Gleaming, shining (que brilla). || Dazzling (que deslumbra).

coruscar v. intr. To shine.

corva f. ANAT. Back of the knee, ham.

corvadura f. Curvature. || ARQ. Curve, arch.

corvar v. tr. (Ant.). To bend.

corvejón m. Hock (de animal). || Spur (espolón de las aves). || ZOOL. Cormorant (cuervo marino). || FAM. *Meter la pata hasta el corvejón*, to put one's foot right in it, to make a huge blunder.

corvejos m. pl. Hock, *sing.*

corveta f. DEP. Curvet (en equitación).

corvetear v. intr. To curvet.

corvina f. Corvina (pez).

corvo, va adj. Crooked, bent, curved. || Hooked: *nariz corva*, hooked nose.

corzo, za m. y f. Roe deer (nombre genérico), roebuck (macho), doe (hembra).

cosa f. Thing: *llévese sus cosas de aquí*, take your things away from here; *toma las cosas demasiado en serio*, he takes things too seriously. || Affair, business (asunto): *meterse en cosas ajenas*, to poke one's nose into other people's business *o* affairs. || — *A cosa hecha*, on purpose (adrede). || *Alguna cosa*, something. || *¿Alguna cosa más?*, anything else? || *Así están las cosas*, that's how *o* the way things are. || *Así las cosas que un día...*, and so it was that one day... || *Cada cosa en su tiempo, y los nabos en adviento*, there is a time and place for everything. || *Como cosa tuya*, as if it were your idea. || *Como si tal cosa*, just like that. || *Cosa de*, about: *cosa de dos horas, de cinco millas*, about two hours, about five miles. || *Cosa igual*, such a thing, anything like it. || *Cosa nunca vista*, something unheard of, something surprising. || *Amer. Cosa que*, so that (no vaya a ser que): *iré a verle mañana cosa que no vaya a pensar que lo he olvidado*, I'll go and see him tomorrow so that he won't think I've forgotten him. || *Cualquier cosa*, anything. || *Decirle a uno cuatro cosas*, to tell s.o. a thing or two. || *Decir una cosa por otra*, to say one thing and mean another. || *Dejar como cosa perdida*, to give up as lost. || *Dos semanas o cosa así*, two weeks or thereabouts. || *Entre unas cosas y otras*, what with one thing and another. || *Esa es la cosa*, that's the crux of the matter. || *Es cosa de empezar a hacer las maletas*, it's time to start packing the cases. || *Es cosa de unos meses, de unos años*, it is a matter of a few months, a few years. || *Es cosa de ver, de oír*, you must see it, hear it; it's worth seeing, hearing. || *Es cosa fácil*, it's easy. || *Eso es otra cosa*, that's another matter. || *Este niño es una cosa mala*, this boy is a little horror. || *Esto es cosa mía*, this is my business. || *La cosa es que...*, the thing is that... || *Las cosas de la vida*, that's life, such is life. || FIG. *Las cosas de palacio van despacio*, it all takes time. || *Lo que son las cosas*, much to my surprise. || *Ni cosa que valga*, nothing of the kind. || *No es cosa de broma*, it's no laughing matter. || *No es cosa del otro jueves* or *del otro mundo*, it's nothing to write home about, it's nothing to make a fuss about (no es ninguna maravilla), there's nothing to it (no es difícil). || *No es cosa de que dejes de ir tú*, it doesn't mean you don't have to go. || *No es gran cosa*, it's not important. || *No hace cosa buena*, he doesn't do anything worthwhile. || *¡No hay tal cosa!*, nothing of the sort! || *No sea cosa que*, in case. || *No vale gran cosa*, it's not worth much. || *Otra cosa*, something else. || *Otra cosa sería si*, things would be different if. || *Poquita cosa*, nothing much. || *Por una cosa o por otra*, for one reason or another. || *¿Qué cosa?*, what's that?, what did you say? || *¡Qué cosa más estúpida!*, how utterly stupid! || *¡Qué cosas tienes!*, the things you come out with! || *Ser cosas de*, to be just like: *son cosas de Juan*, that's just like John. || *Ser poca cosa*, not to be much. || *Tengo otras cosas en que pensar*, I have other things on my mind. || *¡Vaya una cosa!*, marvellous!, wonderful! (irónico). || *Y, cosa rara, nadie lo había hecho*, and, oddly enough, nobody had done it.

cosaco, ca adj./s.m. Cossack. || FIG. *Beber como un cosaco*, to drink like a fish.

cosario, ria adj. Beaten (camino).
— M. Carrier (paquetes), messenger (mensajes).

coscoja f. BOT. Kermes *o* scarlet oak (encina). | Dry leaf of the kermes oak (hoja).

coscojal o **coscojar** m. Oak grove.

coscojo m. Kermes berry, kermes-oak gall.

coscorrón m. Blow on the head. || FIG. *Darse coscorrones*, to suffer hard knocks (reveses).

cosecante f. MAT. Cosecant.

cosecha f. AGR. Harvest, harvesting (recolección). | Crop, harvest (lo recogido). | Yield (producción). | Harvest, harvest time (temporada). || Vintage (del vino). || FIG. Collection, crop (acopio). || — *De su (propia) cosecha*, home-grown (comestibles), of his own invention (ideas, pensamientos). || *Es de la última cosecha*, it's the latest. || *Hacer la cosecha*, to harvest (general), to reap (cereales).

cosechador, ra m. y f. Harvester, reaper.

cosechadora f. Combine harvester, combine (máquina).

cosechar v. intr. AGR. To harvest, to reap.
— V. tr. To harvest (general), to reap, to gather (cereales). || To pick (frutas, flores). || To grow: *aquí cosechan manzanas*, they grow apples here. || FIG. To win, to reap: *cosechar laureles*, to reap *o* to win laurels *o* glory; *cosechó innumerables galardones*, he won innumerable awards.

cosechero, ra m. y f. Harvester, reaper.

cosedora f. Sewing machine (máquina de coser). || Stitching machine (máquina de coser libros).

coselete m. Corslet, corselet (armadura, tórax de los insectos).

coseno m. MAT. Cosine.

cosepapeles m. inv. Stapler.

coser v. tr. To sew [up]: *coser un vestido*, to sew a dress. || To sew on: *coser un botón*, to sew on a button. || To stitch (dar puntadas en). || MED. To stitch up. || FIG. To join, to unite (reunir). || — *Coser a balazos*, to riddle with bullets. || *Coser a puñaladas*, v. PUÑALADA. || *Coser con grapas*, to staple (papeles). || FIG. y FAM. *Eso es coser y cantar*, it's as easy as pie *o* as A.B.C., it's child's play. || *Máquina de coser*, sewing machine.
— V. intr. To sew.
— V. pr. FIG. *Coserse a uno*, to stick [close] to s.o.

cosi adv. *Amer.* That is, I mean.

cosido, da adj. Sewn. || *Cosido a mano*, hand-sewn.
— M. Sewing.

cosijoso, sa adj. *Amer.* Grumpy, grouchy, peevish.

cosmético, ca adj./s.m. Cosmetic.

cósmico, ca adj. Cosmic: *rayos cósmicos*, cosmic rays.

cosmogonía f. Cosmogony.

cosmogónico, ca adj. Cosmogonic.

cosmografía f. Cosmography.

cosmográfico, ca adj. Cosmographic.

cosmógrafo m. y f. Cosmographer.

cosmología f. Cosmology.

cosmológico, ca adj. Cosmological.

cosmonauta m. y f. Astronaut, cosmonaut.

cosmopolita adj./s. Cosmopolitan, cosmopolite.

cosmopolitismo m. Cosmopolitanism.

cosmorama m. Cosmorama.

cosmos m. inv. Cosmos.

coso m. Enclosure (recinto). || Bullring (plaza de toros). || Street (calle). || ZOOL. Deathwatch beetle, woodworm (insecto).

cospel m. Blank (de moneda).
cosque o **cosqui** m. FAM. Blow on the head.
cosquillar v. tr. To tickle.
cosquillas f. pl. Tickles, tickling, *sing.* || — FIG. *Buscarle a uno las cosquillas*, to rub s.o. up the wrong way. || *Hacer cosquillas*, to tickle (físicamente), to tickle s.o.'s fancy (gustarle a alguien algo). || *Tener cosquillas*, to be ticklish. || *Tener malas cosquillas*, to be touchy.
cosquillear v. tr. To tickle.
cosquilleo m. Tickling [sensation].
cosquilloso, sa adj. Ticklish. || FIG. Touchy, easily offended.
costa f. Coast: *la costa cantábrica*, the Cantabrian coast. || — GEOGR. *Costa de Marfil*, Ivory Coast. | *Costa de Oro*, Gold Coast. || *Navegar costa a costa*, to coast.
costa f. Cost (gasto). || — Pl. JUR. Costs (gastos judiciales): *reserva de costas*, award of costs; *condenar en* or *a costas*, to order to pay costs. || — *A costa ajena*, at someone else's expense. || *A costa de*, at the expense of: *a costa de su familia*, at his family's expense; by dint of, by means of, by, through: *se hizo rico a costa de mucho trabajo*, he became rich by dint of hard work; at the cost of: *a costa de su salud*, at the cost of his health; to one's cost: *me enteré a costa mía de que*, I found out to my cost that. || *A costa de su vida*, at the cost of his life. || *A poca costa*, with little effort. || *A toda costa*, at all costs. || *Vivir a costa de uno*, to live off s.o.
costado m. Side: *tendido de costado*, lying on his side. || MIL. Flank (de un ejército). || MAR. Side (de un barco). || — Pl. Lineage, *sing.*, ancestry, *sing.* (genealogía). || — *Dar el costado*, to be broadside on (en un combate), to careen, to heave over (para carenar o limpiar un barco). || *Dolor* or *punto de costado*, stitch. || *Por los cuatro costados*, through and through, a hundred percent.
costal adj. Costal, pertaining to the ribs (de las costillas).
— M. Sack. || Frame [of an adobe wall]. || FIG. y FAM. *El costal de los pecados*, the human body. | *Eso es harina de otro costal*, that's another kettle of fish. | *Ser un costal de huesos*, to be nothing but skin and bone, to be a bag of bones. | *Vaciar el costal*, to unburden o.s.
costalada f. o **costalazo** m. Fall, sidelong fall (caída). || Bump (golpe). || *Pegarse una costalada*, to fall flat [on one's side].
costalero m. Porter (mozo de cordel). | Bearer [of "pasos" in Holy Week].
costana f. Steep hill (cuesta). || MAR. y AVIAC. Rib (cuaderna).
costanera f. Slope (cuesta). || — Pl. ARQ. Rafters (vigas).
costanero, ra adj. Sloping (inclinado). || Coastal: *navegación costanera*, coastal navegation.
costanilla f. Steep little street.
costar* v. tr. e intr. To cost: *cuesta cien pesetas*, it costs a hundred pesetas. || FIG. To cost: *las promesas cuestan poco*, promises cost nothing; *este trabajo me ha costado muchos esfuerzos*, this work has cost me a great deal of effort. | To be difficult, to find it difficult: *me cuesta mucho confesarlo*, it is very difficult for me to confess it, I find it very difficult to confess; *cuesta creerlo*, it is difficult to believe. || — *Costar barato*, to be cheap, not to cost much: *este libro cuesta barato*, this book is cheap, this book does not cost much. || *Costar caro*, to be expensive, to cost a lot: *esta sortija cuesta muy cara*, this ring is very expensive; to pay dearly for: *esta tontería le costará cara*, he will pay dearly for this foolishness. || *Costarle la vida a uno*, to cost s.o. his life. || *Costar trabajo*, to take a lot, to be difficult, to find it difficult: *me ha costado trabajo rehusar*, it took a lot to refuse it, it was difficult for me to refuse; *me cuesta trabajo creerlo*, it takes a lot of believing, I find it difficult to believe. || FIG. y FAM. *Costar un ojo de la cara* or *un riñón*, to cost a fortune *o* a mint. || *¿Cuánto cuesta?*, how much is it?, how much does it cost? || *Cueste lo que cueste*, at all costs, at any cost, whatever the cost. || *El trabajo me costó dos horas*, the job took me two hours. || FIG. y FAM. *Nos costó Dios y ayuda echarle fuera*, we had terrible trouble getting rid of him.
Costa Rica n. pr. f. GEOGR. Costa Rica.
costarricense o **costarriqueño, ña** adj./s. Costa Rican.
costarriqueñismo m. Word or expression typical of Costa Rica.
coste m. Cost, price: *el coste de un coche*, the price of a car. || — *Coste, seguro y flete*, c.i.f. [cost, insurance, freight]. || *Coste de la vida*, cost of living. || *Coste de producción*, production cost. || *Precio de coste*, cost price.

— OBSERV. *Coste* and *costo* are often confused. *Coste* represents the money price (*coste de un mueble*, the price of a piece of furniture). *Costo* is applied to large undertakings and is a term used in economics (*costo de un puente, de una carretera*, cost of a bridge, of a road).

costear v. tr. To pay for, to defray the expenses of: *costear los estudios a un niño*, to pay for a child's education. || To finance (financiar). || MAR. To coast. || *Amer.* To graze (el ganado).
— V. pr. To pay for itself: *este negocio apenas se costea*, this business hardly pays for itself. || FAM. To buy o.s. [sth.]: *costearse un coche*, to buy o.s. a car. || *Amer.* To pull s.o.'s leg (burlarse).
costeño, ña adj. Coastal.
costeo m. Financing. || *Amer.* Grazing (del ganado). | Banter, leg-pulling (burla).
costero, ra adj. Coastal.
— M. Flitch [of timber] (tabla). || MAR. Coaster (barco). || TECN. Wall. || — F. Side (de paquete). || Coast (costa). || Fishing season (temporada de pesca). || Slope (pendiente).
costilla f. ANAT. Rib: *costilla verdadera, falsa, flotante*, rue, false, floating rib. || Chop, cutlet (chuleta). || MAR. AVIAC. Rib. || FIG. y FAM. Better half, wife: *ven a cenar con tu costilla*, come to dinner and bring your better half. || — Pl. FAM. Back, *sing.*, shoulders (espalda). || — FIG. *A las costillas de*, at the expense of. | *Llevar sobre las costillas*, to carry on one's shoulders. | *Medirle a uno las costillas*, to give s.o. a good hiding.
costillaje o **costillar** m. Ribs, *pl.*
costo m. Cost: *costo de la vida*, cost of living.

— OBSERV. V. COSTE.

costosamente adv. Expensively, dearly.
costoso, sa adj. Costly, expensive.
costra f. Crust (corteza). || Scab (en las heridas). || Snuff (de una vela). || MED. *Costra láctea*, milk crust.
costreñir v. tr. V. CONSTREÑIR.
costroso, sa adj. Crusty. || Scabby (herida). || FAM. Scruffy (sucio).
costumbre m. Custom, habit: *cada país tiene sus usos y costumbres*, every country has its manners and customs. || Habit, custom, practice: *tiene la costumbre de levantarse temprano*, he is in the habit of getting up early, it is his custom *o* practice to get up early. || JUR. Usage. || — *Como de costumbre*, as usual (como siempre). || *De costumbre*, usual (adjetivo), usually, generally (adverbio). || *La costumbre es una segunda naturaleza*, habit is second nature. || *La costumbre tiene fuerza de ley* or *hace ley*, custom has the force of law. || *Mujer de malas costumbres*, loose woman. || *Novela de costumbres*, novel of manners. || *Perder la costumbre*, to lose the habit. || *Persona de buenas costumbres*, respectable person. || *Por costumbre*, through force of habit, out of habit. || *Según costumbre*, according to custom, in accordance with usual practice.
costumbrismo m. Literature of manners.
costumbrista adj. Of manners (literatura).
— M. y f. Writer of literature of manners.
costura f. Sewing (acción y efecto). || Seam: *la costura está deshecha*, the seam is undone; *sentar las costuras*, to press the seams. || Dressmaking: *se gana la vida con la costura*, she makes her living from dressmaking. || Scar (cicatriz). || — *Alta costura*, haute couture, high fashion. || *Cesto de la costura*, sewing basket. || *Medias sin costura*, seamless stockings. || FIG. *Meter a uno en costura*, to bring s.o. to reason, to make s.o. see reason.
costurera f. Seamstress, dressmaker (modista).
costurero m. Sewing case, sewing kit (estuche). || Workbox (mueble).
costurón m. Heavy stitching. || FIG. Noticeable scar.
cota f. Doublet (vestido antiguo). || Tabard (túnica de los heraldos). || Bench mark (cifra). || Height above sea level (altura). || *Cota de mallas*, coat of mail.
cotangente f. MAT. Cotangent.
cotarro m. Night lodging for the poor and destitute, night shelter, doss house (*fam.*) [U.S., flophouse (*fam.*)]. || Side [of a ravine] (ladera). || — FIG. y FAM. *Alborotar el cotarro*, v. ALBOROTAR. | *Dirigir el cotarro*, to rule the roost.
cotejable adj. Comparable.
cotejar v. tr. To compare: *si cotejamos las dos situaciones*, if we compare both situations. || To compare, to collate (textos).
cotejo m. Comparison. || Collation, comparison (textos).
coterráneo, a adj. From the same country or region.
— M. y f. Fellow countryman, fellow countrywoman, compatriot.
cotí m. Ticking (tela para colchones).
cotidianamente adv. Daily, every day.
cotidiano, na adj. Daily, everyday.
cotila f. ANAT. Socket (de un hueso).
cotiledón m. BOT. Cotyledon.
cotilla f. Stays, *pl.*, corset (faja antigua). || — M. y f. FAM. Gossip, tattler (chismoso).
cotillear v. intr. FAM. To gossip.
cotilleo m. FAM. Gossip, gossiping (habladuría).
cotillero, ra m. y f. Gossip, tattler (chismoso).
cotillo m. Hammerhead (del martillo).
cotillón m. Cotillion (baile).
cotizable adj. Quotable.
cotización f. Quotation, price (en la Bolsa). || Dues, *pl.* (cuota). || *Cotización al cierre*, closing price.
cotizado, da adj. Quoted (en la Bolsa). || FIG. Esteemed, valued (apreciado). | Sought-after (que tiene mucha demanda). | Popular.
cotizante adj. Subscription-paying.
— M. Subscription-paying member.

cotizar v. tr. To quote, to price (en la Bolsa). || To pay (pagar). || To fix (fijar). || FIG. *Estar cotizado*, to be highly valued (valorarse).
— V. intr. To pay a subscription.
— V. pr. To be quoted: *valores que se cotizan*, stocks that are quoted. || To sell for, to fetch: *éstas son las manzanas que se cotizan más*, these are the apples which fetch the highest price. || FIG. To be valued, to be highly esteemed.
— OBSERV. The use of *cotizar* in the intransitive form is a Gallicism.
coto m. Enclosure (terreno). || Preserve (terreno acotado). || Boundary mark, boundary stone (mojón). || Limit (límite). || Rate, price (precio). || ZOOL. Miller's thumb (pez). || FIG. Stop, end: *tengo que poner coto a sus excesos*, I have to put a stop to his excesses. || *Amer.* MED. Goitre (bocio). || *Coto de caza*, game preserve.
cotón m. Printed cotton (tela). || *Amer.* Work shirt (camisa). | Vest, undershirt (camiseta).
cotona f. *Amer.* Chamois *o* leather jacket (chaqueta). | Cotton shirt (camisa). | Cotton vest, undershirt (camiseta).
cotonada f. Cotton fabric (tejido).
cotorra f. ZOOL. Parrot (loro). | Magpie (urraca). || FIG. y FAM. Chatterbox, windbag (persona habladora). || FAM. *Hablar como una cotorra*, to chatter like a magpie.
cotorrear v. intr. FIG. y FAM. To chatter, to prattle away.
cotorreo m. FIG. y FAM. Chatter, prattle, chattering.
cotorro m. *Amer.* V. COTARRO.
cotorrón, ona m. y f. Old person affecting youthfulness *o* pretending to be young.
cotúa m. *Amer.* Cormorant (mergo).
cotudo, da adj. Fluffy, furry, cottony. || FAM. Mean, tightfisted (tacaño). | Stubborn, pigheaded, obstinate (cabezón). || *Amer.* Goitrous (con bocio).
cotufa f. BOT. Tuber of the Jerusalem artichoke. || Titbit, delicacy (golosina). || Chufa, earth almond.
coturno m. Buskin, cothurnus (zapato). || — FIG. *Calzar el coturno*, to put on the buskin. | *De alto coturno*, of high degree, lofty.
cotutela f. JUR. Joint guardianship.
cotutor m. JUR. Joint guardian.
covacha f. Small cave (cueva pequeña). || FAM. Shanty, hut (zaquizamí). || *Amer.* Greengrocer's shop (tienda). | Stone bench (poyo). | Cubbyhole under the stairs, boxroom (aposento).
covachuela f. FAM. Ministry. | Office (oficina). || Small cellar (bodega pequeña).
— OBSERV. The first meaning derives from the fact that the offices of the former "Secretariats of the Universal Office" — the equivalent of modern ministries — were situated in the cellars (*covachas*) of the Royal Palace in Madrid.
covachuelista o **covachuelo** m. FAM. Pen-pusher, office worker (chupatintas).
covadera f. *Amer.* Guano deposit.
cow-boy m. Cowboy (vaquero).
coxalgia f. MED. Coxalgia.
coxcojilla o **coxcojita** f. Hopscotch. || *A coxcojita*, on one foot.
coxis m. inv. ANAT. Coccyx.
coy m. MAR. Hammock.
coyote m. Coyote, prairie wolf (lobo americano).
coyunda f. Strap *o* rope for yoking oxen, tether (del yugo). || FIG. Yoke, subjection (sujeción). || FAM. Bonds (*pl.*) of marriage, yoke.
coyuntura f. ANAT. Joint, articulation (articulación). || FIG. Opportunity (oportunidad). | Occasion, moment, juncture (circunstancia). | Situation, circumstances, *pl.* (situación).
coyuntural adj. Of the situation, in the context of the situation, arising from the situation.
coz f. Kick (de un caballo). || Backward kick (de una persona). || Recoil, kick (de un arma de fuego). || Butt (culata de fusil). || — FIG. *Dar* or *tirar coces contra el aguijón*, to kick *o* to struggle in vain. || *Tirar* or *dar* or *pegar coces*, to kick, to lash out. || FIG. *Tratar a la gente a coces*, to kick people around.
crac m. Crash, bankruptcy (quiebra comercial).
— Interj. Crack!, snap!
crácking m. QUÍM. Cracking (del petróleo).
Cracovia n. pr. GEOGR. Cracow.
crampón m. Crampon, climbing iron (de alpinista).
cran m. IMPR. Nick (de un carácter).
craneal o **craneano, na** adj. Cranial: *bóveda craneana*, cranial vault.
cráneo m. ANAT. Cranium, skull. || FAM. *¡Vas de cráneo!*, you are fighting a losing battle.
craneología f. Craniology.
craneólogo, ga m. y f. Craniologist.
crápula f. Debauchery, dissipation (libertinaje). || Drunkenness, crapulence (borrachera).
crapuloso, sa adj. Debauched, dissipated (libertino). || Drunken, crapulous (borracho).
— M. Debauchee, dissipated person (libertino). || Drunkard (borracho).
craquear v. tr. QUÍM. To crack.
craqueo m. QUÍM. Cracking.
crascitar v. intr. To caw, to croak (graznar).
crasis f. inv. GRAM. Crasis.
craso, sa adj. Greasy (lleno de grasa). || Fat (gordo). || Crass, gross: *ignorancia crasa*, crass ignorance.
cráter m. Crater (de un volcán, etc.): *cráter de explosión*, breached crater.
crátera f. Crater (vasija).
craticula f. Small window [through which nuns receive Holy Communion].
crawl m. Crawl (natación).
creación f. Creation.
creador, ra adj. Creative.
— M. y f. Creator (que crea). || Inventor (que inventa). || *El Creador*, the Creator.
crear v. tr. To create. || To make: *ser creado cardenal*, to be made a cardinal. || To invent (inventar). || To establish, to set up, to institute (establecer). || To found (un hospital, una institución).
— V. pr. To make, to make for o.s., to create for o.s.: *crearse enemigos*, to make enemies for o.s.; *crearse una posición*, to make a position for o.s.; *te estás creando problemas por gusto*, you are creating problems for yourself for no reason. || To create for o.s. [in the imagination], to imagine: *los niños se crean un mundo imaginario*, children create an imaginary world for themselves.
creativo, va adj. Creative.
crecedero, ra adj. Growing (que puede crecer). || Which allows for growth (ropa de niños).
crecer* v. intr. To grow (personas, plantas, etc.): *su hija ha crecido mucho*, his daughter has grown a lot; *la hierba ha crecido mucho*, the grass has grown very high; *le ha empezado a crecer el pelo*, his hair has begun to grow. || To grow, to increase, to become *o* get bigger: *crece el malestar general*, the general uneasiness is growing; *crecía la mancha*, the stain got bigger; *crece la fuerza del viento*, the force of the wind is increasing. || To wax (la Luna). || To draw out, to get longer (días). || To rise, to swell: *crece el río*, the river is rising. || — FIG. *Crecer como hongos*, v. HONGO. | *Crecer como la cizaña*, to grow like weeds. || *Dejar crecer el bigote*, to grow a moustache.
— V. pr. FIG. To become vain *o* conceited, to become too sure of o.s. (engreírse). | To take courage [from sth.], to be encouraged [by sth.], to be braced [by sth.]: *los revolucionarios, crecidos por su victoria, atacaron la ciudad*, the revolutionaries, encouraged by their victory, attacked the city.
creces f. pl. Increase (*sing.*) in volume. || FIG. Interest, *sing.*: *pagar con creces*, to pay with interest. || — *Con creces*, amply, more than, with interest: *su éxito compensó con creces a su madre por los sacrificios que había hecho*, his success more than repaid his mother for her self-sacrifice. || *Devolver con creces*, to repay *o* to return a hundredfold.
crecida f. Spate, flood, freshet (de un río).
crecidamente adv. More than enough, more than amply.
crecido, da adj. Large, considerable: *una cantidad crecida*, a large amount. || High, large (proporción, porcentaje): *una crecida proporción*, a high proportion. || Grown: *un niño crecido*, a grown boy. || In flood, in spate (río). || FIG. Proud, conceited (engreído).
creciente adj. Growing (que crece). || Increasing (que aumenta). || — *Cuarto creciente*, first quarter (de la Luna). || *Luna creciente*, crescent *o* waxing moon.
— M. HERÁLD. Crescent. || — F. Spate, flood, freshet (crecida). || Yeast (levadura).
crecimiento m. Growth (acción de crecer). || Increase (aumento). || Waxing (de la Luna). || Flooding, rising (de un río).
credencial adj. Credential. || *Cartas credenciales*, letter (*sing.*) of credence, letters credential, credential letters.
— F. pl. Credentials.
credibilidad f. Credibility.
crediticio, cia adj. Credit.
crédito m. Credit, credence: *dar crédito a*, to give credit to. || FIG. Reputation: *goza de gran crédito*, he has a very good reputation. | Authority (autoridad). | Prestige (prestigio). || COM. Credit: *crédito a corto plazo, a largo plazo*, short-term, long-term credit; *apertura de crédito*, opening of credit. || — *Abrir un crédito a uno*, to open a credit account in s.o.'s favour. || *A crédito*, on credit. || *Carta de crédito*, letter of credit. || *Crédito hipotecario*, debt secured by a mortgage. || *Crédito inmobiliario*, credit on real estate *o* property. || *Dar crédito*, to give credit, to credit (acreditar). || FIG. *No doy crédito a mis ojos* or *mis oídos*, I can't believe my eyes *o* ears. | *Tener crédito*, to have a good reputation.
credo m. Creed (oración). || FIG. Creed (convicción). || FIG. *En menos que se dice un credo*, in a jiffy, before you can say Jack Robinson.
credulidad f. Credulity.
crédulo, la adj. Credulous.
— M. y f. Dupe.
creederas f. pl. FAM. Credulity, *sing.* || FAM. *Tener buenas creederas*, to be credulous, to believe everything. | *Tener malas creederas*, to be incredulous.
creedero, ra adj. Believable (verosímil).
creedor, ra adj. Credulous (crédulo).
creencia f. Belief (pensamiento). || Belief, conviction (convicción). || Belief, faith (religión). || *En la creencia de que*, in the belief that.

creer* v. tr. e intr. To believe: *creer en Dios*, to believe in God; *creer en la virtud*, to believe in virtue. || To believe: *creo de mi deber hacerlo*, I believe it is my duty to do it; *créame*, believe me. || To think (pensar): *así lo creo*, that is what I think: *cree saberlo todo*, he thinks he knows everything. || — *Creer a ciencia cierta*, to be convinced of. || *Creer a pies juntillas, a ojos cerrados*, to believe firmly, blindly. || *Creer bajo* or *sobre palabra*, to take s.o.'s word for it: *lo creo bajo* or *sobre tu palabra*, I take your word for it. || *Creo que no*, I don't think so. || *Creo que sí*, I think so. || *Cualquiera creería que*, anyone would think that. || *Hacer creer algo a uno*, to make s.o. believe sth. || *Hay que verlo para creerlo*, you have to see it to believe it, it has to be seen to be believed. || *No vayas a creer que*, don't go thinking that. || *¡Quién lo hubiera creído!*, who would have thought it! || *Según yo creo*, to the best of my belief. || *Si se le cree*, according to him. || FAM. *¡Ya lo creo!*, of course!, naturally!, I should say so!, I should think so!
— V. pr. To believe *o* to think [o.s.] to be: *se cree un escritor*, he thinks he is a writer. || — *Creérlesas*, to be self-satisfied. || *¡Es para no creérselo!*, it's unbelievable! || *No me lo creo*, I don't *o* I can't believe it. || FAM. *¿Qué se cree?*, who does he think he is? | *¡Que te crees!* or *¡que te crees tú eso!* or *¡que te lo has creído!*, that's what you think! | *¿Qué te has creído?*, who do you think you are?
creíble adj. Credible, believable.
creído, da adj. Confident (confiado). || Credulous (crédulo). || Conceited, arrogant, vain (presumido). || *Creído de sí mismo*, self-satisfied, complacent.
crema f. Cream (nata, cosmético, licor): *crema hidratante*, moisturizing cream; *crema de belleza*, beauty cream. || Custard (relleno de pastelería). || [Shoe] cream, shoe polish (betún). || FIG. Cream, élite (lo mejor). || GRAM. Diaeresis. || — *Crema batida*, whipped cream. || *Crema de chocolate*, chocolate cream. || *Crema dental*, dental cream, toothpaste.
— Adj. Cream (color).
cremación f. Cremation (incineración).
cremallera f. TECN. Rack. || Zip, zip fastener [U.S., zipper] (para abrochar la ropa). || *Ferrocarril de cremallera*, rack railway.
crematístico, ca adj. Monetary, chrematistic.
— F. Political economy, chrematistics, *pl.* || FAM. Money matters, *pl.*, money (dinero).
crematorio, ria adj. Crematory. || *Horno crematorio*, crematorium, crematory.
cremería f. *Amer.* Creamery, dairy.
crémor o **crémor tartárico** m. Cream of tartar.
cremoso, sa adj. Creamy.
crencha f. Parting (raya del cabello). || Hair on each side of parting (pelo).
creosol m. QUÍM. Creosol (aceite de creosota).
creosota f. QUÍM. Creosote. || *Aceite de creosota*, creosol.
creosotado m. TECN. Creosoting.
creosotar v. tr. TECN. To creosote.
crepe f. CULIN. Pancake.
crepé m. Crêpe paper (papel). || Crêpe, crape (tela). || Crêpe [rubber]: *suelas de crepé*, crêpe soles.
crepitación f. Crackling, crepitation. || MED. Crepitation.
crepitante adj. Crackling, crepitant.
crepitar v. intr. To crackle, to crepitate. || MED. To crepitate.
crepuscular adj. Twilight, crepuscular.
crepúsculo m. Twilight, dusk.
cresa f. Eggs (*pl.*) of queen bee. || Larva (de cualquier insecto). || Maggot (larva de la moscarda).
crescendo adv./s.m. MÚS. Crescendo.
Creso n. pr. m. Croesus.
cresol m. QUÍM. Cresol.
crespo, pa adj. Frizzy, fuzzy, kinky (pelo). || Crinkled, curly (hojas). || FIG. Involved, obscure (estilo). | Irritated, angry (enfadado).
crespón m. Crêpe, crape (tela): *crespón de China*, crêpe de Chine. || *Crespón tupido*, crepon.
cresta f. Crest, comb (de las aves). || Tuft (copete). || Crest (de las montañas, de las olas). || MED. Crest: *cresta occipital*, occipital crest. || — FIG. y FAM. *Alzar* or *levantar la cresta*, to give o.s. airs. || *Cresta de explanada*, crest of the glacis (de fortificación). || BOT. *Cresta de gallo*, cockscomb. || FIG. y FAM. *Dar a alguien en la cresta*, to take s.o. down a peg or two (humillarle).
crestería f. ARQ. Battlements, *pl.*, crenellation (de fortificación). | Crenellation (remate calado).
crestomatía f. Anthology, chrestomathy.
crestón m. Crest (de la celada). || MIN. Outcrop (de un filón).
creta f. Chalk (carbonato de cal).
Creta n. pr. f. GEOGR. Crete.
cretáceo, a adj./s.m. GEOL. Cretaceous.

— OBSERV. El sustantivo se escribe siempre con mayúscula en inglés.

cretense o **crético, ca** adj./s. Cretan.
cretinismo m. Cretinism (enfermedad). || Cretinism, idiocy, stupidity (estupidez).
cretino, na adj. Cretinous.
— M. y f. Cretin.
cretona f. Cretonne (tela).
creyente adj. Believing.
— M. y f. Believer.
cría f. Breeding: *cría intensiva*, intensive breeding. || Litter (camada de mamíferos), brood (de ovíparos). || Infant, baby (niño de pecho). || Young (de un animal): *la cría de la loba se llama el lobezno*, the young of the wolf is called a [wolf] cub.
criada f. Maid, maidservant. || — *Criada para todo*, all-purpose *o* general-purpose maid. || *Le salió la criada respondona*, he got more than he bargained for.
criadero m. Nursery (de plantas). || Breeding place (para animales). || Hatchery (de peces). || MIN. Seam, vein (yacimiento). || *Criadero de ostras*, oyster bed.
criadilla f. CULIN. Bull's testicle | (Ant.). Small round roll (panecillo). || *Criadilla de tierra*, truffle (trufa).
criado m. Servant, manservant.
criado, da adj. Brought up, bred: *bien, mal criado*, well, badly brought up (niño). || Bred, reared (animal).
criadona o **criadota** f. FAM. Skivvy, drudge.
criador m. Breeder (de animales). || — *Criador de vino*, winegrower, viniculturist. || *El Criador*, the Creator, God (el Creador).
criandera f. *Amer.* Wet nurse (nodriza).
crianza f. Breeding (de animales). || Nursing, suckling (de niños de pecho). || FIG. Upbringing, breeding: *buena, mala crianza*, good, bad upbringing.
criar v. tr. To suckle, to nurse (amamantar). || To feed (niño de pecho). || To rear, to breed, to raise (animales). || To grow (plantas). || To bring up, to rear, to educate (educar). || To produce, to grow: *la tierra cría plantas*, the earth produces plants. || To have, to grow: *los gatos crían pelo y las aves plumas*, cats have fur and birds have feathers. || To elaborate (el vino). || FIG. To engender, to beget (engendrar). | To create, to cause, to bring about, to provoke (ocasionar). || — FIG. *Cría buena fama y échate a dormir*, v. FAMA. || *Criar al pecho*, to breast-feed. || *Criar con biberón*, to bottle-feed. || FAM. *Criar grasas*, to get fat, to become fat. || *Dios los cría y ellos se juntan*, birds of a feather flock together. || *Los alimentos tapados crían moho*, covered food goes mouldy. || *No críes motivos para que te castigue*, do not give me cause to punish you, don't provoke me. || *Zapatos que crían ampollas*, shoes that give blisters.
— V. pr. To be brought up, to grow up (niños): *los niños que se crían al aire libre*, children that are brought up in the open air. || To feed o.s. (alimentarse). || To be reared, to be raised (animales). || To grow (plantas). || To form, to take form (cosas). || FIG. *Criarse en buena cuna*, to be born with a silver spoon in one's mouth.
criatura f. Creature (cosa creada). || Infant, baby (niño de pecho). || FIG. Child, baby, kid (fam.): *llorar como una criatura*, to cry like a baby.
criba f. Sieve, screen. || — FIG. y FAM. *Estar como una criba*, to be riddled like a sieve. | *Pasar por la criba*, to screen (seleccionar).
cribado m. Sieving, sifting, screening. || *Amer.* Openwork embroidery (bordado calado).
cribador, ra adj. Sieving, sifting, screening.
— M. y f. Siever, sifter, screener.
cribaduras f. pl. Siftings, screenings.
cribar v. tr. To sieve, to sift, to screen.
cric m. TECN. Jack (gato).
cricket m. DEP. Cricket.
cricoides adj./s.m. inv. ANAT. Cricoid (cartílago de la laringe).
Crimea n. pr. f. GEOGR. Crimea.
crimen m. Crime.
criminación f. Crimination (acusación).
criminal adj./s. Criminal.
criminalidad f. Criminality. || Crime rate: *la criminalidad aumenta muy rápidamente*, the crime rate is increasing very rapidly.
criminalista m. Criminologist (especialista). || Criminal lawyer (abogado).
criminar v. tr. To criminate, to accuse, to charge (incriminar). || To censure (censurar).
criminología f. Criminology.
criminológico, ca adj. Criminological.
criminologista o **criminólogo, ga** m. y f. Criminologist.
crin f. Mane (del caballo). || Horsehair (relleno de colchones, etc.). || *Crin vegetal*, vegetable fibre.
crineja f. *Amer.* Plait, tress (trenza).
crinoideo m. ZOOL. Crinoid.
crinolina f. Crinoline.

— OBSERV. This word is a Gallicism for *miriñaque*.

crío m. FAM. Baby (niño de pecho). | Child, kid, little one: *vino con todos sus críos*, he came with all his children.
criógeno m. Cryogen.
criolita f. MIN. Cryolite.
criollo, lla adj./s. Creole.

— OBSERV. In Latin America the noun and the adjective *criollo* often denote what is indigenous and national as opposed to what is foreign. Thus. *un manjar criollo* is a typical dish; *un caballo criollo* is a native horse of a breed peculiar to the country in question. In Argentina *un buen criollo* means a good Argentinian, an Argentinian of good stock.

crioscopia f. FÍS. Cryoscopy, cryometry.
cripta f. Crypt.
criptógamo, ma adj. BOT. Cryptogamous.
— F. Cryptogam.
criptografía f. Cryptography (escritura secreta).
criptográfico, ca adj. Cryptographic.
criptógrafo, fa m. y f. Cryptographer.
criptograma m. Cryptogram.
criptón m. QUÍM. Krypton (gas).
criquet m. DEP. Cricket.
cris m. Kris, creese (puñal malayo).
crisálida f. ZOOL. Chrysalis.
crisantemo m. BOT. Chrysanthemum.
crisis f. Crisis (de una enfermedad). || Fit (ataque): *crisis de llanto, de furia*, fit of weeping, of rage. || Crisis (momento decisivo): *crisis financiera, ministerial*, financial, cabinet crisis. || — *Crisis de la vivienda*, housing shortage. || *Crisis nerviosa*, nervous breakdown. || *Hacer crisis*, to reach crisis point (una enfermedad). || *Llegar a una crisis*, to reach crisis point.
crisma m. Chrism (aceite consagrado). || FAM. Head. || — FAM. *Romper la crisma a alguien*, to smash s.o.'s head in. | *Romperse la crisma*, to crack *o* to split one's head open.
crismas m. Christmas card.
crisol m. TECN. Crucible, melting pot. | Hearth (de un horno). || FIG. Melting pot.
crisólito m. Chrysolite (piedra preciosa).
crispadura f. o **crispamiento** m. Muscular contraction.
crispar v. tr. To contract, to tense (músculo). || To twitch (inconscientemente). || To contort: *tenía el rostro crispado por el dolor*, his face was contorted with pain. || To irritate, to get on s.o.'s nerves: *este niño me crispa*, this child gets on my nerves. || *Crispar los nervios*, to get on s.o.'s nerves.
— V. pr. To contract, to tense, to twitch (músculos). || To contort (cara). || To get all on edge (nervios).
cristal m. Crystal (cuerpo cristalizado): *cristal de roca*, rock crystal. || Crystal (vidrio fino): *cristal de Bohemia*, Bohemian crystal. || Pane of glass (de una ventana, etc.). || Glass (vidrio): *el cristal de un reloj*, the glass of a watch; *cristal ahumado*, smoked glass; *cristal tallado*, cut glass; *cristal esmerilado*, ground glass. || Lens (lente): *cristal de contacto*, contact lens. || AUT. Window. || Mirror, looking glass (espejo). || FIG. y POÉT. Water: *el cristal de la fuente*, the water of the fountain. || *Amer.* [Drinking] glass (vaso). || — Pl. Windows (ventanas). || — *Cristal de aumento*, magnifying glass. || *Cristal trasero*, rear window (automóvil). || *De cristal*, glass. || *Limpiar los cristales*, to clean the windows. || *Puerta de cristales*, glass door.
cristalera f. Display cabinet (armario con cristales). || Glazed door (puerta). || Window (ventana).
cristalería f. Glasswork, glass making (arte). || Glassworks (fábrica). || Glass shop, glassware shop (tienda de vasos, etc.). || Glass service (juego de vasos, etc.). || Glassware (objetos de cristal).
cristalero, ra m. y f. Glazier (que arregla los cristales). || Glassworker, glassmaker (que trabaja en cristal). || Glassblower (soplador de vidrio).
cristalino, na adj. FÍS. Crystalline. || FIG. Limpid, clear.
— M. ANAT. Crystalline lens (del ojo).
cristalizable adj. Crystallizable.
cristalización f. Crystallization.
cristalizador, ra adj. Crystallizing.
— M. Crystallizer.
cristalizante adj. Crystallizing.
cristalizar v. tr. e intr. To crystallize. || FIG. To crystallize (concretarse): *el descontento de los trabajadores cristalizó en una huelga general*, the workers' discontent crystallized into a general strike.
— V. pr. To crystallize.
cristalografía f. Crystallography.
cristalográfico, ca adj. Crystallographic.
cristaloide adj./s.m. Crystalloid.
cristaloideo, a adj. Crystalloidal.
cristianar v. tr. FAM. To christen. || FAM. *Los trapitos de cristianar*, one's Sunday best, one's Sunday clothes (los vestidos más elegantes).
cristiandad f. Christendom (conjunto de los cristianos). || Christianity (fe cristiana).
cristiania m. Christiania, christy (esquí).
cristianismo m. Christianity.
cristianización f. Christianization.
cristianizar v. tr. To christianize.
cristiano, na adj./s. Christian. || — *Cristiano nuevo*, Moor, Jew, etc. converted to Christianity. || *Cristiano viejo*, Christian having no Moorish or Jewish ancestors. || FIG. *Hablar en cristiano*, to speak plain Spanish, to speak clearly. | *Vino cristiano*, unwatered wine (sin agua). || — M. FAM. Soul, person: *por la calle no pasa un cristiano*, there's not a soul in the street. || FAM. *No hay cristiano que lo entienda*, no one could understand it, it's utterly incomprehensible.
Cristina n. pr. f. Christine.
cristino, na adj./s. Supporter of Isabel II against the Carlists, under the regency of Maria Cristina.
Cristo m. Christ. || Crucifix: *un cristo de marfil*, an ivory crucifix. || — *Antes de Cristo*, before Christ, B.C. || *Después de Cristo*, A.D., anno domini (en las fechas). || FIG. y FAM. *Donde Cristo dio las tres voces*, miles from anywhere, at the back of beyond. | *Estar hecho un Cristo*, to be a pitiful sight. | *¡Ni Cristo que lo fundó!*, impossible! | *¡Voto a Cristo!*, by the Lord! (exclamación de enfado).
Cristóbal n. pr. m. Christopher. || *Cristóbal Colón*, Christopher Columbus.
cristus m. Christ cross, crisscross (cruz que se ponía al principio del abecedario). || Alphabet (abecedario). || Primer (librito para aprender a leer).
criterio m. Criterion (regla o norma). || Discernment, judgment (discernimiento). || Point of view, viewpoint (punto de vista): *juzgó los cuadros con un criterio clásico*, he judged the paintings from a classical point of view. || Approach (enfoque). || Opinion: *en mi criterio*, in my opinion.
crítica f. Criticism (evaluación de calidades). || Review, notice, critique (reseña). || The critics (conjunto de los críticos). || Criticism, faultfinding, censure (censura). || *Dirigir* or *hacer críticas*, to criticize. || *¿Qué crítica puedes hacerme?*, what can you reproach me?
criticable adj. Criticizable, open to criticism.
criticador, ra adj. Critical.
— M. y f. Critic, faultfinder.
criticar v. tr. To criticize.
criticastro m. Criticaster, petty critic.
criticismo m. FIL. Critical philosophy [of Kant].
crítico, ca adj. Critical (propio de la crítica). || Critical (propio de la crisis). || Critical, crucial (decisivo): *en el momento crítico*, at the crucial moment.
— M. Critic : *crítico de arte*, art critic.
criticón, ona adj. Critical, faultfinding, hypercritical.
— M. y f. Faultfinder, criticizer.
crizneja f. Plait, braid (de pelo). || Rope, plait of esparto (de soga).
croar v. intr. To croak (las ranas).
croata adj./s. Croatian, Croat.
crocitar v. intr. To croak, to crow, to caw (el cuervo).
croché o **crochet** m. Crochet (ganchillo).
cromado m. TECN. Chromium-plating.
cromar v. tr. TECN. To chromium-plate, to chrome. | *Cromado*, chromium-plated, chrome.
cromático, ca adj. FÍS. y MÚS. Chromatic: *escala cromática*, chromatic scale.
cromatina f. BIOL. Chromatin.
cromatismo m. Chromatism (defecto de los instrumentos ópticos). || MÚS. Chromaticism.
cromato m. QUÍM. Chromate.
crómico, ca adj. QUÍM. Chromic.
crómlech m. Cromlech (monumento megalítico).
cromo m. Chromium, chrome (metal). || Chromo, chromolithograph, coloured print (cromolitografía). || Picture card: *coleccionar cromos*, to collect picture cards. || FAM. *Estar hecho un cromo*, to look very smart.
cromolitografía f. Chromolithography (imprenta). || Chromolithograph (estampa).
cromolitógrafo m. Chromolithographer.
cromosfera f. ASTR. Chromosphere.
cromosoma m. BIOL. Chromosome.
crónica f. Chronicle (anales). || Page (en un periódico): *crónica teatral*, theatre page. || *Crónica de sociedad*, society *o* social column.
cronicidad f. Chronicity.
cronicismo m. MED. Chronicity (de una enfermedad).
crónico, ca adj. Chronic.
cronicón m. Short chronicle.
cronista m. Chronicler (autor de anales). || Columnist (periodista que escribe crónicas).
crónlech m. Cromlech.
cronógrafo m. Chronographer (persona). || Chronograph (aparato).
cronología f. Chronology.
cronológico, ca adj. Chronological.
cronologista o **cronólogo** m. Chronologist, chronologer.
cronometrador m. Timekeeper.
cronometraje m. Timing, timekeeping.
cronometrar v. tr. To time.
cronometría f. Chronometry.
cronométrico, ca adj. Chronometric, chronometrical.
cronómetro m. Chronometer. || DEP. Stopwatch.
croquet m. Croquet (juego).
croqueta f. CULIN. Croquette, rissole: *croqueta de pescado*, fish croquette.
croquis m. Sketch (dibujo).
cross o **cross-country** m. DEP. Cross-country race (carrera).
crótalo m. Crotalum (castañuela antigua). || ZOOL. Rattlesnake (serpiente de cascabel). || — Pl. POÉT. Castanets.
croupier m. Croupier (en el juego).
crownglass m. Crown glass (vidrio corona).
cruce m. Crossing (acción de cruzar). || Crisscross, crisscrossing (acción de cruzarse en varios sentidos). || Junction, crossroads, *pl.* [U.S., intersection] (de calles), crossroads, *pl.* [U.S., intersection] (de carreteras). || Pedestrian crossing (paso). || Crossed line (interferencia en las comunicaciones telefónicas). || Crossing, crossbreeding (de razas diferentes). || Cross, crossbreed (ser híbrido). || ELECTR. Short circuit (cortocircuito). || — *Hay un cruce*, the lines are crossed (teléfono). || AUT. *Luces de cruce*, dipped headlights.

cruceiro m. Cruzeiro (moneda brasileña).
crucería f. ARQ. Ogives, *pl.*, ribs, *pl.* || *Bóveda de crucería*, groined *o* ribbed vault.
crucero m. ARQ. Transept (en los templos). || Junction [U.S., intersection] (de calles), crossroads, *pl.* [U.S., intersection] (de carreteras). || MAR. Cruiser (barco de guerra). | Cruise (viaje por mar). | Cruiser, passenger cruiser (navío). || Crossbearer (en las procesiones). || ASTR. Southern Cross (constelación). || IMPR. Fold (de una hoja). | Crossbar (listón que divide el molde). || ARQ. Crossbeam, crosspiece. | Window bar (de ventana). || Cleavage (de un mineral). || *Velocidad de crucero*, cruising speed.
cruceta f. Cross [in cross-stitch] (punto de cruz, de cruceta). || MAR. Crosstree. || ARQ. Crossbeam, crosspiece (crucero). || TECN. Crosshead.
crucial adj. Crucial, cross-shaped: *incisión crucial*, crucial incision. || FIG. Crucial, critical (decisivo): *momento crucial*, crucial moment.
cruciferario m. Crossbearer (el que lleva la cruz). || Member of the religious order of the Holy Cross.
crucífero, ra adj. BOT. Cruciferous.
— F. BOT. Crucifer. || — Pl. BOT. Cruciferae.
crucificado, da adj. Crucified.
— M. *El Crucificado*, the Crucified, Jesus Christ.
crucificar v. tr. To crucify. || FIG. y FAM. To torment, to torture.
crucifijo m. Crucifix.
crucifixión f. Crucifixion.
cruciforme adj. Cruciform.
crucigrama m. Crossword [puzzle].
crucigramista o **cruciverbista** m. y f. Person who does crosswords.
crudeza f. Coarseness, crudeness (realismo brutal). || Rude thing (palabra grosera). || Harshness (rigor): *la crudeza del clima, del invierno*, the harshness of the climate, of the winter. | Severity: *la crudeza de las heladas*, the severity of the frost. || Hardness (del agua). || Bluntness (franqueza, brusquedad). || Rawness (de lo que no está cocido). || Unripeness (de lo que no está maduro). || — Pl. Undigested food, *sing.*
crudo, da adj. Raw (no cocido). || Unripe, green (no maduro). || Crude: *petróleo crudo*, crude oil. || Hard (agua). || Hard to digest (difícil de digerir). || Unbleached (sin blanquear). || Untreated (no elaborado). || Raw : *seda cruda*, raw silk. || FIG. Coarse, crude (excesivamente realista): *un chiste crudo*, a coarse joke. || Harsh, severe (tiempo, clima). || Harsh, cruel (cruel). || Inexperienced, raw (torero, artista, etc.). || Beige (beige). || *Amer.* Suffering from a hangover (después de una borrachera). || *En crudo*, raw: *tomate en crudo*, raw tomato; bluntly (bruscamente).
cruel adj. Cruel: *un tirano cruel*, a cruel tyrant. || *Mostrarse cruel*, to be cruel: *el destino se muestra cruel con él*, fate is cruel to him.
crueldad f. Cruelty.
cruentamente adv. Bloodily.
cruento, ta adj. Bloody.
crujía f. ARQ. Bay, space between two walls. | Corridor, gallery (pasillo). || MAR. Midship gangway. || Ward (sala de hospital). || Passage between choir and sanctuary (en algunas catedrales). || FIG. y FAM. *Pasar* or *sufrir una crujía*, to be going through a bad time *o* a rough patch.
crujido m. Rustle (de la seda, de las hojas secas). || Creak (de una puerta, de una rama gruesa, de los muelles de un sillón, etc.). || Grinding, gnashing (de los dientes). || Crackle (de la madera al arder, del papel al arrugarse). || Crack (de los nudillos).
crujiente adj. Rustling (seda, hojas secas). || Creaky (puerta, rama gruesa, muelles de un sillón, etc.). || Grinding, gnashing (dientes). || Crackling (madera al arder, papel al arrugarse). || Cracking (nudillos). || Crusty, crisp (pan). || Crisp, crunchy (galleta).
crujir v. intr. To rustle (seda, hojas secas). || To creak (puerta, rama gruesa, muelles de un sillón, etc.). || To grind, to gnash (dientes). || To crackle (madera al arder, papel al arrugarse). || To crunch (grava). || To crack (nudillos). || *Allí será el llorar y el crujir de dientes*, there will be weeping and gnashing of teeth.
crúor m. POÉT. Blood. || MED. Cruor, blod clot (sangre coagulada).
crup m. Croup (enfermedad).
crural adj. ANAT. Crural (del muslo).
crustáceo, a adj./s.m. ZOOL. Crustacean. || — Pl. ZOOL. Crustacea.
cruz f. Cross (patíbulo, figura). || Cross (condecoración): *gran cruz de Isabel la Católica*, grand cross of Isabella I. || MAR. Crown (del ancla). || Tails, *pl.* (de la moneda): *¿cara o cruz?*, heads or tails? || Withers, *pl.* (de los caballos). || Fork (de un árbol). || ASTR. Cross: *Cruz del Sur*, Southern Cross (constelación). || Crotch (de los pantalones). || Hilt (de una espada). || HERÁLD. Cross. || FIG. Cross (carga): *cada uno lleva su cruz*, everyone has his own cross to bear. || — *Con los brazos en cruz*, with one's arms outstreched, with one's arms spreadeagled. || *Cruz de San Andrés*, Saint Andrew's Cross. || *Cruz de Lorena*, Cross of Lorraine. || *Cruz de los Caídos*, monument to the dead, war memorial. || *Cruz de Malta*, Maltese cross. || *Cruz gamada*, swastika. || *Cruz griega, latina*, Greek, Latin cross. || HERÁLD. *Cruz potenzada*, cross potent. || *Cruz Roja*, Red Cross. || FIG. y FAM. *Cruz y raya*, that's the end of that, that's that. | *De la cruz a la fecha*, from beginning to end. || *En cruz*, crosswise, crossed: *dos espadas en cruz*, two crossed swords; cross-shaped (que tiene forma de cruz). || FIG. *Es la cruz y los ciriales*, one has the devil's own job. || *Firmar con una cruz*, to make one's mark. || *Hacerse cruces*, to cross o.s. (santiguarse), to be speechless, to be dumbfounded (quedarse perplejo). || FIG. *Llevar la cruz a cuestas*, to have one's cross to bear. || *Por esta cruz* or *por éstas que son cruces*, I swear by this cross *o* by all that is holy. || *Quedarse en cruz y en cuadro*, to be reduced to poverty. || *Señal de la cruz*, sign of the cross.
cruzada f. HIST. Crusade. || (P. us.). Crossroads, *pl.* (encrucijada). || FIG. Crusade, campaign, drive: *una cruzada contra la ignorancia*, a crusade against ignorance; *cruzada antialcohólica*, temperance campaign.
cruzado, da adj. Crossed. || Double-breasted: *abrigo cruzado*, double-breasted coat. || Twilled: *tela cruzada*, twilled cloth. || COM. Crossed: *cheque cruzado*, crossed cheque. || Crossbred (animales, plantas). || MIL. *Fuegos cruzados*, cross fire. || *Palabras cruzadas*, crossword [puzzle], *sing.*
— M. Crusader (participante en una cruzada). || Cross, crossbreed (animal). || Twill weave (de una tela). || Cross (en la danza). || — Pl. Hatching, *sing.* (en el dibujo).
cruzamiento m. Crossing (acción de cruzar). || Crossing, crossbreeding (de animales).
cruzar v. tr. To cross: *cruzar las piernas*, to cross one's legs. || To cross (atravesar): *cruzar la calle*, to cross the street; *el puente cruza el río aquí*, the bridge crosses the river here. || To lay *o* to place across: *cruzar el camino con un árbol*, to lay a tree across the road. || To draw across: *cruzar la página con una raya*, to draw a line across the page. || To lie across (estar cruzado). || COM. To cross (un cheque). || To invest [with the insignia of an order]. || AGR. To plough a second time. || To cross, to crossbreed (plantas y animales). || — *Cruzar a nado*, to swim across. || *Cruzar apuestas*, to make a bet, to bet. || FIG. y FAM. *Cruzar a uno la cara*, to hit s.o. across the face, to slap s.o.'s face. || MIL. *Cruzar la espada con*, to cross swords with (pelearse). || *Cruzar los brazos*, to fold one's arms. || FIG. *Cruzar unas palabras con uno*, to exchange a few words with s.o. (conversar brevemente), to have words with s.o. (disputar). || *Cruzar por la imaginación*, to cross one's mind. || *Nunca había cruzado una palabra con él*, I had never exchanged a word with him.
— V. intr. MAR. To cruise.
— V. pr. To cross: *nuestras cartas se han cruzado*, our letters crossed. || To exchange (palabras, regalos, etc.). || To pass: *me crucé con él por la calle*, I passed him in the street. || To intersect, to cross: *dos carreteras que se cruzan*, two roads which cross. || — *Cruzarse de brazos*, to fold one's arms. || *Cruzarse de palabras*, to quarrel, to have words (disputar). || *Cruzarse de piernas*, to cross one's legs. || FIG. *Cruzarse en el camino de alguien*, to cross s.o.'s path.
cruzeiro m. Cruzeiro (moneda brasileña).
çu f. Q, name of the letter *q*.
cuaba f. *Amer.* Torchwood, candlewood (árbol).
cuacar v. intr. *Amer.* To please, to suit.
cuácara f. *Amer.* Jacket (chaqueta). | Workman's blouse (blusa de mahón). || Frock coat (levita).
cuaco m. *Amer.* Horse (caballo).
cuaderna f. Double fours [in game resembling backgammon]. || MAR. y AVIAC. Frame: *cuaderna maestra*, midship frame. || MAR. Rib. || *Cuaderna vía*, verse form with four alexandrines (estrofa).
cuadernal m. MAR. Block and tackle.
cuadernillo m. IMPR. Quinternion (cinco pliegos de papel). || Booklet (cuaderno pequeño). || Liturgical calendar (añalejo). || Packet of cigarette paper (de papel de fumar). || *Cuadernillo de sellos*, book of stamps.
cuaderno m. Exercise book, copy book. || FAM. Pack of cards (baraja). || MAR. *Cuaderno de bitácora*, logbook.
cuadra f. Stable (caballeriza). || Stable (conjunto de caballos *o* de automóviles de un propietario). || FIG. Pigsty (lugar muy sucio). || Croup, rump (grupa). || Large hall (sala grande). || Ward (de hospital). || Hut (de cuartel). || *Amer.* Block [of houses] (manzana de casas): *vivo a tres cuadras*, I live three blocks away. || Quarter of a Roman mile (medida itineraria). || MAR. Quarter. || MAR. *Navegar a la cuadra*, to sail with the wind on the quarter.
cuadrada f. MÚS. Breve (nota).
cuadradillo m. Square-sectioned ruler (regla). || Square-sectioned iron bar (barra de hierro). || Gusset (de camisa). || Lump, cube [of sugar]: *azúcar de cuadradillo*, lump sugar.
cuadrado, da adj. Square: *una vela cuadrada*, a square sail; *raíz cuadrada*, square root. || Stocky, broad-shouldered (persona). || Full-face (retrato). || Perfect, complete (perfecto, cabal).
— M. MAT. Square (figura). | Square: *el cuadrado de la hipotenusa, de un número*, the square of the hypotenuse, of a number. || Square-sectioned iron bar (barra de hierro). || Square-sectioned ruler (regla).

|| Gusset (de camisa). || IMPR. Quadrat, quad (para espacios). || Die (para monedas).
cuadragenario, ria adj./s. Quadragenarian.
Cuadragésima f. Quadragesima: *domingo de la Cuadragésima*, Quadragesima Sunday.
cuadragesimal adj. Lenten (relativo a la cuaresma).
cuadragésimo, ma adj./s. Fortieth.
cuadrangular adj. Quadrangular.
cuadrángulo, la adj. Quadrangular.
— M. Quadrangle.
cuadrante m. Quadrant (de círculo). || Sundial (reloj de sol). || Dial (dispositivo indicador). || Face (del reloj). || Quadrant (instrumento). || MAR. Quarter (del horizonte). || List of masses (tablilla de las misas).
cuadrar v. tr. To square, to make square (dar forma cuadrada). || MAT. To square (un número, una figura). || IMPR. To lay out. || To divide into squares (cuadricular un dibujo). || TAUR. To line up [the bull].
— V. intr. To agree, to tally, to square: *nuestras cuentas no cuadran con las suyas*, our accounts do not tally with yours. || To suit, to go with: *esta alfombra cuadra con los muebles*, this carpet suits the furniture. || To suit (convenir): *esa hora no me cuadra*, that time doesn't suit me. || To suit (la ropa).
— V. pr. MIL. To stand to attention. || To stop short (el caballo). || FIG. y FAM. To dig one's heels in: *se ha cuadrado y no hay nada que hacer*, he has dug his heels in and there is nothing we can do.
cuadrático, ca adj. MAT. Quadratic.
cuadratín m. IMPR. Quadrat, quad.
cuadratura f. Quadrature.
cuadrero, ra adj. *Amer.* Fast, quick (caballo).
— F. *Amer.* Stable (cuadra).
cuadríceps adj./s.m. Quadriceps (músculo).
cuadrícula f. Grid, cross ruling.
cuadriculado, da adj. Grid: *mapa cuadriculado*, grid map. || *Papel cuadriculado*, squared paper, graph paper.
— M. Grid, cross ruling.
cuadricular adj. Gridded, squared.
cuadricular v. tr. To grid, to square, to divide into squares.
cuadridimensional m. FÍS. Four-dimensional.
cuadrienal adj. Quadrennial.
cuadrienio m. Quadrennium.
cuadriga f. Quadriga.
cuadrigémino adj. m. ANAT. Quadrigeminal.
cuadril m. ANAT. Hip bone (hueso). | Hip, haunch (cadera). | Rump (de los animales).
cuadrilátero, ra adj. MAT. Quadrilateral.
— M. Quadrilateral (polígono). || Ring (boxeo).
cuadrilongo, ga adj. MAT. Rectangular, oblong.
— M. Rectangle, oblong (rectángulo).
cuadrilla f. TAUR. "Cuadrilla" [team assisting the matador in the bullring]. || Gang, band (de malhechores). || Gang, party (de amigos). || Team, gang (de obreros). || Quadrille (baile). || HIST. Company of bowmen of the "Santa Hermandad" [in charge of hunting criminals].
cuadrillero m. Foreman (capataz). || HIST. Bowman of the "Santa Hermandad".
cuadrimotor adj. Four-engined.
— M. Four-engined plane (avión).
cuadripartido, da o **cuadripartito, ta** adj. Quadripartite: *convenio cuadripartito*, quadripartite convention.
cuadriplicado, da adj. Quadruplicate.
cuadriplicar v. tr. e intr. To quadruplicate, to quadruple.
cuadrisílabo, ba adj. Quadrisyllabic.
— M. Quadrisyllable.
cuadrito m. CULIN. Cube. || *Cortar en cuadritos*, to dice.
cuadrivalente adj. QUÍM. Tetravalent, quadrivalent.
cuadrivio m. Quadrivium.
cuadro, dra adj. (P. us.). Square (cuadrado).
— M. Square (cuadrado). || Picture, painting (pintura). || IMPR. Platen. || Patch, bed (de un jardín): *cuadro de flores*, flower bed. || TEATR. Scene. || Sight, scene: *la ciudad bombardeada ofrecía un cuadro desolador*, the bombed city was a sorry sight. || Description, picture (descripción). || Staff (conjunto del personal). || Table, chart (gráfico). || MIL. Officers and noncommissioned officers. | Square (formación). || Frame (de una bicicleta). || *Amer.* Slaughterhouse (matadero). || — *Cuadro de costumbres*, study of manners. || *Cuadro de distribución*, switchboard. || *Cuadro de instrumentos* or *de mandos*, dashboard, instrument panel (de un coche), instrument panel (de un avión). || *Cuadro facultativo* or *médico*, medical staff. || *Cuadro sinóptico*, chart, diagram. || *Cuadro sueco*, crossbeam for attaching gymnastic apparatus. || *Cuadro vivo*, tableau vivant. || *Dentro del cuadro de*, in the framework of. || *En cuadro*, in a square: *sillas dispuestas en cuadro*, chairs arranged in a square. || FIG. *Quedarse en cuadro*, to be left friendless (estar abandonado), to be greatly reduced in numbers (de un conjunto de personas), to be left with officers only (de una unidad militar). || *Tela de cuadros*, check *o* checked cloth. || FAM. *¡Vaya un cuadro!*, what a sight!
cuadrumano, na adj. ZOOL. Quadrumanous.
— M. Quadrumane.
cuadrupedal adj. Quadrupedal.
cuadrúpedo, da adj./s. Quadruped.
cuádruple adj. Quadruple, fourfold.
cuadruplicación f. Quadruplication.
cuadruplicado, da adj. Quadruplicate. || *Por cuadruplicado*, in quadruplicate.
cuadruplicar v. tr. e intr. To quadruple.
cuádruplo, pla adj. Quadruple, fourfold.
— M. Quadruple.
cuaima f. *Amer.* Poisonous snake of Venezuela. || FIG. y FAM. Snake, viper (persona astuta y cruel).
cuajada f. Curd (de la leche). || Cottage cheese (requesón).
cuajado, da adj. Curdled (leche). || Clotted (sangre). || FIG. Dumbfounded, astonished (asombrado). | Asleep (dormido): *quedarse cuajado*, to fall asleep. || *Cuajado de*, v. CUAJAR.
— M. CULIN. Mincemeat dish.
cuajadura f. Curdling (de la leche). || Clotting (de la sangre). || Coagulation, congealing. || Curd (cuajada). || Solidification.
cuajaleche m. BOT. Cheese rennet, yellow bedstraw.
cuajamiento m. Curdling. || Clotting, coagulation.
cuajar m. ZOOL. Abomasum, rennet stomach.
cuajar v. tr. To coagulate, to congeal (en general). || To clot (la sangre). || To curdle (la leche). || To set (la gelatina). || To congeal (las grasas). || To cover: *cuajar un vestido de perlas*, to cover a dress with pearls. || To fill with: *cuajar un libro de ilustraciones*, to fill a book with illustrations.
— V. intr. To settle (nieve). || FIG. y FAM. To work out: *su negocio no cuajó*, his business didn't work out. | To catch on: *esta moda no cuajó*, this fashion did not catch on. | To fit in (en un trabajo). | To get away with: *tales mentiras no cuajan*, one cannot get away with lies like that. | To come off (planes). | To materialize (concretarse). | To develop, to grow: *sus ideas cuajaron en una gran obra*, his ideas grew into a great work. | To become: *no cabe duda que algún día cuajará en un gran artista*, there is no doubt that some day he will become a great artist. | To be acceptable (propuesta). || — *Cuajado de*, full of: *Londres está cuajado de extranjeros*, London is full of foreigners; covered with: *un balcón cuajado de flores*, a balcony covered with flowers; bursting with: *un libro cuajado de ilustraciones*, a book bursting with illustrations; studded with: *un cielo cuajado de estrellas*, a sky studded with stars, a star-studded sky.
— V. pr. To coagulate, to congeal (ponerse gelatinoso). || To curdle (leche). || To clot, to congeal (sangre). || To set (gelatina). || To take (mayonesa, etc.). || FIG. To fill up (llenarse). | To go to sleep (dormirse).
cuajarón m. Clot.
cuajo m. Rennet (sustancia que cuaja la leche). || Curdling (de la leche). || Clotting (de la sangre). || ZOOL. Abomasum, rennet stomach (cuajar del rumiante). || FIG. y FAM. Patience, phlegm (calma). || — *Añadir cuajo*, to add rennet, to curdle. || *Arrancar de cuajo*, to uproot (un árbol), to wrench off (puerta, etc.), to uproot, to eradicate (cosas malas). || FIG. *Tener cuajo*, to be sluggish (ser lento), to be patient (paciente).
cuakerismo m. Quakerism (cuaquerismo).
cuákero, ra m. y f. Quaker.
cual pron. rel. (pl. *cuales*). — PRECEDIDO DE ARTÍCULO. Who, whom (personas), which (cosas): *llamó al portero, el cual dormía*, he called the porter, who was asleep; *quitó las piedras, las cuales le obstruían el camino*, he removed the stones which were obstructing his path. || — *Al cual, a la cual, a los cuales, a las cuales*, to whom (personas), to which (cosas) [complemento indirecto]: *la mujer a la cual mandé la carta*, the woman to whom I sent the letter; whom (personas) [complemento directo]: *el hombre al cual yo vi esta mañana*, the man whom I saw this morning. || *Bajo el cual*, under whom (persona), under which (cosa). || *Con lo cual*, at *o* upon which, whereupon (entonces), with which (con lo que). || *Del cual, de la cual, de los cuales, de las cuales*, of whom (personas), of which (cosas): *el hombre del cual hablé*, the man of whom I spoke; *cinco chicos dos de los cuales son bandidos*, five boys two of whom are bandits; *nueve planetas de los cuales la Tierra es uno*, nine planets of which the Earth is one. || *De lo cual*, which: *ha conseguido lo que quería, de lo cual me alegro mucho*, he got what he wanted which makes me very glad; from which: *de lo cual podemos inferir que*, from which we can infer that; whereof: *en fe de lo cual*, in witness whereof. || *Después de lo cual*, after which. || *En el cual*, in which, where: *el sitio en el cual nací*, the place where I was born. || *Lo cual*, which: *ya no nos habla, lo cual indica que está enfadado con nosotros*, he no longer speaks to us, which means he is angry with us. || *Por lo cual*, for which reason, because of which, whereby. || *Sin lo cual*, without which.
— SIN ARTÍCULO. Such as: *epidemias cuales se propagaban en la Edad Media ya no habrá más*, there will be no more epidemics such as those which were rife in the Middle Ages. || POÉT. Like: *cual las flores del naranjo*, like orange blossoms. || — *Allá cada cual*, every man to his own taste. || *Cada cual*, everyone (todos): *cada cual tiene sus problemas*, everyone has his problems; each, each one: *a cada cual lo suyo*, to each his own. || *Cual o cual*, a few: *entre la asistencia*

había cual o cual aficionado, among the audience, there were a few devotees.
— Adv. Like, as (como). || Just as: *cual se lo cuento*, just as I am telling you. || *Cual... tal*, like... like: *cual el padre, tal el hijo*, like father, like son.
cuál adj. y pron. interrog. Which, what: *no sé cuál será su decisión*, I do not know what his decision will be; *¿cuál es el camino más corto?*, which is the shortest way? || Which, which one: *¿cuál de los tres llegará primero?*, which of the three will arrive first? || — *Estaban gritando a cuál más*, they were trying to outshout each other. || *Los dos trabajan a cuál mejor*, the two work equally well, it is hard to say which of the two works better. || *Son a cuál más estúpidos*, they are each as stupid as the other.
— Pron. indef. Some: *todos se quejaban, cuáles de la comida, cuáles de la cama*, they all complained, some about the food, some about the beds. || *Todos contribuyeron, cuál más, cuál menos, a su éxito*, they all contributed in varying degrees to his success.
— Adv. Imagine!: *¡cuál fue su sorpresa!*, imagine his surprise! || How: *¡cuál gritan!*, how they shout!
cualesquier, cualesquiera pron. indef. pl. V. CUALQUIER, CUALQUIERA.
cualidad f. Quality, attribute (de personas). || Property (de cosas). || Quality: *la generosidad es una cualidad*, generosity is a quality.
cualificado, da adj. Skilled (obrero).
cualitativo, va adj. Qualitative.
cualquier adj. indef. Apocope of *cualquiera*. V. CUALQUIERA.

— OBSERV. The apocope of *cualquiera* is used before a masculine or feminine noun in the singular, even if the noun is preceded by an adjective: *cualquier hombre, cualquier otra mujer*. The form *cualquiera* is sometimes used before a feminine noun in the singular.

cualquiera pron. indef. Anyone, anybody: *cualquiera haría lo mismo*, anyone would do the same. || Any one, one (interrogativo), any one (afirmativo): *cualquiera de ustedes*, any one of you. || Whatever: *cualquiera que sea su excusa no le perdono*, whatever his excuse may be, I will not forgive him. || Nobody (nadie): *¡cualquiera lo creería!*, nobody would believe that! || Whichever, whichever one (personas y cosas): *cualquiera que quieras*, whichever you like. || Whoever (personas): *cualquiera que lo diga*, whoever says so. || — *Cualquiera que sea*, whoever he is (persona), whichever it is (cosa). || *Cualquiera lo diría*, one would think so, anyone would say so. || *Una cualquiera*, a loose woman (mujer desvergonzada), a woman of no account, a nobody (mujer sin importancia). || *Un cualquiera*, a man of no account, a nobody. || *Unos cualquieras*, people of no account, nobodies.
— Adj. indef. Any: *en cualquier momento* y *a cualquier hora*, at any moment, at any time; *cualquier hombre inteligente lo sabe*, any intelligent man knows that. || Whatever: *cualquier excusa que me des, no te creo*, I won't believe you whatever excuse you give me. || Whichever, any (cosas y personas): *puedes escoger cualquier plato [que quieras]*, you can choose any *o* whichever dish you like, you can choose any dish. || Ordinary: *un día cualquiera*, an ordinary day. || — *Cualquier cosa*, anything: *es capaz de hacer cualquier cosa*, he is capable of anything. || *Cualquier cosa que*, whatever: *cualquier cosa que haga*, whatever he does. || *Cualquier otro*, anyone else (personas): *cualquier otro menos yo*, anyone else but me; any other one (cosas). || *Cualquier persona que*, anybody who, whoever, anyone who: *cualquier persona que lo diga es un embustero*, anybody who says that is a fibber, whoever says that is a fibber; anyone who, anybody who: *admiro a cualquier persona que sepa hacerlo*, I admire anyone who can do it. || *En cualquier otra parte*, anywhere else. || *En cualquier sitio*, anywhere. || *Por cualquier parte que vaya*, wherever he goes.

— OBSERV. Pl. *cualesquiera* (*cualesquiera de ustedes*, any of you).

cuan adv. How: *no puedes imaginarte cuán cansada estoy*, you cannot imagine how tired I am. || How (exclamativo): *¡cuán pronto pasan los años!*, how quickly the years go by! || — *Cayó cuan largo era*, he fell full length. || *Tan... cuan*, as... as: *el castigo será tan grande cuan grave fue la culpa*, the punishment will be as severe as the offence was serious; *cuan bueno era el padre, tan malo es el hijo*, the son is as bad as the father was good.

— OBSERV. *Cuan* is the apocope of *cuanto* and is only used before adjectives and adverbs. It is accented in exclamatory and interrogative sentences.

cuando conj. When (en el tiempo en que): *será de noche cuando lleguemos a casa*, it will be night when we arrive home; *cuando joven, yo creía...*, when I was young, I believed... || Whenever (en cualquier momento): *estoy dispuesto a ayudarte cuando quieras*, I am ready to help you whenever you like. || Even though, even if, although (aunque): *cuando lo dijeras mil veces*, even if you said it a thousand times. || Since (puesto que): *cuando lo dices será verdad*, it must be true since you say so. || If: *cuando llueve llevo paraguas, cuando no, lo dejo en casa*, if it rains I take an umbrella, if not I leave it at home. || — *Aun cuando*, even if: *aun cuando llueva*, even if it rains; *aun cuando lo supiese me callaría*, even if I knew it I would not say anything. || *Cuando más* or *cuando mucho*, at the most (a lo sumo). || *Cuando mayor*, when I am [you are, he is, etc.] grown up *o* old enough: *cuando mayor compraré un coche*, when I am old enough I shall buy a car. || *Cuando menos*, at least: *tiene treinta años cuando menos*, he is thirty at least. || *Cuando no*, if not, otherwise (si no). || *Cuando quiera que*, whenever: *cuando quiera que venga me regala algo*, whenever he comes he brings me a present. || *De cuando en cuando* or *de vez en cuando*, from time to time, now and again. || *Entonces es cuando*, it was then that, that was when. || *Hasta cuando*, until.
— Adv. When: *vendrás, pero ¿cuándo?*, you will come, but when?; *no sé cuándo iré*, I don't know when I shall go. || — *Cuándo... cuándo*, at times... at times. || *Cuando quiera*, whenever you like. || *¿De cuándo acá?* or *¿desde cuándo?*, since when? || *¿Para cuándo?*, when?
— Prep. During: *cuando la guerra*, during the war. || At the time of: *cuando la última huelga*, at the time of the last strike.
— M. *El cómo y el cuándo*, the why and the wherefore.

— OBSERV. There is an accent on *cuando* in exclamatory and interrogative sentences.

cuanta m. pl. Quanta.

— OBSERV. En inglés el singular de *quanta* es *quantum*.

cuantía f. Quantity (cantidad). || Extent (extensión, alcance): *desconocemos la cuantía de los daños*, we don't know the extent of the damage. || Amount (importe). || Distinction, importance (de una persona). || Importance (importancia). || *Persona de mayor, de menor cuantía*, distinguished *o* important person, undistinguished *o* unimportant person.
cuántico, ca adj. Quantum, quantic: *teoría cuántica*, quantum theory.
cuantificación f. FIL. Quantification. || FÍS. Quantization.
cuantificar v. tr. FIL. To quantify. || FÍS. To quantize.
cuantimás adv. FAM. All the more [so].
cuantioso, sa adj. Abundant (abundante). || Numerous (numeroso). || Considerable, substantial (grande).
cuantitativo, va adj. Quantitative: *análisis cuantitativo*, quantitative analysis.
cuanto, ta adj. How much: *¿cuánto dinero tiene?*, how much money has he? || What a lot of: *¡cuánta gente!*, what a lot of people! || — Pl. How many: *¿cuántas manzanas quieres?*, how many apples do you want? || What, so many, what a lot of (exclamación): *¡cuántos problemas!*, what problems!, so many problems! || All: *empeñó cuantos libros tenía*, he pawned all his books. || — *Cuanto más... más*, the more... the more: *cuanto más dinero tiene, más quiere*, the more money he has the more he wants. || *Cuanto más frío hace, menos salgo*, the colder it is, the less I go out. || *Cuanto menos trabajo tiene, más se aburre*, the less work he has, the more bored he is. || *Cuantos... tantos*, as many... as: *cuantas cabezas, tantos pareceres*, as many opinions as there are individuals. || *Perdió no sé cuántos libros*, he lost I don't know how many books. || *Tanto... cuanto*, v. TANTO. || *Tanto más... cuanto que*, v. TANTO. || *Unos cuantos, unas cuantas*, a few: *tengo unos cuantos amigos*, I have a few friends.
— Pron. How much: *¿cuánto queda?*, how much is left? || All, as much as: *tome cuanto quiera*, take as much as you like. || All, everything: *¡si supieras cuánto me contó!*, if you knew all he told me! || — Pl. All who, everybody who: *cuantos vayan allí serán castigados*, all who go *o* everybody who goes there will be punished. || How many: *¿cuántos han muerto?*, how many have died? || — *Cuantos más, mejor*, the more the merrier. || *El señor no sé cuántos*, Mr. So-and-So. || *Tenemos que vender cuantos nos mandan*, we must sell all they send us *o* as many as they send us. || *Todo cuanto*, everything (cosas): *te dará todo cuanto quieras*, he will give you everything you want. || *Todos cuantos*, everybody, everyone, all (personas), all (cosas): *el cuadro les gusta a todos cuantos lo ven*, everybody who sees the painting likes it. || *Unos cuantos, unas cuantas*, a few, some.
— Adv. How much (de qué manera): *no sabes cuánto le odio*, you do not know how much I hate him. || How: *¡cuánto ha cambiado!*, how he has changed! || How much (cantidad): *¿cuánto vale esto?*, how much is this worth? || How long: *¿cuánto dura este disco?*, how long does this record play? || — *¿A cuánto estamos?* or *¿a cuántos estamos?*, what date is it? (fecha). || *¿Cada cuánto?*, every how often? || *Cuanto a* or *en cuanto a*, as for: *en cuanto a mí*, as for me. || *Cuanto antes*, as soon as possible. || *Cuanto más*, all the more (a mayor abundamiento), at the most: *esto vale cuanto más cien pesetas*, this is worth a hundred pesetas at the most. || *Cuanto más... más*, the more... the more: *cuanto más le conozco, más le quiero*, the more I know him the more I like him. || *Cuanto más mejor*, the more the better *o* the merrier. || *Cuanto más... menos*, the more... the less: *cuanto más lo miro, menos lo comprendo*, the more I look at it the less I understand it. || *En cuanto*, as soon as: *en cuanto le vi le sonreí*, as soon as I saw him I smiled at him; as: *ella, en cuanto estudiante*, she, as a student. || *Por cuanto*, since, inasmuch as.

— OBSERV. *Cuanto, cuanta* are written with an accent in exclamatory and interrogative sentences.
cuanto m. FÍS. Quantum.
cuaquerismo m. Quakerism (doctrina religiosa).
cuáquero, ra m. y f. Quaker.
cuarcita f. MIN. Quartzite.
cuarenta adj. Forty: *tengo cuarenta alumnos*, I have forty pupils.
— M. Forty. || Fortieth: *es el cuarenta de la clase*, he is the fortieth in the class.
— F. pl. Forty points gained by a player in the game of "tute" when he has the "rey" and the "caballo" of trumps. || FAM. *Cantar a uno las cuarenta*, to tell s.o. a few home truths, to give s.o. a piece of one's mind.
cuarentavo, va adj./s. Fortieth.
cuarentena f. Forty. || Lent (cuaresma). || Quarantine (medida de sanidad). || — *Poner en cuarentena*, to quarantine, to put in quarantine (sentido propio), to send to Coventry (no hablar a). || *Una cuarentena de*, about forty, forty-odd, some forty.
cuarentón, ona adj. Forty-year-old, in one's forties.
— M. y f. Forty-year-old, person in his [*o* her, etc.] forties.
cuaresma m. Lent.
cuaresmal adj. Lenten.
cuarta f. Quarter, fourth (cuarta parte). || Point (de la brújula). || Span (palmo). || Quart, quarte (en naipes). || ASTR. Quadrant. || Quarte, quart (en esgrima). || MÚS. Fourth. || *Amer.* Whip (látigo). || FAM. *No levanta una cuarta del suelo*, he's a shorty.
cuartana f. MED. Quartan.
cuartanal adj. MED. Quartan.
cuartear v. tr. To divide into four, to quarter (dividir en cuatro). || To cut into joints, to quarter (descuartizar). || To crack (fragmentar). || To zigzag along (carretera).
— V. intr. TAUR. To arch one's body [to put in the banderillas].
— V. pr. To crack, to split (agrietarse). || FIG. To crack, to weaken suddenly: *las estructuras de esta organización se han cuarteado*, the structures of this organization have suddenly weakened. || *Amer.* To go back on one's word.
cuartel m. MIL. Quarters, *pl.* (provisional). | Barracks, *pl.* (permanente). || Quarter (gracia concedida al vencido): *dar cuartel a*, to give quarter to. || (P. us.). Quarter (cuarta). || Quarter, district, area (barrio). || Bed (cuadro de jardín). || Lot, plot (de terreno). || HERÁLD. Quarter. || MAR. Hatch. || — *Cuartel general*, headquarters. || MIL. *Estar de cuartel*, to be unassigned and on half pay. || *Amer. Golpe de cuartel*, putsch. || *Guerra sin cuartel*, all out war. || FIG. *No dar cuartel a*, to be merciless to. || *Sin cuartel*, merciless: *lucha sin cuartel*, merciless fight.
cuartelada f. Putsch.
cuartelado, da adj. HERÁLD. Quartered.
cuartelar v. tr. HERÁLD. To quarter.
cuartelazo m. Putsch.
cuartelero adj. m. Barracks.
— M. MIL. Soldier on dormitory guard duty, orderly.
cuarteo m. Side step (del cuerpo). || Crack (grieta).
cuarterón, ona m. y f. Quadroon (mulato). || — M. Fourth, quarter (cuarta parte). || Quarter of a pound (peso de 125 gramos). || Shutter (de ventana). || Panel (de puerta).
cuarteta f. Quatrain (redondilla).
cuartete o **cuarteto** m. Quatrain (poema). || MÚS. Quartet, quartette: *cuarteto de cuerda*, string quartet.
cuartilla f. Sheet (de papel). || Pastern (de un animal).
cuartillo m. Half litre (1/2 litro). || Quarter of a *real* (antigua moneda).
cuartilludo, da adj. Long-pasterned [horse].
cuarto, ta adj. Fourth (que sigue al tercero). || Fourth: *Enrique IV* (cuarto), Henry IV [the fourth]. || — *Cuarta parte*, quarter, fourth part: *tres es la cuarta parte de doce*, three is a quarter *o* the fourth part of twelve. || *En cuarto lugar*, fourthly, in fourth place.
— M. Quarter: *un cuarto de hora*, a quarter of an hour; *son las dos y cuarto*, it's a quarter past two; *las ocho menos cuarto*, a quarter to eight. || Room: *estoy en mi cuarto*, I'm in my room; *este piso tiene dos cuartos y una cocina*, this flat has two rooms and a kitchen, this is a three-room flat. || Flat [U.S., apartment] (piso): *cuarto amueblado*, furnished flat. || Line, ancestors, *pl.* (línea de descendencia). || Quarter (de un vestido). || Quarter (de un animal). || Portion, plot (de un terreno). || ASTR. Quarter: *cuarto creciente*, first quarter; *cuarto menguante*, last quarter. || MIL. Watch: *estar de cuarto*, to be on watch. || VET. Crack (del casco del caballo). || — Pl. FAM. Cash, *sing.*, dough, *sing.*: *tener muchos cuartos*, to have a lot of dough. || — FAM. *Afloja los cuartos*, cough up, fork up. || *Botella de a cuarto*, quarter-litre bottle. || *Cuarto de banderas*, guardroom. || *Cuarto de baño*, bathroom. || *Cuarto de dormir*, bedroom. || *Cuarto de estar*, living room [U.S., living room, family room]. || *Cuarto delantero*, forequarter. || *Cuarto delantero derecho*, right front (de un vestido). || *Cuarto de prevención*, detention room. || *Cuarto oscuro*, darkroom (de fotógrafo). || DEP. *Cuartos de final*, quarter finals. || *Cuarto trasero*, hindquarter. || *Cuarto trastero* or *de los trastos*, lumber room. || *Cuatro cuartos*, very little: *ganó cuatro cuartos*, he won very little; a bit of money: *la gente cuando tiene cuatro cuartos*, people, when they get a bit of money; a song: *lo vendió por cuatro cuartos*, he sold it for a song. || FAM. *Dar un cuarto al pregonero*, to shout it from the rooftops. | *Dejar sin un cuarto*, to leave broke. | *De tres al cuarto*, cheap, of little value: *un vestido de tres al cuarto*, a cheap dress; third-rate: *un político de tres al cuarto*, a third-rate politician. | *Echar su cuarto a espadas*, to butt in, to put one's oar in. || *En cuarto*, quarto (encuadernación). || FAM. *Estar sin un cuarto*, to be broke. | *Manejar los cuartos*, to hold the purse strings. | *No andar bien de cuartos*, to be hard up for money. | *No tener un cuarto*, to be penniless, to be broke, not to have a penny. || *Poner a uno las peras a cuarto*, to clamp down on s.o. | *¡Qué... ni qué ocho cuartos!*, ... my foot!: *¡qué fantasmas ni qué ocho cuartos!*, ghosts my foot! || *Tres cuartos*, three-quarter-length: *manga, abrigo tres cuartos*, three-quarter-length sleeve, overcoat; three-quarter [back] (rugby). || *Tres cuartos de hora*, three quarters of an hour. || FAM. *Tres cuartos de lo mismo* or *de lo propio*, exactly the same: *hizo tres cuartos de lo mismo*, he did exactly the same.
cuartogénito, ta adj. Fourth-born.
— M. y f. Fourth-born, fourth child.
cuartucho m. FAM. Hovel (habitación mala).
cuarzo m. Quartz (piedra). || — *Cuarzo ahumado*, smoky quartz. || *Cuarzo hialino*, rock crystal.
cuarzoso, sa adj. GEOL. Quartzous, quartzose.
cuasi adv. (P. us.). Almost, quasi.
cuasia f. BOT. Quassia.
cuasicontrato m. JUR. Quasi contract.
cuasidelito m. JUR. Technical offence, quasi delict.
Cuasimodo n. pr. m. Quasimodo Sunday.
cuate, ta adj. *Amer.* Twin (gemelo). | Similar (semejante).
— M. y s. *Amer.* Twin (gemelo). | Mate: *¿qué me cuentas, cuate?* whats new, mate?
cuaternario, ria adj./s.m. Quaternary: *era cuaternaria*, Quaternary era.
cuaternio o **cuaternión** m. MAT. Quaternion.
cuatralbo, ba adj. With four white feet (caballo).
cuatreño, ña adj. Four-year-old (toro).
cuatrero, ra n. y f. Horse thief (de caballos), cattle thief (de vacas). || *Amer.* Rascal (bribón). || *Amer.* FAM. Jester, joker (guasón).
cuatrienal adj. Quadrennial.
cuatrifolio m. ARQ. Quatrefoil.
cuatrillizos, zas m. y f. pl. Quadruplets (niños).
cuatrillo m. Quadrille (juego de naipes).
cuatrillón m. Quadrillion [U.S., septillion].
cuatrimestral adj. Four-monthly (que ocurre cada cuatro meses). || Four-month (que dura cuatro meses).
cuatrimestre m. Four-month period.
cuatrimotor adj. m. Four-engined.
— M. Four-engined plane.
cuatrirreactor adj. m. Four-engined
— M. Four-engined jet.
cuatrisílabo, ba adj. Four-syllable, quadrisyllabic.
— M. Quadrisyllable.
cuatro adj. Four: *cuatro pesetas*, four pesetas. || Fourth: *Alejandro nació el día cuatro de marzo*, Alexander was born on the fourth of March.
— M. Four (número). || Fourth (fecha): *el 4* (*cuatro*) *de enero*, the fourth of January, January the fourth; 4 January, January 4th (encabezamiento de cartas). || Four (naipes): *el cuatro de corazones*, the four of hearts. || MÚS. Vocal quartet. || *Amer.* Four-string guitar (guitarra). | Blunder (disparate). || — FAM. *Cuatro gatos*, hardly a soul (casi nadie). || *Cuatro ojos ven más que dos*, two heads are better than one. || *De cuatro en cuatro*, every four (cada cuatro), four at a time (en grupos de a cuatro). || MÚS. *De cuatro por ocho*, four-eight. || *Las cuatro*, four o'clock: *son las cuatro*, it's four o'clock. || FIG. y FAM. *Más de cuatro*, several people, lots of people: *más de cuatro se equivocan*, lots of people make mistakes. | *Trabajar por cuatro*, to work like a slave.
cuatrocientos, tas adj./s.m. Four hundred.
cuba f. Vat, tub (tina). || Barrel, cask (barril). || FIG. y FAM. Potbelly (barrigón). | Drunkard (borracho). || — FIG. y FAM. *Beber como una cuba*, to drink like a fish. | *Cada cuba huele al vino que tiene*, every tub smells of the wine it holds. | *Estar* (*borracho*) *como una cuba*, to be plastered, to be sozzled, to be sloshed.
Cuba n. pr. GEOGR. Cuba. || — *Cuba libre*, rhum and coke. || FIG. *Más se perdió en Cuba*, worse things have happened at sea.
cubaje m. *Amer.* Cubage (cubicación).
cubanismo m. Cubanism.
cubano, na adj./s. Cuban. || — F. Loose-fitting shirt (guayabera).
cubero m. Cooper. || FIG. y FAM. *A ojo de buen cubero*, v. OJO.
cubertería f. Cutlery.
cubeta f. Small cask (tonel). || Pail, bucket (cuba pequeña). || FÍS. Bulb (del barómetro). || Tank, dish, tray (de laboratorio).
cubicación f. Cubage (acción de cubicar).
cubicar v. tr. MAT. To cube (elevar al cubo). | To cube (evaluar el volumen).

cúbico, ca adj. Cubic: *metro cúbico*, cubic metre. || Cube: *raíz cúbica*, cube root.
cubículo m. Cubicle.
cubierta f. Cover, covering. || Cover (de libro). || Cover, covering (funda). || Tyre, casing (del neumático). || Roof (tejado). || Bedspread (de la cama). || MAR. Deck: *cubierta de popa*, poop deck; *cubierta de proa*, front deck; *cubierta de vuelos*, flight deck. || Cover, wrapping (de un cable). || FIG. Pretext, cover. || *Amer.* Envelope (de una carta).
cubiertamente adv. Covertly.
cubierto, ta adj. Covered. || Overcast (cielo). || Filled (una vacante).
— M. Place setting (para comer). || Menu: *cubierto turístico*, tourists' menu. || Cover (abrigo): *ponerse a cubierto*, to take cover. || — Pl. Cutlery, *sing.* || — *A cubierto* or *bajo cubierto*, under cover: *ponerse a cubierto*, to get under cover. || *A cubierto de*, safe from. || *Juego de cubiertos*, canteen of cutlery. || *Poner los cubiertos*, to set the table. || *Precio del cubierto*, cover charge.
cubil m. Den, lair (de animales salvajes).
cubilete m. Mould (molde). || Ice cube (hielo). || Goblet (vaso de metal). || Conjurer's goblet (de prestidigitador). || Dicebox (para guardar los dados). || Cup (para echar los dados). || *Amer.* Top hat (sombrero de copa). | Plot, scheme (intriga). || *Bandeja para los cubiletes de hielo*, ice tray.
cubiletear v. intr. To scheme, to intrigue.
cubileteo m. Scheming, shady dealing.
cubilote m. Cupola (crisol).
cubismo m. Cubism (pintura y escultura).
cubista adj./s. Cubist.
cubital adj. ANAT. Cubital (del codo).
cubito m. Cube: *cubito de hielo*, ice cube. || Bucket (de niño).
cúbito m. ANAT. Cubitus, ulna (hueso).
cubo m. Pail, bucket (recipiente portátil). || Small vat *o* tank (cuba pequeña). || Socket, holder (de bayoneta). || Hub (de rueda). || Millpond (de un molino). || Drum, barrel (de reloj). || Round tower (de fortaleza). || MAT. Cube. || — *Cubo de la basura*, V. BASURA. || *Elevar al cubo*, to cube.
cuboflash m. FOT. Flashcube.
cuboides adj. inv. Cuboid (hueso).
cubrecadena m. Chain guard [of a bicycle].
cubrecama m. Counterpane, bedspread, coverlet.
cubrecorsé m. Camisole.
cubrefuego m. Curfew (queda).
cubrejuntas m. inv. TECN. Butt strap.
cubrepiés m. inv. Foot coverlet [U.S., foot blanket].
cubrerradiador m. Radiator muff.
cubretetera m. Tea cosy.
cubretiestos m. inv. Flowerpot cover.
cubrir v. tr. To cover: *cubrir algo con un velo*, to cover sth. with a veil. || To shroud, to cloak (la niebla, etc.). || To roof, to put a roof on (una casa). || FIG. To satisfy, to meet: *cubrir las necesidades*, to satisfy needs. | To cover, to meet (sufragar los gastos). | To cover: *los ingresos cubren los gastos*, the returns cover the expenses. | To drown: *su voz cubre todas las demás*, his voice drowns all the others. | To cover, to do (una distancia). | To repay (una deuda). | To fill: *cubrir una vacante*, to fill a vacancy. | To shield, to cover, to protect: *está cubierto por una persona importante*, he is being shielded by an important person. | To cover up, to hide, to mask (ocultar). || MIL. To cover (proteger): *cubrir la retirada*, to cover the retreat. || To cover, to mate with (un animal). || — *Cubrir carrera*, to line the route. || *Cubrir de besos*, to smother with kisses. || *Cubrir de gloria*, to cover with glory. || *Cubrir de alabanzas, de improperios*, to shower praise, insults on. || *Cubrir las apariencias* or *las formas*, to keep up appearances. || *Cubrir una demanda*, to meet a demand.
— V. pr. To put on one's hat (ponerse el sombrero). || To cloud over, to become overcast (el cielo). || FIG. To cover o.s.: *cubrirse de un riesgo con un seguro*, to cover o.s. for a risk with an insurance policy. | To be filled: *sólo pudieron cubrirse dos vacantes*, only two vacancies could be filled. || *Cubrirse de gloria*, to cover o.s. with glory.
cuca f. BOT. Ground almond, chufa (chufa). || ZOOL. Caterpillar (cuco). || Sweet (confite). || *Amer.* Kind of heron (zancuda).
cucamonas f. pl. FAM. Cajolery, *sing.*, sweet talk, *sing.* (carantoñas).
cucaña f. Greasy pole (diversión). || FIG. y FAM. Cinch, easy job (cosa fácil de conseguir).
cucañero, ra adj. Smart, resourceful.
— M. y f. Smart customer, resourceful person.
cucar v. tr. To wink (guiñar).
cucaracha f. Cockroach, blackbeetle (fam.). || Snuff (tabaco). || *Amer.* Trailer (de tranvía). | Old crock, jalopy (coche viejo).
cucarachero m. *Amer.* Smart customer, resourceful person.
cuclillas (en) loc. adv. Crouching, squatting. || *Ponerse en cuclillas*, to crouch, to squat.
cuclillo m. Cuckoo (ave).
cuco, ca adj. FIG. y FAM. Nice, cute, pretty (mono). | Crafty, sly, cunning (astuto).
— M. y f. Crafty *o* cunning person, wily bird. || Cheat, trickster (jugador tramposo). || — M. ZOOL. Cuckoo (pájaro). | Caterpillar (oruga). || — Pl. Panties (prenda de mujer). || *Reloj de cuco*, cuckoo clock.
cucú m. Cuckoo (canto del cuco).
cucufato m. *Amer.* Sanctimonious person, bigot.
cucuiza f. *Amer.* Agave fibre.
cuculí m. *Amer.* Wild pigeon.
cucúrbita f. BOT. Cucurbit. || QUÍM. Retort (retorta).
cucurbitáceo, a adj. Cucurbitaceous.
cucurucho m. Cone, cornet (envase). || Penitent's hood (caperuza). || *Amer.* Peak, summit, top.
cuchara f. Spoon (de mesa): *cuchara de café*, coffee spoon; *cuchara sopera*, soup spoon; *cuchara de palo*, wooden spoon; *cuchara de postre*, dessert spoon. || Ladle (cucharón para servir). || Ladle (para metales). || Spoon bait, trolling spoon (para la pesca). || MAR. Bailing scoop (achicador). || TECN. Bucket, scoop (de pala mecánica). || *Amer.* Trowel (llana). || — *Cuchara autoprensora*, grab bucket. || FIG. y FAM. *Meterle a alguien una cosa con cuchara*, to drum something into s.o. *o* into s.o.'s head. | *Meter su cuchara*, to put one's oar in.
cucharada f. Spoonful (cabida de la cuchara).
cucharadita f. Teaspoonful, teaspoon: *una cucharadita de café*, a teaspoonful of coffee.

— OBSERV. El plural de *teaspoonful* es *teaspoonfuls* o *teaspoonsful.*

cucharetear v. intr. FAM. To stir [with a spoon]: *cucharetear en algo*, to stir sth. [with a spoon]. || FIG. To poke one's nose into other people's affairs, to meddle in other people's affairs (entremeterse).
cucharilla f. Teaspoon (cuchara pequeña). || MIN. Fluke (para barrenos). || *Cucharilla de café*, coffee spoon.
cucharón m. Ladle (para servir). || TECN. Bucket, scoop.
cuche m. *Amer.* Pig.
cuché adj. m. *Papel cuché*, surface-coated paper, art paper.
cuchí m. *Amer.* Pig.
cuchichear v. intr. To whisper.
cuchicheo m. Whispering.
cuchichiar v. intr. To call, to cry (la perdiz).
cuchifrito m. Roast piglet.
cuchilla f. Kitchen knife (cuchillo grande) || Chopper, cleaver (de carnicero). || Blade (de guillotina). || Guillotine (del encuadernador). || Razor blade (hoja de afeitar). || Blade (de un arma blanca, de patín). || Coulter [U.S., colter] (de arado). || POÉT. Sword, blade (espada). || *Amer.* Mountain crest (cumbre). | Knife-edged ridge (montaña abrupta). | Mountain range (cadena). | Line of hills (colinas). || — FIG. *Cara cortada con una cuchilla*, hatchet face. || *Patines de cuchilla*, ice skates.
cuchillada f. Slash (golpe). || Stab wound (herida profunda). || Slash, gash (herida larga). || Slash (de vestidos). || — FIG. *Andar a cuchilladas*, to be at daggers drawn. || *Dar una cuchillada*, to stab. || *Dar de cuchilladas a uno*, to stab s.o. || *Matar a alguien a cuchilladas*, to stab s.o. to death.
cuchillazo m. Knife wound (herida). || *Dar un cuchillazo a alguien*, to stab s.o., to knife s.o.
cuchillería f. Cutlery (oficio). || Cutler's shop (tienda).
cuchillero m. Cutler. || *Amer.* Wrangler, troublemaker, quarrelsome person.
cuchillo m. Knife (instrumento cortante): *cuchillo de monte, de trinchar, de postre*, hunting knife, carving knife, dessert knife. || Knife-edge (de la balanza). || ZOOL. Lower tusk (del jabalí). || Gore (de un vestido). || FIG. Power, authority (jurisdicción). || ARQ. Gable frame. || MAR. Lateen sail. || — *Cuchillo bayoneta*, bayonet. || FIG. *Cuchillo de aire*, draught. || *Cuchillo de guillotina*, guillotine blade. || *Pasar a cuchillo a alguien*, to put s.o. to the sword. || FIG. *Tener el cuchillo en la garganta*, to have the knife at one's throat.
cuchipanda f. FAM. Feed (comilona). | Spree (juerga). || FAM. *Ir de cuchipanda*, to go on a spree (ir de juerga), to have a good feed (darse una comilona).
cuchitril m. Hovel, hole, squalid room (habitación sucia). || Den, hole, cubbyhole (habitación pequeña).
cuchufleta f. FAM. Joke (broma). || *Gastar cuchufletas a uno*, to pull s.o.'s leg.
cuchufletear v. intr. FAM. To tell *o* to crack jokes.
cuchufletero, ra m. y f. FAM. Joker, tease, leg-puller.
cueca f. Popular dance of Chile.
cuelgacapas m. inv. Coat rack (en la pared), coat stand (en un soporte).
cuelgaplatos m. inv. Plate rack.
cuellicorto, ta adj. Short-necked.
cuellilargo, ga adj. Long-necked.
cuello m. Neck (del cuerpo): *alargar el cuello*, to stretch *o* to crane one's neck. || Throat: *cortar el cuello a uno*, to cut s.o.'s throat. || Neck (de botella, retorta, etc.). || Collar (de un vestido, de una camisa): *cuello almidonado, duro*, starched, stiff collar. || Neck (de un diente). || Collar size (número de cuello de una camisa). || Collar, collarette (de encaje). || — *Agarrar* or *agarrarse a uno del cuello* or *por el cuello*, to grab *o* to seize s.o. by the scruff of the neck. || *Cuello alechugado* or *escarolado*, ruff. || *Cuello de pajarita* or *de palomita*, wing collar. || *Cuello de pico*, V-neck. || *Cuello*

postizo, detachable collar. || *Cuello vuelto*, roll neck, polo neck [U.S., turtleneck]. || FIG. *Estar metido en algo hasta el cuello*, to be in it up to one's neck. | *Hablar para el cuello de su camisa*, to talk to o.s. || FIG. y FAM. *Me juego el cuello a que*, I bet anything you like that. | *Meter el cuello*, to put one's nose to the grindstone, to put one's back into it.

cuenca f. Wooden bowl (escudilla). || Socket (del ojo). || GEOGR. Basin: *la cuenca del Ebro*, the Ebro basin. | Valley (valle). | Field: *cuenca petrolífera*, oil field.

cuenco m. Earthenware bowl (recipiente de barro).

cuenta f. Account. || Counting (acción de contar). || Count (resultado de contar). || Bill [U.S., check] (factura): *la cuenta de la electricidad*, the electricity bill; *¡mozo, traiga la cuenta, por favor!*, waiter, the bill, please! || DEP. Count (boxeo). || COM. Account: *cuenta bancaria*, bank account. || Bead (de rosario o collar). || FIG. Affair, business (cuidado): *eso es cuenta tuya*, that's your affair.

— *Abonar en cuenta*, V. ABONAR. || *Abrir una cuenta*, to open an account. || *A cuenta, a buena cuenta*, on account: *dar cierta cantidad a cuenta*, to give a certain amount on account; *cien pesetas a cuenta de las mil que usted me debe*, a hundred pesetas on account of the thousand that you owe me. || *¿A cuenta de qué?*, why on earth?, why?, for what reason? || *A fin de cuentas*, when all is said and done, all things considered, taking everything into account (finalmente). || *Caer en la cuenta de que*, to realize that. || COM. *Cargar algo en cuenta a uno*, to debit s.o.'s account with sth.: *...valor que le hemos cargado en cuenta,...* and we have debited your account with this amount; to charge sth. to s.o.'s account (en un almacén, etc.). || *Cerrar una cuenta*, to close an account. || *Con cuenta y razón*, carefully. || *Cuenta atrás*, countdown. || *Cuenta corriente*, current account [U.S., checking account]. || *Cuenta de efectos impagados*, bills payable account. || FAM. *Cuenta de la vieja*, counting on one's fingers. || *Cuenta pendiente*, outstanding account. || *Cuenta redonda*, round sum. || FIG. *Cuentas galanas* or *del Gran Capitán*, exorbitant and fictitious accounts. || *Dar buena cuenta de sí*, to give a good account of o.s. || *Dar cuenta de*, to give an account of (dar a conocer), to give account of (explicar), to tell about *o* to inform of (comunicar), to polish off: *dar cuenta de una tortilla*, to polish off an omelette. || *Dar en la cuenta*, to realize. || *Darse cuenta de*, to realize. || *De cuenta*, of importance, important. || *Dejar de cuenta*, to ignore. || *Echar la cuenta* or *las cuentas*, to reckon up. | *En resumidas cuentas*, in short, in a word. || *Entrar en cuenta*, to come into it, to enter into account. || *Estar fuera de cuenta*, to have reached one's time (una mujer). || *Estar lejos de la cuenta*, to be wide of the mark, to be very much mistaken. || *Esto corre de* or *por mi cuenta*, I'm taking charge of this, I'm seeing to this (encargarse de), I'm bearing the cost of it (pagar), this one's on me (pagar una copa). || *Habida cuenta de*, taking into account. || FIG. *Hacer las cuentas de la lechera*, to count one's chickens before they are hatched. || *Hacerse cuenta de*, to imagine, to think, to suppose. || *Hacer sus cuentas*, to do one's accounts. || FIG. *Las cuentas claras y el chocolate espeso*, let's keep the books straight. || *Las cuentas son las cuentas*, business is business. || FIG. *Le voy a ajustar las cuentas*, I've a bone to pick with him. || *Llevar las cuentas*, to keep the accounts. || *Más de la cuenta*, too much, too many. || *Me salen mal las cuentas*, I've miscalculated (por calcular mal), my figures don't tally (por olvidar una cifra, etc.). || FIG. *No querer cuentas con uno*, to want nothing to do with s.o. | *No tener que dar cuentas a nadie*, not to be answerable to anyone. || *Pasar las cuentas del rosario*, to tell one's beads. || *Pedir cuentas a uno*, to call s.o. to account (preguntar), to have it out with s.o. (reprender). || *Perder la cuenta de*, to lose count of. || *Por cuenta de*, on behalf of (en nombre de), for (para). || *Por cuenta y riesgo de uno*, at one's own risk. || *Por la cuenta que le trae*, in his own interest: *ya se preocupará de llegar a tiempo, por la cuenta que le trae*, he'll make sure he gets here on time in his own interest. || *Por mi cuenta*, for my part, as for me. || *Por su propia cuenta*, for o.s. (para sí), by o.s. (solo). || *Saldar una cuenta*, V. SALDAR. || *Salirle a cuenta a uno*, to be worth one's while. || *Si echamos la cuenta*, all things considered, taking everything into account. || *Tener cuenta*, to be advantageous *o* profitable (provechoso), to be worthwhile (conveniente). || *Tener en cuenta*, to bear in mind, to consider, to take into account *o* consideration: *tengamos en cuenta sus proposiciones*, let us take his proposals into consideration; *tenga usted en cuenta que*, bear in mind that. || COM. *Tomar cuentas*, to audit the accounts. || *Tomar en cuenta*, to take into account, to bear in mind (tomar en consideración), to mind: *no tomes en cuenta que no venga a visitarte*, don't mind if I don't come and visit you. || *Trabajar por cuenta de alguien*, to work for s.o. || *Trabajar por su cuenta* or *por cuenta propia*, to work for o.s., to be self-employed, to be one's own boss. || *Traer cuenta a uno*, to be to one's advantage, to be profitable (provechoso), to be worth one's while (conveniente). || *Vamos a cuentas*, let's settle the matter, let's get things straight, let's clear this up. || *Vivir a cuenta de*, to live at the expense of. || *Ya caigo en la cuenta*, now I get it, the penny has dropped.

cuentacorrentista m. y f. Current-account holder (titular de una cuenta corriente).

cuentagotas m. inv. Dropper. || FIG. *Dar una cosa con cuentagotas*, to give sth. little by little.

cuentahílos m. inv. Counting glass, thread counter.

cuentakilómetros m. inv. AUT. Mileage recorder, milometer (para contar la distancia recorrida). | Speedometer (velocímetro).

cuentarrevoluciones o **cuentavueltas** m. inv. Revolution counter, rev. counter.

cuentista adj. Story-writing (autor de cuentos). || FIG. y FAM. Gossipy (chismoso). | Storytelling, fibbing (mentiroso). | Exaggerating (exagerado).

— M. y f. Storywriter (autor de cuentos). || FIG. y FAM. Gossip (chismoso). | Fibber, storyteller (mentiroso). | Exaggerator (exagerado).

cuento m. Story, tale, (relato): *contar un cuento de hadas*, to tell a fairy tale. || Tip (de bastón, etc.). || FAM. Gossip, tittle-tattle (chisme). | Fib, story (mentira): *no me vengas con cuentos*, don't come to me with fibs. | Tall story, yarn (cosa increíble). | Trouble (disgusto). | Fuss (exageración).

— *A cuento de*, with regard to, concerning. || *¿A cuento de qué?*, why? || *¡Aplíquese el cuento!*, you might take a lesson from it yourself. || *Cuento chino* or *tártaro*, cock-and-bull story. || *Cuento de viejas*, old wives' tale. || *Dejarse de cuentos*, to come to the point. || *¡Déjate de cuentos!*, stop beating about the bush, get to the point (no andar con rodeos), stop telling fibs!, don't tell tales! (un niño), get away with you!, come off it! (no mentir). || *Es cuento largo*, it's a long story. || *Es el cuento de nunca acabar*, there's no end to it, it goes on and on. || *Eso es el cuento de la lechera*, don't count your chickens before they're hatched. || FIG. *Estar en el cuento*, to be in the picture, to be well-informed. || *Esto parece cuento*, it's unbelievable. || *Ir con el cuento a alguien*, to go and tell s.o. || *Nada de cuentos*, no fuss (a un niño), don't come that with me (a una persona mayor). || *No venir a cuento*, to be irrelevant, to have nothing to do with it (no ser pertinente). || *¡Puro cuento!*, a likely story!, all lies! || *Sin cuento*, numberless, countless, innumerable. || *Tener mucho cuento*, to be always having people on (engañar), to put on airs, to give o.s. airs (presumir), to make a lot of fuss, to exaggerate (exagerar). || *Traer a cuento*, to bring up (mencionar). || *¡Váyase con el cuento a otra parte!*, tell that to the marines! || *Venir a cuento*, to be opportune (ser oportuno), to be relevant (ser pertinente).

cuera f. *Amer.* Legging (polaina). | Smack, spank (azotaina). | Leather jacket (chaqueta).

cuerazo m. *Amer.* Lash (latigazo).

cuerda f. Rope: *cuerda de cáñamo*, hemp rope. || Cord (de tamaño medio). || String (bramante). || Measuring tape (en topografía). || ANAT. Chord: *cuerdas vocales*, vocal chords. || Chain (del reloj antiguo). || Spring (muelle). || Chain gang (presos). || Fuse (mecha). || DEP. Rails, *pl.* (de la pista de un hipódromo). | Inside (de la pista de un estadio). || MAT. Chord. || MÚS. Voice (voz). | Range (extensión de la voz). | String (de la guitarra, del violín). || — Pl. DEP. Ropes (del ring). || MÚS. Strings (instrumentos). | Voices (voces).

— FIG. *Acabársele a uno la cuerda*, to be at the end of one's tether. | *Aflojar la cuerda*, to ease up. | *Andar* or *bailar en la cuerda floja*, to walk the tightrope. | *Apretar la cuerda*, to clamp down, to tighten up. || *Cuerda de plomada*, plumbline. || *Cuerda de tripas*, catgut. || *Cuerda floja*, tightrope. || FIG. *Dar cuerda a algo*, to prolong sth. | *Dar cuerda a uno*, to encourage s.o. [to speak], to start s.o. off [speaking]. || FIG. *Dar cuerda a un reloj*, to wind [up] a clock. || *Estar con la cuerda al cuello*, to have one's neck in a noose. | *No ser de la misma cuerda*, not to be of the same opinion (tener opiniones distintas). | *Obrar bajo cuerda*, to act in an underhand way. | *Parece que a éste le han dado cuerda*, he's away, he's off, he's started. | *Siempre se rompe la cuerda por lo más delgado*, the weakest goes to the wall. | *Tener cuerda para rato*, to have still a long way to go. | *Tirar de la cuerda*, to go too far (abusar). | *Tocar la cuerda sensible*, to touch s.o.'s soft spot.

cuerdamente adv. Prudently, wisely, sensibly.

cuerdo, da adj. Sane (sano de juicio). || Wise, prudent, sensible (sensato).

— M. y f. Sane *o* rational person (sano de juicio). || Wise *o* prudent *o* sensible person (sensato). || *De cuerdo y loco todos tenemos un poco*, every man has a fool up his sleeve.

cuereada f. *Amer.* Beating, thrashing (paliza).

cuerear v. tr. *Amer.* To skin, to flay (desollar). || To prepare [hides]. | To beat, to thrash (golpear). | To denigrate, to vilify (hablar mal de uno).

cueriza f. *Amer.* FAM. Beating, thrashing (paliza).

cuerna f. Horns, *pl.* (cornamenta). || Antlers, *pl.* (del ciervo). || Horn (recipiente). || Hunting horn (trompa).

cuerno m. Horn (asta). || Antler (del ciervo). || Horn (materia): *peine de cuerno*, horn comb. || Horn (del caracol). || Feeler, antenna (de los insectos). || Cusp (de la Luna). || ANAT. Cornu (de médula). || MÚS. Horn. || — FIG. Coger *el toro por los cuernos*, to take

the bull by the horns. || *Cuerno de caza*, hunting horn. || *Cuerno de la abundancia*, horn of plenty, cornucopia. || FIG. y FAM. *Estar en los cuernos del toro*, to be in the lion's mouth, to have the tiger by the tail. | *Irse al cuerno*, to fall through (un proyecto). | *Levantar* or *poner en los cuernos de la Luna*, to praise to the skies. | *Mandar a uno al cuerno*, to send s.o. packing, to send s.o. about his business. | *No valer un cuerno*, not to be worth a farthing. | *Poner a uno en los cuernos del toro*, to put s.o. in a dangerous situation. | *Poner los cuernos a*, to be unfaithful to, to cuckold (hacer cornudo). | *Saber a cuerno quemado*, to be distasteful, to make a disagreeable impression (desagradable), to be suspicious (sospechoso). | *¡Váyase al cuerno!*, go to the devil!, go to blazes!
— Interj. *¡Cuerno!*, golly!, gosh!, blimey! (con asombro, admiración), darn it!, dash it! (con enfado).

cuero m. Hide, skin (piel). || Leather: *zapatos de cuero*, leather shoes. || Wineskin (odre). || Washer (del grifo). || *Amer.* Whip (látigo). || — *Amer.* FAM. *Arrimar el cuero* or *dar* or *echar cuero a uno*, to give s.o. a hiding *o* a beating. || *Cuero adobado*, tanned skin. || *Cuero cabelludo*, scalp. || FAM. *En cueros*, naked, in one's birthday suit. | *En cueros vivos*, stark naked, starkers. | *Estar hecho un cuero*, to be canned *o* sozzled. | *Quedarse en cueros*, to be cleaned out (quedarse sin nada).

cuerpear v. intr. *Amer.* To dodge.

cuerpo m. Body: *el cuerpo humano*, the human body. || Body, figure: *tiene un cuerpo fabuloso*, she's got a fabulous figure. || Body (de un tejido, de un vino, de una salsa). || Bodice, body (de un vestido). || Body (cadáver). || Section, part, piece: *armario de dos cuerpos*, two-piece wardrobe, wardrobe in two sections *o* parts. || Stage: *nave espacial de un solo cuerpo*, single-stage spaceship. || Volume (libro): *biblioteca de mil cuerpos*, library with a thousand volumes. || Corps: *cuerpo diplomático*, diplomatic corps; *cuerpo de sanidad*, medical corps. || Body: *cuerpo legislativo*, legislative body. || Body, staff (personal): *cuerpo docente*, teaching body. || ANAT. Corpus, body: *cuerpo amarillo*, corpus luteum, yellow body. || ASTR. Body: *cuerpo celeste*, heavenly body. || DEP. Length: *ganar por medio cuerpo*, to win by half a length. || ARQ. Main part *o* body [of a building]. || JUR. Corpus, body (compilación). || IMPR. Body, size (de una letra). || MIL. Body, corps. || QUÍM. FÍS. y MAT. Body. || FIG. Main part (parte principal).
— *A cuerpo* or *a cuerpo gentil*, without a coat, not wearing a coat. || *A cuerpo descubierto*, exposed, unprotected (sin protección), defenceless, unarmed (sin armas), without *o* not wearing a coat *o* cloak. || *A cuerpo limpio*, defenceless, unarmed (sin armas). || *A medio cuerpo*, up to the waist. || *Bañador de cuerpo entero*, one-piece bathing costume. || *Bañador de medio cuerpo*, bathing trunks, *pl.* || *Cuerpo a cuerpo*, hand-to-hand: *combate cuerpo a cuerpo*, hand-to-hand combat; hand-to-hand fight: *un cuerpo a cuerpo encarnizado*, a fierce hand-to-hand fight. || *Cuerpo a tierra*, on one's stomach, flat on one's face. || QUÍM. *Cuerpo compuesto*, compound. || TEATR. *Cuerpo de baile*, corps de ballet. || *Cuerpo de bomberos*, fire brigade. || *Cuerpo de casa*, housework (limpieza), maid (criada). || *Cuerpo de guardia*, guard (soldados), guardhouse (edificio). || JUR. *Cuerpo del delito*, corpus delicti. || *Cuerpo electoral*, constituent body. || *Cuerpo facultativo*, medical profession, doctors, *pl.* || MAR. *Cuerpo muerto*, mooring buoy. || QUÍM. *Cuerpo simple*, element. || *Dar con el cuerpo en tierra*, to fall down. || *Dar cuerpo*, to give body, to thicken (a un líquido). || *De cuerpo entero*, full-length (retrato), real, true (auténtico). || *De cuerpo presente*, in person (en persona), laid out (un cadáver), lying in state (un personaje importante). || *De medio cuerpo*, half-length: *retrato de medio cuerpo*, half-length portrait; up to the waist, up to one's waist: *entrar en el agua de medio cuerpo*, to go into the water up to one's waist. || FIG. y FAM. *En cuerpo y alma*, heart and soul, totally. | *Estar a cuerpo de rey*, to live like a king. || *Formar cuerpo con*, to form one *o* a whole with. || FAM. *Hacer de* or *del cuerpo*, to empty the bowels. || *Hurtar el cuerpo*, to dodge, to swerve (fintar). || FAM. *Me pide el cuerpo hacerlo*, I'm dying to *o* longing to do it. | *Mi cuerpo serrano*, yours truly. | *No quedarse con nada en el cuerpo*, to confess everything, to get it off one's chest. || *No tener nada en el cuerpo*, to have an empty stomach. || FIG. *Pertenecer a alguien en cuerpo y alma*, to belong to s.o. body and soul. || FAM. *Sacarle a uno algo del cuerpo*, to get sth. out of s.o., to make s.o. tell sth. | *Saltar a cuerpo limpio*, to clear, to jump over. | *Tener buen cuerpo*, to have a good figure (una mujer). | *¡Tengo un miedo en el cuerpo!*, I'm scared stiff! | *Tomar* or *cobrar cuerpo*, to take shape (un proyecto), to thicken (una salsa). || FIG. *Tratar a uno a cuerpo de rey*, to treat s.o. like a king.

cuervo m. ZOOL. Crow. | Raven. || — FIG. *Cría cuervos y te sacarán los ojos*, a dog bites the hand that feeds it. | *Criar cuervos*, to nourish a viper in one's bosom. || — ZOOL. *Cuervo marino*, cormorant (mergo). | *Cuervo merendero*, rook.

cuesco m. Stone (hueso de fruta). || POP. Fart (pedo).

cuesta f. Slope, hill (pendiente). || GEOGR. Cuesta, escarpment. || — *A cuestas*, on one's back: *llevar un bulto a cuestas*, to carry a bundle on one's back; on one's shoulders (una responsabilidad). || *A la mitad de la cuesta*, halfway up [the hill]. || FIG. *Cuesta de enero*, money problems (*pl.*) due to Christmas spending. || *En cuesta*, on a slope, sloping. || FIG. *Este trabajo se me ha hecho cuesta arriba*, I've found this work hard going. || *Ir cuesta abajo*, to go downhill (bajar), to go downhill, to decline (decaer). || *Ir cuesta arriba*, to go uphill. || FIG. *Tener a uno a cuestas*, to have s.o. in one's charge *o* care.
— OBSERV. The Spanish word *cuesta* is recognized in international geographical language as denoting an escarpment.

cuestación f. Collection.

cuestión f. Subject, topic, question (tema): *una cuestión interesante*, an interesting topic; *poner una cuestión sobre el tapete*, to bring up a subject [for discussion]. || Matter, question: *es cuestión de vida o muerte*, it's a matter of life and death; *es cuestión de un cuarto de hora*, it's a question of a quarter of an hour. || Dispute, quarrel (riña). || Fuss, trouble, bother (dificultad, lío): *no quiero cuestiones con nadie*, I want no fuss from *o* trouble with anyone. || JUR. Question (tormento). || — *Cuestión batallona*, vexed *o* much-debated question, moot point. || *Cuestión candente*, burning question. || *Cuestión previa*, previous question. || *En cuestión*, in question (de que se trata), at issue: *la controversia en cuestión*, the controversy at issue. || *En cuestión de*, as regards, in the matter of (en materia de), in a matter of: *en cuestión de quince días*, in a matter of a fortnight. || *Eso es cuestión mía*, that's my affair *o* business. || *Eso es otra cuestión*, that's a different kettle of fish, that's another matter. || *La cuestión es que*, the thing is that. || *La cuestión está en saber si*, the question is whether.

cuestionable adj. Debatable, questionable (discutible).

cuestionar v. tr. (P. us.). To debate, to question, to discuss (discutir).
— V. intr. To argue.

cuestionario m. Questionnaire (en una encuesta). || Question paper, questions, *pl.* (en un examen).

cuestor m. Quaestor (magistrado). || Collector (el que pide para una cuestación).

cuestura f. Quaestorship (oficio del cuestor).

cueto m. Fortified peak. || High crag, rocky peak.

cueva f. Cave: *las cuevas de Altamira*, the caves of Altamira. || Cellar (subterráneo, cabaret). || *Cueva de ladrones*, den of thieves.

cuévano m. Pannier (cesto grande).

cueza f. o **cuezo** m. Trough (de albañil).

cúfico, ca adj. Kufic, cufic (escritura).

cuí m. *Amer.* Guinea pig (conejillo de Indias).

cuica f. *Amer.* Earthworm (lombriz).

cuicacoche f. *Amer.* Kind of thrush.

cuico m. *Amer.* Foreigner (extranjero). || *Amer.* FAM. Copper, cop (agente de policía).

cuidado m. Care, caution (atención). || Care, charge (dependencia). || Affair, concern: *eso es cuidado tuyo*, that's your affair; *correr al cuidado de uno*, to be s.o.'s concern. || Care, worry (preocupación): *vivir libre de cuidados*, to live free from worries. || — Pl. Care, *sing.*, attention, *sing.* (del médico). ||
— *Al cuidado de*, in *o* under the care of, in the charge *o* hands of (cargo). || *Al cuidado del Sr. Pérez*, care of Mr. Pérez (en cartas). || *Andar* or *ir con cuidado*, to be careful, to go carefully, to watch one's step. || *Bajo el cuidado de*, in *o* under the care of. || *¡Cuidado!*, look out!, watch out!, be careful!, careful! || *Cuidado con*, mind (atención): *¡cuidado con el coche!*, mind the car!; *¡cuidado con la pintura!*, mind the paint!; beware of: *¡cuidado con el perro!*, beware of the dog!; what (para censurar): *¡cuidado con el niño!*, what a brat! || *¡Cuidado con Juan, qué pesado es!*, how tiresome that John is! || *De cuidado*, seriously, gravely: *está enfermo de cuidado*, he is seriously ill; shocking: *un catarro de cuidado*, a shocking cold. || *Dejar a uno el cuidado de hacer algo*, to leave it to s.o. to do sth. || *Estar al cuidado de*, to be in *o* under the care of (persona), to be in the charge *o* hands of (cargo). || *Hombre de cuidado*, dangerous man, man to be wary of. || FAM. *Me tiene* or *me trae sin cuidado*, I don't care, I don't give a damn, I couldn't care less. || *No hay cuidado* or *pierda cuidado*, don't worry. || *Poner cuidado en*, to take care in, to be careful in. || *Poner fuera de cuidado a un enfermo*, to pull a patient through. || *Salir de cuidado*, to be delivered of a child (en un parto), to pull through (en una enfermedad). || *Ser de cuidado*, to be dangerous (peligroso), to be unreliable *o* untrustworthy (poco seguro), to be serious: *esta herida es de cuidado*, this wound is serious. || *Sin cuidado*, carelessly, without care. || *¡Ten cuidado!*, be careful! || *Tener cuidado con*, to be careful of.

cuidador, ra adj. Careful, cautious.
— M. Trainer (en rugby, fútbol, etc.), second (en boxeo). || — F. *Amer.* Nurse (enfermera). | Nursemaid, nanny (niñera).

cuidadosamente adv. Carefully, with care, painstakingly (con aplicación). || Cautiously, carefully, prudently, warily (con precaución).

cuidadoso, sa adj. Careful (aplicado). || Concerned, anxious (atento): *cuidadoso del resultado*, anxious about the outcome. || Cautious, wary, prudent

(prudente). || Particular, attentive: *cuidadoso de los detalles*, particular about details, attentive to detail.
cuidar v. tr. To look after, to care for, to nurse (asistir): *cuidar a un enfermo*, to look after a sick person. || To look after, to take care of: *en esta pensión me cuidan mucho*, in this boardinghouse I am well looked after *o* well taken care of; *cuidar la casa*, to look after the house; *cuidar su ropa*, to take care of one's clothes. || MED. To attend. | To nurse (una herida). || FIG. To pay attention to: *cuidar los detalles*, to pay attention to details.
— V. intr. *Cuidar de*, to look after, to take care of: *cuidar de su salud, de los niños*, to take care of one's health, to look after the children; to fuss over, to wait on [s.o.] hand and foot (asistir solícitamente). || *Cuidar de que*, to take care that, to see that, || *Cuidar de sus obligaciones*, to fulfil one's obligations.
— V. pr. To take care of o.s., to look after o.s. (la salud). || — *Cuidarse bien de hacer algo*, to take good care not to do sth. || *Cuidarse de*, to take care of, to look after (la salud, etc.), to bother about, to worry about: *no se cuida del qué dirán*, he does not worry about what people will say; to mind, to watch, to be careful of: *cuídate de lo que dices*, mind what you say; to take care of, to look after (ocuparse de). || *Cuidarse mucho*, to take great care of o.s., to mollycoddle o.s. (fam.). || *Dejar de cuidarse*, to let o.s. go.
cuido m. Care, minding.
cuija f. *Amer.* Small lizard (lagartija). | FIG. Skinny woman (mujer flaca).
cuita f. Worry, trouble (preocupación). || Sorrow, grief (pena). || *Amer.* Bird dropping, birdlime. || *Las cuitas del joven Werther*, the sorrows of Werther (de Goethe).
cuitado, da adj. Worried, troubled (preocupado). || Bashful, shy, timid (apocado).
cuja f. (P. us.). Bedstead (armazón de la cama). || Lance *o* standard bucket (para la lanza *o* la bandera). || *Amer.* Bed (cama).
culada f. Fall on one's backside.
culantrillo m. BOT. Maidenhair.
culantro m. BOT. Coriander.
culata f. Cylinder head, head (de motor). || Breech (del cañón). || Butt (de escopeta). || FIG. Rear, back (parte posterior). || Croup [of horse] (anca). || MIN. Collet (de la talla de un diamante).
culatazo m. o **culatada** f. Blow with the butt [of a gun] (golpe). || Kick, recoil (retroceso de un arma).
culazo m. Fall on one's backside.
culear v. intr. FAM. To wiggle.
culebra f. ZOOL. Snake. || Worm (del alambique). || FIG. y FAM. Disturbance, din (alboroto). || — ZOOL. *Culebra de cascabel*, rattlesnake. || FIG. y FAM. *Saber más que las culebras*, to be as sly *o* as cunning as a fox.
culebrear v. intr. To slither (en el suelo). || To snake, to meander, to wind, to zigzag (un río, un camino). || To zigzag, to stagger (una persona).
culebreo m. Slither (de la serpiente). || Winding, twisting, zigzag (de un río, de un camino). || Zigzagging (una persona).
culebrilla f. MED. Tetter (herpes). || Young of a snake (cría de culebra). || BOT. Green dragon. || Crack (en un cañón). || *Papel de culebrilla*, tissue paper.
culebrina f. Culverin (cañón). || Lightning (relámpago).
culera f. Stain left on a baby's nappy (mancha). || Seat (de pantalón), patch (remiendo).
culero, ra adj. Lazy, sluggish, slothful.
— M. Baby's nappy [U.S., diaper].
culi m. Coolie.
culibajo, ja adj. FAM. Dumpy.
culiblanco m. ZOOL. Wheatear.
culinario, ria adj. Culinary (de cocina).
culmen m. Summit, peak (cumbre).
culminación f. ASTR. Culmination. || FIG. Culmination, crowning *o* culminating point.
culminante adj. Culminating.
culminar v. intr. To culminate. || ASTR. To culminate. || FIG. *Su carrera culminó en la presidencia*, his career culminated in his becoming president.
culo m. FAM. Backside, bottom, arse (pop.) [U.S., ass] (asentaderas): *caer de culo*, to fall on one's backside. || FIG. Bottom (de algunos objetos): *el culo de una botella*, the bottom of a bottle. | End (extremo). || — IMPR. *Culo de lámpara*, tailpiece, cul-de-lampe. || FAM. *Culo* or *culillo de mal asiento*, fidget, fidget breeches, fidgety *o* restless person. || FIG. y FAM. *Culo de pollo*, pucker, ill-mended part in stockings or clothes. || *Culo de vaso*, bottom of a glass (de una copa), imitation precious stone (piedra falsa). || FAM. *Ir de culo* to go downhill. | *Poner los labios de culo* or *de culito de pollo*, to purse the lips. | *Vamos de culo*, things are going very badly for us.
culombio m. ELECTR. Coulomb.
culón, ona adj. FAM. Broad-bottomed, big-bottomed, broad in the beam (persona).
— M. (Ant.). Disabled soldier (soldado).
culote m. Base (casquillo).
culpa f. Fault: *es culpa suya*, it's his fault; *¿de quién es la culpa?*, whose fault is it? || Blame: *echar la culpa de algo a uno*, to throw *o* to put the blame for sth. on s.o. || — Pl. Sins: *pagar las culpas ajenas*, to pay for s.o. else's sins.
— *Echar la culpa de*, to blame for, to throw *o* to put the blame [on s.o.] for: *me ha echado la culpa de su fracaso*, he has blamed me for his failure. || *Es culpa mía*, I'm to blame, it's my fault. || *La culpa es de David*, it is David's fault, David is to blame, the fault lies with David. || *No tengo la culpa*, it's not my fault, I'm not to blame. || *Por culpa de*, because of, through: *por culpa de lo que dijiste*, because of what you said. || *Por culpa tuya*, because of *o* through you, thanks to you, through fault of yours. || *Tener la culpa de*, to be to blame for, to be guilty of.
culpabilidad f. Culpability. || JUR. Guilt. || — JUR. *Declaración de no culpabilidad*, declaration of innocence. | *Solicitar la declaración de culpabilidad*, to plead guilty.
culpable adj. Guilty, culpable, to blame, at fault. || JUR. Guilty. || — *Declarar culpable*, to find guilty. || *Declararse culpable*, to plead guilty.
— M. y f. JUR. Culprit, guilty party, offender. || Culprit (persona responsable). || *Él es el culpable de todo*, he is to blame for everything.
culpación f. Inculpation, accusation.
culpado, da adj. Guilty. || Accused (acusado).
— M. y f. Accused, culprit, guilty party, offender.
culpar v. tr. To accuse (de un delito, etc.). || To accuse: *yo no culpo a nadie*, I accuse no one. || To blame: *le culpo de nuestra derrota*, I blame him for our defeat; *culpar al padre de los daños causados por su hijo*, to blame the father for the damage caused by his son.
— V. pr. To blame o.s., to accuse o.s.
cultalatiniparla f. FAM. Euphuistic language, preciosity. | Bluestocking (mujer pedante).
cultamente adj. Elegantly, in a refined manner (de modo culto). || FIG. In an affected manner (con afectación).
culteranismo m. Gongorism. || Affected style (afectación).
culterano, na adj. Euphuistic, euphuistical, affected.
— M. y f. Euphuist, affected person.
cultiparlista adj. Euphuistic, euphuistical, affected (culterano).
— M. y f. Euphuist, affected person.
cultismo m. Gongorism (culteranismo). || Learned word (palabra culta).
cultivable adj. Cultivable, cultivatable, arable.
cultivado, da adj. Cultured.
cultivador, ra adj. Farming.
— M. y f. Farmer (agricultor). || Cultivator, grower (de plantas). || — F. Cultivator (máquina).
cultivar v. tr. AGR. To cultivate, to farm, to till (la tierra). | To cultivate, to grow, to farm (las plantas). || FIG. To cultivate (las bellas artes, la amistad, etc.). | To train, to develop (la memoria).
cultivo m. AGR. Cultivation, farming: *cultivo extensivo, intensivo*, extensive, intensive cultivation. | Growing, cultivation, farming (de plantas). | Crop: *rotación de cultivos*, rotation of crops. || FIG. Cultivation: *el cultivo de las ciencias*, the cultivation of the sciences. || BIOL. Culture: *cultivo de tejidos*, tissue culture. || — *Caldo de cultivo*, culture fluid, culture medium. || *Cultivo de hortalizas*, market gardening. || *Cultivo de regadío*, irrigation farming. || *Cultivo de secano*, dry farming. || *Cultivo en bancales* or *de terrazas*, terrace cultivation. || *Cultivo frutícola*, fruit growing. || *Cultivo migratorio* shifting cultivation. || *Poner en cultivo*, to cultivate.
culto, ta adj. AGR. Cultivated. || FIG. Cultured, cultivated, educated (instruido). | Learned: *palabra culta*, learned word. | Euphuistic, affected (afectado).
— M. REL. Worship (veneración): *culto a los santos*, worship of the saints; *libertad de cultos*, freedom of worship. | Cult (ritos). || Cult (estimación extraordinaria). || — *Culto a la personalidad*, personality cult. || *Culto de hiperdulía*, hyperdulia. || *Culto de latría*, latria. || *Culto de los antepasados*, ancestor worship. || *Rendir culto a*, to worship (un santo, una persona), to pay homage *o* tribute to: *rendir culto a la valentía de una persona*, to pay homage to a person's courage.
cultura f. Culture: *hombre de gran cultura*, man of great culture; *cultura clásica, física*, classical, physical culture.
cultural adj. Cultural.
cumbarí m. *Amer.* Chili (ají).
cumbre f. Summit, top (cima). || FIG. Height, zenith, pinnacle: *la cumbre de la gloria*, the pinnacle of glory. || *Conferencia en la cumbre*, summit conference.
cumbrera f. ARQ. Ridge (de un tejado). | Lintel (dintel). || *Amer.* Summit, top (cumbre).
cúmel m. Kummel (bebida).
cumpa m. *Amer.* FAM. Chum, pal.
cúmplase m. Official approval [enforcing a decree or nomination].
cumpleaños m. inv. Birthday: *feliz cumpleaños*, happy birthday.
cumplidamente adv. Duly (como es debido). || Sufficiently, amply (ampliamente). || Completely (completamente).
cumplidero, ra adj. Expiring, which expires (plazo).
cumplido, da adj. Fulfilled: *una profecía cumplida*, a fulfilled prophecy. || Full, complete: *pago cumplido*, full payment. || Perfect (perfecto): *un cumplido caballero*, a perfect gentleman; *un modelo cumplido de virtudes*, a perfect model of virtue. || Accomplished: *un cumplido jinete*, an accomplished horseman. ||

Complete, utter: *un cumplido bribón*, an utter scoundrel. || Ample, large, big: *un abrigo demasiado cumplido*, too large an overcoat. || Polite, courteous (bien educado): *persona muy cumplida*, very polite person. || — *Soldado cumplido*, soldier who has completed his service. || *Tener veinte años cumplidos*, to have turned twenty, to be all of twenty.
— M. Compliment (alabanza): *basta de cumplidos*, enough of your compliments. || — Pl. Politeness, *sing.*, courtesy, *sing.*, attentions: *deshacerse en cumplidos*, to be profuse in [one's] attentions. || — *Andarse con* or *hacer cumplidos*, to stand on ceremony. || *De cumplido*, courtesy: *visita de cumplido*, courtesy visit. || *Devolverle el cumplido a uno*, to return s.o.'s compliment. || *Es una señora de mucho cumplido*, she is a stickler for ceremony. || *Ir a algún sitio por cumplido*, to go somewhere out of a sense of duty. || *Por cumplido*, out of courtesy, out of pure politeness. || *Sin cumplidos*, informal: *cena sin cumplidos*, informal dinner; informally: *recibir a alguien sin cumplidos*, to receive s.o. informally.

cumplidor, ra adj. Dependable, reliable, trustworthy (de fiar): *un muchacho cumplidor*, a dependable boy. || Who fulfils: *persona cumplidora de sus obligaciones*, person who fulfils his obligations. || *Hombre cumplidor de sus promesas*, man of his word.
— M. y f. Reliable *o* dependable person.

cumplimentar v. tr. To congratulate, to compliment (felicitar). || To pay a courtesy call to, to go and pay one's respects to (ir a saludar). || To execute, to carry out (órdenes). || *El ministro fue cumplimentado por el gobernador*, the minister was paid a complimentary visit by the governor.

cumplimiento m. Execution, carrying out: *cumplimiento de una orden*, execution of an order. || Enforcement, application: *el cumplimiento de un decreto*, the application of a decree. || Observance (acatamiento): *cumplimiento de los requisitos legales*, observance of statutory provisions. || Fulfilment [U.S., fulfillment] honouring: *cumplimiento de los compromisos*, fulfilment of one's commitments. || Fulfilment [U.S., fulfillment] (de los deseos). || Courtesy, politeness (cortesía). || Ceremony (ceremonia). || FIG. Completion (de una obra). | Expiry (vencimiento). || Complement (complemento). || — *Cumplimiento pascual*, Easter duty. || *Dar cumplimiento a los nuevos estatutos*, to put the new statutes into operation, to enforce the new statutes. || *En cumplimiento de*, in accordance with, in pursuance of, in compliance with. || *Por cumplimiento*, out of courtesy, out of politeness.

cumplir v. tr. To do (hacer): *cumplir su deber*, to do one's duty; *cumplir el servicio militar*, to do one's military service. || To execute, to carry out (ejecutar): *cumplir una orden*, to carry out an order. || To keep, to carry out: *cumplir una promesa*, to keep a promise. || To fulfil, to fulfill: *cumplir un deseo*, to fulfil a desire. || To honour, to fulfil: *cumplir sus compromisos*, to honour one's obligations. || To turn: *ha cumplido veinte años*, he has turned twenty. || To be, to reach the age of: *hoy cumple cinco años*, today he is five [years old], today he has reached the age of five; *cuando cumplas 21 años*, when you are 21. || To observe, to abide by (una ley). || To comply with (lo estipulado). || — *Cumplir condena*, to serve one's time [in prison]. || *Hoy cumple años Pedro*, it's Peter's birthday today.
— V. intr. To keep *o* to fulfil one's word *o* one's promise. || To do *o* to carry out *o* to perform one's duty (su deber), to honour *o* to fulfil one's obligations. || To do, to carry out, to perform: *cumplir con su deber*, to perform one's duty. || To fulfil, to honour: *cumplir con sus obligaciones*, to fulfil one's obligations. || To observe, to abide by: *cumplir con los requisitos legales*, to observe *o* to abide by the statutory provisions. || To expire (un plazo). || To fall due (un pago): *el pagaré cumple mañana*, the bill falls due tomorrow. || MIL. To finish one's military service (soldado). || — *Cumple a Juan hacer esto*, it is for John to do this, John should do this, John is supposed to do this, it behoves John to do this (ant.). || *Cumplir con la Iglesia* or *con Dios* or *con sus deberes religiosos*, to fulfil one's religious obligations. || *Cumplir con los requisitos*, to fulfil the requirements. || *Cumplir con su palabra*, to keep one's word. || *Cumplir con todos*, to fulfil one's duty to everyone, not to fail in one's duty to anyone. || *Para cumplir* or *por cumplir*, as a mere formality.
— V. pr. To be fulfilled, to come true: *se cumplieron sus vaticinios*, his prophecies were fulfilled. || To expire (un plazo). || *Este año se cumple el centenario de su nacimiento*, this year is the centenary of his birth.

cúmquibus m. FAM. Dough (dinero).

cumulativo, va adj. Cumulative.

cúmulo m. Accumulation, pile, heap (de cosas). || Cumulus (nube). || FIG. Load, lot: *un cúmulo de disparates*, a load of rubbish. | Concurrence, conjunction: *un cúmulo de circunstancias*, a concurrence of circumstances.

cumulonimbo m. Cumulonimbus.

cumuloso, sa adj. Cumulous.

cuna f. Cradle (cama). || Foundling hospital (inclusa). || FIG. Cradle: *Grecia, cuna de la civilización*, Greece, the cradle of civilization. | Birth, origin, lineage (origen de una persona): *de ilustre cuna*, of illustrious birth. | Birthplace (lugar de nacimiento). | Early childhood (niñez). || Cradle (del cañón). || Space between the horns (de un toro). || Rustic rope bridge (puente). || — *Canción de cuna*, lullaby, cradlesong. || *Casa cuna*, foundling hospital. || *Criarse en buena cuna*, to be born with a silver spoon in one's mouth. || *Cuna colgante*, swing cot. || *El juego de la cuna*, cat's cradle.

cundir v. intr. To spread, to become widespread: *cundió la noticia, el pánico*, the news, the panic spread. || To go a long way (rendir): *esa pierna de cordero cundió mucho*, that leg of lamb went a very long way. || To swell, to increase in volume: *el arroz cunde al cocer*, rice swells when cooked. || To progress (un trabajo). || To increase, to mulitply (multiplicarse). || To spread: *las manchas de aceite cunden rápidamente*, oil stains spread rapidly. || — *Cunde la voz que*, rumour has it that, it is rumoured that. || *El tiempo no me cunde*, time is too short, I haven't enough time. || *Le cunde el trabajo*, he gets through a lot of work.

cunear v. tr. To rock, to cradle (mecer).
— V. pr. To rock, to sway, to swing.

cuneco, ca m. y f. Youngest son *o* daughter (hijo menor).

cuneiforme adj. Cuneiform: *escritura cuneiforme*, cuneiform writing.

cuneo m. Rocking (mecedura).

cunero, ra adj. Foundling, abandoned (expósito). || Unpedigreed (toro). || External *o* alien and patronized by the Government [deputy, candidate]. || FAM. Of a little-known make *o* brand (de una marca insignificante), bearing no trademark (sin marca): *una estilográfica cunera*, a fountain pen bearing no trademark. | Second-class, second-rate (de poca categoría).
— M. y f. Foundling (expósito). || — M. Unpedigreed bull (toro). | External *o* alien deputy *o* candidate patronized by the government.

cuneta f. Ditch (de una carretera). || Hard shoulder (arcén). || Gutter (de una calle). || Cunette (fortificación).

cuña f. Wedge, chock (para detener una rueda). || Wedge (para rajar la madera). || Wedge heel, wedge [of shoe] (para un pie más corto que el otro). || Wedge-shaped reinforcement for worn part of shoe (refuerzo). || IMPR. Quoin. || FIG. y FAM. Influence (apoyo). || ANAT. Cuneiform bone, tarsal bone. || — MAT. *Cuña esférica*, segment. || FIG. *No hay peor cuña que la de la misma madera*, a man's worst enemies are often those of his own house. | *Tener cuña*, to have influential friends, to have friends at court.

cuñado, da m. y f. Brother-in-law (hombre), sister-in-law (mujer).

cuño m. Die (para monedas). || Stamp (huella que deja el cuño). || FIG. Mark, impression: *dejar el cuño de su personalidad*, to leave the mark of one's personality. || — FIG. *De buen cuño*, of the right stamp. | *De nuevo cuño*, new, modern.

cuota f. Quota, share (parte proporcional): *pagar su cuota*, to pay one's share. || Fees *pl.*, subscription: *ha subido la cuota del club*, the club fees have gone up. || Contribution (contribución). || Cost (gastos): *la cuota de instalación de teléfono*, the cost of installing a telephone. || *Amer.* Instalment, payment (de una compra a plazos). | Tariff (tarifa). || *Amer. Venta por cuotas*, hire-purchase [U.S., installment plan].

cuotidiano, na adj. (P. us.). Daily.

cupé m. Coupé (coche).

cupido m. FIG. y FAM. Lady-killer, Cassanova.

Cupido n. pr. m. Cupid.

cupla f. *Amer.* Couple, pair (par).

cuplé m. Variety song, music-hall song (copla).

cupletista m. y f. Variety singer, music-hall singer.

cupo m. Quota, share (cuota). || MIL. Contingent, quota (reclutas). || COM. Quota. || *Amer.* Capacity, content (cabida).

cupón m. Coupon (de un título de renta). || Ticket (de lotería). || Reply coupon (para un concurso). || Coupon, form: *cupón de pedido*, order coupon. || *Cupón de cartilla de racionamiento*, ration voucher, coupon.

cupresáceas f. pl. BOT. Cupressaceae.

cúprico, ca adj. QUÍM. Cupric.

cuprífero, ra adj. Cupriferous.

cuprita f. MIN. Cuprite.

cuproníquel m. QUÍM. Cupronickel.

cuproso, sa adj. QUÍM. Cuprous.

cúpula f. ARQ. Cupola, dome (bóveda). || BOT. Cupule. || MAR. y MIL. Turret, cupola (blindaje).

cupulíferas f. pl. BOT. Cupuliferae.

cupulino m. ARQ. Lantern (de una cúpula).

cuquillo m. Cuckoo (cuclillo).

cura m. Parish priest (sacerdote). || FAM. [Roman Catholic] priest (sacerdote católico). | Spray (de saliva). || *Amer.* Avocado, alligator pear (aguacate). || — *Casa del cura*, presbytery. || *Cura párroco*, parish priest. || FAM. *Este cura*, yours truly (yo).

cura f. Care: *curas médicas*, medical care. || Treatment (tratamiento). || Cure: *hacer una cura de aguas*, to undergo a water cure. || Dressing [of a wound] (apósito). || — *Cura de almas*, care of souls. || FAM. *No tener cura*, to be incorrigible. || *Ponerse en cura*,

to undergo treatment. || *Primera cura*, first aid. || *Tener cura*, to be curable.
curabilidad f. Curability.
curable adj. MED. Curable.
curaca f. *Amer.* Indian chief, chief, headman (cacique).
curación f. MED. Cure (cura). | Recovery (restablecimiento). | Healing (de una herida). | Treatment (tratamiento). | Dressing (apósito). || *Curación milagrosa.* miracle healing.
curado, da adj. FIG. Hardened, inured, accustomed to hardship (persona). || Cured: *jamón curado*, cured ham. || Tanned (pieles). || *Amer.* Drunk, intoxicated (ebrio). || FIG. *Estoy curado de espanto*, nothing can shock me any more, I've known worse.
curador, ra adj. JUR. Guardian, tutor (tutor).
— M. y f. Guardian, tutor (tutor). || — M. Quack healer, charlatan (curandero). || Caretaker, curator (administrador).
curaduría f. JUR. Guardianship, tutorage, tutorship (cargo de tutor).
curalotodo m. Cure-all.
curandería f. o **curanderismo** m. Quackery, charlatanry, charlatanism.
curandero, ra m. y f. Quack, quack doctor, charlatan (de enfermedades).
curar v. intr. MED. To heal [up] (una herida). | To get well, to recover (una persona). || FIG. To be cured (de un mal moral).
— V. tr. MED. To cure (sanar). | To get rid of, to cure: *pastillas que curan la gripe*, tablets which cure flu. | To treat: *curar a un enfermo con antibióticos*, to treat a patient with antibiotics. | To dress: *curar una herida*, to dress a wound. || To cure (carne, pescado). || To tan (pieles). || To season (pipa). || To bleach (hilos, lienzos). || FIG. To remedy. || *Amer. Curar un mate*, to season a maté.
— V. pr. To be treated: *esta enfermedad se cura con penicilina*, this disease is treated with penicillin. || To get well *o* better, to recover [one's health]: *si quieres curarte tienes que guardar cama*, if you want to get well you must stay in bed; *se está curando*, he's getting better. || To heal up (una herida). || *Amer.* FAM. To get sozzled (emborracharse). || — *Curarse de*, to take care of. || FIG. *Curarse en salud*, V. SALUD.
curare m. Curare, curari (veneno).
curasao m. Curaçao (licor).
curativo, va adj. Curative.
curato m. Office of a parish priest, priesthood (cargo). || Parish (parroquia).
Curazao n. pr. GEOGR. Curaçao (isla).
curco, ca o **curcuncho, cha** adj. *Amer.* Hunchbacked, humpbacked.
— M. y f. Hunchback, humpback. || — F. Hunch, hump (joroba).
curcusilla f. Rump (rabadilla de un ave).
curda f. FAM. Drunkenness, intoxication (borrachera). || FAM. *Coger una curda*, to get sozzled.
— Adj. FAM. Sozzled, sloshed, canned: *estoy curda*, I'm sozzled.
curdo, da adj. Kurdish (del Curdistán).
— M. y f. Kurd.
cureña f. Gun carriage (del cañón). || Gunstock, stock (del mortero).
cureta f. MED. Curette.
curia f. HIST. Curia (de los romanos). || Curia (de la Iglesia). || Legal profession, Bar (abogados, procuradores, funcionarios). || JUR. Court of Litigation. || — *Curia Romana*, Curia Romana. || *Gente de curia*, legal profession.
curial adj. Curial (de la curia).
— M. HIST. Officer of the Curia Romana. || Court clerk (subalterno).
curialesco, ca adj. Legalistic.
curiana f. Cockroach, blackbeetle (fam.) [cucaracha].
curie f. FÍS. Curie (unidad de radioactividad).
curieterapia f. MED. Curietherapy, radiotherapy.
curio m. QUÍM. Curium (elemento).
curiosamente adv. Curiously (con curiosidad). || Neatly, cleanly, tidily (con limpieza). || Carefully, painstakingly (cuidadosamente).
curiosear v. intr. FAM. To poke one's nose into *o* to pry into other people's affairs (entremeterse). || To pry, to nose about *o* around, to ferret about: *está curioseando por toda la casa*, he's prying all around the house. || To browse: *curiosear por una librería*, to browse around *o* through a bookshop.
— V. tr. To poke one's nose into, to pry into, to nose into (fisgonear). || *Los chicos curioseaban los cuartos de la casa*, the children were ferreting *o* nosing about in the rooms of the house.
curiosidad f. Curiosity (deseo de conocer). || Cleanliness, tidiness, neatness (limpieza). || Inquisitiveness (indiscreción). || Care, carefulness (cuidado, esmero). || Curio, curiosity (cosa curiosa): *es aficionado a curiosidades*, he is interested in curios. || — *Mirar con curiosidad*, to look at curiously. || *Tener curiosidad por saber*, to be curious to know.
curioso, sa adj. Curious (que tiene curiosidad): *ser curioso por naturaleza*, to be curious by nature, to be naturally curious; *curioso por conocer la verdad*, curious to know the truth. || Inquisitive (indiscreto). || Clean, tidy, neat (limpio). || Careful (cuidadoso). || Curious, odd, peculiar, unusual, strange (raro). || *Curioso de noticias*, eager for news.
— M. y f. Onlooker, spectator (mirón). || Busybody, nosy person (persona indiscreta).
curista m. y f. Person taking water cures (agüista).
curling m. Curling (deporte).
currelar v. intr. FAM. To toil, to slog away (trabajar).
curriculum vitae m. Curriculum vitae (historial).
curruca f. ZOOL. Whitethroat.
curruscante adj. Crunchy, crispy, crisp: *pan curruscante*, crispy bread.
curruscar v. intr. To crunch.
currutaco, ca adj. Dandyish, foppish [U.S., dudish] (hombre). || Over-fashionable (mujer).
— M. Dandy, fop [U.S., dude] (petimetre). || Nobody (hombre insignificante). || — F. Over-fashionable woman.
curry m. Curry.
cursado, da adj. Experienced. || Versed (instruido).
cursante adj. Who follows a course of study.
— M. y f. Student.
cursar v. tr. To study, to take [a course on], to follow a course on: *cursar literatura*, to study literature. || To deal with, to see to (una solicitud). || To transmit, to convey, to pass (órdenes). || To send (cartas). || *Cursar estudios*, to study, to take a course.
cursi adj. FAM. Pretentious, showy: *un piso muy cursi*, a very pretentious flat. | Affected (amanerado). | Genteel (exageradamente refinado). | Pretentious (presumido). | Snobbish.
— M. y f. Affected person (amanerado). || Genteel person (exageradamente refinado). || Pretentious person (presumido). || Snob.

— OBSERV. The correct plural is *cursis*, not *cursiles*.

cursilada o **cursilería** f. FAM. Pretentiousness, showiness (presunción). | Affectation (afectación). | Vulgarity (vulgaridad). | Gentility (refinamiento exagerado). | Snobbishness, snobbery. | Pretentious *o* showy *o* flashy object.
cursilón, ona adj./s. V. CURSI.
cursillista m. y f. Student on a short course (estudiante). || Trainee (de un período de prácticas). || *Profesor cursillista*, student teacher.
cursillo m. Short course (de corta duración). || Course of lectures (conferencias). || — REL. *Cursillo de cristiandad*, religious instruction. || *Cursillo de capacitación*, training course. || *Un cursillo de vuelo sin visibilidad*, a course on blind flying.
cursivo, va adj. Cursive. || *Letra cursiva*, italics, *pl.*
— F. Italics, *pl.* (letra).
curso m. Course: *el curso de un río, de un astro, de la historia, de los acontecimientos*, the course of a river, of a heavenly body, of history, of events. || Course (clase, tratado): *dar un curso de filosofía*, to give a course on philosophy. || School year (para la enseñanza primaria y media), academic year (para la enseñanza superior). || Direction. || COM. Tender: *este billete tiene curso legal*, this note is legal tender. || Course: *en el curso de la semana*, during the course of the week. || Course, progress (de una enfermedad). || — *Apertura de curso*, beginning of term. || *Curso acelerado, por correspondencia*, crash, correspondence course. || *Dar curso a*, to give rein *o* vent to: *dar libre curso a su cólera*, to give free rein to *o* full vent to one's anger; to deal with, to see to, to take appropriate action concerning (ocuparse de): *dar curso a una solicitud*, to deal with a request. || *Dar libre curso a su fantasía*, to give free rein *o* free play to one's imagination, to let one's imagination run wild. || *En curso*, under way, in process: *la construcción de esta casa está en curso*, the building of this house is in process; under way: *este proyecto está en curso*, this plan is under way; current: *el año en curso*, the current year; in hand: *asuntos en curso*, matters in hand; in circulation (monedas). || *En curso de realización*, under construction (construyéndose), under way (un trabajo). || *Tercer curso*, third year (en enseñanza).
cursor m. TECN. Slide [of mathematical instrument].
curtido, da adj. FIG. Experienced: *militar curtido*, experienced soldier; *una persona curtida en negocios*, a person experienced in business. | Hardened: *estar curtido contra el frío*, to be hardened to the cold. | Sunburnt, tanned (por el sol), weather-beaten (por el tiempo). || Tanned (cuero).
— M. Tanning (del cuero). || *Industria de curtidos*, tanning industry.
curtidor m. Tanner (de cueros).
curtiduría f. Tannery.
curtiembre f. *Amer.* Tannery.
curtiente adj. Tanning.
curtimiento m. Tanning.
curtir v. tr. To tan (el cuero). || FIG. To tan (la piel). | To harden, to inure (acostumbrar a la vida dura).
— V. pr. To become tanned (por el sol), to become weather-beaten (por el tiempo). || To become hardened *o* inured (acostumbrarse a la vida dura). || To become experienced, to accustom o.s. (avezarse).
curul adj. Curule (magistrado y silla).
curva f. Curve (línea). || Bend, curve: *curva peligrosa*, dangerous bend; *curva cerrada*, sharp bend; *curva muy cerrada*, hairpin bend; *tomar la curva muy cerrada*, to take the bend tightly; *sortear una curva*, to take a bend. || Bend, turn (de un río). || FAM.

Curve (del cuerpo). || — *Curva de natalidad*, birth-rate curve. || *Curva de nivel*, contour line. || *Curva de temperatura*, temperature curve.
curvar v. tr. To curve, to bend.
curvatura f. Curvature (cualidad, estado). || Bending (acción).
curvilíneo, a adj. Curvilinear, curvilineal. || Curvaceous, shapely (mujer).
curvímetro m. Curvometer.
curvo, va adj. Curved, bent. || *Línea curva*, curved line.
cusca f. FAM. *Hacer la cusca a*, to bother (fastidiar).
cuscurrante adj. Crunchy, crispy, crisp.
cuscurrear v. intr. To crunch.
cuscurro o **cuscurrón** m. Crust (de pan).
cuscús m. Couscous (alcuzcuz).
cusí cusí adv. *Amer.* So-so (así así).
cusma f. *Amer.* V. CUZMA.
cúspide f. Peak, summit (cima, cumbre). || ANAT. BOT. Cusp. || MAT. Apex: *cúspide de la pirámide*, apex of the pyramid. || FIG. Zenith, pinnacle, height: *llegar a la cúspide de la gloria*, to reach the height of glory.
custodia f. Custody, care, safekeeping (vigilancia): *bajo la custodia de*, in the custody of. || Custodian, guardian (vigilante). || REL. Monstrance (vaso sagrado).
custodiar v. tr. To guard, to take care of (conservar). || To guard, to watch over (vigilar). || To defend, to uphold (proteger).
custodio adj. m./s.m. Guardian: *ángel custodio*, guardian angel. || — M. Custodian, guardian.
cusumbe o **cusumbo** m. *Amer.* Coati.
cususa f. *Amer.* Tafia (ron).
cutáneo, a adj. Cutaneous. || *Enfermedad cutánea*, skin disease.
cúter m. MAR. Cutter.
cuti f. MED. Skin test (cutirreacción).
cutí m. Ticking (tela).
cutícula f. Cuticle (epidermis).
cutirreacción f. Skin test: *ha sido sensible a la cutirreacción*, his skin test has proved positive.
cutis m. inv. Skin, complexion, cutis.
cutre adj. Mean, miserly, stingy (tacaño).
— M. y f. Miser.
cuy m. *Amer.* Guinea pig.
cuyo, ya pron. rel. Whose, of which (de cosas): *la casa cuyo tejado es de tejas*, the house whose roof *o* the roof of which *o* of which the roof is tiled; *el cuarto en cuyo fondo está la chimenea*, the room at the back of which is the fireplace. || Whose, of whom (de personas): *el niño cuyos padres están en Madrid*, the child whose parents *o* the parents of whom are in Madrid; *el amigo a cuya generosidad debo esto*, the friend to whose generosity *o* to the generosity of whom I owe this. || (P. us.). Whose: *¿cuya es esta capa?*, whose is this cape? || — *A cuyo efecto, con cuyo objeto, para cuyo fin*, to which end, for which. || *En cuyo caso*, in which case. || *Por cuya causa*, because of which.
— M. FAM. (P. us.). Lover (enamorado).
¡cuz, cuz! interj. Here boy! (para llamar un perro).
cuzcuz m. Couscous (alcuzcuz).
cuzma f. *Amer.* Long sleeveless shirt.
cuzquear v. tr. *Amer.* To court, to woo (galantear).
czar m. Czar, tsar (soberano).
czarda f. Czardas (danza).
czarevitz m. Czarevitch, tsarevitch.
czarina f. Czarina, tsarina.

— OBSERV. In Spanish the more usual spellings of *czar, czarevitz* and *czarina* are *zar, zarevitz* and *zarina.*

CH

ch f. Ch.

— OBSERV. *Ch* is a letter in its own right in Spanish and is completely independent of the letter *c*. It comes between the letters *c* and *d* in the alphabet. It is pronounced like *ch* in *church*.

chabacanada f. V. CHABACANERÍA.
chabacanamente adv. Crudely rudely, in a vulgar way. || Tastelessly (sin gusto).
chabacanear v. intr. To behave in a coarse *o* vulgar *o* rude way.
chabacanería f. Coarse *o* vulgar *o* rude thing: *decir una chabacanería*, to say sth. rude. || Vulgarity, tastelessness (falta de gusto)
chabacano, na adj. Common, plain, ordinary: *una mujer chabacana*, a common woman. || Vulgar, coarse, common, uncouth: *tiene un aspecto chabacano*, he looks uncouth. || Rude, coarse, crude, vulgar: *un chiste chabacano*, a crude joke.
chabola f. Hut, shack, shanty (choza). || Shed (caseta). || *Las chabolas*, the shanty town (barrio de las latas).
chabolismo m. Shanty towns, *pl.*, slums, *pl.*: *hay que terminar con el chabolismo*, we must clear the slums.
chacal m. ZOOL. Jackal.
chacalín m. *Amer.* Shrimp (camarón).
chácara f. *Amer.* Farm (chacra). | Bag (bolsa). | Sore (llaga).
chacarero, ra adj./s. *Amer.* Peasant, farmer. || — F. Peasant dance [in Argentina, Uruguay and Bolivia].
chacina f. Pork sausage meat (carne). || Pork sausages, *pl.* (conjunto de los embutidos).
chacinería f. Porkbutcher's shop (tienda).
chacinero, ra m. y f. Pork butcher.
chacó m. Shako (morrión).
chacolí m. "Chacoli" [a Basque wine].
chacolotear v. intr. To clatter (la herradura).
chacoloteo m. Clatter, clattering.
chacona f. MÚS. Chaconne.
chacota f. Joking, banter. || — FAM. *Echar* or *tomar a chacota, hacer chacota de*, to make fun of (burlarse de). | *Estar de chacota*, to be in a joking mood. | *Tomar a chacota*, to take as a joke (no tomar en serio).
chacotear v. intr. To make fun [of everything] (burlarse). || To mess about, to clown around (hacer *o* decir tonterías).
— V. pr. To make fun: *chacotearse de una persona*, to make fun of s.o.
chacoteo m. Messing about, clowning, kidding, ragging, joking (regocijo). || Mockery (burla).
chacotero, ra adj. FAM. Mocking, teasing, jesting, fun-loving.
— M. y f. Joker, tease, wisecrack.
chacra f. *Amer.* Farm.
chacuaco, ca adj. *Amer.* Clumsy, careless (chapucero). | Coarse, rough (grosero).
— M. Cigarette end *o* butt (colilla). || Badly-made cigar (puro malhecho). || Smelting furnace (horno).
chacha f. FAM. Maid, nursemaid (niñera). | Girl, lass (muchacha). | Maid (criada).
cháchara f. FAM. Small talk, chatter (charla). || — Pl. *Amer.* Trinkets, baubles (baratijas). || FAM. *Estar de cháchara*, to chatter, to gossip, to chat.
chacharear v. intr. FAM. To chatter, to gossip, to chat.
chacharero, ra adj. FAM. Talkative.
— M. y f. FAM. Chatterbox, chatterer.
chacharón, ona m. y f. FAM. Chatterbox.
chachi adj./ adv. V. CHANCHI.
chacho, cha m. y f. FAM. Boy, lad, kid (muchacho), girl, lass (muchacha): *¡ven acá, chacho!*, come here, lad! || *Amer.* Servant.
chafaldete m. Clew line.
chafalonía f. Scrap gold (oro) *o* silver (plata).
chafalote adj. *Amer.* Uncouth, vulgar, coarse (grosero).
— M. *Amer.* Kind of scimitar (alfanje).
chafallar v. tr. FAM. To botch, to make a mess of.
chafallo m. FAM. Botched job, mess.
chafallón, ona adj. FAM. Careless, slapdash, amateurish, shoddy (chapucero).
— M. y f. Botcher, shoddy worker, careless worker.
chafar v. tr. To flatten, to squash, to crush (aplastar). || To crease, to crumple (arrugar). || To flatten (el peinado). || To dent (un coche). || FIG. To nonplus, to floor, to stump, to cut [s.o.] short (en una discusión). | To shatter (abatir). | To ruin: *la lluvia me ha chafado el plan*, the rain has ruined my plans.
— V. pr. To be squashed, to be crushed (ser aplastado).
chafarote m. Kind of scimitar (alfanje).
chafarrinar v. tr. To daub, to smear, to spot.
chafarrinón m. Daub, smear, stain.
chafe m. *Amer.* FAM. Copper, cop, bobby (policía).
chaflán m. Bevel, chamfer (bisel). || Cant (de un edificio). || *Casa que hace chaflán*, corner house.
chaflanar v. tr. To bevel, to chamfer (abiselar).

chagra m. *Amer.* Peasant. || — F. *Amer.* Farm (chacra).
chaguar v. tr. To wring [out] (la ropa). || *Amer.* To milk (ordeñar).
chah m. Shah (soberano de Irán).
chahuistle f. *Amer.* Mildew, rust, blight (roya).
chaina f. *Amer.* Goldfinch (jilguero). | Mexican flute (flauta).
chaira f. Steel, sharpener (para afilar cuchillos). || Paring knife (de zapatero).
chajá m. *Amer.* Chaja, crested screamer (ave).
chal m. Shawl (mantón).
chala f. *Amer.* Husk, shuck (del maíz).
chalado, da adj. FAM. Dotty, round the bend, touched. | Crazy, mad: *está chalado por Ana, por la música de jazz,* he's crazy about Anna, about jazz.
— M. y f. FAM. Nut.
chaladura f. FAM. Fancy *o* crazy idea: *le ha dado la chaladura de dejarse crecer la barba,* he's got the fancy idea of growing a beard. | Craze (manía). | Stupid thing (tontería). | Crush (enamoramiento).
chalán m. Horse dealer (comerciante en caballos). || Sharp dealer (que engaña). || *Amer.* Horse breaker, broncobuster (domador).
chalana f. MAR. Barge, wherry, lighter (gabarra).
chalanear v. intr. FAM. To be a sharp dealer.
— V. tr. *Amer.* To train, to break (adiestrar).
chalaneo m. Sharp practice *o* dealing (en los negocios). || *Amer.* Horsebreaking.
chalanería f. V. CHALANEO.
chalanesco, ca adj. Sharp, tricky, wily (del chalán).
chalar v. tr. FAM. To drive crazy, to drive round the bend (enloquecer).
— V. pr. To go mad (perder la cabeza). || To get a crush, to be crazy: *chalarse por,* to get a crush on, to be crazy about.
chalaza f. Chalaza.
chalcha f. *Amer.* Double chin (papada).
chalchihuite m. *Amer.* Kind of rough emerald. | Trinket (baratija).
chalé m. [Detached] house (casa con jardín). || Country house (en el campo). || Chalet (suizo). || Villa (casa lujosa). || Bungalow (en la playa).

— OBSERV. *Chalé* is a more common form than *chalet;* it becomes *chalés* in the plural.

chaleco m. Waistcoat [U.S., vest]. || — *Chaleco antibalas,* bullet-proof vest. || *Amer. Chaleco de fuerza,* straightjacket. || *Chaleco de punto,* pullover. || *Chaleco salvavidas,* life jacket.
chalet m. V. CHALÉ.
chalina f. Cravat (corbata).
chalón m. *Amer.* Shawl.
chalote m. BOT. Shallot (cebolla).
chaludo, da adj. *Amer.* FAM. Wealthy, well-to-do (que tiene mucho dinero).
chalupa f. Launch, shallop, boat (lancha). || *Amer.* Maize tortilla [kind of pancake]. | Canoe (canoa).
challenger m. Challenger (candidato).
chamaco, ca m. y f. *Amer.* Boy, lad, kid (muchacho), girl, lass (muchacha).
chamada f. Brushwood (leña menuda). || Blaze (llama). || FAM. Streak *o* run of bad luck (mala racha).
chamagoso, sa adj. *Amer.* Greasy, grimy, dirty (mugriento). | Common, vulgar (vulgar).
chamal m. *Amer.* Blanket used by the Araucanian Indians as a cape.
chamanto m. *Amer.* Kind of poncho.
chámara o **chamarasca** f. Brushwood (leña menuda). || Blaze (llama).
chamarilear v. tr. To swap, to barter, to exchange.
chamarileo m. Secondhand dealing, junk dealing.
chamarilero, ra m. y f. Junk dealer, secondhand dealer.
chamariz m. Greenfinch (pájaro).
chamarra f. Sheepskin jacket (chaqueta).
chamarro m. *Amer.* Serape [kind of shawl].
chamba f. FAM. Fluke, lucky break (en el billar). || FIG. y FAM. Fluke (casualidad): *he aprobado por chamba,* it was a fluke that I passed, I passed by a fluke. || *Amer.* Turf (césped). | Job (trabajo). | Deal (trato).
chambelán m. Chamberlain.
chambergo adj. m. *Sombrero chambergo,* v. SOMBRERO.
chambón, ona adj. FAM. Jammy, lucky (suertudo). | Awkward, clumsy (torpe).
— M. y f. FAM. Jammy *o* lucky person (con suerte). | Bungler (torpe).
chambonada f. FAM. Awkwardness, clumsiness (torpeza). | Fluke (suerte). | Blunder (pifia).
chambra f. Camisole (prenda femenina).
chambrana f. Casing (de puerta, ventana, etc.). || *Amer.* Din, row, racket (jaleo).
chamelicos m. pl. *Amer.* Things, belongings (cachivaches).
chamicado, da adj. *Amer.* Taciturn (taciturno). | Tipsy, merry (achispado).
chamicera f. Patch of burnt land (monte quemado).
chamico m. *Amer.* Stramonium, thorn apple (planta). || *Amer.* FIG. *Dar chamico a uno,* to bewitch s.o.
chamiza f. Chamiso [graminaceous plant whose stalk may be used for thatching]. || Brushwood (leña menuda). || V. CHAMIZO.
chamizo m. Thatched hut (choza). || Hovel (casucha). || FAM. Gambling den, gambling joint (garito). | Half-burned log *o* tree (tronco quemado).
chamorra f. FAM. Shaved *o* shorn head.
chamorro, rra adj. Shaved, shorn (rapado). || V. TRIGO.
— M. y f. Person with a shaved *o* shorn head.
champa f. *Amer.* Piece of turf, sod (hierba con tierra). | Tangle (cosa enmarañada).
champán m. Champagne (vino). || Sampan (embarcación).
champaña m. Champagne.
champiñón m. Mushroom.
champú m. Shampoo.

— OBSERV. Pl. *champúes* or *champús.*

champurrar v. tr. To mix (licores).
chamuchina f. *Amer.* Rabble, riffraff (chusma).
chamullar v. tr. FAM. To speak, to talk (hablar). | To speak a little *o* a few words of, to have a smattering of: *yo chamullo el inglés,* I speak a little English.
chamuscar v. tr. To singe (el pelo, un pollo, etc.). || To scorch (papel, madera, etc.).
chamusquina f. Singeing (acción de chamuscar). || Smell of burning (olor a quemado). || FIG. y FAM. Fight (camorra). || FIG. y FAM. *Esto huele a chamusquina,* it smacks of heresy (una herejía), it looks like trouble (va a ocurrir algo grave), it smells fishy, it seems doubtful (esto es sospechoso).
chamuyo m. *Amer.* Argentinian slang.
chancaca f. *Amer.* Loaf sugar (azúcar).
chancadora f. Mineral crusher (de minerales).
chancar v. tr. *Amer.* To crush (minerales). || To grind (triturar).
chance m. Chance (posibilidad). || Good luck (suerte).
chancear v. intr. To joke, to fool, to crack jokes.
— V. pr. To make fun: *chancearse de,* to make fun of.
chancero, ra adj. Fond of a joke, jocose.
chanciller m. Chancellor (canciller).
chancillería f. Chancery.
chancla f. Old shoe (zapato viejo). || Slipper (zapatilla): *en chanclas,* in one's slippers.
chancleta f. Old shoe (zapato viejo). || Slipper (zapatilla). || *Amer.* FAM. Baby girl (niña). || — M. y f. *Amer.* FIG. y FAM. Good-for-nothing, nincompoop (inepto).
chancletear v. intr. To shuffle [about].
chanclo m. Clog (sandalia de madera). || Galosh, overshoe (de goma).
chancro m. MED. Chancre. || BOT. Canker.
chancha f. *Amer.* Sow (cerda). || *Amer.* FIG. y FAM. Slovenly woman, filthy woman. || *Amer. Hacer la chancha,* to play truant [U.S., to play hooky].
chanchada f. *Amer.* FAM. Dirty trick (cochinada).
cháncharras máncharras f. pl. Beating about the bush, *sing.* || FAM. *No andemos en cháncharras máncharras,* let's not beat about the bush.
chanchería f. *Amer.* Pork butcher's.
chanchero, ra m. y f. *Amer.* Pork butcher.
chanchi adj./adv. FAM. Great, terrific, fantastic: *el plan nos ha salido chanchi,* our plan turned out great; *el málaga es un vino chanchi,* Malaga is a terrific wine.
chancho, cha adj. *Amer.* Dirty, filthy (sucio).
— M. *Amer.* Pig (cerdo). | Boar (macho). || Blocked pawn (en el ajedrez). || — F. V. CHANCHA.
chanchullero, ra adj. FAM. Fiddling, crooked.
— M. y f. FAM Fiddler, crook, twister.
chanchullo m. FAM. Wangle, fiddle: *andar en chanchullos,* to be on the fiddle.
chandal m. DEP. Track suit.
chanelar v. intr. FAM. To understand, to get (comprender). | To understand, to be up on (saber): *yo chanelo de este asunto,* I'm up on this subject.
chanfaina f. Offal stew.
changa f. *Amer.* Joke (broma). | Work of a porter.
changador m. *Amer.* Porter.
changar v. intr. *Amer.* To do odd jobs.
chango m. *Amer.* Monkey.
changuear v. intr. *Amer.* To joke (bromear).
changuero, ra adj. *Amer.* Fond of a joke, jocose.
— M. y f. *Amer.* One for a joke, joker.
changüí m. FAM. Joke (broma). || Trick, hoax (engaño). || *Dar changüí a uno,* to play a joke on s.o. (gastar una broma), to trick *o* to hoax s.o. (engañar).
chanquete m. Very small type of edible fish.
chantaje m. Blackmail. || *Hacer chantaje a uno,* to blackmail s.o.
chantajista m. y f. Blackmailer.
chantre m. REL. Precentor.
chanza f. Joke: *gastar chanzas,* to crack jokes. || — *De chanza,* jokingly, in fun. || FIG. *Entre chanzas y veras,* half jokingly, half in earnest.
chanzoneta f. FAM. Joke (chanza).
¡chao! interj. FAM. Bye-bye!, cheerio!, so long!, ciao!
chapa f. Plate, sheet (de metal). || AUT. Bodywork. || Panel (de madera), veneer (enchapado). || Metal top, cap (de una botella). || Iron: *chapa ondulada,* corrugated iron. || Tray (del horno). || Tag, tally, check (contraseña en un guardarropa). || Plywood (contrachapado). || Rouge (en las mejillas). || FIG. y FAM. Common sense (seriedad). || *Amer.* Lock (cerradura). || — Pl. Game of tossing up coins (juego). || *Chapa de estarcir,* stencil.

chapadanza f. *Amer.* Joke (chanza).
chapado, da adj. TECN. Veneered (cubierto con chapas de madera). || Plated: *reloj chapado de oro*, gold-plated watch. || FIG. *Chapado a la antigua*, old-fashioned.
chapalear v. intr. To splash about (chapotear). || To clatter (chacolotear).
chapaleo m. Splashing about (chapoteo). || Clatter (chacoloteo).
chapaleta f. Flap valve, clack valve (válvula).
chapaleteo m. Lap, lapping (del agua en la orilla). || Pitter-patter, pattering (de la lluvia).
chapapote m. *Amer.* Bitumen, asphalt.
chapar v. tr. TECN. To plate (metal). | To veneer (madera). | To tile (pared). || FIG. To come out with, to let out (encajar).
chaparral m. Chaparral, thicket.
chaparrazo m. *Amer.* Downpour, cloudburst (chaparrón).
chaparreras f. pl. *Amer.* Chaps (pantalones de piel).
chaparro m. Ilex, holm oak, holly oak (carrasca). || Kermes oak (coscoja). || Chaparro (planta malpigiácea). || Chaparral (chaparral). || FIG. Tubby *o* chubby *o* plump person (rechoncho).
chaparrón m. Downpour, cloudburst: *cayó un chaparrón*, there was a downpour. || FIG. y FAM. Shower (de preguntas, etc.). || *Llover a chaparrones*, to pour, to pour down, to rain cats and dogs.
chape m. *Amer.* Plait (trenza).
chapeado, da adj. Plated (de metal). || Veneered (de madera). || *Amer.* Rich (rico).
— M. TECN. Plating (de metal). || Veneering (de madera).
chapear v. tr. TECN. To plate (metal). | To veneer (madera). | To tile (pared). || *Amer.* To clear [the land] (limpiar la tierra).
— V. intr. To clatter (chacolotear).
chapeca f. o **chapecán** m. *Amer.* Plait (trenza).
chapecar v. tr. *Amer.* To plait (trenzar).
chapeleta f. TECN. Valve (válvula).
chapeo m. Hat (sombrero).
chapería f. TECN. Veneering (ebanistería).
chapeta f. V. CHAPA. || FIG. Rosy cheek.
chapetón, ona adj./s. *Amer.* European recently settled in Latin America. || Novice (bisoño). || — M. Downpour, cloudburst (chaparrón).
chapetonada f. "Chapetonada" [illness which Europeans contracted on first arriving in Latin America]. || *Amer.* FIG. Blunder (novatada).
chapetonear v. intr. *Amer.* To make blunders through inexperience.
chapín m. Chopine (calzado). || Coffer fish (pez). || *Amer.* Guatemalan (guatemalteco).
chapino, na adj. *Amer.* Which cuts itself as it walks (un caballo).
chápiro m. Hat (sombrero). || FAM. *¡Por vida del chápiro* or *del chápiro verde!*, *¡Voto al chápiro!*, confound it!, darn it!
chapista m. Sheet metal worker. || AUT. Panel beater. || *Taller de chapista*, body repair shop (para coches).
chapistería f. Sheet metal work. || AUT. Panel beating.
chapitel m. ARQ. Spire (de torre). | Capitel (de columna). || Cap (de brújula).
chapodar v. tr. AGR. To prune, to trim.
chapón m. Ink blot (borrón).
chapopote m. *Amer.* Bitumen, asphalt.
chapotear v. tr. To moisten, to sponge, to dampen, to damp [with a sponge] (mojar).
— V. intr. FAM. To splash about (en el agua). || To squelch about (en el barro). || *Ir chapoteando*, to paddle.
chapoteo m. Sponging, moistening (acción de mojar). || Splashing (en el agua). || Squelching (en el barro).
chapuceado, da adj. Careless, slapdash, amateurish, shoddy (frangollado).
chapucear v. tr. To botch, to make a mess of, to make a shoddy job of (hacer muy de prisa y mal). || *Amer.* To deceive (engañar).
chapuceramente adv. Shoddily, in an amateurish way.
chapucería f. Botched job, shoddy *o* amateurish piece of work (trabajo mal hecho). || Patching up (arreglo rápido). || Shoddiness (mala calidad).
chapucero, ra adj. Careless, slapdash, amateurish, shoddy: *un trabajo chapucero*, a shoddy piece of work.
— M. y f. Careless worker, shoddy worker, botcher (frangollón). || Liar (mentiroso). || — M. Blacksmith (herrero).
chapulín m. *Amer.* Grasshopper (saltamontes).
chapurrar v. tr. V. CHAPURREAR.
chapurrear v. tr. To speak a little, to speak a few words of, to have a smattering of (hablar imperfectamente un idioma): *chapurrear el francés*, to speak a little French, to have a smattering of French. || To mix (los licores).
chapurreo m. Jabbering.
chapuz m. o **chapuza** f. Odd job (trabajo de poca importancia). || Botched job, shoddy *o* amateurish piece of work (trabajo mal hecho). || Patching up (arreglo rápido). || Spare-time job (trabajo hecho fuera de las horas de jornal). || Ducking (en el agua).
chapuzar v. tr. To duck.
— V. intr. To dive.
— V. pr. To dive [in] (tirarse de cabeza). || To have a dip (bañarse).
chapuzón m. Dive (zambullida). || Dip, swim (baño corto). || *Darse un chapuzón*, to have a dip (en el mar).
chaqué o **chaquet** m. Tailcoat, morning coat.

— OBSERV. *Chaqué* is the most common form of the word, and becomes *chaqués* in the plural.

chaquense o **chaqueño, ña** adj. Of *o* from El Chaco.
— M. y f. Inhabitant *o* native of El Chaco.
chaqueta f. Jacket: *con chaqueta*, wearing a jacket, with one's jacket on; *chaqueta de smoking*, dinner jacket. || — FAM. *Cambiarse la chaqueta*, to change sides, to turn one's coat (cambiar de opinión o de partido). | *Ser más vago que la chaqueta de un guardia*, to be bone idle. || *Traje de chaqueta*, V. TRAJE.
chaquete m. Backgammon (juego).
chaquetear v. intr. FIG. To change sides, to be a turncoat (cambiar de opinión). | To back down, to go back on one's word (rajarse). | To flee (huir).
chaqueteo m. FIG. Flight, running away (huida). || Change (cambio).
chaquetero m. Turncoat.
chaquetilla f. Short jacket, bolero (de los toreros, camareros). || Bolero (para mujeres).
chaquetón m. Donkey jacket, pea jacket, three-quarter coat (para hombres). || Three-quarter coat (para mujeres).
charada f. Charade (juego).
charal m. Small Mexican fish (pez). || FIG. y FAM. *Estar hecho un charal*, to be as thin as a rake.
charamusca f. *Amer.* Brushwood (leña menuda). | Row, din (alboroto). | Candy twist (dulce).
charanga f. Brass band (orquesta).
charango m. *Amer.* "Charango" [small guitar].
charanguero m. Careless worker, shoddy worker, botcher (chapucero). || Pedlar, hawker, street salesman (buhonero). || Coaster (barco).
charca f. Pond, pool.
charco m. Puddle, pool. || FIG. y FAM. *Cruzar* o *pasar el charco*, to cross the water (cruzar el mar), to cross the herring pond (ir a América).
charcutería f. Pork butcher's.
charla f. FAM. Chat, talk (conversación). || Talk (conferencia informal). || ZOOL. Missel thrush, stormcock (cagaaceite).
charlador, ra adj. FAM. Talkative, garrulous (hablador). | Gossipy (murmurador).
— M. y f. FAM. Chatterbox (hablador). | Gossip (murmurador).
charladuría f. Chatter, prattle, small talk (conversación). || Gossip (crítica).
charlar v. intr. FAM. To chat, to talk (hablar). | To chatter, to prattle (hablar demasiado). || FAM. *Charlar por los codos*, to be a real chatterbox.
charlatán, ana adj. Talkative, garrulous (que habla mucho). || Gossipy (chismoso).
— M. y f. Chatterbox (que habla mucho). || Gossip, gossipmonger (chismoso). || Quack, charlatan (curandero). || Hawker, pedlar (vendedor callejero). || Trickster, swindler (engañador).
charlatanear v. intr. To chatter, to prattle (hablar mucho). || To gossip (hablar indiscretamente).
charlatanería f. Talkativeness, verbosity (cualidad de charlatán). || Gossip (chismorreo). || Spiel (del vendedor callejero, etc.).
charlatanesco, ca adj. Charlatanic.
charlatanismo m. Charlatanism.
charleston m. Charleston (baile).
charlista m. y f. Lecturer.
charlotear v. intr. FAM. To chatter, to prattle.
charloteo m. FAM. Chatter, prattle. | Chat (charla). || FAM. *Gustarle mucho a uno el charloteo*, to be a real chatterbox.
charnela o **charneta** f. Hinge (bisagra). || ZOOL. Hinge (de algunos moluscos).
charol m. Varnish (barniz). || Patent leather (cuero barnizado): *zapatos de charol*, patent leather shoes. || *Amer.* Tray (bandeja). || FIG. *Darse charol*, to boast, to brag, to blow one's trumpet.
charola f. *Amer.* Tray (bandeja). || — Pl. FAM. *Amer.* Big eyes.
charolado, da adj. Varnished, polished (barnizado). || Shiny, bright (lustroso).
charolar v. tr. To varnish (recubrir con charol).
charpa f. Pistol belt (tahalí). || MED. Sling (cabestrillo).
charque m. *Amer.* V. CHARQUI.
charqueada f. *Amer.* Curing, jerking, drying.
charquear v. tr. *Amer.* To cure, to jerk, to dry, to make into charqui (la carne). || To slice (rebanar). || FIG. To carve up, to wound badly.
charqueo m. *Amer.* Curing, drying, jerking.
charqui m. *Amer.* Charqui, charque, jerked meat (tasajo). | Dried fruit (fruta seca). | Dried vegetables (legumbres).
charquicán m. *Amer.* Stew made mainly from charqui.
charra f. Peasant woman. || *Amer.* Broad-brimmed hat.
charrada f. Boorishness, uncouthness (torpeza). || "Charro" dance (baile). || FIG. Gaudy ornament (adorno tosco).
charrán m. Rascal, rogue, scoundrel (granuja).

charranada f. FAM. Dirty trick, low-down trick (granujada).
charranería f. FAM. Dirty trick, low-down trick (acción). | Roguery, knavery (comportamiento).
charretera f. MIL. Epaulette, epaulet.
charro, rra adj. Of the peasants of Salamanca. || FIG. y FAM. Coarse, common, uncouth, ill-bred (rústico). | Flashy, gaudy, jazzy, loud (llamativo).
— M. y f. Salamanca peasant. || — M. *Amer.* Charro, Mexican horseman. | Sombrero, wide-brimmed hat (sombrero).
— OBSERV. The *charro*, with his wide-brimmed sombrero, his superb horsemanship and his richly adorned outfit, represents the traditional Mexican.
¡chas! interj. Pow!, wham!
chasca f. Brushwood (leña menuda). || *Amer.* Mop of tangled hair (pelo).
chascar v. intr. To click one's tongue (la lengua). || To snap (los nudillos). || To crack (madera, látigo). || To crunch (un manjar duro).
— V. tr. To click (la lengua). || To crack (látigo, etc.). || To crunch (un manjar duro). || To snap (los nudillos).
chascarrillo m. Joke.
chascás m. MIL. Schapska (casco).
chasco m. Joke (broma), trick (engaño): *dar un chasco a uno*, to play a joke on s.o., to play a trick on s.o. || Disappointment (decepción). || — *Dar un chasco a uno*, to pull s.o.'s leg (broma y engaño), to disappoint s.o., to let s.o. down (decepcionar). || *Llevarse un chasco*, to be disappointed, to get a big disappointment (estar decepcionado).
chasis m. AUT. Chassis. || FOT. Plate holder, frame. || FIG. y FAM. *Quedarse en el chasis*, to be all skin and bone.
chasponazo m. Bullet mark, graze (de proyectil).
chasquear v. tr. To play a trick on (engaño). || To play a joke on (broma). || To disappoint, to let down (decepcionar). || To crack (el látigo). || To click (la lengua). || To snap (los dedos). || To crunch (un manjar duro). || To break (promesa). || *Chasquear a alguien*, to pull s.o.'s leg (burla y engaño).
— V. intr. To crack (la madera, el látigo) || To click one's tongue (con la lengua). || To snap (con los dedos). || To crunch (un manjar).
— V. pr. To be disappointed (sufrir un desengaño). || To come to nothing (fracasar).
chasqui m. *Amer.* Mail (correo). | Messenger (mensajero).
chasquido m. Crack (de madera, látigo): *cuando se rompe una rama seca se oye un chasquido*, when you break a dry branch you hear a crack. || Click (de la lengua). || Snap (de los dedos). || Crunch (de un manjar duro). || Bang (de aviones y proyectiles).
chata f. Barge (chalana). || Bedpan (orinal). || Truck (vagón).
chatarra f. Scrap iron, scrap (hierro viejo). || FIG. Scrap. | Slag (escoria). || — Pl. FAM. Scrap metal, *sing.*, junk, *sing.*, medals (condecoraciones).
chatarrero m. Scrap-iron merchant, scrap-metal merchant, scrap merchant, scrap dealer.
chatear v. intr. FAM. To have a few [drinks].
chateo m. FAM. *Ir de chateo*, to go drinking *o* on a pub crawl [U.S., to go barhopping].
chato, ta adj. Snub, flat: *nariz chata*, snub nose. || Snub-nosed, pug-nosed: *persona chata*, snub-nosed person. || FIG. Shallow, flat (barco). | Blunt, flattened (objeto). | Low (torre, etc.). || *Amer.* Poor (pobre). || — FAM. *Chata mía*, my dear, my darling. | *Dejar chato a uno*, to stop s.o. short, to take the wind out of s.o.'s sails. | *Quedarse chato*, to be dumbfounded *o* flabbergasted (pasmado), to fail (fracasar).
— M. FAM. [Small] glass: *un chato de vino*, a glass of wine.
chatre adj. *Amer.* Smart, elegant, richly dressed.
chatungo, ga adj. Snub-nosed, pug-nosed.
¡chau! interj. *Amer.* FAM. Bye-bye!, cheerio!, so long!, ciao!
chaucha adj. inv. *Amer.* Insipid, dull (deslucido).
— F. *Amer.* Coin [of small value]. | French bean (judía verde). || *Amer. Pelar la chaucha*, to brandish a knife.
chauffeur m. V. CHÓFER.
chauvinismo m. Chauvinism (patriotería).
chauvinista adj. Chauvinist, chauvinistic.
— M. y f. Chauvinist.
chaval, la m. y f. FAM. Lad, boy, youngster, kid (muchacho), girl, youngster, lass (muchacha). || FAM. *Estar hecho un chaval*, to look (parecer) *o* to feel (sentirse) very young.
chavalería f. FAM. Kids, *pl.*, kiddies, *pl.*, children, *pl.*
chavea m. FAM. Kid, lad, boy.
chaveta f. TECN. Key, cotter (clavija). | Cotter pin (clavo hendido). || — FIG. y FAM. *Estar chaveta*, to be off one's rocker, to be round the bend, to have a screw loose. | *Perder la chaveta*, to go off one's rocker, to go round the bend, to go mad. | *Perder la chaveta por*, to be crazy about.
chavo m. FAM. Brass coin, farthing (ochavo). || FAM. *No tener un chavo*, not to have a brass farthing [U.S., not to have a red cent].
chavó m. FAM. Kid, lad, boy (chaval).
chayote m. BOT. Chayote (fruto y planta).
chayotera f. BOT. Chayote (planta).
che f. Name of the letter *ch*.
— Interj. *Amer.* Hey!
checar v. tr. *Amer.* V. CHEQUEAR.
checo, ca adj./s. Czech, Czechoslovak, Czechoslovakian (checoslovaco).
checoslovaco, ca adj./s. Czechoslovak, Czechoslovakian.
Checoslovaquia n. pr. f. GEOGR. Czechoslovakia.
chécheres m. pl. *Amer.* Things, bits and pieces, odds and ends, stuff, *sing.*, belongings.
cheira f. V. CHAIRA.
chele adj. *Amer.* Blonde, blond.
— M. *Amer.* Rheum, sleep (legaña).
chelín m. Shilling (moneda).
chelo, la adj./s. *Amer.* Blonde, blond (rubio). || — M. MÚS. Cello (instrumento). | Cellist (músico).
chepa f. FAM. Hump (joroba). || — M. Hunchback (persona).
cheque m. Cheque [U.S., check]: *extender un cheque de mil pesetas*, to write a cheque *o* to make out a cheque for a thousand pesetas. || — *Cheque al portador*, bearer cheque, open cheque, cheque payable to bearer. || *Cheque cruzado*, crossed cheque. || *Cheque de viaje* or *de viajero*, traveller's cheque. || *Cheque en blanco*, blank cheque. || *Cheque nominal*, cheque to order, order cheque. || *Cheque sin fondos* or *sin provisión*, cheque without cover, dud cheque, N.S.F. cheque, worthless cheque, cheque that bounces (fam.). || *Cobrar un cheque*, to cash a cheque. || *Talonario de cheques*, chequebook [U.S., checkbook].
chequear v. tr. To check (averiguar). || To compare (cotejar). || To check (refrenar). || MED. To give a checkup to.
chequeo m. MED. Checkup (examen médico). || Check (averiguación). || Comparison (comparación).
chequera f. *Amer.* Chequebook [U.S., checkbook].
chester m. Cheshire cheese (queso).
cheurón o **cheurrón** m. HERÁLD. Chevron.
cheuronado, da adj. HERÁLD. Chevronny.
cheviot m. Cheviot (tejido).
chibalete m. IMPR. Composing frame *o* stand.
chibcha adj. Chibchan.
— M. y f. Chibcha.
chibola f. *Amer.* Bump (chichón).
chibuquí m. Chibouque, chibouk (pipa turca).
chic adj. inv. Chic, elegant.
— M. Chic, stylishness, elegance.
chica f. Girl (muchacha). || Maid, servant (criada). || *Chica para todo*, maid.
chicada f. Childish trick *o* prank.
chicana f. *Amer.* Chicanery, quibbling.
chicanear v. tr. e intr. *Amer.* To chicane.
chicanero, ra adj. *Amer.* Crafty, tricky.
— M. y f. *Amer.* Chicaner.
chicano, na adj. "Chicano" (mexicano que ha emigrado a los Estados Unidos).
chicar v. tr. To chew (mascar tabaco).
chicarrón, ona m. y f. FAM. Strapping lad, sturdy boy (hombre), strapping lass, sturdy girl (mujer).
chicle m. Chewing gum (goma de masticar). || Chicle (gomorresina). || *Amer.* Dirt, filth (suciedad). || *Chicle de globo*, bubble gum.
chiclear v. intr. *Amer.* To chew, to chew gum (mascar). | To extract gum (extraer el chicle).
chicler m. Jet (del carburador).
chico, ca adj. Small, little: *un libro chico*, a small book. || — FIG. y FAM. *Dejar a uno chico*, to put s.o. in the shade, to make s.o. look small. | *Una perra chica*, a five-cent piece.
— M. y f. Boy (hombre), girl (mujer): *un buen chico*, a good boy; *una chica guapa*, a pretty girl. || Son, boy (hijo), daughter, girl (hija). || — F. FAM. Small coin [of little value] (moneda). || — M. Child, youngster: *dar la merienda a los chicos*, to give the children their tea. || Measure of capacity (medida). || — *Chico con grande*, big and small alike, no matter what size: *a diez pesetas la docena, chico con grande*, ten pesetas a dozen, big and small alike. || *Chico de la calle*, street urchin (golfillo). || *Chico de los recados*, office boy (de oficina), errand boy (para cualquier establecimiento). || *Es buen chico*, he's a good lad. || *¡Oye, chico!*, listen here, my old son; listen here, my friend. || FAM. *Tan feliz como un chico con zapatos nuevos*, as happy as a sandboy.
chicolear v. intr. FAM. To say nice things, to pay compliments (decir frases amables). | To flirt (coquetear).
— V. pr. *Amer.* FAM. To enjoy o.s.
chicoleo m. FAM. Compliment, flirtatious remark (requiebro). | Flirting (coqueteo). || *Amer.* Childish thing. || *Decir chicoleos*, to say nice things, to pay compliments (decir frases amables), to flirt.
chicoria f. BOT. Chicory.
chicotazo m. Jet (chorro). || *Amer.* Lash (latigazo).
chicote, ta m. y f. FAM. Fine *o* strapping lad (hombre), fine girl (mujer). || — M. MAR. End of cable, rope end (de cuerda). || FIG. y FAM. Cigar [stub] (puro). || *Amer.* Whip (látigo).
chicotear v. tr. *Amer.* To whip (azotar).
chicozapote m. BOT. Sapodilla, chicozapote (zapote).
chicuelo, la adj. Very small.
— M. y f. Urchin, kid, youngster.

chicha adj. MAR. *Calma chicha*, dead *o* absolute calm.
— F. Chicha, maize liquor [U.S., corn liquor] (bebida alcohólica). || [Fruit] liquor (hecha con fruta). || Juice (zumo). || Meat [in children's language]. || — FIG. y FAM. *De chicha y nabo*, run-of-the-mill, nondescript, ordinary. | *Esas son economías de chicha y nabo*, that is cheeseparing [economy]. | *No ser ni chicha ni limonada*, to be neither one thing nor the other, to be neither fish nor fowl. | *Sacarle la chicha a alguien*, to make s.o. sweat. | *Tener pocas chichas*, to be all skin and bone, to have no meat on one (flaco), to have no go (pocas fuerzas).
chícharo m. Pea (guisante). || Chick-pea (garbanzo).
chicharra f. Cicada (cigarra). || FIG. y FAM. *Hablar como una chicharra*, to be a real chatterbox.
chicharrero m. FAM. Oven, hothouse (sitio muy caluroso). | Suffocating heat (calor sofocante).
chicharro m. Horse mackerel, caranx (pez).
chicharrón m. Piece of crackling (residuo muy frito de pella de cerdo). || — Pl. Crackling, *sing.* || FIG. *Estar hecho un chicharrón*, to be burnt to a cinder (carne), to be as brown as a berry (persona).
chiche m. *Amer.* FAM. Knick-knack (chuchería). | Toy (juguete). | Jewel (joya). | Breast (pecho). | Nurse, wet nurse (nodriza). | Meat (carne).
— Adj. Easy (fácil).
chichería f. *Amer.* Chicha shop. | Tavern, bar.
chichi f. *Amer.* FAM. Breast (pecho). | Nurse, wet nurse (nodriza).
chichimeca o **chichimeco, ca** adj. Chichimecan.
— M. y f. Chichimec, Chichimeca, Chichimeco.
chichinabo (de) loc. adv. V. CHICHA (*De chicha y nabo*).
chichisbeo m. Gallant, suitor (hombre). || Flattery, gallantry (atenciones).
chicholo m. *Amer.* Sweetmeat wrapped in maize leaf.
chichón m. Bump (en la cabeza o en la frente).
chichonear v. intr. *Amer.* To joke.
chichonera f. Helmet.
chifla f. Whistling (silbido). || Whistle (silbato, pito). || Skiver, parer, whitening knife (para adelgazar las pieles). || Hissing, catcalls, *pl.* (de protesta). || *Menuda chifla se llevó*, he was booed *o* hissed by everyone.
chifladera f. Whistle (silbato).
chiflado, da adj. FAM. Cracked, touched, daft, barmy (loco, tocado). || — FAM. *Estar chiflado*, to be round the bend, to be barmy. | *Estar chiflado por* or *con*, to be mad on *o* about, to be crazy on *o* about: *estar chiflado por la música*, to be mad on music; to be head over heels in love with, to be mad *o* crazy about (enamorado): *está chiflado por Juana*, he's mad about Joan.
— M. y f. FAM. Nut, crackpot (loco). || — M. FAM. Fan: *los chiflados del fútbol*, football fans.
chifladura f. Whistle, whistling (silbido). || FAM. Daftness, craziness (estado de loco). | Craze (afición exagerada). | Whim (capricho). | Infatuation (amor exagerado).
chiflar v. intr. To whistle (silbar).
— V. tr. To skive, to pare (el cuero). || To hiss, to boo, to give the bird to (a un actor). || FAM. To swig, to knock back, to down, to gulp down (vino, etc.). || — *Cazar es lo que le chifla*, he's mad about hunting. || *Ese chico me chifla*, I am crazy about that boy. || *Esto me chifla*, I think this is great *o* fantastic, I love this.
— V. pr. To be crazy *o* mad about, to have a crush on (por una persona), to be mad on, to have a craze on *o* for (por una cosa): *chiflarse por una actriz*, to be mad about a film star; *chiflarse por el cine*, to be mad on films.
chiflato m. Whistle (silbato).
chifle m. Whistle (silbato). || Decoy (reclamo). || Powder horn (para la pólvora).
chiflete m. Whistle (silbato).
chiflido m. Whistle (ruido). || Whistling (acción).
chiflo m. Whistle (silbato).
chiflón m. Draught (corriente de aire). || *Amer.* Waterfall (cascada). | Drain (canal). | Rockfall (derrumbe).
chigua f. *Amer.* Hamper.
chihuahua m. Chihuahua (perro).
chiita m. y f. Shiah, Shiite.
chilaba f. Jellaba, djellaba, jelab (de los árabes).
chilacayote m. BOT. Chilacayote, chilicojote (planta cucurbitácea).
chilar m. *Amer.* Chili field, chile field.
chile m. Chili, chile, chilli.
Chile n. pr. m. GEOGR. Chile.
chilenismo m. Chilean word *o* expression.
chilenizar v. tr. To make Chilean.
chileno, na adj./s. Chilean.
chilindrina f. FAM. Trifle (cosa insignificante). | Anecdote, story (anécdota). | Joke (chiste).
chilindrinero, ra adj. Witty, funny, fond of a joke.
— M. y f. Joker, witty person.
chilindrón m. Pope Joan (juego de baraja). || CULIN. *Pollo al chilindrón*, chicken garnished with tomatoes and peppers.
chilmole m. *Amer.* Sauce made from peppers.
chiltepe o **chiltipiquín** m. *Amer.* Chili, chile, chilli (pimiento).
chilla f. Decoy (reclamo para la caza). || Lath (tabla). || Long thick fur (de animal) *o* hair (de hombre). || Down (de las plantas). || *Amer.* Poverty (pobreza).
chillado m. Roof made from laths (techo de listones y tablas).
chillador, ra adj. Screaming, shrieking, yelling.
— M. y f. Screamer.
chillante adj. Loud, gaudy, lurid (color). || Shrieking (voz).
chillar v. intr. To scream, to shriek (gritar): *el niño no para de chillar*, the child is always screaming. || To cry, to wail (llorar). || To howl (gato). || To squeak (ratón). || To squawk, to screech (ave). || To squeal (cerdo). || To creak (chirriar): *la puerta chilla*, the door creaks. || To blare (radio). || To screech, to squeal (frenos). || To call (la caza). || FIG. To be loud *o* gaudy (un color), to clash (detonar varios colores). || *Amer.* To protest, to complain (protestar). || *Fue chillado por el público*, he was booed *o* hissed by the audience.
— V. pr. *Amer.* To get angry *o* annoyed (enojarse).
chillería f. Screaming, yelling, shouting, howling (alboroto de gritos). || Dressing down, talking-to, scolding (regaño).
chillido m. Scream, yell, cry, howl (grito de persona). || Howl (de gato). || Squeak (de ratón). || Squawk, screech (de ave). || Creak, creaking: *el chillido de una puerta*, the creaking of a door.
chillo m. Decoy (reclamo).
chillón, ona adj. Noisy, screaming: *un niño chillón*, a noisy child. || FIG. Loud, gaudy, lurid (color). || Shrill, screechy, strident (sonido): *una voz chillona*, a shrill voice.
— M. y f. Noisy person. || TECN. Lath nail (clavo).
chimar v. tr. *Amer.* To annoy (fastidiar).
— V. pr. *Amer.* To hurt o.s. (lastimarse).
chimba f. *Amer.* Opposite bank (orilla). | Ford (vado). | Noncentral part of town.
chimbar v. tr. *Amer.* To ford (vadear).
chimenea f. Chimney (de casa, de fábrica). || Chimney [U.S., smokestack] (de locomotora). || Funnel, stack (de barco). || Fireplace (hogar para calentarse). || Shaft (en una mina, etc.). || Nipple (de armas de fuego). || — *Chimenea de campana*, canopy fireplace. || *Chimenea de paracaídas*, parachute vent. || *Chimenea de tiro*, chimney. || *Chimenea de ventilación*, air shaft, air well. || *Chimenea estufa*, closed stove. || *Chimenea francesa*, fireplace. || *Chimenea volcánica*, throat *o* vent *o* chimney of a volcano. || FIG. *Fumar como una chimenea*, to smoke like a chimney.
chimiscolear v. intr. *Amer.* To wander about, to hang about (vagar). | To gossip (chismear).
chimó m. *Amer.* Plug of tobacco and natron paste [as chewed by Indians].
chimpancé m. ZOOL. Chimpanzee.
china f. Pebble (piedrecita). || China (porcelana). || China silk (tejido). || FIG. y FAM. Money (dinero). || — *Echar algo a chinas*, to draw lots for sth. || *Jugar a las chinas*, to play a guessing game. || FIG. *Poner chinas a uno*, to put difficulties *o* obstacles in s.o.'s way. | *Tocarle a uno la china*, to win the draw.
china f. *Amer.* V. CHINO (2.° artículo).
China n. pr. f. GEOGR. China.
chinampa f. "Chinampa", floating garden [near Mexico City].
chinampero, ra adj. Grown in the "chinampa".
— M. Keeper of a "chinampa".
chinazo m. Stone (piedra). || Blow with a pebble (golpe).
chincaste m. *Amer.* Brown sugar (azúcar).
chincol o **chincolito** m. *Amer.* Brandy mixed with water, brandy and soda (agua con aguardiente).
chincual m. *Amer.* Measles (sarampión).
chincha f. *Amer.* Bug (chinche). | Drawing pin [U.S., thumbtack]. | Skunk (mofeta).
chinchal m. *Amer.* Small shop (tenducho).
chinchar v. tr. FAM. To pester, to annoy, to bug (molestar). | To annoy: *me chincha tener que hacerlo*, it annoys me to have to do it. | To do in, to kill (matar).
— V. pr. FAM. To get on with it: *tú lo querías, así que chínchate*, you wanted it, so get on with it. || FAM. *Chínchate* or *para que te chinches*, so there: *me lo dieron a mí, ¡para que te chinches!*, they gave it to me, so there!
chincharrero m. Bug-infested place (nido de chinches). || *Amer.* Small fishing boat (barco).
chinche f. ZOOL. Bug. || Drawing pin [U.S., thumbtack] (clavito). || — M. y f. FIG. y FAM. Nuisance, bore, pest (pesado). || FIG. y FAM. *Morir, caer como chinches*, to die, to fall *o* to drop like flies.
chinchel m. *Amer.* Bar, pub, eating house.
chincheta f. Drawing pin [U.S., thumbtack] (clavito).
chinchibí m. *Amer.* Ginger beer.
chinchilla f. Chinchilla (animal y piel).
chinchín m. FAM. Blare, pom pom pom: *el chinchín de la banda*, the pom pom pom of the band. || *Amer.* Drizzle (llovizna). | Rattle (sonajero).
chinchona f. BOT. y MED. Quinine.
chinchorrera f. FIG. y FAM. Nuisance, annoyance (molestia). | Hairsplitting, quibbling, overfussiness (minuciosidad exagerada). | Gossip (chisme).
chinchorrero, ra adj. Fussy (difícil de contentar). || Gossipy (chismoso).

— M. y f. Fussy person (difícil de contentar). || Gossip, scandalmonger (chismoso).
chinchorro m. MAR. Seine, sweep net (red). | Dinghy (bote).
chinchoso, sa adj. FIG. y FAM. Tiresome, annoying (cargante).
— M. y f. FIG. y FAM. Nuisance, drag (*fam.*).
chinchulines m. pl. *Amer.* Grilled tripe, *sing.*
chiné adj. Chiné (de colores).
— M. Chiné (tejido).
chinear v. tr. *Amer.* To carry in one's arms (en los brazos), to carry on one's back (a cuestas). | To flirt with (requebrar). | To spoil (mimar).
chinela f. Slipper (zapatilla). || Clog (chanclo).
chinería f. o **chinerío** m. *Amer.* Riffraff, rabble.
chinero m. Dresser (mueble).
chinesco, ca adj. Chinese. || *Sombras chinescas,* shadow theatre.
— M. MÚS. Pavillon chinois, Chinese crescent, jingling Johnny.
chinga f. *Amer.* ZOOL. Skunk. | FAM. Drunkenness (borrachera). | Fag end (colilla de cigarro).
chingada o **chingadura** f. FAM. Bother. || *Amer.* Failure, flop (fracaso).
chingana f. *Amer.* Drive, club (tabernucha). | Festival with drinking and dancing (fiesta). | Underground cave *o* passage.
chinganear v. intr. *Amer.* To go on a spree.
chingar v. tr. FAM. To down, to put away, to drink a lot of (beber mucho). | To annoy, to get on [s.o.'s] nerves (dar la lata). || *Amer.* To cut off the tail of (cortar el rabo). | To joke (bromear). || *Amer.* POP. To fuck, to screw (tener relaciones sexuales con).
— V. pr. FAM. To get annoyed (enfadarse). | To get sloshed *o* sozzled (emborracharse). || *Amer.* To fail (fracasar). | To fizzle out (fuego artificial).
chingaste m. *Amer.* Sediment (poso).
chingo, ga adj. *Amer.* Small (pequeño). | Short (corto). | Tailless (rabón). | Flat (chato): *nariz chinga,* flat nose.
chinguirito m. *Amer.* Rum (aguardiente).
chino, na adj. Chinese (de China). || — *Tinta china,* Indian ink, [U.S., India ink].
— M. Chinese, Chinaman (hombre). || Chinese (idioma). || — F. Chinese, Chinese woman (mujer). || — FAM. *Engañar a uno como a un chino,* to take s.o. for a ride. | *Eso es chino para mí,* that's Greek to me. || *Los chinos,* the Chinese. || FIG. y FAM. *Trabajar como un chino,* to work like a slave.
chino, na adj./s. *Amer.* Indian (indio). | Half-breed, half-caste (mestizo). | Mulatto (mulato). | Darling, dear (calificativo cariñoso). || — Adj. *Amer.* Angry (airado). | Curly (pelo). | Yellowish (amarillento). || — M. *Amer.* Kid, youngster (niño). | Servant (criado). | Curl (rizo). || — F. *Amer.* Peasant girl (campesina). | Maid (criada). | Companion (compañera). | Nursemaid (niñera). | Girl friend (novia). | Mistress (amante). | Spinning top (peonza).
chipa f. *Amer.* Fruit basket (cesto). | Pad (rodete). || *Amer.* FAM. Clink, prison (cárcel).
chipá m. *Amer.* Manioc cake.
chipe o **chipén** o **chipendi (de)** loc. adv. FAM. Great, marvellous, super, smashing (de órdago). || — FAM. *Hemos comido de chipén,* we've had a great *o* super *o* smashing meal. || FAM. *La chipén,* the truth.
chipichape m. FAM. Fight (zipizape). | Blow (golpe).
chipichipi m. *Amer.* Drizzle (llovizna).
chipirón m. Squid (calamar): *chipirones fritos,* fried squid.
Chipre n. pr. GEOGR. Cyprus.
chipriota o **chipriote** adj./s. Cypriot, Cypriote.
chiqueadores m. pl. *Amer.* Headache plasters.
chiquear v. tr. *Amer.* To pamper, to mollycoddle (mimar). | To flatter (adular).
— V. pr. *Amer.* To swagger, to strut (contonearse).
chiqueo m. *Amer.* Pampering, mollycoddling (mimo). | Piece of flattery (adulación).
chiquero m. Pigsty (pocilga). || TAUR. Toril, bullpen (toril). || *Amer.* Cow shed (establo).
chiquichaque m. Sawyer (aserrador).
chiquilicuatro FAM. Whippersnapper, runt (mequetrefe).
chiquilín m. Small boy.
chiquillada f. Childish prank *o* trick (niñería). || Foolish *o* childish thing (acción poco sensata). || *Hacer chiquilladas,* to behave childishly.
chiquillería f. Kids, *pl.*, children, *pl.*
chiquillo, lla m. y f. Lad, boy, kid (muchacho), girl, kid (muchacha). || *Los chiquillos,* the kids.
— Adj. Stupid, childish: *no seas chiquillo,* don't be stupid.
chiquirritico, ca o **chiquirritillo, lla** o **chiquirrito, ta** o **chiquitín, ina** adj. Tiny, teeny (fam.).
chiquitear v. intr. FAM. To have a few [drinks].
chiquiteo m. Pub crawl, going drinking from bar to bar. || *Ir de chiquiteo,* to go drinking *o* on a pub crawl [U.S., to go barhopping].
chiquito, ta adj. Tiny, small.
— M. y f. Kid, child, youngster (chico, chica). || FAM. *No andarse con chiquitas,* not to beat about the bush, not to mess about, not to hem and haw (no vacilar), to be generous (no escatimar nada). || — M. FAM. Glass, glass of wine, wine (vaso de vino): *vamos a tomar unos chiquitos,* let's have a few glasses of wine.
chiribita f. Spark (chispa). || — Pl. Spots before the eyes (de la vista). || FIG. y FAM. *Echar chiribitas,* to fume, to blow one's top, to be furious.
chiribitil m. Garret. attic (desván). || Small room, den, cubbyhole (cuchitril).
chirigota f. FAM. Joke (chanza, broma). || FAM. *A chirigota,* as a joke, lightly: *tomar algo a chirigota,* to take sth. as a joke.
chirigotero, ra adj. Fond of a joke, funny, jocose.
— M. y f. Joker.
chirimbolo m. FAM. Thing (chisme). | Contraption (cosa de forma complicada). || — Pl. FAM. Things, gear, *sing.*, stuff, *sing.*, odds and ends (trastos). | Tools, gear, *sing.*, things (utensilios).
chirimía f. MÚS. Chirimia, chirimilla, shawn.
chirimoya f. Cherimoya fruit, soursop (fruto).
chirimoyo m. Cherimoya (árbol).
chirinada f. *Amer.* Failure (fracaso).
chirinola f. Quarrel (gresca). || Lively discussion (conversación). || Skittles, *pl.* (juego). || FIG. Trifle (cosa insignificante). || *De chirinola,* in a good mood.
chiripa f. Fluke (en el billar). || FIG. y FAM. Fluke, stroke of luck (suerte). || — FIG. y FAM. *De* or *por chiripa* or *por pura chiripa,* by a fluke, by sheer luck. | *He aprobado por chiripa,* it was a fluke that I passed, I passed by sheer luck *o* by a fluke.
chiripá m. *Amer.* Chiripa [garment].
chiripear v. intr. To win points by a fluke (en billar).
chiripero m. Lucky *o* fluky person.
chirivía f. BOT. Parsnip (pastinaca). || Wagtail (ave).
chirla f. Clam (almeja).
chirlar v. intr. FAM. To jabber.
chirle adj. FAM. Tasteless, wishy-washy, insipid (sin gracia).
— M. Droppings, *pl.*
chirlo m. Gash, slash (herida). | Scar (cicatriz). || *Amer.* Lash (latigazo).
chirola f. *Amer.* Coin [of little value].
chirona f. FAM. Clink, nick, prison: *meter en chirona,* to put in clink. || FAM. *Estar en chirona,* to be inside, to be in clink *o* in the nick.
chirote m. *Amer.* FAM. Idiot, fool (tonto).
chirriador, ra o **chirriante** adj. Creaking (que rechina). || Crackling, sizzling (al freírse una cosa). || Cheeping (pájaro). || FIG. Shrill, piercing (voz).
chirriar v. intr. To creak (gozne, eje de carro, etc.). || To sizzle, to crackle (al freír). || To cheep (los pájaros). || To chirp (el grillo). || To screech, to squeal (frenos). | To chirp (grillo). || FIG. y FAM. To sing out of tune, to sing badly (cantar mal). | To bawl, to yell (gritar). || *Amer.* To go drinking, to go on a spree (ir de juerga). | To shiver (tiritar).
chirrido m. Chirp, chirping, cheeping (pájaros). || Creak, creaking (ruido desagradable): *el chirrido de la puerta,* the creaking of the door. || Screech, squeal (de los frenos). || Crackling (del fuego). || Sizzling (de una cosa al freírse). || FIG. y FAM. Yell, shriek (grito). || *El chirrido del grillo,* the chirping of the cricket.
chirrión m. Heavy cart (carro). || *Amer.* Leather whip (látigo). | Chat (conversación).
chirumen m. FAM. Common sense, intelligence.
chirusa o **chiruza** f. *Amer.* Coarse *o* uncouth woman.
¡chis! interj. Ssh!, hush! (chitón).
chischás m. Clash (ruido de las espadas al entrechocarse).
chisgarabís m. FAM. Whippersnapper, runt (mequetrefe). | Busybody, meddler (entrometido).
chisguete m. FAM. Drink, swig (trago): *echar un chisguete,* to have a swig. | Jet, spurt, squirt (chorro). || *Amer.* Rubber tube (tubo).
chisguetear v. intr. FAM. To have a drink (beber).
chisme m. Piece of gossip (hablilla). || FAM. Knick-knack (objeto sin importancia). | Thingumajig, thing (cosa): *¡qué chisme tan raro!,* what a funny thing! | Gadget (dispositivo). || — Pl. Gossip, *sing.* (chismorreo). | Things, stuff, *sing.*, odds and ends (trastos). || — *El cuarto de los chismes,* the lumber room, the box room, the glory hole. || *Los vecinos andan siempre con chismes,* the neighbours are always gossiping. || *Meter* or *traer chismes,* to gossip, to tell tales.
chismear v. intr. To gossip, to tell tales.
chismería f. Gossip, piece of gossip (chisme).
chismero, ra adj. Fond of telling tales, gossipy, gossiping.
— M. y f. Gossip, scandalmonger.
chismografía f. FAM. Gossiping, gossip (habladuría).
chismorrear v. intr. To gossip (chismear).
chismorreo m. Gossip, gossiping.
chismoso, sa adj. Fond of telling tales, gossipy, gossiping.
— M. y f. Gossip, scandalmonger.
chispa f. Spark: *chispa eléctrica,* electric spark; *echar chispas,* to give off sparks. || Flash (relámpago). || Sparkle, glitter (en una cosa brillante). || Small diamond (diamante pequeño). || Drop, small drop (de lluvia). || FIG. Crumb, scrap (pedazo de una cosa): *no sobró ni una chispa de pan,* there wasn't a scrap of bread left. | A little (un poquito): *una chispa, nada más,* just a little. | Drop (gota). | Spark, glimmer: *una chispa de inteligencia,* a glimmer of intelligence. | Liveliness

(viveza). | Wit (gracia). || FAM. Drunkenness (borrachera). || *Amer.* Lie (mentira). || — *Caen chispas,* it's drizzling (llueve). || *De chispa,* flint (escopeta). || FIG. y FAM. *Echar chispas,* to be hopping mad [U.S., to spit fire]. | *Ni chispa,* nothing (nada), at all: *no me gusta ni chispa,* I don't like it at all. | *No tiene ni chispa de gracia,* it's not funny at all, it's not a bit funny. | *Ser una chispa,* to be lively (ser muy vivo). | *Tener chispa,* to be witty *o* funny, to be a live wire (persona graciosa), to be funny (cosa graciosa), to be lively (ser muy vivo).
— Interj. Goodness me!
chisparse v. pr. FAM. To get drunk (emborracharse). || *Amer.* To run away (escaparse).
chispazo m. Spark: *le saltó un chispazo a la cara,* a spark flew into his face. || Burn (quemadura). || FIG. Spark: *los primeros chispazos de la guerra,* the first sparks of the war. || FAM. Piece of gossip (chisme). || FIG. *Chispazo de ingenio,* flash of genius.
chispeante adj. Which gives off sparks (que echa chispas). || Sparkling: *ojos chispeantes,* sparkling eyes. || FIG. *Tener un ingenio chispeante,* to sparkle with wit.
chispear v. intr. To give off sparks, to spark (echar chispas). || To spark (echar una chispa). || FIG. To sparkle: *chispear de alegría,* to sparkle with joy. | To be brilliant: *su discurso chispeó,* his speech was brilliant. | To spit, to drizzle (lloviznar).
chispero m. Blacksmith (herrero). || FIG. y FAM. Man from the lower classes of Madrid.
chispo, pa adj. FAM. Merry, tipsy.
— M. FAM. Swig, drink (trago).
chispoleto, ta adj. Bright, wide-awake, sharp (listo).
chisporroteante adj. Crackling (fuego).
chisporrotear v. intr. To crackle: *el fuego chisporrotea,* the fire is crackling. || To spit, to sizzle (aceite). || RAD. To crackle.
chisporroteo m. Crackling (de la leña). || Spitting, sizzling (del aceite). | RAD. Crackling (ruido parásito).
chisquero m. Tinder lighter.
¡chist! interj. Ssh!, hush!
chistar v. intr. To speak, to open one's mouth, to say a word: *no chistó mientras estuvimos allí,* he didn't say a word whilst we were there. || — *Sin chistar,* without saying a word, without opening one's mouth (sin decir nada), without turning a hair (sin protestar). || FAM. *Sin chistar ni mistar,* without a word.
chiste m. Joke, funny story (cuento gracioso): *contar un chiste,* to tell a joke. || — *Caer en el chiste,* to get the joke, to get it. || *Con chiste,* wittily, in a funny way. || *Chiste verde,* dirty joke *o* story. || *Esto tiene chiste,* that's not funny, some joke (irónico). || *Es una cosa sin chiste,* it's not funny. || *Hacer chiste de algo,* to make a joke of sth., to take sth. as a joke. || *Hacer chiste de uno,* to make fun of s.o. || *No le veo el chiste a lo que ha dicho,* I don't see what's funny in what he said. || *Tener chiste,* to be funny.
chistera f. Creel, angler's basket (cesta de pescador). || FIG. y FAM. Top hat, topper (sombrero de copa). || Basket (para jugar a la pelota).
chistoso, sa adj. Funny, witty, fond of a joke, jocose (persona). || Funny: *una anécdota muy chistosa,* a very funny anecdote. || — *Es chistoso que siempre me pida a mí que lo haga,* it's getting beyond a joke that he always asks me to do it. || *Lo chistoso,* the funny part (extraño o gracioso).
— M. y f. Laugh, comic (persona graciosa).
chistu m. Basque flute.
chistulari m. Basque flute player.
¡chit! interj. Ssh!, hush!
chita f. ANAT. Anklebone (hueso). || Quoits, *pl.* (juego). || *Amer.* Net bag (bolsa de red). || — FIG. y FAM. *A la chita callando,* on the quiet, on the sly: *le hizo una mala jugada a la chita callando,* he played a dirty trick on him on the quiet. | *Me acerqué a él a la chita callando,* I crept up on him, I approached him stealthily. | *Se marchó a la chita callando,* he slipped away, he left quietly.
chiticalla m. y f. FAM. Discreet person, clam (fam.).
chiticallando adv. FAM. V. CHITA (*A la chita callando*).
chito m. Kind of quoits, *pl.* (juego).
¡chito! o **¡chitón!** interj. FAM. Ssh!, hush!
chiva f. Kid, young she-goat (cabrita). || *Amer.* Blanket (manta). | Goatee (perilla). | Drunkenness (borrachera). | Rage (berrinche). | Minx (mujer inmoral).
chivar v. tr. FAM. To annoy, to get on s.o.'s nerves.
— V. pr. FAM. To tell, to split (entre niños): *chivarse de algo al maestro,* to tell the teacher *o* to split to the teacher about sth.; *¡cuidado, que me voy a chivar!,* look out or I'll tell! | To inform (soplonear): *me voy a chivar a la policía de las actividades de Juan,* I'm going to inform the police about John's activities.
chivata f. Shepherd's stick.
chivatazo m. FAM. Telling, informing (delación). || FAM. *Dar el chivatazo,* to spill the beans, to split, to inform (delatar).
chivatear v. intr. FAM. To inform, to split, to tell tales (soplonear). || *Amer.* To scream, to shout (gritar).
chivateo m. FAM. Telling, splitting, informing.
chivato, ta m. y f. FAM. Informer (delator). | Telltale (acusica). || — M. Kid, young goat (chivo).
chivo m. Kid, young goat (cría de la cabra). || *Chivo emisario* or *expiatorio,* scapegoat (entre los judíos).
chocante adj. Shocking, offensive: *unas costumbres chocantes,* shocking habits. || Surprising, startling, striking (sorprendente). || Unpleasant: *voz chocante,* unpleasant voice. || Odd, strange (raro). || *Lo chocante es que,* the striking thing is that.
chocar v. intr. To hit, to run (*con,* into), to collide (*con,* with): *el coche chocó con* or *contra la farola,* the car ran into *o* collided with *o* hit the lamppost. || To collide, to run into each other (dos) *o* one another (más de dos), to hit each other *o* one another: *chocaron dos trenes,* two trains collided, two trains ran into each other. || To hit: *la pelota chocó contra la pared,* the ball hit the wall. || FIG. To clash (pelear): *los ejércitos chocaron en esta ciudad,* the armies clashed in this town. | To shock: *me chocó mucho su contestación,* his reply really shocked me. | To argue (reñir): *chocar con uno,* to argue with s.o. | To be surprising (sorprender). || — *Coches que chocan,* dodgems [U.S., bumper cars]. || *Chocar de frente,* to hit head on.
— V. tr. To clink (vasos). || To shake: *chocar la mano con,* to shake hands with. || To surprise (sorprender). || *¡Chócala!,* shake!, shake on it!
chocarrear v. intr. To tell dirty *o* coarse *o* rude *o* crude jokes.
chocarrería f. Dirty *o* coarse *o* crude *o* rude joke.
chocarrero, ra adj. Dirty, coarse, crude, rude.
— M. y f. Coarse comic, person who tells dirty jokes.
choclo m. Clog (chanclo). || *Amer.* Cob of tender corn (maíz). | Food made mainly from tender corn (alimento). | FIG. y FAM. Worry (preocupación), burden, responsibility (carga). || *Amer.* FAM. *¡Qué choclo!,* what a nuisance!
choco, ca adj. *Amer.* One-legged (con una pierna). | One-eared (con una oreja). | One-eyed (con un ojo). | Curly-haired (de pelo rizado).
— M. Small cuttlefish (jibia). || *Amer.* Water spaniel (perro de aguas). | Stump (muñón).
chocolate m. Chocolate: *pastilla de chocolate,* piece *o* square of chocolate; *tableta de chocolate,* bar *o* slab *o* tablet of chocolate. || Drinking chocolate, cocoa: *jícara de chocolate,* cup of drinking chocolate. || — *Chocolate a la taza, con leche,* drinking chocolate, milk chocolate. || *Chocolate para crudo,* plain *o* dark chocolate. || FIG. *Esas son economías del chocolate del loro,* that is cheeseparing [economy]. | *Hacer economías del chocolate del loro,* to count every penny, to overeconomize. || FIG. y FAM. *Las cosas claras y el chocolate espeso,* let's get things clear. || *Amer. Sacar chocolate,* to make [s.o.'s] nose bleed (hacer sangrar las narices).
— Adj. Chocolate-coloured (color).
chocolatera f. Chocolate pot. || FAM. Old crock (coche viejo). | Old tub, hulk (barco).
chocolatería f. Chocolate factory (fábrica). || Chocolate shop (tienda).
chocolatero, ra adj. Chocolate-loving, fond of chocolate.
— M. y f. Chocolate maker (fabricante). || Chocolate seller (vendedor). || Chocolate lover, chocolate eater (aficionado al chocolate).
chocolatín m. o **chocolatina** f. Bar of chocolate (alargado), chocolate (redondo).
chocha o **chochaperdiz** f. ZOOL. Woodcock (ave).
chochear v. intr. To dodder, to be in one's dotage, to be senile (tener debilitadas las facultades mentales). || *El amor hace chochear con frecuencia a los hombres,* love often makes men soft.
chochera o **chochez** f. Dotage, senility (cualidad de chocho). || FAM. Doting (admiración excesiva).
chocho m. Lupin seed (altramuz). || Cinnamon sweet (confite). || Sweet [U.S., candy] (golosina).
chocho, cha adj. Doddering, doddery, senile (un anciano). || — *Estar chocho por,* to be soft on, to have a crush on. || *Viejo chocho,* old dodderer.
chochocol m. *Amer.* Pitcher, jug.
chófer m. Chauffeur (al servicio particular de alguien). || Driver (conductor). || *Chófer de camión,* lorry driver [U.S., truck driver, trucker].
chofes m. pl. Lights, lungs (bofes).
chola f. FAM. V. CHOLLA.
cholada f. o **cholerío** m. *Amer.* Group of half-breeds, group of mestizos.
cholo, la adj. *Amer.* Half-breed, mestizo (mestizo).
— M. y f. *Amer.* Half-breed, mestizo. | Civilized Indian. | One of the common people (plebeyo).
cholla f. FAM. Nut, block, head (cabeza). | Brains, *pl.* (inteligencia). || *Amer.* Wound, injury (llaga). | Laziness (pereza). || FAM. *No le queda un solo pelo en la cholla,* he hasn't got a hair on his head.
chollar v. tr. *Amer.* To injure, to wound (herir).
chollo m. FAM. Soft *o* cushy job, good number (trabajo fácil). | Bargain (ganga). | Luck (suerte).
chonchón m. *Amer.* Kind of kite (cometa). | Bird of ill omen (ave fatídica). | Undesirable person (persona despreciable).
chongo m. *Amer.* Curl (rizo). | Bun (moño). | Milk and syrup sweet (dulce). | Joke (broma). | Blunt knife (cuchillo que no corta).
chonguear v. intr. *Amer.* To joke.
chonta f. *Amer.* Palm tree (palmera). | Black snake (serpiente).
chontal adj. *Amer.* Coarse, rough, uneducated (inculto). | Uncivilized (indio).

chopazo m. *Amer.* Punch (puñetazo).
chope m. *Amer.* Kind of hoe (azadón). | Punch (puñetazo).
chopera f. Poplar grove.
chopo m. BOT. Poplar (álamo). | Black poplar (álamo negro). || FAM. Rifle, gun (fusil).
choque m. Shock: *amortiguar un choque*, to absorb a shock. || FIG. Shock: *la muerte de su hija fue un choque muy fuerte para ella*, the death of her daughter was a great shock for her. || Impact, collision (colisión). || Jolt (de un coche en movimiento). || Crash, smash (coches, trenes). || ELECTR. Shock. || FIG. Clash (de dos ejércitos, personas, etc.). || MED. Shock: *choque operatorio*, postoperative shock. || Clinking, clink (de vasos). || Clatter (de platos). || — *Choque de frente*, head-on collision. || *Precio de choque*, bargain price.
choquezuela f. ANAT. Patella, kneecap (rótula).
chorear v. intr. *Amer.* FAM. To grumble, to moan.
choricería f. Sausage shop (salchichería).
choricero, ra m. y f. Sausage maker (fabricante). || Sausage seller (vendedor).
chorizo m. Sausage [seasoned with red peppers], "chorizo". || FAM. Thief (ladrón). || Balancing pole (balancín). || *Amer.* Loin (lomo). | Daub (para revocar). | Idiot (mentecato).
chorlito m. Plover (pájaro). || FIG. y FAM. *Cabeza de chorlito*, scatterbrain.
chorote m. *Amer.* Chocolate pot (chocolatera). | Chocolate (chocolate).
choroy m. *Amer.* Small parrot (pájaro).
chorra f. FAM. Luck, jam (suerte). || FAM. *Tener mucha chorra*, to be very lucky, to be jammy.
chorrada f. Extra measure (de líquido). || FAM. Stupid thing: *soltar chorradas*, to say stupid things. | Unnecessary adornment (adorno superfluo).
chorreado, da adj. Striped (animal). || *Amer.* Dirty, stained (sucio).
chorreadura f. Dripping (chorreo). || Stain [caused by dripping] (mancha).
chorrear v. intr. To flow, to run: *líquido que chorrea*, flowing liquid. || To drip (gotear): *la ropa está chorreando*, the washing is dripping. || — FAM. *Estar chorreando*, to be soaking, to be dripping wet. || *Estar chorreando de sudor*, to be dripping with sweat.
— V. tr. To pour: *chorrear agua por el suelo*, to pour water on the floor. || To drip with: *el cuerpo chorreando sudor*, his body dripping with sweat. || FIG. y FAM. To give in dribs and drabs (dar poco a poco).
— V. pr. *Amer.* FAM. To pinch (robar): *chorrearse algo*, to pinch sth.
chorreo m. Dripping, trickle (en gotas), gush, gushing (en chorro): *el chorreo del agua*, the dripping of water. || FIG. Flow, flood: *un chorreo de gente, de turistas*, a flood of people, of tourists. | Constant drain (gasto).
chorreón m. Dripping (chorreadura). || Squirt, dash: *echar un chorreón de aceite en la ensalada*, to add a dash of oil to the salad. || Stain (mancha).
chorrera f. Channel (sitio). || Mark left by dripping water (señal). || Rapids, *pl.* (de un río). || Frill, jabot (de camisa). || *Amer.* String: *una chorrera de desatinos*, a string of stupid things.
chorretada f. Spurt, gush, squirt, jet (chorro). || Extra measure (chorrada).
chorrillo m. Spurt, squirt, small jet (de un líquido). || Small jet (de gas). || Dash, squirt: *un chorrillo de aceite*, a dash of oil. || FIG. Trickle (cantidad pequeña). || AGR. *Sembrar a chorrillo*, to sow in a straight line.
chorro m. Jet, spurt, gush, squirt, spout (de un líquido). || Jet (de gas). || Jet, stream (de áridos). || Trickle (caudal muy pequeño). || FIG. Shower, flood, stream: *un chorro de pesetas*, a shower of pesetas. | Stream, torrent: *un chorro de palabras*, a stream of words. | Flood: *un chorro de luz*, a flood of light. || AVIAC. Jet. || — *A chorros*, in plenty. || *Avión de chorro*, jet plane. || *Beber a chorro*, to pour drink into one's mouth [without touching the bottle or glass with the lips]. || TECN. *Chorro de arena*, sandblasting. || *Chorro de vapor*, steam jet. || *De propulsión a chorro*, jet-propelled. || FIG. *Hablar a chorros*, to gabble, to jabber. || *Llover a chorros*, to pour down. || FIG. *Estar (limpio) como los chorros de oro*, to be as clean as a whistle. || *Salir a chorros*, to squirt out. || FIG. *Soltar el chorro de la risa*, to burst out laughing. || *Sudar a chorros*, to drip with sweat.
chotacabras f. inv. Nightjar (pájaro).
chote m. *Amer.* Chayote (chayote).
chotearse v. pr. FAM. To make fun (*de*, of), to take the mickey (*de*, out of) [burlarse].
choteo m. FAM. Teasing (zumba). || FAM. *Tomárselo todo a choteo*, to take everything as a joke.
chotis m. Schottische (danza).
choto, ta m. y f. Kid, young goat (cabrito). || Calf (ternero). || FAM. *Estar como una chota*, to be round the bend, to be barmy.
chotuno, na adj. Of a kid, of a young goat. || FAM. *Oler a chotuno*, to stink to high heaven.
chova f. Chough (ave).
choza f. Hut: *choza de paja*, straw hut. || Shack, shanty (cabaña).
chozo m. Small hut.
christmas m. inv. Christmas card.
chubasco m. Squall, heavy shower, downpour (aguacero). || MAR. Squall (lluvia). || FIG. Setback, cloud, adversity (adversidad).
chubascoso, sa adj. Squally, stormy.
chubasquero m. Oilskins, *pl.* (de marinero). || Oilskin raincoat (impermeable).
chubesqui m. Stove, heater (estufa).
chúcaro, ra adj. *Amer.* Wild (animales). | Shy (personas).
— M. y f. *Amer.* Wild mule.
chucero m. Pikeman (soldado).
chucha f. FAM. Bitch (perra). | Peseta. || *Amer.* Maraca (maraca). | Opossum (zarigüeya). || *¡Chucha!*, shoo!, scat!, go on!, go home! (dirigiéndose a un perro).
chuchear v. intr. To whisper (cuchichear). || To hunt with traps (cazar con trampas) *o* decoys (con señuelos). || FAM. To nibble sweets.
chuchería f. Knick-knack, trinket (fruslería). || Titbit, sweet [U.S., piece of candy] (golosina). || Hunting with traps (trampas) *o* decoys (señuelos).
chucho m. Hound, dog (perro). || *Amer.* Malaria (paludismo). | Shiver (escalofrío).
— Interj. Shoo!, scat!, go on!, go home! (al perro).
chuchoca f. *Amer.* Roasted maize.
chuchurrido, da adj. FAM. Faded: *flores chuchurridas*, faded flowers. | Wrinkled (arrugado). | Wizened: *una vieja chuchurrida*, a wizened old woman.
chueca f. Ball (de un hueso). || Stump (tocón). || Game resembling hockey (juego). || FIG. y FAM. Joke (chasco).
chueco, ca adj. *Amer. Piernas chuecas*, bowlegs, bandy legs.
chufa f. BOT. Chufa, earth almond (planta). || *Horchata de chufas*, orgeat made from chufas.
chufar o **chufear** v. intr. To mock, to make fun (*de*, of).
chufla o **chufleta** f. FAM. Joke (broma). || FAM. *Gastar chufletas a uno*, to pull s.o.'s leg.
chuflarse o **chuflearse** v. pr. FAM. To make fun (*de*, of). || FAM. *Chuflearse de uno*, to pull s.o.'s leg.
chuflay m. *Amer.* Toddy, alcoholic drink.
chufletear v. intr. FAM. To joke, to jest (bromear).
chufletero, ra adj. FAM. Fond of a joke (bromista). | Fond of leg-pulling (burlón).
— M. y f. FAM. Joker, laugh, comic (bromista). | Leg-puller, tease (burlón).
chulada f. FAM. Coarse *o* vulgar thing (cosa grosera). | Funny thing (agudeza). | Cheek, cheekiness, barefacedness, insolence (insolencia). | Showing off, show-off (jactancia). || FAM. *Decir una chulada, hacer chuladas*, to be cheeky (desfachatez), to brag, to show off (jactancia).
chulapo, pa o **chulapón, ona** m. y f. FAM. Dandy, spiv, beau (hombre), elegant young woman from the lower classes of Madrid (mujer).
— Adj. Cheeky, cocky (chulo).
chulé m. FAM. Five peseta piece.
chulear v. tr. To get cocky with (ponerse chulo): *a mí no me chulea nadie*, nobody gets cocky with me. || To touch for: *me ha chuleado veinte duros*, he's touched me for a hundred pesetas. || *Amer.* To flirt with (decir piropos).
— V. pr. To make fun (*de*, of), to pull the leg of: *chulearse de uno*, to pull s.o.'s leg. || FAM. To show off (presumir).
chulería f. FAM. Cheek, cheekiness, barefacedness, insolence (insolencia). | Showing off, show-off (jactancia). | Saucy wit (donaire). || FAM. *Obrar con chulería*, to be cheeky *o* cocksure.
chulesco, ca adj. FAM. Cheeky, barefaced (descarado): *gesto chulesco*, cheeky manner. || Flashy (propio del chulo madrileño).
chuleta f. Chop, cutlet (costilla): *chuleta empanada*, chop fried in breadcrumbs; *chuleta de cerdo*, pork chop. || FIG. y FAM. Slap (bofetada). | Crib [U.S., trot] (de los estudiantes). || — M. FAM. Cheeky *o* barefaced individual.
chulo, la adj. FAM. Cheeky, barefaced, cocky, impudent, saucy, insolent: *un gesto chulo*, an insolent gesture; *si se pone usted chulo le expulsamos*, if you get cheeky, we'll throw you out. | Flashy, natty (vistoso). || From the lower classes of Madrid, lower class Madrid: *la manera de hablar chula de Madrid*, the lower class Madrid way of speaking. || *Amer.* Nice, pretty (bonito). || FAM. *Ir muy chulo*, to swagger along, to show off: *iba muy chulo con su traje nuevo*, he was swaggering along with his new suit.
— M. Souteneur, pimp (rufián). || Typical Madrilenian (equivalent to cockney). || FAM. Ruffian (de mala vida). | Spiv, dandy, beau (petimetre). || TAUR. Bullfighter's assistant. || FAM. *Chulo de putas*, pimp, pander.
chulpa o **chullpa** f. *Amer.* Stone tomb (tumba).
chullo m. *Amer.* "Chullo", woollen cap.
chuma f. *Amer.* Drunkenness (borrachera).
chumacera f. TECN. Bearing. || MAR. Strengthening plate [to receive rowlock].
chumarse v. pr. *Amer.* To get drunk.
chumbe m. *Amer.* Sash.
chumbera f. BOT. Prickly pear.
chumbo, ba adj. *Higuera chumba*, prickly pear. || *Higo chumbo*, prickly pear.
— M. *Amer.* Bullet (bala).
chunga f. FAM. Joke (broma). || — FAM. *Estar de chunga*, to be in a joking mood. | *Por chunga*, jokingly. | *Tomar a* or *en chunga*, to take as a joke.

chungarse o **chunguearse** v. pr. FAM. To joke (bromear). | To make fun (*de*, of) [burlarse].
chungueo m. V. CHUNGA.
chuño m. *Amer.* Potato starch.
chupa f. Kind of tight-fitting waistcoat (prenda). || *Amer.* Drunkenness (borrachera). || FIG. *Poner a uno como chupa de dómine*, to call s.o. all the names under the sun (insultar), to haul s.o. over the coals (reprender).
chupacirios m. y f. inv. FAM. Sanctimonious man (hombre) *o* woman (mujer) [beato].
chupada f. Puff, drag (fam.) [de cigarro]: *dar una chupada al cigarro*, to have a puff at the cigarette. || Suck (de una sustancia). || — *Dar chupadas a un cigarro*, to puff at a cigarette. || *El niño dio una chupada al pirulí*, the child sucked the lollipop.
chupado, da adj. FAM. Skinny, thin (flaco). | Tight: *falda chupada*, tight skirt. || *Amer.* Tight, drunk (borracho). || — FIG. y FAM. *Con la cara chupada*, hollow-cheeked. | *Está chupado*, it's as easy as ABC, it's as easy as pie. | *Mejillas chupadas*, hollow cheeks.
chupador, ra adj. Sucking (que chupa). || BOT. Sucker. || ZOOL. Suctorial.
— M. Dummy [U.S., pacifier] (chupete). || Teat (de biberón). || BOT. Sucker root. || ZOOL. Sucker, suctorial organ. || *Amer.* Drinker (bebedor). | Smoker (fumador).
chupadura f. Suck, sucking.
chupaflor m. *Amer.* Hummingbird (pájaro).
chupar v. tr. To suck: *chupar un limón*, to suck a lemon. || To absorb, to take in, to suck up: *las raíces chupan la humedad del suelo*, the roots absorb the humidity from the ground. || To puff at (cigarro). || To lick (lamer). || To sip (beber). || To suck (un caramelo). || ZOOL. To suck. || To suck, to feed from (mamar). || To soak up, to absorb (absorber): *el papel secante chupa la tinta*, blotting paper soaks up ink. || To lick, to moisten (un sello de correo). || FIG. y FAM. To bleed (dinero): *chuparle a uno el dinero*, to bleed s.o. of his money. || *Amer.* To smoke (fumar). | To drink (beber). || — FIG. *Chuparle la sangre a uno*, to bleed s.o. white *o* dry. | *Tanto trabajo le chupa la salud*, all that work is undermining his health.
— V. intr. To suck.
— V. pr. To lick (lamerse): *chuparse los dedos*, to lick one's fingers. || FIG. y FAM. To go thin, to lose weight (ir enflaqueciendo). | To spend: *chuparse seis meses de prisión*, to spend six months in prison. || *Amer.* To drink (beber). || — FAM. *¡Chúpate esa!*, put that in your pipe and smoke it. || *Amer. Chuparse un insulto*, to swallow an insult.
chupatintas m. y f. inv. FAM. Pen-pusher.
chupe m. FAM. Dummy [U.S., pacifier] (chupete). || *Amer.* Stew (guiso).
chupendo m. FAM. Strong suck.
chupeta f. Small tight-fitting waistcoat (chupa). || MAR. Roundhouse, cabin (en la popa). || *Amer.* Dummy [U.S., pacifier] (chupete).
chupete m. Dummy [U.S., pacifier] (para niños). || Teat (de biberón). || *Amer.* Lollipop (pirulí).
chupetear v. intr. To suck at, to suck away at.
chupeteo m. Sucking, sucking away at.
chupetón m. Strong suck.
chupinazo m. Loud bang; starting signal (fuegos artificiales). || FAM. Hard kick (en el balón).
chupo o **chupón** m. *Amer.* Boil.
chupón, ona adj. Sucking (que chupa). || FIG. y FAM. Parasitic, sponging (que vive de otros).
— M. y f. Sucker (que chupa). || FIG. Parasite, sponger, leech (que vive de otros). || — M. BOT. Sucker, shoot (brote). || Puff (chupada). || Strong suck (chupendo). || Plunger (desatrancador neumático). || ZOOL. Live feather. || TECN. Piston, sucker (de bomba). || Lollipop (pirulí). || Teat (de biberón). || Dummy [U.S., pacifier] (chupete). || *Amer.* Boil.
chupóptero m. FAM. Parasite, sponger, leech.
churra f. Sandgrouse (ortega).
churrasco m. *Amer.* Barbecued steak, "churrasco" (carne asada).
churrasquear v. intr. *Amer.* To have a barbecue (comer churrasco). | To barbecue, to roast (hacer un churrasco).
churrasquería f. *Amer.* Steak house.
churre m. TECN. Wool grease (de la lana). || FIG. y FAM. Filth, grime, grease (suciedad).
churrear v. intr. *Amer.* To have diarrhoea.
churrería f. "Churro" shop, "churrería".
churrero, ra m. y f. "Churro" seller. || — F. Utensil for shaping "churros".
churrete o **churretón** m. Mark, streak (en la cara). || *Amer.* FAM. Poor bloke.
churretoso, sa adj. Dirty, filthy (sucio).
churri adj. FAM. Worthless, useless.
churriento, ta adj. Dirty, filthy, grimy.
churrigueresco, ca adj. ARQ. Churrigueresque (estilo). || FIG. Overelaborate, florid (recargado).

— OBSERV. The churrigueresque style (from the name of the architect José de Churriguera, 1665-1723) was a feature of Spanish architecture at the end of the 17th and the beginning of the 18th centuries. It is an exuberant baroque style approaching rococo.

churro, rra adj. Coarse (lana). || Coarse-wooled (ganado).
— M. Cruller, twist of batter deep-fried, "churro" (masa frita). || FAM. Shoddy piece of work, amateurish job (chapuza). | Dead loss, flop: *esta película es un churro*, this picture is a flop. || — FAM. *Salirle a uno un churro*, to make a complete mess of: *me ha salido un churro*, I've made a complete mess of it. | *Ser un churro*, to be a fluke (chiripa): *este gol ha sido un churro*, that goal was a fluke; to be useless, to be a dead loss (fracaso).

— OBSERV. "Churros", an extremely popular Spanish sweetmeat, are made from a type of stiff batter squeezed out into sticks or rings and deep-fried. They are sprinkled with sugar and eaten for breakfast or as a snack often accompanied by coffee or drinking chocolate.

churroso, sa adj. *Amer.* Suffering from diarrhoea.
churruscarse v. pr. To burn (el pan, un guiso, etc.).
churrusco m. Piece of burnt toast.
churumbel m. FAM. Kid, nipper.
churumbela f. MÚS. Sort of hornpipe. || *Amer.* "Bombilla", tube for drinking maté (bombilla).
chus ni mus (no decir) loc. Not to say a word.
chuscada f. Funny thing: *decir chuscadas*, to say funny things.
chuscamente adv. In a funny way, wittily, funnily.
chusco, ca adj. Funny (gracioso y sorprendente). || *Amer.* Mongrel (perro). | Pretty (bonito).
— M. y f. Joker, wit. || — M. MIL. Ration bread (pan).
chusma f. Gang of galley slaves (de galeotes). || Rabble, riffraff (gentuza).
chusmaje m. *Amer.* FAM. Rabble, riffraff (gentuza).
chuspa f. *Amer.* Leather bag.
chusquero m. FAM. Ranker (en el ejército).
chut m. Shot, kick (puntapié).
chutar v. intr. To shoot (fútbol). || — FAM. *Este asunto va que chuta*, things are going very well, things are coming along nicely. | *¡Y va que chuta!*, and that's fine!
chuza f. *Amer.* Strike (boliche). | Pike (lanza).
chuzo m. Metal-tipped stick (del sereno). || Pike (arma). || *Amer.* Leather whip (látigo). || FIG. *Llover a chuzos* or *caer chuzos de punta*, to pour down, to pour, to rain cats and dogs.

D

d f. D (letra). || D., D.ª, abbreviation of *Don, Doña*.

— OBSERV. At the beginning of a breath group or when preceded by *l* or *n*, the Spanish *d* is pronounced in approximately the same way as the English *d*. When in a final or intervocalic position, it is similar to the voiced *th* in *the*, and sometimes it is barely pronounced at all, as the final *d* in *Madrid*.

daca contraction of *da acá*. Give me: *daca el dinero*, give me the money. || *A toma y daca*, v. TOMAR.
dacio, cia adj./s. Dacian.
dación f. JUR. Dation, giving (acción de dar).
dactilar adj. Finger, digital. || *Huellas dactilares*, fingerprints.
dáctilo m. Dactyl (verso).
dactilografía f. Typewriting, typing.
dactilográfico, ca adj. Typewriting (para escribir a máquina). || Typewritten (escrito a máquina).
dactilógrafo, fa m. y f. Typist.
dactiloscopia f. Fingerprint identification
dadaísmo m. Dadaism.

dadaísta adj./s. Dadaist.
dádiva f. Donation (donación). || Present, gift (regalo).
dadivosidad f. Generosity.
dadivoso, sa adj. Generous.
dado m. Die (pl. *dice*): *echar los dados*, to throw the dice. || ARQ. Dado, die (de un pedestal). || TECN. Block. || — *Cargar los dados*, to load the dice. || FIG. y FAM. *Correr el dado*, to be in luck *o* lucky. || *Echarlo a los dados*, to throw [the dice] for it, to decide it by throwing the dice.
dado, da adj. Given (v. DAR): *en un caso dado*, in a given case. || Addicted, given (inclinado): *dado a la bebida*, given to drinking. || Gone, past: *son las once dadas*, it's past eleven o'clock. || — *Dado*, in view of: *dada su timidez*, in view of his shyness. || *Dado que*, as, since. || FAM. *Ir dado*, to be in for trouble: *¡vas dado con esos obreros!*, you're in for trouble with those workmen! || *Ser dado a*, to be given to, to be fond of: *es muy dado a criticar a sus amigos*, he is very fond of criticizing his friends, he is much given to criticizing his friends.
dador, ra m. y f. Giver. || — M. Bearer (el que entrega una carta). || COM. Drawer (de una letra de cambio).
Dafne n. pr. f. Daphne.
Dafnis n. pr. m. Daphnis.
daga f. Dagger (puñal). || *Amer.* Machete.
daguerrotipia f. Daguerreotypy.
daguerrotipo m. Daguerreotype (aparato o imagen). || Daguerreotypy (arte).
Dahomey n. pr. m. GEOGR. Dahomey.
dahomeyano, na adj./s. Dahoman.
daifa f. Mistress.
dalai lama m. REL. Dalai Lama.
dalia f. BOT. Dahlia.
Dalila n. pr. f. Delilah.
Dalmacia n. pr. f. GEOGR. Dalmatia.
dálmata adj./s. Dalmatian (de Dalmacia). || — M. Dalmatian (perro).
dalmática f. Dalmatic (vestidura).
daltoniano, na adj. MED. Daltonian, colour blind.
— M. y f. MED. Person who suffers from colour blindness, daltonian.
daltonismo m. MED. Colour blindness [U.S., color blindness], daltonism.
dalla f. o **dalle** m. Scythe (guadaña).
dallar v. tr. To scythe.
dama f. Lady (señora). || Lady-in-waiting (de cámara). || (P.us.) Mistress (manceba). || King (del juego de damas): *hacer dama*, to make a king. || Queen [in chess]. || MAR. Rowlock, oarlock. || — Pl. Draughts [U.S., checkers] (juego). || — *Dama cortesana*, courtesan (mujer liviana). || *Dama de honor*, lady-in-waiting (de una reina), bridesmaid (en una boda). || TEATR. *Dama joven*, ingénue. | *Primera, segunda dama*, leading lady, supporting role. || *Ser una dama*, to be a lady. || *Tablero de damas*, draughtboard [U.S., checkerboard].
damaceno, na adj. V. DAMASCENO.
damajuana f. Demijohn.
damán m. ZOOL. Marmot (marmota).
damasana f. *Amer.* Demijohn (damajuana).
damascado, da adj. Damasked, damask.
damasceno, na adj./s. Damascene (de Damasco). || *Ciruela damascena*, damson.
damasco m. Damask (tela).
Damasco n. pr. m. GEOGR. Damascus. || REL. *Camino de Damasco*, road to Damascus.
damasquillo m. Light fabric resembling damask. || Apricot (albaricoque).
damasquina f. BOT. French marigold.
damasquinado m. Damascene [work].
damasquinar v. tr. To damascene, to damask.
damasquino, na adj. Damascene (de Damasco). || Damask (tela). || *Sable damasquino*, Damascus blade.
damisela f. Young miss, young lady, damsel (irónico). || Courtesan (cortesana).
damnificado, da adj. Injured, harmed (persona). || Damaged (cosa).
— M. y f. Victim: *los damnificados por la inundación*, the victims of the flood.
damnificador, ra adj. Harmful, injurious.
damnificar v. tr. To harm, to injure (persona). || To damage (cosa).
Damocles n. pr. m. Damocles: *espada de Damocles*, Damocles' sword.
Danaides n. pr. f. MIT. Danaids.
dáncing m. Dance hall, ballroom.
dandi o **dandy** m. Dandy.
dandismo o **dandysmo** m. Dandyism.
danés, esa adj. Danish.
— M. y f. Danishman (hombre), Danishwoman, (mujer), Dane (hombre o mujer). || — M. Great Dane (perro). || Danish (idioma).
danta f. ZOOL. Elk (anta). | Tapir (tapir).
dante adj. Giving (que da).
— M. y f. Giver (el que da).
dantellado, da adj. HERÁLD. Dentelated.
dantesco, ca adj. Dantesque, Dantean.
Danubio n. pr. m. GEOGR. Danube.
danza f. Dance: *una danza ritual*, a ritual dance. || FAM. [Shady] deal (negocio sucio): *¿por qué te metiste en tal danza?*, why did you get mixed up in such a deal? | Mess (lío). | Deal: *¿cómo va la danza?*, how's the deal getting on? | Row (riña). || — *Danza de espadas*, sword dance. || *Danza de la muerte* or *danza macabra*, dance of death, danse macabre.
danzador, ra adj. (P.us.). Dancing.
— M. y f. Dancer.
danzante adj. Dancing: *procesión danzante*, dancing procession.
— M. y f. Dancer (en una procesión). || FIG. y FAM. Featherbrain (casquivano). | Meddler, busybody (entrometido).
danzar v. tr. To dance (bailar). || FAM. To poke *o* to stick one's nose [*en*, into] (intervenir): *¿qué danza usted en este asunto?*, what are you doing sticking your nose into this affair?
— V. intr. To dance (bailar). || FIG. To wander, to roam: *va danzando por las bibliotecas*, he wanders from library to library. | To lie around: *no me gusta que mis libros estén danzando por aquí*, I don't like to see my books lying around here. | To shuttle: *ahora la tienen danzando de un servicio a otro*, they keep shuttling her from one department to another.
danzarín, ina m. y f. Dancer.
danzón m. Cuban dance derived from the *habanera*.
dañable adj. Harmful (perjudicial). || (P.us.). Condemnable (malo).
dañado, da adj. Spoiled (que empieza a pudrirse). || Damaged (fruta). || Damaged: *ciudades dañadas por la guerra*, towns damaged by the war. || Evil, wicked (malo): *hombre muy dañado*, very wicked man.
dañador, ra adj. Harmful, injurious.
dañar v. tr. To damage, to spoil, to harm: *el granizo ha dañado las cosechas*, hail has spoiled the harvest. || To injure, to harm, to hurt (a una persona). || To damage (fruta). || FIG. To harm, to damage, to stain, to mar: *eso dañará su reputación*, that will stain his reputation; *dañarle a uno en su honra*, to mar s.o.'s good name. | To condemn (condenar).
— V. pr. To spoil, to get damaged (estropearse). || To go bad (fruta, comestibles).
dañino, na adj. Harmful, destructive. || *Animales dañinos*, pests, vermin, *sing.*
daño m. Wrong, injury, harm: *reparar el daño que se ha hecho*, to redress the wrong *o* harm that has been done, to redress the injury that has been caused. || Damage: *el daño causado* or *los daños causados por el granizo*, the damage caused by hail. || MED. Trouble (mal). || — JUR. *Daños y perjuicios*, damages. || *Hacer daño*, to hurt (doler): *me hace daño el pie*, my foot hurts; to harm: *hará daño al país*, it will harm the country; to be bad for: *el chocolate te hace daño*, chocolate is bad for you. || *Hacerse daño*, to hurt o.s.
— OBSERV. La palabra *damage* se utiliza siempre en singular salvo en el sentido jurídico de "daños y perjuicios".
dañoso, sa adj. Harmful (*para*, to), injurious (*para*, to).
dar* v. tr. To give: *dar una propina, noticias, un consejo, batalla*, to give a tip, some news, a piece of advice, battle. || To deal (naipes). || To give: *dar una bofetada, un puntapié*, to give a slap, a kick. || To hit (pegar): *darle a uno en la cabeza*, to hit s.o. on the head. || To give (proporcionar): *dar trabajo a uno*, to give s.o. work. || To strike: *el reloj da las dos, la media*, the clock strikes two, the half-hour. || To produce, to bear, to yield (fruta). || To produce: *el rosal da rosas*, the rosebush produces roses. || To give, to cause, to produce (sentimiento). || To give: *la vaca da leche*, the cow gives milk. || To show (en el cine): *hoy dan una película de miedo*, they are showing a horror film today. || To put on, to perform (en el teatro). || To play (obra de música). || To give (grito, suspiro). || To say: *dar los buenos días, las buenas tardes*, to say hello, good afternoon. || To set (ejemplo). || To go for: *dar un paseo en coche*, to go for a ride in a car. || To take (paseo, paso). || To give, to hand, to pass: *¿me puede dar el pan, por favor?*, could you pass me the bread, please? || To bear, to give: *su mujer le dio dos hijos*, his wife bore him two children. || To give off (desprender): *dar un olor*, to give off a smell. || To give, to grant (permiso, etc.). || To show (mostrar): *dar señales de*, to show signs of. || To yield, to bear (interés).
— FAM. *Ahí me las den todas*, v. AHÍ. || *Al dar las diez*, on the stroke of ten. || *Da gusto* or *da gloria verlo*, it is a joy to behold, it is a delight to see. || *¡Dale!*, hit him! (pégalo), go on! (¡anda!), not again! (¡otra vez!). || *Dale que dale, dale que te pego*, not again! (¡otra vez!), on and on: *y siguió dale que te pego hablando de su familia*, and he kept on and on talking about his family; *está todo el día dale que dale al piano*, he goes on and on all day playing the piano. || *Da lo mismo* or *lo mismo da*, it doesn't matter, it's all the same, it makes no difference. || *Dar algo por*, to give anything for: *yo daría algo por tenerlo*, I would give anything to have it. || *Dar a luz*, to give birth to. || *Dar celos a uno*, to make s.o. jealous. || *Dar clase*, v. CLASE. || *Dar como*, to consider: *dar como falso*, to consider [to be] false. || *Dar cuerda* a, v. CUERDA. || *Dar de comer a*, v. COMER. || *Dar de lado*, to discard (una cosa), to cold-shoulder, to desert (a una persona). || *Dar gusto*, to be nice *o* good *o* a joy: *da gusto ver cómo se divierten los niños*, it is nice to see the children enjoying themselves. || *Dar la mano a alguien*, to shake hands with s.o. || *Dar las gracias por*, to say thank you for, to thank for. || *Darle a uno calentura*, un

ataque, to have a temperature, an attack. || *Darle a uno un dolor en*, to feel a pain in. || FAM. *Darle el día a uno*, not to give s.o. a minute's peace all day. | *Darle la noche a uno*, not to give s.o. a minute's peace all night, not to let s.o. get a wink of sleep all night: *el niño me ha dado la noche*, the child didn't give me a minute's peace all night, the child didn't let me get a wink of sleep all night. || *Dar muerte a*, to kill. || *Dar por*, to assume: *le dan por muerto*, he is assumed dead; to consider (considerar): *dar por hecha* or *concluida una cosa*, to consider sth. finished. || *Dar por perdida una cosa*, to give sth. up as lost. || *Dar prestado*, to lend. || *Dar que hablar* or *que decir*, to give people sth. to talk about, to set tongues wagging: *están dando que hablar con sus reuniones*, they are giving people sth. to talk about with their meetings. || *Dar que hacer*, to make a lot of work for: *los niños te darán que hacer*, the children will make a lot of work for you. || *Dar que pensar* o *dar en que pensar*, to set thinking: *sus palabras me dieron que pensar*, what he said set me thinking; to give food for thought: *lo que voy a decir les dará a todos que pensar*, what I'm about to say will give you all food for thought. || *Dar recuerdos*, to give regards *o* love: *da recuerdos a tu madre de mi parte*, give my regards to your mother. || *Dar saltos*, to jump up and down. || FIG. *Dársela a alguien*, to take s.o. in, to fool s.o. || *Dar testimonio de*, to testify to, to bear witness to. || *Dar voces*, to shout. || FAM. *Donde las dan las toman*, tit for tat. || *Me da no sé qué*, it upsets me, it troubles me: *me da no sé qué ver al pobre mendigo*, it upsets me to see the poor beggar; I don't like, I feel awkward: *me da no sé qué pedirle un favor*, I don't like to ask a favour of him, I feel awkward about asking him a favour. || *¿Qué más da?*, what does it matter?, what difference does it make?

— V. intr. To hit: *dar a la pelota con un palo*, to hit the ball with a stick; *le dio una bala perdida*, he was hit by a stray bullet, a stray bullet hit him. || To strike: *dan las tres*, it is striking three. || To press: *dar al botón*, to press the button. || To turn: *dar a la manilla*, to turn the doorhandle. || To start: *dar a la máquina*, to start the machine. || To shine: *el sol me daba en la cara*, the sun was shining in my face. || To blow: *el viento me daba en la cara*, the wind was blowing in my face. || To be in: *el sol y el viento me daban en la cara*, the sun and wind were in my face.

— FIG. *Ahora le ha dado por ahí*, that's his latest craze. || *Da igual*, it doesn't matter, it's all the same, it makes no difference: *me da igual*, it's all the same to me, it makes no difference to me. || *Dar a*, to look [out] onto, to overlook: *la ventana da al patio*, the window looks onto *o* overlooks the yard; to face: *la casa da al norte*, the house faces north. || *Dar a la luz*, to put *o* to turn *o* to switch the light on. || *Dar con*, to come across (una cosa), to find: *no conseguí dar con él en todo el día*, I couldn't find him all day; to find, to hit on: *dar con la solución*, to find the solution; to meet (encontrar a uno), to bump into, to run into (tropezar): *al salir di con él*, I bumped into him as I went out; to knock with (llamar): *dar con la aldaba*, to knock with the doorknocker; to bang, to bump, to hit: *dar con la cabeza contra la pared*, to bang one's head against the wall. || *Dar con algo en el suelo*, to drop sth. || *Dar consigo en el suelo*, to fall on the floor (dentro), to fall on the ground (fuera). || *Dar consigo en una ciudad*, to end up in a city (ir a parar). || FAM. *Dar con sus huesos*, to end up: *dio con sus huesos en la cárcel*, he ended up in prison. || *Dar de*, to fall flat on: *dar de espaldas*, to fall flat on one's back. || *Dar de barniz* or *de betún a*, to varnish, to polish. || *Dar de cuchilladas, de patadas, de puñetazos a uno*, to stab s.o., to kick s.o., to punch s.o. || *Dar de sí*, to stretch, to give (estirarse), to go a long way (el dinero, la comida, etc.). || *Dar en*, to get, to understand, to grasp: *dar en el chiste*, to get the joke; to find, to hit on: *dar en la solución*, to find the answer; to persist in: *ha dado en decir que no hay que ir*, he persists in saying we shouldn't go; to hit, to strike: *dar en el blanco*, to hit the target. || *Dar en creer que*, to get it into one's head that. || *Darle a algo*, to work at sth. (trabajar): *darle fuerte a las matemáticas*, to work hard at mathematics. || *Dar para*, to be enough for (ser suficiente). || *Dar para más*, to get more from: *este negocio no da para más*, you won't get any more from this business. || *Dar por*, to take to: *a Juan le ha dado por el vino, por viajar*, John has taken to drinking, to travelling; to [suddenly] decide: *de vez en cuando le da por no estudiar*, every so often he decides that he won't do any work. || *Dar por tierra con algo*, to floor, to ruin (proyectos, etc.), to refute, to prove wrong, to put an end to (teoría). || *Este día no me ha hado de sí*, I haven't been able to do *o* to get through all I wanted to today. || *Le dio un ataque*, he had a fit. || *Le dio un resfriado, una pulmonía*, he caught *o* got a cold, he caught *o* got pneumonia. || *Me va a dar algo*, I'm going to go out of my mind, I'm going to have a fit. || *Tener para dar y tomar*, to have [sth.] to spare: *tiene orgullo para dar y tomar*, he has pride to spare.

— V. pr. To surrender, to give o.s. up, to give in (entregarse). || To give oneself over *o* up, to take to: *darse a la bebida*, to give o.s. over to drink, to take to drinking. || To devote o.s. to: *se da toda a sus hijos*, she devotes herself entirely to her children. || To bump: *darse con* or *contra un árbol*, to bump into a tree. || To matter: *¿y a mí qué se me da de todo esto?*, what does all that matter to me? || AGR. To grow (crecer): *se da bien el tabaco en esta provincia*, tobacco grows well in this province. || To be found, to grow (cultivarse): *el tabaco no se da aquí*, tobacco is not found here, tobacco doesn't grow here.

— *Darse a*, to make o.s., to become: *darse a conocer*, to make o.s. known, to become known. || *Dársele bien, mal algo a uno* to be good, bad at: *la natación se me da muy bien*, I am very good at swimming; *el latín se me da mejor que las matemáticas*, I am better at Latin than at mathematics; to turn out well, bad: *se le ha dado muy bien la conferencia*, his lecture turned out very well; to have a knack for, not to have the knack of: *se le da bien coser*, she has a knack for sewing. || *Darse con la cabeza contra*, to bang *o* to knock *o* to hit one's head against. || FIG. *Dárselas de*, to make [o.s.] out to be: *dárselas de valiente*, to make o.s. out to be brave; to fancy o.s. as: *se las daba de duquesa*, she fancied herself as a duchess. || *Darse por*, to consider o.s.: *darse por contento*, to consider o.s. lucky. || *Darse por aludido*, V. ALUDIDO. || *Darse por ofendido*, to take offence. || *Que darse pueda*, that could be, imaginable: *es la persona más estúpida que darse pueda*, he is the most stupid person that could be, he is the most stupid person imaginable. || *Si se diese el caso de que*, should it happen that.

Dardanelos n. pr. m. pl. GEOGR. Dardanelles.

dardo m. Spear (arma arrojadiza). || Dart, arrow (flecha). || FIG. Dig, cutting remark (dicho satírico). || ZOOL. Sting (aguijón). | Bleak, dace (pez).

dares y tomares loc. FAM. Give and take. || FAM. *Andar en dares y tomares*, to bicker, to quarrel.

Darío n. pr. m. Darius.

dársena f. MAR. Dock, basin.

darviniano, na adj. Darwinian.

darvinismo m. Darwinism.

darvinista adj./s. Darwinist.

data f. (P.us.). Date (fecha). || COM. Item. || Regulated outlet (orificio).

datar v. tr. To date, to put a date on (fechar). || COM. To credit, to enter.

— V. intr. To date: *este castillo data del siglo XV*, this castle dates from the 15th century *o* dates back to the 15th century.

dátil m. Date (fruto). || Date mussel, date shell (molusco). || — Pl. FAM. Fingers (dedos).

datilera adj. f. Date: *palmera datilera*, date palm.

— F. Date palm.

dativo, va adj. GRAM. Dative. || JUR. Dative: *tutor dativo*, tutor dative.

— M. GRAM. Dative: *en dativo*, in the dative.

dato m. Fact, piece of information, datum (información). || — Pl. Data, facts, information, *sing.*: *por falta de datos*, through lack of data. || MAT. Information, *sing.*, data (de un problema). || — *Datos personales*, personal details. || *Procesamiento* or *proceso de datos*, data processing.

daza f. BOT. Sorghum.

D.D.T. m. (abreviatura de *diclorodifeniltricloretano*). DDT (insecticida).

de f. D (letra).

de prep.

1. Posesión y pertenencia. — **2.** Origen, procedencia. — **3.** Composición. — **4.**. Contenido. — **5.** Introduce el agente. — **6.** Aposición. — **7.** Uso. — **8.** Suposición. — **9.** Causa. — **10.** Introduce un adverbio de lugar. — **11.** Precio, medida. — **12.** Con el verbo "ser" (seguido por un número). — **13.** Característica. — **14.** Descripción. — **15.** Introduce oraciones sustantivadas. — **16.** Modo. — **17.** Tiempo. — **18.** Locuciones diversas.

1. POSESIÓN Y PERTENENCIA. — Of: *el lomo del libro*, the spine of the book. || Genitivo sajón ('s): *el lápiz de Juan*, John's pencil; *los lápices de los alumnos*, the pupils' pencils; *la casa es de Pablo*, the house is Paul's. || In: *los muebles del cuarto*, the furniture in the room; *comprar acciones de una compañía*, to buy shares in a company; *una subida de precios*, a rise in prices.

2. ORIGEN, PROCEDENCIA. — From: *soy de Barcelona*, I'm from *o* I come from Barcelona; *ir de Madrid a Londres*, to go from Madrid to London. || From: *este tren viene de Madrid*, this train comes from Madrid; *el avión procedente de Londres*, the plane arriving from London. || Of: *cinco de los nuestros*, five of our men. || Of: *los descendientes de los Incas*, the descendants of the Incas; *su carta de hace dos años*, his letter of two years ago. || From: *lo conozco de cuando estuvo aquí*, I know him from when he was here; *de esto se deduce que*, from this one can deduce that. || As: *la conocí de pequeña*, I knew her as a child. || By: *tiene una hija de su primera mujer* or *de su primer matrimonio*, he has a daughter by his first wife *o* by his first marriage.

3. COMPOSICIÓN. — Sin traducción: *una camisa de seda*, a silk shirt; *una mesa de madera*, a wooden table. || In, made of, sin traducción (con el verbo "to be"): *esta mesa es de nogal*, this table is walnut *o* made of walnut *o* in walnut. || In (con los demás verbos): *lo compré de madera*, I bought it in wood; *lo hicieron de cristal*, they made it in glass.

4. CONTENIDO. — Of: *una caja de naranjas*, a box of oranges; *un vaso de vino*, a glass of wine.

5. INTRODUCE EL AGENTE. — By: *acompañado de dos mujeres*, accompanied by two women; *respetado de todos*, respected by all; *un libro de Cervantes*, a book by Cervantes.

6. APOSICIÓN. — Of: *el mes de junio*, the month of June; *la ciudad de Madrid*, the city of Madrid. || Sin traducción: *pobrecillo de mi hermano*, my poor little brother; *¡pobre de mí!*, poor old me!, woe is me! || For: *¿qué hay de postre?*, what is there for dessert? || *La ciudad de Méjico*, Mexico City.

7. USO. — Sin traducción: *máquina de coser*, sewing machine; *salida de emergencia*, emergency exit; *hoja de afeitar*, razor blade.

8. SUPOSICIÓN. — If: *de haberlo sabido antes, no hubiera venido*, if I had known earlier, I shouldn't have come.

9. CAUSA. — Because: *lo sé de haberlo oído antes*, I know because I have already heard it. || Because of: *del dolor que tenía no pude dormir*, I couldn't sleep because of the pain. || So: *de tanto frío como hacía, no pude salir*, it was so cold that I couldn't go out. || With: *llorar de alegría*, to cry with joy. || Of: *morir de hambre, de miedo, de frío*, to die of hunger, of fright, of cold. || *No vino de la vergüenza que tenía*, he was so ashamed that he did not come, he did not come out of shame, he was too ashamed to come.

10. INTRODUCE UN ADVERBIO DE LUGAR. — Sin traducción: *la casa de al lado del río*, the house by the river; *el piso de arriba*, the flat above; *los vecinos de al lado*, the next-door neighbours.

11. PRECIO, MEDIDA. — Sin traducción: *un libro de a diez pesetas*, a ten-peseta book; *manzanas de a dos pesetas el kilo*, apples at two pesetas a kilo: *una moneda de [a] cinco pesetas*, a five-peseta piece; *una botella de [a] litro*, a litre bottle. || *Una carretera de veinte kilómetros*, a road twenty kilometres long.

12. CON EL VERBO "SER" (seguido por un número). — Sin traducción: *la velocidad máxima del coche es de 120 kilómetros por hora*, the maximum speed of the car is 120 kilometres an hour; *el número de electores es de cinco millones*, the number of electors is *o* totals five million.

13. CARACTERÍSTICA. — With: *la señora de las gafas*, the lady with the glasses; *un hombre de tez morena*, a man with a dark complexion. || Sin traducción: *avión de reacción*, jet plane; *nuestra profesora de búlgaro*, our Bulgarian teacher; *barco de vapor*, steamship. || Of: *una playa de arena fina*, a beach of fine sand.

14. DESCRIPCIÓN. — In: *ciego de un ojo*, blind in one eye; *mejor de salud*, better in health; *cinco kilómetros de largo*, five kilometres in length. || By: *es médico de profesión*, he's a doctor by profession. || — *Con cara de español*, with a Spanish-looking face. || *De piernas largas*, long in the leg, long-legged. || *De baja estatura*, short. || *Era pequeño de cuerpo*, he had a small body.

15. INTRODUCE ORACIONES SUSTANTIVADAS. — That *o* sin traducción: *estoy seguro de que vendrá*, I am sure [that] he will come; *es una prueba de que estaba*, it is proof [that] he was there; *yo tenía miedo de que muriera*, I was afraid [that] he would die.

16. MODO. — In: *de paisano*, in civilian clothes; *vestido de blanco*, dressed in white; *el oficial iba de gala*, the officer was in dress uniform; *de luto*, in mourning. || In: *hacer algo de mala manera*, to do sth. in a bad way; *de moda*, in fashion; *de buen humor*, in a good mood. || Sin traducción: *ir de falda corta*, to wear a short skirt. || As: *me lo dieron de regalo*, they gave it to me as a present. || In: *de un trago*, in one gulp. || As: *trabajar de camarero*, to work as a waiter. || With: *de un golpe, de un salto*, with one blow, with one bound. || In, with: *cubierto de nieve*, covered in snow.

17. TIEMPO. — In: *a las dos de la tarde, de la mañana*, at two o'clock in the afternoon, in the morning. || At: *a las diez de la Noche*, at ten o'clock at night.

18. LOCUCIONES DIVERSAS. — *Coger a uno de la mano*, to take s.o. by the hand, to take hold of s.o.'s hand, to hold s.o.'s hand. || *Compañero de clase*, classmate. || *De a caballo*, mounted, on horseback: *tropas de a caballo*, mounted troops, troops on horseback. || *De a pie*, foot: *soldados de a pie*, foot soldiers. || *De cabeza*, headfirst: *tirarse de cabeza*, to dive headfirst. || *De cara a*, facing: *estar de cara al sol*, to be facing the sun. || *De casa en casa*, from house to house, from one house to the next. || *De día, de noche*, by day, in the daytime, by night, at night. || *De dos en dos*, two by two, in twos. || *De él, de ella, de ellos* or *de ellas*, v. ÉL, etc. || *De hecho*, in fact (en realidad). || *De madrugada*, early in the morning (temprano), in the small hours (hasta las cuatro). || *De mal en peor*, from bad to worse. || *De no ser así*, if it were not so, were it not so. || *De puro cansancio*, out of sheer tiredness. || *De que, de quien*, about which, about whom: *la mujer de quien te hablé*, the woman about whom I spoke to you. || *De usted a mí*, between you and me. || *De verdad* or *de veras*, really, truly. || *De vez en cuando*, from time to time, occasionally. || *El camino de Londres*, the road to London, the London road. || *El mejor del mundo*, the best in the world. || *El tiempo de siempre*, the usual weather, the same old weather. || *Es de los que lucharon en la segunda guerra mundial*, he is one of those who fought in the Second World War. || *Está de paseo*, he has gone for a walk, he is taking a walk. || *Estar de*, to work as: *está de conserje en el casino*, he is working as a doorman in the casino. || *Fácil de hacer, de decir*, easy to do, to say. || *Hablar de*, to talk about. || *Hacer de*, to act as: *yo hice de cobaya*, I acted as guinea pig; to play, to take the part of: *ese actor hace de Otelo*, that actor plays Othello. || *Hombre de treinta años [de edad]*, man thirty years of age, man thirty years old, thirty-year-old man, man of thirty. || *Hora de comer*, lunchtime. || *Más de*, more than. || *Muy de las mujeres, de los niños*, typical of women, of children. || *Pidió del pastel que estaba en la mesa*, he asked for some of the cake which was on the table. || *Ser de día*, to be light, to be daylight. || *Ser de noche*, to be dark. || *Silencio de muerte*, deathly silence. || *Un libro de geografía*, a geography book. || *Uno de cada tres*, one out of [every] three, one in three. || *Vamos a casa de Fernando*, we are going to Fernando's.

— OBSERV. In Spain after her marriage a woman keeps her maiden name and adds her husband's name preceded by *de*, e.g. *Doña María López de Velasco*. In English she would be called Mrs. María Velasco, her maiden name being López. In conversation, the form *Señora de Velasco*, Mrs. Velasco, is often used. *Señores de Velasco* is translated by Mr. and Mrs. Velasco.
— The *de* and *del* in names such as *Miranda de Ebro* and *Francfort del Meno* are equivalent to the English use of *on* and *upon* (Upton-upon-Severn).
— La mayor parte de los nombres geográficos compuestos como *Francfort del Meno* se suelen dejar en inglés en su ortografía original: *Frankfurt am Main*.

dé pres. del subj. V. DAR.

deambular v. intr. To stroll, to saunter (andar, pasear).

deambulatorio m. ARQ. Ambulatory.

deán m. Dean.

deanato o **deanazgo** m. Deanery.

debacle f. Disaster.

— OBSERV. The word *debacle* is a Gallicism.

debajo adv. Underneath: *estar debajo*, to be underneath. || — *Debajo de*, under, underneath, beneath, below: *debajo de la mesa*, under the table. || *El, la de debajo*, the one underneath, the one below: *mi libro es el de debajo*, my book is the one underneath *o* below. || *Por debajo*, underneath: *¡pasa por debajo!*, go underneath. || *Por debajo de*, below: *la producción anual está por debajo de lo normal*, the annual production is below normal; *el equipo estuvo por debajo de sus posibilidades*, the team was below form; under, underneath, beneath, below: *el avión pasó por debajo del puente*, the plane flew under the bridge.

— OBSERV. *Debajo de* expresses the concrete meanings of *under, beneath*, etc., whilst *bajo* is usually reserved for the more abstract cases: *bajo la República*, under the Republic.

debate m. Debate, discussion.

debatir v. tr. To debate, to discuss. || *Hoy se debatió el proyecto de ley de reforma de la enseñanza*, today there was a debate on the education reform bill.

debe m. COM. Debit side: *una partida del debe*, an entry on the debit side. | Debit: *el debe y el haber*, the debit and credit.

debelación f. (P.us.) MIL. Victory.

debelar v. tr. (P.us.). MIL. To defeat (vencer).

— OBSERV. This word is used mostly in Latin America.

deber m. Duty: *yo he cumplido con mi deber*, I've carried out *o* done my duty. || Obligation (obligación). || — Pl. Homework, *sing.* || — *Creo mi deber permanecer aquí*, I feel it [is] my duty to stay here. || *Cumplir (con) los deberes militares*, to do one's National Service. || *Es mi deber decírselo*, it is my duty to tell you.

deber v. tr. e intr. To owe: *te debo cincuenta pesetas*, I owe you fifty pesetas; *le debo carta*, I owe him a letter; *¿a qué debo tan grata visita?*, to what do I owe the pleasure of your visit? || Must, to have to, to have got to (obligación presente y futura): *debo marcharme a las seis*, I must go at six, I have to go at six, I have got to go at six; *debes hacerlo ahora*, you must do it now. || Should, ought to (obligación pasada): *debía haberlo hecho ayer*, you should have done it yesterday, you ought to have done it yesterday. || Must, should, ought to (obligación moral): *no debes fumar tanto*, you shouldn't smoke so much. || — FAM. *Deber a medio mundo*, to owe money right and left. || *Deber de*, must (probabilidad): *debe de ser rico*, he must be rich; *no lo encuentro aquí, debe de estar en mi casa*, I can't find it here, it must be at home; should: *el tren debe de llegar de un momento a otro*, the train should arrive any time now; can, must (en frase negativa): *no debe de estar porque no veo su coche*, he can't be there because I can't see his car. || *Debería haber ido, debía haber ido, hubiera debido ir*, I ought to have gone, I should have gone. || *Debería ir, debía ir*, I ought to go, I should go. || *Debía ir*, I was to go, I was meant to go (pensaba ir). || *Debo de haberlo visto, he debido haberlo visto, he debido verlo*, I must have seen it. || FAM. *Quien debe y paga no debe nada*, out of debt, out of danger. || *Ser debido a*, to be due to: *el accidente fue debido al mal tiempo*, the accident was due to the bad weather.

— V. pr. To have a duty towards: *deberse a la patria*, to have a duty towards one's country. || To be due to: *esto se debe a su ignorancia*, it is due to his ignorance. || — *¿A qué se debe esto?* what's the reason for this?, why is this so? || *Reclamar lo que se le debe a uno*, to claim one's due from s.o.

debidamente adv. Properly: *portarse debidamente*, to behave properly. || Duly (en debida forma).

debido, da adj. Due: *la suma debida*, the sum due; *con el debido respeto*, with due respect. || Proper, fitting: *comportamiento debido*, proper behaviour. || Right: *pagar a su debido precio*, to pay the right price for. || — *A su debido tiempo*, v. TIEMPO. || *Como es debido*, properly, as is proper: *habla como es debido*, speak properly; good, proper, real: *vamos a hacer una fiesta como es debido*, let's have a real party. || *Debido a*, due to, because of, through: *debido a la lluvia no pude salir*, due to the rain I couldn't go out. || *Debido a que*, because: *no ha salido bien debido a que cuando lo hicimos ya era de noche*, it didn't work because it was already dark when we did it. || *En debida forma*, in due form. || *Más de lo debido*, too much.

débil adj. Weak: *está un poco débil todavía*, he is still a little weak. || Feeble, weak: *un niño débil*, a weak child; *una luz débil*, a feeble light. || Weak (sin voluntad): *es muy débil con sus alumnos*, he is very weak with his pupils. || Faint: *ruido débil*, faint noise. || Weak (corriente eléctrica). || Halfhearted, feeble, weak: *débil esfuerzo*, halfhearted effort. || Weak (en fonética).
— M. y f. Weak person. || — *Débil mental*, mentally retarded *o* mentally deficient person. || *Los débiles*, the weak.

debilidad f. Weakness, feebleness, debility: *la debilidad de un convaleciente*, a convalescent's weakness. || Faintness (de un sonido). || Weakness (de una corriente eléctrica). || FIG. Weakness: *la música de jazz es su debilidad*, jazz is his weakness. | Soft spot, weakness: *tengo debilidad por mi hijo menor*, I have a soft spot for my younger son. || — *Caerse de debilidad*, to be dropping on one's feet, to be faint with weakness. || MED. *Debilidad mental*, mental deficiency.

debilitación f. o **debilitamiento** m. Weakening, debilitation. || Weakening (en fonética). || Falling (de las cotizaciones en la Bolsa).

debilitador, ra o **debilitante** adj. Weakening, debilitating (que debilita).

debilitar v. tr. To weaken: *la enfermedad le ha debilitado*, the illness has weakened him. || MED. To debilitate. || To weaken (en fonética).
— V. pr. To weaken, to get *o* to become weak: *me he debilitado mucho con la enfermedad*, I have become very weak from the illness. || FIG. To weaken: *su voluntad se ha debilitado*, his willpower has weakened.

debilucho, cha adj. Weakly, delicate, frail (enclenque). || Weak, feeble (excesivamente débil).
— M. y f. Weakling.

debitar v. tr. *Amer.* To debit (cargar en cuenta).

débito m. Debit (debe). || Debt (deuda).

debut m. Début (primera actuación).

— OBSERV. This word, like *debutante* and *debutar*, is a Gallicism.

debutante m. y f. Beginner, newcomer (principiante). || *El debutante Rafael Vargas tuvo una actuación lucida*, Rafael Vargas, making his début *o* his first appearance, performed brilliantly. || — F. Débutante (en una fiesta de sociedad).

debutar v. intr. To make one's début, to make one's first appearance.

década f. Decade (diez años). || Period of ten days (diez días).

decadencia f. Decadence, decline, decay: *decadencia moral*, moral decadence. || — *Caer en decadencia*, to fall into decline *o* decay. || *La decadencia del Imperio Romano*, the decline of the Roman Empire.

decadente adj. Decadent.
— M. y f. Decadent. || — M. pl. Decadents (escritores y artistas de la escuela simbolista).

decaedro m. MAT. Decahedron.

decaer* v. intr. To decline (venir a menos). || COM. To fall off, to decline, to dwindle: *el negocio decae*, business is falling off. || To fall off, to flag: *el interés no decayó*, interest didn't flag. || To weaken, to flag (fuerzas). || To drop: *el viento decae*, the wind is dropping. || To decay (costumbres). || To go down (fiebre). || To go down, to lose, to deteriorate: *ha decaído mucho, ya no es el hombre que era*, he has gone down a lot, he is no longer the man he was. || To become low-spirited: *antes era muy divertido, pero ha decaído mucho*, he was very funny before, but now he has become very low-spirited. || MAR. To drift off course (separarse de su rumbo). || — *Ha decaído en belleza, en inteligencia*, she has lost her good looks, her intelligence. || *Su ánimo no decae a pesar de tantas dificultades*, he doesn't lose heart in spite of so many difficulties.

decagonal adj. Decagonal.

decágono m. Decagon.

decagramo m. Decagram, decagramme.

decaído, da adj. Weak (débil). || Depressed, discouraged, downhearted, crestfallen (sin ánimos). || COM. Slack (Bolsa, mercado).

decaimiento m. Weakness, weakening (físico). || COM. Falling-off. || Decline, decay (decadencia). || Dejection, low spirits, *pl.* (desaliento).

decalitro m. Decalitre [U.S., decaliter].

decálogo m. Decalogue [U.S., decalog].

decámetro m. Decametre [U.S., decameter].

decampar v. intr. MIL. To strike *o* to break camp, to decamp.

decanato m. Deanery, deanship (cargo). || Deanery (despacho).

decano, na m. y f. Dean (de universidad, etc.). || Doyen, senior member (miembro más antiguo).

decantación f. Decantation, decanting. || *Depósito de decantación*, sedimentation basin.

decantador m. Decanter.

decantar v. tr. To decant, to pour off (un líquido). || To praise, to laud: *decantar las proezas de un héroe*, to praise the prowess of a hero.

decapado m. TECN. Scaling (de los metales).

decapante adj. TECN. Scaling. || *Producto decapante*, scaler.
— M. TECN. Scaler (para los metales). | Remover (para la pintura).

decapar v. tr. To scale, to descale (desoxidar). || To remove [the paint] from, to strip (quitar la pintura).

decapitación f. Beheading, decapitation.

decapitar v. tr. To behead, to decapitate.

decápodo m. ZOOL. Decapod.

decasílabo, ba adj./s.m. Decasyllabic, decasyllable.

decatlón m. DEP. Decathlon.

deceleración f. Deceleration.

decelerar v. intr. To decelerate.

decena f. Ten: *¿cuántas decenas tiene la centena?*, how many tens are there in a hundred? || Ten or so, about ten: *una decena de personas*, ten or so people. || — *Decenas de miles*, tens of thousands. || *Hace una decena de años*, some ten years ago, about ten years ago. || *Por decenas*, in tens.

decenal adj. Decennial. || *Período decenal*, period of ten years.

decenario m. Decennary (diez años). || Decade (de rosario).

decencia f. Honesty (honradez). || Decency: *la decencia de un bañador, de una mujer*, the decency of a bathing costume, of a woman. || *Con decencia*, decently.

decenio m. Decade (diez años).

deceno, na adj. Tenth (décimo).

decentar* v. tr. To start, to break into (empezar).
— V. pr. To become sore (la piel).

decente adj. Honest, honourable, upright (honrado). || Decent: *un nivel de vida decente*, a decent standard of living. || Decent, modest, seemly, proper: *un bañador decente*, a decent bathing costume. || Decent, respectable, modest: *una mujer decente*, a decent woman. || Decent, good: *este abrigo está todavía decente*, this coat is still decent. || Clean, tidy (limpio).

decenvir o **decenviro** m. Decemvir (magistrado).

decepción f. Disappointment, disenchantment: *en su vida se llevó grandes decepciones*, he suffered great disappointments in his life.

decepcionante adj. Disappointing.

decepcionar v. tr. To disappoint: *el resultado me ha decepcionado*, the result has disappointed me.

deceso m. Decease (muerte).

decibel o **decibelio** m. FÍS. Decibel.

decible o **decidero, ra** adj. Which can be said, utterable, mentionable. || *No es decible lo que me aburrí*, there are no words to express how bored I was, I can't express how bored I was.

decididamente adv. Determinedly, resolutely, with determination: *lanzarse decididamente*, to go at it with determination. || Definitely (realmente).

decidido, da adj. Determined, resolute: *adversario decidido*, determined opponent; *entró con paso decidido*, he went in with determined steps. || — *Apoyo decidido*, solid support. || *Está decidido a hacerlo*, he is determined *o* resolved to do it, he has made up his mind to do it.

decidir v. tr. To settle, to decide (una cuestión, un asunto, etc.). || To decide, to convince, to persuade (incitar, convencer). || To decide: *decidieron salir*, they decided to go out. || To resolve (resolución categórica): *decidió quedarse*, he resolved to stay.
— V. intr. To decide, to choose: *decidir entre dos candidatos*, to decide between two candidates. || To decide: *decidir del futuro de la humanidad*, to decide the future of humanity; *decidir en una cuestión*, to decide on a question. || *Decidir sobre qué conviene más*, to decide what is more suitable.
— V. pr. To make up one's mind: *hay que decidirse*, we've got to make up our minds. || To decide, to make up one's mind: *decidirse a hacer algo*, to make up one's mind to do sth., to decide to do sth. || *Decidirse por*, to decide on, to choose: *decidirse por un sistema*, to decide on a system, to choose a system.

decidor, ra adj. Witty, lively (gracioso).
— M. *Es un decidor*, he's got the gift of the gab.

decigramo m. Decigram, decigramme.

decilitro m. Decilitre [U.S., deciliter].

décima f. Tenth, tenth part (una de las diez partes). || Tithe (diezmo). || Stanza of ten octosyllabic lines (composición poética). || FAM. *Tener décimas*, to have a slight temperature.

decimal adj./s. m. Decimal.
decimar v. tr. (Ant.). To decimate (diezmar).
decímetro m. Decimetre [U.S., decimeter].
décimo, ma adj. Tenth. || The tenth: *Alfonso X* (décimo), Alfonso X [the tenth]. || *En décimo lugar*, tenthly, in the tenth place.
— M. y f. Tenth. || — M. Tenth part [of a lottery ticket] (lotería). || Small ten-cent silver coin of Colombia and Ecuador.
decimoctavo, va adj./s. Eighteenth.
decimocuarto, ta adj./s. Fourteenth.
decimonónico, ca adj. Nineteenth-century: *edificio decimonónico*, nineteenth-century building.
decimonono, na o **decimonoveno, na** adj./s. Nineteenth.
decimoquinto, ta adj./s. Fifteenth.
decimoséptimo, ma adj./s. Seventeenth.
decimosexto, ta adj./s. Sixteenth.
decimotercero, ra o **decimotercio, cia** adj./s. Thirteenth.
decir m. Saying. || Short mediaeval poem. || — *Al decir de Juan*, according to John, according to what John says. || *Al decir de todos*, by all accounts. || *Es un decir*, it's a manner of speaking. || *Los decires*, rumours, hearsay, *sing*.
decir* v. tr. e intr. To say (pronunciar palabras): *has dicho algo que no me gusta*, you have said sth. I don't like; *dice que va a llover*, he says that it's going to rain. || To tell (contar): *dime lo que piensas de esto*, tell me what you think of this; *decir mentiras, un secreto*, to tell lies, a secret. || To tell (revelar): *su expresión dice que no está contento*, his expression tells you he isn't happy; *decirle a alguien la buena ventura*, to tell s.o.'s fortune. || To call (llamar): *le dicen Juan*, they call him John. || To speak, to tell (verdad). || To mention, to tell, to say: *no me habías dicho nada de esto*, you hadn't mentioned anything of it to me, you hadn't told me anything about it, you hadn't said anything to me about it. || To speak: *esto dice mal de la cortesía de los ingleses*, this speaks poorly of English politeness. || To think (opinar): *¿qué dice de este cuadro?*, what do you think of this picture? || To tell (ordenar): *le dijo que hiciese el trabajo*, he told him to do the job. || To recite: *decir un poema*, to recite a poem. || To read, to say: *el texto dice lo siguiente*, the text reads as follows *o* says the following. || — *A decir verdad*, to tell the truth. || *Al decir esto*, with these words. || *¿Cómo diríamos?*, how shall I put it? || *Como quien dice* or *como si dijéramos*, as it were, so to speak. || *Como quien no dice nada*, nonchalantly, as if it were the most natural thing in the world. || *Con eso queda todo dicho*, the rest goes without saying. || *¿Decía Vd.?*, *¿decías?*, you were saying? || *Decir adiós a*, to say good-bye to (una persona, una cosa). || *Decir agudezas*, to be witty. || *Decir bien*, to be right. || *Decirle a uno cuatro frescas*, v. FRESCA. || *Decirle a uno cuatro verdades* or *las verdades del barquero*, v. VERDAD. || *Decir lo que uno piensa*, to say what one is thinking, to speak one's mind. || FIG. *Decirlo todo*, to speak volumes: *una mirada que lo dice todo*, a look which speaks volumes. || *Decir mal*, to be wrong, to be mistaken. || *Decir misa*, to say Mass. || *Decir para sí* or *para su capote* or *para su coleto* or *para sus adentros*, to say to o.s. || *Decir que no, que sí*, to say no, yes. || *De paso diremos que*, let me say in passing that. || *Dicho de otro modo*, in other words. || *Dicho sea de paso*, let it be said in passing. || *Dicho sea* or *sea dicho entre nosotros*, between you and me. || *Dicho y hecho*, no sooner said than done. || *¿Diga?* or *¿dígame?*, hello? (teléfono), yes? (¿qué desea?). || *¡Dígamelo a mí!*, you're telling me!, you can say that again! || *Digamos*, say, let's say. || *Digámoslo así*, so to speak, as it were. || *Digan lo que digan* or *dígase lo que se diga*, whatever they say. || *¡Digo!*, *¡digo!*, well now! || *Digo yo*, that's what I think. || *Dime con quién andas y te diré quién eres*, a man is known by the company he keeps. || *Dirá Vd.* or *querrá Vd. decir*, you must mean. || *El qué dirán*, what people say *o* think. || *Es decir*, that is to say. || *Es fácil decirlo*, it is easy to say, it is easily said. || *Es mucho decir*, that's saying a lot, that's going a bit far. || *Esto me dice algo*, that rings a bell. || *Esto se dice pronto*, it is easily said. || *¡Haberlo dicho!*, you should have said so! || *He dicho lo que tenía que decir*, I've had my say. || *Huelga decir que*, needless to say. || *Lo dicho, dicho*, what's said is said (no se puede negar lo dicho), a promise is a promise (hay que cumplir las promesas). || *Lo dije sin querer*, I didn't mean to say it. || *Lo que tú digas*, whatever you say, it's up to you. || *Mandar decir a alguien que*, to send word to s.o. that. || *Me permito decir que*, I submit that, I venture to say that. || *Ni que decir tiene*, it goes without saying, needless to say, doubtless, undoubtedly (como aprobación). || *No decir esa boca es mía* or *no decir ni pío*, not to say a word, not to open one's mouth. || *No hay más que decir*, there's nothing more to be said, the rest goes without saying. || *No he dicho nada*, forget what I said (olvida lo dicho). || *No le dejaron decir una palabra*, they wouldn't let him get a word in [edgeways]. || *No lo digo por ti*, I'm not referring to you. || *¡No me diga!*, go on!, you don't say!, get away! || *¡No se lo diré dos veces!*, I shan't tell you again!, I shan't tell you twice! || *No te digo más*, you know what I mean, need I say more?, you can see what I'm getting at. || *O mejor dicho*, or rather. || *Para decirlo con otras palabras*, to put it in other words. || *Para que no se diga*, for the sake of appearances. || *Por decirlo así*, so to speak, as it were. || *Por* or *según lo que se dice*, according to what people say. || *Por más que diga*, whatever he says, in spite of all he says. || *Que digamos*, particularly, to speak of: *no es rico que digamos*, he is not particularly rich. || *¿Qué me dice?*, what did you say? || *...¡Que no te digo nada!* or *...¡ya me dirá usted!*, marvellous, fantastic: *te traigo un pastel que no te digo nada*, I've brought you a marvellous cake. || *Querer decir*, to mean (significar). || *¿Quién lo diría?*, who would have thought so? || *Se lo dije bien claro*, I told you so. || *Te digo que no*, I've told you, no; I said no. || *Usted dirá*, it's up to you (para una decisión), go ahead, I'm listening (lo escucho), say when (al echar vino, comida, etc.). || *¡Ya me dirás!*, you bet! (¡ya lo creo!), you'll see, you'll find out (ya lo verás). || *¡Y no digamos...!*, not to mention... || *¡Y que lo digas!*, *¡y usted que lo diga!*, you bet!
— V. pr. To be said: *esto se dice mucho en inglés*, that is said a lot in English; *se dice que es el asesino*, he is said to be the murderer; *se dice que es hija ilegítima del Rey*, it is said that she is the King's illegitimate daughter. || — *¿Cómo se dice esto en español?*, how do you say this in Spanish?, what is the Spanish for this? || *Fue lo que se dice un éxito clamoroso*, it was what you would call *o* what you call a resounding success. || *Lo menos que puede decirse*, the least one can say. || *Lo que se dice*, what you would really call: *criminal, lo que se dice criminal, no es*, he isn't what you would really call a criminal. || *Se dicen tantas cosas*, people say so many things. || *Sé lo que me digo*, I know what I'm saying, I know what I'm talking about. || *Se me ha dicho que*, I have been told that.
decisión f. Decision: *el Gobierno ha tomado una decisión*, the Government has taken *o* made a decision. || Determination, resolution, decision: *mostrar decisión*, to show determination. || *Con decisión*, determinedly, resolutely.
decisivo, va adj. Decisive: *un acontecimiento decisivo en la historia*, a decisive event in history. || *Tiene motivos decisivos para marcharse*, he has reasons which force him to go.
declamación f. Declamation (arte). || Recitation.
declamador, ra m. y f. Declaimer. || Reciter.
declamar v. tr. e intr. To declaim, to recite: *declamar versos*, to declaim poetry.
declamatorio, ria adj. Declamatory, bombastic.
declaración f. Statement, declaration: *el Presidente ha hecho una declaración a la Prensa*, the President has made a statement to the Press. || Declaration (anuncio importante). || Declaration, return: *declaración de renta*, income tax declaration. || Declaring, declaration (en las aduanas). || JUR. Statement, evidence, deposition: *hacer una declaración*, to make a statement *o* deposition, to give evidence. | Evidence, testimony: *prestar declaración*, to give evidence *o* testimony. || Bid, call (en el bridge). || — Pl. Statement, *sing.*, declaration, *sing.*: *hacer declaraciones*, to make a statement. || Comment, *sing.*, statement, *sing.* (comentario): *se negó a hacer declaraciones*, he refused to make any comment. || — *Declaración de amor*, declaration of love. || *Declaración de guerra*, declaration of war. || *Declaración de no culpabilidad*, verdict of not guilty. || *Declaración de quiebra*, declaration of bankruptcy (por la autoridad competente), filing of petition in bankruptcy (por el quebrado). || *Declaración de siniestro*, claim (de seguros). || JUR. *Prestar una declaración jurada*, to testify under oath.
declaradamente adv. Openly, manifestly.
declarado, da adj. Open, professed.
declarante adj. Who declares. || JUR. Who gives evidence, testifying.
— M. y f. Declarer, declarant. || JUR. Deponent, witness.
declarar v. tr. To declare, to state (manifestar). || To declare: *el jurado le declaró vencedor*, the jury declared him the winner; *declarar la guerra a un país*, to declare war on a country; *les declaró lo que ganaba*, he declared his earnings to them; *¿tiene algo que declarar?*, have you anything to declare? || To bid, to declare, to call (en el bridge). || JUR. To find: *declarar culpable*, to find guilty.
— V. intr. To declare. || JUR. To testify, to give evidence.
— V. pr. To declare o.s. || To break out (epidemia, fuego, etc.). || To come out, to start (una enfermedad). || To declare one's love (declarar su amor). || — *Declararse a favor de* or *por un candidato*, to declare o.s. in favour of a candidate, to come out on the side of a candidate. || JUR. *Declararse culpable*, to plead guilty. || *Declararse enfermo*, to report sick. || *Declararse en huelga*, to go on strike. || *Declararse en quiebra*, to file one's petition.
declaratorio, ria adj. Declaratory.
declinable adj. GRAM. Declinable.
declinación f. ASTR. Declination. || GRAM. Declension. || FIG. Decline (decadencia). || *Declinación magnética*, declination, magnetic variation.
declinante adj. Declining: *poder declinante*, declining power.

declinar v. intr. To decline, to slope downwards (inclinarse). || To vary from the true meridian (una brújula). || FIG. To decline, to diminish (las fuerzas). | To decay (decaer). | To diminish, to abate (fiebre). || To draw to a close: *está declinando el día, la batalla*, the day, the battle is drawing to a close. || To sink, to decline (el sol). || FIG. To fade, to fail, to fall off, to decline, to be on the wane (belleza). | To get weaker (debilitarse): *ha declinado mucho desde la última vez que le vi*, he has got a lot weaker since the last time I saw him. | To depart: *declinar del camino derecho*, to depart from the straight and narrow. || ASTR. To decline.
— V. tr. To decline, to refuse (rechazar). || GRAM. To decline.
declive m. Slope, incline, declivity (cuesta). || FIG. Decline (decadencia). || *En declive*, sloping, on a slope (inclinado).
decocción f. Decoction. || MED. Amputation.
decoloración f. Fading. || Bleaching (del pelo).
decolorante m. Bleaching agent.
decolorar v. tr. To discolour, to fade (rebajar o quitar el color): *cortinas decoloradas por el sol*, curtains faded by the sun. || To bleach (dejar blanco): *pelo decolorado*, bleached hair.
— V. pr. To fade, to become discoloured (perder el color). || To be bleached (quedar blanco).
decomisar v. tr. To confiscate, to seize.
decomiso m. Confiscation, seizure (acción). || Confiscated article (objeto confiscado).
decoración f. Decoration (acción). || Decoration, décor (efecto): *la decoración de una habitación*, the decoration of a room. || TEATR. Scenery, set (decorado). || *Decoración de escaparates*, window dressing.
decorado m. TEATR. Scenery, set. || Decoration (acción). || Decoration, décor (efecto).
decorador, ra adj. Decorating. || — *Decorador de escaparates*, window dresser. || *Pintor decorador*, painter and decorator.
— M. y f. Decorator. || TEATR. Stage *o* set designer.
decorar v. tr. To decorate, to adorn (adornar). || To decorate (una casa).
decorativo, va adj. Decorative, ornamental. || Fairly attractive (una chica). || — *Artes decorativas*, decorative arts. || FIG. y FAM. *Hacer de figura decorativa*, to play a minor part, to be mere decoration.
decoro m. Dignity (dignidad). || Decorum, propriety (honra). || Respect (respeto): *guardar el decoro a uno*, to show respect for s.o. || Decorum, decency (decencia). || — *Acabar con decoro*, to finish off in splendour. || *Con decoro*, decently: *con menos dinero no se puede vivir con decoro*, you can't live decently on less money; decently, modestly (con pudor): *comportarse con decoro*, to behave decently; decent, modest: *una mujer con decoro*, a modest woman. || *Sin decoro*, indecent (adj.), indecently (adv.) [sin pudor].
decorosamente adv. With dignity (con dignidad). || With decorum (como se debe). || Decently (decentemente).
decoroso, sa adj. Proper, seemly, decorous (conveniente). || Honourable: *una profesión decorosa*, an honourable profession. || Decent (decente): *un sueldo decoroso*, a decent wage. || Decent, modest, decorous (conforme al pudor): *una mujer decorosa*, a decent woman. || Respectable (digno). || *Tener un final muy decoroso*, to finish off in splendour.
decrecer* v. intr. To decrease. || To diminish, to dwindle (disminuir). || To go down, to subside (aguas). || To get shorter, to draw in (días).
decreciente adj. Decreasing, decrescent.
decrecimiento m. Decrease. || Diminution (disminución). || Subsiding (de las aguas).
decremento m. MAT. y ELECTR. Decrement.
decrepitar v. intr. To decrepitate.
decrépito, ta adj. Decrepit: *anciano decrépito*, decrepit old man.
decrepitud f. Decrepitude.
decrescendo adj./adv./s. m. MÚS. Decrescendo (de una melodía).
decretal f. Decretal (decisión del Papa).
decretar v. tr. To decree (por decreto). || To ordain, to order (ordenar).
decreto m. Decree, order. || Enactment (para poner en ejecución las leyes). || Decree (del papa). || *Decreto ley*, decree-law, [equivalent of] order in council.
decúbito m. MED. Decubitus: *decúbito supino, prono*, dorsal *o* supine, prone decubitus.
decuplar o **decuplicar** v. tr. To decuple, to increase tenfold.
— V. pr. To decuple, to increase tenfold.
décuplo, pla adj. Tenfold, decuple, ten times [as much as]: *cuarenta es décuplo de cuatro*, forty is decuple four, forty is tenfold four, forty is ten times four.
— M. Decuple.
decurrente adj. BOT. Decurrent.
decurso m. Course: *el decurso de los años*, the course of the years.
dechado m. Model (modelo). || Sampler (en costura). || Model, perfect example, paragon (arquetipo): *este libro es un dechado de armonía*, this book is a model of harmony; *dechado de virtudes*, a paragon of virtue. || *Ser un dechado de perfecciones*, to be perfect in every way, to be a model of perfection.
dedada f. Fingerful (cantidad que se coge con el dedo): *una dedada de mermelada*, a fingerful of jam. || Fingermark (mancha). || FIG. *Dedada de miel*, consolation.
dedal m. Thimble (para coser).
dedalera f. BOT. Foxglove.
dédalo m. Labyrinth, maze (laberinto).
Dédalo n. pr. m. MIT. Daedalus.
dedicación f. Dedication, consecration (de una iglesia). || Devotion, dedication (entrega): *su dedicación al partido*, his devotion to the party. || Devotion (de tiempo, dinero, esfuerzos, etc.). || — *De dedicación exclusiva* or *de plena dedicación*, full-time: *empleo de dedicación exclusiva*, full-time job. || *Le consagra una dedicación completa*, he devotes all his time to it.
dedicar v. tr. To dedicate, to consecrate (una iglesia, etc.). || To dedicate (un libro). || To inscribe, to dedicate (cada ejemplar de un libro, fotografía, etc.). || To devote (dinero, tiempo, esfuerzos, etc.): *cada día hay que dedicar una hora a los estudios*, you must devote an hour every day to studying. || To give over: *dedicó una parte de su tierra a pastos*, he gave over part of his land to grazing. || To address (palabras). || To have, to show: *le dedica mucha admiración*, he has great admiration for him. || *Emisión dedicada a España*, programme about Spain, programme devoted to Spain.
— V. pr. To devote o.s., to dedicate o.s.: *dedicarse al estudio*, to devote o.s. to study. || To dedicate one's life, to give up one's life: *dedicarse a los enfermos*, to dedicate one's life to the sick. || To spend one's time, to go in for (con el infinitivo): *se dedica a cazar*, he spends his time hunting. || *¿A qué se dedica usted?*, what do you do [for a living]?, what is your line of business?
dedicatoria f. Dedication, inscription (de un libro, objeto de arte, etc.).
dedicatorio, ria adj. Dedicatory.
dedil m. Fingerstall: *dedil de goma*, rubber fingerstall.
dedillo m. *Al dedillo*, at one's fingertips: *saber algo al dedillo*, to have sth. at one's fingertips.
dedo m. Finger (de la mano). || Toe (del pie). || Finger, fingerbreadth, digit (medida). || — *Beber un dedo de vino*, to have a drop of wine. || *Contar con los dedos*, to count on one's fingers. || FIG. *Cogerse los dedos*, to get caught. || *Chuparse el dedo*, to suck one's thumb (un niño). || FIG. *Dale un dedo y se tomará hasta el codo*, give him an inch and he'll take a mile. || *Dedo anular*, third finger, ring finger. || *Dedo del pie*, toe. || *Dedo gordo*, thumb. || *Dedo gordo del pie*, big toe. || *Dedo índice*, forefinger, index, index finger. || *Dedo medio* or *del corazón*, middle finger. || *Dedo meñique* or *pequeño*, little finger. || *Dedo pulgar*, thumb. || FAM. *Es* or *está para chuparse los dedos*, it's delicious (comida), it's great (cosa). || FIG. *Estar a dos dedos de*, to be on the point *o* on the verge of, to be inches away from. | *Meter los dedos a uno*, to worm sth. out of s.o., to make s.o. talk. || *Meterse los dedos en la nariz*, to pick one's nose, to put one's fingers up one's nose. || FIG. *Morderse los dedos*, to regret it, to kick o.s. : *decidió no irse de vacaciones y ahora se muerde los dedos*, he decided not to go on holiday and now he regrets it *o* and now he could kick himself. | *No chuparse* or *no mamarse el dedo*, not to have been born yesterday. | *Nombrar a dedo*, to handpick. | *No mover un dedo de la mano*, not to lift a finger. | *No tener dos dedos de frente*, to be as thick as two planks. || *Poner a uno los cinco dedos en la cara*, to slap s.o. across the face, to give s.o. a slap across the face. || MÚS. *Poner bien los dedos*, to play an instrument well. || FIG. *Poner el dedo en la llaga*, to touch on a sore point. || *Señalar a uno con el dedo*, to point at s.o. (dirigir el dedo hacia uno), to put the finger on s.o. (destacar). || *Tocar algo con el dedo*, to put one's finger on sth. || *Yema* or *punta del dedo*, fingertip.
deducción f. Deduction, inference. || COM. Deduction (acción de descontar). || MÚS. Diatonic scale. || *Deducción del salario*, deduction from one's salary.
deducible adj. Deducible, inferable. || COM. Deductible.
deducir* v. tr. To deduce, to infer: *deduzco de* or *por ello que no lo vas a hacer*, from that I deduce that you are not going to do it. || COM. To deduct: *deducir los gastos de las ganancias*, to deduct expenses from the earnings; *deducir algo del salario*, to deduct sth. from one's salary. || JUR. To adduce, to present, to allege (pruebas, razones), to claim, to assert (derechos).
— V. pr. To follow.
deductivo, va adj. Deductive.
defalcar v. tr. To deduct (rebajar). || To embezzle, to misappropriate (robar).
defasado, da adj. ELECTR. Out of phase.
defasaje m. ELECTR. Phase shift, dephasing, phase difference. || FIG. Difference, gap.
defasar v. tr. ELECTR. To dephase.
defecación f. Defecation, defaecation.
defecar v. tr. To defaecate, to defecate.
defección f. Defection, desertion.
defectivo, va adj. Defective (defectuoso). || GRAM. Defective (verbo).
— M. GRAM. Defective verb.
defecto m. Defect, fault (físico, de una máquina, etc.). || Imperfection, flaw (de una joya). || Fault, defect, shortcoming (moral): *esta persona tiene muchos*

defectos, this person has a lot of faults. || Flaw (en un argumento). || Lack, absence (falta). || IMPR. Oddment, waste sheet. || — *A defecto de*, for want of. || *Defecto de pronunciación*, speech defect, speech impediment. || *Defecto físico*, physical defect.

defectuosidad f. Defectiveness, faultiness, unsoundness. || Defect, flaw, imperfection (defecto).

defectuoso, sa adj. Defective, faulty.

defendedor, ra adj. Defending, who defends.
— M. y f. Defender.

— OBSERV. In football *defender* is translated by *defensa* which is masculine and can also mean *back*.

defender* v. tr. To defend (*contra*, against; *de*, from): *defender la patria contra el enmigo*, to defend one's country against the enemy. || To protect (*contra*, against; *de*, from) [proteger]: *la montaña defiende la ciudad del viento norte*, the mountain protects the town from the north wind. || To defend, to uphold (argumento, ideas, etc.). || JUR. To argue, to plead: *defender una causa*, to argue a cause. | To defend (al acusado).
— V. pr. To defend o.s. || FIG. y FAM. To get along, to manage, not to do badly (no dársele mal): *se defiende en ruso*, he gets along in Russian.

defendible adj. Defensible. || Justifiable, defensible (justificable).

defendido, da adj. JUR. Defendant.
— M. y f. JUR. Defendant.

defenestración f. Defenestration.

defensa f. Defence [U.S., defense]: *defensa de una ciudad, de una idea*, defence of a town, of an idea. || JUR. Defence: *conceder la palabra a la defensa*, to call upon the defence to speak. | Speech for the defence (discurso). || MIL. y MAR. Defence: *defensa pasiva*, passive defence. || Leg guard (moto). || MAR. Fender (de barco). || DEP. Defence, defenders, *pl.* (jugadores). | Pad (protección para las piernas). || — Pl. Tusks (colmillos). || — *En defensa de*, in defence of. || *En defensa mía* or *propia*, in self-defence. || *Legítima defensa*, self-defence [U.S., self-defense]. || *Salir en defensa de alguien*, to come out in defence of s.o.

defensa m. DEP. Back, fullback: *defensa izquierda, derecha, central*, left, right, centre back. | Defender (cada jugador que no es delantero).

defensiva f. Defensive: *estar, ponerse a la defensiva*, to be, to go on the defensive. || DEP. *Jugar a la defensiva*, to play a defensive game.

defensivo, va adj. Defensive: *táctica defensiva*, defensive tactics.

defensor, ra adj. Defending, who defends. || JUR. *Abogado defensor*, counsel for the defence [U.S., counsel for the defense].
— M. y f. Defender. || JUR. Counsel for the defence. || *Defensor de la fe*, Defender of the Faith.

deferencia f. Deference, regard: *por* or *en deferencia a*, in *o* out of deference to, out of regard for.

deferente adj. Deferential (atento). || ANAT. *Conducto deferente*, deferent conduit.

deferir* v. intr. To defer: *deferir al dictamen ajeno*, to defer to s.o. else's judgment.
— V. tr. JUR. To refer, to transfer, to delegate: *deferir una causa a un tribunal*, to transfer a case to a court.

deficiencia f. Insufficiency, lack (insuficiencia). || Deficiency: *deficiencia de salud*, health deficiency. || Defectiveness, faultiness (imperfección). || Defect (defecto). || Shortcoming: *las deficiencias de un equipo*, the shortcomings of a team. || MED. *Deficiencia mental*, mental deficiency.

deficiente adj. Deficient: *salud deficiente*, deficient health. || Insufficient, lacking (insuficiente). || Defective, faulty (defectuoso). || Poor: *alumno deficiente*, poor pupil; *trabajo deficiente*, poor piece of work.
— M. y f. MED. *Deficiente mental*, mentally retarded person, mentally deficient person.

deficientemente adv. Insufficiently. || Poorly: *trabajo hecho deficientemente*, work poorly done.

déficit m. Deficit. || FIG. Shortage (carencia).

— OBSERV. Pl. *déficits*.

deficitario, ria adj. Showing a deficit: *balance deficitario*, balance showing a deficit.

definible adj. Definable.

definición f. Definition. || TECN. Definition (telescopio, televisión). || *Por definición*, by definition: *el hombre es egoísta por definición*, man is selfish by definition.

definido, da adj. Definite: *artículo definido*, definite article. || *Bien definido*, well-defined.

definir v. tr. To define: *definir claramente una palabra*, to define a word clearly. || To determine (actitud, postura). || To put the finishing touches to (una pintura).

definitivamente adv. Finally: *las obras están definitivamente terminadas*, the road works have finally been finished. || For good, once and for all: *marcharse definitivamente*, to go for good. || Decisively.

definitivo, va adj. Final, definitive: *el proyecto definitivo*, the final plan. || Permanent: *poner un puente provisional mientras se construye el definitivo*, to put up a temporary bridge while the permanent one is being built. || *En definitiva*, really: *no sé aún lo que voy a hacer en definitiva*, I still don't really know what to do; all things considered (considerándolo todo): *en definitiva, esto no me interesa*, all things considered, this doesn't interest me; in short (en resumen): *en definitiva, todo sigue igual*, in short, everything is still the same.

deflación f. Deflation.

deflacionista adj. Deflationary.

deflagración f. Deflagration.

deflagrador m. Detonator, igniter (para barrenos).

deflagrar v. intr. To deflagrate.

deflector m. TECN. Deflector, baffle. || Quarter light (de coche).

defoliación f. BOT. Defoliation.

deformación f. Deformation. || FÍS. Deformation, strain. || Distortion (televisión). || TECN. Warping (alabeo). || *Deformación profesional*, occupational idiosincracy.

deformar v. tr. To deform: *deformar un miembro*, to deform a limb; *deformar el carácter de una persona*, to deform a person's character. || To put out of shape, to deform: *la lluvia ha deformado el sombrero*, the rain has put the hat out of shape. || To distort: *el flemón le ha deformado la cara*, the gumboil has distorted his face; *deformar la verdad, una imagen*, to distort the truth, a picture. || To twist, to warp (la conciencia). || FÍS. To strain. || TECN. To warp (alabear).
— V. pr. To be deformed (un miembro, etc.). || To go out of shape, to lose one's shape: *los zapatos se deforman con la lluvia*, shoes lose their shape in the rain. || To be distorted (cara, imagen, conciencia). || TECN. To warp (alabearse).

deforme adj. Deformed (miembro). || Distorted (cara, imagen). || Misshapen, shapeless (cosa).

deformidad f. Deformity, malformation: *una deformidad física*, a physical deformity. || FIG. Moral shortcoming, perversion.

defraudación f. FIG. Disappointment (decepción). || Fraud (fraude). || Swindle (estafa). || *Defraudación fiscal*, tax evasion.

defraudado, da adj. FIG. Disappointed (decepcionado). | Frustrated (esperanzas).

defraudador, ra adj. Disappointing (decepcionante). || Deceiving, cheating (que engaña).
— M. y f. Evader: *defraudador fiscal*, tax evader. || Swindler (estafador).

defraudar v. tr. To disappoint (decepcionar). || To frustrate, to dash (esperanzas). || To defraud, to cheat: *defraudar a sus acreedores*, to defraud one's creditors. || To swindle (estafar). || To evade: *defraudar al fisco*, to evade taxes. || *Defraudar la confianza de alguien*, to betray s.o.'s confidence.

defunción f. Decease, demise (fallecimiento). || Death: *esquela de defunción*, death announcement, notification of death; *partida de defunción*, death certificate. || *Cerrado por defunción*, closed due to bereavement.

degeneración f. Degeneration (de las células). || Degeneracy, degeneration (moral).

degenerado, da adj./s. Degenerate.

degenerante adj. Degenerative, degenerating. || ARQ. Flat (arco).

degenerar v. intr. To degenerate (persona, animal, cosa). || FIG. To degenerate: *partido de fútbol que degeneró en batalla campal*, football match which degenerated into a pitched battle.

degenerativo, va adj. Degenerative.

deglución f. Deglutition, swallowing.

deglutir v. tr. e intr. To swallow.

degollación f. Throat cutting (degüello). || Decapitation, beheading (decapitación). || *La degollación de los Inocentes*, the Slaughter of the Innocents.

degolladero m. Throat, windpipe [of animals to be slaughtered]. || Slaughterhouse (matadero). || Scaffold (cadalso). || FIG. *Llevar al degolladero*, to lead to the slaughterhouse.

degollador, ra adj. Cutthroat.
— M. y f. Executioner, beheader (verdugo).

degolladura f. Cut [in the throat] (herida). || Joint (entre ladrillos).

degollar* v. tr. To cut the throat of (cortar la garganta). || To behead, to decapitate (decapitar). || FIG. To ruin, to spoil (arruinar): *esto degüella todos mis proyectos*, that ruins all my plans. | To murder (representar mal una obra, etc.). || TAUR. To kill badly, to butcher. || MAR. To slash (una vela).

degollina f. FAM. Slaughter, massacre (matanza). || FAM. *El profesor hizo una degollina en los exámenes*, the teacher was very severe in his exam marking.

degradación f. Demotion, degradation (de un militar). || FIG. Degradation, debasement (envilecimiento). | Depravity (depravación). || ARTES. Gradation.

degradador m. FOT. Vignetter (desvanecedor).

degradante adj. Degrading: *conducta degradante*, degrading conduct.

degradar v. tr. To degrade. || To demote, to degrade: *degradar a un militar*, to demote a soldier. || FIG. To degrade, to debase: *el abuso del alcohol degrada al hombre*, too much drink degrades a man. || ARTES. To gradate (el color). || FÍS. To degrade.
— V. pr. To lower o.s., to degrade o.s.

degüello m. Throat cutting (acción de cortar el cuello). || Beheading, decapitation (decapitación). || Massacre, slaughter (matanza). || — MIL. *Entrar a degüello*, to massacre, to slaughter, to put to the sword: *entraron a degüello en la ciudad*, they massacred the city, they put the city to the sword. || FIG. *Tirar a uno a degüello*, to have one's knife in s.o., to be gunning for s.o.

degustación f. Tasting.
degustar v. tr. To taste (probar, catar).
dehesa f. Pasture, meadow.
dehiscente adj. BOT. Dehiscent.
deicida adj. Deicidal.
— M. y f. Deicide.
deicidio m. Deicide.
deidad f. Deity, god (dios): *las deidades griegas*, the Greek deities. || Deity (divinidad).
deificación f. Deification.
deificar v. tr. To deify.
deísmo m. Deism.
deísta adj. Deistic.
— M. y f. Deist.
dejación f. Surrender, relinquishment, cession, renunciation: *dejación de bienes*, surrender of property.
dejada f. Surrender, relinquishment. || DEP. Drop shot (en tenis).
dejadez f. Neglect, slovenliness (falta de cuidado). || Negligence, carelessness, slackness (negligencia). || Laziness (pereza).
dejado, da adj. Slovenly, untidy (descuidado). || Negligent, slack, careless (negligente). || Lazy (perezoso). || Dejected, depressed, listless (desanimado). || *Dejado de la mano de Dios*, godforsaken.
— M. y f. Sloven, slovenly person (descuidado).
dejamiento m. Neglect, slovenliness (falta de cuidado). || Negligence, slackness, carelessness (negligencia). || Laziness (pereza). || Relinquishment (dejación). || Dejection, despondency (decaimiento).
dejar v. tr. To leave, to forget: *lo he dejado en casa*, I've left it at home. || To leave: *le ha dejado algo por* or *sin hacer*, he has left you sth. to do; *déjalo tranquilo*, leave him alone: *dejar a uno el cuidado de hacer algo*, to leave it to s.o. to do sth.; *dejar improductivo un capital*, to leave capital uninvested; *dejar para mañana*, to leave till tomorrow. || To leave, to bequeath (la herencia). || To drop, to put down, to leave (depositar): *el coche te dejará en la estación*, the car will drop you at the station. || To leave, to abandon, to forsake (abandonar): *dejar a su mujer*, to leave one's wife. || To give up, to leave (un empleo). || To stop, to finish: *dejo de trabajar a las seis*, I finish work at six o'clock. || To stop, to leave off: *dejó de escribirme*, he stopped writing to me. || To bring in, to make (dar): *este negocio deja mucho dinero*, this business brings in a lot of money. || To yield, to produce, to bring in (beneficios). || To lend (prestar): *déjame veinte duros*, lend me a hundred pesetas. || To forget, to leave out, to omit (omitir). || To drop: *dejemos esta discusión*, let's drop this argument. || To let, to allow (permitir): *no dejo salir a mi hija* or *que salga mi hija después de las diez*, I don't let my daughter go out *o* allow my daughter to go out later than ten o'clock. || To let (permitir): *déjalo trabajar en paz*, let him work in peace; *si el chico quiere salir, déjalo*, if the boy wants to go out, let him; *déjalo jugar* or *que juegue*, let him play. || To put down: *deje ese libro y coja otro*, put that book down and get another. || To leave alone: *deja eso y no lo toques*, leave that alone and don't touch it. || To make: *me ha dejado los zapatos como nuevos*, he has made my shoes as good as new; *la ducha me ha dejado como nuevo*, that shower has made a new man of me. || To keep: *deja tus observaciones para cuando te las pidan*, keep your remarks until you are asked for them. || To wait (esperar): *deja que pase la tormenta*, wait until the storm has passed. || — REL. *Dejad que los niños se acerquen a mí*, suffer the little children to come unto me. || FAM. *¡Déjalo!*, stop it (no hagas eso), forget it, don't worry (no te preocupes). || *¡Déjame!* or *¡déjame en paz!*, leave me alone!, leave me in peace!, go away! || *Dejando a salvo* or *si dejamos a salvo*, with the exception of, except for. || *Dejar al descubierto*, to expose (un ejército): *dejar al descubierto un flanco*, to expose a flank. || *Dejar aparte*, to leave aside. || *Dejar atrás*, to leave behind, to outstrip, to outdistance. || *Dejar a un lado* or *de lado*, to leave aside (apartar), to omit, to pass over (omitir). || FIG. *Dejar caer*, to drop, to slip: *dejó caer en la conversación que quería irse a España*, he slipped it into the conversation that he wanted to go to Spain; to drop (un objeto). | *Dejar chiquito*, to put in the shade (superar): *este nuevo modelo deja chiquito al anterior*, this new model puts the former one in the shade. || *Dejar dicho*, to say: *como dejo dicho*, as I have said; to leave word: *he dejado dicho que no me despierten*, I have left word that I don't want to be awakened. || FAM. *Dejar en la estacada*, to leave in the lurch. || *Dejar entrar*, to let in. || FAM. *Dejar fresco*, to leave cold: *eso me deja fresco*, that leaves me cold. || *Dejar mucho que desear*, to leave a lot to be desired. || *Dejar (el) paso libre*, to get out of the way of: *dejar el paso libre a los bomberos*, to get out of the way of the firemen; to let pass: *los aduaneros dejaron paso libre al automovilista*, the customs officers let the motorist pass; to keep the way clear (no obstruir el paso). || FAM. *Dejar plantado*, v. PLANTADO. || *Dejar por heredero a uno*, to name *o* to leave s.o. as one's heir. || *Dejar por imposible*, to give up as impossible. || *Dejar salir*, to let out (alguien que está encerrado, animal), to allow out (persona). || *Dejar tiempo al tiempo*, to wait, to let things take their time. || *Dejar tirado a alguien*, to leave s.o. in the lurch (dejar en la estacada), to leave s.o. miles behind (en una carrera). || *¡Déjeme paso!*, let me get past!, let me through! || *Dejémoslo así*, let's leave it there, let's leave it at that. || *No dejarle a uno un hueso sano*, v. HUESO. || FIG. *No dejar piedra por mover*, to leave no stone unturned. || *No dejes para mañana lo que puedes hacer hoy*, do not put off till tomorrow what you can do today.
— V. intr. — *Dejar de*, to stop: *no dejó de hablar*, he didn't stop talking; to give up, to stop: *ha dejado de jugar al fútbol*, he has given up playing football. || *No dejar de*, not to fail to, not to neglect to: *no dejes de venir*, don't fail to come. || *No deja de extrañarme su conducta*, his behaviour never fails to surprise me. || *No por eso deja de ser un disparate*, it is still stupid. || *No por eso dejaré de ir*, that won't stop me going. || *No puedo dejar de extrañarme*, I cannot but be surprised, I can't help being surprised.
— V. pr. To make o.s.: *la influencia de la literatura moderna se deja sentir*, the influence of modern literature is making itself felt. || To let o.s., to allow o.s.: *no te dejes explotar*, don't you let yourself be exploited. || To let o.s. go, to neglect o.s. (abandonarse). || To leave, to forget (olvidar): *me he dejado el libro en casa*, I've left my book at home. || To forget: *te has dejado este ejercicio sin hacer*, you have forgotten to do this exercise. || To be: *se deja convencer fácilmente*, he is easily convinced. || — *Consentir sin dejarse rogar*, to consent readily. || *Dejarse abatir*, to get depressed. || *Dejarse caer*, to drop, to fall, to flop: *se dejó caer en el sillón*, he flopped into the armchair; to drop in, to pop in: *me dejé caer por su casa a las ocho*, I dropped in to see him at eight o'clock. || FIG. y FAM. *Dejarse caer con*, to come up *o* out with: *dejarse caer con una noticia sensacional*, to come up with a sensational piece of news. || *Dejarse crecer la barba*, to grow a beard. || *Dejarse de*, to stop: *déjate de historias*, stop beating about the bush; *déjese de llorar*, stop crying. || *Dejarse de cuentos* or *de rodeos*, not to beat around *o* about the bush, to get [straight] to the point. || *Dejarse ir*, to let o.s. go. || *Dejarse llevar por*, to be carried away with: *dejarse llevar por la cólera*, to be carried away with anger; to be influenced by: *dejarse llevar por los demás*, to be influenced by others. || *Dejarse oír*, to be [able to be] heard, to make o.s. heard. || *Dejarse querer*, to like attention. || *Dejarse rogar*, to play hard to get. || *¡Déjate de bromas!*, that's enough of your joking!, stop your clowning! || *Déjate de tonterías*, don't be silly. || *Este vinillo se deja beber*, this is a very drinkable *o* nice little wine. || *Se deja sentir el frío*, you can feel the cold.
— OBSERV. *Dejar* followed by the past participle of a verb is equivalent to the same verb used in its finite form. The difference lies in the emphasis this construction gives to the verb: *dejar a uno asombrado* (asombrar), to amaze s.o.; *dejar desamparado* (desamparar), to forsake.
deje m. [Slight] accent, lilt (modo de hablar).
dejillo m. [Slight] accent, lilt (modo de hablar). || Aftertaste (sabor). || *Este vino tiene un dejillo amargo*, this wine leaves a bitter taste in your mouth.
dejo m. [Slight] accent, lilt (modo de hablar). || Aftertaste (sabor). || Slackness (dejadez). || Abandonment, surrender (abandono). || End, termination (fin). || *Una victoria con un dejo amargo*, a victory which leaves a nasty taste in one's mouth.
del art. [contraction of *de* and *el*]. Of the, from the, etc. (V. DE.).
delación f. Denunciation, accusation.
delantal m. Apron (sin peto). || Pinafore (con peto). || Smock (babero).
delante adv. In front, ahead (con movimiento): *ir delante*, to walk in front. || In front (sin movimiento): *lleva las botones delante*, the buttons are in front. || — *De delante*, in front: *el de delante*, the one in front; *el coche de delante*, the car in front; front: *la puerta de delante*, the front door. || *Delante de*, in front of, ahead of, before (con movimiento): *andaba delante de mí*, he was walking in front of me; in front (sin movimiento): *hay un árbol delante de mi casa*, there is a tree in front of my house; outside: *me estaba esperando delante del cine*, he was waiting for me outside the cinema. || *Por delante*, in front: *abierto por delante*, open in front. || FIG. *Se lleva todo por delante*, he lets nothing stand in his way. || *Tenemos dos días por delante*, we still have two days to go. || *Tenemos esa lista delante mientras trabajamos*, we have that list in front of us while we work. || FAM. *Tener algo delante de sus narices*, to have sth. under one's nose. || *Tener mucho trabajo por delante*, to have a lot of work in front of one, to have a lot of work ahead of one.
delantera f. Front, front part (de casa, de prenda de vestir, etc.). || Front row (fila de teatro, etc.). || Front row seat (asiento). || Lead (ventaja): *tomar la delantera*, to take the lead; *llevar mucha delantera*, to be well in the lead. || Forward line, forwards, *pl.*: *la delantera de un equipo de fútbol*, the forward line of a football team. || — *Coger* or *tomar a uno la delantera*, to take the lead over s.o., to get ahead of s.o. (en una carrera), to get there before s.o., to beat s.o. to it (anticiparse): *fui a solicitar un trabajo pero me cogieron la delantera*, I went for a job but s.o. beat me to it.
delantero, ra adj. Front: *parte, fila, rueda delantera*, front part, row, wheel. || SP. Forward. || *Pata delantera*, foreleg, front leg.

— M. DEP. Forward: *delantero centro*, centre forward. || Front (de un jersey, vestido, etc.).
delatar v. tr. To denounce, to inform on: *delatar a los cómplices*, to denounce one's accomplices. || FIG. To give away: *el ruido que hizo lo delató y lo cogieron*, the noise he made gave him away and they caught him.
delator, ra adj. Who informs, who denounces.
— M. y f. Informer, delator.
delco m. AUT. Distributor.
dele o **deleátur** m. IMPR. Dele.
deleble adj. Delible.
delectación f. Delight, delectation.
delegación f. Delegation (acción de delegar). || Office (cargo y oficina). || Local office: *delegación de Hacienda*, local tax office. || Branch: *la compañía tiene una delegación en Madrid*, the company has a branch in Madrid. || Delegation (conjunto de delegados). || *Delegación sindical*, union delegation (conjunto de delegados), local union [office] (en España).
delegado, da adj. Delegated.
— M. y f. Delegate. || COM. Representative (de una sucursal). || *Delegado de Hacienda*, chief tax inspector.
delegar v. tr. To delegate: *delegar sus poderes a* or *en una persona*, to delegate one's powers to s.o.
delegatorio, ria adj. Delegatory.
deleitable adj. Delightful, delectable, enjoyable. || Delicious (delicioso).
deleitación f. o **deleitamiento** m. Delight, pleasure, delectation.
deleitante adj. V. DELEITABLE.
deleitar v. tr. To delight, to please: *la música deleita el oído*, music delights the ear.
— V. pr. To delight, to take delight *o* great pleasure: *deleitarse en la lectura*, to delight in reading, to take great pleasure in reading; *deleitarse con* or *en la contemplación de*, to delight in the contemplation of.
deleite m. Delight, pleasure, joy: *leer con deleite*, to read with delight. || *El clima de Mallorca es un verdadero deleite*, Majorca's climate is really delightful.
deleitoso, sa adj. Delightful, enjoyable, delectable.
deletéreo, a adj. Noxious, poisonous, deleterious: *gas deletéreo*, noxious gas.
deletrear v. tr. To spell, to spell out: *deletree su apellido*, spell your name. || FIG. To decipher: *deletrear jeroglíficos*, to decipher hieroglyphics.
deletreo m. Spelling, spelling out (de palabras o sílabas). || Deciphering (desciframiento).
deleznable adj. Crumbly, friable: *arcilla deleznable*, crumbly clay. || Slippery (resbaladizo). || FIG. Fragile, frail, ephemeral (que dura poco). | Weak: *razones deleznables*, weak reasons. | Unstable (inestable).
delfín m. Dolphin (cetáceo). || Dauphin (príncipe).
delfina f. Dauphiness, dauphine (esposa del delfín de Francia).
Delfos n. pr. GEOGR. Delphi.
delgadez f. Slimness, slenderness (esbeltez). || Thinness (flacura): *la delgadez de un enfermo*, the thinness of a sick person. || *Delgadez cadavérica*, emaciation.
delgado, da adj. Thin: *una lámina de metal muy delgada*, a very thin sheet of metal. || Slim, slender (esbelto): *una mujer delgada*, a slim woman. || Thin (flaco): *este niño no come lo suficiente y se ha quedado muy delgado*, this child doesn't eat enough and is very thin. || FIG. Sharp (agudo, ingenioso). || Poor (tierra de cultivo). || — FIG. *Hilar delgado*, to split hairs. || ANAT. *Intestino delgado*, small intestine. || *Ponerse delgado*, to lose weight, to get thin (ponerse flaco): *se ha puesto delgado durante el servicio militar*, he has lost weight in the army; to lose weight, to slim (a propósito): *su hermana se ha puesto muy delagada*, his sister has lost a lot of weight *o* has slimmed a lot.
— M. pl. Flanks (de un animal).
delgaducho, cha adj. FAM. Skinny, thin: *niño delgaducho*, skinny child.
deliberación f. Deliberation.
deliberadamente adv. Deliberately, on purpose, intentionally.
deliberado, da adj. Deliberate, intentional.
deliberante adj. Deliberative: *asamblea deliberante*, deliberative assembly.
deliberar v. intr. To deliberate (*sobre*, on).
— V. tr. To decide.
deliberativo, va adj. Deliberative.
deliberatorio, ria adj. Deliberative.
delicadeza f. Delicacy (de máquina, situación, etc.). || Delicacy, frailty (de salud). || Squeamishness (remilgos). || Hypersensitivity (sensibilidad excesiva). || Tactfulness (tacto). || Delicacy, daintiness (de rasgos, etc.). || Refinement (de modales). || Exquisiteness (de un manjar). || — *Con delicadeza*, delicately, gently (suavemente), tactfully (con tacto). || *Falta de delicadeza*, lack of refinement (en los modales), tactlessness (falta de tacto). || *Fue una delicadeza de su parte*, it was a nice gesture on his part. || *Tener mil delicadezas con*, to make a great fuss of, to devote all one's attention to. || *Tuvo la delicadeza de*, he was thoughtful enough to.
delicado, da adj. Delicate: *una máquina delicada*, a delicate machine; *una situación delicada*, a delicate situation: *un color delicado*, a delicate colour. || Delicate, frail (enfermizo): *es delicado de salud*, his health is delicate. || Very sensitive, hypersensitive (muy sensible). || Fussy, particular, fastidious, hard to please (exigente). || Squeamish (remilgado). || Dainty, delicate, exquisite: *los rasgos delicados de un rostro*, the dainty lines of a face. || Exquisite (un manjar). || Refined, polite (cortés). || Sharp, subtle (sutil). || Tactful (que tiene tacto). || Refined: *Eduardo tiene gustos muy delicados*, Edward has very refined tastes. || Considerate, thoughtful (atento). || — *Hacerse el delicado*, to be overfussy. || *Manjar delicado*, delicacy.
delicaducho, cha adj. FAM. Delicate, frail, weakly, sickly.
delicia f. Delight: *Juanito es la delicia de sus padres*, Johnny is his parents' delight. || — *El jardín de las delicias*, the Garden of Earthly Delights. || *Hacer las delicias de*, to delight: *los columpios hacen las delicias de los niños*, the swings delight the children. || *No hay delicia comparable a*, there is nothing like. || *Pensar con delicia en*, to delight in the idea *o* in the thought of. || *Su casa es una delicia*, his house is delightful, he has a delightful house.
delicioso, sa adj. Delightful (deleitable). || Delicious (sabor, etc.). || Charming, delightful (encantador): *es una mujer deliciosa*, she is a charming woman. || FAM. Funny (gracioso).
delictivo, va o **delictuoso, sa** adj. Criminal, punishable.
delicuescencia f. Deliquescence.
delicuescente adj. Deliquescent.
delimitación f. Delimitation.
delimitar v. tr. To delimit, to delimitate, to mark the boundaries of. || To define (atribuciones, etc.).
delincuencia f. Delinquency: *delincuencia juvenil*, juvenile delinquency.
delincuente m. y f. Delinquent, offender. || — *Delincuente sin antecedentes penales*, first offender. || *Delincuente juvenil, joven delincuente*, juvenile delinquent.
— Adj. Delinquent.
delineación f. Delineation, outlining.
delineante m. Draughtsman, draftsman. || *Delineante proyectista*, designer (que idea los proyectos).
delinear v. tr. To delineate, to sketch, to outline. || *Relieve bien delineado*, well-defined relief.
delinquir v. intr. To commit an offence, to break the law.
deliquio m. Faint, fainting fit (desmayo). || Ecstasy (éxtasis).
delirante adj. Delirious. || Frenzied, delirious: *imaginación, ovaciones delirantes*, delirious imagination, ovation.
delirar v. intr. To be delirious. || FIG. To talk nonsense, to rave (desatinar). | To rave (*por*, about, over) [estar entusiasmado].
delirio m. Delirium (desvarío). || FIG. Ravings, *pl.* (ilusión). | Stupid thing, nonsense (disparate). || — *Con delirio*, madly. || *Delirio de grandezas*, delusions of grandeur. || *Delirio de la persecución*, persecution mania. || FIG. y FAM. *¡El delirio!*, it was great! || *Estar en delirio*, to be delirious. || FIG. y FAM. *Tener delirio por*, to be crazy about.
delírium tremens m. MED. Delirium tremens.
delito m. Crime, offence [U.S., offense]. || — *Cogido en flagrante delito*, caught red-handed. || *Delito común*, crime, offence [in common law]. || *Delito de lesa majestad*, lese majesty, lèse majesté. || *Delito flagrante*, flagrante delicto. || *Delito político*, political crime *o* offence. || *El cuerpo del delito*, the corpus delicti.
delta f. Delta (letra griega). || — M. GEOGR. Delta.
deltaico, ca adj. Deltaic.
deltoideo, a adj. ANAT. Deltoid, deltoidal.
deltoides adj. inv. ANAT. Deltoid, deltoidal.
— M. inv. ANAT. Deltoid.
demacración f. Emaciation (adelgazamiento).
demacrado, da adj. Emaciated: *rostro demacrado*, emaciated face.
demacrarse v. pr. To waste away, to become emaciated.
demagogia f. Demagogy.
demagógico, ca adj. Demagogic, demagogical.
demagogo m. Demagogue [U.S., demagog, demagogue].
demanda f. JUR. Petition, claim (petición). | Lawsuit, action (acción). || COM. Demand: *la ley de la oferta y la demanda*, the law of supply and demand; *este artículo tiene mucha demanda*, there is a large demand for this article. || Request, appeal (petición): *rechazar una demanda*, to turn down a request. || Quest, search (busca). || — *En demanda de*, asking for (pidiendo): *en demanda de ayuda*, asking for help; in search of, seeking (buscando). || JUR. *Estimar una demanda*, to allow a claim. | *Presentar una demanda contra uno*, to bring an action against s.o., to sue s.o., to take legal proceedings against s.o.

— OBSERV. The Spanish word *demanda* is used mostly as a legal term: "demand" is normally translated by *reclamación, exigencia*.

demandado, da adj. JUR. *Parte demandada*, defendant.
— M. y f. JUR. Defendant.
demandante adj. JUR. *Parte demandante*, plaintiff.
— M. y f. Plaintiff.
demandar v. tr. JUR. To sue, to file a suit against, to bring an action against: *demandar a una persona*, to sue s.o. || (P.us.). To request (pedir). | To desire (desear). || JUR. *Demandar a uno por daños y perjuicios*, to sue s.o. for damages.
demaquillador m. Makeup remover.

demarcación f. Demarcation, demarkation. || District (territorio). || *Línea de demarcación*, demarcation line, line of demarcation.
demarcador, ra adj. Demarcating, of demarcation.
demarcar v. tr. To demarcate, to delimit, to mark out. || MAR. To take a ship's bearings.
demás adj./pron. indef. Other, rest of the: *la demás gente*, the rest of the people, the other people; *los demás invitados*, the other guests, the rest of the guests; *poco importa lo que piensan los demás*, it matters little what the others *o* the rest [of them] think. || — *Lo demás*, the rest. || *Por lo demás*, otherwise, apart from that: *es díscolo, pero por lo demás muy buen chico*, he is mischievous, but otherwise a very good boy.
— Adv. Besides, moreover (además). || — *Por demás*, no good, in vain: *está por demás que le escribas*, it is no good your writing to him, you are writing to him in vain; too (con adjetivo), too much of a (con sustantivo) [demasiado]: *es por demás cobarde*, he is really too much of a coward. || *Y demás*, et cetera, etc.: *visitamos el Tate Gallery, la torre de Londres y demás*, we visited the Tate Gallery, the Tower of London, etc.

— OBSERV. In the plural the adjective is not always preceded by the article: *Andrés y demás alumnos*, Andrew and the other pupils.

demasía f. Surplus, excess (que sobra). || Outrage, disregard (atropello, abuso). || Insolence, audacity, lack of respect (falta de respeto). || — *Cometer demasías*, to commit outrages *o* excesses, to go too far. || *En* or *con demasía*, in excess, excessively.
demasiado, da adj. Too much, *sing.*, too many, *pl.*: *demasiada agua*, too much water; *demasiados libros*, too many books; *¿tienes bastantes revistas? — Tengo demasiadas*, have you got enough magazines? — I have got too many. || Excessive: *la demasiada confianza es perjudicial*, excessive familiarity is dangerous.
— Adv. Too: *es demasiado buena*, she is too good. || Too much: *pides demasiado*, you are asking too much. || Too much, excessively: *bebe demasiado*, he drinks excessively. || *Sería demasiado*, that would be too much.
demasiarse v. pr. To go too far.
demencia f. Madness, insanity, dementia. || MED. *Demencia precoz*, dementia praecox.
demente adj. Mad, insane, demented.
— M. y f. Lunatic, mental patient (de hospital).
demérito m. Demerit.
demiurgo m. FIL. Demiurge.
democracia f. Democracy.
demócrata adj. Democratic.
— M. y f. Democrat.
democratacristiano, na adj. Christian Democratic.
— M. y f. Christian Democrat.
democrático, ca adj. Democratic.
democratización f. Democratization.
democratizar v. tr. To democratize.
— V. pr. To democratize.
democristiano, na adj./s. V. DEMOCRATACRISTIANO.
Demócrito n. pr. m. Democritus.
demografía f. Demography.
demográfico, ca adj. Demographic. || Population: *explosión demográfica*, population explosion; *crecimiento demográfico*, population increase.
demógrafo m. Demographer.
demoledor, ra adj. Demolishing (herramienta). || FIG. Devastating: *crítica demoledora*, devastating criticism.
— M. y f. Housebreaker [U.S., wrecker] (de edificios).
demoler* v. tr. To demolish, to pull down. || FIG. To demolish (una organización, etc.).
demolición f. Demolition.
demoniaco, ca adj. Demoniac, demoniacal, demonic, possessed of the devil.
— M. y f. Demoniac (endemoniado).
demonio m. Devil, demon. || — FAM. *A demonios*, ghastly, horrible: *oler, saber a demonios*, to smell, to taste ghastly. | *¿Cómo demonios...?*, how the devil...? | *Como el demonio*, like hell. | *Darse a todos los demonios*, to fly off the handle. | *De mil demonios* or *de todos los demonios*, a hell of a: *una casa, un resfriado de mil demonios*, a hell of a house, a hell of a cold; devilish, hellish: *hacía un frío de todos los demonios*, it was hellish cold. | *¡Demonio!* or *¡demonios!*, well, I'll be blowed! (sorpresa), hell!, damn! (disgusto). || *¡Demonio de niño, estate quieto!*, keep still, you little devil! | *Ese demonio de hombre*, that devil of a man. || *Estar poseído por el demonio*, to be possessed of the devil. || FAM. *¡Ni qué demonios!*, like hell!, my foot!: *¡qué abogado ni qué demonios!*, like hell he's a lawyer!, a lawyer my foot! || *Ponerse como un demonio*, to go mad, to get mad, to fly off the handle. || FAM. *¡Qué demonios!* or *¡qué demonio!*, damn it!: *si nadie va a trabajar, yo tampoco, ¡qué demonios!*, if no one is going to work, then I'm not either, damn it! | *¿Qué demonios?* what the hell?: *¿qué demonios estás haciendo?*, what the hell are you doing? || *¡Que me lleve el demonio si...!*, I'll be hanged *o* blowed if...!, the devil take me if...!: *¡que me lleve el demonio si comprendo algo de esto!*, I'll be blowed if I can understand any of this; cross my heart and hope to die: *¡que me lleve el demonio si es mentira!*, it's true, cross my heart and hope to die. || *¿Quién demonios...?*, who the devil...? || *Ser el mismo demonio*, to be a real devil (un niño), to be a sly *o* crafty devil (muy hábil). || *Tener el demonio en el cuerpo*, to have the devil in one, to be full of devilment, to be possessed of the devil, to be full of the devil.
demontre m. FAM. Demon, devil. || FAM. *¡Qué demontre!*, V. DEMONIO.
demora f. Delay: *demora en la entrega de un pedido*, delay in the delivery of an order. || Wait: *¿qué demora tiene una conferencia telefónica con Manchester?*, how long is the wait for a call to Manchester? || *Sin demora*, without delay.
demorar v. tr. To delay, to put off (retrasar): *tuve que demorar el viaje*, I had to delay the journey. || To delay, to hold up: *no quiero demorarte más*, I don't want to delay you any longer. || To hold up: *el barco fue demorado por el mal tiempo*, the boat was held up by the bad weather.
— V. intr. To stay on, to linger on (detenerse).
— V. pr. To take time, to be a long time, to take a long time: *perdóname, me he demorado un poco*, forgive me, I've been rather a long time *o* I've taken rather a long time.
Demóstenes n. pr. m. Demosthenes.
demostrable adj. Demonstrable.
demostración f. Demonstration: *hacer una demostración de cómo funciona un aparato*, to give a demonstration of how a piece of equipment works. || Show, display, demonstration: *demostración de fuerza, de cariño*, show of strength, of affection. || Sign: *las lágrimas son una demostración de dolor*, tears are a sign of grief. || Display: *una demostración gimnástica*, a gymnastic display. || MAT. Proof. || Demonstration, proof (de una proposición, etc.). || MIL. Demonstration. || *Hacer la demostración de*, to demonstrate.
demostrador, ra adj. Demonstrating, who *o* which demonstrates.
— M. y f. Demonstrator.
demostrar* v. tr. To show, to prove: *lo mal que vive demuestra que no tiene mucho dinero*, the poor way in which he lives shows he hasn't much money. || To show: *demostrar su ignorancia en la materia*, to show one's ignorance on the subject. || To prove: *su respuesta demuestra su inteligencia*, his answer proves his intelligence. || To show: *demostrar interés*, to show interest; *el prestidigitador nos demostró varios trucos*, the conjurer showed us a few tricks. || To demonstrate, to show (hacer una demostración). || MAT. To prove. || To prove (una teoría, etc.).
demostrativo, va adj./s. m. GRAM. Demonstrative.
demótico, ca adj. Demotic.
demudación f. o **demudamiento** m. Paling (del color de la cara). || Change (de la expresión).
demudar v. tr. To turn pale (el color de la cara). || To change (la expresión). || *Tenía el rostro demudado por la cólera*, his face was distorted with anger.
— V. pr. To change (la expresión). || To pale (el color). || To be distorted (la cara).
denantes adv. FAM. Before.
denario, ria adv. Denary (decimal).
— M. Denarius (moneda).
dendrita f. MIN. y BIOL. Dendrite.
denegación f. Refusal, rejection (rechazo). || Denial (negación). || — JUR. *Denegación de demanda*, dismissal. | *Denegación de paternidad*, disowning of offspring.
denegar* v. tr. To refuse, to reject (rehusar). || To deny (negar). || JUR. To reject (un recurso). | To dismiss: *denegar una demanda a uno*, to dismiss s.o.'s claim.
dengoso, sa adj. Affected, finicky (melindroso).
dengue m. Affectation (melindre). || Kind of shawl (mantón). || MED. Dengue [fever] (enfermedad tropical). || *No me vengas con dengues*, don't act like a spoilt child, don't be silly, don't be so finicky.
denguear v. intr. To put on airs, to be affected.
denguero, ra adj. Affected.
denier m. TECN. Denier.
denigración f. Denigration, disparagement.
denigrador, ra o **denigrante** adj. Disparaging (insultante). || Denigrating (deshonroso).
— M. y f. Denigrator, disparager.
denigrar v. tr. To denigrate, to run down, to disparage. || To insult (injuriar).
denodadamente adj. Valiantly, bravely, boldly (valientemente). || Stoutly, with determination (esforzadamente).
denodado, da adj. Valiant, brave, bold, intrepid, courageous (valiente). || Determined, resolute: *un esfuerzo denodado*, a determined effort.
denominación f. Denomination, naming (acción). || Denomination, name (nombre). || *Denominación de origen*, "appellation d'origine" (de los vinos).
denominado, da adj. MAT. *Número denominado*, compound number.
denominador, ra adj. Denominative.
— M. MAT. Denominator: *el mínimo común denominador*, the least *o* the lowest common denominator.
denominar v. tr. To name, to denominate, to call.
denominativo, va adj. Denominative.
denostador, ra adj. Insulting.
denostar* v. tr. To insult.
denotar v. tr. To denote, to indicate, to reveal, to show: *su manera de hablar denota una baja cultura*, the way he speaks denotes a low level of education. || To mean (significar).

densidad f. Density. || Fís. Density. || Darkness, blackness (de la noche). || Thickness, denseness (de la niebla, de un bosque).
densificar v. tr. To densify. || To thicken (espesar).
densímetro m. Fís. Densimeter.
denso, sa adj. Fís. Dense. || Dense (población, multitud). || Dense, thick: *humo denso*, thick smoke; *bosque denso*, dense wood. || Fig. Black, dark: *noche densa*, dark night. | Dense: *discurso denso*, dense speech.
dentado, da adj. Toothed (que tiene dientes). || Cogged, toothed (rueda). || Serrated (cuchillo). || Bot. Dentate: *hoja dentada*, dentate leaf. || Heráld. Indented.
— M. Perforation: *el dentado de un sello*, the perforation of a stamp. || — F. *Amer.* Bite (dentellada).
dentadura f. Teeth, *pl.*, set of teeth: *tiene una dentadura muy bonita*, he has very nice teeth, he has a very nice set of teeth. || *Dentadura postiza*, false teeth, *pl.*, denture, dentures, *pl.*
dental adj. Dental: *prótesis dental*, dental prothesis. || *Crema dental*, toothpaste. || — Adj./s. f. Dental. || *Consonante dental*, dental consonant. || — M. Agr. Sole (del arado).
dentar* v. tr. To provide with teeth *o* cogs (una rueda). || To provide with teeth (una sierra). || To serrate (un cuchillo). || To perforate (un sello).
— V. intr. To teethe, to cut teeth (un niño).
dentario, ria adj. Dental.
dentelaria f. Bot. Plumbago, leadwort.
dentellada f. Snap of the jaws (movimiento). || Bite (mordisco). || Toothmark (señal). || — *A dentelladas*, with one's teeth. || *Dar dentelladas a algo*, to bite sth. || *Morder a dentelladas*, to bite.
dentellado, da adj. Heráld. Engrailed. || V. dentado.
dentellar v. intr. *Dentellaba de miedo*, his teeth were chattering with fear.
dentellear v. tr. To nibble, to nibble at (mordiscar).
dentellón m. Arq. Tooth (de la adaraja). | Dentil, denticle (dentículo).
dentera f. Setting on edge (en los dientes). || Fig. y fam. Envy (envidia). || *Dar dentera a uno*, to make s.o. green with envy (dar envidia), to set s.o.'s teeth on edge: *ese ruido me da dentera*, that noise sets my teeth on edge.
dentición f. Teething, cutting of the teeth, dentition (acción de dentar) || Set of teeth, dentition (de los niños). || Set of teeth (serie completa de dientes): *primera, segunda dentición*, first, second set of teeth.
denticulado, da adj. Arq. Denticulate, denticulated.
dentículo m. Arq. Dentil, denticle.
dentífrico, ca adj. Tooth. || *Pasta dentífrica*, toothpaste.
— M. Toothpaste, dentifrice (p.us.).
dentina f. Dentine [U.S., dentin] (de los dientes).
dentista m. Dentist: *ir al dentista*, to go to the dentist's.
dentón, ona adj./s. V. dentudo.
dentro adv. Inside: *está dentro*, he is inside. || Indoors, inside (en casa): *hace frío, vamos a jugar dentro*, it's cold, let's play indoors. || — *Ahí dentro*, in there (de una casa), indoors, inside (de la casa). || *De* or *desde dentro*, from inside. || *Dentro de*, in, inside, within (p.us.): *dentro de la casa*, in the house; in, inside: *meter algo dentro de una caja*, to put sth. in a box; in, in...'s time (tiempo fijo): *venga a verme dentro de un día, dos semanas*, come and see me in a day *o* in a day's time, in two weeks *o* in two weeks' time. || *Dentro de lo posible*, V. posible. || *Dentro de poco*, soon, shorthy, within a short time. || *Está* or *entra dentro de lo posible*, it is possible. || *Ir hacia dentro* or *para dentro*, to go indoors *o* inside (en casa). || *Llevo el patriotismo muy dentro*, I feel patriotism deep down *o* deep inside. || *Meter hacia dentro*, to push in (algo que sobresale), to pull in: *meter el estómago hacia dentro*, to pull one's stomach in. || *Por dentro*, inside, on the inside (en el interior), inwardly, inside: *sentirse muy triste por dentro*, to feel very sad inwardly. || *Tener los pies hacia dentro*, to be pigeon-toed.
dentudo, da adj. Toothy, goofy.
— M. y f. Toothy *o* goofy person.
denudación f. Geol. Denudation.
denudar v. tr. Geol. To denude, to lay bare.
denuedo m. Bravery, courage.
denuesto m. Insult.
denuncia f. Reporting (acción de denunciar un delito). || Report (documento). || Denunciation (delación). || Accusation: *denuncia falsa*, false accusation. || Denunciation, notice of termination (de un tratado). || Denunciation, censure (crítica severa). || Jur. *Presentar una denuncia contra alguien*, to lodge a complaint against s.o., to bring an action against s.o.
denunciable adj. Which can be reported (delito).
denunciación f. V. denuncia.
denunciador, ra o **denunciante** adj. Who reports [a crime, etc.]. || Denunciative.
— M. y f. Informer. || Person who reports: *el denunciador del robo*, the person who reported the theft.
denunciar v. tr. To report: *denunciar un robo a la policía*, to report a theft to the police. || To denounce: *el periódico denunció la invasión de anglicismos*, the newspaper denounced the invasion of Anglicisms. || To expose (exponer). || To indicate, to betray (indicar). || To denounce, to give notice of the termination of (un tratado). || To denounce (delatar). || *Denunciar una mina*, to apply for a mining concession, to register a claim to a mine.
denunciatorio, ria adj. Who reports [a crime]. || Denouncing (que delata o condena).
deontología f. Deontology.
deontológico, ca adj. Deontological.
deparar v. tr. To give, to afford: *este libro me deparó una satisfacción enorme*, this book afforded me a great deal of pleasure. || To give, to provide with: *tu visita me ha deparado la oportunidad de explicarte una cosa*, your visit has provided me with the opportunity of explaining sth. to you. || To cause: *su enfermedad me deparó un gran disgusto*, his illness caused me great grief. || To bring: *veamos lo que nos depara el año nuevo*, let us see what the new year brings. || To provide (solución). || — *¡Dios te la depare buena!*, and the best of luck to you!, the best of British luck [to you]! || *Entré en el primer cine que me deparó la suerte*, I went into the first cinema I chanced upon.
departamental adj. Departmental.
departamento m. Province, district, department, administrative district (división territorial). || Department, section (división administrativa, de un almacén). || Compartment (de un tren). || Compartment, section (de una caja, etc.),
— Observ. Certain Latin American countries are divided into *departamentos* (Bolivia, Colombia, Perú, Uruguay, etc.).
departir v. intr. To talk, to converse.
depauperación f. Impoverishment. || Med. Weakening (debilitación).
depauperar v. tr. To impoverish (empobrecer). || Med. To weaken (debilitar).
dependencia f. Dependence, dependance, reliance: *la dependencia de una persona con respecto a otra*, the dependence of one person on another. || Dependency (país). || Department, section (sección de una oficina, etc.). || Branch [office] (sucursal). || — Pl. Outbuildings: *las dependencias de un castillo*, the outbuildings of a castle. || — *Dependencia asistencial*, small clinic [giving free medical aid]. || *Estar bajo la dependencia de*, to be dependent on.
depender v. intr. To depend. || — *Depender de*, to depend on: *lo que gasto depende de lo que gano*, what I spend depends on what I earn; to be under (estar bajo la autoridad de uno): *veinte empleados dependen de él*, twenty employees are under him; to be dependent on: *todavía el chico depende de sus padres*, the boy is still dependent on his parents; to turn on, to depend on: *todo depende de su contestación*, everything turns on his answer. || *Depende de ti*, it rests with you, it is up to you. || *En lo que de mí* [*de nosotros*, etc.] *depende*, as far as I [we, etc.] am concerned. || *Eso depende*, it depends.
dependienta f. Shop assistant, sales assistant, salesgirl, saleslady, saleswoman.
dependiente adj. Dependent (*de*, on).
— M. Shop assistant, salesman [U.S., clerk].
depilación f. Depilation.
depilar v. tr. To depilate.
— V. pr. To pluck (las cejas): *las mujeres se depilan las cejas*, women pluck their eyebrows. || To depilate (las piernas, etc.).
depilatorio, ria adj./s. m. Depilatory.
deplorable adj. Deplorable, lamentable, regrettable.
deplorar v. tr. To deplore, to regret deeply: *deploramos su muerte*, we regret his death deeply. || To deplore, to lament (lamentar).
deponente adj. Jur. Testifying, giving evidence. || Gram. Deponent (verbo).
— M. y f. Jur. Deponent, witness. || — M. Gram. Deponent, deponent verb.
deponer* v. tr. To lay down: *deponer las armas*, to lay down one's arms. || To remove from office: *deponer a un cónsul de su cargo*, to remove a consul from office. || To depose (al rey). || Jur. To give evidence of, to testify: *deponer algo ante el tribunal*, to give evidence of sth. before the court. || Fig. To banish: *deponer el temor*, to banish fear.
— V. intr. Jur. To give evidence. || To defecate (defecar). || *Amer.* To vomit.
deportación f. Deportation.
deportado, da adj. Deported.
— M. y f. Deported person, deportee.
deportar v. tr. To deport.
deporte m. Sport: *deportes de invierno*, winter sports; *campo de deportes*, sports ground; *hacer deporte*, to practise sport. || — *Deporte de remo*, rowing. || *Deporte de vela*, yachting (con yate, en los Juegos Olímpicos), sailing (como recreo).
deportismo m. Sport, practice of sport (práctica). || Enthusiasm for sport (afición).
deportista adj. Keen on sport, sporty.
— M. Sportsman (que practica deporte). || Sports fan (aficionado). || — F. Sportswoman (que practica deporte). || Sports fan (aficionada).
deportividad f. o **deportivismo** m. Sportsmanship.
deportivo, va adj. Sports (relativo a los deportes): *periódico deportivo*, sports paper; *club deportivo*, sports club; *coche deportivo*, sports car; *campo deportivo*, sports ground; *chaqueta deportiva*, sports jacket. || Sporty, sporting (aficionado a los deportes).

DEPORTES, m. — SPORTS

I. Generalidades, f. — General terms.

monitor *m.*	instructor
manager *m.*	manager
guía *m.*	guide
entrenador *m.*	trainer
árbitro *m.*	referee; umpire (en tenis, béisbol)
juez (*m.*) de línea	linesman; touch judge (rugby)
competidor, ra	contestant, competitor
forma *f.*	form
aficionado, da	enthusiast, fan (entusiasta), amateur (que juega por afición)
profesional *m.* y *f.*	professional
jugador, ra	player
favorito *m.*	favourite [U.S., favorite]
outsider *m.*	outsider
campeonato *m.*	championship
campeón, ona	champion
récord *m.*, plusmarca *f.*	record
recordman *m.*, plusmarquista *m.* y *f.*	record holder
as *m.*	ace
Juegos (*m. pl.*) Olímpicos, Olimpiada *f.*	Olympic Games *pl.*, Olympics *pl.*
Olimpiada (*f.*) de invierno	Winter Olympics *pl.*
estadio *m.*	stadium
pista *f.*	track
ring *m.*, cuadrilátero *m.*	ring
terreno *m.*, campo *m.* [*Amer.*, cancha *f.*]	ground; field, pitch (de fútbol, rugby)
campo *m.* [*Amer.*, cancha *f.*]	court (de tenis)
equipo *m.*	team, side

II. Atletismo, m. — Athletics.

carrera *f.*	race
carrera (*f.*) de medio fondo	middle-distance race
corredor (*m.*) de fondo	long-distance runner
sprint *m.*	sprint [U.S., dash]
los 400 metros vallas	the 400 metre hurdles
maratón *m.*	marathon
decatlón *m.*	decathlon
carrera (*f.*) a campo traviesa, cross-country	cross-country race
salto *m.*	jump (uno), jumping (actividad)
salto (*m.*) de altura	high jump
salto (*m.*) de longitud	long jump [U.S., broad jump]
triple salto *m.*	triple jump, hop step and jump
salto (*m.*) con pértiga [*Amer.*, salto con garrocha]	pole vault
lanzamiento *m.*	throw (uno), throwing (actividad)
lanzamiento (*m.*) de peso	putting the shot, shot put
lanzamiento (*m.*) de disco, de martillo, de jabalina	throwing the discus, the hammer, the javelin
marcha *f.*	walk

III. Deportes (m.) individuales. — Individual sports.

gimnasia *f.*	gymnastics
aparatos (*m. pl.*) de gimnasia	gymnastic apparatus *sing.*
barra (*f.*) fija	horizontal bar
(barras) paralelas *f. pl.*	parallel bars
anillas *f. pl.*	rings
trapecio *m.*	trapeze
cuerda (*f.*) de nudos	knotted rope
espalderas *f. pl.*	wall bars
potro (*m.*) con arzón	side *o* pommelled horse
halterofilia *f.*	weight-lifting
pesas *f. pl.*, halteras *f. pl.*	weights
boxeo *m.*	boxing
peso (*m.*) pesado	heavyweight
peso (*m.*) medio	middleweight
peso (*m.*) gallo	bantamweight
peso (*m.*) mosca	flyweight
lucha (*f.*) grecorromana	Graeco-Roman wrestling
llave *f.*	hold, lock
judo *m.*	judo
esgrima *f.*	fencing
deportes (*m. pl.*) de invierno	winter sports
esquí *m.*	skiing (actividad), ski (plancha)
carrera (*f.*) de descenso	downhill race
slalom *m.*, habilidad *f.*	slalom
concurso (*m.*) de saltos	ski jumping competition
trampolín *m.*	ski jump
patinaje (*m.*) sobre hielo	ice skating
patinaje (*m.*) artístico	figure skating
patinaje (*m.*) sobre ruedas	roller skating
bobsleigh *m.*	bobsleigh, bobsled
hockey (*m.*) sobre hielo	ice hockey

IV. Juegos (m.) y competiciones, f. — Games and competitions.

fútbol *m.*	football
marcar un gol	to score a goal
portero *m.*	goalkeeper
balón (*m.*) de fútbol	football
saque (*m.*) de centro, de puerta	centre, goal kick
saque (*m.*) de banda	throw in
rugby *m.*	rugby
transformar un ensayo	to convert a try
saque (*m.*) de banda	line-out
criquet, *m*, cricquet *m*, cricket *m.*	cricket
béisbol *m.*	baseball
bateador *m.*	batsman (criquet), batter (béisbol)
baloncesto *m.* [*Amer.*, basket-ball *m.*]	basketball
balonvolea *m.* [*Amer.*, voleibol *m.*]	volleyball
balonmano *m.* [*Amer.*, hand ball *m*]	handball
hockey *m.*	hockey
golf *m.*	golf
tenis *m.*	tennis
simple (*m.*) caballeros	men's singles
en los dobles mixtos	in the mixed doubles

V. Deportes (m.) acuáticos. — Water sports.

piscina *f.* [*Amer.*, pileta *f.*]	swimming pool
natación *f.*	swimming
estilo (*m.*) libre	freestyle
relevo (*m.*) estilos	medley relay
crawl *m.*	crawl
braza *f.*	breaststroke
estilo (*m.*) espalda	backstroke
estilo (*m.*) mariposa	butterfly [stroke]
concurso (*m.*) de saltos	diving competition
water-polo *m.*, polo (*m.*) acuático	water polo
esquí (*m.*) náutico	water skiing
el remo *m.*	rowing (deporte)
kayac *m.*	kayak
canca *f.*	canoe
fuera borda *m.*	outboard boat
regata *f.*	boat race (carrera)
deporte (*m.*) de vela	sailing
yate *m.*	yacht

VI. Bicicleta, f., moto, f. auto, m. — Bicycle, motorcycle, car.

velódromo *m.*	velodrome, cycling stadium
carrera (*f.*) en carretera	road race
carrera (*f.*) de velocidad	race
carrera (*f.*) de persecución	chase
motocicleta *f.*, moto *f.*	motorcycle, motorbike
coche (*m.*) de carreras	racing car
piloto (*m.*) de carreras	racing driver
rallye *m.*	rally

VII. Hipismo, m. — Riding and horse racing.

equitación *f.*	riding
hipódromo *m.*	racecourse, racetrack
jockey *m.*; jinete *m.*	jockey; rider
concurso (*m.*) de saltos	show jumping competition
carrera (*f.*) de obstáculos	steeplechase
valla *f.*	fence
polo *m.*	polo
trotón *m.*	trotter

deposición f. Deposition, deposal (de un rey). ‖ Removal from office, deposition: *la deposición del cónsul*, the removal of the consul from office. ‖ JUR. Testimony, evidence, deposition. ‖ Excretion, defecation (evacuación del vientre).

depositador, ra m. y f. Depositor.

depositante adj. Who deposits.
— M. y f. Depositor.

depositar v. tr. To deposit: *depositar fondos en el banco*, to deposit money in the bank; *depositó los diamantes en la caja de caudales*, he deposited the diamonds in the safe. ‖ To place, to deposit: *depositó los libros en el suelo*, he placed the books on the floor. ‖ FIG. To place: *la madre tiene depositada en él toda su esperanza*, his mother has placed all her hope in him. ‖ To deposit, to leave: *el vino deposita heces*, wine leaves a sediment. ‖ To deposit, to store: *depositar las mercancías en un almacén*, to store goods in a warehouse. ‖ *Depositar algo en manos de uno*, to entrust s.o. with sth., to entrust sth. to s.o.
— V. pr. To settle (líquido, polvo, etc.).

depositaría f. Depository, depositary.

depositario, ria m. y f. Depositary, depository, trustee (de dinero, etc.). ‖ Repository (de secreto, confianza, etc.). ‖ *Hacer de uno depositario de un secreto*, to confide in s.o., to make s.o. the repository of a secret. ‖ — M. Cashier (cajero). ‖ Treasurer (tesorero).

depósito m. Deposit (de una suma). ‖ Store, depot, warehouse (almacén). ‖ Dump, depot (de municiones). ‖ Tank: *depósito de gasolina*, petrol tank. ‖ Depot, yard: *depósito de madera, de carbón*, timber, coal yard.

|| Tip, dump (de basuras). || Scale (en una caldera, conducto, etc.). || Deposit, sediment (sedimento). || — *Casco en depósito*, returnable bottle. || *Depósito de aceite combustible*, fuel tank. || *Depósito de agua*, water tank, cistern. || *Depósito de cadáveres*, morgue, mortuary. || *Depósito de decantación*, sedimentation basin. || *Depósito de equipajes*, left-luggage office [U.S., checkroom]. || *Depósito de locomotoras*, engine shed [U.S., roundhouse]. || *Depósito de objetos perdidos*, lost-property office. || *En depósito*, in bond: *mercancías en depósito*, goods in bond.

depravación f. Depravity, depravation.

depravado, da adj. Depraved.
— M. y f. Depraved person, degenerate.

depravador, ra adj. Depraving, which depraves.
— M. y f. Depraver.

depravar v. tr. To deprave.
— V. pr. To become depraved.

deprecación f. Prayer, deprecation.

deprecar v. tr. To beg, to implore.

deprecatorio, ria adj. Deprecatory, imploring.

depreciación f. Depreciation.

depreciador, ra adj. Depreciating, depreciatory.
— M. y f. Depreciator.

depreciar v. tr. To depreciate.
— V. pr. To depreciate.

depredación f. Pillaging, depredation (saqueo).

depredador, ra adj. Depredatory.
— M. y f. Pillager, depredator.

depredar v. tr. To pillage, to depredate.

depresión f. Depression, hollow (concavidad). || Depression (del ánimo). || Depression, slump (económica). || — *Depresión atmosférica*, atmospheric depression. || *Depresión nerviosa*, nervous breakdown.

depresivo, va adj. Depressing (deprimente). || MED. Depressive.

depresor, ra adj. Depressing.
— M. MED. Depressor (en general). | Tongue depressor (para la lengua). || ANAT. Depressor (músculo).

deprimente adj. Depressing.

deprimir v. tr. To depress. || FIG. To depress (quitar los ánimos). || *Frente deprimida*, receding forehead.
— V. pr. To get depressed.

deprisa adv. V. PRISA (DE).

de profundis m. inv. De profundis.

depuesto, ta p. p. V. DEPONER.

depuración f. Purification, depuration (del agua). || Cleansing (de la sangre). || FIG. Purge, purging.

depurador, ra adj. Purifying: *planta* or *estación depuradora*, purifying plant.
— M. Depurative (sustancia). || Purifier (aparato).

depurar v. tr. To purify, to depurate: *depurar el agua*, to purify the water. || To cleanse (la sangre). || FIG. To purify (refinar). | To purge (en política). || FIG. *Estilo depurado*, pure *o* purified style.

depurativo, va adj./s. m. Depurative.

depuratorio, ria adj. Depurative, purifying, cleansing.

deque adv. FAM. When, as soon as (en cuanto).

derecha f. Right hand (mano). || Right (lado): *aquél de la derecha*, that one on the right. || — *A la derecha*, on the right, on the right-hand side. || *La derecha*, the right wing, the right (en política). || *No hacer nada a derechas*, not to do anything right, to do nothing right. || *Torcer a la derecha*, to turn right, to turn to the right.

derechamente adv. Straight, directly: *fue derechamente hacia él*, he went straight to him; *ir derechamente al asunto*, to go straight to the point. || FIG. Properly: *obrar derechamente*, to act properly.

derechazo m. TAUR. "Muleta" pass with the right hand. || Right (boxeo).

derechismo m. Rightist policy.

derechista adj. Rightist, right-wing (política).
— M. y f. Rightist, right-winger (en política).

derecho m. JUR. Law: *derecho administrativo, canónico, civil, consuetudinario, internacional, marítimo, mercantil, penal, político*, administrative, canon, civil, consuetudinary *o* customary [en Inglaterra, common], international, maritime, commercial, criminal, constitutional law; *estudiar derecho*, to read *o* to study law. || Right, claim: *su derecho al trono*, his right to the throne. || Right: *los derechos civiles*, civil rights; *los derechos de una persona*, a person's rights. || Right side: *el derecho de una tela, de un calcetín*, the right side of a material, of a sock. || — Pl. Fees (de un notario, etc.). || Duties, taxes (impuestos). || — *Conforme al derecho*, in accordance with the law. || *Con derecho a*, with the right to. || *Con derecho o sin derecho*, rightly or wrongly. || *¿Con qué derecho?*, what right?: *¿con qué derecho has hecho eso?*, what right did you have to do that? || *Corresponder de derecho a uno*, to be s.o.'s right: *le corresponde de derecho pedirlo*, it is his right to ask for it. || *Dar derecho*, to entitle, to give the right to: *billete que da derecho [a uno] a entrar*, ticket which gives you the right to go in *o* which entitles you to go in. || *De derecho*, by right: *te corresponde de derecho*, it is yours by right. || *De pleno derecho*, full: *miembro de pleno derecho*, full member. || *Derecho al voto*, the right to vote, the vote. || *Derecho del más fuerte*, the rule of the survival of the fittest. || *Derecho de paso*, right of way. || *Derecho divino*, divine right. || *Derecho habiente*, rightful claimant. || *Derechos aduaneros* or *arancelarios* or *de aduana*, customs duties. || *Derechos de autor*, royalties. || *Derechos de entrada*, import duties. || *Derechos del Hombre* or *Derechos Humanos*, Rights of Man: *declaración de los Derechos del Hombre*, Declaration of the Rights of Man. || *Derechos de matrícula*, enrolment *o* registration fees. || *Derechos de peaje*, toll duties. || *Derechos de puerto*, harbour dues [U.S., harbor dues]. || *Derecho sucesorio*, death duty, death tax. || *Estar en su derecho*, to be within one's rights, to be in the right. || *Hacer algo con todo* or *con pleno derecho*, to have every right to do sth., to be within one's rights to do sth. || *No hay derecho*, it's not fair. || *Por derecho propio*, in one's own right. || *Reservado el derecho de admisión*, the management reserves the right to refuse admission. || *Reservados todos los derechos*, copyright, all rights reserved. || *Según derecho*, in accordance with the law (ley), by rights (con razón). || *Tener derecho*, to have the right, to be entitled: *cada uno de los niños tiene derecho a una porción de pastel*, each of the children is entitled to a piece of cake *o* has the right to a piece of cake; to be entitled, to have a *o* the right: *tengo derecho a quejarme*, I have a right *o* the right to complain, I am entitled to complain. || *Usar de su derecho*, to exercise one's right.

derecho adv. Straight: *andar derecho*, to walk straight; *fue derecho a su casa*, he went straight home. || *Siga* or *vaya (todo) derecho*, carry *o* go straight on.

derecho, cha adj. Right: *el brazo derecho*, the right arm. || Straight, upright, erect: *aunque es viejo, todavía va muy derecho*, although he is old, he is still very upright; *ponerse derecho*, to stand up straight. || Upright: *un poste derecho*, an upright pole. || — *Derecho como una vela*, as straight as a die. || *Es un hombre hecho y derecho*, he is a man in every sense of the word, he is a real man.

derechohabiente m. Rightful claimant.

derechura f. Straightness. || Uprightness (verticalmente). || *En derechura*, straight.

deriva f. MAR. Drift, leeway. || — *A la deriva*, drifting, adrift. || MAR. y FIG. *Ir a la deriva*, to drift. || AVIAC. *Plano de deriva*, rudder.

derivable adj. Derivable.

derivación f. Derivation (de una palabra). || Origin (origen). || Change, deviation (cambio). || Diversion (de un canal, etc.). || MAT. Derivation (de una derivada). || ELECTR. Shunt.

derivado, da adj. Derived, derivative (palabra).
— M. Derivative (palabra). || QUÍM. Derivative, by-product. || — F. MAT. Derivative [of a function].

derivar v. intr. To incline, to drift, to derive, to tend: *desde pequeño su interés derivó hacia la pintura*, from a child his interest inclined towards painting. || To stem, to spring, to come, to arise: *de ahí deriva su amistad*, that is where their friendship stems from. || MAR. To drift. || To be derived, to derive: "*librero*" *deriva de* "*libro*", "librero" is derived from "libro".
— V. tr. To direct, to divert: *no pude derivar la conversación hacia otro asunto más agradable*, I couldn't divert the conversation to a pleasanter subject. || To divert, to tap: *derivar de un río un canal de riego*, to tap a river for an irrigation channel, to divert an irrigation channel from a river. || To derive: *derivar una palabra del griego*, to derive a word from the Greek. || MAT. To calculate (función derivada). || ELECTR. To shunt.
— V. pr. To change, to drift (*hacia*, to) [conversación, etc.]. || To come out of (salir). || To be derived: *esta palabra se deriva del griego*, this word is derived from the Greek. || To result, to stem, to arise (*de*, from) [resultar].

derivativo, va adj./m. Derivative.

dermatitis f. inv. MED. Dermatitis.

dermatoesqueleto m. Exoskeleton, dermoskeleton.

dermatología f. MED. Dermatology.

dermatólogo m. MED. Dermatologist.

dermatosis f. inv. MED. Dermatosis.

dérmico, ca adj. ANAT. Dermal, dermic, skin.

dermis f. inv. ANAT. Dermis, derm, cutis.

dermitis f. inv. MED. Dermatitis.

dermorreacción f. Skin test.

derogable adj. Repealable, which can be annulled.

derogación f. JUR. Repeal, repealing, derogation, abolition (de una ley).

derogar v. tr. JUR. To repeal, to derogate, to annul, to abolish (ley). || To rescind, to cancel (contrato, etc.).

derogatorio, ria adj. JUR. Abolishing, annulling, repealing.

derrama f. Assessment, distribution, apportionment, sharing out (de impuestos). || Special tax (contribución).

derramadero m. Spillway (de agua). || Tip, rubbish dump (de residuos).

derramamiento m. Spilling (involuntario). || Overflowing (rebosamiento). || Pouring out (de líquido). || Scattering (de una familia, de un pueblo). || Flowing (chorreo). || Spreading, spread (de una noticia). || — *Derramamiento de sangre*, bloodshed, spilling of blood. || *Revolución sin derramamiento de sangre*, bloodless revolution. || *Sin derramamiento de sangre*, without bloodshed, without a drop of blood being spilt (función adverbial).

derramar v. tr. To spill (involuntariamente): *derramar un vaso de agua*, to spill a glass of water. || To pour, to pour out: *derramar arena al* or *en* or *por el suelo*, to

pour sand on *o* over the floor. || FIG. To spread: *derramar una noticia*, to spread a piece of news. | To overflow with: *derramar ternura*, to overflow with tenderness. || To share out, to distribute (los impuestos). || — *Derramar lágrimas*, to shed tears. || *Derramar sangre*, to shed blood, to spill blood.
— V. pr. To spill (agua, etc.). || To pour out, to spill out (arena, etc.). || To scatter, to spread (esparcirse). || To spread (una noticia). || To be shed, to be spilt (sangre). || To overflow (rebosar).

derrame m. Spilling (involuntario). || Pouring out (voluntario). || Shedding, spilling (de sangre). || Leakage, waste (pérdida). || Overflow (rebosamiento). || MED. Discharge (externo). | Extravasation, effusion (interno). || Fork, forking (de un valle). || ARQ. Splay (de puertas y ventanas). || Slope, incline (declive). || Spreading, scattering (esparcimiento). || MED. *Derrame sinovial*, water on the knee.

derramo m. ARQ. Splay (derrame).

derrapar v. intr. AUT. To skid (patinar).
— OBSERV. This word is a Gallicism.

derredor m. Surroundings, *pl.*, surrounding part (que rodea). || *Al* or *en derredor*, V. ALREDEDOR.

derrelicción f. Dereliction (abandono).

derrelicto, ta adj./s.m. Derelict.

derrengadura f. Exhaustion (cansancio). || Sprained back (del espinazo).

derrengar v. tr. To sprain the back of (lastimar el espinazo). || To twist (torcer). || FIG. y FAM. To exhaust, to wear out, to shatter (cansar): *estoy derrengado*, I'm shattered, I'm worn out.
— V. pr. To sprain one's back. || FIG. y FAM. To wear o.s. out, to knock o.s. out, to exhaust o.s. (cansarse).

derretido, da adj. Melted (hielo, nieve, mantequilla, etc.). || Melted, molten: *sebo derretido*, melted tallow; *plomo derretido*, molten lead. || FIG. Madly in love, crazy: *está derretido por ella*, he is madly in love with her, he is crazy about her.

derretimiento m. Melting, thawing (de nieve). || Melting (de hielo, mantequilla, metal, etc.). || FIG. Squandering, wasting (de una fortuna). | Passionate love (amor).

derretir* v. tr. To melt (manteca, sebo etc.). || To thaw, to melt (hielo, nieve). || To melt down (metales). || FIG. To waste, to squander (derrochar). | To exasperate (exasperar).
— V. pr. To melt (manteca, sebo, etc.): *la mantequilla se derrite con el calor*, butter melts with the heat. || To melt, to become molten (metales). || To thaw, to melt (hielo, nieve). || FIG. To be crazy (*por*, about) [estar enamorado]. | To fall madly in love (*por*, with) [enamorarse]. | To burn (*de*, with) [de amor, de impaciencia]. | To fret, to worry, to be worried stiff (inquietarse).

derribador m. Feller (que derriba). || FIG. Overthrower.

derribar v. tr. To knock down, to pull down, to demolish: *derribar una muralla*, to knock down a wall. || To batter down (una puerta). || To knock over, to upset (una silla). || To knock down: *el conductor derribó a un transeúnte*, the driver knocked a pedestrian down. || To floor, to throw (en la lucha). || To throw: *el caballo derribó al jinete*, the horse threw its jockey. || To blow down (el viento). || To shoot down, to bring down: *derribar un avión*, to shoot a plane down. || To bring down, to knock down (al perseguir a alguien): *derribó al criminal*, he brought the criminal down. || FIG. To overthrow, to bring down (gobierno). | To remove *o* to oust from office, to topple (a un ministro, etc.). | To obtain the dismissal of (a un empleado).
— V. pr. To fall down, to throw o.s. to the ground (tirarse al suelo). || To fall down (caer).

derribo m. Demolition, pulling down, knocking down (demolición). || Demolition site (lugar). || — Pl. Rubble, *sing.* (materiales): *construir con derribos*, to build with rubble. || *Materiales de derribo*, rubble, *sing.*

derrocamiento m. Hurling down. || Demolition (de un edificio). || FIG. Overthrow (de un rey, de un gobierno). | Removal from office, toppling (de un ministro, etc.).

derrocar v. tr. To hurl down (despeñar). || FIG. To knock down, to pull down, to demolish (un edificio). | To overthrow, to bring down: *derrocar la monarquía, el gobierno*, to overthrow the king, the government. | To remove *o* to oust from office, to topple (a un ministro, etc.).

derrochador, ra adj. Spendthrift, wasteful, squandering.
— M. y f. Spendthrift, wasteful person, squanderer.

derrochar v. tr. To squander, to waste: *derrochar su fortuna*, to squander one's fortune. || FIG. To be brimming with *o* full of (salud, energía, simpatía).

derroche m. Waste, squandering (despilfarro). || FIG. Profusion, abundance: *un derroche de luces*, a profusion of lights. | Burst: *un derroche de energía*, a burst of energy. || *Hacer un derroche de energía en*, to put a lot of energy into (hacer un gran esfuerzo), to waste energy in (despilfarrar).

derrochón, ona adj./s. V. DERROCHADOR.

derrota f. Defeat: *su derrota en las elecciones fue un golpe duro para el partido*, his defeat in the elections was a hard blow to the party; *la derrota del equipo nacional*, the defeat of the national team. || Failure, setback: *las derrotas en la vida*, life's setbacks. || MIL. Defeat, rout: *sufrir una derrota*, to suffer a defeat. | Débâcle, debacle (en todos los frentes). || Path (camino). || MAR. Course (rumbo).

derrotado, da adj. Defeated. || FIG. Ragged, in tatters (andrajoso). | Shabby (persona, muebles).

derrotar v. tr. To defeat: *en las elecciones el candidato de la oposición derrotó al del gobierno*, the opposition candidate defeated the government candidate in the elections. || To beat, to defeat: *el equipo nacional derrotó a su oponente por 2 a 1*, the national team beat their opponents 2-1. || MIL. To defeat. | To rout, to put to flight (hacer huir). || TAUR. To butt, to gore: *toro que derrota por la izquierda*, bull which butts to the left. || To squander (su fortuna). || To ruin (salud).
— V. pr. MAR. To drift off course.

derrote m. TAUR. Butt (con los cuernos).

derrotero m. MAR. Course (rumbo). | Book of sailing directions, pilot book (libro). || FIG. Course, plan of action (para llegar a un fin).

derrotismo m. Defeatism.

derrotista adj./s. Defeatist.

derrubiar v. tr. To erode, to undermine, to wash away (las aguas corrientes): *el agua derrubia las orillas*, water washes away the banks.

derrubio m. Erosion, undermining, washing away. || Alluvium (tierra).

derruido, da adj. In ruins (ruinoso).

derruir* v. tr. To knock down, to pull down, to demolish (derribar).

derrumbadero m. Precipice, cliff (despeñadero). || FIG. Pitfall, hazard, danger.

derrumbamiento m. Collapse, falling down (desplome). || Demolition, knocking down (demolición). || Caving-in, falling in (del techo). || Headlong fall (caída). || FIG. Overthrow (derrocamiento). | Collapse, fall: *el derrumbamiento del Imperio Romano*, the collapse of the Roman Empire. | Collapse, sharp fall (de precios). || MIN. Cave-in (en la mina). || *Derrumbamiento de tierra*, landslide.

derrumbar v. tr. To throw down, to hurl down (despeñar). || To knock down, to pull down, to demolish: *derrumbar una casa*, to pull a house down. || To knock over (volcar).
— V. pr. To collapse, to fall down: *la casa se derrumbó*, the house collapsed. || To fall in, to cave in (techo). || FIG. To collapse. | To flop, to fall, to collapse (en un asiento). || FIG. *Se derrumbaron todas mis esperanzas*, all my hopes were shattered.

derrumbe m. V. DERRUMBADERO, DERRUMBAMIENTO.

derrumbo m. Precipice.

derviche m. Dervish.

desabastecer v. tr. To leave short of supplies, to deprive of supplies. || *Desabastecido de carbón*, short of *o* out of coal.

desabastecimiento m. Shortage.

desabollar v. tr. To smooth out, to remove the dents from: *desabollar una cacerola*, to remove the dents from a pan.

desabonarse v. pr. To withdraw one's subscription.

desabono m. Withdrawal of subscription. || Discredit (descrédito).

desaborido, da adj. Insipid, tasteless. || FIG. y FAM. Dull, wet: *una chica desaborida*, a dull girl.
— M. y f. Dull *o* wet person.
— OBSERV. Often pronounced *esaborío* in Andalusia.

desabotonar v. tr. To unbutton, to undo (ropa).
— V. intr. To open out, to blossom [out], to bloom (las flores).
— V. pr. To unbutton one's clothes (desabrocharse). || To come undone (una prenda).

desabridamente adv. Insipidly. || Gruffly: *contestar desabridamente*, to reply gruffly.

desabrido, da adj. Bad tasting (de mal sabor). || Insipid, tasteless (soso). || Unpleasant (tiempo). || Surly: *tiene un carácter desabrido*, he has a surly character. || Abrupt (estilo). || Harsh, sharp, gruff (tono, frase). || Bitter (discusión).

desabrigado, da adj. Uncovered (sin abrigo). || FIG. Unprotected, defenceless (sin amparo). || Open, exposed to the wind (expuesto a los vientos). || *Vas muy desabrigado con el frío que hace*, you're not wrapped up well enough for this cold weather.

desabrigar v. tr. To uncover (descubrir). || To take off some of the clothes of: *desabrigar a un niño*, to take off some of a child's clothes. || To leave without shelter (dejar sin refugio).
— V. pr. To take some *o* any clothes off, to take one's warm clothing off: *no debe uno desabrigarse cuando está sudando*, you should not take any clothes off when you are sweating. || To uncover o.s. || To throw off one's bedcovers (en la cama).

desabrigo m. Uncovering (acción). || Lack of covering *o* shelter, exposure (falta de protección). || FIG. Desertion, destitution, abandonment (abandono).

desabrimiento m. Unpleasant taste (sabor desagradable). || Insipidness, insipidity, tastelessness (insipidez). || Unpleasantness (tiempo). || Surliness (del carácter, etc.). || Abruptness (del estilo). || Harshness, sharpness, gruffness (del tono, etc.). || Bitterness (de discusión). || Grief (pena). || *Contestar con desabrimiento*, to reply gruffly.

desabrir v. tr. To give an unpleasant taste to (dar mal sabor). || To make insipid *o* tasteless, to take the taste away from. || FIG. To distress (apenar). | To annoy (enfadar).
— V. pr. FIG. To be annoyed (enfadarse).

desabrochar v. tr. To undo, to unfasten: *desabrochar la camisa a un niño*, to undo a child's shirt. || To unfasten *o* to undo the clothes of: *desabrochó al niño*, she undid the child's clothes. || FIG. To open (abrir).
— V. pr. To undo *o* to unfasten one's clothes: *los niños no saben desabrocharse*, children don't know how to undo their clothes. || To come undone, to come unfastened (una prenda). || FIG. y FAM. To unbosom o.s. (*con*, to). || *Desabrocharse la chaqueta*, to undo *o* to unfasten one's coat.

desacalorarse v. pr. To cool down, to cool off (refrescarse). || FIG. To calm down, to cool down (calmarse).

desacatador, ra adj. Insolent, impertinent, impudent (insolente). || Disrespectful (falto de respeto).
— M. y f. Insolent person. | Disrespectful person.

desacatamiento m. V. DESACATO.

desacatar v. tr. To have *o* to show no respect for, to be disrespectful to: *desacatar a sus padres*, to be disrespectful to one's parents. || Not to observe, not to respect, to disobey: *desacatar las órdenes*, to disobey orders.

desacato m. Lack of respect (*a*, for), disrespect (*a*, for). || JUR. Disrespect (*a*, for), contempt (*a*, of) [las leyes]. || JUR. *Desacato a la autoridad*, contempt.

desaceitado, da adj. Lacking oil.

desaceitar v. tr. To remove the oil from. || To scour (lana).

desacerar v. tr. To take the steel off.

desacerbar v. tr. To sweeten, to temper (templar).

desacertadamente adv. Wrongly, mistakenly (erróneamente). || Unfortunately (inadecuadamente). || Poorly, clumsily (torpemente). || Tactlessly (sin tino).

desacertado, da adj. Ill-advised, unwise (poco recomendable). || Unsuccessful (de mal resultado). || Unfortunate (inadecuado): *respuesta desacertada*, unfortunate reply. || Poorly chosen (mal elegido). || Wrong, mistaken (erróneo). || Not fitting, unwise: *sería desacertado que fueses a verlo ahora*, it would not be fitting *o* it would be unwise for you to go and see him now. || Poor, clumsy: *una jugada desacertada de la defensa*, a poor piece of play by the defence. || Tactless (sin tacto): *observación desacertada*, a tactless remark.

desacertar* v. intr. To be wrong, to be mistaken (errar). || To lack tact, to be tactless (no tener tacto).

desacierto m. Mistake (error): *ha sido un desacierto comprar la casa*, it was a mistake buying the house. || Lack of tact (falta de tacto). || Unfortunate *o* tactless remark (al hablar). || Bad *o* poor choice: *el título del libro fue un desacierto*, the title of the book was a bad choice.

desaclimatado, da adj. Unacclimatized.

desacobardar v. tr. To encourage, to reassure.

desacomodado, da adj. Badly off, poor (por falta de dinero). || Unemployed, out of work (sin empleo). || Uncomfortable (incómodo). || Inconvenient (molesto). || *Amer.* Untidy (desordenado).

desacomodamiento m. Discomfort (incomodidad). || Inconvenience (molestia).

desacomodar v. tr. To inconvenience, to put out (molestar). || To discharge, to dismiss (despedir).
— V. pr. To lose one's job (quedarse sin empleo).

desacomodo m. Discomfort (incomodidad). || Inconvenience (molestia). || Discharge, dismissal (de un criado).

desacompañar v. tr. To leave.

desaconsejable adj. Inadvisable.

desaconsejado, da adj. Unwise, not advisable: *está desaconsejado bañarse después de comer*, it is unwise to go swimming after a meal. || Foolish (imprudente).
— M. y f. Fool (imprudente).

desaconsejar v. tr. To advise against, to dissuade: *quería marcharse a América pero se lo desaconsejé*, he wanted to go to America but I advised him against it.

desacoplamiento m. TECN. Uncoupling, disconnecting, disconnection. || Lack of coordination (de un equipo).

desacoplar v. tr. TECN. To remove: *desacoplar una rueda del eje*, to remove a wheel from the axle. | To uncouple, to disconnect (dos piezas de un mecanismo). || ELECTR. To disconnect. || To uncouple (un vagón del tren). || To upset the coordination of (un equipo). || To upset, to disrupt (trastornar).

desacordado, da adj. MÚS. Out of tune. || Discordant, clashing (sin armonía).

desacordar* v. tr. MÚS. V. DESAFINAR.

desacorde adj. Discordant: *instrumentos desacordes*, discordant instruments. || FIG. Conflicting, discordant, clashing (opiniones). || Clashing (colores).

desacostumbrado, da adj. Unusual, uncommon.

desacostumbrar v. tr. To break of the habit of *o* from the habit of: *desacostumbrar a uno del tabaco*, to break s.o. of the habit of smoking.
— V. pr. To break o.s. of the habit of, to give up: *me he desacostumbrado de la bebida*, I have given up drinking. || To get out of *o* to get rid of the habit of.

desacreditar v. tr. To run down, to disparage, to discredit (denigrar). || To bring discredit on, to bring into discredit, to discredit, to disgrace: *este producto desacredita al fabricante*, this product brings discredit on the manufacturer, this product brings the manufacturer into discredit.
— V. pr. To disgrace o.s., to let o.s. down, to discredit o.s. || To become discredited.

desacuerdo m. Disagreement, discord: *estar en desacuerdo*, to be in disagreement. || *Estar en desacuerdo con*, to be in disagreement with: *esta copia está en desacuerdo con el original*, this copy is in disagreement with the original version; not to be in keeping with: *su conducta está en desacuerdo con lo que predica*, his conduct is not in keeping with what he preaches; not to match (no hacer juego).

desadornar v. tr. To strip of ornaments, to unadorn.

desadvertido, da adj. Inadvertent.

desadvertimiento m. Inadvertence.

desadvertir* v. tr. To fail to notice.

desafear v. tr. To improve the looks of.

desafección f. Disaffection.

desafecto, ta adj. Opposed, disaffected. || *Las personas desafectas al gobierno*, the people hostile to the government *o* opposed to the government.
— M. Lack of affection, coldness: *mostrar desafecto a uno*, to show coldness *o* a lack of affection towards s.o.

desaferrar v. tr. To let go, to release (soltar). || MAR. To weigh (las anclas). || FIG. To dissuade, to bring round (disuadir).
— V. pr. To let go, to release one's grip (soltarse). || To change one's mind, to come around.

desafiador, ra adj. V. DESAFIANTE.
— M. y f. Challenger.

desafiante adj. Challenging (que reta). || Defiant: *actitud desafiante*, defiant attitude.

desafiar v. tr. To challenge (retar): *les desafiaron a un partido de fútbol*, they challenged them to a game of football. || To dare: *desafiar a alguien a hacer algo*, to dare s.o. to do sth. || To challenge [to a duel] (por el honor). || To defy: *desafió la ira de su padre*, he defied his father's anger. || To brave, to defy, to face: *desafiar el peligro*, to defy danger.
— V. pr. To challenge each other.

desafición f. Lack of affection, coldness.

desaficionar v. tr. To make s.o. dislike, to turn s.o. against *o* off: *desaficionar a uno del tabaco*, to make s.o. dislike smoking.
— V. pr. To come to dislike, to go off: *desaficionarse de algo*, to come to dislike sth.

desafilar v. tr. To blunt, to dull (el filo).
— V. pr. To lose its edge, to get blunt.

desafinación f. o **desafinamiento** m. MÚS. Dissonance, being out of tune (estado). | Going out of tune. | Putting out of tune.

desafinadamente adv. Out of tune.

desafinado, da adj. Out of tune.

desafinar v. intr. MÚS. To be out of tune: *este piano desafina*, this piano is out of tune. | To go out of tune: *el violín desafinó hacia el final del concierto*, the violin went out of tune towards the end of the concert. | To play out of tune (tocar). | To sing out of tune (cantar). || FIG. y FAM. To ramble (desvariar). | To speak out of turn (decir algo inoportuno).
— V. tr. MÚS. To put out of tune.
— V. pr. MÚS. To go out of tune.

desafío m. Challenge (reto). || Duel (duelo). || Defiance (provocación). || Competition, rivalry (competencia).

desaforadamente adv. In a disorderly fashion (atropelladamente). || Outrageously (de una manera escandalosa). || Excessively: *comer desaforadamente*, to eat excessively. || Furiously (con furia). || *Gritar desaforadamente*, to shout one's head off

desaforado, da adj. Unbounded, boundless: *ambición desaforada*, unbounded ambition. || Huge, enormous (gigantesco). || Terrible, terrifying, mighty: *dar voces desaforadas*, to give terrible shouts. || Outrageous (escandaloso). || Ardent: *partidario desaforado de una reforma*, ardent supporter of a reform. || Illegal, lawless (contra fuero). || *Gritar como un desaforado*, to shout one's head off.

desaforar* v. tr. To encroach on *o* upon the rights of (violar los fueros). || To deprive of one's privileges (abolir los fueros).
— V. pr. To go too far, to act outrageously. || To get worked up (irritarse).

desafortunado, da adj. Unlucky, unfortunate (desgraciado). || Unfortunate (desacertado).

desafuero m. Infringement of the laws, lawlessness (violación de las leyes). || Infringement of *o* encroachment upon rights (violación de los fueros). || Deprivation of a right (derecho) *o* privilege (privilegio). || FIG. Liberty, improper act (desacato). | Outrage, excess (abuso). || *Cometer un desafuero*, to break *o* to infringe the law (violar la ley), to commit an outrage (cometer un abuso).

desagraciado, da adj. Ungraceful, graceless, lacking charm.

desagraciar v. tr. To spoil, to spoil the beauty of.

desagradable adj. Unpleasant, disagreeable.

desagradar v. tr. To displease. || — *Este libro me desagrada*, I don't like this book. || *Me desagrada hacerlo*, I don't like doing it. I dislike doing it. || *Que desagrada*, unpleasant: *palabra que desagrada*, unpleasant word.
— V. intr. To be unpleasant.
— OBSERV. El inglés suele emplear el verbo *not to like*, y el sujeto del verbo español viene a ser el complemento del verbo inglés: *esto me desagrada*, I don't like this.
desagradecer* v. tr. To be ungrateful for, to show ingratitude for. || *Desagradece todo el bien que se le ha hecho*, he shows no gratitude for all the good that has been done for him.
desagradecido, da adj. Ungrateful: *desagradecido con* or *para su bienhechor*, ungrateful towards one's benefactor. || *Mostrarse desagradecido*, to be ungrateful *o* unappreciative, to show ingratitude.
— M. y f. Ungrateful person, ingrate.
desagradecimiento m. Ingratitude, ungratefulness.
desagrado m. Displeasure: *mostrar desagrado*, to show displeasure. || — *Con desagrado*, reluctantly, against one's will: *lo hace, pero con desagrado*, he does it, but reluctantly. || *Esta noticia me causó desagrado*, I didn't welcome this news, I didn't like this news.
desagraviar v. tr. To make amends to: *desagraviar a uno de una ofensa*, to make amends to s.o. for an insult. || To indemnify (indemnizar). || To apologize to (disculparse).
desagravio m. Amends, *pl.*, atonement, satisfaction (acción). || Compensation, indemnification, satisfaction (indemnización). || — *Acto de desagravio*, act of atonement. || *En desagravio de*, to make amends for, in amends for. || *Exigir un desagravio*, to demand satisfaction.
desagregación f. Disintegration.
desagregar v. tr. To disintegrate, to break up. || FIG. To break up.
— V. pr. To disintegrate, to break up. || FIG. To break up.
desaguadero m. Drain (desagüe). || FIG. Drain.
desaguador m. Drain, drainpipe (conducto). || Drain (canal).
desaguar v. tr. To drain, to empty, to run off. || FIG. To dissipate, to squander.
— V. intr. To drain, to drain away *o* off (un líquido). || To flow *o* to drain into: *el río desagua en el mar*, the river flows into the sea. || To drain (un depósito).
— V. pr. To drain. || FIG. To vomit (vomitar). | To relieve o.s. (orinar).
desagüe m. Drainage, draining (acción). || Drain, outlet (orificio, canal). || — *Conducto* or *tubo de desagüe*, downspout, drainpipe (canalón), overflow pipe (para el agua sobrante). || *Desagüe del radiador*, radiator overflow pipe. || *Desagüe directo*, direct-to-sewer drainage.
desaguisado, da adj. Illegal, unlawful (contra la ley). || Outrageous, unreasonable (hecho sin razón).
— M. Offence (delito). || Insult (insulto). || Outrage, injustice (atropello). || — *Hacer desaguisados*, to get up to mischief (niño). || *Hacer desaguisados en*, to damage. || *Ocurrió un desaguisado en*, sth. went wrong in.
desahogadamente adv. Easily: *aquí caben desahogadamente dos coches*, two cars can easily fit in here. || Comfortably, easily: *viven desahogadamente con su sueldo*, they can live comfortably on his wage. || Freely, at ease (fácilmente). || Impudently, brazenly (con insolencia).
desahogado, da adj. Spacious, roomy (espacioso): *habitación desahogada*, spacious room. || Uncluttered (desembarazado). || Wide (ancho). || Comfortable, well-to-do, well-off (adinerado): *una familia desahogada*, a comfortable family, a family which is well-off. || Well-paid, comfortable (situación). || Loose, roomy (ropa). || FIG. Impudent, brazen, shameless, barefaced (descarado). || — *Existencia desahogada*, comfortable existence. || *Vida desahogada*, easy life. || *Vivir desahogado*, to live comfortably, to be comfortably off.
desahogar v. tr. To relieve (aliviar). || To comfort, to console (consolar). || To ease (dolor). || FIG. To vent: *desahogar su ira con uno*, to vent one's anger on s.o. | To pour out, to open: *desahogar su corazón*, to pour out one's heart. | To take a weight *o* a load off: *las lágrimas desahogan el corazón*, tears take a weight off your heart.
— V. pr. To make o.s. comfortable (ponerse cómodo). || To relax, to take it easy (esparcirse): *después de haber trabajado mucho hace falta desahogarse*, one needs to relax after a hard day's work. || To rid *o* to free o.s. [from obligations, work, debt, etc.]. || FIG. To unbosom o.s., to confide, to open one's heart (confiarse): *desahogarse con* or *a un amigo*, to unbosom o.s. to a friend, to confide in a friend, to open one's heart to a friend. | To get sth. off one's chest (descargarse de una preocupación). | To let off steam (desfogarse): *todo esto lo hace para desahogarse*, he does all that just to let off steam.
desahogo m. Relief (alivio). || FIG. Comfort, ease (holgura económica). | Space, room: *quitar un mueble para tener más desahogo*, to take away a piece of furniture so as to have more space. | Outlet, vent (expansión). | Relaxation (descanso). | Impudence, barefacedness, brazenness (descaro). || Liberty, freedom (libertad). || — *Expresarse con desahogo*, to speak one's mind, to say what one really thinks. || *Le sirve de desahogo*, it helps him to let off steam. || *Vivir con desahogo*, to be comfortably off, to live comfortably.
desahuciadamente adv. Without hope, hopelessly.
desahuciado, da adj. Evicted, ejected (de una casa). || Hopeless (enfermo).
desahuciar v. tr. To deprive of all hope (quitar toda esperanza). || To give up hope for (declarar sin esperanza): *han desahuciado al enfermo*, they have given up hope for the patient. || To evict, to eject (a un inquilino).
desahucio m. Eviction, ejection (de un inquilino).
desairadamente adv. Ungracefully (sin garbo). || Rudely (descortésmente): *contestar desairadamente*, to answer rudely.
desairado, da adj. Spurned: *pretendiente desairado*, spurned suitor. || Unattractive, ungraceful (sin garbo). || Humiliating (humillante). || Awkward (molesto): *situación desairada*, awkward situation. || *Hacer un papel desairado* or *quedar desairado*, to be unsuccessful, to come off badly (quedar mal).
desairar v. tr. To snub, to spurn (desdeñar). || To slight (ofender): *acepté su invitación para no desairarle*, I accepted his invitation so as not to slight him. || To rebuff, to reject (rechazar).
desaire m. Slight, snub, rebuff (desprecio). || Ungracefulness, lack of charm (falta de gracia). || — *Hacer el desaire a uno de rechazar una oferta*, to snub s.o. by refusing an offer. || *Hacer un desaire a uno*, to snub s.o., to slight s.o., to rebuff s.o. || *Sufrir un desaire*, to be snubbed, to suffer a rebuff.
desajustar v. tr. To upset the adjustment of, to put out of order (una máquina). || To pull apart (dos piezas). || FIG. To spoil, to upset: *esto desajusta mis planes*, that upsets my plans. || *Me desajustó el tiro*, he made me miss.
— V. pr. To go wrong, to break down, to get out of working order (una máquina). || To come apart (dos piezas). || To break (romper un contrato).
desajuste m. Breakdown (avería). || Maladjustment (cuando está mal ajustada la máquina). || Pulling apart (de dos piezas). || Breaking (de un acuerdo). || FIG. Upsetting.
desalabear v. tr. TECN. To straighten *o* to flatten out, to unwarp (enderezar). | To surface (allanar).
desalabeo m. TECN. Straightening out, flattening out, unwarping (enderezamiento). | Surfacing (allanamiento).
desalación f. Desalination (del agua de mar).
desalado, da adj. Unsalted (sin sal). || Wingless (sin alas). || Anxious (ansioso). || — *Correr desalado a un sitio*, to hurry *o* to dash *o* to rush to a place. || *Ir desalado*, to be in a hurry (tener prisa).
desalar v. tr. To remove the salt from, to desalt, to unsalt (quitar la sal). || To desalinate (el agua de mar). || To clip *o* to remove the wings of (quitar las alas).
— V. pr. To hurry, to rush (apresurarse). || FIG. To long to, to yearn to: *se desalaba por conseguir una buena colocación*, he longed to obtain a good job.
desalazón f. Removal of salt, desalting.
desalbardar v. tr. To remove the packsaddle from.
desalbardillar v. tr. To remove the coping from (un muro).
desalentadamente adv. Dispiritedly, unenthusiastically.
desalentador, ra adj. Discouraging, disheartening: *una noticia desalentadora*, a discouraging piece of news.
desalentar* v. tr. To leave *o* to make breathless, to put out of breath. || FIG. To discourage, to dishearten (desanimar): *el fracaso le ha desalentado*, the failure has discouraged him.
— V. pr. To get discouraged, to lose heart: *no debemos desalentarnos ante la adversidad*, we must not lose heart in the face of adversity.
desalfombrar v. tr. To remove *o* to take up the carpets of: *desalfombrar una casa*, to take up the carpets of a house.
desalforjar v. tr. To take from the saddlebag (sacar de las alforjas). || To remove the saddlebags from (quitar las alforjas).
desalhajar v. tr. To empty, to strip, to remove the furnishings from (una habitación).
desaliento m. Discouragement, loss of heart.
desalinear v. tr. To put out of line.
— V. pr. To fall out of line (salirse de la línea). || To go out of line.
desalinización f. Desalination.
desalinizar v. tr. To desalinate.
desaliñadamente adv. Scruffily, untidily.
desaliñado, da adj. Scruffy, slovenly, dishevelled, untidy: *tiene un aspecto desaliñado*, he looks scruffy. || Slovenly, down-at-heel (siempre descuidado): *es una persona desaliñada*, he is a slovenly person. || FIG. Slipshod, slovenly, careless (estilo).
desaliñar v. tr. To disarrange (desarreglar). || To dirty (ensuciar). || To make untidy, to mess up (fam.). || To crease (arrugar): *desaliñar un vestido*, to crease a dress.
desaliño m. Scruffiness, slovenliness, untidiness (descuido). || Carelessness (del estilo). || *Ir vestido con desaliño*, to be scruffily dressed.
desalmado, da adj. Wicked (malvado). || Cruel, heartless (cruel).

— M. y f. Wicked person, scoundrel (malvado). || Heartless person (cruel).
desalmarse v. pr. To long *o* to crave (*por*, for).
desalmenar v. tr. To remove the battlements from.
desalmidonar v. tr. To remove the starch from.
desalojado, da adj. Evicted (inquilino). || Homeless (sin hogar).
— M. y f. Homeless person (sin vivienda). || *Los desalojados*, the homeless.
desalojamiento m. Eviction, ejection (expulsión). || MIL. Dislodging. || Removal, moving house (cambio de residencia). || Evacuation, abandonment (abandono).
desalojar v. tr. MIL. To dislodge: *desalojar al enemigo del fortín*, to dislodge the enemy from the fort. | To evacuate, to abandon, to move out of (marcharse de): *desalojar un pueblo*, to evacuate a town. || To evict, to eject: *desalojar a una persona de su casa*, to eject s.o. from his house. || To vacate (marcharse): *desalojar una casa*, to vacate a house. || To clear, to evacuate (hacer salir a la gente): *desalojaron el bar*, they cleared the bar. || MAR. To have a displacement of, to displace (desplazar): *el barco desaloja tantas toneladas*, the boat has a displacement of so many tons.
— V. intr. To move house, to move out (mudarse): *el vecino desaloja*, our neighbour is moving house. || FAM. To clear off, to clear out (irse).
desalojo m. V. DESALOJAMIENTO.
desalquilado, da adj. Vacant, unrented (un piso).
desalquilar v. tr. To stop renting. || To vacate (dejar libre).
— V. pr. To become vacant.
desalquitranar v. tr. To remove the tar from (quitar el alquitrán de). || To clean the tar off (para limpiar).
desamarrar v. tr. MAR. To cast off, to unmoor (largar las amarras). || To untie (desatar).
desambientado, da adj. Out of place: *en un país extranjero uno se encuentra desambientado*, in a foreign country one feels out of place. || *Esta sala de baile está muy desambientada*, this ballroom really lacks atmosphere *o* is really lacking in atmosphere.
desamontonar v. tr. To unpile.
desamor m. Coldness, indifference, lack of affection (frialdad): *su desamor a los padres*, his coldness *o* indifference towards his parents, his lack of affection for his parents. || Lack of affection (falta de amor). || Dislike (antipatía).
desamorado, da adj. Cold, indifferent.
desamortizable adj. Alienable, disentailable: *bienes desamortizables*, alienable property.
desamortización f. Alienation, disentailment.
desamortizar v. tr. To alienate, to disentail.
desamparadamente adv. Without protection.
desamparado, da adj. Forsaken, abandoned (abandonado). || Helpless, unprotected (sin protección). || Open, exposed to the wind (desabrigado). || Lonely (solo, aislado). || *Niño desamparado*, waif.
desamparar v. tr. To abandon, to forsake, to desert: *desamparar a un niño*, to desert a child. || To leave (un sitio). || JUR. To renounce, to relinquish. || MAR. To dismantle.
desamparo m. Helplessness, lack of protection. || Desertion, abandonment (abandono). || Distress (aflicción). || *En desamparo*, helpless, forsaken, deserted, abandoned: *un anciano en desamparo*, a forsaken old man.
desamueblado, da adj. Unfurnished: *piso desamueblado*, unfurnished flat.
desamueblar v. tr. To remove the furniture from, to strip *o* to clear of furniture.
desanclar o **desancorar** v. intr. MAR. To weigh anchor.
desandar* v. tr. *Desandar el camino* or *lo andado*, to retrace one's steps, to go back.
desangelado, da adj. Insipid, dull, lacking in charm (persona). || Insipid (cosa).
desangrado, da adj. *Está desangrado*, he has lost blood. || *Morir desangrado*, to bleed to death.
desangramiento m. Bleeding (pérdida de sangre). || Draining (desagüe).
desangrar v. tr. To bleed (sangrar). || To drain (un lago). || FIG. To bleed white (empobrecer): *desangrar a los contribuyentes*, to bleed the taxpayers white.
— V. pr. To bleed (perder la sangre). || To bleed to death (morir).
desangre m. Bleeding.
desanidar v. intr. To leave the nest (las aves).
— V. tr. FIG. To oust, to dislodge (desalojar).
desanimado, da adj. Low-spirited, downhearted, dejected (sin ánimo). || Lifeless, dull (fiesta).
desanimar v. tr. To depress: *este tiempo me desanima*, this weather depresses me. || To discourage: *el fracaso le ha desanimado*, the failure has discouraged him.
— V. pr. To be discouraged, to lose heart (desalentarse). || To get depressed (abatirse). || *¡No se desanime!*, don't be discouraged!, don't lose heart.
desánimo m. Discouragement, despondency, dejection (desaliento). || Depression (abatimiento). || Dullness, lifelessness (falta de animación).
desanudar v. tr. To untie, to undo, to unknot: *desanudar una corbata*, to undo a tie. || FIG. To clear up, to straighten *o* to sort out (una situación confusa).
desapacibilidad f. Surliness, harshness, unpleasantness (del genio). || Unsettled nature, unpleasantness, inclemency (del tiempo). || Harshness, unpleasantness (de un sonido).
desapacible adj. Harsh, unpleasant, surly: *tono desapacible*, harsh tone; *persona desapacible*, surly person. || Unpleasant, unsettled (tiempo). || Harsh, unpleasant (sonido). || Bitter, heated (discusión).
desapadrinar v. tr. (P.us.). FIG. To disapprove of (desaprobar). || To withdraw one's support from (retirar el apoyo).
desapareado, da adj. Odd: *calcetín desapareado*, odd sock.
desaparear v. tr. To lose one of.
desaparecer* v. intr. To disappear. || To vanish, to disappear (de repente). || To wear off: *el efecto ha desaparecido*, the effect has worn off. || — FAM. *Desaparecer del mapa*, to disappear completely, to vanish from the face of the earth. || *Hacer desaparecer*, to hide (ocultar), to smooth out, to get rid of (una arruga), to remove, to make off with (llevarse).
desaparecido, da adj. Missing.
— M. y f. Missing person. || — Pl. Missing: *los desaparecidos*, the missing; *hay veinte desaparecidos*, there are twenty missing.
desaparecimiento m. Disappearance.
desaparejar v. tr. To unharness (quitar los arreos). || MAR. To unrig.
desaparición f. Disappearance.
desapasionadamente adv. Dispassionately, objectively, impartially.
desapasionado, da adj. Dispassionate, objective, impartial.
desapasionar v. tr. To make [s.o.] lose interest in: *desapasionar a uno de algo*, to make s.o. lose interest in sth.
— V. pr. To lose interest, to become indifferent: *desapasionarse por alguien*, to lose interest in s.o., to become indifferent to s.o. || To lose interest *o* enthusiasm, to become indifferent: *desapasionarse del juego*, to lose interest in gambling, to become indifferent to gambling. || To overcome one's passion for (haciendo un esfuerzo).
desapegar v. tr. FIG. To estrange, to separate, to alienate (hacer perder el afecto).
— V. pr. FIG. To lose interest in, to turn away from, to go off (desaficionarse, perder el cariño).
desapego m. FIG. Coldness, indifference: *mostrar desapego a una persona*, to show indifference towards a person. | Estrangement, separation (de dos personas). || Lack of interest, indifference, dislike: *desapego a los estudios*, lack of interest in *o* indifference towards one's studies, dislike for *o* of studying.
desapercibidamente adv. Without being seen (sin ser visto): *aproximarse desapercibidamente*, to approach without being seen.
desapercibido, da adj. Unprepared, unready (no preparado). || Unnoticed: *pasar desapercibido*, to go unnoticed. || — *Coger desapercibido*, to catch unawares, to take by surprise. || *No me ha pasado desapercibido lo que ha dicho*, I didn't miss what he said.
desapercibimiento m. Unpreparedness.
desapestar v. tr. To disinfect.
desaplacible adj. Unpleasant, disagreeable.
desaplicación f. Lack of application, slackness, laziness (falta de aplicación).
desaplicadamente adv. Without application, lazily.
desaplicado, da adj. Slack, lazy: *alumno desaplicado*, slack pupil.
— M. y f. Lazybones, idler.
desapoderamiento m. Dispossession (privación). || Deprivation of power (poder) *o* authority (autoridad). || FIG. Rage, fury, wildness (desenfreno).
desapoderar v. tr. To deprive of one's power (poder) *o* authority (autoridad). || To dispossess (quitar).
desapolillar v. tr. To get rid of the moths from: *desapolillar la ropa*, to get rid of the moths from one's clothes.
— V. pr. FIG. y FAM. To get rid of the cobwebs: *salió a desapolillarse*, he went out to get rid of the cobwebs.
desaposentar v. tr. To evict, to throw out (de una habitación). || FIG. To cast aside.
desapoyar v. tr. To withdraw one's support.
desapreciar v. tr. To underestimate (infraestimar).
desaprender v. tr. To forget, to unlearn (olvidar).
desaprensar v. tr. To free (soltar). || To take the gloss *o* finish off (una tela).
desaprensión f. Unscrupulousness, lack of scruples.
desaprensivo, va adj. Unscrupulous, inconsiderate.
— M. y f. Unscrupulous person.
desapretar*, desapretarse v. tr. y pr. To loosen.
desaprobación f. Disapproval.
desaprobador, ra adj. Disapproving, of disapproval: *mirada desaprobadora*, look of disapproval, disapproving look. || Unfavourable, adverse: *juicio desaprobador*, adverse judgment.
desaprobar* v. tr. To disapprove, to disapprove of, to frown on: *desaprueba mi conducta*, he disapproves of my conduct. || To reject (rechazar). || *Desaprueba que yo vaya*, he disapproves of my going, he does not think it right that I should go.
desaprobatorio, ria adj. V. DESAPROBADOR.

desapropiar To deprive (*de*, of).
— V. pr. To give up, to surrender, to cede, to abandon: *desapropiarse de un bien*, to give up a possession.
desaprovechado, da adj. Slack, who does not make the best use of his possibilities, who could do better: *alumno desaprovechado*, pupil who does not make the best use of his possibilities. || Wasted (tiempo, dinero, comida, oportunidad). || FIG. Fruitless, unprofitable (infructuoso).
desaprovechamiento m. Wasting, waste, misuse (del tiempo, del dinero, etc.). || Lack of progress (falta de progresos).
desaprovechar v. tr. Not to take advantage of, to waste, to fail to make the best use of: *desaprovechar el buen tiempo, sus dotes, una influencia*, not to take advantage of the fine weather, one's talents, s.o.'s influence. || To waste: *desaprovechar el tiempo, el dinero, la comida*, to waste time, money, food. || *Desaprovechar una ocasión*, to miss *o* to waste *o* to throw away an opportunity.
desapuntalar v. tr. To remove the shores *o* props from.
desarboladura f. MAR. Dismasting.
desarbolar v. tr. MAR. To dismast.
— V. pr. To lose her mast.
desarenar v. tr. To remove sand from, to clear of sand.
desarmado, da adj. V. DESARMAR. || In pieces (desmontado).
desarmador m. Trigger (de un arma).
desarmadura f. o **desarmamiento** m. V. DESARME.
desarmar v. tr. To disarm (un país, una bomba, una persona, etc.). || To dismantle, to take to pieces, to take apart, to strip down (un motor). || To dismantle, to take to pieces, to take apart: *desarmar un reloj*, to dismantle a watch. || To dismantle, to take down (una tienda de campaña). || MAR. To lay up (un buque). || FIG. To unarm, to disarm: *su respuesta me desarmó*, his reply disarmed me. | To calm, to appease: *desarmar la cólera de uno*, to calm s.o.'s anger. | To stump, to floor (confundir). || — *Desarmar un arco*, to unstring a bow. || MIL. *Desarmar pabellones*, to unpile arms.
— V. intr. y pr. MIL. To disarm. || To come apart, to come to pieces (deshacerse).
desarme m. Disarmament: *conferencia sobre* or *para el desarme*, disarmament conference. || Dismantling, taking apart (de una máquina).
desarmonizar v. tr. To disharmonize.
desarraigado, da adj. Uprooted (árbol). || FIG. Uprooted, rootless (persona). | Eradicated, wiped out (vicio, etc.).
desarraigar v. tr. To uproot, to deracinate: *desarraigar un árbol*, to uproot a tree. || FIG. To uproot: *desarraigar un pueblo*, to uproot a people. | To wipe out, to eradicate: *desarraigar el vicio*, to wipe out vice. | To extirpate (extirpar).
— V. pr. *Desarraigarse de su patria*, to break all ties with one's country, to abandon one's country.
desarraigo m. Uprooting, rooting up (de un árbol). || FIG. Uprooting (de un pueblo, etc.). | Eradication (de un vicio, etc.). | Extirpation.
desarrapado, da adj./s. V. DESHARRAPADO.
desarregladamente adv. Unmethodically (sin método). || Untidily (sin orden).
desarreglado, da adj. Untidy: *una habitación desarreglada*, an untidy room. || Slovenly, untidy (aspecto): *una chica desarreglada*, a slovenly girl. || Disorderly (desordenado): *una vida desarreglada*, a disorderly life. || Out of order, faulty: *reloj desarreglado*, clock which is out of order, faulty clock. || Upset (estómago).
desarreglar v. tr. To mess up, to upset, to disturb, to make untidy, to disarrange: *desarreglar la casa, el peinado*, to make the house untidy, to mess up one's hairdo. || To spoil, to upset: *la lluvia ha desarreglado mis planes*, the rain has spoilt my plans. || To put out of order: *desarreglar un reloj*, to put a clock out of order.
desarreglo m. Disorder, confusion, mess, chaos: *en el más completo desarreglo*, in total confusion, in a terrible mess. || Faulty condition, trouble (de un mecanismo). || Untidiness (de la ropa). || Upset, disorder (del estómago).
desarrendar* v. tr. To stop leasing (dejar de arrendar). || To stop renting (dejar de alquilar). || To unbridle (una caballería).
desarrimar v. tr. To move away (apartar): *desarrimar el armario de la pared*, to move the wardrobe away from the wall. || FIG. To dissuade (disuadir).
desarrollable adj. Developable, which can be developed (expresión, industria, teoría, etc.). || Which can be spread out (superficie).
desarrollado, da adj. Developed. || *País desarrollado*, developed country.
desarrollar v. tr. To unroll, to unfold: *desarrollar un mapa*, to unroll a map. || To develop: *la lluvia y el sol desarrollan la semilla*, the rain and sun develop the seed. || To develop: *desarrollar el cuerpo, la industria*, to develop one's body, industry. || To expound, to explain, to develop (una teoría). || To carry out (realizar). || MAT. To expand, to develop (una expresión algebraica). || MÚS. To develop. || — *Desarrollar actividades subversivas*, to carry on subversive activities. || *Desarrollar una inteligencia enorme*, to show great intelligence. || *Desarrollar una velocidad de...*, to develop a speed of...
— V. pr. To unroll, to unfold (un mapa). || To develop: *la industria de este país se ha desarrollado mucho*, this country's industry has developed a lot. || To develop fully (alcanzar la madurez): *esta planta se desarrolla en dos meses*, this plant takes two months to develop fully. || To take place (tener lugar). || To happen, to take place (suceder). || To go off: *la entrevista se desarrolló como previsto*, the interview went off as planned.
desarrollo m. Development: *niño en pleno desarrollo*, child at the most rapid stage of development; *el desarrollo de una planta, de la industria*, the development of a plant, of industry. || DEP. Run, course (de un partido, etc.). || MAT. Expansion (de una expresión algebraica). | Development (geometría). || Unrolling (de un papel). || FIG. Development, course, unfolding: *el desarrollo de los acontecimientos*, the development of events. || TECN. Distance covered by bicycle for each revolution of pedal. || MÚS. Development. || — *Índice de desarrollo*, growth rate. || *Industria en pleno desarrollo*, rapidly developing industry. || *Niño que está en la edad del desarrollo*, child going through puberty. || *Países en vías de desarrollo*, developing countries. || *Plan de Desarrollo*, Development Plan.
desarropar v. tr. To uncover (descubrir). || To uncover (en la cama). || To undress (desnudar). || To take some clothes off (quitar parte de la ropa).
— V. pr. To take some clothes off: *no te desarropes, que estás sudando*, don't take any clothes off, you're perspiring. || To get undressed (desnudarse). || To remove *o* to throw off the blankets (en la cama). || *Hace demasiado frío para desarroparse*, it is too cold to wear lighter clothing.
desarrugar v. tr. To smooth, to smooth out (alisar). || To get the creases out of: *voy a colgar el traje para desarrugarlo*, I'm going to hang up the dress to get the creases out. || *Desarrugar el entrecejo*, to stop frowning.
— V. pr. To become smooth (quitarse las arrugas). || *Voy a colgar el traje para que se desarrugue*, I'm going to hang up the dress so that the creases will drop out *o* come out *o* to get the creases out.
desarrumar v. tr. MAR. To unstow.
desarticulación f. Putting out of joint, disarticulation, dislocation (de los huesos). || Disconnection (de dos piezas). || FIG. Breaking up: *desarticulación de un partido*, breaking up of a party.
desarticulado, da adj. Disjointed.
desarticular v. tr. To put out of joint, to disarticulate, to disjoint, to dislocate (huesos). || To disconnect (dos piezas). || To take apart, to take to pieces (dividir en partes). || FIG. To break up (un partido, un complot, etc.). | To spoil, to upset: *la lluvia ha desarticulado mis planes*, the rain has spoilt my plans.
desartillar v. tr. To deprive of artillery.
desarzonar v. tr. To throw, to unseat, to unsaddle.
desasar v. tr. To break the handle of.
desaseado, da adj. Untidy, dirty (sucio). || Slovenly, scruffy, untidy, unkempt (descuidado).
— M. y f. Scruff, untidy person.
desasear v. tr. To dirty, to soil (ensuciar). || To mess up (desordenar).
desasentar* v. tr. To move.
desaseo m. Dirtiness, uncleanliness (suciedad). || Untidiness, slovenliness, scruffiness (falta de aseo). || Mess (desorden).
desasimiento m. Release, releasing (acción de soltar). || Detachment (acción de desprender). || Relinquishment (acción de ceder). || Loosening (acción de soltarse). || FIG. Disinterestedness, unselfishness (desinterés).
desasimilación f. Dissimilation.
desasimilar v. tr. To dissimilate.
desasir* v. tr. To release, to let go, to loose (soltar). || To detach (desprender).
— V. pr. To come off (desprenderse). || *Desasirse de*, to give up, to part with (ceder), to rid o.s. of, to get rid of (deshacerse de), to rid o.s. of, to free o.s. of (liberarse).
desasistencia f. Desertion, abandonment.
desasistir v. tr. To desert, to abandon, to forsake (abandonar). || *Estar desasistido*, to be neglected: *estaba muy desasistido en el hospital*, he was rather neglected in hospital.
desasnar v. tr. FIG. y FAM. To polish up, to teach civilized manners to, to refine.
desasociar v. tr. To dissociate, to disassociate.
desasosegadamente adv. Uneasily, restlessly, anxiously.
desasosegado, da adj. Uneasy, restless, anxious.
desasosegar* v. tr. To disturb, to make restless *o* uneasy, to disquiet.
— V. pr. To become uneasy *o* restless.
desasosiego m. Uneasiness, anxiety, disquiet, restlessness (inquietud). || Unrest (malestar).
desastradamente adv. Dirtily (suciamente). || Scruffily, untidily, slovenly (descuidadamente). || In tatters (con andrajos).
desastrado, da adj. Dirty (sucio). || Scruffy, untidy, slovenly (descuidado). || In tatters, ragged (harapiento): *traje desastrado*, ragged dress, dress which is in tatters. || Unfortunate (desgraciado). || Disorderly: *llevar una vida desastrada*, to lead a disorderly life.
— M. y f. Scruff, tramp.

desastre m. Disaster (catástrofe). || MIL. Defeat (derrota). || FIG. Disaster, complete failure: *el baile fue un desastre*, the dance was a disaster. | Absolute mess: *esta falda es un desastre*, this skirt is an absolute mess. || — *Correr al desastre*, to court disaster. || FIG. *Este niño es un verdadero desastre*, this child is absolutely hopeless. | *¡Qué desastre!*, what a calamity! | *Un desastre de hombre*, a dead loss, a disaster.

desastrosamente adv. Disastrously.

desastroso, sa adj. Disastrous, calamitous.

desatado, da adj. Undone. || FIG. Wild, mad (sin contención). |Uncontrolled (pasiones, etc.). || FIG. *Está desatado*, there's no holding him (desenfrenado).

desatadura f. Undoing, unfastening, untying (acción de desatar). || FIG. Clearing up, solving (aclaración). | Outburst (desencadenamiento).

desatar v. tr. To untie, to undo, to unfasten: *desatar un nudo*, to undo a knot. || To untie, to undo: *desatar un paquete*, to undo a parcel. || To unbutton (desabotonar). || To unleash, to let go: *desatar el perro*, to let the dog go. || FIG. To loosen (la lengua). | To unleash, to let loose (las pasiones). | To unleash (represiones). | To spark off, to give rise to (provocar). | To clear up, to unravel, to untangle: *desatar una intriga*, to clear up an intrigue. || REL. *Atar y desatar*, to do and to undo.
— V. pr. To come undone, to come untied, to come unfastened (lo atado). || To undo, to unfasten, to untie: *desatarse los zapatos*, to undo one's shoes. || To get free (prisionero). || To get loose, to break loose (perro). || FIG. To lose one's temper, to get worked up (encolerizarse). | To get carried away (hablar con exceso). | To get out (de un compromiso). | To get carried away, to go too far, to forget o.s., to lose one's head (perder los estribos). | To begin to rage: *los elementos se desataron*, the elements began to rage. | To break, to burst: *la tempestad se desató*, the storm broke. | To explode: *su cólera, odio, entusiasmo se desató*, he exploded with anger, hatred, enthusiasm. | To break out (revolución, motín). || — FIG. *Desatarse en injurias* or *en improperios*, to pour out a stream of insults. | *Se le desató la lengua*, he began to talk.

desatascador m. Plunger (para tuberías).

desatascamiento m. Clearing, unblocking (de una tubería).

desatascar v. tr. To pull out of the mud (sacar de un atascadero). || To clear, to unblock (una cañería). || FIG. y FAM. To get out of a jam *o* of a scrape (sacar de un apuro).

desatasco m. Clearing, unblocking (de una cañería).

desatavío m. Untidiness, disarray, scruffiness.

desatención f. Inattention, lack of attention (distracción). || Disrespect, discourtesy, impoliteness, rudeness (descortesía). || Neglect (negligencia).

desatender* v. tr. To neglect: *desatender a sus huéspedes*, to neglect one's guests. || Not to pay attention to, to disregard, to ignore: *desatender lo que se dice*, not to pay attention to what is being said. || To neglect: *desatender sus deberes, las órdenes*, to neglect one's duties, orders. || To slight (ofender). || *Dejar una tienda desatendida*, to leave a shop unattended.

desatentado, da adj. Foolish, wild, rash, reckless. || Extreme, excessive, severe (riguroso).

desatentamente adv. Inattentively, without paying attention (sin prestar atención). || Impolitely, rudely (descortésmente).

desatento, ta adj. Inattentive: *un alumno desatento*, an inattentive pupil. || Careless (descuidado). || Impolite, discourteous, unmannerly (grosero). || *Está desatento en clase*, he doesn't pay attention in class.

desatinadamente adv. Wildly, madly, rashly (insensatamente). || Foolishly, recklessly, rashly (de manera imprudente). || Clumsily, stupidly, awkwardly (torpemente).

desatinado, da adj. Foolish, silly (tonto). || Rash, unwise (imprudente). || Wild, reckless, rash (sin juicio).

desatinar v. tr. To exasperate, to bewilder (exasperar). || To make lose one's head (atolondrar).
— V. intr. To talk nonsense, to rave (decir desatinos). || To blunder, to make blunders (cometer desaciertos).

desatino m. Silly thing, absurdity (dislate). || Mistake, blunder (equivocación). || Lack of tact, tactlessness (falta de tacto). || Foolishness, silliness (falta de cordura). || — Pl. Nonsense, *sing.*, silly things: *decir desatinos*, to talk nonsense, to say silly things. || Silly things: *cometer desatinos*, to do silly things. || — *Cometer un desatino*, to do sth. silly, to do a silly thing (hacer una tontería). || *Discurso lleno de desatinos*, speech full of absurdities *o* nonsense.

desatolondrarse v. pr. To come to one's senses, to gather one's wits.

desatollar v. tr. To pull out of the mud.

desatontarse v. pr. To come to, to come to one's senses, to gather one's wits.

desatoramiento m. Clearing, unblocking.

desatorar v. tr. To clear, to unblock (desatascar). || MAR. To unstow (la estiba). || MIN. To clear.

desatornillador m. Screwdriver.

desatornillar v. tr. To unscrew (destornillar).

desatracar v. tr. MAR. To push off, to cast off, to unmoor (separar del atracadero).
— V. intr. MAR. To move away, to shove off.

desatraillamiento m. Unleashing (de un perro). || Uncoupling (de un conjunto de perros).

desatraillar v. tr. To unleash (perro). || To uncouple (conjunto de perros).

desatrancador m. Plunger.

desatrancar v. tr. To unbar (una puerta). || To clear, to unblock (una cañería). || To clean out (pozo).

desatufarse v. pr. FIG. To calm down, to cool off (calmarse). | To get some fresh air (tomar el fresco).

desaturdir v. tr. To wake up, to bring to one's senses.
— V. pr. To wake up, to come round, to come to one's senses.

desautoridad f. Lack of authority.

desautorización f. Denial (mentís). || Disapproval (desaprobación). || Discredit (descrédito).

desautorizadamente adv. Without authorization.

desautorizado, da adj. Unauthorized. || Denied (desmentido). || Forbidden (prohibido).

desautorizar v. tr. To deny (desmentir): *el ministro desautorizó el rumor*, the minister denied the rumour. || To forbid (prohibir). || To declare unauthorized, to disallow (declarar que no se autoriza). || To disapprove, to disapprove of (desaprobar). || To discredit (desacreditar).

desavenencia f. Disagreement, discord (desacuerdo). || Row, quarrel (riña).

desavenido, da adj. Incompatible. || On bad terms, who have fallen out (reñidos): *familias desavenidas*, families on bad terms, families who have fallen out. || Contrary, opposing (opuesto). || *Países desavenidos*, countries which are in disagreement.

desavenir* v. tr. To cause a rift between, to cause to break up *o* to quarrel, to split: *desavenir a dos amigos*, to cause two friends to quarrel.
— V. pr. To quarrel, to have a difference of opinion, to fall out (fam.): *desavenirse con alguien*, to have a difference of opinion with s.o.

desaventajado, da adj. At a disadvantage (en situación desventajosa). || Disadvantageous, unfavourable, which has its drawbacks (poco ventajoso).

desaviar v. tr. To put out, to inconvenience (molestar). || To send the wrong way (desviar). || To deprive of necessities (desproveer).

desavío m. Inconvenience: *hacer desavío*, to cause inconvenience. || Misleading (desvío).

desavisado, da adj. Reckless, foolish (incauto).

desayunado, da adj. Who has had breakfast: *estoy desayunado*, I have had [my] breakfast.

desayunar v. intr. To have breakfast, to breakfast: *esta mañana he desayunado muy temprano*, this morning I had breakfast very early. || *Desayunar con pan y café*, to have bread and coffee for breakfast, to breakfast on bread and coffee.
— V. tr. To breakfast on, to have for breakfast.
— V. pr. To have breakfast, to breakfast: *aún no me he desayunado*, I haven't had breakfast yet. || — FIG. *Desayunarse de*, to get the first news of (enterarse). | *Ahora me desayuno*, it's the first I hear *o* I've heard of it.

desayuno m. Breakfast.

desazogar v. tr. To remove the mercury *o* quicksilver from.

desazón f. Tastelessness (insipidez). || AGR. Poverty (falta de sazón). || FIG. Uneasiness, anxiety, restlessness (desasosiego). | Grief (pesadumbre). || — FIG. *Le causa desazón no saber dónde va a trabajar*, it worries him not knowing where he is going to work. || *Sentir una desazón en el estómago*, to have an upset stomach.

desazonado, da adj. Insipid, tasteless (soso). || AGR. Poor (la tierra). || FIG. Uneasy, restless, anxious (intranquilo).

desazonar v. tr. To take away the taste of, to make tasteless *o* insipid (hacer insípido). || FIG. To upset, to annoy (disgustar). | To make uneasy, to worry, to disturb, to upset (inquietar).
— V. pr. FIG. To get angry (enfadarse). | To worry (preocuparse). | To feel off-colour, not to feel well (sentirse mal de salud).

desbabar v. tr. To clean, to remove the slime from (los caracoles).
— V. intr. y pr. To slobber, to drivel, to dribble, to drool.

desbancar v. tr. To take the bank from (en el juego). || FIG. To supplant, to replace (suplantar).
— V. intr. To break the bank (en el juego).

desbandada f. Scattering. || MIL. Rout, stampede. || — *A la desbandada*, in disorder, in confusion. || *Hubo una desbandada general*, everybody scattered.

desbandarse v. pr. MIL. To flee in disorder, to disband, to disperse in confusion: *las tropas se desbandaron*, the troops fled in disorder. || To disperse, to scatter (dispersarse). || To remain aloof (apartarse).

desbarajustar v. tr. To throw into confusion (causar confusión en). || To upset (poner en desorden). || *Está todo desbarajustado*, everything is in a mess *o* is upside down.

desbarajuste m. Confusion, disorder, chaos. || — *Hay tal desbarajuste en la casa que no encuentro nada*, the house is in such a mess that I can't find anything. || *¡Qué desbarajuste!*, what a mess!

desbaratado, da adj. Wrecked, ruined (estropeado). || Broken, ruined (roto). || FIG. y FAM. Dissipated, wild (disipado). || MIL. In confusion.

desbaratamiento m. Disorder, confusion (desorden). || Waste, squandering (derroche). || Wrecking, destruction. || Spoiling, frustration (de proyectos, planes, etc.). || Raving (disparates). || Thwarting, foiling, frustration (de intriga). || MIL. Rout.
desbaratar v. tr. To spoil, to mess up: *el viento desbarató su peinado*, the wind messed up her hairdo. || To wreck, to ruin (destrozar). || To put out of order, to ruin, to break: *desbaratar un reloj*, to ruin a watch. || To spoil, to thwart, to ruin: *desbaratar los planes de uno*, to spoil s.o.'s plans. || To thwart, to foil, to frustrate (hacer fracasar): *desbaratar una intriga*, to frustrate a plot. || To demolish (un razonamiento). || To waste, to squander (derrochar): *desbaratar una fortuna*, to squander a fortune. || MIL. To put to flight, to rout, to throw into confusion: *desbaratar a los adversarios*, to rout the enemy.
— V. intr. To talk nonsense (disparatar).
— V. pr. To fall apart. || FIG. To blow up, to go off the deep end (irritarse), to get carried away (pasarse de la raya).
desbarbado m. TECN. Trimming, removal of the rough edges.
desbarbar v. tr. To trim the rootlets off (quitar las raíces). || To trim (papel). || To trim, to remove the rough edges from (metal). || FAM. To shave (afeitar).
— V. pr. FAM. To shave.
desbarbillar v. tr. AGR. To trim the rootlets off.
desbardar v. tr. To remove the brambles from [a wall].
desbarnizar v. tr. To remove the varnish from.
desbarrancadero m. *Amer.* Precipice.
desbarrar v. intr. To slip (resbalar). || FIG. To talk nonsense (decir disparates). | To do silly *o* stupid things (hacer tonterías).
desbarro m. Slip (resbalón). || FIG. Silly thing, absurdity (disparate).
desbastador m. TECN. Roughing chisel (herramienta). | Roughing mill (laminador).
desbastadura f. TECN. V. DESBASTE.
desbastar v. tr. TECN. To rough down, to rough-plane (madera). | To rough down (metal). | To roughhew, to scabble (piedra). || To smooth down (suavizar). || FIG. To knock the rough corners off, to teach civilized manners to, to polish: *desbastar a un palurdo*, to knock the rough corners off a yokel.
— V. pr. FIG. To acquire some polish.
desbaste m. TECN. Roughing-down, rough-planing (de madera). | Roughing-down (de metal). | Roughhewing, scabbling (de piedra). | Bloom (pieza de acero). || FIG. Polishing, refinement (de una persona). || *En desbaste*, roughly-worked, roughhewn.
desbautizar v. tr. To take away the name of (quitar el nombre). || To change the name of, to rename (poner otro nombre).
— V. pr. To lose one's temper (encolerizarse).
desbloquear v. tr. COM. To unfreeze, to unblock. || TECN. To free. || MIL. To raise the blockade on.
desbloqueo m. COM. Unfreezing, unblocking. || MIL. Raising of the blockade. || TECN. Freeing.
desbocado, da adj. Runaway (caballo). || FIG. Wild: *imaginación desbocada*, wild imagination. | Uncontrollable, wild: *hoy los niños están desbocados*, the children are uncontrollable today. || Bell-mouthed, wide-mouthed (arma de fuego). || With a chipped rim (vasija de boca mellada). || With a broken rim (de boca rota). || Overflowing (río). || FIG. y FAM. Foulmouthed (malhablado). | Cheeky (descarado).
— M. y f. Foulmouthed person (malhablado). | Cheeky person (descarado).
desbocamiento m. Bolting (de un caballo). || FIG. y FAM. Cheek, insolence (descaro). | Coarse language (grosería). | Insults, *pl.*, abuse.
desbocar v. tr. To chip the rim of (mellar). || To break the rim of (romper).
— V. intr. V. DESEMBOCAR.
— V. pr. To bolt, to run away (caballo). || FIG. To blow up, to go off the deep end (irritarse). | To go too far, to get carried away (pasarse de la raya). | To let out a stream of abuse (insultar).
desbordamiento m. Overflowing: *el desbordamiento de un río*, the overflowing of a river. || MIL. Outflanking, envelopment. || FIG. Excitement (exaltación). | Explosion, outbreak, outburst (de cólera, etc.).
desbordante adj. Overflowing, bursting: *el cine estaba desbordante de gente*, the cinema was overflowing with people; *persona desbordante de entusiasmo*, person overflowing with enthusiasm. || Unrestrained, boundless, unbounded: *alegría desbordante*, unbounded joy.
desbordar v. intr. To overflow, to brim over: *el cesto desbordaba de naranjas*, the basket was overflowing with oranges. || To overflow, to flood: *el río desbordó por los campos*, the river overflowed into the fields. || FIG. To overflow, to bubble over: *su alegría desborda*, he is overflowing with joy, he is bubbling over with joy. | To burst with (entusiasmo). || To project, to protrude, to jut out (sobresalir).
— V. tr. To overflow: *el río desbordó su cauce*, the river overflowed its banks. || FIG. To burst through, to overwhelm: *desbordaron las líneas enemigas*, they overwhelmed the enemy lines. | To pass, to go beyond (superar). | To exceed, to surpass (exceder). || — FIG. *Esto desborda mi capacidad de comprensión*, that is beyond me. | *Esto desborda mi paciencia*, that is more than I can stand.
— V. pr. To overflow its banks, to flood, to run over: *el río se desbordó*, the river overflowed its banks. || To overflow: *la piscina se desborda*, the pool is overflowing. || To spill over, to brim over, to overflow: *se desborda el agua del vaso*, the glass is brimming over with water. || FIG. To go wild, to get carried away (exaltarse). | To burst: *su corazón se desborda de alegría*, his heart is bursting with joy.
desborde m. *Amer.* V. DESBORDAMIENTO.
desborrar v. tr. To burl (limpiar el paño).
desbotonar v. tr. To remove the buds from (plantas). || To take the button off (un florete).
desbravador m. Horsebreaker, broncobuster (de caballos).
desbravar v. tr. To tame, to train (animal). || To break in (caballo).
— V. intr. y pr. To become less wild (hacerse más sociable). || To calm down, to become calm (calmarse): *el mar se desbrava*, the sea is becoming calm. || To lose its strength (un licor).
desbravecer* v. intr. y pr. V. DESBRAVAR.
desbridar v. tr. To unbridle (una caballería). || MED. To debride (los tejidos).
desbriznar v. tr. To mince (la carne). || To chop finely (las verduras, etc.). || To remove the stamens from [the crocus] (el azafrán).
desbroce m. V. DESBROZO.
desbrozar v. tr. To clear of weeds (la hierba). || To clear of undergrowth (matorrales). || To clear, to grub (un terreno). || FIG. To clear (camino). | To do the spadework on (un tema).
desbrozo m. Clearing of weeds (de la hierba). || Clearing of undergrowth (de matorrales). || Clearing, grubbing (del terreno). || Rubbish (desechos). || Prunings, *pl.* (ramas). || FIG. Spadework.
desbulla f. Oyster shell (concha). || Shelling (acción de abrir una ostra).
desbullador m. Oyster fork (tenedor). || Oyster opener (cuchillo). || Oyster sheller (persona).
desbullar v. tr. To shell [oysters].
descabal adj. Odd (no cabal). || Incomplete.
descabalado, da adj. Incomplete (incompleto). || Odd: *guante descabalado*, odd glove.
descabalamiento m. Spoiling.
descabalar v. tr. To spoil, to leave incomplete (dejar incompleto). || To split, to separate (desemparejar).
descabalgar v. intr. To dismount.
descabellado, da adj. FIG. Wild, crazy: *ideas, teorías descabelladas*, wild ideas, theories; *es descabellado hacer tal cosa*, it's crazy to do such a thing.
descabellar v. tr. To ruffle *o* to tousle the hair of (despeinar): *mujer descabellada*, woman with ruffled hair. || TAUR. To kill the bull with a "descabello".
descabello m. TAUR. "Descabello" [a sharp stab with the sword between the first and second cervical vertebrae, designed to kill the bull after an unsuccessful "estocada"]. | Sword used for the "descabello".
descabezado, da adj. Decapitated, beheaded, headless (decapitado). || Headless (cosa desprovista de cabeza). || FIG. Wild, crazy, reckless (insensato). | Absurd, ridiculous (absurdo). | Forgetful, absentminded (desmemoriado).
descabezamiento m. Decapitation, beheading (decapitación). || Pollarding, cutting the top off (árbol).
descabezar v. tr. To behead, to decapitate (a una persona). || To take the head off (una cosa): *descabezar un clavo*, to take the head off a nail. || To cut the top off, to pollard, to lop (un árbol). || To top (plantas). || FIG. To remove the head of: *descabezar una organización*, to remove the head of an organization. || MIL. To change the direction of (hacer cambiar de dirección). || — FIG. y FAM. *Descabezar una dificultad*, to start to surmount *o* to get over a difficulty. | *Descabezar un sueño*, v. SUEÑO.
— V. pr. To shed grain (las espigas). || FIG. To rack one's brains (persona).
descachalandrado, da adj. *Amer.* Scruffy, untidy (desharrapado).
descacharrante adj. FAM. Hilarious, killing (muy divertido).
descacharrar v. tr. To break (romper). | To ruin, to spoil, to mess up (estropear).
descaecer* v. intr. V. DECAER.
descaecimiento m. V. DECAIMIENTO.
descafeinar v. tr. To decaffeinate, to decaffeinize: *café descafeinado*, decaffeinated coffee.
descaimiento m. V. DECAIMIENTO.
descalabazarse v. pr. FIG. y FAM. To rack one's brains.
descalabrado, da adj. With a head injury, injured in the head (herido en la cabeza). || FIG. Injured (herido). || FIG. *Salir descalabrado de un negocio*, to come out of a business the worse for wear.
descalabradura f. Head injury, head wound. || Scar (cicatriz).
descalabrar v. tr. To injure the head of, to injure in the head (herir en la cabeza): *descalabrar a uno*, to injure s.o.'s head, to injure s.o. in the head. || To injure (herir). || FIG. To give a rough time to, to knock about (maltratar). | To harm (perjudicar). | To defeat (al enemigo).
— V. pr. To injure one's head.

descalabro m. Setback, blow, misfortune: *sufrir muchos descalabros en la vida*, to undergo many setbacks in one's life. || MIL. Defeat (derrota). || Disaster (desastre): *esta derrota fue un descalabro*, this defeat was a disaster.
descalaminado m. TECN. Removing of calamine.
descalaminar v. tr. To remove the calamine from.
descalce m. Undermining (socava).
descalcificación f. MED. Decalcification.
descalcificar v. tr. MED. To decalcify.
— V. pr. MED. To become decalcified.
descalificación f. Disqualification: *descalificación de un equipo*, a team's disqualification. || Discredit (descrédito).
descalificar v. tr. To disqualify: *descalificar a un equipo de fútbol*, to disqualify a football team. || To bring discredit on (desacreditar).
descalzar v. tr. To take off [s.o.'s] shoes (quitar el calzado). || To remove the wedge *o* the chocks from (quitar el calzo). || AGR. To dig under, to undermine (socavar).
— V. pr. To take off one's shoes (quitarse los zapatos). || To lose *o* to cast a shoe (caballo). || To take off (los guantes, las gafas). || FIG. To become a discalced Carmelite (fraile).
descalzo, za adj. Barefoot, barefooted, shoeless: *ir descalzo*, to go barefoot. || FIG. Badly shod (mal provisto de calzado). | Poor, destitute, down and out (pobre). || Discalced (fraile).
descamación f. MED. Desquamation, peeling.
descamar v. tr. MED. To desquamate.
— V. pr. MED. To desquamate, to scale off.
descambiar v. tr. To change back [again].
descaminadamente adv. *Ir descaminadamente*, to be on the wrong track, to go the wrong way.
descaminar v. tr. To mislead, to misdirect, to send the wrong way, to put on the wrong road (hacer perder el camino). || FIG. To lead astray, to mislead, to lead off the straight and narrow: *las malas compañías lo descaminaron*, bad company led him astray. || — FIG. *Andar* or *estar* or *ir descaminado*, to be on the wrong road, to have the wrong idea, to be on the wrong track. || *Ir descaminado*, to be on the wrong road. || FIG. *No andas muy descaminado*, you're not far wrong.
— V. pr. To take the wrong road, to go the wrong way. || FIG. To go astray, to go the wrong way, to go off the straight and narrow.
descamino m. Losing one's way (desorientación). || FIG. Error.
descamisado, da adj. Shirtless, without a shirt (sin camisa). || FIG. In rags, ragged (desharrapado). | Wretched (muy pobre).
— M. Tramp (desharrapado). || Wretch (pobre). || — Pl. HIST. Descamisados (Spanish liberals who took part in the 1820 revolution. In Argentinian history, the name given to supporters of General Perón and his wife).
descamisar v. tr. To take the shirt off. || *Amer.* FIG. To ruin (arruinar). | To rob (robar).
descampado, da adj. Open (un terreno).
— M. Open piece of ground, open field. || *Al* or *en descampado*, in the open country.
descampar v. intr. To clear up, to stop raining (escampar).
descansadamente adv. Without effort, effortlessly, without tiring o.s. [out]: *nadar descansadamente*, to swim effortlessly. || In a leisurely manner (sin prisa).
descansadero m. Resting place.
descansado, da adj. Rested: *ya estoy descansado*, I'm rested now. || Relaxed (relajado). || Easy, carefree: *vida descansada*, easy life. || Effortless, easy: *trabajo descansado*, easy job. || Restful, peaceful, quiet (tranquilo). || — *Este trabajo es mucho más descansado que el otro*, this job is much less tiring than the other. || *Puede usted estar descansado que*, you can rest assured that. || *Tiene un negocio descansado*, his is a cushy business.
descansapiés m. inv. Footrest (reposapiés).
descansar v. intr. To rest (reparar las fuerzas): *está descansando de su viaje*, he is resting after his journey. || To sleep (dormir); *¡que descanse!*, sleep well; *¿qué tal ha descansado usted?*, did you sleep well? || To lie down (echarse). || To take a rest, to have a break (en el trabajo). || To rest, to be supported: *la viga descansa en la pared*, the beam rests upon the wall, the beam is supported by the wall. || To find relief (después de un dolor, pena). || To be idle, to be out of work (holgar). || To rest, to lie (muertos): *aquí descansa...*, here lies... || To be based on (basarse): *este razonamiento descansa sobre una base falsa*, this argument is based on a false premise. || To abate (tempestad). || To lie fallow, to rest (la tierra). || To relax (relajarse). || To rely on (contar con): *puede usted descansar en mí*, you can rely on me. || — *No descanso en todo el día*, I don't have a moment's rest all day, I never stop all day. || *Que en paz descanse*, may he rest in peace.
— V. tr. To rest: *para descansar la vista*, to rest your eyes; *descansar la cabeza en* or *sobre la almohada*, to rest one's head on the pillow. || To rest, to lean (apoyar). || To help, to give a hand to (ayudar). || MIL. To order: *descansar las armas*, to order arms. || MIL. *¡Descansen armas!*, order arms.
— V. pr. To rest, to relax. || To sleep (dormir). || To rely, to count (contar con): *descansarse en alguien*, to rely on *o* to count on s.o.
descansillo m. Landing (rellano).
descanso m. Rest: *tomar un rato de descanso*, to take a moment's rest. || Halt, stop (en la marcha). || Break: *en la oficina tenemos un descanso a las diez*, we have a break in the office at ten o'clock. || Leave: *descanso por enfermedad*, sick leave. || Landing (descansillo de escalera). || Half time, interval (en un partido de fútbol): *en el descanso*, at half time, during the interval. || Interval (cine, teatro). || TECN. Support, seat. || FIG. Relief, comfort (alivio). || *Amer.* Toilet (retrete). || — *Descanso de maternidad*, maternity leave. || *Descanso eterno*, last sleep. || *Descanso semanal*, day off. || *Día de descanso*, day off (del trabajo), day of rest (domingo), rest day (en una competición, etc.), day on which there is no performance (en el teatro). || *No dar el menor descanso*, not to give a minute's peace. || *Sin descanso*, without a break.
descantillar o **descantonar** v. tr. To chip (desportillar). || FIG. To deduct (rebajar).
— V. pr. To get chipped (desportillarse).
descañonar v. tr. To pluck (desplumar). || To shave close (afeitar). || FIG. y FAM. To fleece (en el juego).
descaperuzar v. tr. To unhood.
descapirotar v. tr. To unhood.
descapotable adj./s. m. Convertible (coche).
descapotar v. tr. To put the [car's] hood down.
descapsulador m. Bottle opener.
descaradamente adv. Barefacedly, shamelessly.
descarado, da adj. Cheeky, impudent, insolent (insolente): *niño descarado*, cheeky boy. || Blatant, shameless, barefaced (falto de recato). || *Mentira descarada*, barefaced lie.
— M. y f. Scoundrel (granuja). || Cheeky devil (insolente).
descaramiento m. V. DESCARO.
descararse v. pr. To be cheeky *o* insolent *o* impudent (obrar con insolencia): *descararse con un anciano*, to be cheeky to an old man. || To be barefaced (obrar con cinismo). || *Se descaró a pedir...*, he had the nerve to ask for..., he was cheeky enough to ask for....
descarbonatar v. tr. QUÍM. To decarbonate (quitar el ácido carbónico).
descarburación f. TECN. Decarbonization, decarburization, decarbonizing, decarburizing.
descarburante adj. TECN. Decarbonizing, decarburizing.
— M. TECN. Decarbonizer, decarburizer.
descarburar v. tr. TECN. To decarbonize, to decarburize.
descarga f. Unloading (acción de descargar): *descarga de un barco*, unloading of a boat. || Firing, discharge (de armas). || Salvo, volley (fuego simultáneo de armas). || ELECTR. Discharge: *tubo de descarga*, discharge tube. || ARQ. Relieving (aligeramiento). || *Descarga cerrada*, volley, salvo (de armas de fuego).
descargadero m. Wharf, landing stage, unloading dock.
descargado, da adj. Flat (una batería).
descargador m. Docker, stevedore (que descarga barcos). || Unloader (en general). || Wormer, wad hook (de arma).
descargar v. tr. To unload, to discharge: *descargar una barcaza*, to unload a barge; *descargar el azúcar de un barco*, to unload the sugar from a boat. || MIL. To fire, to discharge, to shoot (disparar un arma). | To disarm, to unload (quitar la carga). || ELECTR. To discharge. | To run down (una batería). || To deal: *descargar golpes*, to deal blows. || To evacuate (el vientre). || FIG. To give vent to, to vent: *descargar uno la ira en contra de alguien*, to give vent to one's wrath on s.o., to vent one's anger on s.o. | To relieve, to free, to release (*de*, from) [de una obligación, preocupación]. | To free (de una deuda). | To clear, to absolve, to acquit (*de*, of) [de culpa]. | To unburden (el corazón). | To ease, to relieve (aliviar). || — *Las nubes descargaron lluvia*, the clouds burst, the rain came pouring down. || *Descargar un golpe sobre* or *contra uno*, to hit out at s.o., to let fly at s.o.
— V. intr. To flow (*en*, into) [río]. || To break: *una tempestad descargó sobre Madrid*, a storm broke over Madrid. || To burst (las nubes). || ELECTR. To discharge.
— V. pr. ELECTR. To discharge. || To shift, to unload: *descargarse de sus obligaciones en* or *sobre un colega*, to unload one's responsibilities onto a colleague. || To resign (dimitir). || To unburden o.s. (de penas, etc.). || To blow one's top, to blow up (desahogarse). || JUR. To clear o.s. (*de*, of).
descargo m. Unloading (descarga). || COM. Credit (abono en cuenta). | Receipt, voucher (recibo). || FIG. Relief (alivio). || JUR. Acquittal, discharge (de acusación). || Release (de obligación). || — Pl. Excuse, *sing.* (disculpa). || JUR. Plea, *sing.* (del acusado). | Evidence, *sing.* (pruebas). || — *En descargo de conciencia*, for conscience's sake. || JUR. *En* or *para su descargo*, in his defence. | *Pliego de descargo*, evidence for the defence. | *Testigo de descargo*, witness for the defence.
descargue m. Unloading (descarga).
descarnadamente adv. Frankly, plainly, to the point (sin rodeos).

descarnado, da adj. Lean, thin, scrawny: *cara descarnada*, lean face. || Clean (hueso). || FIG. Plain, bare (escueto). | Frank, straightforward, candid (sincero). || Straightforward, plain: *estilo descarnado*, straightforward style.
descarnador m. Scraper (del dentista).
descarnadura f. Removal of flesh (acción de quitar carne). || FIG. Emaciation.
descarnar v. tr. To strip the flesh from (hueso). || FIG. To lay bare, to strip (descubrir). | To wear away: *rocas descarnadas por la acción de las olas*, rocks worn away by the action of waves.
— V. pr. To lose flesh, to waste away.
descaro m. Cheek, impudence, insolence, nerve, impertinence (insolencia): *su descaro me asombra*, his cheek amazes me. || Effrontery, barefacedness (cinismo). || — *¡Qué descaro!*, what cheek!, what a nerve! || *Tuvo el descaro de venir a mi casa*, he had the cheek *o* the nerve to come to my house.
descarozar v. tr. *Amer.* To stone, to pit (fruta).
descarriamiento m. V. DESCARRÍO.
descarriar v. tr. To send the wrong way, to misdirect, to put on the wrong road (descaminar). || To separate from the herd (una res). || FIG. To lead astray. || FIG. *Oveja descarriada*, lost sheep.
— V. pr. To get lost, to go the wrong way. || To stray, to wander, to stray from the herd (res). || FIG. To go astray, to go the wrong way, to go off the straight and narrow.
descarrilamiento m. Derailment: *no hubo heridos en el descarrilamiento del tren París-Roma*, no one was injured in the derailment of the Paris-Rome train.
descarrilar v. intr. To be derailed, to run off the rails (un tren). || FIG. To get off the track.
descarrío m. Losing one's way. || FIG. Going astray. | Error.
descartar v. tr. To discard, to put aside, to reject: *descartar un proyecto*, to discard a plan. || To discard, to throw away, to throw down (los naipes). || — *Descartar una posibilidad*, to eliminate *o* to dismiss *o* to rule out a possibility. || *Quedar descartado*, to be left out.
— V. pr. *Descartarse de*, to discard, to throw away, to throw down (naipes), to get out of (un compromiso).
descarte m. Discarding, throwing-away, discard (acción). || Discarded cards, *pl.*, discard (naipes descartados). || Discarding, ruling out (acción de desechar). || Rejection (acción de rechazar). || FIG. Excuse (excusa).
descasar v. tr. To annul *o* to dissolve the marriage of (anular un matrimonio). || To estrange, to separate (separar). || FIG. To upset: *descasar los sellos de una colección*, to upset the stamps in a collection. | To separate (dos cosas).
— V. pr. To separate. || To get divorced (divorciarse).
descascar o **descascarar** v. tr. To shell (nuez, grano de café, huevo duro, etc.). || To peel (naranja, limón).
descascarillado m. Husking (acción de quitar la cascarilla). || Peeling-off, flaking (de pintura, esmalte).
descascarillar v. tr. To husk, to remove the husk from. || *Arroz descascarillado*, husked rice.
— V. pr. To peel off, to flake off.
descaspar v. tr. To remove the dandruff *o* the scurf from (quitar la caspa).
descastado, da adj. Unaffectionate, cold (poco cariñoso).
descatolización f. Dechristianization.
descatolizar v. tr. To dechristianize.
descebar v. tr. To unprime (un arma).
descendencia f. Descent (*de*, from). || Descendants, *pl.*, offspring (hijos): *su descendencia vive en Madrid*, his descendants live in Madrid. || *Morir sin descendencia*, to die without issue.
descendente adj. Descending, downward: *curso descendente*, downward course. || Of descent: *línea descendente* (*del árbol genealógico*), line of descent. || Diminishing (que disminuye). || MAT., ASTR. y MED. Descending. || Outgoing (marea). || MÚS. Falling (escala). || *Tren descendente*, down train.
descender* v. intr. To descend, to go down, to come down (bajar): *descender de una cima*, to descend from a summit. || To go down: *ha descendido mucho en mi estima*, he has gone down a lot in my esteem. || To go down, to fall, to drop (fiebre, temperatura, nivel, etc.): *el nivel del mercurio ha descendido*, the mercury level has gone down. || To hang (las cortinas). || — FIG. *Descender a*, to lower o.s. to, to stoop to (rebajarse a). || *Descender de*, to descend from, to be descended from, to issue from: *todos descendemos de Adán y Eva*, we are all descended from Adam and Eve; to come from (proceder).
— V. tr. To take down, to get down, to bring down, to lower. || To go down, to descend: *descender la escalera*, to go down the stairs.
descendiente adj. Descending (que desciende). || — *Se cree descendiente de la pata del Cid*, v. CID. || *Ser descendiente de*, to come from, to be a descendant of: *era descendiente de una familia linajuda*, he came from a noble family, he was a descendant of a noble family.
— M. y f. Descendant: *un descendiente de Newton*, a descendant of Newton. || — Pl. Issue, *sing.*, progeny, *sing.*, descendants.
descendimiento m. V. DESCENSO. || Descent: *Descendimiento de la Cruz*, Descent from the Cross. || MED. Prolapse (de un órgano).
descenso m. Descent, going down, coming down (acción de descender). || Fall, drop (de fiebre, temperatura). || Fall (de paracaídas). || DEP. Downhill race (esquí). || MED. Prolapse. || Fall, subsidence: *descenso del nivel de un río*, fall in the level of a river, subsidence of a river. || Decline, drop, fall, falling-off (desnivel, disminución). || Fall (de los precios). || Demotion (degradación). || Slope (declive). || Way down: *el descenso hacia el río*, the way down to the river. || FIG. Decline (decadencia). || *Descenso a segunda división*, relegation to the second division (fútbol).
descentración f. Putting off centre (acción). || Eccentricity (resultado).
descentrado, da adj. Eccentric, off centre. || FIG. All at sea, bewildered, lost: *me encuentro descentrado en esta ciudad*, I feel lost in this town. | Unbalanced (desequilibrado). | Out of focus (problema, etc.).
— M. Putting off centre (acción). || Eccentricity (resultado).
descentralización f. Decentralization.
descentralizado, da adj. Decentralized.
descentralizador, ra adj. Decentralizing.
— M. y f. Decentralizer.
descentralizar v. tr. To decentralize.
descentramiento m. Putting off centre (acción). || Eccentricity (resultado). || FIG. Confusion, bewilderment (desorientación). | Unbalanced state (desequilibrio).
descentrar v. tr. To put off centre. || FIG. To unbalance (desequilibrar).
desceñir* v. tr. To loosen, to undo (soltar).
— V. pr. To come loose (aflojarse). || To loosen (aflojar). || To take off (quitarse).
descepar v. tr. To uproot (planta). || FIG. To wipe out, to eradicate (extirpar).
descercado, da adj. Open, unfenced.
descercar v. tr. To relieve (ciudad). || To remove the wall from (quitar la muralla). || To remove the fence from (quitar la cerca).
descerezar v. tr. To pulp (el café).
descerrajado, da adj. Forced (cerradura). || FIG. Licentious, loose, corrupt (de mal vivir).
descerrajadura f. Forcing (de una cerradura).
descerrajar v. tr. To force, to break open (una cerradura, una puerta). || FIG. y FAM. To fire, to let off: *descerrajar un tiro*, to fire a shot. | To drop, to say (decir). | To ask (preguntar).
descifrable adj. Decipherable (signo con sentido oculto). || Legible (letra).
descifrado m. Deciphering (de una escritura). || Decoding (con clave). || MÚS. Sight reading.
descifrador, ra adj. Deciphering.
— M. y f. Decipherer (de signo con sentido oculto). || Decoder (de mensaje).
desciframiento m. Deciphering (de una escritura). || Decoding (con clave).
descifrar v. tr. To decipher (signo con sentido oculto). || To decode (conociendo la clave). || FIG. To solve, to figure out (un misterio).
descifre m. Deciphering (de una escritura). || Decoding (con clave).
descinchar v. tr. To ungirth, to remove the girth from (quitar la cincha). || To slacken the girth of (aflojar la cincha).
desclavador m. Nail puller, nail wrench.
desclavar v. tr. To unnail, to remove the nails from (algo sujeto con clavos). || To unstick (algo pegado).
descoagulante adj. Liquefying.
descoagular v. tr. To liquefy, to dissolve.
descobajar v. tr. To stem, to remove the stem from (los racimos de uvas).
descocado, da adj. Forward, brazen: *una mujer descocada*, a brazen woman. || Cheeky, impudent (descarado).
descocamiento m. Brazenness, forwardness (atrevimiento). || Cheek, impudence (descaro).
descocar v. tr. AGR. To remove the insects from.
descocarse v. pr. FAM. To be brazen *o* forward (ser atrevido). | To be cheeky *o* impudent (descararse).
descoco m. Brazenness, forwardness (atrevimiento). || Cheek, impudence (descaro).
descogotar v. tr. To kill [with a blow on the back of the neck] (acogotar). || To cut off the antlers of [stag] (el venado).
descolar v. tr. To dock the tail of.
descolgadura f. o **descolgamiento** m. Taking down (de un cuadro, etc.). || Lowering, letting down (desde una posición alta). || Lifting (del teléfono).
descolgar* v. tr. To take down: *descolgar un cuadro*, to take down a picture. || To lift, to pick up (el teléfono). || To let down, to lower (desde una posición alta). || *Dejar el teléfono descolgado*, to leave the telephone off the hook.
— V. pr. To come down: *se ha descolgado el cuadro*, the picture has come down. || To lower o.s., to let o.s. down (bajar por una cuerda): *descolgarse de* or *por una pared*, to lower o.s. down *o* to let o.s. down a wall. || To slip, to slide [*por*, down] (bajar escurriéndose). || To come down, to rush down (bajar rápidamente): *las tropas se descolgaron de las montañas*, the troops

rushed down the mountains. || FIG. y FAM. To drop, to turn, to pop: *a veces se descuelga por casa a la hora de comer*, he sometimes drops in *o* turns up *o* pops in at our house at lunchtime. | To come up, to come out: *se descolgó con una noticia sensacional*, he came up with a sentational piece of news. | To surprise: *su tío se descolgó con mil pesetas*, his uncle surprised him with a thousand pesetas. | To descend, to turn up: *se descolgó pidiéndome dinero*, he descended on me asking for money. || FIG. y FAM. *Descolgarse con*, to come out with, to blurt out (decir, soltar).

descolocado, da adj. Unemployed, jobless, out of work.

descolonización f. Decolonization.

descolonizar v. tr. To decolonize.

descoloración f. Bleaching (del cabello).

descolorado, da adj. Discoloured [U.S., discolored]. || Faded (tela, color).

descoloramiento m. Discolouration [U.S., discoloration]. || Fading (de una tela, de un color). || Bleaching (del pelo).

descolorante adj. Bleaching.
— M. Bleaching agent.

descolorar v. tr. To discolour [U.S., to discolor] (hacer perder el color). || To fade (tela, color): *el sol descolora todos los vestidos*, the sun fades all clothes. || To bleach (el cabello).
— V. pr. To lose colour [U.S., to lose color] (perder el color). || To fade (una tela, un color). || To be bleached (quedar blanco). || To bleach one's hair (una persona).

descolorido, da adj. Discoloured [U.S., discolored]. || Faded (tela, color). || Pale (pálido). || FIG. Dull, lifeless, colourless [U.S., colorless] (estilo).
— M. Discolouration [U.S., discoloration]. || Fading (de una tela, de un color). || Bleaching (del pelo).

descolorimiento m. V. DESCOLORIDO.

descolorir v. tr. V. DESCOLORAR.

descolladamente adv. Brilliantly, outstandingly: *siempre ha intervenido descolladamente en las sesiones del Parlamento*, he has always spoken brilliantly in parliamentary debates.

descollamiento m. Superiority.

descollante adj. Outstanding.

descollar* v. intr. To stand out, to excel: *este alumno descuella mucho entre los demás*, this pupil stands out a great deal amongst the others. || To stand out, to be outstanding: *no hay nada que descuelle en su vida*, there is nothing which stands out in his life. || To distinguish o.s., to excel: *ha descollado en la pintura de frescos*, he has distinguished himself in fresco painting. || To rise, to stand out (una montaña, etc.).

descombrar v. tr. To clear (despejar).

descombro m. Clearing.

descomedidamente adv. Rudely, insolently (con insolencia): *hablar descomedidamente*, to speak rudely. || Excessively, to excess, immoderately: *beber descomedidamente*, to drink excessively.

descomedido, da adj. Rude, insolent (insolente). || Excessive, immoderate (desmedido). || Extreme (extremoso).

descomedimiento m. Rudeness, insolence (insolencia). || Excess (exceso).

descomedirse* v. pr. To go too far (excederse). || To be rude *o* insolent (faltar al respeto).

descompaginar v. tr. To upset, to disarrange (descomponer). || FIG. To upset, to disrupt: *la huelga descompagina todos mis proyectos*, the strike upsets all my plans.

descompás m. Disproportion, lack of proportion.

descompasadamente adv. Out of time (sin ritmo). || Excessively, immoderately (con exceso). || Rudely (con insolencia).

descompasado, da adj. Out of time (sin ritmo). || Disproportionate, immoderate (desproporcionado). || Rude (insolente).

descompasarse v. pr. To be rude *o* insolent (faltar al respeto). || To go too far (excederse).

descompensación f. Decompensation.

descomponer* v. tr. To decompose, to rot, to decay: *descomponer un cuerpo*, to decompose a body. || QUÍM. To decompose. || FÍS. To resolve (una fuerza). || MAT. To split up (una fracción). || GRAM. To split up (una frase). || To break down: *descomponer en partes una teoría*, to break down a theory into parts. || To break, to put out of order (un mecanismo): *descomponer un reloj*, to break a watch; *descomponer un motor*, to put an engine out of order. || To disturb, to mess up, to upset (los proyectos). || To spoil: *me has descompuesto el peinado*, you have spoiled my hairdo. || To disarrange, to disrupt, to upset (el orden). || FIG. To upset, to disturb: *me descompone ver tantas injusticias*, it upsets me to see so much injustice. | To annoy, to irritate, to put out (irritar). | To distort, to convulse: *el miedo descompuso sus rasgos*, fear distorted his features. || *Descomponerle a uno el intestino* or *el vientre*, to upset s.o.'s stomach.
— V. pr. To decompose, to decay, to rot: *el cadáver se ha descompuesto*, the corpse has decomposed. || QUÍM. To decompose. || FÍS. To resolve (fuezas). || GRAM. y MAT. To split up (una frase, una fracción). || To get out of order, to break down (mecanismo). || FIG. To get angry *o* annoyed, to get worked up, to lose one's temper (irritarse). | To get upset: *me descompongo cuando veo todo lo que tengo que hacer*, I get upset when I see all that I have to do. | To be distorted (rasgos, cara, etc.). | To go to pieces (estropearse). || *Se me descompuso el intestino* or *el vientre*, I had an upset stomach, my stomach was upset.

descomponible adj. Decomposable.

descomposición f. Decay, rotting, decomposition (acción de pudrirse). || QUÍM. Decomposition. || FÍS. Resolution (de fuerzas). || MAT. Factoring, factorizing (de un número). || GRAM. Construing (de una frase). || FIG. Decadence, decline: *la descomposición del Imperio Romano*, the decadence of the Roman Empire. | Distortion, discomposure, convulsion (de la cara). | Breakdown, failure (de un mecanismo). || *Descomposición intestinal* or *del vientre*, diarrhoea (diarrea).

descompostura f. Breaking (rotura). || Breakdown (de un motor). || Slovenliness, untidiness, carelessness (desaliño). || Impudence, rudeness, brazenness (descaro). || Lack of modesty (falta de pudor). || Discomposure, distorsion (del rostro). || Disorder (desorden).

descompresión f. Decompression.

descompresor m. Reducing valve (válvula). || AUT. Decompressor.

descomprimir v. tr. To decompress. || To depressurize.

descompuesto, ta adj. Decomposed, decayed, rotten (podrido). || QUÍM. Decomposed. || Broken: *reloj descompuesto*, broken watch. || Broken down, out of order: *motor descompuesto*, broken down engine. || FIG. Upset (trastornado). | Brazen, impudent (descarado). | Distorted, convulsed: *rostro descompuesto*, distorted face. | Angry: *gritos descompuestos*, angry shouts. || Untidy (desordenado). | Slovenly (desaliñado). || — *Estar descompuesto*, to have diarrhoea (tener diarrea). || FIG. *Tener el cuerpo descompuesto*, not to feel well. || *Tener el vientre descompuesto*, to have diarrhoea (tener diarrea), to have an upset stomach.

descomunal adj. Enormous, huge, colossal: *estatura descomunal*, huge stature; *mentira descomunal*, huge lie. || FIG. y FAM. Fantastic, magnificent: *una película descomunal*, a fantastic film.

descomunalmente adv. Extremely, extraordinarily, tremendously. || Excessively, to excess, too much: *beber descomunalmente*, to drink excessively. || FAM. Magnificently, superbly, tremendously well (muy bien).

desconcentración f. Decentralization.

desconcentrar v. tr. To decentralize, to break up.

desconceptuar v. tr. To misjudge (juzgar mal). || To discredit (desacreditar).

desconcertadamente adv. In a confused *o* disorderly way.

desconcertador, ra adj. Disconcerting, upsetting.

desconcertante adj. Disconcerting, upsetting.

desconcertar* v. tr. FIG. To disconcert, to upset, to put out (perturbar). | To confuse, to disconcert (desorientar): *lo hago para desconcertar al adversario*, I do it to confuse my opponent; *mi pregunta lo ha desconcertado*, my question has confused him. || To dislocate (hueso).
— V. pr. FIG. To be disconcerted *o* put out (turbarse). | To lose one's temper (enfadarse). | To be upset (el estómago). | To break down, not to work (un mecanismo). | To be dislocated (huesos). || *Yo no me desconcierto por cualquier cosa*, I don't let anything upset me.

desconcierto m. FIG. Disorder, confusion (desorden): *sembrar el desconcierto en el país*, to cause disorder in the country. | Disagreement, discord (desavenencia). | Confusion, perplexity, bewilderment (confusión).

desconchado m. o **desconchadura** f. Peeling, flaking (de una pared). || Bare patch (parte sin enlucido). || Chipping (de la loza). || Chip, nick (parte desconchada de la loza).

desconchar v. tr. To make peel *o* flake, to peel off: *la humedad ha desconchado la pared*, the damp has made the wall flake. || To chip (la loza). || *Pared desconchada*, flaking *o* peeling wall.
— V. pr. To peel off, to flake off (una pared). || To get chipped, to chip (la loza).

desconchón m. Bare patch, patch of flaking paint: *la pared tiene desconchones*, there are bare patches on the wall. || Chip (en la loza).

desconectar v. tr. ELECTR. To disconnect. | To switch off, to turn off (la radio, etc.). | To take out, to pull out (el enchufe). | To unplug (desenchufar). || FIG. *Estar desconectado de*, not to have contact with, not to be in contact with.
— V. pr. To become disconnected.

desconexión f. ELECTR. Disconnexion, disconnection. || FIG. Disconnection.

desconfiado, da adj. Distrustful: *una persona desconfiada*, a distrustful person. || Unsure, suspicious (que tiene sospechas): *estar desconfiado*, to be suspicious.
— M. y f. Wary *o* distrustful person.

desconfianza f. Distrust, mistrust, wariness, suspicion (falta de confianza).

desconfiar v. intr. To distrust, not to trust, to have no confidence: *desconfío de ese hombre*, I do not trust that man, I have no confidence in that man. || To be distrustful (ser desconfiado). || To doubt, not to be sure (no creer): *desconfío de que las ostras estén frescas*, I doubt that the oysters are fresh. || To suspect (sos-

pechar). || — *¡Desconfíe!*, beware! || *Desconfíe de las imitaciones*, beware of imitations.
desconforme adj. V. DISCONFORME.
desconformidad f. V. DISCONFORMIDAD.
descongelación f. Unfreezing (de créditos). || Defrosting (de la nevera).
descongelar v. tr. To defrost (nevera). || To unfreeze: *descongelar créditos*, to unfreeze credits.
descongestión f. Relieving of congestion, clearing.
descongestionar v. tr. To relieve congestion in: *descongestionar la cabeza, una calle*, to relieve congestion in the head, in a street. || FIG. To clear (despejar).
desconocer* v. tr. Not to know, not to be acquainted with: *desconozco a esta persona*, I do not know this person. || Not to know, to be unaware of, to be ignorant of: *desconozco su punto de vista*, I do not know his point of view. || Not to recognize: *tanto ha cambiado que lo desconocí*, he has changed so much that I didn't recognize him. || To deny (negar): *desconozco esas afirmaciones*, I deny those statements. || To disown: *desconoció a su hijo*, he disowned his son. || Not to recognize: *desconoce los méritos de los demás*, he does not recognize other people's merits.
desconocido, da adj. Unknown: *un pintor, un país desconocido*, an unknown painter, country; *desconocido de* or *para todos*, unknown to everyone. || Unrecognizable (que ha cambiado): *desde su enfermedad está desconocido*, since his illness he is unrecognizable. || Unrecognized: *méritos desconocidos*, unrecognized merits. || Strange, unfamiliar (que no se conoce). || Ungrateful (desagradecido). || *Vivir desconocido*, to live unnoticed.
— M. y f. Stranger, unknown person. || Newcomer (recién llegado). || — *Lo desconocido*, the unknown. || *Un ilustre desconocido*, a nobody.
desconocimiento m. Ignorance (*de*, of), disregard (*de*, for) (ignorancia). || Repudiation (de los deberes). || Ingratitude.
desconsideración f. Lack of consideration, thoughtlessness, inconsiderateness.
desconsideradamente adv. Inconsiderately, without consideration, thoughtlessly.
desconsiderado, da adj. Inconsiderate, thoughtless.
desconsiderar v. tr. To be inconsiderate towards, to lack consideration for.
desconsoladamente adv. Sadly, disconsolately, sorrowfully.
desconsolado, da adj. Unconsoled (que no recibe consuelo). || Disconsolate, distressed, grieved (afligido). || Sad (triste). || Dejected (desanimado).
desconsolador, ra adj. Distressing, heartbreaking, grievous.
desconsolar* v. tr. To distress, to grieve.
desconsuelo m. Distress, grief, affliction (pena). || Sadness, sorrow (tristeza).
descontado, da adj. V. DESCONTAR.
descontaminación f. Decontamination.
descontaminar v. tr. To decontaminate.
descontar* v. tr. To deduct: *descontar el diez por ciento*, to deduct ten per cent. || Not to count: *descontando las vacaciones y los domingos quedan más de doscientos cincuenta días de trabajo*, not counting holidays and Sundays there are more than two hundred and fifty working days left. || FIG. To discount, to disregard: *hay mucho que descontar en las alabanzas que le tributan*, you must discount a lot in people's praises for him. || To take for granted (considerar seguro). || COM. To discount (un efecto a pagar). || — *Dar por descontado*, to take for granted: *doy por descontado su éxito*, I am taking his success for granted. || *Descontarse años*, to make out that one is younger than one is. || *Por descontado*, of course.
descontentadizo, za adj. Hard to please, fastidious.
descontentar v. tr. To displease, to make discontent.
— V. pr. To be displeased.
descontento, ta adj. Discontented, unhappy, displeased, dissatisfied: *descontento con su propia suerte, de sí mismo*, unhappy with one's lot, with o.s.
— M. y f. Discontented *o* dissatisfied person. || *Los descontentos declararon una huelga*, the discontented *o* the dissatisfied declared a strike. || — M. Displeasure, dissatisfaction. || Discontent, unrest (de la población).
descontrolado, da adj. Uncontrolled.
desconvenir* v. intr. Not to agree, to disagree (en las opiniones). || Not to go together, not to match (cosas).
descorazonadamente adv. FIG. Dejectedly, dishearenedly, downheartedly (sin ánimo).
descorazonador, ra adj. Discouraging, disheartening.
descorazonamiento m. FIG. Disheartenment, discouragement, dejection.
descorazonar v. tr. FIG. To dishearten, to get down, to discourage (desanimar): *este tiempo me descorazona*, this weather disheartens me. || (P.us.). To tear out the heart of (arrancar el corazón de).
— V. pr. To lose heart, to get discouraged.
descorchador m. Bark stripper [of cork trees] (obrero). || Corkscrew (sacacorchos).
descorchar v. tr. To strip the bark from [cork trees] (los alcornoques). || To uncork (una botella). || FIG. To force (abrir por la fuerza).
descorche m. Bark stripping (de los alcornoques). || Uncorking (de una botella).
descordar* v. tr. MÚS. To remove the strings from [an instrument]. || TAUR. V. DESCABELLAR.
descornar* v. tr. To dehorn (arrancar los cuernos de).
— V. pr. FIG. y FAM. To rack one's brains (pensar). | To slog away (trabajar).
descoronar v. tr. To discrown, to depose (a un rey).
descorrer v. tr. To draw, to open: *descorrer las cortinas*, to draw the curtains. || To remove (un velo). || *Descorrer el cerrojo*, to unbolt the door.
descortés adj. Impolite, rude, discourteous.
descortesía f. Impoliteness, rudeness, discourtesy.
descortezadura f. Piece of bark (trozo de corteza). || Bare patch (parte descortezada).
descortezamiento m. Bark stripping, decortication (de los árboles). || Peeling (de la fruta).
descortezar v. tr. To strip the bark from, to decorticate (árboles). || To cut the crust off (el pan). || To peel (la fruta). || FIG. y FAM. To knock the rough edges off *o* the corners off, to refine (desbastar).
descosedura f. V. DESCOSIDO.
descoser v. tr. To unpick, to unstitch (las costuras).
— V. pr. To come undone *o* unstitched.
descosido, da adj. Unpicked, unstitched (en costura). || Undone, unstitched (estado accidental). || FIG. Disjointed, disconnected: *discurso descosido*, disjointed speech. | Talkative, indiscreet (indiscreto).
— M. Open seam, seam which has come undone *o* unstitched (costura). || — FIG. y FAM. *Beber como un descosido*, to drink like a fish. | *Comer como un descosido*, to eat like a horse. | *Correr como un descosido*, to run like the devil. | *Hablar como un descosido*, to talk nineteen to the dozen. | *Reír como un descosido*, to laugh one's head off, to split one's sides laughing.
descostillarse v. pr. To fall flat on one's back (caerse).
descostrar v. tr. To cut the crust off.
descotado, da adj./s. m. V. ESCOTADO.
descotar v. tr. V. ESCOTAR.
descote m. V. ESCOTE.
descoyuntamiento m. MED. Dislocation. || Dislocation (de cosas). || Exhaustion, fatigue (malestar).
descoyuntar v. tr. MED. To dislocate. || To dislocate (cosas). || FIG. To twist, to force the sense of (desvirtuar). || FIG. *Estar descoyuntado*, to be double-jointed (un artista de circo).
— V. pr. To dislocate: *descoyuntarse la cadera*, to dislocate one's hip. || To get dislocated: *se descoyuntó la articulación*, his joint got dislocated. || FIG. y FAM. *Descoyuntarse de risa*, to split one's sides laughing.
descrédito m. Disrepute, discredit: *caer en descrédito*, to fall into disrepute. || *Ir en descrédito de*, to be to the discredit of, to damage the reputation of.
descreído, da adj. Disbelieving, unbelieving.
— M. y f. Disbeliever, unbeliever.
descreimiento m. Disbelief, unbelief.
descremar v. tr. To skim (la leche).
descrestar v. tr. To cut off the crest of. || FIG. To deceive (engañar).
describible adj. Describable.
describir v. tr. To trace, to describe (trazar): *describir una órbita*, to trace an orbit. || To describe: *describir un paisaje*, to describe a landscape.
descripción f. Tracing, describing, description (acción de trazar). || Description: *una hermosa descripción*, a beautiful description.
descriptible adj. Describable.
descriptivo, va adj. Descriptive: *geometría, anatomía descriptiva*, descriptive geometry, anatomy.
descrismar v. tr. FAM. To smash *o* to bash [s.o.'s] face in (pegar).
— V. pr. FAM. To break one's neck (romperse la cara). || FIG. y FAM. To fly off the handle (encolerizarse). | To slog away, to work o.s. to death, to wear o.s. out (trabajar). | To rack one's brains (pensar).
descristianización f. Dechristianization.
descristianizar v. tr. To turn away from Christianity, to dechristianize.
descrito, ta adj. Described, traced (trazado). || Described (narrado).
descruzar v. tr. To uncross: *descruzar los brazos*, to uncross one's arms.
descuadernar v. tr. To unbind, to remove the binding from (un libro). || FIG. To confuse, to upset (turbar).
— V. pr. To come apart, to come unbound (un libro).
descuadrillado, da adj. VET. Hipshot (caballo).
— M. VET. Sprained haunch (del caballo).
descuajar v. tr. To liquefy, to dissolve (poner líquido). || FIG. y FAM. To dishearten, to discourage (desanimar). || AGR. To uproot (desarraigar). || FIG. To wipe out, to eradicate (extirpar).
— V. pr. To liquefy, to dissolve.
descuajaringar v. tr. FAM. To take *o* to pull to pieces (descomponer). || FAM. *Estar descuajaringado*, to be exhausted *o* worn out (de cansancio).
descuaje o **descuajo** m. AGR. Uprooting.
descuartizamiento m. Quartering (suplicio). || Cutting into joints, quartering, cutting up (de un animal).
descuartizar v. tr. To quarter (en un suplicio). || To cut into joints, to quarter [the carcass of], to cut up: *descuartizar un ternero*, to cut a calf into joints. || FAM. To pull to pieces, to tear apart.

descubierta f. MIL. Scouting, reconnoitering, reconnaissance. || MAR. Inspection of the rigging. || — *A la descubierta*, openly (sin disfraz), in the open (sin protección). || MIL. *Ir a la descubierta*, to scout, to reconnoitre.

descubiertamente adv. Openly.

descubierto, ta adj. Discovered. || Uncovered (no cubierto). || Clear: *el cielo estaba descubierto*, the sky was clear. || Exposed, open (expuesto). || Open (automóvil). || Open, bare, treeless (terreno). || Bareheaded, hatless, without a hat (persona). || Bare (cabeza). || *Iban descubiertos*, they were not wearing hats.
— M. COM. Deficit (de cuenta corriente). | Bears, *pl.*, shorts, *pl.* (en Bolsa). | Shortage (en el presupuesto). || Open space (lugar). || REL. Exposition [of the Sacrament]. || — *Al descubierto*, openly (sin disfraz), in the open (sin protección). || *En todo lo descubierto*, in the whole world. || *Estar en descubierto*, to be overdrawn, to be in the red (ser deudor), to be stuck for words (quedarse cortado). || *Quedar al descubierto*, to come out into the open, to be exposed.

descubridor, ra adj. Discovering. || MAR. Reconnaissance, scouting (embarcación).
— M. y f. Discoverer. || — M. MIL. Scout (batidor).

descubrimiento m. Discovery: *el descubrimiento de América*, the discovery of America; *la época de los descubrimientos*, the age of discovery. || Unveiling (de una estatua, lápida).

descubrir v. tr. To uncover (quitar lo que cubre). || To take the lid off (una cacerola). || To discover: *descubrir un país*, to discover a country; *descubrir un nuevo antibiótico*, to discover a new antibiotic. || To unveil: *descubrir una estatua*, to unveil a statue. || To find (un tesoro, minas de oro, etc.). || To reveal (revelar): *descubrir sus intenciones*, to reveal one's intentions. || To bring to light (un crimen). || To detect (un criminal, un fraude). || To discover, to find out (una conjuración). || To unmask (un impostor). || To be able to see, to make out (divisar): *desde la ventana descubríamos todo el valle*, from the window we could see the whole valley. || To bare (la cabeza). || To expose, to lay down (los naipes). || MAR. To sight (la tierra). || MIL. To expose (la retaguardia). || REL. To expose [the Sacrament]. || — FIG. *Descubrir América* or *el Mediterráneo*, to force an open door. || *Descubrir su juego*, to show one's hand *o* one's cards.
— V. pr. To be discovered. || To take off one's hat (quitarse el sombrero). || To raise one's hat (para saludar). || To clear (el cielo). || To come into sight (verse). || FIG. To come out, to come to light (un crimen, un secreto, la verdad). | To confide, to open one's heart: *descubrirse con alguien*, to confide in *o* to open one's heart to s.o. || To reveal o.s., to show o.s. (mostrarse). || To lower one's guard (en esgrima, boxeo). || FAM. *¡Hay que descubrirse!*, bravo!, well done!

descuento m. Deduction (acción de descontar). || COM. Discount: *con descuento*, at a discount. | Discount, reduction: *conceder un descuento a un cliente*, to give a discount *o* a reduction to a client. || Stoppage: *descuento del salario*, wage stoppage. || — *Descuento por no declaración de siniestro*, no-claims bonus. | *Descuento racional* or *matemático*, true *o* arithmetical discount. || *Tipo de descuento*, discount rate (privado), bank rate (de un Estado).

descuerar v. tr. To skin (reses). || *Amer.* To pull to pieces, to criticize (criticar).

descuidadamente adv. Carelessly, negligently (sin cuidado). || In a slovenly way, untidily (con desaseo). || Rashly, thoughtlessly, without thinking, carelessly (sin pensarlo). || Nonchalantly, carefree, casually (sin preocupación).

descuidado, da adj. Careless, negligent, thoughtless (negligente). || Untidy, slovenly (en su aseo personal). || Casual, easygoing, carefree: *es muy descuidado, no se preocupa por nada*, he's very casual, he doesn't worry about a thing. || Unprepared (desprevenido). || Neglected: *libro, niño descuidado*, neglected book, child. || — *Coger descuidado*, to catch unawares *o* napping *o* off guard. || *Estar descuidado*, to relax, not to worry, to rest assured (no preocuparse): *puedes estar descuidado*, you can relax, you need not worry.

descuidar v. tr. To neglect: *descuidar sus deberes*, to neglect one's duties. || To free, to release (de una obligación). || To distract (distraer).
— V. intr. Not to worry: *¡descuida!*, don't worry. || To forget (*de*, to), to neglect (*de*, to).
— V. pr. To neglect: *descuidarse de su trabajo*, to neglect one's work. || To be careless (no prestar atención). || To let o.s. go, to neglect o.s. (en el atavío). || Not to be careful, not to watch out: *si te descuidas, te roban la cartera*, if you are not careful, you will have your wallet stolen. || Not to bother, not to worry (no preocuparse): *siempre se descuida de todo*, he never bothers about anything. || To neglect one's health: *se ha descuidado y ahora tiene gripe*, he has neglected his health and now he has influenza. || — *En cuanto se descuida usted*, if you are not careful, if you do not watch out. || *Me descuidé un momento y tropecé con un árbol*, my attention wandered for a minute and I bumped into a tree. || *Si me descuido*, if I am not careful (presente), if I hadn't been careful (pasado).

descuidero m. Sneak thief, pickpocket.

descuido m. Negligence, carelessness, neglect (negligencia): *el accidente ocurrió por un descuido del automovilista*, the accident happened because of negligence on the part of the motorist. || Absentmindedness, inadvertence, inattention (falta de atención): *un momento de descuido*, a moment's inadvertence. || Slip, mistake (error): *hay muchos descuidos en ese libro*, there are many mistakes in that book. || Slovenliness, untidiness (en el arreglo personal). || — *Al descuido*, negligently, carelessly (sin cuidado), casually, nonchalantly (con descuido afectado). || *Al menor descuido*, if my [your, his, etc.] attention wanders [wandered, etc.] for a minute. || *Con descuido*, without thinking. || *En un descuido*, when least expected. || *Por descuido*, inadvertently.

descular v. tr. To break the bottom of.

desde adv. Since (tiempo): *desde el año cero*, since the year dot. || From (lugar): *desde Madrid hasta Londres*, from Madrid to London. || — *Desde abajo*, from below. || *Desde ahora*, from now on. || *Desde arriba*, from above. || *Desde ayer acá*, since yesterday. || *¿Desde cuándo?*, since when? || *Desde entonces*, since then, from that time on: *no le volví a ver desde entonces*, I haven't seen him again since then. || *¿Desde hace cuánto tiempo?*, how long?: *¿desde hace cuánto tiempo está lloviendo?*, how long has it been raining? || *Desde hace poco*, for a short time, not for long: *tiene un coche desde hace poco*, he has had a car for a short time, he hasn't had a car for long. || *Desde hace tiempo* or *mucho tiempo* for a long time: *está allí desde hace mucho tiempo*, he has been there for a long time. || *Desde hace* (*hacía*) *un mes*, for a month, it is [was] a month since: *no le he visto desde hace un mes*, I haven't seen him for a month, it is a month since I saw him; *no le había visto desde hacía un mes*, I hadn't seen him for a month, it was a month since I had seen him. || *Desde... hasta*, from... to, from... until: *desde las ocho hasta las diez*, from eight o'clock to ten. || *Desde lejos*, from afar, from a long way off. || *Desde lo alto de*, from the top of. || *Desde luego*, of course, certainly. || *Desde mi punto de vista*, as I see it, as far as I can see. || *Desde niño*, since I (you, he, etc.) was (were, etc.) a child, from childhood. || *Desde que*, since. || *Desde siempre*, for ever. || *Amer. Desde ya*, from now on (de ahora en adelante), right now (ahora mismo).

desdecir* v. intr. To be unworthy of, to let down: *desdecir de su familia*, to be unworthy of one's family, to let one's family down. || Not to go, not to match: *su corbata desdice de su traje*, his tie does not go with his suit. || To be inconsistent (*de*, with) [no concordar]. || — *Desdecir de su pasado*, to decline, to degenerate, to go downhill. || *Desdecir uno de otro*, not to match (colores).
— V. pr. To take back what one has said (retractarse). || To go back, to retract, to withdraw: *desdecirse de su promesa*, to go back on one's promise, to retract one's promise. || To repudiate, to disown: *desdecirse de sus opiniones*, to repudiate one's opinions. || To contradict o.s. (contradecirse).

desdén m. Contempt, scorn, disdain (desprecio). || *Al desdén*, casually, nonchalantly.

desdentado, da adj. Toothless. || ZOOL. Edentate.
— M. pl. ZOOL. Edentata.

desdentar* v. tr. To remove the teeth of.

desdeñable adj. Insignificant, negligible (insignificante). || Despicable, contemptible (despreciable). || *No desdeñable*, far from negligible.

desdeñar v. tr. To scorn, to disdain: *desdeña a sus compañeros*, he scorns his companions. || To turn one's nose up at, to scorn: *desdeña mis ofertas*, he turns his nose up at my offers. || To forget, to ignore (ignorar).
— V. pr. Not to deign: *desdeñarse de hablar*, not to deign to speak.

desdeñoso, sa adj. Scornful, disdainful, contemptuous.

desdibujado, da adj. Blurred: *contornos desdibujados*, blurred outlines.

desdibujarse v. pr. FIG. To fade, to become faint *o* blurred (borrarse).

desdicha f. Misfortune (desgracia): *sufrir continuas desdichas*, to suffer continuous misfortunes. || Unhappiness, wretchedness, misfortune, misery (infelicidad). || — *Para colmo de desdichas*, to top it all. || *Por desdicha*, unfortunately.

desdichado, da adj. Unfortunate, poor, pitiful, unlucky (desgraciado). || Unhappy (triste). || Wretched, despicable (despreciable).
— M. y f. Poor devil, poor wretch (pobre desgraciado). || Wretch (persona despreciable). || *¡Desdichado de mí, de ti*, woe is me, woe is you.

desdoblamiento m. Straightening (de un alambre, etc.). || Unfolding (de una sábana, etc.). || Splitting (conversión en dos). || FIG. Explanation, elucidation (aclaración). || *Desdoblamiento de la personalidad*, split personality.

desdoblar v. tr. To straighten (un alambre, etc.). || To unfold: *desdoblar un mapa*, to unfold a map. || To split (convertir en dos).

desdorar v. tr. To remove the gilt from. || FIG. To tarnish (la reputación de uno).

desdoro m. Tarnishing. || FIG. Stain, blot. || *Sin desdoro de*, without tarnishing *o* harming: *puedes hacerlo sin*

desdoro de tu fama, you can do it without tarnishing your reputation.
deseable adj. Desirable. || *Poco deseable*, undesirable.
deseado, da adj. Desired.
deseador, ra adj. Desirous.
desear v. tr. To want (querer): *deseo que hable*, I want you to speak; *¿qué desea de mí?*, what do you want of me? || To desire, to long for, to wish for: *deseamos la libertad*, we desire liberty. || To wish: *desearía que me ayudases*, I wish you would help me; *desearía ser*, I wish I were. || To wish, to desire, to want: *desear hacer algo*, to wish to do sth. || To long for: *estoy deseando que llegue mi amigo*, I am longing for my friend to arrive. || To wish: *le deseo mucho éxito*, I wish you every success. || — *Cuanto más se tiene más se desea*, the more you have, the more you want. || *Dejar bastante que desear*, to leave a lot to be desired. || *Desear con ansia*, to long *o* to yearn for. || *Desearía tener amigos*, I should like to have friends. || *Es de desear*, it is to be hoped. || *Hacerse desear*, to make o.s. wanted, to keep people waiting. || *¿Qué desea?*, what would you like? (qué quiere), what can I do for you? (en qué puedo servirle).
desecación f. Drying, desiccation (de comestibles). || Drying (natural). || Withering (de plantas). || Draining, drainage, reclaiming: *desecación de una marisma*, draining of marsh.
desecado, da adj. Dried, desiccated.
— M. V. DESECACIÓN.
desecador, ra adj. Drying. || QUÍM. Desiccative, desiccating.
— M. Desiccator.
desecamiento m. V. DESECACIÓN.
desecante adj. Drying. || QUÍM. Desiccative, desiccating, desiccant.
desecar v. tr. To dry up: *el calor deseca la tierra*, heat dries up the earth. || To drain: *desecar un estanque*, to drain a pond. || QUÍM. To desiccate.
— V. pr. To dry up.
desecativo, va adj. Drying. || QUÍM. Desiccative, desiccating, desiccant.
desechable adj. Disposable, throw-away.
desechar v. tr. To discard, to throw away *o* out (tirar): *desechar un traje viejo*, to discard an old suit. || To put aside, to get rid of, to cast aside: *debes desechar estos malos pensamientos*, you should put aside these bad thoughts. || To reject: *desechar un consejo, una proposición*, to reject advice, a suggestion. || To drop, to discard (una idea, un proyecto). || To refuse, to turn down (un empleo, una dignidad).
desecho m. Castoff (prenda de vestir): *armario lleno de desechos*, wardrobe full of castoffs. || Piece of rubbish, throw-out (cosa tirada). || Throw-out, reject (después de elegir lo bueno). || Offal (de carnicero). || FIG. Contempt, scorn (desprecio). | Scum, dregs, *pl.* (lo peor). | Dead loss (persona inútil). || — Pl. Rubbish, *sing.*: *el desván está lleno de desechos*, the attic is full of rubbish. || Castoffs (vestidos). || Waste, *sing.* (de una industria). || Rejects, throw-outs (después de elegir lo bueno). || — *De desecho*, cast-off (vestidos), scrap (máquina), waste (producto). || TAUR. *Desecho de tienta*, bull that has not proved brave enough in the "tienta" [test]. (It is either slaughtered for meat or used in a *becerrada* or a *novillada*.) || *Desechos de metal*, scrap metal. || *Desechos radiactivos*, radioactive waste.
deselectrizar v. tr. ELECTR. To discharge.
desellar v. tr. To unseal.
desembalaje m. Unpacking.
desembalar v. tr. To unpack: *desembalar una máquina*, to unpack a machine.
desembaldosar v. tr. To remove the tiles *o* flagstones from, to untile, to unpave.
desembanastar v. tr. To take out of a basket. || FIG. To chatter about (hablar). || To draw (un arma).
desembarazadamente adv. Easily, with ease (fácilmente). || Freely, with ease (con soltura).
desembarazado, da adj. Free, clear (libre). || Free and easy (desenvuelto). || Uncluttered, unencumbered (desahogado).
desembarazar v. tr. To clear (un camino). || To empty, to clear (un piso).
— V. pr. To rid o.s. of, to get rid of: *desembarazarse de algo, de alguien*, to rid o.s. of sth., of s.o., to get rid of sth., of s.o.
desembarazo m. Clearing. || Self-confidence, ease (desenfado). || *Amer.* Childbirth (parto).
desembarcadero m. Landing stage, pier, wharf.
desembarcar v. tr. To unload, to disembark: *desembarcar mercancías*, to unload merchandise. || To land, to put ashore (personas).
— V. intr. To disembark, to land, to go ashore, to debark (p.us.): *desembarcamos en el puerto por la noche*, we disembarked in the port at night. || To disembark (de un avión). || FIG. y FAM. To lead (*en*, to) (una escalera). | To land (llegar).
desembarco m. Landing, disembarkation (de personas). || Landing (de tropas): *el desembarco de Normandía*, the Normandy landing. || Landing (de escalera).
desembargar v. tr. To clear (desembarazar). || JUR. To lift *o* to raise the embargo on (suprimir el embargo).
desembargo m. JUR. Lifting *o* raising of an embargo.
desembarque m. Disembarkation, landing (de pasajeros). || Unloading, disembarkation (de mercancías). || Disembarkation (de un avión). || *Tarjeta de desembarque*, landing card.
desembarrancar v. tr. To refloat (un barco).
desembarrar v. tr. To clear the mud from, to clean the mud off (quitar el barro).
desembaular v. tr. To take out (sacar). || To unpack (desembalar). || FIG. y FAM. To get [sth.] off one's chest (desahogarse).
desembelesarse v. pr. To recover, to come to one's senses (salir de su embeleso).
desembocadero m. V. DESEMBOCADURA.
desembocadura f. Mouth, outlet (de un río, de una cañería). || Opening, end (de una calle).
desembocar v. intr. To flow, to run: *este río desemboca en el Océano Atlántico*, this river flows into the Atlantic Ocean. || To meet, to join, to lead into: *esta avenida desemboca en la calle mayor*, this avenue meets the main street. || FIG. To lead, to end: *disturbios que pueden desembocar en la guerra*, disturbances which can lead to war *o* end in war; *razonamientos que no desembocan en nada*, reasoning which leads to nothing *o* leads nowhere. || *El río Mersey desemboca en Liverpool*, the mouth of the river Mersey is in Liverpool, the river Mersey ends in Liverpool.
desembojar v. tr. To remove [the silk cocoons] from the bushes.
desembolsado, da adj. Paid-up: *acciones desembolsadas*, paid-up shares (en la Bolsa). || Spent: *cantidad desembolsada*, sum spent.
desembolsar v. tr. To pay (pagar). || FIG. To lay out (gastar).
desembolso m. Payment (pago). || Payment, instalment [U.S., installment] (cada uno de los pagos). || — Pl. Expenses, costs (gastos). || *Desembolso inicial*, down payment (al comprar a plazos), initial outlay (gastos iniciales).
desemboque m. V. DESEMBOCADURA.
desemborrachar v. tr. To sober up.
desembotar v. tr. FIG. To sharpen [s.o.'s wits].
desembozar v. tr. To uncover, to reveal, to unmask (quitar el embozo de). || FIG. To uncover, to bring out into the open (descubrir).
desembragar v. tr. To disengage, to disconnect. || AUT. To release (el embrague).
— V. intr. AUT. To declutch, to put the clutch out.
desembrague m. Disengaging, disconnecting. || AUT. Declutching. | Clutch pedal (pedal).
desembravecer* v. tr. To tame (animales). || FIG. To calm.
— V. pr. To become tame (animales). || FIG. To calm down.
desembriagar v. tr. To sober up.
— V. pr. To sober up.
desembridar v. tr. To unbridle.
desembrollar v. tr. FAM. To sort out, to clear up, to clarify (aclarar). || To unravel, to disentangle (una madeja, etc.).
desembrozar v. tr. V. DESBROZAR.
desembrujar v. tr. To remove a spell from [s.o.], to free [s.o.] from a spell.
desembuchar v. tr. To disgorge (los pájaros). || FIG. y FAM. To come out with, to let out (revelar).
— V. intr. FIG. y FAM. To spill the beans (confesar). || *¡Desembucha!*, out with it!
desemejante adj. Dissimilar, different.
desemejanza f. Dissimilarity, difference.
desemejar v. intr. Not to be alike, to differ, to be dissimilar, to be unlike.
— V. tr. To alter, to change (cambiar).
desempacar v. tr. To unpack.
desempachar v. tr. To relieve from indigestion.
— V. pr. To be relieved from indigestion (el estómago). || FIG. To come out of one's shell (perder la timidez).
desempacho m. Relief from indigestion (del estómago). || FIG. Self-confidence, ease (soltura).
desempalagar v. tr. To restore one's appetite, to settle one's stomach.
— V. pr. To recover one's appetite, to feel better.
desempañar v. tr. To take the nappy off (a un niño). || To clean, to polish (un cristal).
desempapelar v. tr. To take the paper off, to unwrap (un paquete). || To strip the walls of: *desempapelar una habitación*, to strip the walls of a room.
desempaque o **desempaquetado** m. Unpacking, unwrapping.
desempaquetar v. tr. To unpack, to unwrap.
desemparejado, da adj. Odd: *tengo un calcetín desemparejado*, I've got an odd sock. || Without a partner, odd (desparejado).
desemparejar v. tr. To separate, to lose one of (un par de calcetines, etc.). || To leave without a partner (en un baile, etc.).
desempastar v. tr. To remove the filling from.
desempaste m. Removal of a filling (de un diente).
desempatar v. tr. To break the tie between: *desempatar los votos*, to break the tie between the votes.
— V. intr. DEP. To take the lead (en un partido). | To play off, to play a deciding match (jugar un partido de desempate).
desempate m. Play-off (en fútbol). || — DEP. *Gol de desempate*, deciding goal. | *Jugar un partido de desempate*, to play off, to play a deciding match.

desempedrado m. Removal of paving.
desempedrador m. Paving remover.
desempedrar* v. tr. To take up the paving of, to unpave.
desempeñar v. tr. To take out of pawn, to redeem (de una casa de empeño): *desempeñar sus alhajas*, to take one's jewels out of pawn. || To free from debt, to pay the debts of (pagar las deudas): *desempeñó a Juan*, he freed John from debt, he paid John's debts. || To carry out, to fulfil: *desempeñar una misión peligrosa*, to carry out a dangerous mission. || To fill, to occupy, to hold (un cargo). || To discharge, to fulfil, to carry out (el deber). || TEATR. y CINEM. To play: *desempeñar el papel de Desdémona*, to play the part of Desdemona; *desempeñar un papel muy importante*, to play an important role. || To get out of a fix *o* of difficulty (sacar de apuro).
— V. pr. To get out of debt, to free o.s. from debt. || To get out of a fix *o* of difficulty (salir de apuro).
desempeño m. Redeeming, redemption (de una prenda empeñada). || Discharge, carrying out, fulfilment (de un deber). || Carrying out, fulfilment, performance (de un cargo, etc.). || Freeing from *o* paying of debts (para otra persona). || Paying (de sus propias deudas). || Playing, acting, performance (de un papel).
desemperezar v. intr. To make an effort, to shake o.s., to pull o.s. together.
— V. pr. To make an effort, to shake o.s., to pull o.s. together.
desempleado, da adj. Unemployed, out of work.
— M. y f. Unemployed man, unemployed woman. || *Los desempleados*, the unemployed.
desempleo m. Unemployment.
desemplumar v. tr. To pluck.
desempolvadura f. Dusting.
desempolvar v. tr. To dust (quitar el polvo). || FIG. To revive, to unearth: *desempolvar viejos recuerdos*, to revive old memories.
desemponzoñar v. tr. To detoxicate, to detoxify (a una persona). || To remove the poison from (una cosa).
desempuñar v. tr. To let go.
desencabestrar v. tr. To untangle [a horse's] feet from the halter (el caballo).
desencadenamiento m. Unchaining, unleashing (de un perro). || FIG. Outbreak (de un ataque). | Outburst (de protestas, de hilaridad).
desencadenar v. tr. To unchain (quitar las cadenas). || To unleash (un perro). || FIG. To start, to spark off: *desencadenar una guerra*, to start a war. | To unleash (las pasiones). | To give rise to: *desencadenar aplausos, protestas*, to give rise to applause, to protests. || FIG. *Desencadenar la hilaridad*, to set everyone off laughing, to raise a storm of laughter.
— V. pr. FIG. To break out (ovaciones, guerra): *los aplausos se desencadenaron*, applause broke out. | To burst, to break: *la tempestad se desencadenó*, the storm broke. | To break loose, to explode (la cólera). | To rage (viento, pasión). || To break loose (soltarse).
desencajado, da adj. Twisted, contorted, distorted (cara). || Wild (ojos). || Dislocated (huesos). || Disconnected (desconectado).
desencajamiento m. Dislocation (de los huesos). || Distortion (del rostro). || Disconnection.
desencajar v. tr. To dislocate (los huesos). || To disjoint (separar). || To disconnect, to disengage (desconectar). || To unwedge, to free, to unblock (liberar una pieza). || To distort (demudar).
— V. pr. To become distorted (el rostro). || To look wild (los ojos). || To come apart (deshacerse). || To come off (una pieza).
desencajonamiento m. TAUR. Removal [of the bull] from the transport crate. || Unpacking.
desencajonar v. tr. To unpack, to uncrate. || ARQ. To remove the coffering from (un pozo). | To remove the timbering from (una galería). || TAUR. To remove [the bull] from the transport crate.
desencalladura f. o **desencallamiento** m. Refloating.
desencallar v. tr. To refloat.
desencaminar v. tr. V. DESCAMINAR.
desencanallar v. tr. To put back on the straight and narrow.
desencantador, ra adj. Disenchanting.
desencantamiento m. Disenchantment.
desencantar v. tr. To remove a spell from, to disenchant (quitar el hechizo). || To disillusion, to disappoint (decepcionar).
— V. pr. To be disappointed *o* disillusioned.
desencanto m. Disappointment, disillusionment (desengaño). || Freeing from a spell, disenchantment (desencantamiento). || *Sufrir un desencanto*, to be disappointed.
desencapillar v. tr. MAR. To unrig.
desencapotar v. tr. (P.us.). To uncloak, to take the cloak off. || FIG. To uncover, to uncloak (descubrir).
— V. pr. To take off one's cloak. || To clear (el cielo). || FIG. To brighten up.
desencaprichar v. tr. To rid [s.o.] of a whim *o* fancy.
desencarcelar v. tr. To release from prison, to free.
desencargar v. tr. To cancel an order for.
desenclavar v. tr. To unnail (desclavar).
desenclavijar v. tr. To remove the pegs from.
desencofrado m. Removal of shuttering *o* formwork (del hormigón). || MIN. Removal of timbering.
desencofrar v. tr. To remove the shuttering *o* formwork from (el hormigón). || To remove the timbering from (una galería).
desencoger v. tr. To stretch out (extender). || To unfold (desdoblar).
— V. pr. FIG. To come out of one's shell.
desencogimiento m. Self-confidence, ease.
desencoladura f. Ungluing, unsticking.
desencolar v. tr. To unglue, to unstick.
— V. pr. To come unglued *o* unstuck.
desencolerizar v. tr. To calm [down], to pacify.
— V. pr. To calm down, to cool down *o* off.
desenconar v. tr. To relieve the inflammation of. || FIG. To calm, to soothe (la cólera).
— V. pr. To calm down, to cool off (calmarse). || To control one's temper (contenerse).
desencono m. MED. Relief of inflammation. || Calming, pacification (acción de calmar). || Calm (calma). || Restraint, control (contención).
desencordar* v. tr. To unstring (un instrumento).
desencordelar v. tr. To untie (desatar).
desencorvar v. tr. To straighten.
desencuadernar v. tr. To unbind, to remove the binding from.
— V. pr. To come apart, to come unbound. || *El libro se desencuadernó*, the binding came off the book.
desenchufar v. tr. To unplug, to disconnect.
desenchufe m. Unplugging.
desendemoniar o **desendiablar** v. tr. To drive the evil spirits from, to exorcise.
desendiosar v. tr. FIG. To take down a peg or two (humillar). | To show up in one's true light, to show up for what one really is: *desendiosar a un gran personaje*, to show a great man up in his true light.
desenfadadamente adv. With ease *o* self-assurance, confidently.
desenfadaderas f. pl. Resourcefulness, *sing.* || *Tiene desenfadaderas*, he is resourceful.
desenfadado, da adj. Self-confident, self-assured, confident (desenvuelto). || Carefree, free and easy, easy, easygoing (despreocupado): *hablar con un tono desenfadado*, to speak in a carefree tone.
desenfadar v. tr. To calm down, to quieten.
desenfado m. Openness, frankness, ease (franqueza). || Self-confidence, assurance (desenvoltura). || Ease (facilidad). || Freedom from care (despreocupación).
desenfardar o **desenfardelar** v. tr. To unpack.
desenfilada f. MIL. Defilade.
desenfilar v. tr. MIL. To defilade, to cover from enemy fire (poner a cubierto).
desenfocado, da adj. Out of focus.
desenfocar v. tr. To put out of focus (fotografía). || FIG. To approach from the wrong angle (un problema).
desenfoque m. *El desenfoque es muy grande*, it is right out of focus.
desenfrenado, da adj. Wild, frantic: *baile desenfrenado*, wild dance. || Unbridled, uncontrolled, ravenous: *apetito desenfrenado*, unbridled appetite. || Unrestrained, unbridled, wild, frantic (pasiones).
desenfrenamiento m. V. DESENFRENO.
desenfrenar v. tr. To unbridle (el caballo).
— V. pr. FIG. To be let *o* to break loose (pasiones). | To give o.s. over to vice (caer en el desenfreno). | To break, to burst (tempestad). | To rage (viento). | To run riot, to go wild (la multitud).
desenfreno m. Wantonness, licentiousness (vicio). || Unleashing, unbridling (de las pasiones).
desenfundar v. tr. To remove from its case. || To draw (un arma). || To uncover (un mueble).
desenfurecer* v. tr. To calm *o* to quieten down, to pacify.
desenfurruñar v. tr. To calm down, to pacify.
desengalgar v. tr. To unchock (una rueda).
desenganchar v. tr. To unhook. || To take off: *desenganchar un abrigo de una percha*, to take a coat off a coat hanger. || To unhitch (caballerías). || To uncouple (vagones). || TECN. To disengage (piezas).
desenganche m. Unhitching (de las caballerías). || Uncoupling (de dos vagones). || Unhooking.
desengañado, da adj. Disillusioned (desilusionado): *estar desengañado de* or *con*, to be disillusoned by *o* with. || Disappointed (decepcionado). || *Amer.* Hideous, ugly (muy feo).
desengañador, ra adj. Disillusioning (que desilusiona). || Disappointing (que decepciona).
desengañar v. tr. To enlighten, to open the eyes of, to undeceive: *le creía inteligente pero sus profesores me han desengañado*, I thought he was intelligent but his teachers have enlightened me *o* have opened my eyes. || To disillusion (desilusionar). || To disappoint (decepcionar).
— V. pr. To realize the truth (ver la realidad). || To be disillusioned (desilusionarse). || To be disappointed (decepcionarse). || To realize: *¿te has desengañado de que no era verdad?*, have you realized that it was not true? || — *¡Desengáñate!*, don't you believe it! || *Desengañarse de sus ilusiones*, to lose one's illusions.
desengaño m. Enlightenment. || Eye-opener (cosa que abre los ojos a uno). || Disillusion, disillusionment

(desilusión). || Disappointment (decepción). || *Llevarse* or *sufrir un desengaño*, to be disillusioned, to be disappointed.

desengarzar v. tr. To unthread (quitar el hilo). || To unstring (perlas). || To remove from its setting, to unset (joyas).

desengastar v. tr. To remove from its setting, to unset (una piedra preciosa).

desengaste m. Unsetting, removal of a jewel from its setting.

desengomado m. o **desengomadura** f. Ungluing. || Boiling off (de seda).

desengomar v. tr. To unglue. || To boil off (tejidos).

desengoznar v. tr. To unhinge.

desengranar v. tr. To disengage.

desengrasado m. Removal of the grease. || Scouring (de la lana).

desengrasador m. Cleaner.

desengrasadora f. Scourer (de la lana).

desengrasar v. tr. To degrease, to remove the grease from (limpiar). || To scour (la lana).
— V. intr. FAM. To lose weight (adelgazar).

desengrase m. Removal of grease. || Scouring (de la lana).

desengrosar* v. tr. To make thin (enflaquecer). || To slim (adelgazar).
— V. intr. To lose weight (perder peso). || To slim, to grow thin (adelgazar).

desenguantarse v. pr. To take off one's gloves.

desenhebrar v. tr. To unthread (una aguja).
— V. pr. To come unthreaded.

desenhornamiento m. Taking out of the oven *o* of the kiln.

desenhornar v. tr. To take out of the oven (horno pequeño). || To take out of the kiln (horno grande).

desenjaezar v. tr. To unharness (quitar los jaeces).

desenjalmar v. tr. To take the packsaddle off, to unsaddle.

desenjaular v. tr. To let out of a cage, to release, to uncage.

desenlace m. Ending, denouement (de una obra literaria). || Ending (final). || Outcome, result (resultado).

desenladrillar v. tr. To remove *o* to dig up *o* to take up the bricks from.

desenlatar v. tr. To open, to take out [of a tin].

desenlazar v. tr. To unfasten, to undo, to untie (desatar). || FIG. To clear up, to unravel (un asunto). | To solve (un problema).
— V. pr. To come undone (desatarse). || *La obra se desenlaza muy mal*, the work has a very poor ending *o* denouement.

desenlodar v. tr. To clean the mud from.

desenlosar v. tr. To take up the tiles from. || To take up the paving stones from *o* the flags from. (V. ENLOSAR [Observ.].)

desenlutar v. tr. To bring out of mourning, to make [s.o.] give up mourning.
— V. pr. To give up mourning.

desenmarañar v. tr. To untangle, to unravel, to disentangle. || FIG. To unravel, to clarify, to clear up, to sort out (un asunto).

desenmascaradamente adv. Openly.

desenmascarar v. tr. To unmask (quitar la máscara). || FIG. To unmask, to expose: *desenmascarar a un hipócrita*, to unmask a hypocrite.

desenmohecer* v. tr. To remove the rust from. || To remove the mildew *o* the mould from.

desenmudecer* v. tr. To loosen the tongue of (hacer hablar). || To cure from tongue-tie (devolver el sentido de la palabra).
— V. intr. To recover from tongue-tie, to recover one's speech. || FIG. To break one's silence.

desenojar v. tr. To calm down, to soothe (desenfadar).
— V. pr. To calm down. || FIG. To amuse o.s. (entretenerse).

desenojo m. Calm (calma).

desenredar v. tr. To untangle, to unravel, to disentangle (desenmarañar). || FIG. To clear up, to unravel, to disentangle (una intriga, etc.). | To straighten out, to sort out (arreglar).
— V. pr. FIG. To extricate o.s. (salir de apuro).

desenredo m. Disentanglement, unravelling (de una madeja, etc.). || Disentanglement, solution, clearing-up (de un problema). || Way out (de un apuro). || Ending, denouement (desenlace). || Ending, outcome (de una situación crítica).

desenrollar v. tr. To unroll. || To unwind (hilo).

desenroscar v. tr. To unscrew (destornillar). || To unwind, to uncoil (un hilo, etc.).
— V. pr. To unwind, to uncoil (serpiente, hilo, etc.).

desensamblar v. tr. To take apart, to take to pieces (desmontar). || To separate (separar).

desensañar v. tr. To calm down, to appease.

desensartar v. tr. To unthread, to unstring (soltar cosas ensartadas): *desensartar un collar*, to unstring a necklace. || To unthread (desenhebrar): *desensartar una aguja*, to unthread a needle.

desensibilización f. Desensitization.

desensibilizar v. tr. To desensitize.

desensillar v. tr. To unsaddle (un caballo).

desensoberbecer* v. tr. To humble, to make less arrogant *o* conceited.

desensortijado, da adj. Straightened, straight (pelo).

desentarimar v. tr. To take up the parquet flooring of (un suelo).

desentenderse* v. pr. To want nothing to do, to want no part: *me desentiendo por completo de ese negocio*, I want absolutely nothing to do with that business, I want absolutely no part in that business. || To pretend not to know (*de*, about) [afectar ignorancia].

desentendido, da adj. (Ant.). Ignorant. || *Hacerse el desentendido*, to turn a deaf ear, to pretend not to hear *o* to notice.

desenterrado, da adj. Exhumed (un cadáver). || Unearthed, disinterred, dug up (un objeto).

desenterrador m. Gravedigger, exhumer.

desenterramiento m. Exhuming, disinterment (de un cadáver). || Unearthing, digging up, disinterment.

desenterrar* v. tr. To exhume, to disinter (un cadáver). || To dig up, to unearth, to disinter (un objeto). || FIG. To revive, to recall.

desentierramuertos m. y f. inv. FIG. y FAM. Scandalmonger, backbiter.

desentoldar v. tr. To remove the awning *o* sunshade from (una calle, etc.). || To take the drapes down from (quitar los adornos).

desentonación f. V. DESENTONO.

desentonadamente adv. Out of tune: *cantar desentonadamente*, to sing out of tune.

desentonamiento m. V. DESENTONO.

desentonar v. intr. To sing out of tune, to be out of tune (cantar falso). || To be out of tune (instrumento). || To be inharmonious (la música). || FIG. Not to match (colores). | To be out of place: *el chico desentonó en la reunión*, the boy was out of place at the meeting. | Not to fit in, to clash: *modales que desentonan con su educación*, manners which do not fit in with *o* which clash with his upbringing.
— V. pr. To be rude *o* insolent (*con*, *contra*, with *o* to). || To raise one's voice (*contra*, to) [alzar la voz].

desentono m. Poor intonation. || Dissonance (disonancia). || FIG. Rudeness, insolence.

desentorpecer* v. tr. To take the numbness *o* the stiffness out of: *desentorpecer el brazo*, to take the stiffness out of one's arm. || FIG. To smarten up, to knock the edges off (a un necio). || *Desentorpecer las piernas*, to stretch one's legs
— V. pr. To come back to life (la pierna, etc.). || To smarten up, to brighten up (una persona).

desentrampar v. tr. FAM. To get out of debt.
— V. pr. FAM. To get out of debt, to pay off one's debts.

desentrañar v. tr. (P.us.). To disembowel, to eviscerate. || FIG. To figure out, to work out: *ha conseguido desentrañar el misterio*, he has managed to figure out the mystery.
— V. pr. To give one's all.

desentrenado, da adj. Out of training.

desentrenamiento m. Lack of training.

desentrenarse v. pr. To get *o* to be out of training.

desentumecer* v. tr. To revive the feeling in, to take the numbness *o* the stiffness out of: *desentumecer el brazo*, to revive the feeling in one's arm. || DEP. To loosen up. || *Desentumecer las piernas*, to stretch one's legs.

desentumecimiento m. Recovery of feeling.

desentumir v. tr. V. DESENTUMECER.

desenvainar v. tr. To unsheathe, to draw: *desenvainar el sable*, to draw one's sword. || FIG. To bare, to show [its claws] (un animal).

desenvergar v. tr. MAR. To unbend.

desenvoltura f. Ease, grace, naturalness (en los movimientos). || Self-confidence, assurance (falta de timidez): *en la reunión habló con desenvoltura*, at the meeting he spoke with assurance. || Rudeness, insolence, boldness, forwardness (descaro). || Brazenness, shamelessness (de una mujer). || Carefreeness (despreocupación).

desenvolver* v. tr. To unwrap (un paquete). || To unwind (hilo). || To unroll (desenrollar). || FIG. To develop, to expound (una idea, una teoría). | To disentangle, to clear up (aclarar). | To expand (un negocio).
— V. pr. To come unwrapped (un paquete). || To develop, to evolve (desarrollarse). || To expand (crecer). || To prosper (prosperar). || FIG. To fend for o.s., to look after o.s.: *desenvolverse en la vida*, to fend for o.s. in life. | To manage (arreglárselas): *con ochenta libras al mes me desenvuelvo muy bien*, I manage very well with eighty pounds a month. | To go [off]: *el partido se desenvolvió sin incidente*, the game went [off] without incident.

desenvolvimiento m. Unwrapping (de un paquete). || Development, expansion (desarrollo). || Exposition, development (de una idea, etc.). || Disentanglement, clearing up (aclaración).

desenvueltamente adv. Gracefully, naturally, with ease (en los movimientos). || Confidently, naturally, with assurance (sin timidez). || Rudely, insolently, boldly (descaradamente). || Brazenly, shamelessly (una mujer). || Openly (abiertamente).

desenvuelto, ta adj. FIG. Graceful, natural, agile (en los movimientos). | Eloquent (al hablar). | Confident, assured, natural (sin timidez). | Carefree, free and easy,

easygoing (despreocupado). | Brazen, forward (descarado). | Resourceful (ingenioso).
desenzarzar v. tr. To pull out of the brambles (sacar de las zarzas). || FIG. y FAM. To pull apart, to separate (a personas que riñen).
deseo m. Desire, want, wish: *satisfacer los deseos de alguien*, to satisfy s.o.'s wishes. || Desire (cosa deseada). || Wish, desire (aspiración): *según sus deseos*, according to his wishes. || Wish: *deseos de felicidad*, wishes for happiness. || Vow (voto): *formular un deseo*, to make a vow. || — *A medida de mi deseo*, to my liking. || *Arder en deseos de*, to burn with desire for, to long for, to yearn for. || *Buenos deseos*, good intentions. || *Es nuestro mayor deseo*, it is our dearest wish. || *Tener deseo de algo*, to want sth. || *Tener deseo de hacer algo*, to want to do sth., to feel like doing sth.
deseoso, sa adj. Desirous, eager, anxious. || Longing, wishful: *mirada deseosa*, longing look. || — *Estar deseoso de hacer algo*, to be eager *o* anxious to do sth., to desire to do sth. || *Estar deseoso de una cosa*, to long for *o* to yearn for sth., to be eager *o* anxious for sth.
desequilibrado, da adj. Off balance, unbalanced. || FIG. Unbalanced (persona, mente).
— M. y f. Unbalanced person.
desequilibrar v. tr. To put off *o* to throw off *o* to knock off balance, to unbalance. || FIG. To unbalance: *la guerra ha desequilibrado las mentes de muchos hombres*, the war has unbalanced the minds of many men. | To unbalance mentally (a una persona).
— V. pr. To lose one's balance (perder el equilibrio). || FIG. To become mentally unbalanced.
desequilibrio m. Lack of balance. || FIG. Unbalance (de la mente). | Unbalanced mind (de una persona). | Imbalance: *suprimir el desequilibrio entre las importaciones y las exportaciones*, to correct the imbalance between imports and exports.
deserción f. Desertion (del ejército). || FIG. Abandoning, abandonment, desertion (abandono). || JUR. Dropping [of proceedings].
desertar v. intr. To desert: *desertar del ejército*, to desert from the army. || FIG. To abandon, to desert: *desertar de un círculo*, to desert a circle. | To neglect (los deberes). || JUR. To drop [proceedings]. || *Desertar al campo contrario*, to go over to the enemy.
— V. tr. To desert.
desértico, ca adj. Desert, barren (como un desierto). || Deserted (vacío). || GEOGR. Desert.
desertor m. Deserter.
desescalada f. De-escalation.
desescalar v. tr. To de-escalate.
desescombrar v. tr. To clear up, to clear of rubbish.
deseslabonar v. tr. To unlink (cadena).
desespaldar v. tr. To break the back of.
— V. pr. To break one's back.
desespañolizar v. tr. To take away the Spanish qualities *o* characteristics of.
— V. pr. To lose one's Spanish qualities.
desesperación f. Despair (desesperanza total). || Desperation: *estar loco de desesperación*, to be out of one's mind with desperation. || Exasperation (rabia). || — *Con desesperación*, desperately. || *Me da* or *me causa desesperación*, it exasperates me. || *Ser la desesperación de*, to be the despair of. || *Ser una desesperación*, to be exasperating, to be unbearable.
desesperado, da adj. Desperate, despairing (sin esperanza). || Exasperated (exasperado). || Hopeless: *una situación desesperada*, a hopeless situation. || MED. Hopeless (caso). || Furious (esfuerzo). || — *Estar desesperado*, to be desperate, to have lost hope, to despair. || *Me tiene desesperado*, he exasperates me (irritar), he makes me despair (desanimar).
— M. y f. Desperate person. || — *A la desesperada*, in desperation, as a last hope. || *Correr como un desesperado*, to run like mad.
desesperante adj. Exasperating. || Hopeless (persona). || FIG. Discouraging (descorazonador).
desesperanza f. Hopelessness, despair, desperation.
desesperanzar v. tr. To make despair, to drive to despair.
— V. pr. To despair, to lose hope.
desesperar v. tr. To make despair, to drive to despair. || To exasperate (irritar).
— V. intr. To have lost hope, to despair: *desespero de que venga*, I have lost hope that he will come, I despair of his coming; *desespero de verle un día*, I have lost hope of ever seeing him.
— V. pr. To despair, to lose hope: *me desespero por no recibir noticias suyas*, I despair at not hearing from him. || To become desperate (no tener esperanza alguna). || To be exasperated (irritarse).
desespero m. Despair.
desesterar v. tr. To take up the mats from.
desestero m. Removal of mats.
desestima f. Lack of respect *o* esteem, disrespect.
desestimación f. Lack of respect *o* esteem, disrespect. || JUR. Refusal, rejection: *desestimación de una demanda*, refusal of a claim.
desestimar v. tr. To have no respect for, to have a low opinion of, to hold in low esteem (despreciar). || To underestimate (menospreciar). || JUR. To reject, to refuse: *han desestimado mi demanda*, they have rejected my claim.
desfacedor, ra m. y f. Undoer. || FAM. *Desfacedor de entuertos*, righter *o* redresser of wrongs.
desfachatado, da adj. FAM. Cheeky, insolent, brazen, barefaced.
desfachatez f. FAM. Cheek, nerve: *tiene una desfachatez inmensa*, he's got a fantastic cheek.
desfalcador, ra m. y f. Embezzler, defaulter.
desfalcar v. tr. To embezzle, to defalcate: *desfalcar fondos*, to embezzle funds. || To remove a part of (quitar una parte).
desfalco m. Embezzlement, defalcation (malversación).
desfallecer* v. intr. To weaken (perder las fuerzas). || To faint (desmayarse). || To fail (la voz).
— V. tr. To weaken (debilitar).
desfallecido, da adj. Faint (desmayado). || Weak (débil).
desfalleciente adj. Faint (que se desmaya). || Weakening, failing (que se debilita).
desfallecimiento m. Weakening (debilidad). || Faint (desmayo).
desfasado, da adj. FIG. Behind the times (anticuado). | Out of place (fuera de su ambiente). || TECN. Out of phase.
desfasaje m. ELECTR. Phase shift, phase difference.
desfasar v. tr. To phase out.
desfase m. ELECTR. Phase shift, phase difference. || FIG. Imbalance (desequilibrio). | Gap (diferencia).
desfavorable adj. Unfavourable.
desfavorecer* v. tr. To put at a disadvantage, to be disadvantageous to, to disadvantage (perjudicar). || To have a low opinion of (tener mala opinión de). || Not to flatter, not to suit, not to do anything for: *este color te desfavorece*, this colour does not flatter you.
desfibrado m. o **desfibración** f. TECN. Removal of fibres. | Shredding (fabricación del papel).
desfibradora f. TECN. Shredding (máquina).
desfibrar v. tr. TECN. To shred (fabricación del papel). | To remove the fibre from (quitar las fibras).
desfiguración f. Disfiguring, disfiguration (de una persona). || Distortion (de los hechos). || Defacement (de una estatua, etc.).
desfigurado, da adj. Disfigured (persona). || Distorted (noticia, etc.). || Defaced (estatua, etc.).
desfiguramiento m. V. DESFIGURACIÓN.
desfigurar v. tr. To disfigure: *una cicatriz ancha le desfigura*, a large scar disfigures him. || To distort: *desfigurar la verdad, los hechos*, to distort the truth, the facts. || To deface (un monumento, etc.). || To blur (las formas). || FIG. To disguise, to alter (la voz).
— V. pr. To be disfigured.
desfiladero m. Narrow pass, defile (paso estrecho).
desfilar v. intr. MIL. To march in files. || To walk in file (andar en fila). || To march, to parade: *durante la manifestación desfilaron dos mil personas*, two thousand people marched in the demonstration. || To march past: *los soldados desfilaron ante el presidente*, the soldiers marched past in front of the president. || FAM. To file by (pasar). | To file out (irse).
desfile m. MIL. March-past, parade: *desfile de la victoria*, victory parade. || Procession, parade: *un desfile de carruajes*, a procession of carriages. || March (en una manifestación): *había un desfile para protestar contra las reformas*, there was a march to protest against the reforms. || *Desfile de modelos* or *de modas*, fashion show, fashion parade.
desflecadura f. Fraying, fringing.
desflecar v. tr. To fray, to fringe.
desflemar v. intr. MED. To cough up phlegm.
desfloración f. o **desfloramiento** m. Defloration, deflowering. || Fading, withering (ajamiento).
desflorar v. tr. To strip the flowers from, to deflower (hacer caer la flor). || To deflower (a una mujer). || To spoil, to tarnish (estropear). || FIG. To skim over, to touch lightly on (no profundizar).
desflorecer* v. intr. To wither, to lose its bloom.
desflorecimiento m. Loss of bloom (de una planta).
desfogar v. tr. To give vent to, to vent: *desfogó su cólera en* or *con su hermano*, he vented his anger on his brother. || To slake (la cal).
— V. intr. MAR. To break, to burst (una tormenta).
— V. pr. To let off steam, to give vent to one's anger: *después de la bronca que le habían echado se desfogó con nosotros*, after the telling off they gave him, he let off steam on us. || To let off steam: *de vez en cuando los niños necesitan desfogarse*, children need to let off steam now and again.
desfogue m. Vent (del fuego). || Outburst, venting, vent (de una pasión). || Letting-off [of] steam (acción de desfogarse). || *Amer.* Outlet [of a pipe].
desfondamiento m. V. DESFONDE.
desfondar v. tr. To go through *o* to break the bottom of (romper el fondo de). || AGR. To plough deeply (la tierra). || To damage the bottom of, to bilge (un barco).
— V. pr. MAR. To bilge. || FIG. To wear o.s. out (de cansancio). || *El sillón se ha desfondado*, the bottom *o* the seat has come out of the armchair.
desfonde m. Breaking of the bottom: *el desfonde de un tonel*, the breaking of the bottom of a barrel. || MAR. Bilging. || FIG. Exhaustion (cansancio).
desformar v. tr. To deform.
desfosforar v. tr. TECN. To dephosphorize.
desfruncir v. tr. To take the gathers out of, to ungather. || To unfold, to unfurl (desplegar).
desgaire m. Nonchalance (descuido). || Slovenliness, carelessness (en el vestir). || Scornful gesture (gesto de

desprecio). || — *Al desgaire*, nonchalantly (con descuido afectado), carelessly, sloppily (con descuido). || *Andar con desgaire*, to walk nonchalantly. || *Vestir con desgaire*, to dress untidily *o* scruffily.

desgajar v. tr. To tear off, to break off: *desgajar las ramas de un árbol*, to tear off the branches of a tree. || To tear up (desarraigar). || To tear out: *desgajar la hoja de un cuaderno*, to tear out a leaf of an exercise book. || To break (romper). || To tear *o* to rip apart *o* to pieces (desgarrar). || FIG. To uproot (personas). — V. pr. To come off, to break off. || FIG. *Desgajarse de su patria*, to abandon one's country, to break all ties with one's country.

desgalichado, da adj. FAM. Gawky, ungainly.

desgana f. Reluctance, unwillingness (disgusto). || Lack of appetite (falta de apetito). || — *Comer con desgana*, to eat without appetite *o* reluctantly. || *Hacer una cosa a* or *con desgana*, to do sth. reluctantly.

desganado, da adj. Without appetite (sin apetito). || Halfhearted, unenthusiastic (sin entusiasmo). || Reluctant (poco entusiasta). || — *El equipo jugó desganado*, the team played halfheartedly *o* unenthusiastically. || *Estoy desganado*, I have no appetite, I'm not hungry.

desganar v. tr. To spoil the appetite of (cortar el apetito). || To turn [s.o.] off (quitar las ganas).
— V. pr. To lose one's appetite (el apetito). || To get bored (*de*, with), to go off (cansarse).

desgañitarse v. pr. To shout one's head off. || *Gritar hasta desgañitarse*, to shout o.s. hoarse.

desgarbado, da adj. Ungainly, ungraceful, gawky.

desgarbo m. Gawkiness, ungainliness, lack of grace.

desgargantarse v. pr. FAM. To shout one's head off, to shout at the top of one's voice.

desgarrador, ra adj. Heartrending, heartbreaking: *oíanse gritos desgarradores*, you could hear heartrending cries. || Bloodcurdling (que da mucho miedo).

desgarradura f. o **desgarramiento** m. Rip, tear, rent (de una tela). || Tear (de un músculo).

desgarrar v. tr. To rip, to tear, to rend: *desgarrar un vestido*, to rip a dress. || FIG. To break, to rend (afligir): *sus desgracias me desgarran el corazón*, his misfortunes break my heart. | To rend: *la tos le desgarraba el pecho*, his cough rent his chest.
— V. pr. To rip, to tear. || FIG. *Desgarrarse uno a otro*, to make each other suffer.

desgarro m. Tear (muscular). || Tear, rip, rent (de una tela, etc.). || Grief (aflicción). || FIG. Rudeness, effrontery, insolence (descaro). | Forwardness, shamelessness (de una mujer). | Boasting, bragging (jactancia). || *Amer.* Spittle (escupitajo).

desgarrón m. Rip, tear. || Tatter (jirón). || Tear (muscular).

desgastamiento m. V. DESGASTE.

desgastar v. tr. To wear away (gastar progresivamente). || To wear out: *un niño que desgasta mucho la ropa*, a child who wears out his clothes quickly. || To erode (una roca). || To corrode (un metal). || To fray, to chafe, to wear (una cuerda, etc.). || FIG. To weaken (debilitar).
— V. pr. To wear away (ropa, objeto). || FIG. To weaken (debilitarse). | To wear o.s. out (agotarse).

desgaste m. Wearing away, erosion: *el desgaste de una roca*, the wearing away of a rock. || Wear (de un objeto, motor, vestido, etc.). || Chafing, fraying (de una cuerda, etc.). || Deterioration, damage, spoiling (deterioro). || Corrosion (de un metal). || FIG. Weakening (debilitación). | Waste (desperdicio). || *Guerra de desgaste*, war of attrition.

desglosador, ra m. y f. Cutter (de una película).

desglosar v. tr. To detach (un escrito de otro). || CINEM. To cut, to edit (una película). || To break down (gastos). || JUR. To sever (dos causas).

desglose m. CINEM. Cutting, editing. || Breakdown: *desglose de los gastos*, breakdown of expenses. || JUR. Severance. || Removal (de páginas, etc.). || *Hacer el desglose de*, to break down.

desgobernado, da adj. Dissolute (disoluto). || Disorderly, undisciplined (poco disciplinado).

desgobernar* v. tr. To upset (perturbar). || To misgovern, to misrule (governar mal). || To mismanage (llevar mal). || To dislocate (huesos). || MAR. To steer badly (un barco).
— V. pr. To become dislocated (huesos).

desgobierno m. Mismanagement (de la casa). || Misgovernment, misrule (en un país). || Disorderliness (en la vida). || Bad handling, mishandling (en los gastos).

desgolletar v. tr. To break the neck of (botella).

desgomar v. tr. To degum (una tela).

desgonzar o **desgoznar** v. tr. To unhinge.

desgracia f. Misfortune: *ser* or *verse perseguido por la desgracia*, to have nothing but misfortune; *labrarse la propia desgracia*, to bring about one's own misfortune. || Blow: *el accidente ha sido una desgracia*, the accident was a blow. || Mishap (contratiempo). || Disfavour, disgrace (pérdida de favor). || Bad luck (mala suerte). || Lack of charm *o* grace, awkwardness (torpeza). || — *Caer en desgracia*, to lose favour, to fall into disgrace. || *En la desgracia se conoce a los amigos*, a friend in need is a friend indeed. || *Las desgracias nunca vienen solas*, it never rains but it pours. || *No ha habido que lamentar desgracias personales*, there were no casualties, no one was hurt. || *Para colmo de desgracias* or *para mayor desgracia*, to top everything. || *Por desgracia*, unfortunately. || *¡Qué desgracia!*, what a shame! || *Ser la desgracia de la familia*, to be the disgrace of one's family. || *Tener la desgracia de*, to be unfortunate enough to.

desgraciadamente adv. Unfortunately.

desgraciado, da adj. Unfortunate, unlucky: *desgraciado en el juego*, unlucky in gambling. || Unhappy (infeliz): *era desgraciada en el matrimonio*, she was unhappy in her marriage. || Unfortunate: *un suceso desgraciado*, an unfortunate event. || Poor (pobre). || Unattractive, graceless (sin atractivo). || Unpleasant (desagradable). || Wretched (miserable): *una vida desgraciada*, a wretched life; *¡qué desgraciado soy!*, how wretched I am!
— M. y f. Unlucky *o* unfortunate person (infortunado). || Unhappy person (infeliz). || Wretch (miserable). || Rotter, scoundrel (mala persona). || — *¡Desgraciado de ti si...!* woe betide you if...! || *Los desgraciados*, the poor (pobres). || *Pobre desgraciado*, poor devil, poor wretch, unlucky devil (infortunado), wretch (sentido despectivo).

desgraciar v. tr. To spoil (estropear): *las arrugas desgracian su vestido*, the creases spoil your dress. || To damage (un mecanismo). || To maim (lisiar). || To deflower, to dishonour (a una mujer).
— V. pr. To be ruined (estropearse). || To turn out badly, to fail (malograrse). || To fall through, to collapse (un proyecto). || To quarrel, to fall out (desavenirse). || — *Si no se desgracia*, all being well: *si no se desgracia, la cosecha será buena*, all being well the harvest will be good. || *Su niño se desgració antes de nacer*, she had a miscarriage.

desgramar v. tr. To remove the bermuda grass from.

desgranador, ra adj. Shelling. || Threshing, shelling.
— M. Sheller (de maíz, de guisantes, etc.). || Thresher (de trigo, etc.). || — F. Sheller (de maíz). || Threshing machine (de trigo).

desgranamiento m. Shelling (de maíz, de guisantes, etc.). || Threshing, shelling (de trigo). || Picking of grapes (de un racimo de uvas).

desgranar v. tr. AGR. To shell (maíz, guisantes). | To thresh, to shell (trigo). || To pick the grapes off (un racimo de uvas). || To pick the seeds out of (una granada). || To tell: *desgranar las cuentas de un rosario*, to tell one's beads. || FIG. To reel off (decir, soltar).
— V. pr. To lose its corn (maíz). || To lose its grain (trigo). || To lose its grapes (uva). || To come unstrung (cuentas). || *Amer.* To separate (desbandarse).

desgrane m. V. DESGRANAMIENTO.

desgranzar v. tr. AGR. To separate [grain] from the chaff. || To carry out the first grinding on (colores).

desgrasar v. tr. V. DESENGRASAR.

desgrase m. V. DESENGRASE.

desgravación f. Reduction of taxes. || Reduction of duties (en las aduanas).

desgravar v. tr. To reduce the tax on. || To reduce the duties on (en las aduanas).

desgreñado, da adj. Dishevelled, tousled, ruffled. || *Tenía el pelo desgreñado*, his hair was dishevelled *o* tousled *o* ruffled, he was dishevelled.

desgreñar v. tr.To dishevel *o* to ruffle *o* to tousle the hair of (despeinar).
— V. pr. To get ruffled *o* dishevelled *o* tousled (el pelo). || To ruffle *o* to dishevel *o* to tousle one's hair: *la niña se desgreñó*, the girl ruffled her hair. || FIG. To argue, to quarrel (reñir).

desguace m. MAR. Breaking-up, shipbreaking (de un barco). || Roughhewing (de un madero). || Taking-down, pulling-down (de una estructura). || Car breaking (de automóviles).

desguarnecer* v. tr. To take the trimmings off, to untrim (quitar los. adornos de). || To dismantle (una máquina, una plaza fuerte). || To unharness (una caballería). || To strip: *desguarnecer de cuerdas un violín*, to strip a violin of its strings, to strip the strings off a violin.

desguazar v. tr. To roughhew (un madero). || To break up (un barco, un automóvil). || To take *o* to pull down (una estructura).

desguince m. V. ESGUINCE.

desguindar v. tr. MAR. To haul down, to lower.
— V. pr. MAR. To slide down: *desguindarse de un mastelero*, to slide down a mast.

desguinzado m. Rag cutting.

desguinzadora f. TECN. Rag-cutting machine.

desguinzar v. tr. To cut [rags].

deshabillé m. Negligé [U.S., negligee] (salto de cama).

deshabitado, da adj. Uninhabited, unoccupied: *una casa deshabitada*, an uninhabited house.

deshabitar v. tr. To leave, to vacate, to abandon (abandonar). || To leave without inhabitants, to depopulate: *la guerra deshabitó la provincia*, the war left the province without inhabitants.

deshabituación f. Loss of habit.

deshabituar v. tr. To break [s.o.] from *o* of the habit.
— V. pr. To get out of the habit, to lose the habit.

deshacedor, ra adj. (P.us.). Undoing.
— M. *Deshacedor de agravios* or *de entuertos*, righter *o* redresser of wrongs.

deshacer* v. tr. To destroy (destruir). || To damage (estropear). || To undo, to unpick: *deshacer una* *costura*, to undo a seam. || To take apart *o* to pieces (desmontar). || To upset (desordenar). || To retrace (pasos, camino). || To melt (derretir): *el sol ha deshecho la nieve*, the sun has melted the snow. || To wear down (metales). || To dissolve (disolver). || To ruin, to spoil: *deshacer los proyectos de uno*, to ruin s.o.'s plans. || To spoil, to damage (la vista). || To beat, to defeat (ganar). || TECN. To take to pieces (un motor). || To undo, to unpack, to unwrap (un paquete). || To unpack (una maleta). || To undo, to unfasten, to untie: *deshacer un nudo*, to undo a knot. || To unmake, to strip (la cama). || To unknit, to ravel (un tejido de punto). || To cancel, to annul (un contrato). || To break (un tratado). || To divide up (dividir). || To break off (un casamiento). || To frustrate, to thwart: *deshacer una intriga*, to frustrate a plot. || To right (los males). || To wear out: *el trabajo me ha deshecho*, the work has worn me out. || To prove the undoing of, to ruin (arruinar): *la guerra ha deshecho el país*, the war has ruined the nation. || MIL. To rout, to put to flight (vencer). || — *Deshacer agravios* or *entuertos*, to right *o* to redress wrongs. || *Es él quien hace y deshace*, he's the boss, he rules the roost.

— V. pr. To get rid, to rid o.s.: *deshacerse de algo*, to get rid of sth. || To break: *el vaso se deshizo al caer*, the glass broke when it fell. || To come undone *o* untied *o* unfastened (nudo, etc.). || To come unsewn (una costura). || To come to pieces (un objeto). || To melt (derretirse): *el hielo se ha deshecho*, the ice has melted. || To dissolve: *el azúcar se deshace en el agua*, sugar dissolves in water. || To break up (una reunión). || To break *o* to rid o.s. of (de una costumbre). || To disappear (desvanecerse). || To go to pieces (moralmente): *cuando murió su mujer el pobre hombre se deshizo*, the poor man went to pieces when his wife died. || To wear o.s. out, to tire o.s. out (agotarse): *deshacerse trabajando, en esfuerzos baldíos*, to tire o.s. out working, with vain efforts. || To do one's utmost, to try one's hardest (hacer todo lo posible): *se deshizo por terminar pronto*, he did his utmost to finish quickly. || To go out of one's way: *deshacerse por uno, por agradar a uno*, to go out of one's way for s.o., to please s.o. || To be mad: *se deshace por las antigüedades*, he is mad about antiques. || — *Deshacerse como el humo*, to disappear *o* to vanish into thin air. || FIG. *Deshacerse en*, to dissolve into. || *Deshacerse en alabanzas, en cumplidos*, to be full of praise, of compliments, to dissolve into praise, into compliments. || *Deshacerse en atenciones con alguien*, to lavish attention on s.o. || *Deshacerse en excusas*, to apologize profusely. || *Deshacerse en imprecaciones*, to curse vehemently. || *Deshacerse en lágrimas*, to burst into tears. || *Deshacerse en llanto*, to sob one's heart out. || *Deshacerse en suspiros*, to heave deep sighs.

desharrapado, da adj. Tattered, ragged, shabby.
— M. y f. Shabby person, tramp.

desharrapamiento m. Raggedness (de la ropa). || Poverty, misery (pobreza).

deshebillar v. tr. To unbuckle.

deshebrar v. tr. To ravel, to undo (una tela). || To unthread (una aguja). || To remove the strings from (judías verdes). || To tear into shreds (deshacer en briznas).

deshechizar v. tr. To remove the spell from, to break the spell on.

deshecho, cha adj. Destroyed (destruido). || Undone, untied, unfastened (nudo, lazos, etc.). || Unsewn (costura). || Melted (hielo, nieve). || Dissolved: *deshecho en agua*, dissolved in water. || In pieces (desmontado). || Defeated, beaten (vencido). || Unpacked (maleta). || Open, unwrapped (paquete). || Ruined (arruinado, estropeado). || Dishevelled (los pelos). || Discomposed (rostro). || Worn-out, tired out, exhausted (rendido de cansancio). || Worn-out: *zapatos deshechos*, worn-out shoes. || Broken (salud). || Violent (tempestad). || Strong (lluvia). || — *Con los nervios deshechos*, at one's wits' end. || *Estar deshecho*, to have gone to pieces: *desde la muerte de su mujer el pobre hombre está deshecho*, since the death of his wife the poor man has gone to pieces; to be upset *o* troubled (consternado).

deshelador m. Deicer.

deshelamiento m. Deicing (de coche, de avión).

deshelar* v. tr. To thaw out: *deshelar una cañería*, to thaw out a pipe. || To deice (coche, avión). || To defrost (una nevera). || To melt, to thaw (derretir).
— V. pr. To thaw out (descongelarse). || To melt, to thaw (río).

desherbaje m. Weeding.

desherbar* v. tr. To weed.

desheredación f. Disinheritance, disinheriting.

desheredado, da adj. Disinherited. || FIG. Underprivileged: *gente desheredada*, underprivileged people.
— M. y f. Disinherited person. || FIG. Underprivileged person. || *Ayudar a los desheredados*, to help the underprivileged.

desheredamiento m. Disinheritance, disinheriting.

desheredar v. tr. To disinherit.

desherencia f. Disinheritance, disinheriting.

deshermanado, da adj. Odd: *un calcetín deshermanado*, an odd sock.

deshermanar v. tr. To separate.
— V. pr. To forsake one's brother, to behave in an unbrotherly way. || To separate, to be split up.

desherradura f. Bruised hoof (de los caballos).

desherrar* v. tr. To unshoe (a una caballería). || To unchain, to unshackle (a un prisionero).
— V. pr. To throw a shoe (una caballería). || To break free from one's chains *o* shackles (un prisionero).

desherrumbrar v. tr. To remove the rust from.

deshidratación f. Dehydration.

deshidratado, da adj. Dehydrated.

deshidratar v. tr. To dehydrate.
— V. pr. To become dehydrated.

deshidrogenación f. Dehydrogenation.

deshidrogenar v. tr. To dehydrogenate, to dehydrogenize.

deshielo m. Thaw (del tiempo). || Deicing (de un coche, un avión). || Defrosting (de una nevera). || Thawing (de un río). || Thawing-out (de una cañería, etc.). || FIG. Thawing: *el deshielo de las relaciones internacionales*, the thawing of international relations.

deshijar v. tr. *Amer.* To trim shoots off [plants]. | To take the young away from (animales).

deshilachado o **deshilachadura** f. Ravelling. || Fraying (acción de deshilacharse).

deshilachar v. tr. To ravel.
— V. pr. To fray.

deshilado, da adj. In single file (en fila india). || Frayed: *la solapa está deshilada*, the lapel is frayed. || *A la deshilada*, in single file.
— M. Openwork (bordado).

deshilar v. tr. To ravel. || To draw threads from (para bordar). || FIG. To cut into thin pieces.
— V. pr. To fray (deshilacharse).

deshilvanado, da adj. Untacked (costura). || FIG. Disjointed, disconnected: *estilo, discurso, juego deshilvanado*, disjointed style, speech, play.

deshilvanar v. tr. To take the tacking out of, to untack.

deshinchado, da adj. Flat (neumáticos). || Deflated (globo, balón, etc.). || *Tengo el brazo deshinchado*, the swelling in my arm has gone down.

deshinchadura f. o **deshinchamiento** m. o **deshinchazón** f. Deflation, letting down: *deshinchadura de un neumático*, deflation of a tyre. || Reduction of swelling (de un miembro). || Going down (acción de deshincharse).

deshinchar v. tr. To deflate, to let down: *deshinchar un globo, un neumático*, to deflate a balloon, a tyre. || To reduce the swelling in, to make the swelling go down in (un miembro, etc.). || FIG. To give vent to, to vent (la cólera).
— V. pr. To go flat, to go down, to deflate (un neumático). || To go down (la hinchazón): *se te ha deshinchado la pierna*, the swelling in your leg has gone down. || FIG. y FAM. To get down from one's high horse (perder la presunción). | To climb down (rajarse).

deshipnotizar v. tr. To dehypnotize.

deshipotecar v. tr. To free from mortgage, to pay off the mortgage on.

deshojado, da adj. Leafless (árbol). || Stripped of its petals (flor).

deshojadura f. o **deshojamiento** m. Stripping of leaves, defoliation (de un árbol, etc.). || Stripping of petals (de una flor).

deshojar v. tr. To strip of leaves, to defoliate (un árbol). || To strip of petals (una flor). || To tear the pages out of (un libro).
— V. pr. To lose its leaves (árbol) *o* its petals (flor).

deshoje m. Fall of leaves.

deshollejar v. tr. To peel (la fruta, etc.).

deshollinadera f. Wall brush (escobón).

deshollinador, ra adj. Who sweeps chimneys (que deshollina). || FIG. y FAM. Nosey, inquisitive.
— M. y f. FIG. y FAM. Busybody, nosey parker (fisgón). || — M. Chimney sweep, sweep (persona). || Chimney sweep's brush (cepillo). || Wall brush (escobón).

deshollinar v. tr. To sweep, to clean (chimeneas). || To clean [the walls and ceilings of] (la casa). || FIG. y FAM. To scrutinize, to examine closely.

deshonestidad f. Dishonesty (cualidad de no honesto). || Indecency, immodesty, impropriety (indecencia).

deshonesto, ta adj. Dishonest (no honesto). || Indecent, immodest, improper (obsceno).

deshonor m. Disgrace, dishonour [U.S., dishonor] (pérdida del honor). || Disgrace: *es el deshonor de su familia*, he is the disgrace of his family; *vivir en el deshonor*, to live in disgrace. || Insult (afrenta). || Disgrace (cosa que deshonra): *ser pobre no es ningún deshonor*, it's no disgrace to be poor.

deshonorar v. tr. To disgrace, to dishonour [U.S., to dishonor].

deshonra f. Disgrace, dishonour [U.S., dishonor] (pérdida del honor). || Disgrace (vergüenza). || *Tener a deshonra*, to find below one's dignity, to consider shameful.

deshonradamente adv. Dishonourably [U.S., dishonorably].

deshonrar v. tr. To disgrace, to dishonour [U.S., to dishonor], to bring disgrace on: *deshonrar (a) la familia*, to disgrace one's family. || To dishonour [U.S., to dishonor] (a una mujer). || To insult (afrentar).
— V. pr. To disgrace o.s.

deshonrosamente adv. Disgracefully, dishonourably.

deshonroso, sa adj. Disgraceful, shameful, dishonourable: *acto deshonroso*, disgraceful act.
deshora f. Inconvenient time. || *A deshora* or *a deshoras*, at an untimely *o* inconvenient moment (a hora inoportuna), at an unusual time (a hora desacostumbrada), very late, at an unreasonable hour (muy tarde).
deshornar v. tr. To take out of the oven (pequeño horno). || To take out of the kiln (horno grande).
deshuesado, da adj. Boned, off the bone (carne). || Stoned, pitted (fruta).
deshuesadora f. Stoning *o* pitting machine (para fruta). || Boning machine (para carne).
deshuesamiento m. Stoning, pitting (de fruta). || Boning (de carne).
deshuesar v. tr. To stone, to pit (fruta). || To bone (carne).
deshumanizar v. tr. To dehumanize.
deshumano, na adj. Inhuman.
deshumedecer* v. tr. To dry up, to dehumidify.
— V. pr. To dry up.
desiderata m. pl. Desiderata.
desiderativo, va adj. Desiderative (verbo).
desiderátum m. Desideratum.
desidia f. Negligence, slovenliness, laziness. || Slovenliness (al vestir).
desidioso, sa adj. Negligent, lazy, slovenly. || Slovenly (al vestir).
desierto, ta adj. Deserted, uninhabited (deshabitado). || Desolate, bleak: *llanura desierta*, desolate plain. || GEOGR. Desert. || Void: *el premio Nóbel ha sido declarado desierto*, the Nobel prize has been declared void. || FIG. Deserted: *calle desierta*, deserted street. || *Isla desierta*, desert island.
— M. Desert. || FIG. *Predicar* or *clamar en el desierto*, to preach in the wilderness.
designación f. Appointment, designation (para un empleo). || Representation, indication, designation (representación). || Designation, name (nombre).
designar v. tr. To appoint, to designate, to assign (nombrar): *designar a alguien para un puesto*, to appoint s.o. to a post. || To point out (señalar). || To represent, to indicate, to designate (representar). || To appoint, to decide on, to fix: *designar la hora de una cita*, to decide on the time of an appointment.
designio m. Intention: *con el designio de*, with the intention of. || Design, project, plan (proyecto).
desigual adj. Unequal, uneven: *batalla desigual*, unequal battle. || Different: *dos hermanas muy desiguales*, two very different sisters. || Unfair, inequitable (tratamiento). || Changeable (cambiadizo): *persona, tiempo desigual*, changeable person, weather. || Uneven, rough, rugged (terreno). || Uneven (escritura, estilo): *letra desigual*, uneven writing. || Inconsistent: *un alumno desigual*, an inconsistent pupil. || FIG. y FAM. *Salir desigual*, to come out *o* to be different: *las dos figuras me salieron completamente desiguales*, the two figures were completely different.
desigualar v. tr. To make unequal (dos cosas). || To make different (una cosa de otra). || To make unequal *o* uneven: *desigualar una lucha*, to make a fight unequal *o* uneven. || To make uneven *o* rough (terreno).
— V. pr. To excel (aventajar). || To get ahead (adelantarse).
desigualdad f. Inequality: *desigualdades sociales*, social inequalities. || Roughness, unevenness, ruggedness (de terreno). || Changeableness (del tiempo, del carácter). || Unevenness (de la letra, del estilo). || Inconsistency (inconsistencia). || Difference, inequality: *desigualdad entre los salarios agrícolas e industriales*, difference between *o* inequality of agricultural and industrial wages. || MAT. Inequality.
desigualmente adv. Unequally: *en ese país la renta está dividida desigualmente*, the income is unequally divided in that country. || Unevenly: *la carretera está asfaltada desigualmente*, the road is unevenly asphalted. || Inconsistently: *este futbolista juega muy desigualmente*, this footballer plays very inconsistently. || Unevenly (letra, estilo).
desilusión f. Disappointment (decepción): *sufrir una desilusión*, to suffer a disappointment. || Disillusion, disillusionment (pérdida de ilusiones).
desilusionado, da adj. Disappointed (decepcionado). || Disillusioned (sin illusiones).
desilusionante adj. Disappointing, disillusioning.
desilusionar v. tr. To disappoint (decepcionar). || To disillusion (quitar las ilusiones).
— V. pr. To be disappointed. || To get disillusioned.
desimanación f. Demagnetization.
desimanar v. tr. To demagnetize.
desimantación f. Demagnetization.
desimantar v. tr. To demagnetize.
desimpresionar v. tr. To enlighten, to undeceive, to open the eyes of (desengañar).
— V. pr. To be enlightened, to have one's eyes opened.
desincrustación f. Descaling, unscaling.
desincrustante adj. Water-softening.
— M. Water softener.
desincrustar v. tr. To descale, to unscale.
desinencia f. GRAM. Ending, desinence (p.us.).
desinencial adj. GRAM. Desinential.
desinfartar v. tr. MED. To cure of an infarct.
desinfección f. Disinfection.
desinfectante adj./s. m. Disinfectant.
desinfectar o **desinfestar** v. tr. To disinfect.
desinficionar v. tr. To disinfect.
desinflacionista adj. Disinflationary, deflationary.
desinflado o **desinflamiento** m. Deflation, letting down (de un neumático).
desinflamación f. Reduction of inflammation.
desinflamar v. tr. MED. To reduce the inflammation in.
— V. pr. MED. *Se le ha desinflamado la herida*, the inflammation in his wound has gone down, his wound has become less inflamed.
desinflar v. tr. To deflate, to let down (un neumático).
— V. pr. To go flat, to go down, to deflate (un neumático). || FAM. To climb down (rajarse). | To climb down from one's high horse (perder la presunción).
desinsectación f. Fumigation, disinfection.
desinsectar v. tr. To fumigate, to disinfect.
desintegración f. Disintegration (en fragmentos). || Breaking up, disintegration: *la desintegración de un sindicato*, the breaking up of a union. || FÍS. Disintegration, fission, splitting: *desintegración atómica, nuclear*, atomic disintegration, nuclear fission.
desintegrar v. tr. To disintegrate: *desintegrar una roca*, to disintegrate a rock. || FIG. To break up: *desintegrar un grupo de amigos*, to break up a group of friends. || FÍS. To split (el átomo).
— V. pr. To disintegrate. || FIG. To break up. || FÍS. To split (el átomo).
desinterés m. Disinterestedness, impartiality (imparcialidad). || Unselfishness, altruism, generosity (generosidad). || (P.us.). Lack of interest (falta de interés).
desinteresadamente adv. Disinterestedly, impartially (imparcialmente). || Unselfishly, altruistically, generously (generosamente).
desinteresado, da adj. Not interested. || Disinterested, unbiased, unprejudiced (consejo). || Unselfish, altruistic (motivo). || Unselfish, altruistic, disinterested (persona). || Impartial (imparcial).
desinteresarse v. pr. To lose interest: *se ha desinteresado de la pintura*, he has lost interest in painting. || To take no interest: *se desinteresó completamente de las conversaciones*, he took no interest in the talks.
desintoxicar v. tr. MED. To detoxicate, to detoxify.
— V. pr. FIG. y FAM. To get away from: *desintoxicarse de la rutina cotidiana*, to get away from the routine of everyday life.
desistimiento m. Desistance, giving up. || JUR. Waiving [of a right].
desistir v. intr. To give up, to desist: *desistió de su empresa*, he gave up his undertaking, he desisted from the undertaking. || To give up the idea: *he desistido de encontrarlo*, I have given up the idea of finding it. || JUR. To waive [a right]. || To stand down, to withdraw (candidato).
desjarretar v. tr. To hamstring.
desjarrete m. Hamstringing.
desjuiciado, da adj. Senseless, unwise, injudicious.
desjuntar v. tr. To separate, to divide.
deslabonamiento m. Unlinking (de una cadena).
deslabonar v. tr. To unlink (una cadena).
desladrillar v. tr. To remove the bricks from.
deslastrar v. tr. To unballast, to remove the ballast from.
deslavado m. o **deslavadura** f. Rinsing, rinse. || Washing out, fading (acción de desteñir).
deslavar v. tr. To rinse through. || To wash out, to fade (desteñir).
deslavazado, da adj. Faded, washed out (desteñido). || Limp (lacio). || Insipid (comida). || FIG. Disjointed, disconnected (estilo). | Colourless (insípido).
deslavazar v. tr. To fade, to wash out (desteñir). || To rinse through (aclarar). || To make limp (volver lacio). || To make insipid (una comida).
deslave m. *Amer.* Erosion (acción). | Alluvion (tierra).
desleal adj. Disloyal: *desleal con su hermano*, disloyal to his brother. || Unfair (entre comerciantes).
deslealtad f. Disloyalty. || Unfairness (entre comerciantes).
desleidura f. o **desleimiento** m. Dissolving (de un sólido en líquido). || Dilution (de un líquido espeso).
desleír* v. tr. To dissolve (un sólido). || To dilute (un líquido espeso). || To thin down (una salsa). || FIG. To dilute.
— V. pr. To dissolve (un sólido). || To be diluted (un líquido espeso). || To thin out (una salsa).
deslendrar v. tr. To clean the nits from.
deslenguado, da adj. FIG. Cheeky, insolent, rude (insolente). | Foulmouthed, coarse (grosero).
deslenguamiento m. FIG. y FAM. Cheek, insolence (insolencia). | Foul *o* bad language (lenguaje grosero).
deslenguar v. tr. To cut out the tongue of.
— V. pr. FIG. y FAM. To be cheeky *o* insolent *o* rude (con insolencia). | To swear, to curse, to use foul *o* bad language (hablar groseramente). | To talk too much (hablar mucho).
desliar v. tr. To open (un paquete). || To unfasten, to undo, to untie (desatar). || To unwrap (desenvolver). || To separate lees from (mosto).
— V. pr. To come undone *o* unfastened *o* untied.
desligado, da adj. Loose, free.
desligadura f. o **desligamiento** m. Untying, unfastening, unbinding. || FIG. Freeing (de una obliga-

ción). | Detachment (desapego). | Separation (separación). | Disentanglement, clearing up (desenredo).

desligar v. tr. To untie, to unfasten, to unbind (desatar). || FIG. To free (liberar). | To excuse, to release: *desligar a alguien de una promesa*, to release s.o. from a promise. | To separate, to detach (separar). | To clear up, to sort out, to disentangle (desenredar). || MÚS. To detach.
— V. pr. To break away, to separate: *se desligó de su familia*, he broke away from his family. || To free o.s., to excuse o.s., to release o.s.: *desligarse de un compromiso*, to free o.s. from an obligation. || To come undone *o* loose (desatarse).

deslindador m. Land surveyor.

deslindamiento m. Marking of boundaries, delimitation, demarcation (de un terreno, etc.). || FIG. Defining, demarcation. | Explanation, definition (explicación).

deslindar v. tr. To mark the boundaries of, to mark out, to fix the limits of, to demarcate, to delimitate, to delimit: *deslindar un jardín*, to mark the boundaries of a garden. || To mark the boundary between (dos cosas). || FIG. To define the limits of, to demarcate: *deslindar las actividades de dos organizaciones*, to define the limits of two organizations' activities. | To outline (delimitar): *deslindar un problema*, to outline a problem.

deslinde m. V. DESLINDAMIENTO.

desliz m. Slipping, slip (de personas). || Sliding (de cosas). || Gliding (sobre agua). || FIG. y FAM. Slip, mistake, error (equivocación). | Lapse, slip, error (indiscreción). || *Cometer* or *tener un desliz*, to go wrong, to slip up, to make a slip.

deslizable adj. Slippery (que se desliza). || Sliding (corredizo).

deslizadero m. Slippery spot. || TECN. Slide, chute.

deslizadizo, za adj. Slippery, slippy.

deslizamiento m. Slipping, slip (de personas). || Sliding (de cosas). || *Deslizamiento de tierra*, landslide.

deslizante adj. Slippery, slippy. || Sliding (corredizo).

deslizar v. tr. To slide: *deslizó la mano por el pasamanos*, he slid his hand along the handrail. || To slip: *deslizó un billete en su bolsillo*, he slipped a ticket into his pocket; *deslizar unas críticas en un discurso*, to slip a few criticisms into a speech. || To let slip (un secreto).
— V. intr. To slide, to slip.
— V. pr. To slide: *el trineo se deslizó sobre* or *en* or *por el hielo*, the sledge slid over the ice. || To slip (caerse uno). || To glide (sobre el agua). || To slither (una serpiente). || To run, to flow: *la arena se deslizó entre sus dedos*, the sand ran through his fingers. || To flow (una corriente líquida). || To slip by, to pass, to glide past (tiempo). || FIG. To slip away, to slip off (escaparse): *deslizarse de un sitio*, to slip away from a place. | To slip: *se deslizó en la sala*, he slipped into the room. | To slip out (un secreto). | To slip in (una falta, un error). | To weave, to slip away: *deslizarse por entre la muchedumbre*, to weave through *o* to slip away through the crowd. | To go wrong, to make a slip, to slip up (cometer una falta). || *Deslizarse entre las manos de uno*, to slip through one's hands.

deslomado, da adj. Worn-out, exhausted.

deslomadura f. Exhaustion.

deslomar v. tr. To exhaust, to wear out, to break s.o.'s back (derrengar). || To break s.o.'s back (romper la espalda). || *Deslomar a uno a palos*, to beat s.o. black and blue, to beat s.o. up.
— V. pr. FAM. To wear o.s. out, to break one's back (trabajar demasiado). || To put one's back out, to hurt one's back.

deslucidamente adv. Unimpressively (sin brillo). || Shabbily, dowdily: *vestir deslucidamente*, to dress shabbily. || Ungracefully, gracelessly (sin gracia).

deslucido, da adj. Unimpressive, tarnished, uninspiring: *el torero tuvo una deslucida actuación*, the bullfighter gave an unimpressive performance. || Shabby, dowdy: *sillón, vestido deslucido*, shabby armchair, dress. || Dull, lacklustre (sin gracia). || Undistinguished (poco distinguido). || Lifeless, lacklustre (sin vida, sin brillo). || Unsuccessful (fracasado).

deslucimiento m. Unimpressiveness, insignificance (falta de brillantez). || Shabbiness, dowdiness (de vestidos, de muebles, etc.). || Dullness (falta de gracia). || Lifelessness (falta de vitalidad). || Failure, unsuccessfulness (fracaso).

deslucir* v. tr. To spoil, to ruin (estropear). || To tarnish (quitar el brillo a). || To tarnish [the reputation of], to discredit (desacreditar). || To dull (quitar brillantez).
— V. pr. FIG. To fail, to be unsuccessful (fracasar). || To become tarnished *o* dull (perder el brillo). || To be discredited.

deslumbrador, ra o **deslumbrante** adj. Dazzling (luz, actuación, etc.). || Overwhelming (que asombra).

deslumbramiento m. Dazzle, dazzling.

deslumbrar v. tr. To dazzle. || FIG. To dazzle: *nos deslumbró con sus promesas, con su habilidad*, he dazzled us with his promises, with his skill.

deslustrado, da adj. Dull, tarnished (sin lustre). || Frosted, ground (vidrio). || Unglazed (loza).
— M. Steaming (de los paños de lana). || V. DESLUSTRE.

deslustrar v. tr. To tarnish, to dull, to take the shine off (quitar el lustre). || To grind, to frost (el vidrio). || TECN. To steam (los paños de lana). | To remove the finish from (los paños de algodón). | To unglaze (el papel, la loza). | To mat, to dull (oro, plata). || FIG. To tarnish [the reputation of] (desacreditar). | To dull, to tarnish (la brillantez). | To disgrace (deshonrar).

deslustre m. Dullness, lack of shine (falta de lustre). || Steaming (del paño de lana). || Removal of finish (del paño de algodón). || Unglazing (del papel). || Grinding, frosting (del vidrio). || Matting, dulling (del oro, de la plata). || FIG. Stain, spot (mancha). | Discredit (descrédito). | Disgrace (deshonra).

desmadejado, da adj. FIG. Weak, run-down, exhausted (sin energía). | Lanky, gawky, ungainly (desgarbado).

desmadejamiento m. FIG. Weakness, exhaustion (falta de energía). | Lankiness, gawkiness, ungainliness (desgarbo).

desmadejar v. tr. FIG. To weaken, to exhaust (debilitar).

desmadrar v. tr. To take [an animal] from its mother.

desmagnetización f. TECN. Demagnetization.

desmagnetizar v. tr. TECN. To demagnetize.

desmajolar* v. tr. To clear of young vines (un campo). || To unfasten, to untie (los zapatos).

desmalezar v. tr. *Amer.* To weed.

desmallar v. tr. To ladder (una media). || To break the mesh of (una red). || To break the mail of (una cota de malla). || To unravel (un tejido de punto).
— V. pr. To ladder (una media).

desmán m. Outrage, abuse, excess (ultraje): *cometer desmanes*, to commit outrages. || Misfortune, mishap (desdicha). || ZOOL. Desman, muskrat.

desmanarse v. pr. To stray from the flock (ovejas). || To stray from the herd (vaca, caballo).

desmanchar v. tr. *Amer.* To clean, to get the marks off.
— V. pr. *Amer.* To go one's own way.

desmandado, da adj. Insubordinate, rebellious, out of hand (indómito). ||Uncontrollable (incontrolable). || Unruly, unbridled (desenfrenado). || Disobedient, unruly, intractable (desobediente). || Runaway (caballo). || Stray (otros animales). || *Muchedumbre desmandada*, crowd that has got out of hand *o* out of control.

desmandamiento m. Countermand, revoking (revocación de una orden). || Insubordination, disobedience (desobediencia). || Insolence, impudence, impertinence (falta de cortesía).

desmandar v. tr. To countermand, to revoke.
— V. pr. To go too far, to forget o.s. (descomedirse). || To get out of hand *o* out of control: *el profesor debe cuidar que sus alumnos no se desmanden*, the teacher must be careful that his pupils don't get out of hand. || To rebel (rebelarse). || To behave badly (portarse mal). || To be disobedient (desobedecer): *como te desmandes te metemos en un internado*, if you are disobedient we'll send you to a boarding shool. || To run wild, to get out of hand (animales). || To bolt (caballo). || FIG. To go one's own way (separarse).

desmangado, da adj. Handleless, with no handle.

desmangar v. tr. To take the handle off.

desmano (a) loc. adv. Out of reach. || *Me coge a desmano*, it's out of my way.

desmantecar v. tr. To skim (la leche). || To remove the fat *o* grease from (quitar la grasa). || *Leche desmantecada*, skim milk.

desmantelado, da adj. Dismantled. || MAR. Dismasted (desarbolado). | Unrigged (desaparejado).

desmantelamiento m. Dismantling. || MAR. Dismasting. | Unrigging.

desmantelar v. tr. To dismantle (una fortificación). || To dismantle (una estructura). || MAR. To dismast, to unmast (desarbolar). | To unrig (desaparejar). || To strip [down], to dismantle: *desmantelar una máquina*, to strip a machine. || To clear, to empty, to dismantle (un local, una casa). || FIG. To disband: *desmantelar una organización*, to disband an organization.

desmaña f. Clumsiness.

desmañado, da adj. Clumsy, bungling, hamfisted.
— M. y f. Clumsy person, bungler.

desmaquillador m. Cleansing cream *o* milk, makeup remover.

desmarcaje m. DEP. *Esperar el desmarcaje de un compañero de equipo*, to wait until a teammate is unmarked. | *Provocar el desmarcaje de un compañero*, to allow a teammate to get into an unmarked position.

desmarcar v. tr. To remove the marks from. || DEP. To allow to get into an unmarked position, to leave unmarked.
— V. pr. DEP. To get into an unmarked position.

desmarque m. V. DESMARCAJE.

desmarrido, da adj. Downhearted, dejected, crestfallen (alicaído). || Exhausted, weak (desmadejado).

desmaterialización f. Dematerialization.

desmayado, da adj. Unconscious, who has fainted (sin sentido). || Dejected, dismayed, disheartened (desanimado). || Exhausted, worn-out (agotado). || Faint with hunger (hambriento). || Dull, wan, washed-out (color).

desmayar v. tr. To make faint: *la noticia le desmayó*, the news made him faint.
— V. intr. FIG. To lose heart, to be dismayed.
— V. pr. To faint, to swoon (p. us.).

desmayo m. Faint, fainting fit, swoon (p. us.). || Unconsciousness (estado). || BOT. Weeping willow (sauce llorón). || FIG. Depression, dismay, downheartedness (desánimo). | Faltering, flagging (de la voz). || — *Sin desmayo*, unfaltering, without flinching: *siguió trabajando sin desmayo*, he worked on unfaltering. || *Tener un desmayo*, to faint.
desmedido, da adj. Excessive (excesivo). || Immoderate, disproportionate (inmoderado). || Unbounded, boundless, limitless: *ambición desmedida*, unbounded ambition.
desmedirse* v. pr. To go too far, to forget o.s.
desmedrado, da adj. Puny, emaciated (enclenque).
desmedrar v. intr. To fall off, to decline, to go down, to deteriorate: *este negocio ha desmedrado mucho*, this business has greatly declined *o* deteriorated, this business has fallen off a lot *o* gone down a lot. || MED. To grow weak.
— V. tr. To impair (perjudicar).
— V. pr. To fall off, to decline, to go down, to deteriorate (deteriorarse). || To waste away (de salud).
desmedro m. Decline, deterioration (decaimiento). || Wasting away, puniness (de una persona). || Impairment (perjuicio).
desmejora f. V. DESMEJORAMIENTO.
desmejoramiento m. Deterioration, decline (de la salud). || Deterioration, spoiling.
desmejorar v. tr. To spoil, to impair, to damage, to deteriorate (menoscabar).
— V. intr. y pr. To lose one's health, to deteriorate *o* to decline in health (una persona). || To deteriorate, to get worse: *la situación se ha desmejorado rápidamente*, the situation has quickly deteriorated.
desmelenado, da adj. Dishevelled, tousled, with ruffled hair.
desmelenar v. tr. To dishevel, to tousle the hair of, to ruffle the hair of.
desmembración f. o **desmembramiento** m. Dismemberment. || FIG. Division, dismemberment (división). | Separation (separation).
desmembrar* v. tr. To dismember. || FIG. To divide up, to break up: *desmembrar un imperio*, to divide up an empire. | To separate (separar).
desmemoriado, da adj. Forgetful, absentminded. || *Ser desmemoriado*, to have a bad memory, to be forgetful *o* absentminded.
desmemoriarse v. pr. To become forgetful, to lose one's memory.
desmentida f. o **desmentido** m. Denial. || Contradiction (contradicción).
desmentidor, ra adj. Denying.
desmentir* v. tr. To deny: *el ministro desmintió el rumor*, the minister denied the rumour. || To contradict, to give the lie to, to belie: *desmentir a alguien*, to contradict s.o. || To prove wrong, to refute (teoría, sospecha, indicios). || To go against (una conducta, una palabra dada). || To belie (temores, promesas).
— V. pr. To contradict o.s. || To go back on one's word (desdecirse).
desmenuzable adj. Crumbly.
desmenuzamiento m. Crumbling.
desmenuzar v. tr. To crumble (pan, etc.). || To chop up (carne). || To break into small pieces. || FIG. To examine minutely, to sift, to scrutinize.
— V. pr. To crumble.
desmerecedor, ra adj. Unworthy.
desmerecer* v. tr. Not to deserve, to be unworthy of.
— V. intr. To be inferior, to compare unfavourably: *el cuadro desmerece de* or *al lado de los otros de la exposición*, the painting is inferior to *o* compares unfavourably with the rest in the exhibition. || To deteriorate, to decline, to get worse (decaer). || To lose: *este verde desmerece al ponerlo al lado del rojo*, this green loses when it is put next to red. || *No desmerecer*, to compare favourably.
desmerecimiento m. Demerit.
desmesura f. Immoderacy, immoderation, lack of moderation. || Disproportion.
desmesuradamente adv. Uncommonly, extremely: *ojos desmesuradamente grandes*, uncommonly large eyes. || Excessively, inordinately, extremely (excesivamente). || Disproportionately, inordinately.
desmesurado, da adj. Excessive, inordinate, disproportionate (desmedido). || Unbounded, boundless, inordinate, limitless: *ambición desmesurada*, unbounded ambition. || Insolent, impudent, cheeky (descarado).
desmesurarse v. pr. To go too far, to forget o.s.
desmigajar o **desmigar** v. tr. To crumble.
— V. pr. To crumble.
desmilitarización f. Demilitarization.
desmilitarizar v. tr. To demilitarize.
desmineralización f. Demineralization.
desmineralizar v. tr. To demineralize.
desmirriado, da adj. FAM. Weedy, puny.
desmochar v. tr. To pollard, to lop (los árboles). || To blunt the horns of (una res). || FIG. To cut (una obra, un texto).
desmoche m. Pollarding, lopping (de árboles). || Blunting of the horns (de una res).
desmonetización f. Demonetization.
desmonetizar v. tr. To demonetize.
desmontable adj. That can be dismantled *o* taken to pieces, dismountable [U.S., knockdown] (máquina). || Collapsible: *armario desmontable*, collapsible wardrobe. || Detachable (que se quita). || ARQ. Portable, sectional (construcción).
— M. *Desmontable para neumáticos*, tyre lever.
desmontaje m. Removal (de una rueda, etc.). || TECN. Dismounting, disassembling (de una máquina). || Uncocking (de un arma de fuego).
desmontar v. tr. To remove, to take off: *desmontar una rueda*, to remove a wheel. || To dismantle, to take to pieces, to disassemble, to dismount (un mecanismo). || To strip (un motor). || To dismantle, to take down: *desmontar un andamio*, to take down a scaffold. || To unset, to unmount (un diamante, una piedra). || To unhinge (una puerta). || To unstitch (un traje). || MAR. To unship (el timón). || MIL. To dismount (un cañón). || To uncock (arma de fuego). || To dismount, to unhorse, to throw (el caballo al jinete). || To clear (cortar árboles). || To level (allanar).
— V. intr. To dismount (apearse).
— V. pr. To come to pieces (deshacerse). || To dismount (apearse).
desmonte m. Clearing [of trees] (tala de árboles). || Levelling (nivelación). || Clearing (terreno sin árboles). || Levelled ground (terreno allanado). || Cutting (para ferrocarriles). || Rubble, excavated soil (escombros).
desmoralización f. Demoralization. || Corruption.
desmoralizador, ra adj. Demoralizing. || Corrupting (que corrompe).
— M. y f. Demoralizer. || Corrupter (el que corrompe).
desmoralizante adj. Demoralizing. || Corrupting (que corrompe).
desmoralizar v. tr. To demoralize (desalentar). || To corrupt, to deprave (corromper).
— V. pr. To become demoralized. || To become corrupt *o* depraved.
desmoronadizo, za adj. Crumbly.
desmoronamiento m. Decay, crumbling: *desmoronamiento de un muro*, crumbling of a wall. || FIG. Destruction (ruina). | Crumbling, decaying, decline: *desmoronamiento de un régimen*, crumbling of a régime.
desmoronar v. tr. To wear away. || FIG. To corrode, to erode (arruinar lentamente).
— V. pr. To crumble, to decay, to fall to pieces: *esta casa se desmorona*, this house is crumbling. || FIG. To crumble (imperio, proyectos). | To decline (decaer).
desmotadera f. TECN. Cotton gin.
desmotador, ra m. y f. Burler (de lana). || Ginner (de algodón). || — F. Cotton gin.
desmotar v. tr. To burl (lana). || To gin (algodón).
desmovilización f. Demobilization, demob (fam.).
desmovilizar v. tr. To demobilize, to demob (fam.).
desmultiplicación f. TECN. Gearing down.
desmultiplicador adj. TECN. Reducing, reduction: *engranaje desmultiplicador*, reducing gear.
desmultiplicar v. tr. TECN. To gear down.
desnacionalización f. Denationalization.
desnacionalizar v. tr. To denationalize.
desnarigado, da adj. Noseless (sin narices). || Snub-nosed (chato).
desnarigar v. tr. To cut off the nose of. || To knock off the nose of (con un golpe).
desnatadora f. Cream separator, skimmer.
desnatar v. tr. To skim, to separate the cream from (la leche). || FIG. To take the cream of (tomar lo mejor). || *Leche sin desnatar*, whole milk.
desnaturalización f. Denaturalization. || Corruption, perversion (del carácter, de una persona). || Misrepresentation, distortion, adulteration (de un hecho, de la verdad). || Adulteration (de la leche).
desnaturalizado, da adj. Denaturalized (sin nacionalidad). || Corrupt, perverted (corrompido). || Misrepresented, distorted; adulterated (un hecho, la verdad, etc.). || Adulterated (leche). || Unnatural: *padre desnaturalizado*, unnatural father. || QUÍM. Denatured: *alcohol desnaturalizado*, denatured alcohol.
desnaturalizar v. tr. To denaturalize (quitar la naturalización). || To corrupt, to pervert (corromper). || To misrepresent, to distort, to adulterate: *desnaturalizar los hechos*, to misrepresent the facts. || To adulterate, to change the nature of (leche, alcohol, etc.). || QUÍM. To denature.
— V. pr. To give up one's nationality, to become stateless.
desnicotinizar v. tr. To denicotinize (tabaco).
desnitrar v. tr. Denitrate.
desnitrificación f. Denitrification, denitration.
desnitrificar v. tr. To denitrify.
desnivel m. Unevenness. || Slope (pendiente). || Depression (depresión). || FIG. Difference, inconsistency, inequality: *desnivel cultural entre las regiones*, cultural difference between the districts. || *Hay un desnivel entre estos puntos*, these points are not level *o* not on a level.
desnivelación f. Unevenness (desigualdad). || Unlevelling (acción). || Difference of level (entre dos puntos).
desnivelado, da adj. Uneven: *terreno desnivelado*, uneven ground. || Which are not on a level *o* not level: *puntos desnivelados*, points which are not on a level. || FIG. Uneven, unequal.

desnivelar v. tr. To make uneven: *desnivelar un campo*, to make a field uneven. || To put on different levels: *desnivelar varias cosas*, to put several things on different levels. || FIG. To unbalance, to throw out of balance (un presupuesto). || To tip (una balanza).
desnucar v. tr. To break the neck of.
— V. pr. To break one's neck.
desnudamente adv. Openly, clearly (abiertamente).
desnudamiento m. Stripping, undressing. || FIG. Denudation.
desnudar v. tr. To undress, to strip (quitar la ropa a). || To bare (un arma, una espada). || FIG. To strip: *desnudar a alguien de sus bienes*, to strip s.o. of his possessions; *el viento desnudó los árboles de sus hojas*, the wind stripped the trees of their leaves. | To lay bare (descubrir). | To ruin (arruinar). | To fleece, to clean out (fam.) [en el juego].
— V. pr. To strip, to get undressed (quitarse la ropa): *desnudarse hasta la cintura*, to strip to the waist. || FIG. To lose, to shed: *el árbol se está desnudando de hojas*, the tree is losing its leaves. | To rid o.s., to cast aside: *desnudarse de sus defectos*, to rid o.s. of *o* to cast aside one's faults.
desnudez f. Nakedness, nudity.
desnudismo m. Nudism.
desnudista adj./s. Nudist.
desnudo, da adj. Undressed, naked, nude, bare (desvestido). || Naked: *el hombre nace desnudo*, man is born naked. || FIG. Bare: *una pared desnuda*, a bare wall. | Bare, naked, drawn (espada). | Bare, naked: *los árboles están desnudos*, the trees are bare. | Devoid (falto de): *desnudo de méritos*, devoid of merits. | Clear, apparent (patente). | Penniless, destitute (pobre). | Ruined (arruinado). || — *Con las piernas desnudas*, bare-legged. || *La verdad desnuda*, the plain truth, the naked truth.
— M. ARTES. Nude.
desnutrición f. Malnutrition, undernourishment.
desnutrido, da adj. Undernourished.
desnutrirse v. pr. To suffer from malnutrition, to be undernourished.
desobedecer* v. tr. To disobey: *desobedecer la ley, a sus padres*, to disobey the law, one's parents.
desobediencia f. Disobedience.
desobediente adj. Disobedient.
— M. y f. Disobedient person.
desobligar v. tr. To free [from an obligation]. || To offend, to disoblige (causar disgusto a).
desobstrucción f. Removal of obstructions, clearing (de un camino). || Unblocking (de un conducto, etc.).
desobstruir* v. tr. To remove the obstructions from, to clear (un camino, etc.). || To unblock (un conducto).
desocupación f. Vacation (de una casa). || MIL. Evacuation. || Leisure, idleness (ocio). || Unemployment (desempleo).
desocupado, da adj. Idle (ocioso). || Unoccupied: *alquilar un piso desocupado*, to rent an unoccupied flat. || Empty, vacant, unoccupied (terreno, asiento, etc.). || Spare, free (tiempo). || Unemployed, out of work (sin empleo). || *Estar desocupado*, to have nothing to do, to be idle, to be at a loose end (fam.).
— M. y f. Idler (ocioso). || Unemployed person (sin empleo).
desocupar v. tr. To vacate: *desocupar una casa*, to vacate a house. || MIL. To evacuate. || To clear (desobstruir). || To empty (vaciar).
— V. pr. To become empty (quedar vacío). || To free o.s., to get away (de una ocupación).
desodorante adj./s. m. Deodorant.
desodorización f. Deodorization.
desodorizar v. tr. To deodorize.
desoír* v. tr. Not to listen to, to ignore, to take no notice of: *desoí los consejos de mi padre*, I didn't listen to *o* I took no notice of my father's advice. || To take no notice of: *desoyó la prescripción médica*, he took no notice of the doctor's orders.
desojar v. tr. To break the eye of (una aguja).
desolación f. Desolation. || FIG. Distress, grief.
desolado, da adj. Desolate (desierto). || Desolated, devastated (devastado). || Disconsolate, heartbroken, distressed (afligido).
desolador, ra adj. Desolating (que aflige). || Devastating, ravaging, desolating: *una epidemia desoladora*, a devastating epidemic.
desolar* v. tr. To desolate, to distress, to grieve (afligir). || To devastate, to ravage, to lay waste, to desolate (devastar).
— V. pr. To be distressed *o* grieved.
desoldar* v. tr. To unsolder.
desolidarizarse v. pr. To break away, to break with: *desolidarizarse de sus compañeros*, to break away from *o* to break with one's companions.
desolladero m. Slaughterhouse (matadero).
desollado, da adj. FAM. Insolent, impudent, cheeky (descarado). || FAM. *Salir desollado*, to be pulled to pieces, to be slated (ser muy criticado).
— M. y f. Insolent *o* cheeky person.
desollador m. Skinner (en el matadero). || FIG. Flayer (criticón). | Fleecer (en el juego). || ZOOL. Butcher-bird (alcaudón).
desolladura f. Skinning, flaying (de las reses). || Graze (arañazo).
desollar* v. tr. To skin, to flay: *desollar un conejo*, to skin a rabbit. || To skin, to graze (arañar). || FIG. y FAM. To fleece (hacer pagar muy caro). | To flay, to slate (criticar). || — FIG. *Desollar a uno vivo*, to make s.o. pay through the nose, to fleece s.o. (vender caro), to clean s.o. out (en el juego), to pull s.o. to pieces, to slate s.o., to flay s.o. (criticar). | *Queda el rabo por desollar*, the worst is yet to come.
desollón m. FAM. Graze (arañazo).
desorbitado, da adj. Exhorbitant: *precios desorbitados*, exhorbitant prices. || Exaggerated (exagerado). || *Tener los ojos desorbitados*, to be wide-eyed.
desorbitar v. tr. To exaggerate: *un periódico que desorbita los hechos*, a newspaper which exaggerates the facts.
— V. pr. To bulge (los ojos). || FIG. To lose one's sense of proportion. || To leave its orbit (satélite).
desorden m. Disorder, confusion: *reinaba gran desorden en la administración*, complete disorder reigned in the administration. || Muddle, mess: *la habitación está en desorden*, the room is in a mess. || FIG. Disorderliness (de la conducta). || — Pl. Disturbances, riots, disorder, *sing.*: *desórdenes estudiantiles*, student disturbances. || Disorders: *el alcohol puede ocasionar desórdenes en el estómago*, alcohol can cause stomach disorders. || Excesses (excesos). || — *Con el pelo en desorden*, with untidy *o* ruffled *o* tousled hair. || *Poner en desorden*, to upset, to muddle, to mix up, to disarrange.
desordenadamente adv. In disorder, in confusion: *huyeron desordenadamente*, they fled in disorder. || Disjointedly, confusedly: *hablar desordenadamente*, to speak disjointedly.
desordenado, da adj. Untidy (persona, habitación, trabajo). || Muddled, jumbled, disordered (objetos). || FIG. Disorderly: *vida desordenada*, disorderly life. || Unruly (revoltoso).
desordenamiento m. Disorder, confusion.
desordenar v. tr. To upset, to disarrange: *desordenar un cajón*, to upset a drawer. || To make a mess in, to make untidy (una habitación). || To mix up, to jumble (mezclar). || To throw into confusion (causar confusión).
— V. pr. To become untidy (una habitación, etc.). || To get into a muddle, to get muddled up: *los papeles se desordenaron*, the papers got muddled up. || To get out of order *o* out of control.
desorejado, da adj. Without handles (vasija). || TAUR. Earless [after the bullfight].
desorejar v. tr. To cut the ears off.
desorganización f. Disorganization, lack of organization.
desorganizadamente adv. In a disorganized way.
desorganizador, ra adj. Disorganizing.
— M. y f. Disorganizer.
desorganizar v. tr. To disorganize, to disrupt: *desorganizar una fábrica*, to disorganize a factory. || To disband, to break up, to disperse (desagregar).
desorientación f. Disorientation, loss of one's bearings (acción de perderse). || FIG. Confusion.
desorientado, da adj. Lost. || FIG. Confused.
desorientador, ra adj. Confusing, misleading, disorientating.
desorientar v. tr. To make lose one's bearings *o* one's way, to mislead, to disorientate: *el letrero me desorientó*, the sign made me lose my bearings, the sign disorientated me. || FIG. To confuse, to throw: *mi pregunta lo desorientó*, my question confused him.
— V. pr. To lose one's way, to get lost. || To get confused *o* mixed up (confundirse).
desorillar v. tr. To cut the selvedge off (una tela). || To cut the edge off (papel).
desornamentado, da adj. Plain, not decorated, bare.
desosar* v. tr. To bone (pescado, carne). || To stone, to pit (fruta).
desovar v. intr. To oviposit, to lay eggs (insectos). || To spawn (peces, anfibios).
desove m. Spawning (de los peces, los anfibios). || Ovipositing, egg-laying (de los insectos). || Spawning *o* egg-laying season (temporada).
desovillar v. tr. To unwind, to unravel.
desoxidación f. Deoxidization. || Cleaning, removal of oxide (de un metal).
desoxidante adj. Deoxidizing.
— M. Deoxidizer.
desoxidar v. tr. To deoxidize. || To clean, to remove the oxide from (limpiar los metales).
— V. pr. To be deoxidized.
desoxigenar v. tr. QUÍM. To deoxygenate, to deoxidize.
desoxirribonucleico, ca adj. QUÍM. Deoxyribonucleic, desoxyribonucleic.
despabiladeras f. pl. Snuffers.
despabilado, da adj. Wide-awake (despierto). || FIG. Quick, alert, sharp, smart (despejado): *un niño muy despabilado*, a very quick child. || FIG. *Ser despabilado*, to have one's wits about one.
despabilador m. Snuffer (en el teatro). || Snuffers, *pl.* (despabiladeras).
despabilar v. tr. To snuff (una vela). || To trim (una mecha). || FIG. y FAM. To wake up (despertar). | To brighten *o* to smarten up, to wake up (avivar el ingenio de): *hay que despabilar a ese alumno*, we shall have to brighten up that pupil. | To eat up, to finish: *despabiló*

dos raciones de calamares fritos, he ate up two helpings of fried squid. | To squander: *despabilar una fortuna*, to squander a fortune. | To rush off: *despabiló el trabajo*, he rushed off the work. | To pinch, to knock off, to steal (robar). | To kill, to do in (matar).
— V. pr. Fig. To wake up (despertarse). | To liven up, to wake up, to pull o.s. together, to get a move on: *¡despabílate que nos tenemos que ir!*, wake up, we've got to go! || *Amer*. To leave, to go away (marcharse).
despacio adv. Slowly: *hable más despacio*, speak more slowly, speak slower. || Quietly (silenciosamente). || Gradually, slowly (poco a poco).
— Interj. Take it easy!, easy does it!
despacioso, sa adj. Slow, sluggish.
despacito adv. Fam. Slowly.
— Interj. Fam. Take it easy!, easy does it!
despachaderas f. pl. Surliness, *sing.*, curtness, *sing.* (brusquedad). || Cheek, insolence (insolencia). || Resourcefulness, *sing.* (recursos). || Fig. *Tener buenas despachaderas*, to be on the ball.
despachado, da adj. Fam. Cheeky, rude, insolent, impudent (descarado). || Efficient, resourceful, on the ball (rápido). || *Ir bien despachado de*, to have a lot of, to be well off for.
despachante m. *Amer*. Customs officer (aduanero).
despachar v. tr. To settle, to dispatch, to finish (terminar). || To deal with, to attend to: *despachar la correspondencia*, to deal with the mail. || To see to, to attend to, to serve: *me despachó este dependiente*, this salesman served me. || To sell (vender): *despachar localidades*, to sell tickets. || To send, to dispatch: *despachar un recadero*, to send an errand boy. || To send, to dispatch (cartas, paquetes). || To dismiss, to sack (despedir): *despachó a la criada*, he dismissed the maid. || To send off, to send packing: *vino pidiendo limosna y lo despaché*, he come begging and I sent him packing. || To settle (un negocio, un problema, un convenio). || Fam. To polish off, to dispatch: *despachar un bocadillo, una botella de vino*, to polish off a sandwich, a bottle of wine. | To get through, to get out of the way: *el orador despachó su conferencia en media hora*, the speaker got through his lecture *o* got his lecture out of the way in half an hour. | To dispatch, to do in (matar). | To reel off (una historia).
— V. intr. To hurry, to hurry up (apresurarse). || To attend to business: *el director despachará mañana*, the manager will attend to business tomorrow. || To do business: *no despachamos los días de fiesta*, we don't do business on holidays. || To serve (en una tienda).
— V. pr. To get rid, to rid o.s.: *despacharse de algo*, to get rid of sth. || To finish (terminar): *suele despacharse a las seis*, he usually finishes at six. || To get out of the way: *quiso despacharse del asunto*, he wanted to get the matter out of the way. || To hurry, to hurry up (darse prisa). || — Fig. y fam. *Despacharse a su gusto*, to let go, to go the whole way. | *Despacharse a su gusto con uno*, to tell s.o. what one thinks of him, to give s.o. a piece of one's mind.
despacho m. Dispatch, sending (envío). || Sale (venta). || Store, shop (tienda): *despacho de vinos*, wine store. || Office (oficina): *el despacho del jefe*, the boss's office. || Study (en una casa). || Settlement (de un negocio, un convenio). || Dispatch (de un asunto). || Dispatch: *despacho diplomático*, diplomatic dispatch. || Message: *un despacho telefónico*, a telephone message. || Mil. Commission (título de oficial). || Office: *despacho de billetes, de localidades*, ticket, box office. || *Amer*. Grocery shop (tienda de comestibles). || *Despacho telegráfico*, telegram.
despachurramiento o **despachurro** m. Squashing.
despachurrar v. tr. Fam. To squash, to flatten.
despajar v. tr. Agr. To winnow. || Min. To sieve, to sift, to riddle (la tierra).
despaldar v. tr. To break the shoulder of.
despaldillar v. tr. To break (romper) *o* to dislocate (dislocar) the shoulder of.
despalillar v. tr. To strip (el tabaco). || To remove the stalks from (las uvas). || *Amer*. To kill (matar).
despampanadura f. Agr. Trimming, pruning.
despampanante adj. Fam. Stunning.
despampanar v. tr. Agr. To trim, to prune. || Fig. y fam. To astonish, to stun (sorprender).
— V. pr. Fig. y fam. To fall and hurt o.s.
despampanillar v. tr. To trim, to prune (las vides).
despanchurrar o **despanzurrar** v. tr. Fam. To disembowel (romper la panza de). | To squash (aplastar). | To burst (reventar). | To tear apart: *casa despanzurrada por los obuses*, house torn apart by shells.
desparejado, da adj. Odd: *un zapato desparejado* an odd shoe. || Without a partner, odd (en un baile).
desparejar v. tr. To separate.
desparejo, ja adj. Odd: *los dos guantes son desparejos*, the two gloves are odd.
desparpajado, da adj. Self-confident, sure of o.s. (desenvuelto). || Cheeky, rude, impudent (descarado). || Brisk, prompt, alert (rápido).
desparpajar v. tr. To spoil, to ruin (estropear). || To mess up, to disarrange (desordenar). || To scatter, to spread (desparramar).
— V. intr. To talk one's head off, to prattle away.
desparpajo m. Self-confidence, ease (desenvoltura). || Cheek, impudence (descaro). || Briskness, ease (soltura). || *Amer*. Fam. Disorder, confusion.
desparramado, da adj. Scattered: *flores desparramadas por el suelo*, flowers scattered over the floor. || Spilt (un líquido). || Fig. Scattered, sprawling (que se extiende mucho): *una ciudad muy desparramada*, a very scattered town.
desparramamiento m. Scattering. || Sprinkling (de gotas). || Spilling (de un líquido). || Spreading (de una noticia). || Fig. Squandering (de dinero). | Disorder (desorden).
desparramar v. tr. To scatter: *desparramar flores en el suelo*, to scatter flowers on the ground. || To spread (una noticia). || To sprinkle (un líquido en gotas). || To spill, to splash: *desparramó la leche por la mesa*, he spilled the milk all over the table. || Fig. To squander: *desparramó su fortuna*, he squandered his fortune. || Fig. *Desparramar la atención*, to divide one's attention amongst too many things.
— V. pr. To scatter. || To spread (una noticia). || To splash, to spill (un líquido). || Fig. To let o.s. go, to let one's hair down, to enjoy o.s. (divertirse).
desparramo m. *Amer*. V. DESPARRAMAMIENTO.
desparvar v. tr. Agr. To pile up [cereals].
despatarrada f. Fam. Splits, *pl.* (en algunas danzas).
despatarrar v. tr. Fam. To make [s.o.] open his legs wide. || Fig. To astonish, to astound, to flabbergast (asombrar). || Fig. *Dejar a uno despatarrado*, to astonish *o* to astound *o* to flabbergast s.o.
— V. pr. To open one's legs wide (separar las piernas). || Fig. To go sprawling (caerse). | To be astonished *o* astounded *o* flabbergasted.
despatillado m. Tenon (carpintería).
despatillar v. tr. To tenon (en carpintería). || To shave off the sideboards *o* sideburns of (quitar las patillas a).
despavesaderas f. pl. *Amer*. Snuffers.
despavesar v. tr. To snuff (una vela). || To trim (la mecha). || To blow the ashes off [embers].
despavonar v. tr. Tecn. To remove the bluing from.
despavoridamente adv. In terror.
despavorido, da adj. Terrified.
despavorirse* v. pr. To be terrified.
despeado, da adj. Footsore.
despearse v. pr. To be footsore, to have sore feet (al andar). || Vet. To bruise its hooves (el caballo). | To have foot rot (corderos).
despectivamente adj. Disparagingly, contemptuously, scornfully. || Gram. Pejoratively.
despectivo, va adj. Contemptuous, disparaging, derogatory, scornful: *hablar con tono despectivo*, to speak in a disparaging tone. || Gram. Pejorative: *sentido despectivo*, pejorative sense.
despechar v. tr. Fam. To wean (destetar). || To vex, to make resentful *o* indignant (causar despecho a).
— V. pr. To get angry (enfadarse). || To despair (estar desesperado).
despecho m. Spite. || Indignation. || Despair (desesperación). || Fam. Weaning (destete). || — *A despecho de*, in spite of, despite. || *A despecho suyo*, in spite of o.s. || *Por despecho*, out of spite.
despechugado, da adj. Fam. Bare breasted.
despechugar v. tr. To cut the breast off (un ave).
— V. pr. Fig. y fam. To bare one's breast (descubrir el pecho). | To open one's collar (abrir el cuello).
despedazamiento m. Tearing *o* pulling to pieces (por la fuerza). || Falling to pieces (al deshacerse algo). || Smashing, shattering (de una vasija, etc.).
despedazar v. tr. To tear to pieces *o* to shreds: *el león despedazaba su presa*, the lion was tearing its prey to pieces. || To smash, to shatter (romper). || Fig. To break: *despedazarle el corazón a uno*, to break s.o.'s heart.
— V. pr. To fall to pieces (caerse). || To smash (una vasija, etc.).
despedida f. Good-bye, farewell: *una despedida conmovedora*, a touching good-bye; *cena de despedida*, farewell dinner. || Farewell, send-off (antes de un viaje). || Closing formula (en una carta). || Envoi, last verse (de un canto). || Dismissal (de un trabajo).
despedir* v. tr. To give off *o* out, to emit: *el sol despide rayos de luz*, the sun gives off light rays. || To eject, to throw out: *la fuerza del golpe le despidió de su asiento*, the force of the blow threw him out of his seat. || To throw (el caballo al jinete). || To send out, to eject: *despedir un chorro de agua*, to send out a jet of water. || To give out (jugo). || To shoot out: *en este juego el resorte despide la bola*, in this game the spring shoots the ball out. || To say good-bye to, to see off: *despedir a uno en la estación*, to see s.o. off at the station. || To see out: *por favor, despide tú a los invitados*, could you see the guests out, please? || To dismiss, to sack (fam.) [a un empleado]. || To throw out (echar): *despedir a un invitado descortés*, to throw out an impolite guest. || To evict (a un inquilino). || To get rid of (librarse de). || To dismiss (una idea). || *Salir despedido*, to be thrown out: *salió despedido de su asiento*, he was thrown out of his seat.
— V. pr. To say good-bye, to take one's leave: *se fue sin despedirse de su hermano*, he went without saying good-bye to his brother. || To see [s.o.] off (en la estación, terminal, etc.). || To leave: *despedirse de un empleo*, to leave a job. || Fig. To say good-bye: *te puedes despedir del libro que le prestaste*, you can say good-bye to the book you lent him. || — Fig. *Despedirse a la*

francesa, to take French leave. || *Me despido de usted con un saludo afectuoso*, yours sincerely (en una carta). || *Se despide de usted su seguro servidor q.e.s.m.*, yours faithfully (en una carta).
despegado, da adj. Unstuck. || Which has come unstuck: *un sello despegado*, a stamp which has come unstuck. || FIG. Detached, cold (poco afectuoso).
despegadura f. Unsticking. || FIG. Detachedness, detachment, coldness.
despegamiento m. Detachment, coldness (despego).
despegar v. tr. To unstick: *despegar dos cosas, un sobre*, to unstick two things, an envelope. || To take off, to detach: *despegar la etiqueta de una botella*, to take the label off a bottle. || To take out (descoser). || FIG. *No despegar los labios*, not to open one's mouth, not to say a word.
— V. intr. AVIAC. To take off: *el avión para Manchester despega en seguida*, the plane for Manchester will take off immediately. | To blast off (un cohete).
— V. pr. To come unstuck. || FIG. To break away, to separate: *despegarse de sus padres*, to break away from one's parents. | To become separated (por las circunstancias).
despego m. Detachment, alienation (separación). || Indifference, coldness (falta de cariño). || Indifference (indiferencia).
despegue m. AVIAC. Takeoff. | Blast-off (de un cohete). || FIG. Launching. || *Pista de despegue*, runway.
despeinado, da adj. Unkempt, dishevelled, tousled.
despeinar v. tr. To dishevel, to tousle, *o* to ruffle the hair of.
despejado, da adj. Confident, sure of o.s. (seguro de sí). || Quick, clever, sharp, bright (listo). || Clear (camino, vista). || Open, clear: *un campo despejado*, an open field. || Clear, cloudless (cielo). || Broad (frente). || Spacious, uncluttered: *una plaza despejada*, a spacious square. || Wide-awake, awake (sin sueño).
despejar v. tr. To clear: *la policía despejó el local, el camino*, the police cleared the premises, the way; *despejar la calle de escombros*, to clear the street of rubble. || FIG. To clear up, to clarify, to sort out (aclarar). | To explain, to clarify (explicar). | To get rid of: *despejar las dificultades*, to get rid of the difficulties. | To clear: *el portero despejó la pelota*, the goalkeeper cleared the ball. || MAT. To find: *despejar la incógnita*, to find the unknown quantity. | To solve (resolver). || FIG. *Despejar el terreno*, to clear the ground *o* the way.
— V. intr. To clear the way, to move away: *¡despejen!*, clear the way! || DEP. To clear.
— V. pr. To clear up (el tiempo). || To clear (el cielo). || To abate (la fiebre). || To gain self-confidence (adquirir soltura). || To become clearer (un misterio) || To wake up, to brighten up (espabilarse). || To enjoy o.s., to let o.s. go (esparcirse). || To clear one's head, to wake o.s. up: *dar un paseo para despejarse*, to go for a walk to clear one's head.
despeje m. Clearance (en el fútbol).
despejo m. Clearing.
despelotado, da adj. FAM. Stark-naked.
despelotarse v. pr. FAM. To strip naked. | To take care of o.s., to fend for o.s. (arreglárselas).
despeluchar v. tr. To ruffle the hair of.
despeluzar o **despeluznar** v. tr. To ruffle the hair of (despeinar). || To make s.o.'s hair stand on end (erizar). || To terrify, to scare (aterrar). || *Amer.* To clean out, to fleece (en el juego).
— V. pr. To ruffle one's hair, to mess one's hair up (el pelo). || To be scared (aterrarse).
despellejadura f. Skinning (desolladura).
despellejar v. tr. To skin: *despellejar un conejo*, to skin a rabbit. || FIG. To flay, to slate, to pull to pieces (criticar). | To ruin, to fleece (arruinar).
despenar v. tr. To console. || FAM. To kill (matar).
despensa f. Pantry, larder (para guardar las provisiones). || Provisions, *pl.*, supplies, *pl.* (provisiones). || Storeroom, pantry (de una nave). || Post of steward *o* pantryman (oficio de despensero).
despensería f. Post of steward *o* pantryman.
despensero, ra m. y f. Pantryman, steward (hombre), pantrywoman (mujer).
despeñadero, ra adj. Steep, precipitous (abrupto).
— M. Precipice, cliff. || FIG. Risk, danger, hazard (riesgo).
despeñamiento m. o **despeño** m. Fall, headlong fall (caída). || MED. Diarrhoea.
despeñar v. tr. To hurl, to throw: *despeñar a alguien por un precipicio*, to hurl s.o. down from a cliff, to throw s.o. over a cliff.
— V. pr. To hurl *o* to throw o.s. [down]: *despeñarse por una roca*, to hurl o.s. [down] from a cliff. || To fall [down], to fall headlong (involuntariamente).
despepitar v. tr. To remove the pips from, to pit.
— V. pr. To bawl, to shout, to rant (gritar). || To be rash, to forget o.s. (hablar o actuar descomedidamente). || *Despepitarse por algo*, to be dying for sth. (desear mucho), to be mad about sth. (apreciar).
desperdiciado, da adj. Wasted, squandered, gone to waste.
desperdiciador, ra adj. Wasteful (con cosas). || Spendthrift, wasteful (con dinero).
— M. y f. Spendthrift, waster (persona).
desperdiciar v. tr. To waste: *despediciar el tiempo, la comida*, to waste time, food. || To waste, to squander (dinero). || To miss, to throw away, to waste: *desperdiciar una ocasión*, to miss an opportunity. || *Ha desperdiciado todos mis consejos*, he has not taken any of my advice.
desperdicio m. Waste: *desperdicio de tiempo*, waste of time. || — Pl. Rubbish, *sing.* (basura). || Waste, *sing.*: *desperdicios de comida, de papel*, waste food, paper. || — *Desperdicios de cocina*, kitchen scraps. || *Este trozo no tiene desperdicio*, there is no waste on this piece of meat. || FIG. y FAM. *No tener desperdicio*, to be faultless (una obra de arte), to be good in all that he *o* she does (una persona), to be good all the way through (un libro, una película).
desperdigar v. tr. To scatter, to disperse: *mis hermanos andan desperdigados por el mundo entero*, my brothers are scattered all over the world. || To divide, to dissipate (la atención, la actividad).
— V. pr. To scatter, to disperse. || To become scattered *o* dispersed.
desperecer* v. tr. To perish (perecer).
— V. pr. To be dying, to crave, to yearn (desear).
desperezarse v. pr. To stretch (estirarse).
desperezo m. Stretch.
desperfecto m. Flaw, blemish: *hay un desperfecto en la tela*, there is a flaw in the cloth. || Damage (deterioro). || Imperfection. || *Sufrir desperfectos*, to be *o* to get damaged.
despernada f. Splits, *pl.* (en el baile).
despernado, da adj. Lame (animal). || FIG. Footsore, weary (cansado).
despernar* v. tr. To lame.
despersonalizar v. tr. To depersonalize.
despertador, ra adj. Awakening, arousing.
— M. Alarm clock (reloj). || — M. y f. Knocker-up, waker-up (persona).
despertar* v. tr. To wake up, to wake, to awaken, to awake: *el ruido me despertó*, the noise woke me up. || FIG. To rouse, to stir up, to awake (deseo, pasión, sentimiento). | To arouse, to awaken (la esperanza, el apetito). | To revive, to recall (recordar): *esto despierta recuerdos de mi niñez*, this revives memories of my childhood. | To wake up, to brighten up (espabilar).
— V. intr. y pr. To wake up, to wake, to awake, to awaken: *se despertó a las seis de la mañana*, he woke up at six in the morning. || FIG. To wake up, to brighten up, to liven up (espabilarse).
despertar m. Awakening: *el despertar de un pueblo*, the awakening of a people.
despestañar v. tr. To pluck out the eyelashes of.
— V. pr. FIG. To strain one's eyes.
despezuñarse v. pr. To damage its hooves (un animal). || *Amer.* To rush (apresurarse).
despiadado, da adj. Pitiless, merciless, remorseless: *una crítica despiadada*, pitiless criticism. || Heartless, inhuman, merciless (persona).
despicar v. tr. To calm down, to appease.
— V. pr. To get one's own back, to take one's revenge, to get even.
despichar v. tr. To dry (secar). || To exude, to give out (escurrir). || *Amer.* To squash (aplastar).
— V. intr. FAM. To kick the bucket, to snuff it (morir).
despido m. Dismissal, discharge. || *Notificación previa de despido*, notice.
despiertamente adv. Cleverly.
despierto, ta adj. Awake. || FIG. Quick, sharp, bright: *una muchacha muy despierta*, a very bright girl. | Lively (vivaz). | Alert (alerto).
despilfarrado, da adj. V. DESPILFARRADOR.
despilfarrador, ra adj. Spendthrift, wasteful (con dinero). || Wasteful (con cosas, comida, etc.).
— M. y f. Spendthrift, squanderer, waster (con dinero). || Waster (con cosas).
despilfarrar v. tr. To waste, to squander (dinero). || To waste (cosas, comida, etc.).
— V. pr. To waste *o* to squander one's money.
despilfarro m. Wasting, squandering (acción de despilfarrar): *el despilfarro de una fortuna*, the wasting of a fortune. || Wastefulness, wasteful spending: *el despilfarro es la ruina de la economía de un país*, wasteful spending is the ruin of a country's economy. || Extravagance: *no pienso pagar todos tus despilfarros*, I don't intend to pay for all your extravagances. || *Hacer un despilfarro*, to throw away one's money, to squander one's money.
despimpollar v. tr. AGR. To trim, to prune (la vid).
despinochar v. tr. To remove the husk from (el maíz).
despintar v. tr. To take the paint off (quitar pintura). || FIG. To misrepresent, to change (un suceso).
— V. intr. To be worse: *éste no despinta de los demás*, this one is no worse than the rest.
— V. pr. To fade (lo teñido). || FIG. To fade from the memory of: *despintarse a alguien*, to fade from s.o.'s memory. || *Aquel hombre no se me despintará nunca*, I shall never forget that man.
despiojar v. tr. To delouse (quitar los piojos a). || FIG. y FAM. To pull out of the gutter (sacar de la miseria).
despique m. Revenge, satisfaction (desquite).
despistado, da adj. Absentminded (distraído). || Unpractical (poco práctico). || Lost (desorientado):

estoy despistado, I'm lost. || Confused, bewildered, muddled (confuso).
— M. y f. Scatterbrain, absentminded person. || *Hacerse el despistado*, to act dumb (hacerse el tonto), to pretend not to see s.o. (para no saludar).

despistar v. tr. To throw off the scent: *la liebre despistó a los perros*, the hare threw the dogs off the scent. || To put off the track, to shake off (fam.): *despistar a la policía*, to put the police off the track. || To mislead, to make lose one's way, to put on the wrong road: *el letrero mal puesto me despistó*, the badly placed sign misled me. || FIG. To mislead: *lo que me dijiste me despistó*, what you told me misled me.
— V. intr. To be misleading: *el problema es tan fácil que despita*, the problem is so easy that it is misleading.
— V. pr. To get lost, to lose one's way (extraviarse). || To put off the track, to shake off (fam.): *el ladrón se ha despistado de la policía*, the thief has put the police off the track. || To leave the road *o* the track (un coche). || FIG. *Se despistó y cogió mi cartera en vez de la suya*, he absentmindedly *o* unthinkingly picked up my briefcase instead of his own.

despiste m. Leaving the road (de un coche). || FIG. Absentmindedness (distracción). | Confusion, bewilderment (confusión). | Mistake, slip (error). || — *Momento de despiste*, moment's inattentiveness. || *Tener un despiste enorme*, to be terribly absentminded, to have one's head in the clouds (ser despistado), to be terribly bewildered *o* muddled *o* confused (estar despistado). || *Tiene tanto despiste que nunca sabe qué camino tomar*, he has such a poor sense of direction that he never knows which way to go.

desplacer m. Displeasure.

desplacer* v. tr. To displease (disgustar). || To grieve (afligir).

desplantación f. AGR. Uprooting, taking up.

desplantador m. Trowel (utensilio).

desplantar v. tr. AGR. To uproot, to pull up, to take up: *desplantar tomates*, to pull up tomatoes.

desplante m. Bad stance (en esgrima, danza). || Act of defiance or insolence (acción descarada). || Boast (jactancia). || TAUR. Defiant stance [assumed in front of the bull]. (V. ADORNO [Observ.]) || *Hacer un desplante a uno*, to defy s.o.

desplatar v. tr. TECN. To desilverize, to desilver, to remove the silver from.

desplatear v. tr. *Amer.* To desilver, to desilverize (lo plateado). || *Amer.* FAM. To get money out of (sacar dinero a).

desplazado, da adj. Out of place: *me encuentro desplazado aquí*, I feel out of place here.

desplazamiento m. MAR. y FÍS. Displacement. || Moving, removal (acción de trasladar). || Travelling, journey (viaje): *gastos de desplazamiento*, travelling expenses. || Shifting (cambio de sitio). || Movement (de tropas). || Transference, swing (de votos).

desplazar v. tr. To move, to shift: *desplazar una mesa*, to move a table. || To remove (quitar). || TECN. To displace, to move: *desplazar un eje tres milímetros*, to displace an axle three millimetres. || FÍS. y MAR. To displace: *este cuerpo desplaza una mayor cantidad de agua*, this body displaces a larger quantity of water. || To displace, to replace: *en aquella fábrica los jóvenes han desplazado a las personas mayores*, in that factory young people have displaced the older people. || To transfer, to move (tropas).
— V. pr. To move (una cosa). || To travel: *tiene que desplazarse seis kilómetros cada día*, he has to travel six kilometres every day. || To swing (votos, tendencias).

desplegable m. Folder, brochure, pamphlet.

desplegadura f. Unfolding, spreading out. || Unfurling.

desplegar* v. tr. To unfold (lo plegado): *desplegar el mantel*, to unfold the tablecloth. || To unfold, to open out (un periódico). || To spread out, to open out: *desplegar un mapa*, to spread out a map. || To spread (las alas). || To stretch out (los brazos). || To unfurl (una bandera). || To spread, to unfurl (las velas). || FIG. To display, to show: *desplegar inteligencia, celo*, to show intelligence, zeal. || To clarify, to elucidate (aclarar). || MIL. To deploy (tropas).
— V. pr. To spread, to unfold (las alas). || To fly, to unfurl (bandera). || MIL. To deploy, to spread out.

despliegue m. MIL. Deployment. || Unfolding, opening (abertura). || Unfurling (de una bandera). || Display, show (ostentación).

desplomar v. tr. To put off the vertical *o* out of plumb. || *Amer.* To scold, to reprimand (regañar).
— V. pr. To lean, to tilt (inclinarse). || To topple over, to fall down, to collapse (derrumbarse): *la torre se desplomó*, the tower toppled over. || To drop (una cosa pesada). || To collapse (una persona): *su madre se desplomó al oír la noticia*, his mother collapsed when she heard the news. || To tumble, to drop (precios).

desplome m. Collapse, fall (caída). || ARQ. Overhang (saledizo).

desplumadura f. Plucking.

desplumar v. tr. To pluck: *desplumar un ganso*, to pluck a goose. || FIG. To fleece, to clean out (sacar el dinero).
— V. pr. To moult [U.S., to molt] (ave).

despoblación f. Depopulation. || — *Despoblación del campo*, rural depopulation, drift from the land *o* to the cities. || *Despoblación de un río*, unstocking. || *Despoblación forestal*, deforestation, clearing.

despoblado, da adj. Depopulated (con pocos habitantes). || Uninhabited (sin habitantes). || Deserted (desierto). || — *Despoblado de árboles*, deforested. || *Frente despoblada*, receding hairline.
— M. Wilderness, deserted place. || *En despoblado*, in the wilds.

despoblamiento m. V. DESPOBLACIÓN.

despoblar* v. tr. To depopulate: *la peste ha despoblado el país*, the plague has depopulated the country. || To clear (despojar): *despoblar un campo de hierbas*, to clear a field of grass. || FIG. To lay waste, to ravage (devastar). || *Despoblar de árboles*, to deforest, to clear.
— V. pr. To become depopulated *o* deserted (un lugar).

despoetizar v. tr. To take all poetry out of: *despoetizar la vida*, to take all poetry out of life.

despojar v. tr. To deprive, to strip, to despoil (p. us.), to divest: *despojar a uno de todo lo que posee, de sus derechos*, to deprive s.o. of all he possesses, of his rights; *despojaron la iglesia de todas sus obras de arte*, they stripped the church of all its works of art. || To strip, to divest: *despojar a uno de sus vestidos*, to strip s.o. of his clothes. || To strip: *despojar un árbol de su corteza*, to strip a tree of its bark. || FAM. To clean out, to fleece (quitarle todo el dinero). || JUR. To dispossess.
— V. pr. To give up, to forsake: *despojarse de sus bienes*, to give up one's wealth. || To take off: *despojarse de su abrigo*, to take off one's coat. || BOT. To shed (de hojas). || FIG. To put aside: *despojarse de su orgullo*, to put aside one's pride.

despojo m. Depriving, divestment, divestiture. || Stripping. || Dispossession (desposeimiento). || Plundering, despoiling (robo). || Booty, plunder, spoils, *pl.* (botín). || — Pl. Offal, *sing.* (de animales). || Leftovers (de comida). || Remains (cadáver). || Rubble, *sing.* (de un edificio). || *Despojos mortales*, mortal remains.

despolarización f. FÍS. Depolarization.

despolarizador, ra adj. FÍS. Depolarizing.
— M. FÍS. Depolarizer.

despolarizar v. tr. FÍS. To depolarize.

despopularizar v. tr. To make unpopular.
— V. pr. To lose popularity.

desportilladura f. o **desportillamiento** m. Chipping (acción). || Chip (en un jarro, etc.).

desportillar v. tr. To chip (una vasija).

desposado, da adj. Newly married. || Handcuffed (preso).
— M. y f. Newlywed (recién casado).

desposar v. tr. To marry, to wed (casar).
— V. pr. To get engaged (contraer esponsales): *desposarse con*, to get engaged to. || To get married (*con*, to), to marry (casarse).

desposeer v. tr. To dispossess: *desposeer a un propietario de su casa*, to dispossess an owner of his house. || To oust (de un cargo). || To remove (de la autoridad).
— V. pr. To give up, to renounce.

desposeído, da m. y f. *Los desposeídos*, the have-nots.

desposeimiento m. Dispossession.

desposorios m. pl. Engagement, *sing.*, betrothal, *sing.* (ant.) [esponsales]. || Marriage, *sing.* (matrimonio). || Wedding, *sing.*, marriage ceremony, *sing.* (boda).

déspota m. Despot: *Nerón fue un déspota cruel*, Nero was a cruel despot; *el niño es un verdadero déspota*, the child is a real despot.

despóticamente adv. Despotically.

despótico, ca adj. Despotic: *un gobierno, un marido despótico*, a despotic government, husband.

despotismo m. Despotism: *el despotismo ilustrado*, enlightened despotism.

despotizar v. tr. *Amer.* To tyrannize, to oppress.

despotricar v. intr. FAM. To rant on, to carry on (hablar sin reparo). || FIG *Despotricar contra alguien*, to run s.o. down.

despotrique m. FAM. Carrying on, ranting on.

despreciable adj. Despicable, contemptible: *una persona despreciable*, a despicable person. || Negligible (insignificante): *un error despreciable*, a negligible error. || Worthless, paltry (de poca monta).

despreciador, ra adj. Scornful, contemptuous.

despreciar v. tr. To despise, to scorn: *despreciar a un empleado*, to despise an employee. || To depreciate, to disparage, to belittle (menospreciar). || To neglect, to ignore (no hacer caso de): *no hay que despreciar esta posibilidad*, we should not neglect this possibility. || To ignore: *despreciar un peligro*, to ignore a danger. || To snub, to slight, to spurn (desairar).

despreciativo, va adj. Scornful, contemptous: *un gesto despreciativo*, a scornful gesture.

desprecio m. Scorn, contempt, disdain: *con desprecio de las convenciones*, with contempt for convention. || Slight, snub (desaire). || *Con desprecio de su propia vida*, without a thought for his own life, with disregard for his own life.

desprender v. tr. To remove, to detach: *desprender un sello del sobre*, to remove a stamp from an envelope. || To release, to loosen (soltar). || To take off: *desprender una manga de una chaqueta*, to take a sleeve off a jacket. || To give off: *esta flor desprende un olor agradable*, this flower gives off a pleasant smell. || To throw off (chispas). || To give off (gas).
— V. pr. To come off *o* away: *la etiqueta se ha des-*

prendido de la botella, the label has come off the bottle. || To come out *o* off: *la manga se desprendió de su vestido*, the sleeve came out of her dress *o* came off her dress. || To be given off, to emanate (olor). || MED. To be detached (la retina). || To fly off, to fly out, to shoot out (chispas). || To be given off, to issue (el gas). || To shed (la piel). || FIG. To part with, to forsake, to give up: *se tuvo que desprender de sus joyas*, she had to part with her jewels. | To get rid of, to do away with: *desprenderse de lo que no le interesa a uno*, to get rid of everything that doesn't interest one. | To get free (de estorbos). | To cast *o* to put aside: *desprenderse de sus escrúpulos*, to cast aside one's scruples. || To follow, to be implied (deducirse): *de todo aquello se desprenden dos conclusiones*, two conclusions follow from all that, two conclusions are implied by all that. || — *De aquí se desprende que*, it can be deduced from this that, from this it follows that, this implies that. || *Por lo que se desprende de*, judging by, going by.

desprendido, da adj. Loose, detached (una pieza). || Generous, unselfish, altruistic (generoso). || Disinterested (desinteresado).

desprendimiento m. Unselfishness, generosity (generosidad). || Disinterestedness (desinterés). || Unsticking (despegadura). || Separation (de cápsula de cohete). || Giving off, emission (de un olor, del gas). || Shedding (de la piel). || ARTES. Deposition (de Cristo). || — MED. *Desprendimiento de la retina*, detachment of the retina. || *Desprendimiento de tierras*, landslide.

despreocupación f. Lack of care, unconcern (falta de preocupación). || Carelessness, negligence (descuido). || Impartiality, freedom from bias, open-mindedness (imparcialidad). || Unconcernedness, indifference.

despreocupado, da adj. Carefree, unconcerned (sin preocupación). || Unworried (sin inquietud). || Careless, negligent (descuidado). || Unconcerned, indifferent (indiferente). || Impartial, unbiased (imparcial). ||Casual: *despreocupado en el vestir*, casual in his dress.

despreocuparse v. pr. To be neglectful, not to bother (descuidarse). || To stop worrying (dejar de preocuparse). || To be unconcerned *o* indifferent (ser indiferente). || *Despreocuparse de*, to forget.

desprestigiar v. tr. To discredit, to cause [s.o.] to lose prestige, to ruin [s.o.'s] reputation: *su comportamiento lo ha desprestigiado*, his behaviour has ruined his reputation. || To discredit, to disparage, to decry (criticar): *desprestigiar a sus colegas*, to discredit one's colleagues; *una marca injustamente desprestigiada*, an unjustly disparaged brand.
— V. pr. To lose prestige, to lose one's reputation, to fall into discredit: *el rey se desprestigió completamente*, the king lost all prestige.

desprestigio m. Loss of reputation *o* prestige, discredit (descrédito).

desprevenidamente adv. Without warning, unexpectedly (sin previo aviso). || Unawares, by surprise (de improviso).

desprevenido, da adj. Improvident (imprevisor). || Unawares, unprepared, off guard: *coger a una persona desprevenida*, to catch a person unawares.

desproporción f. Disproportion, lack of proportion.

desproporcionado, da adj. Disproportionate, disproportional, disproportioned, out of proportion.

desproporcionar v. tr. To disproportion.

despropósito m. Irrelevant remark, nonsense, rubbish: *decir muchos despropósitos*, to make a lot of irrelevant remarks, to talk a lot of nonsense. || Blunder (metedura de pata). || *Con despropósito*, irrelevantly.

desproveer v. tr. To deprive.

desprovisto, ta adj. Lacking, without, devoid: *desprovisto de interés*, lacking interest, devoid of interest. || *Estar desprovisto de*, to lack, to be lacking.

despueble o **despueblo** m. Depopulation.

después adv. Afterwards, later: *no tengo tiempo ahora, después hablaremos*, I haven't got time now, we'll have a talk afterwards; *varios días después*, several days later. || Then, next, afterwards (a continuación): *después fuimos a la playa*, then we went to the beach; *hay un pasillo y después una habitación grande*, there is a corridor and then a large room. || — *Después de*, after: *después de la guerra*, after the war; *después de cenar*, after supper; *mi nombre viene después del tuyo en la lista*, my name comes after yours on the list; from, since: *después de esa fecha no la ha vuelto a ver*, since that date he hasn't seen her; from, after: *después de hoy no habrá reuniones*, from today there will be no meetings; (con participio pasado) once: *después de hecho*, once done; *después de cerrada la ventana*, once the window was *o* had been closed. || *Después de hacerlo* or *después de haberlo hecho*, having done it, after doing it. || *Después de todo*, after all. || *Después que*, after: *llegó después que yo*, he arrived after me; after, when: *después que saliste, lo hicimos*, we did it when *o* after you [had] left; *después que llegue hablaremos de ello*, we shall talk about it when he arrives *o* when *o* after he has arrived. || (Ant.). *Después que*, since (desde que). || *El año después, el día después*, the year after *o* the next year *o* the following year, the day after *o* the next day *o* the following day. || *Poco después*, shortly after, soon after.

despulmonarse v. pr. FAM. To shout o.s. hoarse (desgañitarse).

despulpador m. TECN. Pulper.

despulpar v. tr. To pulp. || *Máquina de despulpar*, pulper.

despumar v. tr. To skim (espumar).

despuntado, da adj. Blunt.

despuntador m. *Amer.* Pick, pickaxe [of miner].

despuntar v. tr. To blunt, to break off the point of (embotar). || MAR. To round (pasar una punta, un cabo). || To cut away the empty combs of [a beehive].
— V. intr. To bud (las flores), to sprout (las plantas). || FIG. To break (la luz del día): *el alba despunta*, the dawn breaks. | To show intelligence *o* wit (manifestar inteligencia). | To excel, to stand out: *este niño despunta entre los demás*, this child stands out amongst the rest; *despuntó por sus cualidades de orador*, he excelled for his qualities as an orator. | *Al despuntar el alba*, at daybreak.

despunte m. Blunting (embotadura). || *Amer.* Twig, sprig (rama).

desquebrajar v. tr. To crack, to split (resquebrajar).

desquejar v. tr. AGR. To slip.

desqueje m. AGR. Slipping.

desquiciado, da adj. FIG. Unbalanced, unsettled, deranged: *una persona desquiciada*, an unbalanced person. | Unsettled, topsy-turvy, mad: *vivimos en un mundo desquiciado*, we live in an unsettled world.

desquiciador, ra adj. Distressing, disturbing (que turba). || Unsettling (que trastorna).

desquiciamiento m. FIG. Unsettling, perturbation (perturbación). | Unsettled state, unsettledness (desequilibrio). | Disturbance (trastorno).

desquiciar v. tr. To unhinge (una puerta). || FIG. To distress, to disturb (perturbar). | To upset (trastornar). | To unsettle, to unhinge: *la guerra ha desquiciado a muchos hombres*, the war has unsettled many men. | To unbalance, to unhinge, to derange, (afectar profundamente).
— V. pr. To come off its hinges (una puerta). || To be disturbed (perturbarse).

desquicio m. *Amer.* V. DESQUICIAMIENTO.

desquijerar v. tr. ARQ. To tenon.

desquitar v. tr. To compensate: *desquitar a uno por los estropicios producidos*, to compensate s.o. for the damage caused.
— V. pr. To make good, to recoup: *desquitarse de una pérdida*, to make good a loss. || To make up for it: *hoy no he dormido mucho pero me desquitaré mañana*, I haven't slept much today but I'll make up for it tomorrow. || To take [one's] revenge, to get one's revenge, to get even: *el equipo se desquitó*, the team got its revenge.

desquite m. Revenge: *tomar un desquite*, to take revenge. || Compensation (compensación). || DEP. Return match. || *En desquite*, in return, in retaliation.

desramar v. tr. To prune, to lop (podar).

desrame m. Pruning, lopping.

desratización f. Deratting, deratization.

desratizar v. tr. To derat, to clear of rats.

desrazonable adj. FAM. Unreasonable.

desrielar v. intr. *Amer.* To derail, to run off the rails.

desriñonar v. tr. To break the back of, to cripple (derrengar).

desrizar v. tr. To take the curls out of (el pelo).

desrodrigar v. tr. AGR. To remove the prop from.

destacado, da adj. Distinguished, prominent, outstanding (notable): *persona destacada*, distinguished person. || Outstanding, remarkable: *un trabajo destacado*, an outstanding piece of work || Outstanding: *los hechos más destacados*, the most outstanding events. || Choice: *ocupar un lugar destacado en la jerarquía eclesiástica*, to occupy a choice position in the ecclesiastical hierarchy.

destacamento m. MIL. Detachment, detail.

destacar v. tr. MIL. To detach, to detail (tropas): *destacar unos soldados para una expedición peligrosa*, to detach some soldiers for a dangerous expedition. || FIG. To underline, to point out, to emphasize: *conviene destacar la importancia de esta decisión*, it is appropriate to underline the importance of this decision. | To make [sth.] stand out, to highlight, to bring out: *el pintor quiso destacar a sus personajes*, the painter wished to make his characters stand out. | To honour, to confer an honour upon: *destacar a una persona por los servicios prestados*, to honour a person for services rendered.
— V. intr. y pr. To stand out: *destaca por su inteligencia*, he stands out for his intelligence.
— V. pr. To stand out, to be highlighted (cosas colores): *la silueta de la torre se destacaba en el cielo*, the silhouette of the tower stood out against the sky. || To break away, to draw ahead (corredor). || To stand out (descollar).

destajador m. TECN. Blacksmith's hammer.

destajar v. tr. To settle the conditions for [a job]. || To cut (naipes). || *Amer.* To cut up (cortar).

destajero, ra o **destajista** m. y f. Pieceworker.

destajo m. Piecework. || — *A destajo*, by the job, by the piece: *pagado a destajo*, paid by the piece. || FAM. *Hablar a destajo*, to talk nineteen to the dozen. || *Precio a destajo*, piecework price. || *Trabajar a destajo*, to be on piecework (por piezas), to work hard (trabajar mucho). || *Trabajo a destajo*, piecework.

destalonar v. tr. To wear down the heel of: *destalonar el calzado*, to wear down the heels of one's shoes. || To detach, to tear off [leaves from a stub book].
destapado m. o **destapadura** f. Uncorking (tapón), opening, uncapping (chapa), removal of [the] lid (tapadera).
destapar v. tr. To uncork (quitar el tapón). || To take the top *o* cap off, to uncap, to open (quitar la chapa). || To take the lid off, to open, to remove the lid from (quitar la tapa). || To open (abrir). || To uncover: *destapar al niño*, to uncover the child. || *Destapar la cama*, to pull the covers back.
— V. pr. To throw off one's bedclothes (en la cama). || To uncover o.s., to get uncovered (descubrirse). || FIG. To unbosom o.s., to open one's heart: *se destapó con su amigo*, he opened his heart to his friend. | To reveal *o* to show one's real *o* true self (revelarse). | To turn up: *se destapó con un regalo estupendo*, she turned up with a fantastic present.
destapiar v. tr. To pull down the walls of.
destaponar v. tr. To uncork (una botella). || To unplug, to unstop.
destarar v. tr. To deduct the tare on (de un peso).
destartalado, da adj. Rambling, ramshackle: *una casa destartalada*, a rambling house. || Rickety (coche).
destejar v. tr. To untile the roof of: *destejar una casa*, to untile the roof of a house. || FIG. To expose, to leave unprotected (descubrir).
destejer v. tr. To unweave, to undo, to unravel: *Penélope destejía por la noche la tela que tejía durante el día*, Penelope unwove at night the cloth that she wove during the day. || FIG. To undo.
destellar v. intr. To flash (con luz repentina). || To sparkle, to glitter (piedra preciosa, etc.). || To twinkle (estrellas).
— V. tr. To flash, to give *o* to send off: *destellar rayos de luz*, to flash rays of light.
destello m. Twinkling (de las estrellas). || Flash, flash of light (luz repentina). || Sparkle, glitter (de una piedra preciosa). || FIG. Scrap, bit (atisbo). | Flash, glimmer, spark: *destello de genio*, flash of wit.
destemplado, da adj. Harsh, angry, gruff (irritado): *con voz destemplada*, in a harsh voice. || Bad-tempered, irritable (carácter). || Unsettled, unpleasant (tiempo). || MÚS. Out-of-tune, out of tune, untuned: *una guitarra destemplada*, an out-of-tune guitar; *la guitarra está destemplada*, the guitar is out of tune. | Inharmonious, dissonant (voz, música). || MED. Feverish, a little feverish, off colour. || ARTES. Inharmonious (cuadro). || TECN. Untempered, softened, weakened (acero).
destemplanza f. Unsettledness (del tiempo). || Intemperance, lack of moderation (abuso). || FIG. Irascibility, irritability (impaciencia). | Lack of moderation *o* restraint (falta de moderación). || MED. Slight fever. || MÚS. Inharmoniousness (de voz, música). | Dissonance (de un instrumento).
destemplar v. tr. MÚS. To put out of tune, to untune. || To unsettle (el tiempo). || To untemper (el acero). || MED. To give a slight fever. || To infuse (en infusión).
— V. pr. To become unsettled (el tiempo). || MÚS. To go *o* to get out of tune (un instrumento). || MED. To have a touch of fever. || To become *o* to get angry (irritarse). || TECN. To lose its temper (acero). || *Amer.* To have one's teeth on edge (sentir dentera).
destemple m. MÚS. Dissonance (de un instrumento). | Inharmoniousness (de voz, música). || TECN. Loss of temper, untempering (del acero u otros metales).
desteñir* v. tr. To discolour [U.S., to discolor], to fade: *el sol ha desteñido la cortinas*, the sun has faded the curtains. || To discolour: *la camisa roja ha desteñido la sábana*, the red shirt has discoloured the sheet. || *Esta tela no destiñe*, this fabric will not run.
— V. pr. To lose its colour [U.S., to lose its color], to discolour [U.S., to discolor] to fade: *desteñirse con el uso*, to lose its colour with use.
desternillarse v. pr. *Desternillarse de risa*, to split one's sides laughing. || *Es cosa de desternillarse de risa*, it's a scream, it's enough to make you die laughing.
desterrado, da adj./s. Exile.
desterrar* v. tr. To banish, to exile (término político y jurídico). || To remove the earth from [roots of plants, minerals] (quitar la tierra). || FIG. To banish, to expel: *desterrar la tristeza*, to banish sadness. | To abolish, to do away with (abolir).
— V. pr. To go into exile (exilarse), to leave one's country (abandonar su país).
desterronadora f. AGR. Clod crusher (arado).
desterronar v. tr. To break up *o* to crush the clods in.
desterronamiento m. Breaking-up *o* crushing of [the] clods.
destetar v. tr. To wean.
— V. pr. To be weaned.
destete m. Weaning.
destiempo (a) adv. Inopportunely, at an inopportune moment, at the wrong moment: *lo hace todo a destiempo*, he does everything at the wrong moment.
destierro m. Exile, banishment: *vivir en el destierro*, to live in exile. || Place of exile (lugar).
destilación f. Distillation. || Secretion, exudence (de humores).
destiladera f. Still, alembic (alambique).
destilado m. Distillate (producto de la destilación).
destilador, ra adj. Distilling.
— M. Still, alembic (alambique). || Filter (filtro). || Distiller (persona).
destilar v. tr. To distil, to distill: *destilar vino*, to distil wine. || To exude, to secrete: *destilar pus, veneno*, to exude pus, venom. || To filter, to filtrate (filtrar). || FIG. To exude: *este libro destila una profunda amargura*, this book exudes a profound bitterness.
— V. intr. To trickle, to drip (gotear). || To ooze, to seep, to exude (rezumar).
— V. pr. To be distilled: *la gasolina se destila del petróleo*, petrol is distilled off petroleum. || To filter (filtrarse).
destilería f. Distillery.
destinación f. Destination.
destinar v. tr. To destine: *destinar un buque al transporte de carbón*, to destine a boat for the transportation of coal; *destinar a su hijo al foro*, to destine one's son for the bar. || To appoint, to assign: *lo han destinado al consulado de España*, he has been appointed to the Spanish consulate. || To send: *fue destinado a Madrid de cónsul*, he was sent to Madrid as consul. || To post, to station: *militar destinado en Burgos*, soldier posted in Burgos. || COM. To allot, to earmark, to assign, to appropriate: *destinar una cantidad*, to earmark a sum of money. || To address: *un paquete destinado a ti*, a parcel addressed to you.
— V. pr. To intend to take up, to intend to enter (pensar dedicarse).
destinatario, ria m. y f. Addressee (de una carta). || Consignee: *el destinario de un paquete*, the consignee of a parcel. || Payee (de un giro).
destino m. Destiny, fate, lot, fortune (hado): *un destino desgraciado*, a hapless fate. || Function, use: *este edificio ha cambiado de destino*, this building has changed function. || Destination: *el destino de un barco*, the destination of a ship. || Post, station (de un militar). || Position, post (colocación, empleo). || Earmarking (de dinero). || — *Con destino a*, bound for, going to: *barco con destino a África*, ship bound for Africa; to (tren), going to, for (viajeros), to, addressed to: *cartas con destino a Madrid*, letters to Madrid. || FIG. *Dar destino a*, to find a home for, to put to use. || *Estación o lugar de destino*, destination. || *Llegar a destino*, to arrive at *o* to reach one's destination. || *Salir con destino a*, to leave for.
destitución f. Dismissal, removal from office *o* from one's post, discharge: *destitución de un ministro*, removal of a minister from office.
destituidor, ra adj. Who *o* which dismisses.
destituir* v. tr. To dismiss, to remove from office *o* from one's post, to discharge: *destituir a un jefe de Estado*, to remove a Head of State from office. || To deprive (privar).
destocar v. tr. (P. us.). To ruffle the hair of (despeinar).
— V. pr. To take off one's hat [*o* one's scarf, etc.] (descubrirse).
destorcer* v. tr. To untwist: *destorcer un cable*, to untwist a cable. || To straighten [out] (enderezar): *destorcer una varilla*, to straighten a stick.
— V. pr. To become untwisted, to untwist. || To straighten [out]. || MAR. To drift off course, to drift (salirse un barco de su ruta).
destornillado, da adj. FAM. Screwy, nutty, dotty (atolondrado).
destornillador m. Screwdriver.
destornillamiento m. Unscrewing.
destornillar v. tr. To unscrew: *destornillar una bisagra*, to unscrew a hinge.
— V. pr. To come unscrewed. || FAM. To go round the bend *o* round the twist *o* off one's rocker (perder el juicio).
destrabar v. tr. To unfetter, to untie. || To separate, to disconnect (cosas).
— V. pr. To get loose *o* free, to free o.s. (liberarse). || To come apart *o* away (separarse).
destral m. Hatchet, small axe.
destramar v. tr. To unweave, to undo the weft of.
destrenzar v. tr. To unbraid, to unplait.
destreza f. Skill (habilidad). || Dexterity (agilidad). || (Ant.). Fencing [sport]. || — *Este prestidigitador tiene mucha destreza*, this magician is very skilful. || *Obrar con destreza*, to act skilfully *o* deftly.
destripado o **destripamiento** m. Gutting (del pescado). || Disembowelling.
destripador, ra adj. Ripper.
destripar v. tr. To gut (el pescado). || To disembowel (un animal, una persona). || To rip open (una cosa): *destripar un colchón*, to rip open a mattress. || To crush, to squash (despachurrar). || FIG. To ruin, to ruin the effect of [joke, etc.]. || AGR. *Destripar los terrones*, to crush *o* to break up [the] clods.
destripaterrones m. inv. FIG. y FAM. Clodhopper.
destrísimo, ma adj. Very dextrous *o* skilful.
destronamiento m. Dethronement. || FIG. Overthrow.
destronar v. tr. To dethrone, to depose. || FIG. To overthrow (un gobierno), to supplant (a una persona).
destroncar v. tr. To chop *o* to cut down, to fell (un árbol). || FIG. To maim, to mutilate (lastimar). | To upset, to ruin, to spoil, to thwart (proyectos). | To clip [s.o.'s] wings (a una persona). | To tire out, to wear out,

to exhaust (cansar). | To interrupt (un discurso). | To mutilate, to retrench [a text] (cortar). || *Amer.* To uproot (descuajar).

destroyer m. MAR. Destroyer (destructor).

destrozar v. tr. To break [into pieces], to smash, to shatter (romper). || To tear up, to tear to shreds: *destrozar un libro*, to tear up a book. || To ruin, to spoil, to smash, to dash (estropear). || MIL. To wipe out, to smash, to crush (deshacer un ejército). | To rout (derrotar). || FIG. To break: *destrozar el corazón de alguien*, to break s.o.'s heart. | To ruin, to mar: *destrozar la carrera, la salud de alguien*, to ruin s.o.'s career, health. | To ruin, to upset, to spoil: *su llegada ha destrozado mis planes*, his arrival has ruined my plans. | To dissipate (una fortuna). | To shatter, to tire out, to wear out, to exhaust: *estoy destrozado de tanto andar*, I'm shattered from all this walking. | To shatter: *la triste noticia lo ha destrozado*, the sad news has shattered him.
— V. pr. To break [into pieces], to smash, to shatter.

destrozo m. Destruction. || Rout (derrota). || — Pl. Damage, *sing.* (daño). || Ruins, debris, *sing.* (pedazos).

destrozón, ona adj. Destructive (que lo rompe todo). || Hard on one's clothes (que rompe la ropa).
— M. y f. Destructive person.

destrucción f. Destruction.

destructible adj. Destructible.

destructividad f. Destructiveness.

destructivo, va adj. Destructive.

destructor, ra adj. Destructive.
— M. y f. Destructive person. || — M. MAR. Destroyer (buque).

destruible adj. Destructible.

destruir* v. tr. To demolish, to destroy: *destruir una casa*, to demolish a house. || To destroy: *destruir un país, un ejército*, to destroy a country, an army. || FIG. To destroy, to dash (esperanza). | To destroy, to ruin, to wreck (proyecto). | To demolish, to refute (argumento).
— V. pr. MAT. To cancel [each other] out.

desuello m. FIG. Effrontery, impudence (descaro). || Skinning, flaying.

desuerar v. tr. To drain the whey from [milk].

desuero m. Draining of the whey.

desuncir v. tr. To unyoke [oxen].

desunidamente adv. Separately.

desunión f. Separation, disunion, disjunction. || Discord, disunity, dissension: *la desunión de los países, de una familia*, the discord between countries, in a family.

desunir v. tr. To separate, to disunite, to disjoin. || To disunite, to bring about discord between: *la cuestión de la esclavitud desunió a los norteamericanos*, the question of slavery disunited the Americans.

desusadamente adv. Behind the times, out of date (anticuadamente). || Uncommonly.

desusado, da adj. Out of date, antiquated, old-fashioned (anticuado): *modos desusados*, antiquated ways. || Obsolete, archaic (caído en desuso): *palabra desusada*, obsolete word. || Uncommon, rare (poco usado). || Unusual, strange (extraño): *hablar en tono desusado*, to speak in a strange tone of voice.

desuso m. Disuse, obsolescence, desuetude (p. us.): *caer en desuso*, to fall into disuse. || *Expresión caída en desuso*, obsolete expression.

desvaído, da adj. Pale, dull, faded (descolorido). || Vague, blurred (borroso). || FIG. Dull, spiritless (de poca personalidad). | Lanky (desgarbado).

desvainadura f. Shelling [of peas, etc.].

desvainar v. tr. To shell (legumbres).

desvalido, da adj. Destitute, needy.
— M. y f. Destitute *o* needy person. || *Socorrer a los desvalidos*, to help the needy *o* the destitute.

desvalijador, ra m. y f. Robber, thief (ladrón). || Burglar (saqueador).

desvalijamiento m. o **desvalijo** m. Theft, robbery.

desvalijar v. tr. To rob (robar a alguien). || To steal (robar algo). || To burgle (saquear). || FIG. To strip [bare]: *cuando vienen sus nietos le desvalijan la despensa*, when his grandchildren come they strip his larder bare.

desvalimiento m. Destitution, need.

desvalorar v. tr. To devalue, to devaluate (moneda). || To depreciate (una cosa). || To discredit (desacreditar).

desvalorización f. Depreciation, fall in value (de una (cosa). || Devaluation (de la moneda).

desvalorizar v. tr. To depreciate, to reduce the value of (una cosa). || To devalue, to devaluate (la moneda).

desván m. Attic, garret, loft.

desvanecedor m. FOT. Vignetter, mask.

desvanecer* v. tr. To dispel, to make disappear, to disperse, to dissipate: *el viento desvanece el humo*, the wind dispels smoke. || To tone down (colores). || To blur (los contornos). || FIG. To dispel, to remove, to banish, to dismiss (temores, sospechas, etc.). || FOT. To vignette, to mask. || RAD. To fade.
— V. pr. To disperse, to dissipate, to be dispelled (el humo, etc.). || FIG. To disappear, to vanish (desaparecer). | To faint, to swoon (desmayarse). | To fade, to die (recuerdos). | To lose its flavour (perder el sabor). | To pride o.s. (enorgullecerse).

desvanecidamente adv. Vainly, conceitedly (vanido samente). || Presumptuously (con presunción).

desvanecido, da adj. Vain, conceited (vanidoso). || Smug, complacent, self-satisfied (presumido). || MED. Faint: *caí desvanecido*, I fell in a faint.

desvanecimiento m. Dispersal, dissipation (del humo). || Toning-down (de los colores). || Dispelling, driving-away, removal (de sospechas, dudas, temores). || Disappearance (desaparición). || MED. Fainting fit, faint, swoon (desmayo). || FIG. Smugness, complacency, self-satisfaction (presunción). | Arrogance, haughtiness (altanería). || RAD. Fading [of signals].

desvarar v. tr. MAR. To refloat.
— V. intr. To slide, to slip (resbalar).

desvariar v. intr. To be delirious, to rave (enfermo o loco). || To talk nonsense (desatinar).

desvarío m. Delirium, raving (enfermo o loco). || FIG. Foolish remark, piece of nonsense (desatino). | Wandering, raving: *los desvaríos de una imaginación enfermiza*, the wanderings of an unhealthy imagination. | Act of folly *o* madness: *la compra de esta casa ha sido un desvarío*, buying this house was an act of madness. | Vicissitude: *los desvaríos de la fortuna*, the vicissitudes of fortune. | Whim (capricho).

desvelado, da adj. Awake, unable to sleep: *se quedó desvelado toda la noche*, he stayed awake all night, he was unable to sleep all night.

desvelar v. tr. To prevent [s.o.] *o* to stop [s.o.] from sleeping, to keep [s.o.] awake: *el café desvela*, coffee keeps you awake; *las preocupaciones desvelan a todo el mundo*, worries keep everyone awake.
— V. pr. To stay awake (no poder dormir). || FIG. To devote o.s., to dedicate o.s.: *una madre que se desvela por sus hijos*, a mother who devotes herself to her children. || *Desvelarse por que todo esté bien*, to take great pains to see that everything is right.

desvelo m. Insomnia. || Trouble, pains, *pl.* (trabajo): *todos sus desvelos resultaron inútiles*, all his trouble was *o* all his pains were of no avail. || Effort (esfuerzo): *merced a mis desvelos*, thanks to my efforts. || Worry, care (preocupación). || Devotion, dedication: *el desvelo por la causa común*, dedication to the common cause.

desvenar v. tr. To remove the veins from [meat] (de la carne). || MIN. To extract [ore] from a vein. || To strip, to remove the strings *o* veins from (el tabaco).

desvencijado, da adj. Insecure, unsteady, shaky: *una puerta desvencijada*, an insecure door. || Ramshackle, tumbledown, dilapidated: *una casa desvencijada*, a ramshackle house. || Rickety: *una silla desvencijada*, a rickety chair. || Broken-down, ramshackle: *una máquina desvencijada*, a broken-down machine.

desvencijar v. tr. To put out of action (un mecanismo). || To break (romper). || To ruin (estropear). || To weaken (debilitar). || To dilapidate (una casa, etc.). || To exhaust (agotar).
— V. pr. To come *o* to fall apart, to come *o* to fall to pieces (puerta, silla, máquina). || To dilapidate, to fall apart, to go to ruin (una casa).

desvendar v. tr. To remove a bandage from, to unbandage (quitar una venda).

desventaja f. Disadvantage: *en su desventaja*, to his disadvantage. || Drawback, disadvantage: *las desventajas de una política*, the drawbacks of a policy. || Handicap: *su peso es una desventaja*, his weight is a handicap. || — *Estar en desventaja*, to be at a disadvantage. || *Tener una desventaja de dos goles*, to be two goals down, to be losing by two goals.

desventajoso, sa adj. Disadvantageous, unfavourable [U.S., unfavorable]. || Disadvantageous, which has its drawbacks. || Unprofitable (no provechoso).

desventura f. Misfortune, [piece of] bad luck (des gracia). || Misery, unhappiness (infortunio).

desventuradamente adj. Unfortunately.

desventurado, da adj. Unfortunate, wretched (desgraciado). || Poor (pobre). || Spiritless, timid (tímido). || Ill-fated, disastrous: *un día desventurado*, one ill-fated day. || Unlucky (de poca suerte).
— M. y f. Poor wretch, poor devil. || *Socorrer a los desventurados*, to help the unfortunate.

desvergonzadamente adv. Impudently, cheekily (descaradamente). || Insolently, rudely (insolentemente).

desvergonzado, da adj. Impudent, cheeky (descarado). || Insolent, shameless (sinvergüenza).
— M. y f. Impudent *o* cheeky person. || Insolent *o* shameless person.

desvergonzarse* v. pr. To go to the bad, to get into bad ways, to go downhill (perder la vergüenza). || To swallow one's shame (vencer la vergüenza): *desvergonzarse a hacer algo*, to swallow one's shame and do sth. || To be rude, to be insolent: *desvergonzarse con uno*, to be rude to s.o.

desvergüenza f. Impudence, nerve, effrontery, cheek (descaro): *tuvo la desvergüenza de pedírmelo*, he had the cheek to ask me for it. || Insolence (insolencia). || Dissoluteness, wantonness, shamelessness (mala conducta). || Rude thing, shameless remark: *decir desvergüenzas*, to say rude things, to make shameless remarks.

desvestir* v. tr. To strip, to lay bare (una cosa). || To unclothe, to undress, to strip (a una persona). || FIG.

Desvestir un santo para vestir otro, to rob Peter to pay Paul.
— V. pr. To undress, to take off one's clothes.
desviación f. Deviation, deflection: *desviación de la luz, de la aguja imantada*, deviation of light, of a magnetic needle. || Curvature: *desviación de la columna vertebral*, curvature of the vertebral column. || Diversion, detour: *hay una nueva desviación en la carretera*, there is a new diversion in the road. || Departure, deviation (de principios). || Deflection (de un golpe).
desviacionismo m. Deviationism.
desviacionista adj./s. Deviationist.
desviar v. tr. To deviate, to deflect: *desviar una línea*, to deflect a line. || To deflect, to turn aside, to ward off: *desviar un golpe*, to deflect a blow. || To deflect (el balón). || To parry (en esgrima). || To divert (un río). || To divert (un avión, un barco, etc.): *desviar a uno de su ruta*, to divert s.o. from his route. || FIG. To dissuade, to put off: *desviar a uno de un proyecto*, to put s.o. off a plan, to dissuade s.o. from a plan. | To keep *o* to steer clear of *o* away from: *desviar a uno de las malas compañías*, to steer s.o. clear of bad company. | To change, to turn: *desviar la conversación*, to change the subject. || *Desviar la mirada*, to look aside *o* away, to turn away.
— V. pr. To be deflected *o* deviated (una línea). || To be deflected *o* turned aside *o* warded off (un golpe). || To change *o* to alter [its] course (un barco, un avión). || To drift, to go *o* to sail off course (un barco). || To go *o* to fly off course (un avión) [a causa de una tempestad, etc.]. || To take a detour: *se desviaron para evitar el tráfico*, they took a detour to avoid the traffic. || To go astray, to lose one's way (descaminarse). || To stray: *desviarse de su camino*, to stray from one's route. || FIG. To stray, to wander, to get away from: *desviarse del tema*, to stray from the point. | To deviate (de los principios).
desvinculación f. Freeing, releasing, discharging (de un compromiso). || Cutting-off, separation.
desvincular v. tr. To free, to release, to discharge: *desvincular a uno de un compromiso*, to free s.o. from a commitment. || To cut off, to separate: *desvinculado de su familia*, cut off from his family. || *Desvincularse con*, to break one's links with, to lose contact with.
desvío m. Deviation, deflection (desviación). || Diversion, detour (en una carretera). || Coldness, indifference (frialdad).
desvirgar v. tr. To deflower, to devirginate.
desvirtuar v. tr. To impair, to spoil (estropear). || To adulterate, to spoil (adulterar). || FIG. To detract from (quitar valor a): *tu argumento no desvirtúa mi razonamiento*, your argument doesn't detract from my reasoning. | To distort (viciar): *desvirtuar el sentido de una palabra*, to distort the meaning of a word. | To misrepresent, to distort: *desvirtuar los hechos*, to misrepresent the facts.
— V. pr. To spoil, to go off (el vino, el café).
desvitalizar v. tr. To devitalize.
desvitrificación f. Devitrification.
desvitrificar v. tr. To devitrify.
desvivirse v. pr. To be dying, to long: *desvivirse por ir al teatro*, to be dying to go to the theatre. || To be madly in love, to be head over heels in love: *desvivirse por una chica*, to be madly in love with a girl. || To do one's utmost, to strive: *desvivirse por hacer el bien*, to strive to do good. || To devote o.s. to, to dedicate o.s. to, to live for: *una madre que se desvive por sus hijos*, a mother who devotes herself to her children.
desyemar v. tr. AGR. To disbud.
desyerbar v. tr. To weed.
detal o **detall** m. *Vender al detall*, to retail, to sell retail.
— OBSERV. *Al detall* is a Gallicism for *al por menor*.
detalladamente adv. In detail.
detallar v. tr. To relate in detail, to detail, to give the details of (contar con detalles). || COM. To retail, to sell retail.
detalle m. Detail. || Kind thought, nice gesture *o* thought (cosa amable): *eso fue un detalle de su parte*, that was a nice thought on his part. || *Amer.* Retailing. || — *Ahí está el detalle*, that's the secret. || COM. *Al detalle*, retail. || *Con todo detalle*, in full detail, in great detail. || *No meterse en detalles*, not to go into details. || *No perder detalle*, not to miss a thing, to miss nothing. || *¡Qué detalle!*, how thoughtful!, how considerate! || *Sin entrar en detalles*, without going into details. || *Tener muchos detalles con una persona*, to be very considerate towards s.o. *o* with s.o. || *Tuvo el detalle de traerme flores*, he was thoughtful enough to bring me flowers. || *Un mal detalle*, a rotten thing to do.
detallista m. y f. Retailer (comerciante).
detección f. Detection.
detectar v. tr. To detect: *detectar aviones enemigos*, to detect enemy aircraft.
detective m. Detective.
detector m. Detector: *detector de incendios*, fire detector; *detector de mentiras*, lie detector; *detector de minas*, mine detector. || Scanner, monitor (de radar).
— Adj. Detecting.
detención f. Stopping, halting (acción de parar). || Stoppage, standstill (estancamiento). || Stop, halt (alto). || Holdup, delay (retraso). || Care, thoroughness (cuidado). || Delay (dilación): *lo llamé y vino sin detención*, I called him and he came without delay. || JUR. Arrest (acción de detener). | Detention, confinement (prisión). || DEP. Stoppage (en el juego). || *Examinar con detención*, to examine carefully *o* thoroughly.
detenedor, ra adj. Stopping (que para). || Delaying (que retrasa). || Detaining.
detener* v. tr. To stop, to halt (parar): *detuvo el coche*, he stopped the car. || JUR. To arrest: *detener a un asesino*, to arrest a murderer. | To detain (encarcelar). || To hold up, to delay (paralizar): *detener las negociaciones*, to hold up [the] negotiations. || To delay, to detain, to keep, to hold up (retrasar): *no quiero detenerle más*, I don't want to keep you any longer. || To keep, to retain (guardar). || *Detener la mirada en*, to settle one's gaze upon.
— V. pr. To stop: *detenerse mucho tiempo en un paraje*, to stop for a long time in one place. || To dwell: *detenerse en una idea*, to dwell upon an idea. || To stop off: *detenerse en casa de un amigo*, to stop off at a friend's house. || To stay, to linger (quedarse).
detenidamente adv. Carefully, closely: *mirar detenidamente algo*, to look closely at sth. || Carefully, in detail, thoroughly: *estudiar detenidamente un problema*, to study a problem carefully.
detenido, da adj. JUR. Detained, in custody (mantenido preso). | Under arrest: *queda Vd. detenido*, you are under arrest. || Careful, thorough, detailed (minucioso): *un estudio detenido*, a detailed study.
— M. y f. Prisoner (preso).
detenimiento m. V. DETENCIÓN.
detentación f. JUR. Unlawful *o* illegal possession, detainer, deforcement (posesión ilegal).
detentador, ra adj. JUR. Who is in unlawful possession, who holds unlawfully.
— M. y f. Unlawful holder, deforciant. || Holder (de un récord).
detentar v. tr. JUR. To be in unlawful possession of, to hold unlawfully, to have illegal possession of (poseer). || To hold (un récord).
detente m. HIST. Talisman, emblem representing the Sacred Heart of Jesus bearing the motto "*detente, bala*" [halt, bullet] worn for protection by Carlist soldiers.
detentor, ra m. y f. JUR. Unlawful holder. || Holder (de un récord).
detergente adj./s.m. Detergent, detersive.
deterger v. tr. To deterge (limpiar): *deterger una herida*, to deterge a wound.
deterioración f. V. DETERIORO.
deteriorado, da adj. Damaged (mercancías, etc.).
deteriorar v. tr. To damage, to impair, to spoil (estropear). || To wear out (desgastar).
— V. pr. To be damaged *o* impaired *o* spoilt (estropearse). || To wear out (desgastarse). || FIG. To deteriorate.
deterioro f. Deterioration, damage, spoiling. || Wear and tear (con el uso). || FIG. Impairment, damage, harm (daño). | Deterioration (empeoramiento).
determinable adj. Determinable.
determinación f. Fixing, settling: *la determinación de una fecha*, the fixing of a date. || Decision, resolution: *tomar una determinación*, to take a decision, to make a resolution. || Determination, resolution: *mostrar determinación*, to show determination. || *Tener poca determinación*, to be irresolute, to lack determination.
determinado, da adj. Resolute, determined, firm (resuelto). || Definite (definido). || Specific, particular (preciso). || Appointed (día, etc.). || Decided, determined: *disposiciones determinadas de antemano*, measures determined beforehand. || MAT. Determinate. || GRAM. Definite (artículo).
determinante adj. Determining, decisive, determinant.
— M. MAT. Determinant.
determinar v. tr. To determine: *determinar las causas de un accidente*, to determine the causes of an accident. || To fix, to set, to appoint: *determinar la fecha*, to fix the date. || To decide, to make up one's mind, to determine, to resolve: *eso me determinó a hacerlo*, that decided me to do it; *determinaron firmar la paz*, they decided to sign a peace treaty. || To stipulate, to lay down, to specify: *la ley determina que*, the law stipulates that. || To cause, to bring about (causar).
— V. pr. To decide, to determine, to make up one's mind, to resolve (decidir).
determinativo, va adj./s.m. GRAM. Determinative.
determinismo m. FIL. Determinism.
determinista adj./s. FIL. Determinist.
detersión f. Detersion, cleansing.
detersivo, va o **detersorio, ria** adj./s.m. Detersive, detergent.
detestable adj. Detestable, hateful, loathsome: *una persona detestable*, a detestable person. || Horrible, awful (tiempo, sabor, gusto).
detestación f. Detestation, hatred, horror.
detestar v. tr. To detest, to hate, to loathe: *detestar a una persona, los viajes*, to detest a person, travelling.
detonación f. Detonation, explosion.
detonador m. Detonator (fulminante).
detonante adj. Detonating, explosive: *mezcla detonante*, explosive mixture.
— M. Explosive.

detonar v. intr. To detonate, to explode.
detracción f. Denigration, defamation, disparagement (murmuración). || Withdrawal (retiro).
detractar v. tr. To denigrate, to defame, to disparage.
detractor, ra adj. Denigrating, defamatory, disparaging.
— M. y f. Denigrator, defamer, disparager.
detraer* v. tr. To denigrate, to defame, to disparage (desacreditar). || To withdraw (quitar).
detrás adv. Behind: *las chicas iban delante y los chicos detrás*, the girls went in front and the boys behind. || On the back: *la carpeta del disco trae la letra detrás*, the record sleeve has the words on the back. || After (después). || — *Detrás de*, behind: *detrás de la casa*, behind the house; *dejó un buen recuerdo detrás de él*, he left a good memory behind him; behind one's back (a espaldas). || *Por detrás*, on the back (en la parte posterior), behind, round the back: *pasar por detrás*, to go behind; from behind: *se acercaron a mí por detrás*, they approached me from behind; behind one's back: *por detrás hablan mal de él*, they speak ill of him behind his back. || *Por detrás de*, behind.
detrimento m. Detriment: *en detrimento de*, to the detriment of; *sin detrimento de*, without detriment to. || Damage, harm, injury (daño).
detrito o **detritus** m. GEOL. Detritus.
deuda f. Debt: *tener una deuda con uno* or *estar en deuda con uno*, to be in debt to s.o.; *pagar una deuda*, to pay [off] a debt. || REL. Trespass: *perdónanos nuestras deudas*, forgive us our trespasses. || — *Contraer deudas*, to contract debts, to run into debt. || *Deuda a largo plazo*, long-term debt. || *Deuda consolidada*, funded *o* consolidated debt. || *Deuda flotante*, floating debt. || *Deuda morosa*, bad debt. || *Deuda pública*, national *o* public debt. || FIG. *Estar en deuda con uno*, to be indebted to s.o., to be in s.o.'s debt. || *Lo prometido es deuda*, a promise is a promise.
deudo, da m. y f. Relative, relation. || — M. Relationship, kinship (parentesco).
deudor, ra adj. Indebted. || — *Saldo deudor*, debit balance. || FIG. *Ser deudor de una persona*, to be indebted to a person.
— M. y f. Debtor.
deuterio m. QUÍM. Deuterium.
deuterón m. FÍS. Deuteron.
Deuteronomio n. pr. m. Deuteronomy.
devaluación f. Devaluation (moneda).
devaluar v. tr. To devaluate, to devalue.
devanadera f. Reel, spool, bobbin (bobina). || Winder, winding frame (utensilio para devanar).
devanado m. ELECTR. Winding, coiling (del alambre).
devanador, ra adj. Winding.
— M. y f. Winder. || — M. Reel, spool, bobbin (carrete). || *Amer.* Winder (devanadera).
devanamiento m. Reeling, winding (del hilo). || Winding (de la lana). || Winding, coiling (del alambre).
devanar v. tr. To reel, to wind (un hilo). || To coil, to wind (un alambre). || FAM. *Devanarse los sesos*, to rack one's brains.
devanear v. intr. To be delirious, to rave, to talk nonsensically.
devaneo m. Flirtation (amorío). || Delirium, raving, nonsensical utterings, *pl.* (delirio). || Frivolity, time-wasting pastime *o* action (fruslería).
devastación f. Devastation, destruction.
devastador, ra adj. Devastating, destructive.
— M. y f. Devastator.
devastar v. tr. To devastate, to ravage, to lay waste, to destroy (destruir): *casa devastada*, devastated house. || *Regiones devastadas*, devastated areas (después de la guerra).
devengado, da adj. COM. Due, outstanding. || *Intereses devengados*, outstanding *o* accrued interest.
devengar v. tr. To be owed, to have due (tener que cobrar). || To yield, to bear, to bring in (intereses).
devengo m. Amount due.
devenir* v. intr. (P. us.). To happen, to occur (suceder). || FIL. To become (cambiarse en).
devenir m. FIL. Flux.
deviación f. V. DESVIACIÓN.
devoción f. Devotion: *La Devoción de la Cruz*, The Devotion to the Cross (obra de Calderón). || Devotion, devoutness (piedad). || Devotion, strong attachment (afición). || Habit, custom (costumbre): *tengo por devoción pasear todos los días*, I am in the habit of going *o* it is my custom to go for a walk every day. || — Pl. Devotions (oraciones, etc.). || — *Con devoción*, devoutly. || FIG. *Estar a la devoción de uno*, to be at s.o.'s disposal. | *Miguel no es santo de mi devoción* or *a Miguel no le tengo mucha devoción*, I'm not exactly fond of Michael.
devocionario m. Prayer book.
devolución f. Return, giving-back. || Refund, repayment: *devolución del importe de una entrada*, refund of an entrance fee. || COM. Returning, return (de una mercancía). || JUR. Devolution (de propiedades). || DEP. Return (de la pelota). || Return (correo): *devolución al remitente*, return to sender. || — *No se admiten devoluciones*, no goods returnable (recuperando el dinero), no goods exchanged (cambiando el artículo por otro). || *Sin devolución*, nonreturnable.
devolver* v. tr. To return, to give back: *devolver un libro prestado*, to return a borrowed book. || To return, to send back (correo): *devolver una carta*, to return a letter. || To return, to put back: *devolver algo a su sitio*, to put sth. back in its place, to return sth. to its place. || To return, to take *o* to send back (una mercancía). || To repay, to refund: *devolver el importe de la entrada*, to refund the entrance fee. || FIG. To give back, to restore: *la operación le devolvió la vista*, the operation gave him back his sight *o* restored his sight. || To restore: *devolver algo a su antiguo estado*, to restore sth. to its former state. || To return, to pay back (un favor, una visita, un cumplido). || DEP. To return (la pelota). || To free from, to release from: *devolverle la palabra a uno*, to free s.o. from his promise. || FAM. To bring up, to throw up (vomitar). || — *Devolver (el) bien por (el) mal*, to repay evil with good. || *Devolver la palabra*, to give back the floor (a un orador). || FIG. *Devolver la pelota a uno*, to give s.o. tit for tat. || *Devuélvase al remitente*, return to sender (en el correo).
— V. pr. *Amer.* To return, to go back (volver).
devoniano, na o **devónico, ca** adj./s.m. GEOL. Devonian.
devorador, ra o **devorante** adj. Devouring, consuming (fuego, pasión, etc.). || *Hambre devoradora*, ravenous hunger.
devorar v. tr. To devour: *el lobo devoró al cordero*, the wolf devoured the lamb. || To devour, to wolf, to gobble [up] (comer ávidamente). || FIG. To devour, to consume: *el fuego lo devoró todo*, the fire devoured everything; *esta pasión que me devora*, this passion which devours me. | To destroy (destruir). | To squander, to dissipate (disipar su fortuna). | To devour, to swallow up: *el juego ha devorado toda mi fortuna*, gambling has swallowed up all my fortune. || To devour: *devorar una novela*, to devour a novel; *devorar a uno con los ojos*, to devour s.o. with one's eyes.
devoto, ta adj. Devout, pious (piadoso). || Of devotion, devotional: *imagen devota*, devotional image. || Devoted: *devoto de su amo*, devoted to his master. || *Su muy devoto*, your devoted servant.
— M. y f. Devotee, devout *o* pious person. || Enthusiast, devotee (aficionado).
devuelto, ta p. p. V. DEVOLVER.
dextrina f. QUÍM. Dextrin.
dextrógiro, ra adj. FÍS. Dextrorotatory [U.S., dextrorotary].
dextrorso, sa adj. Dextrorse.
dextrosa f. QUÍM. Dextrose.
dey m. Dey (príncipe musulmán).
deyección f. MED. Defecation, defaecation. || — Pl. GEOL. Debris, *sing.* (de roca). | Ejecta (de un volcán). || MED. Dejecta.
deyector m. Apparatus for preventing the formation of fur inside steam boilers.
día m. Day: *noche y día*, night and day, day and night; *el día que llegues*, the day you arrive; *un día hermoso, soleado*, a lovely, sunny day. || Daytime (las horas de luz). || Name day (día del santo). || Birthday (día del cumpleaños). || Weather, day: *hace buen día*, it's fine *o* nice weather, it's a fine *o* nice day. || — Pl. Days (vida): *hasta el fin de sus días*, until the end of his days; *mis días de corredor*, my days as a runner. || — *A días*, some days, at times. || *A la luz del día*, in daylight, in the daytime, in the light of day. || *Al día*, up to date (sin retraso): *poner al día*, to bring up to date; up to date (moderno), in the know, informed, up to date: *estar al día de lo que pasa*, to be informed on what is happening; from hand to mouth (con estrechez): *vivir al día*, to live from hand to mouth; daily, everyday, day-to-day (cotidiano): *la vida madrileña al día*, daily life in Madrid; in fashion, fashionable (de moda), per day, a day: *dos litros al día*, two litres per day; by the day: *alquilar una habitación al día*, to rent a room by the day. || *A los pocos días*, a few days later, within a few days. || *A los pocos días de*, a few days after, within a few days of. || *Al otro día* or *al día siguiente*, on the next day, [the] next day, [on] the following day, the day after. || *Al romper* or *al despuntar* or *al rayar el día*, at daybreak, at break of day. || *A tantos días vista* or *fecha*, v. VISTA. || *¡Buenos días!* good morning!, good day! || *Cada día más...* (seguido de un adjetivo), more and more..., more... each day, more... every day [v. OBSERV.]: *es cada día más complicado*, it gets more and more complicated, it gets more complicated every day *o* each day; (seguido de un sustantivo), more and more like, more like... each day, more like... every day: *es cada día más su padre*, he is more like his father every day. || *Cada día menos...* (seguido de un adjetivo o de un sustantivo en singular), less and less, less... each day, less... every day; (seguido de un sustantivo en plural), fewer and fewer, fewer each day, fewer every day, less and less: *hay cada día menos solicitudes*, there are fewer applications each day. || *Cada dos días*, every other day, every two days. || *Cada tres días*, every three days. || *Cierto día*, one fine day, one day. || *Como de la noche al día* or *como del día a la noche*, as different as night and day. || *Cualquier día*, any day: *ven cualquier día*, come any day. || *Dar los buenos días*, to say good morning. || *Dar los días a uno*, to wish s.o. [a] happy birthday; to congratulate s.o. on his name day. || *De cada día*, daily, everyday, day-to-day. || *De día*, by day. || *De día en día*, from day to day. || *Dejar para el día del juicio final*, to put off until judgment day.

|| *Del día*, today's, fresh (fresco, reciente), latest (moda). || *De un día a* or *para otro*, any day now. || *Día a día*, day by day. || *Día civil*, civil day. || *Día D*, D day. || *Día de Año Nuevo*, New Year's Day. || *Día de asueto*, day off. || *Día de ayuno*, fast day. || *Día de carne*, meat day, meat-eating day. || *Día de descanso*, v. DESCANSO. || *Día de fiesta* or *festivo*, feast day, holiday. || *Día de la banderita*, flag day. || *Día de la Madre*, Mother's Day. || *Día del Corpus*, Corpus Christi. || *Día del juicio final*, judgment day, doomsday. || *Día de recibo*, at-home day. || *Día de Reyes*, Epiphany. || *Día de trabajo*, working day, workday. || *Día de vigilia* or *de viernes* or *de pescado*, day of abstinence, fish day. || *Día entre semana*, weekday. || *Día feriado* or *festivo*, holiday. || *Día laborable* or *hábil*, working day, workday. || *Día tras día*, day after day. || *El día de hoy* today (hoy), nowadays (actualmente). || *El día de mañana*, tomorrow (mañana), one day soon, in the near future (en tiempo venidero). || *El día de San Pablo*, Saint Paul's day. || *El día siete*, [on] the seventh (del mes). || *El mejor día* or *el día menos pensado*, any day, when least expected, some fine day, one of these days. || *En los días de*, in the days of, in the time of. || *En mis días...*, in my time..., in my day... || *En pleno día*, in broad daylight. || *En su día*, in due time *o* course, at the proper time. || *En sus mejores días*, in his heyday. || *Es de día*, it's daylight. || *Hacerse de día*, to break [the day], to dawn: *se está haciendo de día*, the day is breaking, it is dawning. || FAM. *Hay más días que longanizas*, there's no hurry, there's no rush, there's all the time in the world. || *Hoy día* or *hoy en día* or *en nuestros días*, nowadays, these days, at the present time, today. || *Hoy, día 22 de febrero*, today, the 22nd of February; today, February 22nd. || *Amer. Los otros días*, the other day. || *Mañana será otro día*, tomorrow is another day. || *No todos los días son iguales*, who knows what tomorrow holds. || *Ocho días*, a week. || *Otro día*, some other day, another day: *lo haremos otro día*, we'll do it some other day. || *¿Qué día es hoy?*, what's the date today? || *Quince días*, a fortnight. || *Romper el día*, to break [the day], to dawn. || *Si algún día*, if ever: *si algún día le encuentras*, if ever you meet him. || *Tener días*, to have one's good days and one's bad days, to have one's on days and one's off days. || *Tiene contados los días*, his days are numbered. || FAM. *Todo el santo día*, all day long, all the livelong day. || *Todos los días*, every day. || *Un buen día*, one fine day. || *Un día de éstos*, one of these days. || *Un día señalado*, a great day, an important day, a red-letter day. || *Un día sí y otro no*, every other day, every two days, on alternate days.

— OBSERV. Las formas *more and more, more each day* y *more every day* se sustituyen por el comparativo en *-er* cuando el adjetivo que sigue la expresión "cada día más" se traduce en inglés por una palabra corta: *es cada día más mona* she gets prettier and prettier, she gets prettier every day.

diabetes f. MED. Diabetes.
diabético, ca adj./s. MED. Diabetic.
diabla f. FAM. She-devil. || Two-wheeled carriage, cabriolet (coche). || FAM. *A la diabla*, any old how, any old way (de cualquier modo).
diablear v. intr. FAM. To get up to mischief, to get up to one's tricks, to play up (un niño).
diablejo m. Little devil, imp.
diablesa f. She-devil.
diablesco, ca adj. Diabolical, diabolic, devilish.
diablillo m. FIG. y FAM. Little devil, little imp, mischief-maker (persona traviesa).
diablo m. Devil, demon. || FIG. Devil, little devil, scamp: *este niño es un diablo*, this child is a devil. | Rogue (canalla). | Monster (monstruo). || *Amer.* Two-wheeled cart (carromato).
— *Al diablo*, to the devil. || *Anda el diablo en Cantillana*, there's trouble afoot. || *¿Cómo diablos...?*, how the devil...? || *Cuando el diablo no tiene que hacer con el rabo mata moscas*, the devil finds work for idle hands. || *Del diablo* or *de todos los diablos*, the devil of a: *un problema de todos los diablos*, the devil of a problem. || *¡Diablos!*, by Jove!, golly! (admiración, sorpresa, etc.). || *El abogado del diablo*, the devil's advocate. || *El Diablo*, the Devil, Satan. || *El diablo cojuelo*, The Devil on Two Sticks (título de una obra literaria). || *El diablo encarnado* or *hecho carne*, a real devil (un niño), the devil himself, the devil in person (un hombre). || *El diablo que lo entienda*, I'll be blowed *o* damned if I understand. || *Enviar al diablo*, to send to the devil. || *Más sabe el diablo por viejo que por diablo*, nothing like the old horse for the hard road. || *No es tan feo el diablo como lo pintan*, the devil is not so black as he is painted. || *¿Qué diablos...?*, what the devil...? what the deuce...?, what the blazes? || *¡Qué diablos!*, damn it!, hang it! || *Tener el diablo en el cuerpo* or *ser de la piel del diablo*, to be a little devil (travieso). || *¡Váyase al diablo!*, go to the devil!, go to hell!, go to blazes!
diablura f. Mischief: *las diabluras de los niños*, the children's mischief. || Practical joke, prank (travesura). || Wonder, miracle: *este malabarista hace diabluras con sus aros*, this juggler works wonders *o* performs miracles with his hoops. || *Hacer diabluras*, to get up to mischief, to get up to one's tricks.
diabólico, ca adj. Diabolical, diabolic, devilish.
diábolo m. Diabolo (juguete).
diaconado m. Diaconate, deaconate, deaconship.
diaconal adj. REL. Diaconal.
diaconato m. Diaconate, deaconate, deaconship.
diaconía f. Deaconry.
diaconisa f. Deaconess.
diácono m. Deacon: *ordenar de diácono*, to ordain deacon.
diacrítico, ca adj. GRAM. Diacritic, diacritical. || MED. Diagnostic.
diadema f. Diadem (corona).
diafanidad f. Diaphaneity, diaphanousness, transparency.
diáfano, na adj. Diaphanous, filmy, transparent. || FIG. Transparent.
diafragma m. Diaphragm.
diafragmar v. tr. TECN. To diaphragm.
diafragmático, ca adj. Diaphragmatic.
diagnosis f. inv. MED. Diagnosis.
diagnosticar v. tr. To diagnose.
diagnóstico, ca adj. MED. Diagnostic.
— M. MED. Diagnosis, diagnostic (calificación de una enfermedad). | Diagnostic, diagnostics (ciencia).
diagonal adj. Diagonal.
— F. Diagonal. || *En diagonal*, diagonally.
diagrama m. Diagram.
dial m. Dial (de radio).
dialectal adj. Dialectal.
dialectalismo m. Dialectalism.
dialéctica f. Dialectics.
dialéctico, ca adj. Dialectic, dialectical.
— M. y f. Dialectician.
dialecto m. Dialect.
dialectología f. Dialectology.
diálisis f. QUÍM. Dialysis.
dializar v. tr. QUÍM. To dialyze.
dialogar v. intr. To dialogue, to dialogize, to hold a dialogue. || To talk (hablar).
— V. tr. To write in dialogue form, to set down as a dialogue.
diálogo m. Dialogue [U.S., dialogue, dialog].
dialoguista m. y f. Dialogist, dialogue writer.
diamagnetismo m. ELECTR. Diamagnetism.
diamantado, da adj. Diamond-like [like a diamond]
diamantar v. tr. To diamond, to make sparkle.
diamante m. Diamond: *diamante en bruto*, rough *o* uncut diamond. || Diamond (naipe). || FIG. *Bodas de diamante*, diamond wedding. || *Edición diamante*, midget *o* miniature edition.
diamantífero, ra adj. Diamantiferous, diamond-bearing, diamond-yielding. || *Zona* or *región diamantífera*, diamond field.
diamantino, na adj. Diamond-like. || Diamond (de diamante). || FIG. POÉT. Adamantine.
diamantista m. Diamond cutter (que labra diamantes). || Diamond merchant (vendedor).
diametral adj. Diametral, diametric, diametrical.
diametralmente adj. Diametrically.
diámetro m. MAT. Diameter. || Bore (de cilindro de motor).
diana f. MIL. Reveille: *tocar diana*, to sound the reveille. | Bull's-eye, bull (blanco): *hacer diana*, to hit the bull's-eye *o* bull, to score a bull.
¡dianche! o **¡diantre!** interj. FAM. Hang it!, damn it! (enfado). | By Jove!, golly! (sorpresa, admiración).
diapasón m. MÚS. Tuning fork, diapason (para afinar). | Diapason, range (notas que abarca un instrumento). | Fingerboard (del violín). || FIG. *Bajar, subir el diapasón*, to lower, to raise one's tone [of voice].
diapositiva f. FOT. Slide, transparency.
diariamente adv. Daily, every day.
diario, ria adj. Daily, everyday.
— M. Daily newspaper, daily, paper (periódico). || Diary (relación de acontecimientos). || COM. Journal, daybook. || Daily expenses, *pl.* (gasto diario). || — *A* or *de diario*, daily, every day. || MAR. *Diario de a bordo*, logbook. || *Diario de la mañana* or *diario matinal*, morning paper, morning daily. || *Diario de la noche* or *diario vespertino*, evening paper. || *Diario de sesiones*, parliamentary report, report of proceedings in Parliament. || *Diario hablado*, news bulletin, news. || *Traje de diario*, everyday dress.
diarismo m. *Amer.* Journalism (periodismo).
diarista m. y f. Diarist (persona que escribe un diario). || *Amer.* Journalist.
diarquía f. Diarchy, dyarchy.
diarrea f. MED. Diarrhoea.
diastasa f. BIOL. Diastase (fermento).
diástole f. ANAT. Diastole (dilatación del corazón). || GRAM. Diastole (cambio de una sílaba).
diastólico, ca adj. Diastolic.
diatermia f. Diathermy.
diátesis f. Diathesis.
diatómico, ca adj. Diatomic.
diatónico, ca adj. MÚS. Diatonic.
diatriba f. Diatribe: *lanzar* or *dirigir una diatriba*, to pronounce a diatribe.
diávolo m. Diabolo (juquete).
diazoico, ca adj. Diazo: *compuestos diazoicos*, diazo compounds.
dibásico, ca adj. QUÍM. Dibasic.
dibujante adj. Who draws *o* sketches, drawing, sketching.

— M. y f. Sketcher, drawer. || Designer (de moda). || Cartoonist (de dibujos animados, caricaturas, etc.). || TECN. Draughtsman, draftsman (de dibujo lineal).
dibujar v. tr. To draw: *dibujar con* or *a pluma, con* or *a lápiz, a mano alzada, del natural*, to draw in ink, in pencil, freehand, from nature. || To sketch (bosquejar). || To design (diseñar). || FIG. To describe, to outline, to depict (describir). | To describe, to sketch (un carácter).
— V. pr. To stand out, to be outlined: *a lo lejos se dibuja una torre contra el cielo*, in the distance a tower is outlined against the sky. || FIG. To take shape, to materialize (concretarse). | To be written, to show: *en su cara se dibuja el dolor*, pain is written across his face.
dibujo m. Drawing: *dibujo al carbón, a lápiz, a pluma, a mano alzada*, charcoal, pencil, ink, freehand drawing. || Drawing, sketching (arte). || Sketch (bosquejo). || TECN. Design. || Cartoon (en un periódico). || Pattern, design (de papel, de una tela). || FIG. Outline (del paisaje, del rostro). | Description, depiction (descripción). || — *Academia de dibujo*, art school, school of art. || *Dibujo del natural*, drawing from nature *o* life. || *Dibujo lineal*, draughtsmanship, draftsmanship, mechanical drawing. || *Dibujos animados*, cartoons.
dicción f. Diction (pronunciación). || Word (palabra).
diccionario m. Dictionary, lexicon.
diccionarista m. y f. Lexicographer.
díceres m. pl. *Amer.* Gossip, *sing.*
diciembre m. December: *el 25 de diciembre*, December 25 *o* 25th, the 25th of December.
dicotiledón o **dicotiledóneo, a** adj. BOT. Dicotyledonous.
— F. Dicotyledon. || — Pl. Dicotyledoneae.
dicotomía f. Dichotomy.
dicroísmo m. Fís. Dichroism (coloración doble).
dicromático, ca adj. Dichromatic.
dicromatismo m. Dichromatism.
dictado m. Dictation: *hacer un dictado*, to do a dictation; *dictado musical*, musical dictation; *escribir al dictado*, to take dictation. || Title, epithet (calificativo). || — Pl. FIG. Dictates: *los dictados de la conciencia*, the dictates of conscience.
dictador m. Dictator.
dictadura f. Dictatorship.
dictáfono m. Dictaphone.
dictamen m. Opinion: *abundo en su dictamen*, I wholeheartedly agree with your opinion; *dar un dictamen desfavorable*, to give an unfavourable opinion. || Advice (consejo). || Report (informe): *dictamen de las comisiones*, commissions' report; *dictamen facultativo*, medical report. || — *Dictamen médico*, diagnosis. || *Dictamen pericial*, expert advice.
dictaminar v. tr. To consider, to hold the opinion, to be of the opinion: *el grafólogo dictamina que la letra es la de un tímido*, the graphologist considers that the handwriting is that of a timid person. || To prescribe (un médico). || JUR. To report (en un juicio).
— V. tr. e intr. To advise, to give one's advice (dar consejo). || To give *o* to express one's opinion: *han dictaminado sobre el proyecto de ley*, they have given their opinion on the bill. || JUR. To pass judgment.
díctamo m. BOT. Dittany.
dictar v. tr. To dictate: *dictar una carta*, to dictate a letter. || To enact, to decree (leyes). || To promulgate, to issue, to proclaim (decreto). || To give, to issue (órdenes). || To suggest, to say, to dictate, to advise (aconsejar). || To give (clases). || To deliver (conferencias). || JUR. To pronounce (sentencia). || — *Dictar condiciones*, to dictate terms. || *Dictar disposiciones*, to take *o* to adopt measures. || *Dictar la ley*, to lay down the laws.
dictatorial adj. Dictatorial.
dicterio m. Insult.
dicha f. Happiness (felicidad). || Joy (alegría). || Good luck (buena suerte). || — *Nunca es tarde si la dicha es buena*, better late than never. || *Por dicha*, happily, fortunately, luckily, by chance. || *Ser un hombre de dicha*, to be a lucky *o* a fortunate man.
dicharachero, ra adj. Witty, racy, spicy, funny (gracioso). || Talkative, chatty, loquacious (parlanchín).
— M. y f. Joker, wag, tease, character (gracioso). || Chatterbox (parlanchín).
dicharacho m. Rude language (lenguaje inconveniente). || Racy remark *o* joke (observación).
dicho, cha p.p. de *decir* y adj. V. DECIR. || — *Dicho de otro modo*, in other words, to put it another way. || *Dicho está*, it's settled. || *Dicho esto*, this said. || *Dicho sea de paso*, let it be said in passing. || *Dicho y hecho*, no sooner said than done. || *Mejor dicho*, rather: *alto, o mejor dicho gigantesco*, tall, or rather, gigantic.
— Adj. dem. This (pl. *these*), the said: *dicha ciudad*, this city.
— M. Expression, saying: *un dicho de Cicerón*, one of Cicero's sayings. || Remark, statement: *un dicho desacertado*, an unfortunate remark. || Proverb, saying, adage (refrán). || FAM. Insult (insulto). | Rude expression (expresión desvergonzada). || JUR. Statement, declaration (de un testigo). || — Pl. Betrothal pledge, *sing.* (compromiso matrimonial). || Engagement, *sing.*, betrothal, *sing.* (esponsales). || — FIG. *Del dicho al hecho hay mucho* or *un gran trecho*, there's many a slip twixt the cup and the lip, saying and doing are different things. || *Dicho de las gentes*, rumour, gossip. || *Dicho gracioso*, witty remark, witticism. || *Lo dicho*, what has been said *o* decided, what was said *o* decided: *lo dicho ayer vale todavía*, what was said yesterday still goes. || *Lo dicho, dicho está*, what was said *o* what has been said still stands. || *Tomarse los dichos*, to become engaged *o* betrothed.
dichosamente adv. Happily, fortunately, luckily.
dichoso, sa adj. Happy, content: *dichoso con su suerte*, content with his lot. || Lucky, fortunate (afortunado). || FIG. y FAM. Tiresome, wearisome, boring: *¡dichosa visita!*, what a tiresome visit! | Cursed, damned, blessed, confounded, blasted: *ese dichoso individuo*, that blasted fellow; *ese dichoso trabajo me impide salir*, that cursed work stops me going out.
didáctico, ca adj. Didactic.
— F. Didactics, *pl.*
diecinueve adj. Nineteen: *hay diecinueve personas*, there are nineteen people. || Nineteenth: *el siglo XIX (diecinueve)*, the 19th [nineteenth] century.
— M. Nineteen: *juego siempre el diecinueve*, I always play nineteen. || Nineteenth: *hoy estamos a 19 de febrero*, today is the 19th *o* nineteenth of February, today is February 19th *o* the nineteenth.
diecinueveavo, va adj./s. Nineteenth.
dieciochavo, va adj./s. Eighteenth. || *En dieciochavo (en 18.º)*, in eighteenmo, in 18.º, in eighteens (libro).
dieciochesco, ca adj. Eighteenth-century *o* 18th-century, of the eighteenth *o* 18th century: *pintura dieciochesca*, eighteenth-century painting.
dieciocho adj. Eighteen. || Eighteenth: *el siglo XVIII (dieciocho)*, the 18th [eighteenth] century.
— M. Eighteen: *tres por seis, dieciocho*, three times six makes eighteen. || Eighteenth: *llegaron el 18 de enero*, they arrived on the eighteenth of January.
dieciséis adj. Sixteen. || Sixteenth: *el siglo XVI (dieciséis)*, the 16th [sixteenth] century.
— M. Sixteen: *dieciséis es el cuadrado de cuatro*, sixteen is the square of four. || Sixteenth: *el 16 de julio*, July 16th, the sixteenth of July.
dieciseisavo, va adj./s. Sixteenth. || *En dieciseisavo (en 16.º)*, in sixteenmo, in 16º, in sixteens (libro).
diecisiete adj. Seventeen. || Seventeenth: *el siglo XVII (diecisiete)*, the 17th [seventeenth] century.
— M. Seventeen: *el diecisiete es un número primo*, seventeen is a prime number. || Seventeenth: *me voy el 17*, I'm leaving on the 17th [seventeenth].
diecisieteavo, va adj./s. Seventeenth.
diedro adj. m. Dihedral: *ángulo diedro*, dihedral angle.
— M. Dihedron.
diego m. BOT. Marvel of Peru, four o'clock flower.
Diego n. pr. m. James (Jaime).
dieléctrico, ca adj./s.m. Dielectric.
diente m. Tooth: *dientes de leche*, milk teeth; *diente picado*, bad *o* decayed tooth. || Tooth (de un peine, de una sierra). || Prong (de un bieldo, rastrillo, tenedor). || ARQ. Toothing stone (adaraja). || BOT. Tooth, serration (de una hoja). | Clove (de ajo). || TECN. Cog (de rueda dentada).
— FIG. y FAM. *Aguzarse los dientes*, to get one's hand in, to cut one's teeth. | *Alargársele a uno los dientes*, to be filled with longing (desear). | *Armado hasta los dientes*, armed to the teeth. || *Con todos sus dientes*, greedily, hungrily (morder). || FIG. *Crujirle* or *rechinarle a uno los dientes*, to have one's teeth set on edge (por una sensación desagradable), to gnash *o* to grind one's teeth (de rabia). || *Da diente con diente* or *le castañetean los dientes*, his teeth are chattering. || FIG. *Decir de dientes afuera* o *para fuera*, to say insincerely. || *Diente canino* or *columelar*, canine tooth (de personas), fang (de animales). || *Diente de león*, dandelion (planta). || TECN. *Diente de lobo*, burnisher. || FIG. *Diente por diente*, tooth for tooth. || *Dientes postizos*, false teeth. || *Echar los dientes* or *salirle a uno los dientes*, to cut one's teeth, to teethe (un niño). || FIG. *Enseñar* or *mostrar los dientes*, to bare *o* to show one's teeth. | *Hablar entre dientes*, to mumble, to mutter (mascullar). || FIG. y FAM. *Hincar el diente en*, V. HINCAR. || *Amer. Pelar el diente*, to smile falsely, to give a false smile. || FIG. y FAM. *Ponerle a uno los dientes largos*, to make one's mouth water (un plato apetitoso), to make s.o. green with envy (darle envidia). | *Reír de dientes afuera*, to force a smile, to give a sickly smile. | *Tener a uno entre dientes*, not to be able to stand *o* bear *o* stomach s.o. | *Tener buen diente*, to be a hearty eater. | *Tener los dientes largos*, to have an itching palm.
diéresis f. GRAM. y MED. Diaeresis.
diesel adj. Diesel.
— M. Diesel engine, diesel (motor).
diesi f. MÚS. Sharp (sostenido).
diestra f. Right hand.
diestramente adv. Cleverly, skilfully, deftly.
diestro, tra adj. Right: *la mano diestra*, the right hand. || Clever, skilful [U.S., skillful], deft: *diestro en hablar*, a skilful speaker; *diestro en su oficio*, skilful at his job. || Shrewd (astuto). || HERÁLD. Dexter. || — *A diestro y siniestro*, right and left (por todas partes), at random (sin método). || *Golpear a diestro y siniestro*, to hit out *o* to lash out left right and centre.
— M. TAUR. Matador. || Bridle (correa), halter (rienda). || (Ant.). Swordsman.

dieta f. HIST. Diet (congreso). || MED. Diet: *poner a dieta*, to put on a diet; *dieta láctea alta en calorías*, calory-rich milk diet. || — Pl. Emoluments [of a member of parliament] (de diputados). || Per diem allowance, *sing.*, per diem, *sing.* (de un empleado que está de viaje). || Emoluments, fees (de un juez).
dietario m. Account book.
dietético, ca adj. Dietetic. || *Médico dietético*, dietician, dietitian.
— F. Dietetics, *pl.*
diez adj. num. Ten: *diez pesetas*, ten pesetas. || Tenth (ordinal): *el (día) 10 (diez) de mayo*, the 10th [tenth] of May, May 10th [the tenth]; *el siglo X (diez)*, the 10th [tenth] century.
— M. Ten. || Decade (del rosario). || Paternoster [bead] (cuenta gruesa del rosario). || Ten (naipes). || — FIG. y FAM. *Estar en las diez de últimas*, to be at death's door, to have one foot in the grave. | *Hacer las diez de últimas*, to queer one's own pitch, to damage one's own cause. || *Las diez de últimas*, ten points which go to the winner of the last trick (naipes). || *Son las diez*, it is 10 o'clock. || *Unos diez libros*, about ten books.

— OBSERV. The cardinal numbers from 16 to 19 can be written in two ways: *diez y seis* or *dieciséis*, *diez y siete* or *diecisiete*, etc.

diezmar v. tr. To decimate.
— V. intr. To pay the tithe (pagar el diezmo).
diezmilésimo, ma adj./s. Ten thousandth.
diezmilímetro m. Tenth of a millimetre.
diezmillonésimo, ma adj./s. Ten millionth.
diezmo m. Tithe (impuesto). || Tenth [part].
difamación f. Defamation, slander (hablando). || Defamation, libel (por escrito).
difamador, ra m. y f. Defamer, slanderer (de palabra). || Defamer, libeller [U.S., libeler] (por escrito).
— Adj. V. DIFAMATORIO.
difamante adj. V. DIFAMATORIO.
difamar v. tr. To defame, to slander (hablando). || To defame, to libel (por escrito).
difamatorio, ria adj. Defamatory, slanderous (de palabra). || Defamatory, libellous [U.S., libelous] (por escrito).
difásico, ca adj. FÍS. Two-phase, diphase.
diferencia f. Difference: *la diferencia de edad*, the difference in age, the age difference. || Difference [of opinion], disagreement, dispute: *arreglar una diferencia*, to settle a dispute. || — *A diferencia de*, unlike, contrary to. || *Pagar la diferencia*, to pay the difference. || *Partir la diferencia*, to split the difference.
diferenciación f. Differentiation.
diferencial adj. Differential: *ecuación, cálculo diferencial*, differential equation, calculus.
— F. MAT. Differential. || — M. TECN. Differential.
diferenciar v. tr. To differentiate. || To distinguish (distinguir). || MAT. To differentiate.
— V. intr. To differ [in opinion], to disagree, not to be of *o* not to hold the same opinion (de opinión): *en este punto diferenciamos*, we disagree on this point.
— V. pr. To differ [in opinion], to disagree, to hold different *o* differing opinions; *en esta cuestión nos diferenciamos mucho*, on this matter we differ greatly [in opinion], we hold vastly different *o* widely differing opinions on this matter. || To differ, to be different (ser diferente). || To stand out, to distinguish o.s. (distinguirse): *esta chica se diferencia de sus compañeras*, this girl stands out from her friends.
diferendo m. *Amer.* Difference, quarrel, disagreement.
diferente adj. Different: *diferente a* or *de*, different to *o* from. || *Diferentes veces*, several times.
diferible adj. Deferable, deferrable.
diferido, da adj. Deferred, postponed, put off. || *Emisión diferida*, recorded transmission.
diferir* v. tr. To defer, to postpone, to put off (aplazar): *han diferido la reunión*, they have postponed the meeting. || JUR. To reserve (un fallo).
— V. intr. To differ, to be different (ser diferente).
difícil adj. Difficult, hard: *difícil de decir*, hard to say; *cada vez más difícil*, more and more difficult; *hacer difícil*, to make *o* to render difficult. || Difficult (carácter). || Hard: *difícil de contentar*, hard to please. || FIG. Unpleasant, odd, disagreeable (cara). || — *Difícil de llevar*, wayward, ungovernable: *un niño difícil de llevar*, a wayward child; difficult to run *o* manage: *esta empresa es difícil de llevar*, this firm is difficult to manage; difficult to keep (cuenta), difficult to wear: *este traje es difícil de llevar*, this dress is difficult to wear; difficult to follow: *un compás difícil de llevar*, a beat difficult to follow. || *Es difícil que venga*, it is unlikely that he will come. || *No es muy difícil que digamos*, it's not exactly difficult.
difícilmente adv. Hardly: *difícilmente se puede creer*, you'd hardly believe it. || With difficulty.
dificultad f. Difficulty: *vencer dificultades*, to surmount difficulties; *sin dificultad alguna*, without the least difficulty. || Trouble (molestia). || Obstacle (obstáculo). || Problem, difficulty (problema). || Inconvenience (inconveniente). || — Pl. Difficulties: *poner dificultades a todo*, to create difficulties in everything; *ponerle dificultades a uno*, to present s.o. with difficulties. || Trouble, *sing.*: *dificultades mecánicas*, mechanical trouble. || Objections: *poner dificultades*, to raise objections. || *Tener dificultad para andar*, to have difficulty in walking.
dificultador, ra adj. Difficult, fussy (dificultoso).
dificultar v. tr. To make *o* to render difficult, to hinder, to obstruct, to hamper.
dificultosamente adv. With difficulty.
dificultoso, sa adj. Difficult, hard: *trabajo dificultoso*, difficult work. || FIG. y FAM. Unpleasant, disagreeable (rostro). || Fussy, difficult (exigente).
difluir* v. intr. To be diffused, to disperse, to spread out.
difracción f. FÍS. Diffraction.
difractar v. tr. FÍS. To diffract.
difractivo, va o **difrangente** adj. FÍS. Diffractive.
difteria f. MED. Diphtheria.
diftérico, ca adj. MED. Diphtheric, diphtheritic.
difuminación f. Stumping.
difuminar o **difumar** v. tr. To stump.
difumino m. Stumping (acción). || Stump (lápiz). || *Dibujo al difumino*, stump drawing.
difundir v. tr. To spread: *las ratas difunden las epidemias*, rats spread epidemics. || To diffuse: *difundir la luz*, to diffuse light. || To disseminate (diseminar). || To broadcast, to transmit: *difundir una emisión radiofónica*, to broadcast a radio transmission, to transmit a radio broadcast. || To spread, to radiate: *difundir la felicidad*, to spread happiness. || To spread, to divulge: *difundir una noticia*, to spread a piece of news. || To disseminate, to propagate (una doctrina).
— V. pr. To diffuse, to be diffused: *la transpiración se difunde por los poros*, perspiration diffuses through the pores. || To [be] spread, to be propagated (una doctrina). || To spread (una noticia).
— OBSERV. The verb *difundir* has two past participles: the regular *difundido* is used to form compound tenses, and the irregular *difuso* is used as an adjective.
difunto, ta adj./s. Deceased, defunct. || — Adj. Late: *mi difunto padre*, my late father. || — M. Casualty (víctima). || — *Día de (los) Difuntos*, All Souls' Day. || FIG. y FAM. *Oler a difunto*, to smell fusty *o* musty (una habitación), to look as if one is not long for this world (antes de morir uno).
difusible adj. Diffusible.
difusión f. Spreading (de una epidemia, etc.). || Diffusion (de luz, calor, agua). || RAD. Broadcasting, transmission (acción), broadcast (programa). || Diffusion, spreading, dissemination, propagation (de una noticia).
difuso, sa adj. Diffuse, wordy (explicación, estilo). || Wide (extenso).
difusor, ra adj. Propagating, disseminating, who *o* which propagates *o* disseminates (de una doctrina). || Spreading (de una noticia). || Diffusive, diffusing, who *o* which diffuses (del agua, de la luz). || RAD. Broadcasting, transmitting.
— M. y f. Propagator, disseminator (de una doctrina). || — M. TECN. Diffuser. || — F. RAD. Broadcasting station.
digerible adj. Digestible.
digerir* v. tr. To digest (la comida). || FIG. To suffer, to endure, to stand, to bear (una ofensa). | To digest, to assimilate: *no ha digerido la lección*, he has not digested the lesson. || FAM. *No poder digerir a uno*, not to be able to stand *o* to bear s.o.
— V. pr. To digest.
digestibilidad f. Digestibility.
digestible adj. Digestible.
digestión f. Digestion.
digestivo, va adj./s.m. Digestive.
digesto m. JUR. Digest.
digestónico, ca adj./s.m. Digestive.
digitación f. MÚS. Fingering, digitation.
digitado, da adj. BOT. y ZOOL. Digitate.
digital adj. Digital. || Finger (dactilar). || *Huellas digitales*, fingerprints.
— F. BOT. Foxglove, digitalis. || MED. Digitalis.
digitalina f. Digitalin (medicina).
digitiforme adj. Digitiform.
digitígrado, da adj./s.m. ZOOL. Digitigrade.
dígito m. MAT. Digit.
dignamente adv. With dignity.
dignarse v. pr. To deign, to condescend: *no se dignó contestarme*, he did not deign to answer me. || — *Dígnese usted hacer lo que le pido*, [will you] be so good *o* kind as to do what I ask of you. || *Señor, dígnate aceptar este sacrificio*, Lord, accept this sacrifice (oración).
dignatario m. Dignitary.
dignidad f. Dignity. || Self-respect, dignity (de uno mismo). || Office, post, rank (cargo).
dignificante adj. Dignifying (gracia).
dignificar v. tr. To dignify.
digno, na adj. Worthy, deserving: *digno de admiración*, worthy of admiration. || Fitting, appropriate: *el digno castigo*, the fitting punishment. || Worthy, honourable, meritorious (que merece respeto): *hombre digno*, honourable man; *conducta digna*, worthy conduct. || Decent (decente, decoroso): *viviendas, condiciones de trabajo dignas*, decent houses, working conditions. || — *Digno de compasión*, pitiable, pitiful. || *Digno de encomio*, praiseworthy. || *Digno de ser mencionado*, worth mentioning. || *Digno de verse*, worth seeing. || *Ejemplo digno de imitación*, example worth emulating. || *Él, muy digno, rehusó*, he, with great dignity, refused.

digresión f. Digression.
dije m. Trinket, locket; charm: *esta pulsera tiene muchos dijes*, this bracelet has many trinkets. || FIG. y FAM. Treasure, jewel, gem: *esta criada es un dije*, this maid is a treasure. || — Pl. FAM. Bragging, *sing.*, boasting, *sing.*, bravado, *sing.* (bravuconerías).
dilaceración f. Dilaceration, laceration. || MED. Tearing (músculo).
dilacerar v. tr. To dilacerate, to lacerate, to tear asunder. || To tear (un músculo). || FIG. To hurt, to harm, to wound (el orgullo, etc.).
dilación f. Delay, delaying (retraso). || Delay (demora). || *Sin dilación*, without delay, immediately.
dilapidación f. Squandering, wasting, dissipation.
dilapidador, ra adj. Squandering, wasteful.
— M. y f. Squanderer, waster.
dilapidar v. tr. To squander, to waste, to dissipate.
dilatabilidad f. FÍS. Expansibility, expandability. || Dilatability (de la pupila).
dilatable adj. Expansible, expandable (un metal, etc.). || Dilatable (pupila).
dilatación f. FÍS. Expansion. || Dilation (de la pupila). || MED. Dilatation, dilation. || Protraction, prolongation (del tiempo).
dilatadamente adv. Extensively, widely (extensamente). || At length, diffusely, long-windedly: *hablar dilatadamente de algo*, to speak at length on sth.
dilatado, da adj. FÍS. Expanded. || Dilated (la pupila). || Extensive, vast (extenso). || Long: *un dilatado período de tiempo*, a long period of time. || FIG. Unlimited, wide: *horizontes dilatados*, unlimited prospects, wide horizons.
dilatador, ra adj. MED. Dilative, which dilates. || FÍS. Which causes expansion, which expands, expanding.
— M. MED. Dilator.
dilatar v. tr. To expand: *el calor dilata los metales*, heat expands metals. || MED. To dilate. || FIG. To postpone, to delay, to put off, to defer (retrasar): *dilató su regreso por un año*, he postponed his return by a year. | To enlarge, to widen (ampliar). | To prolong, to protract, to drag out (prolongar). || *Dilatar un asunto*, to drag out an affair.
— V. pr. To expand: *el agua se dilata al congelarse*, water expands on freezing. || MED. To dilate. || To dilate (la pupila). || FIG. To be diffuse (al hablar). | To drag on (un relato). | To extend, to stretch: *la llanura se dilataba hasta el horizonte*, the plain extended as far as the horizon. || *Amer.* To take *o* to be long *o* a long time, to be slow, to linger, to tarry, to delay (tardar): *no te dilates para salir*, don't be slow leaving.
dilatorio, ria adj. JUR. Dilatory, delaying.
— F. Delay. || *Andar* or *venir con dilatorias*, to delay, to drag things out, to waste time.
dilección f. Love, affection.
dilecto, ta adj. Dearly beloved, beloved: *mi dilecto amigo*, my dearly beloved friend.
dilema m. Dilemma.
diletante m. Dilettante (aficionado).
diletantismo m. Dilettantism.
diligencia f. Diligence, application, care (cuidado). || Speed, rapidity (rapidez). || Step, measure: *hacer diligencias para*, to take steps to, to take the necessary steps *o* measures to. || [Piece of] business, job, affair (gestión). || Diligence, stagecoach (coche). || JUR. Proceeding. || — JUR. *Diligencias previas*, inquiry. || *Tengo que ir a unas cuantas diligencias*, I have a few things to see to, I have some business to see to.
diligenciar v. tr. To take the necessary steps *o* measures to obtain, to go through the necessary procedures to obtain: *diligenciar un pasaporte*, to take the necessary steps to obtain a passport.
diligente adj. Diligent. || Quick, speedy (rápido).
dilucidación f. Elucidation, explanation.
dilucidador, ra adj. Elucidatory, explanatory.
— M. y f. Elucidator, explainer.
dilucidar v. tr. To elucidate, to explain (aclarar). || To solve, to clear up (un misterio, etc.).
dilución f. Dissolution, dissolving (de un sólido en un líquido). || Dilution (entre dos líquidos).
diluente adj. Diluting, solvent.
diluir* v. tr. To dissolve (un sólido en un líquido). || To dilute (líquidos). || To thin (salsas). || FIG. To water down.
— V. pr. To become diluted, to dilute.
diluvial adj. Diluvial.
— M. Diluvium.
diluviano, na adj. Diluvian: *lluvia diluviana*, diluvian rain.
diluviar v. intr. To pour with rain, to pour down, to teem (llover mucho).
diluvio m. Deluge, flood. || FIG. Flood, storm, torrent: *un diluvio de protestas*, a storm of protest; *un diluvio de injurias*, a torrent of abuse. || FIG. *Tras mí, el diluvio*, I'm all right, Jack.
dimanar v. intr. To flow, to run (el agua). || FIG. To emanate, to issue, to derive, to originate: *el poder dimana del pueblo*, power emanates *o* issues *o* derives from the people, power originates in the people. || To arise, to follow, to result (resultar).
dimensión f. Dimension. || Magnitude, size (tamaño). || — Pl. Dimensions, size, *sing.*: *de grandes dimensiones*, of great size. || — *Dimensiones exteriores*, overall *o* external dimensions. || *Tomar las dimensiones de*, to measure out, to take the measurements of.
dimensional adj. Dimensional.
dimes y diretes loc. FAM. Bickering, quibbling, argument. || *Andar en dimes y diretes*, to bicker, to quibble, to argue.
diminución f. Diminution, diminishing, reduction.
diminuendo adj./s.m. MÚS. Diminuendo.
diminuir v. tr. To diminish, to reduce (disminuir).
diminutivo, va adj./s.m. Diminutive.

— OBSERV. *Diminutives* are much more commonly used in Spanish than in English. Besides implying the idea of smallness they are often used affectionately. They are formed as follows:
1.° With the suffix *-ito*, for polysyllables ending in *a*, *o* or a consonant other than *n* and *r* (*mesita, librito, españolito*);
2.° With the suffix *-cito*, for polysyllables ending in *e*, *n* or *r* (*pajecito, silloncito, lunarcito*);
3.° With the suffix *-ecito*, for monosyllables or for disyllables containing an accented diphthong or a final diphthong (*panecito, cuerpecito, indiecito*);
4.° The same rules apply for the suffixes *-illo, -cillo, -ecillo; -uelo, -zuelo, -ezuelo; -ico, -cico, -ecico* (*mesilla, libruelo, panecico*).

diminuto, ta adj. Tiny, minute, diminutive.
dimisión f. Resignation: *presentar su dimisión*, to hand in *o* to tender one's resignation. || *Hacer dimisión de un cargo*, to resign from *o* to resign a post.
dimisionario, ria adj. Resigning, outgoing.
— M. y f. Resigner.
dimisorias f. pl. Dimissory letters.
dimitente adj./s. V. DIMISIONARIO.
dimitir v. tr. e intr. To resign, to resign from: *dimitir (de) un cargo*, to resign a post.
dimorfo, fa adj. Dimorphous, dimorphic.
din m. (P. us.). Money, dough. || FIG. *Poco importa el don sin el din*, a lord without riches is a soldier without arms.
dina f. FÍS. Dyne (unidad de fuerza).
Dinamarca n. pr. f. GEOGR. Denmark.
dinamarqués, esa adj. Danish.
— M. y f. Dane.
dinámico, ca adj. Dynamic.
— F. FÍS. Dynamics.
dinamismo m. Dynamism.
dinamista adj. Dynamistic.
— M. y f. Dynamist.
dinamita f. Dynamite || — *Voladura con dinamita*, dynamiting. || *Volar con dinamita*, to dynamite.
dinamitar v. tr. To dynamite.
dinamitazo m. Explosion, blast.
dinamitero, ra m. y f. Dynamiter.
dinamo o **dínamo** m. ELECTR. Dynamo.
dinamoeléctrico, ca adj. Dynamoelectric, dynamo-electrical.
dinamometría f. Dynamometry.
dinamómetro m. Dynamometer.
dinar m. Dinar (moneda).
dinastía f. Dynasty.
dinástico, ca adj. Dynastic, dynastical.
dinerada f. o **dineral** m. Fortune, great deal *o* large sum of money: *costó un dineral*, it cost a fortune.
dinerillo m. FAM. A little [money], a bit [of money]. || Pocket money (dinero para gastos menudos).
dinero m. Money: *dinero para gastos menudos* or *de bolsillo*, pocket money; *andar escaso de dinero*, to be short of money; *hacer algo por dinero*, to do sth. for money. || Denarius (moneda antigua *o* denario): *Judas vendió a Jesucristo por treinta dineros*, Judas betrayed Christ for thirty denarii. || FIG. y FAM. Money, wealth (riqueza).
— *De dinero*, rich, wealthy, moneyed: *familia, hombre de dinero*, wealthy family, man. || *De dineros y bondad quita siempre la mitad* or *de dinero y calidad, la mitad de la mitad*, believe only half of what you hear of a man's wealth and goodness. || *Dinero acuñado*, minted money. || *Dinero contante y sonante*, hard cash. || *Dinero de San Pedro*, Peter's pence. || *Dinero efectivo*, or *en metálico*, cash. || *Dinero líquido*, ready money. || *Dinero suelto*, change, loose change (moneda suelta): *no tengo dinero suelto*, I have no change. || *Dineros son calidad*, you're nobody without money. || *(El) dinero llama (al) dinero*, money makes money. || *El dinero no tiene olor*, money is welcome though it comes in a dirty clout. || *Estar mal de dinero*, to be hard up, to be short of money. || FIG. y FAM. *Ganar dinero a espuertas*, to make tons of money, to make a pile. | *Hacer dinero*, to make money. || *Invertir dinero*, to invest money. || *Poderoso caballero es don Dinero*, money talks. || *Por dinero baila el perro*, V. PERRO. || *Sacar dinero de las piedras*, to be a skinflint. || *Sacarle jugo al dinero*, to make the most of one's money, to get one's money's worth, to get value for money. || *Tirar el dinero por la ventana*, to throw money down the drain.
dingo m. Dingo (perro de Australia).
dinosaurio m. Dinosaur.
dintel m. ARQ. Lintel (parte superior de las puertas). | Overdoor (decoración). | Threshold (umbral).
diñar v. tr. POP. To give (dar). || POP. *Diñarla*, to kick the bucket.
diocesano, na adj./s. Diocesan.
diócesis o **diócesi** f. Diocese.

diodo m. Diode.
dionisiaco, ca o **dionisíaco, ca** adj. Dionysiac, dionysian.
— F. pl. Dionysia.
Dioniso o **Dionisos** n. pr. m. Dionysus, Dionysos.
dioptra f. Fís. Diopter, alidade.
dioptría f. Fís. Med. Diopter, dioptre.
dióptrico, ca adj. Fís. Dioptric, dioptrical.
— F. Dioptrics.
diorita f. Min. Diorite.
dios m. Rel. God. || — Pl. Gods: *los dioses del Olimpo*, the gods of Olympus.
— *¡A Dios!*, good-bye, farewell, adieu. (V. ADIÓS [Observ.]). || *¡A Dios gracias!* or *¡gracias a Dios!*, thank God!, thank heaven! || *A Dios rogando y con el mazo dando*, God helps those who help themselves. || *¡Alabado sea Dios!*, God be praised!, praise be to God! || *A la buena de Dios*, in a slapdash way, any old how, at random. || *¡Anda* or *vete con Dios!*, farewell!, God be with you!, God go with you!, adieu! || *Armar la de Dios es Cristo*, to raise hell. || *¡Ay Dios!*, God!, my God! || *¡Bendito sea Dios!*, God be praised! || *Clamar a Dios*, to cry out to heaven. || *Como Dios le da a entender*, as best one can, [in] one's [own] way: *hágalo como Dios le dé a entender*, do it as best you can, do it your way. || *Como Dios manda*, properly: *vestido como Dios manda*, properly dressed; according to the rules: *jugar como Dios manda*, to play according to the rules; as it should be (como se debe). || Fam. *¡Con Dios!*, good-bye! || *Dar gracias a Dios*, to thank God, to give thanks to God, to thank one's lucky stars. || *Digan, que de Dios dijeron*, say what you like, it doesn't worry me. || *Dios aprieta pero no ahoga*, God tempers the wind to the shorn lamb. || *Dios da ciento por uno*, God repays a hundredfold. || *¡Dios dirá!*, time will tell!, we shall see! || *Dios es testigo que...*, God *o* heaven knows... || *Dios Hijo, Dios hecho Hombre*, God the Son, God made Man. || *¡Dios le ampare!*, God protect you! || *¡Dios le asista* or *le ayude!*, God help you! || *¡Dios le bendiga!*, God bless [you]! || *Dios le ha dejado de su mano*, God has forsaken him. || *¡Dios lo quiera!* or *¡quiera Dios!*, let us hope so!, would to God! || *Dios los cría y ellos se juntan*, birds of a feather flock together. || *¡Dios me confunda!*, damn! || *Dios mediante*, God willing. || *¡Dios me libre!*, God *o* heaven forbid! || *¡Dios (mío)!*, good heavens!, my God! || *Dios no le ha llamado por el camino de*, he's not cut out for. || *¡Dios proveerá!*, God will provide! || *Dios sabe* or *sabe Dios*, God *o* Heaven knows (con un complemento), God *o* Heaven only knows (al final). || *¡Dios santo!*, good God!, my God!, good heavens! || *¡Dios se lo pague!*, God bless you! || *Dios Todopoderoso*, almighty God. || *Estaba de Dios*, God [had] willed it, it was inevitable. || *Hay que dar a Dios lo que es de Dios y al César lo que es del César*, render therefore unto Caesar the things which are Caesar's and unto God the things that are God's. || *Jurar por todos los dioses*, to swear by all the gods. || Fam. *No había ni Dios*, there wasn't a soul [there]. || *No (lo) quiera Dios*, God *o* Heaven forbid. || *No temer ni a Dios ni al diablo*, to fear neither man nor beast. || *Pasar la de Dios es Cristo*, to have a rough time of it, to suffer great hardship, to go through hell. || *Poner a Dios por testigo*, to swear by Heaven above, to swear by almighty God. || *¡Por Dios!*, for goodness' sake!, for God's sake! || *¡Que Dios le guarde!*, God protect you! || *Que Dios le tenga en su (santa) gloria*, may his soul rest in peace. || *Que Dios me perdone, pero...*, [may] God *o* Heaven forgive me, but... || *Que Dios nos asista* or *nos coja confesados*, God *o* Lord help us. || *Quiera Dios que*, if only, would to God that. || *Sea lo que Dios quiera*, God's will be done. || *Se va a armar la de Dios es Cristo*, v. ARMAR. || *Si Dios quiere*, God willing. || *¡Válgame Dios!*, by Jove!, bless my soul! (sorpresa), Lord, give me strength! || *¡Vaya con Dios!*, farewell!, God be with you!, God go with you! || *¡Vaya por Dios!*, good God!, my God! || *¡Vive Dios!* or *¡Voto a Dios!* (ant.), zounds!, gadzooks!
diosa f. Goddess.
diplodoco m. Diplodocus (fósil).
diploma m. Diploma.
diplomacia f. Diplomacy.
diplomado, da adj. Qualified, having a diploma, who holds a diploma.
— M. y f. Diplomate, qualified person. || Graduate (en la Universidad). || *Diplomada en belleza*, qualified beautician.
diplomar v. tr. *Amer.* To grant a diploma to.
— V. pr. To graduate (en la Universidad).
diplomática f. Diplomatics.
diplomático, ca adj. Diplomatic: *cuerpo diplomático*, diplomatic corps; *valija diplomática*, diplomatic bag. || Fig. y Fam. Diplomatic, tactful (sagaz).
— M. Diplomat, diplomatist.
dipsomanía f. Dipsomania (sed violenta).
dipsómano, na adj. Dipsomaniacal, dipsomaniac.
— M. y f. Dipsomaniac.
díptero, ra adj. Arq. Dipteral: *un templo díptero*, a dipteral temple. || Zool. Dipterous, dipteran.
— M. Zool. Dipteran. || — Pl. Zool. Diptera.
díptico m. Diptych.
diptongación f. Gram. Diphthongization.
diptongar v. tr. Gram. To diphthongize.
— V. pr. Gram. To diphthongize.
diptongo m. Gram. Diphthong.
diputación f. Deputation (delegación). || Post of member of parliament (en Gran Bretaña). || Post of congressman (en Estados Unidos). || Post of member of the Spanish Cortes (en España). || *Amer.* Town hall (ayuntamiento). || *Diputación provincial*, county council.
diputado m. Representative, delegate, deputy (delegado). || Member of parliament (en Gran Bretaña). || Congressman (en Estados Unidos). || Member of the Cortes *o* of the Spanish parliament (en España). || *Diputado provincial*, county councillor.
diputar v. tr. To deputize, to delegate.
dique m. Mar. Dike, breakwater, mole, jetty (muro). | Dry dock (en la dársena). | Dike (en Holanda). || Fig. Check, rein (obstáculo): *poner un dique a las pasiones*, to put a check *o* rein on passions. || Geol. Dike (filón volcánico vertical). || — *Dique de carena*, dry dock. || *Dique de contención*, dam. || *Dique flotante*, floating dock. || *Dique seco*, dry dock. || *Entrar en dique*, to dock. || Fig. *Poner un dique a*, to restrain, to curb, to check, to repress (contener).
diquelar v. tr. Fam. To look at (mirar). | To see, to get (entender).
dirección f. Direction: *le confiaron la dirección de la obra*, they entrusted him with the direction of the work. || Direction, way: *vamos en la misma dirección*, we're going in the same direction, we're going the same way. || Address (señas): *mi dirección es Calle Mayor 13*, my address is 13 Calle Mayor. || Managership, directorship (función de director). || Management, board of directors: *por orden de la dirección*, by order of the management. || Tecn. Steering (de coche, avión, etc.): *dirección asistida*, servo-assisted steering. || Leadership (de un partido). || Headship (de una escuela). || Editorship (de un periódico). || Office (de la administración pública). || Teatr. Production. || Cinem. Direction. || Mar. Course, route (rumbo). || — *Calle de dirección única*, one-way street. || *Dirección escénica*, production (teatro), direction (cine). || *Dirección general*, head office, headquarters, *pl.* || *Dirección general de producción*, executive direction (cine). || *Dirección por radio*, radio control. || *Dirección prohibida*, no entry. || *En dirección a*, in the direction of, towards. || *Llevar la dirección de*, to direct.
directamente adv. Directly. || *Fuimos allí directamente*, we went straight there.
directivo, va adj. Directive. || Managerial, managing (de la dirección de una empresa). || Guiding: *principio directivo*, guiding principle. || *Junta directiva*, board of directors, directors, *pl.*
— M. Director, board member. || — F. Board [of directors]. || Guideline, directive, instruction: *no me dio ninguna directiva*, he gave me no instructions.
directo, ta adj. Direct. || Direct, straight (línea). || Lineal (herencia). || Gram. Direct. || — *Emisión en directo*, live transmission. || *Tren directo*, through *o* direct train.
— M. Straight (boxeo): *directo de izquierda, de derecha*, straight left, right. || — F. Top gear (coche): *poner la directa*, to go into *o* to engage top gear.
director, ra adj. Governing, steering (junta, asamblea). || Guiding, master (idea). || Directive (función). || Master (plan). || Guiding (principio). || Tecn. Controlling (fuerza).
— M. y f. Director, head (hombre), directress, head (mujer) [administración]. || Director, manager (hombre), directress, manageress (mujer) [de sociedad]. || Headmaster (hombre), headmistress (mujer) [de un colegio]. || President (de una Academia). || Governor, warden (de prisión). || Editor (hombre), editress (mujer) [de periódico]. || Manager (hombre), manageress (mujer) [de hotel]. || — *Director de cine*, film director. || *Director de emisión*, producer. || *Director de escena*, producer (teatro), director (cine). || *Director de orquesta*, conductor. || *Director de producción*, director of production. || *Director espiritual*, spiritual director. || *Director general*, director general. || *Director gerente*, managing director.
directoral adj. Directorial.
directorio, ria adj. Directive, directorial, directory.
— M. Directory (de direcciones, de normas). || Governing body (asamblea directiva).
Directorio m. Hist. Directory (en Francia).
directriz adj. f. Mat. Dirigent, describing (línea).
— F. Mat. Directrix. || — F. pl. Instructions, guidelines: *les he dado directrices perfectamente claras*, I have given them perfectly clear instructions.
dirigente adj. Directing, leading. || — *Clase dirigente*, ruling class. || *Personal dirigente*, executives, *pl.*
— M. y f. Leader. || Manager (director).
dirigible adj./s.m. Aviac. Dirigible.
dirigir v. tr. To direct, to point, to aim, to level (un arma): *dirigió la pistola hacia el ladrón*, he pointed the pistol at the thief. || To direct, to point, to aim: *dirigir un telescopio hacia la Luna*, to direct a telescope at the moon. || To drive, to steer (un coche). || To steer, to pilot (un avión, barco). || To address (una carta). || To direct, to address: *dirigir una observación*, to address a remark. || To direct: *me dirigió a la estación*, he directed me to the station. || To manage (una empresa). || To run (negocio, escuela). || To control (el tráfico). || To administer (los asuntos públicos). || To edit (un periódico). || To conduct, to lead (una

orquesta). || To direct, to conduct (operaciones, negociaciones). || To lead, to head (una sublevación, expedición). || To dedicate: *dirigió todos sus esfuerzos a terminar sus estudios*, he dedicated all his efforts to finishing his studies. || To level, to make (una acusación). || To bend (los pasos). || To turn (la mirada). || To guide (guiar). || To direct, to supervise: *dirigir un seminario*, to supervise a seminary. || To superintend (obras). || To direct, to guide: *dirigir espiritualmente a uno*, to direct s.o. spiritually. || TEATR. To produce. || CINEM. To direct. || — FIG. *Dirigir el baile*, to rule the roost, to run the show. || *Dirigir la mirada*, to direct *o* to turn one's gaze, to look. || *Dirigir por radio*, to radio-control.

— V. pr. To make one's way, to go: *dirigirse a su casa*, to make one's way homewards. || To be managed (una empresa). || To address, to speak: *dirigirse a uno*, to address s.o., to speak to s.o. || To write (escribir): *me dirijo a usted*, I am writing to you. || To apply (para solicitar algo). || To aim, to be aimed at (crítica, acusación, etc.). || To turn (la mirada).

dirigismo m. State control.

dirigista adj. Of State control: *política dirigista*, policy of State control.

— M. y f. Advocate of State control.

dirimente adj. JUR. Diriment, nullifying.

dirimir v. tr. To settle (una contienda). || To annul, to dissolve, to declare void: *dirimir el matrimonio, un contrato*, to annul the marriage, a contract.

discernible adj. Discernible.

discernidor, ra adj. Discerning.

discernimiento m. Discernment, perception. || Discernment, discrimination. || Discernment, judgment (criterio): *actuar con discernimiento*, to act with discernment. || JUR. Appointment (designación).

discernir* v. tr. To discern, to distinguish: *discernir el bien del mal*, to discern good from evil. || JUR. To appoint [s.o.] as guardian.

— OBSERV. This verb is sometimes used with the meaning *to award*, which is better expressed by *conceder*.

disciplina f. Discipline (sometimiento a reglas). || Doctrine (doctrina). || Subject (asignatura). || Scourge whip, discipline (azote).

disciplinadamente adv. With discipline.

disciplinado, da adj. Disciplined. || FIG. Variegated, marbled (jaspeado).

disciplinante m. y f. Flagellant, disciplinant (en Semana Santa).

disciplinar v. tr. To discipline (un ejército, sus instintos). || To scourge, to whip, to discipline (azotar). || To teach, to instruct (instruir).

— V. pr. To discipline o.s.

disciplinario, ria adj. Disciplinary: *castigo, batallón disciplinario*, disciplinary punishment, batallion.

discípulo, la m. y f. Disciple (el que sigue a un maestro). || Pupil, student [of a teacher] (escolar, alumno): *un discípulo aplicado*, a studious pupil.

disco m. Discus: *lanzamiento del disco*, throwing the discus. || Disk, disc: *disco de Newton*, Newton's disc. || Record, disc (de fonógrafo): *poner un disco*, to play a record. || Light (en las calles): *disco rojo, verde*, red, green light. || Signal (de ferrocarriles). || Dial (del teléfono). || TECN. Disk, disc (del freno). | Plate, disc (del embrague). || MED. Disk, disc (de las vértebras). || FAM. Bore, drag (cosa pesada): *¡qué disco ir allí*, what a bore going there! | Same old story *o* song, same string: *siempre estás con el mismo disco*, you're always telling the same old story, you're always singing the same old song, you're always harping on the same string, it's the same old story *o* song. || — FIG. y FAM. *Cambiar el disco*, to change the record. || *Disco de control*, parking disc. || *Disco de señales*, [disc] signal (ferrocarril). || *Disco selector*, dial (teléfono). || *Pasar con el disco cerrado, abierto*, to go through a red light, to proceed on green.

discóbolo m. Discobolus, discus thrower.

discófilo, la m. y f. Record fan, discophile.

discoidal o **discoideo, a** adj. Discoid, discoidal.

díscolo, la adj. Disobedient, ungovernable, wayward.

disconforme adj. Not in agreement, in disagreement: *estoy disconforme contigo*, I am not in agreement with you. || Differing, disagreeing (diferente).

disconformidad f. Disagreement (desacuerdo). || Difference, nonconformity, divergence: *disconformidad de opiniones*, difference of opinions.

discontinuación f. Discontinuation, discontinuance.

discontinuar v. tr. e intr. To discontinue, to cease.

discontinuidad f. Discontinuity, lack of continuity.

discontinuo, nua adj. Discontinuous. || MAT. *Función discontinua*, discontinuous function.

disconveniencia f. Incongruity.

disconvenir* v. intr. Not to agree, to disagree (en las opiniones). || Not to go together, not to match (cosas).

discordancia f. MÚS. Discordance, dissonance. || Clashing, incongruity (de colores). || Difference, divergence, nonconformity (de opiniones). || Disagreement, discordance, nonconformity: *discordancia entre los dichos y los hechos*, disagreement between the statements and the facts. || Discord (discordia).

discordante adj. MÚS. Discordant, dissonant. || Clashing, incongruous (colores). || Differing, divergent, nonconforming (opiniones). || Disagreeing, discordant, nonconforming (que no coinciden).

discordar* v. intr. MÚS. To be discordant *o* dissonant. || To clash (colores). || To disagree, not to agree, to be in disagreement, to differ [in opinion] (no estar de acuerdo). || To differ: *discordamos en pareceres*, we differ in opinion. || Not to tally *o* agree (no coincidir).

discorde adj. MÚS. Discordant, dissonant. || Clashing (colores). || Differing, diverging (opiniones). || In disagreement, not in agreement: *estamos discordes*, we are not in agreement. || Disagreeing, discordant (que no coinciden).

discordia f. Discord, dissension: *sembrar la discordia*, to sow discord. || — *Manzana de la discordia*, apple of discord. || *Tercero en discordia*, arbitrator.

discoteca f. Record collection (colección). || Record library: *la discoteca de la B.B.C.*, the record library of the B.B.C. || Record rack (soporte). || Discothèque (salón de baile).

discreción f. Discretion, prudence, tact, circumspection (prudencia, tacto). || Discretion (no divulgación). || Wit (ingenio). || — *A (la) discreción de*, at the discretion of, at [s.o.'s] discretion. || MIL. *¡Descanso a discreción!*, stand easy! || *Vino a discreción*, as much wine as one wants, unlimited wine.

discrecional adj. Discretionary, discretional: *poder discrecional*, discretionary power. || Optional (facultativo). || Request: *parada discrecional*, request stop. || *Servicio discrecional*, private, special (autobuses).

discrecionalmente adv. At one's discretion.

discrepancia f. Discrepancy: *discrepancia de ideas, de dos textos*, discrepancy between ideas, between two texts. || Disagreement, difference of opinion (desacuerdo).

discrepante adj. Discrepant. || Disagreeing, differing.

discrepar v. intr. To differ: *nuestras opiniones discrepan*, our opinions differ. || To disagree, to differ in opinion, to hold differing opinions (dos o más personas). || To disagree (no estar de acuerdo).

discretear v. intr. To try to be witty (dárselas de ingenioso).

discreteo m. Show of wit (ingenio).

discreto, ta adj. Discreet (reservado). || Unobtrusive, modest (poco visible). || Discreet, prudent, cautious, tactful, circumspect (cuerdo). || Witty (ingenioso). || Moderate, reasonable, average: *una inteligencia discreta*, an average intelligence. || Sober (traje). || Subdued, sober (color). || MAT. y MED. Discrete.

— M. y f. Discreet person (reservado). || Discreet *o* prudent *o* tactful *o* circumspect person (cuerdo). || Witty person, wit (ingenioso). || Superior's assistant and adviser (en una comunidad religiosa).

discriminación f. Discrimination.

discriminante m. MAT. Discriminant.

discriminar v. tr. To discriminate (distinguir). || To discriminate against (por motivos raciales, etc.).

discriminatorio, ria adj. Discriminatory.

disculpa f. Apology (por una ofensa). || Excuse: *tiene disculpa por ser joven*, he has the excuse of being young, his excuse is that he's young; *esta falta no tiene disculpa*, there is no excuse for this mistake. || — *Dar disculpas*, to make excuses. || *Pedir disculpas a alguien*, to apologize to s.o., to offer one's apologies to s.o.

disculpable adj. Excusable, pardonable.

disculpar v. tr. To excuse, to forgive: *disculpe mi retraso*, forgive my delay. || To excuse: *su inexperiencia le disculpa*, his inexperience excuses him.

— V. pr. To apologize, to excuse o.s.: *disculparse por su retraso*, to apologize for one's delay.

discurrir v. intr. To think, to reflect, to ponder, to meditate (reflexionar): *discurrir en*, to think about, to reflect on, to ponder, to meditate on. || To speak, to discourse (hablar). || To roam, to walk [about] (andar). || To flow, to run (líquidos). || To pass (tiempo). || To go by (la vida). || To go on (una reunión).

— V. tr. To invent, to think up, to devise (inventar).

discursante m. Speaker.

discursar v. intr. To discourse (*sobre*, on), to speak (*sobre*, about).

discursear v. intr. FAM. To spout, to make a speech.

discursista m. y f. Windbag (parlanchín).

discursivo, va adj. Thoughtful, reflective, meditative. || Discursive: *método discursivo*, discursive method.

discurso m. Speech: *pronunciar un discurso en el Parlamento*, to deliver a speech in Parliament. || Ratiocination, reasoning (raciocinio). || Discourse, dissertation (escrito). || Course (del tiempo). || Meditation (meditación).

discusión f. Discussion (normal). || Argument, dispute (muy fuerte): *una discusión acalorada*, a heated argument. || — *En discusión*, in debate (debatido), under discussion, pending, at issue (sin decidir). || *Eso no admite discusión*, there can be no argument about that.

discutible adj. Debatable, disputable. || Questionable, doubtful (dudoso).

discutido, da adj. Controversial.

discutidor, ra adj. Fond of discussion (aficionado a la discusión). || Argumentative (que lo discute todo).

— M. y f. Arguer.

discutir v. tr. To discuss, to debate: *discutir el pro y el contra de una propuesta*, to discuss the pros and cons of a proposal. || To argue about *o* over (argumentar): *discutir el precio del coche*, to argue over the price of the car. || To question, to contest: *discutir las órdenes de alguien*, to question s.o.'s orders. || *Un*

libro muy discutido, a much-discussed *o* much-talked-about book.
— V. intr. To discuss, to talk about: *discutir de* or *sobre política*, to discuss politics. || To argue (argumentar). || *¡No discutas!*, don't argue!
disecación f. Dissection. || Stuffing (de un animal muerto).
disecador, ra m. y f. Dissector. || Taxidermist (el que conserva animales).
disecar v. tr. To dissect (un cadáver, una planta). || To stuff (conservar un animal muerto). || FIG. To dissect, to analyse (analizar).
disección f. Dissection. || Stuffing (de un animal muerto).
disector m. Dissector. || Taxidermist (el que conserva animales).
diseminación f. Dissemination, spreading.
diseminar v. tr. To disseminate, to scatter, to spread.
— V. pr. To spread.
disensión f. Dissidence, disagreement, dissent (disentimiento). || Quarrel (riña). || — Pl. Discord, *sing.*, strife, *sing.*, dissension, *sing.*
disenso m. Dissidence, disagreement.
disentería f. MED. Dysentery.
disentérico, ca adj. MED. Dysenteric.
— M. y f. Person suffering from dysentery.
disentimiento m. Dissidence, disagreement, dissent (desacuerdo).
disentir* v. intr. To disagree, to differ: *disentimos en esto*, we disagree on that. || To dissent, to disagree: *disentir de la opinión general*, to dissent from *o* to disagree with general opinion. || To differ: *nuestras opiniones disienten*, our opinions differ.
diseñador, ra m. y f. Designer.
diseñar v. tr. To design.
diseño m. Design, sketch. || [Brief] description, outline, sketch (por palabra).
disertación f. Dissertation, lecture, discourse (conferencia). || Dissertation, disquisition (escrito).
disertador, ra o **disertante** adj. Dissertative.
— M. y f. Lecturer, discourser (conferenciante).
disertar v. intr. To discourse, to dissert, to lecture (hablar). || To discourse, to dissertate (escribir).
diserto, ta adj. Fluent, eloquent.
disfasia f. Dysphasia (dificultad en el habla).
disforme adj. Deformed (deformado). || Shapeless (sin forma). || Enormous (enorme). || Disproportionate, out of proportion (desproporcionado).
disfraz m. Disguise. || Fancy dress (traje). || Mask (máscara). || FIG. Disguisement, dissimulation (disimulación). | Pretence, appearance (apariencia): *bajo el disfraz de*, under the pretence of. || — *Baile de disfraces*, fancy dress ball. || *Sin disfraz*, plainly: *hablar sin disfraz*, to speak plainly.
disfrazado, da adj. *Disfrazado de*, disguised as.
disfrazar v. tr. To disguise. || FIG. To disguise: *disfrazar la voz*, to disguise one's voice. | To conceal, to hide, to disguise (la verdad). | To dissemble (con malos designios). | To disguise, to dissimulate, to hide, to conceal (los sentimientos, etc.). || *Asesinato disfrazado de suicidio*, murder made to look like suicide.
— V. pr. To disguise o.s., to dress up: *disfrazarse de chino*, to disguise o.s. as a Chinaman.
disfrutar v. tr. To own, to possess, to enjoy (poseer). || To receive (una renta). || To enjoy (la salud). || To make the most of: *¡disfrútelo!*, make the most of it!; *disfrutar sus vacaciones*, to make the most of one's holidays.
— V. intr. To enjoy, to have the benefit of (sacar provecho): *disfrutar de* or *con la renta de una finca*, to enjoy the income from a property. || To enjoy, to have, to possess (de salud, favor, herencia). || To enjoy o.s., to have a good time: *he disfrutado mucho en esta ciudad*, I've enjoyed myself immensely *o* I've had a very good time in this city. || To enjoy (gozar de): *madre que disfruta de la compañía de sus hijos*, mother who enjoys the company of her children. || *Disfrutar con la música*, to enjoy listening to music, to take pleasure in listening to music.
disfrute m. Enjoyment. || Benefit (provecho). || Use (uso). || Possession.
disfumar v. tr. To stump (difumar).
disfumino m. Stump (difumino).
disgregación f. Disintegration (desintegración). || Dispersion, breaking-up (dispersión).
disgregante adj. Disintegrating. || Dispersing.
disgregar v. tr. To disintegrate: *rocas disgregadas por las heladas*, rocks disintegrated by the frosts. || To disperse, to break up: *disgregar la muchedumbre*, to disperse the crowd.
— V. pr. To disintegrate. || To disperse, to break up.
disgustado, da adj. Angry, annoyed, displeased: *disgustado con* or *de uno*, angry with s.o.; *disgustado con* or *de una cosa*, angry about sth. || Disappointed (decepcionado): *disgustado con la actitud del ministro*, disappointed by the minister's attitude. || FAM. *Estoy disgustado con este coche*, I'm not pleased with this car.
disgustar v. tr. To displease: *tu carta me disgustó*, your letter displeased me. || To annoy (contrariar). || To anger, to make angry (enfadar). || *Me disgusta este olor*, I don't like this smell, I dislike this smell.
— V. pr. To get *o* to become angry: *disgustarse con uno por una tontería*, to get angry with s.o. over a trifle. || To fall out, to make each other angry (enfadarse dos personas). || To be annoyed: *se disgustará si no la invita*, she'll be annoyed if you don't invite her. || To be displeased (molestarse). || To have had enough, to be tired (hartarse).
disgusto m. Annoyance, anger (enfado): *no pudo ocultar su disgusto*, he was unable to hide his annoyance. || Displeasure (desagrado). || Misfortune, [piece of] bad luck (revés): *ha tenido muchos disgustos*, he has suffered many misfortunes, he has had a lot of bad luck. || Trouble, difficulty (molestia). || Sorrow, pain, grief, blow (pesadumbre): *la muerte de su madre le dio un gran disgusto*, the death of his mother caused him great sorrow *o* grief, his mother's death was a great blow to him. || Repugnance, repulsion (tedio, repulsión). || Quarrel, argument, row (desavenencia). || — *A disgusto*, unwillingly, against one's will, reluctantly, with displeasure. || *Estar* or *hallarse a disgusto en*, to be ill at ease in, to be unhappy in. || *Llevarse un gran disgusto*, to be very upset. || FIG. y FAM. *Matar a disgustos a uno*, to drive s.o. mad, to make one's life a misery. || *Tener disgustos con uno*, to have trouble *o* difficulty with s.o.
disidencia f. Dissidence, disagreement. || REL. Dissent.
disidente adj. Dissident, dissentient.
— M. y f. Dissident (en política, etc.). || Dissenter, nonconformist (en religión).
disidir v. intr. To dissent.
disilábico, ca o **disílabo, ba** adj. Disyllabic, dissyllabic.
— M. Disyllable, dissyllable.
disimetría f. Dissymmetry.
disimétrico, ca adj. Dissymmetric, dissymmetrical.
disímil adj. Dissimilar.
disimilación f. Dissimilation.
disimilar v. tr. To dissimilate.
disimilitud f. Dissimilitude, dissimilarity.
disimulable adj. Concealable (ocultable). || Excusable, pardonable (disculpable).
disimulación f. Dissimulation, hiding, concealment, disguising (ocultación). || Excusing, pardoning, pardon (disculpa).
disimuladamente adv. Furtively.
disimulado, da adj. Dissembling, who dissembles (hipócrita). || Hidden (oculto). || — *A lo disimulado* or *a la disimulada*, furtively. || *Hacerse el disimulado*, to feign ignorance, to act dumb.
disimulador, ra adj. Dissimulating, dissembling.
— M. y f. Dissimulator, dissembler.
disimular v. tr. To hide, to conceal (ocultar). || To disguise, to dissimulate, to dissemble, to hide, to conceal: *disimular su alegría*, to hide one's joy. || To excuse, to pardon, to overlook (disculpar).
— V. intr. To dissemble, to pretend.
— V. pr. To conceal o.s. || To be concealed.
disimulo m. Hiding, concealment (ocultación). || Indulgence, leniency, tolerance. || Dissimulation, disguising (fingimiento). || — *Con disimulo*, furtively. || *Hablar sin disimulo*, to speak plainly.
disipable adj. Dispersable (nubes). || Easily dispelled (ilusiones). || Easily squandered (una fortuna).
disipación f. Dissipation, squandering, wasting (del dinero). || Dissipating, dispersion (de nubes). || Dispelling (de ilusiones). || Dissipation (libertinaje).
disipado, da adj. Dissipated. || Dissipated, dissolute (persona, vida). || Restless, unruly (alumno). || Wasteful (derrochador).
disipador, ra adj. Squandering, wasteful, prodigal.
— M. y f. Spendthrift, squanderer.
disipar v. tr. To dissipate, to disperse, to scatter, to dispel: *el sol disipó las nubes*, the sun dissipated the clouds. || To dispel (dudas, temores, ilusiones). || To destroy (las esperanzas). || To squander, to fritter away, to dissipate (una fortuna). || To waste (energía). || To clear up (un malentendido). || To allay (las sospechas).
— V. pr. To dissipate, to disperse, to be dispelled (nubes, etc.). || To clear up, to dissipate (una tormenta). || To vanish (el humo). || To be dispelled, to vanish (ilusiones, sospechas, dudas). || To be squandered, to be frittered away (fortuna). || To fail, to flag (energías).
dislate m. Blunder, bloomer (disparate). || Absurdity (absurdo).
dislocación f. Dislocation (de huesos). || FIG. Dismembering, dismemberment (de un imperio, un estado, etc.). || Breaking-up (de una reunión, un cortejo, etc.). || Distortion, misrepresentation (de hechos). || GEOL. Slip, fault.
dislocadura f. V. DISLOCACIÓN.
dislocar v. tr. To dislocate, to put out of joint (los huesos). || FIG. To dismember: *dislocar un imperio*, to dismember an empire. | To distort, to misrepresent (desfigurar). || FIG. y FAM. *Estar dislocado de alegría*, to be beside o.s. with joy.
— V. pr. To dislocate: *dislocarse el brazo*, to dislocate one's arm. || To be dislocated, to come out of joint (los huesos). || To break up (separarse).
disloque m. FAM. Tops, top notch, first rate (muy bueno): *esta película es el disloque*, this film is first rate *o* is the tops. | Last straw, end, limit (el colmo): *es el disloque*, that's the end.

disminución f. Fall, drop, decrease (de temperatura). || Decrease, reduction (de velocidad). || Reduction, diminution (de las dimensiones). || Decrease, fall (de población). || Cutting down, diminution (de cargas financieras, de raciones). || Decrease, diminution (de las fuerzas de uno). || Reduction, drop, fall, lowering (de precios). || Depreciation (del valor). || MED. Assuagement (del dolor). | Abatement (de la fiebre). || *Ir en disminución*, to diminish (las fuerzas), to fall (la temperatura, los precios), to decrease (la velocidad, la población).

disminuir* v. tr. To lower, to cause to fall *o* drop (la temperatura). || To reduce, to decrease (la velocidad). || To reduce, to diminish (las dimensiones). || To decrease, to cause a decrease in (la población). || To cut down, to curtail, to reduce (las cargas financieras, las raciones). || To decrease, to diminish (las fuerzas de uno). || To reduce, to lower, to bring down (los precios). || To lower, to bring down (el valor). || To relieve, to assuage (el dolor). || To diminish, to weaken (la autoridad, el prestigio). || To lighten (la pena). || To damp, to diminish (el entusiasmo).

— V. intr. To diminish (en altura, las raciones, las fuerzas). || To fall, to drop, to go down (la temperatura, los precios). || To slacken (la velocidad). || To decrease (la población). || To relax (el frío). || To grow shorter (el día). || To decline (la luz). || To fall off, to dwindle (el número, los beneficios). || To abate (la fiebre). || To decline (las fuerzas, la salud). || To fail (la memoria, la vista). || To wane (la fama).

disnea f. MED. Dyspnoea [U.S., dyspnea].

disociable adj. Dissociable.

disociación f. Dissociation.

disociar v. tr. To dissociate.

disolubilidad f. QUÍM. Solubility, dissolubility.

disoluble adj. Soluble, dissoluble.

disolución f. Dissolution (de un cuerpo, de un matrimonio, de una sociedad, del parlamento). || Breaking-up (de una manifestación, asociación, reunión). || AUT. Rubber solution (para un neumático). || FIG. Dissoluteness, profligacy (de las costumbres). || QUÍM. Solution, dissolution.

disoluto, ta adj. Dissolute, profligate.

— M. y f. Dissolute person, debauchee.

disolvente adj. Dissolvent, solvent.

— M. QUÍM. Dissolvent, solvent. || Thinner (para pinturas).

disolver* v. tr. To dissolve (cuerpo, matrimonio, sociedad, parlamento). || FIG. To break up (manifestación, reunión). || To annul (contrato).

— V. pr. To dissolve. || To be dissolved (una sociedad). || To break up (reunión).

disonancia f. MÚS. Dissonance. || FIG. Dissonance, lack of harmony, disharmony (falta de armonía). | Discord, disagreement (desacuerdo).

disonante adj. MÚS. Dissonant, discordant. || FIG. Out of keeping, discordant.

disonar* v. intr. MÚS. To be dissonant *o* discordant, to be out of tune. || FIG. To lack harmony (no armonizar). | To disagree (no estar de acuerdo).

dispar adj. Unlike, different, disparate.

disparada f. *Amer.* Flight (fuga). || — *Amer.* FAM. *A la disparada*, full pelt, flat out, hell for leather (a todo correr). | *De una disparada*, straight away, at once (inmediatamente). | *Tomar la disparada*, to take to one's heels.

disparadamente adv. Hurriedly, precipitously (rápidamente). || Suddenly (de pronto). || Foolishly (disparatadamente). || *Salió disparadamente*, he was off like a shot, he dashed *o* bolted out.

disparado, da adj. V. DISPARAR.

disparador m. Firer (el que dispara). || Trigger (en las armas). || Shutter release (de cámara fotográfica). || Escapement (de reloj). || FIG. y FAM. *Poner a uno en el disparador*, to push s.o. too far, to provoke s.o.

disparar v. tr. To fire: *disparar un cañón, un tiro*, to fire a cannon, a shot. || To fire, to shoot (un arco, una flecha). || To fire *o* to shoot at: *disparar a alguien*, to fire at s.o. || To hurl, to throw (arrojar una piedra, etc.). || DEP. To shoot at goal (el balón). || — FIG. y FAM. *Estar disparado*, to be [all] on edge. | *Salir disparado*, to go off like a shot [from a gun], to bolt *o* to fly *o* to dart *o* to dash off (salir corriendo), to fly, to be flung *o* hurled: *salir disparado de su asiento*, to fly out of one's seat.

— V. intr. To fire, to shoot: *disparar contra el enemigo*, to fire at *o* on the enemy, to shoot at the enemy. || FIG. To talk nonsense (decir tonterías), to act foolishly, to blunder (hacer tonterías). || *Amer.* To dash off, to bolt.

— V. pr. To go off (un arma de fuego). || To shoot *o* to rush *o* to dash off (arrojarse). || To bolt, to run away (un caballo). || To fly off, to shoot off (desprenderse violentamente). || To race (un motor). || FIG. y FAM. To fly off the handle (enfadarse).

disparatadamente adv. Foolishly, absurdly, senselessly.

disparatado, da adj. Foolish, absurd, senseless (absurdo). || FAM. Absurd, excessive (excesivo).

disparatar v. intr. To talk nonsense (decir disparates). || To blunder, to act foolishly (hacer un disparate).

disparate m. Silly thing, foolish *o* senseless act, act of folly (acción irreflexiva). || Blunder, mistake, bloomer (fam.), boob (fam.): *libro lleno de disparates*, book full of blunders. || Silly thing, foolish remark: *soltar un disparate*, to say sth. silly, to make a foolish remark. || — Pl. Nonsense, *sing.*: *decir disparates*, to talk nonsense. || — *¡Qué disparate!*, how absurd!, how ridiculous! || FIG. *Un disparate*, a heck of a lot (mucho).

disparejo, ja adj. Different, disparate, unlike (distinto). || Uneven, unequal (desigual).

disparidad f. Disparity, difference, dissimilarity.

disparo m. Firing (acción de disparar un arma). || Shot (tiro). || Shot (en el fútbol). || FIG. Silly thing, foolish *o* senseless act (disparate). | Attack: *los disparos de los periodistas se centraron en él*, the newspapermen's attacks were directed against him || MAR. *Disparo de aviso* or *de advertencia*, warning shot.

dispendio m. Waste, squandering.

dispendioso, sa adj. Expensive, costly (caro).

dispensa f. Exemption, dispensation (*de*, from). || REL. Dispensation. || *Dispensa de edad*, waiving of age limit.

dispensable adj. Exemptable. || REL. Dispensable. || Pardonable, excusable (perdonable).

dispensación f. Dispensation, exemption.

dispensar v. tr. To confer (honores). || To grant, to bestow (mercedes). || To show (interés). || To have (admiración). || To pay (atención). || To give (recibimiento, ayuda). || To dispense, to administer (justicia, asistencia médica). || To exempt, to excuse (eximir). || REL. To dispense. || To forgive, to excuse, to pardon: *dispénseme por llegar tan tarde*, forgive me for arriving so late. || — *Dispensar a uno [de] algo*, to excuse s.o. from sth. || *Dispense usted*, forgive me, excuse me, [I'm] sorry.

dispensaría f. *Amer.* Clinic.

dispensario m. Clinic, dispensary (consultorio).

dispepsia f. MED. Dyspepsia.

dispéptico, ca adj./s. Dyspeptic.

dispersar v. tr. To disperse, to scatter (diseminar). || To disperse (rayos luminosos). || To break up, to disperse (una manifestación). || MIL. To disperse, to scatter, to put to flight. || FIG. To divide (esfuerzos, atención, actividad, etc.).

— V. pr. To disperse, to scatter. || To break up, to disperse (una muchedumbre). || MIL. To spread out, to deploy (desplegarse).

dispersión f. Dispersion. || FIG. Division (de la atención, actividad, etc.)

dispersivo, va adj. Dispersive.

disperso, sa adj. Dispersed, scattered. || MIL. *En orden disperso*, in disorder, in disarray.

displacer* v. tr. To displease.

displicencia f. Indifference, coolness, coldness (en el trato). || Indifference, lack of enthusiasm (desgana). || Nonchalance (descuido). || Despair, discouragement (desaliento). || *Trabajar con displicencia*, to work unenthusiastically *o* reluctantly.

displicente adj. Unpleasant, disagreeable: *tono displicente*, unpleasant tone. || Indifferent, unenthusiastic (desganado).

disponer* v. tr. To arrange, to dispose: *disponer las naves en orden de batalla*, to arrange the ships in battle order. || To set out, to lay out: *disponer los platos en la mesa*, to set out the plates on the table. || To prepare, to get ready (preparar). || To order (ordenar). || To provide, to stipulate: *la ley dispone que*, the law provides that. || MIL. To form up, to line up. || *Disponer la mesa*, to set *o* to lay the table.

— V. intr. To have, to have at one's disposal, to have available: *no disponemos de mucho tiempo*, we haven't a lot of time. || To have the use, to have at one's disposal: *todavía no puede disponer de sus bienes*, he cannot yet have the use of his goods. || To dispose (vender, dar, etc.): *disponer de una finca*, to dispose of an estate. || To order: *disponer de la vida de uno*, to order one's own life. || — *Disponer de dinero*, to have money in hand *o* at one's command. || *Disponga de mí a su gusto*, I am entirely at your disposal. || *Los medios de que dispone*, the means available to him.

— V. pr. To prepare, to get ready: *disponerse a* or *para marcharse*, to prepare to leave. || MIL. To form up.

disponibilidad f. Availability. || — Pl. COM. Resources, financial assets, available funds, cash (*sing.*) on hand (dinero). | Available stocks (mercancías). || *En disponibilidad*, unattached, unassigned (empleado).

disponible adj. Available, at [s.o.'s] disposal (utilizable). || Unoccupied, unengaged, disengaged, free (libre). || Spare, free (tiempo). || On hand, available (dinero). || Available, vacant: *dos plazas disponibles*, two available seats. || Vacant (puesto). || Unattached, on call (militar, empleado).

disposición f. Arrangement, disposition, disposal (arreglo). || Layout: *la disposición de los cuartos de un piso*, the layout of the rooms of a flat. || JUR. Ordinance, order, decree (ley). | Provision (cláusula). || FIG. Natural aptitude, gift, talent, disposition (don): *tener disposición para la música*, to have a gift for music. | Disposition, bent, inclination (propensión). | Disposition (de ánimo). || Disposal: *tener la libre disposición de sus bienes*, to have one's goods entirely at one's disposal. || MIL. Formation (de tropas). || — Pl. Arrangements, preparations. | Steps (medidas). || — *A la disposición de*, at the disposal of. || *A su disposición*, at your service, at your disposal. || *A su libre disposición*, [I am] entirely at your service *o* disposal. || *Disposición de ánimo*, attitude, frame of mind, disposition. || *Disposición escénica*, stage positioning [of actors]. || *Disposiciones legales*, statutory provisions. || *Disposiciones testamentarias*, dispositions of a will. || *Estar* or *hallarse en disposición de*, to be ready to. || *Estoy a la dispocisión de usted* or *a su disposición*, I am at your service *o* disposal. || *Salvo disposición contraria*, unless otherwise provided. || *Tener la libre disposición de*, to be free to dispose of. || *Tomar las disposiciones para*, to make preparations *o* arrangements for (con sustantivo), to take steps to (con verbo). || *Última disposición*, last will and testament.

dispositivo m. Device (de una máquina). || Appliance, device, gadget (aparato).

dispuesto, ta adj. Ready (listo): *dispuesto para la marcha*, ready to leave. || Arranged, disposed (arreglado). || Disposed, inclined, prepared, willing (inclinado). || Helpful, who is always willing to help (servicial). || Clever, go-ahead (vivo, hábil). || — *Bien, mal dispuesto con uno*, well-disposed, ill-disposed towards s.o. || *Lo dispuesto*, the provisions, what is stipulated: *en cumplimiento de lo dispuesto en el artículo*, in accordance with the provisions of *o* with what is stipulated in the article. || *Poco dispuesto a*, unwilling to, reluctant to.

disputa f. Dispute, argument (discusión). || Dispute, controversy (controversia). || — *Sin disputa*, indubitably, indisputably, undoubtedly (indudablemente). || *Tener una disputa*, to quarrel, to have an argument.

disputable adj. Disputable, open to dispute, debatable, questionable.

disputador, ra adj. Disputatious, argumentative, quarrelsome.

— M. y f. Disputer, disputatious person, wrangler.

disputar v. tr. To contend *o* to compete for, to dispute: *disputar el primer puesto a uno*, to contend with s.o. for the first place. || DEP. To play (jugar).

— V. intr. To dispute, to argue: *disputar por*, to dispute, to argue about *o* over.

— V. pr. To contend *o* to compete for, to dispute: *se disputan el premio*, they are contending for the prize. || To be debated, to be discussed (discutirse). || To be contested, to be disputed (ser disputado). || DEP. To be played (jugarse).

disquisición f. Disquisition. || — Pl. Digressions.

disruptor m. ELECTR. Circuit breaker, spark breaker, cutout.

distancia f. Distance: *a dos kilómetros de distancia*, at a distance of two kilometres. || Difference (diferencia): *hay* or *va mucha distancia de las promesas a los hechos*, there's a lot of difference between promises and actions. || FIG. Distance: *guardar las distancias*, to keep one's distance. || — *Acortar las distancias*, to cut down *o* to reduce the distance. || *A distancia* or *a la distancia*, at *o* from a distance. || *A respetable* or *respetuosa distancia*, at *o* from a respectable distance. || *Avión de larga distancia*, long-haul *o* long distance aeroplane. || *Distancia focal*, focal length. || *Mantener* or *tener a distancia*, to keep at a distance.

distanciado, da adj. Remote (remoto). || Distant (distante). || Separated (separado). || Isolated (aislado). || Far apart (muy separados).

distanciamiento m. Spacing out (espaciamiento). || Remoteness, isolation (aislamiento). || FIG. Distance.

distanciar v. tr. To place farther apart *o* at a distance, to separate (separar, apartar). || To cause a rift between (reñir). || To leave behind, to outdistance (dejar atrás): *un corredor que distancia a su rival*, a runner who leaves his rival behind. || — *Acompañarte a tu casa me distancia de mi camino*, accompanying you to your house takes me out of my way. || *Estar distanciado de su familia*, to be estranged from one's family, to no longer see one's family.

— V. pr. To become separated. || To get ahead (de un seguidor). || To fall out (disgustarse). || To become estranged, to drift away, to no longer see: *se ha distanciado de sus amigos*, he has become estranged from his friends, he has drifted away from his friends.

distante adj. Distant, far (espacio). || Distant, remote, far-off (espacio y tiempo): *en época distante*, in a distant epoch. || FIG. Distant. || *La ciudad está distante de cincuenta kilómetros*, the town is fifty kilometres away *o* is fifty kilometres distant.

distar v. intr. To be distant, to be away: *distar dos leguas*, to be two leagues distant. || To be after: *su llegada no distó de la mía más de cinco días*, his arrival was no more than five days after mine. || FIG. To be far, to be a long way: *dista mucho de ser bueno*, he's a long way from being a good man.

distender* v. tr. To slacken, to loosen (aflojar). || MED. To strain, to pull (músculo). | To distend (piel).

— V. pr. To distend, to be distended (hincharse). || To slacken (aflojarse). || To be strained (un músculo).

distensión f. Distension. || Strain (de un músculo). || Slackening (aflojamiento). || *Tener* or *sufrir una distensión*, to pull a muscle.

distico m. POÉT. Distich.

distinción f. Distinction: *hacer distinción entre*, to make a distinction between. || Distinction, honour [U.S., honor] (honor). || Distinction, refinement (refinamiento). || Deference, consideration, respect, regard, esteem (miramiento): *tratar a un superior con distinción*, to treat a superior with deference. || — *A distinción de*, unlike, in contrast to, as distinct from. || *Distinción honorífica*, honour. || *De gran distinción*, highly distinguished. || *Sin distinción*, without distinction. || *Sin distinción de edades*, irrespective of age. || *Sin distinción de personas*, without respect to persons. || *Sin distinción de raza*, without any racial discrimination.

distingo m. Reservation, qualification (salvedad). || Distinction.

distinguible adj. Distinguishable.

distinguido, da adj. Distinguished: *un escritor distinguido*, a distinguished writer. || Distinguished, refined (modales, persona). || Gentlemanly (caballero).

distinguir v. tr. To distinguish: *distinguir una cosa de otra*, to distinguish one thing from another. || To distinguish, to tell (reconocer). || To distinguish, to differenciate (diferenciar). || To mark out, to distinguish (singularizar). || To discern, to distinguish (discernir). || To pay honour *o* tribute to: *el general le distinguió ascendiéndole a coronel*, the general paid honour to him by raising him to the rank of colonel. || To honour: *me ha distinguido con su amistad*, he has honoured me with his friendship. || To show a preference for (preferir). || *Saber distinguir*, to be a good judge [of].

— V. intr. To distinguish, to discriminate.

— V. pr. To be distinguished, to differ (diferenciarse). || To distinguish o.s.: *distinguirse por su valor*, to distinguish o.s. for one's valour. || To be noticeable, to stand out: *se distingue por su belleza*, she is noticeable for her beauty. || To be audible (oírse). || To be visible (verse). || *A lo lejos se distinguía una torre*, far off a tower could be distinguished.

distintivo, va adj. Distinguishing, distinctive, characteristic: *signo distintivo*, distinguishing mark.

— M. Symbol: *el caduceo es el distintivo de la profesión médica*, the caduceus is the symbol of the medical profession. || Badge, emblem (emblema). || Distinctive *o* distinguishing feature *o* quality (cualidad). || Distinguishing mark (aspecto).

distinto, ta adj. Distinct (claro). || Different: *distinto a* or *de*, different from; *quiero uno distinto*, I want a different one. || — Pl. Different, various, diverse, several (varios).

distorsión f. Distortion.

distracción f. Recreation, distraction, pastime: *mi distracción favorita es la pesca*, my favourite recreation is fishing. || Form of amusement: *el cine es una distracción muy criticada*, the cinema is a much-criticized form of amusement. || Amusement, diversion, entertainment: *hay muchas distracciones en esta ciudad*, there are many amusements in this city. || Inattention, distraction, absentmindedness (descuido). || Dissipation, debauchery (libertinaje).

distraer* v. tr. To distract (apartar la atención). || To amuse, to entertain (entretener). || To take s.o.'s mind off (de una pena, dolor): *distraer a uno de su preocupación*, to take s.o.'s mind off his worry. || To take [s.o.] away from, to divert (de un trabajo). || To embezzle, to misappropriate (fondos). || MIL. *Distraer al enemigo*, to distract the enemy.

— V. intr. To be relaxing, to be entertaining.

— V. pr. To amuse *o* to enjoy o.s. (divertirse). || To enjoy: *distraerse con la lectura*, to enjoy reading. || To pass the time (pasar el tiempo): *mientras esperaba se distrajo leyendo una revista*, while he waited he read a magazine to pass the time. || To be inattentive, to let one's mind wander, not to pay attention (descuidarse).

distraído, da adj. Amusing, entertaining (divertido): *una película distraída*, an amusing film. || Casual: *una mirada distraída*, a casual glance. || Absentminded (persona). || Inattentive, absentminded (desatento). || Dissolute (disoluto). || *Amer.* Untidy, slovenly (desaseado).

— M. y f. Absentminded person, scatterbrain. || *Hacerse el distraído*, to pretend not to notice.

distribución f. Distribution. || Delivery (del correo, etc.): *distribución de la leche*, milk delivery. || Giving out (de prospectos). || AUT. e IMPR. Distribution. || Layout (plano de una casa). || Service, supply (del agua, del gas). || Sharing out (de dividendos, del trabajo). || *Distribución de premios*, prizegiving.

distribuidor, ra adj. Distributing, distributive.

— M. y f. Distributor. || — M. AUT. Distributor. || Dealer, agent (de un producto comercial). || *Distribuidor automático*, slot machine [U.S., vending machine].

distribuir* v. tr. To distribute (repartir): *distribuir dinero entre los pobres*, to distribute money among the poor. || To deliver: *distribuir el correo*, to deliver the mail. || To allot: *distribuir trabajo a los obreros*, to allot work to the workers. || To award, to give out (premios). || To design, to lay out (la disposición de una casa). || To give out (prospectos). || To deal out (golpes). || To supply (el agua, el gas).

distributivo, va adj. Distributive.

distributor, ra o **distribuyente** adj. Distributing.

— M. y f. Distributor.

distrito m. District. || *Distrito postal, federal*, postal, federal district.

distrofia f. MED. Dystrophy.
disturbar v. tr. To disturb.
disturbio m. Disturbance (alteración de la tranquilidad). || Disturbance, trouble (desorden).
disuadir v. tr. To dissuade (*de*, from).
disuasión f. Dissuasion. || MIL. *Fuerza* or *poder de disuasión*, striking force (capacidad), deterrent (arma).
disuasivo, va adj. Dissuasive. || MIL. *Fuerza disuasiva* or *poder disuasivo*, striking force (capacidad), deterrent (arma).
disuasorio, ria adj. V. DISUASIVO.
disuelto, ta adj. Dissolved.
disúrico, ca adj. MED. Dysuric.
disyunción f. Disjunction.
disyuntiva f. Alternative. || *No tengo otra disyuntiva*, I have no other choice *o* alternative.
disyuntivo, va adj. Disjunctive.
disyuntor m. ELECTR. Circuit breaker, cutout.
dita f. Surety, bond (garantía). || *Amer.* Debt (deuda) || *Vender a dita*, to sell on credit.
ditirámbico, ca adj. Dithyrambic.
ditirambo m. Dithyramb.
diuresis f. MED. Diuresis.
diurético, ca adj./s.m. MED. Diuretic.
diurno, na adj. Diurnal, daily.
— M. REL. Diurnal (libro).
diuturnidad f. Diuturnity.
diva f. POÉT. Goddess. || MÚS. Diva, prima donna.
divagación f. Digression (al hablar). || — Pl. Wanderings.
divagador, ra adj. Digressive. || Wandering.
divagar v. intr. To wander, to roam. || To digress, to ramble (al hablar).
diván m. Divan, couch (canapé). || Diwan, divan (consejo y gobierno turco). || Diwan, divan (poesía oriental).
divergencia f. Divergence.
divergente adj. Divergent. || FIG. Divergent, differing.
divergir v. intr. To diverge. || FIG. To diverge, to differ. || To diverge, to fork (carreteras).
diversidad f. Diversity, variety.
diversificación f. Diversification. || Diversity (diversidad).
diversificar v. tr. To diversify, to vary.
— V. pr. To be diversified. || To vary (variar).
diversiforme adj. Diversiform.
diversión f. Recreation, distraction, pastime: *la caza es su diversión preferida*, hunting is his favourite pastime. || Amusement, diversion, entertainment: *hay pocas diversiones en este pueblo*, there are few amusements in this town. || MIL. Diversion. || *Servir de diversión*, to keep one amused, to be a pastime.
diverso, sa adj. Diverse. || Different (diferente). || — Pl. Several, different, various: *en diversas oportunidades*, on several occasions; *artículos de diversas categorías*, articles of different kinds. || Varied (variado): *el orador habló sobre los temas más diversos*, the orator spoke on the most varied themes. || Miscellaneous (extractos). || Sundry (gastos). || Several, various (razones). || *Artículos diversos*, sundries.
divertido, da adj. Amusing, entertaining, funny: *una película divertida*, an entertaining film. || Funny (chiste). || Funny, amusing (persona).
divertimento m. MÚS. Divertissement.
divertimiento m. (P. us.). Diversion, amusement.
divertir* v. tr. To amuse, to entertain: *ese cuento me divirtió muchísimo*, that tale amused me immensely. || To distract, to divert (distraer la atención): *una estratagema para divertir al enemigo*, a stratagem to distract the enemy.
— V. pr. To amuse o.s. (distraerse): *divertirse pintando*, to amuse o.s. painting. || To enjoy o.s., to have a good time (pasarlo bien): *divertirse a costa de uno*, to enjoy o.s. at s.o.'s expense. || To be diverted *o* distracted (la atención, etc.).
dividendo m. MAT. y COM. Dividend. || — COM. *Dividendo acumulado, provisional*, accrued, interim dividend. | *Sin dividendos*, ex-dividend.
dividir v. tr. To divide: *dividir 60 por 6*, to divide 60 by 6. || To divide, to separate: *los Pirineos dividen España de Francia*, the Pyrenees separate Spain from France. || To divide, to disunite. || To split, to divide: *dividir un pastel en cuatro porciones*, to divide a cake into four portions; *el asunto dividió el pueblo en dos bandos*, the affair divided the population into two camps. || To divide [out], to split, to share [out] (repartir): *dividir un pastel entre cuatro personas*, to share a cake out between four people. || *Divide y vencerás*, divide and conquer.
dividivi m. BOT. Divi-divi.
divieso m. Boil, furuncle (furúnculo).
divinatorio, ria adj. Divinatory.
divinidad f. Divinity, deity (del paganismo). || God (Dios). || Divinity, godhead (naturaleza). || — FIG. *¡Qué divinidad!*, how divine! | *¡Es una divinidad!*, it's (she's, etc.) gorgeous *o* divine!
divinización f. Deification. || Glorification (ensalzamiento).
divinizar v. tr. To deify. || FIG. To exalt, to glorify.
divino, na adj. Divine: *castigo divino*, divine punishment. || FIG. Divine, lovely, gorgeous (precioso).
divisa f. Emblem, ensign: *el águila es la divisa del país*, the eagle is the country's emblem. || COM. Currency: *el dólar es una divisa muy fuerte*, the dollar is a very strong currency. || HERÁLD. Motto (lema). | Device (emblema). || TAUR. Owner's coloured rosette fixed to bull's neck. || — Pl. COM. Foreign exchange *o* currency: *control de divisas*, foreign exchange control.
divisar v. tr. To make out, to distinguish, to discern.
divisibilidad f. Divisibility.
divisible f. Divisible.
división f. Division. || GRAM. Hyphen, dash (guión). || MIL. Division. || FIG. Difference, division, divergence: *división de opiniones*, a divergence of opinion. | Discord: *sembrar la división en una familia*, to sow discord within a family. | Split (de un partido).
divisional o **divisionario, ria** adj. Divisional.
diviso, sa adj. Divided, split.
divisor, ra adj. Dividing.
— M. Divider. || MAT. Divisor. | Factor: *máximo común divisor*, highest common factor.
divisorio, ria adj. Dividing: *pared divisoria*, dividing wall. || *Línea divisoria de las aguas*, watershed [U.S., divide].
divo, va adj. POÉT. Divine.
— M. y f. FIG. Star (figura principal). || — M. Pagan god, deity (divinidad). || — F. V. DIVA.
divorciado, da adj. Divorced.
— M. y f. Divorcee.
divorciar v. tr. To divorce.
— V. pr. To get *o* to be divorced. || *Divorciarse de uno*, to divorce s.o., to get a divorce from s.o.
divorcio m. Divorce. || FIG. Disagreement.
divulgación f. Divulging, disclosure, divulgation (revelación). || Extension: *divulgación agrícola*, agricultural extension. || Popularizing, spreading (de una canción). || Spreading, circulation (propagación).
divulgador, ra adj. Divulging, revealing.
— M. y f. Divulger, revealer.
divulgar v. tr. To divulge, to disclose (revelar). || To spread, to circulate (propagar): *divulgar una noticia*, to spread a piece of news. || To disseminate, to spread, to popularize: *la radio ha divulgado la música clásica*, radio has popularized classical music.
— V. pr. To come out.
divulsión f. MED. Divulsion.
do m. MÚS. Do, doh (de la solfa). | C (primera nota de la escala diatónica). || — *Do de pecho*, high C. || FIG. y FAM. *Dar el do de pecho*, to surpass o.s.
— Adv. POÉT. Where (donde). | Whence (de donde).
dobladillo m. Hem (costura). || Turnup [U.S., cuff] (de los pantalones).
doblado, da adj. Doubled, double. || Bent (encorvado). || Folded (plegado). || FIG. Stocky, thickset (estatura). | Deceitful, two-faced (engañoso). || FIG. y FAM. Dead beat (agotado).
doblaje m. CINEM. Dubbing.
doblar v. tr. To fold: *doblar un papel en dos*, to fold a piece of paper in two. || To turn up (los bajos de un pantalón). || To double (duplicar): *doblar un sueldo*, to double a salary. || To bend: *doblar la rodilla, el codo*, to bend one's knee, one's elbow; *doblar una vara de hierro*, to bend an iron bar. || To turn, to go round: *doblar una esquina*, to turn a corner. || MAR. To round: *doblar un cabo*, to round a cape. || FIG. To subdue, to reduce to submission (dominar). | To make [s.o.] change his mind, to bring [s.o.] round (hacer cambiar de parecer). || To double (en el bridge). || CINEM. To dub (una película). | To double for: *en esta escena un jinete experto dobla a la estrella*, in this scene an expert horseman doubles for the star. || FIG. y FAM. To wear out (cansar mucho). || *Amer.* To shoot down (matar). || — FIG. y FAM. *Doblar a uno a palos* or *a golpes*, to beat s.o. up. || *Doblar el pico de una página*, to turn down the corner of a page. || *Le doblo la edad*, I'm twice as old as he is, I'm twice his age.
— V. intr. To double (duplicarse): *sus fuerzas doblaron en dos meses*, his strength doubled in two months. || To turn: *doblar a la derecha*, to turn right; *en ese punto la carretera dobla hacia el río*, at that point the road turns towards the river. || To toll (tocar a muerto): *las campanas están doblando por alguien*, the bells are tolling for s.o. || FIG. To give in, to yield, to submit (ceder). | TAUR. To collapse, to crumple up (el toro al morir). || To double, to play two roles (un actor).
— V. pr. To fold (plegarse). || To double (duplicarse). || To bend, to give, to buckle: *las ramas se doblan bajo el peso del fruto*, the branches give beneath the weight of the fruit. || To stoop, to bend down (persona). || FIG. To give in, to yield (ceder). || FAM. *Doblarse por la cintura*, to be in stitches (de risa).
doble adj. Double: *esta casa es doble de alta que ésa*, this house is double the height of that one; *un doble error*, a double error; *un geranio doble*, a double geranium; *doble sentido*, double meaning. || Dual (mando, nacionalidad, etc.). || Stocky, thickset (rechoncho). || Thick (fuerte): *una tela muy doble*, a very thick cloth. || FIG. Two-faced, deceitful (disimulado) || — *Con* or *de doble sentido*, ambiguous. || COM. *Contabilidad por partida doble*, double-entry bookkeeping. || *De doble fondo*, double-bottomed. || *En doble ejemplar*, in duplicate.
— M. Double: *has pagado el doble de lo que vale*, you payed double what it's worth. || Duplicate: *el doble de un acta*, the duplicate of a deed. || Carbon

copy (con papel carbón). || Fold, crease (pliegue). || Knell, toll (toque de campana). || DEP. Doubles, *pl.*: *doble caballeros* or *masculino*, men's doubles (tenis); *doble damas*, ladies' doubles; *doble mixto*, mixed doubles. || Double (cantidad doble de whisky, cerveza). || Double (en los naipes). || Double (sosia). || CINEM. Double, stand-in. || — *Doble contra sencillo*, two-to-one (apuesta). || CINEM. *Doble especial*, stunt man. || *Doble o nada*, double or quits (juego). || *El doble*, twice as much: *costar el doble*, to cost twice as much. || *El doble de la distancia*, twice *o* double the distance. || *El doble que*, twice as much as: *come el doble que tú*, he eats twice as much as you.

— Adv. Double: *ver doble*, to see double. || *Al doble*, twofold.

doblegable adj. FIG. Pliable, pliant: *carácter muy doblegable*, very pliable character.

doblegar v. tr. To fold (doblar). || To bend (curvar). || To twist (torcer). || To brandish (un arma). || FIG. To make [s.o.] give in (hacer ceder). | To humble.

— V. pr. To fold (doblarse). || To bend (encorvarse). || To twist (torcerse). || FIG. To yield, to give in (ceder).

doblemente adv. Doubly: *doblemente magnánimo*, doubly magnanimous. || FIG. Deceitfully, two-facedly (con falsedad): *actuar doblemente*, to act deceitfully.

doblete adj. Medium, medium-thick.

— M. GRAM. Doublet. || Doublet (piedra falsa).

doblez m. Fold (pliegue). || Hem (dobladillo). || — F. Deceitfulness, two-facedness, duplicity, double-dealing (falsedad).

doblón m. Doubloon (moneda antigua).

doce adj. Twelve: *los doce apóstoles*, the twelve apostles. || Twelfth: *Pío XII* (*doce*), Pius XII [the twelfth].

— M. Twelve: *en la lotería ha salido el doce*, twelve has come up in the lottery. || Twelfth: *el doce de agosto*, the twelfth of August.

— F. pl. *Las doce de la noche*, midnight, twelve o'clock at night. || *Son las doce* (*del día*), it's twelve o'clock, it's twelve noon, it's midday *o* noon.

docena f. Dozen: *una docena de ostras*, a dozen oysters. || — *A docenas*, by the dozen (venta), in dozens, by the dozen: *llegaban a docenas*, they were arriving in dozens. || FIG. *La docena del fraile*, the baker's dozen. || *Por docenas*, by the dozen.

doceno, na adj. Twelfth (duodécimo).

docente adj. Teaching: *cuerpo, personal docente*, teaching body, staff. || Educational, teaching: *centro docente*, educational centre.

dócil adj. Docile, meek, mild: *dócil de condición*, of a docile nature. || Obedient: *me gustan los niños dóciles*, I like obedient children.

docilidad f. Docility, meekness, mildness. || Obedience.

dócilmente adv. Docilely, meekly, mildly. || Obediently.

dock m. Dock (dársena). || Warehouse (almacén).

dócker m. Docker (descargador).

doctamente adv. Learnedly.

docto, ta adj. Learned, erudite (sabio). || *Muy docto en historia*, well versed in history.

— M. y f. Scholar, learned person (erudito).

doctor, ra m. y f. Doctor: *la señora de Jáuregui es doctora en filosofía*, Mrs. Jáuregui is a doctor of philosophy; *la mujer del farmacéutico es doctora*, the chemist's wife is a doctor. || — REL. *Doctor de la Iglesia*, doctor of the Church. || *Doctor honoris causa*, honorary doctor.

doctorado m. Doctorate.

doctoral adj. Doctoral. || Pompous, pedantic: *habla siempre en tono doctoral*, he always speaks in a pompous tone.

doctorando m. Candidate for a doctor's degree.

doctorar v. tr. To confer a doctor's degree on.

— V. pr. To take one's doctorate (hacer el doctorado). || To receive one's doctorate (obtener el doctorado).

doctorear v. intr. FAM. To talk pompously.

doctrina f. Doctrine: *la doctrina aristotélica, budista*, Aristotelian, Buddhist doctrine. || Teaching (enseñanza). || Knowledge, learning (ciencia). || Catechism (catecismo).

doctrinal adj. Doctrinal.

doctrinar v. tr. To teach (enseñar). || FIG. To indoctrinate (convencer).

doctrinario, ria adj./s. Doctrinaire.

doctrinarismo m. Doctrinairism.

doctrinero m. Catechist. || *Amer.* Parish priest.

doctrino m. Orphan, child raised in an orphanage.

documentación f. Documentation. || Papers, *pl.* (de identidad). || — *Documentación del buque*, ship's papers. || *Documentación del coche*, car licence and insurance papers of a car.

documental adj. Documentary: *prueba documental*, documentary proof.

— M. CINEM. Documentary.

documentar v. tr. To document: *una causa bien documentada*, a well-documented case.

— V. pr. To gather documentary evidence. || — *Documentarse para un libro*, to gather material for a book. || *Documentarse sobre un tema*, to read up on *o* to do some research on a subject.

documento m. Document. || — Pl. Papers (de identidad). || — *Documento de identidad*, proof of identity. || *Documento justificativo*, voucher, certificate. || *Documento Nacional de Identidad*, national identity card.

dodecaedro m. MAT. Dodecahedron.

dodecafónico, ca adj. MÚS. Dodecaphonic.

dodecafonismo m. MÚS. Dodecaphony.

dodecágono, na adj. MAT. Dodecagonal.

— M. Dodecagon.

dodecasílabo, ba adj. Alexandrine, twelve-syllable, dodecasyllabic.

— M. Alexandrine, dodecasyllable.

dogal m. Halter (para atar un animal). || Noose, hangman's rope (para ahorcar). || FIG. y FAM. *Estar con el dogal al cuello*, to be in a tight spot, to have one's neck in a noose.

dogaresa f. Dogaressa.

dogma m. Dogma.

dogmático, ca adj. Dogmatic.

— M. y f. Dogmatist. || — F. Dogmatics.

dogmatismo m. Dogmatism. || Dogma.

dogmatista m. Dogmatist.

dogmatizador, ra o **dogmatizante** m. y f. Dogmatizer, dogmatist.

dogmatizar v. intr. To dogmatize.

dogo m. Bulldog (perro).

doladera f. TECN. Cooper's adze (herramienta).

doladura f. Hewing (desbastadura). || Shaving (viruta).

dolaje m. Wine absorbed by the cask.

dólar m. Dollar.

dolencia f. Complaint, ailment (achaque). || Ache, pain (dolor).

doler* v. intr. To hurt: *me duele la cabeza*, my head is hurting; *sus insultos me han dolido mucho*, I was very hurt by his insults. || To have a pain: *me duele el estómago*, I have a pain in my stomach. || To ache (producir un dolor continuo): *me duele la cabeza, el estómago*, my head, my stomach aches. || To grieve, to pain, to distress (afligir): *me duele ver tanta injusticia*, it grieves me to see so much injustice. || To hurt, to pain, to be sorry: *me duele tener que decirle esto*, I am sorry to have to tell you this, it hurts me to have to tell you this. || — FIG. *Ahí le duele*, that's where the shoe pinches. || *Estar dolido*, to be hurt (ofendido), to be grieved (afligido).

— V. pr. To feel the effects of: *dolerse del golpe*, to feel the effects of the blow. || To regret: *dolerse de haber dicho tales cosas*, to regret having said such things. || To sympathize with, to pity, to have pity on (compadecer). || To complain (quejarse): *se duele de lo mal que lo han tratado*, he complains about how badly he has been treated. || To grieve (*de*, at, over; *por*, for) [afligirse]. || *Dolerse de sus pecados*, to repent of one's sins.

dolicocefalia f. Dolichocephalism, dolichocephaly.

dolicocéfalo, la adj. Dolichocephalic.

— M. y f. Dolichocephal.

doliente adj. Sick, ailing, poorly (que tiene dolencia). || Aching (que duele). || Sad, sorrowful (triste).

— M. y f. Mourner (en entierro). || MED. Sick person.

dolmán m. Dolman.

dolmen m. Dolmen.

dolo m. JUR. Wilful misrepresentation (en contrato, trato). | Fraud, dolus (fraude).

Dolomitas n. pr. f. pl. GEOGR. Dolomites.

dolomítico, ca adj. GEOL. Dolomitic.

dolor m. Pain: *sintió un dolor repentino en el brazo*, he felt a sudden pain in his arm. || Ache: *tengo un dolor latente en la espalda*, I have a nagging ache in my back. || FIG. Sorrow, grief, regret (pena): *con harto dolor de mi parte*, with great regret. || — FIG. *Causar dolor*, to pain, to grieve. || *Dolor de cabeza*, headache. || FIG. *Dolor de corazón*, remorse. || *Dolor de costado*, stitch; (ant.) pneumonia. || *Dolor de muelas, de oído, de tripas, de vientre*, toothache, earache, bellyache, stomachache. || *Dolores del parto*, labour pains. || *Dolor sordo*, dull ache. || *Estar con los dolores*, to be in labour (mujer).

— OBSERV. *Ache* es un dolor que suele ser continuo e interno, y no causado por una herida. *Pain* es más general y puede ser continuo o repentino, interno o externo.

dolora f. Short poem on a philosophical theme of the type composed by Campoamor.

dolorido, da adj. Painful, aching, sore: *tengo la pierna dolorida del golpe de ayer*, my leg is sore from the knock I received yesterday. || FIG. Pained, grieved, grief-stricken (afligido). | Sad, sorrowful (triste).

doloroso, sa adj. Painful: *una operación, una decisión dolorosa*, a painful operation, decision. || FIG. Painful, grievous, distressing (afligente). | Pitiable, pitiful (que inspira compasión).

— F. ARTES. Madonna (representación de la Virgen). || FAM. *Tráigame la dolorosa, por favor*, what's the damage? (al pedir la cuenta).

doloso, sa adj. Dolose, fraudulent.

doma f. Taming (de fieras). || Breaking in (de caballerías). || Training (adiestramiento). || FIG. Taming, mastering, control (de las pasiones). || *La doma de la bravía*, The Taming of the Shrew (de Shakespeare).

domable adj. Tamable. || Trainable (para el circo, etc.).

domador, ra m. y f. Tamer (que amansa animales salvajes). || Trainer (que los adiestra). || *Domador de caballos*, horsebreaker, broncobuster. || *Domador de leones*, lion tamer.

domadura f. V. DOMA.

domar v. tr. To tame, to domesticate (fieras). || To break in (una caballería). || To train (adiestrar). || FIG. To break in: *domar zapatos nuevos*, to break in new shoes. | To tame, to bring under control (a alguien). | To tame, to master, to control (las pasiones).
domeñable adj. Tamable. || Trainable (adiestrable). || FIG. Controllable, tamable (pasiones, persona).
domeñar v. tr. To subdue, to reduce to obedience (a una persona). || To subdue, to control, to master (las pasiones). || *Domeñar la resistencia de uno*, to break down s.o.'s resistance.
domesticable adj. Domesticable, tamable (que se puede amansar). || Trainable (que se puede adiestrar).
domesticación f. Domestication. || Taming (domadura). || Training (adiestramiento).
domesticar v. tr. To domesticate, to tame: *domesticar un ratón*, to domesticate a mouse. || To train (adiestrar): *domesticar un elefante, pulgas*, to train an elephant, fleas. || FIG. To subdue, to reduce to submission (domar a alguien). | To educate (educar a alguien).
— V. pr. To become domesticated (un animal). || FIG. To become sociable (una persona).
domesticidad f. Domesticity.
doméstico, ca adj. Domestic: *servicio, animal doméstico*, domestic service, animal. || Domestic, home: *economía doméstica*, domestic economy; *artes domésticas*, domestic arts.
— M. y f. Servant, domestic.
domiciliación f. Domiciliation.
domiciliado, da adj. Living, resident, domiciled (p. us.): *está domiciliado en el 4 de la calle de Alcalá*, he is resident at nº 4 calle de Alcalá.
domiciliar v. tr. To domicile.
domiciliario, ria adj. Domiciliary. || House: *arresto domiciliario*, house arrest.
— M. y f. Inhabitant, resident, tenant.
domicilio m. Residence, home, domicile (p. us.), abode (p. us.): *eligir domicilio*, to take up residence *o* one's domicile *o* one's abode, to make a home; *domicilio particular*, private residence. || — *A domicilio*, home. || *Domicilio social*, head office, registered office. || *Entrega a domicilio*, home delivery service. || *Sin domicilio fijo*, of no fixed abode.
dominación f. Domination. || Dominion, rule, power, control. || MIL. Commanding position, high ground [dominating an area]. || Pull-up (en gimnasia). || — Pl. REL. Dominions, dominations (ángeles).
dominador, ra adj. Dominating (dominante). || Domineering (persona).
dominante adj. Dominating, dominant, ruling: *el poder dominante*, the dominant power. || Dominant (altura). || Commanding, dominant, dominating (posición, situación). || Prevailing, predominating (viento, color, opinión). || Governing, leading, master (idea). || Predominant (interés). || Domineering (despótico): *tiene una mujer muy dominante*, he has a very domineering wife. || MÚS. Dominant. || *Carácter dominante*, domineering *o* dominant character.
— F. Dominant feature *o* characteristic. || BIOL. MÚS. Dominant.
dominar v. tr. To dominate, to rule, to control: *Napoleón quiso dominar Europa*, Napoleon wanted to rule Europe. || To control: *dominar un caballo, un barco, los nervios*, to control a horse, a boat, one's nerves. || To overpower (a un adversario). || To put down, to subdue (una revolución, rebelión). || To control, to contain, to check (una epidemia, un incendio). || To control, to master, to restrain (las pasiones). || To get over (una pena). || To have a good *o* sound knowledge of, to master (un tema): *dominar la química*, to have a good knowledge of chemistry. || To have a good command of, to master, to know well, to be fluent in (idioma). || To rise above (el ruido). || To dominate, to tower over: *el ayuntamiento domina la plaza*, the city hall towers over the square. || To command, to overlook: *la casa domina toda la bahía*, the house commands the whole bay. || — *Desde ese pico se domina toda la ciudad*, you can see the whole city from that peak. || *Dominar la situación*, to master the situation, to have the situation under control. || *Te domina la envidia*, you are ruled by envy.
— V. intr. To dominate. || To predominate. || To stand out (un color, etc.)
— V. pr. To restrain o.s., to control o.s., to keep o.s. under control.
dominatriz adj. f. Dominating. || Domineering (mujer).
— F. Domineering woman.
dómine m. Latin teacher. || FIG. Pedant.
domingo m. Sunday: *vendré el domingo*, I shall come on Sunday. || — *Domingo de Carnaval*, Shrove Sunday. || *Domingo de Cuasimodo*, Low Sunday. || *Domingo de Ramos*, Palm Sunday. || *Domingo de Resurrección*, Easter Sunday. || *Hacer domingo*, to have a day off. || *Traje de los domingos*, Sunday best.
Domingo n. pr. m. Dominic.
Domingo (Santo) n. pr. m. GEOGR. Santo Domingo [Dominican Republic].
dominguejo m. Tumbler (juguete). || *Amer*. Nonentity (persona insignificante).
dominguillo m. Tumbler (juguete). || FIG. y FAM. *Traer a uno como un dominguillo*, to twist s.o. round one's little finger (manejar), to have s.o. running round at one's beck and call (mandar de un lado a otro).
Dominica n. pr. f. Dominique. || GEOGR. *La Dominica*, Dominica (Antillas).
domínica f. REL. Sunday, the Sabbath. | Sunday office (textos).
dominical adj. Sunday, dominical. || *La oración dominical*, the Lord's Prayer.
dominicano, na adj./s. Dominican (religioso y persona de la República Dominicana). || *República Dominicana*, Dominican Republic.
dominico, ca adj./s. Dominican (religioso).
dominio m. Authority, control (autoridad): *tener bajo su dominio*, to have under one's authority; *un maestro que tiene dominio sobre sus alumnos*, a teacher who has control over his pupils. || Dominion, power (soberanía). || Domination (predominancia). || Domain (territorio). || Dominion (en el Commonwealth). || Supremacy: *dominio del aire, de los mares*, air, sea supremacy. || FIG. Good knowledge, mastery: *tiene un gran dominio de las matemáticas*, he has a very good knowledge of mathematics. | Good command (de un idioma). | Control, restraint (de las pasiones). || JUR. Ownership, dominion (de bienes). || — *Con pleno dominio de sus facultades*, in full control of one's faculties. || *Dominio de sí mismo*, self-control. || *Dominio público*, public property. || *Recobrar el dominio de sí mismo*, to pull o.s. together. || *Ser del dominio público*, to be common knowledge.
dominó m. Dominoes, *pl.* (juego). || Set of dominoes (conjunto de las fichas). || Domino (disfraz).
domo m. ARQ. Dome, cupola (cúpula).
don m. Gift, present (regalo). || Donation (a una institución, etc.). || [Natural] gift, talent (talento): *el don de lenguas*, a gift for languages, a talent for languages. || Wish (en cuentos y leyendas): *el hada le concedió varios dones*, the fairy granted him several wishes. || — *Don de acierto*, knack for doing the right thing, savoir faire. || *Don de errar*, knack for doing the wrong thing. || *Don de mando*, qualities (*pl.*) of a leader. || *Tener don de gentes*, to have charm *o* magnetism, to get on well with people, to have a way with people. || *Tener el don de la palabra*, to have a way with words, to have the gift of the gab (fam.).
don m. Mr: *Don Fulano de Tal*, Mr So-and-So. || — *Don Juan*, don Juan (Tenorio) [personaje literario], womanizer, lady-killer, Casanova, don Juan (mujeriego). || *Señor Don* (*Sr. D. or Sr. Dn.*), Esquire [Esq.]: *Sr. Dn. Martín Rodríguez*, Martín Rodríguez Esq. (en un sobre).

— OBSERV. *Don* is only used before the Christian name, which may or may not be followed by the surname.
— Cuando *don* va seguido simplemente por el nombre de pila, no se traduce en inglés (*don Tomás*, Thomas).

donación f. Donation (a una institución, etc.). || Gift, present (regalo). || Bequest (en testamento). || JUR. *Donación entre vivos*, donation inter vivos.
donador, ra adj./s. V. DONANTE.
donaire m. Grace, poise, elegance: *andar con mucho donaire*, to walk with great poise. || Wit (en el hablar). || Witticism, bon mot (agudeza).
donante adj. Donating.
— M. y f. Donor. || *Donante de sangre*, blood donor.
donar v. tr. To donate, to give, to bestow.
donatario, ria m. y f. Donee, donatory.
donativo m. Donation.
doncel m. (Ant.). Young nobleman *o* squire (joven noble). || King's pageboy, donzel (paje). || Young nobleman in the king's army. || Chaste youth (muchacho virgen).
doncella f. Virgin, maid, maiden (virgen). || Maiden, damsel (ant.), girl (chica). || Maid, housemaid (criada). || Doncella, wrasse (pez). || *Amer*. Whitlow (panadizo). || *La Doncella de Orleáns*, the Maid of Orleans (Juana de Arco).
doncellez o **doncellería** f. Virginity, maidenhood.
donde adv. Where: *¿dónde estás?*, where are you?; *lo compré donde tú me dijiste*, I bought it where you told me; *¿de dónde vienes?*, where have you come from? || Where, in which: *es un sitio donde abundan los peces*, it is a spot where there are plenty of fish *o* in which there are plenty of fish. || (Ant.). Whence (de donde). || At *o* to the house of: *voy donde Juan*, I am going to John's [house]. || — *A donde*, where: *¿a dónde vas?*, where are you going? || *De* or *desde donde*, where from, whence (ant.). || *Donde no*, otherwise. || *Donde sea*, anywhere. || *El pueblo de donde viene*, the village he comes from. || *En donde*, where, in which, wherein (ant.): *la casa en donde nací*, the house in which I was born. || *Estés donde estés*, wherever you are. || *Hacia donde*, towards which, where. || *Hasta donde*, up to which. || *¿Hasta dónde?*, how far? || FIG. *¡Mira por dónde!*, fancy that! || *Por donde*, where: *el sitio por donde paseaba*, the place where he was walking; through which: *la ciudad por donde pasé*, the city which I passed through; whereupon, from which: *por donde se infiere que*, whereupon *o* from which it follows that; by which, through which; *la ventana por donde entré*, the window through which I got in. || *¿Por dónde?*, why? (por qué), where?, whereabouts? (en qué sitio), which way? (por qué camino).

— OBSERV. The interrogative adverb *dónde* always bears an accent.

dondequiera adv. Anywhere (en cualquier parte). || Everywhere (en todas partes). || *Dondequiera que*, wherever, anywhere.
dondiego m. BOT. Marvel-of-Peru, four o'clock. || — *Dondiego de día*, morning glory. || *Dondiego de noche*, marvel of Peru, four o'clock.
donjuán m. BOT. Marvel of Peru, four o'clock.
donjuanesco adj. m. Fond of women, donjuanesque.
donjuanismo m. Philandering, womanizing, donjuanism.
donosamente adj. Wittily: *habla muy donosamente*, he speaks very wittily. || Gracefully, elegantly, with great poise.
donosidad f. V. DONOSURA.
donoso, sa adj. Witty (divertido): *una observación donosa*, a witty remark. || Light (estilo). || Graceful, elegant, poised (elegante). || Fine (con ironía): *¡donosa pregunta!*, that's a fine thing to ask! || — *¡Donosa ocurrencia!*, what a bright idea! || *Donosa cosa es que*, the best part of it is that.
donostiarra adj. [Of *o* from] San Sebastián.
— M. y f. Native *o* inhabitant of San Sebastián.
donosura f. Wit (gracia, humor). || Witticism, bon mot (agudeza). || Grace, poise, elegance (elegancia). || Lightness (del estilo).
doña f. Mrs, mistress (ant.), madam (p. us.): *doña Dolores Valdés*, Mrs Dolores Valdés. || *Señora Doña (Sra. Dª)*, Mrs (en un sobre).
— OBSERV. *Doña* indicates a married woman or a widow and is only used before the Christian name, which may be followed by the surname or not.
— Cuando *doña* va seguido simplemente por el nombre de pila, no se traduce o se emplea la fórmula anticuada *mistress* (*doña María*, Mary, mistress Mary).
dopar v. tr. To drug, to dope (drogar con estimulante).
doping m. Doping, drugging.
doquier o **doquiera** adv. Anywhere. || *Por doquier*, everywhere.
dorada f. Gilthead (pez).
doradilla f. BOT. Scale fern. || Gilthead (dorada).
dorado, da adj. Golden (de color de oro). || Gilt (cubierto de oro). || FIG. Golden: *edad, juventud dorada*, golden age, golden years of youth; *el siglo dorado*, the golden age. || Bay (caballo). || *Libro de cantos dorados*, gilt-edged book.
— M. Gilding (acción de dorar). || Gilt (capa de oro). || Dorado (pez).
Dorado (El) m. pr. m. El Dorado (país legendario).
dorador, ra adj. Gilding.
— M. y f. Gilder.
doradura f. Gilding (acción de dorar).
dorar v. tr. To gild, to cover with gold. || To gold-plate (un objeto de metal). || — FIG. y FAM. *Dorar la píldora*, to gild the pill. || CULIN. *Hacer dorar*, to brown.
— V. pr. To turn brown *o* golden.
dórico, ca adj. Dorian (de los dorios). || ARQ. Doric: *orden dórico*, Doric order.
— M. Doric (dialecto griego).
Dórida o **Dóride** n. pr. f. GEOGR. Doris.
dorífera o **dorífora** f. ZOOL. Colorado beetle.
dorio, ria adj./s. Dorian (de Dóride).
dormán m. Dolman (chaqueta).
dormición f. Dormition (de la Virgen).
dormida f. Short sleep, nap.
dormidero, ra adj. Soporific, sleep-inducing.
dormido, da adj. Asleep: *estar medio dormido*, to be half asleep. || Sleepy (con sueño). || — *Quedarse dormido*, to fall asleep (dormirse), to oversleep (pegársele a uno las sábanas). || FIG. *Tengo la pierna dormida*, my leg has gone dead *o* has gone to sleep.
dormilón, ona adj. Sleepy-headed, fond of one's bed *o* of sleeping, lazy.
— M. y f. Sleepyhead. || — F. Earring (arete). || Comfortable armchair [used for taking a nap].
dormir* v. intr. To sleep. || To spend *o* to pass the night (pernoctar): *dormimos en Madrid*, we spent the night in Madrid. || FIG. To hang fire (un asunto). || — *¡A dormir!*, to bed! || *Dormir al raso* or *al sereno* or *con cortinas verdes*, to sleep outdoors *o* in the open *o* under the stars. || FIG. *Dormir como un lirón* or *como un tronco* or *a pierna suelta* or *como una marmota*, to sleep like a log, to sleep soundly. | *Dormir con un ojo abierto*, to sleep with one eye open. || *Dormir de un tirón*, to sleep soundly all night. || *Dormir doce horas de un tirón*, to sleep for twelve hours solid. || *Echarse a dormir*, to go to bed. || *Ganas de dormir*, sleepiness. || *Quien duerme cena*, he who sleeps forgets his hunger. || *Ser de mal dormir*, to sleep badly, to be a very light sleeper.
— V. tr. To put *o* to send *o* to lull to sleep: *dormir a un niño*, to put a child to sleep. || To send to sleep: *esta música me duerme*, this music sends me to sleep. || To put *o* to send to sleep (anestesiar). || — *Dormir el sueño de los justos*, to sleep the sleep of the just. || *Dormir el último sueño*, to be at rest. || FAM. *Dormir la mona*, to sleep it off. || *Dormir la siesta*, to have a siesta *o* a nap.
— V. pr. To go to sleep, to fall asleep, to drop off [to sleep]. || FIG. To go to sleep, to go dead: *se me ha dormido la pierna*, my leg has gone to sleep. || MAR. To heel *o* to list badly (inclinarse el barco). || *Dormirse sobre los laureles*, to rest on one's laurels.
dormitar v. intr. To doze, to snooze.
dormitorio m. Bedroom (alcoba). || Dormitory (en una escuela, etc.).
dornajo o **dornillo** m. Round bowl (artesa).
dorsal adj. Dorsal, back: *músculos dorsales*, dorsal muscles. || GRAM. Dorsal (consonante).
— M. Number (en la espalda de un atleta).
dorso m. Back (de un animal). || Back: *el dorso de una carta*, the back of a letter. || *Véase al dorso*, see over, please turn over [P.T.O.].
dos adj./s.m. Two: *dos y dos son cuatro*, two and two are four; *el dos de bastos*, the two of clubs. || Second (segundo): *el 2 (dos) de enero*, 2nd [the second of] January. || Second, [number] two: *el tomo dos*, the second volume, volume [number] two. || — *A dos pasos de aquí*, a few steps away, a short way away, nearby. || *Cada dos días*, every other day, every two days. || *Cada dos por tres*, every five minutes. || *De dos en dos*, in twos, two by two: *llegaban de dos en dos*, they arrived in twos; into twos, into groups of two: *dividir de dos en dos*, to divide into twos. || *Dos a dos*, two by two, in twos: *los alumnos andaban dos a dos*, the pupils were walking in twos. || *Dos por dos*, two by two, two times two, two twos (multiplicación), in twos, two by two (dos a dos), in twos (en grupos de dos). || *Dos tes*, double t. || *Dos veces*, twice. || *Ellos dos* or *entre los dos*, between the two of them, both of them. || FAM. *En un dos por tres*, in a jiffy, in a flash, before you can say Jack Robinson. || *Es para los dos*, it's for both of you. || *Hacer un trabajo entre dos*, to share a job. || *Las dos*, two o'clock. || *Los dos*, both: *vinieron los dos*, they both came; *los dos chicos son estudiantes*, both boys are students. || *No hay dos sin tres*, misfortune always comes in threes. || *Para nosotros dos*, for us two. || *Una de dos*, one of the two.
dosalbo, ba adj. With two white feet (caballo).
doscientos, tas adj./s.m. Two hundred: *dos mil doscientos*, two thousand two hundred; *había doscientas personas en la sala*, there were two hundred people in the room. || Two hundredth (ordinal). || *Mil doscientos*, one thousand two hundred, twelve hundred.
dosel m. Canopy, baldachin (p. us.), dais (ant.) [sobre altar, trono, cama, etc.].
dosificación f. Dosage. || QUÍM. Titration.
dosificador m. Dosimeter.
dosificar v. tr. To dose (un medicamento). || QUÍM. To titrate. || FIG. To measure out, to apportion.
dosis f. inv. MED. Dose: *a* or *en pequeña dosis*, in a small dose, in small doses. || QUÍM. Proportion. || FIG. Dose (cantidad). | Admixture (de un defecto). || — || MED. *Dosis de recuerdo*, booster (de una vacuna). || FIG. *En pequeñas dosis*, in small doses. | *Tener una buena dosis de*, to have one's share of.
dotación f. Endowment: *dar cien libras como dotación*, to give an endowment of a hundred pounds. || MAR. Crew, complement (tripulación). || Personnel, staff (en oficina, etc.). || Dowry (de una mujer).
dotado, da adj. Gifted. || Endowed (*de*, with). || Equipped, fitted (una máquina).
dotal adj. Dowry, dotal.
dotar v. tr. To give a dowry, to give as a dowry, to dower (p. us.): *dotó a su hija con medio millón*, he gave his daughter a dowry of half a million *o* half a million as a dowry. || To endow, to provide: *dotar a un pueblo de una escuela*, to endow a town with a school; *la naturaleza le ha dotado de buena vista*, nature endowed him with good eyesight. || To provide funds for, to assign money to (subvencionar). || To equip (equipar). || To staff (oficina). || To man (tripular un barco).
dote f. Dowry, marriage portion. || Portion brought by a nun on entering a convent or by a monk on entering a monastery. || — Pl. Talent, *sing*, gift, *sing.*: *tiene dotes para la música*, he has a talent for music. || — *Dotes de mando*, qualities of a leader. || *Es un niño de excelentes dotes*, he is a very gifted child.
dovela f. ARQ. Voussoir (cuña de piedra). | Soffit (superficie).
dovelar v. tr. ARQ. To hew [a stone] into a voussoir, to make wedge-shaped.
dozavo, va adj./s. Twelfth (duodécimo). || IMPR. *En dozavo*, in duodecimo *o* twelvemo.
dracma f. Drachma (moneda). || Dram (peso).
draconiano, na adj. Draconian, drastic.
draga f. Dredge, dredging machine (para limpiar). || Drag (para buscar). || Dredger (barco).
dragado m. Dredging (para limpiar o excavar). || Dragging (para encontrar algo perdido).
dragador, ra adj. Dredging.
— M. Dredger (boat).
dragaje m. V. DRAGADO.
dragaminas m. inv. MAR. Minesweeper.
dragar v. tr. To dredge (limpiar o excavar). || To drag (para encontrar algo perdido). || To sweep (minas).
dragea f. (Ant.). Sugar-coated pill (píldora).
drago m. BOT. Dragon tree.
dragomán m. Dragoman, interpreter (intérprete).
dragón m. Dragon (animal fabuloso). || MIL. Dragoon (soldado). || ZOOL. Flying dragon (reptil). | Greater weever (pez). || BOT. Snapdragon. || TECN. Mouth, throat (de un horno).
dragona f. MIL. Epaulette (charretera). | Sword knot (de la espada).
dragoncillo m. BOT. Tarragon.

dragonear v. intr. *Amer.* To pose, to pass o.s. off: *dragonear de médico*, to pose *o* to pass o.s. off as a doctor. | To boast (jactarse).
drama m. TEATR. Drama: *drama lírico*, lyric drama. | Drama, play (obra de teatro). || FIG. Drama.
dramática f. Dramatic art, dramaturgy (arte de escribir). || Drama (género teatral).
dramático, ca adj. Dramatic.
— M. Dramatist (autor).
dramatismo m. Dramatism, drama.
dramatizar v. tr. To dramatize.
dramaturgia f. Dramatic art, dramaturgy.
dramaturgo, ga m. y f. Playwright, dramatist, dramaturge (p. us.), dramaturgist (p. us.).
dramón m. FAM. Melodrama.
drapeado m. ARTES. Drapery.
drapear v. tr. To drape.
drástico, ca adj. MED. Drastic. || Drastic (acción, medidas, etc.).
— M. MED. Drastic purgative.
drávida m. y f. Dravidian.
drenaje m. Drainage (de un campo, un absceso, etc.). || — *Colector de drenaje*, main drain. || *Tubo de drenaje*, drain, drainpipe.
drenar v. tr. To drain (un terreno, un absceso, etc.).
dríada o **dríade** f. Dryad.
driblar v. intr. DEP. To dribble (regatear en el fútbol).
drible m. DEP. Dribble (regate).
dril m. Drill, duck (tela).
drive m. DEP. Drive (tenis, golf).
driza f. MAR. Halyard.
drizar v. tr. To hoist.
droga f. Drug. || FIG. y FAM. Story, tale, fib (mentira). | Trick (engaño). | Practical joke (broma). || FAM. Bother, nuisance (lata). || *Amer.* Bad debt (deuda).
drogadicto, ta adj./s. Drug addict.
drogado, da adj. Drugged, doped.
— M. y f. Drug addict. || — M. Doping.
drogar v. tr. To drug, to dope.
— V. pr. To drug o.s.
drogmán m. Dragoman, interpreter (intérprete).
droguería f. Drysaltery, chandler's (ant.) [U.S., drugstore].
droguero, ra m. y f. Drysalter [U.S., druggist]. || *Amer.* Swindler.
droguista m. y f. Drysalter [U.S., druggist]. || *Amer.* Swindler.
dromedario m. ZOOL. Dromedary.
druida m. Druid.
drupa f. BOT. Drupe.
drusa f. MIN. Druse.
dual adj. Dual. || — Adj./m. GRAM. Dual.
dualidad f. Duality. || MIN. Dimorphism. || *Amer.* Tie, draw (empate).
dualismo m. Dualism.
dualista adj. Dualistic.
— M. y f. Dualist.
dubitación f. Doubt.
dubitativo, va adj. Doubting, dubitative, doubtful (que expresa duda). || Dubitative (conjunción).
Dublín n. pr. GEOGR. Dublin.
ducado m. Duchy, dukedom (territorio). || Dukedom (título). || Ducat (moneda).
ducal adj. Ducal: *palacio ducal*, ducal palace.
ducentésimo, ma adj./s. Two hundredth.
duco m. Thick paint, lacquer.
dúctil adj. Ductile (metal, arcilla, etc.). || FIG. Ductile, pliant, pliable (persona).
ductilidad f. Ductility.
ducha f. Shower: *tomar* o *darse una ducha*, to take *o* to have a shower. || Douche (para una parte del cuerpo). || FIG. y FAM. *Esto vino como una ducha de agua fría*, this put the damper on everything.
duchar v. tr. To give a shower. || MED. To douche. || FAM. To douse, to dowse (mojar).
— V. pr. To have *o* to take a shower. || To douche.
ducho, cha adj. Expert, skilful, well up: *ducho en latín*, expert *o* skilful at Latin, well up in *o* on Latin. || *Estar ducho en la materia*, to be well up on the subject.
duda f. Doubt: *sin la menor duda*, without the slightest doubt; *sin duda alguna*, without any doubt; *sin sombra de duda*, without the shadow of a doubt; *fuera de duda*, beyond doubt. || — *En duda*, in question. || *En la duda abstente*, when in doubt, don't; **when in doubt, abstain.** || *Entrar en la duda*, to begin to have doubts. || *Estar en la duda*, to be doubtful, to be in doubt. || *No cabe duda* or *no hay duda* or *sin lugar a dudas*, there is no doubt. || *Poner en duda*, to question, to doubt. || *Sacar de dudas a uno*, to dispel s.o.'s doubts. || *Salir de dudas*, to shed one's doubts. || *Sin duda*, no doubt, undoubtedly, without a doubt.
dudable adj. Doubtful, dubious.
dudar v. intr. y tr. To doubt, to have doubts, to be in doubt: *estoy dudando*, I'm having doubts. || To doubt, to have doubts about: *lo dudo*, I doubt it; *dudo haber dicho eso*, I doubt having said that. || — *Dudar de* or *sobre* or *acerca de algo*, to doubt sth., to be in doubt *o* to have doubts about *o* as to sth.: *dudo de su honradez*, I have doubts about his honesty; to question (poner en tela de juicio), to suspect (sospechar): *la policía duda del cajero*, the police suspect the cashier. || *Dudar en*, to hesitate to: *dudo en salir por si acaso vienen*, I hesitate to go out lest they should arrive. || *Dudar entre* (con infinitivo), to be not sure *o* not certain whether to [with infinitive]: *dudo entre ir por avión o ir en tren*, I am not sure whether to go by plane or train; (con sustantivo), to be unable to decide *o* to make up one's mind between: *dudo entre los dos*, I can't decide between the two. || *Dudar que*, to doubt whether *o* if: *dudo que sea tan tacaño*, I doubt whether he is such a skinflint; *dudo que pueda venir tan tarde*, I doubt whether he can come *o* whether he will be able to come so late. || *Dudar si*, to doubt whether *o* if: *dudo si llegaré a tiempo*, I doubt if I will get there on time; to be not sure *o* not certain whether: *dudo si he cerrado bien la puerta*, I am not certain whether I closed the door properly. || *No dudo de ello*, I don't doubt it, I have no doubt about it.
dudosamente adv. Doubtfully (sin certeza). | Hesitantly (vacilando). || Dubiously (sospechosamente).
dudoso, sa adj. Doubtful, uncertain: *la fecha de su llegada es dudosa*, the date of his arrival is doubtful. || Hesitant, undecided (vacilante). || Dubious (sospechoso): *un tipo dudoso*, a dubious character. || Questionable (discutible).
duela f. Stave (de tonel).
duelista m. Duellist [U.S., duelist].
duelo m. Duel (combate): *batirse en duelo*, to fight a duel. || Sorrow, grief, affliction (dolor). || Mourning (luto). || Mourners, *pl.* (los dolientes). || Funeral procession (cortejo). || — Pl. Toils, labours, trials (trabajos). || — CULIN. *Duelos y quebrantos*, fried dish made with eggs and brains, bacon, etc. || FAM. *Los duelos con pan son menos*, money lessens the blow. || *Presidir el duelo*, to lead the mourning, to be chief mourner.
duende m. Goblin, elf, imp (espíritu). || FIG. Imp, mischievous child (niño travieso). | Magic: *el duende de una persona*, a person's magic. || — Pl. FIG. Magic, *sing.*: *los duendes del flamenco*, the magic of flamenco. || — *Andar como un duende* or *parecer un duende*, to be a will-o'-the-wisp, to be always popping up all over the place. || *Tener duende*, to have sth. on one's mind (estar preocupado), to have a certain magic (persona, sitio, etc.).
dueña f. Owner (propietaria). || Owner, mistress (de un perro, gato, etc.). || Owner, proprietress (de un negocio). || Landlady (de una pensión). || Mistress, lady (de una casa). || Matron, married woman (señora). || (Ant.). Duenna, governess (dama de compañía). || FIG. Mistress (dominadora). || — *Dueña de honor*, lady-in-waiting. || FIG. y FAM. *Ponerle a uno cual digan dueñas*, to abuse s.o. (insultarle), to drag s.o.'s name through the mud (insultarle a espaldas suyas).
dueño m. Owner (propietario). || Owner, master (de un perro, gato, etc.). || Owner, proprietor (de un negocio): *es dueño de un bar*, he is the proprietor of a bar. || Landlord (de una taberna, una pensión). || Master, head of the household (cabeza de familia). || FIG. Master: *ser dueño de la situación*, to be the master of the situation. || — *Dueño y señor*, lord and master. || *Hacerse dueño de*, to take command of, to master (una situación, etc.), to take possession of. || *Ser dueño de sí mismo*, to be one's own master, to be free to do as one pleases (ser libre), to be master of o.s., to have self-control (dominarse). || *Ser dueño de sus pasiones*, to be master of *o* in control of one's passions. || *Ser muy dueño de*, to be entirely free *o* at liberty to: *es usted muy dueño de aceptar o rehusar*, you are entirely free to accept or refuse.
Duero n. pr. m. GEOGR. Douro, Duero.
duetista m. y f. Duettist.
dueto m. MÚS. Short duet.
dulce adj. Sweet: *el café está muy dulce*, the coffee is very sweet; *la música dulce de la flauta*, the sweet music of the flute; *el dulce placer de la vuelta al hogar*, the sweet joy of a homecoming. || Mild, gentle (carácter, clima, voz). || Soft (viento, brisa). || Loving, soft (palabras). || Gentle, tender (mirada). || Fresh (agua). || Soft (metal).
— M. Sweet [U.S., candy]. || Preserved *o* candied fruit (fruta). || — Pl. Sweetmeats, sweets, sweet things (golosinas). || — *A mí me gustan los dulces*, I am fond of sweet things, I have a sweet tooth. || FIG. *A nadie le amarga un dulce*, v. AMARGAR. || *Dulce de fruta*, candied fruit. || *Amer. Dulce de leche*, custard cream. || *Dulce de membrillo*, quince preserve. || *En dulce*, candied (confitado): *fruta en dulce*, candied fruit; in syrup: *melocotón en dulce*, peaches in syrup.
dulcera f. Preserve dish, sweet dish.
dulcería f. Confectionery, confectioner's [U.S., candy store].
dulcero, ra adj. Sweet-toothed (goloso). || *Ser dulcero*, to have a sweet tooth.
— M. y f. Confectioner.
dulcificación f. Sweetening. || FIG. Soothing.
dulcificante adj. Sweetening. || FIG. Soothing.
dulcificar v. tr. To sweeten. || FIG. To soften, to soothe.
— V. pr. To become milder (el tiempo).
Dulcinea f. Sweetheart, lady-love, Dulcinea.
dulía f. REL. Dulia, veneration of angels and saints.
dulzaina f. MÚS. "Dulzaina", pipe [popular folk instrument similar to the *chirimía* and usually played to the accompaniment of the *tamboril*]. || FAM. Sweet stuff, sweet things, *pl.* (palabras melosas).

dulzarrón, ona o **dulzón, ona** adj. Sickly, oversweet: *una pequeña tarta dulzarrona*, a sickly little tart. || FIG. Sickly (persona).
dulzor m. Sweetness (del azúcar, de una sonrisa, etc.). || Gentleness, sweetness (del carácter).
dulzura f. Sweetness: *la dulzura de la miel, de su sonrisa*, the sweetness of honey, of her smile. || Gentleness, sweetness (del carácter). || Mildness (del clima).
duma f. Duma (asamblea en Rusia zarista).
dum-dum f. Dumdum (bala explosiva).
dumping m. COM. Dumping.
duna f. Dune.
dundeco, ca adj. *Amer.* V. DUNDO.
dundera f. *Amer.* Silliness, stupidity, foolishness.
dundo, da adj. *Amer.* Silly, stupid, foolish.
— M. y f. Fool, dolt, ass.
dúo m. MÚS. Duet, duo.
duodecimal adj. Duodecimal.
duodécimo, ma adj./s Twelfth. || *En duodécimo lugar*, twelfth, in twelfth place.
duodenal adj. MED. Duodenal.
duodenitis f. inv. MED. Duodenitis.
duodeno, na adj. (P. us.). Twelfth.
— M. ANAT. Duodenum.
dúplex adj./s.m. TECN. Duplex. || Duplex, duplex telegraphy: *enlace dúplex*, duplex line *o* link. || Split-level flat, maisonette [U.S., duplex] (piso).
dúplica f. JUR. Rejoinder.
duplicación f. Duplication (de documentos, etc.). || Doubling: *la duplicación de la producción*, the doubling of output.
duplicado m. Duplicate, copy: *el duplicado de un acta*, the copy of a deed. || Duplicate: *el duplicado de una llave*, a duplicate key.
— Adj. In duplicate. || Double (doblado). || A: *calle Miracruz número 17 duplicado*, nº. 17A, Miracruz Street. || *Por duplicado*, in duplicate.
duplicador, ra adj. Duplicating.
— M. Duplicator (máquina).
duplicar v. tr. To duplicate (reproducir): *duplicar un documento*, to duplicate a document. || To double (multiplicar por dos): *duplicar la producción*, to double production. || JUR. To answer [the plaintiff's reply].
— V. pr. To double: *la población se ha duplicado*, the population has doubled.
duplicativo, va adj. Duplicative.
duplicidad f. Duplicity, double-dealing, two-facedness.
duplo, pla adj./s.m. Double. || *Ocho es el duplo de cuatro*, eight is twice four, eight is double four.
duque m. Duke (título): *el señor duque*, his Grace the Duke.
duquesa f. Duchess: *la señora duquesa*, her Grace the Duchess.
durabilidad f. Durability.
durable adj. Durable, lasting.
duración f. Duration, length: *la duración de nuestra estancia en España*, the length of our stay in Spain; *la duración del día, de la película*, the length of the day, of the film. || Life (de un coche, una bombilla, una pila, etc.). || — *De corta* or *poca duración*, short-lived: *moda, felicidad de poca duración*, short-lived fashion, happiness; short: *una visita de poca duración*, a short visit. || *De larga duración*, long-lasting, lengthy (enfermedad), long-life (pila, bombilla, etc.), long (estancia, vacaciones, etc.), lasting (éxito, placer), long-playing (disco). || *Duración media de la vida*, average life span, average life expectancy.
duraderamente adv. Durably.
duradero, ra adj. Durable, lasting. || Lasting: *paz duradera*, lasting peace.
duraluminio m. Duralumin (aleación).
duramadre o **duramáter** f. ANAT. Dura mater.
duramen m. BOT. Duramen.
duramente adv. Hard: *trabajar duramente*, to work hard. || Harshly, severely: *la vida le trató duramente*, life treated him very harshly.
durante prep. During: *durante las vacaciones*, during the holidays. || In: *durante el día*, in the daytime. || For: *vivió en España durante diez años*, he lived in Spain for ten years.
durar v. intr. To last, to continue, to go on for: *el mitin duró cuatro horas*, the rally lasted four hours. || To remain (permanecer). || To last, to wear [well] (ropa): *esos zapatos le durarán mucho*, those shoes will last him a long time *o* will wear well. || *¿Cuánto duró su estancia en Buenos Aires?*, how long was your stay in Buenos Aires?
duraznero m. BOT. Peach tree (melocotonero).
duraznillo m. BOT. Persicaria, lady's thumb.
durazno m. BOT. Peach (fruto). | Peach tree (árbol).
Durero n. pr. Dürer.
dureza f. Hardness (de agua, hierro, oído, etc.). || Toughness (de alimentos). || Stiffness (de un mecanismo). || Hardheartedness, insensitivity (insensibilidad). || Harshness, severity (severidad). || Obstinacy, stubbornness (obstinación). || Difficulty (dificultad). || Harshness (luz, sonido). || Toughness, strength (resistencia). || Steeliness (de la mirada). || MED. Callosity, hard patch. || *Dureza de corazón*, hardheartedness, hardness.
durita f. (nombre registrado). AUT. Hose, radiator hose.
durmiente adj. Sleeping: *La Bella durmiente del bosque*, Sleeping Beauty.
— M. ARQ. Sleeper (madero para sostener). || Sleeper [U.S., tie] (traviesa de ferrocarril).
duro, ra adj. Hard: *el acero es duro*, steel is hard. || Tough (alimentos): *la carne está dura*, the meat is tough. || Stale, old (pan). || Hardhearted, insensitive (insensible). || Harsh, severe, hard, tough: *un clima duro*, a harsh climate; *una dura reprimenda* a severe reprimand; *un juez, un dictador duro*, a severe judge, dictator. || Stony, stern (mirada). || Stony, hard (corazón). || Hard, difficult, tough: *una subida dura*, a hard climb; *un problema duro*, a tough problem. || Stiff (cerradura, puerta, mecanismo, palanca, cuello, etc.). || Harsh: *luz dura, sonido duro*, harsh light, sound. || Tough, strong (capaz de aguantar mucho): *un coche duro*, a tough car. || Hardy, tough, strong (persona, raza, planta que aguanta). || Stubborn, obstinate (terco). || DEP. Rough (juego). || Rough, bumpy (aterrizaje). || — *Agua dura*, hard water. || *De facciones duras*, hard-featured. || FIG. *Duro de corazón*, hardhearted. | *Duro de cabeza*, V. CABEZA. | *Duro de roer* or *de tragar*, hard to swallow. | *Estar a las duras y a las maduras*, to take the rough with the smooth. || *Hacer algo a duras penas*, to do sth. with great difficulty. || *Huevo duro*, hard-boiled egg. || FIG. *Más duro que una piedra*, as hard as nails. | *Ser duro de casco*, to be obstinate *o* stubborn. | *Ser duro de mollera*, V. MOLLERA. || *Ser duro de oído*, to be hard of hearing. || FIG. *Ser duro de pelar*, to be a hard nut. || *Sufrir dura prueba*, to have a bad time of it, to suffer great hardships.
— Adv. Hard: *pegar duro*, to hit hard; *trabajar duro, darle duro al trabajo*, to work hard.
— M. Five pesetas, five-peseta coin (dinero). || FAM. Tough guy (persona). || *Vale veinte duros*, it costs a hundred pesetas.
duunvir o **dunnviro** m. HIST. Duumvir.
duunvirato m. HIST. Duumvirate.
dux m. HIST. Doge.
duz adj. Sweet (dulce). || Mild, gentle. || — *Caña duz*, sugar cane. || *Palo duz*, liquorice root.

E

e f. E: *una e mayúscula*, a capital e.
— OBSERV. The pronunciation of the Spanish *e* is similar to that of the first *e* in the English word *element*.
e conj. And.
— OBSERV. The conjunction *e* replaces *y* before words beginning with *i* or *hi* (vocalic *i*): *Federico e Isabel*, Frederick and Elizabeth; *madre e hija*, mother and daughter. However, at the beginning of an interrogative or exclamatory sentence, or before a word beginning with *y* or *hi* followed by a vowel (consonantal *i*), the *y* is retained: *¿y Ignacio?*, and Ignatius?; *vid y hiedra*, vine and ivy; *tú y yo*, you and I.
¡ea! interj. Come on! (para animar). || So what! (para terminar una discusión).
ebanista m. Cabinetmaker.
ebanistería f. Cabinetmaking (arte). || Cabinetmaker's workshop (taller). || Cabinetwork (muebles).
ébano m. Ebony (madera). || Ebony [tree] (árbol). || FIG. *Ébano vivo*, black ivory.

ebenáceas f. pl. BOT. Ebenaceae.
ebonita f. Ebonite (caucho endurecido).
ebriedad f. Drunkenness, intoxication, inebriation. || *En estado de ebriedad*, inebriated, intoxicated.
ebrio, a adj. Drunk, inebriated, intoxicated (embriagado). || FIG. Blind: *ebrio de ira*, blind with anger. | Drunk: *ebrio de poder*, power drunk. | Beside o.s.: *estaba ebrio de alegría*, I was beside myself with happiness.
— M. y f. Drunkard, drunk.
Ebro n. pr. m. GEOGR. Ebro.
ebullición f. Boiling, ebullition (de un líquido). || FIG. Ebullience. || — FIG. *Estar en ebullición*, to be boiling over [with excitement]. || *Punto de ebullición*, boiling point.
ebúrneo, a adj. Eburnean, ivory-like.
eccehomo o **ecce homo** m. Ecce homo. || FIG. *Estar hecho un eccehomo*, to cut a sorry figure.
eccema m. MED. Eczema.
eccematoso, sa adj. Eczematous.
eclampsia f. MED. Eclampsia.
eclecticismo m. Eclecticism.
ecléctico, ca adj./s. Eclectic.
eclesiastés n. pr. m. Ecclesiastes (libro de la Biblia).
eclesiástico, ca adj. Ecclesiastical, ecclesiastic.
— M. Ecclesiastic, clergyman (clérigo). || Ecclesiasticus (libro de la Biblia).
eclipsar v. tr. ASTR. To eclipse. || FIG. To eclipse, to outshine, to overshadow (deslucir).
— V. pr. To be eclipsed (desaparecer).
eclipse m. ASTR. Eclipse: *eclipse de Luna* or *lunar*, *de Sol* or *solar*, lunar, solar eclipse. || FAM. Eclipse, disappearance.
eclipsis f. GRAM. Ellipsis.
eclíptico, ca adj./s. f. Ecliptic.
eclisa f. TECN. Fishplate (vía).
eclosión f. Hatching (de un huevo). || Opening, blooming (de una flor). || FIG. Appearance (aparición).
eco m. Echo (acústica). || Distant sound, echo: *oía el eco de su voz*, I could hear the distant sound of his voice. || Echo (del radar, en poesía). || FIG. Word: *no tenemos eco de lo ocurrido*, we have no word of what has happened. | Rumour (noticia imprecisa). | Echo (persona que repite o repetición servil). || — *Ecos de sociedad*, society news, *sing.*, society column, *sing.* || *Hacerse eco de*, to echo. || *Tener eco*, to make news (tener difusión), to catch on (ser adoptado), to get a response (obtener una reacción).
ecología f. BIOL. Ecology.
ecológico, ca adj. Ecological.
ecologista adj. Ecological.
— M. y f. Ecologist.
ecólogo m. Ecologist.
economato m. Discount store, cooperative store.
econometría f. Econometrics. || *Especialista en econometría*, econometrician.
economía f. Economics: *estudiar economía*, to study economics. || Economy: *economía planificada*, planned economy. || Economy (de esfuerzo, de palabras). || Saving (ahorro): *hacer una economía de cien pesetas*, to make a saving of one hundred pesetas; *una economía de quince minutos*, a saving of fifteen minutes. || Economy, thrift (moderación en los gastos). || — Pl. Savings (ahorros). || — *Economía política*, political economy. || FAM. *Esas son economías de chicha y nabo* or *del chocolate del loro*, that's cheeseparing [economy]. || *Hacer economías*, to economize.
económico, ca adj. Economic: *Comunidad Económica Europea*, European Economic Community. || Economic, financial: *crisis económica*, financial crisis. || Economical, cheap, inexpensive: *restaurante económico*, economical restaurant. || Economical, thrifty (persona). || — *Año* or *ejercicio económico*, financial *o* fiscal year. || *Cocina económica*, wood-fired stove.
economista m. y f. Economist.
economizar v. tr. To save, to economize (dinero, esfuerzos, tiempo).
— V. intr. To economize, to save: *economizar para las vacaciones*, to save for the holidays.
ecónomo, ma m. y f. Treasurer, bursar.
ectodermo m. BIOL. Ectoderm.
ectoparásito, ta adj. Ectoparasitic.
— M. Ectoparasite.
ectoplasma m. BIOL. Ectoplasm.
ecuación f. MAT. Equation: *ecuación de segundo grado*, quadratic equation; *ecuación de primer grado*, simple equation. || — *Raíz de una ecuación*, root of an equation. || *Sistema de ecuaciones con varias incógnitas*, simultaneous equations.
ecuador m. Equator. || — FAM. *El paso del ecuador*, halfway point [in a course of study]. || *Pasar el ecuador*, to cross the line.
Ecuador (El) n. pr. m. GEOGR. Ecuador.
ecuánime adj. Impartial, fair, unprejudiced (imparcial). || Calm, composed, level-headed (equilibrado).
ecuanimidad f. Impartiality, fairness (justicia): *la ecuanimidad de un juez*, the fairness of a judge. || Equanimity, composure (serenidad).
ecuatoreñismo m. V. ECUATORIANISMO.
ecuatorial adj. Equatorial.
— M. ASTR. Equatorial.
ecuatorianismo m. Word *o* expression characteristic of the Spanish of Ecuador, Ecuadorianism.
ecuatoriano, na adj./s. Ecuadorian, Ecuadoran, Ecuadorean.
ecuestre adj. Equestrian: *estatua ecuestre*, equestrian statue.
ecumene m. Ecumene, oecumene.
ecuménico, ca adj. Ecumenical, oecumenical.
ecumenismo m. Ecumenicalism, ecumenism, oecumenicalism, oecumenism.
eczema m. MED. Eczema.
eczematoso, sa adj. MED. Eczematous.
echada f. Throw (lanzamiento). || Length (en una carrera): *ganar por tres echadas*, to win by three lengths. || *Amer.* Boast (mentira).
echado, da adj. Lying down (tumbado). || FAM. *Un hombre echado para adelante*, a bold *o* fearless man.
echador, ra adj. Throwing (que echa). || *Amer.* Boastful (fanfarrón).
— M. y f. Thrower (que tira). || — F. *Echadora de buenaventura* or *de cartas*, fortune-teller.
echamiento m. Throw.
echar v. tr. e intr.

1. Tirar, arrojar. — **2.** Despedir, expulsar. — **3.** Brotar, salir. — **4.** Poner, aplicar. — **5.** Decir. — **6.** Otros sentidos. — **7.** Con preposición. — **8.** Locuciones diversas. — **9.** Verbo pronominal.

1. TIRAR, ARROJAR. — To throw: *echar un hueso a un perro*, to throw a bone to a dog; *echar por la borda*, to throw overboard. || To give off: *echar chispas*, to give off sparks; *estas flores echan un olor agradable*, these flowers give off a nice smell. || To put (poner): *echar leña al fuego*, to put wood on the fire. || To pour: *echar agua en un vaso*, to pour water into a glass. || To serve, to give (comida). || To shed: *echar lágrimas*, to shed tears. || To post [U.S., to mail]: *echar una carta*, to post a letter. || To add, to put in: *echar sal*, to add salt. || To toss (una moneda). || To throw (los dados). || To deal (los naipes). || To cast (redes, ancla, anzuelo).
2. DESPEDIR, EXPULSAR. — To throw out, to turn out, to eject: *le echaron de la sala*, he was thrown out of the room; *me han echado del piso*, they have turned me out of my flat. || To throw out, to sack: *le han echado de su trabajo*, he has been thrown out of his job, he has been sacked from his job. || To throw out, to expel (de una sociedad, club, etc.). || To bring on, to send on: *¡que echen el toro!*, send on the bull! || To take off, to send [off]: *echar el toro al corral*, to send the bull to the pen.
3. BROTAR, SALIR. — To put out, to sprout (raíces, hojas). || To grow (pelo). || To cut (dientes): *el niño está echando los dientes*, the baby is cutting his teeth.
4. PONER, APLICAR. — To put on, to apply: *echar un remiendo*, to put on a patch. || To spread (mantequilla). || To impose: *echar una multa*, to impose a fine. || To put on, to apply (el freno). || To put on, to bet, to wager (apostar). || To mate (aparear).
5. DECIR. — To tell: *echar la buenaventura a alguien*, to tell s.o.'s fortune. || To recite: *echar versos*, to recite poetry. || To hurl (blasfemias). || To give: *echar un sermón, una reprimenda*, to give a sermon, a reprimand. || To give, to make (un discurso).
6. OTROS SENTIDOS. — To do: *echar cálculos*, to do calculations. || To play, to have (jugar): *echar una partida de cartas*, to play a game of cards. || To have, to take: *echar una mirada a algo*, to have a look at sth. || To give, to throw: *me echó una mirada furibunda*, he gave me a furious look. || To have, to take (tener): *echar una siesta*, to have a siesta. || To give: *¿qué edad le echas?*, what age would you give him? || To push, to move: *echó la silla hacia atrás*, he pushed the chair backwards. || To put on, to show: *echar una película*, to put on a film. || To add up (la cuenta). || To have, to smoke (un cigarrillo). || To lay (los cimientos). || To take: *echo una hora en ir de Madrid a Toledo*, I take an hour *o* it takes me an hour to go from Madrid to Toledo. || To turn (la llave). || To shoot (el cerrojo). || To slide (el pestillo). || To put to bed: *voy a echar al niño*, I'm going to put the child to bed.
7. CON PREPOSICIÓN. — *Echar a* (con infinitivo), to begin, to start: *echar a llorar*, to begin crying, to begin to cry. || *Echar a volar*, to take wing, to fly away *o* off (un pájaro). || *Echar de comer, de beber*, to feed, to water. || *Echar por*, to take: *echar por la primera calle*, to take the first street; to bear: *echar por la derecha*, to bear right.
8. LOCUCIONES DIVERSAS. — *Echando por largo*, at the outside, at the very most. || *Echar abajo* or *por tierra*, to pull down, to demolish (derribar), to ruin (reputación), to bring down, to overthrow (un gobierno), to break down (una puerta). || *Echar a broma*, to turn into a joke, to take as a joke. || *Echar a cara y cruz*, to toss for. || FIG. *Echar agua en el mar*, to carry coals to Newcastle. || *Echar a la calle*, to turn out, to chuck out (fam.). || *Echar a la lotería*, to play the lottery. || *Echar a perder*, to spoil, to ruin: *echar a perder un vestido*, to ruin a dress; to waste (no aprovechar). || *Echar a pique*, V. PIQUE. || *Echar atrás*, to set back. || *Echar barriga* or *vientre*, to get a potbelly,

to put on weight. || *Echar bolas*, to tell fibs *o* lies (mentir). || *Echar bravatas*, to brag, to boast. || *Echar carnes*, to put on weight. || *Echar de menos*, to miss: *echo de menos (a) mi pueblo*, I miss my home town. || *Echar de ver*, to notice. || *Echar el cerrojo*, to bolt the door, to lock the door (cerrar). || FIG. y FAM. *Echar el guante a uno*, to catch hold of s.o., to get hold of s.o. | *Echar el resto*, V. RESTO. | *Echar en cara a alguien*, to throw in s.o.'s face. | *Echar fuego por los ojos*, to look daggers. || *Echar humo*, to smoke, to give off smoke. || *Echar juramentos*, to swear. || *Echar la bendición*, to bless, to give one's blessing. || FIG. *Echar la casa por la ventana*, V. CASA. || *Echar las bases de*, to lay the foundations for. || *Echar las bendiciones*, to marry. || *Echar (las) cartas*, to deal the cards (repartir), to tell fortunes by cards (adivinar). || *Echar las cortinas*, to draw *o* to pull the curtains. || *Echarle gracia a una cosa* or *echarle sal y pimienta*, to add character to sth., to add that certain something to sth. || FIG. *Echar leña al fuego*, to add fuel to the fire. || *Echar los brazos al cuello de alguien*, to fling one's arms round s.o.'s neck. || FIG. *Echarlo todo a rodar*, to ruin everything (estropear), to give up (abandonar). || *Echar mano a*, to reach for (alargar la mano), to go for (un arma), to get hold of, to lay one's hands on (agarrar). || *Echar mano de*, to make use of, to fall back on: *echar mano de las reservas*, to fall back on the reserves; to turn to (persona). || FIG. *Echar pajas*, to draw straws. | *Echar pestes de alguien*, to heap abuse on s.o., to drag s.o. through the mud, to run s.o. down (criticar mucho). || *Echar sangre*, V. SANGRE. || *Echar suertes*, V. SUERTE. || FIG. *Echar tierra a un asunto*, to hush up an affair. | *Echar una mano a alguien*, to give *o* to lend s.o. a hand. || FAM. *Echar un bocado, un trago*, to have a bite *o* sth. to eat, to have sth. to drink. || FIG. *Echar un capote a uno*, to give s.o. a helping hand, to help s.o. out. | *Echar un párrafo*, to have a chat. | *No lo eche usted en saco roto*, take good note of that. | *¿Qué (película) echan en el Astoria?*, what's on at the Astoria?

9. VERBO PRONOMINAL. — To throw o.s. (arrojarse): *echarse en brazos de alguien*, to throw o.s. into s.o.'s arms. || To lie down (tumbarse): *échate en la cama*, lie down on the bed. || To sit, to brood (aves). || To die down, to drop (el viento). || To put (ponerse). || To get o.s. (una novia). || To have, to smoke (un cigarrillo). || To have (una siesta). || FIG. To become addicted to, to take to: *echarse a la bebida*, to take to drink. | To treat o.s. to (regalarse): *se ha echado un abrigo de visón*, she has treated herself to a mink coat. || MAR. To settle on her beam-ends. || *Amer.* To wear, to have on: *echarse zapatos*, to have shoes on. || — *Echarse a dormir*, to go to bed *o* to sleep. || FAM. *Echarse algo al cuerpo*, to have sth. (comer): *echarse al cuerpo una buena comida*, to have a good feed. | *Echarse al monte*, to take to the hills. | *Echarse a morir* or *a temblar*, to be panic-stricken. || *Echarse a perder*, to go bad (alimentos), to go to the dogs (personas), to be ruined *o* spoiled (estropearse). || *Echarse atrás*, to lean back (inclinarse hacia atrás), to throw o.s. back (para evitar algo), to back down (arrepentirse). || *Echarse a un lado*, to move aside. || *Echarse de ver*, to be obvious. || *Echarse encima*, V. ENCIMA. || *Echárselas de enfermo*, to sham *o* to feign illness, to pretend to be ill. || *Echárselas de héroe*, to play the hero.

echarpe m. Shawl (chal).

echazón f. Throw (acción). || MAR. Jettison.

echón, ona adj. *Amer.* Boastful, swaggering.

echona o **echuna** f. *Amer.* Sickle (hoz).

edad f. Age: *diez años de edad*, ten years of age; *a la edad de 10 años*, at the age of 10; *no aparentar su edad*, not to look one's age. || Age (época): *la Edad de Piedra*, the Stone Age; *Edad de Oro*, Golden Age; *Edad Moderna*, Modern Age; *Edad de Bronce*, Bronze Age. || Time, date, period: *por aquella edad*, at that time. || — *A mi edad*, at my age. || *De cierta edad*, elderly. || *De corta* or *poca edad*, of tender years, young. || *De edad* or *de edad avanzada*, elderly: *persona de edad*, elderly person. || *De edad provecta*, elderly. || *De edad temprana*, of tender years. || *De más edad*, older, elder. || *De mediana edad*, middle-aged. || *De menor edad*, younger. || *Edad crítica*, puberty (adolescencia), change of life, menopause (de una mujer). || *Edad de la razón* or *del juicio*, age of reason. || *Edad del pavo* or *del chivateo* (Amer.), awkward age. || *Edad Media*, Middle Ages. || *Edad núbil*, nubility. || *En edad de*, old enough to. || *En edad escolar*, of school age. || *En su edad temprana*, in his early years, in his childhood. || *Entrado en edad*, elderly. || *Llegar a la mayoría de edad*, to come of age. || *Menor edad*, minority, nonage, infancy (minoría de edad). || *Primera edad*, infancy, childhood. || *¿Qué edad le das* or *le echas?*, how old do you think he is?, what age would you give him? || *¿Qué edad tienes?*, how old are you? || *Representar la edad que se tiene*, to look one's age. || *Ser mayor de edad*, to be of age. || *Ser menor de edad*, to be under age, to be a minor. || *Tener edad para*, to be old enough to. || *Un chico de diez años de edad*, a ten-year-old boy. || *Un mayor de edad, un menor de edad*, a major, a minor (personas).

edecán m. Aide-de-camp.

edelweiss m. BOT. Edelweiss.

edema f. MED. Edema, oedema.

edematoso, sa adj. MED. Edematous, oedematous.

Edén m. Eden. || FIG. *Aquello era un Edén*, it was a garden of Eden.

edénico, ca adj. Edenic.

edición f. Edition (de un libro): *primera edición*, first edition; *edición en rústica*, paperbound *o* paperback edition. || Edition, issue edition (de periódico, revista). || — *Ediciones Larousse*, Larousse Publications. || *Edición príncipe*, editio princeps.

edicto m. Edict, decree.

edificación f. Construction, building. || FIG. Edification.

edificador, ra m. y f. Builder, constructor.
— Adj. Building, construction. || FIG. Edifying.

edificante adj. Edifying: *un ejemplo edificante*, an edifying example.

edificar v. tr. To build, to construct: *edificar en la arena*, to build on sand. || FIG. To edify: *edificar con el ejemplo*, to edify by one's example.
— V. pr. To be built [up]: *las grandes fortunas se edifican con el trabajo*, great fortunes are built [up] on hard work.

edificativo, va adj. Edifying.

edificatorio, ria adj. Building, construction.

edificio m. Building, edifice: *el Prado es un edificio hermoso*, the Prado is a magnificent building. || FIG. Structure, edifice: *el edificio social*, the social structure.

edil m. Aedile, edile (magistrado romano). || Municipal official, town councillor.

Edimburgo n. pr. GEOGR. Edinburgh.

Edipo n. pr. m. Oedipus.

editar v. tr. To publish: *editar un libro*, to publish a book.

editor, ra adj. Publishing: *casa editora*, publishing house.
— M. y f. Publisher (persona). || — F. Publishing house (casa).

editorial adj. Editorial. || Publishing.
— M. Editorial, leading article (artículo de fondo). || — F. Publishing house.

editorialista m. Editorialist, leader writer.

edredón m. Eiderdown.

eduardiano, na adj. Edwardian.

Eduardo n. pr. m. Edward.

educable adj. Educable, teachable.

educación f. Education (enseñanza). || Upbringing (crianza). || [Good] manners, *pl.*, politeness, breeding (modales): *no tiene educación*, he has no manners. || — *Educación física*, physical education *o* training. || *Mala educación*, bad manners. || *Ministerio de Educación y Ciencia*, Ministry of Education. || *¡Qué falta de educación!*, how rude!, what bad manners!

educacionista m. y f. Educationist, educationalist, educator.

educado, da adj. Educated. || Well-mannered, polite (formal). || — *Bien educado*, well-bred, well-mannered. || *Mal educado*, ill-bred, bad-mannered, rude.

educador, ra m. y f. Educator.
— Adj. Educating.

educando, da m. y f. Pupil, student.

educar v. tr. To educate (dar instrucción). || To bring up: *educar con* or *en buenos principios*, to bring up on good principles. || To train, to educate, (el oido, los miembros). || To educate, to develop (el gusto). || To bring up, to rear (criar).
— V. pr. To be brought up. || To be educated.

educativo, va adj. Educative, educational (que sirve para educar). || Educative, instructive.

educción f. Eduction.

edulcoración f. Sweetening.

edulcorar v. tr. To edulcorate, to sweeten.

efe f. F [name of the letter *f*].

efebo m. Ephebe.

efectismo m. Sensationalism, striving for effect (en arte y literatura). || Trompe-l'oeil.

efectista adj. Sensationalist. || Trompe-l'oeil: *pintura efectista*, trompe-l'oeil painting.

efectivamente adv. Really, in fact (en realidad). || Indeed, exactly (por supuesto).

efectividad f. Effectiveness,

efectivo, va adj. Effective. || Real (verdadero). || Permanent, regular (empleo). || — *Dinero efectivo*, cash, ready money. || *Hacer efectivo un cheque*, to cash a cheque. || *Hacerse efectivo*, to take effect, to come into effect. || TECN. *Potencia efectiva*, brake horsepower.
— M. Cash: *efectivo en caja*, cash in hand; *pagar en efectivo*, to pay [in] cash. || — Pl. MIL. Effective [force], *sing.*, total strength, *sing.* (de un ejército).

efecto m. Effect, result (resultado): *la escasez de alimentos fue uno de los efectos de la guerra*, the food shortage was one of the effects of the war. || Effect, impression, impact (impresión hecha en el ánimo): *la noticia le hizo gran efecto*, the news made a great impression on him. || Spin (picado): *dar efecto a la pelota*, to put a spin on the ball. || ARTES. Trompe-l'œil. || COM. Document. | Bill (letra de cambio). || — Pl. Goods (mercancías). || Belongings, effects (cosas personales). || Effects, property, *sing.*, possessions (bienes). || — *A este* or *a tal efecto*, for that purpose, to that end. || *A efectos de*, with the object of. || *Con efecto retroactivo*, retroactive. || *Dar efecto*, to implement (a unas disposiciones). || *Efecto retardado*, delayed action. || *Efectos de consumo*, consumer goods. || CINEM. *Efectos especiales*, special effects. || *Efectos mobiliarios*, chattels. || *Efectos sonoros*, sound effects (cine, teatro, radio). || *Efecto útil*, output. || *En efecto*, in fact, really, as a matter of fact, in effect (efectivamente), indeed (por supuesto). || *Eso hace buen efecto*, that looks well. || *Hacer efecto*, v. TENER y SURTIR EFECTO. || FAM. *Hacer un efecto bárbaro*, to have a great effect. || *Lanzar con efecto una pelota*, to spin a ball. || *Llevar a efecto*, to put into effect, to carry out. || *Ser de buen, de mal efecto*, to create a good, bad effect *o* impression. || *Surtir efecto*, v. SURTIR. || *Tener efecto*, to take effect, to come *o* go into effect *o* operation (entrar en vigor): *el nuevo horario tendrá efecto a partir de mañana*, the new timetable will go into effect tomorrow; to take place (celebrarse): *mañana tendrá efecto la inauguración del estadio*, the opening of the stadium will take place tomorrow. || *Tener por efecto*, to result in, to have as a result.

efectuar v. tr. To effect, to carry out, to do, to perform: *efectuar una multiplicación*, to do a multiplication. || To make: *efectuar una detención, una visita, un viaje*, to make an arrest, a visit, a journey.
— V. pr. To take place (celebrarse).

efedrina f. Ephedrine.

efemérides f. pl. ASTR. Ephemerides (almanaque astronómico). || Ephemeris, *sing.* (ant.), diary, *sing.* (diario). || List of the day's anniversaries which appears in a newspaper (en un periódico).

— OBSERV. This word is often used in the singular (una *efeméride* or una *efemérides*) although only the plural is accepted by the Academy.

eferente adj. ANAT. Efferent.

efervescencia f. Effervescence, effervescency. || FIG. Excitement, agitation, effervescence.

efervescente adj. Effervescent. || Fizzy (bebidas).

Éfeso n. pr. GEOGR. Ephesus.

eficacia f. Efficacy, effectiveness (de cosas). || Efficiency (de personas).

eficaz adj. Efficacious, efficient, effective (que produce el efecto deseado). || Efficient (eficiente). || *Con su eficaz ayuda*, with your able assistance.

— OBSERV. *Efficient, efficacious* y *effective* significan todos *que logra un efecto determinado; efficient* significa además *que anda bien* o, tratándose de una máquina, *que produce gran rendimiento*.

eficiencia f. Efficiency.

eficiente adj. Efficient.

efigie f. Effigy, image.

efímera f. ZOOL. Ephemera, mayfly.

efímero, ra adj. Ephemeral.

eflorescencia f. Efflorescence.

eflorescente adj. Efflorescent.

efluvio m. Effluvium, exhalation. || *Los primeros efluvios de la primavera*, the first breath of spring.

efracción f. Effraction.

efugio m. Subterfuge, evasion.

efusión f. Effusion. || FIG. Effusion. || — *Con efusión*, effusively. || *Efusión de sangre*, bloodshed.

efusivo, va adj. Effusive. || GEOL. Effusive, extrusive.

Egeo n. pr. m. GEOGR. *Mar Egeo*, Aegean [Sea].

Egeria n. pr. f. Egeria.

égida o **egida** f. Aegis. || *Bajo la égida de*, under the aegis *o* the auspices *o* the sponsorship of.

egipcio, cia adj./s. Egyptian.

Egipto n. pr. m. GEOGR. Egypt.

egiptología f. Egyptology.

egiptólogo, ga m. y f. Egyptologist.

égira f. Hegira, hejira (hégira).

Egisto n. pr. m. Aegisthus.

eglantina f. BOT. Eglantine.

égloga f. Eclogue, short pastoral poem.

ego m. FIL. Ego.

egocéntrico, ca adj. Egocentric, egocentrical, self-centred [U.S., self-centered].

egocentrismo m. Egocentrism, egocentricity, self-centredness [U.S., self-centeredness].

egoísmo m. Selfishness, egoism, egotism. || FIL. Egoism.

egoísta adj. Selfish, egoistic, egotistic, egoistical. || FIL. Egoistic.
— M. y f. Egoist, egotist, selfish person. || FIL. Egoist.

ególatra adj. Self-worshipping.

egolatría f. Self-worship.

egotismo m. Egotism.

egotista adj. Egotistic, egotistical, egoistic.
— M. y f. Egotist.

egregio, gia adj. Illustrious, eminent.

egresado, da adj./s. Graduate.

egresar v. intr. *Amer.* To pass out (de una academia militar). | To leave, to graduate (terminar sus estudios).

egreso m. Passing-out (de una academia militar). || Graduation (de una universidad). || Expenditure.

eh interj. Eh!, hey! (para llamar la atención). || O. K.?, understood?, all right?: *que no vuelva a ocurrir, ¿eh?*, don't let it happen again, understood? || — *Esto es muy malo, ¿eh?*, this is very bad, isn't it? || *Y ahora te vas a la cama, ¿eh?*, and now you'll go to bed, won't you?

eider m. Eider (pato).

einstenio m. QUÍM. Einsteinium.

eirá m. Eyra (especie de puma).

Eire n. pr. m. GEOGR. Eire.

eje m. TECN. Axle (de una rueda): *eje trasero, delantero*, rear, front axle. | Shaft (árbol). || Axis: *eje del mundo*, earth's axis. || MAT. y FÍS. Axis: *eje de revolución, de simetría*, axis of rotation, of symmetry; *eje óptico*, optical axis. || FIG. Hub, core, crux (de un argumento). || — TECN. *Caja del eje*, axle box. | *Chaveta del eje*, axle pin. | *Eje de levas*, camshaft. || MAT. *Eje de ordenadas, de abscisas*, y-axis, x-axis. || *El Eje* (Berlín-Roma), the Axis. || *El eje de una calle, de un río*, the centre line of a street, of a river. || *Idea eje*, central idea. || TECN. *Manga del eje*, axle arm, axle journal. || FAM. *¡Me parte por el eje!*, it's a big nuisance!

ejecución f. Execution, carrying-out: *la ejecución de un proyecto*, the execution of a plan. || Execution (de un condenado). || MÚS. y TEATR. Performance, interpretation. || JUR. Distraint, distress (de un deudor). | Seizure, attachment (embargo). || — *Pelotón de ejecución*, firing squad. || *Poner en ejecución*, to put into execution, to carry out.

ejecutable adj. Practicable, feasible (factible). || MÚS. y TEATR. Performable.

ejecutante m. y f. Executor [one who carries out a plan]. || MÚS. Executant, performer. || — M. JUR. Distrainor.

ejecutar v. tr. To execute, to carry out (un proyecto, una orden, etc.). || To execute (a un condenado). || MÚS. y TEATR. To perform, to interpret. || JUR. To distrain upon (deudor). | To seize, to attach (embargar).
— V. intr. To act. || *Usted manda y yo ejecuto*, you give the orders and I carry them out.

ejecutivamente adv. Promptly, quickly. || JUR. By distraint.

ejecutivo, va adj. Executive (que ejecuta): *consejo ejecutivo*, executive council; *el poder ejecutivo*, the executive power. || Expeditious, prompt (rápido).
— M. The executive (poder). || Executive (director).

ejecutor, ra m. y f. Executant, executor. || — *Ejecutor de la justicia*, executioner. || *Ejecutora testamentaria*, executrix. || *Ejecutor testamentario*, executor.

ejecutoria f. Letters (*pl.*) patent of nobility. || FIG. Record, accomplishments, *pl.* (historial). || JUR. Writ of execution (acto que confirma un juicio).

ejecutoría f. Executorship.

ejecutoriar v. tr. To confirm (un juicio). || To verify (comprobar).

ejecutorio, ria adj. JUR. Executory.

¡ejem! interj. Ahem!, hum!

ejemplar adj. Exemplary: *conducta ejemplar*, exemplary behaviour; *castigo ejemplar*, exemplary punishment.
— M. Copy (unidad): *una tirada de diez mil ejemplares*, a run of ten thousand copies; *ejemplar gratuito*, free copy. || Number, issue (de una revista). || Specimen, example: *un ejemplar magnífico de mariposa*, a magnificent example of a butterfly. || FAM. *¡Menudo ejemplar!*, sly bird!, wily bird!

ejemplaridad f. Exemplariness, exemplarity.

ejemplarizar v. tr. To set an example to, to exemplify.

ejemplificación f. Exemplification, illustration.

ejemplificar v. tr. To exemplify, to illustrate.

ejemplo m. Example: *un diccionario sin ejemplos es un esqueleto*, a dictionary without examples is a mere skeleton. || Model, epitome: *es un ejemplo de generosidad*, he is a model of generosity, he is the epitome of generosity. || — *A ejemplo de*, after the example of, after the manner of. || *Dar ejemplo*, to set an example. || *Por ejemplo*, for example, for instance. || *Predicar con el ejemplo*, to set an example (actuando). || *Servir de ejemplo*, to serve as an example. || FIG. *Sin ejemplo*, unprecedented. || *Tomar ejemplo de alguien*, to follow s.o.'s example, to take a leaf out of s.o.'s book. || *Tomar por ejemplo* or *como ejemplo*, to take as an example.

ejercer v. intr. To practise, to be in practice: *es abogado pero ya no ejerce*, he is a lawyer but no longer practises *o* is no longer in practice.
— V. tr. To exert (influencia, poder). || To exercise (ejercitar). || To exercise, to use: *ejercer el derecho de voto*, to use one's right to vote. || To exercise (autoridad). || To practise: *ejercer la medicina*, to practise medicine. || To perform (unas funciones).

ejercicio m. Practice: *el ejercicio de la medicina*, the practice of medicine. || Exercise, use (de un derecho). || Exertion (de una influencia, de un poder). || Performance (de una función). || Exercise: *ejercicios de latín*, Latin exercises. || Homework (trabajos para hacer en casa). || Test (examen o prueba): *ejercicio escrito, oral*, written, oral test. || Exercise (esfuerzo corporal): *hacer ejercicios*, to do exercises. || MIL. Training, exercise, drill, practice. || — *Ejercicio económico*, financial *o* fiscal year. || REL. *Ejercicios espirituales*, spiritual retreat. || *En ejercicio*, practising: *un abogado en ejercicio*, a practising lawyer. || *Presidente en ejercicio*, acting chairman (de una reunión).

ejercitación f. Practice (de una profesión). || Exercise (de un derecho, de la autoridad).

ejercitado, da adj. Trained.

ejercitante adj. Training.
— M. y f. Person in spiritual retreat.

ejercitar v. tr. To exercise. || To practise (una profesión). || To drill: *ejercitar a un alumno en latín*, to drill a pupil in Latin. || MIL. To drill, to train.

— V. pr. To train, to practise: *ejercitarse en el tiro al arco*, to practise archery *o* to train in archery.
ejército m. Army. || — *Ejército del Aire*, Air Force. || *Ejército de Salvación*, Salvation Army.
ejido m. Common [land] (de un pueblo).
ejote m. *Amer.* Runner bean, green bean.
el art. def. m. sing. The: *el pozo*, the well. || The one: *el de Málaga está enfermo*, the one from Málaga *o* the Málaga one is ill. || — *El del abrigo negro*, the one in the black coat, the one with the black coat. || *El de las gafas*, the one with spectacles. || *El de usted*, yours. || *El que*, he who, the one who (personas, sujeto): *el que vino ayer*, the one who came yesterday; the one whom, the one that, the one (personas, complemento): *el que veré mañana*, the one I'll see tomorrow; the one which, the one that, the one (cosas). || *¡El ... que ...!*, what a ...!: *¡el susto que me dio!*, what a fright it gave me! || *El tuyo es mejor*, yours is better. || *En el año 1979*, in 1979. || *No es mi libro sino el de tu padre*, it is not my book but your father's. || *Ser ... el que*, to be the one that *o* the one which (cosas), to be the one who (personas): *es el avión del general el que está despegando*, the one which *o* the one that is taking off is the general's plane; *soy yo el que ha de decidir*, I'm the one who has to decide.

— OBSERV. *El* debe traducirse a menudo por el adjetivo posesivo en inglés: *llevaba el sombrero puesto*, he had his hat on; *extendió el brazo*, he stretched out his arm. Cuando antecede un día de la semana, se traduce por *on* (*vino el lunes, me iré el viernes*, he came on Monday, I shall leave on Friday), excepto en casos similares a los siguientes: *el lunes pasado, el lunes que viene*, last Monday, next Monday; *el lunes es mal día*, Monday is a bad day. Tampoco se suele usar el artículo en inglés delante de los nombres de países (*el Japón, el Perú*, Japan, Peru), y en otros muchos casos (*me gusta el té*, I like tea; *está en el hospital*, he is in hospital: *en el Madrid actual*, in present-day Madrid; *el capitán X*, captain X).

— In proper names like *El Greco, El Escorial*, the article is never contracted to *al* or *del* (*un cuadro de El Greco, voy a El Escorial*).

— *El* replaces the feminine article before a word beginning with accentuated *a* or *ha* (*el ala, el hacha*).

él pron. pers. m. sing. He (personas): *él viene*, he is coming. || He, him (enfático): *es él*, it is he, it is him (v. OBSERV.). || Him (complemento, si se trata de personas): *hablo de él*, I am talking about him; *trabajo con él*, I work with him. || It (cosas): *se me olvidó el pañuelo y no puedo prescindir de él*, I forgot my handkerchief and I can't manage without it. || — *De él*, his (persona), its (cosa) [suyo]: *el coche de él*, his car; *este coche es de él*, this car is his. || *Él mismo*, himself: *lo dijo él mismo*, he said it himself.

— OBSERV. *Él*, as the subject, is usually omitted before the verb ([*él*] *se marchó*, he left). It is generally only included either to avoid ambiguity or to add emphasis: the latter may be conveyed in English by stressing *he* (*él se fue,yo me quedé*, he left, I remained).

— Cuando *él* se emplea con el verbo *ser* se traduce frecuentemente en inglés por el pronombre complemento *him* aunque sea incorrecto desde un punto de vista puramente gramatical.

elaboración f. Elaboration, processing (de una materia prima). || Working (de metal, madera). || Production, manufacture (de un producto). || Production: *la elaboración de la miel*, honey production. || Elaboration, preparation, working-out: *la elaboración de una ley*, the preparation of a law.
elaborar v. tr. To elaborate, to process (materia prima). || To work (la madera, el metal). || To manufacture, to make, to produce (producto): *elaborar chocolate*, to manufacture chocolate. || To make, to produce: *la seda es elaborada por un gusano*, silk is produced by a worm. || To elaborate, to prepare, to work out: *elaborar un proyecto*, to prepare a plan.
elan m. FIL. *El elan vital*, the élan vital.
elástica f. Vest [U.S., undershirt] (camiseta). || DEP. Singlet [U.S., athletic jersey].
elasticidad f. Elasticity (en general). || Stretch (de tejidos). || FIG. Flexibility, elasticity (de un horario, reglamento, etc.).
elástico, ca adj. Elastic (en general). || Stretch, elastic (tejidos). || FIG. Flexible, elastic: *un horario elástico*, a flexible timetable.
— M. Elastic, elastic band (cinta). || Welt (banda de punto extensible). || — Pl. Braces [U.S., suspenders] (tirantes).
elatérido, da adj. ZOOL. Elaterid.
Elba n. pr. m. GEOGR. Elbe (río). || — F. Elba (isla).
Eldorado n. pr. m. Eldorado, El Dorado.
ele f. L [name of the letter *l*].
eléboro m. BOT. Hellebore.
elección f. Choice, choosing, selection: *la elección de una carrera*, the choice of a career. || Choice, alternative (posibilidad de elegir). || Election: *la elección del Presidente de la República*, the election of the President of the Republic; *presentarse a una elección*, to stand for an election. || — Pl. Election, *sing.*: *elecciones generales*, general election; *convocar a elecciones*, to call *o* hold an election. || — *A elección de*, at the choice of, to suit: *a elección del cliente*, to suit the client. || *Tierra de elección*, the country of one's choice.
electivo, va adj. Elective.
electo, ta adj. Elect: *el presidente electo*, the president-elect.

— OBSERV. The adjective *electo* is the irregular past participle of the verb *elegir*. It is only applied to a successful candidate who has not yet taken up his post. The perfect tense of *elegir* is formed with the regular past participle, *elegido*.

elector, ra adj. Electing.
— M. y f. Elector, voter (en elecciones, referéndum, etc.). || — M. HIST. Elector (antiguo príncipe alemán).
electorado m. Electorate, electoral body, voters, *pl.* || HIST. Electorate: *el Electorado de Maguncia*, the Electorate of Mainz.
electoral adj. Electoral: *censo electoral*, electoral roll; *colegio electoral*, electoral college.
Electra n. pr. f. Electra.
electricidad f. Electricity: *electricidad estática*, static electricity.
electricista adj. Electrical: *ingeniero electricista*, electrical engineer.
— M. y f. Electrician.
eléctrico, ca adj. Electric, electrical. || — *Azul eléctrico*, electric blue. || *Manta eléctrica*, electric blanket. || *Silla eléctrica*, electric chair.
— M. FAM. Electrician (electricista).

— OBSERV. *Electric* y *electrical* son sinónimos. Sin embargo *electric* es mucho más corriente y se aplica generalmente a los objetos que funcionan con electricidad (*electric lamp, electric car, electric train*). *Electrical* se utiliza sobre todo en términos de física o mecánica (*electrical conductivity, electrical drainage, electrical engineering*).

electrificación f. Electrification.
electrificado ,da adj. Electrified.
electrificar v. tr. To electrify: *electrificar un ferrocarril*, to electrify a railway. (V. ELECTRIZAR [Observ.].)
electriz f. Electress.
electrizable adj. Electrifiable.
electrización f. Electrification.
electrizador, ra o **electrizante** adj. Electrifying.
electrizar v. tr. To electrify (cargar de electricidad). || FIG. To electrify: *electrizar una asamblea*, to electrify a meeting.

— OBSERV. *Electrificar* and *electrizar* are not synonymous but are both rendered by the English *electrify*. *Electrificar* means to convert to electric power (e.g. a machine), *electrizar* means to produce an electric charge or current in.

electroacústica f. FÍS. Electroacoustics.
electroanálisis m. QUÍM. Electroanalysis.
electrobomba f. Electric pump.
electrocardiografía f. Electrocardiography.
electrocardiógrafo m. Electrocardiograph.
electrocardiograma m. MED. Electrocardiogram.
electrocauterio m. MED. Electrocautery.
electrocinética f. Electrokinetics.
electrocoagulación f. MED. Electrocoagulation.
electrocución f. Electrocution.
electrocutar v. tr. To electrocute.
— V. pr. To be electrocuted.
electrochoque m. MED. Electric shock, electroshock.
electrodinámico, ca adj. FÍS. Electrodynamic.
— F. Electrodynamics.
electrodinamómetro m. Electrodynamometer.
electrodo m. FÍS. Electrode.
electrodoméstico, da adj. Electrical household: *aparatos electrodomésticos*, electrical household appliances.
— M. pl. Electrical household appliances.
electroencefalografía f. Electroencephalography.
electroencefalógrafo m. Electroencephalograph.
electroencefalograma m. Electroencephalogram.
electrófono m. Record player.
electróforo m. FÍS. Electrophorus.
electrógeno, na adj. Generating, generator: *grupo electrógeno*, generator set.
— M. Electric generator.
electroimán m. FÍS. Electromagnet.
electrólisis f. QUÍM. Electrolysis.
electrolítico, ca adj. QUÍM. Electrolytic.
electrólito m. QUÍM. Electrolyte.
electrolización f. QUÍM. Electrolysis.
electrolizar v. tr. To electrolyze.
electromagnético, ca adj. FÍS. Electromagnetic: *onda electromagnética*, electromagnetic wave.
electromagnetismo m. FÍS. Electromagnetism.
electromecánico, ca adj. Electromechanical.
— F. Electromechanics (ciencia).
electrometalurgia f. Electrometallurgy.
electrometría f. FÍS. Electrometry.
electrómetro m. Electrometer.
electromotor, ra adj. FÍS. Electromotive.
— M. Electromotor, electric motor.
electromotriz adj. f. Electromotive: *fuerza electromotriz*, electromotive force.
electrón m. FÍS. Electron.
electronegativo, va adj. FÍS. Electronegative.
electrónico, ca adj. Electronic. || — *Microscopio electrónico*, electron microscope. || *Tubo electrónico*, thermionic valve, electron tube
— F. Electronics.
electronvoltio m. Electron volt.
electropositivo, va adj. FÍS. Electropositive.
electroquímico, ca adj. QUÍM. Electrochemical.
— F. Electrochemistry.
electroscopio m. FÍS. Electroscope.

electrostático, ca adj. FÍS. Electrostatic.
— F. Electrostatics.
electrotecnia f. FÍS. Electrotechnics, electrical engineering.
electrotécnico, ca adj. Electrotechnical.
electroterapia f. MED. Electrotherapy.
electrotermia f. Electrothermy.
electrotérmico, ca adj. FÍS. Electrothermic.
— F. Electrothermy.
electuario m. Electuary.
elefancia f. MED. Elephantiasis.
elefanciaco, ca o **elefanciaco, ca** adj. Elephantiasic.
elefanta f. Female elephant, cow elephant.
elefante m. Elephant. || *Elefante marino*, sea elephant, elephant seal.
elefantiásico, ca adj. MED. Elephantiasic.
elefantiasis f. MED. Elephantiasis.
elegancia f. Elegance, style.
elegante adj. Elegant, stylish, smart. || Well-turned (frase).
— M. Man of fashion, dandy. || — F. Fashionable woman.
elegantemente adv. Elegantly, stylishly, smartly, fashionably.
elegantizar v. tr. To make elegant, to make stylish, to make smart.
elegantón, ona adj. FAM. Smart: *el novio iba muy elegantón*, the bridegroom looked very smart.
elegía f. Elegy.
elegíaco, ca adj. Elegiac.
elegibilidad f. Eligibility.
elegible adj. Eligible.
elegido, da adj. Chosen, elected: *elegido por la mayoría*, chosen by the majority. || Favourite, preferred (predilecto). || Select, choice (selecto). || *El presidente elegido*, the president-elect.
— M. y f. Elected person. || One chosen (escogido). || One chosen by God, predestinate. || — M. pl. The elect.
elegir* v. tr. To choose, to select (escoger). || To elect (por voto). || — *Dos platos a elegir entre los siguientes*, choice of two dishes from the following (en un menú). || *Te toca a ti elegir*, the choice is yours.
elemental adj. Elementary: *eso es elemental*, that's elementary. || Basic, elementary: *una gramática elemental*, a basic grammar. || Elemental (de los elementos).
elemento m. Element (parte de una cosa). || Part, component (de una máquina). || Section, unit (muebles): *una biblioteca de siete elementos*, a seven-section bookcase. || Member: *los elementos de una junta*, the members of a board; *un buen elemento del equipo*, a good member of the team, a good team-member. || Constituent, ingredient (ingrediente). || FIG. y FAM. Individual, type, character: *reunirse con elementos sospechosos*, to join up with suspicious characters. || FIG. Factor: *elementos que contribuyen al desorden*, factors which contribute to the confusion. || MAT. Element. || ELECTR. Cell (de una batería). || QUÍM. y BIOL. Element. || *Amer.* Fool, idiot (tonto). || — Pl. Elements, basic principles: *elementos de geometría*, basic principles of geometry. || Means (medios) || — *Elementos de juicio*, facts to formulate an opinion: *no tengo bastantes elementos de juicio*, I have insufficient facts to formulate an opinion. || *El líquido elemento*, the sea (mar), water (agua). || FIG. *Estar en su elemento*, to be in one's element. || *La furia de los elementos*, the fury of the elements. || FAM. *¡Menudo elemento!*, wily o sly bird!
Elena n. pr. f. Helen.
elenco m. Catalogue [U.S., catalog], list. || CINEM. y TEATR. Cast (reparto). | Company, troupe.
elevación f. Raising, lifting (de un peso). || Erection (de un edificio). || Raising, rise, increase (de precios). || Raising (de la voz). || Elevation, height (de una montaña). || Rise in the ground, hill (eminencia). || FIG. Raising (de protestas). | Elevation: *su elevación a la nobleza*, his elevation to the peerage. | Ascent (en una jerarquía). | Loftiness, grandness, elevation (del estilo, etc.). | Raising: *la elevación del tono en una discusión*, the raising of voices in a discussion. | Ecstasy, rapture, transport (del alma). || MAT. Raising (a una potencia). || ARQ., ASTR. y REL. Elevation.
elevadamente adv. Elevatedly, loftily.
elevado, da adj. High: *un precio, un edificio elevado*, a high price, building. || High, elevated, (rango, etc.). || Elevated, lofty, grand (estilo). || — MAT. *Elevado a*, [raised] to the power of: *diez elevado a tres es mil*, ten [raised] to the power of three is a thousand. || *Elevado al cuadrado*, squared: *dos elevado al cuadrado*, two squared.
elevador, ra adj. Elevating. || ANAT. *Músculo elevador*, elevator muscle.
— M. Lift, service lift, goods lift, hoist (montacargas). || *Amer.* Lift [U.S., elevator] (ascensor). || ANAT. Elevator (músculo). || ELECTR. Step-up transformer: *elevador-reductor*, step-up-step-down transformer. || TECN. Jack: *elevador de rosca* or *de tornillo*, screw jack. | Ramp: *elevador hidráulico*, hydraulic ramp. || *Elevador de voltaje*, booster.
elevamiento m. FIG. Ecstasy, rapture, transport.
elevar v. tr. To raise, to lift (un peso). || To erect, to put up (un monumento, un edificio). | To raise, to increase, to put up (precios). || To raise (la voz). || FIG. To promote, to raise: *elevar a alguien a un alto cargo*, to promote s.o. to a high position. | To raise, to elevate (a una dignidad). | To elevate, to raise (el tono). | To elevate (el estilo). || MAT. To raise: *elevar a la enésima potencia*, to raise to the power of n. || *Elevar al cuadrado, al cubo*, to square, to cube. || FIG. *Elevar protestas*, to make a protest, to raise a protest.
— V. pr. To rise [up], to ascend: *elevarse por los aires*, to rise into the air; *elevarse en la jerarquía*, to ascend in the hierarchy. || To go up, to increase, to rise (precio). || FIG. To raise o.s., to elevate o.s. || To amount to: *el total se eleva a*, the total amounts to. || To become vain *o* conceited (engreírse). || To be transported, to be enraptured (enajenarse). || — *El pico más alto se eleva a cinco mil metros*, the highest peak rises to *o* reaches five thousand metres. || *Los edificios más grandes de la ciudad se elevan en esta calle*, the city's largest buildings stand in this street.
elevón m. AVIAC. Elevator, aileron.
elfo m. Elf.
elidir v. tr. To weaken. || GRAM. To elide.
— V. pr. To elide, to be elided.
eliminación f. Elimination.
eliminador, ra adj. Eliminating, eliminative.
— M. y f. Eliminator.
eliminar v. tr. To eliminate: *eliminar a un concursante*, to eliminate a competitor. || To eliminate, to remove, to exclude: *le han eliminado del equipo*, they have excluded him from the team. || To get rid of, to cast aside, to expel: *tenemos que eliminar estos temores*, we must cast aside these fears. || MED. To eliminate, to expel (cualquier sustancia nociva). || MAT. *Eliminar una incógnita*, to eliminate an unknown quantity.
eliminatorio, ria adj. Eliminatory: *un examen eliminatorio*, an eliminatory examination.
— F. DEP. Heat, qualifying round (en atletismo). | Preliminary round (en otros deportes).
elinvar m. Elinvar (aleación de níquel y cromo).
elipse f. MAT. Ellipse.
elipsis f. inv. GRAM. Ellipsis.
elipsoidal adj. MAT. Ellipsoidal.
elipsoide m. MAT. Ellipsoid.
elíptico, ca adj. Elliptic, elliptical.
elisabetiano, na adj. Elizabethan.
Elíseo n. pr. m. MIT. Elysium.
elíseo, a adj. MIT. Elysian. || MIT. *Campos Elíseos*, Elysian Fields.
elisión f. GRAM. Elision.
élite f. Elite: *la élite de la nación*, the nation's élite.
— OBSERV. This word is a commonly used Gallicism.
élitro m. ZOOL. Elytrum, elytron (de insecto).
elixir m. Elixir.
elocución f. Elocution (manera de hablar). || *Tiene la elocución fácil*, he has the gift of the gab.
elocuencia f. Eloquence.
elocuente adj. Eloquent. || Telling, significant: *un silencio elocuente*, a telling silence.
elogiable adj. Praiseworthy, laudable.
elogiador, ra adj. Laudatory, eulogistic.
— M. y f. Praiser, eulogist.
elogiar v. tr. To praise, to laud, to eulogize. || *Discurso muy elogiado*, highly praised speech.
elogio m. Eulogy, praise. || — *Deshacerse en elogios*, to be lavish in one's praise. || *Está por encima de todo elogio*, he is beyond praise. || *Hacer elogios de*, to sing the praises of, to eulogize. || *Hacer un caluroso elogio de*, to praise highly.
elogiosamente adv. Eulogistically, with great praise.
elogioso, sa adj. Eulogistic, laudatory: *habló de él en términos elogiosos*, he spoke about him in laudatory terms. || Laudable (digno de elogio): *una acción elogiosa*, a laudable act.
elongación f. ASTR. y MED. Elongation.
elote m. *Amer.* Ear of green corn (mazorca de maíz).
elucidación f. Elucidation, explanation.
elucidar v. tr. To elucidate, to explain (aclarar).
elucubración f. Lucubration.
elucubrar v. tr. To lucubrate.
— OBSERV. *Elucubración* and *elucubrar* are Gallicisms used for *lucubración* and *lucubrar*.
eludible adj. Avoidable, evadable, eludible.
eludir v. tr. To avoid, to elude, to evade: *eludir una pregunta*, to avoid a question. || To avoid: *eludió mirarme a la cara*, he avoided looking me in the face.
elzevir o **elzevirio** m. Elzevir (libro).
ella pron. pers. f. sing. She (sujeto, personas): *ella viene*, she is coming. || Her, herself (enfático, personas): *es ella*, it's her; *lo hizo ella*, she did it [herself]. || Her (con prep., personas): *hablo de ella*, I am talking about her; *lo hice por ella*, I did it for her. || It (sujeto o con prep., cosas). || — FAM. *Allí fue ella*, then the trouble began. || *De ella*, hers (persona): *mi libro y el de ella*, my book and hers; its (cosa). || *Ella misma*, [she] herself. || FAM. *Mañana será ella*, there will be trouble tomorrow.
— OBSERV. The subject pronoun *ella* is only used in Spanish to avoid ambiguity or when emphasis is required; the latter may be conveyed in English by stressing "she"
ellas pron. pers. pl. V. ELLOS.
elle f. Ll [name of the letter *ll*].
ello pron. pers. neutro. It: *no pienses más en ello*, don't think about it any more. || — FAM. *Aquí* or *allí*

fue ello, then the trouble began. || *Ello es que*, the fact is that, the thing is that. || *Por ello me gusta*, that's why I like it. || *¡Vamos a ello!*, let's get on with it!
ellos, ellas pron. pers. pl. They (sujeto). || Them, themselves (complemento). || — *¡A ellos!* or *¡a por ellos!*, forward!, at them! (para atacar). || *De ellos, de ellas*, theirs. || *Ellos mismos, ellas mismas*, themselves: *ellos mismos lo han hecho*, they have done it themselves.
emaciación f. Emaciation.
emaciado, da adj. Emaciated.
emanación f. Emanation.
emanante adj. Emanating.
emanar v. intr. To emanate: *el olor que emana de la panadería*, the smell emanating from the bakery. || To emanate, to be sent out: *la orden emana del gerente*, the order emanates from *o* is sent out by the manager. || To arise, to result: *esta obligación emana del contrato*, this obligation arises from the contract.
emancipación f. Emancipation.
emancipado, da adj. Emancipated.
emancipador, ra adj. Emancipatory.
— M. y f. Emancipator.
emancipar v. tr. To emancipate.
— V. pr. To become emancipated. || To free o.s., to liberate o.s. (liberarse).
emarginado, da adj. BOT. Emarginate.
emasculación f. Emasculation.
emascular v. tr. To emasculate (mutilar).
embabiamiento m. FAM. Absentmindedness.
embadurnador, ra adj. Daubing, smearing.
— M. y f. Dauber [inferior artist].
embadurnar v. tr. To daub, to smear: *embadurnar con* or *de pintura*, to daub with paint.
— V. pr. To smear o.s., to plaster o.s.: *embadurnarse de grasa*, to plaster o.s. with grease.
embaimiento m. Deception, trickery.
embaír* v. tr. To deceive, to trick, to mislead.
— OBSERV. This verb is defective, existing only in the forms whose endings begin with *i*.
embajada f. Embassy. || Ambassadorship (función del embajador). || FIG. Errand, job (encargo). | Message (mensaje). || FAM. *No me vengas ahora con esa embajada*, don't come to me with these stories.
embajador, ra m. y f. Ambassador (hombre), ambassadress (mujer): *embajador en* or *cerca de*, ambassador in *o* to.
embalador, ra m. y f. Packer, wrapper, packager.
embalaje o **embalamiento** m. Packing, packaging. || *Papel de embalaje*, wrapping paper, brown paper.
embalar v. tr. To pack, to package (muebles, etc.). || To rev (un motor).
— V. intr. To race (un motor).
— V. pr. To race (un motor). || To sprint (correr). || To gabble (hablar de prisa). || To get worked up, to get excited (entusiasmarse).
embaldosado, da adj. Tiled.
— M. Tiled floor (suelo). || Tiling.
embaldosar v. tr. To tile (con baldosas).
embalsadero m. Bog, quagmire.
embalsamador, ra adj. Embalming.
— M. Embalmer.
embalsamamiento m. Embalmment, embalming. || Perfuming, scenting, embalming (perfume).
embalsamar v. tr. To embalm (un cadáver). || To perfume, to scent, to embalm (perfumar).
embalsar v. tr. To dam, to dam up (agua). || MAR. To sling, to hoist (izar).
— V. pr. To be dammed up.
embalse m. Damming, damming-up (acción de embalsar). || Dam (presa). || Reservoir, dam (lago artificial). || Collecting (de una cantidad de agua). || MAR. Slinging, hoisting.
emballenado, da adj. Boned, stiffened.
— M. Boning, stiffening.
emballenar v. tr. To bone, to stiffen (con ballenas).
embanastar v. tr. To put in a basket. || FIG. To pack, to crowd, to cram (a la gente).
embancarse v. pr. MAR. To run aground (encallarse). || *Amer.* To silt up, to block, to become blocked (río o lago). || *Amer.* TECN. To adhere to the furnace walls.
embanderar v. tr. To adorn *o* to deck with flags *o* bunting.
embanquetado m. *Amer.* Pavement [U.S., sidewalk].
embanquetar v. tr. *Amer.* To build a pavement on.
embarazada adj. f. Pregnant (mujer): *estar embarazada de seis meses*, to be six months pregnant; *quedarse embarazada*, to become pregnant; *dejar embarazada a una mujer*, to get a woman pregnant. || FIG. Embarrassed (confusa).
— F. Pregnant woman, expectant mother.
embarazadamente adv. With embarrassment, in an embarrassed way (con confusión). || With difficulty (con dificultad).
embarazado, da adj. Embarrassed (persona). || Hampered, hindered (estorbado). || Inconvenienced, troubled (molesto). || Blocked, obstructed (obstruido).
embarazador, ra adj. Embarrassing (que pone en un apuro). || Hampering, hindering, encumbering (que estorba). || Obstructive (que obstruye).
embarazar v. tr. To embarrass (hacer pasar un apuro). || To hinder, to hamper, to encumber: *su abrigo le embaraza*, his overcoat hampers him; *esto embaraza sus movimientos*, this hampers his movements. || To inconvenience, to trouble (molestar). || To block, to obstruct: *embarazar el paso*, to block the way. || To make pregnant (a una mujer).
— V. pr. To get embarrassed (estar confuso). || To be hindered *o* hampered (molestarse). || To get blocked, to become obstructed (obstruirse). || To become pregnant (quedarse encinta).
embarazo m. Embarrassment (apuro). || Hindrance, encumbrance (estorbo). || Obstacle, obstruction (obstáculo). || Pregnancy (de la mujer).
embarazosamente adv. V. EMBARAZADAMENTE.
embarazoso, sa adj. Embarrassing: *una pregunta embarazosa*, an embarrassing question. || Hampering, encumbering, hindering (molesto). || Obstructive (que obstruye).
embarbillado m. TECN. Rabbeting (acción). | Rabbet (ensambladura).
embarbillar v. tr. TECN. To rabbet.
embarcación f. Boat, craft: *embarcación de pesca, de recreo*, fishing, pleasure boat. || Embarkation, embarcation (embarco). || Voyage (viaje).
embarcadero m. MAR. Landing stage (plataforma). | Quay, jetty, pier (muelle para viajeros). | Dock, wharf (muelle para mercancías). || *Amer.* Goods station, loading platform (de ferrocarriles).
embarcar v. tr. To embark (pasajeros). || To ship aboard (mercancías). || FAM. To involve: *embarcar a alguien en un asunto*, to involve s.o. in an affair.
— V. pr. To embark, to go aboard: *embarcarse en un vapor*, to go aboard a steamer; *mañana me embarco a las nueve*, I embark tomorrow at nine o'clock. || FAM. y FIG. To embark upon, to launch into, to engage in (un negocio, un pleito, etc.).
embarco m. Embarkation, embarcation (de personas).
embardar v. tr. To top with spikes *o* barbed wire *o* broken glass (una pared).
embargador m. One who lays an embargo. || JUR. Distrainer, distrainor.
embargar v. tr. FIG. To overcome (la emoción, el dolor). || JUR. To seize, to distrain, to sequestrate. || MAR. To lay an embargo upon (un barco). || (P. us.). To hinder, to hamper (estorbar).
embargo m. JUR. Seizure, sequestration, distraint. || MAR. Embargo. || MED. Indigestion. || FIG. Access (de una emoción). || — JUR. *Ejecución de embargo*, distress, execution. | *Embargo de bienes litigiosos*, seizure under a prior claim. | *Embargo de la cosecha en pie*, distraint by seizure of crops. | *Embargo de retención*, attachment. || *Sin embargo*, however, nevertheless.
embarnizamiento m. Varnishing.
embarnizar v. tr. To varnish.
embarque m. Loading, shipment (de mercancías).
embarrada f. *Amer.* Blunder (patochada).
embarrado, da adj. Muddy.
embarrancar v. intr. MAR. To go *o* to run aground (encallarse). || FIG. To get bogged down.
— V. pr. MAR. To go *o* to run aground. || To get stuck, to get bogged down (atascarse).
embarrar v. tr. To cover *o* to splash with mud (salpicar de barro). || To daub, to smear (embadurnar). || *Amer.* FIG. To sling mud at (envilecer). | To involve (a una persona en un asunto).
— V. pr. To get dirty, to get covered with mud. || To take refuge in the trees (perdices).
embarrilado o **embarrilamiento** m. Casking, barrelling.
embarrilar v. tr. To cask, to barrel.
embarullador, ra adj. Muddling. || FAM. Slapdash, careless, bungling (chapucero).
— M. y f. Muddler, muddlehead. || FAM. Bungler, slapdash *o* careless person.
embarullar v. tr. To muddle, to mix up. || FAM To do in a careless *o* in a slapdash manner, to bungle (chapucear).
embasamiento m. ARQ. Foundation.
embastar v. tr. To baste, to tack (hilvanar). || To put in an embroidery frame (una tela). || To quilt (un colchón). || To put a packsaddle on, to load (las caballerías).
embaste m. Tacking, basting.
embastecer* v. intr. To grow stout, to grow fat (engordar).
— V. pr. To become rude *o* coarse.
embate m. MAR. Dashing, breaking (de olas). || Sea breeze (viento). || FIG. Sudden attack (acometida).
embaucador, ra adj. Deceptive, deceiving (que engaña). || Cajoling (engatusador).
— M. y f. Trickster, swindler, cheater (timador). || Cajoler (engatusador).
embaucamiento m. Deception, deceit, cheating (engaño). || Cajolery (seducción).
embaucar v. tr. To deceive, to cheat, to dupe (engañar): *embaucar a uno con promesas*, to deceive s.o. with promises. || To cajole, to wheedle (seducir).
embaulado, da adj. FIG. Packed, crammed (apretado).
embaular v. tr. To pack [in a trunk]. || FIG. y FAM. To pack, to cram (personas o cosas). | To put away, to gorge, to guzzle (engullir).
embebecer* v. tr. To delight, to fascinate (embelesar).
— V. pr. To be delighted, to be fascinated.
embebecimiento m. Delight, fascination.

embeber v. tr. To absorb, to soak up: *la esponja embebe el agua*, a sponge absorbs water. || To soak, to saturate, to drench: *embeber algo en agua*, to soak sth. in water. || To fit in, to insert (encajar). || To take in (acortar). || To contain (contener).
— V. intr. To shrink (encogerse). || To be absorbent (el lienzo pintado al óleo).
— V. pr. FIG. To absorb o.s., to immerse o.s., to become absorbed: *embeberse en un libro*, to become absorbed in a book. | To soak o.s. (en alcohol, etc.).
embebimiento m. Shrinking.
embelecador, ra adj. Deceptive, deceiving (engañador). || Cajoling, wheedling (engatusador).
embelecamiento m. Deception, deceit (engaño).
embelecar v. tr. To deceive, to cheat, to dupe (engañar). || To cajole, to wheedle (seducir).
embeleco m. Deceit, deception (engaño).
embelesador, ra adj. Charming, enchanting (encantador). || Bewitching (hechicero).
embelesamiento m. V. EMBELESO.
embelesar v. tr. To delight, to charm, to enchant (encantar). || To fascinate, to enrapture, to enthrall (maravillar). || FIG. To bewitch (embrujar).
— V. pr. To be delighted, to be fascinated: *embelesarse con un espectáculo*, to be delighted by a show.
embeleso m. Delight, enchantment (encanto). || Fascination, rapture, enthrallment. || FIG. Bewitchment (embrujo). || BOT. Plumbago, leadwort.
embellaquecerse* v. pr. To go to the bad, to become a rogue.
embellecedor m. AUT. Hubcap (tapacubos).
embellecer* v. tr. To embellish, to beautify, to adorn. || FIG. To idealize.
— V. intr. To improve in looks (naturalmente).
— V. pr. To beautify o.s. (adornándose).
embellecimiento m. Embellishment.
embermejar o **embermejecer*** v. tr. To make red, to redden. || To make blush (sonrojar).
— V. intr. To redden, to turn red. || To blush (cara).
— V. pr. To blush.
emberrenchinarse o **emberrincharse** v. pr. FAM. To fly into a tantrum.
embestida f. Attack, assault, onslaught. || Charge: *la embestida del toro*, the bull's charge. || FIG. y FAM. Touch [for a loan].
embestidor, ra adj. Attacking. || Charging (toro).
embestidura f. V. EMBESTIDA.
embestir* v. tr. To attack, to assail, to assault (asaltar). || To charge: *el toro embistió al matador*, the bull charged the matador. || FIG. y FAM. To smash (un coche). || FIG. y FAM. *Embestir a alguien*, to go at s.o., to throw o.s. at s.o.
— V. intr. To attack.
embetunar v. tr. To black, to polish (zapatos). || To tar, to asphalt (asfaltar).
embicar v. tr. MAR. To luff (orzar). || *Amer.* To insert (una cosa en otra).
— V. intr. *Amer.* To head straight for the coast.
embizcar v. intr. To become cross-eyed.
emblandecer* v. tr. To soften.
— V. pr. To soften, to grow soft. || FIG. To soften up, to relent.
emblanquecer* v. tr. To bleach, to whiten.
— V. pr. To turn white, to bleach.
emblanquecimiento m. Bleaching, whitening.
emblema m. Emblem. || Badge (insignia).
emblemático, ca adj. Emblematic.
embobado, da adj. Agape, dumbfounded, flabbergasted (boquiabierto). || Dazed, stupefied, bewildered (sin reacción).
embobamiento m. Fascination, amazement. || Stupefaction, bewilderment (estupefacción).
embobar v. tr. To amaze, to dumbfound, to astound (atontar). || To stupefy, to bewilder (dejar sin reacción). || To fascinate.
— V. pr. To be amazed *o* astounded *o* stupefied *o* fascinated.
embobecer* v. tr. To make *o* to turn silly *o* stupid.
embobecimiento m. Stupefaction.
embocado, da adj. Smooth (vino).
embocadura f. Mouth (de un río, de un canal). || Taste (de vino). || Bit (de freno de caballo). || TEATR. Proscenium arch. || MÚS. Mouthpiece (boquilla).
embocar v. tr. To put in the mouth. || To enter: *el barco embocó el canal*, the ship entered the canal. || To insert. || MÚS. To put to one's lips (un instrumento). || To catch in the mouth (coger con la boca). || FIG. y FAM. To make believe *o* swallow (hacer creer). | To scoff, to guzzle, to bolt (engullir).
— V. pr. To squeeze in (meterse en un lugar estrecho).
embocinado, da adj. Trumpet-shaped.
embodegar v. tr. To store [in the cellar] (vino, etc.).
embojar v. tr. To put on branches to encourage the formation of cocoons (gusanos de seda).
embojo m. Branches, *pl.* [used for silkworms]. || Putting [silkworms] on branches (acción).
embolado m. Bull with protective wooden balls on the horns (toro). || TEATR. Minor role. || FIG. y FAM. Story, fib (engaño). | Thankless task, irksome job (trabajo). || FAM. *¡Pues vaya un embolado!*, what a job!
embolar v. tr. TAUR. To put protective wooden balls on [the horns of a bull]. || *Amer.* To black, to polish (shoes).
— V. pr. *Amer.* To get drunk.
embolia f. Clot, embolism.
embolismar v. tr. FAM. To gossip about.
émbolo m. TECN. Piston.
embolsar v. tr. To pocket.
embonar v. tr. *Amer.* To manure (con abonos). || To suit (ir bien). | To join (juntar).
emboñigar v. tr. To cover in cow dung.
emboquillado, da adj. Filter-tipped, tipped, filter (cigarrillos).
emboquillar v. tr. To tip, to filter-tip (un cigarrillo). || MIN. To open up, to make an entrance to (una galería, un túnel).
emborrachador, ra adj. Intoxicating.
emborrachamiento m. Intoxication, drunkenness.
emborrachar v. tr. To intoxicate, to make drunk (embriagar). || To get drunk: *emborrachar a alguien*, to get s.o. drunk.
— V. pr. To get drunk, to become intoxicated: *emborracharse con* or *de coñac*, to get drunk on brandy.
emborrascarse v. pr. To become stormy (el tiempo). || To fail, to go wrong (negocios, etc.). || To get angry *o* annoyed (irritarse). || *Amer.* To become exhausted (una mina).
emborrizar v. tr. To card (la lana). || To coat (en pan rallado, harina, azúcar, etc.): *emborrizar un pescado en harina*, to coat a fish in *o* with flour.
emborronador, ra m. y f. *Emborronador de cuartillas* or *de papel*, hack, scribbler, second-rate author (escritor), scribbler (garrapateador).
emborronar v. tr. To scribble (escribir mal). || To scribble on (llenar de garabatos). || To blot (con borrones).
emboscada f. Ambush: *tender una emboscada*, to lay an ambush. || FIG. Trap.
emboscado m. MIL. Soldier under cover *o* in ambush.
emboscar v. tr. MIL. To place under cover *o* in ambush.
— V. pr. To lie in ambush, to ambush. || FIG. To get a cushy job.
embosquecer* v. intr. To become wooded.
embotado, da adj. Dull, blunt.
embotadura f. o **embotamiento** m. Blunting (acción). || Bluntness, dullness (estado). || FIG. Dulling (de los sentidos).
embotar v. tr. To blunt, to dull (una herramienta, etc.). || FIG. To dull, to deaden (los sentidos). | To enervate (a una persona). || To pack in a jar (el tabaco).
— V. pr. To become blunt *o* dull || FIG. To become enervated (persona). | To be dulled, to be deadened (sentidos). || FAM. (P. us.). To put on one's boots.
embotellado, da adj. Bottled. || FIG. Jammed, blocked (circulación). | Stored in one's mind, learnt by heart (aprendido de memoria). | Prepared in advance (discurso, conferencia). || MAR. Blocked, bottled up.
— M. Bottling.
embotellador m. Bottler.
embotelladora f. Bottling machine.
embotellamiento m. Bottling (en botellas). || Jam (en la vía pública): *un embotellamiento de coches*, a traffic jam.
embotellar v. tr. To bottle (poner en botellas). || FIG. To jam, to block (la circulación). | To learn by heart, to memorize (aprender). || MAR. To block, to bottle up (no dejar salir un barco enemigo).
— V. pr. To learn by heart: *se embotelló todo el código civil*, he learned all the civil code by heart.
embotijar v. tr. To put in jugs.
— V. pr. FIG. y FAM. To swell (hincharse). | To become angry *o* annoyed (encolerizarse).
embovedar v. tr. ARQ. To arch, to vault [over].
embozadamente adv. Secretly.
embozar v. tr. To cover [the lower part of the face], to muffle up (con la capa, etc.). || To muzzle (poner un bozal). || FIG. To conceal, to cloak, to disguise (ocultar).
— V. pr. To wrap *o* to muffle o.s. up, to cover one's face: *embozarse en la capa*, to cover one's face with one's cloak.
embozo m. Fold, flap (de una capa). || Turnover, fold (de una sábana). || FIG. Disguise (disfraz), covering-up, concealment, dissimulation (disimulo). || — FIG. y FAM. *Hablar con embozo*, to talk equivocally *o* ambiguously. | *Quitarse el embozo*, to take off one's mask, to reveal one's intentions.
embragar v. tr. TECN. To connect, to engage.
— V. intr. TECN. To engage the clutch, to let the clutch in.
embrague m. TECN. Engaging of the clutch (acción de embragar). | Clutch: *embrague automático, de disco, de fricción, magnético, hidráulico*, automatic, disc, friction, magnetic, hydraulic clutch.
embravecer* v. tr. To enrage, to infuriate, to incense.
— V. pr. To become furious *o* enraged (una persona). || To grow wild (el mar). || To flourish, to thrive (plantas).
embravecido, da adj. Furious, incensed (persona). || Raging, wild, rough (el mar). || Wild (el viento).
embravecimiento m. Fury, rage.
embrazadura f. Handle (de escudo).
embrazar v. tr. To take up [a shield].

embreado m. o **embreadura** f. Tarring.
embrear v. tr. To tar.
embriagado, da adj. Intoxicated, drunk.
embriagador, ra o **embriagante** adj. Intoxicating.
embriagamiento m. Intoxication, inebriation.
embriagar v. tr. To intoxicate, to inebriate (emborrachar). || FIG. To enrapture (enajenar). | To elate, to intoxicate, to make drunk: *embriagado por el éxito*, intoxicated with success.
— V. pr. To become intoxicated, to get drunk. || FIG. To become elated *o* intoxicated *o* drunk (*de*, with).
embriaguez f. Drunkenness, intoxication, inebriation (borrachera). || FIG. Elation, intoxication. | Rapture (enajenación).
embridar v. tr. DEP. To bridle (poner la brida). | To make [a horse] carry its head well (con las riendas).
embriología f. BIOL. Embryology.
embriológico, ca adj. Embryologic, embryological.
embriólogo m. Embryologist.
embrión m. BIOL. Embryo. || FIG. Embryo (principio). || *En embrión*, embryonic, in embryo.
embrionario, ria adj. In embryo, embryonic.
embrocación f. MED. Embrocation.
embrocar v. tr. To decant (un líquido). || To turn upside down (poner boca abajo). || TECN. To wind on to a bobbin (el hilo). | To nail on (la suela de un zapato). || TAUR. To catch between the horns.
embrochalar v. tr. ARQ. To support with a header beam.
embrolladamente adv. Confusedly, in a confused fashion: *hablar embrolladamente*, to talk confusedly.
embrollador, ra adj. Confusing, muddling.
— M. y f. Troublemaker.
embrollar v. tr. To muddle, to tangle up, to mix up (enmarañar). || To confuse, to mix up, to muddle (confundir). || To involve (en un asunto).
— V. pr. To get mixed up, to get tangled *o* muddled (enmarañarse). || To get confused, to get mixed up, to get in a muddle (confundirse). || To get involved (meterse en un asunto).
embrollo m. Tangle (enredo): *un embrollo de hilo*, a tangle of thread. || FIG. Jumble, muddle, mess (confusión). | Mess: *¡en menudo embrollo se ha metido!*, he's got himself into a fine mess! | Trick, lie (embuste).
embrollón, ona adj. Confusing, muddling.
— M. y f. Troublemaker.
embromado, da adj. *Amer. Estar embromado*, to be in a fix.
embromador, ra adj. Fond of joking.
— M. y f. Joker, wag.
embromar v. tr. To make fun of, to tease (burlarse de). || To hoax, to fool (engañar). || *Amer.* To annoy (fastidiar). | To damage (perjudicar). | To delay (entretener, retrasar).
embroquelarse v. pr. V. ABROQUELARSE.
embroquetar v. tr. To skewer (un ave para asarla).
embrujado, da adj. Bewitched (persona). || Haunted (sitio).
embrujador, ra adj. Bewitching.
— M. y f. Sorcerer (hombre), sorceress (mujer).
embrujamiento m. Bewitchment.
embrujar v. tr. To cast a spell on, to bewitch (persona). || To haunt (sitio). || FIG. To enchant, to bewitch (encantar).
embrujo m. Bewitchment (embrujamiento). || Curse, spell (maleficio). || FIG. Spell, charm (encanto).
embrutecedor, ra adj. Brutalizing.
embrutecer* v. tr. To brutalize, to bestialize, to brutify (volver bruto). || To besot (por al alcohol). || To stupefy, to deaden, to dull (por la sorpresa).
— V. pr. To become brutalized. || To grow stupid, to become dull (volverse tonto).
embrutecimiento m. Brutishness, sottishness. || Degradation.
embuchado m. Sausage (embutido). || FIG. Ad-libbing (añadidura a un texto). | Rigging of an election (fraude).
embuchar v. tr. To cram, to force-feed (un ave). || To stuff [with sausage meat] (para hacer embutidos). || FAM. To gulp down, to gobble (engullir).
embudar v. tr. To put a funnel into. || FIG. To trick (engañar).
embudo m. Funnel (para trasegar líquidos). || FIG. Trick, deception (engaño). || Crater (de bomba, meteorito, etc.).
embullo m. *Amer.* Bustle, noise.
emburujar v. tr. FAM. To heap together (amontonar). | To jumble (mezclar). || *Amer.* To mix up (confundir).
— V. pr. *Amer.* To muffle up, to wrap o.s. up (arrebujarse).
embuste m. Lie: *una sarta de embustes*, a string of lies. || Trick (engaño).
embustería f. Lying (mentiras). || Deceit (engaño).
embustero, ra adj. Lying (mentiroso). || Deceitful (engañoso).
— M. y f. Liar.
embutición f. Stamping, pressing.
embutidera f. TECN. Nail set, cupping machine.
embutido m. Sausage. || Stuffing (acción de embutir). || Inlay, marquetry (taracea). || TECN. Stamping, pressing (de las chapas). || *Amer.* Insertion (bordado).
— OBSERV. *Embutido* is a generic term including all types of sausage.
embutir v. tr. To stuff [with sausage meat] (para hacer embutidos). || To stuff, to pack (rellenar): *embutir lana en una almohadilla*, to stuff a cushion with wool, to stuff wool into a cushion. || To insert (introducir). || TECN. To inlay (taracea). | To stamp, to press (metal). || FIG. y FAM. To drive in (meter en la cabeza). || FIG. y FAM. *Embutido en un abrigo*, wrapped *o* muffled up in an overcoat.
— V. tr. y pr. FAM. To wolf down, to bolt down, to gulp down (engullir).
eme f. M [name of the letter *m*]
emergencia f. Emergence (acción de emerger). || Emergency: *en caso de emergencia*, in case of emergency, in an emergency. || — *Estado de emergencia*, state of emergency. || *Salida de emergencia*, emergency exit. || *Solución de emergencia*, emergency solution.
emergente adj. Emergent (que emerge). || FIG. Resulting, resultant (que resulta).
emerger v. intr. To emerge (de un líquido). || To surface (submarino). || To come into view, to emerge, to appear (aparecer). || To project, to jut out: *la roca emerge en medio del río*, the rock juts out in the middle of the river. || FIG. To result.
emérito, ta adj. Emeritus [retired].
emersión f. ASTR. Emersion.
emético, ca adj./s.m. MED. Emetic.
emétrope adj. Emmetropic (de vista normal).
— M. y f. Emmetrope.
emetropía f. MED. Emmetropia.
emigración f. Emigration: *fomentar la emigración a Australia*, to encourage emigration to Australia. || Migration (de un pueblo, de aves, etc.). || FIG. *Emigración de capitales*, outflow *o* flight of capital.
emigrado, da m. y f. Emigrant, political exile, émigré.
emigrante adj./s. Emigrant.
emigrar v. tr. To emigrate: *emigrar a la Argentina*, to emigrate to Argentina. || To migrate (un pueblo, las aves, etc.).
emigratorio, ria adj. Emigratory, migratory.
eminencia f. Hill, height, eminence (elevación de terreno). || FIG. Eminent figure (persona). || — FIG. *Eminencia gris*, grey eminence, éminence grise. | *Su Eminencia*, His Eminence (tratamiento eclesiástico).
eminente adj. FIG. Eminent, outstanding, distinguished. || High, eminent (alto).
eminentemente adv. Eminently.
eminentísimo adj. Most eminent.
emir m. Emir (jefe árabe).
emirato m. Emirate.
emisario, ria m. y f. Emissary (enviado).
emisión f. Emission. || RAD. Transmission, broadcasting (acción de emitir) | Broadcast (programa): *la emisión de la tarde*, the afternoon broadcast. || Issue (de papel moneda, sellos, valores, etc.). || RAD. *Director de emisión*, producer.
emisivo, va adj. Emissive.
emisor, ra adj. Issuing: *banco emisor*, issuing bank. || RAD. *Centro emisor* or *estación emisora*, transmitter, broadcasting station.
— M. Issuer. || RAD. Transmitter (aparato). | Station (de radar). || *Emisor receptor*, walkie-talkie. || — F. Transmitter, radio station, broadcasting station.
emitir v. tr. To emit: *emitir luz, sonidos*, to emit light, sounds. || To give off (olor). || To issue (poner en circulación). || FIG. To express, to give: *emitir un juicio*, to express an opinion. || To give, to cast (un voto). || RAD. To transmit, to broadcast: *emitir en onda corta*, to transmit on short wave. || *Sufragios emitidos*, votes cast.
— V. intr. RAD. To transmit.
emoción f. Emotion (sentimiento profundo). || Excitement, thrill: *la emoción de la aventura*, the excitement of adventure. || *¡Qué emoción!*, how exciting!
emocionado, da adj. Moved, touched: *emocionado con sus lágrimas*, moved by her tears. || Upset (perturbado).
emocional adj. Emotional.
emocionante adj. Moving, touching (conmovedor). || Exciting, thrilling: *un libro, una película emocionante*, an exciting book, film.
emocionar v. tr. To move, to touch (conmover): *me emocionó su bondad*, I was moved by his kindness. || To excite, to thrill: *una excursión al mar siempre emociona a los niños*, a trip to the coast always thrills the children. || To upset (perturbar): *le emociona ver sangre*, the sight of blood upsets him.
— V. pr. To be moved, to be touched. || To be *o* to get excited *o* thrilled: *se emocionó tanto*, he got so excited. || To be *o* to get upset, to upset o.s.
emoliente adj./s.m. MED. Emollient.
emolumento m. Emolument.
emotividad f. Emotionality.
emotivo, va adj. Emotional: *una niña emotiva*, an emotional little girl. || Emotive (que suscita emoción). || Moving, touching (conmovedor).
empacador, ra adj. Packing.
— M. y f. Packer, baler. || — F. Baler, baling machine, packing machine.
empacamiento m. *Amer.* Packing. | Obstinacy.
empacar v. tr. To pack (empaquetar). || To bale (el algodón, etc.).

— V. pr. *Amer.* To get stubborn *o* obstinate (obstinarse). | To get confused (turbarse). | To stop dead, to balk [un animal] (plantarse).

empacón, ona adj. *Amer.* Stubborn, obstinate. | Balky (caballo, etc.).

empachado, da adj. Clumsy, awkward (torpe). || *Estar empachado*, to have indigestion (del estómago), to be fed up, to be sick (estar harto).

empachar v. tr. To surfeit, to satiate (saciar). || To give indigestion (a una persona). || To upset (el estómago). || FIG. To hinder, to impede (estorbar). | To embarrass (hacer pasar un apuro). | To hide, to conceal (ocultar). | To sicken, to weary (fastidiar).

— V. pr. To have indigestion. || FIG. To get mixed up *o* confused (turbarse). | To be embarrassed *o* ashamed (avergonzarse). | To get fed up, to get sick (hartarse).

empacho m. Indigestion. || (P. us.). Hindrance, obstacle (estorbo). || FIG. Embarrassment (embarazo). | Bashfulness, shame (vergüenza). | Confusion. || — *¡Qué empacho de niño!*, what a troublesome child! || FIG. *Tener un empacho de*, to have had one's fill of.

empachoso, sa adj. Heavy, indigestible, cloying (alimento). || FIG. Sickly, sugary (empalagoso). | Troublesome, annoying (pesado). | Embarrassing, shameful (vergonzoso). | Confusing.

empadrarse v. pr. To become excessively attached to one's father *o* to one's parents.

empadronador m. Keeper of the electoral roll. || Census taker.

empadronamiento m. Enrolment [in the register of electors]. || Census (censo).

empadronar v. tr. To take a census of (la población). || To register in a census *o* on the electoral roll.

— V. pr. To have one's name registered on the electoral roll *o* in a census.

empajar v. tr. To cover with straw (un semillero, etc.). || To stuff with straw (rellenar con paja). || To bottom with straw (un asiento). || *Amer.* To thatch (techar con paja). | To mix with straw (el barro).

— V. pr. *Amer.* To produce much straw and little fruit (cereales).

empalagamiento m. V. EMPALAGO.

empalagar v. tr. e intr. To cloy, to surfeit, to satiate (los alimentos). || FIG. To annoy, to sicken, to weary (fastidiar).

— V. pr. FIG. To get fed up, to get sick.

empalago m. Sickness (malestar). || Surfeit (exceso). || Disgust, repugnance (asco). || FIG. Annoyance, boredom.

empalagoso, sa adj. Sickly, cloying (alimento). || FIG. Cloying, sickening, mawkish (zalamero). | Sugary, sickly (película, novela, voz, etc.). | Wearisome, trying (fastidioso).

empalamiento m. Impalement.

empalar v. tr. To impale (atravesar con un palo).

— V. pr. *Amer.* To be persistent *o* obstinate (obstinarse). | To become numb *o* stiff (envararse).

empalizada f. MIL. Palisade, stockade (estacada). || Fence (valla).

empalizar v. tr. MIL. To palisade, to stockade. || To fence (vallar).

empalmadura f. V. EMPALME.

empalmar v. tr. To connect, to join, to fit together (unir). || To butt join, to join (en carpintería). || To splice (cuerda, película). || DEP. To kick on the volley (la pelota). || FIG. To link up (ideas, planes).

— V. intr. To fit (encajar). || To join, to meet, to connect (caminos, líneas de ferrocarril). || To connect (trenes, autocares). || *Empalmar con*, to follow, to succeed (seguir).

empalme m. Joint, join, connection (conexión). || Joint, butt joint (en carpintería). || Splice (de cuerda, película cinematográfica). || Junction (de líneas de ferrocarril). || Intersection, junction (de carreteras). || Connection (de trenes, autocares). || Kick on the volley (en fútbol).

empalletado m. MAR. Mat.

empamparse v. pr. *Amer.* To get lost in the pampas. | To lose one's way (extraviarse).

empampirolado, da adj. FAM. Conceited, vain.

empanada f. CULIN. Turnover, pie. || FIG. Fraud.

empanadilla f. CULIN. Turnover (de carne, pescado *o* dulce).

empanado, da adj. CULIN. Covered in breadcrumbs, breaded.

empanar v. tr. To coat in breadcrumbs, to bread.

empantanado, da adj. Flooded, swampy.

empantanar v. tr. To flood, to swamp (inundar). || To bog down (meter en un barrizal). || FIG. To bog down, to hold up (detener): *empantanar un asunto*, to bog down an affair.

— V. pr. To be *o* to become flooded: *la carretera se empantanó*, the highway was flooded. || To get bogged down: *la carreta se empantanó*, the cart got bogged down. || FIG. To be held up *o* bogged down: *se empantanó el plan*, the plan was held up. | To mark time (persona). | To make no headway: *asunto que se empantana*, affair which makes no headway.

empañado, da adj. Misty, steamy (un cristal). || Faint (voz). || Tarnished, blemished (la honra).

empañar v. tr. To put a nappy on [U.S., to diaper], to swaddle (ant.) [a un niño]. || To steam up, to cloud, to mist: *el vapor empañó el cristal*, the steam clouded the glass. || To dull, to tarnish (quitar el brillo). || FIG. To tarnish, to blemish, to sully (la reputación). || — FIG. *Empañar el honor de alguien*, to cast a stain *o* a slur on s.o.'s honour. | *Voz empañada por la emoción*, voice choked with emotion.

— V. pr. To get steamed up, to mist up (cristales). || To falter (la voz).

empapamiento m. Soaking, steeping (de la ropa al lavar). || Soaking, saturation, drenching (por la lluvia, etc.). || Absorption (absorción). || Mopping-up (acción de enjugar).

empapar v. tr. To soak, to steep (mojar completamente): *empapar sopas en vino*, to soak crumbs in wine; *empapar la ropa sucia*, to soak the dirty linen. || To soak, to saturate, to drench: *la lluvia me empapó*, the rain drenched me. || To saturate, to soak: *empapar una esponja en agua*, to saturate a sponge with water. || To absorb, to soak up (absorber): *la tierra empapa la lluvia*, the earth absorbs the rain. || To sponge up, to mop up (enjugar): *empapar la leche vertida con un trapo*, to mop the spilt milk up with a rag. || FIG. To soak. || — *Estar empapado*, to be drenched *o* sodden *o* soaked. || *Estar empapado en sudor*, to be drenched in sweat, to be dripping with perspiration *o* sweat.

— V. pr. To be soaked, to be steeped: *el pan se empapa en leche*, the bread is steeped in milk. || To be *o* to become *o* to get soaked *o* drenched *o* saturated: *me empapé con la lluvia*, I got soaked in the rain. || To be *o* to become saturated *o* soaked: *el papel secante se empapó de tinta*, the blotting paper became saturated with ink. || To be absorbed *o* soaked up: *la tinta se empapa en el papel secante*, the ink is absorbed by the blotting paper. || FIG. To become imbued *o* pervaded *o* possessed with: *empaparse de ideas nuevas*, to become imbued with new ideas. | To soak o.s.: *se empapó de obras revolucionarias*, he soaked himself in revolutionary literature. | To get into one's head: *empápate bien esta regla*, get this rule into your head. || FIG. y FAM. To stuff o.s. (saciarse).

empapelado m. Wallpaper (papel para las paredes). || Wallpapering, papering, paperhanging (colocación del papel). || Lining (de un baúl, etc.).

empapelador m. Paperhanger (de paredes).

empapelar v. tr. To paper, to wallpaper (las paredes). || To line with paper (un baúl, etc.). || To wrap in paper (envolver). || FIG. y FAM. To have up (formar causa criminal a uno).

empapirotarse v. pr. FAM. To dress up, to put on one's Sunday best.

empaque m. Packing (acción de empaquetar). || Packing (materiales empleados). || FAM. Bearing, presence (de una persona). | Gravity (solemnidad). | *Amer.* Cheek, impudence, effrontery (descaro). || *Un caballo de mucho empaque*, a good stepper.

empaquetado o **empaquetamiento** m. Packing.

empaquetador, ra m. y f. Packer.

empaquetadura f. Packing.

empaquetar v. tr. To package, to pack up, to make into a parcel, to parcel up (embalar). || To pack (colocar apretadamente). || FIG. To pack *o* to cram together (a personas).

emparamarse v. pr. *Amer.* To freeze to death.

emparedado, da adj. Walled in, immured. || Confined, imprisoned (prisionero). || In reclusion (ermitaño).

— M. y f. Prisoner, captive (por castigo). || Recluse, hermit (por propia voluntad). || — M. Sandwich.

emparedamiento m. Immurement. || Confinement (de un prisionero). || Reclusion (de un ermitaño).

emparedar v. tr. To immure, to wall in. || To confine, to imprison (encerrar).

emparejadura f. o **emparejamiento** m. Matching. || Levelling.

emparejar v. tr. To match: *emparejar dos candelabros*, to match two candelabra. || To make level, to bring to the same level (poner una cosa a nivel con otra). || To level [off], to smooth, to flush, to make even (alisar). || To level [off] (tierra).

— V. intr. To match: *su blusa empareja con su falda*, her blouse matches her skirt. || To catch up, to draw level: *el coche aceleró y emparejó con la moto*, the car speeded up and drew level with the motorbike. || To catch up: *emparejó con sus rivales*, he caught up with his rivals.

— V. pr. To match (dos cosas). || To catch up, to draw level (ponerse juntos). || To pair off (dos personas).

emparentado, da adj. Related.

emparentar* v. intr. To become related by marriage. || To be related (ser pariente). || *Emparentar con*, to marry into (una familia).

emparrado m. Trained vine (parra). || Arbour [U.S., arbor], bower (bóveda de jardín). || Trellis, trelliswork, latticework (armazón).

emparrandarse v. pr. *Amer.* FAM. To go on a spree *o* on a binge (ir de parranda).

emparrar v. tr. To train (una planta).

emparrillado m. Grillage, grating.

emparrillar v. tr. To grill (asar en la parrilla). || ARQ. To reinforce with a grillage *o* a grating.

emparvar v. tr. AGR. To lay for threshing (la mies).

empastador m. Paste brush (pincel). || *Amer.* Bookbinder (encuadernador).

empastado, da adj. Filled, stopped (muela). || Clothbound (libro).
empastar v. tr. To paste (cubrir de pasta). || To bind (encuadernar). || To fill, to put a filling in, to stop (un diente). || ARTES. To impaste. || *Amer.* To turn into pasture, to pasture (un terreno).
— V. pr. To be filled *o* stopped (muelas). || *Amer.* To suffer from meteorism (el ganado). | To become covered in weeds (un terreno).
empaste m. Filling (de un diente). || Bookbinding (encuadernación). || ARTES. Impasto, impasting. || *Amer.* Meteorism (del ganado).
empastelar v. tr. FIG. y FAM. To find a way out of [a difficulty] (para salir del paso). || IMPR. To pie (mezclar fundiciones distintas). | To transpose accidentally, to mix up (composición tipográfica).
— V. pr. IMPR. To become pied. | To become transposed, to get mixed up.
empatar v. intr. To draw, to tie: *los dos candidatos empataron*, the two candidates drew; *empatar a dos*, to draw two all [U.S., to tie two to two] || DEP. To equalize: *Gómez empató en el minuto diecisiete*, Gómez equalized in the seventeenth minute. | To tie, to have a dead heat (en las carreras de caballos). || *Amer.* To fit (empalmar). || — *Empatados a dos*, two all [U.S., two to two] (fútbol). || *Estar empatados*, to be equal *o* tying. || *Salir* or *quedar empatados*, to draw, to tie.
empate m. Draw, tie (en un partido, un concurso, una elección). || Dead heat (en una carrera). || Division (de opiniones). || *Amer.* Joint, connection. || — *El gol de empate*, the equalizing goal, the equalizer. || *Empate a dos*, two all (tanteo), two all draw (resultado) [U.S., tie two to two]. || *Empate a quince*, fifteen all (tenis).
empavesado, da adj. Dressed (buque). || Decked, decorated (calles). || Veiled (monumento).
— M. Dressing, bunting (del buque). || — F. MAR. Hammock cloth (para los coyes). || MIL. Pavis.
empavesar v. tr. To dress (un buque). || To deck, to decorate (las calles). || To veil (un monumento).
empavonado o **empavonamiento** m. TECN. Blueing (de un metal).
empavonar v. tr. To blue (los metales). || *Amer.* To grease.
empecatado, da adj. Incorrigible, wicked (malvado). || Cursed, wretched (maldito): *ese empecatado crío me exaspera*, that wretched brat is driving me round the bend. || Unlucky, ill-fated (desgraciado).
empecer* v. intr. *Lo que no empece*, which does not prevent.
empecinado, da adj. Obstinate, stubborn (terco). || *El Empecinado*, nickname of Martín Díaz [a hero of the Spanish War of Independence].
empecinamiento m. Obstinacy, stubbornness.
empecinarse v. pr. To be *o* to become obstinate *o* stubborn.
empedarse v. pr. *Amer.* FAM. To get drunk.
empedernido, da adj. FIG. Heavy, confirmed, inveterate (bebedor, fumador, jugador). | Hardened, confirmed (criminal). || Confirmed (solterón). || Inveterate (mentiroso, odio). || Callous, unfeeling, hardhearted (insensible).
empedernir* v. tr. To harden, to toughen (volver duro). || FIG. To harden, to toughen up (curtir el cuerpo). | To make hardhearted *o* callous *o* unfeeling (insensibilizar).
— V. pr. To become hard, to harden. || FIG. To toughen o.s. up, to get fit (para los deportes, para un trabajo duro). | To become hardhearted *o* callous *o* unfeeling (insensibilizarse).
— OBSERV. This verb is defective, and exists only in the forms whose endings begin with *i* (*empederní, empedernía, empederniera*, etc.).
empedrado, da adj. Paved (con adoquines). || Cobbled (con guijarros). || Dappled (color de caballerías). || Pockmarked (cara).
— M. Paving (adoquinado). || Cobbles, *pl.* (enguijarrado).
empedrador m. Paver.
empedramiento m. V. EMPEDRADO.
empedrar* v. tr. To pave (con adoquines). || To cobble (con guijarros). || FIG. To sprinkle, to lard: *empedrar un discurso de galicismos, de citas*, to lard a speech with Gallicisms, quotations.
empega f. Pitch (pez). || Pitch mark made on sheep (señal).
empegado m. Tarpaulin.
empegar v. tr. To pitch, to coat with pitch. || To mark with pitch (el ganado lanar).
empeine m. Instep (del pie, de un zapato). || Groin (parte baja del vientre). || MED. Impetigo (en la piel). || BOT. Hepatica, liverwort.
empelotarse v. pr. FAM. To squabble, to row (reñir). || *Amer.* FAM. To strip, to undress (desnudarse). || *Amer.* FAM. *Empelotarse por*, to be *o* to become crazy *o* mad about (chiflarse).
empeltre m. AGR. Shield graft (injerto de escudete).
empellada f. Push, shove.
empellar o **empeller** v. tr. To push, to shove.
empellón m. Push, shove (empujón). || — *A empellones*, V. EMPUJÓN. || *Dar empellones*, to shove, to jostle. || *Hablar a empellones*, to gabble.
empenachar v. tr. To plume, to adorn with plumes.
empenaje m. AVIAC. Empennage, tail unit.
empeñadamente adv. Insistently, steadfastly.
empeñado, da adj. Vehement, heated: *una discusión empeñada*, a heated argument. || Determined (decidido). || Insistent, persistent (porfiado). || In debt: *empeñado hasta los ojos*, up to one's neck in debt. || In pawn, pawned (en el Monte de Piedad).
empeñar v. tr. To leave *o* to give as security, to pledge (dar como fianza). || To pawn (en el Monte de Piedad). || To plege, to plight: *empeñar su palabra, la fe*, to pledge one's word, one's faith. || To bind, to commit [s.o. to sth.] (obligar a alguien a una cosa). || To engage in, to begin (una lucha). || To begin, to start (una discusión). || To involve, to embroil: *empeñaron el país en una guerra sangrienta*, they embroiled the country in a bloody war. || FAM. *Empeñar hasta la camisa*, to stake one's shirt.
— V. pr. To commit *o* to bind o.s. [to] (obligarse a una cosa). || To begin, to start (una discusión). || To engage in (una lucha). || To get involved *o* embroiled: *se han empeñado en una discusión sobre fútbol*, they've got embroiled in an argument about football. || To persist, to insist: *empeñarse en hacer algo*, to persist in doing sth., to insist on doing sth.; *puesto que te empeñas, te lo diré*, since you insist, I'll tell you. || To be determined to (estar decidido a). || To endeavour, to strive, to take pains (esforzarse): *me empeñaba en hacerlo lo mejor posible*, I endeavoured to do it as well as possible. || To get into debt (endeudarse). || *Empeñarse por alguien*, to intercede for s.o.
empeñero, ra m. y f. *Amer.* Pawnbroker.
empeño m. Pledging (acción de empeñar). || Pawning (en el Monte de Piedad). || Obligation (obligación). || Embroilment, involvement (participación). || Eagerness, zeal (afán). || Desire, aim (objetivo). || Determination: *su empeño en hacerlo*, his determination to do it. || Insistence, persistence (insistencia). || Backer, patron (apoyo, relación). || — *Casa de empeños*, pawnshop. || *En empeño*, in pawn. || *Papeleta de empeño*, pawn ticket. || *Poner* or *tomar empeño en*, to take pains to. || *Tengo empeño en que este trabajo esté acabado hoy*, I am determined that this work be finished today, I am eager for this work to be finished today.
empeñoso, sa adj. *Amer.* Persevering.
empeoramiento m. Deterioration, worsening.
empeorar v. tr. To worsen, to make worse, to deteriorate.
— V. intr. y pr. To worsen, to get worse, to deteriorate: *la situación se ha empeorado rápidamente*, the situation has rapidly deteriorated. || To get worse (un enfermo).
empequeñecer* v. tr. To make smaller, to diminish, to reduce (hacer más pequeño). || FIG. To dwarf, to make look small: *el nuevo rascacielos empequeñece los demás edificios*, the new skyscraper dwarfs the other buildings. | To put in the shade, to overshadow: *nos empequeñece con todas sus hazañas*, he puts us in the shade with all his achievements. | To belittle, to disparage (desprestigiar).
empequeñecimiento m. Diminution, reduction (disminución). || FIG. Belittling, disparagement (desprestigio).
emperador m. Emperor. || Swordfish (pez espada).
emperatriz f. Empress.
— OBSERV. The form *emperadora* is archaic.
emperejilarse o **emperifollarse** v. pr. FAM. To doll o.s. up, to dress up.
empernar v. tr. TECN. To bolt [down *o* together].
empero conj. (P. us.). But (pero). || Nevertheless, none the less (sin embargo).
— OBSERV. The use of this conjunction is generally restricted to literary contexts.
emperramiento m. FAM. Mulishness, stubbornness (obstinación). | Insistence, determination. | Rage, anger (rabia).
emperrarse v. pr. FAM. To be dead set (obstinarse): *se emperró en hacerlo como él quería*, he was dead set on doing it his own way. || To insist, to be determined (estar decidido). || To be obsessed *o* infatuated (*con*, with) [encapricharse]. || To flare up, to lose one's temper (irritarse).
empezar* v. tr. To begin, to start: *empezó su discurso hablando de la guerra*, he began *o* he started his speech by talking about the war; *empezamos la semana con una discusión*, we started the week with an argument. || To start: *¿has empezado la botella de coñac?*, have you started the bottle of brandy? || *Empezar de nuevo* or *volver a empezar*, to start again *o* afresh, to begin again.
— V. intr. To begin, to start: *empezar a trabajar*, to start working, to start to work; *empezaré por abrir todas las ventanas*, I shall begin by opening all the windows; *todo empezó cuando cayó enfermo*, everything started when he fell ill; *empezamos a las nueve*, we begin at nine; *empezó a tiros*, he started shooting; *empezó recordándome que*, he began by reminding me that. || — *Al empezar*, at the beginning.

|| *Empezar con*, to open with, to start with. || *Haber empezado con nada*, to have started from nothing. || *Para empezar*, to begin with. || *Todo es empezar*, the first step is the hardest.

empicarse v. pr. To become infatuated (*por*, with). || *Empicarse en el juego*, to get the gambling itch.

empicotar v. tr. To pillory, to put in the pillory.

empiece m. FAM. Beginning, start.

empiezo m. *Amer*. Beginning, start (comienzo).

empilar v. tr. To pile, to pile up, to stack.

empinado, da adj. Erect, upright (erguido). || Steep: *camino empinado*, steep path. || Very high (alto). || On tiptoe (persona). || Rearing (caballo). || FIG. Haughty, stuck-up (orgulloso).

empinadura f. o **empinamiento** m. Standing up, setting straight (enderezamiento). || Rearing [up] (del caballo). || Standing on tiptoe. || AVIAC. Zooming.

empinar v. tr. To stand [up], to set straight (poner derecho o vertical). || To raise, to tip up (una botella para beber). || FAM. *Empinar el codo*, v. CODO.
— V. pr. To rear [up] (caballo). || To stand on tiptoe (ponerse de puntillas). || To tower, to rise up (árbol, edificio, montaña, etc.). || AVIAC. To zoom.

empingorotado, da adj. FIG. Upper-class, of high social standing. || Haughty, stuck-up (orgulloso).

empingorotarse v. pr. To climb, to go up (subirse). || FIG. To become haughty *o* stuck-up (engreírse).

empiparse v. pr. FAM. To stuff o.s. (*de*, with), to gorge (*de*, on) [atracarse].

empíreo, a adj. Empyreal.
— M. Empyrean (cielo).

empírico, ca adj. Empirical, empiric.
— N. Empiric, empiricist.

empirismo m. Empiricism.

empitonar v. tr. TAUR. To gore, to catch with the horns (cornear).

empizarrado, da adj. Covered with slates.
— M. Slate roof (tejado).

empizarrar v. tr. To cover *o* to roof with slates, to slate.

emplasto m. MED. Plaster. || FIG. Makeshift arrangement, unsatisfactory compromise (componenda). || *Amer*. Bore (aburrido).

emplazado, da adj. HIST. *Fernando IV el Emplazado*, Ferdinand IV the Summoned.

emplazamiento m. JUR. Summons. || MIL. Positioning: *emplazamiento de una batería*, positioning of a battery. | Emplacement (posición). || Location (situación). || *Emplazamiento arqueológico*, archaeological site.

emplazar v. tr. JUR. To summon. || To locate, to situate (colocar). || MIL. To position.

empleable adj. Usable, employable.

empleado, da m. y f. Employee. || Clerk (oficinista): *empleado de banco*, bank clerk. || *Empleados del Estado*, civil servants.

empleador, ra adj. Employing.
— M. y f. Employer.

emplear v. tr. To use: *emplear un utensilio, una palabra*, to use a tool, a word; *ha empleado toda su astucia para conseguir este puesto*, he has used all his cunning to get this job. || To employ: *esta fábrica emplea a mil obreros*, this factory employs a thousand workers. || To spend, to occupy, to employ (tiempo). || To invest: *emplear su fortuna en fincas*, to invest one's fortune in real estate. || — *Bien empleado le está* or *lo tiene bien empleado*, he deserves it, it serves him right. || *Dar por bien empleado*, to consider well spent (tiempo, dinero). || *Emplear mal*, to misuse.
— V. pr. To be used: *esa palabra ya no se emplea*, that word is no longer used. || To be employed.

empleita f. Plaited esparto.

empleo m. Job, post: *tiene un buen empleo*, he has a good job; *busco un empleo*, I am looking for a job. || Employment: *pleno empleo*, full employment. || Spending, use (del tiempo). || Use (uso): *modo de empleo*, instructions for use; *el empleo de una palabra*, the use of a word. || Investment (del dinero). || MIL. Rank. || — *Sin empleo*, unemployed. || *Solicitud de empleo*, application for a job. || *Suspender a uno del empleo*, to relieve s.o. of his duties.

empleomanía f. FAM. Eagerness to hold public office.

emplomado m. Leading (de una ventana). || Lead covering, lead lining (revestimiento). || Lead roof (tejado). || Lead seal (sello).

emplomar v. tr. To cover with lead, to line with lead (revestir). || To roof with lead (tejado). || To lead, to join with lead (vidrieras). || To seal with lead (precintar). || *Amer*. To fill (dientes).

emplumar v. tr. To feather (una flecha). || To put feathers on, to put a feather on, to plume. || *Amer*. To deceive (engañar). || *Amer*. FAM. *Emplumarlas*, to beat it, to skedaddle (huir).
— V. intr. To grow feathers, to fledge (pájaro). || *Amer*. To beat it, to skedaddle (huir). || *Serpiente emplumada*, plumed serpent.

emplumecer* v. intr. To grow feathers, to fledge (pájaro).

empobrecer* v. tr. To impoverish.
— V. intr. y pr. To become poor *o* impoverished.

empobrecimiento m. Impoverishment.

empodrecer* v. intr. To rot (pudrir).

empolvado, da adj. Dusty (cubierto de polvo). || Powdered (cubierto de polvos).
— M. Powdering.

empolvar v. tr. To cover with dust (ensuciar). || To cover: *el viento empolva la ropa con arena*, the wind covers the clothes in sand. || To powder (cara, pelo).
— V. pr. To become covered in dust, to get dusty (los muebles). || To powder one's face (la cara).

empolvoramiento m. Covering with dust. || Layer *o* deposit *o* accumulation of dust (capa de polvo).

empolvorar o **empolvorizar** v. tr. V. EMPOLVAR.

empollado, da adj. FAM. Well up: *está empollado en matemáticas*, he is well up on mathematics.
— M. y f. FAM. Brainbox.

empolladura f. Brood of bees.

empollar v. tr. To brood (huevos). || FAM. To mug up, to swot up [U.S., to bone up] (estudiar mucho): *empollar química*, to mug up chemistry.
— V. intr. To sit, to brood (aves). || To breed (los insectos). || FAM. To mug up, to swot up [U.S., to bone up] (estudiar).
— V. pr. FAM. To mug up, to swot up [U.S., to bone up] (una lección). || *Amer*. To get *o* to develop blisters (levantar ampollas).

empollón, ona adj. FAM. Swot, grind.

emponchado, da adj. *Amer*. Wearing a poncho, in a poncho. | FIG. Suspicious.

emponcharse v. pr. *Amer*. To put on a poncho.

emponzoñador, ra adj. Poisoning, poisonous. || FIG. Harmful (perjudicial).
— M. y f. Poisoner.

emponzoñamiento m. Poisoning.

emponzoñar v. tr. To poison (envenenar). || FIG. To poison: *país emponzoñado por el vicio*, country poisoned by vice. | To embitter (riña, discusión).

empopar v. intr. MAR. To sail before the wind. | To be low in the stern (calar).

emporio m. Emporium, mart, market *o* trade centre (centro comercial). || Centre [U.S., center]: *emporio de las artes*, artistic centre. || *Amer*. Store, department store.

empotrado, da adj. Built-in, fitted (alacena).

empotramiento m. Embedding, bedding (con cemento). || Building-in, fitting (de un armario, etc.).

empotrar v. tr. To embed, to bed (fijar con cemento). || To build in, to fit: *armario empotrado*, built-in *o* fitted cupboard.

empotrerar v. tr. *Amer*. To pasture, to put out to pasture (el ganado).

empozar v. tr. To put in a well (echar en un pozo). || To ret (el lino o el cáñamo).
— V. intr. *Amer*. To stagnate (estancarse).
— V. pr. FIG. To be shelved, to be forgotten (un asunto).

emprendedor, ra adj. Enterprising, go-ahead.

emprender v. tr. To undertake (un trabajo, una tarea). || To embark upon, to set out on (un viaje). || To start (empezar). || To attack (atacar). || — *Emprender el regreso*, to go back, to turn back. || *Emprender el vuelo*, v. VUELO. || FAM. *Emprenderla con uno*, to pick a quarrel *o* a fight with s.o. || *Emprender la retirada*, to retreat.

empresa f. Enterprise, undertaking, venture: *la subida al Everest fue una empresa atrevida*, the ascent of Everest was a daring venture. || Enterprise: *empresa privada*, private enterprise. || Company, firm, concern (sociedad). || Management (dirección): *la empresa no es responsable de los objetos perdidos*, the management accepts no responsibility for lost articles. || Emblem, device (emblema). || — *Empresa funeraria*, undertaker's. || *Jurado de empresa*, works council.

empresariado m. Employers, *pl*.

empresarial adj. Management, managerial (del empresariado): *dificultades empresariales*, management difficulties. || *La clase empresarial*, the employers.

empresario, ria m. y f. Employer (empleador). || Operator (explotador). || Contractor: *empresario de obras públicas*, public works contractor. || Manager (director, gerente). || — M. TEATR. Impresario. || DEP. Manager (de un equipo, de un boxeador, etc.). || *Empresario de pompas fúnebres*, undertaker, funeral director.

emprestar v. tr. (P. us.). To lend (prestar). | To borrow (pedir prestado).

empréstito m. Loan: *un empréstito al 3 por ciento*, a loan at 3 percent interest. || Government *o* public loan (del Estado). || *Lanzar* or *hacer un empréstito*, to float a loan.

empringar v. tr. To grease, to cover *o* to smear with grease (untar). || To stain *o* to spot with grease (ensuciar).

empujar v. tr. To push, to shove (mover). || TECN. To thrust. || To press (el timbre, etc.). || FIG. To urge, to push (incitar).
— V. intr. To push, to shove.

empuje m. Push, shove (empujón). || Pressure (presión). || ARQ., AVIAC. y FÍS. Thrust. || FIG. Energy, go, drive: *tiene mucho empuje*, he has got a lot of go. || FIG. *Hombre de empuje*, man of action.

empujón m. Push, shove: *dar un empujón a uno*, to give s.o. a push. || — *Abrirse paso a empujones*, to push one's way through. || *A empujones*, roughly, violently (bruscamente), by force (a la fuerza), in *o* by fits and

starts (con interrupciones). || *Dar empujones,* to push, to shove, to jostle. || FIG. y FAM. *Dar un empujón a algo,* to give sth. a push forward. || *Entrar, salir, avanzar a empujones,* to push one's way in, out, forward.
empulgadura f. Notching, nocking (de una ballesta).
empulgar v. tr. To brace [a crossbow].
empulguera f. Nock, notch (de una ballesta). || — Pl. Thumbscrew, *sing.* (suplicio).
empuñadura f. Hilt (de espada, etc.): *le clavó la daga hasta la empuñadura,* he drove the dagger in him up to the hilt. || Handle (de paraguas, etc.). || Grip, handle (de una herramienta).
empuñar v. tr. To seize, to grasp, to take hold of (asir). || To take up (la pluma, la espada, etc.). || FIG. To land (un empleo).
empuñidura f. MAR. Earing.
emú m. Emu (ave).
emulación f. Emulation.
emulador, ra adj. Emulative, emulating.
— M. y f. Emulator, rival.
— OBSERV. *Emulador* suggests jealousy while *émulo* does not.
emular v. tr. To emulate.
émulo, la adj. Emulous.
— M. y f. Emulator, rival.
emulsión f. QUÍM. Emulsion.
emulsionar v. tr. To emulsify.
emulsivo, va adj. Emulsive.
emulsor m. Emulsifier (aparato).
en prep.

1. Lugar. — **2.** Tiempo. — **3.** Modo. — **4.** Locuciones diversas.

1. LUGAR. — In: *en Francia, en Madrid,* in France, in Madrid; *en la Francia de hoy,* in present-day France; *en el Perú,* in Peru; *en la Plaza Mayor,* in the main square; *en la jaula,* in the cage; *estar en la cama,* to be in bed; *sentarse en una butaca,* to sit in an armchair. || In, into: *poner algo en una caja,* to put sth. in *o* into a box. || On: *el libro está en la mesa, en el suelo,* the book is on the table, on the floor; *sentarse en una silla, en la cama,* to sit on a chair, on the bed; *en la carretera de Ávila,* on the Avila road; *en la página trece,* on page thirteen; *hay un buen programa en el primer canal,* there's a good programme on channel one. || Into: *entrar en,* to go into. || At: *estar en casa,* to be at home; *en casa de Juan,* at John's house; *en la estación,* at the station. || *En donde,* where: *¿en dónde nos hemos de reunir?,* where are we to meet?
2. TIEMPO. — In: *en 1980, en el año 1980,* in 1980, in the year 1980; *en el 45,* in 45; *en el siglo XX,* in the 20th century; *en invierno, en septiembre,* in winter, in September; *terminó la novela en dos semanas,* he finished his novel in two weeks; *en mi juventud,* in my youth; *en tiempos de,* in the time of; *en mi tiempo, en mis tiempos,* in my time; *en mi vida he visto tal cosa,* I've never seen such a thing in my life. || On: *en el día 18,* on the 18th; *sucedió en domingo,* it happened on a Sunday; *en una tarde calurosa,* on a hot afternoon; *en vísperas de,* on the eve of. || At: *en esa época,* at that time; *en ese momento,* at that moment. || — *De hoy en ocho días,* a week [from] today. || *El año en que te conocí,* the year [in which] I met you. || *En cuanto,* as soon as. || *En esto,* thereupon. || *En llegando el general, disparó la artillería,* upon the general's arrival, the artillery fired (v. OBSERV.). || *En tanto que,* v. TANTO. || *No he dormido en toda la noche,* I haven't slept a wink all night.
3. MODO. — In: *en voz alta,* in a loud voice; *en mangas de camisa,* in shirt sleeves; *escribir en verso,* to write in verse. || By: *le conocí en el andar,* I recognized him by his gait; *ir en bicicleta, en tren,* to go by bicycle, by train; *aumentar en un diez por ciento,* to increase by ten percent. || — *En broma,* as a joke, jokingly: *lo dije en broma,* I said it jokingly. || *En guerra,* at war. || *En haciendo lo que te digo triunfarás,* if you do what I tell you you'll succeed (v. OBSERV.). || *Hábil en manejar las armas,* skilful at handling arms. || *Lento en obrar,* slow to act, slow in acting. || *Ponerse en círculo,* to form a circle. || *Vender en veinte pesetas,* to sell for twenty pesetas.
4. LOCUCIONES DIVERSAS. — *Convertir en,* to turn into. || *De casa en casa,* from house to house. || *Doctor en ciencias, en medicina,* doctor of science, of medicine. || *En cambio,* v. CAMBIO. || *En cuanto a,* as regards, regarding, with respect to. || *¿En qué quedamos?,* what is it to be?, what shall we do? (¿qué hacemos?), so (entonces). || *Pensar en,* to think of *o* about.
— OBSERV. When *en* precedes the gerund this indicates that the action expressed by the gerund takes place immediately before the action expressed in the main clause (*en diciendo estas palabras, se marchó,* upon saying these words, he left) or is a prerequisite (*en tomando tú el coche, te acompañaré,* if you take the car, I'll go with you).
enaceitar v. tr. To oil.
— V. pr. To go rancid (ponerse rancio). || To become oily (ponerse aceitoso).
enagua f. Petticoat, underskirt.
— Pl. Petticoat, *sing.*, underskirt, *sing.*
enaguachar v. tr. To soak, to drench, to flood.
enaguar v. tr. To soak, to drench, to flood.
enaguazar v. tr. To soak, to flood (la tierra).
enaguillas f. pl. Short petticoat, *sing.* short underskirt, *sing.* || Fustanella, *sing.* (del traje nacional griego).
enajenable adj. Alienable.
enajenación f. Alienation (cesión). || FIG. Panic (turbación). | Rapture (éxtasis). | Absentmindedness (distracción). || *Enajenación mental,* mental derangement, alienation, insanity.
enajenador, ra m. y f. Alienator, alienor.
enajenamiento m. V. ENAJENACIÓN.
enajenar v. tr. To alienate, to transfer (bienes). || FIG. To drive mad (volver loco): *el dolor le enajenaba,* the pain was driving him mad. | To drive to distraction (distraer). | To estrange, to alienate (una amistad). | To intoxicate, to make drunk (embriagar): *enajenado por el éxito,* intoxicated with success. | To enrapture (extasiar). || *Enajenado por el furor, la alegría, la inquietud,* beside o.s. with rage, joy, worry.
— V. pr. FIG. To be driven mad (volverse loco). | To lose one's self-control (no poder dominarse). | To become drunk *o* intoxicated (por el poder, el éxito, etc.). | To go *o* to fall into rapture *o* ecstasy (extasiarse). || *Enajenarse la amistad de uno,* to lose s.o.'s friendship, to become estranged *o* alienated from s.o.
enalbardar v. tr. To put a packsaddle on (poner la albarda). || CULIN. To coat [in batter *o* in breadcrumbs]. | To lard (un ave).
enaltecer* v. tr. To ennoble, to do [s.o.] credit, to be a credit [to s.o.]: *esta acción le enaltece,* this action does him credit. || To praise, to exalt, to extol, to glorify (alabar).
enaltecimiento m. Ennobling, ennoblement. || Praise, exaltation, extolling, glorification (alabanza).
enamoradizo, za adj. Who is always falling in love.
enamorado, da adj. In love: *está perdidamente enamorado de ella,* he is madly in love with her. || Amorous (amoroso).
— M. y f. Sweetheart, lover. || Lover: *es un enamorado de Mozart,* he is a lover of Mozart; *los enamorados de los deportes de invierno,* winter sports lovers. || *Una pareja de enamorados,* a courting couple.
enamorador, ra adj. Winning.
— M. Ladykiller.
enamoramiento m. Falling in love. || Love (amor).
enamorar v. tr. To win the heart of. || To court (cortejar).
— V. pr. To fall in love (*de,* with).
enamoriscarse o **enamoricarse** v. pr. FAM. To take a fancy (*de,* to).
enanismo m. Nanism, dwarfism.
enanito, ta m. y f. Dwarf.
enano, na adj./s. Dwarf. || FAM. *Trabajar como un enano,* to work like a Trojan.
enantes adv. (Ant.). Before, previously (antes).
enarbolar v. tr. To hoist (una bandera). || To brandish (una espada). || MAR. To fly: *enarbolar bandera argentina,* to fly the Argentinian flag.
enarcar v. tr. To arch (arquear). || To hoop (toneles). || To raise: *enarcar las cejas,* to raise one's eyebrows.
enardecedor, ra adj. Exciting (excitante). || Inflaming (que enfervoriza).
enardecer* v. tr. To inflame (las pasiones, una discusión, etc.).
— V. pr. To become inflamed *o* excited (una persona). || To become inflamed (una parte del cuerpo).
enardecimiento m. Inflaming, excitation (acción de enardecer). || Excitement (excitación). || Inflammation (del cuerpo).
enarenamiento m. Sanding.
enarenar v. tr. To sand, to cover with sand (cubrir de arena). || To cover with gravel (cubrir de gravas). || MIN. To mix [ore] with sand.
— V. pr. MAR. To run aground (encallar).
enastar v. tr. To put a handle *o* shaft on (un arma, etc.).
encabalgadura f. TECN. Overlap, overlapping.
encabalgamiento m. TECN. Support of crossbeams. || MIL. Gun carriage (cureña). || POÉT. Enjambment.
encabalgar v. intr. TECN. To rest, to lean (una viga en otra). || To mount a horse.
— V. tr. To overlap. || To provide with horses.
encaballado m. IMPR. Pieing.
encaballadura f. TECN. Overlap, overlapping.
encaballar v. tr. TECN. To overlap (tejas). || IMPR. To pie, to mix up.
— V. intr. TECN. To rest, to lean (una viga).
— V. pr. IMPR. To become pied, to get mixed up.
encabestramiento m. Entanglement in the halter.
encabestrar v. tr. To put a halter on, to halter. || TAUR. To lead [a bull] with an ox.
— V. pr. To get tangled in the halter.
encabezamiento f. Headline, title, heading, caption (en un periódico). || Form of address (fórmula). || Heading (al principio de una carta). || Preamble (preámbulo). || Epigraph (epígrafe). || Registration in the census. || Census (padrón). || Tax roll (impuestos).
encabezar v. tr. To lead, to head (una rebelión, etc.). || To title, to head (un periódico). || To head (una carta). || To lead (una carrera). || To head (una lista). || To introduce: *encabezó su libro con la frase siguiente,*

he introduced his book with the following sentence. || To open, to start off: *encabezar una suscripción*, to open a subscription. || To take a census of (empadronar). || To include in a census (registrar). || To fortify (el vino con alcohol). || TECN. To join (tablones o vigas).
encabritarse v. pr. To rear. || To nose up (un avión).
encabuyar v. tr. *Amer.* To tie (atar). | To wrap (envolver).
encachado m. TECN. Stone *o* concrete lining.
encachar v. tr. TECN. To line with stones *o* concrete (el cauce de un río).
encadenación f. V. ENCADENAMIENTO.
encadenado m. ARQ. Buttress, pier. || CINEM. Dissolve.
encadenamiento m. Chaining. || FIG. Connection, linking, concatenation.
encadenar v. tr. To chain, to shackle, to fetter (a un prisionero). || To chain up (a una persona, un perro, una cosa). || FIG. To tie down, to chain down: *sus tareas domésticas la encadenan a la casa*, her housework ties her down in the house. | To connect, to link up (razonamientos, pruebas, ideas). || CINEM. To fade in.
encajador m. Enchaser (persona). || Enchasing tool (herramienta). || FAM. Boxer who can take punishment (boxeador).
encajadura f. Setting (de un hueso). || Socket (hueco).
encajar v. tr. To fit, to insert (ajustar): *encajar una pieza en otra*, to fit one part into another. || To join, to fit together (juntar). || To set (un hueso). || FIG. To suffer, to bear: *encajar críticas*, to suffer criticism. | To stand, to take (soportar): *encajar un golpe*, to take a blow. | To pocket, to swallow (una afrenta). | To drop (una indirecta). | To hurl (un insulto). | To palm off on, to foist off on, to unload on, to pass off on: *le encajaron diez billetes falsos*, they palmed off ten forged banknotes on him. | To land, to strike: *le encajó un golpe*, he landed him a blow. || TECN. To enchase. | To join, to dovetail (dos maderos). || FIG. *Nos encajó un sermón* he made us listen to *o* sit through a sermon.
— V. intr. To fit: *la puerta no encaja bien con la humedad*, because of the damp, the door doesn't fit properly; *dos piezas que encajan perfectamente*, two parts which fit perfectly. || FIG. To fit: *este ejemplo encaja con mi hipótesis*, this example fits my hypothesis. | To fit in: *Pedro no encaja en el grupo de amigos que tengo*, Peter does not fit in with my circle of friends; *eso encaja en mis proyectos*, that fits in with my plans. | To correspond [to], to fit in [with], to tally [with]: *su versión de lo que pasó no encaja con la del testigo ocular*, his version of what happened does not tally with that of the eyewitness. | To suit, to go with: *ese atavío no encaja con la solemnidad del acto*, that getup doesn't go with the solemnity of the ceremony. | To take punishment, to be able to stand a lot of punishment (un boxeador). || — FIG. *Encajar bien en un papel*, to suit the part. | *Está ya encajado en su nuevo destino*, he has now settled down in his new job. || *La puerta no está bien encajada*, the door is not properly shut.
— V. pr. To jam, to stick, to get stuck: *la rueda se encajó entre dos piedras*, the wheel got stuck between two stones. || To squeeze in (introducirse). || To slip on, to pull on: *encajarse un gabán*, to slip on an overcoat. || To put on (un sombrero). || FIG. y FAM. To go (ir). | To settle down (llevar una vida ordenada).
encaje m. Lace: *una blusa de encaje*, a lace blouse. || Fitting, insertion (acción de encajar). || Joining together (acción de juntar). || Setting (de un hueso). || Joint (empalme). || TECN. Socket (hueco de un hueso o en una pieza). | Housing (caja). || *Amer.* COM. Reserve. || *Encaje de blonda*, blonde lace.
encajero, ra m. y f. Lace maker, laceworker.
encajetar v. tr. V. ENCAJAR.
encajonado, da adj. Incised: *un río profundamente encajonado*, a deeply incised river. || Hemmed in, boxed in: *una calle encajonada entre edificios altos*, a street hemmed in by tall buildings. || *Estar encajonado*, to run through a cutting (una carretera, un ferrocarril).
— M. ARQ. Cofferdam (ataguía). | Mud wall (tapia).
encajonamiento m. Narrowness (de un río, una carretera). || Boxing, casing, crating, packing (acción de poner en un cajón). || ARQ. Coffering (de un pozo). | Shuttering (de una galería). || TAUR. Crating (de un toro para transportarlo).
encajonar v. tr. To box, to case, to crate, to pack (poner en un cajón). || To squeeze in (meter en un sitio estrecho). || ARQ. To coffer (un pozo). | To put up shuttering for (una galería). || TAUR. To crate (un toro).
— V. pr. To narrow.
encalabrinar v. tr. To irritate, to exasperate (exasperar). || To go to one's head (olor, vino).
— V. pr. To become infatuated *o* obsessed (*con*, with) [encapricharse]. || To be *o* to become obstinate *o* stubborn (empeñarse).
encalado m. Whitewashing (de paredes). || Whitening (de pieles). || AGR. Liming.
encalador m. Whitewasher.
encaladura f. V. ENCALADO.
encalamocar v. tr. *Amer.* To stun.
— V. pr. *Amer.* To be stunned.
encalar v. tr. To whitewash (blanquear). || AGR. To lime.
encalmarse v. pr. To become calm, to calm down (el mar). || To drop (el viento). || To calm down, to regain one's composure (una persona). || VET. To be overheated. || *Mercado encalmado*, slack *o* quiet market (en la Bolsa).
encalvecer* v. intr. To go bald.
encalladero m. MAR. Sandbank, shoal, reef.
encalladura f. o **encallamiento** m. MAR. Running aground, grounding, stranding.
encallar v. intr. MAR. To run aground. || FIG. To founder.
— V. pr. To harden (un alimento).
encallecer* v. intr. To become callous *o* hard (la piel).
— V. pr. To become callous *o* hard (la piel). || To harden. || FIG. To become callous *o* hardhearted *o* unfeeling (insensibilizarse). | To become hardened (en un trabajo o vicio).
encallecido, da adj. V. EMPEDERNIDO.
encamarse v. pr. To confine o.s. to bed, to take to one's bed (un enfermo). || To hide, to couch (la caza). || AGR. To bend over, to droop (las mieses).
encaminamiento m. Guiding, guidance, direction (dirección). || FIG. Guidance (orientación).
encaminar v. tr. To direct, to put on the right road (poner en camino). || To direct, to guide (orientar). || To route (expedición). || — *Asunto bien encaminado*, affair that is going well. || *Encaminar sus esfuerzos a* [followed by infinitive], *hacia* [followed by noun], to direct *o* to channel one's efforts towards, to concentrate one's efforts on (con sustantivo o gerundio). || *Medidas encaminadas a reducir los gastos públicos*, measures aimed at reducing public spending.
— V. pr. To make one's way, to head (*a*, *hacia*, towards): *encaminarse a un pueblo*, to head towards a town. || To be aimed at (con sustantivo o gerundio), to be intended to (con infinitivo) [tener como objetivo].
encamisar v. tr. To put a shirt on. || To cover up, to put a cover on (enfundar). || FIG. To disguise.
— V. pr. To put one's shirt on.
encamotarse v. pr. *Amer.* FAM. To fall in love.
encampanado, da adj. Bell-shaped (acampanado).
encampanarse v. pr. To widen out at the mouth. || To flare out, to be flared (una falda). || TAUR. To stand defiantly with the head raised (el toro). || *Amer.* To swagger, to strut (pavonearse).
encanallamiento m. Debasement, degradation.
encanallar v. tr. To corrupt, to debase.
— V. pr. To go to the dogs, to degrade o.s., to become corrupted.
encanastar v. tr. To put in a basket.
encandecer* v. tr. To make white-hot.
encandelar v. intr. To blossom with catkins.
encandilado, da adj. FAM. Erect (erguido). || *Mirar con ojos encandilados*, to gaze starry-eyed at.
encandilar v. tr. To dazzle. || FIG. To bewilder (dejar pasmado). | To stimulate (estimular). | To dazzle (deslumbrar). || FAM. To stir, to poke (la lumbre).
— V. pr. To light up (los ojos, el rostro).
encanecer* v. intr. To go grey (el cabello, una persona). || To grow old (envejecer): *encanecer en el oficio*, to grow old in service *o* in the job.
encanijado, da adj. Puny, weak (canijo).
encanijamiento m. Puniness, weakness.
encanijarse v. pr. To grow *o* to become puny *o* weak.
encanillar v. tr. To wind on [a spool *o* bobbin].
encantación f. V. ENCANTAMIENTO.
encantado, da adj. Enchanted, charmed, delighted. || FIG. y FAM. Absentminded (distraído). | Haunted: *casa encantada*, haunted house. || *Encantado [de conocerle]*, pleased to meet you.
encantador, ra adj. Charming, delightful, enchanting: *una niña encantadora*, a charming little girl. || Fascinating (belleza, mirada). || Glamorous (noche). || Bewitching (sonrisa). || Lovely (lugar).
— M. y f. Charmer, enchanter (hombre), enchantress (mujer). || — *Encantador de serpientes*, snake charmer. || *Merlín el Encantador*, Merlin, the Magician.
encantamiento m. Magic (magia): *como por encantamiento*, as if by magic. || Bewitchment, witchcraft (hechizo). || Spell, charm, incantation (invocación mágica). || Delight, enchantment.
encantar v. tr. To bewitch, to cast a spell on (con magia). || To charm, to delight: *estoy encantado con tu regalo*, I am delighted with your present. || *Me encanta su manera de cantar*, I love the way she sings; *me encanta trasnochar*, I love staying up late.
encante m. Auction (subasta): *vender muebles al encante*, to sell furniture by auction. || Auction room, saleroom (lugar).
encanto m. Magic: *como por encanto*, as if by magic. || Spell, charm, enchantment (invocación mágica). || Delight, enchantment. || Charm (atractivo): *¡qué encanto tiene esta mujer!*, what charm this woman has! || — Pl. Charms. || — *El niño es un encanto*, the child is a treasure *o* a jewel. || *El sitio es un encanto*, the place is beautiful *o* delightful *o* lovely. || *La casa es un encanto*, the house is a dream. || *¡Ven aquí, encanto!*, come here, darling!
encañada f. Gorge, ravine (entre dos montes).
encañado m. Piping, tubing (canalización). || AGR. Trellis (para las plantas). | Drainage pipe (tubo de desagüe). | Drainage, draining (avenamiento). || TECN. Lathing, lathwork.

encañar v. tr. To pipe (agua). || To channel (por conductos). || AGR. To drain (un terreno húmedo). | To stake, to prop up (los tallos de algunas plantas). || To wind on [a bobbin *o* spool] (hilo, seda).
encañizada f. Crawl, weir made of reeds (para la pesca). || AGR. Trellis.
encañizado m. Wire netting, fence.
encañonado m. Goffering, crimping (planchado).
encañonar v. tr. To pipe (agua). || To channel (encauzar). || To wind on a bobbin, to quill (enrollar). || To aim at, to point at (con un arma). || To goffer, to crimp (una pechera).
— V. intr. To grow feathers, to fledge (los pájaros).
encaparazonar v. tr. To caparison (un caballo).
encaperuzado, da adj. Hooded.
encapilladura f. MAR. Top-rigging.
encapillar v. tr. MAR. To rig. || MIN. To enlarge [a gallery]. || To hood (un ave). || To send to the prison chapel [a condemned man].
— V. pr. FAM. To slip on over the head (un vestido).
encapirotado, da adj. Hooded.
encapirotar v. tr. To hood (un halcón).
encapotado, da adj. Overcast, cloudy: *cielo, tiempo encapotado,* cloudy sky, weather. || Cloaked (con capa o capucha).
encapotadura f. o **encapotamiento** m. Frown (ceño). || Clouding-over (acción de encapotarse el cielo). || Cloudiness (nubosidad).
encapotar v. tr. To cloak, to put a cloak on.
— V. pr. To put a cloak on. || To cloud over, to become overcast *o* cloudy (el cielo). || To frown (mostrar descontento). || To hold its head too low (el caballo).
encaprichamiento m. Infatuation. || Whim, fancy (capricho).
encapricharse v. pr. To take it into one's head to, to set one's mind on: *el niño se ha encaprichado con ir al circo,* the child has set his mind on going to the circus. || FAM. *Encapricharse por* or *con,* to become infatuated with *o* mad about (enamorarse), to take a fancy to (encariñarse).
encapuchar o **encapuzar** v. tr. To hood, to put a hood on.
— V. pr. To put one's hood on.
encarado, da adj. *Bien encarado,* good-looking, nice-looking, pleasant-looking. || *Mal encarado,* nasty-looking, evil-looking.
encaramar v. tr. To put high up (colocar muy alto) || FIG. To elevate *o* to promote to a high position.
— V. pr. To climb (subir): *encaramarse a* or *en un árbol,* to climb a tree. || FIG. To reach a high position (alcanzar un puesto elevado). || *Amer.* To blush (avergonzarse).
encaramiento m. Encounter, confrontation (de personas). || Facing (de una dificultad).
encarapitarse v. pr. *Amer.* To climb.
encarar v. tr. To face [up to], to confront (una dificultad). || To aim (un arma).
— V. pr. To face [up to], to confront: *encararse con un peligro,* to face a danger; *encararse con uno,* to face up to s.o. || To be faced *o* confronted with: *nos encaramos con un problema muy grave,* we are faced with a very serious problem.
encarcelación f. o **encarcelamiento** m. Imprisonment, incarceration. || *Registro* or *asiento de encarcelamiento,* prison register.
encarcelar v. tr. To imprison, to jail, to put in prison, to incarcerate (p. us.). || TECN. To embed *o* to set in mortar (asegurar con yeso). | To clamp (dos piezas de madera). || *Estar encarcelado,* to be in prison *o* in jail.
encarecedor, ra adj. Praising, extolling.
— M. y f. Praiser, extoller.
encarecer* v. tr. To raise *o* to put up the price of (hacer más caro). || FIG. To praise, to extol (elogiar). | To emphasize, to stress [the importance of]: *encareció la importancia de llegar puntualmente,* he emphasized the importance of arriving on time. | To recommend earnestly, to urge: *le encareció que trabajase,* he urged him to work, he earnestly recommended him to work. || *Se lo encarezco,* I beg of you, please.
— V. intr. To go up, to rise in price, to become dearer: *la vida ha encarecido,* the cost of living has gone up.
encarecidamente adv. Earnestly: *se lo ruego encarecidamente,* I earnestly beg of you. || Insistently (con insistencia). || *Elogiar algo encarecidamente,* to praise sth. warmly *o* highly.
encarecido, da adj. Highly recommended *o* praised (persona). || Warm (elogio).
encarecimiento m. Rise *o* increase in the price, price increase, rise *o* increase in the cost: *el encarecimiento del pan,* the rise in the price *o* in the cost of bread; *el encarecimiento de la vida,* the rise in the cost of living. || Extolling (alabanza). || Stressing, emphasis (acentuación). || Recommendation (recomendación). || *Con encarecimiento,* v. ENCARECIDAMENTE.
encargado, da m. y f. Person in charge. || Manager (de un negocio). || Employee, clerk, attendant (empleado). || — *Encargado de negocios,* chargé d'affaires. || *Encargado de relaciones públicas,* public relations officer. || *Encargado de un surtidor de gasolina,* pump attendant. || *Pilar fue la encargada de la comida,* Pilar was in charge of the meal.
— Adj. In charge.
encargar v. tr. To entrust with, to put in charge of: *encargar un asunto a uno,* to entrust s.o. with an affair; *encargar a alguien del teléfono,* to put s.o. in charge of the telephone. || To instruct, to ask (pedir): *le encargué a usted que escribiera,* I instructed you to write. || To order: *encargó un almuerzo para diez personas,* he ordered lunch for ten. || To order, to have made (mandar hacer): *encargar un vestido,* to have a dress made. || To advise, to recommend (aconsejar): *me encargó mucho que tratase de conseguirlo,* he strongly advised me to try and get it.
— V. pr. To take charge of, to undertake responsibility for: *encargarse de la venta* or *de vender,* to take charge of sales *o* of selling. || To look after, to attend to: *me encargo de la biblioteca,* I look after the library. || To take care of, to see about: *yo me encargaré del vino,* I'll take care of the wine. || To be in charge of (ser responsable de). || To order, to have made: *encargarse un traje,* to order a suit. || FAM. To deal with, to see to, to attend to: *¡ya me encargaré yo de él!,* I'll deal with him!
encargo m. Errand (recado): *hacer encargos,* to run errands. || Job, assignment, mission: *cumplir un encargo,* to carry out a job, to fulfil an assignment. || Responsibility. || COM. Order: *hacer un encargo,* to place an order. || — FIG. *Como hecho de encargo,* as if made to measure. || *De encargo,* to measure (a la medida), to order (a petición).
encariñado, da adj. Attached.
encariñar v. tr. To endear, to arouse affection in.
— V. pr. To become fond of, to take a liking to, to get attached to, to take to: *me he encariñado mucho con él,* I have become very fond of him, I have taken a strong liking to him.
encarna f. Fleshing of the hounds (caza).
encarnación f. Incarnation. || Flesh colour. || FIG. *Es la encarnación de la bondad,* he is the soul *o* the epitome of kindness, he is kindness itself *o* personified.
encarnado, da adj. Incarnate: *el diablo encarnado,* the devil incarnate. || Red, incarnadine (p. us.) [color]. || Ruddy (complexion). || Ingrowing (uña).
— M. Red (rojo) || Flesh colour (color de carne).
encarnadura f. Wound (herida). || Fleshing (del perro de caza). || — *Buena encarnadura,* skin with good healing qualities *o* which heals well. || *Mala encarnadura,* skin with poor healing qualities *o* which does not heal easily.
encarnamiento m. MED. Healing, closing-up (de una herida).
encarnar v. intr. To become incarnate (el Verbo Divino). || MED. To be ingrowing (una uña). | To heal [over], to close up (cicatrizarse). || To penetrate the flesh (un arma).
— V. tr. To personify, to embody: *personaje que encarna la justicia,* character who personifies justice. || To flesh (los perros). || To bait (colocar el cebo en el anzuelo). || ARTES. To give flesh colour to, to incarnadine. || TEATR. To play (un papel).
V. pr. To feed on the entrails of game (los perros de caza). || FIG. To join, to mix (mezclarse).
encarne m. Fleshing of the hounds.
encarnecer* v. intr. To put on weight, to put on flesh, to get fat (engordar).
encarnizadamente adv. Brutally, cruelly, bitterly, fiercely, mercilessly (luchar).
encarnizado, da adj. Bloody, bitter, fierce, hard-fought (batalla). || Furious, bitter (riña). || Bloodshot (ojos).
encarnizamiento m. Bitterness, fierceness, cruelty (en la lucha).
encarnizar v. tr. To flesh (los perros de caza). || To brutalize, to make brutal *o* cruel *o* savage: *la guerra encarniza a los hombres,* war makes men brutal.
— V. pr. To become fierce *o* savage (una batalla). || To treat cruelly (con su víctima). || To turn nasty *o* savage [*con,* with] (de palabra). || *Encarnizarse en la lucha,* to fight bitterly.
encarpetar v. tr. To put in a file *o* in a portfolio. || *Amer.* FIG. To shelve, to pigeonhole (dejar un asunto sin resolver).
encarrilamiento m. FIG. Guidance, orientation.
encarrilar v. tr. To put back on the rails (un vehículo descarrilado). || FIG. To direct, to guide (encaminar un carro, un coche, etc.). | To guide, to direct, to put on the right road (dar una buena orientación). | To orient, to orientate: *encarrilar su vida,* to orientate one's life. || *Hemos encarrilado mal el asunto,* we got off to a bad start, we started off on the wrong track.
— V. pr. MAR. To get fouled in the sheave (una cuerda).
encarroñar v. tr. To rot.
— V. pr. To decay, to rot (pudrirse).
encarrujarse v. pr. To curl (rizarse).
encartar v. tr. To proscribe, to outlaw (proscribir). || To summon (emplazar). || To register [for taxes] (incluir en un padrón). || To insert: *encartar una página suplementaria en un libro,* to insert an extra page in a book. || To involve, to implicate: *las personas encartadas en este asunto,* the people involved in this affair. || To lead (naipes).
— V. intr. FIG. y FAM. To be suitable, to do (ser conveniente): *eso no encarta,* that won't do. | To fit in,

to go: *eso no encarta con mis proyectos*, that doesn't fit in with my plans.
— V. pr. FIG. y FAM. *Si se encarta*, should the occasion arise.
encarte m. Lead (naipes). || Order of the cards (orden de los naipes). || IMPR. Insert, inset.
encartonar v. tr. To bind with cardboard (los libros). || To cover with cardboard.
encascabelar v. tr. To adorn with bells.
encasillable adj. Classifiable.
encasillado m. Grid, table, squares, *pl.* (cuadro con casillas). || Pigeonholes, *pl.* (casillero).
encasillar v. tr. To set out in a table *o* grid, to tabulate (cifras, datos, etc.). || To pigeonhole (distribuir en casillas). || To class, to classify (clasificar): *en seguida le encasillé entre los comunistas*, I immediately classed him with the communists *o* as a communist. || To typecast (a un actor). || To designate as a government candidate (en las elecciones para diputados).
— V. pr. FIG. To limit o.s.
encasquetar v. tr. To put on, to pull down (el sombrero). || FIG. To get *o* to put into s.o.'s head (idea, opinión). || FIG. *Nos encasquetó un discurso interminable*, he made us listen to an endless speech, he forced us to sit through an endless speech.
— V. pr. To put on, to pull down (el sombrero). || FIG. *Se le encasquetó la idea de estudiar ruso*, he got the idea of studying Russian into his head.
encasquillador m. *Amer.* Farrier, blacksmith.
encasquillamiento m. Jamming (de un arma).
encasquillar v. tr. *Amer.* To shoe (el caballo).
— V. pr. To jam (arma de fuego).
encastillado, da adj. Fortified [with castles]. || FIG. Obstinate. | Haughty, lofty (soberbio).
encastillamiento m. (P. us.). Fortification. || FIG. Isolation, detachment (aislamiento). | Obstinacy.
encastillar v. tr. (P. us.). To fortify with castles (un lugar). || To pile, to pile up (apilar). || To provide with scaffolding, to erect scaffolding round (una obra).
— V. pr. To take refuge in a castle. || To take refuge [in the hills, etc.]. || FIG. To stick to one's opinion *o* to one's guns, to persist obstinately in one's views (emperrarse). | To withdraw into one's shell, to become withdrawn (retirarse). || *Encastillarse en su dignidad*, to wrap o.s. in one's dignity.
encastrar v. tr. To imbed, to embed, to fit in, to set in. || TECN. To mesh, to engage (endentar).
encauchar v. tr. To rubberize.
encausar v. tr. To prosecute.
encausticar v. tr. To polish, to beeswax.
encáustico, ca adj. Encaustic.
— M. Polish, beeswax.
encausto m. Encaustic: *pintura al encausto*, encaustic painting.
encauzamiento m. Channeling, canalization. || Embanking (para que no se salga un río). || FIG. Guidance, orientation.
encauzar v. tr. To channel, to canalize. || To embank (poner dique). || FIG. To direct, to channel, to guide (un asunto, una discusión, investigaciones).
encebollado m. CULIN. Stew flavoured with onions.
encebollar v. tr. To flavour *o* to cook with onions.
encefalalgia f. MED. Cephalalgia, headache.
encefálico, ca adj. ANAT. Encephalic.
encefalitis f. MED. Encephalitis.
encéfalo m. ANAT. Encephalon.
encefalografía f. MED. Encephalography.
encefalograma m. MED. Encephalogram, encephalograph.
encefalomielitis f. MED. Encephalomyelitis.
encelamiento m. Jealousy (celos).
encelar v. tr. To make jealous.
— V. pr. To become jealous. || To rut, to be in rut *o* on heat (animales).
encella f. Cheese mould (molde).
encellar v. tr. To mould (el queso).
encenagado, da adj. Muddy (lleno de lodo). || Silted up (puerto). || Bogged down, stuck in the mud (atascado). || Covered in mud (sucio). || FIG. Wallowing (en el vicio).
encenagamiento m. Sticking *o* sinking in the mud (atascamiento). || Silting up (de un puerto). || FIG. Wallowing (en el vicio).
encenagarse v. pr. To get stuck *o* bogged down (atascarse). || To become boggy *o* muddy (un terreno). || To get covered in mud, to get muddy (ensuciarse). || To silt up (un puerto). || To wallow in mud (revolcarse). || FIG. To wallow (envilecerse en el vicio, en la ignorancia).
encendajas f. pl. Kindling, *sing.*
encendedor m. Lighter: *encendedor de gas*, gas lighter. || Lamplighter (persona).
encender* v. tr. To light: *encender una vela, un cigarrillo, el fuego*, to light a candle, a cigarette, the fire. || To ignite: *encender una mezcla combustible*, to ignite a combustible mixture. || To set on fire, to set fire to, to set alight (pegar fuego a): *encender el rastrojo, un montón de basura*, to set fire to the stubble, to a pile of rubbish. || To turn on, to switch on, to put on (la radio, la luz eléctrica). || To light, to put on (el gas). || To strike, to light (una cerilla). || FIG. To inflame, to kindle (una discordia, un conflicto, las pasiones). | To arouse (el entusiasmo). | To spark off (una guerra). | To awake (los celos, el odio, etc.). || — *La fiebre encendía sus mejillas*, her cheeks were burning with fever. || *Me encendía el odio*, hatred was burning me up.
— V. pr. To light: *esta vela, este cigarrillo, la cocina no quiere encenderse*, this candle, this cigarette, the cooker will not light. || To ignite, to catch fire: *sería muy peligroso si el gas que ha escapado se encendiera*, it would be very dangerous if the gas which has escaped were to ignite. || To burn up, to flare up (una llama). || FIG. To light up: *su cara se encendió*, her face lit up. | To get excited (inflamarse). | To blush, to get red (ruborizarse). | To break out (un conflicto). || *Encenderse de ira*, to flare up with rage.
encendidamente adv. Ardently, passionately. || Enthusiastically.
encendido, da adj. Lit (el fuego, un cigarrillo). || On, switched on: *la luz está encendida*, the light is on. || Burning, on fire (incendiado). || FIG. Bright red (rojo). | Fiery: *una mirada encendida*, a fiery glance. | Flushed, red: *tener la cara encendida*, to have a flushed face. | Crimson, purple: *tiene la cara encendida por la ira*, his face is purple with rage. || FIG. *Encendido como la grana* or *como un pavo*, as red as a beetroot.
— M. Lighting: *el encendido de los faroles*, the lighting of the lamps. || AUT. Ignition: *avance en el encendido*, ignition advance. || Firing (de un cohete). || *Encendido de alta tensión*, high-tension ignition.
encendimiento m. Burning. || FIG. Redness. | Blushing (de la cara). | Ardour (de una pasión).
encenizar v. tr. To cover with ashes.
encentadura f. o **encentamiento** m. Beginning, start.
encentar* v. tr. To start, to begin (empezar).
encepar v. intr. To take root (una planta).
— V. tr. To pillory, to put in the stocks (a un prisionero). || To stock, to fit with a stock (un arma, un ancla). || TECN. To join.
encepe m. AGR. Rooting, taking root.
encerado adj. Waxed, polished (suelo, mueble). || Wax-coloured.
— M. Waxing, polishing (del suelo, de un mueble). || Wax (capa de cera). || Blackboard (pizarra para escribir). || Oilcloth (tela para proteger una mesa), oilskin (tela para las prendas). || MAR. Tarpaulin.
encerador, ra adj. Waxing, polishing.
— M. y f. Floor polisher *o* waxer (persona). || — F. Floor polisher *o* waxer (aparato).
enceramiento m. Waxing, polishing.
encerar v. tr. To wax, to polish (dar cera). || To spot, to soil with wax (las velas). || To thicken (la argamasa).
— V. intr. y pr. To turn yellow (las mieses).
encerotar v. tr. To wax.
encerradero m. Pen, fold (aprisco). || TAUR. Bullpen.
encerrar* v. tr. To shut in, to shut up: *encerrar a alguien*, to shut s.o. up; *encerrar un perro*, to shut a dog up. || To lock in, to lock up, to put under lock and key (con llave): *encerrar a un prisionero, un objeto precioso*, to put a prisoner, a valuable object under lock and key. || To put: *encerrar una frase entre comillas, en un paréntesis*, to put a sentence in inverted commas, in brackets. || FIG. To contain, to include: *este libro encierra unas agudezas muy graciosas*, this book includes some very amusing witticisms. | To contain: *sus palabras encierran un profundo significado*, his words contain deep significance; *el museo encierra unas magníficas obras de arte*, the museum contains some magnificent works of art. | To involve: *el proyecto encierra grandes dificultades*, the project involves serious difficulties. | To block (en el ajedrez). || *Encerrar en la cárcel*, to put in jail.
— V. pr. To shut o.s. in *o* up, to lock o.s. in. || FIG. To go into retreat *o* seclusion. || FIG. *Encerrarse en una idea*, to stick obstinately to an idea.
encerrona f. FAM. Retreat, seclusion (retiro). || TAUR. Private bullfight. || FIG. Trap. || FIG. y FAM. *Le prepararon una encerrona para que votase a su favor*, they trapped him into voting for them.
encespedamiento m. Turfing.
encespedar v. tr. To turf, to cover with turf.
encestar v. intr. To score a basket [U.S., to make a basket] (in basketball).
enceste m. Basket (en el baloncesto): *marcar un enceste*, to score a basket.
encía f. ANAT. Gum.
encíclico, ca adj./s.f. Encyclical.
enciclopedia f. Encyclopedia, encyclopaedia. || FIG. *Esa chica es una enciclopedia* or *una enciclopedia viviente*, that girl is a walking encyclopedia.
enciclopédico, ca adj. Encyclopedic, encyclopaedic, encyclopedical, encyclopaedical.
enciclopedismo m. Encyclopedism, encyclopaedism.
enciclopedista adj./s. Encyclopedist, encyclopaedist.
encierro m. Confinement (de una persona). || Seclusion, retreat (retiro). || Penning (del ganado vacuno), folding (del ganado lanar). || Pen, fold (corral). || Cell (calabozo). || TAUR. Driving of the bulls into the pen before a bullfight. | Bullpen (toril). | "Encierro".
— OBSERV. The *encierro* is part of the fiestas of San Fermin which begin on 7th July in Pamplona. In the *encierro* the bulls chase young men through the town to the bullring, where they are then shut in the "toriles".
encima adv. Above: *encima hay un reloj colgado en la pared*, above, there is a clock hanging on the wall.

|| On top: *un edificio enorme con dos grúas encima*, a huge building with two cranes on top; *llevaba un jersey y el abrigo encima*, I was wearing a pullover and my overcoat on top; *queso con una lonja de jamón encima*, cheese with a slice of ham on top. || Overhead, above: *teníamos encima la Estrella Polar*, we had the Pole Star overhead. || In addition, as well, on top of that (además): *le dio diez pesos y otros dos encima*, he gave him ten pesos and another two as well. || FAM. On top of that: *le insultaron y encima le pegaron*, they insulted him, and on top of that they hit him; *es caro y encima feo*, it's expensive, and on top of that ugly. || — *Ahí encima*, over there on [the] top. || *Aquí está su cama con la foto colgada encima*, here is his bed with the picture above it. || *De encima*, on top, top: *quieres pasarme el libro de encima*, will you pass me the top book *o* the book on top. || *Echarse encima*, to throw o.s. onto *o* at (atacar): *se echaron encima del enemigo*, they threw themselves at the enemy; to bear down on: *se nos echó encima el camión*, the lorry bore down on us; to overtake: *la noche se nos echó encima*, nightfall overtook us; to take upon o.s., to undertake (encargarse de): *echarse encima un trabajo*, to undertake a job; to shoulder (una responsabilidad), to set against o.s. (indisponer): *se echo encima a todos los críticos*, he set all the critics against him. || *Encima de*, on, on top of (sobre): *encima de la mesa*, on the table; above, over (más arriba): *la nariz está encima de la boca*, the nose is above the mouth; in addition to (además de). || *Encima de (que)*, besides, as well as: *encima de ser o de que es perezoso, es mentiroso*, as well as [his] being lazy he is a liar. || *Encima mía* or *de mí*, above me. || *Llevar encima*, to have on one: *no llevo dinero encima*, I haven't any money on me. || FIG. *Pasar por encima*, v. PASAR. || *Por encima*, on top (sobre), above, over, overhead (más arriba), quickly, superficially: *leer algo por encima*, to read through sth. quickly. || *Por encima de*, above: *está por encima de los demás alumnos*, he is above the other pupils; *el jefe está por encima de todos los problemas menores de la empresa*, the boss is above all the petty problems of the firm; beyond: *el problema está por encima de él, por encima de su inteligencia*, the problem is beyond him, beyond his intelligence; over: *pasó por encima del arroyo*, he stepped *o* strode over the stream; in spite of (a pesar de). || *Por encima de todo*, above all (sobre todo). || *Puso el sombrero en la silla y luego se sentó encima*, he put his hat on the chair and then sat on it. || *Quitarse de encima*, to clear o.s. of (deudas), to get out of (un problema, dificultades), to get rid of (una cosa), to get rid of, to shake off (una persona): *creía que no podría nunca quitármelo de encima*, I thought I would never be able to get rid of him. || *Ya están encima las vacaciones*, the holidays are almost here.

— OBSERV. *Encima* is used in preference to *sobre* when one object is placed on another at some distance from the ground, e.g. *encima del armario, del tejado*.

encimar v. tr. To put on top. || To add to [a stake] (en el juego del tresillo). || *Amer*. To throw in (añadir algo más a lo estipulado).
— V. pr. To rise [above].

encimero, ra adj. Top, on [the] top: *la sábana encimera*, the top sheet.
— F. *Amer*. Leather saddle cover.

encina f. BOT. Holm oak, ilex.

encinal o **encinar** m. Grove of holm oaks.

encinchar v. tr. *Amer*. To girth, to cinch (un caballo).

encino m. V. ENCINA.

encinta adj. f. Pregnant.

encintado m. Kerb [U.S., curb] (de la acera).

encintar v. tr. To beribbon, to adorn with ribbon. || To put a kerb on, to kerb [U.S., to curb] (una acera).

encizañar v. tr. e intr. To sow discord, to cause trouble (sembrar discordia). || *Encizañar contra*, to incite against.

enclaustrar v. tr. To cloister, to shut up in a convent. || FIG. To cloister, to shut up.
— V. pr. FIG. To shut o.s. up *o* in.

enclavar v. tr. To enclave (territorio). || To situate, to locate, to place (situar). || To nail (clavar). || To pierce, to transfix (traspasar). || VET. To prick.

enclave m. Enclave (territorio). || Setting, situation (emplazamiento).

enclavijar v. tr. To peg.

enclenque adj. Sickly (enfermizo). || Skinny (delgaducho).
— M. y f. Sickly person. || Skinny person.

enclítico, ca adj./s.f. Enclitic.

enclocar* o **encloquecer*** v. intr. To become broody (la gallina).

encocorante adj. FAM. Annoying.

encocorar v. tr. FAM. To get on s.o.'s nerves, to annoy.

encofrado m. TECN. Formwork, shuttering (para el hormigón). | Timbering (en una mina).

encofrar v. tr. TECN. To put up shuttering for (el hormigón). | To timber, to plank (galería de mina).

encoger v. tr. To shrink (estrechar): *el lavado encoge ciertos tejidos*, washing shrinks certain fabrics. || To contract (contraer). || FIG. To intimidate (dar miedo).
— V. intr. To shrink (tela).
— V. pr. To shrink (tela). || To hunch up (el cuerpo). || FIG. To feel small (achicarse). || — *Encogerse de hombros*, to shrug one's shoulders. || *Se le encogió el corazón*, his heart stood still (de miedo, sorpresa), his heart sank (de tristeza).

encogido, da adj. Shrunk, shrunken (tela). || Hunched up (el cuerpo). || FIG. Timid, bashful, shy (tímido). | Fainthearted (pusilánime). || — FIG. *Tenía el estómago encogido*, his stomach was in knots. | *Tenía el corazón encogido*, his heart was in his mouth (de miedo), he had a heavy heart (de tristeza).

encogimiento m. Shrinkage (de una tela). || Hunching (del cuerpo). || FIG. Bashfulness, shyness, timidity (timidez). || *Encogimiento de hombros*, shrug [of the shoulders].

encolado, da adj. *Amer*. FIG. Stuck-up (vanidoso).
— M. Clarification (del vino). || Gluing, gumming, sticking (con cola). || Sizing (para pintar).

encoladora f. TECN. Slasher (textiles). | Splicer (cine).

encoladura f. o **encolamiento** m. Gluing, gumming, sticking. || Sizing (para pintar). || Clarification (del vino).

encolar v. tr. To glue, to gum, to stick (pegar). || To size (antes de pintar). || To clarify (el vino).

encolerizar v. tr. To anger, to infuriate, to exasperate.
— V. pr. To get angry, to lose one's temper.

encomendar* v. tr. To commend, to entrust (confiar): *le encomiendo a usted mi hijo*, I entrust *o* commend my child to you, I entrust you with my child; *le encomiendo esta misión*, I entrust you with this mission. || To commend: *encomendar algo a la memoria*, to commend sth. to memory.
— V. pr. To commend o.s., to entrust o.s.: *encomendarse a la bondad de alguien*, to commend o.s. to s.o.'s good graces. || — *Encomendarse a Dios*, to commend one's soul to God. || *En vuestras manos me encomiendo*, I put myself in your hands. || FIG. *No saber a qué santo encomendarse*, v. SANTO.

encomendero m. HIST. "Encomendero", master of an "encomienda". (V. ENCOMIENDA.)

encomiador, ra adj. Laudatory, praising.
— M. y f. Praiser, extoller.

encomiar v. tr. To praise, to extol, to laud.

encomiasta m. Praiser, extoller, eulogist.

encomiástico, ca adj. Eulogistic, laudatory.

encomienda f. Assignment (encargo). || Commandery (antigua dignidad). || HIST. "Encomienda" (v. OBSERV.). || *Amer*. Packet, package, parcel: *encomienda postal*, postal packet.

— OBSERV. *Encomiendas* (concessions, holdings) were estates granted to Spanish settlers in Latin America in the colonial era. The Indians living on the land were put into the service of their *encomendero* or had to pay him taxes. For his part, the *encomendero* was supposed to look after the interests of the Indians in his territory and convert them to Christianity.

encomio m. Praise, eulogy.

encomioso, sa adj. Eulogistic, laudatory.

encompadrar v. intr. FAM. To become friends, to pal up.

enconado, da adj. Inflamed (inflamado). || Infected (infectado). || Passionate, ardent, eager: *bibliófilo enconado*, passionate booklover; *partidario enconado*, ardent supporter. || Bitter, fierce: *adversario enconado*, bitter opponent; *lucha enconada*, fierce struggle. || Angry (enfadado).

enconadura f. o **enconamiento** m. Inflammation (inflamación), infection (infección). || FIG. V. ENCONO.

enconar v. tr. To inflame (inflamar), to infect (infectar). || FIG. To inflame (una disensión, una lucha). | To anger (enfadar).
— V. pr. To become inflamed (inflamarse), to become infected (infectarse). || FIG. To grow bitter (una lucha, una discusión). | To get angry (enfadarse).

encono m. Rancour [U.S., rancor], ill will (rencor). || Bitterness, fierceness (en una lucha, una discusión).

encontradizo, za adj. *Hacerse el encontradizo con alguien*, to pretend to meet s.o. by chance.

encontrado, da adj. Opposing, contrary: *intereses encontrados*, opposing interests.

encontrar* v. tr. To find: *encontrar una solución*, to find a solution; *la encontré anegada en lágrimas*, I found her crying her eyes out. || To find, to come across: *encontré un libro muy interesante*, I came across a very interesting book. || To meet, to come across, to bump into (fam.) [tropezar con]: *acabo de encontrar a Rafael en la calle*, I've just met Raphael in the street. || To encounter, to come across, to find (dificultades). || To see: *no sé lo que encuentras en ella*, I don't know what you see in her. || To think of (parecer): *¿cómo encuentras mi anillo?*, what do you think of my ring? || To find: *¿cómo has encontrado la película?*, how did you find the film? || — FIG. *Encontrar la horma de su zapato*, v. HORMA. || *No encuentro palabras para expresarle mi agradecimiento*, I can't tell you how grateful I am.
— V. pr. To meet, to meet each other, to bump into (fam.), to bump into each other (fam.): *se encontraron en la plaza*, they bumped into each other in the square; *me encontré con él en el bulevar*, I met him in the boulevard. || To collide (chocar). || To be (estar): *se encuentra en el Brasil*, he is in Brazil. || To meet (reunirse): *quedaron en encontrarse en el bar*, they arranged to meet in the bar. || FIG. To be, to feel: *me encuentro mucho mejor*, I feel much better. | To clash (ser

contrarias las opiniones, etc.). || — *Encontrarse con*, to meet (a alguien), to run into (tropezar con), to encounter, to run up against (problemas). || *Encontrarse con ánimo para*, to feel up to. || FAM. *No me encuentro entre gente tan presumida*, I don't feel right among such pretentious people.
encontrón o **encontronazo** m. Collision, crash.
encopetado, da adj. Upper-crust, upper-class (de alto copete). || Haughty, conceited (presumido).
encopetarse v. pr. To put on airs (engreírse).
encorajar v. tr. To encourage.
— V. pr. To get angry.
encorajinar v. tr. To provoke, to make angry.
— V. pr. To lose one's temper, to get angry, to see red (encolerizarse). || To pluck up courage (animarse).
encorchar v. tr. To hive (abejas). || To cork (botella).
encorchetar v. tr. To fit with a clasp *o* hook and eye (poner un corchete). || To fasten with a hook and eye *o* with a clasp (abrochar). || To cramp (piedras).
encordar* v. tr. To string (un instrumento de música, una raqueta de tenis). || To tie with laces.
— V. pr. To rope up (alpinismo).
encordelar v. tr. To tie up (atar).
encordonar v. tr. To tie up (atar).
encornado, da adj. Horned. || *Toro bien encornado*, bull with good horns.
encornadura f. Horns, *pl.* (de un toro). || Antlers, *pl.* (del venado). || Shape *o* position of the horns.
encornar v. tr. To gore (cornear).
encorozar v. tr. To put a cone-shaped cap on (a un condenado).
encorralar v. tr. To pen (animales).
encorsetar v. tr. To corset. || FIG. To straightjacket (paralizar).
— V. pr. To put on a corset.
encorvado, da adj. Curved, bent (en curva). || Stooped, bent (por la edad). || Bent over (agachado).
encorvadura f. o **encorvamiento** m. Bending, curving (acción). || Bend, curve (curva). || Stoop (de una persona de edad).
encorvar v. tr. To bend, to curve: *tiene la espalda encorvada por la edad*, his back is bent with age.
— V. pr. To curve, to bend. || To become stooped, to become bent (una persona). || To bend down, to bend over (agacharse). || To warp (madera). || To give, to bend, to buckle (bajo una carga). || To buck (caballo).
encostalar v. tr. To put in sacks *o* bags, to bag (ensacar).
encostrar v. tr. To cover with a crust. || To put a crust on (un pastel).
— V. pr. To form a crust. || To form a scab, to scab over (una herida).
encrasar v. tr. To thicken (espesar). || AGR. To fertilize, to manure (la tierra).
encrespado, da adj. Curly (el pelo). || Choppy, rough (el mar).
encrespamiento m. Tight curling, frizzing (del pelo). || Erection (del plumaje). || Bristling (del pelo, por miedo). || Roughness, choppiness (del mar). || FIG. Excitement (de las pasiones). | Irritation, provocation (irritación). | Entanglement (enredo).
encrespar v. tr. To curl tightly, to frizz (rizar): *cabello encrespado*, tightly curled hair. || To set [one's hair] on end (erizar el pelo). || To erect (el plumaje). || To make rough *o* choppy (el agua). || FIG. To work up, to excite (las pasiones). | To irritate, to provoke, to infuriate (irritar).
— V. pr. To become rough *o* choppy (el mar). || To curl up, to go frizzy (el cabello). || To stand on end, to bristle (erizarse). || FIG. To boil, to become heated (las pasiones). | To become entangled *o* mixed up (enredarse). | To become irritated, to get cross (enfadarse).
encristalar v. tr. To glaze.
encrucijada f. Crossroads, intersection. || FIG. Crossroads: *la encrucijada de la vida*, the crossroads of life; *París, encrucijada de Europa*, Paris, crossroads of Europe. | Dilemma.
encrudecer* v. tr. FIG. To irritate.
— V. intr. y pr. To grow worse *o* colder (el tiempo).
encruelecer* v. tr. To make cruel.
— V. pr. To become cruel.
encuadernación f. Bookbinding (oficio). || Binding (de un libro): *encuadernación en tela, en cuero*, cloth, leather binding. || *Taller de encuadernación*, bindery.
encuadernador, ra m. y f. Bookbinder.
encuadernar v. tr. To bind. || — *Libro encuadernado en rústica*, paperback. || *Sin encuadernar*, unbound.
encuadramiento m. CINEM. Framing. || FIG. Frame, framework (límite). || MIL. Officering (de tropas).
encuadrar v. tr. To frame (encerrar en un marco). || To fit in, to insert (encajar). || FIG. To surround (rodear). | To put in, to incorporate (en un grupo): *han encuadrado a los nuevos reclutas en el primer batallón*, the new recruits have been incorporated into the first batallion. || CINEM. To frame (la imagen). || MIL. To officer (proveer de oficiales).
encuadre m. CINEM. Framing. || Setting (situación). || FIG. Frame, framework (límite). || MIL. Officering (de tropas).
encuartelar v. tr. *Amer.* To quarter in barracks (acuartelar). | To confine to barracks (recluir).
encubamiento m. Vatting.
encubar v. tr. To vat (el vino).
encubierta f. Fraud.
encubiertamente adv. Secretly, in secret. || Fraudulently (fraudulentamente).
encubierto, ta adj. Hidden, concealed, secret (oculto). || Fraudulent, underhand (fraudulento). || — FIG. *Hablar con palabras encubiertas*, to talk cryptically *o* guardedly. || *Paro encubierto*, underemployment.
encubridor, ra adj. Hiding, concealing.
— M. y f. JUR. Receiver, fence (fam.) [de mercancías robadas]. | Accessory after the fact (que encubre un delito o a un delincuente). | Harbourer [U.S., harborer] (de un criminal). || Procurer (hombre), procuress (mujer) [alcahuete].
encubrimiento m. Hiding, concealment (ocultación). || JUR. Receiving (de lo robado). | Harbouring [U.S., harboring], concealment (de un criminal).
encubrir v. tr. To hide, to conceal (ocultar). || JUR. To receive (mercancías robadas). | To harbour [U.S., to harbor], to conceal (a un delincuente).
encuentro m. Meeting (reunión, entrevista): *un encuentro casual*, a chance meeting. || Rendezvous (cita): *el encuentro de los astronautas en el espacio*, the astronauts' rendezvous in space. || Discovery (descubrimiento). || Collision (colisión). || Meeting (coincidencia). || DEP. Match (partido). | Meeting, clash (entre dos personas, campeones). | Meeting: *encuentro deportivo*, sports meeting. || FIG. Find (hallazgo). | Clash (de ideas, de intereses). || ANAT. Armpit (axila). || ARQ. Angle. || MIL. Skirmish, encounter, clash (lucha).
— Pl. Wing joint *sing.*, (en las aves). || Withers (de una caballería). || IMPR. Blanks *o* spaces [left for printing in another colour]. || — *Ir al encuentro de*, to go to meet. || *Salir al encuentro de*, to go to meet (ir a buscar), to contradict (contradecir), to oppose, to make a stand against (oponer), to anticipate (anticiparse), to face (afrontar una dificultad).
encuerado, da adj. *Amer.* Naked, nude.
encuerar v. tr. *Amer.* To strip, to undress (desnudar). || *Amer.* FIG. To fleece, to rob, to skin (en el juego).
— V. pr. To get undressed (desnudarse).
encuesta f. Poll, opinion poll, survey (sobre la opinión pública): *hacer una encuesta*, to carry out an opinion poll. || Inquiry, investigation (investigación).
encuestador, ra m. y f. Pollster.
encumbrado, da adj. Of high social standing, upper-class (socialmente). || Eminent, distinguished (eminente). || High, lofty (alto).
encumbramiento m. Rise, raising, elevation. || Exaltation, eminence (exaltación). || Praise, extolling (ensalzamiento). || Climbing (de un monte). || Height (altura).
encumbrar v. tr. To raise, to elevate (levantar). || FIG. To honour, [U.S., to honor], to exalt, to dignify (elevar). | To extol, to praise (ensalzar): *encumbrar hasta las nubes*, to praise to the skies.
— V. pr. To rise. || FIG. To rise to a high social position. | To put on airs, to be haughty (envanecerse).
encunar v. tr. To put in the cradle (poner en la cuna). || TAUR. To catch between its horns (el toro al torero).
encureñar v. tr. To mount (un cañón).
encurtidos m. pl. Pickles (pepinillos, cebollas, etc.).
encurtir v. tr. To pickle (pepinillos, etc.). || *Amer.* To tan (curtir).
enchalecar v. tr. POP. To pocket (robar). || *Amer.* To put [s.o.] into a straightjacket.
— V. pr. POP. To pocket (embolsarse).
enchancletar v. tr. To put on (poner zapatillas). || To drag [one's shoes] like slippers (arrastrar los zapatos).
— V. pr. To put slippers on.
enchapado m. Veneer (chapa de madera). || Veneering (acción). || Plating (de metal).
enchapar v. tr. To veneer (con madera). || To plate (con metal).
encharcado, da adj. Flooded, swamped.
encharcamiento m. Flooding, swamping (de un terreno).
encharcar v. tr. To flood, to swamp (un terreno).
— V. pr. To be flooded (un terreno). || To become bloated (el estómago).
enchicharse v. pr. *Amer.* To get drunk [on corn liquor].
enchilada f. *Amer.* Rolled corn omelette spiced with chili.
enchilado, da adj. *Amer.* Spiced with chili. || Red (rojo). | FIG. Hot-tempered.
— M. *Amer.* Stew spiced with chili.
enchilar v. tr. *Amer.* To season with chili. | FIG. To annoy (molestar).
— V. pr. *Amer.* FIG. To become irritated *o* angry.
enchinar v. tr. To pave with pebbles *o* cobbles. || *Amer.* To curl (rizar).
enchiqueramiento m. TAUR. Shutting in the bullpen. || FIG. y FAM. Imprisonment (en la cárcel).
enchiquerar v. tr. TAUR. To shut in the bullpen. || FIG. y FAM. To put in clink *o* in the nick (encarcelar).
enchironar v. tr. FAM. To put in clink *o* in the nick.

enchufado, da adj. FAM. Well in (recomendado). | Who has a sinecure *o* a cushy job. || FAM. *Estar enchufado*, to have friends in the right places *o* useful contacts, to be well in (estar recomendado), to have a cushy job (tener una colocación buena).
— M. y f. FAM. Person who has succeeded through contacts, wirepuller. | Slacker (soldado).
enchufar v. tr. ELECTR. To plug in, to connect. || To fit together, to couple (tubos). || FIG. y FAM. To pull wires for (ejercer influencia).
— V. pr. FAM. To get a cushy job.
enchufe m. ELECTR. Socket, plug, point (hembra): *enchufe para la luz relámpago*, flash socket. | Plug (macho). || Joint, connection (de dos tubos). || FIG. y FAM. Wirepulling (influencia). | Contacts, *pl.* (relaciones). | Cushy job (puesto). || — *Enchufe flexible*, adapter. || FIG. y FAM. *Tener enchufe*, to have a cushy job (tener una colocación buena), to have friends in the right places *o* useful contacts (tener relaciones).
enchufismo m. FIG. y FAM. Wirepulling.
ende adv. (Ant.). There. || *Por ende*, therefore, hence.
endeble adj. Weak, frail, feeble (persona, argumento). || Puny, sickly (enclenque). || Flimsy, fragile, (cosa).
endeblez f. Weakness, frailty, feebleness (de personas, argumentos). || Flimsiness, fragility (de cosas).
endecágono, na adj. MAT. Hendecagonal.
— M. Hendecagon.
endecasílabo, ba adj. Hendecasyllabic.
— M. Hendecasyllable.
endecha f. Lament, dirge (lamento). || POÉT. Quatrain with lines of six or seven syllables, usually assonant. || *Endecha real*, quatrain of three usually heptasyllabic lines followed by one hendecasyllable.
endeja f. ARQ. Toothing (adaraja).
endemia f. MED. Endemic disease, endemic.
endémico, ca adj. MED. Endemic, endemical. || FIG. Chronic.
endemoniado, da adj. Possessed [of the devil]. || Evil, wicked (malo). || Devilish, mischievous (travieso). || Diabolical, terrible: *un olor endemoniado*, a diabolical smell. || Furious, wild (irritado). || Damned, wretched, cursed (maldito): *ese endemoniado disco me vuelve loco*, that wretched record drives me mad. || Wild, frenzied: *un ritmo endemoniado*, a frenzied rhythm.
— M. y f. Person possessed. || FIG. *Chillar como un endemoniado*, to shriek like a madman.
endemoniar v. tr. To bedevil, to possess with an evil spirit *o* with the devil. || To anger, to infuriate (enojar).
endenantes adv. FAM. Before (antes). | Previously, formerly (en otro tiempo).
endentar* v. tr. TECN. To tooth (poner dientes a una rueda). | To mesh (ruedas dentadas). || To interlock (encajar).
endentecer* v. intr. To cut one's teeth, to teethe.
enderezado, da ajd. Favourable, appropriate, suitable (propicio).
enderezador, ra m. y f. Righter, redresser (de entuertos).
enderezamiento m. Straightening [out *o* up] (de algo torcido). || Reerection (de algo tendido). || Righting, redressing (de un entuerto, de una situación).
enderezar v. tr. To straighten [out *o* up], to put straight (poner derecho). || To reerect, to set upright again (algo que estaba tendido). || To right (un barco). || FIG. To put right, to right, to redress (entuertos, una situación). | To direct (encaminar). | To reform (enmendar).
— V. intr. To head, to make one's way (dirigirse).
— V. pr. To straighten [out *o* up]. || To be directed *o* aimed (*a*, at) [encaminarse a]. || To stand up straight (una persona).
endeudarse v. pr. To get *o* to run *o* to fall into debt (entramparse). || FIG. To become indebted (*con*, to) [tener que estar agradecido].
endiabladamente adv. Evily, wickedly. || Mischievously, devilishly (de modo travieso). || Furiously, angrily.
endiablado, da adj. Possessed [of the devil]. || Evil, wicked (malo). || Mischievous, devilish (travieso). || Diabolical, terrible: *tiene un sabor endiablado*, it tastes terrible, it has a terrible taste. || Furious, wild (irritado). || Blessed, wretched, cursed (maldito). || Wild, frenzied: *un ritmo endiablado*, a frenzied rhythm. || Ugly, horrible (feísimo).
endiablar v. tr. To bedevil, to possess with the devil *o* with an evil spirit (endemoniar).
endibia f. BOT. Endive.
endilgar v. tr. FAM. To palm off, to lumber: *no me endilgues ese trabajo*, don't palm that job off on me, don't lumber that job on me. | To land, to deal (una bofetada). | To send off, to dispatch (mandar). || FAM. *Le endilgué todo mi poema*, I made him listen to *o* sit through my whole poem.
endino, na adj. FAM. Wicked.
endiñar v. tr. POP. To land, to deal (un golpe). | To fetch (un tortazo).
endiosado, da adj. Conceited, stuck-up (vanidoso). || Deified (considerado como un dios).
endiosamiento m. FIG. Pride, vanity, conceit.
endiosar v. tr. To deify.
— V. pr. To become proud *o* stuck-up *o* conceited.
enditarse v. pr. *Amer.* To run *o* to fall *o* to get into debt (endeudarse).
endocardiaco, ca adj. ANAT. Endocardial.
endocardio m. ANAT. Endocardium.
endocarditis f. MED. Endocarditis.
endocarpio m. BOT. Endocarp.
endocráneo m. ANAT. Endocranium.
endocrino, na adj. BIOL. Endocrine, endocrinal, endocrinic, endocrinous. || *Glándula endocrina*, endocrine gland.
endocrinología f. MED. Endocrinology.
endocrinólogo, ga m. y f. Endocrinologist.
endodermo m. BIOL. Endoderm.
endodermis f. BIOL. Endodermis.
endoesqueleto m. ANAT. Endoskeleton.
endogamia f. Endogamy, inbreeding.
endogénesis f. BIOL. Endogeny.
endógeno, na adj. Endogenous.
endomingar v. tr. To dress up in one's Sunday best.
— V. pr. To put on one's Sunday best.
endoparásito, ta adj. Endoparasitic.
— M. Endoparasite.
endoplasma m. Endoplasm.
endosador, ra o **endosante** adj. COM. Endorsing.
— M. y f. Endorser.
endosar v. tr. COM. To endorse. || FIG. To shoulder, to lumber (una responsabilidad, una carga). | To palm off, to foist (un trabajo a otro).
endosatario, ria m. y f. COM. Endorsee.
endoscopia f. MED. Endoscopy.
endoscopio m. MED. Endoscope.
endoselar v. tr. To provide with a canopy.
endosmómetro m. BIOL. Endosmometer.
endósmosis o **endosmosis** f. QUÍM. Endosmosis.
endosmótico, ca adj. Endosmotic.
endoso m. COM. Endorsement, endorsing.
endosperma m. BOT. Endosperm.
endotelio m. ANAT. Endothelium.
endotérmico, ca adj. QUÍM. Endothermic, endothermal.
endotoxina f. BIOL. Endotoxin.
endrino, na adj. Blue-black.
— M. BOT. Blackthorn, sloe (arbusto). || — F. BOT. Sloe (fruto).
endrogarse v. pr. *Amer.* To get into debt.
endulzar v. tr. To sweeten: *endulzar con miel*, to sweeten with honey. || FIG. To soften, to alleviate, to ease (el sufrimiento). | To brighten up: *las visitas de sus nietos endulzaron su vejez*, her grandchildren's visits brightened up her old age. || ARTES. To tone down, to soften (las tintas y contornos).
endurecer* v. tr. To harden, to make hard (poner duro). || FIG. To harden, to toughen, to inure: *la vida militar endurece a los hombres*, life in the army hardens men.
— V. pr. To harden, to become hard. || FIG. To become inured *o* hardened (volverse resistente). | To become hardhearted (volverse insensible).
endurecimiento m. Hardening (acción). || Hardness (estado). || FIG. Hardening, inurement (del cuerpo, de las emociones). | Hardheartedness (insensibilidad). | Obstinacy.
ene f. N [name of the letter *n*]. || X: *hace ene años*, X years ago.
enea f. BOT. V. ANEA.
Eneas n. pr. m. Aeneas.
enebro m. BOT. Juniper (árbol).
Eneida n. pr. f. Aeneid.
eneldo m. BOT. Anethum, dill.
enema m. (Ant.). MED. Ointment (ungüento). | Enema (ayuda).
— OBSERV. In its second sense the word *enema* can be either masculine or feminine. The Academy prefers the feminine.
enemiga f. Ill will (antipatía): *tenerle enemiga a alguien*, to bear s.o. ill will. || Enmity, hostility (enemistad).
enemigo, ga adj. Enemy, hostile: *el ejército enemigo*, the enemy army. || FIG. *Ser enemigo de*, to dislike.
— M. y f. Enemy, adversary, foe. || MIL. Enemy. || — FIG. *Al enemigo que huye puente de plata*, let sleeping dogs lie. | *Enemigo malo*, devil. | *Hacerse enemigos*, to make enemies. | *No hay enemigo pequeño*, do not underrate your enemy. || *Pasarse al enemigo*, to go over to the enemy.
enemistad f. Enmity.
enemistar v. tr. To make enemies of, to set at odds: *enemistar a dos personas*, to set two people at odds.
— V. pr. To become enemies. || To fall out (enfadarse).
energético, ca adj. Energy.
— F. Energetics. || — M. pl. Fuels.
energía f. FÍS. Energy: *energía cinética, potencial, química*, kinetic, potential, chemical energy. || Energy, power: *energía nuclear, eléctrica*, nuclear, electric power. || Energy, vitality, vigour [U.S., vigor] (fuerzas): *una persona de mucha energía*, a person with lots of energy. || Spirit (ánimo). || *Energía hidráulica*, water-power.
enérgico, ca adj. Energetic, spirited, vigorous (carácter). || Forceful (decisión, medida). || Strenuous (esfuerzo). || Vigorous, strong (ataque). || Emphatic

(negativa). || Forcible, strong (palabras). || MED. Powerful, drastic (medicina).
energúmeno, na m. y f. Madman (hombre), madwoman (mujer): *comportarse como un energúmeno*, to behave like a madman. || Fanatic. || Energumen (persona poseída del demonio).
enero m. January: *el 5 de enero*, the 5th of January, January 5th.
enervación f. o **enervamiento** m. Enervation. || Effeminacy.
enervador, ra o **enervante** adj. Enervating.
enervar v. tr. To enervate. || FIG. To weaken.
enésimo, ma adj. MAT. Nth, n: *elevar a la enésima potencia*, to raise to the nth power *o* to the power of n. || *Te lo digo por enésima vez*, I'm telling you for the nth time *o* for the umpteenth time.
enfadadizo, za adj. Irritable, touchy.
enfadar v. tr. To annoy, to irritate, to get on s.o.'s nerves (disgustar). || To anger, to infuriate, to madden (enojar).
— V. pr. To be *o* to become irritated *o* annoyed. || To get angry *o* mad, to lose one's temper: *se enfada por cualquier cosa*, he gets mad about anything. || *Enfadarse con uno*, to get angry *o* cross with s.o. (enojarse), to fall out with s.o. (enemistarse).
enfado m. Annoyance, irritation (descontento). || Anger (enojo). || Quarrel, tiff (disgusto). || *Causar enfado*, v. ENFADAR.
enfadosamente adv. Annoyingly, irritatingly. || Unpleasantly (de manera desagradable). || Unwillingly, begrudgingly (a regañadientes).
enfadoso, sa adj. Annoying, irritating, irksome (molesto). || Unpleasant, disagreeable (desagradable).
enfangar v. tr. To cover with mud.
— V. pr. To cover o.s. in mud, to get covered in mud (llenarse de fango). || FIG. y FAM. To dirty one's hands (en negocios vergonzosos). | To wallow in vice (en placeres). | To degrade o.s. (deshonrarse). || MAR. To stick in the mud.
enfardadora f. AGR. Baler, baling machine.
enfardar v. pr. To wrap up, to parcel up (empaquetar). || AGR. To bale.
énfasis m. Emphasis, stress (insistencia). || Emphasis (en retórica). || *Dar énfasis a algo*, to give sth. emphasis, to emphasize sth., to put *o* to lay stress on sth., to stress sth.
enfático, ca adj. Emphatic
enfatizar v. tr. To emphasize.
enfatuarse v. pr. To become conceited.
enfebrecido, da adj. *Amer.* Febrile, feverish.
enfermar v. intr. To fall ill, to be taken ill. || *Enfermar del pecho*, to contract a chest complaint.
— V. tr. To make ill. || FIG. To make sick, to make ill (irritar): *las injusticias me enferman*, injustice makes me sick. | To weaken (debilitar).
enfermedad f. Illness, disease (afección): *su enfermedad era muy grave*, his illness was very serious. || Illness, ill health, sickness (indisposición): *a consecuencia de enfermedad*, through illness *o* ill health. || FIG. Malady. || — *Ausentarse por enfermedad*, to be away ill *o* sick. || *Enfermedad azul, contagiosa, de Parkinson, profesional*, blue, contagious, Parkinson's, occupational disease. || *Enfermedad del hígado*, liver complaint. || *Enfermedad del sueño*, sleeping sickness. || *Enfermedad infantil*, child's complaint. || *Enfermedad mental* or *nerviosa*, mental illness *o* disease. || *Salir de una enfermedad*, to recover from an illness. || *Una enfermedad larga*, a long illness.
enfermería f. Infirmary, sick bay (de un colegio, etc.). || Hospital.
enfermero, ra m. y f. Male nurse (hombre), nurse (mujer).
enfermizo, za adj. Sickly: *persona enfermiza*, sickly person. || Unhealthy, morbid: *pasión enfermiza*, unhealthy obsession. || Unhealthy (alimento, comarca).
enfermo, ma adj. Ill, sick: *ponerse* or *caer enfermo*, to fall ill, to be taken ill. || — *Enfermo de amor*, lovesick. || *Enfermo de gravedad*, seriously ill. || *Fingirse enfermo*, to pretend to be ill, to malinger. || FIG. *Poner enfermo a alguien*, to make s.o. ill *o* sick, to give s.o. a pain in the neck: *su conversación me pone enfermo*, his conversation makes me sick.
— M. y f. Sick person, invalid. || Patient (en el hospital). || *Enfermo de aprensión*, hypochondriac.
enfermucho, cha adj. Ailing, sickly.
enfervorizar v. tr. To encourage (animar). || To enthuse: *su discurso enfervorizó al público*, his speech enthused the audience.
enfeudación f. o **enfeudamiento** m. HIST. Enfeoffment, infeudation.
enfeudar v. tr. To enfeoff.
enfiebrecido, da adj. Febrile, feverish.
enfilada f. MIL. Enfilade. || MIL. *Tiro de enfilada*, raking *o* enfilading fire.
enfilado m. Stringing, threading (de perlas).
enfilar v. tr. To string, to thread (ensartar): *enfilar perlas*, to string pearls. || To align, to line up (colocar en fila). || To take, to go along (una calle). || To direct, to point, to train (apuntar): *enfilar un cañón*, to point a gun. || MIL. To enfilade, to rake.
enfisema m. MED. Emphysema.
enfisematoso, sa adj. Emphysematous.
enfistolarse v. pr. MED. To turn into fistula.
enfiteusis f. JUR. Long lease, emphyteusis.
enfiteuta m. y f. JUR. Emphyteuta.
enfitéutico, ca adj. JUR. Emphyteutic.
enflaquecer* v. tr. To make thin (adelgazar). || FIG. To weaken (debilitar).
— V. intr. To lose weight, to get thin (adelgazar). || FIG. To lose heart (desanimarse).
enflaquecimiento m. Losing weight, slimming (acción de enflaquecer). || Loss of weight (pérdida de peso). || FIG. Weakening (debilitación).
enflatarse v. pr. *Amer.* To become sad.
enflautada f. *Amer.* Absurdity.
enflautado, da adj. FIG. Bombastic, high-flown.
enflautar v. tr. FAM. To deceive, to cheat (engañar). | To inflate (hinchar). || *Amer.* FAM. To unload on.
enfocar v. tr. To shine on: *le enfocó con su linterna*, he shone his torch on him. || To focus (una lente, cámara, etc.). || To point, to train (gemelos). || FIG. To approach, to consider, to look at (una cuestión): *enfocar un asunto desde el punto de vista religioso*, to consider a subject from the religious point of view. || FIG. *Enfocar algo de distinta manera*, to see sth. from a different point of view, to have a different view of sth.
— V. intr. y pr. To focus.
enfoque m. FOT. Focusing, focussing (acción de enfocar). | Focus (resultado obtenido). || FIG. Point of view, approach (óptica).
enfrascamiento m. FIG. Absorption.
enfrascar v. tr. To put in a flask, to bottle (embotellar).
— V. pr. To enter into a thicket (en una maleza). || FIG. To get involved *o* engrossed *o* absorbed (en una ocupación). || FIG. *Estaba enfrascado en la lectura*, he was buried in a book.
enfrentar v. tr. To face, to confront (un peligro, adversidades, etc.). || To bring face to face, to confront (poner frente a frente): *enfrentar a una persona con otra*, to bring two people face to face, to confront two people, to confront one person with another.
— V. pr. To meet, to confront, to encounter: *nuestro ejército se enfrentó a* or *con el ejército enemigo*, our army encountered the enemy army. || To face up to, to face (arrostrar): *tendrás que enfrentarte con muchas dificultades*, you will have to face up to many difficulties. || To meet, to encounter, to come up against (encontrar): *al día siguiente se enfrentó con la primera dificultad*, on the next day he met the first difficulty. || To meet (equipos): *el equipo del Real Madrid se enfrentó con el del Manchester United*, Real Madrid met Manchester United; *los dos equipos se enfrentaron en Madrid*, the two teams met in Madrid. || To stand up to, to face up to: *se enfrentó conmigo*, he stood up to me. || To antagonize: *se ha enfrentado con sus amigos*, he has antagonized his friends. || To meet (satisfacer): *enfrentarse con las necesidades de*, to meet the needs of.
enfrente adv. Opposite, in front, facing: *enfrente de mi casa*, opposite my house; *enfrente mía*, opposite me. || Against: *incluso su propia madre se le puso enfrente*, even his own mother sided against him. || — *Allí enfrente*, over there, there in front of [me, you, him, etc.]. || *En la página de enfrente*, on the opposite *o* facing page. || *Tu casa y la suya están una enfrente de otra*, your house and his are opposite each other.
enfriadera f. Cooler [for drinks].
enfriadero m. Cold room.
enfriador, ra adj. Cooling.
— M. Cooler (aparato). || Cold room (fresquera).
enfriamiento m. Cooling (acción de enfriar). || MED. Cold, chill (catarro).
enfriar v. tr. To cool, to cool down: *enfriar un líquido*, to cool a liquid. || FIG. To cool down (una pasión, etc.). | To dampen: *enfriar el entusiasmo de uno*, to dampen s.o.'s enthusiasm. || *Amer.* To kill (matar).
— V. intr. To cool, to cool down, to cool off (ponerse frío). | To go *o* to get cold.
— V. pr. To cool, to cool down, to cool off (ponerse frío). || To go cold, to get cold: *se está enfriando el té*, your tea is going cold. || To catch a cold (acatarrarse). || FIG. To cool off, to grow cold (pasiones, etc.): *se enfrió el entusiasmo*, the enthusiasm cooled off.
enfundadura f. Casing. || Sheathing (de espada, puñal, etc.). || Covering (de un mueble).
enfundar v. tr. To put in its case: *enfundar una cosa*, to put sth. in its case. || To sheathe (envainar la espada, el puñal, etc.). || To holster (una pistola). || To cover (un mueble). || TECN. To case, to sheathe.
enfurecer* v. tr. To make mad, to infuriate, to enrage, to madden. || *Mar enfurecido*, stormy *o* raging sea.
— V. pr. To lose one's temper, to fly into a rage, to become furious: *enfurecerse con*, to lose one's temper with. || To get rough, to start to rage (el mar).
enfurecimiento m. Fury, rage.
enfurruñamiento m. FAM. [Slight] anger.
enfurruñarse v. pr. FAM. To sulk (enfadarse). | To cloud over (el cielo).
enfurtido m. Fulling (del paño). || Felting (del fieltro).
enfurtir v. tr. To full (el paño). || To felt (el fieltro).
engafar v. tr. MAR. To hook.
engaitar v. tr. FAM. To take in, to trick (engañar). | To wheedle, to coax (engatusar).
engalanar v. tr. To adorn, to dress up, to deck out (adornar): *engalanar con*, to deck out with. || To

decorate (decorar). || To dress up, to deck out [in fine clothes]: *estar muy engalanada*, to be really dressed up. || MAR. To dress, to deck out.
— V. pr. To be decked out, to be adorned, to be dressed up (adornarse). || To dress up, to deck o.s. out [in fine clothes].
engalgar v. tr. To chock, to scotch (una rueda). || To set on the track of (un perro).
engallado, da adj. FIG. Arrogant, haughty (presumido). | Daring (envalentonado).
engalladura f. Cicatricule, tread (galladura).
engallamiento m. FIG. Arrogance.
engallarse v. pr. FIG. To put on airs and graces, to be arrogant (envalentonarse). || To hold up its head (el caballo).
enganchador, ra adj. Which hooks, hooking.
— M. Recruiter (reclutador).
enganchamiento m. Hooking. || MIL. Enrolment, enlistment, recruitment.
enganchar v. tr. To hook (coger con un gancho): *enganchar un pez*, to hook a fish. || To hang [up]: *enganchar la gabardina en la percha*, to hang up one's raincoat on the coat hanger. || To harness, to hitch (las caballerías a un carruaje). || To hitch (un remolque). || To couple (dos vagones). || MIL. To enlist, to recruit (reclutar). || TECN. To engage (engranar). | To couple, to connect (empalmar). || FIG. y FAM. To get round, to wheedle, to persuade, to rope in (atraer a una persona). | To hook (un marido). | To catch: *la policía enganchó al ladrón*, the police caught the thief. || TAUR. To catch (coger).
— V. pr. To get caught: *se le enganchó el pantalón en un clavo*, his trousers got caught on a nail. || To get hooked up (en un gancho). || MIL. To enlist, to enrol, to sign on, to join up.
enganche m. Hook (gancho). || Hooking [up]. || Coupling (de vagones). || Hitching-up (de remolques). || Harnessing (de las caballerías). || TECN. Engaging (trinquete). | Connection (empalme). || MIL. Recruitment, enlistment, enrolment.
enganchón m. Snag (desgarrón en una prenda).
engañabobos m. inv. Confidence trickster, swindler [U.S., con man] (persona). || Confidence trick, con (engaño). || ZOOL. Nightjar (chotacabras).
engañadizo, za adj. Gullible, easily taken in.
engañador, ra adj. Deceitful, deceiving, deceptive.
— M. y f. Deceiver, trickster.
engañar v. tr. To deceive, to trick: *engañar a un cliente*, to deceive a customer. || To take in, to fool, to dupe (ocultar la verdad): *a él nadie le engaña*, there's no fooling him. || To cheat, to swindle, to trick (estafar). || To be unfaithful to (adulterio). || To mislead: *me engañó con sus consejos falsos*, he misled me with his false advice; *le engaña su buena voluntad*, he is misled by his good will. || FIG. To deceive: *me engaña la vista*, my eyes are deceiving me. | To stave off, to stay, to ward off: *engañar el hambre*, to stave off hunger. | To kill, to while away: *engañar el tiempo*, to while away the time, to kill time. || FAM. *¡A mí no me engañan!*, they can't fool me!, I wasn't born yesterday!
— V. intr. To be deceptive, to be misleading. || *Las apariencias engañan*, appearances are deceptive, you can't judge by appearances.
— V. pr. To be mistaken, to be wrong (equivocarse): *se engaña Ud.*, you are mistaken. || To make a mistake: *engañarse con uno*, to make a mistake about s.o. || To deceive o.s., to delude o.s. (no querer admitir la verdad). || *Si no me engaño*, if I'm not mistaken.
engañifa f. FAM. Deceit, deception. | Swindle, fraud (estafa).
engaño m. Mistake (equivocación): *salir del engaño*, to realize one's mistake. || Deceit, deception, trickery (acción de engañar). || Fraud, trick, swindle (timo). || Deception, trick (lo que engaña). || TAUR. Muleta (muleta). | Cape (capa). || Bait (para pescar). || — *Deshacer un engaño*, to establish the truth. || *Llamarse a engaño*, to claim that one has been deceived.
engañoso, sa adj. Deceptive: *apariencias engañosas*, deceptive appearances. || Deceitful (con malicia): *palabras engañosas* deceitful words. || Misleading: *consejo engañoso*, misleading piece of advice.
engarabatar v. tr. To hook (con un garabato).
engarabitarse v. pr. To climb (trepar).
engaratusar v. tr. *Amer.* V. ENGATUSAR.
engarce m. Threading, stringing (acción de engarzar perlas). || String (hilo de un collar, etc.). || Setting, mounting (de una piedra). || FIG. Linking, connection (de ideas, etc.).
engargantar v. tr. To cram (las aves).
— V. intr. To mesh, to engage (engranar).
engargolado m. TECN. Groove-and-tongue joint (ensambladura). | Groove (de una puerta de corredera).
engargolar v. tr. TECN. To fit with a groove-and-tongue joint.
engarzador, ra adj. Who threads *o* strings (de perlas). || Mounting, setting (de piedras).
engarzadura f. V. ENGARCE.
engarzar v. tr. To thread, to string (las cuentas o las perlas de un collar). || To set, to mount (joyas). || To curl (rizar). || FIG. To link, to connect (enlazar).
— V. pr. To get tangled (enredarse).

engastador, ra adj. Setting, mounting.
— M. Setter, mounter (de joyas).
engastadura f. V. ENGASTE.
engastar v. tr. To set, to mount, to enchase (piedras preciosas): *engastar un diamante en oro*, to set a diamond in gold.
engaste m. Setting, mounting, enchasing (acción). || Setting (cerco de metal que sujeta la piedra). || Imperfect pearl (perla).
engatillar v. tr. ARQ. To clamp, to cramp.
engatusador, ra adj. Coaxing, wheedling.
— M. y f. Coaxer, wheedler.
engatusamiento m. Coaxing, wheedling.
engatusar v. tr. FAM. To get round: *engatusó a sus acreedores*, he got round his creditors. | To coax, to wheedle: *engatusar a alguien para que haga algo*, to coax *o* to wheedle s.o. into doing sth.
engavillar v. tr. AGR. To sheave, to bind into sheaves.
engendrador, ra adj. Begetting, engendering.
engendramiento m. Begetting, engendering.
engendrar v. tr. To engender, to beget. || FIG. To give rise to, to engender: *engendrar la duda en una persona*, to engender doubt in s.o.'s mind. | To cause (provocar). | To produce: *engendrar una corriente eléctrica*, to produce an electric current.
engendro m. Foetus (feto). || Deformed child, stunted child (criatura informe). || Freak, monster (monstruo). || FIG. Botched job, bad piece of work (algo mal hecho). | Brainchild, wild plan (proyecto). || FIG. y FAM. *¡Mal engendro!*, little monster!
englobar v. tr. To include (comprender). || To bracket, to lump together (incluir).
engolado, da adj. FIG. Presumptuous, arrogant (persona). | High-flown, bombastic (estilo).
engolamiento m. Presumption, arrogance.
engolfar v. intr. MAR. To lose sight of land, to make for the open sea.
— V. pr. MAR. To make for the open sea. || FIG. To become lost *o* absorbed *o* engrossed: *engolfarse en la meditación*, to become lost in thought.
engolillado, da adj. FIG. y FAM. Straitlaced, old-fashioned.
engolosinador, ra adj. Tempting, enticing.
engolosinar v. tr. To tempt, to entice.
— V. pr. To acquire *o* to develop a taste: *engolosinarse con algo*, to develop a taste for sth.
engolletarse v. tr. FAM. To give o.s. airs.
engomado m. o **engomadura** f. Gluing, gumming (acción de engomar). || Gum, glue (pegamento). || Sizing (de los tejidos).
engomar v. tr. To glue, to gum (pegar). || To size (los tejidos). || *Papel engomado*, sticky *o* adhesive paper.
engorda f. *Amer.* Fattening (ceba). | Fattening animals, *pl.* (ganado).
engordadero m. Fattening sty (sitio). || Fattening period (tiempo). || Fattening fodder (alimento).
engordar v. tr. To make fat, to fatten (a una persona). || To fatten [up] (los animales).
— V. intr. To get fatter, to put on weight: *has engordado mucho*, you have got much fatter, you have put on a lot of weight. || To be fattening: *el pan engorda*, bread is fattening.
engorde m. Fattening [up] (de los animales).
engorro m. Nuisance, bother (molestia). || FAM. Snag, difficulty, catch (dificultad): *asunto lleno de engorros*, matter full of snags.
engorroso, sa adj. Annoying, trying, bothersome (molesto): *asunto engorroso*, annoying affair.
engoznar v. tr. To hinge.
engranaje m. TECN. Gear: *engranaje diferencial*, differential gear; *engranaje de distribución*, timing gear. | Cogs, *pl.*, gear teeth, *pl.* (conjunto de dientes). | Gears, *pl.*, gearing (conjunto): *el engranaje de una máquina*, the gearing of a machine. | Cogwheels, *pl.* (de un reloj). || Engaging, meshing, gearing (transmisión). || FIG. Connection, linking. || FIG. *Estar preso en el engranaje*, to be caught up in the machinery.
engranar v. tr. e intr. TECN. To engage, to mesh, to gear. || FIG. To connect, to link (enlazar).
engrandecer* v. tr. To enlarge, to make bigger (hacer mayor). || FIG. To enhance, to exalt (enaltecer). | To praise, to exalt (alabar). | To promote, to raise (elevar). | To widen, to broaden: *la lectura engrandece el espíritu*, reading widens the mind. | To magnify (exagerar).
— V. pr. FIG. To rise, to be promoted.
engrandecimiento m. Enlargement (agrandamiento). || FIG. Enhancement, exaltation (enaltecimiento). | Praise, exaltation (alabanza). | Promotion. | Magnification (exageración).
engranujarse v. pr. To become pimply (llenarse de granos). || To become a rogue (hacerse granuja).
engrapado m. ARQ. Cramping. || Stapling (de papeles).
engrapar v. tr. ARQ. To cramp (fijar con grapas). || To staple (papeles).
engrasado m. Greasing, lubrication.
engrasador, ra adj. Greasing.
— M. Grease gun.
engrasamiento m. V. ENGRASE.
engrasar v. tr. TECN. To grease, to lubricate: *engrasar un coche*, to grease a car. || To oil (aceitar). || To oil up (las bujías). || To make greasy, to stain with grease (ensuciar). || AGR. To manure, to fertilize (abonar).

— V. pr. TECN. To get oiled up (una bujía de motor).
engrase m. Greasing, lubrication (con grasa). || Oiling, lubrication (con aceite). || Oiling-up (de una bujía). || Lubricant (materia lubricante).
engreído, da adj. Presumptuous, conceited, arrogant. || *Amer.* Spoiled (mimado). || *Engreído de sí mismo*, fond of o.s., full of self-importance, blown-up.
engreimiento m. Presumptuousness, conceit, arrogance, self-importance.
engreír* v. tr. To make conceited, to make presumptuous *o* arrogant. || *Amer.* To spoil (mimar).
— V. pr. To become conceited *o* presumptuous *o* arrogant (envanecerse). || *Amer.* To become fond (encariñarse). | To get spoiled (con mimos).
engrescar v. tr. To cause trouble between, to cause an argument between, to antagonize.
— V. pr. To quarrel, to argue (disputarse).
engrifarse v. pr. FAM. To drug o.s., to take drugs.
engrillar v. tr. To fetter, to shackle (poner grilletes).
engringarse v. pr. *Amer.* To adopt foreign ways.
engrosamiento m. Fattening (de una persona). || Increase, enlargement (de una cosa). || Thickening (espesamiento).
engrosar* v. tr. To increase (aumentar). || To enlarge (agrandar). || To swell (un río). || To thicken (espesar).
— V. intr. To get fatter, to put on weight (una persona). || To swell (un río).
— V. pr. To increase. || To enlarge.
engrudamiento m. Pasting (de papeles).
engrudar v. tr. To paste (papeles).
engrudo m. Paste.
engruesar v. intr. V. ENGROSAR.
engrumecerse* v. pr. To clot (la sangre). || To curdle (la leche). || To go lumpy (hacerse grumos).
enguachinar v. tr. To soak, to flood (enaguazar).
engualdrapar v. tr. To put a horsecloth on.
enguantado, da adj. Gloved: *una mano enguantada*, a gloved hand. || *Iban todos enguantados*, they all had gloves on, they were all wearing gloves.
enguantarse v. pr. To put on one's gloves.
enguatar v. tr. To pad.
enguedejado, da adj. Long-haired (persona). || Long (pelo).
enguijarrado m. Pebbling (acción). || Cobbles, *pl.* (pavimento).
enguijarrar v. tr. To pebble, to cobble.
enguirnaldar v. tr. To garland, to wreathe.
engullimiento m. Gobbling, gulping.
engullir* v. tr. To gobble up, to gulp down.
engurruñar v. tr. To crease, to wrinkle, to crumple.
— V. pr. FAM. To get sad.
enhacinar v. tr. To pile up, to heap up.
enharinar v. tr. To flour (cubrir con harina). || To sprinkle with flour (echar harina). || To whiten [the face].
enhebrado o **enhebramiento** m. Threading.
enhebrar v. tr. To thread (una aguja). || To string, to thread (perlas). || FIG. To link, to connect (ideas). || — FIG. *Enhebrar una mentira tras otra*, to reel off a string of lies. | *Una cosa es enhebrar, otra es dar puntadas*, it is easy to criticize.
enhiesto, ta adj. Erect, upright, straight.
enhilar v. tr. V. ENHEBRAR.
enhorabuena f. Congratulations, *pl.* || — *Dar a uno la enhorabuena*, to congratulate s.o. || *Estar de enhorabuena*, to be very happy. || *Mi más cordial enhorabuena*, my very best wishes.
— Adv. Thank heavens that, thank God: *¡que se vaya enhorabuena!*, thank God he is going! || Very good (de acuerdo). || *Venga usted enhorabuena*, you're welcome to come.
enhoramala adv. Inopportunely: *enhoramala habló*, he spoke inopportunely. || *Haber nacido enhoramala*, to be born under an unlucky star. || *¡Iros enhoramala!*, good riddance!
enhornar v. tr. To put into the oven.
enigma m. Riddle, enigma (dicho). || Puzzle, mystery: *su comportamiento es un enigma para mí*, his behaviour is a puzzle to me.
enigmático, ca adj. Enigmatic, puzzling, mysterious.
enilismo m. Alcoholism [produced by wine].
enjabonado m. o **enjabonadura** f. Soaping.
enjabonar v. tr. To soap. || FIG. y FAM. To give [s.o.] a dressing down, to give [s.o.] a telling off (reprender). | To soft-soap, to butter up (adular).
enjaezamiento m. Harnessing.
enjaezar v. tr. To harness.
enjalbegado m. Whitewashing (de una pared).
enjalbegador m. Whitewasher.
enjalbegadura f. Whitewashing.
enjalbegar v. tr. To whitewash (blanquear). || FIG. To paint (el rostro).
enjalma f. Packsaddle (albarda).
enjalmar v. tr. To put a packsaddle on (albardar).
enjambrar v. tr. e intr. To swarm, to hive.
enjambrazón m. Swarming.
enjambre m. Swarm (de abejas). || FIG. Swarm, crowd, throng. || ASTR. Cluster (de estrellas).
enjaquimar v. tr. To halter, to put the halter on (una caballería).
enjarciar v. tr. MAR. To rig (un barco).
enjaretado m. Lattice screen, latticework.
enjaretar v. tr. To thread through a hem (cordón, cinta). || FIG. y FAM. To reel off, to spill out: *nos enjaretó unos versos*, he reeled some poetry off to us. | To palm off, to lumber: *enjaretar a uno un trabajo molesto*, to palm off an annoying job on s.o. | To rush through (hacer rápidamente).
enjaulamiento m. Caging.
enjaular v. tr. To put into a cage, to cage (meter en una jaula). || FAM. To put inside, to put in [the] clink, to lock up, to jail (encarcelar).
enjebe m. Alum (alumbre). || Lye, bleach (lejía). || Lying, bleaching (de los tejidos). || Whitewashing (de las paredes).
enjoyar v. tr. To decorate *o* to adorn with jewels (cosas). || To dress *o* to deck with jewels *o* jewellery (a una persona). || FIG. To adorn, to beautify (embellecer). || TECN. To set with precious stones (engastar).
enjuagadientes m. inv. Mouthwash.
enjuagadura f. Rinsing (lavado). || Rinsing water (líquido).
enjuagar v. tr. To rinse (la ropa).
— V. pr. To rinse out [one's mouth].
enjuague m. Rinsing (lavado). || Rinsing water (líquido). || Finger bowl (lavafrutas). || Mouthwash (enjuagadientes). || FIG. Plot, scheme (estragema).
enjugador m. Clothes drier. || TECN. Drier.
enjugamanos m. inv. *Amer.* Towel (toalla).
enjugar v. tr. To dry (secar). || To wipe up, to mop up (un líquido). || To dry, to wipe: *enjugar los platos*, to dry the dishes. || To wipe away: *enjugar el llanto de alguien*, to wipe away s.o.'s tears. || To mop, to wipe (la frente). || FIG. To cancel, to wipe out: *enjugar un déficit*, to cancel a deficit.
— V. pr. To dry, to wipe.
— OBSERV. This verb has two past participles, *enjugado* which is used to form compound tenses and *enjuto*, used as an adjective (*han enjugado la deuda; dama enjuta*).
enjuiciamiento m. JUR. Trial, prosecution (criminal). | Lawsuit (civil). | Procedure (procedimiento). || Judgment (acción de juzgar).
enjuiciar v. tr. JUR. To sue (civil). | To prosecute (criminal). | To try (someter a juicio). || To judge, to examine (juzgar).
enjulio o **enjullo** m. TECN. Beam, roller (de un telar).
enjundia f. Fat (grasa). || FIG. Substance: *un libro de mucha enjundia*, a book with a lot of substance | Force, vitality, strength (vigor). | Character: *una persona de mucha enjundia*, a person with a lot of character.
enjundioso, sa adj. Fatty (grasiento). || FIG. Substantial (sustancioso). | Full of character (persona).
enjuta f. ARQ. Spandrel. | Pendentive (de una cúpula).
enjutar v. tr. ARQ. To fill up.
enjuto, ta adj. Lean, skinny (flaco). [V. ENJUGAR.]
enlace m. Connection, connexion, relationship, link (relación): *hay un enlace entre las dos ideas*, there is a link between the two ideas. || Marriage, union (casamiento). || Linking (de dos familias). || Liaison (en la pronunciación). || Junction (de vías férreas). || Connection (de tren, autobús). || Meeting, rendezvous (encuentro). || MIL. Liaison. || ELECTR. Linkage. || QUÍM. Bond. || — MIL. *Agente de enlace*, liaison officer. || *Carretera de enlace*, link road, connecting road. || *Enlace matrimonial*, marriage. || *Enlace sindical*, shop steward [U.S., union delegate].
enladrillado m. Brick floor, brick paving.
enladrillador m. Bricklayer.
enladrillar v. tr. To pave with bricks.
enlardar v. tr. To coat with grease, to baste, to lard.
enlatado, da adj. Canned, tinned (en lata).
— M. Canning, tinning.
enlatar v. tr. To can, to tin (en botes de lata).
enlazadura f. o **enlazamiento** m. V. ENLACE.
enlazar v. tr. To tie together, to bind (unir con lazos). || To tie, to fasten (atar). || FIG. To connect, to relate, to link (trabar): *enlazar una idea con otra*, to link one idea with another. || To lasso (un animal). || To connect (dos ciudades, etc.).
— V. intr. To connect (avión, tren, etc.).
— V. pr. To link [up] to be linked (unirse). || To get married, to marry (novios). || To become linked by marriage (dos familias). || To be connected *o* linked *o* related (dos ideas).
enlistonado m. TECN. Laths, *pl.*
enlodar o **enlodazar** v. tr. To muddy, to cover with mud (cubrir de lodo). || To splash *o* to splatter with mud (manchar de lodo). || FIG. To stain, to besmirch (la fama).
— V. pr. To get muddy.
enloquecedor, ra adj. Maddening.
enloquecer* v. tr. To drive mad, to madden, to drive crazy (turbar). || To drive mad *o* insane (volver loco). || *Me enloquece la pintura*, I am mad about painting.
— V. intr. y pr. To go mad *o* insane.
enloquecimiento m. Madness, insanity.
enlosado m. Tiling (de baldosas). || Paving (de losas).
enlosar v. tr. To tile (con baldosas). || To pave, to flag (con losas).
— OBSERV. *To tile* se emplea para las baldosas que se ponen en las casas y *to pave* o *to flag* para las losas más grandes que se ven en las iglesias, los jardines, etc.

enlucido, da adj. Plastered (pared). || Whitewashed (blanqueado). || Polished (armas).
— M. Plaster, coat of plaster (de una pared).
enlucidor m. Plasterer (de paredes). || Polisher (de armas).
enlucimiento m. Plastering (de las paredes). || Polishing (de las armas).
enlucir* v. tr. To plaster (una pared). || To polish (armas).
enlutado, da adj. In mourning.
enlutar v. tr. To dress in mourning (vestir de luto). || To cast into mourning, to bereave: *la catástrofe enlutó a numerosas familias*, the disaster cast many families into mourning. || FIG. To sadden (entristecer). | To darken (oscurecer).
— V. pr. To wear mourning, to dress in mourning (vestirse de luto).
enllantado m. TECN. Rimming (de una rueda).
enllantar v. tr. To rim (poner llantas).
enmaderado o **enmaderamiento** m. Timbering, woodwork (obra de madera). || Wooden panelling (revestimiento de madera). || Floorboards, *pl.* (del suelo).
enmaderar v. tr. To panel (revestir una pared). || To lay the floorboards of (revestir el suelo). || To timber, to build the wooden framework of (construir el maderamen).
enmadrarse v. pr. To become excessively attached to one's mother (un niño).
enmalezarse v. tr. To get overgrown with weeds.
enmaniguarse v. pr. *Amer.* To get overgrown with trees.
enmarañamiento m. Tangle, entanglement (de cosas). || FIG. Muddle, confusion (de un asunto).
enmarañar v. tr. To tangle up, to entangle (enredar). || FIG. To muddle up, to confuse, to make more involved (un asunto).
— V. pr. To get into a tangle, to get entangled, to get tangled. || FIG. To get muddled *o* confused, to get more involved (un asunto).
enmarcar v. tr. To frame (en un marco). || To surround (rodear).
enmaridar, enmaridarse v. intr. y pr. To get married, to marry [a woman].
enmarillecerse* v. pr. To turn yellow.
enmaromar v. tr. To tie up [with a rope], to rope.
enmascarado, da m. y f. Masked person.
enmascaramiento m. MIL. Camouflage.
enmascarar v. tr. To mask. || MIL. To camouflage.
— V. pr. To put on a mask, to mask o.s. (ponerse una careta). || To masquerade as (disfrazarse de).
enmasillar v. tr. To putty (poner masilla).
enmendador, ra adj. Correcting. || Amending.
enmendadura f. Correction.
enmendar* v. tr. To correct, to reform (corregir): *enmendar un texto*, to correct a text. || JUR. To amend (una ley). | To revise (un juicio). || To repare, to put right (un daño). || To correct, to rectify: *enmendar un defecto*, to rectify a fault. || To make amends for, to compensate for (compensar). || AGR. To improve, to fertilize (la tierra). || MAR. To alter, to change (el rumbo, el fondeadero).
— V. pr. To change *o* to mend one's ways, to reform: *era un criminal pero se ha enmendado*, he was a criminal but he has changed his ways. || To correct: *enmendarse de una equivocación*, to correct one's mistake. || TAUR. To move: *dio cinco pases sin enmendarse*, he made five passes without moving.
enmienda f. Correction, amendment: *hacer muchas enmiendas en un texto*, to make many corrections in a text. || Repair, indemnity, compensation (de un daño). || Amendment (de textos oficiales, de un juicio, de una ley). || Correction, rectification, amendment (de un defecto). || AGR. Fertilizer (fertilizante). | Fertilizing, improvement (acción de abonar). || — *Enmienda de la vida*, mending *o* changing of one's ways. || *No tener enmienda*, to be incorrigible. || *Poner enmienda*, to amend, to correct. || *Tener propósito de enmienda*, to resolve to do better.
enmohecer* v. tr. To rust (el metal). || To make mouldy (materia orgánica). || FIG. To make rusty (embotar).
— V. intr. FIG. To get rusty, to rust up (embotarse).
— V. pr. To get rusty, to rust (el metal). || To get mouldy (materia orgánica). || FIG. To get rusty, to rust up (embotarse).
enmohecimiento m. Rusting (acción), rustiness (estado) [metales]. || Mouldering (acción), mouldiness (estado) [materias orgánicas]. || FIG. Rustiness (embotamiento).
enmudecer* v. tr. To silence, to make quiet. || FIG. To dumbfound, to leave speechless (por el temor, etc.).
— V. intr. To become dumb, to lose one's voice *o* speech (perder el habla). || FIG. To be dumbfounded, to be speechless (por el miedo, la sorpresa, etc.). | To keep quiet, to be silent, to say nothing (callar).
ennegrecer* v. tr. To blacken, to turn black (poner negro). || FIG. To darken (oscurecer).
— V. intr. y pr. To turn black, to go black. || FIG. To be dark, to darken.
ennegrecimiento m. Blackening.
ennoblecer* v. tr. To ennoble (dar título de nobleza). || FIG. To add an air of distinction to: *estas cortinas ennoblecen la habitación*, these curtains add an air of distinction to the room. | To do honour to, to be a credit to: *esas ideas le ennoblecen*, those ideas do him honour, those ideas are a credit to him.
ennoblecimiento m. Ennobling, ennoblement. || FIG. Distinction.
enojadizo, za adj. Irritable, touchy, short-tempered, quick-tempered.
enojado, da adj. Angry: *estar enojado con uno*, to be angry with s.o. || Cross, angry (ligeramente enfadado).
enojar v. tr. To make angry, to anger (enfadar). || To annoy, to irritate (molestar). || To offend.
— V. pr. To get angry: *enojarse con sus criados*, to get angry with one's servants. || To get irritated *o* annoyed (molestarse): *se enoja al ver todos los papeles en el suelo*, he gets annoyed when he sees all the papers on the floor. || To get cross *o* angry (enfadarse ligeramente): *enojarse con los niños*, to get cross with the children. || To get rough, to grow rough (el mar). || To get stronger (el viento).
enojo m. Anger (ira). || Annoyance, irritation (molestia). || *Causar enojo a*, to anger, to make angry.
enojosamente adv. Angrily.
enojoso, sa adj. Annoying, irritating, troublesome.
enología f. Oenology (ciencia de los vinos).
enológico, ca adj. Oenological.
enólogo, ga m. y f. Oenologist.
enorgullecer* v. pr. To make proud, to fill with pride.
— V. pr. To be proud, to pride o.s.: *enorgullecerse de* or *con sus éxitos*, to be proud of *o* to pride o.s. on one's successes.
enorgullecimiento m. Pride (orgullo). || Filling with pride (acción de enorgullecer).
enorme adj. Enormous, massive, gigantic, huge: *una casa enorme*, a massive house. || Enormous, great, huge: *la diferencia es enorme*, the difference is enormous. || FIG. Horrible, wicked (muy malo).
enormemente adv. Extremely, tremendously.
enormidad f. Enormity, hugeness. || Enormity, wickedness (de un pecado). || Monstrous thing (monstruosidad). || Ridiculous *o* gross mistake: *un libro lleno de enormidades*, a book full of gross mistakes. || Stupidity (estupidez). || — *Es una enormidad dejar a los niños solos en casa*, it is a crime to leave children alone in the house. || *Me gusta una enormidad*, I love it, I like it tremendously.
enquiciar v. tr. To put [a door] on, to put [a window] in.
enquillotrarse v. pr. (P. us.). To become conceited (engreírse). || FAM. To fall in love (enamorarse).
enquistado, da adj. MED. Encysted.
enquistamiento m. BIOL. Encystment.
enquistarse v. pr. MED. To encyst. || FIG. To become embedded (una cosa). || FIG. *Estar enquistado en una familia*, to impose on *o* to be an intruder in a family.
enrabiar v. tr. To infuriate, to enrage.
— V. pr. To be furious, to rage, to get enraged.
enraizar v. intr. To take root.
enramada f. Branches, *pl.* (conjunto de ramas). || Bower, arbour [U.S., arbor] (cobertizo). || Decoration *o* garland made of branches (adorno).
enramado m. MAR. Frames, *pl.*
enramar v. tr. To decorate with branches (adornar). || To put an arbour over (para sombra). || MAR. To fit the frames to [a ship].
— V. intr. To put out branches (un árbol).
enrarecer* v. tr. To rarefy (aire, etc.). || To make scarce (hacer escaso).
— V. intr. y pr. To rarefy (el aire). || To become scarce (escasear).
enrarecido, da adj. Rarefied.
enrarecimiento m. Rarefaction. || Scarcity (escasez).
enrasar v. tr. To make flush *o* level: *enrasar una cosa con otra*, to make a thing flush with another. || To smooth (allanar). || To level up (un líquido).
— V. intr. To be at the same level.
enrase m. Levelling [U.S., leveling].
enredadera adj. f. Climbing: *planta enredadera*, climbing plant.
— F. BOT. Bindweed. || BOT. *Enredadera de campanillas*, convolvulus.
enredador, ra adj. Mischievous: *un niño enredador*, a mischievous child. || Troublemaking (que causa riñas). || Gossipy (chismoso). || *Es una mujer enredadora*, she is a busybody (que se entromete).
enredar v. tr. To tangle up, to entangle (enmarañar). || FIG. To confuse, to complicate: *enredar un asunto*, to confuse matters. | To involve, to implicate, to mix up: *enredar a una persona en un negocio peligroso*, to mix a person up in a dangerous business. | To cause trouble, to sow discord: *enredar a dos personas*, to cause trouble between two people; *enredó a su familia*, he sowed discord in his family. || To net, to catch in a net (coger con una red).
— V. intr. To get into mischief, to play about: *este niño siempre está enredando en clase*, this child is always getting into mischief at school. | To mess about, to play about (desordenar): *no enredes con esos papeles*, do not mess about with those papers.
— V. pr. To get into a tangle, to get entangled *o*

tangled up (enmarañarse). || To catch on (engancharse). || FIG. To become muddled *o* confused *o* complicated (un asunto). | To get involved *o* implicated *o* mixed up (en un mal negocio). || FAM. To get involved, to have an affair (amancebarse).
enredijo m. FAM. Tangle (enredo).
enredista adj. *Amer.* V. ENREDADOR.
enredo m. Tangle (maraña): *un enredo de alambres*, a tangle of wires. || FIG. Muddle, confusion, complication (confusión). | Mess, mix-up, muddle (situación inextricable): *¡qué enredo!*, what a mix-up! | Shady business (asunto poco claro): *no se meta en aquel enredo*, do not get mixed up in that shady business. | Mischief (travesura). | Deceit (engaño). | Plot (de un libro). | Affair, love affair (amancebamiento). || Intrigue: *comedia de enredo*, comedy of intrigue. || — Pl. Stuff, *sing.*, things (trastos). || Mischievous stories (mentiras).
enredoso, sa adj. Complicated, involved (complicado). || FIG. Mischievous (niño). | Troublemaking (que provoca desavenencias).
enrejado m. Railings, *pl.* (rejas). || Bars, *pl.* (de una jaula, una celda). || Wire netting (alambrada). || Trellis (de un jardín). || Lattice, trellis (de ventana). || Openwork (bordado). || Grating, grille (para la ventilación).
enrejar v. tr. To surround with railings, to rail off (cerrar con rejas). || To put bars on (una ventana). || To put wire netting on (con alambrada). || To fix a grating to (para la ventilación). || AGR. To fit the share to [the plough]. | To wound the feet of [with a ploughshare].
enrevesado, da adj. Intricate, complicated: *un nudo enrevesado*, an intricate knot. || Difficult, complicated: *este crucigrama es muy enrevesado*, this crossword is very difficult.
enriado m. o **enriamiento** m. Retting.
enriar v. tr. To ret (el lino, el cáñamo).
enrielar v. tr. To make into ingots (un metal). || To pour into an ingot mould (echar en la rielera). || *Amer.* To put on the rails (encarrilar). | FIG. To put on the right track (un negocio).
enripiar v. tr. To fill with rubble.
Enrique n. pr. m. Henry.
enriquecer* v. tr. To enrich, to make rich. || FIG. To enrich: *enriquecer la tierra*, to enrich the land. | To embellish (una cosa).
— V. intr. y pr. To get rich. || *Enriquecerse a costa ajena*, to get rich at other people's expense.
enriquecimiento m. Enrichment.
enriscado, da adj. Rocky, rugged (escarpado).
enriscar v. tr. FIG. To raise, to lift.
— V. pr. To take refuge *o* to hide among the rocks.
enristrar v. tr. To string, to make a string of (ensartar). || To couch (la lanza).
enristre m. Couching (de la lanza).
enrocar v. tr. To castle (en el ajedrez).
enrodrigar o **enrodrigonar** v. tr. AGR. To stake, to prop up.
enrojecer* v. tr. To turn red, to redden (poner rojo). || FIG. To turn red, to flush: *la cólera enrojecía su rostro*, anger turned his face red. || To heat red-hot (el hierro).
— V. intr. y pr. To turn red, to redden (ponerse rojo). || To turn red, to blush (persona). || To become red-hot (el hierro).
enrojecimiento m. Reddening, glowing (del metal). || Blush (del rostro).
enrolamiento m. Signing-up, enrolment [U.S., enrollment] (reclutamiento). || MIL. Enlistment.
enrolar v. tr. To sign up, to enrol, to enroll (reclutar). || MIL. To enlist.
enrollable adj. Roll-up.
enrollamiento m. Rolling up (de papel). || Winding (del hilo). || Coiling (de cables).
enrollar v. tr. To roll up (papel). || To wind (hilo). || To coil (cables). || To wrap up (una persona en algo). || To cobble (empedrar).
— V. pr. To be wound, to be rolled [*en*, round]. || To wrap o.s. (una persona).
enronquecer* v. tr. To make hoarse *o* husky: *el frío le enronqueció*, the cold made him hoarse.
— V. intr. y pr. To go hoarse: *se ha enronquecido con tanto hablar*, he has gone hoarse from talking so much.
enronquecido, da adj. Hoarse, husky.
enronquecimiento m. Hoarseness, huskiness.
enroque m. Castling (ajedrez).
enroscadura f. o **enroscamiento** m. Coiling.
enroscar v. tr. To coil, to wind [*en*, round] (arrollar). || To screw in (atornillar).
— V. pr. To wind o.s., to coil o.s. [*en*, round] (una serpiente, etc.).
enrostrar v. tr. *Amer.* To reproach (echar en cara).
enrular v. tr. *Amer.* To curl.
ensabanar v. tr. To cover with a sheet.
ensacado m. Sacking, bagging, putting into sacks.
ensacador, ra m. y f. Sacker, bagger.
— F. Sacking *o* bagging machine (máquina).
ensacar v. tr. To sack, to put into sacks, to bag.
ensaimada f. Spiral pastry.
ensalada f. Salad. || FIG. Mess, mix-up, muddle (lío): *armar una ensalada*, to make a mess. || MÚS. Medley, potpourri. || — *Ensalada de fruta*, fruit salad. || *Ensalada rusa*, Russian salad.
ensaladera f. Salad bowl.
ensaladilla f. Diced vegetable salad. || FIG. Mess, mix-up, muddle (lío). || *Ensaladilla rusa*, Russian salad.
ensalivación f. Insalivation.
ensalivar v. tr. To moisten with saliva.
ensalmador, ra m. y f. Quack (curandero). || Bonesetter (de los huesos).
ensalmar v. tr. To set (los huesos). || To cure, to heal (un curandero).
ensalmo m. Quack remedy (de curandero). || Incantation (conjuro). || *Como por ensalmo*, as if by magic.
ensalzador, ra adj. Of praise, praising: *palabras ensalzadoras*, words of praise.
— M. y f. Praiser, exalter.
ensalzamiento m. Exaltation (engrandecimiento). || Praise, exaltation (elogio).
ensalzar v. tr. To exalt (enaltecer). || To praise, to exalt, to extol (alabar).
— V. pr. To boast.
ensamblado m. Joint.
ensamblador m. Joiner.
ensambladura f. o **ensamblaje** m. Joining (acción). || Joint: *ensambladura de cola de milano*, dovetail joint.
ensamblar v. tr. To join.
ensamble m. V. ENSAMBLADURA.
ensanchador, ra adj. Widening.
— M. Glove stretcher.
ensanchamiento m. Widening, broadening. || Expansion, enlargement (de una ciudad).
ensanchar v. tr. To widen, to broaden: *ensanchar una carretera*, to widen a road. || To enlarge, to expand: *ensanchar una ciudad*, to enlarge a city. || To widen, to make bigger: *ensanchar una abertura*, to make an opening bigger. || To stretch (la tela). || To let out (una prenda). || FIG. To gladden, to cheer (alegrar).
— V. pr. To get wider. || FIG. To become conceited (envanecerse). || To stretch (dar de sí).
ensanche m. Widening, broadening: *ensanche de la acera*, widening of the pavement. || Enlargement, expansion: *ensanche de una ciudad*, enlargement of a city. || New district, area of expansion, new development area, extension (barrio nuevo). || Widening, extension, enlargement (de un edificio). || Tuck (costura).
ensangrentado, da adj. Bloodstained.
ensangrentar* v. tr. To stain with blood (manchar). || FIG. To steep *o* to bathe in blood, to cause great bloodshed in: *la guerra ensangrentó el país*, the war caused great bloodshed in the country.
— V. pr. To get stained with blood (mancharse). || FIG. To fly into a temper (enfurecerse). || FIG. *Ensangrentarse con* or *contra*, to treat brutally, to be merciless with.
ensañamiento m. Mercilessness, cruelty, brutality. || Rage, fury (cólera).
ensañar v. tr. To infuriate, to enrage.
— V. pr. To be merciless, to treat brutally: *ensañarse con su víctima*, to be merciless with one's victim, to treat one's victim brutally.
ensartador, ra m. y f. Threader.
ensartar v. tr. To thread, to string: *ensartar perlas*, to string pearls. || To thread: *ensartar una aguja*, to thread a needle. || To run through (atravesar). || FIG. To reel off, to rattle off: *ensartar una serie de disparates*, to reel off a string of nonsense.
ensayador m. Assayer (de metales).
ensayar v. tr. To test, to try out: *ensayar un prototipo*, to test a prototype. || To assay (metales). || To rehearse (un espectáculo). || To try out, to try: *ensayar un nuevo sistema*, to try out a new system. || To train (un animal).
— V. intr. TEATR. To rehearse.
— V. pr. To practise [U.S., to practice], to rehearse: *ensayarse a* or *para cantar*, to practise singing.
ensaye m. Assay (de metales).
ensayista m. Essayist (autor de ensayos).
ensayo m. Test, testing, trial: *el ensayo de una máquina*, the trial of a machine. || Trial: *ensayo de un nuevo método*, trial of a new method. || Test: *vuelo de ensayo*, test flight. || Essay (obra literaria). || Try (rugby). || Assay (de metales). || QUÍM. Test: *tubo de ensayo*, test tube. || FIG. Attempt (intento). || TEATR. Rehearsal: *ensayo general*, dress rehearsal. || *A modo de ensayo*, as an experiment.
ensebar v. tr. To grease.
enseguida o **en seguida** adv. At once, immediately, straight away [U.S., right away].
ensenada f. GEOGR. Inlet, cove. || *Amer.* Enclosure.
enseña f. Standard, emblem, ensign.
enseñable adj. Teachable. || That can be shown, showable (mostrable).
enseñado, da adj. *Bien, mal enseñado*, well-bred, ill-bred. || *Perro enseñado*, house-trained dog.
enseñanza f. Teaching: *dedicarse a la enseñanza*, to devote o.s. to teaching. || Education: *enseñanza laboral* or *técnica*, technical education. || Training (instrucción). || FIG. Lesson. || — *Enseñanza superior*, higher education. || *Escuela de primera enseñanza*, primary school. || *Primera enseñanza* or *enseñanza primaria*, primary education. || *Segunda enseñanza* or *enseñanza media*, secondary education.

ENSEÑANZA, *f.* — EDUCATION

I. Generalidades, *f.* — General terms.

instrucción *f.*	instruction, education
cultura *f.*	culture
enseñanza (*f.*) primaria, secundaria *or* media, superior	primary, secondary, higher education
primeras letras *f. pl.*	the three R's
curso (*m.*) *or* año (*m.*) escolar	school year
trimestre *m.*	term, trimester
semestre *m.*	semester
día (*m.*) lectivo	school day
vacaciones (*f. pl.*) escolares	school holidays
programa *m.*	curriculum
asignatura *f.*	subject
disciplina *f.*	discipline
horario *m.*	timetable
clase *f.*; lección *f.*	class; lesson
deberes *m. pl.*	homework *sing.*
ejercicio *m.*	exercise
dictado *m.*	dictation
falta (*f.*) de ortografía	spelling mistake
cursillo *m.*	[short] course
seminario *m.*	seminar
prueba *f.*, test *m.*	test
recreo *m.*; descanso *m.*	playtime; break
hacer rabona *or* novillos	to play truant *o* hooky
carrera *f.*	course [of study]
alumno *m.*, discípulo *m.*	pupil
alumnado *m.*	student body
colegial *m.*; colegiala *f.*	schoolboy; schoolgirl
estudiante *m.* y *f.*	student
compañero (*m.*) de clase	classmate, schoolmate
oyente *m.*	auditor
empollón *m.*	swot, grind
antiguo alumno *m.*	old boy
beca *f.*	grant; scholarship, fellowship
becario *m.*	holder of a grant; scholar, fellow
uniforme (*m.*) del colegio	school uniform
maestro *m.*, maestra *f.*	primary school teacher
profesor *m.*, profesora *f.*	teacher (de segunda enseñanza), lecturer (de universidad)
adjunto *m.*, auxiliar *m.*	assistant
profesor (*m.*) de educación física	games master, gym teacher *o* instructor
catedrático *m.*	professor
cuerpo (*m.*) docente, magisterio *m.*	teaching staff; teachers *pl.*
ayudante (*m.* y *f.*) de laboratorio	laboratory *o* lab assistant
bedel *m.*	beadle, porter
director *m.*; directora *f.*	headmaster; headmistress
subdirector *m.*	deputy headmaster *o* head (*fam.*)
rector *m.*	rector
decano *m.*	dean
preceptor *m.*, ayo *m.*	private tutor
pedagogo *m.*	pedagogue
escolaridad *f.*	schooling
de edad escolar	of school age
matrícula *f.*	matriculation
matricularse	to enrol, to enroll
apertura (*f.*) de curso	beginning of term
dar clase	to take lessons (alumno); to teach (profesor)
estudiar	to study
aprender de memoria	to learn by heart
repasar	to revise, to go over
tomar la lección	to test
bachillerato *m.*	General Certificate of Education [U.S., high school diploma]
estar en primero de bachillerato	to be in the first year
bachiller *m.*	holder of the General Certificate of Education [U.S., holder of a high school diploma]
examen (*m.*) oral, escrito	oral, written examination
convocatoria *f.*	convocation notice
examinador *m.*	examiner
tribunal (*m.*) de exámenes	board of examiners
examinarse, presentarse a un examen	to take *o* to sit *o* to do an examination
pregunta *f.*	question
papeleta (*f.*) de examen	question paper
chuleta *f.*	crib [U.S., trot]
aprobar un examen	to pass an examination *o* exam (*fam.*)
aprobado *m.*	pass, passing grade
reparto (*m.*) de premios	prizegiving
ser suspendido en un examen	to fail an examination
suspenso *m.*	failure
repetir curso	to repeat a year
licenciatura *f.*	degree
licenciado *m.*	graduate
licenciarse	to graduate
tesina *f.*; tesis *f.*	project; thesis
doctorado *m.*	doctorate
doctor *m.*	doctor
oposición *f.*	competitive examination

II. Establecimientos (*m.*) de enseñanza. — Educational establishments.

jardín (*m.*) de la infancia	kindergarten
colegio (*m.*) de párvulos	infant school
escuela (*f.*) primaria	primary *o* junior school
escuela (*f.*) secundaria	secondary school
colegio *m.*	school
instituto *m.*	high school, secondary school
internado *m.*	boarding school
externado *m.*	day school
mediopensionista *m.* y *f.*	day student who has lunch at school
escuela (*f.*) de comercio	business school
escuela (*f.*) de artes y oficios	technical school
escuela (*f.*) técnica	technical college
ciudad (*f.*) universitaria	[university] campus
universidad *f.*	university
facultad *f.*; academia *f.*	faculty; academy
colegio (*m.*) mayor, residencia (*f.*) universitaria	hall of residence
aula *f.*, sala (*f.*) de clase	classroom
aula (*f.*) magna, anfiteatro *m.*, paraninfo *m.*	lecture theatre [U.S., lecture theater], amphitheatre [U.S., amphitheater]
sala (*f.*) de los profesores	staff room
despacho (*m.*) del director	headmaster's study *o* office
salón (*m.*) de actos	[assembly] hall
biblioteca *f.*	library
patio *m.*	playground
pupitre *m.*, banco *m.*	desk
tarima *f.*	platform

III. Material (*m.*) escolar. — Equipment.

libro (*m.*) de texto	text book
diccionario *m.*	dictionary
enciclopedia *f.*	encyclopedia
atlas *m.*	atlas
cartera *f.*	satchel
pizarra *f.*, encerado *m.*	blackboard
(una) tiza *f.*	[a piece of] chalk
pizarrín *m.*	slate pencil
mapa (*m.*) mural, mudo	wall, skeleton map
globo (*m.*) terráqueo	globe
cuaderno *m.*	exercise book
borrón *m.*, borrador *m.*	rough note book [U.S., scribbling pad]
papel (*m.*) secante	blotting paper
papel (*m.*) de calco	tracing paper
papel (*m.*) cuadriculado	squared *o* graph paper
pluma (*f.*) estilográfica	[fountain] pen
bolígrafo *m.*, boli *m.* (fam.)	biro, ballpoint [pen]
lápiz *m.*	pencil
portaminas *m. inv.*	propelling pencil
sacapuntas *m. inv.*	pencil sharpener
tinta *f.*; tintero *m.*	ink; inkwell
goma (*f.*) de borrar	rubber, eraser
regla *f.*	ruler, rule
regla (*f.*) de cálculo	slide rule
cartabón *m.*	set square
transportador *m.*	protractor
compás *m.*	compass, pair of compasses

enseñar v. tr. To teach: *enseñar a uno a hablar*, to teach s.o. to speak; *enseñar latín en la universidad*, to teach Latin in the university. ‖ To show (mostrar): *enseñar el camino*, to show the way; *me enseñó como funcionaba*, he showed me how it worked. ‖ *Enseñar con el dedo*, to point at.

enseñoramiento m. Taking over, taking possession.

enseñorearse v. pr. To take over, to take possession: *se enseñoreó de mi casa*, he took over my house.

enseres m. pl. Equipment, *sing.*, goods: *enseres domésticos*, household equipment. ‖ Tools (herramientas). ‖ Utensils (utensilios).

enseriarse v. pr. *Amer.* To turn *o* to become serious.

ensilado o **ensilaje** o **ensilamiento** m. AGR: Ensilage.

ensilar v. tr. AGR. To silo, to ensilage, to ensile, to store in a silo.

ensillado, da adj. Saddled. ‖ Saddlebacked (caballo).

ensilladura f. Saddling (acción de ensillar). ‖ Back (lomo del caballo). ‖ Curvature (de la columna vertebral).

ensillar v. tr. To saddle (el caballo).

ensimismado, da adj. Deep in thought, pensive (absorto). ‖ *Ensimismado en la lectura, en sus pensamientos*, lost *o* engrossed *o* absorbed in a book, in his thoughts.

ensimismamiento m. Pensiveness, absorption, deep thought. ‖ *Amer.* Conceit.

ensimismarse v. pr. To become lost *o* absorbed *o* engrossed (en algo). ‖ To become lost *o* absorbed *o* deep in thought (quedarse abstraído). ‖ *Amer.* To become conceited *o* full of conceit (envanecerse).

ensoberbecer* v. tr. To make proud, to make conceited.

— V. pr. To become proud, to grow conceited. ‖ FIG. To become rough (el mar).

ensombrecer* v. tr. To darken. ‖ FIG. To darken: *esta desgracia ensombreció su vida*, this misfortune darkened his life. | To overshadow (ocultar).

— V. pr. To darken (oscurecer). ‖ FIG. To turn gloomy (entristecerse).

ensombrerado, da adj. FAM. With a hat on, wearing a hat.

ensoñador, ra adj. Dreamy.

— M. y f. Dreamer.

ensopar v. tr. To dunk (empapar).

ensordecedor, ra adj. Deafening.

ensordecer* v. tr. To deafen: *nos ensordecía con sus gritos*, he deafened us with his shouts. || To make deaf, to deafen (provocar sordera). || To deafen, to muffle (amortiguar): *ensordecer un sonido*, to muffle a sound.
— V. intr. To turn deaf, to go deaf (quedarse sordo). || FIG. To pretend not to hear.
ensordecimiento m. Deafening (acción). || Deadening, muffling (de un sonido). || Deafness (sordera).
ensortijamiento m. Curling (de los cabellos). || Curls, *pl.* (rizos). || Coiling (de hilo).
ensortijar v. tr. To curl (los cabellos). || To coil, to wind (enrollar).
— V. pr. To curl (los cabellos).
ensuciamiento m. Dirtying, soiling (acción). || Dirtiness, dirt (suciedad).
ensuciar v. tr. To dirty, to soil: *ensuciar algo con lodo*, to dirty sth. with mud. || To dirty, to make dirty: *el humo de la fábrica ensucia los cristales*, the smoke from the factory dirties the windows. || To get dirty, to dirty: *no te ensucies el vestido*, don't get your dress dirty. || To stain (manchar). || FIG. To sully, to tarnish, to besmirch, to stain (el honor, la reputación, etc.).
— V. intr. FAM. To make a mess, to mess (necesidades corporales).
— V. pr. To get dirty. || FAM. To make a mess, to mess (necesidades corporales). || FIG. To sully *o* to tarnish *o* to besmirch *o* to stain one's reputation. || FIG. *Ensuciarse por dinero*, to accept bribes.
ensueño m. Dream (durante el sueño). || FIG. Dream: *país de ensueño*, dream country. | Dream, fantasy (ilusión). || *¡Ni por ensueño!*, never!, not likely!
ensullo m. TECN. Beam, roller (de un telar).
entabicar v. tr. To partition off.
entablado m. TECN. Boarding, planking, planks, *pl.* (conjunto de tablas). || Wooden floor (suelo). || Floorboards, *pl.* (tablas del suelo).
entabladura f. Boarding, planking, planks, *pl.*
entablamento m. ARQ. Entablature.
entablar v. tr. To begin, to start (empezar): *intentó entablar conversación*, he tried to begin a conversation; *entablaron una discusión*, they began a discussion. || To begin, to engage (un combate). || To open, to begin, to enter into: *entablar negociaciones*, to open negotiations. || To start, to begin, to open: *entablar conversaciones*, to begin talks. || JUR. To bring, to file: *entablar un pleito*, to file a suit. || To establish, to set up: *entablar relaciones*, to establish relations. || To place, to set out [the pieces] (en juegos). || To board up, to plank (poner tablas). || MED. To put in a splint, to splint (entablillar). || *Amer.* To train [livestock] to stay in a herd. || — *Entablar amistad*, to become friends. || *Entablar amistad con*, to strike up friendship with, to make friends with.
— V. intr. *Amer.* To draw (empatar). | To boast, to brag (fanfarronear).
— V. pr. To begin, to start (empezar). || *Amer.* To settle (el viento). | To refuse to turn (el caballo).
entablerarse v. pr. TAUR. To stay close to the barrier.
entablillar v. tr. MED. To put in a splint, to splint. *entablillar un brazo*, to put an arm in a splint.
entalegar v. tr. To put into a bag (meter en un saco). || FAM. To hoard, to save (ahorrar dinero). | To pocket (embolsar).
— V. pr. FAM. To make (ganar). | To pocket (embolsarse).
entalingadura f. MAR. Clinch.
entalingar v. tr. MAR. To clinch.
entalla f. Notch.
entalladura f. o **entallamiento** m. Notch (corte). || TECN. Mortising. | Mortise, notch (muesca). || Sculpture (en mármol). || Carving (en madera). || Engraving (grabado).
entallamiento m. V. ENTALLADURA. || Fitting, tailoring (de un vestido).
entallar v. tr. To notch (hacer un corte). || To tap (un árbol para sacar resina). || TECN. To mortise, to mortice. || To sculpture (el mármol). || To carve (la madera). || To engrave (grabar). || To tailor, to fit (un vestido).
— V. intr. To be tailored, to fit: *este vestido entalla bien*, this dress is well tailored *o* fits well.
entallecer* v. intr. To sprout, to shoot, to grow shoots (las plantas).
entarimado m. Parquet, parquetry. || Parquet laying (acción). || *Entarimado de espinapez*, herringbone parquet.
entarimador m. Parquet layer.
entarimar v. tr. To parquet.
entarquinar v. tr. AGR. To fertilize with silt. || To splatter with mud (manchar).
entarugado m. Wooden paving.
entarugar v. tr. To pave in wood.
éntasis f. ARQ. Entasis (de una columna).
ente m. Being, entity (ser). || Firm, company (comercial). || Organization, body, institution (organismo). || FAM. Specimen (persona notable o ridícula). || *Ente de razón*, imaginary being.
enteco, ca adj. Puny.
entechar v. tr. *Amer.* To roof.
entejar v. tr. *Amer.* To roof with tiles, to tile (tejar).
entelarañado, da adj. Covered with cobwebs.
entelequia f. FIL. Entelechy.
entena f. MAR. Lateen yard.

entendederas f. pl. FAM. Brains. || FAM. *Ser duro de entendederas*, to be slow on the uptake, to be slow.
entendedor, ra adj. Well-up: *es muy entendedor de esas cosas*, he is very well-up on those things. || Intelligent, clever (listo).
— M. y f. Expert. || FIG. *Al buen entendedor con pocas palabras basta* or *al buen entendedor pocas palabras bastan*, a word to the wise is enough.
entender* v. tr. To understand (comprender): *entender un problema*, to understand a problem; *no entiendo nada*, I don't understand anything; *tengo que confesar que no te entiendo*, I must confess that I don't understand you; *ahora entiendo por qué no vino*, now I understand why he did not come; *entender el inglés*, to understand English; *es difícil entender a los niños*, it is difficult to understand children. || To believe, to think (creer): *entiendo que sería mejor callarse*, I believe it would be better to keep quiet. || To mean, to intend, to want (querer): *entiendo que se me obedezca*, I mean to be obeyed. || To understand, to take it: *¿debo entender que quiere que me marche?*, am I to take it that you want me to leave? || To mean: *¿qué entiende usted por esta palabra?*, what do you mean by this word? || — *Dar a entender*, to hint, to insinuate (insinuar), to let it be known (manifestar), to mean (significar). || *Entender a medias palabras*, to read between the lines. || *Entender mal*, to misunderstand. || *Hacer como quien lo entiende todo*, to act as if one understands, to pretend to understand. || *Hacerse entender*, to make o.s. understood. || FAM. *No entender ni jota* or *ni pizca*, not to understand a thing. || *¿Qué debo entender por eso?*, what is that supposed to mean?
— V. intr. To understand, to know about: *usted entiende mucho de esto*, you understand a lot about this, you know all about this; *entiendo poco de cocina*, I know little about cooking. || — *A mi, tu, su entender*, to my, your, his mind. || *Entender en*, to know about (conocer una materia determinada), to be in charge of, to deal with: *entender en un asunto*, to deal with a matter. || *Ya entiendo*, I see now, now I understand.
— V. pr. To make o.s. understood: *entenderse por señas*, to make o.s. understood by signs. || To be understood (comprenderse): *se entiende que será así*, it is understood that it will be like that. || To be meant (significar). || To understand each other (dos personas). || To agree, to come to an agreement (ponerse de acuerdo): *entenderse con sus socios*, to agree with one's associates. || To get on *o* along (llevarse bien): *no se entiende con su hermano*, he does not get on with his brother. || To get in touch (ponerse en relación): *te entenderás con él para este trabajo*, you will get in touch with him about this work. || To have an affair (relación amorosa). || — *Allá se las entienda*, let him work it out for himself. || *Yo me entiendo*, I know what I am saying (lo que digo) *o* doing (lo que hago).
entendidamente adv. Cleverly, intelligently.
entendido, da adj. Understood (comprendido). || Agreed (de acuerdo). || Well up, well informed: *es entendido en coches*, he is well up on *o* he is well informed about cars. || Well up: *es muy entendido en matemáticas*, he is very well up in mathematics. || Clever, skilled (hábil). || Clever, intelligent (inteligente). || — *Bien entendido que*, on the understanding that. || *No darse por entendido*, to pretend not to have heard *o* understood, to turn a deaf ear. || *Según tenemos entendido*, as far as we know. || *Tenemos entendido que*, we understand that, we gather that.
— M. y f. Expert, authority, connoisseur (enterado): *según los entendidos*, according to the experts.
— Interj. All right!, agreed!, right!, O.K.! (de acuerdo), understood! (comprendido).
entendimiento m. Understanding (comprensión). || Judgment, understanding, sense (juicio). || Intelligence, understanding (inteligencia). || Mind (mente). || — *Ser corto de entendimiento* or *tener el entendimiento limitado*, to be slow to understand, to be slow. || *Un hombre de entendimiento*, a wise *o* judicious man.
entenebrecer* v. tr. To darken.
— V. pr. To darken, to get dark (oscurecerse). || FIG. To darken.
entente f. Entente: *entente cordial*, entente cordiale.
enterado, da adj. Aware (que sabe). || Well up, well informed: *enterado de asuntos comerciales*, well up on *o* well informed about commercial matters. || Knowledgeable: *un profesor muy enterado*, a very knowledgeable teacher. || *Amer.* Haughty, arrogant (orgulloso). || — *Darse por enterado de algo*, to be well aware of sth. || *Dese por enterado*, don't make me tell you again. || *Estar enterado de una noticia*, to be aware of *o* to know about *o* to have been informed about a piece of news. || *No darse por enterado*, to pretend not to have heard *o* understood, to turn a deaf ear.
— M. y f. Expert, authority, connoisseur. || FAM. Know-all [U.S., know-it-all] (sabelotodo).
enteralgia f. MED. Enteralgia.
enteramente adv. Completely, entirely, fully.
enterar v. tr. To inform. || *Amer.* To pay (pagar). | To complete (completar).
— V. pr. To find out, to get to know: *enterarse de lo que ha pasado*, to find out what has happened. || To learn, to hear, to become aware: *me enteré de la muerte de tu tío*, I heard about your uncle's death. || To realize, to be aware (darse cuenta): *pasaba las páginas*

sin enterarme de lo que leía, I turned the pages without realizing what I was reading. || To pay attention, to take note (prestar atención): *entérate de lo que te digo,* take note of what I am telling you. || FAM. *¿Te enteras?,* have you got it?, do you understand?

entercarse v. pr. To persist, to insist.

entereza f. Integrity, uprightness (integridad). || FIG. Firmness (firmeza). | Strength: *entereza de carácter,* strength of character. | Force, energy (energía). | Strictness (observancia perfecta).

enteritis f. MED. Enteritis.

enterizo, za adj. Whole (entero). || In one piece (de una pieza).

enternecedor, ra adj. Touching, moving.

enternecer* v. tr. To soften (ablandar). || To make tender (la carne). || FIG. To touch, to move (conmover).
— V. pr. FIG. To be moved *o* touched (conmoverse). | To relent (ceder).

enternecidamente adv. Tenderly.

enternecimiento m. Tenderness (cariño). || Pity (compasión).

entero, ra adj. Whole, in one piece (no roto). || Entire, whole, complete: *leerse el libro entero,* to read the whole book. || Full, whole: *un saco entero de naranjas,* a whole sack of oranges. || Whole, entire: *viajar por el mundo entero,* to travel the whole world over. || Complete: *a mi entera satisfacción,* to my complete satisfaction. || FIG. Firm (firme). | Strong: *carácter entero,* strong character. | Fair, just (justo). | Upright (honrado). | Robust, strong (fuerte). || Strong, thick (telas). || Entire, uncastrated (no castrado). || Pure, virginal (virgen). || MAT. Whole (número). || *Amer.* FAM. Identical (parecido). || — *Darse por entero a,* to give o.s. up to, to devote o.s. entirely to. || *Por entero,* entirely, completely.
— M. Point (Bolsa): *estas acciones han perdido muchos enteros,* these shares have lost many points. || MAT. Whole number, integer (número). || *Amer.* Payment (remesa de dinero). | Balance (saldo).

enterrador m. Gravedigger. || ZOOL. Burying beetle.

enterramiento m. Burial, interment (entierro). || Grave (tumba). || Burying, burial (de una cosa).

enterrar* v. tr. To bury, to inter (una persona). || To bury: *enterrar un tesoro,* to bury a treasure. || FIG. To bury, to abandon, to give up, to forget (olvidar): *enterrar sus ilusiones,* to give up one's dreams. || To outlive, to bury (sobrevivir a): *nos enterrará a todos,* he will outlive us all. | To drive in, to sink (clavar).
— V. pr. FIG. To bury o.s., to hide away: *enterrarse en un convento,* to bury o.s. in a convent.

entesar* v. tr. To tighten, to stretch (poner tieso). || To strengthen (reforzar).

entibación f. o **entibado** m. MIN. Timbering, shoring. || Timbering (de pozos).

entibador m. Timberman.

entibar v. tr. MIN. To timber, to shore. || To timber (un pozo).

entibiar v. tr. To make lukewarm (poner tibio). || FIG. To cool down, to moderate, to temper (las pasiones).
— V. pr. To become lukewarm (un líquido). || FIG. To cool down.

entibo m. ARQ. y MIN. Prop, shore. || Buttress (de una bóveda).

entidad f. Society, firm, concern: *entidad privada,* private concern. || Company: *entidad de seguros,* insurance company. || Organization, body (organización). || FIG. Significance, importance: *un asunto de poca entidad,* a matter of little significance. || FIL. Entity.

entierro m. Burial, interment (acción). || Funeral (ceremonia): *asistí al entierro,* I went to the funeral. || Grave (sepulcro). || FAM. Buried treasure. || — FIG. *¿Quién te dio vela en este entierro?,* v. VELA. | *Ser más triste que un entierro de tercera,* to be like death warmed-up (una persona), to be like [being at] a funeral (fiesta).

entintado m. IMPR. Inking.

entintador, ra adj. IMPR. Inking: *rodillo entintador,* inking roller.

entintar v. tr. IMPR. To ink (aplicar tinta). || To stain with ink (manchar). || FIG. To dye (teñir).

entoldado m. Awnings, *pl.*

entoldamiento m. Covering with an awning.

entoldar v. tr. To put an awning over: *entoldar una calle,* to put an awning over a street.
— V. pr. To become overcast, to cloud over (el cielo).

entomófago, ga adj. ZOOL. Entomophagous.

entomofilia f. Entomophily.

entomología f. Entomology.

entomológico, ca adj. Entomological, entomologic.

entomólogo m. Entomologist.

entonación f. Intonation (música, fonética). || FIG. Arrogance, haughtiness, presumption, conceit.

entonado, da adj. Arrogant, haughty, presumptuous, conceited (presumido). || In tune: *tiene la voz entonada* his voice is in tune. || FIG. On form (en forma). | Brisk (Bolsa).

entonador m. MÚS. Organ blower.

entonamiento m. V. ENTONACIÓN.

entonar v. tr. MÚS. To intone (cantar): *entonar un salmo,* to intone a psalm. | To work the bellows of (el órgano). | To give, to pitch (una nota). || FIG. To put right, to tone up: *este ponche me ha entonado,* this punch has put me right. | To brighten up (alegrar). | To sound (alabanzas). | To match (colores). || FIG. *Entonar el yo pecador,* to confess one's sins.
— V. intr. MÚS. To intone. | To sing in tune. || FIG. To match, to be in tune: *este azul no entona con el rojo,* this blue does not match the red. | To be in tune, to harmonize (armonizar). | To put one right, to tone one up (animar).
— V. pr. To be arrogant *o* conceited (engreírse). || To recover (fortalecerse). || FIG. To tone o.s. up.

entonces adv. Then: *llamó a la puerta y entonces entró,* he knocked at the door and then he came in. || At that time, then (en aquel tiempo). || So, then (en ese caso). || — *Desde entonces,* since then. || *El entonces presidente,* the then president. || *En* or *por aquel entonces,* at that time, then. || *¿Entonces?,* so? || *Entonces fue cuando entró,* it was then that he came in. || *Hasta entonces,* till *o* until then. || *La gente de entonces,* people of that time.

entonelado o **entonelamiento** m. Casking (en un barril), barrelling (en un tonel).

entonelar v. tr. To cask (en un barril), to barrel (en un tonel).

entono m. Presumption, arrogance, conceit, haughtiness (engreimiento). || MÚS. Intonation.

entontecer* v. tr. V. ATONTAR.

entontecimiento m. V. ATONTAMIENTO.

entorchado m. Braid (para bordar). || MIL. Braid, braiding. || FIG. Title (título): *consiguió el entorchado de internacional a los 25 años,* he got the international title when he was twenty-five. || MÚS. Bass string.

entorchar v. tr. To twist (un hilo). || To braid (galones). || *Columna entorchada,* wreathed column.

entornado, da adj. Half-closed.

entornar v. tr. To half-close, to leave ajar (puerta, ventana). || To half-close (ojos).
— V. pr. To half-close.

entorpecedor, ra adj. Numbing (que embota). || FIG. Hindering, hindersome (que molesta). | Dulling, deadening, numbing (que adormece).

entorpecer* v. tr. To numb: *el frío entorpece las manos,* the cold numbs one's hands. || FIG. To hinder, to obstruct (estorbar). | To delay (retrasar). | To dull, to deaden, to numb (la imaginación, etc.)
— V. pr. To grow numb (los miembros). || FIG. To be dulled *o* deadened *o* numbed. | To be delayed. || To get stuck (un mecanismo).

entorpecimiento m. Numbness (estado), numbing (acción) [de un miembro]. || FIG. Dullness, numbness (estado), dulling, deadening, numbing (acción) [del entendimiento, etc.]. | Hindering, obstructing (acción), hinderance, obstruction (estado) [estorbo]. | Delay (retraso). || Sticking (de un mecanismo).

entozoario m. ZOOL. Entozoan.

entrada f. Entry, entrance: *entrada triunfal,* triumphal entry. || Entrance, entry: *entrada principal,* main entrance; *entrada a la ciudad,* entry to the city. || Hall (vestíbulo). || Entry, admittance: *se prohibe la entrada al almacén,* no entry into the store, no admittance into the store. || Way in, entrance (de parque). || Entrance (de un cine, teatro, museo, etc.). || Beginning: *la entrada del invierno,* the beginning of winter. || Entrée (en una comida). || Beginning (de una carrera, libro, discurso, etc.). || Entrance (examen de ingreso). || Admission (en una academia, club, etc.). || Entrance (salida a escena). || Cue (de un actor de teatro). || Influx (de turistas, etc.). || Audience, house: *anoche hubo una gran entrada en el teatro,* last night there was a large audience at the theater. || Crowd, spectators, *pl.* (público de un encuentro deportivo). || Takings, *pl.,* receipts, *pl.* (lo recaudado en un espectáculo). || Gate (lo recaudado en un partido de fútbol, etc.). || Admission: *¿cuánto cuesta la entrada en este museo?,* how much is the admission to this museum?; *derecho de entrada,* right of admission; *entrada gratis,* admission free. || Ticket: *fui a sacar las entradas del cine,* I went to get the tickets for the cinema; *entrada de favor,* complimentary ticket. || COM. Incomings, *pl.: las entradas y las salidas,* incomings and outgoings. | Receipts, *pl.: entrada bruta,* gross receipts. | Earnings, *pl.* (ingresos). || Incoming (de cables del teléfono). || Down payment: *al comprar este piso tuve que pagar una entrada de doscientas libras,* when I bought this flat I had to make a down payment of 200 pounds. || Inning (en béisbol). || TECN. Intake, inlet (de aire). || MIL. Invasion. || Admission, acceptance (de una palabra en un diccionario). || Entry (artículo tratado en un diccionario). || — *Dar entrada a,* to lead into (conducir), to admit (admitir). || *De entrada,* straight away, right away, from the outset. || *De primera entrada,* at first sight. || *Entrada en materia,* introduction. || *Entrada general,* standing room. || *Entrada prohibida,* no admittance, no entry. || *Hacer su entrada,* to make one's entry. || *Media entrada,* half-price ticket (precio), half-capacity crowd (público). || *Puerta de entrada,* front door (de una casa), main door (de un edificio grande). || *Se prohibe la entrada,* no admittance, no entry. || FIG. *Tener entrada en una casa,* to be always welcome in a house. || *Tiene entradas en la frente,* his hair is receding.

entramado m. Lattice, trellis (de un tabique). || Half-timbering, wooden framework (de un muro). || Framework (de un puente).

entramar v. tr. To make a lattice *o* a framework for.

entrambos, bas adj. y pron. ind. pl. Both: *lo hicieron entrambos hermanos*, both brothers did it; *entrambos vinieron*, they both came. || FIG. *Lo mío, mío, y lo tuyo de entrambos*, what's yours is mine and what's mine is my own.

entrampar v. tr. To trap, to snare (un animal). || FIG. To trap, to catch out (engañar). | To muddle, to mess up (un negocio). || *Estar entrampado*, to be up to one's eyes in debt.
— V. pr. To fall into a trap. || To fall *o* to get into debt (contraer deudas).

entrante adj. Incoming, entering (que entra). || Coming, next: *el año entrante*, the coming year, next year. || Incoming: *el presidente entrante*, the incoming president. || — MAT. *Ángulo entrante*, re-entering *o* re-entrant angle. || *Guardia entrante*, new *o* relieving *o* relief guard.
— M. y f. Person who is entering, incomer, ingoer: *los entrantes y los salientes*, the incomers and outgoers. || — M. ARQ. Recess. || Inlet (ensenada).

entraña f. ANAT. Entrails, *pl.*, bowels, *pl.* || FIG. Core, root (lo esencial). || — Pl. ANAT. Entrails, bowels. || FIG. Bowels: *las entrañas de la Tierra*, the bowels of the earth. | Feelings, heart, *sing.* (ternura): *no tener entrañas*, to have no feelings. | Nature, *sing.* (índole). || — FIG. y FAM. *Arrancársele a uno las entrañas*, to break s.o.'s heart. | *De malas entrañas*, callous. | *Echar las entrañas*, to spew, to puke, to be as sick as a dog (vomitar), to put all one has into it, to give it everything one has got (echar el resto). | *¡Entrañas mías!* or *¡hijo de mis entrañas!* my little love! | *Sacar las entrañas*, to disembowel, to rip open. | *Ser de buenas entrañas*, to be big-hearted.

entrañable adj. Dear: *amigo entrañable*, dear friend. || Dearly loved, beloved: *Soria, lugar entrañable de Castilla*, Soria, a dearly loved spot in Castile. || Deep, dear: *los más entrañables deseos*, the deepest wishes.

entrañablemente adv. Deeply, dearly.

entrañar v. tr. To involve (implicar). || To entail (acarrear). || To contain, to carry within (contener). || To bury deep (introducir).
— V. pr. To penetrate *o* to go deeply (penetrar). || FIG. To become very fond *o* very attached (*con*, to).

entrar v. intr. To enter, to go in, to come in (v. OBSERV. I): *entrar por la puerta*, to enter through the door, to go in through the door; *¡entre!*, come in!; *entró llorando*, he came in crying. || To enter, to go, to come (*en*, into) [v. OBSERV. I]: *entramos en un bar*, we went into a bar; *entramos en un período de crisis*, we are entering a period of crisis; *entró sonriendo en la habitación*, he came into the room smiling. || To go in, to enter: *el estoque entró hasta la empuñadura*, the sword went in up to the hilt. || To fit, to go (caber, encajar): *este abrigo no entra en la maleta*, this coat doesn't fit in the suitcase; *el anillo no le entra en el dedo*, the ring doesn't fit on his finger; *esta pieza no entra en la otra*, this piece doesn't fit in the other. || To get, to fit: *no entro en su coche*, I can't get in his car, I don't fit in his car. || To fit: *esta sortija no me entra*, this ring doesn't fit me (v. OBSERV. II). || To begin, to start: *ya ha entrado el invierno*, winter has begun. || To join: *entrar en el ejército, en un club*, to join the army, a club. | To take up: *entrar en una profesión*, to take up a profession. || To open, to begin: *la carta entra diciendo*, the letter opens saying; *el libro entra tratando de*, the book begins by dealing with. || To take part [in] (participar). || FIG. To get [into], to enter [into]: *entrar en malas costumbres*, to get into bad habits. | To enter, to come: *esto no entra en mis atribuciones*, this does not enter into my duties; *esto no entra en mis planes*, this does not enter into my plans. | To come over: *le entró calentura, frío, sueño, miedo*, fever, cold, sleep, fear came over him. | To reach: *entrar en los sesenta*, to reach sixty. | To go: *en la paella entran arroz y carne*, rice and meat go into paella. || To flow into, to join (ríos). || AUT. To engage: *no entra la tercera*, third gear will not engage. || MÚS. To enter, to come in. || TAUR. To charge: *el toro no entra*, the bull will not charge. || To invade (invadir). || To be the bidder (en los juegos de cartas). || — *El año que entra*, next year, the coming year. | *Entrado en años*, elderly. || *Entrar a escena*, to go off [stage]. || *Entrar a servir con uno*, to start working for s.o., to enter s.o.'s service. || FIG. *Entrar bien*, to be appropriate (ser oportuno). | *Entrar como un torbellino*, to burst in. | *Entrar con buen pie*, to start off on the right foot *o* footing. || MIL. *Entrar de guardia*, to come on watch. || *Entrar en años*, to be getting on in years. || MIL. *Entrar en campaña*, to take the field, to begin a campaign. || *Entrar en contacto con uno*, to get in touch with s.o., to contact s.o. || *Entrar en cólera*, to get angry. || *Entrar en conversaciones*, to start *o* to begin talks. || *Entrar en detalles*, to go into details. || *Entrar en el marco de*, to be within the framework of. || *Entrar en las miras de*, to have in view *o* in mind: *este proyecto entra en sus miras*, he has this plan in view *o* in mind. || *Entrar en materia*, to give an introduction. || MIL. *Entrar en posición*, to be brought into position (cañones). || *Entrar en religión*, to enter a religious order. || *Entrar en servicio*, to go into service. || FAM. *Entrar por los ojos a uno*, to catch s.o.'s eye. || *Hacer entrar a uno en el despacho*, to show s.o. into the office. || *Hacer entrar en razón a alguien*, to make s.o. see sense. || *Hasta muy entrada la noche*, until late at night. || FAM. *Le entra la prisa* (*por hacer algo*), he gets the urge [to do sth.]. | *Me entra bien esa chica*, I think that girl is nice, I quite like that girl. || *Me entran ganas de*, I feel like. || FAM. *No entro ni salgo*, I want nothing to do with it. | *No me entra ese tío*, I can't stand *o* I can't bear that bloke. | *No me entra la comida*, I can't eat. | *No me entra la geometría*, I can't get the hang of geometry. | *Por un oído me entra y por otro me sale*, it goes in one ear and out of the other. || *Una vez bien entrado el mes de mayo*, once we are well into May.
— V. tr. To put: *entrar el coche en el garaje*, to put the car in the garage. || To bring in, to take in (v. OBSERV. I): *entrar el carbón para la calefacción*, to bring coal in for the heating. || To show in, to bring in (introducir a uno). || To smuggle (de contrabando). || To invade, to attack (invadir). || To take in (en costura). || MAR. To overtake.
— V. pr. To get in (con una idea de esfuerzo).
— OBSERV. I. El verbo *entrar* se traduce por *to go in, to take in* o *to come in, to bring in* según que la persona que habla se encuentre fuera o dentro del lugar considerado.
— II. Cuando *entrar* significa *caber* se suele emplear el verbo auxiliar *will* antes de la traducción del verbo (*este abrigo no entra en la maleta*, this coat will not fit in the suitcase).

entre prep. Between: *vacilar entre dos partidos*, to hesitate between two parties; *llegaron entre las dos y las tres*, they arrived between two and three. || Among, amongst: *entre mis amigos*, amongst my friends; *entre (los) romanos*, amongst the Romans. || Among, amongst, in the midst of: *entre la muchedumbre*, amongst the crowd, in the midst of the crowd. || In: *lo cogió entre sus manos*, he took it in his hands; *entre paréntesis*, in brackets. || In: *tuvo que conducir entre la niebla*, he had to drive in the fog. || Half ... half: *entre dulce y amargo*, half sweet half bitter; *una mirada entre cariñosa y hostil*, a half affectionate half hostile look. || — *De entre*, out of, from among. || *Dividir algo entre dos personas, entre cuatro personas*, to divide sth. between two people, between *o* amongst four people. || *Entre gris y negro*, midway between grey and black, of some colour between grey and black. || *Entre el ruido y el frío no he dormido*, what with the noise and the cold I haven't slept. || *Entre ellos se quieren mucho*, they love each other a great deal. || *Entre esto y lo otro*, what with one thing and another. || *Entre jóvenes y viejos serán unos veinte*, counting the young people and the old people there will be about twenty. || *Entre los cuatro hicieron el trabajo*, the four of them did the work together, they did the work between the four of them. || *Entre nosotros* or *dicho sea entre nosotros, entre tú y yo*, between ourselves, between the two of us, between you and me. || *Entre otras cosas*, amongst other things; namely (en particular). || *Entre que*, while, whilst. || *Entre tanto*, in the meanwhile, meanwhile, in the meantime. || *Entre todos había 50 personas*, there were 50 people in all. || *Entre unas cosas y otras*, what with one thing and another. || *Estar entre la vida y la muerte*, to be at death's door. || *Pensar entre sí*, to think to o.s. || *Por entre*, amongst, among; through (a través de).

entreabierto, ta adj. Half-open. || Half-open, ajar (puerta, ventana).

entreabrir v. tr. To half-open: *entreabrir los ojos*, to half-open one's eyes. || To half-open, to leave ajar (puerta).
— V. pr. To half-open, to be ajar.

entreacto m. Interval, entr'acte (intermedio).

entreayudarse v. pr. To help one another.

entrebarrera f. TAUR. Passageway [for spectators].

entrecalle f. ARQ. Quirk.

entrecanal m. ARQ. Fillet (de columna).

entrecano, na adj. Greying: *pelo entrecano*, greying hair. || With greying hair, who is going grey (persona).

entrecejo m. Space between the eyebrows. || — *Fruncir* or *arrugar el entrecejo*, to frown. || *Mirar a uno con entrecejo*, to frown at s.o., to give s.o. a frown.

entrecerrar* v. tr. *Amer.* To half-close (entornar).

entreclaro, ra adj. Fairly light, fairly clear.

entrecomillar v. tr. To put in inverted commas *o* in quotation marks.

entrecoro m. Chancel (de una iglesia).

entrecortado, da adj. Faltering, broken: *voz entrecortada*, faltering voice. || Laboured, difficult: *respiración entrecortada*, laboured breathing.

entrecortar v. tr. To make a partial cut in, to cut partially. || FIG. To cut off, to interrupt: *los sollozos entrecortaban su discurso*, his sobs interrupted his speech. | To cause to falter (la voz).

entrecote m. Sirloin.

entrecruzamiento m. Interlacing, intertwining. || Intersection (de carreteras).

entrecruzar v. tr. To interlace, to intertwine.
— V. pr. To intersect (carreteras).

entrecubierta f. MAR. Between decks.

entredicho, cha adj. Interdicted, under interdict.
— M. Prohibition. || REL. Interdict (censura eclesiástica): *poner en entredicho a alguien*, to lay s.o. under an interdict. || — FIG. *Estar en entredicho*, to be in question. | *Poner algo en entredicho*, to question sth.
entredós m. Insertion (en costura). || Dresser (mueble).
entrefilete m. Short article, paragraph (en un periódico).
entrefino, na adj. Medium quality.
entrega f. Handing over: *la entrega de las llaves*, the handing over of the keys. || Delivery (de géneros, compras, periódico): *entrega contra reembolso*, cash on delivery. || Fascicle, instalment (fascículo). || Devotion: *entrega a una causa*, devotion to a cause. || Surrender (rendición). || Pass (en fútbol). || ARQ. End of beam [embedded in wall]. || — *Entrega de los premios*, presentation of the prizes (a los galardonados), prizegiving (ceremonia). || *Hacer entrega de*, to hand over (dar), to deliver (cartas, paquetes, etc.), to present (premios). || *Novela por entregas*, serialized novel, novel by instalments.
entregamiento m. V. ENTREGA.
entregar v. tr. To deliver: *entregar un pedido*, to deliver an order. || To give (dar): *me entregó esta carta*, he gave me this letter. || To hand over: *entregar los poderes*, to hand over the powers; *le entregó la carta en propia mano*, he handed the letter over to him personally. || To surrender (rendir). || To betray (por traición): *entregar una ciudad*, to betray a city. || To hand in, to give in [U.S., to turn in]: *entregar al profesor los ejercicios*, to hand in one's exercises to the teacher. || FIG. To surrender, to give over: *entregar a alguien a su suerte*, to surrender s.o. to his fate. || — *Entregar a la voluntad de*, to leave at the mercy of. || *Entregar el alma*, to pass away, to breathe one's last, to give up the ghost. || *Para entregar*, care of (carta): *señor Taylor para entregar a la señora Rodríguez*, Mrs. Rodríguez, care of Mr. Taylor.
— V. pr. To surrender, to give o.s. up (rendirse). || FIG. To devote o.s.: *entregarse al estudio*, to devote o.s. to studying. | To give o.s. over *o* up: *entregarse a la bebida*, to give o.s. over to drink. | To sink into: *entregarse al sueño*, to sink into sleep. | To give in, to give up (ceder). | To confide in people (confiarse). || *Entregarse al lujo*, to indulge in luxury.
entrehierro m. ELECTR. Air gap.
entrejuntar v. tr. To assemble.
entrelargo, ga adj. Medium length.
entrelazamiento m. Intertwining, interlacing.
entrelazar v. tr. To intertwine, to interlace.
entrelínea f. Interlineation (añadido).
entrelinear v. tr. To interline.
entrelistado, da adj. Striped, with coloured stripes.
entremedias adv. In between, halfway (en medio). || In the meanwhile *o* meantime, meanwhile (mientras tanto). || *Entremedias de*, between.
entremés m. CULIN. Hors d'œuvre. || TEATR. Interlude, short comedy.
entremeter v. tr. To mix (mezclar). || To insert, to put between (poner entre).
— V. pr. To interfere, to meddle: *no te entremetas en eso*, do not interfere in that. || To butt in (en una conversación).
entremetido, da adj. Interfering, meddlesome: *una persona entremetida*, an interfering person.
— M. y f. Busybody, meddler, interferer.
entremetimiento m. Interfering, meddling.
entremezcladura f. Mixture.
entremezclar v. tr. To intermingle, to mix.
entrenador, ra m. y f. DEP. Trainer, coach. || — M. AVIAC. Simulator.
entrenamiento m. DEP. Training, coaching.
entrenar v. tr. DEP. To train, to coach. || *Estar entrenado*, to be fit, to be in training.
— V. pr. To train.
entreoír* v. tr. To hear vaguely, to half-hear.
entrepaño m. ARQ. Bay (entre columnas o huecos). || Panel (de puerta). || Shelf (estante).
entrepierna f. Crotch, crutch, fork. || — Pl. Crotch, *sing.*, crutch, *sing.*, fork, *sing.* (de cuerpo, pantalón).
entrepiso m. MIN. Space between galleries. || *Amer.* Mezzanine, entresol (entresuelo).
entrepuente m. MAR. Between decks.
entrerrenglonadura f. Interlineation, writing between the lines.
entrerrenglonar v. tr. To interline (escribir entre dos renglones).
entrerriano, na adj. *Amer.* Of *o* from Entre Ríos [province of Argentina].
— M. y f. Native *o* inhabitant of Entre Ríos.
entrerriel m. Gauge.
entresacar v. tr. To pick out, to select (escoger). || To prune (un árbol). || To thin (el pelo, un bosque). || To thin out (plantas).
entresijo m. ANAT. Mesentery (mesenterio). || FIG. Secret, mystery (misterio). | Difficulty, snag (dificultad). || — FIG. *Conocer todos los entresijos*, to know all the ins and outs. | *Tener muchos entresijos*, to be very complicated, to be full of complications (una cosa), to be mysterious (una persona).
entresuelo m. Mezzanine, entresol [floor between first floor and ground floor].
entresurco m. AGR. Space between furrows.
entretallar v. tr. To carve in bas-relief. || To do openwork on (hacer calados en). || FIG. To stop.
entretanto adv. Meanwhile, meantime, in the meantime, in the meanwhile (mientras tanto). || *En el entretanto*, in the meantime, in the meanwhile.
entretecho m. *Amer.* Attic, loft (desván).
entretejedor, ra adj. Interweaving (que entreteje).
entretejedura f. Interweaving.
entretejer v. tr. To interweave (hilos). || To intertwine, to interlace (entrecruzar). || To mix (mezclar). || FIG. To weave into (un escrito).
entretejido m. Interweaving, intertwining, interlacing.
entretela f. Interlining (para reforzar). || Buckram (tela gruesa). || IMPR. Surfacing.
— Pl. FAM. Heart, *sing.*
entretenedor, ra adj. Entertaining, amusing.
— M. y f. Entertainer.
entretener* v. tr. To entertain, to amuse (recrear). || To occupy, to keep occupied (distraer): *mientras uno le entretenía el otro le robó*, while one kept him occupied the other robbed him. || To keep: *no quiero entretenerle demasiado*, I don't want to keep you too long. || To keep busy *o* occupied: *estas gestiones me han entretenido toda la mañana*, these transactions have kept me busy all morning. || To put off, to delay, to hold up (dar largas): *están entreteniendo la resolución de la cuestión*, they are putting off the solution of the question. || FIG. To stave off, to ward off: *entretener el hambre*, to ward off hunger. | To keep at bay, to delay: *entretener la muerte*, to keep death at bay, to delay death. | To relieve, to allay (el dolor). | To ward off, to divert (el enemigo). | To while away, to pass (el tiempo). | To keep alive: *entretener una esperanza*, to keep a hope alive. | To keep alive *o* going: *entretener el fuego*, to keep the fire going. | To put off, to deceive: *entretener con promesas*, to put off with promises. || To maintain (cuidar). || — FIG. *Entretener a alguien con esperanzas*, to keep s.o. hoping, to keep s.o.'s hopes up. | *Entretener la soledad de una persona*, to keep s.o. company.
— V. pr. To pass the time, to amuse o.s.: *entretenerse en leer* or *leyendo*, to pass the time reading. || FIG. To waste one's time (perder el tiempo). | To linger, to loiter, to dally, to hang about (fam.): *entretenerse en casa de alguien*, to linger at s.o.'s house. || *Por entretenerse*, for amusement, to amuse o.s.
entretenido, da adj. Entertaining, amusing (divertido). || Demanding (que requiere mucho tiempo). || Busy, occupied (ocupado).
entretenimiento m. Entertainment, amusement (recreo). || Amusement: *en el jardín hay entretenimientos para los niños*, in the garden there are amusements for children. || Pastime (pasatiempo). || Maintenance, upkeep: *gastos de entretenimiento*, maintenance costs. || Conversation, talk (conversación). || Delaying, putting off (acción de dar largas). || Diversion (del enemigo).
entretiempo m. Between-season [used in spring or autumn]: *traje de entretiempo*, between-season suit.
entreventana f. ARQ. Pier.
entrever* v. tr. To be able to make out, to make out: *allá entreveía unos árboles*, over there he could make out some trees. || To foresee: *entreveo esa posibilidad*, I can foresee that possibility. || To guess (vislumbrar).
entreverado m. *Amer.* Roasted offal (asadura). || *Tocino entreverado*, streaky bacon.
entreverar v. tr. To intermingle, to mingle, to mix.
entrevero m. *Amer.* Crowd (gentío). | Muddle, confusion (mezcla). | Hand-to-hand fight [between horse soldiers] (lucha).
entrevía f. Gauge.
entrevista f. Meeting (entre varias personas). || Interview: *tuve una entrevista con el director*, I had an interview with the director. || Interview (de periodista). || *Hacer una entrevista a*, to interview.
entrevistador, ra m. y f. Interviewer (periodista). || Pollster (encuestador).
entrevistar v. tr. To interview.
— V. pr. To have a meeting *o* an interview: *el presidente se entrevistó con el ministro*, the president had a meeting with the minister. || To interview: *el periodista se entrevistó con el actor*, the journalist interviewed the actor.
entripado, da adj. Intestinal.
— M. Stuffing (relleno de un asiento). || FIG. Bitterness, resentment (encono). || *Amer.* Concealed anger (enfado).
entristecedor, ra adj. Saddening.
entristecer* v. tr. To sadden, to make sad, to grieve (contristar). || To sadden, to make sad (dar aspecto triste).
— V. pr. To be sad, to grieve: *entristecerse con* or *de* or *por algo*, to be sad about sth., to grieve about *o* over sth. || FIG. To cloud over (cielo, rostro).
entristecimiento m. Sadness (estado). || Saddening (acción).
entrojar v. tr. To garner.
entrometer v. tr. V. ENTREMETER.
entrometido, da adj./s. V. ENTREMETIDO.
entrometimiento m. V. ENTREMETIMIENTO.

entromparse v. pr. Pop. To get sozzled *o* stewed *o* canned (emborracharse). || *Amer.* To get angry (enfadarse).
entronar v. tr. To enthrone.
entroncamiento m. Relationship (parentesco). || Relationship by marriage (parentesco que se contrae). || Fig. Relationship. || *Amer.* Junction (ferrocarril).
entroncar v. tr. To establish a relationship between, to link, to connect.
— V. intr. To be related: *mi familia entronca con la tuya*, my family is related to yours. || To become related by marriage (contraer parentesco): *sus familias entroncaron en el siglo XVIII*, their families became related by marriage in the eighteenth century. || To marry (emparentar): *entroncar con una familia*, to marry into a family. || *Amer.* To join [railway lines].
— V. pr. *Amer.* To join [railway lines].
entronización f. **entronizamiento** m. Enthroning, throning (acción). || Enthronement (estado).
entronizar v. tr. To throne, to enthrone, to put on the throne (colocar en el trono). || Fig. To worship, to exalt (adorar).
entronque m. V. ENTRONCAMIENTO.
entruchada f. o **entruchado** m. Fam. Plot: *armar una entruchada*, to hatch a plot. | Trick (trampa).
entruchar v. tr. Fam. To trick, to lure (engañar).
entubación f. Tecn. Piping, tubing. || Med. Tubing.
entubado m. Tecn. Tubing, casing (de sondeo). || Med. Tubing.
entubar v. tr. Tecn. To pipe, to tube (poner tubos). | To tube, to case (para sondear). || Med. To tube.
entuerto m. Injury (daño). || Offence, insult (agravio). || Wrong: *deshacer* or *enderezar entuertos*, to right wrongs. || — Pl. Med. Afterpains.
entullecer* v. intr. y pr. To become paralyzed.
entumecer* v. tr. To numb, to make numb: *el frío entumece los dedos*, the cold numbs one's fingers.
— V. pr. To get *o* to go numb (por el frío). || Fig. To surge (mar).
entumecido, da adj. Numb.
entumecimiento m. Numbness (adormecimiento). || Swelling, swell (hinchazón).
entumirse v. pr. To go *o* to get numb (entumecerse).
enturbiar v. tr. To make cloudy, to cloud: *enturbiar el agua con barro*, to cloud the water with mud. || Fig. To cloud (estropear). | To mix up, to muddle up, to confuse (enredar). | To dampen (la alegría).
entusiasmar v. tr. To inspire, to excite, to fire with enthusiasm. || *Le entusiasma la música*, he is mad about *o* very keen on music, he loves music.
— V. pr. To be very keen *o* mad, to love: *se entusiasma con el teatro*, he is very keen on *o* mad about the theatre, he loves the theatre. || To get enthusiastic, to get excited (tener entusiasmo): *se entusiasman con* or *por cualquier cosa*, they get enthusiastic about anything. || To be delighted (estar encantado).
entusiasmo m. Enthusiasm. || Excitement || *Con entusiasmo*, enthusiastically.
entusiasta adj. Enthusiastic: *un público muy entusiasta*, a very enthusiastic audience.
— M. y f. Enthusiast, fan (fam.).
entusiástico, ca adj. Enthusiastic: *un recibimiento entusiástico*, an enthusiastic welcome.
enucleación f. Med. Enucleation: *la enucleación de un ojo, de un tumor*, the enucleation of an eye, of a tumour.
enuclear v. tr. Med. To enucleate.
enumeración f. Enumeration. || Summary, summing-up (resumen). || Jur. Census (de población).
enumerar v. tr. To enumerate.
enumerativo, va adj. Enumerative.
enunciación f. o **enunciado** m. Enunciation. || Declaration, statement (de hechos). || Wording (de ideas, de un problema).
enunciar v. tr. To enounce, to enunciate (una teoría). || To declare, to state (una condición). || To explain (un problema). || To state, to express (una idea). || To word (formular).
enunciativo, va adj. Enunciative. || Gram. Declarative (oración).
envainador, ra adj. Bot. *Hoja envainadora*, sheath.
envainar v. tr. To sheathe.
envalentonamiento m. Boldness, daring, courage (valor). || Encouragement (estímulo).
envalentonar v. tr. To make bold *o* daring *o* brave *o* courageous (dar valor). || To encourage (estimular).
— V. pr. To get brave *o* bold *o* daring, to pluck up courage. || To be encouraged: *se envalentonó con aquellas palabras elogiosas*, he was encouraged by those words of praise. || To boast (presumir).
envanecer* v. tr. To make conceited *o* vain, to fill with conceit *o* vanity (poner vanidoso). || To make proud, to fill with pride (causar orgullo legítimo a).
— V. pr. To be conceited *o* vain (ponerse vanidoso): *envanecerse con* or *de* or *por sus éxitos*, to be conceited about one's successes. || To be proud (con orgullo legítimo): *puede envanecerse de su hijo*, he can be proud of his son.
envanecimiento m. Vanity, conceit (vanidad). || Pride (orgullo).
envaramiento m. Numbness (entumecimiento). || Stiffness (tiesura).
envarar v. tr. To make numb, to numb (entumecer). || To stiffen, to make stiff (poner tieso). || To hinder *o* to restrict the movements of: *esta chaqueta le envara*, this jacket hinders his movements.
— V. pr. To go numb (entumecerse). || To go stiff (ponerse tieso).
envasado, da adj. Tinned, canned (frutos, pescado, etc.). || Bottled (líquidos). || In cylinders (butano). || In barrels (en toneles). || Packed (empaquetado).
— M. Tinning, canning (en latas, etc.). || Bottling (en botella). || Putting in cylinders (de gas butano). || Packing (empaquetado). || Sacking (de granos).
envasador m. Tinner, canner (que pone en latas). || Bottler (que pone en botella). || Packer (empaquetador). || Large funnel (embudo grande).
envasar v. tr. To put into a container (poner en un recipiente). || To tin, to can (poner en latas). || To bottle (líquidos). || To barrel (poner en toneles). || To put in cylinders (gas butano). || To pack (empaquetar). || To put in sacks (poner en sacos).
envase m. V. ENVASADO. || Container (recipiente). || Tin, can (lata). || Box (caja). || Bottle (botella). || Sack (saco). || Packing, package (embalaje): *envase de materia plástica*, plastic packing. || Cylinder (de gas butano). || *Leche en envase de cartón*, milk in a carton.
envejecer* v. tr. To make old, to age: *los sufrimientos le han envejecido*, suffering has made him old *o* has aged him. || Fig. To make look older, to age: *este vestido negro te envejece*, this black dress makes you look older *o* ages you.
— V. intr. To get old, to age: *ha envejecido mucho*, he has got very old, he has aged a lot. || To age (el vino). || Fig. To become out-of-date.
— V. pr. To get old, to age (de modo natural). || To make o.s. look older (aparentar ser más viejo de lo que se es).
envejecido, da adj. Aged, old. || Fig. Old-looking (aspecto). | Out-of-date (pasado de moda). | Obsolete (anticuado). | Experienced.
envejecimiento m. Aging, ageing.
envenenador, ra adj. Poisonous.
— M. y f. Poisoner.
envenenamiento m. Poisoning. || Pollution (contaminación): *el envenenamiento del aire*, the pollution of the air. || Fig. Poisoning.
envenenar v. tr. To poison. || To pollute (el aire). || Fig. To embitter, to poison, to envenom: *la envidia ha envenenado su vida*, envy has embittered his life. | To misconstrue, to interpret wrongly: *envenenar las palabras de una persona*, to misconstrue a person's words, to interpret a person's words wrongly. | To turn sour, to embitter (relaciones, discusiones).
— V. pr. To poison o.s., to take poison. || Fig. To become envenomed, to grow bitter.
enverar v. intr. To begin to ripen (las frutas).
envergadura f. Mar. Breadth, spread [of a sail]. || Wingspan, span, spread (de las aves). || Aviac. Wingspan, span. || Fig. Importance. | Scope (de un programa). || Reach (de un boxeador). || — *De mucha envergadura*, very important, of great importance. || *De poca envergadura*, unimportant, of little importance.
envergar v. tr. Mar. To bend (una vela).
envergue m. Mar. Roband.
envés m. Wrong side, back (de tela). || Back, flat (de una espada). || Verso, reverse, back (de una página). || Bot. Reverse. || Fam. Back (espalda).
enviada f. V. ENVÍO.
enviado, da adj. Sent.
— M. y f. Representative. || Envoy (de un gobierno): *enviado extraordinario*, envoy extraordinary. || Messenger (mensajero). || *Enviado especial*, special correspondent (de un periódico).
enviar v. tr. To send: *me envió un ramo de flores*, he sent me a bouquet of flowers; *ha enviado a su hijo a España*, he has sent his son to Spain. || — Fam. *Enviar a uno al diablo* or *a paseo*, to send s.o. packing. || *Enviar de*, to send as: *le enviaron de embajador*, they sent him as [an] ambassador. || *Le envió por unos libros*, he sent him for some books.
enviciar v. tr. To corrupt, to lead astray: *enviciar a un adolescente*, to corrupt an adolescent, to lead an adolescent astray.
— V. intr. To be addictive, to be habit-forming (un vicio). || To produce too much foliage (un árbol). || *Está enviciado en el juego, en los deportes, en la droga*, he is addicted to gambling, to sports, to drugs.
— V. pr. To be corrupted, to acquire bad habits, to go astray: *se ha enviciado con el contacto de las malas compañías*, he has been corrupted by bad company. || To become *o* to get addicted: *enviciarse en la bebida*, to become addicted to drink.
envidada f. Raise [in cards].
envidar v. intr. To raise the wager [in cards]. || *Envidar en falso*, to bluff.
envidia f. Envy *la envidia es uno de los siete pecados capitales*, envy is one of the seven deadly sins; *con una mirada de envidia*, with a look of envy. || Jealousy (celos). || Emulation, rivalry (emulación). || — *Dar envidia*, to make jealous *o* envious. || *Muerto de envidia*, green with envy. || *Se lo comía la envidia*, he was eaten up with envy. || *Tener envidia a uno*,

to envy s.o. || *Te tengo envidia de haber hecho este viaje*, I envy you that journey you made.
envidiable adj. Enviable: *una posición envidiable*, an enviable position.
envidiar v. tr. To envy, to be envious of: *envidiar a uno*, to envy s.o., to be envious of s.o.; *envidia tu tranquilidad*, he envies your tranquillity, he is envious of your tranquillity. || To envy: *envidiar el cargo a uno, envidiar a uno por su cargo*, to envy s.o. his post. || *Más vale ser envidiado que envidioso*, better to be envied than envious.
envidioso, sa adj. Envious: *envidioso de la felicidad ajena, de su hermano*, envious of other people's happiness, of his brother. || Jealous (celoso): *envidioso de su amigo*, jealous of his friend.
— M. y f. Envious *o* jealous man, envious *o* jealous woman.
envido m. Raise [in cards].
envigado m. ARQ. Beams, *pl.*, rafters, *pl.*
envigar v. tr. To put the beams *o* the rafters in.
envilecedor, ra adj. Degrading, debasing.
envilecer* v. tr. To degrade, to debase (hacer vil). || To devalue, to depreciate (depreciar).
— V. pr. To degrade o.s., to debase o.s.
envilecimiento m. Degradation, debasement.
envinado, da adj. *Amer.* Wine-coloured (color).
envinagrar v. tr. To put vinegar on.
envinar v. tr. To pour wine into [water].
— V. pr. *Amer.* To get drunk (emborracharse).
envío m. Sending, dispatch (acción de enviar). || Shipment (expedición de mercancías). || Consignment (remesa). || Remittance (de dinero). || Letter (carta). || Package, parcel (paquete). || — *Envío contra reembolso*, cash on delivery. || *Gastos de envío*, post and packing.
enviscar v. tr. To smear with birdlime, to birdlime (untar con liga). || To tease [dogs] (azuzar).
— V. pr. To get stuck in birdlime.
envite m. Raise [in cards]. || FIG. Push, shove (empujón). | Offer (ofrecimiento). || — *Aceptar el envite*, to see [cards]. || *Al primer envite*, right away, from the outset, at the beginning, in the first place.
enviudar v. intr. To become a widow, to be widowed (mujer). || To become a widower (hombre).
envoltijo o **envoltorio** m. Wrapper, wrapping (envoltura de papel). || Cover (cubierta). || Bundle (lío, fardo).
envoltura f. Wrapping (acción). || Wrapper, wrapping (de papel). || Cover (cubierta). || Coating (de medicamentos). || BIOL. y BOT. Envelope. || — Pl. Swaddling clothes (pañales).
envolvedor m. Wrapping, wrapper (lo que envuelve). || Table [for dressing a baby] (mesa).
envolvente adj. MIL. Encircling, outflanking: *movimiento envolvente*, encircling movement. || MAT. Enveloping: *línea envolvente*, enveloping line.
— F. MAT. Envelope.
envolver* v. tr. To wrap, to wrap up: *envolver algo en un papel*, to wrap sth. *o* to wrap sth. up in a piece of paper. || To wrap, to muffle up: *envuelto en una capa*, wrapped in a cloak. || To wind: *envolver hilo en un carrete*, to wind thread onto a spool. || To cover, to coat: *envolver una avellana en chocolate*, to coat a hazelnut with chocolate. || To coat (medicamentos). || To wrap, to swathe, to swaddle (a los niños). || To envelop, to enshroud: *la niebla envuelve la casa*, the fog envelops the house. || FIG. To envelop, to shroud: *el misterio que envuelve el asunto*, the mystery which shrouds the matter. | To involve, to get involved, to implicate, to mix up: *le han envuelto en el proceso*, they have involved him in *o* they have got him involved in the trial, they have mixed him up in the trial. | To imply: *sus palabras envuelven una crítica*, his words imply criticism. | To stump, to floor (liar en una discusión). || MIL. To encircle, to surround. || *Papel de envolver*, brown paper, wrapping paper.
— V. pr. To wrap up, to wrap o.s. up: *envolverse en* or *con una manta*, to wrap up in a blanket. || To be wrapped: *el chocolate suele envolverse en papel de estaño*, chocolate is usually wrapped in silver paper. || FIG. To get involved *o* mixed up *o* implicated. | To wrap o.s. up: *envolverse en su dignidad*, to wrap o.s. up in one's dignity.
envolvimiento m. Wrapping. || Winding (enrollamiento). || Coating (de medicamentos). || MIL. Encircling, encirclement, surrounding.
envuelto, ta adj. Wrapped, wrapped up: *envuelto en papel*, wrapped in paper. || Wound (en un carrete). || Coated (medicamentos). || FIG. Envelopped, shrouded: *envuelto en misterio*, shrouded in mystery. | Involved, mixed up, implicated: *envuelto en una serie de robos*, involved in a series of robberies.
— M. *Amer.* Rolled tortilla (tortilla).
enyerbarse v. pr. *Amer.* To get *o* become overgrown with grass. | To poison o.s. (envenenarse).
enyesado m. o **enyesadura** f. Plastering. || MED. Plaster, plaster cast (escayolado).
enyesar v. tr. To plaster: *enyesar una pared*, to plaster a wall. || MED. To put in plaster *o* in a plaster cast: *enyesar una pierna rota*, to put a broken leg in plaster.
enyugar o **enyuntar** v. tr. To yoke.
enzarzar v. tr. To cover with brambles (una tapia). || FIG. To cause trouble among (engrescar).
— V. pr. To get caught [in brambles]. || FIG. To get mixed up, to get involved (enredarse en un asunto). | To get involved (en una discusión).
enzima f. BIOL. Enzyme.
enzootia f. Enzootic (enfermedad de animales).
enzunchar v. tr. TECN. To bind with hoops *o* rings.
eñe f. Name of the letter *ñ*.
eoceno adj./s.m. GEOL. Eocene.
eólico, ca o **eolio, lia** adj. Aeolian.
eolito m. Eolith.
Eolo n. pr. m. MIT. Aeolus.
¡epa! interj. *Amer.* Hello! (¡hola!). | Come on! (¡ea!).
eparca m. Eparch.
epazote m. *Amer.* BOT. Wormseed, Mexican tea.
epeira f. Epeira (araña).
epéntesis f. GRAM. Epenthesis.
eperlano m. ZOOL. Sparling (pez).
epiblasto m. BIOL. Epiblast.
épica f. Epic poetry.
epicarpio m. BOT. Epicarp.
epiceno adj. m. GRAM. Epicene.
epicéntrico, ca adj. Epicentral.
epicentro m. GEOL. Epicentre [U.S., epicenter].
epicíclico, ca adj. Epicyclic.
epiciclo m. ASTR. Epicycle.
epicicloidal adj. Epicycloidal.
epicicloide f. MAT. Epicycloid.
épico, ca adj. Epic: *poema épico*, epic poem.
epicureísmo m. FIL. Epicureanism, epicurism.
epicúreo, a adj. Epicurean.
— M. y f. Epicurean.
Epicuro n. pr. m. Epicurus.
epidemia f. Epidemic. || FIG. Plague, wave, epidemic (oleada).
epidémico, ca adj. Epidemic, epidemical.
epidérmico, ca adj. Epidermic, epidermal.
epidermis f. ANAT. Epidermis. || FIG. y FAM. *Tener la epidermis fina*, to be thin-skinned.
epidídimo m. ANAT. Epididymis.
Epifanía f. REL. Epiphany.
epifenomenismo m. Epiphenomenalism.
epifenómeno m. Epiphenomenon.
epífisis f. ANAT. Epiphysis.
epifito, ta adj. BOT. Epiphytic, epiphytical.
— M. BOT. Epiphyte.
epigástrico, ca adj. Epigastric.
epigastrio m. ANAT. Epigastrium.
epigénesis f. BIOL. Epigenesis.
epigenético, ca adj. Epigenetic.
epigeo, a adj. BOT. Epigeal, epigean, epigeous.
epiglotis f. ANAT. Epiglottis.
epígono m. Epigone.
epígrafe m. Epigraph.
epigrafía f. Epigraphy.
epigráfico, ca adj. Epigraphic, epigraphical.
epigrafista m. y f. Epigraphist.
epigrama m. Epigram (pieza satírica).
epigramático, ca adj. Epigrammatic, epigrammatical.
epigramatista o **epigramista** m. Epigrammatist.
epilepsia f. MED. Epilepsy.
epiléptico, ca adj./s. MED. Epileptic.
epilogación f. Epilogue (epílogo).
epilogal adj. Compendious, summary.
epilogar v. tr. To summarize, to sum up (resumir). || To round off, to round out (terminar).
epílogo m. Epilogue (conclusión). || Summary (compendio).
episcopado m. REL. Episcopate, episcopacy, bishopric (dignidad). | Episcopacy, episcopate (obispos).
episcopal adj. Episcopal.
episcopalismo m. REL. Episcopalism.
episcopalista adj./s. REL. Episcopalian.
episódico, ca adj. Episodic, episodical.
episodio m. Episode.
episternón m. ANAT. Episternum.
epístola f. Epistle.
epistolar adj. Epistolary.
epistolario m. Collection of letters. || Epistolary (libro litúrgico).
epitafio m. Epitaph.
epitalámico, ca adj. Epithalamic, epithalamial.
epitalamio m. Epithalamium, epithalamion (canto).
epitelial adj. Epithelial: *tejidos epiteliales*, epithelial tissues.
epitelio m. ANAT. Epithelium.
epitelioma m. MED. Epithelioma (tumor maligno).
epíteto m. Epithet.
epítome m. Epitome, summary.
epizootia f. VET. Epizootic.
época f. Epoch, age, era, time: *en la época del cine mudo*, in the epoch of silent films. || Time (temporada): *época de la siembra*, sowing time. || Period: *la época entre fines del siglo XV y principios del XVII*, the period between the end of the 15th century and the beginning of the 17th. || — *De los que hacen época*, to beat all...: *un gol de los que hacen época*, a goal to beat all goals; epoch-making (de mucha resonancia). || *En esta época*, at this time. || *En la época de Felipe II*, at the time of Philip II. || *En mi época*, in my day. || *Hacer época*, to make history, to mark an era *o* epoch.

|| *Muebles de época*, period furniture. || *Ser de su época*, to be up to date, to be with the times.
epodo m. Epode.
epónimo, ma adj. Eponymous, eponymic.
— M. Eponym.
epopeya f. Epic poem, epopee (poema). || Epic poetry, epopee (poesía). || FIG. Epic.
épsilon f. Epsilon.
eptágono, na adj. MAT. Heptagonal.
— M. MAT. Heptagon.
equiángulo, la adj. MAT. Equiangular.
equidad f. Equity, fairness (justicia).
equidistancia f. Equal distance, equidistance.
equidistante adj. Equidistant.
equidistar v. intr. MAT. To be equidistant.
équido, da adj./s.m. Equine.
equilátero, ra adj./s.m. MAT. Equilateral: *triángulos equiláteros*, equilateral triangles.
equilibrado, da adj. Balanced. || FIG. Sensible (sensato): *una persona equilibrada*, a sensible person. | Balanced: *espíritu equilibrado*, balanced mind.
equilibrador m. Balancing device.
equilibrar v. tr. To balance: *equilibrar la carga de un camión*, to balance a lorry's load. || To equilibrate, to counterbalance: *equilibrar un peso con otro*, to equilibrate one weight with another. || To balance (un presupuesto, la mente, etc.)
— V. pr. To balance (objetos). || To equilibrate, to counterbalance (fuerzas). || FIG. To recover one's balance (mente).
equilibrio m. FÍS. Equilibrium. || Balance: *perder el equilibrio*, to lose one's balance. || Counterbalance, counterpoise (contrapeso). || FIG. Poise, calmness, composure (serenidad). | Balance, harmony (armonía). || — FIG. *Equilibrio político*, balance of power. | *Hacer equilibrios*, to perform miracles (con el dinero). || *Mantener el equilibrio*, to keep one's balance: *mantuvo el equilibrio sobre la cuerda*, he kept his balance on the rope; to maintain the balance: *mantener el equilibrio entre la demanda y la oferta*, to maintain the balance between supply and demand. || *Mantener en equilibrio*, to balance: *mantener algo en equilibrio sobre la cabeza*, to balance sth. on one's head. || *Mantenerse en equilibrio*, to keep one's balance.
equilibrismo m. Acrobatics, *pl.* || Rope-walking (del funámbulo).
equilibrista m. y f. Acrobat, equilibrist. || Ropewalker, tightrope walker, equilibrist (funámbulo).
equimolecular adj. QUÍM. Equimolecular.
equimosis f. MED. Ecchymosis.
equino, na adj. Equine, horse (relativo al caballo). || FIG. Equine.
— M. Sea urchin, echinus (erizo de mar). || ARQ. Echinus (moldura).
equinoccial adj. Equinoctial.
— F. Equinoctial line.
equinoccio m. ASTR. Equinox.
equinodermo m. ZOOL. Echinoderm.
equinoideo m. Echinoid.
equipaje m. Luggage, baggage: *viajar con mucho equipaje*, to travel with a lot of luggage. || MAR. Crew (tripulación). || — *Equipaje de mano*, hand luggage. || *Exceso de equipaje*, excess baggage.
equipar v. tr. To equip: *equipar el ejército de* or *con armamento moderno*, to equip the army with modern arms. || To fit out (de ropa). || MAR. To fit out (un barco).
equiparable adj. Comparable (*con*, to).
equiparación f. Comparison.
equiparar v. tr. To compare, to put on the same level: *equiparar Alejandro a* or *con César*, to compare Alexander with Caesar.
equipo m. Team: *equipo de colaboradores*, team of collaborators; *equipo de fútbol*, football team. || Shift (de trabajadores). || Equipment, kit, gear: *el equipo de un alpinista, de un soldado*, a mountaineer's, a soldier's equipment. || Instruments, *pl.* || Equipment: *equipo eléctrico*, electrical equipment. || Outfit (de colegial). || Trousseau (de novia). || — *Bienes de equipo*, capital goods. || *Compañero, compañera de equipo*, team member (jugador), team mate (en relación uno con otro). || *Equipo quirúrgico*, surgical instruments, *pl.* (colección de instrumentos), surgical unit (en un hospital).
equiponderar v. intr. To be equal in weight.
equis f. X [name of the letter *x*]. || MAT. X [any number].
equitación f. Horse riding, riding, equitation (p. us.) [acción]: *al niño le gusta la equitación*, the child likes riding. || Horsemanship, equitation (p. us.) [arte].
equitativo, va adj. Equitable, fair (justo).
equivalencia f. Equivalence, equivalency.
equivalente adj./s.m. Equivalent.
equivaler* v. intr. To be equivalent, to be equal, to be the equivalent: *tres duros equivalen a quince pesetas*, three "duros" are equal to *o* are equivalent to *o* are the equivalent of fifteen pesetas. || To mean: *eso equivaldría a un fracaso*, that would mean failure. || *Eso equivale a decir que*, that amounts to saying that, that means that: *eso equivale a decir que no quiere ir*, that amounts to saying that he does not want to go.
equivocación f. Mistake, error: *cometer* or *tener una equivocación*, to make a mistake. || Misunderstanding (malentendido). || *Por equivocación*, by mistake, in error.
equivocadamente adv. By mistake, mistakenly.
equivocado, da adj. Wrong, mistaken: *un juicio equivocado*, a wrong judgment; *estar equivocado*, to be wrong, to be mistaken.
equívocamente adv. Ambiguously, equivocally.
equivocar v. tr. To get wrong, to mistake: *equivoqué la fecha*, I got the date wrong, I mistook the date. || To get mixed up: *equivocar los abrigos de los niños*, to get the children's coats mixed up. || To confuse, to get mixed up: *si hablas mientras estoy contando me equivocas*, if you talk while I'm counting, you get me mixed up. || To mislead: *su respuesta me equivocó*, his answer misled me.
— V. pr. To be mistaken, to make a mistake, to mistake, to get wrong: *equivocarse de fecha*, to be mistaken about *o* to make a mistake about the date, to mistake the date, to get the date wrong. || To make a mistake, to be mistaken, to be wrong (no tener razón): *reconozco que me equivoqué*, I admit that I was mistaken. || To make a mistake: *equivocarse en un cálculo*, to make a mistake in a calculation. || To be mistaken (juzgar mal): *me equivoqué con ese chico*, I was mistaken about that boy. || — *Equivocarse de casa*, to go to the wrong house. || *Equivocarse de camino*, to take the wrong road. || *Si no me equivoco*, if I'm not mistaken.
equívoco, ca adj. Ambiguous, equivocal: *frase equívoca*, ambiguous sentence. || Misleading (engañoso). || Strange, queer (persona).
— M. Ambiguity, ambiguous *o* equivocal expression *o* word: *discurso lleno de equívocos*, speech full of ambiguities. || Misunderstanding, mistake (malentendido). || *Andar con equívocos*, to play on words.
era f. Era: *la era cristiana*, the Christian era. || FIG. Age, era: *la era atómica*, the atomic age. || AGR. Threshing floor: *trillar en la era*, to thresh grain on the threshing floor. | Patch (para hortalizas). | Bed (para flores). || MIN. Pithead.
eral m. Bullock [less than two years old].
erario m. Treasury, funds, *pl.* || *Erario público*, treasury, public funds, *pl.*, exchequer.
erasmismo m. Erasmianism.
erasmista adj./s. Erasmian.
Erasmo n. pr. m. Erasmus.
erbio m. Erbium (metal).
ere f. R [name of the Spanish single *r*].
erección f. Erection, raising (de un monumento). || FIG. Setting-up, establishment (de una institución). || Erection (en fisiología).
eréctil adj. Erectile.
erecto, ta adj. Erect.
erector, ra adj. Erecting.
— M. Erector.
eremita m. Hermit, eremite (ermitaño).
eremítico, ca adj. Hermitical, eremitic: *vida eremítica*, hermitical life.
eretismo m. MED. Erethism.
erg o **ergio** m. FÍS. Erg.
ergosterol m. MED. Ergosterol.
ergotismo m. MED. Ergotism. || Sophistry.
ergotizar v. intr. To argufy, to quibble (fam.).
erguimiento m. Raising, lifting-up.
erguir* v. tr. To raise, to lift up: *erguir la cabeza*, to raise one's head.
— V. pr. To rise: *la montaña se yergue a lo lejos*, the mountain rises in the distance. || To straighten up (enderezarse). || FIG. To swell with pride (envanecerse).
erial adj. Uncultivated, untilled (tierra).
— M. Uncultivated *o* untilled land.
erigir v. tr. To erect, to raise, to set up (un monumento). || To build, to construct (un edificio). || FIG. To establish, to set up, to found (una institución).
— V. pr. To set o.s. up: *erigirse en juez*, to set o.s. up as judge.
Erín n. pr. f. (Ant.) Erin (Irlanda).
erisipela f. MED. Erysipelas.
eritema m. MED. Erythema (inflamación).
Eritrea n. pr. f. GEOGR. Eritrea.
eritroblasto m. Erythroblast (célula).
eritrocito m. BIOL. Erythrocyte (glóbulo rojo).
erizado, da adj. Bristly, prickly: *erizado de espinas*, bristly with thorns. || FIG. *Problema erizado de dificultades*, thorny *o* prickly problem, problem bristling with difficulties.
erizar v. tr. To bristle (un animal). || FIG. *El miedo le erizó el pelo*, fear made his hair stand on end.
— V. pr. To stand on end: *se me erizó el pelo*, my hair stood on end. || To bristle: *se le erizó el pelo al perro*, the dog's fur bristled.
erizo m. Hedgehog (animal). || Bur, burr (envoltura de la castaña). || FIG. y FAM. Surly person, prickly customer (persona arisca). || Row of spikes (defensa de púas en un muro). || BOT. Burr, prickly plant. || Globefish (pez). || *Erizo de mar*, sea urchin.
ermita f. Hermitage.
ermitaño m. Hermit (hombre). || ZOOL. Hermit crab.
erogación f. Distribution. || *Amer.* Expenditure (gasto). | Payment (pago). | Contribution.

erogar v. tr. To distribute (distribuir). || *Amer.* To pay (pagar). | To spend (gastar). | To contribute (contribuir).
erógeno, na adj. Erogenous.
Eros n. pr. m. Eros.
erosión f. Erosion: *erosión eólica, glacial, pluvial,* wind, glacial, pluvial erosion. || MED. Graze.
erosionar v. tr. To erode.
erosivo, va adj. Erosive.
erótico, ca adj. Erotic.
erotismo m. Erotism, eroticism.
erotomanía f. MED. Erotomania.
erotómano, na adj. Erotic.
— M. y f. Erotomaniac.
errabundo, da adj. Wandering, roving.
erradamente adv. Mistakenly, by mistake.
erradicación f. Eradication.
erradicar v. tr. To uproot (un árbol, una planta). || FIG. To eradicate, to uproot: *erradicar un vicio,* to eradicate a vice.
errado, da adj. Wrong, mistaken (equivocado).: *estar errado,* to be mistaken. || Wide of the mark (tiro). || *Golpe, tiro errado,* miss.
erraj m. Fuel made from crushed olive stones.
errante adj. Wandering, roaming, roving. || Nomadic (nómada). || MED. Erratic. || Stray (animal). || *Estrella errante,* planet.
errar* v. intr. To wander, to rove, to roam (vagar). || To make a mistake, to be mistaken, to be wrong (equivocarse). || To err, to go astray: *errar es humano,* to err is human. || FIG. To wander (la imaginación).
— V. tr. To miss: *errar el blanco,* to miss the target. || FIG. To miss. || — *Errar el camino,* to take the wrong road (en un viaje), to miss one's vocation *o* one's calling (en la vida). || *Errar el golpe,* to miss. || *Errar el tiro,* v. TIRO. || *Errar la respuesta,* to give the wrong answer, to get the answer wrong.
errata f. Erratum. || *Fe de erratas,* errata.
errático, ca adj. Wandering. || GEOL. y MED. Erratic.
errátil adj. Variable, inconstant.
erre f. R [name of the Spanish *rr* and the initial *r*]. || — FAM. *Erre que erre,* stubbornly. | *Tropieza en las erres,* his speech is slurred (un borracho).
erróneamente adj. Mistakenly, erroneously.
erróneo, a adj. Erroneous, incorrect, mistaken (falso). || *Identificación errónea,* mistaken identity.
error m. Mistake, error (engaño, equivocación): *cometer un error* or *incurrir en un error,* to make a mistake. || Mistake, fault: *un texto lleno de errores,* a text full of mistakes. || Mistake: *ha sido un error obrar de esta manera,* it was a mistake to do that. || MAT. Mistake, fault. || — *Caer en un error,* to fall into error, to make a mistake. || *Error de imprenta,* misprint. || *Error de máquina,* typing mistake *o* error. || JUR. *Error judicial,* miscarriage of justice. || *Estar en un error,* to be mistaken, to be wrong. || *Por error,* by mistake. || *Salvo error u omisión,* errors and omissions excepted.
eructar v. intr. To belch, to eructate, to burp (fam.).
eructo m. Belch, eructation, burp (fam.).
erudición f. Learning, erudition, scholarship. || Knowledge (conocimientos).
eruditamente adv. Learnedly, eruditely, knowledgeably.
erudito, ta adj. Scholarly, erudite, knowledgeable, learned: *un hombre muy erudito,* a very scholarly man.
— M. y f. Scholar, erudite. || — FAM. *Erudito a la violeta,* pseudo-intellectual. || *Erudito en,* widely read in, well up in. || *Los eruditos en la materia,* those who are expert in this subject.
erupción f. Eruption (volcánica). || MED. Rash, eruption (cutánea). | Eruption (de los dientes). || FIG. Eruption, outbreak. || — *Entrar en erupción,* to erupt. || *Estar en erupción,* to be erupting.
eruptivo, va adj. Eruptive.
esa, ésa adj./pron. V. ESE, ÉSE.
esbeltez f. Slenderness, litheness, svelteness.
esbelto, ta adj. Slender, lithe, svelte.
esbirro m. Bailiff (alguacil). || FIG. Henchman (ayudante).
esbozar v. tr. To sketch: *esbozar un dibujo a lápiz,* to sketch a drawing in pencil. || To rough out, to outline (un proyecto). || *Esbozar una sonrisa,* to give a faint smile.
esbozo m. Sketch, outline.
escabechado, da adj. In a marinade, pickled, soused: *atún escabechado,* tuna in a marinade.
— M. Preservation in a marinade.
escabechar v. tr. To marinate, to preserve in a marinade, to pickle, to souse (conservar). || FIG. y FAM. To bump off, to kill (matar). | To fail, to plough (en un examen).
escabeche m. Marinade, pickle, souse: *atún en escabeche,* tuna in a marinade. || Pickled fish, fish in a marinade (pescado escabechado).
escabechina f. FIG. y FAM. Massacre, slaughter (matanza): *la batalla fue una escabechina,* the battle was a massacre. | Trail of destruction, wholesale destruction (de cosas). || FIG. FAM. *El profesor ha hecho una escabechina en los exámenes,* the teacher has failed a lot of students in the exams.
escabel m. Footstool (para los pies). || Stool (asiento).
escabiosa f. BOT. Scabious.
escabioso, sa adj. MED. Scabious.
escabro m. VET. Scab, mange (de las ovejas).
escabrosamente adv. Crudely.
escabrosidad f. Roughness, unevenness, ruggedness (del terreno). || FIG. Difficulty, toughness, thorniness (dificultad). | Crudeness, scabrous nature, dirtiness (inmoralidad). | Harshness (del carácter).
escabroso, sa adj. Rough, uneven, rugged (terreno). || FIG. Difficult, tough, thorny (difícil). | Crude, dirty, scabrous: *historia escabrosa,* crude story. | Harsh (carácter).
escabullirse* v. pr. To slip away. || *Escabullirse por,* to slip through.
escacharrar v. tr. FAM. To break, to bust (romper). | To spoil, to ruin (estropear).
— V. pr. FAM. To break, to bust (romperse). | To be spoilt *o* ruined (estropearse).
escafandra f. o **escafandro** m. Diving suit. || *Escafandra autónoma,* scuba.
escafoides adj./s.m. ANAT. Scaphoid.
escala f. Scale (graduación, proporción): *la escala de un mapa, de un termómetro,* the scale of a map, of a thermometer. || Ladder (escalera de mano). || Intermediate stop, stopover (de avión). || Port of call (de barco). || MIL. Promotion roster *o* list. || MÚS. Scale: *escala mayor, menor, cromática,* major, minor, cromatic scale. || Range (gama). || — *A escala,* to scale: *dibujar algo a escala,* to draw sth. to scale. || *A escala internacional,* on an international scale. || *A gran, a pequeña escala,* large-scale, small-scale: *mapa a gran escala,* large-scale map. || *En gran, en pequeña escala,* on a large, on a small scale. || *Escala de cuerda,* rope ladder. || MIL. *Escala de reserva,* inactive list, reserve of officers. || *Escala móvil,* sliding scale: *escala móvil salarial,* sliding wage scale. || **MAR. *Escala real,* accommodation ladder.** || *Hacer escala en,* to call in at, to stop in. || *Vuelo sin escala,* non-stop flight.
escalabrar v. tr. V. DESCALABRAR.
escalada f. Climbing (de una montaña). || Scaling (de una pared, un acantilado). || Escalade (con una escalera). || Break-in (de una casa). || MIL. Escalation. || Escalade (de la guerra, de precios, etc.).
escalador, ra m. y f. Climber, mountaineer (montañero). || Climber (ciclista). || Burglar, housebreaker (ladrón).
escalafón m. Promotion list, promotion roster, roll (de empleados, de soldados, etc.). || Table, list (cuadro). || *Seguir el escalafón,* to work one's way up.
escalamiento m. Scaling (de una pared, un acantilado). || Escalade (con una escalera). || Climbing (de una montaña). || Break-in (de una casa). || MIL. Escalation.
escálamo m. MAR. Thole, tholepin.
escalar v. tr. To scale (una pared, un acantilado). || To escalade (con una escalera). || To climb (una montaña). || To break into, to burgle (una casa). || To lift [a sluice gate].
— V. intr. To climb. || To escalate (en la guerra, los precios, etc.).
escalar adj. MAT. y FÍS. Scalar.
Escalda n. pr. m. GEOGR. Scheldt.
escaldado, da adj. Scalded. || FIG. Wary, cautious (receloso).
— M. Scalding.
escaldadura f. Scald (quemadura). || Scalding (acción). || FIG. Lesson.
escaldar v. tr. To scald (con agua caliente). || To make red hot (poner al rojo). || FIG. To teach a lesson: *aquella experiencia te escaldó,* that experience taught you a lesson.
— V. pr. To scald o.s., to get scalded.
escaleno adj./s. m. MAT. Scalene.
escalera f. Staircase, stairway: *escalera de caracol,* spiral staircase; *escalera excusada* or *falsa,* private staircase. || Stairs, *pl.*: *subir, bajar la escalera,* to go up, to go down the stairs. || Straight (en el póker), sequence (naipes). || — *Escalera abajo,* downstairs, down the stairs: *cayó escalera abajo,* he fell downstairs. | *Escalera de color, real,* straight, royal flush. || *Escalera de gancho,* scaling ladder. || *Escalera de incendios,* fire escape. || *Escalera de mano,* ladder. || *Escalera de servicio,* service stairs, backstairs. || *Escalera de tijera,* stepladder, steps, *pl.* || *Escalera mécanica* or *automática,* escalator. || FIG. *Gente de escaleras abajo,* servants, *pl.*
escalerilla f. Sequence of three cards (tres naipes seguidos). || Small staircase (escalera). || Small ladder (escala). || MAR. Gangway (de barco). || Steps, *pl.* (de avión). || VET. Metal instrument for keeping horse's mouth open.
escalfado, da adj. Poached (huevo). || Blistered (pared).
escalfador m. Hot-water container (de barbero). || Chafing dish (para calentar). || Poacher (para los huevos).
escalfar v. tr. To poach (los huevos).
escalinata f. Flight of steps.
escalo m. Scaling (acción de escalar). || *Robo con escalo,* burglary, housebreaking.
escalofriante adj. Bloodcurdling.

escalofrío m. Chill, shiver (de fiebre). || Shiver (de frío). || FIG. Shiver (de miedo, etc.). || *Tener escalofríos*, to shiver.
escalón m. Step, stair (de escalera). || Rung (de escala). || FIG. Step (en una jerarquía). | Stepping stone (para progresar). || MIL. Echelon. || *Cortar el pelo en escalones*, to cut hair unevenly.
escalonado, da adj. Spread out, spaced out. || Graded (en serie ascendente o descendente). || Staggered (huelga, vacaciones). || In stages (por etapas): *aprendizaje escalonado*, apprenticeship in stages.
escalonamiento m. Spreading out, spacing out. || Staggering: *escalonamiento de las vacaciones*, staggering of holidays.
escalonar v. tr. To spread out, to space out: *escalonar soldados*, to space out soldiers. || To grade: *escalonar las dosis*, to grade the doses. || To stagger (huelga, producción, vacaciones). || To do *o* to carry out in stages (hacer por etapas). || To terrace (land).
escalonia o **escaloña** f. BOT. Shallot (chalote).
escalope m. Veal cutlet, escalope.
escalpar v. tr. To scalp.
escalpe o **escalpo** m. Scalp.
escalpelo m. MED. Scalpel.
escama f. Scale (de pez, de serpiente). || MED. Flake, scale (de la piel). || BOT. Scale. || FIG. Suspicion, mistrust, wariness (desconfianza). || *Jabón en escamas*, soap flakes.
escamado, da adj. FAM. Suspicious, wary.
escamadura f. Scaling (del pescado).
escamar v. tr. To scale (quitar las escamas). || FIG. y FAM. To make suspicious *o* wary: *la experiencia le ha escamado*, the experience has made him wary. || FIG. y FAM. *Esto me ha escamado siempre*, I have always been suspicious about this, I have always been wary about this.
— V. pr. FIG. y FAM. To become wary *o* suspicious.
escamón, ona adj. Suspicious, wary.
escamonda f. Pruning.
escamondadura f. Pruned branches, *pl.*
escamondar v. tr. AGR. To prune (podar). || FIG. To prune, to cut down (lo superfluo). | To clean (limpiar). | To wash (lavar).
escamondo m. Pruning.
escamoso, sa adj. Scaly (que tiene escamas). || Flaky, scaly (piel). || FIG. Suspicious, wary.
escamotable adj. Retractable (tren de aterrizaje).
escamotar v. tr. V. ESCAMOTEAR.
escamoteador, ra m. y f. Conjuror, conjurer (prestidigitador). || FIG. y FAM. Thief, swindler (ladrón).
escamotear v. tr. To make disappear, to make vanish: *el prestidigitador escamoteó las cartas*, the magician made several cards vanish. || FIG. y FAM. To pinch, to lift, to take (robar). | To skip (una dificultad).
escamoteo m. Sleight of hand, conjuring (de un prestidigitador). || Vanishing, disappearing (desaparición). || FIG. y FAM. Lifting, pinching (robo). | Skipping (de una dificultad). || AVIAC. Retraction (de las ruedas).
escampada f. Clear spell (de la lluvia).
escampar v. impers. To stop raining, to clear up: *espera que escampe*, wait till it stops raining.
escampavía f. MAR. Scout (barco que acompaña a otro). | Coastguard vessel, revenue cutter [U.S., coastguard cutter] (para vigilar las costas).
escanciador m. Wine waiter. || HIST. Cupbearer (de los reyes).
escanciar v. tr. To serve, to pour (vino).
— V. intr. To drink wine.
escandalera f. FAM. V. ESCÁNDALO.
escandalizador, ra adj. Shocking, scandalizing.
— M. y f. Scandalous person.
escandalizar v. tr. To shock, to scandalize: *su conducta me escandaliza*, his conduct shocks me.
— V. intr. To make a fuss (armar un escándalo).
— V. pr. To be shocked *o* scandalized: *se escandalizó de tu conducta*, he was shocked by your conduct. || To protest, to be scandalized (protestar).
escándalo m. Scandal: *este crimen fue el mayor escándalo del año*, this crime was the biggest scandal of the year. || Row, racket, uproar, din (alboroto). || JUR. Disturbance of the peace. || — *Armar un escándalo*, to make a row *o* a racket *o* a din, to cause an uproar (hacer ruido), to make a scene (hacer una escena), to cause a scandal (provocar indignación). || *Armar* or *formar un escándalo a uno*, to give s.o. a dressing down *o* a telling off. || *Causar escándalo*, to cause a scandal. || *Con gran* or *con el consiguiente escándalo de*, to the indignation of. || *Piedra de escándalo*, cause of the scandal. || *Ser un escándalo*, to be scandalous *o* disgusting *o* shocking: *es un escándalo cómo suben los precios*, it is scandalous the way prices are rising.
escandalosa f. V. ESCANDALOSO.
escandalosamente adv. Scandalously, shockingly. || Noisily (ruidosamente). || Flagrantly (claramente).
escandaloso, sa adj. Scandalous, outrageous, shocking (que causa escándalo): *injusticia escandalosa*, scandalous injustice. || Rowdy, noisy (que mete jaleo). || Scandalous, notorious: *una vida escandalosa*, a notorious life. || Flagrant (a la vista de todos): *crimen escandaloso*, flagrant crime. || Uproarious (risa). || Loud (colores chillones).
— M. y f. *Mi vecina es una escandalosa*, my neighbour is always kicking up a fuss. || — F. MAR. Gaff, topsail (vela). || FIG. y FAM. *Echar la escandalosa a uno*, to give s.o. a telling off *o* a piece of one's mind.
escandallar v. tr. MAR. To sound. || COM. To fix the price of (determinar el precio). | To sample (para comprobar la calidad).
escandallo m. MAR. Sounding lead. || COM. Price fixing, pricing (de mercancías). | Sampling (prueba).
Escandinavia n. pr. f. GEOGR. Scandinavia.
escandinavo, va adj./s. Scandinavian.
escandio m. QUÍM. Scandium.
escandir v. tr. To scan (versos).
escantillón m. TECN. Template, templet, pattern.
escaño m. Bench (banco). || Seat (de diputado).
escapada f. Escape, flight (acción de escapar). || Escapade (travesura). || Breakaway (de un ciclista). || Quick trip (excursión). || *Hacer una escapada al campo*, to escape to the country, to slip away to the country, to make a quick trip to the country.
escapado, da adj. *Irse, volver escapado*, to rush off, to rush back.
escapamiento m. Escape, flight.
escapar v. intr. To escape: *escapar de un peligro, de una enfermedad*, to escape a danger, an illness; *escapar del naufragio*, to escape from the shipwreck. || To escape: *escapar de la cárcel, de la jaula*, to escape from prison, from the cage. || To escape, to run away, to flee (huir). || To break away (un ciclista, etc.). || — *¡De buena hemos escapado!*, we had a narrow escape! || *Dejar escapar*, to let out: *dejó escapar un suspiro*, he let out a sigh; to let go: *dejar escapar una oportunidad*, to let an opportunity go. || *Escapar bien*, to get off lightly. || *Escapar con vida de un accidente*, to survive an accident. || *Eso escapó a mi vista*, I missed that, that escaped my notice.
— V. tr. To run *o* ride hard (un caballo).
— V. pr. To escape, to get out: *el canario se ha escapado de la jaula*, the canary has escaped from the cage *o* got out of the cage. || To escape, to run away, to flee (huir). || To slip away (irse discretamente). || To leak, to escape (gas, líquido). || To escape (no llegar a comprenderse): *este sentido se te escapa*, this meaning escapes you. || To break away (en deportes). || — *Escapársele de las manos a alguien*, to slip out of s.o.'s hands: *el plato se le escapó de las manos*, the plate slipped out of his hands. || *Escaparse por un pelo* or *por tablas*, to have a narrow escape *o* a close shave, to escape by the skin of one's teeth. || *Se le escapó la mano*, he let fly. || *Se le escapó un suspiro*, he let out a sigh. || *Se me escapó la lengua*, I couldn't keep my mouth shut. || *Se me escapó la palabra*, the word slipped out, I let the word slip out. || *Su cumpleaños se me ha escapado*, his birthday slipped my mind.
escaparate m. Window: *¿quiere enseñarme la corbata que está en el escaparate?*, will you show me the tie that is in the window? || Shop window: *los escaparates están todos iluminados*, the shop windows are all lit up. || Showcase, display cabinet (vitrina). || *Amer.* Wardrobe (armario). || *Decorador, decoradora de escaparates*, window dresser.
escaparatista m. y f. Window dresser.
escapatoria f. Way out (salida): *es la única escapatoria*, it is the only way out. || Loophole, means of evasion (para eludir una obligación, etc.). || Excuse, subterfuge (excusa). || Trip (escapada). || Escape, flight (huida). || *No me venga usted con escapatorias*, don't try to worm your way out of it, don't try to put me off with excuses.
escape m. Escape (huida). || Leak, escape (de gas). || FIG. Way out (salida). || TECN. Exhaust (de motor): *tubo de escape*, exhaust pipe. | Exhaust valve (válvula). | Escapement (de reloj). || — *A escape*, at full speed: *correr a escape*, to run at full speed. || FIG. *Puerta de escape*, way out.
escápula f. ANAT. Scapula, shoulder blade.
escapular adj. Scapular (del hombro).
escapulario m. REL. Scapular, scapulary.
escaque m. Square (del tablero de ajedrez). || HERÁLD. Square. || — Pl. Chess, *sing.* (ajedrez).
escaqueado, da adj. Checked, checkered.
escara f. MED. Eschar, scab.
escarabajear v. intr. FIG. To mill around (moverse). || FAM. To worry, to bother (preocupar): *este problema me escarabajea*, this problem bothers me. || FIG. To scrawl, to scribble (escribir mal).
escarabajeo m. FAM. Worry, bother. || FIG. Scrawling, scribbling (garabateo).
escarabajo m. Beetle (insecto coleóptero). || FIG. y FAM. Dwarf, stunted person (persona de mal aspecto). || TECN. Flaw (en un tejido). || Fault in the bore (de un cañón). || — Pl. FIG. Scrawl, *sing.*, scribble, *sing.* (al escribir).
escaramucear v. intr. To skirmish.
escaramujo m. BOT. Dog rose (rosal silvestre). | Hip (fruto). || ZOOL. Barnacle (crustáceo).
escaramuza f. MIL. Skirmish. || FIG. Brush (fricción).
escaramuzar v. intr. To skirmish.
escarapela f. Rosette, cockade (insignia). || FIG. Quarrel (riña).

escarbadientes m. inv. Toothpick (mondadientes).
escarbador, ra adj. Scratching.
— M. Poker (para el fuego). || AGR. Scraper.
escarbaorejas m. inv. Earpick.
escarbar v. tr. e intr. To scratch: *las gallinas escarban la tierra*, hens scratch the ground. || To pick (dientes, oídos). || To poke (la lumbre). || FIG. To forage in, to rummage in: *escarbar (en) los archivos*, to forage in the archives. | To delve: *escarbar (en) un asunto*, to delve into a matter. || AGR. To scrape.
escarbo m. Scratching.
escarcear v. intr. *Amer.* To prance, to caracole.
escarcela f. Pouch (bolsa de cazador). || Purse (para el dinero). || Cap (cofia). || Cuisse (de armadura).
escarceo m. MAR. Ripple. || — Pl. Prances, caracoles, prancing, *sing.* (del caballo). || FIG. Wanderings, ramblings (rodeos). || — FIG. *Escarceos amorosos*, flirtation, *sing.* || *Hacer escarceos*, to prance, to caracole (el caballo).
escarcha f. Frost (rocío congelado). || Frost, hoarfrost (niebla condensada).
escarchado, da adj. Frost-covered, frosty, frosted: *árbol escarchado*, frost-covered tree. || Candied, crystallized: *fruta escarchada*, candied fruit. || Frosted, iced: *pastel escarchado*, frosted cake. || *Aguardiente escarchado*, brandy containing crystallized anise branch.
— M. Silver embroidery (de plata), gold embroidery (de oro). || Crystallizing, candying (de frutas).
escarchar v. impers. To freeze: *anoche ha escarchado*, it froze last night. || *Escarcha*, it's frosty.
— V. tr. To crystallize, to candy (frutas). || To ice, to frost (pasteles). || To crystallize an anise branch in [brandy] (el aguardiente).
— V. intr. To become frosty *o* covered with frost.
escarda f. AGR. Weeding hoe (instrumento). | Weeding (acción). | Weeding time (época).
escardadera f. AGR. Weeding hoe.
escardador, ra m. y f. Weeder (persona). || — M. Weeding hoe (instrumento).
escardadura f. AGR. Weeding.
escardar v. tr. AGR. To weed [out]. || FIG. To weed out. || FIG. y FAM. *Mandar a uno a escardar cebollinos*, to send s.o. packing, to tell s.o. to jump in the lake.
escardilla f. AGR. Weeding hoe.
escardillar v. tr. To weed [out] (escardar).
escardillo m. Weeding hoe (herramienta).
escariado m. TECN. Reaming.
escariador m. TECN. Reamer.
escariar v. tr. TECN. To ream (un agujero).
escarificación f. MED. Scarification.
escarificador m. Scarifier.
escarificar v. tr. AGR. y MED. To scarify.
escarlata f. Scarlet (color y tela). || MED. Scarlet fever.
— Adj. Scarlet.
escarlatina f. MED. Scarlet fever.
escarmenador m. V. CARMENADOR.
escarmenar v. tr. V. CARMENAR.
escarmentado, da adj. *Estar escarmentado*, to have learnt one's lesson, to have learnt from experience.
— M. y f. *De los escarmentados salen los avisados*, once bitten, twice shy.
escarmentar* v. tr. To teach a lesson: *escarmentar a un niño*, to teach a child a lesson.
— V. intr. To learn one's lesson: *no escarmienta nunca*, he never learns his lesson. || — *¡Así escarmentarás!*, that'll teach you! || *Escarmentar en cabeza ajena*, to learn from s.o. else's mistakes. || *Hacer escarmentar a uno*, to teach s.o. a lesson. || *Nadie escarmienta en cabeza ajena*, one only learns by one's own mistakes.
escarmiento m. Lesson (lección). || Punishment (castigo). || *Servirle de escarmiento a uno*, to be a lesson *o* a warning to s.o.
escarnecedor, ra adj. Jeering, scoffing, mocking (burlón). || Shameful (vergonzoso).
— M. y f. Jeerer, scoffer, mocker (burlón).
escarnecer* v. tr. To jeer at, to scoff at, to mock.
escarnecimiento o **escarnio** m. Mockery, scoffing, jeering, jeers, *pl.* (burla). || Derision, ridicule (ridículo). || Shame (vergüenza): *para mayor escarnio mío*, to my great shame.
escarola f. Endive (verdura). || (Ant.). Ruff (cuello alechugado).
escarpa f. Steep slope, escarpment, scarp (cuesta empinada). || Escarpment, scarp (de fortificación).
escarpado, da adj. Steep, sheer, precipitous: *orillas escarpadas*, steep banks. || Craggy, cragged (montaña, peñón). || Sheer, steep (pendiente).
escarpadura f. Steep slope, escarpment, scarp.
escarpar v. tr. To escarp (subir). || TECN. To rasp.
escarpia f. Hook (alcayata).
escarpidor m. Large-toothed comb (peine).
escarpín m. Pump (zapato). || Slipper (calzado interior).
escarzano adj. m. ARQ. Segmental (arco).
escasamente adv. Scarcely, barely, hardly: *trabajó escasamente una hora*, he worked scarcely an hour. || Only just (por muy poco): *los liberales ganaron escasamente*, the liberals only just won. || — *Cielo escasamente nublado*, sky with scattered clouds. || *Vivir escasamente*, to make ends meet.
escasear v. tr. To be sparing with, to be mean with (escatimar). || TECN. To bevel.
— V. intr. To be scarce (ser poco abundante): *escasea el arroz*, rice is scarce.
escasez f. Shortage, scarcity: *escasez de agua, de mano de obra*, shortage of water, of manpower. || Lack, shortage: *escasez de dinero*, lack of money. || Want, need (pobreza). || Scantiness: *la escasez de sus recursos*, the scantiness of his resources. || Stinginess, meanness (tacañería). || — *Año de escasez*, lean year. || *Con escasez*, hardly, scarcely, barely (apenas), stingily, meanly (con mezquindad), in need, on a shoestring (fam.): *vivir con escasez*, to live in need.
escaso, sa adj. Scarce (poco abundante). || Very little: *escaso tiempo*, very little time. || Poor, meagre: *escasa recompensa*, poor recompense. || Poor, low: *escaso salario*, poor wage; *escasa visibilidad*, poor visibility. || Only just, hardly, barely, scarcely: *dos días escasos*, hardly two days; *una hora escasa*, only just an hour. || Low: *los víveres son escasos*, provisions are low. || Thin, sparse (cosecha). || Low: *escasas lluvias*, low rainfall. || Scant, scanty, very little: *escasa vegetación*, scant vegetation. || Scanty, scant, meagre: *una comida escasa*, a scanty meal. || Scanty, very limited: *recursos escasos*, scanty resources. || Few (pocos): *escasos visitantes*, few visitors. || Small (reducido): *un público escaso*, a small audience. || Slight, slim, slender (alguna): *una escasa posibilidad*, a slight possibility. || Only a few: *desplazamiento de escasos milímetros*, displacement of only a few millimetres. || Miserly, mean, stingy (tacaño). || — *Andar escaso de*, to be short of. || *Andar escaso de dinero*, to be short of money. || *La comida va a resultar escasa*, there won't be enough food. || *Ser escaso de inteligencia*, to have a low intelligence.
escatimar v. tr. To be mean *o* stingy with, to skimp on (ser poco generoso con): *escatimar la comida*, to be mean with the food, to skimp on the food. || To be sparing with: *escatima hasta las sonrisas*, he is sparing even with his smiles; *hay que escatimar el azúcar porque ya no queda mucho*, we'll have to be sparing with the sugar because there is not much left. || To stint: *no escatimaba sus elogios*, he did not stint his praise. || To save: *escatimar sus energías*, to save one's strength. || *No escatimar esfuerzos, gastos*, to spare no effort, no expense.
escatología f. Scatology. || FIL. Eschatology.
escatológico, ca adj. Scatological (excrementicio). || FIL. Eschatological.
escayola f. Plaster of paris (yeso). || Stucco (estuco). || MED. Plaster.
escayolado, da adj. MED. In a plaster cast, in plaster (miembro).
— M. Plastering.
escayolar v. tr. MED. To put in a plaster cast *o* in plaster: *escayolar un brazo*, to put an arm in a plaster cast.
escena f. TEATR. Scene (subdivisión de un acto). | Stage (escenario): *salir a escena*, to go on stage. | Scene (lugar de la acción), | Theatre [U.S., theater] (arte dramático). || FIG. Scene: *una escena conmovedora*, a moving scene. || — *Director de escena*, producer (teatro). || *Escena retrospectiva*, flashback (en cine). || FIG. *Hacer una escena*, to make a scene. || *Poner en* or *llevar a la escena*, to stage. || *Puesta en escena*, staging. || *Su vocación es la escena*, his vocation is the stage. || *Volver a la escena*, to make one's comeback.
escenario m. TEATR. Stage: *estar en el escenario*, to be on stage; *nunca volvió a pisar un escenario*, he never set foot on a stage again. || Set (plató de cine). || FIG. Scene, setting: *ese lugar fue escenario de una batalla*, that place was the setting of a battle. | Surroundings, *pl.* (ambiente).
escénico, ca adj. Scenic.
escenificación f. Dramatizing, adaptation for the stage (de una obra literaria). || Staging (presentación).
escenificar v. tr. To dramatize, to adapt for the stage: *escenificar una novela*, to dramatize a novel, to adapt a novel for the stage. || To stage (poner en escena).
escenografía f. Scenography (arte). || Scenery (conjunto de decorados).
escenográfico, ca adj. Scenographical, scenographic.
escenógrafo, fa m. y f. Producer.
escepticismo m. Scepticism [U.S., skepticism].
escéptico, ca adj./s. Sceptic [U.S., skeptic].
Escila n. pr. GEOGR. Scylla. || FIG. *Estar entre Escila y Caribdis*, to be between Scylla and Charybdis. | *Librarse de Caribdis y caer en Escila*, to jump out of the frying pan into the fire.
escinco m. Skink (lagarto).
escindible adj. Divisible. || FÍS. Fissionable.
escindir v. tr. To divide, to split. || FÍS. To split (the atom).
— V. pr. To split.
Escipión n. pr. m. Scipio: *Escipión el Africano*, Scipio Africanus.
escisión f. Splitting, scission (acción). || Split, division: *la escisión de un partido político*, the split in a political party. || FÍS. Fission (of the atom): *escisión nuclear*, nuclear fission. || MED. Excision.

Escitia n. pr. f. GEOGR. Scythia.
esclarecer* v. tr. FIG. To throw light on, to clarify, to elucidate (una cosa dudosa). | To enlighten (explicar). | To ennoble (ennoblecer). | To make illustrious.
— V. intr. *Ya esclarece*, the day is breaking, it is getting light.
esclarecidamente adj. Illustriously.
esclarecido, da adj. Illustrious, distinguished, outstanding.
esclarecimiento m. Elucidation, elucidating (acción de esclarecer). || Enlightenment (información). || FIG. Illustriousness (celebridad). | Ennoblement (ennoblecimiento).
esclava f. V. ESCLAVO.
esclavina f. Short cape (capa). || Large collar (de capa).
esclavista adj. Pro-slavery.
— M. y f. Slavery supporter.
esclavitud f. Slavery: *vivir en la esclavitud*, to live in slavery. || FIG. Slavery: *este trabajo es una esclavitud*, this job is pure slavery.
esclavizar v. tr. To enslave. || FIG. To overwork, to slave-drive (hacer trabajar mucho): *el jefe esclaviza a todos los empleados*, the boss slave-drives all the employees. | To dominate (dominar).
esclavo, va m. y f. Slave. || FIG. Slave: *un esclavo de la bebida, del trabajo*, a slave to drink, to work. || — F. Bracelet, bangle (pulsera).
— Adj. Enslaved. || FIG. Tied: *ser esclavo de la casa, del despacho*, to be tied to the house, to the office. | Devoted (entregado): *ser esclavo de sus amigos*, to be devoted to one's friends. | Addicted: *es esclavo de la bebida*, he is addicted to drink. || — *Esclavo de su palabra*, faithful to one's word. || *Ser esclavo de su deber*, to be a slave to one's duties.
esclerosis f. MED. Sclerosis (endurecimiento). || FIG. Paralysis (de una industria, etc).
escleroso, sa adj. MED. Sclerotic, sclerosed.
esclerótica f. ANAT. Sclerotic, sclera.
esclusa f. Lock, sluice (de un canal). || Floodgate (compuerta). || *Esclusa de aire*, airlock.
esclusero, ra m. y f. Lockkeeper.
escoba f. Broom (utensilio). || Broomstick (de bruja). || BOT. Broom. || — DEP. *Camión escoba*, support vehicle. || *Pasar la escoba*, to sweep up.
escobajo m. Old broom. || Stalk (del racimo de uvas).
escobazo m. Blow with a broom. || — *Le dio un escobazo en la cabeza*, she hit him on the head with the broom. || FIG. y FAM. *Lo echaron a escobazos*, they booted him out.
escobén m. MAR. Hawsehole.
escobero, ra m. y f. Broom dealer.
escobilla f. Brush (cepillo). || Small broom (escoba pequeña). || TECN. Brush (de dinamo). || BOT. Teasel (cardencha). | Heather (brezo).
escobillar o **escobillear** v. tr. To brush.
— V. intr. *Amer.* To do shuffling steps (baile).
escobillón m. MIL. Swab.
escobina f. Filings, *pl.* (de un metal). | Sawdust (de la madera).
escobón m. Large broom. || Wall brush (de mango largo). || Short broom (de mango corto). || Chimney-sweeping brush (deshollinador).
escobonazo m. V. ESCOBAZO.
escocedor, ra adj. Painful, hurtful.
escocedura f. Sore (en la piel). || Sting, smarting, soreness (de una herida). || FIG. Hurt feelings, *pl.* (en el sentimiento).
escocer* v. intr. To smart, to sting (irritar): *me escuece la herida*, my wound stings. || FIG. To hurt the feelings of, to hurt: *su falta de respeto me escoció*, his lack of respect hurt me *o* hurt my feelings.
— V. tr. To chafe: *tengo la piel escocida*, my skin is chafed.
— V. pr. To get sore (la piel, etc.). || — *El niño se ha escocido* or *está escocido*, the baby is all sore. || FIG. *Se escoció por lo que le dije*, he was hurt *o* his feelings were hurt by what I said to him.
escocés, esa adj. Scottish, Scots (persona). || Scotch (comida, whisky). || *Tela escocesa*, tartan, plaid.
— M. y f. Scotsman, Scot (hombre), Scotswoman, Scot (mujer). || — M. Scottish, Scots (lengua).
Escocia n. pr. f. GEOGR. Scotland. || *Nueva Escocia*, Nova Scotia.
escocimiento m. V. ESCOCEDURA.
escoda f. TECN. Stonecutter's hammer, bushhammer.
escodar v. tr. TECN. To cut [with a hammer]. || To rub (el ciervo).
escofia o **escofieta** f. Cap, coif (cofia).
escofina f. TECN. Rasp: *escofina de mediacaña*, half-round rasp.
escofinar v. tr. TECN. To rasp.
escoger v. tr. To choose, to pick, to select: *escoger una manzana de una cesta*, to choose an apple from a basket. || To choose: *escoge entre estos dos colores*, choose between these two colours; *escoger entre muchas cosas*, to choose from many things. || — *A escoger*, to choose from: *hay cinco platos a escoger*, there are five plates to choose from. || *Escoger a bulto* or *al buen tuntún*, to choose at random. || *Escoger como* or *para* or *por mujer*, to choose as one's wife. || *Muchos son los llamados y pocos los escogidos*, many are called but few are chosen. || *Tener de sobra donde escoger*, to have more than enough to choose from. || *Tener donde escoger*, to have a good choice *o* selection.
escogidamente adv. Discerningly (con discernimiento). || Perfectly (muy bien).
escogido, da adj. Chosen, selected. || Selected: *obras escogidas*, selected works. || Choice, select (de calidad): *mercancías escogidas*, choice goods. || MIL. *Tropas escogidas*, crack troops.
escogimiento m. Choice, selection.
escolanía f. Choir school (escuela). || Choirboys, *pl.* (escolanos).
escolano m. Choirboy, chorister.
escolapio m. Monk who teaches in a charity school (religioso). || Charity school pupil (alumno).
escolar adj. School, scholastic: *edad escolar*, school age; *curso escolar*, school year. || — *Comportamiento escolar*, conduct in school. || *Libro escolar*, school book (para estudiar), report book (para consignar las notas).
— M. y f. Schoolboy, pupil (muchacho), schoolgirl, pupil (muchacha).
escolaridad f. Schooling: *se exige un mínimo de escolaridad*, a minimum of schooling is required; *escolaridad obligatoria*, compulsory schooling. || *Prolongar la escolaridad hasta los dieciséis años*, to raise the school-leaving age to sixteen.
escolarización f. Schooling.
escolástica f. o **escolasticismo** m. Scholasticism.
escolástico, ca adj. Scholastic: *doctrina escolástica*, Scholastic doctrine.
— M. y f. Scholastic.
escolio m. Scholium (nota). || MAT. Scholium.
escoliosis f. MED. Scoliosis.
escolopendra f. ZOOL. Scolopendrid, scolopendra, centipede (ciempiés). || BOT. Scolopendrium, hart's-tongue (lengua de ciervo).
escolta f. Escort. || MAR. Escort (barco). || *Dar escolta a*, to escort.
escoltar v. tr. To escort.
escollar v. intr. *Amer.* To run aground (encallarse). | FIG. To fail (malograrse).
escollera f. Breakwater (rompeolas).
escollo m. Reef (arrecife). || FIG. Difficulty, stumbling block: *tropezar en un escollo*, to come up against a difficulty. | Danger (peligro).
escombrar v. tr. To clear (quitar los escombros de).
escombrera f. Rubbish dump, tip. || Tip (de mina de carbón). || Slag heap (de escoria).
escombro m. Mackerel (pez).
escombros m. pl. Debris, *sing.*, rubble, *sing.* (de un edificio, etc.). || Slag, *sing.* (escoria).
esconce m. Recess (ángulo entrante). || Corner, angle (ángulo saliente).
escondedero m. Hiding place (escondrijo).
esconder m. Hide-and-seek (escondite).
esconder v. tr. To hide: *el niño escondió la muñeca en el cajón*, the child hid the doll in the drawer. || To hide, to conceal: *su sonrisa esconde su tristeza*, his smile conceals his sadness.
— V. pr. To hide: *esconderse de uno*, to hide from s.o. || To hide o.s., to hide: *se escondió en el armario*, he hid himself in the cupboard. || To lurk, to hide, to be concealed *o* hidden: *en su alma se esconde la tristeza*, sadness lurks in his soul.
escondidamente adv. Secretly, on the sly.
escondidas f. pl. *Amer.* Hide-and-seek (juego).
— Adv. *A escondidas*, secretly. || *Hacer algo a escondidas de alguien*, to do sth. without s.o.'s knowledge.
escondido m. *Amer.* Hide-and-seek (escondite).
escondite m. Hiding place (escondrijo). || Hide-and-seek (juego de niños): *jugar al escondite*, to play [at] hide-and-seek.
escondrijo m. Hiding place.
escopeta f. Shotgun, rifle: *escopeta de dos cañones*, double-barrelled shotgun. || — FIG. y FAM. *Aquí te quiero ver, escopeta*, let's see what you can do, show us what you can do. || *Escopeta de aire comprimido*, air gun, air rifle.
escopetazo m. [Shotgun] shot, gunshot (disparo). || Shotgun wound (herida). || FIG. Piece of bad news, blow.
escopetear v. tr. To shoot at with a shotgun *o* rifle.
— V. intr. To fire a shotgun.
— V. pr. FIG. To shower each other with compliments *o* with flattery (lisonjearse). | To shower each other with insults (con insultos). | To fire questions at each other (con preguntas).
escopeteo m. [Shotgun] shooting. || FIG. y FAM. *Un escopeteo de insultos, de cortesías, de preguntas*, a shower of insults, of politeness, of questions.
escopetería f. MIL. Gunshots, *pl.* || Men (*pl.*) armed with shotguns *o* rifles, riflemen, *pl.* (hombres).
escopetero m. Soldier armed with a shotgun, rifleman (soldado). || Man armed with a shotgun (hombre). || Gunsmith (fabricante). || ZOOL. Bombardier beetle.
escopladura o **escopleadura** f. TECN. Cut made with a chisel (corte). | Chiselling (acción).
escoplear v. tr. To chisel.
escoplo m. TECN. Chisel.
escora f. MAR. Level line (línea del fuerte). | Stanchion, prop (puntal). | List (inclinación del barco).

escorar v. tr. MAR. To stanchion, to prop (apuntalar).
— V. intr. MAR. To list (un barco): *escora a estribor*, she is listing to starboard.
escorbútico, ca adj. MED. Scorbutic.
escorbuto m. MED. Scurvy.
escoria f. Slag (de mina). || Slag, dross, scoria (de alto horno). || Scoria (de volcán). || FIG. Scum, dregs, *pl.*: *la escoria de la sociedad*, the scum of society.
escoriáceo, a adj. Scoriaceous.
escoriación f. Chafing, excoriation (p. us.).
escorial m. Slag heap.
Escorial (El) n. pr. m. El Escorial.
escoriar v. tr. To chafe, to excoriate (p. us.).
— V. pr. To chafe.
escorificación f. Slagging, scorification.
escorificar v. tr. To slag, to scorify.
Escorpio o **Escorpión** m. ASTR. Scorpio.
escorpión m. Scorpion. || FIG. *Lengua de escorpión*, evil tongue.
escorzado m. V. ESCORZO.
escorzar v. tr. ARTES. To foreshorten.
escorzo m. ARTES. Foreshortening (acción y efecto). | Foreshortened figure (figura).
escorzonera f. BOT. Viper's grass, scorzonera.
escota f. MAR. Sheet.
escotado, da adj. Low-necked, low-cut (vestido). || Wearing a low-necked *o* a low-cut dress (persona). || *Iba muy escotada*, she was wearing a very low-necked dress.
— M. [Low] neck, [low] neckline (escotadura).
escotadura f. Scooping-out (corte). || [Low] neck, [low] neckline (abertura del cuello). || Armhole (de una manga). || TEATR. Large trapdoor.
escotar v. tr. To scoop out *o* to cut out the armhole in (para la manga). || To scoop out *o* to cut out the neckline in (para el cuello). || To lower the neckline of (para ensanchar). || To cut to fit (para ajustar). || To divert water from [a river]. || To contribute: *todos escotaron su parte*, everybody contributed his share.
— V. intr. y pr. To chip in, to pay one's share *o* way (pagar su cuota). || To go Dutch (una pareja). || To club together, to chip in: *vamos a escotarnos para comprarle un regalo*, let's club together to buy him a present.
escote m. Neck, neckline (corte del cuello). || Low neck, low neckline, décolleté, décolletage (abertura grande alrededor del cuello). || Armhole (para la manga). || Lace frill (adorno). || Neck (parte del cuerpo descubierta). || Share, contribution (cuota). || — *Comprar algo a escote*, to club together to buy sth. || *Pagar a escote*, to go Dutch (una pareja). || *Pagar algo a escote*, to chip in to pay for sth. (entre varias personas). || *Pagar su escote*, to pay one's share *o* one's way, to chip in, to make one's contribution, to contribute: *cada chico pagó su escote*, each boy paid his share, each boy made his contribution *o* contributed.
escotilla f. MAR. Hatchway.
escotillón m. MAR. y TEATR. Trapdoor.
escozor m. V. ESCOCEDURA.
escriba m. Scribe.
escribana f. Notary's wife.
escribanía f. Portable writing case (caja portátil). || Writing desk (mueble). || Writing materials, *pl.* (recado de escribir). || Notary's position (oficio de notario). || Notary's office (despacho del notario). || Clerkship (oficio de secretario judicial). || Clerk's office (despacho del secretario judicial).
escribano m. Clerk, secretary (escribiente). || Clerk of the court (secretario judicial). || Notary (notario). || ZOOL. Whirligig beetle.
escribido, da adj. FAM. *Ser muy leído y escribido*, to be well read, to be very knowledgeable (presumir de sabio).
escribidor m. FAM. Hack writer.
escribiente m. y f. Clerk.
escribir v. tr. To write: *escribe cuentos para niños*, he writes children's stories. || To write, to compose (música). || To spell (ortografiar): *no sabe escribir esta palabra*, he cannot spell this word. || To write to tell: *me ha escrito que vendrá mañana*, he has written to tell me that he is coming tomorrow. || — *Escribir algo a mano*, to write by hand. || *Escribir algo a máquina*, to type sth. || *Escribir algo de su puño y letra*, to write sth. by hand, to do sth. in one's own handwriting. || *Máquina de escribir*, typewriter. || *Papel de escribir*, writing paper, notepaper.
— V. intr. To write: *me escribe cada mes*, he writes to me every month.
— V. pr. To be spelt, to spell: *¿cómo se escribe la palabra?*, how is the word spelt?, how do you spell the word? || *Se escriben cada semana*, they write to each other every week.
escriño m. Straw basket (cesta). || Coffer (cofrecito).
escrito, ta adj. Written: *examen escrito*, written examination; *avaricia escrita en su cara*, greed written on his face. || — *Escrito a mano*, handwritten. || *Escrito a máquina*, typewritten, typed: *una carta escrita a máquina*, a typewritten letter. || FIG. *Estaba escrito*, it was inevitable. || *Lo arriba escrito*, what has been said above, the above. || FIG. *Lo escrito está*, it's down in writing, it's down in black and white.
— M. Writing, work: *los escritos de Ortega*, the works of Ortega. || Letter: *le mandó un escrito*, he sent him a letter. || Document (documento). || Written exam (examen). || Writing: *había un escrito en la pared*, there was some writing on the wall. || JUR. Writ. || *Poner por escrito*, to put down *o* to put in writing, to write down.
escritor, ra m. y f. Writer.
escritorio m. Bureau [U.S., secretary] (mueble). || Office (despacho). || — *Gastos de escritorio*, stationery expenses. || *Objetos de escritorio*, stationery, *sing.*, writing materials.
escritorzuelo, la m. y f. Third-rate writer, hack writer.
escritura f. Writing: *la escritura de una carta*, the writing of a letter; *la escritura griega*, Greek writing. || Script: *escritura fonética*, phonetic script. || Writing, handwriting (letra). || Document (documento). || JUR. Deed: *escritura de propiedad*, title deed; *escritura notarial*, notarial deed. | Bill: *escritura de venta*, bill of sale. || *La Sagrada Escritura*, the Holy Scripture.
escriturar v. tr. To legalize with a written document, to execute by deed, to notarize. || To book, to engage (a un artista).
escriturario, ria adj. Notarial.
— M. Bible scholar, scripturalist.
escrófula f. MED. Scrofula.
escrofuloso, sa adj. MED. Scrofulous.
escroto m. ANAT. Scrotum.
escrúpulo m. Scruple: *tener escrúpulos*, to have scruples. || Scrupulousness, conscientiousness, extreme care (escrupulosidad): *hacer algo con escrúpulo*, to do sth. with extreme care. || Stone [in one's shoe] (piedrecilla). || — *Escrúpulos de conciencia*, qualms of conscience. || *Me da escrúpulo beber en el vaso de otro*, I have qualms about drinking from another person's glass. || *Un hombre de negocios sin escrúpulos*, an unscrupulous businessman.
escrupulosidad f. Scrupulousness, extreme care.
escrupuloso, sa adj. Scrupulous (que tiene escrúpulos de conciencia). || Scrupulous, conscientious (concienzudo). || Scrupulous, meticulous: *con escrupulosa atención*, with meticulous care. || Fussy, particular: *no me gusta invitar a esa gente porque es demasiado escrupulosa*, I don't like inviting those people because they are too fussy.
escrutador, ra adj. Scrutinizing, examining. || Searching: *mirada escrutadora*, searching look.
— M. y f. Teller (en una asamblea). || Scrutineer (que comprueba la validez de los votos).
escrutar v. tr. To scrutinize, to examine. || To count (votos).
escrutinio m. Count, counting of the votes (recuento). || Examination, scrutiny (averiguación): *hacer el escrutinio de una cosa*, to carry out an examination on sth. || *Efectuar* or *hacer el escrutinio*, to count the votes.
escuadra f. Square (instrumento). || Angle iron (pieza para consolidar). || MIL. Squad. | Rank of corporal (cargo de cabo). || FIG. Gang (de obreros). || MAR. Squadron, fleet. || DEP. Angle (fútbol). || — *A escuadra*, at right angles. || *Corte a escuadra*, squaring. || *Escuadra de agrimensor*, surveyor's cross. || *Falsa escuadra* or *escuadra móvil*, bevel square. || *Fuera de escuadra*, on the bevel. || *Labrar a escuadra*, to square.
escuadrar v. tr. To square.
escuadreo m. Squaring (medición por áreas).
escuadrilla f. MAR. y AVIAC. Squadron.
escuadrón m. MIL. Squadron.
escualidez f. Skinniness, thinness (delgadez). || Squalour [U.S., squalor], filth (suciedad).
escuálido, da adj. Skinny, thin (delgado). || Filthy, squalid (sucio).
escualo m. ZOOL. Shark (pez).
escucha f. Listening (acción de escuchar). || Nun acting as a chaperon (monja). || Listening-in (de comunicaciones). || — *Estación de escucha*, listening-in station. || *Estar a la escucha*, to be listening. || *Ponerse a la escucha*, to listen.
— M. MIL. Scout (centinela). || Monitor (sistema de detección). || Listener (radioyente).
escuchador, ra m. y f. Listener.
escuchar v. tr. To listen to: *escuchar música*, to listen to music. || To hear (oír). || To listen to, to pay attention to (un consejo).
— V. intr. To listen: *escuchar detrás de las puertas*, to listen at doors.
— V. pr. To like to hear o.s. talk.
escuchimizado, da adj. Thin, puny.
escudar v. tr. To shield, to protect with a shield. || FIG. To shield, to protect (proteger).
— V. pr. To shield o.s., to protect o.s. with a shield. || FIG. To hide, to use as an excuse: *siempre se escuda con el trabajo para no ayudarme*, he always hides behind his work *o* he always uses his work as an excuse so that he doesn't have to help me.
escudería f. Squiredom, position as squire. || AUT. Stable (de coches).
escuderil adj. Squire's, of a squire.

escudero m. Squire (paje). || Nobleman (hidalgo). || Lady's page (servidor de señora). || Shield maker (fabricante).
escudete m. Small shield (escudo pequeño). || Gusset (costura). || Escutcheon (de una cerradura). || AGR. Shield. *injerto de escudete*, shield grafting. || BOT. Water lily.
escudilla f. Bowl (recipiente). || Bowlful (contenido). || *Amer.* Large cup (tazón).
escudo m. Shield (arma defensiva). || Escudo (moneda). || HERÁLD. Coat of arms. || Escutcheon (de una cerradura). || Gun shield (del cañón). || MAR. Escutcheon (espejo de popa). || AGR. Shield. || FIG. Shield, protection (defensa, protección). || Shoulder (del jabalí). || *Escudo de armas*, coat of arms.
escudriñador, ra adj. Examining, scrutinizing, investigating (que examina). || Curious, inquisitive, nosey (fam.) [curioso].
— M. y f. Examiner, scrutinizer, investigator. || Inquisitive person, nosey parker (fam.) [curioso].
escudriñamiento m. Investigation, inquiry, examination (investigación). || Search, scanning (del horizonte, etc.). || Scrutinizing, examination (acción de mirar cuidadosamente).
escudriñar v. tr. To investigate, to inquire into, to examine (examinar): *escudriñar la vida de alguien*, to investigate *o* to inquire into s.o.'s life. || To search, to scan: *escudriñar el horizonte*, to scan the horizon. || To scrutinize, to examine: *escudriñar un mapa para encontrar una pequeña calle*, to examine a map to find a small street.
escuela f. School: *escuela de párvulos*, infant school; *escuela de equitación*, riding school; *escuela de Bellas Artes*, Art School. || Training (instrucción): *tiene buena disposición para el clarinete, pero le falta escuela*, he's well suited for the clarinet, but he needs training. || Teaching (métodos de enseñanza). || FIG. School: *escuela racionalista, holandesa*, rationalist, Dutch school. || — *Alta escuela*, higher horsemanship (equitación). || *Escuela de artes y oficios*, technical school. || *Escuela de comercio*, business school. || *Escuela de Ingenieros Agrónomos*, Agricultural College. || *Escuela de primera enseñanza, de enseñanza secundaria* or *media*, primary, secondary school. || *Escuela nocturna*, night school. || *Escuela Normal*, teachers' training college [U.S., Normal School]. || *Formar escuela*, to found a school. || *La vieja escuela*, the old school. || *Tener buena escuela*, to be well trained.
escuerzo m. Toad (sapo). || FIG. Rake, bean pole (persona flaca).
escueto, ta adj. Concise, (conciso): *un informe muy escueto*, a very concise report. || Simple, unadorned: *lenguaje, estilo escueto*, simple language, style. || Plain: *la verdad escueta*, the plain truth.
Esculapio n. pr. m. Aesculapius.
esculpidor m. Sculptor.
esculpir v. tr. To sculpture: *esculpir una estatua en piedra*, to sculpture a statue in stone. || To engrave (grabar). || To carve (madera).
escultor, ra m. y f. Sculptor (hombre), sculptress (mujer): *escultor en mármol*, sculptor of marble.
escultórico, ca adj. Sculptural.
escultura f. Sculpture. || Carving (de madera). || Engraving (grabado).
escultural adj. Sculptural. || FIG. Statuesque (cuerpo de una mujer).
escupida f. *Amer.* Spit (salivajo).
escupidera f. Spittoon, cuspidor (para escupir). || Chamber pot (orinal).
escupidor, ra adj. Who is always spitting (que escupe).
— M. y f. Spitter. || — M. *Amer.* Spittoon, cuspidor (escupidera).
escupidura f. Spit, spittle (esputo). || Phlegm (flema). || Cracking [of the lips] (en los labios).
escupir v. intr. To spit: *se prohibe escupir*, no spitting. || FIG. To blot, to make blots (una pluma). || FAM. To cough up (pagar). || — FAM. *Escupir a uno*, to spit in s.o.'s face. | *Es su padre escupido*, he is the spit and image of his father, he is the spitting image of his father. | *Si escupes al cielo, en la cara te caerá*, chickens and curses come home to roost.
— V. tr. To spit, to spit out: *escupir sangre*, to spit blood. || FIG. To belch out: *el volcán escupía lava*, the volcano was belching out lava. | To throw out: *escupir metralla*, to throw out shrapnel. | To spit out (injurias, etc.). || FAM. To fork out, to cough up (dinero). || *Esta pluma escupe tinta*, this fountain pen blots *o* makes blots.
escupitajo m. o **escupitina** f. o **escupitinajo** m. o **escupo** m. Spit, spittle.
escurialense adj. Of *o* from El Escorial.
escurrebotellas m. inv. Draining rack [for bottles].
escurreplatos m. inv. Plate rack, dish rack.
escurridero m. Draining rack (de botellas). || Plate rack, dish rack (de vajilla). || Draining board (del fregadero).
escurridizo, za adj. Slippy, slippery (resbaladizo). || FIG. Elusive: *idea escurridiza*, elusive idea. | Slippery: *problema escurridizo*, slippery problem; *persona escurridiza*, slippery person. || FAM. *Hacerse el escurridizo*, to slip off *o* away, to sneak off *o* away.
escurrido, da adj. Narrow-hipped, slim-hipped (de caderas). || Wearing a tight skirt (una mujer). || *Amer.* Ashamed (avergonzado).
escurridor m. Dish rack, plate rack (escurreplatos). || Draining board (del fregadero). || Colander (colador). || Wringer (para la ropa).
escurriduras f. pl. Dregs (de un vaso o botella). || Drips: *escurriduras de pintura*, paint drips.
escurrimiento m. Draining (de platos, manjares). || Dripping (de la ropa). || FIG. Slip (desliz).
escurrir v. tr. To drain. || To wring (la ropa). || FAM. *Escurrir el bulto*, V. BULTO.
— V. intr. To drip (líquidos, ropa). || To be slippery (ser resbaladizo): *este suelo escurre*, this floor is slippery.
— V. pr. To slip: *escurrirse en el hielo*, to slip on the ice; *escurrirse de* or *entre las manos de alguien*, to slip out of s.o.'s hands. || To drip (líquidos, ropa). || FIG. y FAM. To slip off *o* away, to sneak off *o* away (escabullirse). | To give o.s. away (en la conversación). | To make a slip (equivocarse).
esdrujulizar v. tr To accentuate the antepenultimate syllable of.
esdrújulo, la adj. Proparoxytone, accented on the antepenultimate syllable.
— M. Proparoxytone, word accented on the antepenultimate syllable.
ese f. S [name of the letter *s*]. || Zigzag: *las eses de la carretera*, the zigzags in the road. || S-hook (gancho). || Sound hole (de violín, etc.). || — *Andar haciendo eses*, to stagger (dando traspiés), to zigzag (zigzaguear). || *Hundir el puñal hasta la ese*, to push a dagger in up to the hilt. || *La carretera hace eses*, the road twists and turns.
ese, esa (pl. **esos, esas**) adj. dem. That [pl. those]: *esa mujer*, that woman, *esos libros son tuyos*, those books are yours.

— OBSERV. *Ese* denotes proximity to the person spoken to (see AQUEL and ESTE). When placed after the noun *ese* often has a pejorative meaning: *¡qué pesado es el niño ese!*, what a nuisance that child is!

ése, ésa (pl. **ésos, ésas**) pron. dem. That one [pl. those]: *me gusta más esta casa que ésa*, I like this house more than that one; *ésos son tus poderes*, those are your powers. || The former (el último). || He, she, that one [pl. they, those, those ones] (v. OBSERV.): *ése lo sabe*, he knows; *ésos se quedan*, they stay. || Him, her, that one [pl. them, those, those ones] (v. OBSERV.): *se lo he dado a ése*, I've given it to him. || — FIG. y FAM. *¡Conque ésas tenemos!*, so that's it! | *¡Choque usted ésa!*, shake on it! || *En una de ésas*, one of these days. || *Ése que*, that one who: *ése que vino ayer*, that one who came yesterday. || *Llegaré a ésa mañana*, I shall arrive in your town tomorrow. || FAM. *Ni por ésas*, even so: *ni por ésas lo consiguió*, even so he didn't get it. | *¡No me vengas con ésas!*, don't come to me with that story.

— OBSERV. According to the Spanish Academy the accents on the pronouns *ése, ésa, ésos ésas* are optional. The accent on the pronouns was originally intended to distinguish them from adjectives. Now it may be omitted in all cases where no confusion is possible.
— Cabe señalar que los pronombres *ése, ésa, ésos* se traducen por *he, she, it, they* cuando tienen la función de sujeto, y por *him, her, it, them* cuando tienen la función de complemento directo o indirecto. Cuando *ése y ésa* tienen un sentido despectivo equivalen a *that one.* (V. ESE [Observ.].)

esecilla f. TECN. Small S-hook (alacrán).
esencia f. Essence: *esencia del liberalismo*, essence of liberalism. || Essence, entity (entidad). || Essence (extracto concentrado): *esencia de café*, coffee essence. || Perfume: *un frasco de esencia*, a bottle of perfume. || QUÍM. Essence, essential oil. || FIG. Heart, core, essence (de un problema). || — FIG. *Contar algo en esencia*, to give a brief outline of sth. | *En esencia*, essentially, in essence (esencialmente). || *Quinta esencia*, quintessence.
esencial adj. Essential: *la aplicación es esencial en los estudios*, application is essential in studying; *aceite esencial*, essential oil. || — *En lo esencial*, in the main. || *Lo esencial*, the main *o* the essential thing: *lo esencial es ser honrado*, the main thing is to be honest. || *No esencial*, non-essential, inessential.
esfenoidal adj. ANAT. Sphenoidal.
esfenoideo, a adj. ANAT. Sphenoidal.
esfenoides adj./s.m. ANAT. Sphenoid.
esfera f. Sphere: *esfera armilar*, armillary sphere; *esfera celeste*, celestial sphere. || Dial, face (de reloj). || TECN. Dial. || Circle, sphere (ambiente): *salirse de su esfera*, to leave one's circle. || Field, sphere: *esfera de actividad*, field of action. || — *Esfera terrestre*, [terrestrial] globe. || *Las altas esferas*, high circles: *se dice en las altas esferas que*, it is being said in high circles that.
esfericidad f. Sphericity.
esférico, ca adj. MAT. Spherical.
— M. FAM. Ball (balón).
esferoidal adj. MAT. Spheroidal.
esferoide m. MAT. Spheroid.
esferómetro m. Spherometer.

esfinge f. Sphinx. || ZOOL. Hawkmoth (mariposa nocturna). || FIG. Sphinx.
esfínter m. ANAT. Sphincter.
esforzado, da adj. Courageous, valiant (valiente). || Vigorous, energetic (vigoroso).
esforzar* v. tr. (P. us). To encourage.
— V. pr. To make an effort, to exert o.s. (hacer un esfuerzo físico): *el niño tuvo que esforzarse para levantar la silla*, the child had to make an effort *o* the child had to exert himself to lift the chair. || To strive: *se esfuerza en* or *por llevar una vida moral*, he strives to lead a moral life. || To try hard, to make an effort (intentar): *esfuérzate por* or *en* or *para aprenderlo*, try hard to learn it. || To do one's best (hacer todo lo posible): *me esforzaré en* or *por darle satisfacción*, I'll do my best to please you. || MED. To strain o.s.
esfuerzo m. Effort: *redoblar los esfuerzos*, to double one's efforts. || Effort, endeavour, attempt (intento). || TECN. Stress (en mecánica). || — *Aplicar la ley del mínimo esfuerzo*, to make the least effort possible. || *Hacer esfuerzos* or *un esfuerzo*, V. ESFORZARSE. || *Sin esfuerzo*, effortlessly.
esfumación f. Stumping, toning down.
esfumar v. tr. To stump, to tone down.
— V. pr. To fade away, to disappear.
esfuminar v. tr. To stump.
esfumino m. Stump (lápiz). || Stump drawing (dibujo).
esgrima f. Fencing: *maestro de esgrima*, fencing master. || *Practicar la esgrima*, to fence.
esgrimidor, ra m. y f. Fencer.
esgrimir v. tr. To brandish: *esgrimir un palo*, to brandish a stick. || To wield (una espada). || FIG. To use [as a weapon]: *esgrimir un argumento*, to use an argument.
— V. intr. To fence.
esgrimista m. y f. *Amer.* Fencer.
esguince m. MED. Sprain, twist (torcedura). || Swerve, dodge (del cuerpo). || (P. us.). Frown (gesto de desagrado). || *El accidente le produjo un esguince en el tobillo*, he sprained his ankle in the accident.
eslabón m. Link (de cadena). || Steel (para sacar chispas). || Steel (para afilar). || ZOOL. Scorpion (alacrán). || FIG. Link. || VET. Splint. || MAR. *Eslabón giratorio*, swivel.
eslabonamiento m. Linking.
eslabonar v. tr. To link together. || FIG. To link, to interlink, to connect.
— V. pr. FIG. To be linked.
eslavizar v. tr. To slavicize.
eslavo, va adj. Slav, slavonic.
— M. y f. Slav (persona). || — M. Slavonic (lengua).
eslinga f. MAR. Sling (cabo).
eslogan m. Slogan.
eslora f. MAR. Length (de un barco): *eslora total*, overall length. || — Pl. MAR. Binding strakes (brazolas).
esmaltado m. Enamelling.
esmaltador, ra m. y f. Enameller.
esmaltar v. tr. To enamel. || To varnish, to paint (las uñas). || FIG. To be scattered over: *flores de varios colores esmaltan el prado*, flowers of several colours are scattered over the meadow. | To adorn, to sprinkle: *esmaltar una conversación con* or *de citas latinas*, to adorn a conversation with Latin quotations.
esmalte m. Enamel: *esmalte campeado*, champlevé enamel. || Enamel (de los dientes). || Enamelling (decoración, arte). || Enamelled object (objeto esmaltado). || Smalt (color). || HERÁLD. Tincture. || *Esmalte de* or *para uñas*, nail varnish, nail enamel, nail polish.
esmeradamente adv. Carefully, with great care (con cuidado). || Elegantly (con elegancia).
esmerado, da adj. Carefully done, neat (bien hecho): *un ejercicio esmerado*, a carefully done exercise. || Careful, painstaking: *una criada esmerada*, a careful maid. || Elegant.
esmeralda f. Emerald.
esmerar v. tr. To tidy up, to clean up (limpiar).
— V. pr. To take pains, to take care (esforzarse): *esmerarse en el trabajo*, to take pains over one's work. || To do one's best (hacer todo lo posible).
esmeril m. Emery (piedra). || *Papel de esmeril*, emery paper.
esmerilado, da adj. TECN. Ground (vidrio). | Polished with emery (pulido). || *Papel esmerilado*, emery paper.
— M. TECN. Grinding. | Polishing (acción de pulir).
esmerilar v. tr. TECN. To grind: *esmerilar una válvula, vidrio*, to grind a valve, glass. | To polish with emery (pulir).
esmero m. Care: *trabajar, escribir con esmero*, to work, to write with care. || Neatness (aseo). || — *Estar vestido con esmero*, to be neatly dressed. || *Poner esmero en*, to take pains over, to take care over: *puso mucho esmero en esta carta*, he took great pains over this letter.
Esmirna n. pr. f. GEOGR. Smyrna, Izmir.
esmirriado, da adj. Puny, thin (escuchimizado). || FIG. Scraggy: *árbol esmirriado*, scraggy tree.
esmoquin m. Dinner jacket [U.S., tuxedo].
esmorecerse v. pr. To faint.
esnob adj. Snobbish.
— M. y f. Snob.
esnobismo m. Snobbery, snobbishness.
esnórquel n. MAR. Snorkel.
eso pron. dem. neutro. That: *eso no me gusta*, I don't like that; *antes, después de eso*, before, after that. || — *A eso de*, at about: *a eso de las nueve*, at about nine o'clock. || *A pesar de eso*, in spite of that. || *En eso*, at that moment, at that point. || *¡Eso!* or *¡eso es!*, that's it. || *Eso de no tener salud es muy fastidioso*, [the fact of] being unhealthy is very annoying. || *Eso de tu accidente no es más que...*, all that about your accident is just... || *Eso mismo*, just that, exactly. || *¡Eso no!*, certainly not!: *¿vienes? — ¡Eso no!*, are you coming? — Certainly not! || *Eso que me contaste ayer*, that story you told me yesterday. || *Eso que me dijiste me parece excelente*, what you told me sounds excellent. || *¡Eso sí!*, of course!, certainly! || *¡Eso sí que es...!*, that certainly is...!: *¡eso sí que es una buena acción!*, that certainly is a good deed! || *¡Eso sí que no!*, certainly not! || *Hace diez años de eso*, it's ten years since then (diez años han transcurrido), ten years before that (diez años antes de ese acontecimiento). || *¡Nada de eso!*, none of that! || *¿No es eso?*, isn't that right?, isn't that so? || *No es eso ni mucho menos*, it's not that at all, it's nothing like that. || *Por eso*, that's why: *por eso lo hice*, that's why I did it; therefore (por consiguiente). || *¿Qué es eso?*, what's that? || *Y eso que*, although, in spite of the fact that: *habla mal el inglés, y eso que ha vivido en Londres*, he speaks English badly although he has lived in London.
esos, esas adj. dem. pl. V. ESE.
ésos, ésas pron. dem. pl. V. ÉSE.
esófago m. ANAT. Oesophagus [U.S., esophagus].
Esopo n. pr. m. Aesop.
esotérico, ca adj. Esoteric (oculto, secreto).
esoterismo m. Esoterism, esotericism.
esotro, tra, esotros, tras adj. dem. [contraction of *ese* and *otro*]. That other, those others.
— Pron. That other one, those other ones.

— OBSERV. Like *ese*, *esotro* can have a pejorative meaning.

espabiladeras f. pl. Snuffers.
espabilado, da adj. V. DESPABILADO.
espabilar v. tr. V. DESPABILAR.
espaciador m. Space bar, spacer (en una máquina de escribir).
espacial adj. Space: *vuelo espacial*, space flight; *encuentro espacial*, space rendezvous. || — *Nave espacial*, spaceship. || *Vehículos espaciales*, spacecraft.
espaciamiento m. Spacing (distancia). || Staggering (escalonamiento).
espaciar v. tr. To space out, to spread out (poner espacio entre). || To stagger, to space out: *espaciar los pagos*, to stagger payments. || IMPR. To space: *espaciar los renglones*, to space lines of type. || To spread (divulgar).
— V. pr. To spread (divulgarse). || FIG. To expatiate: *espaciarse en una carta*, to expatiate in a letter. | To enjoy o.s. (distraerse).
espacio m. Space: *espacio entre dos cosas*, space between two things; *viaje por el espacio*, space journey. || Room, space: *este armario ocupa mucho espacio*, this wardrobe takes up a lot of room. || Space, period (de tiempo). || Distance (distancia). || IMPR. y MÚS. Space. || FIG. Slowness (tardanza). || Programme [U.S., program] (en televisión). || — *A doble espacio*, double-spaced. || *Espacio aéreo*, air space. || *Espacio publicitario*, advertising spot. || *Espacio tiempo*, space-time. || *Espacio vital*, living space. || *Por espacio de*, during, for.
espacioso, sa adj. Spacious, roomy (amplio): *un cuarto espacioso*, a spacious room. || Slow (lento).
espachurrar v. tr. FAM. To squash.
espada f. Sword: *traer la espada al cinto*, to be wearing one's sword. || FIG. Swordsman (persona): *ser buena espada*, to be a good swordsman. | Authority, important figure: *es una de las primeras espadas en su profesión*, he is one of the biggest authorities *o* he is one of the most important figures in his profession. || — Pl. "Espadas" [corresponds to spades in the English pack of cards]. || — *Cruzar la espada con alguien*, to cross swords with s.o. || *De capa y espada*, cloak and dagger. || *Desenvainar* or *desnudar la espada*, to unsheathe *o* to draw one's sword. || FIG. y FAM. *Echar su cuarto a espadas*, V. CUARTO. || *Envainar la espada*, to sheathe one's sword. || *Espada de dos filos*, two-edged sword (espada), double-edged argument (argumento). || FIG. *Estar entre la espada y la pared*, to be between the devil and the deep blue sea. || *Meter la espada hasta la guarnición*, to plunge one's sword in up to the hilt. || *Pez espada*, swordfish. || FIG. *Quienes matan con la espada por la espada morirán*, he who lives by the sword will die by the sword.
espada m. TAUR. Matador.
espadachín m. Good swordsman (buen esgrimidor). || Bully (bravucón).
espadaña f. BOT. Bulrush. || ARQ. Bell gable.
espadín m. Ceremonial sword. || Sprat (pez).

espaguetis m. pl. Spaghetti, *sing.*
espalda f. Back. || DEP. Backstroke: *200 metros espalda*, 200 metres backstroke. || — Pl. Back, *sing.* (de persona, de cosa). || MIL. Rearguard. || — *A espaldas de alguien*, behind s.o.'s back. || *A las espaldas*, in one's back: *con el sol a las espaldas*, with the sun in one's back. || *Anchura de espaldas*, width of shoulders. || *Caer* or *caerse* or *dar de espaldas*, to fall [flat] on one's back. || *Cargado de espaldas*, round-shouldered: *este joven es cargado de espaldas*, this young man is round-shouldered. || *Dar* or *volver la espalda a uno*, to turn one's back on s.o. || *De espaldas*, from behind: *sólo le vi de espaldas*, I only saw him from behind. || FAM. *Echarse algo a las espaldas*, to forget about sth. | *Echarse entre pecho y espalda*, to put away, to tuck away (comida, bebida). | *Echarse una cosa sobre las espaldas*, to take sth. on, to take sth. upon o.s. || *En la espalda*, in one's back. || FAM. *Esta noticia me tiró de espaldas*, this news knocked me flat. || *Estar de espaldas*, to have one's back turned. || *Estar tendido de espaldas*, to be lying on one's back. || FIG. *Guardar las espaldas*, to keep sth. in reserve. || *Guardar las espaldas de alguien*, to back s.o. || FIG. y FAM. *Hablar por las espaldas*, to talk behind people's backs. || *Herir a uno por la espalda*, to injure s.o. in the back (con un arma), to stab s.o. in the back (con una mala acción). || FIG. *Medirle a uno las espaldas*, to give s.o. a beating, to beat s.o. up. || *Nadar de espalda*, to swim backstroke, to swim on one's back. || *Poner de espaldas*, to pin (en la lucha). || *Por la espalda*, from behind. || *Ser ancho de espaldas*, to be broad-shouldered. || FIG. *Tener buenas espaldas* or *anchas espaldas*, to be easygoing. | *Tener guardadas las espaldas*, to be well backed. | *Tener muchos años a la espalda*, to have a lot of years behind one. || *Volver la espalda*, V. VOLVER.
espaldar m. Back plate (de coraza). || Back (de un asiento, del cuerpo). || AGR. Espalier.
espaldarazo m. Accolade [of a knight]: *dar el espaldarazo a*, to give the accolade to. || FIG. Backing (apoyo).
espaldera f. AGR. Espalier. || — Pl. DEP. Wall bars.
espaldilla f. Shoulder blade (omóplato). || Shoulder (de reses).
espantada f. Bolt (del caballo). || Running away (huida). || Stampede (de un grupo). || Sudden scare, sudden fear (miedo). || *Dar una* or *la espantada*, to run away, to take to one's heels (huir), to bolt (el caballo), to stampede (un grupo), to get cold feet, to get scared (desistir).
espantadizo, za adj. Shy (caballo). || Easily frightened, scary, timorous, shy (persona).
espantado, da adj. Frightened, scared, terrified.
espantador, ra adj. Frightening, scaring. || *Amer.* Shy (espantadizo).
espantajo m. Scarecrow (espantapájaros). || FIG. Sight (persona fea). | Bogeyman (coco). | Deterrent (cosa que infunde miedo): *este argumento sirve de espantajo*, this argument is a deterrent.
espantalobos m. inv. BOT. Bladder senna.
espantamoscas m. inv. Fly whisk, flyswatter.
espantapájaros m. inv. Scarecrow.
espantar v. tr. To frighten, to scare (dar miedo a). || To frighten away *o* off, to scare away (ahuyentar): *espantar a un caballo, a un ladrón*, to frighten off a horse, a robber. || To drive away, to shoo away: *espantar las moscas*, to drive away the flies. || FIG. To ward off (miedo, sueño, etc.). | To terrify, to frighten: *me espantan los exámenes*, examinations terrify me. | To horrify, to disgust (horrorizar).
— V. pr. To be frightened away *o* off, to be scared away (ahuyentarse): *el caballo se espantó con el tiro*, the horse was frightened away by the shot. || To be frightened *o* scared (asustarse): *espantarse de* or *por algo*, to be frightened about sth; *los caballos se espantan fácilmente*, horses are easily frightened *o* scared. || To be astonished *o* amazed (admirarse).
espanto m. Fright, terror: *causar espanto*, to be a source of fright; *llenar de espanto*, to fill with fright. || Threat (amenaza). || Astonishment (asombro). || Horror, disgust (horror). || Ghost (fantasma). || — *De espanto*, frightening, terrifying (que da miedo), horrible, terrible (feo). || FAM. *Estoy curado de espanto*, nothing can shock me any more, I have known worse. | *Ser un espanto*, to be frightening *o* appalling *o* dreadful: *es un espanto lo cara que está la carne ahora*, it's frightening how expensive meat is now.
espantoso, sa adj. Frightening, terrifying (que causa espanto). || Frightening, appalling, dreadful: *un aumento de precios espantoso*, a dreadful rise in prices. || Terrible, dreadful: *un ruido espantoso*, a terrible noise. || Horrible, disgusting (horroroso). || Incredible (pasmoso).
España n. pr. f. GEOGR. Spain. || *La España de pandereta*, the tourist's Spain, typical Spain.
español, la adj. Spanish. || *A la española*, in the Spanish way.
— M. y f. Spaniard. || — M. Spanish (lengua). || — Pl. Spanish, Spaniards (gente, pueblo).
españolado, da adj. Spanish-like.
— F. Exaggerated portrait of Spain (espectáculo). || Typically Spanish idea *o* mannerism *o* action.
españolismo m. Spanish nature, Spanishness (carácter español). || Love of Spain (amor a lo español). || Hispanicism (hispanismo).
españolizar v. tr. To make Spanish, to hispanicize.
— V. pr. To adopt Spanish ways.
esparadrapo m. MED. Sticking plaster.
esparaván m. Sparrow hawk (gavilán). || VET. Spavin.
esparavel m. Casting net (red). || TECN. Mortarboard (de albañil).
esparceta f. BOT. Sainfoin (pipirigallo).
esparciata adj./s. Spartan (de Esparta).
esparcidamente adv. Separately.
esparcido, da adj. Scattered: *flores esparcidas por el campo*, flowers scattered over the field. || FIG. Widespread: *una noticia muy esparcida*, a very widespread piece of news. || Gay, merry (alegre).
esparcidora f. Spreader.
esparcimiento m. Spreading (de un líquido). || Scattering (dispersión). || AGR. Spreading (de abonos). || FIG. Spreading (de una noticia, etc.). | Merriness, gaiety (alegría). | Relaxation: *tomarse unas horas de esparcimiento*, to take a few hours relaxation. | Amusement, diversion (recreo).
esparcir v. tr. To scatter: *esparcir flores por el camino*, to scatter flowers over the road. || To spread (derramar). || AGR. To spread (abono). || FIG. To spread (una noticia).
— V. pr. To scatter, to be scattered (desparramarse). || To spread (derramarse). || FIG. To spread: *la noticia se esparció como una mancha de aceite*, the news spread like wildfire. | To relax, to take it easy (descansar). | To amuse o.s. (recrearse).
espárrago m. BOT. Asparagus. || Post (palo). || Peg ladder (escalera). || TECN. Stud. || FAM. Lanky person (flacucho). || — FAM. *Estar hecho un espárrago*, to be as thin as a rake. | *Mandar a uno a freír espárragos*, to send s.o. packing. || CULIN. *Puntas de espárragos*, asparagus tips. || FAM. *¡Vete a freír espárragos!*, go jump in the lake!
esparraguera f. Asparagus [plant] (planta). || Asparagus patch (plantación). || Asparagus dish (plato).
esparraguina f. MIN. Apatite.
esparrancado, da adj. Straddling, with one's legs wide apart (persona). || Too wide apart (cosas).
esparrancarse v. pr. FAM. To open *o* to spread one's legs.
Esparta n. pr. GEOGR. e HIST. Sparta.
espartano, na adj./s. Spartan (de Esparta).
espartería f. Esparto workshop (taller). || Esparto work (oficio).
espartero, ra m. y f. Esparto worker.
esparto m. BOT. Esparto (planta).
espasmo m. Spasm.
espasmódico, ca adj. Spasmodic: *tos espasmódica*, spasmodic cough.
espata f. BOT. Spathe.
espatarrarse v. pr. To open one's legs wide.
espático, ca adj. MIN. Spathic.
espato MIN. Spar: *espato de Islandia*, Iceland spar. || *Espato flúor*, fluorspar, fluorite.
espátula f. Spatula (paleta). || Palette knife (de pintor). || Spoonbill (ave). || *Espátula de modelar*, drove.
espatulado, da adj. Spatular. || BOT. Spatulate.
especería f. V. ESPECIERÍA.
especia f. Spice.
especiado, da adj. Spiced, spicy.
especial adj. Special. || *En especial*, especially.
especialidad f. Speciality, specialty.
especialista adj./s. Specialist: *un especialista en neurología*, a neurology specialist. || *Médico especialista*, specialist.
especialización f. Specialization.
especializado, da adj. Specialized: *obrero especializado*, specialized worker.
especializar v. tr. To specialize.
— V. pr. To specialize: *especializarse en historia romana*, to specialize in Roman history.
especie f. Species: *especie humana*, human species; *la propagación de la especie*, the propagation of the species. || Kind, sort, type (género, clase). || Matter, affair (asunto). || Piece of news (noticia): *propagar una especie falsa*, to spread a false piece of news. || — *En especie*, in kind: *pagar en especie*, to pay in kind. || REL. *Especies sacramentales*, species.
especiería f. Grocer's shop [U.S., grocery store] (tienda). || Spices, *pl.*, spicery (especias).
especiero, ra m. y f. Spice dealer. || — M. Spice box.
especificación f. Specification.
especificamente adv. Specifically.
especificar v. tr. To specify.
especificativo, va adj. Specifying.
específico, ca adj. Specific: *peso específico*, specific gravity.
— M. MED. Specific (medicamento para tratar una enfermedad determinada). | Patent medicine.
espécimen m. Specimen.

— OBSERV. Pl. *especímenes.*

especiosidad f. Speciosity.
especioso, sa adj. Specious (engañoso). || (P. us.). Beautiful.
espectacular adj. Spectacular.

espectáculo m. Entertainment (diversión): *el circo es un espectáculo que gusta a los niños*, circus is a popular entertainment among children. || Show: *espectáculo de variedades*, variety show. || Performance: *ver el espectáculo de la tarde*, to see the afternoon performance. || Spectacle, sight: *el espectáculo grandioso de las cataratas del Niágara*, the imposing spectacle of Niagara falls. || — Pl. Entertainments: *guía de espectáculos*, entertainments guide; *durante el festival dieron buenos espectáculos*, during the festival they provided some good entertainments. || — *Dar el espectáculo en la calle*, to make a scene *o* to cause a scandal in the street. || *Sala de espectáculos*, theatre [U.S., theater] (teatro), cinema (cine).

espectador, ra m. y f. Spectator (en teatro, cine, deportes). || Onlooker: *miraba como espectador*, he was an onlooker. || — Pl. Audience, *sing.* (público). || Spectators (en deportes). || *Sala que tiene cabida para dos mil espectadores*, theatre with seating for two thousand *o* that seats two thousand.

espectral adj. Ghostly: *luz espectral*, ghostly light. || FÍS. Spectral: *análisis espectral*, spectral analysis.

espectro m. Spectre [U.S., specter], ghost. || FÍS. Spectrum. || FIG. Spectre: *el espectro de la guerra*, the spectre of war. | Ghost (persona cadavérica).

espectrografía f. FÍS. Spectrography.

espectrógrafo m. FÍS. Spectrograph.

espectrograma m. FÍS. Spectrogram.

espectroscopia f. FÍS. Spectroscopy.

espectroscópico, ca adj. FÍS. Spectroscopic.

espectroscopio m. FÍS. Spectroscope.

especulación f. Speculation: *especulación en la Bolsa*, speculation on the Stock Exchange. || Speculation, contemplation, meditation (meditación). || Conjecture, speculation (conjetura).

especulador, ra adj. Speculating.
— M. y f. Speculator.

especular v. intr. To speculate: *especular en la Bolsa, en cereales*, to speculate on the Stock Exchange, in cereals; *especula con la concesión de los permisos*, he speculates with the granting of licences.

especulativo, va adj. Speculative.
— F. Intellect, understanding (facultad del espíritu).

espéculo m. MED. Speculum.

espejear v. intr. To shine, to gleam.

espejeo m. Gleaming shining (brillo). || Mirage (espejismo).

espejería f. Mirror shop.

espejero m. Mirror maker *o* seller.

espejismo m. Mirage (fenómeno de óptica). || FIG. Illusion, mirage (ilusión engañosa).

espejo m. Mirror, looking glass (ant.): *mirarse en el espejo*, to look at o.s. in the mirror; *el espejo de las aguas*, the mirror of the waters. || FIG. Reflection: *el teatro es el espejo de la vida*, the theatre is the reflection of life. | Model (dechado). || — *Espejo de cuerpo entero*, full-length mirror. || *Espejo retrovisor*, driving mirror, rear-view mirror. || FÍS. *Espejo ustorio*, burning glass. || FIG. *Mirarse en uno como en un espejo*, to model o.s. on s.o. (imitar), to be very fond of s.o. (querer). | *Mírate en este espejo*, let this be an example to you.

espejuelo m. MIN. Selenite (yeso cristalizado). | Flake of talc (hoja de talco). || Lark mirror (para cazar). || FIG. Bait (atractivo). || Crystallized citron (confitura). || VET. Chestnut (excrecencia córnea de los caballos). || — Pl. Spectacle lenses (cristales). || Glasses, spectacles (anteojos).

espeleología f. Speleology, potholing.

espeleológico, ca adj. Speleological.

espeleólogo m. Speleologist.

espeluznante adj. FAM. Hair-raising, horrifying.

espeluznar v. tr. To make [s.o.'s] hair stand on end: *la idea de la muerte me espeluzna*, the thought of death makes my hair stand on end.

espeluzno m. Shiver, shudder.

espeque m. MAR. Handspike. || Prop (puntal).

espera f. Wait: *la espera fue muy larga*, the wait was very long. || Waiting: *sala de espera*, waiting room. || JUR. Respite, stay (plazo). || Patience (paciencia). || — *Cazar a espera*, to lie in wait for game. || *Compás de espera*, v. COMPÁS. || *En espera de*, while waiting for: *en espera de tu llegada se puso a leer una novela*, while waiting for you to arrive he started reading a novel; awaiting: *en espera de su respuesta*, awaiting your reply. || *Estar a la espera*, to be waiting.

esperantista adj./s. Esperantist.

esperanto m. Esperanto (lengua).

esperanza f. Hope (virtud): *la esperanza consuela a los infelices*, hope consoles unhappy people. || Hope (confianza): *la esperanza en el éxito*, hope of *o* for success. || Hope, prospect (perspectiva): *ahora hay esperanzas de paz*, there are now hopes of peace. || Faith (fe): *esperanza en Dios, en uno*, faith in God, in s.o. || Expectation: *defraudar las esperanzas de alguien*, to disappoint s.o.'s expectations; *esperanza de vida*, life expectation. || — *Abrigar esperanzas*, to foster hopes. || *Alimentarse de esperanzas*, to live on hope *o* on hopes. || *Como última esperanza*, as a last hope. || *Con la esperanza de* or *de que*, in the hope of *o* that. || *Dar esperanzas de* or *de que*, to give hope for *o* that. || *La esperanza es lo último que se pierde*, one should never lose hope, we must hope against hope. || *Llenar la esperanza de uno*, to fulfil s.o.'s hopes *o* expectations. || *Mientras hay vida, hay esperanza*, whilst there is life, there is hope. || *No hay esperanza*, there is no hope. || *Tener esperanza*, to have a hope; *tiene esperanza de obtener el premio*, he has a hope of winning the prize; to have hopes: *tengo esperanza de que venga mañana*, I have hopes that he will come tomorrow. || *Tener muchas esperanzas*, to have high hopes. || *Tener pocas esperanzas*, to have little hope. || *Vivir de esperanzas*, to live on hope.

esperanzador, ra adj. Encouraging: *resultados esperanzadores*, encouraging results.

esperanzar v. tr. To give hope to. || *Estar esperanzado*, to be hopeful.

esperar v. tr. To wait for (aguardar): *te esperaré hasta las ocho*, I shall wait for you until eight o' clock; *estaba esperando que le recibieran*, he was waiting for them to see him. || To hope (desear): *espero que vendrás*, I hope [that] you will come; *espero sacar un premio en la lotería*, I hope to win a prize in the lottery. || To hope for: *esperemos días mejores*, let us hope for better days. || To expect (contar con la llegada de): *esperamos a muchos espectadores para el partido*, we expect a lot of spectators for the match; *estar esperando una llamada*, to be expecting a call. || To expect (creer): *¡yo que esperaba que hiciera buen tiempo!*, and I expected the weather to be fine! || To await, to be in store for: *mal día nos espera*, a bad day is in store for us *o* awaits us. || To be expecting (un bebé). || — *Ahí lo espero*, I'll get him there. || *Esperar como agua de mayo* or *como el santo advenimiento*, to be longing for. || *Estar esperando familia*, to be expecting a baby. || FAM. *Espéreme sentado*, don't hold your breath! || FIG. y FAM. *Te espero fuera*, I'll deal with you later, I'll see you outside.
— V. intr. To wait: *esperaré a que vengas para comer*, I will wait until you come to eat. || — *Esperar en Dios*, to put one's faith in God, to trust in God. || *Esperar en Dios que*, to hope to God that. || *Esperar en uno*, to trust in s.o. | *Espero que sí, que no*, I hope so, I hope not. || *Hacer esperar a uno*, to keep s.o. waiting, to make s.o. wait. || *Hacerse esperar*, to keep people waiting. || *Nada se pierde con esperar*, we shall lose nothing by waiting. || *Quien espera desespera*, a watched pot never boils.
— V. pr. To expect: *no me esperaba tantos éxitos*, I didn't expect so many successes. || To wait: *¡espérate un momento!*, wait a minute! || — *Cuando menos se lo esperaban*, when least expected. || FAM. *¡Espérate sentado!*, you could wait for ever!, don't hold your breath! || *La producción no fue tan alta como se esperaba*, production was not so high as expected. || *Se espera que*, it is hoped that.

esperma f. Sperm. || *Amer.* Candle. || *Esperma de ballena*, spermaceti, sperm oil.

espermaceti m. Spermaceti, sperm oil.

espermático, ca adj. Spermatic.

espermatocito m. Spermatocyte.

espermatofita f. BOT. Spermatophyte.

espermatogénesis f. Spermatogenesis.

espermatógeno, na adj. Spermatogenetic.

espermatozoide m. Spermatozoid.

espermatozoo m. Spermatozoon.

esperpento m. FAM. Fright, sight (persona o cosa fea): *¡qué esperpento!*, what a fright! | Nonsense, absurdity (disparate).

espesado o **espesamiento** m. Thickening.

espesar m. Thicket (espesura).

espesar v. tr. To thicken: *espesar una salsa*, to thicken a sauce. || To weave tighter (un tejido). || To press together (apretar).
— V. pr. To thicken (chocolate, salsa). || To thicken, to get thicker (hierba). || To get thicker *o* bushier (árbol). || To get denser *o* thicker (bosque).

espeso, sa adj. Thick: *tejido, caldo espeso*, thick material, soup. || Dense, thick: *bosque espeso*, dense wood. || Stiff: *pasta espesa*, stiff dough. || Bushy, thick (árbol). || Dirty (sucio).

espesor m. Thickness. || — *De mucho espesor*, very thick. || *Espesor de nieve*, depth of snow.

espesura f. Thickness (de un tejido, un caldo, una salsa, etc.). || Stiffness (de la pasta). || Denseness, thickness (de un bosque). || Bushiness, thickness (de un árbol). || Thicket (matorral). || Dirtiness (suciedad).

espetar v. tr. To spit (con un asador largo). || To skewer (con una broqueta). || FIG. To run through, to skewer (traspasar). || FIG. y FAM. To make sit through, to make listen to (encajar): *nos espetó un discurso aburrido*, he made us sit through a boring speech. | To spring, to pop (con brusquedad): *nos espetó una pregunta*, he sprang a question on us. | To rap out (una orden).

espeto m. Spit (asador). || Skewer (broqueta).

espetón m. Spit (asador). || Skewer (broqueta).

espía m. y f. Spy. || *Espía doble*, double agent. || — F. MAR. Warping (acción de espiar). | Warp (cabo).

espiar v. tr. To keep watch on (observar, acechar): *espiar las acciones de los demás*, to keep watch on other people's movements. || To spy on: *espiar el ejército enemigo*, to spy on the enemy army.
— V. intr. To spy. || MAR. To warp (remolcar).

espícula f. Spicule.

espichar v. tr. To prick. || FAM. *Espicharla*, to kick the bucket (morir).
— V. intr. FAM. To kick the bucket (morir). || *Amer.* To make a speech (hacer un discurso).
— V. pr. *Amer.* To lose weight (adelgazar). | To be ashamed (avergonzarse).
espiche m. Peg, plug (para caños, toneles, etc.). || MAR. Plug. || *Amer.* Speech.
espiga f. BOT. Ear, spike. || Herringbone (dibujo en un tejido). || Tang (de espada). || Tenon (de un madero). || Pin, peg (clavija). || MAR. Masthead.
espigadera f. Gleaner.
espigado, da adj. Which has gone to seed (planta). || FIG. Tall and graceful, slender: *una muchacha espigada*, a tall and graceful girl.
espigadora f. Gleaner (espigadera).
espigar v. tr. AGR. To glean. || FIG. To collect, to glean (en libros). || TECN. To tenon.
— V. intr. To ear, to produce ears *o* spikes (cereales). || AGR. To glean. || FIG. To glean *o* to collect data (en libros). | To shoot up (personas).
— V. pr. To shoot up (personas): *esta muchacha se ha espigado mucho este año*, this girl has shot up a lot this year. || To run to seed (hortalizas).
espigón m. Point (punta). || Jetty, pier, breakwater (dique). || Ear [of corn] (mazorca). || Peak (cerro).
espigueo m. Gleaning.
espiguilla f. Herringbone (dibujo): *tela de espiguillas*, herringbone material. || BOT. Spikelet.
espín m. Porcupine (puerco espín). || FÍS. Spin (momento cinético del electrón).
espina f. Thorn (de vegetal): *clavarse una espina en el dedo*, to get a thorn in one's finger. || Splinter (astilla). || Bone [of a fish] (de los peces). || ANAT. Spine, backbone (espinazo). || FIG. Difficulty (dificultad). || — FIG. y FAM. *Eso me da mala espina*, I don't like the look of that. || BOT. *Espina blanca*, cotton thistle. || *Espina dorsal*, spine, backbone. || BOT. *Espina Santa*, Christ's-thorn. || FIG. *Problema lleno de espinas*, thorny problem. | *Sacarse la espina*, to remove the thorn from one's side (salir de apuro), to get even (desquitarse). | *Tener clavada una espina en el corazón*, to have a thorn in one's side.
espinaca f. BOT. Spinach. || — Pl. CULIN. Spinach, *sing.*
espinal adj. Spinal: *médula espinal*, spinal marrow.
espinapez m. *Entarimado de espinapez*, herringbone parquet *o* flooring.
espinar m. Hawthorn bushes, *pl.* (espinos). || Thorny thicket (matorral). || FIG. Jam, thorny situation (enredo). | Difficulty.
espinar v. tr. To prick (herir). || AGR. To protect with thorn branches (los árboles). || FIG. To hurt, to offend (zaherir).
espinazo m. ANAT. Spine, backbone. || CULIN. Chine. || ARQ. Keystone (clave). || — FIG. y FAM. *Doblar el espinazo*, to bow down. | *Romperse el espinazo*, to break one's back (cayendo, trabajando).
espinela f. Stanza with ten octosyllabic lines [named after the Spanish poet Espinela].
espineta f. MÚS. Spinet (clavicordio).
espingarda f. Small cannon (cañón). || Arab shotgun (escopeta de los moros). || FIG. Beanpole (mujer).
espinilla f. ANAT. Shinbone (tibia). || Blackhead, spot (en la piel).
espinillera f. Greave (de la armadura). || DEP. Shinpad, shin guard.
espino m. BOT. Hawthorn. || — BOT. *Espino albar* or *blanco*, [English] hawthorn. || *Espino artificial*, barbed wire. || BOT. *Espino cerval*, purging buckthorn (arbusto). | *Espino majoleto*, [English] hawthorn. | *Espino negro*, blackthorn.
espinoso, sa adj. Thorny (planta). || Bony (pescado). || FIG. Thorny (difícil).
espionaje m. Espionage, spying. || *Novela de espionaje*, spy story.
espira f. ARQ. Surbase (de columna). || MAT. Spire (de una espiral). | Spiral (espiral). || ZOOL. Spire, whorl. || ELECTR. Turn.
Espira n. pr. GEOGR. Speyer.
espiración f. Breathing out, expiration, exhalation.
espirador adj. m. ANAT. Expiratory: *músculo espirador*, expiratory muscle.
espiral adj. Spiral: *escalera espiral*, spiral staircase. || *Muelle espiral*, hairspring (de reloj).
— F. Hairspring (de reloj). || MAT. Spiral. || Spiral (de humo). || *En espiral*, corkscrew: *rabo en espiral*, corkscrew tail; spiral: *muelle, escalera en espiral*, spiral spring, staircase.
espirante adj./s. f. Spirant (fricativa).
espirar v. tr. To breathe out, to exhale, to expire (el aire). || To give off (un olor).
— V. intr. To breathe out, to exhale, to expire. || FIG. To blow gently (el viento).
espiritado, da adj. Possessed [of the Devil]. || FIG. y FAM. Thin, skinny (flaco).
espiritismo m. Spiritualism, spiritism.
espiritista adj. Spiritualistic, spiritualist.
— M. y f. Spiritualist.
espiritoso, sa adj. Spirited (vivo). || Spirituous (vino).
espíritu m. Spirit, soul (alma). || Spirit (ser): *los ángeles son espíritus*, angels are spirits. || Spirit, ghost (aparecido): *creer en los espíritus*, to believe in ghosts; *comunicación de los espíritus*, spirit rapping. || Spirit (energía): *espíritu de lucha*, fighting spirit. || Spirit (disposición): *espíritu de justicia, de trabajo*, spirit of justice, of work. || Spirit (adhesión): *espíritu de clase, de partido*, class, party spirit. || Mind (mente, persona): *tener el espíritu vivo*, to have a lively mind; *un gran espíritu de nuestra época*, a great mind of our time. || Spirit (sentido): *espíritu de una ley, de un siglo*, spirit of a law, of a century. || Wit (vivacidad del ingenio). || Breathing (signo gráfico griego). || — Pl. Demons (demonios). || — *Dar* or *exhalar* or *entregar* or *rendir el espíritu*, to give up the ghost. || *Espíritu de contradicción*, contrariness. || *Espíritu de cuerpo*, esprit de corps, corporate feeling. || *Espíritu de equipo*, team spirit. || *Espíritu de profecía*, gift of prophecy (don sobrenatural). || QUÍM. *Espíritu de sal*, spirits of salt. || *Espíritu de vino*, spirit *o* spirits of wine. || *Espíritu maligno*, evil spirit. || REL. *Espíritu Santo*, Holy Ghost, Holy Spirit. || *Firmeza de espíritu*, firmness. || *Grandeza de espíritu*, noble heartedness. || *Levantar el espíritu*, to cheer up. || *Levantar el espíritu a alguien*, to raise s.o.'s spirits, to cheer s.o. up. || *Pobre de espíritu*, poor in spirit. || *Tener espíritu de contradicción*, to be contrary.
espiritual adj. Spiritual: *pasto, vida espiritual*, spiritual food, life. || Witty (ingenioso). || *Patria espiritual*, spiritual home.
espiritualidad f. Spirituality: *la espiritualidad del alma*, the spirituality of the soul. || Wittiness (ingenio).
espiritualismo m. Spiritualism.
espiritualista adj. Spiritualistic.
— M. y f. Spiritualist.
espiritualización f. Spiritualization.
espiritualizar v. tr. To spiritualize.
espiritualmente adv. Spiritually (con el espíritu). || Wittily (ingeniosamente).
espirituoso, sa adj. Witty, funny (ingenioso). || Spirituous (bebida).
espiroidal o **espiroideo, a** adj. Spiral, spiroid.
espirómetro m. MED. Spirometer.
espiroqueta f. ZOOL. Spirochaete [U.S., spirochete].
espita f. Faucet, spigot (de tonel). || FIG. y FAM. Drunkard, boozer (borracho).
esplender v. intr. To shine.
esplendidez f. Splendour [U.S., splendor], magnificence (magnificencia). || Beauty (belleza). || Generosity, lavishness (generosidad).
espléndido, da adj. Splendid, magnificent (magnífico). || Beautiful (bello). || Generous, lavish (generoso). || Resplendent (resplandeciente).
esplendor m. Splendour [U.S., splendor], magnificence: *el esplendor del día*, the splendour of the day. || Splendour, magnificence, lavishness: *el esplendor de la ceremonia*, the lavishness of the ceremony. || Grandeur, glory, splendour (apogeo, nobleza): *una época de esplendor*, an age of splendour. || Resplendence, shining (resplandor).
esplendorosamente adv. Resplendently (con resplandor). || Splendidly, magnificently, lavishly.
esplendoroso, sa adj. Resplendent (resplandeciente). || Splendid, magnificent, lavish (magnífico).
esplénico, ca adj. Splenic, splenetic.
esplenio m. ANAT. Splenius (músculo).
espliego m. BOT. Lavender.
esplín m. Melancholy, spleen (tedio).
espolada f. o **espolazo** m. Prod with a spur.
espoleadura f. Spur wound.
espolear v. tr. To spur (el caballo). || FIG. To spur on, to stimulate (estimular): *espolear a uno para que haga algo*, to spur s.o. on to do sth.
espoleo m. Spurring.
espoleta f. Fuse (de proyectil): *espoleta de percusión*, percussion fuse. || Wishbone (clavícula del ave). || *Quitar la espoleta de*, to defuse, to disarm.
espolio m. Effects, *pl.* [of a dead bishop].
espolique m. Footman.
espolón m. Spur (de ave). || Fetlock (de caballo). || Cutwater (de puente, de barco). || Spur (de montaña). || Levee (de río). || Sea wall (malecón). || Promenade (paseo a orillas del mar). || ARQ. Buttress (contrafuerte). || Ram (de barco antiguo). || FAM. Chilblain (sabañón). || MAR. *Embestir con el espolón*, to ram.
espolonazo m. Blow with the spur (de gallo). || Ramming (de barco).
espolvoreadora f. AGR. Sprayer.
espolvorear v. tr. To sprinkle (esparcir algo hecho polvo). || To dust (quitar el polvo de).
espondaico, ca adj. Spondaic.
espondeo m. Spondee.
espongiarios m. pl. ZOOL. Spongiae.
esponja f. Sponge: *esponja sintética, de platino*, synthetic, platinum sponge. || Towelling (tejido). || FIG. y FAM. Sponger (gorrón). || — FIG. y FAM. *Beber como una esponja*, to drink like a fish. | *Pasemos la esponja por eso*, let us say no more about it, let bygones be bygones. | *Ser una esponja*, to be a heavy drinker, to drink like a fish (beber mucho), to be able to hold *o* to take one's drink (aguantar). | *Tirar* or *arrojar la esponja*, to throw in the towel *o* the sponge.
esponjado, da adj. Spongy. || Fluffy (lana, pelo).
— M. Sugar bar (azucarillo).

esponjadura f. Fluffiness (de la lana). || Sponginess (esponjosidad).
esponjar v. tr. To make spongy. || To soften (la tierra). || To fluff up, to make fluffy (la lana).
— V. pr. To become spongy. || To become fluffy, to fluff up (la lana). || FIG. To become puffed up with pride, to assume a pompous air (engreírse). | To glow with health (rebosar de salud).
esponjera f. Sponge holder, sponge rack.
esponjosidad f. Sponginess. || Fluffiness (de la lana).
esponjoso, sa adj. Spongy.
esponsales m. pl. Engagement, *sing.*, betrothal, *sing.* (ant.) [desposorios]. || *Contraer esponsales*, to get engaged, to become betrothed (ant.).
espontanearse v. pr. To open up one's heart, to unbosom o.s. (franquearse).
espontaneidad f. Spontaneity.
espontáneo, a adj. Spontaneous: *generación, combustión espontánea*, spontaneous generation, combustion. || Spontaneous, unbidden: *ayuda espontánea*, spontaneous help. || Wild, spontaneous (plantas). || Spontaneous, natural: *es una persona muy espontánea*, he is a very natural person.
— M. TAUR. "Espontáneo" [spectator who tries to join in a bullfight].
espora f. BOT. y BIOL. Spore.
esporadicidad f. Sporadicalness.
esporádico, ca adj. Sporadic. || MED. Isolated.
esporangio m. BOT. Sporangium, spore case.
esporidio m. BOT. Sporidium.
esporozoario o **esporozoo** m. ZOOL. Sporozoan.

— OBSERV. El pl. de *sporozoan* es *sporozoa*.

esportada f. Basketful, frailful (cantidad que cabe en una espuerta). || FIG. y FAM. *A esportadas*, in abundance, by the ton.
esportear v. tr. To carry *o* to transport in frails *o* baskets.
esportilla f. Small basket, small frail.
esportillero m. Street porter.
esportillo m. Esparto basket.
esportón m. Large basket. || FIG. y FAM. *A esportones*, in abundance, by the ton.
esporulación f. BOT. Sporulation.
esposa f. Wife, spouse (ant.) [mujer]. || *Amer.* Episcopal ring. || — Pl. Handcuffs (de un preso): *poner las esposas a uno*, to put handcuffs on s.o.
esposado, da adj. Newly married (recién casado). || Handcuffed (un preso).
— M. y f. Newlywed.
esposar v. tr. To handcuff, to put handcuffs on.
esposo m. Husband, spouse (ant.). || *Los esposos*, the husband and wife, the couple.
esprint m. DEP. Sprint.
esprintar v. intr. To sprint.
esprinter m. y f. Sprinter.
espuela f. Spur (del jinete). || FIG. Spur, incentive, stimulus (estimulo). || *Amer.* Spur (del gallo). | — FIG. *Aguijoneado por la espuela del deseo*, spurred on by desire. | *Echar* or *tomar la espuela*, to have one for the road (tomar la última copa). | *El miedo pone espuelas*, fear gives wings to the feet. || *Picar (con las dos) espuelas, dar espuelas a*, to spur, to put the spurs to [a horse]. || FIG. *Poner espuelas*, to spur on (estimular).
espuerta f. [Two-handled] basket, frail. || FIG. y FAM. *Tener dinero a espuertas*, to have bags *o* loads *o* lots *o* tons of money.
espulgar v. tr. To delouse, to rid of fleas *o* lice (quitar las pulgas). | FIG. To examine closely, to scrutinize.
espulgo m. Delousing, ridding of lice *o* fleas (de pulgas). | FIG. Close examination, scrutiny (examen).
espuma f. Foam (en el mar). || Froth (en las bebidas). || Head (en un vaso de cerveza). || Lather (de jabón). || Scum (espuma acompañada de impurezas). || Foam (tejido). || FIG. y FAM. Cream (lo mejor). || MAR. Spray (en el aire). || — FIG. *Crecer como la espuma*, to shoot up, to grow like wildfire. || *Espuma de caucho*, foam rubber. || MIN. *Espuma de mar*, meerschaum. || *Hacer espuma*, to foam (las olas), to froth (las bebidas), to lather (el jabón).
espumadera f. Skimmer (para quitar la espuma). || Slice (paleta).
espumado m. Skimming.
espumador, ra m. y f. Skimmer.
espumajear o **espumajar** v. intr. To foam *o* to froth at the mouth. || FIG. *Espumajear de ira*, to foam with rage, to foam at the mouth.
espumajo m. V. ESPUMARAJO.
espumajoso, sa adj. Frothy, foamy.
espumante adj. Foaming, frothing. || Sparkling (vino).
espumar v. tr. To skim (quitar la espuma).
— V. intr. To foam (el mar). || To froth (la cerveza). || To lather (el jabón). || To sparkle (el vino).
espumarajo m. Scum (en el agua). | Foam, froth (arrojado por la boca). || FIG. y FAM. *Echar espumarajos por la boca*, to foam with rage, to foam at the mouth.
espumeante adj. V. ESPUMANTE.
espumosidad f. Foaminess, frothiness. || Sparkles, *pl.* (del champán, etc.).
espumoso, sa adj. Foamy, frothy: *una ola espumosa*, a foamy wave. || Sparkling (vino). || Lathery (jabón).
espúreo, a o **espurio, ria** adj. Illegitimate, bastard (bastardo): *hijo espúreo*, illegitimate child. || Spurious, false (falso). || Adulterated (adulterado).

— OBSERV. The form *espúreo* is a barbarism but is more common than the original form *espurio*.

espurrear o **espurriar** v. tr. To spray, to sprinkle (por la boca).
esputar v. tr. To spit, to expectorate.
esputo m. Spit, spittle (saliva). || MED. Sputum.
esqueje m. AGR. Cutting, slip.
esquela f. Note, short letter (carta breve). || Invitation (para invitar). || Notice, announcement (para avisar). || — *Esquela amorosa*, love letter. || *Esquela mortuoria* or *de defunción*, obituary notice.
esquelético, ca adj. Skeletal, of the skeleton (del esqueleto). || FIG. Very thin, bony, like a skeleton.
esqueleto m. ANAT. Skeleton. || FIG. Outline, sketch, skeleton (de una novela, discurso, etc.). | Framework (armazón). || *Amer.* Preliminary plan. | Form (formulario). || FIG. y FAM. *Estar hecho un esqueleto*, to be like a skeleton.
esquema m. Outline, sketch (bosquejo). || Diagram (diagrama). || Outline, plan, sketch (de un proyecto, un discurso, etc.). || REL. y FIL. Schema.
esquemático, ca adj. Schematic, diagrammatic.
esquematización f. Schematization.
esquematizar v. tr. To schematize. || To outline, to sketch (esbozar).
esquí m. Ski: *un esquí metálico*, a metal ski. || Skiing (deporte): *esquí náutico* or *acuático*, water-skiing.

— OBSERV. Pl. *esquíes* o *esquís*.

esquiador, ra m. y f. Skier.
esquiar v. intr. To ski.
esquife m. Skiff (barco).
esquila f. Bell, cowbell (cencerro). || Handbell, small bell (campanilla). || Shearing, clipping, sheepshearing (esquileo). | BOT. Squill (cebolla albarrana). || ZOOL. Squill, squilla, mantis prawn (camarón).
esquilador, ra m. y f. Sheepshearer (persona). || — F. Sheepshearer (tijeras).
esquilar v. tr. To shear, to clip.
esquileo Shearing, clipping, sheepshearing (acción). || Shearing time (época).
esquilmar v. tr. AGR. To harvest (cosechar). | To exhaust (el suelo). | FIG. To impoverish (empobrecer). || FIG. y FAM. To fleece (despojar).
Esquilo n. pr. m. Aeschylus.
esquilón m. Large bell. | Large cowbell.
esquimal adj./s. Eskimo.
esquina f. Corner: *doblar la esquina*, to turn the corner; *calle Velázquez, esquina Goya*, on the corner of the "calle Velázquez" and the "calle Goya". || — FIG. *A la vuelta de la esquina*, just round the corner (muy cerca). | *Encontrarse a la vuelta de la esquina*, to be two a penny [U.S., to be a dime a dozen]. || *Hacer esquina*, to be on the corner, to be on a corner (un edificio), to join, to meet (dos calles). || ***Las cuatro esquinas*, puss in the corner (juego).**

— OBSERV. The word *esquina* is used to indicate a projecting corner such as between two streets. *Rincón* is the word for a recessed corner such as in a room.

esquinado, da adj. Angular (anguloso). | On the corner, on a corner (que forma esquina). || FIG. Bad-tempered, prickly, difficult to get on with (persona), prickly, unpleasant (carácter).
esquinar v. tr. To put in the *o* in a corner (poner en la esquina). | To form a corner with (formar esquina). || FIG. To set against, to estrange (enemistar): *esquinar a dos personas*, to set two people against each other. || TECN. To square (un madero).
— V. intr. To be on the corner (*con*, of) [estar en la esquina]. | To form a corner, to join, to meet (formar esquina).
— V. pr. To sulk (enfurruñarse), to fall out (enfadarse).
esquinazo m. FAM. Corner. || *Amer.* Serenade. || — FAM. *Dar esquinazo a alguien*, to stand s.o. up (no acudir a una cita), to walk out on s.o. (dejar plantado), to shake s.o. off, to give s.o. the slip (deshacerse de alguien).
Esquines n. pr. m. Aeshines.
esquinzar v. tr. TECN. To cut (trapos).
esquirla f. Splinter (astilla).
esquirol m. FAM. Blackleg, scab, strikebreaker.
esquisto m. MIN. Schist. || — *Aceite de esquisto*, shale oil. || *Esquisto bituminoso*, bituminous shale.
esquistoso, sa adj. MIN. Schistose.
esquivar v. tr. To avoid, to evade (evitar). || To dodge, to avoid: *esquivar un golpe*, to dodge a blow.
— V. pr. To make o.s. scarce (irse). || To dodge (de un golpe). || To back out (para no cumplir algo).
esquivez f. Aloofness, coldness, disdain (frialdad). || Shyness, bashfulness (timidez). || Unsociability (falta de sociabilidad).
esquivo, va adj. Aloof, cold, disdainful (desdeñoso). || Shy, bashful (huraño). || Unsociable (carácter).
esquizofrenia f. MED. Schizophrenia.
esquizofrénico, ca adj./s. MED. Schizophrenic.
esquizoide adj./s. MED. Schizoid.
esta, ésta adj./pron. V. ESTE, ÉSTE.

estabilidad f. Stability. || Balance, equilibrium: *recuperó su estabilidad*, he regained his balance.
estabilización f. Stabilization. || Balancing (equilibrio). || AVIAC. *Planos de estabilización*, stabilizers.
estabilizador, ra adj. Stabilizing.
— M. Stabilizer. || AVIAC. *Estabilizador giroscópico*, gyrostabilizer.
estabilizar v. tr. To stabilize (barco, avión, precios).
— V. pr. To become stable, to become stabilized.
estable adj. Stable: *un edificio, una situación estable*, a stable building, situation. || Balanced (equilibrado).
establecedor, ra adj. Establishing, founding.
— M. y f. Founder (fundador). || Creator (creador).
establecer* v. tr. To establish, to set up, to found (una monarquía, una sucursal, una universidad, una fundación). || To settle (colonos). || To take up, to establish (el domicilio). || To take (un censo). || To make (investigaciones). || To establish (la verdad, una relación, un precedente). || To prepare, to draw up (planos). || To set up (un récord). || To lay down (una regla). || *Establecer un campamento*, to pitch camp, to set up camp.
— V. pr. To settle down, to set up (instalarse): *se ha establecido en Roma*, he has settled down in Rome. || To set [o.s.] up, to set up on one's own: *se ha establecido de abogado*, he has set himself up as a lawyer. || To set up [in business] on one's own: *estaba antes de dependiente en una tienda pero ahora se ha establecido*, he was a shop assistant before, but now he has set up on his own.
establecido, da adj. Established. || Customary (habitual). || — *Conforme a lo establecido en el artículo 43*, according to the provisions of article 43. || *Dejar establecido*, to establish.
establecimiento m. Establishment, setting up, foundation (de una sucursal, monarquía, etc.). || Establishment (de la verdad, de una relación). || Preparation, drawing up (de planos, etc.). || Establishment (local): *establecimiento comercial*, commercial establishment. || Settlement (colonia).
establo m. Cowshed, stall. || MIT. *Establos de Augias*, Augean stables.
estabulación f. Stabling.
estabular v. tr. To stable.
estaca f. Stake, post (que se clava en el suelo). || Stick, cudgel (para apalear). || AGR. Cutting (rama). || TECN. Spike (clavo de hierro). || *Amer.* Mineral concession. | Spur (espolón).
estacada f. Palisade, fence, picket fence (valla). || Palisade, stockade (fortificación). || MAR. Breakwater, pier. || — FIG. y FAM. *Dejar a uno en la estacada*, to leave s.o. in the lurch. | *Quedarse en la estacada*, to be left dead on the field (morir), to be beaten (ser vencido), to be floored (en una disputa), to be left in the lurch (en una situación apurada), to fail miserably (fracasar).
estacado m. Duelling ground.
estacar v. tr. To stake out (señalar los límites). || To fence with stakes (vallar). || MIL. To stockade, to palisade. || To picket, to stake (un animal). || *Amer.* To stake out on the ground (pieles).
— V. pr. FIG. To freeze to the spot (quedarse inmóvil). || *Amer.* To get a splinter (clavarse una astilla). | To balk (un caballo).
estacazo m. Blow with a stick *o* a stake. || FIG. Blow.
estación f. Season (del año): *las cuatro estaciones*, the four seasons. || Season (temporada): *la estación de las lluvias*, the rainy season. || Station (de ferrocarril, de metro). || [Research] station: *una estación agronómica*, an agricultural research station. || Station: *estación de radio, repetidora*, radio, relay station. || REL. Station: *estaciones del Vía Crucis*, stations of the Cross. || Time (época): *en la estación actual*, at the present time. || Resort: *estación veraniega*, summer resort. || Position (estado): *estación vertical*, vertical position. || — *Estación balnearia*, spa, watering place (medicinal), seaside resort (en el mar). || *Estación clarificadora*, filter plant *o* station. || *Estación de apartado* or *de clasificación*, marshalling yard. || *Estación de empalme*, junction. || *Estación de mercancías*, goods station. || *Estación depuradora*, purifying plant. || *Estación de seguimiento*, tracking station (espacial). || *Estación de servicio*, service station. || RAD. *Estación emisora*, broadcasting station, transmitter. || *Estación espacial*, space station. || *Estación meteorológica*, weather station.
estacional adj. Seasonal. || ASTR. Stationary.
estacionamiento m. Parking (acción de aparcar): *prohibido el estacionamiento*, no parking. || Parking place *o* space (lugar). || Stationing (de tropas).
estacionar v. tr. To station. || To park (un coche).
— V. pr. To remain stationary (permanecer estacionario). || To come to a standstill (dejar de progresar). || To park (coche). || To loiter (personas).
estacionario, ria adj. Stationary (inmóvil). || COM. Slack. || *Mar estacionario*, slack sea.
estada f. Stay (estancia).
estadía f. Stay (estancia). || Sitting (ante un pintor, etc.). || Stadia [rod] (topografía). || MAR. Lay day (plazo). | Demurrage (indemnización).
estadio m. Stadium: *estadio olímpico*, olympic stadium. || Stadium, (*pl.* stadia) [medida antigua]. || Stage, phase (período).
estadista m. Statesman (hombre de Estado). || Statistician (estadístico). || FAM. *Los estadistas de café*, armchair politicians.
estadística f. Statistics (ciencia). || Statistic (dato).
estadístico, ca adj. Statistical: *estudio estadístico*, statistical survey.
— M. y f. Statistician.
estado m. State, condition (condición): *estado físico*, physical condition. || State: *estado sólido*, solid state. || Order, condition: *una bicicleta en buen, en mal estado*, a bicycle in good, in bad condition; *en estado de funcionamiento*, in working order. || State (gobierno, nación): *secretos de Estado*, State secrets; *razón de Estado*, reason of State. || Status: *estado civil*, marital *o* civil status. || HIST. Estate (clase en la Europa medieval). || Statement: *estado de cuenta*, statement of account. || — Pl. Lands, states (de un señor). || — *Estado de alma* or *de ánimo*, state of mind, mood. || *Estado de cosas*, state of affairs. || *Estado de emergencia* or *de excepción, de sitio*, state of emergency, state of siege. || REL. *Estado de gracia*, state of grace. || *Estado de la nieve*, snow report. || *Estado de soltero*, celibacy, bachelorhood. || *Estado de viuda, de viudo*, widowhood, widowerhood. || *Estado llano* or *común*, third estate, commons. || MIL. *Estado mayor*, staff. || *Estar en estado de merecer*, to be eligible *o* marriageable. || *Estar en estado (interesante)*, to be expecting *o* pregnant. || *Hombre de Estado*, Statesman. || (Ant.). *Ministerio de Estado*, Foreign Office (en Gran Bretaña), State Department (en Estados Unidos). || *Tomar estado*, to marry (casarse), to take holy orders (entrar en religión).
Estados Unidos n. pr. m. pl. GEOGR. United States, *sing.*

— OBSERV. The abbreviation for *Estados Unidos* is EE. UU. or E.U.

estadounidense adj. American, United States.
— M. y f. American, United States citizen.
estafa f. Swindle. || Racket (fraude organizado).
estafador, ra m. y f. Swindler. || Racketeer.
estafar v. tr. To swindle, to cheat: *estafar dinero a alguien*, to swindle s.o. out of money.
estafermo m. HIST. Quintain (muñeco). || FAM. Simpleton, dumbbell (necio).
estafeta f. Courier (correo). || Sub-post office [U.S., branch post office] (de correos). || Diplomatic bag (correo diplomático). || *Estafeta móvil*, mobile post office.
estafilococo m. MED. Staphylococcus.
estagnación f. *Amer.* V. ESTANCAMIENTO.
estalactita f. Stalactite.
estalagmita f. Stalagmite.
estallar v. intr. To explode, to blow up: *la mina, el avión estalló*, the mine, the plane blew up. || To burst (un neumático). || To shatter (el cristal). || To crack (el látigo). || To break (una ola). | To crash (el trueno). | FIG. To break (un escándalo). | To break out (la guerra, una revolución, una epidemia, un incendio). | To split (un vestido). | To blow up [with rage], to fly off the handle: *estas palabras le hicieron estallar*, these words made him blow up. || — FIG. *Estallar de alegría, de risa, en aplausos*, to leap with joy, to burst out laughing, to burst into applause. | *Estallar en llanto*, to burst into tears. || *Hacer estallar*, to explode (una mina), to burst (un neumático), to shatter (un cristal), to split (un vestido), to spark off, to trigger off (una rebelión).
estallido m. Explosion (de una bomba, un polvorín, etc.). || Bursting (de neumático). || Crack (de látigo). || Clap (de trueno). || Splitting (de madera, etc.). || Shattering (del cristal). || Outbreak (de la guerra, revolución, etc.). || Outburst, burst (de ira, de risa, de alegría, de aplausos). || *Dar un estallido*, to burst (neumático).
estambre m. Long-fibred wool (mechón). || Worsted yarn (hilo). || Worsted (tela). || Warp (urdimbre). || BOT. Stamen.
Estambul n. pr. GEOGR. Istanbul.
estamento m. Each of the four estates in the "Cortes" of Aragon. || Either of the two legislative bodies in nineteenth-century Spain. || Class, stratum (clase). || State (estado).
estameña f. Serge, worsted, estamene (tela).
estaminífero, ra adj. BOT. Staminiferous, staminate.
estampa f. IMPR. Print (imagen). | Plate (en un libro). | Lithograph (litografía). | Engraving (grabado). | Printing (imprenta). || Picture: *a los niños les gustan los libros con estampas*, children like books with pictures in. || FIG. Look, appearance: *tiene estampa de malvado*, he has the look of a villain. | Hallmark, mark: *la estampa del genio*, the hallmark of genius. | Image: *es la viva estampa de su padre*, he is the very image of his father. || — *Dar a la estampa*, to print (imprimir), to publish (publicar). || FIG. y FAM. *¡Maldita sea su estampa!*, damn him!, blast him! | *Romper la estampa a uno*, to do s.o. in. || *Sección de estampas*, print room (de una biblioteca). || FAM. *Tener estampa de*, to look [like]: *tiene estampa de torero*, he looks a bullfighter. | *Una persona de buena, mala estampa*, a decent-looking, shady-looking person. | *Un toro de buena, mala estampa*, a fine-looking, poor-looking bull.

estampación f. Stamping. || Printing (impresión). || Engraving (grabado). || Embossing (del cuero, etc.). || Corrugating (del papel). || Punching *o* stamping out (recortado). || Tooling (de la encuadernación).
estampado adj. Stamped. || Printed (impreso). || Engraved (grabado). || Embossed (cuero). || Corrugated (papel). || Stamped *o* punched out (recortado). || Printed: *tela estampada*, printed material. || Print, printed (traje). || Tooled (encuadernación).
— M. V. ESTAMPACIÓN. || Cotton print (tela).
estampador m. Stamper. || Embosser (de cuero).
estampar v. tr. To stamp (sacar relieve). || To emboss (el cuero). || To stamp out, to punch out (recortar): *estampar arandelas*, to punch out washers. || To print (imprimir): *estampar grabados, el tejido*, to print engravings, cloth. || To tool (la encuadernación). || To engrave (grabar). || To stamp: *estampar el pie en la arena*, to stamp one's foot in the sand. || FIG. To imprint, to stamp (inculcar). || FIG. y FAM. To fling, to hurl: *estampó la botella contra la pared*, he hurled the bottle against the wall. | To deal, to give (una bofetada). | To plant (un beso).
estampía (de) loc. adv. *Entrar de estampía*, to burst *o* to rush in. || *Salir de estampía*, to go *o* to be off like a shot *o* like a rocket.
estampida f. Explosion, bang (estampido). || *Amer.* Stampede.
estampido m. Explosion, bang. || *Dar un estampido*, to bang.
estampilla f. Rubber stamp (sello de goma). || Seal (precinto). || *Amer.* Stamp (sello de correos). | Revenue stamp (sello fiscal).
estampillado m. Rubber-stamping (con sello de goma). || Sealing (con precinto).
estampillar v. tr. To rubber-stamp (con sello de goma). || To seal (con precinto).
estampita f. Print.
estancación f. o **estancamiento** m. Checking of the flow (de la sangre). || Damming [up] (embalse). || Stagnation, stagnancy (del agua). || FIG. Stagnation (de un asunto). | Standstill (de negociaciones). || State monopolization, State monopoly (de mercancías).
estancado, da adj. Stagnant (agua). || FIG. Bogged down, stagnant (asunto). | At a standstill, bogged down (negociaciones).
estancar v. tr. To check *o* to stem *o* to stop the flow of (la sangre). || To dam [up]: *estancar un río*, to dam up a river. || To turn into a State monopoly (monopolizar). || FIG. To block, to delay, to hold up: *estancar una transacción*, to hold up a deal. | To bring to a standstill (negociaciones).
— V. pr. To stagnate, to become stagnant (líquidos). || FIG. To stagnate, to get bogged down, to make no headway (un asunto, un negocio). | To come to a standstill, to get bogged down (negociaciones).
estancia f. Stay: *después de diez días de estancia en Madrid, se marchó*, after ten days' stay *o* after a ten-day stay in Madrid, he left. || Day [spent in a hospital]. || Abode, dwelling (morada). || Room (habitación). || POÉT. Stanza. || *Amer.* "Estancia", farm, ranch (hacienda).
estanciero m. *Amer.* Farmer, rancher.
estanco, ca adj. Watertight: *compartimientos estancos*, watertight compartments.
— M. State tobacco shop, tobacconist's [U.S., cigar store] (tienda donde se venden tabaco y sellos). || State monopoly: *el estanco del tabaco*, the State tobacco monopoly. || (Ant.). Archives, *pl.*
estandard o **estándar** m. V. STANDARD.
estandardización o **estandarización** f. V. STANDARDIZACIÓN.
estandardizar o **estandarizar** v. tr. V. STANDARDIZAR.
estandarte m. Standard, banner.
estannato m. QUÍM. Stannate.
estánnico, ca adj. QUÍM. Stannic (de estaño).
estannífero, ra adj. Stanniferous, tin-bearing.
estanque m. [Ornamental] lake (en jardines). || Reservoir (para el riego). || Pond, pool (pequeño).
estanqueidad f. Watertightness.
estanquero, ra o **estanquillero, ra** m. y f. Tobacconist.
estanquidad f. Watertightness.
estante m. Shelf [pl. *shelves*] (anaquel). || Bookcase (para libros). || Stand (soporte para máquina, etc.). || *Amer.* Stay, prop (puntal).
estantería f. Shelving, shelves, *pl.* (anaquel). || Bookcase (para libros).
estantigua f. Ghost, phantom (fantasma). || FIG. y FAM. Scarecrow (persona desgarbada y mal vestida).
estañado m. Tin-plating (acción y efecto de estañar). || Soldering (acción y efecto de soldar).
estañador m. Tinsmith.
estañadura f. Tin-plating (acción y efecto de estañar). || Soldering (acción y efecto de soldar).
estañar v. tr. To tin, to tin-plate. || To solder (soldar).
estañero m. Tinsmith.
estaño m. Tin (metal). || ARTES. Pewter.
estañoso, sa adj. QUÍM. Stannous.
estaqueada f. *Amer.* Beating, thrashing (paliza).
estaquear v. tr. *Amer.* To stake out on the ground.
estaquilla f. Peg, pin (de madera). || Brad (de metal). || Spike (clavo largo).

estar* v. intr.

> **1.** Posición espacial o temporal. — **2.** Estado transitorio. — **3.** Pasivo. — **4.** Forma reflexiva. — **5.** Con gerundio. — **6.** Seguido de una preposición. — **7.** Locuciones diversas.

1. POSICIÓN ESPACIAL O TEMPORAL. — To be: *está en Sevilla, en casa*, he is in Seville, at home; *la señora de la casa, el libro no está*, the landlady is not in *o* at home, the book is not here; *si no estoy*, if I'm not there (sin indicación del lugar hay que añadir un adverbio); *estamos en verano*, it is summer. || To be, to stay: *estuve seis días en Córdoba*, I was *o* stayed in Cordoba for six days.
2. ESTADO TRANSITORIO. — To be: *el suelo está húmedo*, the ground is damp; *mi tío está enfermo*, my uncle is ill; *¿cómo estás?*, how are you?; *estar bien, malo, mejor*, to be well, ill, better (de salud). || To look: *estás muy favorecida hoy*, you look very nice today.
3. PASIVO. — To be [describing the state resulting from an action]: *la puerta está cerrada*, the door is closed; *estos libros están bien impresos*, these books are well printed.
4. FORMA REFLEXIVA. — To remain, to stay: *os podéis estar con nosotros unos días*, you can stay with us a few days; *ahí se estuvo hasta la vuelta de su hermana*, there he remained until his sister came back. || To keep: *¡estaos quietos!*, keep still!
5. CON GERUNDIO. — To be: *está escribiendo una novela*, he is writing a novel; *estaba muriéndose* or *se estaba muriendo*, he was dying. || *Le estuve esperando dos horas*, I waited for him two hours, I spent two hours waiting for him.
6. SEGUIDO DE UNA PREPOSICIÓN. — *Estar a.* — To be, to cost: *las patatas están a cinco pesetas*, potatoes are five pesetas. || — *¿A cuánto* or *cuántos estamos?*, what is the date? || *Estamos a 22 (ventidós) de febrero*, it is 22nd [the twenty-second of] February.
Estar de. — To be (más gerundio): *estar de paso, de caza, de mudanza, de vacaciones*, to be passing through, hunting, moving house, on holiday. || To be: *estar de buen humor*, to be in a good mood. || To be[working as]: *está de camarero en un hotel*, he is working as a waiter in a hotel. || To be [dressed] in: *estar de uniforme, de paisano, de etiqueta*, to be in uniform, in civilian clothes, in formal dress. || *Estar de rodillas*, to be on one's knees.
Estar en. — To understand (entender): *estoy en lo que usted dice*, I understand what you say. || To know (saber, estar enterado de): *tú no estás en nada*, you don't know anything. || To think, to believe (creer): *estoy en que vendrá Juanita*, I think Jean will come. || To intend to (tener la intención de hacer algo): *está en venir cuanto antes*, he intends to come as soon as possible. || To agree to (estar conforme con). || To be up to (depender de): *está en ti hacerlo*, it is up to you to do it. || To stand at: *el récord está en 10 segundos*, the record stands at 10 seconds. || — *El problema está en la fecha*, the problem lies in the date. || *Todo está en que él pueda venir para entonces*, everything depends on *o* hangs on whether he can make it then.
Estar para. — To be about to: *el Presidente está para llegar de un momento a otro*, the President is about to arrive any minute. || To be in the mood for, to feel like: *no estoy para frivolidades*, I am in no mood for frivolities. || To be in a state *o* condition for: *no estoy para emprender largos viajes*, I am in no state for making long journeys. || *Estamos para servirles*, we are at your service, we are here to serve you.
Estar por. — To remain to be, to have yet to be: *la historia de esa época está por escribir*, the history of that period remains to be written *o* has yet to be written; *eso está por ver*, that remains to be seen. || To be about to (estar a punto de). || To be tempted to (estar tentado de hacer algo): *estoy por venir contigo*, I'm tempted to come with you. || To be in favour of, to favour, to be for: *todos están por él*, everyone is for him; *yo estoy por hacerlo así*, I'm in favour of doing it like this.
Estar sin. — To be without. || *La casa está sin vender*, the house is unsold *o* has not been sold.
7. LOCUCIONES DIVERSAS. — *Aquí estoy y aquí me quedo*, here I am and here I'll stay. || FIG. *Como estamos aquí tú y yo*, as sure as I'm standing here. || *Déjame estar*, let me be, leave me alone. || *Está bien*, it's all right (bien hecho), all right (de acuerdo). || FAM. *Está hasta en la sopa*, v. SOPA. || *¿Estamos?*, right? (comprender), right?, ready? (estar listo). || *Estamos todavía a tiempo de*, we are still in time to. || *Estar (a) bien, (a) mal con uno*, to be on good, on bad terms with s.o. || *Estar a la que salga*, to be always ready to seize an opportunity. || *Estar al caer*, to be about to strike: *están al caer las diez*, ten is about to strike; to be imminent: *la guerra está al caer*, war is imminent. || *Estar al corriente* or *al tanto de*, v. CORRIENTE y TANTO. || *Estar a matar*, to be at loggerheads *o* at daggers drawn. || *Estar a oscuras*, to be in the dark (sin luz o no enterado). || *Estar a pan y agua*, to be on bread and water. || *Estar a punto*

de or *a pique de*, to be about to, to be on the point of. || *Estar bueno*, to be edible *o* eatable *o* all right (comestible), to be nice *o* tasty (sabroso), to be well (de salud). || *Estar con gripe*, to have flu. || Fig. *Estar con uno*, to be [in agreement] with s.o. (estar de acuerdo). || *Estar de más* or *de sobra*, to be unnecessary *o* superfluous (superfluo), to be unwanted *o* in the way (importuno). || *Estar en todo*, to look after everything, to keep an eye on everything (ocuparse), to think of everything (pensar), to have a finger in every pie (meterse). || *Estar fuera*, v. fuera. || *Estar fuera de sí* (*de ira*, etc.), to be beside o.s. [with rage, etc.] (estar muy enojado). || *Estar hecho*, to be, to have turned into, to have become: *el caballo está hecho una ruina*, the horse is a wreck. || *Estarle* [followed by an adjective] *a uno* (una prenda de vestir), to be too (más adjetivo) for s.o.: *este sombrero me está ancho*, this hat is too big for me. || *Estarle bien a uno*, to suit (ropa). || *Estar para todo*, to take care of *o* to look after everything. || *Estar siempre sobre uno*, to be always hovering over s.o. (vigilar). || Fam. *Estoy que me subo por las paredes*, I'm going up the wall. || *Estoy que no puedo ni moverme*, I'm in such a state I can't even move. || *Si estuviese en tu lugar*, if I were you, if I were in your place *o* in your shoes. || *Ya está*, that's it. || *¡Ya está bien!*, that'll do!, that's enough! (¡basta!). || *Ya que estamos*, while we're here, while we're at it.

estarcido m. Stencil (dibujo).
estarcir v. tr. To stencil.
estasis f. Med. Stasis.
estatal adj. State.
estático, ca adj. Static. || Fig. Dumbfounded (pasmado).
— F. Tecn. Statics.
estatificar v. tr. To nationalize (nacionalizar).
estatismo m. Statism, State control. || Immobility.
estator m. Tecn. Stator.
estatorreactor m. Aviac. Ramjet.
estatoscopio m. Fís. Statoscope.
estatua f. Statue: *estatua yacente, ecuestre*, recumbent, equestrian statue. || Fig. *Quedarse hecho una estatua*, to be dumbfounded (pasmado) *o* transfixed (con admiración) *o* petrified (con miedo).
estatuario, ria adj. Statuary: *arte, mármol estatuario*, statuary art, marble. || Taur. *Pase estatuario*, statuesque pass [made without moving the body].
— M. Statuary, sculptor. || — F. Statuary (arte).
estatuilla f. Statuette.
estatuir* v. tr. To enact, to decree. || To provide (disponer). || To establish (establecer).
estatura f. Stature, height (de una persona).
estatutario, ria adj. Statutory.
estatuto m. Statute. || *Estatuto formal*, protocol.
estay m. Mar. Stay. || *Estay mayor*, mainstay.
este m. East. || East wind, easterly (viento). || — *Del este*, eastern: *las provincias del este*, the eastern provinces; east: *Alemania del Este*, East Germany; east, easterly: *viento del este*, easterly wind. || Mar. *Este cuarta al nordeste, al sudeste*, east by north, by south.
— Adj. East: *el ala este de la casa*, the east wing of the house. || Easterly: *rumbo este*, easterly direction. || Easterly, east (wind).
este, esta (pl. **estos, estas**) adj. dem. m. y f. This [pl. these]: *no conozco a esta mujer*, I am not acquainted with this woman.
éste, ésta (pl. **éstos, éstas**) pron. dem. m. y f. This, this one [pl. these, these ones]: *me gusta más esa casa que ésta*, I prefer that house to this one. || He, she, [pl. they] (v. ése [Observ.]): *nadie me lo dijo, aunque ésta lo sabía*, nobody told me, although she knew. || Him, her [pl. them] (v. ése [Observ.]): *se lo he dado a éste*, I've given it to him. || The latter: *Juan y Carlos estaban sentados; éste se levantó y aquél se quedó*, John and Charles were seated; the latter got up and the former remained seated. || *Ésta*, the place in which a document or letter is signed: *hecho en ésta* (Madrid) *a 10 de octubre*, Madrid, 10th October. || Fam. *Ésta y nunca* or *no más*, never again (nunca más), this is the very last time (por última vez).

— Observ. The written accent may be omitted where no confusion with the adjectives *este, esta*, etc. is possible.

estearato m. Quím. Stearate.
esteárico, ca adj. Quím. Stearic.
estearina f. Stearin. || *Amer.* Candle.
esteatita f. Min. Steatite, soapstone.
esteba f. Mar. Steeve (pértiga para apretar la carga).
estela f. Wake (de un barco). || Trail (de un avión, un cohete). || Trail (de una estrella fugaz). || Stele (monumento). || Fig. Wake: *dejar una estela de descontento*, to leave a wake of discontent. || Bot. Stele. || *Estela de condensación*, contrail, vapour trail.
estelar adj. Astr. Stellar. || Fig. Star: *combate estelar*, star bout (boxeo).
estelión m. Zool. Gecko (salamanquesa). || Toadstone (piedra fabulosa).
estelionato m. Stellionate, fraud in real estate deals.
estenio m. Sthene (unidad de fuerza).
estenocardia f. Med. Stenocardia, angina pectoris.
estenografía f. Stenography, shorthand.
estenografiar v. tr. To take down in shorthand, to write in shorthand, to stenograph.
estenográfico, ca adj. Stenographic, stenographical, in shorthand (escritura).
estenógrafo, fa m. y f. Stenographer, shorthand writer.

— Observ. *Taquígrafo, taquígrafa* are more common.

estenordeste m. East-northeast.
estenotipia f. Stenotypy (arte). || Stenotype (máquina).
estenotipista m. y f. Stenotypist.
estenotipo m. Stenotype.
estentóreo, a adj. Stentorian: *voz estentórea*, stentorian voice.
estepa f. Steppe (llanura). || Bot. Rockrose (jara).
estepario, ria adj. Steppe.
éster m. Quím. Ester.
estera f. Matting (tejido): *estera de juncos*, rush matting. || Mat (alfombra). || Doormat (felpudo). || *Darle a uno más palos que a una estera*, to give s.o. a good beating *o* thrashing.
esterar v. tr. To cover with mats *o* matting.
estercoladura f. o **estercolamiento** m. Agr. Manuring.
estercolar v. tr. To manure (la tierra).
— V. intr. To dung (los animales).
estercolero m. Dunghill, manure heap. || Fig. Pigsty (sitio muy sucio).
estéreo m. Stere, cubic metre (medida para madera).
— Adj. Stereo: *un disco estéreo*, a stereo record.
estereóbato m. Arq. Stereobate.
estereofonía f. Stereophony, stereo.
estereofónico, ca adj. Stereophonic, stereo.
estereografía f. Stereography.
estereograma m. Stereogram, stereograph.
estereometría f. Stereometry.
estereómetro m. Stereometer.
estereoquímica f. Stereochemistry.
estereoscopia f. Stereoscopy.
estereoscópico, ca adj. Stereoscopic, stereoscopical.
estereoscopio m. Stereoscope.
estereotipado m. Stereotyping.
estereotipado, da adj. Stereotyped. || Fig. Stereotyped: *sonrisa, actitud estereotipada*, stereotyped smile, attitude. | Hackneyed, stereotyped: *expresión estereotipada*, hackneyed phrase.
estereotipar v. tr. To stereotype.
estereotipia f. Stereotypy (proceso). || Stereotype (máquina). || Med. Stereotypy (repetición).
estereotipo m. Stereotype.
estereotomía f. Stereotomy.
estereríа f. Mat shop (tienda). || Mat workshop (taller).
esterero m. Mat layer (colocador). || Mat maker (fabricante). || Mat dealer (comerciante).
esterificación f. Quím. Esterification.
esterificar v. tr. Quím. To esterify.
estéril adj. Sterile, barren, infertile (terreno). || Sterile, infertile (mujer). || Sterile (hombre). || Barren (animal). || Sterile (aséptico). || Fig. Futile, unfruitful, fruitless: *conversaciones estériles*, futile talks.
esterilidad f. Sterility, barrenness, infertility (de un terreno). || Sterility, infertility (de una mujer). || Sterility (de un hombre). || Barrenness (de un animal). || Sterility (asepsia). || Fig. Futility, unfruitfulness, fruitlessness.
esterilización f. Sterilization.
esterilizador, ra adj. Sterilizing.
— M. Sterilizer (aparato).
esterilizar v. tr. To sterilize.
esterilla f. Small mat (alfombrilla). || Rush matting (de juncos). || Gold *o* silver braid (trencilla). || *Esterilla de baño*, bath mat.
esterlina adj. f. Sterling: *libra esterlina*, pound sterling.
esternón m. Anat. Sternum, breastbone.
estero m. Mat laying (colocación de esteras). || Estuary (de un río). || *Amer.* Bog, swamp (pantano).
esterol m. Quím. Sterol.
estertor m. Death rattle (al morir). || Med. Stertor. || *Estar en los últimos estertores*, to be at the point of death, to be in the article of death.
estertoroso, sa adj. Med. Stertorous.
estesudeste m. East-southeast.
esteta m. y f. Aesthete.
esteticismo m. Aestheticism.
estético, ca adj. Aesthetic, esthetic: *desde el punto de vista estético*, from the aesthetic point of view. || Artistic, beautiful (bello). || *Cirugía estética*, cosmetic *o* plastic surgery.
— M. Aesthetician. || — F. Aesthetics.
estetoscopia f. Med. Stethoscopy.
estetoscopio m. Med. Stethoscope.
esteva f. Plough handle [U.S., plow handle].
estevado, da adj. Bowlegged, bandy-legged.
— M. y f. Bowlegged person.
estiaje m. Low water (de un río).
estiba f. Mar. Stowing, stowage (colocación de la carga). | Trimming (distribución de los pesos). || Place for packing wool in bags.
estibador m. Mar. Stevedore.
estibar v. tr. To pack tight, to compress (apretar). || Mar. To stow (colocar la carga). | To trim (equilibrar la carga).

estiércol m. Dung, manure. || *Jugo de estiércol*, liquid manure.
estigio, gia adj. Stygian. || MIT. *Laguna Estigia*, Styx.
estigma m. BOT., ZOOL. y MED. Stigma. || FIG. Stigma, disgrace: *el estigma de la quiebra*, the stigma attached to bankruptcy. | Stigma, brand (señal). || — Pl. REL. Stigmata (en el cuerpo de algunos santos).
estigmatismo m. Stigmatism (óptica).
estigmatización f. Branding (de un animal, un esclavo, etc.). || FIG. Branding, stigmatization. || REL. Stigmatization, marking with stigmata.
estigmatizar v. tr. To brand (con hierro candente). || FIG. To brand, to stigmatize. || REL. To stigmatize, to mark with stigmata.
estilar v. tr. JUR. To draw up [in due form] (un documento). || To be in the habit of (acostumbrar).
— V. intr. y pr. To be used, to be in use (emplearse): *esta palabra no se estila aquí*, this word is not used here. || To be in fashion *o* fashionable, to be worn (estar de moda): *los botines ya no se estilan*, spats are no longer fashionable. || To be normal *o* customary *o* usual (ser corriente): *no se estila llevar sombrero de paja en invierno*, it is not customary to wear a straw hat in winter. || To be the done thing: *son costumbres sociales que ya no se estilan*, these social customs are no longer the done thing.
estilete m. Style (para escribir, de un aparato grabador). || Stiletto (puñal). || MED. Stylet, probe.
estilismo m. Stylism (en el arte, la literatura).
estilista m. y f. Stylist (escritor). || Stylist, designer: *estilista de coches*, car designer.
estilístico, ca adj. Stylistic.
— F. Stylistics.
estilización f. Stylizing, stylization.
estilizado, da adj. Stylized. || Streamlined (aerodinámico). || Slender (esbelto).
estilizar v. tr. To stylize.
estilo m. Style, stylus (para escribir). || Style (en arte, literatura). || Style, manner (manera). || Style, fashion (moda): *es el último estilo*, it's the latest style. || FIG. Style: *tiene mucho estilo*, he has a lot of style. || BOT. Style. || DEP. Stroke: *estilo mariposa*, butterfly stroke. || Type: *vino espumoso estilo champán*, sparkling wine, champagne type. || Gnomon, style (de reloj de sol). || — *A* or *al estilo de*, in the style of, in the ... style: *al estilo de España, de su país*, in the Spanish style, in the style of his country. || *Carrera de 400 metros estilos*, 400-metres medley race (natación). || *De buen, mal estilo*, in good, bad taste: *una broma de mal estilo*, a joke in bad taste; the done thing, not the done thing: *es de buen estilo ir a ese restorán*, it is the done thing to go to that restaurant. || *Estilo de vida*, way of life. || GRAM. *Estilo directo*, direct speech. || *Estilo libre*, freestyle (natación). || *Por el estilo*, of the kind, of that sort. || *Todo está por el estilo*, it's all very much the same.
estilográfico, ca adj. Stylographic. || *Pluma estilográfica*, fountain pen.
— F. Fountain pen, pen.
estima f. Esteem, respect: *le tengo poca estima*, I have little respect for him; *tener en gran estima a uno*, to hold s.o. in high *o* great esteem. || MAR. Dead reckoning.
estimabilidad f. Estimableness.
estimabilísimo, ma adj. Highly estimable.
estimable adj. Estimable. || FIG. Considerable (grande).
estimación f. Estimation, valuation (evaluación comercial). || Estimate: *estimación presupuestaria*, budget estimate. || Esteem, respect (estima). || — JUR. *Estimación de una demanda*, admittance of a claim. || *Estimación propia*, self-esteem, self-respect. || *Según estimación común*, according to general opinion.
estimado, da adj. Esteemed, respected. || Dear: *Estimado señor*, Dear Sir.
estimador m. Valuer, appraiser (tasador).
estimar v. tr. To esteem, to respect, to hold in esteem, to have respect for: *estimar (en) mucho a uno*, to hold s.o. in great esteem, to have great respect for s.o., to respect s.o. highly. || To value: *estimaron la sortija en mil libras*, they valued the ring at a thousand pounds. || To consider, to think, to deem, to esteem (juzgar): *no lo estimo necesario*, I don't think it necessary. || FAM. To like, to be fond of: *le estimo, pero no le quiero*, I am fond of him but I am not in love with him. || JUR. *Estimar una demanda*, to admit a claim.
— V. pr. To hold each other in esteem, to respect each other (dos personas). || To have a high opinion of o.s. (uno mismo). || To be valued (un objeto). || — *Ninguna persona que se estime haría eso*, no self-respecting person would do that. || *Se estima que la temperatura es hoy de cinco grados*, today's temperature is estimated at five degrees.
estimativa f. Judgment (juicio). || Instinct (instinto).
estimatorio, ria adj. Estimative.
estimulación f. Stimulation.
estimulante adj. Encouraging, stimulating: *una noticia estimulante*, an encouraging piece of news. || Stimulative: *remedio estimulante*, stimulative drug.
— M. MED. Stimulant. || FIG. Stimulus, incentive.
estimular v. tr. To encourage: *estimula a su hijo a estudiar*, he encourages his son to study. || To promote, to encourage: *el gobierno quiere estimular la industria y las artes en esta región*, the government wishes to encourage industry and the arts in this area. || To stimulate (el apetito). || To incite, to stir, to urge: *los agitadores estimularon a los estudiantes a sublevarse*, the agitators incited the students to rebel.
estímulo m. Stimulant, stimulus (estimulante): *sus palabras fueron un estímulo para mí*, his words acted as a stimulus for me. || Encouragement, stimulation: *un poco de estímulo de parte de la dirección no estaría de más*, a little encouragement from the management would not be amiss. || Incentive (incentivo). || BIOL. Stimulus.
estinco m. Skink (reptil).
estío m. Summer (verano).
— OBSERV. The use of *estío* is restricted to literary contexts.
estipendiar v. tr. To pay a stipend to, to remunerate.
estipendio m. Remuneration, pay, stipend (salario).
estípite m. ARQ. Pedestal [in the form of an inverted pyramid]. || BOT. Stipe, stalk (de palmera, etc.).
estíptico, ca adj./s. m. Styptic.
estipulación f. Stipulation.
estipular v. tr. To stipulate.
estirable adj. Stretchable.
estiradamente adv. Scarcely *o* hardly *o* barely enough: *tener estiradamente para vivir*, to have barely enough to live on.
estirado, da adj. Stretched. || FIG. Dressed to kill (acicalado). | Lofty, haughty (presumido). | Stiff, starchy (tieso). || FIG. y FAM. Stingy, miserly, tight-fisted (avaro). || *Andar estirado*, to walk stiffly.
— F. Dive (en fútbol). || *Hacer una estirada*, to dive. || — M. Straightening (del pelo). || TECN. Drawing (del metal, de fibras). || Facelift (de la piel).
estirador, ra adj. TECN. *Máquina estiradora*, wire drawer (para el metal), drawing frame (para tejidos).
estiraje m. TECN. Drawing (de metales o de fibras).
estiramiento m. Stretching.
estirar v. tr. To stretch (alargar). || To tauten, to draw tight (poner tenso). || To stretch out: *estirar el brazo*, to stretch out one's arm. || To pull up (las medias). || To pull down (la falda). || TECN. To draw (el metal, las fibras). || FIG. To stretch out, to spin out (un ensayo, un discurso, etc.). | To stretch, to eke out (el dinero). || MAR. To run out (un cable). || *Amer.* FAM. To bump off (matar). || — *Estirar con la plancha*, to run an iron over (la ropa). || FIG. y FAM. *Estirar la pata*, to kick the bucket, to snuff it (morir). | *Estirar las piernas*, to stretch one's legs.
— V. pr. To stretch. || To stretch out (tumbarse).
estireno o **estiroleno** m. QUÍM. Styrene.
estirón m. Pull, tug, jerk (tirón). || Sudden rapid growth (crecimiento rápido). || FIG. y FAM. *Dar un estirón*, to shoot up (crecer rápidamente).
estirpe f. Stock (origen de una familia): *es de buena estirpe*, he comes of a sound stock. || Lineage, ancestry (descendencia). || FIG. *No niega su estirpe*, he takes after his parents.
estival adj. Summer, estival (p. us.): *calor, ropa estival*, summer heat, clothing; *solsticio estival*, summer solstice.
esto pron. dem. neutro. This: *yo quiero esto*, I want this; *esto es verdad*, this is true. || — *En esto*, at that point, then (entonces), thereupon (inmediatamente después). || *Esto* ... (cuando se vacila), er ... || *Esto es*, right (de acuerdo), that is [to say] (o sea). || *No hay como esto para darte ánimo*, there's nothing like this to cheer you up. || *Y en esto*, when (cuando): *estaba nadando tranquilamente y en esto apareció un tiburón*, I was happily swimming when a shark appeared; whereupon (y luego): *me enfadé y en esto él se marchó*, I got angry, whereupon he left.
estocada f. Thrust, lunge, stab (acción). || Stab, stab wound (herida). || TAUR. [Sword] thrust, "estocada": *una estocada en lo alto*, a well-placed "estocada."
estocafís m. Stockfish (pescado).
Estocolmo n. pr. GEOGR. Stockholm.
estofa f. Brocade (tela). || Quality (de una cosa). || Type, class: *no queremos nada con gente de su estofa*, we don't want anything to do with [people of] his type. || *De baja estofa*, low-class (personas), low quality (cosas).
estofado, da adj. CULIN. Stewed. || Quilted (acolchado).
— M. CULIN. Stew: *estofado de vaca*, beef stew.
estofar v. tr. To stew (guisar). || To quilt (acolchar).
estoicismo m. Stoicism (escuela). || FIG. Stoicism.
estoico, ca adj. Stoic, stoical: *la doctrina estoica*, the Stoic doctrine. || FIG. Stoic, stoical: *estoico ante la desgracia*, stoic in the face of misfortune.
— M. y f. Stoic: *Séneca fue un estoico*, Seneca was a Stoic. || FIG. Stoic: *es un verdadero estoico*, he's a real stoic.
estola f. Stole.
estolidez f. Stupidity.
estólido, da adj. Stupid.
estolón m. BOT. Stolon, sucker, runner. || Large stole (de sacerdote).
estoma m. BOT. y ZOOL. Stoma.

estomacal adj./s.m. Stomachic. || *Trastorno estomacal*, stomach upset.
estomagante adj. Indigestible. | FIG. Sickening.
estomagar v. tr. To give indigestion (empachar). || FIG. To sicken.
estómago m. Stomach: *con el estómago vacío*, on an empty stomach. || — *Boca del estómago*, pit of the stomach. || *Dolor de estómago*, stomachache. || FIG. *Hacerse el estómago a algo, a alguien*, to get used to sth., to s.o. | *Revolver el estómago a uno*, to turn s.o.'s stomach (causar repugnancia). | *Tener a uno cogido por el estómago*, to have s.o. where one wants him. | *Tener a uno sentado en el estómago* or *en la boca del estómago*, to be unable to stomach s.o. | *Tener el estómago en los pies* or *tener el estómago pegado al espinazo*, to be faint with hunger, to be starving. | *Tener estómago* or *mucho* or *buen estómago*, to be able to stand a lot, to be tough (aguantar mucho), to have guts (tener valor), not to be over-scrupulous (ser poco escrupuloso). | *Tener los ojos más grandes que el estómago*, to have eyes bigger than one's belly. | *Tener un estómago de piedra*, to have a cast-iron stomach. | *Tener un vacío en el estómago* or *el estómago vacío*, to have an empty stomach, to feel empty *o* hungry.
estomatitis f. MED. Stomatitis.
estomatología f. MED. Stomatology.
estomatólogo, ga m. y f. MED. Stomatologist.
estopa f. Tow (fibra). || Burlap (tela). || MAR. Oakum. || *Estopa de acero*, steel wool.
estopilla f. Cheesecloth, lawn (tela).
estopor m. MAR. Stopper (del ancla).
estoque m. Rapier, tuck (ant.) [espada]. || TAUR. Matador's sword, "estoque". || BOT. Gladiolus.
estoqueador m. TAUR. Matador.
estoquear v. tr. TAUR. To stab [with the sword].
estoraque m. Styrax, storax (árbol). || Storax (resina).
estorbar v. tr. To hinder, to hamper, to impede, to get in the way of: *el abrigo me estorba para correr*, the overcoat gets in my way when I run. || To thwart, to frustrate (frustrar): *la lluvia estorbó nuestros planes*, the rain thwarted our plans. || To annoy, to bother, to trouble (molestar). || To block, to obstruct: *estorbar el paso*, to block the way; *estorbar el tráfico*, to block the traffic. || To hold up (negociaciones, etc.).
— V. intr. To be in the way.
estorbo m. Hindrance, encumbrance (molestia): *este paquete es un estorbo*, this parcel is a hindrance. || Obstacle (obstáculo). || Obstruction. || Nuisance (molestia).
estornino m. Starling (ave).
estornudar v. intr. To sneeze.
estornudo m. Sneeze.
estos, estas, éstos, éstas adj. y pron. dem. m. y f. pl. These. V. ESTE y ÉSTE.
estovar v. tr. CULIN. To cook in butter or oil on a low flame.
estrábico, ca adj. Strabismal, strabismic, strabismical.
estrabismo m. MED. Strabismus, squint.
estradivario m. Stradivarius (violín).
estrada f. Road, highway.
estrado m. Stage, platform (tarima). || (Ant.). Drawing room (sala). | Drawing-room furniture (mobiliario). || — Pl. JUR. Court rooms.
estrafalariamente adv. Outlandishly, eccentrically, bizarrely (de modo extraño). || In a slovenly fashion (desaliñadamente).
estrafalario, ria adj. Outlandish, eccentric, bizarre (extraño). || Slovenly (desaliñado).
— M. y f. Eccentric.
estragador, ra adj. Destroying, devastating. || Corrupting (corruptor).
estragamiento m. Devastation, ravage.
estragar v. tr. To devastate, to ruin, to ravage (causar estragos). || To corrupt, to deprave (corromper). || To spoil (estropear): *estragar el apetito*, to spoil one's appetite. || *Tener el gusto* or *el paladar estragado*, to have a jaded palate.
estrago m. Destruction, devastation, ruin (destrucción). || Damage: *el terremoto ha causado muchos estragos*, the earthquake has caused a lot of damage. || Corruption, perversion (en las costumbres). || FIG. Ravage: *los estragos de los años*, the ravages of time. || *Causar* or *hacer estragos*, to work havoc: *el torbellino, la epidemia ha causado estragos en todo el país*, the whirlwind, epidemic has wrought havoc throughout the whole country.
estragón m. BOT. y CULIN. Tarragon.
estrambote m. Extra verses, *pl.* [added to a poem].
estrambóticamente adv. Outlandishly, bizarrely.
estrambótico, ca adj. Outlandish, bizarre, weird.
estramonio m. BOT. Thorn apple, stramonium.
estrangulación f. Strangulation, strangling. || MED. Strangulation.
estrangulado, da adj. Strangled. || MED. Strangulated: *hernia estrangulada*, strangulated hernia.
estrangulador, ra adj. Strangling. || MED. Strangulating.
— M. y f. Strangler (persona). || — M. AUT. Choke.
estrangulamiento m. Strangling. || MED. Strangulation. || FIG. Bottleneck (en la carretera).
estrangular v. tr. To strangle (ahogar). || MED. To strangulate. || AUT. To choke. || TECN. To throttle.
— V. pr. To strangle o.s. (matarse).
estrapada f. Strappado (suplicio).
estraperlear v. intr. FAM. To deal in black-market goods.
estraperleo m. FAM. Blackmarketing.
estraperlista m. y f. FAM. Blackmarketeer.
— Adj. Black-market.
estraperlo m. FAM. Black market: *vender de estraperlo*, to sell on the black market.
estrás m. Strass (vidrio).
estratagema f. Stratagem.
estratega m. MIL. Strategist. || FAM. *Los estrategas de café*, armchair strategists.
estrategia f. Strategy.
estratégicamente adv. Strategically.
estratégico, ca adj. Strategic.
— M. y f. Strategist.
estratificación f. Stratification.
estratificado, da adj. Stratified.
estratificar v. tr. To stratify.
— V. pr. To stratify, to be stratified.
estrato m. GEOL. y BIOL. Stratum. || Stratus (nube). || FIG. Stratum: *estratos sociales*, social strata.
estratocumulo m. Stratocumulus.
estratosfera f. Stratosphere.
estratosférico, ca adj. Stratospheric.
estrave m. MAR. Stem.
estraza f. Rag, shred. || *Papel de estraza*, brown paper.
estrechamente adv. Narrowly. || Tightly (con poco espacio). || FIG. Closely: *estrechamente vinculados*, closely linked. || — FIG. *Estrechamente unidos*, very close (personas). | *Vivir estrechamente*, to live poorly *o* meagrely (con poco dinero), to live in cramped conditions (en poco espacio).
estrechamiento m. Taking-in (de la ropa). || Narrowing (acción de estrecharse un valle, una carretera, etc.). || Narrow point, narrow part (punto estrecho). || FIG. Tightening: *estrechamiento de los lazos económicos entre ambos países*, tightening of the economic links between the two countries. || — *Estrechamiento de carretera*, road narrows (señal de tráfico). || *Estrechamiento de manos*, handshake.
estrechar v. tr. To take in, to make smaller: *estrechar un vestido*, to take in a dress. || To make narrower, to narrow: *están estrechando la carretera*, they are making the road narrower. || To squeeze (apretar). || FIG. To bring closer together: *la desgracia estrecha a las familias*, misfortune brings families closer together. | To tighten: *estrechar los lazos de amistad*, to tighten the bonds of friendship. || FIG. To compel, to oblige (obligar, forzar). | To harass (acosar). || — *Estrechar a uno entre los brazos*, to embrace s.o., to hug s.o. || *Estrechar la mano a uno*, to shake s.o.'s hand, to shake hands with s.o. || MIL. *Estrechar las filas*, to close the ranks.
— V. pr. To become narrower, to narrow: *en el valle la carretera se estrecha*, in the valley the road becomes narrower. || To squeeze together *o* up: *estrechaos un poco para que yo entre*, squeeze up a bit so as I can get in. || FIG. To grow tighter (lazos económicos, etc.). | To make economies, to cut down, to tighten one's belt (reducir los gastos). | To become close *o* closer (intimar). || To shake (las manos).
estrechez f. Narrowness (anchura). || Tightness (poco espacio). || FIG. Tight spot (apuro). | Poverty, want, need (falta de dinero): *vivir con mucha estrechez*, to live in great poverty. || Closeness, intimacy (intimidad). || Strictness, rigidity (lo estricto). || Austerity (austeridad). || MED. Stricture. || — *Estrechez de espíritu* or *de conciencia* or *de miras*, narrow-mindedness. | *Pasar estrecheces*, to be hard up. | *Vivir con estrechez*, to live poorly *o* meagrely (con poco dinero), to live in cramped conditions (en poco espacio).
estrecho, cha adj. Narrow: *calle estrecha*, narrow street. || Tight (demasiado pequeño): *zapato estrecho*, tight shoe. || Cramped, small: *una habitación estrecha*, a cramped room. || Tight, short (de dinero). || Packed: *íbamos los seis muy estrechos en el coche*, there were six of us tightly packed in the car. || FIG. Close: *amistad, relación estrecha*, close friendship, relationship; *estrechos vínculos*, close links. | Narrow: *espíritu estrecho*, narrow mind. | Strict, rigid: *una moral estrecha*, strict morals. | Stingy, miserly, tight (avaro). || *De espíritu estrecho* or *de miras estrechas*, narrow-minded.
— M. GEOGR. Straits, *pl.*, strait: *el estrecho de Gibraltar*, the Straits of Gibraltar. || FIG. Tight spot (apuro). || *Lo estrecho*, v. ESTRECHEZ.
estrechura f. V. ESTRECHEZ.
estregadera f. Scrubbing brush (cepillo). || Footscraper (para los zapatos).
estregadura f. o **estregamiento** m. Rubbing (con un trapo). || Scrubbing (con un cepillo). || Scouring (con un abrasivo).
estregar* v. tr. To rub (frotar con la mano, un trapo, etc.). || To scrub (con un cepillo). || To scour (con abrasivo).
— V. pr. To rub o.s.
estregón m. Hard rubbing.
estrella f. ASTR. Star: *estrella fugaz*, shooting star. || Star, blaze, white mark (de caballo). || IMPR. Asterisk, star. || MIL. Star, pip (en el uniforme).

|| FIG. Fate, destiny: *lo quiso mi estrella*, fate willed it. | Star: *es una estrella de cine*, he's a movie star. || — *Dormir bajo las estrellas*, to sleep under the stars. || ZOOL. *Estrella de mar*, starfish. || *Estrella errante*, planet. || *Estrella matutina* or *del alba*, morning star. || *Estrella polar*, pole star. || *Estrella vespertina*, evening star. || FIG. y FAM. *Haber nacido con buena estrella*, to be born under a lucky star. | *Levantarse con las estrellas*, to get up before daybreak. | *Poner por* or *sobre las estrellas*, to praise to the skies. | *Tener mala estrella*, to be unlucky. | *Ver las estrellas*, to see stars.

estrellado, da adj. Starry, star-spangled (cielo). || Star-shaped, stellate (en forma de estrella). || With a star *o* a blaze *o* white mark on its forehead (caballo). || CULIN. Fried (huevos). || FIG. Smashed, shattered (con un porrazo).

estrellamar m. ZOOL. Starfish. || BOT. Plantain.

estrellar adj. Stellar.

estrellar v. tr. To smash, to dash, to shatter (romper): *estrelló un vaso contra la pared*, he smashed a glass against the wall. || CULIN. To fry (huevos). || To stud *o* to spangle *o* to cover with stars.
— V. pr. To smash, to shatter (romperse). || To crash: *el coche se estrelló contra el parapeto*, the car crashed into *o* against the parapet. || To dash: *las olas se estrellaban contra el rompeolas*, the waves dashed against the breakwater. || FIG. To fail (fracasar). || — FIG. *Estrellarse con una dificultad*, to run into a difficulty. | *Estrellarse con uno*, to run into s.o., to come up against s.o.

estrellato m. Stardom: *ese disco le lanzó al estrellato*, that record launched him into stardom.

estrellón m. Star-shaped firework. || *Amer.* Crash.

estremecedor, ra adj. Startling (que asusta). || Blood-curdling (espeluznante). || Violent (violento).

estremecer* v. tr. To shake (sacudir): *el terremoto estremeció la casa*, the earthquake shook the house. || To startle, to make [s.o.] jump (asustar): *el escopetazo me estremeció*, the rifle shot startled me. || FIG. To shake: *nuevas ideas que estremecen los cimientos de la sociedad*, new ideas which shake the foundations of society. | To make [s.o.] shudder (el miedo, etc.).
— V. pr. To shake, to shudder: *las ventanas se estremecen cuando truena*, the windows shake when it thunders. || To jump, to start (sobrecogerse). || To tremble, to shake, to quiver (*de*, with) [emoción, miedo]. || To tremble (de ilusión, alegría). || To tremble, to shiver (de frío). || FIG. To shudder: *se estremece uno al pensar en la posibilidad de una epidemia*, one shudders at the thought of a possible epidemic. | To come into question: *se estremece la moral tradicional*, traditional morals are coming into question. || *Se estremeció al oír un ruido*, a noise made him start *o* jump.

estremecimiento m. Shaking, shuddering (acción de sacudir). || Shake, shudder (sacudida). || Start, jump (sobresalto). || Trembling, shaking, quivering (acción), tremble, shake, quiver (hecho) [de emoción]. || Shivering (acción), shiver (hecho) [de frío].

estrenar v. tr. To use for the first time: *estrenar un nuevo bolígrafo*, to use a new ball-point for the first time. || To wear for the first time (un traje, zapatos, etc.). || TEATR. To perform for the first time (una comedia). || CINEM. To show for the first time, to release, to put on release (una película). || *Estrenar un piso*, to give a housewarming party.
— V. pr. To make one's début: *estrenarse como futbolista*, to make one's début as a footballer. || TEATR. To open. || CINEM. To have its première || COM. To make one's first sale of the day (un vendedor).

estreno m. First use. || First time on (ropa). || Début: *su estreno como vendedor fue un desastre*, his début as a salesman was a disaster. || TEATR. y CINEM. Première, first night. | New play (comedia), new release, new film (película). | Début, first appearance (de un actor). || *Cine de estreno*, first-run cinema.

estreñido, da adj. MED. Constipated, costive. || FIG. Mean, stingy (avaro).

estreñimiento m. MED. Constipation.

estreñir* v. tr. MED. To constipate.
— V. pr. MED. To become constipated.

estrépito m. Din, racket (ruido fuerte). || Clatter, crash (ruido brusco). || FIG. Flourish, fuss, ostentation: *lo hace todo con mucho estrépito*, he does everything with lots of flourish.

estrepitosamente adv. Noisily, with a din *o* racket.

estrepitoso, sa adj. Noisy, deafening, clamorous: *una pita estrepitosa*, deafening jeers. || Noisy, rowdy (persona). || FIG. Resounding: *un fracaso, un éxito estrepitoso*, a resounding failure, success.

estreptococia f. MED. Streptococcosis.

estreptococo m. BIOL. Streptococcus.

estreptomicina f. Streptomycin (antibiótico).

estría f. Groove (ranura). || ARQ. Flute, fluting. || Rifling (de arma de fuego). || GEOL. Stria, striation.

estriación f. o **estriado** m. Grooving. || ARQ. Fluting. || Rifling (de arma de fuego). || GEOL. Striation.

estriar v. tr. To groove (hacer ranuras). || ARQ. To flute (una columna). || To rifle (el cañón de un arma de fuego). || GEOL. To striate.

estribación f. GEOGR. Spur. || — Pl. Foothills.

estribadero m. Support.

estribar v. intr. To rest: *el depósito estriba en cuatro pilares*, the tank rests on four pillars. || FIG. To lie: *la belleza de la sala estriba en su altura*, the beauty of the room lies in its height; *su éxito estriba en su poder de persuasión*, his success lies in his power of persuasion. | To be based on (fundarse).

estribillo m. Refrain (en poesía). || Chorus (en canciones). || Catchphrase, pet word *o* phrase (muletilla).

estribo m. Stirrup. || Step (de carruaje). || Running board (de coche). || ANAT. Stirrup bone, stapes. || ARQ. Buttress (contrafuerte). | Abutment (de un puente). || GEOGR. V. ESTRIBACIÓN. || FIG. Foundation, basis (fundamento). || — FIG. *Con el pie en el estribo*, V. PIE. || *Hacer estribo con las manos a uno*, to give s.o. a leg up. || FIG. *Perder los estribos*, to lose one's temper, to fly off the handle (perder el control), to lose one's head (perder la serenidad).

estribor m. MAR. Starboard.

estricnina f. Strychnine.

estricto, ta adj. Strict.

estridencia f. Stridency, stridence, shrillness.

estridente adj. Strident, shrill, grating (ruido).

estridor m. Stridor, strident sound (ruido estridente). || Stridulation, chirring, chirping (de los insectos). || MED. Stridor.

estridulación f. Stridulation, chirring, chirping (de saltamontes, etc.).

estridular v. intr. To stridulate, to chirr, to chirp.

estro m. Inspiration: *estro poético*, poetic inspiration. || ZOOL. Oestrus, heat, rut (celo). | Botfly (insecto).

estroboscopio m. Stroboscope.

estrofa f. Verse, stanza, strophe.

estrógeno, na adj. BIOL. Œstrogenic [U.S., estrogenic]. —M. BIOL. Œstrogen [U.S., estrogen].

estroncio m. QUÍM. Strontium (metal).

estropajo m. Scourer (para fregar). || Loofah [U.S., luffa] (planta y esponja vegetal). || FIG. Useless person, dead loss (persona). | Useless thing, piece of rubbish (cosa). || *Estropajo de aluminio*, scouring pad.

estropajoso, sa adj. Tough, leathery (alimentos). || Ragged (andrajoso). || Slovenly (desaseado). || Stammering (que pronuncia mal). || *Tener la lengua estropajosa*, to have a pasty tongue.

estropear v. tr. To damage, to ruin, to spoil (poner en mal estado o volver inservible): *las heladas han estropeado la cosecha*, the frosts have ruined the harvest; *he estropeado mi traje al caer*, I ruined my suit when I fell over. || To break, to damage, to ruin (un mecanismo): *los niños han estropeado la máquina de escribir, el ascensor*, the children have damaged the typewriter, the lift. || To spoil, to ruin (proyectos). || To hurt, to injure (lastimar). || To maim, to cripple (lisiar). || To age (envejecer) || To mix, to wet (el mortero). || — *Estar estropeado*, to be broken down o out of action *o* out of order (no funcionar), to be ruined (deteriorado). || *Tengo el estómago estropeado*, my stomach is out of order, I have an upset stomach.
— V. pr. To be *o* to get damaged *o* ruined *o* spoilt. || To break down: *el coche se ha estropeado*, the car has broken down. || To spoil, to go bad (la fruta, etc.). || To go wrong, to fail (proyectos).

estropicio m. Clatter, crash (rotura estrepitosa): *se armó un gran estropicio en la cocina*, there was a loud crash in the kitchen. || Damage (destrozo). || Mess (desorden): *hacer un estropicio en la mesa*, to make a mess on the table. || Rumpus (jaleo).

estructura f. Structure: *estructura social, celular, de hormigón*, social, cellular, concrete structure. || Framework, frame (armazón).

estructuración f. Structuring, organization, construction.

estructural adj. Structural.

estructuralismo m. Structuralism.

estructurar v. tr. To organize, to construct, to structure.

estruendo m. Roar, din: *el estruendo de las cataratas, de los motores*, the roar of the waterfall, of engines. || Din, racket (ruido fuerte). || Clatter, crash (ruido brusco). || Tumult, uproar (de una muchedumbre). || Show, pomp, ostentation (fausto).

estruendoso, sa adj. Thunderous, deafening (muy fuerte): *aplausos estruendosos, voz estruendosa*, thunderous applause, voice. || Noisy (ruidoso).

estrujadora f. Squeezer, lemon squeezer.

estrujadura f. o **estrujamiento** m. Squeezing (de limón). || Pressing (de uva).

estrujar v. tr. To squeeze (exprimir): *estrujar un limón*, to squeeze a lemon. || To press (uva). || To screw up, to crumple up: *estrujó la carta con ira*, he screwed the letter up with rage. || To wring (la ropa, el cuello). || FIG. To bleed dry: *el gobierno está estrujando al pueblo con impuestos*, the government is bleeding the country dry with taxation. | To exploit (explotar). | To get everything one can out of (sacar el mejor rendimiento).
— V. pr. To crowd, to press, to throng: *los aficionados se estrujaban a la puerta del estadio*, the fans were crowding at the gates of the stadium. || FIG. y FAM. *Estrujarse los sesos*, to rack one's brains.

estrujón m. Squeezing. || Pressing.

Estuardo n. pr. Stuart.
estuario m. Estuary.
estucado m. Stucco, stuccowork.
estucador m. Stucco plasterer, stucco worker.
estucar v. tr. To stucco.
estuco m. Stucco.
estuche m. Case: *estuche de gafas, de violín, de peine*, glasses case, violin case, comb case. || Set (conjunto): *estuche de instrumentos*, set of instruments. || Sheath (vaina). || Casket (cofrecito). || — *Estuche de joyas*, jewel case, jewel box. || *Estuche de tocador*, makeup case. || FIG. *Ser un estuche*, to be a jack-of-all-trades.
estuchista m. Case *o* box maker.
estudiado, da adj. Studied, elaborate: *una indiferencia estudiada, un gesto estudiado*, studied indifference, a studied gesture. || Mannered (amanerado). || — *Precio estudiado*, rock-bottom price. || *Vehículo bien estudiado*, carefully designed vehicle.
estudiantado m. Students, *pl.*, student body.
estudiante m. y f. Student: *estudiante de Derecho*, law student; *estudiante de medicina*, medical student.

— OBSERV. *Estudianta* is sometimes used in spoken language instead of the correct feminine form *estudiante*.

estudiantil adj. Student.
estudiantina f. Student band.
estudiantino, na adj. FAM. Student.
estudiar v. tr. e intr. To study: *estudiar filosofía, español, un proyecto*, to study philosophy, Spanish, a plan. || To read, to study (en la universidad): *estudia geografía en Cambridge*, he's reading geography at Cambridge. || To work, to study: *ayer me quedé toda la noche estudiando*, I stayed up all last night working. || To think about, to consider (una proposición). || — *Estudiar de memoria*, to learn by heart. || *Estudiar para cura, para maestro*, to study to be a priest, to be a schoolteacher.
estudio m. Study: *aplicarse en los estudios*, to work hard at one's studies; *un estudio sobre la desnutrición*, a study on malnutrition. || Survey, research (encuesta): *un estudio del mercado*, a market survey. || Investigation (investigación). || MÚS. Étude, study. || ARTES. Study (dibujo). || Study (despacho). || Studio: *estudio cinematográfico, de artista, de fotógrafo*, film, artist's, photographer's studio. || Bed-sitter, bed-sitting-room (piso). || — *Cursar* or *hacer estudios*, to study. || *Dar estudios a uno*, to pay for s.o.'s studies, to finance s.o.'s schooling. || *Estar en estudio*, to be under consideration. || *Estudio del mercado*, marketing, market research. || *Estudios mayores*, advanced studies. || *Hacer estudios* to study. || *Tener estudios*, to be well educated.
estudioso, sa adj. Studious.
— M. Scholar, specialist.
estufa f. Stove, heater (para la calefacción). || Fire (de gas, de electricidad). || Hothouse, greenhouse (invernadero de plantas). || Steam room (para baños de vapor). || Heat cabinet (para secar, evaporar, etc.). || Small brasier, foot warmer (estufilla). || — FIG. *Criar en estufa*, to mollycoddle. | *Esta habitación es una estufa*, this room is like an oven, it's like an oven in this room. || *Estufa de desinfección*, sterilizer.
estufilla f. Small brasier, foot warmer (brasero). || Muff (manguito).
estulticia f. Stupidity, foolishness (necedad).
estulto, ta adj. Stupid, foolish.
estupefacción f. Astonishment, stupefaction, amazement.
estupefaciente adj. Astonishing, amazing, stupefying (que produce estupefacción). || Narcotic (sustancia).
— M. MED. Drug, narcotic.
estupefacto, ta adj Astonished, amazed, stupefied, flabbergasted: *estupefacto con la noticia*, astonished at *o* by the news. || *Dejar estupefacto*, to astonish, to amaze, to stupefy, to flabbergast.
estupendamente adv. Wonderfully, marvellously, fantastically: *el coche funciona estupendamente*, the car runs marvellously.
estupendo, da adj. Marvellous, wonderful, fantastic, stupendous (bueno). || Beautiful (hermoso). || — FAM. *¡Estupendo!*, great! | *Un tío estupendo*, a great chap.
estupidez f. Stupidity, silliness. || — *Cometer una estupidez*, to do sth. stupid. || *Eso es una estupidez*, that's a stupid thing to do (haciendo), that's a stupid thing to say (hablando).
estúpido, da adj. Stupid, silly.
— M. y f. Idiot.
estupor m. Astonishment, amazement, stupefaction (asombro). || Stupor.
estuprar v. tr. To rape.
estupro m. Rape (violación).
estuque m. Stucco (estuco).
estuquista m. Stucco plasterer, stucco worker.
esturión m. Sturgeon (pez).
esvástica f. Swastika.
esviaje m. ARQ. Skew, obliqueness (oblicuidad).
eta f. Eta (letra griega).
etalaje m. Bosh (de alto horno).
etano m. QUÍM. Ethane.
etapa f. Stage: *hacer un viaje en dos etapas*, to make a journey in two stages; *una etapa de cuarenta kilómetros*, a stage of forty kilometres. || Leg, stage (en una carrera). || Stop, stage: *nuestra primera etapa fue Londres*, our first stop was London. || FIG. Stage, phase (fase). || Stage (cuerpo de cohete). || MIL. Halt, stop (lugar de parada). || — *Por etapas*, in stages. || FIG. *Quemar etapas*, to get on in leaps and bounds.
etcétera f. Et cetera, etc. || *Etcétera, etcétera*, and so on and so forth; et cetera, et cetera.
éter m. Ether, aether. || POÉT. Sky, heavens, *pl.*
etéreo, a adj. Ethereal (del éter). || POÉT. *La bóveda etérea*, the ethereal vault.
eterificar v. tr. QUÍM. To etherify.
eterismo m. MED. Etherism.
eterizar v. tr. MED. To etherize.
eternidad f. Eternity: *por* or *para toda la eternidad*, for all eternity.
eternizar v. tr. To eternalize, to eternize, to make eternal. || FIG. To make everlasting (hacer durar). | To immortalize.
— V. pr. To be endless, to drag on (fam.): *la discusión se eternizaba*, the discussion was endless. || To stay for ages: *me eternizaría aquí*, I could stay here for ages. || To take ages: *esta chica se eterniza arreglándose*, this girl takes ages to get ready.
eterno, na adj. Eternal: *la vida eterna*, eternal life. || FIG. Endless, everlasting: *amistad eterna*, endless friendship. || *Padre Eterno*, Eternal Father.
eterómano, na adj. Addicted to ether.
— M. y f. Ether addict.
ético, ca adj. Ethical (moral). || FIG. Skinny (muy flaco). || MED. Consumptive.
— M. Moralist. || — F. Ethics (conjunto de principios): *ética profesional*, professional ethics. || Ethics (parte de la filosofía).
etileno m. QUÍM. Ethylene.
etílico, ca adj. Ethylic. || *Alcohol etílico*, ethyl alcohol.
etilismo m. MED. Alcoholism.
etilo m. QUÍM. Ethyl.
etimología f. Etymology.
etimológico, ca adj. Etymological.
etimologista m. y f. Etymologist.
etimologizar v. intr. To etymologize.
etimólogo, ga m. y f. Etymologist.
etiología f. Aetiology, etiology.
etiológico, ca adj. Aetiological, etiological.
etíope o **etiope** adj./s. Ethiopian.
Etiopía n. pr. f. GEOGR. Ethiopia.
etiópico, ca adj. Ethiopian.
etiqueta f. Ceremonial, ceremony, etiquette: *la etiqueta de la Corte*, the Court ceremonial. || Pomp, ceremony: *recibir a uno con mucha etiqueta*, to entertain s.o. with great ceremony. || Label (marbete, rótulo). || Tag (inscripción atada a un paquete). || — *De etiqueta*, formal: *baile de etiqueta*, formal ball. || *Se ruega* or *se suplica etiqueta*, formal dress. || *Traje de etiqueta*, formal dress. || *Vestirse de etiqueta*, to wear formal dress.
etiquetado m. Labelling.
etiquetadora f. Labelling machine.
etiquetar v. tr. To label.
etiquetero, ra adj. Ceremonious, formal.
etmoidal adj. Ethmoidal.
etmoides adj./s.m. Ethmoid (hueso del cráneo).
etnarca m. Ethnarch.
etnarquía f. Ethnarchy.
etnia f. Ethnos.
étnico, ca adj. Ethnic.
etnografía f. Ethnography.
etnográfico, ca adj. Ethnographic, ethnographical.
etnógrafo m. Ethnographer.
etnología f. Ethnology.
etnológico, ca adj. Ethnologic, ethnological.
etnólogo m. Ethnologist.
etrusco, ca adj./s. Etruscan.
eucalipto m. BOT. Eucalyptus.
eucaliptol m. Eucalyptol.
Eucaristía f. Eucharist.
eucarístico, ca adj. Eucharistic, Eucharistical: *congreso eucarístico*, Eucharistic congress.
Euclides n. pr. m. Euclid: *postulado de Euclides*, Euclid's postulate.
euclidiano, na adj. Euclidean (de Euclides).
eudemonismo m. Eudemonism, eudaemonism.
eufemismo m. Euphemism.
eufemístico, ca adj. Euphemistic.
eufonía f. Euphony.
eufónico, ca adj. Euphonic, euphonious.
euforbio m. BOT. Euphorbia (planta). || Euphorbium (resina).
euforia f. Euphoria.
eufórico, ca adj. Euphoric.
eufuismo m. Euphuism.
eufuista adj./s. Euphuist.
eufuístico, ca adj. Euphuistic.
eugenesia f. BIOL. Eugenics.
eugenésico, ca adj. Eugenic.
eulogia f. Eulogia.
eunuco m. Eunuch.
eupatorio m. BOT. Eupatorium.
eupéptico, ca adj. MED. Eupeptic.
Eurasia n. pr. f. GEOGR. Eurasia.
eurasiático, ca adj./s. Eurasian.
¡eureka! interj. Eureka!
Eurípides n. pr. m. Euripides.

euritmia f. Eurythmy (movimiento armonioso). || Eurythmics (rítmica).
eurítmico, ca adj. Eurythmic, eurythmical.
Europa n. pr. f. GEOGR. Europe.
europeísmo m. Europeanism.
europeísta adj. Pro-European, in favour of Europeanism.
— M. y f. Pro-European, supporter of Europeanism *o* of European unity.
europeización f. Europeanization.
europeizante adj./s. Pro-European.
europeizar v. tr. To Europeanize.
— V. pr. To become Europeanized.
europeo, a adj./s. European.
europio m. QUÍM. Europium.
Eurovisión n. pr. f. Eurovision.
éuscaro, ra adj./s. Euskarian, Basque.
Eustaquio n. pr. m. Eustachius. || ANAT. *Trompa, válvula de Eustaquio*, Eustachian tube, valve.
eutanasia f. Euthanasia.
eutrapelia f. (P.us.). Moderation [in one's pastimes] (moderación). || Innocent pastime (distracción). || Lighthearted joke (broma).
Eva n. pr. f. Eve.
evacuación f. Evacuation.
evacuado, da m. y f. Evacuee.
evacuante adj./s.m. MED. Evacuant.
evacuar v. tr. To evacuate: *la policía evacuó el local*, the police evacuated the premises; *los habitantes evacuaron la ciudad*, the inhabitants evacuated the town. || To evacuate (expeler del cuerpo). || To carry out (llevar a cabo).
evacuativo, va adj./s.m. MED Evacuant.
evacuatorio, ria adj. MED. Evacuant.
— M. Public lavatory.
evadido, da adj. Escaped.
— M. y f. Escapee, fugitive.
evadir v. tr. To avoid, to evade: *evadir una dificultad*, to avoid a difficulty; *evadió hablar del asunto*, he avoided talking about the matter. || To escape, to avoid, to evade (un peligro). || To shirk (responsabilidad).
— V. pr. To escape: *el preso se evadió*, the prisoner escaped.
evaluación f. Evaluation.
evaluar v. tr. To evaluate, to assess: *evaluar algo en cien libras*, to evaluate sth. at a hundred pounds.
evanescente adj. Evanescent.
evangeliario m. Gospel book.
evangélico, ca adj. Evangelical, evangelic.
evangelio m. REL. Gospel: *el Evangelio según San Juan*, the Gospel according to Saint John. || FIG. Gospel truth (verdad): *esto es el evangelio*, this is the Gospel truth.
evangelismo m. Evangelism.
evangelista adj./s. Evangelist. || *Amer.* Letter writer (memorialista). || *San Juan Evangelista*, Saint John the Evangelist.
evangelización f. Evangelization, evangelizing.
evangelizador, ra adj. Evangelizing.
— M. y f. Evangelist.
evangelizar v. tr. To evangelize, to preach the Gospel to.
evaporable adj. Evaporable.
evaporación f. Evaporation.
evaporador m. Evaporator.
evaporar v. tr. To evaporate.
— V. pr. To evaporate. || FIG. To disappear, to vanish, to evaporate.
evaporizar v. tr. e intr. To vaporize.
— V. pr. To vaporize.
evasión f. Escape (fuga). || Excuse, dodge, evasion (evasiva). || Flight: *evasión de capitales*, capital flight. || Evasion: *evasión fiscal*, tax evasion.
evasiva f. Excuse. || *Andarse con evasivas*, to hedge.
evasivo, va adj. Evasive.
evección f. ASTR. Evection.
evento m. Event (acontecimiento). || *A todo evento*, at all events.
eventual adj. Possible (posible): *un viaje eventual*, a possible journey. || Temporary, casual, provisional (provisional). || Fortuitous (casual). || Incidental (gastos).
eventualidad f. Eventuality, possibility.
eventualmente adv. By chance (por casualidad). || Possibly (probablemente).
evicción f. JUR. Eviction.
evidencia f. Obviousness, clearness (cualidad de evidente). || Certainty (certidumbre). || JUR. Evidence, proof. || — *Con toda evidencia*, obviously. || *Poner en evidencia*, to show, to make obvious *o* evident, to demonstrate: *el experimento puso en evidencia la verdad de la teoría*, the experiment showed *o* demonstrated the truth of the theory, the experiment made the truth of the theory obvious; to show up (persona): *le puso en evidencia delante de su mujer*, he showed him up in front of his wife. || *Ponerse en evidencia*, to become clear *o* obvious (cosas, hechos), to show o.s. up, to reveal o.s. (personas).
evidenciar v. tr. To show, to demonstrate, to make obvious *o* evident: *esto evidencia su inteligencia*, this shows his intelligence.
— V. pr. To be obvious *o* evident: *se evidencia la necesidad de ensanchar esa calle*, it is obvious that that street needs widening. || To stand out, to be evident: *su talento se evidencia en sus obras*, his talent stands out in his works.
evidente adj. Obvious, clear, evident.
evidentemente adv. Obviously, clearly, evidently.
evitable adj. Avoidable. || That can be prevented *o* avoided (que se puede impedir).
evitación f. Avoiding, avoidance. || Preventing, prevention, avoiding (acción de impedir). || Saving, sparing (de una molestia, un sufrimiento, etc.).
evitar v. tr. To avoid (eludir): *evitó hablar conmigo*, he avoided speaking to me. || To escape, to avoid, to evade: *evitar un peligro*, to escape a danger. || To save, to spare (ahorrar): *no pude evitarle este sufrimiento*, I couldn't spare him this suffering. || To avoid, to prevent (impedir): *no pudo evitar el accidente*, he couldn't avoid the accident. || To shun (las tentaciones).
evocable adj. Evocable.
evocación f. Evocation, recalling, conjuring up (acción). || Evocation, recollection (descripción): *evocación de su niñez*, evocation of his childhood.
evocador, ra adj. Evocative, evocatory.
evocar v. tr. To evoke, to recall, to call forth, to conjure up: *evocar recuerdos*, to recall memories. || To evoke: *una casa que evoca las del siglo XVIII*, a house which evokes those of the 18th century. || To invoke (a los espíritus).
evocativo, va adj. Evocative.
evocatorio, ria adj. Evocatory.
evolución f. Evolution. || Development, evolution (de ideas, del pensamiento). || MIL. Evolution, manoeuvre. || Evolution, turn (vuelta).
evolucionado, da adj. Fully-developed: *pueblo evolucionado*, fully-developed nation.
evolucionar v. intr. To evolve. || To evolve, to change, to develop (ideas, pensamiento, etc.). || MIL. To manoeuvre, to carry out evolutions. || To turn (dar vueltas).
evolucionismo m. Evolutionism.
evolucionista adj./s. Evolutionist.
evoluta f. Evolute (curva).
evolutivo, va adj. Evolutionary, evolutional.
evolvente f. MAT. Involute.
ex pref. Ex , former: *ex ministro*, ex-minister, former minister. || — *El Congo ex belga*, the former Belgian Congo. || *Ex alumno*, v. EXALUMNO. || *Los ex combatientes*, the ex-servicemen [U.S., the veterans].
— OBSERV. En inglés siempre hay un guión entre *ex* y el nombre.
ex abrupto adv. Abruptly, sharply.
exabrupto m. FAM. Abrupt *o* sharp remark.
exacción f. Exaction: *exacción de tributos*, exaction of taxes. || Extortion, exaction (abuso).
exacerbación f. o **exacerbamiento** m. Exasperation. || Exacerbation, aggravation (de enfermedad, dolor). || Exacerbation (de sentimientos).
exacerbante adj. Irritating, exasperating.
exacerbar v. tr. To exasperate, to irritate (irritar). || To exacerbate, to aggravate (enfermedad, dolor, etc.). || To exacerbate (los sentimientos).
exactitud f. Exactness. || Accuracy (de copia, cálculo, versión, etc.). || Precision. || Correctness, truth (verdad).
exacto, ta adj. Exact: *la hora exacta*, the exact time. || Faithful, exact, accurate: *una copia exacta*, a faithful copy. || Accurate, correct: *cálculo exacto*, accurate calculation; *versión exacta del accidente*, correct version of the accident. || Correct, true, right (verdadero). || Punctual (puntual). || — *En cumplimiento exacto de sus órdenes*, assiduously carrying out his orders. || *Es un exacto cumplidor de*, he carries out assiduously *o* scrupulously. || *Tres metros exactos*, exactly three metres.
— Adv. Exactly.
exageración f. Exaggeration. || *Eso es una exageración*, that's going too far, that's overdoing it, that's exaggerating.
exageradamente adv. Exaggeratedly. || Exceedingly, extremely: *es un hombre exageradamente amable*, he is an exceedingly kind man.
exagerado, da adj. Exaggerated, farfetched: *relato exagerado*, exaggerated story. || Excessive (excesivo): *severidad exagerada*, excessive severity. || Exorbitant, outrageous (precio). || Overdemonstrative (persona). || — *Confianza exagerada*, over-confidence. || *Ser exagerado*, to overdo it, to go too far, to exaggerate.
exagerar v. tr. To exaggerate: *exagerar lo ocurrido*, to exaggerate what happened. || To overdo, to go too far with: *no exageres el entrenamiento*, don't overdo your training.
— V. intr. To overdo, to go too far with: *exagerar con los baños de sol*, to overdo one's sunbathing. || To overdo it, to go too far, to exaggerate: *tú exageras*, you are overdoing it, you are going too far.
exaltación f. Extolling, exalting, praising: *exaltación de la virtud*, extolling of virtue. || Elation, exaltation (alegría). || Exaltation, overexcitement (por una pasión). || Exaltation, promotion: *exaltación al grado de general*, exaltation to the rank of general. || Extremism (politics). || *Exaltación de la Santa Cruz*, Exaltation of the Holy Cross.
exaltado, da adj. Exalted, extolled, praised (alabado). || Extreme (político). || Excitable, hotheaded: *un chico*

muy exaltado, a very excitable boy. || Worked up, overexcited: *hoy está exaltado*, he's worked up today.
— M. y f. Hothead. || Extremist (político).

exaltador, ra o **exaltante** adj. Exalting.

exaltar v. tr. To extol, to exalt, to praise (enaltecer). || To work up, to overexcite (excitar). || To elate (con alegría). || To exacerbate, to increase (pasión). || To exalt, to raise (elevar).
— V. pr. To be extolled *o* exalted *o* praised (enaltecerse). || To get worked up *o* overexcited *o* carried away (excitarse): *¡no te exaltes tanto!*, don't get so worked up! || To increase, to run high (pasión). || To get heated (en una pelea). || To be exalted *o* raised (elevarse).

exalumno, na m. y f. Old boy (chico), old girl (chica) [de un colegio]. || Former student (de la universidad).

examen m. Examination, exam: *tener un examen*, to sit *o* to take *o* to do an examination; *aprobar un examen*, to pass an exam. || Examination, consideration, study (de un problema, una situación). || Survey (indagación). || — *Examen de conciencia*, self-examination. || *Examen de ingreso*, entrance examination. || JUR. *Examen de testigos*, interrogation *o* examination of witnesses. || *Examen médico*, medical examination *o* checkup. || *Libre examen*, personal interpretation [of the Bible]. || *Presentarse a un examen*, to take *o* to sit an exam. || *Someter a examen*, to examine. || *Sufrir un examen*, to take *o* to sit *o* to do an exam.

examinador, ra adj. Examining.
— M. y f. Examiner.

examinando, da m. y f. Candidate, examination candidate, examinee.

examinante adj. Examining.

examinar v. tr. To examine. || To consider, to study, to examine: *examinar un documento*, to consider a document. || To examine (a un candidato, a un enfermo).
— V. pr. To take *o* to sit *o* to do an examination: *examinarse de historia*, to take a history examination *o* an examination in history.

exangüe adj. Bloodless, exsanguine (falto de sangre). || FIG. Exhausted, worn-out (sin fuerzas). | Dead (muerto).

exánime adj. Dead (muerto). || Lifeless, inanimate (inanimado). || Exhausted, worn-out (sin fuerzas).

exantema m. MED. Exanthema, exanthem (erupción).

exarca m. Exarch.

exarcado m. Exarchate.

exasperación f. Exasperation.

exasperador, ra adj. Exasperating (irritante).

exasperante adj. Exasperating.

exasperar v. tr. To exasperate.
— V. pr. To get exasperated.

excarcelación f. Release [from prison] (liberación).

excarcelar v. tr. To release [from prison] (liberar).

ex cátedra adj./adv. Ex cathedra.

excavación f. Excavation, digging: *excavación de zanjas*, digging of ditches. || Excavation: *hacer excavaciones en Egipto*, to carry out excavations in Egypt.

excavador, ra adj. Excavating, digging.
— M. y f. Excavator (persona). || — F. Digger, excavator. || — *Excavadora de mandíbulas*, grab. || *Excavadora mecánica*, mechanical digger *o* shovel.

excavar v. tr. To dig, to excavate: *excavar una zanja*, to dig a ditch. || To excavate, to dig up: *excavar el suelo*, to excavate the ground. || To excavate (en arqueología). || AGR. To clear the soil around [plants].

excedencia f. Leave (de funcionario, de militar): *pedir la excedencia por un año*, to ask for a year's leave. || Leave pay (sueldo). || Sabbatical leave (de profesor). || *Excedencia por un año*, sabbatical year (de profesor).

excedente adj. Excess, surplus (que sobra). || Excessive (excesivo). || On leave (funcionario, soldado). || On sabbatical leave (profesor).
— M. Surplus: *excedente de productos en un país*, a country's surplus products. || What is left (sobra): *quédate con el excedente*, keep what is left. || *Excedentes agrícolas*, agricultural surplus.

exceder v. intr. To exceed, to surpass, to be more than: *los ingresos exceden a los gastos en cien libras*, income exceeds *o* surpasses expenditure by a hundred pounds, income is a hundred pounds more than expenditure. || To surpass, to excel: *mi coche excede al tuyo en velocidad*, my car surpasses yours in speed. || To be beyond: *el trabajo excede a su capacidad*, the work is beyond his capacity.
— V. pr. To exceed: *se excedió en sus funciones*, he exceeded his duty. || To overdo, to go too far *o* to the extreme (exagerar): *se han excedido en el castigo*, they have overdone the punishment, they have gone to the extreme *o* too far with the punishment. || To be extremely kind [friendly, generous, etc.]: *se excedieron conmigo*, they were extremely kind to me. || — *Excederse a sí mismo*, to excel o.s. || *No se han excedido conmigo*, they weren't overkind to me, they weren't exactly kind to me.

excelencia f. Excellence. || Excellency (tratamiento honorífico). || — *Por excelencia*, par excellence. || *Su Excelencia*, His Excellency.

excelente adj. Excellent.

excelentísimo, ma adj. Most excellent.

excelsitud f. Sublimity, sublimeness, loftiness.

excelso, sa adj. Sublime, lofty.
— M. *El Excelso*, the Most High.

excentricidad f. MAT. Eccentricity: *la excentricidad de una elipse*, the eccentricity of an ellipse. || FIG. Oddity, eccentricity, peculiarity (cosa rara, extravagancia). | Eccentricity (de una persona).

excéntrico, ca adj. MAT. Eccentric. || FIG. Eccentric, odd.
— M. y f. Eccentric. || — F. TECN. Eccentric.

excepción f. Exception: *ser una excepción a la regla*, to be an exception to the rule. || — *A* or *con excepción de*, except for, with the exception of: *me gustan todos los vestidos a excepción del rojo*, I like all the dresses with the exception of the red one. || *Estado de excepción*, state of emergency. || *Hacer excepción de*, not to include. || *Hacer una excepción*, to make an exception. || *La excepción confirma la regla*, the exception proves the rule. || *Si se hace excepción de*, except for, apart from, with the exception of: *si se hace excepción de dos o tres, todos vienen*, apart from *o* with the exception of *o* except for two or three, they are all coming.

excepcional adj. Exceptional (extraordinario): *un libro excepcional*, an exceptional book. || Unusual, exceptional (raro): *una coincidencia excepcional*, an unusual coincidence.

excepto prep. Except for, excepting, apart from: *excepto eso, todo va bien*, except for that, everything is going well. || Except, except for, apart from: *vienen todos, excepto Pedro*, they are all coming except Peter; *salgo todos los días, excepto cuando llueve*, I go out every day, except when it rains.

exceptuar v. tr. To except, to exclude, not to include, to leave out: *exceptuaron a los niños de esta regla*, they excepted children from this rule. || JUR. To exempt. || *Exceptuando a los niños*, children excepted, except for children.
— V. pr. To be excepted *o* excluded, not to be included. || *Se vacunará a todos los niños, pero se exceptúa a los de menos de un año*, all children will be vaccinated except *o* except for *o* apart from those under one year of age.

excesivo, va adj. Excessive: *una carga excesiva*, an excessive load.

exceso m. Excess. || Excess, surplus (excedente). || Surfeit (de comida). || FIG. Excess: *pagar los excesos de su juventud*, to pay for the excesses of one's youth. || — *Cometer excesos en la bebida*, to drink too much, to drink to excess. || *Cometer excesos en la comida*, to overeat, to eat to excess. || *Con exceso*, too much: *fumar con exceso*, to smoke too much. || *El exceso de ejercicio es malo*, too much *o* excessive excercise is bad. || *En exceso*, excessively, in excess. || *Exceso de comida, de peso*, overeating, overweight. || *Exceso de equipaje*, excess baggage. || *Exceso de velocidad*, speeding.

excipiente m. MED. Excipient.

excisión f. MED. Excision.

excitabilidad f. Excitability.

excitable adj. Excitable, easily worked up. || Temperamental (nervioso). || Excitable (en fisiología).

excitación f. Rousing, stirring up, inciting, exciting (incitación). || Rousing, stirring up, stimulation (de una pasión). || Restlessness, uneasiness, agitation (agitación). || Excitement (de alegría, entusiasmo). || Activation (activación). || Stimulation (del apetito, etc.). || ELECTR. Excitation.

excitador m. FÍS. y ELECTR. Exciter.

excitante adj. Exciting. || Stimulating, excitant: *una bebida excitante*, a stimulating drink.
— M. Stimulant, excitant.

excitar v. tr. To rouse, to incite, to stir up, to excite: *excitar a un pueblo a la rebelión*, to rouse a nation to rebellion. || To arouse, to stir up, to excite, to stimulate: *excitar la ira, el deseo*, to arouse anger, desire. || To get worked up, to put on edge, to make restless *o* uneasy (poner en estado de nerviosismo o impaciencia). || To excite, to get worked up (con alegría, entusiasmo). || To activate (activar). || To stimulate (el apetito, la circulación de la sangre). || ELECTR. To excite: *excitar una dinamo*, to excite a dynamo. || *Excitarle los nervios a alguien*, to put s.o.'s nerves on edge.
— V. pr. To get excited. || To get worked up *o* carried away *o* excited (por alegría, entusiasmo). || To get worked up *o* restless *o* uneasy (por nerviosismo, impaciencia). || To be roused *o* incited *o* stirred up *o* excited (a la rebelión, etc.).

excitativo, va adj. Exciting, excitative (excitante).

exclamación f. Exclamation. || Cry (grito). || Exclamation mark (signo de admiración).

exclamar v. tr. e intr. To exclaim.

exclamativo, va o **exclamatorio, ria** adj. Exclamatory, exclamative (ant.).

exclaustración f. Secularization.

exclaustrado, da m. y f. Secularized monk (monje), secularized nun (monja).

exclaustrar v. tr. To secularize (mandar abandonar el claustro a un religioso).

excluir* v. tr. To exclude (no incluir). || To exclude, to shut out (de un círculo, etc.). || To throw out (expulsar). || To reject (rechazar).

exclusión f. Exclusion. || *Con exclusión de*, excluding, to the exclusion of.
exclusiva f. Exclusive *o* sole right (privilegio): *dar la exclusiva a un editor*, to give the sole right to a publisher. || Exclusive (en un periódico). || — *En exclusiva*, exclusively. || *Venta en exclusiva*, exclusive sale.
exclusive adv. Exclusively (únicamente). || Exclusive: *desde el dos hasta el diez de abril exclusive*, from the second to the tenth of April exclusive.
exclusividad f. Exclusiveness (cualidad de exclusivo). || Exclusive *o* sole right (exclusiva).
exclusivismo m. Exclusivism.
exclusivista adj./s. Exclusivist.
exclusivo, va adj. Exclusive, sole: *agente exclusivo*, sole agent.
excogitar v. tr. To excogitate.
excombatiente m. Ex-serviceman [U.S., veteran].
excomulgado, da adj. Excommunicate, excommunicated.
— M. y f. Excommunicant, excommunicated person.
excomulgar v. tr. To excommunicate: *excomulgar a un hereje*, to excommunicate a heretic. || FIG. To ban.
excomunión f. Excommunication. || Excommunication order (decreto): *fulminar una excomunión*, to fulminate an excommunication order.
excoriación f. Chafing, rubbing, excoriation. || Graze (desolladura).
excoriar v. tr. To chafe, to rub, to excoriate (la piel). || To graze (desollar).
— V. pr. To be chafed.
excrecencia f. Excrescence.
excreción f. Excretion.
excrementar v. intr. To excrete, to defecate, to defaecate.
excrementicio, cia adj. Excremental.
excremento m. Excrement.
excrementoso, sa adj. Full of roughage (alimento). || Excremental (excrementicio).
excrescencia f. Excrescence.
excretar v. tr. To excrete.
excretor, ra o **excretorio, ria** adj. ANAT. Excretory: *conducto excretor*, excretory duct.
exculpación f. Exculpation, exoneration. || JUR. Acquittal.
exculpar v. tr. To exculpate, to exonerate (descargar de culpa). || JUR. To acquit (absolver).
excursión f. Trip, excursion, outing: *ir de excursión, hacer una excursión*, to go on a trip, to go on an excursion.
excursionismo m. Outings, *pl.*, excursions, *pl.* || Hiking (a pie).
excursionista m. y f. Excursionist, tripper. || Hiker (a pie).
excusa f. Excuse (pretexto): *¡nada de excusas!*, no excuses! || Apology, excuse (disculpa). || — *Dar excusas*, to make excuses. || *Deshacerse en excusas*, to apologize profusely. || *Presentar sus excusas a*, to apologize to, to give one's apologies to, to excuse o.s. to, to make one's excuses to.
excusable adj. Excusable, pardonable.
excusadamente adv. Unnecessarily.
excusado, da adj. Excused, pardoned (perdonado). || Unnecessary, superfluous, needless (inútil). || Exempt (exento): *excusado de ir*, exempt from going. || Concealed: *puerta excusada*, concealed door. || Private, reserved (reservado). || *Excusado es decir que*, needless to say that.
— M. Toilet (retrete).
excusar v. tr. To excuse, to pardon (disculpar). || To avoid, to prevent (impedir): *excusar disturbios*, to avoid disturbances. || To save, to spare: *esto te excusa venir*, this saves your coming. || To have no need: *excusas venir*, you have no need to come. || To exempt (eximir). || To dodge, to shirk: *excusar responsabilidades*, to dodge responsibilities. || *Excúsame con tu madre*, apologize to your mother for me, give my apologies to your mother.
— V. pr. To excuse o.s. || To apologize: *excusarse con uno*, to apologize to s.o.; *excusarse de* or *por haber hecho algo*, to apologize for having done sth. || *El que se excusa, se acusa*, to excuse o.s. is to accuse o.s.
exeat m. inv. Discharge, exeat (permiso de salida).
execrable adj. Abominable, loathsome, execrable.
execración f. Execration. || Curse: *proferir execraciones*, to utter curses.
execrar v. tr. To loathe, to detest, to execrate (odiar). || To execrate, to curse (maldecir).
exégesis f. Exegesis.
exegeta m. Exegete.
exegético, ca adj. Exegetic, exegetical.
exención f. Exemption.
exentar v. tr. (P.us.). To exempt.
exento, ta adj. Exempt. || Free: *exento de toda obligación*, free from any obligation. || Open (descubierto). || — *Exento de aduanas*, duty-free: *productos exentos de aduanas*, duty-free goods. || *No exento de riesgos*, not without dangers.
exequátur m. inv. Exequatur.
exequias f. pl. Funeral rites, funeral ceremony, *sing.*, obsequies, exequies.
exergo m. Exergue (de una medalla).
exfoliación f. Exfoliation.
exfoliador m. *Amer.* Tear-off calendar (calendario de taco).
exfoliar v. tr. To exfoliate.
exfoliativo, va adj. Exfoliative.
exhalación f. Exhalation, giving off (acción de exhalar). || Exhalation, effluvium (efluvio). || Vapour, exhalation (vapor). || Shooting star (estrella fugaz). || Flash of lightning (rayo). || — FIG. *Irse como una exhalación*, to be gone in a flash. | *Pasar como una exhalación*, to flash past.
exhalar v. tr. To exhale, to give off *o* out: *exhalar un olor*, to give off a smell. || FIG. To breathe, to heave: *exhalar suspiros*, to heave sighs. | To utter (quejas). || *Exhalar el último suspiro*, to heave one's last sigh, to breathe one's last.
— V. pr. To run quickly.
exhaustivo, va adj. Exhaustive (completo). || *Tratar un tema de modo exhaustivo*, to deal exhaustively with a subject.
exhausto, ta adj. Exhausted, worn-out (muy cansado). || Exhausted (agotado).
exheredar v. tr. To disinherit.
exhibición f. Exhibition, show (demostración, exposición). || Presentation, show, exhibition (de modelos de alta costura). || Showing (en un cine). || *Exhibición de fieras*, menagery.
exhibicionismo m. Exhibitionism.
exhibicionista m. y f. Exhibitionist.
exhibidor, ra adj. Showing.
— M. CINEM. Cinema owner [U.S., exhibitor].
exhibir v. tr. To put on show (mostrar). || To exhibit (cuadros, etc.) || To show: *exhibió su pasaporte*, he showed his passport. || To present, to show (modelos de alta costura). || To show (en un cine). || FIG. To show off (mostrar con orgullo). | To let show (hacer alarde). || *Amer.* To pay (pagar).
— V. pr. To make an exhibition of o.s., to show o.s. (mostrarse en público).
exhortación f. Exhortation.
exhortador, ra adj. Exhorting.
exhortar v. tr. To exhort.
exhortativo, va adj. Exhortative.
exhortatorio, ria adj. Exhortatory.
exhorto m. JUR. Letters rogatory, *pl.*
exhumación f. Exhumation.
exhumar v. tr. To exhume. || FIG. To dig up: *exhumar el pasado*, to dig up the past.
exigencia f. Exigency, demand. || Requirement (lo necesario). || — *Él tiene muchas exigencias*, he is very demanding. || *Según las exigencias del caso*, as the situation requires.
exigente adj. Demanding, exacting, exigent. || *Es muy exigente conmigo*, he asks a lot of me, he is very demanding with me.
exigibilidad f. Liability to be demanded.
exigible adj. Demandable, exactable, exigible. || Payable on demand (una deuda).
exigir v. tr. To demand, to exact: *exigir un pago*, to demand a payment. || To insist upon, to ask for, to demand: *exigir ropa de buena calidad*, to insist upon good quality clothing. || To require, to call for: *medidas exigidas por las circunstancias*, measures required by the circumstances. || To demand, to call for: *crimen que exige venganza*, crime which calls for revenge. || *Exiges demasiado*, you are very demanding.
exigüidad f. Smallness: *la exigüidad de un cuarto*, the smallness of a room. || Meagerness, scantiness, exiguity: *la exigüidad de sus recursos*, the meagerness of his resources.
exiguo, gua adj. Small, tiny, exiguous (casa, etc.). || Meager, exiguous, scanty (cantidad, recursos, etc).
exilado, da o **exiliado, da** adj. Exiled, in exile.
— M. y f. Exile.
exilar o **exiliar** v. tr. To exile.
— V. pr. To go into exile..
exilio m. Exile (destierro): *enviar al exilio*, to send into exile; *gobierno en el exilio*, government in exile.
eximente adj. JUR. Absolving, absolutory.
eximio, mia adj. Renowned, distinguished, eminent: *el eximio poeta*, the distinguished poet.
eximir v. tr. To exempt (de impuestos, de servicio militar). || To free (liberar): *esto le exime de cualquier obligación conmigo*, this frees him from any obligation to me.
— V. pr. To free o.s. (liberarse).
existencia f. Existence. || — Pl. COM. Stock, *sing.*, stocks: *liquidación de existencias*, clearance sale of stock; *las existencias de un género*, the stock of an article. || COM. *Renovar las existencias*, to restock.
existencial adj. Existential.
existencialismo m. Existentialism.
existencialista adj./s. Existentialist.
existente adj. Existent, existing. || Existing, in stock (reservas).
existir v. intr. To exist (ser). || — *Aún existe uno*, there is still one left. || *Existe desde hace cien años*, it has existed *o* has been in existence for a hundred years.
éxito m. Success: *esta película ha sido un éxito clamoroso*, this film was an overwhelming success. || Success, hit (canción, novela, obra de teatro, etc.). || Outcome, result (resultado). || — *Con éxito*, successfully. || *Éxito de taquilla*, box-office success. || *No tener éxito*, to

fail, not to succeed. || *Novela de gran éxito editorial*, best seller. || *Tener éxito*, to succeed: *tener éxito en la vida*, to succeed in life; to be successful: *este actor tiene mucho exito*, this actor is very successful; to be popular (tener muchos admiradores): *esta chica tiene mucho éxito*, this girl is very popular.
exitosamente adv. *Amer.* Successfully.
exitoso, sa adj. *Amer.* Successful.
ex libris m. Ex libris, bookplate.
exocrino, na adj. Exocrine.
éxodo m. Exodus: *éxodo rural*, rural exodus.
exoftalmía f. MED. Exophthalmus, exophthalmos.
exogamia f. Exogamy.
exógamo, ma adj. Exogamic, exogamous.
exógeno, na adj. Exogenous.
exoneración f. Freeing, exoneration. || *Exoneración de base*, basic [tax] abatement (en un impuesto).
exonerar v. tr. To free, to exonerate (de una obligación). || To exempt (de impuestos). || To dismiss (de un cargo). || *Exonerar el vientre*, to relieve o.s.
exorbitancia f. Exorbitance, exorbitancy.
exorbitante adj. Exorbitant.
exorcismo m. Exorcism.
exorcista m. Exorcist, exorciser, exorcizer.
exorcizar v. tr. To exorcize, to exorcise.
exordio m. Exordium, introduction, preamble (preámbulo). || FAM. Beginning.
exornar v. tr. To adorn, to embellish.
exósmosis f. Exosmosis.
exotérico, ca adj. Exoteric.
exotérmico, ca adj. Exothermic.
exótico, ca adj. Exotic.
exotismo m. Exoticism.
expandir v. tr. To expand (desarrollar, dilatar). || To spread (propagar).
— V. pr. To expand (extenderse). || To spread: *la noticia se ha expandido por todo el país*, the news has spread throughout the country.
expansibilidad f. FÍS. Expansibility, expandability. || FIG. Expansiveness.
expansible adj. Expansible, expandable.
expansión f. Expansion (dilatación). || Spreading (de una idea, de un uso, de una noticia). || Relaxation (recreo). || Expansion: *expansión industrial, colonial*, industrial, colonial expansion. || Expansion, increase (aumento). || FIG. Openness, frankness, expansiveness (franqueza).
expansionar v. tr. To expand.
— V. pr. To expand (dilatarse). || To open one's heart: *expansionarse con uno*, to open one's heart to s.o. || To relax (recrearse).
expansionismo m. Expansionism.
expansionista adj./s. Expansionist.
expansivo, va adj. Open, frank, expansive (franco). || Expansible, expandable (expansible).
expatriación f. Expatriation (exilio). || Emigration.
expatriado, da adj./s. Expatriate.
expatriar v. tr. To banish, to expatriate.
— V. pr. To leave one's country, to go into exile (exiliarse). || To emigrate (emigrar).
expectación f. Expectation, expectancy, anticipation: *había gran expectación en la ciudad ante la llegada de la reina*, the queen's arrival caused great expectation in the city. || Excitement (emoción). || Waiting (espera).
expectante adj. Expectant.
expectativa f. Expectation, expectancy. || Prospect (perspectiva). || Hope (esperanza). || *Estar a la expectativa de algo*, to be on the lookout for sth., to be on the watch for sth.
expectoración f. MED. Expectoration. | Sputum (esputo).
expectorante adj./s. m. MED. Expectorant.
expectorar v. tr. e intr. MED. To expectorate.
expedición f. Expedition (excursión). || Party, expedition: *expedición de salvamento*, search party, rescue expedition. || Dispatch, shipping, sending (envío de mercancías). || Shipment (mercancías enviadas). || Sending (de un paquete). || Dispatch (de un asunto).
expedicionario, ria adj. Sending, dispatching (que envía). || Expeditionary: *cuerpo expedicionario*, expeditionary force.
— M. y f. Sender (expedidor). || Member of an expedition (que participa en una expedición).
expedidor, ra adj. Sending, dispatching, shipping, forwarding (de mercancías). || Sending (de un paquete, etc.).
— M. y f. Sender, dispatcher, shipper, forwarding agent (de mercancías). || Sender (de un paquete, etc.).
expedientado, da adj. Under enquiry.
expedientar v. tr. To place under enquiry. || To make a file on (la policía).
expediente adj. Expedient.
— M. Expedient, means (medio): *un hábil expediente*, a clever expedient. || JUR. Case, proceedings, *pl.*: *instruir un expediente*, to open a case *o* proceedings. || File, dossier (documentos): *tiene un expediente cargado en la policía*, the police have a full file on him. || Enquiry: *formar* or *instruir expediente a un funcionario*, to open an enquiry on a civil servant. || Record: *expediente académico, profesional*, academic, professional record. || — Pl. Proceedings (trámites). || — FIG. *Cubrir el expediente*, to do one's duty. || *Dar expediente a un asunto*, to dispose of *o* to expedite a matter. || *Tener recurso al expediente de*, to resort to [the device of].
expedienteo m. Red tape (papeleo).
expedir* v. tr. To send, to dispatch, to forward, to ship (enviar mercancías). || To send (un paquete, etc.). || JUR. To draw up: *expedir un contrato*, to draw up a contract. || To issue: *pasaporte expedido en París*, passport issued in Paris. || To deal with (un asunto). || FIG. To dispose of, to dispatch (hacer rápidamente).
expeditar v. tr. *Amer.* To solve (un asunto).
expeditivo, va adj. Expeditious.
expedito, ta adj. Clear, free: *la vía quedó expedita*, the road was clear. || Expeditious, speedy, quick, prompt: *expedito para obrar*, expeditious to act.
expelente adj. Expelling. || *Bomba expelente*, force pump.
expeler v. tr. To expel (a uno). || To give out, to throw out, to eject: *el volcán expele rocas*, the volcano throws out rocks. || MED. To spit out (mucosidades). | To eliminate (cálculo).
expendedor, ra adj. Spending.
— M. y f. Dealer, retailer (vendedor al detalle). || Ticket agent (de localidades). || Tobacconist [U.S., dealer in tobacco] (de tabaco). || Person who spreads counterfeit money (de moneda falsa). || *Expendedor automático*, vending machine.
expendeduría f. Retail store (tienda). || Retailing (venta). || Ticket office (de localidades para espectáculos). || Ticket office (de lotería). || *Expendeduría de tabaco*, tobacconist's [U.S., cigar store].
expender v. tr. To retail (vender al por menor). || To spend (gastar). || To circulate, to pass [counterfeit money] (moneda falsa).
expendio m. *Amer.* V. EXPENDEDURÍA.
expensar v. tr. *Amer.* To pay the expenses of.
expensas f. pl. Expenses (gastos). || JUR. Costs. || *A expensas de*, at the expense of.
experiencia f. Experience: *tener experiencia*, to have experience. || FÍS. y QUÍM. Experiment (experimento). || — *Por experiencia*, from experience. || *Saber por propia experiencia*, to know from one's own experience.
experimentación f. Testing, experimenting, experimentation: *la experimentación de un nuevo procedimento de televisión*, the testing of a new television process. || Experiment (experimento).
experimentado, da adj. Experienced (persona). || Tested, tried (método, etc.).
experimentador, ra adj. Experimenting.
— M. y f. Experimenter.
experimental adj. Experimental.
experimentar v. tr. To carry out experiments on, to test, to try out (científicamente). || To test: *experimentar un nuevo método*, to test a new method. || To experience (probar). || To have, to experience (dificultades). || To have, to experience, to feel (sentir): *experimentar una sensación desagradable*, to experience an unpleasant sensation. || To feel (una emoción). || To show (un aumento). || To suffer (sufrir). || To suffer, to sustain: *experimentar una derrota*, to suffer a defeat. || To undergo, to experience: *experimentar una renovación completa*, to undergo a complete renovation.
experimento m. Experiment: *un experimento de química*, a chemistry experiment. || Experimenting, experimentation (acción de experimentar).
expertamente adv. Expertly, skilfully.
experto, ta adj./s. Expert. || *Ser experto en la materia*, to be an expert in the matter *o* on the subject.
expiable adj. Expiable.
expiación f. Expiation, atonement.
expiar v. tr. To expiate, to atone for (un pecado). || To serve (una pena).
expiativo, va o **expiatorio, ria** adj. Expiatory.
expiración f. Expiration.
expirante adj. Expiring.
expirar v. intr. To die, to expire, to breathe one's last (morir). || JUR. To expire (contrato, etc.). || FIG. To expire: *su pena ha expirado ya*, his sentence has now expired.
explanación f. Levelling (de un terreno). || FIG. Explanation, elucidation (aclaración).
explanada f. Esplanade. || Glacis, esplanade (fortificación).
explanar v. tr. To level (un terreno). || FIG. To explain, to elucidate, to clear up (aclarar).
explayar v. tr. To spread out, to extend.
— V. pr. To be long-winded, to speak at length, to expatiate: *explayarse en un discurso*, to be long-winded in a speech. || To open one's heart, to confide (confiarse): *se explayaba en sus cartas a sus amigos*, in his letters he opened his heart to his friends, in his letters he confided in his friends. || *Explayarse al gusto de uno*, to talk one's head off.
expletivo, va adj. Expletive.
explicable adj. Explicable, explainable. || Justifiable.
explicación f. Explanation. || Reason, explanation: *sin dar ninguna clase de explicaciones*, without giving any reason at all. || Excuse, explanation (excusa). || *Tener una explicación con alguien*, to come to an explanation with s.o., to have it out with s.o.

explicaderas f. pl. FAM. Way (*sing.*) of explaining. || FAM. *Tener buenas explicaderas*, to have a way of explaining things.

explicar v. tr. To explain: *explícame cómo ha ocurrido*, explain to me how it happened. || To lecture in, to teach (enseñar). || To expound, to explain, to explicate: *explicar una teoría*, to expound a theory. || To explain, to comment upon (un texto). || To justify (justificar): *explicó su intervención*, he justified his intervention. || *Explicar algo con pelos y señales*, to explain sth. in the minutest detail.
— V. pr. To explain o.s. || To understand, to make out, to be able to understand: *no me explico cómo he podido perderlo*, I can't understand how I could have lost it. || To express o.s. (expresarse). || To explain o.s. (justificarse). || *Eso se explica difícilmente*, this is difficult to explain.

explicativo, va adj. Explanatory, explicative.

explícito, ta adj. Explicit.

exploración f. Exploration (de un territorio, de una herida). || Prospecting (de minas). || Scanning (radar, televisión): *línea de exploración*, scanning line. || MIL. Reconnaissance, scouting. || *Exploración submarina*, underwater exploration (investigaciones), skin diving (deporte).

explorador, ra adj. Exploring, exploratory. || TECN. Scanning (en televisión, radar): *haz explorador*, scanning beam. || MIL. Scouting: *barco explorador*, scouting vessel.
— M. y f. Explorer. || — M. MIL. Scout. || Boy scout (niño). || TECN. Scanner (radar, televisión). || MED. Probe. || — F. Girl guide [U.S., girl scout] (niña).

explorar v. tr. To explore: *explorar la costa africana*, to explore the African coast. || To prospect (minas). || TECN. To scan (con un haz electrónico). || MED. To explore, to probe. || MIL. To scout, to reconnoitre. || FIG. To explore, to examine. || — *Explorar con la vista*, to scan. || FIG. *Explorar el terreno*, to see how the land lies.

exploratorio, ria adj. Exploratory: *conversaciones exploratorias*, exploratory talks. || MED. Exploratory, probing.

explosión f. Explosion, blowing up: *la explosión de una bomba*, the explosion of a bomb. || Bursting (de un balón). || Outburst, blast (detonación). || FIG. Outburst: *explosión de entusiasmo, de ira*, outburst of enthusiasm, of anger. || — *Explosión demográfica*, population explosion. || *Hacer explosión*, to explode. || *Motor de explosión*, internal combustion engine.

explosionar v. tr. To explode.
— V. intr. To explode, to blow up.

explosivo, va adj./s.m. Explosive. || — Adj./s. f. GRAM. Plosive, explosive (consonante).

explotable adj. Workable, exploitable (mina). || Which can be cultivated *o* farmed (terreno).

explotación f. Working, exploitation (de una mina): *explotación a cielo abierto*, opencast working. || Cultivation, farming (de un terreno). || Tapping, exploitation: *la explotación de los recursos naturales*, tapping of natural resources. || Commercial use, exploitation, working (de un bosque, etc.). || Operating, running, operation (de una fábrica, de una línea de comunicaciones, etc.). || Management (de un negocio). || Plant (conjunto de instalaciones): *explotación industrial*, industrial plant. || Exploitation (abuso): *la explotación de los obreros*, the exploitation of the workers. || — *Explotación agrícola*, farm (granja), farming (organización agrícola). || *Explotación forestal*, timber farm. || *Explotación minera*, mine (mina), mining (industria). || *Gastos de explotación*, operating costs.

explotador, ra adj. Operating: *compañía explotadora*, operating company. || AGR. Working, farming. || Exploiting (que abusa).
— M. y f. Operator (el que explota). || AGR. Exploiter, farmer, cultivator (cultivador). || Worker (de una mina). || Exploiter (el que abusa).

explotar v. tr. To work, to exploit (una mina). || To cultivate, to farm (terreno). || To tap, to exploit (recursos). || To manage (un negocio). || To put to commercial use, to exploit (comercializar). || To operate, to run (una fábrica, una línea de trenes, autobuses, etc.). || To exploit (abusar): *explota su bondad*, he exploits his kindness. || To exploit (a los obreros). || To explode (una bomba).
— V. intr. To explode, to blow up (una bomba, etc.).

expoliación f. Despoiling, spoliation.

expoliador, ra adj. Despoiling (persona). || Spoliatory (medida).
— M. y f. Despoiler, spoliator.

expoliar v. tr. To despoil, to spoliate (despojar).

exponencial adj. MAT. Exponential.

exponente adj. Exponent, expounding (que expone).
— M. MAT. Exponent, index. || Exponent (representante): *Cervantes es el máximo exponente de la literatura española*, Cervantes is the greatest exponent of Spanish literature. || Proof, example (prueba): *nuestras exportaciones son un magnífico exponente de la vitalidad de la industria nacional*, our exports are a magnificent proof of the vitality of the national industry.

exponer* v. tr. To expound: *exponer una teoría*, to expound a theory. || To put forward: *exponer una propuesta*, to put forward a proposal. || To set out, to state, to set forth (hechos). || To explain (explicar): *exponer su pensamiento*, to explain one's thought. || To show, to exhibit, to put on show: *exponer un cuadro*, to put a painting on show. || To display: *el comerciante expone su mercancía en el escaparate*, the dealer displays his goods in the window. || To expose (al aire, al sol, al viento). || To risk, to expose (arriesgar). || FOT. To expose. || REL. To expose (el Santísimo Sacramento). || To abandon (un niño). || *Exponer mucho*, to take great risks *o* a lot of risks, to run a lot of risks.
— V. pr. To expose o.s. || To run the risk, to take the risk: *exponerse a un fracaso, a que se enfade*, to run the risk of a failure, of his getting angry.

exportable adj. Exportable.

exportación f. Exportation, exporting (acción de exportar). || Export: *las exportaciones han aumentado*, exports have increased; *comercio de exportación*, export trade; *artículo de exportación*, export item; *exportaciones de naranjas*, orange exports.

exportador, ra adj. Exporting: *país exportador*, exporting country.
— M. y f. Exporter.

exportar v. tr. To export: *exportar naranjas de España*, to export oranges from Spain.

exposición f. Exhibition (de cuadros, etc.). || Show: *exposición del automóvil*, motor show. || Display (de mercancías). || Exposition (de una teoría). || Putting forward (de una propuesta). || Exposition, disclosure (de ideas). || Exposition, statement (declaración). || Explanation, exposé: *este periódico hace una exposición clara de los hechos*, this paper gives a clear explanation of the facts. || Exposition (en literatura y música). || Exposing (al aire, al sol, al viento). || Exposition (de una casa). || Risk, danger (riesgo). || FOT. Exposure. || REL. Exposition. || — FOT. *Exceso de exposición*, overexposure. || JUR. *Exposición de motivos*, motivation. || *Exposición Universal*, Universal Exhibition, World Fair. || FOT. *Falta de exposición*, underexposure. || *Sala de exposición*, showroom. || FOT. *Tiempo de exposición*, exposure time.

exposímetro m. FOT. Exposure meter.

expositivo, va adj. Explanatory, expositive, expository.

expósito, ta adj. Abandoned.
— M. y f. Foundling: *casa de expósitos*, home for foundlings.

expositor, ra adj./s. Exponent. || — M. y f. Exhibitor (en una exposición).

exprés m. Express (tren). || Espresso (café).

expresado, da adj. Expressed (expreso). || Mentioned, above-mentioned (mencionado).

expresamente adv. Specifically, expressly, especially (concretamente). || Purposely, on purpose (a propósito). || Explicitly (explícitamente).

expresar v. tr. To express: *expresar una idea*, to express an idea. || To show, to express (un sentimiento): *expresar alegría*, to show happiness. || To convey (comunicar).
— V. pr. To express o.s.: *no me expreso bien*, I don't express myself well. || To be expressed (cosa, sentimiento, idea). || To state: *como se expresa más adelante*, as is stated below.
— OBSERV. *Expresar* has two past participles. One regular, *expresado*, which is used with *haber* and *tener*, and one irregular, *expreso*, which is used only as an adjective.

expresión f. Expression. || — Pl. Regards, greetings (recuerdos): *dale expresiones de mi parte*, give him my regards. || — *Perdone* or *válgame la expresión*, pardon the expression. || *Reducir a la mínima expresión*, to reduce to the simplest expression, to reduce to the lowest terms (una fórmula), to reduce to almost nothing, to make as small as possible (un objeto).

expresionismo m. Expressionism.

expresionista adj./s. Expressionist.

expresivamente adv. Expressively. || Affectionately, warmly (con cariño).

expresivo, va adj. Expressive: *un gesto muy expresivo*, a very expressive gesture. || Significant: *silencio expresivo*, significant silence. || Sincere: *mi más expresivo agradecimiento*, my sincerest thanks. || Affectionate, warm (cariñoso).

expreso, sa adj. Expressed (dicho). || Express (especificado): *por orden expresa de la autoridad*, by express order of the authority. || Express: *tren expreso*, express train.
— M. Express (tren). || Express messenger (mensajero).

exprimelimones m. inv. Lemon squeezer.

exprimidera f. o **exprimidero** m. V. EXPRIMIDOR.

exprimidor m. Squeezer, lemon squeezer.

exprimir v. tr. To squeeze (extraer el jugo de). || FIG. To exploit, to get the most out of (explotar): *su patrón trata de exprimirle al máximo*, his boss is trying to exploit him as much as he can *o* to get the most he can out of him. | To bleed dry (sacar dinero). || FIG. *Exprimirse el cerebro*, to rack one's brains.

ex profeso adv. Specifically, especially, purposely.

expropiación f. Expropriation.

expropiador, ra adj. Expropriating.
— M. y f. Expropriator.

expropiar v. tr. To expropriate.

expuesto, ta adj. On display, on show, displayed: *las prendas estaban expuestas en el escaparate*, the garments were on display in the window. | Exhibited, on show: *los cuadros expuestos*, the exhibited pictures, the pictures on show. || Exposed: *una casa expuesta al viento*, a house exposed to the wind. || Dangerous (peligroso). || Expounded (teoría). || Explained, shown (explicado). || *Estar expuesto a*, to be exposed to, to be open to (una persona): *estar expuesto a las críticas*, to be open to criticism.

expugnar v. tr. MIL. To take by storm.

expulsar v. tr. To eject, to throw out, to expel (echar). || To expel (de un colegio, instituto, etc.). || To send down [U.S., to expel] (de la universidad). || To expel, to eject (del cuerpo). || MED. To bring up, to spit out. || DEP. To send off (fútbol).

expulsión f. Ejection, expulsion. || Expulsion (de un colegio, instituto, .etc.). || Sending down [U.S., expulsion] (de la universidad). || Expulsion, ejection (del cuerpo). || MED. Bringing-up, spitting-out. || DEP. Sending-off. || AVIAC. Ejection (eyección).

expulsivo, va adj. Expulsive. || MED. Expellant.

expulsor m. Ejector (de armas).

expurgación f. Expurgation (de un libro, texto, etc.). || FIG. Purging, purgation, purge.

expurgar v. tr. To expurgate: *expurgar una novela*, to expurgate a novel. || FIG. To purge.

expurgatorio, ria adj. Expurgatory. || FIG. Purging.

expurgo m. Expurgation (de un libro, etc.). || Purge.

exquisitamente adv. Exquisitely.

exquisitez f. Exquisiteness. || Refinement, exquisiteness (delicadeza).

exquisito, ta adj. Exquisite: *belleza exquisita*, exquisite beauty. || Exquisite, delicious (sabor). || Delightful, exquisite (lugar). || Refined, exquisite: *gusto, hombre exquisito*, refined taste, man.

extasiar v. tr. To enrapture, to send into raptures.
— V. pr. To go into raptures *o* ecstasies: *extasiarse con algo*, to go into raptures over sth.

éxtasis f. inv. Ecstasy, rapture (de alegría, admiración, etc.). || REL. Ecstasy. || *Estar sumido en éxtasis*, to be in ecstasy *o* raptures.

extático, ca adj. Ecstatic, enraptured.

extemporal o **extemporáneo, a** adj. Unseasonable: *lluvia extemporal*, unseasonable rain. || Ill-timed, untimely, inappropriate: *respuesta extemporánea*, ill-timed reply.

extender* v. tr. To spread: *el ave extendió las alas*, the bird spread its wings; *extender el mantel sobre la mesa*, to spread the tablecloth over the table. || To spread out: *extender un mapa*, to spread out a map; *extender una manta en el suelo*, to spread a blanket out on the ground. || To spread out (esparcir). || To spread (mantequilla, pintura). || To spread (una noticia, etc.). || To extend: *extender su influencia*, to extend one's influence; *extender una red de autopistas*, to extend a network of motorways. || To extend (ampliar): *extendieron la ley a otros casos*, they extended the law to other cases. || To draw up (documento, contrato). || To issue (un certificado). || To make out (cheque, recibo).
— V. pr. To spread: *la epidemia se ha extendido*, the epidemic has spread; *la mancha de tinta se ha extendido*, the ink stain has spread. || To go, to range, to extend: *hasta ahí no se extienden mis conocimientos*, my knowledge does not extend that far. || To enlarge: *extenderse sobre un tema*, to enlarge on a subject. || To expatiate. || To stretch, to extend (ocupar espacio): *el campo se extendía hasta el horizonte*, the countryside stretched to the horizon; *el bosque se extiende desde el río hasta la ciudad*, the wood stretches from the river to the city. || To stretch out, to lie: *la llanura se extendía delante del ejército*, the plain lay before the army. || To extend, to last (durar): *su reinado se extendió desde el año 1533 hasta el año 1603*, her reign extended from 1533 to 1603. || To stretch out (echarse): *extenderse en el suelo*, to stretch out on the ground. || — *El fuego se extendió al tejado*, the fire spread to *o* reached the roof. || *Extenderse en consideraciones sobre algo*, to expound sth. at length.

extendidamente adv. V. EXTENSAMENTE.

extendido, da adj. Spread out, extended. || Widespread: *una costumbre muy extendida*, a very widespread custom. || Outstretched: *con los brazos extendidos*, with arms outstretched.

extensamente adv. At length: *trató el tema extensamente*, he dealt with the subject at length. || Widely (ampliamente).

extensibilidad f. Extensibility.

extensible adj. Extensible, extendible, extensile. || *Mesa extensible*, extending table.

extensión f. Extension (acción de ampliar). || Spreading (de las alas). || Spreading out (de un mapa, de una manta, etc.). || Area (superficie): *la extensión de un país*, the area of a country. || Size (tamaño). || Length, duration: *la extensión de un discurso, de la vida*, the length of a speech, of life. || Length (de una carta, de un escrito, etc.). || Extent: *la extensión de mis conocimientos*, the extent of my knowledge. || Expanse (del mar). || Range (de una voz, de un instrumento). || MAT. Extension. || GRAM. Extension: *por extensión*, by extension. | Application, extension: *el término "fruta" tiene más extensión que "manzana"*, the term "fruit" has a wider application than "apple". || Extension (del teléfono). || *En toda la extensión de la palabra*, in every sense of the word.

extensivo, va adj. Extendable, extendible: *la ley es extensiva a otros casos*, the law is extendable to other cases. || — AGR. *Cultivo extensivo*, extensive cultivation. || *Hacer extensivo algo a alguien*, to extend sth. to s.o. || *Ser extensivo a*, to extend to, to apply to.

extenso, sa adj. Extensive, vast (amplio): *un extenso país*, an extensive country. || Large, sizeable (grande): *una sala extensa*, a large room. || Widespread (conocimientos). || Long (largo): *viaje, discurso extenso*, long journey, speech. || Full, extensive (reportaje). || *Por extenso*, at length, in detail, in full.

extensor adj. Extending. || ANAT. *Músculo extensor*, extensor muscle.
— M. DEP. Chest expander.

extenuación f. Exhaustion (agotamiento). || Weakening (debilitación). || Emaciation (enflaquecimiento).

extenuado, da adj. Exhausted (agotado). || Weak (débil). || Emaciated (delgado).

extenuante adj. Exhausting.

extenuar v. tr. To exhaust (agotar). || To weaken (debilitar).
— V. pr. To exhaust o.s.

extenuativo, va adj. Exhausting.

exterior adj. Outer, external, exterior: *la parte exterior de un mueble*, the outer part of a piece of furniture. || Outward, external: *aspecto exterior*, outward appearance. || Outside: *ventana, habitación exterior*, outside window, room. || Foreign: *asuntos exteriores*, foreign affairs; *comercio exterior*, foreign trade. || *Dimensiones exteriores*, overall *o* external dimensions.
— M. Outside, exterior: *el exterior de un edificio*, the outside of a building. || Appearance (apariencia). || — Pl. CINEM. Exteriors. || — *Al exterior*, out, outside. || *Noticias del exterior*, overseas news, news from abroad.

exterioridad f. Outward *o* external appearance.

exteriorización f. Showing, manifestation, externalization, revelation.

exteriorizar v. tr. To show, to manifest, to externalize, to reveal.

exteriormente adv. Externally, outwardly.

exterminación f. Extermination, wiping out (supresión). || Destruction.

exterminador, ra adj. Exterminating.
— M. y f. Exterminator.

exterminar v. tr. To exterminate, to wipe out (suprimir). || To destroy.

exterminio m. Extermination, wiping out (supresión). || Destruction.

externado m. Day school.

externamente adv. Outwardly, externally.

externo, na adj. External: *medicamento de uso externo*, medicine for external use. || Outward: *signos externos de riqueza*, outward signs of richness. || External, outer: *parte externa*, outer part. || Exterior: *ángulo externo*, exterior angle. || Day: *alumno externo*, day pupil. || *En la parte externa*, on the outside.
— M. y f. Day pupil (alumno), day student (estudiante).

extinción f. Extinction (del fuego). || Wiping out, obliteration (de una epidemia). || Extinction, dying out (de una raza).

extinguible adj. Extinguishable (fuego, luz).

extinguido, da adj. V. EXTINTO.

extinguir v. tr. To extinguish, to put out (fuego, luz). || To wipe out, to obliterate, to make extinct (una raza). || To wipe out, to obliterate (una epidemia). || To put down (rebelión). || To wipe out (deuda).
— V. pr. To die out, to go out (fuego). || To go out (luz). || To die away: *su amor se extinguió*, his love died away. || To become extinct, to die out (una raza). || To die (morirse).

extinto, ta adj. Extinguished, out (fuego, luz). || Extinct: *raza extinta*, extinct race; *volcán extinto*, extinct volcano. || Wiped out, obliterated (epidemia). || *Amer.* Dead (muerto).

extintor, ra adj. Extinguishing.
— M. y f. Extinguisher. || — M. Extinguisher: *extintor de incendios*, fire extinguisher.

extirpable adj. Extirpable (tumor). || FIG. Eradicable.

extirpación f. Uprooting (de plantas). || Extraction, pulling (de un diente). || Extirpation, excision, removal (de un tumor). || FIG. Eradication, stamping out, wiping out.

extirpador, ra adj. Extirpating.
— M. AGR. Cultivator.

extirpar v. tr. To uproot (planta, árbol). || To extract, to pull out (diente). || To extirpate, to excise, to remove (tumor). || FIG. To eradicate, to stamp out, to wipe out: *extirpar los vicios*, to eradicate vices.

extorsión f. Extortion, exaction (despojo). || FIG. Inconvenience: *causarle mucha extorsión a uno*, to cause great inconvenience to s.o.

extorsionar v. tr. To extort, to exact (despojar). || FIG. To inconvenience.

extra adj. FAM. Extra. | Best-quality: *vino extra*, best-quality wine. || *Horas extras*, overtime.
— M. FAM. Extra. || CINEM. y TEATR. Extra.
extracción f. Extraction: *la extracción de un diente*, the extraction of a tooth; *extracción de una raíz cuadrada*, extraction of a square root; *la extracción del carbón*, the extraction of coal. || FIG. Extraction, descent: *de humilde extracción*, of humble descent.
extracorriente f. ELECTR. Self-induced current.
extractar v. tr. To summarize (compendiar).
extractivo, va adj. Extractive.
extracto m. Extract, excerpt (trozo de una obra). || Summary (resumen). || Extract (de una sustancia). || *Extracto de cuentas*, statement [of account].
extractor m. Extractor.
extradición f. Extradition. || *Aplicar la extradición a*, to extradite.
extradós m. ARQ. Extrados.
extraer* v. tr. To extract (sacar): *extraer una muela*, to extract a molar. || MAT. To extract (una raíz). || QUÍM. To extract (algo de una sustancia). || To take out (líquido de un recipiente). || To excerpt (trozos de una obra).
extraescolar adj. Out-of-school.
extrafino, na adj. Superfine, best-quality, best.
extraíble adj. Extractable, extractible.
extrajudicial adj. Extrajudicial.
extralegal adj. Extralegal.
extralimitación f. Abuse.
extralimitarse v. pr. To overdo, to overstep, to go too far: *come bien sin extralimitarse en nada*, he eats well without overdoing it *o* overstepping the mark *o* going too far. || To take liberties, to go too far (ir demasiado lejos). || To abuse (en sus atribuciones).
extramuros adv. Outside the city.
extranjería f. Alienage, alienism (condición).
extranjerismo m. Foreign expression, foreignism.
extranjerizante adj. Fond of foreign things.
extranjerizar v. tr. To introduce foreign customs into (un país).
extranjero, ra adj. Foreign, alien (de otro país).
— M. y f. Foreigner (sentido general): *le gusta hablar con extranjeros*, he likes talking to foreigners. || Alien, foreigner (término oficial y jurídico): *los extranjeros tienen los mismos derechos que los naturales del país*, aliens have the same rights as nationals. || — M. Foreign countries, *pl.* || — *Del extranjero*, from abroad. || *En* or *por el extranjero*, abroad. || *Ir al extranjero*, to go abroad.
extranjis adv. FAM. *De extranjis*, secretly, on the sly (de tapadillo).
extrañación f. Banishment.
extrañamente adv. Strangely.
extrañamiento m. Banishment. || Astonishment, surprise (asombro).
extrañar v. tr. To surprise (sorprender): *le extrañó que no se lo hubiese dicho*, he was surprised that you should not have told him. || Not to be used to, to find strange (sentir la novedad de): *extraña la cama en el hotel*, he is not used to the hotel bed, he finds the hotel bed strange. || To be shy: *el niño extraña a los desconocidos*, the child is shy with strangers. || To banish (de una comunidad, de un país). || *Amer.* To miss (echar de menos). || — *Eso me extraña*, I'm surprised at that, that's a surprise to me, that surprises me. || *Me extraña que haya venido*, I'm surprised *o* it surprises me that he has come. || *Me extraña tu presencia*, I am surprised at your being here. || *Me extraña verte aquí*, I'm surprised *o* it surprises me to see you here. || *Me extraña verte con ese peinado*, it's funny to see you with that hairstyle. || *No es de extrañar que*, it is not surprising that, no wonder that.
— V. intr. To be strange *o* funny (ser extraño): *extraña oírle cantar*, it is strange to hear him singing. || To be surprising (ser sorprendente): *extraña ver a tanta gente aquí*, it is surprising to see so many people here.
— V. pr. To leave one's country, to go into exile (de un país). || To leave (de una comunidad, un grupo). || To be surprised: *extrañarse de algo, de que no esté*, to be surprised at sth., that he is not in.
extrañeza f. Strangeness (cualidad de extraño). || Surprise (asombro). || *Causar extrañeza a*, to surprise.
extraño, ña adj. Strange, odd, peculiar (raro). || Foreign: *cuerpo extraño*, foreign body. || Extraneous, outside: *influencias extrañas*, extraneous influences. || — *El nuevo sistema me es extraño*, I am not used to the new system. || *Hace extraño verte sin gafas*, it's funny *o* strange to see you without glasses. || *No es extraño que*, no wonder that, it is not surprising that. || *Ser extraño a*, to have nothing to do with: *soy extraño a esta discusión*, I have nothing to do with this argument. || *Una persona extraña*, a stranger.
— M. y f. Stranger: *es un extraño en su familia*, he is a stranger in his family. || — M. Shying (del caballo). || *Hacer un extraño*, to shy (el caballo).
extraoficial adj. Unofficial, nonofficial.
extraordinariamente adv. Extremely, extraordinarily. || Extremely well (muy bien).
extraordinario, ria adj. Extraordinary: *un suceso extraordinario*, an extraordinary event; *embajador extraordinario*, ambassador extraordinary. || Uncommon, unusual, rare (poco común). || Queer, odd, singular (raro). || Surprising (sorprendente). || Wonderful (maravilloso). || Additional (añadido): *gastos extraordinarios*, additional expenses. || Bonus: *pagas extraordinarias*, bonus payments. || Special (edición). || *Horas extraordinarias*, overtime.
— M. Special delivery (correo especial). || Extra dish (plato suplementario). || Special issue (de periódico).
extrapolación f. MAT. Extrapolation.
extrapolar v. tr. e intr. To extrapolate.
extrarradio m. Suburbs, *pl.*, outskirts, *pl.*
extrasensible adj. Extrasensory.
extraterreno, na o **extraterrestre** adj. Extramundane, extraterrestrial.
extraterritorial adj. Extraterritorial.
extraterritorialidad f. Extraterritoriality.
extrauterino, na adj. Extrauterine.
extravagancia f. Extravagance, eccentricity, oddness (cualidad de extravagante). || Eccentricity, oddity (cosa, costumbre, etc.). || *Decir, hacer extravagancias*, to say, to do odd *o* eccentric things.
extravagante adj. Eccentric, odd (raro). || Extravagant: *lenguaje extravagante*, extravagant language.
— M. y f. Eccentric.
extravasar v. tr. To extravasate.
— V. pr. MED. To extravasate.
extravenarse v. pr. MED. To extravasate (sangre).
extraversión f. Extraversion, extroversion.
extravertido, da adj. Extraverted, extroverted.
— M. y f. Extravert, extrovert.
extraviado, da adj. Lost, mislaid (perdido): *departamento de objetos extraviados*, lost property department. || Stray, lost, missing: *niño, perro extraviado*, lost child, dog. || Out of the way, isolated (lugar). || Vacant: *ojos extraviados*, vacant eyes. || FIG. y FAM. Touched (algo loco): *está algo extraviado*, he's slightly touched. || — *Estar extraviado*, to have gone astray, to be lost, to have lost one's way (haber perdido el camino). || *Un hombre extraviado*, a man who has gone astray (de mala vida).
extraviar v. tr. To make lose one's way, to make get lost (desorientar): *el mapa era tan malo que me extravió*, the map was so bad that it made me lose my way. || To mislead: *su falso argumento me extravió*, his false argument misled me. || To misplace, to mislay, to lose: *he extraviado las tijeras*, I have misplaced the scissors. || To lead astray (pervertir).
— V. pr. To get lost: *me extravié en el bosque*, I got lost in the wood. || To be missing, to get mislaid: *se han extraviado dos libros*, two books are missing, two books have got mislaid. || FIG. To go astray (llevar mala vida). | To wander (la mirada). | To be mistaken (equivocarse). | To go slightly weak in the head (volverse un poco loco). || *Se me han extraviado los papeles*, I have misplaced *o* mislaid the papers.
extravío m. Misplacing, mislaying, loss (de una cosa). || Misleading (de una persona). || Losing one's way, getting lost (acción de perderse una persona). || FIG. Leading astray (acción de pervertir). | Going astray (acción de pervertirse). | Mistake (error). | Error: *los extravíos de la juventud*, the errors of youth. | Misconduct (mala conducta).
extremadamente adv. Extremely.
extremado, da adj. Extreme.
Extremadura n. pr. f. GEOGR. Estremadura.
extremar v. tr. To carry to an extreme, to go to an extreme with, to overdo: *extremar las precauciones*, to carry precautions to an extreme.
— V. pr. To take great pains, to do one's utmost.
extremaunción f. REL. Extreme unction.
extremeño, ña adj. [Of *o* from] Estremadura.
— M. y f. Native *o* inhabitant of Estremadura.
extremidad f. End, extremity (extremo). || — Pl. Extremities.
extremismo m. Extremism.
extremista adj./s. Extremist.
extremo, ma adj. Extreme: *frío extremo*, extreme cold; *extrema derecha en política*, extreme right wing in politics. || Furthest (más alejado). || Extreme, utmost: *amabilidad extrema*, utmost kindness. || Dire, utmost: *necesidad extrema*, dire necessity. || Last (último). || — *El Extremo Oriente*, the Far East. || *El punto extremo de una península*, the tip of a peninsula. || *En caso extremo*, as a last resort.
— M. End: *el extremo de un palo*, the end of a stick. || Point, pitch (situación extremada): *llegó a tal extremo que quiso matarse*, he got to such a point that he wanted to kill himself. || Extreme, extent (colmo): *está preocupado hasta el extremo de no comer*, he is worried to the extreme that he doesn't eat. || MAT. Extreme. || Point, question, item: *sobre ese y otros extremos no se pusieron de acuerdo*, on this and several other points no agreement was reached. || Wing, winger (en fútbol). || — *Con* or *en extremo*, in the extreme, extremely. || *De extremo a extremo*, from one end to the other, from end to end. || *En último extremo*, as a last resort. || DEP. *Extremo derecha, izquierda*, outside-right, outside-left (fútbol), right wing, left wing (hockey). || FIG. *Los extremos se tocan*, extremes meet. | *Pasar de un extremo a otro*, to go from one extreme to the other.
extremoso, sa adj. Demonstrative, effusive. || Extreme, excessive (excesivo).
extrínseco, ca adj. Extrinsic.

extrorso, sa adj. BOT. Extrorse.
extroversión f. Extroversion.
extrovertido, da adj./s. V. EXTRAVERTIDO.
extrusión f. TECN. Extrusion.
exuberancia f. Exuberance, abundance (abundancia). || Exuberance (carácter demostrativo).
exuberante adj. Exuberant, abundant (abundante). || Exuberant (demostrativo).
exudación f. Exudation.
exudado m. Exudate.
exudar v. tr. e intr. To exude (transpirar).
exultación f. Exultation.
exultar v. intr. To exult, to rejoice.
exvoto m. REL. Ex-voto, votive offering.
eyaculación f. Ejaculation.
eyacular v. tr. To ejaculate.
eyección f. Ejection.
eyectable adj. Ejectable. || *Asiento eyectable*, ejector *o* ejection seat.
eyectar v. tr. To eject.
eyector m. Ejector.
Ezequías n. pr. m. Hezekiah.

F

f f. F (letra): *una f mayúscula*, a capital f.
fa m. MÚS. F: *clave de fa*, F clef. | Fa (en la escala de do).
fabada f. Asturian dish made of beans, pork sausage and bacon.
fabla f. Imitation of Old Spanish.
fablar v. intr. y sus derivados V. HABLAR.
fabordón m. MÚS. Faux-bourdon.
fábrica f. Factory: *trabaja en una fábrica*, he works in a factory. || Factory, works, *pl.*: *fábrica siderúrgica, de jabón*, iron and steel, soap factory. || Mill (de textiles, papel, aceite, azúcar). || Manufacture (fabricación). || Plant (instalación). || Building (edificio). || Fabric (estructura). || ARQ. Masonry. || Fabric (bienes de una iglesia). || — *De fábrica*, stonework: *construcción de fábrica*, stonework construction. || *Fábrica de cerveza*, brewery. || *Fábrica de conservas*, canning plant. || *Fábrica de harina*, flour mill. || *Fábrica de hilados*, spinning mill. || *Fábrica de montaje*, assembly plant. || *Fábrica de muebles*, furniture factory. || *Marca de fábrica*, trademark. || *Precio de fábrica*, factory price, ex-works price.
fabricación f. Manufacture: *fabricación de bicicletas* bicycle manufacture. || Manufacture, making, fabrication: *fabricación defectuosa*, faulty manufacture. || — *De fabricación casera*, home-made. || *Estar en fabricación*, to be in production. || *Fabricación en serie*, mass production.
fabricador, ra m. y f. Fabricator (de mentiras, etc).
fabricante m. y f. Manufacturer, maker.
fabricar v. tr. To manufacture, to make: *fabricar automóviles*, to manufacture cars. || To build, to construct (edificar). || FIG. To fabricate, to invent: *fabricar una mentira*, to fabricate a lie. | To make (hacer): *fabricó solo su fortuna*, he made his fortune by himself. || — *Fabricado en España*, made in Spain. || *Fabricar cerveza*, to brew beer. || *Fabricar en serie*, to mass-produce.
fabril adj. Manufacturing: *industria fabril*, manufacturing industry.
fabriquero m. REL. Churchwarden.
fábula f. Fable: *las fábulas de La Fontaine*, the fables of La Fontaine. || FIG. Fable, invention (mentira): *esta historia es una fábula*, this story is an invention. | Laughingstock (hazmerreír). | Piece of gossip (habladuría). | Plot (argumento). || FIG. *Es algo de fábula*, it's fabulous.
fabulario m. Collection of fables.
fabulista m. Fabulist, fable writer, writer of fables.
fabuloso, sa adj. Fabulous, fabled (de las fábulas). || FIG. Fabled, fictitious (inventado). | Incredible (inverosímil). | Fabulous (enorme): *una fortuna fabulosa*, a fabulous fortune.
faca f. Large knife [with curved blade].
facción f. Faction: *una facción autonomista*, an autonomist faction. || Band, gang (bando). || — Pl. Features (rasgos de la cara): *hermosas facciones*, beautiful features. || MIL. *Estar de facción*, to be on guard [duty].
faccioso, sa adj. Factious, rebellious, seditious (rebelde).
— M. y f. Factious person, rebel (rebelde). || Troublemaker, agitator (revoltoso).
faceta f. Facet: *las facetas de un diamante*, the facets of a diamond. || FIG. Facet, side: *una faceta desconocida de España*, an unknown facet of Spain; *otra faceta del asunto*, another side of the affair. || *Tallar* or *labrar en facetas*, to facet.
facial adj. Facial: *nervio, ángulo facial*, facial nerve, angle. || — *Técnica facial*, beauty treatment. || *Técnico facial*, beautician.
facies f. inv. MED. Facies, *inv.*
fácil adj. Easy: *problema fácil*, easy problem; *criticar es fácil*, it is easy to criticize; *una vida muy fácil*, a very easy life; *fácil de hacer*, easy to do. || Simple, easy (sencillo). || Likely, probable: *es fácil que venga hoy*, it is likely that he will come today. || Easygoing, compliant: *este hombre es muy fácil, se entiende con todos*, this man is very easygoing, he gets on with everyone. || Good, well-behaved, easy to bring up (niño). || Loose, of easy virtue (mujer). || — *De puro fácil*, so easy: *de puro fácil que es, no hay que explicarlo*, it is so easy that there is no need to explain it. || *Fácil de creer*, easy to believe, easily believed. || *Fácil de digerir*, easy to digest, easily digested. || *Soy fácil de contentar*, I am easy to please. || *Soy fácil de hacer reír*, it is easy to make me laugh.
— Adv. Easily.
facilidad f. Easiness, facility: *la facilidad de su trabajo*, the easiness of his work. || Ease: *hacer algo con la mayor facilidad*, to do sth. with the greatest of ease. || Simplicity (sencillez). || Complaisance, docility, easygoing nature (docilidad). || Wantonness, looseness (de una mujer). || Fluency: *facilidad de palabra*, fluency in speech. || Gift, aptitude, talent: *tener facilidad para el estudio, para los idiomas*, to have a gift for studying, for languages. || Facility: *aquí no hay facilidades para practicar deportes*, there are no facilities here for practising sport. || Facility (condición favorable): *facilidades de crédito*, credit facilities. || — *Facilidades de pago*, easy terms. || *Tener facilidad para acatarrarse*, to catch a cold easily. || *Tener facilidad para olvidar*, to be forgetful.
facilillo, lla adj. FAM. As easy as winking *o* as pie.
facilitación f. Facilitation. || Provision (acción de proporcionar).
facilitar v. tr. To facilitate, to make easy (hacer fácil). || To make easier, to facilitate (hacer más fácil). || To get: *la agencia le facilitó el piso*, the agency got him the flat. || To provide (proporcionar): *facilitar informaciones a uno*, to provide s.o. with information. || To arrange: *facilitar una entrevista*, to arrange an interview.
fácilmente adv. Easily: *lo hizo fácilmente*, he did it easily; *tendrá fácilmente cincuenta años*, he is easily fifty years old.
facilón, ona adj. FAM. Dead easy, rather simple: *un problema facilón*, a dead easy problem.
facineroso, sa adj. Criminal. || Wicked (malévolo).
— M. y f. Criminal. || Robber (ladrón). || Wicked person, villain (persona malévola).
facistol m. Lectern (atril).
facón m. *Amer.* Dagger, large knife [used by "gauchos"]. || *Amer. Pelar el facón*, to unsheathe one's knife.
facsímil o **facsímile** m. Facsimile.
factible adj. Feasible, possible (posible). || Workable (realizable).
facticio, cia adj. Factitious, artificial.
factor m. Factor (elemento): *el factor humano*, the human factor. || BIOL. Factor: *factor Rhesus*, rhesus factor. || MAT. Factor. || Luggage and goods clerk (de ferrocarril). || Agent, factor (de comercio).
factoría f. Trading post (establecimiento de comercio). || Factorage, position of agent *o* factor (cargo de factor). || Agency (agencia). || Factory (fábrica).
factorial f. MAT. Factorial.
factótum m. Factotum.
factura f. COM. Bill: *me dio la factura de la reparación*, he gave me the repair bill. | Invoice (de géneros vendidos): *factura pro forma*, pro forma invoice.

|| Manufacture (hechura). || — *Extender una factura*, to make out a bill *o* an invoice. || *Según factura*, as per invoice.
facturación f. COM. Invoicing (de géneros vendidos). | Bill: *facturación por mil pesetas*, bill for a thousand pesetas. | Turnover (volumen de negocios). || Registration (en ferrocarril).
facturador, ra m. y f. Invoice clerk (empleado).
facturar v. tr. COM. To invoice (géneros vendidos). | To charge for: *facturarle a uno el transporte*, to charge s.o. for the transport. || To register [U.S., to check] (en ferrocarril).
fácula f. ASTR. Facula (del Sol).
facultad f. Faculty (poder): *facultad de hablar, de sentir*, faculty of speech, of feeling. || Faculty, school (en la universidad): *facultad de Derecho*, faculty of Law; *facultad de Filosofía y Letras*, faculty of Arts. || MED. Strength, resistance. || Ability (capacidad). || FIG. Power (derecho): *tener facultad para*, to have the power to. || — Pl. Faculties, powers: *en pleno uso de sus facultades*, in possession of his faculties; *facultades mentales*, mental powers. || — *En la plenitud de sus facultades*, at one's peak. || *Tener facultad para*, to be authorized to.
facultar v. tr. To authorize, to empower, to give the power to: *facultar a alguien para*, to authorize s.o. to, to give s.o. the power to.
facultativo, va adj. Optional, facultative (no obligatorio). || Medical: *cuadro facultativo*, medical staff; *parte facultativo*, medical bulletin. || Faculty (de una facultad universitaria). || Professional. || MED. *El Cuerpo facultativo*, the doctors, the Faculty.
— M. Doctor (médico). || Surgeon (cirujano).
facundia f. Gift for talking, gift of the gab (fam.) [verbosidad]: *tener facundia*, to have a gift for talking, to have the gift of the gab. || Eloquence.
facundo, da adj. Talkative (parlanchín). || Eloquent.
facha f. FAM. Appearance, look, looks, *pl.*: *me gusta la facha de este chico*, I like the look of this boy. | Mess, sight: *estar hecho una facha*, to look a mess. || — MAR. *Estar en facha*, to heave to. || FAM. *Tener buena facha*, to be good-looking.
— M. Mess, sight (adefesio).
fachada f. ARQ. Façade, front. | Frontage (dimensión). || FIG. Show, façade, front: *la prosperidad del país era pura fachada*, the country's prosperity was nothing but show *o* nothing but a façade. || Title page (de un libro). || — *Con fachada a*, facing: *una casa con fachada al mar*, a house facing the sea. || *Hacer fachada con*, to be opposite to, to face.
fachear v. intr. MAR. To heave to.
fachenda f. FAM. Swanking, bragging, showing off (presunción). || — M. FAM. Show-off, swank (fachendoso).
fachendear v. intr. FAM. To swank, to show off.
fachendista o **fachendón, ona** o **fachendoso, sa** adj. FAM. Swanky, snooty.
— M. y f. Show-off, swank.
fachinal m. *Amer.* Marsh (pantano).
fachoso, sa o **fachudo, da** adj. Odd-looking (extraño). || *Amer.* FAM. Swanky, snooty (fachendoso).
fading m. RAD. Fading (de las ondas).
faena f. Task, job: *las faenas diarias*, the daily tasks. || Work: *tengo mucha faena*, I've got a lot of work. || TAUR. "Faena" [series of passes with the muleta]. || MIL. Fatigue. || MAR. Fishing. || FIG. y FAM. Dirty trick: *hacer una faena a alguien*, to play a dirty trick on s.o. || — *Estar en plena faena*, to be hard at work. || *Las faenas de la casa*, the household chores, the housework. || *Las faenas del campo*, agricultural work. || MIL. *Uniforme de faena*, fatigue dress. || FAM. *¡Vaya faena!* or *¡qué faena!*, that was a dirty trick!
faenar v. intr. MAR. To fish.
faenero m. *Amer.* Agricultural labourer, farmhand.
faetón m. Phaeton (coche).
fafarachero, ra m. y f. *Amer.* Boaster, braggart.
— Adj. Boastful.
fagocitario, ria o **fagocítico, ca** adj. Phagocytic.
fagocito m. BIOL. Phagocyte.
fagocitosis f. BIOL. Phagocytosis.
fagot m. MÚS. Bassoon (instrumento). | Bassoonist (músico).
fagotista m. MÚS. Bassoonist.
fahrenheit adj. inv. Fahrenheit.
faisán m. Pheasant (ave).
faisana f. Hen pheasant (ave).
faja f. Strip, belt: *faja de terreno*, strip of land. || Girdle, corset (de mujer): *faja de embarazo*, maternity girdle. || MED. Belt: *faja abdominal*, body belt. || Bandage (para niños). || Sash, cummerbund (de vestido, de traje). || Wrapper (de periódico). || Band (de puro, de un libro). || Sash (insignia). || ARQ. Fascia (moldura). || FIS. Band. || HERÁLD. Fesse, fess. || *Faja braga*, pantie girdle.
fajada f. *Amer.* Attack.
fajado, da adj. Bandaged (con venda). || Swaddled (niño). || TAUR. With a light coloured band round its body.
— M. MIN. Prop (madero).
fajadura f. o **fajamiento** m. Swaddling (de un niño). || Bandaging (con vendas). || MAR. Tarred outer covering [for underwater cables].
fajar v. tr. To gird, to put a sash on (ceñir con una faja). || To wrap (envolver). || To bandage (con venda). || To swaddle (a un niño). || To swathe (un miembro). || To put a wrapper on, to wrap up (un periódico). || *Amer.* To give: *fajar una bofetada*, to give a slap. | To beat (golpear). || *Amer. Fajar con uno*, to attack s.o.
— V. pr. To put one's sash on. || To fight (luchar).
fajilla f. *Amer.* Wrapper (de periódico).
fajín m. Sash (de militar).
fajina f. AGR. Shock. || Bundle of firewood *o* of faggots *o* of kindling (hacecillo). || Job, task, chore (faena). || MIL. Fascine (haz de ramas). | Mess call (toque). || FAM. *Meter fajina*, to ramble on.
fajo m. Bundle (haz). || Wad: *un fajo de billetes de banco*, a wad of bank notes. || — Pl. Swaddling clothes (de un niño).
fakir m. Fakir (faquir).
falacia f. Deceit (engaño). || Deceitfulness, falseness. || Fallacy (cosa falsa).
falange f. ANAT. Phalanx, phalange. || HIST. Phalanx. || Falange (en la política española).
falangero m. ZOOL. Phalanger.
falangeta f. ANAT. Third phalanx.
falangina f. ANAT. Second phalanx.
falangio m. ZOOL. Harvestman, harvest spider, daddy longlegs.
falangista adj./s. Falangist.
falangismo m. Falangism.
falaz adj. Fallacious, false (engañoso). || Deceitful: *una persona falaz*, a deceitful person.
falda f. Skirt: *falda acampanada, tubo*, bell, straight skirt. || Side (de una montaña). || Skirt (de la armadura). || Skirt, cover (de una mesa camilla). || Brim (de un sombrero). || Lap, knees, *pl.*: *tener un niño en la falda*, to have a child on one's lap. || Brisket (de las reses). || — Pl. Skirt, *sing.* (faldillas). || — FIG. y FAM. *Andar siempre entre faldas*, to be always with the girls. | *Es un asunto de faldas*, there are women mixed up in it. | *Estar pegado* or *cosido a las faldas de su madre*, to be tied to one's mother's apron strings. || *Falda pantalón*, culotte skirt, divided skirt. || *Falda de colina* or *de monte*, hillside. || *Falda escocesa*, kilt. || FIG. y FAM. *Le gustan mucho las faldas*, he is a one for the girls *o* ladies, he is very fond of the girls.
faldear v. tr. To skirt (un monte, etc.).
faldellín m. Short skirt (falda corta). || *Amer.* Christening gown (de bautizo).
faldero, ra adj. Skirt (de la falda). || — FIG. *Hombre faldero*, one for the girls *o* ladies. | *Niño faldero*, mother's child. || *Perro faldero*, lapdog.
faldicorto, ta adj. Short-skirted, wearing a short skirt.
faldillas f. pl. Skirt, *sing.* (que cuelgan de un vestido).
faldón m. Skirt (faldillas). || Tail (de un frac, de una camisa). || ARQ. Gable (de un tejado). | Mantelpiece (de chimenea). || *Estar colgado de* or *agarrado a los faldones de uno*, to be always at s.o.'s heels.
falena f. ZOOL. Phalaena, moth.
falibilidad f. Fallibility.
falible adj. Fallible: *memoria falible*, fallible memory.
fálico, ca adj. Phallic.
falo m. Phallus.
falsario, ria adj. V. FALSEADOR.
falsarregla f. Bevel square (falsa escuadra). || Underlines, *pl.* (falsilla).
falseador, ra adj. Falsifying (que adultera). || Forging, counterfeiting (que fabrica algo falso). || Lying (embustero).
— M. y F. Falsifier. || Forger, counterfeiter. || Liar (embustero).
falseamiento m. Falsification.
falsear v. tr. To falsify (adulterar). || To distort: *han falseado mis declaraciones*, they have distorted my statements. || To forge, to counterfeit (fabricar algo falso). || To bevel (un madero, una piedra).
— V. intr. ARQ. To sag (viga). || To buckle (pared). || MÚS. To be out of tune.
falsedad f. Falseness, hypocrisy (hipocresía). || Falseness, falsity (carácter de falso). || Falsehood, lie (mentira). || JUR. Forgery (falsificación).
falseo m. ARQ. Bevel, bevelling.
falseta f. MÚS. Flourish [on the guitar].
falsete m. Bung (de tonel). || Joining door (puerta). || MÚS. Falsetto: *voz de falsete*, falsetto voice.
falsía f. Falseness, hypocrisy (falsedad).
falsificación f. Forgery, forging, counterfeiting (acción): *falsificación de moneda*, money counterfeiting. || Forgery, forging, faking (de una firma). || Falsification (adulteración). || Forgery, counterfeit (objeto falsificado): *falsificación de escritura pública*, forgery of a public document.
falsificado, da adj. Forged, counterfeit. || Fake (falso).
falsificador, ra adj. Forging, counterfeiting (que fabrica algo falso). || Falsifying (que adultera).
— M. y f. Forger, counterfeiter (el que fabrica algo falso). || Falsifier (el que adultera). || Faker.
falsificar v. tr. To forge, to counterfeit (moneda, documento). || To forge, to fake (una firma). || To falsify (adulterar). || To adulterate (un líquido). || To fake (un objeto antiguo).
falsilla f. Underlines, *pl.*

falso, sa adj. False: *noticia falsa*, false piece of news. || False, deceitful, untrustworthy: *una persona falsa*, a false person. || Untrue, not true, false: *esto es falso*, this is untrue. || Unfounded, false (sin fundamento). || Unsound (argumento). || Wrong, incorrect, inexact: *una medida falsa*, an incorrect measurement. || False, counterfeit (moneda). || Fake, imitation (piedra preciosa). || False (nota de música). || False (forzado). || BOT. False: *acacia falsa*, false acacia. || Vicious (caballo). || — *Este Renoir es falso*, this Renoir is a fake. || *Falsa alarma*, false alarm. || *Falsa puerta*, concealed door. || *Más falso que Judas*, false to the core. || *Monedero falso*, counterfeiter.
— M. Reinforcement (de tela). || Lining (forro de un vestido). || — *Dar un golpe en falso*, to miss one's mark. || *Dar un paso en falso*, to stumble, to trip (fallar al andar), to make a wrong move (cometer un error). || *Envidar en falso*, to bluff. || *Estar en falso*, to be overhanging, to be out of plumb. || *Jurar en falso*, to commit perjury. || *Lo falso*, falsehood: *distinguir lo falso de lo verdadero*, to distinguish truth from falsehood. || *Tachar algo de falso*, to indict sth. as false, to deny sth.

falta f. Lack (privación): *falta de dinero*, lack of money. || Shortage (escasez): *falta de obreros*, shortage of workmen. || Absence (ausencia). || Need (necesidad). || Fault, defect (defecto de una cosa). || Fault, shortcoming, failing (defecto de una persona). || Lack: *falta de respeto, de tacto*, lack of respect, of tact. || Mistake (error): *falta de ortografía*, spelling mistake; *tiene cinco faltas*, he has made five mistakes. || Fault (culpa): *fue falta tuya*, it was your fault. || DEP. Foul. | Fault (en tenis). || Diminution of weight (de las monedas). || Misdeed (mala acción). || JUR. Misdemeanour [U.S., misdemeanor] (infracción).
— *A falta de* or *por falta de*, for want of, for lack of: *a falta de otra cosa*, for want *o* for lack of sth. better. || *A falta de pan buenas son tortas*, half a loaf is better than none. || *Coger a uno en falta*, to catch s.o. at fault. || *Cometer una falta*, to make a mistake. || *Echar en falta*, to miss: *echa en falta a su hija*, he misses his daughter. || *Falta de educación*, bad manners, *pl.* || *Falta de imprenta*, misprint. || *Falta de pago*, nonpayment. || *Hace falta tener mucha paciencia*, you need [to have] a lot of patience, one must have a lot of patience. || *Hace falta que vengas ahora*, you must come now. || *Hace falta una cuerda*, we need a rope, a rope is necessary. || *Hace falta una lámpara aquí*, a lamp is wanting *o* is needed here. || *Incurrir en falta*, to commit a foul (deportes), to make a mistake (cometer un error). || *Me hace falta tu presencia*, I need you. || *Me hacen falta diez libras*, I need ten pounds. || *No hay falta sin perdón*, everything can be forgiven. || *Notar la falta de*, to miss: *notó mucho la falta de su coche cuando estaba estropeado*, he missed his car a lot when it was broken down. || *Poner falta a*, to mark absent. || *Sacar faltas a alguien*, to point out s.o.'s defects. || *Sacar* or *poner faltas*, to find fault: *a todo le pone faltas*, he finds fault with everything. || DEP. *Sacar una falta*, to take a free kick (fútbol), to take a free hit (hockey). || *Ser una falta*, to be bad manners, to be impolite: *fue una falta no contestarle*, it was bad manners not to answer him. || *Si hace falta*, if necessary. || *Sin falta*, without fail. || *Si no fui, no fue por falta de ganas*, if I didn't go, it was not because I didn't want to.

faltar v. intr. To be missing: *faltan dos libros en la biblioteca*, two books are missing from the library. || To be lacking, to be wanting, to be needed, not to be enough: *aquí falta luz*, light is lacking here, there is not enough light here. || To lack (v. OBSERV.): *la chica es muy guapa, pero le falta carácter*, the girl is very pretty but she lacks character. || To need (v. OBSERV.): *me falta un cuchillo para cortarlo*, I need a knife to cut it; *me faltan diez pesetas más*, I need ten more pesetas. || To miss, not to go (no ir): *faltó a clase*, he missed school. || To stay away, not to go: *faltó a la oficina*, he didn't go to the office, he stayed away from the office. || To be missing *o* absent (estar ausente). || To fail (no cumplir): *faltar a un deber, a sus compromisos*, to fail in a duty, in one's obligations. || To fail (arma, mecanismo). || To be direspectful (desmandarse): *le faltó a su padre*, he was disrespectful to his father. || To be unfaithful (mujer). || To betray: *ha faltado a nuestra confianza, a nuestra amistad*, he has betrayed our confidence, our friendship. || — *El jersey está casi terminado, sólo falta una manga*, the jumper is almost finished, there is only one sleeve to do. || *Falta mucho para Navidad*, Christmas is a long way off. || *Faltan tres días para mi cumpleaños*, my birthday is three days off, there are three days to go to my birthday. || *Faltan veinte segundos para las tres*, it is twenty seconds to three o'clock. || *Falta por*, there is still... to be: *falta por coser una manga*, there is still a sleeve to be sewn. || *Falta por hacer*, it remains to be done, it has yet to be done. || *Falta por ver si él aceptará*, whether he will accept remains to be seen. || *Falta que lo pruebes*, you still have to prove it. || *Faltar a la verdad*, to lie, not to tell the truth. || *Faltar al honor*, to forfeit one's honour. || *Faltar al respeto a uno*, to lack respect for s.o. || *Faltar a su palabra, a una promesa*, to break one's word, one's promise; not to keep one's word, one's promise. || *Faltar a una cita*, to miss an appointment, to fail to keep an appointment. || *Faltar de palabra a uno*, to insult *o* to offend s.o. || *Falta y pasa*, manque and passe (en la ruleta). || *Me falta tiempo para hacerlo*, I haven't the time to do it, I am short of time to do it. || *Mucho falta*, far from it. || *Nada* or *poco faltó para que*, almost, nearly: *poco faltó para que se cayera*, he almost fell. || *¡No faltaba más!* or *¡lo que faltaba!* or *¡sólo faltaba eso!*, that's all we needed!, that tops it all!, that crowns it all! || *¡No faltaría más!* or *¡no faltaba más!*, of course (naturalmente), don't mention it (no hay de qué).
— OBSERV. In these cases the subject of the Spanish verb becomes the object of the English verb and vice versa.

falto, ta adj. Lacking, wanting (*de*, in): *falto de cortesía*, lacking in politeness; *espíritu falto de ideas*, mind lacking in ideas. || Without (sin): *falto de recursos*, without resources. || Short: *estaba falto de dinero*, I was short of money. || (P. us.). Short: *una libra falta*, a short pound.

faltón, ona adj. *Amer.* Disrespectful (irrespetuoso). | FAM. Unreliable (que no es de fiar).

faltoso, sa adj. Lacking, wanting (necesitado). || Incomplete (incompleto). || Quarrelsome (peleón).

faltriquera f. Pocket (bolsillo). || Purse (monedero). || Fob (de chaleco). || Small box (palco). || FAM. *Rascarse la faltriquera*, to dig into one's pocket.

falúa f. MAR. Launch.

falucho m. Felucca (embarcación).

falla f. Faille (tela). || GEOL. Fault (grieta). || Defect, fault (defecto). || *Amer.* Bonnet (gorrito). || "Falla" [in Valencia, grotesque and humourous scenes made up of cardboards figures]. || — Pl. "Fallas" [celebrations in Valencia on the feast of St. Joseph].

fallar v. tr. To ruff (naipes). || JUR. To pronounce: *fallar una sentencia*, to pronounce sentence. || — *Fallar el golpe*, to miss (al disparar, etc.), to miss one's target (no alcanzar el objetivo). || *Fallar un premio literario*, to award a literary prize.
— V. intr. To fail: *le falló el corazón*, his heart failed him; *me falló la memoria*, my memory failed me. || To give way: *la viga ha fallado*, the beam has given way; *le fallaron las piernas*, his legs gave way. || To fail, to let down: *mi amigo me ha fallado*, my friend has let me down. || To fail (fracasar): *ha fallado su proyecto*, his plan has failed. || To miss (un golpe, un tiro). || To miss (un motor). || To fail (frenos, arma). || Not to work properly, to have sth. wrong with it (mecanismo). || To prove wrong, to be wrong: *sus pronósticos fallaron*, his forecasts proved wrong. || JUR. To pass judgment, to pronounce sentence. || *Sin fallar*, without fail.

falleba f. Espagnolette, hasp (dispositivo). || Handle [of an espagnolette] (manivela).

fallecer* v. intr. To die: *falleció a los ochenta años*, he died at the age of eighty.

fallecido, da adj. Deceased, late.
— M. y f. Deceased.

fallecimiento m. Death, demise, decease.

fallero, ra adj. Of the "fallas" [en Valencia].
— M. y f. "Falla" maker (fabricante), "fallas" organizer (el que organiza). || — *Fallera mayor*, queen of the "fallas". || *Fallero mayor*, king of the "fallas" (v. FALLA).

fallido, da adj. Vain, frustrated: *esfuerzos fallidos*, vain efforts; *esperanzas fallidas*, vain hopes. || Unsuccessfull: *resultó fallido su proyecto*, his plan turned out unsuccessful. || Bad, unsuccessful (tiro). || Bad, poor: *cosecha fallida*, bad harvest. || COM. Bankrupt (que ha quebrado). | Irrecoverable (incobrable). | Bad (deuda).
— M. Bankrupt (comerciante).

fallo, lla adj. Void (en naipes): *estoy fallo de corazones*, I am void in hearts.
— M. JUR. Judgment, sentence: *emitir un fallo*, to pass judgment, to pronounce sentence. || Ruff (en naipes). || Miss (de un golpe, un tiro). || Awarding (de un premio). || Failure (del corazón, de las fuerzas). || Giving way (de una viga, etc.). || FIG. Decision (decisión). | Failure (fracaso). | Shortcoming, fault: *es un buen sistema, sin embargo tiene muchos fallos*, it is a good system, however it has many shortcomings. | Fault (falta). || TECN. Failure (de los frenos). || — TECN. *Fallo del motor*, engine failure *o* trouble. || *Tener fallo a espadas*, to be void in spades (en naipes). || *Tiene fallos de memoria*, he has lapses of memory.

falluto, ta adj. *Amer.* Failed.

fama f. Fame, renown (celebridad). || Reputation: *tener buena fama, mala fama*, to have a good reputation, a bad reputation. || — *Buena fama*, good name *o* reputation. || *Cobra* or *cría buena fama y échate a dormir*, build yourself a good reputation and you can sit back and relax. || *Conquistar fama*, to become famous. || *Dar fama a*, to make famous. || *De buena fama*, of good repute. || *De fama*, well-known, famous, renowned (afamado). || *De mala fama*, of ill repute, ill-famed. || *Es fama que*, it is rumoured that, they say that. || *Mala fama*, bad name *o* reputation. || *Tener fama de*, to have a reputation for, to have the reputation of being: *ese hombre tiene fama de cruel*, that

man has a reputation for cruelty. || *Tener mucha fama*, to be very well-known *o* very famous.
famélico, ca adj. Starving, famished.
familia f. Family: *de buena familia*, of a good family. || BOT. y ZOOL. Family. || GRAM. Family (de palabras, etc.). || Children, *pl.*, family: *tiene mucha familia*, he has a lot of children *o* a big family; *tiene poca familia*, he has not many children, he has a small family; *tener familia*, to have children *o* a family. || Servants, *pl.*, domestic staff (servidumbre). || Household (los que viven en la casa). || — *En familia*, with one's family. || FIG. y FAM. *Estábamos en familia*, there was hardly anybody there. || *La familia política*, the in-laws. || REL. *La Sagrada Familia*, the Holy Family. || *Pedro debe ser su hermano porque tiene un parecido de familia*, Peter must be his brother because there's a family likeness *o* resemblance about him. || *Ser como de la familia*, to be one of the family. || *Venir de familia*, to run in the family.
familiar adj. Family (relativo a la familia): *lazos familiares*, family ties; *parecido familiar*, family resemblance *o* likeness; *subsidio familiar*, family allowance. || Colloquial, familiar: *expresión familiar*, colloquial expression. || Informal: *estilo familiar*, informal style. || Familiar (conocido): *su cara me es familiar*, his face is familiar to me. || Familiar: *sus respuestas son a veces demasiado familiares*, at times his answers are too familiar. || — *Demonio familiar*, familiar spirit. || *El inglés le es muy familiar*, he is very familiar with English.
— M. Relative, relation (pariente). || Intimate *o* good friend (amigo). || (P.us.). Servant (criado). || Familiar (eclesiástico). || — Pl. Suite, *sing.*, attendants, entourage, *sing.*: *los familiares del rey*, the king's suite. || *Familiar del Santo Oficio*, Inquisition officer.
familiaridad f. Familiarity. || *Tomar familiaridades con*, to get familiar with.
familiarizar v. tr. To familiarize.
— V. pr. To familiarize o.s., to make o.s. familiar.
familión m. FIG. Large family.
famoso, sa adj. Famous: *un artista famoso*, a famous artist. || FAM. Fantastic, great, famous, fabulous.
fámula f. FAM. Maid, servant.
fámulo m. FAM. Manservant, servant.
fanal m. MAR. Lantern, lamp (farol). || Bell glass (para proteger del polvo). || Glass shade [for lamp or lantern]. || — Pl. Big eyes (ojos).
fanático, ca adj. Fanatic, fanatical.
— M. y f. Fanatic.
fanatismo m. Fanaticism.
fanatizar v. tr. To make a fanatic.
fandango m. MÚS. Fandango (baile). || FAM. Row, rumpus (jaleo).
fandanguero, ra m. y f. Reveller.
fandanguillo m. Dance similar to the fandango.
fanega f. Fanega [unit of capacity which varies between 22,5 litres and 55,5 litres according to the district]. || *Fanega de tierra*, fanega [unit of area approximately equal to 6.600 square metres].
fanerógamo, ma adj. BOT. Phanerogamic, phanerogamous.
— F. Phanerogam.
fanfarrear v. intr. V. FANFARRONEAR.
fanfarria f. V. FANFARRONADA. || MÚS. Fanfare (de trompetas).
fanfarrón, ona adj. Swanky, boastful.
— M. Show-off, swank, braggart, swaggerer.
fanfarronada f. Showing-off, swanking, bragging, boasting, swaggering (acción). || Brag, boast (dicho). || Swankiness, boastfulness (cualidad de fanfarrón).
fanfarronear v. intr. To show off, to swank, to brag, to boast, to swagger (presumir).
fanfarronería f. V. FANFARRONADA.
fangal o **fangar** m. Bog, mudpit, mudhole (lodazal).
fango m. Mud (barro). || FIG. Degradation (deshonor). | Dirt, grime, slime (suciedad).
fangoso, sa adj. Muddy.
fantaseador, ra adj. Daydreaming, dreaming (que sueña). || Imaginative, fanciful (imaginativo).
fantasear v. intr. To daydream, to dream (soñar). || To romance (imaginar).
fantaseo m. *Amer.* Dreaming, daydreaming, imagining.
fantasía f. Imagination, fantasy, fancy (imaginación): *un relato lleno de fantasía*, a story full of imagination. || Fantasy, fancy, dream: *estos viajes son fantasías suyas*, these journeys are only his fantasies. || Fantasy, fancy: *esto es pura fantasía*, this is pure fantasy. || FAM. Vanity, conceit (presunción). || Whim, fancy (capricho). || MÚS. Fantasia. || *De fantasía*, fancy: *artículos, chaleco de fantasía*, fancy goods, waistcoat; imitation, fancy: *una joya de fantasía*, a piece of imitation jewellery.
fantasioso, sa adj. Stuck-up (fam.), conceited (presumido). || Imaginative (fantaseador).
— M. y f. Show-off, swank, braggart (presumido). || Imaginative person (fantaseador).
fantasista m. Variety artist.
fantasma m. Ghost, phantom (espectro). || Ghost, phantasm (aparecido). || FIG. y FAM. Show-off, conceited person (vanidoso).
— Adj. Ghost, phantom: *buque fantasma*, ghost ship.
fantasmagoría f. Phantasmagoria.
fantasmagórico, ca adj. Phantasmagoric.
fantasmal adj. Ghostly, phantasmal (irreal). || Phantasmal (de los fantasmas).
fantasmón, ona adj. FAM. Stuck-up, conceited.
fantástico, ca adj. Fantastic, fanciful (quimérico): *un relato fantástico*, a fantastic story. || Fantastic, great, fabulous, terrific: *una casa, una memoria fantástica*, a terrific house, memory. || Phantasmal, ghostly (fantasmal).
fantochada f. FIG. Invention, bright idea: *es otra fantochada del alcalde*, it's another invention of the mayor's.
fantoche m. Puppet, marionette (títere) || FIG. Puppet (persona manejable). | Storyteller (cuentista). | Popinjay, swank, show-off, braggart, swaggerer (presumido). || Nincompoop (persona inútil).
faquir m. Fakir.
farad m. ELECTR. Farad.
faraday m. ELECTR. y QUÍM. Faraday.
farádico, ca adj. Faradic.
faradio m. ELECTR. Farad.
faradización f. Faradism, faradization.
faralá m. Flounce, frill (de un vestido). || — Pl. FAM. Frills, flounces (adornos de mal gusto). || *Traje de faralaes*, frilly dress (vestido andaluz).
— OBSERV. Pl. The plural form of *faralá* is *faralaes*.
farallón m. Rock [jutting out of the sea].
faramalla f. FAM. Patter, claptrap (charla). | Piece of trumpery (cosa sin valor). || *Amer.* Bragging, swanking, swaggering (fanfarronada). || — M. y f. Bamboozler, trickster.
faramallear v. intr. *Amer.* To brag, to show off, to swank, to swagger (farolear).
faramallero, ra o **faramallón, ona** adj. Bamboozling, cajoling (engatusador). || *Amer.* Swanky, boastful (fanfarrón).
— M. y f. Bamboozler, trickster.
farándula f. Theatre [U.S. theater], acting, stage (trabajo de los cómicos). || Troupe of strolling players (compañía). || FIG. y FAM. Patter, claptrap (charla).
farandulero, ra m. y f. Strolling player (farsante). || FAM. Swindler, trickster, bamboozler (estafador).
faraón m. Pharaoh.
faraónico, ca adj. Pharaonic.
faraute m. Messenger, herald (mensajero). || FIG. y FAM. Busybody (entrometido).
farda f. Bundle (lío pequeño). || Bale (bala). || Parcel (paquete). || TECN. Mortise (en carpintería).
fardar v. tr. To dress, to outfit.
— V. intr. FAM. To be classy: *tener un coche deportivo farda mucho*, it's very classy to have a sports car. | To show off, to swank (presumir).
fardo m. Bundle (lío pequeño). || Bale (bala). || Parcel (paquete).
fardón, ona adj. FAM. Classy, flashy (cosa). | Boastful, conceited (persona).
— M. y f. FAM. Show-off, swank (presumido).
farfalá f. Flounce, frill (faralá).
farfallón, ona adj. V. FARFULLERO.
fárfara f. Inner shell membrane (binza del huevo). || *En fárfara*, without shell (huevo), unfinished, incomplete (incompleto).
farfolla f. Husk (del maíz). || FIG. Baubie, piece of trumpery (oropel).
farfulla f. FAM. Jabbering, spluttering. || — M. y f. Jabberer, gabbler.
— Adj. Jabbering, gabbling, spluttering (persona).
farfullador, ra adj. Jabbering, gabbling, spluttering.
— M. y f. Jabberer, gabbler.
farfullar v. tr. To jabber, to gabble, to splutter (hablar mal). || FIG. y FAM. To scamp, to botch (trabajo).
— V. intr. To jabber, to gabble, to splutter.
farfullero, ra adj. FAM. Jabbering, gabbling, spluttering (que habla mal). || FIG. y FAM. Careless, slapdash, shoddy (chapucero). || *Ser muy farfullero*, to jabber *o* to gabble a lot (hablar muy mal).
— M. y f. FAM. Jabberer, gabbler (que habla mal). || Slapdash *o* shoddy *o* careless worker (chapucero).
farináceo, a adj. Farinaceous.
faringe f. ANAT. Pharynx.
faríngeo, a adj. ANAT. Pharyngeal, pharyngal.
faringitis f. MED. Pharyngitis.
fariña f. *Amer.* Coarse manioc flour (harina).
fario m. FAM. *Traer mal fario*, to be a jinx.
farisaico, ca adj. Pharisaic, pharisaical.
farisaísmo o **fariseísmo** m. Pharisaism, phariseeism.
fariseo m. Pharisee. || FIG. Hypocrite, pharisee.
farmacéutico, ca adj. Pharmaceutical, pharmaceutic.
— M. y f. Pharmacist (título universitario). || Chemist [U.S., druggist, pharmacist] (en una tienda). || Pharmacist (en un laboratorio).
farmacia f. Pharmacy (estudios). || Chemist's, chemist's shop [U.S., drugstore, pharmacy] (tienda). || Pharmacy (de un hospital, una empresa, etc.).
fármaco m. Medicine (medicamento).
farmacología f. Pharmacology.
farmacológico, ca adj. Pharmacological.
farmacólogo, ga m. y f. Pharmacologist, pharmacist.
farmacopea f. Pharmacopoeia.
farniente m. Idleness (ociosidad).

faro m. Lighthouse (torre). || Beacon (señal luminosa). || Light, lantern (farol). || AUT. Headlight, headlamp. || FIG. Guiding light.

farol m. Lantern (luz). || Streetlamp, gas lamp (en las calles). || Light (de locomotora). || FIG. y FAM. Bluff (en el juego). | Swank, show-off (farolero). | Showing off, swanking (faroleo). || TAUR. "Farol" [pass which the bullfighter ends with a flourish of the cape above his head]. || *Amer.* Balcony (balcón). || — FAM. *¡Adelante con los faroles!*, carry on!, keep it up!, come on then! || *Farol a la veneciana*, Chinese lantern. || MAR. *Farol de popa, de proa*, stern, bow light. || FAM. *Tirarse* or *marcarse* or *echarse un farol*, to spin a yarn, to swank, to show off.

farola f. Streetlamp (del alumbrado público). || Gas lamp (de gas). || Lantern, lamp (fanal). || FAM. Lighthouse, beacon (de la costa).

farolear v. intr. FAM. To brag, to boast, to swank, to show off. | To bluff (en los naipes).

faroleo m. FAM. Boasting, showing off.

farolería f. Swankiness, boastfulness.

farolero, ra adj. FIG. y FAM. Swanky, boastful (presumido). | Bluffing (en el juego).
— M. y f. FIG. y FAM. Swank, show-off (presumido). | Bluffer (en el juego). || — M. Lantern maker (el que hace faroles). || Lamplighter (el que enciende las farolas).

farolillo o **farolito** m. Chinese lantern (de papel). || BOT. Canterbury bell (campánula). || FIG. *El farolillo rojo*, the last one (en una carrera, una clasificación).

farra f. ZOOL. Lavaret (pez). || FAM. *Ir de farra*, to go on a binge *o* a spree.

fárrago m. Jumble, hotchpotch, mess.

farragoso, sa adj. Involved, confused (discurso, escrito). || Fussy (decoración).

farrear v. intr. *Amer.* To go on a binge *o* a spree.

farrista m. y f. *Amer.* Fun lover, reveller [U.S., reveler].
— Adj. Fun-loving.

farruco, ca m. y f. Galician *o* Asturian emigrant.
— Adj. FAM. Defiant, bold (desafiante). | Cocky (muy seguro de sí mismo). | Proud, pleased with o.s.: *iba muy farruco con su traje nuevo*, he was very pleased with himself in his new suit, he looked very proud of his new suit.

farruto, ta adj. *Amer.* Puny, weak, sickly (enclenque).

farsa f. Farce (comedia). || Theatre [U.S. theater], stage (teatro). || FIG. Sham, make-believe (simulación, engaño). | Farce: *este sistema parlamentario es una farsa*, this parliamentary system is a farce.

farsante m. Actor. || FIG. Humbug, charlatan, sham.

farsear v. intr. *Amer.* To joke.

fas o por nefas (por) loc. adv. FAM. Rightly or wrongly, by hook or by crook.

fascículo m. Fascicle.

fascinación f. Fascination.

fascinador, ra o **fascinante** adj. Fascinating.

fascinar v. tr. To fascinate: *los juguetes fascinan a los niños*, toys fascinate children.

fascismo m. Fascism.

fascista adj./s. Fascist.

fase f. Phase, stage (etapa): *las fases de una enfermedad*, the phases of an illness. || ASTR. Phase: *las fases de la Luna*, the Moon's phases. || ELECTR. Phase. || TECN. Stage: *la primera fase de un cohete*, the first stage of a rocket. || Stage (de una obra): *entrega de la primera fase en 1980*, handing over of the first stage in 1980.

fastidiar v. tr. To spoil s.o.'s plans, to upset s.o.'s plans: *me fastidió la lluvia*, the rain spoiled my plans. || To upset, to spoil, to mess up: *esto fastidia todos los proyectos*, this spoils all the plans. || To annoy, to be a nuisance for, to bother: *me fastidia tener que ir a pie*, it annoys me having to walk, it's a nuisance for me to have to walk; *deja de fastidiarme*, stop bothering me, stop being a nuisance. || To get on the nerves of, to annoy: *me fastidia este niño con sus gritos*, this child gets on my nerves with his shouting. || To disgust (causar asco). || To damage, to ruin, to spoil (poner en mal estado o volver inservible): *el granizo ha fastidiado la cosecha*, the hail has ruined the harvest; *he fastidiado mi traje al caer*, I spoilt my suit when I fell over. || To break, to damage, to ruin (un mecanismo). || To injure, to hurt (una parte del cuerpo). || — *Estar fastidiado*, to be broken down *o* out of action (no funcionar), to be damaged (funcionar mal), to be spoilt (estar deteriorado). || *Me fastidia esa chica*, I can't stand that girl. || FAM. *¡No fastidies!*, you're kidding! || *Tengo el estómago fastidiado*, I have an upset stomach, my stomach is out of order.
— V. pr. To get bored, to get fed up (fam.): *fastidiarse con la charla de uno*, to get bored with s.o.'s chatter. || To put up with (aguantarse): *para que tú te vayas él tiene que fastidiarse*, he has to put up with staying here so that you can go; *si habéis tenido mala suerte esta vez, os fastidiáis*, if you have been unlucky this time you will just have to put up with it. || To be damaged *o* ruined *o* spoilt: *se ha fastidiado la cosecha con el granizo*, the harvest has been ruined by the hail; *el traje se fastidió con la lluvia*, the suit was ruined in the rain. || To break down, to be damaged, to be ruined (un mecanismo). || To hurt, to injure (una parte del cuerpo). || — FAM. *¡Fastídiate!*, that's your hard luck! | *¡Para que te fastidies!*, so there! | *¡Que se fastidie!*, that's his hard luck!

fastidio m. Nuisance, bother (molestia): *es un fastidio tener que quedarnos aquí*, it's a nuisance having to stay here. || Nuisance: *es un fastidio que llueva ahora*, it's a nuisance that it's raining now. || Annoyance (enfado de poca importancia). || Boredom (aburrimiento). || — *Este olor me causa fastidio*, this smell makes me feel sick. || *¡Qué fastidio!*, what a nuisance!, how annoying *o* tiresome!

fastidioso, sa adj. Troublesome, trying, annoying: *un niño fastidioso*, a troublesome child. || Annoying, irksome: *acontecimiento fastidioso*, annoying event. || Tedious, boring, irksome: *trabajo fastidioso*, tedious work.

fasto, ta adj. Fortunate, happy, auspicious, lucky: *día fasto*, fortunate day.
— M. Pomp, display, splendour (fausto). || — Pl. Annals, archives (anales).

fastuosidad f. Splendour, pomp, lavishness.

fastuoso, sa adj. Splendid, pompous, lavish (ceremonia). || Lavish, ostentatious (persona).

fatal adj. Inevitable, fateful. || Fatal: *fatales circunstancias*, fatal circumstances; *una caída fatal*, a fatal fall. || FIG. Horrible, terrible, lousy, rotten (pésimo): *una película fatal*, a lousy film. || — FAM. *Estar fatal*, to feel terrible *o* awful: *estoy fatal*, I feel terrible; to be seriously ill: *el enfermo está fatal*, the patient is seriously ill. || *Mujer fatal*, vamp, femme fatale. || FAM. *Tener una suerte fatal*, to have rotten luck.
— Adv. Very badly: *esquía fatal*, he skis very badly.

fatalidad f. Fate, fatality (destino). || Misfortune (desgracia).

fatalismo m. Fatalism.

fatalista adj. Fatalistic.
— M. y f. Fatalist.

fatalmente adv. Inevitably: *había de suceder aquello fatalmente*, that inevitably had to happen. || Unfortunately (desafortunadamente). || Very badly (mal).

fatídico, ca adj. Ominous, fateful: *signo fatídico*, ominous sign. || Fatidical: *número fatídico*, fatidical number. || Fatal: *momento fatídico*, fatal moment.

fatiga f. Fatigue, tiredness, weariness (cansancio). || Laboured breathing (respiración dificultosa). || Fatigue (de metales). || — Pl. Troubles, difficulties (dificultades). || Troubles (penas). || Nausea, *sing.*, sickness, *sing.* (náusea). || FAM. *Me da fatiga pedirle dinero prestado*, I feel ashamed to borrow *o* I don't like to borrow money from him.

fatigar v. tr. To tire, to weary (cansar). || To tire: *fatigar un caballo*, to tire a horse. || To make breathless, to take away the breath of: *la altitud me fatiga*, altitude makes me breathless *o* takes my breath away. || To annoy (molestar).
— V. pr. To tire, to get tired: *fatigarse corriendo*, to get tired running.

fatigosamente adv. With difficulty, painfully.

fatigoso, sa adj. Tiring, fatiguing (que cansa). || Painful (trabajoso). || Tiresome (fastidioso). || Laboured (respiración). || Breathing heavily, wheezing (jadeante).

fatuidad f. Fatuity, fatuousness.

fatuo, tua adj. Fatuous (necio). || Vain, conceited, fatuous (engreído). || *Fuego fatuo*, v. FUEGO.

fauces f. pl. ANAT. Fauces. || Mouth (de un animal).

fauna f. Fauna.

fauno m. MIT. Faun.

Fausto n. pr. m. Faust.

fausto, ta adj. Fortunate, happy, lucky, auspicious.
— M. Pomp, display, splendour (esplendor).

fautor, ra m. y f. Accomplice, abettor, abetter (cómplice). || Instigator (autor).

fauvismo m. ARTES. Fauvism.

favo m. MED. Favus.

favor m. Favour [U.S., favor], good turn: *prestar* or *hacer un favor a uno*, to do s.o. a favour. || Favour: *solicitar un favor a alguien*, to ask a favour of s.o. || Favour, grace: *buscar el favor del rey*, to seek the favour of the king. || Favour (cinta). || Favour (de una mujer). || — *A favor de*, in favour of: *testamento a favor de su hijo*, will in favour of one's son; with the aid of, thanks to (gracias a), in favour of: *estar a favor de la pena de muerte*, to be in favour of capital punishment. || *De favor*, complimentary (billete). || *En favor de*, in favour of (a beneficio de). || *Ganarse el favor de alguien*, to come into favour with s.o. || *Gozar del favor de alguien*, to be in s.o.'s favour *o* in favour with s.o. || *Haber perdido el favor de alguien*, to be out of favour with s.o. || *Hacer el favor de*, to be so kind as to: *haga el favor de salir ahora*, would you be so kind as to go out now?; to do the pleasure *o* favour: *hágame el favor de cenar conmigo*, do me the pleasure of dining with me. || *Hacer favor a uno*, to be kind to s.o. || *Haga el favor de esperar*, please wait. || *Pedir algo por favor a uno*, to ask s.o. for sth. politely (cortésmente), to beg sth. of s.o. (suplicar). || *Por favor*, please: *¿qué hora es, por favor?*, what time is it please? || *Tener algo, tener a alguien a* or *en su favor*, to have sth., to have s.o. in one's favour.

favorable adj. Favourable [U.S., favorable], suitable: *condiciones favorables para*, suitable conditions for. || Favourable (propicio): *viento favorable*, favourable wind. || Optimistic: *diagnóstico favorable*, optimistic diagnosis. || *Mostrarse favorable a algo*, to be in favour of sth., to favour sth.

favorecedor, ra adj. Favouring [U.S., favoring], favourable [U.S., favorable]. || Flattering: *un retrato favorecedor*, a flattering portrait. || Becoming: *un peinado favorecedor*, a becoming hairdo.
— M. y f. Client, customer (cliente).

favorecer* v. tr. To favour [U.S., to favor]: *esta reforma favorece las injusticias*, this reform favours injustice; *la fortuna favorece a los audaces*, fortune favours the brave. || To be in the favour of: *las circunstancias me han favorecido*, circumstances were in my favour. || To help (ayudar). || To flatter, to favour: *esta foto, este vestido te favorece*, this photo, this dress flatters you. || *Ser favorecido con*, to win, to be awarded: *ha sido favorecido con el premio gordo*, he has won the first prize.
— V. pr. *Favorecerse dè*, to avail o.s. of, to fall back on (valerse de).

favorecido, da adj. Favoured [U.S., favored]. || *Cláusula del país más favorecido*, most-favoured-nation clause.
— F. *Amer.* Letter (carta).

favoritismo m. Favouritism [U.S., favoritism].

favorito, ta adj. Favourite [U.S., favorite]: *mi deporte favorito*, my favourite sport.
— M. y f. Favourite.

faya f. Faille (tela).

faz f. Face: *la faz de la tierra*, the face of the earth. || Obverse, head (de una moneda). || — *A la faz de*, in front of. || *Faz a faz*, face to face. || *La Sacra* or *Santa Faz*, the Holy Face.

fe f. Faith: *la fe cristiana*, the Christian faith; *tener fe en el porvenir*, to have faith in the future. || Certificate (documento): *fe de bautismo, de matrimonio*, baptism, marriage certificate. || Faithfulness (fidelidad): *fe conyugal*, faithfulness between husband and wife. || — *A fe de*, on the word of: *a fe de caballero*, on the word of a gentleman. || *A fe mía* or *por mi fe*, on my honour, upon my faith. || *Buena, mala fe*, honesty, dishonesty. || *Dar fe de*, to attest, to certify. || *De buena fe*, with good intentions, in good faith. || *De mala fe*, in bad faith. || *En fe de lo cual*, in witness whereof. || *Fe de erratas*, list of errata. || *Fe de vida*, document to prove that a person is still alive. || *Hacer fe*, to certify, to attest. || *Prestar fe a*, to believe in, to have faith in. || *Profesión de fe*, profession of faith. || *Tener buena, mala fe*, the be honest, dishonest. || *Tener una fe ciega en*, to have blind faith in.

fealdad f. Ugliness. || FIG. Unseemliness: *la fealdad de su conducta*, the unseemliness of his behaviour.

feamente adv. In an ugly manner. || FIG. Unseemingly, indecorously. || *Mató al toro feamente*, he killed the bull very badly.

feble adj. Feeble, weak (débil). || Too light (moneda).

Febo n. pr. m. Phoebus (el Sol).

febrero m. February: *ocurrió el 27 de febrero*, it happened on the 27th. of February.

febrífugo, ga adj./s.m. Febrifuge: *la quinina es un febrífugo*, quinine is a febrifuge.

febril adj. Feverish.

febrilidad f. Feverishness.

fecal adj. Faecal [U.S., fecal].

fécula f. Starch.

feculencia f. Starchiness. || Feculence (impureza).

feculento, ta adj. Starchy. || Feculent (impuro).
— M. Starchy food.

fecundable adj. Fertilizable.

fecundación f. Fertilization, fecundation.

fecundador, ra o **fecundante** adj. Fertilizing, fecundating.

fecundar v. tr. To fertilize, to fecundate. || To make fertile (un terreno).

fecundidad f. Fertility, fecundity. || FIG. Productivity, fruitfulness (productividad).

fecundizar v. tr. To fertilize, to fecundate. || To make fertile (un terreno).

fecundo, da adj. Fertile, fecund. || FIG. Prolific (prolífico). | Fruitful (fructífero). | Productive (productivo). | Fertile, rich (imaginación). | Full: *fecundo en consecuencias*, full of consequence.

fecha f. Date: *¿cuál es la fecha de hoy?*, what is the date today?, what is today's date? || Day: *mi carta tardó tres fechas*, my letter took three days. || — *A estas fechas*, now, by now. || *A fecha fija*, on a fixed date. || *A partir de esta fecha*, from today. || *A tres días fecha*, three days after sight. || *Con fecha del 10*, dated the 10th. || *De fecha de*, dated: *una carta de fecha 3*, a letter dated the 3rd. || *De fecha reciente*, recent. || COM. *De larga fecha*, long-dated. || *En fecha próxima*, at an early date, in the near future. || *Fecha tope*, final *o* closing date. || *Hasta la fecha*, so far. || *Poner la fecha en una carta*, to put the date on a letter, to date a letter. || *Por estas fechas*, this time: *el año pasado por estas fechas hubo un terremoto*, this time last year there was an earthquake. || *Señalar fecha*, to fix a date. || *Sin fecha*, undated.

fechador m. Date stamp (matasellos).

fechar v. tr. To date, to put the date on.

fecho, cha adj. (Ant.). V. HECHO.

fechoría f. Misdeed, misdemeanour [U.S., misdemeanor]: *cometer fechorías*, to commit misdeeds. || Mischief: *los niños hicieron fechorías*, the children got up to mischief. || *Le han hecho una fechoría con el traje*, they have ruined his suit.

federación f. Federation.

federado, da adj. Federate, federated.
— M. Federate.

federal adj./s.m. Federal.

federalismo m. Federalism.

federalista adj./s. Federalist.

federalizar v. tr. To federate.

federar v. tr. To federate.
— V. pr. To federate.

federativo, va adj. Federative.

Federico n. pr. m. Frederick.

féferes m. pl. *Amer.* Things, bits and pieces, paraphernalia (trastos).

fehaciente adj. Authentic, reliable (documento). || Irrefutable: *prueba fehaciente*, irrefutable proof.

feldespático, ca adj. MIN. Feldspathic.

feldespato m. MIN. Feldspar, feldspath.

feldmariscal m. Field marshall (mariscal del campo).

felice adj. POÉT. Happy.

felicidad f. Happiness, felicity (p.us.). || Prosperity, success (prosperidad). || — FAM. *Deseos de felicidad*, best wishes. | *La curva de la felicidad*, potbelly, paunch (tripa). || *Felicidades* or *muchas felicidades*, congratulations (acontecimiento feliz), best wishes, Happy New Year (Año Nuevo), many happy returns, happy birthday (cumpleaños), best wishes (santo). || FIG. *Hicieron el viaje con toda felicidad*, their journey went off without a hitch, their journey went off very smoothly. || *Os deseo toda clase de felicidades*, I wish you every happiness.

felicitación f. Congratulation: *mis mejores felicitaciones por su éxito*, my sincere congratulations on your success. || Compliment: *mis felicitaciones por tu peinado*, my compliments on your hairdo. || Greeting, wish (escrito, expresión): *ha recibido muchas felicitaciones*, he has received a lot of greetings.

felicitar v. tr. To congratulate: *le felicité por el nacimiento de su hijo*, I congratulated him on the birth of his son. || To congratulate: *te felicito por el gusto con que te peinas*, I congratulate you on your taste in hairstyles. || To compliment, to congratulate: *todo el mundo la felicitó por su cocina*, everyone complimented her on her cooking. || — *Felicitar a uno*, to wish s.o. a Happy New Year (Año Nuevo). || *Felicitarle a uno (por) su santo, (por) su cumpleaños, (por) las Navidades o las Pascuas, (por) el Año Nuevo*, to wish s.o. a happy name day, a happy birthday, a Happy Christmas, a Happy New Year. || *¡Te felicito!*, congratulations!
— V. pr. To be happy *o* glad: *me felicito de que haya tenido éxito*, I am glad that he has been successful. || To congratulate o.s.

félido m. ZOOL. Felid. || — Pl. ZOOL. Felidae.

feligrés, esa m. y f. Parishioner.

feligresía f. Parish (parroquia). || Parishioners, *pl.*, parish (feligreses).

felino, na adj./s.m. ZOOL. Feline.

Felipe n. pr. m. Philip (nombre actual). || Philippe (nombre de los reyes de Francia). || FIG. *Se lo ponen como a Felipe II (segundo)*, he gets everything handed to him on a plate.

feliz adj. Happy: *feliz con su suerte*, happy with one's lot; *existencia feliz*, happy existence. || Clever (acertado): *una decisión feliz*, a clever decision. || Fortunate, lucky (afortunado). || Felicitous, happy (expresión). || Good: *fue un viaje muy feliz*, it was a very good journey. || Successful (que tiene éxito). || — *Desearle a uno un feliz Año Nuevo*, to wish s.o. a Happy New Year. || *¡Felices Pascuas!*, the season's greetings!, compliments of the season! || *¡Feliz Año Nuevo!*, Happy New Year! || *Feliz con saber algo*, happy to know sth. || *Feliz desenlace*, happy ending. || *¡Feliz viaje!*, have a good journey!, bon voyage! || *Más feliz que nadie*, as happy as the day is long *o* as a king. || *No me hace feliz tener que viajar de noche*, I'm not happy about having to travel by night.

felizmente adj. Fortunately (por fortuna): *felizmente la tempestad fue de poca duración*, fortunately the storm was short. || Uneventfully, smoothly, without a hitch (sin ninguna pega): *la fiesta terminó felizmente*, the celebrations finished uneventfully. || Happily: *vivieron muchos años felizmente*, they lived happily for many years. || Successfully (con éxito).

felón, ona adj. Treacherous, villainous, perfidious.
— M. y f. Traitor, villain.

felonía f. Treachery, perfidy, betrayal (traición).

felpa f. Plush (tela parecida al terciopelo). || Towelling, terry cloth (tela para toallas, manoplas, etc.). || FIG. y FAM. Beating, hiding (paliza). | Dressing down, telling off (reprensión severa): *darle* or *echarle una felpa a uno*, to give s.o. a telling off. || *Oso de felpa*, teddy bear.

felpar v. tr. To cover with plush.
— V. pr. FIG. To be carpeted *o* covered (*de*, with).

felpilla f. Chenille (cordón felpudo).

felpudo, da adj. Plushy, plush-like, velvety.
— M. Doormat (esterilla).

femenil adj. Feminine, womanly.

femenino, na adj. Feminine: *gracia femenina*, feminine grace; *terminación femenina*, feminine ending. || BIOL. y BOT. Female: *sexo femenino*, female sex. || *Equipo femenino*, women's team.
— M. GRAM. Feminine.
fementido, da adj. False, treacherous, perfidious.
feminidad f. Femininity (de una mujer). || Effeminacy (afeminación).
feminismo m. Feminism.
feminista adj./s. Feminist.
femoral adj. Femoral.
— F. Femoral artery.
fémur m. ANAT. Femur.
fenecer* v. intr. To die, to pass away (morir). || To perish (perecer). || To come to an end (terminarse).
— V. tr. To settle, to finalize, to finish.
fenecimiento m. Passing away, death, decease (muerte). || Close, end (de un plazo). || End, finish (final).
fenestración f. MED. Fenestration.
fenestrado, da adj. Fenestrate.
fenianismo m. HIST. Fenianism.
feniano m. HIST. Fenian.
Fenicia n. pr. f. GEOGR. Phoenicia, Phenicia.
fenicio, cia adj./s. Phoenician, Phenician.
fenilo m. Phenyl.
fénix m. inv. Phoenix, phenix.
fenol m. QUÍM. Phenol.
fenomenal adj. Phenomenal. || FIG. Extraordinary, phenomenal: *un talento fenomenal*, an extraordinary talent. | Fantastic, wonderful (magnífico). | Huge, colossal (enorme).
fenomenalismo o **fenomenismo** m. Phenomenalism.
fenómeno m. Phenomenon: *los fenómenos de la naturaleza*, the phenomena of nature. || FIG. Freak: *enseñan fenómenos en el circo*, they are showing freaks in the circus. | Phenomenon (suceso, cosa).
— Adj. FAM. Fantastic, great, terrific: *este chico es fenómeno*, this boy is great. || FAM. *Pasarlo fenómeno*, to have a terrific *o* a great time.
— Interj. FAM. Great!, fantastic!, terrific!
fenomenología f. Phenomenology.
fenomenólogo m. Phenomenologist.
feo, a adj. Ugly: *una persona fea*, an ugly person. || Awful, terrible: *una película fea*, an awful film. || Not nice: *es feo mentir*, it is not nice to lie. || Unbecoming, unseemly (poco decoroso): *es feo fumar en la calle*, it is unbecoming to smoke in the street. || Unsightly (repugnante). || Dirty, nasty: *una acción fea*, a dirty action. || Foul, nasty: *hace un tiempo feo*, the weather is nasty. || Serious, nasty (situación). || — *La cosa se está poniendo fea*, things are taking a nasty turn. || *Más feo que Picio* or *de un feo que asusta*, as ugly as sin. || FIG. *Tocarle a uno bailar con la más fea*, to get the short end of the stick.
— M. Insult, slight, affront (afrenta). || Ugliness (fealdad). || *Hacer un feo a alguien*, to offend s.o., to slight s.o.
— Adv. *Amer.* Nasty, awful: *saber, oler feo*, to taste, to smell nasty.
feracidad f. Fertility, fecundity.
feral adj. (P.us.). Fierce, feral.
feraz adj. Fertile (fértil).
féretro m. Coffin (ataúd). || Bier (andas).
feria f. Fair: *feria del campo, de ganado*, agricultural, livestock fair. || Fair, carnival (verbena). || REL. Feria (día de la semana). || Holiday, day of rest (día de descanso). || *Amer.* Tip (propina). || — Pl. Gifts (regalos). || — FIG. *Cada uno habla de la feria según le va en ella*, everyone sees things in his own way. || *Feria de muestras*, trade fair, trade exhibition.
feriado adj. m. *Día feriado*, holiday.
ferial adj. Fair (de la feria). || REL. Ferial (de los días).
— M. Fairground (de una feria).
feriante m. y f. Fairgoer (el que va a la feria). || Exhibitor (en una feria de muestras).
feriar v. tr. To buy at the fair (comprar). || To trade (comprar o vender).
— V. intr. To be on holiday (no trabajar).
ferino, na adj. Ferine, feral. || MED. *Tos ferina*, whooping cough, hooping cough.
fermentable adj. Fermentative.
fermentación f. Fermentation.
fermentar v. tr. e intr. To ferment.
fermento m. Ferment.
fermio m. QUÍN. Fermium.
Fernando o **Fernán** n. pr. m. Ferdinand.
ferocidad f. Ferocity, fierceness, ferociousness.
ferodo m. Brake lining (forro de freno).
feróstico, ca adj. FAM. Unruly, wild (rebelde). | Irritable (irritable). | Ugly (feo).
feroz adj. Ferocious, fierce (animal). || Fierce, savage (persona). || Fierce, raging (tempestad, viento). || Fierce, ferocious: *feroz resistencia*, fierce resistance. || Terrible (tremendo). || — *El lobo feroz*, the big bad wolf. || *Tener un hambre feroz*, to be ravenous.
ferrar v. tr. To cover with iron (cubrir). || To trim with iron (guarnecer).
ferrato m. QUÍM. Ferrate.
férreo, a adj. Ferreous, ferrous (of or like iron). || FIG. Of iron, iron: *voluntad férrea*, iron will, will of iron. || *Vía férrea*, railway [U.S., railroad].
ferrería f. Forge (forja). || Ironworks (fábrica).
ferrete m. Copper sulfate. || Iron punch (punzón).
ferretería f. Ironmonger's shop, ironmongery, hardware shop (tienda). || Ironmongery, hardware (profesión).
ferretero m. Ironmonger, hardware dealer.
ferricianuro m. QUÍM. Ferricyanide.
férrico, ca adj. QUÍM. Ferric.
ferrífero, ra adj. QUÍM. Ferriferous.
ferrita f. MIN. Ferrite.
ferrito m. QUÍM. Ferrite (sal).
ferrobús m. Railcar, monorail car.
ferrocarril m. Railway [U.S., railroad]: *ferrocarril de cremallera*, rack railway. || *Por ferrocarril*, by rail, by train.
ferrocarrilero, ra adj./s. *Amer.* V. FERROVIARIO.
ferrocianuro m. QUÍM. Ferrocyanide.
ferromagnético, ca adj. Ferromagnetic.
ferromagnetismo m. Ferromagnetism.
ferromanganeso m. Ferromanganese.
ferroníquel m. Ferronickel.
ferroprusiato m. Ferroprussiate.
ferroso, sa adj. QUÍM. Ferrous.
ferroviario, ria adj. Railway, rail [U.S., railroad]: *red ferroviaria*, rail network.
— M. Railwayman, railway worker, railway employee (empleado). || *Huelga de ferroviarios*, rail strike.
ferruginoso, sa adj. Ferruginous.
ferry boat m. Ferryboat, train ferry (transbordador).
fértil adj. Fertile. || FIG. Fertile: *imaginación fértil*, fertile imagination. | Rich: *año fértil en* or *de acontecimientos*, year rich in events.
fertilidad f. Fertility, fecundity.
fertilizable adj. Fertilizable.
fertilización f. Fertilization.
fertilizante adj. Fertilizing.
— M. Fertilizer: *fertilizantes nitrogenados*, nitrate fertilizers.
fertilizar v. tr. To fertilize.
férula f. BOT. Ferula. || Cane, ferule (del maestro). || FIG. *Estar bajo la férula de uno*, to be under s.o.'s thumb *o* under s.o.'s rule.
férvido, da adj. Fervent, fervid, ardent: *defensor férvido*, fervent defender.
ferviente adj. Fervent, ardent.
fervor m. Fervour [U.S., fervor].
fervorín m. Short prayer.
fervorizar v. tr. V. ENFERVORIZAR.
fervoroso, sa adj. Fervent, fervid, ardent.
festejar v. tr. To celebrate: *festejar un aniversario*, to celebrate an anniversary. || To wine and dine, to feast, to entertain: *festejar a un huésped*, to wine and dine a guest. || To court (cortejar). || *Amer.* To beat, to thrash (azotar).
festejo m. Entertainment, feast (de un huésped). || Celebration. || Courting, wooing (cortejo). || — Pl. Festivities, rejoicings (regocijos, fiestas).
festín m. Banquet, feast.
festival adj. Festive, feast (festivo).
— M. Festival: *festival de cine*, film festival.
festivamente adv. Wittily (chistosamente).
festividad f. Festivity, celebration (fiesta alegre). || Ceremony (acto solemne). || Feast day (fiesta). || Festivity, gaiety (alegría). || Wit, humour (agudeza).
festivo, va adj. Feast, festive: *día festivo*, feast day. || Festive, joyful (alegre): *estar de un humor festivo*, to be in a festive mood. || Witty, humorous (chistoso).
festón m. Festoon, garland (guirnalda). || Scallop (adorno).
festoneado m. Festoonry.
festonear v. tr. To festoon. || To scallop (en costura).
fetal adj. Foetal [U.S., fetal]: *vida fetal*, foetal life.
fetén adj. FAM. Fantastic, great, terrific (formidable). | Hundred per cent, genuine, through and through: *un madrileño fetén*, a hundred per cent *o* a genuine Madrilenian, a Madrilenian through and through.
feticidio m. Foeticide [U:S., feticide].
fetiche m. Fetish.
fetichismo m. Fetishism.
fetichista adj. Fetishistic, fetishist.
— M. y f. Fetishist.
fetidez f. Foetidness [U.S., fetidness], foetidity [U.S., fetidity], foulness, stench.
fétido, da adj. Foetid [U.S., fetid], foul-smelling, stinking. || *Bomba fétida*, stink bomb.
feto m. Foetus [U.S., fetus]. || FIG. y FAM. Monster (persona contrahecha).
feúco, ca o **feúcho, cha** adj. FAM. Plain.
feudal adj. Feudal: *señor feudal*, feudal lord.
feudalidad f. Feudality.
feudalismo m. Feudalism.
feudatario, ria adj./s. Feudatory.
feudo m. Fief, feud (territorio). || Vassalage (vasallaje). || — *Dar en feudo*, to enfeoff. || *Feudo alodial*, alodium.
fez m. Fez.
fi f. Phi (letra griega).
fiabilidad f. Reliability.
fiable adj. Trustworthy, reliable (seguro). || Solvent.
fiado, da adj. Trusting (confiado). || On credit: *comprar fiado*, to buy on credit. || *Al fiado*, on credit.
fiador, ra m. y f. JUR. Guarantor, surety. || — M. Snap fastener, press stud (presilla de capa). || Sword knot (del sable). || TECN. Safety catch (de la escopeta).

| Tumbler (cerrojo). | Pin, clip (garfio). | Bracket (de los canalones). || Fam. Buttocks, *pl.* (nalgas). || *Amer.* Chin strap (barboquejo). || Jur. *Salir* or *ser fiador de*, to go bail for, to stand surety for (pagar fianza), to vouch for (garantizar).

fiambre adj. Cold (alimentos). || Fig. y fam. Stale, old: *una noticia fiambre*, stale news.
— M. Cold meat [U.S., cold cuts] (alimento frío). || Fam. Stiff (cadáver). || *Amer.* Funeral, boring party (reunión desanimada). || — Fam. *Dejar fiambre*, to kill, to do in (matar). | *Está (hecho) fiambre*, he has kicked the bucket (ha muerto). || *Fiambres variados*, assorted cold meats [U.S., assorted cold cuts].

fiambrera f. Lunch box [U.S., dinner pail *o* bucket] (para llevar los alimentos). || *Amer.* Meat safe, food safe (fresquera).

fiambrería f. *Amer.* Coldmeat store, sausage store.

fianza f. Deposit (dinero): *dejar como fianza*, to leave as a deposit. || Surety, security (objeto). || Guarantor, surety (fiador). || — Jur. *Contrato de fianza*, security. || *Dar fianza*, to pay a deposit (dinero). || *Fianza de arraigo*, mortgage. || *Libertad bajo fianza*, release on bail.

fiar v. tr. To guarantee (garantizar). || Jur. To go bail for, to stand surety for (salir fiador por). || To confide: *fiarle a uno un secreto*, to confide a secret to s.o. || To sell on credit (vender). || — *Cuán largo me lo fiáis*, I've got a long time to think about that.
— V. intr. To trust: *fiar en una cosa*, to trust sth., to trust in sth. || *No es persona de fiar*, he's not a person to be trusted, he's not a trustworthy *o* a reliable person.
— V. pr. To trust: *fiarse de* or *en uno*, *de* or *en algo*, to trust s.o. *o* to trust in s.o., to trust sth. *o* to trust in sth. || — *Fiarse de las apariencias*, to trust appearances. || *No se fía*, no credit given (letrero colocado en ciertas tiendas).

fiasco m. Fiasco, failure (fracaso): *ser un fiasco*, to be a fiasco.

fíat m. Fiat, blessing: *dar el fiat*, to give one's blessing.

fibra f. Fibre [U.S., fiber]: *fibra textil*, textile fibre. || Grain (de madera). || Fig. Push, go, energy, vigour (vigor). || *Fibra de vidrio*, fibreglass [U.S., fiberglass]. || *Fibras artificiales*, artificial *o* man-made fibres.

fibrana f. Staple fibre [U.S., staple fiber].

fibrilación f. Med. Fibrillation.

fibrilla adj. Anat. Fibril, fibrilla.

fibrina f. Biol. y Quím. Fibrin.

fibrinógeno m. Fibrinogen.

fibrocemento m. Fibrocement.

fibroma m. Med. Fibroma.

fibroso, sa adj. Fibroid, fibrous.

fíbula f. Fibula (broche, peroné).

fibular adj. Fibular.

ficción f. Fiction. || — Jur. *Ficción de derecho* or *legal*, legal fiction. || *La realidad y la ficción*, fact and fiction.

ficomiceto m. Bot. Phycomycete.

ficticio, cia adj. Fictitious: *nombre ficticio*, fictitious name. || False: *amabilidad ficticia*, false kindness.

ficha f. Index card, file *o* filing card (tarjeta). || Counter (en los juegos). || Chip (en los juegos de naipes). || Piece, man (de ajedrez). || Domino. || Token (para el teléfono). || Registration form (en los hoteles). || Record: *ficha policiaca*, police record. || Fig. Rogue, villain (pillo). || — Cinem. *Ficha técnica*, credit titles, *pl.*, credits, *pl.* || *Sacar fichas*, to make file cards.

fichaje m. Signing-up [of a player with a team].

fichar v. tr. To put on an index card (apuntar en una ficha). || To file, to index (clasificar). || To draw up a dossier on, to put in the files (hacer la ficha antropométrica). || To sign on, to sign up (un futbolista). || Fig. To size up, to tape: *le tengo fichado*, I've got him sized up *o* taped. || — *Estar fichado por la policía*, to be in the police records *o* files, to have a criminal record. || Fig. *Estar fichado por un jefe*, to be on a boss's black list.
— V. intr. To sign up, to sign on: *fichar por un equipo*, to sign up with a team. || To clock in (en una empresa).

fichero m. File, filing cabinet (mueble). || Card index (fichas). || Records, *pl.* (de la policía).

fichú m. Fichu, headscarf (toquilla).

fidedigno, na adj. Reliable, trustworthy: *fuentes fidedignas*, reliable sources.

fideicomisario, ria m. y f. Jur. Trustee, fiduciary.
— Adj. Trust, fiduciary.

fideicomiso m. Jur. Trusteeship: *en* or *bajo fideicomiso*, in trusteeship.

fidelidad f. Faithfulness, fidelity. || Accuracy (exactitud). || Rad. *Alta fidelidad*, high fidelity.

fideo m. Noodle. || Fam. Skinny person (persona flaca). || Fam. *Estar como un fideo*, to be as thin as a rake [U.S., as thin as a rail].

fiduciario, ria adj. Fiduciary: *moneda fiduciaria*, fiduciary money.
— M. Fiduciary, trustee.

fiebre f. Med. Fever: *fiebre álgida*, *amarilla*, *intermitente*, *tifoidea*, algid, yellow, intermittent, typhoid fever. || Fig. Fever: *fiebre electoral*, election fever. || — *Fiebre láctea*, milk fever. || *Fiebre palúdica*, malaria. || *Tener fiebre*, to have a temperature *o* a fever. || *Tener mucha fiebre*, to run a very high temperature *o* a high fever.

fiel adj. Faithful, loyal: *fiel a su juramento*, faithful to one's oath; *fiel a* or *con* or *para con sus amigos*, faithful to one's friends; *fiel al rey*, loyal to the king. || Reliable: *memoria fiel*, reliable memory. || Faithful, accurate, exact: *un relato fiel de los sucesos*, a faithful report of the events. || Honest (honrado).
— M. Faithful person (cristiano). || Inspector, supervisor (verificador). || Needle, pointer (de balanza). || Screw (de las tijeras). || — Fig. *Inclinar el fiel de la balanza*, v. balanza. || *Los fieles*, the faithful.

fielato m. Tollhouse.

fieltro m. Felt (tejido). || Felt hat (sombrero). || *Ponerse como el fieltro*, to felt (una prenda de lana).

fiemo m. Manure (estiércol).

fiera f. Wild animal. || Taur. Bull. || Fig. Beast, brute (hombre cruel). | Dragon, vixen (mujer cruel e irritable). | Bad-tempered devil (hombre irritable). || — *Casa de fieras*, menagerie. || Fig. *Estar hecho una fiera*, to be wild, to be in a rage. | *Luchar como una fiera*, to fight like a tiger. | *Ser una fiera para*, to be a fiend for.

fierabrás m. Fig. Rebel (rebelde). | Little devil, imp (niño travieso).

fierecilla f. *La fierecilla domada*, the Taming of the Shrew (obra de Shakespeare).

fiereza f. Fierceness, ferocity (ferocidad). || Cruelty (crueldad). || Wildness (cualidad de no domesticado).

fiero, ra adj. Fierce, ferocious (feroz). || Cruel (cruel). || Wild (no domesticado). || Fig. Terrible, frightful (horrible). | Ugly (feo). | Huge, enormous (enorme).
— M. pl. Boasting, *sing.*, swanking, *sing.*, bragging, *sing.* (fanfarroneo). || *Echar fieros*, to boast, to brag, to swank.

fierro m. Iron (hierro).

fiesta f. Party (en una casa particular): *dar una fiesta*, to give a party. || Party, celebration: *hicieron una fiesta con motivo del bautizo de su hijo*, they held a celebration *o* they gave a party for their son's baptism. || Rel. Holy day, feast. || Holiday: *el dos de mayo es fiesta*, May 2nd is a holiday. || Ceremony (acto solemne). || Fig. Treat: *tu carta fue una fiesta para mí*, your letter was a treat for me. || — Pl. Celebrations, festivities: *las fiestas de Valencia*, the festivities in Valencia. || Holidays: *las fiestas de Navidad*, the Christmas holidays. || Soothing words, flattering words (palabras cariñosas).
— Fig. *Aguar la fiesta*, to be a wet blanket *o* a killjoy, to spoil the fun. | *Estar de fiesta*, to be in a festive mood (alegre), to be celebrating (celebrando), to be on holiday (no trabajar). || Rel. *Fiesta de guardar* or *de precepto*, day of obligation. || *Fiesta de la banderita*, flag day. || *Fiesta de la Raza*, Columbus day. || *Fiesta del Trabajo*, Labour Day. || *Fiesta fija*, immovable *o* fixed feast. || *Fiesta movible* or *móvil*, movable feast. || *Fiesta nacional*, bank holiday (en Inglaterra), national *o* public holiday (en los demás países). || *Guardar* or *hacer fiesta*, to take a day off. || *Hacer fiestas*, to play about (bromear). || *Hacer fiestas a uno*, to make a fuss of s.o. || *La fiesta brava*

FIESTAS (*f.*) RELIGIOSAS — FEAST DAYS

Adviento *m.*	Advent
Anunciación *f.*	Lady Day, Annunciation
Ascensión *f.*	Ascension Day
Asunción *f.*	Assumption
Candelaria (la) *f.*	Candlemas
Circuncisión (*f.*) *or* día (*m.*) de Año Nuevo	New Year, New Year's Day
Corpus Christi *m.*	Corpus Christi
Cuadragésima *f.*	Quadragesima
Cuaresma *f.*	Lent
Cuasimodo *m.*	Low *o* Quasimodo Sunday
Difuntos (día [*m.*] de los)	All Souls' Day
Domingo (*m.*) de Ramos	Palm Sunday
Domingo (*m.*) de Resurrección	Easter Sunday, Easter
Epifanía (*f.*) *or* Reyes *m. pl.*	Epiphany, Twelfth Day
fiesta (*f.*) de guardar *or* de precepto	day of obligation
Jueves (*m.*) Santo	Maundy Thursday
Martes (*m.*) de Carnaval	Shrove Tuesday
Miércoles (*m.*) de Ceniza	Ash Wednesday
Natividad (*f.*) de la Virgen	Nativity of the Virgin
Navidad *f.*	Christmas
Nochebuena *f.*	Christmas Eve
Nochevieja *f.*	New Year's Eve
Pascua (*f.*) Florida *or* de Resurrección	Easter
Pentecostés *m.*	Whitsun, Whitsuntide
Quincuagésima *f.*	Quinquagesima
Ramadán *m.*	Ramadan
Rogativas *f. pl.*	Rogation Days
Sábado (*m.*) israelita	Sabbath
Sagrado Corazón *m.*	Feast of the Sacred Heart
San Juan (día [*m.*] de)	Midsummer Day
Semana (*f.*) de Pasión	Passion Week
Semana (*f.*) Santa *or* grande *or* Mayor	Holy Week
Septuagésima *f.*	Septuagesima
Sexagésima *f.*	Sexagesima
Témporas *f. pl.*	Ember Days
Todos los Santos (fiesta [*f.*] de)	All Saints' Day
Trinidad *f.*	Trinity Sunday, Trinity
Viernes (*m.*) Santo	Good Friday
Visitación *f.*	Visitation

or *nacional*, bullfighting. || FIG. *No estar para fiestas*, to be in no mood for jokes. | *Tengamos la fiesta en paz*, let's have less of that, cut that out. | *Y como fin de fiesta*, to round everything off.

fiestero, ra adj. FAM. Party-loving, fun-loving (a quien le gustan las fiestas). | Gay (alegre).

fifiriche m. *Amer.* Fop, dandy (elegantón). | Puny person, weakling (enclenque).

fígaro m. Barber (barbero). || Bolero (chaquetilla).

figón m. Eating house, cheap restaurant (tasca).

figonero, ra m. y f. Keeper of an eating house *o* of a cheap restaurant.

figulino, na adj. Earthenware, fictile (de arcilla).

figura f. Shape, form (forma): *¿qué figura tiene?*, what shape is it? || Figure (de persona): *en el cuadro hay una figura de mujer*, on the picture there is a figure of a woman. || Shape: *figuras de madera*, wooden shapes. || (Ant.). Face (rostro). || Figure (tipo): *tener buena figura*, to have a good figure. || FIG. Personality, figure (personaje): *ser una gran figura*, to be an important figure. | Character (de una obra teatral). || GRAM. Figure: *figura de construcción*, figure of speech. || MÚS. Note. || Chessman (de ajedrez). || Court card, face card (naipe). || Figure (de una danza). || MAT. Figure. || — *Figura central*, central figure (en un drama). || *Figura de bulto*, statue, figure. || *Hacer figuras*, to pull faces. || *Ser la figura de la fiesta*, to be the central figure at a party (el más importante), to be the life and soul of the party (ser el alma de la fiesta).

figuración f. Imagination (acción de figurarse). || *Eso son figuraciones tuyas*, these are figments of your imagination.

figuradamente adv. Figuratively, with a figurative meaning.

figurado, da adj. Figurative. || *En sentido figurado*, figuratively, with a figurative meaning.

figurante m. y f. TEATR. Extra, supernumerary, walker-on.

figurar v. tr. To simulate, to feign (fingir). || To represent, to depict: *esta esfera figura la Tierra*, this sphere represents the Earth. || To outline (delinear).

— V. intr. To act, to figure: *figurar como* or *de profesor*, to act as the teacher. || To appear, to figure, to be: *su nombre figura en la lista*, his name appears on the list. || To be important (ser importante): *es la persona que más figura en la alta sociedad*, he is the most important person in high society. || To show off (presumir).

— V. pr. To imagine, to think: *se figuraba que era el único en su caso*, he imagined he was the only one in his condition. || — *Figúrate, figúrese*, just imagine. || *¿Qué te has figurado?*, what do you think this is? || *Ya me lo figuraba*, I thought as much.

figurativo, va adj. Figurative: *arte figurativo*, figurative art.

figurín m. Sketch, design (dibujo). || Fashion magazine (revista). || FIG. y FAM. Fop, dandy (elegantón).

figurinista m. y f. Costume designer.

figurón m. FIG. y FAM. Show-off, swank, swaggerer (presumido). || Character actor (actor). || — MAR. *Figurón de proa*, figurehead. || *Comedia de figurón*, comedy of character.

fijacarteles m. inv. Billposter.

fijación f. Setting, fixing: *fijación de una fecha*, fixing of a date. || Fastening, fixing: *la fijación del lienzo en el bastidor*, the fixing of the canvas to the frame. || Sticking (de un sello). || Posting, putting up (de un cartel). || Securing (acción de asegurar). || FOT. Fixing: *baño de fijación*, fixing bath. || QUÍM. Fixation. || *La fijación del impuesto*, tax assessment.

fijado m. FOT. Fixing.

fijador, ra adj. Fixative.

— M. Fixative (para el pelo). || Pointer (en albañilería). || ARTES. Fixative. || FOT. Fixer, fixative.

fijamente adv. Fixedly.

fijapelo m. Fixative.

fijar v. tr. To fix, to fasten: *fijar un lienzo en el bastidor*, to fasten a canvas to the frame. || To stick: *fijar un sello en un sobre*, to stick a stamp on an envelope. || To post, to put up (un cartel). || To fix: *fijar un poste en tierra*, to fix a post in the ground. || To secure (asegurar). || To fix, to set: *fijar un precio*, to fix a price; *fijar la fecha de un viaje*, to fix the date of a journey. || To determine: *fijar un reglamento*, to determine regulations. || To draw up: *fijar un plan*, to draw up a plan. || To install (puerta, ventana). || To point (ladrillos). || FOT. y QUÍM. To fix. || — *Fijar domicilio en*, to take up residence in. || *Fijar la atención* or *el pensamiento en*, to fix one's attention on, to concentrate on. || *Fijar la mirada* or *los ojos en*, to fix one's eyes on, to stare at. || *Prohibido fijar carteles* or *anuncios*, post *o* stick no bills.

— V. pr. To settle (establecerse): *el dolor se ha fijado en el brazo*, the pain has settled in his arm. || FIG. To take notice: *fíjate en todo lo que vas a ver para contármelo luego*, take notice of everything you see so that you can tell me about it later. | To notice: *¿no te has fijado en mi vestido nuevo?*, haven't you noticed my new dress? | To look: *fíjate como ha crecido el niño*, look how the child has grown. | To pay attention, to be careful: *fíjate en lo que dices*, pay attention to what you are saying, be careful what you are saying. || — *¡Con que fíjate!*, just imagine!, just think! || *¡Fíjate!*, look (¡mira!), imagine!, just think! (¡te das cuenta!). || *Se ha estado fijando en ella toda la noche*, he has had his eyes on her all night.

fijativo, va adj. Fixative.

— M. ARTES. Fixative. || FOT. Fixer, fixative.

fijeza f. Fixity, firmness (estabilidad). || Fastness (de colores). || Certainty (seguridad). || — *Mirar algo con fijeza*, to stare at sth. || *Saber algo con fijeza*, to know sth. for certain.

fijo, ja adj. Fastened, fixed (sujeto). || Steady, stable, firm, secure: *no subas porque la escalera no está bien fija*, don't go up because the ladder is not very steady. || Settled: *estoy fijo en París*, I am settled in Paris. || Fixed: *fiesta fija*, fixed feast. || Definite: *ya saben el día fijo de la boda*, now they know the definite date of the wedding. || Fixed: *una renta fija*, a fixed income. || Permanent: *un empleo fijo*, a permanent job. || Fast (color). || Stationary (inmóvil). || QUÍM. Fixed: *un ácido fijo*, a fixed acid. || — *Con la mirada fija en algo*, staring at sth. || *De fijo*, for certain, for sure. || *Mirada fija*, fixed gaze, stare. || *Sueldo fijo*, fixed salary.

— Adv. *Mirar fijo*, to stare at.

— M. Fixed salary (sueldo).

fila f. File: *en fila india* or *en fila de a uno*, in single *o* Indian file. || Row (teatro, cine): *en primera fila*, in the front row. || Line, queue (de gente esperando). || MIL. Rank. || — MIL. *Alistarse en filas*, to sign up. | *Alistarse en las filas de*, to sign up for. | *Cerrar* or *estrechar las filas*, to close the ranks. | *Estar en filas*, to be in the army *o* in the ranks *o* on active service. | *Llamar a filas*, to call up. || *Ponerse en fila*, to line up. || MIL. *¡Rompan filas!*, fall out!, dismiss! | *Romper filas*, to break ranks. || FAM. *Tenerle fila a uno*, to have sth. against s.o.

Filadelfia n. pr. GEOGR. Philadelphia.

filamento m. Filament.

filamentoso, sa adj. Filamentous.

filantropía f. Philanthropy.

filantrópico, ca adj. Philanthropic, philanthropical.

filántropo, pa adj. Philanthropic, philanthropical.

— M. y f. Philanthropist.

filaria f. MED. Filaria (parásito).

filariasis o **filariosis** f. MED. Filariasis, filariosis.

filarmonía f. Love of music.

filarmónico, ca adj. MÚS. Philharmonic.

filatelia f. Philately, stamp collecting.

filatélico, ca adj. Philatelic.

filatelista m. y f. Philatelist, stamp collector.

filete m. Sirloin (solomillo). || Fillet (trozo de carne, de pescado). || Fillet (moldura). || Edging (ribete de la ropa). || Snaffle bit, snaffle (embocadura del caballo). || IMPR. Fillet (adorno). || TECN. Thread (de un tornillo).

fileteado m. TECN. Thread (rosca de un tornillo).

filetear v. tr. To fillet, to decorate with fillets (adornar). || To thread (un tornillo).

filfa f. FAM. Hoax (engaño): *¡eso es pura filfa!*, this is all a hoax. | Fib, lie (mentira).

filhelénico, ca adj. Philhellenic.

filhelenismo m. Philhellenism (amor a los griegos).

filheleno, na adj. Philhellenic.

— M. y f. Philhellene, philhellenist.

filiación f. Particulars, *pl.* (datos personales). || Description (señas personales). || Filiation (procedencia). || Affiliation (afiliación). || MIL. Record card.

filial adj. Filial: *amor filial*, filial love, filial piety. || COM. Subsidiary, affiliated.

— F. COM. Branch (sucursal): *establecer una filial en Londres*, to set up a branch in London. | Subsidiary (empresa dirigida por otra).

filiar v. tr. To take the particulars of.

— V. pr. MIL. To sign up, to enlist (engancharse). || To affiliate (*a*, with).

filibusterismo m. Filibustering.

filibustero m. Filibuster, freebooter (pirata).

filiforme adj. Filiform. || FIG. Skinny (persona). | Thread-like (cosa).

filigrana f. Filigree (obra de orfebrería). || Watermark (en el papel). || Delicately worked object (objeto).

Filipenses n. pr. m. pl. Philippians: *Epístola a los Filipenses*, Epistle to the Philippians.

filípica f. Philippic.

filipino, na adj./s. Philippine, Filipino. || FAM. *Es un punto filipino*, he is a scoundrel *o* a rogue.

Filipinas n. pr. f. pl. GEOGR. Philippines. || *Las Islas filipinas*, The Philippine Islands.

Filipo n. pr. m. HIST. Philip (rey de Macedonia).

filisteo, a adj./s. HIST. Philistine. || — M. FIG. y FAM. Colossus, Goliath, giant (hombre corpulento). | Philistine (inculto).

film m. Film, picture [U.S., movie] (película).

filmación f. Filming, shooting (rodaje).

filmar v. tr. To film, to shoot (rodar).

filme m. V. FILM.

fílmico, ca adj. Film.

filmología f. Study of the influence of cinema on social and moral matters.

filmoteca f. Film library.

filo m. Edge, cutting edge: *el filo de la navaja*, the edge of a razor. || BIOL. Phylum. || *Amer.* Hunger (hambre).

|| — *Al filo de la medianoche*, on the stroke of midnight. || *Al filo del mediodía*, on the stroke of twelve, at midday. || FIG. *Arma de dos filos*, double-edged argument, argument which cuts both ways. || *Dar* or *sacar filo a*, to sharpen. || FIG. *Dormir hasta en el filo de una navaja*, to be able to sleep anywhere. || MAR. *Filo del viento*, direction of the wind. || *Pasar al filo de la espada*, to put to the sword.
filodendrón m. BOT. Philodendron.
filología f. Philology.
filológico, ca adj. Philological, philologic.
filólogo m. Philologist.
filón m. MIN. Vein, seam. || FIG. y FAM. Cushy job (ganga). | Gold mine (fuente de riquezas).
filosofador, ra m. y f. Philosophizer.
filosofal adj. Philosopher's, philosophers': *piedra filosofal*, philosopher's stone.
filosofar v. intr. To philosophize.
filosofastro m. Philosophaster.
filosofía f. Philosophy. || FIG. *Tomar algo con filosofía*, to be philosophical about sth., to accept sth. philosophically.
filosófico, ca adj. Philosophic, philosophical.
filosofismo m. Philosophism.
filósofo, fa adj. Philosophic, philosophical.
— M. y f. Philosopher.
filoxera f. BOT. Phylloxera.
filtración f. Filtration. || FIG. Misappropriation (malversación). | Leak (indiscreción). || FIG. *La decisión se conoció por una filtración*, the decision leaked out.
filtrado, da adj. Filtered. || QUÍM. *Líquido filtrado*, filtrate.
filtrador m. Filter (filtro).
filtrante adj. Filtering. || Porous: *papel, piedra filtrante*, porous paper, stone.
filtrar v. tr. e intr. To filter.
— V. pr. To filter: *filtrarse a través de* or *por un papel*, to filter through a paper. || FIG. To disappear (dinero, bienes). | To leak out: *los secretos se han filtrado*, the secrets have leaked out. | To filtrate: *elementos revolucionarios se han filtrado en el país*, revolutionary elements have filtrated into the country.
filtro m. Filter. || Philtre [U.S., philter], love potion (bebida mágica). || FOT. Filter. || — *Cigarrillo con filtro*, V. CIGARRILLO. || AUT. *Filtro de aceite, de gasolina*, oil, petrol filter. | *Filtro de aire*, air filter, air cleaner.
fimo m. Manure (estiércol).
fimosis f. MED. Phimosis.
fin m. End: *el fin del mundo*, the end of the world; *el fin del carrete*, the end of the reel. || Objective, aim, end, purpose (objetivo): *conseguir sus fines*, to achieve one's aims. || Finish (acabado). || — *A fin de*, in order to, so as to: *a fin de terminarlo*, in order to finish it. || *A fin de que*, so that, in order that: *date prisa a fin de que podamos salir*, hurry up so that we can go out. || *A fines de*, at the end of. || *Al fin*, at last, finally. || *Al fin y al cabo*, after all, when all is said and done. || *Con buen fin*, with good intentions: *lo hizo con buen fin*, he did it with good intentions. || *Con el fin de*, with the purpose *o* the aim of. || *Con el solo* or *el único fin de*, with the sole object of *o* purpose of, merely for the purpose of. || *Con este fin* or *para este fin*, to this end, with this aim. || *Dar* or *poner fin a*, to put an end to, to end. || *El fin justifica los medios*, the end justifies the means. || *En fin*, in short (en resumen), well (bueno). || *En fin de cuentas*, after all, when all is said and done. || *Fin de semana*, weekend. || *Llegar* or *tocar a su fin*, to come to an end, to reach its end. || *Noche de fin de año*, New Year's Eve. || *Por fin*, finally. || *¡Por fin!*, at last! || *Sin fin*, endless: *correa, tornillo sin fin*, endless belt, screw. || *Tener fin*, to end. || *Un sin fin de cosas*, no end of things, piles *o* loads of things.
finado, da m. y f. Deceased, defunct.
— Adj. Late, deceased.
final adj. Final, last: *la letra final de una palabra*, the last letter of a word. || Final: *decisión final*, final decision. || GRAM. Final: *conjunción final*, final conjunction. || *El Juicio Final*, the Last Judgment.
— M. End: *hasta el final*, until the end. || End (muerte): *un trágico final*, a tragic end. || Ending: *película con final feliz*, film with a happy ending. || Conclusion. || MÚS. Finale. || — *Al final*, in the end. || *Al final del año*, at the end of the year. || — F. Final: *la final de copa*, the cup final; *cuartos de final*, quarter finals. || *Final de línea*, terminus, terminal (transportes).
finalidad f. FIG. Objective, aim, purpose, object (propósito). || FIL. Finality.
finalismo m. FIL. Finalism.
finalista adj. In the final: *el equipo finalista*, the team in the final.
— M. y f. Finalist.
finalización f. Termination, conclusion.
finalizar v. tr. e intr. To conclude, to finish, to end. || *Finalizaba el invierno*, winter was drawing to a close.
finalmente adv. Finally.
finamente adv. Finely: *escribir finamente*, to write finely. || In a refined manner: *hablar finamente*, to speak in a refined manner. || Acutely, shrewdly (con agudeza). || Delicately (delicadamente).
finamiento m. Demise, death (fallecimiento).
financiación f. o **financiamiento** m. Financing.
financiar v. tr. To finance. || *Amer.* To buy on credit.
financiero, ra adj. Financial. || *Compañía financiera*, finance company.
— M. Financier.
finanzas f. pl. Finance, *sing.* (hacienda).
finar v. intr. To die, to pass away.
— V. pr. To long, to yearn (*por*, for).
finca f. Property, real estate (propiedad). || Estate (tierras): *una finca rústica* or *de campo*, a country *o* rural estate. || Farm (granja). || *Finca urbana*, building.
fincar v. intr. To buy property *o* real estate (comprar fincas). || *Amer.* To lie, to rest (la dificultad).
finés, esa adj. Finnic (del pueblo antiguo o de la subfamilia de lenguas finesas). || Finnish (finlandés).
— M. y f. Finn (persona). || — M. Finnic (subfamilia de lenguas). || Finnish (lengua actual de Finlandia).
fineza f. Fineness (cualidad de fino). || Refinement, courtesy, politeness (refinamiento, cortesía). || Kindness (amabilidad). || Nice thing (cosa agradable). || Gift (obsequio).
fingidamente adv. Falsely, feignedly.
fingido, da adj. False, feigned, sham. || *Nombre fingido*, false *o* assumed name.
fingidor, ra adj. False, fake.
— M. y f. Fake, sham.
fingimiento m. Feigning, pretence [U.S., pretense], simulation.
fingir v. tr. e intr. To feign, to simulate: *fingir sorpresa, alegría* to feign surprise, happiness. || To simulate, to represent: *con luces rojas finge el fuego*, he simulates fire with red lights. || To pretend: *finge que duerme*, he is pretending to be asleep, he is pretending he is asleep; *fingir creer algo*, to pretend to believe sth., to pretend one believes sth.
— V. pr. To pretend to be, to sham: *fingirse amigos*, to pretend to be friends, to sham friendliness; *fingirse muerto*, to pretend to be dead, to sham death.
finiquitar v. tr. COM. To close, to settle (una cuenta). || FIG. y FAM. To bump off (matar).
finiquito m. COM. Settlement, closing (de una cuenta). | Final discharge (documento). || *Dar finiquito a una cuenta*, to settle *o* to close an account.
finito, ta adj. Finite. || *Lo finito y lo infinito*, the finite and the infinite.
finlandés, esa adj. Finnish.
— M. y f. Finn. || — M. Finnish (idioma).
Finlandia n. pr. f. GEOGR. Finland.
fino, na adj. Fine (papel, hilo, lluvia, piel). || Delicate (facciones). || Slender: *talle fino*, slender waist. || Fine, sharp (punta). || Keen, sharp, acute: *olfato, oído fino*, keen sense of smell, keen hearing. || Thin: *una lonja fina*, a thin slice. || Refined, polite (cortés, bien educado). || Shrewd, acute (inteligencia). || Subtle (ironía, humor). || Elegant. || Choice (alimentos): *vino fino*, choice wine. || Pure, fine (oro). || Fine (gusto, tela). || Select (tabaco). || — *Bailar por lo fino*, to do ballroom dancing. || *Jerez fino*, dry sherry. || *Piedra fina*, semi-precious stone.
finolis adj. FAM. Genteel, affected (afectado).
finta f. Feint (boxeo, esgrima, etc.).
fintar v. intr. To feint.
finura f. Fineness. || Slenderness (del talle, etc.). || Sharpness, keenness (del oído, olfato). || Sharpness (de una punta). || Delicacy (delicadeza). || Politeness, refinement (cortesía). || Acuteness, shrewdness (agudeza). || Subtlety (sutileza). || Elegance. || Excellence, high quality (de alimentos). || *Bailó con gran finura*, she danced very gracefully.
fiord o **fiordo** m. Fiord, fjord.
fique m. *Amer.* Agave fibre.
firma f. Signature: *firma en blanco*, blank signature. || Signing (acto). || Firm (empresa). || FIG. *Llevar la firma de*, to represent, to act for.
firmamento m. Firmament.
firmante adj. Signatory: *los países firmantes*, the signatory countries.
— M. y f. Signatory: *los firmantes de un acuerdo*, the signatories to an agreement. || — *El abajo firmante*, the undersigned, I the undersigned. || *Los abajo firmantes*, the undersigned.
firmar v. tr. e intr. To sign: *firmar un cheque (en blanco)*, to sign a [blank] cheque.
firme adj. Firm, secure, steady, stable (estable). || Solid (sólido). || Rigid (rígido). || Hard (duro). || Straight, erect (erguido): *mantenerse firme*, to keep straight. || Fast (color). || Settled (tiempo). || COM. Steady, strong (mercado). | Steady, firm (precios). | | Firm: *oferta firme*, firm offer. || FIG. Firm: *amistad, idea, creencia firme*, firm friendship, idea, belief. | Firm, unswerving, steadfast: *firme en sus ideas*, steadfast in one's ideas. || — *Andar con paso firme*, to walk with a determined step. || *Andar con pie firme* or *tener el pie firme*, to walk steadily. || *A pie firme*, with a firm step, steadfastly. || *Esperar a pie firme*, to wait resolutely. || MIL. *Estar firmes*, to stand at attention. | *¡Firmes!*, attention! || FIG. *Mantenerse firme*, to stand fast, to hold one's ground. || MIL. *Ponerse firme*, to come to attention. || JUR. *Sentencia firme*, final judgment. || *Tierra firme*, terra firma.
— M. Solid *o* firm ground. || Foundation (de edificio).

|| Roadbed, foundation (cimientos de carretera). || Surface (pavimento de carretera): *firme deslizante*, slippery surface.
— Adv. Hard: *trabajar, estudiar, pegar firme*, to work, to study, to hit hard. || — *De firme*, hard: *trabajar de firme*, to work hard; *llueve de firme*, it is raining hard. || COM. *Vender en firme*, to make a firm sale.
firmemente adv. Firmly, solidly: *clavado firmemente en hormigón*, firmly set in concrete. || Firmly, strongly: *lo creo firmemente*, I strongly believe it. || FIG. Firmly, steadfastly (resueltamente).
firmeza f. Firmness, stability, steadiness (estabilidad). || Solidity (solidez). || Rigidity (rigidez). || FIG. Firmness: *firmeza de creencias, de convicciones, de carácter*, firmness in one's beliefs, in one's convictions, of character. | Firmness, steadfastness (resolución). || COM. Steadiness. || *Amer.* Old Argentinian folk dance (baile).
firuletes m. pl. *Amer.* Adornments, ornaments.
fiscal adj. Fiscal, treasury (del fisco). || Financial (financiero). || Tax (de los impuestos).
— M. JUR. Public prosecutor [U.S., district attorney]. || Treasury official (empleado del fisco). || FIG. y FAM. Snooper (entremetido).
fiscalía f. JUR. Public prosecutor's office [U.S., district attorney's office]. || *Fiscalía de tasas*, rationing department.
fiscalización f. Supervision (vigilancia). || Inspection (inspección). || FIG. Prying, snooping.
fiscalizador adj. FIG. Prying, snooping.
— M. y f. FIG. Snooper.
fiscalizar v. tr. To supervise (controlar). || FIG. To pry into (curiosear). | To keep an eye on, to inspect, to check up on (vigilar): *siempre está fiscalizando nuestro trabajo*, he is always checking up on our work. | To criticize (criticar).
fisco m. Treasury, exchequer.
fisga f. Banter, raillery, chaff (mofa).
fisgador, ra adj. Prying, snooping (curioso). || Mocking, bantering (burlador).
— M. y f. Snooper, busybody (entremetido). | Banterer (burlador).
fisgar v. tr. To pry into (un asunto). || To spy on (una persona). || To harpoon (pescar con arpón).
— V. intr. To pry, to snoop.
— V. pr. To mock, to scoff, to make fun: *fisgarse de uno*, to make fun of *o* to scoff at *o* to mock s.o.
fisgón, ona adj./s. V. FISGADOR.
fisgonear v. tr. To pry into (un asunto). || To spy on (el vecino, etc.).
— V. intr. To snoop, to pry.
fisgoneo m. Snooping, prying.
fisible adj. Fissile.
física f. Physics: *física nuclear*, nuclear physics.
físicamente adv. Physically.
físico, ca adj. Physical: *un cambio físico en una sustancia*, a physical change in a substance; *geografía, imposibilidad física*, physical geography, impossibility. || *Amer.* Affected, finicky (remilgado).
— M. Physique (forma del cuerpo). || Face, features, *pl.* (cara). || Appearance, looks, *pl.* (aspecto). || (Ant.). Physician (médico). || *Tener un físico agradable*, to be pleasant-looking. || — M. y f. Physicist (científico).
fisicoquímico, ca adj. Physicochemical.
— F. Physical chemistry.
físil adj. Fissile.
fisiócrata m. y f. Physiocrat.
fisiografía f. Physiography.
fisiógrafo m. Physiographer.
fisiología f. Physiology.
fisiológico, ca adj. Physiological, physiologic.
fisiólogo, ga m. y f. Physiologist.
fisión f. FÍS. y BIOL. Fission.
fisionable adj. Fissionable.
fisionomía f. V. FISONOMÍA.
fisioterapeuta m. y f. Physiotherapist.
fisioterapia f. Physiotherapy.
fisirrostro adj. ZOOL. Fissirostral.
fisonomía f. Physiognomy, face, features, *pl.* (cara). || Aspect, appearance (aspecto).
fisonómico, ca adj. Physiognomical, physiognomic.
fisonomista o **fisónomo, ma** m. y f. Physiognomist. || *Ser buen, mal fisonomista*, to be good, no good at remembering faces.
fístula f. MED. Fistula: *fístula lagrimal*, lachrymal fistula. || Pipe, tube (conducto). || MÚS. Fistula.
fistular o **fistuloso, sa** adj. Fistular, fistulous.
fisura f. MED. y MIN. Fissure.
fitófago, ga adj. Phytophagous, plant-eating.
fitografía f. Phytography [descriptive botany].
fitología f. Phytology [botany].
fitozoario m. ZOOL. Phytozoon. || — Pl. ZOOL. Phytozoa.
flabelo m. Flabellum.
flacidez o **flaccidez** f. Flabbiness, limpness, flaccidity.
flácido, da o **fláccido, da** adj. Flabby, limp, flaccid: *músculos fláccidos*, flabby muscles.
flaco, ca adj. Thin, lean, skinny (muy delgado). || Weak, feeble (sin fuerzas). || FIG. Weak, weak-willed (poco resistente a las tentaciones): *la carne es flaca*, the flesh is weak. | Bad, short (memoria). || — *Argumento flaco*, weak argument. || *Punto flaco*, weak point, weak spot: *la ortografía es su punto flaco*, spelling is his weak point; *la conclusión ofrece varios puntos flacos*, the conclusion has several weak points; *su punto flaco es la afición a la bebida*, his weak point is drink.
— M. Weak point, weak spot (punto flaco): *conozco su flaco*, I known his weak point.
flacucho, cha adj. FAM. Very thin, skinny.
flacura f. Thinness, leanness, skinniness (delgadez). || Weakness, feebleness (debilidad).
flagelación f. Whipping, scourging, flagellation.
flagelado, da adj. Flagellate.
— M. pl. ZOOL. Flagellatae.
flagelador, ra adj. Whipping, scourging, flagellant.
— M. y f. Flagellant, scourger, flagellator.
flagelante adj./s. REL. Flagellant (penitente).
flagelar v. tr. To whip, to lash, to scourge, to flagellate. || FIG. To revile, to flay (censurar).
flagelo m. Whip, scourge, lash (azote). || FIG. Scourge (calamidad). || BIOL. Flagellum (filamento).
flagrancia f. Flagrancy.
flagrante adj. Flagrant. || *En flagrante delito*, in the act, red-handed (in fraganti).
flamante adj. (Ant.). Blazing, flaming (llameante). || FIG. Splendid, magnificent (brillante). | Brand-new (nuevo): *un coche flamante*, a brand-new car.
flameado, da adj. CULIN. Flambé: *plátanos flameados*, flambé bananas.
— M. Flaming.
flameante adj. Flamboyant.
flamear v. intr. To flame, to blaze, to burn (llamear). || To flutter (bandera, etc.). || MAR. To flap (vela).
— V. tr. To flame, to sterilize (esterilizar). || CULIN. To flame.
flamenco, ca adj. Flemish (de Flandes). || Flamenco: *guitarra flamenca*, flamenco guitar; *cante flamenco*, flamenco singing. || Andalusian gypsy (gitano). || *Amer.* Thin, lean (flaco). || FIG. y FAM. *Ponerse flamenco*, to get cocky (chulo).
— M. y f. Fleming (persona de Flandes). || — M. Flemish (lengua). || Flamenco (cante y baile). || ZOOL. Flamingo (ave). || *Amer.* Dagger (facón).
flamenquería f. Cheekiness, cockiness (chulería).
flamenquismo m. Cheekiness, cockiness (chulería). || Love of flamenco (afición al flamenco).
flamígero, ra adj. POÉT. Flaming, blazing. || ARQ. Flamboyant.
flámula f. Pennant, streamer (gallardete).
flan m. CULIN. Caramel custard (crema). | Baked custard (pastel). || *Flan de arena*, sand pie.
flanco m. Flank, side (de persona). || MIL. Flank: *atacaron por el flanco derecho*, they attacked on the right flank.
Flandes n. pr. m. GEOGR. Flanders. || FAM. *Ser de mantequilla de Flandes*, to be a weakling.
flanero m. Custard mould [U.S., custard mold].
flanqueado, da adj. Flanked: *flanqueado por montañas*, flanked by mountains.
flanquear v. tr. To flank.
flanqueo m. Flanking.
flap m. AVIAC. Flap (alerón).
flaquear v. intr. To weaken, to flag: *me flaquean las fuerzas*, my strength is flagging; *su resistencia, su entusiasmo flaqueaba*, his resistance, enthusiasm was weakening. || To fail, to flag (el valor). || To slacken, to flag (esfuerzos). || To flag, to become tired (cansarse). || To fail (salud, vista, memoria). || To lose heart (abatirse). || To give way (viga, contrafuerte, piernas, etc.): *me flaquearon las piernas*, my legs gave way.
flaqueza f. Thinness, leanness (delgadez). || Weakness (debilidad). || FIG. Weakness (punto flaco): *la afición al alcohol es una de sus flaquezas*, one of his weaknesses is drink. | Frailty: *la flaqueza humana*, human frailty.
flash m. FOT. Flash, flashlight. || RAD. Flash, newsflash (boletín corto).
flato m. Wind, flatus (gas intestinal). || *Amer.* Melancholy, sadness. || (Ant.). Wind (viento). || *Echar flatos*, to have wind, to burp (niño).
flatulencia f. Flatulence.
flatulento, ta adj. Flatulent.
flatuosidad f. Flatulence, wind (fam.).
flauta f. MÚS. Flute: *flauta travesera*, transverse *o* German flute. || — FIG. *Cuando pitos, flautas, cuando flautas, pitos*, if it's not one thing it's another. | *Entre pitos y flautas*, what with one thing and another. || *Flauta de Pan*, pipes (*pl.*) of Pan. || *Amer.* FAM. *¡La gran flauta!*, good Lord!, good heavens! || FAM. *Y sonó la flauta por casualidad*, how lucky can you get!
— M. Flautist (flautista).
flautado, da adj. Flute-like.
— M. MÚS. Flute (de órgano).
flautero m. Flute maker.
flautín m. MÚS. Piccolo.
flautista m. MÚS. Flautist, flutist.
flebitis f. MED. Phlebitis.
flebotomía f. MED. Phlebotomy.
fleco m. Fringe (adorno). || Fringe, bang [U.S., bangs, *pl.*] (flequillo). || Frayed edge, fraying (borde desgastado).
flecha f. Arrow (de arco), dart (más pequeña). || Bolt (de ballesta). || AUT. Direction indicator, trafficator (indicador de dirección). || MAT. Sagitta. || ARQ.

Rise (de arco). | Spire, fleche (en una torre, etc.). || — FIG. *Correr como una flecha*, to run like the wind. || *Salir como una flecha*, to fly *o* to shoot out.
flechador m. Archer, bowman.
flechar v. tr. To draw [the bow] (estirar la cuerda). || To shoot with an arrow (asaetear). || FIG. y FAM. To inspire love at first sight in, to make a hit with (enamorar a alguien). || — FAM. *Ir flechado*, to fly, to rush, to hurry, to dart. | *Voy flechado a por tabaco*, I'm going to nip out for some cigarettes.
— V. pr. FAM. To fall in love at first sight (enamorarse).
flechaste m. MAR. Ratline.
flechazo m. Arrow shot. || Arrow wound (herida). || FIG. y FAM. Love at first sight.
flechero m. Archer, bowman (arquero).
flechilla f. Dart, small arrow.
flegma f. V. FLEMA.
flegmático, ca adj. (Ant.). V. FLEMÁTICO.
flegmón m. (Ant.). V. FLEMÓN.
fleje m. TECN. Metal strip *o* band (para ceñir). | Hoop (de tonel).
flema f. Phlegm (humor, mucosidad). || FIG. Phlegm, calm, coolness, imperturbability (imperturbabilidad). | Sluggishness (torpeza).
flemático, ca adj. Phlegmatic, stolid, stoic, imperturbable.
fleme m. VET. Fleam (lanceta).
flemón m. MED. Phlegmon, abscess. | Gumboil (en las encías).
flequillo m. Fringe, bang [U.S. bangs, *pl.*] (de pelo).
fletador m. MAR. y AVIAC. Charterer, freighter, shipper. || Hirer.
fletamento o **fletamiento** m. MAR. y AVIAC. Chartering (acción de fletar). | Charter party (contrato).
fletante m. *Amer.* Shipowner. | Person who has animals of burden for hire.
fletar v. tr. MAR. y AVIAC. To charter (alquilar). | To freight, to load (embarcar mercancías). || *Amer.* FAM. To hire (un vehículo, un animal de carga, etc.). || *Vuelo fletado*, charter flight.
— V. pr. *Amer.* FAM. To skedaddle, to beat it (largarse).
flete m. MAR. y AVIAC. Freight, cargo (carga). | Freightage (precio). || *Amer.* Load (carga en cualquier vehículo). | Haulage, transportation charge (precio). | Packhorse (caballo). || *Contrato de flete*, charter party.
fletero, ra adj. *Amer.* For hire.
— M. y f. Owner of vehicles for hire.
flexibilidad f. Flexibility. || FIG. Adaptability, pliability (de persona). | Flexibility (de reglamento, etc.).
flexible adj. Flexible. || Soft (sombrero). || FIG. Adaptable, pliable: *carácter flexible*, adaptable character. | Flexible (reglamento, etc.). | Compliant (persona).
— M. ELECTR. Flex, wire [U.S., electric cord]. || Soft hat (sombrero).
flexión f. Flexion. || GRAM. Inflection, inflexion.
flexor m. ANAT. Flexor (músculo). || *Músculo flexor*, flexor, flexor muscle.
flint-glass o **flintglas** m. TECN. Flint glass.
flirt m. Flirtation, flirting (galanteo). || Flirtation (amorío). || Boyfriend (hombre), girlfriend (mujer). || *Es un antiguo flirt suyo*, she's an old flame of his.
flirtear v. intr. To flirt.
flirteo m. Flirting, flirtation (galanteo). || Flirtation (amorío).
flit m. FAM. Insecticide spray.
floculación f. QUÍM. Flocculation.
flocular v. intr. QUÍM. To flocculate.
floculento, ta adj. Flocculent.
flóculo m. QUÍM. Floc, floccule. || ASTR. Flocculus.
flogisto m. HIST. Phlogiston.
flojamente adv. Loosely (sin apretar). || Weakly, feebly (débilmente). || Lightly (ligeramente). || Poorly (mal). || Lazily, indolently (perezosamente). || Carelessly (sin cuidado).
flojear v. intr. To ease up, to let up, to slacken: *el calor, el viento empieza a flojear*, the heat, the wind is beginning to ease up. || To fall off, to go down (disminuir): *la producción ha flojeado*, production has fallen off. || To grow weak, to weaken (debilitarse). || To slack (no trabajar como es debido).
flojedad f. Slackness, looseness (de nudo, cuerda, etc.). || Flabbiness, limpness, flaccidity (flaccidez). || Weakness (debilidad). || Slackness (del mercado). || Lightness, slackness (del viento). || Slackness, laziness (pereza). || Carelessness (descuido). || *Flojedad de voluntad*, spinelessness, lack of spirit.
flojel m. Down (vello de las aves). || Fluff (que se desprende del paño). || *Pato de flojel*, eider.
flojera f. FAM. Laziness, slackness (pereza). | Weakness (debilidad).
flojo, ja adj. Slack, loose: *nudo, cable flojo*, slack knot, cable. || Flabby, limp, flaccid (fláccido). || Weak: *tela, cerveza floja*, weak material, beer. || Weak, poor: *excusa floja*, weak excuse; *estilo flojo*, poor style; *película floja*, poor film; *flojo en matemáticas*, weak at mathematics. || Light, slack (viento). || Poor, meagre (escaso): *producción floja*, meagre output. || Weak, feeble (débil). || Slack (inactivo): *la Bolsa estaba floja*, things were slack at the Stock Exchange. || Slack, lazy, idle, indolent (holgazán): *estudiante, obrero flojo*, slack student, workman. || CULIN. Low (horno). || *Amer.* Cowardly. || *Flojo de voluntad*, spineless, spiritless.
flor f. BOT. Flower: *cultivar flores*, to grow flowers. | Flower, bloom: *planta en flor*, plant in flower *o* in bloom. | Blossom (de árbol frutal): *flor de azahar*, orange blossom; *en flor*, in blossom. | Bloom (capa en las uvas, ciruelas, etc.). || Flowers, *pl.* (del vino). || QUÍM. Flowers, *pl.*: *flor de azufre*, flowers of sulphur. || Grain side (de pieles curtidas). || FAM. Compliment: *decirle* or *echarle flores a una chica*, to pay a girl compliments. || FIG. Flower (lo más selecto). || *Amer.* White spot (de la uña).
— *A flor de*, at ... level: *a flor de tierra*, at ground level. || *A flor de agua*, awash (submarino, roca). || *A flor de piel*, skin-deep. || TECN. *Ajustado a flor*, flush (a nivel). || FIG. *En la flor de la edad* or *de la vida*, in the prime of life. | *En la flor de la juventud*, in the flower of youth. || *Flor artificial*, artificial flower. || *Flor de harina* or *harina de flor*, wheatmeal, pure wheaten flour. || *Flor de la Pasión*, passionflower. || BOT. *Flor de la Trinidad*, pansy. || *Flor de lis*, fleur-de-lis, fleur-de-lys (emblema heráldico), amaryllis (planta). || FIG. *La flor y nata*, the cream, the pick, the best, the flower: *la flor y nata de la sociedad londinense*, the cream of London society. || *No se admiten flores ni coronas*, no flowers, by request (en un entierro). || *Tienda de flores*, florist's [shop].
flora f. Flora.
floración f. Flowering, blooming (planta), blossoming (árbol frutal). || Flowering time, blooming time, blossoming time (época).
floral adj. Floral.
florar v. intr. To flower, to bloom. || To blossom (árbol frutal).
floreado, da adj. Flowered, flowery, decorated with flowers: *cortinas floreadas*, flowered curtains. || FIG. Flowery, florid (estilo). || *Pan floreado*, fine wheaten bread.
florear v. tr. To decorate with flowers (adornar con flores). || To sift out the finest flour from (la harina).
— V. intr. To brandish a sword (con la espada). || MÚS. To play in arpeggio (la guitarra). || FAM. To pay compliments (echar flores). || FIG. To elaborate: *florear sobre un tema*, to elaborate on a theme.
florecer* v. intr. To flower, to bloom (una planta). || To blossom (un árbol frutal). || To flourish, to thrive, to prosper (prosperar): *las ciencias florecían en esa época*, the sciences flourished during that period. || To flourish: *Dryden floreció en el siglo XVII*, Dryden flourished in the 17th century.
— V. pr. To mildew, to go mouldy [U.S., to go moldy] (cubrirse de moho).
floreciente adj. BOT. Flowering, blooming. || FIG. Flourishing, prosperous.
florecimiento m. Flowering, blooming (de una planta). || Blossoming (de un árbol frutal). || FIG. Flourishing, prospering, thriving. || Moulding [U.S., molding], mildewing (enmohecimiento).
florentino, na adj/s. Florentine.
floreo m. Idle wordplay (conversación de pasatiempo). || Witty remark (dicho frívolo). || Flourish (en esgrima, música, escritura). || Caper (en el baile). || FIG. *Andarse con floreos*, to beat about the bush.
florería f. Florist's, florist's shop.
florero, ra m. y f. Florist (vendedor). || — M. [Flower] vase.
florescencia f. BOT. Florescence. || QUÍM. Efflorescence.
floresta f. Wood, thicket, grove (bosque). || Glade (lugar frondoso y agradable). || FIG. Anthology (florilegio).
floretazo m. Hit with a foil.
florete m. Foil (espadín). || Fencing with the foil (esgrima).
— Adj. Superfine (muy fino).
floretista m. Foilsman, fencer.
floricultor, ra m. y f. Flower grower, floriculturist.
floricultura f. Flower growing, floriculture.
floridez f. Floweriness: *la floridez de la primavera*, the floweriness of spring. || FIG. Floridity, floweriness.
florido, da adj. Flowery, full of flowers: *un jardín florido*, a flowery garden. || FIG. Select (selecto). | Flowery, florid (lenguaje, estilo). || — *Gótico florido*, flamboyant Gothic. || FIG. *Lo más florido*, the cream. || *Pascua florida*, Easter.
florilegio m. Anthology, florilegium (antología).
florín m. Florin (moneda).
floripondio m. BOT. Datura. || FIG. Gaudy flower (flor grande de mal gusto): *cortinas salpicadas de enormes floripondios rojos*, curtains bespattered with huge gaudy red flowers.
florista m. y f. Florist (que tiene una tienda de flores). || Flower maker (que fabrica flores artificiales). || *Florista callejera*, flower seller.
florón m. Large flower. || ARQ. Rosette, fleuron (en el techo). || HERÁLD. Fleuron. || IMPR. Tailpiece.
flósculo m. BOT. Floret.
flota f. Fleet: *flota pesquera, aérea*, fishing, air fleet. || *Flota mercante*, merchant navy [U.S., merchant marine].

flotabilidad f. Buoyancy, floatability (capacidad de flotar). || Floatability (de una vía fluvial).
flotable adj. Buoyant, floatable (capaz de flotar). || Floatable: *río flotable*, floatable river.
flotación f. Floating, floatation, flotation (acción de flotar). || Fluttering, flapping (de una bandera). || MIN. Floatation, flotation. || Floating (de la moneda).
flotador, ra adj. Floating.
— M. Float (de caña de pescar, carburador, hidroavión, etc.). || Water wings, *pl.* (para nadar). || Ball (en depósitos). || *Flotador de alarma*, boiler float.
flotante adj. Floating: *costillas, riñones flotantes*, floating ribs, kidneys; *ancla, dique, eje flotante*, floating anchor, dock, axle; *moneda, deuda flotante*, floating currency, debt. || Loose (capa). || Flowing (cabellos, etc.).
flotar v. intr. To float. || To flutter, to float, to wave (bandera, gallardete, etc.). || To stream: *su cabellera flotaba al viento*, her hair streamed in the wind. || To float (la moneda).
flote m. Floating, floatation, flotation (flotación). || — *A flote*, afloat: *estar a flote*, to be afloat; on one's feet (fuera de apuro): *ponerse a flote*, to get back on one's feet. || *Poner a flote*, to set afloat, to float (una embarcación). || *Sacar a flote*, to refloat, to set afloat (un barco), to put on its feet (un negocio). || *Salir a flote*, to get back on one's feet, to get out of difficulty (después de un apuro), to become solvent again, to get out of the red (fam.) [después de una crisis financiera].
flotilla f. Flotilla, fleet of small ships.
fluctuación f. Fluctuation: *fluctuaciones del mercado*, market fluctuations. || FIG. Vacillation, irresolution, hesitation, wavering (vacilación).
fluctuar v. intr. To fluctuate: *el precio fluctúa entre nueve y diez libras*, the price fluctuates between nine and ten pounds. || FIG. To oscillate: *su humor fluctúa entre el abatimiento y la exaltación*, his mood oscillates between dejection and exaltation. | To vacillate, to waver, to hesitate (entre dos soluciones). || To bob [up and down] (sobre el agua).
fluente adj. Fluid (fluido). || Flowing (que fluye).
fluidez f. Fluidity. || FIG. Fluency.
fluidificar v. tr. To fluidify. || FIG. *Fluidificar el tráfico*, to make the traffic flow.
fluido, da adj. Fluid. || FIG. Fluent (lenguaje, manera de expresarse). | Flowing, fluent (estilo).
— M. FÍS. Fluid. || ELECTR. Current. || *Mecánica de los fluidos*, fluid mechanics.
fluir* v. intr. To flow, to run.
flujo m. Flow, stream: *flujo de sangre, de palabras*, flow of blood, of words. || MAR. Flow, rising tide. || MED. Discharge (de un humor). || QUÍM. y FÍS. Flux. || — MED. *Flujo blanco*, leucorrhoea, whites, *pl.* (fam.). | *Flujo de vientre*, diarrhoea. || *Flujo magnético*, magnetic flux. || *Flujo y reflujo*, ebb and flow.
fluminense adj. [Of *o* from] Rio de Janeiro.
— M. y f. Native *o* inhabitant of Rio de Janeiro.
flúor m. QUÍM. Fluorine. || *Espato flúor*, fluorspar.
fluoración f. Fluoridation.
fluorescencia f. Fluorescence.
fluorescente adj. Fluorescent.
fluorhidrato m. QUÍM. Hydrofluoride.
fluorhídrico, ca adj. QUÍM. Hydrofluoric.
fluorita f. MIN. Fluorite.
fluoruro m. QUÍM. Fluoride.
fluvial adj. Fluvial, river: *tráfico fluvial*, river traffic; *residuos fluviales*, fluvial deposits. || *Vía fluvial*, waterway.
flux m. inv. Flush (en los naipes). || *Amer.* Suit (traje). || FIG. y FAM. *Hacer flux*, to blow *o* to squander one's money.
fluxión f. MED. Congestion (de la nariz). | Fluxion.
fobia f. Phobia.
foca f. ZOOL. Seal. || Sealskin (piel).
focal adj. Focal: *distancia focal*, focal length.
focalización f. FÍS. Focalization.
focalizar v. tr. FÍS. To focalize.
focense adj./s. Phocian.
foco m. FÍS. y MAT. Focus. || FIG. Focus, focal point, centre [U.S., center]: *el foco de la civilización griega*, the focus of Greek civilization. | Seat (de un incendio). || Spotlight, floodlight (lámpara potente). || MED. Focus, seat (de un trastorno). | Centre: *foco de infección*, centre of infection. || — FOT. *Foco fijo*, fixed focus. | *Fuera de foco*, out of focus (desenfocado). | *Profundidad de foco*, depth of focus.
fofo, fa adj. Spongy, soft (esponjoso, poco denso). || Flabby: *carne fofa*, flabby flesh.
fogarada f. Bonfire (hoguera). || Blaze (llamarada).
fogata f. Bonfire (hoguera). || Blaze (llamarada). || Small land mine (explosivo). || *Fogata de San Juan*, Midsummer Day bonfire.
fogón m. Hearth (hogar). || Kitchen range (cocina de carbón). || Cooker, stove: *fogón de gas*, gas cooker. || Firebox (de caldera). || Vent (de arma de fuego).
fogonadura f. MAR. Mast hole.
fogonazo m. Flash. || FOT. Flash.
fogonero m. Stoker, fireman (de máquina de vapor).
fogosidad f. Fire, ardour, [U.S., ardor], spirit (ardor). || Dash (ímpetu). || Fieriness (de un caballo).
fogoso, sa adj. Fiery, spirited (lleno de ardor): *corcel fogoso*, fiery steed.
fogueado, da adj. Experienced, hardened.
foguear v. tr. To harden *o* to accustom [men, horses] to war. || To inure, to harden, to accustom (a una cosa desagradable). || To train (formar para un trabajo). || TAUR. To place "banderillas de fuego" in [the bull]. || VET. To cauterize.
— V. pr. To become hardened *o* inured.
fogueo m. Training (de caballos para la guerra). || — *Cartucho de fogueo*, blank cartridge. || *Tiro de fogueo*, firing with blank cartridges.
foja f. Coot (ave). || *Amer.* JUR. Leaf, page (página de documento, libro), sheet (hoja suelta).
folía f. (Ant.). Madness. || "Folia" [dance of Portugese origin, song of the Canary Isles].
foliáceo, a adj. BOT. Foliaceous.
foliación f. Foliation. || IMPR. Foliation, page numbering.
foliado, da adj. Foliated, numbered (páginas). || BOT. Foliate.
foliar adj. BOT. Foliar.
foliar v. tr. To foliate, to number (paginar).
foliatura f. Foliation.
folicular adj. Follicular.
foliculario m. Pamphleteer.
foliculina f. Folliculin.
foliculitis f. MED. Folliculitis.
folículo m. BOT. ZOOL. Follicle.
folio m. Leaf (hoja). || IMPR. Folio (hoja, número). | Running head, running title (encabezamiento). || — FIG. *De a folio*, enormous (disparate, tontería). || IMPR. *En folio*, folio, in folio: *edición en folio*, folio edition, edition in folio. | *Folio atlántico*, atlas size. | *Folio explicativo*, running head, running title.
folíolo m. BOT. Foliole.
folklore m. Folklore.
folklórico, ca adj. Folk, popular, folkloric (p.us): *baile folklórico*, folk dance.
folklorista m. y f. Folklorist.
follada f. Small puff pastry pie. || POP. *Tener mala follada*, to be a damned nuisance (ser un pesado), to be unlucky (tener mala suerte).
follaje m. Foliage, leaves, *pl.* (fronda). || FIG. Adornments, *pl.*, ornamentation, decoration (adornos). | Verbiage, verbosity (palabrería).
follar* v. tr. To blow with bellows (soplar).
— V. tr. e intr. POP. To fuck (practicar el coito).
— V. pr. POP. To drop a silent one (ventosear).
folletín m. Newspaper serial (novela por entregas en un periódico). || FIG. Melodrama.
folletinesco, ca adj. Melodramatic. || Unlikely (inverosímil).
folletinista m. y f. Serial writer.
folletista m. y f. Pamphleteer.
folleto m. Pamphlet, brochure: *folleto turístico*, tourists' brochure. || Folder, leaflet (desplegable). || Handout (de publicidad). || *Folleto explicativo*, instruction booklet.
follón, ona adj. (P.us.). Lazy, indolent, slothful (vago). || Arrogant (arrogante). || Blustering (fanfarrón). || Cowardly (cobarde).
— M. y f. Good-for-nothing, loafer (vago). || Arrogant person, blusterer (arrogante). || Coward, poltroon (ant.) [cobarde]. || — M. Silent rocket (cohete). || FAM. Row, shindy, rumpus (alboroto): *armaron un follón en la calle*, they kicked up a rumpus in the street. | Chaos (situación confusa): *fue un follón cuando las luces fallaron*, it was chaos when the lights failed. | Jumble (montón desordenado): *un follón de libros en la mesa*, a jumble of books on the table. | Mess (situación enmarañada): *está metido en un follón*, he has got himself into a mess, he is in a mess. | Bore, drag (persona o cosa pesada). || POP. Silent fart (ventosidad).
fomentador, ra adj. Fomenting (de disturbios, etc.). || Promoting (de la industria, etc.).
— M. y f. Fomenter (de odio, etc.). || Promoter (de la industria, etc.).
fomentar v. tr. To warm (calentar suavemente). || To incubate, to brood (huevos). || MED. To foment, to put a poultice on (en un tumor, etc.). || FIG. To encourage, to promote, to foster: *fomentar el comercio entre dos países*, to encourage trade between two countries. | To foment (la rebelión, el odio, etc.).
fomento m. Warmth (calor). || Warming (acción de calentar). || Incubation (de huevos). || MED. Fomentation. | Poultice (compresa caliente). || FIG. Promotion, encouragement, fostering: *fomento de las ventas*, sales promotion. | Fomentation (de una rebelión, etc.). || — *Banco de fomento*, development bank [promoting the development of industry, agriculture, etc.]. || (Ant.) *Ministerio de Fomento*, Ministry of Public Works and the Economy.
fon m. FÍS. Phon (unidad de potencia sonora).
fonación f. Phonation.
fonda f. Tavern (ant.), inn (ant.), small restaurant (restaurante barato). || Boardinghouse (hospedería). || Buffet (en las estaciones).
fondeadero m. MAR. Anchorage.
fondeado, da adj. Anchored, at anchor. || *Amer.* Rich, wealthy (rico).

fondear v. tr. To anchor (un barco). || To sound, to take soundings in (sondear). || To search (registrar una embarcación). || FIG. To get to the bottom of (una cuestión). | To sound out (una persona).
— V. intr. MAR. To anchor, to cast *o* to drop anchor.
— V. pr. *Amer.* To get rich.

fondeo m. MAR. Search, searching (del cargamento). | Anchoring.

fondero m. *Amer.* V. FONDISTA.

fondillos m. pl. Seat, *sing.* (de pantalones).

fondista m. Innkeeper (ant.), restaurant owner (de restaurante). || Boardinghouse keeper (de pensión).

fondo m. Bottom (parte más baja): *el fondo de un valle, de una taza, de un saco,* the bottom of a valley, of a cup, of a sack. || Bottom, end (parte más lejana): *el fondo de un pasillo, de una calle,* the bottom of a corridor, of a street. || Back: *en el fondo del salón, del escenario,* at the back of the lounge, of the stage. || Bottom, bed, floor: *fondo del mar,* bottom of the sea, sea bed, sea floor. || Background: *el fondo de un cuadro,* the background of a painting; *una tela con fondo azul,* a fabric with a blue background; *música de fondo,* background music. || Depth (profundidad): *la piscina tiene cinco metros de fondo,* the depth of the swimming pool is five metres; *la casa tiene poca fachada pero veinte metros de fondo,* the house has a short frontage but a depth of twenty metres. || Fund: *Fondo Monetario Internacional,* International Monetary Fund; *fondo de amortización,* sinking fund; *fondo para la construcción,* building fund. || Money, resources, *pl.* (dinero). || Collection (de una librería, una biblioteca). || FIG. Substance (de un libro, un discurso, etc.): *forma y fondo,* form and substance. | Bottom: *vayamos al fondo del asunto,* let's get to the bottom of the matter; *el fondo de un problema,* the bottom of a problem. | Stock, fund (caudal): *tener un fondo de sabiduría,* to possess a stock of knowledge *o* a fund of wisdom. | Stamina (resistencia). || Head, bottom (de tonel). || Lunge (en la esgrima). || — Pl. Funds: *fondos disponibles,* available funds; *estar en fondos,* to be in funds.
— *A fondo,* thoroughly: *estudiar un asunto a fondo,* to study a question thoroughly; thorough: *una limpieza a fondo,* a thorough cleaning. || *Al fondo de,* at the bottom of. || *Artículo de fondo,* leading article, leader. || *Bajos fondos,* scum, dregs (de la sociedad). || *Cheque sin fondos,* v. CHEQUE. || MAR. *Dar fondo,* to drop *o* to cast anchor, to anchor. || *De bajo fondo,* shallow. || *De cuatro en fondo,* in column of fours (término militar), four abreast (término normal). || *De fondo,* long-distance: *corredor, carrera de fondo,* long-distance runner, race. || *De medio fondo,* middle-distance. || *Doble fondo,* false bottom (fondo falso), ballast tank (de un barco). || *Echar a fondo,* to sink, to send to the bottom (un barco). || FIG. *En el fondo,* deep down, at heart: *parece un poco tacaño pero en el fondo es muy generoso,* he seems a bit of a skinflint but deep down he is very generous; really, basically: *en el fondo tiene usted razón,* basically you are right. || COM. *Fondo de operaciones,* working capital. | *Fondo de rotación,* revolving fund. | *Fondo perdido,* life annuity. | *Fondos bloqueados,* frozen assets. || *Fondos públicos,* public funds, government stock, *sing.* || MAR. *Irse a fondo,* to sink, to go down. || *Maquillaje de fondo,* foundation. || *Mar de fondo,* ground swell (marejada), undercurrent of tension (tensión latente). || *Reunir fondos,* to raise funds. || FIG. *Tener buen fondo,* to be good-natured. || *Tirarse a fondo,* to lunge (esgrimidor).

fondón, ona adj. FAM. Big-bottomed.

fonducho n. Cheap eating house, cheap restaurant.

fonema m. Phoneme.

fonémico, ca adj. Phonemic.
— F. Phonemics.

fonendoscopio m. Stethoscope.

fonético, ca adj. Phonetic.
— F. Phonetics.

fonetista m. y f. Phonetician, phonetist.

foniatra m. MED. Phoniatrician.

foniatría f. MED. Phoniatrics.

fónico, ca adj. Phonic.

fonio o **fono** m. FÍS. Phon (fon).

fonocaptor m. TECN. Pickup.

fonográfico, ca adj. Phonographic.

fonógrafo m. Phonograph.

fonograma m. Phonogram.

fonolita f. MIN. Phonolite.

fonolocalización f. Sound ranging.

fonología f. Phonology.

fonólogo, ga m. y f. Phonologist.

fonometría f. Phonometry.

fonómetro m. Phonometer.

fonoteca f. Record library.

fontana f. POÉT. Spring, fountain.

fontanal adj. Spring: *aguas fontanales,* spring water.

fontanal o **fontanar** m. Spring.

fontanela f. ANAT. Fontanel, fontanelle.

fontanería f. Plumbing.

fontanero m. Plumber.

foque m. MAR. Jib (vela): *foque volante,* flying jib.

forajido, da adj. Outlawed.
— M. y f. Outlaw.

foral adj. Relative to the "fueros" or privileges, statutory.

foralmente adv. According to the "fueros" or privileges.

foráneo, a adj. Strange (extraño). || Foreign, alien (extranjero).
— M. y f. Stranger (forastero). || Foreigner, alien (extranjero).

forastero, ra adj. Strange (extraño). || Foreign, alien (extranjero). || Outside (de fuera).
— M. y f. Stranger (desconocido). || Outsider (persona que viene de fuera): *muchos forasteros vinieron para la feria del pueblo,* a lot of outsiders came to the village fair.

forcejar o **forcejear** v. intr. To struggle, to wrestle (para deshacerse de una sujeción). || To struggle (luchar). || To strive (afanarse).

forcejeo m. Struggle, struggling.

fórceps m. inv. MED. Forceps.

forense adj. Forensic: *medicina forense,* forensic medicine. || Strange (forastero).
— M. MED. Forensic surgeon. || Stranger (forastero).

forero, ra adj. Relative to a "fuero" or privilege, statutory.

forestación f. *Amer.* Reafforestation [U.S., reforestation].

forestal adj. Forest. || — *Guarda forestal,* forester [U.S., forest ranger]. || *Patrimonio forestal del Estado,* State forests, *pl.* || *Repoblación forestal,* reafforestation [U.S., reforestation].

forja f. Forge (fragua). || Ironworks, foundry (ferrería). || Forging (acción y arte de forjar). || Mortar (argamasa).

forjado, da adj. Wrought (hierro). || FIG. Made-up, invented (inventado). | Made (hecho). | Built-up (ilusiones, etc.).

forjador m. Forger.

forjar v. tr. To forge: *forjar en frío,* to forge cold. || To forge, to make, to form (formar). || FIG. To fabricate, to make up (mentiras, una excusa). | To make (un proyecto). | To hatch (un complot). | To build up, to create (sueños, ilusiones, etc.). || — *Forjar palabras nuevas,* to coin new words. || *Hierro forjado,* wrought iron.
— V. pr. To forget o.s.: *forjarse una buena reputación, un porvenir,* to forge o.s. a good reputation, a future. || *Forjarse ilusiones,* to build up false hopes.

forma f. Shape; *la forma de un coche, de un edificio,* the shape of a car, of a building; *tiene forma redonda,* it has a round shape. || Form: *se publicó en forma de libros,* it was published in book form; *forma y fondo,* form and substance; *su discurso tomó la forma de una charla amistosa,* his speech took the form of a friendly chat. || Form, manner, method: *forma de pago,* form of payment. || Way: *hay varias formas de decirlo,* they are several ways of saying it. || Way, means (modo): *no hay forma de hacerlo,* there is no means of doing it. || GRAM. y FIL. Form. || JUR. Form (de un acto o sentencia). || Mould [U.S., mold], form (horma). || Block (de sombrerero). || Last (de zapatero). || IMPR. Format (formato). | Form (molde). || DEP. Form. || — Pl. Conventions (reglas sociales). || Manners (modales): *buenas formas,* good manners. || Figure, *sing.* (silueta). || — *Dar forma a,* to shape (un objeto), to put into shape (una idea), to formulate, to express (expresar). || *De esta forma,* in this way. || *De forma que,* so, so that: *había huelga, de forma que tuvimos que ir a pie,* there was a strike, so we had to walk. || *De todas formas,* anyway, at any rate, in any case. || *En debida forma,* in due form. || *En forma de,* -shaped: *en forma de hongo,* mushroom-shaped. || *Es pura forma,* it's just for form's sake, it's a mere matter of form. || *Estar en baja forma* or *no estar en forma,* to be off form. || *Estar en forma,* to be in good form. || *Estar en plena forma,* to be on the top of one's form. || *Guardar las formas,* to keep up appearances. || *No veo la forma de evitarlo,* I see no way of avoiding it. || *Ponerse en forma,* to get fit. || REL. *Sagrada forma,* host, consecrated wafer.

formación f. Formation: *formación geológica,* geological formation. || MIL. Formation: *formación en orden cerrado,* close-order formation; *formación de a tres,* formation in threes. || Upbringing (educación). || Education (enseñanza): *se recibe una buena formación en ese colegio,* they give you a good education at that school; *formación universitaria,* university education. || Training: *formación profesional,* vocational training; *centro de formación obrera,* workers' training centre.

formal adj. Formal: *requisito, petición formal,* formal requisite, request. || Formal, express (promesa). || FIG. Reliable, dependable, responsible (persona de fiar). | Serious, serious-minded (persona seria): *es una chica muy formal,* she is a very serious-minded girl. | Correct (correcto). || *Ser formal,* to behave o.s. (niños).

formaldehído m. QUÍM. Formaldehyde.

formalidad f. Formality (requisito): *hay que pasar por muchas formalidades para entrar,* one must go through a lot of formalities to get in. || FIG. Reliability (confianza, fiabilidad). | Seriousness (seriedad). | Good behaviour (de los niños). || *Hablemos con formalidad,* let's talk seriously.

formalina f. QUÍM. Formalin, formaline.
formalismo m. Formalism.
formalista adj. Formalistic.
— M. y f. Formalist.
formalizar v. tr. To formalize (hacer formal): *formalizar un noviazgo*, to formalize an engagement. || To put into proper form, to legalize (dar forma legal): *formalizar un contrato*, to put a contract into proper form. || To put in order (regularizar una situación, etc.).
— V. pr. To become serious. || To take offence (ofenderse).
formalote adj. Serious, formal.
formar v. tr. To form: *formar un equipo, un círculo*, to form a team, a circle. || To make: *formar una bola de nieve*, to make a snowball. || To fashion, to shape: *formar una escultura con barro*, to fashion a sculpture out of clay. || To form: *formar una frase*, to form a sentence. || To constitute, to form, to make up: *tres hombres forman el comité de acción*, three men make up the action committee; *las ocho provincias que forman Andalucía*, the eight provinces forming Andalusia. || To build up (reservas). || To make up, to lay (un proyecto). || FIG. To bring up (educar). | To educate (enseñar). | To train (entrenar): *formar a los nuevos reclutas*, to train the new recruits. | To form, to shape (el carácter). || MIL. To muster (tropas). || — *Formar filas*, to fall into line *o* into rank, to fall in (militares), to line up (personas). || *Formar parte de*, to be *o* to form a part of (algo), to be a member of (ser miembro), to be attached to (depender). || *Una mujer bien formada*, a well-formed woman.
— V. intr. MIL. To form up, to fall in: *el escuadrón formó en el patio del cuartel*, the troop formed up on the parade ground. || MIL. *¡A formar!*, fall in!
— V. pr. To form, to be formed: *se formó un círculo, un comité*, a circle, a committee was formed. || To be trained, to be educated (educarse). || To form: *nubes empezaban a formarse*, clouds began to form. || To take shape (tomar forma). || To develop: *su estilo se está formando*, his style is developing. || To form (una opinión). || DEP. To line up. || MIL. To form up, to fall in. || — *Formarse una idea falsa de*, to get the wrong idea about. || FAM. *¡Menudo lío se formó!*, it was a right mess!
formativo, va adj. Formative: *los años formativos de la vida*, the formative years of life. || Educational: *una película formativa*, an educational film. || GRAM. Formative (sufijo, etc.).
formato m. IMPR. Format. || Size (tamaño).
formero m. ARQ. Supporting arch (de una bóveda).
formicación f. MED. Formication.
fórmico adj. m. QUÍM. Formic. || *Aldehído fórmico*, formaldehyde, formic aldehyde.
formidable adj. Formidable: *una tarea formidable*, a formidable task. || Enormous, huge, tremendous (muy grande). || Marvellous, terrific, wonderful, fantastic (muy bueno). || *¡Formidable!*, great!
formol m. QUÍM. Formol.
formón m. TECN. Firmer chisel (herramienta).
Formosa n. pr. f. GEOGR. Formosa.
fórmula f. Formula: *fórmula de cortesía*, courtesy formula; *la fórmula para una medicina*, the formula for a medicine. || Method (método). || Solution. || MAT. y QUÍM. Formula. || CULIN. Recipe. || MED. Prescription (receta). || AUT. Formula: *coche de fórmula uno*, formula one car. || *Por fórmula*, as a matter of form, for form's sake.
formulación f. Formulation.
formular v. tr. To formulate: *formular una teoría*, to formulate a theory. || To make: *formular quejas, una petición*, to make complaints, a request. || To express: *formular críticas*, to express criticism; *formular un deseo*, to express a wish. || To ask (una pregunta). || — *Formular una reclamación*, to make a claim, to put in a claim. || *Formular votos por*, to express one's sincere wishes for.
formulario m. Formulary (reunión de fórmulas). || Form: *formulario de inscripción*, application form; *llenar un formulario*, to fill in a form.
formulismo m. Formulism.
fornicación f. Fornication.
fornicador, ra m. y f. Fornicator.
fornicar v. intr. To fornicate.
fornido, da adj. Strong, robust, hefty.
fornituras f. pl. MIL. Cartridge belt, *sing.*
foro m. HIST. Forum. || Court of justice, lawcourt (tribunal). || Bar (ejercicio de la abogacía). || TEATR. Back (del escenario). || — *Desaparecer por el foro*, to disappear into the background.
forofo, fa m. y f. FAM. Fan, supporter.
forraje m. Fodder, forage: *forraje verde, mixto*, green, mixed fodder; *carro de forraje*, forage wagon. || Foraging (acción de forrajear). || FIG. y FAM. Hodgepodge (fárrago).
forrajeador m. MIL. Forager.
forrajear v. tr. e intr. To forage.
forrajero, ra adj. Fodder: *plantas forrajeras*, fodder crops.
— F. Forage rope *o* net (cuerda o red). || Braid (cordón del uniforme).
forrar v. tr. To line (interiormente): *forrar un abrigo, un cajón, cortinas con* or *de seda*, to line a coat, a drawer, curtains with silk. || To cover (exteriormente): *forrar una puerta con* or *de chapas de acero*, to cover a door with steel sheets; *forrar un sillón*, to cover an armchair. || To sheathe (el casco de un barco). || To back [a book] (para protección). || TECN. To line, to cover (revestir). || FIG. *Estar forrado de oro* or *estar bien forrado*, to be rolling in money.
— V. pr. FAM. To stuff o.s. [with food] (comer mucho). | To feather one's nest (enriquecerse), to line one's pockets (por medios deshonestos).
forro m. Lining: *forro de un vestido, de un armario, de un canal*, lining of a dress, of a cupboard, of a canal. || Cover (funda): *forro de sillón*, chair cover. || Cover (de un libro). || MAR. Sheathing (del casco). | Plating (conjunto de chapas de metal). | Planking (conjunto de tablones). || TECN. Liner (de cilindro, etc.). | Lining (revestimiento): *forros de freno*, brake linings. || — FAM. *Ni por el forro*, not in the slightest, not at all. | *No conoce la medicina ni por el forro*, he doesn't know the slightest thing about medicine. | *No conoce el latín ni por el forro*, he doesn't know a word of Latin.
forsythia f. BOT. Forsythia.
fortachón, ona adj. FAM. Strong, hefty, tough.
fortalecedor, ra adj. Fortifying.
fortalecer* v. tr. To fortify, to strengthen (una persona, un lugar). || To give strength, to fortify (dar fortaleza espiritual).
— V. pr. To fortify o.s. || To become stronger (una creencia).
fortalecimiento m. Fortification, fortifying (fortificación). || Strengthening: *el fortalecimiento de la economía*, the strengthening of the economy.
fortaleza f. Strength, vigour [U.S., vigor] (de una persona). || Fortitude (fuerza moral). || MIL. Fortress, stronghold (recinto fortificado). || AVIAC. *Fortaleza volante*, flying fortress.
forte adv. m. MÚS. Forte.
— Interj. MAR. Avast!
fortepiano m. MÚS. Piano, pianoforte.
fortificación f. Fortification, fortifying (de la salud, un lugar, una posición, etc.). || Strengthening (de una construcción). || — Pl. Fortifications.
fortificante adj. Fortifying.
— M. Fortifier, tonic.
fortificar v. tr. To fortify: *fortificar la salud, una ciudad*, to fortify the health, a town. || To strengthen, to fortify (una construcción). || *Plaza fortificada*, stronghold, fortified town *o* place.
— V. pr. To gain strength (fortaleza moral). || To build up one's strength (fortaleza física). || To build fortifications (para defenderse).
fortín m. MIL. Small fort. | Blockhouse, pillbox (emplazamiento para armas). | Bunker (refugio).
fortiori (a) loc. adv. A fortiori, all the more.
fortísimo, ma adj. Very strong, extremely strong. || MÚS. Fortissimo.
— Adv. MÚS. Fortissimo.
fortuito, ta adj. Fortuitous, chance: *un encuentro fortuito*, a chance meeting. || *Caso fortuito*, accidental case, accident (imprevisto), act of God (jurídico).
fortuna f. Fortune, fate, destiny (destino): *la rueda de la fortuna*, the wheel of fortune. || Luck, fortune (suerte): *buena fortuna*, good luck; *golpe de fortuna*, stroke of luck. || Fortune (bienes): *fue a América del Sur para hacer fortuna*, he went to South America to make his fortune. || Storm, squall (borrasca). || — MAR. *Correr fortuna*, to weather a storm. || *Mala fortuna*, misfortune. || *Por fortuna*, fortunately, luckily. || *Probar fortuna*, to try one's luck. || *Tener la fortuna de*, to have the good fortune to.
fortunón m. FAM. Immense fortune. | Stroke of luck (suerte).
forúnculo m. MED. Boil, furuncle.
forzadamente adv. Forcibly, by force (por fuerza). || Forcedly, in a forced way (no naturalmente). || With difficulty (con dificultad). || *Sonreír forzadamente*, to force a smile.
forzado, da adj. Hard: *trabajos forzados*, hard labour. || Forced: *sonrisa forzada*, forced smile. | Farfetched, contrived (rebuscado): *un chiste forzado*, a contrived joke. | Compulsory (obligatorio). || — MIL. *A marcha forzada*, by forced march. || FIG. *A marchas forzadas*, in double quick time (acabar algo), at a rapid pace, against the clock (trabajar).
— M. HIST. Galley slave (galeote).
forzamiento m. Forcing.
forzar* v. tr. To force: *forzar una llave*, to force a key; *forzar una sonrisa*, to force a smile. || To force, to oblige, to compel: *forzar a alguien a hacer algo* or *a que haga algo*, to force s.o. to do sth. || To force, to pick, to break open (una cerradura, un cajón, etc.). || To break into, to force one's way into (una casa, un edificio). || To break down, to break open, to force (una puerta). || To rape, to ravish (violar a una mujer). || AGR. To force. || MIL. To take by force. || — *Forzar el paso*, to force *o* to quicken one's pace. || *Forzar la mano a uno*, to force s.o.'s hand.
— V. pr. To force o.s.

forzosamente adv. Unavoidably, inevitably, inescapably (inevitablemente). || Necessarily (necesariamente). || Compulsorily (obligatoriamente).
forzoso, sa adj. Unavoidable, inevitable, inescapable (inevitable): *consecuencia forzosa,* inevitable consequence. || Obligatory, compulsory: *la asistencia es forzosa,* attendance is obligatory. || Necessary (necesario) || — *Aterrizaje forzoso,* forced landing. || *Es forzoso que...,* it is inevitable that... || *Forzoso es reconocer que...,* one must admit that... || *Heredero forzoso,* heir apparent. || *Trabajos forzosos,* v. TRABAJO.
forzudo, da adj. Strong, tough.
— M. Strong man, tough guy (fam.).
fosa f. Grave: *fosa común,* common grave. || Pit (hoyo). || ANAT. Fossa: *fosas nasales,* nasal fossae. || — *Fosa oceánica,* ocean deep. || *Fosa séptica,* septic tank.
fosca f. Haze, mist (calina).
fosco, ca adj. Sullen, surly, gruff (hosco). || Dark (oscuro).
fosfatado, da adj. Phosphatized.
— M. AGR. Fertilizing with phosphates, phosphatizing.
fosfatar v. tr. To add phosphate to, to phosphatize. || AGR. To fertilize with phosphates, to phosphatize.
fosfático, ca adj. QUÍM. Phosphatic.
fosfato m. QUÍM. Phosphate: *fosfato de cal,* phosphate of lime, calcium phosphate.
fosfeno m. Phosphene.
fosfito m. QUÍM. Phosphite.
fosforado, da adj. Phosphoretted, phosphuretted [U.S., phosphoreted, phosphurèted].
fosforar v. tr. To phosphorate.
fosforecer* o **fosforescer*** v. intr. To phosphoresce.
fosforera f. Matchbox. || Matchbox holder (estuche). || Match factory (fábrica).
fosforero, ra adj. Match-manufacturing, match: *industria fosforera,* match industry.
— M. y f. Match seller (vendedor). || — F. Matchbox (caja de cerillas).
fosforescencia f. Phosphorescence.
fosforescente adj. Phosphorescent.
fosfórico, ca adj. QUÍM. Phosphoric.
fosforismo m. MED. Phosphorism.
fósforo m. QUÍM. Phosphorus. || Match (cerilla).
fosforoso, sa adj. Phosphorous.
fosgeno m. QUÍM. Phosgene.
fósil adj./s.m. Fossil. || FIG. y FAM. Fossil (persona).
fosilización f. Fossilization.
fosilizarse v. pr. To fossilize, to become fossilized.
foso m. Ditch, trench (zanja). || Hole, pit (hoyo). || Fosse, moat (en fortificaciones). || Inspection pit (en un garaje). || TEATR. Pit, below-stage (del escenario). | Pit: *foso de orquesta,* orchestra pit. || DEP. Pit (de arena). | Dugout (emplazamiento del entrenador). || AGR. Ditch, trench.
fot m. FÍS. Phot (unidad de iluminación).
foto f. Photo, photograph: *sacar fotos,* to take photos. || FÍS. Phot (fot).
fotocalco m. Photoprint.
fotocomposición f. Phototypesetting.
fotoconductor, ra adj. Photoconductive.
fotocontrol m. Photocontrol.
fotocopia f. Photocopy.
fotocopiadora f. Photocopier.
fotocopiar v. tr. To photocopy.
fotocromía f. Photochromy (procedimiento), photochrome (prueba).
fotoelasticidad f. FÍS. Photoelasticity.
fotoelectricidad f. FÍS. Photoelectricity.
fotoeléctrico, ca adj. FÍS. Photoelectric. || — *Célula fotoeléctrica,* photoelectric cell, photocell. || *Corriente fotoeléctrica,* photocurrent. || *Tubo fotoeléctrico,* phototube.
fotoelectrón m. FÍS. Photoelectron.
fotoemisión f. FÍS. Photoemission.
fotoforesis f. FÍS. Photophoresis.
fotóforo m. Photophore.
fotogénico, ca adj. Photogenic.
fotógeno, na adj. Photogenic.
fotograbado m. Photogravure, photoengraving.
fotograbador m. Photoengraver.
fotograbar v. tr. To photoengrave.
fotografía f. Photography: *fotografía aérea,* aerial photography. || Photograph: *sacar una fotografía,* to take a photograph. || — *Fotografía instantánea,* snapshot, snap. || *Sacarse una fotografía,* to have one's photograph taken. || *Sale mal en las fotografías,* he doesn't photograph well.
fotografiar v. tr. To photograph, to take a photograph of. || *Máquina de fotografiar,* camera.
fotográfico, ca adj. Photographic. || *Máquina fotográfica,* camera.
fotógrafo, fa m. y f. Photographer: *fotógrafo callejero,* street photographer.
fotograma m. Photogram. || CINEM. Still.
fotogrametría f. Photogrammetry.
fotólisis f. Photolysis.
fotolito m. Photolith, photolitho.
fotolitografía f. Photolithography (procedimiento). || Photolitograph (prueba).
fotolitografiar v. tr. To photolithograph.
fotolitográfico, ca adj. Photolithographic.
fotoluminescencia f. FÍS. y QUÍM. Photoluminescence.
fotomecánico, ca adj. IMPR. Photomechanical.
— F. Process engraving.
fotometría f. FÍS. Photometry.
fotométrico, ca adj. Photometric, photometrical.
fotómetro m. Photometer, exposure meter.
fotomicrografía f. Photomicrography (procedimiento), photomicrograph (prueba).
fotomontaje m. Photomontage.
fotón m. FÍS. Photon.
fotoquímica f. Photochemistry.
fotosensible adj. Photosensitive.
fotosfera f. Photosphere.
fotosíntesis f. Photosynthesis.
fotostático, ca adj. Photostatic.
fotostato m. FOT. Photostat.
fototeca f. Photograph library.
fototerapia f. MED. Phototherapy.
fototipia f. IMPR. Phototypy.
fototipo m. IMPR. Phototype.
fototipografía f. IMPR. Phototypography.
fototropismo m. BOT. Phototropism.
foul m. DEP. Foul.
fox terrier m. Fox terrier (perro raposero).
fox trot m. Fox-trot (baile).
foyer m. TEATR. Foyer.
frac m. Dress coat, tails, *pl.*
— OBSERV. Pl. *fraques* or *fracs.*
fracasado, da adj. Unsuccessful.
— M. y f. Failure.
fracasar v. intr. To fail, to be unsuccessful: *el ataque fracasó,* the attack failed; *les negociaciones fracasaron,* the negotiations were unsuccessful. || To fall through, to fail (proyectos).
fracaso m. Failure: *el fracaso del experimento,* the failure of the experiment; *la obra fue un fracaso,* the play was a failure; *sufrir un fracaso,* to meet with failure; *como médico es un fracaso,* as a doctor he is a failure. || — *Fracaso amoroso,* disappointment in love. || *Ir a un fracaso,* to court failure *o* disaster.
fracción f. Breaking [into pieces], fraction (ant.): *la fracción del pan,* the breaking of the bread, the fraction of the bread. || Part, portion, fraction (parte). || Faction, group (dentro de un partido). || MAT. Fraction (quebrado): *fracción continua, decimal, impropia, propia,* continued, decimal, improper, proper fraction. || QUÍM. Fraction.
fraccionamiento m. Breaking-up, division. || TECN. Cracking (del petróleo). || QUÍM. Fractionation.
fraccionar v. tr. To break up, to break into pieces, to divide. || To fraction, to fractionize (dividir en fracciones). || TECN. To crack (petróleo). || QUÍM. To fractionate. || FIG. To divide, to split: *el asunto fraccionó la opinión pública,* the affair divided public opinion. || QUÍM. *Destilación fraccionada,* fractional distillation.
fraccionario, ria adj. MAT. Fractional. || *Se ruega moneda fraccionaria,* v. MONEDA.
fractura f. Break, fracture (rotura). || GEOL. y MED. Fracture: *fractura concoidea,* conchoidal fracture; *fractura complicada, conminuta, en tallo verde,* compound, comminuted, greenstick fracture. || JUR. *Robo con fractura,* burglary, housebreaking.
fracturar v. tr. To fracture, to break: *fracturar el cráneo a uno,* to fracture s.o.'s skull. || To force (una cerradura).
— V. pr. To fracture, to break: *fracturarse la pierna,* to break one's leg.
fraga f. Rough ground covered in brambles. || BOT. Raspberry bush (frambueso).
fragancia f. Fragrance.
fragante adj. Fragrant, sweet-smelling. || Flagrant (flagrante). || *En fragante,* in the act, red-handed (en flagrante delito).
fraganti (in) adv. In the act, red-handed.
fragata f. MAR. Frigate. || Frigate bird (ave).
frágil adj. Fragile, delicate: *un vaso, un mecanismo frágil,* a fragile glass, mechanism. || FIG. Delicate, frail, fragile (salud, persona). | Weak (memoria). | Weak (con poca fortaleza moral).
fragilidad f. Fragility, delicacy (de una cosa). || FIG. Frailty (de la salud, una persona). | Weakness (debilidad).
fragmentación f. Fragmentation. || Fragmentation, division (de terrenos).
fragmentar v. tr. To fragment. || To fragment, to divide up (terrenos).
fragmentario, ria adj. Fragmentary.
fragmento m. Fragment. || Passage, excerpt (de un discurso). || Snatch (de conversación, canción).
fragor m. Din (estrépito): *en el fragor de la batalla,* amid the din of battle. || Rumble (del trueno). || Roar (de la tempestad).
fragoroso, sa adj. Deafening, thunderous.
fragosidad f. Rough ground covered in brambles (terreno lleno de malezas). || Roughness, unevenness (del terreno). || Thickness, denseness (de la selva).
fragoso, sa adj. Rough, uneven (terreno), brambly (con malezas). || Dense (selva). || Deafening, thunderous (ruidoso).
fragua f. Forge.
fraguado m. Setting (del cemento).

fraguador, ra m. y f. Schemer. || — *Fraguador de líos*, troublemaker. || *Fraguador de mentiras*, liar, story-teller.
fraguar v. tr. To forge (hierro). || FIG. To fabricate, to concoct (mentiras). | To hatch (complot). | To make, to cause: *fraguar un lío*, to cause trouble. || *Fraguar quimeras*, to daydream.
— V. intr. To set, to harden (cemento).
fraile m. Friar, monk. || IMPR. Friar. || — FIG. *Fraile de misa y olla*, ignorant friar. || *Meterse a fraile*, to become a friar.
frailecillo m. Puffin (ave).
frailengo, ga o **fraileño, ña** adj. FAM. Monkish, monk-like.
frailería f. FAM. Friars, *pl.* monks, *pl.* | Priests, *pl.* (curas).
frailero, ra o **frailesco, ca** adj. FAM. Monkish, monk-like.
frailuco m. Insignificant little monk *o* priest.
frailuno, na adj. FAM. Monkish, monk-like.
framboyán m. BOT. Royal poinciana, flamboyant.
frambuesa f. BOT. Raspberry.
frambueso m. BOT. Raspberry bush.
francachela f. FAM. Spread, feast (comilona). | Good time, spree, binge (juerga): *estar de francachela*, to be on a binge *o* on a spree, to be having a good time.
francés, esa adj. French. || — *A la francesa*, in the French way *o* style, French-style. || *De habla francesa*, French-speaking. || FIG. y FAM. *Despedirse a la francesa*, to take French leave. || *Tortilla a la francesa*, plain *o* French omelette.
— M. French (idioma): *francés antiguo*, Old French. || Frenchman (hombre). || — F. Frenchwoman (mujer). || *Los franceses*, the French.
francesada f. Napoleonic invasion of Spain. || Typically French turn of phrase *o* action, etc.
francesilla f. BOT. Buttercup.
Francia n. pr. f. GEOGR. France.
francio m. QUÍM. Francium (elemento).
francisca f. HIST. Frankish battle-axe (segur).
Francisca n. pr. f. Frances.
franciscano, na o **francisco, ca** adj./s. Franciscan.
Francisco n. pr. m. Francis, Frank.
francmasón m. Freemason (masón).
francmasonería f. Freemasonry (masonería).
franco, ca adj. Frank, candid (sincero): *mirada franca*, frank looks. || Open (abierto): *franco con* or *para todos*, open with everybody. || Clear, obvious (patente). || Exempt, free (exento): *franco de impuestos*, free from taxation, tax-free. || Free: *puerto franco*, free port; *entrada franca*, free entry. || HIST. Frankish. || Franco (prefijo que significa *francés*): *franco-belga*, Franco-Belgian. || — *Franco de aduana*, duty-free. || *Franco de gastos*, free of expenses. || *Tener mesa franca*, to keep open house.
— M. y f. HIST. Frank. || — M. Frankish (idioma de los francos). || Franc (unidad monetaria): *franco belga*, Belgian franc.
— Adv. Free: *franco a bordo*, free on board, f.o.b. || — *Franco de porte*, carriage-paid (transporte), post-paid, postfree (correos). || *Franco de porte y embalaje*, post and package free.
francoespañol, la adj. Franco-Spanish.
francófilo, la adj./s. Francophile.
francófobo, ba adj./s. Francophobe.
francofonía f. French-speaking countries, *pl.*
francófono, na adj. French-speaking.
— M. y f. French-speaking person.
francote, ta adj. FAM. Extremely frank *o* open, outspoken, forthright.
francotirador m. Sniper (guerrillero).
franchute, ta m. y f. FAM. Frog, froggy, Frenchy.
franela f. Flannel (tela).
frangollar v. tr. FIG. y FAM. To hurry over, to scamp, to botch, to bungle, to do carelessly (un trabajo).
frangollo m. Porridge, boiled cereal (trigo cocido). || FIG. y FAM. Scamping, bungling, botching (de un trabajo). | Botch, mess, sloppy piece of work (trabajo mal hecho). || *Amer.* Sweet made from green bananas (dulce de las Antillas). | Swill (comida mal hecha). | Hodgepodge, jumble (revoltijo).
frangollón, ona adj. Slapdash, bungling.
— M. y f. Slapdash *o* careless *o* sloppy worker, bungler.
franja f. Trimming, border (adorno). || Fringe (de flecos). || Band, stripe (banda). || Strip (de tierra). || Fringe (de árboles). || FÍS. *Franja de interferencia*, interference fringe.
franjar o **franjear** v. tr. To trim, to border (poner una franja), to fringe (poner flecos).
franqueable adj. Which can be crossed *o* passed, passable, crossable. || Breachable (barrera). || Fordable (río). || Surmountable (obstáculo).
franqueadora adj. f. *Máquina franqueadora*, franking machine.
franqueamiento m. Crossing (de un río, etc.). || Surmounting (de obstáculos). || Franking, stamping (de carta). || Enfranchisement, freeing (de esclavo).
franquear v. tr. To free, to clear (desembarazar): *franquear el pasillo, el paso*, to clear the corridor, the way. || To exempt, to free: *franquear a uno de un tributo*, to exempt s.o. from a tax. || To cross, to pass *o* to go through *o* across *o* over, to clear: *franquear un puerto, el umbral*, to go over a pass, to cross the threshold. || To overcome, to surmount (un obstáculo). || To frank, to stamp (una carta). || To free, to enfranchise, to liberate (un esclavo). || To grant (conceder). || — *Franquear un río a nado*, to swim across a river. || *Máquina de franquear*, franking machine.
— V. pr. To unbosom o.s., to open one's heart: *franquearse con un amigo*, to unbosom o.s. to a friend.
franqueo m. Franking, stamping (acción de franquear una carta). || Postage (cantidad que se paga). || *Franqueo concertado*, postage paid.
franqueza f. Frankness, candidness (sinceridad): *dispense mi franqueza*, pardon my frankness. || Openness (carácter abierto). || Familiarity, intimacy (confianza). || Generosity (generosidad). || — *Con franqueza*, frankly. || *Tiene bastante franqueza con él para decirle la verdad*, he is on intimate enough terms with him to tell him the truth.
franquía f. MAR. Searoom. || FIG. *Estar en franquía*, to be in the clear.
franquicia f. Exemption (exención): *franquicia aduanera, postal*, exemption from customs duty, from postal charges.
franquista adj./s. Francoist.
fraque m. V. FRAC.
frasco m. Small bottle: *un frasco de agua de Colonia*, a small bottle of eau de Cologne. || Flask (para licor, de laboratorio). || MIL. Powder flask (para la pólvora). || FAM. *¡Toma del frasco!*, put that in your pipe and smoke it!
frase f. Sentence (oración): *la estructura de la frase*, the structure of the sentence. || Phrase, expression (expresión). || MÚS. Phrase. || — *Frase hecha* or *acuñada*, set phrase *o* expression. || *Frase proverbial*, proverbial phrase, proverb, saying. || FAM. *Gastar frases*, to speak in flowery *o* pretentious language.
frasear v. tr. e intr. To phrase.
fraseo m. MÚS. Phrasing.
fraseología f. Phraseology.
frasquera f. Flask *o* bottle carrier.
frasquete m. Phial, small flask (frasco pequeño).
fratás m. Trowel (utensilio de albañilería).
fraterna f. Dressing down, lecture (reprensión).
fraternal adj. Fraternal, brotherly.
fraternidad f. Fraternity, brotherhood.
fraternización f. Fraternization.
fraternizar v. intr. To fraternize.
fraterno, na adj. Fraternal, brotherly.
fratría f. HIST. Phratry.
fratricida adj. Fratricidal.
— M. y f. Fratricide (persona).
fratricidio m. Fratricide (acto).
fraude m. Fraud. || Cheating, dishonesty: *ha habido fraude en los exámenes*, there has been cheating in the examinations.
fraudulencia f. Fraudulence.
fraudulentamente adv. Fraudulently, by fraud.
fraudulento, ta adj. Fraudulent: *quiebra fraudulenta*, fraudulent bankruptcy.
fraustina f. Dummy head (cabeza de madera).
fray m. Brother, friar [only used before names].
frazada f. Blanket (manta).
freático, ca adj. Phreatic. || *Capa freática*, water table, groundwater table.
frecuencia f. Frequency: *la frecuencia de sus visitas*, the frequency of his visits. || RAD. Frequency: *baja, alta frecuencia*, low, high frequency; *emisora de frecuencia modulada*, frequency modulation transmitter. || — *Con frecuencia*, frequently. || *Con mucha frecuencia*, very frequently.
frecuencímetro m. Frequency meter.
frecuentación f. Frequentation, frequenting.
frecuentador, ra adj. Frequenting, who frequents.
— M. y f. Regular customer, frequenter, habitué.
frecuentar v. tr. To frequent, to visit frequently. || REL. *Frecuentar los sacramentos*, to frequent the sacraments.
frecuentativo, va adj./s.m. GRAM. Frequentative.
frecuente adj. Frequent. || Common (corriente).
frecuentemente adv. Frequently, often.
fregadero m. Sink (en la cocina).
fregado m. Washing (del suelo, de los cristales, etc.). || Washing up (de la vajilla). || Scouring (de las cacerolas). || FIG. y FAM. Rumpus, shindy (alboroto): *¡menudo fregado armaron!*, they kicked up a right shindy! | Mess (lío): *meterse en un fregado*, to get into a mess. || — FIG. y FAM. *Lo mismo sirve para un fregado que para un barrido*, he is a jack-of-all-trades. | *Tener un fregado con alguien*, to have a row with s.o.
— Adj. *Amer.* Obstinate, stubborn (obstinado). | Annoying (molesto).
fregador, ra m. y f. Dishwasher. || — M. Sink (fregadero). || Dishcloth (estropajo), scouring pad (de aluminio).
fregadura f. V. FREGADO.
fregamiento m. *Amer.* Rub, rubbing (fricción).
fregar* v. tr. To rub (frotar). || To scrub (limpiar con cepillo), to scour (con abrasivo, estropajo metálico): *fregar las cacerolas*, to scour the saucepans. || To wash up (platos). || To mop, to scrub (el suelo). || *Amer.* To annoy, to bother (fastidiar). || — *Agua de*

fregar, dishwater. || *Fregar la loza* or *los platos*, to do the washing up, to wash the dishes, to wash up.
fregona f. Dishwasher (fregadora). || Skivvy (sirvienta).
fregotear v. tr. To give a quick wipe.
fregoteo m. Quick wipe.
freidora f. Fryer.
freidura f. Frying.
freiduría f. Fish shop.
freimiento m. Frying.
freír* v. tr. CULIN. To fry. || FIG. y FAM. To bother, to exasperate. || — FIG. *Al freír será el reír*, he who laughs last laughs longest. || FAM. *Freír a preguntas*, to bombard *o* to plague with questions.
— V. pr. CULIN. To fry. || FIG. *Freírse de calor*, to be boiling hot *o* baking hot.

— OBSERV. *Freír* has two past participles, the regular (*freído*), and the more common (*frito*). [V. FRITO.]

fréjol m. Bean, kidney bean (judía).
frenado o **frenaje** m. Braking.
frenar v. tr. To brake, to apply the brake to. || FIG. To check, to restrain: *frenar la producción*, to check production. | To stop, to restrain: *su marido le frena para que no coma demasiado*, her husband stops her from eating too much.
frenazo m. Sudden braking. || *Dar un frenazo*, to brake hard, to jam on *o* to slam on the brakes.
frenesí n. Frenzy.
frenético, ca adj. Frenetic, frenzied, frantic. || Mad, furious, wild (colérico): *ponerse frenético*, to go mad.
frenetismo m. Frenzy.
frénico, ca adj. ANAT. Phrenic.
frenillo m. ANAT. Frenum. || — *No tener frenillo en la lengua*, to speak one's mind, not to mince one's words. || *Tener frenillo*, to lisp, to be tongue-tied.
freno m. Bit (de caballería). || Brake (de coche, etc): *freno de pedal*, foot brake; *freno de tambor, de disco, asistido*, drum, disc, power brake; *freno delantero, trasero*, front, back brake. || FIG. Check, curb. || *Amer.* Hunger (hambre). || — *Echar los frenos*, to brake, to put the brakes on. || *Freno de mano*, handbrake. || *Poner el freno*, to put the brake on. || FIG. *Poner freno a*, to curb, to check, to bridle: *este contratiempo puso freno a sus ambiciones*, this setback curbed his ambitions. || *Potencia al freno*, brake horsepower. || *Soltar el freno*, to release the brake. || FIG. y FAM. *Tascar el freno*, V. TASCAR.
frenología f. Phrenology.
frenólogo m. Phrenologist.
frental adj. ANAT. Frontal (de la frente).
frente f. ANAT. Forehead, brow. || FIG. Head: *con la frente alta*, with one's head held high. || *Frente a frente*, face to face. || *Frente calzada*, low forehead.
— M. Front (parte delantera de una cosa). || Façade, front (fachada de un edificio). || MIL. Front: *frente de batalla*, battle front. || MIN. Face: *frente de corte*, working face. || Front (agrupación política): *frente popular*, popular front. || GEOGR. Front (entre dos zonas atmosféricas): *frente frío, cálido*, cold, warm front. || Top, head (de una página): *al frente*, at the top. || — *Al frente*, at the head: *al frente de su compañía iba el capitán*, the captain was riding at the head of his company; forward: *dos pasos al frente*, two steps forward. || *Atacar de frente*, to make a frontal attack. | *De frente*, forward (no oblicuamente): *entrar de frente y no de lado*, to go in forward and not sideways; abreast (uno al lado del otro), head on (en un choque): *los coches chocaron de frente*, the cars hit each other head on; resolutely (con determinación). || MIL. *¡De frente!, ¡ar!*, forward, march! | *De frente en columna de a tres*, forward in threes. || *En frente*, opposite (enfrente). || *En frente de*, opposite, facing, in front of. || *Frente a*, as opposed to (en comparación con). || *Frente a* or *frente de*, opposite, opposite to, facing (enfrente de), faced with, confronted with (un problema). || *Frente por frente*, opposite. || *Hacer frente a*, to face, to stand up to. || *Hacer frente común*, to make common cause. || *Mirar a uno frente a frente*, to look s.o. straight in the face. || FIG. y FAM. *No tener dos dedos de frente*, V. DEDO. || *Poner frente a frente*, to confront.
fresa f. BOT. Strawberry plant, strawberry (planta): *fresa silvestre*, wild *o* wood strawberry. | Strawberry (fruto). || TECN. Milling cutter (herramienta). | Drill (de dentista).
fresado m. TECN. Milling.
fresador, ra m. y f. Miller, milling-machine operator. || — F. TECN. Milling machine.
fresal m. Strawberry patch, strawberry field.
fresar v. tr. TECN. To mill.
fresca f. Fresh *o* cool air: *tomar la fresca*, to get some fresh air. || Cool [of the day, of the evening]: *pasear con la fresca de la tarde*, to stroll in the cool of the evening. || FIG. y FAM. Home truth (verdad): *decirle cuatro frescas a uno*, to tell s.o. a few home truths. | Cheeky *o* impertinent remark *o* comment (impertinencia): *soltar frescas*, to make cheeky remarks. | Cheeky girl *o* woman (mujer descarada). | Brazen *o* shameless woman (mujer liviana).
frescachón, ona adj. FAM. Healthy, robust (robusto). | Buxom (mujer). | Cheeky (descarado). || MAR. *Viento frescachón*, brisk wind.
frescales m. y f. inv. FAM. Cheeky devil *o* monkey.
frescamente adv. Freshly, newly, recently (recientemente). || FIG. Cheekily, impertinently (descaradamente).
fresco, ca adj. Cool, fresh: *viento fresco*, cool wind. || Fresh: *pescado fresco*, fresh fish. || New-laid, fresh (huevos). || Fresh, new (pan). || Cold (agua). || Cool (ropa, bebida). || FIG. Fresh, new (reciente): *noticias frescas*, fresh news. | Fresh: *tez fresca*, fresh complexion; *después de una noche de viaje llegó tan fresco*, after travelling all night he arrived as fresh as a daisy. || FIG. y FAM. Calm, cool, unruffled (sereno): *se quedó tan fresco con la noticia*, he was quite unruffled by the news, he remained calm on hearing the news. | Cheeky, impudent, saucy, fresh (descarado). | Shameless (desvergonzado). || Thin, light (telas). || — FIG. y FAM. *Está fresco si cree que se lo voy a hacer*, he'll be lucky *o* he's got a hope if he thinks I'll do it for him, if he thinks I'll do it for him he's got another think coming. | *¡Estamos frescos!*, we're in a fine pickle *o* in a fine mess! || *Hacer fresco*, to be chilly *o* cool. || *Ponerse fresco*, to put on light clothes (vestirse ligeramente). || FAM. *¡Qué fresco!*, what a nerve! || FIG. *Sentirse fresco como una rosa*, to feel as fresh as a daisy.
— M. Fresh air, cool air: *tomar el fresco*, to get some fresh air. || Cool: *con el fresco de la tarde muchos salen a pasear*, a lot of people go out for a stroll in the cool of the evening. || ARTES. Fresco: *pintura al fresco*, painting in fresco. || FIG. Fresco: *un vasto fresco histórico*, a vast historical fresco. || FIG. y FAM. Cheeky *o* impudent person, shameless person. || *Amer.* Cool drink (refresco). || — *Al fresco*, in the cool, out of the heat: *pon las bebidas al fresco*, put the drinks in the cool; in the open air: *comimos al fresco en la terraza*, we ate in the open air on the terrace. || FIG. y FAM. *Mandar a tomar el fresco*, to send packing.
frescor m. Coolness, freshness. || ARTES. Pinkness, freshness (de la carne).
frescote, ta adj. FIG. y FAM. Healthy, ruddy, radiant with health (saludable). | Buxom (mujer). | Cheeky (descarado).
frescura f. Coolness, freshness (temperatura): *la frescura del agua*, the coolness of the water. || Freshness (del pan, de los huevos, del rostro, etc.). || FIG. y FAM. Cheek, nerve, sauce: *con mucha frescura me pidió dinero*, he had the nerve to ask me for money; *¡qué frescura!*, what a nerve!; *¡vaya una frescura que tiene usted!*, you've got a cheek! | Cheeky *o* impertinent remark *o* comment (impertinencia): *soltar frescuras*, to come out with impertinent comments. | Calmness, calm, coolness (serenidad). || — *Con la mayor frescura*, with the greatest unconcern. || FAM. *Tomar las cosas con frescura*, to take things calmly *o* without batting an eyelid.
fresneda f. Ash grove (bosque de fresnos).
fresnillo m. BOT. Fraxinella.
fresno m. BOT. Ash, ash tree.
fresón m. BOT. Strawberry.
fresquera f. Meat safe, food safe.
fresquería f. *Amer.* Refreshment bar.
fresquero, ra m. y f. Fresh-fish seller, fishmonger.
fresquete o **fresquito, ta** adj. Chilly.
freudiano, na adj./s. Freudian.
freudismo m. Freudianism.
freza f. Dung (estiércol). || Spawn (huevos de los peces). || Spawning (desove). || Spawning season (período del desove). || Hole made by an animal.
frezar v. intr. To dung (evacuar excrementos los animales). || To spawn (los peces). || To root (hozar).
friabilidad f. Friability.
friable adj. Friable.
frialdad f. Coldness (de la temperatura). || FIG. Indifference, coldness (indiferencia): *la frialdad del público*, the indifference of the audience. | Coldness: *la frialdad de su estilo, de su tono*, the coldness of his style, of his tone. | Coldness, coolness (desapego). || MED. Frigidity (sexual). || FIG. *Recibir a alguien con frialdad*, to receive s.o. coldly *o* cooly, to give s.o. a cool reception.
fríamente adv. Coldly, coolly. || *Recibir a uno fríamente*, to receive s.o. coldly *o* cooly, to give s.o. a cool reception.
Friburgo n. pr. GEOGR. Freiburg.
fricandó m. CULIN. Fricandeau.
fricativo, va adj./s.f. GRAM. Fricative.
fricción f. Rub, rubbing (friega). || Massage (masaje): *darse una fricción en el cuero cabelludo*, to give o.s. a scalp massage. || TECN. Friction (roce). || FIG. Friction, trouble, discord: *fricción entre varios grupos étnicos*, friction between different ethnic groups.
friccionar v. tr. To rub (frotar). || To massage (dar masajes).
friega f. Rub, rubbing. || MED. Massage. || *Amer.* Beating, thrashing (zurra). || *Dar friegas*, to massage.
friegaplatos m. y f. inv. Dishwasher.
Frigia n. pr. f. GEOGR. Phrygia.
frigidez f. Coldness, frigidity. || MED. Frigidity.
frígido, da adj. Cold, frigid. || MED. Frigid.
frigio, gia adj./s. Phrygian: *gorro frigio*, V. GORRO.
frigoría f. FÍS. Kilocalorie.
frigorificación f. Refrigeration.
frigorífico, ca adj. Refrigerating: *mezcla, máquina frigorífica*, refrigerating mixture, machine. || Refrig-

erator: *vagón, camión frigorífico*, refrigerator car, lorry. || — *Armario frigorífico*, refrigerator. || *Cámara frigorífica*, cold-storage room.
— M. Refrigerator, fridge (fam.) [doméstico]. || Cold-storage room (cámara). || Cold-storage plant (establecimiento industrial).
frigorista m. Refrigerating engineer.
frigorizar v. tr. To refrigerate.
frijol o **frijol** m. *Amer*. Bean, kidney bean. || — Pl. *Amer*. Boasting, *sing.*, bragging, *sing.* (fanfarronería).
frijón m. Bean, kidney bean.
frío, a adj. Cold: *una comida fría*, a cold meal; *un día frío*, a cold day. || FIG. Cold (carente de sensibilidad). | Cold, cool, unfriendly: *un recibimiento frío*, a cold reception. | Indifferent, cold (falto de entusiasmo). | Cold, detached, objective (desapasionado). | Cool (sereno). | Cold (lejos de la cosa buscada). | Cold (muerto). | Frigid (poco amoroso). || ARTES. Cold (colores). || — FIG. *Dejar frío*, to leave cold (dejar indiferente), to dumbfound (dejar pasmado). || *Guerra fría*, cold war. || FIG. *Más frío que el hielo*, as cold as ice. | *Quedarse frío como el mármol*, to be left cold (indiferente), to be dumbfounded (pasmado).
— N. Cold. || — *Coger frío*, to catch cold. || *En frío*, cold, when cold; dispassionately (desapasionadamente). || FIG. *Esto no me da ni frío ni calor*, it's all the same to me, it leaves me quite cold *o* indifferent. || *Hace mucho frío*, it is very cold. || FAM. *Hace un frío que pela* or *un frío de perros*, it is freezing cold, it is icy. || *¡Qué frío!*, isn't it cold! || *Pasar* or *tener frío*, to be cold. || *Tener mucho frío*, to be very cold.
friolento, ta adj. V. FRIOLERO.
friolera f. Trifle, trinket, bauble (cosa de poco valor). || *La moto le costó la friolera de mil libras*, the motorbike cost him a mere thousand pounds (irónico).
friolero, ra adj. Sensitive to the cold, chilly.
frisa f. Frieze (tela). || Fraise (en fortificaciones).
frisadora f. Friezing machine.
frisar v. tr. To frieze, to frizz (los tejidos). || To seal, to pack (las junturas).
— V. tr. e intr. To be getting on for, to be close on: *frisa (en) los ochenta años*, he is getting on for eighty.
Frisia n. pr. f. GEOGR. Friesland.
frisio, sia adj./s. Frisian (de Frisia). || *Islas Frisias*, Frisian Islands.
friso m. ARQ. Frieze.
frisón, ona adj./s. Frisian (de Frisia).
frita f. TECN. Frit.
fritada f. Fried dish, fry. || *Fritada de tomates*, fried tomatoes.
fritado o **fritaje** m. TECN. Fritting.
fritanga f. Fried dish, fry (fritura). || Greasy mess (fritura mala).
fritar v. tr. TECN. To frit (sinterizar).
frito, ta adj. Fried: *huevos fritos*, fried eggs. || — FAM. *Estar frito*, to be exasperated (exasperado), to be fed up (harto), to be done for (perdido). | *Estar frito de calor*, to be baking hot *o* boiling hot. | *Estar frito por hacer algo*, to be dying to do sth. | *Me tiene* or *me trae frito con sus preguntas*, I'm sick to death of *o* sick and tired of him and his questions. || *Patatas fritas*, chips [U.S., french fries]. || FAM. *Quedarse frito*, to fall asleep, to nod off (dormirse).
— M. Fried dish, fry (fritura).
fritura f. Fried dish, fry. || RAD. Crackling (ruido). || *Fritura de sesos*, fried brains.
frivolidad f. Frivolity.
frívolo, la adj. Frivolous.
fronda f. Frond (hoja), foliage, leaves, *pl.* (follaje). || — Pl. Foliage, *sing.*, leaves (follaje).
Fronda n. pr. f. HIST. Fronde.
frondosidad f. Leafiness (cualidad de frondoso). || Luxuriance (de la vegetación). || Foliage, leaves, *pl.* (follaje).
frondoso, sa adj. Leafy (árbol). || Luxuriant (vegetación). || Close, thick (bosque).
frontal adj. ANAT. Frontal.
— M. Frontal (de altar). || ANAT. Frontal bone. || *Amer*. Browband, headband (del caballo).
frontalera f. Browband, headband (del caballo). || Yoke pad (de los bueyes).
frontalero, ra adj. Frontier (fronterizo).
frontera f. Frontier, border (de un Estado). || FIG. Limit, bounds, *pl.*: *no hay frontera para su generosidad*, there is no limit to his generosity, his generosity knows no bounds. | Borderland (área sin límites precisos). || *Sus ademanes están en la frontera de lo ridículo*, his gestures border on the ridiculous.
fronterizo, za adj. Frontier, border: *ciudad fronteriza*, frontier town. || Opposite (colocado enfrente). || *España y Portugal son fronterizos*, Portugal borders on Spain, Portugal has a common border with Spain.
frontero, ra adj. Opposite, facing: *casa frontera a la mía*, house facing mine.
— Adv. Opposite: *frontero a la iglesia*, opposite the church.
frontis m. V. FRONTISPICIO.
frontispicio m. ARQ. Façade, ornamental front (fachada). | Pediment, frontispiece (frontón). || Frontispiece (de libro).
frontón m. ARQ. Pediment, fronton. || DEP. Pelota court. | Wall of a pelota court (pared). || Cliff (en la costa).

frotación f. Rubbing, rub. || TECN. Friction.
frotador, ra adj. Rubbing.
— M. y f. Rubber. || — M. ELECTR. Brush, sliding contact (escobilla), shoe (para riel eléctrico).
frotadura f. o **frotamiento** m. Rubbing, rub. || TECN. Friction.
frotar v. tr. To rub. || To strike (una cerilla).
— V. pr. To rub. || *Frotarse las manos*, to rub one's hands.
frote m. Rub, rubbing.
fructífero, ra adj. BOT. Fructiferous, fruit-bearing. || FIG. Fruitful: *un viaje fructífero*, a fruitful trip.
fructificación f. Fructification.
fructificar v. intr. To fructify, to bear fruit. || FIG. To be productive *o* fruitful.
fructosa f. QUÍM. Fructose.
fructuoso, sa adj. Fruitful (fructífero).
frufrú m. Frou-frou.
frugal adj. Frugal: *una comida, una vida frugal*, a frugal meal, life.
frugalidad f. Frugality.
frugívoro, ra adj. Frugivorous, fructivorous, fruit-eating: *animales frugívoros*, frugivorous animals.
fruición f. Enjoyment, pleasure, delight. || *Hacer algo con fruición*, to enjoy doing sth. (disfrutar), to do sth. with great pleasure (hacerlo con gusto).
frumentario, ria o **frumenticio, cia** adj. Frumentaceous.
frunce m. Gather, shirr (pliegue). || Gathers, *pl.*, gathering (arrugas en la tela). || *Con frunces*, gathered, shirred.
fruncido, da adj. Gathered, shirred: *una falda fruncida*, a gathered skirt. || Wrinkled (arrugado). || *Con el ceño fruncido*, frowning.
— M. Gathers, *pl.*, gathering, shirrs, *pl.*, shirring (de una tela). || Wrinkling (del entrecejo). || Pursing, puckering (de los labios).
fruncimiento m. Gathering, shirring (de vestidos). || Pursing, puckering (de los labios). || *Fruncimiento del entrecejo*, frown.
fruncir v. tr. To gather, to shirr: *fruncir una tela*, to gather a fabric. || To purse, to pucker (los labios). || *Fruncir el entrecejo* or *el ceño*, to frown, to knit one's brow.
fruslería f. Trifle, trinket (chuchería). || Titbit, sweet [U.S., piece of candy] (golosina). || Triviality, silly thing (tontería). || Mere nothing (nadería).
frustración f. Frustration.
frustrado, da adj. Frustrated, thwarted: *frustradas sus esperanzas*, his hopes frustrated. || Unsuccessful: *un golpe de estado frustrado*, an unsuccessful coup d'état. || — *Es un escritor frustrado*, as a writer he is a failure. || *Sentirse frustrado*, to feel frustrated (insatisfecho), to be disappointed (defraudado).
frustrar v. tr. To frustrate, to thwart. || To disappoint (defraudar): *quedar frustrado*, to be disappointed.
— V. pr. To fail, to come to nothing (fracasar): *su intento se ha frustrado*, his attempt has failed. || To be frustrated: *sus esperanzas se frustraron*, his hopes were frustrated.
fruta f. Fruit: *la pera es una fruta sabrosa*, the pear is a delicious fruit; *no como nunca fruta*, I never eat fruit. || FIG. Fruit. || *Amer*. Apricot (albaricoque). || — *Fruta bomba*, papaya, papaw (papaya). || *Fruta del tiempo*, fresh fruit, fruit in season (fruta de la temporada), seasonal feature (cosa propia de una época). || *Fruta de sartén*, fritter. || *Fruta escarchada*, candied fruit. || FIG. *Fruta prohibida*, forbidden fruit. || *Frutas confitadas*, comfits [U.S., preserved fruit]. || *Fruta seca*, dried fruit. || *Fruta temprana*, early fruit.
— OBSERV. The word *fruta* is used for the edible fruits such as pears, cherries, strawberries, etc. In the singular form it can signify fruit in general: *a mí me gusta la fruta*, I like fruit, I am fond of fruit.
— La palabra *fruit* se puede aplicar al conjunto de las frutas.
frutal adj. Fruit: *árboles frutales*, fruit trees.
— M. Fruit tree (árbol).
frutería f. Fruiterer's.
frutero, ra adj. Fruit: *industria frutera*, fruit industry. || *Plato frutero*, fruit dish, fruit bowl.
— M. y f. Fruiterer (vendedor de fruta). || — M. Fruit dish, fruit bowl (recipiente).
frutilla f. *Amer*. Strawberry (fresa).
frutillar m. *Amer*. Strawberry patch, strawberry field.
fruto m. Fruit: *frutos carnosos, secos*, fleshy, dry fruits. || FIG. Fruit: *los frutos del trabajo, de una mala educación*, the fruits of one's work, of a bad upbringing. | Fruit, produce (*inv.*): *el fruto de la tierra*, the fruit of the land. | Offspring, child (hijo). | Profit, benefit (beneficio): *sacar fruto de*, to derive benefit from. | Result: *el trabajo no ha dado ningún fruto*, the work hasn't given any result. || — *Dar fruto*, to bear fruit, to bear fruit (plantas), to bear fruit, to be fruitful (ser provechoso). || REL. *El fruto de tu vientre*, the fruit of thy womb. | *Fruto prohibido*, forbidden fruit. || JUR. *Frutos civiles*, unearned income. || *Frutos industriales*, earnings. || FIG. *No dar fruto*, to be fruitless. | *Por el fruto se conoce el árbol*, the tree is known by its fruit. | *Sacar fruto de algo*, to derive benefit from sth., to profit from sth. | *Sin fruto*, fruitless: *trabajo sin fruto*, fruitless work; fruitlessly:

trabajar sin fruto, to work fruitlessly. | *Trabajar con fruto*, to work successfully *o* profitably.

— OBSERV. *Fruto* is a botanical term referring to the large reproductive body of a seed plant.

ftaleína f. QUÍM. Phthalein.

fu m. Hiss [noise made by an angry cat]. || — *¡Fu!*, ugh! (repugnancia), huh!, phooey! (desprecio). || *Hacer fu a*, to snub, to give the cold shoulder to (a personas), to pooh-pooh (a cosas). || *Ni fu ni fa*, so-so.

fucilar v. intr. POÉT. To fulgurate, to flash (fulgurar).

fucilazo m. POÉT. Flash of sheet lightning.

fuco m. BOT. Fucus.

fucsia f. BOT. Fuchsia (arbusto).

fucsina f. QUÍM. Fuchsine, fuchsin.

fuego m. Fire: *encender un fuego de leña*, to light a wood fire; *apagar el fuego*, to put out the fire; *atizó el fuego*, he poked the fire. || Fire (incendio): *hay fuego en el pueblo*, there is a fire in the town. || Light (lumbre): *¿tiene usted fuego, por favor?*, have you got a light, please? || Burner, ring (de cocina de gas). || Home (hogar): *una aldea de diez fuegos*, a village with ten homes. || MIL. Fire (de arma de fuego): *abrir fuego contra*, to open fire on; *estar bajo el fuego*, to be under fire. || MAR. Beacon. || MED. Rash (erupción). || FIG. Ardour, zeal: *trabajar con fuego*, to work with zeal. | Fire, passion (pasión). | Heat: *en el fuego de la discusión*, in the heat of the discussion. || — *A fuego lento*, on a low flame (en cocina), slowly (lentamente). || *A fuego y sangre*, mercilessly. || *¡Alto el fuego!*, v. ALTO. || MIL. *Apagar los fuegos*, to silence the enemy guns. || *Arma de fuego*, firearm. || FIG. *Atizar el fuego de la discordia*, to stir up discord. || CULIN. *Cocer a fuego lento*, to cook on a low flame, to cook slowly *o* gently (gas), to cook slowly *o* gently (electricidad). | *Cocer a fuego vivo*, to cook quickly (electricidad), to cook on a high flame (gas). || FIG. *Echaba fuego por los ojos*, he was looking daggers, his eyes glared. | *Echar leña al fuego*, to add fuel to the fire. | *Estar entre dos fuegos*, to be between two fires, to be caught in a cross fire. || *¡Fuego!*, fire! || *Fuego a discreción*, fire at will. || *Fuego cruzado*, cross fire. || *Fuego de campamento*, campfire. || *Fuego de San Telmo*, Saint Elmo's fire, corposant. || *Fuego fatuo*, will-o'-the-wisp, Jack-o'-lantern. || MIL. *Fuego graneado*, running fire. || *Fuego griego*, Greek fire. || MIL. *Fuego nutrido*, heavy fire. | *Fuego por descarga*, volley. || *Fuegos artificiales*, fireworks. || MIL. *Hacer fuego*, to fire (*sobre*, at, on). || CULIN. *Hervir a fuego lento*, to simmer. || FIG. *Jugar con fuego*, to play with fire. | *Mantener el fuego sagrado*, to keep enthusiasm alive. || *Marcar a fuego*, to brand (reses). || FIG. *Matar a fuego lento*, to torture to death. | *Meter fuego*, to add spice (animar). || *Meter* or *pegar* or *prender fuego a*, to set on fire, to set fire to. || FIG. *Poner las manos en el fuego por*, to stake one's life on. || *Prueba del fuego*, trial by fire. || MIL. *Romper fuego*, to open fire. || *Tocar a fuego*, to ring the fire alarm.

fueguero m. *Amer.* Pyrotechnist.

fueguino, na adj./s. Fuegian [of Tierra del Fuego].

fuel o **fuel-oil** m. Fuel oil. || *Calefacción por fuel-oil*, oil-fired central heating.

fuelle m. Bellows, *pl.* (de órgano, para el fuego, de máquina fotográfica, acordeón, etc.). || Accordion pleats, *pl.* (en la ropa, un bolso, una cartera). || Folding hood, folding top (de carruaje). || Bag (de gaita). || Connecting corridor (de tren). || FIG. y FAM. Telltale (soplón). || FIG. *Tener mucho fuelle*, to have good wind.

fuente f. Fountain: *una fuente monumental*, a monumental fountain. || Drinking fountain (para beber). || Spring (manantial): *una fuente cristalina*, a clear spring. || Dish, serving dish [U.S., platter] (plato grande y su contenido): *una fuente de verduras*, a dish of vegetables. || Source (de un río). || FIG. Source: *fuente de divisas, de suministro, de infección*, source of foreign currency, supply, infection. | Origin. || MED. Exutory (exutorio). || — FIG. *Beber en buenas fuentes*, to have a reliable source of information, to be well-informed. | *De fuente desconocida*, from an unknown source. | *De fuentes bien informadas* or *fidedignas*, from reliable sources. || *Fuente bautismal*, baptismal font. || *Fuente de horno*, v. HORNO.

fuer m. V. FUERO. || *A fuer de*, as a: *a fuer de hombre honrado*, as an honest man.

fuera adv. Out: *echar fuera a alguien*, to throw s.o. out; *cenar fuera*, to dine out. || Outside: *la calma reina en el país, pero no fuera*, calmness reigns in our country but not outside. || Abroad (en el extranjero). || — *Aquí fuera, allí fuera*, out here, out there. || *Con la lengua fuera*, with one's tongue hanging out. || *De fuera*, outside, outer. || *Desde fuera*, from [the] outside (desde el exterior), from abroad (desde el extranjero). || DEP. *El equipo de fuera*, the away team. || *Estar fuera*, to be away from home, to be away (de viaje), to be out (haber salido), to be abroad *o* out of the country (en otro país), to be out (en deporte). || *Estar fuera de sí*, to be beside o.s. || *Esto esta fuera de la cuestión*, this is irrelevant. || *Esto está fuera de lo común* or *de lo corriente*, this is unusual *o* out of the ordinary. || *Esto está fuera de su competencia*, that does not come within his province, that is outside his scope. || *¡Fuera!*, out!, get out! go away! || *Fuera de*, outside of, outside: *vivo fuera de la ciudad*, I live outside the city; out of: *fuera del contexto*, out of context; except for, besides, apart from (exceptuando): *fuera de ti, no conozco a nadie aquí*, except for you I don't know anybody here; besides, as well as (además de). || *Fuera de alcance*, out of reach, beyond one's reach. || *¡Fuera de aquí!*, get out of here!, out of here!, away from here! || *Fuera de casa*, away from home. || JUR. *Fuera de causa*, irrelevant. || *Fuera de combate*, out of action; knocked out (en boxeo). || *Fuera de concurso*, not competing. || *Fuera de duda*, beyond doubt. || *Fuera de esto*, besides this, in addition to this. || DEP. *Fuera de juego*, v. JUEGO. || *Fuera de lo normal*, out of the ordinary, unusual. || *Fuera de lugar*, out of place, inappropriate: *su observación está fuera de lugar*, his comment is out of place. || *Fuera de moda*, out of fashion. || *Fuera de peligro*, out of danger. || *Fuera de propósito*, v. PROPÓSITO. || *Fuera de que*, besides the fact that, apart from the fact that. || *Fuera de serie*, out of the ordinary, unusual. || *Ir fuera*, to go out. || *Jugar fuera*, to play away (un equipo). || *Lámina fuera de texto*, plate. || *Persona fuera de la ley*, outlaw. || *Por fuera*, outside (exteriormente), on the outside (en apariencia). || FIG. *Poner fuera de sí*, to drive crazy.

fuera borda o **fuera bordo** m. inv. MAR. Outboard (motor, canoa).

fuero m. JUR. Law [special law in a certain region, city]. | "Fuero", code of laws (compilación de leyes). | Privilege (privilegio). | Jurisdiction. || — Pl. FAM. Arrogance, *sing.*, conceit, *sing.* || — *A fuero*, according to regional law and custom. || *En mi, tu, su fuero interno* or *interior*, in my, your, his heart of hearts, deep down. || *Fueros municipales*, municipal code of laws. || *No tenga tantos fueros*, don't put on such airs.

fuerte adj. Strong: *un hombre fuerte*, a strong man. || Strong (olor, viento, bebida). || Loud (voz, ruido). || Strong, resistant: *una tela muy fuerte*, a very strong fabric. || Intense (calor, frío, color). || Heavy (abundante): *una fuerte nevada*, a heavy snowfall. || Strong: *una nación fuerte*, a strong nation. || Heavy: *un golpe fuerte*, a heavy blow. || Strong (moneda). || High (fiebre). || Severe: *un fuerte resfriado*, a severe chill. || Great (dolor). || Strong: *nudo fuerte*, strong knot. || Hard (duro). || Great, large: *una fuerte cantidad de dinero*, a great sum of money. || Heavy, big (comida). || Important (importante). || FIG. Good, well up: *estar fuerte en latín*, to be good at *o* well up in Latin. | Strong (palabras). | Risqué (chiste). || — *Fuerte como un roble* or *un toro*, as strong as an ox. || *Hacerse fuerte en*, to entrench o.s. on *o* in (fortificarse), to remain firm in (mantener su actitud). || *Plato fuerte*, main course (manjar), main attraction (atracción principal). || *Plaza fuerte*, stronghold. || *Precio fuerte*, full price.

— M. Strong: *proteger al débil contra el fuerte*, to protect the weak from the strong. || MIL. Fort, fortress, stronghold. || FIG. Strong point, forte: *la música es su fuerte*, music is his forte.

— Adv. Hard: *jugar, trabajar, pegar, apretar fuerte*, to play, to work, to hit, to squeeze hard. || Heavily: *beber fuerte*, to drink heavily. || Loudly: *hablar fuerte*, to speak loudly. || — *Comer fuerte*, to eat a lot, to eat too much. || *¡Más fuerte!*, speak up, louder (a un orador).

fuertemente adv. Strongly. || Loudly: *hablar fuertemente*, to speak loudly.

fuerza f. Strength: *la fuerza de un atleta*, the strength of an athlete. || Force: *recurrir a la fuerza*, to resort to force. || Power: *la fuerza de una máquina*, the power of a machine. || Strength: *la fuerza de un ácido*, the strength of an acid. || Resistance (resistencia). || FÍS. Force: *fuerza centrífuga, electromotriz*, centrifugal, electromotive force; *fuerza de gravedad, de inercia*, force of gravity, of inertia. | Power: *fuerza motriz*, motive power; *fuerza hidráulica*, water power. | Energy (energía). | Power (electricidad). || FIG. Force, strength: *la fuerza de un argumento*, the force of an argument. | Strength, force (de carácter). || — Pl. MIL. Forces: *las fuerzas españolas*, the Spanish forces. || Strength, *sing.* (de una persona): *recobrar fuerzas*, to regain *o* to recover strength. || — FAM. *A éste se le va la fuerza por la boca*, he is all words and no action. || *A fuerza de*, by dint of, by force of: *ha llegado a fuerza de trabajo*, he has arrived by dint of hard work; by means of: *hace sus traducciones a fuerza de diccionarios*, he does his translations by means of dictionaries. || *A la fuerza*, of necessity, perforce (por necesidad): *tiene que pasar por aquí a la fuerza*, he has to pass here of necessity; by force, forcibly: *tuvieron que hacerle entrar en la cárcel a la fuerza*, they had to get him into prison by force; compulsively (por obligación). || FIG. *A la fuerza ahorcan*, I [*o* you *o* he, etc.] have no choice *o* alternative. || *A viva fuerza*, by main *o* sheer force. || JUR. *Caso de fuerza mayor*, v. CASO. || *Con todas sus fuerzas*, with all of one's energy, with all one's might. || *De grado o por fuerza*, willy-nilly. || *Es fuerza confesarlo*, one must admit *o* confess. || *Es fuerza hacerlo*, it's necessary to do it. || *Fuerza bruta*, brute force. || *Fuerza de disuasión* or *disuasoria*, deterrent.

|| *Fuerza de la costumbre*, force of habit. || *Fuerza de sustentación*, lift (de un avión). || JUR. *Fuerza mayor*, force majeure, act of God. || *Fuerza pública*, police force. || *Fuerzas aéreas*, Air Force, *sing.* || *Fuerzas armadas*, armed forces. || *Fuerzas terrestres*, land forces. || *Hacer fuerza sobre* or *a uno para que*, to put pressure on s.o. to. || *La fuerza de la edad*, the prime of life. || *La fuerza de la sangre*, the call of blood. || *Por fuerza*, by force, forcibly (usando la fuerza), of necessity, perforce (necesariamente). || *Restar fuerzas a*, to weaken. || *Sacar fuerzas de flaqueza*, to muster up one's courage, to take one's courage in both hands. || *Sacar fuerzas para*, to find the energy to. || *Sentirse con fuerzas para*, to feel up to. || *Tener fuerzas para*, to have the strength to, to be strong enough to.

fuete m. *Amer.* Whip (látigo).

fuga f. Flight: *poner en fuga*, to put to flight; *darse a la fuga*, to take [to] flight. || Escape (evasión). || Elopement (de un hombre y una mujer). || Leak (de gas, etc.). || MÚS. Fugue. || FIG. Flight: *fuga de capitales*, flight of capital. | Ardour (impetuosidad). || — FIG. *Fuga de cerebros*, brain drain. || *Ponerse en fuga*, to flee, to take [to] flight.

fugacidad f. Fugacity.

fugarse v. pr. To escape, to flee: *fugarse de la cárcel*, to escape from jail. || To run away: *fugarse de casa*, to run away from home. || To elope (un hombre y una mujer).

fugaz adj. Fleeting, brief, transient, fugacious (p.us.). || *Estrella fugaz*, shooting star.

fugitivo, va adj. Fugitive, fleeing (que se fuga). || Fleeting, brief, transient, fugacious (p.us.) [fugaz]. || Fugitive (efímero).

— M. y f. Fugitive, runaway.

fuguillas m. y f. inv. FAM. Fidget.

fuina f. ZOOL. Stone *o* beech marten (garduña).

ful adj. FAM. Bogus, sham, phony (cosa). | Phony (persona). | Phony, sham (fiesta, recepción).

fulano, na m. y f. So-and-so, what's his name: *he visto a Fulano*, I have seen what's his name. || — *Don Fulano de Tal*, John Smith, Mr. So-and-So, Mr. what's his name. || *Ese fulano*, that fellow. || *Fulano, Mengano y Zutano*, Tom, Dick and Harry. || *Una fulana*, a whore, a tart (prostituta). || *Un fulano*, a fellow.

fular m. Foulard (tela y pañuelo para el cuello).

fulastre o **fulastrón, ona** adj. FAM. Rotten (malo). | Bungling (chapucero). | Slapdash, shoddy (mal hecho). | Poor-quality, shoddy (de poca calidad).

— M. y f. Bungler.

fulcro m. TECN. Fulcrum (de la palanca).

fulero adj. Bungling.

— M. y f. Bungler.

fulgente o **fúlgido, da** adj. Brilliant, resplendent.

fulgir v. intr. To shine, to glow (brillar). || To glitter, to sparkle (centellear).

fulgor m. Brilliance, shine, glow (brillo). || Glitter, sparkle (centelleo). || FIG. Splendour.

fulguración f. Brilliance, flash. || Fulguration (p.us.).

fulgurante adj. Flashing, shining, fulgurant, brilliant (luz). || Withering (mirada).

fulgurar v. intr. To flash (intermitentemente). || To shine, to glow (brillar). || To glitter, to sparkle (centellear).

fúlica f. Coot (ave).

fuliginoso, sa adj. Fuliginous, smoky, sooty.

fulmicotón m. Guncotton (algodón pólvora).

fulminación f. Fulmination (explosión). || Lightning stroke (por el rayo).

fulminado, da adj. Struck by lightning.

fulminador, ra adj. Fulminating.

fulminante adj. Fulminating: *pólvora fulminante*, fulminating powder. || MED. Fulminant: *apoplejía fulminante*, fulminant apoplexy. || FIG. Staggering (éxito). || FIG. *Mirada fulminante*, withering look.

— M. Fuse, detonator (mecha). || Cap (cápsula).

fulminar v. tr. To strike by lightning (matar por el rayo). || To hurl (bomba). || FIG. To thunder forth, to fulminate (excomuniones, amenazas). | To strike down: *fulminado por la enfermedad*, struck down by illness. || — FIG. *Fulminar con la mirada*, to cast a withering look at, to look daggers at. || *Morir fulminado*, to be struck by lightning.

— V. intr. To explode, to fulminate.

full m. Full house (en el póker).

fullear v. intr. To cheat (en los naipes).

fullerear v. intr. *Amer.* To gabble (farfullar). | To swank (presumir).

fullería f. Cardsharping, cheating (naipes). || Trick (trampa). || Guile (astucia). || *Hacer fullerías*, to cheat.

fullero, ra adj. Cheating, crooked.

— M. y f. Cardsharper [U.S., cardsharp], cheat.

fumable adj. Smokable. || FIG. y FAM. Acceptable.

fumada f. Puff (de humo).

fumadero m. Smoking room. || Smoking den (de opio, etc.).

fumador, ra adj. Smoking.

— M. y f. Smoker.

fumante adj. QUÍM. Fuming.

fumar v. tr. e intr. To smoke: *fumar en pipa*, to smoke a pipe. || — FAM. *Fumar como una chimenea*, to smoke like a chimney. || *Papel de fumar*, cigarette paper. || *Se prohibe fumar*, no smoking.

— V. pr. To smoke: *fumarse un pitillo*, to smoke a cigarette. || FAM. To squander (gastar): *fumarse la paga del mes*, to squander one's monthly salary. | *Fumarse una clase*, V. CLASE.

fumarada f. Puff of smoke (de humo). || Pipeful, pipe (de tabaco).

fumarola f. Fumarole.

fumigación f. Fumigation.

fumigador m. Fumigator.

fumigar v. tr. To fumigate.

fumigatorio, ria adj. Fumigatory.

— M. Perfume brazier.

fumígeno, na adj. Smoking, smoke-producing.

fumista m. Stove *o* heater repairman. || *Amer.* Joker (bromista).

fumistería f. Stove *o* heater shop (tienda). || Stove *o* heater repairing (oficio).

funambulesco, ca adj. Relating to ropedancing.

funámbulo, la m. y f. Tightrope walker, ropewalker, ropedancer, funambulist.

función f. Function: *la función de la fuerza pública*, the function of the police force. || Duty, function: *desempeñar las funciones de secretario*, to carry out secretarial duties. || ANAT. Function: *funciones del corazón*, functions of the heart. || TEATR. Perfomance, show (espectáculo). || REL. Religious ceremony, function. || Party (fiesta). || MAT., QUÍM. y GRAM. Function. || FAM. Scene: *armar una función*, to make a scene. || — *En función de*, in terms of. || *Entrar en funciones*, to take office, to take up one's duties. || *Estar en funciones*, to be in office. || *Función benéfica*, charity performance. || *Función de gala* or *de etiqueta*, gala performance. || *Función de la tarde*, matinée. || *Función de noche*, late performance. || *No hay función*, no performance (teatro, espectáculos, etc.). || *Presidente en funciones*, acting president.

funcional adj. Functional.

funcionamiento m. Functioning. || TECN. Operation, working, running (de motor, máquina). | Performance (cualidades técnicas). || — *Mal funcionamiento*, malfunction. || *Poner en funcionamiento*, to put into operation.

funcionar v. intr. To operate, to run, to work, to function: *está máquina funciona bien*, this machine operates well. || — *Hacer funcionar*, to operate, to work, to run. | *No funciona*, out of order (teléfono, ascensor, etc.).

funcionario, ria m. y f. Civil servant, official, functionary: *funcionario público*, public official.

funda f. Cover (de tela, plástico). || Case, slip (de almohadón, etc.). || Case (de violín, gafas, fusil). || Sheath (de puñal, espada, cable). || Cover (de un paraguas). || — *Funda de almohada*, pillowcase, pillowslip. || *Funda de arzón*, [saddle] holster.

fundación f. Foundation.

fundacional adj. Constituent: *acta fundacional*, constituent act.

fundadamente adv. With good reason.

fundado, da adj. Founded, well-founded, justified.

fundador, ra m. y f. Founder. || *Miembro fundador*, foundation member [U.S., charter member].

fundamentación f. Foundation.

fundamental adj. Fundamental.

fundamentalmente adv. Fundamentally, basically.

fundamentar v. tr. To found, to establish (establecer). || To lay the foundations of (sentar las bases de). || To base, to found (*en*, on).

— V. pr. To be based, to be founded: *esto se fundamenta en principios sólidos*, this is based on sound principles.

fundamento m. Foundation (de un edificio). || FIG. Foundation, basis, grounds, *pl.* (base). | Reason (razón). | Reliability (confianza). | Seriousness (seriedad). || *Sin fundamento*, unfounded, groundless.

fundar v. tr. To found (edificar). || To set up, to establish (crear). || FIG. To found, to base: *fundar sus sospechas en*, to base one's suspicions on.

— V. pr. To be based, to rest (estribar): *el arco se funda en los pilares*, the arch rests on the pillars. || FIG. To be based, to be founded (fundamentarse). | To base one's opinion: *¿en qué te fundas para decir esto?*, what do you base your opinion on?

fundente adj. Melting.

— M. Flux.

fundible adj. Fusible, easily melted.

fundición f. Melting (acción de fundir). || Smelting, casting (de los metales). || Cast iron (hierro colado). || Foundry, smelting works (lugar donde se funde). || IMPR. Fount, font (de letras). || TECN. *Fundición de acero*, steelworks.

fundido n. CINEM. Fade-in; fade-out.

fundidor m. Founder, smelter, caster (obrero).

fundir v. tr. To found, to cast (campana, cañón). || To smelt: *fundir hierro*, to smelt iron. || To melt (plomo, nieve). || To cast (vaciar una estatua). || To blend (colores). || To merge, to amalgamate (fusionar). || To unite, to join (unir). || ELECTR. To fuse (una bombilla, etc.).

— V. pr. To melt (volverse líquido). || To merge, to amalgamate (unirse). || To seize up (una biela). || To go, to burn out (bombilla). || To blow, to burn out (fusible). || To blend (colores). || *Amer.* FAM. To be ruined, to ruin o.s. (arruinarse).

fundo m. JUR. Piece of real estate, country estate (finca rústica).
fúnebre adj. Funeral: *canto fúnebre*, funeral chant. || FIG. Mournful, gloomy, funereal (triste). || — *Coche fúnebre*, hearse. || *Pompas fúnebres*, v. POMPA.
funeral adj. Funeral.
— M. Memorial service (en el aniversario). || Funeral (entierro). || — Pl. Funeral, *sing.* (exequias).
funerala (a la) loc. adv. With reversed arms, with arms inverted (fusiles). || FAM. *Ojo a la funerala*, black eye, shiner.
funerario, ria adj. Funerary.
— F. Undertaker's [U.S., funeral parlor]. || — M. Undertaker [U.S., mortician].
funesto, ta adj. Fatal, ill-fated: *un día funesto*, a fatal day. || Fatal, unfortunate: *una batalla funesta*, a fatal battle. || Disastrous, fatal: *consejo funesto*, disastrous advice. || Baneful: *influencia funesta*, baneful influence.
fungible adj. JUR. Fungible.
fungicida adj. Fungicidal.
— M. Fungicide.
fungir v. intr. *Amer.* To act.
fungo m. MED. Fungus.
fungosidad f. Fungosity.
fungoso, sa adj. Fungous.
funicular adj./s.m. Funicular (tren). || *Funicular aéreo*, cable car (teleférico).
furcia f. POP. Tart, whore (prostituta).
furgón m. Van, wagon. || Luggage van, goods wagon [U.S., boxcar] (de tren). || *Furgón de cola*, guard's van.
furgoneta f. Van. || *Furgoneta familiar*, station wagon, estate car.
furia f. Fury, rage: *hablar con furia*, to speak with fury. || Violence (violencia). || Frenzy (frenesí). || Fury: *la furia del mar*, the fury of the sea. || FIG. Fury (mujer enfadada). || — *Amer. A toda furia*, like fury. || *Estar hecho una furia*, to be in a fury *o* rage. || *Ponerse hecho una furia*, to become furious, to fly into a rage.
Furias n. pr. f. pl. MIT. Furies.
furibundo, da adj. Furious, enraged: *miradas furibundas*, furious looks. || *Batalla furibunda*, furious battle, raging battle.
furiosamente adv. Furiously.
furioso, sa adj. Furious. || FIG. Furious, raging: *viento furioso*, furious wind. | Tremendous, enormous: *un gasto furioso*, a tremendous expense. || *Ponerse furioso*, to become *o* to get furious *o* livid.
furor m. Fury, rage: *gritar con furor*, to scream with rage. || FIG. Furor, ardour [U.S., ardor]: *el furor de la juventud*, the furor of youth. | Fever: *el furor del juego*, gambling fever. || — *Con furor*, madly, ardently. || *Furor uterino*, nymphomania. || FIG. *Hacer furor*, to be all the rage.
furriel m. Quartermaster.
furtivo, va adj. Furtive, sly, stealthy: *mirada furtiva*, furtive look. || — *Caza* or *pesca furtiva*, poaching. || *Cazador* or *pescador furtivo*, poacher.
furúnculo m. MED. Furuncle, boil.
furunculosis f. MED. Furunculosis.
fusa f. MÚS. Demisemiquaver.
fuselaje m. AVIAC. Fuselage.
fusibilidad f. Fusibility.
fusible adj. Fusible.
— M. Fuse (electricidad).
fusil m. Gun, rifle. || — *Echarse el fusil a la cara* or *encararse el fusil*, to aim one's rifle, to put one's rifle to one's shoulder. || *Fusil ametrallador*, automatic rifle. || *Fusil con alza automática*, rifle with automatic sight. || *Fusil de aguja, de chispa*, needle gun, flintlock. || *Fusil de repetición*, repeater, magazine rifle.
fusilamiento m. Execution, shooting. || FIG. Plagiarism (plagio). || *Fusilamiento en masa*, mass execution.
fusilar v. tr. To execute [by shooting], to shoot. || FAM. To plagiarize (plagiar).
fusilería f. Rifles, *pl.* (fusiles). || Fusiliers, *pl.* (fusileros). || *Descarga* or *fuego de fusilería*, fusillade.
fusilero m. Fusilier, fusileer, rifleman.
fusión f. Fusion, melting (de los metales). || Melting, thawing (de la nieve). || Merger, amalgamation (de sociedades).
fusionamiento m. Merger, amalgamation.
fusionar v. tr. To fuse (unir). || COM. To merge, to amalgamate (varias sociedades).
— V. pr. To fuse. || COM. To merge, to amalgamate: *los bancos se han fusionado*, the banks have merged.
fusta f. Brushwood, twigs, *pl.* (varas). || Riding whip (látigo).
fustán m. Fustian (tela). || *Amer.* White petticoat (enaguas blancas).
fuste m. Shaft (de lanza). || Saddletree (de la silla de montar). || ARQ. Shaft. || Wood, timber (madera). || FIG. Importance, consequence: *negocio de poco fuste*, business of little importance. | Substance, essence (fundamento). || *Gente de fuste*, important people, people of consequence.
fustigación f. Whipping, lashing. || FIG. Sharp reprimand, censure (censura).
fustigar v. tr. To whip, to lash. || FIG. To reprimand sharply, to censure.
fútbol m. DEP. Football, soccer.
futbolín m. Table football (juego de mesa).
futbolista m. Footballer, football *o* soccer player.
futbolístico, ca adj. Football: *un torneo futbolístico*, a football tournament.
futesa f. FAM. Trifle.
fútil adj. Futile, trivial, pointless, trifling: *hablar de cosas fútiles*, to talk about futile things.
futileza f. V. FUTILIDAD.
futilidad f. Futility, triviality (falta de sustancia): *la futilidad de una conversación*, the futility of a conversation. || Frivolity (de una persona). || Worthlessness (inutilidad): *la futilidad del argumento*, the worthlessness of the argument. || Triviality, trifle (cosa insustancial). || *Hablar de futilidades*, to talk trivia, to talk piffle.
futre m. *Amer.* FAM. Dandy, toff, fop.
futura f. FAM. Bride-to-be, intended, fiancée (novia).
futurismo m. Futurism.
futurista adj. Futuristic.
— M. y f. Futurist.
futuro, ra adj. Future. || — *En lo futuro*, in [the] future. || *En los años futuros*, in the years to come. || *La vida futura*, the life to come.
— M. Future. || FAM. Intended, fiancé (novio). || — Pl. COM. Futures (entregas a plazo). || — *En un futuro próximo*, in the [very] near future. || GRAM. *Futuro imperfecto*, future. | *Futuro perfecto* or *anterior*, future perfect.

G

g f. G: *una g minúscula*, a small g.
— OBSERV. Followed by *e* or *i*, the *g* is pronounced as the Spanish *j*. Followed by a consonant or *a*, *o*, *u*, it is similar in sound to the hard English *g*, as in *gun*.
gabacho, cha adj./s. [French] Pyrenean (montañés de los Pirineos franceses). || FAM. Frog, froggy, Frenchy. || — Adj. Feather-legged (paloma). || — M. FAM. Frenchified Spanish [language].
gabán m. Overcoat, topcoat.
gabardina f. Gabardine (tela). || Gabardine raincoat (impermeable hecho con esta tela). || Mac, mackintosh, raincoat (impermeable en general).
gabarra f. Barge, lighter (embarcación).
gabarrero m. Bargee, lighterman [U.S., bargeman].
gabarro m. Flaw (defecto de un tejido). || Nodule (nódulo). || VET. Tumour [U.S., tumor] (del caballo). | Pip (pepita de las gallinas). || FIG. Error, mistake.
gabazo m. Husks, *pl.*
gabela f. Tax, duty (impuesto). || FIG. Burden. || *Amer.* Advantage (ventaja).
gabinete m. Study (para recibir visitas). || Room (sala): *gabinete de lectura*, reading room. || Section (conjunto de salas): *gabinete de historia natural*, natural history section. || Museum (museo). || Laboratory (laboratorio). || Consulting room (de médico). || Boudoir (de una señora). || Cabinet (de ministros). || FIG. *Estrategas de gabinete*, armchair strategists.
gablete m. ARQ. Gable.
Gabón n. pr. m. GEOGR. Gabon.
Gabriel, ela n. pr. m. y f. Gabriel, Gabriella.
gabrieles m. pl. FAM. Chick-peas (garbanzos).
gacela f. ZOOL. Gazelle.

gaceta f. Gazette (periódico). || (Ant.). Official gazette [in Spain]. || FIG. Gossip, gossipmonger (correveidile). || TECN. Sagger. || FIG. y FAM. *Mentir más que la gaceta*, to lie one's head off (una persona), to be a pack of lies: *este libro miente más que la gaceta*, this book is a pack of lies.
gacetero m. Gazette writer, newspaper writer, journalist (periodista).
gacetilla f. Gossip column (noticias sobre personas conocidas). || Section of short news items (noticias breves). || FIG. Gossip, gossipmonger (correveidile).
gacetillero m. Writer of short news items, gossip columnist (escritor de gacetillas). || Newshound (reportero).
gacetista m. FAM. Avid gazette reader.
gacha f. Porridge, pap (papilla). || FIG. Paste, mush (masa blanda). || *Amer.* Bowl, basin. || — Pl. Porridge, *sing.*, pap, *sing.* (papilla). || FAM. Cajolery, *sing.*, blandishments. || FIG. y FAM. *Hacerse unas gachas*, to get mushy.
gaché o **gachó** m. Name given by gypsies to Andalusians. || FAM. Bloke, guy, fellow: *un gachó poco recomendable*, not a very recommendable bloke.
gacheta f. TECN. Spring catch (de cerradura).
gachí f. FAM. Bird, chick (mujer, muchacha).

— OBSERV. Pl. *gachís*.

gacho, cha adj. Bowed (la cabeza). || Drooping (orejas de un animal): *el cócker tiene las orejas gachas*, the cocker spaniel has drooping ears. || Downturned (cuerno). || With downturned horns (buey o vaca). || Which tends to hold its head too low (caballo). || — *A gachas*, on all fours. || *Sombrero gacho*, slouch hat. || FIG. y FAM. *Volver con las orejas gachas*, to return with one's tail between one's legs.
gachó m. V. GACHÉ.
gachón, ona adj. FAM. Sweet, charming, nice (atractivo). | Spoilt, spoiled (mimado).
— F. FAM. Bird, chick (mujer). || — M. pl. Blokes, guys, fellows (gachós).
gachumbo m. *Amer.* Shell (cáscara del coco).
gachupín m. *Amer.* Spanish immigrant [living in South America]. | Spaniard (español).
gádido, da adj./s.m. Gadid, gadoid.
gaditano, na adj. Gaditan, of *o* from Cádiz.
— M. y f. Gaditan, native *o* inhabitant of Cádiz.
gadolinio m. Gadolinium (metal).
gaélico, ca adj. Gaelic (céltico).
— M. y f. Gael. || — M. Gaelic (lengua).
gafa f. MAR. Hook (garfio). || Clamp (grapa). || — Pl. Glasses, spectacles (anteojos): *llevar gafas de oro*, to wear gold-framed spectacles; *calarse las gafas*, to put on one's glasses. || Goggles (submarinas, de motorista). || — *Gafas bifocales*, bifocals, bifocal spectacles. || *Gafas de sol*, sunglasses.
gafar v. tr. To hook, to seize with a hook (con un gancho), to grasp with the nails (con las uñas) to grasp with the claws (un animal). || MAR. To hook. || FAM. To bring [s.o.] bad luck, to bring bad luck upon, to jinx (a una persona). | To bring bad luck upon, to jinx: *gafar las cartas a alguien*, to jinx s.o.'s cards.
gafe m. FAM. Jinx. || FAM. *Ser gafe*, to be a jinx, to bring *o* to be bad luck (para otras personas), to be jinxed, to have bad luck (para sí mismo).
gafedad f. Claw hand. || Leprosy causing claw hand (lepra).
gafete m. Hook and eye.
gafo, fa adj. Claw-handed. || Leprous (leproso). || *Amer.* Footsore (caballerías).
gag m. Comic situation, gag (situación cómica).
gaita f. MÚS. Bagpipes, *pl.*, bagpipe (gallega), Breton bagpipes, *pl.*, Breton pipes, *pl.* (en Bretaña). | Flageolet [type of chirimía] (flauta). | Hurdy-gurdy (zanfonía). || FIG. y FAM. Neck (pescuezo): *estirar la gaita*, to crane one's neck. | Nuisance, drag, bother: *es una gaita tener que escribir esta carta*, it's a nuisance having to write this letter. | Job, right game: *aparcar allí es una gaita*, it's a right game parking there. || — *Alegre como una gaita*, as happy as a lark, chirpy as a cricket. || FAM. *No me vengas con gaitas*, don't bother me with all that. | *Templar gaitas*, to pour oil on troubled waters, to smooth things out.
gaitero, ra adj. FAM. Gaudy, loud, flashy (vestido). | Buffoonish, clownish (bufo).
— M. y f. Buffoon, clown (bufo). || MÚS. Bagpiper, piper.
gajes m. pl. Emoluments, remuneration, *sing.* (salario). || FAM. *Los gajes del oficio*, the occupational hazards.
gajo m. Branch, broken-off branch (rama). || Small bunch *o* cluster (de frutas). || Segment (de naranja, limón). || Prong, tine (de horcas, bieldos, etc.).
gal m. FÍS. Gal (unidad de aceleración).
gala f. Best clothes, *pl.*, Sunday best (vestido). || Elegance, grace, poise, gracefulness (garbo). || Flower, jewel, pride: *la gala del pueblo*, the flower of the village || Cream, flower: *la gala de la sociedad*, the cream of society. || *Amer.* Tip (propina). || — Pl. Finery, *sing.*, regalia (vestidos), jewellery, *sing.* (joyas), decorations, regalia (condecoraciones). || Wedding presents (regalos de boda). || — MIL. *Con traje* or *uniforme de gala*, in full-dress uniform, in dress uniform, in ceremonial dress, in full regimentals. || *Estar en traje de gala*, to be in full dress. || *Función, baile de gala*, gala performance, gala ball. || *Galas de novia*, bridal attire. || *Hacer gala de*, to glory in, to take pride in (gloriarse), to make a show of, to show off: *hacer gala de sus riquezas*, to make a show of one's wealth; to show, to display: *hacer gala de una gran habilidad*, to show great skill. || *La ciudad está de gala*, the town is bedecked (adornada). || *Tener a gala*, to pride o.s. on: *tiene a gala hacerlo todo por sí mismo*, he prides himself on doing it all by himself.
galáctico, ca adj. ASTR. Galactic.
galactómetro m. Lactometer.
galactosa f. QUÍM. Galactose.
galalita f. Galalith.
galaico, ca adj. Galician (gallego).
galán m. Gallant, beau (galante), lover (enamorado). || Suitor (pretendiente). || Handsome man, handsome young man (apuesto, bien parecido). || TEATR. Leading man, lead. || — BOT. *Galán de día, de noche*, day, night jasmine. || TEATR. *Galán joven*, juvenile lead [U.S., juvenile]. | *Segundo galán*, second lead.
galancete m. Handsome young man. || TEATR. Juvenile lead [U.S., juvenile].
galanía f. Elegance (galanura).
galano, na adj. Smartly-dressed, smart, spruce (bien vestido). || Elegant, nicely-turned (frase), elegant, polished (estilo). || Good-looking (de hermoso aspecto). || *Amer.* Mottled (una vaca).
galante adj. Gallant [attentive to women]. || Polite (cortés). || Flirtatious, fond of male attention (que gusta de galanteos), loose, licentious (de costumbres licenciosas).
galantear v. tr. To pay compliments to, to say flattering *o* nice things to (requebrar). || To flirt with (coquetear). || To court, to woo (cortejar).
galanteo m. Flattery (requiebro). || Flirting, flirtation (coqueteo). || Courting, wooing (cortejo).
galantería f. Gallantry (caballerosidad). || Politeness (cortesía). || Gallantry, compliment (expresión obsequiosa), gallant deed, act of gallantry (hecho). || Elegance (elegancia). || Generosity (generosidad).
galantina f. CULIN. Galantine.
galanura f. Elegance (de estilo, de concepto). || Gracefulness, elegance (al andar). || *Vestir con galanura*, to dress elegantly.
galapagar m. Place full of turtles.
galápago m. Turtle (tortuga). || MIL. Testudo, tortoise. || Slade, sole (del arado). || TECN. Ingot, pig (lingote). | Tile mould (para tejas). || MED. Bandage (vendaje). || Light saddle (silla de montar). || VET. Grease *o* greasy heel (úlcera del caballo). || MAR. Cleat.
Galápagos (Islas) f. pl. GEOGR. Galápagos Islands.
galardón m. Reward.
galardonado, da adj. [Who has been] rewarded. || Prizewinning, who has won a prize.
— M. y f. Prizewinner.
galardonar v. tr. To reward (recompensar). || To award a prize to: *ha sido galardonado por su novela*, he has been awarded a prize for his novel. || *Galardonar con una medalla*, to award a medal to.
galaxia f. ASTR. Galaxy.
galbana f. FAM. Laziness, sloth, slackness (pereza).
galdosiano, na adj. Of Pérez Galdós.
galeaza f. MAR. Galleass, galliass.
galena f. MIN. Galena, lead sulphide [U.S., lead sulfide].
galeno, na adj. MAR. Gentle, soft (viento).
— M. FAM. Quack [U.S., medic] (médico).
galeón m. MAR. Galleon (barco).
galeota f. Galliot (barco).
galeote m. Galley slave (forzado).
galeoto n. Pimp, procurer (alcahuete).

— OBSERV. This word, taken from a play by Echegaray, *El gran Galeoto*, has no connection with *galeote*.

galera f. MAR. Galley. || Four-wheeled covered wagon (carro). || Ward (crujía de hospital). || Women's prison (cárcel). || MAT. Two perpendicular lines separating divisor from dividend in a division. || IMPR. Galley. | Galley, galley proof (prueba). || MIN. Crucible furnace. || ZOOL. Squilla. || *Amer.* Top hat (sombrero). | Shed (cobertizo). || — Pl. Galleys (condena): *condenar a galeras*, to condemn to the galleys.
galerada f. Wagonload (carga). || IMPR. Galley, galley proof (prueba).
galería f. Gallery (en una casa, de pinturas, de mina, militar). || TEATR. Gallery (localidades, público). || MAR. Stern gallery (de popa). || Pelmet, valance (para cortinajes). || FIG. Gallery: *para la galería*, to the gallery. || *Galería de tiro*, shooting gallery.
galerín m. IMPR. Small galley.
galerna f. MAR. Strong north-west wind (viento).
galerón m. *Amer.* Shed (cobertizo). | Popular song and dance [in Venezuela].
Gales n. pr. GEOGR. Wales. || *El País de Gales*, Wales.
galés, esa adj. Welsh.
— M. y f. Welshman (hombre), Welshwoman (mujer). || — M. Welsh (lengua). || *Los galeses*, the Welsh.
galga f. Boulder (piedra). || Strap (cinta del zapato). || Millstone (del molino). || MED. Rash (erupción

cutánea). || TECN. Hub brake [which presses on waggon axle] (freno). | Gauge (calibrador).
galgo, ga m. y f. ZOOL. Greyhound (perro). || — FIG. *Correr como un galgo*, to run like a hare. | *De casta le viene al galgo el ser rabilargo*, like father, like son. || FAM. *¡Échale un galgo!*, some hopes!
— Adj. *Amer.* Sweet-toothed (goloso).
Galia n. pr. f. HIST. Gaul.
galibar v. tr. MAR. To trace [using a template].
gálibo m. TECN. Gauge (galga). || MAR. Template, templet, pattern. || ARQ. Perfect proportion.
galicado, da adj. Full of Gallicisms, gallicized.
galicanismo m. Gallicanism.
galicano, na adj. Gallic (de los galos). || Gallican (adepto al galicanismo).
Galicia n. pr. f. GEOGR. Galicia [Spain].
galicismo m. Gallicism.
galicista adj. Fond of using Gallicisms.
— M. y f. Lover of Gallicisms, person fond of using Gallicisms.
gálico, ca adj. Gallic (de los galos). || QUÍM. Gallic.
— M. MED. Syphilis.
Galilea n. pr. f. GEOGR. Galilee.
galileo, a adj./s. Galilean (de Galilea).
galillo m. ANAT. Uvula.
galimatías m. FAM. Gibberish, nonsense.
galio m. Gallium (metal).
galiparla f. Language full of Gallicisms.
galiparlista m. y f. Person who uses many Gallicisms.
galipote m. MAR. Galipot, gallipot.
Galitzia n. pr. f. GEOGR. Galicia (Polonia).
galo, la adj. HIST. Gallic.
— M. y f. Gaul.
galocha f. Wooden *o* iron clog (calzado).
galón m. Braid (cinta). || MIL. Stripe. || Gallon (medida).
galonear v. tr. To trim with braid, to braid.
galonista m. Outstanding pupil in a military academy.
galop m Galop (baile). || *Bailar el galop*, to galop.
galopada f. Gallop.
galopante adj. Galloping. || MED. Galloping.
galopar v. intr. To gallop.
galope m. Gallop: *galope sostenido* or *medio galope*, hand gallop. || — *A* or *de galope*, at a gallop (un caballo), quickly, speedily, in a rush (muy rápidamente). || *A galope tendido*, at full gallop (un caballo), at full speed, with utmost haste (muy rápidamente). || *Ir a* or *de galope*, to gallop.
galopear v. intr. To gallop (galopar).
galopín m. Ragamuffin, urchin (niño). || Rogue (bribón). || MAR. Ship's boy, cabin boy.
galorromano, na adj. Gallo-Roman.
galpón m. *Amer.* Shed (cobertizo). | (Ant.). Slaves' quarters (*pl.*) on a "hacienda".
galucha f. *Amer.* Gallop (galope).
galuchar v. intr. *Amer.* To gallop (galopar).
galvánico, ca adj. FÍS. Galvanic.
galvanismo m. FÍS. Galvanism.
galvanización f. FÍS. Galvanization.
galvanizar v. tr. FÍS. To galvanize. || FIG. To galvanize.
galvano m. Electrotype.
galvanocauterio m. MED. Galvanocautery.
galvanómetro m. FÍS. Galvanometer.
galvanoplastia f. Galvanoplasty, galvanoplastics.
galvanoplástico, ca adj. Galvanoplastic.
galvanotipar v. tr. To electrotype.
galvanotipia f. Electrotyping.
galladura f. Cicatricle (del huevo).
gallarda f. Galliard (danza). || IMPR. Brevier (carácter).
gallardamente adv. Elegantly, gracefully (airosamente). || Gallantly, valiantly, bravely (con valentía). || Nobly (con nobleza).
gallardear v. intr. To strut (pavonearse).
gallardete m. Pennant.
gallardía f. Elegance, poise, gracefulness (bizarría). || Gallantry, valour, bravery (valor). || Nobleness (nobleza).
gallardo, da adj. Elegant, charming, debonair (airoso). || Gallant, valiant, brave (valeroso). || Noble (noble). || FIG. Excellent (excelente).
gallareta f. ZOOL. Coot.
gallarón m. ZOOL. Little bustard (sisón).
gallear v. tr. To tread (el gallo).
— V. intr. FIG. y FAM. To show off (presumir). | To brag (fanfarronear). | To strut (pavonearse). || TECN. To flaw [on cooling] (metales).
gallegada f. Word *o* phrase *o* action typical of a Galician. || Galician dance (baile).
gallego, ga adj./s. Galician (de Galicia). || — M. Galician (lengua). || *Amer.* Dago (español).
galleguismo m. Galician word *o* expression *o* idiom.
galleo m. TECN. Flaw (de un metal fundido). || TAUR. Swerve [of the body to avoid the bull's horns]. || FIG. Showing off (presunción). | Bragging (jactancia).
gallera o **gallería** f. *Amer.* Cockpit, cockfight arena.
galleta f. CULIN. Biscuit (bizcocho). | Ship's biscuit, hardtack (de marinero). || FAM. Slap (bofetada). || Nuts, *pl.* (carbón). || *Amer.* Recipient for drinking maté. | Brown bread (pan). || *Amer.* FAM. *Colgar la galleta*, to sack, to fire (despedir).
gallina f. Hen, chicken (ave). || — FIG. *Acostarse con las gallinas*, to go to bed early. || *Caldo de gallina*, chicken broth. || FIG. *Dar con la gallina que pone los huevos de oro*, to find the goose that lays the golden eggs. | *En casa de Gonzalo más puede la gallina que el gallo*, the wife wears the trousers in that house. | *Estar como gallina en corral ajeno*, to be like a fish out of water. | *Gallina ciega*, blindman's buff (juego). || *Gallina clueca*, broody hen. || *Gallina de agua*, coot (foja), moorhen (polla de agua). || *Gallina de Guinea*, Guinea fowl. || *Gallina de río*, coot. || *Gallina ponedora*, layer, laying hen. || *Gallina sorda*, woodcock. || FIG. *Gallina vieja da buen caldo*, V. CALDO. | *Matar la gallina de los huevos de oro*, to kill the goose that lays the golden eggs.
— M. y f. FIG. y FAM. Coward, chicken. || *Es un gallina*, he wouldn't say boo to a goose.
gallináceo, a adj. ZOOL. Gallinaceous.
— F. Gallinacean. || — Pl. Gallinaceae.
gallinaza f. Turkey buzzard (gallinazo). || Hen droppings, *pl.* (estiércol).
gallinazo m. Turkey buzzard (buitre de América).
gallinería f. Hens, *pl.* (conjunto de gallinas). || Poultry shop (tienda). || FIG. Cowardice (cobardía).
gallinero m. Henhouse, henroost, coop (recinto para aves de corral). || Poulterer, poultry dealer (vendedor de gallinas). || Hen basket, poultry basket (cesto para transportar). || TEATR. Gods, *pl.* || FIG. Madhouse (sitio ruidoso). || — FIG. y FAM. *Dejar a uno como palo de gallinero*, to drag s.o. through the mud. | *Más sucio que el palo de un gallinero*, V. SUCIO.
gallineta f. ZOOL. Coot (fúlica). | Woodcock (chocha). || *Amer.* Guinea fowl (pintada).
gallito m. ZOOL. Cockerel, young cock. || *Amer.* Cock of the rock (gallito de roca). | Dart (rehilete). || — FIG. *Gallito de pueblo*, cock of the walk. || *Gallito del rey*, wrasse (budión).
gallo m. ZOOL. Cock, rooster (ave). | John dory, dory (pez). || FIG. y FAM. Squawk (nota falsa): *soltar un gallo*, to let out a squawk. | Boss (el que manda). | Cock of the walk (persona mandona). | Cocky person (presumid bravucón). || POP. Spit, phlegm (esputo). || — FAM. *Alzar el gallo*, to get on one's high horse. | *En menos que canta un gallo*, in a flash, before you can say Jack Robinson. || *Entre gallos y media noche*, at an unearthly time. || *Gallo de monte* or *gallo silvestre*, cock of the wood, capercaillie (urogallo). || FIG. *Gallo de pueblo*, cock of the walk. || *Gallo de riña* or *de pelea*, gamecock, fighting cock. || *Gallo de roca*, cock of the rock. || *Misa del gallo*, midnight Mass. || FIG. *Otro gallo cantara*, it would have been quite different. || DEP. *Peso gallo*, bantamweight (boxeo), || FAM. *Ser engreído como gallo de cortijo*, to be too big for one's boots. || *Amer.* *Ser muy gallo*, to be very courageous.
gallofero, ra o **gallofo, fa** m. y f. Beggar (pordiosero). || Vagabond, tramp (vagabundo).
gallón m. Clod (terrón), piece of turf (de césped). || ARQ. Ovolo (ornamento).
gallup m. Gallup poll (sondeo de la opinión pública).
gama f. ZOOL. Doe (hembra del gamo). || MÚS. Scale (escala): *hacer gamas en el piano*, to play scales on the piano. || FIG. Range, scale, gamut (serie).
gamada adj. f. *Cruz gamada*, swastika, gammadion, gammation, fylfot.
gamarra f. Martingale (correa).
gamba f. Variety of prawn.
gamberrada f. Act of hooliganism, piece of loutish behaviour. || Act of vandalism (vandalismo).
gamberrear v. intr. To act like a hooligan, to behave loutishly.
gamberrismo m. Hooliganism, vandalism: *ola de gamberrismo*, wave of vandalism. || Libertinism, dissolution (libertinaje).
gamberro, rra adj. Loutish (mal educado, grosero). || Vandalistic (vandálico). || Rakish, dissolute (libertino).
— M. y f. Hooligan, lout (golfo). || Vandal (vándalo). || Libertine (libertino). || — F. Tart, whore (ramera).
gambeta f. Cross step (en la danza). || Curvet (corveta). || DEP. Dribble. || *Amer.* Dodge (esguince). | Excuse (excusa).
gambetear v. intr. To cross-step (en la danza). || To curvet (caballo). || DEP. To dribble.
gambeteo m. DEP. Dribbling.
gambito m. Gambit (en el ajedrez).
gamella f. Half of the yoke [on each ox's neck]. || Feeding trough (artesa).
gameto m. BIOL. Gamete.
gamezno m. ZOOL. Fawn (cría del gamo).
gamma m. Gamma (letra griega). || FÍS. *Rayos gamma*, gamma rays.
gamo m. ZOOL. Fallow deer, buck. || FIG. *Correr como un gamo*, to run like a hare.
gamón m. BOT. Asphodel.
gamonal m. Asphodel field. || *Amer.* Cacique, chief.
gamonalismo m. *Amer.* Caciquism.
gamopétalo, la adj. BOT. Gamopetalous.
gamosépalo, la adj. BOT. Gamosepalous.
gamusino m. Imaginary animal [invented by hunters to hoax novices].
gamuza f. Pyrenean chamois, izard (animal). || Chamois (piel). || Duster (trapo).
gamuzado, da adj. Chamois-coloured, buff-coloured.
gana f. Desire, wish, (deseo): *la gana* or *las ganas de bañarse en el mar*, the desire to go for a swim in the sea. || Longing (vivo deseo). || — Pl. Appetite, *sing.*,

hunger, *sing.* (hambre). || — *Abrir las ganas a*, to give an appetite to, to make hungry. || *Comer con ganas*, to eat heartily. || *Comer sin ganas*, to pick at one's food, to eat without appetite. || *Como te dé la gana*, just as you wish. || *Darle ganas a uno de*, to like to, to feel like: *me dan ganas de bailar*, I feel like dancing, I'd like to dance. || *De buena gana*, with pleasure, willingly (con gusto), willingly (con buena voluntad). || *De buena o mala gana*, like it or not. || *De mala gana*, reluctantly, unwillingly. || *Amer. Es gana*, it's impossible, there's no chance. || *Ganas locas*, wild desire, mad urge. || *Hace lo que le da la gana*, he does just what he likes. || *Hacer algo con poca gana*, to do sth. reluctantly. || *Le dieron ganas de saltar*, he felt like leaping about, he could have leaped about. || FAM. *Lo haré cuando me dé la real gana*, I'll do it when I feel like it *o* when I want to. || *Me dejaron* or *me quedé con las ganas*, I had to go without *o* to do without, I just had to forget the idea, I didn't get what I wanted. || *Morirse de ganas de*, to be dying to. || *No me da la gana*, I don't feel like it, I don't want to. || *Quitar las ganas*, to stop [s.o.'s] wanting, to make [s.o.] stop wanting: *el accidente me ha quitado las ganas de comprar un coche*, the accident has stopped my wanting to buy a car; to take away *o* to spoil the appetite (quitar el hambre). || *Tener ganas de*, to be longing to, to want (anhelar, desear): *tengo ganas de verte*, I'm longing to see you; to feel like, to fancy (apetecer): *tengo ganas de comer un pastel*, I feel like eating a cake; to have a mind to: *tengo ganas de decirle lo que pienso de él*, I have a mind to tell him what I think of him. || FIG. *Tenerle ganas a uno*, to bear a grudge against s.o. || *Tener muchas ganas* or *unas ganas locas de*, to really fancy, to really feel like: *tengo unas ganas locas de ir al teatro*, I really fancy going to the theatre. || *Tener pocas ganas de*, not to really want to (con infinitivo), not to really feel like (con gerundio).

ganadería f. Cattle raising, stockbreeding (cría del ganado). || Stock farm, cattle farm (sitio donde se cría). || Strain, breed (raza): *ganadería de toros de lidia*, strain of fighting bulls. || Cattle, livestock (ganado).

ganadero, ra adj. Cattle, cattle-raising, stockbreeding: *región ganadera*, cattle-raising region. || Cattle, livestock. (del ganado).
— M. y f. Cattle raiser, stockbreeder, stock farmer.

ganado m. Cattle, livestock, stock (en general): *ganado en pie*, cattle on the hoof; *cabeza de ganado*, head of cattle. || Hive, hiveful (de abejas). || FIG. y FAM. Crowd, people (gente). || — *Ganado caballar*, horses, *pl.* || *Ganado cabrío*, goats, *pl.* || *Ganado de cerda* or *moreno* or *porcino*, pigs, *pl.* || *Ganado de engorde*, fattening livestock. || FIG. *Ganado humano*, [human] chattels (esclavos). || *Ganado lanar*, sheep. || *Ganado mayor*, bovine cattle, horses and mules. || *Ganado menor*, sheep, goats and pigs. || *Ganado ovino*, sheep. || *Ganado vacuno*, cattle, bovine cattle.

ganador, ra adj. Winning.
— M. y f. Winner. || *Jugar a ganador*, to bet [on a horse] to win.

ganancia f. Gain, profit (beneficio): *obtener ganancia*, to make a profit. || *Amer.* Bonus, extra (adehala). || — Pl. Earnings: *compré un coche con las ganancias del año pasado*, I bought a car on last year's earnings. || Winnings (en el juego, etc.). || — FAM. *No le arriendo la ganancia*, I wouldn't like to be in his shoes, rather him than me, I don't envy him. || COM. *Pérdidas y ganancias*, profit and loss.

ganancial adj. JUR. *Bienes gananciales*, V. BIEN.

ganancioso, sa adj. Lucrative, profitable (lucrativo). || Gainful (que produce ganancia). || Winning (ganador). || *Salir ganancioso*, to end up with a profit, to come out better off (salir ganando), to be the winner (vencer).
— M. y f. Winner.

ganapán m. Casual odd-jobber, casual odd-jobman. || Porter (que lleva cargas). || Messenger (recadero).

ganapierde m. Giveaway (juego de damas).

ganar v. tr. To earn, to make, to get: *ganar con que vivir*, to earn enough to live on; *gana mucho dinero*, he earns a lot of money. || To win (una apuesta, una batalla, una carrera, un pleito, un premio). || To win, to gain (la estima, la fama). || To beat, to defeat (vencer): *ganar a uno al ajedrez*, to beat s.o. at chess. || To surpass (superar): *ganar a uno en inteligencia*, to surpass s.o. in intelligence. || To outstrip (aventajar, adelantar). || To reach, to arrive at (alcanzar): *ganar la meta en segundo lugar*, to reach the finish in second position. || MIL. To take, to capture: *ganar a los romanos la ciudad*, to take the city from the Romans. || To win over: *ganar a uno para la causa*, to win s.o. over to the cause. || To get, to obtain, to win: *ganar el apoyo del gobierno*, to obtain the support of the government. || To reclaim (tierras). || — FIG. y FAM. *¡A idiota no hay quien te gane!*, you're a prize idiot! || *Ganar el premio gordo*, to win the first prize. || FIG. *Ganar la partida a uno* or *ganarle a uno por la mano*, to beat s.o. to it. || *Ganarle a uno en fuerza*, to be stronger than s.o. || *Ganar terreno*, to gain ground: *con la campaña publicitaria hemos ganado mucho terreno*, we have gained a lot of ground with the advertising campaign; to gain, to gain ground: *el corredor ganó terreno a su rival*, the runner gained on his rival. || *Ganar tiempo*, to gain time. || *Le gané cinco libras al póker*, I won five pounds from him at poker. || *No hay quien le gane a Pedro al ajedrez*, Peter has no equal at chess, there's no one to touch Peter at chess. || *Nunca me dejo ganar por el pesimismo*, I never let pessimism get the better of me. || *Pedro le gana a Juan estudiando*, Peter is a better student than John.
— V. intr. To improve (mejorar): *ganar en salud*, to improve in health. || To win (vencer): *ganar por un largo*, to win by a length. || To earn: *ganar bien*, to earn well. || — *Gana con el trato*, he's quite nice once you get to know him. || *Ganar en peso*, to put on *o* to gain weight. || DEP. *Ir ganando*, to lead, to be winning: *ir ganando por tres a uno*, to lead *o* to be leading *o* winning three-one. || FIG. *Llevar las de ganar*, V. LLEVAR. | *Salir ganando*, to come out better off, to come out ahead.
— V. pr. To earn: *ganarse la vida*, to earn one's living *o* one's livelihood. || To earn o.s., to earn: *me gané mil pesetas*, I earned myself a thousand pesetas. || To deserve (merecer): *se lo ha ganado*, he deserved it. || To win, to gain, to earn: *ganarse el respeto de todos*, to gain everyone's respect. || To bring upon o.s., to incur: *ganarse el desprecio general, un castigo*, to bring general disdain upon o.s., to incur a punishment. || — FIG. y FAM. *Ganarse una bofetada* or *una torta*, to get a slap in the face. || FAM. *Hay que ganarse el puchero*, a man must earn a living. | *¡La que se va a ganar!*, he's going to cop it! || *¡Se lo ha ganado a pulso!*, he's earned it!

ganchero m. Raftsman (el que guía los maderos).

ganchete m. *Amer. A medio ganchete*, half. | *De ganchete*, arm in arm. | *De medio ganchete*, about *o* ready to fall (a punto de caer).

ganchillo m. Crochet hook (aguja de gancho para labores). || Crochet, crochet work (labor). || Hairpin (horquilla). || — *Hacer ganchillo*, to crochet.

gancho m. Hook, crook (instrumento corvo). || Hook, hanger (para colgar). || Hook (de carnicero). || Crochet, crochet work (crochet). || Crook (cayado). || Snag (de una rama que se rompe), stub (rama cortada). || DEP. Hook (boxeo). || FIG. y FAM. Enticer, coaxer (el que convence a otro). | Decoy (asistente de charlatán). | Pimp, procurer (alcahuete). | Sex appeal, attractiveness: *mujer que tiene gancho*, woman who has sex appeal. || *Amer.* Hairpin (horquilla). | Lady's saddle (silla de montar). | Help, aid (auxilio). || — FAM. *Echar el gancho a*, to hook. | *Mujer de gancho*, club hostess.

ganchoso, sa o **ganchudo, da** adj. Hooked.

gándara f. Low wasteland.

gandinga f. MIN. Fine washed ore.

gandul, la adj. FAM. Good-for-nothing (inútil). | Idle, lazy (perezoso).
— M. y f. FAM. Good-for-nothing (inútil). | Lazybones (perezoso).

gandulear v. intr. To idle, to loaf.

gandulería f. Idleness, laziness.

gandumbas m. inv. FAM. Lazybones.

gang m. Gang (banda).

ganga f. ZOOL. Sandgrouse. || FIG. y FAM. Bargain, gift (cosa buena y barata). | Cushy *o* soft job (buena situación). || MIN. Gangue (del mineral). || — *Andar a caza de gangas*, to go bargain hunting. | *Aprovechar una ganga*, to snap up a bargain (en las rebajas). || *¡Menuda ganga!, ¡vaya una ganga!*, what a bargain!, it's a giveaway! (cosa buena y barata), what a cushy job! (buena situación). || *Precio de ganga*, bargain price, giveaway price.

Ganges n. pr. m. GEOGR. Ganges.

ganglio m. ANAT. y MED. Ganglion.

gangosear v. intr. V. GANGUEAR.

gangoso, sa adj. Nasal (voz). || *Hablar gangoso*, to speak through one's nose *o* with a twang.

gangrena f. MED. Gangrene.

gangrenarse v. pr. MED. To gangrene.

gangrenoso, sa adj. Gangrenous.

gángster m. Gangster (atracador).

gangsterismo m. Gangsterism.

ganguear v. intr. To speak through one's nose *o* with a twang.

gangueo m. Nasal intonation, nasal accent, twang.

gánguil m. MAR. Hopper (draga). | Fishing barge (barco de pesca). | Sweep net (red).

ganoso, sa adj. Desirous (*de*, of), anxious (*de*, to).

gansada f. FAM. Silly *o* daft thing (hecho y dicho).

gansarón m. Goose (ganso).

gansear v. intr. To do *o* to say daft things.

ganseria f. Silly *o* daft thing (gansada).

ganso, sa m. y f. Goose (hembra), gander (macho). || FIG. y FAM. Goose, simpleton, dope (persona poco inteligente). || — *Hablar por boca de ganso*, V. BOCA. || *Hacer el ganso*, to act the goat. || *Los gansos del Capitolio*, the geese of the Capitol. || MIL. *Paso de ganso*, goose step. || *Ser muy ganso*, to be a silly goose, to be as daft as a brush.

Gante n. pr. m. GEOGR. Ghent.

gantés, esa adj. Ghent, of *o* from Ghent.
— M. y f. Native *o* inhabitant of Ghent.

ganzúa f. Picklock (garfio). || FIG. y FAM. Picklock, thief (ladrón). | Inquisitive person, prying sort

(sonsacador). || — *Abrir con ganzúa*, to pick. || *Ladrón de ganzúa*, picklock, housebreaker.
gañán m. Farmhand (en una hacienda). || FIG. y FAM. Big brute (hombre fuerte y tosco).
gañanía f. Farmhands, *pl.* (gañanes). || Farmhands' quarters, *pl.* (local).
gañido m. Yelp, yelping (de perro). || Caw, cawing, croak, croaking (de aves). || FIG. y FAM. Scream, shriek (chillido). | Wheeze (voz ronca).
gañir* v. intr. To yelp (aullar). || To caw, to croak (aves). || FIG. y FAM. To scream, to shriek (chillar). | To croak, to wheeze (con voz ronca).
gañote m. FAM. Gullet, throat (garganta). || FAM. *De gañote*, free, gratis.
garabatear v. intr. To sling a hook *o* hooks (para asir con un garabato). || To scribble, to scrawl (garrapatear). || FIG. y FAM. To beat about the bush (andar con rodeos).
— V. tr. To scribble, to scrawl (palabras), to scribble on, to scrawl over (hojas, cuartillas, etc.).
garabateo m. Scribbling (acción), scribble, scrawl (escritura). || FIG. Beating about the bush.
garabato m. Hook (gancho). || Meat hook, butcher's hook (de carnicero). || Scribble (garrapato, dibujo mal hecho), scrawl, scribble (mala letra). || FIG. y FAM. Attractiveness, sex appeal (en la mujer). || — Pl. Exaggerated gestures *o* finger movements (ademanes). || Scrawl, *sing.*, scribble, *sing.* (mala letra).
garaje m. Garage.
garajista m. Garage owner (propietario), garage attendant (encargado).
garambaina f. Frippery (adorno). || — Pl. FAM. Ridiculous grimaces (muecas). | Scribble, *sing.*, scrawl, *sing.* (garabateo).
garandumba f. *Amer.* Barge, large raft (embarcación). | FIG. y FAM. Big woman (mujer corpulenta).
garante adj. Acting as guarantor, responsible.
— M. y f. Guarantor, guarantee (fiador).
garantía f. Guarantee, warranty (de la calidad de un objeto). || JUR. Security, guarantee (fianza). | Pledge (de cumplimiento de un contrato). || Assurance, guarantee: *la autoridad ha dado garantías de que el orden público no será alterado*, the authorities have given their assurance that the peace will not be disturbed. || — *Certificado de garantía*, guarantee, certificate of guarantee. || *Garantías constitucionales*, constitutional rights.
garantir* v. tr. V. GARANTIZAR.
garantizado, da adj. Guaranteed, under guarantee: *garantizado por un año*, guaranteed for a year, under a year's guarantee. || Warranted: *oro de 18 quilates garantizado*, warranted 18-carat gold.
garantizar v. tr. To guarantee, to warrant: *garantizar un reloj por un año*, to guarantee a clock for a year. || To assure, to guarantee: *le garantizo que es la pura verdad*, I assure you it is the honest truth. || To act as guarantor for, to vouch for (avalar).
garañón m. Stud jackass (asno). || *Amer.* Stallion (semental).
garapiña f. Frozen state (de un líquido). || Browning in boiling sugar (de las almendras). || Braid (galón). || *Amer.* Pineapple-skin drink (bebida).
garapiñado, da adj. Frozen (helado). || *Almendra garapiñada*, praline.
garapiñar v. tr. To freeze (helar). || To brown in boiling sugar (las almendras).
garapullo m. Dart (rehilete). || TAUR. Banderilla.
garba f. AGR. Sheaf (haz de mieses).
garbancero, ra adj. Chick-pea (relativo al garbanzo), suitable for chick-pea growing (terreno, tiempo).
garbanzal m. Chick-pea field.
garbanzo m. BOT. Chick-pea. || — Pl. FIG. y FAM. Bread and butter, *sing.*, daily bread, *sing.* || — FIG. y FAM. *Contar los garbanzos*, to count every penny. | *En toda tierra de garbanzos*, v. TIERRA. | *Garbanzo negro*, black sheep.
garbear v. intr. To strut (al andar).
— V. pr. FAM. To take a stroll, to go for a stroll: *voy a garbearme por el parque* I'm going to go for a stroll in the park. | To fend for o.s., to manage, to get along, to get by (componérselas).
garbeo m. FAM. Stroll (vuelta): *darse un garbeo*, to go for a stroll, to take a stroll. | Tour, trip (viaje): *me voy a dar un garbeo por España*, I'm going to go on a tour of Spain *o* a trip round Spain.
garbillar v. tr. To sieve (granos). || To riddle, to screen (minerales).
garbillo m. Esparto sieve (para granos). || Riddle, screen (para minerales).
garbo m. Gracefulness, poise, graceful deportment, fine bearing (al andar). || Gracefulness and ease, poise, grace (airosidad). || Attractiveness (atractivo). || Elegance (del estilo). || FIG. Generosity. || *Andar con garbo*, to walk gracefully.
garbosamente adv. Gracefully (con gracia). || Proudly and gracefully (airosamente). || Elegantly (con elegancia). || FIG. Generously (con generosidad).
garboso, sa adj. Graceful (andar), elegant, graceful (persona). || Attractive (atractivo). || Elegant (estilo). || FIG. Generous.
garceta f. ZOOL. Egret (ave). || Antler (mogote del venado). || Sidelock (pelo).
gardenal m. Gardenal.
gardenia f. BOT. Gardenia.
garden-party f. Garden party.
garduña f. ZOOL. Stone marten, beech marten.
garduño m. FAM. Sneak thief, pickpocket (ratero).
garete (irse al) loc. MAR. To drift, to go adrift.
garfear v. intr. To throw a hook *o* hooks.
garfio m. Hook (gancho). || Grapnel, grapple (con varias puntas).
gargajear v. intr. To spit [phlegm] (escupir). || To hawk (carraspear).
gargajeo m. Spitting.
gargajo m. FAM. Spit, gob.
garganta f. f. ANAT. Throat (exterior), throat, gullet (interior). || FIG. Instep (del pie). || ARQ. Neck. || GEOGR. Gorge. || Groove (de polea). || — *Agarrar por la garganta*, to seize by the throat. || *Dolerle a uno la garganta*, to have a sore throat. || FIG. y FAM. *Lo tengo atravesado en la garganta*, he *o* it sticks in my throat *o* in my gullet. || FIG. *Tener* or *atravesársele a uno un nudo en la garganta*, to have *o* to feel a lump in one's throat. | *Tener buena garganta*, to have a good voice.
gargantear v. intr. To warble [in singing].
garganteo m. Warbling.
gargantilla f. Short necklace (collar).
Gargantúa n. pr. m. Gargantua.
gárgara f. Gargling, gargle. || — *Hacer gárgaras*, to gargle. || FIG. y FAM. *Mandar a uno a hacer gárgaras*, to send s.o. packing.
gargarismo m. Gargling, gargle (tratamiento). || Gargle (líquido).
gargarizar v. intr. To gargle.
gárgol m. Groove.
gárgola f. ARQ. Gargoyle. || Boll [of flax] (baga).
garguero o **gargüero** m. Throat, gullet, windpipe.
garita f. Box (caseta). || Sentry box (de centinela). || Porter's lodge (de portero). || Watchtower, lookout turret (en un castillo). || Lavatory (retrete).
garitero m. Gambling-house keeper (amo). || Gambler, frequenter of gambling houses (jugador).
garito m. Gambling den, gambling house, gaming house (casa de juego). || Gambling profits, *pl.*, winnings, *pl.* (ganancia sacada del juego).
garitón m. *Amer.* City gate (puerta de la ciudad).
garla f. FAM. Chatter, gossip.
garlar v. intr. FAM. To chatter, to gossip.
garlito m. Fish trap (red de pescar). || FIG. y FAM. Trap (trampa): *caer en el garlito*, to fall into the trap.
garlopa f. TECN. Jack plane.
garlopín m. TECN. Trying plane.
garnacha f. Gown, robe (de magistrado). || Judge (juez). || Purplish grape (uva roja amoratada), "garnacha" wine (vino). || *Amer.* Meat turnover || *Gente de garnacha*, gentlemen (*pl.*) of the robe.
Garona n. pr. m. GEOGR. Garonne.
garra f. Claw (uña de animal). || Talon (de las aves de rapiña). || FIG. y FAM. Claw, paw, hand (de una persona). || MAR. Hook. || *Amer.* Hard, wrinkled piece of leather (pedazo de cuero). || — Pl. Rags, tatters (harapos). || — FIG. y FAM. *Caer en las garras de uno*, to fall into s.o.'s clutches. | *Echar la garra a uno*, to lay one's hands on s.o.
garrafa f. Carafe, decanter. || Demijohn (damajuana).
garrafal adj. Producing large, tasty cherries (cerezo). || FIG. y FAM. Enormous, huge (error), whopping (mentira). || — *Cereza garrafal*, bigarreau cherry. || *Una falta garrafal*, an enormous blunder.
garrafón m. Large carafe. || Demijohn (damajuana).
garrapata f. Tick (insecto). || FAM. Hack, crock (mal caballo).
garrapateador, ra m. y f. Scribbler, scrawler.
garrapatear v. intr. To scribble, to scrawl.
garrapato m. Scribble, scribbling. || — Pl. Scrawl, *sing.*, scribble, *sing.* (escarabajos).
garrar v. intr. MAR. To drag, to drag anchor.
garrear v. intr. MAR. To drag, to drag anchor. || *Amer.* To live at s.o. else's expense.
— V. tr. *Amer.* To steal (robar).
garrete m. *Amer.* Back of the knee (del hombre). | Hock (del caballo).
garrido, da adj. Good-looking (mozo), pretty (moza).
garrocha f. Barbed lance, pike (vara). || Goad (aguijada). || TAUR. Pike, lance (en las tientas). || *Amer.* Pole: *salto con garrocha*, pole vault.
garrochazo m. TAUR. Thrust with the lance (golpe). | Lance wound (herida).
garrochear v. tr. TAUR. To weaken [the bull] with the lance.
garrochista m. TAUR. Picador. || Herdsman armed with a goad (en las fincas).
garrotazo m. Cudgel blow, blow with a club *o* stick.
garrote m. Club, cudgel, stick (palo). || Garotte, garrotte [U.S., garrote] (ejecución e instrumento), garotting, garrotting [U.S., garroting] (acción de dar garrote). || MED. Tourniquet. || Bulge, bulging (pandeo de una pared). || *Amer.* Brake (freno). || *Dar garrote a*, to garotte, to garrotte [U.S., to garrote].
garrotear v. tr. *Amer.* To club, to cudgel (apalear).
garrotillo m. MED. Croup.
garrotín m. Popular late 19th century Spanish dance.
garrucha f. Pulley (polea).
garrulador, ra adj. V. GÁRRULO.
garrulería f. Garrulity, loquacity (garrulidad). || Prattle, chatter (charla).

garrulidad f. Garrulity, loquacity.
gárrulo, la adj. Twittering, chirping (aves). || FIG. Garrulous, talkative, loquacious (hablador). || POÉT. Babbling, purling (agua): *un arroyo gárrulo*, a babbling brook. | Sighing (viento).
garúa f. *Amer.* Drizzle (llovizna).
garuar v. impers. *Amer.* To drizzle (lloviznar).
garufa f. *Amer.* FAM. Spree, binge (juerga).
garujo m. Concrete (hormigón).
garulla f. Loose grapes (uva desgranada). || Rascal, scoundrel (granuja, pillo). || FIG. y FAM. Mob, rabble, disorderly crowd (muchedumbre).
garza f. ZOOL. Heron (ave). || — *Garza imperial*, purple heron. || *Garza real*, grey heron [U.S., gray heron].
garzo, za adj. Blue: *ojos garzos*, blue eyes. || Blue-eyed (persona).
garzota f. ZOOL. Tufted heron (ave). || Aigrette, plume (adorno).
gas m. FÍS. y QUÍM. Gas: *gas de alumbrado*, illuminating *o* coal gas; *gas hilarante, lacrimógeno*, laughing, tear gas. || *Amer.* Petrol [U.S., gas] (gasolina). || — Pl. Exhaust, *sing.*, exhaust fumes (de escape). || — *Asfixiar con gas*, to gas. || *A todo gas*, flat out, at full speed: *correr a todo gas*, to run flat out. || *Cámara de gas*, gas chamber. || *Cocina, estufa, hornillo de gas*, gas cooker, fire, ring. || *Contador de gas*, gas meter. || *Gas de agua*, water gas. || *Gas de combate* or *asfixiante*, asphyxiating *o* lethal *o* poison gas. || *Gas de los pantanos*, marsh gas. || *Gas pobre*, producer gas. || *Mechero de gas*, gas lighter (encendedor), gas burner (de laboratorio). || FIG. *Pérdida de gas*, loss of speed.
gasa f. Gauze (tela). || MED. Gauze. || Crêpe, crepe, crape (de luto).
gascón, ona adj./s. Gascon.
Gascuña n. pr. f. GEOGR. Gascony.
gaseoso, sa adj. Gaseous. || Aerated, carbonated: *agua gaseosa*, aerated water. || Fizzy (espumoso). — F. Lemonade (bebida).
gasfitero m. *Amer.* Gas fitter, gasman (gasista). | Plumber (fontanero).
gasificación f. Gasification.
gasificar v. tr. To gasify.
gasista m. Gas fitter, gasman (empleado del gas).
gasoducto m. Gas pipeline.
gasógeno m. Gasogene, gazogene (en vehículos).
gas-oil o **gasóleo** m. Gas oil. || Diesel oil (para motores diesel).
gasolina f. QUÍM. y AUT. Petrol [U.S., gas, gasoline, gasolene]. || — *Gasolina-plomo*, high-grade petrol [U.S., high-octane gasoline]. || *Surtidor de gasolina*, petrol pump [U.S., gasoline *o* gas pump], petrol station [U.S., gas station].
gasolinera f. Motorboat (lancha). || Petrol station [U.S., gas station] (estación de gasolina).
gasómetro m. TECN. Gasometer [U.S., gasholder].
gastable adj. Expendable, spendable (dinero).
gastado, da adj. Worn [away]: *piedras gastadas por las olas*, stones worn away by the waves. || Worn-out, worn-away (neumáticos, telas, madera, metales), worn-out (zapatos, vestidos): *zapatillas gastadas*, worn-out slippers. || Worn-out, broken, weary (personas). || Spent: *dinero bien gastado*, money well spent. || FIG. Hackneyed, trite (tema). || FIG. *Gastado por los placeres*, pleasure-worn.
gastador, ra adj. Spendthrift, wasteful.
— M. y f. Spendthrift. || — M. MIL. Pioneer. || Convict (en los presidios).
gastamiento m. Wearing away (de piedras), wearing out, wearing away (de neumáticos, madera, telas, metales, etc.), wearing out (de zapatos, vestidos).
gastar v. tr. To spend (dinero). || To expend, to lay out (invertir dinero). || To use, to consume (consumir): *mi coche gasta mucha gasolina*, my car uses a lot of petrol. || To spend: *gastar el tiempo, las fuerzas*, to spend time, effort. || To waste (emplear mal o en vano): *gastar palabras*, to waste words. || To use up (agotar). || To wear away (piedras). || To wear out *o* away (neumáticos, telas, madera, metales, etc.). || To wear out (zapatos, vestidos): *gastó sus pantalones en el tobogán*, he wore out his trousers on the helter-skelter. || To wear, to have: *gastar bigote, gafas, sombrero*, to wear a moustache, glasses, a hat. || To have, to run (coche). || — *Gastar bromas*, to play practical jokes. || FAM. *Gastarlas*, to behave, to act: *así las gastas tú*, so that's how you behave. || *Gastar mal humor*, to be bad-tempered, to have a bad temper. || *Gastar saliva*, to waste one's breath. || *Hacer gastar mucha tinta*, to cause much ink to flow. || *No gastar ni medio*, not to spend a penny. || FIG. y FAM. *Ya sé cómo las gasta usted*, I know what you're like. | *Ya verá cómo las gasto*, you'll see what stuff I'm made of.
— V. intr. To spend: *a mi mujer le gusta gastar*, my wife likes to spend.
— V. pr. To wear out (deteriorarse las telas, los zapatos, etc.), to wear away (piedras), to wear out *o* away (neumáticos, madera, metales, etc.). || To run out (agotarse). || To wear o.s. out (arruinarse la salud). || FAM. To be worn: *esa clase de peinado ya no se gasta*, that kind of hairstyle isn't worn any more.
gasterópodos m. pl. ZOOL. Gasteropods.
gasto m. Expense, expenditure, expenses, *pl.*, outlay (cantidad de dinero que se gasta): *el gasto diario*, daily expenses. || Spending, expenditure (acción de gastar): *gasto de dinero, de energía*, spending of money, of energy. || FÍS. Output, volume of flow (de agua, electricidad, gas, etc.). || Consumption (consumo): *elevado gasto de gasolina*, high petrol consumption. || — Pl. Expenses, costs, cost, *sing.*: *gastos de mantenimiento*, maintenance costs. || — *Con poco gasto*, at little cost *o* expense. || *Cubrir gastos*, to cover costs *o* expenses. || *Dinero para gastos menudos*, pocket money, petty cash. || *Gastos accesorios*, incidental expenses, contingencies. || *Gastos corrientes*, running expenses. || *Gastos de escritorio*, stationery expenses. || *Gastos de representación*, entertainment allowance. || *Gastos e ingresos*, outgoings and incomings, expenditure and income. || *Gastos generales*, overheads, overhead expenses. || *Hacer el gasto de la conversación*, to do all the talking. || *Meterse en gastos*, to go to expense.
gastoso, sa adj. Spendthrift, wasteful, extravagant.
gastralgia f. MED. Gastralgia.
gástrico, ca adj. Gastric: *jugo gástrico*, gastric juice.
gastritis f. MED. Gastritis.
gastroenteritis f. MED. Gastroenteritis.
gastroenterología f. MED. Gastroenterology.
gastronomía f. Gastronomy.
gastronómico, ca adj. Gastronomic, gastronomical.
gastrónomo, ma m. y f. Gastronome, gastronomist.
gastrópodo m. ZOOL. Gastropod.
gata f. Cat, tabby, she-cat (animal). || Hill cloud (nubecilla). || FAM. Madrilenian girl *o* woman. || *Amer.* Maid, servant (sirvienta). | Crank (manubrio).
gatas (a) loc. adv. On all fours. || *Amer.* Scarcely, hardly (apenas). || — *Andar a gatas*, to go on all fours, to crawl (cualquier persona), to crawl (un niño). || FAM. *Salir a gatas de un apuro*, to squeeze out of a scrape. | *Ser más viejo que andar a gatas*, to be as old as the hills. | *¡Y lo que anduvo a gatas!*, and the rest! [to s.o. who says he is younger than he really is].
gatazo m. Large tomcat (gato). || FAM. Swindle (engaño). || FAM. *Dar gatazo a*, to swindle.
gatear v. intr. To clamber, to climb (trepar). || FAM. To go on all fours, to crawl (andar a gatas). || *Amer.* To go womanizing.
— V. tr. To scratch (arañar). || FAM. To pinch, to swipe (robar). || *Amer.* To flirt with, to make advances to (requebrar).
gatera f. Cathole (para un gato). || MAR. Cathole (escobén). || FAM. Young pickpocket (ratero). | Urchin (golfillo). || *Amer.* Market stallholder (vendedora).
gatero, ra adj. Frequented by cats (lugar). || Catloving (aficionado a los gatos).
— M. y f. Catlover (aficionado a los gatos). || Cat dealer (vendedor).
gatillazo m. Click of the trigger [when gun is fired].
gatillo m. Trigger (de un arma de fuego): *con el dedo en el gatillo*, with one's finger on the trigger. || Forceps (de dentista). || Part of the neck between the nape and the withers (de ciertos animales). || TECN. Clamp (de carpintero). | Jack (para levantar cargas).
gatito m. Small cat, kitten.
gato m. Cat, tomcat: *gato callejero*, alley cat, stray cat. || FIG. Hoard (dinero que se guarda), money bag (bolso o talego). || TECN. Jack (para levantar cargas). | Clamp (de carpintero). || FAM. Madrilenian (madrileño). | Pickpocket (ratero). | Fox (hombre astuto). || *Amer.* Fleshy part of the arm (del brazo). | Popular dance (baile). | Open-air market (mercado). | Servant (criado). || — FIG. y FAM. *Buscarle tres pies al gato*, v. PIE. | *Caer de pie como los gatos*, to fall on one's feet. | *Cuando el gato no está los ratones bailan*, when the cat's away the mice will play. | *Cuatro gatos*, hardly a soul, hardly anybody. | *Dar gato por liebre a uno*, to take s.o. in, to sell s.o. a pig in a poke (engañar). | *Defenderse como gato panza arriba*, to defend o.s. like a demon *o* like demons. || *El gato con botas*, Puss in Boots. || FIG. y FAM. *Eso lo sabe hasta el gato*, everyone knows that. || ZOOL. *Gato cerval*, lynx. || FIG. *Gato con guantes no caza ratones*, a cat in mittens catches no mice. || ZOOL. *Gato de algalia*, civet cat. | *Gato de Angora*, Angora cat. || FIG. y FAM. *Gato escaldado del agua fría huye*, once bitten twice shy. || *Gato montés*, wildcat. || *Gato romano*, tabby. || *Gato siamés*, Siamese cat. || FIG. y FAM. *Hay gato encerrado*, I smell a rat, there's a nigger in the woodpile. | *Llevarse como el perro y el gato*, to fight like cat and dog. | *Llevarse el gato al agua*, to bring it off. | *No hay ni un gato*, there isn't a soul. | *No hay perro ni gato que no lo sepa*, it's common knowledge.
gatuno, na adj. Catlike, feline.
gatuña f. BOT. Cammock, restharrow.
gatuperio m. Hotchpotch, hodgepodge (mezcla). || Imbroglio (embrollo). || Intrigue (intriga). || Deceit (engaño). || Dirty business (negocio sucio).
gauchada f. Typical gaucho act. || *Amer.* Favour: *hacer una gauchada a uno*, to do s.o. a favour.
gauchaje m. Group of gauchos, gauchos, *pl.*
gauchear v. intr. To live like a gaucho.
gauchesco, ca adj. Gaucho (relativo al gaucho): *vida gauchesca*, gaucho life. || Gaucho-like, like a gaucho (parecido al gaucho). || *Poema gauchesco*, poem about gauchos and the pampas.

gauchismo m. "Gauchismo" [Argentinian literary movement of the second half of the 19th century. Its authors, notably H. Ascasubi, Estanislao del Campo and J. Hernández, described gaucho life on the pampas].
gaucho, cha adj. Gaucho: *un payador gaucho*, a gaucho minstrel. || *Amer.* Pleasant, nice (bonito). | Rough, boorish (grosero). | Cunning, crafty (astuto). | Good, expert (jinete).
— M. Gaucho. || *Amer.* Wide-brimmed straw hat.
gaudeamus m. FAM. Beano (festín). || FAM. *Andar de gaudeamus*, to whoop it up.
gauderio m. (Ant.). *Amer.* Gaucho. | Lazy (holgazán).
gauss m. FÍS. Gauss.
gavanza f. BOT. Dog rose [flower].
gavanzo m. BOT. Dog rose [plant].
gaveta f. Drawer (cajón).
gavia f. Ditch (zanja). || (P.us.). Padded cell (para locos furiosos). || MAR. Topsail (vela). | Top (cofa). || ZOOL. Seagull (ave). || — Pl. Mental asylum, *sing.* (manicomio).
gavial m. ZOOL. Gavial (cocodrilo).
gaviero m. MAR. Topman.
gavieta f. MAR. Mizen crow's nest (sobre la mesana), bowsprit crow's nest (sobre el bauprés).
gavilán m. Sparrow hawk (ave). || FIG. Hawk (persona). || Quillon (de la espada). || Flourish, stroke [at the end of a letter] (de una letra). || Nib (división de la plumilla). || BOT. Thistle flower. || MAR. Boathook. || *Amer.* Ingrowing nail (uñero).
gavilla f. Sheaf (de cereales). || Bundle (de sarmientos, etc.). || FIG. Gang, band: *gavilla de ladrones*, band of thieves. || *La gente de gavilla*, the underworld.
gavión m. MIL. Gabion. || FAM. Large hat (sombrero).
gaviota f. ZOOL. Seagull, gull (ave).
gavota f. Gavotte (baile y música).
gaya f. Coloured stripe [U.S., colored stripe] (lista). || Victor's sash (insignia). || (P.us.). Magpie (urraca).
gayadura f. Coloured stripes, *pl.* (del vestido).
gayar v. tr. To adorn with coloured stripes.
gayo, ya adj. Gay, merry (alegre). || Showy (vistoso). || *Gaya ciencia*, gay science, poetry.
gayola f. Cage (jaula). || FIG. y FAM. Clink, jail (cárcel).
gaza f. MAR. Eye splice, loop, bight.
gazapa f. FAM. Fib, lie.
gazapo m. Young rabbit (conejillo). || FIG. y FAM. Sly customer, fox (hombre astuto). | Slip (lapso). | Bloomer (enlace vicioso en la pronunciación de dos letras). | Blunder, bloomer (disparate). | IMPR. Printing error, misprint (error en un impreso).
gazmoñada o **gazmoñería** f. Prudery, priggishness (modestia afectada). || Sanctimoniousness, religious hypocrisy (santurronería).
gazmoñero, ra o **gazmoño, ña** adj. Prudish, priggish (de virtud fingida). || Sanctimonious (devoto fingido).
— M. y f. Prude, prig. || Sanctimonious person.
gaznápiro, ra adj. FAM. Dense, stupid (palurdo).
— M. y f. FAM. Blockhead, simpleton.
gaznate m. Throat, gullet, windpipe (garguero). || *Amer.* Sweet of pineapple and coconut. || FAM. *Refrescarse el gaznate*, to wet one's whistle.
gazpacho m. CULIN. "Gazpacho", cold soup of bread, tomatoes, garlic, salt, vinegar and oil.
gazpachuelo m. Egg soup seasoned with vinegar or lemon.
gazuza f. FAM. Ravenous hunger (hambre). || *Tener gazuza*, to be starving *o* famished *o* ravenous.
ge f. G [name of the letter *g*].
gehena f. Gehenna, hell (infierno).
géiser m. GEOGR. Geyser.
geisha f. Geisha.
gel m. QUÍM. Gel.
gelatina f. QUÍM. Gelatine, gelatin. || Jelly (de carne).
gelatinoso, sa adj. Gelatinous.
gélido, da adj. POÉT. Gelid, icy.
gelificarse v. pr. QUÍM. To gel.
gelignita f. QUÍM. Gelignite.
gema f. MIN. Gem, precious stone. || BOT. Bud, gemma. || *Sal gema*, rock salt.
gemación f. Gemmation.
gemebundo, da adj. Wailing, moaning, groaning.
gemelo, la adj./s. Twin. || — *Alma gemela*, kindred spirit. || *Hermanos gemelos*, twin brothers. || ANAT. *Músculos gemelos*, gemelli. || — M. pl. Binoculars (anteojos). || Cufflinks (de camisa). || ASTR. Gemini, the Twins (Géminis). || *Gemelos de campaña, de teatro*, field, opera glasses.
gemido m. Groan, moan. || Wail (lamento).
gemidor, ra adj. Groaning, moaning. || Wailing (que se lamenta).
geminado, da adj. Geminate.
Géminis n. pr. m. pl. ASTR. Gemini, the Twins.
gémino, na adj. Geminate.
gemiquear v. intr. *Amer.* To whimper, to snivel.
gemir* v. intr. To moan, to groan. || To wail (lamentarse). || To whine (animales). || To howl, to moan (el viento).
gemonías f. pl. Humiliating punishment, *sing.*
Gemonías f. pl. HIST. Gemonies (en Roma).
gen m. BIOL. Gene.
genciana f. BOT. Gentian.
gendarme m. Gendarme (en Francia).
gendarmería f. Gendarmerie, gendarmery.
gene m. BIOL. Gene.
genealogía f. Genealogy.
genealógico, ca adj. Genealogical. || *Árbol genealógico*, family tree, genealogical tree (de una persona), pedigree (de un animal).
genealogista m. y f. Genealogist.
generación f. Generation. || (P.us.). Descent (descendencia). || *Generación espontánea*, spontaneous generation, abiogenesis.
generador, ra adj. Generating.
— M. TECN. Generator.
general adj. General: *parálisis general*, general paralysis; *la opinión general*, the general opinion. || Common (común, corriente). || — *En general*, in general. || *Por lo general*, generally.
— M. MIL. General. || REL. General. || — MIL. *General de división, de brigada*, major general, brigadier [U.S., brigadier general]. | *General en jefe*, supreme commander.
generala f. General's wife. || MIL. *Tocar generala*, to call to arms.
generalato m. Generalship, office of general.
generalidad f. Generality: *limitarse a generalidades*, to confine o.s. to generalities. || Majority (mayoría). || HIST. "Generalidad" [autonomous government of Catalonia]. || *Con generalidad*, in broad outline: *tratar una cosa con generalidad*, to treat sth. in broad outline.
generalísimo m. Generalissimo, supreme commander.
generalización f. Generalization. || Widening, escalation (de un conflicto).
generalizado, da adj. Generalized. || Widespread: *la opinión más generalizada*, the most widespread opinion.
generalizador, ra adj. Generalizing.
generalizar v. tr. e intr. To generalize.
— V. pr. To become general. || To widen, to escalate (un conflicto).
generalmente adv. Generally.
generar v. tr. To generate: *generar una corriente eléctrica*, to generate an electric current. || (Ant.). To generate, to procreate (procrear). || FIG. To engender (tener como resultado).
generativo, va adj. Generative.
generatriz f. MAT. Generatrix.
genérico, ca adj. Generic.
género m. Race (raza). || Sort, type, kind (clase): *los distintos géneros de automóviles*, the different kinds of motorcars. || Style, manner, way (manera). || ARTES. Genre: *pintor de género*, genre painter. || BIOL. Genus (grupo taxonómico). || Article, piece of merchandise (mercancía). || Material, fabric, cloth (tela). || GRAM. Gender: *género masculino, femenino, neutro*, masculine, feminine, neuter gender. || — Pl. Goods, merchandise, *sing.*, articles. || — *Género chico*, genre comprising one-act comedies and "zarzuelas" [at the end of 19th century]. || *Género humano*, human race, mankind. || *Géneros de punto*, knitted goods, knitwear, *sing.* || *Vendedor, fabricante de géneros de punto*, dealer in knitted garments, knitwear manufacturer.
generosidad f. Generosity. || *No peca de generosidad*, he's not overgenerous.
generoso, sa adj. Generous (propenso a dar). || Magnanimous, noble (magnánimo). || Generous, noble (acciones, palabras). || Noble (estirpe). || Generous, liberal (liberal). || Fertile (fértil). || Valiant, courageous (valiente). || Generous, full-bodied (vino). || Excellent (excelente).
genésico, ca adj. Genetic.
génesis f. Genesis (origen).
Génesis n. pr. m. Genesis (libro de la Biblia).
genética f. Genetics.
genético, ca adj. BIOL. Genetic.
genetista o **geneticista** m. y f. Geneticist.
genial adj. Full of genius, inspired, brilliant (dotado de genio creador). || Outstanding, brilliant, of genius: *una obra genial*, a brilliant work. || Brilliant (idea). || Witty (gracioso, ocurrente). || Genial, pleasant (agradable). || Characteristic (característico).
genialidad f. Genius (genio). || Stroke of genius, brilliant idea: *eso fue una genialidad*, that was a stroke of genius. || Genial *o* brilliant work (obra). || Eccentricity (excentricidad). || Originality.
geniazo m. FAM. Foul *o* violent temper: *tener un geniazo horrible*, to have a horribly violent temper.
genio m. Nature, disposition (carácter). || Temper, mood: *estar de mal genio*, to be in a bad temper. || Bad temper (mal carácter). || Genius (facultad creadora). || Genius (persona dotada de dicha facultad): *Shakespeare fue un genio*, Shakespeare was a genius. || Genius (espíritu de un país, de una época, etc.): *el genio de la lengua*, the genius of the language. || Genie, jinn (ser sobrenatural). || Spirit (espíritu). || — *Corto de genio*, spiritless, timid. || *De mal genio*, bad-tempered. || *Genio del mal*, evil spirit. || *Genio y figura hasta la sepultura*, the leopard cannot change his spots. || *Genio vivo*, quick temper. || *Pronto* or *vivo de genio*, quick-tempered. || *Tener el genio atravesado*, to have a foul temper. || *Tener mal genio*, to be bad-tempered *o* ill-natured.
genioso, sa adj. *Amer. Mal genioso*, ill-natured, bad-tempered.
genital adj. Genital.
— M. pl. Genitals, genitalia.

genitivo m. GRAM. Genitive.
genitor adj. m. Generating, begetting.
— M. Begetter.
genitourinario, ria adj. ANAT. Genitourinary.
genízaro m. Janizary, janissary (soldado turco).
genocidio m. Genocide.
genol m. MAR. Futtock.
genotipo m. BIOL. Genotype.
Génova n. pr. GEOGR. Genoa.
— OBSERV. Do not confuse *Geneva* (Ginebra) with *Genoa* (Génova).
genovés, esa adj./s. Genoese (de Génova).
gente f. People, *pl.*: *había mucha gente en la calle*, there were a lot of people in the street; *¡había una de gente!*, there were no end of people there!; *gente joven*, young people; *la gente del campo*, [the] country people; *¿qué dirá la gente?*, what will people say? || People, nation (nación). || FAM. Folks, *pl.*, relatives, *pl.*: *¿cómo está tu gente?*, how are your folks? || Retinue (seguidores de un soberano). || Tribe: *la gente alada*, the feathered tribe. || MIL. Men of a unit. || *Amer.* Upper-class people. || — Pl. Gentiles: *el Apóstol de las gentes*, the Apostle of the gentiles. || Followers (seguidores, partidarios).
— *De gente en gente*, from generation to generation. || JUR. *Derecho de gentes*, law of nations. || *Gente armada* or *de guerra*, men (*pl.*) in arms, armed troops, *pl.* || *Gente baja*, low-class people. || *Gente bien*, the best people (de la alta sociedad), nice people (respetable). || *Gente copetuda* or *de alto copete*, upper-crust *o* high-class people, *pl.* || *Gente de baja estofa*, low-class people, people of low degree. || *Gente de bien*, honest people, decent folk. || *Gente de capa parda*, countryfolk, *pl.*, rustics, *pl.* || *Gente de color*, coloured people. || *Gente de cuidado* or *de mala vida* or *de mal vivir* or *maleante*, bad people, shady characters, *pl.* || *Gente de Iglesia*, clergy. || *Gente de la ciudad*, townspeople, *pl.* || *Gente de mar*, seamen, *pl.* || *Gente de medio pelo* or *de poco más o menos*, people of no account. || *Gente de negocios*, businessmen, business people. || *Gente de paz*, friend, friends: *¿quién va?* — *¡Gente de paz!*, who goes there? — Friend! || *Gente gorda*, people of influence *o* standing, bigwigs, *pl.* || *Gente de pluma*, writers, *pl.* (escritores), clerks, *pl.*, penpushers, *pl.* (escribanos). || *Gente de vida airada*, libertines, *pl.* || *Gente humilde* or *modesta*, humble people. || *Gente menuda*, children, *pl.*, little ones, *pl.* (niños), people of small means (plebe). || *Hacer gente*, to make a crowd. || *La gente en general*, people at large. || *La mayoría de la gente*, most people. || *Ser gente*, to be somebody (ser importante).
gentecilla o **gentezuela** f. FAM. Rabble, riffraff.
gentil adj. Heathen, pagan (pagano). || Gentile (que no es judío). || Attractive (atractivo). || Pleasant (agradable). || Charming: *una gentil doncella*, a charming young girl. || Graceful, elegant: *de gentil porte*, of graceful deportment. || FAM. Huge (enorme).
— M. Heathen, pagan (pagano). || Gentile (no judío).
gentileza f. Gracefulness, elegance, poise (garbo). || Charm (encanto). || Kindness, goodness (amabilidad): *tuvo la gentileza de prestarme cien libras*, he had the kindness to lend me a hundred pounds. || Politeness, courtesy (cortesía). || *¿Tendría usted la gentileza de...?*, would you be so kind as to...?
gentilhombre m. Gentleman: *gentilhombre de cámara*, gentleman in waiting. || (P. us.). Handsome young man (buen mozo).
— OBSERV. Pl. *gentileshombres*.
gentilicio, cia adj. Gentilic, gentile (de una nación): *nombre, adjetivo gentilicio*, gentilic noun, adjective.
— M. Gentilic, name of an inhabitant *o* of inhabitants of a country, region or city.
gentílico, ca adj. Gentile (no judío). || Heathen, pagan (pagano).
gentilidad f. o **gentilismo** m. Gentilism, heathenism, paganism (religión de los gentiles). || Heathendom, gentiles, *pl.* (conjunto de gentiles).
gentilmente adv. Gracefully, elegantly (con gracia): *bailar gentilmente*, to dance gracefully. || Kindly (amablemente).
gentío m. Crowd, throng, mob (multitud). || *¡Qué gentío!*, what a lot of people!.
gentleman m. Gentleman.
— OBSERV. Pl. *gentlemen* in both languages.
gentualla o **gentuza** f. Rabble, riffraff (populacho).
genuflexión f. Genuflexion, genuflection.
genuino, na adj. Genuine, true: *un genuino representante del pueblo*, a genuine representative of the people. || Pure: *en genuino inglés*, in pure English. || Genuine, real, authentic: *un caso genuino de esquizofrenia*, a genuine case of schizophrenia.
geocéntrico, ca adj. ASTR. Geocentric.
geoda f. GEOL. Geode.
geodesia f. Geodesy.
geodésico, ca adj. Geodetic, geodesic.
— F. Geodetics, geodesy.
geofísico, ca adj. Geophysical.
— M. Geophysicist. || — F. Geophysics.
geografía f. Geography.
geográfico, ca adj. Geographical: *latitud geográfica*, geographical latitude. || Geographic: *milla geográfica*, geographic mile.
geógrafo m. Geographer.
geoide m. GEOGR. Geoid.
geología f. Geology.
geológico, ca adj. Geological, geologic.
geólogo m. Geologist.
geomagnético, ca adj. Geomagnetic.
geómetra m. Geometer, geometrician.
geometral adj. Geometric, geometrical.
geometría f. Geometry: *geometría plana, descriptiva, del espacio*, plane, descriptive, solid geometry.
geométrico, ca adj. Geometric: *progresión geométrica*, geometric progression. || Geometrical: *construcción geométrica*, geometrical construction.
geomorfología f. Geomorphology.
geopolítica f. Geopolitics.
Georgia n. pr. f. GEOGR. Georgia.
georgiano, na adj./s. Georgian.
geórgico, ca adj. Georgic (agrícola).
— F. pl. Georgics (de Virgilio).
geosinclinal adj. GEOL. Geosynclinal.
— M. Geosyncline, geosynclinal.
geranio m. BOT. Geranium.
Gerardo n. pr. m. Gerard, Gerald.
gerbo m. ZOOL. Gerbil, gerbille (roedor).
gerencia f. Management (gestión). || Manager's office (oficina). || Managership (cargo).
gerente m. Manager, director: *gerente de publicidad*, advertising manager *o* director. || *Gerente de una tienda*, shop manager.
geriatra m. y f. MED. Geriatrician.
geriatría f. MED. Geriatrics.
gerifalte m. ZOOL. Gerfalcon (ave). || FIG. y FAM. Bigwig, big shot (personaje importante).
germanesco, ca adj. Slang. || HIST. Relative to the "Germanías".
Germania n. pr. f. HIST. Germania (antigua región).
germanía f. Thieves' slang, cant (jerga). || HIST. "Germanía" [revolutionary movement in Valencia at the beginning of the 16th century]. || (P.us.). Concubinage (amancebamiento).
germánico, ca adj./s.m. Germanic.
germanio m. QUÍM. Germanium (elemento metálico).
germanismo m. Germanism.
germanista m. y f. Germanist, German scholar.
germano, na adj. German, Germanic, Teutonic.
— M. y f. German, Teuton.
germanófilo, la adj./s. Germanophile.
germanófobo, ba adj./s. Germanophobe.
germen m. BIOL. Germ. || FIG. Origin, germ.
germicida adj. Germicidal.
— M. Germicide.
germinación f. Germination.
germinal adj. BOT. Germinal.
germinar v. intr. To germinate.
germinativo, va adj. Germinative.
gerontocracia f. Gerontocracy.
gerontología f. MED. Gerontology.
gerontólogo, ga m. y f. Gerontologist.
gerundense adj. [Of *o* from] Gerona.
— M. y f. Native *o* inhabitant of Gerona.
gerundio m. GRAM. Gerund (en español, latín). | Present participle (en inglés).
gesta f. Heroic deed, exploit. || *Cantar de gesta*, chanson de geste.
gestación f. BIOL. Gestation.
Gestapo f. Gestapo.
gestar v. tr. To gestate.
gestatorio, ria adj. Gestatorial: *silla gestatoria*, gestatorial chair.
gestear v. intr. V. GESTICULAR.
gestero, ra adj. V. GESTICULADOR.
gesticulación f. Grimace, face (mueca). || Gesticulation (ademán).
gesticulador, ra adj. Given to grimacing *o* pulling faces (que hace muecas). || Gesticulative, given to gesticulating (que hace ademanes).
gesticular v. intr. To grimace, to pull faces *o* a face (hacer muecas). || To gesticulate (hacer ademanes).
gestión f. Step, measure (trámite): *hacer gestiones*, to take steps. || Management, conduct (administración). || — Pl. Business, *sing.* (asunto).
gestionar v. tr. [To take steps] to acquire *o* to procure: *gestionar un pasaporte, un permiso*, to take steps to acquire a passport, a permit. || To negotiate: *gestionar una transacción, una venta, un empréstito*, to negotiate a deal, a sale, a loan. || To manage, to conduct: *su agente gestiona sus asuntos durante su ausencia*, his agent manages his affairs while he is away.
gesto m. Expression (expresión del rostro): *un gesto de alegría*, an expression of joy. || Face (rostro): *torcer el gesto de dolor*, to twist one's face with pain. || Grimace, face, wry face (mueca). || Gesture, gesticulation (con las manos). || FIG. Gesture: *su donación al asilo fue un gesto generoso*, his donation to the home was a generous gesture. || — *Estar de buen, de mal gesto*, to be in a good, in a bad mood. || *Fruncir el gesto*, to frown, to scowl. || *Hacer gestos*, to pull *o* to make faces (cara), to gesticulate (manos). || *Me hizo un gesto para que me callase*, he gestured to me to be silent. || *Poner mal gesto* or *torcer el gesto*, to pull a face (hacer una mueca), to scowl (estar enfadado). || *Poner un gesto de enfado*, to scowl.

GEOGRAFÍA, *f.* — GEOGRAPHY

I. Términos (*m.*) generales. — General terms.

geografía (*f.*) física	physical geography
geografía (*f.*) económica	economic geography
geopolítica *f.*	geopolitics
geología *f.*	geology
geodesia *f.*	geodesy
etnografía *f.*	ethnography
cosmografía *f.*	cosmography
cosmología *f.*	cosmology
toponimia *f.*	toponymy
oceanografía *f.*	oceanography
meteorología *f.*	meteorology
orografía *f.*	orography
hidrografía *f.*	hydrography
vegetación *f.*	vegetation
relieve *m.*	relief
clima *m.*	climate
Tierra *f.*	Earth
Universo *m.*; cosmos *m.*	Universe; cosmos
mundo *m.*	world
globo *m.*	globe
globo (*m.*) terráqueo, esfera (*f.*) terrestre	earth, globe
continente *m.*	continent
tierra (*f.*) firme	terra firma
costa *f.*	coast
litoral *m.*	littoral, coast, shore
archipiélago *m.*	archipelago
península *f.*	peninsula
isla *f.*	island
llanura *f.*	plain
valle *m.*	valley
pradera *f.*	meadow (pequeña), prairie (grande)
lago *m.*	lake
estanque *m.*	pond
pantano *m.*; ciénaga *f.*	marsh; bog, swamp
laguna *f.*	small lake; lagoon (de atolón)
landa *f.*	moor, moorland
desierto *m.*	desert
duna *f.*	dune
oasis *m.*	oasis
sabana *f.*	savanna, savannah
selva (*f.*) virgen	virgin forest
estepa *f.*	steppe
tundra *f.*	tundra

II. Cartografía, *f.* — Cartography.

mapa *m.*	map
mapamundi *m.*	map of the world
planisferio *m.*	planisphere
mapa (*m.*) mural, mudo	wall, skeleton map
plano *m.*	map, plan, chart
atlas *m.*	atlas
carta (*f.*) marina	chart
catastro *m.*	cadastre
escala *f.*	scale
topografía *f.*	topography
fotogrametría *f.*	photogrammetry

III. Orientación, *f.* — Orientation.

puntos (*m. pl.*) cardinales	cardinal points
rosa (*f.*) de los vientos	compass rose
meridiano *m.*	meridian
paralelo *m.*	parallel
longitud *f.*; latitud *f.*	longitude; latitude
ecuador *m.*	equator
trópico (*m.*) de Cáncer, de Capricornio	Tropic of Cancer, of Capricorn
línea (*f.*) equinoccial	equinoctial line
Polo (*m.*) Norte, Sur	North, South pole
círculo (*m.*) polar	polar circle
boreal	northern
austral	southern
zona (*f.*) glacial, templada, tórrida	glacial, temperate, torrid zone
cenit *m.*	zenith
altura (*f.*) sobre el nivel del mar	height above sea level

IV. Mar (*m.* y *f.*) y río, *m.* — Sea and river.

mar *m.* y *f.*	sea
alta mar *f.*	high seas, open sea
océano *m.*	ocean
brazo (*m.*) de mar	inlet
bahía *f.*	bay
golfo *m.*	gulf
cala *f.*, caleta *f.*	cove, creek
ensenada *f.*	cove, inlet
cabo *m.*; promontorio *m.*	cape; promontory, headland
acantilado *m.*	cliff
puerto *m.*	port, harbour [U.S., harbor]
rada *f.*	bay, roadstead
banco *m.*, bajío *m.*	sandbank
playa *f.*	beach, shore
estrecho *m.*	strait
istmo *m.*	isthmus
escollo *m.*	reef
cayo *m.*	key
barra *f.*	sandbar
marea *f.*	tide
resaca *f.*	undertow
ola *f.*	wave
tempestad *f.*	tempest
mar (*m.*) de fondo	ground swell
maremoto *m.*	seaquake
estiaje *m.*	low water
aguas (*f. pl.*) jurisdiccionales	territorial waters
corriente *f.*	current
banco (*m.*) de hielo	ice floe
iceberg *m.*, témpano *m.*	iceberg
ribera *f.*, orilla *f.*	shore (de mar), bank (río)
estuario *m.*, estero *m.*	estuary
delta *m.*	delta
desembocadura *f.*, embocadura *f.*	mouth
fiordo *m.*	fiord
ría *f.*	ria
corriente (*f.*) de agua	watercourse
arroyo *m.*	stream, brook
torrente *m.*	torrent
rápido *m.*, rabión *m.*	rapids *pl.*
nacimiento *m.*, cabecera *f.*	source
manantial *m.*	spring
lecho *m.*, cauce *m.*	bed
caudal *m.*	flow
cuenca *f.*	basin
salto (*m.*) de agua, cascada *f.*	waterfall, falls *pl.*, cascade
catarata *f.*	cataract
afluente *m.*	tributary
confluente *m.*	confluent
meandro *m.*	meander
canal *m.*	canal
ued *m.*	wadi, wady
crecida *f.*, avenida *f.*	swelling, freshet, flood
inundación *f.*	flood

V. Montaña, *f.* — Mountain.

cordillera *f.*, cadena (*f.*) de montañas	mountain range *o* chain
nudo *m.*	knot
monte *m.*, sierra *f.*	mountain; mount
macizo *m.*	massif
cuchilla *f.*	mountain range (cadena), mountain crest (cumbre)
cumbre *f.*, cima *f.*, cresta *f.*	summit, top, crest
pico *m.*	peak
puerto *m.*	mountain pass, col
punto (*m.*) culminante	highest peak *o* mountain
estribación *f.*, contrafuerte *m.*	spur, ridge
ladera *f.*, falda *f.*	slope, side
volcán *m.*	volcano
quebrada *f.*, cañón *m.*	ravine, canyon
desfiladero *m.*	narrow pass
garganta *f.*	gorge, ravine
falla *f.*, grieta *f.*	crevice
precipicio *m.*	precipice
glaciar *m.*, ventisquero *m.*, nevero *m.*	glacier
meseta *f.*	plateau, tableland
altiplanicie *f.* [*Amer.*, altiplano *m.*]	high plateau
colina *f.*	hill
cerro *m.*	hill, hillock
altonazo *m.*, collado *m.*, otero *m.*, loma *f.*	hillock, knoll
peñón *m.*, roca *f.*	rock

gestor, ra m. y f. Agent (que gestiona). || Manager, administrator (administrador). || Manager (gerente de una empresa).
— Adj. Managing. || Negotiating.

gestoría f. Agency.

gestudo, da adj. FAM. Grumpy.
— M. y f. FAM. Grouse.

Getsemaní n. pr. Gethsemane.

geyser m. GEOGR. Geyser.

ghanés, esa adj./s. Ghanaian.

ghetto m. Ghetto.

giba f. Hump (del camello). || Hump, hunch, humpback, hunchback (de una persona). || FIG. y FAM. Nuisance, bore, bother (molestia).

gibado, da adj. Humpbacked, hunchbacked, gibbous [p.us.] (corcovado).
— M. y f. Humpback, hunchback.

gibar v. tr. To curve, to bend, to arch. || FIG. y FAM. To annoy, to bother, to give the hump (fastidiar).

gíbaro, ra adj./s. V. JÍBARO.

gibón m. ZOOL. Gibbon (mono).

gibosidad f. Hump, gibbosity (giba).

giboso, sa adj./s. V. GIBADO.

Gibraltar n. pr. Gibraltar: *el peñón, el estrecho de Gibraltar*, the Rock, the Straits of Gibraltar.

gibraltareño, ña adj. [Of *o* from] Gibraltar.
— M. y f. Gibraltarian.

giga f. Jig (danza y música).

giganta f. Giantess. || BOT. Sunflower (girasol).

gigante adj. Giant, gigantic.
— M. Giant.

gigantesco, ca adj. Gigantic, giant.

gigantez f. Gigantic size.

gigantismo m. Gigantism, giantism.

gigantón, ona m. y f. Giant [in a procession]. || — M. *Amer.* Sunflower (girasol).

gigolo m. Gigolo.

gigote m. Minced meat stew.

gijonense o **gijonés, esa** adj. [of *o* from] Gijón.
— M. y f. Native *o* inhabitant of Gijón.

gilí adj./s. FAM. V. JILÍ.

gilipolla m. y f. POP. V. JILIPOLLA.

gilipollada f. POP. V. JILIPOLLADA.

gilipollez f. POP. V. JILIPOLLEZ.

gimnasia f. Gymnastics. || Physical training (educación física). || FAM. *Confundir la gimnasia con la magnesia*, not to know one's left hand from one's right.
gimnasio m. Gymnasium (para hacer gimnasia). || Gymnasium, grammar school [U.S., high school] (colegio en Alemania).
gimnasta m. y f. Gymnast.
gimnástico, ca adj. Gymnastic.
— F. Gymnastics (gimnasia).
gimnosperma f. BOT. Gymnosperm.
gimoteador, ra adj. Whining, snivelling, whimpering.
— M. y f. Whiner, sniveller, whimperer.
gimotear v. intr. To whimper, to whine, to snivel.
gimoteo m. Whimpering, whining, snivelling.
gindama f. FAM. Jitters: *tener gindama*, to have the jitters.
ginebra f. Gin (licor). || MÚS. Xylophone (xilófono). || FIG. Confusion (confusión). | Hubbub (ruido).
Ginebra n. pr. GEOGR. Geneva
ginebrés, esa o **ginebrino, na** adj./s. Genevan, Genevese.
gineceo m. HIST. Gynaeceum. || BOT. Gynoecium [U.S., gynecium].
ginecología f. MED. Gynaecology [U.S., gynecology].
ginecológico, ca adj. MED. Gynaecological [U.S., gynecological].
ginecólogo, ga m. y f. MED. Gynaecologist [U.S., gynecologist].
gineta f. ZOOL. Genet (jineta).
gingival adj. ANAT. Gingival.
gingivitis f. MED. Gingivitis.
Gioconda (La) n. pr. f. The Mona Lisa, the Gioconda.
gira f. Picnic, outing, excursion (excursión): *ir de gira*, to go on an outing *o* an excursion, to go for a picnic. || Tour (viaje por varios sitios). || Tour (de un artista).
girado, da m. y f. COM. Drawee.
girador, ra m. y f. COM. Drawer.
giralda f. Weather vane, weathercock (veleta).
giraldilla f. Weather vane, weathercock (veleta). || Popular Asturian dance (baile). || TAUR. Type of pass with the "muleta".
girándula f. Girandole.
girar v. intr. To rotate, to revolve, to go round: *las ruedas giran*, the wheels go round. || To rotate, to revolve, to gyrate (alrededor de un eje). || To spin (un trompo, etc.). || To revolve: *la Tierra gira alrededor del Sol*, the Earth revolves around the Sun. || FIG. To turn on, to center on: *la conversación giraba alrededor de la eutanasia*, the conversation turned on euthanasia. || To turn: *la carretera gira a la izquierda*, the road turns to the left. || To swing, to turn: *la puerta gira en sus goznes*, the door swings on its hinges. || COM. To do business: *girar bajo la razón social de*, to do business under the name of. || TECN. To rotate || — AUT. *Coche que gira bien*, car with a good *o* a small turning circle, car with a good lock. || FIG. *Girar alrededor de*, to be approximately *o* around *o* in the region of: *el número de las víctimas gira alrededor de cien mil*, the number of victims is in the region of a hundred thousand. || *Hacer girar la llave en la cerradura*, to turn the key in the lock.
— V. tr. To spin: *girar un trompo*, to spin a top. || To turn: *girar el volante*, to turn the steering wheel. || COM. To draw (una letra de cambio). | To transfer (enviar por giro postal). || *Girar una visita oficial*, to make an official visit.
girasol m. BOT. Sunflower. || MIN. Girasol, girasole. || Sycophant (adulador).
giratorio, ria adj. Gyratory: *un movimiento giratorio*, a gyratory movement. || Revolving: *puerta giratoria*, revolving door. || — *Placa giratoria*, turntable (ferrocarriles). || *Puente giratorio*, swing bridge. || *Silla giratoria*, swivel chair.
giro m. Turn, turning, spinning (acción de girar). || Turn (vuelta). || Rotation, revolution (revolución). || FÍS. Gyration. || FIG. Course (curso). | Turn: *su carrera ha tomado un nuevo giro*, his career has taken a new turn. || Turn of phrase (locución): *un giro arcaico*, an archaic turn of phrase. || COM. Draft. | Bill of exchange (letra de cambio). | Transfer (de una persona a otra). || — AUT. *Ángulo de giro*, steering lock. || *Giro postal*, money order, postal order. || *Giro telegráfico*, telegraphic money order. || AUT. *Radio de giro*, turning circle.
giro, ra adj. *Amer.* Yellow (gallo).
girocompás m. Gyrocompass.
girola f. ARQ. Apse aisle, ambulatory.
Gironda n. pr. m. GEOGR. Gironde.
girondino, na adj./s. HIST. Girondist (partido de la Revolución francesa).
giropiloto m. AVIAC. Gyropilot.
giroscópico, ca adj. Gyroscopic. || *Estabilizador giroscópico*, gyrostabilizer.
giroscopio m. Gyroscope.
giróstato m. Gyrostat.
gitanada m. Gipsy-like action, gipsy-like trick. || FIG. Cajolery, wheedling (zalamería).
gitanear v. intr. To cajole to wheedle.
gitanería f. Gipsy-like action, gipsy-like trick (gitanada). || Wheedling, cajolery (zalamería). || Band of gipsies (grupo de gitanos).
gitanesco, ca adj. Gipsy (de gitano). || Gipsy-like (parecido a los gitanos).
gitanismo m. Gipsy way of life, gipsy customs, *pl.* || Gipsy expression *o* phrase *o* word (giro, palabra).
gitano, na adj. Gipsy, gypsy. || FIG. Cajoling, wheedling.
— M. y f. Gipsy, gypsy: *una familia de gitanos*, a family of gipsies.
glabro, bra adj. Glabrous (lampiño).
glaciación f. GEOL. Glaciation.
glacial adj. Glacial: *zonas glaciales*, glacial zones; *período glacial*, glacial period. || FIG. Icy: *recibimiento, viento glacial*, icy reception, wind.
glaciar m. GEOL. Glacier.
— Adj. Glacial: *depósitos glaciares*, glacial deposits.
glaciología f. Glaciology.
glacis m. Glacis (en fortificaciones).
gladiador m. HIST. Gladiator.
gladio o **gladiolo** o **gladíolo** m. BOT. Gladiolus.
glande m. ANAT. Glans penis.
glándula f. Gland: *glándula lagrimal*, lachrymal gland; *glándula de secreción interna*, ductless gland.
glandular adj. Glandular.
glanduloso, sa adj. Glandulous.
glaseado, da adj. Glazed, glossy.
— M. Glazing (de cuero, papel, tela, repostería, etc.).
glasear v. tr. To glaze.
glasto m. BOT. Woad.
glauco, ca adj. Glaucous.
glaucoma m. MED. Glaucoma.
gleba f. Clod [of earth turned over by the plough]. || HIST. *Siervo de la gleba*, serf.
glena f. ANAT. Glenoid cavity.
glenoideo, a adj. ANAT. Glenoid.
glicemia f. MED. Glucemia.
glicérido m. QUÍM. Glyceride.
glicerina f. QUÍM. Glycerin, glycerine, glycerol.
glicerofosfato m. QUÍM. Glycerophosphate.
glicerol m. QUÍM. Glycerol.
glicina f. BOT. Wistaria.
glicógeno m. QUÍM. Glycogen (glucógeno).
glicol m. QUÍM. Glycol.
glifo m. ARQ. Glyph.
glíptica f. ARTES. Glyptic.
gliptodonte m. ZOOL. Glyptodon, glyptodont.
gliptografía f. ARTES. Glyptography.
global adj. Global: *vista global*, global view; *método global*, global method. || Overall (de conjunto). || Comprehensive: *un estudio global*, a comprehensive study. || Total, aggregate (cantidad). || Lump (suma).
globalmente adv. As a whole, all in all.
globo m. Globe, sphere (esfera). || Spherical lampshade (de lámpara). || Balloon (aeróstato): *montar en globo*, to go up in a balloon. || Balloon (juguete). || — DEP. *Dar un globo*, to lob the ball (en tenis). || *En globo*, as a whole, all in all (en conjunto). || *Globo aerostático*, balloon, aerostat. || *Globo cautivo*, captive balloon. || MIL. *Globo de barrera*, barrage balloon. || *Globo dirigible*, dirigible. || ANAT. *Globo ocular*, eyeball. || *Globo sonda*, sounding balloon. || *Globo terráqueo* or *terrestre*, globe, earth.
globoso, sa adj. Globose, globate, spherical.
globular adj. Globular.
globulina f. BIOL. Globulin.
glóbulo m. Globule. || ANAT. Corpuscle: *glóbulos rojos, blancos*, red, white corpuscles.
globuloso, sa adj. Globular, globulous.
gloria f. Glory (fama alcanzada): *cubrirse de gloria*, to cover o.s. in glory *o* with glory. || Glory (que causa honor): *Cervantes es una de las glorias de España*, Cervantes is one of the glories of Spain. || Glory (majestad, magnificencia): *la gloria de Dios*, the glory of God. || ARTES. Glory, aureole, gloria (aureola). | Gloria (representación del cielo). || Delight (cosa que produce gran placer): *es una gloria* or *da gloria ver a los niños tan felices*, it is a delight to see the children so happy. || REL. Heaven, paradise, glory (cielo). || CULIN. Custard tart. || — *A gloria* heavenly, divine: *oler, saber a gloria*, to smell, to taste divine *o* heavenly. || *Dios le tenga en su gloria*, God rest his soul. || FIG. *Estar en la gloria*, to be in seventh heaven *o* in one's glory. || *Ganarse la Gloria*, to go to Heaven. || *¡Que Santa Gloria goce!*, God rest his soul.
— M. REL. Gloria (cántico o rezo).
gloriarse v. pr. To glory: *gloriarse de sus hazañas*, to glory in one's achievements. || To boast (vanagloriarse).
glorieta f. Arbour [U.S., arbor], bower (cenador). || Roundabout (encrucijada). || Square (plaza ajardinada).
glorificación f. Glorification.
glorificar v. tr. To glorify, to praise.
— V. pr. To glory (gloriarse): *glorificarse de haber hecho algo*, to glory in having done sth. || To boast (*de, en*, of) [vanagloriarse].
glorioso, sa adj. Glorious. || Blessed: *la gloriosa Virgen María*, the blessed Virgin Mary. || Vainglorious (vanidoso).
— F. The blessed Virgin Mary. || HIST. Spanish revolution of 1868.
glosa f. Gloss, marginal note (comentario, explicación de un texto). || FIG. Comment, note. || Gloss (composición poética). || MÚS. Variation.
glosador, ra m. y f. Glossarist, glossator.

glosar v. tr. To gloss (un texto). || FIG. To comment on (comentar). | To put an unfavourable interpretation on, to gloss (interpretar en mala parte).
glosario m. Glossary.
glose m. Glossing (acción de glosar).
glosopeda f. VET. Foot-and-mouth disease.
glótico, ca adj. ANAT. Glottal, glottic.
glotis f. inv. ANAT. Glottis.
glotón, ona adj. Gluttonous, greedy.
— M. y f. Glutton. || — M. ZOOL. Glutton.
glotonear v. intr. To guzzle, to devour, to eat greedily (comer con avidez).
glotonería f. Gluttony, greed, greediness.
glucemia f. MED. Glucemia.
glúcido m. QUÍM. Glucide.
glucinio m. QUÍM. Glucinium, glucinum.
glucógeno m. ANAT. Glycogen.
glucómetro m. Glucometer.
glucosa f. QUÍM. Glucose.
glucósido m. QUÍM. Glucoside.
gluglú m. Gurgle (del agua). || Gobble (del pavo). || *Hacer gluglú*, to gurgle (agua), to gobble (pavo).
gluglutear v. intr. To gobble (el pavo).
gluten m. Gluten.
glúteo, a adj. ANAT. Gluteal.
— M. Gluteus (músculo).
glutinoso, sa adj. Glutinous, viscous.
gneis m. GEOL. Gneiss.
gnómico, ca adj. Gnomic.
gnomo m. Gnome (duende).
gnomon m. Gnomon (instrumento astronómico o índice de reloj de sol).
gnosis f. FIL. Gnosis.
gnosticismo m. FIL. Gnosticism.
gnóstico, ca adj./s. FIL. Gnostic.
gnu m. ZOOL. Gnu.
gobernable adj. Governable (país). || Manageable (negocio). || Steerable (barco).
gobernación f. Government. || *Ministerio de la Gobernación*, Ministry of the Interior [in Spain].
— OBSERV. El "Ministerio de la Gobernación" es el equivalente del *Home Office* en Gran Bretaña y del *Department of the Interior* en los Estados Unidos.
El "Ministro de la Gobernación" corresponde al *Home Secretary* en Gran Bretaña y al *Secretary of the Interior* en los Estados Unidos.
gobernador, ra adj. Governing: *junta gobernadora*, governing board.
— M. Governor: *gobernador del Banco de España*, governor of the Bank of Spain. || — *Gobernador civil*, provincial governor. || *Gobernador general*, governor-general. || — F. Governor's wife.
gobernalle m. MAR. Rudder, helm (timón).
gobernante adj. Governing, ruling.
— M. y f. Ruler, governor (dirigente). || — M. FAM. Self-appointed head.
gobernar* v. tr. To govern (un país). || To run, to manage, to control, to direct, to conduct, to handle (dirigir). || To lead (una procesión, la danza, etc.). || MAR. To steer.
— V. intr. To govern. || MAR. To steer.
gobernativo, va adj. V. GUBERNATIVO.
gobierno m. Government (de un país): *gobierno federal, totalitario*, federal, totalitarian government. || Governorship (cargo de gobernador y duración). || Running, management, direction (administración): *el gobierno de un negocio*, the running of a business. || Guidance: *se lo digo a usted para su buen gobierno*, I am telling you for your own guidance. || MAR. Rudder, helm (timón). | Steering (docilidad al timón). || — *Gobierno civil*, provincial government (institución), civil governorship (cargo), government office *o* house (edificio). || *Gobierno de la casa*, housekeeping. || *Gobierno interino*, caretaker government. || *Servir de gobierno*, to be a guide.
gobio m. ZOOL. Gudgeon (pez de agua dulce).
goce m. Enjoyment (disfrute): *el goce de un privilegio*, the enjoyment of a privilege. || Pleasure: *goces materiales, sensuales*, material, sensual pleasures.
godo, da adj. Gothic.
— M. HIST. Goth. || (Ant.). FIG. Noble. || *Amer.* Dago, Spaniard [used contemptuously].
gofo, fa adj. Coarse, rough, uncouth.
gofrado m. TECN. Embossing (del cuero). | Corrugating (del papel). | Goffering (de la tela).
gofradora f. TECN. Embosser (para el cuero). | Goffer (para la tela).
gofrar v. tr. TECN. To emboss (el cuero). | To corrugate (el papel). | To goffer, to gauffer (la tela).
gol m. DEP. Goal (tanto): *marcar* or *meter un gol*, to score a goal. || — DEP. *Área de gol*, goal area. | *Gol average*, goal average. | *Tiro a gol*, shot.
gola f. FAM. Gullet (garganta). || MIL. Gorget (pieza de armadura). || Ruff (cuello alechugado). || ARQ. Cyma, ogee. || MAR. Channel, narrows, *pl.* (paso).
goleada f. DEP. Very high score. || FAM. *Ganar por una goleada*, to walk away with the match.
goleador m. DEP. Goal scorer.
golear v. tr. DEP. To score a series of goals against.
— V. intr. DEP. To score.
goleta f. MAR. Schooner.
golf m. Golf (juego). || — *Jugador de golf*, golfer. || *Palo de golf*, golf club. || *Terreno de golf*, golf course, golf links, *pl.*
golfa f. FAM. Little hussy, shameless hussy (mala). | Tart (prostituta).
golfear v. intr. To live like a ragamuffin, to roam the streets (un pilluelo). || To behave like a scoundrel, to get up to no good (un granuja). || To loiter *o* to loaf about (vagabundear).
golfería f. Gang of urchins *o* scoundrels (conjunto de golfos). || Mischief, mischievous *o* naughty trick (acción de un pilluelo). || [Piece of] roguery (de un granuja). || Vandalism, hooliganism (gamberrismo).
golfillo m. Street urchin.
golfista m. y f. Golfer, golf player.
golfo m. GEOGR. Gulf: *el golfo de México*, the Gulf of Mexico. | Bay: *el golfo de Vizcaya*, the Bay of Biscay. || Urchin, ragamuffin (pilluelo). || Scoundrel, rogue (granuja). || Loafer (holgazán).
Gólgota n. pr. m. GEOGR. Golgotha.
goliardo, da adj. Debauched, immoderate.
— M. HIST. Goliard (clérigo o estudiante vagabundo).
Goliat n. pr. m. Goliath (gigante).
golilla f. Ruff (gola). || Starched white collar (de magistrado). || Ruff [of poultry]. || TECN. Collar, flange (empalme). || *Amer.* [Peasant's] scarf *o* neckerchief.
— M. FIG. y FAM. Lawyer. || — Pl. FIG. y FAM. Legal fraternity, *sing.*
golondrina f. ZOOL. Swallow (ave). || MAR. Motorboat (lancha). || — *Golondrina de mar*, tern (ave), swallow fish (pez). || FIG. *Una golondrina no hace verano*, one swallow does not make a summer. || FIG. y FAM. *Voló la golondrina*, the bird has flown.
golondrino m. ZOOL. Young swallow (pollo de la golondrina). | Swallow fish (pez). || (P.us.). FIG. Rolling stone (vagabundo). | Deserter (soldado desertor). || MED. FAM. Boil *o* tumour in the armpit. || FIG. y FAM. *Voló el golondrino*, the bird has flown.
golosear v. intr. To nibble at *o* to eat sweets.
golosina f. Titbit, delicacy (manjar delicado). || Sweet (dulce). || FIG. Desire, longing (vivo deseo). | Greed, greediness (gula).
golosinar o **golosinear** v. intr. V. GOLOSEAR.
goloso, sa adj. Sweet-toothed, fond of sweets *o* of delicacies. || Greedy (que come mucho). || Appetizing, inviting (apetitoso). || FIG. Attractive, inviting (atractivo). || *Ser goloso*, to have a sweet tooth.
— M. y f. Gourmand. || *Tener muchos golosos*, to arouse envy.
golpazo m. Heavy *o* violent blow (golpe fuerte). || Violent impact (choque violento). || *Cerrar la puerta de un golpazo*, to slam the door.
golpe m. Blow, knock: *recibió un golpe en la cabeza*, he received a blow on the head. || Bump, collision (choque): *los coches chocaron con un golpe fuerte* the cars collided with a violent bump, the cars hit each other in a violent collision. || Jolt (sacudida). || Gust (de viento). || Beat (latido). || DEP. Shot, stroke (con un palo, una raqueta). | Kick, shot (en el fútbol). | Punch, blow (en el boxeo): *golpe bajo*, low punch. | Stroke (con un remo). || Crowd, throng (gran cantidad de gente). || FIG. Blow: *sufrió un golpe duro con la muerte de su madre*, he suffered a severe blow when his mother died. | Shock (sorpresa). | Witty remark, stroke of wit, flash of wit (agudeza). | Coup (acción astuta y afortunada): *dar un buen golpe*, to pull off a successful coup. | Job (acción realizada por malhechores). | Fit, attack, access: *un golpe de risa, de tos*, a fit of laughter, of coughing. || TECN. Spring lock (de cerradura). | Stroke (de émbolo). || Flap (cartera de bolsillo). || AGR. Hole for planting (hoyo). || — *Abrir de golpe*, to fling open. || *Abrirse de golpe*, to fly open. || *Acusar el golpe*, to feel the blow. || *A golpe de*, by means of. || *A golpes*, by force (con golpes), intermittently, in fits and starts (intermitentemente). || *A golpe seguro*, surely (sin duda), without any risk (sin riesgo). || *¡Buen golpe!*, well done! || *Cerrar de golpe*, to slam (una puerta). || FIG. y FAM. *Dar el golpe*, to cause a sensation, to be a hit: *con ese sombrero vas a dar el golpe*, you'll cause a sensation with that hat on. || *Dar golpes en*, to beat [on], to hammer [on], to knock [on]. || *Dar* or *asestar un golpe a alguien*, to deal *o* to strike s.o. a blow. || *Darse golpes de pecho*, to beat one's chest. || *Darse un golpe en el brazo*, to bang *o* to knock *o* to hit one's arm. || *De golpe*, suddenly, all of a sudden. || FAM. *De golpe y porrazo*, suddenly (de repente), very hurriedly (precipitadamente). || *De un golpe*, at one go, at one fell swoop (de una vez). || *Errar el golpe*, to miss. || *Golpe bien dado*, hit. || *Golpe de efecto*, coup de théâtre. || *Golpe de Estado*, coup d'état. || *Golpe de fortuna*, stroke of luck *o* of fortune. || *Golpe de gracia*, coup de grâce, death blow. || ARTES. *Golpe de luz*, highlight. || MIL. *Golpe de mano*, raid, sudden attack. || *Golpe de mar*, huge wave. || FIG. *Golpe de pecho*, confession [of one's sins], mea culpa. || *Golpe de suerte*, stroke of luck. || *Golpe de vista*, glance: *al primer golpe de vista*, at first glance. || *Golpe doble*, double hit (esgrima). || DEP. *Golpe franco*, free kick. || *Golpe maestro*, master stroke. || *Más fue el susto que el golpe*, I [you, he, etc.] was more frightened than hurt. || FAM. *No dar (ni) golpe*, not to do a stroke. || *Tener buenos golpes* or *cada golpe*, to be very witty, to be always coming out with witty remarks.

golpeador, ra adj. Beating, knocking.
— M. y f. Beater, knocker. || — M. Door knocker (aldaba).
golpeadura f. Knocking, banging (en la puerta). || Beating (de una persona, de la lluvia).
golpear v. tr. To hit, to strike, to knock (dar un golpe). || To beat, to pound, to hammer (dar varios golpes). || To punch (dar con el puño). || To bang (dar golpes fuertes). || To tap (golpetear). || To beat against: *la lluvia golpeaba los cristales*, the rain beat against the windowpanes.
— V. intr. To knock.
golpeo m. Knocking, banging (en la puerta). || Beating (de una persona, de la lluvia).
golpetazo m. Violent blow (golpe violento). || Violent collision (choque fuerte). || *Cerrar la puerta de un golpetazo*, to slam the door.
golpete m. Door *o* window catch [to keep the door or window open].
golpetear v. tr. e intr. To pound, to beat, to hammer (dar repetidos golpes). || To tap, to beat lightly, to drum (dar pequeños golpes). || To pitter-patter (la lluvia). || To rattle, to bang: *el postigo estuvo golpeteando toda la noche*, the shutter banged *o* rattled all night.
golpeteo n. Tapping, drumming, beating. || Pitter-patter (de la lluvia). || Rattling (de un postigo, puerta, etc.). || Knocking, knock (de un motor).
golpiza f. *Amer.* Beating (paliza).
gollería f. Delicacy, titbit (golosina). || FIG. Nicety, dainty *o* fancy thing (delicadeza). || FIG. *Pedir gollerías*, to ask for the moon and stars.
golletazo Blow on the neck of a bottle [in order to break it]. || TAUR. Sword thrust into the neck of the bull which pierces the animal's lungs. || FIG. *Dar un golletazo a un asunto*, to cut a matter short, to put an end to a matter.
gollete m. Throat, neck (cuello). || Neck (de botella). || FIG. y FAM. *Estar hasta el gollete*, to be fed up, to have had enough (estar harto), to be full [up] (haber comido mucho).
goma f. Gum, glue (para pegar). || Rubber (caucho): *suelas de goma*, rubber soles. || Rubber band (para sujetar objetos). || Elastic (en costura). || MED. Gumma. || POP. Rubber (condón). || — *Borrar con goma*, to rub out, to erase. || Amer. FAM. *Estar de goma*, to have a hangover (tener resaca). || *Goma adragante*, tragacanth. || *Goma arábiga*, gum arabic. || *Goma de borrar*, rubber, eraser. || *Goma de mascar*, chewing gum. || *Goma de pegar*, glue. || *Goma espuma*, foam rubber. || *Goma guta*, gamboge. || *Goma laca*, shellac.
gomal m. *Amer.* Rubber plantation.
gomero, ra adj. Rubber. || Gum.
— M. *Amer.* Rubber plantation worker (obrero). | Rubber planter (plantador). | Gum tree, rubber tree (árbol).
gomespuma f. Foam rubber.
gomina f. Hair dressing, hair cream.
gomita f. Rubber band.
Gomorra n. pr. HIST. Gomorrah.
gomorresina f. Gum resin.
gomosidad f. Gumminess, viscosity.
gomoso, sa adj. Gummy, viscous. || MED. Gummatous.
— M. FAM. Dandy, fop (pisaverde).
gónada f. ANAT. Gonad.
góndola f. Gondola (embarcación). || Gondola (de aeronave, globo). || *Amer.* Omnibus. | Wagon (coche).
gondolero m. Gondolier.
gonfalón m. Gonfalon, banner, standard (bandera).
gonfalonero m. Gonfalonier, standard bearer.
gong m. Gong.
gongorino, na o **gongorista** adj. Gongoristic, gongoresque (culterano).
— M. y f. Gongorist, euphuist, cultist.
gongorismo m. Gongorism, euphuism (culteranismo).
goniometría f. Goniometry.
goniómetro m. Goniometer.
gonococo m. MED. Gonococcus.
gonorrea f. MED. Gonorrhoea [U.S., gonorrhea].
gordal adj. Big, fat, large.
gordana f. Animal fat.
gordiano adj. Gordian.
gordiflón, ona o **gordinflón, ona** adj. FAM. Chubby, podgy.
— M. y f. FAM. Chubby person, fatty.
gordo, da adj. Fat (persona): *un hombre gordo*, a fat man. || Big (cosa): *una manzana muy gorda*, a very big apple. || Thick: *hilo gordo*, thick thread. || Thick, coarse (tela). || Thick: *una rama gorda*, a thick branch. || Fat, fatty: *tocino gordo*, fatty bacon. || FIG. y FAM. Huge (enorme) | Important, big (acontecimiento). || — *Agua gorda*, hard water. || FAM. *Algo gordo ha ocurrido*, sth. really big has happened. || *Dedo gordo del pie*, big toe. || FAM. *De los gordos, de las gordas*, enormous, huge: *es una equivocación de las gordas*, it is an enormous error. || FIG. *Hacer la vista gorda*, v. VISTA. || *Lengua gorda*, furry tongue. || FAM. *Me cae gordo*, he gets on my nerves, I can't stand him. || FIG. y FAM. *Peces gordos* or *gente gorda*, bigwigs, big shots, V.I.P.'s. | *Premio gordo*, first prize, grand prize (lotería). || FIG. y FAM. *Reventar de gordo*, to be as fat as a pig. | *Vacas gordas*, v. VACA.
— M. Fat: *no me gusta la carne con gordo*, I don't like meat with fat on. || FAM. First prize, grand prize: *le ha caído* or *tocado el gordo*, he has won the grand prize. || — F. FAM. Ten-cent piece (moneda). || — FAM. *Armar la gorda*, to cause a rumpus *o* a ruckus. | *Estoy sin una gorda*, I don't have a penny to my name. | *Se va a armar la gorda*, there is going to be [big] trouble.
gordolobo BOT. Mullein (verbasco).
gordura f. Fat (grasa). || Corpulence. || *Amer.* Cream.
gorgojarse o **gorgojearse** v. pr. AGR. To be infested with weevils (semillas).
gorgojo m. Weevil (insecto). || FIG. y FAM. Midget, dwarf, small person.
Gorgona n. pr. f. MIT. Gorgon.
gorgoritos m. pl. MÚS. Roulades, warble, *sing.* || Quaver, *sing.*, warble, *sing.* (de la voz al hablar).
gorgotear v. intr. To gurgle.
gorgoteo m. Gurgle.
gorguera f. Ruff (cuello). || Gorget (armadura). || BOT. Involucre.
gori m. FAM. Row, racket, ruckus: *armar gori*, to make a racket, to kick up a row.
gorigori m. FAM. Dirge, funeral chant.
gorila m. ZOOL. Gorilla.
gorjal f. Bands, *pl.* (de la ropa sacerdotal). || Gorget (de armadura).
gorjeador, ra o **gorjeante** adj. Warbling, chirping, twittering.
gorjear v. intr. To chirp, to warble, to twitter (los pájaros). || MÚS. To sing roulades, to warble.
— V. pr. To gurgle (los niños).
gorjeo m. Warbling, chirping, twittering (de los pájaros). || Roulade, warble (canto). || Gurgle (balbuceo de los niños).
gorra f. Peaked cap, cap with visor. || Bonnet (de niños). || Cap (de jockey). || MIL. Bearskin, busby (de granaderos). || *Gorra de plato*, peaked cap.
— M. FIG. y FAM. Sponger, scrounger, cadger (gorrón). || — FAM. *Comer de gorra*, to have a buckshee meal. | *De gorra*, free (gratis). | *Pasar la gorra*, to pass the hat. | *Vivir de gorra*, to sponge, to cadge, to scrounge.
gorrear v. intr. *Amer.* To sponge, to cadge, to scrounge.
gorrero, ra m. y f. Maker *o* seller of caps. || — M. FAM. Sponger, scrounger, cadger (gorrón).
gorrinada o **gorrinería** f. Piggishiness (porquería). || Dirty trick (mala jugada).
gorrino, na m. y f. Sucking pig (cerdo de menos de cuatro meses), piglet, pigling (cerdo pequeño). || Pig, hog (cerdo). || FAM. Pig (sucio).
gorrión m. ZOOL. Sparrow (pájaro). || *Amer.* Colibri, hummingbird.
gorriona f. Female sparrow.
gorrista adj. FAM. Sponging, cadging.
— M. y f. FAM. Sponger, scrounger, cadger (gorrón).
gorro m. Cap: *gorro militar, de baño*, military, swimming *o* bathing cap. || Bonnet (de niños). || Hat (de cocinero). || — FAM. *Estar hasta el gorro de algo*, to be fed up with sth. || *Gorro de dormir*, nightcap. || *Gorro frigio*, cap of liberty, Phrygian cap. || FAM. *Poner el gorro a uno*, to embarrass s.o. (molestar), to deceive (ser infiel).
gorrón m. Pebble (guijarro). || Silkworm that does not complete its cocoon (gusano de seda). || TECN. Pivot, gudgeon.
gorrón, ona adj. Sponging, cadging. || *Pasa gorrona*, big raisin.
— M. y f. Sponger, scrounger, cadger.
gorronear v. intr. To sponge, to scrounge, to cadge.
gorronería f. Sponging, cadging.
gota f. Drop (de líquido). || ARQ. Gutta. || MED. Gout. || FIG. Drop (pequeña cantidad): *una gota de vino*, a drop of wine. || — *Caer gota a gota*, to drip. || *Gota a gota*, drop by drop. || MED. *Gota coral*, epilepsy. || *Gota militar*, gleet. || FIG. *La última gota hace rebasar la copa*, it's the last straw that breaks the camel's back. | *No ver ni gota*, to be as blind as a bat (estar medio ciego), not to be able to see one's hand in front of one's face (a causa de la oscuridad). | *Parecerse como dos gotas de agua*, to be as like as two peas in a pod. | *Sudar la gota gorda*, v. SUDAR. || *Transfusión gota a gota*, drip transfusion.
goteado, da adj. Spotted, speckled.
gotear v. intr. To drip, to dribble (caer gota a gota): *el agua gotea del tejado*, the water drips from the roof. || To leak (salirse un líquido). || To gutter (las velas).
goteo m. Dripping.
gotera f. Gutter (canalón). || Leak, leakage (en un techo). || Stain resulting from dripping water (mancha). || Valance (de cama). || — Pl. FIG. Aches and pains (achaques). || *Amer.* Outskirts, environs (afueras).
gotero m. *Amer.* Dropper (cuentagotas).
goterón m. ARQ. Throat. || Big raindrop (de lluvia).
gótico, ca adj. Gothic: *lengua, letra gótica*, gothic language, type. || FIG. Noble. || FAM. *Niño gótico*, show-off.
— M. Gothic: *gótico flamígero*, flamboyant gothic.
gotita f. Droplet. || FIG. Drop, little drop (pequeña cantidad).
gotoso, sa adj. MED. Gouty.
— M. y f. Person with gout.
goyesco, ca adj. Characteristic *o* in the style of Goya.
gozar v. intr. To enjoy. || To be delighted (alegrarse): *gozo con su visita*, I am delighted by your visit.

|| *Gozar del beneficio de la duda*, to have *o* to enjoy the benefit of the doubt.
— V. tr. To enjoy: *gozar buena salud*, to enjoy good health. || FAM. *Gozarla*, to have a good time, to enjoy o.s. (divertirse).
— V. pr. To enjoy, to rejoice in: *gozarse en hacer daño*, to enjoy doing harm.
gozne m. Hinge.
gozo m. Joy (alegría): *saltar de gozo*, to jump for joy. || Pleasure, enjoyment (placer). || Delight (regocijo). || — Pl. Poem (*sing.*) in honour of the Virgin. || — *Mi gozo en un pozo*, that's just my luck. || *No caber en sí de gozo*, to be beside o.s. with joy.
gozoso, sa adj. Joyful, delighted (alegre).
gozque o **gozquejo** m. Little yapping dog.
grabación f. Recording (discos, etc.). || *Grabación en una cinta magnetofónica*, tape recording.
grabado m. Engraving: *grabado punteado*, stipple engraving. || Picture, illustration (estampa): *un libro con muchos grabados*, a book with many pictures. || Recording (discos, cinta magnetofónica, etc.). || — *Grabado al agua fuerte*, etching. || *Grabado en cobre* or *en dulce*, copperplate. || *Grabado en hueco*, intaglio. || *Grabado en madera*, woodcut.
grabador, ra adj. Recording.
— M. y f. Engraver. || — F. *Amer.* Recorder: *grabadora de cinta*, tape recorder. || — *Grabador al agua fuerte*, etcher. || *Grabador de cinta*, tape recorder.
grabadura f. Engraving.
grabar v. tr. To engrave: *grabar al buril*, to engrave with a burin. || To carve, to engrave (madera). || To record (discos, cintas magnetofónicas). || FIG. To engrave, to imprint: *grabar en la memoria*, to engrave on one's mind *o* on one's memory. || — *Grabar al agua fuerte*, to etch. || *Grabar en relieve*, to emboss.
gracejo m. Wit, humour (humor). || Bantering manner (modo de decir festivo).
gracia f. Grace (divina). || Favour: *conceder una gracia*, to concede *o* to grant a favour. || Pardon, mercy (indulto). || Grace, gracefulness (atractivo, donaire). || Charm (atractivo): *no es guapa pero tiene cierta gracia*, she isn't pretty but she has a certain charm. || Grace (título). || Joke (broma), witty remark (dicho chistoso): *siempre está diciendo gracias*, he is always telling jokes, he is always making witty remarks. || Wit, humour (humor). || FAM. Favour, dirty trick (mala pasada): *me hizo una gracia que me ha costado cien mil pesetas*, he did me a favour *o* he played a dirty trick on me that has cost me a hundred thousand pesetas. || Name (nombre de pila). || — Pl. Thanks (agradecimiento): *miles de gracias*, a thousand thanks. || MIT. Graces: *las Tres Gracias*, the Three Graces.
— REL. *Acción de gracias*, thanksgiving. || *Ahí está la gracia*, that's what's funny about it, that's where the humour is. || *Caer en gracia a uno*, to make a hit with s.o. || *Dar gracias al cielo* or *a Dios*, to give thanks to God. || *Dar las gracias a*, to thank, to say thank you to, to give thanks to. || *De gracia*, free (gratis). || REL. *En estado de gracia*, in a state of grace. || *En gracia a*, because of (a causa de). || *Estar en gracia cerca de alguien*, to be in s.o.'s good graces. || *¡Gracias!*, thank you, thanks (fam.). || *Gracias a*, thanks to. || *¡Gracias a Dios!* or *¡A Dios gracias!*, thank God!, thank Heaven! || *Gracias a que*, thanks to the fact that. || *Gracias por*, thank you for, thanks for: *gracias por haber venido*, thanks for coming, thanks for having come. || *Hacer gracia*, to like (gustar): *este hombre no me hace gracia*, I don't like this fellow; to strike as funny, to amuse: *este chiste no me hace gracia*, this joke doesn't strike me as funny. || *Hacer gracia de*, to spare: *le hago gracia de todos los detalles*, I shall spare you all the details. || *¡Maldita la gracia que tiene esto!* or *¡menuda gracia tiene!* or *¡tiene muy poca gracia!*, it's not a bit funny! || *Más vale caer en gracia que ser gracioso*, charm can do more than merit. || *Me hace poca gracia hacerlo ahora*, I'm not keen on doing it now, I don't exactly feel like doing it now. || *¡Muchas gracias!*, thank you very much, thanks very much, many thanks, thanks a lot (fam.). || *No estar para gracias*, not to be in the mood for jokes. || *No le veo la gracia* I don't see what's funny. || *No tener ni pizca de gracia*, not to be a bit funny. || *Por la gracia de Dios*, by the grace of God. || FIG. *Por obra y gracia del Espíritu Santo*, as if by magic. || *¡Qué gracia tiene!*, how funny! || *Sin gracia*, graceless: *facciones sin gracia*, graceless features. || *Tener gracia*, to be funny: *tiene mucha gracia*, it is very funny. || *Tener toda la gracia*, to be really funny. || COM. *Un día de gracia*, a day's grace. || *Y gracias si*, and be thankful if.
graciable adj. Gracious (amable). || Affable (afable). || Easily granted (que se puede otorgar).
grácil adj. Gracile, slender, slim (delgado). || Slender: *árboles gráciles*, slender trees. || Delicate (delicado).
gracilidad f. Slenderness, slimness.
graciosamente adv. Gracefully, graciously (con garbo). || Amusingly, funnily (divertidamente). || Gratuitously, free (gratis).
graciosidad f. Gracefulness, grace (encanto).
gracioso, sa adj. Funny, amusing (divertido): *un chico muy gracioso*, a very funny boy. || Witty (agudo). || Comical (cómico). || Charming, graceful, gracious (encantador). || Gratuitous, free (gratuito). || *Su Graciosa Majestad*, His *o* Her Gracious Majesty.
— M. TEATR. "Gracioso", comic character [buffoon in Spanish comedy]. || — FAM. *Hacerse el gracioso*, to clown around. || *Lo gracioso de la cosa* or *lo gracioso del caso*, the funny thing about it. || — F. TEATR. Soubrette.
grada f. Step, stair (peldaño). || Row (línea de asientos). || Tier (de anfiteatro, estadio). || Step (al pie del altar). || Grille, grill (celosía, verja de locutorio). || AGR. Harrow. || MAR. Slip, slipway (para construir un barco). || — Pl. Flight (*sing.*) of steps (escalinata).
gradación f. Gradation. || Climax (figura retórica).
gradar v. tr. AGR. To harrow.
gradería f. o **graderío** m. Steps, *pl.*, flight of steps. || Rows, *pl.* (teatro). || Tiers, *pl.* (anfiteatro, estadio). || *Gradería cubierta*, grandstand (tribuna).
gradiente n. FÍS. Gradient. || *Amer.* Gradient (declive).
gradilla f. Small stepladder (escalerilla). || TECN. Brick mould [U.S., brick mold] (molde para ladrillos).
grado m. Degree: *la temperatura es de diez grados bajo cero*, the temperature is ten degrees below zero. || Degree (parentesco). || Degree, grade (jerarquía). || Degree (porcentaje): *grado de humedad*, degree of humidity. || Content (contenido). || Degree (nivel): *grado de invalidez*, degree of disablement. || Stage, step (fase): *los diferentes grados de la evolución de las especies*, the different stages of the evolution of the species. || MIL. Rank. || Degree (título universitario). || Year, form [U.S., grade]: *alumno del segundo grado*, second year student. || GRAM., MAT. y FÍS. Degree. || Step (peldaño). || Willingness (voluntad). || — *De grado, de buen grado*, willingly. || *De grado o por fuerza* or *de buen o mal grado*, willy-nilly. || *De mal grado*, unwillingly. || MAT. *Ecuación de segundo grado*, quadratic equation, equation of the second degree. || *En sumo* or *en último* or *en alto grado* or *en grado superlativo*, in the extreme, extremely. || *Mal de mí, de tu, de su grado*, against my, your, his *o* her will, unwillingly. || *Primo en tercer grado*, third cousin, cousin three times removed. || *Vino que tiene once grados*, wine which is eleven degrees proof.
graduable adj. Adjustable: *tirantes graduables*, adjustable braces. || That can be graduated.
graduación f. Graduation. || QUÍM. Strength (porcentaje de alcohol). | Determination of the strength (evaluación de este porcentaje). || MIL. Rank. || FIG. Progression.
graduado, da adj. Graduated: *escala graduada*, graduated scale. || Graduate: *graduado en la Universidad de París*, graduate of the University of Paris. || *Vaso graduado*, graduated flask.
— M. y f. Graduate.
graduador m. TECN. Gauge, graduator (utensilio). | Adjusting screw (tornillo).
gradual adj. Gradual.
— M. REL. Gradual.
graduando, da m. y f. Undergraduate.
graduar v. tr. To graduate (termómetro). || To regulate, to set, to adjust: *graduar la temperatura*, to regulate the temperature. || To measure *o* to determine the strength of (alcohol, vino). || To measure (medir). || To calibrate (calibrar). || To test (la vista). || To confer the rank of, to commission as: *graduar de capitán a uno*, to confer the rank of captain on s.o. || To confer a degree on: *graduar a un estudiante de doctor*, to confer a doctor's degree on a student. || To grade (escalonar).
— V. pr. MIL. To take a commission, to receive the rank of: *graduarse de capitán*, to take a commission as captain. || To graduate (*de*, as) to receive the degree (*de*, of): *graduarse de doctor en filosofía*, to graduate as a doctor of philosophy.
grafía f. Sign or signs representing the sound of a word. || Spelling (ortografía).
gráfica f. V. GRÁFICO.
gráfico, ca adj. Graphic. || FIG. Graphic, vivid: *me hizo una descripción muy gráfica*, he gave me a very graphic description. || *Artes gráficas*, graphic arts.
— M. y f. MAT. Graph. || Chart (de la temperatura). || Diagram (esquema).
gráfila f. Milled edge (de una moneda).
grafilar v. tr. To mill, to knurl.
grafismo m. Writing.
grafito m. MIN. Graphite, black lead.
grafología f. Graphology.
grafólogo m. Graphologist.
gragea f. Sugar-coated pill (medicamento). || Sugar almond [U.S., Jordan almond].
graja f. ZOOL. Rook, crow.
grajo m. ZOOL. Rook, crow (graja). || *Amer.* Body odour [U.S., body odor] (mal olor).
grama f. BOT. Bermuda grass.
gramática f. Grammar: *gramática comparada, histórica*, comparative, historical grammar. || FAM. *Gramática parda*, gumption.
gramatical adj. Grammatical: *análisis gramatical*, grammatical analysis.
gramático, ca adj. Grammatical.
— M. y f. Grammarian.
gramil m. Gauge, marking gauge (herramienta).
gramilla m. Brake (agramadera). || BOT. Brake (agramadera).

gramíneo, a adj. BOT. Gramineous, graminaceous.
— F. pl. BOT. Gramineae, graminaceae.
gramo m. Gramme, gram.
gramófono m. Gramophone [U.S., phonograph].
gramola f. Gramophone [U.S., phonograph].
gran adj. V. GRANDE.
grana f. Seeding (acción de granar). || Seeding time (época). || Seed (semilla). || ZOOL. Cochineal (cochinilla). || Kermes (quermes). || Scarlet (color). || Scarlet cloth (tela). || — *Dar grana*, to go to seed (las plantas). || *Ponerse rojo como la grana*, to turn as red as a lobster *o* as a beetroot.
— Adj. Scarlet (color).
granada f. BOT. Pomegranate. || MIL. Grenade: *granada de mano*, hand grenade. | Shell (de cañón): *granada de mortero*, mortar shell.
Granada n. pr. GEOGR. Granada.
granadero m. MIL. Grenadier (soldado).
granadilla f. Passionflower, granadilla, grenadilla.
granadino, na adj. [Of *o* from] Granada.
— M. y f. Inhabitant *o* native of Granada. || — F. Grenadine (jarabe). || Beverage made with grenadine syrup (bebida). || Flamenco song from Granada.
granado m. BOT. Pomegranate tree (arbusto).
granado, da adj. Grainy (espiga). || Ripe (trigo). || FIG. Notable, distinguished (notable). | Select (escogido). | Mature (maduro). | Tall (alto). || FIG. *Lo más granado*, the most select, the pick.
granalla f. Granular metal.
granar v. intr. BOT. To seed. || FIG. To mature (los jóvenes).
granate m. MIN. Garnet. || *Granate almandino*, almandine, almandite.
— Adj. Garnet (color).
granazón f. Seeding. || FIG. Maturity (de las personas).
Gran Bretaña n. pr. f. GEOGR. Great Britain.
grande adj. Big, large: *una casa muy grande*, a very big house. || Big, tall (alto): *es un chico muy grande*, he is a very big boy. || Great, big: *oímos un gran ruido*, we heard a great noise. || Great, high (elevado): *el avión vuela a gran altura*, the aeroplane flies at great altitude; *gran velocidad*, high speed. || Great, large: *un gran número de gente*, a large number of people. || FIG. Great: *un gran hombre*, a great man. | Grand, great: *ha dado una gran fiesta*, he gave a grand party. | Eminent (eminente). || *Amer*. Middle-aged (de cierta edad). || — *A lo grande*, on a grand scale, in a big way: *vivir a lo grande*, to live on a grand scale. || *En grande*, as a whole (en conjunto). || *Le queda grande este vestido*, this dress is too big *o* too large for you. || GEOGR. *Los Grandes Lagos*, the Great Lakes. || FIG. y FAM. *¡Mira que esto es grande!*, that's the limit!, that's the last straw! | *Pasarlo en grande*, to have a whale of a time, to have a fabulous time (divertirse mucho). | *¡Sería una gran cosa!*, that would be great! || *Venir grande*, to be too big. || FIG. *Ver las cosas en grande*, to see things on a grand scale *o* in a big way.
— M. Grandee: *grande de España*, Spanish grandee. || Eldest (niño mayor). || *Los Cuatro Grandes*, the Big Four.
— OBSERV. The apocopated form of *grande*, *gran*, is used before singular nouns of both genders.
grandeza f. Greatness, magnitude: *la grandeza de un proyecto*, the greatness of a project. || Size (tamaño). || Grandeur, splendour [U.S., splendor], magnificence (esplendor). || Greatness, grandeur, nobleness (nobleza de sentimientos). || Status of grandee (dignidad de grande de España). || Grandees, *pl.* (conjunto de los grandes).
grandilocuencia f. Grandiloquence.
grandilocuente o **grandílocuo, cua** adj. Grandilocuent.
grandiosidad f. Grandeur, magnificence, splendour [U.S., splendor]: *la grandiosidad del espectáculo*, the grandeur of the spectacle.
grandioso, sa adj. Magnificent, grand. || Grandiose (más ostentoso).
grandor m. Size (tamaño). || Magnitude.
grandote, ta adj. FAM. Very big.
grandullón, ona adj. FAM. Very big, oversized.
graneado, da adj. Granulated (granulado). || MIL. *Fuego graneado*, running fire.
— M. Grain (del cuero, tejido).
granear v. tr. To sow (sembrar el grano). || TECN. To stipple (para el grabado al humo). | To grain (piedra litográfica).
granel (a) loc. adv. In bulk: *cereales, colonia a granel*, cereals, cologne in bulk. || Loose: *naranjas a granel*, loose oranges. || FIG. In abundance, galore (en abundancia).
granero m. Granary, barn.
granillo m. [Small] pimple (en la piel). || Small tumour (de los pájaros).
granítico, ca adj. Granitic, granite.
granito m. MIN. Granite. || MED. Granule (en la piel). | Pimple (acné). || Small grain (grano pequeño). || FIG. *Echar su granito de sal en la conversación*, to put a word in [the conversation].
granívoro, ra adj. Granivorous, grain-eating.
granizada f. Hailstorm, hail (tormenta de granizo). || FIG. Hail: *una granizada de golpes*, a hail of blows. || Iced drink (bebida).

granizado m. Iced drink. || *Granizado de limón*, iced lemon.
granizar v. intr. To hail.
granizo m. Hail. || Hail, hailstones, *pl.* (granos de la granizada).
granja f. Farm: *granja modelo*, model farm; *granja avícola*, poultry farm.
granjear v. intr. (P.us.). To trade, to deal. || MAR. To gain, to fetch: *granjear a barlovento*, to gain the wind, to fetch to windward.
— V. tr. *Amer*. To steal (robar).
— V. pr. To gain, to win, to earn (conquistar): *granjearse la confianza de*, to gain the confidence of; *se granjeó su afecto*, he won his affection. || To earn (una reputación).
granjería f. Profits, *pl.*, gains, *pl.* (ganancia).
granjero, ra m. y f. Farmer.
grano m. Grain (de los cereales). || Seed (semilla). || Grape (de uva). || Bean (de café). || Grain (partícula): *grano de arena, de sal*, grain of sand, of salt. || MED. Pimple, spot (tumorcillo). || Grain (estructura): *madera de grano grueso*, coarse-grained wood, wood with a coarse grain. || FOT. Grain. || — Pl. Grain, *sing.*, cereals. || — FIG. *Apartar el grano de la paja*, to separate the wheat from the tares. || *Grano de pimienta*, peppercorn. || FAM. *Ir al grano*, to get to the point, to go straight to the point. *No es grano de anís*, it is no trifle, it is no small matter. || FIG. *Un grano no hace granero pero ayuda al compañero*, many a mickle makes a muckle, every little bit helps.
granoso, sa adj. Granular. || Grainy: *cuero granoso*, grainy leather.
granuja f. Loose grapes, *pl.* (uva). || Pips, *pl.*, seeds, *pl.* (semillas). || FAM. Gang (banda de granujas). || — M. Rogue, scoundrel, knave, rascal (canalla). || Ragamuffin, urchin (pilluelo).
granujada o **granujería** f. Gang of rogues *o* of urchins (conjunto de granujas). || FIG. Roguish *o* knavish trick, piece of roguery *o* of knavery.
granujiento, ta adj. Pimply.
granujilla m. FAM. Rascal.
granulación f. Granulation.
granulado, da adj. Granulated.
— M. Granulation.
granular adj. Granular. || Pimply (granujiento).
granular v. tr. To granulate.
— V. pr. To granulate. || To break out in pimples (cubrirse de granos).
gránulo m. Granule. || MED. Small pill.
granuloso, sa adj. Granular.
granza f. BOT. Madder (rubia). || — Pl. Chaff, *sing.* (de las semillas). || Dross, *sing.*, slag, *sing.* (del metal).
grao m. Beach, shore (playa). || *El Grao*, the port of Valencia (España).
grapa f. Staple. || Cramp, clamp (para la madera). || ARQ. Cramp (para sujetar). | Keystone (adorno). || MED. Stitch. || — Pl. VET. Grapes. || — *Coser con grapas*, to staple. || *Sujeción con grapas*, stapling.
grasa f. Fat (cuerpo graso). || Grease (sustancia grasienta). || Grease (mugre, suciedad). || Grease, lubricating oil (lubricante). || — Pl. MIN. Slag, *sing.* (de metal). || FAM. *Criar grasa*, to get fat.
grasera f. Container for grease *o* fat *o* drippings (para conservar la grasa). || Dripping pan (para recoger la grasa).
grasiento, ta adj. Greasy, oily. || Grimy, filthy (sucio). || Greasy (resbaladizo).
graso, sa adj. Fatty. || *Cuerpo graso*, fatty body.
grasoso, sa adj. Fatty (graso). || Greasy, oily (grasiento).
gratar v. tr. TECN. To burnish (la plata o el oro).
gratén m. CULIN. Gratin: *lenguado al gratén*, sole au gratin.
gratificación f. Reward (recompensa). || Gratuity, tip (propina). || Bonus (sobresueldo). || Bounty (subvención). || Gratification (agrado, satisfacción).
gratificador, ra adj. Rewarding (que compensa). || Gratifying (que satisface).
— M. y f. Rewarder.
gratificar v. tr. To reward (recompensar). || To tip, to give a gratuity to (dar una propina). || To give a bonus to (dar sobresueldo). || To gratify (satisfacer).
grátil o **gratil** m. MAR. Foreleech, head (de la vela).
gratín m. CULIN. Gratin.
gratis adv. Gratis, free, for nothing.
gratitud f. Gratitude.
grato, ta adj. Pleasing, agreeable: *grato al paladar*, pleasing to the taste. || Pleasant, pleasing, agreeable: *grato de oír*, pleasant to hear; *recuerdo grato*, pleasing memory. || Welcome, appreciated (apreciado). || *Amer*. Grateful (agradecido). || — *En espera de sus gratas noticias*, hoping to hear from you soon. || *Me es grato anunciar que*, I am pleased to announce that.
gratuidad f. Gratuitousness. || FIG. Gratuitousness, lack of foundation. || *La gratuidad de las clases*, the fact that the classes are free.
gratuitamente adv. Free, for nothing (gratis). || FIG. Gratuitously, unfoundedly.
gratuito, ta adj. Free: *entrada gratuita*, free entrance. || FIG. Uncalled-for, unwarranted, gratuitous: *afirmación gratuita*, gratuitous remark.
grava f. Gravel.

gravamen m. Obligation (obligación). || Tax (impuesto). || Burden (carga, peso). || Encumbrance (estorbo). || Inconvenience (molestia).
gravar v. tr. To tax (imponer contribución): *gravar las importaciones*, to tax the imports. || To levy, to impose (un impuesto). || To burden, to encumber (imponer gravamen): *gravar un país con impuestos*, to burden a country with taxes. || To burden: *tener un coche grava mucho un pequeño presupuesto*, having a car heavily burdens a small budget.
grave adj. Serious, grave: *enfermedad, situación grave*, grave illness, situation. || Grave: *una persona grave*, a grave person. || Grave, serious (mistake). || Serious (herida). || Low, deep: *una voz grave*, a low voice. || Solemn, serious: *estilo grave*, solemn style. || MÚS. Low, deep. || FÍS. Heavy, weighty (atraído por la tierra). || GRAM. Paroxytone (palabra). | Grave: *acento grave*, grave accent. || *Estar grave*, to be seriously ill.
— M. FÍS. Heavy body. || MÚS. Bass.
gravedad f. Gravity, seriousness (de una enfermedad, una falta, un accidente). || Solemnity, seriousness: *la gravedad de sus palabras*, the solemnity of his words. || Seriousness, gravity (de un personaje). || FÍS. Gravity: *leyes de la gravedad*, laws of gravity; *centro de gravedad*, centre of gravity. || MÚS. Depth. || — *Enfermo de gravedad*, seriously *o* gravely ill. || *Herido de gravedad*, seriously *o* badly hurt *o* wounded.
grávido, da adj. Gravid, pregnant.
gravilla f. [Fine] gravel. || *Cubrir una carretera con gravilla*, to gravel a road.
gravimetría f. Gravimetry.
gravitación f. FÍS. Gravitation: *gravitación universal*, universal gravitation.
gravitar v. intr. FÍS. To gravitate. || FIG. *Gravitar sobre*, to rest on (apoyarse), to rest upon, to lie upon (recaer), to weigh on, to burden down (pesar): *gravitaba sobre él toda la responsabilidad*, all the responsibility weighed on him *o* burdened him down; to hang over (una amenaza).
gravoso, sa adj. Costly (costoso). || Onerous (oneroso). || Burdensome, heavy (pesado). || Boring, tiresome (molesto).
graznador, ra adj. Cawing (cuervo). || Squawking (aves en general). || Quacking (pato), cackling, gaggling (ganso).
graznar v. intr. To caw (cuervo). || To quack (pato). || To squawk (aves en general). || To cackle, to gaggle (ganso).
graznido m. Caw, cawing (cuervo). || Quack, quacking (pato). || Squawk, squawking (aves en general). || Cackle (ganso).
greba f. Greave (armadura).
greca f. ARQ. Fret.
Grecia n. pr. f. GEOGR. Greece.
grecismo m. Grecism, hellenism.
greco, ca adj. (Ant.). Greek, Grecian.
— M. y f. (Ant.). Greek (griego).
grecolatino, na adj. Greco-Latin.
grecorromano, na adj. Greco-Roman.
greda f. MIN. Fuller's earth, clay.
gredal m. Clay pit.
gredoso, sa adj. Clayey.
gregario, ria adj. Gregarious. || *Instinto gregario*, herd instinct.
— M. FAM. Teammate who helps the team leader during a race (en ciclismo).
gregoriano, na adj. Gregorian: *canto, calendario gregoriano*, Gregorian chant, calendar.
Gregorio n. pr. m. Gregory.
greguería f. Hubbub, uproar (algarabía). || "Greguería" [a type of aphorism created by the Spanish writer Ramón Gómez de la Serna].
gregüescos m. pl. Breeches (calzones).
grelos m. pl. Turnip tops.
gremial adj. HIST. Guild. || Union (de una asociación).
— M. HIST. Guildsman. || Union member. || REL. Gremial (paño del obispo).
gremio m. HIST. Guild (individuos de igual oficio). || Association, society, union (asociación): *gremio de panaderos*, Association of Bakers. || Brotherhood, fraternity (fraternidad).
greña f. Mop *o* shock *o* mat of hair (cabellera descuidada). || Tangle, entanglement (maraña). || FAM. *Andar a la greña*, to tear each other's hair, to fight (pelear), to squabble, to argue (discutir).
greñudo, da adj. Dishevelled, unkempt (mal peinado).
gres m. GEOL. Sandstone. || Potter's clay (mezcla para hacer cerámica). || Stoneware: *vasija de gres*, stoneware pot. || — *Gres cerámico*, stoneware. || *Gres flameado*, glazed earthenware.
gresca f. Hubbub, uproar (ruido): *armar* or *meter gresca*, to create an uproar. || Row (jaleo). || Quarrel, row, fight (riña): *andar a la gresca*, to look for a fight.
grey f. Flock, herd (rebaño). || FIG. Group (individuos de igual raza o nación). | Congregation, flock (fieles).
grial m. Grail (vaso místico). || *El Santo Grial*, the Holy Grail.
griego, ga adj. Greek, Grecian.
— M. y f. Greek. || — M. Greek (idioma). || — FAM. *Eso es griego para mí*, that's Greek to me, that's double Dutch to me. | *Hablar en griego*, to speak gibberish, to talk double Dutch.
grieta f. Crack, fissure, crevice (en el suelo). || Crack, crevice (en el hielo de un glaciar). || Crack, chink, cranny (en una pared). || MED. Chap (en la piel).
grieteado, da adj. Cracked. || — M. TECN. Crackle.
grietearse v. pr. To crack. || To crackle (cerámica). || To get chapped (la piel).
grifa f. *Amer.* Claw (garra). || FAM. Marijuana.
grifería f. Plumbing (grifos y accesorios). || Manufacture of plumbing materials (fabricación).
grifo, fa adj. Dishevelled (desgreñado), curly (rizado), kinky (crespo).
— M. Griffin, griffon (animal fabuloso). || Tap [U.S., faucet] (llave o caño). || Spigot (de barril). || *Amer.* Petrol-pump [U.S., gas pump] (surtidor de gasolina).
grifón m. Griffon (perro).
grilla f. ZOOL. Female cricket. || *Amer.* Row (riña).
grillera f. Cricket hole (agujero). || Cricket cage (jaula). || FIG. y FAM. Bedlam.
grillete m. MAR. Shackle, fetter. || — Pl. Shackles, fetters (cadena de los presos).
grillo m. ZOOL. Cricket. || BOT. Shoot, sprout. || — Pl. Shackles, fetters (grilletes). || FIG. Shackles. || ZOOL. *Grillo cebollero* or *real*, mole cricket.
grima f. Annoyance, displeasure (disgusto). || Disgust (repulsión). || Horror (horror). || *Dar grima a uno*, to get on one's nerves (irritar): *me da grima verle*, it gets on my nerves to see him; to give one the shivers (horrorizar).
grímpola f. Pennant (gallardete).
gringada f. Action typical of a "gringo".
gringo, ga adj. Foreign.
— M. y f. Foreigner. || *Amer.* Yankee (norteamericano). || *Amer. Hablar en gringo*, to speak gibberish, to speak double Dutch.
— OBSERV. The word *gringo* is used contemptuously and applies primarily to North Americans.
griñón m. Wimple (de monjas). || BOT. Nectarine.
gripa f. *Amer.* MED. Influenza, flu.
gripal adj. MED. Flu, grippy.
gripe f. MED. Influenza, flu: *coger la gripe*, to catch the flu; *estar con gripe*, to have the flu.
griposo, sa adj. MED. *Estar griposo*, to have the flu.
gris adj. Grey [U.S., gray] (color). || FIG. Dull, gloomy (triste).
— M. Grey [U.S., gray] (color). || ZOOL. Miniver (ardilla). || FAM. Cop (policía). || Cold wind: *hace gris*, there's a cold wind. || *Gris perla*, pearl grey [U.S., pearl gray].
grisáceo, a adj. Greyish [U.S., grayish].
grisalla f. Grisaille.
grisgris m. Amulet (amuleto).
grisú m. Firedamp: *explosión de grisú*, firedamp explosion.
grita f. Shouting, screaming, uproar, clamour (gritería). || Booing, hooting (reprobación general).
gritar v. intr. To shout, to yell: *gritar desaforadamente*, to shout like mad *o* at the top of one's lungs. || To scream, to cry out (con voz estridente). || *Gritar a voz en cuello*, to shout at the top of one's voice.
— V. tr. To shout at: *gritar a alguien*, to shout at s.o. || To boo, to jeer at, to hoot (silbar): *gritar a un actor*, to boo an actor.
gritería f. o **griterío** m. Shouting, uproar, din, screaming. || Outcry (protesta). || Booing, hooting (en el teatro).
grito m. Shout, yell (de dolor, de sorpresa, etc.). || Shriek, scream, cry (más agudo). || Shout (de aclamación). || Boo, hoot (de desaprobación). || Cry (de guerra). || Cry (de los animales). || — *A grito herido* or *pelado* or *limpio* or *a voz en grito*, at the top of one's voice, at the top of one's lungs (en muy alta voz). || *Alzar el grito*, to raise one's voice (gritar). || *Andar a gritos*, to be always arguing (reñir). || *Asparse a gritos*, to shout o.s. hoarse (desgañitarse). || *Cantar a voz en grito*, to sing at the top of one's voice. || *Dar gritos*, to shout. || FIG. *El último grito*, the latest thing *o* craze. || *Estar en un grito*, not to be able to take any more [from constant pain]. || *Pedir a gritos*, to clamour for. || FAM. *Pegarle a uno cuatro gritos*, to haul s.o. over the coals. || *Poner el grito en el cielo*, to raise the roof, to raise an outcry, to kick up a fuss.
gritón, ona adj. FAM. Shouting, screaming (que grita). | Noisy (ruidoso).
— M. y f. Shouter, screamer.
groenlandés, esa adj. Greenlandic.
— M. y f. Greenlander.
Groenlandia n. pr. f. GEOGR. Greenland.
grog m. Grog, rum punch (bebida).
groggy adj. Groggy (boxeador). || FIG. Groggy.
groom m. Page boy [U.S., bellboy, bellhop] (botones).
grosella f. BOT. Currant (fruto). || — *Grosella espinosa*, gooseberry. || *Grosella negra*, black currant. || *Grosella roja*, redcurrant.
grosellero m. BOT. Currant bush (planta). || — *Grosellero espinoso*, gooseberry bush. || *Grosellero negro*, blackcurrant bush.
grosería f. Coarseness, rudeness, crudeness, vulgarity (falta de educación, acción inconveniente). || Coarse thing, rude thing, crude thing, vulgar thing (palabra inconveniente). || Roughness, coarseness (tosquedad). || Stupidity (ignorancia). || *Decir una grosería*, to say sth. rude.

grosero, ra adj. Coarse, rude, crude, vulgar: *¡qué tipo más grosero!*, what a crude fellow! || Rude, ill-bred, ill-mannered (descortés). || Coarse, rough (basto). || Gross: *error grosero*, gross error.
grosor m. Thickness.
grosso modo loc. adv. Roughly.
grosura f. Fat (grasa), suet (sebo). || *Comer grosura*, to eat meat.
grotesco, ca adj. ARTES. Grotesque. || Bizarre, absurd, grotesque (ridículo).
— M. ARTES. Grotesque (grutesco).
grúa f. Crane: *grúa de pórtico, de puente*, gantry, bridge crane. || Derrick.
grueso, sa adj. Thick, heavy: *hilo grueso*, heavy thread. || Thick (espeso). || Fat, stout, big: *una mujer gruesa*, a fat woman. || Heavy, thick, big: *un palo grueso*, a heavy stick. || Thick: *cristales gruesos*, thick glasses. || Heavy: *líneas gruesas*, heavy lines. || Coarse: *tela gruesa*, coarse fabric. || MAR. Heavy: *mar gruesa*, heavy sea. || FIG. Dense, dull (poco agudo). || *Intestino grueso*, large intestine.
— M. Thickness (volumen, espesor). || Main body: *el grueso del ejército*, the main body of the army. || Downstroke (de una letra). || Heaviness, thickness (grosor): *el grueso de un alambre, del papel*, the heaviness of a wire, of paper. || Depth (en geometría). || — F. Gross (doce docenas). || MAR. *Préstamo a la gruesa*, bottomry loan.
— Adv. Big: *escribir grueso*, to write big. || *En grueso*, in bulk, in gross.
gruir* v. intr. To cry (las grullas).
gruista m. Crane driver *o* operator.
grujidor m. TECN. Glass cutter.
grujir v. tr. To trim [glass] (el vidrio).
grulla f. ZOOL. Crane (ave).
grullo, lla adj. *Amer.* Dark grey (caballo).
— M. *Amer.* Dark grey horse (caballo). | Peso (dinero).
grumete m. Cabin boy (marinero).
grumo m. Curd (leche coagulada). || Clot, grume (sangre). || Lump, clot (líquido). || Cluster, bunch (de cosas apiñadas). || Wing tip (del ave).
grumoso, sa adj. Curdled, clotted (sangre). || Lumpy, clotted (líquido).
gruñido m. Grunt (cerdo), growl, snarl (perro, etc.). || FIG. Grumble, grunt (refunfuño).
gruñidor, ra adj. Grunting (cerdo), growling, snarling (perro, etc.). || FIG. Grumbling, grouchy, grumpy.
— M. y f. Grumbler, grouch (refunfuñador).
gruñir* v. intr. To grunt (cerdo). || To growl, to snarl (perro, etc.). || FIG. To grumble (refunfuñar). | To creak (una puerta).
gruñón, ona adj. FAM. Grumpy, grouchy, grumbling.
— M. y f. FAM. Grumbler, grouch.
grupa f. Hindquarters, *pl.*, croup, rump (parte trasera del caballo). || Crupper: *llevar a la grupa*, to take on the crupper. || — *Montar a la grupa*, v. MONTAR. || FIG. *Volver grupas*, to turn back (volverse atrás).
grupera f. Pillion (de la silla de montar). || Crupper (baticola).
grupo m. Group. || Cluster, clump (de árboles). || TECN. Unit, set: *grupo electrógeno*, generator set. || — *Grupo de presión*, pressure group. || *Grupo sanguíneo*, blood group [U.S., blood type].
gruta f. Grotto, cavern, cave (cueva).
grutesco, ca adj./s.m. Grotesque.
gruyere m. Gruyère (queso).
¡gua! interj. *Amer.* Oh!
guaca f. *Amer.* Indian tomb (sepultura). | Buried treasure (tesoro). | Money box (hucha).
guacal m. *Amer.* Wooden crate *o* hamper (cesta). || Calabash tree (árbol). || Calabash, gourd (fruto y vasija).
guacamaya f. o **guacamayo** m. Macaw (ave).
guacamol o **guacamole** m. *Amer.* Guacamole [salad of chopped avocado, tomato, onion and spices].
guacamote m. *Amer.* Yucca.
guacarnaco, ca adj. *Amer.* Fool.
guaco m. BOT. Guaco. || ZOOL. Curassow (ave). || *Amer.* Pre-Columbian pottery.
— Adj. *Amer.* Harelipped (labihendido). | Twin (mellizo).
guachacai m. *Amer.* Very bad quality liquor.
guachalomo m. *Amer.* Sirloin (solomillo).
guachapear v. tr. To splash with the feet (el agua). || FIG. y FAM. To botch, to bungle (chapucear). || *Amer.* To steal, to rob.
— V. intr. To rattle, to clatter, to clank.
guacho, cha adj. *Amer.* Orphaned (huérfano). | Odd (descabalado).
— M. Fledgling (pollo de pájaro). || *Amer.* Furrow (surco).
guadal m. *Amer.* Swamp, bog.
guadalajarense adj. [Of *o* from] Guadalajara.
— M. y f. Native *o* inhabitant of Guadalajara (México).
guadalajareño adj. [Of *o* from] Guadalajara.
— M. y f. Native *o* inhabitant of Guadalajara (España).
guadaloso, sa adj. *Amer.* Swampy, boggy.
Guadalupe n. pr. f. GEOGR. Guadeloupe (isla).
guadamací o **guadamecí** m. Embossed leather.
guadaña f. Scythe.
guadañador, ra m. y f. Mower. || — F. Mowing machine, mower (máquina).
guadañar v. tr. To mow, to scythe.
guadañero o **guadañil** m. Mower.
guadarnés m. Harness room (lugar). || Harness keeper (guardia). || Armory (armería).
guagua f. Trifle (cosa baladí). || *Amer.* Baby. | Bus (autobús). || — FAM. *De guagua*, free, gratis. | *¡Qué guagua!*, what a bargain!
guaica f. *Amer.* Glass bead (abalorio). | Rosary bead (cuenta de rosario).
guaico m. *Amer.* Basin, hollow (hondonada). | Rubbish dump [U.S., garbage dump] (vertedero).
guaira f. *Amer.* Smelting furnace (hornillo). || MAR. Triangular sail. || *Amer.* Indian panpipe.
guajá f. *Amer.* Heron.
guaje adj./s. *Amer.* Fool (tonto). || — M. *Amer.* Calabash, gourd (calabaza). | Trinket (baratija).
guajiro, ra m. y f. *Amer.* Cuban peasant. || — F. Cuban peasant song.
guajolote m. *Amer.* Turkey (pavo). | FAM. Jackass, fool (bobo).
gualda f. BOT. Dyer's weed, weld.
gualdado, da adj. Yellow.
gualdera f. Cheek (del cañón).
gualdo, da adj. Yellow (amarillo): *la bandera roja y gualda*, the red and yellow flag.
gualdrapa f. Housing, trappings, *pl.*, caparison (manta para el caballo). || FAM. Tatter, rag (harapo).
gualdrapazo m. Flap [of sail against the mast].
gualdrapear v. intr. To flap (las velas).
gualicho o **gualichú** m. *Amer.* Devil, evil spirit [to "gauchos"]. | Talisman.
guama f. BOT. Guama tree (árbol), guama fruit (fruta). || *Amer.* Lie (mentira).
guamo m. BOT. Guama tree (árbol).
guanábana f. Soursop (fruto).
guanábano m. BOT. Soursop (árbol). || *Amer.* Fool (tonto).
guanaco m. ZOOL. Guanaco.
guanajo, ja adj. Foolish (tonto).
— M. y f. Fool. || — M. *Amer.* Turkey (pavo).
guanche adj./s. Guanche [first inhabitants of the Canary Islands].
guanear v. tr. *Amer.* To fertilize with guano.
guanero, ra adj. Guano.
guano m. Guano [fertilizer]. || *Amer.* FAM. Dough (dinero). || FAM. *¡Véte al guano!*, go to hell!
guantada f. o **guantazo** m. FAM. Slap.
guante m. Glove: *guantes de boxeo*, boxing gloves. || FIG. y FAM. Bribe (gratificación). || — FIG. *Arrojar el guante a uno*, to throw down the gauntlet (desafiar). | *Dar un guante a uno*, to bribe s.o., to grease s.o.'s palm (untar la mano). | *De guante blanco*, formal (reunión). | *Echar el guante a alguien*, to seize *o* to get hold of s.o. | *Echar el guante a una cosa*, to seize sth., to grab sth. | *Estar* or *ponerse más suave que un guante*, to be *o* to become as meek as a lamb. | *Recoger el guante*, to take up the gauntlet, to take up the challenge. | *Sentar como un guante*, to fit like a glove.
guantear v. tr. To slap.
guantelete m. Gauntlet (manopla).
guantería f. Glove factory (taller), glove shop (tienda).
guantero, ra m. y f. Glover. || — F. Glove box, glove compartment (en el coche).
guapear v. intr. FAM. To show bravery *o* courage (ser valiente). | To dress showily (hacer alarde de gusto). || *Amer.* To brag, to boast (fanfarronear).
guapetón, ona adj. FAM. Very good-looking, handsome (guapo). | Dashing (garboso). | Flashy (ostentoso).
guapeza f. FAM. Boldness, bravery, dash (ánimo). | Showiness, flashiness (en el vestir). || Handsomeness, good looks, *pl.* (de un hombre guapo). || Prettiness, attractiveness (de una mujer guapa).
guapo, pa adj. Good-looking, handsome (hombre). || Pretty, attractive, good-looking (mujer): *una muchacha guapa*, a pretty girl. || Smart (elegante). || Flashy, showy (ostentoso). || Bold, brave, dashing (valiente).
— M. Braggart, boaster (fanfarrón). || Bully (pendenciero). || FAM. Lover, gallant (galán). || Good-looking young man (joven apuesto). || *Echárselas* or *dárselas de guapo*, to brag, to boast (fanfarronear), to boast of being a lover *o* a Don Juan (presumir).
— Interj. Love: *¡ven aquí, guapa!*, come over here, love!
guapote, ta adj. FAM. Good-looking, handsome (hombre). | Good-looking, pretty (mujer). || Good-natured (de buen carácter).
guapura f. FAM. Good looks, *pl.*
guaraca f. *Amer.* Sling.
guaracha f. *Amer.* Antillean song and dance.
guarache m. *Amer.* Indian sandal.
guaragua f. *Amer.* Swinging (contoneo). | Roundabout way, beating about the bush (al hablar). || — Pl. *Amer.* Trinkets, baubles (perifollos).
guaraní adj./s. Guarani.
guarapo m. Sugar-cane juice (zumo de la caña de azúcar). || Sugar-cane liquor (bebida).
guarda m. y f. Guard (vigilante). || Keeper (en un jardín zoológico, parque, museo). || Custodian (de edificio público, monumento histórico). || *Amer.* Tram conductor (cobrador). || — *Ángel de la Guarda*, guardian angel. || *Guarda de caza*, gamekeeper [U.S., game warden]. || *Guarda de noche* or *nocturno*, night

watchman. || *Guarda de pesca*, water bailiff [U.S., fish warden]. || *Guarda de ribera*, river police. || *Guarda forestal*, forester [U.S., forest ranger]. || *Guarda jurado*, rural policeman. || — F. Custody (custodia). || Protection, safekeeping (protección): *la guarda de sus derechos*, the protection of his rights. || Observance (de una ley). || Guard (de la espada). || Endpaper, flyleaf (de un libro). || — Pl. Wards (de una cerradura). || Outer ribs (de un abanico).

guardabarrera m. y f. Crossing keeper.

guardabarros m. inv. Mudguard [U.S., fender].

guardabosque m. Forester [U.S., forest ranger], gamekeeper [U.S., game warden].

guardabrisa f. Lantern shade (fanal). || Windscreen [U.S., windshield] (parabrisas).

guardacabo m. MAR. Thimble.

guardacabras m. y f. inv. Goatherd.

guardacadena m. Chain guard.

guardacantón m. Spur stone, corner post.

guardacoches m. inv. Parking attendant.

guardacostas m. inv. MAR. Coastguard vessel, revenue cutter [U.S., coastguard cutter].

guardador, ra adj. Careful, provident (que guarda bien sus posesiones). || Observant (que observa una ley, una orden). || Stingy, miserly (tacaño).

— M. y f. Keeper. || Observer (de una ley). || Miser (avaro). || Careful person.

guardaespaldas m. inv. Bodyguard.

guardafrenos m. inv. Brakeman (de ferrocarril).

guardagujas m. inv. Switchman (de ferrocarril).

guardainfante m. Farthingale.

guardalmacén m. Warehouseman, storekeeper.

guardalodos m. inv. Mudguard [U.S., fender].

guardamalleta f. Valance (para ventanas).

guardamano m. Guard (de espada).

guardameta m. DEP. Goalkeeper.

guardamonte m. Trigger guard (de arma de fuego). || Gamekeeper [U.S., game warden] (guarda de caza). || *Amer.* Chaps, *pl.* (de jinete).

guardamuebles m. inv. Furniture warehouse, furniture repository.

guardapelo m. Locket (medallón).

guardapiés m. inv. Skirt (falda). || Petticoat (refajo).

guardapolvo m. Dustcoat (prenda de vestir). || Overall (de niño, de dependiente). || Housecoat [U.S., duster] (bata de ama de casa). || Dust cover, dust sheet (funda contra el polvo). || Small roof (tejadillo). || Inner lid (de un reloj).

guardar v. tr. To keep: *guardar algo con* or *bajo llave*, to keep sth. under lock and key; *guardar un secreto*, to keep a secret. || To guard, to keep: *guardar las puertas de la ciudad*, to keep the gates of the city. || To protect (proteger). || To take care of (cuidar). || To tend, to guard: *guardar un rebaño de ovejas*, to tend a flock of sheep. || To guard, to watch over (los presos). || To put aside, to save, to keep: *guardó la copia de su artículo*, he saved the copy of his article. || To put away: *guarda el dinero en tu bolso*, put the money away in your handbag. || To put by, to lay by (poner de lado). || To save, to keep: *guárdame sitio en la cola*, save me a place in the queue. || To have: *guarda un buen recuerdo de su estancia en Londres*, he has pleasant memories of his stay in London. || To observe (una ley, etc.). || To keep (mandamientos). || To show, to have (respeto, atenciones, etc.). || To keep (conservar): *te guardaré la cena caliente*, I'll keep the dinner warm for you. || — *¡Dios guarde la Reina!*, God save the Queen! || *Fiesta de guardar*, day of obligation. || *¡Guarda!*, look out!, watch out!, be careful! || *Guardar cama*, to be confined to bed. || *Guardar con siete llaves*, to keep under lock and key. || *Guardar la derecha*, to keep right, to keep to the right. || *Guardar las distancias*, to keep one's distance. || *Guardar silencio*, to keep *o* to be quiet, to keep *o* to be silent. || *Guardar su palabra*, to keep one's word. || *No me guardes rencor*, don't resent me. || *Si Dios le guarda*, God willing.

— V. pr. To look out for o.s., to be on one's guard (preservarse). || To avoid, to refrain from, to guard against (con gerundio), to be careful not to (con infinitivo): *guárdate de hacer tal cosa*, avoid doing such a thing, be careful not to do such a thing. || To keep: *guardarse un libro prestado*, to keep a borrowed book. || FAM. *Guardársela a uno*, to have it in for s.o., to bear a grudge against s.o.

guardarropa m. y f. Cloakroom attendant (persona encargada de la ropa), wardrobe (en la casa real). || TEATR. Wardrobe keeper. || — M. Wardrobe (armario y ropa). || Cloakroom [U.S., checkroom] (en establecimientos públicos).

guardarropía f. TEATR. Wardrobe (para la ropa), props, *pl.* (para los accesorios). || FIG. *De guardarropía*, fake, sham, make-believe.

guardarruedas m. inv. Spur stone, corner post.

guardasellos m. inv. (Ant.). Keeper of the Seals.

guardasilla f. Chair rail.

guardatimón m. MAR. Stern chaser (cañón).

guardavallas m. inv. *Amer.* DEP. Goalkeeper.

guardavela m. *Amer.* Furling line.

guardavía m. Linesman [U.S., trackman].

guardería f. Guard. || *Guardería infantil*, day nursery.

guardia f. Guard (cuerpo de tropa). || Custody, care (custodia). || MAR. Watch: *estar de guardia*, to keep watch, to be on watch. || Guard (boxeo, esgrima). || — Pl. Wards (de la cerradura). || — *Cuerpo de guardia*, guardroom, guardhouse. || *Entrar de guardia*, to go on guard. || *Estar de guardia*, to be on duty, to be on guard. || FIG. *Estar en guardia*, to be on one's guard. || *Guardia baja*, low guard (boxeo). || *Guardia civil*, civil guard. || *Guardia entrante, saliente*, new *o* relieving guard, outgoing guard. || *Guardia municipal* or *urbana*, municipal police. || MIL. *Hacer guardia, montar la guardia*, to mount guard. || *Poner en guardia a uno*, to put s.o. on his guard. || *Ponerse en guardia*, to put o.s. on guard. || *Relevar la guardia*, to change the guard. || *Salir de guardia*, to come off guard.

— M. MIL. Guard, guardsman. || Policeman (del tráfico, del orden público). || — *Guardia civil*, Spanish civil guard (policía), dragon, bossy woman (mujer autoritaria). || *Guardia de corps*, bodyguard. || *Guardia marina*, midshipman. || *Guardia de tráfico*, traffic policeman. || *Jugar a guardias y ladrones*, to play cops and robbers. || FAM. *Ser más vago que la chaqueta de un guardia*, to be bone idle.

guardiamarina m. Midshipman.

guardián, ana m. y f. Guardian, keeper. || Keeper (de jardín zoológico, parque). || Caretaker (de un edificio). || Watchman (encargado de vigilar). || Warder (de prisiones). || — M. MAR. Hawser (cable). || REL. Guardian (de convento franciscano).

guardilla f. Attic, garret (buhardilla).

guardín m. MAR. Tiller rope (del timón).

guarecer* v. tr. To protect (proteger). || To shelter, to take in, to give shelter to (abrigar). || To nurse, to treat (a un enfermo).

— V. pr. To take shelter *o* refuge (refugiarse). || To take refuge, to protect o.s., to shelter, to take shelter: *guarecerse de la lluvia*, to take refuge from the rain.

guarida f. Den, lair (de los animales). || FIG. Haunt, hideout (de ladrones), hangout, haunt (de amigos), refuge, shelter (refugio).

guarismo m. Number, figure (número).

guarnecer* v. tr. To equip, to provide: *guarnecer un barco de velas*, to equip a boat with sails. || To adorn, to decorate, to embellish: *guarnecer una ventana con cortinas*, to decorate a window with curtains. || To trim (un vestido). || MIL. To be garrisoned in: *el regimiento de Covadonga guarnece Alcalá*, the Covadonga regiment is garrisoned in Alcalá. | To garrison (establecer una guarnición). || To plaster, to stucco (revocar). || CULIN. To garnish. || TECN. To line (frenos). | To set: *guarnecer una sortija de* or *con diamantes*, to set a ring with diamonds.

guarnecido m. Stucco, plaster. || Plastering, stuccoing.

guarnés m. Harness room (guadarnés).

guarnición f. Adornment (adorno). || Trimming, binding (de un traje). || Guard (de espada). || Provision, equipment (avío). || MIL. Garrison. || CULIN. Garnish. || Harness (arreos). || TECN. Lining (del freno). | Setting (para piedras preciosas). | Stuccoing, plastering (revoque). || *Estar de guarnición en una ciudad*, to be garrisoned *o* in garrison in a city.

guarnicionar v. tr. MIL. To garrison.

guarnicionería f. Harness shop.

guarnicionero m. Harness maker.

guarnir v. tr. MAR. To rig.

guarrada f. V. GUARRERÍA.

guarrazo m. FAM. Fall. || FAM. *Darse un guarrazo*, to fall, to come a cropper.

guarrería f. FAM. Dirtiness, filthiness (cualidad de sucio). | Filth, muck (suciedad). | Mess: *¡qué guarrería está haciendo este niño!*, what a mess this child is making! | Obscenity (indecencia). | Dirty trick, foul trick, lousy trick (mala pasada). || — FAM. *Decir guarrerías*, to use foul language, to have a foul tongue *o* a foul mouth. | *Este libro es una guarrería*, this book is obscene *o* disgusting.

guarro, rra m. Pig, hog (macho), sow (hembra). || FAM. Pig, dirty pig.

— Adj. Dirty, filthy (muy sucio).

guasa f. Joke (broma). || Joking (acción de bromear). || Teasing (burla). || Irony, banter, sarcasm (ironía): *la guasa andaluza*, Andalusian sarcasm. || Dullness (sosería). || — *Con* or *en* or *de guasa*, in fun, for fun, jokingly. || *Estar siempre de guasa*, to be always joking. || FIG. *Es una guasa hacer esto*, it's a pain in the neck *o* it's a nuisance doing this. || *Hablar en guasa*, to speak jokingly. || *Sin guasa*, without joking, seriously, joking aside. || *Tomar a guasa*, to take as a joke, not to take seriously.

guasada f. *Amer.* Crudeness.

guasca f. *Amer.* Strap, thong (correa). | Whip (látigo). || *Amer. Dar guasca*, to whip.

guascazo m. *Amer.* Lash.

guasearse v. pr. FAM. To joke, to tease, to kid (bromear). | To make fun, to scoff: *se guasea de todo*, he makes fun of everything, he scoffs at everything.

guaseo m. Leg-pull (mofa). || FAM. *Traerse un guaseo con uno*, to pull s.o.'s leg.

guasería f. *Amer.* Crudeness, rudeness.

guasipongo m. V. HUASIPONGO.

guaso, sa adj. *Amer.* Coarse, crude, rude.

— M. y f. *Amer.* Chilean peasant.

guasón, ona adj. Jocular, humorous, fond of joking (bromista). || Sarcastic (sarcástico).

— M. y f. Joker, banterer, wag.

guasquear v. tr. *Amer.* To whip.

guata f. Raw cotton (algodón en rama). || Padding, (para acolchados). || *Amer.* Belly, paunch (vientre). | Bulging, warping (pandeo).
guate m. *Amer.* Maize plantation [for fodder].
guatear v. tr. To pad, to quilt.
Guatemala n. pr. f. GEOGR. Guatemala.
guatemalteco, ca adj./s. Guatemalan.
Guatepeor n. pr. FAM. *Salir de Guatemala y meterse* or *entrar en Guatepeor*, to jump *o* to fall out of the frying pan into the fire.
guateque m. Party (fiesta).
guatusa f. *Amer.* Agouti.
guau m. Bow-wow (del perro).
¡guay! interj. Alas!, woe! || — *¡Guay de los vencidos!*, woe betide the conquered! || *¡Guay de mí!*, woe is me!
guaya f. Complaint, lament.
guayaba f. BOT. Guava (fruto). || Guava jelly (dulce). || Pretty young girl (jovencita). || *Amer.* Fib, lie (mentira). | Hoax (embuste).
guayabal m. Guava grove.
guayabero, ra adj. *Amer.* Lying.
— F. Lightweight jacket.
guayabo m. BOT. Guava.
guayaca f. *Amer.* Tobacco pouch (para tabaco). | Amulet (amuleto).
guayacán o **guayaco** m. BOT. Guaiacum.
guayacol m. Guaiacol.
Guayana n. pr. f. GEOGR. Guiana.
guayaquileño, ña adj. [Of *o* from] Guayaquil (Ecuador).
— M. y f. Native *o* inhabitant of Guayaquil.
gubernamental adj. Governmental.
— M. y f. Loyalist.
gubernativamente adv. Officially.
gubernativo, va adj. Governmental.
gubernista adj. *Amer.* Governmental.
gubia f. TECN. Gouge.
guedeja f. Long hair. || Mane (del león).
guedejón, ona o **guedejoso, sa** o **guedejudo, da** adj. Long-haired.
güegüecho, cha adj. *Amer.* Goitrous (con bocio). | Stupid, silly, foolish (tonto).
— M. *Amer.* Goitre [U.S., goiter] (bocio).
Güeldres n. pr. f. GEOGR. Gelderland, Guelders.
Guernesey n. pr. GEOGR. Guernsey.
güero, ra adj. *Amer.* Blond, fair.
guerra f. War (conflicto): *guerra civil*, civil war; *guerra fría, de nervios, nuclear*, cold war, war of nerves, nuclear war; *consejo de guerra*, war council. || Warfare (sistema, método): *guerra bacteriológica, atómica, nuclear, de guerrillas, de trincheras*, germ, atomic, nuclear, guerrilla, trench warfare. || Hostility (hostilidad). || — FAM. *Dar mucha guerra*, to be a nuisance to, to annoy. || *Declarar la guerra a*, to declare war on. || FAM. *Esta paella está pidiendo guerra*, this paella is just crying out to be eaten. || *Estar en guerra*, to be at war. || *Guerra a muerte*, war *o* fight to the death. || *Guerra mundial*, world war. || *Guerra relámpago*, lightning war. || *Guerra sin cuartel*, merciless war *o* fight. || *Hacer la guerra a*, to wage war on, to make war on. || *Tenerle declarada la guerra a uno*, to be openly at war with s.o.
guerrear v. intr. To war, to wage war, to fight. || FIG. To resist.
guerrero, ra adj. Warring. || Warlike, martial. || Fighting (belicoso). || FIG. y FAM. Mischievous, troublesome (travieso). || *Danza guerrera*, war dance.
— M. y f. Warrior, soldier. || — F. Tunic (del uniforme militar).
guerrilla f. MIL. Guerrilla band (partida). | Guerrilla warfare (tipo de guerra). | Line of riflemen (línea de tiradores). || Beggar-my-neighbour (juego de naipes). || MIL. *Marchar en guerrilla*, to march in skirmishing *o* extended order.
guerrillear v. intr. To wage guerrilla warfare, to skirmish.
guerrillero m. Guerrilla, guerrilla fighter, partisan.
guía m. y f. Guide (de museo, de montaña, etc.). || Courier, guide (de un grupo de turistas). || — M. MIL. Guide. || FIG. Guide, adviser (que da consejos). || — F. Guidance (orientación). || Handlebar (de bicicleta). || [Telephone] directory (de teléfono). || Timetable (de ferrocarriles). || Street guide (de calles). || Guidebook (libro). || BOT. Main stem. || COM. Waybill (hoja de ruta). || MIN. Leader (vetilla). || MAR. Fairleader. || TECN. Guide. | Curtain rail (de cortina). || Leader (caballo). || — Pl. Reins (riendas). || Ends (del bigote).
guiadera f. TECN. Guide.
guiahílos m. inv. Thread guide (de máquina de coser).
guiar v. tr. To guide: *guiar a unos turistas*, to guide some tourists. || To lead (llevar): *las huellas les guiaron hasta la cueva*, the tracks led them to the cave. || To drive (conducir): *guiar un coche*, to drive a car. || MAR. To steer. || AVIAC. To pilot. || To train (una planta). || FIG. To guide, to drive, to move, to motivate: *le guía sólo el interés*, he is driven only by personal interest. | To advise, to direct, to guide (aconsejar): *guiar a uno en sus estudios*, to direct s.o. in his studies.
— V. pr. To be guided *o* ruled by, to go by: *se guiaba por su instinto*, he was guided by his instinct; *me guiaré por sus consejos*, I will go by your advice.
Guido n. pr. m. Guy.
guija f. Pebble, small stone (china). || BOT. Vetch.
guijarral m. Stony place.
guijarreño, ña adj. V. GUIJARROSO.
guijarro m. Pebble, stone (piedra). || Cobblestone, cobble (para carreteras). || — Pl. Shingle, *sing.*, pebbles (en una playa).
guijarroso, sa adj. Stony, pebbly (terreno). || Shingly, pebbly (playa).
guijo m. Gravel. || *Amer.* Shaft (eje).
guilda f. Guild.
guillado, da adj. FAM. Nutty, crazy.
guilladura f. FAM. Madness, craziness.
guillame m. TECN. Rabbet plane (de carpintero).
guillarse v. pr. FAM. To become crazy *o* nutty (*por*, about) [chiflarse por]. || FAM. *Guillárselas*, to beat it, to run away (largarse).
Guillermo n. pr. m. William.
guillotina f. Guillotine (para decapitar). || Paper cutter, guillotine (para papel). || *Ventana de guillotina*, sash window.
guillotinamiento m. Guillotining (acción).
guillotinar v. tr. To guillotine. || To cut, to guillotine (papel).
guimbalete m. TECN. Pump handle (de la bomba).
guimbarda f. TECN. Router plane, grooving plane (cepillo de carpintero).
guinchar v. tr. To goad, to prod, to prick.
güinche m. *Amer.* Crane, derrick (grúa). | Winch (cabrestante).
guinda f. Sour cherry, morello cherry (fruta). || Maraschino cherry (en pastelería). || MAR. Height (de la arboladura).
guindaleta f. MAR. Hemp rope.
guindaleza f. MAR. Hawser.
guindar v. tr. To hoist, to hang up high. || FAM. To swipe: *guindar un empleo a uno*, to swipe a job from s.o.; *guindarle la novia a uno*, to swipe s.o.'s girlfriend. | To hang (ahorcar).
guindaste m. MAR. Windlass (cabria).
guindilla f. BOT. Red pepper. || — M. FAM. Cop (guardia).
guindo BOT. Sour cherry tree, morello cherry tree.
guindola f. MAR. Boatswain's chair (andamio para limpiar el casco). | Life buoy (boya). | Log chip (de la corredera).
guinea f. Guinea (antigua moneda inglesa).
Guinea n. pr. f. GEOGR. Guinea.
guineo, a adj./s. Guinean.
guinga f. o **guingán** m. Gingham (tela).
guiñada f. Wink (del ojo). || MAR. Yaw.
guiñapo m. Rag, tatter (harapo). || FIG. Reprobate (persona despreciable). || — FIG. *Estar hecho un guiñapo*, to feel as limp as a rag (estar muy débil), to have no backbone (no tener voluntad). | *Poner a uno como un guiñapo*, to haul s.o. over the coals, to give s.o. a dressing down (reprender), to call s.o. all the names under the sun (insultar).
guiñaposo, sa adj. Ragged, tattered (haraposo).
guiñar v. tr. To wink at: *le guiñó*, he winked at her. || *Guiñar el ojo*, to wink.
— V. intr. To wink. || MAR. To yaw.
— V. pr. To wink at each other.
guiño m. Wink. || *Hacer guiños a uno*, to wink at s.o. (hacer señas con los ojos), to make eyes at s.o. (para conquistar a una persona).
guiñol m. Puppet show.
guión m. MIL. Guidon (estandarte). || REL. Processional cross, processional banner. || Royal standard (estandarte). || Outline (esquema). || CINEM. Script, scenario (de una película). || Hyphen (raya en las palabras compuestas o cortadas). || Dash (raya en el diálogo o como paréntesis). || Leader (el que dirige).
guionista m. CINEM. Scriptwriter, scenarist.
guipar v. tr. FAM. To see (mirar). | To get (understand).
guipur m. Guipure (encaje).
guipuzcoano, na adj. [Of *o* from] Guipúzcoa.
— M. y f. Native *o* inhabitant of Guipúzcoa.
güira f. BOT. Calabash (árbol y fruto). || *Amer.* FAM. Nut (cabeza).
guirigay m. FAM. Hubbub, hullabaloo, fuss, commotion (jaleo). | Gibberish (lenguaje ininteligible).
— OBSERV. Pl. *guirigays, guirigayes.*
guirlache m. Almond brittle.
guirlanda o **guirnalda** f. Garland. || Wreath (de forma redonda). || Chaplet, wreath (en la cabeza). || BOT. Globe amaranth.
güiro m. *Amer.* Calabash (árbol), calabash, gourd (fruto). || Musical instrument made from a gourd (instrumento de música). | Stalk of unripe maize (tallo de maíz).
guisa f. Manner, way: *obrar a su guisa*, to work in one's own way. || — *A guisa de*, as, for (a manera de). || *De tal guisa* or *en tal guisa*, in such a manner, in such a way.
guisado m. Stew: *guisado de cordero*, lamb stew.
guisante m. BOT. Pea (planta y legumbre). || — *Guisante de olor*, sweet pea. || *Guisante mollar*, sugar pea.
guisar v. intr. To cook.
— V. tr. To cook (cocinar), to stew (un estofado). || FIG. To prepare, to arrange (preparar). || — *Ellos se lo guisan y ellos se lo comen*, as you make your

bed so you must lie on it. || *La comida está guisada*, lunch *o* dinner is ready, lunch *o* dinner is served.

guiso m. CULIN. [Cooked] dish: *echar a perder un guiso*, to spoil a dish. || Stew: *guiso de patatas*, potato stew. || — Pl. Dishes, cooking, *sing.*: *me gustan los guisos españoles*, I like Spanish cooking.

guisote m. FAM. Poorly made stew.

guisotear v. tr. To cook, to prepare, to make.
— V. intr. To cook.

guita f. Twine (cuerda). || FAM. Dough (dinero).

guitarra f. MÚS. Guitar. || TECN. Beater (del yesero). || FIG. y FAM. *Tener bien, mal templada la guitarra*, to be in a good, in a bad mood.

guitarrear v. intr. To play the guitar.

guitarreo m. Strumming on the guitar.

guitarrero m. Guitar maker *o* seller. || Guitarist.

guitarrillo m. Small four-string guitar.

guitarrista m. y f. Guitarist.

guitarrón m. Large guitar. || FAM. Sly rascal (tunante).

güito m. FAM. Hat (sombrero).

gula f. Gluttony: *pecado de gula*, sin of gluttony.

gules m. pl. HERÁLD. Gules.

gulusmear v. intr. To sniff and taste what is cooking. || To nibble titbits (comer golosinas). || To snoop around (curiosear).

gumía f. Moorish dagger.

guripa m. FAM. Soldier, private (soldado raso). | Rogue, scoundrel (golfo).

gurriato o **gurripato** m. ZOOL. Young sparrow. || FAM. Youngster, kid (niño).

gurrumino, na adj. FAM. Mean (ruin). | Weak, puny, sickly (enclenque).
— M. FAM. Uxorious man (que idolatra a su mujer). | Henpecked husband, henpeck (que se deja dominar).
— M. y f. FAM. Youngster, kid. || — F. FAM. Uxoriousness (idolatría).

gusanear v. intr. To swarm, to teem (hormiguear).

gusanera f. Worms, *pl.* (conjunto de gusanos). || Breeding ground for worms (sitio donde se crían). || FIG. Great passion.

gusanillo m. Small worm. || FIG. y FAM. Bug (afición): *le entró el gusanillo de la afición a los toros*, he got the bullfight bug. || — FIG. y FAM. *Gusanillo de la conciencia*, remorse, nagging conscience. | *Matar el gusanillo*, to take a nip first thing in the morning (beber aguardiente por la mañana).

gusano m. ZOOL. Worm. | Earthworm (lombriz). | Maggot (larva de mosca doméstica). | Caterpillar (oruga). || FIG. Worm (persona despreciable). || — FIG. y FAM. *Criar gusanos*, to be pushing up daisies. || *Gusano blanco*, grub (larva de abejorro). || FIG. y FAM. *Gusano de la conciencia*, nagging conscience, remorse. || *Gusano de luz*, glowworm. || *Gusano de seda*, silkworm.

gusanoso, sa adj. Wormy, maggoty (lleno de gusanos). || Worm-eaten (carcomido por los gusanos).

gusarapiento, ta adj. Wormy, maggoty.

gusarapo m. Small worm (gusanillo). || Little creature, tiny animal (animalillo).

gustación f. Tasting, sampling, gustation (p.us.).

gustar v. tr. To taste, to try, to sample (probar).
— V. intr. To please, to be pleasing. || To like: *me gusta mucho este escritor*, I like this author very much; *a Juan no le gusta leer novelas policíacas*, John doesn't like reading detective novels; *no me gusta su hermano*, I don't like his brother. || — *¡Así me gusta!*, that's what I like. || *Como le guste*, as you like, as you wish. || *Cuando le guste*, whenever you wish, whenever you like. || *Gustar de*, to like, to enjoy: *gusto de leer*, I like to read, I enjoy reading; *no gusto de su compañía*, I don't like *o* I don't enjoy your company. || *Una novela que gusta*, a novel which is popular *o* that people like. || *¿Usted gusta?*, would you like some?
— OBSERV. The intransitive verb *gustar* is construed like the English verb *to please*: *eso me gusta*, that pleases me. However the verb "to like" is more commonly used, in which case the subject of *gustar* becomes the object of "like": *eso me gusta*, I like that: *a María no le gustan los pasteles*, Mary does not like pastries.

gustativo, va adj. Gustative.

gustazo m. FAM. Great pleasure, immense pleasure: *me ha dado un gustazo ver lo que le ocurría*, it gave me great pleasure to see what happened to him. || — FAM. *Darse el gustazo de*, to treat o.s. to: *me di el gustazo de ir al teatro*, I treated myself to the theatre; to allow o.s. the great pleasure of: *me di el gustazo de decirle cuatro verdades*, I allowed myself the great pleasure of giving him a piece of my mind. || *Un gustazo por un trancazo*, a great pleasure is worth any price.

gustillo m. Aftertaste (regusto). || Tang, slight taste: *esta sopa tiene un gustillo extraño*, this soup has a strange tang *o* a slightly strange taste. || Slight pleasure (placer).

gusto m. Taste, flavour (sabor). || Taste (sentido). || Taste: *hombre de buen gusto*, man of good taste; *una cosa de buen gusto*, a thing in good taste. || Pleasure: *tengo el gusto de acogerle aquí*, I have the pleasure of welcoming you here. || Fancy, whim (capricho). || Liking (afición). || Style, fashion (estilo). || — *A gusto*, at ease, comfortable: *estoy muy a gusto con estas personas*, I feel very comfortable with these people, I am very much at ease with these people; comfortable: *estoy a gusto en este sillón*, I am comfortable in this armchair; happily, with pleasure: *lo haría muy a gusto*, I would do it happily; easily: *pesa muy a gusto sus cien kilos*, he very easily weighs one hundred kilos. || *A gusto de*, to the liking of, to the taste of: *a gusto de todos*, to everybody's liking. || *Al gusto del consumidor*, according to the client's taste. || *Canta que da gusto*, he sings magnificently, his singing is a delight. || *Coger* or *tomar el gusto a algo*, to take a liking to, to acquire *o* to develop a taste for. || *Con gusto*, with pleasure: *con mucho gusto*, with great pleasure; *con sumo gusto*, with the greatest pleasure; willingly: *estudia con gusto*, he studies willingly; heartily: *come con gusto*, he eats heartily. || *Dar gusto a*, to please, to give pleasure to. || *Darse el gusto de*, to allow o.s. the pleasure of, to treat o.s. to. || *Despacharse a su gusto*, V. DESPACHAR. || *El gusto es mío*, the pleasure is mine. || *Encontrar algo al gusto de uno*, to find sth. to one's taste. || *Encontrar gusto en*, to find pleasure in, to enjoy. || *En la variedad está el gusto*, variety is the spice of life. || *Hay gustos que merecen palos*, some people have no taste, there is no accounting for tastes. || *Hay para todos los gustos*, there is sth. for everyone *o* sth. to suit every taste. || *Mal a gusto*, uncomfortable, ill at ease. || *Mucho gusto* or *tanto gusto en conocerle*, how do you do?, pleased to meet you. || *No hay gusto sin disgusto*, there is no rose without a thorn. || *No tener gusto para nada*, not to feel like anything (no querer comer), not to feel like doing anything, not to be in the mood for anything (no querer hacer nada). || *Por gusto*, for the pleasure of it, for the sake of it, because one likes to. || *Que da gusto*, marvellously, beautifully (adv.), lovely, wonderful (adj.). || *Se está más a gusto aquí*, we are better here, we are more comfortable here. || *Sobre* or *de gustos no hay nada escrito*, everyone to his own taste, there's no accounting for tastes. || *Tener gusto a*, to taste of, to taste: *tiene gusto a naranja*, it tastes of orange, it tastes orangy. || *Tener mucho gusto en*, to be very pleased to *o* glad to. || *Tomar gusto a*, to take a liking to, to develop a taste for. || *Tonto que da gusto*, a prize idiot (tonto de remate).

gustosamente adv. With pleasure, gladly (con placer). || Tastefully.

gustoso, sa adj. Tasty, savoury [U.S., savory]: *fruta gustosa*, tasty fruit. || Pleasant, delightful, agreeable. || — *Gustoso le escribo a usted*, I have the pleasure of writing to you. || *Hacer una cosa muy gustoso*, to do sth. with great pleasure. || *Lo haré gustoso*, I'll do it with pleasure, I'll do it gladly.

gutagamba f. Gamboge.

gutapercha f. Gutta-percha.

gutiámbar f. Gamboge.

gutural adj./s. f. Guttural.

Guyana n. pr. f. GEOGR. Guyana.

gymkhana f. Gymkhana.

H

h f. H. || — *La hora H*, zero hour. || *Por H o por B*, for one reason or another.
— OBSERV. This letter is not usually sounded. However in popular Andalusian speech it is sometimes pronounced rather like the Spanish *j*.

¡ha! interj. Aha!, ah!

haba f. BOT. Broad bean. | Bean (de cacao, de café). || Voting ball (para votar). || MED. Bruise (cardenal). | Swelling (bulto). || MIN. Nodule (nódulo). || VET. Tumour on a horse's palate (tumor). || — *Echar las habas a*, to cast a spell on. || *En todas partes cuecen habas*, it's the same the whole world over. || *Esas* *son habas contadas*, it's a certainty, it's a sure thing. || *Haba de las Indias*, sweet pea (guisante de olor). || *Haba panosa* or *menor*, horsebean. || *Haba tonca*, tonka bean.

Habana (La) n. pr. GEOGR. Havana.

habanera f. Habanera [Afro-Cuban dance or music].

habanero, ra adj./s. Havanan (de La Habana).

habano, na adj. Havanan, Havana, of Havana. || — Adj./s. Havanan (habitante). || — M. Havana [cigar].

habar m. Bean field.

hábeas corpus m. JUR. Habeas corpus.

haber m. COM. Assets, *pl.*, credit [side]: *debe y haber*, liabilities and assets, debit and credit. || — Pl. Assets, property, *sing.*, estate, *sing.* (bienes). || Income, *sing.*, salary, *sing.* (retribución). || — FIG. *Tener en su haber*, to be to one's credit: *tiene en su haber una gran generosidad*, his great generosity is to his credit. || *Tengo miles de pesetas en mi haber*, I have thousands of pesetas in my account *o* to my credit.

haber* v. tr. To have (tener) [V. OBSERV.] || To catch (detener): *hubieron al ladrón*, they caught the thief.

— V. auxil. To have: *he dicho*, I have said; *lo hubieras encontrado*, you would have found it; *de haberlo hecho yo*, if I had done it.

— V. impers. To be: *ayer hubo fiesta en el pueblo*, yesterday there was a celebration in the village; *las había muy hermosas antes*, there were very lovely ones before. || — FAM. *¡Allá te las hayas!*, that's your problem! || *¡Bien haya quien!*, blessed be he who. || *¿Cuánto hay de aquí a León?*, how far is it from here to León? || *Era el más valiente si los hay*, if anyone, he was the bravest. || *Es de lo que no hay*, there are few like him. || FIG. *Esto es lo que hay*, that's all there is. || *Es un cobarde como hay pocos*, there are few as cowardly as he, he is a coward the likes of which I've rarely seen before. || *Haber de*, to have to: *han de salir mañana*, they have to leave tomorrow; *no sabía que habías de salir*, I didn't know that you had to leave; must (presente): *se han de pronunciar bien todas las letras*, one must pronounce all the letters well; might (pasado): *hubo de pensar que*, he might have thought that; will: *he de decírselo mañana*, I will tell him tomorrow; to be to: *¿cómo había de saberlo?*, how was I to know?; can: *¿cómo había de ser de otro modo?*, how could it be otherwise? || *Haber que*, to be necessary to, to have to, must: *hay que comer para vivir*, one must eat *o* one has to eat to live, it's necessary to eat to live. || *Habérselas con uno*, to have it out with s.o., to deal with s.o. (tener que discutir con), to be up against s.o. (estar opuesto). || *¡Había que verlo!*, you should have seen it! || *Habidos y por haber*, past, present and future. || *Habrá quince días que ha llegado*, it must be fifteen days since he arrived, it must have been fifteen days ago that he arrived, he must have arrived about fifteen days ago. || *¡Habráse visto!*, have you ever seen such a thing? || *Hay*, there is (*sing.*), there are (*pl.*): *hay poca gente aquí*, there are few people here. || *¿Hay manzanas?*, have you any apples?, are there any apples? || *Lo que hay es que*, the fact is that. || *Los hay que*, there are some who, there are those who. || *No hay de qué*, don't mention it, not at all [U.S., you're welcome]. || *No hay más que hablar*, there is nothing more to be said. || *No hay más que pedir*, one couldn't expect more *o* ask for more. || *No hay nada como el té para quitar la sed*, there's nothing like tea for quenching one's thirst. || *No hay para*, there is no reason to. || *No hay tal cosa*, there is no such thing. || *Poco tiempo ha*, a short time ago. || *¿Qué hay?*, how are you?, what's new? (¿qué tal?), what's up?, what's the matter? (¿qué pasa?). || *¿Qué hay de nuevo?*, what's new? || *¿Qué le he de hacer?*, what can I do? || *Simón, que Dios haya en su gloria*, Simon, God rest his soul. || *Ya no hay más*, there's nothing more, there's no more.

— OBSERV. *Haber* retains the antiquated transitive meaning in expressions such as: *los hijos habidos de ese matrimonio*, the children from that marriage; *¡mal haya quien!*, woe betide he who; *haber menester de*, to need, to have need of.
— *Haber de* is sometimes, in the present and imperfect, a substitute for the future and conditional: *¿ha de venir mañana?*, will he come tomorrow?; *¿quién había de decirme que iba a ser millonario?*, who could have told me that he was going to be a millionaire?

habichuela f. Bean (judía). || *Habichuelas verdes*, French beans, green beans.

habiente adj. Having. || JUR. *Habiente* or *habiente derecho* or *derecho habiente*, rightful claimant *o* owner, beneficiary, interested party.

hábil adj. Skilful [U.S., skillful]: *un cirujano hábil*, a skilful surgeon. || Proficient, expert, good (perito). || Capable (capaz). || Clever, skilful: *una maniobra hábil*, a clever manœuvre. || Good, suitable, adequate (adecuado): *una sala hábil para conferencias*, a good room for meetings. || JUR. Competent, qualified: *hábil para testar*, competent to make a will. || — *Días hábiles*, working days. || *En tiempo hábil*, duly, at the proper time. || *Hábil para un empleo*, fit for *o* qualified for a job. || *Ser hábil en*, to be good at.

habilidad f. Skill, ability, expertise, dexterity (destreza): *tener mucha habilidad*, to have a great deal of skill; *la habilidad de un político*, the skill of a politician. || Expertise, expertness (pericia). || JUR. Capacity, competency, competence: *habilidad para suceder*, capacity to succeed. || Feat, trick: *hace muchas habilidades en el trampolín*, he does a lot of feats on the trampoline. || Talent: *la niña tuvo que lucir todas sus habilidades delante de la familia*, the girl had to display all of her talents before the family. || DEP. *Prueba de habilidad*, slalom (esquí).

habilidoso, sa adj. Skilfull, clever, capable, able.

habilitación f. JUR. Qualification (acción de habilitar). || Authorization. || Paymastership (cargo de habilitado). || Paymaster's office (oficina). || Financing (financiación). || Fitting out (de una casa).

habilitado m. Paymaster.

habilitador, ra adj. JUR. Qualifying.
— M. Qualifier (que habilita). || COM. Backer.

habilitar v. tr. JUR. To qualify, to entitle: *habilitar a uno para suceder*, to qualify s.o. to succeed. | To enable (permitir). | To empower (dar poderes). || COM. To provide: *habilitar con fondos*, to provide with funds. | To finance. || To set up, to fit out: *habilitar una casa*, to set up a house. || *Local habilitado para establecimiento comercial*, suitable premises for a commercial establishment.

habitabilidad f. Habitability.

habitable adj. Habitable, inhabitable.

habitación f. Dwelling, habitation (morada). || Habitation, residence (hecho de vivir en un sitio). || Room: *piso con cinco habitaciones*, apartment with five rooms; *habitación individual*, single room; *habitación doble*, double room. || Bedroom (cuarto de dormir). || Habitat (de vegetales o animales).

habitáculo m. POÉT. Dwelling. || Cabin (de astronave).

habitante m. y f. Inhabitant: *ciudad de un millón de habitantes*, city of a million inhabitants.

habitar v. tr. To live in, to inhabit, to dwell in (un país, una ciudad). || To live in, to reside in, to occupy (una casa).
— V. intr. To live.

habitat o **hábitat** m. Habitat.

hábito m. Habit (vestidura de los religiosos). || Habit (costumbre): *tener malos hábitos*, to have bad habits. || — FIG. y FAM. *Ahorcar* or *colgar los hábitos*, to give up the cloth. || FIG. *El hábito no hace al monje*, it is not the cowl that makes the monk, clothes don't make the man. || *Tomar el hábito*, to take holy orders, to take the habit, to take vows (un hombre), to take the veil, to become a nun (una mujer).

habituación f. Habituation.

habituado, da m. y f. Habitué, regular [customer].

— OBSERV. This word is a Gallicism used in place of *aficionado* or *parroquiano*.

habitual adj. Habitual, customary (acostumbrado). || Usual, normal (usual). || Regular: *un cliente habitual*, a regular customer.

habitualmente adv. Habitually.

habituar v. tr. To habituate, to accustom (*a*, to).
— V. pr. *Habituarse a*, to become accustomed to, to get used to.

habitud f. Relation, connection [between two things]. || Habit (costumbre).

habla f. Speech (facultad de hablar). || Language (lengua, idioma): *el habla española*, the Spanish language. || Dialect, speech: *la gente de esta región tiene un habla especial*, the people in this region have a special dialect. || Talk: *el habla de los niños*, baby talk. || Speech, discourse, address (discurso). || — MAR. *Al habla*, within hail. || *¡Al habla Miguel!*, Michael speaking! (al teléfono). || *De habla española*, Spanish-speaking: *países de habla española*, Spanish-speaking countries. || *Estar al habla* or *en habla con*, to be in contact with, to be in touch with. || *Negarle el habla a uno*, not to be on speaking terms with s.o. || *Perder el habla*, to become speechless. || *Ponerse al habla con*, to get in touch with (entrar en contacto), to speak to (al teléfono). || *Prensa de habla francesa*, French-language newspapers, *pl.*

habladas f. pl. *Amer.* Boasting, *sing.*, bragging, *sing.*

hablado, da adj. Spoken: *una lengua mal hablada*, a poorly-spoken language. || — *Bien hablado*, well-spoken. || *Cine hablado*, talking cinema, talkies, *pl.* (fam). || *Mal hablado*, rude, foulmouthed.

hablador, ra adj. Talkative (que habla mucho). || Gossipy (chismoso).
— M. y f. Chatterbox, talker (parlanchín). || Gossip (chismoso).

habladuría f. Rumour [U.S., rumor], piece of gossip (chisme). || — Pl. Gossip, *sing.* (cotilleo).

hablanchín, ina adj. FAM. Talkative.
— M. y f. FAM. Talker, chatterbox.

hablante adj. Speaking.
— M. y f. Speaker.

hablar v. intr. To speak, to talk: *hablar con el vecino*, to speak with the neighbour *o* to the neighbour; *estuvo hablando de ti ayer*, he was speaking of you yesterday, he talked about you yesterday. || FIG. To go out: *habló dos años con Carmen*, he went out with Carmen for two years. || — *¿Con quién se cree usted que está hablando?*, who do you think you are talking to? || *Dar mucho que hablar*, to cause a lot of talk. || *Dejar hablar a uno*, to let s.o. speak. || *El hablar bien no cuesta dinero*, good words cost nothing but are worth much. || *Eso es hablar*, now you're talking.

|| *Estar hablando*, to be almost alive (un retrato, una estatua). || *Hablando del rey de Roma por la puerta asoma*, talk of the devil [and he will appear]. || *Hablar al alma*, to touch one's heart. || *Hablar alto, hablar bajo*, to speak up *o* loudly, to speak softly *o* in a low voice. || *Hablar a medias palabras*, to speak cryptically. || *Hablar a solas*, to speak to o.s. || *Hablar a tontas y a locas*, to talk without rhyme or reason. || *Hablar bien, mal de uno*, to speak well, ill *o* badly of s.o. || *Hablar clara y llanamente*, to speak plainly and frankly. || *Hablar como los indios*, V. INDIO. || *Hablar como quien habla a la pared* or *como si lo hiciese a la pared*, to be like talking to a brick wall: *estoy hablando como quien habla a la pared*, it is like talking to a brick wall. || *Hablar como una verdulera*, to speak like a fishwife. || *Hablar como un carretero*, to swear like a trooper. || *Hablar como un libro*, to speak like a book. || *Hablar con el corazón en la mano*, V. CORAZÓN. || *Hablar con la nariz*, to speak through one's nose. || *Hablar con soltura*, to speak fluently *o* with fluency. || *Hablar de negocios, de política*, to talk [about] business, [about] politics. || *Hablar de todo un poco*, to talk about this, that and the other. || *Hablar de trapos*, to talk about clothes. || *Hablar de tú, de usted a alguien*, V. TÚ Y USTED. || *Hablar en broma*, to be joking. || *Hablar en crudo*, to speak one's mind, to speak straight from the shoulder. || *Hablar en plata*, to put it plainly. || *Hablar entre dientes*, to mumble, to mutter. || *Hablar en voz alta*, to speak up *o* loudly. || *Hablar en voz baja* or *queda*, to speak in a low voice. || *Hablar largo y tendido de algo*, V. LARGO. || *Hablar más que siete* or *más que un papagayo*, to talk nineteen to the dozen, to be a real chatterbox, to talk the hind leg off a donkey. || *Hablar para su coleto* or *para el cuello de su camisa* or *para sí* or *solo*, to talk to o.s. || *Hablar por boca de ganso*, V. BOCA. || *Hablar por hablar*, to talk for the sake of talking. || *Hablar por los codos*, V. CODO. || FIG. *Hablar por sí mismo*, to speak volumes. || *Hablar sin rodeos*, not to mince one's words. || *Hablar sin ton ni son*, to talk without rhyme or reason. || *Hablemos poco y bien*, let's get straight to the point, let's be brief. || *Habló el buey y dijo mu*, what can you expect from a pig but a grunt? || *Miente más que habla*, he lies like a thief. || FAM. *¡Ni hablar!*, out of the question! || *No hay más que hablar*, there's nothing more to be said. || *¡Puede hablar!*, you're through! (al teléfono). || *¿Quién habla?*, who's speaking? (al teléfono). || *Quien mucho habla, mucho yerra*, least said soonest mended, the less said the better. || *Sin hablar de*, without mentioning, not to mention. || *Sólo le falta hablar*, it almost speaks, it seems almost alive (retrato), it does everything but talk (animal).

— V. tr. To speak: *hablar (el) francés*, to speak French. || Talk (decir): *hablar disparates*, to talk nonsense. || *Sin hablar palabra*, without saying a word, without a word.

— V. pr. To converse, to speak, to talk. || To be spoken: *en México se habla español*, Spanish is spoken in Mexico. || — FIG. *Pedro ya no se habla con Juana*, Peter does not speak to Jane, Peter is not on speaking terms with Jane. || *Se está hablando de una reforma*, there's some talk about a reform. || *Se habla español*, Spanish spoken (en un letrero).

hablilla f. Rumour [U.S., rumor], piece of gossip. || — Pl. Gossip, *sing.* (cotilleo).

hablista m. y f. Purist [of language].

Habsburgo n. pr. Hapsburg, Habsburg.

hacecillo m. BOT. Fascicle. || Small bunch *o* bundle *o* sheaf (de mieses).

hacedero, ra adj. Feasible, practicable.

hacedor, ra m. y f. Creator, maker. || *El Sumo* or *el Supremo Hacedor*, the Creator, the Maker.

hacendado, da adj. Landed, property-owning: *un hombre hacendado*, a landed man.

— M. y f. Landowner (terrateniente). || *Amer.* Farmer [U.S., rancher] (ganadero).

hacendar* v. tr. To make over *o* to give property to.

— V. pr. To settle: *hacendarse en Argentina*, to settle in Argentina.

hacendero, ra adj. Industrious, hard-working.

hacendista m. Economist, financial expert.

hacendístico, ca adj. Of the public treasury.

hacendoso, sa adj. Industrious, hard-working. || *Hacendoso como una hormiga*, as busy as a bee.

hacer*

1. Fabricar, ejecutar, componer. — **2.** Causar. — **3.** Acostumbrar. — **4.** Otros sentidos. — **5.** Para sustituir otro verbo. — **6.** Locuciones diversas. — **7.** Convenir, concordar. — **8.** Hacer de. — **9.** Hacer para, por, como. — **10.** Hacer, con infinitivo. — **11.** Impers. — **12.** V. pr.

1. FABRICAR, EJECUTAR, COMPONER, v. tr. — To make: *hacer muebles, un pastel, la cama*, to make furniture, a cake, one's bed; *hacer una lista*, to make a list; *hacer planes*, to make plans. || To do: *hacer sus deberes*, to do one's homework; *haz lo que te dijeron*, do as they told you. || To make, to create (crear). || To write, to compose, to make up: *hacer un poema*, to write a poem. || To write (un libro). || To work, to do: *hacer un milagro, maravillas*, to work a miracle, wonders. || To draw up: *hacer un contrato*, to draw up a contract. || To make, to build (una casa). || To pack (la maleta). || To make, to deliver (un discurso). || To pay (una visita). || To wage (la guerra). || To make (un error).

2. CAUSAR, v. tr. — To make: *hacer humo*, to make smoke; *el retraso hizo que perdiésemos el tren*, the delay made us miss the train. || To give, to cast: *hacer sombra*, to give shade, to cast a shadow.

3. ACOSTUMBRAR, v. tr. — To accustom: *hacer su cuerpo a la fatiga*, to accustom one's body to fatigue.

4. OTROS SENTIDOS, v. tr. — To hold, to contain: *esta botella hace un litro*, this bottle holds a litre. || To make (nombrar): *le hicieron presidente*, they made him [their] president; *hacerle a alguien heredero*, to make s.o. one's heir. || To think, to believe, to suppose (pensar): *yo te hacía en Montevideo*, I thought you were in Montevideo; *le hacía estudiando*, I thought he was studying. || To do (la barba, el pelo). || To cut (las uñas). || To do, to make (guisar). || To make (obligar): *hizo que la señora se sentara*, he made the lady sit down. || To make (volver): *esto lo hace más fácil*, this makes it easier. || To make (sumar): *esto hace veinte*, this makes twenty. || TEATR. To act, to play the part of (representar un papel).

5. PARA SUSTITUIR OTRO VERBO, v. tr. — To do: *salió y los demás hicieron lo mismo*, he went out and the others did the same.

6. LOCUCIONES DIVERSAS, v. tr. — *A lo hecho pecho*, it is no use crying over spilt milk, what is done is done. || *¡Buena la has hecho!*, you've done it now! || *Dar que hacer*, to give a lot to do, to give trouble. || *El que la hace la paga*, one must face the music, one must face the consequences. || *Hacer agua*, V. AGUA. || FAM. *Hacer aguas*, V. AGUA. || *Hacer alarde de*, V. ALARDE. || *Hacer bien*, to do the right thing. || AUT. y AVIAC. *Hacer cien kilómetros por hora*, to do *o* to go a hundred kilometres per hour. || FOT. *Hacer una copia*, to make a print. || *Hacer daño*, to hurt, to harm. || *Hacer de su hijo un médico*, to make one's son a doctor. || *Hacer el amor*, to court (cortejar), to make love. || *Hacer el bobo*, to act the clown. || *Hacer el papel de*, V. PAPEL. || *Hacer las veces de*, to act as, to serve as. || FAM. *Hacerle la pascua* or *hacerle un pie agua a uno*, V. PASCUA Y PIE. || *Hacerle la vida imposible a uno*, to make life impossible for s.o. || *Hacer otro tanto*, to do the same thing. || *Hacer pedazos*, to tear to pieces (desgarrar), to smash to pieces, to break to pieces (romper). || *Hacer polvo*, V. POLVO. || *Hacer presente*, to let know, to notify, to inform, to tell (avisar), to state (declarar). || *Hacer recados*, to run errands. || FAM. *Hacer sus necesidades*, V. NECESIDAD. || *Hacer tiempo*, to kill time. || *Hacer todo lo posible para*, to do everything possible to, to do one's best to. || *Hacer trizas*, V. TRIZA. || *Hacer una apuesta*, to lay a bet. || *Hacer una cosa arrastrando*, to do sth. against one's will *o* unwillingly. || *Hacer una cosa con los pies*, V. PIE. || *Hacer una de las suyas*, to be up to one's [old] tricks. || *Hacer una objeción*, to make *o* to raise an objection. || *Hacer una pregunta a*, to ask a question, to put a question to. || COM. *Hacer una rebaja*, to give a reduction. || *Hacer un favor a alguien*, to do s.o. a favour. || *Hacer uso de la palabra*, to take the floor, to speak (en una conferencia, etc.). || *Hacer vida ascética*, to lead an ascetic life. || *Haga lo que quiera*, do as you please. || *Haz bien y no mires a quien*, do well and dread no shame. || *Mandar hacer un vestido*, to have a dress made. || *Más hace el que quiere que el que puede*, where there's a will there's a way. || *Me hace falta*, V. FALTA. || *No tener nada que hacer*, not to have anything to do. || *Por más que haga* or *haga lo que haga*, whatever he does. || *¿Qué hemos de hacer?*, what can we do? || *¿Qué le vamos a hacer?*, what are we going to do? || *¿Qué quiere que haga?*, what do you want me to do? || *¿Qué tiempo hace?*, what is the weather like? || FIG. *Ser el que hace y deshace*, to rule the roost, to be the boss. | *¡Ya la hizo!*, now you've done it!

7. CONVENIR, CONCORDAR, v. intr. — To go: *esto hace con aquello*, this goes with that. || To be suitable, to be fitting (convenir). || — *Eso no le hace*, that has no importance, that doesn't matter. || *Mil dólares más o menos no le hace*, a few thousand dollars don't matter to him. || *No hace al caso*, it has nothing to do with it.

8. HACER DE. — To work as: *hace de portero*, he works as a caretaker. || To act as, to serve as: *hacer de madre para alguien*, to act as a mother to s.o. || To act: *hacer de tonto*, to act the fool. || To act, to pretend to be (simular): *hace de valiente*, he acts brave. || To do: *hacer de todo un poco*, to do a little of everything. || TEATR. To act as, to play the part of, to do: *hace de Hamlet*, he plays the part of Hamlet.

9. HACER PARA, POR, COMO. — To do one's best to (hacer todo lo posible): *hizo para venir*, he did his best to come. || To try to (intentar). || — *Hacer como que* or *si*, to pretend [that], to act as if: *hace como que no sabe nada*, he acts as if he knows nothing. || FIG. y FAM. *Hacer por la vida*, to eat.

10. HACER, CON INFINITIVO. — To make: *hacer reír, llorar a alguien*, to make s.o. laugh, cry. || To make (obligar): *la hizo venir*, he made her come.

|| — JUR. *Hacer comparecer*, to summon to appear. || *Hacer entrar, subir a uno*, to bring *o* to send *o* to ask s.o. in, up. || *Hacerle esperar a uno*, to keep s.o. waiting. || *Hacer saber*, to inform, to let know, to tell. || *Hacer saltar las lágrimas a uno*, to make s.o. cry, to bring tears to s.o.'s eyes. || FAM. *Hacer sudar a alguien*, to give s.o. a lot of trouble. || *No hice más que* or *sino decírselo*, I only told him, all I did was tell him.

11. IMPERS. — To be: *hace calor, frío, mucho calor, mucho frío*, it is hot, cold, very hot, very cold. || ...ago (tiempo): *hace tres días*, three days ago; *hace mucho tiempo*, a long time ago; *¿cuánto tiempo hace?*, how long ago? || — *¿Cuánto tiempo hace que?*, how long has it been since?, how long is it since? || *Desde hace dos años*, for two years: *no le veo desde hace dos años*, I haven't seen him for two years.

12. V. PR. *a*) VOLVERSE. — To become: *hacerse sacerdote*, to become a priest; *el Verbo se hizo carne*, the Word became flesh; *hacerse un atleta*, to become an athlete; *el ruido se hizo demasiado fuerte*, the noise became too loud; *hacerse rico*, to become wealthy *o* rich. || To become, to change into: *el vino se hizo vinagre*, the wine changed into vinegar. || To get, to become, to grow: *hacerse tarde*, to get late; *hacerse viejo*, to grow old. || To mature, to ripen: *el vino se hace*, wine matures.
b) ACOSTUMBRARSE. — To become accustomed, to get used: *hacerse al calor*, to become accustomed to the heat; *no me hice a vivir solo*, I couldn't get used to living alone.
c) ESTAR HECHO. — To be made: *el pan se hace con harina*, bread is made with flour.
d) LOCUCIONES DIVERSAS. — *Hacerse a la mar*, to put to sea. || *Hacerse a la vela*, to set sail. || *Hacerse a sí mismo*, to be a self-made man. || *Hacerse atrás*, to move back. || *Hacerse a un lado*, v. LADO. || *Hacerse cortar el pelo*, to have one's hair cut. || *Hacerse de* or *con*, to get (conseguir), to get hold of (tomar), to make off with (apropiarse): *se ha hecho con mi libro*, he has made off with my book; to get hold of (en deporte): *se hizo con el balón*, he got hold of the ball. || *Hacerse de nuevo con*, to regain: *hacerse de nuevo con el poder*, to regain power. || *Hacerse de rogar*, v. ROGAR. || *Hacerse el* or *la*, to act like, to pretend to be (fingir, blasonar). || FAM. *Hacerse el remolón*, v. REMOLÓN. || *Hacerse fuerte en*, v. FUERTE. || *Hacerse indispensable*, to make o.s. indispensable. || *Hacerse el olvidadizo*, to pretend to be forgetful. || *Hacerse pasar por*, to pass o.s. off as. || *Hacerse tres mil dólares al mes*, to make three thousand dollars a month. || *Se me hace que va a llover*, it seems to me that it is going to rain, I think that it is going to rain.

haces m. pl. V. HAZ.

hacia prep. Towards, toward: *hacia la derecha*, towards the right. || Near (cerca de). || At about: *hacia las dos*, at about two o'clock. || Towards (para con). || — *Hacia abajo*, down, downwards. || *Hacia acá*, this way, here, over here. || *Hacia adelante*, forwards. || *Hacia arriba*, up, upwards. || *Hacia atrás*, backwards. || *Hacia casa*, homeward, towards home, home. || *Hacia donde*, where, wither. || *Vamos hacia allá*, let's start making our way there, let's go over there.

hacienda f. Country property (propiedad rural). || Hacienda, ranch (en América del Sur). || Property, fortune, possessions, *pl.* (bienes). || *Amer.* Livestock, cattle (ganado). || — *Hacienda pública*, public treasury. || *Ministerio de Hacienda*, Exchequer (en Gran Bretaña), Treasury (en Estados Unidos), Ministry of Finance (en los demás países). || *Ministro de Hacienda*, Chancellor of the Exchequer (en Gran Bretaña), Secretary of the Treasury (en Estados Unidos), Minister of Finance (en los demás países).

hacina f. Stack, rick (conjunto de haces). || FIG. Heap, pile.

hacinación f. o **hacinamiento** m. Stacking, piling, heaping.

hacinar v. tr. To stack (colocar en hacinas). || FIG. To stack [up], to pile [up] (amontonar): *hacinar las pruebas contra un culpable*, to stack up proof against a guilty person.
— V. pr. To be crowded, to be piled, to be huddled: *la familia se hacinaba en una choza*, the family was crowded into a hut.

hacha f. o **hachón** m. Torch (antorcha). || Large candle (de cera).

hacha f. Axe [U.S., ax]: *un hacha de armas*, a battle-axe. || Hatchet (más pequeña). || FIG. y FAM. Ace [U.S., whiz]: *ser un hacha en matemáticas*, to be an ace at mathematics; *es un hacha del volante*, he is an ace driver, he is an ace at the wheel.

hachazo m. Axe blow, stroke with an axe, hack. || Lunge (de un toro).

hache f. Aitch (nombre de la letra h). || — FIG. y FAM. *Llámele usted hache*, call it what you like, it's all the same.

hachear v. tr. e intr. To chop, to hew.

hachero m. Torch stand (candelero). || Candlestick (para vela). || Woodcutter, lumberjack (leñador).

hachís m. Hashish.

hacho m. Torch (antorcha). || Beacon, beacon hill *o* head (altozano).

hachón m. V. HACHA.

hachuela f. Hatchet.

hada f. Fairy. || *Cuento de hadas*, fairy tale.

Hades n. pr. m. MIT. Hades (Plutón).

hado m. Fate, destiny.

hagiografía f. Hagiography (vida de los santos).

hagiográfico, ca adj. Hagiographic.

hagiógrafo m. Hagiographer.

hagiología f. Hagiology.

haiga m. FAM. Superluxurious limousine.

Haití n. pr. m. GEOGR. Haiti.

haitiano, na adj./s. Haitian (de Haití).

¡hala! interj. Come on!, go on!

halagador, ra adj. Flattering.

halagar v. tr. To flatter. || To please, to gratify: *me halaga tu propuesta*, your proposal pleases me. || To cajole (adular).

halago m. Flattery (lisonja). || Cajolery (adulación). || *Palabras de halago*, flattering words.

halagüeño, ña adj. Flattering (lisonjero). || Promising (alentador): *perspectivas halagüeñas*, promising prospects. || Pleasing, gratifying (agradable). || Attractive (atractivo).

halar v. tr. MAR. To haul, to pull, to heave (un cabo). || To tow (una gabarra).

halcón m. Falcon, hawk (ave). || FIG. Hawk. || — *Halcón campestre*, domesticated falcon. || *Halcón niego*, eyas. || *Halcón palumbario*, goshawk. || *Halcón peregrino*, peregrine falcon. || *Halcón zahareño*, haggard hawk.

halconería f. Falconry, hawking (caza con halcón).

halconero m. Falconer.

¡hale! interj. Get going!, come on!, go on!

haleche m. Anchovy (boquerón).

halibut m. ZOOL. Halibut.

haliéutico, ca adj. Halieutic.
— F. Halieutics.

hálito m. Breath (aliento). || POET. Breath of wind, zephyr, gentle breeze.

halo m. Halo.

halógeno, na adj. QUÍM. Halogenous.
— M. QUÍM. Halogen.

halografía f. QUÍM. Halography.

haloideo, a adj. QUÍM. Haloid.
— M. QUÍM. Haloid.

haltera f. DEP. Dumbbell.

halterofilia f. DEP. Weight-lifting, weightlifting.

halterófilo, la adj. Weight-lifting, weightlifting.
— M. y f. Weight-lifter.

hall m. Hall [U.S., entrance hall].

hallado, da adj. Found, discovered. || — FIG. *Bien hallado*, at ease, in one's element. || *Mal hallado*, uneasy, ill at ease, out of one's element.

hallador, ra adj. Finding, discovering.
— M. y f. Finder, discoverer.

hallar v. tr. To find (encontrar): *quien busca halla*, seek and ye shall find. || To discover (descubrir). || To come across, to run across (topar). || To find, to locate (una persona).
— V. pr. To be (encontrarse): *hallarse en Madrid*, to be in Madrid. || To be: *hallarse muy enfermo*, to be very sick. || — *Hallarse con una cosa*, to find sth. || *Hallarse en todo*, to have a hand in everything. || *No hallarse*, to feel out of place, to feel like a fish out of water.

hallazgo m. Discovery, finding (descubrimiento). || Find, finding (cosa descubierta). || Find: *esta expresión es un hallazgo*, this expression is a find.

hamaca f. Hammock (cama). || Deck chair [U.S., canvas lawn chair] (tumbona). || Palanquin (vehículo). || *Amer.* Swing (columpio).

hamadría f. o **hamadríada** f. MIT. Hamadryad.

hámago m. Propolis, bee glue (de las abejas).

hamaquear v. tr. *Amer.* To rock, to swing (mecer).

hambre f. Hunger: *aplacar el hambre*, to satisfy one's hunger. || Famine. || Starvation (escasez): *salario de hambre*, starvation salary. || FIG. y FAM. Hunger, longing, desire (deseo). || — *A buen hambre no hay pan duro*, hunger is the best sauce. || *Confundir el hambre con las ganas de comer*, to confuse the chaff with the grain. || *El hambre aguza el ingenio*, hunger sharpens the wit. || FIG. *El hambre es mala consejera*, hunger is a poor adviser. || *Engañar el hambre*, to stave off hunger. || *Huelga del hambre*, hunger strike. || FIG. y FAM. *Juntarse el hambre con las ganas de comer*, to combine [two circumstances]. || *Matar a uno de hambre*, to starve s.o. to death. || *Matar el hambre*, to stave off hunger. || *Morir* or *morirse de hambre*, to starve to death, to die from starvation (morir), to starve (estar hambriento). || *Pasar hambre*, to be hungry, to go hungry. || FIG. y FAM. *Ser más listo que el hambre*, to be [as] sharp as a needle. || *Tener hambre*, to be hungry (de comida), to hunger: *tiene hambre de riquezas*, he hungers for riches. || FAM. *Tengo un hambre que no veo* or *un hambre canina*, I am hungry enough to eat a horse, I am starving, I am as hungry as a wolf, I am ravenously hungry.
— OBSERV. The word *hambre*, although feminine, is preceded by the masculine article *el* to avoid hiatus.

hambriento, ta adj. Hungry, starving, famished. || FIG. *Hambriento de*, longing for, hungry for.
— M. y f. Starving person. || — M. pl. The hungry, the starving, starving people.

hambrina o **hambruna** f. *Amer.* Ravenous hunger.
hambrón, ona adj. FAM. Famished, starving.
— M. y f. Glutton [never satisfied]. || Starving person (persona hambrienta).
Hamburgo n. pr. GEOGR. Hamburg.
hamburgués, esa adj. Hamburg.
— M. y f. Native *o* inhabitant of Hamburg. || — F. Hamburger, hamburg steak, hamburger steak.
hampa f. Underworld: *el hampa de Chicago*, the Chicago underworld.
hampesco, ca adj. Underworld, of the underworld.
hampón, ona adj. Bullying, rowdy (pendenciero). || Roguish, shady (bribón).
— M. Thug, tough.
hámster m. ZOOL. Hamster (roedor).
handicap m. DEP. Handicap: *sufrir un handicap*, to have a handicap.
hangar m. AVIAC. Hangar (cobertizo).
hansa f. Hanse.
hanseático, ca adj. Hanseatic.
haragán, ana adj. Idle, lazy.
— M. y f. Idler, lazybones.
haraganear v. intr. To idle, to loaf around, to lounge.
haraganería f. Idleness, laziness.
harakiri m. Hara-kiri.
harapiento, ta adj. Ragged, tattered, in rags.
harapo m. Rag, tatter (andrajo). || Weak *o* low grade alcohol (aguardiente). || *Andar hecho un harapo*, to be in rags.
haraposo, sa adj. Ragged, tattered, in rags.
haraquiri m. Hara-kiri.
harca f. Morrocan military expedition. || Band of Morrocan rebels.

— OBSERV. The initial *h* is aspirate.

hardware m. Hardware (de una computadora).
harem m. o **harén** m. Harem.
harina f. Flour: *el pan se hace con harina*, bread is made with flour. || Meal, flour: *harina de pescado*, fish meal. || Powder (polvo menudo). || — *Almacén de harina*, granary. || FAM. *Donde no hay harina, todo es mohina*, when poverty comes in the door love flies out of the window. | *Eso es harina de otro costal*, that's another kettle of fish. || *Fábrica de harina*, flour mill. || *Harina de avena*, oatmeal. || *Harina de flor*, wheatmeal. || *Harina de maíz*, cornflour. || *Harina lacteada*, malted milk. || *Metido en harina*, doughy, heavy (pan), engrossed, absorbed (absorto), busy (ocupado), stout, fat (gordo).
harinero, ra adj. Flour. || *Molino harinero*, flour mill.
harinoso, sa adj. Floury: *pan harinoso*, floury bread. || Farinaceous (farináceo).
harmonía f. y sus derivados. V. ARMONÍA.
harnero m. Sifter, sieve (criba).
harpa f. MÚS. Harp.
harpía f. V. ARPÍA.
harpillera f. Sacking, sackcloth (tela).
hartada f. V. HARTAZGO.
hartar v. tr. To satiate, to satisfy (calmar el hambre). || FIG. To satisfy (un deseo). | To weary, to bore, to tire (cansar). | To annoy (fastidiar). || *Hartar de palos*, to shower blows on.
— V. pr. To eat one's fill (comer bastante). || To gorge o.s., to stuff o.s. (comer demasiado): *hartarse de pasteles*, to stuff o.s. with cakes, to gorge o.s. on cakes. || FIG. To get tired (*de*, of), to get fed up (*de*, with): *hartarse de esperar*, to get tired of waiting. || — FAM. *Hartarse de dormir*, to have one's fill of sleep. || *Hasta hartarse*, one's fill: *comer hasta hartarse*, to eat one's fill; until one has had enough, until one is fed up.
hartazgo m. Bellyful (fam.) [exceso, demasía]. || — *Darse un hartazgo*, to eat one's fill (comer bastante), to overeat, to eat too much, to get indigestion (comer demasiado), to have one's fill of: *nos dimos un hartazgo de música anoche*, we had our fill of music last night; to have a bellyful (fam.): *me he dado un hartazgo de cine*, I've had a bellyful of the pictures.
harto, ta adj. Full, satiated (de comer). || FIG. Tired, fed up (cansado). || — FIG. y FAM. *Estar harto de*, to be fed up with, to be sick of: *estoy harto de oír tus quejas*, I am fed up with listening to your complaints.
— Adv. Enough (bastante). || Very, quite (muy).
hartón m. FAM. Bellyful (hartazgo). || *Amer.* Glutton.
hartura f. Satiety (de comer). || Abundance. || FIG. Fulfilment [U.S., fulfillment], satisfaction (de un deseo). || — FIG. y FAM. *Me entró tal hartura que*, I got so fed up that. | *¡Qué hartura!*, what a drag!, what a bore! || *Tener una hartura de*, to be fed up with, to have had one's fill of: *tengo una hartura de cine*, I am fed up with the cinema, I have had my fill of the pictures.
hasta prep. Up to, as far as: *hasta allí*, as far as there; *hasta aquí*, up to here. || To: *desde París hasta Madrid*, from Paris to Madrid. || Until, till: *no vendrá hasta mañana*, he won't come until tomorrow; *no se levantó hasta terminar su lectura*, he didn't get up until he had finished reading. || — *Es malo hasta más no poder*, he is as evil as can be. || *Hasta ahora, hasta la fecha*, until now, up to now, so far, to date. || *¡Hasta ahora!*, see you later!, see you! || *¿Hasta cuándo?*, until when?, how long? || *¿Hasta dónde?*, how far?, up to where? || *Hasta el punto que*, to such a point that. || *Hasta entonces*, until then, until that time, up to then. || *¡Hasta la vista!*, see you!, good-bye! || *¡Hasta luego!, ¡hasta después!, ¡hasta pronto!*, see you later!, see you!, see you soon [U.S., so long!]. || *¡Hasta mañana!*, see you tomorrow. || *Hasta más no poder*, as much [hard, fast, etc.] as one can, as much as can be *o* as possible: *correr hasta más no poder*, to run as fast as one can. || *Hasta que*, until, till. || *Hasta tal punto que*, to such a point that. || *¡Hasta más ver!*, I'll be seing you! [U.S., so long!]
— Adv. Even: *hasta los niños saben esto*, even children know this; *hasta dice que*, he even says that; *hasta se burla de nosotros*, he even mocks us.
hastiado, da adj. Disgusted (*de*, with) [asqueado]. || Tired (*de*, of) [cansado].
hastial m. Gable end. || FIG. Lout (hombre tosco). || MIN. Lateral wall of an excavation.

— OBSERV. When *hastial* means "lout" the *h* is aspirate.

hastiar v. tr. To disgust, to sicken (asquear). || To annoy (fastidiar). || To bore, to weary (aburrir).
— V. pr. To get fed up (*de*, with), to get tired (*de*, of).
hastío m. Disgust (asco). || Weariness, boredom (tedio). || — *Causar hastío*, to bore (aburrir), to sicken, to disgust (dar asco). || *Sentir hastío de un trabajo*, to be fed up with a job, to be sick of a job.
hatajo m. Small herd *o* flock (rebaño). || FIG. y FAM. Heap, bunch, lot: *un hatajo de disparates*, a lot of nonsense.
hatijo m. Cover of beehive entrance.
hatillo m. Small flock *o* herd (rebaño). || Bundle [of belongings] (paquetito). || FAM. *Tomar* or *coger su hatillo*, to pack one's bags.
hato m. Flock, herd (rebaño). || Provisions, *pl.* (víveres). || Belongings, *pl.*, things, *pl.* (efectos). || FIG. Band, gang: *hato de pícaros*, band of rogues. | Lot, heap, bunch (de cosas). || *Amer.* Cattle ranch (hacienda). || — FAM. *Andar con el hato a cuestas*, to be a rover, to roam about. | *Liar el hato*, V. LIAR.
Hawai n. pr. GEOGR. Hawaii.
hawaiano, na adj./s. Hawaiian.
haya f. BOT. Beech, beech tree.
Haya (La) n. pr. GEOGR. The Hague.
hayaca f. *Amer.* Turnover made of corn and filled with meat or fish then wrapped in a banana leaf.
hayal m. o **hayedo** m. Beech grove.
hayo m. BOT. Coca. || Coca leaves [chewed by Indians].
hayucal m. Beech grove.
hayuco m. Beechnut (fruto del haya).
haz m. Bundle, bunch (de cosas). || FÍS. Beam (de rayos luminosos). || Sheaf (de trigo). || Truss (de paja). || Faggot, bundle (de leña). || Bundle (fajo). || — Pl. Fasces, *pl.* (de los lictores). || — F. Face (rostro). || Right side (lado opuesto al envés). || Surface, face: *la* or *el haz de la Tierra*, the face of the earth.
haza f. Plot of arable land.
hazaña f. Exploit, feat, deed: *las hazañas del Cid*, the feats of El Cid.
hazañería f. Fuss.
hazmerreír m. Laughingstock: *ser el hazmerreír del pueblo*, to be the laughingstock of the village.
¡he! interj. Hey!
he adv. dem. Used with the adv. *aquí* or *allí* and with the pron. *me, te, le, la, lo*, etc: *he aquí*, here is, here are; *he allí*, there is; *heme aquí*, here I am; *hete aquí*, here you are; *hele aquí*, here he is; *he aquí las consecuencias de su comportamiento*, these are the consequences of your behaviour.
hebdomadario, ria adj. Weekly.
hebén adj. Type of large, white grape (uva).
hebijón m. Tongue *o* pin of a buckle (de una hebilla).
hebilla f. Buckle, clasp: *hebilla de cinturón*, belt buckle.
hebra f. Thread (hilo). || Length of thread (trozo de hilo). || Fibre [U.S., fiber], string (de verduras). || Sinew (de carne). || Filament (filamento). || Grain (de madera). || Thread (de araña, gusano de seda). || FIG. Thread (del discurso). || MIN. Vein. || — Pl. POÉT. Hair. || — *Amer. De una hebra*, all at once, in one breath. || FAM. *Pegar la hebra*, to start a conversation (entablar una conversación), to chat (estar charlando).
hebraico, ca adj. Hebraic.
hebraísmo m. Hebraism.
hebraísta o **hebraizante** m. y f. Hebraist.
hebreo, a adj./s. Hebrew.
Hébridas n. pr. f. pl. GEOGR. Hebrides.
hecatombe f. Hecatomb. || FIG. Hecatomb, slaughter (matanza). | Disaster (desastre).
heces f. pl. Faeces (excrementos).
hectárea f. Hectare (medida).
héctico, ca adj. MED. Hectic, consumptive.
hectogramo m. Hectogramme [U.S., hectogram].
hectolitro m. Hectolitre [U.S., hectoliter].
hectómetro m. Hectometre [U.S., hectometer].
hectovatio m. ELECTR. Hectowatt.
hecha f. Date (fecha). || *De esta, aquella hecha*, from now, then on.
hechicería f. Witchcraft, sorcery. || FIG. Enchantment, charm, spell (seducción).
hechicero, ra adj. Magic, bewitching, enchanting. || FIG. Charming, enchanting, bewitching: *mujer, mirada hechicera*, bewitching woman, look.

— M. Sorcerer, wizard (brujo). || Charmer, enchanter. || Witch doctor (en África, etc.). || — F. Witch, sorceress (bruja).
hechizar v. tr. To cast a spell on, to bewitch. || FIG. To bewitch, to enchant, to fascinate.
hechizo m. Magic, sorcery, witchcraft (hechicería). || Charm, spell (sortilegio). || FIG. Enchantment, fascination, spell, charm (encanto). | Charmer (persona que hechiza).
hecho, cha p. p. de *hacer*. || — *Bien hecho*, well made, well done (cosa), well-proportioned, shapely (mujer), well-built (hombre). || *¡Bien hecho!*, well done! || *Dicho y hecho*, no sooner said than done. || FIG. *Está hecho un monstruo*, he is a monster. | *Estar hecho*, to be like (parecer), to have become (haberse vuelto). || *¡Hecho!*, agreed!, done!, all right! || *Hecho a la medida*, v. MEDIDA. || *Hecho a mano*, hand-made. || *Hecho a máquina*, machine-made. || *Lo hecho hecho está*, what is done is done. || *Mal hecho*, badly made, badly done (cosa), oddly-shaped (persona). || *Ropa hecha*, ready-made clothes, ready-to-wear clothes.
— Adj. Mature: *hombre hecho*, mature man. || Finished (terminado). || — *Hecho y derecho*, real, in every sense of the word: *un hombre hecho y derecho*, a real man. || *Muy hecho*, overdone (carne). || *Poco hecho*, underdone (carne).
— M. Act, deed (acción). || Feat: *hecho de armas*, feat of arms. || Fact: *debido al hecho de que*, due to the fact that. || Matter (cuestión). || Event (suceso). || — *De hecho*, in fact, as a matter of fact, actually (en realidad), de facto (sentido jurídico). || *Del dicho al hecho hay mucho* or *gran trecho*, v. DICHO. || *El hecho es que*, the fact is that. || *Es un hecho que*, it's a fact that. || *Hecho consumado*, fait accompli, accomplished fact. || REL. *Hechos de los Apóstoles*, Acts of the Apostles. || *Hechos y milagros*, doings, exploits. || *No hay que tomar las palabras por hechos*, one should not take words at their face value. || *Vías de hecho*, acts of violence, assault and battery. || *Volvamos al hecho*, let's get back to the matter in hand.
hechura f. Making (fabricación). || Making-up, confection (confección de un traje). || Cut (forma de la ropa). || Form, shape (forma de un objeto). || Workmanship (calidad de la fabricación). || Build, form, shape (del cuerpo). || FIG. Creation, doing (obra). || Creature: *somos hechuras de Dios*, we are creatures of God. || FIG. *Entre sastres no se pagan hechuras*, what's a favour between friends?
heder* v. intr. To stink, to reek (oler mal).
hediente o **hediento, ta** adj. Stinking, reeking, fetid.
hediondez f. Stench, stink, reek, fetidness (hedor).
hediondo, da adj. Stinking, foul-smelling, smelly, fetid (pestilente). || FIG. Repulsive, revolting.
hedonismo m. Hedonism.
hedonista adj. FIL. Hedonistic, hedonic.
— M. y f. Hedonist.
hedor m. Stench, stink, reek, fetidness.
hegelianismo m. FIL. Hegelianism.
hegeliano, na adj./s. Hegelian.
hegemonía f. Hegemony.
hégira o **héjira** f. Hegira, hejira (era mahometana).
helada f. Freeze (fenómeno atmosférico). || Frost (escarcha). || *Helada blanca*, hoarfrost.
heladera f. [Ice-cream] freezer (para hacer helados). || *Amer.* Refrigerator.
heladería f. Ice-cream stall *o* parlour *o* shop.
heladero m. Ice-cream man.
heladizo, za adj. Easily frozen.
helado, da adj. Frozen, icy. || Freezing cold, icy (muy frío). || Frozen, as cold as ice, freezing: *tengo los pies helados*, my feet are frozen. || Iced (café). || — *Estoy helado*, I am chilled to the bone, I am freezing [cold]. || FIG. *Quedarse helado*, to be dumbfounded *o* flabbergasted (sorpresa), to be scared stiff (miedo).
— M. Ice cream: *un helado de vainilla*, a vanilla ice cream. || *Helado de corte*, wafer.
helador, ra adj. Freezing, icy.
heladora f. [Ice-cream] freezer (para hacer helados). || Refrigerator, icebox (nevera).
heladura f. Crack.
helamiento m. Freezing.
helar* v. tr. To freeze: *el frío hiela el agua de los ríos*, the cold freezes the water in the rivers. || To harden, to set, to congeal (aceite, grasa). || To ice, to chill (enfriar mucho). || FIG. To dumbfound (dejar pasmado). | To daunt, to discourage (desanimar). || *Hace un frío que hiela las piedras*, it's freezing cold.
— V. pr. To freeze, to congeal (líquidos). || To harden, to set, to congeal (aceite, grasa). || To become frozen, to freeze over (un estanque, etc.). || To freeze (motor). || To ice up (alas, carriles). || To be frostbitten (plantas). || FIG. To freeze to death: *en invierno se hiela uno*, in winter one freezes to death. || FIG. *Se me heló la sangre*, my blood curdled *o* ran cold.
— V. impers. To freeze: *ayer heló*, it froze yesterday.
helechal m. Fern-covered ground.
helecho m. BOT. Fern.
Helena n. pr. f. Helen.
helénico, ca adj. Hellenic, Greek (griego).
helenio m. BOT. Elecampane.
helenismo m. Hellenism.
helenista adj. Hellenistic.
— M. y f. Hellenist.
helenístico, ca adj. Hellenistic.
helenización f. Hellenization.
helenizar v. tr. To hellenize.
heleno, na adj. Hellenic, Greek.
— M. y f. Hellene, Greek (griego).
helera f. *Amer.* Refrigerator.
helero m. Glacier (ventisquero). || Snow cap (capa de nieve). || Ice sheet (masa de hielo).
helgadura f. Gap (entre los dientes).
heliaco, ca adj. ASTR. Heliacal.
hélice m. Propeller, airscrew (de avión). || Propeller, screw (de barco). || ANAT. Helix (de la oreja). || MAT. Helix. || ZOOL. Helix (caracol). || Spiral (espiral).
helicoidal adj. Helicoidal.
helicoide m. MAT. Helicoid.
helicón m. MÚS. Helicon.
helicóptero m. AVIAC. Helicopter.
heliocéntrico, ca adj. ASTR. Heliocentric.
heliocromía f. IMPR. Heliochromy, colour photography.
heliogábalo m. Glutton. || *Comer como un heliogábalo*, to eat like a horse.
Heliogábalo n. pr. m. Heliogabalus.
heliograbado m. IMPR. Heliogravure, photoengraving.
heliograbador m. IMPR. Photoengraver.
heliografía f. Heliography.
heliógrafo m. Heliograph.
heliómetro m. Heliometer (telescopio).
helión m. FÍS. Helium nucleus.
helioscopio m. Helioscope.
helioterapia MED. Heliotherapy.
heliotipia f. Heliotype.
heliotropina f. QUÍM. Heliotropin.
heliotropismo m. BOT. Heliotropism.
heliotropo m. BOT. y MIN. Heliotrope.
helipuerto m. Heliport.
helmintiasis f. MED. Helminthiasis.
helminto m. ZOOL. Helminth.
Helvecia n. pr. f. GEOGR. Helvetia [Switzerland].
helvecio, cia adj./s. Helvetian, Swiss.
helvético, ca adj. Helvetic, Helvetian.
— M. y f. Helvetian.
hemático, ca adj. Haematic [U.S., hematic].
hematíe m. ANAT. Red corpuscle (glóbulo rojo).
hematina f. Haematin [U.S., hematin, hematine].
hematites f. MIN. Haematite [U.S., hematite].
hematocito m. Haematocyte, haemocyte [U.S., hematocyte, hemocyte].
hematología f. MED. Haematology [U.S., hematology].
hematólogo m. MED. Haematologist [U.S., hematologist].
hematoma m. MED. Hematoma.
hematosis f. BIOL. Haematosis [U.S., hematosis].
hematozoario m. ZOOL. Haematozoan, haematozoon [U.S., hematozoan, hematozoon].
hematuria f. MED. Haematuria [U.S., hematuria].
hembra f. Female, she (de los animales): *la yegua es la hembra del caballo*, the mare is the female horse *o* the she-horse. || Female, hen (de las aves). || FAM. Girl: *tiene tres hijos, dos hembras y un varón*, he has three children, two girls and one boy. | Woman: *una buena hembra*, a good-looking woman. || TECN. Female. | Clasp (de broche). | Eye (de corchete). | Socket (de enchufe). | Nut (de tornillo).
— Adj. Female. || Feminine (femenino). || *Una mujer muy hembra*, a real woman.
hembraje m. *Amer.* Female stock.
hembrilla f. TECN. Female (de ciertas piezas). | Eyebolt (armella).
hembruno, na adj. Female.
hemeroteca f. Newspaper library.
hemiciclo m. Hemicycle. || Floor (del Parlamento).
hemiedro, dra adj. Hemihedral.
hemiplejía f. MED. Hemiplegia.
hemipléjico, ca adj./s. MED. Hemiplegic.
hemíptero, ra adj. ZOOL. Hemipterous.
— M. ZOOL. Hemipteran [U.S., hemipteron]. || — Pl. ZOOL. Hemiptera.
hemisférico, ca adj. Hemispheric, hemispherical.
hemisferio m. Hemisphere.
hemistiquio m. Hemistich (en poesía).
hemofilia f. MED. Haemophilia [U.S., hemophilia].
hemofílico, ca adj. Haemophilic [U.S., hemophilic].
— M. y f. Haemophiliac [U.S., hemophiliac].
hemoglobina f. BIOL. Haemoglobin [U.S., hemoglobin].
hemólisis f. MED. Haemolysis [U.S., hemolysis].
hemoptisis f. MED. Haemoptysis [U.S., hemoptysis].
hemorragia f. MED. Haemorrhage, hemorrhage. || FIG. Drain. || *Hemorragia nasal*, nosebleed.
hemorrágico, ca adj. MED. Haemorrhagic [U.S., hemorrhagic].
hemorroidal adj. MED. Haemorrhoidal [U.S., hemorrhoidal].
hemorroides f. pl. MED. Haemorrhoids [U.S., hemorrhoids], piles (almorranas).
hemostático, ca adj./s.m. MED. Haemostatic [U.S., hemostatic].
henal m. AGR. Hayloft.
henar m. Hayfield (prado). || Hayloft (henil).
henchidura f. o **henchimiento** m. Filling, stuffing.

henchir* v. tr. To fill [up], to stuff, to cram (llenar). || To fill: *henchir de aire los pulmones*, to fill one's lungs with air.
— V. pr. To stuff o.s. (de comida). || FIG. *Henchirse de orgullo*, to swell with pride.
hendedura f. V. HENDIDURA.
hender* v. tr. To cleave, to split (cortar). || To crack, to split (partir). || FIG. To cleave (el aire, el agua). | To make one's way through, to elbow one's way through (abrirse paso).
— V. pr. To split, to crack.
hendible adj. Cleavable.
hendido, da adj. Cloven: *pie hendido*, cloven hoof.
hendidura f. Split, cleft (corte). || Crack, fissure (grieta). || Crevice (ancha grieta). || Slot (ranura). || Groove (de una polea). || GEOL. Fissure, rift.
hendimiento m. Splitting, cleaving, cracking.
hendir* v. tr. (P.us.). V. HENDER.
henequén m. *Amer.* Henequen (pita).
henificación f. AGR. Haymaking.
henificar v. tr. To ted, to toss (el heno).
henil m. AGR. Hayloft.
heno m. Hay (hierba cortada y seca): *segar el heno*, to reap hay.
henrio m. FÍS. Henry (unidad).
hepático, ca adj. Hepatic, liver.
— F. BOT. Liverwort, hepatica (flor).
hepatitis f. MED. Hepatitis.
heptacordo o **heptacordio** m. MÚS. Heptachord.
heptaedro m. MAT. Heptahedron.
heptagonal adj. MAT. Heptagonal.
heptágono, na adj. MAT. Heptagonal.
— M. Heptagon.
heptámetro m. Heptameter (verso).
heptarquía f. Heptarchy (forma de gobierno).
heptasílabo, ba adj. Heptasyllabic.
— M. Heptasyllable.
Heracles n. pr. m. Heracles (Hércules).
heráldico, ca adj. Heraldic (relativo al blasón).
— M. Heraldist (heraldista). || — F. Heraldry.
heraldista m. Heraldist.
heraldo m. Herald.
herbáceo, a adj. BOT. Herbaceous.
herbajar v. tr. To put out to pasture, to graze.
herbaje m. Herbage, grass, pasture (conjunto de hierbas). || Grazing fee, herbage (derecho de pastoreo).
herbario, ria adj. Herbal.
— M. Herbarium (colección de plantas). || Herbal (libro). || Herbalist (persona que colecciona plantas). || Botanist (botánico). || Rumen (de un rumiante).
herbazal m. Grassland.
herbecer* v. intr. To become green [with grass] (los campos), to begin to grow, to come up (la hierba).
herbero m. Rumen (de los rumiantes).
Herberto n. pr. m. Herbert.
herbicida adj./s.m. Weed killer, herbicide.
herbívoro, ra adj. Herbivorous, grass-eating.
— M. y f. Herbivore. || — M. pl. Herbivora.
herbolario m. Herbalist, herborist. || Herbalist's shop (tienda).
herboristería f. Herbalist's shop.
herborización f. Herborization.
herborizar v. intr. To gather herbs. || To herborize, to botanize (un herbolario).
herboso, sa adj. Grassy.
herciniano, na adj. GEOL. Hercynian.
hercio m. FÍS. Hertz.
hercúleo, a adj. Herculean.
hércules m. FAM. Hercules (hombre fuerte).
Hércules n. pr. m. Hercules.
heredable adj. Inheritable.
heredad f. Country estate *o* farm *o* property.
heredado, da adj. Landed, property-owning.
heredar v. intr. To inherit: *heredar a* or *de un tío*, to inherit from an uncle.
— V. tr. To inherit: *heredar una fortuna*, to inherit a fortune; *heredar una casa de su padre*, to inherit a house from one's father. || FIG. *Heredar las virtudes de sus padres*, to inherit the virtues of one's parents.
heredero, ra adj. Inheriting.
— M. Heir (*de*, to), inheritor (*de*, of). || — F. Heiress, inheritor, inheritress. || — *Heredero forzoso*, heir apparent. || *Heredero universal*, general devisee, general legatee. || *Instituir heredero* or *por heredero a uno*, to appoint s.o. as one's heir. || *Presunto heredero*, heir presumptive. || *Príncipe heredero*, crown prince.
hereditario, ria adj. Hereditary: *enfermedad hereditaria*, hereditary disease.
hereje m. y f. Heretic. || FIG. Rascal (sinvergüenza).
herejía f. Heresy. || FIG. Heresy: *herejía científica*, scientific heresy. | Insult. | Dirty trick (mala jugada).
herencia f. Inheritance: *recibir una herencia*, to receive an inheritance. || Legacy (legado). || FIG. Heritage. || BIOL. Heredity. || — JUR. *Adición de la herencia*, acceptance of an inheritance. || *Herencia yacente*, unclaimed estate, estate in abeyance. || FAM. *Lo tiene de herencia*, it runs in the family.
heresiarca m. Heresiarch.
herético, ca adj. Heretical.
herida f. Injury. || Wound (de soldado, combatiente, etc.). || Wound (llaga). || FIG. Insult, outrage (ofensa). | Injury, wound (del alma, etc.). || — *Herida contusa*, contusion. || FIG. *Hurgar en la herida*, to turn the knife in the wound. | *Renovar la herida*, to open up an old wound. | *Tocar en la herida*, to put one's finger on the sore spot.
herido, da adj. Wounded, injured, hurt: *herido de gravedad* or *mal herido*, seriously *o* badly wounded; *herido de muerte*, mortally wounded. || FIG. Hurt, wounded (ofendido).
— M. Injured person, wounded person. || MIL. *Los heridos*, the wounded.
herir* v. tr. To hurt, to injure: *herir a uno en el brazo*, to injure s.o.'s arm, to injure s.o. in the arm. || To wound: *herir a uno con la espada*, to wound s.o. with a sword. || To fall on, to strike, to hit (los rayos de sol). || To beat down on (el sol). || MÚS. To play, to pluck (pulsar, tocar). || FIG. To hurt, to offend (ofender). | To hurt: *este ruido hiere mi oído*, this noise is hurting my ears. | To hurt, to wound: *herir a alguien en su amor propio*, to hurt s.o.'s pride. | To offend: *esta palabra hiere mi oído*, this word offends my ears. || — *Herir a alguien por la espalda*, to knife *o* to shoot s.o. in the back. || *Herir de muerte*, to mortally wound. || *Herir el aire con sus gritos*, to rend the air with one's screams. || FIG. *Herir en carne viva*, V. CARNE. || *Herir en lo vivo*, to touch *o* to cut *o* to hurt to the quick. || *Herir la vista*, to hurt one's eyes.
— V. pr. To injure o.s., to hurt o.s.
hermafrodita adj. Hermaphroditic, hermaphrodite, hermaphroditical.
— M. y f. Hermaphrodite.
hermafroditismo m. Hermaphroditism.
hermana f. Sister: *hermana mayor*, eldest sister, big sister. || REL. Sister: *hermana de la Caridad*, Sister of Charity. || FIG. Other half (de un par). || — *Hermana gemela*, twin sister. || *Hermana política*, sister-in-law. || *Media hermana*, half sister. || *Prima hermana*, first cousin.
hermanable adj. Brotherly, fraternal. || Compatible. || Matching (que hace juego).
hermanado, da adj. FIG. Similar: *conceptos hermanados*, similar ideas. || Matched (que hace juego). || Twin (ciudad).
hermanal adj. Brotherly, fraternal.
hermanamiento m. Fraternal *o* brotherly union. || Twinning [of towns] (de ciudades).
hermanar v. tr. To match (reunir las cosas parecidas). || To join (unir). || To combine (combinar). || To twin: *han hermanado a León con San Francisco*, they twinned León and San Francisco.
— V. pr. To match (dos o varias cosas). || To become brothers in spirit (dos o varias personas).
hermanastra f. Stepsister. || Half sister (media hermana).
hermanastro m. Stepbrother. || Half brother (medio hermano).
hermandad f. Fraternity, brotherhood (entre hermanos), fraternity, sisterhood (entre hermanas). || Brotherhood (cofradía). || Association, league (asociación): *hermandad de ganaderos*, association of cattlemen. || FIG. Similarity, likeness (semejanza). || HIST. Spanish militia formed about the XIIth century to maintain public order. || *Convenio de hermandad*, twin city agreement.
hermano, na adj. Similar (semejante). || Brother: *pueblos hermanos*, brother peoples || Sister (lengua).
— M. Brother: *el hermano mayor*, the eldest brother; *tengo dos hermanos mayores y uno menor*, I have two older brothers and a younger one. || REL. Brother: *hermano lego*, lay brother. || — *Hermano carnal*, full brother. || *Hermano de leche*, foster brother. || *Hermano de trabajo*, porter (ganapán). || *Hermano de madre* or *uterino*, half brother on the mother's side. || *Hermano de padre*, half brother on the father's side. || *Hermano gemelo*, twin brother. || *Hermano político*, brother-in-law (cuñado). || REL. *¡Hermanos!*, brothers!, brethren! || *Hermanos siameses*, Siamese twins. || *Medio hermano*, half brother. || *Primo hermano*, first cousin.
hermenéutico, ca adj. Hermeneutic, hermeneutical.
Hermés n. pr. m. Hermes (Mercurio).
herméticamente adv. Hermetically.
hermeticidad f. Airtightness, watertightness. || FIG. Impenetrability. | Watertightness (de una teoría).
hermético, ca adj. Hermetic, airtight, watertight. || FIG. Impenetrable (impenetrable). | Watertight: *razonamiento hermético*, watertight reasoning.
hermetismo m. Hermeticism, hermetism. || FIG. Impenetrability. | Watertightness (de un razonamiento). | Secrecy, secretiveness (carácter reservado).
hermosamente adv. Beautifully, handsomely. || FIG. Admirably, perfectly.
hermoseamiento m. Beautifying, embellishment.
hermosear v. tr. To beautify, to embellish (embellecer). || To adorn (adornar).
hermoso, sa adj. Beautiful, lovely: *una mujer hermosa*, a beautiful woman. || Handsome (hombre). || Bonny (niño). || Beautiful (cosa): *un hermoso edificio*, a beautiful building. || Splendid (espléndido). || — *¡Hermoso día!*, fine *o* lovely *o* beautiful day! || *Más hermoso que un sol*, as pretty as a picture, divine (chica, niño), fine-looking, handsome (adolescente).
hermosura f. Beauty: *la hermosura del paisaje*, the beauty of the landscape. || Beauty, loveliness (de una mujer). || Handsomeness (de un hombre). || — *Este*

HERRAMIENTAS, *f.* — TOOLS

I. Herramientas (*f.*) de carpintero. — Carpenter's tools.

caja (*f.*) de herramientas	toolbox
banco *m.*	bench
torno (*m.*) *or* tornillo (*m.*) de banco	vice [U.S., vise], clamp
cárcel *f.*, mordaza *f.*	clamp
sierra *f.*	saw
sierra (*f.*) de arco	bow saw
sierra (*f.*) circular	circular saw [U.S., buzz saw]
sierra (*f.*) de contornear	compass *o* scroll saw
segueta *f.*, sierra (*f.*) de calar	fretsaw
serrucho *m.*	handsaw, saw
cincel *m.*, escoplo *m.*, bedano *m.*, formón *m.*	chisel
cortafrío *m.*; buril *m.*	cold chisel; burin
gubia *f.*	gouge
formón (*m.*) de mediacaña	firmer gouge
cepillo *m.*	plane
cepillo (*m.*) bocel	moulding plane
garlopa *f.*	jack plane
guillame *m.*	rabbet plane
plana *f.*	drawknife
raedera *f.*	scraper
escofina *f.*	rasp
lima *f.*	file
escuadra *f.*	square
inglete *m.*	miter
punta (*f.*) de trazar	scriber
cartabón *m.*	set square, triangle
berbiquí *m.*	brace
taladradora (*f.*) de mano	hand drill
barrena *f.*, taladro *m.*	drill, bit (sin mango), gimlet, auger (con mango)
broca *f.*	drill, bit
avellanador *m.*	countersink
gramil *m.*	gauge, marking gauge
martillo *m.*	hammer
mazo *m.*	mallet
clavo *m.*	nail
puntilla *f.*	brad
tachuela *f.*	tack, stud
tornillo *m.*	screw
destornillador *m.*	screwdriver
macho (*m.*) de aterrajar	screw tap
sacaclavos *m. inv.*	nail puller
metro *m.*	ruler (regla), tape measure (cinta).
metro (*m.*) plegable	folding ruler
papel (*m.*) de lija *or* esmerilado	sandpaper, emery paper

II. Herramientas (*f.*) de mecánico. — Mechanic's tools.

llave *f.*	spanner [U.S., wrench]
llave (*f.*) plana de doble boca	double-ended spanner
llave (*f.*) inglesa	adjustable spanner, monkey wrench
llave (*f.*) de tubo	box spanner [U.S., socket wrench]
pie (m.) de rey	calipers *pl.*
tenazas *f. pl.*	pincers, tongs
cizallas *f. pl.*	shears
cortaalambres *m. inv.*	wire cutters *pl.*
alicates (*m. pl.*) universales	multipurpose *o* universal pliers
alicates (*m. pl.*) de boca graduable	adjustable pliers
punzón *m.*, sacabocados *m. inv.*	punch
broca *f.*, trépano *m.*	drill
mandril *m.*	chuck
raspador *m.*	scraper
escariador *m.*	reamer
calibrador (*m.*) de mordazas	calliper gauge
sierra (*f.*) de metales	hacksaw
remache *m.*, roblón *m.*	rivet
tuerca *f.*	nut
contratuerca *f.*	locknut
perno *m.*	bolt
clavija *f.*	pin, peg, dowel
arandela *f.*	washer
grapa *f.*	staple
bomba (*f.*) de engrase, engrasadora *f.*	grease gun
aceitera *f.*	oil can
gato *m.*	jack

III. Herramientas (*f.*) de jardinería. — Gardening tools.

laya *f.*; laya (*f.*) de dientes	spade; fork
pala *f.*	shovel
horca *f.*, horquilla *f.*	fork
rastrillo *m.*	rake
rodillo *m.*	roller
plantador *m.*	dibble
carretilla *f.*	wheelbarrow
regadera *f.*	watering can
manguera *f.*	garden hose, hosepipe
cortacéspedes *m. inv.*	lawnmower
tijeras *f. pl.*	shears, garden shears
podadera *f.*	pruning shears *pl.* (tijeras), pruning knife (cuchillo).
hoz *f.*	sickle
guadaña *f.*	scythe
desplantador *m.*	trowel
almocafre *m.*, escardillo *m.*, escardadera *f.*	weeding hoe
azada *f.*, azadón *m.*, binador *m.*	hoe
sembradora *f.*	seed drill

IV. Herramientas (*f.*) de decorador. — Decorator's tools.

escalera *f.*	stepladder
caballete *m.*	trestle
paleta *f.*, palustre *m.*	trowel
llana *f.*	float
espátula *f.*	spatula
cubo *m.*	bucket, pail
brocha *f.*	brush (en general), paintbrush, brush (para pintar)
rodillo *m.*	roller
tijeras *f. pl.*	scissors

V. Otras herramientas, *f.* — Other tools.

navaja *f.*	penknife
cortavidrio *m.*, diamante *m.*, grujidor *m.*	glass cutter
plomada *f.*	plumb line
nivel (*m.*) de agua	spirit level
piocha *f.*, piqueta *f.*	pickaxe [U.S., pickax]
el hacha *f.*	the axe [U.S., the ax]
almádena *f.*, almádana *f.*	sledgehammer
escoda *f.*	bushhammer
pisón *m.*	rammer
yunque *m.*	anvil
bigornia *f.*	beakiron, bickiron, two-beaked anvil
fuelle *m.*	bellows *pl.* & *sing.*
lezna *f.*	awl
compás (*m.*) de vara	beam compass, trammel
palanca *f.*	lever
desmontable (*m.*) para neumáticos	tyre lever
cigüeñal *m.*	crank
soldador *m.*	soldering iron
soplete *m.*	blowlamp [U.S., blowtorch]
troquel *m.*	die
terraja *f.*	diestock
máquinas (*f. pl.*) herramientas	machine tools
torno *m.*	lathe
torno (*m.*) revólver	turret lathe
fresa *f.*	milling cutter
fresadora *f.*	milling machine
taladradora (*f.*) eléctrica	electric *o* power drill
trituradora *f.*	grinder, crusher
remachadora *f.*	riveter
laminadora *f.*	rolling mill
prensa *f.*	press
pilón *m.*	drop hammer
martillo (*m.*) pilón	pile hammer, drop hammer
martillo (*m.*) neumático	air hammer, pneumatic hammer
martinete *m.*	pile hammer

coche es una hermosura, this car is a beauty. || *¡Qué hermosura!*, what a beauty!

hernia f. MED. Hernia, rupture. || MED. *Hernia estrangulada*, strangulated hernia.

herniado, da adj. Ruptured. || Suffering from a hernia *o* rupture.
— M. y f. Person suffering from a hernia.

herniario, ria adj. MED. Hernial.

herniarse v. pr. To rupture o.s.

hernioso, sa adj. MED. Hernial.
— M. y f. Person suffering from a hernia.

Herodes n. pr. m. Herod. || *Andar* or *ir de Herodes a Pilatos*, to fall out of the frying pan into the fire.

Herodoto o **Heródoto** n. pr. m. Herodotus.

héroe m. Hero.

heroicamente adv. Heroically.

heroicidad f. Heroism (heroísmo). || Heroic deed, exploit (hazaña).

heroico, ca adj. Heroic. || FIG. Heroic: *medicamento heroico*, heroic remedy. || *Verso heroico*, heroic verse.

heroicocómico, ca adj. Heroicomic, mock-heroic.

heroína f. Heroine. || MED. Heroin (alcaloide).

heroísmo m. Heroism. || *Acto de heroísmo*, heroic deed.

herpe m. y f. MED. Herpes.
— OBSERV. This word is often used in the plural form.

herpético, ca adj. MED. Herpetic.

herpetismo m. MED. Herpetism.

herpetología f. Herpetology.

herrada f. Bucket.

herradero m. Branding (acción de marcar el ganado). || Branding place (sitio). || Branding time (temporada).

herrador m. Blacksmith, farrier [who shoes horses].

herradura f. Horseshoe. || — ARQ. *Arco de herradura*, horseshoe arch, Moorish arch. || *Camino de herradura*, bridle path. || *Mostrar las herraduras*, to kick (dar coces), to show a clean pair of heels, to take to one's heels (huir).

herraj m. Charcoal fuel made from the stones of pressed olives (erraj).

herraje m. Metal *o* iron fittings, *pl.*, ironwork. || *Amer.* Horseshoe (herradura).

herramental m. Tools, *pl.*, set of tools, tool kit (herramientas). || Toolbox (caja). || Toolbag (bolsa). || Tool rack (de un carpintero).
herramienta f. Tool. || Tools, *pl.*, tool kit, set of tools (conjunto de herramientas). || FIG. FAM. Horns, *pl.* (de un toro). | Weapon (arma). | Teeth, *pl.* (dentadura). || *Bolsa de herramientas*, toolbag.
herrar* v. tr. To shoe (una caballería). || To brand (el ganado). || To trim with iron.
herrería f. Blacksmithing (oficio). || Smithy, forge, blacksmith's workshop (taller). || Ironworks, *pl.* (fábrica siderúrgica). || FIG. Uproar, racket (ruido).
herrerillo m. ZOOL. Great tit (ave).
herrero m. Blacksmith.
herreruelo m. ZOOL. Coal tit, coletit.
herrete m. Metal tip, tag (de cordones, cintas, etc.).
herretear v. tr. To put a metal tip on, to tip (poner herretes). || (Ant.) To brand (marcar con hierro).
herrín m. Rust (herrumbre).
herrumbrar v. tr. To rust (aherrumbrar).
herrumbre f. Rust (orín). || Iron taste (sabor a hierro).
herrumbroso, sa adj. Rusty.
hertz o **hertzio** m. FÍS. Hertz.
hertziano, na adj. FÍS. Hertzian: *onda hertziana*, hertzian wave.
hervidero m. Boiling, bubbling, seething (de un líquido). || Bubbling spring (manantial). || FIG. Swarm, throng (de gente). | Hotbed: *un hervidero de intrigas*, a hotbed of intrigue.
hervidor m. Kettle, pot, pan (para hervir líquidos). || TECN. Heater (de caldera).
hervir* v. tr. e intr. To boil: *el agua hierve a 100 grados*, water boils at 100 degrees. || To bubble, to seethe (borbotear). || To seethe, to surge (el mar). || FIG. To boil (la sangre, de enfado). | To swarm, to teem, to seethe: *la plaza hierve de gente*, the square is swarming with people. || — *Hervir a fuego lento*, to simmer. || FIG. *Hervir en cólera*, to boil *o* to seethe with anger. | *Hervir en deseos de*, to be consumed with desire to, to have a burning desire to.
hervor m. Boiling, seething (acción de hervir). || Bubbling, seething, bubble (burbujeo). || FIG. Ardour, fire (fogosidad).
hervoroso, sa adj. Impetuous, fiery, ardent (ardoroso). || Boiling, seething (hirviente).
hesitar v. intr. (P.us.). To hesitate (dudar).
Hespérides n. pr. f. pl. MIT. Hesperides.
hetaira o **hetera** f. Hetaera, hetaira (cortesana).
heteróclito, ta adj. Heteroclite.
heterodino, na adj./s.m. ELECTR. Heterodyne.
heterodoxia f. Heterodoxy.
heterodoxo, xa adj. Heterodox, unorthodox.
heterogamia f. BIOL. y BOT. Heterogamy.
heterógamo, ma adj. Heterogamous.
heterogeneidad f. Heterogeneity.
heterogéneo, a adj. Heterogeneous.
heterogenia f. Heterogenesis.
heteronomía f. Heteronomy.
heterónomo, ma adj. Heteronomous.
heterosexual adj./s. Heterosexual.
hético, ca adj. MED. Consumptive, hectic (tísico). || Emaciated (flaco).
hetiquez f. MED. Consumption, tuberculosis.
heurístico, ca adj. Heuristic.
hevea m. BOT. Hevea.
hexacordo m. MÚS. Hexachord.
hexaédrico, ca adj. Hexahedral, six-sided.
hexaedro m. Hexahedron.
hexagonal adj. Hexagonal, six-sided.
hexágono m. Hexagon.
hexámetro, tra adj. Hexametrical (verso).
— M. Hexameter.
hez f. Sediment, dregs, *pl.*, lees, *pl.* || FIG. Dregs, *pl.*, scum. || — Pl. Excrement, *sing.*, faeces (excrementos). || *Heces fecales*, faeces.
hi m. y f. Son (hijo).
— OBSERV. Only employed in the composition of the word *hidalgo* and its derivatives, and in certain insulting expressions such as *hi de perro*, son of a bitch.
hialino, na adj./s. f. MIN. Hyaline.
hialita f. MIN. Hyalite.
hiato m. GRAM. Hiatus.
hibernación f. Hibernation.
hibernal adj. Winter (frío, etc.). || Wintry (tiempo). || Hibernal (que tiene lugar durante el invierno).
hibernante adj. Hibernating.
hibernar v. intr. To hibernate.
hibisco m. BOT. Hibiscus.
hibridación f. Hybridization.
hibridismo m. Hybridism, hybridity.
hibridizar v. tr. To hybridize.
híbrido, da adj./s.m. Hybrid.
hico m. *Amer.* Clew.
hicotea f. *Amer.* Hicatee, hicotee.
hidalgo m. Hidalgo, nobleman, noble [Spanish noble]. || — *Hidalgo de bragueta*, noble who acquired his title by siring seven male children in succession. || *Hidalgo de cuatro costados*, noble descended from four noble grandparents. || *Hidalgo de ejecutoria*, noble who has documentary proof of his noble ancestry. || *Hidalgo de gotera*, noble of little account whose title was only valid in his home town. || *Hidalgo de privilegio*, noble who purchased his title.
— Adj. Noble. || FIG. Noble, generous. | Gentlemanly (caballeroso).
— OBSERV. In the plural, the noun *hidalgo* becomes *hijosdalgo*, and the adjective becomes *hidalgos*.
hidalguez o **hidalguía** f. Nobility. || FIG. Nobleness, generosity. | Gentlemanliness, chivalry (caballerosidad).
hidátide f. MED. Hydatid.
hidra f. MIT. y ZOOL. Hydra.
hidrácido m. QUÍM. Hydracid.
hidrargirismo m. MED. Hydrargyriasis, hydrargyrism.
hidrargiro m. QUÍM. Hydrargyrum.
hidrartrosis f. MED. Hydrarthrosis.
hidratable adj. QUÍM. Hydratable.
hidratación f. QUÍM. Hydration.
hidratante adj. Moisturizing: *crema hidratante*, moisturizing cream.
hidratar v. tr. QUÍM. To hydrate.
hidrato m. QUÍM. Hydrate. || *Hidrato de carbono*, carbohydrate.
hidráulico, ca adj. Hydraulic: *prensa hidráulica*, hydraulic press; *freno hidráulico*, hydraulic brake; *cemento hidráulico*, hydraulic cement. || — *Fuerza hidráulica*, hydraulic power, waterpower. || *Rueda hidráulica*, waterwheel.
— F. Hydraulics (ciencia).
hídrico, ca adj. Hydric.
hidroavión m. Seaplane, flying boat.
hidrocarbonato m. QUÍM. Hydrocarbonate.
hidrocarburo m. QUÍM. Hydrocarbon.
hidrocefalia f. MED. Hydrocephalus.
hidrocéfalo, la adj./s. MED. Hydrocephalic.
hidrocele f. MED. Hydrocele.
hidrocloruro m. QUÍM. Hydrogen chloride.
hidrodinámico, ca adj. FÍS. Hydrodynamic.
— F. Hydrodynamics.
hidroeléctrico, ca adj. ELECTR. Hydroelectric.
hidroelectricidad f. Hydroelectricity.
hidrófilo, la adj. Hydrophilic. || Absorbent: *algodón hidrófilo*, absorbent cotton.
— M. ZOOL. Water beetle.
hidrofobia f. Hydrophobia (horror al agua). || Rabies (rabia).
hidrófobo, ba adj. Hydrophobic.
— M. y f. Hydrophobic person, hydrophobe.
hidrófugo, ga adj. Waterproof, water-repellent, dampproof. || *Hacer hidrófugo*, to waterproof.
hidrogel m. QUÍM. Hydrogel.
hidrogenación f. Hydrogenation.
hidrogenado, da adj. Hydrogenated, hydrogenized, hydrogenous.
hidrogenar v. tr. To hydrogenate, to hydrogenize.
hidrógeno m. Hydrogen. || *Hidrógeno pesado*, heavy hydrogen, deuterium.
hidrografía f. Hydrography.
hidrográfico, ca adj. Hydrographic.
hidrógrafo, fa m. y f. Hydrographer.
hidrólisis f. QUÍM. Hydrolysis.
hidrolizar v. tr. QUÍM. To hydrolyze, to hydrolyse.
hidrología f. Hydrology.
hidrológico, ca adj. Hydrologic, hydrological.
hidrólogo m. Hydrologist.
hidromecánico, ca adj. Hydromechanical.
— F. Hydromechanics.
hidromel m. Hydromel (aguamiel).
hidrometría f. Hydrometry.
hidrométrico, ca adj. Hydrometric, hydrometrical.
hidrómetro m. Hydrometer.
hidroneumático, ca adj. Hydropneumatic.
hidropedal m. Paddle boat, pedal boat (embarcación de recreo).
hidropesía f. MED. Dropsy, hydrops, hydropsy.
hidrópico, ca adj. MED. Hydropic, dropsical.
— M. y f. Person suffering from dropsy.
hidroplano m. MAR. Hydroplane. || Seaplane, flying boat (hidroavión).
hidroscopio m. Hydroscope.
hidrosfera f. GEOL. Hydrosphere.
hidrosilicato m. QUÍM. Hydrosilicate.
hidrostático, ca adj. FÍS. Hydrostatic.
— F. Hydrostatics.
hidroterapia f. MED. Hydrotherapy.
hidroterápico, ca adj. MED. Hydrotherapeutic, hydrotherapeutical.
hidróxido m. QUÍM. Hydroxide.
hidroxilo m. QUÍM. Hydroxyl.
hidrozoario m. Hydrozoan.
hidruro m. QUÍM. Hydride.
hiedra f. BOT. Ivy.
hiel f. ANAT. Bile, gall. || FIG. Bitterness, gall (amargura). || — Pl. Sorrows, troubles. || — FIG. y FAM. *Echar* or *sudar la hiel*, to sweat blood. | *No hay miel sin hiel*, no rose without a thorn.
hielo m. Ice: *hielo en barras*, blocks of ice. || Frost (escarcha). || FIG. Coldness, indifference (frialdad). || — *Estar cubierto de hielo*, to be icy (un camino). || FIG. y FAM. *Estar hecho un hielo*, to be frozen, to be freezing cold. || FIG. *Romper el hielo*, to break the ice. | *Ser más frío que el hielo* or *como un pedazo de hielo*, to be as cold as ice.
hiemal adj. Wintry.
hiena f. ZOOL. Hyena, hyaena. || FIG. Brute (persona cruel).

hierático, ca adj. Hieratic.
hieratismo m. Hieratic attitude.
hierba f. Grass. || Herb: *hierbas medicinales*, medicinal herbs. || Flaw (defecto en la esmeralda). || — Pl. Grass, *sing.*, pastureland, *sing.* (pasto). || Poison, *sing.* [from herbs]. || Years (de los animales): *este toro tiene tres hierbas*, this bull is three years old. || — *En hierba*, green: *cebada en hierba*, green oats. || CULIN. *Finas hierbas*, herbs for seasoning. || BOT. *Hierba buena*, mint (hierbabuena). | *Hierba del Paraguay* or *hierba mate*, maté, Paraguay tea. || *Hockey sobre hierba*, field hockey. || *Mala hierba*, weed (planta dañina), evil people, bad lot (mala gente). || FIG. *Mala hierba nunca muere*, ill weeds grow apace. | *Pañuelo de hierba*, checquered handkerchief. | *Sentir crecer la hierba*, to be a deep one. | *Y otras hierbas*, and others, and so forth.
hierbabuena f. BOT. Mint.
hierbajo m. Weed.
hierbal m. *Amer.* Grassland.
hierbecilla f. FAM. Grass.
hierofanta o **hierofante** m. Hierophant.
hieroglífico, ca adj. Hieroglyphic.
— M. pl. Hieroglyphics.
hierra f. *Amer.* Branding.
hierro m. Iron (metal): *hierro forjado, candente*, wrought, red-hot iron. || Branding iron (para marcar el ganado, etc.). || Brand (marca). || Head, point (de una lanza, etc.). || FIG. Steel, weapon, blade (arma). | Iron (resistencia). || — Pl. Irons, chains (grillos, esposas, etc.). || — *A hierro y fuego*, to fire and sword. || FIG. y FAM. *Al hierro candente batir de repente*, strike while the iron is hot. | *Comer* or *mascar hierro*, to court an Andalusian girl through the grille of her window. | *De hierro*, [of] iron, cast iron: *voluntad de hierro*, will of iron, iron will. || *Hierro albo*, white-hot iron. || *Hierro colado* or *fundido*, cast iron. || *Hierro comercial*, merchant iron. || *Hierro cuadradillo* or *cuadrado*, square iron bar. || *Hierro de doble T*, I bar. || *Hierro dulce*, soft iron. || *Hierro en lingotes*, pig iron. || *Hierro palanquilla*, billet. || *Hierro redondo*, round iron. || *Hierro viejo*, old iron, scrap iron. || FIG. *Machacar en hierro frío*, to bang one's head against a brick wall. | *Quien a hierro mata a hierro muere*, he who lives by the sword dies by the sword.
higa f. [Fist-shaped] amulet. || FIG. Scorn, contempt (desprecio). | Derision, mockery (burla). || (Ant.) Nose-thumbing, fig (ant.) [gesto de burla]. || — FIG. *Dar una higa, dar higas, hacer la higa*, to thumb one's nose, to fig (ant.), to cock a snook (burlarse). | *No daría dos higas por*, I wouldn't give tuppence [U.S., two cents] for. | *No me importa una higa*, I don't give a fig *o* a damn *o* a hang.
higadilla f. o **higadillo** m. Liver [of small animals, birds]. || — FIG. y FAM. *Comerse los higadillos*, v. COMER. | *Echar los higadillos*, to work one's fingers to the bone. | *Sacar hasta los higadillos a uno*, to bleed s.o. white.
hígado m. ANAT. Liver. || — Pl. FIG. y FAM. Guts (valentía): *¡qué hígados tiene!*, what guts he has! || — FIG. y FAM. *Echar los hígados*, to work one's fingers to the bone. | *Hay que tener muchos hígados para trabajar con él*, you need a lot of guts *o* a strong stomach to work with him.
higiene f. Hygiene.
higiénico, ca adj. Hygienic. || Sanitary: *paños higiénicos*, sanitary towels. || *Papel higiénico*, toilet paper *o* tissue.
higienista m. Hygienist.
higo m. BOT. Fig: *higo seco*, dried fig. || — FIG. y FAM. *De higos a brevas*, once in a blue moon, once in a while. | *Hecho un higo*, wizened (muy arrugado). || BOT. *Higo chumbo* or *de tuna* or *de pala*, prickly pear. || FAM. *Más seco que un higo*, as dry as a bone (no húmedo), completely wizened (flaco). || *No dársele a uno un higo de algo*, not to care a fig *o* a rap about sth. | *No valer un higo*, not to be worth a brass farthing [U.S., two cents].
higroma m. MED. Hygroma.
higrometría f. Hygrometry.
higrométrico, ca adj. Hygrometric, hygrometrical.
higrómetro m. Hygrometer.
higroscopia f. Hygrometry.
higroscópico, ca adj. Hygroscopic.
higroscopio m. Hygroscope.
higuera f. BOT. Fig tree. || — FIG. *Caer de la higuera*, to come back to earth. || BOT. *Higuera chumba* or *de Indias* or *de pala*, prickly pear. || FIG. *Estar en la higuera*, to be in the clouds, to be in another world.
hija f. Daughter: *tiene un hijo y dos hijas*, he has a son and two daughters. || Child. || — *¡Hija mía!*, my dear, my child, my daughter. || *Hija política*, daughter-in-law.
hijastro, tra m. y f. Stepchild (hijo o hija). || Stepson (hijo). || Stepdaughter (hija).
hijo m. Son: *hijo mayor*, eldest son; *hijo menor*, youngest son. || Child: *tiene tres hijos*, he has three children; *hijos crecidos*, grown children. || Son, native son: *los hijos de España*, the sons of Spain. || — Pl. Children, sons and daughters. || Descendants, offspring, *sing.* (descendientes).
— FAM. *Cualquier* or *todo hijo de vecino*, everyone, anyone, every mother's son. || *El hijo del Hombre* or *de Dios*, the Son of Man *o* of God. || *Es hijo de su padre*, he's a chip off the old block, he's a son who takes after his father. || *Hacerle a una un hijo*, to get s.o. pregnant. || *Hijo adoptivo*, adopted son *o* child. || *Hijo bastardo* or *espurio*, bastard [child]. || *Hijo de bendición* or *legítimo*, legitimate child. || *Hijo de buena familia*, boy from a very good family. || *Hijo de ganancia* or *natural*, bastard, illegitimate *o* natural child. || *Hijo del diablo*, child of the devil. || *Hijo de leche*, foster child. || *Hijo de papá*, daddy's boy. || POP. *Hijo de puta*, bastard, son of a bitch. || *Hijo incestuoso*, child of an incestuous relationship. || *Hijo mío*, son, my boy (a un chico), old chap, man, old boy (a un hombre). || *Hijo político*, son-in-law. || *Hijo predilecto*, favourite child *o* son (de una familia), favourite son (de una comunidad). || *Hijo pródigo*, prodigal son. || *Hijo único*, only child. || *José García, hijo*, José García junior. || *Nombrar hijo predilecto de la ciudad*, to give the freedom of the city.
hijodalgo m. Hidalgo, nobleman.

— OBSERV. Pl. *hijosdalgo*.

hijuela f. Piece of material added to enlarge a garment (añadido). || Branch (dependencia). || Small mattress (colchoneta). || Small irrigation ditch (acequia). || Secondary path (camino). || JUR. Portion [of an inheritance] (de una herencia). | Document stating the inheritance of one of several inheritors (documento). || BOT. Palm seed (semilla). || REL. Pall. || *Amer.* Small inherited portion of a farm.
hijuelo m. BOT. Shoot (retoño).
hila f. Row, line (hilera). || Thin gut (tripa delgada). || Spinning (acción de hilar). || — Pl. Lint, *sing.* [for dressing wounds] (para vendar heridas). || *A la hila*, in a line, in file, in a row.
hilacha f. o **hilacho** m. Ravelled thread (hilo que se desprende). || Shred, thread (brizna de hilo). || — Pl. Rags, tatters (andrajos).
hilada f. Row, line (hilera). || ARQ. Course (hilera horizontal de piedras).
hiladillo m. Ferret, floss silk (hilo de seda). || Band, braid (cinta).
hilado m. Spinning (acción de hilar). || Thread, yarn (materia textil hilada). || *Fábrica de hilados*, spinning mill.
hilador, ra m. y f. Spinner (persona que hila). || — F. Spinning machine (máquina).
hilandería f. Spinning (trabajo de artesanía). || Spinning mill (fábrica).
hilandero, ra m. y f. Spinner (persona que hila).
hilar v. tr. To spin (hilo). || FIG. To reflect on, to think about (cavilar). | To infer (deducir). | To hatch, to weave (tramar): *hilar una intriga*, to hatch a plot. || — FIG. y FAM. *Hilar delgado* or *muy fino*, to split hairs. || *Máquina de hilar*, spinning machine.
hilarante adj. Hilarious. || *Gas hilarante*, laughing gas.
hilaridad f. Hilarity, laughter, mirth: *causar la hilaridad*, to cause laughter.
hilatura f. Spinning. || Spinning mill (fábrica).
hilaza f. Yarn, thread (hilado). || Coarse thread *o* yarn (hilo grueso). || Thread (de una tela). || — FIG. y FAM. *Descubrir la hilaza*, to show one's true colours *o* one's true nature. | *Se le ve la hilaza*, he is showing his true colours.
hilera f. Row, line: *una hilera de árboles, de espectadores*, a row of trees, of spectators. || Fine thread (hilo fino). || TECN. Drawplate. || ARQ. Ridgepole, ridgepiece. || MIL. Rank, file. || *En hilera*, in line.
hilo m. Thread, yarn: *hilo de coser*, sewing thread; *hilo de hilvanar*, basting thread. || Linen (tejido): *sábanas de hilo*, linen sheets. || ELECTR. y TECN. Wire. | Thin beam (de luz). || Trickle (de agua). || Thin column *o* line (de humo). || String (de un collar). || Thread (de araña). || BOT. Fibre [U.S., fiber], string. || FIG. Course: *el hilo de la vida*, the course of life. | Thread: *el hilo de la narración*, the thread of the story; *cortar el hilo del discurso*, to break the thread of the speech. | Train (de pensamiento). || — *Al hilo*, on the straight, on the grain (tela), on the grain (madera). || FIG. *El hilo siempre se rompe por lo más delgado*, a chain is only as strong as its weakest link. | *Estar con el alma en un hilo*, v. ALMA. | *Estar cosido con hilo gordo*, to be obvious, to be transparent. | *Estar hecho un hilo*, to be as thin as a rake. | *Estar pendiente de un hilo*, to be hanging by a thread. || *Hilo de bramante*, twine. || FIG. *Hilo de voz*, thin *o* tiny voice. | *Írsele a uno el hilo*, to lose the thread. | *Mover los hilos*, to pull the strings. | *Por el hilo se saca el ovillo*, it is just a question of putting two and two together. || *Telegrafía sin hilos*, wireless telegraphy.
hilván m. Tacking, basting. || Tacking *o* basting stitch (punto). || *Amer.* Hem (dobladillo).
hilvanado, da adj. Tacked, basted.
— M. Tacking, basting. || Tacking *o* basting stitch (punto).
hilvanar v. tr. To tack, to baste. || FIG. To outline (bosquejar). || FIG. y FAM. To throw together (hacer muy de prisa).
Himalaya n. pr. m. GEOGR. Himalayas, *pl.*
himen m. ANAT. Hymen, maidenhead.
himeneo m. Wedding, marriage. || Epithalamium.

himenóptero, ra adj. ZOOL. Hymenopterous.
— M. Hymenopteran [U.S., hymenopteron]. || — Pl. ZOOL. Hymenoptera.
himnario m. Hymnbook, hymnal.
himno m. Anthem: *el himno nacional*, the national anthem. || Hymn (cántico).
himplar v. intr. To roar, to growl (pantera, onza).
hincada f. *Amer.* Sinking, driving, thrusting (hincadura). | Genuflection (genuflexión).
hincadura f. Driving, thrusting, sinking.
hincapié m. Firm footing. || *Hacer hincapié en*, to insist on, to stress, to emphasize: *hacer hincapié en la necesidad de una reforma*, to insist on the necessity of a reform.
hincar v. tr. To drive [in], to sink (clavar): *hincar un clavo*, to sink a nail. || To sink (los dientes.) || To drive, to thrust, to push, to plunge: *hincar un puñal en el corazón de alguien*, to plunge a dagger into s.o.'s heart. || To set firmly (el pie). || — FIG. *Hincar el diente en*, to get one's teeth into, to grapple with (emprender), to slate [U.S., to cut down] (criticar), to put the bite on (sacar provecho). || FAM. *Hincar el pico*, to kick the bucket, to peg out (morir), to throw in the sponge, to give in (darse por vencido). || *Hincar la rodilla*, to kneel [on one knee].
— V. pr. To sink [*en*, into]. || *Hincarse de rodillas*, to kneel [down].
hincha f. FAM. Grudge (odio). || FAM. *Tener hincha a alguien*, to have it in for s.o., to bear a grudge against s.o.
— M. Fan, supporter [U.S., rooter] (de un club deportivo): *los hinchas del fútbol*, football fans.
hinchada f. *Amer.* FAM. Fans, *pl.*, supporters, *pl.* [U.S., rooters].
hinchado, da adj. Blown up, inflated: *globo hinchado de gas*, balloon blown up with gas. || Swollen [up], puffed up (la piel), swollen, distended (el vientre). || FIG. Swollen, puffed up (orgulloso). | Pompous, high-flown, bombastic (estilo).
hinchamiento m. Swelling.
hinchar v. tr. To blow up (con la boca), to inflate (con la boca o una bomba), to pump up (con una bomba): *hinchar un globo*, to blow up a balloon. || To swell, to distend (el vientre). || To swell up, to puff up (la piel, el cuerpo). || FIG. To inflate, to exaggerate: *hinchar un acontecimiento*, to exaggerate an event. | To make pompous *o* high-flown *o* bombastic (el estilo). || FAM. *Hincharle a uno la cabeza con*, to stuff s.o. with.
— V. pr. To swell [up], to puff up (el cuerpo y la piel). || MED. To swell [up]: *se le había hinchado la rodilla*, his knee had swollen. || To swell: *el río se hincha con las lluvias*, the river swells with the rains. || FIG. To become *o* to get bigheaded *o* conceited *o* puffed up: *hincharse con sus éxitos*, to get conceited about one's success. | To have one's fill, to be satiated (hartarse). || FAM. To line one's pockets (ganar mucho dinero). || — FIG. y FAM. *Hincharse* or *hincharse de comer*, to gorge *o* to stuff o.s. with food. | *Hincharse como un pavo*, to be as proud as a peacock. | *Hincharse de correr, de reír*, to run, to laugh a lot. | *Se le hinchan las narices*, he flares up [U.S., he gets his dander up].
hinchazón f. Swelling: *hinchazón de la cara*, swelling of the face. || Lump, bump (protuberancia). || Distension, swelling (del vientre). || Swelling, puffiness (de las carnes, de carácter morboso). || FIG. Vanity, conceit (vanidad). | Pomposity, bombast (del estilo).
hindi m. Hindi (idioma).
hindú adj./s. Indian (de la India). || Hindu (que practica el hinduismo).
hinduismo m. REL. Hinduism.
hiniesta f. BOT. Broom, genista (retama).
hinojal m. Fennel bed, fennel field.
hinojo m. BOT. Fennel. || — Pl. Knees (rodillas). || — *De hinojos*, on one's knees, kneeling. || *Hinojo marino*, sea fennel, samphire. || FAM. *¡Hinojos!*, oh my goodness! || *Ponerse de hinojos*, to kneel [down].
hioideo, a adj. Hyoid.
hioides adj./s.m. inv. ANAT. Hyoid.
hipar v. intr. To hiccup, to hiccough (tener hipo). || To pant (los perros que corren). || To whimper, to whine (gimotear). || FIG. *Hipar por*, to long to, to yearn to: *está hipando por ir al teatro*, he is longing to go to the theatre; to long for, to yearn for (algo).

— OBSERV. The initial *h* of *hipar* is aspirate when the meaning is *to whimper, to whine.*

Hiparco n. pr. m. Hipparchus.
hiperacidez f. MED. Hyperacidity.
hipérbaton m. GRAM. Hyperbaton.

— OBSERV. The Spanish word has two plurals: *hiperbatones* o *hipérbatos.*

hipérbola f. MAT. Hyperbola.
hipérbole f. GRAM. Hyperbole (exageración).
hiperbólico, ca adj. Hyperbolic, hyperbolical.
hiperboloide m. MAT. Hyperboloid.
hiperbóreo, a o **hiperboreal** adj. Hyperborean.
hiperclorhidria f. MED. Hyperchlorhydria.
hipercrisis f. MED. Grave crisis.
hipercrítico, ca adj. Hypercritical.
hiperdulía f. REL. Hyperdulia.
hiperfocal adj. Hyperfocal [distance].
hipermétrope adj. MED. Hypermetropic, longsighted.
hipermetropía f. Hypermetropia, longsightedness.
hipermnesia f. MED. Hypermnesia.
hipernervioso, sa adj. Hypernervous.
hipersecreción f. MED. Hypersecretion.
hipersensibilidad f. Hypersensitivity.
hipersensible adj. Hypersensitive.
hipertensión f. MED. Hypertension, high blood pressure.
hipertenso, sa adj. Suffering from high blood pressure, hypertensive.
hipertermia f. Hyperthermia.
hipertiroidismo m. MED. Hyperthyroidism.
hipertónico, ca adj. Hypertonic.
hipertrofia f. MED. Hypertrophy.
hipertrofiar v. tr. MED. To hypertrophy.
— V. pr. To hypertrophy.
hipertrófico, ca adj. MED. Hypertrophic.
hipervitaminosis f. MED. Hypervitaminosis.
hipiátrico, ca adj. Veterinary.
— F. Veterinary (veterinaria).
hípico, ca adj. Horse: *concurso hípico*, horse show. || Equine. || *Club hípico*, riding club.
hipido m. Whimper, sob, whine (gimoteo).

— OBSERV. The initial *h* of *hipido* is aspirate.

hipismo m. Horse racing.
hipnosis f. MED. Hypnosis.
hipnótico, ca adj./s.m. MED. Hypnotic.
hipnotismo m. MED. Hypnotism.
hipnotizador, ra adj. Hypnotizing.
— M. y f. Hypnotist, hypnotizer.
hipnotizar v. tr. To hypnotize.
hipo m. Hiccup, hiccough: *tener hipo*, to have [the] hiccups. || FIG. Longing, yearning (deseo muy vivo). | Grudge (animadversión). || FAM. *Quitar el hipo*, to take one's breath away (dejar estupefacto).
hipocampo m. Sea horse (caballo marino).
hipocausto m. Hypocaust.
hipocentro m. Hypocentre [U.S., hypocenter].
hipoclorhidria f. MED. Hypochlorhydria.
hipoclorito m. QUÍM. Hypochlorite.
hipocloroso, sa adj. Hypochlorous.
hipocondría f. MED. Hypochondria.
hipocondríaco, ca adj./s. Hypochondriac.
hipocondrio m. ANAT. Hypochondrium.
hipocorístico, ca adj. *Nombre hipocorístico*, pet name (nombre cariñoso), diminutive.
Hipócrates n. pr. m. Hippocrates.
hipocrático, ca adj. Hippocratic.
hipocratismo m. Hippocratism.
hipocresía f. Hypocrisy.
hipócrita adj. Hypocritical.
— M. y f. Hypocrite.
hipodérmico, ca adj. Hypodermic: *inyección hipodérmica*, hypodermic injection.
hipodermis f. ANAT. Hypodermis.
hipódromo m. Racetrack (para carreras de caballos). || HIST. Hippodrome.
hipofagia f. Hippophagy.
hipofágico, ca adj. Hippophagous, hippophagistical. || *Carnicería hipofágica*, horsemeat butcher's shop.
hipófago, ga adj. Hippophagous.
hipófisis f. ANAT. Hypophysis.
hipogástrico, ca adj. ANAT. Hypogastric.
hipogastrio m. ANAT. Hypogastrium.
hipogeo m. Hypogeum, hypogaeum (subterráneo).
hipogrifo m. MIT. Hippogriff, hippogryph.
hipomóvil adj. Horse-drawn.
hipopótamo m. ZOOL. Hippopotamus.
hipóstilo, la adj. ARQ. Hypostyle.
hiposulfito m. QUÍM. Hyposulphite, thiosulphate.
hipotálamo m. ANAT. Hypothalamus.
hipoteca f. Mortgage: *levantar una hipoteca*, to raise a mortgage.
hipotecable adj. Mortgageable.
hipotecar v. tr. To mortgage.
hipotecario, ria adj. Mortgage: *contrato hipotecario*, mortgage deed.
hipotensión f. Hypotension, low blood pressure.
hipotenso, sa adj. Hypotensive.
hipotenusa f. MAT. Hypotenuse.
hipotermia f. MED. Hypothermia.
hipótesis f. inv. MAT. Hypothesis. || Hypothesis, supposition (supuesto).
hipotético, ca adj. Hypothetical, hypothetic.
hipotiroidismo m. MED. Hypothyroidism.
hipotónico, ca adj. MED. Hypotonic.
hipsometría f. Hypsometry (medida de las alturas).
hipsómetro m. FÍS. Hypsometer.
hirco m. Wild goat.
hiriente adj. Offensive (arma, objeto). || FIG. Offensive, wounding, cutting (palabras).
hirsuto, ta adj. Shaggy, hirsute. || Bristly (erizado). || FIG. Surly, brusque, rough (persona, carácter).
hirviente adj. Boiling, seething.
hisopada o **hisopadura** f. Aspersion.
hisopar o **hisopear** v. tr. To sprinkle [with holy water].
hisopazo m. Aspersion.
hisopo m. BOT. Hyssop. || REL. Aspergillum, sprinkler (para el agua bendita). || *Amer.* Paintbrush (para pintar). | Shaving brush (para afeitarse).

hispalense adj./s. Sevillan, Sevillian (de Sevilla).
Hispalis n. pr. HIST. Hispalis [Roman name of Seville].
Hispania n. pr. f. HIST. Hispania [Roman name for Iberian Peninsula].
hispánico, ca adj. Hispanic, Spanish.
hispanidad f. Spanishness (cualidad de español). || Spanish *o* Hispanic world (conjunto de los pueblos hispanos). || *Día de la Hispanidad*, Columbus Day.
hispanismo m. Love of Spain (afición a España). || Hispanicism (giro español).
hispanista m. y f. Hispanicist, hispanist (que estudia la cultura española). || Lover of Spain (aficionado a España).
hispanizar v. tr. To hispanicize, to hispanize.
hispano, na adj. Spanish.
— M. y f. Spaniard.
Hispanoamérica n. pr. f. GEOGR. Spanish America, Hispano-America.

— OBSERV. *Hispanoamérica* refers to those countries of North, Central, and South America where Spanish is spoken. It therefore excludes Brazil. The English expression *Latin America* (i.e. including Brazil) may be rendered by *Iberoamérica, América latina*, or even simply *América*.

hispanoamericanismo m. Spanish Americanism, Hispano-Americanism.
hispanoamericanista m. y f. Spanish Americanist, Hispano-Americanist.
hispanoamericano, na adj./s. Spanish American, Hispano-American.
hispanoárabe adj. Hispano-Arabic.
— M. y f. Spanish Arab.
hispanofilia f. Love of Spain, fondness for Spanish things.
hispanófilo, la adj. Fond of Spain.
— M. y f. Hispanophile, lover of Spain.
hispanofobia f. Hispanophobia.
hispanófobo, ba adj. Hispanophobic.
— M. y f. Hispanophobe.
hispanohablante adj. Spanish-speaking.
— M. pl. Spanish-speaking people.
hispanojudío, a adj. Hispano-Jewish.
— M. y f. Spanish Jew.
híspido, da adj. Hispid.
histamina f. BIOL. Histamine.
histéresis f. FÍS. Hysteresis.
histeria f. MED. Hysteria. || Hysterics.
histérico, ca adj. Hysteric, hysterical.
histerismo m. Hysteria. || FIG. Hysterics.
histología f. BIOL. Histology.
histológico, ca adj. BIOL. Histological.
histólogo, ga m. y f. Histologist.
historia f. History: *las lecciones de la historia*, the lessons of history; *la historia de la literatura, de la aviación*, the history of literature, of aviation. || Story, tale (relato): *contar la historia de su vida*, to tell the story of one's life. || Past, history (de una persona): *una mujer con historia*, a woman with a past. || FAM. Story, tale, fib (cosa inventada): *no me vengas con historias*, don't come telling stories to me. | Gossip, tale (chisme). | Trouble (lío, problema). || — FAM. *Armar historias*, to make trouble. || *¡Así se escribe la historia!*, that's the way history is written! || FAM. *Dejarse de historias*, to get to the point. || *Historia natural*, natural history. || REL. *Historia Sacra* or *Sagrada*, sacred history, Bible history, Holy Scripture. || FIG. *La historia de siempre*, the same old story, the same old song. || *Pasar a la historia*, to go down in history.
historiado, da adj. Historiated: *letra historiada*, historiated letter. || Storied (friso, tapiz, etc.). || FIG. Overornate (recargado).
historiador, ra m. y f. Historian.
historial m. Historical record, account (reseña). || Curriculum vitae (profesional). || Background (pasado). || DEP. Record.
historiar v. tr. To tell the history *o* the story of. || To depict (representar).
historicidad f. Historical authenticity, historicity.
histórico, ca adj. Historical (relativo a la historia o sucedido realmente): *una novela, una figura histórica*, a historical novel, figure; *exactitud histórica*, historical accuracy. || Historic (de gran importancia o que figura en la historia): *un acontecimiento histórico*, a historic event; *una fecha histórica*, a historic date; *fue un momento histórico en su vida*, this was a historic moment in his life. || GRAM. *Presente histórico*, historical present.
historieta f. Anecdote, short story, tale. || Strip cartoon, comic strip (ilustrada con dibujos).
historiografía f. Historiography.
historiógrafo, fa m. y f. Historiographer.
histrión m. Histrion, actor. || FIG. Buffoon, clown.
histriónico, ca adj. Histrionic.
histrionismo m. Histrionics, *pl.*, theatrical behaviour. || Acting world, theatre [U.S., theater] (mundo de los actores).
hita f. TECN. Small headless nail. || Boundary stone, milestone (v. HITO).
hitita adj./s. HIST. Hittite.
hito m. Boundary stone (para marcar un límite), milestone (para indicar distancias). || Bull's eye (del blanco). || FIG. Target, aim, goal (objetivo). | Milestone, landmark: *acontecimiento que será un hito en la historia*, event which will be a milestone in history. || Quoits, *pl.* (juego). || — FIG. *Dar en el hito*, to hit the mark, to hit the nail on the head. | *Mirar de hito en hito*, to stare at.
hobby m. Hobby (entretenimiento).
hocicada f. V. HOCICAZO.
hocicar v. tr. To root among *o* in.
— V. intr. FAM. To fall on one's face (caerse). | To hit one's face: *hocicar con* or *en la pared*, to hit one's face against the wall. || FIG. To come up against, to run into (con un obstáculo, una dificultad). | To bow one's head, to bow down (ceder, humillarse). || MAR. To pitch (hundirse la proa). || FAM. To smooch, to kiss (besarse).
hocicazo m. FAM. Fall on one's face (caída). || FAM. *Darse un hocicazo con el suelo, con la puerta*, to fall flat on one's face, to hit one's face against the door.
hocico m. Snout (de porcinos, etc.). || Muzzle (de perro, lobo, oso). || FIG. y FAM. Blubber lips, *pl.* (labios abultados). | Snout (cara de persona). | Pout (mueca). || — FAM. *Caer* or *darse de hocicos con el suelo, con la puerta*, to fall flat on one's face, to hit one's face against the door. | *¡Cierra el hocico!*, shup up! | *Dar con la puerta en los hocicos de uno*, to slam the door in s.o.'s face. | *Dar de hocicos contra*, to bump into. | *Estar de* or *hacer* or *poner hocico*, to pout. | *Meter el hocico en todo*, to poke one's nose into everything. | *Romperle a uno los hocicos*, to smash s.o.'s face in.
hocicón, ona u **hocicudo, da** adj. Big-snouted (animal). || FIG. y FAM. Thick-lipped, blubber-lipped (con labios abultados). | Big-nosed (de nariz saliente).
hocino m. Billhook (para cortar). || Trowel (herramienta para transplantar). || Narrows, *pl.* (angostura de un río). || Valley shoulder (entre río y montaña).
hociquear v. intr. V. HOCICAR.
hociquera f. *Amer.* Muzzle (de la cabezada).
hockey m. DEP. Hockey: *hockey sobre hielo*, ice hockey; *hockey sobre ruedas* or *patines*, hockey on skates; *hockey sobre hierba*, field hockey.
hodierno, na adj. Modern.
hogaño adv. Nowadays (hoy en día). || (P.us.). This year.
hogar m. Hearth, fireplace (de la chimenea), firebox (de cocina, de locomotora). || TECN. Furnace (de caldera). | Hearth (de horno). || FIG. Home: *sin casa ni hogar*, without house or home; *fundar un hogar*, to establish a home. || — Pl. Home, *sing.*: *volver a sus hogares*, to return home. || — *Hogar del soldado*, soldier's home *o* institute. || *La vida del hogar*, home *o* family life. || *Sin hogar*, homeless.
hogareño, na adj. Home, family: *vida hogareña*, home life. || Home-loving, stay-at-home (persona).
hogaza f. Large loaf [of bread].
hoguera f. Bonfire: *encender una hoguera*, to light a bonfire. || FIG. Blaze. || — *Hoguera de San Juan*, midsummer bonfire [lit on 24th June]. || FIG. *La casa era una verdadera hoguera*, the house was a blazing inferno. || *Morir en la hoguera*, to die at the stake.
hoja f. BOT. Leaf (*pl.* leaves): *hoja aovada, caduca*, ciliate, deciduous leaf; *hoja seca*, dead leaf. | Petal (pétalo de flor). || Sheet (de metal, madera). || Sheet, leaf (de papel). || Leaf (de un libro): *hoja suelta* or *volante*, loose *o* mobile leaf. || Handout, leaflet (prospecto). || Blade (de espada, cuchillo, patines, etc.): *hoja de afeitar*, razor blade. || POÉT. Blade, sword, steel (espada). || Leaf (puerta, ventana, biombo, tríptico). || Flap, leaf (de mesa). || Piece [of armour] (de la armadura). || AGR. Fallow land (barbecho). || Newspaper (periódico). || Form, sheet (formulario). || Side, flitch (de tocino). || TECN. Leaf (de un muelle). || — *De hoja caduca*, deciduous. || *De hoja perenne*, evergreen. || *Hoja de lata*, tinplate, tin. || MIL. *Hoja de movilización*, call-up papers, *pl.* [U.S., draft card]. || *Hoja de paga*, payroll, pay sheet. || *Hoja de parra*, fig leaf. || COM. *Hoja de ruta*, waybill. || *Hoja de servicios*, v. SERVICIO. || *Hoja suelta*, leaflet (prospecto). || FIG. *No tiene vuelta de hoja*, v. VUELTA. | *Temblar como una hoja*, to shake like a leaf. | *Tener hoja*, to ring false (una moneda). | *Volver la hoja*, to change the subject (cambiar de conversación), to turn over a new leaf (cambiar de vida).
hojalata f. Tinplate, tin. || *Un bote de hojalata*, a tin can.
hojalatería f. Tinsmith's workshop (taller), tinsmith's shop (tienda). || Tinware (objetos). || Tinwork (oficio).
hojalatero m. Tinsmith.
hojaldrado, da adj. CULIN. Puff, flaky: *pasta hojaldrada*, puff pastry. || *Pastel hojaldrado*, puff.
— M. Rolling out to make puff pastry.
hojaldrar v. tr. CULIN. To make into puff pastry, to roll out into flaky pastry (pasta).
hojaldre m. CULIN. Puff pastry (pasta). || *Pastel de hojaldre*, puff.
hojarasca f. Dead *o* fallen leaves, *pl.* || Excessive foliage (de las plantas). || FIG. Verbiage, wordiness (palabrería). | Rubbish (cosas inútiles). || FIG. *Tus promesas son hojarasca*, your promises are just a lot of wind.
hojear v. tr. To turn the pages of, to leaf through (pasar las hojas de un libro). || To glance through (leer superficialmente).

hojoso, sa u **hojudo, da** adj. Leafy.
hojuela f. BOT. Leaflet, small leaf (hoja pequeña). | Leaflet, foliole (de una hoja compuesta). || CULIN. Pancake (tortita). || Pressed olive skins, *pl.* (de las aceitunas). || Foil (de oro, plata, etc.). || FAM. *Miel sobre hojuelas*, so much the better, better still.
¡hola! interj. FAM. Hello!, hallo!, hullo! (expresión de saludo o de sorpresa). || *Amer.* Hello!, hallo!, hullo! (teléfono).
Holanda n. pr. f. GEOGR. Holland (provincia), the Netherlands, Holland (país).

— OBSERV. El nombre oficial del país es *The Netherlands*, pero en el lenguaje corriente se emplea más *Holland*.

holandés, esa adj. Dutch. || *A la holandesa*, quarter-bound (encuadernación).
— M. Dutchman. || Dutch (idioma). || — Pl. Dutch (habitantes). || — F. Dutchwoman. || Sheet of paper 21 × 27 cm.
holding m. COM. Holding company.
holgadamente adv. Easily (con holgura): *caben cinco personas holgadamente*, five people fit in easily. || Comfortably (cómodamente). || *Vivir holgadamente*, to be well-off.
holgado, da adj. Loose, full: *una chaqueta holgada*, a loose jacket. || Baggy (demasiado ancho). || Big (demasiado grande): *esos zapatos me están un poco holgados*, those shoes are rather big for me. || Roomy (espacioso). || FIG. Comfortable: *vida holgada*, comfortable life. | Comfortably-off, well-off: *familia holgada*, well-off family. | Idle (desocupado). || — FIG. *Estar holgado de tiempo*, to have time to spare. || *Estar muy holgado en un sitio*, to have plenty of room to spare in a place.
holganza f. Idleness (ociosidad). || Rest (descanso). || Leisure (ocio). || Enjoyment, pleasure, fun, entertainment (diversión).
holgar* v. intr. To rest (descansar). || Not to work, to have a day off: *huelgo los jueves*, I don't work on Thursdays. || To be idle (estar ocioso). || To be out of use (estar sin uso). || To be unnecessary (estar de más). || (Ant.). To enjoy o.s. (divertirse). || — *Huelga añadir que*, there is no need to add that. || *Huelga decir que...*, needless to say [that]... || *¡Huelgan los comentarios!*, no comment!
— V. pr. To amuse o.s., to enjoy o.s. (divertirse). || To be pleased (alegrarse): *me huelgo de* or *con su visita*, I am pleased by your visit.
holgazán, ana adj. Lazy, idle.
— M. y f. Loafer, lazybones, idler.
holgazanear v. intr. To loaf, to laze, to idle.
holgazanería f. Laziness, idleness.
holgorio m. FAM. V. JOLGORIO.
holgura f. Looseness, fullness: *la holgura de un abrigo*, the looseness of a coat. || Bagginess (amplitud excesiva). || Roominess (espacio). || FIG. Affluence (bienestar económico). || (Ant.). Enjoyment (diversión). | Merriment (regocijo). || TECN. Play. || — *Cabemos los tres con holgura*, the three of us fit in with ease *o* with room to spare. || FIG. *Vivir con holgura*, to live comfortably, to be well-off.
holmio m. QUÍM. Holmium.
holocausto m. HIST. Holocaust, burnt sacrifice *o* offering. || FIG. Sacrifice. || *Ofrecerse en holocausto*, to sacrifice o.s.
holoédrico, ca adj. Holohedral.
holoturia f. ZOOL. Holothurian (cohombro de mar).
holladura f. Treading (acción de pisar). || Trampling (acción de pisotear). || FIG. Trampling. || (Ant.). Toll levied for the passing of livestock.
hollar* v. tr. To tread on, to tread (pisar): *hollar la alfombra*, to tread on the carpet. || To trample down (pisotear). || To tread: *hollar regiones desconocidas*, to tread unknown regions. || FIG. To trample on *o* underfoot: *hollar los derechos de uno, la memoria de uno*, to trample on s.o.'s rights, on s.o.'s memory. | To humiliate (humillar).
hollejo u **hollejuelo** m. Skin, peel (de uva, etc.).
hollín m. Soot (tizne). || V. JOLLÍN.
hombrada f. Manly action.
hombradía f. Manliness, virility.
hombre m. Man: *los hombres y las mujeres*, men and women; *el sistema digestivo en el hombre*, man's digestive system. || Mankind, man (la especie humana). || FAM. Man (marido, amante). || — *Buen hombre*, good fellow. || *Como un hombre*, like a man. || *Como un solo hombre*, as one man. || *De hombre a hombre*, man-to-man. || *El abominable hombre de las nieves*, the abominable snowman. || *El hombre de la calle*, the man in the street. || *El hombre del día*, the man of the moment *o* of the day. || *El hombre fuerte*, the strong man. || *El hombre medio*, the average man. || *El hombre propone y Dios dispone*, Man proposes, God disposes. || *Es el hombre para el caso*, he's the man for the job, he's our man. || *Está ya hecho un hombre*, he's quite a young man already (un niño). || *Gran hombre*, great man. || *Hacer un hombre*, to make a man of: *el ejército le hará un hombre*, the army will make a man of him. || *Hombre anuncio*, sandwich man. || FAM. *Hombre de agallas*, man with guts. || *Hombre de armas*, man-at-arms. || *Hombre de bien*, honest man. || *Hombre de Estado*, statesman. || *Hombre de las cavernas*, caveman. || *Hombre de letras*, man of letters. || *Hombre del tiempo*, weatherman. || *Hombre de mar*, seafaring man, seaman. || *Hombre de mundo*, man of the world. || *Hombre de negocios*, businessman. || *Hombre de paja*, man of straw. || *Hombre de palabra*, man of his word. || FAM. *Hombre de pelo en pecho*, real man. || FIG. *Hombre de peso*, man of influence. || *Hombre de pro*, upright man, honest man. || *Hombre de puños*, strong man. || *Hombre prevenido vale por dos*, forewarned is forearmed. || *Hombre público*, politician. || *Hombre rana*, frogman. || *Hombre serpiente* or *de goma*, contortionist. || *Nuestro hombre*, our hero (en un cuento). || *Pobre hombre*, nobody (don nadie), poor devil (hombre desgraciado). || *Poco hombre*, not much of a man. || *Portarse como un hombre*, to act like a man. || *Ser hombre para*, to be man enough to *o* for. || *Ser muy hombre*, to be a real man. || *Ser otro hombre*, to be a different *o* changed man.
— Interj. My boy!, man! (al dirigirse a una persona). || My dear fellow! (expresión de cariño): *¡hombre! ¡No sabía que estuvieras aquí!*, my dear fellow! I didn't know you were here! || Good heavens!, I never! (sorpresa). || You bet! (confirmación): *¿te hace ilusión ir al teatro? — ¡Hombre!*, are you excited about going to the theatre? — You bet [I am]! || Well (pues): *hombre, tal vez*, well, perhaps. || Dear me! (compasión). || Come now! (protesta). || — *¡Hombre al agua* or *a la mar!*, man overboard! || *¡Pero hombre!*, but my dear fellow!, but really!; heavens, man! (enfado).

— OBSERV. The exclamation *¡hombre!* is very common in conversation and may express many different shades of meaning. It may also be used when addressing a woman.

hombrear v. intr. To play *o* to act the man (dárselas de hombre). || To push with the shoulders (empujar). || *Amer.* To behave like a man (una mujer). || *Hombrear con*, to try to keep up with.
hombrera f. Epaulet, epaulette (tira de tela en el hombro). || Shoulder plate, épaulière (de armadura). || Shoulder pad (almohadilla). || Shoulder strap (tirante).
hombretón m. Well-built fellow.
hombría f. Manliness, virility. || *Hombría de bien*, integrity, honesty.
hombro m. Shoulder: *hombros caídos*, drooping shoulders. || — *A* or *en hombros*, on the shoulders; shouldered (arma). || MIL. *¡Arma al hombro!*, shoulder *o* slope arms! || FIG. *Arrimar* or *meter el hombro*, to put one's shoulder to the wheel (trabajar mucho), to lend a hand (ayudar). | *Echarse al hombro algo*, to shoulder sth., to take sth. upon o.s. (encargarse de algo). || *Encogerse de hombros*, to shrug one's shoulders. || *Estar hombro a hombro* or *hombro contra hombro* or *hombro con hombro*, to be shoulder to shoulder. || FIG. *Estar hombro a hombro con alguien*, to rub shoulders with s.o. | *Hurtar el hombro*, to shirk [work, a responsibility, etc.]. || *Llevar a hombros*, to carry on one's shoulders (transportar), to carry shoulder-high (en triunfo). || *Mirar por encima del hombro*, to look down on, to look down one's nose at. || *Sacar a hombros a uno*, to carry s.o. shoulder-high (a un torero, etc.). || *Salir a hombros*, to be carried out shoulder-high. || FIG. *Tener la cabeza sobre los hombros*, to have one's head squarely on one's shoulders.
hombruno, na adj. Mannish, masculine (una mujer).
homenaje m. JUR. Homage: *rendir homenaje al rey*, to pay homage to the king. | Allegiance (juramento de fidelidad). || FIG. Tribute: *rendir homenaje a*, to pay a tribute to. || — *Banquete en homenaje al presidente*, banquet in honour of *o* in homage to the president. || *Torre del homenaje*, keep.
homeópata adj. MED. Homeopathic.
— M. Homeopath.
homeopatía f. MED. Homeopathy.
homeopático, ca adj. MED. Homeopathic.
homérico, ca adj. Homeric.
Homero n. pr. m. Homer.
homicida adj. Homicidal. || Murderous, murder: *arma homicida*, murder weapon.
— M. Homicide, murderer (asesino). || — F. Homicide, murderess (asesina).
homicidio m. JUR. Homicide, murder (voluntario). | Manslaughter (involuntario).
homilía f. Homily (sermón).
homocentro m. MAT. Homocentre.
homofonía f. Homophony.
homófono, na adj. Homophonous, homophonic.
— M. Homophone.
homogeneidad f. Homogeneity.
homogeneización f. Homogenization.
homogeneizar v. tr. To homogenize.
homogéneo, a adj. Homogeneous.
homografía f. Homography.
homógrafo, fa adj. GRAM. Homographic.
— M. Homograph.
homologación f. Homologation, confirmation.
homologar v. tr. To confirm.
homología f. Homology.
homólogo, ga adj. QUÍM. y MAT. Homologous.
homonimia f. Homonymy.
homónimo, ma adj. Homonymous.
— M. Homonym.
homosexual adj./s. Homosexual.

homosexualidad f. Homosexuality.
homotecia f. MAT. Similarity.
homotético, ca adj. MAT. Homothetic.
homúnculo m. Homunculus. || FIG. Runt, squirt.
honcejo m. Billhook (hocino).
honda f. Sling (arma).
hondear v. tr. To sound (sondar). || To unload (descargar una embarcación).
— OBSERV. Do not confuse with *ondear*, to wave.
hondero m. Slinger.
hondo, da adj. Deep: *un recipiente hondo*, a deep vessel; *raíces hondas*, deep roots. || Low, low-lying (terreno). || FIG. Profound, deep, intense (sentimientos). || — *Cante hondo*, "cante hondo", flamenco song. || *En lo hondo de su alma*, in the depths of his heart. || *Plato hondo*, soup plate *o* dish.
— M. Bottom. || Depth (profundidad). || *Tiene unos cinco metros de hondo*, it is about five metres deep.
hondonada f. Depression, hollow, dip (depresión en el terreno). || Ravine (valle encajonado).
hondura f. Depth. || FIG. *Meterse en honduras*, to get out of one's depth, to get into deep water.
Honduras n. pr. f. GEOGR. Honduras.
hondureñismo m. Word *o* turn of phrase characteristic of Honduras.
hondureño, ña adj./s. Honduran.
honestamente adv. In an upright *o* an honourable way, honestly. || Decently, decorously (decorosamente). || Modestly (con pudor). || Fairly (con justicia).
honestidad f. Uprightness, honourableness, honesty (honradez). || Decency, decorum (decoro). || Modesty (pudor). || Fairness (justicia).
honesto, ta adj. Upright, honourable, honest (honrado). || Decent, decorous (decoroso). || Reasonable, fair (justo). || Modest (púdico). || *Estado honesto*, celibacy (de una mujer).
hongo m. BOT. Fungus. | Mushroom (comestible). | Toadstool (venenoso). || Bowler hat [U.S., derby] (sombrero). || — FIG. *Crecer como hongos*, to spring up *o* to grow like mushrooms, to mushroom. | *Hongo atómico*, mushroom cloud. || *Hongo yesquero*, tinder fungus.
honor m. Honour [U.S., honor]: *hombre de honor*, man of honour; *su honor está en juego*, his honour is at stake; *su visita ha sido un gran honor para mí*, his visit has been a great honour for me. || Reputation, good name, honour (reputación): *una mancha en el honor*, a stain on one's reputation. || Virtue, honour, purity (de una mujer). || — Pl. Honours: *aspirar a los honores*, to aspire to honours; *honores de guerra*, war honours; *con todos los honores militares*, with full military honours. || Honorary titles *o* positions. || — *A gran señor gran honor*, honour where honour is due. || *Campo de honor*, field of honour. || *Dama de honor*, V. DAMA. || *En honor a la verdad*, for truth's sake. || *En honor de*, in honour of. || *Hacer honor a*, to honour. || *Hacer los honores de la casa*, to do the honours. || *Hicimos los honores al almuerzo*, we did justice to the lunch. || *Jurar por su honor*, to swear on one's honour. || *Lance de honor*, challenge. || *Legión de Honor*, Legion of Honour. || *Palabra de honor*, word of honour. || *¡Palabra de honor!*, on my honour! || *Rendir honores a*, to do *o* to pay honour to. || *Tener el honor de*, to have the honour to. || *Tener honores de bibliotecario*, to be an honorary librarian.
honorabilidad f. Honourableness [U.S., honorableness], honour [U.S., honor].
honorable adj. Honourable [U.S., honorable], honest.
honorar v. tr. To honour [U.S., to honor] (honrar).
honorario, ria adj. Honorary: *miembro honorario*, honorary member.
— M. pl. Fees, fee, *sing.*, honorarium, *sing.*, emoluments.
honorífico, ca adj. Honorific. || *Mención honorífica*, honourable mention.
honra f. Honour [U.S., honor]: *luchó en defensa de su honra*, he fought to defend his honour. || Dignity (dignidad). || Reputation, good name, honour (buena fama). || Honour, virtue (de una mujer). || Honour: *ser la honra de su país*, to be an honour to one's country. || — Pl. Last honours (por un difunto). || — *Tener a honra hacer algo*, to be proud to do sth., to deem *o* to regard it an honour to do sth. || *Tener una cosa a mucha honra*, to be proud of sth. || *¡Y a mucha honra!*, and [I'm] proud of it!
honradez f. Honesty, integrity, uprightness.
honrado, da adj. Honest (que es de fiar). || Honourable [U.S., honorable] (que cumple con sus deberes). || Upright (recto).
honrar v. tr. To honour [U.S., to honor], to do honour to: *honrar a una persona con su amistad, con su presencia*, to honour s.o. with one's friendship, with one's presence; *honrar a su país*, to do honour to one's country. || To honour (premiar). || COM. To honour (una deuda, etc.). || To honour (venerar): *honrar a Dios*, to honour God; *honrar padre y madre*, to honour one's father and mother. || To do credit: *su comportamiento le honra*, his behaviour does him credit. || *Muy honrado con* or *por su visita*, I am highly honoured by your visit.
— V. pr. To be honoured: *me honro con su amistad*, I am honoured by his friendship.
honrilla f. Concern for one's reputation. || *Por la negra honrilla*, out of concern for one's reputation.
honroso, sa adj. Honourable [U.S., honorable].
hontanar m. Springs, *pl.*, place with springs.
hopear v. intr. To wag the tail (menear la cola). || To run about (corretear).
hopo m. Shock of hair (mechón). || Bushy tail, brush (rabo).
— Interj. Out!, hop it!, scram!
— OBSERV. When *hopo* means "tail", the *h* is aspirate.
hora f. Hour: *una hora tiene sesenta minutos*, there are sixty minutes in an hour; *hace tres horas*, three hours ago.; *una hora y media*, an hour and a half. || Time: *¿a qué hora?*, at what time?; *¿qué hora es?*, what time is it?, what is the time?; *la hora de comer*, dinner time. || Hour: *la hora fatal*, the fateful hour; *horas de visita*, visiting hours. || Time (momento de la muerte): *le llegó su hora*, his time came. || League (medida de distancia). || — Pl. REL. Hours. || — *¡A buena hora!*, about time! (al llegar ya tarde algo o alguien). || *¡A buena hora me lo dices!*, now you tell me! || FAM. *¡A buena hora mangas verdes!*, too late!, it's no good shutting the stable door after the horse has bolted! || *A cualquier hora*, at any hour, at any time of the day. || *A estas horas*, now, by now: *a estas horas debe de haber recibido la carta*, he must have received the letter by now. || *A la hora*, punctually, on time (puntualmente), hourly, per hour: *cien pesetas a la hora*, a hundred pesetas per hour. || *A la hora de ahora*, at this time of day. || *A la hora en punto*, right on time, on the hour. || *Altas horas de la noche* or *de la madrugada*, small hours. || *A primera hora*, first thing in the morning. || *A todas horas*, all the time, at all hours (incesantemente). || *A última hora*, at the end: *ven a última hora de la tarde*, come at the end of the afternoon; at the last minute *o* moment: *llegó a última hora*, he arrived at the last minute; last thing at night (muy tarde por la noche). || *Dar hora*, to fix a time, to make an appointment (concertar cita), to give an appointment: *el médico me dio hora para las tres*, the doctor gave me an appointment for three. || *Dar la hora*, to strike the hour (reloj). || *De hora en hora*, hour by hour. || *De última hora*, last-minute. || *En buena hora*, at the right time (en el momento oportuno), fortunately (afortunadamente). || *En mala hora*, at the wrong time (inoportunamente), unluckily (desafortunadamente). || *Entre horas*, between meals: *comer entre horas*, to eat between meals. || *Es hora de*, it's time to: *es hora de que me vaya*, it's time for me to go. || *¡Es la hora!*, time's up! || *Ésta es la hora en que no sé si voy a ir de excursión o no*, I still don't know *o* I don't yet know whether I am going picnicking or not. || *Ganar horas* or *ganar las horas*, to save time. || FIG. *Ha llegado su hora*, his time has come. || *Hora de almorzar*, lunchtime. || *Hora de comer*, mealtime. || *Hora de Greenwich*, Greenwich Mean Time. || *Hora de la verdad*, moment *o* hour of truth. || *Hora de mayor afluencia* or *de mayor aglomeración*, *hora punta*, rush hour, peak hour (transportes). || *Hora de mayor consumo*, peak hour (electricidad, gas). || *Hora de verano*, summer time. || *Hora H*, zero hour. || *Hora legal* or *oficial*, civil *o* standard *o* official time. || *Horas de menor consumo* or *de menor afluencia*, off-peak hours. || *Horas de oficina*, office *o* business hours. || *Horas de trabajo*, working hours. || *Horas enteras*, hours on end. || *Horas extraordinarias*, overtime, *sing.* || *Horas libres*, free time, *sing.*, spare time, *sing.* || *Horas muertas*, wasted time, *sing.*, wasted hours. || *Hora suprema*, supreme moment. || *Horas y horas*, hours and hours. || *La hora de irse a la cama*, bedtime. || *Media hora*, half an hour, half hour: *dentro de media hora*, within a half hour, within half an hour. || FAM. *No da ni la hora*, he wouldn't even give you the time of day (tacaño). || *No tener una hora libre*, to have no time to o.s. || *Noticias de última hora*, stop press, *sing.* (en periódico), latest news (televisión, etc.). || FIG. *No ver la hora de*, to look forward to. || *Pasar las horas en blanco*, to have a sleepless night (no dormir), to waste one's time, to spend one's time doing nothing (no hacer nada). || *Pedir hora*, to request an appointment, to make an appointment (*a*, with). || *Poner en hora*, to set (un reloj). || *Por hora*, per hour, an hour: *cien kilómetros por hora*, a hundred kilometres per hour; hourly, per hour: *salario por hora*, hourly wage, wage per hour; *dos libras por hora*, two pounds per hour, two pounds hourly. || *Por horas*, by the hour: *trabajar por horas*, to work by the hour; *estoy pagado por horas*, I am paid by the hour. || *¿Qué horas son éstas para llegar?*, what sort of time do you think this is to arrive? || FIG. *Suena la hora de que lo haga*, the time has come for him to do it. | *Sus horas están contadas*, his days are numbered. || *Tener hora*, to have an appointment (cita). || FIG. *Tener muchas horas de vuelo*, to be all there. || *¿Tiene usted hora?*, have you got the time? || *Una hora escasa*, scarcely *o* barely an hour. || *Una hora larga*, a good hour. || *Una jornada de ocho horas*, an eight-hour day. || *¡Vaya unas horas para salir!*, what a fine time to go out! || *¡Ya era hora!*, and about time too! || *Ya es hora de que*, it's high time [that]: *ya es hora de que aprendas la lección*, it's high time you learnt the lesson.

— Adv. (P.us.). Now (ahora).
Horacio n. pr. m. Horace.
horadación f. Boring, drilling, piercing.
horadador, ra adj. Boring, drilling, piercing.
— M. Drill (máquina). || Driller (persona).
horadar v. tr. To bore [through], to drill (taladrar). || To pierce, to perforate (perforar). || *Horadar un túnel en*, to tunnel through, to open a tunnel in.
horario, ria adj. Hour: *ángulo horario*, hour angle. || Time: *huso horario*, time zone. || Hourly (cada hora). || *Círculo horario*, hour circle, meridian.
— M. Timetable (de clases, trenes, aviones, etc.): *horario de verano*, summer timetable. || Hour hand (de reloj). || Hours, *pl.* (horas de trabajo).
horca f. Gallows, gibbet (para ahorcar a los condenados). || Gibbet (para los ajusticiados). || AGR. Fork. | Winnowing fork (herramienta para aventar). | Pitchfork (para amontonar paja, etc.). | Forked prop (horquilla). | Yoke (para cerdos, perros, etc.). || String (de ajos, cebollas). || *Amer.* Gift, present (regalo). || — *Merecer la horca*, to deserve to be hanged. || *Pasar por las horcas caudinas*, to pass under the yoke. || *Señor de horca y cuchillo*, feudal lord invested with civil and criminal jurisdiction (sentido propio), Grand Panjandrum (sentido irónico, déspota).
horcadura f. Fork (de árbol).
horcajadas (a) loc. adv. Astride, astraddle.
horcajadura f. ANAT. Crotch, fork.
horcajo m. Yoke (de mula). || GEOGR. Fork (de dos ríos). | Gully (entre dos vertientes).
horchata f. Orgeat, cold drink made of almonds or chufas. || FIG. *Tener sangre de horchata*, V. SANGRE.
horchatería f. Milk bar, orgeat shop.
horchatero, ra m. y f. Orgeat seller *o* maker.
horda f. Horde.
horizontal adj./s. f. Horizontal.
horizontalidad f. Horizontality.
horizonte m. Horizon: *en el horizonte*, on the horizon. || FIG. Horizon, outlook: *ampliar los horizontes*, to broaden one's horizons *o* outlook; *tiene horizontes muy estrechos*, he has very narrow horizons. || *Línea del horizonte*, skyline.
horma f. Form (molde). || Last (para fabricar zapatos). || Shoe tree, boot tree (para conservar la forma). || Hat block (para sombreros). || Dry-stone wall (muro). || FIG. *Encontrar la horma de su zapato*, to find just what the doctor ordered (lo deseado), to find Mr *o* Miss Right, to meet one's perfect match (a un novio o novia conveniente), to meet one's match (a alguien con quien medirse).
hormiga f. ZOOL. Ant. || MED. Formication (enfermedad). || — *Hormiga blanca*, white ant. || *Hormiga león*, ant lion. || FAM. y FIG. *Ser una hormiga*, to be industrious and thrifty.
hormigón m. Concrete: *hormigón armado*, *pretensado* or *precomprimido*, reinforced, prestressed concrete.
hormigonado m. Concreting.
hormigonera f. Cement mixer, concrete mixer.
hormigueamiento m. V. HORMIGUEO.
hormiguear v. intr. To swarm, to teem (bullir). || *Me hormiguea la pierna*, I have got pins and needles in my leg, my leg is tingling.
hormigueo m. Swarming, teeming. || Pins and needles, *pl.*, tingling sensation (sensación cutánea): *sentir hormigueo en la pierna*, to have pins and needles in one's leg. || FIG. Anxiety (desasosiego).
hormiguero m. Ant's nest (donde viven las hormigas). || Anthill (montoncito). || FIG. Swarm [of people]. | Anthill, place swarming with people. || — *La salida del estadio era un hormiguero*, the exit of the stadium was swarming with people. || *Oso hormiguero*, anteater.
hormiguilla f. Pins and needles, *pl.*, tingling sensation (cosquilleo). || FIG. Nagging conscience. || FIG. *Ser una hormiguilla*, to be industrious and thrifty.
hormiguillo m. Pins and needles, *pl.*, tingling sensation (hormigueo). || Chain (para pasar algo de mano en mano). || VET. Founder (enfermedad del casco). || FIG. y FAM. *Parece que tiene hormiguillo*, he's got ants in his pants.
hormiguita f. FIG. *Ser una hormiguita*, to be industrious and thrifty.
hormona f. BIOL. Hormone.
hormonal adj. BIOL. Hormonal.
hornablenda f. MIN. Hornblende.
hornacina f. ARQ. Niche.
hornacho m. MIN. Excavation.
hornada f. Batch: *hornada de pan*, batch of bread.
hornaguera f. Coal.
hornaza f. TECN. Silversmith's crucible (horno pequeño). | Light yellow glazing (para vidriar).
hornear v. tr. e intr. To bake.
hornería f. Baking.
hornero, ra m. y f. Baker. || — F. Oven floor (suelo de un horno). || — M. *Amer.* Ovenbird (ave).
hornija f. Firewood [for heating the oven].
hornilla f. u **hornillo** m. Cooker, stove: *hornillo de gas*, gas stove. || Ring (con una sola placa): *hornillo portátil de gas*, portable gas ring. || Ring, burner (de cocina de gas), hotplate, ring (de cocina eléctrica): *cocina con cuatro hornillos*, cooker with four rings. || MIN. Blast hole. || MIL. Land mine. || Bowl (de pipa). || *Hornillo de atanor*, athanor (horno de alquimista).
horno m. Oven: *horno de panadero*, baker's oven. || TECN. Kiln (para ladrillos, cerámica, etc.): *horno de esmalte*, enamel kiln. | Furnace (para la fundición): *alto horno*, blast furnace; *horno de hogar abierto*, open-hearth furnace; *horno de reverbero*, reverberatory furnace; *horno de arco*, arc furnace. || — *Fuente de horno*, ovenproof *o* fireproof dish [U.S., ovenproof platter]. || *Horno crematorio*, crematory, crematorium. || FIG. y FAM. *No está el horno para bollos* or *para tortas*, this is not the right time, the time is not right.
Hornos n. pr. GEOGR. *Cabo de Hornos*, Cape Horn.
horóscopo m. Horoscope: *hacer un horóscopo*, to cast a horoscope. || Astrologer (adivino).
horqueta f. AGR. Pitchfork, winnowing fork (horca). || Fork (de árbol). || *Amer.* Bend (de río).
horquilla f. AGR. Fork, pitchfork, winnowing fork (horca). || Fork (bifurcación). || Forked prop (palo bifurcado para sostener árboles, etc.). || Hairpin (para sujetar el moño), hair clip (para sujetar el peinado). || Wishbone (de ave). || MED. Split ends, *pl.* (enfermedad del pelo). || Forks, *pl.* (de bicicleta).
horrendamente adv. V. HORROROSAMENTE.
horrendo, da adj. V. HORROROSO.
hórreo m. Granary (granero).
horribilidad f. Horribleness, dreadfulness.
horrible adj. Horrible, dreadful, awful.
hórrido, da adj. V. HORROROSO.
horrificar v. tr. To horrify.
horrífico, ca adj. Horrific.
horripilación f. Horripilation (estremecimiento). || Horror, dread, terror (miedo).
horripilante adj. Hair-raising, terrifying.
horripilar v. tr. To make one's hair stand on end, to terrify, to horrify, to give the creeps (fam.): *es un cuento que horripila*, it is a tale which makes your hair stand on end.
horrísono adj. Dreadful, terrible, blood-curdling (ruido).
horro, ra adj. Enfranchised (esclavo). || Free, exempt (exento). || Lacking (carente): *horro de vigor*, lacking in energy. || Sterile (estéril).
horror m. Horror, dread, terror (miedo intenso): *pálido de horror*, pale with horror. || Horror (que causa miedo): *los horrores de la guerra*, the horrors of war. || Atrocity (atrocidad). || Horrible thing: *dice horrores de los franceses*, he says horrible things about the French. || — *Da horror verle tan flaco*, it is horrible *o* it horrifies me to see him so thin. || *Divertirse horrores*, to have a whale of a time, to have a jolly good time. || *Me gusta horrores*, I like it very much, I love it. || *¡Qué horror!*, how horrible!, how awful! || *Querer horrores a uno*, to be madly in love with s.o. (estar enamorado). || *Tener horror a la mentira*, to hate *o* to detest lies, to have a horror of lies. || *Un horror de gente*, masses (*pl.*) of people.
horrorizar v. tr. To horrify, to terrify. || *Estar horrorizado*, to be horrified, to be aghast, to be horror-stricken.
— V. pr. To be horrified *o* horror-stricken, to be aghast.
horrorosamente adv. Horribly: *horrorosamente desfigurado*, horribly disfigured. || FAM. Awfully, dreadfully, terribly, frightfully: *es horrorosamente difícil*, it's frightfully difficult.
horroroso, sa adj. Horrible, horrifying, frightful, horrid (que da horror). || Hideous, horrible, terribly ugly (muy feo). || Horrible, terrible, awful (muy malo): *hace un tiempo horroroso*, the weather is awful. || *Tengo un hambre horrorosa*, I'm terribly *o* awfully hungry.
hortaliza f. Vegetable: *hortalizas tempranas*, early vegetables.
hortelano, na adj. Market-gardening: *una región hortelana*, a market-gardening region.
— M. y f. Gardener (jardinero). || Market gardener (que cultiva para la venta). || — M. Ortolan (ave).
hortense adj. Market-garden, vegetable: *producción hortense*, vegetable production.
hortensia f. BOT. Hydrangea.
hortera f. Wooden bowl. || — M. FAM. Shop assistant (dependiente de comercio). | Flashy type (hombre atildado).
hortícola adj. Horticultural.
horticultor m. Horticulturist.
horticultura f. Horticulture.
hosanna m. REL. Hosanna.
hosco, ca adj. Surly, sullen: *tenía una expresión hosca*, he looked surly. || Dark, gloomy: *el cielo cobró un aspecto hosco*, the sky began to look gloomy. || Dark, dark-skinned, swarthy (muy moreno).
hospedaje u **hospedamiento** m. Lodging (acción de alojar). || Rent (alquiler): *pagar poco hospedaje*, to pay a a low rent. || Lodgings, *pl.*: *mi hospedaje está lejos de aquí*, my lodgings are a long way from here. || *Tomar hospedaje en un hotel*, to lodge in a hotel, to put up at a hotel.
hospedar v. tr. e intr. To put up, to lodge: *hospedar a un invitado*, to put a guest up.
— V. pr. To lodge, to stay, to put up: *hospedarse en casa de un amigo*, to lodge at a friend's house.
hospedera f. Innkeeper, landlady (de un establecimiento). || Landlady (de casa de huéspedes).

hospedería f. Hostelry, inn (establecimiento). || Guest room (habitación). || REL. Hospice. || Lodging (hospedaje).
hospedero, ra m. y f. Innkeeper, landlord (de un establecimiento). || Landlord (de una pensión).
hospiciano, na m. y f. Inmate of an orphanage or a poorhouse.
hospiciante m. y f. *Amer.* V. HOSPICIANO.
hospicio m. REL. Hospice (para peregrinos, viajeros). || Poorhouse (para los pobres). || Orphanage (para huérfanos).
hospital m. Hospital. || (Ant.). Hospice. || — *Buque hospital*, hospital ship. || MIL. *Hospital de sangre*, field hospital. || *Tren hospital*, hospital train.
hospitalario, ria adj. Hospitable (acogedor). || Hospital: *instalaciones hospitalarias*, hospital facilities. || *Caballero hospitalario*, Knight Hospitaller [U.S., Knight Hospitaler].
— M. REL. Hospitaller [U.S., hospitaler].
hospitalero, ra m. y f. Hospital manager *o* administrator. || REL. Hospitaller [U.S., hospitaler].
hospitalidad f. Hospitality: *dar hospitalidad a una persona*, to show s.o. hospitality.
hospitalización f. Hospitalization.
hospitalizar v. tr. To hospitalize, to send *o* to take to hospital.
— V. pr. To go into hospital.
hosquedad f. Surliness, sullenness (del rostro). || Gloominess, darkness, (de un lugar, del cielo, etc.). || Darkness, swarthiness (de la piel).
hostal m. Hostelry, inn.
hostelero, ra m. y f. Innkeeper.
hostería f. Inn, hostelry.
hostelería f. Hotel-keeping, hotel management: *escuela de hostelería*, school of hotel management. || Hotel business *o* trade: *la hostelería española está en pleno desarrollo*, the Spanish hotel trade is developing fast.
hostia f. REL. [Communion] wafer, host. || POP. Blow, bash (golpe). | Pain in the neck (pesado). || POP. *Pegarle una hostia a alguien*, to give s.o. a belting.
— Interj. POP. Damn it!, hell! (de enfado). | Christ! (de sorpresa, admiración).
hostiario m. Wafer box.
hostigador, ra adj. Annoying, tiresome (molesto). || Harassing (fastidioso). || Urging (incitador).
hostigamiento m. Whipping (del caballo). || FIG. Harassment, pestering, plaguing (acción de molestar). | Encouragement, urging (incitación).
hostigar v. tr. To whip (fustigar). || FIG. To urge: *le hostigué para que trabajase más de prisa*, I urged him to work faster. | To plague, to harass, to pester (fastidiar). || MIL. To harass (al enemigo).
hostigoso, sa adj. *Amer.* Cloying, sickening (empalagoso). | Annoying, tiresome, bothersome (molesto).
hostil adj. Hostile.
hostilidad f. Hostility: *romper, reanudar las hostilidades*, to begin, to renew hostilities.
hostilizar v. tr. To antagonize. || MIL. To harass.
hotel m. Hotel: *alojarse en un hotel*, to put up at a hotel. || Villa, house (casa particular).
hotelero, ra adj. Hotel: *industria hotelera*, hotel trade, hotel industry.
— M. y f. Hotelkeeper.
hotelito m. Villa, house (casa particular).
hotentote, ta adj./s. Hottentot.
hoy adv. Today: *hoy estamos a viernes*, today is Friday. || Now, nowadays, today (en la actualidad). || — *De hoy a mañana*, at any moment. || *De hoy en adelante*, from now on, henceforth, as of today. || *De hoy en quince días*, today fortnight, a fortnight today. || *Desde hoy*, from now on, as of today. || *En el día de hoy*, today. || *Hoy día, hoy en día*, nowadays. || *Hoy por hoy*, for the time being (de momento), nowadays (actualmente). || *Hoy por la mañana, por la tarde*, this morning, this afternoon. || *Hoy por mí y mañana por ti*, today me, tomorrow thee. || *No dejes para mañana lo que puedes hacer hoy*, do not put off till tomorrow what you can do today.
hoya f. Pit, ditch, hole. || Grave (sepultura). || GEOGR. Valley, dale. || AGR. Seedbed (semillero). || — AGR. *Plantar a hoya*, to plant in holes. || FIG. *Tener un pie en la hoya*, to have one foot in the grave.
hoyada f. Depression, hollow, dip (hondonada).
hoyar v. tr. *Amer.* To dig *o* to make holes in.
hoyo m. Hole. || Pockmark (de las viruelas). || Grave (fosa). || Dimple (hoyuelo). || DEP. Hole (golf). || FAM. *El muerto al hoyo, el vivo al bollo*, let the dead bury the dead.
hoyuelo m. Dimple (en la barbilla y las mejillas).
hoz f. AGR. Sickle, scythe. || Gorge, ravine (valle). || FIG. *Meter la hoz en mies ajena*, to poach on s.o.'s preserves.
hozada f. Stroke of the sickle.
hozadero m. Rooting place.
hozador, ra adj. Rooting.
hozar v. tr. To root [up].
huaca f. V. GUACA.
huacal m. V. GUACAL.
huaco m. V. GUACO.
huahua m. y f. *Amer.* V. GUAGUA.
huaico m. *Amer.* V. GUAICO.
huarache m. *Amer.* V. GUARACHE.
huarapón m. *Amer.* Wide-brimmed hat.
huaro m. *Amer.* Tafia, rum (aguardiente de caña).
huasca f. *Amer.* Strap (correa). | Whip (látigo). || *Amer. Dar huasca a uno*, to whip s.o.
huascazo m. *Amer.* Whipping, flogging.
huasipongo o **huasipungo** m. *Amer.* Land given to Ecuadorian workers in addition to their salaries.
huaso, sa m. y f. *Amer.* Chilean peasant.
huasquear v. tr. *Amer.* To whip.
huata f. *Amer.* V. GUATA.
huatón, ona adj. *Amer.* Potbellied.
hucha f. Moneybox, piggy bank (alcancía). || Chest (arca). || FIG. Savings, *pl.*, nest egg (fam.) [ahorros].
huebra f. AGR. Day's ploughing [U.S., day's plowing] (tierra labrada en un día). | Pair of mules and driver [hired by the day]. | Fallow land (barbecho).
hueca f. Spiral groove in a spindle.
hueco, ca adj. Hollow: *árbol hueco*, hollow tree. || Concave (cóncavo). || Empty (vacío). || Deep: *voz hueca*, deep voice. || Hollow: *sonido hueco*, hollow sound. || FIG. Empty: *estilo hueco*, empty style. | Vain, conceited (presumido). || Spongy (esponjoso). || Fluffy (mullido). || Loose: *tierra hueca*, loose earth.
— M. Hollow: *algo que cabe en el hueco de la mano*, sth. that fits in the hollow of one's hand. || Hole (agujero). || Spare time (tiempo libre). || Interval, lapse (intervalo). || Empty space (sitio libre). || ARQ. Opening. || FIG. y FAM. Vacancy (empleo vacante). | Gap: *su jubilación dejó un hueco en el equipo*, his retirement left a gap in the team. || — *El hueco de la escalera*, the stairwell, the stair well. || *El hueco del ascensor*, the lift *o* elevator shaft. || *El hueco de una puerta*. the doorway. || *Grabado en hueco*, intaglio. || FIG. *Hacer su hueco*, to make o.s. a place. | *Sonar a hueco*, to sound hollow.
huecograbado m. Photogravure.
huecú m. *Amer.* Grass-covered swamp *o* bog.
huélfago m. VET. Heaves, *pl.* (de los caballos).
huelga f. Strike: *declararse en huelga* or *declarar la huelga*, to declare o.s. on strike, to go on strike; *estar en huelga*, to be on strike. || Good time, amusement, enjoyment (recreo). || — *Huelga de brazos caídos* or *de brazos cruzados*, down tools, sit-down strike. || *Huelga del hambre*, hunger strike. || *Huelga escalonada* or *alternativa* or *por turno*, staggered strike. || *Huelga intermitente*, go-slow [U.S., slow-down]. || *Huelga por solidaridad*, sympathetic strike. || *Subsidio de huelga*, strike pay.
huelgo m. Breath (aliento). || TECN. Play (juego).
huelguista m. y f. Striker.
huelguístico, ca adj. Strike. || *Movimiento huelguístico en las minas*, wave of strikes in the mines.
huella f. Footprint, footstep, track (del pie, de una persona): *se ven huellas en la nieve*, footprints can be seen in the snow. || Track (de animales, vehículos). || Trace, mark (señal): *el tiempo ha dejado huellas en su rostro*, time has left its mark on his face. || Tread (de un escalón). || — *Dejar huellas*, to leave one's mark: *hecho que dejará sus huellas en la historia*, event that will leave its mark on history. || *Huella digital* or *dactilar*, fingerprint. || *No encontrar huellas de*, not to find a trace of. || *Seguir la huellas de alguien*, to follow s.o.'s tracks *o* trail, to trail s.o. (seguir el rastro), to follow in s.o.'s footsteps (hacer lo mismo).
huello m. Step, pace (de un caballo). || Sole (del casco del caballo). || Surface (superficie). || Path, track (camino).
huérfano, na adj. Orphaned, orphan. || *Huerfano de*, devoid of, without, lacking.
— M. y f. Orphan. || — *Asilo de huérfanos*, orphanage. || *Huérfano de guerra*, war orphan. || *Huérfano de madre*, motherless child. || *Huérfano de padre*, fatherless child.
huero, ra adj. FIG. Empty: *un discurso huero*, an empty speech. || Rotten (podrido). || *Amer.* Blond, blonde (rubio). || FIG. *Salir huero*, to be a failure.
huerta f. Large kitchen garden, large vegetable garden (para cultivo de hortalizas). || "Huerta", irrigated and cultivated plain (tierra de regadío, especialmente en Valencia y Murcia). || Orchard (de árboles frutales). || Market garden [U.S., truck garden] (de cultivo para la venta). || *Productos de la huerta*, market-garden produce.

— OBSERV. *La huerta* is generally much larger than *el huerto* and more vegetables than fruits are grown there.

huertano, na adj. Pertaining to an inhabitant of the "Huerta." || Market-garden (de la huerta).
— M. y f. Inhabitant of the "Huerta".
huertero, ra m. y f. *Amer.* Gardener.
huerto m. Orchard (de árboles frutales). || Vegetable garden, kitchen garden (de hortalizas). || Market garden [U.S., truck garden] (de cultivo para la venta).
huesa f. Grave: *tener un pie en la huesa*, to have one foot in the grave.
huesillo m. *Amer.* Sun-dried peach.
hueso m. ANAT. Bone: *los huesos del pie*, the bones of the foot. || Stone [U.S., pit] (de una fruta). || Bone (sustancia): *botones de hueso*, buttons made of bone. || FIG. y FAM. Hard work, drudgery: *el latín para mí es un hueso*, Latin is hard work *o* a drudgery for me. | Pain in the neck: *¡éste tío es un hueso!*, that fellow is a pain in the neck! | Snag (dificultad). || — Pl. Bones (restos de una persona).
— FIG. *A otro perro con ese hueso*, v. PERRO. || *Calado*

hasta los huesos, soaked to the skin, wet through, drenched. || FAM. *¡Choca esos huesos!*, it's a deal!, put it there! | *Dar con los huesos en el suelo*, to come a cropper, to fall flat. | *Dar con sus huesos*, to end up: *dio con sus huesos en la cárcel*, he ended up in jail. | *Dar en (un) hueso* or *tropezar con un hueso*, to hit a snag. | *Darle a la sin hueso*, to tongue-wag. | *En carne y hueso*, in the flesh. | *Estar* or *quedarse en los huesos*, to be nothing but skin and bone, to be a bag of bones. | *Este profesor es un hueso* or *un rato hueso* or *muy hueso*, this teacher is a stickler. | *Estoy por sus huesos*, I'm head-over-heels in love with him. || *Hueso de la alegría* or *de la suegra*, funny bone. || *Hueso sacro*, sacrum. || FIG. y FAM. *La sin hueso*, the tongue. | *No dejarle a uno un hueso sano*, to break every bone in s.o.'s body, to make mincemeat of s.o. (pegándole), to pull *o* to pick s.o. to pieces (criticar mucho). | *No llegará a hacer huesos viejos*, he won't make old bones, he will not live long. | *No poder uno con sus huesos*, to be done in, to be all in. | *Romperle a uno los huesos* or *un hueso*, to beat s.o. to a pulp. | *Ser un hueso duro de roer*, to be a hard nut to crack. | *Tener los huesos duros*, to be too old [for certain types of work] (ser demasiado viejo), to be as hard as nails (aguantar mucho). | *Tener los huesos molidos*, to be all in *o* bushed *o* shattered.
huesoso, sa adj. Bony.
huésped, da m. y f. Host (hombre que invita), hostess (mujer que invita). || Guest (invitado): *estar de huésped en casa de*, to be a guest in the house of. || Innkeeper (mesonero). || BIOL. y BOT. Host. || — *Casa de huéspedes*, boardinghouse. || *Cuarto de huéspedes*, guest room. || FIG. *Hacérsele a uno los dedos huéspedes*, to imagine things (imaginarse cosas), to count one's chickens (crearse ilusiones). || *Huésped de una pensión*, boarder, lodger. || FIG. y FAM. *No contar con la huéspeda*, to reckon without one's host.
hueste f. (Ant.). Host, army (ejército). || Followers, *pl.* (partidarios).
huesudo, da adj. Big-boned, bony (persona). || Bony: *manos huesudas*, bony hands.
hueva f. Roe, fish eggs, *pl.*, spawn.
huevar v. intr. To begin to lay (las aves).
huevería f. Egg shop *o* store.
huevero, ra m. y f. Egg dealer. || — F. Eggcup (para comer los huevos). || Egg stand (para servir los huevos). || ANAT. Oviduct (de las aves).
huevo m. Egg (de ave, etc.): *poner un huevo*, to lay an egg. || Darning egg (para zurcir). || POP. Ball (testículo). || — FIG. y FAM. *Andar* or *ir pisando huevos*, to walk carefully. || POP. *Costar un huevo*, to cost the earth, to cost a fortune. || *Huevo de Colón*, sth. that seems at first to be difficult but has a simple solution. || *Huevo de Pascuas*, Easter egg. || *Huevo duro*, hard-boiled egg. || *Huevo escalfado*, poached egg. || *Huevo estrellado* or *frito* or *al plato*, fried egg. || *Huevo fresco*, new-laid egg. || *Huevo huero*, wind egg. || *Huevo pasado por agua*, boiled *o* soft-boiled egg. || *Huevos batidos a punto de nieve*, egg whites beaten stiff. || *Huevos moles*, dessert of egg-yolk and sugar. || *Huevos revueltos*, scrambled eggs. || *Amer. Huevo tibio*, boiled *o* soft-boiled egg. || FIG. *No es tanto por el huevo sino por el fuero*, it's a matter of principle. | *Parecerse como un huevo a otro huevo*, to be as like as two peas in a pod. | *Parecerse como un huevo a una castaña*, to be as different as chalk and cheese. || POP. *Se lo puse a huevo*, I handed it to him on a plate [U.S., I gave it to him on a silver platter]. | *Tener huevos*, to have guts.
Hugo n. pr. m. Hugh, Hugo.
hugonote, ta adj./s. Huguenot.
huida f. Flight, escape (acción de huir). || EQUIT. Shy.
huidero, ra adj. Fleeting.
— M. Cover, shelter (de los animales).
huidizo, za adj. Shy (tímido). || Elusive (esquivo). || Fleeting (fugaz). || Shy (animal).
huido, da adj. Fugitive. || Shy of people, withdrawn.
huilón, ona adj. *Amer.* Inclined to flee (que huye). | Cowardly (cobarde).
huincha f. *Amer.* Ribbon (cinta). | Tape measure (para medir).
huinche m. *Amer.* Winch.
huipil m. *Amer.* Woman's tunic.
huir* v. intr. y tr. To flee, to escape: *huir de la cárcel*, to flee from jail. || To flee, to run away: *huir del vicio*, to flee from vice. || To run away: *huir a* or *de una persona*, to run away from s.o. || To fly: *¡cómo huyen las horas!*, how time flies! || *Huir de* (con el infinitivo), to avoid, to shun: *huir de ir a hacer visitas*, to avoid making visits.
hule m. Oilcloth (para mesa, etc.). || Oilskin (para ropa). || Rubber sheet (para recién nacidos). || *Amer.* Rubber (caucho). || — FIG. *Ayer hubo hule en la corrida de toros*, there was an accident in yesterday's bullfight. | *Ayer hubo hule en la calle*, there was fighting *o* trouble in the street yesterday.
hulería f. *Amer.* Plantation of rubber trees.
hulero m. *Amer.* Rubber worker.
hulla f. Coal. || — *Hulla blanca*, water power, white coal. || *Mina de hulla*, coal mine, colliery.
hullero, ra adj. Coal: *cuenca hullera*, coal bed.
humanamente adv. Humanly: *hacer lo humanamente posible*, to do what is humanly possible. || Humanely (tratar, etc.).
humanar v. tr. To humanize (humanizar).
— V. pr. To become more human. || To become man (Dios). || *Amer.* To condescend (condescender).
humanidad f. Mankind, humanity (género humano). || FIG. Humanity, humaneness. || FAM. Corpulence. || — Pl. Humanities: *estudiar humanidades*, to study humanities. || FIG. y FAM. *Este cuarto huele a humanidad*, this room smells stuffy.
humanismo m. Humanism.
humanista m. y f. Humanist.
humanístico, ca adj. Humanistic.
humanitario, ria adj. Humane (humano). || — Adj./s. Humanitarian.
humanitarismo m. Humanitarianism.
humanización f. Humanization.
humanizar v. tr. To humanize.
— V. pr. To become more human.
humano, na adj. Human: *el cuerpo humano*, the human body. || Humane: *tiene un trato muy humano con sus empleados*, he has a very humane relationship with his employees. || *Todo cabe en lo humano*, anything is possible.
— M. Human, human being.
humarada o **humareda** f. Cloud of smoke.
humarazo m. Dense smoke.
humazo m. Dense smoke. || Fumigation.
humeada f. *Amer.* Puff of smoke.
humeante adj. Smoking, smoky (cenizas, etc.). || Steaming: *sopa humeante*, steaming soup.
humear v. intr. To smoke: *carbón, chimenea que humea*, coal, chimney that smokes. || To be steaming hot: *sopa que humea*, soup that is steaming hot. || FIG. Not to be completely settled (riña). | To be conceited (presumir).
— V. tr. *Amer.* To fumigate (fumigar).
humectación f. Humidification, moistening.
humectador m. Humidifier.
humectante adj. Moistening.
humectar v. tr. V. HUMEDECER.
humedad f. Humidity, dampness, damp, moisture. || FÍS. Humidity: *humedad relativa*, relative humidity.
humedecedor m. Humidifier.
humedecer* v. tr. To moisten, to dampen, to humidify.
— V. pr. To become moist *o* wet *o* damp. || *Se le humedecieron los ojos*, his eyes became watery, tears filled his eyes.
humedecimiento m. Moistening, dampening, humidification.
húmedo, da adj. Humid, moist, damp (clima). || Damp: *ropa húmeda*, damp clothes; *suelo húmedo*, damp ground. || Wet (mojado).
humera f. FAM. Drunkenness (borrachera).

— OBSERV. The "*h*" is aspirate.

humeral adj. ANAT. Humeral.
— M. REL. Humeral [veil].
humero m. Chimney, smokestack.
húmero m. ANAT. Humerus.
húmido, da adj. POET. Humid, moist.
humildad f. Humility: *con toda humildad*, with all humility. || Humbleness, lowliness (de nacimiento).
humilde adj./s. Humble: *la gente humilde*, the humble people. || FIG. Humble, lowly: *de humilde cuna*, of humble birth. || — *A mi humilde parecer*, in my humble opinion. || *Favorecer a los humildes*, to favour the humble.
humillación f. Humiliation.
humilladero m. Calvary (cruz al entrar en un pueblo).
humillador, ra o **humillante** adj. Humiliating.
humillar v. tr. To humiliate: *humillar a un hombre*, to humiliate a man. || To humble: *humillar a los enemigos*, to humble the enemy. || To bow (bajar): *humillar la frente*, to bow one's head. || To bend (la rodilla). || TAUR. *Humillar la cabeza*, to lower its head (el toro).
— V. intr. To lower its head (el toro).
— V. pr. To humble o.s.
humillo m. FIG. Conceit, airs, *pl.*, vanity (vanidad). || VET. Disease of sucking pigs.
humo m. Smoke. || Steam, vapour [U.S., vapor] (vapor). || Fumes, *pl.* (gas nocivo). || — Pl. Hearths, homes. || FIG. Conceit, *sing.*, airs (orgullo). || — FIG. y FAM. *A humo de pajas*, thoughtlessly. | *Bajarle los humos a uno*, to take s.o. down a peg, to put s.o. in his place. || *Cortina de humo*, smoke screen. || FIG. y FAM. *¡Cuántos humos tiene!*, how presumptuous he is! || *Curar al humo*, to smoke [ham, fish, etc.]. || *Echar* or *hacer humo*, to smoke: *la chimenea echa humo*, the chimney smokes. || FIG. *Hacer humo a uno*, to ignore s.o. || *Amer. Hacerse humo*, to vanish into thin air (desaparecer). || *Irse todo en humo*, to go up in smoke. || FIG. *Quedar en humo de pajas*, to come to nothing. | *Se le bajaron los humos*, he was put in his place. | *Se le subieron los humos a la cabeza*, he got on his high horse, he became conceited. | *Tener muchos humos*, to put on airs, to think a lot of o.s.
humor m. Mood, temper, humour [U.S., humor]: *buen, mal humor*, good, bad mood. || Character, nature, temper (índole). || ANAT. Humour: *humor ácueo, vítreo*, aqueous, vitreous humour. || FIG. Wit, humour (agudeza). || Humour (gracia): *tiene sentido del humor*, he has a sense of humour. || — *Estar de buen* or *mal humor*, to be in a good *o* bad mood,

to be in a good *o* bad temper. || FAM. *Humor de todos los diablos*, very bad temper. || *No estoy de* or *no tengo humor para bromas*, I'm in no mood for jokes. || *Remover los humores*, to disturb. || *Seguirle el humor a uno*, to go along with s.o., to humour s.o. || *Si estás de humor*, if you like, if you feel like it.
humorada f. Joke (broma). || Fancy, caprice, whim (capricho). || Gall, nerve: *tuvo la humorada de decirme esto*, he had the gall to tell me that.
humorado, da adj. *Bien humorado*, good-humoured [U.S., good-humored], good-tempered. || *Mal humorado*, bad-humoured, bad-tempered.
humoral adj. ANAT. Humoral.
humorismo m. Humour [U.S., humor], humorousness.
humorista adj. Humorous, humoristic.
— M. y f. Humorist.
humorístico, ca adj. Humoristic, humorous.
humoso, sa adj. Smoky.
humus m. AGR. Humus (mantillo).
hundible adj. Sinkable.
hundido, da adj. Sunken: *barco hundido*, sunken boat. || Hollow, sunken (mejillas). || Deep-set, sunken: *ojos hundidos*, deep-set eyes. || *Hundido en sus pensamientos*, sunk in thought.
hundimiento m. Sinking (acción de hundir). || Cave-in (del terreno, socavón). || Collapse (de una casa). || Depression (de la moral). || Collapse, fall, downfall (de un imperio). || Crash (de la Bolsa). || Slump (de los precios, cotizaciones). || Sinking (de un barco).
hundir v. tr. To sink: *hundir un barco*, to sink a ship. || To cause to sink *o* to subside: *la lluvia hunde el suelo*, the rain causes the ground to sink. || To plunge, to immerse (sumergir). || To drive, to thrust (un puñal). || To drive, to sink (una estaca). || FIG. To confound (confundir). | To depress (deprimir). | To overwhelm (abrumar). | To ruin (arruinar). | To squander (una fortuna).
— V. pr. To fall down, to tumble down, to collapse (un edificio). || To subside, to cave in (el terreno). || To sink (irse al fondo). || To fall, to collapse (un imperio). || To sink, to flag (la moral). || To collapse (la economía). || To crash (la Bolsa). || To slump (los precios, cotizaciones). || To come to nothing (proyectos). || To become hollow *o* sunken (las mejillas, los ojos). || MAR. To sink (un barco, un avión): *el avión se hundió en el mar*, the plane sank into the sea.
húngaro, ra adj./s. Hungarian.
Hungría n. pr. f. GEOGR. Hungary.
huno m. HIST. Hun.
huracán m. Hurricane.
huracanado, da adj. Hurricane, tempestuous: *viento huracanado*, hurricane wind.
huraño, ña adj. Unsociable (insociable), surly (arisco), shy (tímido).
hurgador m. Poker (persona, utensilio).
hurgar v. tr. To poke, to stir (el fuego). || To rummage in, to poke around in (en un bolso, papeles). || FIG. To incite, to stir up (incitar). || — FIG. *Hurgar en la herida*, V. HERIDA. || FAM. *Peor es hurgallo*, better leave it alone.
— V. pr. FAM. To pick: *hurgarse las narices, los dientes*, to pick one's nose, one's teeth.
hurgón m. Poker (persona, utensilio).
hurgonada f. Poking.
hurgonazo m. Thrust *o* jab with a poker.
hurgonear v. tr. To poke, to stir (el fuego).
hurgonero m. Poker (utensilio).
hurguillas m. y f. inv. Busybody (bullebulle).
hurí f. Houri.
hurón m. ZOOL. Ferret (animal). || FIG. y FAM. Prier, snooper, busybody (persona entrometida). | Unsociable person (persona huraña).
hurón, ona adj./s. Huron (indio de América del Norte). || — Adj. Shy, reserved (tímido). || Unsociable (poco sociable).
hurona f. Female ferret.
huronear v. intr. To ferret, to hunt with a ferret (cazar). || FIG. y FAM. To pry, to ferret, to snoop (escudriñar).
huronera f. Ferret hole. || FIG. y FAM. Hiding place, hideout (escondrijo). | Den, hideout (para maleantes).
huronero m. Ferreter, ferret keeper.
¡hurra! interj. Hurrah!
hurraca f. Magpie (urraca).
hurtadillas (a) loc. adv. Stealthily, on the sly.
hurtar v. tr. To steal (robar). || To cheat, to give short measure (engañar en el peso). || FIG. To wash *o* to wear *o* to eat away (tierras). | To plagiarize, to lift (plagiar). || *Hurtar el cuerpo*, to dodge.
— V. pr. FIG. To hide: *hurtarse a los ojos de uno*, to hide from s.o. | To shirk, to evade: *hurtarse a las responsabilidades*, to evade responsibilities.
hurto m. Petty theft *o* larceny (robo). || Loot, stolen object (cosa robada).
husada f. Spindleful (de hilo).
húsar m. MIL. Hussar.
husillo m. Screw, worm [of a press] (de molino). || Drain (conducto). || Small spindle (huso). || TECN. Spindle.
husita adj./s. HIST. Hussite.
husma f. Snooping, prying. || FAM. *Andar a la husma*, to go snooping around.
husmeador, ra adj. FAM. Prying, snooping.
— M. y f. Prier, snooper.
husmear v. tr. To scent, to smell out. || FIG. y FAM. To pry into, to snoop into (indagar). | To smell (presentir): *husmear el peligro*, to smell danger.
— V. intr. To smell bad *o* off (las carnes). || To snoop around (curiosear).
husmeo m. Scenting. || FIG. Snooping, prying.
husmo m. Bad *o* rotten smell (olor).
huso m. Spindle (para hilar). || Fuselage (de los aviones). || Spindle (de torno). || HERÁLD. Lozenge. || — MAT. *Huso esférico*, lune. || *Huso horario*, time zone. || FIG. y FAM. *Ser más derecho* or *tieso que un huso*, to be as straight *o* as stiff as a poker.
¡huy! interj. Ouch! (dolor). || Well! (sorpresa).

I

i f. I: *una i mayúscula*, a capital i. || FIG. *Poner los puntos sobre las íes*, to dot the i's and cross the t's.
Iberia n. pr. f. GEOGR. Iberia.
ibérico, ca o **iberio, ria** adj./s. Iberian: *la península ibérica*, the Iberian Peninsula.
ibero, ra o **íbero, ra** adj./s. Iberian.
Iberoamérica n. pr. f. GEOGR. Latin America.
iberoamericano, na adj./s. Latin-American.
— OBSERV. V. LATIN-AMERICAN.
íbice m. ZOOL. Ibex (cabra montés).
ibicenco, ca adj./s. Ibizan (de Ibiza).
ibídem adv. lat. Ibidem (en el mismo lugar).
— OBSERV. Abreviación: *ibid* or *ib.* en ambos idiomas.
ibis m. Ibis (ave).
Ibiza n. pr. GEOGR. Ibiza.
icaco m. BOT. Icaco, coco plum, cocoa plum.
icáreo, a o **icario, ria** adj. Icarian.
Ícaro n. pr. m. MIT. Icarus.
iceberg m. Iceberg.
icefield m. Icefield.
icneumón m. ZOOL. Ichneumon, mongoose (mamífero). | Ichneumon [fly] (insecto).
icono m. Icon.
iconoclasia f. Iconoclasm.
iconoclasta adj. Iconoclastic.
— M. y f. Iconoclast.
iconografía f. Iconography.
iconográfico, ca adj. Iconographic.
iconógrafo m. Iconographer.
iconolatría f. Iconolatry, image worship.
iconología f. Iconology.
iconoscopio m. RAD. Iconoscope.
icor m. MED. Ichor.
icoroso, sa adj. MED. Ichorous (purulento).
icosaedro m. MAT. Icosahedron.
ictericia f. MED. Icterus, jaundice.
ictérico, ca adj. MED. Icteric, suffering from jaundice.
— M. y f. MED. Person suffering from jaundice.
ictiocola f. Ichthyocolla, fish glue, isinglass.
ictiofagia f. Ichthyophagy.
ictiófago, ga adj. Ichthyophagous.
— M. y f. Ichthyophagist.
ictiol m. QUÍM. Ichthyol.
ictiología f. Ichtyology.
ictiólogo m. Ichthyologist.

ictiosauro m. Ichthyosaur.
ictus m. MED. Ictus. || Ictus (acento).
ida f. Going, outward journey: *me gusta la ida, pero no la vuelta*, I like the going, but not the coming back. || Departure (salida): *¿a qué hora es la ida?*, what time is the departure? || FIG. Impulsive action, impetuous action (ímpetu). || Attack (esgrima). || Track, trail (caza). || — *Billete de ida y vuelta* [*Amer., de ida y llamada*], return ticket [U.S., round-trip ticket]. || *Idas y venidas*, comings and goings. || *Perdimos una hora en la ida*, we lost an hour going, we lost an hour on the outward journey. || *Viaje de ida*, outward journey. || *Viaje de ida y vuelta*, round trip, return trip *o* journey.
idea f. Idea: *idea preconcebida*, preconceived idea; *tengo una idea*, I've [got] an idea. || Memory, thought (recuerdo): *no puedo borrar su idea de la mente*, I cannot erase his memory *o* the thought of him from my mind. || Intention (intención): *lo hizo con buena idea, pero...*, his intentions were good *o* he did it with good intention, but... || Concept, idea (concepto). || Opinion, impression: *tener buena idea de uno*, to have a good opinion of. s.o. || Idea, belief (creencia): *una idea muy extendida por el mundo*, an idea widely spread throughout the world. || Idea, outline (esquema). || Idea (habilidad): *no tiene mucha idea para pintar*, he hasn't much idea of *o* about painting.
— *Cambiar* or *mudar de idea*, to change one's mind. || *Dar idea de*, to give an idea of. || *Darle* or *ocurrírsele a uno la idea de*, to get the idea of, to take it into one's head to: *le dio súbitamente la idea de escalar el Mont Blanc*, he suddenly took it into his head to climb Mont Blanc. || *Formarse una idea*, to form *o* to get an idea. || *Hacer algo con mala idea*, to do sth. with ill intentions. || *Hacerse a la idea de que*, to get used to the idea that. || *Hacerse una idea de*, to get an idea of. || *Idea eje*, central idea. || *Idea fija*, obsession, fixed idea, idée fixe. || *Idea general* or *de conjunto*, general idea, general outline. || *Idea genial* or *luminosa*, brilliant idea, brain wave [U.S., brain storm]. || *Idea vacía*, empty idea. || *Llevar* or *tener idea de*, to intend to, to have the intention of. || *Metérsele a uno una idea en la cabeza*, to get an idea into one's head. || *¡Ni idea!*, no idea! || FIG. *No tener idea buena*, to be always up to no good. || *No tengo ni la más ligera* or *remota idea*, I'haven't a clue, I haven't the slightest *o* the remotest idea. || *¿Qué idea tienes del director?*, what impression do you have of the director? || *Tener idea*, to have an idea *o* the idea: *se ve que tiene idea*, he has obviously got an idea. || *Tener mala idea*, to be malicious *o* ill-intentioned. || FIG. *Tener una idea en la cabeza*, to be up to sth., to have sth. up one's sleeve.
ideal adj. Ideal (de la idea o de las ideas). || Imaginary, hypothetical, ideal (imaginado, supuesto). || Ideal: *sueña con un mundo ideal*, he dreams of an ideal world. || Gorgeous, lovely (muy bonito): *lleva un traje ideal*, she is wearing a gorgeous dress.
— M. Ideal: *hombre de ideales*, man of ideals. || *Lo ideal*, the ideal thing.
idealidad f. Ideality. || *Su vestido es una idealidad*, her dress is gorgeous.
idealismo m. Idealism.
idealista adj. Idealistic.
— M. y f. Idealist.
idealización f. Idealization.
idealizador, ra adj. Idealizing, who idealizes.
idealizar v. tr. To idealize.
idear v. tr. To think up, to conceive (concebir). || To invent, to devise, to contrive: *un aparato ideado por un ingeniero*, an appliance devised by an engineer. || To design: *ha sido ideado para ir a quinientos por hora*, it is designed to do five hundred miles per hour.
ideario m. Ideology.
ideático, ca adj. *Amer.* Eccentric (venático). | Ingenious (ingenioso).
ídem adv. Idem, ditto. || *Carlos es un vago y un embustero y su padre ídem de ídem*, Charles is an idler and a liar, and his father is the same *o* and the same goes for his father.
idéntico, ca adj. Identical.
identidad f. Identity: *tarjeta* or *documento* or *carnet de identidad*, identity card. || FIG. Identity (semejanza): *identidad de pareceres*, identity of opinions.
identificable adj. Identifiable.
identificación f. Identification.
identificar v. tr. To identify.
— V. pr. To identify o.s., to identify (*con*, with). || *Identificarse plenamente con su papel*, to identify with one's role, to really live the part.
ideograma m. Ideograph, ideogram.
ideología f. Ideology.
ideológico, ca adj. Ideological, ideologic.
ideólogo m. Ideologist.
idílico, ca adj. Idyllic.
idilio m. Idyll, idyl. || Amorous talk (coloquio amoroso). || Amorous relationship, romance (relaciones).
idioma m. Language, tongue: *el idioma inglés*, the English language. || Parlance, idiom, language: *idioma de la corte*, language of the Court, Court parlance *o* idiom. || FIG. *No hablamos el mismo idioma*, we just don't speak the same language, we're not on the same wavelength.
idiomático, ca adj. Idiomatic. || *Expresión idiomática*, idiom, idiomatic expression.
idiopatía f. Idiopathy.
idiosincrasia f. Idiosyncrasy.
idiosincrásico, ca adj. Idiosyncratic.
idiota adj. Idiotic, stupid, foolish.
— M. y f. Idiot, fool. || *¡Idiota!*, you idiot!
idiotez f. Idiocy, foolishness (cualidad). || Idiotic thing (hecho, dicho). || — *Decir idioteces*, to talk nonsense. || *Hacer idioteces*, to fool about, to be silly.
idiotismo m. GRAM. Idiom. || Ignorance (falta de instrucción).
idiotizar v. tr. To idiotize.
ido, da adj. FAM. Miles away (distraído): *perdóname, estaba ido*, I'm sorry, I was miles away. | Touched, cracked (chiflado).
idólatra adj. Idolatrous.
— M. y f. Idolater (hombre), idolatress (mujer).
idolatrar v. tr. To worship. || FIG. To idolize: *idolatrar a sus padres*, to idolize one's parents.
idolatría f. Idolatry.
idolátrico, ca adj. Idolatrous: *culto idolátrico*, idolatrous cult. || FIG. Idolatrous.
ídolo m. Idol. || FIG. Idol: *hacerse el ídolo de*, to become the idol of.
idoneidad f. Suitability, fitness (conveniencia). || Ability, capability (capacidad).
idóneo, a adj. Suitable, fit (*para*, for) [conveniente]. || Capable, competent, able (capaz).
idos o **idus** m. pl. Ides.
íes f. pl. Véase I.
iglesia f. Church (edificio). || Church: *Iglesia militante, purgante, triunfante*, Church militant, suffering, triumphant. || (Ant.). Sanctuary (inmunidad). || — *Acogerse a la Iglesia* or *entrar en la Iglesia*, to enter the Church, to take holy orders. || FIG. y FAM. *Casarse por detrás de la iglesia*, v. CASAR. || *Casarse por la Iglesia*, to get married in church. || FIG. *¡Con la Iglesia hemos topado!*, now we are really up against it! || *Cumplir con la Iglesia*, to fulfil one's religious duties *o* obligations. || *El seno de la Iglesia*, the bosom of the Church. || *Iglesia Anglicana*, Church of England, Anglican Church. || *Iglesia parroquial*, parish church. || *Llevar a la Iglesia a una mujer*, to lead a woman to the altar. || *Los Padres de la Iglesia*, the Fathers of the Christian Church. || *Santa Madre Iglesia*, Mother Church.
iglú m. Igloo.
Ignacio n. pr. m. Ignatius.
ignaro, ra adj. Ignorant.
— M. y f. Ignoramus.
ígneo, a adj. Igneous.
ignición f. Ignition. || Combustion, burning.
ignícola adj. Fire-worshipping.
— M. y f. Fire worshipper (adorador del fuego).
ignifugación f. Fireproofing.
ignifugar v. tr. To fireproof.
ignífugo, ga adj. Fireproof, fire-resisting.
ignominia f. Ignominy, disgrace (deshonra). || Humiliation, degradation (humillación). || Injustice (injusticia). || Crime, shame: *sería una ignominia cortarle sus hermosos rizos*, it would be a crime to cut off her beautiful curls.
ignominioso, sa adj. Ignominious.
ignorancia f. Ignorance: *ignorancia crasa* or *supina*, crass ignorance. || *La ignorancia de la ley no exime su cumplimiento*, ignorance of the law is no excuse.
ignorante adj. Ignorant (que carece de instrucción). || Uninformed, unaware (que no ha sido informado).
— M. y f. Ignoramus (que carece de instrucción). || Dunce, ignoramus (estúpido).
ignorantismo m. Ignorantism, obscurantism.
ignorantista m. y f. Obscurantist.
ignorantón, ona adj. FAM. Very ignorant.
— M. y f. FAM. Ignoramus, dunce.
ignorar v. tr. Not to know, to be unaware *o* ignorant of: *ignoraban su presencia*, they were unaware of his presence. || To ignore (no tener en cuenta, no prestar atención). || *No ignorar que*, to be fully aware that.
igual adj. Even, level, smooth: *terreno, borde igual*, even ground, edge. || Steady, even, smooth: *la marcha igual del tren*, the steady motion of the train. || Alike, similar: *los dos hermanos son iguales*, the two brothers are alike. || Equal: *dos cantidades iguales*, two equal quantities. || The same: *nuestros pareceres son prácticamente iguales*, our opinions are practically the same; *tengo uno igual que el tuyo*, I have one the same as yours; *¿cómo está el enfermo? — Igual*, how is the patient? — Still the same. || Constant, even: *temperatura igual*, constant temperature. || Equable: *clima igual*, equable climate. || Even, equable (carácter). || The same (indiferente): *todo le es* or *le da igual*, it is all the same to him. || — *Es igual*, it makes no difference, it doesn't matter. || *Ir iguales*, to be level, to be even (en una carrera). || *Nunca he visto cosa igual*, I've never seen the like of it *o* anything like it. || DEP. *Quince iguales* or *iguales a quince*, fifteen all. || *Su coche es igual que el mío*, his car is like mine *o* is the same as mine. || MAT. *X igual a Y*, X equals Y.
— Adv. Easily: *igual podías haberte matado*, you could easily have killed yourself. || *Igual han tenido algún problema con el coche*, they might [well] have had trouble with the car.

— M. Equal: *es su igual*, he is your equal. || MAT. Equal sign. || — Pl. Lottery ticket [on behalf of the "Organización Nacional de Ciegos" in Spain]. || — *Al igual que*, [just] like, the same as, just as. || *De igual a igual*, as [to] an equal, as [to] one's equal, as [to] one's equals, as equals: *hablar a uno, tratar a uno de igual a igual*, to speak to s.o. as to one's equal, to treat s.o. as an equal. || *El sin igual cantante X*, the incomparable singer X. || *Igual ocurre con Y*, the same with Y, the same holds good of Y, so it is with Y. || *Igual que*, [the same] as: *igual que antes*, as before; *igual que yo*, the same as me. || *No tiene (otro) igual*, he has no equal, there isn't another like him. || *Por igual*, evenly, equally (uniformemente). || *Sin igual*, unequalled, unparalelled, unique, without equal.

iguala f. Equalization (igualación). || Agreed fee (cuota pagada al médico, veterinario, etc.) || Agreement, contract (ajuste). || FAM. Friendly society (igualatorio). || Rule (de albañil). || TECN. Smoothing.

igualación f. Equalization, equalizing. || Levelling (de terreno). || Planing, smoothing (de madera). || Smoothing (de cuero, metal). || FIG. Agreement, contract (convenio). || MAT. Equating.

igualado, da adj. Smooth (césped). || Similar, alike (semejante). || Level (en situación muy semejante): *todos los caballos entraron en la meta muy igualados*, all the horses came home very level. || Even: *un partido muy igualado*, a very even game.

igualador, ra adj. Equalizing, who *o* which makes equal (que iguala).

igualamiento m. Equalization, equalizing (igualación). || Agreement, contract (convenio).

igualar v. tr. To equal (ser igual): *nada iguala la belleza de este paisaje*, there is nothing to equal the beauty of this scenery. || To make equal, to equalize (volver igual). || To consider equal, to place on an equal footing (a dos o más personas). || To even out, to adjust (ajustar). || To level off *o* out, to level (el terreno). || To trim (el césped). || TECN. To plane, to smooth (madera). | To smooth off (cuero, metal). || MAT. To equate. || To match (la pintura). || To conclude (por un contrato): *igualar una venta*, to conclude a sale.
— V. intr. To be equal (ser igual). || To match (colores). || DEP. To equalize. || *Igualar a 2*, to bring the score to 2-2, to make it 2-2 (durante un partido), to draw 2-2 (al final de un partido).
— V. pr. To be equal, to equal each other *o* one another: *se igualan en fuerza*, they are equal in strength. || To become equal *o* the same (en magnitud). || To become level (nivelarse). || *Igualarse con uno*, to place o.s. on an equal footing with s.o.

igualatorio m. Friendly society (asociación). || Medical centre (centro médico).

igualdad f. Equality: *igualdad de oportunidades*, equality of opportunity. || Sameness: *igualdad de opiniones*, sameness of opinions. || Similarity (semejanza). || Smoothness (de la madera). || Evenness, levelness (del terreno). || Evenness, equableness (del carácter). || — DEP. *A igualdad de tanteo*, in the event of a tie. || *En igualdad de condiciones*, on equal terms. || *En un pie de igualdad*, on an equal footing. || *Igualdad de salario*, equal pay.

igualitario, ria adj./s. Equalitarian.

igualmente adv. Equally. || The same, in the same way: *las dos van igualmente vestidas*, they both dress the same. || Likewise, also (además, también). || *¡Qué te diviertas mucho! — Igualmente*, have a good time! — The same to you!

iguana f. ZOOL. Iguana.

iguanodonte m. ZOOL. Iguanodon.

ijada f. Flank (de un animal). || Loin (del hombre).

ijar m. Flank (de un animal). || Loin (del hombre).

ilación f. Illation, deduction (deducción). || Connection (enlace de las ideas). || Cohesion (de un discurso).

ilativo, va adj. Illative. || GRAM. Illative (conjunción).

ilegal adj. Illegal.

ilegalidad f. Illegality.

ilegibilidad f. Illegibility.

ilegible adj. Illegible: *firma ilegible*, illegible signature.

ilegitimar v. tr. To illegitimate.

ilegitimidad f. Illegitimacy.

ilegítimo, ma adj. Illegitimate: *hijo ilegítimo*, illegitimate son. || Illegitimate, illegal, illicit (ilícito).

íleo m. MED. Ileus (cólico).

ileocecal adj. ANAT. Ileocecal.

íleon m. ANAT. Ileum (intestino).

ilerdense adj. [Of *o* from] Lérida.
— M. y f. Native *o* inhabitant of Lérida.

ilergete adj. Of *o* from a region that comprised part of the provinces of Huesca, Zaragoza and Lérida.

ileso, sa adj. Unhurt, unscathed, unharmed, uninjured: *el conductor resultó* or *salió ileso*, the driver was unhurt; *salir ileso de un accidente*, to come out of an accident unscathed.

iletrado, da adj./s. Illiterate (analfabeto).

iliaco, ca o **ilíaco, ca** adj. ANAT. Iliac: *hueso iliaco*, iliac bone.

Ilíada n. pr. f. Iliad (de Homero).

ilicitano, na adj. [of *o* from] Elche [formerly *Ilici*].
— M. y f. Native *o* inhabitant of Elche.

ilícito, ta adj. Illicit (ilegal).

ilicitud f. Illicitness.

ilimitable adj. Unlimitable, illimitable.

ilimitado, da adj. Unlimited, limitless, illimited.

ilion m. ANAT. Ilium, iliac bone (hueso).

iliterato, ta adj. Illiterate.

ilógico, ca adj. Illogical.

ilogismo m. Illogicality, illogicalness.

ilota m. Helot (esclavo en Esparta).

ilotismo m. Helotism.

iluminación f. Illumination (acción de iluminar). || Lighting (alumbrado): *iluminación artificial, indirecta*, artificial, indirect lighting. || Floodlighting (de un estadio). || Illumination (de estampas, letras, libro). || FIG. Enlightenment. || FÍS. Illumination, illuminance. || — Pl. Illuminations.

iluminado, da adj. Illuminated. || FIG. Enlightened. || *La casa está iluminada*, the house is lit up.
— M. y f. Illuminist (visionario). || — M. pl. Illuminati.

iluminador, ra m. y f. Illuminator (de estampas).

iluminancia f. FÍS. Illuminance, illumination.

iluminar v. tr. To illuminate, to light up (alumbrar): *iluminar un monumento*, to illuminate a monument. || To light, to illuminate: *cuarto iluminado por cuatro velas*, room lit by four candles. || To illuminate (adornar con luces). || To floodlight (un estadio). || To colour, to illuminate (estampas, letras, etc.). || To illuminate (un libro, una página, etc.). || To provide [prints, engravings] with a coloured background (con fondo de color). || FIG. To illuminate, to light up: *una amplia sonrisa iluminó su rostro*, a broad smile illuminated her face. | To illuminate, to enlighten (ilustrar el entendimiento). | To illuminate, to throw light upon, to enlighten (un asunto, un problema, etc.). || To illuminate (teología).
— V. pr. To light up: *su cara se iluminó*, his face lit up.

iluminarias f. pl. Lights, illuminations.

iluminismo m. Illuminism.

ilusamente adv. Mistakenly, erroneously: *creía ilusamente en las buenas intenciones de su amigo*, he mistakenly believed in his friend's good intentions.

ilusión f. Illusion: *ilusión óptica*, optical illusion. || Dream: *su ilusión era ir a París*, his dream was to go to Paris; *vivir de ilusiones*, to live on dreams. || FIG. Thrill, pleasure, joy (alegría). | Hopefulness, hopeful anticipation (esperanza): *esperar el resultado con cierta ilusión*, to await the outcome with a certain hopefulness. || Illusion, illusory hope *o* belief, delusion (esperanza vana). || — *Con ilusión*, hopefully. || *Forjarse* or *hacerse ilusiones*, to build up one's hopes (*de*, of), to cherish hopes (*de*, of), to indulge in wishful thinking. || *Hacerse la ilusión de que*, to imagine that. || *Me hace mucha ilusión ir a Acapulco*, I'm so looking forward *o* I'm really looking forward to going to Acapulco. || *¡Qué ilusión ir esta noche al teatro!*, how thrilling to be going to the theatre tonight! || *Tener ilusión por*, to be looking forward to. || *Trabajar con ilusión*, to work with a will. || *Tu visita me hizo mucha ilusión*, I was thrilled by your visit.

ilusionar v. tr. To build up [s.o.'s] hopes, to deceive (hacer concebir esperanzas). || — *Estar ilusionado con*, to be thrilled with (presente), to be thrilled *o* excited about (futuro). || *Me ilusiona el viaje*, I'm looking forward to the journey, I'm thrilled about the journey.
— V. pr. To have hopes for: *los padres se ilusionan mucho con el primer hijo*, the parents have great hopes for their first son. || To be *o* to become thrilled *o* excited: *se ilusionó cuando le hablé del viaje*, he was thrilled when I spoke to him about the journey. || To have unfounded hopes (tener esperanzas infundadas). || *No te ilusiones mucho*, don't build your hopes too high.

ilusionismo m. Illusionism.

ilusionista m. y f. Illusionist, conjurer (prestidigitador).

iluso, sa adj. Dreamy, who indulges in flights of fancy (soñador). || Easily deceived *o* duped (inocentón).
— M. y f. Dreamer (soñador). || Dupe (inocentón).

ilusorio, ria adj. Illusory (hopes). || Imaginary (imaginario). || False, empty (promesas).

ilustración f. Erudition, learning (instrucción). || Illustration, picture (grabado). || Illustration (conjunto de grabados). || Illustrated magazine (publicación). || HIST. *La Ilustración*, the Enlightenment.

ilustrado, da adj. Erudite, cultured, learned (docto). || Illustrated (con dibujos, citas, etc.). || Enlightened: *el despotismo ilustrado*, the enlightened despotism.

ilustrador, ra adj. Illustrative.
— M. y f. Illustrator (dibujante).

ilustrar v. tr. To explain, to make clear, to enlighten: *eso me ilustró sobre sus intenciones*, that explained his intentions to me, that made his intentions clear to me. || To illustrate: *ilustrar con dibujos, con citas*, to illustrate with drawings, by means of quotations. || To make illustrious, to make famous (hacer ilustre). || To enlighten (el entendimiento).
— V. pr. To acquire knowledge (*sobre*, of). || To learn (*sobre*, about). || To become famous (personas).

ilustrativo, va adj. Illustrative.

ilustre adj. Illustrious, famous (célebre, famoso). || Distinguished.

ilustrísimo, ma adj. Most illustrious. || *Su Ilustrísima*, His Lordship, His Grace.

imagen f. Image: *imagen religiosa*, religious image. || Statue, image (p.us.): *una imagen de bronce*, a bronze statue. || Picture (en televisión). || Image (símbolo, metáfora). || Fís. Image: *imagen invertida, real, virtual*, inverted, real, virtual image. || Mental picture (en la mente). || — *Dios creó al hombre a su imagen y semejanza*, God created man after His own image and likeness. || FIG. y FAM. *Quedarse para vestir imágenes*, to be left on the shelf, to remain an old maid. || FIG. *Ser la imagen viva de*, to be a picture of: *es la imagen viva de la desesperación*, she is a picture of despair. | *Ser la viva imagen de alguien*, to be the living *o* the spitting image of s.o.
imaginable adj. Imaginable.
imaginación f. Imagination (facultad). || FIG. Fancy (fantasía). || — *Eso no es verdad, son imaginaciones tuyas*, that's not true, you're imagining things *o* it's all in your imagination. || *No se le pasó por la imaginación*, it never occurred to him. || *¡No te dejes llevar por la imaginación!*, don't let your imagination run away with you!
imaginar v. tr. To imagine. || To think up (idear).
— V. pr. To imagine: *me imagino lo que te habrá costado*, I can imagine what it must have cost you. || To picture, to imagine (representarse). || — *Imagínate lo que ha pasado hoy*, guess what happened today. || *Me imagino que sí*, I suppose so, I imagine so. || *Me lo imagino*, I can just imagine.
imaginaria f. MIL. Reserve guard.
imaginario, ria adj. Imaginary. || *Lo imaginario*, the imaginary.
imaginativo, va adj. Imaginative: *facultad imaginativa*, imaginative power.
— F. Imagination, imaginativeness (facultad de imaginar). || Common sense (sentido común).
imaginería f. REL. Religious imagery. || Embroidery (bordado).
imaginero m. [Religious] image maker.
imán m. Magnet (hierro imantado): *imán artificial*, artificial magnet. || FIG. Magnetism, charm (atractivo). || Imam, imaum (sacerdote mahometano). || *Imán de herradura*, horseshoe magnet.
imanación f. Magnetization.
imanar v. tr. To magnetize.
— V. pr. To become magnetized.
imanato m. Imanate (dignidad del imán).
imantación f. Magnetization.
imantar v. tr. To magnetize.
— V. pr. To become magnetized.
imbatible adj. Unbeatable, invincible.
imbatido, da adj. Unbeaten.
imbebible adj. Undrinkable.
imbécil adj. MED. Imbecile. || Stupid, silly (tonto).
— M. y f. MED. Imbecile. || Idiot, imbecile (tonto). || *¡Imbécil!*, you idiot!, you imbecile!
imbecilidad f. Imbecility (falta de inteligencia). || Stupidity, silliness (tontería). || *Decir imbecilidades*, to talk nonsense.
imberbe adj. Beardless.
imbibición f. Absorption, soaking-up, imbibing.
imbornal m. MAR. Scupper.
imborrable adj. Indelible, ineffaceable (indeleble). || Indelible, unforgettable: *recuerdo imborrable*, indelible memory.
imbricación f. Imbrication, overlapping.
imbricado, da adj. Imbricate, imbricated, overlapping.
imbricar v. tr. To imbricate, to overlap.
imbuido, da adj. Imbued, steeped: *imbuido de su importancia*, imbued with *o* steeped in one's own importance.
imbuir* v. tr. To imbue, to inculcate, to instil (infundir): *imbuir a uno ideas falsas*, to imbue s.o. with false ideas, to inculcate *o* to instil false ideas into s.o.
— V. pr. To become imbued *o* inculcated (*de*, with).
imitable adj. Imitable.
imitación f. Imitation. || Pastiche (en literatura). || TEATR. Imitation, impersonation. || — *A imitación de*, in imitation of. || *Bolso imitación cocodrilo*, imitation crocodile bag. || *Imitación fraudulenta*, forgery (de billetes de banco, etc.), fraudulent imitation (de cualquier cosa). || *Joyas de imitación*, imitation jewelry.
imitador, ra adj. Imitating, imitative.
— M. y f. Imitator. || Writer of pastiches (escritor).
imitamonos m. inv. FIG. Copycat.
imitar v. tr. To imitate.
imitativo, va adj. Imitative: *armonía imitativa*, imitative harmony; *artes imitativas*, imitative arts.
impaciencia f. Impatience.
impacientar v. tr. To make [s.o.] lose patience, to exasperate, to make [s.o.] impatient.
— V. pr. To grow impatient: *impacientarse por no recibir noticias*, to grow impatient at the lack of news. || To lose one's patience, to get impatient (con alguien).
impaciente adj. Impatient: *impaciente por salir*, impatient to go out. || Anxious, restless (intranquilo). || *Impaciente con* or *por la tardanza*, impatient at *o* made impatient by the delay.
impacto m. Impact: *punto de impacto*, point of impact. || Impact mark (huella). || MIL. Hit (en el blanco). || FIG. Impact: *causar un impacto*, to cause *o* to have an impact. | Incidence (repercusión).
impagable adj. Unpayable (no pagable). || FIG. Invaluable (inestimable).
impagado, da adj. Unpaid.
impago, ga adj. *Amer.* Unpaid.
impalpabilidad f. Impalpability.
impalpable adj. Impalpable.
impar adj. Odd, uneven: *número impar*, odd number. || Unpaired: *órgano impar*, unpaired organ.
imparable adj. Unstoppable (en deporte).
imparcial adj. Impartial (justo): *un juez imparcial*, an impartial judge. || Unbiased (objetivo).
imparcialidad f. Impartiality.
impartir v. tr. To impart (otorgar). || — JUR. *Impartir auxilio*, to demand assistance. || *Impartir su bendición*, to give one's blessing.
impás o **impase** m. Finesse (bridge).
impasibilidad f. Impassiveness, impassivity, impassibility.
impasible adj. Impassive, impassible (insensible).
impavidez f. Fearlessness, dauntlessness, courage (arrojo). || Impassiveness, imperturbability (impasibilidad). || *Amer.* Barefacedness, cheek (descaro).
impávido, da adj. Fearless, dauntless, courageous (atrevido). || Impassive (impasible). || *Amer.* Barefaced, insolent, cheeky (descarado). || *Recibió impávido la noticia*, he remained impassive at the news, he was unmoved by the news.
impecabilidad f. Impeccability.
impecable adj. Impeccable.
impedancia f. ELECTR. Impedance.
impedido, da adj. Disabled, crippled (tullido). || *Impedido de las dos piernas*, disabled in both legs, without the use of both legs.
— M. y f. Disabled person, cripple.
impedidor, ra adj. Preventive, preventing (que no permite). || Hindering, obstructive (que obstaculiza).
impedimenta f. MIL. Impedimenta, *pl.*
impedimento m. Prevention: *en caso de impedimento*, in case of prevention. || Hindrance, impediment, obstacle (traba). || JUR. *Impedimento dirimente*, diriment impediment.
impedir* v.tr. To prevent, to stop: *la lluvia le impidió que saliera*, the rain prevented him from going out. || To impede, to hinder (el movimiento). || To obstruct, to block (el paso). || — *Eso no impide que*, that does not alter the fact that. || *Me veo impedido para venir*, it is impossible for me to come, I'm afraid I cannot come.
impeditivo, va adj. Preventive.
impelente adj. Impellent, impelling, propelling, driving: *fuerza impelente*, impelling force. || *Bomba impelente*, force pump.
impeler v. tr. To propel, to drive forward, to impel: *el viento impelió la barca*, the wind drove the boat forward. || TECN. To drive, to propel. || FIG. To drive, to impel: *impelido a la venganza*, driven to vengeance. || *Los Cruzados, impelidos por su fe...*, the Crusaders, driven on by their faith...
impenetrabilidad f. Impenetrability.
impenetrable adj. Impenetrable: *coraza impenetrable*, impenetrable armour. || Unfathomable, impenetrable (misterio, enigma, etc.).
impenitencia f. Impenitence.
impenitente adj. Impenitent, unrepentant. || FIG. Inveterate, confirmed (bebedor, jugador). || Confirmed (criminal). || Inveterate (mentiroso).
impensable adj. Unthinkable.
impensadamente adv. Unexpectedly (llegar). || Without thinking, inadvertently, unintentionally (decir una cosa).
impensado, da adj. Unexpected (imprevisto). || Spontaneous (respuesta).
impepinable adj. FAM. Certain, sure, undeniable, beyond doubt. || FAM. *Eso es impepinable*, there's no doubt about that, that's for sure.
imperante adj. Ruling (dinastía). || Prevailing (viento, tendencia).
imperar v. intr. To reign, to rule (un emperador). || FIG. To reign: *impera una atmósfera de pesimismo*, there reigns an atmosphere of pessimism. | To prevail, to predominate: *impera el viento norte*, the north wind prevails. | To be current (precios).
imperativo, va adj. Imperious (persona). || Imperative (tono). || Imperative, imperious (urgente). || GRAM. Imperative: *modo imperativo*, imperative mood.
— M. GRAM. Imperative. || FIG. Imperative (necesidad absoluta). | Consideration, imperative: *imperativos económicos*, economic considerations.
imperatorio, ria adj. Imperatorial.
imperceptibilidad f. Imperceptibility.
imperceptible adj. Imperceptible: *sonido, diferencia imperceptible*, imperceptible sound, difference.
impercuso, sa adj. Badly struck (moneda).
imperdible adj. Unlosable, that cannot be lost.
— M. Safety pin (alfiler).
imperdonable adj. Unpardonable, unforgivable.
imperecedero, ra adj. Imperishable, undying. || FIG. Immortal, eternal (inmortal).
imperfección f. Imperfection. || Defect, fault (defecto).
imperfecto, ta adj. Imperfect. || Defective, faulty (defectuoso). || GRAM. *Pretérito imperfecto*, imperfect.
imperforación f. MED. Imperforation.

imperial adj. Imperial (del emperador, del imperio): *corona imperial*, imperial crown.
— F. Top deck, upper deck, imperial (de un carruaje).
imperialismo m. Imperialism.
imperialista adj. Imperialistic.
— M. y f. Imperialist.
impericia f. Unskilfulness (inhabilidad). || Inexperience (falta de experiencia).
imperio m. Empire: *el Sacro Imperio*, the Holy Roman Empire. || Emperorship (cargo, dignidad del emperador). || FIG. Domination, authority, power (poder). | Pride, haughtiness (orgullo). || MIL. Mess.
— Adj. Empire: *estilo Imperio*, Empire style.
imperioso, sa adj. Imperious, overbearing (persona). || Imperative, imperious: *necesidad, orden imperiosa*, imperative need, command.
imperito, ta adj. Inexpert, unskilled.
impermeabilidad f. Impermeability. || TECN. Imperviousness. | Watertightness (estanquidad).
impermeabilización f. Waterproofing.
impermeabilizar v. tr. To waterproof, to make waterproof.
impermeable adj. Impermeable, impervious. || Waterproof: *una tela impermeable*, a waterproof fabric.
— M. Raincoat, mackintosh, mac.
impermutable adj. Unexchangeable.
impersonal adj. Impersonal.
impersonalidad f. Impersonality.
impersonalizar v. tr. To use [a verb] impersonally.
impertérrito, ta adj. Imperturbable (de carácter). || Impassive, unmoved (en un momento dado).
impertinencia f. Impertinence (cualidad). || Impertinent remark (dicho). || *Con impertinencia*, impertinently.
impertinente adj. Impertinent (insolente). || Impertinent, irrelevant (no pertinente).
— M. y f. Impertinent fellow (hombre), impertinent woman (mujer). || — M. pl. Lorgnette, *sing*.
imperturbabilidad f. Imperturbability.
imperturbable adj. Imperturbable.
impétigo m. MED. Impetigo.
impetración f. Impetration, entreaty, beseeching (petición). || Impetration, obtaining by entreaty (consecución).
impetrador, ra o **impetrante** adj. Impetrating.
— M. y f. Impetrator.
impetrar v. tr. To ask for, to entreat, to beseech, to impetrate (solicitar): *impetrar la protección divina*, to impetrate divine protection. || To impetrate, to obtain by entreaty (obtener).
ímpetu m. Violence (de las olas, ataques, etc.). || Energy (brío, energía). || Impetuosity (fogosidad). || Impetus, momentum, impulse (impulso).
impetuosidad f. Violence: *la impetuosidad de un ataque*, the violence of an attack. || Impetuosity, impulsiveness (fogosidad).
impetuoso, sa adj. Violent (olas, viento, ataques, etc.). || Impetuous, impulsive (fogoso). || *Torrente impetuoso*, rushing torrent.
impiedad f. Impiety.
impío a adj. Impious, irreligious, godless (falto de fe religiosa). || Irreligious, irreverent (irreverente).
— M. y f. Infidel.
implacabilidad f. Implacability, relentlessness (del odio, de un enemigo, etc.). || Inexorability (de un juez, un adversario, etc.).
implacable adj. Implacable, relentless: *enemigo, odio implacable*, implacable enemy, hatred; *la furia implacable del mar*, the sea's relentless fury. || Inexorable: *un juez implacable*, an inexorable judge.
implantación f. Implantation (de costumbres, ideas). || Introduction (de una moda, de reformas). || MED. Implantation.
implantar v. tr. To implant (costumbres, ideas). || To introduce (una moda, reformas). || MED. To implant.
— V. pr. To be *o* to become implanted (costumbres, ideas). || To be introduced (moda, reformas).
implicación f. Implication. || Contradiction.
implicancia f. *Amer*. Legal impediment. | Incompatibility (incompatibilidad).
implicante adj. Involving, implicating (que envuelve). || Implying (que lleva en sí).
implicar v. tr. To implicate, to involve (envolver): *está implicado en un delito*, he is implicated in a crime. || To imply (llevar en sí). || To mean (entrañar): *la derrota del equipo implicaría el descenso inmediato*, the team's defeat would mean instant relegation.
implicatorio, ria adj. Implicative, implicatory.
implícitamente adv. Implicitly.
implícito, ta adj. Implicit, implied.
imploración f. Supplication, entreaty.
implorante adj. Imploring, entreating.
implorar v. tr. To implore, to beseech, to beg, to entreat: *implorar perdón*, to implore forgiveness.
implosivo, va adj. GRAM. Implosive.
implume adj. Featherless.
impolíticamente adv. Discourteously, impolitely, uncivilly (con descortesía). || Impolitically, tactlessly (sin tacto). || Impolitically, inexpediently, ill-advisedly, unwisely (con imprudencia).
impolítico, ca adj. Impolite, discourteous (descortés). || Impolitic, tactless (falto de tacto). || Inexpedient, ill-advised, unwise (imprudente): *una medida impolítica*, an inexpedient measure.
impoluto, ta adj. Unpolluted.
imponderabilidad f. Imponderability.
imponderable adj. Imponderable. || FIG. Invaluable (inapreciable).
— M. Imponderable.
imponente adj. Imposing: *persona imponente*, imposing person. || FAM. Sensational, terrific: *una chica, un coche imponente*, a sensational girl, car. || Tremendous (enorme). || *Hace un frío imponente*, it's freezing cold.
imponer* v. tr. To impose (disciplina, multa, obligación, tributo, silencio, voluntad). || To set (una tarea). || To exact, to demand (requerir). || To lay down, to impose (una condición). || FIG. To inspire (el temor). | To command (el respeto, la obediencia). | To impute [falsely] (atribuir falsamente). || To impose, to lay: *imponer las manos sobre*, to impose one's hands on. || To deposit: *imponer dinero en un banco*, to deposit money in a bank. || To give: *imponer un nombre a*, to give a name to. || To award: *imponer una condecoración a un militar*, to award a soldier a medal. || To instruct (enseñar): *imponer a uno en contabilidad*, to instruct s.o. in bookkeeping. || To acquaint, to inform: *imponer a alguien de los hechos*, to acquaint s.o. with the facts, to inform s.o. of the facts. || IMPR. To impose [type].
— V. intr. To command *o* to inspire respect (respeto). || To inspire admiration (admiración). || To inspire fear (miedo). || To be impressive *o* imposing (edificios).
— V. pr. To be imposed. || To be imperative *o* necessary (ser necesario). || To show authority (*a*, over), to assert o.s. (*a*, over), to impose one's authority (*a*, on) [hacerse obedecer]. || To command respect (*a*, from) [hacerse respetar]. || To show one's superiority (*a*, over) [mostrar su superioridad]. || To take on (comprometerse a hacer). || To get on (situarse): *imponerse por su mérito*, to get on through one's own merit. || To acquaint o.s. (*de*, with), to find out (*de*, about) [instruirse]. || To dominate: *imponerse a las circunstancias*, to dominate the circumstances. || To prevail (prevalecer).
imponible adj. Taxable: *riqueza imponible*, taxable wealth. || — *Base imponible*, taxable income. || *No imponible*, tax-free.
impopular adj. Unpopular.
impopularidad f. Unpopularity.
importable adj. Importable.
importación f. Importation, importing (acción). || — Pl. Imports (cosas importadas). || — *Bienes de importación*, imported goods. || *Licencia de importación*, import licence.
importador, ra adj. Importing: *país importador*, importing country.
— M. y f. Importer.
importancia f. Importance: *conceder* or *dar importancia a*, to attach *o* to give importance to. || Size, magnitude. || — *Darse uno importancia*, to give o.s. airs, to put on airs. || *De importancia*, important, of importance. || *De gran* or *mucha importancia*, of great importance, very important *o* significant. || *Herido de importancia*, seriously wounded. || *No tiene la menor importancia*, it's not important, it has not the slightest importance, it doesn't matter in the least. || *Sin importancia*, unimportant, insignificant.
importante adj. Important: *modificaciones importantes*, important modifications. || Considerable, sizeable: *una suma importante de dinero*, a considerable sum of money. || — *Dárselas* or *echárselas de importante*, to be full of self-importance, to think too much of o.s. || *Lo importante*, what is important, the important *o* main thing. || *Poco importante*, unimportant.
importar v. tr. To import (de un país extranjero): *importar arroz*, to import rice. || To cost (valer): *el libro importa cien pesetas*, the book costs a hundred pesetas. || To come to, to amount to: *la cuenta importa cien pesetas*, the bill comes to one hundred pesetas. || FIG. To mean, to bring about, to cause (acarrear). | To entail (llevar consigo). | To involve, to imply (implicar).
— V. intr. e impers. To be important, to be of importance: *importa hacerlo*, it is important that it be done *o* for it to be done. || To matter: *no importa lo que digas*, it doesn't matter what you say. || To interest: *lo que más me importaba de él era su erudición*, what interested me most about him was his erudition. || To concern (afectar). || — *A Juan nada le importa*, John does not care about anything. || *¿Le importaría traerme ese libro?*, would you mind bringing me that book? || FIG. y FAM. *Me importa un comino* or *tres pepinos* or *un bledo* or *un pito* or *un adarme*, I don't give a damn *o* a hang, I couldn't care less. || *No importa*, it doesn't matter, never mind. || *¿Qué importa?*, what does it matter?, what difference does it make? || *¿Y a ti qué te importa?*, what's it to you?, what's it got to do with you?, what concern is it of yours?
importe m. Price, cost (valor). || Total amount, total (total): *hasta el importe de cien pesetas*, up to

a total of a hundred pesetas. || Amount: *el importe de una factura*, the amount of a bill.
importunamente adv. Inopportunely (de manera inoportuna). || In a bothersome *o* tiresome way (de manera importuna).
importunar v. tr. To importune, to bother, to pester.
importunidad f. Importunity, importuning, pestering (molestia). || Bothersomeness, troublesomeness (pesadez). || Nuisance, bother, importunity (cosa importuna).
importuno, na adj. Inopportune, ill-timed (que no es oportuno). || Bothersome, troublesome, tiresome, trying, annoying (fastidioso). || Importunate, importune (que molesta con peticiones).
imposibilidad f. Impossibility. || Inability (de una persona).
imposibilitado, da adj. Disabled, crippled (inválido): *tras el accidente se quedó imposibilitado para toda la vida*, the accident left him crippled for life. || Prevented, unable: *estuvo imposibilitado de salir*, he was prevented from going out, he was unable to go out.
imposibilitar v. tr. To make impossible: *la lluvia imposibilitó el ataque*, the rain made attack impossible. || To prevent, to stop (impedir): *la lluvia me imposibilitó salir*, the rain prevented my going out. || To disable (físicamente).
— V. pr. To be *o* to be left disabled *o* crippled.
imposible adj. Impossible: *nada es imposible en la vida*, nothing in life is impossible; *se ha puesto imposible*, he has become impossible. || FIG. Terrible, awful (muy malo): *hacía un tiempo imposible*, the weather was terrible. || Filthy, dirty (sucio).
— M. Impossible: *pedir un imposible*, to ask the impossible. || — *Dios no pide imposibles*, you cannot expect s.o. to do the impossible. || *Hacer lo imposible*, to perform *o* to do the impossible (hacer algo que no parecía posible), to do one's utmost (hacer todo lo posible). || *¡Me parece imposible que estés aquí!*, I can hardly believe you're here! || *¡Parece imposible!*, I don't *o* I can hardly believe it!
imposición f. REL. Imposition, laying on (de manos). || Imposition (de una condición, disciplina, multa, obligación, tributo, silencio, voluntad). || Setting (de una tarea). || Deposit (cantidad en depósito). || Tax, imposition (impuesto). || IMPR. Imposition. || *Imposición de condecoraciones*, investiture.
impositivo, va adj. Tax, of taxes. || *Sistema impositivo*, taxation, tax system.
impositor m. IMPR. Typesetter.
imposta f. ARQ. Impost.
impostergable adj. Unpostponable, that cannot be put off *o* delayed.
impostor, ra m. y f. Impostor (suplantador). || Slanderer (calumniador).
impostura f. Imposture. || Slander, slur (calumnia).
impotable adj. Not drinkable, undrinkable, unsuitable for drinking.
impotencia f. Powerlessness, impotence, helplessness: *la impotencia del gobierno contra la rebelión*, the government's powerlessness in the face of the rebellion. || Inability (incapacidad). || MED. Impotence.
impotente adj. Powerless, impotent, helpless (sin fuerza suficiente). || Unable (incapaz). || MED. Impotent.
impracticabilidad f. Impracticability.
impracticable adj. Impracticable, unfeasible: *proyecto impracticable*, impracticable plan. || Impassable (carretera).
imprecación f. Imprecation, curse.
imprecar v. tr. To imprecate, to curse.
imprecatorio, ria adj. Imprecatory.
imprecisión f. Lack of precision, vagueness, imprecision (falta de precisión).
impreciso, sa adj. Imprecise, vague.
impregnable adj. That can be impregnated, impregnable.
impregnación f. Impregnation.
impregnar v. tr. To impregnate: *impregnar en* or *de*, to impregnate with. || FIG. To cover: *cara impregnada de tristeza*, face covered in sadness.
— V. pr. To become impregnated.
impremeditación f. Unpremeditation.
impremeditadamente adv. Unpremeditatedly.
impremeditado, da adj. Unpremeditated.
imprenta f. Printing (arte y actividad). || Printing house (taller). || FIG. Press: *libertad de imprenta*, freedom of the press. || Printed matter (cosas impresas). || — *Dar a la imprenta*, to send to press, to submit for printing. || *Escribir en letras de imprenta*, to print.
imprescindible adj. Essential, indispensable.
imprescriptibilidad f. Imprescriptibility.
imprescriptible adj. Imprescriptible.
impresentable adj. Unpresentable, not presentable.
impresión f. Impression, impressing, imprinting (de una marca en un sitio). || Impression, imprint (huella, marca). || IMPR. Printing. | Printing, print: *una impresión deficiente hace desagradable la lectura*, faulty print *o* a faulty printing makes for unpleasant reading. || Edition: *una impresión de veinte ejemplares*, an edition of twenty copies. || FOT. Print. || Impression: *hacerle buena, mala impresión a alguien*, to make a good, a bad impression on s.o. || Recording (en disco o en cintas magnetofónicas). || — *Cambiar impresiones con*, to exchange views with. || *Causar impresión en*, to make an impression on. || *Causar la impresión de que*, to give the impression that. || *Impresión dactilar* or *digital*, fingerprint. || *La primera impresión es la que vale*, it is the first impression that counts. || *Me da la impresión de que*, I get the impression that. || *Tener la impresión de que*, to have the impression that.
impresionabilidad f. Impressionability.
impresionable adj. Impressionable.
impresionante adj. Impressive (que causa impresión). || Amazing (sorprendente).
impresionar v. tr. To impress, to make an impression on (causar impresión). || To move, to touch (conmover): *me impresiona su generosidad*, I am touched by his generosity. || To record (los sonidos). || To cut (un disco). || FOT. To expose. || — *Quedarse bien, mal impresionado*, to have *o* to be left with a good, a bad impression. || FOT. *Rollo sin impresionar*, unexposed film.
— V. intr. To impress.
— V. pr. To be impressed. || To be moved *o* touched (conmovido).
impresionismo m. Impressionism.
impresionista m. Impressionist.
impreso, sa adj. Printed.
— M. Printed sheet *o* paper (papel). || Printed book (libro). || Form (formulario): *impreso de solicitud*, application form. || — Pl. Printed matter, *sing*.
impresor m. Printer.
imprevisible adj. Unforeseeable, unpredictable.
imprevisión f. Lack of foresight.
imprevisor, ra adj. Unforeseeing, lacking in foresight.
imprevisto, ta adj. Unforeseen, unexpected (que no se ha previsto): *suceso imprevisto*, unexpected event. || — *Lance imprevisto*, coup de théâtre. || *Lo imprevisto*, the unforeseen, the unexpected. || *Si ocurre algo imprevisto*, if anything unexpected turns up *o* happens.
— M. pl. Incidental expenses.
imprimación f. ARTES. Priming (acción de imprimar).
— OBSERV. Do not confuse with *impresión*.
imprimar v. tr. To prime (lienzos).
imprimátur m. Imprimatur.
imprimible adj. Printable.
imprimir v. tr. To impress, to imprint, to stamp (una marca). || IMPR. To print (un libro, etc.). || FIG. To impart, to transmit (comunicar): *imprimir un movimiento a un cuerpo*, to impart motion to a body. | To impress, to imprint (en la mente). | To write: *la desesperación estaba impresa en su rostro*, despair was written across his face.
— OBSERV. The past participle of *imprimir* is irregular: *impreso*. *Imprimido* is archaic.
improbabilidad f. Improbability, unlikelyhood.
improbable adj. Improbable, unlikely.
improbidad f. Improbity, dishonesty, lack of integrity.
ímprobo, ba adj. Dishonest, lacking integrity (sin probidad). || Very hard, laborious (muy duro): *labor ímproba*, very hard work. || Strenuous (esfuerzo).
improcedencia f. Unseemliness (inconveniencia). || Inappropriateness, unsuitability (inadecuación). || JUR. Irrelevancy. | Inadmissibility.
improcedente adj. Improper, unseemly (inconveniente). || Inappropriate, unsuitable (inadecuado). || JUR. Irrelevant. | Inadmissible (protesta, etc.).
improductividad f. Unproductiveness.
improductivo, va adj. Unproductive (esfuerzo, terreno). || Unproductive, unprofitable (negocio).
impromptu m. Impromptu.
impronta f. [Relief] impression (reproducción). || FIG. Impression, mark, stamp (huella).
impronunciable adj. Unpronounceable.
improperio m. Insult, abusive remark. || — Pl. REL. Reproaches. || *Llenar a uno de improperios*, to shower s.o. with abuse.
impropiedad f. Unsuitability (inadecuación). || Impropriety (de comportamiento, lenguaje, etc.). || Impropriety, incorrectness (inexactitud).
impropio, pia adj. Unsuited, unsuitable, inappropriate, improper (inadecuado): *es un sitio impropio para el cuadro*, it's an unsuitable *o* inappropriate *o* improper place for the picture, it's a place unsuited to the picture. || Unbecoming, unfitting, improper: *comportamiento impropio de su edad*, unbecoming behaviour for [a man of] his age. || Improper, incorrect (no exacto): *uso impropio de una palabra*, improper use of a word. || MAT. Improper (fracción).
improrrogable adj. That cannot be prolonged *o* extended *o* protracted.
impróvido, da adj. Unprepared, improvident.
improvisación f. Improvisation.
improvisadamente adv. Unexpectedly, without warning, suddenly.
improvisado, da adj. Improvised, impromptu: *discurso improvisado*, improvised speech. || Rough-and-ready, makeshift: *una reparación improvisada*, a makeshift repair. || MÚS. Extempore, impromptu.
improvisador, ra m. y f. Improviser.
improvisar v. tr. To improvise. || To get ready, to knock up: *improvisó una cena en un cuarto de hora*, she got some dinner ready in a quarter of an hour. || MÚS. To extemporize.

improviso, sa adj. Unforeseen, unexpected. || — *Al* or *de improviso*, unexpectedly, suddenly, without warning. || *Coger de improviso*, to catch unawares.
improvisto, ta adj. Unforeseen, unexpected. || — *A la improvista*, unexpectedly, suddenly, without warning. || *De improvisto*, unexpectedly, suddenly.
imprudencia f. Imprudence. || Indiscretion (indiscreción). || JUR. *Imprudencia temeraria*, negligence.
imprudente adj. Imprudent, unwise (poco juicioso). || Rash (atrevido, peligroso). || Careless (conductor, etc.). || Indiscreet (indiscreto).
impúber o **impubero, ra** adj. Impubic, under the age of puberty.
— M. y f. Child under the age of puberty.
impublicable adj. Unpublishable, unprintable.
impudencia f. Impudence (al hablar). || Shamelessness, immodesty, impudence (desvergüenza).
impudente adj. Impudent (en el habla). || Shameless, immodest, impudent (desvergonzado).
impudicia o **impudicicia** f. Impudicity, immodesty (falta de pudor). || Shamelessness (desvergüenza).
impúdico, ca adj. Immodest. || Shameless (desvergonzado).
impudor m. Impudicity, immodesty (falta de pudor). || Shamelessness (desvergüenza).
impuesto, ta adj. Imposed. || FIG. *Estar impuesto de* or *en*, to be acquainted with *o* informed of.
— M. Tax (tributo): *impuesto de utilidades* or *sobre la renta*, income tax; *impuesto territorial*, land tax; *exento de impuesto*, free of tax. || Rate, tax (sobre una propiedad). || Duty (derecho): *impuesto del timbre*, stamp duty. || — *Gravar con un impuesto*, to levy a tax on, to impose a tax on. || *Impuesto concertado*, composition tax. || *Impuesto de circulación*, Road [Fund] tax. || *Impuesto degresivo*, degressive taxation. || *Impuesto de lujo*, luxury tax. || *Impuesto de plusvalía*, capital gains tax. || *Impuesto sobre los espectáculos públicos*, entertainment tax. || *Impuesto sobre sucesiones*, death tax *o* duty.
impugnable adj. Impugnable, refutable (refutable). || Challengeable, contestable, impugnable (que puede combatirse). || JUR. Challengeable, contestable.
impugnación f. Impugnment, impugnation, refutation (refutación). || Challenge, contestation, impugnment. || JUR. Challenge, challenging, contestation.
impugnador, ra adj. Impugning, refuting (refutador). || Challenging, contesting, opposing, impugning. || JUR. Challenging.
— M. y f. Refuter.
impugnante adj. V. IMPUGNADOR.
impugnar v. tr. To challenge, to contest, to oppose (combatir). || To refute, to impugn: *impugnar un argumento*, to refute an argument. || JUR. To challenge, to contest (una sucesión, un jurado).
impugnativo, va adj. Impugning, challenging. || Refuting.
impulsar v. tr. To impel, to drive forward (empujar). || FIG. To impel, to drive (incitar). | To promote, to give an impulse to: *impulsar el comercio*, to promote trade.
impulsión f. Impulsion. || TECN. Drive (empuje). | Momentum, impetus (fuerza existente). | Impulse: *impulsión específica*, specific impulse. | Impulse (corriente). || FIG. Impulse (impulso).
impulsividad f. Impulsiveness, impulsivity.
impulsivo, va adj. Impulsive.
impulso m. Impulse, impulsion, thrust, push, drive: *el impulso del émbolo se transmite a las ruedas de la locomotora por medio de las bielas*, the piston thrust is transmitted to the wheels of the locomotive through the connecting rods. || Momentum, impetus: *el gran impulso del coche hizo que no pudiera detenerse a tiempo*, the car's momentum prevented it from stopping in time. || FIG. Impulse, prompting: *impulsos del corazón*, promptings of the heart. || Impulse (en fisiología). || RAD. Pulse. || ELECTR. Impulse. || — *A impulsos de*, driven by, prompted by. || *En el impulso del momento*, on the spur of the moment. || *Hacer una cosa llevado por un impulso*, to do sth. on impulse. || *Por propio impulso*, on one's own initiative. || *Tomar impulso*, to [take a] run up (deportes).
impulsor, ra adj. TECN. Impelling, driving. || Instigating.
— M. Instigator.
impune adj. Unpunished: *el crimen quedó impune*, the crime went unpunished.
impunemente adv. With impunity.
impunidad f. Impunity.
impureza f. Impurity. || FIG. Immorality, impurity.
impurificar v. tr. To adulterate, to make impure.
impuro, ra adj. Impure. || FIG. Immoral, impure.
imputabilidad f. Imputability.
imputable adj. Imputable, chargeable.
imputación f. Imputation, charge.
imputador, ra adj. Imputing, who imputes.
— M. y f. Imputer.
imputar v. tr. To impute, to charge with (acusar). || To impute, to attribute (atribuir). || COM. To allocate, to assign (asignar).
imputrescibilidad f. Imputrescibility (de la carne, de la fruta). || Rot resistance (de la madera).
imputrescible adj. Imputrescible, imperishable (la carne, la fruta). || Rotproof (la madera).

inabarcable adj. Too wide, too large: *un programa inabarcable*, too wide a programme.
inabordable adj. Unapproachable, inaccessible.
inacabable adj. Interminable, endless.
inaccesibilidad f. Inaccessibility. || Unapproachability, inaccessibility (de una persona).
inaccesible adj. Inaccessible. || Unapproachable, inaccessible (persona). || FIG. Prohibitive, inaccessible (precio).
inacción f. Inaction, inactivity.
inacentuado, da adj. Unaccented, unaccentuated, unstressed.
inaceptable adj. Unacceptable.
inacostumbrado, da adj. Unaccustomed.
inactividad f. Inactivity.
inactivo, va adj. Inactive.
inadaptable adj. Inadaptable, unadaptable.
inadaptación f. Maladjustment. || Failure to adjust.
inadaptado, da adj. Maladjusted.
— M. y f. Misfit.
inadecuación f. Inadequacy (insuficiencia). || Unsuitability (impropiedad).
inadecuado, da adj. Unsuitable, inappropriate (inapropiado). || Inadequate (insuficiente).
inadmisibilidad f. Inadmissibility. || Intolerability. || Incredibility (incredibilidad). || JUR. Irreceivability.
inadmisible adj. Inadmissible. || Intolerable (intolerable). || Incredible (increíble). || JUR. Irreceivable (demanda).
inadoptable adj. Unadoptable.
inadvertencia f. Inadvertence, inadvertency, inattention. || Inadvertence, oversight (error). || *Por inadvertencia*, inadvertently.
inadvertidamente adv. Inadvertently.
inadvertido, da adj. Unnoticed, unobserved, unseen (no visto). || Inadvertent, inattentive (distraído). || *Pasar inadvertido*, to escape notice, to pass unnoticed.
inagotable adj. Inexhaustible (bondad, fuente, mina, paciencia, etc.). || Endless (conversación). || Tireless, indefatigable: *un atleta inagotable*, a tireless athlete.
inaguantable adj. Unbearable, intolerable.
inalámbrico, ca adj. Wireless (telégrafo).
in albis adv. FAM. V. ALBIS.
inalcanzable adj. Unreachable, unattainable. || Beyond [s.o.'s] understanding *o* grasp *o* reach: *concepto inalcanzable para el hombre medio*, concept beyond the grasp of the average man.
inalienabilidad f. Inalienability.
inalienable adj. Inalienable.
inalterabilidad f. Inalterability, unalterability. || Unchangingness, immutability (de un paisaje, un régimen político). || Fastness (de un color). || FIG. Impassivity (de una persona, un rostro, etc.). | Immutability (de la serenidad, etc.). | Constancy (de una amistad). | Imperishability (de alimentos).
inalterable adj. Inalterable, unalterable. || Unchanging, immutable (paisaje, régimen político). || Permanent, fast (color). || FIG. Impassive (persona, rostro, etc.). | Immutable (serenidad). | Undying (amistad). | Imperishable (alimentos).
inalterado, da adj. Unaltered. || Unchanged (paisaje, régimen político). || FIG. Impassive, unmoved (persona, rostro, etc.). | Unaffected: *alimentos inalterados por el calor*, foodstuffs unaffected by the heat.
inamovible adj. Irremovable.
inamovibilidad f. Irremovability.
inane adj. Inane, empty, insubstantial.
inanición f. MED. Inanition. || Starvation: *morir de inanición*, to die of starvation.
inanidad f. Inanity, emptiness, insubstantiality.
inanimado, da adj. Inanimate.
inánime adj. Lifeless: *cuerpo inánime*, lifeless body.
inapagable adj. Inextinguishable. || FIG. Unquenchable (sed). | Inextinguishable (pasión).
inapelable adj. Without appeal, unappealable.
inapercibido, da adj. Unperceived, unnoticed.
— OBSERV. This word is a Gallicism for *inadvertido*.
inapetencia f. Inappetence, lack of appetite.
inapetente adj. Inappetent, having no appetite.
inaplazable adj. Unpostponable, undeferable. || Urgent, pressing: *necesidad inaplazable*, pressing need.
inaplicable adj. Inapplicable.
inaplicación f. Lack of application.
inaplicado, da adj. Slack (desaplicado).
inapolillable adj. Mothproof (tejido).
inapreciable adj. Inappreciable, imperceptible: *diferencia inapreciable*, imperceptible difference. || Inestimable, invaluable (inestimable).
inapropiado, da adj. Inappropriate.
inaprovechado, da adj. Unused. || Undeveloped (tierras).
inaptitud f. Incapability, inaptitude (incapacidad). || Unsuitability (inadecuación).
inapto, ta adj. Incapable (incapaz). || Unsuitable (*para*, for), unsuited (*para*, to) [inadecuado].
inarmonía f. Inharmony.
inarmónico, ca adj. Inharmonic, inharmonious.
inarrugable adj. Crease-resistant (ropa).
inarticulado, da adj. Inarticulate.
in articulo mortis adv. In articulo mortis.
inasequible adj. Out of reach (fuera del alcance). || Unattainable (ambición, esperanza). || Unapproachable, inaccessible (persona). || Prohibitive,

inaccessible (precio). || Incomprehensible (incomprensible). || *Conceptos inasequibles al entendimiento*, concepts beyond comprehension.
inasimilable adj. Unassimilable.
inasistencia f. Absence.
inastillable adj. Shatterproof (cristal).
inatacable adj. Unattackable, unassailable (posición). || FIG. Irrefutable (teoría). || Incorrodible (metal).
inatención f. Inattention. || Discourtesy (descortesía).
inaudible adj. Inaudible.
inaudito, ta adj. Unheard-of (nunca oído). || Unprecedented, extraordinary (extraordinario). || Outrageous (ultrajante).
inauguración f. Inauguration. || Unveiling (de una estatua). || Opening (de una reunión). || — *Inauguración de una casa particular*, housewarming. || *Inauguración de una exposición de arte*, varnishing day, vernissage.
inaugurador, ra adj. Inaugurating.
— M. y f. Inaugurator.
inaugural adj. Inaugural, opening: *discurso inaugural*, inaugural speech. || MAR. Maiden (viaje).
inaugurar v. tr. To inaugurate, to open: *inaugurar una escuela*, to inaugurate a school. || To open (una exposición). || To unveil (una estatua). || *Inaugurar una casa particular*, to have a housewarming.
inaveriguable adj. Unascertainable (hecho, resultado).
inca adj./s. Inca. || — M. (Ant.). Inca [Peruvian gold coin].
incaico, ca adj. Inca, Incan.
incalculable adj. Incalculable.
incalificable f. Unqualifiable. || Indescribable, unspeakable (crimen).
incambiable adj. Unchangeable (situación). || Unexchangeable (mercancías).
incandescencia f. Incandescence. || *Lámpara de incandescencia*, incandescent lamp.
incandescente adj. Incandescent.
incansable adj. Tireless, indefatigable, untiring.
incansablemente adj. Tirelessly, indefatigably.
incantable adj. Unsingable.
incapacidad f. Incapacity, incapability. || Incapacity, unfitness: *incapacidad para gobernar*, incapacity to govern. || Incapacity, inefficiency, inability, incompetence (incompetencia). || Disability (física). || FIG. Dullness, stupidity (rudeza). || JUR. *Incapacidad legal*, legal incapacity, disability.
incapacitado, da adj. JUR. Incapacitated. | Disqualified (sujeto a interdicción).
incapacitar v. tr. To incapacitate, to make unfit, to disqualify: *su edad le incapacita para la guerra*, his age incapacitates him for war. || To incapacitate, to disable: *incapacitado por la enfermedad*, incapacitated by illness. || JUR. To incapacitate, to declare incapable.
incapaz adj. Incapable: *incapaz de matar una mosca*, incapable of harming a fly. || Incapable, unfit: *incapaz de gobernar*, incapable of *o* unfit for governing, unfit to govern. || Incapable, inefficient, incompetent (incompetente). || JUR. Incompetent, incapable. || *Amer*. Unbearable, insufferable (fastidioso).
— M. y f. *Es un incapaz*, he's good for nothing.
incasable adj. Unmarriable, unmarriageable.
incásico, ca adj. Inca, Incan.
incautación f. JUR. Seizure, confiscation.
incautamente adv. Incautiously, unwarily.
incautarse v. pr. JUR. To seize, to confiscate: *la policía se incautó de todos los ejemplares del libro*, the police seized all copies of the book.
incauto, ta adj. Incautious, unwary (imprudente). || Gullible (fácil de engañar).
incendajas f. pl. Kindling, *sing*. (para prender fuego).
incendiado, da adj. Which is on fire, burning (que arde). || Burnt-out (destruido por un incendio).
incendiar v. tr. To set on fire, to set fire to, to set alight.
— V. pr. To catch fire.
incendiario, ria adj. Incendiary (bomba, persona). || FIG. Incendiary, inflammatory: *discurso incendiario*, incendiary speech. || *Mirada incendiaria*, fiery glance (con enfado).
— M. y f. Incendiary.
incendio m. Fire: *provocar un incendio*, to start a fire. || FIG. Fire (de las pasiones). || — *Incendio premeditado*, arson, fire-raising. || *Los damnificados por un incendio*, the fire victims.
incensar* v. tr. REL. To cense, to incense. || FIG. To flatter (lisonjear).
incensario m. Censer, thurible, incensory. || FAM. *Romperle a uno el incensario en las narices*, to shower flattery *o* praise upon s.o., to butter s.o. up.
incensurable adj. Irreproachable, uncriticizable, not open to criticism (conducta, defecto, etc.).
incentivo m. Incentive (estímulo): *el interés es un incentivo potente*, interest is a powerful incentive. || Attraction (atractivo). || *El incentivo de la ganancia*, the lure *o* incentive of gain.
incertidumbre f. Uncertainty, incertitude.
incesable o **incesante** adj. Incessant, unceasing, uninterrupted.
incesantemente adv. Incessantly, unceasingly.
incesto m. Incest.
incestuoso, sa adj. Incestuous.
incidencia f. Incident (incidente). || Fís. Incidence: *ángulo de incidencia*, angle of incidence. || FIG. Repercussion, implication, consequence (consecuencia). || *Por incidencia*, by chance, accidentally.
incidental adj. Incidental: *observación incidental*, incidental remark. || GRAM. Parenthetic (oración).
— F. GRAM. Parenthetic clause.
incidentalmente adv. Incidentally, in passing.
incidente adj. Fís. y JUR. Incident. || Incidental.
— M. Incident: *un incidente diplomático*, a diplomatic incident. || *Una vida llena de incidentes*, a life full of incident.
incidentemente adv. Incidentally, in passing.
incidir v. intr. To fall (*en*, into) [una falta, un error]. || Fís. To fall, to strike: *el rayo incide en la superficie con un ángulo de 45 grados*, the ray falls upon *o* strikes the surface at an angle of 45 degrees. || To affect: *el impuesto incide más en nosotros*, the tax affects us worst. || To influence (influir). || MED. To make an incision, to incise.
incienso m. Incense. || Frankincense (término bíblico). || FIG. Flattery, incense [lisonja]. || FIG. *Echar incienso a*, to flatter.
inciertamente adv. Uncertainly.
incierto, ta adj. Uncertain, doubtful (dudoso). || Unsteady: *con mano incierta*, with [an] unsteady hand. || Hesitant (paso). || Unsettled (tiempo). || Indistinct (perfil). || Unknown (desconocido).
incineración f. Incineration. || Cremation (de cadáveres).
incinerador m. Incinerator.
incinerar v. tr. To incinerate. || To cremate (cadáveres).
incipiente adj. Dawning: *el día incipiente*, the dawning day. || Budding: *un poeta incipiente*, a budding poet. || Incipient: *parálisis incipiente*, incipient paralysis.
incircunciso, sa adj. Uncircumcised.
incircunscrito, ta adj. Uncircumscribed.
incisión f. Incision. || Caesura (en un verso).
incisivo, va adj. Incisive (diente). || Incisive, incisory (instrumento). || FIG. Incisive, biting, trenchant.
— M. Incisor (diente).
inciso, sa adj. Jerky (estilo).
— M. GRAM. Incidental clause (frase corta). | Comma (coma). | Sub-subparagraph. || *A modo de inciso*, in passing, incidentally.
incisura f. MED. Incision.
incitación f. Incitation, incitement: *incitación al crimen*, incitement to crime.
incitador,ra adj. Inciting.
— M. y f. Inciter.
incitamento o **incitamiento** m. Incitement.
incitante adj. Inciting. || Provocative (provocativo).
incitar v. tr. To incite, to stir (estimular): *incitar al pueblo a la rebelión*, to incite the people to rebellion. || FIG. To incite, to urge: *incitar al gasto*, to urge to spend. | To encourage (animar).
incitativo, va adj. Inciting.
incivil adj. Rude, uncivil (grosero).
incivilidad f. Incivility, rudeness.
incivilizable adj. Uncivilizable.
incivilizado, da adj. Uncivilized.
inclasificable adj. Unclassifiable, nondescript.
inclaustración f. Entry into a convent *o* monastery.
inclemencia f. Inclemency.
inclemente adj. Inclement.
inclinación f. Inclination, inclining, slanting, sloping, tilting (acción). || Inclination, slant, slope (posición oblicua). || Inclination, bow (saludo con la cabeza). || Nod (señal de asentimiento). || Pitch, slant, slope (de un tejado). || List (de un barco). || ASTR. Inclination. || Gradient, incline, slope, inclination (ferrocarriles, carretera). || GEOL. Dip. || Fís. Dip, inclination: *inclinación magnética*, magnetic dip. || FIG. Inclination, propensity, tendency (propensión). | Inclination, penchant, liking (afición): *tener inclinación hacia la música*, to have an inclination towards *o* a penchant for music. || FIG. *De malas inclinaciones*, evilly inclined.
inclinador, ra o **inclinante** adj. Inclining, slanting, sloping.
inclinar v. tr. To incline, to slant, to slope, to tilt (ladear). || To bow, to bend: *árbol inclinado por el viento*, tree bowed by the wind. || To incline, to bow (saludar con la cabeza). || To nod (asentar con la cabeza). || FIG. To incline, to induce, to dispose: *razones que me inclinan a aceptar*, reasons which incline me to accept. || *Plano inclinado*, inclined plane (en un dibujo), incline (pendiente).
— V. intr. To lean, to slope: *inclinar a* or *hacia la derecha*, to lean to the right.
— V. pr. To lean, to slope, to slant, to incline: *inclinarse hacia adelante*, to lean forward. || To stoop down, to bend down (para coger algo del suelo). || To bow (al saludar). || MAR. To list. || — *Inclinarse a*, to be inclined to: *me inclino a creerle*, I'm inclined to believe him; to be similar to, to resemble (parecerse). || FIG. *Inclinarse ante*, to bow to.
ínclito, ta adj. Illustrious.
incluido, da adj. Included: *todo está incluido*, everything is included. || Enclosed (en cartas). || — *Precio todo incluido*, inclusive *o* all-in price. || *Todo incluido*, all *o* everything included, all in.
incluir* v. tr. To include (en precios, en una lista, etc.). || To enclose (en cartas). || To insert (introducir).

|| To contain (contener). || To comprise (comprender). || *Sin incluir*, not including, not included.
inclusa f. Foundling home.
inclusero, ra adj. *Niño inclusero*, foundling.
— M. y f. Foundling.
inclusión f. Inclusion. || (P.us.). Friendship (amistad). || *Con inclusión de*, including.
inclusivamente o **inclusive** adv. Inclusive: *de domingo a sábado inclusive*, Sunday to Saturday inclusive. || — *Hasta el lunes inclusive*, up to and including Monday. || *Los niños inclusive*, including the children, the children included.
inclusivo, va adj. Inclusive.
incluso, sa adj. Included (en precios, una lista, etc.). || Enclosed: *la carta inclusa*, the enclosed letter.
— Adv. Including, included: *todos vinieron incluso los niños*, everyone came, including the children *o* the children included. || Even: *incluso le hablé*, I even talked to him.
incoación f. Inchoation, commencement, inception.
incoado, da adj. JUR. Inchoate.
incoagulable adj. Incoagulable.
incoar v. tr. To commence, to initiate, to begin (empezar). || To initiate, to institute: *incoar expediente contra*, to initiate proceedings against.
incoativo, va adj. Inchoate, inchoative, incipient, inceptive, initial (que empieza). || Inchoative (verbo).
incobrable adj. Irrecoverable.
incoercibilidad f. Incoercibility.
incoercible adj. Incoercible.
incógnita f. MAT. Unknown, unknown quantity: *despejar la incógnita*, to find the unknown quantity. || FIG. Mystery (cosa misteriosa). | Hidden motive (razón oculta).
incógnito, ta adj. Unknown: *regiones incógnitas*, unknown regions.
— M. Incognito: *guardar el incógnito*, to preserve one's incognito. || *De incógnito*, incognito: *viajar de incógnito*, to travel incognito.
incognoscible adj. Not knowable, unknowable.
incoherencia f. Incoherence, incoherency.
incoherente adj. Incoherent.
íncola m. Inhabitant.
incoloro, ra adj. Colourless [U.S., colorless]. || FIG. Colourless [U.S., colorless], dull, insipid.
incólume adj. Unharmed, unhurt, safe [and sound].
incombustibilidad f. Incombustibility.
incombustible adj. Incombustible.
incomestible adj. Inedible, uneatable.
incomible adj. Uneatable, inedible.
incomodar v. tr. To inconvenience, to incommode (causar incomodidad). || To annoy, to vex, to anger (disgustar). || To bother, to annoy, to trouble, to pester, to incommode (fastidiar).
— V. pr. To get angry *o* vexed *o* annoyed (enfadarse). || To bother, to put o.s. out, to trouble o.s.: *no te incomodes, que lo haré yo*, don't bother, I'll do it.
incomodidad f. Discomfort, uncomfortableness (falta de comodidad). || Inconvenience, annoyance, bother, nuisance (molestia). || Discontent, displeasure (disgusto). || Unrest, uneasiness (malestar). || Vexation (desazón). || Inconvenience, discomfort (inconveniente): *una casa con muchas incomodidades*, a house with many inconveniences.
incómodo, da adj. Uncomfortable: *calor incómodo*, uncomfortable heat; *postura incómoda*, uncomfortable position; *silla incómoda*, uncomfortable chair; *encontrarse incómodo en una silla*, to feel uncomfortable in a chair. || Uncomfortable, awkward, ill at ease: *me siento incómodo en su compañía*, I feel uncomfortable in his company. || Awkward, cumbersome (que abulta mucho). || Bothersome (molesto).
incomparable adj. Incomparable (sin puntos comunes). || Incomparable, matchless, beyond compare (sin par).
incomparado, da adj. Incomparable.
incomparecencia f. JUR. Default, nonappearance (ausencia). || DEP. Walk over.
incompartible adj. Unsharable, unshareable.
incompasivo, va adj. Incompassionate, unsympathetic (sin compasión). || Incompassionate, merciless, pitiless (cruel).
incompatibilidad f. Incompatibility: *incompatibilidad de caracteres*, incompatibility of character.
incompatible adj. Incompatible.
incompetencia f. Incompetence.
incompetente adj./s. Incompetent.
incompleto, ta adj. Incomplete. || Unfinished: *la Sinfonía Incompleta*, the Unfinished Symphony.
incomprehensible adj. Incomprehensible.
incomprendido, da adj. Misunderstood. || Unappreciated (no apreciado).
— M. y f. Misunderstood person. || *El poeta era un gran incomprendido*, the poet was grossly misunderstood.
incomprensibilidad f. Incomprehensibility.
incomprensible adj. Incomprehensible.
incomprensión f. Incomprehension.
incomprensivo, va adj. Incomprehensive.
incompresibilidad f. Incompressibility.
incompresible o **incomprimible** adj. Incompressible.
incomprobable adj. Unverifiable.
incomunicabilidad f. Incommunicability.
incomunicable adj. Incommunicable.
incomunicación f. JUR. Solitary confinement. || Lack of communication (falta de comunicación). || Isolation (aislamiento).
incomunicado, da adj. Incommunicado, in solitary confinement (preso). || Isolated, cut off, without means of communication (aislado): *varios pueblos quedaron incomunicados después del terremoto*, several towns remained cut off after the earthquake.
incomunicar v. tr. To place in solitary confinement (a un preso). || To cut off, to deprive of [means of] communication, to isolate (aislar). || To shut off (una habitación).
— V. pr. To cut *o* to shut o.s. off, to isolate o.s.
inconcebible adj. Inconceivable.
inconciliable adj. Inconciliable, irreconcilable.
inconcluso, sa adj. Unfinished.
inconcuso, sa adj. Indubitable, unquestionable, undeniable, incontrovertible.
incondicional adj. Unconditional. || Absolute, unfailing (amistad, obediencia, etc.). || Staunch (adepto, amigo). || Unquestioning, total (fe). || Wholehearted (apoyo).
— M. y f. Staunch follower *o* supporter.
inconexión f. Disconnection (falta de conexión). || Incoherence.
inconexo, xa adj. Disconnected, unconnected (sin conexión). || Incoherent.
inconfesable adj. Unconfessable, shameful, disgraceful, unspeakable (vergonzoso).
inconfeso, sa adj. Unconfessed (reo).
inconformista m. y f. Nonconformist.
inconfortable adj. Uncomfortable.
inconfundible adj. Unmistakable. || Unique (único).
incongelable adj. Uncongealable, unfreezable.
incongruencia f. Incongruence, incongruity, incongruousness (cualidad de incongruente). || Incongruity (cosa incongruente).
incongruente adj. Incongruent, incongruous: *respuesta incongruente*, incongruous reply.
incongruidad f. Incongruity.
incongruo, grua adj. Incongruous, incongruent (incongruente). || REL. Inadequate [emolument]. | Who does not receive an adequate emolument [priest].
inconmensurabilidad f. Incommensurability.
inconmensurable adj. Incommensurable. || MAT. Incommensurate. || FAM. Immense, vast, enormous (inmenso). | Fantastic, marvellous, great (fantástico).
inconmovible adj. Firm, solid (cimientos). || Firm (amistad, principios). || Inexorable (ante súplicas). || Unshakable, unyielding (ante amenazas).
inconmutabilidad f. Immutability. || Incommutability.
inconmutable adj. Immutable (inmutable). || Incommutable (no conmutable).
inconquistable adj. Unconquerable, invincible. || Impregnable (fuerte, castillo, etc.). || FIG. Incorruptible. | Unyielding (que no se deja convencer).
inconsciencia f. Unconsciousness (de un acto). || Unconsciousness (pérdida del conocimiento). || Unawareness, unconsciousness: *inconsciencia del riesgo*, unawareness of the risk. || Thoughtlessness, irresponsibility (irreflexión).
inconsciente adj. Unconscious. || Unconscious: *dejar inconsciente a uno*, to knock s.o. unconscious. || Unconscious, unaware: *inconsciente del peligro*, unaware of the danger. || Thoughtless, irresponsible (irreflexivo). || Subconscious (subconsciente).
inconsecuencia f. Inconsistency (falta de concordancia): *inconsecuencia entre los principios y la conducta*, inconsistency between principles and conduct. || Inconsequence, inconsistency (falta de lógica). || Inconsistency (acción inconsecuente).
inconsecuente adj. Inconsistent: *inconsecuente en sus ideas políticas*, inconsistent in one's political ideas. || Inconsequent, inconsequential (sin lógica).
— M. y f. Inconsistent person.
inconsideración f. Inconsiderateness, thoughtlessness (cualidad). || Inconsiderate act (acción).
inconsistencia f. Inconsistency (de una sustancia). || FIG. Insubstantiality: *la inconsistencia de un argumento*, the insubstantiality of an argument.
inconsistente adj. Inconsistent (sustancia). || FIG. Insubstantial: *argumento inconsistente*, insubstantial argument.
inconsolable adj. Unconsolable, inconsolable.
inconstancia f. Inconstancy. || Inconstancy, fickleness (de una persona).
inconstante adj. Inconstant. || Inconstant, fickle (que cambia de opinión, etc.). || Changeable, variable (tiempo).
— M. y f. Fickle person.
inconstitucional adj. Unconstitutional.
inconstitucionalidad f. Unconstitutionality.
inconstruible adj. Inconstructible.
inconsulto, ta adj. *Amer.* Inconsiderate.
inconsútil adj. Seamless.
incontable adj. Countless, innumerable (muy numeroso): *incontables granos de arena*, countless grains of sand. || Untellable (que no puede ser narrado).
incontaminado, da adj. Uncontaminated, unpolluted.

incontenible adj. Unrestrainable, uncontrollable, irrepressible (cólera, risa). || Uncheckable, unrestrainable, uncontrollable (ímpetu). || Uncontrollable (llanto). || Uncontainable (alegría, entusiasmo).
incontestabilidad f. Incontestability, indisputability.
incontestable adj. Incontestable, indisputable, unquestionable (indiscutible). || Undeniable (innegable).
incontestado, da adj. Uncontested, unquestioned, undisputed. || Undenied (no negado). || Unanswered (pregunta).
incontinencia f. Incontinence. || Incontinence, unchastity (falta de castidad). || MED. *Incontinencia de orina*, incontinence of urine.
incontinente adj. Incontinent. || Incontinent, unchaste (falto de castidad). || MED. Incontinent.
— Adv. Instantly, immediately.
incontinenti adv. Instantly, immediately, forthwith.
incontrarrestable adj. Irresistible: *la incontrarrestable furia del viento*, the wind's irresistible fury.
incontrastable adj. Indisputable, undeniable, unquestionable (indiscutible). || Invincible, unconquerable (invencible). || Unshakable, unyielding (que no cede).
incontrito, ta adj. Uncontrite.
incontrolable adj. Uncontrollable.
incontrovertible adj. Incontrovertible, uncontrovertible, indisputable.
incontrovertido, da adj. Undisputed, uncontroverted.
inconvencible adj. Inconvincible.
inconveniencia f. Inconvenience, disadvantage: *ésas son las inconveniencias de tener tantos hijos*, those are the inconveniences of having so many children. || Unsuitability, inappropriateness (inoportunidad). || Inadvisability (imprudencia). || Impropriety, unseemliness, indecorousness (indecoro). || Crude *o* coarse remark (grosería). || Insolent remark, insolence (insolencia).
inconveniente adj. Inconvenient: *llegó a una hora inconveniente*, he arrived at an inconvenient time. || Unsuitable, inappropriate (inapropiado). || Inadvisable (imprudente). || Improper, unseemly, indecorous (poco decoroso): *conducta inconveniente*, improper behaviour. || Impolite, uncivil (descortés). || Coarse, crude (grosero).
— M. Objection: *no tengo inconveniente en que usted salga*, I've no objection to your going out. || Drawback, disadvantage (desventaja). || Obstacle (dificultad). || Trouble, difficulty: *el inconveniente es que sea tan tarde*, the trouble is that it is too late. || *¿Tienes algún inconveniente en venir?*, do you mind coming?
inconvertible adj. Inconvertible.
incoordinación f. Incoordination.
incordiar v. tr. FAM. To bother, to pester. || *¡No incordies!*, behave yourself!, don't be such a nuisance! (¡no seas molesto!).
incordio m. MED. Bubo. || FIG. y FAM. Nuisance, bother (molestia, persona molesta).
incorporable adj. Incorporable.
incorporación f. Incorporation (acción de incorporar). || Sitting-up (en la cama). || MIL. Induction.
incorporado, da adj. Incorporated. || Sitting up (en la cama). || TECN. Built-in.
incorporal adj. Incorporeal. || Impalpable (al tacto).
incorporar v. tr. To incorporate: *incorporar Saboya a Francia*, to incorporate Savoy with France; *incorporar artículos en una lista*, to incorporate items in *o* into a list. || To mix (ingredientes). || MIL. To induct. || *Incorporar a uno*, to help s.o. to sit up (en la cama).
— V. pr. To incorporate. || To join (una sociedad, un regimiento, etc.). || To sit up (cuando se está acostado): *se incorporó en la cama*, he sat up in his bed. || — MIL. *Incorporarse a filas*, to join the ranks. || *Incorporarse a su cargo*, to start one's job (por primera vez), to go back to one's job (volver).
incorporeidad f. Incorporeity.
incorpóreo, a adj. Incorporeal.
incorrección f. Incorrectness, inaccuracy (inexactitud). || Impropriety, unseemliness: *la incorrección de su conducta*, the impropriety of his behaviour. || Discourtesy (descortesía). || Impropriety (acción). || *Cometiste una grave incorrección*, that was very rude of you, that was a very improper thing for you to do.
incorrecto, ta adj. Incorrect, inaccurate (inexacto). || Improper, indecorous, incorrect (conducta). || Impolite, discourteous (descortés).
incorregibilidad f. Incorrigibility.
incorregible adj. Incorrigible: *pereza incorregible*, incorrigible laziness.
incorruptibilidad f. Incorruptibility.
incorruptible adj. Incorruptible.
incorrupto, ta adj. Uncorrupted, incorrupt (no podrido): *el cuerpo incorrupto del santo*, the uncorrupted body of the saint. || FIG. Uncorrupted, incorrupt (moralmente). || Pure, chaste (mujer).
incredibilidad f. Incredibility.
incredulidad f. Incredulity. || REL. Unbelief.
incrédulo, la adj. Incredulous. || REL. Unbelieving.
— M. y f. Unbeliever.
increíble adj. Incredible, unbelievable.
incrementar v. tr. To increase: *incrementar una renta, las exportaciones*, to increase an income, exports. || To promote: *incrementar las relaciones económicas*, to promote economic relations.
incremento m. Increase: *el incremento de una renta*, the increase of an income. || Growth: *el incremento de un negocio*, the growth of a business. || MAT. Increment. || *Incremento térmico*, rise in temperature.
increpación f. Rebuke.
increpador, ra adj. Scolding, rebuking.
increpar v. tr. To scold, to rebuke (reñir). || To insult (insultar).
incriminable adj. Chargeable, accusable.
incriminación f. Incrimination. || Charge, accusation (acusación).
incriminar v. tr. To incriminate, to accuse: *su prueba incriminó al médico*, his evidence incriminated the doctor.
inconsiderado, da adj. Inconsiderate, thoughtless (irreflexivo). || Hasty, rash (precipitado).
— M. y f. Inconsiderate person.
incrustación f. Incrustation, inlay. || Incrustation (con una costra). || Scale (depósito en una caldera).
incrustar v. tr. To incrust, to inlay: *incrustado con piedras preciosas*, incrusted with gems. || To incrust (cubrir con una costra). || FIG. To engrave: *incrustado en la mente*, engraved upon the mind.
— V. pr. To embed itself: *la bala se le incrustó en el cerebro*, the bullet embedded itself in his brain. || To scale (una caldera). || FIG. To dig o.s. in. || FIG. *Incrustarse algo en la cabeza*, to get sth. into one's head.
incubación f. Incubation: *período de incubación*, incubation period.
incubador, ra adj. Incubative.
— F. Incubator.
incubar v. tr. To incubate (los huevos). || MED. To be getting, to be sickening for, to incubate: *estoy incubando las paperas*, I'm getting the mumps. || FIG. To hatch (tramar).
— V. intr. To incubate.
incuestionable adj. Unquestionable, indisputable.
inculcación f. Inculcation.
inculcador, ra m. y f. Inculcator.
inculcar v. tr. To inculcate, to instil [U.S., to instill]. || IMPR. To compose [type] too close together.
inculpabilidad f. Inculpability, guiltlessness, blamelessness. || JUR. *Veredicto de inculpabilidad*, verdict of not guilty.
inculpable adj. Inculpable, guiltless, blameless.
inculpación f. Inculpation (acción de inculpar). || Accusation, charge (cosa de que se acusa a alguien).
inculpado, da adj./s. Accused.
inculpar v. tr. To accuse (*de*, of), to charge (*de*, with) [acusar]. || To inculpate, to incriminate, to accuse (incriminar).
incultivable adj. Uncultivable, uncultivatable.
inculto, ta adj. Uncultured, uneducated (sin cultura). || Uncouth, coarse (tosco). || Unrefined (poco refinado). || Uncultivated, untilled (terreno).
— M. y f. Ignoramus.
incultura f. Lack of culture, ignorance (falta de cultura). || Uncouthness (tosquedad).
incumbencia f. Line, province, field: *la crítica teatral no es de mi incumbencia*, theatre criticism is not in my line *o* is not my province. || Incumbency, obligation, duty (obligación). || JUR. Jurisdiction.
incumbir v. tr. To be incumbent on *o* upon, to be the duty *o* the obligation of: *te incumbe a ti*, it is incumbent on you, it is your duty. || JUR. To be within the jurisdiction (*a*, of).
incumplido, da adj. Unfulfilled.
incumplimiento m. Nonfulfilment (de un deber). || Failure to keep: *incumplimiento de la palabra dada*, failure to keep one's word. || Nonexecution (de una orden). || Nonobservance (de un reglamento). || Breach (de un contrato, de una promesa).
incumplir v. tr. Not to fulfill, to fail to fulfill. || To break (contrato, compromiso): *incumplir una promesa*, to break a promise. || To fail to observe (una regla), to fail to carry out (una orden).
incunable adj. Incunabular.
— M. Incunable, incunabulum. || — Pl. Incunabula.
incurabilidad f. Incurability.
incurable adj. Incurable. || FIG. Irremediable, hopeless, incurable.
— M. y f. Incurable: *hospital de incurables*, home for incurables.
incuria f. Carelessness, negligence.
incurrir v. intr. To incur: *incurrir en la desgracia del rey, en castigo, en odio*, to incur the king's disfavour, punishment, hatred. || To fall: *incurrir en un error*, to fall into error. || To commit: *incurrir en falta, en delito*, to commit a fault, a crime. || *Incurrir en olvido*, to forget.

— OBSERV. The verb *incurrir* has an irregular past participle: *incurso*.

incursión f. Incursion, raid. || *Incursión aérea*, air raid
incurso, sa adj. Guilty, culpable.
indagación f. Investigation, inquiry. || JUR. Inquiry, inquest.
indagador, ra adj. Investigating, inquiring
— M. y f. Investigator.
indagar v. tr. To investigate, to inquire into (investigar): *indagar las causas de la explosión*, to investigate the causes of the explosion.

indagatorio, ria adj. JUR. Investigatory. || *Comisión indagatoria*, board of inquiry.
— F. JUR. Unsworn statement.
indebidamente adv. Unduly. || Wrongly (injustamente). || Improperly, unduly (desconsideradamente). || Unlawfully, illegally (ilegalmente).
indebido, da adj. Undue. || Improper, undue (desconsiderado): *una respuesta indebida*, an improper answer. || Unlawful, illegal, undue (ant.) [ilegal].
indecencia f. Indecency. || Obscenity (obscenidad). || *Su vestido es una indecencia*, her dress is indecent.
indecente adj. Indecent, obscene: *vestido indecente*, indecent dress; *película, lenguaje indecente*, obscene film, language. || FIG. Foul, wretched (muy malo): *fue una comida indecente*, it was a foul meal. | Miserable: *tiene un salario indecente*, he has a miserable wage. | Squalid, wretched (miserable): *viven en un cuartucho indecente*, they live in a squalid little room. || — *Es una persona indecente*, he is a wretched sort. || *La casa está indecente de polvo*, the house is terribly dusty.
indecible adj. Unspeakable, inexpressible, indescribable. || *He sufrido lo indecible*, I can't tell you how I've suffered.
indecisión f. Indecision, irresolution, hesitancy.
indeciso, sa adj. Undecided, not yet determined: *los resultados de la elección son todavía indecisos*, the election results are still undecided. || Indecisive: *batalla indecisa*, indecisive battle. || Indecisive, irresolute, hesitant (que vacila): *hombre indeciso*, irresolute man. || Indistinct, vague (contorno).
indeclarable adj. Undeclarable.
indeclinable adj. GRAM. Indeclinable, undeclinable. || That cannot be declined *o* refused, unavoidable (que no se puede rechazar).
indecoro m. Indecorum, indecorousness, unseemliness. || Indecency, immodesty (indecencia).
indecoroso, sa adj. Indecorous, unseemly. || Indecent, immodest: *vestido indecoroso*, indecent dress.
indefectibilidad f. Indefectibility.
indefectible adj. Indefectible, unfailing.
indefectiblemente adv. Indefectibly, unfailingly. || *Y llevará indefectiblemente el traje azul oscuro*, and he'll be wearing the inevitable dark blue suit.
indefendible o **indefensible** adj. Indefensible.
indefenso, sa adj. Defenceless [U.S., defenseless]. || Helpless (desamparado).
indefinible adj. Indefinable, undefinable.
indefinido, da adj. Indefinite: *límite, período de tiempo indefinido*, indefinite boundary, period of time. || GRAM. Indefinite: *artículo, adjetivo, pronombre indefinido*, indefinite article, adjective, pronoun.
indeformable adj. That keeps its shape.
indehiscente adj. BOT. Indehiscent.
indelebilidad f. Indelibility.
indeleble adj. Indelible.
indeliberación f. Indeliberation.
indeliberado, da adj. Unintentional, indeliberate (no intencionado). || Irreflexive (irreflexionado).
indelicadeza f. Indelicacy.
indelicado, da adj. Indelicate: *fue un acto muy indelicado invitarnos y no invitaros a vosotros*, it was very indelicate of them to invite us and not you. || Unscrupulous (falto de escrúpulo).
indemne adj. Unhurt, unharmed, uninjured (persona). || Undamaged (cosa).
indemnidad f. Indemnity, insurance (seguridad). || Indemnity, immunity (inmunidad).
indemnizable adj. That can be indemnified.
indemnización f. Indemnification (acción de indemnizar). || Indemnity, compensation (compensación). || *Indemnización por despido*, severance pay.
indemnizado, da adj. Indemnified, compensated.
indemnizar v. tr. To indemnify, to compensate.
indemorable adj. That cannot be deferred (pago) *o* postponed (mitin, viaje, etc.).
indemostrable adj. Indemonstrable, undemonstrable.
independencia f. Independence. || — *Con independencia de*, independently of. || *Conseguir la independencia*, to gain independence.
independiente adj./s. Independent.
independientemente adv. Independently. || Irrespectively, regardless (aparte de, además de).
independista adj./s. Independent.
independizar v. tr. To make independent, to free.
— V. pr. To become independent.
indescifrable adj. Indecipherable. || FIG. Impenetrable.
indescriptible adj. Indescribable.
indeseable adj./s. Undesirable.
indesmallable adj. Ladderproof, runproof (medias).
indesmontable adj. Noncollapsible: *cama indesmontable*, noncollapsible bed.
indestructibilidad f. Indestructibility.
indestructible adj. Indestructible.
indeterminable adj. Indeterminable, undeterminable.
indeterminación f. Indetermination.
indeterminado, da adj. Indeterminate (indefinido). || Imprecise, vague: *contornos indeterminados*, vague outlines. || Indeterminate, irresolute (persona). || GRAM. Indefinite (artículo, pronombre).
indeterminismo m. Indeterminism.
indeterminista adj./s. Indeterminist.
índex m. Index, index finger, forefinger (dedo índice).
India n. pr. f. GEOGR. India.
indiada f. *Amer*. Crowd *o* group of Indians. | Typically Indian saying (dicho) *o* action (acto).
indiana f. Printed calico (tela).
indianismo m. Indianism.
indianista m. y f. Indianist.
indiano, na adj./s. Latin American (natural de América). || West Indian (antillano). || — M. Spanish emigrant returned from Latin America. || FIG. Spanish emigrant who returns to Spain after having made a fortune in Latin America.

— OBSERV. *Indiano* is better replaced by *indio* when meaning a native of Latin America.

Indias n. pr. f. pl. GEOGR. Indies: *Indias Occidentales, Orientales*, West, East Indies.

— OBSERV. At the time of the colonization *Indias* was the term used to designate America. The name is still to be found in the denomination of such institutions as *los Archivos de Indias, el Consejo de Indias*, etc.

indicación f. Indication, sign (señal). || Suggestion: *fui a ese dentista por indicación de tu padre*, I went to that dentist at your father's suggestion. || Hint (clave). || Directions, *pl.*: *le pregunté el camino del museo pero me dio una falsa indicación*, I asked him the way to the museum but he gave me the wrong directions. || Note: *una indicación al margen*, a note in the margin. || Direction, instruction: *indicaciones sobre el manejo de una máquina*, directions for the use of a machine. || Remark, observation (observación).
indicado, da adj. Suitable, good (adecuado): *la persona más indicada para la tarea*, the best *o* the most suitable person for the job; *el día más indicado*, the best *o* the most suitable day. || Recommended, advised (aconsejado). || — *En el momento menos indicado*, at the worst possible moment. || *Tú eres el menos indicado para protestar*, you are the last person who should complain. || *Un comentario poco indicado*, an inopportune comment. || *Un sitio muy indicado para descansar*, a very good place *o* an ideal place to go for a rest. || *Un traje indicado para la ocasión*, a dress suited to *o* suitable for the occasion.
indicador, ra adj. Indicating, indicatory. || *Lámpara indicadora*, warning light.
— M. Indicator. || Store guide (en un almacén). || — AUT. *Indicador de carretera*, road sign. | *Indicador de dirección*, indicator (en general), trafficator (mecánico), indicator, flasher, blinker, winker (intermitente). || *Indicador de escape de gas*, [gas-] leak detector. || *Indicador de fichero*, file divider (para clasificar). || *Indicador de horarios*, timetable (de trenes). || AUT. *Indicador del nivel de aceite, del nivel de gasolina*, [oil] dipstick, petrol gauge [U.S., fuel gauge]. | *Indicador de presión del aceite*, oil-pressure gauge. | *Indicador de velocidad*, speedometer.
indicar v. tr. To point out, to show: *indicar el camino a uno*, to show s.o. the way. || To indicate, to tell: *indíqueme lo que piensa de esto*, tell me what you think about this. || To indicate, to denote, to betoken (revelar): *un gesto que indica impaciencia*, a gesture that indicates impatience. || To advise (aconsejar). || To indicate, to suggest, to intimate: *les indicó que su presencia no era grata*, he indicated that their presence was undesirable. || To show, to read (un termómetro). || TECN. To indicate, to register, to show (un indicador). || — *A la hora indicada*, at the scheduled *o* specified time. || *Indicar con el dedo*, to point out. || *Indicar el día*, to name the day.
indicativo, va adj./s.m. Indicative.
indicción f. Indiction. || Convocation.
índice m. Indication, sign, index (indicio). || Index, table (tabla). || Table of contents, index (de un libro). || Catalogue, index (de una biblioteca). || Index finger, index, forefinger (dedo de la mano). || Pointer, needle, hand (de un cuadrante), index, gnomon (de un reloj de sol). || FÍS. y MAT. Index: *índice de refracción*, refractive index. || Percentage: *índice de alcohol*, percentage of alcohol. || Rate (coeficiente): *índice de natalidad*, birth rate; *índice de incremento*, rate of increase. || Index: *índice del coste de vida*, cost-of-living index; *índice de precios*, price index. || REL. Index: *meter* or *poner en el Índice*, to put on the Index. || — *Índice de compresión*, compression ratio. || AUT. *Índice de octano*, octane number.
— Adj. Index (dedo).
indiciar v. tr. To indicate (indiçar). || To suspect (sospechar).
indicio m. Indication, sign: *es indicio de mala educación*, it is a sign of bad manners. || Trace: *descubrir indicios de albúmina*, to discover traces of albumin. || Trace, sign: *no hay el menor indicio del libro*, there is no sign of the book. || JUR. Piece of evidence. || — Pl. JUR. Evidence, *sing*.
indicioso, sa adj. Suspicious.
índico, ca adj. Indian: *Océano Índico*, Indian Ocean.
indiferencia f. Indifference.
indiferente adj. Indifferent: *dejar indiferente*, to leave indifferent. || Indifferent, apathetic (apático). || *Me es indiferente el color que escojas*, the colour you choose is indifferent to me, it makes no difference to me *o* it's all the same to me *o* it's immaterial to me what colour you choose.
indiferentismo m. Indifferentism.
indígena adj. Indigenous (*de*, to), native (*de*, of).
— M. y f. Native.

indigencia f. Poverty, destitution, need, indigence: *estar en la indigencia más completa,* to be in direst poverty.
indigenismo m. Indianism [Latin-American politico-literary movement in favour of the Indians].
indigenista adj./s. Indigenist.
indigente adj. Destitute, poverty-stricken, needy, poor, indigent.
— M. y f. *Los indigentes,* the needy, the poor.
indigestarse v. pr. To cause *o* to give indigestion (producir indigestión). || To get indigestion (tener indigestión). || — *La comida se me indigestó,* the meal gave me indigestion. || FIG. y FAM. *Se me indigesta ese tío,* I can't stomach that fellow.
indigestibilidad f. Indigestibility.
indigestión f. Indigestion.
indigesto, ta adj. Undigested (no digerido). || Indigestible (difícil de digerir). || FIG. Unbearable (persona). || *Estar* or *sentirse indigesto,* to have indigestion.
indignación f. Indignation, anger.
indignado, da adj. Indignant, angry.
indignante adj. Infuriating, outrageous (que indigna).
indignar v. tr. To infuriate, to anger, to make angry *o* indignant, to rouse to indignation.
— V. pr. To be *o* to get indignant, to feel indignation: *indignarse por algo, con alguien,* to get indignant at *o* about sth., with s.o. || *¡Es para indignarse!,* it's infuriating!, it's maddening!
indignidad f. Unworthiness (cualidad de indigno). || Indignity (afrenta). || Dirty trick (canallada).
indigno, na adj. Unworthy (*de,* of). || Contemptible, despicable (merecedor de desprecio).
índigo m. Indigo (color, planta).
indilgar v. tr. V. ENDILGAR.
indino, na adj. FAM. Mischievous, naughty (travieso). | Bad (malo).
indio, dia adj./s. Indian (de la India, de América). || — FIG *En fila india,* in single file, in Indian file. || FAM. *Hablar como los indios,* to speak pidgin Spanish [*o* English, etc.], to speak broken Spanish [*o* English, etc.]. | *Hacer el indio,* to act the fool (hacer el tonto).
— M. Indium (metal).
indiófilo, la adj. Who admires the Indians and their customs.
indirecta f. Allusion, insinuation, hint: *tirar* or *soltar una indirecta,* to drop a hint. || — FAM. *Indirecta del padre Cobos,* broad hint. || *Lanzaron* or *tiraron indirectas sobre la infidelidad de su esposa,* they alluded to *o* insinuated *o* hinted at his wife's infidelity.
indirecto, ta adj. Indirect.
indiscernible adj. Indiscernible, imperceptible.
indisciplina f. Indiscipline, lack of discipline.
indisciplinado, da adj. Undisciplined, unruly.
indisciplinarse v. pr. To become undisciplined *o* unruly.
indiscreción f. Indiscretion (acto). || Tactless remark (dicho). || — *Cometer la indiscreción de,* to be so tactless as to. || *Si no es indiscreción,* without being indiscreet.
indiscreto, ta adj. Indiscreet, tactless.
— M. y f. Indiscreet person.
indisculpable adj. Inexcusable, unpardonable, unforgivable.
indiscutible adj. Indisputable, unquestionable, incontrovertible: *prueba indiscutible,* incontrovertible proof. || Undisputed: *jefe, verdad indiscutible,* undisputed leader, truth.
indisolubilidad f. Indissolubility.
indisoluble adj. Indissoluble.
indispensable adj. Indispensable, essential.
indisponer* v. tr. To indispose, to make unwell, to upset (hacer enfermar). || FIG. *Indisponer a una persona con otra,* to set a person against another.
— V. pr. To become indisposed, to fall ill (ponerse enfermo). || FIG. *Indisponerse con uno,* to fall out with s.o.
indisponibilidad f. Unavailability.
indisponible adj. Unavailable.
indisposición f. Indisposition.
indispuesto, ta adj. Indisposed, slightly ill, unwell (ligeramente enfermo). || *Está indispuesto con su hermano,* he has fallen out with his brother, he is on bad terms with his brother.
indisputable adj. Indisputable, unquestionable.
indistinguible adj. Indistinguishable, undistinguishable.
indistintamente adv. Indistinctly (poco claramente). || Indifferently (indiferentemente).
indistinto, ta adj. Indistinct.
individuación f. Individuation.
individual adj. Individual. || Single: *habitación individual,* single room.
— M. Singles, *pl.* (tenis): *individual caballeros,* men's singles.
individualidad f. Individuality.
individualismo m. Individualism.
individualista adj. Individualistic.
— M. y f. Individualist.
individualización f. Individualization.
individualizar v. tr. To individualize.
individuar v. tr. To individuate.
individuo, dua adj. Individual.
— M. Individual (ser, vegetal o animal). || Member (de una corporación, de una academia). || Member, fellow (de una sociedad). || FAM. Individual, fellow, person (hombre indeterminado). || *Cuidar bien de su individuo,* to take good care of o.s.
indivisibilidad f. Indivisibility.
indivisible adj. Indivisible.
indivisión f. Indivision. || JUR. Co-ownership, joint ownership.
indiviso, sa adj. JUR. Undivided, joint: *bienes indivisos,* joint estate.
Indo n. pr. m. GEOGR. Indus.
indo, da adj./s. Hindu (cuya religión es el hinduismo). || Indian (indio).
indócil adj. Indocile, headstrong, unruly (difícil de educar). || Disobedient (desobediente).
indocilidad f. Indocility, unruliness.
indoctamente adv. Ignorantly.
indocto, ta adj. Unlearned, uneducated, ignorant.
indocumentado, da adj. Without [identification] papers.
— M. y f. Person without identification papers. || FAM. *Es un indocumentado,* he's a duffer.
Indochina n. pr. f. GEOGR. Indochina.
indochino, na adj./s. Indochinese, Indo-Chinese.
indoeuropeo, a adj./s. Indo-European.
indofenol m. QUÍM. Indophenol.
indogermánico, ca adj./s. Indo-Germanic.
índole f. Nature, disposition: *de índole perezosa,* of a lazy disposition. || Kind, sort: *regalos de toda índole,* gifts of all kinds. || Nature: *dada la índole de nuestra revista,* given the nature of our magazine. || *Personas de la misma índole,* people of the same stamp, birds of a feather (fam.).
indolencia f. Indolence.
indolente adj. Indolent.
— M. y f. Idler.
indoloro, ra adj. Indolent, painless.
indomable adj. Untamable (animal). || Unbreakable (caballo). || Ungovernable, unsubmissive, unruly (pueblo). || Ungovernable, unmanageable, uncontrollable, unruly (niño). || Uncontrollable, indomitable (pasión). || Indomitable (orgullo, valor).
indomado, da adj. Untamed, wild (animal). || Unbroken (caballo). || Uncontrolled (pasión).
indomeñable adj. Untamable (animal). || Ungovernable, unruly (pueblo). || Uncontrollable, indomitable (pasión).
indomesticable adj. Untamable.
indomesticado, da adj. Undomesticated, untamed, wild.
indómito, ta adj. Untamed (no domado). || Untamable (indomesticable). || Unsubmissive, unruly (persona).
Indonesia n. pr. f. GEOGR. Indonesia.
indonesio, sia adj./s. Indonesian.
Indostán n. pr. m. GEOGR. Hindustan. || India.
indostanés, esa o **indostano, na** adj./s. Hindustani.
indostaní m. Hindustani (lengua).
indostánico, ca adj. (P.us.). Hindustani.
indubitable adj. Indubitable, doubtless, certain.
indubitado, da adj. Certain, doubtless.
inducción f. Induction. || ELECTR. *Bobina* or *carrete de inducción,* induction coil.
inducido, da adj. ELECTR. Induced.
— M. Armature.
inducidor, ra adj. Inducing.
— M. y f. Inducer.
inducimiento m. Inducement.
inducir* v. tr. To lead: *inducir a error,* to lead into error. || To induce, to lead (mover a): *condiciones que habían inducido a mucha gente a emigrar,* conditions which had induced many people to emigrate. || To induce, to infer (inferir). || ELECTR. To induce.
inductancia f. ELECTR. Inductance.
inductivo, va adj. Inductive.
indúctil adj. Fís. Inductile.
inductor, ra adj. Inducing. || ELECTR. Inductive.
— M. y f. Inducer. || — M. ELECTR. y QUÍM. Inductor.
indudable adj. Indubitable, doubtless, certain. || *Es indudable que,* there is no doubt that.
indulgencia f. Indulgence, leniency. || REL. Indulgence: *indulgencia plenaria,* plenary indulgence.
indulgenciar v. tr. REL. To indulgence.
indulgente adj. Indulgent, lenient: *indulgente con* or *hacia,* indulgent towards, lenient with.
indultar v. tr. To pardon (de una pena). || To excuse, to exempt (de una obligación, de un pago).
indulto m. Mercy (compasión). || Reprieve, pardon (de un reo). || Exemption (de un pago). || Indult (concedido por el Papa).
indumentaria f. Clothing, clothes, *pl.*, garments, *pl.* (ropa). || Historical study of costume (estudio). || *Lleva la indumentaria más extravagante que te puedas imaginar,* he dresses up in the most extravagant garb *o* apparel imaginable.
indumento m. Clothing, clothes, *pl.*, garments, *pl.*
induración f. MED. Induration.
indurar v. tr. To indurate.
industria f. Industry: *industria clave,* key industry; *industria pesada,* heavy industry; *industria siderúrgica,* iron and steel industry.
industrial adj. Industrial.
— M. Industrialist, industrial.

industrialismo m. Industrialism.
industrialización f. Industrialization.
industrializar v. tr. To industrialize.
— V. pr. To become industrialized.
industriar v. tr. To instruct, to train.
— V. pr. To find means *o* a way: *industriarse para conseguir algo*, to find means *o* a way of obtaining sth., to find a way to obtain sth. || To manage, to get along *o* by (arreglárselas).
industrioso, sa adj. Industrious (trabajador, diligente). || Ingenious, skilful [U.S., skillful] (ingenioso).
inecuación f. MAT. Inequation, inequality.
inédito, ta adj. Unpublished. || FIG. Unknown (desconocido).
ineducable adj. Ineducable.
ineducación f. Impoliteness, unmannerliness, ill-breeding (malos modales). || Lack of education (falta de educación).
ineducado, da adj. Impolite, unmannerly, ill-bred (mal educado). || Uneducated (sin educar).
inefabilidad f. Ineffability, inexpressibility.
inefable adj. Ineffable, inexpressible, indescribable.
ineficacia f. Inefficacy, ineffectiveness.
ineficaz adj. Inefficacious, inefficient, ineffective, ineffectual.
ineficiencia f. Inefficiency.
ineficiente adj. Inefficient.
inejecutable adj. Inexecutable. || MÚS. Unperformable, uninterpretable, unplayable.
inejecución f. Inexecution, non-execution.
inelegancia f. Inelegance, inelegancy.
inelegibilidad f. Ineligibility.
inelegible adj. Ineligible.
ineluctable adj. Ineluctable, inevitable, inescapable.
ineludible adj. Ineludible, inescapable.
inembargable adj. JUR. Not attachable *o* distrainable *o* seizable.
inenarrable adj. Indescribable, inexpressible.
inencogible adj. Nonshrink.
inepcia o **ineptitud** f. Inability (incapacidad). || Ineptitude, inaptitude, incompetence (incompetencia). || Ineptitude, foolishness (necedad).
inepto, ta adj. Incapable (incapaz). || Inept, inapt, incompetent (incompetente). || Unsuitable, inapt (inadecuado). || Inept, foolish, preposterous (necio).
— M. y f. Incompetent, dead loss (fam.).
inequívoco, ca adj. Unequivocal, unmistakable: *inequívocas señales de embriaguez*, unmistakable signs of inebriation.
inercia f. TECN. Inertia. || Inertia, lifelessness (falta de vivacidad). || *Fuerza de inercia*, inertial force.
inerme adj. BOT. y ZOOL. Without prickles or spines. || Unarmed (sin armas). || Defenceless (sin defensa).
inerte adj. Inert. || Inert, lifeless (falto de energía o vivacidad). || Inert (gas).
inervación f. Innervation.
inervar v. tr. To innervate.
Inés n. pr. f. Agnes.
inescrutabilidad f. Inscrutability.
inescrutable o **inescudriñable** adj. Inscrutable (insondable): *los caminos del Señor son inescrutables*, the ways of the Lord are inscrutable.
inesperadamente adv. Unexpectedly.
inesperado, da adj. Unexpected, unforeseen.
inestabilidad f. Instability.
inestable adj. Unstable, instable, unsteady.
inestético, ca adj. Inaesthetic.
inestimable adj. Inestimable, invaluable. || *De inestimable valor*, priceless.
inestimado, da adj. Unestimated, unappraised (no tasado). || Underestimated (subestimado).
inevitabilidad f. Inevitability.
inevitable adj. Inevitable, unavoidable.
inexactitud f. Inexactitude, inexactness, inaccuracy (falta de precisión). || Inexactitude, incorrectness (falsedad).
inexacto, ta adj. Inexact, inaccurate (impreciso). || Inexact, incorrect (erróneo). || Untrue (falso).
inexcusable adj. Inexcusable, unforgivable (imperdonable). || Inevitable, unavoidable (inevitable).
inexcusabilidad f. Inexcusability.
inexigibilidad f. Nonexigibility.
inexigible adj. Inexigible.
inexistencia f. Inexistence, nonexistence.
inexistente adj. Nonexistent, inexistent.
inexorabilidad f. Inexorability.
inexorable adj. Inexorable.
inexperiencia f. Inexperience (falta de experiencia). || Unskilfulness, inexpertness (falta de habilidad).
inexperimentado, da adj. Inexperienced.
inexperto, ta adj. Inexperienced (falto de experiencia). || Inexpert (falto de habilidad).
inexpiable adj. Inexpiable.
inexpiado, da adj. Unexpiated.
inexplicable adj. Inexplicable.
inexplicado, da adj. Unexplained.
inexplorable adj. Unexplorable.
inexplorado, da adj. Unexplored. || Uncharted (indicación en un mapa).
inexplotable adj. Unexploitable.
inexplotado, da adj. Unexploited.
inexpresable adj. Inexpressible.
inexpresivo, va adj. Inexpressive.
inexpugnable adj. Inexpugnable, impregnable.
inextensible adj. Inextensible.
inextenso, sa adj. Unextended.
in extenso loc. adv. In extenso, at full length.
inextinguible adj. Inextinguishable. || Unquenchable (sed). || Eternal (amor).
inextirpable adj. Inextirpable, ineradicable.
in extremis loc. adv. In extremis.
inextricable adj. Insolvable, inextricable (problema). || Inextricable (laberinto). || Impenetrable.
infalibilidad f. Infallibility: *infalibilidad pontificia*, papal infallibility.
infalible adj. Infallible. || Certain, sure, inevitable: *éxito infalible*, certain success.
infaliblemente adv. Infallibly. || Certainly, surely (seguramente).
infalsificable adj. Unfalsifiable. || Unforgeable (moneda).
infamador, ra adj. Defamatory, slanderous.
— M. y f. Slanderer, defamer (difamador). || Discreditor, detractor (el que desacredita).
infamante adj. Shameful (castigo).
infamar v. tr. To defame, to slander, to infame (ant.) [difamar, ofender]. || To discredit, to dishonour [U.S., to dishonor] (desacreditar).
infamatorio, ria adj. Defamatory, slanderous (que difama). || Discrediting (que desacredita).
infame adj. Infamous, odious, wicked, vile (vil). || Infamous (de mala fama). || FIG. Vile, foul, odious: *tiempo infame*, vile weather. | Thankless, odious (tarea).
— M. y f. Infamous *o* wicked person.
infamia f. Infamy.
infancia f. Infancy, childhood. || Children, *pl.* (niños). || FIG. Infancy (principio): *en la infancia del mundo*, in the world's infancy. || — *En la primera infancia*, in one's early childhood. || *Ha vuelto a la infancia*, he is in his second childhood. || FIG. *No estás en la primera infancia*, you're not a child any more.
infanta f. Infanta, princess (hija del rey o esposa de un infante). || Infant, little girl (niña).
infantado m. Appanage, apanage, territory assigned to an infante *or* to an infanta.
infante m. Infante, prince (hijo del rey). || Infant, little boy (niño). || Infantryman (soldado).
infantería f. MIL. Infantry: *infantería motorizada*, motorized infantry. || MIL. *La infantería de marina*, the marines, *pl.*
infanticida adj. Infanticidal.
— M. y f. Infanticide, child killer.
infanticidio m. Infanticide (asesinato).
infantil adj. Infantile: *enfermedad infantil*, infantile disease. || Child's: *tamaño infantil*, child's size. || Infantile, childish (aniñado): *comportamiento infantil*, infantile behaviour. || Childlike: *una cara infantil*, a childlike face. || — *Literatura infantil*, children's literature. || DEP. *Prueba para infantiles*, infants' *o* children's event.
infantilidad f. Childishness (niñería).
infantilismo m. Infantilism (anormalidad).
infanzón, ona m. y f. Nobleman *o* noblewoman [member of the lowest rank of the nobility].
infarto m. MED. Infarct: *infarto del miocardio, pulmonar*, infarct of the myocardium, of the lungs. | Engorgement (hinchazón).
infatigable adj. Indefatigable, tireless, untiring.
infatuación f. Conceit, vanity, pride (engreimiento).
infatuar v. tr. To make conceited.
— V. pr. To become conceited: *infatuarse con un éxito*, to become conceited about one's success.
infausto, ta adj. Unfortunate, unlucky, unhappy.
infebril adj. Without fever, feverless.
infección f. Infection.
infeccionar v. tr. To infect (inficionar).
infeccioso, sa adj. Infectious: *una enfermedad infecciosa*, an infectious disease.
infectar v. tr. To infect: *herida infectada*, infected wound.
— V. pr. To become infected.
infecto, ta adj. Infected, contaminated. || Foul (repugnante).
infecundidad f. Infecundity, sterility (esterilidad).
infecundo, da adj. Infertile, infecund, barren, sterile (suelo). || Infecund, sterile (mujeres).
infelice adj. POÉT. Unfortunate, unhappy (infeliz).
infelicidad f. Unhappiness, misfortune, infelicity.
infeliz adj. Unhappy, unfortunate (desgraciado). || Miserable, wretched (miserable). || FAM. Good-natured, kind-hearted (bondadoso). | Gullible (inocente).
— M. y f. Poor devil. || FAM. Good-natured fellow. | Simpleton (inocentón).
infelizote m. Good-natured fellow (buena persona). || Simpleton (inocentón).
inferencia f. Inference.
inferior adj. Lower: *la mandíbula inferior*, the lower jaw; *la parte inferior*, the lower part. || Inferior: *este libro es inferior al otro*, this book is inferior to the other; *de calidad inferior*, of inferior quality; *no ser inferior a nadie*, to be inferior to none. || Less: *veinte es inferior a treinta*, twenty is less than thirty. || — *El lado inferior*, the underside, the underneath. || *Una cantidad inferior*, a lesser *o* smaller quantity. || *Un número inferior a treinta*, a number under thirty *o* less than thirty.

— M. Inferior.
inferioridad f. Inferiority: *complejo de inferioridad*, inferiority complex.
inferir* v. tr. To infer, to deduce (sacar una conclusión): *de ello infiero que*, from this I infer that. || To cause: *inferir daños*, to cause damage. || To inflict (una herida).
infernáculo m. Hopscotch (juego).
infernal adj. Infernal. || FIG. Devilish, infernal: *niño infernal*, devilish child; *un ruido infernal*, an infernal din *o* racket. || — *Fuego infernal*, hellfire. || *Máquina infernal*, infernal machine.
infernillo m. Stove.
infestar v. tr. To infest (causar estragos). || To overrun, to swamp, to invade (llenar). || To infect (corromper).
infeudar v. tr. To enfeoff (enfeudar).
inficionar v. tr. To infect (infectar). || To contaminate (contaminar). || FIG. To corrupt: *inficionar a la juventud con malos ejemplos*, to corrupt youth by bad examples.
infidelidad f. Infidelity, unfaithfulness: *infidelidad conyugal*, infidelity in marriage. || REL. Unbelief. | Infidels, *pl.*, unbelievers, *pl.* (los infieles).
infiel adj. Unfaithful: *marido infiel*, unfaithful husband; *persona infiel con* or *a* or *para con sus promesas*, person unfaithful to his promises. || Disloyal, faithless: *un amigo infiel*, a disloyal friend. || Inaccurate, inexact: *nos dio una versión infiel de lo que pasó*, he gave us an inaccurate version of what happened. || REL. Infidel, unbelieving. || FIG. *La memoria me fue infiel*, my memory failed me.
— M. y f. REL. Infidel, unbeliever.
infiernillo m. Stove: *infiernillo de alcohol*, spirit stove.
infierno m. Hell: *ir al infierno*, to go to hell. || FIG. y FAM. Hell. || TECN. Tank [in olive production]. || — Pl. MIT. Hades. || — FAM. *¡Anda* or *vete al infierno!*, go to hell! || FIG. *El camino del infierno está empedrado de buenas intenciones*, the road to hell is paved with good intentions. || FAM. *En el quinto infierno* or *en los quintos infiernos*, miles from anywhere, in the middle of nowhere, at the back of beyond.
infijo m. GRAM. Infix.
infiltración f. Infiltration.
infiltrado m. MED. Infiltrate.
infiltrar v. tr. To infiltrate.
— V. pr. To infiltrate (*en*, into). || FIG. To infiltrate.
ínfimo, ma adj. Lowest (muy bajo). || Worst, poorest (peor). || Ridiculously low (precios).
infinidad f. Infinity: *la infinidad del universo*, the infinity of the universe. || — *En infinidad de ocasiones*, on countless *o* innumerable occasions, time and again. || *Había infinidad de gente*, there were countless people *o* an awful lot of people there. || *Me tuvo allí una infinidad de tiempo*, he kept me there for ages. || *Te lo he dicho infinidad de veces*, I've told you time and again *o* over and over *o* I don't know how many times. || *Tengo infinidad de cosas que hacer*, I've got a million things to do *o* countless things to do. || *Una infinidad de*, countless, innumerable, an infinity of.
infinitesimal adj. Infinitesimal.
infinitésimo, ma adj. Infinitesimal.
infinito, ta adj. Infinite. || *A lo infinito*, ad infinitum.
— M. Infinite. || MAT. y FÍS. Infinity.
— Adv. Infinitely, extremely: *se lo agradezco infinito*, I am infinitely grateful.
infinitud f. Infinitude, infinity.
infirmación f. Invalidation.
infirmar v. tr. JUR. To invalidate.
inflación f. Inflation: *inflación monetaria*, monetary inflation; *inflación galopante*, runaway inflation. || FIG. Conceit, vanity. || Swelling (hinchamiento).
inflacionario, ria adj. Inflationary.
inflacionismo m. Inflationism, inflation.
inflacionista adj. Inflationary.
— M. y f. Inflationist.
inflado m. Inflation.
inflador m. Inflator, air pump.
inflamabilidad f. Inflammability.
inflamable adj. Inflammable.
inflamación f. Inflammation. || MED. Inflammation.
inflamar v. tr. To set on fire, to inflame. || FIG. To inflame, to arouse.
— V. pr. To catch fire. || FIG. To become inflamed. || MED. To become inflamed.
inflamatorio, ria adj. Inflammatory.
inflamiento m. Swelling, inflation.
inflar v. tr. To inflate, to swell, to fill out: *el viento infla las velas*, the wind swells the sails. || To inflate, to blow up: *inflar un globo, un neumático*, to inflate a balloon, a tyre. || To puff out (los carrillos). || FIG. To exaggerate, to blow up (exagerar): *inflar un suceso*, to exaggerate an event. | To swell up, to make conceited (envanecer).
— V. pr. To fill out, to swell (las velas de un barco). || To inflate (globo, neumático, etc.). || To puff out (los carrillos). || FIG. To get conceited: *inflarse con un éxito*, to get conceited about a success. || FIG. *Inflarse de orgullo*, to swell with pride.
inflexibilidad f. Inflexibility.
inflexible adj. Inflexible. || FIG. Inelastic, inflexible (reglas). | Unyielding, inflexible, unbending (que no cede). | Strict, inflexible (severo).
inflexión f. Inflection, inflexion.
infligir v. tr. To inflict: *infligir un castigo a uno*, to inflict punishment upon s.o.; *infligir una derrota a*, to inflict defeat on *o* upon.
influencia f. Influence. || — *Ejercer una influencia sobre uno*, to have an influence upon *o* over s.o., to influence s.o. || *Persona de mucha influencia*, very influential person. || *Valerse de sus influencias*, to use one's influence.
influenciable adj. Easily influenced, impressionable.
influenciar v. tr. To influence (influir).
influenza f. MED. Influenza, flu (fam.).
influir* v. intr. To influence, to have an influence: *el clima influye en* or *sobre la vegetación*, the climate influences the vegetation, the climate has an influence on the vegetation. || To bear (*en*, upon): *influyó en un amigo suyo para que me diera el puesto*, he bore upon a friend of his to give me the post.
— V. tr. To influence.
influjo m. Influence (influencia). || Rising tide (flujo de la marea). || Impulse: *influjo nervioso*, nerve impulse.
influyente adj. Influential.
infolio m. inv. Folio (libro).
información f. Information. || JUR. Inquiry (investigación). | Report, account (informe). || MIL. Intelligence. || Section, news (en un periódico): *información financiera*, financial section *o* news. || Data, *pl.*: *tratamiento de la información*, data processing. || — Pl. News, *sing.* (en radio, televisión). || Directory inquiries (teléfono). || References (de un empleado). || — *A título de información*, by way of information. || *Información secreta*, classified *o* top-secret information. || JUR. *Información sumaria*, summary proceedings. || *Para su información*, for your information. || MIL. *Servicio de información*, intelligence service. || *Una información*, a piece of news, some news.
informado, da adj. Informed: *fuentes bien informadas*, well-informed sources. || With references: *se necesita un empleado bien informado*, an employee with references is needed.
informador, ra adj. Informing.
— M. y f. Informant. || — M. *Amer.* Rapporteur (ponente).
informal adj. Unmannerly, incorrect (conducta). || Unreliable, untrustworthy (poco de fiar): *persona informal*, unreliable person. || Irregular (no normal). || Bad-mannered (mal educado).
informalidad f. Unmannerliness, incorrectness (de la conducta). || Unreliability, untrustworthiness (de una persona). || Irregularity (irregularidad). || Bad manners, *pl.* (incorrección).
informante adj. Informing.
— M. Informant (que informa). || Rapporteur (de una comisión).
informar v. tr. To inform, to tell, to make known to. || To report: *los cosmonautas informaron que todo iba bien*, the astronauts reported that all was well.
— V. intr. JUR. To enquire (investigar): *informar sobre algo*, to enquire into sth. | To plead (un abogado). | To inform (denunciar). | To report: *informar de las decisiones de una comisión*, to report on the decisions of a commission.
— V. pr. To enquire, to inquire: *infórmense en nuestras oficinas*, enquire in our offices; *informarse sobre algo*, to enquire into sth.; *informarse sobre un empleado*, to enquire about an employee. || To find out (*de*, about) [enterarse]. || *Informarse sobre un asunto*, to look into a matter.
informática f. Computer science.
informativo, va adj. Informative. || Information: *servicios informativos*, information services.
informe adj. Formless, shapeless.
— M. Report (de policía, de una sociedad, etc.): *el informe de la comisión*, the commission's report; *informe anual*, annual report. || Piece of information (información). || JUR. Pleading (exposición). | Dossier (expediente). || — Pl. References: *se necesita cocinero con buenos informes*, cook with good references needed. || Information, *sing.*: *pedir informes sobre* or *de*, to request information about; *tomar informes*, to get information.
infortunado, da adj. Unfortunate.
— M. y f. Unfortunate person, unfortunate (p.us.).
infortunio m. Misfortune.
infosura f. VET. Founder.
infracción f. Infraction, infringement. || AUT. Offence.
infractor, ra m. y f. Offender, infractor.
infradotado, da adj. MED. Handicapped (físicamente). | Subnormal (mentalmente).
infraestructura f. Infrastructure.
in fraganti loc. adv. In the act, red-handed: *coger a uno in fraganti*, to catch s.o. red-handed.
infranqueable adj. Impassable. || FIG. Insurmountable.
infraoctava f. REL. Octave.
infrarrojo, ja adj. FÍS. Infrared.
— M. Infrared radiation, infrared.
infrascripto, ta o **infrascrito, ta** adj./s. Undersigned: *Yo, el infrascrito*, I the undersigned. || Hereinafter mentioned (mencionado más adelante).
infrasonido m. FÍS. Infrasonic wave.
infravalorar v. tr. To undervalue, to underestimate.
infrecuente adj. Infrequent.
infringir v. tr. To infringe, to transgress, to break.

infructífero, ra adj. Unproductive: *campo infructífero*, unproductive field. || FIG. Fruitless, unfruitful.
infructuosidad f. Unfruitfulness, fruitlessness.
infructuoso, sa adj. Unfruitful, fruitless, vain, useless: *esfuerzo infructuoso*, unfruitful effort.
ínfulas f. pl. Infulae (antiguo ornamento sacerdotal, cintas de la mitra episcopal). || FIG. Pretension, *sing.*, conceit, *sing.* || FIG. *Darse* or *tener muchas ínfulas*, to put on airs.
infumable adj. Not smokable, unsmokable. || FAM. Unbearable (insoportable).
infundado, da adj. Unfounded, groundless.
infundio m. FAM. Lie, story, tale: *circulan infundios sobre ti*, people are spreading lies about you.
infundioso, sa adj. False, untrue.
infundir v. tr. To instil, to infuse, to inspire: *infundir terror, respeto, ánimo, ideas*, to instil fear, respect, courage, ideas. || To cause: *infundir sospechas, dudas*, to cause suspicion, doubt. || To inject: *infundir un espíritu nuevo a una empresa*, to inject new life into a firm.
infusión f. Infusion.
infuso, sa adj. Inspired: *ciencia infusa*, inspired knowledge. || FAM. *Tener la ciencia infusa*, to be a born genius.
infusorios m. pl. ZOOL. Infusoria.
ingeniar v. tr. To invent, to conceive, to devise, to think up.
— V. pr. To manage to: *ingeniarse para vivir decentemente*, to manage to live decently. || *Ingeniárselas*, to manage: *siempre se las ingenia para no trabajar*, he always manages to get out of work.
ingeniería f. Engineering (ciencia). || *Ingeniería civil*, civil engineering.
ingeniero m. Engineer. || — *Ingeniero agrónomo*, agriculturist. || *Ingeniero civil*, civil engineer. || *Ingeniero consultor*, consulting engineer. || *Ingeniero de Caminos, Canales y Puertos*, civil engineer. || *Ingeniero de minas*, mining engineer. || *Ingeniero de montes*, forestry expert. || *Ingeniero de sonido*, sound technician *o* engineer. || *Ingeniero militar*, army engineer. || *Ingeniero naval*, naval architect. || *Ingeniero químico*, chemical engineer.
ingenio m. Ingenuity, ingeniousness, genius (talento). || Inventiveness, creativeness (inventiva). || Wit, humour (agudeza). || Genius (persona). || Appliance, machine (aparato o máquina). || Device (militar). || TECN. Cutter (máquina de encuadernación). || — *Aguzar el ingenio*, to sharpen one's wits. || *Ingenio de azúcar*, sugar mill. || *Ingenio espacial*, space missile. || *Tener ingenio*, to be witty.
ingeniosidad f. Ingenuity, ingeniousness: *la ingeniosidad de un mecanismo, de un razonamiento*, the ingenuity of a mechanism, of a reasoning. || FIG. Bright idea (genialidad).
ingenioso, sa adj. Ingenious (máquina, idea, etc.). || Ingenious, resourceful (persona). || Witty (agudo). || *Echárselas de ingenioso*, to try to be witty.
ingénito, ta adj. Innate, inborn (innato). || Unbegotten (no engendrado).
ingente adj. Enormous, huge.
ingenuidad f. Ingenuousness, naïveté.
ingenuo, nua adj. Naïve, ingenuous.
— M. y f. Naïve person. || — F. TEATR. Ingénue.
ingerencia f. Interference.
ingerir* v. tr. To ingest, to take [in], to consume, to eat: *ingerir alimentos*, to ingest food. || To take [in], to consume, to drink (beber). || To insert, to introduce (introducir).
— V. pr. To inferfere: *ingerirse en los asuntos ajenos*, to interfere in other people's affairs.
ingestión f. Ingestion.
Inglaterra n. pr. f. GEOGR. England.
ingle f. ANAT. Groin.
inglés, esa adj. English. || *Patatas fritas a la inglesa*, crisps [U.S., potato chips].
— M. Englishman. || English [language] (idioma): *hablar inglés*, to speak English. || — F. Englishwoman || English (letra).

— OBSERV. *Inglés* is often used by Spanish speakers to mean "British."

inglesismo m. Anglicism.
inglete m. Forty-five degree angle (ángulo). || Mitre joint [U.S., miter joint] (en la escuadra). || TECN. *Caja de ingletes*, mitre box [U.S., miter box].
ingobernable adj. Ungovernable (en política). || Uncontrollable.
ingratitud f. Ingratitude, ungratefulness. || *Mostrar ingratitud*, to be ungrateful.
ingrato, ta adj. Ungrateful, ingrate (ant.): *ingrato con* or *para con*, ungrateful to *o* towards. || Disagreeable, unpleasant (desagradable): *tiempo ingrato*, disagreeable weather. || Unrewarding, thankless: *una labor ingrata*, an unrewarding task. || Unproductive: *un terreno ingrato*, an unproductive field. || *Hijo ingrato*, ungrateful child.
— M. y f. Ungrateful person, ingrate (ant.). || *De ingratos está lleno el mundo*, the world is full of ungrateful people, one can't trust anybody.
ingravidez f. Weightlessness, lightness (carencia de peso). || Absence *o* lack of gravity (falta de gravedad).
ingrávido, da adj. Weightless, light (sin peso). || Lacking gravity (sin gravedad).
ingrediente m. Ingredient.
ingresado, da adj. Deposited (dinero). || Entrant (persona).
ingresar v. intr. To come in, to enter (dinero, fondos): *hoy han ingresado cinco millones de pesetas en el banco*, five million pesetas have come into the bank today. || To enrol, to register, to enter (en una escuela, universidad, etc.). || To be admitted: *falleció a poco de ingresar en el hospital*, he died shortly after being admitted to the hospital; *ingresar en la Academia*, to be admitted to the Academy. || To join, to become a member of (en una sociedad, un club). || MIL. To enlist, to join: *ingresar en el ejército*, to enlist in the army, to join the army.
— V. tr. To deposit, to pay: *ingresar dinero en el banco*, to deposit money in the bank; *ingresar una cantidad en cuenta*, to pay an amount into one's account.
— V. pr. *Amer.* To enlist (alistarse).
ingreso m. Entrance (entrada). || Admission (en una academia, escuela, hospital). || COM. Receipt, entry (de dinero). | Deposit (depósito). || — Pl. Income, *sing.*: *los ingresos de un abogado*, the income of a lawyer. || Revenue, *sing.* (del Estado). || *Examen de ingreso*, entrance examination.
inguinal o **inguinario, ria** adj. Inguinal.
ingurgitación f. MED. Ingurgitation.
ingurgitar v. tr. To ingurgitate (engullir).
inhábil adj. Unskilful [U.S., unskillful]: *costurera inhábil*, unskilful seamstress. || Incompetent (incompetente). || JUR. Incompetent: *abogado inhábil*, incompetent lawyer; *inhábil para testificar*, incompetent to testify. || — *Día inhábil*, holiday. || *Hora inhábil*, closing time. || *Inhábil para el trabajo* or *para trabajar*, unfit for work *o* to work.
inhabilidad f. Unskilfulness [U.S., unskillfulness]. || Incompetence (falta de competencia). || JUR. Incompetence.
inhabilitación f. Incapacitation, disablement, disqualification.
inhabilitar v. tr. To disable, to incapacitate, to disqualify.
inhabitable adj. Uninhabitable.
inhabitado, da adj. Uninhabitated (deshabitado).
inhabitual adj. Unusual.
inhacedero, ra adj. Unfeasible.
inhalación f. Inhalation.
inhalador, ra adj. Inhalant.
— M. Inhaler.
inhalar v. tr. To inhale.
inherencia f. Inherence.
inherente adj. Inherent: *responsabilidad inherente a un cargo*, inherent responsibility of a job, responsibility inherent in a job.
inhibición f. Inhibition (fisiológica o psíquica).
inhibidor m. QUÍM. Inhibitor.
inhibir v. tr. To inhibit (un proceso fisiológico o psicológico). || JUR. To inhibit.
— V. pr. To be inhibited (fisiológica o psicológicamente). || To keep out: *inhibirse en un asunto*, to keep out of a matter.
inhibitorio, ria adj. Inhibitory.
inhospitalario, ria adj. Inhospitable.
inhospitalidad f. Inhospitality.
inhóspito, ta adj. Inhospitable.
inhumación f. Inhumation, burial.
inhumanidad f. Inhumanity.
inhumano, na adj. Inhuman.
inhumar v. tr. To inhume, to bury.
iniciación f. Introduction: *iniciación a la filosofía*, introduction to philosophy. || Initiation: *iniciación religiosa*, religious initiation; *ceremonia de iniciación*, initiation ceremony. || Beginning (principio).
iniciado, da adj. Initiated.
— M. y f. Initiate.
iniciador, ra adj. Initiatory.
— M. y f. Initiator. || FIG. Pioneer (pionero).
inicial adj. Initial: *la velocidad inicial de un proyectil*, the initial velocity of a missile.
— F. Initial (letra).
iniciar v. tr. To initiate: *iniciar a uno en la masonería*, to initiate s.o. into freemasonry. || To begin, to start: *iniciar las negociaciones*, to begin negotiations.
— V. pr. To learn by o.s.: *iniciarse en el arte de tocar la guitarra*, to learn to play the guitar by o.s. || To begin: *se inició el debate el lunes*, the debate began on Monday.
iniciativa f. Initiative: *tomar la iniciativa*, to take the initiative; *persona de mucha iniciativa*, person with a lot of initiative; *obrar por propia iniciativa*, to act upon one's own initiative.
iniciativo, va adj. Initiative.
inicio m. Beginning.
inicuo, cua adj. Iniquitous, wicked.
inigualado, da adj. Unequalled, unequaled.
in illo témpore adv. Formerly.
inimaginable adj. Unimaginable.
inimitable adj. Inimitable.
ininflamable adj. Uninflammable.
ininteligente adj. Unintelligent.
ininteligible adj. Unintelligible.
ininterrupción f. Uninterruption.
ininterrumpido, da adj. Uninterrupted.

iniquidad f. Iniquity, wickedness.
injerencia f. Interference.
injeridura f. Graft.
injerir v. tr. To insert, to introduce (introducir una cosa en otra). || AGR. To graft.
— V. pr. To interfere: *injerirse en los asuntos ajenos*, to interfere in other people's affairs.
injertable adj. That can be grafted.
injertador m. Grafter.
injertar v. tr. AGR. y MED. To graft.
injerto m. AGR. Graft: *injerto de corona*, crown graft. | Graft, scion (yema implantada). || MED. Graft: *un injerto de piel*, a skin graft. || — AGR. *Injerto de aproximación*, inarching. | *Injerto de escudete*, shield grafting.
injuria f. Insult (insulto). || Offence [U.S., offense] (ofensa). || MED. Injury. || FIG. Ravage: *las injurias del tiempo*, the ravages of time. || — *Delito de injurias al jefe del Estado*, crime of slander against the Head of State. || *Injurias y actos de violencia*, slander and acts of violence.
injuriador, ra adj. Offensive.
— M. y f. Offender.
injuriante adj. Offensive.
injuriar v. tr. To offend, to insult, to abuse (ofender). || To injure, to harm (producir un daño material).
injurioso, sa adj. Offensive.
injusticia f. Injustice. || Unfairness (falta de equidad). || *Con injusticia*, unjustly.
injustificable adj. Unjustifiable.
injustificado, da adj. Unjustified.
injusto, ta adj. Unjust. || Unfair (*para*, *con*, to, with) [sin equidad].
inmaculado, da adj. Immaculate.
— F. *La Inmaculada*, the Immaculate Conception.
inmadurez f. Immaturity.
inmaduro, ra adj. Unripe. || FIG. Immature, unripe.
inmanejable adj. Unmanageable. || *Amer.* Undriveable (automóvil).
inmanencia f. Immanence.
inmanente adj. Immanent.
inmanentismo m. Immanentism.
inmarcesible o **inmarchitable** adj. Unwithering, unfading: *la gloria inmarcesible*, unfading glory.
inmaterial adj. Immaterial.
inmaterialidad f. Immateriality.
inmaterialismo m. Immaterialism.
inmaturo, ra adj. V. INMADURO.
inmediación f. Immediacy (carácter de lo inmediato). || — Pl. Environs, neighbourhood, *sing.*: *Alcalá de Henares está en las inmediaciones de Madrid*, Alcalá de Henares is in the environs of Madrid.
inmediatamente adv. Immediately, at once. || *Inmediatamente después de cenar* or *inmediatamente que cenemos*, immediately after dinner.
inmediato, ta adj. Near, close to (cercano): *un pueblo inmediato a Londres*, a town near London. || Next (contiguo): *en el cuarto inmediato al mío*, in the next room to mine, in the room next to mine. || Immediate: *una medicina de efecto inmediato*, a medicine with immediate effect. || *Amer. De inmediato*, immediately, at once.
inmejorable adj. Unsurpassable, unimprovable. || Excellent (excelente). || Unbeatable (precios).
inmemorial adj. Immemorial: *desde tiempo inmemorial*, from time immemorial.
inmensidad f. Immensity, vastness.
inmenso, sa adj. Immense, huge, vast: *llanura inmensa*, immense plain; *fortuna inmensa*, immense fortune. || FIG. y FAM. Fabulous (magnífico). || — *Me dio una pena inmensa*, I was terribly upset. || FIG. y FAM. *Pasarlo inmenso*, to have a fabulous time, to have a ball.
inmensurable adj. Immeasurable, unmeasurable.
inmerecidamente adv. Undeservingly.
inmerecido, da adj. Unmerited, undeserved.
inmergir v. tr. To immerse (sumergir).
inmersión f. Immersion. || Dive (de un hombre rana).
inmerso, sa adj. Immersed (sumergido).
inmigración f. Immigration.
inmigrado, da adj./s. Immigrant.
inmigrante adj./s. Immigrant.
inmigrar v. intr. To immigrate.
inmigratorio, ria adj. Immigratory.
inminencia f. Imminence, imminency.
inminente adj. Imminent (a punto de ocurrir). || Impending (amenaza, peligro).
inmiscuir v. tr. (P.us.). To mix.
— V. pr. To interfere, to meddle: *inmiscuirse en un asunto*, to interfere in a matter.
inmobiliario, ria adj. Real estate, property. || — *Agente inmobiliario*, estate agent [U.S., real estate broker]. || *Sociedad inmobiliaria*, real estate company.
— F. Real estate company.
inmoble adj. Motionless (que no se mueve). || Unmovable (que no se puede mover). || FÍS. Firm.
inmoderado, da adj. Immoderate.
inmodestia f. Immodesty.
inmodesto, ta adj. Immodest.
inmolación f. Immolation, sacrifice.
inmolador m. Immolator.
inmolar v. tr. To immolate, to sacrifice.
— V. pr. To immolate o.s., to sacrifice o.s.
inmoral adj. Immoral.
inmoralidad f. Immorality.
inmoralismo m. Immoralism.
inmoralista m. y f. Immoralist
inmortal adj./s. Immortal.
inmortalidad f. Immortality.
inmortalizar v. tr. To immortalize.
inmotivadamente adv. For no reason.
inmotivado, da adj. Unmotivated. || Groundless (infundado).
inmovible adj. V. INMOBLE.
inmóvil adj. Motionless, still, immobile: *permanecer inmóvil*, to remain motionless.
inmovilidad f. Immobility.
inmovilismo m. Opposition to progress, ultraconservatism.
inmovilización f. Immobilization. || COM. Tying up (del capital).
inmovilizar v. tr. To immobilize. || To paralyse, to bring to a standstill (una fábrica, la industria, un país). || COM. To tie up (el capital).
inmudable adj. Immutable.
inmueble adj. JUR. *Bienes inmuebles*, real estate, *sing.*, immovables.
— M. Building (edificio).
inmundicia f. Dirtiness, squalor (suciedad). || — Pl. Rubbish, *sing.*, refuse, *sing.* (basura). || FIG. Filth.
inmundo, da adj. Dirty, filthy, squalid. || Unclean (impuro). || FIG. Foul (language). || *El espíritu inmundo*, the spirit of evil (el demonio).
inmune adj. MED. Immune: *estar inmune al cólera*, to be immune to cholera.
inmunidad f. Immunity: *inmunidad contra una enfermedad*, immunity to a disease; *inmunidad parlamentaria*, parliamentary immunity.
inmunización f. Immunization.
inmunizador, ra adj. Immunogenic, immunizing.
inmunizar v. tr. To immunize.
inmutabilidad f. Immutability.
inmutable adj. Immutable.
inmutación f. Alteration, change.
inmutar v. tr. To alter, to change.
— V. pr. To change. || — *No inmutarse*, to be unperturbed, not to flinch, not to bat an eyelid (fam.). || *Se inmutó al leer la carta*, his face fell upon reading the letter.
innato, ta adj. Innate, inborn.
innavegable adj. Unnavigable (río, mar). || Unseaworthy (barco).
innecesario, ria adj. Unnecessary.
innegable adj. Undeniable.
innoble adj. Ignoble.
innominable adj. Unnamable, unnameable.
innominado, da adj. Unnamed, nameless, innominate. || *Hueso innominado*, innominate bone.
innovación f. Innovation. || Novelty, new thing (novedad).
innovador, ra adj. Innovative, innovatory.
— M. y f. Innovator.
innovar v. tr. e intr. To innovate.
innumerabilidad f. Innumerability.
innumerable adj. Innumerable, countless.
inobediencia f. Disobedience.
inobediente adj. Disobedient.
inobservable adj. Unobservable.
inobservado, da adj. Unobserved.
inobservancia f. Inobservance, inobservancy.
inobservante adj. Inobservant, unobservant.
inocencia f. Innocence: *con toda inocencia*, in all innocence.
Inocencio n. pr. m. Innocent.
inocentada f. FAM. Practical joke (broma): *dar una inocentada a uno*, to play a practical joke on s.o. | Naïve remark (dicho ingenuo). | April Fool's joke (el día de los Inocentes).
— OBSERV. In Spain these practical jokes take place on the 28th of December, Innocents' day, and not on the 1st of April as in England and the United States.
inocente adj. Innocent: *alma inocente*, innocent soul; *broma inocente*, innocent joke. || Innocent, naïve (ingenuo).
— M. y f. Innocent, innocent person (no culpable). || Simpleton (bobo). || — *Hacerse el inocente*, to play innocent. || *Los Santos Inocentes*, the Holy Innocents.
inocentón, ona adj. Credulous, gullible, naïve.
— M. y f. Simpleton.
inocuidad f. Innocuousness, harmlessness.
inoculación f. Inoculation.
inocular v. tr. To inoculate: *inocular un virus a uno*, to inoculate s.o. with a virus. || FIG. To infect, to inoculate (ideas nocivas, etc.).
inocultable adj. Inconcealable.
inocuo, cua adj. Innocuous, harmless: *una droga inocua*, an innocuous drug.
inodoro, ra adj. Odourless, inodorous.
— M. *Amer.* Toilet, lavatory.
inofensivo, va adj. Inoffensive.
inoficioso, sa adj. JUR. Inofficious.
inolvidable adj. Unforgettable.
inoperable adj. Inoperable: *tumor inoperable*, inoperable tumour.
inoperante adj. Inoperative.

inopia f. Poverty, impecuniousness. || FIG. *Estar en la inopia*, to be in the clouds (estar distraído).
inopinado, da adj. Unexpected.
inoportunidad f. Inopportuneness, untimeliness. || Inconvenience (molestia).
inoportuno, na adj. Inopportune, untimely, ill-timed. || Inconvenient (molesto).
inorgánico, ca adj. Inorganic.
inoxidable adj. Inoxidizable, rustless. || *Acero inoxidable*, stainless steel.
in péctore loc. adv. In petto.
in promptu loc. adv. Impromptu.
inquebrantable adj. Unbreakable (irrompible). || FIG. Unyielding: *fe inquebrantable*, unyielding faith.
inquietador, ra adj. Disturbing, worrying.
inquietante adj. Disturbing, alarming, worrying.
inquietar v. tr. To disturb, to worry, to trouble. || MIL. To harass.
— V. pr. To worry: *inquietarse por*, to worry about.
inquieto, ta adj. Restless (agitado): *niño, mar inquieto*, restless child, sea. || Worried, anxious: *su madre está inquieta*, his mother is worried.
inquietud f. Anxiety, worry, uneasiness (preocupación). || Restlessness (desasosiego).
inquilinaje m. *Amer.* Tenants, *pl.* (inquilinos).
inquilinato m. Lease (arrendamiento). || *Impuesto de inquilinato*, rates, *pl.*
inquilino, na m. y f. Tenant. || ZOOL. Inquiline.
inquina f. FAM. Ill will, dislike, grudge: *tenerle inquina a alguien*, to bear ill will towards s.o., to have a dislike for *o* a grudge against s.o. || *Tomarle inquina a alguien*, to take a dislike to s.o.
inquiridor, ra adj. Inquiring, enquiring, investigating.
— M. y f. Inquirer, enquirer, investigator.
inquirir* v. tr. e intr. To inquire *o* to enquire [into], to investigate: *la policía inquirió (sobre) la muerte del joyero*, the police enquired into the jeweller's death.
inquisición f. HIST. Inquisition (antiguo tribunal eclesiástico). || Inquiry, enquiry, investigation (averiguación).
inquisidor, ra adj. Inquiring, inquisitive: *mirada inquisidora*, inquiring glance.
— M. Inquisitor (juez de la Inquisición).
inquisitivo, va adj. Inquisitive: *le lanzó una mirada inquisitiva*, he gave her an inquisitive glance.
inquisitorial adj. Inquisitorial, inquisitional.
inquisitorio, ria adj. Inquisitive.
inri m. Inri (en la Cruz). || FIG. Insult (afrenta). || — FIG. *Ponerle el inri a uno*, to insult s.o. | *Y para mayor inri*, and to make it worse.
insaciabilidad f. Insatiability.
insaciable adj. Insatiable.
insalivación f. BIOL. Insalivation.
insalivar v. tr. BIOL. To insalivate.
insalubre adj. Insalubrious, unhealthy.
insalubridad f. Insalubrity, unhealthiness.
insalvable adj. Insurmountable (invencible).
insanable adj. Incurable.
insania f. Insanity (locura).
insano, na adj. Insane (loco). || Unhealthy (insalubre).
insatisfacción f. Dissatisfaction.
insatisfecho, cha adj. Unsatisfied, dissatisfied. || Unsatisfied: *venganza insatisfecha*, unsatisfied revenge.
inscribible adj. Registrable. || MAT. Inscribable.
inscribir v. tr. To inscribe (grabar). || To register, to enroll: *inscribir a alguien en un registro*, to enroll s.o. in a register. || To enter: *inscribir a alguien en una lista*, to enter s.o.'s name on a list. || To write down (escribir). || To register: *inscribir una declaración en las actas de una conferencia*, to register a declaration in a conference record. || To include, to place: *inscribir en el orden del día*, to include in *o* to place on the agenda. || MAT. To inscribe.
— V. pr. To register, to enroll, to enter [one's name]: *me he inscrito en el concurso*, I have entered for the competition. || To write one's name (apuntar su nombre).
inscripción f. Enrolment, registration. || Inscription: *había una inscripción sobre la tumba*, there was an inscription over the grave.
inscrito, ta adj. Registered, enrolled, entered: *inscrito en un registro*, entered *o* enrolled in a register. || Inscribed (grabado). || MAT. Inscribed: *polígono inscrito*, inscribed polygon.
insecticida adj. Insecticidal, insecticide.
— M. Insecticide.
insectívoro, ra adj. ZOOL. Insectivorous.
— M. Insectivore. || — Pl. Insectivora.
insecto m. Insect.
inseguridad f. Insecurity (sentimiento). || Uncertainty (duda). || Unsafety (peligro). || Unsteadiness, instability (inestabilidad).
inseguro, ra adj. Insecure (sentimiento, condición). || Unsafe (peligroso). || Uncertain (dudoso). || Unsteady, unstable, insecure (inestable).
inseminación f. Insemination: *inseminación artificial*, artificial insemination.
inseminar v. tr. To inseminate.
insensatez f. Foolishness, stupidity, folly. || FIG. Folly (tontería): *es una insensatez ir a verle a estas horas de la noche*, it's folly to go to see him at this time of night. | Foolish remark (dicho estúpido).
insensato, ta adj. Foolish, stupid, senseless.
— M. y f. Senseless person, fool.
insensibilidad f. MED. Insensibility. || Insensitiveness, insensitivity (ante las emociones).
insensibilización f. Anaesthetization, anesthetization.
insensibilizador, ra adj./s.m. MED. Anaesthetic, anesthetic. || *Un agente insensibilizador*, an anaesthetizing agent.
insensibilizar v. tr. MED. To anaesthetize, to anesthetize. || FIG. To make insensitive.
insensible adj. MED. Insensible. || Insensitive, unfeeling (a las emociones). || Imperceptible (imperceptible).
inseparabilidad f. Inseparability.
inseparable adj. Inseparable.
insepulto, ta adj. Unburied.
inserción f. Insertion.
insertable adj. Insertable.
insertar v. tr. To insert: *insertar una cláusula en un tratado*, to insert a clause in a treaty. || To include (incluir).
— V. pr. BOT. y ANAT. To be inserted *o* attached.
inserto, ta adj. Inserted.
inservible adj. Unserviceable, useless.
insidia f. Trap, snare (trampa). || Maliciousness (mala intención).
insidioso, sa adj. Insidious, treacherous. || FIG. Insidious: *enfermedad insidiosa*, insidious disease.
— M. y f. Insidious person.
insigne adj. Famous, renowned, distinguished.
insignemente adv. Notably.
insignia f. Badge: *el policía lleva una insignia blanca*, the policeman wears a white badge. || Banner: *el teniente llevaba la insignia del regimiento*, the lieutenant carried the banner of the regiment. || MAR. Pennant. || — Pl. Insignia. || *Buque insignia*, flagship.
insignificancia f. Insignificance. || Trifle: *el regalo que me hizo era una insignificancia*, the gift that he gave me was a trifle; *el reloj me costó una insignificancia*, my watch cost me a trifle.
insignificante adj. Insignificant, unimportant. || Trifling: *una cantidad insignificante de dinero*, a trifling amount of money. || Insignificant, unimportant: *una persona insignificante*, an insignificant person.
insinceridad f. Insincerity.
insincero, ra adj. Insincere.
insinuación f. Insinuation, hint: *es una insinuación inadmisible*, it is an inadmissible insinuation. || Suggestion (sugerencia).
insinuante adj. Insinuating, suggestive.
insinuar v. tr. To insinuate, to hint at: *¿qué es lo que insinúas?*, what are you insinuating? || To insinuate, to hint: *insinuó que conocía el culpable*, he insinuated he knew who the culprit was. || To suggest (proponer): *insinúo que vayamos al campo*, I suggest that we go to the country.
— V. pr. To make advances: *insinuarse a una mujer*, to make advances to a woman. || To gradually work one's way into (infiltrarse en).
insinuativo, va adj. Insinuating, insinuative.
insipidez f. Insipidity, insipidness.
insípido, da adj. Insipid, tasteless: *un alimento insípido*, a tasteless food. || FIG. Dull, insipid: *una comedia insípida*, an insipid play.
insistencia f. Insistence: *la miró con insistencia*, he looked at her with insistence. || Persistence: *la insistencia de la lluvia*, the persistence of the rain.
insistente adj. Insistent (persona). || Persistent (lluvia, quejas, etc.).
insistentemente adv. Insistently, with insistence. || Persistently.
insistir v. intr. To insist: *insistir en* or *sobre un punto*, to insist on *o* upon a point; *insistir en hablar*, to insist on *o* upon talking; *insiste en que los inquilinos abandonen la casa*, he insists that the tenants leave the house; *insisto en que tienes la culpa*, I insist that you are at fault. || To stress, to emphasize (hacer hincapié): *insistió en la importancia de*, he stressed the importance of. || To persist.
insobornable adj. Incorruptible.
insociabilidad f. Unsociability.
insociable adj. Unsociable.
insocial adj. Unsociable.
insolación f. Sunstroke, insolation (p.us.): *coger una insolación*, to get sunstroke. || Insolation (en meteorología).
insolar v. tr. To insolate, to expose to the sun's rays.
— V. pr. To get sunstroke.
insolencia f. Insolence. || *Decir insolencias*, to be insolent.
insolentar v. tr. To make insolent.
— V. pr. To be *o* to become insolent.
insolente adj. Insolent (descarado). || Haughty, contemptuous (arrogante).
— M. y f. Insolent person. || Haughty *o* contemptuous person.
insólito, ta adj. Unusual, unaccustomed.
insolubilidad f. Insolubility.
insoluble adj. Insoluble (no soluble). || Unsolvable (imposible de resolver).
insolvencia f. Insolvency: *certificación de insolvencia*, report of insolvency.
insolvente adj./s. Insolvent.

insomne adj. Insomnious, sleepless.
— N. Insomniac.
insondable adj. Unsoundable, unfathomable (muy profundo). || FIG. Unfathomable, inscrutable.
insonoridad f. Soundlessness.
insonorización f. Soundproofing.
insonorizado, da adj. Soundproof.
insonorizar v. tr. To soundproof.
insonoro, ra adj. Insonorous, soundless.
insoportable adj. Unbearable, intolerable.
insoslayable adj. Inevitable, unavoidable (inevitable).
insospechable adj. Unexpected (sorprendente). || Beyond suspicion (que no puede ser sospechado).
insospechado, da adj. Unsuspected.
insostenible adj. Unsustainable. || Untenable, indefensible, unmaintainable: *posición insostenible*, untenable position.
inspección f. Inspection, examination. || Control. || — *Inspección ocular*, visual inspection *o* examination. || *Inspección sanitaria*, hygiene inspection.
inspeccionar v. tr. To inspect, to examine.
inspector, ra adj. Inspecting.
— M. y f. Inspector.
inspectoría f. *Amer.* Central police station.
inspiración f. Inspiration. || Inhalation, inspiration, breathing in (del aire).
inspirado, da adj. Inspired.
inspirador, ra adj. Inspirational, inspiring (que inspira). || Inspiratory: *músculos inspiradores*, inspiratory muscles.
— M. y f. Inspirer.
inspirar v. tr. To inspire. || To inhale, to inspire, to breathe in (aire).
— V. pr. To be inspired: *el escritor se inspiró en la obra de Cervantes*, the writer was inspired by Cervantes' works.
instabilidad f. Instability.
instable adj. Unstable.
instalación f. Installation, instalment (acción). || Installation: *instalación frigorífica*, refrigerator installation. || Plant (fábrica). || Equipment (equipo). || Laying: *instalación de la primera piedra*, laying of the foundation stone. || *Instalación sanitaria*, plumbing.
instalador m. Fitter.
instalar v. tr. To install: *instalar la electricidad, el gas*, to install electricity, gas. || To fit out (proveer del equipo necesario). || To install, to settle: *han instalado a cien familias pobres en el barrio*, they have installed a hundred poor families in the neighbourhood. || To set up (tienda de campaña).
— V. pr. To settle, to install o.s.
instancia f. Request, petition (petición): *presentar una instancia*, to present a request; *ceder a las instancias de uno*, to give in to *o* to concede s.o.'s request. || JUR. Instance: *tribunal de primera instancia*, court of first instance. || Application form (solicitud). || — JUR. *A instancia de*, at the petition of. || *A instancias de*, at the request of. || FIG. *De primera instancia*, first of all (en primer lugar). | *En última instancia*, as a last resort. || JUR. *Fallo en primera instancia*, appealable judgment.
instantáneamente adv. Instantaneously.
instantaneidad f. Instantaneity.
instantáneo, a adj. Instantaneous. || Instant: *café instantáneo*, instant coffee.
— F. FOT. Snapshot, snap: *sacar instantáneas*, to take snapshots.
instante adj. Insistent.
— M. Instant, moment: *en el mismo instante*, in the same instant. || — *A cada instante*, all the time, constantly. || *Al instante*, immediately, right away, at once. || *Dentro de un instante*, in a moment, in an instant. || *Desde el instante en que*, from the moment that *o* when. || *En este (mismo) instante*, at this [very] moment. || *Por instantes*, incessantly, all the time: *la multitud crecía por instantes*, the crowd grew larger all the time. || *Por un instante te confundí con tu hermano*, for an instant *o* for one moment I took you for your brother.
instar v. tr. To urge, to press: *le instó a que se decidiese*, he urged him to decide. || (Ant.). To refute (impugnar).
— V. intr. To be urgent *o* pressing: *insta que vayas a verla*, it is urgent that you go to see her.
instauración f. Establishment.
instaurador, ra adj. Establishing.
— M. y f. Establisher.
instaurar v. tr. To establish, to set up (establecer).
instigación f. Instigation. || *A instigación de*, at *o* on the instigation of.
instigador, ra adj. Instigative, instigating.
— M. y f. Instigator.
instigar v. tr. To instigate, to incite (incitar).
instilar v. tr. To instil [U.S., to instill] (líquidos). || To instil [U.S., to instill], to infuse: *instilar ideas en la mente de alguien*, to instil ideas into s.o.'s head.
instintivo, va adj. Instinctive.
instinto m. Instinct: *hombre de malos instintos*, man of evil instincts; *instinto de conservación*, self-preservation instinct; *instinto materno*, maternal instinct. || Urge, desire: *instinto sexual*, sexual urge. || *Por instinto*, by instinct, instinctively.
institución f. Institution, establishment (acción de instituir). || Institution (organismo, entidad): *institución benéfica*, charitable *o* welfare institution. || — Pl. Institutions: *es un hombre que no respeta las instituciones*, he is a man who does not respect institutions. || — JUR. *Institución de heredero*, appointment of an heir. || FIG. y FAM. *Pedro es una institución en su pueblo*, Peter is an institution in his town.
institucional adj. Institutional, institutionary.
institucionalización f. Institutionalization.
institucionalizar v. tr. To institutionalize.
instituido, da adj. Instituted.
instituidor, ra adj. Founding.
— M. y f. Institutor, founder.
instituir* v. tr. To institute, to establish (entidad, principios, etc.). || To found, to institute (un premio). || To appoint: *instituir un heredero*, to appoint an heir.
instituta f. pl. Institutes [Roman civil law].
instituto m. Institute (institución): *instituto geográfico*, geographical institute. || Grammar school [U.S., high school], secondary school (de segunda enseñanza). || Rule, principle (regla). || — *Instituto de belleza*, beauty salon, beauty parlour [U.S., beauty parlor]. || *Instituto de la Vivienda*, housing office. || *Instituto de Moneda Extranjera*, foreign money exchange. || *Instituto Laboral*, technical school.
institutor, ra adj. Instituting, institutive, founding.
— M. y f. Institutor, founder. || *Amer.* Schoolmaster.
institutriz f. Governess.
instituyente adj. Instituting, institutive, founding.
instrucción f. Instruction (acción de instruir). || Education: *instrucción primaria, pública*, primary, public education. || Knowledge (ciencia). || MIL. Drill, training: *instrucción de las tropas*, training of troops. || JUR. Preliminary investigation. || DEP. Training, coaching. || — Pl. Instructions: *dar a uno instrucciones sobre algo*, to give s.o. instructions on *o* about sth. || — *Instrucciones para el uso*, instructions, directions. || *Juez de instrucción*, examining magistrate. || *Recibir instrucciones antes de llevar a cabo una misión*, to be briefed before a mission.
instructivo, va adj. Instructive: *libro instructivo*, instructive book. || Educational (película, viaje, etc.).
instructor, ra adj. Instructing. || *Juez instructor*, examining magistrate.
— M. Instructor (en el cuartel). || — M. y f. DEP. Coach, trainer.
instruido, da adj. Educated, well-educated.
instruir* v. tr. To educate, to teach (enseñar). || To instruct: *instruir a uno en el manejo de un arma*, to instruct s.o. in the use of an arm. || MIL. To train, to drill. || DEP. To coach, to train. || To inform: *me instruyó de* or *sobre lo ocurrido*, he informed me of *o* about what had happened. || JUR. *Instruir una causa*, to investigate a case.
— V. pr. To teach o.s.
instrumentación f. MÚS. Instrumentation, orchestration.
instrumental adj. Instrumental: *música instrumental*, instrumental music. || JUR. Documentary: *prueba instrumental*, documentary evidence. || *Testigo instrumental*, witness to a deed.
— M. Instruments, *pl.*
instrumentalismo m. Instrumentalism.
instrumentar v. tr. To orchestrate, to instrument.
instrumentista m. y f. Instrumentalist (músico). || Instrument maker (fabricante).
instrumento m. Instrument: *instrumento músico*, musical instrument; *tocar un instrumento*, to play an instrument. || Instrument, tool (herramienta): *instrumentos de precisión*, precision instruments. || Instrument (documento). || FIG. Instrument, tool: *servir de instrumento a la venganza de uno*, to serve as an instrument of s.o.'s revenge. || — MÚS. *Instrumento de cuerda, de metal, de percusión, de viento*, string, brass, percussion, wind instrument. || AVIAC. *Instrumentos de mando*, controls.
insubordinación f. Insubordination.
insubordinado, da adj. Insubordinate.
— M. Rebel.
insubordinar v. tr. To stir up, to make unruly *o* rebellious, to incite to rebellion.
— V. pr. To become insubordinate, to rebel.
insubstancial adj. Insubstantial. || || FIG. Empty, shallow, trite (conversación, etc.). | Shallow, superficial (persona).
insubstancialidad f. Insubstantiality. || FIG. Emptiness, shallowness, triteness (de una conversación, etc.). | Shallowness, superficiality (de una persona).
insubstancialmente adv. Insubstantially.
insubstituible adj. Irreplaceable.
insuficiencia f. Insufficiency, inadequacy, scarcity, shortage (escasez). || Incompetency, inability, insufficiency (p.us.): *la insuficiencia de un empleado*, the incompetency of an employee. || MED. Insufficiency: *insuficiencia mitral*, mitral insufficiency. | Failure: *insuficiencia cardiaca*, heart failure.
insuficiente adj. Insufficient, inadequate (escaso). || Incompetent.
insuflación f. Insufflation.
insuflador m. Insufflator.
insuflar v. tr. To insufflate.
insufrible adj. Insufferable, unbearable, intolerable (inaguantable).
ínsula f. Island (isla).

insular adj. Insular, island: *provincias insulares*, island provinces. || MED. Insular.
— M. y f. Islander.

insularidad f. Insularity.

insulina f. Insulin.

Insulindia n. pr. GEOGR. Indian Archipelago.

insulinoterapia f. Treatment by insulin.

insulsez f. Insipidity, tastelessness (falta de sabor). || FIG. Dullness, insipidness (falta de gracia). | Insipid *o* flat remark (dicho sin gracia).

insulso, sa adj. Insipid, tasteless (comida, guiso, etc.). || FIG. Dull, insipid (conversación, tema).

insultador, ra adj. Insulting.
— M. y f. Insulter.

insultante adj. Insulting, offensive.

insultar v. tr. To insult.

insulto m. Insult.

insumergible adj. Insubmersible, insubmergible.

insumisión f. Insubordination.

insumiso, sa adj. Unsubmissive, insubordinate.

insumo m. COM. Input.

insuperable adj. Unsurpassable (calidad, hazaña, trabajo, etc.). || Insurmountable: *una dificultad insuperable*, an insurmountable difficulty. || *Precios insuperables*, unbeatable prices.

insurgente adj. Insurgent.
— M. y f. Insurrectionist, insurgent, rebel.

insurrección f. Insurrection, revolt, rebellion.

insurreccional adj. Insurrectional, insurrectionary.

insurreccionar v. tr. To incite to rebellion.
— V. pr. To rebel, to rise in revolt.

insurrecto, ta adj. Insurgent.
— M. y f. Insurrectionist, insurgent, rebel.

insustancial adj. V. INSUBSTANCIAL.

insustancialidad f. V. INSUBSTANCIALIDAD.

insustituible adj. Irreplaceable.

intacto, ta adj. Untouched (no tocado). || Whole (entero). || Intact, undamaged: *la casa salió intacta del bombardeo*, the house remained undamaged after the bombing. || FIG. Intact, undamaged (reputación, etc.). || *Un tema que ha quedado intacto*, a subject which has not been touched upon.

intachable adj. Irreproachable, blameless.

intangibilidad f. Intangibility.

intangible adj. Intangible.

integrable adj. MAT. Integrable.

integration f. Integration. || *Integraciones bancarias*, bank mergers.

integracionista m. y f. Integrationist.

integrador, ra adj. Integrative.
— M. Integrator.

integral adj. Integral. || — *Cálculo integral*, integral calculus. || *Pan integral*, wholemeal bread.
— F. MAT. Integral.

integralmente adv. Wholly, entirely, completely.

integrante adj. Integral, integrant.

integrar v. tr. To compose, to make up: *varios estados integran la federación*, several states make up the federation. || To integrate: *integrar a los pobres en la sociedad*, to integrate the poor into society. || To complete, to make whole (completar). || To repay, to reimburse (reintegrar). || MAT. To integrate. || *Amer.* To pay (pagar). || *La Asamblea General estará integrada por todos los miembros de la organización*, the General Assembly shall be composed of all the members of the organization.

integridad f. Integrity. || Whole: *la integridad de su sueldo*, the whole of his salary. || Integrity, uprightness (rectitud). || Virginity (virginidad).

integrismo m. Late nineteenth century Spanish political party which advocated the preservation of national traditions.

íntegro, gra adj. Whole, entire, complete. || FIG. Upright (honrado). || *En versión íntegra*, in an unabridged version.

intelecto m. Intellect.

intelectual adj./s. Intellectual.

intelectualidad f. Intellectuality. || Intellectuals, *pl.*, intelligentsia.

intelectualismo m. Intellectualism.

intelectualista adj. Intellectualist, intellectualistic.
— M. y f. Intellectualist.

intelectualizar v. tr. To intellectualize.

inteligencia f. Intelligence: *dar pruebas de inteligencia*, to show signs of intelligence. || Knowledge (conocimiento). || Comprehension. || — *En la inteligencia de que*, on the understanding that. || *Los ladrones del expreso estaban en inteligencia con el guardafrenos*, the robbers of the express were in league with the brakeman. || *Tener inteligencia para los negocios*, to have a good head for business. || *Vivir en buena inteligencia con alguien*, to live in harmony with s.o.

inteligenciado, da adj. Informed.

inteligente adj. Intelligent (dotado de inteligencia). || Intelligent, clever (de mucha inteligencia): *un chico inteligente*, a clever boy.
— M. y f. Intelligent person.

inteligibilidad f. Intelligibility.

inteligible adj. Intelligible, understandable (comprensible). || Audible.

intelligentsia f. Intelligentsia.

intemerata f. FAM. Boldness (atrevimiento). || — FAM. *Formar la intemerata*, to cause a rumpus. | *Saber la intemerata*, to know a hell of a lot.

intemperancia f. Intemperance. || Immoderation: *el director no pudo soportar más las intemperancias de la actriz*, the producer could no longer tolerate the immoderations of the actress.

intemperante adj. Intemperate, immoderate.

intemperie f. Inclemency (del tiempo). || — *Dormir a la intemperie*, to sleep out of doors *o* in the open. || *Estar a la intemperie*, to be out in the open (estar fuera), to be at the mercy of the elements (sin protección de la lluvia, etc.).

intempestivamente adv. Inopportunely.

intempestivo, va adj. Inopportune, untimely.

intemporal adj. Intemporal.

intemporalidad f. Non-temporality.

intención f. Intention: *con la intención de*, with the intention of. || Plan, intention (proyecto): *éstas son mis intenciones*, these are my plans. || Will, testament: *las últimas intenciones del moribundo*, the last testament of the dying man. || JUR. Intent: *intención delictiva*, criminal intent. || MED. Intention: *cura de* or *por primera intención*, healing by first intention. || — *Buena intención*, good will, benevolence, good intention. || *Con intención*, intentionally, on purpose, deliberately. || MED. *Curar de primera intanción a*, to administer first aid to. || *De intención*, bad-tempered (animal). || *De primera intención*, straightaway, right away. || *Mala intención*, ill will, malevolence, ill intention. || FIG. *Primera intención*, frankness, candour: *obrar con primera intención*, to act with frankness. || *Segunda intención*, underhandedness, duplicity, deceitfulness. || *Tener (la) intención de*, to intend to. || *Tener malas intenciones*, to bear ill will, to be ill-intentioned. || *Tener una segunda intención*, to have an ulterior motive.

intencionadamente adv. Intentionally, on purpose, deliberately.

intencionado, da adj. Intentioned, deliberate (intencional). || *Mal intencionado*, ill-intentioned, malevolent.

intencional adj. Intentional, deliberate.

intencionalidad f. Intentionality.

intendencia f. Intendance, intendancy (funciones de intendente). || Service Corps [U.S., Quartermaster Corps] (en el ejército).

intendenta f. Intendant's wife.

intendente m. Intendant (de un servicio administrativo del Estado). || MIL. Quartermaster general.

intensidad f. Intensity. || ELECTR. Strength. || FÍS. Intensity.

intensificación f. Intensification.

intensificar v. tr. To intensify.
— V. pr. To intensify, to strengthen (relaciones, etc.). || To intensify, to increase (comercio, etc.).

intensivo, va adj. Intensive: *curso intensivo*, intensive course. || GRAM. Intensive. || AGR. *Cultivo intensivo*, intensive cultivation *o* farming.

intenso, sa adj. Intense. || Acute (dolor). || ELECTR. Strong (light, current).

intentar v. tr. To try, to attempt: *intentar salir de un mal paso*, to try to get out of a tight spot. || JUR. To institute [proceedings]. | To bring [an action]. || *Con intentarlo no se pierde nada*, nothing is lost by trying.

intento m. Intent. || Intention (intención). || Attempt: *al primer intento*, at the first attempt. || — *Como de intento*, as if intentionally. || *De intento*, intentionally, on purpose. || *Intento de suicidio*, attempted suicide. || *No pasar del intento*, to fail in one's attempt. || *Tener intento de*, to intend to.

intentona f. FAM. Rash *o* foolhardy attempt.

interacción f. Interaction, interplay.

interaliado, da adj. Interallied.

interamericano, na adj. Interamerican.

interandino, na adj. Interandean.

intercadencia f. Intercadence (del pulso).

intercadente adj. Intercadent (pulso).

intercalación f. Intercalation, insertion.

intercalar adj. Intercalary: *día intercalar*, intercalary day.

intercalar v. tr. To intercalate, to insert.

intercambiable adj. Interchangeable.

intercambiar v. tr. To interchange, to exchange. || To swap (trocar). || COM. To exchange.

intercambio m. Exchange, interchange: *intercambio de cartas*, exchange of letters. || Exchange: *intercambio cultural*, cultural exchange. || *Intercambios comerciales*, international trade, *sing.*

interceder v. intr. To intercede: *interceder con* or *cerca de alguien por otro*, to intercede with s.o. on behalf of another.

intercelular adj. Intercellular.

intercepción f. Interception.

interceptación f. Interception. || Blockage (del tráfico, de la carretera, etc.).

interceptador m. Interceptor (avión).

interceptar v. tr. To intercept. || To block: *carretera interceptada*, blocked road. || To hold up, to block, to interrupt (la circulación): *continúa interceptada la circulación*, the traffic is still held up.

intercesión f. Intercession.

intercesor, ra adj. Intercessory, interceding.
— M. y f. Intercessor.

intercesoriamente adv. Intercessorily, by intercession.

intercolumnio o **intercolunio** m. ARQ. Intercolumniation.
intercomunicación f. Intercommunication.
intercomunicador m. Intercommunication system, intercom (fam.).
intercomunicarse v. pr. To intercommunicate.
interconectar v. tr. ELECTR. To interconnect.
interconexión f. Interconnection.
intercontinental adj. Intercontinental.
intercostal adj. ANAT. Intercostal: *músculos intercostales*, intercostal muscles.
interdecir v. tr. To prohibit, to forbid.
interdental adj. Interdental.
interdepartamental adj. Interdepartmental.
interdependencia f. Interdependence.
interdependiente adj. Interdependent.
interdicción f. Interdiction, prohibition. || — JUR. *Interdicción civil*, judicial restraint, civil interdiction (por locura o imbecilidad), suspension of civil rights (pena accesoria). || *Interdicción de residencia* or *de lugar*, prohibition from entering a specified area.
interdicto m. Interdiction, prohibition. || REL. Interdict.
interdigital adj. Interdigital (músculo, membrana, espacio).
interés m. Interest: *este libro no tiene interés alguno*, this book has no interest whatsoever; *en interés de*, in the interest of. || Self-interest: *dejarse guiar por el interés*, to allow o.s. to be guided by self-interest. || FIG. Interest (inclinación): *despertar el interés de alguien*, to arouse s.o.'s interest. || COM. Interest (rédito): *interés compuesto*, *simple*, compound, simple interest; *colocar dinero a interés*, to invest money at interest; *un interés del diez por ciento* or *de un diez por ciento*, a ten per cent interest, an interest of ten per cent. || — Pl. COM. Interests (capital invertido en una industria). | Interests (propiedades, bienes de fortuna). || — COM. *Devengar intereses*, to bear interest. || *Merecer interés*, to be interesting. || *Mostrar interés en* or *por*, to show an interest in. || *Poner interés en*, to take an interest in. || *Prestar con interés*, to lend at interest. || *Prestar especial interés a*, to show special interest in. || *Ser de gran interés*, to be of great interest, to be very interesting. || *Tener interés en* or *por*, to be interested in (interesarse), to be anxious for *o* that (desear): *tengo interés en que vengan*, I am anxious for them to come *o* that they should come; to be in one's interest: *tienes interés en llevarte bien con el director*, it is in your interest to keep on the right side of the manager. || COM. *Tener intereses en*, to hold shares in. || *Tomarse interés por algo, por uno*, to take an interest in sth., in s.o. || *Un tema de interés*, a topic of interest.
interesado, da adj. Interested: *interesado en un negocio*, interested in a business. || Biassed, prejudiced (parcial). || Selfish, self-interested (egoísta). || *Obrar de una manera interesada*, to act out of self-interest.
— M. y f. Interested [person]: *los interesados se servirán pasar por nuestras oficinas*, those [persons] interested please call in at our offices. || Applicant (en una solicitud). || *Los interesados*, those concerned, those interested.
interesante adj. Interesting. || *Hacerse el interesante*, to try to attract attention.
interesar v. tr. To interest: *interesar a uno en una empresa*, to interest s.o. in an enterprise. || To concern, to be of interest to: *es un caso que nos interesa a todos*, it's a case which concerns us all. || MED. To affect. || To take into, to give an interest in: *interesar a uno en un negocio*, to take s.o. into a business. || — *Este libro me interesa mucho*, this book interests me a great deal. || *¿Le interesa el deporte?*, are you interested in sport?
— V. intr. To be of interest: *interesa saber si*, it is of interest to know whether. || *Mi propuesta no interesó*, no one was interested in *o* by my proposal, my proposal interested no one.
— V. pr. To be interested, to take an interest: *interesarse por* or *en*, to be interested *o* to take an interest in.
interestelar adj. Interstellar.
interfecto, ta adj. JUR. Murdered.
— M. y f. JUR. Murder victim. || FAM. Person in question.
interferencia f. FÍS. Interference (en radio, televisión): *franjas de interferencia*, interference fringes *o* rings. | Jamming (para impedir la escucha, etc.). || FIG. Interference, intervention.
interferente adj. Interfering.
interferir* v. intr. To interfere (*en*, *con*, in, with).
— V. tr. RAD. To interfere with: *interferir una emisión*, to interfere with a broadcast. | To jam (para impedir la escucha, etc.).
interfono m. Intercom (en oficinas, etc.).
interglacial adj. Interglacial.
intergubernamental adj. Intergovernmental.
ínterin m. Interim, meantime: *en el ínterin*, in the meantime.
— Adv. Meanwhile, in the meantime (mientras tanto). || *Por ínterin*, temporarily.
interinamente adv. Meanwhile, in the meantime, in the interim (mientras tanto). || Temporarily (temporalmente).
interinar v. tr. To occupy temporarily (un cargo). || *Interinar el cargo de presidente*, to be acting president *o* acting chairman.
interinato m. *Amer.* Interim (tiempo). || Temporary post (cargo).
interinidad f. Temporariness. || Temporary employment.
interino, na adj. Interim. || Provisional, interim, temporary (provisional): *una solución interina*, a provisional solution. || Acting: *presidente interino*, acting president *o* chairman.
— M. y f. Person who executes a duty in the absence of another. || Acting president *o* acting chairman (presidente). || Deputy, stand-in (sustituto). || — F. Charwoman (asistenta).
interior adj. Interior, inside: *patio interior*, inside patio. || Inner (más cerca del centro): *la parte interior de una rueda*, the inner part of a wheel. || Inner (pensamientos). || Domestic, internal: *política interior*, domestic policy. || GEOGR. Inland. || — *En la parte interior*, on the inside, inside. || *Ropa interior*, underclothing, underclothes, *pl.*
— M. Inside, interior. || GEOGR. Interior. || DEP. Inside forward (fútbol). || Local (en un sobre). || — Pl. Insides, entrails (entrañas). || — *Dijo para su interior*, he said to himself. || DEP. *Interior derecha*, inside right. | *Interior izquierda*, inside left.
interioridad f. Interiority, inwardness. || — Pl. Personal affairs: *meterse en las interioridades de los demás*, to interfere in other people's personal affairs. || FIG. Interior *o* inside aspects (de un asunto, etc.). | Ins and outs (pormenores).
interiormente adv. Inwardly, inside.
interjección f. GRAM. Interjection.
interjectivo, va adj. Interjectional.
interlínea f. Space between lines (espacio). || PRINT. Lead (regleta).
interlineación f. o **interlineado** m. Interlineation, interlining.
interlineal adj. Interlinear.
interlinear v. tr. To interline.
interlocución f. Interlocution (conversación).
interlocutor, ra m. y f. Interlocutor. || *Su interlocutor*, the person he was speaking to (persona a quien se habla), the person who spoke to him (persona que habla a otra).
interlocutorio, ria adj. JUR. Interlocutory: *formar auto interlocutorio*, to award an interlocutory decree.
intérlope adj. Interloping (fraudulento).
interludio m. Interlude.
intermaxilar adj. ANAT. Intermaxillary.
intermediar v. intr. To intermediate, to mediate.
intermediario, ria adj. Intermediary.
— M. y f. Mediator, intermediary, go-between. || COM. Middleman.
intermedio, dia adj. Intermediate, medium. || Intervening: *los años intermedios*, the intervening years. || *Precio intermedio*, moderate price.
— M. Interval (intervalo). || Recess (Parlamento). || Interlude (televisión). || Intermission (cine). || Interval (teatro). || — *En el intermedio*, in the meantime. || *Por intermedio de*, through, by means of.
intermezzo m. MÚS. Intermezzo.
interminable adj. Interminable, endless.
interministerial adj. Interministerial: *reunión interministerial*, interministerial meeting.
intermisión f. Intermission.
intermitencia f. Intermittence, intermittency. || — *Con* or *por intermitencia*, intermittently. || MED. *Intermitencia de la fiebre*, intermittence of fever.
intermitente adj. Intermittent: *luz intermitente*, intermittent light.
— M. AUT. Indicator, blinker, winker.
intermolecular adj. Intermolecular.
intermuscular adj. Intermuscular.
internación f. Internment (en una cárcel). || Confinement (en un hospital). || Penetration (en un país).
internacional adj. International.
— M. y f. International (deportista). || — F. International (asociación). || Internationale (himno).
internacionalidad f. Internationality.
internacionalismo m. Internationalism.
internacionalista adj./s. Internationalist.
internacionalización f. Internationalization.
internacionalizar v. tr. To internationalize.
internado, da adj. Interned: *los prisioneros internados en el campo de concentración*, prisoners interned in the concentration camp. || Confined (en un hospital). || *Los ancianos internados en el asilo*, the old people in the home.
— M. Boarding school (colegio). || Boarders, *pl.* [living in a boarding school]. || MIL. Internee. || — F. DEP. Breakthrough.
internamente adv. Internally, inside.
internamiento m. Internment.
internar v. tr. To intern (un prisionero). || To commit (*en*, to) [en un manicomio]. || To confine (en un hospital). || To put in a home (a un anciano).
— V. pr. To penetrate (por la fuerza): *los moros se internaron en España*, the Moors penetrated into Spain. || FIG. To go deeply (*en*, into) [profundizar]. | To intrude (en la intimidad de uno). || DEP. To break through: *el extremo se internó por la izquierda*, the

winger broke through on the left. | *Internarse en*, to go into the interior of (un país), to go into (un bosque).
internista adj. *Médico internista*, internist.
— M. y f. Internist.
interno, na adj. Internal, interior. || Domestic, internal (del país). || Boarding (estudiante). || *Por vía interna*, internally.
— M. y f. Intern (de un hospital). || Boarder, boarding student (en un colegio). || *Poner* or *meter a un niño interno*, to put *o* to place a child in a boarding school.
inter nos loc. lat. FAM. Between ourselves, between you and me.
internuncio m. REL. Internuncio. || Interlocutor. || Spokesman (portavoz).
interoceánico, ca adj. Interoceanic.
interpaginar v. tr. To interpage.
interparietal adj. ANAT. Interparietal.
interparlamentario, ria adj. Interparliamentary.
interpelación f. Interpellation. || Appeal, plea (ruego).
interpelador, ra o **interpelante** adj. Interpellant.
— M. y f. Interpellator, interpellant.
interpelar v. tr. To interpellate (en el parlamento). || To appeal to, to implore, to beseech (rogar).
interpenetración f. Interpenetration.
interplanetario, ria adj. Interplanetary.
interpolación f. Interpolation.
interpolador, ra adj. Interpolating.
— M. y f. Interpolator.
interpolar v. tr. To interpolate (intercalar).
interponer* v. tr. To interpose. || JUR. *Interponer recurso de apelación*, to give notice of appeal.
— V. pr. To intervene.
interposición f. Interposition. || Intervention. || JUR. Lodging of an appeal.
interpósita persona (por) loc. adv. By an intermediary.
interpretable adj. Interpretable.
interpretación f. Interpretation. || Interpreting (profesión). || MÚS. y TEATR. Performance, interpretation. || *Mala interpretación*, misinterpretation.
interpretador, ra adj. Interpreting.
— M. y f. Interpreter.
interpretar v. tr. To interpret. || To sing, to perform (una canción). || TEATR. To play, to act, to interpret (un papel). | To perform (una obra). || To perform, to interpret (una obra de música).
interpretariado m. Interpreting.
interpretativo, va adj. Interpretative.
intérprete m. y f. Interpreter: *intérprete de conferencia*, conference interpreter; *intérprete jurado*, sworn interpreter. || Exponent, interpreter (de música). || Performer, artist (de una obra de teatro). || Singer (de una canción).
interprofesional adj. Interprofessional.
interpuesto, ta adj. Interposed.
interregno m. Interregnum.
interrogación f. Question, interrogation (pregunta). || Questioning, interrogation (acción de preguntar). || GRAM. *Signo de interrogación*, question *o* interrogation mark.
interrogador, ra adj. Interrogating. || Inquisitive: *una mirada interrogadora*, an inquisitive look.
— M. y f. Interrogator, questioner.
interrogante adj. Interrogating, questioning. || *Punto interrogante*, question *o* interrogation mark.
— M. Question (pregunta). || FIG. Question mark: *quedan muchos interrogantes todavía*, there are still a lot of question marks.
interrogar v. tr. To interrogate, to question: *interrogar a alguien acerca de*, to interrogate s.o. about; *interrogaron al testigo*, they interrogated the witness.
interrogativo, va adj. Interrogative.
interrogatorio m. Interrogation.
interrumpir v. tr. To interrupt: *interrumpir a uno con una pregunta*, to interrupt s.o. with a question. || To block, to obstruct, to interrupt: *el coche averiado interrumpía el tráfico*, the broken-down car blocked the traffic. || To stop temporarily (parar provisionalmente). || To cut off (el abastecimiento, etc.): *interrumpieron la corriente para reparar la avería*, they cut off the current in order to repair the fault. || To cut short, to interrupt, to curtail: *tuvieron que interrumpir sus vacaciones*, they had to cut their holiday short.
interrupción f. Interruption: *sin interrupción*, without interruption. || Interruption, break (para descansar).
interruptor, ra adj. Interrupting.
— M. ELECTR. Switch. || *Interruptor eléctrico automático*, automatic time switch.
intersecarse v. pr. To intersect.
intersección f. Intersection.
intersexual adj. Intersexual.
intersideral adj. ASTR. Interstellar.
intersindical adj. Inter-trade-union.
intersticial adj. Interstitial: *tejido intersticial*, interstitial tissue.
intersticio m. Interstice (espacio). || Interval (intervalo).
intertrigo m. MED. Intertrigo.
intertropical adj. Intertropical.
interurbano, na adj. Interurban. || — *Central interurbana* or *teléfono interurbano*, interurban telephone exchange. || *Poner una conferencia interurbana*, to make a long distance call *o* a trunk call.
intervalo m. Interval (tiempo). || Gap (espacio). || MÚS. Interval. || *A intervalos*, at intervals.
intervención f. Intervention. || Tapping (del teléfono). || Auditing, audit (de cuentas). || Participation (en una conversación). || Control (de los precios). || — MED. *Intervención quirúrgica*, operation. || *Política de no intervención*, nonintervention policy.
intervencionismo m. Interventionism.
intervencionista adj. Interventionist.
— M. y f. Interventionist.
intervenir* v. intr. To intervene: *el ejército intervino en la batalla*, the army intervened in the battle. || To intervene, to intercede (interceder). || To interfere (entrometerse): *intervenir en un asunto familiar*, to interfere in a family matter. || To participate, to take part (tomar parte): *¿en cuántas películas has intervenido?*, in how many films have you taken part? || To happen, to occur (acontecer).
— V. tr. To control (precios). || To audit (cuentas). || To tap (teléfono). || MED. To operate on, to perform an operation on.
interventor m. Supervisor, inspector (inspector). || Controller (verificador). || *Interventor de cuentas*, auditor.
interviú f. Interwiew. || *Hacer una interviú a uno*, to interwiew s.o.
interviuvar v. tr. To interwiew (entrevistar).
interyacente adj. Interjacent.
intestado, da adj./s. Intestate.
intestinal adj. Intestinal: *lombrices intestinales*, intestinal worms.
intestino, na adj. Internal, intestine: *luchas intestinas*, internal conflicts.
— M. ANAT. Intestine. || — ANAT. *Intestino ciego*, caecum. | *Intestino delgado*, small intestine. | *Intestino grueso*, large intestine.
intimación f. Notification (mandato). || JUR. *Intimación judicial*, judicial notice.
intimar v. tr. To notify, to summon: *le intiman a que pague la multa*, they notify him to pay the fine. || To order (mandar).
— V. intr. To become intimate *o* very friendly: *intimar con uno*, to become intimate with s.o.
intimatorio, ria adj. Intimating, notifying.
intimidación f. Intimidation.
intimidad f. Intimacy (con alguien). || Privacy, private life (vida privada). || — *En la intimidad*, privately, in private. || *Una persona de su intimidad*, one of his circle.
intimidar v. tr. To intimidate: *intimidar a uno con amenazas*, to intimidate s.o. with threats. || To scare (asustar).
intimista adj./s. Intimist.
íntimo, ma adj. Intimate. || Private (vida, boda, etc.). || Close, intimate (amistad, relaciones). || Innermost (pensamientos).
— M. Close friend, bosom friend: *un íntimo de la casa*, a close friend of the family.
intitular v. tr. To entitle.
— V. pr. To be entitled.
intocable adj./s. Untouchable.
intolerable adj. Intolerable.
intolerancia f. Intolerance.
intolerante adj./s. Intolerant.
intonso, sa adj. With uncut hair, long-haired. || Uncut (libro). || FIG. Ignorant.
intoxicación f. Intoxication, poisoning. || Food poisoning (debida a la comida).
intoxicado, da adj. Intoxicated, poisoned (envenenado). || Intoxicated, drunk (borracho).
— M. y f. Intoxicated person.
intoxicar v. tr. To intoxicate, to poison (envenenar).
— V. pr. To be intoxicated *o* poisoned.
intracelular adj. Intracellular.
intradérmico, ca adj. Intradermic.
intradós m. ARQ. Intrados.
intraducible adj. Untranslatable.
intramuros adv. Within the city, intramurally.
intramuscular adj. Intramuscular: *inyección intramuscular*, intramuscular injection.
intranquilidad f. Restlessness, uneasiness, worry.
intranquilizador, ra adj. Disquieting, worrying.
intranquilizar v. tr. To disquiet, to worry.
intranquilo, la adj. Restless, uneasy, worried.
intranscendencia f. Insignificance, unimportance.
intranscendente adj. Insignificant, unimportant.
intransferible adj. Untransferable, not transferable, nontransferable.
intransigencia f. Intransigence.
intransigente adj. Intransigent, uncompromising.
intransitable adj. Impassable.
intransitivo, va adj./s.m. GRAM. Intransitive.
intransmisible adj. Intransmissible.
intransportable adj. Not transportable, untransportable.
intranuclear adj. Intranuclear.
intrascendencia f. Insignificance, unimportance.
intrascendente adj. Insignificant, unimportant.
intrasmisible adj. Intransmissible.

intratable adj. Intractable, unmanageable (difícil de tratar). || Unsociable (poco sociable).
intrauterino, na adj. MED. Intrauterine.
intravenoso, sa adj. Intravenous: *inyección intravenosa*, intravenous injection.
intrepidez f. Intrepidity, boldness, daring, fearlessness.
intrépido, da adj. Intrepid, bold, daring, fearless.
intriga f. Intrigue: *intrigas palaciegas*, court intrigues. || *Tramar* or *urdir intrigas*, to plot, to intrigue, to scheme.
intrigante adj. Intriguing.
— M. Intriguer, intrigant. || — F. Intriguer, intrigante.
intrigar v. intr. To intrigue, to plot, to scheme.
— V. tr. To intrigue, to puzzle (dejar perplejo): *su conducta me intriga*, his conduct intrigues me. || To intrigue, to fascinate (suscitar interés).
intrincación f. Intricacy.
intrincado, da adj. Intricate, involved, complicated (problema, asunto). || Dense (bosque).
intrincamiento m. Intricacy.
intrincar v. tr. To complicate, to confuse.
intríngulis m. inv. FAM. Ulterior *o* hidden motive (razón oculta). | Snag, difficulty: *ahí está el intríngulis*, there's the snag. | Enigma, mystery: *el intríngulis de un asunto*, the enigma of a matter.
intrínseco, ca adj. Intrinsic, intrinsical.
introducción f. Introduction.
introducir* v. tr. To insert, to introduce: *introducir el dedo en un agujero*, to insert one's finger into a hole. || To introduce: *introducir a uno en la alta sociedad*, to introduce s.o. into high society. || To introduce, to bring in: *introducir una nueva moda*, to introduce a new fashion. || To show into: *la criada nos introdujo en el salón*, the maid showed us into the living room. || To cause, to create, to bring on (provocar): *introducir el desorden, la discordia*, to bring on disorder, discord.
— V. pr. To get into (meterse). || To interfere (entremeterse).
introductor, ra adj. Introductory.
— M. *Introductor de embajadores*, head of the Protocol Section of the Foreign Affairs department.
introductorio, ria adj. Introductory, introductive.
introito m. REL. Introit (oración). || Prologue (principio, prólogo).
intromisión f. Meddling, interfering (entrometimiento). || JUR. Intromission.
introspección f. Introspection.
introspectivo, va adj. Introspective.
introversión f. Introversion.
introverso, sa adj. Introversive.
introvertido, da adj. Introverted, introvert.
— N. Introvert.
intrusión f. Intrusion.
intruso, sa adj. Intrusive, intruding.
— M. y f. Intruder.
intubación f. MED. Intubation.
intubar v. tr. MED. To intubate.
intuición f. Intuition.
intuicionismo m. Intuitionism.
intuir* v. tr. To sense: *avanza hacia el pueblo que intuye cercano*, he moves towards the town which he senses to be near. || To feel: *se intuye la palpitación del campo en su poesía*, one feels the palpitation of the country in his poetry. || To have a sense of, to have a feeling for: *este niño intuye la música*, this child has a feeling for music. || To intuit: *intuir el porvenir*, to intuit the future.
intuitivo, va adj. Intuitive.
intumescencia f. Intumescence, swelling.
intumescente adj. Intumescent.
inundable adj. Inundable, easily flooded.
inundación f. Inundation, flooding (acción). || Flood (efecto). || FIG. Flood.
inundar v. tr. To flood. || FIG. To flood, to swamp, to inundate: *inundar el mercado de productos extranjeros*, to flood the market with foreign products.
inurbano, na adj. Inurbane, discourteous.
inusitado, da adj. Unusual, uncommon.
inútil adj. Useless (inservible): *¿por qué guardas tantas cosas inútiles?*, why do you keep so many useless things? || Unnecessary, needless: *es inútil decirlo*, it's unnecessary to say it. || Vain, fruitless (esfuerzo). || Unfit: *inútil para el servicio militar*, unfit for military service. || Good-for-nothing (incapaz). || *Es inútil que grites*, it's no good your shouting, it's useless for you to shout.
— M. y f. FAM. *Un* or *una inútil*, a good-for-nothing.
inutilidad f. Uselessness, unusefulness. || Incompetence (de una persona). || Fruitlessness (de unos esfuerzos).
inutilizable adj. Unusable.
inutilizar v. tr. To make unusable, to put out of action: *el niño ha inutilizado la máquina de escribir*, the child has made the typewriter unusable. || To disable, to put out of action: *los aviones inutilizaron uno de los barcos*, the planes disabled one of the ships. || To cancel (sello). || To spoil, to ruin (estropear, echar a perder).
invadir v. tr. To invade. || FIG. To encroach upon (los derechos ajenos). | To overcome: *le invadió una gran tristeza*, he was overcome by deep sadness.
invaginación f. MED. Invagination.
invaginar v. tr. MED. To invaginate.
invalidación f. Invalidation.
invalidable adj. That may be invalidated.
invalidar v. tr. To invalidate. || JUR. To invalidate, to nullify, to annul (anular).
invalidez f. Invalidity.
inválido, da adj. MED. Invalid, disabled. || JUR. Invalid, void, null.
— M. y f. MED. Invalid. || MIL. Disabled soldier.
invar m. Invar (metal).
invariabilidad f. Invariability.
invariable adj. Invariable.
invariadamente adv. Invariably.
invariado, da adj. Unvaried, unchanged.
invasión f. Invasion.
invasor, ra adj. Invading.
— M. Invader.
invectiva f. Invective: *fulminar invectivas contra uno*, to thunder invectives against s.o. || *Lanzar invectivas contra*, to inveigh against.
invencibilidad f. Invincibility.
invencible adj. Invincible. || Unsurmountable (obstáculos). || *La Armada Invencible*, The Spanish Armada.
invención f. Invention. || — *De su propia invención*, of his own invention. || REL. *La Invención de la Santa Cruz*, the finding of the true Cross. || *Patente de invención*, patent.
invendible adj. Unsalable, unmarketable, unsellable.
invendido, da adj. Unsold.
inventar v. tr. To invent. || To make up (mentiras, etc.). || To invent, to think up (imaginar).
inventariar v. tr. To inventory, to make an inventory of, to take stock of.
inventario m. Inventory: *hacer un inventario*, to make an inventory. || Inventory, stocktaking (acción).
inventivo, va adj. Inventive, creative (capaz de crear). || Resourceful (ingenioso).
— F. Inventiveness, creativeness (capacidad para crear). || Resourcefulness (ingeniosidad).
invento m. Invention.
inventor, ra m. y f. Inventor.
invernación f. Hibernation.

— OBSERV. This word is a barbarism used for *hibernación*.

invernáculo m. Greenhouse, hothouse.
invernada f. Wintertime, winter (invierno). || *Amer.* Winter pasture.
invernadero m. Greenhouse, hothouse (para las plantas). || Winter quarters, *pl.* (refugio de invierno). || Winter pasture (pasto).
invernal adj. Wintry, wintery.
— M. Winter shed, winter stable.
invernar* v. intr. To winter, to hibernate (pasar el invierno). || ZOOL. To hibernate.
invernizo, za adj. Wintry, wintery, winter.
inverosímil adj. Improbable, unlikely, implausible: *un relato inverosímil*, an improbable story.
inverosimilitud f. Improbability, unlikelihood.
inversión f. Inversion. || COM. Investment.
inversionista m. COM. Investor.
inverso, sa adj. Inverted: *la imagen inversa de un objeto*, the inverted image of an object. || Inverse, reverse: *en orden inverso*, in inverse order. || Opposite: *venía en sentido inverso*, he was coming in the opposite direction. || — *A* or *por la inversa*, the other way round (inversamente), on the contrary (al contrario). || *A la inversa de*, unlike (a diferencia de). || *Y a la inversa*, and vice versa.
inversor m. FÍS. Reversing device.
invertebrado, da adj./s.m. ZOOL. Invertebrate. || — Pl. Invertebrata.
invertido, da adj. Inverted, reversed. || *Azúcar invertido*, invert sugar.
— M. y f. Homosexual, invert.
invertir* v. tr. To invert, to change, to reverse (cambiar): *invertir los papeles*, to change roles. || To put upside down, to put the other way round (poner al revés). || To invert (sistemáticamente): *invertir la imagen de un objeto*, to invert the image of an object. || To reverse: *invertir el sentido de una corriente*, to reverse the direction of a current. || To spend: *invirtieron 30 minutos en el recorrido*, they spent 30 minutes on the journey. || COM. To invest (capitales). || MAT. To invert.
investidura f. Investiture.
investigación f. Investigation, inquiry (policiaca, fiscal). || Research: *investigación científica*, scientific research. || — *Consejo Superior de Investigaciones Científicas*, Council for Scientific Research. || *Investigación de mercados*, market research, marketing. || *Investigación de la paternidad*, affiliation suit.
investigador, ra adj. Investigating. || Inquiring, inquisitive: *mirada investigadora*, inquiring look.
— M. y f. Investigator. || Researcher, research worker (científico).
investigar v. intr. To investigate (la policía, etc.). || To do research (científicos).
— V. tr. To investigate, to inquire into, to look into: *investigar los móviles de un crimen*, to inquire into the causes of a crime. || To find out: *tengo que investigar quién ha dicho esto*, I have to find out who said this. || To do research on (los científicos).
investir* v. tr. To invest (conferir una dignidad).
inveterado, da adj. Inveterate.

invicto, ta adj. Unconquered, unbeaten.
invierno m. Winter (estación): *en lo más crudo del invierno,* in the dead of winter. || Winter, wintertime (período). || *Amer.* Rainy season (en las regiones ecuatoriales).
inviolabilidad f. Inviolability. || *Inviolabilidad parlamentaria,* parliamentary privilege.
inviolable adj. Inviolable.
inviolado, da adj. Inviolate.
invisibilidad f. Invisibility.
invisible adj. Invisible.
invitación f. Invitation.
invitado, da adj. Invited.
— M. y f. Guest: *mañana tenemos invitados,* we are expecting guests tomorrow.
invitador, ra o **invitante** adj. Inviting.
— M. y f. Host (hombre), hostess (mujer).
invitar v. tr. To invite: *invitar a uno a una cena,* to invite s.o. to dinner. || To call on: *invitar a alguien a hablar,* to call on s.o. to speak. || FIG. To tempt, to invite (impulsar). || — *El tiempo invita a ir de excursión,* it is tempting *o* inviting weather to go on an excursion. || *Invitar a una copa,* to buy a drink, to stand a drink.
invitatorio m. REL. Invitatory.
invocación f. Invocation.
invocador, ra adj. Invoking.
— M. y f. Invoker.
invocar v. tr. To invoke (a Dios, etc.). || To invoke, to beg for: *invocar la piedad de,* to invoke the mercy of, to beg for mercy. || To invoke, to refer to (alegar).
invocatorio, ria adj. Invocatory.
involución f. Involution.
involucrado, da adj. Involucrate.
involucrar v. tr. To introduce, to bring in (introducir). || To involve (entrañar, implicar).
involuntario, ria adj. Involuntary. || Unintentional (no intencionado).
involuta f. MAT. Involute.
invulnerabilidad f. Invulnerability.
invulnerable adj. Invulnerable.
inyección f. Injection: *poner una inyección a,* to give an injection to. || Injection: *motor de inyección,* injection engine.
inyectable adj. Injectable.
— M. Injectable substance, injection.
inyectado, da adj. Injected. || *Ojos inyectados en sangre,* bloodshot eyes.
inyectar v. tr. To inject: *inyectar agua,* to inject water; *inyectar algo a alguien,* to inject s.o. with sth.
inyector m. Injector. || TECN. *Inyector de aire,* jet blower (de alto horno).
ion m. FÍS. y QUÍM. Ion.
iónico, ca adj. FÍS. y QUÍM. Ionic.
ionización f. FÍS. y QUÍM. Ionization.
ionizar, ionizarse v. tr. y pr. FÍS. y QUÍM. To ionize.
ionosfera f. Ionosphere.
iota f. Iota (letra griega).
ipecacuana f. BOT. Ipecac, ipecacuanha.
iperita f. Yperite, mustard gas (gas).
ipsilon f. Upsilon (letra griega).
ipso facto loc. lat. Ipso facto (por ese mismo hecho). || Immediately (en el acto).
ir*

> **1.** Sentidos generales del v. intr. — **2.** Ir, con el gerundio. — **3.** Ir, con el participio pasivo. — **4.** Ir, seguido de preposiciones. — **5.** Locuciones. — **6.** V. pr.

1. SENTIDOS GENERALES. — To go: *ir al campo,* to go to the country; *el tren va de Madrid a Barcelona,* the train goes from Madrid to Barcelona; *esta calle va del bulevar a la avenida,* this street goes from the boulevard to the avenue; *vaya donde vaya no se escapará,* he will not escape, wherever he goes *o* go where he may. || To be becoming, to suit: *no te va muy bien este sombrero,* this hat does not suit you very well *o* is not very becoming. || To fit (por el tamaño). || To be coming along, to get along *o* on: *¿cómo te va en el nuevo trabajo?,* how is your new job coming along?, how are you getting on in your new job? || To be: *no sabe por dónde va en su trabajo,* he does not know where he is with his work. || To be, to be getting along: *¿cómo va el enfermo hoy?,* how is the patient [getting along] today? || To be: *va bien vestido,* he is well dressed. || To bet (apostar): *¿cuánto va a que yo llego primero?,* how much do you bet that I arrive first? || To go, to lead (en juegos de cartas).
2. IR, CON EL GERUNDIO. — Indicates that the action is being realized or is just beginning: *vamos andando,* we are walking; *su salud iba empeorando,* his health was deteriorating; *va haciendo calor,* it's getting hotter; *iba anocheciendo,* it was beginning to get dark. || *¡Vamos andando!,* let's walk!
3. IR, CON EL PARTICIPIO PASIVO. — Indicates the result of an action: *van escritas siete cartas,* I have written seven letters, seven letters have been written; *ya van vendidos diez cuadros,* ten paintings have already been sold.
4. IR, SEGUIDO DE PREPOSICIONES. — *Ir a,* to go to: *voy a Madrid,* I am going to Madrid; *voy al médico,* I am going to the doctor's; *voy a hacerlo mañana,* I'm going to do it tomorrow; to be about to, to be just going to (estar a punto de): *iba a decir lo mismo,* I was about to say the same thing. || — *Ir a caballo,* to ride. || *Ir a dar a,* to end at, to lead to: *camino que va a dar a la carretera,* road that ends at the highway. || *Ir a la ruina,* to go to wrack and ruin. || *Ir a parar,* to get at: *¿dónde quiere usted ir a parar?,* what are you getting at?; to get to, to be: *¿dónde ha ido a parar este libro?,* where is that book?, where has that book got to?; to end up, to land up: *el hombre fue a parar a la cárcel,* the man ended up in jail. || *Ir a lo suyo,* v. SUYO. || *Ir a pie,* to walk, to go on foot. || FIG. *No irle a uno a la zaga,* v. ZAGA. | *Si vamos a eso* for that matter.
— *Ir con,* to go with: *ir con su madre al cine,* to go to the cinema with one's mother; *el azul va bien con el blanco,* blue goes well with white; to be: *ir con cuidado, con miedo,* to be careful, afraid.
— *Ir contra,* to go against: *va contra sus principios, su dignidad,* it goes against his principles, his dignity.
— *Ir de,* to go for: *ir de paseo,* to go for a walk; to go on: *ir de viaje,* to go on a trip; to go: *ir de caza, de pesca,* to go hunting, fishing; *ir de compras,* to go shopping; *ir de juerga,* to go and have a good time [U.S., to go have a blast]; to be [dressed] in, to be wearing: *ir de uniforme,* to be in uniform. || — *Esto va de veras,* this is serious, this is no joke. || *Ir del brazo,* to go arm in arm. || *Las noticias iban de boca en boca,* the news spread *o* went from mouth to mouth.
— *Ir en,* to go by (viajar): *ir en coche, en avión, en tren,* to go by car, by plane, by train; to be at stake (estar en juego): *en eso le va la salud,* his health is at stake here; *te va en ello el honor,* your honour is at stake. || — *Ir en bicicleta,* to cycle. || *¿Qué le va en ello?,* what does it matter to you? || *Va mucho en ello,* a lot is at stake, a lot depends on it.
— *Ir para,* to be almost, to be getting on for, to be pushing (fam.): *va para doce años,* he is almost twelve years old; *va para los cincuenta,* he's getting on for fifty, he's pushing fifty. || — *Ir para largo,* to drag on. || *Ir para viejo,* to be getting old. || *Va para médico,* he's going to be a doctor.
— *Ir por,* to go for, to go and fetch: *ir por vino a la bodega,* to go to the cellar for wine; *ir por el médico,* to go for the doctor; to be about: *María iba por los quince años,* Mary was about fifteen years old. || — *Eso no va por usted,* I wasn't referring to you. || *¡Vaya por...!,* here's to... (brindis).
— *Ir tras,* to run after (correr), to pursue, to chase (perseguir), to be behind (estar detrás), to follow (seguir), to chase after (una chica).
5. LOCUCIONES. — FAM. *A eso voy* or *vamos,* I'm coming to that. || *Ahí van cien pesetas,* here are *o* here you have a hundred pesetas. || *¡Allá va!,* catch! || *¿Cómo le va?* or *¿Cómo va eso?,* how are you?, how's it going? || *Con éste van veinte,* that makes twenty. || *De diez a quince van cinco,* ten from fifteen leaves five. || *En lo que va de año,* so far this year. || FAM. *Estar ido,* to be crazy (chiflado), to be daydreaming (distraído). | *Esto no me va ni me viene,* that doesn't interest me (no me interesa), it's all the same to me (me da igual). | *Esto no va contigo,* this doesn't concern you. || FIG. *Ir adelante,* to make progress. || *Ir bien,* to go well, to do well, to get on well: *los negocios van bien,* business is going well. || *Ir descalzo,* to go barefoot. || *Ir descaminado,* v. DESCAMINAR. || FIG. *Ir lejos,* to go far, to go a long way. || *Ir sin sombrero,* to go hatless, to go bareheaded. || FIG. *Ir sobre ruedas,* to run *o* to go smoothly. | *Ir tirando* or *viviendo,* to manage, to get along, to get by. | *Ir zumbando,* v. ZUMBAR. | *¡Lo que va de ayer a hoy!,* how times have changed! | *¡Lo que va del padre al hijo!,* what a difference there is between father and son! | *No vaya a ser que,* so as not to, in order not to, in case: *ponte el abrigo, no vaya a ser que te enfríes,* put on your coat in case you catch a cold. | *¡Qué va!,* nonsense!, rubbish!, nothing of the sort! || *¿Quién va?* or *¿quién va allá?,* who goes there?, who is there? || *Vamos,* well (vacilación): *es guapa, vamos no es fea,* she's pretty, well, she isn't ugly. || *¡Vamos, anda!,* v. ANDAR. || *Vamos a ver,* let's see. || FAM. *¡Vamos despacio!,* slowly does it! | *¡Vamos, una sonrisita!,* come on, just a little smile! | *¡Vaya!* or *¡Vamos!,* fancy that!, you don't say!, come on now! (incredulidad), fancy that!, well, well! (indignación, sorpresa), let's go!, come on! (impaciencia), in short, when you come right down to it (al final de una frase): *es buen chico, ¡vaya!,* when you come right down to it, he's a good lad. | *¡Vaya calor!,* this heat! | *¡Vaya equipo!,* what a team! | *¡Vaya susto que me has dado!,* what a fright you gave me!, good grief, you scared me! || *Voy y vengo,* I'll be right back. || *¡Ya voy!,* I'm coming!
6. V. PR. — To go away, to leave: *se fue ayer,* he left yesterday; *¡idos!,* go away!; *¡vete!,* go away! || FIG. To pass away, to die (morirse). || To lose, to slip: *se le fueron los pies,* his feet slipped, he lost his footing. || To leak (un recipiente, un líquido, un gas). || To go, to disappear (gastarse): *¡cómo se va el dinero!,* how money goes! || To drop (un punto): *se le fue un punto,* she dropped a stitch. || To fade (un color, la luz). || To go away (un dolor, una mancha, etc.). || To wear out, to fall apart (desgarrarse, destrozarse). || POP.

To let off, to fart [U.S., to cut one] (ventosear). || — FIG. y FAM. *¡Allá se van los dos!*, those two make a pretty pair!, those two are tarred with the same brush. | *¡Anda y vete por ahí!*, push off!, clear off! || FIG. *Irse abajo*, to collapse. || *Irse al otro mundo*, to pass away. || *Irse a pique*, v. PIQUE. || *Irse como se había venido*, to leave the same way one came [in]. || *Irse de*, to discard (en el juego de naipes). || *Irse de la lengua* or *írsele a uno la lengua*, v. LENGUA. || *Irse de la memoria*, to slip one's mind, to escape one: *su nombre se me ha ido de la memoria*, his name has slipped my mind. || *Írsele a uno de las manos*, v. MANO. || FAM. *Irse uno que se las pela*, v. PELAR. || *Por aquí se va a mi casa*, this is the way to my house. || *¿Por dónde se va?*, which is the way?, which way is it? || *¡Vámonos!*, let's go! || FAM. *¡Váyase lo uno por lo otro!*, one thing compensates the other. | *¡Vete (iros) a paseo!* or *¡vete (iros) al diablo!*, go to blazes!, go to the devil! | *¡Vete a saber!*, who knows?, goodness knows.

— OBSERV. The construction *ir y* followed by a verb occurs frequently in everyday language to express a sense of determination. It may sometimes be rendered in English by *to up and* or *to go and* (*cuando me insultó, fui y le di una torta*, when he insulted me, I upped and slapped him; *fue y se tiró al río*, he went and jumped in the river).

ira f. Wrath, anger, ire (ant.): *la ira es mala consejera*, wrath is a bad advisor; *en un arrebato de ira*, in a fit of anger. || FIG. Fury, wrath (de los elementos). || — *Descargar la ira en uno*, to vent one's wrath *o* spleen on s.o. || FAM. *¡Ira de Dios!*, by thunder!
iracundia f. Irascibility. || Ire, wrath (ira).
iracundo, da adj. Irascible. || Irate (enfadado). || FIG. y POÉT. Raging, wrathful (los elementos).
Irak o **Iraq** n. pr. m. GEOGR. Iraq.
Irán n. pr. m. GEOGR. Iran.
iraní o **iranio, nia** o **iranés, esa** adj./s. Iranian.

— OBSERV. The plural of the word *iraní* is *iraníes*.

iraqués, esa o **iraquí** adj./s. Iraqi, Iraqian.

— OBSERV. The plural of the word *iraquí* is *iraquíes*.

irascibilidad f. Irascibility.
irascible adj. Irascible, choleric, irritable.
Irene n. pr. f. Irene.
iribú m. *Amer.* Urubu, black vulture (aura).
iridáceas f. pl. BOT. Iridaceae.
iridio m. Iridium (metal).
iridiscencia f. Iridescence.
iridiscente adj. Iridescent.
iris m. Rainbow (meteoro). || ANAT. Iris (del ojo). || MIN. Noble opal (ópalo). || *Arco iris*, rainbow.
irisación f. Iridescence.
irisado, da adj. Rainbow-hued, iridescent.
irisar v. intr. To iridesce, to be iridescent.
— V. tr. To make iridescent.
Irlanda n. pr. f. GEOGR. Ireland. || — *De Irlanda*, Irish, of Ireland. || *Irlanda del Norte*, Northern Ireland.
irlandés, esa adj. Irish.
— M. Irishman (hombre). || Irish (idioma). || — F. Irishwoman (mujer). || *Los irlandeses*, the Irish.
ironía f. Irony.
irónicamente adv. Ironically.
irónico, ca adj. Ironic.
ironista m. y f. Ironist (persona irónica).
ironizar v. tr. To ridicule, to treat ironically.
irracional adj. Unreasoning, irrational (carente de razón). || Irrational (contrario a la razón). || MAT. Irrational.
irracionalidad f. Irrationality.
irracionalismo m. Irrationalism.
irracionalista adj./s. Irrationalist.
irradiación f. Irradiation.
irradiar v. intr. y tr. To irradiate, to radiate. || FIG. To radiate (cultura).
irrazonable adj. Unreasonable.
irreal adj. Unreal.
irrealidad f. Unreality.
irrealismo m. Unrealism.
irrealizable adj. Unrealizable. || Unattainable (imposible de conseguir o de alcanzar).
irrebatible adj. Irrefutable.
irreconciliable adj. Irreconcilable.
irreconocible adj. Irrecognizable, unrecognizable.
irrecuperable adj. Irrecoverable, irretrievable. || Unrecoverable, irrecoverable (crédito, etc.).
irrecusable adj. Unchallengeable, unimpeachable.
irredentismo m. Irredentism.
irredentista adj./s. Irredentist.
irredento, ta adj. Unredeemed (territorio).
irredimible adj. Irredeemable.
irreducible adj. Irreducible: *fractura irreducible*, irreducible fracture.
irreductibilidad f. Irreducibility.
irreductible adj. Irreducible: *fracción irreductible*, irreducible fraction. || Incompatible: *dos tendencias irreductibles*, two incompatible tendencies. || Unyielding (inflexible).
irreembolsable adj. Nonreturnable (sin reembolso).
irreemplazable adj. Irreplaceable.
irreflexión f. Irreflection, rashness, impetuosity.
irreflexivamente adv. Thoughtlessly, rashly.
irreflexivo, va adj. Thoughtless, unreflecting, rash.
irrefragable adj. Irrefragable, undeniable, irrefutable.
irrefrenable adj. Irrepressible, uncontrollable.
irrefutable adj. Irrefutable, indisputable: *argumento irrefutable*, irrefutable argument.
irregular adj. Irregular: *polígono, pulso, verbo irregular*, irregular polygon, pulse, verb. || Abnormal (anormal). || FIG. Dissolute: *una vida irregular*, a dissolute life.
irregularidad f. Irregularity. || FIG. Disorder.
irreligión f. Irreligion, impiety.
irreligiosidad f. Irreligiousness, impiety.
irreligioso, sa adj. Irreligious, impious.
— M. y f. Irreligious *o* impious person.
irremediable adj. Irremediable. || Incurable (que no se puede curar).
irremisible adj. Irremissible, unpardonable, unforgivable.
irreparable adj. Irreparable.
irreprensible adj. Irreprehensible, irreproachable.
irrepresentable adj. Unpresentable.
irreprimible adj. Irrepressible.
irreprochable adj. Irreproachable.
irrescatable adj. Ransomless.
irresistible adj. Irresistible.
irresoluble adj. Unsolvable (que no se puede resolver).
irresolución f. Irresolution.
irresoluto, ta adj. Irresolute, indecisive (persona). || Unresolved (problema).
— M. y f. Indecisive *o* irresolute person.
irrespetuoso, sa adj. Disrespectful.
irrespirable adj. Irrespirable, unbreathable.
irresponsabilidad f. Irresponsibility.
irresponsable adj. Irresponsible.
irresuelto, ta adj. Irresolute (persona).
irretroactividad f. Nonretroactive character.
irreverencia f. Irreverence, disrespect.
irreverenciar v. tr. To treat irreverently. || To profane (profanar).
irreverente adj. Irreverent, disrespectful.
irreversibilidad f. Irreversibility.
irreversible adj. Irreversible, nonreversible.
irrevocabilidad f. Irrevocability.
irrevocable adj. Irrevocable.
irrigable adj. Irrigable.
irrigación f. Irrigation. || MED. Irrigation.
irrigador m. MED. Irrigator.
irrigar v. tr. To irrigate. || MED. To irrigate.
irrisible adj. Laughable, ludicrous, absurd, ridiculous.
irrisión f. Derision, ridicule. || Laughingstock (objeto de burla): *ser la irrisión del pueblo*, to be the laughingstock of the town. || *Hacer irrisión de uno*, to hold s.o. up to ridicule.
irrisorio, ria adj. Ridiculous, derisory, derisive: *oferta irrisoria*, ridiculous offer. || Giveaway (precio).
irritabilidad f. Irritability.
irritable adj. Irritable (persona). || JUR. Which can be annulled.
irritación f. Irritation (enfado). || MED. Irritation. || JUR. Invalidation, annulment.
irritado, da adj. Irritated. || POÉT. *El mar irritado*, the angry *o* turbulent sea.
irritamiento m. V. IRRITACIÓN.
irritante adj. Irritating. || MED. Irritant, irritating. || *Agente irritante*, irritant.
irritar v. tr. To irritate, to anger, to exasperate (enfadar). || FIG. To excite (las pasiones). || MED. To irritate. || JUR. To annul, to void.
— V. pr. To get angry, to lose one's temper: *irritarse con* or *por algo*, *con* or *contra alguien*, to get angry about *o* at sth., with s.o.
írrito, ta adj. JUR. Null and void, null, void, invalid.
irrogar v. tr. To cause, to occasion [harm or damages].
irrompible adj. Unbreakable.
irrumpir v. intr. *Irrumpir en*, to burst into.
irrupción f. Irruption.
Isaac n. pr. m. Isaac.
Isabel n. pr. f. Isabel, Elizabeth. || Elizabeth (refiriéndose a las reinas de Inglaterra).
isabelino, na adj. Elizabethan (relativo a Isabel I de Inglaterra). || Stamped with the bust of Isabella II [coin]. || Pearl-coloured, whitish-yellow (color). || — Adj./s. Isabelline (en España).
Isaías n. pr. m. Isaiah.
isba f. Isba (casa rusa de madera).
isidoriano, na adj. Isidorian.
— M. Person of the order of Saint Isidore.
Isidoro o **Isidro** n. pr. m. Isidore.
isidro, dra m. y f. Country bumpkin [U.S., hick].

— OBSERV. This word is employed exclusively in Madrid to designate a person from the provinces who comes to the capital for special occasions.

Isis n. pr. f. MIT. Isis.
isla f. Island, isle. || Block [of houses] (de casas). || Island (en una calle). || *Amer.* Grove (bosquecillo). | Flood plain (cerca de un río). || — *Islas Anglonormandas*, Channel Islands. || *Islas Baleares*, Balearic Islands. || *Islas Británicas*, British Isles. || *Islas Canarias*, Canary Islands. || *Islas Filipinas*, Philippine Islands.
islam m. Islam.
islámico, ca adj. Islamic.
islamismo m. Islamism, Mohammedanism (religion). || Moslem world (pueblos musulmanes).

islamita adj./s. Islamite.
islamización f. Islamization.
islamizar v. tr. To islamize.
islandés, esa adj. Icelandic.
— M. y f. Icelander. || — M. Icelandic (lengua).
Islandia n. pr. f. GEOGR. Iceland.
isleño, ña adj. Island.
— M. y f. Islander.
isleta f. Islet, small island. || Island (en la calle).
islote m. Islet, small island.
Ismael n. pr. m. Ishmael.
ismaelita adj./s. Ishmaelite.
ismo m. Ism.
isobara f. Isobar (línea isobárica).
isobárico, ca adj. Isobaric: *líneas isobáricas*, isobaric lines.
isoclinal o **isoclino, na** adj. GEOL. Isoclinal.
isocromático, ca adj. Isochromatic.
isócrono, na adj. Isochronous.
isogamia f. BIOL. Isogamy.
isógamo, ma adj. BIOL. Isogamous.
isoglosa f. Isogloss.
isógono adj. Isogonic, isogonal.
isomería f. QUÍM. Isomerism.
isómero, ra adj. Isomeric, isomerous.
— M. Isomer.
isométrico, ca adj. Isometric, isometrical.
isomorfismo m. Isomorphism.
isomorfo, fa adj. Isomorphic, isomorphous.
isópodo, da adj./s.m. ZOOL. Isopod.
isósceles adj. Isosceles: *triángulo isósceles*, isosceles triangle.
isotérmico, ca adj. Isothermic, isothermal: *vagón isotérmico*, isothermic wagon.
isotermo, ma adj. Isothermal.
— F. Isotherm.
isotonía f. FÍS. Isotonicity.
isotónico, ca o **isótono, na** adj. FÍS. Isotonic.
isotopía f. QUÍM. Isotopy.
isotópico, ca adj. QUÍM. Isotopic.
isótopo m. QUÍM. Isotope.
isotropía BIOL. y FÍS. Isotropy.
isótropo, pa adj. BIOL. y FÍS. Isotropous, isotropic.
— M. Isotropous body.
isquemia f. MED. Ischemia.
isquion m. ANAT. Ischium (hueso).
Israel n. pr. m. GEOGR. Israel.
israelí adj./s. Israeli (del estado de Israel).
— OBSERV. The plural of *israelí* is *israelíes*.
israelita adj./s. Israelite.
israelítico, ca adj. Israelite, Israelitish.
istmeño, ña adj. Isthmian (en general). || Panamanian (de Panamá).
ístmico, ca adj. Isthmic, isthmian: *juegos ístmicos*, isthmic games.
istmo m. Isthmus: *Istmo de Panamá*, Isthmus of Panama. || ANAT. Isthmus.
Italia n. pr. f. GEOGR. Italy.
italianismo m. Italianism.
italianista m. y f. Italianist.
italianización f. Italianization.
italianizar v. tr. To italianize.
— V. pr. To italianize.
italiano, na adj./s. Italian. || *A la italiana*, Italian style.
itálico, ca adj. Italic.
ítalo, la adj./s. POÉT. Italian.
itapá f. *Amer.* Raft (balsa).
ítem adv. lat. Item, likewise (además).
— M. Article, item (artículo).
iteración f. (P.us.). Iteration, repetition.
iterar v. tr. To iterate, to repeat.
iterativo, va adj. Iterative, repetitive.
iterbio m. Ytterbium (metal).
itinerante adj. Itinerant, roving, travelling: *embajador itinerante*, itinerant ambassador. || Itinerant, floating: *campamento itinerante*, floating camp.
itinerario, ria adj./s.m. Itinerary.
itria f. MIN. Yttria.
itrio m. MIN. Yttrium.
izar v. tr. To hoist, to haul up, to heave.
izquierda f. Left hand (mano). || Left (lado, dirección). || Left wing (política). || — *A la izquierda*, left, to the left (con movimiento), on the left (sin movimiento). || *De izquierdas*, left-wing. || MIL. *¡Izquierda, ar!*, left face! || *Mantenerse a la izquierda*, keep left, keep to the left (aviso). || FIG. y FAM. *Ser un cero a la izquierda*, to be a nobody. || *Un hombre de izquierda*, a leftist, a man of the left, a left winger.
izquierdismo m. Leftism.
izquierdista adj. Leftist, left-wing.
— M. y f. Leftist, left winger.
izquierdo, da adj. Left: *mano izquierda*, left hand. || Knock-kneed (caballo). || Left-handed (zurdo).
— M. y f. Left-hander, southpaw (fam.) [zurdo]. || V. IZQUIERDA.

J

j f. J: *una j mayúscula*, a capital j.
— OBSERV. The *jota* sound is similar to the Scottish *ch* [as in *loch*].
jabado, da adj. *Amer.* Parti-coloured (gallo).
jabalcón m. ARQ. Brace, strut (puntal).
jabalconar v. tr. ARQ. To brace, to strut (apuntalar).
jabalí m. ZOOL. Wild boar, boar: *jabalí alunado*, long-tusked boar.
— OBSERV. Pl. *jabalíes*.
jabalina f. Wild sow, female wild boar (hembra del jabalí). || Javelin (en deportes, arma): *lanzamiento de la jabalina*, throwing the javelin.
jabato m. Young wild boar. || FIG. *¡Es un jabato!*, he's as bold as a lion! (valiente).
jábega f. Sweep net, dragnet (red). || Fishing boat (embarcación).
jabegote m. Sweep-net fisherman.
jabeguero, ra adj. Sweep-net (pesca).
— M. y f. Sweep-net fisherman.
jabeque m. Xebec (embarcación). || FIG. y FAM. Wound, gash (herida).
jabí m. *Amer.* Quebracho (árbol).
jabirú m. ZOOL. Jabiru (pájaro).
jable n. TECN. Croze (de los toneles).
jabón m. Soap: *pompa de jabón*, soap bubble; *jabón de afeitar, de tocador or de olor*, shaving, toilet soap. || Bar of soap (pastilla de jabón). || FIG. y FAM. Dressing down, ticking off (reprensión): *dar* or *echar un jabón a alguien*, to give s.o. a dressing down. | Soft soap, flattery (lisonja). || *Amer.* Fright, scare (susto). || — FIG. y FAM. *Dar jabón a uno*, to soft-soap s.o. (lisonjear). || *Jabón blando*, soft soap. || *Jabón de Marsella*, household soap. || *Jabón de piedra*, hard soap. || *Jabón de sastre*, soapstone, steatite, French chalk. || *Jabón en escamas*, soap flakes. || *Jabón en polvo*, soap powder, washing powder.
jabonado m. Soaping (jabonadura). || Washing, wash, laundry (ropa que se lava). || FAM. Dressing down, ticking off (reprensión).
jabonadura f. Soaping. || — Pl. Soapy water, *sing.* || Lather, *sing.*, soapsuds (espuma). || FAM. Ticking off (reprensión). || *Dar una jabonadura a alguien*, to give s.o. a ticking off.
jabonar v. tr. To soap, to wash (la ropa). || To lather (la barba). || FIG. y FAM. To give [s.o.] a dressing down *o* a ticking off, to tell [s.o.] off (reprender).
jaboncillo m. Bar of toilet soap (para lavarse). || BOT. Soapberry (árbol). || *Amer.* Soap powder (jabón en polvo), liquid soap (líquido). || *Jaboncillo de sastre*, soapstone, steatite, French chalk.
jabonera f. Soapdish (caja). || BOT. Soapwort.
jabonería f. Soapworks, soap factory (fábrica). || Soap shop (tienda).
jabonero, ra adj. Soap. || Off-white (toro).
— M. y f. Soap manufacturer, soap maker (fabricante), soap dealer (vendedor).
jabonoso, sa adj. Soapy.
jaborandi m. BOT. Jaborandi.
jabotí m. *Amer.* Large tortoise.
jaca f. Pony, small horse (caballito). || Horse (en general). || *Amer.* Small mare (yegua). | Fighting cock (gallo de pelea).
jacamar m. o **jacamara** f. *Amer.* Jacamar (ave).
jácara f. Picaresque ballad (romance). || Spanish popular dance and its music (danza y música). || Band of night revellers (juerguistas). || FIG. y FAM. Bother,

annoyance (molestia). | Tale, fib (embuste): *contar jácaras*, to tell tales. || — *Estar de jácara*, to be very merry (alegre), to be living it up (de juerga). || *No estoy para jácaras*, I'm not in the mood for jokes.
jacarandá m. BOT. Jacaranda.
jacarandoso, sa adj. FAM. Jolly, sprightly, lively, gay (alegre). || Vain (presumido).
jacaré m. *Amer.* Alligator.
jacarear v. intr. To go singing through the streets. || To sing picaresque ballads.
jacarero o **jacarista** m. Merrymaker, reveller.
— Adj. Merry.
jácena f. ARQ. Summer (viga maestra).
jacinto m. BOT. Hyacinth. || Hyacinth, jacinth (piedra preciosa). || — *Jacinto de Ceilán*, zircon. || *Jacinto occidental*, topaz. || *Jacinto oriental*, ruby.
Jacinto n. pr. m. Hyacinth.
jaco m. Hack, nag (caballo malo). || Young horse (caballo joven). || Short-sleeved coat of mail (cota).
Jacob n. pr. m. Jacob.
jacobeo, a adj. Of Saint James. || *Peregrinación jacobea*, pilgrimage to Santiago de Compostela.
jacobinismo m. Jacobinism.
jacobino, na adj./s. Jacobin.
jacobita adj. Jacobitical, Jacobite.
— M. Jacobite.
Jacobo n. pr. m. James.
jactancia f. Boastfulness (cualidad). || Boasting, bragging (acción).
jactanciosamente adv. Boastfully.
jactancioso, sa adj. Boastful.
— M. y f. Boaster, braggart.
jactarse v. pr. To boast, to brag (vanagloriarse): *jactarse de su fuerza*, to boast of one's strength.
jaculatorio, ria adj. Ejaculatory, brief and fervent.
— F. Ejaculation (oración breve).
jade m. Jade (piedra).
jadeante adj. Panting, gasping.
jadear v. intr. To pant, to gasp, to puff [and blow]. || *Llegar jadeando*, to arrive out of breath.
jadeo m. Panting, gasping, breathlessness.
jaenés, esa adj./s. V. JIENNENSE.
jaez m. Harness (del caballo). || FIG. Character, nature (carácter). | Mood: *estar de mal jaez*, to be in a bad mood. | Kind, sort (índole). | Sort (despectivo): *no se mezcle con gente de ese jaez*, don't get mixed up with that sort of people. || — Pl. Trappings (del caballo).
jaguar m. ZOOL. Jaguar.
jagüel o **jagüey** m. *Amer.* Pool, pond (charco).
jai alai m. "Jai alai", pelota (pelota vasca). || Pelota court (frontón).
jaiba f. *Amer.* Crab (cangrejo).
Jaime n. pr. m. James.
jaique m. Haik, haick (almalafa).
¡ja, ja, ja! interj. Ha, ha, ha!
jalapa f. BOT. Jalap.
jalapeño, ña adj. Jalapa, Jalapan [Guatemala and Mexico].
— M. y f. Jalapan.
jalar v. tr. FAM. V. JAMAR.
jalbegar v. tr. To whitewash (enjalbegar).
jalea f. Jelly. || — FIG. y FAM. *Hacerse* or *volverse una jalea*, to turn *o* to go sweet. || *Jalea de cidra*, citron jelly. || *Jalea real*, royal jelly.
jaleador, ra adj. Noisy, rowdy (que hace ruido). || Encouraging, cheering (que anima).
jalear v. tr. To urge on [dogs] (caza). || To encourage [by clapping and shouting], to cheer on: *el público jaleó a la bailarina*, the audience cheered on the dancer. || *Amer.* To pester (fastidiar).
jaleo m. Shouting [to urge on dogs] (en la caza). || Cheering and clapping (para bailarines, cantantes, etc.). || Popular Andalusian dance. || FAM. Binge, good time (juerga). | Row, din, racket (alboroto): *armar jaleo*, to kick up a racket. | Jumble: *un jaleo de cifras y letras*, a jumble of figures and letters. | Row (riña): *armar un jaleo con*, to start a row with. | Fuss, to-do, commotion (escándalo): *se armó* or *hubo un jaleo enorme*, there was a right to-do.
jaleoso, sa adj. Noisy, rowdy.
jalifa f. Supreme authority representing the sultan in the former Spanish protectorate of Morocco.
jalifato m. Dignity and jurisdiction of the "jalifa".
jalisciense adj. [Of *o* from] Jalisco (México).
— M. y f. Native *o* inhabitant of Jalisco.
jalisco adj. m. *Amer.* Drunk.
jalma f. Packsaddle (enjalma).
jalón m. Range pole (estaca). || FIG. Milestone: *el viaje del escritor a Inglaterra constituyó un jalón en su vida*, the writer's trip to England was a milestone in his life. | Stage (etapa). || *Amer.* Pull (tirón). | Stretch, distance (distancia): *nos falta todavía un gran jalón*, we still have a long stretch ahead of us. || *Jalón de mira*, target levelling rod, level rod.
jalonamiento m. Staking *o* marking *o* laying out.
jalonar v. tr. To stake out, to mark out, to lay out. || FIG. To mark, to dot: *estar jalonado de*, to be dotted with.
Jamaica n. pr. f. GEOGR. Jamaica.
jamaicano, na adj./s. Jamaican.
jamancia f. FAM. Grub, nosh (comida).
jamar v. tr. FAM. To stuff o.s. with, to tuck in to, to nosh [U.S., to chow] (comer).
— V. intr. FAM. To nosh, to tuck in (comer).
jamás adv. Never: *jamás lo haré de nuevo*, I shall never do it again, never shall I do it again; *jamás lo he visto* or *no lo he visto jamás*, I've never seen it. || Ever: *¿has visto jamás una cosa parecida?*, have you ever seen such a thing? || — *La mejor película que jamás se haya hecho*, the best film that has ever been made, the best film ever made. || *Jamás de los jamases*, never ever, never on your life. || *Nunca jamás*, never ever: *nunca jamás lo haré de nuevo*, I shall never ever do it again. || *Para siempre jamás*, for ever and ever.
jamba f. ARQ. Jamb. || TECN. Post, jamb: *jamba de puerta*, doorpost, doorjamb.
jambaje m. ARQ. Doorframe (de puerta). || Window-frame (de ventana).
jámbico, ca adj. Iambic (verso).
jamboree m. Jamboree (de exploradores).
jamelgo m. Hack, jade, nag (caballo malo).
jamón m. Ham: *jamón ahumado*, smoked ham; *huevos con jamón*, ham and eggs. || — *Codillo de jamón*, knuckle of ham. || *Jamón en dulce*, ham boiled in white wine. || *Jamón serrano*, cured ham. || *Manga de jamón*, leg-of-mutton sleeve. || *Ser una mujer jamón*, to be a knockout. || FAM. *¡Y un jamón!* or *¡y un jamón con chorreras!*, not on your life!, you've got a hope!, nothing doing!
jamona adj. f. FAM. Meaty, buxom.
jamúas o **jamuga** f. o **jamugas** f. pl. Sidesaddle.
jangada f. MAR. Raft, float (balsa). || *Amer.* Jangada [Brazilian boat]. | Timber raft (armadía). | FAM. Daft thing, silly remark (tontería). | Mean *o* dirty trick (trastada).
jansenismo m. Jansenism.
jansenista adj. Jansenistic, Jansenist.
— M. y f. Jansenist.
Japón n. pr. m. GEOGR. Japan.
japonés, esa adj./s. Japanese: *los japoneses*, the Japanese.
japuta f. Pomfret (pez).
jaque m. Check (ajedrez). || FAM. Bully (valentón). || — *Dar jaque*, to check. || *Dar jaque y mate*, to checkmate. || *Estar en jaque*, to be in check. || *Jaque al rey*, check. || *Jaque mate*, checkmate. || *Jaque perpetuo*, perpetual check. || FIG. *Tener* or *traer en jaque*, to hold a threat over (sujetar bajo una amenaza), to harass, to worry (hostigar).
jaquear v. tr. To check (en ajedrez). || FIG. To harass (hostigar). | To hold a threat over (amenazar).
jaqueca f. Migraine (dolor de cabeza). || FIG. y FAM. Bother, nuisance, pain in the neck: *¡qué jaqueca tener que hacer esto!*, what a bother having to do this! || — FIG. y FAM. *Dar jaqueca a*, to bother, to pester. | *¡Qué tío jaqueca!*, what a pest!
jaquecazo m. Violent migraine.
jaquecoso, sa adj. Suffering from migraine (con jaqueca). || FIG. Bothersome (fastidioso).
jáquima m. Headstall (de caballos). || *Amer.* FAM. *Coger una jáquima*, to get sozzled (emborracharse).
jaquimón m. *Amer.* Headstall (jáquima).
jara f. BOT. Rockrose. || Spear (arma).
jarabe m. Syrup: *jarabe para la tos*, cough syrup. || Popular Mexican dance (baile). || — FIG. y FAM. *Dar jarabe a uno*, to butter s.o. up, to soft-soap s.o. | *Dar a uno jarabe de palo*, to give s.o. a hiding. | *Estar hecho un jarabe*, to go sweet. | *Jarabe de pico*, blarney, mere words, *pl.*: *eso es todo jarabe de pico*, that is a lot of blarney; gift of the gab: *tiene mucho jarabe de pico*, he has really got the gift of the gab.
jaral m. Place full of rockroses.
jaramago m. BOT. Hedge mustard (sisimbrio).
jarana f. FAM. Spree, binge (juerga): *ir de jarana*, to go on a spree. | Rumpus, racket, din (alboroto): *armar jarana*, to kick up a rumpus. | Trick (trampa). | Deceit, trickery (engaño). || *Amer.* Joke (chanza). | Debt (deuda). | Small guitar (guitarra). | Dance (baile).
jaranear v. intr. To go on a binge *o* on a spree (ir de juerga). || To make merry, to amuse o.s., to have a good time (divertirse).
— V. pr. To go on a binge *o* on a spree (irse de juerga). || To laugh (*de*, at) [reírse, no tomar en serio].
jaranero, ra adj. Fun-loving (a quien le gusta divertirse). || Rowdy, noisy (ruidoso). || *Amer.* Tricky, deceitful, cheating (tramposo).
— M. y f. Reveller.
jaranista adj. *Amer.* V. JARANERO.
jarca f. V. HARCA.
jarcia f. MAR. Rigging, ropes, *pl.* (cabos y aparejos). | Fishing tackle (para pescar). || FIG. Jumble, mess (mezcolanza). || — Pl. MAR. Rigging, *sing.* || MAR. *Jarcia muerta*, standing rigging.
jarciar v. tr. MAR. To rig [a ship].
jardín m. Garden: *jardín colgante*, hanging garden. || MAR. Latrine, head (fam.) [retrete de un navío]. || TECN. Flaw (mancha en una esmeralda). || — *Jardín botánico*, botanical garden. || *Jardín de la infancia*, kindergarten.
jardinaje m. Gardening.
jardinera f. [Woman] gardener. || Jardinière, flower stand (para tiestos de flores). || Window box (en una

ventana). || Open carriage (coche). || Open tramcar (coche de tranvía).
jardinería f. Gardening.
jardinero m. Gardener. || *Jardinero paisajista*, landscape gardener.
jareta f. Hem (dobladillo). || MAR. Cable, rope (cabo). | Netting (empalletado). || FAM. Chatter (charla). || FAM. *Dar jareta*, to [have a] chat.
jaretón m. Wide hem.
jarillo m. BOT. Arum (aro).
jarocho, cha adj. Uncouth, rude (tosco).
— M. y f. Uncouth *o* rude person. || Peasant from Veracruz.
jarope m. Syrup (jarabe).
jarra f. Jug, pitcher. || Churn (de leche). || Beer mug, tankard (de cerveza). || Ancient Aragonese order of chivalry (orden antigua en Aragón). || *De jarras* or *en jarra* or *en jarras*, hands on hips, arms akimbo.
jarrazo m. Blow with a jug *o* pitcher.
jarrete m. Back of the knee (del hombre). || Hock (corvejón de una res, de un caballo).
jarretera f. Garter (liga). || Order of the Garter.
jarro m. Jug, jar, pitcher (recipiente). || Jar, jug, jarful, jugful (contenido). || Beer mug, tankard (para cerveza). || — FIG. y FAM. *A jarros*, buckets, cats and dogs (llover). | *Echar un jarro de agua fría a*, to pour cold water on.
jarrón m. ARQ. [Ornamental] vase *o* urn. || Vase (para flores).
jartar v. tr. e intr. FAM. V. HARTAR.
Jartum n. pr. GEOGR. Khartoum.
jaspe m. Jasper (piedra). || Veined marble (mármol).
jaspeado, da adj. Marbled, mottled, streaked, veined. || Variegated (hojas).
— M. Marbling, mottling. || Marbling (de un libro).
jaspear v. tr. To marble, to mottle, to vein, to streak.
Jauja n. pr. FIG. Promised land, paradise. || — *¡Esto es Jauja!*, this is the life! || *Tierra de Jauja*, land of milk and honey, land of plenty, Never-Never land.

— OBSERV. The Spanish noun *Jauja* is used in allusion to the Peruvian town and province of *Jauja*, noted for its wealth and the clemency of its climate.

jaula f. Cage (para animales). || Padded cell (para locos). || Crate (embalaje). || Lockup (en un garaje). || Playpen (para niños). || MIN. Cage. || Cage, car (de un ascensor). || ELECTR. *Jaula de ardilla*, squirrel cage.
jauría f. Pack [of hounds] (perros de caza). || FIG. Pack: *jauría de acreedores*, pack of creditors.
Java n. pr. GEOGR. Java.
javanés, esa adj./s. Javanese.
Javier n. pr. m. Xavier.
jazmín m. BOT. Jasmine: *jazmín de España* or *real*, Spanish *o* Catalonian jasmine.
jazz m. Jazz (música).
jazz-band m. Jazz band.
jebe m. Alum (alumbre). || *Amer.* Rubber (caucho).
jedive m. Khedive.
jeep m. Jeep (coche todo terreno).
jefa f. Boss. || Head (de un departamento). || [Lady] president (presidenta). || Manageress (directora). || Leader (de partido, etc.).
jefatura f. Leadership: *bajo la jefatura de*, under the leadership of. || Managership, management (dirección). || Position of head (de un departamento, de una familia). || Chieftaincy (de una tribu). || *Jefatura de policía*, police headquarters.
jefe m. Boss (de un empleado, etc.): *mi jefe*, my boss. || Manager (director). || Leader (de un partido, de un sindicato, de una banda, etc.). || Head (de un departamento, de familia). || Chief, chieftain, headman (de una tribu). || MIL. Officer in command. || Scoutmaster (de exploradores). || Foreman (de un jurado). || HERÁLD. Chief. || — *Comandante en jefe*, commander-in-chief. || *Jefe de camareros*, head waiter. || *Jefe de cocina*, chef, head cook. || *Jefe de comedor*, head waiter, maître d'hôtel. || *Jefe de cordada*, leader, first on the rope, head of the rope. || *Jefe de escuadra*, squadron commander. || *Jefe de estación*, stationmaster. || *Jefe de Estado*, head of State. || *Jefe de Estado Mayor*, Chief of Staff. || *Jefe de gobierno*, head of [the] government. || *Jefe de negociado*, chief clerk, departmental head. || *Jefe de redacción*, editor-in-chief. || *Jefe de taller*, foreman. | *Jefe de ventas*, sales manager. || *Jefe supremo*, commander-in-chief. || *Redactor jefe*, editor-in-chief. || FIG. *Ser el jefe*, to be the boss.
Jehová m. Jehovah (Dios).
¡je, je, je! interj. Ha, ha, ha!, tee, hee, hee!
jején m. *Amer.* Gnat (mosquito). | FIG. Lot, great number.
jemiquear v. intr. To snivel, to whimper.
jengibre m. BOT. Ginger.
jeniquén m. Henequen (henequén).
jenízaro, ra adj. FIG. Mixed, hybrid (mezclado). || *Amer.* Born of mixed parentage (de padres de distinta nacionalidad). | Born of half-bred father and Chinese mother *o* vice versa.
— M. Janizary, Janissary (soldado).
jenneriano, na adj. Jennerian.
jenny f. Spinning jenny, jenny (máquina de hilar algodón).
Jenofonte n. pr. m. Xenophon.
jeque m. Sheikh, sheik (jefe árabe).
jerarca m. Hierarch (de una sociedad). || REL. Hierarch, dignitary. || Chief, leader (jefe). || Important person.
jerarquía f. Hierarchy: *jerarquía administrativa, angélica, social*, administrative, angelic, social hierarchy. || Scale: *jerarquía de valores*, scale of values. || Hierarch, dignitary: *el arzobispo y otras jerarquías eclesiásticas*, the archbishop and other ecclesiastical hierarchs. || *Elevarse en la jerarquía*, to rise *o* to ascend in the hierarchy.
jerárquico, ca adj. Hierarchic, hierarchical.
jerarquización f. Hierarchization.
jerarquizar v. tr. To hierarchize.
jerbo m. ZOOL. Jerboa.
jeremiada f. Jeremiad.
jeremías m. y f. inv. Whiner, whimperer.
Jeremías n. pr. m. Jeremy. || Jeremiah (en la Biblia).
jeremiquear v. intr. To snivel, to whimper.
jeremiqueo m. Snivelling, whimpering.
jerez m. Sherry (vino): *jerez fino*, dry sherry.
jerezano, na adj. [Of *o* from] Jerez.
— M. y f. Native *o* inhabitant of Jerez.
jerga f. Coarse woollen cloth, sackcloth (tela). || Straw mattress (colchón). || Jargon, slang, cant (lenguaje): *la jerga estudiantil*, student jargon. || Gibberish, double Dutch (galimatías). || MIN. Jargon, jargoon (gema). || *Hablar en jerga*, to talk gibberish, to talk double Dutch.
jergal adj. Jargonistic, slangy.
jergón m. Straw mattress (colchón).
jergueta f. Coarse cloth (tela).
jerguilla f. Serge-like cloth (tela).
jeribeque m. Face, grimace (mueca). || Blink (guiño).
Jericó n. pr. GEOGR. Jericho.
jerifato o **jerifazgo** m. Dignity of *o* territory under a sherif.
jerife m. Sherif (jefe árabe).
jerifiano, na adj. Sherifian.
jerigonza f. Jargon, slang (jerga). || Gibberish, double Dutch (galimatías).
jeringa f. Syringe (para inyecciones). || Gun (para aceite). || FAM. Annoyance, bother (aburrimiento).
jeringador, ra adj. FAM. Annoying, bothersome.
— M. y f. FAM. Pest, nuisance (latoso).
jeringar v. tr. To inject, to syringe (inyectar). || To syringe (para limpiar). || FIG. y FAM. To bother, to annoy, to pester (molestar).
jeringazo m. Squirt [from a syringe]. || Syringe, syringeful (contenido).
jeringuilla f. BOT. Mock orange. || Small syringe (para inyecciones).
Jerjes n. pr. m. HIST. Xerxes.
jeroglífico, ca adj. Hieroglyphic.
— M. Hieroglyphic, hieroglyph. || Rebus, picture puzzle (juego). || — Pl. Hieroglyphics.
jerónimo, ma adj./s. Hieronymite.
Jerónimo n. pr. m. Jerome, Hieronymus.
jersey m. Jersey, pullover, sweater.

— OBSERV. Pl. *jerseys* or *jerseis*.

Jerusalén n. pr. GEOGR. Jerusalem.
Jesucristo m. Jesus Christ.
jesuita adj./s. Jesuit.
jesuítico, ca adj. Jesuitic, jesuitical. || FIG. Jesuitical.
jesuitismo m. Jesuitism.
Jesús m. Jesus: *Jesús Nazareno*, Jesus of Nazareth. || — *El Niño Jesús*, the Infant Jesus (Jesús niño), the Bambino (imagen). || FIG. y FAM. *En un decir Jesús* or *en un Jesús*, in the twinkling of an eye, before you can *o* could say Jack Robinson, in a jiffy. || FIG. *Sin decir Jesús*, very suddenly (morir).
— Interj. Good heavens!, gracious! || *¡Jesús!* or *¡Jesús, María y José!*, bless you! (al estornudar).

— OBSERV. *Jesús* is a common Spanish Christian name.

jeta f. Snout (hocico de cerdo). || Thick lips, *pl.* (labios abultados). || FAM. Mug, face (cara). || — *Amer.* FAM. *Estirar la jeta*, to kick the bucket (morir). || FAM. *Le voy a romper la jeta*, I'm going to smash his face in. | *Poner jeta*, to pull a face.
jetudo, da adj. Thick-lipped.
jíbaro, ra adj. *Amer.* Country, rural, rustic (campesino). | Jivaroan (jívaro).
— M. y f. *Amer.* Rustic, peasant (campesino). | Jivaro (indio).
jibia f. ZOOL. Cuttlefish, sepia (molusco). || Cuttlebone (jibión).
jibión m. Cuttlebone.
jícara f. Cup: *una jícara de chocolate*, a cup of chocolate. || *Amer.* Calabash, gourd.
jicarazo m. Blow with a cup. || FIG. *Dar jicarazo a*, to poison.
jicote m. *Amer.* Hornet, big wasp (abejorro).
jicotera f. *Amer.* Wasp's nest (nido).
jiennense adj. [Of *o* from] Jaén.
— M. y f. Native *o* inhabitant of Jaén.
jifero m. Cleaver (cuchillo de carnicero). || Slaughterer (el que mata las reses).
jigote m. V. GIGOTE.
¡ji, ji, ji! interj. Hee, hee, hee!, tee, hee! (risa).
jijona f. Variety of large-grained yellowish wheat.
— M. Almond sweetmeat [made in Jijona].
jilguero m. Goldfinch (ave).

jilí m. FAM. Cretin, idiot, imbecile.
jilipolla o **jilipollas** m. POP. Twit, berk, cretin, idiot.
jilipollada f. POP. Stupid thing to do (acción). | Stupid thing to say (dicho).
jilipollez f. POP. Stupid thing to do (acción). | Stupid thing to say (dicho). || — POP. *Eso son jilipolleces*, that's a load of old cobblers, that's a load of [old] rot. | *¡Qué jilipollez!*, how stupid can you get!
jilote m. *Amer.* Spike of maize [U.S., spike of corn].
jimelga f. MAR. Fish (refuerzo de madera).
jimia f. She-ape.
jimio m. Ape, simian.
jinda o **jindama** f. FAM. Fear, funk (miedo). || Fright (susto).
jineta f. Horsewoman, rider (mujer que monta a caballo). || Short lance [former insignia of infantry captains] (lanza corta). || [Sergeant's] epaulette (hombrera). || ZOOL. Genet. || *A la jineta*, with short stirrups and knees bent.
jinete m. Horseman, rider (caballista). || MIL. Cavalryman. || Saddle horse (caballo). || Thoroughbred horse (caballo de pura sangre). || *Venía jinete en un caballo negro*, he approached riding a black horse.
jinetear v. intr. To ride around [on horseback] (pasearse a caballo). || To show off one's horsemanship (presumir).
— V. tr. *Amer.* To break in [horses].
jingoísmo m. Jingoism.
jingoísta adj. Jingoistic, jingo.
— M. y f. Jingoist, jingo.
jínjol m. BOT. Jujube [berry] (azufaifa).
jinjolero m. Jujube [tree] (azufaifo).
jipar v. intr. To hiccough, to hiccup (hipar). || To heave, to pant (jadear).
jipi m. FAM. Panama hat, straw hat (sombrero).
jipido m. FAM. Hiccough, hiccup (hipo).
jipijapa f. Jipijapa (planta). || Fine strip of straw [from jipijapa leaf]. || — M. Panama hat, straw hat (sombrero).

— OBSERV. *Jipijapa* is a town in Ecuador where the so-called Panama hat actually orginated.

jiquilete m. Indigo plant (añil).
jira f. Strip [of cloth] (tira). || Shred of cloth (jirón). || Picnic (merienda campestre). || Excursion. || Tour: *hacer una jira por España*, to go on a tour of Spain, to make a tour of Spain.
jirafa f. Giraffe (animal). || Boom (de micrófono).
jirafista m. Boom operator.
jirón m. Shred, tatter (pedazo): *hacer jirones*, to tear to shreds. || FIG. Scrap, bit, piece (porción pequeña). || Facing (de una falda). || HERÁLD. Gyron. || *Hecho jirones*, in rags, in tatters, in shreds.
jitomate m. *Amer.* Tomato.
jiu-jitsu m. Jujitsu, jujutsu.
jíbaro, ra adj. Jivaroan (indio).
— M. y f. Jivaro.
Joaquín n. pr. m. Joachim.
Job n. pr. m. Job. || *Tener más paciencia que (el santo) Job*, to have the patience of Job.
jockey m. Jockey.
jocosamente adv. Jocularly, humorously.
jocoserio, ria adj. Tragicomic, seriocomic.
jocosidad f. Humour [U.S., humor], humorousness (gracia). || Jocularity, humour [U.S., humor] (de una persona). || Pleasantry, joke (chiste).
jocoso, sa adj. Humorous, amusing, funny, comical, jocular (cómico): *libro jocoso*, humorous book.
jocundidad f. Jocundity, cheerfulness, gaiety.
jocundo, da adj. Jocund, cheerful, gay.
joder v. tr. e intr. POP. To fuck (tener relaciones íntimas con). || FIG. y POP. To pester (importunar). | To get on [s.o.'s] nerves, to annoy (fastidiar, molestar): *ese maldito ruido me está jodiendo*, that bloody noise is getting on my nerves. | To be a drag *o* a bind (ser una pesadez): *jode mucho tener que levantarse tan temprano*, it's a drag having to get up so early. | To bugger up, to mess up, to ruin (estropear). || — FIG. y POP. *¡La jodiste!*, you've made a right mess of things!, you've ruined everything! | *¡No me jodas!*, stop pestering me! (no me des la lata), come off it! (no me digas).
— V. pr. FIG. y POP. To be a flop (fracasar). | To be ruined *o* spoilt *o* messed up: *la excursión se jodió con la lluvia*, the trip was ruined by rain. || — FIG. y POP. *¡Hay que joderse!*, to hell with it all! | *¡Que se joda!*, to hell with him! [*o* her *o* it, etc.]. | *¡Que te jodas!*, go to hell!
joder interj. Shit!, hell!, damn!
jodido, da adj. FIG. y POP. Shagged, shattered (rendido): *estoy jodido*, I'm shagged. | Bloody (maldito): *este jodido coche*, this bloody car. | Bloody awful (malísimo): *un trabajo jodido*, a bloody awful job. | Ruined (estropeado, fastidiado). || — FIG. y POP. *Esta radio está jodida*, this radio has had it. | *Todo está jodido*, everything's gone to pot, everything's ruined.
jofaina f. Washbasin.
jolgorio m. FAM. Rave, spree, binge, merrymaking (fiesta). || Fun, merriment, gaiety (alegría). || — *Ir de jolgorio*, to go on a binge *o* a spree. || *¡Qué jolgorio!*, what fun!
¡jolín! o **¡jolines!** interj. Damn!, hell!
jollín m. FAM. Row, set-to (disputa).
Jonás n. pr. m. Jonah.
Jonatán o **Jonatás** n. pr. m. Jonathan.
Jonia n. pr. f. GEOGR. Ionia.
jónico, ca adj. Ionic, Ionian. || ARQ. Ionic: *orden jónico*, Ionic order.
— M. y f. Ionian. || — M. Ionic (en poesía).
jonio, nia adj./s. Ionian.
jopo m. Tail (rabo).
¡jopo! interj. FAM. Hop it!, scram!, beat it!, scat!
jordán m. FIG. Fountain of Youth. || FIG. y FAM. *Ir al jordán*, to be rejuvenated, to rejuvenate (remozarse), to convalesce, to pick up (convalecer).
Jordán n. pr. m. GEOGR. Jordan [river].
Jordania n. pr. f. GEOGR. Jordan [kingdom].
jordano, na adj./s. Jordan, Jordanian.
Jorge n. pr. m. George.
jornada f. Working day (día de trabajo): *una jornada de ocho horas*, an eight-hour working day. || Journey (viaje). || Day's journey (camino recorrido en un día). || Stage (etapa): *hice el viaje en tres jornadas*, I did the journey in three stages. || FIG. Lifetime. || MIL. Day, battle (batalla). | Expedition (expedición). || TEATR. Act [in Spanish classical plays]. || CINEM. Part, episode: *película en tres jornadas*, film in three parts. || Royal journey (viaje de la familia real). || Royal visit (estancia). || IMPR. Sheets (*pl.*) printed in a day. || *Trabajo de media jornada, de jornada entera*, part-time, full-time work.
jornal m. Daily *o* day's wage, daily *o* day's wages, *pl.* (retribución). || Day's work (día de trabajo). || Land measure (medida agraria). || — *A jornal*, by the day: *trabajar a jornal*, to work *o* to be paid by the day. || *Gana un buen jornal*, he earns a good wage.
jornalero, ra m. y f. Day labourer [U.S., day laborer].
joroba f. Hump, hunch, hunched back (giba). || FIG. y FAM. Bind, drag (molestia).
jorobado, da adj. Hunchbacked, humpbacked.
— M. y f. Hunchback, humpback.
jorobadura f. FAM. Bind, drag (molestia).
jorobar v. tr. FIG. y FAM. To get on one's nerves (poner nervioso): *este calor me está jorobando*, this heat is getting on my nerves. | To bother (fastidiar). || — FIG. y FAM. *Está jorobado*, he's got the hump (de mal humor). | *¡No me jorobes!*, get away with you!
— V. pr. FAM. To get fed up (hartarse). || *¡Hay que jorobarse!*, damn it all!
jorobeta m. FAM. Hunchback, humpback.
jorongo m. [Mexican] poncho.
joropo m. *Amer.* Popular dance of the Colombian and Venezuelan lowlanders.
jorrar v. tr. To drag, to haul [a net].
Josafat n. pr. GEOGR. Jehoshaphat: *el Valle de Josafat*, the Valley of Jehoshaphat.
José n. pr. m. Joseph.
Josefa o **Josefina** n. pr. f. Josephine.
josefino, na adj. HIST. Supporting Joseph Bonaparte. || *Amer.* Belonging to the Chilean clerical party (clerical). | [Of *o* from] San José (Costa Rica y Uruguay).
— M. y f. HIST. Partisan of Joseph Bonaparte. || *Amer.* Member of the Chilean clerical party. | Native *o* inhabitant of San José.
Josué n. pr. m. Joshua.
jota f. J (nombre de la letra *j*). || Jota [popular Aragonese, Valencian and Navarrese dance and its music]. || Jack, knave (en la baraja inglesa). || FIG. Iota, jot, bit, scrap (cosa mínima). || Vegetable soup (potaje). || *Amer.* Sandal (ojota). || — FIG. y FAM. *No decir ni jota*, not to say a word. | *No entiendo ni jota*, I don't understand a word of it *o* a thing. | *No falta una jota*, not an iota *o* not one iota is wanting. | *No sabe ni jota* or *no sabe jota de pintura*, he doesn't know the first thing about painting. | *No se ve una jota*, you can't see a thing. | *Sin faltar una jota*, without missing a single detail.
joule m. FÍS. Joule (julio).
joven adj. Young: *de muy joven se fue a Madrid*, he went to Madrid when still very young; *un país joven* a young country; *todavía la noche es joven*, the night is still young; *es dos años más joven que yo*, he is two years younger than I. || Youthful, young: *rostro joven*, youthful face. || *De aspecto joven*, young-looking, youthful in appearance.
— M. Young man, youth (hombre). || — F. Young woman, girl (mujer). || *Los jóvenes*, young people, youth.
jovencito, ta o **jovenzuelo, la** adj. Rather young, quite young, youngish (bastante joven), very young (muy joven).
— M. y f. Youngster, young boy (hombre), young girl (mujer).
jovial adj. Jovial, jolly, cheerful (alegre). || Jovian (relativo a Júpiter).
jovialidad f. Joviality, jollity, cheerfulness.
jovialmente adv. Cheerfully, jovially.
joviano, na adj. Jovian (relativo a Júpiter).
joya f. Jewel (alhaja). || Piece of jewellery (objeto de adorno). || Jewelled brooch (brocamantón). || Gift, present (regalo). || FIG. Jewel, gem, treasure (cosa o persona): *la niña es una joya*, the child is a jewel. | Treasure (persona valiosa): *el nuevo empleado es una joya*, the new clerk is a treasure. || ARQ. Astragal. || — Pl. Trousseau, *sing.* (de la novia). || Jewellery,

sing. [U.S., jewelry], jewels: *joyas de imitación* or *de fantasía*, imitation jewellery. || *Joya de familia*, family heirloom.

joyel m. Small jewel.

joyería f. Jewellery [U.S., jewelry] trade *o* business (comercio). || Jeweller's [U.S., jeweler's], jeweller's shop, jewellery shop (tienda).

joyero m. Jeweller [U.S., jeweler] (fabricante o comerciante). || Jewel box, jewel case (estuche).

Juan n. pr. m. John: *Juan Bautista*, John the Baptist. || — M. *Amer.* FAM. Private, footslogger (soldado de línea). || — FAM. *Juan Lanas*, simpleton (tonto), good sort (bonachón). || *Yo soy Juan Palomo, yo me lo guiso y yo me lo como*, I'm all right, Jack.

Juana n. pr. f. Jean, Joan, Jane. || *Juana de Arco*, Joan of Arc.

juanete m. Prominent cheekbone (pómulo abultado). || Bunion (callosidad). || MAR. Topgallant [sail]: *juanete mayor, de proa*, main, fore topgallant.

juanetero m. MAR. Topgallantman.

juanetudo, da adj. With prominent cheekbones (pómulo). || Suffering from bunions (que tiene callos).

juarista adj. Supporting Juárez [in Mexico].
— M. y f. Partisan of Juárez.

jubete m. Coat of mail.

jubilación f. Retirement, pensioning-off (acción de jubilar). || Retirement (acción de jubilarse, retiro). || Pension (renta). || Jubilation (alegría).

jubilado, da adj. Retired, in retirement, pensioned off.
— M. y f. Pensioner, retired person.

jubilar adj. Jubilee (relativo al jubilco).

jubilar v. tr. To retire, to pension off (a un trabajador). || FIG. y FAM. To scrap, to ditch, to get rid of (una cosa). | To ditch, to get rid of (una persona).
— V. intr. To jubilate, to be jubilant, to rejoice (alegrarse).
— V. pr. To retire, to go into retirement (un trabajador). || To jubilate, to be jubilant, to rejoice (regocijarse). || *Amer.* To become skilled, to acquire practice (instruirse).

jubileo m. REL. Jubilee. || FIG. Comings and goings, *pl.* (idas y venidas).

júbilo m. Jubilation. || Joy: *no caber en sí de júbilo*, to be beside o.s. with joy. || — *Con júbilo*, with jubilation, joyfully, jubilantly. || *Mostrar júbilo*, to jubilate, to be jubilant.

jubiloso, sa adj. Jubilant, joyful.

jubón m. Jerkin, doublet (vestidura). || Bodice (de mujer). || Sleeved vest (de niño).

Judá n. pr. m. Judah.

judaico, ca adj. Jewish, Judaic.

judaísmo m. Judaism.

judaizante adj. Judaizing.
— M. y f. Judaizer, Judaist.

judaizar v. intr. To Judaize.

judas m. FIG. Judas (traidor). | Effigy of Judas burnt during Holy Week (muñeco). || FIG. y FAM. *Estar hecho* or *parecer un Judas*, to be dressed in rags.

Judas n. pr. m. Judas: *Judas Iscariote*, Judas Iscariot.

Judea n. pr. f. GEOGR. Judaea, Judea.

judeoalemán m. Yiddish, Judaeo-German (lengua).

judeocristiano, na adj./s. Judaeo-Christian.

judeoespañol adj./s. Judaeo-Spanish.

judería f. Jewish quarter, Jewry (barrio judío). || Jewry (conjunto de judíos). || Ancient tax (impuesto).

judía f. BOT. Bean. || — *Judía blanca*, haricot bean. || *Judía escarlata*, runner bean. || *Judía verde*, French bean, green bean.

judiada f. FAM. Dirty trick (mala jugada). | Extortion (lucro).

judicatura f. Judicature (cargo). || Term of office of a judge, judgeship (mandato). || Judicature, judiciary (conjunto de jueces).

judicial adj. Judicial, juridical. || — *Partido judicial*, judicial district (de una provincia). || *Recurrir a la vía judicial*, to have recourse to the law.

judiciario, ria adj. Judicial.
— M. Astrologer (astrólogo).

judío, a adj. Jewish.
— M. y f. Jew.

Judit n. pr. f. Judith.

judo m. Judo (lucha).

judoka m. Judoka (luchador).

juego m. Game (recreo). || Sport (deporte). || Game (en tenis). || Court (terreno donde se juega). || Game: *juegos de azar*, games of chance; *juego de cartas* or *de naipes*, card game. || Gambling: *ha perdido mucho dinero en el juego*, he has lost a lot of money gambling; *casa de juego*, gambling house. || Rubber (en bridge). || Play: *juego limpio*, fair play; *juego sucio*, foul play. || FIG. Game: *sé muy bien su juego*, I know what his game is. | Play: *el juego de luces en el espejo*, the play of light on the mirror. || Set: *juego de cepillos, de útiles*, set of brushes, of tools. || Service, set: *juego de café, de té*, coffee, tea service. || Set (de botones, de chimenea, de diamantes, de neumáticos). || Suite (de muebles): *juego de comedor*, dining-room suite. || TECN. Play (holgura, movimiento): *hay juego entre estas dos piezas*, there is play between these two parts. || — Pl. Games: *Juegos Olímpicos*, Olympic Games.
— *Afortunado en el juego, desgraciado en amores*, lucky at cards, unlucky in love. || *A juego*, matching: *corbata y pañuelo a juego*, matching tie and handkerchief. || FIG. *Dar juego*, to make work: *el escándalo dio mucho juego a los periodistas*, the scandal made a lot of work for the newspapermen. | *Entrar en el juego* or *hacer el juego de alguien*, to play into s.o.'s hands (inconscientemente), to play s.o.'s game (conscientemente). | *Entrar en juego*, to be at work (intervenir). | *Entre bobos anda el juego*, they are as thick as thieves. || *Estar en juego*, to be in play (un balón), to be at stake (fortuna, intereses). || *Estar fuera de juego*, to be offside (persona), to be out [of the court] (pelota), to be out of play (el balón en fútbol, rugby, etc.). || FIG. *Hacer doble juego*, to be two-faced, to play a double game, to run with the hare and hunt with the hounds. || *Hacer juego*, to match: *estos dos candelabros hacen juego*, the two candelabras match. || *Hacer juegos de ojos*, to roll one's eyes. || *Hacer juegos malabares*, V. MALABAR. || *¡Hagan juego!*, place your bets! || *Juego de Bolsa*, speculation. || *Juego de damas*, [game of] draughts [U.S., checkers]. || *Juego de envite*, gambling game. || *Juego de la oca*, snakes and ladders. || *Juego de las canicas*, marbles. || *Juego de manos*, sleight of hand. || *Juego de palabras*, pun, play on words. || DEP. *Juego de piernas*, footwork (de un boxeador, etc.). || *Juego de prendas*, game of forfeits. || *Juegos atléticos*, sports, athletic sports. || *Juegos florales*, poetry competition. || *Juegos malabares*, juggling. || FIG. *No ser cosa de juego*, to be no laughing matter. || *Poner en juego*, to bring into play, to put at stake : *poner en juego su posición*, to put one's position at stake; to make use of (influencias, relaciones). || *Por juego*, for fun. || *Queda poco tiempo de juego*, there is little time left to play. || FIG. *Seguirle el juego a alguien*, to play along with s.o. | *Ser juego de niños*, to be child's play. || *Tener buen juego*, to have a good hand (naipes). || FIG. *Verle a uno el juego*, to be on to s.o., to see through s.o.

juerga f. FAM. Binge, spree, good time [U.S., blast]. || — FAM. *Estar de juerga*, to be living it up *o* whooping it up. | *Irse de juerga*, to go on a spree, to go and have a good time [U.S., to go have a blast]. | *Llevar una vida de juerga*, to lead a wild life. | *Tener ganas de juerga*, to feel like a bit of fun. | *¡Vaya juerga que nos corrimos!*, what a time we had!, what a laugh!

juerguearse v. pr. FAM. To live it up, to have a good time, to enjoy o.s. (divertirse). | Not to take [sth.] seriously (no tomar en serio). | To make fun [*de*, of] (burlarse).

juergueo m. FAM. V. JUERGA.

juerguista adj. FAM. Fun-loving.
— M. y f. FAM. Reveller.

jueves m. Thursday: *el jueves que viene, el jueves pasado*, next Thursday, last Thursday. || — *Jueves Santo*, Maundy Thursday, Holy Thursday. || FAM. *No es cosa* or *nada del otro jueves*, there's nothing to it (no es difícil), it's nothing to write home about, it's nothing to make a fuss about (no es ninguna maravilla). | *Parece que lo has aprendido en jueves*, don't you know how to say anything else?

juez m. Judge. || — Pl. Judges, Bench, *sing.* || — REL. *El Juez Supremo*, the Divine Judge. || *Juez de Instrucción*, examining magistrate. || DEP. *Juez de línea* or *de banda*, linesman. || *Juez de menores*, judge sitting in juvenile court. || FAM. *Juez de palo* or *lego*, incompetent judge. || *Juez de paz*, justice of the peace. || *Juez de primera instancia*, country court judge, judge of the court of first instance. || *Amer.* DEP. *Juez de raya*, finish line judge (en las carreras de caballos). || DEP. *Juez de salida*, starter (carreras). | *Juez de silla*, umpire (tenis).

jugada f. Throw (flechas, dados, bolos). || Stroke (golf, tenis). || Move (ajedrez, damas). || Shot, stroke (billar, croquet). || Piece of play, play (en general). || FIG. Dirty trick: *me hizo una jugada*, he played a dirty trick on me. || — *Jugada de Bolsa*, piece of speculation. || FIG. *Mala jugada*, dirty trick. || *Una buena jugada*, a good move (buena táctica), a nice piece of play, a nice move (en deportes), a dirty trick (jugarreta).

jugador, ra m. y f. Player. || Gambler (de casa de juego). || — *Jugador de Bolsa*, speculator on the Stock Exchange. || *Jugador de fútbol*, footballer, football player. || *Jugador de manos*, magician, conjurer. || *Jugador de ventaja*, cardsharp (fullero).

jugar* v. intr. To play: *los niños juegan a los indios en el patio*, the children are playing [at] cowboys and indians in the courtyard; *nuestro equipo jugará mañana*, our team will play tomorrow; *jugar al tenis*, to play tennis. || To play: *jugar a la Bolsa*, to play the Stock Exchange. || To bet (apostar). || TECN. To play, to have play (moverse). || — *Eso no es jugar limpio*, that isn't fair play, that isn't cricket. || *Jugar a cartas vistas*, to play with the cards on the table. || *Jugar a ganador, a colocado*, to bet [on a horse] to win, to bet [on a horse] to place. || *Jugar al alza, a la baja*, to bull, to bear the market. || *Jugar algo a cara o cruz*, to toss for sth. || *Jugar a pídola*, to play leapfrog. || FIG. *Jugar con dos barajas*, to double-deal. | *Jugar con fuego*, to play with fire. | *Jugar con su salud*, to play with one's health. | *Jugar con uno*, to play with s.o., to use s.o. || *Jugar fuerte* or *grueso*, to play *o* to bet heavy. || *Jugar limpio*, to play fair *o* fairly. || *Jugar sucio*, to play dirty, to

play foul. || *¿Quién juega?*, whose go is it, whose turn is it? || FIG. *Solamente está jugando con ella*, he is just trifling *o* playing with her.
— V. tr. To play: *jugar un partido, una partida, una carta*, to play a match, a game, a card. || To stake (dinero). || To wield: *jugar la espada*, to wield one's sword. || — *Jugar doble contra sencillo*, to bet two to one. || *Jugar una mala pasada* or *partida a uno*, to play a dirty trick on s.o.
— V. pr. To risk (arriesgar): *jugarse la vida, el honor*, to risk one's life *o* neck, one's honour. || To bet, to stake: *jugarse mil pesetas en*, to stake a thousand pesetas on. || — FIG. *El país se juega su futuro en las próximas elecciones*, the forthcoming elections put the future of the country in the balance. | *Jugarse el pellejo*, to risk one's neck *o* one's skin. | *Jugarse hasta la camisa, el alma*, to stake one's shirt. | *Jugársela a alguien*, to play a dirty trick on s.o. | *Jugárselo todo a una carta* or *jugarse el todo por el todo*, to stake everything one has (apostar), to go the whole hog, to take the plunge (tomar una acción drástica). | *Me juego la cabeza a que*, I'd stake my life that. | *Se juega su felicidad en eso*, his happiness is at stake.
jugarreta f. FAM. Bad move, bad play. || FIG. y FAM. Dirty trick (trastada): *le hizo una jugarreta*, he played a dirty trick on him.
juglar m. Minstrel (trovador). || Juggler (malabarista).
juglaresco, ca adj. Pertaining to minstrels. || *Poesía juglaresca*, poetry of the minstrels, minstrel poetry.
juglaría o **juglería** f. Minstrelsy.
jugo m. Juice: *jugo de limón*, lemon juice; *jugo de carne*, juice of the meat; *jugo gástrico, pancreático*, gastric, pancreatic juice. || CULIN. Gravy. || FIG. Essence, substance, pith (lo esencial). || — FIG. y FAM. *Sacar el jugo de un libro*, to get the pith and marrow out of a book. | *Sacarle el jugo a alguien*, to bleed s.o. white, to bleed s.o. dry. | *Sacarle jugo al dinero*, V. DINERO.
jugosidad f. Juiciness, succulence. || FIG. Substance.
jugoso, sa adj. Juicy: *una fruta jugosa*, a juicy fruit. || FIG. Lucrative, profitable (provechoso). | Substantial, meaty, worthwhile, pithy (sustancioso). | Rich (colores).
juguete m. Toy. || TEATR. Skit. || — FIG. *Ser el juguete de alguien*, to be s.o.'s plaything. || *Un coche de juguete*, a toy car.
juguetear v. intr. To play (jugar). || To play, to toy: *está jugueteando con su pulsera*, she is toying with her bracelet. || To romp, to frolic (retozar).
jugueteo m. Playing (diversión). || Romping, frolicking.
juguetería f. Toyshop (tienda). || Toy trade, toy business (comercio).
juguetón, ona adj. Playful: *niño, perro juguetón*, playful child, dog. || Frolicsome, frisky (retozón).
juicio m. Judgment, judgement: *tener el juicio recto*, to have sound judgment. || Mind, reason, sanity, senses, *pl.*: *perder el juicio*, to lose one's mind. || Common sense (sentido común): *tiene poco juicio*, he lacks common sense. || Good sense, sensibleness (sensatez). || Judgment: *emitir un juicio sobre alguien*, to make a judgment about s.o. || JUR. Trial (pleito). || — *A juicio de*, in the opinion of. || *A juicio de peritos*, according to expert opinion. || *A mi juicio*, in my opinion. || *Asentar el juicio*, to come to one's senses. || *Dejar algo a juicio de uno*, to leave sth. to s.o.'s discretion. || *Estar en su juicio* or *en su cabal juicio*, to be in one's right mind. || *Estar fuera* or *falto de juicio*, to be out of one's mind. || REL. *Juicio de Dios*, trial by ordeal. || JUR. *Juicio definitivo* or *sin apelación*, decree absolute. | *Juicio en rebeldía*, judgment in contumacy, judgment by default. || REL. *Juicio Final*, Last Judgment. || *La edad del juicio*, the age of reason. || *Muela del juicio*, wisdom tooth. || *No estar en su sano juicio*, not to be in one's right mind. || *Poner en tela de juicio*, V. TELA. || *Quitar el juicio a alguien*, to drive s.o. out of his mind. || *Someter al juicio pericial*, to submit to expert opinion. || *Volver en su juicio*, to come to one's senses, to regain consciousness.
juicioso, sa adj. Judicious, wise (sensato). || FIG. Appropriate, sensible (atinado).
jujeño, ña adj. [Of *o* from] Jujuy (Argentina).
— M. y f. Native *o* inhabitant of Jujuy.
julepe m. MED. Julep (poción). || Sort of card game (juego de naipes). || FIG. y FAM. Dressing down, scolding (reprimenda). || *Amer.* Scare, fright (miedo). || — *Dar julepe a alguien*, to leave s.o. without a trick (naipes). || FIG. y FAM. *Darse un julepe*, to work like a dog *o* like the devil (trabajar mucho). || *Amer. Dar un julepe a uno*, to scare s.o., to give s.o. a fright.
julepear v. tr. *Amer.* To scare (asustar). | To hurry up (dar prisa). | To tire (fatigar).
Julián n. pr. m. Julian.
juliana f. BOT. Rocket, damewort, dame's violet. || CULIN. Julienne soup (sopa).
Juliana n. pr. f. Juliana.
juliano, na adj. Julian: *calendario juliano*, Julian calendar; *era juliana*, Julian era.
Julieta n. pr. f. Juliet.
julio m. July (mes): *el 5 de julio*, the 5th of July. || FÍS. Joule (unidad de trabajo).
Julio n. pr. m. Jules.
jumá o **juma** f. FAM. V. JUMERA.
jumado, da adj. FAM. Drunk, canned.
jumarse v. pr. FAM. To get drunk *o* canned.
jumento, ta m. y f. Ass, donkey.
jumera f. FAM. *Agarrar una jumera*, to get drunk *o* canned.
juncáceas f. pl. BOT. Juncaceae.
juncal adj. Willowy (esbelto). || Shapely (talle).
juncal o **juncar** m. BOT. Rush bed, rushes, *pl.*
juncia f. BOT. Sedge.
junco m. BOT. Rush. || Cane, stick (bastón). || MAR. Junk (embarcación china). || — BOT. *Junco de Indias*, rattan. | *Junco florido*, flowering rush. | *Junco oloroso*, camel grass.
jungla f. Jungle.
juniense adj. [Of *o* from] Junín (Perú).
— M. y f. Native *o* inhabitant of Junín.
junino, na adj. [Of *o* from] Junín (Argentina).
— M. y f. Native *o* inhabitant of Junín.
junio m. June (mes): *el 24 de junio*, the 24th of June.
júnior m. REL. Novice (monje). || Junior (el más joven, deportista).
junípero BOT. Juniper (enebro).
junquera f. BOT. Rush (junco). | Rush bed (juncal).
junqueral m. Rush bed, rushes, *pl.*
junquillo m. BOT. Jonquil. | Rattan (junco de Indias). || R ttan [walking stick] (bastón). || Strip of wood (varilla). || ARQ. Beading (moldura).
junta f. Meeting, assembly: *junta general*, general meeting. || Session, sitting (sesión). || Board, council: *junta administrativa*, administrative board. || Council: *junta de empresa*, works council. || Board: *junta de beneficencia*, charity board; *junta directiva*, board of directors; *ser miembro de una junta*, to serve on a board. || Junta (en los países ibéricos): *junta militar*, military junta. || ARQ. Jointing seam. || MAR. Seam (entre tablones). || TECN. Joint: *junta estanca*, watertight joint. || — Pl. *Amer.* Junction, *sing.* (de dos ríos). || — *Celebrar junta*, to hold a meeting, to sit. || TECN. *Junta de culata*, gasket. | *Junta universal*, universal joint, cardan joint.
juntamente adv. Together, jointly (conjuntamente). || At the same time, together (al mismo tiempo).
juntar v. tr. To unite, to join: *juntar dos tablas*, to join two boards. || To put together, to assemble (varias piezas). || To unite: *la amistad les junta*, friendship unites them. || To join, to put together (poner juntos). || To gather together: *juntar amigos en su casa*, to gather friends together in one's home. || To collect, to raise (dinero). || To collect, to gather (sellos, documentos, etc.).
— V. pr. To join [up with], to meet: *me juntaré al grupo en Madrid*, I will join the group in Madrid. || To join (dos ríos). || To meet, to assemble, to gather [together] (congregarse). || To join [forces with]: *Pedro se ha juntado con Antonio para fundar una empresa*, Peter has joined Anthony to start a business. || To join together, to join forces (aunar sus fuerzas). || To live with (vivir con). || To live together (vivir juntos). || *Dios los cría y ellos se juntan*, V. DIOS.
juntillas V. PIE (*a pie juntillas*).
junto, ta adj. Joined, united: *dos tablas juntas*, two joined boards. || Side by side (uno al lado de otro). || Together: *vivían juntos*, they were living together; *las niñas jugaban juntas*, the girls were playing together; *todo junto* or *todos juntos*, all together. || Put together: *un territorio tan extenso como seis provincias juntas*, a territory as large as six provinces put together. || — *Demasiado juntos*, too close. || *Muy juntos*, very close together.
— Adv. *Aquí junto*, near by, close by. || *Demasiado junto*, too close. || *En junto* or *por junto*, in all, in total, all together. || *Junto a*, close to, near, next to (cerca de), next to (al lado de), against (contra). || *Junto con*, together with. || *Muy junto*, very close, very near.
juntura f. Junction, join. || ANAT. Joint. || TECN. Joint, coupling. || ANAT. *Juntura serrátil*, serrated suture (articulación fija).
Júpiter n. pr. m. MIT. Jupiter, Jove.
jupiterino, na o **jupiteriano, na** adj. Jovian, relative to Jupiter.
jura f. Oath (acción). || Swearing in (ceremonia). || *Jura de (la) bandera*, pledge of allegiance to the flag.
jurado, da adj. Sworn. || Sworn, sworn-in (que ha prestado juramento). || FIG. *Enemigo jurado*, sworn enemy.
— M. Jury (tribunal). | Juryman (miembro del tribunal). || Panel of judges, jury (en un concurso). || — *Jurado de cuentas*, chartered accountant [U.S., certified public accountant]. || *Jurado de empresa*, works council.
juramentado, da adj. Sworn, sworn-in: *traductor juramentado*, sworn-in translator.
juramentar v. tr. To swear in, to put on oath.
— V. pr. To take an oath, to be sworn in.
juramento m. Oath: *prestar juramento*, to take the oath. || Oath, curse, blasphemy (blasfemia). || — *Bajo juramento*, on *o* under oath. || *Juramento asertorio*, assertory oath. || *Juramento falso*, perjury. || *Juramento promisorio*, promissory oath. || *Soltar juramentos*, to curse, to blaspheme. || *Tomar juramento a alguien*, to put s.o. on oath, to swear s.o. in.
jurar v. tr. e intr. To swear, to take an oath: *jurar sobre el Evangelio*, to swear on the Gospel. || To swear: *te juro que te he dicho la verdad*, I swear that I have

VOCABULARIO (*m.*) JURÍDICO — LEGAL TERMINOLOGY

I. Derecho, *m.* — Law.

ley *f.*	law
anteproyecto *m.*	draft
proyecto (*m.*) de ley	Government bill
adoptar una ley	to pass *o* to carry a bill
promulgar una ley	to enact *o* to promulgate a law
ratificación *f.*	ratification, confirmation
aplicación (*f.*) de la ley	law enforcement
entrar en vigor	to come into force
decreto *m.*	decree
cláusula *f.*	clause
actas *f. pl.*	minutes
atestado *m.*	report
codificación *f.*	codification
legislación *f.*	legislation
legislador *m.*	legislator
jurista *m.*	jurist
jurisprudencia *f.*	jurisprudence
legitimación *f.*	legitimation
legalidad *f.*	legality, lawfulness
legal	legal, lawful
fuera de la ley	outlaw, outside the law
quebrantar *or* transgredir *or* contravenir una ley	to contravene *o* to infringe *o* to break a law
contraventor *m.*	offender
abolir	to abolish
revocación *f.*	revocation
rescisión *f.*	rescission, annulment
anulación *f.*	repeal, revocation, annulment (de una ley), cancellation, annulment, invalidation (de un contrato), cancellation (de un cheque), annulment (de un testamento), repeal, rescission (de un fallo)
inmunidad *f.*	immunity
incapacidad *f.*	disability, legal incapacity
irretroactividad *f.*	nonretroactive character
prescripción *f.*	prescription
privación (*f.*) de derechos cívicos	attainder
derecho (*m.*) canónico	canon law
derecho (*m.*) consuetudinario	common law
derecho (*m.*) penal, administrativo, civil	criminal, administrative, civil law
derecho (*m.*) mercantil *or* comercial	commercial *o* mercantile law
derecho (*m.*) político *or* constitucional	constitutional law
derecho (*m.*) de gentes	law of nations
derecho (*m.*) internacional	international law
derecho (*m.*) natural	natural law
derecho (*m.*) del trabajo *or* laboral	labour laws *pl.*
derecho (*m.*) fiscal	fiscal law
derechos (*m. pl.*) civiles	civil rights
derecho (*m.*) de asilo	right of asylum
derechos (*m. pl.*) del hombre	human rights, rights of man
derechos (*m. pl.*) arancelarios	[customs] duties
derechos (*m. pl.*) de sucesión	death duty *sing.*, death tax *sing.*
derechos (*m. pl.*) de autor	royalties
código (*m.*) civil	code of civil law
código (*m.*) penal	penal code
código (*m.*) de comercio	code of mercantile law

II. Tribunales, *m.* — Courts.

Tribunal (*m.*) de primera instancia	court of first instance
Audiencia (*f.*) de lo criminal	criminal court
Tribunal (*m.*) civil	civil court
Audiencia (*f.*) territorial, Tribunal (*m.*) de apelación	regional court, Court of Appeal
Tribunal (*m.*) de Casación	Court of Cassation
Tribunal (*m.*) Supremo	High Court [U.S. Supreme Court]
Tribunal (*m.*) Internacional de Justicia	International Court of Justice
Magistratura (*f.*) del Trabajo	conciliation board in industrial disputes
Tribunal (*m.*) de arbitraje	arbitration tribunal, court of arbitration
Tribunal (*m.*) de Menores	juvenile court
Consejo (*m.*) de guerra	court-martial
Palacio (*m.*) de Justicia	Law Courts *pl.*
Tribunal (*m.*) de cuentas	National Audit Office [U.S., Committee on Public Accounts]
ser de la competencia de un tribunal	to fall within the competence of a court

III. Funciones, *f.* — Functions.

foro *m.*, colegio (*m.*) de abogados	The Bar
juez *m.*	judge
presidente *m.*	presiding judge
asesor (*m.*) jurídico	legal adviser
juez (*m.*) de instrucción	examining magistrate
juez (*m.*) de apelación	judge in appeal
juez (*m.*) de menores	juvenile court judge
fiscal *m.*, procurador (*m.*) de la República	public prosecutor [U.S., district attorney]
procurador (*m.*) general	attorney general
jurado *m.*	jury (tribunal), juror (miembro)
abogado *m.*	lawyer, solicitor (consejero), barrister [U.S., attorney, lawyer] (en el tribunal)
pasante (*m.*) de abogado	assistant lawyer
procurador *m.*	attorney
defensor *m.*	counsel for the defence
notario *m.*	notary

IV. Instrucción, *f.* — Preliminary investigation.

investigación *f.*, indagación *f.*, diligencias (*f. pl.*) previas	inquiry
audiencia *f.*, vista *f.*	hearing
autos *m. pl.*	proceedings
sumario *m.*	summary
interrogatorio *m.*	interrogatory, examination
antecedentes (*m. pl.*) penales	criminal record *sing.*
audición (*f.*) de testigos	hearing of witnesses
responsabilidad *f.*	responsibility, liability
testigo (*m.*) ocular	eyewitness
visita (*f.*) domiciliaria	domiciliary visit, house search
piezas (*f. pl.*) de convicción	evidence *sing.*, exhibits
circunstancias (*f. pl.*) atenuantes, agravantes, eximentes	extenuating, aggravating, exculpatory *o* exonerating circumstances
coartada *f.*	alibi
auto (*m.*) *or* orden (*f.*) de comparecencia, requerimiento *m.*, intimación *f.*, conminación *f.*	summons
orden (*f.*) de detención	warrant for arrest
detener	to arrest
arresto *m.*, detención *f.*	arrest
en libertad vigilada	on probation
libertad (*f.*) provisional *or* bajo fianza	release on bail
citar ante los tribunales	to sue, to prosecute
citar a uno de testigo	to call s.o. to witness

V. Procedimiento (*m.*) judicial, enjuiciamiento, *m.* — Proceedings, *pl.*, procedure.

justicia *f.*	justice
juzgar	to judge
pleito *m.*	lawsuit
entablar un pleito	to institute proceedings
proceso *m.*	trial
incoación (*f.*) de un proceso	institution of proceedings

told you the truth. || To swear, to curse (blasfemar). || — *Jurar el cargo*, to take the oath of office. || *Jurar en falso*, to commit perjury, to bear false witness. || *Jurar (la) bandera*, to pledge allegiance to the flag. || *Jurar por Dios que*, to swear to God that. || *Jurar por la salud de uno*, to swear on one's mother's grave. || *Jurar por lo más sagrado* or *por todos los dioses*, to swear by all that is sacred *o* to swear by all the gods. || *Lo juraría*, I would swear to it. || *No jurar el santo nombre de Dios en vano*, thou shalt not take the name of the Lord thy God in vain (mandamiento). || *Te lo juro*, I swear it.
— V. pr. *Jurársela a uno*, to swear to get even with s.o., to swear vengeance on s.o.

jurásico, ca adj./s.m. GEOL. Jurassic (del Jura).

jurel m. ZOOL. Horse mackerel, jack mackerel, scad, jurel, saurel (pez).

jurídico, ca adj. Legal, juridical: *problemas jurídicos*, juridical problems. || *Persona jurídica*, V. PERSONA.

jurisconsulto m. Jurisconsult, legal expert.

jurisdicción f. Jurisdiction. || FIG. *Caer bajo la jurisdicción de uno*, to fall *o* to come under s.o.'s jurisdiction.

jurisdiccional adj. Jurisdictional. || *Aguas jurisdiccionales*, territorial waters.

jurispericia f. Jurisprudence.

jurisperito m. Jurist, legal expert, jurisprudent.

jurisprudencia f. Jurisprudence. || Case law (precedentes). || *Sentar jurisprudencia*, to be a test case.

jurisprudencial adj. Jurisprudential.

jurista m. Jurist, lawyer.

juro m. Right of perpetual ownership. || Pension (renta).

justa f. Joust, tilt (combate). || FIG. Contest, competition (certamen). || *Justa poética*, poetry contest.

justamente adv. Precisely, just, exactly: *es justamente lo que quería*, it is exactly what I wanted. || Just enough: *tiene justamente para vivir*, he has just enough to live on. || Justly, fairly (con justicia). || — *Eso es, justamente*, that's just it. || *¡Justamente!*, precisely!

justicia f. Justice: *la justicia está cumplida*, justice has been done. || Justice, fairness: *no hay justicia en el mundo*, there is no justice in the world. || Execution (de un condenado a muerte). || — *Administrar (la) justicia*, to administer justice. || *De justicia*, justly,

causa *f.*	cause, suit
denuncia *f.*	accusation
presentar una denuncia	to lodge a complaint
querella *f.*	complaint
acción *f.*; demanda *f.*	action; claim
presentar una demanda	to institute proceedings, to bring a lawsuit,
demanda (*f.*) pública	prosecution
demanda (*f.*) por daños y perjuicios	claim for damages
petición (*f.*) de indemnización	claim for compensation
demandante *m.* y *f.*	plaintiff
la parte contraria	the opposing party, the other side
citación *f.*	writ of summons, citation
alegar	to plead, to claim
alegato *m.*	plea
deposición *f.*	deposition, evidence
informe (*m.*) del fiscal	indictment, charge
cargo (*m.*) de acusación	count of indictment
acta (*f.*) de acusación	indictment
declararse culpable	to plead guilty
declaración (*f.*) jurada	sworn statement
bajo juramento	on oath
acusador *m.*	accuser
acusado *m.*, procesado *m.*	accused, defendant
delincuente *m.* y *f.*	delinquent, offender
reo *m.* y *f.*	accused, defendant
culpable *m.* y *f.*	guilty party, culprit
reincidente *m.* y *f.*	recidivist
cómplice *m.* y *f.*	accomplice
complicidad *f.*	complicity
encubridor *m.*	harbourer [U.S., harborer] (de personas), receiver (de mercancías).
en flagrante delito	in flagrante delicto
con premeditación	with malice aforethought
audiencia (*f.*) pública	public hearing
a puerta cerrada	in camera
testigo (*m.*) de cargo, de descargo	witness for the prosecution, for the defence
prueba *f.*	proof, evidence
barra *f.*	witness box [U.S., witness stand]
banquillo (*m.*) de los acusados	dock
legítima defensa *f.*	self-defence [U.S., self-defense]
fuerza (*f.*) mayor	force majeure, act of God
pronunciar un fallo	to pronounce sentence
error (*m.*) judicial	miscarriage of justice
condena *f.*	sentence
condenado *m.*	convict
condena (*f.*) en rebeldía	judgment by default
ser condenado en costas	to be ordered to pay costs
absolución *f.*	acquittal
veredicto (*m.*) absolutorio	verdict of not guilty
petición (*f.*) de indulto	petition for a reprieve
sobreseimiento *m.*	stay of proceedings (provisional), nonsuit (definitivo)
apelar, recurrir, interponer recurso	to appeal, to lodge an appeal

VI. Infracciones, *f.* **— Infractions.**

delito *m.*	crime, offence [U.S., offense]
ofensa *f.*	offence [U.S., offense]
crimen *m.*	crime
tentativa *f.*, conato *m.*	attempt
incumplimiento *m.*	unfulfilment
inobservancia *f.*	nonobservance
injusticia *f.*	injustice
amenaza *f.*	threat, menace
alta traición *f.*	high treason
adulterio *m.*	adultery
falsificación *f.*	forgery, forging, counterfeiting
perjurio *m.*	perjury
levantar falso testimonio	to bear false witness, to commit perjury
atentado *m.*	attempted murder (contra personas), offence [U.S., offense] (contra la ley)
asesinato *m.*	assassination, murder
homicidio *m.*	homicide
infanticidio *m.*	infanticide, child murder
lesiones *f. pl.*	assault and battery
rapto *m.*, secuestro *m.*	kidnapping, abduction
secuestro *m.*	highjacking (de aviones)
piratería *f.*	piracy
violación *f.*	rape, violation
conspiración *f.*	conspiracy, plot
robo *m.*	theft, larceny
robo (*m.*) a mano armada	armed robbery
robo (*m.*) con fractura	housebreaking, burglary
contrabando *m.*	contraband, smuggling
estafa *f.*, timo *m.*	swindle
malversación (*f.*) de fondos, desfalco *m.*	embezzlement
prevaricación *f.*	prevarication
soborno *m.*	bribery, suborning
ruptura (*f.*) de contrato	breach of contract
fraude *m.*	fraud
fraude (*m.*) fiscal	tax evasion
abuso (*m.*) de autoridad	misuse of authority
corrupción *f.*	corruption
usurpación *f.*	usurpation
chantaje *m.*	blackmail
calumnia *f.*	calumny, slander
estado (*m.*) de embriaguez	intoxication
alteración (*f.*) del orden público	disturbance of the peace

VII. Penas, *f.* **— Punishment,** *sing.*, **penalty,** *sing.*

pena (*f.*) de muerte	death sentence *o* penalty
prisión *f.*	imprisonment
cárcel *f.*	prison, gaol [U.S., jail]
cadena (*f.*) perpetua	life imprisonment
trabajos (*m. pl.*) forzados *or* forzosos	hard labour [U.S., hard labor]
multa *f.*	fine
embargo *m.*	embargo
interdicción (*f.*) de residencia	local banishment
interdicción (*f.*) civil	attainder
pensión (*f.*) alimenticia	alimony, allowance
indemnización *f.*	indemnity, indemnification, compensation
extradición *f.*	extradition

VIII. Otros términos, *m.* **— Other terms.**

fe (*f.*) de bautismo	baptismal certificate
partida (*f.*) de nacimiento, de matrimonio, de defunción	birth, marriage, death certificate
certificado (*m.*) de penales	extract from police records
escritura (*f.*) notarial	notarial deed
escritura (*f.*) de venta	bill of sale
arrendamiento *m.*,	lease
propiedad *f.*	proprietorship, ownership
nuda propiedad *f.*	ownership without usufruct *o* use
bienes (*m. pl.*) muebles	personal property *sing.*, movables
bienes (*m. pl.*) raíces *or* inmobiliarios	real estate
propiedad (*f.*) artística y literaria	copyright
propiedad (*f.*) industrial	patent rights *pl.*
propiedad (*f.*) inmobiliaria	real estate
registro (*m.*) de la propiedad	Land Register
alienación *f.*, enajenación *f.*	alienation, transfer, assignment
enajenación (*f.*) mental	mental derangement, alienation, insanity
huella (*f.*) dactilar *or* digital	fingerprint
cadáver *m.*	corpse
depósito (*m.*) de cadáveres	mortuary, morgue
autopsia *f.*	autopsy
expediente *m.*	file, dossier
naturalización *f.*	naturalization
testamento *m.*	will
codicilo *m.*	codicil
heredero *m.*; lega ario; *m.*	heir; legatee
herencia *f.*	inheritance
emancipación *f.*	emancipation
llegar a la mayoría de edad	to come of age
denegación (*f.*) de la paternidad	disowning of offspring
tutela *f.*	tutelage, guardianship
tutor *m.*	tutor, guardian
casamiento (*m.*) por poderes	marriage by proxy
pedir el divorcio	to sue for divorce

deservedly, duly. || *Ejecutor de la justicia*, executioner. || *Es de justicia que*, it is just that, it is right that. || *Hacer justicia*, to do justice. || *Ir por justicia*, to go to law, to bring an action. || *Justicia distributiva*, distributive justice. || *Justicias y ladrones*, cops and robbers (juego). || *Ministerio de Justicia*, Lord High Chancellor's Office [U.S., Department of Justice]. || *Pedir en justicia*, to go to court. || *Pedir justicia*, to demand justice. || *Tomarse la justicia por su mano*, to take the law into one's own hands.
— M. *Justicia mayor*, supreme magistrate [in Aragon].

justiciable adj. Justiciable, actionable.

justiciar v. tr. *Amer.* To execute (ajusticiar). | To condemn (condenar).

justiciero, ra adj. Just, fair. || *Espíritu justiciero*, sense of justice.
— M. y f. Just *o* fair person.

justificable adj. Justifiable.

justificación f. Justification. || IMPR. Justification.

justificado, da adj. Justified, just, right.

justificador, ra adj. Justifying, justificatory.
— M. Justifier.

justificante adj. Justifying.
— M. Voucher, voucher copy (comercio). || JUR. Document in proof, relevant paper.

justificar v. tr. To justify. || IMPR. To justify. || *Sin razón que lo justifique*, without justifiable reason.
— V. pr. To clear o.s., to justify o.s.: *justificarse con alguien*, to justify o.s. with s.o.

justificativo, va adj. Justifying, justificatory.

justillo m. Jerkin (prenda de vestir).

Justiniano n. pr. m. Justinian.

justipreciación f. Appraisal, estimate, evaluation.

justipreciar v. tr. To appraise, to evaluate, to estimate (apreciar).

justiprecio m. Appraisal, estimate, evaluation.

justo, ta adj. Just, fair, right. || Tight (apretado): *me está muy justo*, it's very tight. || Exact, right, correct (exacto). || Sufficient, just enough (suficiente). || Deserved, condign (castigo). || Legitimate (cólera). || Fair (trato). || Right (cálculo, hora). || Right, accurate, exact (palabra, dicho). || Sound (razonamiento). || — *Justo es que*, it is just that, it is right that. || || *Llegamos al lugar justo del incidente*, we arrived at the very place of the incident. || *Más de lo justo*, more

than enough. || *Mil pesetas justas,* exactly one thousand pesetas.
— M. Righteous person. || — *Lo justo y lo injusto,* right and wrong. || *Los justos,* the righteous. || *Pagan justos por pecadores,* the innocent must often pay for the guilty.
— Adv. Just, exactly. || — *Llegar justo,* to arrive just in [the nick of] time (a tiempo), to arrive just: *llegó justo cuando me iba,* he arrived just as I was leaving. || *Tener justo para vivir,* to have just enough to live on. || *Vivir muy justo,* to scrape a bare living.
jutía f. *Amer.* Hutia (mamífero).
Jutlandia n. pr. f. GEOGR. Jutland.
juvenil adj. Young, youthful, juvenile: *aspecto juvenil,* youthful appearance. || Youthful, young: *un traje juvenil,* a youthful suit. || *En los años juveniles,* in one's youth.
— M. y f. DEP. Junior.
juventud f. Youth (edad). || Youthfulness: *ha conservado su juventud,* she has conserved her youthfulness. || Youth, young people (gente joven).
juzgado, da adj. Judged.
— M. Court, tribunal. || Judicature (judicatura).
juzgador, ra adj. Judging.
— M. y f. Judge.
juzgar v. tr. To judge: *juzgar a un reo,* to judge a criminal. || To judge, to consider, to deem, to think: *yo no juzgo oportuno hacer esto,* I don't think it fitting *o* right to do this. || — *A juzgar por,* judging by, judging from: *a juzgar por su apariencia,* judging from his appearance. || *Juzgar mal,* to misjudge. || *Juzgar por las apariencias* or *a la vista,* to judge by appearances. | *No se puede juzgar por las apariencias,* one can't judge a book by its cover. || *¡Y juzgue mi sorpresa cuando le vi!,* and just imagine my surprise when I saw him!

K

k f. K: *una k mayúscula, minúscula,* a capital, a small k.
— OBSERV. The Spanish *k* is pronounced like the English k as in *kite.*
ka f. K [name of the letter *k*].
kabila adj./s. Kabyle (cabila).
kainita f. QUÍM. Kainite (sal).
káiser m. Kaiser.
kakatoes m. ZOOL. Cockatoo.
kaki adj. Khaki (color).
— M. Kaki, Japanese persimmon (árbol y fruto). || Khaki (color). || FAM. Khakies, *pl.* (uniforme militar).
kaleidoscopio m. Kaleidoscope (caleidoscopio).
kamikase m. Kamikaze (avión suicida).
kan m. Khan (príncipe). || Caravanserai (caravasar y mercado público).
kanato m. Khanate.
kantiano, na adj./s. Kantian.
kantismo m. Kantianism.
kapoc m. Kapok.
kappa f. Kappa (letra griega).
kaqui adj./s.m. V. KAKI.
karakul m. ZOOL. Karakul, caracul (caracul).
karate m. DEP. Karate.
kart m. Go-kart (vehículo).
karting m. Karting [U.S., go-kart racing].
katangueño, ña adj./s. Katanganese.
kayac m. Kayak (embarcación).
kéfir m. Kefir (bebida).
kenotrón m. Kenotron (tubo).
kepí o **kepis** m. Kepi (quepis).
kermes m. Kermes (quermes).
kermesse f. Charity fair.
kerosén m. V. QUEROSENO.
khedive m. Khedive.
kibutz m. Kibbutz. || — Pl. Kibbutzim.
— OBSERV. The plural of *kibutz* is *kibutzim.*
kieselgur m. Kieselguhr, kieselgur (silíceo).
kieserita f. MIN. Kieserite.
kif m. Kif (polvo de cáñamo).
kilo m. Kilo, kilogram, kilogramme (kilogramo).
kilocaloría f. FÍS. Kilocalorie.
kilociclo m. Kilocycle.
kilográmetro m. Kilogram-metre [U.S., kilogram-meter].
kilogramo m. Kilogramme, kilogram.
kilojulio m. Kilojoule.
kilolitro m. Kilolitre [U.S., kiloliter].
kilometraje m. Distance in kilometres. || Mileage (de un coche).
— OBSERV. La palabra *mileage* se refiere a la distancia recorrida en millas.
kilometrar v. tr. To measure in kilometres.
kilométrico, ca adj. Kilometric. || FIG. y FAM. Endless, interminable: *un pasillo kilométrico,* an endless corridor. || *Mojón kilométrico,* milestone [indicating distance in kilometres].
— OBSERV. For long train journeys in Spain, one can obtain *un billete kilométrico,* in coupon form. Each coupon is valid for a certain distance in kilometres. There is a reduction in proportion to the number of kilometres travelled.
kilómetro m. Kilometre [U.S., kilometer]: *kilómetro cuadrado,* square kilometre.
kilotón m. Kiloton.
kilovatio m. Kilowatt.
kilovatio-hora m. Kilowatt-hour.
kilovoltio m. Kilovolt.
kilt m. Kilt (falda escocesa).
kimono m. Kimono.
kindergarten m. Kindergarten.
kinesiterapeuta m. y f. Masseur (hombre), masseuse (mujer) [masajista].
kinesiterapia f. Massage, kinesitherapy, massage (curación por medio de masajes).
kiosco m. Kiosk. || Bandstand (de música). || *Kiosco de periódicos,* newsstand, newspaper stall.
— OBSERV. The Spanish spelling *quiosco* is preferred.
kirie m. Kyrie. || FIG. y FAM. *Llorar los kiries,* to cry ones eyes out.
kirieleisón m. Kyrie eleison. || FAM. Funeral chant, dirge. || FIG. y FAM. *Cantar el kirieleisón,* to beg for mercy.
kirsch m. Kirsch (aguardiente de cereza).
kiwi m. ZOOL. Kiwi.
klaxon m. Horn, hooter (bocina). || *Tocar el klaxon,* to sound *o* to honk the horn.
knock-out m. inv. Knockout. || *Dejar* or *poner a alguien knock-out,* to knock s.o. out.
knut m. Knout (látigo).
koala m. ZOOL. Koala.
kola f. Kola *o* cola nut.
koljoz m. Kolkhoz (en Rusia).
kopek m. Copeck, kopeck, kopek (moneda rusa).
kraft m. Kraft (papel).
krausismo m. Philosophy of Krause.
— OBSERV. *Krausismo* had a great influence on Spain in the nineteenth century.
krausista adj. Krause: *doctrina krausista,* Krause doctrine.
— M. y f. Follower of Krause.
kriptón m. Krypton (gas).
kronprinz m. Crown prince (de Prusia).
kulak m. Kulak (campesino).
kumis m. Koumiss, kumiss (bebida).
kummel m. Kümmel (licor).
kurdo, da adj. Kurdish, Kurd.
— M. y f. Kurd.

L

l f. L (letra): *una l mayúscula*, a capital l.

— OBSERV. Pronounced like the English *l*.

la m. MÚS. La (nota de la escala vocal). | A (de la escala instrumental): *la sostenido*, A sharp. || *Dar el la*, to give the tuning A (a una orquesta).

la art. f. sing. The: *la cabeza*, the head.

— OBSERV. When feminine nouns begin with a stressed *a* or *ha*, for euphonic reasons *la* is replaced by *el* (*el agua, el alma, el hambre*).
— El artículo *la* debe traducirse en inglés por el adjetivo posesivo cuando se refiere a una parte del cuerpo (*dame la mano*, give me your hand). Se omite delante de los nombres de países (*la Argentina*, Argentina), excepto si se trata de una República (*la República Argentina*, the Republic of Argentina). El uso popular de *la* delante del nombre existe en español pero no en inglés (*la María me lo dijo*, Mary told me).

la pron. pers. Her (persona): *yo la saludo*, I greet her. || You (cuando corresponde a "usted"): *la vi a usted ayer*, I saw you yesterday. || It (cosa): *la leo*, I read it. || The one: *la del tercer piso*, the one on the third floor. || — FAM. *La de*, the quantity of, the amount of: *si vieras la de vino que bebimos*, you should have seen the quantity of wine we drank; the number of: *si vieras la de platos que pedimos*, you should have seen the number of dishes we ordered. || *La del abrigo negro*, the one in the black coat, the one with the black coat. || *La de Martínez*, Mrs. Martínez. || *La de Miguel es más grande*, Michael's one *o* Michael's is bigger. || *La de usted*, yours. || *La que*, the one who, she who, she that (persona, sujeto): *la que vino ayer*, the one who came yesterday; the one whom, the one that, the one (persona, complemento): *la que veré mañana*, the one I'll see tomorrow; the one which, the one that, the one (cosas): *la que quiero*, the one I want. || *Son... las que*, it is ... that: *son las de arriba las que están rotas*, it is the upper ones that are broken; it is ... who: *son María y Carola las que vienen*, it is Mary and Carol who are coming.

— OBSERV. *La* should not be used instead of *le* in the dative : *le hablé dos palabras, le di la mano*, not *la hablé dos palabras, la di la mano*. This improper use of *la* is called *laísmo*.

label m. Label (etiqueta de garantía).

laberíntico, ca adj. Labyrinthine, labyrinthian.

laberinto m. Labyrinth, maze. || FIG. Tangle, maze (asunto embrollado).

labia f. FAM. Glibness. || *Tener mucha labia*, to have the gift of the gab.

labiado, da adj. BOT. Labiate.
— F. BOT. Labiate.

labial adj./s. f. Labial.

labialización f. Labialization.

labializar v. tr. To labialize.

labihendido, da adj. Harelipped.

labio m. ANAT. Lip: *labio superior abultado*, heavy upper lip. | Labium, lip (de vulva). || Edge, rim, lip (de recipiente). || BOT. Lip, labrum, labium (lóbulo). || — Pl. FIG. Lips: *nunca le ofendieron mis labios*, my lips have never uttered a word against him. || Lips (de una llaga). || — *Apretar los labios*, to clench *o* to screw up one's lips. || FIG. *Cerrar* or *sellar los labios*, to keep one's lips sealed, to keep one's mouth shut. | *Estar pendiente de los labios de alguien*, to hang on to s.o.'s every word. | *Hablar con el corazón en los labios*, to speak frankly *o* with an open heart. || *Labio belfo*, thick lower lip. || MED. *Labio leporino*, harelip. || FIG. *Lamerse los labios*, to lick one's lips. | *Morderse los labios*, to bite one's lip. | *No despegar* or *no descoser los labios*, not to open one's mouth, not to say a word. | *No morderse los labios*, to speak one's mind, to be outspoken. | *Sellarle a uno los labios*, to seal s.o.'s lips, to silence s.o.

labiodental adj./s. f. GRAM. Labiodental.

labiovelar adj./s. f. Labiovelar.

labor f. Job, work, piece of work: *una labor productiva*, a profitable piece of work. || Labour [U.S., labor], work (tarea). || Thousand tiles *o* bricks (tejas o ladrillos). || Manufactured tobacco. || MIN. Excavation, workings, *pl.* || — *Caballo de labor*, workhorse. || *Cesta de labores*, sewing basket (de costura), knitting bag (de punto). || *Dar dos labores a un campo*, to plough a field twice. || *Labor de equipo*, teamwork. || *Labores de aguja*, needlework, sewing, embroidery. || *Labores de ganchillo*, crochet. || *Labores de la casa*, housework. || *Labores del campo*, farm work (en general), tilling, ploughing [U.S., plowing] (labranza). || *Labores de punto*, knitting. || *Sus labores*, unemployed (solteras), housewife (casadas). || *Tierra de labor*, arable land.

— OBSERV. The phrase *sus labores*, abbreviated *S.L*, represents the full expression *que hace sus labores en casa* and applies to all woman who do not work except in their own homes.

laborable adj. Working, work: *día laborable*, working day. || AGR. Arable, tillable, workable.

laboral adj. Labour [U.S., labor]: *conflictos laborales*, labour disputes. || — *Accidente laboral*, industrial accident. || *Enseñanza laboral*, technical education. || *Instituto laboral*, technical college.

laborar v. tr. To work, to till, to plough (la tierra).
— V. intr. To work: *labora por el bien de su país*, he is working for the good of his country.

laboratorio m. Laboratory. || *Ayudante de laboratorio*, laboratory *o* lab assistant *o* technician.

laborear v. tr. To work. || AGR. To work, to till, to plough. || MIN. To work [a mine].
— V. intr. MAR. To reeve.

laboreo m. AGR. Tilling, ploughing [U.S., plowing] (arado). | Cultivation, working (de la tierra). || Exploitation, working (de minas). || MAR. Reeving.

laboriosidad f. Laboriousness, industry.

laborioso, sa adj. Laborious, hard-working, industrious: *estudiante laborioso*, hard-working student. || Laborious, difficult: *parto laborioso*, *digestión laboriosa*, laborious delivery, difficult digestion. || Arduous, laborious (tarea).

laborismo m. Labour Party (partido político). || Labour movement (movimiento).

laborista adj. Labour [U.S., labor]: *partido laborista*, Labour Party.
— M. y f. Labour Party member, Labour member *o* supporter. || *Los laboristas*, Labour (partido).

labra f. Cutting, carving (de piedra, madera).

labrado, da adj. Worked (trabajado). || Worked, ploughed [U.S., plowed] (tierras). || Cut, carved (piedra). || Carved (madera). || Wrought (metales). || Worked (artesanía). || Embroidered (tejido).
— M. Cutting, carving (de piedra). || Carving (de madera). || Working (de metales). || Embroidery (de tejidos). || — Pl. Cultivated fields.

labrador, ra adj. Farming, farm: *población labradora*, farming population.
— M. y f. Peasant (campesino). || — M. Farmer (dueño). || Farm labourer, farm worker [U.S., farmhand] (obrero agrícola). || Ploughman [U.S., plowman] (que ara). || *Sindicato de labradores*, farm worker's union.

labradorita f. MIN. Labradorite.

labrantío, a adj. Arable, tillable.
— M. Arable *o* tillable land.

labranza f. Farming, cultivation (de la tierra). || Farmland (campo). || Work (trabajo). || *Aperos* or *instrumentos de labranza*, farming tools *o* implements.

labrar v. tr. To work (trabajar). || To carve (madera). || To cut, to carve (piedra). || To work (los metales). || To plough [U.S., to plow], to work, to till (arar). || To cultivate (cultivar). || To build (edificar). || To cut (piedras preciosas). || To embroider (bordar). || FIG. To work for, to forge: *labrar la felicidad de uno*, to work for s.o.'s happiness; *labraremos la grandeza del país*, we shall forge the greatness of our country. | To cause, to bring about (causar): *labrar su propia ruina*, to cause one's own ruin. || — *Labrar chocolate*, to manufacture *o* to produce chocolate. || *Labrar moneda*, to coin money.
— V. intr. To work: *labrar en madera, en mármol*, to work in wood, in marble.
— V. pr. To make, to build, to forge: *labrarse un porvenir*, to build one's future.

labriego, ga m. y f. Peasant (campesino). || Farm labourer *o* worker [U.S., farmhand] (obrero agrícola). || Farmer (dueño).

labro m. Labrum (en los insectos). || Wrasse (pez).

laca f. Lac (resina). || Lacquer (mueble). || Lacquer, shellac (barniz). || Lacquer, hair spray (para el pelo). || — *Barnizar con laca*, to varnish with shellac. || *Dar laca, pintar con laca*, to lacquer. || *Goma laca*, shellac. || *Laca para uñas*, nail varnish *o* polish. || *Poner laca en, echar laca a*, to lacquer *o* to spray [with hair spray] (el pelo).

lacayo m. Lackey, lacquey (criado), footman (de a pie), groom (de a caballo). || FIG. Lackey, flunkey, toady (persona servil).

laceador m. *Amer.* Lassoer.

lacear v. tr. To trim *o* to adorn with bows (adornar con cintas). || To lasso (coger con lazo). || To snare (la caza menor). || To drive [game] into range (disponer la caza).

Lacedemonia n. pr. f. GEOGR. Lacedaemon.

laceración f. Laceration.

lacerado, da adj. Unhappy, unfortunate, unlucky (infeliz). || Wounded (herido). || Lacerated (desgarrado). || Leprous (leproso).
— M. y f. Leper (leproso). || (Ant.). Miser.

lacerante adj. Wounding (palabras). || Sharp (dolor). || Heart-rending, harrowing (grito).

lacerar v. tr. To lacerate, to tear (desgarrar). || FIG. To damage, to harm, to injure (la reputación). | To rend, to lacerate (el corazón).
laceria f. Misery, poverty, want.
lacería f. Bows, *pl.*, ornamental bows, *pl.* (bordados). || ARQ. Interlacing arches.
lacero m. Lassoer (para toros, etc.). || Poacher [using snares] (cazador furtivo). || Dogcatcher (empleado municipal).
Lacio n. pr. m. GEOGR. Latium.
lacio, cia adj. Withered, faded (marchito). || Lank, straight: *con los cabellos lacios*, with lank hair. || FIG. Limp, languid (flojo).
lacolito m. GEOL. Laccolith, laccolite.
lacón m. Shoulder of pork.
Laconia n. pr. f. GEOGR. Laconia.
lacónico, ca adj. Laconic, terse (conciso).
laconismo m. Laconicism, terseness (concisión).
lacra f. Mark, scar [left by illness]. || FIG. Blemish, stain, blot (de la reputación). | Defect, flaw, fault (defecto). | Scourge, blight, bane: *la miseria es una lacra que traspasa las fronteras*, poverty is a scourge which knows no frontiers. || *Amer.* Sore, wound (llaga). | Scab (postilla).
lacrado m. Sealing [with wax] (de una carta).
lacrar v. tr. To seal [with wax] (cerrar con lacre). || To strike (afligir a uno una enfermedad). || To contaminate (contagiar).
lacre m. Sealing wax. || — *Barra de lacre*, stick of sealing wax. || *Cerrar con lacre*, to seal with wax.
— Adj. Red (rojo).
lácrima christi m. Lachryma *o* lacrima christi (vino).
lacrimal adj. Lachrymal, lacrimal, tear: *conductos lacrimales*, tear ducts.
lacrimatorio, ria adj./s. m. Lachrymatory, lacrimatory (vaso).
lacrimógeno, na adj. Tear-producing. || FIG. Sentimental, tearful (comedia). || *Gas lacrimógeno*, tear gas.
lacrimoso, sa adj. Tearful, weeping. || Watering (ojos). || *Una voz lacrimosa*, a tearful voice.
lactancia f. Lactation, nursing, suckling.
lactante adj. Nursing, suckling (niño, madre).
— M. Suckling, unweaned baby (niño).
lactar v. tr. To nurse, to breast-feed, to suckle (amamantar). || To bottle nurse, to bottle feed.
— V. intr. To feed on milk, to nurse, to suckle.
lactasa f. QUÍM. Lactase.
lactato m. QUÍM. Lactate.
lacteado, da adj. Mixed with milk. || *Harina lacteada*, malted milk.
lácteo, a adj. Milky, lacteous. || Milk: *dieta láctea*, milk diet. || — *Productos lácteos*, milk products, dairy products. || *Vasos lácteos*, lacteal vessels. || ASTR. *Vía Láctea*, Milky Way.
lactescente adj. Lactescent.
láctico, ca adj. QUÍM. Lactic (ácido).
lactífero, ra adj. ANAT. Lactiferous.
lactona f. QUÍM. Lactone.
lactosa f. QUÍM. Lactose, milk sugar.
lacunario m. ARQ. Lacunar (artesonado).
lacustre adj. Lake, lacustrine: *vivienda lacustre*, lake dwelling; *aldea lacustre*, lake village.
lacha f. Anchovy (boquerón). || — *Me da lacha*, I feel *o* I am ashamed. || *Tener poca lacha*, to be shameless.
ladear v. tr. To lean, to tilt, to slant, to incline, to tip (inclinar). || To tilt, to incline to one side (la cabeza). || To bend (doblar): *ladear un clavo*, to bend a nail. || FIG. To avoid (evitar). | To avoid, to evade, to get round (una dificultad). || — *El cuadro está ladeado*, the picture is lopsided. || *Ladear una montaña*, to go round *o* to skirt a mountain.
— V. intr. To lean, to tilt, to slant, to incline. || AVIAC. To bank. || FIG. To go off the straight and narrow (salir del camino recto).
— V. pr. To lean, to incline [to one side] (una persona, un árbol, un edificio). || To bend (doblarse). || AVIAC. To bank. || To swerve (echarse a un lado). || FIG. To be equal (*con*, to) [igualarse]. || *Amer.* To fall in love (enamorarse).
ladeo m. Leaning, inclination, tilt (acción de inclinar o inclinarse). || Bending (acción de doblarse). || AVIAC. Banking. || FIG. Inclination.
ladera f. Slope, side, hillside (de una colina), slope, side, mountainside (de una montaña).
ladi f. Lady.
ladilla f. Crab louse (insecto). || Variety of barley (especie de cebada). || FIG. y FAM. *Pegarse como una ladilla*, to cling *o* to stick like a leech.
ladillo m. Door panel (de coche). || IMPR. Marginal note.
ladino, na adj. Astute, shrewd, cunning, wily (astuto). || Multilingual, poliglot. || Rhaeto-Romanic (rético). || *Amer.* Spanish-speaking [Indian]. | Of Spanish-Indian descent, half-breed. || *Lengua ladina*, Spanish language [as opposed to Arabic].
— M. Ladin, Rhaeto-Romanic (retorromano). || Ladino, Judeo-Spanish, Sephardic.
lado m. Side: *el lado izquierdo*, the left side, the left-hand side. || Side: *pariente mío por el lado paterno*, a relation on my father's side. || Room (sitio): *déjame un lado*, make room for me. || MAT. Side: *un triángulo tiene tres lados*, a triangle has three sides. || Side (del cuerpo). || Edge, side (en el perímetro de una cosa). || MIL. Flank. || DEP. End: *cambiar de lado*, to change ends. || FIG. Hand: *por un lado*, on the one hand. | Way (camino): *me fui por otro lado*, I went off by another way. | Side, aspect: *un lado nuevo del asunto*, a new side to *o* a new aspect of the matter. | Patronage, protection (favor, protección). | Side (opinión, punto de vista): *yo estoy de su lado*, I am on his side. || — Pl. Aids, helpers, assistants (ayudantes), protectors, patrons (protectores), advisers (consejeros), set, *sing.* (íntimos).
— *Al lado*, close by, nearby, near. || *Al lado de*, at *o* by the side of, beside, next to (posición), next door to: *vivo al lado de tu casa*, I live next door to your house *o* to you; compared to *o* with, next to (comparación). || *Al otro lado de*, on the other side of, over. || *A mi lado* or *al lado mío*, at *o* by my side, beside me, next to me. || *Cada uno por su lado*, in different directions. || FIG. *Cada uno tira* or *va por su lado*, each goes his own way. | *Dar de lado*, to cold-shoulder, to desert (a alguien), to discard (algo). || *De al lado*, next door: *la casa de al lado*, the house next door. || *Dejar de lado* or *dejar a un lado*, to leave *o* to put *o* to set aside, to leave *o* to put *o* to set to one side (colocar), to omit, to pass over (descartar). || *De lado*, aslant, to one side: *llevar el sombrero de lado*, to wear one's hat aslant; sideways, sidewards, to one side: *volverse de lado*, to turn sideways; crosswise, from the side: *el viento sopla de lado*, the wind is blowing crosswise. || *Del lado de*, on the side of (en una lucha), near (cerca de). || *De un lado para otro*, up and down: *andar de un lado para otro en una habitación*, to walk up and down a room; to and fro (por todas partes): *vagar de un lado para otro*, to wander to and fro. || *De uno y otro lado*, on *o* from both sides. || *Echar a un lado*, to cast aside. || FIG. *El lado bueno*, the right side. || *Hacer lado*, to leave *o* to make room. || *Hacerse* or *echarse a un lado*, to step *o* to stand aside, to make way, to move over (una persona), to draw *o* to pull to one side (un vehículo). || *Ir lado a lado*, to go side by side (ir juntos), to go hand in hand, to go together (estar unidos). || *Irse* or *tirar* or *echar por otro lado*, to go off another way (ir por otro camino), to try another way, to try sth. else (utilizar otro medio). || *Lado débil* or *flaco*, weak point, weak spot. || FIG. *Mirar de lado* or *de medio lado*, to look down on (con desprecio), to look at out of the corner of one's eye, to look askance at (con disimulo). || FIG. *Poner a un lado*, to put aside *o* on one side. || *Ponerse del lado de*, to side with, to take sides with. || *Por el lado de*, in the direction of. || *Por todos lados*, on all sides. || *Por un lado..., por otro (lado)...*, on the one hand..., on the other [hand]... || *Una figura de tres lados*, a three-sided figure. || *Ver el lado bueno de las cosas*, to look on the bright side.
ladrador, ra adj. Barking.
ladrar v. intr. To bark (el perro). || To yap (perro pequeño). || FIG. y FAM. To growl, to bark. || — FIG. y FAM. *Hoy está que ladra*, he's in a nasty mood today. | *Ladrar a la Luna*, to bay [at] the moon. | *Me ladra el estómago*, my stomach is rumbling.
— V. tr. FIG. To bark [out] (órdenes, etc.).
ladrería f. Lazaretto (para leprosos).
ladrido m. Bark. || Yap (agudo). || FIG. y FAM. Growl (respuesta áspera, etc.).
ladrillado m. Brick floor. || Tiled floor (de azulejos).
ladrillal o **ladrillar** m. Brickworks, brickyard.
ladrillar v. tr. To brick, to pave with bricks. || To tile (con azulejos).
ladrillazo m. Blow with a brick. || FIG. *Caer como un ladrillazo*, to be heavy on the stomach (un alimento).
ladrillera f. Brick mould (molde). || Brickworks (fábrica).
ladrillero, ra adj. Brickmaking: *industria ladrillera*, brickmaking industry.
— M. y f. Brickmaker (que hace ladrillos). || Brick dealer (que vende ladrillos).
ladrillo m. Brick: *ladrillo hueco, macizo*, hollow, solid brick. || Tile (azulejo). || FIG. Block (de chocolate). | Check (en las telas). || — FAM. *Caer como un ladrillo*, to be heavy on the stomach (la comida). || *Color ladrillo*, brick red, brick. || FIG. y FAM. *Es un ladrillo*, he *o* it is deadly dull *o* deadly boring. || *Fábrica de ladrillos*, brickworks. || *Horno de ladrillos*, brick kiln. || *Ladrillo azulejo*, tile. || *Ladrillo refractario* or *de fuego*, firebrick. || *Ladrillo visto*, mock brick.
ladrón, ona adj. Thieving, light-fingered.
— M. y f. Thief, robber. || — M. Sluice gate (portillo para el agua). || ELECTR. Multiple socket. || Thief (de vela). || — *¡Al ladrón!* or *¡ladrones!*, stop thief! || *Cueva de ladrones*, den of thieves. || *El buen, el mal ladrón*, the penitent, the impenitent thief (del Evangelio). || FIG. *Ladrón de corazones*, ladykiller. | *La ocasión hace al ladrón*, opportunity makes the thief. | *Piensa el ladrón que todos son de su condición*, we all judge others by our own standards.
ladronear v. intr. To thieve, to steal.
ladronera f. Den of thieves (guarida).
ladronería f. Thieving, robbery, theft.
ladronesco, ca adj. Thievish.
— F. FAM. Gang of thieves.
ladronzuelo, la m. y f. Small-time *o* petty thief.
lady f. Lady.
lagaña f. Sleep, rheum (en los ojos).

lagar m. Press house (local). || Wine *o* apple *o* olive press (prensa).
lagarejo m. Small press house. || Small wine *o* apple *o* olive press. || *Hacerse lagarejo*, to be bruised *o* squashed (la uva).
lagarta f. ZOOL. Female lizard. | Gipsy moth (mariposa). || FIG. y FAM. Sly minx (mujer astuta y mal intencionada). || POP. Tart (prostituta).
lagartear v. tr. *Amer.* To pinion, to hold by the arms.
lagarterano, na adj. [Of *o* from] Lagartera [in the province of Toledo]. || *Manteles lagarteranos*, Lagartera-embroidered tablecloths.
— M. y f. Native *o* inhabitant of Lagartera.
lagartija f. [Small] lizard. || FIG. *Moverse más que el rabo de una lagartija*, to have ants in one's pants, to be fidgety.
lagartijero, ra adj. Lizard-hunting (animal). || TAUR. *Media lagartijera*, short but effective sword thrust.
lagarto m. ZOOL. Lizard (reptil). || ANAT. Biceps (músculo). || FIG. y FAM. Sly devil, crafty fellow (hombre astuto). || Red sword of the order of Santiago (insignia). || *Amer.* Alligator. || *Lagarto de Indias*, alligator.
— Interj. Touch wood! [superstitious exclamation].
lagartón, ona adj. FIG. y FAM. Sly, wily, crafty.
— M. Sly devil. || — F. Sly minx.
lago m. Lake: *lago de agua salada*, saltwater lake. || FIG. Sea: *lago de sangre*, sea of blood.
lágrima f. Tear: *bañado en lágrimas*, bathed in tears; *le corrían las lágrimas*, tears streamed down his face. || Drop of sap [exuding from vine or tree]. || Drop (caramelo redondeado). || FAM. Drop (pequeña cantidad). || — *Beberse las lágrimas*, to hold back one's tears. || *Con lágrimas en los ojos*, with tears in his eyes. || *Derramar lágrimas*, to shed tears. || *Enjugarse las lágrimas*, to dry one's eyes *o* one's tears. || *Estar hecho un mar de lágrimas*, V. MAR. || *Hacer saltar las lágrimas*, to bring tears to one's eyes, to make one cry. || *Lágrimas de cocodrilo*, crocodile tears. || *Lo que no va en lágrimas va en suspiros*, she does nothing but weep and sigh. || *Llorar a lágrima viva*, to sob one's heart out, to cry one's eyes out. || FIG. *Llorar lágrimas de sangre*, to weep tears of blood. || *Se me saltaron las lágrimas a los ojos*, tears came to my eyes. || FIG. *Ser el paño de lágrimas de alguien*, to give s.o. a shoulder to cry on, to be s.o.'s consoler.
lagrimal adj. Lachrymal.
— M. ANAT. Corner of the eye.
lagrimar v. intr. To weep, to cry.
lagrimear v. intr. To water (los ojos). || To weep, to shed tears (una persona).
lagrimeo m. Watering (de los ojos). | Weeping, tears, *pl.* (de persona).
lagrimón, ona adj. Tearful.
— M. Big tear.
lagrimoso, sa adj. Watery (ojos). || Tearful, lachrymose (persona).
laguna f. Small lake (lago pequeño), tarn (en el monte). || Lagoon (de un atolón). || FIG. Gap, lacuna: *las lagunas de mi educación*, the gaps in my education. | Gap, hiatus, lacuna (en un texto).
lagunar m. ARQ. Coffer, lacunar (de techo).
lagunoso, sa adj. Full of lagoons.
laicado m. Laity.
laical adj. Lay, laical.
laicalización f. *Amer.* Laicization.
laicalizar v. tr. *Amer.* To laicize.
laicidad f. Secularity, laicism.
laicismo m. Laicism.
laicización f. Laicization.
laicizar v. tr. To laicize.
laico, ca adj. Lay, secular, laical: *escuela laica*, secular school.
laísmo m. Use of *la* and *las* as indirect objects instead of *le* and *les*: *la dijeron*, they told her [instead of *le dijeron*]; *las sucedió*, it happened to them [instead of *les sucedió*].
laísta adj. Who uses *la* and *las* as indirect objects.
— M. y f. Person who uses *la* and *las* as indirect objects.
laja f. Flat stone, stone slab. || MAR. Shoal.
lakismo m. Lake School (escuela poética inglesa).
lakista m. y f. Lake poet.
lama f. Slime, mud, silt (cieno). || — M. REL. Lama.
lamaísmo m. REL. Lamaism.
lamaísta adj./s. REL. Lamaist.
lamasería f. REL. Lamasery.
lambda f. Lambda (letra griega).
lambdacismo m. Lambdacism.
lambel m. HERÁLD. Label.
lamé m. Lamé (tejido).
lameculos m. y f. inv. POP. Bootlicker (cobista).
lamedor adj. Licking (que lame).
— M. Syrup (jarabe). || FIG. Flattery, cajolery(halago).
lamedura f. Licking, lick.
lamelibranquio m. ZOOL. Lamellibranch. || — Pl. ZOOL. Lamellibranchia (clase de moluscos).
lamelicornio adj./s.m. ZOOL. Lamellicorn. || — Pl. ZOOL. Lamellicornia.
lamelirrostros m. pl. Lamellirostres (aves).
lamentable adj. Lamentable, deplorable, pitiful: *en un estado lamentable*, in a deplorable state. || Regrettable.
lamentación f. Lamentation, lament, lamenting.
lamentador, ra adj. Lamenting. || Grumbling, whining (quejumbroso).
lamentar v. tr. To be sorry, to regret: *lamento que no hayas podido venir*, I am sorry you could not come. || To be sorry about: *lamento este accidente*, I am sorry about this accident. || To lament, to mourn: *tuvimos que lamentar muchas pérdidas*, we had to mourn many losses. || To lament, to grieve (sentir un dolor profundo). || *Es de lamentar que*, it is to be regretted that, it is regrettable that.
— V. pr. To complain (*de*, about): *siempre te estás lamentando*, you are always complaining. || To lament, to bewail: *lamentarse de las desgracias de su familia*, to lament the misfortunes of one's family.
lamento m. Lament, lamentation (por un dolor moral). || Wail, moan (por un dolor físico).
lamentoso, sa adj. Plaintive, mournful (quejumbroso). || Lamentable, deplorable, pitiful (lamentable).
lamer v. tr. To lick. || To lap: *el agua lame la orilla*, the water is lapping the bank.
lametada f. o. **lamentazo** o **lametón** m. Lick. || Lap (de ola, etc.).
lameteo m. FAM. Licking (acción de lamer).
lamido, da adj. Licked. || FIG. Thin, scrawny (flaco). | Dandified, done up (relamido). | Spick and span, spruce (aseado). | Finical, finicky (estilo, pintura). | (P.us.). Worn-out (desgastado).
— M. Licking.
lámina f. Sheet, plate, lamina (de metal). || Sheet (de madera, de vidrio, de mármol). || FOT. e IMPR. Plate. || ANAT. y BOT. Lamina. || FIG. Appearance (de caballo, etc.).
laminable adj. Rollable.
laminación f. Rolling (del acero, etc.). || Splitting, lamination (división en hojas). || Lamination (revestimiento con láminas). || TECN. *Tren de laminación*, rolling mill.
laminado, da adj. Laminated, laminate. || Rolled (metal): *laminado en caliente*, hot-rolled. || *Acero laminado*, sheet steel, rolled steel.
— M. Rolling (de metal): *laminado en frío*, cold rolling. || Laminate (producto para revestir).
laminador m. Rolling mill (laminadora). || Roller, rolling mill operator (obrero).
— Adj. Rolling: *cilindros laminadores*, rolling mills.
laminadora f. Rolling mill (máquina).
laminar adj. Laminar: *estructura laminar*, laminar structure; *corriente laminar*, laminar flow.
laminar v. tr. To roll [into sheets], to roll out (metal, etc.). || To split [into sheets], to laminate (dividiendo). || To laminate, to surface (cubrir con láminas): *laminar una mesa con plástico*, to laminate a table with plastic.
laminilla f. Thin sheet. || BOT. y ANAT. Lamella.
laminoso, sa adj. Laminose, laminous, lamellar.
lampacear v. tr. MAR. To swab, to mop.
lampalagua f. ZOOL. Anaconda.
lampante adj. Lamp: *aceite lampante*, lamp oil.
lampar v. intr. To long, to crave, to yearn: *lampar por algo, por hacer algo*, to long for sth., to do sth.
— V. pr. To long, to crave, to yearn.
lámpara f. Lamp, light: *lámpara eléctrica, de gas*, electric, gas lamp. || Bulb, lamp (bombilla). || RAD. Valve. || FAM. Oil *o* grease stain (mancha). || — *Lámpara colgante*, hanging lamp. || *Lámpara de aceite*, oil lamp. || *Lámpara de alcohol*, spirit lamp. || *Lámpara de arco*, arc lamp. || *Lámpara de incandescencia* or *incandescente*, incandescent lamp. || *Lámpara de minero or de seguridad*, miner's *o* safety lamp. || *Lámpara de pie*, standard lamp. || *Lámpara de rayos infrarrojos, de rayos ultravioleta*, infrared, ultraviolet lamp. || AUT. *Lámpara de techo*, interior light. || *Lámpara de vapor de mercurio*, mercury vapour lamp. || *Lámpara indicadora*, pilot *o* warning light. || *Lámpara para la mesilla de noche*, reading lamp. || FOT. *Lámpara relámpago*, flash. || *Lámpara solar*, sunray lamp.
lamparería f. Lamp works (taller). || Lamp shop (tienda).
lamparero m. Lamp maker (que hace lámparas). || Lamp dealer (que las vende).
lamparilla f. Small lamp. || Nightlight (mariposa).
lamparista m. V. LAMPARERO.
lamparón m. Large lamp. || FAM. Large grease stain (mancha en la ropa). || MED. Scrofula (escrófula).
lampazo m. BOT. Burdock. || MAR. Swab. || *Amer.* FAM. Lash (latigazo).
lampiño, ña adj. Beardless (sin barba). || Hairless (con poco pelo o vello). || BOT. Glabrous (sin vello). | Awnless (trigo).
lampista m. Lampmaker (que hace lámparas). || Lamp dealer (que las vende).
lampistería f. V. LAMPARERÍA.
lampo m. POÉT. Refulgence, fulguration, effulgence.
lamprea f. Lamprey (pez).
lamprear v. tr. To cook [meat] with wine, spices, and honey or sugar.
lampreazo m. FAM. Lash (latigazo).
lamprehuela o **lampreílla** f. River lamprey (pez).
lana f. Wool. || Fleece, wool (del carnero vivo). || — Pl. FAM. Hair, *sing.*, mop, *sing.*: *voy a que me esquilen las lanas*, I'm going to get my mop cut. || — *Batir la lana*, to shear the sheep. || FIG. y FAM.

Cardarle a uno la lana, to give s.o. a good telling off. || *De lana*, wool, woolen: *tejido de lana*, woolen fabric. || FIG. *Ir por lana y volver trasquilado*, to go for wool and come home shorn. || *Lana de esquileo*, shorn wool. || *Lana de vidrio*, glass wool.
lanada f. Sponge, cleaning rod (para los cañones).
lanado, da adj. BOT. Lanate.
lanar adj. Wool-bearing. || *Ganado lanar*, sheep.
Lancaster n. pr. Lancashire (condado). || Lancaster (ciudad y dinastía).
lance m. Throw, cast (lanzamiento). || Cast, casting (de la red de pesca). || Catch (pesca que se saca). || Episode, incident, event (suceso). || Critical moment *o* juncture (trance crítico). || Move, stroke (jugada). || TAUR. Pass with the cape. || — *De lance*, secondhand: *libros de lance*, secondhand books. || *Lance apretado*, tight spot, jam (fam.). || *Lance de amor*, amorous adventure. || *Lance de fortuna*, stroke of fortune. || *Lance de honor*, question of honour; challenge (desafío).
lancear v. tr. To spear, to lance. || TAUR. To play [the bull] using simple passes with the cape.
Lancelote n. pr. m. Lancelot, Launcelot.
lanceolado, da adj. BOT. Lanceolate, lanceolar. || ARQ. Lancet (arco).
lancero m. Lancer. || — Pl. Lancers (baile).
lanceta f. MED. Lancet. || *Amer*. Sting (aguijón).
lancetada f. o **lancetazo** m. MED. Lancing.
lancetero m. Lancet case.
lanciforme adj. Lanciform, lance-shaped.
lancinante adj. Stabbing, piercing (dolor).
lancinar v. intr. To pierce, to stab (un dolor).
lancha MAR. Boat (barco). | Motor launch, motorboat (con motor). | Pinnace (barca dependiente de un buque o de servicio portuario). || Lighter, barge (barcaza). || Flat stone, stone slab (piedra). || Partridge trap (para coger perdices). || — MAR. *Lancha bombardera* or *cañonera* or *obusera*, gunboat. | *Lancha de desembarco*, landing craft. | *Lancha de socorro* or *de auxilio*, lifeboat. | *Lancha motora* or *rápida*, motorboat, speedboat. | *Lancha neumática*, rubber dinghy. | *Lancha salvavidas*, lifeboat (que lleva un barco). | *Lancha torpedera*, torpedo boat.
lanchada f. Boatful, boatload.
lanchaje m. MAR. Lighterage (transporte, coste).
lanchar m. Quarry (cantera).
lanchero m. Boatman. || Lighterman, bargee (de la barcaza).
lanchón m. Lighter, barge.
landa f. Moor, moorland, heathland.
landgrave m. HIST. Landgrave.
landgraviato m. HIST. Landgraviate.
landó m. Landau (coche).
landrecilla f. Small fleshy lump.
lanería f. Wool shop.
lanero, ra adj. Wool: *industria lanera*, wool industry. — M. y f. Wool dealer, wool seller (persona). || — M. Wool warehouse (almacén).
langor m. (Ant.). V. LANGUIDEZ.
langosta f. ZOOL. Locust (insecto). | [Spiny] lobster (crustáceo). || FIG. Scourge (plaga).
langostero m. Lobster boat. || Lobster fisherman.
langostino m. Prawn (crustáceo).
langostón m. Grasshopper (insecto).
langucia f. *Amer*. Hunger.
languidecer* v. intr. To languish.
languidez f. Languor, languidness. || Lassitude, listlessness (falta de energía).
lánguido, da adj. Languid, languorous: *una mirada lánguida*, a languid look. || Listless (sin energía).
lanífero, ra adj. POÉT. Laniferous, woolly, lanigerous.
lanificación f. o **lanificio** m. Woolwork, woollen manufacture. || Woollen goods, *pl.* [U.S., woolen goods, *pl.*] (cosas hechas de lana).
lanilla f. Nap (pelillo en tejidos de lana). || Flannel (tela fina de lana). || MAR. Bunting.
lanolina f. Lanolin, lanoline.
lanosidad f. Down (pelusa).
lanoso, sa adj. V. LANUDO.
lansquenete m. HIST. Lansquenet (soldado).
lantano m. QUÍM. Lanthanum (metal).
lanudo, da adj. Woolly, fleecy (que tiene mucha lana). || Downy, furry (que tiene vello). || *Amer*. FAM. Coarse, uncouth (tosco).
lanuginoso, sa adj. Lanuginous, downy.
lanza f. Lance, spear (arma). || Shaft, thill (de carruaje). || Nozzle (de una manga de riego). || Lancer (soldado). || — *Correr lanzas*, to joust. || *Estar con la lanza en ristre*, to have one's lance at the ready (afianzada en el ristre), to be ready for action (preparado). || FIG. *Medir lanzas con alguien*, to cross swords with s.o. | *No romper lanzas con nadie*, not to argue with anybody. | *Romper una lanza en defensa de*, to fight for, to defend.
lanzable adj. *Asiento lanzable*, ejector seat.
lanzabombas adj. inv. MIL. *Dispositivo lanzabombas*, bomb release gear (de avión).
— M. MIL. Bomb release gear (de avión etc.). | Mortar (de trinchera).
lanzacabos adj. inv. MAR. *Cañón lanzacabos*, life-saving gun. | *Cohete lanzacabos*, life-saving rocket.
lanzacohetes m. inv. MIL. Rocket launcher.
lanzada f. Lance thrust, spear thrust (golpe). || Lance wound, spear wound (herida).
lanzadera f. Shuttle (del telar). || Marquise (anillo).
lanzado, da adj. Determined (decidido). || *Ir lanzado*, to speed *o* to tear along: *la moto iba lanzada*, the motorbike was tearing along.
— M. *Pesca al lanzado*, spinning, casting.
lanzador, ra adj. Throwing.
— M. y f. Thrower. || DEP. Bowler (en el cricket). | Pitcher (béisbol). | Thrower (de jabalina, disco). || Promoter (promotor).
lanzafuego m. (Ant.). MIL. Linstock (botafuego).
lanzagranadas m. inv. MIL. Grenade launcher.
lanzallamas m. inv. Flamethrower.
lanzamiento m. Throw, fling, hurl: *con su primer lanzamiento batió el récord*, with his first throw he beat the record. || Throwing, flinging, hurling: *el lanzamiento de almohadillas está prohibido*, the throwing of cushions is forbidden. || DEP. Put (del peso). | Ball (en el cricket). | Pitch (béisbol). | Throw (del disco, de la jabalina). || Firing: *lanzamiento de un proyectil, de un torpedo*, firing of a missile, of a torpedo. || Launching: *lanzamiento de un barco*, launching of a ship; *lanzamiento de una sonda lunar*, launching of a moon probe. || Dropping (de una bomba). || Drop (de paracaidistas). || Jump (salto de un paracaidista). || Release (de un ave). || COM. Launching (de una campaña, etc.). || FIG. Launching (de un ataque, etc.).
lanzaminas m. inv. MIL. Minelayer.
lanzaplatos m. inv. DEP. Trap (del tiro al plato).
lanzar v. tr. To throw: *lanzar una pelota*, to throw a ball. || To fling, to hurl (con violencia). || To fire (una flecha, un proyectil, un torpedo, etc.): *lanzar un cohete de un avión*, to fire a rocket from an aircraft. || To launch (un satélite, etc.): *lanzar un cohete de la plataforma de lanzamiento*, to launch a rocket from the launching pad. || To drop, to release (una bomba). || To drop (paracaidistas). || To release (un ave). || DEP. To throw (el disco, la jabalina). | To put (el peso). | To bowl (en cricket). | To pitch (béisbol). || MAR. To launch (botar). || JUR. To dispossess (*de*, of). || FIG. To launch: *lanzar un libro, un producto, una nueva línea, un ataque*, to launch a book, a product, a new line, an attack. | To utter (un grito, un gemido). | To hurl (un insulto, una maldición). | To heave (un suspiro). | To cast, to give (una mirada). | To make (una acusación). | To throw down, to throw out (un desafío). | To bring up (vomitar).
— V. pr. To rush, to hurl o.s., to fling o.s., to throw o.s.: *lanzarse contra alguien*, to rush at s.o., to hurl o.s. at s.o.; *lanzarse contra la pared*, to hurl o.s. against the wall. || To rush, to hurtle: *lanzarse al ataque*, to rush into the attack. || To jump: *se lanzó al vacío desde el décimo piso*, he jumped into the void from the tenth floor; *lanzarse al agua*, to jump into the water. || To dive (tirarse de cabeza). || AVIAC. To jump (paracaidista), to bale out (en caso de emergencia). || FIG. To launch o.s.: *lanzarse a los negocios*, to launch o.s. in *o* into business. | To embark upon (emprender). || *Lanzarse en persecución de una persona*, to dash off in pursuit of s.o.
Lanzarote n. pr. m. Lancelot, Launcelot.
lanzatorpedos adj./s.m. inv. (*Tubo*) *lanzatorpedos*, torpedo tube.
lanzazo m. V. LANZADA.
laña f. Clamp (grapa). || Green coconut (coco verde).
lañador m. Clamper.
lañar v. tr. To clamp (sujetar con lañas). || To clean [for salting] (el pescado).
Laodicea n. pr. f. GEOGR. Laodicea.
Laos n. pr. m. GEOGR. Laos.
laosiano, na adj./s. Laotian.
lapa f. ZOOL. Limpet (molusco). || Vegetal film [on the surface of liquids]. || BOT. Burdock. || FAM. Hanger-on (persona pegajosa). || FIG. y FAM. *Pegarse como una lapa*, to stick like glue *o* like a leech.
lapicera f. *Amer*. Penholder (palillero). | V. LAPICERO.
lapicero m. Propelling pencil (instrumento en que se pone la mina). || Pen (pluma), pencil (lápiz de mina), crayon (de color). || *Amer*. Penholder (palillero).
lápida f. Memorial tablet *o* stone. || — *Lápida conmemorativa*, memorial *o* commemorative stone *o* tablet. || *Lápida sepulcral* or *mortuoria*, gravestone, tombstone.
lapidación f. Stoning [to death], lapidation.
lapidar v. tr. To stone [to death], to lapidate. || *Amer*. To cut (piedras preciosas).
lapidario, ria adj. Lapidary: *estilo lapidario*, lapidary style.
— M. Lapidary (de piedras preciosas). || Monumental mason (de lápidas).
lapidificación f. Petrification, lapidification.
lapidificar v. tr. To petrify, to lapidify.
— V. pr. To lapidify.
lapilli m. pl. GEOL. Lapilli.
lapislázuli m. MIN. Lapis lazuli.
lápiz m. Lead, graphite (grafito). || Pencil: *escribir a lápiz* or *con lápiz*, to write in pencil; *lápiz estilográfico* or *de mina*, propelling pencil. || — *Dibujo a lápiz*, pencil drawing. || *Lápiz de color*, coloured pencil, crayon. || *Lápiz de labios*, lipstick. || *Lápiz de los ojos*, eyebrow pencil. || *Lápiz plomo* or *de plomo*, graphite pencil, lead pencil.
lapizar m. Graphite mine.

lapo m. Lash (latigazo). || Blow (golpe). || Swig, swallow (trago). || FAM. Spit (escupitajo). || *Amer.* Slap (bofetada). | Mug [U.S., sucker] (inocentón).
lapón, ona adj. Lapp.
— M. y f. Lapp, Laplander (persona). || — M. Lapp (lengua).
Laponia n. pr. f. GEOGR. Lapland.
lapso m. Lapse, space (de tiempo). || Slip, lapse (lapsus).
lapso, sa adj. REL. Lapsed.
lapsus m. Slip, lapse. || *Lapsus cálami, linguae,* slip of the pen, of the tongue.
laque m. *Amer.* Bola (tipo de lazo).
laquear v. tr. To lacquer. || *Amer.* To lasso with the bola.
lar m. Lar (divinidad de la casa): *los dioses lares,* the lares. || Hearth (fogón). || FIG. Home (hogar): *el lar paterno,* the family home. || — Pl. FIG. Home, *sing.* (hogar).
— OBSERV. The plural form of this word in both languages is *lares.*
lardar o **lardear** v. tr. To baste, to lard (la carne).
lardero adj. m. *Jueves lardero,* the Thursday before Lent.
lardo m. Bacon fat, pork fat (tocino). || Animal fat (grasa).
larense adj. [Of *o* from] Lara (en Venezuela).
— M. y f. Native *o* inhabitant of Lara.
larga f. Lengthening piece joined to the last (en la elaboración de zapatos). || Longest billiard cue (billar). || Flourish with the cape [to draw the bull away from the picador]. || — Pl. Delay, *sing.* (dilación). || — *A la larga,* in the end, in the long run (al final). || *Dar largas a un asunto,* to put off a matter, to delay a matter.
largamente adv. At length, for a long time: *hablar largamente de una cuestión,* to talk about a matter at length. || Generously (con generosidad).
largar v. tr. To let go, to release (soltar). || To slacken, to loosen, to ease off (ir soltando poco a poco). || To unfurl (una bandera). || FAM. To land, to deal, to give (una bofetada, un golpe). | To give: *le largué una buena propina,* I gave him a good tip | To utter (una exclamación, una palabrota, un suspiro, una imprecación, etc.). | To throw out, to see off (echar): *largó a la criada,* he threw the maid out; *le largaron del hotel,* he was thrown out of the hotel, he was seen off from the hotel. | To drive out (expulsar): *largar los demonios,* to drive out the evil spirits. | To get rid of, to unload (deshacerse de): *largó el perro al vecino,* he got rid of the dog *o* he unloaded the dog on his neighbour. | To give, to make [s.o.] sit through: *les largó un discurso interminable,* he made them sit through an endless speech. | To throw (arrojar). || MAR. To let out (las amarras). | To unfurl, to spread (velas). | To launch (una barca). | To discharge (lastre).
— V. pr. FAM. To push off, to beat it, to hop it, to clear off (marcharse). || MAR. To put to sea (zarpar), to bear off (apartarse de otra embarcación). || *Amer.* To begin (*a,* to) [comenzar]. || FAM. *¡Lárgate con viento fresco!,* clear off!
larghetto adv./s.m. MÚS. Larghetto.
largo, ga adj. Long, lengthy: *una carretera larga,* a long road; *un viaje, un libro largo,* a long journey book. || Long: *largo tiempo,* a long time. || Prolonged, long, lengthy: *retraso largo,* prolonged delay; *visita larga,* prolonged visit. || Tall (persona alta). || Too long: *esta falda te está larga,* this skirt is too long for you. || GRAM. Long (vocal, sílaba). || Good: *una hora larga,* a good hour; *catorce millones largos de turistas,* a good fourteen million tourists. || Good, long: *dos largas millas,* two long miles. || FIG. Quick-witted, sharp (astuto). | Generous, liberal (generoso). || MAR. Slack, loose. || RAD. Long (onda). || — *A la larga,* in the long run, in the end. || *A largo plazo,* long-term: *previsiones a largo plazo,* long-term forecasts. || *A lo largo,* lengthwise, lengthways (longitudinalmente): *partir un tablón a lo largo,* to split a plank lengthwise; in the distance (a lo lejos). || *A lo largo de,* along: *anduvimos a lo largo del andén,* we walked along the platform; all... long, throughout, all through: *a lo largo del día, del año,* all day long, all year long; throughout (por dentro). || *A lo largo y a lo ancho,* up and down, to and fro. || *A lo largo y a lo ancho de,* all over: *hay ríos trucheros a lo largo y a lo ancho de toda la región,* there are trout rivers all over the area. || *A lo más largo,* at the most, at the outside. || *Caer cuan largo es uno,* to fall full length. || *De largo a largo,* from one end to the other. || *Es largo de contar,* it's a long story. || *Hacerse largo,* to drag. || *Ir para largo,* to drag on. || *Largos años,* many years, many a long year. || FIG. *Más largo que un día sin pan,* very long. || *Pasar de largo,* to go straight past, to pass by (sin pararse), to pass over (un detalle). || *Poner cara larga,* V. CARA. || *Ponerse* or *vestirse de largo,* to wear a long dress (para salir de noche), to come out, to make one's début in society (sentido figurado). || FIG. *Poner* or *vestir de largo a su hija,* to launch one's daughter into society, to give one's daughter her début. | *Puesta de largo,* coming out, début (de una chica en la sociedad). | *Tener una cara larga* or *así de larga,* to have a long face. | *Tirar largo* or *de largo,* V. TIRAR.
— M. Length (longitud): *el largo de un vestido,* the length of a dress. || Length: *hace falta tres largos de tela,* three lengths of cloth are needed. || DEP. Length: *diez largos de la piscina,* ten lengths of the pool; *ganar por un largo,* to win by a length. || MÚS. Largo. || *Tiene un metro de largo,* it is one metre long.
— Adv. Far (lejos): *muy largo de aquí,* very far from here. || At length: *hablar largo de un asunto,* to talk about a matter at length. || Abundantly (abundantemente). || — *Hablar largo y tendido de algo,* to talk sth. over. || *¡Largo!, ¡largo de aquí!, ¡largo de ahí!,* get away!, get out!, get out of my sight!
largucho, cha adj. FAM. V. LARGUIRUCHO.
larguero m. TECN. Longitudinal beam *o* girder. || Jamb (de puerta). || Side (de cama). || Bolster (travesaño). || DEP. Crossbar (barra horizontal), goal post (barra vertical). || Extension leaf (de una mesa). || AVIAC. Spar (del ala), longeron (del fuselaje). || AUT. Side member. || *Mesa con largueros,* extending table, draw-leaf table.
largueza f. Generosity. || Length (longitud).
larguirucho, cha adj. FAM. Gangling, lanky (alto).
largura f. Length (longitud).
laringe f. ANAT. Larynx.
laringectomía f. MED. Laryngectomy.
laríngeo, a adj. Laryngeal.
laringitis f. MED. Laryngitis.
laringología f. MED. Laryngology.
laringólogo m. MED. Laryngologist.
laringoscopia f. MED. Laryngoscopy.
laringoscopio m. MED. Laryngoscope.
laringotomía f. MED. Laryngotomy.
larva f. MIT. y ZOOL. Larva. || — Pl. Larvae.
larvado, da adj. MED. Larval, larvate.
larval adj. Larval.
larvícola adj. Larvicolous.
las art. def. f. pl. The: *ir a las Islas Británicas,* to go to the British Isles. || Not translated: *le gustan mucho las patatas,* he is very fond of potatoes; *todas las mujeres tienen cierta intuición,* all women have a certain amount of intuition. || — *Las García,* the García girls, the García women, the Garcías. || *Son las diez,* it is ten o'clock.
— Pron. pers. f. pl. Them: *las vi,* I saw them. || Those, the ones: *las de Madrid son las mejores,* the ones *o* those from Madrid are best; *las que he comprado,* the ones [which] I have bought, those [which] I have bought. || Not translated, or translated by "some" (con *haber* impersonal): *¿hay cartas? — Las hay,* are there any letters? — There are [some]. || — *Las de usted,* yours. || *Las de Víctor son viejas,* Victor's are old. || *¿Las hay?,* are there any? || *Las hay que,* there are those who, there are some who (personas), there are those that (cosas): *las hay que siempre están hablando,* there are those who are always talking. || *Las que,* those who, the ones who (personas, sujeto), those whom, the ones that (personas, complemento), those [which], the ones [which], the ones [that] (cosas). || *Son ellas las que lo dijeron,* it is they who said it, they are the ones who said it. || *Son mis hermanas las que vienen,* it is my sisters that are coming, my sisters are the ones who are coming. || *Una canción de las de los años 1930,* a song typical of the 1930's.
— OBSERV. The dative form of *las* is *les: les dije,* I said to them. « Laísmo » (*las dije*) should be avoided.
— *Las* is often translated by the possessive adjective: *tienes las manos sucias,* your hands are dirty.
lasca f. Chip [of stone]. || Slice (loncha).
lascar v. tr. MAR. To slacken (aflojar). || *Amer.* To chip (desconchar). | To scrape, to scratch (lastimar).
lascivia f. Lasciviousness, lechery, lewdness.
lascivo, va adj. Lascivious, lecherous, lewd. || Playful, frisky (juguetón, alegre).
laser m. TECN. Laser: *rayo laser* laser beam.
lasitud f. (P.us.). Lassitude (cansancio).
laso, sa adj. Tired, weary (cansado). || Weak (débil). || Languid (lánguido). || TECN. Floss (seda).
lástex m. Lastex (nombre registrado).
lástima f. Pity, compassion, sympathy (compasión): *siento lástima por él,* I feel pity for him. || Complaint, lamentation, tale of woe: *déjame de lástimas,* I've had enough of your tales of woe. || Pity, shame: *¡qué lástima que no puedas venir!,* what a shame you cannot come!; *es una lástima que se haya roto el disco,* it is a pity the record got broken. || — *Dar lástima,* to be pitiful: *da lástima verle así,* it is pitiful to see him like that. || *Él me da lástima,* I feel sorry for him. || *Es digno de lástima por su mala suerte,* he is to be pitied for his bad luck. || *Estar hecho una lástima,* to be in a pitiful state, to be a sorry sight. || *Llorar lástimas,* to moan and groan, to feel sorry for o.s. || *Que da lástima,* pitifully: *es tan tonto que da lástima,* he is pitifully stupid. || *¡Qué lástima!,* what a pity!, what a shame! || *Tener lástima de,* to feel sorry for.
lastimado, da adj. Hurt (por un golpe, un insulto).
lastimador, ra adj. Injurious, harmful. || FIG. Hurtful (insulto, etc.).
lastimadura f. Injury (acción y efecto de hacer daño).
lastimar v. tr. To hurt, to injure (herir): *le lastimaron en el brazo,* they hurt his arm. || To hurt (hacer daño): *estos zapatos me lastiman,* these shoes hurt. || FIG. To hurt, to offend: *le lastimó en su amor propio,* it

hurt his pride; *me lastimó su falta de consideración*, I was hurt by his lack of consideration. || To pity, to feel sorry for, to sympathize with (compadecer). || — FIG. *Lastimar el oído* or *los oídos*, to hurt one's ears. | *Un color que lastima*, a harsh *o* glaring colour.
— V. pr. To hurt o.s., to injure o.s. || — *Lastimarse de*, to pity, to feel sorry for, to sympathize with (compadecer), to complain about (quejarse). || *Lastimarse la mano* to hurt one's hand.
lastimero, ra adj. Plaintive, doleful (palabras, etc.). || Injurious (que hace daño).
lastimoso, sa adj. Pitiful, piteous (digno de lástima): *el estado de la casa es lastimoso*, the house is in a pitiful state; *una situación lastimosa*, a pitiful situation; *una pérdida lastimosa de tiempo*, a pitiful waste of time. || Lamentable: *un accidente lastimoso*, a lamentable accident.
lastra f. Flat stone, stone slab, flagstone (piedra).
lastrado m. MAR. Ballasting.
lastrar v. tr. MAR. To ballast. || To weigh down.
lastre m. MAR. Ballast: *en lastre*, in ballast; *largar* or *echar* or *soltar lastre*, to discharge ballast. || FIG. Steadiness (equilibrio). | Nuisance (estorbo). | Ballast, dead weight (cosa inútil).
lata f. Tinplate (hojalata). || Tin, can (envase): *una lata de melocotones*, a tin of peaches. || Lath (de madera). || FIG. y FAM. Drag, nuisance, bore, bind (cosa pesada): *es una lata tener que salir ahora*, it's a drag having to go out now. | Bore, pest, drag, nuisance (persona pesada). || — *Barrio de las latas*, shanty town. || FIG. y FAM. *Dar la lata*, to be a nuisance (persona), to be a drag *o* a bore (cosa). || *En lata*, tinned, canned. || *Amer. Estar en la lata* or *no tener ni una lata*, to be broke *o* penniless. | *¡Qué lata!* or *¡vaya una lata!*, what a drag *o* a nuisance *o* a bore *o* a bind! || *Sonar a lata*, to sound tinny (un ruido).
latamente adv. Amply (extensamente). || Broadly speaking (en sentido lato).
latazo m. Blow with a tin *o* a can. || FIG. y FAM. Drag, nuisance, bore, bind (lata).
latente adj. Latent: *calor latente*, latent heat; *en estado latente*, in a latent state.
lateral adj. Side, lateral: *calle lateral*, side street; *nave lateral*, side aisle. || Lateral (en fonética).
— M. Side. || Side, wing (del escenario).
lateranense adj. Lateran: *concilio lateranense*, Lateran Council.
latero, ra adj. Annoying, boring, tiresome.
— M. Tinsmith (hojalatero).
látex m. BOT. Latex.
latido m. Beating (acción de latir el corazón, etc.), beat (cada sonido o movimiento). || Throbbing (de una herida). || Yelping (del perro), yelp (cada ladrido).
latiente adj. Beating (pulso). || Throbbing (herida). || Yapping, yelping (perro).
latifundio m. Latifundium, large landed estate.

— OBSERV. The plural of *latifundio* is *latifundios* (most common) or *latifundia*.

latifundismo m. Latifundium system, ownership of latifundia.
latifundista m. y f. Owner of a large estate.
latigazo m. Lash [with a whip]. || Crack of a whip (chasquido). || FIG. Verbal lashing, tongue lashing, harsh reprimand (reprimenda). || FAM. Drink, swig (trago): *darse un latigazo*, to have a drink. || *Dar latigazos a*, to whip, to lash.
látigo m. Whip: *hacer restallar el látigo*, to crack the whip. || Riding whip (de jinete). || Whip (en parque de atracciones). || Cord (cuerda). || Strap (correa). || *Amer.* Lash (latigazo).
latiguear v. intr. To crack one's whip. || *Amer.* To lash, to whip.
latigueo m. Crack of a whip.
latiguillo m. Small whip. || BOT. Runner (estolón). || Overacting, hamming (de un actor). || Platitude, empty phrase: *un discurso lleno de latiguillos*, a speech full of platitudes.
latín m. Latin: *aprender latín*, to learn Latin. || Latin word *o* phrase, Latinism: *echar latines*, to come out with Latin phrases. || — *Bajo latín*, Low Latin. || FAM. *Latín de cocina* or *macarrónico*, dog Latin. || *Latín rústico* or *vulgar*, Vulgar Latin. || FIG. y FAM. *Sabe latín* or *mucho latín*, he is nobody's fool, there are no flies on him.
latinajo m. FAM. Dog Latin. | Latin word *o* phrase, Latinism: *echar latinajos*, to come out with Latin words.
latinar v. intr. To speak *o* to write in Latin.
latinear v. intr. To speak *o* to write in Latin. || To use Latinisms, to Latinize.
latinidad f. Latinity. || Latin countries, *pl.* || Latin (latín).
latiniparla f. Latinized language, language larded with Latinisms.
latinismo m. Latinism.
latinista m. y f. Latinist.
latinización f. Latinization.
latinizar v. tr. e intr. To Latinize.
latino, na adj./s. Latin. || — Adj. MAR. Lateen: *vela latina*, lateen sail. || *Cruz latina*, Latin cross. || *La Iglesia latina*, the Latin *o* Western Church.
Latinoamérica n. pr. f. GEOGR. Latin America.
latinoamericano, na adj./s. Latin-American.
latir v. intr. To beat (el corazón, el pulso). || To throb (una herida). || To yelp (el perro).
latitud f. Width, breadth (anchura). || Extent, area (extensión). || ASTR. y GEOGR. Latitude: *a 40° de latitud*, at latitude 40°. || FIG. Latitude, freedom (libertad): *las reglas me permiten cierta latitud para obrar*, the rules allow me a certain degree of latitude within which to act.
latitudinal adj. Latitudinal.
latitudinario, ria adj./s. Latitudinarian.
latitudinarismo m. Latitudinarianism (doctrina).
lato, ta adj. Broad, wide (ancho). || Extensive, ample (extenso). || FIG. *En el sentido lato de la palabra*, in the broad sense of the word.
latón m. Brass.
Latona n. pr. f. MIT. Latona.
latonería f. Brassworks (taller). || Brassware shop.
latonero m. Brassworker, brazier.
latoso, sa adj. Annoying, boring, tiresome.
— M. y f. Bore, drag, nuisance (persona pesada).
latría f. REL. Latria.
latrocinar v. intr. To rob, to steal.
latrocinio m. Robbery, theft.
laucha f. *Amer.* Mouse (ratón). | Nonentity, nobody (persona insignificante).
laúd m. MÚS. Lute. || MAR. Catboat. || ZOOL. Leatherback (tortuga). || *Tañedor de laúd*, lutanist, lutenist.
laudable adj. Laudable, praiseworthy.
láudano m. Laudanum (medicamento).
laudar v. tr. JUR. To pronounce sentence on, to render a decision on.
laudatoria f. o **laudatorio** m. Panegyric, eulogy.
laudatorio, ria adj. Laudatory, eulogistic.
laude f. Engraved tombstone. || — Pl. REL. Lauds.
laudo m. JUR. Decision, finding.
laureado, da adj. Prizewinning, award-winning (premiado). || Honoured [U.S., honored] (honrado). || Decorated with the Cross of Saint Ferdinand (un militar). || *Poeta laureado*, poet laureate.
— M. y f. Laureate, recipient of an honour *o* of an award. || Holder of the Cross of Saint Ferdinand. || — F. Cross of Saint Ferdinand [the highest decoration in Spain].
laurear v. tr. To crown with laurels. || To decorate with the Cross of Saint Ferdinand (a un militar). || FIG. To honour, to reward.
laurel m. BOT. Laurel. || — Pl. FIG. Laurels (recompensa). || — FIG. *Cargado de laureles*, laden with laurels. | *Cosechar* or *conquistar laureles*, to win *o* to reap laurels. | *Dormirse en los laureles*, to rest on one's laurels. || BOT. *Laurel cereza* or *real*, cherry laurel. | *Laurel rosa*, rosebay, oleander. || FIG. *Mancillar sus laureles*, to cast a stain on one's laurels.
laurencio m. QUÍM. Lawrencium.
láureo, a adj. Laurel.
lauro m. (P.us.). V. LAUREL.
lauroceraso m. Cherry laurel (arbusto).
lava f. Lava (del volcán). || MIN. Washing (de los metales).
lavable adj. Washable.
lavabo m. Washbasin (lavamanos). || Washstand (con soporte). || Washroom (cuarto de aseo). || Toilet, lavatory (retrete). || REL. Lavabo (lavatorio).
lavacoches m. inv. Car washer (persona).
lavacristales m. inv. Window cleaner.
lavada f. Washing, wash (lavado).
lavadero m. Washing place (público, al aire libre). || Wash house (edificio). || Laundry (en una casa). || MIN. Place where gold-bearing sands are panned.
lavadientes m. inv. (P.us.) Mouthwash (enjuague).
lavado m. Washing, wash (de ropa, coche, persona, metales). || Washing out (del estómago). || Wash (dibujo). || Shampoo (de cabeza). || MED. Lavage. || — FIG. y FAM. *Dar un buen lavado a uno*, to give s.o. a good talking-to. || FAM. *Lavado de cerebro*, brainwashing. || *Lavado en seco*, dry cleaning.
lavador, ra adj. Washing. || *Oso lavador*, racoon.
— M. Washer. || *Amer.* Great anteater (oso hormiguero). || *Lavador de oro*, gold washer. || — F. Washing machine, washer (para la ropa).
lavadura f. Washing (lavado). || Dirty water (agua sucia).
lavafrutas m. inv. Finger bowl.
lavaje m. Washing (de la lana).
lavamanos m. inv. Washbasin, washstand.
lavamiento m. Enema. || Washing (lavado).
lavanco m. Wild duck.
lavanda f. BOT. Lavender (espliego).
lavandería f. Laundry. || Launderette [U.S., laundromat] (automática).
lavandero, ra m. y f. Laundryman, launderer (hombre), laundress, washerwoman (mujer).
lavándula f. Lavender (espliego).
lavaojos m. inv. Eyebath [U.S., eyecup].
lavaparabrisas m. inv. AUT. Windscreen washer [U.S., windshield washer].
lavaplatos m. y f. inv. Dishwasher, washer-up. || *Máquina lavaplatos*, dishwashing machine, dishwasher. || — M. Sink (fregadero).
lavar v. tr. To wash: *lavar la ropa*, to wash clothes. || To paint in water colour (dibujo). || To clean (pescado, etc.). || — *Lavar en seco*, to dry-clean. || FIG. *Lavar la ofensa con sangre*, to avenge an insult

with blood. || *Lavar y marcar*, to shampoo and set (en la peluquería). || *Máquina de lavar*, washing machine, washer (para la ropa), dishwasher (para los platos).
— V. pr. To wash [o.s.], to have a wash. || To wash: *lavarse la cabeza*, to wash one's hair. || FIG. *¡De eso me lavo las manos!*, I wash my hands of that.
lavativa f. MED. Enema. || FIG. y FAM. Nuisance, bind, bore (molestia).
lavatorio m. Washing (lavado). || REL. Maundy (ceremonia religiosa). | Lavabo (de la misa). || MED. Lotion. || *Amer.* Washbasin (lavamanos).
lavavajillas m. inv. Dishwasher.
lavazas f. pl. Dishwater, *sing.*, dirty water, *sing.*
lavotear v. tr. To wash quickly and badly.
— V. pr. To have a quick wash.
lavoteo m. Quick *o* hurried wash.
laxación f. o **laxamiento** m. Laxation, loosening, slackening. || Laxity (laxitud).
laxante adj./s.m. Laxative.
laxar v. tr. To loosen, to slacken (aflojar). || To loosen [the bowels] (vientre).
laxativo, va adj./s.m. Laxative.
laxidad f. Laxity.
laxismo m. Laxism.
laxitud f. Laxity. || Slackness (de una cuerda).
laxo, xa adj. Slack, loose, lax (no tenso). || FIG. Lax, loose (moral, costumbres).
lay m. Lay (poema).
laya f. Sort, kind: *ser de la misma laya*, to be of the same sort. || Quality (calidad). || AGR. Spade. || *Laya de dientes*, fork.
layar v. tr. To dig with a spade.
lazada f. Bow, knot.
lazar v. tr. To lasso, to rope (un animal).
lazareto m. Lazaretto, lazaret.
lazarillo m. Blind man's guide.

— OBSERV. This word comes from the picaresque hero in Spanish literature, « Lazarillo de Tormes ».

lazarino, na adj. Leprous.
— M. y f. Leper.
lazarista m. Lazarist.
Lázaro n. pr. m. Lazarus.
lázaro m. Ragged beggar. || Leper (leproso).
lazo m. Knot (nudo): *atar un lazo*, to tie a knot. || Bow (con una cinta). || Snare, trap (para cazar): *coger con lazo*, to catch in a snare. || Lasso (para sujetar caballos, etc.). || Loop, bend (de un camino). || Rope (cordel). || FIG. Tie, bond (vínculo): *los lazos de la amistad*, the bonds of friendship. | Link: *España sirve de lazo entre Europa y América del Sur*, Spain serves as a link between Europe and South America. | Trap (trampa). || ARQ. Interlaced design (ornamento). || Figure (en el baile). || — FIG. y FAM. *Caer en el lazo*, to fall into the trap. || *Lazo cerrado*, loop (en el ferrocarril). || *Lazo corredizo*, slipknot. || *Lazo de zapato*, shoelace. || FIG. *Tender un lazo*, to set a trap.
lazulita f. MIN. Lazulite (lapislázuli).
le pron. Him, to him, her, to her (personas), it, to it (cosas) [dativo]: *le dije*, *le doy*, I said to him, I give [to] him. || Him, her (acusativo): *le veo*, I [can] see him (V. OBSERV.). || You, to you (cuando corresponde a "usted"): *le vi ayer pero no le pude hablar*, I saw you yesterday but I could not speak to you. || [For] him, [for] her, [for] it, [for] you (para él, para ella, etc.): *cómprale éste*, buy him this one, buy this one for him. || From him, from her, from it, from you (de él, etc.): *le tomó el dinero*, he took the money from him. || *Le pregunté a mi hermano si...*, I asked my brother if...

— OBSERV. The Spanish Academy acknowledges the use of *le* instead of *lo* in the accusative case of the third person masculine singular, but esteems it preferable to reserve this pronoun for the dative case. This use of *le* is far more common in Spain than in South America.

leal adj. Loyal: *un corazón leal*, a loyal heart; *sentimientos leales*, loyal sentiments. || Faithful, loyal (partidario del gobierno). || Faithful, trustworthy, loyal (criado). || Faithful (animal).
— M. Loyalist.
leala f. FAM. Peseta.
lealtad f. Loyalty. || Loyalty, faithfulness, trustworthiness (de criado). || Faithfulness (de animal).
leandra f. FAM. Peseta.
lebrada f. Hare stew.
lebrato m. Leveret.
lebrel m. Greyhound. || *Perro lebrel*, greyhound.
lebrero, ra adj. Harehunting.
— M. Greyhound (lebrel).
lebrillo m. Glazed earthenware bowl (gran recipiente). || Earthenware pot (pequeño recipiente).
lección f. Lesson. || Reading (lectura). || Lesson, class (clase). || Lecture (en la Universidad). || REL. Lesson, lection, reading (de la Biblia). || — FIG. *Dar a uno una lección*, to teach s.o. a lesson. || *Dar la lección*, to recite a lesson (discípulo). || *Dar lección*, to give a lesson (el profesor). || *Dar lecciones*, to teach, to give lessons (enseñar). || *Servir de lección*, to serve as *o* to be a lesson: *esto le servirá de lección por haberse fiado de la gente*, let this be a lesson to you for having trusted people. || *Tomarle la lección a un niño* to make a child say his lesson.
lectivo, va adj. School: *año lectivo*, school year.
lector, ra m. y f. Reader (que lee). || Assistant (profesor). || — M. REL. Lector.
lectorado m. Assistantship. || REL. Lectorate.
lectoría f. Assistantship in a university.
lectura f. Reading. || Reading matter (texto). || Culture, knowledge (conocimiento). || IMPR. Pica, twelve-point type (carácter). || — *Dar lectura a*, to read. || *Una persona de mucha lectura*, a well-read person.
lecha f. Milt, roe (de los peces).
lechada f. Whitewash (albañilería). || TECN. Paste. | Pulp (de papel). || Milk-like *o* milky liquid (líquido blanco). || *Lechada de cal*, milk of lime.
lechal adj. Sucking (animal): *cordero lechal*, sucking lamb. || BOT. Lactiferous, milky (planta).
— M. Milky sap (de árboles). || Suckling (cordero).
lechaza f. Milt, roe (de los peces).
leche f. Milk: *leche cuajada, sin desnatar, desnatada, en polvo, condensada, homogeneizada*, curdled, unskimmed, skim *o* skimmed, powdered, condensed, homogenized milk; *la leche se ha cortado*, the milk has turned *o* curdled *o* gone sour. || BOT. Milky sap (látex). || POP. Spunk, semen. || — *Ama de leche*, wet nurse. || *Café con leche*, [white] coffee. || *Cochinillo de leche*, v. COCHINILLO. || FIG. *Como una leche*, like jelly. || *Dientes de leche*, milk teeth. || FIG. y FAM. *Estar con* or *traer* or *tener la leche en los labios*, to be still wet behind the ears. || POP. *Estar de mala leche*, to be in a stinking *o* in a foul mood. || *Gota de leche*, centre where milk is given free. || POP. *Hacer algo con mala leche*, to do sth. for the hell of it. || *Hermano, hermana de leche*, foster brother, foster sister [two people nursed by the same wet nurse]. || FIG. y FAM. *Mamar una cosa en la leche*, to have been brought up with sth. || POP. *¡Leche!*, hell! | *Tener mala leche*, to be spiteful *o* twisted, to be a nasty piece of work. || *Ternera de leche*, calf. || *Vaca de leche*, milch cow, milk cow.
lechecillas f. pl. Sweetbreads (molleja). || Offal, *sing.* (asadura).
lechera f. Dairymaid, milkmaid (vendedora). || Milk churn [U.S., milk can] (recipiente grande), milk can (recipiente pequeño de metal). || Milk jug (jarro). || *Amer.* Milk cow, milch cow (vaca de leche).
lechería f. Dairy, creamery (tienda).
lechero, ra adj. Milk, dairy (industria): *industria lechera*, milk industry. || FIG. y FAM. Stingy, tight-fisted. || — *Central lechera*, dairy centre (cooperativa). || *Vaca lechera*, milk cow, milch cow.
— M. Milkman (que reparte). || Dairyman (en una granja). || — F. Milkmaid (que ordeña). || Dairywoman (en una granja).
lechigada f. Brood (de aves). || Litter (de animales).
lecho m. Bed (cama): *estar en un lecho de rosas*, to be on a bed of roses. || Bed (de un río). || Bottom (fondo). || ARQ. Base (de una piedra o columna). || GEOL. Layer (estrato). || — *Abandonar el lecho*, to get up, to get out of bed. || *En el lecho de la muerte*, on one's deathbed. || TECN. *Lecho de colada*, pig bed. || *Lecho de roca*, bedrock. || *Lecho mortuorio*, deathbed.

— OBSERV. *Cama* is the usual word for *bed*, the word *lecho* being more literary.

lechón m. Sucking pig (cochinillo). || Hog, swine (puerco).
lechona f. Young sow (cerda). || FIG. y FAM. Pig, filthy woman (mujer sucia).
— Adj. f. FIG. y FAM. Filthy (sucia).
lechoncillo m. Sucking pig.
lechoso, sa adj. Milky.
lechuga f. Lettuce (planta): *ensalada de lechuga*, lettuce salad. || Ruff (cuello). || Pleat, flute, crimp (pliegue en una tela). || — FIG. y FAM. *Como una lechuga*, as fresh as a daisy. || *Lechuga romana*, cos-lettuce [U.S., romaine lettuce]. || FIG. y FAM. *Ser más fresco que una lechuga*, to be as cool as a cucumber.
lechuguilla f. Ruff (cuello). || Wild lettuce (lechuga silvestre).
lechuguina f. FIG. y FAM. Elegant young woman.
lechuguino m. Young lettuce (lechuga). || Plot of small lettuce (plantío). || FIG. y FAM. Dandy, beau (elegante).
lechuza f. Owl (ave). || FIG. y FAM. Hag (mujer fea).
lechuzo m. FIG. y FAM. Owl (hombre muy feo).
leer v.tr. e intr. To read: *leer en voz alta*, to read aloud *o* out loud; *leer en voz baja*, to read quietly; *leer música*, to read music. || To teach, to lecture (enseñar un profesor). || — MÚS. *Leer a primera vista*, to read at sight, to sight-read. || *Leer de corrido*, to read fluently. || *Leer de un tirón*, to read straight through *o* in one go. || FIG. *Leer en los ojos* or *en la mirada de alguien*, to read in s.o.'s eyes. | *Leer entre líneas*, to read between the lines. || *Leerle la mano a uno*, to read s.o.'s palm.
lega f. Lay sister.
legacía f. Legateship (dignidad de legado).
legación f. Legation.
legado m. Legacy (manda testamentaria). || Legate (del Papa, de los romanos). || FIG. Legacy, bequest.
legajo m. Bundle of papers. || Dossier, file (carpeta).
legal adj. Legal (establecido por la ley): *procedimientos legales*, legal procedures. || Lawful, legal: *contrato legal*, lawful contract. || Scrupulous, honest, fair (en el ejercicio de sus poderes).

legalidad f. Legality, lawfulness (conformidad con la ley). || *Salirse de la legalidad*, to break the law.
legalismo m. Legalism.
legalista adj. Legalistic.
— M. y f. Legalist.
legalizable adj. Legalizable.
legalización f. Legalization. || Authentication (de documentos).
legalizar v. tr. To legalize. || To authenticate (documentos). || *Copia legalizada*, certified copy.
legalmente adv. Legally, lawfully (conforme con la ley). || Loyally (lealmente).
légamo m. Slime, ooze (cieno). || Loam (arcilla).
legamoso, sa adj. Slimy, oozy (cenagoso). || Loamy (arcilloso).
Leganés n. pr. GEOGR. Leganes [a town near Madrid where there was a well known psychiatric hospital]. || FAM. *Bueno para ir a Leganés*, ready for the madhouse (loco).
legaña f. Sleep, rheum (en los ojos).
legañoso, sa adj. Rheumy, bleary.
legar v. tr. To bequeath, to legate (hacer donación por testamento). || To delegate (enviar en legación). || FIG. To bequeath (lengua, cultura).
legatario, ria m. y f. JUR. Legatee, heir: *legatario universal*, general legatee.
legendario, ria adj. Legendary.
— M. Collection *o* book of legends.
leghorn f. Leghorn (raza de gallinas).
legibilidad f. Legibility.
legible adj. Legible.
legión f. Legion. || — *Legión de Honor*, Legion of Honour. || *Legión Extranjera*, Foreign Legion.
legionario, ria adj. Legionary: *fuerzas legionarias*, legionary forces.
— M. Legionary.
legislación f. Legislation.
legislador, ra adj. Legislative.
— M. Legislator.
legislar v. intr. To legislate.
legislativo, va adj. Legislative: *asamblea legislativa*, legislative assembly.
legislatura f. Legislature.
legisperito m. Legal expert, jurist.
legista m. Legist (experto en leyes). || Law student. || *Médico legista*, forensic expert.
legitimación f. Legitimation, legitimization.
legitimador, ra adj. Legitimating.
legitimar v. tr. To legitimize, to legitimate.
legitimidad f. Legitimacy. || Authenticity (de un producto).
legitimismo m. Legitimism.
legitimista adj./s. Legitimist.
legítimo, ma adj. Legitimate: *hijo legítimo*, legitimate child. || Authentic, genuine, real: *champán legítimo*, authentic champagne; *cuero legítimo*, real leather. || Pure: *oro legítimo*, pure gold. || Right (justo).
lego, ga adj. Lay, laic, secular (seglar). || Lay: *hermano lego*, lay brother. || FIG. Ignorant (sin instrucción). | Uninformed. || FIG. y FAM. *Ser lego en la materia*, to know nothing about the subject.
— M. Layman. || REL. Lay brother.
legra f. MED. Raspatory (instrumento). | Curette (de ginecólogo).
legración f. o **legrado** m. o **legradura** f. MED. Scraping, scrape (de un hueso). | Scraping, scrape, curetting (de la matriz).
legrar v. tr. MED. To scrape (huesos). | To scrape, to curette (la matriz).
legua f. League (medida itineraria de 5572 m). || — FIG. *A la legua*, far away, miles away. || *Cómico de la legua*, strolling player. || *Legua cuadrada*, square league. || *Legua de posta*, unit of distance of four kilometres. || *Legua marítima*, marine league (5555 m). || FIG. *Se ve a la legua*, it stands out a mile, you can see it a mile away.
legui m. Legging (polaina).
leguleyo m. Pettifogger [U.S., shyster (fam.)].
legumbre f. BOT. Legume, pod vegetable: *legumbres secas*, dried legumes. || Vegetable (verdura): *legumbres verdes*, green vegetables.
leguminoso, sa adj. Leguminous.
— F. Pulse, leguminous plant.
leíble adj. Legible, readable (legible).
leída f. Reading: *de una leída*, in one reading.
leído, da adj. Well-read (persona). || Read: *una obra muy leída*, a widely read work. || — *Leído y conforme*, read and approved. || FAM. *Ser muy leído y escribido*, V. ESCRIBIDO.
leísmo m. The use of the pronoun *le* in the masculine singular accusative case instead of the pronoun *lo* (*este lápiz no te le doy* instead of *no te lo doy*).
leísta adj. Who uses *le* as direct object.
— M. y f. Person who uses *le* as direct object.
leitmotiv m. Leitmotiv, leitmotif (tema).

— OBSERV. *Leitmotiv* is a Germanism which can be replaced by *tema central* [of a film, opera, novel, etc.].

lejanía f. Distance: *sonido debilitado por la lejanía*, sound weakened by the distance. || Distant *o* remote place (paraje lejano). || *En la lejanía*, in the distance.
lejano, na adj. Distant, remote, far-off: *el Japón es un país lejano*, Japan is a distant country. || Distant: *pariente lejano*, a distant relative. || — *Lejano Oriente*, Far East. || *Un lugar lejano de mi casa*, a place far from my home *o* a long way from my home.
lejía f. Lye (agua alcalina). || Bleach (hipoclorito de sosa). || FIG. y FAM. Dressing down (reprimenda). | Scolding (bronca): *dar a uno una buena lejía*, to give s.o. a good scolding.
lejío m. Dyers' lye.
lejísimos adv. Very far.

— OBSERV. The incorrect form *lejísimo* should be avoided.

lejitos adv. FAM. Fairly far [away], quite far [away].
lejos adv. Far, far away: *¿estaba lejos?*, was it far? || — *A lo lejos*, in the distance: *ver a lo lejos*, to see in the distance. || *De lejos*, from afar, from a distance: *la iglesia se ve de lejos*, the church can be seen from afar; from a distance: *de lejos no veo nada*, from a distance I can't see anything; by far: *es de lejos el mejor*, he's by far the best. || *Desde lejos*, from afar, from a long way off. || FIG. *Ir* or *llegar lejos*, to go far, to go a long way. || *Lejos de*, a long way from, far from: *lejos de Madrid*, a long way from Madrid; far from: *estaba lejos de saber lo que iba a sucederme*, I was far from knowing what was to happen to me; instead of, far from: *lejos de asustarse, el niño se puso a acariciar al león*, instead of getting frightened the boy began to pat the lion. || FIG. *Llevar demasiado lejos*, to carry too far: *llevó el asunto demasiado lejos*, he carried the matter too far. || *Más lejos*, further, further away. || FIG. *Ni de lejos*, far from it. | *Para no ir más lejos*, to take an obvious example. || *Veo muy lejos la terminación del proyecto*, I can't envisage an early completion of the plan.
— M. Appearance from a distance (aspecto). || Background (pintura). || *Tener buen lejos*, to look good from a distance.
lelo, la adj. Silly, stupid, foolish (tonto). || — FAM. *Dejar a uno lelo*, to leave s.o. stupefied, to stun s.o. | *Estar lelo por*, to be crazy about. | *Quedarse lelo*, to be stunned *o* stupefied: *al ver el accidente me quedé lelo*, I was stunned by the sight of the accident.
— M. Ninny, simpleton, fool.
lema m. Motto (en un escudo, en un monumento). || Epigraph (en un libro). || Lemma (en lógica). || Theme, subject (tema). || Assumed name (concurso). || MAT. Lemma. || Slogan (de un partido, etc.). || Watchword (contraseña).
lemming m. Lemming (ratón campestre).
lemnáceas f. pl. Lemnaceae.
lemnisco m. Lemniscus.
lempira m. Lempira (moneda de Honduras).
lémur m. ZOOL. Lemur. || — Pl. MIT. Lemures (almas de los muertos). || FIG. Phantoms, ghosts.
lencería f. Linen (ropa blanca). || Underwear (ropa interior). || Linen goods, *pl.* (géneros de lienzo). || Linen shop, draper's (tienda de ropa blanca). || Linen room (en un hospital).
lencero, ra m. y f. Draper, linen maker *o* dealer.
lendrera f. Toothcomb [U.S., fine-tooth comb] (for removing nits *o* lice).
lengua f. ANAT. Tongue. || Language, tongue (p.us.) [idioma]: *lengua española, inglesa*, Spanish, English language. || Clapper, tongue (badajo). || Neck, spit, tongue (de tierra). || CULIN. Tongue. || — FIG. y FAM. *Andar en lenguas*, to be the talk of the town. | *Atar la lengua a uno*, to silence s.o. | *Buscarle la lengua a uno*, to ask for it, to provoke s.o., to pick a quarrel with s.o. (buscar pelea o discusión), to provoke s.o. to speak (incitar a hablar). | *Calentársele a uno la lengua*, to get worked up *o* steamed up. | *Con la lengua fuera* or *de un palmo*, panting, puffing and panting. | *Darle a la lengua*, to chatter. | *De lengua en lengua*, from mouth to mouth. || *Dominar una lengua*, to master a language. || FIG. y FAM. *Estar con la lengua fuera*, to be dead beat (de cansancio). | *Hacerse lenguas de*, to rave about. | *Hay que darle siete vueltas a la lengua antes de hablar*, one must think twice before speaking. | *Írsele a uno la lengua* or *irse de la lengua*, to blab, to talk too much (de costumbre), to spill the beans (en una ocasión). || *Lengua aglutinante*, agglutinative language. || BOT. *Lengua de buey*, oxtongue. || FIG. *Lengua de estropajo* or *de trapo*, stammerer, stutterer, mumbler (persona). | *Lengua de fuego*, tongue of fire. | *Lengua de gato*, finger biscuit. || *Lengua de oc, de oil*, langue d'oc, d'oïl. || FIG. *Lengua de víbora* or *lengua viperina*, poisonous tongue. | *Lengua larga*, gossip. || *Lengua madre*, parent language [of other languages.] || *Lengua materna* or *nativa*, mother *o* native tongue, native language. || *Lengua muerta*, dead language. || *Lengua pastosa* or *gorda*, coated tongue, furry tongue. || *Lenguas hermanas*, sister tongues. || *Lengua viva*, living language. || FIG. *Ligero de lengua*, loose-tongued. | *Mala lengua*, evil tongue. | *Media lengua*, childish talk *o* language. | *Morderse la lengua*, to hold one's tongue. | *No hay que prestar atención a las malas lenguas*, one should not worry about what people say. | *No morderse la lengua*, not to mince one's words, to speak one's mind. | *No tener pelos* or *pelillos en la lengua*, not to mince one's words, to be outspoken. | *Pegársele a uno la lengua al paladar*, to be unable to speak. | *Sacar la lengua*, to stick out *o* to put out one's tongue (*a*, at) [hacer burla]. | *Se me vino algo a la lengua*, sth. came to my mind.

| *Tener la lengua gorda,* to be drunk (borracho), to have a furry tongue (lengua pastosa). | *Tener uno mala lengua,* to have a vicious tongue. | *Tener uno mucha lengua* or *tener la lengua suelta,* to be outspoken. | *Tenía el nombre en la punta de la lengua,* the name was on the tip of his tongue. | *Tenía la lengua fuera,* his tongue was hanging out. | *Tirarle a uno de la lengua,* to draw s.o. out, to make s.o. talk. | *Tomar lengua* or *lenguas,* to find out, to inquire. | *Trabarse la lengua,* to get tongue-tied: *se me trabó la lengua,* I got tongue-tied. | *Traer en lenguas a uno,* to criticize s.o. | *Tragarse la lengua,* to bite one's lip. | *Venírsele a uno a la lengua una cosa,* to get an idea.

lenguado m. Sole: *lenguado a la parrilla,* grilled sole.

lenguaje m. Language: *lenguaje culto, grosero, cifrado,* cultured, foul, code language. || Idiom (de un autor). || Speech (facultad de hablar). || FIG. Language: *el lenguaje de las flores,* the language of flowers. || Style: *lenguaje literario,* literary style.

lenguaraz adj. Talkative (hablador). || FIG. Slanderous, scurrilous (maldiciente). || Polyglot, multilingual.
— M. y f. Talkative person. || Slanderer (maldiciente). || Polyglot.

lengüeta f. Pointer (de la balanza). || Flap, tongue (de cartera, de bolso, etc.). || Tongue (del calzado). || ANAT. Epiglottis. || MÚS. Reed (de una flauta). || Tenon, tongue (en carpintería). || Barb (de una flecha). || Barb (de anzuelo). || Bit (barrena). || — *Ensambladura de ranura y lengüeta,* tongue-and-groove joint. || *Poner lengüetas,* to reed (un órgano), to barb (una flecha).

lengüetada f. o **lengüetazo** m. Lick.

lengüetear v. intr. To lick. || *Amer.* To chatter.

lengüetería f. Reed stops, *pl.* (de un órgano).

lengüicorto, ta adj. FAM. Timid, shy, quiet.

lengüilargo, ga adj. FAM. Talkative (parlanchín). | Foul-mouthed (deslenguado).

lengüón, ona adj. *Amer.* Talkative (parlanchín). | Gossipy (chismoso).
— M. y f. *Amer.* Chatterbox. | Gossip (chismoso).

lenidad f. Leniency, lenience (indulgencia).

lenificación f. Softening.

lenificar v. tr. To soothe, to alleviate (el dolor). || To alleviate (otro sufrimiento).

lenificativo, va adj. Soothing, alleviating.

leninismo m. Leninism.

leninista adj./s. Leninist.

lenitivo, va adj. Soothing, lenitive.
— M. MED. Lenitive. || FIG. Lenitive, palliative.

lenocinio m. Pimping, procuring. || *Casa de lenocinio,* brothel.

lente m. y f. Lens (óptica): *lente de aumento,* magnifying lens. || Magnifying glass (lupa): *mirar con lente,* to look at through a magnifying glass. || Lens, glass (de gafas). || Monocle (monóculo). || — Pl. Glasses, spectacles (gafas). || Pince-nez, *sing.,* eyeglasses (quevedos). || *Lentes de contacto,* contact lenses.
— OBSERV. The ambiguous gender of this word sometimes causes difficulties, but it is usually masculine when meaning *spectacles (los lentes)* and feminine when it applies to *refractive lenses.*

lenteja f. BOT. Lentil.

lentejar m. Lentil field.

lentejuela f. Sequin, spangle.

lenticular adj. Lenticular.

lentilla f. Contact lens.

lentiscal m. Grove of mastic trees.

lentisco m. BOT. Lentiscus, lentisk, mastic tree.

lentitud f. Slowness, sluggishness.

lento, ta adj. Slow: *lento en actuar,* slow to act; *lento en el trabajo,* a slow worker. || Slow, sluggish (persona). || MED. Viscous, viscid. || *A cámara lenta,* slow-motion (cine), in slow motion (rodar).

leña f. Firewood. || FIG. y FAM. Rough play: *hubo mucha leña durante el partido de fútbol,* there was a lot of rough play during the football match. || — FIG. y FAM. *Añadir* or *echar* or *poner leña al fuego,* to add fuel to the fire. | *Dar* or *repartir leña,* to play rough (deportes), to lash out (pegar). | *Dar leña a alguien,* to give s.o. a beating. || *Leña menuda,* kindling [wood]. || *Leña seca,* deadwood. || FIG. *Llevar leña al monte,* to carry coals to Newcastle.

leñador, ra m. y f. Woodcutter.

leñazo m. FAM. Blow with a stick (garrotazo). | Blow (golpe). || — FAM. *Me dieron un leñazo,* they hit *o* walloped me. | *Me di un leñazo con el coche,* I crashed my car.

¡leñe! interj. POP. Jesus!, Christ!

leñera f. Woodshed (sitio). || Woodpile (montón).

leñero m. Wood seller. || Woodshed (leñera).
— Adj. m. FAM. Rough: *equipo leñero,* rough team.

leño m. Log (trozo de árbol). || Firewood (leña). || FIG. y POÉT. Vessel (embarcación). || FIG. y FAM. Blockhead, thickhead (persona). || FAM. *Dormir como un leño,* to sleep like a log.

leñoso, sa adj. Ligneous.

Leo n. pr. m. ASTR. Leo.

león m. ZOOL. Lion. || Ant lion (hormiga león). || FIG. Lion: *valiente como un león,* as brave as a lion. || HERÁLD. Lion. || *Amer.* Puma. || — *Cachorro del león,* lion cub. || FIG. *La parte del león,* the lion's share. || *León marino,* sea lion (foca). || *Amer. León miquero,* puma. || FIG. *No es tan fiero* or *bravo el león como lo pintan,* he is not as fierce *o* brave as he's made out to be (una persona), it is not as difficult as they make out (una cosa). | *Ponerse como un león,* to get furious.

leona f. Lioness.

leonado, da adj. Fulvous, tawny.

leonera f. Lion's den (foso). || Lion's cage (jaula). || FIG. y FAM. *Este cuarto es* or *está hecho una leonera,* this room is a mess.

leonero m. Lion keeper.

leonino, na adj. Leonine. || — *Contrato leonino,* one-sided contract. || *Hacer un reparto leonino,* to make an unfair distribution, to share sth. out unfairly.

Leonor n. pr. f. Eleanor.

leontina f. Watch chain (de reloj).

leopardo m. ZOOL. Leopard.

leotardo m. Leotard (traje para gimnastas). || — Pl. Tights (medias).

Lepanto n. pr. GEOGR. Lepanto.

Lepe n. pr. *Sabe más que Lepe (Lepijo y su hijo),* he's got no flies on him, he's nobody's fool.

lepidóptero, ra adj. ZOOL. Lepidopterous, lepidopteran.
— M. ZOOL. Lepidopteron, lepidopteran. || — Pl. Lepidoptera.

leporino, na adj. Leporine. || *Labio leporino,* harelip.

lepra f. MED. Leprosy.

leprosería f. Leprosarium, lazaretto.

leproso, sa adj. Leprous.
— M. y f. Leper.

lerdo, da adj. Dull, slow, dim (lento). || Sluggish, lumbering, clumsy (torpe).
— M. Dullard, sluggard.

Lerna n. pr. MIT. Lerna. || *Hidra de Lerna,* Lernaean hydra.

les pron. pers. m. y f. pl. To them, them (a ellos, a ellas), you, to you (a ustedes): *les presto (a ellas) mis joyas,* I lend them my jewels, I lend my jewels to them. || For them, them (para ellos), for you, you (para ustedes): *les traigo un regalo (a ustedes),* I have brought you a present *o* brought a present for you. || From them (de ellos), from you (de ustedes): *les compré un coche,* I bought a car from them.

lesa adj. V. LESO.

lesbianismo m. Lesbianism.

lesbiano, na o **lesbio, bia** adj./s. Lesbian.

Lesbos n. pr. GEOGR. Lesbos.

lesión f. Injury, wound, lesion: *lesión interna,* internal injury; *lesión en la pierna,* wound in the leg. || Damage (daño). || JUR. Injury (perjuicio). || — Pl. JUR. Assault and battery.

lesionado, da adj. Injured, wounded. || Damaged (dañado).
— M. y f. Injured person.

lesionar v. tr. To damage (dañar). || To wound, to injure (herir).
— V. pr. To get hurt, to be injured, to injure *o* to hurt o.s.

lesivo, va adj. Injurious, harmful.

lesna f. Awl.

leso, sa adj. Injured, wronged. || FIG. Disturbed, warped (trastornado). || *Amer.* Stupid (tonto). || JUR. *Crimen de lesa majestad,* high treason, lese majesty.

letal adj. Lethal, deadly (mortífero).

letanía f. REL. Litany. || Supplicatory procession (procesión). || FIG. y FAM. String, long list (sarta).

letárgico, ca adj. MED. Lethargic.

letargo m. MED. Lethargy: *caer en estado de letargo,* to fall into a state of lethargy. || FIG. Lethargy, drowsiness (modorra).

letífero, ra adj. Lethal, deadly (letal).

letón, ona adj. Latvian, Lettish.
— M. y f. Latvian, Lett (habitante). || — M. Latvian, Lettish (idioma).

Letonia n. pr. f. GEOGR. Latvia.

letra f. Letter: *la letra a,* the letter a. || Character, letter (en imprenta). || Handwriting, writing, hand: *tener buena letra,* to have good handwriting. || Lyrics, *pl.,* words, *pl.* (de una canción). || Inscription, motto (lema). || Rondeau (poesía). || COM. Bill of exchange (letra de cambio). || FIG. y FAM. Astuteness, cunning, artfulness (astucia). || — Pl. Letters (literatura). || Arts: *licenciado en Letras,* arts graduate; *Facultad de Letras,* Faculty of Arts. || Line, *sing.,* lines: *te pondré unas letras,* I'll drop you a line, I'll write you a few lines. || — *A la letra* or *al pie de la letra,* to the letter: *cumplió mis instrucciones al pie de la letra,* he carried out my instructions to the letter; literally: *tomó al pie de la letra lo que dije y se enfadó,* he took what I said literally and got angry; word for word: *copió el artículo al pie de la letra,* he copied the article word for word. || *Atenerse a la letra* or *atarse a la letra,* to stick to the literal meaning. || *Bellas* or *buenas letras,* literature, belles lettres. || *Ciencias y Letras,* Arts and Sciences. || *Con todas sus letras,* written out in full. || *De su puño y letra,* by his own hand. || *Escribir en letras de molde,* to print. || *Hombre, mujer de letras,* man, woman of letters. || FIG. y FAM. *La letra con sangre entra,* spare the rod and spoil the child. || *Letra abierta,* letter of credit [for an unlimited amount]. || COM. *Letra a la vista,* sight draft. || *Letra bastardilla,* italic letters, italics. || *Letra corrida* or *cursiva*, cursive writing. || *Letra de cambio*, bill of exchange. || *Letra de imprenta* or *de molde*, print. || *Letra dominical*, dominical letter. || *Letra florida*, ornamental capital, head letter. || *Letra gótica*, Gothic lettering *o* script. || *Letra mayúscula, minúscula*, capital, small letter. || FIG. *Letra muerta*, dead letter. || *Letra negrilla*, bold type, boldface. || *Letra por letra*, word for word. || *Letra redonda* or *redondilla*, round hand. || *Letras divinas* or *sagradas*, The Bible, the Scriptures. || *Letras humanas*, Humanities. || *Letra versalita*, small capital [letter]. || FIG. *Ponerle a uno cuatro letras*, to drop s.o. a line. | *Primeras letras*, three R's. || COM. *Protestar una letra*, to protest a bill. || FIG. *Tener letra menuda*, to be artful *o* cunning.

letrado, da adj. Lettered, learned (instruido). || FAM. Pedantic (presumido).
— M. Lawyer (abogado).

Letrán n. pr. m. Lateran (palacio romano).

letrero m. Notice (anuncio). || Sign (señal). || Poster (cartel). || Label (etiqueta). || Inscription (inscripción). || *Letrero luminoso*, neon sign.

letrilla f. Rondeau (composición poética).

letrina f. Latrine.

leucemia f. MED. Leucaemia [U.S., leucemia], leukaemia [U.S., leukemia].

leucémico, ca adj. Leucaemic [U.S., leucemic], leukaemic [U.S., leukemic].
— M. y f. Leukaemic person. || *Es un leucémico*, he suffers from leukaemia.

leucito m. BOT. Leucite.

leucoblasto m. BIOL. Leucoblast [U.S., leukoblast].

leucocito m. BIOL. Leucocyte [U.S., leukocyte].

leucocitosis f. MED. Leucocytosis [U.S., leukocytosis].

leucoma m. MED. Leucoma [U.S., leukoma].

leucoplasto m. BOT. Leucoplast [U.S., leukoplast].

leucorrea f. MED. Leucorrhoea [U.S., leukorrhea].

leucosis f. Leucosis [U.S., leukosis].

leudar v. tr. To leaven.
— V. pr. To rise (la masa del pan).

leude m. HIST. Leud.

leudo, da adj. Leavened (el pan).

leva f. MAR. Weighing anchor (de un barco). || Levy (reclutamiento). || TECN. Cam. | Vane (álabe). | Lever (palanca). || *Amer.* Trick (engaño). || TECN. *Árbol de levas*, camshaft.

levadizo adj. m. *Puente levadizo*, drawbridge.

levador m. TECN. Vane (álabe).

levadura f. Leaven (para el pan). || Yeast (de la cerveza, etc.). || FIG. Seed (germen). || — *Levadura en polvo*, baking powder. || *Pan sin levadura*, unleavened bread.

levantada f. Getting up, rising (de la cama). || Lift (halterofilia).

levantado, da adj. Lifted up. || FIG. Lofty, elevated, high (elevado). || *Votar por levantados y sentados* to vote by sitting and standing.

levantador, ra adj. Lifting, raising.
— M. y f. Lifter: *levantador de pesos*, weight lifter. || Agitator, insurrectionist (agitador).

levantamiento m. Raising, lifting (acción de levantar). || Erection (de una estatua). || Construction (de un edificio). || Elevation. || Insurrection, uprising (sedición). || TECN. Hoisting, lifting. || GEOL. Upheaval. || Drawing up (de planos). || — *Levantamiento de la veda*, opening of the hunting *o* of the fishing season. || *Levantamiento del cadáver*, removal of the corpse. || *Levantamiento de pesos*, weight-lifting. || *Levantamiento topográfico*, survey, land survey.

levantar v. tr. To raise, to put up: *levantar la mano*, to raise one's hand. || To lift, to lift up: *no puedo levantar este paquete*, I can't lift this parcel. || To set *o* to put up: *levantar una escala*, to set up a ladder. || To throw up (en el aire). || To raise, to lift (alzar): *levantar los ojos*, to raise one's eyes. || To erect, to raise, to construct: *levantar un templo*, to erect a temple. || To set up: *levantar una fábrica*, to set up a factory. || To lift up, to pick up (recoger): *levanta la silla*, pick up the chair. || To cut (en los naipes). || To remove (quitar): *levantar el mantel*, to remove the tablecloth. || To draw up (un plano). || To do (un dibujo). || To put up: *levantar obstáculos*, to put up obstacles. || JUR. To draw up (acta): *levantar un atestado*, to draw up a report. || To weigh: *levantar el ancla*, to weigh anchor. || To lift, to raise (el telón). || To raise (un chichón). || FIG. To turn (trastornar): *levantar el estómago*, to turn one's stomach. | To turn (enemistar): *levantar a un hijo contra su padre*, to turn a son against his father. | To stir up: *levantar al pueblo*, to stir up the people. | To lift (el pensamiento, el corazón): *levantar el corazón a Dios*, to lift one's heart to God. | To raise: *levantar el nivel de vida*, to raise the standard of living. | To put on its feet: *levantar al país, la economía nacional*, to put the country, the national economy on its feet. | To cause, to give rise to, to entail: *la ejecución de un programa político levanta grandes dificultades*, the carrying out of a political programme gives rise to great difficulties. | To found, to institute (fundar). | To bear: *levantar falso testimonio*, to bear false witness. | To raise, to lift (una prohibición). | To adjourn (una sesión). | To take (un censo). | To suspend, to raise (una prohibición): *levantar la excomunión*, to suspend the excommunication. | To raise (la voz). || MIL. To levy, to raise, to recruit (tropas). | To raise (un sitio). || DEP. To rear (el caballo). | To lift (un peso). || To flush out (en la caza). || — FIG. *Levantar cabeza*, to get better (estar mejor). || *Levantar del suelo*, to lift off the ground. || *Levantar el ánimo*, to cheer *o* to buck s.o. up, to lift *o* to raise s.o.'s spirits. || *Levantar el cadáver*, to remove the corpse. || *Levantar el campo*, V. CAMPO. || *Levantar en alto*, to lift up into the air. || *Levantar la baza*, to win the trick (en los naipes). || *Levantar la casa*, to move house. || *Levantar la mano a uno*, to raise one's hand to s.o. || *Levantar la veda*, to open the hunting *o* fishing season. || FAM. *Levantarle a uno la tapa de los sesos*, V. TAPA. || *Levantar polvo*, to raise dust. || JUR. *Levantar un proceso*, to institute proceedings. || *Sin levantar la vista*, without looking up, without raising *o* lifting one's eyes.
— V. pr. To get up: *levantarse temprano*, to get up early. || To stand up, to rise (ponerse de pie). || To stand out, to rise (erguirse). || To come out ahead (salir ganador). || To rise, to come up (el viento). || To lift (la niebla). || FIG. To break out (escándalo, riña). | To rise up, to rise (sublevarse). | To rise, to be adjourned (una sesión). || — *Al levantarse el telón*, when the curtain rose *o* rises. || *Al levantarse la sesión*, when the meeting rose *o* adjourned. || FIG. *Levantarse con*, to make off with (llevarse). || FAM. *Levantarse con el pie izquierdo*, V. PIE. || *Levantarse de la cama*, to get out of bed. || *Levantarse de la mesa, de la silla*, to get up from the table, off *o* from the chair. || *Levantarse del suelo*, to get up off the ground. || *Levantarse en armas*, to rise up in arms. || *Levantarse pronto*, to get up early. || *Se me levantó el estómago al ver la sangre*, the sight of blood made my stomach turn.

levante m. East, Orient. || East wind, levanter (viento).

Levante n. pr. m. GEOGR. Levante [a region in eastern Spain made up of Valencia and Murcia]. || Levant (países al Este del Mediterráneo).

levantino, na adj. Of *o* from "Levante". || Levantine [of the Levant].
— M. y f. Native *o* inhabitant of "Levante" (de España). || Levantine.

levantisco, ca adj. Turbulent, restless.

levar v. tr. MAR. To weigh (el ancla).
— V. pr. MAR. To set sail, to weigh anchor.

leve adj. Light. || FIG. Slight: *una herida leve*, a slight wound. | Slight, trivial, unimportant (error, etc.).

levedad f. Lightness (ligereza). || FIG. Slightness, triviality, unimportance: *la levedad de una ofensa*, the slightness of an offence.

levemente adv. Lightly. || FIG. Slightly

Leviatán n. pr. m. Leviathan.

levigación f. Levigation.

levita m. Levite (de la tribu de Leví). || — F. Frock coat (chaqueta). || FIG. *Tirar de la levita*, V. TIRAR.

levitación f. Levitation.

levítico, ca adj. Levitical. || FIG. Clerical: *ambiente levítico*, clerical atmosphere.

Levítico n. pr. m. Leviticus (libro de Moisés).

léxico, ca adj. Lexical.
— M. Lexicon, dictionary. || Vocabulary.

lexicografía f. Lexicography.

lexicográfico, ca adj. Lexicographic, lexicographical.

lexicógrafo, fa m. y f. Lexicographer.

lexicología f. Lexicology.

lexicológico, ca adj. Lexicologic, lexicological.

lexicólogo, ga m. y f. Lexicologist.

lexicón m. Lexicon, dictionary. || Vocabulary.

ley f. JUR. Law: *respetar la ley*, to respect the law; *ley vigente*, law in force; *ley marcial*, martial law. || Bill, act (en las Cortes): *aprobar una ley*, to pass a bill. || Law: *la ley de la oferta y la demanda*, the law of supply and demand; *leyes de la física*, laws of physics. || Rule, law: *las leyes del juego*, the rules of the game. || Religion: *la ley de los mahometanos*, the religion of the Mahometans. || Quality (calidad), weight (peso), dimension (medida). || Sterling (de la plata). || Purity (de un metal). || Statute (de una asamblea). || Regulations, *pl.* (de un concurso). || Liking (cariño) [with the verbs *cobrar, tener* and *tomar*]: *tomar ley a alguien*, to take a liking to s.o. || — Pl. Law, *sing.*: *estudiar leyes*, to study law.
— *Allá van leyes do* or *donde quieren reyes*, the strong man is a law unto himself. || *Al margen de la ley* or *fuera de la ley*, outside the law. || *Bajar de ley*, to lower the sterling content of, to lessen the purity of (un metal). || *Bajo de ley*, below sterling standard, base (plata). || *Con todas las de la ley*, fully-fledged, real: *ser un médico con todas las de la ley*, to be a fully-fledged doctor; according to the rules (según las reglas); in due form (en debida forma). || *Contra la ley*, against the law. || *De buena ley*, sterling (en sentido propio y figurado). || *Dictar la ley*, to lay down the law. || *Dictar sus propias leyes*, to be a law unto o.s. || FIG. *En buena ley*, rightly, justly. || *Hecha la ley, hecha la trampa*, laws are made to be broken. || *La costumbre hace ley* or *tiene fuerza de ley*, custom has the force of law. || *La ignorancia de la ley no excusa su cumplimiento*, ignorance of the law is no excuse. || REL. *La Ley*, the Law. || FIG. *La ley del embudo*, one law for oneself and one for everyone else. || *Ley natural*, natural law. || *Ley sálica*, salic law. || *Ley seca*, prohibition law [U.S., dry law]. || *Oro de ley*, pure gold, standard gold. || *Plata de ley*, pure

silver, sterling silver. || *Representante de la ley*, officer of the law. || *Según la ley*, according to the law, by law. || *Tener fuerza de ley*, to have force of law. || *Venir contra la ley*, to break the law.

Leyden n. pr. GEOGR. Leyden. || *Botella de Leyden*, Leyden jar.

leyenda f. Legend (vida de santos). || Legend (cuento). || Inscription, legend (de una moneda). || *Leyenda negra*, black legend.

lezna f. Awl (de zapatero).

liana f. BOT. Liana (bejuco).

liar v. tr. To tie, to bind: *liar un paquete con una cuerda*, to tie a parcel with string. || To tie up, to do up: *no puedo liar este paquete*, I can't tie up this parcel. || To wrap [up]: *liar algo en una manta*, to wrap sth. [up] in a blanket. || To roll: *liar un cigarrillo*, to roll a cigarette. || FIG. y FAM. To coax (engatusar). | To take [s.o.] in (engañar). | To mix up, to involve: *no me líes en este asunto*, don't mix me up in this matter. | To muddle up (confundir): *trató de liarme con sus razonamientos*, he tried to muddle me up with his reasoning. | To complicate (volver más complicado). || — FAM. *Liar el hato* or *liarlas*, to do a bunk, to hop it (irse), to kick the bucket (morir). | *Liar los bártulos*, v. BÁRTULOS.

— V. pr. To wrap o.s. [up]: *liarse en una manta*, to wrap o.s. [up] in a blanket. || FIG. y FAM. To get muddled up, to get confused (enredarse). | To become complicated: *el asunto se lió más de lo previsto*, the matter became more complicated than was anticipated. | To get *o* to become involved (meterse). | To interfere (intervenir). || FIG. y POP. To become lovers (dos personas), to become the lover [*con*, of] (amancebarse). || — FAM. *Liarse a palos*, to come to blows (pelearse). || FIG. y FAM. *Liárselas*, to do a bunk, to hop it (irse), to kick the bucket (morir).

lías o **liásico** m. GEOL. Lias.

liásico, ca adj. GEOL. Liassic.

libación f. Libation.

libanés, esa adj./s. Lebanese.

Líbano n. pr. m. GEOGR. Lebanon.

libar v. tr. To suck (chupar).

libelar v. tr. JUR. To word (un documento). | To petition (demandar).

libelista m. y f. Lampoonist (de escritos satíricos). || JUR. Libellist [U.S., libelist].

libelo m. Lampoon (escrito satírico). || JUR. Libel.

libélula f. Dragonfly, libellula (insecto).

líber m. BOT. Inner bark.

liberable adj. Able to be freed *o* liberated.

liberación f. Liberation (de un país, de la servidumbre). || Release, freeing (de presos). || Receipt (recibo). || Remission (perdón, remisión). || Exemption (de una obligación). || *Amer.* Delivery (parto). || *Acto de liberación*, order of release.

liberado, da adj. Liberated, freed: *país liberado*, liberated country. || Exempted (de una obligación). || COM. Paid-up (pagado).

liberador, ra adj. Liberating.

— M. y f. Liberator.

liberal adj./s. Liberal: *liberal con uno*, liberal with s.o. || — *Artes liberales*, liberal arts. || *Los liberales*, the liberals (en política). || *Partido liberal*, liberal party. || *Profesión liberal*, [liberal] profession.

liberalidad f. Liberality.

liberalismo m. Liberalism.

liberalización f. Liberalization.

liberalizar v. tr. To liberalize.

— V. pr. To become liberal.

liberalmente adv. Liberally, freely (con desprendimiento). || *Amer.* Rapidly, quickly (rápidamente).

liberar v. tr. To liberate, to free. || To free: *liberar un dedo cogido en el engranaje*, to free a finger caught in the gears. || FIG. To free, to release: *liberar a uno de su promesa*, to free s.o. from his promise. | To exempt (de una obligación).

liberatorio, ria adj. Liberatory.

Liberia n. pr. f. GEOGR. Liberia.

liberiano, na adj./s. Liberian (de Liberia).

libérrimo, ma adj. Entirely free, completely free, very free. || *Por su libérrima voluntad*, entirely of his own free will.

libertad f. Freedom (palabra general). || Liberty, freedom: *hipotecar su libertad*, to pledge one's liberty. || Familiarity (en el trato). || Ease, freedom (desembarazo). || — Pl. Liberties: *tomarse libertades*, to take liberties. || Liberties, privileges (prerrogativas). || — *Con entera* or *con toda libertad*, with absolute *o* complete liberty. || *En libertad para hacer algo*, free to *o* at liberty to do sth. || *Estar en libertad*, to be free, to be at large. || *Libertad bajo fianza*, bail. || *Libertad bajo palabra*, parole. || *Libertad condicional*, probation. || *Libertad de comercio*, free trade. || *Libertad de conciencia, de cultos, de imprenta* or *de prensa, de palabra* or *de expresión*, freedom of conscience, of worship, of the press, of speech. || *Libertad de reunión*, freedom of assembly. || *Libertad individual*, freedom of the individual. || *Libertad provisional*, bail (bajo fianza), parole (bajo palabra). || *Libertad vigilada*, probation. || *Poner en libertad*, to set free, to release. || *Tener plena libertad de* or *para*, to be free to *o* at liberty to, to have complete liberty to. || *Tomarse la libertad de*, to take the liberty of (con gerundio). || *Una tarde de libertad*, a free afternoon, an afternoon off.

libertador, ra adj. Liberating.

— M. y f. Liberator. || *Amer. El Libertador*, Simón Bolívar.

libertar v. tr. To liberate, to free, to set free. || To exempt, to release (de una deuda, de una obligación). || To emancipate (de la esclavitud). || To save, to deliver (preservar).

libertario, ria adj./s. Libertarian.

libertinaje m. Libertinism, licentiousness.

libertino, na adj./s. Libertine, profligate. || — M. y f. Son or daughter of an emancipated slave (hijo de liberto).

liberto, ta adj. Emancipated.

— M. y f. Freedman (hombre), freedwoman (mujer).

Libia n. pr. f. GEOGR. Libya.

libídine f. Lewdness, libido.

libidinosidad f. Lasciviousness, lewdness, lustfulness.

libidinoso, sa adj. Libidinous, lewd, lustful.

libido f. Libido.

libio, bia adj./s. Libyan.

libra f. Pound (peso, moneda). || *Amer.* Leaf of top quality tobacco. || — FIG. y FAM. *De estos entran pocos en libra*, these are rare, there are few like these, these are few and far between. | *Es un amigo de los que entran pocos en libra*, he is an exceptionally good friend. || *Libra carnicera*, kilogramme. || *Libra esterlina*, pound sterling.

Libra n. pr. f. ASTR. Libra (signo del Zodiaco).

libraco m. FAM. Worthless book (libro).

librador, ra adj. Liberating (que libra).

— M. y f. Liberator, deliverer. || COM. Drawer. || — M. Scoop [used in a grocery shop] (cogedor).

libramiento m. Liberation (acción de libertar). || Deliverance (de un peligro). || Exemption (de un cargo, trabajo). || Order of payment (orden de pago).

librancista m. Bearer (de una letra de cambio).

librante m. Drawer (de una letra de cambio).

libranza f. Order of payment (orden de pago).

librar v. tr. To save, to rescue (de un peligro). || To free, to liberate, to deliver: *librar de la tiranía*, to free from tyranny. || To relieve: *librar a uno de una preocupación*, to relieve s.o. of a worry. || To exempt, to free, to release (de un cargo o trabajo). || To place, to put (la confianza). || To join in, to engage (una batalla, dos ejércitos). || To join, to give: *librar combate por*, to join battle for. || To wage (la guerra). || To draw (letras de cambio, cheques, etc.): *librar un cheque contra alguien*, to draw a cheque on s.o. || To pronounce, to pass (una sentencia). || To issue, to promulgate (un decreto). || — *¡Dios me libre!* or *¡líbreme Dios!*, Heaven forbid! || *Librar su esperanza en Dios*, to place one's hopes in God. || *Salir bien librado*, to come out unscathed *o* well, to get off lightly. || *Salir mal librado*, to come out the worse for wear, to suffer.

— V. intr. To go out to receive visitors (una monja). || To give birh, to be delivered of a child (una mujer). || FAM. To have one's day off (los obreros).

— V. pr. To avoid: *librarse de un golpe*, to avoid a blow. || To escape: *librarse de un peligro*, to escape [from] danger. || To get out (*de*, of) [una cosa molesta]. || To free o.s. (*de*, of) [una obligación, un perjuicio]. || To get rid of: *librarse de una persona molesta*, to get rid of a bothersome person. || — FAM. *Librarse de una buena*, v. BUENO. | *Librarse por los pelos*, to have a narrow escape, to escape by the skin of one's teeth, to have a close shave.

libre adj. Free: *es usted muy libre de ir*, you are completely free to go; *amor, sociedad libre*, free love, society. || Free (que no está preso). || Open: *el aire libre*, the open air. || FIG. Free, clear (sitio desembarazado). | Vacant (no ocupado). | Bold, forward (atrevido). | Familiar. | Outspoken (franco). | Loose, licentious (licencioso). | Independent (independiente). | Free, out: *libre de deudas*, free of debt. | Free, unattached (sin compromiso, suelto). || QUÍM. Free: *oxígeno libre*, free oxygen. || DEP. Freestyle: *los 100 metros libres*, the 100 metres freestyle. || — *Entrada libre*, admission free. || *Es libre en su lenguaje*, he is one for plain speaking. || *Estar libre de alguien*, to be rid of s.o. || *Estudiar por libre*, to be an external student. || *Libre albedrío*, free will. || *Libre bajo palabra*, on parole. || *Libre de*, free from: *libre de penas*, free from worries. || *Libre de cuidado*, out of danger. || *Libre de derechos de aduana*, duty-free, free of duty. || *Libre de impuestos*, tax-free, free of tax, free from tax. || FIG. *Más libre que un pájaro*, as free as a bird. || *Oyente libre*, auditor (en un curso). || *Tener entrada libre en casa de alguien*, to always have the door open to one. || *Traducción libre*, free translation. || *Zona de libre cambio* or *de libre comercio*, free trade area.

librea f. Livery (de un mayordomo). || Coat (de los venados).

librecambio m. Free trade.

librecambismo m. Free trade.

librecambista adj. Free-trade: *política librecambista*, free-trade policy.

— M. y f. Free trader.

librepensador, ra adj. Freethinking.

— M. y f. Freethinker.

librepensamiento m. Free thought.
librería f. Bookshop [U.S., bookstore] (tienda): *librería de ocasión* or *de lance*, secondhand bookshop. || Library (colección de libros). || Bookcase, bookshelf (mueble). || Book trade (industria).
librero, ra m. y f. Bookseller. || — M. *Amer*. Bookcase, bookshelf (mueble).
libresco, ca adj. Acquired from books, book. || *Conocimientos librescos*, book learning.
libreta f. Notebook (cuaderno). || Savings book (de caja de ahorros). || Memorandum, agenda (agenda). || One-pound loaf (pan).
libretista m. y f. Mús. Librettist.
libreto m. Mús. Libretto.
librillo m. Small book, booklet (libro). || Zool. Third stomach, omasum (de los rumiantes). || *Librillo de papel de fumar*, packet of cigarette papers.
libro m. Book (para leer): *libro de cabecera*, bedside book. || Register, record book (para recoger datos). || Notebook (cuaderno). || Book: *libro de señas* or *de direcciones*, address book. || Libretto (teatro). || Zool. Third stomach, omasum (de los rumiantes). || — Pl. Books (contabilidad). || — Fig. y fam. *Ahorcar los libros*, to burn one's books, to throw one's books away (dejar los estudios). || *Hablar como un libro*, to talk like a book. || *Libro amarillo, azul, blanco, rojo, etc.*, yellow, blue, white, red, etc. paper (en diplomacia). || *Libro antifonario*, antiphonal, antiphonary. || *Libro borrador*, daybook. || Com. *Libro copiador*, letter book. || Mar. *Libro de a bordo*, ship's log, ship's register, logbook. || *Libro de actas*, minute book. || *Libro de asiento* or *de contabilidad*, account book. || *Libro de bolsillo*, paperback [U.S., pocket book] (en rústica), pocket edition (edición de bolsillo). || *Libro de caballerías*, book of knight-errantry. || Com. *Libro de caja*, cashbook. || *Libro de cocina*, cookery book [U.S., cookbook]. || *Libro de consulta*, reference book. || *Libro de cuentos*, storybook. || *Libro de familia*, booklet delivered by the priest to a married couple for the registration of births and deaths in the family. || *Libro de horas*, Book of Hours. || Com. *Libro de inventario*, inventory [book]. || *Libro de lectura*, reader. || *Libro de mano*, manuscript. || *Libro de memoria*, memorandum *o* memo [book]. || *Libro de misa*, prayer book. || *Libro de música*, music book. || *Libro de reclamaciones*, complaints book. || *Libro de texto*, textbook. || Com. *Libro diario*, diary. || *Libro empastado* or *encuadernado*, bound book, hardback. || *Libro en rústica*, paperback. || *Libro escolar*, school report. || *Libro mayor*, ledger. || *Libros sagrados*, sacred books. || *Libro talonario*, counterfoil book [U.S., stub book]. || Com. *Llevar los libros*, to keep the accounts, to keep the books. || Fig. *Meterse en libros de caballerías*, to poke one's nose into s.o. else's business. || *Tenedor de libros*, bookkeeper. || *Teneduría de libros*, bookkeeping.
licántropo m. Med. Lycanthrope.
licencia f. Permission, leave, licence [U.S., license]: *con licencia de sus jefes*, with his bosses' permission. || Bachelor's degree: *licencia en derecho, en filosofía y letras*, bachelor's degree in law, in arts. || Permit, licence: *licencia de exportación*, export permit. || || Licence (libertad absoluta). || Licence, permit: *licencia de caza, de pesca*, hunting licence, fishing licence. || Licence (en poesía). || (Ant.). Mil. Leave (temporal). | Discharge (definitiva). || Leave: *licencia por enfermedad*, sick leave. || Mil. *Licencia absoluta*, discharge.
licenciable adj. Dischargeable (soldado).
licenciado, da adj. Graduated (estudiante). || Dismissed, discharged (despedido). || Mil. Discharged. || Priggish (presumido).
— M. y f. Graduate, Bachelor [of Arts, Science, etc.]. || — M. Lawyer (abogado). || Discharged soldier (soldado). || Fam. *Licenciado Vidriera*, timorous person.
licenciamiento m. Dismissal (de empleados). || Graduation (de estudiantes). || Mil. Discharge of soldiers.
licenciar v. tr. To dismiss (echar). || To confer a bachelor's degree upon (a un estudiante). || To licence [U.S., to license], to authorize, to give permission (dar permiso). || To discharge, to demobilize, to demob (un soldado).
— V. pr. To graduate: *licenciarse en derecho, en filosofía y letras*, to graduate in law, in arts. || To become dissolute *o* lewd (volverse licencioso).
licenciatura f. Bachelor's degree (título): *licenciatura de derecho, de ciencias, de filosofía y letras*, bachelor's degree in law, in science, in arts. || Degree [course] (estudios).
licencioso, sa adj. Licentious, dissolute.
liceo m. Literary society. || Grammar school, high school, secondary school (escuela). || Lyceum (en Atenas). || *El Liceo*, the Opera theatre in Barcelona.
— Observ. Grammar school and secondary school in Spanish are more frequently called *instituto* (de segunda enseñanza) except in America where *liceo* is commonly used.
licitación f. Bidding [at an auction] (acción de licitar). || Bid (cada oferta). || *Sacar a licitación*, to put up for auction (un objeto), to put out to tender, to invite tenders for (un trabajo).
licitador m. Bidder.
licitante adj. Bidding.
licitar v. tr. To bid for (pujar un objeto). || To tender for (un trabajo).
lícito, ta adj. Jur. Lawful, legal, licit. || Permissible, allowed.
licitud f. Jur. Lawfulness, legality, licitness.
licor m. Liquid. || Liqueur (alcohólico): *beber un licor después de cenar*, to drink a liqueur after dinner. || — Quím. *Licor de Fehling*, Fehling's solution. | *Licor de Schweitzer*, Schweitzer's reagent.
licorera f. Cocktail cabinet [U.S., liquor cabinet].
licoroso, sa adj. Aromatic (vino).
lictor m. Hist. Lictor.
licuable adj. Liquefiable.
licuación f. Liquefaction. || Tecn. Liquation.
licuador m. o **licuadora** f. *Amer*. Mixer.
licuante adj. Liquefying. || Tecn. Liquating.
licuar v. tr. To liquefy (volver líquido). || Tecn. To liquate.
licuefacción f. Liquefaction.
licuefacer v. tr. To liquefy (licuar).
licuefactible adj. Liquefiable (licuable).
licuefactivo, va adj. Liquefactive, liquefacient.
licuescente adj. Liquescent.
lid f. Combat, fight (pelea). || Fig. Dispute (disputa). || — Fig. *En buena lid*, by fair means. | *Un hombre avezado a estas lides*, an old hand, a man who knows how to handle these matters.
líder m. Leader (jefe de un partido).
— Observ. Pl. *líderes*.
liderato o **liderazgo** m. Leadership.
lidia f. Fight, battle. || Taur. Bullfight. || *Toros de lidia*, fighting bulls.
lidiador, ra m. y f. Fighter. || Fig. Arguer. || — M. Taur. Bullfighter.
lidiar v. tr. Taur. To fight [bulls]. || Fig. To deal with (saber convencer): *sabe lidiar a la gente*, he knows how to deal with people. || Fig. y fam. *Harto de lidiar*, for the sake of peace and quiet.
— V. intr. To fight, to combat. || Fig. To put up (*con*, with) [soportar]: *he tenido que lidiar con* or *contra él*, I have had to put up with him. | To contend (*con*, with) [contender].
liebre f. Hare (animal). || Fig. y fam. Coward, mouse, chicken (cobarde). || Astr. Hare (constelación). || — Fig. y fam. *Agarrar* or *coger una liebre*, to come a cropper. | *Correr como una liebre*, to run like a hare. | *Donde menos* or *cuando menos se piensa, salta la liebre*, things always happen when you least expect them to. | *Levantar la liebre*, to let the cat out of the bag, to spill the beans.
lied m. Mús. Lied.
— Observ. Pl. *lieder* en ambos idiomas.
liendre f. Nit (huevo de piojo). || — Fig. y fam. *Cascarle* or *machacarle a uno las liendres*, to beat s.o. up (aporrear), to give s.o. a telling off (reprender). | *Sacar a uno hasta las liendres*, to bleed s.o. white.
lienzo m. Fabric, material, cloth (tela en general). || Linen (por oposición a la lana, etc.). || Piece of cloth *o* of material (porción de tela). || Handkerchief (pañuelo). || Canvas (tela de un cuadro). || Painting, canvas (cuadro). || Arq. Facade, front [of a building]. | Stretch [of a wall] (de pared). || Curtain (fortificación).
liga f. Garter (de mujeres y hombres). || League (confederación). || Dep. League. || Alloy (aleación). || Mixture (mezcla). || Bot. Mistletoe (muérdago). || Birdlime (materia pegajosa). || — *Hacer buena, mala liga con uno*, to get on *o* along well, badly with s.o. || *Liga Hanseática*, Hanseatic League.
ligación f. Ligation, binding (acción). || Bond, tie (ligadura). || Mixture (mezcla). || Link (enlace).
ligado m. Ligature (de dos letras). || Mús. Ligature.
ligadura f. Ligature, tie, bond. || Soluble mixture (mezcla). || Fig. Bond, tie (vínculo). || Tourniquet (para dar garrote). || Ligature (de una arteria). || Mús. Ligature. || Mar. Lashing.
ligamen m. Undissolved marriage which prevents a second marriage.
ligamento m. Anat. Ligament. || Bond, tie (atadura). || Weave (textiles).
ligamentoso, sa adj. Ligamentous.
ligamiento m. Tying, attaching (acción de ligar o atar). || Fig. Harmony.
ligar v. tr. To tie, to bind, to fasten (atar). || To relate: *ligar una cosa con otra*, to relate one thing to another. || To alloy (los metales). || Fig. To join, to unite: *sólo el interés nos liga*, only interest unites us. | To tie, to bind: *estoy ligado por esta promesa*, I am bound by this promise. || To league (en una liga). || To mix (bebidas). || Med. To ligature (una arteria). || Mús. To slur [notes]. || Culin. To thicken (una salsa). || *Amer*. To pinch, to pilfer (sisar).
— V. intr. To combine cards of the same suit. || Fam. To get on *o* along well (entenderse). | To pick up, to get off with, to flirt with (galantear): *ligar con una chica*, to pick a girl up, to get off with a girl.
— V. pr. To bind o.s., to commit o.s.: *ligarse con* or *por una promesa*, to commit o.s. by a promise. || To unite, to combine (unirse).
ligazón f. Bond, tie, union (enlace). || Mar. Futtock.
ligeramente adv. Lightly (tocar, rozar, etc.). || Slightly (un poco).

ligereza f. Lightness (de peso). || Agility (agilidad). || Swiftness (rapidez). || Flippancy (falta de sensatez). || Inconstancy, fickleness (de carácter). || *Obrar con ligereza*, to act rashly *o* without thinking.

ligero, ra adj. Light: *sueño, metal ligero*, light sleep, metal; *comida ligera*, light meal. || Light, nimble: *paso ligero*, nimble step. || Swift (rápido). || Agile, nimble (ágil). || Weak (bebida). || FIG. Inconstant, fickle (inconstante). | Flippant (poco serio). | Unimportant, superficial (sin importancia). | Slight: *tiene unos conocimientos muy ligeros del chino*, he has a very slight knowledge of Chinese. || — *Ligero de manos*, light-fingered. || *Ligero de pies*, fleet-footed. || *Ligero de ropa*, lightly clad. || *Ligero de tono*, frivolous (conversación). || *Ligero en su conducta*, frivolous. || *Mujer ligera*, loose woman. || *Peso ligero*, lightweight (boxeo). || FIG. y FAM. *Ser ligero de cascos*, to be featherbrained, to be scatterbrained.

— Adv. Fast, rapidly, quickly (de prisa): *hazlo ligero*, do it fast. || — *A la ligera*, lightly, superficially: *tomar algo a la ligera*, to take sth. lightly; superficially: *hacer algo a la ligera*, to do sth. superficially. || *De ligero*, thoughtlessly, rashly (sin reflexión). || *Juzgar a la ligera*, to judge hastily.

ligio adj. m. Liege (feudo).

lignificación f. BOT. Lignification.

lignificarse v. pr. To lignify.

lignito m. Lignite (carbón).

lígnum crucis m. Holy relic [consisting of a piece of wood from the cross of Christ].

ligón, ona adj. Lucky [at cards]. || FAM. *Es una mujer muy ligona*, she is good at picking up men (que liga), she is a flirt (que le gusta ligar).

— M. FAM. Wolf, womanizer (con las mujeres).

liguero m. Suspender [U.S., garter].

— Adj. m. *Campeonato liguero*, league championship.

liguilla f. Narrow garter, narrow ribbon. || Championship in which only a few teams take part (deportes).

ligur adj./s. Ligurian.

ligures m. pl. HIST. Ligures.

Liguria n. pr. f. GEOGR. Liguria.

lija f. Dogfish (pez). || Sandpaper (papel esmerilado). || *Papel de lija*, sandpaper.

lijadora f. Sandpapering machine, sander (pulidor).

lijar v. tr. To sand, to sandpaper (pulir).

lila f. Lilac (arbusto y flor). || Wool (tela). || — M. Lilac (color). || FAM. Fool, simpleton (tonto).

— Adj. FAM. Foolish.

liliáceo, a adj. BOT. Liliaceous.

— F. pl. Liliaceae.

Liliput n. pr. Lilliput.

liliputiense adj./s. Lilliputian.

lima f. File (herramienta): *lima para uñas*, nail file. || Filing (pulido). || BOT. Lime (fruta). | Lime [tree] (árbol). || ARQ. Rafter (madero), hip (ángulo saliente). || FIG. Polish, polishing (enmienda). || — FIG. *Comer como una lima*, to eat like a horse. || ARQ. *Lima hoya*, valley. | *Lima tesa*, hip, arris. || *Lima sorda*, dead-smooth file.

Lima n. pr. GEOGR. Lima.

limado, da adj. Filed.

— M. Filing (acción de limar).

limador, ra adj. Filing.

— M. y f. Filer.

limadura f. Filing (acción de limar). || — Pl. Filings (trocitos de metal).

limalla f. Filings, *pl.*

limar v. tr. To file, to file down. || FIG. To polish (retocar). || FIG. *Limar asperezas*, V. ASPEREZA.

limaza f. Slug (babosa).

limazo m. Sliminess, slime.

limbo m. Limb (de hoja, de astro). || MAT. Limb. || Hem, edge (de vestidura). || Limbo (de las almas). || FIG. y FAM. *Estar uno en el limbo*, to be in the clouds, to be miles away (distraído).

limeño, ña adj. [Of *o* from] Lima.

— M. y f. Native *o* inhabitant of Lima.

limero, ra m. y f. Lime seller. || — M. Lime tree (árbol). || — F. MAR. Rudder hole.

liminal adj. Liminal.

liminar adj. Liminary, introductory. || *Advertencia liminar*, foreward.

limitación f. Limitation. || Limit (límite). || Restriction (restricción). || *Limitación de velocidad*, speed limit.

limitado, da adj. Limited. || Dull-witted (poco inteligente). || *Sociedad limitada*, private company.

limitador, ra adj. Limitative, restrictive (restrictivo).

limitar v. tr. To limit. || FIG. To limit, to cut down, to reduce: *hay que limitar sus prerrogativas*, his prerogatives must be limited.

— V. intr. *Limitar con*, to border on, to be bounded by.

— V. pr. To confine o.s., to limit o.s.: *limitarse a copiar*, to limit o.s. to copying.

limitativo, va adj. Limitative, restrictive.

límite m. Limit. || Ceiling (tope): *el límite presupuestario*, the budget ceiling. || — Pl. Boundaries, borders (fronteras). || — *Todo tiene sus límites*, everything has its limits. || *Velocidad límite*, speed limit.

limítrofe adj. Bordering, neighbouring: *Francia y países limítrofes*, France and its bordering countries.

limnología f. Limnology (estudio de lagos).

limo m. Mud, slime (légamo). || *Amer.* Lime tree (limero).

limón m. Lemon (fruto). || Lemon tree (árbol). || Shaft (de un coche). || ARQ. String (de una escalera). || — FIG. *Estrujar a uno como un limón*, to bleed s.o. white, to bleed s.o. dry. || *Limón natural* or *refresco de limón*, lemonade.

— Adj. inv. *Amarillo limón*, lemon, lemon-yellow.

limonada f. Lemonade (bebida). || FAM. *Ni chicha ni limonada*, neither fish nor fowl, neither one thing nor the other.

— OBSERV. En Inglaterra la palabra *lemonade* corresponde también a la *gaseosa* española.

limonado, da adj. Lemon, lemon-yellow.

limonar m. Lemon grove. || *Amer.* Lemon tree (árbol).

limoncillo m. *Amer.* Small lemon *o* lime.

limonera f. Shaft (de un coche).

limonero, ra adj. Shaft (caballo).

— M. y f. Lemon dealer. || Shaft horse. || — M. Lemon tree (árbol).

limonita f. Limonite, marsh ore (mineral).

limosidad f. Muddiness, sliminess. || Tartar (sarro).

limosna f. Alms, *pl.*: *dar limosna*, to give alms. || — *Pedir limosna*, to beg. || *Vivo de limosna*, I live on charity.

limosnear v. intr. To beg.

limosneo m. Begging.

limosnera f. Alms bag *o* box.

limosnero, ra adj. Charitable, almsgiving (p.us.). || *Amer.* Beggarly (pordiosero).

— M. Person who collects alms (recolector de limosna). || *Amer.* Beggar (mendigo).

limoso, sa adj. Muddy, slimy.

limpia f. Cleaning, cleansing (limpieza). || FIG. Clean-up (purga). || — M. FAM. Bootblack (limpiabotas).

limpiabarros m. inv. Boot scraper.

limpiabotas m. inv. Bootblack.

limpiacristales m. inv. Window cleaner.

limpiachimeneas m. inv. Chimney sweep (deshollinador).

limpiada f. o **limpiado** m. Clean, clean-out, clean-up (limpieza).

limpiador, ra adj. Cleaning, cleansing.

— M. y f. Cleaner (persona): *limpiador de cristales*, window cleaner.

limpiadura f. Cleaning, cleansing (acción de limpiar). || — Pl. Dirt, *sing.*, rubbish, *sing.*, refuse, *sing.* (basura).

limpiamente adv. Cleanly, neatly. || FIG. Skilfully, with ease (con destreza). | Sincerely (con sinceridad). | Honestly (honestamente). | Fairly (jugando limpio).

limpiaparabrisas m. inv. AUT. Windscreen wiper [U.S., windshield wiper].

limpiapipas m. inv. Pipe cleaner.

limpiar v. tr. To clean: *limpiar una habitación*, to clean a room; *limpiar un vestido*, to clean a dress. || To wipe, to wipe off: *limpiar el sudor de la frente*, to wipe the sweat from one's forehead. || To wipe (las narices). || To sweep (la chimenea). || To shine (los zapatos). || FIG. To take out (desembarazar). | To clear (la vía pública). | To prune (podar). | To cleanse: *limpiado de culpas*, cleansed of faults. || FIG. y FAM. To pinch, to nick (robar): *me limpiaron el reloj*, they pinched my watch. | To clean out (quitar todo el dinero). | To groom, to rub down (un caballo). || MIL. To mop up. || *Amer.* To whip (castigar). | To kill (matar). | To beat (azotar). || — *Limpiar el polvo*, to dust. || *Limpiar en seco*, to dry-clean.

— V. intr. To clean.

— V. pr. To clean o.s. || *Limpiarse las narices*, to wipe one's nose.

limpiaúñas m. inv. Nail cleaner.

limpidez f. Limpidity.

límpido, da adj. Limpid, crystal-clear.

limpieza f. Cleanness, cleanliness: *la limpieza de un cuarto*, the cleanness of a room. || Cleaning: *limpieza en seco*, dry cleaning. || Clearing (de la vía pública). || Cleaning: *hacer la limpieza*, to do the cleaning. || Shining (de zapatos). || FIG. Purity, chastity (pureza). | Honesty, integrity (honradez). | Fair play (juego limpio). | Skill (destreza). | Clean-up, clean-out (de maleantes, etc.). || — *Artículos de limpieza*, cleaning products. || *Ejecutar un trabajo con toda limpieza*, to do a good, clean job. || *Hacer la limpieza del comedor, de la habitación*, to clean up *o* to straighten up the dining room, the bedroom. || FIG. y FAM. *Hacer una limpieza general*, to have a good clean-out (tirar lo innecesario), to purge (hacer una purga). || MIL. *Hacer una operación de limpieza*, to mop up. || — FIG. *Limpieza de corazón*, integrity, honesty. || *Limpieza de sangre*, purity of blood. || MIL. *Operación de limpieza*, mopping-up operation.

limpio, pia adj. Clean: *platos limpios*, clean plates; *un niño muy limpio*, a very clean little boy. || Clean, tidy, neat (aseado). || Pure (sangre). || Clean (agua). || Pure (puro): *el alma limpia de los niños*, the pure souls of children. || REL. Clean (alimentos, personas). || Clear, net (sin cargas): *beneficio limpio*, clear profit. || Free, clear: *limpio de toda sospecha*, free of all suspicion. || Clear (foto). || DEP. Clean: *salto limpio*, clean jump. | Fair, clean (jugador). || FIG. y FAM. Clean, broke, penniless: *dejar limpio a uno*, to leave s.o. broke; *estar limpio*, to be clean. || — FIG. y FAM. *A puñetazo limpio*, with bare fists. | *Estaba limpio*

cuando fui al examen, I went to the exam completely unprepared *o* without knowing a single thing [U.S., I went to the exam cold]. || FIG. *Es un asunto poco limpio*, it is a dirty affair. || *Intenciones poco limpias*, dishonourable intentions. || FIG. *Limpio como una patena* or *como un espejo* or *como los chorros del oro*, as clean as a whistle *o* as a new pin. | *Limpio de polvo y paja*, clear, net (precio y sueldo). | *Llamar a grito limpio*, to call at the top of one's voice.
— Adv. Fairly: *jugar limpio*, to play fairly. || — *En limpio*, net, clear: *ganar un millón en limpio*, to win a million net. || *Pasar a limpio* or *poner en limpio*, to make a clean *o* a fair copy of (un escrito). || *Quedar en limpio que*, to be clear that. || *Sacar algo en limpio de*, to get sth. out of: *no he sacado nada en limpio*, I have not got anything out of it.

limusina f. Limousine (coche).

lináceo, a adj. BOT. Linaceous.
— F. pl. Linaceae.

linaje m. Lineage, line (alcurnia). || FIG. Kind, category, type, genre: *este libro y los de su linaje*, this book and those of its kind. || — Pl. Nobility, *sing.* || *El linaje humano*, the human race, mankind.

linajudo, da adj. Highborn.

linaza f. Linseed, flax seed (simiente). || *Aceite de linaza*, linseed oil.

lince m. Lynx (animal). || FIG. y FAM. Sharp-eyed person (persona muy perspicaz). || *Ojos de lince*, sharp eyes.

linchamiento m. Lynching.

linchar v. tr. To lynch.

lindamente adv. Prettily, neatly, elegantly. || FIG. y FAM. *Se quedó lindamente sin la cena*, he was simply left without dinner.

lindante adj. Bordering, adjoining, adjacent: *lindante con el jardín*, bordering on *o* adjacent to *o* adjoining the garden.

lindar v. intr. To border (*con*, on), to adjoin, to be adjacent (*con*, to) [estar contiguo]: *tu jardín linda con el mío*, your garden adjoins mine. || To border, to be bounded: *Francia linda con España*, France borders on Spain, France is bounded by Spain. || FIG. To border: *lindar en la locura*, to border on madness.

linde f. Boundary, limit. || Edge: *la linde del bosque*, the edge of the forest.

— OBSERV. According to the Spanish Academy, *linde* may be either masculine or feminine. It is usually now considered feminine.

lindera o **lindería** f. Boundary, limit.

lindero, ra adj. Bordering, adjoining, adjacent (lindante): *lindero con*, bordering on, adjoining, adjacent to.
— M. Edge (de un bosque). || Edge, border (de un campo o huerto).

lindeza f. Beauty (belleza). || Niceness, graciousness (amabilidad). || Witticism (dicho gracioso). || — Pl. FIG. y FAM. Insults, improprieties (insultos).

lindo, da adj. Pretty, lovely (hermoso): *linda casa*, pretty house. || Pretty, nice, charming (bonito). || Delicate (primoroso). || First-rate (de primera categoría). || FIG. Fine (irónico): *¡lindo amigo!*, a fine friend! || — FAM. *¡Lindas cosas me han dicho de ti!*, I've heard some fine *o* pretty tales about you! | *¡Sería demasiado lindo!*, that would be too good to be true!
— M. FIG. y FAM. Coxcomb, dandy [U.S., dude]. || *Lindo Don Diego*, fop, dandy.
— Adv. *Amer.* Prettily, nicely. || — *De lo lindo*, a lot, a great deal (mucho), perfectly, marvellously, wonderfully (muy bien). || *Lo pasamos de lo lindo*, we had a great *o* fantastic time.

— OBSERV. The adjective *lindo* is used more frequently in America than in Spain, where *bonito, mono, precioso, hermoso* are more common.

lindura f. Prettiness, loveliness, beauty (lindeza). || Pretty thing (cosa bonita). || *¡Qué lindura!*, how lovely!

línea f. Line: *línea recta, quebrada*, straight, broken line. || Line (renglón). || Class, order (clase). || Lineage, line, family (parentesco). || Line, cable (comunicaciones): *línea telegráfica, telefónica*, telegraph, telephone line; *línea de alta tensión*, high-tension cable. || Line (de conducta, de un partido). || MAR. Line (ruta). || MIL. Line: *línea de fuego*, firing line. | Line: *línea Maginot*, Maginot Line. || Line (para pescar). || Figure (esbeltez). || Line (de coche, etc.). || — Pl. Lines (de la mano).
— *Cruzar la línea* to cross the line, to cross the equator. || *En líneas generales*, in broad outline (sin detalle), approximately, roughly (aproximadamente). || *En toda la línea*, all along the line. || *Final de línea*, terminus. || *Guardar la línea*, to keep *o* to watch one's figure. || DEP. *Juez de línea*, linesman. || FIG. *Leer entre líneas*, to read between the lines. || AVIAC. *Línea aérea*, airline. || *Línea de abastecimiento*, supply line. || MAR. *Línea de agua*, waterline. || DEP. *Línea de banda*, touchline, sideline. || *Línea de batalla*, battle line. || *Línea de carga*, load line. || *Línea de conducta*, line of behaviour (comportamiento), policy (norma). || *Línea de demarcación*, line of demarcation, demarcation line. || TECN. *Línea de exploración*, scanning line. || *Línea de flotación*, waterline. || DEP. *Línea de fondo*, base line (en tenis). | *Línea de gol, de puerta*, goal line (fútbol). | *Línea delantera* or *de ataque*, forward line (fútbol). || *Línea de la vida*, life line. || MAR. *Línea del viento*, wind's line, direction of the wind. | *Línea de máxima carga*, Plimsoll line, deep load line. || *Línea de mira*, line of sight. || *Línea de montaje*, assembly line. || ASTR. *Línea de nodos*, line of nodes. || *Línea derivada*, extension (teléfonos). || DEP. *Línea de saque*, service line (tenis). || *Línea divisoria*, dividing line. || *Línea divisoria de las aguas* or *de cresta*, watershed [U.S., divide], crest line. || *Línea férrea*, railway line. || ASTR. *Línea meridiana*, meridional line. || *Línea punteada* or *de puntos*, dotted line. || *Línea saliente*, arris. || FIG. *Poner unas líneas a uno*, to drop s.o. a line. || MIL. *Primera línea*, front line.

lineal adj. Lineal, linear. || *Dibujo lineal*, v. DIBUJO.

lineamento o **lineamiento** m. Lineament.

linear v. tr. To draw lines on. || To sketch, to outline (bosquejar).

linfa f. ANAT. Lymph.

linfangitis f. MED. Lymphangitis.

linfático, ca adj. Lymphatic.

linfatismo m. MED. Lymphatism.

linfocito m. ANAT. Lymphocyte (leucocito).

linfocitosis f. MED. Lymphocytosis.

linfoide adj. Lymphoid.

lingote m. Ingot (barra de metal). || Pig (fundición). || IMPR. Slug. || — *Lingote de primera fusión* or *de arrabio*, pig iron. || *Lingotes de oro*, gold bullion, *sing.*, gold bars.

lingotera f. Ingot mould (molde).

lingual adj./s.f. Lingual.

lingüiforme adj. Linguiform.

lingüista m. y f. Linguist.

lingüístico, ca adj. Linguistic.
— F. Linguistics.

linimento m. Liniment.

lino m. Flax (planta y textil). || Linen (tela). || FIG. Canvas (de barco). || *Amer.* Linseed, flax seed (linaza).

linóleo o **linóleum** m. Linoleum, lino.

linotipia f. IMPR. Linotype.

linotipista m. y f. Linotypist, linotyper.

lintel m. ARQ. Lintel (dintel).

linterna f. Lantern: *linterna mágica, sorda*, magic, dark lantern. || Torch (de bolsillo). || ARQ. Lantern (torrecilla). || TECN. Lantern pinion (piñón).

linternón m. Large lantern. || MAR. Poop lantern.

lío m. Bundle, parcel (paquete). || FIG. y FAM. Muddle, mess (embrollo). | Problem: *Pedro tiene líos con su familia*, Peter has problems with his family. | Trouble: *andar siempre metido en líos*, to be always getting into trouble. | Trouble, jam: *meterse en un lío*, to get into a jam, to get into trouble. | Mess, clutter (desorden). | Headache: *este problema es un lío*, this problem is a headache. | Jumble, hodgepodge (mezcla). | Tale (chisme): *no me vengas con líos*, don't come telling tales to me. | Affair (amancebamiento). || — FIG. y FAM. *Armar un lío*, to make a fuss, to kick up a rumpus (dar un escándalo), to cause confusion (confundir). | *Estar hecho un lío*, to be completely mixed up. | *Formar un lío*, to cause a scandal. | *Hacerse un lío*, to get into a muddle *o* a mess.

liofilizar v. tr. To lyophilize.

Liorna n. pr. GEOGR. Leghorn.

lioso, sa adj. FAM. Troublemaking, scheming (persona). | Tangled, involved (cosa).
— M. y f. Troublemaker. || *Lo lioso*, the hard part, the difficult part, the troublesome part.

lipasa f. Lipase.

lipemanía f. MED. Melancholia.

lípido m. QUÍM. Lipid, lipide (grasa).

lipoide m. Lipoid.

lipoideo, a adj. Lipoid.

lipoma m. MED. Lipoma.

liquefacción f. Liquefaction.

— OBSERV. Es barbarismo por *licuefacción*.

liquelique o **liquilique** m. *Amer.* Blouse.

liquen m. BOT. Lichen.

liquidable adj. Liquefiable (que se puede licuar). || Liquidatable (que puede ser liquidado).

liquidación f. COM. Liquidation. | Clearance sale (en una tienda). | Settlement (de una cuenta). || Liquefaction (acción de licuefacer). || FIG. Liquidation (eliminación). || — JUR. *Liquidación judicial*, liquidation by decision of Court. || *Vender en liquidación*, to sell up.

liquidado, da adj. COM. Liquidated. || Liquefied (licuado).

liquidador, ra adj. COM. Liquidating.
— M. y f. Liquidator.

liquidámbar m. Liquidambar (bálsamo).

liquidar v. tr. To liquefy (convertir en líquido). || COM. To liquidate, to wind up (un negocio). || To sell up, to sell off, to clear: *hay que liquidar todas las mercancías*, all the stock must be sold up. || To settle, to pay off, to clear, to discharge (pagar). || To settle (una cuenta). || To resolve, to clear up, to end (poner fin): *liquidar una situación difícil*, to resolve a difficult situation. || FIG. To liquidate (eliminar). || FAM. To murder, to kill off (matar).

liquidez f. Liquidity.

líquido, da adj./s.m. Liquid: *medidas para líquidos*, liquid measures. || GRAM. Liquid. || COM. Net. || — *Dinero líquido*, ready money, cash. || *El líquido elemento*, [the] water. || *Líquido imponible*, taxable income.
lira f. MÚS. Lyre. || Lira (moneda italiana). || Stanza of five or six lines each of seven or eleven syllables (en poesía). || Lyrebird (ave).
Lira n. pr. ASTR. Lyra.
lírica f. Lyric *o* lyrical poetry.
lírico, ca adj. Lyric, lyrical. || *Amer.* Fantastic, utopian (proyecto). | Dreamy (persona).
— M. Lyric poet, lyrist. || *Amer.* Visionary, utopian.
lirio m. BOT. Iris. || — BOT. *Lirio blanco*, white lily (azucena). | *Lirio cárdeno*, purple iris. | *Lirio de agua*, calla lily. | *Lirio de los valles*, lily of the valley.
lirismo m. Lyricism. || FIG. Effusiveness.
lirón m. ZOOL. Dormouse. || BOT. Water plantain. || FIG. y FAM. Sleepyhead (dormilón). || — FIG. y FAM. *Dormir como un lirón*, to sleep like a log *o* soundly. || *Lirón gris*, garden dormouse.
lirondo, da adj. *Mondo y lirondo*, v. MONDO.
lis f. BOT. Lily. | Iris. || HERÁLD. Fleur-de-lis.
lisa f. ZOOL. Spiny loach (pez). | Grey mullet, striped mullet (mújol).
lisamente adv. Frankly, plainly. || *Lisa y llanamente*, purely and simply (simplemente).
Lisboa n. pr. GEOGR. Lisbon.
lisboeta o **lisbonense** o **lisbonés, esa** adj. [Of *o* from] Lisbon.
— M. y f. Native *o* inhabitant of Lisbon.
lisiado, da adj. Disabled, maimed, crippled (tullido). || Injured (herido). || FAM. Dead tired (cansado).
— M. y f. Disabled *o* maimed person, cripple.
lisiadura f. Injury.
lisiar v. tr. To disable, to cripple, to maim (tullir). || To injure (herir).
lisible adj. Legible.
Lisístrata n. pr. f. Lysistrata.
liso, sa adj. Flat (llano): *carrera de cien metros lisos*, one hundred-metre flat race. || Flat (pecho). || Smooth, even (sin asperezas). || Plain (tela): *camisa lisa*, plain shirt. || Straight (pelo). || Calm (el mar). || *Amer.* Shameless, brazen. || *Pana lisa*, velvet.
— M. MIN. Smooth face [of a rock].
lisonja f. Flattery, piece of flattery (alabanza). || HERÁLD. Lozenge (losange). || — Pl. Flattery, *sing.*
lisonjeador, ra adj. Flattering. || Pleasing (agradable).
— M. y f. Flatterer.
lisonjeante adj. Flattering.
lisonjear v. tr. To flatter (adular). || To delight, to please (deleitar).
lisonjero, ra adj. Flattering. || Gratifying: *un resultado lisonjero*, a gratifying result. || Pleasing, agreeable (agradable).
— M. y f. Flatterer.
lista f. Stripe, band (raya). || Bill of fare, menu (restaurante). || List (enumeración): *borrar de la lista*, to strike off *o* to take off the list. || Catalogue (catálogo). || Roll (recuento): *pasar lista*, to call the roll. || Register, roll (en un colegio). || — *Lista de bajas*, casualty list. || *Lista de correos*, poste restante [U.S., general delivery]. || *Lista de espera*, waiting list. || *Lista de precios*, price list. || *Lista de premios*, prize list, honours list (en el colegio). || *Lista electoral*, register [of voters]. || *Lista negra*, blacklist. || *Pasar lista a los alumnos*, to take *o* to call the register.
listado, da adj. Striped.
listar v. tr. To list (alistar). || To stripe (una tela).
listear v. tr. To stripe.
listel m. ARQ. Fillet, listel (moldura).
listero m. Roll taker. || Timekeeper (en una fábrica).
listeza f. Cleverness (inteligencia). || Alertness, quickness (de entendimiento). || Shrewdness, cunningness (astucia).
listín m. Short list. || Telephone directory *o* book. || *Amer.* Newspaper.
listo, ta adj. Clever (inteligente). || Alert, quick-witted (agudo). || Shrewd, cunning (astuto). || Ready, prepared (preparado): *estoy listo*, I'm ready; *¿listo?*, ready? || — FIG. y FAM. *Echárselas* or *dárselas de listo*, to try to be clever. | *¡Estamos listos!*, we're in a fine fix! | *Listo como una ardilla*, as cunning as a fox. | *Pasarse de listo*, to be too clever by half.
listón m. Lath, strip (carpintería). || Ribbon (cinta). || Listel, fillet (moldura). || DEP. Bar (para saltar).
— Adj. m. With a white stripe down its back [bull].
listonado m. Lathing, lathwork.
listonar v. tr. To lath.
lisura f. Smoothness (ausencia de asperezas). || Evenness (ausencia de elevaciones). || Plane surface (superficie plana). || Straightness (del pelo). || FIG. Frankness, sincerity (sinceridad).
lite f. JUR. Lawsuit (pleito).
litera f. Litter (vehículo). || Berth, bunk (en barco, en tren). || Bunk bed, bunk (en un cuarto).
literal adj. Literal: *traducción literal*, literal translation.
— *Amer.* Paragraph.
literalmente adv. Literally, to the letter. || *Traducir literalmente*, to translate literally *o* word for word.
literario, ria adj. Literary. || *La República literaria*, the republic of letters.
literato, ta adj. Lettered.
— M. Writer, man of letters. || — F. Woman of letters.
literatura f. Literature: *la literatura española*, Spanish literature. || FIG. Culture (instrucción general).
lítico, ca adj. Lithic.
litigación f. Litigation, lawsuit (pleito). || Pleading (alegato).
litigante adj./s. Litigant: *las partes litigantes*, the litigant parties.
litigar o **litigiar** v. intr. JUR. To litigate. || To contend, to dispute. || *Litigar por pobre*, to file an appeal in forma pauperis.
litigio m. Lawsuit, litigation (pleito). || Dispute (contienda). || *En litigio*, in dispute, at stake.
litigioso, sa adj. Litigious.
litio m. Lithium (metal).
litisconsorte m. y f. JUR. Associate in a lawsuit, joint litigant (cointeresado).
litisexpensas f. pl. JUR. Costs [of a lawsuit].
litispendencia f. JUR. Pendency [of a case].
litocromía f. Lithochromy.
litófago, ga adj. ZOOL. Lithophagous.
litófito m. BOT. Lithophyte.
litografía f. Lithography (arte). || Lithograph (reproducción).
litografiar v. tr. To lithograph.
litográfico, ca adj. Lithographic.
litógrafo m. Lithographer.
litoral adj. Littoral, coastal, seaboard.
— M. Littoral, coast, seaboard.
litosfera f. GEOL. Lithosphere.
lítote f. Litotes (atenuación).
litotipografía f. Lithotypography.
litri adj. FAM. Dandified.
litro m. Litre [U.S., liter] (medida).
Lituania n. pr. f. GEOGR. Lithuania.
lituano, na adj./s. Lithuanian.
liturgia f. Liturgy.
litúrgico, ca adj. Liturgical.
livianamente adv. Lightly (sin fundamento). || FIG. Superficially. || Licentiously, lewdly (lascivamente).
liviandad f. Lightness. || Frivolity, triviality. || Lewdness (lascivia).
liviano, na adj. Light (ligero). || Slight (pequeño, sin importancia). || FIG. Inconstant, fickle (superficial, inconstante). | Frivolous, trivial (frívolo). | Loose: *una mujer liviana*, a loose woman.
— M. Lights, *pl.* (bofe, pulmón). || Leading donkey. || — F. Popular Andalusian song.
lividecer v. intr. To become livid.
lividez f. Lividity, lividness.
lívido, da adj. Livid.
living m. Living room.
lixiviar v. tr. To lixiviate, to leach.
liza f. Lists (campo para la lid): *entrar en liza*, to enter the lists. || Contest (lid). || Mullet (pez).
lizo m. Heddle, heddle (de un telar): *lizo bajo*, low heddle. || Warp (de un tejido).
lo pron. pers. neutro. It: *yo lo creo*, I believe it; *no lo es tampoco*, that isn't it either.
— Pron. pers. m. Him: *lo miro*, I look at him. (V. OBSERV).
— Art. def. neutro. *Followed by a qualifying adjective.* The... part, the... thing: *lo mejor*, the best part; *lo triste del caso*, the sad thing about it; the: *lo contrario*, the opposite; what is: *lo útil y lo agradable*, what is useful and agreeable; what: *según lo previsto por la ley*, according to what has been provided in the law. || *Followed by a possessive pronoun.* Mine, yours, his, etc. (lo que pertenece): *esto es lo tuyo*, this is yours; what is mine, yours, etc.: *lo mío es tuyo*, what is mine is yours; what concerns (lo que se refiere): *sólo me ocupo de lo mío*, I only look after what concerns me.
— *A lo*, like: *a lo loco*, like a fool; style: *vestir a lo español*, to dress Spanish style. || *A lo sumo*, at [the] most. || *De lo más*, most: *traje de lo más elegante que hay*, a most elegant suit. || *De lo mejor que hay*, the best there is. || *De lo que*, what: *de lo que se trata aquí es...*, what one is dealing with here is... || *En lo* or *por lo* (followed by an agreeing adjective), because of: *por lo arrugada parecía muy vieja*, because of her wrinkles she seemed very old; *por lo cerrado de su acento me pareció andaluz*, because of his marked accent, I took him to be Andalusian. || *En lo alto*, in *o* at the highest part. || *En lo alto de la casa, de la montaña*, at the top of the house, of the mountain. || *Hacer todo lo posible*, v. POSIBLE. || *Lo caro no siempre es bueno*, expensive things are not always good, what is expensive is not necessarily good. || *Lo cual*, which (sujeto): *lo cual quiere decir*, which means; which (complemento): *lo cual dijo sin intención*, which he said unintentionally. || *Lo de* (con sustantivo), the affair *o* business of, the affair *o* business about: *lo del testamento fue muy desagradable*, the business about the will was very unpleasant; *después de lo de la quiebra, desapareció*, after the affair of the bankruptcy *o* the bankruptcy affair he disappeared; what about?, how about? (en pregunta): *¿y lo de tu viaje a Francia?*, and what about your trip to France? || *Lo de* (con infinitivo), idea, project, business: *lo de vender la casa resulta difícil*, the project of selling the house has created problems; *lo de irse de viaje no le gusta nada*, he doesn't like the idea of going away on a trip. || *Lo más... posible*, as... as possible. || *Lo mismo*, the same [thing].

|| *Lo mucho que*, how much (cuanto), the amount (la cantidad). || *Lo que*, what (sujeto, complemento): *lo que ha de pasar*, what is going to happen; *lo que pienso*, what I think; *si tuviera lo que usted*, if I had what you have; how much (cuanto): *sabes lo que te aprecio*, you know how much I think of you; the same as, like (lo mismo): *hago lo que todos*, I do the same as everyone else, I do like everyone does. || *Lo... que*, how: *no sabes lo cansada que estoy*, you don't know how tired I am. || *¡Lo que cuesta aprender un idioma!*, isn't it difficult to learn a language! || *Lo que sea*, anything [at all] (cualquier cosa), nothing, not... anything (nada). || *Lo sumo*, the most. || *Más... de lo que*, more... than: *es más inteligente de lo que pensaba*, he is more intelligent than I thought. || *Todo lo... que*, as... as: *no ha sido todo lo agradable que hubiera querido*, it hasn't been as pleasant as I would have liked. || *Todo lo que*, everything which *o* that (sujeto), everything (complemento).

— OBSERV. In South America the tendency to use *lo* as the personal pronoun for the 3rd person singular in the accusative case is far more widespread than in Spain, where the pronoun *le* is often used.

loa f. Praise: *cantar loa a* or *hacer loa de*, to sing the praises of. || TEATR. Prologue (prólogo). | Short play presented at the beginning of a performance. || Elegy, eulogy, poem in honour of s.o. (poema).
loable adj. Laudable, praiseworthy.
loar v. tr. To praise (alabar).
lob m. Lob (en tenis).
loba f. She-wolf.
lobagante m. Lobster (bogavante).
lobanillo m. Cyst, wen (tumor). || BOT. Gall.
lobato m. Wolf cub (cachorro del lobo).
lobectomía f. MED. Lobectomy.
lobera f. Wolf's lair (guarida del lobo).
lobero, ra adj. Wolf, wolfish.
— M. Wolf hunter.
lobezno m. Wolf cub (cachorro del lobo).
lobo m. Wolf (animal). || Loach (pez). || Lobe (lóbulo). || Iron instrument for scaling walls. || FIG. y FAM. Drunkenness (borrachera). || FAM. Thief (ladrón). || *Amer.* Fox (zorro), coyote. || — *Caza de lobos*, wolf hunt. || *Cazador de lobos*, wolf hunter. || *El lobo feroz*, the big bad wolf. || FIG. *Está como boca de lobo*, it's pitch-dark. || *Ir a paso de lobo*, to creep along. || *Amer. Lobo acuático*, otter. || *Lobo cerval*, kind of lynx (lince), shark, profiteer (estafador). || FIG. y FAM. *Lobo de mar*, old salt, sea dog. || *Lobo marino*, seal (foca), sea dog (marino experimentado). || FIG. y FAM. *Meter el lobo en el redil*, to let the cat among the pigeons. | *Meterse en la boca del lobo*, v. BOCA. | *Ser un lobo con piel de oveja*, to be a wolf in sheep's clothing. | *Son lobos de la misma camada*, they're tarred with the same brush, they are birds of a feather. | *Un lobo a otro no se muerden*, there is honour among thieves.
Lobo pr. n. ASTR. Wolf.
lobo, ba adj./s. *Amer.* Half-breed (mestizo).
lobotomía f. MED. Lobotomy.
lóbrego, ga adj. Gloomy, dark, murky. || FIG. Gloomy, sad.
lobreguecer* v. tr. To darken, to make dark.
— V. intr. To grow dark (anochecer).
lobreguez f. Gloom, gloominess, darkness, murkiness. || FIG. Gloom, gloominess.
lobulado, da o **lobular** adj. BOT. y ZOOL. Lobulate, lobed, lobular.
lóbulo m. Lobe.
lobuno, na adj. Wolfish, wolf.
locación f. JUR. Lease.
local adj. Local: *color local*, local colour; *costumbres locales*, local customs.
— M. Premises, *pl.* (edificios). || Headquarters, *pl.* (domicilio social): *el local de la Cámara de Comercio*, the headquarters of the Chamber of Commerce. || Site, place (lugar, sitio).
localidad f. Locality (pueblo). || Place (lugar). || Seat, ticket (de un espectáculo): *reservar una localidad*, to book a seat; *sacar una localidad*, to get a ticket. || — *No hay más localidades*, sold out, house full (teatro). || *Reserva de localidades*, booking, advanced booking. || *Venta de localidades*, sale of tickets (acción de vender billetes), box office (taquilla).
localismo m. Regionalism, localism (exclusivismo). || Localism, provincialism (palabra, expresión).
localista adj. Regional, local, of local interest: *problemas localistas*, regional problems. || Parochial: *asuntos localistas*, parochial affairs. || Limited, restricted (visión).
localizable adj. Localizable.
localización f. Localization. || Location (sitio). || Location (encuentro). || Placing, siting (situación).
localizar v. tr. To find, to locate: *localizar un libro*, to locate a book. || To situate (situar). || To locate: *localizar un avión*, to locate an aeroplane. || To track down, to find: *no pude localizarte en todo el día*, I couldn't track you down all day. || To localize: *localizar una epidemia, un fuego*, to localize an epidemic, a fire.
locatis m. y f. FAM. Madcap, nutcase.
locativo, va adj. Renting, letting, leasing. || GRAM. Locative.
— M. GRAM. Locative.
locería f. Crockery, china (cacharrería).
loción f. Lotion, wash. || — *Loción capilar*, hair lotion. || *Loción facial*, face lotion.
lockout m. Lockout (cierre patronal).
loco, ca adj. Insane, mad (alienado). || FAM. Mad, crazy: *empresa loca*, crazy venture; *amor loco*, mad love. | Tremendous, fantastic (tremendo). | Huge, enormous (enorme). || Ridiculous (excesivo, extraordinario): *precio loco*, ridiculous price. || Wild: *avena loca*, wild oats. || TECN. Loose (polea, etc.). | Mad (brújula). || — FIG. y FAM. *A locas* or *a tontas y a locas*, without rhyme or reason. | *A lo loco*, wildly: *estaban bailando a lo loco*, they were dancing wildly; without thinking, lightly; *decisión tomada a lo loco*, decision taken lightly; helter-skelter, any old how: *hacer un trabajo a lo loco*, to do a job helter-skelter. | *Anda loco con su trabajo*, his job is driving him crazy. | *Andar* or *estar como loco*, to act crazily. | *Como loco*, like mad (correr, etc.). | *Es para volverse loco*, it is enough to drive you mad. | *Estar loco de* or *por* or *con*, to be crazy *o* mad *o* wild about: *está loca por él*, she is crazy about him; to be mad keen: *estar loco por hacer una cosa*, to be mad keen on doing sth. | *Estar loco de alegría*, to be overjoyed *o* beside o.s. with joy, to be thrilled to bits. | *Estar loco de contento*, to be blissfully happy. | *Loco de atar* or *de remate* or *rematado* or *como una cabra*, as mad as a March hare *o* as a hatter, as mad as they come. || *Loco perdido* or *furioso*, raving mad, stark mad. || *Risa loca*, hysterical laughter. || FIG. *Tener una suerte loca*, to be ever so lucky. | *Traer* or *volver* or *tener loco a uno*, to drive s.o. crazy *o* mad. || *Volverse loco* or *estar loco*, to go crazy *o* mad, to be crazy *o* mad.
— M. y f. Madman (hombre), madwoman (mujer). || Lunatic (enfermo mental). || — FIG. *Cada loco con su tema*, everyone has his hobbyhorse. || *Casa de locos*, madhouse. || FIG. *Correr como un loco*, to run like mad. | *Gritar como un loco*, to shout like mad *o* like a madman. | *Hacer el loco*, to act the fool. | *Hacerse el loco*, to play dumb. || FIG. y FAM. *La loca de la casa*, the imagination.
locomoción f. Locomotion.
locomotiva f. *Amer.* Locomotive, engine.

— OBSERV. Es galicismo por *locomotora.*

locomotor, ra adj. Locomotive, locomotor.
— F. Locomotive, engine (de un tren).
locomotriz adj. f. Locomotor: *ataxia locomotriz*, locomotor ataxy.
locomovible o **locomóvil** adj. Locomobile.
locro m. *Amer.* Maize and meat stew.
locuacidad f. Loquacity, talkativeness.
locuaz adj. Loquacious, talkative.
locución f. Phrase, turn of phrase, locution, expression. || GRAM. Phrase: *locución adverbial, prepositiva*, adverbial, prepositional phrase.
locuelo, la adj. FAM. Madcap, daft.
— M. y f. FAM. Madcap.
locura f. Madness, insanity, lunacy. || Act of madness *o* folly, mad *o* crazy thing (acción). || Mad passion (cariño, afecto), wild enthusiasm (entusiasmo). || — *Acceso* or *ataque de locura*, fit of madness. || *Con locura*, madly. || *Fue una locura hacer esto*, it was madness *o* folly to do this. || FIG. *Gastar una locura*, to spend a fortune. || *Hacer* or *cometer locuras*, to do foolish things. || *La quiere con locura*, he is crazy about her. || *¡Qué locura!*, it's madness!
locutor, ra m. y f. Announcer (que presenta). || Commentator (que comenta).
locutorio m. Locutory, parlour, visiting room (de un convento), visiting room (de una cárcel). || Telephone box *o* booth (de teléfono).
locha f. Loach (pez).
lodachar o **lodazal** o **lodazar** m. Mire, quagmire, muddy place.
loden m. Loden (tejido).
lodo m. Mud (fango): *baños de lodo*, mud baths. || MIN. Sludge. || — FIG. *Arrastrar por el lodo*, to drag through the mud. || *Poner de lodo a uno*, to fling *o* to sling *o* to throw mud at s.o.
lodoso, sa adj. Muddy (cenagoso).
loess m. GEOL. Loess, löss.
logarítmico, ca adj. Logarithmic.
logaritmo m. MAT. Logarithm. || *Tabla de logaritmos*, logarithm table.
loggia f. ARQ. Loggia (galería).
logia f. Lodge (de masones).
logicial m. Software (en informática).
lógico, ca adj. Logical. || — *Como es lógico*, naturally, of course. || *Ser lógico*, to be logical, to stand to reason.
— M. y f. Logician. || — F. Logic.
logístico, ca adj. Logistic.
— F. MIL. Logistics. || — M. MIL. Logistician.
logógrafo m. Logographer.
logogrifo m. Logogriph (enigma).
logomaquia f. Logomachy.
logos m. FIL. Logos.
logrado, da adj. Successful.
lograr v. tr. To get, to obtain (obtener). || To win, to achieve, to gain (victoria). || To achieve (éxito). || To win, to gain (premio). || To succeed in, to manage to: *logró escaparse*, he succeeded in escaping, he managed to escape. || To realize, to realise, to achieve (ambiciones). || To satisfy, to fulfil (deseos). || *Eso*

lo puedes dar por logrado, you can take that for granted, you can bank on that.
— V. pr. To succeed, to be successful, to turn out well *o* successfully: *el plan de desarrollo se ha logrado*, the development plan has been successful.
logrería f. Usury. || Profiteering.
logrero, ra m. y f. Usurer, moneylender. || Profiteer (aprovechón).
logro m. Winning, achievement (de victoria). || Achievement, attainment (de éxito). || Winning (de un premio). || Success (éxito): *su mayor logro*, his greatest success. || Achievement, accomplishment: *los logros técnicos del siglo XX*, the technical achievements of the 20th century. || Realization (de unas ambiciones). || Satisfaction, fulfilment (de deseos). || Gain, profit (lucro). || Usury (usura). || *Prestar* or *dar a logro*, to lend at a high interest rate.
loísmo m. GRAM. Exclusive use of *lo* instead of *le* in the dative of the personal pronoun *él: lo doy*, instead of *le doy*, I give [to] him. || Exclusive use of *lo* instead of *le* in the accusative: *lo miro*, and not *le miro*, I look at him.
loísta adj. GRAM. Who uses *lo* instead of *le* in the accusative and dative of the masculine pronoun *él*.
— M. y f. Person who uses *lo* and not *le* (V. LOÍSMO).
loma f. Hillock, hill, rise.
lombarda f. Red cabbage (col). || Lombard (cañón).
Lombardía n. pr. f. GEOGR. Lombardy.
lombriguera f. Earthworm *o* worm hole.
lombriz f. Earthworm, worm. || Worm: *lombriz intestinal*, intestinal worm. || *Lombriz solitaria*, tapeworm.
lomera f. Backband (de la guarnición del caballo). || Back, backband (de un libro). || Ridge (caballete de un tejado).
lomo m. Back (de un animal, de un cuchillo). || Spine, back (de un libro). || Fold, crease (doblez). || ANAT. Loin (del hombre). || Chine (carne de cerdo). || Loin (de una colina). || AGR. Ridge [between furrows] (caballón). || — Pl. Ribs (costillas). || — *A lomo de*, on the back of [a mule, donkey, etc.]. || *Arquear el lomo*, to arch its back (el gato). || FIG. *De tomo y lomo*, v. TOMO. || FIG. y FAM. *Pasar la mano por el lomo* or *sobar el lomo*, to soft-soap, to butter up. | *Sacudir el lomo a alguien*, to give s.o. a hiding, to tan s.o.'s hide.
lona f. MAR. Sailcloth (tela). | Sail (vela). || Canvas: *zapatos de lona*, canvas shoes. || Canvas cover, canvas (para cubrir). || Big top (de circo). || — *Ciudad de lona*, canvas town. || *Hacer besar la lona a alguien*, to floor s.o. (boxeo), to bring s.o. down (humillar).
loncha f. Slice: *una loncha de jamón*, a slice of ham. || Slab (de piedra).
londinense adj. Of *o* from London, London.
— M. y f. Londoner (persona).
Londres n. pr. GEOGR. London.
longanimidad f. Forbearance, magnanimity, longanimity.
longánimo, ma adj. Forbearing, magnanimous.
longaniza f. Sausage. || — FIG. y FAM. *Allí no atan los perros con longanizas*, money does not grow on trees there. | *Hay más días que longanizas*, v. DÍA.
longevidad f. Longevity.
longevo, va adj. Long-lived, longevous.
longitud f. Length: *su longitud es de seis metros*, its length is six metres. || ASTR. y GEOGR. Longitude. || — *Longitud de onda*, wavelength. || DEP. *Salto de longitud*, long jump. || *Tener seis metros de longitud*, to be six metres long. || *35° longitud Oeste*, 35° West.
longitudinal adj. Longitudinal.
longui adj./s. FAM. *Hacerse el longui*, to act dumb.
lonja f. Slice: *una lonja de jamón*, a slice of ham. || Rasher, slice (de tocino). || Commodity Exchange (bolsa de comercio). || Wool warehouse (almacén). || Grocer's shop (tienda). || ARQ. Porch, vestibule [of a church]. || Leather strap (correa).
lonjear v. tr. *Amer.* To cut into strips (cortar en lonjas). | To remove the hair from [skins]. | FAM. To whip (azotar). || (Ant.). To warehouse, to store (almacenar).
lontananza f. ARTES. Background. || *En lontananza*, in the distance, far off, far away.
looping m. Looping the loop (ejercicio), loop (rizo).
loor m. Praise (alabanza): *en loor de*, in praise of. || *Decir loores de*, to praise, to sing the praises of, to speak in praise of.
López n. pr. FIG. y FAM. *Esos son otros López*, that's a different kettle of fish.
loquear v. intr. To act *o* to play the fool (hacer), to talk nonsense (decir). || FIG. To make merry (retozar).
loquera f. Padded cell (jaula de locos).
loquería f. *Amer.* Madhouse, lunatic asylum.
loquero m. Lunatic asylum nurse.
lora f. Hen parrot, female parrot. || *Amer.* Parrot (loro).
loran m. MAR. y AVIAC. Loran (ayuda para la navegación a gran distancia).
lord m. Lord: *primer lord del Almirantazgo*, First Lord of the Admiralty. || — *Cámara de los Lores*, House of Lords. || *Lord mayor*, Lord Mayor (de Londres).
lordosis f. MED. Lordosis.
Lorenzo m. Laurence, Lawrence.
loriga f. Lorica, coat of mail, suit of armour [U.S., suit of armor] (de soldado). || Horse armour (de caballo). || TECN. Band [reinforcing axlebox] (del buje de una rueda).
loro, ra adj. Dark brown (color).
— M. Parrot (papagayo). || Cherry laurel (lauroceraso). || FAM. Hag (mujer fea). || FAM. *Más viejo que un loro*, as old as Methuselah.
lorquiano, na adj. Of García Lorca.
los art. def. m. pl. The : *los invitados han llegado*, the guests have arrived; *los Smith*, the Smiths. || Not translated: *los hombres no son inmortales*, men are not immortal; *todos los hombres*, all men.
— Pron. pers. m. pl. Them: *los he visto*, I've seen them. || Those, the ones: *los que he comprado*, those [which] I have bought; *los de mi padre*, those of my father, my father's ones. || Not translated *o* translated by "some" (con *haber*, impersonal): *¿hay libros? — Los hay*, are there any books? — There are [some]. || — *Los de usted*, yours. || *Los de Víctor son viejos*, Victor's are old. || *Los hay que*, there are those who, there are some who (personas), there are those that (cosas): *los hay que no saben nada*, there are those who know nothing. || *Los que*, those who, the ones who (personas, sujeto), those whom, the ones that (personas, complemento), those which, the ones which, the ones that (cosas). || *Los que estáis aquí*, those of you who are here. || *Los que trabajamos*, those of *o* among us who work. || *Son... los que*, it is... who (personas, sujeto), it is... whom (personas, complemento directo), they are... that *o* which (cosas): *son mis libros los que has cogido*, they are my books that you have taken. || *Un traje de los de 1930*, a suit typical of the 1930's.

— OBSERV. The dative form of *los* is *les: les hablo* I speak to them. « Loísmo » (see this word) should be avoided.
— *Los* is often translated by the possessive adjective: *tiene los oídos tapados*, his ears are blocked.

losa f. Stone slab. || Paving stone, flagstone, flag (para pavimentar). || Tile (para cocina, etc.). || — FIG. *Echar* or *poner una losa encima*, to keep it under one's hat. | *Estar bajo la losa*, to be six feet under. || *Losa sepulcral*, tombstone. || FIG. *Yo soy una losa*, my lips are sealed.
losado m. Flagstones, *pl.*, flagging.
losange m. HERÁLD. Lozenge.
loseta f. Small stone slab. || Small paving stone *o* flagstone, small flag (para pavimentar). || Floor tile (baldosa). || Trap (trampa).
lota f. Burbot (pez).
lote m. Share, portion (parte). || Share (de herencia). || COM. Lot (subasta). || Tombola prize (premio). || FIG. y FAM. *Darse un lote de comer higos*, to stuff o.s. with figs.
lotería f. Lottery: *jugar a la lotería*, to play on the lottery. || Lotto (juego de niños). || *Caerle* or *tocarle a uno la lotería*, to win a prize in the lottery (ganar), to strike it lucky (tener suerte).
lotero, ra m. y f. Lottery-ticket seller.
loto m. BOT. Lotus.
Lovaina n. pr. GEOGR. Louvain.
loza f. [Glazed] earthenware, pottery. || Crockery (del ajuar doméstico). || *Fregar la loza*, to wash up, to wash the dishes, to do the washing-up.
lozanía f. Luxuriance, lushness (de la vegetación, de las plantas), freshness (de una flor). || Vigour (vigor). || Robustness (aspecto saludable). || Freshness: *la lozanía de la tez*, the freshness of the complexion. || Sprightliness (de una persona mayor).
lozano, na adj. Luxuriant, lush (vegetación), fresh (verduras, flores). || Robust: *una campesina lozana*, a robust country girl. || Robust, vigorous, lusty (hombre). || Fresh (tez). || Sprightly (persona mayor).
lubina f. [Sea] bass (robalo).
lubricación f. Lubrication.
lubricante adj. Lubricant, lubricating.
— M. Lubricant.
lubricar v. tr. To lubricate.
lubricativo, va adj. Lubricant.
lubricidad f. Lubricity, lewdness, lasciviousness (lujuria). || (P.us.). Slipperiness, lubricity.
lúbrico, ca adj. Lubricous, lewd, lascivious (lujurioso). || (P.us.). Slippery, lubricous.
lubrificación f. Lubrication.
lubrificante adj. Lubricant, lubricating.
— M. Lubricant.
lubrificar v. tr. To lubricate.
Lucas n. pr. m. Luke.
Lucayas n. pr. f. pl. GEOGR. Bahamas.
lucense adj. [Of *o* from] Lugo [Spanish town and province].
— M. y f. Native *o* inhabitant of Lugo.
lucerna f. Chandelier (araña). || Skylight (lumbrera). || Glowworm (luciérnaga).
lucero m. Bright star (estrella). || Evening *o* morning star, Venus (planeta). || Window shutter (postigo). || Star (lunar en la frente del caballo). || FIG. Lustre, brilliance (lustre). || — Pl. Eyes (ojos). || *El lucero del alba* or *de la mañana, de la tarde*, the morning, the evening star (Venus).
luces f. pl. V. LUZ.
lucidez f. Lucidity, clarity.

lucido, da adj. Brilliant: *un discurso lucido*, a brilliant speech. || Successful (que tiene éxito). || Elegant: *un vestido muy lucido*, a very elegant dress. || Generous (liberal). || Splendid, magnificent: *un papel lucido*, a splendid role. || Bonny (saludable): *tienen dos niños muy lucidos*, they have two very bonny children. || — *¡Estamos lucidos!*, we're in a fine mess! || *Estás lucido si...*, you've got another think coming if... || *Las fiestas del pueblo resultaron muy lucidas*, the town festivities were a great success.
lúcido, da adj. Lucid, clear (claro). || MED. *Intervalo lúcido*, lucid interval.
luciérnaga f. Glowworm (insecto).
lucifer m. Lucifer, Venus (lucero). || FIG. Demon.
Lucifer n. pr. m. Lucifer.
luciferino, na adj. Satanic.
lucífero, ra adj. POÉT. Luciferous.
— M. Lucifer, Venus (lucero del alba).
lucimiento m. Lucidity, brilliance (brillo). || Triumph, success (éxito). || — FIG. *Hacer algo con lucimiento*, to do sth. brilliantly. | *Quedar con lucimiento*, to come through [an enterprise] brilliantly *o* with flying colours.
lucio m. Luce, pike (pez).
lucio, cia adj. Shining, bright. || Glossy: *el pelaje lucio del caballo*, the horse's glossy coat.
lucir* v. intr. To shine: *el sol lucía con resplandor*, the sun shone brightly. || To give off light: *una lámpara que luce poco*, a lamp that gives off little light. || To glitter, to sparkle (joyas). || FIG. To shine (sobresalir). | To look nice (un vestido). | To be of benefit, to turn out to advantage (ser de provecho). || FIG. *No le luce lo que come*, the food he eats isn't doing him any good.
— V. tr. To illuminate, to light up (iluminar). || FIG. To show off, to make a show of, to display: *lucir su valor*, to display one's bravery. | To show off: *luciendo las piernas*, showing off her legs. || To sport: *lucía una magnífica corbata verde*, he was sporting a splendid green tie. || To plaster (enlucir).
— V. pr. To dress up, to deck o.s. out (engalanarse). || FIG. To come out brilliantly *o* with flying colours (quedar bien). | To shine, to excel [o.s.], to distinguish o.s. (sobresalir): *Juan se ha lucido en una empresa tan difícil*, John has excelled in such a difficult undertaking. || FAM. To make a fool of o.s. || — *Lucirse en una prueba*, to pass a test with flying colours. || FIG. y FAM. *¡Pues sí que nos hemos lucido!*, we've really gone and done it now!
lucrar v. tr. To gain, to obtain, to win.
— V. pr. To profit: *lucrarse a costa ajena*, to profit at other people's expense.
lucrativo, va adj. Lucrative, profitmaking.
Lucrecia n. pr. f. Lucretia.
Lucrecio n. pr. m. Lucretius.
lucro m. Gain, profit (ganancia). || Benefit, profit (beneficio). || — JUR. *Lucro cesante*, lucrum cessans. || *Lucros y daños*, profit and loss.
luctuoso, sa adj. Sorrowful, sad, mournful.
lucubración f. Lucubration.
lucubrar v. tr. To lucubrate.
lucha f. Fight, struggle. || Conflict (conflicto): *en reñida lucha*, in bitter conflict. || FIG. Dispute (disputa). | War, struggle: *lucha de clases*, class war. || DEP. Wrestling: *lucha libre, grecorromana*, freestyle, Graeco-Roman wrestling. || *Lucha por la existencia*, fight *o* struggle for survival.
luchador, ra m. y f. Fighter. || DEP. Wrestler.
luchar v. intr. To fight, to struggle (combatir). || FIG. To quarrel, to argue, to fight, to dispute (pelearse). | To fight, to struggle: *luchar por la existencia*, to struggle to survive, to fight for survival. || DEP. To wrestle. || *Luchar cuerpo a cuerpo*, to fight hand to hand.
ludibrio m. Shame (vergüenza). || Derision, mockery (mofa). || Contempt, scorn (desprecio). || Laughing-stock (irrisión): *ser el ludibrio del pueblo*, to be the laughingstock of the village. || *Para mayor ludibrio suyo*, to his greater shame.
ludir v. tr. To rub.
luego adv. Then, afterwards (después): *iré luego al cine*, then I'll go to the cinema. || Then, next (después de otra cosa). || Later, later on, afterwards (más tarde). || Soon (pronto). || At once, straightaway, immediately (sin dilación): *vuelvo luego*, I'm coming back at once.
— Conj. Therefore: *pienso, luego existo*, I think, therefore I am. || *Amer.* Sometimes, at times, from time to time (algunas veces). | Near, close by (cerca). || — *Desde luego*, of course, certainly. || *Hasta luego*, see you later [U.S., so long]. || *Luego como* or *que*, as soon as, the moment: *luego que llegues avísame*, let me know the moment you arrive. || *Luego de* [with the infinitive], after, when: *luego de comer se fue*, after eating *o* after he had eaten *o* when he had eaten, he left. || *Luego después*, straight after, immediately [afterwards]. || *Amer. Tan luego*, as well, moreover. | *Tan luego como*, as soon as.
lueguito adv. *Amer.* V. LUEGO.
luengo, ga adj. Long (largo). || *Hace luengos años*, many a long year ago.
lúe f. Syphilis.
lugar m. Place (paraje): *el lugar a donde voy de vacaciones*, the place where I go for my holidays. || Spot, place: *hemos encontrado un lugar precioso*, we found a lovely spot. || Place (sitio de una persona o cosa): *el libro no está en su lugar habitual*, the book is not in its usual place. || Room (espacio): *hacer lugar*, to make room. || Village (pueblo): *en un lugar de la Mancha de cuyo nombre no quiero acordarme*, in a village of La Mancha whose name I do not wish to recall. || Locality, place, spot (localidad). || Part: *en un lugar de la casa*, in one part of the house. || Passage (de un libro): *lo encontrarás en un lugar de tu libro de texto*, you'll find it in a passage in your textbook. || Position, post, office: *ocupa un buen lugar en la empresa*, he holds a good post in the company. || Time, moment (tiempo, oportunidad): *no es el lugar de decirlo*, now is no time to mention it, this is not the [right] moment to mention it. || Time: *no hay lugar para hacer tantas cosas*, there is no time to do so many things. || Cause, reason, motive (motivo). || MAT. Locus. || DEP. Place (posición): *en primer lugar*, in first place.
— *Consérvese en lugar fresco*, keep cool, keep in a cool place (alimentos). || *Dar lugar a*, to give rise to: *esta reforma dio lugar al descontento*, this reform gave rise to unrest; to provoke, to give rise to: *su comportamiento dio lugar a que le criticasen*, his behaviour provoked their criticism. || *Dejar en mal lugar a alguien*, to let s.o. down. || *En cualquier lugar*, anywhere, any place (en cualquier sitio), everywhere, in all places (en todos los sitios). || *En lugar de*, instead of, in place of. || *En lugar seguro*, in a safe place. || *En primer lugar*, in the first place *o* instance, first, firstly. || MIL. *En su lugar ¡descanso!*, stand at ease!, stand easy! || *En tiempo y lugar oportunos*, at the right time, in the right place, in due course. || *En último lugar*, finally, last of all, lastly. || *Fuera de lugar*, out of place (palabras). || JUR. *Ir al lugar del suceso*, to go to the scene of the crime. || *Lugar arqueológico*, archaeological site. || *Lugar común*, commonplace, cliché (tópico). || *Lugar de perdición*, den of iniquity. || *Lugar de señorío*, seigniorial fief. || *Lugar destacado*, prominent place: *ocupar un lugar destacado en la historia*, to occupy a prominent place in history. || *Lugar preferente*, choice *o* first-class position. || *Los Santos Lugares*, the Holy Places. || FIG. *Poner a alguien en su lugar*, to put s.o. in his place. | *Poner las cosas en su lugar*, to put things straight. || *Ponerse uno en lugar de otro*, to put o.s. in s.o. else's place. || JUR. *Providencia de no ha lugar*, nonsuit, nolle prosequi. || *Sin dejar lugar a dudas*, without any doubt. || *Tener lugar*, to take place (suceder), to have room (tener cabida), to have [the] time (tener tiempo). || TEATR. *Unidad de lugar*, unity of place. || *Yo, en tu lugar*, if I were you, if I were in your place.
lugarejo m. Small village, hole (poblacho).
lugareño, ña adj. Village. || Country, rural (rural).
— M. y f. Villager. || Countryman, countrywoman (campesino).
lugartenencia f. Lieutenancy.
lugarteniente m. Lieutenant, deputy.
lugre m. MAR. Lugger (embarcación).
lúgubre adj. Lugubrious, dismal.
luis m. Louis (moneda).
Luis n. pr. m. Louis, Lewis.
Luisa n. pr. f. Louise.
Luisiana n. pr. f. GEOGR. Louisiana.
lujo m. Luxury. || — *Con lujo de*, with great (con abundancia de). || *De lujo*, de luxe: *modelo de lujo*, de luxe model; luxury: *artículos de lujo*, luxury goods. || *Impuesto de lujo*, luxury tax. || *No poder permitirse el lujo de*, to be unable to afford the luxury of. || *Vivir en un lujo asiático*, to live in the lap of luxury.
lujoso, sa adj. Luxurious.
lujuria f. Lust, lechery, lewdness. || FIG. Excess (demasía). | Profusion, abundance (abundancia).
lujuriante adj. Luxurious, lush (vegetación). || Lustful, lecherous, lewd (lascivo).
lujuriar v. intr. To lust, to be lustful *o* lecherous. || To copulate (los animales).
lujurioso, sa adj. Lustful, lecherous, lewd.
— M. y f. Lecher.
lulú m. Pomeranian (perro).
lumbago m. MED. Lumbago.
lumbar adj. ANAT. Lumbar: *región lumbar*, lumbar region.
lumbrada o **lumbrarada** f. Big fire, blaze.
lumbre f. Fire (de la chimenea, etc.): *cerca de la lumbre*, by the fire. || Glow, light (luz del fuego). || Light (luz del sol, candelero, vela, etc.). || Light: *¿tienes lumbre?*, have you got a light? || Luminary, light (luminaria). || ARQ. Light (en una ventana). || Toe (de la herradura). || Battery (de un arma de fuego). || FIG. Brilliance, brightness (lucimiento). | Radiance, splendour (esplendor). | Surface (superficie del agua). || — Pl. Tinderbox, *sing.* || Sparks (chispas). || — *Al amor de la lumbre*, by the fireside, by the fire. || *Dar lumbre a uno*, to give s.o. a light (dar fuego). || *Encender la lumbre*, to light the fire. || *Pedir lumbre*, to ask for a light. || FIG. *Ser la lumbre de los ojos de alguien*, to be the apple of s.o.'s eye.
lumbrera f. Luminary, light (luminaria, cuerpo luminoso). || Skylight (de un buque, abertura en un techo). || Mouth [of plane] (de cepillo). || TECN. Port, vent: *lumbrera de escape*, exhaust port. || FIG. Luminary, leading light (persona muy sabia). || *Amer.* Box (en la plaza de toros). || — Pl. FIG. Eyes (ojos).

lumen m. FÍS. Lumen (unidad de flujo luminoso).
— OBSERV. The plural of the Spanish word should be *lúmenes* although *lumen* is also widely used.
luminar m. Luminary.
luminaria f. Light, lantern [for illuminations]. || Altar light, altar lamp [kept burning before the Holy Sacrament] (en las iglesias). || — Pl. Illuminations.
luminescencia o **luminiscencia** f. Luminescence.
luminescente o **luminiscente** adj. Luminescent.
luminosidad f. Luminosity, brightness.
luminoso, sa adj. Luminous: *cuerpo luminoso*, luminous body. || Bright (bombilla). || Illuminating: *potencia luminosa*, illuminating power. || Illuminated, luminous (p.us.): *fuente luminosa*, illuminated fountain. || FIG. Bright, brilliant: *idea luminosa*, bright idea. | Luminous, crystal-clear (muy claro).
luminotecnia f. Lighting *o* illuminating engineering.
luminotécnico m. Lighting *o* illuminating engineer.
luna f. Moon (astro, satélite). || Moonlight, moon (luz de la luna). || Moon (tiempo): *hace muchas lunas*, many moons ago. || Mirror, glass (espejo). || Window, window pane (de un escaparate). || Lens, glass (cristal de gafas). || FIG. Wanderings (*pl.*) of a madman, fit of lunacy. | Whim, passing fancy (capricho). || — *Amer.* FIG. y FAM. *A la luna de Paita* or *de Payta*, in the lurch. || *Armario de luna*, wardrobe with a mirror. || *Claro de luna*, moonlight. || *Estar de buena, de mala luna*, to be in a good, in a bad mood. || FIG. *Estar en la Luna*, to be miles away. | *Ladrar a la Luna*, to bay [at] the moon. || *Luna creciente*, first quarter, waxing moon, crescent moon. || *Luna de abril*, April moon. || FIG. *Luna de miel*, honeymoon. || *Luna llena*, full moon. || *Luna menguante*, last quarter, waning moon. || *Luna nueva*, new moon. || *Media luna*, half-moon (la mitad), crescent (del astro), Crescent, Turkish Empire (el Imperio turco), demilune (fortificación), butcher's curved knife (cuchilla), crescent-shaped jewel (joya). || FIG. *Pedir la luna*, to ask the earth, to ask for the moon. || *Pez luna*, sunfish, moonfish. || FIG. *Quedarse a la luna de Valencia*, to be left in the lurch. | *Tener lunas*, to be capricious *o* whimsical. | *Vivir en la Luna*, to have one's head in the clouds.
lunación f. Lunation.
lunado, da adj. Lunate, crescent shaped.
lunar adj. Lunar: *año lunar*, lunar year.
— M. Mole, beauty spot (en la piel humana). || Spot (en la piel de los animales, en los tejidos). || FIG. Stain (mancha). | Flaw, blemish (defecto pequeño). || — *Lunar postizo*, beauty spot. || *Vestido de lunares*, spotted dress, polka dot dress.
lunático, ca adj. Lunatic (loco). || Whimsical (caprichoso).
— M. y f. Lunatic (loco). || Whimsical *o* fickle person (caprichoso).
lunch m. Buffet, buffet luncheon.
lunes m. Monday: *vendré el lunes por la mañana*, I shall come [on] Monday morning; *viene los lunes* or *cada lunes*, he comes on Mondays *o* every Monday. || — FIG. *Cada lunes y cada martes*, every day of the week. || *El lunes pasado*, last Monday; *el lunes que viene*, next Monday. || *Amer. Hacer lunes* or *lunes porteño*, to take Monday off. || FIG. y FAM. *Tener lunes*, to have that Monday morning feeling, to be down in the dumps.
luneta f. Lens, glass (de gafas). || Crescent-shaped ornament (adorno). || TEATR. Stall, orchestra seat (butaca). || Backrest (de un torno). || Lunette (fortificación). || ARQ. Front tile (bocateja). | Lunette (bovedilla). || AUT. Rear window (cristal trasero).
luneto m. ARQ. Lunette (bovedilla).
lunfardismo m. Argentinian slang word *o* expression.
lunfardo m. Thief (ladrón). || Buenos Aires slang (jerga).
— Adj. Slang [in Argentina].
lúnula f. MAT. Lunule, lunula, lune. || Half-moon, lunule (de la uña).
lupa f. Magnifying glass, lens: *mirar algo con lupa*, to look at sth. with *o* through a magnifying glass.
lupanar m. Brothel.
lupercales f. pl. Lupercalia (fiestas romanas).
lupino, na adj. Lupine, wolf.
— M. BOT. Lupin [U.S., lupine] (altramuz).
lúpulo m. BOT. Hop, hops.
Lusiadas (Los) n. pr. m. pl. [The] Lusiads.
Lusitania n. pr. f. GEOGR. Lusitania.
lusitanismo m. Portuguese word *o* expression.
lusitano, na o **luso, sa** adj./s. Lusitanian.
lustrabotas m. inv. *Amer.* Bootblack (limpiabotas).
lustración f. Lustration (purificación).
lustrado m. Shine (de los zapatos). || Sheen (de tela).
lustrar v. tr. To polish, to shine (limpiar). || To lustrate (purificar).
lustre m. Lustre [U.S., luster], shine, gloss, polish (brillo). || Sheen, gloss (de telas). || Shoe polish, polish (betún). || FIG. Splendour, distinction, glory (esplendor, distinción). | Splendour: *el lustre de las fiestas*, the splendour of the festivities. || — *Dar* or *sacar lustre a*, to polish, to shine, to put a shine on. || FIG. *Para su mayor lustre*, to his greater glory.
lustrina f. Lustring (tela). || Lamé (tela de oro y plata). || *Amer.* Shoe polish, polish (betún).
lustro m. Lustre [U.S., luster], lustrum (espacio de cinco años). || Hanging lamp (lámpara), lustre, chandelier (araña).
lustroso, sa adj. Shiny, glossy (brillante). || Radiant (rostro). || Healthy looking (animal).
Lutecia n. pr. f. HIST. Lutetia (París).
lutecio m. QUÍM. Lutetium.
luteína f. BIOL. Lutein.
lúteo, a adj. [Of] mud (de lodo). || Luteous, light yellow (color).
luteranismo m. Lutheranism.
luterano, na adj./s. Lutheran.
Lutero n. pr. m. Luther.
luto m. Mourning: *vestirse* or *ponerse de luto*, to go into mourning; *vestir de luto*, to be in mourning. || Grief, sorrow (dolor). || — *Aliviar el luto*, to go into half mourning. || *De luto*, in mourning: *estar de luto*, to be in mourning. || *Luto riguroso*, deep mourning. || *Llevar luto por*, to be in mourning for. || *Medio luto*, half mourning.
lutria f. Otter (nutria).
lux m. FÍS. Lux (unidad de luz).
luxación f. MED. Luxation, dislocation.
Luxemburgo n. pr. m. GEOGR. Luxembourg, Luxemburg.
luxemburgués, esa adj. Luxembourgian, Luxemburgian.
— M. y f. Luxembourger, Luxemburger.
luz f. Light. || Light (lámpara): *tráeme una luz*, bring me a light. || Light, daylight (que se recibe en una casa). || Light, daylight, daytime, day (día). || Lighting (iluminación). || Electricity: *en su casa no hay luz*, there is no electricity in their house; *cortar la luz*, to cut off the electricity. || Electricity bill: *pagar la luz*, to pay the electricity bill. || AUT. Light. || ARQ. Window, light (ventana). | Aperture, opening, light (abertura). | Span (de un puente). || FIG. Light, luminary, guiding light (sabio). | News, information (noticia). || Sparkle (destello de un diamante). || ARTES. Light. || — Pl. Lights: *las luces de la ciudad*, the city lights. || Culture, *sing.* (cultura). || Enlightenment, *sing.*: *el Siglo de las Luces*, the Age of Enlightenment. || Intelligence, *sing.* (inteligencia). || Lights (de un coche). || — FIG. *A buena luz*, in all awareness, aware of *o* in possession of all the facts. | *A dos luces*, ambiguously. | *A la luz de*, by the light of (gracias a la luz de), in the light of (juzgando por). || TEATR. *A la luz de las candilejas*, in the foolights. || *A la luz del día*, v. DÍA. || *Año de luz*, light year. || *Apagar la luz*, to switch off *o* to put off *o* to turn off the light. || *A primera luz*, at daybreak, at first light. || FIG. *Arrojar* or *echar luz sobre*, to shed *o* to throw *o* to cast light on. | *A todas luces*, obviously, evidently, clearly: *su proyecto es a todas luces irrealizable*, your plan is obviously impracticable. | *Claro como la luz del día*, as clear as daylight. | *Corto de luces*, dim, stupid. || *Dar a luz*, to give birth to (parir), to publish, to bring out (publicar). || *Dar (a) la luz*, to turn on *o* to put on *o* to switch on the light. || *Dar luz*, to give [out] light: *una lámpara que da buena luz*, a lamp that gives a good light; to shed *o* to throw light (*sobre*, on) [dar aclaraciones]. || FIG. *De pocas luces*, dim, stupid. || *Encender la luz*, to switch on *o* to put on *o* to turn on the light. || FIG. *En plena luz*, in broad daylight. | *Entre dos luces*, at the break of day, at daybreak, at first light (al amanecer), in the dusk of the evening, at dusk, at twilight, in the twilight (en el crepúsculo), fuddled, tipsy, half-drunk (medio borracho). || *Gusano de luz*, glowworm. || FIG. *Hacer la luz sobre*, to shed *o* to throw light on. || *¡Hágase la luz!*, let there be light! || FIG. *Hombre de luces*, educated *o* cultured man. | *Hombre de pocas luces*, dim-witted man, man of limited intelligence. || *Ingeniero de luces*, lighting engineer. || FIG. *La luz de sus ojos*, the apple of his eye. || *Luces de carretera, de cruce*, headlights on full beam, dipped headlights (coche). || *Luces de tráfico*, traffic lights. || ASTR. *Luz cenicienta*, earthlight, earthshine. || *Luz cenital*, skylight (en una habitación), interior light (en un coche). || *Luz de Bengala*, Bengal light. || AUT. *Luz de ciudad* or *de población* or *de posición*, sidelight: *poner luces de población*, to switch on the sidelights. | *Luz de estacionamiento*, parking light. || *Luz de la Luna*, moonlight. || *Luz del Sol*, sunlight. || FIG. *Luz de mis ojos*, my sweet, my angel. || MAR. *Luz de situación*, riding light, position light. || *Luz eléctrica*, electric light (lámpara), electricity (electricidad). || *Luz intermitente*, indicator, flasher [U.S., winker]. || AUT. *Luz larga*, headlights on full beam. || *Amer. Luz mala*, will-o'-the-wisp, Jack-o'-lantern (fuego fatuo). || *Luz negra*, black light. || AUT. *Luz posterior*, rear light, tail light. || *Luz primaria*, direct light. || *Luz refleja* or *secundaria*, reflection, reflected light. || *Luz relámpago*, flashlight. || *Luz roja*, red light. || *Luz y sombra*, light and shade. || *Luz y sonido*, son et lumière. || *Media luz*, half-light. || *Quitarle la luz a alguien*, to stand in s.o.'s light. || *Sacar a luz*, to bring out, to publish (libro), to bring to light (descubrir). || *Salir a luz*, to come out, to appear, to be published (un libro), to come to light (hacerse patente). || *Tener pocas luces*, to be dim-witted, not to be very bright. || TAUR. *Traje de luces*, bullfighter's costume. || FIG. *Ver la luz*, to see the light of day, to draw one's first breath (nacer).

LL

ll f. Ll: *una ll mayúscula*, a capital ll.

— OBSERV. *Ll* is pronounced like the *li* in the English *battalion*. In many parts of Spain, including Andalusia and Madrid, and in South America, *ll* often approximates to the Spanish *y*, so that, for instance, *pollo* and *poyo* are indistinguishable. This « yeísmo » is considered colloquial and is avoided in educated language.

llaga f. Ulcer, sore (úlcera). || Wound (herida). || FIG. Wound: *renovar la llaga* to reopen the wound. || TECN. Joint (entre ladrillos). || FIG. *Poner el dedo en la llaga*, V. DEDO.

llagar v. tr. To wound, to injure, to hurt.

llama f. Flame: *estallar en llamas*, to burst into flames. || FIG. Flame, burning passion (sentimiento ardiente). || Marsh, swamp (terreno pantanoso). || ZOOL. Llama (animal). || — *En llamas*, in flames, ablaze, burning. || *Llama auxiliar*, pilot light.

llamada f. Call: *hacer una llamada telefónica*, to make a telephone call; *la llamada de la selva*, the call of the wild; *llamada al orden*, call to order. || Knock, ring (en la puerta). || Reference mark (en un libro). || Sign, gesture (ademán). || Invitation to emigrate. || MIL. Fall-in: *tocar llamada*, to sound the fall-in. || — *Amer. Billete de ida y llamada*, return ticket. [U.S., round-trip ticket]. || *Carta de llamada*, letters (*pl.*) of recall (de embajador). || *Da la señal de llamada*, it is ringing (teléfono). || TEATR. *Llamada a escena*, curtain call. || MAR. *Llamada de socorro*, SOS, distress signal. || MIL. *Toque de llamada*, fall-in.

llamadera f. Goad (aguijada).

llamado, da adj. Known as: *Enrique I llamado el Pajarero*, Henry Ist, known as the Fowler. || So-called (supuesto): *los llamados juegos de suerte*, the so-called games of chance. || So-called (que se nombra): *los llamados Picos de Europa*, the so-called "Picos de Europa". || — *Constantinopla, así llamada porque fue fundada por Constantino*, Constantinople, so called because it was founded by Constantine. || *Estar llamado a*, to be destined to.

— M. *Amer.* Call (llamada). || *Muchos son los llamados, pocos los escogidos*, many are called but few are chosen.

llamador, ra m. y f. Caller. || — M. Doorknocker (aldaba). || Doorbell (campana, timbre). || Push-button (botón).

llamamiento m. Call, appeal: *un llamamiento a todos los médicos de la población para que prestasen ayuda*, an appeal for help sent out to all the town's doctors. || Invitation to emigrate. || Calling (de Dios). || JUR. Nomination [of heir, trustee, etc.].

llamar v. tr. To call (nombrar): *¿cómo le llamaremos?*, what shall we call him? || To nickname, to call (dar un apodo): *en el colegio le llaman Enano*, at school they call him Tiny. || To call: *me llamó desde la cocina*, he called me from the kitchen. || To ask for: *¿quién me llama?*, who is asking for me? || To summon, to call (convocar): *llamar a la criada*, to call the maid. || To call for, to call in: *llamar al médico*, to call for the doctor. || To beckon (con un ademán): *llamar a uno con la mano, con la cabeza*, to beckon s.o. with one's hand, with a nod. || To call: *fue llamado al sacerdocio*, he was called to the priesthood. || To appeal (hacer una petición): *llamar a la O.N.U.*, to appeal to the U.N. || To call, to ring up (por teléfono). || To attract (atraer): *Norteamérica llama a muchos científicos europeos*, many European scientists are attracted to North America; *llamar la atención*, to attract attention. || To call (considerar): *lo llamo una estafa*, I call it a swindle. || — FAM. *Llamar a alguien de todo*, to call s.o. names. || TEATR. *Llamar a escena*, to call back on, to give a curtain call. || *Llamar a filas*, to call up (para el ejército). || *Llamar al orden*, to call to order. || *Llamar a uno con un silbido*, to whistle [to] s.o. || *Llamar a voces a uno*, to shout for s.o., to call *o* to shout to s.o. || *Llamar de tú*, to address as "*tú*", to address familiarly. || *Llamar la atención a alguien*, V. ATENCIÓN. || *Llamar por señas*, to signal to. || *Llamar por teléfono*, to telephone, to call [up], to phone, to ring [up]. || *No meterse donde no le llaman*, to mind one's own business. || *Que me llamen a las 3*, get them to *o* have them call me at 3.

— V. intr. To call (dar voces, por teléfono). || To knock, to ring (en la puerta). || *¿Quién llama?*, who is it?, who is there?

— V. pr. To be called: *se llama Carlos*, he is called Charles. || MAR. To haul, to shift (el viento). || — *¿Cómo se llama?*, what is his name? || *¡Eso sí que se llama bailar!*, now that's what I call dancing! || *Me llamo Juan*, my name is John.

llamarada f. Flare-up, sudden blaze (llama rápida). || FIG. Flush (de rubor). | Outburst, flare-up (de entusiasmo, ira, pasión, etc.).

llamativo, va adj. Loud, gaudy, flashy (de color chillón): *una corbata llamativa*, a loud tie. || Ostentatious, flashy, showy (que llama la atención): *llevaba una indumentaria muy llamativa*, he was wearing a very ostentatious outfit. || *Un título llamativo*, an impressive title.

llameante adj. Blazing, flaming: *un bosque, un horizonte llameante*, a blazing wood, horizon.

llamear v. intr. To blaze, to flame: *la casa llameaba todavía*, the house was still blazing; *sus ojos llameaban con ira*, her eyes were blazing with anger.

llamingo m. *Amer.* ZOOL. Llama (llama).

llampo m. *Amer.* Ore (mineral).

llana f. TECN. Float, trowel (de albañil). || Page [of writing] (plana). || Plain (llanura).

llanada f. Flat ground, plain.

llanamente adv. FIG. Naturally, plainly: *comportarse llanamente*, to behave naturally. || Plainly, straightforwardly, frankly (con franqueza). || *Lisa y llanamente*, purely and simply.

llanca f. *Amer.* Copper ore (mineral). | Jewellery made from pebbles. | Earthworm (gusano).

llaneador m. DEP. Rider who is good on the flat (ciclista).

llanear v. intr. DEP. To ride on the flat (ciclista).

llanero, ra m. y f. *Amer.* Plaindweller, lowlander, plainsman (hombre), plainswoman (mujer).

llaneza f. Simplicity, naturalness, plainness (de una persona). || Plainness, straightforwardness, frankness (franqueza). || Informality (falta de ceremonias).

llanito, ta m. y f. FAM. Gibraltarian (gibraltareño).

llano, na adj. Flat, level, even, smooth: *superficie, tierra llana*, flat surface, land. || FIG. Natural, simple, unaffected: *gente llana*, simple people; *modales llanos*, simple manners. | Frank, straightforward, open, plain (al hablar). | Simple, informal (sin ceremonias). || GRAM. Paroxytone [with the penultimate syllable accentuated]. || HIST. Plebeian (pechero). || — FAM. *A la llana*, V. LLANAMENTE. || *A la pata la llana*, without ceremony, simply. || *Canto llano*, V. CANTO. || FIG. *De llano*, plainly. | *En lenguaje llano*, in plain language. | *Estado llano*, V. ESTADO. | *Número llano*, Roman numeral. | *Pueblo llano*, common people.

— M. Plain (llanura). || Flatness, smoothness, evenness (lo llano).

llanote, ta adj. FIG. Plain-spoken (al hablar). | Uncomplicated (sencillo).

llanta f. Iron hoop (de rueda de carro). || Rim (de rueda de automóvil, bicicleta). || *Amer.* Tyre [U.S., tire]: *llanta de goma*, rubber tyre. || BOT. Type of cabbage (col). || *Amer.* Sunshade (quitasol).

llantén m. BOT. Plantain. || — *Llantén de agua*, water plantain. || *Llantén menor*, ribwort [plantain].

llantera f. FAM. Blubber. || FAM. *Coger una llantera*, to start blubbering, to burst into tears.

llantería f. o **llanterío** m. *Amer.* Weeping.

llantina f. FAM. V. LLANTERA.

llanto m. Weeping, crying (acción de llorar): *crisis de llanto*, crying fit. || Tears, *pl.*: *enjugar el llanto de alguien*, to wipe s.o.'s tears. || *Amer.* Plaintive song, lament. || — *Anegarse en llanto*, V. ANEGAR. || *Deshacerse en llanto*, to sob one's heart out. || *Prorrumpir* or *romper en llanto*, to burst into tears.

llanura f. Plain: *la llanura de Flandes*, the plain of Flanders. || Flatness, evenness (cualidad de llano).

llapa f. *Amer.* MIN. Mercury [added to silver ore to aid extraction]. || *Amer.* Extra, bonus (adehala). | Tip (propina). | Thick end (del lazo).

llapango, ga adj. Barefoot (descalzo).

llapar v. intr. *Amer.* MIN. To add mercury [to produce silver amalgam].

— V. tr. To offer as a bonus *o* an extra.

llar m. Hearth (fogón). || — F. pl. Pothanger, *sing.*, pothook, *sing.*

llave f. Key: *llave maestra*, skeleton *o* master key. || Spanner [U.S., wrench] (para las tuercas): *llave de tubo*, box spanner [U.S., socket wrench]. || Tap [U.S., faucet] (de grifo). || ELECTR. Switch (interruptor). || Winder (de reloj). || MÚS. Clef (signo): *llave de fa, de sol*, bass clef, treble clef. | Stop (de órgano). | Valve: *trombón de llaves*, valve trombone. | Key (de clarinete, etc.). || Lock (de arma de fuego). || IMPR. Square bracket (corchete), brace (para abarcar en cuadro sinóptico, etc.). || FIG. Key (de una cifra). | Key: *la llave del éxito*, the key to success. || MED. Dentist's forceps, *pl.* || Wedge (cuña). || DEP. Hold, lock (en lucha). || — *Ama de llaves*, housekeeper. || *Bajo llave*, under lock and key. || *Bajo siete llaves*, safely under lock and key. || *Cerrar con llave*, to lock. || *Cerrar con siete llaves*, to lock and doublelock. || *Echar la llave*, to lock up. || *Llave de contacto*, ignition key. || *Llave de paso*, stopcock (espita). || *Llave inglesa*, [monkey] wrench, adjustable spanner.

llavero, ra m. y f. Keeper of the keys. || Jailer, turnkey (ant.) [de cárcel]. || — M. Key ring (para poner las llaves).

llavín m. Latchkey (llave pequeña).

lleco, ca adj. Uncultivated, virgin (tierra).

llegada f. Arrival. || *A mi llegada a París*, upon my arrival in Paris, when I arrived in Paris, on arriving in Paris.

llegado, da adj. Arrived: *recién llegado*, newly arrived. — M. y f. *Los recién llegados*, the newcomers, the new arrivals.

llegar v. intr. To arrive: *llegaré a Londres mañana*, I shall arrive in London tomorrow; *cuando llegó el buen tiempo*, when the good weather arrived. || To come: *llegará un día en que se arrepienta*, the day will come when he will be sorry; *llegará la paz*, peace will come; *llegó su vez*, his turn came. || To reach: *la escalera, la cuerda no llega*, the ladder, the rope won't reach. || To suffice, to be enough *o* sufficient: *el dinero no llega para repartirlo entre todos*, the money is not sufficient *o* there is not enough money to go round. || To be big enough (ser bastante grande). || To come about, to happen (suceder): *llegó que...*, it came about that... || — FIG. *¿Adónde quiere llegar?*, what's he getting at?, what's he driving at? | *Aquello fue llegar y besar el santo*, V. SANTO. | *Hacer llegar el dinero*, to make one's money last, to eke out one's money. || *Llegar a* (*con infinitivo*), to succeed in, to manage to (conseguir): *llegué a ver al ministro*, I succeeded in seeing *o* I managed to see the minister; to get to, to end up: *llegué a dudar si vendrías*, I got to wondering *o* I ended up wondering if you were coming; *llegó a conocer todas las capitales del mundo*, he got to know *o* he ended up knowing all the capitals of the world; to end up: *llegó a suicidarse*, he ended up committing suicide; to be able to, to have time to: *no llegará a aburrirse porque estará allí poco tiempo*, he will not have time to get bored because he will not be there long. || *Llegar a* (*con sustantivo*), to reach: *el niño no llega al tirador de la puerta*, the child can't reach the door handle; to reach, to arrive in *o* at, to get to: *llegar a Madrid, a la estación, a la cima*, to arrive in Madrid, at the station, at the summit; to reach, to arrive at, to come to: *llegar a un acuerdo, a una conclusión*, to reach an agreement, a conclusion; to attain: *llegar a la mayoría de edad, a la fama*, to attain one's majority, to attain fame; to come to, to amount to: *su salario semanal no llega a dos mil pesetas*, his weekly wage comes to less than two thousand pesetas; *los espectadores llegaban al millar*, the spectators amounted to about a thousand; to become (llegar a ser): *llegó a presidente*, he became president; to last out until (durar): *el nuevo régimen no llegará al año que viene*, the new régime will not last out until next year. || *Llegar a conocer a uno*, to get to know s.o. || *Llegar a la vejez*, to reach old age. || *Llegar al extremo de*, to go as far as to. || *Llegar al poder*, to come to power. || *Llegar a saber*, to find out. || *Llegar a ser*, to become. || FIG. *No llegarle a uno a la suela del zapato* or *a la punta de la bota*, not to hold a candle to s.o. || *No me llega el dinero*, I have not got enough money, I do not have enough money. || *Si llego a saberlo...*, if I had known...
— V. tr. To gather up (reunir). || To draw up, to bring over (acercar).
— V. pr. To go [round], to come [round]: *llégate a casa de tu hermano*, go round to your brother's house. || To approach, to come near (acercarse).

llenado m. Filling.

llenar v. tr. To fill, to fill up: *llenar de vino un tonel*, to fill a barrel with wine; *las bicicletas llenan las calles de la población*, the streets of the town are filled with bicycles. || To fill, to fill up, to satisfy (hartar de comida). || To fill in [U.S., to fill out] (rellenar): *llenar un cuestionario*, to fill in a questionnaire. || To fill in (rellenar): *llenar un hoyo*, to fill in a hole. || FIG. To fill (colmar): *llenar a uno de ira, de confusión*, to fill s.o. with rage, with confusion. | To shower, to overwhelm: *me llenó de elogios, de favores, de injurias*, he showered me with praise, with favours, with insults. || To fulfil, to satisfy (cumplir, satisfacer): *su viaje llena su mayor ambición*, his trip fulfils his greatest ambition. | To fulfil, to carry out (un cometido). || FIG. y FAM. To satisfy, to convince: *el razonamiento de Alberto no me llena*, Albert's reasoning does not convince me. || — *Llenar ciertas condiciones*, to meet certain requirements, to fulfil *o* to satisfy certain conditions. || FIG. y FAM. *Llenar el ojo antes que la barriga* or *la tripa*, to have eyes bigger than one's belly. | *No me llena su nueva película*, I'm not mad about his new film. || *Vuelva a llenar* (*las copas*), the same again.
— V. intr. To be full (la Luna). || To be filling (la comida).
— V. pr. To be *o* to become filled *o* full: *llenarse de humo, de orgullo, de indignación*, to become filled with *o* full of smoke, pride, indignation. || To fill up: *la tina se llenó de agua*, the butt filled up with water. || To fill o.s. up (*de*, with), to eat one's fill (*de*, of) [de alimento]. || To cover: *llenarse los dedos de tinta*, to cover one's fingers with ink. || To get covered with (de polvo, etc.). || *Llenarse completamente* or *hasta los topes*, to be filled to overflowing.

lleno, na adj. Full, filled: *vaso lleno de vino*, glass full of wine; *lleno de enojo, de alegría*, filled with anger, with happiness. || Full, full up (teatro, cine). || Full (preñada). || Covered: *lleno de manchas*, covered with stains; *estar lleno de polvo*, to be covered in dust. || Full, full up (de comida). || FIG. Full, plump (un poco gordo): *tener una cara muy llena*, to be very full in the face. || HERÁLD. Pale. || — *Dar de lleno en*, to flood (el sol). || *Dar de lleno en la cara*, to hit squarely *o* right in the face. || *De lleno* or *de lleno en lleno*, completely. || *Es luna llena*, there is a full moon. || *Lleno de peligro*, fraught with danger. || *Lleno hasta los topes*, full to the brim *o* to overflowing. || *Voz llena*, good *o* strong voice.
— M. Full moon (plenilunio). || Full house, sellout (en el teatro). || FAM. Abundance (abundancia). || FIG. Completion (último complemento de algo). || — Pl. MAR. Rounded hull, *sing.*

lleudar v. tr. To leaven.

llevadero, ra adj. Bearable, tolerable: *un calor llevadero*, a bearable heat. || Wearable (ropa).

llevar v. tr. To carry: *llevar a un niño en brazos*, to carry a child in one's arms; *llevar en la cabeza*, to carry on one's head. || To carry, to transport: *el tren lleva carbón*, the train is transporting coal; *el coche llevaba cuatro personas*, the car was carrying four people. || To carry away (una cosa a lo lejos): *el viento lo llevó todo*, the wind carried it all away. || To get, to win, to take: *este número lleva premio*, this number gets a prize. || To take: *llévame a mi casa*, take me home; *me llevaron al cine*, they took me to the pictures. || To lead (inducir): *esto me lleva a pensar que*, this leads me to think that. || To bring (traer): *voy a llevar a un amigo a casa*, I'm going to bring a friend home; *el paro llevó el hambre a muchas familias*, unemployment brought hunger to many families. || To have: *el cuadro lleva demasiadas flores*, the painting has too many flowers in it; *su vestido no lleva cinturón*, her dress does not have a belt; *el vino lleva muchas heces*, the wine has a lot of lees; *llevar ventaja a*, to have an advantage over. || To wear, to have on: *lleva un sombrero negro*, he has a black hat on, he wears a black hat. || To have [on one] (dinero): *llevo dos libras*, I have two pounds [on me]. || To bear: *llevar una enfermedad con paciencia*, to bear an illness with patience. || To take: *me llevará un día escribir el artículo*, the article will take me a day to write. || To have been: *lleva un mes en la cama*, he has been in bed [for] a month; *lleva cinco años de coronel*, he has been a colonel [for] five years; *el restaurante llevaba abierto diez años*, the restaurant had been open [for] ten years. || To bear (un nombre, un título). || To charge: *no me ha llevado muy caro el sastre*, the tailor has not charged me a great deal. || To take care of, to look after (ocuparse de): *el jefe lleva el asunto*, the boss is looking after the matter. || To run, to manage: *lleva bien su negocio*, he runs his business well; *me lleva la finca*, he runs my property. || To manage, to control (un coche, un caballo). || To lead: *llevar una vida muy ajetreada*, to lead a very hectic life. || To offer, to present (dificultades, problemas). || To keep (las cuentas, los libros). || To lead, to take: *esta calle te lleva al ayuntamiento*, this street leads you to the Town Hall. || To get, to lead (conducir): *¿adónde nos lleva la guerra?*, where does war get us?; *¿adónde nos lleva esta discusión?*, where is this discussion getting us? || To have: *llevar estudiado*, to have studied; *llevo el trabajo hecho*, I have the work finished. || COM. To keep (la contabilidad). || MAT. To carry (un número): *veintitrés, pongo tres y llevo dos*, twenty-three, three down and carry two. || COM. To bear, to carry (un interés). || To be ... older, taller, etc. than (exceder en años, en altura, etc.): *su hijo me lleva dos años, tres centímetros*, his son is two years older than I, three centimetres taller than I. || To lead by, to be ahead of: *su coche me lleva diez kilómetros* (*de ventaja* or *de delantera*), his car is ten kilometres ahead of mine *o* leading mine by ten kilometres; *me lleva diez minutos* (*de ventaja* or *de delantera*), he is ten minutes ahead of me, he is leading me by ten minutes. || To follow (seguir): *¿qué dirección lleva el ladrón?*, what direction is the thief following? || To bear: *este árbol lleva manzanas*, this tree bears apples. || — *¿Cuánto tiempo llevas aquí?*, how long have you been here? || *Dejarse llevar* (*por*), V. DEJAR. || *Llevar a cabo*, V. CABO. || *Llevar a cuestas*, to carry on one's back (un bulto, a una persona), to give a piggyback (a un niño). || *Llevar adelante*, V. ADELANTE. || *Llevar a los tribunales*, to take to court. || *Llevar a uno a aceptar su punto de vista*, to bring s.o. round to one's point of view, to talk s.o. round. || *Llevar camino de ser un buen ingeniero, un buen médico*, to look as if one will make a good engineer, a good doctor. || *Llevar consigo*, to entail, to involve (dificultades, problemas, etc.). || *Llevar de la mano a uno*, to lead s.o. by the hand. || *Llevar el compás*, to beat time (con la mano), to keep time (bailando). || *Llevar el nombre de*, to bear the name of. || *Llevar en peso algo*, to hold sth. at arm's length. || *Llevar idea de*, to intend to. || *Llevar la batuta*, V. BATUTA. || *Llevar la cabeza alta*, to carry *o* to hold one's head high. || *Llevar la casa*, to run the house. || *Llevar la contraria a uno*, V. CONTRARIO. || *Llevar las de ganar*, to hold

all the winning cards, to look like a winner. || *Llevar las de perder*, to be fighting a losing battle, to look like losing. || FIG. *Llevar la voz cantonte*, to rule the roost. | *Llevar los pantalones*, to wear the trousers (una mujer). || *Llevar luto*, to be in mourning. || *Llevar mala, buena conducta*, to behave badly, well. || *Llevar puesto*, to be wearing, to have on (ropa). || FIG. *Llevar su cruz*, to bear one's cross. || *Llevar trazas de durar mucho*, to look as if it will last a long time. || *Llevar ventaja a uno*, to have the advantage over s.o. *o* the edge on s.o. || FAM. *No llevarlas todas consigo*, to have the wind up. | *Ser difícil de llevar*, V. DIFÍCIL.
— V. intr. To lead, to go (conducir): *todos los caminos llevan a Roma*, all roads lead to Rome. || *Llevar y traer*, to go around gossiping.
— V. pr. To take [away], to carry off, to make *o* to run off with: *alguien se ha llevado mi paraguas equivocadamente*, s.o. has taken my umbrella by mistake; *el ratero se llevó mi cartera*, the pickpocket made off with my wallet. || To sweep away (con violencia): *el viento, el agua se llevó todos los detritos*, the wind, the water swept away all the debris. || To carry off, to win, to take (conseguir): *se han llevado el premio*, they have taken the prize. || To get: *se ha llevado el castigo que merece*, he got the punishment he deserved. || To take: *llévate a tu hermano al cine*, take your brother to the pictures. || To be popular, to be fashionable *o* in fashion: *esos sombreros ya no se llevan, esa actitud ya no se lleva*, that type of hat, that attitude is no longer fashionable. || MAT. To carry (en aritmética). || To have, to get (sufrir): *llevarse un susto*, to have a fright. || To receive, to get: *llevarse una patada*, to get a kick. || — *Llevarse bien, mal con alguien*, to get on *o* along with s.o., not to get on *o* along with s.o. || *Llevarse como el perro y el gato*, V. GATO. || *Llevarse la palma*, V. PALMA. || *Llevarse un chasco*, V. CHASCO. || FAM. *No tener qué llevarse a la boca*, not to have a bite to eat. | *¡Que se lo lleve el diablo!*, go to hell! (dirigiéndose a una persona), to hell with it *o* him! (hablando de una cosa o de otra persona). || *Se lleva todo por delante*, he lets nothing stand in his way.
lliclla f. *Amer.* Shawl.
llorado, da adj. Late: *el llorado García Lorca*, the late García Lorca.
lloraduelos m. y f. inv. FIG. y FAM. Moaner, whiner.
llorar v. intr. To cry, to weep: *no lloréis por mí*, don't cry on my account. || To water, to run (los ojos). || — FIG. *El que no llora no mama*, he who doesn't ask doesn't get, you don't get anything unless you ask for it. || *Llorar a lágrima viva* or *a mares* or *a moco tendido*, to cry bitterly, to cry one's eyes out, to sob one's heart out, to weep buckets. || *Romper a llorar*, to begin to cry, to burst into tears.
— V. tr. To shed, to weep (lágrimas). || To be sorry for, to regret: *en el futuro llorará su pereza*, he will be sorry for his laziness in the future. || To mourn, to weep for (la muerte de alguien). || To bemoan: *llorar sus desgracias*, to bemoan one's misfortunes.
llorera f. FAM. [Fit of] crying *o* weeping, blubbering.
llorica o **lloricón, ona** adj. FAM. Blubbering.
— M. y f. FAM. Crybaby, blubberer.
lloriquear v. intr. To whimper, to snivel, to whine.
lloriqueo m. Whimpering, whining, snivelling.
llorisquear v. intr. V. LLORIQUEAR.
lloro m. Crying, weeping, tears, *pl.*
llorón, ona adj. Given to weeping *o* to crying. || Blubbering. || BOT. *Sauce llorón*, weeping willow.
— M. y f. Crybaby (niño). || Tearful person, blubberer (el que llora mucho). || — M. Plume (adorno de sombrero). || — F. Hired mourner (plañidera). || *Amer.* Spur (espuela).
lloroso, sa adj. Tearful, weeping.
llovedera o **llovedero** m. *Amer.* Persistent rain.
llovedizo, za adj. Leaky, leaking (tejado). || *Agua llovediza*, rainwater.
llover* v. impers. To rain: *está lloviendo*, it is raining. || — FIG. *Como llovido* or *como llovido del cielo*, out of the blue, heaven-sent. | *Es como quien oye llover*, it's like talking to a brick wall. | *Habrá llovido para entonces*, a lot of water will have passed under the bridge by then. || *Llover a cántaros* or *a chorros* or *a chuzos* or *a mares*, to rain cats and dogs, to rain buckets, to pour [down]. || FIG. *Llueve sobre mojado*, it never rains but it pours, it's just one thing on top of another. | *Nunca llueve a gusto de todos*, you can't please everybody.
— V. intr. To shower: *en este negocio el dinero te lloverá*, you will be showered with money in this business.
— V. pr. To leak (un tejado).
llovida f. *Amer.* Rain.
llovizna f. Drizzle.
lloviznar v. impers. To drizzle.
llueca adj. f. Broody (gallina).
— F. Brooder, broody hen.
lluvia f. Rain (agua que llueve): *salir bajo la lluvia*, to go out in the rain; *el barómetro indica lluvia*, the barometer shows rain. || Rainfall: *una región de poca lluvia*, a region of limited rainfall. || FIG. Shower: *lluvia de regalos, de piedras, de insultos, de desgracias*, shower of gifts, of stones, of insults, of misfortunes. | Pile, heap (gran cantidad de dinero). || — *Agua de lluvia*, rainwater. || *Día de lluvia*, rainy day. || FIG. *Lluvia de estrellas*, shower of shooting stars. | *Lluvia radiactiva*, radioactive fallout. || *Lluvia torrencial*, torrential rain.
lluvioso, sa adj. Rainy, wet.

M

m f. M (letra): *una m mayúscula*, a capital m.
— OBSERV. The pronunciation of the Spanish *m* is similar to that of the English *m*.
maca f. Bruise (en una fruta). || Stain, spot (de prendas de lana). || FIG. Defect, flaw (defecto). | Trick (engaño).
Macabeo n. pr. m. Maccabee.
macabro, ra adj. Macabre: *danza macabra*, macabre dance.
macaco, ca adj. *Amer.* Ugly, misshapen (feo). | Foolish, idiotic (necio).
— M. ZOOL. Macaque (mono). || FIG y FAM. Ugly man (hombre feo). | Runt, squirt (hombre pequeño). || *Amer.* Bogyman (coco). || *Es un macaco*, he is as ugly as sin. || — F. *Amer.* FAM. Binge, drinking spree [U.S., drunk] (borrachera).
macadam o **macadán** m. Macadam.
macana f. Macana, Indian club or tool (arma). || Heavy club (porra). || FIG. y FAM. Piece of soiled stock (cosa deteriorada). | Old rubbish (antigualla). || *Amer.* Blunder, faux pas (despropósito). | Lie, fib (mentira). | Bad job (trabajo malo). | Joke (broma).
— Interj. *Amer.* FAM. That's a pack of lies! || *¡Que se deje de macanas!*, enough of your stories!
macanada f. *Amer.* Foolishness, stupidity (estupidez). | Nonsense, absurdity (disparate).
macanazo m. Blow with a club. || *Amer.* FAM. Nonsense, absurdity (disparate). | Nuisance (aburrimiento).
macaneador, ra adj. *Amer.* Fond of joking (bromista). | Deceitful (engañoso). | Unreliable (poco de fiar).
— M. y f. Charlatan, storyteller.
macanear v. intr. *Amer.* To boast, to exaggerate (exagerar). | To joke (bromear). | To talk nonsense (disparatar). | To tell tall stories, to fib (contar cuentos). | To work hard (trabajar).
macanudo, da adj. FAM. Terrific, great, fabulous, extraordinary (extraordinario).
macaón m. Swallow-tail butterfly (mariposa).
macaquear v. intr. *Amer.* To act like a monkey, to make faces (gesticular).
macarrón m. Macaroon (pastel). || — Pl. Macaroni (pastas). || MAR. Stanchions.
macarronea f. Macaronic verse, macaronics, *pl.* [burlesque composition, generally in verse, in which Latin words are mixed with others to which Latin endings are added].
macarrónico, ca adj. FAM. Macaronic. || *Latín macarrónico*, pig Latin.
macarronismo m. FAM. Macaronic style.
macarse v. pr. To start to rot *o* to go off, to get bruised (las frutas).
macear v. tr. To hammer, to pound.
— V. intr. To go on (insistir).

macedonia f. CULIN. Salad, macedoine: *macedonia de frutas, de legumbres*, fruit, vegetable salad.
Macedonia n. pr. f. GEOGR. Macedonia.
macedónico, ca o **macedonio, nia** adj./s. Macedonian.
macegual m. *Amer.* Indian peasant.
maceo m. Hammering, pounding.
maceración f. Maceration. || FIG. Mortification.
macerador m. Macerator.
maceramiento m. Maceration.
macerar v. tr. e intr. To macerate. || FIG. To mortify.
— V. pr. To macerate. || FIG. To mortify o.s.
macero m. Mace-bearer, macer, mace.
maceta f. Flowerpot (tiesto). || Mallet, small hammer (mazo pequeño). || Stone hammer (martillo de escultor).
macetero m. Flowerpot stand. || *Amer.* Flowerpot.
macetón m. Large flowerpot, tub (tiesto).
macicez f. Solidity, compactness. || Massiveness.
macilento, ta adj. Wan, lean: *rostro macilento*, wan face || Wan (luz).
macillo m. Hammer (del piano).
macizo, za adj. Solid: *de oro macizo*, of solid gold. || FIG. Solid: *argumento macizo*, solid argument.
— M. Mass (masa). || Massif, mountain mass (de montañas). || Bed (de plantas). || Clump (de árboles). || ARQ. Chimney breast. | Group (de edificios).
macla f. HERÁLD. Mascle. || MIN. Macle.
macolla f. Bunch, cluster (de planta).
macollo m. *Amer.* BOT. Bunch, cluster.
macrobiótico, ca adj. Macrobiotic.
— F. Macrobiotics.
macrocefalia f. MED. Macrocephaly.
macrocéfalo, la adj. MED. Macrocephalic, macrocephalous.
macrocito m. BIOL. Macrocyte.
macrocosmo m. Macrocosm.
macrodáctilo, la adj. Macrodactyl.
macrófago, ga adj. Macrophagic.
— M. Macrophage.
macrofotografía f. Macrophotography.
macrogameto m. BIOL. Macrogamete.
macromolécula f. Macromolecule.
macromolecular adj. Macromolecular.
macrópodo adj. m./s. m. Macropodid.
macroscópico, ca adj. Macroscopic.
macrospora f. BOT. Macrospore.
macrosporangio m. BOT. Macrosporange.
macruro, ra adj. Macrural, macruran.
— M. Macruran.
macuache m. *Amer.* Ignorant *o* illiterate Indian.
macuco, ca adj. *Amer.* Terrific, marvellous (notable). | Cunning, clever crafty (taimado). | Big, strong (grandullón).
mácula f. Spot, stain (mancha). || Macula lutea (del ojo). || IMPR. Mackle. || ASTR. Macula. || FIG. Deception, trick.
macular v. tr. To spot, to stain. || IMPR. To mackle.
maculatura f. IMPR. Blurred sheet, mackle.
macuquero m. Illegal worker of an abandoned mine.
macuquino, na adj. Edgeless, cut down (moneda).
macurca f. *Amer.* Cramp, ache.
macuto m. MIL. Knapsack, haversack. || *Amer.* Alms basket (para limosnas).
mach m. FÍS. Mach.
macha f. *Amer.* Tellina (molusco). || Drunkenness (borrachera). | Mannish woman, virago (marimacho).
machacador, ra adj./s. Crushing, pounding (que machaca). || Grinding, crushing (que muele). || Beating (que bate). || — F. Crushing *o* grinding machine.
machacante m. FAM. Five peseta coin (moneda). || MIL. Sergeant's orderly *o* aid (soldado).
machacar v. tr. To pound, to crush (en un mortero). || To grind, to crush (moler). || MIL. To bombard, to shell (bombardear). | To crush (al enemigo). || FIG. y FAM. To harp on, to go on about, to repeat (repetir) | To crush, to flatten (en una discusión). | To slash (los precios). || — FIG. *Hay que machacar el hierro mientras que está caliente*, [one must] strike while the iron is hot. | *Machacando se aprende el oficio*, practice makes perfect. | *Machacar en hierro frío*, V. HIERRO. | *Machacar los oídos*, to say [the same thing] over and over again.
— V. intr. FIG. y FAM. To be boring, to be a bore *o* a nuisance (aburrir). | To harp on a subject (repetir). | To swot, to cram, to grind (estudiar con ahínco).
— V. pr. FAM. To spend (dinero, tiempo).
machacón, ona adj. FAM. Repetitious, insistent (que repite). | Boring, tiring (pesado). | Hard-working, studious (muy estudioso). || *Con machacona frecuencia*, all the time, constantly, forever.
— M. y f. FAM. Bore, pest, nuisance (pesado). | Swot, crammer (muy estudioso).
machaconería f. FAM. Tiresomeness (pesadez). | Insistence (insistencia). | Harping (sobre un tema).
machada f. Flock of billy goats. || FIG. y FAM. Stupidity (necedad). | Manly action (hombrada).
machamartillo (a) loc. adv. Thoroughly, attentively (concienzudamente). || FIG. Obstinately. || — *Creo a machamartillo*, I firmly believe. || *Cristiano a machamartillo*, confirmed Christian, Christian through and through. || *Cumplir a machamartillo*, to carry out [a task] to the letter. || *Hacer entrar una cosa a machamartillo*, to drive sth. in *o* home. || *Repetir a machamartillo*, to repeat time and again.
machaquear v. tr. V. MACHACAR.
machaqueo m. Pounding, crushing (trituración). || Grinding (molido). || FIG. Bombardment, pounding (bombardeo intenso). || FIG. y FAM. Insistence, stubbornness (insistencia). | Harping (sobre un tema).
machaquería f. V. MACHACONERÍA.
macharse v. pr. *Amer.* To get drunk (emborracharse).
machear v. intr. To beget more males than females. || FAM. To play the tough guy (dárselas de hombre).
machetazo m. Blow with a machete (golpe). || Wound from a machete (herida).
machete m. Machete (espada corta). || Hunting knife (cuchillo).
machetear v. tr. To slash *o* to strike *o* to wound with a machete (espada corta) *o* hunting knife (cuchillo de monte). || To cut down with a machete (la caña de azúcar, etc.).
— V. intr. To drive stakes (clavar estacas). || *Amer.* To persist, to insist. | To work (trabajar). | To cram, to swot hard (empollar).
machetero m. Path clearer, trailblazer, person who clears a way with a machete (que desmonta). || Cane cutter (que corta la caña). || *Amer.* Unskilled labourer (peón). | Swot, crammer (empollón).
machi o **machí** m. *Amer.* Medicine man (curandero).
machiega adj. f. *Abeja machiega*, queen bee.
machihembrado m. Tongue and groove [joint].
machihembrar v. tr. To join with a tongue and groove (carpintería).
machismo m. Machismo, virility *o* masculinity cult. || Virility, manliness, masculinity (virilidad).
macho adj. m. Male: *gorrión macho*, male sparrow. || FIG. Strong (fuerte): *vino macho*, strong wine. | Manly, virile (varonil). || TECN. Male. || *Amer.* Great, terrific (formidable).
— M. Male. || He-mule (mulo). || Hook (de un corchete). || Tassel (borla). || FIG. Numbskull, fool (necio). || ARQ. Pilaster, buttress (pilar). || TECN. Male piece *o* part (pieza que penetra en otra). | Plug (de un enchufe). | Tenon (espiga). | Sledgehammer (maza). | Anvil block (banco de yunque). | Square anvil (yunque). || FAM. He-man, tough guy (hombre varonil). || — *Macho cabrío*, he-goat, billy-goat. || TECN. *Macho de aterrajar* or *de roscar*, screw tap.
machón m. ARQ. Pilaster, buttress (pilar).
machorra f. Sterile *o* barren woman. || FAM. Virago, mannish woman (marimacho).
machota f. Hammer, mallet (mazo). || Brave woman *o* girl (valiente). || FAM. Mannish woman, virago (marimacho).
machote adj. m. Virile, masculine. || Courageous (valiente).
— M. Mallet (mazo). || FAM. He-man, tough guy (hombre varonil). || *Amer.* Rough draft (borrador). | Model (modelo). | Boundary stone (mojón).
machucado m. o **machucadura** f. o **machucamiento** m. Bruising, bruise (de una fruta). || Bump (de un objeto). || Contusion, bruise (herida).
machucar v. tr. To crush (aplastar). || To bruise (una fruta). || To dent, to deform (abollar).
machucón m. *Amer.* V. MACHUCADO.
Madagascar n. pr. GEOGR. Madagascar.
madeja f. Hank, skein (de lana). || FIG. Tuft *o* mass *o* mop of hair (de pelo). || FIG. y FAM. Layabout, loafer (hombre sin vigor). || — FIG. *Enredarse la madeja*, to get complicated. | *Madeja de nervios*, bundle of nerves.
madera f. Wood: *madera seca*, dry wood. || Timber (de construcción). || Horn *o* rind of horse's hoof (del casco de las caballerías). || DEP. Wood (en el golf). || FIG. Stuff (de una persona): *tiene madera de santo*, his is the stuff *o* he is of the stuff saints are made of. || — *A media madera*, scarf (empalme). || *De madera*, wooden, wood. || *Madera anegadiza*, non-floating wood. || *Madera aserradiza, de construcción*, sawn *o* hewn timber, construction timber. || *Madera blanca*, deal. || *Madera contrachapada*, plywood. || *Madera del aire*, horn (de animal). || *Madera en rollo*, rough timber. || *Madera fósil*, lignite. || *Madera plástica*, plastic wood. || *Maderas preciosas* or *exóticas*, fancy woods. || FIG. *Tener buena madera para pintor*, to have what it takes to be a painter, to have it in one to be a painter, to have the makings of a painter. | *Tocar madera*, to touch wood [U.S., to knock on wood].
— M. Madeira (vino).
Madera n. pr. f. GEOGR. Madeira (isla).
maderable adj. Timber-yielding.
maderada f. Raft.
maderaje o **maderamen** m. Wood, timber (madera). || Framework (armazón). || Timberwork, woodwork, timbering (enmaderamiento).
maderero, ra adj. Timber, lumber.
— M. Timber *o* lumber dealer.
madero m. Log, piece of wood. || Piece of timber, log (de construcción). || FIG. Ship, vessel (buque). || FIG. y FAM. Numbskull, blockhead, dolt (necio).
Madianitas m. pl. Midianites (antiguo pueblo de Arabia).
madona f. REL. Madonna.
madrás m. Madras (tejido).

madrastra f. Stepmother. || FIG. Callous *o* cruel mother (madre cruel). | Plague (cosa molesta).
madraza f. FAM. Doting mother, mother hen.
madre f. Mother: *madre de familia*, mother of a family; *futura madre*, expectant mother. || Mother (de los animales): *una leona madre*, a mother lioness. || Matron (de un hospital). || REL. Mother: *madre superiora*, mother superior. || FAM. Old mother (mujer vieja): *la madre Juana*, old mother Jane. || FIG. Mother, origin, cradle (origen): *Grecia, madre de las artes*, Greece, mother of the arts. | Root: *la ociosidad es la madre de todos los vicios*, idleness is the root of all evil. || Matrix, womb (matriz). || Main sewer (cloaca maestra). || Bed (de un río). || Main irrigation ditch (acequia). || Lees, *pl.*, dregs, *pl.* (del vino). || Mother (del vinagre). || Grounds, *pl.*, dregs, *pl.* (del café). || TECN. Main piece, spindle. || — FAM. *Ahí está* or *ésa es la madre del cordero*, v. CORDERO. | *Como su madre lo echó al mundo* or *lo parió*, stark naked, in one's birthday suit. || *Día de la madre*, Mother's Day. || *La Santa Madre Iglesia*, Mother Church. || *Lengua madre de otras lenguas*, mother language of other languages. || *Madre adoptiva*, foster mother. || *¡Madre de Dios!*, good heavens! || *Madre de leche*, wet nurse. || *¡Madre mía!*, good heavens! || *Madre patria*, mother country. || *Madre política*, mother-in-law. || *Madre soltera*, unwed *o* unmarried mother. || *Reina madre*, Queen Mother. || FIG. y FAM. *Sacar de madre a uno*, to make s.o. lose his patience. || *Salirse de madre*, to overflow, to flood its banks, to run over (un río), to lose one's self-control (excederse). || *Su señora madre*, your mother.
madreperla f. Pearl oyster (ostra). || Mother-of-pearl (nácar).
madrépora f. ZOOL. Madrepore, white coral.
madreporarios m. pl. ZOOL. Madreporaria.
madreporita f. Madreporite.
madrero, ra adj. FAM. *Ser muy madrero* or *demasiado madrero*, to be tied to one's mother's apron strings, to be a mother's boy (hombre) *o* girl (mujer).
madreselva f. BOT. Honeysuckle.
Madrid n. pr. GEOGR. Madrid.
madrigal m. POÉT. Madrigal.
madrigalesco, ca adj. Madrigalian. || FIG. Delicate, elegant.
madriguera f. Burrow, hole (de conejos, etc.). || Earth, lair, den (de zorros, tejones). || FIG. Den [of thieves] (guarida).
madrileño, ña adj./s. Madrilenian.
Madriles (Los) n. pr. m. pl. FAM. Madrid.
madrina f. Godmother (de un niño). || Bridesmaid (de boda) [V. OBSERV.]. || FIG. Protectress (protectora). | Sponsor (de un candidato). || Post, pole (poste). || Strap which connects the bits of two horses (correa). || AGR. Lead mare. || MAR. Stanchion. || *Amer.* Herd of tame animals used to lead a wild herd. || *Madrina de guerra*, girl *o* woman who sends letters, gifts, etc. to a soldier during a war.

— OBSERV. In Spain the *madrina* is the woman, generally the mother of the groom, who accompanies the groom into the church and is one of the witnesses to the wedding.

madrinazgo m. Role of godmother. || Sponsorship.
madroñal m. o **madroñera** f. Patch of strawberry trees *o* madrona trees.
madroño m. BOT. Strawberry tree, madrona [tree] (árbol). || Small strawberry (fruta). || Berry-shaped tassel (borlita).
madrugada f. Dawn (alba). || [Early] morning: *a las dos de la madrugada*, at two o'clock in the morning. || Early rising (acción de madrugar). || — *De madrugada*, at daybreak. || *Levantarse de madrugada*, to get up very early.
madrugador, ra adj. Early rising, who gets up early. || *Ser madrugador*, to be an early riser.
— M. y f. Early riser.
madrugar v. intr. To get up early. || — FIG. *A quien madruga, Dios le ayuda*, the early bird catches the worm. *No por mucho madrugar amanece más temprano*, time must take its course.
madrugón, ona adj. Early rising.
— M. Very early riser. || *Darse un madrugón*, to get up very early.
maduración f. Maturation, ripening.
maduradero m. Place for ripening fruit.
maduramiento m. Maturing, ripening, maturation.
madurar v. tr. AGR. To mature, to ripen. || MED. To ripen. || FIG. To think out, to mature (un plan): *madurar un problema*, to think out a problem. | To mature (una persona).
— V. intr. To ripen, to mature (fruta, etc.). || FIG. To mature. || MED. To ripen.
— V. pr. To ripen. || FIG. To mature.
madurez f. Ripeness, maturity. || FIG. Maturity. | Wisdom, prudence (sabiduría).
maduro, ra adj. Ripe, mature (fruta). || FIG. Mature: *juicio maduro*, mature judgment; *edad madura*, mature age. || MED. Ripe (absceso). || — *Pera muy madura*, mellow pear. || *Poco maduro*, unripe, green (fruta), immature (persona).
maelstrom m. Maelstrom.
maesa f. Queen bee.
maese m. (Ant.). Master (maestro): *maese Pedro*, master Peter. || FAM. *Maese Zorro*, Reynard the Fox.
maestoso adv. MÚS. Maestoso.
maestra f. [School] teacher, schoolmistress (de escuela). || Teacher's wife, wife of a teacher (esposa del maestro). || Teacher, instructor: *maestra de piano*, piano teacher. || Girl's school (escuela): *ir a la maestra*, to go to a girl's school. || Queen bee (abeja maestra). || FIG. Teacher: *la desgracia es la mejor maestra del hombre*, misfortune is the best teacher [of man]. || TECN. Guide line (listón que sirve de guía). || *Maestra de escuela* or *de primeras letras*, teacher, schoolteacher, schoolmistress.
maestrante m. Member of a riding club.
maestranza f. Equestrian society of Spanish noblemen (sociedad de equitación). || MAR. Petty officers, *pl.* || MIL. Arsenal (talleres). | Men who work in an arsenal (operarios).
maestrazgo m. Dignity of the grand master of a military order. || Territory under jurisdiction of the grand master of a military order.
maestre m. Master [of a military order]: *el maestre de Santiago*, the master of Santiago; *gran maestre*, grand master.
maestresala m. Headwaiter, maître d'hôtel.
maestrescuela m. Cathedral dignitary who teaches divinity. || Chancellor (en las universidades).
maestría f. Master's degree. || Mastery, skill, talent: *pintar con maestría* to paint with skill.
maestril m. Queen cell (apicultura).
maestrillo m. Insignificant schoolmaster. || FIG. *Cada maestrillo tiene su librillo*, each person has his own way of thinking.
maestro, tra adj. Main, principal: *viga maestra*, main beam. || Skilled, expert (hábil). || Basic, governing (idea). || Trained (adiestrado): *perro maestro*, trained dog. || — *Abeja maestra*, queen bee. || *Clavija maestra*, kingpin, kingbolt. || *Con* or *de mano maestra*, masterfully. || AVIAC. y MAR. *Cuaderna maestra*, midship frame. || *Golpe maestro*, masterstroke. || *Llave maestra*, master key, skeleton key. || *Obra maestra*, masterpiece. || MAR. *Palo maestro*, mainmast.
— M. Master (de un arte): *maestro de armas* or *de esgrima*, fencing master. || Teacher, schoolmaster, schoolteacher (profesor). || Master (práctico): *maestro sastre*, master tailor. || Master: *inspirarse en los maestros*, to take one's inspiration from the masters. || MAR. Mainmast. || MÚS. Maestro. || — *Gran maestro*, grand master. || *Maestro de baile*, dancing master. || *Maestro de capilla*, chapel master, choirmaster. || *Maestro de ceremonias*, master of ceremonies. || *Maestro de cocina*, chef, master cook (cocinero). || *Maestro de escuela*, schoolmaster. || *Maestro de obras*, master builder. || *Ser maestro* or *maestro consumado en el arte de*, to be a master at, to be a master in the art of.
maffia o **mafia** f. Maffia, mafia.
mafioso, sa adj. Of the Maffia.
— M. y f. Member of the Maffia, mafioso.
Magallanes n. pr. HIST. Magellan. || GEOGR. *Estrecho de Magallanes*, Magellan Straits.
magancear v. intr. *Amer.* To loaf about, to laze about, to lead an idle life.
maganza f. *Amer.* FAM. Laziness.
maganzón, ona adj. *Amer.* FAM. Lazy.
— M. y f. *Amer.* FAM. Loafer, lazybones.
magdalena f. Madeleine, small sponge cake (pastel). || FIG. Magdalene, repentant woman.
Magdalena n. pr. f. Magdalene, Magdalen. || FIG. y FAM. *Estar hecho una Magdalena* or *llorar como una Magdalena*, to weep one's heart out.
magdaleniense adj./s.m. Magdalenian.
magenta adj. Magenta. || *Azul magenta*, magenta.
magia f. Magic: *magia blanca, negra*, white, black magic. || FIG. Magic, charm, spell (encanto). || *Por arte de magia*, as if by magic, by magic.
magiar adj./s. Magyar.
mágico, ca adj. Magic, magical: *poder mágico*, magic power. || FIG. Wonderful, marvellous. || *Varita mágica*, magic wand.
— M. y f. Magician (mago). || — F. Magic (magia).
magín m. FAM. Imagination (imaginación). | Mind (mente). | Good sense (sentido común). || — FAM. *Duro de magín*, dense, as thick as a plank, as daft as a brush. | *Idea de su magín*, figment of one's imagination. | *Se lo ha sacado de su magín*, it is a figment of his imagination.
magister m. FAM. Schoolmaster.
magisterial adj. Magisterial, teaching.
magisterio m. Teaching (enseñanza): *se dedicó al magisterio*, he took up teaching. || Teaching staff *o* body, teachers, *pl.* (conjunto de maestros). || Teaching profession (empleo). || FIG. Affected solemnity.
magistrado m. Magistrate.
magistral adj. Magistral, magisterial: *en tono magistral*, with a magisterial tone. || Masterful (excelente).
magistratura f. Magistracy, magistrature. || *Magistratura del Trabajo*, conciliation board in industrial disputes.
magma m. Magma.
magnanimidad f. Magnanimity.
magnánimo, ma adj. Magnanimous.

magnate m. Magnate.
magnesia f. QUÍM. Magnesia.
magnesiano, na adj. QUÍM. Magnesian.
magnésico, ca adj. QUÍM. Magnesic.
magnesífero, ra adj. Magnesiferous.
magnesio m. QUÍM. Magnesium (metal). || Flashlight (de los fotógrafos).
magnesita f. MIN. Magnesite.
magnético, ca adj. Magnetic: *campo, ecuador, polo magnético*, magnetic field, equator, pole; *aguja, inducción, mina, tempestad magnética*, magnetic needle, induction, mine, storm. || *Grabación magnética*, tape recording, magnetic recording.
magnetismo m. Magnetism. || Magnetics (ciencia). || *Magnetismo animal*, animal magnetism (hipnotismo).
magnetita f. MIN. Magnetite.
magnetizable adj. Magnetizable.
magnetización f. Magnetization.
magnetizar v. tr. To magnetize. || To hypnotize. || FIG. To fascinate, to mesmerize, to magnetize.
magneto f. Magneto.
magnetoeléctrico, ca adj. Magnetoelectric.
magnetofón o **magnetófono** m. Tape recorder, magnetophone.
magnetofónico, ca adj. Magnetic. || *Cinta magnetofónica*, magnetic tape, recording tape.
magnetómetro m. Magnetometer.
magnetoscopio m. Magnetoscope.
magnetrón m. TECN. Magnetron.
magnicida m. Assassin, murderer.
magnicidio m. Assassination of an important person.
magnificar v. tr. To magnify.
magníficat m. Magnificat (himno).
magnificencia f. Magnificence, grandeur. || Generosity.
magnificente adj. Magnificent.
magnífico, ca adj. Magnificent. || Generous (generoso). || *El Rector Magnífico*, the Rector.
magnitud f. Magnitude. || Size (tamaño). || Greatness (grandeza). || FIG. Order: *potencia nuclear de primera magnitud*, nuclear power of the first order. | Magnitude: *un proyecto de gran magnitud*, a project of great magnitude. || ASTR. Magnitude.
magno, na adj. Great, grand. || — *Alejandro Magno* Alexander the Great. || *Aula magna*, main amphitheatre. || *Carta Magna*, Magna Carta, Magna charta. || *Magna Grecia*, Magna Graecia.
magnolia f. BOT. Magnolia (árbol, flor).
magnoliáceas f. pl. BOT. Magnoliaceae.
magnolio m. BOT. Magnolia (árbol).
mago, ga adj. Magian. || *Los tres Reyes Magos*, the three Magi, the three Wise Men of the East, the Three Kings.
— M. Magician, wizard (que ejerce la magia). || Magus, sage (sacerdote de la religión de Zoroastro). || *Simón Mago*, Simon Magus.
magra f. Slice of ham.
magrear v. tr. POP. To pet, to paw.
Magreb n. pr. m. GEOGR. Maghreb.
magrez f. Thinness, leanness.
magro, gra adj. Meagre [U.S., meager] (pobre). || Lean, thin, gaunt (persona). || Lean (carne).
— M. Lean meat (carne sin grasa).
maguer o **magüer** conj. Although (aunque).
— OBSERV. *Magüer* is a barbarism.
maguey o **magüey** m. BOT. Maguey (pita).
— OBSERV. *Magüey* is a barbarism.
magulladura f. o **magullamiento** m. Bruise, contusion.
magullar v. tr. To bruise, to contuse (una persona). || To bruise (una fruta).
magullón m. *Amer.* Bruise.
Maguncia n. pr. GEOGR. Mainz.
magyar adj./s. Magyar.
maharajá m. Maharaja, maharajah.
maharaní f. Maharanee, maharani.
mahatma m. Mahatma.
Mahoma n. pr. m. Mohammed, Mahomet.
mahometano, na adj./s. Mohammedan, Mahometan, Muslim.
mahometismo m. Mohammedanism, Islam.
mahometista adj./s. Mohammedan, Muslim.
mahometizar v. intr. To profess Mohammedanism.
mahón m. Nankeen (tela).
mahonesa f. Mayonnaise (salsa).
maicena f. Cornflour [U.S., cornstarch].
maicero m. *Amer.* Maize dealer [U.S., corn dealer].
— Adj. Maize [U.S., corn].
mail-coach m. Four-in-hand (berlina inglesa).
maillechort m. Nickel silver, German silver (metal).
mainel m. ARQ. Mullion (montante vertical), transom (montante horizontal).
maitinada f. Dawn (madrugada). || Aubade, dawn song *o* serenade (serenata).
maitines m. pl. REL. Matins: *llamar* or *tocar a maitines*, to call *o* to ring to matins.
maíz m. BOT. Maize [U.S., corn]: *maíz tostado*, toasted maize. || *Roseta de maíz*, popcorn.
maizal m. Maize field [U.S., cornfield].
maja f. Elegant young girl (mujer). || Pestle (del mortero). || V. MAJO.
majada f. Sheepfold (aprisco). || Animal manure, dung (estiércol). || *Amer.* Flock of sheep (rebaño).
majadal m. Pasture land for sheep (pastizal). || Sheepfold (majada).
majadería f. Nonsense, absurdity (necedad). || *Decir majaderías*, to talk nonsense, to make stupid remarks.
majadero, ra adj. Stupid, foolish (necio).
— M. y f. Fool, clown, idiot (necio). || — M. Pestle (maza). || Lace bobbin (del huso).
majado m. Crushing, pounding, grinding.
majador, ra adj. Crushing, pounding, grinding.
— M. y f. Crusher, pounder, grinder.
majadura f. Crushing, pounding, grinding (machacadura).
majagranzas m. inv. FAM. Bore (pesado). | Clumsy oaf, clod (torpe).
majamiento m. Crushing, pounding, grinding.
majar v. tr. To crush, to pound, to grind: *majar algo en un mortero*, to crush sth. in a mortar. || FIG. y FAM. To bother, to pester, to get on [s.o.'s] nerves (molestar). | To wallop (pegar). | To wipe out, to annihilate: *majar un ejército*, to wipe out an army. || FIG. *Majar a uno a palos*, to beat s.o. up.
majara o **majareta** adj. FAM. Cracked, nuts, nutty, touched (loco).
— M. y f. FAM. Nut.
majestad f. Majesty. || Stateliness, grandeur (grandeza). || — *Su Divina Majestad*, the Divine Majesty (Dios). || *Su Graciosa Majestad*, His Majesty the King, Her Majesty the Queen (de Inglaterra). || *Su Majestad*, Your Majesty, your Highness (dirigiéndose a un soberano), His *o* Her Majesty (hablando de un soberano). || *Su Majestad Católica*, His Catholic Majesty [King of France]. || *Su Majestad Cristianísima*, His Christian Majesty [King of Spain].
majestuosidad f. Majesty, stateliness: *la majestuosidad de su porte*, the majesty of his bearing.
majestuoso, sa adj. Majestic, stately, imposing.
majeza f. FAM. Elegance.
majo, ja adj. Toffish (dicho de gentes del pueblo) [V. OBSERV.] || FAM. Smart, well dressed (compuesto): *ir muy majo*, to be very smart *o* very well dressed. | Nice, sweet, cute (mono). | Pretty, beautiful (hermoso). | Nice (simpático). | Corky (bravucón). | Showy, flashy (vistoso).
— M. y f. Toff, dandy. || *¡Maja!, ¡majo!*, love! [U.S., honey]: *¡anda, majo!*, come on, love!
— OBSERV. *Majo* was applied chiefly to the young men of the 16th century from the lower classes who adopted the elegance and the carefree style of the nobles. They have been frequently represented by Goya in his paintings. Nowadays the usual meaning of the word is *pretty* or *nice*.
majolar m. Grove of hawthorns.
majoleto m. BOT. Hawthorn (majuelo).
majuelo m. BOT. Hawthorn (espino). | Young grapevine (viña joven).
maki m. ZOOL. Maki.
mal adj. [Apocopated form of *malo* used before a masculine sing. noun] Bad: *mal humor*, bad humour. || *Tener mal color*, to look off colour *o* poorly (tener mala cara).
— M. Evil: *los males de la guerra*, the evils of war. || Evil, wrong, wrongdoing: *el bien y el mal*, good and evil, right and wrong. || Harm, hurt, damage, wrong (daño, perjuicio): *para reparar el mal*, to undo the harm, to right the wrong, to repair the damage. || Disease, illness (enfermedad). || Misfortune (desgracia). || Harm, ill: *no le deseo ningún mal*, I don't wish him any harm. || — *Acogerse al mal menor*, to choose the lesser of two evils. || *A grandes males grandes remedios*, desperate ills call for desperate measures. || *Caer en el mal*, to fall into evil ways. || *Combatir el mal*, to fight [against] evil. || *Del mal el menos*, the lesser of two evils; of two evils one must choose the lesser. || *El mal consiste en que...*, the trouble is ... || *Estar a mal con alguien*, to be on bad terms with s.o. || *Hacer mucho mal*, to do a lot of harm *o* evil (hacer daño). || *Llevar a mal una cosa*, to take sth. amiss, to be offended by sth. || *Mal caduco*, epilepsy. || *Mal de la tierra*, homesickness. || *Mal de montaña*, mountain sickness. || *Mal de muchos, consuelo de tontos*, it's a fool's consolation to think everyone is in the same boat. || *Mal de ojo*, the evil eye. || *Mal de piedra*, urinary calculi, *pl.* || *Mal de San Vito*, St. Vitus's dance. || *Mal francés*, syphilis. || *¡Mal haya...!* v. MALHAYA. || *Mal menor*, lesser evil. || *No hay mal que dure cien años*, everything will turn out all right in the end. || *No hay mal que por bien no venga*, every cloud has a silver lining. || *Ser un mal a medias*, to be only half bad. || *Tomar a mal*, to take badly: *tomó a mal mi broma*, he took my joke badly.
mal adv. Badly, poorly: *escribir mal*, to write badly. || Wrongly, badly: *escoger mal*, to choose wrongly. || Bad: *oler mal*, to smell bad. || Hardly, scarcely: *mal puede ayudarme*, he can hardly help me. || — *Caer mal*, v. CAER. || *Decir* or *hablar mal de uno*, to speak badly of s.o., to speak ill of s.o. || *Encontrarse mal*, to feel bad, to feel faint (en un momento). || *Encontrarse mal de salud*, not to feel well, to feel unwell. || *Estar mal de dinero*, to be hard up, to be short of money. || *Estar mal de salud*, to be ill, not to be well. || *Hacer mal*, to do [sth.] badly: *hacer mal su trabajo*, to do one's work badly; to be wrong: *hiciste mal obrando así*, you were wrong to act like that; *hace*

mal en reír, he is wrong to laugh. || *Ir de mal en peor*, to go from bad to worse. || *Mal de mi grado*, against my will. || *Mal que bien*, somehow (de un modo u otro). || *Mal que le pese*, like it or not. || *¡Menos mal!*, what a relief!, thank heavens! || *Menos mal que*, it's a good job that [U.S., it's a good thing that]: *menos mal que has venido*, it's a good job that you came. || *No está (nada) mal*, it's not bad [at all]. || *No estaría mal que viniese*, it wouldn't be bad if he came, it would be a good thing if he came. || *No hice mal en discutirlo con ella*, it was rather a good idea to discuss it with her, I am glad I discussed it with her. || *Oír mal*, not to hear very well. || *Por mal que le vaya*, at the worst. || *Salir mal*, V. SALIR. || *Ser un mal pensado*, to be evil-minded. || *Si mal no recuerdo*, if I remember rightly *o* correctly. || *Venirle mal a uno*, V. VENIR.

mala f. Trunk (baúl). || Mailbag (correo).

malabar adj./s. Malabar. || — *Hacer juegos malabares*, to juggle (en el circo). || FIG. *Hacer juegos malabares con las palabras*, to make plays on words, to pun. || *Juegos malabares*, juggling.

malabarismo m. Juggling. || FIG. Jugglery. || FIG. *Hacer malabarismos con los números*, to juggle with numbers.

malabarista m. y f. Juggler. || *Amer.* Sly thief.

Malaca n. pr. GEOGR. Malacca.

malacate m. Whim, winch (cabrestante). || *Amer.* Spindle (huso).

malacitano, na adj. [Of *o* from] Malaga.
— M. y f. Native *o* inhabitant of Malaga.

malaconsejado, da adj. Ill-advised.

malacopterigio, gia adj./s.m. Malacopterygian (peces).

malacostumbrado, da adj. Who has bad habits. || Ill-bred, ill-mannered (mal criado). || Spoiled (mimado).

malacostumbrarse v. pr. To get into bad habits.

malacrianza f. Bad breeding, lack of breeding, bad manners, *pl.*

málaga m. Malaga wine, Malaga (vino).

Málaga n. pr. GEOGR. Málaga. || FIG. y FAM. *Salir de Málaga para entrar en Malagón*, to jump out of the frying pan into the fire.

malage m. Insipidness, dullness, lack of wit *o* charm. || — *Cantó con malage*, he sang without spirit. || *Es un malage*, he is a bore, there is no life in him.
— OBSERV. This word is an Andalusian deformation of *mal ángel*.

malagradecido, da adj. Ungrateful.

malagueña f. Malaguena [song].

malagueño, ña adj. [Of *o* from] Malaga.
— M. y f. Native *o* inhabitant of Malaga.

malamente adv. FAM. Badly: *lo hice malamente*, I did it badly.

malandante adj. Unfortunate (desafortunado). || Unhappy (infeliz).

malandanza f. Misfortune.

malandrín, ina adj. Malign, perverse.
— M. Scoundrel.

malapata m. y f. FAM. Jinx (gafe). | — F. Bad luck (mala suerte).

malaquita f. MIN. Malachite.

malar adj./s.m. ANAT. Malar.

malaria f. MED. Malaria.

malasangre adj. Evil-minded.
— M. y f. Evil-minded person.

Malasia n. pr. f. GEOGR. Malaysia.

malasio, sia adj./s. Malaysian.

malasombra m. y f. FAM. Bore, pest (persona sosa o molesta). || — F. FAM. Bad luck (mala suerte). || Lack of charm *o* wit, dullness, insipidness (falta de gracia). || FAM. *¡Qué malasombra tiene!*, what a drag he is!

malatería f. Leprosery, leprosarium, lazaretto.

malatía f. Leprosy (lepra).

malavenido, da adj. Incompatible (dos personas).

malaventura o **malaventuranza** f. Misfortune. (desventura).

malaventurado, da adj. Unfortunate, poor.
— M. y f. Poor soul.

malaxación f. Malaxation (de una sustancia). || Massage (masaje).

malaxar v. tr. To malaxate (amasar). || To massage (dar masajes).

malayo, ya adj./s. Malay, Malayan.

Malaysia n. pr. GEOGR. Malaysia.

malbaratador, ra adj. Squandering.
— M. y f. Squanderer, spendthrift.

malbaratar v. tr. To squander (malgastar). || To undersell (malvender).

malcarado, da adj. Grim-faced.

malcasado, da adj. Unfaithful (infiel). || Married to s.o. below one's station (con persona de condición inferior).
— M. y f. Unfaithful person (infiel). || Person married to s.o. below his *o* her station.

malcasar v. tr. To mismatch, to mismate.
— V. pr. To make a bad marriage. || To marry beneath o.s. *o* below one's station.

malcomer v. intr. To eat poorly.

malcomido, da adj. Underfed, undernourished.

malconsiderado, da adj. Inconsiderate, thoughtless.

malcontentadizo, za adj. Hard to please, ill-humoured [U.S., ill-humored].

malcontento, ta adj. Malcontent (contra las autoridades). || Discontented, displeased, unhappy: *malcontento con su suerte*, discontented with his lot.
— M. Malcontent.

malcriadez f. *Amer.* V. MALACRIANZA.

malcriado, da adj. Ill-bred, bad mannered.
— M. y f. Ill-bred *o* bad mannered person.

malcriar v. tr. To raise [a person] badly. || To spoil (mimar).

maldad f. Badness, evil, wickedness (carácter de malo). || Bad thing, evil thing, wicked thing. || *Cometer maldades*, to do evil *o* wrong.

maldecido, da adj. Wicked, evil (malo). || Damned (maldito).
— M. y f. Wicked *o* evil person (persona mala).

maldecidor, ra adj. Backbiting (que calumnia). || Foulmouthed (que blasfema).
— M. y f. Evil-tongued person, backbiter.

maldecir* v. tr. To curse (echar una maldición): *maldijo a su hijo*, he cursed his son. || To curse (renegar de): *maldecir su suerte*, to curse one's luck.
— V. intr. To backbite (murmurar). || To swear, to curse (blasfemar). || *Maldecir de algo* or *alguien*, to speak ill of sth. *o* s.o. (hablar mal de), to curse sth. *o* s.o. (echar maldiciones).

maldiciente adj. Backbiting (que calumnia). || Foulmouthed (que blasfema).
— M. y f. Backbiter, evil-tongued person.

maldición f. Curse, malediction: *una maldición parecía haber caído sobre el pueblo*, it seemed as if a curse had fallen upon the town. || Imprecation (imprecación). || Blasphemy, curse, oath (blasfemia).
— Interj. Damn it!, curse it!, damnation!

maldispuesto, ta adj. Indisposed (de salud). || Ill-disposed, reluctant (sin ganas).

maldita f. FAM. Tongue.

maldito, ta adj. Cursed, damned (condenado). || Damned, confounded, bloody (pop.), cursed: *¡maldito embustero!*, damned liar! || Lousy (fam.), rotten (fam.): *no tengo ni una maldita peseta*, I haven't even got one lousy peseta. || — *Maldita la gana que tengo*, I don't feel like it at all. || *¡Maldita sea!*, damn it! || *Maldito lo que le importa*, he doesn't care a damn. || *No le hago maldito caso*, I don't take a blind bit of notice. || *No sé maldita la cosa de eso*, I know damn all about it. || *No tiene maldita la gracia*, I don't find it the least bit amusing.
— M. Devil (diablo). || TEATR. Extra.

Maldivas n. pr. f. pl. *Islas Maldivas*, Maldive Islands.

maleabilidad f. Malleability.

maleabilizar v. tr. To make malleable.

maleable adj. Malleable.

maleado, da adj. Corrupted, perverted.

maleamiento m. Corruption.

maleante adj. Corrupting (que corrompe). || Perverse (perverso). || Malicious, wicked (maligno). || Shady (poco de fiar).
— M. Evildoer, crook, malefactor (malhechor). || Vagrant (vagabundo).

malear v. tr. To spoil, to ruin (estropear). || FIG. To corrupt, to pervert (pervertir).
— V. pr. To go bad, to be corrupted *o* perverted (pervertirse). || To be spoilt *o* ruined (estropearse).

malecón m. Dike, mole, jetty (dique).

maledicencia f. Evil talk, slander.

malediciente adj./s. V. MALDICIENTE.

maleducado, da adj. Ill-bred, bad-mannered.
— M. y f. Boor, ill-bred *o* bad-mannered person.

maleficencia f. Maleficence, wrongdoing.

maleficiado, da adj. Bewitched, under a spell.

maleficiar v. tr. To harm, to injure (a uno). || To damage (algo). || To curse, to cast a spell on, to bewitch (embrujar).

maleficiente adj. Maleficent.

maleficio m. Evil spell, curse.

maléfico, ca adj. Maleficent, evil, harmful (dañino): *un poder maléfico*, an evil power. || Malefic (en astrología).
— M. y f. Sorcerer (que hace maleficios).

malencarado, da adj. Insolent, bad-mannered.

malentendido m. Misunderstanding.

maléolo m. ANAT. Maleolus.

malespín m. *Amer.* Jargon used by street urchins.

malestar m. Malaise, indisposition: *sentir malestar*, to feel malaise. || FIG. Uneasiness (inquietud). | Unrest (del pueblo por causas políticas, etc.).

maleta f. Suitcase, case (de ropa). || Boot [U.S., trunk] (de coche). || *Amer.* Bundle (lío de ropa). | Saddlebag (de bicicleta, de una montura). || *Hacer la maleta*, to pack one's bags *o* one's suitcase.
— M. Bungler [said especially of bullfighters]. || Despicable person (hombre despreciable).

maletera f. *Amer.* V. MALETA.

maletero m. Suitcase maker (que hace maletas). || Boot [U.S., trunk] (de coche). || Porter, station porter (mozo de estación).

maletilla m. FAM. Novice, youth who aspires to become a bullfighter.

maletín m. Small suitcase, valise (maleta pequeña). || Medical bag (de médico, veterinario). || Briefcase, attaché case (para documentos). || MIL. *Maletín de grupa*, saddlebag.

maletón m. Big suitcase (maleta grande).

malevaje m. *Amer.* Banditry.

malevo, va adj. Malevolent (malévolo).
— M. y f. *Amer.* Malefactor, evildoer.
malevolencia f. Malevolence, ill will.
malévolo, la adj. Malevolent.
maleza f. Weeds, *pl.* (hierbas). || Undergrowth, underbrush, scrub (arbustos). || Brambles, *pl.* (zarzas). || *Amer.* Pus.
malformación f. Malformation.
malgache adj./s. Madagascan, Malagasy. || *República Malgache*, Malagasy Republic.
malgastador, ra adj. Wasteful, squandering.
— M. y f. Squanderer, spendthrift.
malgastar v. tr. To squander, to waste (bienes). || To ruin, to run down (salud). || To waste (tiempo).
malgeniado, da adj. *Amer.* Irritable, bad-tempered.
malhablado, da adj. Foulmouthed.
— M. y f. Foulmouthed person.
malhadado, da adj. Unfortunate, unlucky, ill-fated.
malhaya adj. FAM. Damned, cursed. || — *Malhaya sea quien mal piense*, evil be to him who evil thinks. || *¡Malhaya sea!*, damn it!
malhecho, cha adj. Malformed, deformed, misshapen.
— M. Misdeed, malefaction.
malhechor, ra adj. Wicked, malefactory.
— M. y f. Malefactor, wrongdoer, evildoer.
malherir* v. tr. To wound *o* to injure badly.
malhumor m. Bad temper, ill-humour.
malhumorado, da adj. Bad-tempered, ill-humoured. || *Responder con tono malhumorado*, to reply gruffly.
malhumorar v. tr. To put in a bad mood, to annoy, to upset.
malicia f. Malice, maliciousness, wickedness (perversidad). || Evil intention (maldad). || Slyness, cunning, trickiness (astucia, sutileza). || Mischievousness, mischief (de los niños). || Roguishness, naughtiness (de la mirada, de un dicho). || Viciousness (de un animal). || FIG. y FAM. *Tener la malicia de que*, to suspect that, to have a suspicion that (tener recelo): *tengo la malicia de que no ocurrió así*, I suspect that it didn't happen like that.
maliciable adj. Suspicious (sospechoso). || Corruptible.
maliciarse v. pr. To go bad (malearse). || To have one's suspicions about sth. *o* s.o. (sospechar). || *Algo me malicio en ese lío*, there is sth. fishy about this mess, I smell a rat in this mess.
malicioso, sa adj. Malicious, evil, wicked (malo). || Shrewd, sly, cunning (astuto). || Ill-intentioned (malintencionado). || Roguish, naughty (mirada, chiste).
málico adj. m. QUÍM. Malic (ácido).
malignidad f. Malignity, malignancy.
maligno, gna adj. Malignant: *fiebre maligna*, malignant fever; *tumor maligno*, malignant tumour. || Malicious, malignant, perverse: *intención maligna*, malicious intentions. || Wicked, evil (malo).
malilla f. Manille (en juegos de cartas).
malinas f. Mechlin lace, *sing.* (encaje).
Malinas n. pr. GEOGR. Malines, Mechlin.
malintencionado, da adj. Ill-intentioned, evil-intentioned.
malmandado, da adj. Disobedient.
— M. y f. Disobedient person.
malmaridada adj. f. Unfaithful.
— F. Unfaithful wife.
malmirado, da adj. Ill-considered. || Inconsiderate, discourteous (descortés).
malo, la adj. Bad (que no es bueno): *este vino es malo*, this wine is bad; *una acción mala*, a bad act *o* deed. || Evil, wicked, bad (perverso): *malos pensamientos*, evil thoughts; *tu amigo es malo*, your friend is wicked. || Mean, nasty: *es malo con* or *para con sus hermanos*, he is mean to his brothers. || Naughty, mischievous (aplicado especialmente a los niños). || Bad, nasty (sabor, olor). || Sick, ill (enfermo): *estar malo*, to be sick. || Unpleasant, disagreeable obnoxious (desagradable). || Hard, difficult (dificultoso): *este perro es malo de enseñar*, this dog is hard to train. || Bad, poor (insuficiente): *una mala cosecha*, a bad crop. || FAM. No good (sin habilidad, que no sirve): *soy malo para las matemáticas*, I'm no good at mathematics; *vamos a tirar todo lo que esté malo*, let's throw away everything which is no good. || — FIG. *Andar a malas*, to be on bad terms. || *Dar mala vida a alguien*, to make s.o.'s life a misery. || *En mala hora*, at the wrong time. || FIG. *Estar de malas*, to be down on one's luck (tener mala suerte), to be in a bad mood (de mal humor). | *Estar de malas con la justicia*, to be on the wrong side of the law. || *Los ángeles malos*, the fallen angels. || *Mala jugada*, dirty trick. || *¡Mala suerte!*, bad luck! || *Mala temporada*, wrong season *o* time of year. || *Más vale malo conocido, que bueno por conocer*, better the devil you know than the one you don't know. || FIG. *Ponerse de malas con alguien*, to fall out with s.o. || *Ponerse malo*, to get *o* to fall ill. || *Ponerse malo de risa*, to die laughing, to split one's sides laughing. || *Por las buenas o por las malas*, willy-nilly. || *Por las malas*, by force. || *Tener mala cara*, to look off-colour *o* under the weather *o* unwell. || *Tener mala suerte*, to be unlucky, to have bad luck. || FIG. *Venir de malas*, to be in a bad mood.
— M. *El Malo*, The Devil (el diablo), the villain, the bad guy [fam.] (en una narración, película). || *Lo malo es que...*, the trouble is that...
— Interj. That's bad! (un asunto). || Naughty! (a un niño, etc.). || Boo! (en un espectáculo).
— OBSERV. One should not confuse *ser malo*, to be bad *o* evil, with *estar malo*, to be sick.
— *Malo* is apocopated to *mal* before a masculine singular noun.
maloca f. *Amer.* Attack on Indian territory. | Raid (correría).
malogrado, da adj. Ill-fated, unfortunate [applied to a person who died before reaching the climax of his career] (artista, etc.): *el malogrado poeta García Lorca*, the ill-fated poet García Lorca. || Abortive (proyecto, etc.). || Wasted (esfuerzo).
malograr v. tr. To waste, to lose, to miss (no aprovecharse de): *malograr una oportunidad*, to waste an opportunity. || To spoil, to ruin (estropear). || *Malograr la vida*, to be a failure.
— V. pr. To fail, to fall through, to come to nothing (fracasar): *se malograron sus esperanzas*, his hopes fell through. || Not to come up to s.o.'s expectations (autor, hijo, etc.). || To be wasted, to be lost *o* missed (oportunidad). || To be cut off in one's prime (morir prematuramente). || AGR. To fail (la cosecha).
malogro m. Failure (fracaso). || Untimely end (fin). || AGR. Failure.
maloliente adj. Smelly, foul-smelling, malodorous.
malón m. *Amer.* Surprise attack by Indians, Indian raid.
maloquear v. intr. *Amer.* To make a surprise attack, to raid.
malparar v. tr. To damage, to harm (estropear). || To hurt (maltratar). || — *Dejar algo* or *a alguien malparado*, to leave sth. *o* s.o. in a sorry state: *Francisco dejó malparado a Juan*, Frank left John in a sorry state; *la enfermedad le ha dejado malparado*, his illness has left him in a sorry state. || *Salir malparado de un negocio*, to come off badly in a business deal.
malparida f. Woman who has miscarried.
malparir v. intr. To miscarry, to have a miscarriage.
malparto m. Miscarriage (aborto).
malpensado, da adj. Nasty-minded, evil-minded, malicious.
— M. y f. Nasty-minded person. || — *Es un malpensado*, he is nasty-minded. || *No seas malpensado*, don't be nasty.
malquerencia f. Malevolence, ill will (malevolencia). || Antipathy, dislike (antipatía).
malquerer* v. tr. To dislike.
malquerido, da adj. Disliked, unpopular.
malquistar v. tr. To set at loggerheads, to alienate, to estrange.
— V. pr. To fall out (enfadarse).
malquisto, ta adj. Estranged, alienated (enfadado). || Disliked, unpopular (mal considerado).
malsano, na adj. Unhealthy (malo para la salud). || Sick, morbid (mentalidad, pensamiento).
malsonante adj. Ill-sounding (que suena mal). || Obnoxious, offensive, nasty (palabra).
malsufrido, da adj. Weak (débil). || Impatient.
malta f. Malt (cebada). || *Amer.* Top quality beer (cerveza). || *Fábrica de malta*, malthouse.
Malta n. pr. GEOGR. Malta: *caballero de Malta*, Knight of Malta. || *Cruz de Malta*, Maltese cross.
maltaje m. TECN. Malting.
maltasa f. Maltase.
maltear v. tr. TECN. To malt.
malteado m. TECN. Malting.
maltería f. Malthouse (fábrica).
maltés, esa adj/s. Maltese.
maltosa f. QUÍM. Maltose.
maltraer* v. tr. To maltreat, to ill-treat, to treat badly (tratar mal). || FIG. *Llevar* or *traer a maltraer*, to give s.o. a hard time.
maltraído, da adj. *Amer.* Shabby, badly dressed, untidy, dishevelled (desaseado).
maltratamiento m. Maltreatment, ill-treatment, abuse.
maltratar v. tr. To maltreat, to ill-treat, to treat badly, to mistreat (tratar mal): *no se debe maltratar a los animales*, one should not ill-treat animals. || To spoil, to damage (echar a perder).
maltrato m. Maltreatment, ill-treatment.
maltrecho, cha adj. Battered, wrecked, damaged. || *Dejar algo* or *a alguien maltrecho*, to leave sth. *o* s.o. in a sorry state: *dejar maltrecho al enemigo*, to leave the enemy in a sorry state.
maltusianismo m. Malthusianism.
maltusiano, na adj./s. Malthusian.
malucho, cha adj. FAM. Sickly, out of sorts (algo enfermo): *hoy está malucho*, he is sickly today. | Rather bad (tirando a malo).
malva f. BOT. Mallow. || — FAM. *Estar criando malvas*, to be pushing up the daisies. || BOT. *Malva loca, real* or *rósea*, rose mallow, hollyhock. || FIG. *Ser como una malva*, to be as meek as a lamb.
— Adj. inv./s.m. Mauve (color).
malváceas f. pl. BOT. Malvaceae.
malvadamente adv. Spitefully, nastily (con maldad).
malvado, da adj. Evil, wicked, villainous.
— M. y f. Evildoer, villain, wicked person.
malvaloca o **malvarrosa** f. BOT. Rose mallow, hollyhock.

malvasía f. Malmsey (vino). || Malvasia (uva).
malvavisco m. BOT. Marshmallow.
malvender v. tr. To sell at a loss, to sell off cheap, to sacrifice.
malversación f. Malversation, embezzlement, misappropriation.
malversador, ra adj. Embezzling.
— M. y f. Embezzler.
malversar v. tr. To embezzle, to misappropriate.
Malvinas n. pr. f. pl. GEOGR. *Islas Malvinas*, Falkland Islands.
malvinero, ra adj. Falkland Island.
— M. y f. Native *o* inhabitant of the Falkland Islands.
malvís m. Redwing, song thrush (ave).
malvivir v. intr. To live badly.
malvón m. *Amer.* Geranium.
malla f. Mesh (de una red). || Net, network, mesh (red de hilo). || Mail (de metal): *cota de mallas*, coat of mail. || *Amer.* Bathing costume, swimsuit (bañador). | Tights, *pl.* (de deportista). || — Pl. DEP. Net, *sing.* (de portería). || *Amer. Hacer malla*, to knit.
mallar v. intr. To make meshing *o* netting *o* network.
mallo m. Mallet, maul (mazo). || Mall, pall mall (juego y terreno).
Mallorca n. pr. GEOGR. Majorca.
mallorquín, ina adj./s. Majorcan.
mama f. ANAT. Mamma, mammary gland (teta). | Breast (pecho). || FAM. Mamma, mama, mommy, mom, mummy, mum (madre).
mamá f. FAM. Mummy, mum, mamma, mama, mommy, mom (madre). || *Amer. Mamá señora*, grandmother.
mamacallos m. inv. FIG. y FAM. Fool, simpleton, dolt.
mamacita f. *Amer.* Mommy, mummy.
mamacona f. *Amer.* Incan priestess.
mamada f. Nursing, sucking (acción). || Feeding time [time a child nurses] (tiempo). || *Amer.* FAM. Windfall (ganga). | Booze-up, drinking spree [U.S., drunk] (borrachera). || FAM. *Coger una mamada*, to get drunk.
mamadera f. Breast pump. || *Amer.* Teat [U.S., nipple] (del biberón). | Feeding bottle [U.S., nursing bottle] (biberón).
mamado, da adj. POP. Drunk, plastered, sloshed, canned, stoned (borracho). || *Amer.* Foolish (tonto). || POP. *Esto está mamado*, this is a cinch, this is a piece of cake.
mamador, ra adj. Sucking, nursing.
mamagrande f. *Amer.* Grandmother.
mamaíta o **mamita** f. FAM. Mummy, mommy.
mamancona f. *Amer.* Fat old woman.
mamandurria f. *Amer.* Sinecure (ganga).
mamar v. tr. To suck, to nurse (el niño). || FIG. y FAM. To be suckled on, to grow up in *o* with *o* amidst: *mamar la honradez*, to be suckled on honour. | To learn from childhood, to grow up with: *haber mamado un idioma*, to have learned a language from childhood. | To swallow (engullir).
— V. intr. To suck. || *Dar de mamar*, to suckle, to give suck, to nurse.
— V. pr. FAM. To get drunk *o* stoned *o* canned *o* sloshed *o* plastered (emborracharse). | To wangle, to fiddle, to get (ventajas, etc.). || FAM. To stick, to swallow: *mamarse dos años de cárcel*, to stick two years in prison. || — *Amer. Mamarse a uno*, to get the better of s.o. (aventajar), to cheat s.o., to take s.o. in (engañar), to do s.o. in, to do away with s.o. (matar). || FIG. y FAM. *No se mama el dedo*, there are no flies on him, he wasn't born yesterday.
mamario, ria adj. ANAT. Mammary.
mamarrachada f. FAM. Daub, bad painting (cuadro malo). | Washout, dead loss (libro, película). | Nonsense, tomfoolery (idiotez).
mamarrachista m. y f. FAM. Botcher, dauber (pintor).
mamarracho m. FAM. Ninny, clown, nincompoop (tonto). | Puppet (fantoche). | Horror, sight, hag (fealdad). | Daub, bad painting (cuadro malo). | Washout, dead loss (libro, película malos). || *Iba hecho un mamarracho*, he was dressed like a tramp *o* like a scarecrow.
mambí o **mambís, isa** adj. Rebellious, separatist [in Cuba in 1868].
— M. y f. Rebel, separatist.
Mambrú n. pr. m. Marlborough.
mamela f. FAM. Bribe (comisión extra).
mamelón m. Dug, teat (de animales). || Knoll, hill (colina).
mameluco m. Mameluke. || FIG. y FAM. Dolt, simpleton (necio). || *Amer.* Overalls, *pl.* (prenda para obreros). | Child's sleepsuit, rompers, *pl.* (para niños). | Brazilian mestizo, mameluco.
mamífero, ra adj. Mammalian, mammiferous.
— M. Mammal. || — Pl. Mammalia, mammals.
mamila f. ZOOL. Udder, teat (de la hembra). || ANAT. Nipple (del hombre).
mamilar adj. ANAT. Mammillary.
mamola f. Chuck [under the chin]. || FIG. y FAM. *Hacer a uno la mamola*, to make fun of s.o. (burlarse).
mamón, ona adj. Unweaned, nursing (que mama todavía). || *Diente mamón*, milk tooth.
— M. y f. Unweaned child, suckling (que mama todavía). || — M. BOT. Shoot, sucker (chupón). | Genip (árbol). | *Amer.* Papaw, pawpaw, papaya (árbol y fruta). | Sponge cake (bizcocho). || POP. Runt, squirt (persona despreciable). | Swine (persona mala).
mamotreto m. Notebook, memo book. || FIG. y FAM. Big book (libraco). | Monstrosity (armatoste).
mampara f. Screen (biombo). || Padded door (puerta).
mamparo m. MAR. Bulkhead: *mamparo estanco*, watertight bulkhead.
mamporro m. FAM. Blow, clout, punch (golpe).
mampostear v. tr. ARQ. To make *o* to build of rubble.
mampostería f. Rubblework.
mampostero m. Stonemason, roughsetter (albañil). || Tithe collector (recaudador).
mamut m. ZOOL. Mammoth.
— OBSERV. Pl. *mamutes*.
mana f. *Amer.* Manna. | Source, spring (manantial).
maná m. Manna (del cielo, de los árboles). || FIG. Manna, godsend: *esperar el maná*, to wait for a godsend.
manada f. Flock, herd, drove (rebaño). || Pack (bandada): *manada de lobos*, pack of wolves. || Pride (de leones). || FIG. y FAM. Crowd, mob (de personas). || Handful (de hierbas). || FAM. *A manadas*, in droves, in crowds, in throngs (en tropel).
manager m. Manager (de boxeador, empresa).
Managua n. pr. GEOGR. Managua.
managüense adj. [Of *o* from] Managua (Nicaragua).
— M. y f. Native *o* inhabitant of Managua.
manantial adj. Spring. || *Agua manantial*, spring water, running water.
— M. Source, spring. || FIG. Source, origin (origen).
manar v. intr. To flow, to run: *mana sangre de la herida*, blood is flowing from the wound. || FIG. To abound (abundar).
— V. tr. *La herida manaba sangre*, blood flowed from the wound.
manatí m. Manatee, sea cow (mamífero).
manaza f. FAM. Large hand. || FAM. *Ser un manazas*, to be clumsy.
mancar v. tr. To cripple s.o.'s arms (las manos). || To maim, to cripple (cualquier miembro). || *Amer.* To miss (fallar el tiro).
manceba f. Concubine.
mancebía f. Brothel.
mancebo m. Young man (joven). || Bachelor (soltero). || Clerk (dependiente). || Pharmacist's assistant, dispenser (de farmacia). || — Pl. Young men (mozos).
mancera f. Plough handle, ploughtail (del arado).
mancilla f. FIG. Spot, stain, blemish.
mancillar v. tr. To spot, to stain, to sully.
manco, ca adj. One-handed (de una mano), with both hands missing (de las dos manos). || One-armed (de un brazo), armless (de los dos brazos). || FIG. Halting: *verso manco*, halting verse. || MAR. Without oars (barco). || FAM. Bad: *estas fiestas tampoco son mancas*, these parties aren't bad either. || — *Manco de la izquierda*, maimed in the left arm. || FAM. *No es manco*, he's no fool, he knows what he is doing (es hábil). | *No es cojo ni manco*, v. COJO.
— M. y f. One-armed person (del brazo). || One-handed person (de la mano). || — M. Nag (caballo malo). || *El manco de Lepanto*, Cervantes [who injured an arm in battle there].
mancomún (de) loc. adv. o **mancomunadamente** adv. In agreement, jointly, together, in common.
mancomunar v. tr. To combine, to join, to unite (personas). || To pool (recursos). || To combine (intereses). || JUR. To make [two or more parties] jointly liable.
— V. pr. To become associated: *mancomunarse con otro*, to become associated with s.o. || To unite.
mancomunidad f. Union, association. || Commonwealth (de provincias, etc.). || Pool (de recursos). || Community (de intereses). || Co-property, joint ownership (de una casa).
mancuerna f. Pair [of oxen] tied together by the horns (pareja). || Strap, thong (correa). || — Pl. *Amer.* Cuff inks.
mancha f. Stain, spot: *quitar una mancha*, to remove *o* to take out a stain. || Blot (de tinta). || Bruise (en una fruta). || Flaw, blemish (en una piedra preciosa). || Patch (de vegetación). || FIG. Stain, blemish, stigma, blot (infamia): *hacer una mancha en su honor*, to cast a stain on one's honour. || ANAT. Spot: *mancha amarilla*, yellow spot. || ARTES. Rough sketch (boceto). || ASTR. Spot. || *Amer.* Anthrax (tumor). || — FIG. *Extenderse como mancha de aceite*, to spread like wildfire. || *La mancha ha salido*, the stain has come out (ha desaparecido). || *La mancha ha vuelto a salir*, the stain has come up *o* out again (ha vuelto a aparecer). || *Mancha solar*, sunspot. || *Sin mancha*, unblemished.
Mancha (La) n. pr. f. GEOGR. La Mancha [region of Spain]. || La Manche (departamento de Francia). || The English Channel (canal de la Mancha).
manchado, da adj. Spotted (la piel de un animal). || Spotty (la piel). || Stained, dirty (sucio). || Smudged (una página, etc.).
manchar v. tr. To spot, to stain (hacer una mancha): *manchar con* or *de tinta*, to stain with ink. || To dirty, to soil (ensuciar). || FIG. To stain, to blemish, to tarnish (la reputatión).
— V. pr. To get dirty. || To stain *o* to spot one's clothing

(hacerse una mancha). || To dirty *o* to soil one's hands *o* one's clothing (ensuciarse). || FIG. To stain one's reputation.
manchego, ga adj. [Of *o* from] La Mancha [region of Spain].
— M. y f. Native *o* inhabitant of La Mancha. || — M. Cheese from La Mancha (queso).
manchón m. Large spot *o* stain. || Patch of thick vegetation (de vegetación). || Patch of pastureland (pasto).
manchú, úa adj./s. Manchurian, Manchu.
manda f. Legacy, bequest (legado testamentario).
mandadero, ra m. y f. Messenger, errand boy *o* girl (recadero). || — M. Office boy (botones).
mandado m. Errand (recado): *hacer los mandados*, to do *o* to run errands. || Order (orden). || Mandate (encargo, delegación). || — *Amer. A su mandado*, at your service. || *Bien mandado*, obedient, well-behaved. || *Mal mandado*, disobedient, badly-behaved.
mandamás m. FAM. Big shot, bigwig: *es el mandamás del pueblo*, he's the big shot of the town. | Leader, kingpin: *el mandamás de una rebelión*, the leader of a rebellion.
mandamiento m. Command, order (orden). || REL. Commandment: *los diez mandamientos*, the Ten Commandments. || JUR. Writ, mandate. | Warrant: *mandamiento de arresto* or *de detención*, warrant for arrest. || — Pl. FIG. y FAM. Five fingers of the hand.
mandanga f. FAM. Calmness (flema), sluggishness (lentitud). | Dope, cocaine (droga).
mandante adj. Commanding (que manda).
— M. JUR. Constituent, mandator.
mandar v. tr. To order (ordenar): *me mandó que lo limpiase todo*, he ordered me to clean it all. || To command, to lead: *mandar un ejército*, to command an army. || To send, to mail (enviar por correo): *mandar una carta*, to mail a letter. || To send (enviar): *mandar a uno a la farmacia*, to send s.o. to the chemist's; *mandar recuerdos*, to send one's regards; *mandar buscar*, to send for. || To bequeath, to will, to leave (por testamento). || TECN. To control (un mecanismo). || DEP. To control, to manage [a horse]. || — *Bien, mal mandado*, obedient, disobedient. || *Lo que usted mande* or *¡mande!*, at your service (criados). || FAM. *Mandar a alguien a freír espárragos* or *a freír monas*, to send s.o. packing. || POP. *Mandar a alguien a la mierda*, to tell s.o. to go to hell. || FAM. *Mandar a alguien al infierno*, to tell s.o. to go to blazes *o* to the devil. | *Mandar a alguien a hacer gárgaras* or *a hacer puñetas* or *a la porra* or *al cuerno* or *a paseo* or *a tomar viento fresco* or *con viento fresco*, to send s.o. packing, to tell s.o. to go to blazes, to tell s.o. to go [and] take a running jump, to tell s.o. to go [and] take a long jump off a short pier, to tell s.o. to go [and] jump in the lake. || *Mandar decir que*, to send word that. || *Mandar hacer algo*, to have something done. || FAM. *Mandarlo todo a paseo*, to chuck it all in, to give up. || *Mandar por*, to send for: *mandar por el periódico*, to send for the newspaper. || *Amer. Mandar una bofetada a alguien*, to land s.o. a clout, to clobber s.o. (fam.).
— V. intr. To be in command: *mandar en jefe*, to be chief in command. || TECN. To be in control (un mecanismo). || — *Aquí mando yo*, I give the orders here, I'm the boss here. || *Como Dios manda*, v. DIOS. || *Amer. ¿Mande?*, pardon?, sorry? (¿cómo?).
— V. pr. To move about *o* to get around on one's own (un enfermo). || To communicate, to connect (dos habitaciones). || *Amer.* To please (servirse): *mándese pasar*, please enter. | To go away (irse), to sneak away (solapadamente). || *Amer. Mandarse cambiar* or *mudar*, to make o.s. scarce, to buzz off (fam.).
mandarín m. Mandarin.
mandarina f. Mandarin, mandarine (fruta).
mandarino o **mandarinero** m. BOT. Mandarin (árbol).
mandarino, na adj. Mandarin.
mandatario m. Mandatory. || Chief executive, president (gobernante).
mandato m. Order, command (orden). || Mandate, term of office (de un diputado). || Mandate (procuración, encargo, misión). || Mandate (soberanía). || Maundy (ceremonia religiosa). || — JUR. *Mandato judicial*, writ, warrant, summons. | *Territorio bajo mandato*, mandated territory.
mandíbula f. ANAT. y ZOOL. Mandible. || Jawbone: *mandíbula desencajada*, dislocated jawbone. || Mandibula (de pájaros). || Maxilla (de insectos y crustáceos). || TECN. Jaw. || FAM. *Reír* or *reírse a mandíbula batiente*, to laugh till one's sides ache, to laugh one's head off, to laugh until one's jaws ache.
mandil m. Apron (delantal). || Fine-meshed fishing net (red). || Grooming cloth (para limpiar el caballo).
mandilete m. Tampion, tompion (de un cañón). || Gauntlet (de una armadura).
mandinga adj. *Amer.* Negro (de la raza negra). | Mandingo (raza africana). | Effeminate (afeminado). | Mischievous (travieso).
— M. y f. *Amer.* Mandingo (raza africana). | Negro. || — M. *Amer.* Devil (el diablo). | Imp, goblin (duende). | Imp, little rogue (niño travieso). | Sorcery (brujería).
mandingo m. y f. Mandingo.
mandioca f. Manioc (planta). || Tapioca (fécula).
mando m. Command, control: *el mando del ejército*, command of the army. || Term of office (de un gobernante). || High-ranking officer: *los mandos de un regimiento*, the high-ranking officers of a regiment. || Lead (en una carrera). || TECN. Control, drive (órgano de transmisión). || — Pl. Governing body, *sing.*, authorities: *los mandos del país*, the governing body of the country. || Steering, *sing.*, steerage, *sing.* (de un barco). || Controls (de un avión, de una radio, etc.). || — *Alto mando*, high command. || *Ejercer el mando*, to be in command. || *Entregar el mando*, to hand over command. || *Estar bajo el mando de* or *al mando de un superior*, to be under the command *o* the orders of a superior. || *Mando a distancia*, remote control. || *Mando doble*, dual drive *o* control. || *Palanca de mando*, control lever (de una máquina), control stick, joy stick (de un avión). || *Tablero de mandos*, instrument panel (de un avión), dashboard, fascia (de un coche). || *Tener el mando de* or *estar al mando de*, to be in command of. || FIG. *Tener el mando y el palo* or *la estaca*, to rule the roost. || *Tomar el mando*, to take command. || *Torre de mandos*, control tower (aeropuerto).
mandoble m. Two-handed blow with a sword. || FAM. Large sword (espada grande). || FIG. y FAM. Tongue-lashing, piece of one's mind (reprimenda). | Blow (golpe).
mandolina f. MÚS. Mandolin, mandoline.
mandón, ona adj. Bossy, domineering.
— M. y f. Bossy *o* domineering person. || — M. Boss, big shot (mandamás). || *Amer.* Foreman, boss [of a mine] (de una mina). | Starter (en las carreras de caballos).
mandora f. MÚS. Mandola.
mandrágora f. Mandragora, mandrake.
mandria adj. Worthless (inútil). || Cowardly (cobarde).
— M. y f. Idiot, fool (necio). || Coward (cobarde).
mandril m. ZOOL. Mandrill (mono). || TECN. Mandrel, mandril [of a lathe] (que asegura la pieza labrada). | Chuck (que asegura la herramienta). || TECN. *Mandril del embrague*, splined shaft.
mandrilado m. TECN. Drifting, broaching, boring (calibrado).
mandriladora f. TECN. Boring *o* broaching *o* drifting machine (máquina de calibrar).
mandrilar v. tr. TECN. To bore, to broach, to drift.
mandubí m. *Amer.* Peanut.
manduca f. FAM. Grub, chow (comida).
manducable adj. FAM. Eatable.
manducación f. FAM. Eating.
manducar v. tr. e intr. FAM. To eat, to nosh (comer).
manducatoria f. FAM. Grub, chow (comida).
manea f. Shackle, fetter, hobble (maniota).
manecilla f. Hand (de un reloj). || Clasp, book clasp (de un libro). || Handle, hand lever (palanca). || IMPR. Index (signo tipográfico). || BOT. Tendril.
manejabilidad f. Manageability.
manejable adj. Manageable. || Handy, easy to use (de fácil uso). || Manœuvrable (un coche, avión, etc.).
manejador, ra m. y f. *Amer.* Driver (de un coche).
manejar v. tr. e intr. To handle, to wield: *manejar una espada*, to handle a sword. || To use (utilizar). || To handle (los caballos). || FIG. To manage, to operate, to run (dirigir). | To administer, to administrate (administrar). | To handle (ocuparse de dinero, negocios). | To handle, to manage (dirigir a una persona). || *Amer.* To drive (un automóvil). || — FIG. *Manejar a uno a su antojo*, to lead s.o. by the nose. | *Manejar el tinglado*, to pull the strings. | *Manejar los cuartos*, to hold the purse strings.
— V. intr. *Amer.* To drive (un coche).
— V. pr. To move about *o* to get around on one's own (un enfermo): *ya se maneja un poco*, he is already moving about a bit on his own. || To behave (portarse). || To behave o.s. (portarse bien). || To manage *o* to get on on one's own (arreglárselas).
manejo m. Handling (de un arma, de herramientas, de personas, de un caballo, de fondos). || Running, working, operation (de una máquina). || FIG. Administration, management (de un negocio). | Tricks, *pl.*, tactics, *pl.* (intriga): *conozco su manejo*, I know his tricks. | Use (de la lengua). | Handling (de muchos negocios). || *Amer.* Driving (de un automóvil). || — *De fácil manejo*, easy-to-use. || *Instrucciones de manejo*, directions, instructions.
maneota f. Hobble (maniota).
manera f. Manner, way: *no me gusta su manera de hablar*, I don't like his manner of speaking *o* the way he speaks. || Kind, sort (clase, forma). || ARTES. Manner, style. || — Pl. Manners (modales): *maneras distinguidas*, distinguished manners. || — *A la manera de*, like, in the manner of. || *A manera de*, by way of: *a manera de prólogo*, by way of a prologue. || *A su manera*, in one's own way, as one likes. || *A su manera de ver*, as he sees it, in his view, according to him. || *Cada cual a su manera*, each to his own, each in his own way. || *De cualquier manera*, any old way (fácilmente), anyway (inevitablemente). || *De esta manera*, this way, like this. || *De la misma manera*, in the same way, similarly. || *De mala manera*, badly: *conduce de mala manera*, he drives badly; rudely, discourteously: *me contestó de mala manera*, he answered me rudely.

|| *De manera que*, so that, so (así que). || *De ninguna manera*, not at all, by no means, in no way. || *De otra manera*, otherwise. || *De tal manera que...*, in such a way that... || *De todas maneras*, anyway, at any rate. || *De una manera o de otra*, one way or another, somehow or other. || *En cierta manera*, up to a point, to a certain extent. || *En gran manera*, a lot, a great deal, in great measure, very much: *contribuyó en gran manera al desarrollo*, he contributed a great deal to the development. || *La manera como*, the way, how: *no entiendo la manera como sucedió*, I don't understand how it happened. || *Manera de obrar*, way of going about things, line of conduct, way of doing things. || *Manera de ser*, the way one is: *es su manera de ser*, that's the way he is. || *Manera de ver*, outlook, point of view. || *No hay manera*, there's nothing one can do, there is no way. || *¡Qué manera de...!*, what a way to...! || *Sobre manera*, exceedingly.

Manes m. pl. Manes (almas de los muertos).

Manes o **Maniqueo** n. pr. m. Mani.

manezuela f. Small hand. | Handle (manija). || Small lever (palanquilla). || Clasp, buckle (de un broche).

manflor o **manflora** o **manflorita** m. *Amer.* Pansy, fairy, effeminate man (afeminado).

manga f. Sleeve (del vestido): *manga de jamón* or *afarolada*, leg-of-mutton sleeve. || Hose (de una bomba): *manga de riego*, garden *o* watering hose (para regar), fire hose (de bombero). || Waterspout (tromba). || Arm [of an axletree] (de un carruaje). || Portmanteau (bolso de viaje). || Banner (estandarte). || Cast net, casting net (esparavel). || Net (red): *manga de mariposas*, butterfly net. || Cloth strainer (para filtrar). || Conical strainer (colador). || MAR. Airshaft, ventilation shaft (de ventilación). | Breadth (ancho del buque). || DEP. Game (juego). || MIL. Detachment (destacamento). || BOT. Mango (fruta y árbol). || *Amer.* Cattle chute (paso). | Mob, crowd (multitud). | Poncho (abrigo). || — Pl. Profits, gains (utilidades). || — FIG. y FAM. *¡A buena hora mangas verdes!*, v. HORA. || *De manga corta, larga*, short-sleeved, long-sleeved. || FIG. y FAM. *Ésas son otras mangas*, that's a horse of a different colour, that is quite a different kettle of fish. || *Estar en mangas de camisa*, to be in shirtsleeves. || FIG. y FAM. *Hacer mangas y capirotes de*, to completely ignore, to pay no attention to (no hacer caso). || *Manga acuchillada*, slashed sleeve. || *Manga de agua*, waterspout. || *Manga de aire* or *manga veleta*, wind sock. || *Manga de ventilación*, air vent (de un edificio), ventilation shaft (de una mina). || *Manga de viento*, whirlwind (torbellino). || FIG. y FAM. *Sacarse algo de la manga*, to pull sth. out of one's hat. | *Ser de manga ancha* or *tener la manga ancha*, to be broadminded. || *Sin mangas*, sleeveless. || FIG. y FAM. *Traer algo en la manga*, to have sth. up one's sleeve.

manganato m. QUÍM. Manganate.

manganesa o **manganesia** f. QUÍM. Manganese dioxide, pyrolusite.

manganésico, ca adj. QUÍM. Manganous, manganesian.

manganeso m. QUÍM. Manganese.

mangánico adj. QUÍM. Manganic (ácido).

manganita f. Manganite.

manganoso, sa adj. QUÍM. Manganous.

mangante adj. FAM. Pilfering (que roba). | Cadging [U.S., mooching] (pedigüeño).
— M. y f. FAM. Pilferer (ladrón). | Cadger, sponger [U.S., moocher] (pedigüeño).

mangar v. tr. FAM. To pinch, to knock off, to pilfer (robar). | To sponge, to cadge [U.S., to mooch] (pedir).

manglar m. Mangrove swamp.

mangle m. BOT. Mangrove (árbol).

mango m. Handle (de un instrumento, de la sartén, de un cuchillo). || Crop (de la fusta). || Stock (del látigo). || Helve (del hacha). || Handle, stick (del paraguas). || BOT. Mango (árbol y fruta). || — *Mango de cuchillo*, razor clam (molusco). || *Mango de escoba*, broomstick.

mangoneador, ra adj. Bossy, domineering.

mangonear v. intr. FAM. To run things, to organize, to attend to *o* to see to everything (dirigir). | To boss people about (mandar). | To meddle, to pry (entremeterse). || *Amer.* To use public office for personal gain.

mangoneo m. FAM. Meddling, prying (entremetimiento). | Running (mando). || *Amer.* FAM. Graft.

mangosta f. Mongoose (animal).

mangostán m. BOT. Mangosteen (árbol y fruto).

manguear v. tr. *Amer.* To beat, to flush (la caza). | To pen [U.S., to corral] (el ganado). || FIG. y FAM. To coax.

manguera f. Hose, garden *o* watering hose (manga de riego). || MAR. Pump hose (de bomba). || Air duct, ventilation shaft (ventilador). || Waterspout (tromba). || *Amer.* Corral.

manguero m. Hoseman.

mangueta f. Enema (para lavados intestinales). || ARQ. Tie, beam (tirante). | Strut, prop (jabalcón). || TECN. Lever (palanca). | Steering knuckle spindle (de coche). | U-tube (de los retretes).

manguito m. Muff (de piel). || Glove (manopla). || Oversleeve (para proteger las mangas). || TECN. Bushing (anillo de acero). | Sleeve, joint: *manguito de acoplamiento*, coupling sleeve. | Mantle (incandescente). || *Manguito roscado*, threaded sleeve.

maní m. Peanut (fruto y planta).

manía f. Mania. || Mania, fad (obsesión, capricho). || Craze: *la manía de coleccionar sellos*, the stamp collecting craze. || Idiosyncrasy: *tener manías*, to have idiosyncrasies. || Oddity, eccentricity (rareza). || FIG. Habit: *tiene la mala manía de conducir de prisa*, he has the bad habit of driving fast. || — *Manía de grandezas*, megalomania. || *Manía depresiva*, manic-depressive psychosis. || *Manía persecutoria*, persecution mania *o* complex. || FAM. *Tenerle manía a uno*, not to like s.o.

maniaco, ca adj. Maniacal, maniac, mad.
— M. y f. Maniac.

maniatar v. tr. To tie [s.o.'s] hands, to handcuff. || FIG. To tie hand and foot.

maniático, ca adj. Fussy, finical. || Strange (extraño).
— M. y f. Fussy *o* finical person. || Strange person.

manicero, ra m. y f. *Amer.* Peanut seller.

manicomio m. Mental hospital, mental asylum.

manicorto, ta adj. FIG. y FAM. Stingy, tightfisted (avaro).
— M. y f. FIG. y FAM. Skinflint (avaro).

manicuro, ra m. y f. Manicurist. || — F. Manicure: *hacerle a uno la manicura*, to give s.o. a manicure; *hacerse la manicura*, to give o.s. a manicure (uno mismo), to get a manicure (por otra persona).

manido, da adj. High (carne). || FIG. Trite, hackneyed (trillado, sobado): *un tema manido*, a trite theme.

manierismo m. Mannerism (arte).

manierista adj. Manneristic (arte).
— M. y f. Mannerist.

manifestación f. Manifestation. || Declaration (declaración). || Demonstration, expression, show: *manifestaciones de amistad*, demonstrations of friendship. || [Public] demonstration: *asistir a una manifestación*, to attend a public demonstration. || Political meeting, mass meeting (reunión pública). || *Hacer una manifestación*, to demonstrate.

manifestador, ra adj. Manifesting, demonstrating.
— M. y f. Demonstrator.

manifestante m. y f. Demonstrator.

manifestar* v. tr. To manifest: *manifestar su parecer*, to manifest one's opinion. || To demonstrate, to show (demostrar): *manifestar interés por alguien*, to demonstrate an interest in s.o. || To make known, to declare, to state: *el ministro manifestó que*, the minister declared that. || To express: *no sé cómo manifestarle mi agradecimiento*, I don't know how to express my thanks to him. || REL. To expose (el Santísimo Sacramento).
— V. intr. To demonstrate, to take part in a public demonstration.
— V. pr. To show, to be manifest. || To appear, to come out (mostrarse). || To declare o.s. (declararse). || To make one's opinions known (exteriorizar sus opiniones). || To demonstrate (en una manifestación).

manifiesto, ta adj. Manifest, evident, clear (patente). || Obvious, evident (error). || Manifest (verdad). || *Poner de manifiesto*, to show, to reveal: *el balance pone de manifiesto un beneficio*, the balance shows a profit; to make [sth.] clear (decir claramente).
— M. Manifesto (de carácter político). || MAR. Manifest. || REL. Exposition (del Santísimo Sacramento).

manigua f. o **manigual** m. *Amer.* Brushland (monte bajo). | Forest (selva). || *Amer. Echarse a la manigua*, to take to the hills.

manija f. Handle (de un instrumento). || Hobble (de un animal). || Lever (palanca). || Collar coupling (abrazadera de hierro). || AGR. Workman's glove. || *Amer.* Strap [for fastening a whip to one's wrist].

manila m. Manila, cigar (puro).

Manila n. pr. GEOGR. Manila.

manilargo, ga adj. Long-handed. || FIG. Generous, liberal, openhanded (generoso). | Light-fingered (ladrón): *es muy manilargo*, he is very light-fingered.

manilense o **manileño, ña** adj. [Of *o* from] Manila.
— M. y f. Native *o* inhabitant of Manila.

manilla f. Hand (de reloj). || Handle (de puerta o ventana). || Bracelet (pulsera). || Manacle (de los presos).

manillar m. Handlebar, handlebars, *pl.* (de bicicleta).

maniobra f. Manœuvring [U.S., maneuvering], handling, managing. || TECN. Operation (de una máquina). | Driving (de una grúa, etc.). || MAR. Manœuvring, handling. || MIL. Manœuvre [U.S., maneuver]. || Shunting (de ferrocarriles). || FIG. Move (movimiento). | Manœuvre, move, stratagem (estratagema). || — Pl. MIL. y MAR. Manœuvres. || — MIL. y MAR. *Estar de maniobras*, to be on manœuvres. || *Hacer maniobras*, to manœuvre [U.S., to maneuver].

maniobrabilidad f. Manœuvrability [U.S., maneuverability].

maniobrable adj. Manœuvrable [U.S., maneuverable]. || Easy to handle (de fácil manejo).

maniobrar v. tr. To work, to operate (una máquina). || To drive (una grúa, etc.). || MAR. To manœuvre, to handle (un barco). | To work, to handle (las velas). || To shunt (ferrocarriles). || FIG. To manœuvre [U.S., to maneuver] (a una persona).

— V. intr. To manœuvre [U.S., to maneuver].
maniobrero, ra adj. MIL. Manœuvring [U.S., maneuvering].
maniobrista adj. FAM. Good at manœuvring.
— M. y f. FAM. Good strategist. || MIL. Skilled tactician.
maniota f. Hobble (de un animal).
manipulación f. Manipulation. || Handling (de mercancías).
manipulado m. Handling (de mercancías).
manipulador, ra adj. Manipulating. || Handling (de mercancías).
— M. y f. Manipulator. || — M. ELECTR. Telegraph key, tapper.
manipulante adj. Manipulating.
— M. y f. Manipulator.
manipular v. tr. To manipulate. || To handle (mercancías). || To operate (en telégrafos). || FIG. To manipulate (a una persona).
manípulo m. Maniple.
maniqueísmo m. Manichaeism, Manicheism.
maniqueo, a adj./s. Manichaean, Manichean.
maniquí m. Mannequin, dummy (de sastre, etc.). || FIG. Puppet (persona sin carácter). || — F. Mannequin, model (mujer que presenta).
manir* v. tr. To hang (carne). || FIG. To handle (manosear).
manirroto, ta adj. Lavish, spendthrift, wasteful.
— M. y f. Spendthrift, waster: *es una manirrota*, she is a spendthrift.
manís m. *Amer.* Friend, brother (amigo).
manisero, ra m. y f. *Amer.* Peanut seller.
manitas m. inv. Skilful person, handyman.
manito, ta m. y f. *Amer.* Brother (hermano), sister (hermana). | Mate (amigote). || — F. Hand, small hand. || — *Hacer manitas*, to hold hands. || *Manitas de plata*, clever hands. || — M. Mild laxative.

— OBSERV. The correct diminutive form of *mano* is *manecita.*

manitú m. Manitou.
manivacío, a adj. FAM. Empty-handed.
manivela f. Crank (manubrio).
manjar m. Dish (alimento exquisito). || Food (comestible). || FIG. Recreation, entertainment (deleite). || — CULIN. *Manjar blanco*, blancmange. || *Manjar de (los) dioses*, tasty dish.
mano f. Hand: *la mano derecha*, the right hand. || Hand (de mono). || Forefoot, front foot, front hoof (de caballo, cerdo, vaca, etc.). || Front paw, forepaw (de gato, perro, etc.). || Trotter, foot (de los animales de carnicería): *mano de cerdo*, pig's trotter. || Foot (del ave). || Talon, claw (del ave de rapiña). || Trunk (del elefante). || Hand (manecilla de un reloj). || Pestle (de almirez). || Bunch, hand (de plátanos). || Mano, handstone [for cocoa, maize, etc.] (rodillo de piedra). || Quire (de papel). || Coat (capa de color): *darle una segunda mano de pintura a la pared*, to give the wall a second coat of paint. || Hand (grupo de cartas), hand, round (jugada), game (partido, conjunto de jugadas): *echar una mano de naipes*, to play a game of cards. || Lead, leading hand (jugador que juega el primero): *tú eres mano*, it's your lead. || FIG. Series: *una mano de golpes*, a series of blows. | Reprimand (reprensión). | Side (lado). | Hand (ayuda): *echarle una mano a uno*, to lend *o* to give s.o. a hand. | Authority (autoridad). | Influence (influencia). | Labourer, hand, worker (persona que trabaja): *faltan manos en la agricultura*, there is a shortage of labourers in agriculture. | Hand (persona que ejecuta una cosa): *dos retratos por la misma mano*, two portraits by the same hand. | Hand (destreza): *tener buena mano para la pintura*, to have a good hand for painting. || DEP. Handball (falta en fútbol). || Round (ronda): *una mano de vino*, a round of wine. || Priority, right of way (en la carretera). || MÚS. Scale. || *Amer.* Group of four similar objects. | Batch of thirty-four (panecillos). | Brother (hermano). | Mate (amigo).
— FIG. *Abrir la mano*, to become more lenient *o* tolerant (tolerante), to ease up on restrictions (atenuar las restricciones), to give generously (dar), to spend lavishly (gastar), to accept presents (admitir regalos). || *Alzarle* or *levantarle la mano a uno*, to raise one's hand to *o* against s.o. || *A mano*, all square, quits (iguales), by hand: *hecho a mano*, made by hand, hand-made; *escrito a mano*, written by hand, handwritten; in handwriting, in longhand: *escribir algo a mano*, to do sth. in handwriting, to write sth. in longhand; at hand, to hand, handy (cerca): *tener algo a mano*, to have sth. at hand; on the way *o* route: *la tienda me coge a mano*, the shop is on my way. || *A mano airada*, violently. || *A mano alzada*, freehand (dibujo). || *A mano armada*, armed: *ataque a mano armada*, armed attack. || *A mano derecha, izquierda*, on the right, on the right-hand side, on the left, on the left-hand side. || *A manos de*, at the hands of: *murió a manos de su marido*, she died at the hands of her husband. || FIG. *A manos llenas* or *a mano abierta*, liberally, generously. || *Apretar la mano a*, to shake hands with [para saludar], to clamp down on, to tighten up on (apretar las clavijas). || FIG. *A quien le dan el pie, se toma la mano*, give s.o. an inch and he'll take a mile. || *¡Arriba las manos!* or *¡manos arriba!*, hands up! || FIG. *Atar a uno de manos* or *las manos*, to tie s.o.'s hands: *llevo las manos atadas*, my hands are tied. | *Bajo mano*, underhandedly, secretly, in secret. | *Buena mano*, luck (suerte). | *Caerse de las manos*, to weary, to try one's patience (ser pesado). | *Cambiar de manos*, to change hands. | *Cargar la mano*, to insist, to lay stress (*de*, on) [insistir], to put one's foot down, to crack down (tener rigor), to be too strict (ser demasiado severo), to overcharge (*en*, on) [en los precios], to add too much, to go heavy on [a certain ingredient to a stew, etc.] (con un ingrediente, etc.). | *Cerrar la mano*, to tighten one's belt (restringir los gastos), to be tightfisted (ser mezquino). | *Coger con las manos en la masa*, to catch red-handed. || *Cogidos de la mano*, holding hands, hand in hand. || FIG. y FAM. *Comerse las manos*, to be famished, to be starving. || FIG. *Con el corazón en la mano*, with open heart, from the heart. || *Con las dos manos* or *con ambas manos*, with two hands, with both hands. || *Con las manos en los bolsillos*, hands in pockets, with one's hands in one's pockets. || *Con las manos juntas*, hands together. || *Con las manos vacías*, empty-handed: *volver con las manos vacías*, to go *o* to come back empty-handed. || *Con mano dura*, with a hard *o* heavy hand. || *Con* or *de mano maestra*, masterfully. || *Conocer algo como la palma de la mano*, to know sth. like the back of one's hand. || FIG. *Con una mano atrás y otra delante*, empty-handed. | *Dar de mano*, to stop working, to knock off (fam.) [en el trabajo], to plaster (enlucir), to abandon (dejar). || *Daría mi mano derecha por*, I would give my right arm to *o* for. || *Dar la mano a*, to shake hands with [saludo], to take by the hand: *dar la mano a un niño*, to take a child by the hand; to give *o* to lend a hand (ayudar). || FIG. *Dar la última mano a*, to put the finishing touches to, to finish off. | *Darle una mano de azotes a uno*, to give s.o. a beating *o* a flogging. | *Darse buena mano en una cosa*, to do sth. skilfully. | *Darse la mano*, to shake hands (estrecharse la mano). | *Darse la mano con*, to go hand in hand with (tener relación con). | *Darse las manos*, to join hands (coligarse), to bury the hatchet, to shake hands (reconciliarse). | *Dar su mano*, to give one's hand [in marriage]. | *Dar una mano de jabón a*, to soap, to give a soaping. | *Dejar de la mano una cosa*, to abandon sth., to drop sth. (abandonarla), to neglect sth. (descuidarla), to put sth. down (un libro etc.). || *De la mano*, by the hand: *llevar de la mano*, to hold by the hand; hand in hand, holding hands (cogidos de la mano), under the guidance *o* tutelage (*de*, of). || FIG. y FAM. *De la mano a la boca se pierde la sopa*, there's many a slip 'twixt the cup and the lip. || *De mano*, hand: *equipaje de mano*, hand luggage; *granada de mano*, hand grenade. || *De mano a mano*, directly. || *De mano derecha, izquierda*, right-hand, left-hand (puerta). || *De mano en mano*, from hand to hand. || FIG. *De manos a boca*, suddenly, unexpectedly. | *De primera mano*, firsthand: *informe de primera mano*, firsthand account; *sé de primera mano que*, I have it firsthand that. | *De segunda mano*, secondhand (ventas), at second hand (informaciones). | *Echar mano a, de*, V. ECHAR (LOCUCIONES DIVERSAS). | *En buenas, malas manos*, in good, bad hands. || *En mano*, by hand: *entregar algo en mano*, to deliver sth. by hand. || *En manos de*, into the hands of: *caer en manos de*, to fall into the hands of; in the hands of (al cuidado de). || *En propias manos*, in person, personally (a la persona misma): *se lo entregué en propias manos*, I gave it to him in person *o* personally. || FIG. *Ensangrentarse las manos*, to stain one's hands with blood. | *Ensuciarse las manos*, to soil *o* to dirty one's hands. || FIG. y FAM. *Estar con una mano atrás y otra delante*, to be stony-broke. || FIG. *Estar dejado de la mano de Dios*, to be godforsaken *o* unfortunate (desgraciado), to be a total failure (ser una calamidad). | *Estar de mano* or *ser mano* or *tener la mano*, to have the lead (en el juego). | *Estar en la mano de todo el mundo*, to be within the reach of everyone (fácil). | *Estar en mano de uno*, to lie with s.o., to be up to s.o.: *está en tu mano aceptarlo*, it is up to you to accept. || *Estar mano sobre mano*, to sit twiddling one's thumbs, to sit idle, not to do a hand's turn. || *Estrecharle la mano a uno*, to shake s.o.'s hand, to shake hands with s.o. || FIG. *Forzar la mano a uno*, to force s.o.'s hand. | *Ganar a uno por la mano*, to beat s.o. to it. || MIL. *Golpe de mano*, raid. || *Hablar con* or *por las manos*, to use sign language, to talk with one's hands. || *Hacer lo que está en su mano*, to do all within one's power. || FIG. *Írsele a uno de la mano*, to slip through s.o.'s fingers. || *Írsele a uno de las manos*, to slip out of one's hands: *el plato se le fue de las manos*, the plate slipped out of her hands; to slip from one's hands *o* grasp, to slip through one's fingers: *su autoridad se le va de las manos*, his authority is slipping from his grasp. || FIG. *Írsele* or *escapársele a uno la mano*, to lose control, to let fly. || *Irsele la mano en*, to go heavy on, to add too much (ingredientes), to go too far with (pasarse de la raya). || *Juego de manos*, sleight of hand. || FAM. *Juegos de manos, juegos de villanos*, let's have no horseplay. | *¡Las manos quietas!*, keep your hands to yourself!, hands off! || FIG. *Lavarse las manos del asunto*, to wash one's hands of the affair. || *¡Levante la mano!*, hands up!, raise your hands! || *Listo de manos*, light-fingered. || *Llegar* or *venir a las manos*, to arrive, to

reach: *tu carta llegó a mis manos ayer*, your letter reached me yesterday *o* arrived yesterday; to come to blows (pegarse). || *Llevar de la mano a uno*, to hold *o* to lead s.o. by the hand, to hold s.o.'s hand. || *Llevarse* or *echarse las manos a la cabeza* or *ponerse las manos en la cabeza*, to throw one's hands to one's head [in surprise, alarm]. || *Mano a mano*, together (juntos), on an equal footing, on equal terms (sin ventaja), competition (entre dos rivales), bullfight in which only two matadors take part [instead of three] (corrida), tête-à-tête (entrevista). || FIG. *Mano de hierro en guante de seda*, iron hand in a velvet glove. || *Mano de obra*, labour [U.S., labor], manpower. || FIG. *Mano derecha*, right-hand man: *ser la mano derecha de uno*, to be s.o.'s right-hand man. || FAM. *Mano de santo*, miraculous cure. || *¡Manos a la obra!*, let's get down to work. || JUR. *Manos muertas*, mortmain. || *Me muerdo (me mordía) las manos por haber perdido la oportunidad*, I could kick [could have kicked] myself for missing the chance. || FIG. *Meter las manos en*, to have a hand in (tomar parte), to set one's hand to (emprender). | *Meter mano a*, to lay one's hands on, to seize (coger), to take action against (una persona), to touch (tocar), to touch up (fam.) [indecentemente a una persona]. | *No mover ni pie ni mano*, not to lift a finger. | *No saber uno lo que se trae entre manos*, not to know what one is doing *o* what one is about. | *No se veía la mano*, you could not see your hand in front of you [in the darkness]. || FIG. y FAM. *Nos quitan de las manos nuestras nuevas camisas*, there is a rush on our new shirts, our new shirts are selling like hot cakes. | *Pasar la mano por el lomo a alguien*, to butter s.o. up, to soft-soap s.o. | *Pedir la mano de*, to ask for the hand of. | *Poner en manos de*, to place in the hands of, to entrust to. | *Poner la mano en el fuego por*, to stake one's life on. | *Ponerle a uno la mano encima*, to lay hands on s.o. || *Ponerse de manos*, to sit up and beg (un oso, un perro, etc.), to rear (un caballo). || FIG. *Ponerse en manos de uno*, to place o.s. in s.o.'s hands. | *Poniéndose la mano en el pecho*, hand on heart. || *Por su propia mano*, by one's own hand: *herido por su propia mano*, wounded by his own hand; into one's own hands: *tomarse la justicia por su propia mano*, to take the law into one's own hands. || *¡Que Dios nos tenga en su Santa mano!*, God protect us! || FIG. *Se me fue la mano*, my hand slipped. | *Sentar la mano a uno*, to give s.o. a good hiding (golpear), to fleece, to overcharge (cobrar demasiado). || FIG. *Si a mano viene*, should the occasion arise. | *Sin levantar mano*, without letting up, without respite. | *Soltarse la mano en*, to get one's hand in at. || *Tender la mano*, to offer one's hand (apoyo, saludo, reconciliación), to hold out a [helping] hand (*a*, to) [ayudar]. || FIG. *Tener al alcance de la mano*, to have within one's grasp. | *Tener buena mano para hacer algo*, to be good at doing sth. | *Tener en sus manos*, to be in the hands of: *tienes la decisión, tu porvenir en tus manos*, the decision, your future is in your hands; to have within one's grasp (al alcance de la mano). || *Tener entre manos*, to have in hand. | *Tener las manos largas* or *ser largo de manos*, to be free with one's fists (para pegar), to be free with one's hands (con las mujeres), to be light-fingered (para robar). | *Tener mano con uno*, to have an influence over s.o. | *Tener mano izquierda*, to have one's wits about one, to know what is what. | *Tener manos de trapo*, to be a butterfingers. | *Tener manos de santo*, to work miracles. | *Tener mucha mano*, to be very influential. | *Tocar con la mano*, to have within one's grasp. | *Tomar en sus manos*, to take in hand. || *Tradiciones que han llegado de mano en mano hasta nosotros*, traditions which have been handed down to us. || FIG. *Traer a la mano*, to bring back (caza). | *Traerse* or *traer* or *llevar* or *tener entre manos*, to plan (planear), to plot, to scheme (tramar), to have in hand *o* on one's hands, to be engaged in (estar ocupándose en), to be up to: *¿qué te traes entre manos?*, what are you up to? || FIG. y FAM. *Untarle la mano a uno*, to grease s.o.'s palm. || FIG. *Vivir de sus manos*, to fend for o.s., to make one's living. || *Votación a mano alzada*, vote by show of hands.

mano m. *Amer.* FAM. Chum, pal (amigo). || *¡Eh, mano!*, hey, old pal!

manodescompresor m. TECN. Pressure-control valve [on butane cylinders, etc.].

manojo m. Bunch (haz): *manojo de llaves, de espárragos*, bunch of keys, of asparagus. || Bundle: *un manojo de estacas*, a bundle of stakes. || FIG. Handful (puñado). | Heap, pile (montón). | Bunch (grupo). || — FIG. *A manojos*, in abundance. | *Estar hecho un manojo de nervios*, to be a bundle of nerves.

manoletina f. TAUR. A pass of the *muleta* invented by Manolete, the famous Spanish bullfighter.

manolo, la m. y f. Typical Madrilenian of the popular quarters.

Manolo n. pr. m. (dim. of Manuel) Emmanuel.

manómetro m. FÍS. Manometer, pressure gauge.

manopla f. Gauntlet (de la armadura). || Mitten (guante). || Washing mitten, flannel [U.S., facecloth] (para lavarse). || Working glove (guante de obreros). || Postilion's whip (látigo). || *Amer.* Knuckleduster (arma).

manoseador, ra m. y f. Person fond of handling *o* fingering *o* touching.

manosear v. tr. To handle, to finger, to touch (tocar). || FAM. To paw. || FIG. *Tema manoseado*, well-worn subject.

manoseo m. Handling, fingering, touching.

manotada f. o **manotazo** m. Cuff, slap. || *Quitarle a uno un libro de un manotazo*, to knock a book out of s.o.'s hands.

manotear v. tr. To slap, to cuff (golpear). || *Amer.* To steal (robar).

— V. intr. To gesticulate.

manoteo m. Gesticulation.

manquedad o **manquera** f. Lack of one *o* both hands (las manos), lack of one *o* both arms (los brazos). || FIG. Defect, imperfection.

mansalva (a) loc. adv. Without taking any risk.

mansarda f. Attic.

— OBSERV. *Mansarda* is a Gallicism for *buhardilla.*

mansedumbre f. Gentleness (de una persona). || Tameness (de un animal). || Mildness (del clima).

mansión f. Mansion (casa suntuosa). || *Mansión señorial*, stately home.

manso, sa adj. Gentle: *manso como un cordero*, as gentle as a lamb. || Peaceful (apacible). || Tame (animal domesticado). || Calm, gentle, tranquil (cosas): *aguas mansas*, calm waters.

— M. Bellwether (de un rebaño). || TAUR. Ox used to lead bulls.

mansurrón, ona adj. Very gentle. || Very tame (animales).

manta f. Blanket (de cama, para las caballerías). || Travelling rug [U.S., car blanket] (de viaje). || Poncho (abrigo). || FIG. y FAM. Beating (paliza). || MIL. Mantelet (mantelete). || *Amer.* Bag of agave for carrying ore (costal). | Popular dance (baile). | Cotton cloth (tela de algodón). || — *A manta* or *a manta de Dios*, a great deal: *ha llovido a manta*, it has rained a great deal. || FIG. *Liarse uno la manta a la cabeza*, to take the plunge. || *Manta eléctrica* electric blanket. || *Manta sudadera*, numnah, saddle blanket. || FIG. *Tirar de la manta*, to let the cat out of the bag, to spill the beans.

manteador, ra adj. Tossing.

— M. y f. Tosser.

manteamiento m. Tossing [in a blanket].

mantear v. tr. To toss [in a blanket].

manteca f. Grease, fat (grasa). || Lard (del cerdo). || Butter (mantequilla). || Cream (de leche). || Cocoa butter (de cacao). || Pulp (de fruta). || FAM. Fat, blubber (gordura). | Dough [U.S., green stuff] (dinero). || FIG. Cream (lo mejor). || — FIG. *Derretirse como manteca*, to melt like butter. | *Eso no se le ocurre ni al que asó la manteca*, only a fool would think of doing that. || *Manteca de cacahuete*, peanut butter. || *Manteca de vaca*, butter. || *Manteca requemada*, browned butter. || FIG. *Ser como manteca*, to be as meek as a lamb. | *Tener buenas mantecas*, to be fat (gordo). || *Untar manteca en*, to butter.

mantecada f. Slice of bread and butter. || Butter bun (bollo).

mantecado m. Bun (bollo). || Dairy *o* vanilla ice cream (helado).

mantecón adj. m. FAM. Soft, fond of comfort (delicado). | Fat (gordo).

— M. FAM. Soft person, mollycoddle (delicado). | Fatty [gordo].

mantecoso, sa adj. Creamy (la leche). || Buttery (como la manteca): *bizcocho mantecoso*, buttery sponge.

mantel f. Tablecloth (de la mesa de comer). || Altar cloth (del altar). || *Mantel individual*, table mat [U.S., place mat].

mantelería f. Table linen.

manteleta f. Mantelet, shawl (prenda de mujer).

mantelete m. Mantelet, mantlet (fortificación).

mantenedor m. President (en un torneo, juegos florales, etc.). || *Mantenedor de familia*, breadwinner.

mantenencia f. Maintenance (acción de mantenerse). || Support (apoyo).

mantener* v. tr. To feed, to sustain (alimentar): *mantener a uno con pan y agua*, to feed s.o. on bread and water. || To maintain, to support: *mantener a una familia*, to support a family. || To keep (a una mujer). || To hold up, to support (sostener): *el muro mantiene el techo*, the wall holds up the ceiling. || To keep: *mantener algo en equilibrio*, to keep sth. balanced. || To keep in, to keep going (el fuego). || FIG. To support, to back [up], to stand up for, to stand by (apoyar a una persona, una idea). | To hold, to keep to, to maintain: *mantengo mi opinión*, I maintain my opinion. | To maintain, to affirm: *ella mantiene que*, she maintains that. | To keep up, to maintain (usos, reglas, amistades, etc.). | To keep: *mantener la ley, la paz*, to keep the law, the peace. || To maintain, to keep [sth.] up (conservar en buen estado). || To maintain, to defend, to uphold, to sustain: *mantener sus derechos*, to maintain one's rights. || To hold (celebrar). || To keep (conservar): *mantener la carne fresca*, to keep the meat fresh; *mantener su rango social*, to keep one's social status. || — *Mantener a distancia*, to keep at a distance. || *Mantener al día*, to keep up to date. || *Mantener caliente*, to keep [sth.] hot. || *Man-*

tener correspondencia con, V. CORRESPONDENCIA. || *Mantener despierto a uno*, to keep s.o. awake. || *Mantener la neutralidad*, to stay *o* to remain neutral. || *Mantener los ojos cerrados*, to keep one's eyes shut. || FIG. *Mantener una conversación*, to hold a conversation, to keep up a conversation: *incapaz de mantener una conversación*, incapable of keeping up a conversation; to hold an interview (celebrar una entrevista). | *Mantener un cambio de impresiones, una entrevista*, to have an exchange of ideas, an interview.
— V. pr. To feed o.s. (alimentarse). || To live, to support o.s.: *se mantiene con su trabajo*, he lives by his work. || To remain firm (en una posición, opinión, etc.). || To hold o.s.: *mantenerse derecho*, to hold o.s. straight. || To remain, to keep: *mantenerse tranquilo*, to keep calm. || To remain the same *o* unchanged, to still hold *o* stand: *nuestro trato se mantendrá*, our agreement will still stand. || — *Mantenerse a distancia*, to keep one's distance. || *Mantenerse en contacto con*, to keep in touch with, to keep in contact with. || *Mantenerse en su puesto*, to keep one's job (un trabajo), to know *o* to remember one's place (comportarse según su rango). || *Mantenerse en su sitio*, to know *o* to remember one's place. || FIG. y FAM. *Mantenerse en sus trece*, to stick to one's guns, to stand one's ground. || *Mantenerse firme*, to stand firm, to hold one's ground. || *Mantenerse serio*, to keep *o* to remain serious.
mantenido, da adj. Kept (una persona).
— F. Kept woman.
mantenimiento m. Maintenance (subsistencia). || Sustenance (alimento). || Maintenance, upkeep: *el mantenimiento de una carretera, de una familia*, the upkeep of a road, of a family. || Maintenance, keeping: *el mantenimiento del orden*, maintenance of order.
manteo m. Tossing [in a blanket] (manteamiento). || Long cloak *o* mantle (capa).
mantequera f. Dairywoman (persona). || Butter churn (máquina). || Butter dish (recipiente).
mantequería f. Creamery, dairy (tienda). || Dairy (fábrica). || Butter making (fabricación de la mantequilla).
mantequero, ra adj. Butter: *la industria mantequera*, the butter industry.
— M. Dairyman (persona).
mantequilla f. Butter (manteca de vaca): *mantequilla fresca, salada*, fresh, salted butter; *mantequilla derretida, requemada*, melted, browned butter.
mantequillera f. *Amer.* V. MANTEQUERA.
mantequillero m. *Amer.* Dairyman (vendedor). | Butter dish (recipiente).
mantilla f. Mantilla (de mujer). || Shawl (para los niños). || Trappings, *pl.*, caparison (del caballo). || IMPR. Blanket. || — Pl. Shawl, *sing.* || — FIG. *Estar en mantillas*, to be in one's infancy, to be in nappies [U.S., to be in diapers] (un niño), to be in its infancy (empezar), to be in the dark, not to know anything (ignorar). || FIG. y FAM. *Ya he salido de mantillas*, I wasn't born yesterday.
mantillo m. Vegetable mould, humus (capa del suelo). || Manure (estiércol).
mantisa f. MAT. Mantissa.
manto m. Cloak, mantle (de mujer). || Shawl (chal). || Ceremonial robe (capa de ceremonia). || Mantel (de chimenea). || MIN. Stratum (capa). || ZOOL. Mantle (de los moluscos). || FIG. Cover, cloak, mantle (lo que encubre): *bajo el manto de la indiferencia*, under the cover of indifference. || FIG. *Tapar con un manto*, to cover up.
mantón m. Shawl. || *Mantón de Manila*, embroidered silk shawl.
manuable adj. Manageable, easy to handle.
manual adj. Manual: *trabajo manual*, manual labour *o* work. || Manageable (manejable).
— M. Manual (libro). || COM. Daybook (libro).
manubrio m. Crank (manivela). || Handle (mango). || *Piano de manubrio*, street piano, hurdy-gurdy.
manucodiata f. ZOOL. Bird of paradise (ave).
Manuel n. pr. m. Emmanuel.
manuela f. Open carriage.
manuelino adj. m. *Estilo manuelino*, architectural style prevalent in Portugal during the reign of Manuel I (1469-1521).
manufactura f. Factory, manufactory (fábrica). || Manufacture (fabricación). || Manufactured article.
manufacturable adj. Manufacturable.
manufacturado, da adj. Manufactured: *productos manufacturados*, manufactured goods.
manufacturar v. tr. To manufacture (fabricar).
manufacturero, ra adj. Manufacturing: *industria manufacturera*, manufacturing industry.
manumisión f. JUR. Manumission (del esclavo).
manumitir v. tr. JUR. To manumit, to emancipate.
manuscribir v. tr. To write by hand.
manuscrito, ta adj./s.m. Manuscript.
manutención f. Maintenance (mantenimiento): *la manutención de una familia*, the maintenance of a family. || Maintenance, upkeep (conservación).
manzana f. Apple (fruto). || Block (grupo de casas). || Pommel [of a sword] (de la espada). || Knob (adorno). || *Amer.* Adam's apple (nuez). || — FIG. y FAM. *Estar sano como una manzana* or *más sano que una manzana*, to be as fit as a fiddle. | *Manzana de la discordia*, apple of discord. | *Manzana podrida*, bad egg.
manzanar m. Apple orchard.
manzanilla f. Manzanilla (vino). || BOT. Manchineel berry (fruto). || Chamomile, camomile (planta). || Camomile tea (infusión). || Manzanilla (aceituna). || Pad, cushion (del pie de algunos mamíferos). || Knob (adorno). || Point of the chin (barba).
manzanillo m. BOT. Manchineel (árbol). | Manzanilla-olive tree (olivo).
manzano m. BOT. Apple tree (árbol).
maña f. Skill, ability, know-how (habilidad). || Cunning, astuteness (astucia). || Bad habit (mala costumbre). || Bunch (manojo). || — *Darse maña para*, to manage to, to contrive to. || *Más vale maña que fuerza*, brain is better than brawn. || *Tener maña para* or *en hacer algo*, to have the knack of doing sth., to be good at doing sth.
mañana f. Morning: *esta mañana*, this morning; *a la mañana siguiente*, the following morning; *estudio por la mañana*, I study in the morning. || — *A las tres de la mañana*, at three o'clock in the morning, at three a. m. || *Ayer mañana, ayer por la mañana*, yesterday morning. || *De la mañana a la noche*, from morning to night. || *De la noche a la mañana*, overnight: *de la noche a la mañana ha cambiado*, he has changed overnight; all night long, through the night: *leer de la noche a la mañana*, to read all night long. || *Mañana por la mañana, por la noche*, tomorrow morning, night. || *Tomar la mañana*, to take a nip first thing in the morning (con aguardiente). || — M. Tomorrow, the future (futuro): *no pensar en el mañana*, not to think about tomorrow.
— Adv. Tomorrow: *mañana será domingo*, tomorrow will be Sunday, it is Sunday tomorrow; *saldrá usted mañana mismo*, you will leave tomorrow without fail. || — *A partir de mañana*, starting tomorrow, as from tomorrow. || *De mañana*, early (temprano), in the morning (por la mañana). || *De mañana en ocho días*, a week tomorrow, tomorrow week. || *El mundo de mañana*, the world of tomorrow. || *Hasta mañana*, see you tomorrow (fórmula de despedida). || *Mañana será otro día*, tomorrow is another day. || *Mañana, tarde y noche*, morning, noon and night. || *Muy de mañana*, very early. || *No dejes para mañana lo que puedes hacer hoy*, do not put off till tomorrow what you can do today. || *Pasado mañana*, the day after tomorrow.
— Interj. We'll see!
mañanear v. intr. To rise *o* to get up early.
mañanero, ra adj. Early-rising (madrugador).
mañanita f. FAM. Daybreak, early morning. || Bed jacket (prenda de vestir). || — Pl. Popular Mexican songs sung in honour of s.o. or sth.
maño, ña m. y f. FAM. Aragonese. || — M. *Amer.* Old man, old chap, my friend (expresión de cariño). | Brother (hermano). || — F. *Amer.* My dear (expresión de cariño). | Sister (hermana).
mañoco m. Tapioca. || *Amer.* Indian corn meal.

— OBSERV. The Spanish for *manioc* is *mandioca*.

mañosamente adv. Skilfully, cleverly (con habilidad). || Craftily (con astucia).
mañoso, sa adj. Skilful [U.S., skillful], clever: *es un hombre muy mañoso*, he is a very skilful man. || Clever, crafty, cunning (astuto). || *Amer.* False, deceitful (falso). | Balky, shy (que tiene resabios).
maoísmo adj./s. Maoism.
maoísta m. y f. Maoist.
maorí adj./s. Maori.
mapa m. Map: *el mapa de España*, the map of Spain; *mapa mudo*, skeleton *o* blank map; *levantar un mapa*, to draw up a map. || — FIG. y FAM. *Desaparecer del mapa*, to disappear completely, to vanish from the face of the earth. | *Esto no está en el mapa*, this is way out *o* far out, I've never seen anything like this before. | *Hacer desaparecer una ciudad del mapa*, to wipe a town off the map.
— F. FAM. Best. || FAM. *Llevarse la mapa*, to top the lot, to be tops.
mapache o **mapachín** m. ZOOL. Racoon (mamífero).
mapamundi m. World map, map of the world. || FAM. Backside, bottom, rear (nalgas).
maquear v. tr. To lacquer. || To varnish (barnizar). || FIG. y FAM. *Estar bien maqueado*, to be dressed up.
— V. pr. FAM. To dress up (engalanarse).
maqueta f. Scale model, mock-up, maquette (boceto). || IMPR. Dummy [book].
maquetista m. y f. Maquette maker.
maquiavélico, ca adj. Machiavellian.
maquiavelismo m. Machiavellianism, machiavellism.
Maquiavelo n. pr. m. Machiavelli.
maquila f. Multure (tributo). || Corn measure (para maquilar).
maquilar o **maquilear** v. tr. To collect multure on.
maquilero m. Multurer.
maquillador, ra m. y f. Makeup assistant. || — F. Makeup girl.
maquillaje m. Makeup (productos y arte de maquillarse). || Making-up (acción). || *Maquillaje de fondo*, foundation.
maquillamiento m. Making-up.

maquillar v. tr. To make up. || FIG. To falsify, to cover up (encubrir, falsificar).
— V. pr. To make o.s. up, to put one's makeup on (pintarse). || *No le gusta que me maquille*, he doesn't like me to wear makeup.
máquina f. Machine: *máquina de sumar*, adding machine. || TEATR. Stage machinery (tramoya). || Engine, locomotive (locomotora). || Engine (motor). || Bicycle, machine, bike (bicicleta). || Car, automobile (coche). || Camera (de fotografías). || FIG. Machine: *la máquina del Estado*, the State machine. | Project, idea (proyecto). || — *A toda máquina*, at full speed. || MAR. *Cuarto* or *sala de máquinas*, engine room. || *Entrar en máquina*, to go to press [a newspaper]: *al entrar en máquina esta edición*, as this edition goes to press. || *Escribir a máquina*, to type. || *Escrito a máquina*, typewritten. || *Forzar la máquina*, to overwork the engine (motor), to overwork o.s. (una persona). || *Hecho a máquina*, machine-made. || *Máquina contabilizadora* or *contable*, accounting machine. || *Máquina de afeitar eléctrica*, electric razor. || *Máquina de calcular*, calculator, calculating machine. || *Máquina de coser, de lavar, de volar*, sewing, washing, flying machine. || *Máquina de escribir*, typewriter. || *Máquina de vapor*, steam engine. || *Máquina fotográfica* or *de fotografiar* or *de retratar*, camera. || *Máquina herramienta*, machine tool. || *Máquina infernal*, infernal machine. || *Máquina neumática*, air pump. || *Máquina registradora*, cash register. || *Máquina tragaperras*, slot machine, fruit machine, one-armed bandit (de juego), slot machine, vending machine (expendedora automática).
maquinación f. Machination.
maquinador, ra adj. Machinating.
— M. y f. Machinator. || Schemer, plotter (intrigante).
maquinal adj. Mechanical: *movimientos maquinales*, mechanical movements.
maquinar v. tr. To machinate, to plot.
maquinaria f. Machinery: *maquinaria agrícola*, agricultural machinery. || Machinery, machines, *pl.* (conjunto de máquinas). || Mechanism, workings, *pl.*: *conoce bien la maquinaria de este coche*, he knows the mechanism of this car well. || FIG. Machinery: *la maquinaria burocrática, administrativa*, bureaucratic, administrative machinery.
maquinilla f. Small machine *o* device. || MAR. Winch (chigre). || — *Café de maquinilla*, drip coffee. || *Maquinilla de afeitar*, safety razor. || *Maquinilla para cortar el pelo*, hair clippers, *pl.*
maquinismo m. Mechanization.
maquinista m. Machinist, mechanic. || Engine driver, engineer (del tren). || TEATR. Stagehand. || — F. Machinist (costurera).
maquinizar v. tr. To mechanize.
mar m. y f. Sea: *mar interior*, inland *o* landlocked sea; *mar Mediterráneo*, Mediterranean Sea. || Swell (marejada). || — *Al otro lado del mar*, overseas. || *Alta mar*, high seas, open sea: *en alta mar*, on the high seas. || FIG. y FAM. *Arar en el mar*, to plough the sands. | *Correr a mares*, to stream, to flow: *el sudor corría a mares por su cara*, the sweat streamed down his face; to flow freely: *el vino corría a mares*, the wine flowed freely. || *De alta mar*, seagoing (barco), deep-water (pesca). || FIG. y FAM. *Echar pelillos a la mar*, to let bygones be bygones, to say no more about it, to bury the hatchet. | *Estamos la mar de bien aquí*, it's great [U.S., swell] here. | *Estar hecho un brazo de mar*, to be dressed up to the nines, to be dressed to kill. | *Estar hecho un mar de lágrimas*, to cry a sea of tears (persona), to be bathed in tears (cara). | *Estar la mar de bien*, to feel great (de salud), to look great (de aspecto), to be great (una película, libro, etc.). || *Golpe de mar*, huge wave. || FIG. y FAM. *Hablar de la mar*, to ask for the moon and stars. || MAR. *Hacerse a la mar*, to put to sea. | *Irse* or *hacerse mar adentro*, to stand out to sea, to put to sea. || FIG. y FAM. *La mar*, loads, lots, hoards, swarms: *habiá la mar de niños*, there were loads of children; loads, lots, stacks, no end: *la mar de trabajo*, stacks of work; extremely, ever so, very: *es la mar de guapa*, she is extremely pretty; very much, a lot, a hell of a lot: *me gusta la mar*, I like it a lot. | *La mar de bien*, very well, awfully well, ever so well: *canta la mar de bien*, he sings ever so well. | *Le sienta la mar de bien este vestido*, this dress suits her to a tee *o* suits her down to the ground *o* looks great on her. | *Llover a mares*, to rain cats and dogs, to rain buckets. || *Mar adentro*, offshore, out to sea. || *Mar agitado*, rough sea. || *Mar de arena*, a vast expanse *o* an ocean of sand. || *Mar de fondo*, v. FONDO. || FIG. *Mar de sangre*, bloodbath. || *Mar en bonanza* or *en calma*, calm sea. || *Mar enfurecido*, angry *o* raging *o* stormy sea. || *Mar gruesa*, heavy sea. || *Mar picado, rizado*, choppy sea. || *Por mar*, by sea, by boat. || FIG. *Quien no se arriesga no pasa la mar*, nothing ventured, nothing gained.

— OBSERV. The word *mar* is usually masculine in current speech (*the Red Sea*, el Mar Rojo) but feminine when used by fishermen and seamen and in expressions such as *la alta mar, la mar de cosas*, etc.

marabú m. Marabou, marabout (ave, plumas).
marabunta f. Plague of ants (plaga de hormigas). || FIG. Crowd (muchedumbre).
maraca f. MÚS. Maraca.
maracucho, cha adj. [Of *o* from] Maracay.
— M. y f. Native *o* inhabitant of Maracay.
maracure m. Vine from which curare is extracted.
maragatería f. Group of muleteers.
maragato, ta adj./s. Maragaterian, from Maragatería [in the North of Spain].
— M. Muleteer (arriero).
maraña f. Thicket, brush (maleza). || BOT. Holm oak (encina). || FIG. Tangle, mess (confusión). | Tangle (asunto intrincado). || — *¡Qué maraña!*, what a mess! || *Una maraña de mentiras*, a pack of lies. || *Una maraña de pelo*, a mop of hair, a tangle of hair.
marasmo m. MED. Marasmus. || FIG. Apathy (apatía). | Decline (disminución). | Stagnation (estancamiento).
maratón m. Marathon (carrera).
maravedí m. Maravedi [coin].
maravilla f. Marvel: *éste es una maravilla*, this one is a marvel. || Astonishment, amazement (asombro). || BOT. Marigold (flor anaranjada). | Morning glory (flor azul). | Marvel-of-Peru. || — *A las mil maravillas* or *de maravilla*, marvellously [U.S., marvelously], wonderfully: *hablar a las mil maravillas*, to speak wonderfully; *todo va de maravilla*, everything is going marvellously. || *Contar* or *decir maravillas de*, to speak wonderfully about (de personas o cosas). || *Hacer maravillas*, to do *o* to work wonders: *hace maravillas con la guitarra, en el trapecio*, he does wonders with a guitar, on the trapeze. || *Las siete maravillas del mundo*, the seven wonders of the world. || *¡Qué maravilla!*, marvellous! || *Venirle a uno de maravilla*, to be just what the doctor ordered.
maravillar v. tr. To astonish, to amaze, to surprise (sorprender): *me maravilla su fracaso*, his failure amazes me. || To fill with admiration: *este cuadro maravilla a todos*, this painting fills everyone with admiration. || *Quedarse maravillado*, to marvel (*ante*, at), to be amazed *o* astonished (*ante*, at, by).
— V. pr. To marvel (*con*, at), to wonder (*con*, at), to be amazed (*con*, at, by): *me maravillo con su paciencia*, I marvel at his patience.
maravilloso, sa adj. Marvellous [U.S., marvelous], wonderful (admirable).
marbete m. Label (etiqueta). || Border, edge (borde). || FIG. Label, tag.
marca f. Mark, sign (señal). || Trademark: *marca registrada* or *patentada*, registered *o* patented trademark. || Make, brand: *¿qué marca compra Ud.?*, what brand do you buy? || Make: *¿de qué marca es su coche?*, what make of car has he got? || Scar, mark (cicatriz). || Brand (con hierro candente). || Branding (acción): *la marca del ganado*, the branding of cattle. || Measuring stick (talla). || DEP. Record: *batir* or *mejorar una marca*, to break *o* to beat a record. | Score (resultado). || March (provincia fronteriza). || MAR. Landmark. || — *De marca*, outstanding: *producto, personaje de marca*, outstanding product, person. || FIG. y FAM. *De marca mayor*, first-class (excelente), huge, voluminous (muy grande o voluminoso), first-class: *un imbécil de marca mayor*, a first-class idiot; enormous: *una tontería de marca mayor*, an enormous blunder. || *Marca de fábrica*, trademark. || *Papel de marca*, foolscap paper.
Marca n. pr. f. GEOGR. Marche.
marcadamente adv. Markedly, noticeably. || *Habla con un acento marcadamente español*, he speaks with a marked *o* a noticeable Spanish accent.
marcado, da adj. Marked.
— M. Marking. || Setting (del cabello).
marcador, ra adj. Marking. || Branding (del ganado).
— M. IMPR. Feeder. || Inspector (contraste de pesos y medidas). || Scoreboard (deportes). || Brander (del ganado). || Marker (lápiz). || — DEP. *Abrir* or *hacer funcionar* or *inaugurar el marcador*, to open the scoring. | *Adelantarse* or *ponerse por delante en el marcador*, to go ahead in the scoring. || *Ir por delante en el marcador*, to be ahead in the scoring. || *Marcador de votos*, vote counter.
marcaje m. Marking (deportes).
marcar v. tr. To mark: *marcar la ropa*, to mark the clothes. || To brand (el ganado): *marcar con hierro* or *a fuego*, to brand with an iron. || DEP. To mark: *marcar a un contrario*, to mark an opposing player. | To score: *marcar un gol* or *un tanto*, to score a goal (fútbol); *marcar una canasta*, to score a basket (baloncesto). || To dial (un número de teléfono). || MAR. To take [bearings]. || To underline, to mark (subrayar, destacar). || To indicate, to show, to mark, to point to: *las agujas del reloj marcan las tres*, the hands of the clock indicate three o'clock. || To score (un punto en una discusión). || To show, to register, to record (el termómetro, barómetro, etc.). || To mark out *o* off (delimitar un terreno). || To mark: *la Revolución Francesa marcó el comienzo de una nueva época*, the French Revolution marked the beginning of a new era. || To assign, to set: *el maestro marcó la lección para el día siguiente*, the teacher assigned the lesson for the following day. || To single out (destacar). || To mark (poner el precio). || To bid (los naipes). || To set (el pelo). || IMPR. To feed. || — *Marcar el compás*, to mark the rhythm, to beat time (con la mano o la batuta), to keep time (bailando, cantando). || MIL. *Marcar el paso*, to mark time. || *Marcar el pelo* or *las ondas*, to have one's hair set. || *Marcar las cartas*, to mark the cards.

— V. intr. To make a mark. || DEP. To score (un tanto). | To mark. || To dial (en el teléfono).
— V. pr. To score (apuntarse un tanto). || — *Marcarse un detalle*, to make a nice gesture.
marcasita f. MIN. Marcasite (pirita).
marceño, ña adj. March.
marcial adj. Martial: *ley marcial*, martial law. || Military: *porte marcial*, military air. || Martial, chalybeate (que contiene hierro): *medicamento marcial*, chalybeate medicine.
marcialidad f. Military air.
marciano, na adj./s. Martian (de Marte).
marco m. Frame (de un cuadro, puerta o ventana). || FIG. Framework: *dentro del marco de*, within the framework of. | Setting (lugar): *celebrar algo en un marco adecuado*, to celebrate sth. in an appropriate setting. || Standard (patrón). || Mark (moneda alemana). || Mark (moneda de oro). || Mark (medida antigua de peso). || Goalpost (en deportes).
Marco n. pr. n. Marcus, Mark. || — *Marco Antonio*, Mark Antony. || *Marco Aurelio*, Marcus Aurelius.
Marcos pr. n. m. Mark.
marcha f. March: *organizar una marcha de protesta*, to organize a protest march; *en marcha*, on the march (soldados). || MÚS. March: *marcha fúnebre, nupcial*, funeral, wedding march. || Departure (salida): *¿a qué hora es la marcha?*, what time is the departure? || March, course (paso): *la marcha de los acontecimientos*, the course of events. || Progress (progreso). || Running: *la buena marcha de un negocio*, the smooth running of a business. || Walking (deportes): *marcha atlética*, walking race. || Functioning, working, operation, running (de una máquina). || Speed (velocidad). || AUT. Gear (cambio de velocidades): *marcha directa, atrás*, top, reverse gear. || — *Abrir la marcha*, to be first. || *A marchas forzadas*, at a rapid pace, against the clock: *trabajar a marchas forzadas*, to work against the clock. || *A toda marcha*, at full speed. || *Avanzar a buena marcha*, to advance rapidly. || *Cerrar la marcha*, to bring up the rear. || *Coger la marcha*, to get the hang of it, to get into the swing of things. || *Dar marcha atrás*, to reverse (un coche), to change one's mind (volverse atrás): *a última hora ha dado marcha atrás*, at the last moment he changed his mind. || *¡En marcha!*, let's go (vamos), forward march! (militar). || *Estar en marcha*, to be underway (barco), to be on the move (progresar), to be running, to be working (funcionar). || MAR. y TECN. *La marcha de un motor*, the running of a motor. || *Marcha atrás*, reverse [gear]: *meter la marcha atrás*, to change *o* to go into reverse. || *Marcha forzada*, forced march. || *Marcha moderada*, slow down (señal de tráfico). || *Marcha Real*, National Anthem in Spain. || *Poner en marcha*, to start [up] (un motor, un mecanismo). || *Ponerse en marcha*, to start [off]. || *Sobre la marcha*, on the way, as one goes along.
marchador, ra adj. *Amer.* Walking (andarín). | Pacing, ambling (caballo).
— M. DEP. Walker.
marchamar v. tr. To mark, to stamp (en las aduanas).
marchamo m. Stamp, mark, seal (señal de las aduanas). || FIG. Mark: *un marchamo de elegancia*, a mark of elegance. || *Amer.* Duty charged for each head of cattle killed in the slaughterhouse. || *Un disparo con marchamo de gol*, a shot which looked like a goal all the way.
marchante, ta m. y f. Merchant, dealer. || Customer (parroquiano).
marchapié m. MAR. Footrope.
marchar v. intr. To go, to walk (andar). || To move (moverse). || MIL. To march. || To go, to work (funcionar): *el reloj no marcha*, the clock isn't going. || FIG. To operate: *un negocio que marcha bien*, a business that is operating well. | To go (ir): *todo marcha bien*, everything is going well. || — FIG. *Marchar sobre ruedas* or *rieles*, to run like clockwork. || MIL. *¡Marchen!*, forward march!
— V. pr. To go away, to leave: *¿se marchan?*, are you leaving?; *se marchó a otro lugar*, he went somewhere else, he left for another place. || *Marcharse por las buenas*, to disappear (desaparecer), to leave for good (para no volver más).
marchitable adj. That withers, perishable.
marchitamiento m. Withering, wilting, fading.
marchitar v. tr. To wither, to wilt, to shrivel, to fade (las flores, la hermosura).
— V. pr. To wither, to wilt, to shrivel, to fade.
marchitez f. Wilted *o* withered state *o* condition.
marchito, ta adj. Withered, wilted, faded.
marea f. Tide: *marea creciente, menguante*, rising, ebb tide. || Sea breeze (viento). || Dew (rocío). || Drizzle (llovizna). || FIG. Flood (gran cantidad): *una marea humana*, a flood of people. | Tide. || — FIG. *Contra viento y marea*, V. VIENTO. || *Está alta, baja la marea*, it is high tide, low tide. || *Marea alta, baja*, high, low tide *o* water. || *Marea entrante* or *ascendente*, incoming *o* rising tide. || *Marea saliente* or *descendente*, outgoing tide, ebb tide. || *Marea viva*, spring tide *o* water.
mareado, da adj. Sick (malo): *estoy mareado*, I feel sick. || Seasick (en el mar). || Drunk (bebido). || Dizzy (aturdido).
mareaje m. Navigation, seamanship. || Course (rumbo del navío).
mareamiento m. V. MAREO.
mareante adj. Nauseating, sickening (que marea). || Sailing (navegante). || FIG. y FAM. Boring: *una conversación mareante*, a boring conversation. | Bothersome (molesto).
— M. Navigator.
marear v. tr. MAR. To navigate. || To make feel sick, to upset one's stomach: *ese perfume me marea*, that perfume makes me feel sick. || To make sick, to make feel seasick: *el movimiento del barco me marea*, the movement of the ship makes me sick. || FIG. y FAM. To annoy, to bother (molestar, fastidiar). | To make [s.o.] dizzy: *me mareas con tantas preguntas*, you make me dizzy with so many questions. || CULIN. To cook over a fire in butter or oil (rehogar). || *Aguja de marear*, compass (brújula).
— V. pr. To be *o* to feel sick (tener náuseas). || To be *o* to get seasick (en un barco). || To get *o* to become dizzy (estar aturdido). || FAM. To get a bit drunk (emborracharse un poco). || *Me mareo con tanto ruido*, all this noise makes me dizzy.
marejada f. Swell (del mar). || FIG. Excitement, agitation (agitación). | Wave (oleada). | Rumour (rumor). | Undercurrent (de descontento).
maremagno o **mare mágnum** m. FIG. y FAM. Crowd, multitude (de personas). | Ocean, sea (cosas).
maremoto m. Seaquake.
marengo adj./s. Dark grey (color). || CULIN. *A la marengo*, fricassee (en pepitoria).
mareo m. Sickness, nausea. || Seasickness (en un barco). || Dizziness, vertigo. || FIG. y FAM. Bother, annoyance, nuisance (molestia).
mareógrafo m. Marigraph, mareograph.
mareomotor, triz adj. Tidal. || *Central mareomotriz*, tidal power plant.
marfil m. Ivory. || — *Marfil vegetal*, ivory nut. || *Negro de marfil*, ivory black. || FIG. *Torre de marfil*, ivory tower.
marfileño, ña adj. Ivory. || [Of *o* from] the Ivory Coast.
marga f. MIN. Marl, loam.
margal m. Marlpit.
margar v. tr. AGR. To marl.
margarina f. Margarine.
margarita f. Daisy (flor), marguerite (con flores grandes). || Margarite, pearl (perla). || ZOOL. Mollusc (molusco). | Shellfish (concha cualquiera). || — FIG. *Deshojar la margarita*, to play "she loves me, she loves me not". || FIG. y FAM. *Echar margaritas a los cerdos* or *puercos*, to cast pearls before swine.
Margarita n. pr. f. Margaret.
margen m. y f. Margin (de una página): *dejar margen*, to leave a margin. || Border, edge (borde). || Marginal note (apostilla). || Bank, side (de un río), margin, verge, side (de un camino), edge, border (de un campo). || FIG. Margin: *margen de error, de seguridad*, margin of error, safety margin. | Margin, latitude (libertad): *dejarle margen a uno*, to allow s.o. some margin. | Opportunity (oportunidad). | Pretext, motive, cause, occasion (pretexto). || COM. Margin: *margen de ganancias*, profit margin, margin of profit. || — *Al margen*, in the margin: *firmar al margen*, to sign in the margin; on the fringe: *vivir al margen de la sociedad*, to live on the fringe of society. || FIG. *Dar margen para*, to give occasion for (ocasión). | *Dejar al margen a uno*, to leave s.o. out. | *Mantenerse al margen*, to keep out, to stand aside, to remain on the sidelines. | *Por un escaso margen*, by a narrow margin, narrowly.

— OBSERV. The gender of *margen* varies according to its meaning. It is generally masculine when denoting the space around the text of a page, and feminine when it means the bank of a river, etc.

marginado, da adj. On the fringe.
— M. y f. Dropout.
marginador m. IMPR. Marginal stop.
marginal adj. Marginal: *tecla marginal*, marginal stop.
marginalismo m. Marginalism.
marginar v. tr. To margin, to leave a margin *o* margins on. || To margin, to write notes in the margin *o* margins of (anotar al margen).
margoso, sa adj. Marly, loamy.
margrave m. Margrave. || *Mujer del margrave*, margravine.
margraviato m. Margraviate.
marguera f. Marlpit (cantera), marl deposit (depósito).
María n. pr. f. Mary, Maria.
mariache o **mariachi** m. *Amer.* "Mariachi" [popular music characteristic of the state of Jalisco in Mexico and the band that plays it].
marial adj. Marian, containing canticles to the Virgin Mary (libro).
Mariana n. pr. f. Marian, Marianne, Marion.
Marianas n. pr. f. pl. GEOGR. *Islas Marianas*, Mariana Islands.
marianismo m. Marianism [veneration of the Virgin Mary].
marianista adj./s. Marianist.
mariano, na adj. Marian, of the Virgin Mary.
marica f. Magpie (urraca). || — M. FIG. y FAM. Pansy, fairy (homosexual).
Maricastaña n. pr. f. *En tiempos de Maricastaña*, V. TIEMPO.

maricón m. Pop. Queer, puff (sodomita).
mariconería f. Pop. Homosexualism.
maridaje m. Married life. || Fig. Harmony, close relationship (armonía). | Close understanding (entre personas). | Unnatural alliance (contubernio).
maridar v. intr. To marry (casarse). || To live together as husband and wife, to cohabit (sin estar casados). — V. tr. Fig. To marry (unir, armonizar).
marido m. Husband.
mariguana o **marihuana** o **marijuana** f. Marijuana.
marimacho m. Fam. Mannish woman.
marimandona f. Domineering woman, termagant, battle-axe (fam.).
marimba f. Sort of drum (tambor). || *Amer.* Marimba (xilofón). | Kettledrum (tímpano). | Thrashing, drubbing (paliza). | Cowardly cock (gallo).
marimoños f. inv. Fam. Flirt, coquette.
marimorena f. Fam. Row, squabble. || Fam. *Armar la marimorena*, to kick up a hell of a row.
marina f. Seacoast (costa). || Seascape, seapiece, marine (cuadro). || Navy, marine: *marina mercante*, merchant navy. || Seamanship (arte de navegar). || — *De marina*, nautical. || *Infantería de Marina*, marines, *pl.* || *Marina de guerra*, Navy. || *Ministerio de Marina*, Admiralty [U.S., Department of the Navy]. || *Ministro de Marina*, First Lord of the Admiralty [U.S., Secretary of the Navy]. || *Oficial de Marina*, naval officer. || *Servir en la marina*, to serve in the Navy.
marinar v. tr. To marinate, to marinade (escabechar). || Mar. To man (tripular).
marinear v. intr. To be a sailor.
marinera f. V. MARINERO.
marinería f. Crew (tripulación de un barco). || Seamen, *pl.*, sailors, *pl.* (marineros). || Sailoring (profesión).
marinero, ra adj. Seaworthy: *barco marinero*, seaworthy ship. || Seaboard: *pueblo marinero*, seaboard town. || [Of the] sea: *cuentos marineros*, tales of the sea. || Sailor's, sailors': *traje marinero*, sailor's costume. — M. Sailor, seaman, mariner. || Argonaut (molusco). || — Fig. *Marinero de agua dulce*, landlubber, poor sailor. || *Traje de marinero*, sailor's costume. || — F. Middy blouse (blusa de niño). || Middy blouse, sailor blouse (de mujer). || *Amer.* Marinera [popular dance]. || — *A la marinera*, sailor-fashion (como los marineros). || *Salsa, pescado a la marinera*, matelote.
marinismo m. Marinism (preciosismo).
marinista adj. Seascape, marine.
— M. y f. Seascapist.
marino, na adj. Marine: *vegetación marina*, marine vegetation. || Sea: *brisa marina*, sea breeze. || *Azul marino*, navy blue.
— M. Sailor, seaman: *marino mercante*, merchant seaman. || Nautics expert (experto en náutica).
marioneta f. Marionette, puppet (títere). || — Pl. Puppet show, *sing.* (pantomina).
mariposa f. Butterfly (insecto). || Variety of finch (ave). || Tecn. Butterfly *o* wing nut (tuerca). || Lamp (lamparilla). || *Amer.* Blindman's buff (juego). || — *Braza mariposa*, butterfly (natación). || *Mariposa nocturna*, moth.
mariposeador, ra adj. Inconsistent, fickle, always chopping and changing (inconstante). || Flirtatious (galanteador). || Always hovering around (que está dando vueltas).
— M. y f. Chopper and changer. || Flirt (galanteador).
mariposear v. intr. Fig. To chop and change (ser inconstante). | To flirt (galantear). | To hover around (dar vueltas).
mariposón m. Fam. Romeo, flirt (galanteador). | Pansy (marica).
mariquita f. Ladybird [U.S., ladybug] (coleóptero). || Bug (hemíptero). || Parakeet (perico). || *Amer.* Popular dance (danza). || — M. Fam. Sissy, cissy, pansy (afeminado). || Fam. *Mariquita azúcar*, sissy.
marisabidilla f. Fam. Bluestocking.
mariscal m. Mil. Marshal. || *Mariscal de campo*, field marshal.
mariscala f. Marshal's wife.
mariscalato m. o **mariscalía** f. Marshalship.
mariscador m. Shellfisherman.
mariscar v. tr. To fish for [shellfish].
marisco m. Shellfish, seafood.
marisma f. Salt marsh. || — Pl. *Las Marismas*, marshy region at the mouth of the Guadalquivir.
marismeño, ña adj. Marsh.
marisquería f. Shellfish bar *o* restaurant.
marisquero, ra m. y f. Shellfisherman, shellfisher-woman. || Shellfish seller (vendedor).
marista adj./s. Marist (religioso).
marital adj. Marital. || Husband's: *autorización marital*, husband's authorization. || *Vida marital*, married life.
marítimo, ma adj. Maritime, sea: *navegación marítima*, maritime navigation. || Seaboard (pueblo, etc.). || Shipping, seaborne (comercio). || Harbour (estación). || — *Arsenal marítimo*, naval dockyard. || *Seguro marítimo*, marine insurance.
maritornes f. Fig. y fam. Sluttish servant.
marjal m. Marsh, bog.
marjoleta f. Hawthorn berry, haw.
marjoleto m. Hawthorn.
marketing m. Marketing.
marmita f. [Cooking] pot (olla). || Pressure cooker (para guisar a presión).
marmitón m. Kitchen hand, cook's help, scullion (ant.) [pinche de cocina].
mármol m. Marble: *esculpido en mármol*, sculpted in marble. || Marble (escultura). || — *Cantera de mármol*, marble quarry. || Fig. *De mármol*, stony-hearted, as cold as marble.
marmolería f. Marbles, *pl.*, marblework (conjunto de mármoles). || Marble (obra). || Marble-cutter's workshop (taller).
marmolillo m. Spur stone (guardacantón). || Fig. Idiot, dolt (idiota). || Taur. Indolent bull.
marmolista m. Marble cutter (el que labra). || Marble dealer (vendedor).
marmóreo, a adj. Marmoreal.
marmota f. Zool. Marmot (mamífero). || Worsted cap (gorro). || Fig. y fam. Sleepyhead (dormilón). | Charwoman, maid (criada). || *Dormir como una marmota*, to sleep like a log *o* soundly.
maro m. Bot. Cat thyme, marum.
maroma f. [Thick] rope. || Mar. Cable. || *Amer.* Tightrope walking.
maromear v. intr. *Amer.* To perform on the tightrope. || Fig. To sit on the fence.
maromo m. Fam. Man friend.
maronita adj./s. Maronite.
marplatense adj./s. [Of *o* from] Mar del Plata [Republic of Argentina].
— M. y f. Native *o* inhabitant of Mar del Plata.
marqués m. Marquis, marquess (título). || *Los marqueses*, the marquis and marquise.
marquesa f. Marquise, marchioness (título). || Easy chair (sillón). || — *Dárselas de marquesa*, to put on airs. || *Marquesa de vidrio*, glass canopy [U.S., marquee].
marquesado m. Marquisate, marquessate.
marquesina f. Canopy (cobertizo). || *Marquesina de cristales*, glass canopy [U.S., marquee].
marquesita f. Min. Marcasite (marcasita).
marquetería f. Marquetry, marqueterie, inlaid work. || *Especialista en marquetería*, specialist in marquetry, inlayer.
marquista m. Proprietor of one or more brands of wine.
marra f. Gap, space (espacio). || Lack (falta). || Stone hammer (almádena).
marrajo, ja adj. Mean, vicious (toro). || Fig. Shrewd, cunning (malicioso).
— M. Shark (tiburón).
marrana f. Sow (hembra del cerdo). || Fig. y fam. Slut, trollop, slattern (sucia, indecente). || Tecn. Axle (de una noria).
marranada o **marranería** f. Fig. y fam. Dirty *o* filthy *o* foul *o* rotten trick (cochinada). || Filthy *o* mucky *o* grubby thing (cosa suciamente hecha). || *Este cuarto está hecho una marranada*, this room is like a pigsty.
marrano, na adj. Filthy, dirty.
— M. Hog (cerdo). || Fig. y fam. Swine (mala persona). | Pig, slob (sucio). || Piece securing drum to axle (de noria). || Pressure-distributing board [in oil mills] (de una prensa). || Timber supporting the bottom part of a well (de pozo). || Hist. "Marrano" [converted Jew] (judío).
marrar v. intr. To miss (errar). || To turn out badly, to fail (fallar): *ha marrado el proyecto*, the project has failed. || Fig. To deviate, to branch off (desviarse). || *Marrar el tiro*, to miss: *marrar el tiro a una liebre*, to miss a hare.
marras (de) loc. adv. Fam. Long ago (de antes). || In question: *el asunto, el individuo de marras*, the matter, the individual in question. || *El cuento de marras*, the same old story.
marrasquino m. Maraschino (licor).
marrón adj. Brown (color). || Pseudo-amateur, sham amateur (deportista).
— M. Brown (color).
marroquí adj./s. Moroccan. || — M. Morocco leather (tafilete).
— Observ. Pl. *marroquíes.*
marroquín m. Morocco leather (tafilete).
marroquinería f. Morocco-leather dressing (preparación). || Morocco-leather tannery (taller). || Leather goods, *pl.* (artículos de cuero). || Leather goods store (tienda). || Leather goods industry (industria).
marroquinero m. Morocco-leather dresser (tafiletero).
marrubio m. Bot. Marrubium (p.us.), horehound.
Marruecos n. pr. m. Geogr. Morocco.
marrullería f. Cajolery.
marrullero, ra adj. Cajoling, artful.
— M. y f. Cajoler.
Marsella n. pr. Geogr. Marseilles.
marsopa o **marsopla** f. Porpoise (cetáceo).
marsupial adj./s.m. Marsupial.
marta f. Zool. Marten (mamífero). || Sable (piel). || *Marta cebellina*, sable.
Marte n. pr. m. Mars (planeta). || Mars (dios).
martelo m. Jealousy (celos). | Love, passion (amor).
martes m. inv. Tuesday (día): *vendrá el martes*, he will come on Tuesday; *viene el martes, cada martes*, he comes on Tuesday, every Tuesday. || — *El martes pasado, que viene*, last, next Tuesday. || Fig. *El martes*,

ni te cases ni te embarques, never undertake anything on a Tuesday [an unlucky day like Friday in England]. || *Martes de Carnaval*, Shrove Tuesday.

martiano, na adj. Of José Martí [Cuban writer and hero].

martillada f. Hammer blow.

martillador m. Hammersmith, hammerer.

martillar v. tr. To hammer. || FIG. To torment. || — FIG. *Martillar en hierro frío*, to bang one's head against a brick wall. | *Martillar los oídos*, to hammer *o* to pound on one's ears.

martillazo m. Blow with a hammer. || *A martillazos*, with a hammer.

martillear v. tr. To hammer. || FIG. *Martillear los oídos*, to hammer *o* to pound on one's ears.
— V. intr. To knock (un motor).

martilleo m. Hammering. || Hammering (bombardeo intenso). || FIG. Pounding (ruido).

martillero m. *Amer.* Auctioneer.

martillo m. Hammer (herramienta). || Tuning hammer (templador). || Hammer, striker (reloj). || ANAT. Malleus, hammer (del oído interno). || DEP. Hammer. || ZOOL. Hammer-head shark (tiburón). || Gavel (de presidente de sesión). || FIG. One armed cross of the Order of St. John. || Auction room (para subastas). || — *A macha martillo*, v. MACHAMARTILLO (A). || *A martillo*, with a hammer, by hammering. || *Martillo de fragua*, blacksmith's hammer. || *Martillo de herrador*, shoeing hammer. || *Martillo de picapedrero*, stone hammer, braying hammer. || *Martillo de remachar*, riveting hammer. || *Martillo neumático*, air hammer, pneumatic drill. || *Martillo pilón*, drop *o* steam hammer.

Martín n. pr. m. Martin. || *Día de San Martín*, Martinmas.

martín del río m. ZOOL. Heron.

martín pescador m. ZOOL. Kingfisher.

martinete m. ZOOL. Heron (ave). | Heron plumes, *pl.* (penacho). || Hammer (de piano). || TECN. Drop hammer (martillo pilón). | Pile driver (para clavar estacas). || Andalusian song (cante).

martingala f. Martingale (en el juego). || FIG. Trick (artimaña). || — Pl. Breeches worn under armour.

martiniano, na adj. V. MARTIANO.

Martinica (La) n. pr. f. GEOGR. Martinique.

mártir m. y f. Martyr. || — *Capilla de mártires*, martyry, shrine. || FIG. *Dárselas de mártir*, to make a martyr of o.s.

martirio m. Martyrdom.

martirizador, ra adj. Martyring, persecuting.
— M. Tormentor, torturer, persecutor.

martirizar v. tr. To martyr, to martyrize (hacer sufrir martirio). || FIG. To torture, to torment, to martyrize (hacer padecer).

martirologio m. Martyrology (lista de mártires).

marusiño, ña adj./s. Galician.

marxismo m. Marxism (doctrina): *marxismo-leninismo*, Marxism-Leninism.

marxista adj./s. Marxist.

marzo m. March: *el 17 de marzo de 1915*, 17th March 1915.

mas conj. But (pero).
— M. Farm.

— OBSERV. The conjunction *mas* bears no written accent.

más adv. More: *no te digo más*, I shall say no more; *tengo más trabajo que él*, I have more work to do than he; *escribe más rápidamente que su hermana*, he writes more quickly than his sister; *¿quieres más sopa?*, do you want more soup *o* any more soup?; *este coche es más caro que ése*, this car is more expensive than that one; *nos trajeron más armas*, they brought us more arms [V. OBSERV. I.]. || Most (superlativo): *el chico más listo de la clase*, the most intelligent boy in the class [V. OBSERV. II.]. || Over, more than (con un número): *tengo más de cien libras*, I have over a hundred pounds *o* more than a hundred pounds. || MAT. Plus, and: *dos más dos son cuatro*, two plus two are *o* make four. || After, past (con la hora): *son más de la nueve*, it is after nine, it is past nine. || More of a (con sustantivo): *es más coche*, it is more of a car; *más hombre*, more of a man. || Another, more (después de un sustantivo): *un kilómetro más*, another kilometre, one more kilometre; *deme dos botellas más*, give me two more bottles *o* another two bottles. || Longer: *quédate un poco más*, stay a little longer; *durar más*, to last longer. || FAM. So: *¡estaba más contento!*, he was so happy!; *¡es más buena!*, she is so kind! || As (tan): *es más pobre que las ratas*, he is as poor as a church mouse; *más blanco que la nieve*, as white as snow. || Not translated: *¡qué manera más extraña de comer!*, what a strange way to eat! || — *A cuál más*, v. CUÁL. || *A lo más*, at the most, at most. || *A más* or *a más de*, besides, in addition. || *A más correr*, at full speed. || *A más no poder*, as much [fast, hard, etc.] as possible *o* as can be *o* as one can: *están trabajando a más no poder*, they are working as hard as can be; *correr a más no poder*, to run as fast as possible; *es tonto a más no poder*, he is as silly as can be; *comimos a más no poder*, we ate as much as we could. || *A más tardar*, at the latest. || *A más y mejor*, a lot, a great deal (mucho). || *Cada día más*, v. DÍA. || *Cada vez más*, v. VEZ. || *Como el que más*, as well as anyone, as well as the next man. || *Cuando más*, at the most. || *Cuanto más... más*, the more... the more. || *Cuanto más... menos*, the more... the less. || *De más*, extra, spare (que sobra): *traje uno de más por si acaso*, I brought an extra one just in case; too much, too many (demasiado): *me has dado veinte de más*, you have given me twenty too many; unnecessary, superfluous (superfluo), out of place (poco apto). || *De más en más*, more and more. || *El más allá*, the beyond. || *El que más y el que menos* or *cual más cual menos* or *quien más quien menos sabe algo de matemáticas, tiene sus debilidades*, we all have some knowledge of mathematics, we all have our weaknesses. || *En lo más mínimo*, in the least, in the slightest, at all. || *Es más*, moreover, furthermore. || *Estar de más*, to be in the way (estorbar), not to be needed (innecesario). || *Gustar más*, to prefer, to like better: *me gusta más el pavo que el pollo*, I prefer turkey to chicken. || *Las más de las veces*, usually, most times, more often than not. || *Lo más*, at the most, at most (a lo más). || *Lo más posible*, as much as possible. || *Lo más tarde*, at the latest. || *Más adelante*, further on. || *Más allá de*, beyond, past, further than. || *Más aún*, still more, even more. || *Más bien*, rather. || *Más de, más de lo que*, more than. || *Más de la cuenta*, too much. || *Más de lo regular*, more than usual. || FAM. *¡Más lo eres tú!*, you too!, the same to you! || *Más o menos*, more or less. || *Más que nunca*, more than ever. || *Más tarde o más temprano*, sooner or later. || *Más vale tarde que nunca*, better late than never. || *Más y más*, more and more. || *Mientras más... más*, the more... the more. || *Mucho más*, much more, a lot more. || *Nada más*, v. NADA. || *Nadie más*, nobody else. || *Ni más ni menos*, no more, no less (exactamente), quite simply (simplemente). || *No más*, only: *me dio dos pesetas no más*, he only gave me two pesetas; *ayer no más*, only yesterday; as soon as, no sooner, just: *no más hubo llegado que...*, as soon as he arrived..., no sooner had he arrived than..., he had just arrived when...; no more, that is enough (basta): *¡no más gritos!*, no more shouting!; quite simply: *le dijo no más que era un negado*, he quite simply told him he was useless; please, do (en América): *sírvese no más*, please help yourself; *siéntese no más*, do sit down. || *No... más*, no more *o* not any more: *no quiero más*, I want no more *o* I don't want any more. || *No más de*, no more than. || *No... más que*, only, all, no more than: *no quiero más que veinte libras por semana*, I only want twenty pounds a week *o* all I want is twenty pounds a week *o* I want no more than twenty pounds a week. || *No veo más solución que...*, I see no other solution than... || *Poco más o menos*, more or less. || *Poder más*, to be stronger than, to prevail, to triumph: *el amor pudo más que el odio*, love triumphed over hate. || *Por más* (con sustantivo), whatever, no matter what: *por más esfuerzos que hagas*, whatever efforts you may make. || *Por más* (con adjetivo o adverbio), however, no matter how: *por más robusto que sea*, no matter how strong he may be. || *Por más que* (con verbo), no matter how much, however much: *por más que trabajase, nunca saldría de pobre*, no matter how much he were to work, he would never escape poverty; however fast, however hard, etc.: *por más que corra*, however fast he runs. || *¿Qué más?*, what else? || *¿Qué más da?*, what difference does it make? || *Sin más* or *sin más ni más*, v. SIN. || *Tanto más*, the more, all the more. || *Tanto más... cuanto que*, all the more... since *o* because. || *Todo lo más*, at [the] most (como mucho), at the latest (como muy tarde). || *Una vez más*, one more time, once more, once again. || *Valer más*, to be better: *más vale hacerlo enseguida*, it is better to do it straight away. || *Y lo que es más*, and furthermore. || *¿Y qué más?*, and then what?
— M. MAT. Plus (signo). || — *Hubo sus más y sus menos*, there was a clash of opinion (en una discusión). || *Los más*, most people. || *Los más de, las más de*, the majority of, most: *las más de las mujeres*, the majority of women, most women. || *Tener sus más y sus menos*, to have one's *o* its difficulties (tener sus dificultades).

— OBSERV. I. La mayoría de los adjetivos ingleses toman una forma comparativa : *este coche es más caro que ése*, this car is dearer than that one; *mi casa es más bonita que la tuya*, my house is nicer than yours.
II. La mayoría de los adjetivos ingleses toman una forma superlativa : *el chico más listo de la clase*, the cleverest boy in the class; *el vino más seco que conozco*, the driest wine I know.

masa f. Dough (del pan). || Mortar, plaster (argamasa). || FÍS. Mass: *el gramo es una unidad de masa*, the gram is a unit of mass. || Mass (cantidad, conjunto): *una masa de nieve, de nubes*, a mass of snow, of clouds; *una masa gaseosa*, a gaseous mass. || Masses, *pl.* (gente): *el control del país está en manos de la masa* or *de las masas*, control of the country is in the hands of the masses. || Total: *la masa de bienes*, total fortune. || ELECTR. Earth [U.S., ground]. || — *De masas*, mass: *medios de comunicación de masas*, mass media. || *En la masa de la sangre*, v. SANGRE. || *En masa*, en masse: *llegaron en masa*, they arrived en masse; mass: *manifestación en masa*, mass demonstration. || *Masa coral*, choir, chorale. || FÍS. *Masa crítica*, critical mass. || *Producción en masa*, mass production.

masacre m. Massacre.
— OBSERV. This word is a Gallicism used for *matanza*.
masada f. Farm.
masaje m. Massage. || — *Dar masajes a*, to massage. || *Hacerse dar masajes*, to have o.s. massaged.
masajista m. y f. Masseur (hombre), masseuse (mujer).
mascabado, da adj. Muscovado, unrefined (azúcar). — M. Muscovado.
mascada f. *Amer*. Quid (de tabaco). | Silk neckerchief (pañuelo). | Chewing (mascadura).
mascador, ra adj. Chewing.
— M. y f. Chewer.
mascadura f. Chewing, mastication.
mascar v. tr. To chew, to masticate (masticar). || FIG. y FAM. To mumble (mascullar). || — FIG. y FAM. *Dárselo todo mascado a uno*, to hand it to s.o. on a spoon. | *Estar mascando tierra*, to be pushing up daisies.
— V. intr. To chew.
máscara f. Mask: *máscara antigás*, gas mask. || FIG. Mask, pretence. || Masked figure, mask, masker (persona disfrazada con una máscara). || — Pl. Masquerade, *sing*., masked ball, *sing*. (fiesta). || — *Quitar la máscara a*, to unmask. || *Quitarse la máscara*, to unmask o.s., to take off one's mask, to reveal o.s. || *Traje de máscara*, fancy dress.
mascarada f. Masquerade, masked ball, masque. || FIG. Masquerade.
mascarilla f. Half mask. || Death mask (que se saca de un cadáver). || Face mask (de cirujano). || Face pack (de belleza). || Mask (de oxígeno).
mascarita f. Small mask. || FIG. *Te conozco mascarita aunque vengas disfrazada*, it's easy to see what your little game is.
mascarón m. Large mask. || ARQ. Mascaron, grotesque mask (adorno). || MAR. *Mascarón de proa*, figurehead.
mascota f. Mascot.
mascujar v. tr. V. MASCULLAR.
masculillo m. Bumping (juego de chicos). || FIG. y FAM. Thwack, blow (porrazo).
masculinidad f. Masculinity, manliness.
masculinizar v. tr. GRAM. To make masculine. || To make mannish (a una mujer).
masculino, na adj. Male: *un individuo del sexo masculino*, a person of the male sex; *los órganos masculinos de una flor*, the male organs of a flower. || Masculine, manly (propio de los hombres): *una característica masculina*, a manly characteristic; *un color masculino*, a masculine colour. || Mannish, masculine (mujer). || *Ropa masculina*, men's clothing. || — Adj./s.m. GRAM. Masculine.
mascullar v. tr. To chew with difficulty, to chew badly (mascar mal). || To mumble, to mutter (pronunciar indistintamente).
maser m. FÍS. Maser.
masera f. Trough (artesa). || Type of crab (cangrejo).
masetero m. ANAT. Masseter (músculo).
masía f. Farm (granja).
masilla f. Putty. || *Fijar con masilla*, to putty.
masita f. MIL. Uniform money.
masivo, va adj. Massive: *dosis masiva*, massive dose. || *Manifestación masiva*, mass *o* massive demonstration.
maslo m. Dock (tronco de la cola de un animal). || Stem (de una planta).
masón m. Mason, freemason.
masonería f. Masonry, freemasonry.
masónico, ca adj. Masonic: *logia masónica*, Masonic lodge.
masoquismo m. Masochism.
masoquista adj. Masochistic.
— M. y f. Masochist.
massé m. Massé (billar).
mastaba f. Mastaba (tumba).
mastelerillo m. MAR. Topgallant mast. || — *Mastelerillo de juanete de proa*, fore-topgallant mast. | *Mastelerillo de juanete mayor* or *de popa*, main-topgallant mast.
mastelero m. Topmast. || — *Mastelero de gavia* or *mayor*, main-topmast. || *Mastelero de perico*, mizzen-topgallant mast. || *Mastelero de sobremesana*, mizzen-topmast. || *Mastelero de velacho*, fore-topmast.
masticación f. Chewing, mastication.
masticador adj. Chewing. || ZOOL. Masticatory (aparato, animal).
— M. Salivant bit (del caballo). || Masticator (aparato para triturar). || ZOOL. Masticator.
masticar v. tr. To chew, to masticate. || FIG. To chew over, to ponder over, to ruminate.
masticatorio, ria adj. Masticatory.
— M. Masticatories, *pl.*
mástil m. MAR. Mast, spar. | Topmast (mastelero). || Mast, pole (para sostener una antena, bandera, etc.). || Bedpost (de cama). || MÚS. Neck (de la guitarra, etc.). || Stem (de planta). || Barrel, quill (de una pluma). || Stanchion (sostén).
mastín m. ZOOL. Mastiff (perro). || *Mastín danés*, Great Dane.
mastitis f. MED. Mastitis.
mastodonte m. Mastodon.
mastodóntico, ca adj. FIG. Elephantine.
mastoideo, a adj. ANAT. Mastoid.
mastoides adj./s.f. Mastoid. || ANAT. Mastoid.
mastoiditis f. MED. Mastoiditis.
mastuerzo m. BOT. Cress. || FIG. y FAM. Dolt (necio).
masturbación f. Masturbation.
masturbar v. tr. To masturbate.
— V. pr. To masturbate.
mata f. Plantation, grove (de árboles). || Orchard (de árboles frutales). || Shrub, bush (arbusto). || Mastic tree (lentisco). || Sprig, twig, tuft (trozo arrancado de una planta). || Head of hair (pelo). || TECN. Matte (sulfuro múltiple). || — FIG. y FAM. *A salto de mata*, v. SALTO. || BOT. *Mata de la seda*, milkweed. || FIG. y FAM. *Ser más tonto que una mata de habas*, to be as daft as a brush, to be as mad as a hatter.
matacán m. ARQ. Machicolation.
matadero m. Slaughterhouse, abattoir (de reses). || FIG. y FAM. Backbreaking job, bind (trabajo). || *Amer*. FIG. y FAM. Batchelor's flat. || FIG. *Llevar a uno al matadero*, to lead s.o. to the slaughter.
matador, ra adj. Killing, murderous. || FIG. y FAM. Killing, backbreaking: *el trabajo es matador*, the work is killing. | Deadly (pesado). | Ridiculous, absurd.
— M. Killer, murderer (asesino). || TAUR. Matador, bullfighter. || Trump card [in the game of ombre]. || — F. Killer, murderess (asesina).
matadura f. Harness sore.
matafuego m. Fire extinguisher (extintor). || Fireman (bombero).
mátalas callando m. y f. inv. FAM. Wolf in sheep's clothing.
matalotaje m. MAR. Ship's stores, *pl.* (víveres). || FIG. y FAM. Jumble, mess (desorden).
matalote m. Worn-out nag. || Ship: *matalote de proa, de popa*, next ship ahead, astern.
matambre m. *Amer*. Slice of meat.
matamoros adj. inv. Blustering, arrogant, swashbuckling.
— M. inv. Swashbuckler, braggart.
matamoscas adj. inv. *Papel, bomba matamoscas*, fly paper, fly spray. || *Pala matamoscas*, fly swatter.
— M. inv. Fly killer.
matanza f. Slaughter, slaughtering (de animales). || Massacre, slaughter, butchery, killing (de muchas personas). || Slaughtering season (época de la matanza). || Pork products, *pl.* (productos del cerdo). || *Hacer una matanza de mil personas*, to slaughter *o* to butcher *o* to massacre a thousand people.
mataperrada f. *Amer*. Mischievous prank.
mataperrear v. intr. *Amer*. To get up to mischief.
matapolillas m. inv. Moth killer.
mataquintos m. inv. FAM. Bad tobacco.
matar v. tr. To kill. || To slaughter, to kill (reses). || FIG. To kill: *los excesos le matarán*, his excesses will kill him. | To tire out (de trabajo). | To slake (la cal, el yeso). | To put out (un fuego). | To round, to bevel (una arista). | To lay (el polvo). | To kill, to stave off (el hambre). | To kill (el tiempo, la sed). | To kill, to tone down (apagar un color vivo). | To cancel to obliterate (sello). || DEP. To kill (la pelota). || — FIG. *Así me maten*, for the life of me. || TAUR. *Entrar a matar*, to go in to kill *o* for the kill. || FIG. *Estar a matar con uno* to be at loggerheads *o* at daggers drawn with s.o. | *Matar a disgustos*, v. DISGUSTO. | *Matar a fuego lento*, to torture to death. | *Matar a preguntas*, to plague *o* to bombard with questions. | *Matar de aburrimiento*, to bore to death *o* to tears. || *Matar de hambre*, to starve to death. | *Matar el gusanillo*, v. GUSANILLO. | *Matarlas callando*, to be a wolf in sheep's clothing. | *¡Que me maten si...!*, I'll be damned if...!
— V. intr. To kill. || To mate (en ajedrez).
— V. pr. To kill o.s. (suicidarse). || To be *o* to get killed (en un accidente). || FIG. To kill o.s., to wear o.s. out (en el trabajo): *matarse trabajando*, to kill o.s. working; *matarse por conseguir algo*, to kill o.s. getting sth.
matarife m. Butcher, slaughterer.
matarratas m. inv. Rat killer. || FIG. Rotgut, firewater (aguardiente malo).
matasanos m. inv. FAM. Quack (médico).
matasellar v. tr. To cancel, to postmark, to obliterate.
matasellos m. inv. Canceller (instrumento de correos). || Postmark (marca).
matasiete m. FAM. Braggart, blusterer, bully, boaster.
matasuegras m. inv. Paper serpent (juguete).
matatías m. inv. FAM. Moneylender.
matazón f. *Amer*. Massacre.
match m. Match (encuentro deportivo).
mate adj. Matt, dull (sin brillo). || Dull (sonido).
— M. Checkmate, mate (ajedrez). || *Amer*. Maté, Paraguayan tea (bebida). | Maté (calabaza seca). | Maté (arbusto). | FIG. y FAM. Nut (cabeza). || — *Amer*. *Cebar mate*, to prepare maté. || *Dar jaque mate*, to checkmate. || *Amer*. *Hierba mate*, maté. || *Jaque mate*, checkmate. || *Amer*. *Mate amargo* or *mate cimarrón*, unsweetened maté, bitter maté.
matear v. intr. To grow thickly (el trigo). || To search the undergrowth (caza). || *Amer*. To have a drink of maté.
matemático, ca adj. Mathematical: *lógica matemática*, mathematical logic.
— M. y f. Mathematician. || — F. Mathematics, maths (fam). || — Pl. Mathematics, maths (fam.): *las matemáticas puras, aplicadas*, pure, applied mathematics.

Mateo n. pr. m. Matthew: *evangelio según San Mateo*, Gospel according to Saint Matthew. || FIG. y FAM. *Estar como Mateo con la guitarra*, to be as pleased as Punch *o* as pie.
materia f. Matter: *no se puede destruir la materia*, matter cannot be destroyed; *el espíritu y la materia*, mind and matter. || Material, substance (material). || Matter, question, subject (cuestión): *eso es otra materia*, that is another question. || Subject (asignatura): *estudia ocho materias*, he studies eight subjects. || MED. Matter, pus. || — *En materia de*, in the matter of, as regards. || *Entrar en materia*, to get down to business. || *Índice de materias*, table of contents. || *Materia colorante*, dyestuff, colouring matter. || *Materia de Estado*, affair *o* matter of State. || *Materia gris*, grey matter. || *Materia prima*, raw material.
material adj. Material: *necesidades materiales*, material necessities. || Physical: *presencia, dolor, daño, goce material*, physical presence, pain, damage, pleasure. || Materialistic: *un espíritu demasiado material*, an over-materialistic mind. || Real: *el autor material de un hecho*, the real instigator of a deed. || — FIG. *El tiempo material para algo, para hacer algo*, just enough time for sth., to do sth. | *Error material*, clerical error.
— M. Material: *el vaso es de material plástico*, the glass is made of a plastic material; *materiales de construcción*, building materials. || Equipment: *material deportivo*, sports equipment; *material de oficina*, office equipment. || AGR. Implements, *pl.* (de una granja). || TECN. Plant, equipment (maquinaria). || Leather (de calzado). || — *Material bélico* or *de guerra*, war material. || *Material escolar*, teaching materials, *pl.*, school equipment. || *Materiales de derribo*, rubble, *sing.* || *Material móvil* or *rodante*, rolling stock (ferrocarriles). || *Material publicitario*, advertising material. || TECN. *Material refractario*, heatproof material.
materialidad f. Materiality, material nature. || — *No me importa la materialidad del dinero, sino que se lo llevase ese sinvergüenza*, it is not the money itself which bothers me, but the fact that it was that scoundrel who took it. || *No oye más* que *la materialidad de las palabras*, he is incapable of taking what you say at anything other than its face value.
materialismo m. Materialism.
materialista adj. Materialistic, materialist.
— M. y f. Materialist.
materialización f. Materialization.
materializar v. tr. To materialize.
— V. pr. To materialize.
materialmente adv. Materially. || Physically, utterly, absolutely.
maternal adj. Maternal, motherly.
maternidad f. Maternity, motherhood. || Maternity hospital *o* home (casa de maternidad).
materno, na adj. Motherly, maternal: *amor materno*, motherly love. || Mother, native (lengua). || Maternal: *abuela materna*, maternal grandmother.
matero, ra adj. Fond of maté. || Of maté.
— M. y f. Maté drinker.
matete m. *Amer.* Mixture (mejunje). | Dispute, row (riña). | Confusion, mess (confusión).
matidez f. Dullness (de una superficie, un sonido).
matinal adj. Morning, matinal.
matinée f. TEATR. Matinée.
matiz m. Shade, hue, tint, nuance (de color). || FIG. Shade, nuance (de sentido). | Touch (con ironía).
matización f. Harmonization, matching (de varios colores). || Tingeing, shading, colouring (con un matiz de otra cosa). || Nuances, *pl.*, shades, *pl.* (matices).
matizar v. tr. To harmonize, to match (casar varios colores). || To tinge (un color de otro). || FIG. To vary (introducir variedad): *matizar el tono de voz*, to vary one's tone of voice. | To tinge: *doctrinas matizadas de socialismo*, doctrines tinged with socialism.
matojo m. BOT. Bush, shrub (mata). | Saltwort (planta quenopodiácea).
matón m. FAM. Tough guy, bully.
matonear v. intr. FAM. To play the tough guy.
matonería f. o **matonismo** m. Bullying, terrorizing, loutishness.
matorral m. Brushwood, scrub. || Thicket (conjunto de matas).
matraca f. Rattle (instrumento). || — FIG. y FAM. *Dar la matraca a uno*, to get on s.o.'s nerves, to pester s.o. (dar la lata), to make fun of s.o., to scoff at s.o. (burlarse). | *Ser una matraca*, to be a pest *o* a nuisance.
matraquear v. intr. To rattle, to make a noise with the rattle. || FIG. y FAM. V. MATRACA (*Dar la matraca*).
matraqueo m. Rattling, rattle, noise made with the rattle. || FIG. y FAM. Pestering (molestia). | Banter, scoffing (burla). | Wearisome insistence (insistencia).
matraz m. QUÍM. Matrass, glass vessel.
matrero, ra adj. Cunning, shrewd, astute (astuto). || *Amer.* Suspicious, distrustful (desconfiado).
— M. *Amer.* Bandit, brigand (bandido).
matriarcado m. Matriarchy.
matriarcal adj. Matriarchal.
matricaria f. BOT. Feverfew.
matricida adj. Matricidal.
— M. y f. Matricide (persona).
matricidio m. Matricide (acto).
matrícula f. Register, list, roll (lista). || Registration, enrolment, matriculation (acto de matricularse en una universidad, etc.): *derechos de matrícula*, registration fee. || Roll (número de alumnos o de estudiantes). || MAR. Register (lista de hombres o de embarcaciones). || AUT. Registration number (número), number plate [U.S., license plate] (placa). || — *Matrícula de honor*, prize (universidad). || MAR. *Puerto de matrícula*, port of registry.
matriculación f. Registration (de coche, barco, persona). || Registration, enrolment, matriculation (en un centro de enseñanza).
matriculado, da adj. Registered, enrolled (en la universidad). || Registered (coche, barco).
— M. y f. Registered student.
matricular v. tr. To register (un coche, una embarcación, a una persona). || To enrol, to register, to matriculate (a uno en la universidad, etc.).
— V. pr. To enrol, to matriculate, to register: *matricularse de física en la universidad de Granada*, to matriculate in physics at the university of Granada. || To register: *matricularse como médico*, to register as a doctor.
matrimonial adj. Matrimonial, marital. || — *Capitulaciones matrimoniales*, marriage settlement (*sing.*) *o* contract, *sing.* || *Vida matrimonial*, married life, conjugal life.
matrimoniar v. intr. To marry, to get married.
matrimonio m. Marriage, matrimony. || Married couple: *un joven matrimonio*, a young married couple. || Married state (estado de casado). || Marriage (casamiento, boda): *matrimonio civil*, civil marriage. || — *Cama de matrimonio*, double bed. || *Contraer matrimonio con*, to take in marriage, to contract marriage with, to marry. || *Dar palabra de matrimonio*, to plight one's troth (ant.), to promise to marry. || *Fuera del matrimonio*, out of wedlock. || *Matrimonio de conveniencia* or *de interés*, marriage of convenience. || FAM. *Matrimonio por detrás de la iglesia*, marriage over the broomstick, companionate marriage. || *Matrimonio por poderes*, marriage by proxy. || *Matrimonio rato*, non-consummated marriage. || *Partida de matrimonio*, wedding certificate, certificate of marriage.
matritense adj. [Of *o* from] Madrid, Madrilenian.
— M. y f. Native *o* inhabitant of Madrid, Madrilenian.
matriz f. ANAT. Uterus, womb (de la mujer). || TECN. Die (troquel). | Nut (tuerca). || IMPR. Type mould, matrix. || Stub, counterfoil (de talonario). || Mother record [U.S., master record] (de un disco). || Master copy, original (original de un documento). || MAT. y MIN. Matrix. || TECN. *Matriz de terraja*, extruder.
— Adj. f. *Casa matriz*, motherhouse (de orden religiosa), headquarters, *pl.*, head office (de una empresa).
matrona f. Matron (madre de familia de cierta edad). || Midwife (partera, comadre). || Matron (en una cárcel). || Searcher (en la aduana).
Matusalén n. pr. m. Methuselah: *más viejo que Matusalén*, as old as Methuselah.
matute m. Smuggling, contraband. || Smuggled goods, *pl.*, contraband.
matutear v. intr. To smuggle.
matutero, ra m. y f. Smuggler.
matutino, na adj. Morning, matutinal. || — *Estrella matutina*, morning star. || *Persona matutina*, early riser, early bird.
maula f. Piece of junk, useless thing (cosa inútil). || Remnant (retal). || Ruse, trick (engaño). || — M. y f. FIG. y FAM. Dead loss, good-for-nothing (persona inútil). || Bad payer (mal pagador). || *Un buen maula*, a tricky customer.
maulería f. Remnant shop (tienda de retales). || Trickery, cunning (engaño).
maulero, ra m. y f. Remnant seller (vendedor de retales). || Trickster (tramposo).
maullador, ra adj. Miaowing, mewing.
maullar v. intr. To miaow, to mew.
maullido m. Miaowing, mewing (acción). || Miaow, mew (ruido). || *Dar maullidos*, to miaow, to mew.
Mauricio n. pr. m. Maurice, Morris. || GEOGR. Mauritius (isla).
Mauritania n. pr. f. GEOGR. Mauritania.
mauritano, na adj./s. Mauritanian.
máuser m. Mauser (fusil).
mausoleo m. Mausoleum: *los mausoleos*, the mausoleums, the mausolea.
maxifalda f. Maxiskirt.
maxilar adj. ANAT. Maxillary.
— M. Jaw, jawbone. || *Maxilar superior*, maxilla.
máxima f. Maxim (aforismo). || Maximum temperature: *las máximas del año*, the year's maximum temperatures.
— Adj. V. MÁXIMO.
máximamente adv. [All] the more (máxime).
máxime adv. [All] the more, especially: *estaba muy contento, máxime porque había llegado su hija*, he was very happy, [all] the more as his daughter had come.
máximo, ma adj. Maximum, greatest, highest: *la máxima recompensa*, the highest reward; *el punto máximo*, the highest point; *el máximo esfuerzo*, the

greatest effort; *temperatura máxima*, maximum temperature. || Greatest: *uno de los pintores máximos del mundo*, one of the world's greatest painters. || MAT. *Máximo común divisor*, highest common factor.
— M. Maximum (*pl.* maxima *o* maximums): *ley de los máximos*, law of maxima; *la producción llegó al máximo*, production reached a maximum. || — *Al máximo*, to the maximum, to the utmost. || *Como máximo*, at the most: *hay sitio para cuatro personas como máximo*, there is room for four people at the most; at the latest: *saldremos como máximo a las siete*, we shall leave at seven at the latest. || *Hacer el máximo*, to do one's utmost.
máximum m. Maximum.
maxvelio o **maxwell** m. FÍS. Maxwell (unidad de fluido magnético).
maya f. BOT. Daisy (margarita).
maya adj. Mayan.
— M. y f. Maya, Mayan.
mayar v. intr. To miaow, to mew (maullar).
mayestático, ca adj. Majestic. || GRAM. *El tratamiento mayestático*, the Royal "we".
mayéutica f. FIL. Maieutics.
mayo m. May (mes): *el primero de mayo*, the first of May. || Maypole (palo). || FIG. *Hasta el cuarenta de mayo no te quites el sayo*, ne'er cast a clout till May is out.
mayólica f. Majolica (loza esmaltada).
mayonesa f. CULIN. Mayonnaise (salsa).
mayor adj. Bigger, larger (más grande, comparativo): *mi casa es mayor que la suya*, my house is bigger than his. || Biggest, largest (superlativo): *la mayor ciudad del país*, the biggest city in the country. || Greater (superior, comparativo): *su inteligencia es mayor que la mía*, he is of greater intelligence than I. || Greatest (superlativo): *la mayor falta que ha cometido*, the greatest mistake he has made; *su mayor enemigo*, his greatest enemy. || Older, elder (de más edad, comparativo): *mi amigo es mayor que yo*, my friend is older than I; *mis dos hermanas mayores*, my two elder sisters. || Oldest, eldest (superlativo): *mi hermano mayor*, my eldest brother. || Elderly (de edad): *una señora mayor*, an elderly lady. || Grown-up (adulto): *tiene dos hijas que ya son mayores*, he has two grown-up daughters. || Major, main (principal). || Main (plaza, calle, mástil). || High: *calle, misa mayor*, high street, mass; *altar mayor*, high altar. || MÚS. Major. || FIL. Major (término): *premisa mayor*, major premise. || REL. Major (orden). || — *Al por mayor*, wholesale (comercio). || *Caballerizo mayor*, Master of the Horse. || *Caza mayor*, large game (jabalíes, ciervos, etc.), big game (leones, tigres, etc.). || *Colegio mayor*, hall of residence (residencia de estudiantes). || *En su mayor parte*, mainly, for the most part. || *Estado mayor*, staff: *jefe de estado mayor*, chief of staff. || *Ganado mayor*, v. GANADO. || *Hacerse mayor*, to grow up, to come of age. || GEOGR. *Lago Mayor*, Lake Maggiore. || *La mayor parte*, most, the majority. || *Libro mayor*, ledger. || *Mayor de edad*, elderly (entrado en años), of age (de 21 años o más). || *Mayor edad*, majority (mayoría). || *Montero mayor*, master of the hounds. || MAR. *Palo mayor*, mainmast. || *Por mayores razones*, for imperative reasons.
— M. Head, chief (jefe). || FAM. Grown-up (persona adulta). || Ledger (libro grande empleado en la contabilidad). || — Pl. Ancestors, elders (antecesores). || — F. Major [premise] (en lógica). || — M. y f. Older, oldest, elder, eldest. || — *Mayor de edad*, major, adult, person legally of age. || *Respetar a los mayores*, to show respect for one's elders.

— OBSERV. Se emplea la forma comparativa en inglés cuando se trata de dos personas o cosas: *el mayor de los dos*, the elder of the two; *el mayor de los dos coches*, the bigger of the two cars. Si el número pasa de dos, se utiliza la forma superlativa: *el mayor de los tres coches*, the biggest of the three cars.

mayoral m. Head shepherd (pastor). || AGR. Foreman, overseer (capataz). | Farm manager (de una ganadería). || Coachman (cochero). || *Amer.* Conductor (de tranvía).
mayorazgo m. Primogeniture. || Entailed estate [inherited by primogeniture]. || Heir to an entailed estate (heredero). || (P.us.). Eldest son, first-born son (hijo mayor).
mayordomía f. Catering (de los aviones). || Stewardship (de casa).
mayordomo m. Butler (de una casa). || Steward (de una finca). || Churchwarden (de iglesia). || HIST. *Mayordomo de palacio*, mayor of the palace.
mayoría f. Majority: *tres votos de mayoría*, a majority of three; *mayoría abrumadora*, overwhelming majority; *la mayoría está contenta*, the majority are happy. || Majority, full legal age (de edad). || Majority, most: *la mayoría de los participantes*, most of the participants. || MIL. Sergeant-major's office. || — *En la mayoría de los casos*, in most cases. || *En su mayoría*, in the main. || *La inmensa mayoría*, the great majority. || *La mayoría de las veces*, most times, usually. || *Llegar a la mayoría*, to come of age, to reach one's majority. || *Mayoría absoluta, relativa*, absolute, relative majority. || *Mayoría de edad*, majority, adult age, full legal age.
mayoridad f. Majority (mayoría).
mayorista m. Wholesaler (comerciante).
— Adj. Wholesale (comercio).
mayoritario, ria adj. Majority: *decisión mayoritaria*, majority decision.
mayormente adv. Especially.
mayúsculo, la adj./s.f. Capital (letra). || *Amistad con mayúscula*, friendship with a capital F. || — Adj. FAM. Monumental, enormous: *disparate mayúsculo*, monumental boob. || FAM. *Un susto mayúsculo*, a terrible fright.
maza f. Mace (arma antigua, insignia del macero). || TECN. Pounder (utensilio para machacar, apisonar). | Drop hammer (martinete). | Pile driver (para clavar pilotes). | Monkey (cabeza de martinete). | Brake (para machacar el cáñamo). || Butt (del taco de billar). || MÚS. Drumstick (del bombo). || FIG. y FAM. Bore, pest (persona pesada). || *Amer.* Hub, nave (de rueda).
mazacote m. Soda (sosa). || Concrete (hormigón). || FIG. y FAM. Monstrosity, eye-sore (obra artística fea): *el nuevo monumento es un mazacote*, the new memorial is a monstrosity. | Stodgy mess (plato mal hecho). | Bore, pest (persona pesada). || *Amer.* Mess, mixture (mezcla).
Mazalquivir n. pr. GEOGR. Mers-el-Kebir.
mazamorra f. *Amer.* Boiled maze (gachas). || MAR. Broken biscuit (restos de galleta). || FIG. Crumbs, *pl.* (cosa desmenuzada).
mazapán m. CULIN. Marzipan.
mazazo m. Blow with a mace *o* with a club.
mazdeísmo m. REL. Mazdaism.
mazmorra f. Dungeon (calabozo).
mazo m. Mallet (martillo de madera). || Mallet (de croquet). || Club, bat (en otros deportes). || Bunch (manojo): *mazo de llaves, de plumas*, bunch of keys, of feathers. || Wad (de papeles, de billetes de banco). || FIG. y FAM. Bore, pest (pelma). || MÚS. Drumstick (maza). || FIG. *A Dios rogando y con el mazo dando*, God helps those who help themselves.
mazorca f. AGR. Ear, spike, cob (de maíz). | Cacao pod (del cacao). || Spindle (husada de lino, etc.). || *Amer.* Despots, *pl.*, gang of despots. || *Maíz de* or *en la mazorca*, corn on the cob.
mazorquero, ra adj. *Amer.* Despotic.
— M. Despot.
mazurca f. Mazurka (danza, música).
mazut m. Fuel oil.
me pron. pers. Me (acusativo): *me está usted fastidiando*, you are annoying me; *llévame*, take me. || Me, to me (dativo): *¡dámelo!*, give me it!, give it to me!; *me dijo eso*, he said that to me *o* he told me that. || Myself (reflexivo): *me corté afeitándome*, I cut myself shaving; *me divierto*, I enjoy myself. || For me (para mí). || From me: *me lo quitó*, he took it from me.
mea culpa m. inv. Mea culpa, || *Decir su mea culpa*, to confess one's error.
meada f. POP. Piss: *echar una meada*, to have a piss. | Urine stain (mancha).
meadero m. POP. Loo (fam.), urinal.
meados m. pl. POP. Piss, *sing.*
meandro m. Meander (de río, camino). || ARQ. Meander (adorno). || — Pl. FIG. Meanders.
mear v. intr. FAM. To pee, to piss.
— V. tr. FAM. To piss on.
— V. pr. FAM. To wet o.s. || POP. *Mearse de risa*, to piss o.s. laughing.
meato m. ANAT. y BOT. Meatus.
Meca (La) n. pr. f. GEOGR. Mecca.
¡mecachis! interj. Confound it!, darn it!
mecánica f. Mechanics: *mecánica ondulatoria*, wave mechanics. || Mechanism, works, *pl.*: *la mecánica de un aparato*, the mechanism of an apparatus.
mecanicista m. y f. Mechanist.
mecánico, ca adj. Mechanical (relativo a la mecánica). || Machine-made (hecho con máquina). || FIG. Mechanical.
— M. Mechanic. || Driver (chófer).
mecanismo m. Mechanism. || FIL. Mechanicalism. || MÚS. Technique. || FIG. Mechanism, machinery. || — *Mecanismo administrativo*, administrative machine. || *Mecanismo de disparo, de expulsión*, firing mechanism, ejector mechanism.
mecanización f. Mechanization. || *Mecanización contable*, mechanized accounting.
mecanizado m. TECN. Machining (de una pieza). || Mechanization (de una fábrica, etc.).
mecanizar v. tr. To mechanize: *mecanizar una fábrica*, to mechanize a factory; *contabilidad mecanizada*, mechanized accountancy. || TECN. To machine (una pieza).
mecano, na adj./s. Meccan (de la Meca). || — M. Meccano (juego).
mecanografía f. Typing, typewriting.
mecanografiado, da adj. Typewritten, typed.
mecanografiar v. tr. To type, to typewrite.
mecanográfico, ca adj. Typewriting, typing.
mecanógrafo, fa m. y f. Typist.
mecanoterapia f. MED. Mechanotherapy.
mecapal m. *Amer.* Porter's leather strap.
mecapalero m. *Amer.* Porter.
mecatazo m. *Amer.* Whiplash (latigazo). | Draught, gulp, swig (fam.) [trago].
mecate m. *Amer.* Pita cord *o* string.
mecatear v. tr. *Amer.* To whip (zurrar).

mecedero m. TECN. Stirrer (mecedor).
mecedor, ra adj. Swinging. || Rocking.
— M. Swing (columpio). || Stirrer [for wine in vats, soap in tubs, etc.]. || — F. Rocking chair, rocker (silla).
mecedura f. V. MECIDA.
Mecenas m. Maecenas.
mecenazgo m. Patronage, Maecenatism.
mecer v. tr. To rock (a un niño, la cuna). || To swing (en un columpio). || To shake (un líquido, un recipiente). || To sway, to move to and fro (balancear).
— V. pr. To rock. || To swing (en el columpio). || To sway, to move to and fro (balancearse).
mecida f. o **mecimiento** m. Rock, rocking (de una cuna, una mecedora). || Swing, swinging (de un columpio). || Shaking (de un líquido, de un recipiente). || To and fro motion (balanceo).
mecha f. Wick (de lámpara). || Fuse (de mina). || Match (de arma de fuego). || Pledget, tent (quirúrgica). || CULIN. Lardoon, lardon (tocino). || Lock (de cabellos). || MAR. Spindle (pieza central de un palo), heel (parte inferior). || — FIG. y FAM. *Aguantar mecha*, to grin and bear it. || FAM. *A toda mecha*, at full speed. || *Mecha de seguridad* or *lenta*, safety fuse.
mechar v. tr. CULIN. To lard (la carne).
mechera f. CULIN. Larding needle. || FAM. Shoplifter (ladrona). || *Aguja mechera*, larding needle.
mechero m. Lighter, cigarette lighter, cigar lighter (encendedor). || Burner (de gas): *mechero Bunsen*, Bunsen burner. || Burner, jet (boquilla de lámpara). || Wick holder (canutillo que contiene la mecha). || Socket (de candelero). || FAM. Shoplifter (ladrón).
mechón m. Large wick (de lámpara). || Lock, tuft (de cabellos). || Tuft (de lana).
medalla f. Medal: *conceder una medalla a uno*, *premiar con una medalla a uno*, to award s.o. a medal. || Pendant, medallion (colgada del cuello), medal (religiosa). || Medallion, plaque (placa grande). || FIG. *El reverso de la medalla*, the other side of the coin (el aspecto opuesto), the complete opposite (la antítesis).
medallista m. Medallist [U.S., medalist].
medallón m. Medallion (medalla grande). || Locket (relicario). || ARQ. Medallion. || CULIN. Pat.
médano o **medano** m. [Sand] dune (duna). || Sandbank (banco de arena).
media f. Stocking (para las piernas): *media* or *medias de punto*, net stocking; *ponerse las medias*, to put on one's stockings. || Mean: *media aritmética*, arithmetic mean. || Average (promedio). || Half-back line (deportes). || *Amer.* Sock (calcetín). || — *Hacer media*, to knit. || *Hacer 60 km de media*, to do 60 km on [an] average, to do an average of 60 km. || *Media proporcional*, mean proportional, geometric mean. || *Son las tres y media*, it is half past three. || *Tocar la media*, to strike half past, to strike the half hour.
Media n. pr. f. HIST. Media.
mediacaña f. ARQ. Gorge, cavetto (tipo de moldura). | Listel, fillet (listón). || TECN. Gouge (gubia). | Half-round file (lima). || Curling tongs, *pl.* (tenacillas).
mediación f. Mediation. || *Por mediación de*, through, through the instrumentality *o* agency of.
mediado, da adj. Half full, half empty: *está el jarro mediado*, the jug is half full. || Halfway through: *llevo mediado el diccionario*, I am halfway through the dictionary. || — *A mediados de*, in *o* about the middle of, in mid-: *a mediados de agosto*, in mid-August. || *Mediada la noche*, in the middle of the night, in the dead of night. || *Mediada la tarde*, halfway through the afternoon.
mediador, ra adj. Mediating, mediative. || Intermediary, mediating (intermediario).
— M. y f. Mediator. || Intermediary, mediator.
medialuna f. Croissant.
mediana f. MAT. Median.
medianamente adv. Fairly, moderately.
medianería f. Party wall (pared). || Party fence *o* hedge, fence *o* hedge common to two properties (seto). || Joint ownership of party wall *o* dividing fence, adjacency (condición).
medianero, ra adj. Party, dividing (pared, valla, etc.). || Mediating, interceding (mediador).
— M. y f. Mediator (mediador). || Neighbour [U.S., neighbor], owner of an adjacent house *o* field (vecino). || Métayer, tenant farmer (aparcero).
medianía f. Moderate means, *pl.*, moderate circumstances, *pl.*: *vivir en la medianía*, to live on moderate means *o* in moderate circumstances. || Mean, average (término medio). || FIG. Mediocre person, mediocrity.
mediano, na adj. Middling, medium, average: *inteligencia mediana*, average intelligence; *mediano de cuerpo*, of medium build. || Mediocre, middling, fair (ni bueno ni malo): *cerveza mediana*, mediocre beer. || Mediocre, middling (malo): *un trabajo muy mediano*, a very middling piece of work. || Median: *línea mediana*, median line. || *De tamaño mediano*, medium-sized.
medianoche f. Midnight: *a medianoche*, at midnight. || FIG. Ham sandwich.
mediante prep. By means of, using, with, with the help of: *abrió la caja fuerte mediante una palanca*, he opened the safe by means of a crowbar. || Through, thanks to: *mediante su ayuda*, through his help; *mediante él*, thanks to him. || — *Dios mediante*, God willing. || *Mediante presentación de la tarjeta*, on presentation of the card.
mediar v. intr. To be between [two things]: *entre las dos casas media un jardín*, between the two houses there is a garden. || To be in the middle [*en*, of], to get halfway [*en*, through] (estar en la mitad de). || To pass, to elapse (transcurrir): *entre las dos guerras mediaron veinte años*, twenty years passed between the two wars. || To intervene (ocurrir en el curso de otra cosa). || To mediate: *mediar entre dos enemigos*, to mediate between two enemies; *mediar en un asunto*, to mediate in an affair. || To exist (existir). || To intercede, to plead (rogar): *mediar por* or *en favor de uno*, to intercede for *o* on behalf of. || — *Mediado el mes*, in the middle of the month, halfway through the month. || *Media el hecho de que*, the fact is that, the fact remains that. || *Media un abismo entre*, there is a wide gap between. || *¿Qué diferencia media entre tú y yo?*, what difference is there between you and me?
mediatinta f. Halftone, middletone.
mediatizar v. tr. To mediatize.
mediato, ta adj. Mediate.
mediatriz f. MAT. Perpendicular bisector.
médica f. Woman *o* lady doctor, doctor.
medicación f. Medication, medical treatment (acción de medicar). || Medications, *pl.*, medicaments, *pl.*, medicines, *pl.* (medicamentos).
medical adj. Medical.
medicamentar v. tr. V. MEDICINAR.
medicamento m. Medicament, medicine.
medicamentoso, sa adj. Medicinal.
medicar v. tr. To medicate.
medicastro m. Medicaster, quack (médico malo).
medicina f. Medicine (arte): *estudiar medicina*, to study medicine; *doctor en medicina*, doctor of medicine. || Medicine, medicament (medicamento). || — *Estudiante de medicina*, medical student. || *Medicina legal* or *forense*, forensic medicine.
medicinal adj. Medicinal. || DEP. *Balón medicinal*, medicine ball.
medicinalmente adv. Medicinally.
medicinar v. tr. To treat, to give medicine to, to prescribe medicine for.
— V. pr. To take medicine, to dose o.s.
medición f. Measurement (medida).
médico, ca adj. Medical: *reconocimiento* or *examen médico*, medical examination. || HIST. Median (de los medos). || — *Cuadro médico*, medical staff. || *Receta médica*, medical prescription.
— M. Doctor, physician. || — *Consejero médico*, medical adviser. || *Médico consultor* or *de apelación* or *de consulta*, medical consultant, consultant doctor. || *Médico de cabecera* or *de familia*, family doctor. || *Médico forense*, forensic surgeon. || *Médico general*, general practitioner. || MIL. *Médico militar* or *castrense*, army medical officer. || *Médico rural*, country doctor. || — F. V. MÉDICA.
medicolegal adj. Medico-legal, forensic.
medicucho m. Quack.
medida f. Measuring, measurement (acción de medir): *la medida del tiempo*, the measurement of time. || Measurement (magnitud): *tomarle a uno las medidas*, to take s.o.'s measurements (en costura); *tomar las medidas de la habitación*, to take the measurements of the room. || Measure: *medida de capacidad*, *de superficie*, *de volumen*, liquid *o* dry, square, cubic measure. || Measure (unidad): *pesas y medidas*, weights and measures. || Measure (cosa medida): *tres medidas de vino*, three measures of wine. || Extent, proportion, measure, degree: *en cierta medida*, to some *o* to a certain extent. || FIG. Moderation, restraint, measure (prudencia). || Measure, step (disposición): *medida disciplinaria*, disciplinary measure; *adoptar medidas enérgicas*, to adopt strong measures; *tomar todas las medidas necesarias*, to take all necessary steps. || Metre [U.S., meter], measure (de un verso).
— *A la medida*, to measure, to order [U.S., custom-made]: *pantalón hecho a la medida*, trousers made to measure [U.S., custom-made trousers]. || *A la medida de*, in proportion to, as (proporcionado a). || *A medida de*, in accordance with, according to: *a medida de tus deseos*, in accordance with your wishes. || *A medida que*, as, with, at the same time as. || *Colmar* or *llenar la medida*, to be the limit, to be the last straw. || *En gran medida*, to a great extent, largely. || *En* or *hasta cierta medida*, to a certain extent, up to a point. || *En la medida de lo posible*, as far as possible, insofar as it is possible. || *En la medida en que*, insofar as: *en la medida en que sea posible*, insofar as it is possible; in that, insofar as (ya que), according to, in accordance with (proporcionalmente con). || *En menor medida*, to a lesser extent, on a smaller scale. || *Eso pasa de la medida*, that is the limit, that is the last straw, that is carrying things too far. || *Medida común*, common measure. || *Medida del cuello*, neck size. || *Sin medida*, unbounded.
medidor, ra adj. Measuring.
— M. Measure, measurer (instrumento). || Measurer (persona). || *Amer.* Meter (contador). || *Fiel medidor*, inspector of weights and measures.
mediero, ra m. y f. Stocking maker (que hace medias), hosier, stocking seller (que vende medias). || Métayer, tenant farmer (aparcero).

MEDICINA, *f.* — MEDICINE

I. Términos (*m.*) generales — General terms.

medicina (*f.*) legal *or* forense	forensic medicine
médico *m.*, doctor *m.*	doctor, physician
médico (*m.*) de cabecera	family doctor
pediatra *m.*	pediatrician, pediatrist
ginecólogo *m.*	gynecologist
tocólogo *m.*	tocologist, obstetrician
neurólogo *m.*	neurologist
psiquiatra *m.*, siquiatra *m.*	psychiatrist
oftamólogo *m.*; oculista *m.*	ophthalmologist; oculist
dentista *m.*; odontólogo *m.*	dentist; odontologist
cirujano *m.*	surgeon
anestesista *m.*	anesthetist, anaesthetist
enfermero *m.*, enfermera *f.*	nurse
hospital *m.*	hospital
clínica *f.*	clinic
sanatorio *m.*	sanatorium; clinic
salud *f.*	health
sano, na	healthy (person), wholesome (cosa)
higiene *f.*	hygiene
vacunarse	to get vaccinated
enfermo *m.*	sick person; patient
paciente *m.* y *f.*	patient
estar enfermo *or* malo	to be sick *o* ill
enfermizo, za	sickly
achaque *m.*, dolencia *f.*	ailment, complaint
dolor *m.*	pain
indisposición *f.*	indisposition, slight illness
indispuesto, ta	unwell, indisposed
afección *f.*	affection, disease
úlcera *f.*	ulcer
herida *f.*	wound, injury
lesión *f.*	lesion, injury
llaga *f.*	wound
erupción *f.*, sarpullido *m.*	rash, eruption
grano *m.*	spot, pimple
espinilla *f.*	blackhead, spot
barro *m.*, barrillo *m.*	blackhead
ampolla *f.*, vejiga *f.*	blister
furúnculo *m.*	furuncle, boil
postilla *f.*, costra *f.*	scab
cicatriz *f.*	scar
verruga *f.*	wart
callo *m.*, callosidad *f.*	callus, callosity; corn (en los pies)
sabañón *m.*	chilblain
cardenal *m.*; equimosis *f.*	bruise; ecchymosis
chichón *m.*	bump, swelling
hinchazón *f.*	swelling
contusión *f.*	contusion, bruise
esguince *m.*, torcedura *f.*	sprain, twist
fractura *f.*	fracture
síntoma *m.*	symptom
diagnóstico *m.*	diagnosis
caso *m.*	case
incubación *f.*	incubation
epidemia *f.*	epidemic
contagio *m.*	contagion
calentura *f.*, fiebre *f.*	fever
ataque *m.*, acceso *m.*	attack, access, fit
acceso (*m.*) de tos	coughing fit
acostarse, encamarse	to take to one's bed
estornudar	to sneeze
desmayo *m.*	faint, fainting fit
vértigo *m.*	vertigo; dizziness
estar mareado	to feel sick
perder el conocimiento	to lose consciousness
conmoción (*f.*) cerebral	concussion
coma *m.*	coma
régimen *m.*, dieta *f.*	diet
tratamiento *m.*	treatment
mejorar	to get better, to improve
cura *f.*, curación *f.*	cure
recaída *f.*	relapse

II. Enfermedades, *f.* — Diseases.

anemia *f.*	anemia, anaemia
angina (*f.*) de pecho	angina pectoris
apendicitis *f.*	appendicitis
artritis *f.*	arthritis
bronquitis *f.*	bronchitis
cáncer *m.*	cancer
catarro *m.*	cold, catarrh
ciática *f.*	sciatica
cólera *m.*	cholera
constipado *m.*	[head] cold
desnutrición *f.*	malnutrition
diabetes *f.*	diabetes
difteria *f.*	diphtheria
dolor (*m.*) de cabeza	headache
eczema *m.*	eczema
enfriamiento *m.*	cold
epilepsia *f.*	epilepsy
erisipela *f.*	erysipelas
escarlatina *f.*	scarlet fever
esclerosis *f.*	sclerosis
faringitis *f.*	pharyngitis
fiebre (*f.*) amarilla	yellow fever
fiebre (*f.*) de Malta	Malta fever
fiebre (*f.*) palúdica, paludismo *m.*	malaria, swamp fever
gangrena *f.*	gangrene
gota *f.*	gout
gripe *f.*	flu
hemiplejía *f.*	hemiplegy, hemiplegia
ictericia *f.*	icterus, jaundice
indigestión *f.*	indigestion
infarto (*m.*) del miocardio	miocardial infarction
jaqueca *f.*	migraine, splitting headache
leucemia *f.*	leukemia
locura *f.*	insanity
malaria *f.*	malaria
neumonía *f.*, pulmonía *f.*	pneumonia
neuralgia *f.*	neuralgia
neurastenia *f.*	neurasthenia
paperas *f. pl.*	mumps
parálisis *f.*	paralysis
peritonitis *f.*	peritonitis
poliomielitis *f.*	poliomyelitis
rabia *f.*	rabies
raquitismo *m.*	rickets, rachitis
resfriado *m.*	cold, chill, catarrh
reúma *m.*, reumatismo *m.*	rheumatism
rubéola *f.*	German measles, rubella
sarampión *m.*	measles
sarna *f.*	scabies, itch
septicemia *f.*	septicemia, septicaemia
sífilis *f.*	syphilis
síncope *m.*	syncope
sinusitis *f.*	sinusitis
tétanos *m.*	tetanus
tifus *m.*	typhus
tisis *f.*	phtisis
tortícolis *f.*	torticollis, stiff neck
tos (*f.*) ferina, tosferina *f.*	whooping cough
trombosis *f.*	thrombosis
tuberculosis *f.*	tuberculosis
tumor *m.*	tumour [U.S., tumor]
urticaria *f.*	urticaria, hives
varicela *f.*	chicken pox, varicella
viruela *f.*	smallpox
zona *f.*	zona, shingles

III. Cirugía, *f.* — Surgery.

operación *f.*	operation
anestesia *f.*	anesthesia, anaesthesia
transfusión (*f.*) de sangre	blood transfusion
sondaje *m.*	probing, sounding
amputación *f.*	amputation
traqueotomía *f.*	tracheotomy
trepanación *f.*	trepanation
injerto *m.*; trasplante *m.*	graft; transplant
ligadura *f.*	ligature
puntos *m. pl.*	stitches
cicatrización *f.*	cicatrization
quirófano *m.*	operating theatre [U.S., operating theater]
instrumental *m.*	instruments *pl.*
bisturí *m.*; escalpelo *m.*	bistoury; scalpel
venda *f.*	bandage
vendaje *m.*, apósito *m.*	dressing, bandages *pl.*
gasa *f.*	gauze
compresa *f.*	compress
esparadrapo *m.*	sticking plaster
catgut *m.*	catgut
enyesado *m.*, escayola *f*	plaster
cabestrillo *m.*	sling
cirugía (*f.*) estética *or* plástica	plastic surgery
acupuntura *f.*	acupuncture

medieval adj. Medieval, mediaeval.
medievalismo m. Medievalism, mediaevalism.
medievalista m. y f. Medievalist, mediaevalist.
medievo m. Middle Ages, *pl.*
medio m. Middle (centro): *está en medio*, it is in the middle. || Half (mitad). || Means, *pl.* (procedimiento): *el fin justifica los medios*, the end justifies the means. || Means, *pl.*, way (manera). || Means, *pl.*, way, possibility (posibilidad). || Means, *pl.*, power (capacidad). || Measure (medida): *tomar los medios necesarios*, to take the necessary measures. || Means (recursos, elementos): *medios de producción, de transporte*, means of production, of transport. || Class, set, circle (clase social). || Medium, environment, surroundings, *pl.* (ambiente). || Society (sociedad). || Circle (círculo): *en los medios bien informados*, in well-informed circles. || Middle finger (dedo). || DEP. Halfback, half: *medio derecho, izquierdo*, right, left half. || Medium (médium). || BIOL. Medium. || — Pl. Means (fortuna): *su padre es hombre de pocos medios*, his father is a man of small means. || TAUR. Centre (*sing.*) of the ring. || — *De medio a medio*, completely (enteramente). || *De por medio*, in the middle, in between (en medio), in the way (constituyendo un obstáculo). || *El coche de en medio*, the middle car, the car in the middle, the car in between. || *El justo medio*, the happy medium, the golden mean. || *En los medios allegados a*, in the entourage of. || *En medio de*, in the middle of: *en medio de la calle*, in the middle of the street; among: *estar en medio de mucha gente*, to be among a lot of people; in the face of, in the midst of: *en medio de todos esos inconvenientes*, in the midst of all those drawbacks; *debatirse en medio de muchas dificultades*, to struggle

in the face of many difficulties; in spite of (a pesar de): *en medio de todo*, in spite of everything. || *En su medio*, in one's element. || *Estar corto de medios*, to be short of funds. || *Estar de por medio*, to intervene (intervenir), to be involved (estar en juego). || *Justo en medio*, right in the middle. || *Medio ambiente*, environment. || *Medio de cultivo*, culture medium. || *Meterse* or *ponerse de por medio*, to intervene (en una pelea), to interfere (entremeterse). || *No ahorrar medios*, to spare no expense (gastar dinero), to spare no effort (hacer esfuerzos). || *No hay medio*, there is no way. || *Poner tierra por medio*, to make o.s. scarce. || *Por en medio*, in the way. || *Por medio*, in *o* down the middle: *cortar el pan por medio*, to cut the loaf down the middle. || *Por medio de*, through [the middle of]: *el río pasa por medio del pueblo*, the river passes through the middle of the town; by means of, with the help of (mediante), through (por el intermedio de). || *Por sus propios medios*, of one's own resources. || *Por todos los medios*, by all manner of means, by all possible means. || *Quitar de en medio*, to get *o* to take out of the way (una cosa), to get rid of (a una persona). || *Quitarse de en medio*, to get out of the way (cambiar de sitio): *¡quítate de en medio!*, get out of the way!; to disappear, to make o.s. scarse (irse). || *Vivir pared por medio*, to be neighbours.

medio, dia adj. Half: *dos horas y media*, two and a half hours; *saldré dentro de media hora*, I shall go out in half an hour; *media botella de coñac*, half a bottle of brandy, a half-bottle of brandy. (V. OBSERV.) || Half: *fue a recibirle medio Madrid, media ciudad*, half Madrid, half the city went to greet him. || Middle: *clase media*, middle class; *corredor de medio fondo*, middle-distance runner. || Mean, average: *temperatura media*, mean temperature. || Average: *el español medio*, the average Spaniard. || Central, centre, dividing: *línea media*, centre line. || — *A media cuesta*, halfway up. || *A media luz*, in the half-light. || *A media mañana*, in mid-morning, in the middle of the morning. || *A media pierna*, up to the middle of the calf. || *A media voz*, in a low voice. || *A medio camino*, halfway, halfway there. || *A medio cuerpo*, up to the waist, waist-high. || *De medio cuerpo*, half-length (pintura), up to the *o* one's waist: *entrar en el agua de medio cuerpo*, to go into the water up to one's waist. || *De medio pelo*, of no account, common (gente), mediocre, average, passable (cosa). || *Edad Media*, Middle Ages, *pl.* || *Media lengua*, childish talk *o* language. || *Medio billete*, half, half fare (en el autobús, etc.). || *Medio hermano*, half brother. || *Medio pariente*, distant relation. || DEP. *Medio tiempo*, half time. || *No hay término medio*, there is no middle course. || *Oriente Medio*, Middle East. || *Por término medio*, on the average. || MAT. *Término medio*, average.
— Adv. Half: *medio muerta de frío*, half frozen to death; *una botella medio llena*, a half-full bottle, a bottle half full. || — *A medias*, half: *dormido, satisfecho a medias*, half asleep, satisfied; half-: *medidas, verdad a medias*, half-measures, half-truth; halves, fifty-fifty: *ir a medias en un negocio*, to go halves in a business; *compramos el coche a medias*, we went halves on the car; half and half, half each (cada uno la mitad). || *A medio* (con verbo en infinitivo), half (con participio pasivo): *a medio terminar*, half finished. || *Es un escritor a medias*, he is a writer of sorts. || *Medio loco*, half crazy. || *Solución a medias*, partial solution.

— OBSERV. El inglés suele emplear el artículo indefinido con el adjetivo que equivale a *medio*. Lo coloca sea entre el adjetivo y el sustantivo sea antes del adjetivo: *esperó media hora*, he waited half an hour; *compré medio kilo de garbanzos*, I bought a half kilo of chick-peas.

mediocre adj. Mediocre.
mediocridad f. Mediocrity.
mediodía m. Midday, noon: *llegó a mediodía*, he arrived at midday. || South (sur): *se va al mediodía de Francia*, he is going to the South of France.
medioeval adj. Mediaeval, medieval.
medioevo m. Middle Ages, *pl.*
mediopensionista m. y f. Day pupil, day student, student who has lunch at school.
medir* v. tr. To measure: *medir por litros, con cinta métrica*, to measure in litres, with a tape measure. || To measure out: *medir trigo*, to measure out wheat. || To scan (los versos). || To measure, to be (tener cierta longitud). || FIG. To measure, to gauge (medir las fuerzas, las consecuencias, etc.). | To weigh: *medir las palabras*, to weigh one's words. || — *¿Cuánto mides?*, how tall are you? || *Medir con la vista*, to size up. || FIG. *Medir de arriba abajo*, to look up and down, to give the once-over (con la mirada). | *Medir el suelo*, to fall full-length (caerse). | *Medir las costillas a uno*, to give s.o. a good hiding *o* a beating. | *Medir sus pasos*, to watch one's step.
— V. pr. To measure o.s. || FIG. To measure o.s., to pit o.s.: *medirse con uno*, to measure o.s. against s.o. | To act with moderation, to be moderate (moderarse). || FIG. *Medirse consigo mismo*, to test one's strength.
meditabundo, da adj. Pensive, thoughtful.
meditación f. Meditation.
meditador, ra adj. Meditative.
meditar v. intr. To meditate, to ponder, to think: *meditar en* or *sobre el pasado*, to meditate on *o* upon the past.
— V. tr. To think about, to meditate on, to meditate, to ponder. || To prepare, to plan, to meditate (un proyecto, etc.).
meditativo, va adj. Meditative.
mediterráneo, a adj. Mediterranean: *el clima mediterráneo*, the Mediterranean climate. || *El (mar) Mediterráneo*, the Mediterranean [Sea].
médium m. Medium.
medo, da adj. Median (de Media).
— M. y f. Mede.
medra f. Growth, increase (aumento). || Improvement (mejora). || Prosperity || Progress.
medrar v. intr. To grow, to thrive (plantas, animales). || FIG. To prosper, to thrive. | To improve (mejorar). | To increase, to grow (aumentar). || FAM. *¡Medrados estamos!*, a lot of good that's done us!
medro m. V. MEDRA.
medroso, sa adj. Fearful (miedoso). || Timorous, timid (tímido). || Afraid, frightened (asustado). || Fearsome, frightening (que causa miedo).
médula o **medula** f. ANAT. Medulla, marrow: *médula oblonga*, medulla oblongata. || BOT. Medulla, pith, marrow (pulpa): *médula de saúco*, elder medulla. || FIG. Medulla, pith, marrow, essence. || — FIG. *Hasta la médula*, to the core. || *Médula espinal*, spinal cord. || *Médula ósea*, bone marrow. || FAM. *Me sacarán hasta la médula*, they'll bleed me white, they'll suck me dry.
medular adj. Medullary.
meduloso, sa adj. ANAT. Marrowy. || BOT. Pithy, marrowy.
medusa f. ZOOL. Jellyfish.
Medusa n. pr. f. MIT. Medusa.
Mefistófeles n. pr. m. Mephistopheles.
mefistofélico, ca adj. Mephistophelian.
mefítico, ca adj. Mephitic.
megacéfalo, la adj. Megacephalic.
megaciclo m. Megacycle (unidad de frecuencia).
megafonía f. Public-address system.
megáfono m. Megaphone.
megajulio m. Million joules (unidad de trabajo).
megalítico, ca adj. Megalithic.
megalito m. Megalith.
megalocéfalo, la adj. Megalocephalous, megalocephalic.
megalomanía f. Megalomania.
megalómano, na adj./s. Megalomaniac.
mégano m. V. MÉDANO.
megaterio m. Megathere (mamífero fósil).
megatón m. FÍS. Megaton.
megavatio m. FÍS. Megawatt.
megavoltio m. FÍS. Megavolt.
megohmio m. FÍS. Megohm (unidad de resistencia).
mehala f. MIL. Moroccan regular army corps.
meharista m. Meharist, mehariste.
meiosis f. BIOL. Meiosis.
mejicanismo m. Mexicanism.
mejicano, na adj./s. Mexican.
Méjico n. pr. m. GEOGR. Mexico (país). || Mexico City (la capital).

— OBSERV. V. MÉXICO.

mejido adj. m. Beaten (huevo).
mejilla f. Cheek.
mejillón m. Mussel (molusco). || *Criadero de mejillones*, mussel bed.
mejor adj. Better (comparativo): *este libro es mejor que el otro*, this book is better than the other. || Best (superlativo): *es mi mejor amigo*, he is my best friend. || Highest [bid, bidder] (puja, postor). || — *A falta de otra cosa mejor*, for want of sth. better. || *Encontrar algo mejor*, to find something better. || *En las mejores condiciones*, in the best condition (*para*, for). || *Es lo mejor que hay*, it is the best there is. || *Hace mejor tiempo*, the weather is better. || *Hago lo mejor que puedo*, I do my best, I do the best I can. || *Lo mejor*, the best [thing]: *lo mejor que podemos hacer*, the best thing we can do. || *Lo mejor del caso es que*, the best [part] of it is that. || *Lo mejor del mundo*, the best in the world. || *Lo mejor de lo mejor*, superlative, the tops (fam.) [óptimo], the pick of the bunch (la crema). || *Lo mejor es enemigo de lo bueno*, leave well enough alone. || *Lo mejor posible*, as well as possible (de la mejor manera), as well as one can (todo lo que se puede): *lo hice lo mejor posible*, I did it as well as I could. || *Llevarse lo mejor*, to get the best of it. || *Nunca he visto cosa mejor*, I have never seen anything better. || *Y lo que es mejor*, better still.
— Adv. Better (comparativo): *trabajas mejor que él*, you work better than he. || Best (superlativo de bien): *es el libro mejor escrito de este autor*, it is this author's best-written book. || Rather, sooner: *escogería mejor este abrigo*, I should rather choose this overcoat. || So much the better: *nos vamos en seguida. — ¡Mejor!*, we're going at once. — So much the better! || — *A cuál mejor*, v. CUÁL. || *A lo mejor*, perhaps, maybe, may: *a lo mejor no vendrá*, perhaps *o* maybe he will not come, he might not come. || *Cada vez mejor*, better and better. || *Estar mejor*, to be better. || *Hubiera sido mejor no decir nada*, you would have done better *o* it would have been better to say

nothing. || *Ir mejor*, to feel *o* to be better. || *Mejor dicho*, rather. || *Mejor que mejor*, so much the better. || *Mucho mejor*, much better. || *Nada mejor*, nothing better. || *Querer mejor*, to prefer, to like better. || *Tanto mejor*, so much the better, all the better.
— M. y f. Better (de dos). || Best (de más de dos): *es la mejor de las mujeres*, she is the best of women. || *En el mejor de los casos*, at best.
mejora f. Improvement: *no hay mejora en su situación*, there is no improvement in his situation; *la mejora del suelo*, the improvement of the soil. || Improvement, betterment, progress (adelanto): *las mejoras producidas por la tecnología*, the improvements brought about by technology. || Increase, raise (del sueldo). || Higher bid (puja). || JUR. Improvement *o* betterment of an estate (hecha por un arrendatario). | Additional portion of an inheritance set aside for one of the coheirs (en una herencia).
mejorable adj. Improvable.
mejoramiento m. Improvement.
mejorana f. BOT. Sweet marjoram.
mejorar v. tr. To improve, to better, to ameliorate (volver mejor): *mejorar su situación*, to improve one's situation. || To make better, to bring about an improvement in (a un enfermo): *la cura le ha mejorado mucho*, the cure has made him a lot better *o* has brought about a great improvement in him. || To increase, to raise (un sueldo). || To improve the lot of: *la nueva ley mejora a los funcionarios*, the new law improves the lot of civil servants. || To do better than, to better (superar). || To better (una oferta). || To raise (una puja). || JUR. To will an additional bequest to (en un testamento). || DEP. To beat, to break (un récord). || *Mejorando lo presente*, present company excepted.
— V. intr. To improve, to get better (ponerse mejor, progresar). || To clear up (el tiempo). || — *Mejorar de salud*, to improve, to get better. || *Mejorar de situación*, to improve one's situation. || *¡Que te mejores!*, I hope you get better!, get well soon!
mejorcito, ta adj. [dim. de *mejor*] FAM. A little better, slightly improved: *el niño se encuentra mejorcito*, the child is a little better. | Best: *Juana es la mejorcita de la clase*, Joan is the best in the class. || FAM. *Lo mejorcito*, the very best.
mejoría f. Improvement.
mejunje m. Mixture (mezcla). || FIG. Brew [bebida]. | Fraud, fiddle (superchería).
melancolía f. Melancholy, despondency, gloom: *caer en un estado de melancolía*, to sink into a state of melancholy. || MED. Melancholia, melancholy.
melancólico, ca adj. Melancholic, melancholy, despondent, gloomy. || MED. Melancholiac, melancholic.
— M. y f. Melancholy person, melancholic (ant.). || MED. Melancholiac, melancholic.
Melanesia n. pr. f. GEOGR. Melanesia.
melanesio, sia adj./s. Melanesian.
melar adj. Honey-sweet.
melaza f. Molasses, treacle.
melcocha f. Taffy.
Melchor n. pr. m. Melchior.
melée f. Scrum, scrummage (rugby): *medio de melée*, scrum half.
melena f. Hair (pelo). || Mane (del león). || — Pl. Mop, *sing.*, dishevelled hair, *sing.* (greñas).
melenudo, da adj. Long-haired, shaggy (fam.).
melífero, ra adj. Melliferous.
melificación f. Honey-making.
melificar v. intr. To make honey (las abejas).
melífico, ca adj. Melliferous, honey-producing.
melifluo, flua adj. Mellifluous, honeyed: *palabras melifluas*, mellifluous words.
melillense adj./s. Melillan (de Melilla).
melindre m. Honey fritter (fruta de sartén). || Sugared marzipan cake (de mazapán). || Narrow ribbon (cinta estrecha). || FIG. Affectation (afectación), simpering (por coquetería), fussiness, finickiness (remilgo, delicadeza), priggishness (moral). || *Andarse con melindres, hacer melindres* or *gastar melindres*, to simper (por coquetería), to affect reluctance (hacerse de rogar), to be finicky (ser remilgado), to be priggish (moralmente).
melindrear v. intr. V. MELINDRES (*Andarse con*).
melindrería f. V. MELINDRE.
melindrosamente adv. Affectedly (con afectación), simperingly (por coquetería), fussily (con remilgo), priggishly (moral).
melindroso, sa adj. Affected (afectado), simpering (por coquetería), fussy, finicky (remilgado), prudish, priggish (moral).
melocotón m. BOT. Peach (fruto). | Peach, peach tree (árbol).
melocotonar m. Peach orchard.
melocotonero m. BOT. Peach tree (árbol).
melodía f. Melody, tune. || Melody, melodiousness (calidad).
melódico, ca adj. Melodic.
melodioso, sa adj. Melodious, tuneful.
melodista m. Melodist, melody writer.
melodrama m. Melodrama.
melodramáticamente adv. Melodramatically.
melodramático, ca adj. Melodramatic.
melodramatizar v. tr. To melodramatize.
melomanía f. Melomania.
melómano, na adj. Melomane.
— M. y f. Melomaniac.
melón m. Melon (fruta). || FIG. y FAM. Nut (cabeza). | Noodle (imbécil). || *Melón de agua*, watermelon.
melonada f. FAM. Silly *o* daft thing (bobada).
melonar m. Melon patch.
meloncillo m. Small melon. || ZOOL. [North African] mongoose.
melonero, ra m. y f. Melon grower (que siembra). || Melon dealer (que vende).
melopea f. MÚS. Melopoeia. || FAM. *Coger* or *agarrar* or *tener una melopea*, to get *o* to be canned (emborracharse).
melopeya f. MÚS. Melopoeia.
melosidad f. Sweetness (suavidad). || FIG. Sweetness. | Sugariness (cualidad de almibarado).
meloso, sa adj. Honeyed, sweet. || FIG. Sweet, gentle, mellow. | Sugary (almibarado).
mella f. Notch, nick (rotura, hendedura). || Chip (en un plato). || Gap, hole (hueco). || Gap (en la dentadura). || FIG. Harm, damage, injury (menoscabo). || — FIG. y FAM. *Hacer mella*, to make an impression, to have an effect (impresionar): *las críticas no hacen la menor mella en él*, criticism does not have the slightest effect on him; to cast a slur, to damage, to harm (menoscabar): *hacer mella en la reputación de alguien*, to cast a slur on s.o.'s reputation; to make a hole *o* a dent: *hacer mella en la fortuna de alguien*, to make a hole in s.o.'s fortune. || *Tener dos mellas en la dentadura*, to have two teeth missing.
mellado, da adj. Notched, nicked (desportillado). || Chipped (plato). || Gap-toothed (falto de algún diente): *una vieja mellada*, a gap-toothed old woman.
melladura f. V. MELLA.
mellar v. tr. To notch, to nick. || To chip (un plato). || FIG. V. MELLA (*Hacer*).
— V. pr. To lose one's teeth. || To get chipped (un plato). || FIG. To be harmed *o* injured.
mellizo, za adj./s. Twin. || — M. pl. FIG. y FAM. Pair of cops (policías).
memada f. Silly *o* daft thing.
membrana f. Membrane: *membrana mucosa*, mucous membrane. || Web, membrane (de los palmípedos).
membranoso, sa adj. Membranous.
membrete m. Letterhead, [letter] heading (del remitente). || Addressee's name and address (del destinatario). || Note (anotación).
membrillar m. Quince plantation.
membrillero m. BOT. Quince, quince tree.
membrillo m. BOT. Quince, quince tree (árbol). | Quince (fruto): *carne* or *dulce de membrillo*, quince preserve *o* jelly. || FIG. *Veranillo del membrillo*, Indian summer.
membrudo, da adj. Burly, hefty, brawny (robusto).
memento m. REL. Memento.
memez f. Silly *o* stupid thing (simpleza).
memo, ma adj. Silly, stupid.
— M. y f. Fool, dolt, simpleton.
memorable adj. Memorable.
memorándum o **memorando** m. Memorandum (nota). || Notebook (carnet).
memorar v. tr. (P.us.) To remember, to recall.
memoria f. Memory (facultad): *tener buena memoria*, to have a good memory; *perder la memoria*, to lose one's memory. || Memory, recollection (recuerdo): *guardar memoria de*, to retain the memory of. || Statement, report, account (informe). || Memorandum (nota diplomática). || Essay, report, paper (estudio escrito). || Thesis, dissertation (tesis). || Account (factura). || Memorial, monument (monumento). || Legacy [bequeathed to a foundation perpetuating the legator's memory] (fundación). || Codicil (complemento a un testamento). || TECN. Memory, storage (de computadora). || — Pl. Memoirs (documento). || Regards: *dele usted memorias a su hermano*, give my regards to your brother. || — FIG. *Borrar de la memoria*, to erase *o* to banish from memory. | *Borrarse de la memoria*, to be forgotten (un recuerdo). || *Conservar la memoria de*, to remember. || *De memoria*, by heart: *aprender, saberse de memoria*, to learn, to know by heart; from memory: *hablar de memoria*, to speak from memory. || *En memoria de*, in memory of, to the memory of. || *Falta de memoria*, forgetfulness. || *Flaco de memoria*, forgetful. | FIG. *Hacer memoria de*, to remember, to recall. | *Irse de la memoria*, to slip one's mind, to escape: *el nombre se me ha ido de la memoria*, the name has slipped my mind, the name escapes me. | *Refrescar la memoria*, to refresh one's memory. || *Ser flaco de memoria*, to have a short memory, to be forgetful. || *Si la memoria no me falla* or *si tengo buena memoria*, if my memory serves me well, if I am not mistaken. || FAM. *Tener una memoria como un colador*, to have a head like a sieve. || *Traer a la memoria*, to recall, to bring to mind. | *Venir a la memoria*, to come to mind, to come back to one, to remember: *me vino a la memoria que...*, it came back to me that..., it came to my mind that..., I remembered that...
memorial m. Memorandum book (libro). || Memorial (petición). || Bulletin (publicación).
memorialista m. Memorialist.
memorión m. Good memory (memoria grande). || *Ser un memorión*, to have a good memory.

memorioso, sa adj. Retentive, having a good memory. — M. y f. Retentive person, person with a good memory.
memorista adj./s. V. MEMORIOSO.
memorístico, ca adj. Acquired by memory.
memoriudo, da adj. *Amer.* V. MEMORIOSO.
memorización f. Memorizing, memorization.
memorizar v. tr. To memorize.
mena f. MIN. Ore. || MAR. Size, thickness [of a cable].
ménade f. MIT. Maenad (bacante).
menaje m. Furnishings, *pl.* (de una casa). || Furniture, fittings, *pl.* (de escuela). || Housekeeping (gobierno de la casa). || Kitchen utensils, *pl.*, kitchen equipment (de cocina).
mención f. Mention: *mención honorífica*, honourable mention. || *Hacer mención de*, to make mention of, to mention.
mencionado, da adj. Mentioned, named (personas): *las anteriormente mencionadas*, the above-mentioned. || This, that, in question: *la mencionada batalla*, this battle, the battle in question. || *Anteriormente mencionado*, aforementioned, above-mentioned.
mencionar v. tr. To mention, to name (nombrar). || To point out, to call *o* to draw attention to (señalar). || *Sin mencionar a*, not to mention.
menchevique adj./s. Menshevik.
menda (mi) loc. FAM. Yours truly.
mendacidad f. Mendacity (hábito de mentir). || Untruth, big lie (mentira).
mendaz adj. Lying, untruthful, mendacious.
— M. y f. Liar.
mendelevio m. QUÍM. Mendelevium.
mendelismo m. Mendelism, Mendelianism.
mendicación f. Begging, mendicancy.
mendicante adj./s. Mendicant: *las órdenes mendicantes*, the mendicant orders.
mendicidad f. Mendicity, mendicancy, begging (acción). || Mendicity, mendicancy, beggary (condición).
mendigante m. Beggar, mendicant.
mendigar v. tr. To beg, to beg for. || FIG. To beg: *mendigar una comida*, to beg a meal.
— V. intr. To beg.
mendigo, ga m. y f. Beggar.
mendocino, na adj. [Of *o* from] Mendoza [Argentina].
— M. y f. Native *o* inhabitant of Mendoza.
mendrugo m. y f. FIG. y FAM. Chump (tonto). || — M. Crust, chunk [of hard bread]. || FIG. *Por un mendrugo (de pan)*, for a crust of bread, for a bite to eat.
meneallo V. MENEAR (*Mejor es no meneallo*).
menear v. tr. To move, to shake (la cabeza, la mano, etc.). || To stir (un líquido). || To wag (el rabo). || To wiggle (las caderas). || To waggle (las orejas). || FIG. To handle, to run (un negocio). || — FIG. y FAM. *De no te menees*, a hell of: *una bofetada, una fiesta de no te menees*, a hell of a slap, of a party. | *Mejor es no meneallo* or *peor es meneallo*, the least said the better.
— V. pr. To move, to shake (un miembro). || To sway, to swing (contonearse). || To move about, to fidget: *el niño se menea mucho*, the child is fidgeting a lot. || To toss and turn (en la cama). || To budge, to stir: *no te menees de aquí*, don't budge from here. || FAM. To be on the go, to bustle about (no parar). || *Menéate!*, stir yourself!, get a move on!
menegilda f. FAM. Housemaid, maidservant.
meneo m. Movement, shake, shaking (de la cabeza, de la mano, etc.). || Stir, stirring (de un líquido). || Wag, wagging (del rabo). || Wiggle, wiggling (de las caderas). || Waggle, waggling (de las orejas). || Jerk (sacudida). || FIG. y FAM. Hiding (vapuleo). || — Pl. Ups and downs, vicissitude, *sing.*: *los meneos de la vida*, the ups and downs of life. || — FIG. y FAM. *Darle un meneo a*, to have a go at: *le dio tal meneo a la botella que casi se la bebió*, he had such a go at the bottle that he almost drank it all. || FAM. *Dar un meneo a uno*, to give s.o. a hiding (vapulear), to boo s.o., to hiss s.o. (en un teatro, etc.), to jolt s.o. (sacudir).
menester m. Need, necessity, want (necesidad). || Occupation, work (ocupación). || Work, duty, job (trabajo). || — Pl. Bodily needs (necesidades corporales). || FAM. Gear, *sing.*, tackle, *sing.*, tools (instrumentos de trabajo). || — *Haber* or *tener menester de*, to have need of, to need (una cosa), to need to (con un verbo). || FIG. *Hacer sus menesteres*, to do one's business. || *No ser menester*, not to be necessary, not to have to: *no es menester que vayas ahí*, it is not necessary for you to go there, you do not have to go there. || *Ser menester*, to be necessary, to have to, must: *es menester comer para vivir*, it is necessary to *o* one has to *o* one must eat to live.
menesteroso, sa adj. Needy, in want.
— M. y f. Needy person. || *Los menesterosos*, the needy.
menestra f. Kind of stew (con carne). || Mixed vegetables, *pl.*, vegetable hotchpotch (de verdura). || — Pl. Dried vegetables.
menestral m. Artisan, craftsman (artesano). || Manual worker (trabajador manual).
menestralía f. Artisans, *pl.*, craftsmen, *pl.* (artesanos). || Manual workers, *pl.* (trabajadores manuales).
menfita adj./s. Memphite.
mengano, na m. y f. What's-his-name (hombre), what's-her-name (mujer), so-and-so (hombre o mujer): *Fulano y Mengano*, so-and-so and what's-his-name.
— OBSERV. The noun *mengano* is only used after the word *fulano* to designate a person whose name is not known.
mengua f. Diminution, decrease, lessening, dwindling (en general). || Wane, waning (de la Luna). || Lack, want (falta). || Poverty (pobreza). || FIG. Discredit, disgrace (descrédito). | Sinking, failing (falta de energía). | Decline (intelectual, moral). || *En mengua de*, to the detriment of: *lo hizo en mengua de su honra*, he did it to the detriment of his honour.
menguado, da adj. Decreased, diminished (disminuido). || Spineless, cowardly (cobarde). || Miserable, wretched (desgraciado). || Silly (tonto). || Mean, stingy (avaro). || Paltry, mean (reducido): *ha obtenido tan menguados éxitos*, he has gained such paltry successes. || *Jersey menguado*, fully-fashioned jersey.
— M. y f. Coward (cobarde). || Wretch (desgraciado). || Miser (avaro). || — M. Decreased stitch (punto).
menguante adj. Diminishing, decreasing, dwindling, lessening (que mengua). || Waning, on the wane (la Luna). || Ebb (marea). || *Cuarto menguante*, last quarter (de la Luna).
— F. Fall, falling, subsidence, going-down (de las aguas de un río). || Ebb tide (del mar). || Waning (de la Luna). || FIG. Decline, decadence.
menguar v. intr. To diminish, to decrease, to dwindle, to lessen: *el número de estudiantes en la universidad mengua cada año*, the number of students in the university decreases each year. || To go down (la marea, etc.). || To wane (la Luna). || FIG. To sink, to fail (físicamente), to decline, to go downhill (fam.) [intelectual o moralmente]. | To decrease (en las labores de punto). | To wane, to dwindle, to decrease (fama, gloria, etc.).
— V. tr. To diminish, to decrease, to lessen (en general). || To reduce (la velocidad). || FIG. To diminish, to lessen (la responsabilidad, etc.). | To detract from: *esto no mengua en nada su fama*, this in no way detracts from his reputation.
menhir m. Menhir.
menina f. Maid of honour [U.S., maid of honor].
meninge f. ANAT. Meninx: *las meninges*, the meninges.
meníngeo, a adj. Meningeal.
meningitis f. MED. Meningitis.
meningococo m. MED. Meningococcus (microbio).
menipeo, a adj. Menippean: *sátira menipea*, Menippean satire.
menisco m. FÍS. y ANAT. Meniscus.
menjuí m. BOT. Benzoin.
menjunje o **menjurje** m. V. MEJUNJE.
Meno n. pr. m. GEOGR. Main: *Francfort del Meno*, Frankfurt-am-Main.
menonita m. Mennonite.
menopausia f. MED. Menopause.
menor adj. Smaller (más pequeño, comparativo): *el número de niños en la clase es menor que el de niñas*, the number of boys in the class is smaller than that of girls. || Smallest (superlativo): *la menor habitación de la casa*, the smallest room in the house. || Lesser (más mínimo, comparativo): *es un mal menor*, it is a lesser evil. || Least (superlativo): *el menor ruido le asusta*, the least noise frightens him. || Younger (de menos edad, comparativo): *mis dos hermanas menores*, my two younger sisters. || Youngest (superlativo): *mi hermano menor*, my youngest brother. || Shorter (de menos duración, comparativo): *el mes de febrero es menor que los demás*, the month of February is shorter than the rest. || Shortest (superlativo): *el menor mes del año*, the shortest month in the year. || Minor (de poca importancia): *los profetas menores*, the minor prophets. || Minor: *órdenes menores*, minor orders. || MÚS. Minor: *en la menor*, in A minor. || — *Al por menor*, retail. || *El menor, la menor*, the smallest [one] (superlativo de pequeño): *deme la menor que hay*, give me the smallest there is. || *Hermano, hermana menor*, younger brother, sister (de dos), youngest brother, sister (de tres o más). || GEOGR. *Las Antillas Menores*, the Lesser Antilles. || *Menor de edad*, under age. || *Menor edad*, minority. || MAT. *Menor que*, less than. || *No tengo la menor idea*, I haven't the faintest idea, I haven't the slightest idea. || *Por menor*, in detail, minutely (por extenso), retail (venta). || *Rama menor*, younger branch.
— M. y f. Minor (menor de edad). || Young person (niño). || — *Juez de menores*, juvenile court judge. || *Menor de edad*, minor. || *No apta para menores*, adults only, persons under 21 not admitted, X-certificate (película). || *Tribunal de menores*, juvenile court. || — M. Minorite, Franciscan friar (monje). || — Pl. Juniors (en el colegio). || Elementary grammar class, *sing.* (clase). || — F. Minor premise (segunda proposición del silogismo).
— OBSERV. Se emplea la forma comparativa en inglés cuando se trata de dos personas o cosas: *el menor de los dos*, the younger of the two; *el menor de los dos coches*, the smaller of the two cars. Si el número pasa de dos, se utiliza la forma superlativa: *el menor de los tres coches*, the smallest of the three cars.
Menorca n. pr. GEOGR. Minorca.

menoría f. Minority (minoría).
menorista m. *Amer.* Retailer, retail dealer (minorista).
menorquín, ina adj./s. Minorcan (de Menorca).
menorragia f. MED. Menorrhagia.
menos adv. Less: *menos caro*, less expensive; *menos generoso*, less generous. || Not so: *menos lejos*, not so far. || Less (delante de un sustantivo y con idea de cantidad): *menos viento*, less wind. || Fewer, less (con idea de número): *menos soldados*, fewer soldiers. || Less (después de un sustantivo): *un litro menos*, one litre less. || Less of a: *es menos coche*, it is less of a car. || Least (superlativo de poco): *el alumno menos inteligente de la clase*, the least intelligent pupil in the class. || — *Al menos* or *a lo menos* or *por lo menos*, at least. || *A menos de*, for less than: *a menos de treinta pesetas el kilo*, for less than thirty pesetas a kilo; less than, within: *a menos de diez kilómetros de aquí*, less than ten kilometres from here; unless: *a menos de estar loco*, unless he is mad. || *A menos que*, unless. || *Cada vez menos*, less and less: *le veo cada vez menos*, I see less and less of him. || *Cuando menos*, at least. || *Cuanto menos... menos (más)*, the less... the less [the more]. || *De menos*, short: *me han dado cien gramos de menos*, they have given me a hundred grammes short; missing, short: *hay tres lápices de menos*, there are three pencils missing. || *Dos de menos*, two down (bridge). || *Echar de menos*, to miss: *echo de menos a mi país*, I miss my country. || *En menos*, less, less highly: *valoro en menos su belleza que su encanto*, I value her beauty less than her charm. || *En menos de*, by less than: *la producción ha bajado en menos de un dos por ciento*, production has dropped by less than two per cent; in less than: *lo hizo en menos de una hora*, he did it in less than an hour. || *En menos de nada*, in [less than] no time. || *Es lo menos que puede hacerse*, it is the least that can be done. || *Eso es lo de menos*, that's the least of it. || *Ir a menos*, to lose status *o* social standing, to come down. || *(La cosa) no es para menos*, little wonder. || *Lo de menos es el ruido*, it is not so much the noise. || *Lo menos*, at least: *lo menos había mil personas*, there were at least a thousand people there. || *Menos de* or *menos de lo que* or *menos que*, less than. || *Mientras menos... menos*, the less... the less: *mientras menos se habla, menos se equivoca uno*, the less you speak, the less you are wrong. || *Nada menos que*, v. NADA. || *Ni mucho menos*, far from it. || *No menos de*, no less than. || *No pude menos de preguntarle si...*, I could not help asking him if... || *Poco menos*, a little less: *poco menos de un litro*, a little less than a litre; little less: *es poco menos que tonto*, he is little less than stupid. || *Por menos de*, for less than: *no trabajo por menos de cien libras*, I won't work for less than a hundred pounds. || *Por menos de nada*, v. NADA. || *Por no ser menos*, not to be outdone. || *¿Qué menos?*, it's the least one could expect. || *Ser lo de menos*, to be the least important [thing] (lo menos importante), to be of no importance (no importar). || *Si al menos* or *por lo menos*, if only. || *Son menos de las diez*, it is before ten o'clock. || *Tanto menos*, so much the less, all the less. || *Tener a menos trabajar*, to consider it beneath o.s. to work. || *Tener en menos*, to look down on. || *Tener menos años que*, to be younger than. || *Una familia venida a menos*, a family which has seen better days *o* which has come down in the world. || *Venir a menos*, to lose status, to come down in the world (personas), to go downhill (una empresa).
— Prep. But: *cualquier cosa menos eso*, anything but that. || Except, but: *todos lo hicieron menos él*, everyone did it except him; *todo incluido menos el transporte*, everything included but the transport. || Save (ant.): *todo está perdido menos el honor*, all is lost save honour. || MAT. Minus, less: *cuatro menos uno son tres*, four minus one is three. || *Son las tres menos diez*, it is ten to three.
— M. MAT. Minus (signo). || *Los menos de, las menos de*, the minority of.
menoscabar v. tr. To diminish, to reduce, to lessen (disminuir): *una ley que menoscaba los derechos del propietario*, a law which diminishes the rights of the landlord. || FIG. To impair, to spoil: *menoscabar la belleza, la reputación de uno*, to impair s.o.'s beauty, reputation.
menoscabo m. Reduction, diminishing, lessening (mengua). || Damage (daño). || FIG. Impairment (perjuicio). | Discredit (descrédito). || — *Con menoscabo de*, to the detriment of. || *Sin menoscabo*, unimpaired, unscathed. || *Sufrir menoscabo en su fortuna*, to suffer heavy losses, to see one's fortune dwindle.
menospreciable adj. Despicable, contemptible.
menospreciador, ra adj. Contemptuous, scornful, disdainful.
menospreciar v. tr. To despise, to scorn (despreciar). || To ignore, to spurn, to shun (ignorar). || To underestimate, to underrate, to minimize: *menospreciar la importancia de un acontecimiento*, to underestimate the importance of an event.
menospreciativo, va adj. Contemptuous, disdainful, scornful.
menosprecio m. Contempt, scorn: *con menosprecio de*, in contempt of. || Underestimation, underrating (subestimación). || Disrespect (falta de respeto). || *Hacer menosprecio de*, to make light of, to scoff at.
mensaje m. Message. || *Mensaje de la Corona*, King's *o* Queen's speech.
mensajería f. Transport service (transporte). || Transport office (empresa). || *Mensajería marítima*, sea transport (transporte), shipping line (empresa).
mensajero, ra adj. Messenger, message-carrying. || *Paloma mensajera*, v. PALOMA.
— M. y f. Messenger. || — *Mensajera de la primavera*, harbinger of spring (golondrina). || *Mensajero de malas noticias*, bearer of bad news.
menstruación f. Menstruation.
menstrual adj. Menstrual.
menstruar v. intr. To menstruate.
menstruo m. Menses, *pl.*, menstruation.
mensual adj. Monthly. || A month: *500 pesetas mensuales*, 500 pesetas a month.
mensualidad f. Monthly *o* month's wage (salario): *cobrar su mensualidad*, to draw one's monthly wage. || Monthly payment *o* instalment [U.S., monthly installment] (renta): *pagar en doce mensualidades*, to pay in twelve monthly instalments.
mensualización f. Payment by the month.
mensualizar v. tr. To pay by the month.
ménsula f. ARQ. Console. || Support, bracket (soporte).
mensura f. *Amer.* Measure. | Measurement.
mensurabilidad f. Mensurability.
mensurable adj. Mensurable, measurable.
mensuración f. Mensuration, measurement.
mensurar v. tr. To measure.
menta f. BOT. Mint. || Peppermint (licor). || *Con sabor a menta*, mint-flavoured.
mentado, da adj. Aforementioned, in question (mencionado). || Famous, renowned, well-known (famoso).
mental adj. Mental: *cálculo mental*, mental calculation: || *Ser un atrasado mental*, to be mentally retarded.
mentalidad f. Mentality. || Mind: *tener mentalidad abierta*, to have an open mind.
mentalmente adv. Mentally. || *Hacer una multiplicación mentalmente*, to do a multiplication in one's head *o* mentally.
mentar* v. tr. To mention, to name.
mente f. Mind, intellect, intelligence (inteligencia). || Mind (pensamiento): *tener en la mente*, to have in mind. || Mind, intention (propósito): *no estaba en mi mente hacer eso*, I had no mind to do that, it was not my intention to do that. || — *Irse de la mente*, to slip one's mind. || *Traer a la mente*, to call *o* to bring to mind: *esto me trae a la mente tristes recuerdos*, this calls to mind sad memories. || *Venir a la mente*, to cross one's mind: *la sospecha no me vino a la mente*, the suspicion did not cross my mind; to come to mind: *me vienen a la mente tristes pensamientos*, sad thoughts come to my mind.
mentecatada o **mentecatería** o **mentecatez** f. Half-wittedness, stupidity (falta de sensatez). || Foolishness (necedad). || Foolish *o* silly thing (acción). || Stupid remark (palabras).
mentecato, ta adj. Half-witted, stupid (falto de sensatez). || Foolish (necio).
— M. y f. Simpleton, idiot, fool.
mentidero m. FAM. Gossip corner, gossip shop.
mentir* v. intr. To lie. || To lie, to deceive, to be misleading *o* deceptive (equivocar): *las apariencias mienten*, appearances lie. || — *Mentir sin necesidad* or *por costumbre*, to lie for lying's sake. || FAM. *Miente como un sacamuelas* or *más que habla*, he is an arrant liar, he lies through his teeth, he lies like a thief. || *¡Miento!*, I tell a lie!
mentira f. Lie (embuste): *mentira piadosa*, white lie; *me cogió en una mentira*, he caught me in a lie. || Lie, story, tale: *siempre está contando mentiras*, he is always telling stories. || Story (cosa inventada). || FIG. y FAM. White spot [on fingernail]. || Mistake, error (errata). || — *Aunque parezca mentira*, strange as it may seem. || *Decir mentira por* or *para sacar la verdad*, to angle for the truth with a lie, to try to draw s.o. out. || *De luengas tierras, luengas mentiras*, travellers from afar can lie with impunity. || *¡Eso es mentira!* or *¡mentira!*, that's a lie!, that's not true! || *Parece mentira*, it is unbelievable, it hardly seems possible. || FAM. *Una mentira como una casa*, a whopper, a whopping lie.
mentirijillas (de) o **de mentirillas** loc. adv. As a joke, for fun, in jest, for a laugh.
mentiroso, sa adj. Lying (que miente). || Full of misprints *o* errors (libro). || FIG. Deceitful, false, deceptive (engañoso): *proposiciones mentirosas*, deceitful propositions.
— M. y f. Liar.
mentís m. Denial. || *Dar un mentís a*, to give the lie to.
mentol m. Menthol.
mentolado, da adj. Mentholated. || *Cigarrillos mentolados*, menthol *o* mentholated cigarettes.
mentón m. ANAT. Chin.
mentor m. Mentor.
menú m. Menu, bill of fare (minuta).
— OBSERV. Pl. *menús*.
menudamente adv. Minutely, tinily. || Minutely, in minute detail (detalladamente).

menudear v. tr. To do *o* to repeat frequently. || To recount in detail (contar). || *Amer.* To retail, to sell retail (vender al por menor).
— V. intr. To happen frequently, to be frequent (ocurrir frecuentemente). || FIG. To rain, to fall incessantly: *menudean los castigos sobre los malos,* punishments rain upon the wicked. || To go into detail (contar las cosas detalladamente). || To talk about trivialities (contar menudencias).
menudencia f. Trifle (cosa sin importancia). || || Minuteness, meticulousness (esmero). || Minuteness (pequeñez). || Detail (detalle). || Pettiness (insignificancia).
— Pl. Offal, *sing.* (de las reses), giblets (de las aves).
menudeo m. Retail trade. || *Venta al menudeo,* retailing.
menudillo m. Fetlock joint (del pie de los cuadrúpedos). || — Pl. Giblets (de las aves).
menudo, da adj. Small, tiny, minute (pequeño). || Fine (lluvia). || Slight (delgado). || Small, trifling, petty (insignificante). || Meticulous, scrupulous (exacto). || — *A menudo,* often, frequently. || *¡En menudo estado estaba!,* he was in a fine state! || *La gente menuda,* V. GENTE. || FAM. *¡Menuda profesión!,* what a job! | *¡Menudo cuento!,* a likely story! | *¡Menudo jaleo!,* a tidy old rumpus! | *¡Menudo porrazo!,* what a wallop! | *¡Menudo precio!,* it's daylight robbery!, it's no giveaway! (es muy caro). || *Moneda menuda,* small change. || *Por menudo,* minutely, in minute detail (detalladamente), retail (al por menor).
— M. pl. Offal, *sing.* (de las reses), giblets (de las aves). || Small change, *sing.* (monedas).
meñique adj. Tiny, very small, minute (pequeño). || *Dedo meñique,* little finger.
— M. Little finger (dedo auricular).
meollada f. Brains, *pl.* (de una res).
meollar m. MAR. Spun yarn.
meollo m. Brain, brains, *pl.* (seso). || Marrow (médula). || Crumb (miga del pan). || FIG. Pith, marrow, core, essence (lo principal). | Brains, *pl.,* intelligence (inteligencia). || FIG. *Entrar en el meollo del asunto,* to come to the heart of the matter.
meón, ona adj. FAM. Who is forever weeing.
— M. y f. FAM. Person who is forever weeing. || FIG. Baby (niño).
mequetrefe m. FAM. Whippersnapper.
Mequínez n. pr. GEOGR. Meknès.
meramente adv. Merely, purely, solely.
mercachifle m. Hawker, pedlar (buhonero). || FAM. Small tradesman (comerciante). | Shark, profiteer (negociante rapaz).
mercadear v. intr. To trade, to deal.
mercadeo m. Trade, trading (comercio). || Marketing (estudio de mercados).
mercader m. Merchant, trader, dealer. || — *El Mercader de Venecia,* the Merchant of Venice. || FIG. *Hacer oídos de mercader,* to turn a deaf ear.
mercadería f. Commodity, article (mercancía). || — Pl. Goods, merchandise, *sing.*
mercado m. Market: *mercado de pescado,* fish market; *lanzar un nuevo producto al mercado,* to launch a new product on to the market; *inundar el mercado de,* to flood the market with; *sacar al mercado,* to put on the market. || — *Acaparar el mercado de,* to corner the market in. || *El domingo hay mercado,* Sunday is market day. || *Hay mucho* or *un gran mercado para,* there is a good market for. || *Investigación* or *estudio de mercados,* market research, marketing. || *Ir al mercado,* to go to market. || *Mercado a tanto alzado,* fixed-price market. || *Mercado Común,* Common Market. || *Mercado de cambios,* foreign exchange market. || *Mercado de valores,* stock market. || *Mercado exterior, interior* or *nacional,* overseas, home market. || *Mercado libre, negro, paralelo,* open, black, unofficial market. || *Mercado sostenido, encalmado,* steady, quiet market.
mercancía f. Article, commodity. || — Pl. Merchandise, *sing.,* goods. || *Tren de mercancías,* goods train, freight train.
mercante adj. Merchant: *marina mercante,* merchant navy, merchant marine. || *Barco mercante,* merchant ship, merchantman, merchant boat.
— M. Merchantman, merchant ship (barco).
mercantil adj. Mercantile, commercial: *operaciones mercantiles,* mercantile operations, commercial transactions. || Mercantile, mercenary, money-grabbing (codicioso): *espíritu mercantil,* mercantile mentality. || — *Derecho mercantil,* commercial *o* mercantile law. || *Sociedad mercantil,* trading company.
mercantilismo m. Mercantilism.
mercantilista adj./s. Mercantilist. || Expert in commercial law (experto en derecho mercantil).
mercantilización f. Commercialization.
mercantilizar v. tr. To consider in terms of money (valorar todo en dinero). || To commercialize (comercializar).
mercar v. tr. To buy (comprar).
merced f. Grace, favour (gracia). || (Ant.). Grace, favour: *hágame la merced de...,* do me the grace of... || Recompense, reward (recompensa). || — *A (la) merced de,* at the mercy of. || *La Merced,* Our Lady of Mercy [order]. || *Merced a,* thanks to, by the grace of. || *Muchas mercedes,* many thanks. || *Su* or *vuestra merced,* your grace, your honour (título). || *Tenga la merced de,* please be so kind as to.
— OBSERV. *Vuestra merced* is today contracted to *usted,* itself abbreviated to *Ud.* or *Vd.* [V. USTED.].
mercedario, ria adj. Of the order of Our Lady of Mercy.
— M. y f. Mercedarian. || — Pl. Mercedarians (orden).
mercenario, ria adj. Mercenary: *soldado mercenario,* mercenary soldier. || Mercenary (ant.), done solely for gain (un trabajo). || Mercenary, money-grabbing (codicioso).
— M. y f. Mercenary. || Day worker (jornalero). || Mercedarian (mercedario). || Ghost writer (escritor que hace el trabajo de otro).
mercería f. Haberdashery [U.S., notions trade] (comercio). || Haberdasher's, haberdashery [U.S., notions store] (tienda).
mercerizar v. tr. To mercerize.
mercero, ra m. y f. Haberdasher [U.S., notions dealer].
mercurial adj. Mercurial.
mercúrico, ca adj. QUÍM. Mercuric.
mercurio m. QUÍM. Mercury (metal). || *Lámpara de vapor de mercurio,* mercury-vapour lamp.
Mercurio n. pr. m. MIT. y ASTR. Mercury.
mercurioso adj. m. QUÍM. Mercurous (óxido).
merdellón m. FAM. Status-seeking fop, coxcomb (p.us.) [hortera]. | Grubby servant *o* maid (criado o criada sucios).
merecedor, ra adj. Deserving, worthy. || — *Hacerse merecedor de,* to become worthy of. || *Merecedor de confianza,* trustworthy. || *Ser merecedor de,* to be worthy of, to deserve.
merecer* v. tr. To deserve, to merit, to be worthy of: *merecer un premio,* to merit a prize. || To deserve, to be worth, to merit: *el castillo merece una visita,* the castle deserves a visit. || To deserve, to be worth (con infinitivo): *el cuento merece ser contado,* the tale deserves to be told *o* is worth telling. || To need (tener necesidad): *esta noticia merece ser comprobada,* this piece of news needs to be verified. || To earn, to get (valer): *su insolencia le mereció una bofetada,* his insolence earned him a slap. || — *Lo tiene bien merecido,* he has well deserved it (un premio, etc.), it serves him right (un castigo, etc.). || *Merecer la pena,* V. PENA. || *Tener lo que uno se merece,* to get what one deserves.
— V. intr. To be deserving, to be worthy. || *Mereció bien de la patria,* he served his country well.
— V. pr. To deserve.
merecidamente adv. Deservedly, rightly.
merecido m. Deserts, *pl.,* due, deserved punishment. || — *A cada uno su merecido,* give the devil his due. || FIG. *Dar su merecido,* to settle one's account. || *Llevar* or *tener su merecido,* to get one's deserts *o* one's due, to get what is coming to one.
merecimiento m. Merit, worth.
merendar* v. intr. To have *o* to take an afternoon snack, to have [a light] tea (tomar la merienda). || To picnic (en el campo).
— V. tr. To have as an afternoon snack, to have for tea: *merendar café y galletas,* to have coffee and biscuits for tea.
— V. pr. FIG. y FAM. *Merendarse una cosa,* to land, to get hold of (conseguir). | *Merendarse a,* to get the better of (dominar), to lick, to trounce (derrotar), to rush off (hacer rápidamente), to throw down the drain (una fortuna).
merendero m. Refreshment room, teahouse, snack bar (donde se merienda). || Picnic spot (en el campo).
merendona f. FIG. Spread (merienda abundante). | Picnic (merienda campestre).
merengue m. Meringue (dulce). || FIG. Weakling (débil). || FIG. y FAM. *Durará menos que un merengue en la puerta de una escuela,* it will not last five minutes.
meretriz f. Harlot, prostitute, meretrix.
mergánsar o **mergo** m. ZOOL. Cormorant, merganser.
meridano, na adj. [Of *o* from] Mérida [town in Mexico].
— M. y f. Native *o* inhabitant of Mérida.
merideño, ña adj. [Of *o* from] Mérida [town in Extremadura (Spain), state of Venezuela].
— M. y f. Native *o* inhabitant of Mérida.
meridiano, na adj. Meridian, midday, noon (de mediodía). || Meridian: *altitud, línea meridiana,* meridian altitude, line. || Dazzling, brilliant (luz). || — FIG. *Con claridad meridiana,* with striking clarity, very clearly. | *Ser de una claridad meridiana,* to be as clear as day *o* as clear as crystal *o* crystal clear.
— M. ASTR. y GEOGR. Meridian: *primer meridiano,* prime meridian. || — F. Couch (cama). | Siesta, afternoon nap (siesta).
meridional adj. Meridional (del sur de Europa). || Southern, south (en general): *América meridional,* South America; *Europa meridional,* Southern Europe.
— M. y f. Meridional (del sur de Europa). || Southerner (en general).
merienda f. Afternoon snack, tea (por la tarde). || Lunch, midday meal (del mediodía). || Picnic (campestre). || Packed lunch (provisiones para una excursión), picnic (para una merienda campestre). || — *Ir de merienda* to go for a picnic. || FIG. y FAM.

Juntar meriendas, to join forces. || *Merienda cena*, high tea. || FIG. y FAM. *Merienda de negros*, free-for-all, bedlam.
merino, na adj./s. Merino (carnero, lana, tela).
mérito m. Merit: *obra de poco mérito*, work of little merit. || Worth (valor): *cosa de poco mérito*, thing of little worth. || Desert: *ser recompensado según sus méritos*, to meet with one's deserts. || — *Atribuirse el mérito de*, to take the glory for. || *De mérito*, of merit: *autor de gran mérito*, author of great merit. || FIG. *Hacer méritos para*, to strive to make o.s. deserving of. || *Méritos de guerra*, mention in dispatches. || *Quitar méritos a*, to detract from.
meritorio, ria adj. Meritorious, praiseworthy (cosa). || Of merit, deserving, worthy (persona).
— M. Improver, unpaid trainee (empleado).
Merlín n. pr. m. Merlin. || FIG. *Sabe más que Merlín*, he knows everything.
merlo m. Black wrasse (pez). || *Amer.* Idiot, ass (tonto).
merluza f. Hake (pez). || FIG. y FAM. Ass, idiot (tonto). || FIG. y FAM. *Coger, tener una merluza*, to get *o* to be canned *o* sloshed (emborracharse).
merma f. Decrease, reduction (disminución). || Loss, wastage (pérdida).
mermar v. tr. To decrease, to reduce, to cut down (la paga, las raciones, etc.). || To deplete, to reduce: *capital mermado*, depleted capital. || FIG. To cast a slur on: *mermarle a uno la reputación*, to cast a slur on s.o.'s reputation. || To cause to go down (un líquido).
— V. intr. To decrease, to diminish, to lessen. || To go down (un líquido).
mermelada f. Jam, preserves, *pl.* (frutas cortadas y cocidas con azúcar): *mermelada de fresa*, strawberry jam. || *Mermelada de naranjas amargas*, marmalade.
mero m. Grouper (pez).
mero, ra adj. Mere, pure, simple: *por el mero hecho de*, through the mere fact of; *una mera casualidad*, a pure coincidence. || *Amer.* Real (verdadero): *es el mero amo*, he is the real boss. || — *Amer. Llegó a la mera hora*, he arrived right on time (en el momento preciso). | *Ser el mero malo*, to be wickedness itself. | *Uno mero, una mera*, only one. | *Yo mero*, I myself.
— Adv. *Amer.* Really (verdaderamente). | Exactly: *son mero las dos*, it is exactly two o'clock (en punto).
merodeador, ra adj. MIL. Marauding. || Prowling.
— M. y f. MIL. Marauder. || Prowler.
merodear v. intr. MIL. To maraud. || To prowl, to roam. || *Merodear por*, to scout *o* to snoop around (explorar, curiosear).
merodeo m. MIL. Marauding. || Prowling.
Meroveo n. pr. m. Meroveous, Merovaeous.
merovingio, gia adj./s. HIST. Merovingian.
mes m. Month: *en el mes de mayo*, in the month of May; *dentro de un mes*, within a month, in a month's time; *el mes pasado, que viene*, last, next month; *cobra cien libras al* or *por mes*, he is paid a hundred pounds a month. || Monthly *o* month's pay *o* wage *o* salary, wage for the month (salario): *cobrar el mes*, to draw one's monthly wage *o* one's wage for the month. || Menses, *pl.*, menstruation (menstruo). || — *Alquilar una habitación al* or *por mes*, to rent a room by the month. || *El mes corriente*, the current month. || *Mes civil*, calendar month. || *Mes lunar*, lunar month. || *Pagar por meses*, to pay by the month.
mesa f. Table: *en la mesa*, on the table (encima), at the table (alrededor). || Bureau, desk, writing desk, writing table (escritorio de oficina). || Board, bureau, general committee (de una asamblea). || GEOGR. Tableland, plateau, meseta (meseta). || Landing (de escalera). || Table (de una piedra preciosa). || Flat (de una hoja). || Revenue, income (renta eclesiástica). || FIG. Table (comida): *en casa de mi tía siempre hay buena mesa*, my aunt always keeps a good table. || Game (partida de billar). || — *¡A la mesa!*, lunch [dinner, etc.] is ready! || *Alzar* or *quitar* or *levantar la mesa*, to clear the table. || *A mesa puesta*, with all one's needs provided for. || *Bendecir la mesa*, to say grace. || *De mesa*, table: *vino de mesa*, table wine. || *Estar a mesa y mantel en casa de uno*, to receive free board from s.o. || *Levantarse de la mesa*, to leave the table. || *Mesa camilla*, v. CAMILLA. || *Mesa con largueros*, draw-leaf *o* extension table. || *Mesa de alas*, table with flaps. || *Mesa de altar*, altar. || MÚS. *Mesa de armonía*, soundboard (de piano), belly (de violín). || *Mesa de batalla*, sorting table (correos). || *Mesa de billar*, billiard table. || *Mesa de juego*, gambling *o* gaming table. || *Mesa de noche*, bedside table. || MED. *Mesa de operaciones*, operating table. || *Mesa de tijera* or *plegable*, folding table. || *Mesa electoral*, electoral college. || *Mesa extensible*, extension table. || *Mesa redonda*, common table (de huéspedes mezclados), table d'hôte (en los restaurantes), round table, round-table discussion *o* conference (reunión). || FIG. *Mesa revuelta*, hotchpotch, medley (batiburrillo), miscellany pages (de periódico). || *Mesa y cama*, bed and board. || *Poner la mesa*, to lay *o* to set the table. || *Sentarse a la mesa*, to sit down at the *o* to table, to sit down to lunch [dinner, etc.]. || *Servir la mesa*, to wait at table. || *Tener a uno a mesa y mantel*, to give s.o. free board. || *Tener mesa franca*, to keep open house. || *Tener mesa franca en casa de uno*, to be assured of a place at s.o.'s table.
mesadura f. Tearing [of the hair *o* beard].
Mesalina n. pr. f. Messalina.
mesana f. MAR. Mizen, mizzen, mizenmast, mizzenmast (mástil). | Mizensail, mizzensail (vela).
mesar v. tr. To tear [at] (one's hair o beard).
— V. pr. To tear [at] (one's hair *o* beard).
mescal m. *Amer.* Mescal.
mescolanza f. FAM. V. MEZCOLANZA.
mesenterio m. ANAT. Mesentery.
meseta f. Plateau, tableland, meseta (llanura): *la meseta de Castilla*, the plateau of Castile. || Landing (de escalera).
mesiánico, ca adj. Messianic.
mesianismo m. Messianism.
Mesías m. Messiah.
mesilla f. Small table (mesa pequeña). || Landing (de escalera). || Ledge, sill (de ventana). || Mantelpiece (de chimenea). || Rail, coping (de balaustrada). || — *Mesilla de noche*, bedside table. || *Mesilla de ruedas*, trolley.
mesmedad f. FAM. *Por su propia mesmedad*, by itself.
mesmo, ma adj. (Ant.). FAM. V. MISMO.
mesnada f. Armed retinue. || FIG. Band, group, company (compañía). || — Pl. FIG. Followers (partidarios).
mesnadero m. Man-at-arms, member of an armed retinue.
mesocarpio o **mesocarpo** m. BOT. Mesocarp.
mesocéfalo, la adj. Mesocephalic, mesencephalic.
mesodermo m. ANAT. Mesoderm.
mesolítico, ca adj./s.m. Mesolithic.
mesón m. Inn, tavern, hostelry (posada en tiempos antiguos). || Old-style tavern (establecimiento moderno). || FÍS. Meson.
mesonero, ra m. y f. Innkeeper (hombre o mujer), landlord (hombre), landlady (mujer).
— Adj. Inn, tavern.
Mesopotamia n. pr. f. GEOGR. Mesopotamia.
mesopotámico, ca adj./s. Mesopotamian.
mesosfera f. Mesosphere.
mesotelio m. Mesothelium.
mesotórax m. Mesothorax.
mesotrón m. FÍS. Mesotron.
mesozoico, ca adj. GEOL. Mesozoic.
mesta f. "Mesta" [medieval association of cattle farmers]. || — Pl. Confluence [of streams] (confluente).
mester m. (Ant.). Trade, craft (oficio). || Verse: *mester de clerecía, de juglaría*, clerical, minstrel verse.
mestizaje m. Mestization, crossbreeding.
mestizar v. tr. To crossbreed (cruzar razas).
mestizo, za adj. Half-bred, half-caste (persona). || Crossbred, half-blooded (animal). || Mongrel (perro). || Hybrid (vegetal).
— M. y f. Mestizo (hombre), mestiza (mujer), half-caste, half-breed (hombre o mujer). || Crossbreed, half-blood (animal). || Mongrel (perro). || Hybrid (vegetal).
mesura f. Moderation, restraint, measure (moderación). || Gravity, composure (compostura). || Respect, civility (respeto). || (Ant.). Temperance (templanza).
mesuradamente adv. With moderation *o* restraint.
mesurado, da adj. Moderate, restrained (moderado). || Circumspect (circunspecto). || Temperate (templado). || Grave, composed (sereno).
mesurar v. tr. To moderate, to restrain (moderar). || To consider, to think over (considerar). || *Mesurar sus palabras*, to weigh one's words.
— V. pr. To moderate *o* to restrain o.s., to act with moderation *o* restraint. || *Mesurarse en sus palabras*, to weigh one's words.
meta f. Goal, aim, objective (finalidad): *conseguir su meta*, to reach one's goal. || DEP. Goal (portería). | Finish (en las carreras ciclistas, de automóviles), finish line, tape (en atletismo), winning post (de caballos). || — M. Goalkeeper (guardameta).
metabólico, ca adj. BIOL. Metabolic.
metabolismo m. BIOL. Metabolism.
metacarpiano, na adj. ANAT. Metacarpal.
metacarpo m. ANAT. Metacarpus.
metafase f. BIOL. Metaphase.
metafísico, ca adj. Metaphysical.
— M. y f. Metaphysician. || — F. Metaphysics.
metáfora f. Metaphor.
metafórico, ca adj. Metaphorical, metaphoric.
metaforizar v. tr. To metaphorize, to express metaphorically.
metagoge f. Personification, prosopopoeia.
metal m. Metal. || Brass (latón). || FIG. Timbre, ring (de la voz). | Quality, condition (calidad). || HERÁLD. Metal (oro o plata). || — FAM. *El vil metal*, filthy lucre. || MÚS. *Instrumentos de metal*, brass [instruments]. || *Metal blanco*, white metal, nickel *o* German silver. || *Metal de imprenta*, type metal. || *Metal precioso*, precious metal.
metaldehído m. QUÍM. Metaldehyde.
metálico, ca adj. Metallic.
— M. [Hard] cash, specie (monedas y billetes): *pagar en metálico*, to pay [in] cash. || Coin, specie (monedas).
metalífero, ra adj. Metalliferous, metal-bearing.
metalistería f. Metalwork.
metalización f. Metallization [U.S., metalization].

metalizar v. tr. To metallize [U.S., to metalize]. — V. pr. To become metallized [U.S., to become metalized]. || FIG. To go money-mad.
metaloide m. QUÍM. Metalloid.
metalurgia f. Metallurgy.
metalúrgico, ca adj. Metallurgical, metallurgic. — M. Metallurgist.
metamórfico, ca adj. GEOL. Metamorphic.
metamorfismo m. GEOL. Metamorphism.
metamorfosear v. tr. To metamorphose, to change. — V. pr. To be metamorphosed, to change completely.
metamorfosis o **metamórfosis** f. inv. Metamorphosis, transformation: *sufrir una metamorfosis*, to undergo metamorphosis.
metano m. QUÍM. Methane.
metanol m. QUÍM. Methanol.
metaplasmo m. GRAM. Metaplasm.
metapsíquico, ca adj. Metapsychic, metapsychical. — F. Metapsychology.
metástasis f. MED. Metastasis.
metatarsiano adj./s.m. Metatarsal.
metatarso m. ANAT. Metatarsus.
metate m. Stone [for grinding cacao and maize].
metátesis f. GRAM. Metathesis.
metatórax m. Metathorax (de insectos).
metazoario, ria adj. ZOOL. Metazoan. — M. Metazoan. || — Pl. Metazoa.
metazoo m. ZOOL. Metazoan.
meteco m. Foreigner, alien (extranjero).
metedor m. Napkin [U.S., diaper] (de los niños). || Smuggler, contrabandist (contrabandista). || IMPR. Imposing stone, imposing table.
metedura f. FAM. Putting. || FAM. *Metedura de pata*, blunder, bloomer.
metempsicosis f. Metempsychosis.
meteórico, ca adj. Meteoric.
meteorismo m. VET. Bloat. || MED. Meteorism.
meteorito m. Meteorite.
meteorizar v. tr. VET. To produce bloat in. || MED. To produce meteorism in. — V. pr. VET. To get bloat. || MED. To become affected with meteorism. || AGR. To be affected by atmospheric agents (la tierra).
meteoro m. Meteor.

METALURGIA, *f.* — METALLURGY

industria (*f.*) siderúrgica	iron and steel industry
planta (*f.*) siderúrgica	ironworks
fundición *f.*	foundry
acería *f.*	steelworks, steel mill
coquería *f.*	coking plant
electrometalurgia *f.*	electrometallurgy
metalurgia (*f.*) de polvos	powder metallurgy
alto horno *m.*	blast furnace
tragante *m.*	mouth, throat
tolva *f.*	hopper, chute
cuba *f.*	stack
vientre *m.*	belly
etalaje *m.*	bosh
crisol *m.*	crucible
bigotera *f.*	slag tap
piquera *f.*	taphole
lecho (*m.*) de colada	pig bed
orificio (*m.*) de colada	taphole, drawhole
molde *m.*	mould [U.S., mold]
tobera *f.*	tuyère, nozzle
lingotera *f.*	ingot mould [U.S., ingot mold]
solera *f.*	floor
hogar *m.*	hearth
cargadora *f.*	charger
cuchara *f.*	ladle
separador (*m.*) de polvo	dust catcher
lavador *m.*	washer
convertidor *m.*	converter
montacargas *m. inv.*	hoist
compresor *m.*	compressor
mezclador (*m.*) basculante	tilting mixer
regenerador *m.*	regenerator
cambiador (*m.*) de calor	heat exchanger
depurador (*m.*) de gases	gas purifier
turbocompresor *m.*	turbocompressor
quemador *m.*	burner
caldero (*m.*) de colada	ladle
cubilote *m.*	cupola
vaciador *m.*	emptier
bebedero *m.*	trough
vagoneta *f.*	skip
laminador *m.*, tren (*m.*) laminador	rolling mill
tren (*m.*) blooming	blooming mill
cilindros *m. pl.*	rollers
rodillo *m.*	roller
bancada *f.*	bed
jaula (*f.*) del laminador	rolling-mill housing
banco (*m.*) de estirar	drawbench
hilera *f.*	drawplate
horno (*m.*) de cuba, de refinación, de reverbero, de solera	shaft, refining, reverberatory, hearth furnace
revestimiento (*m.*) refractario	firebrick lining
retorta *f.*	retort
mufla *f.*	muffle
bóveda *f.*	roof, arch
forja *f.*	forge
prensa *f.*	press
martillo (*m.*) pilón	pile hammer, drop hammer
matriz *f.*	die
soplete *m.*	blowlamp [U.S., blowtorch]
trituradora *f.*	crusher
mineral (*m.*) de hierro	iron ore
coque *m.*	coke
bauxita *f.*	bauxite
alúmina *f.*	alumina
criolita *f.*	cryolite
fundente *m.*	flux
castina *f.*	limestone flux
hematites *f.*	haematite [U.S., hematite]
ganga *f.*	gangue
arrabio *m.*, fundición *f.*, hierro (*m.*) colado	cast iron
lingote (*m.*) de arrabio	cast iron ingot
escoria *f.*	slag
hierro (*m.*) dulce	soft iron
hierro (*m.*) en lingotes	pig iron
hierro (*m.*) forjado	wrought iron
hierro (*m.*) tocho	iron ingot
hierro (*m.*) pudelado	puddled iron
hierro (*m.*) redondo	round iron
chatarra *f.*	scrap iron
acero *m.*	steel
acero (*m.*) bruto	crude steel
acero (*m.*) dulce, duro, colado, inoxidable, eléctrico	mild *o* soft, hard, cast, stainless, electric steel
acero (*m.*) rápido	high-speed steel
acero (*m.*) moldeado	cast *o* moulded steel
acero (*m.*) refractario	refractory steel
acero (*m.*) aleado	alloy steel
chapa *f.*	plate, sheet
chapa (*f.*) ondulada	corrugated iron
hojalata *f.*	tinplate, tin
producto (*m.*) acabado	finished product
producto (*m.*) semiacabado, semiproducto *m.*	semifinished product
productos (*m. pl.*) férreos	ferrous products
banda *f.*	coiled sheet
bloom *m.*, desbaste *m.*	bloom
fleje *m.*	metal strip *o* band
palanquilla *f.*	billet
viruta *f.*	shavings *pl.*
barra (*f.*) perfilada	profiled bar
perfil *m.*	shape, section
angular *m.*	angle iron
frita *f.*	frit
alambre *m.*	wire
ferroníquel *m.*	ferronickel
elinvar *m.*	elinvar
ferrita *f.*	ferrite
cementita *f.*	cementite
perlita *f.*	pearlite
carga *f.*	charging, loading
fusión *f.*	fusion, melting, smelting
refundición *f.*	remelting
afino *m.*, afinación *f.*, afinado *m.*	refining
vaciado *m.*, colada *f.*	casting
vaciar, colar	to cast
sangría *f.*	tapping
insuflar, inyectar	to insufflate, to inject
caldeo *m.*	heating
precalentamiento *m.*	preheating
templado *m.*	tempering
temple *m.*	temper
endurecimiento *m.*	hardening
recocido *m.*	annealing
revenido *m.*	tempering
reducción *f.*	reduction
enfriamiento *m.*	cooling
descarburación *f.*	decarbonization, decarburization
coquificación *f.*, coquización *f.*	coking
escorificación *f.*	slagging, scorification
carburación *f.*	carburization
cementación *f.*	case hardening, cementation
fritado *m.*, fritaje *m.*, sinterización *f.*	fritting, sintering
pudelado *m.*, pudelaje *m.*	puddling
pulverización *f.*	pulverization
nitruración *f.*	nitriding
aleación *f.*	alloy
modelaje *m.*	patternmaking
moldeo *m.*, moldeado *m.*	moulding [U.S., molding]
flotación *f.*	floatation, flotation
calcinación *f.*	calcination
amalgamación *f.*	amalgamation
laminación *f.*, laminado *m.*	rolling
estirado *m.*	drawing
extrusión *f.*	extrusion
trefilado *m.*	wiredrawing
embutido *m.*	stamping, pressing
estampación *f.*, estampado *m.*	stamping
matrizado *m.*	die casting
prensado *m.*	pressing
forjado *m.*	forging
torneado *m.*	turning
fresado *m.*	milling
mecanizado *m.*	machining, tooling
soldadura (*f.*) autógena	autogenous *o* fusion welding
soldadura (*f.*) de arco	arc welding
electrólisis *f.*	electrolysis
desbarbado *m.*	trimming
sopladura *f.*	blowhole

meteorología f. Meteorology.
meteorológico, ca adj. Meteorological, meteorologic. || *Parte meteorológico*, weather report.
meteorólogo, ga m. y f. Meteorologist.
meter v. tr.

1. Introducir. — **2.** Causar. — **3.** Otros sentidos. — **4.** Locuciones — **5.** V. pr.

1. INTRODUCIR. — To put: *meter la mano en el bolsillo*, to put one's hand in *o* into one's pocket; *meter en la cama, en la cárcel*, to put to bed, in prison. || To put, to introduce, to insert: *meter un tubo en la tráquea de un enfermo*, to introduce a tube into a patient's windpipe. || To place, to put (colocar). || To squeeze in (en un sitio estrecho). || To smuggle in (en fraude): *meter tabaco*, to smuggle in tobacco. || FIG. To get, to drive: *intenté meterle en la cabeza que...*, I tried to get it into his head that... || To get *o* to find a job (poner a trabajar): *le han metido de carnicero*, they have found him a job as a butcher. || To take, to bring: *meter a su hijo en el negocio familiar*, to bring one's son into the family business. || To send (*en*, to), to put (*en*, in) [a un niño en un colegio]. || FIG. y FAM. To get: *¡en menudo lío me has metido!*, a fine mess you've got me into! | To involve, to get mixed up, to get involved (enredar): *no quiero que me metas en tus asuntos*, I don't want you getting me mixed up in your affairs. || DEP. To pocket [a ball] (en el billar), to hole (en golf), to basket (en baloncesto), to put in (en fútbol). || *Meter a uno a trabajar*, to put s.o. to work, to set s.o. working.
2. CAUSAR.— To make: *meter ruido*, to make a noise. || To make, to kick up (fam.): *meter jaleo*, to kick up a row. || To cause: *meter enredos*, to cause confusion. || — *Meterle a uno un susto*, to give s.o. a fright. || *Meterle miedo a uno*, to frighten *o* to scare s.o. || *Meter un lío*, to make a mess.
3. OTROS SENTIDOS. — To take up (acortar una prenda). || To take in (estrechar una prenda). || To compress, to squeeze *o* to cram together (apretar): *meter los renglones de una plana*, to compress the lines on a page. || To present, to hand in (una solicitud). || To stake, to bet, to put (en el juego, en la lotería). || To put, to invest, to tie up (invertir). || To pay in, to place (en un banco, en una caja de ahorros, etc.). || DEP. To score (un gol). || FAM. To give (un golpe, una paliza). | To tell (embustes). | To spread, to start (chismes). | To give: *nos va a meter el rollo de siempre*, he is going to give us his usual speech. || MAR. To take in [the sails].
4. LOCUCIONES. — FAM. *Anda siempre metido con los golfillos de la calle*, he is always knocking around with the little street urchins. | *A todo meter*, at full speed. || FIG. *Estar muy metido en política*, to be deeply involved in politics. | *Meter baza*, v. BAZA. | *Meter cizaña*, v. CIZAÑA. | *Meter en cintura* or *en vereda*, to make s.o. behave, to bring s.o. into line *o* to heel. || FIG. y FAM. *Meter la nariz* or *las narices en todo*, v. NARIZ. | *Meter la pata*, to put one's foot in it. || AUT. *Meter la primera* (*segunda, etc.*), to change into first [second, etc.]. || *Meter por los ojos*, v. OJO. || *Meter prisa*, to hurry [up], to make haste (uno mismo), to hurry, to rush (a otro). || FIG. *Tener a uno metido en un puño*, to have s.o. in the palm of one's hand.
5. V. pr. — To get: *meterse en la cama*, to get into bed; *se me ha metido una carbonilla en el ojo*, some soot has got in my eye. || FIG. To get: *¿dónde te has metido?*, where did you get to? | To go, to enter, to take: *se metió en una bocacalle*, he went into a side street. | To become: *meterse monja*, to become a nun. | To turn (soldado). | To jut out: *la costa se mete en el mar*, the coast juts out into the sea. || — *¿Dónde se habrá metido mi libro?*, where can my book have got to? || FIG. *Meterse a*, to become (con sustantivo): *meterse a fraile*, to become a monk; to start, to begin (con infinitivo): *meterse a escribir*, to start writing *o* to write. | *Meterse con*, to bother, to annoy (jorobar), to tease (embromar): *meterse con alguien* (*en plan de broma*), to tease s.o.; to pick a quarrel with (buscar pelea), to pick on: *deja de meterte con tu hermanito*, stop picking on your little brother; to attack: *todos los críticos se meten con él*, all the critics attack him. | *Meterse en*, to get into (aventuras, vicios, etc.), to go into (negocio), to get involved in, to get mixed up in: *se ha metido en un asunto poco claro*, he has got involved in some shady deal; to meddle, to interfere: *siempre se mete donde no le llaman*, he always meddles in things that do not concern him; *meterse en todo*, to interfere in everything; to get into: *meterse en dificultades*, to get into difficulties; to enter: *meterse en una discusión*, to enter a discussion; *meterse en unas explicaciones inútiles*, to enter into futile explanations; to go into, to enter: *se metió en una tienda*, he went into *o* he entered a shop; to go: *esta pieza se mete aquí dentro*, this piece goes in here. | *Meterse en gastos*, to go to expense. | *Meterse en sí mismo*, to withdraw into o.s., to go into one's shell. | *Metérsele a uno en la cabeza*, v. CABEZA. | *Métete en lo tuyo* or *en tus cosas* or *en lo que te importa*, mind your own business. | *¿Por qué te metes?*, what's it to you?, what business is it of yours?
meticulosidad f. Meticulousness, meticulosity.
meticuloso, sa adj. Meticulous. || Finicky (exageradamente cuidadoso). || Fearful, meticulous (ant.) [miedoso].
metidito, ta adj. FAM. *Metidita en carnes*, plump, fleshy. | *Metidito en años*, getting on, a little long in the tooth.
metido, da adj. V. METER. || — *Metido en carnes*, plump. || *Metido en años*, advanced in years. || *Pan metido en harina*, bread rich in flour.
— M. Punch (golpe). || Shove (empujón): *darle a uno un metido en la espalda*, to give s.o. a shove in the back. || Material let in, seam (al estrechar), material turned up, hem (al acortar) [en costura]. || Napkin [U.S., diaper] (metedor). || FIG. y FAM. Dressing down (reprensión); *darle a uno un metido*, to give s.o. a dressing down.
metileno m. QUÍM. Methylene. || *Azul de metileno*, methylene blue.
metílico, ca adj. QUÍM. Methylic.
metilo m. QUÍM. Methyl.
metódico, ca adj. Methodical.
metodismo m. REL. Methodism.
metodista adj./s. REL. Methodist.
metodizar v. tr. To methodize.
método m. Method. || Method, course: *método de lectura*, reading method. || — *Con método*, methodically. || *Método de piano*, piano tutor.
metodología f. Methodology.
metomentodo m. y f. FAM. Meddler, busybody.
metonimia f. Metonymy.
metonímico, ca adj. Metonymical.
metopa f. ARQ. Metope.
metraje m. CINEM. Footage, length [of film]. || — *Un corto metraje*, a short film. || *Un largo metraje*, a full-length film, a feature film.
metralla f. Shrapnel (al estallar un proyectil). || Grapeshot (carga). || *Granada de metralla*, frangible shell.
metrallazo m. Discharge of grapeshot.
metralleta f. Tommy gun, submachine gun (arma).
métrica f. POÉT. Metrics.
métrico, ca adj. Metric: *sistema métrico*, metric system. || Metrical (del verso, de la métrica). || *Cinta métrica*, tape measure.
metrificación f. Metrification, versification.
metrificador, ra m. y f. Versifier.
metrificar v. intr. To versify.
— V. tr. To metrify, to versify.
metritis f. MED. Metritis.
metro m. Metre [U.S., meter] (medida): *metro cuadrado, cúbico*, square, cubic metre. || Metre [U.S., meter] (verso). || Ruler (regla). || Tape measure (cinta). || *Medir por metros*, to measure in metres *o* by the metre.

— OBSERV. Como el *metro* no se emplea en los países anglosajones, en algunos casos se puede utilizar como equivalente la *yard*, que mide casi un metro: *¿cuántos metros le hacen falta?*, how many yards do you need? (de una tela).

metro m. Underground, tube [U.S., subway] (transporte). || *Metro aéreo* or *a cielo abierto*, overhead railway.
metrología f. Metrology.
metrónomo m. MÚS. Metronome.
metrópoli f. Metropolis. || Metropolis, mother country (nación).
metropolitano, na adj. Metropolitan.
— M. REL. Metropolitan. || Underground, tube [U.S., subway] (transporte).
mexicano, na adj./s. Mexican.
México n. pr. m. GEOGR. Mexico (país). | Mexico City (ciudad).

— OBSERV. Although *México* (with an *x* instead of a *j*) is the only spelling accepted in Mexico, the pronunciation of the word is not affected.

mezcal m. *Amer.* Mescal (pita, aguardiente).
mezcalina f. Mescaline.
mezcla f. Mixing, mixture, blending (acción de mezclar). || Mixture (resultado): *una mezcla de varios ingredientes*, a mixture of several ingredients. || Mixture, blend, combination: *mezcla de buenas y malas cualidades*, blend of good and bad qualities. || Mortar (argamasa). || CINEM. y RAD. Mixing. || AUT. Mixture. || Mixture, fabric woven with different sorts of thread (tela).
mezclable adj. Mixable.
mezclador, ra m. y f. Mixer. || — F. Mixing machine, mixer (máquina).
mezcladura f. o **mezclamiento** m. Mixture.
mezclar v. tr. To mix: *mezclar una cosa con otra*, to mix one thing with another. || To mix, to blend: *mezclar colores*, to mix colours; *mezclar dos vinos*, to blend two wines. || To mix up (desordenar). || To mix, to mingle (reunir): *mezclar en la misma clase niños de distintas edades*, to mix children of different ages in the same class. || FIG. To mix, to mingle, to combine: *mezclar la amabilidad con la severidad*, to combine kindness with severity. || To shuffle (los naipes).
— V. pr. To mix: *el aceite y el agua no se mezclan*,

oil and water do not mix. || To mingle: *mezclarse con la multitud*, to mingle with the crowd. || FIG. To mix: *no le gusta a su padre la gente con quien se mezcla*, her father does not like the people she mixes with. | To take part (tomar parte). | To meddle, to interfere: *no te mezcles en mis asuntos*, don't meddle in my affairs. | To get mixed up, to get involved (en negocios sucios).
mezclilla f. Mixture, light cloth woven with different sorts of thread (tela).
mezcolanza f. Mixture (mezcla). || FAM. Hotchpotch, jumble [of ideas, etc.] (batiburrillo).
mezquindad f. Meanness, niggardliness, stinginess (tacañería). || Mean thing (acción tacaña). || Paltriness, scantiness (escasez). || Paltry thing (cosa insignificante).
mezquino, na adj. Mean, niggardly, stingy (tacaño). || Wretched, small (pequeño). || Paltry, scanty (escaso): *un salario mezquino*, a paltry wage. || Poor, wretched (pobre). || Petty, narrow, small (mentalidad).
— M. y f. Mean person.
mezquita f. Mosque.
mi m. MÚS. Mi, me, E (nota).
mi, mis adj. poses. de la 1ª pers. My: *mi libro, mi madre, mis zapatos*, my book, my mother, my shoes.
mí pron. pers. de la 1ª pers. del sing. Me [used with a preposition]: *lo trajo para mí*, he brought it for me; *nos acompañó a mi hermano y a mí*, he accompanied my brother and me. || — *¡A mí!*, help! (socorro). || *¡A mí con ésas!*, come off it! || *A mí me toca* or *me corresponde hacerlo*, it is for me to do it. || *En cuanto a mí respecta* or *para mí* or *por mí* or *por lo que a mí respecta*, as for me, as far as I am concerned. || *Por mí mismo*, by myself, on my own. || FAM. *¿(Y) a mí qué?*, what's it to me?, so what?

— OBSERV. *Mí* is not translated in constructions such as: *a mí no me importa*, it's all the same to me; *a mí me gusta el jazz*, I like jazz, etc.

miaja f. Crumb (migaja). || FAM. Bit: *ha heredado una miaja de dinero*, he has come into a bit of money; *espérate una miaja*, hang on a bit. | Scrap: *no tiene una miaja de inteligencia*, he hasn't a scrap of intelligence.
mialgia f. MED. Myalgia.
miasma m. Miasma (pl. *miasmas, miasmata*).

— OBSERV. The use of *miasma* as a feminine noun is incorrect.

miau m. Miaow, mew, meow (del gato).
mica f. MIN. Mica.
mica f. Female long-tailed monkey (mona). || *Amer. Agarrar una mica*, to get sloshed (emborracharse).
micáceo, a adj. MIN. Micaceous.
micado m. Mikado (emperador del Japón).
micción f. Micturition.
micela f. Micelle (partícula).
micelio m. BOT. Mycelium.
Micenas n. pr. GEOGR. Mycenae.
micer m. Messire, sir (título antiguo). || Master (dicho de los abogados).
micifuz m. FAM. Puss, pussy, kitty (gato).
mico m. ZOOL. Monkey (mono). | Long-tailed monkey (mono de cola larga). || FIG. y FAM. Monkey face, ape (persona fea). | Lecher (lujurioso). | Little monkey [affectionate insult to a child] (niño). | Conceited puppy (persona presumida). | Runt (hombre pequeño). || — FIG. y FAM. *Dar* or *hacer un mico a uno*, to stand s.o. up (faltar a una cita). | *Dar el mico*, to disappoint. | *Dejar a uno hecho un mico*, to make a monkey out of s.o., to put s.o. to shame. | *Quedarse hecho un mico*, to be shown up *o* ridiculed, to be made a monkey of. | *Ser el último mico*, not to count, to be the lowest of the low, to be the pip-squeak. | *Volverse mico*, to strive hard, to take pains.
micosis f. MED. Mycosis.
micra f. Micron (micrón).
micro m. FAM. Mike, microphone (micrófono). || *Amer.* Bus (autobús).
microamperio m. Microampere.
microanálisis m. Microanalysis.
microbiano, na adj. Microbic, microbial.
micróbicida m. Microbicide.
microbio m. Microbe.
microbiología f. Microbiology.
microbús m. Minibus (pequeño autobús).
microcefalia f. Microcephaly.
microcéfalo, la adj. Microcephalic, microcephalous.
microclima m. Microclimate.
microcosmo m. Microcosm.
microcósmico, ca adj. Microcosmic.
microfaradio m. FÍS. Microfarad.
microfilm o **microfilme** m. Microfilm.

— OBSERV. The plural in Spanish is *microfilmes*.

microfilmar v. tr. To microfilm.
microfísica f. Microphysics.
micrófono m. Microphone: *hablar por el micrófono*, to speak through *o* over the microphone.
microfotografía f. Microphotography (arte). || Microphotograph (fotografía).
micrografía f. Micrography.
microhmio o **microhm** m. ELECTR. Microhm.
microlentillas f. pl. Contact lenses.
micrométrico, ca adj. Micrometrical, micrometric.
micrómetro m. Micrometer.
micrón m. Micron (micra).
Micronesia n. pr. f. GEOGR. Micronesia.
micronesio, sia adj./s. Micronesian.
microonda f. Microwave.
microómnibus m. Minibus.
microorganismo m. Microorganism.
microscopia f. Microscopy.
microscópico, ca adj. Microscopic, microscopical.
microscopio m. Microscope: *microscopio electrónico*, electron microscope.
microsegundo m. Microsecond.
microsurco adj. m. Microgroove (disco).
— M. Microgroove.
microtaxi m. Minicab.
microteléfono m. Handset [combined hand microphone and receiver].
microtermia f. Microtherm (caloría menor).
micho, cha m. y f. FAM. Puss, pussy, kitty (gato).
midriasis f. MED. Mydriasis.
mieditis f. FAM. Jitters, *pl.*, funk (miedo). || — FAM. *Pasar mieditis*, to have the jitters, to have the wind up. | *Tener mieditis*, to be jittery *o* windy (permanentemente), to have the jitters, to have the wind up (temporalmente).
miedo m. Fear. || — *Dar miedo*, to be frightening. || *Dar miedo a alguien*, to frighten *o* to scare s.o. || FAM. *De miedo*, terrific, fantastic (formidable), awful, ghastly (horroroso), terribly well, marvellously (bien). || *Fue mayor el miedo que el daño* or *tuvimos más miedo que otra cosa*, we were more frightened than hurt, we were more frightened than anything else. || *Meterle miedo a uno*, to frighten *o* to scare s.o. || *Morirse de miedo*, to die of fright (sentido real), to be frightened *o* scared to death *o* out of one's wits (asustarse). || *Pasar mucho miedo*, to be very scared *o* frightened, to be terrified. || *Película de miedo*, horror film. || *Por miedo a*, for fear of. || *Por miedo a* or *de que*, for fear that. || *Que da* or *que mete miedo*, fearsome, frightful (adj.), frighteningly, fearsomely, frightfully, dreadfully (adv.): *de un feo que mete miedo*, dreadfully ugly. || *Sin miedo y sin tacha*, fearless and faultless, fearless and without reproach. || *Temblar de miedo*, to tremble with fear, to quake in one's shoes. || *Tener más miedo que vergüenza* or *que once viejas*, to be scared out of one's wits, to be in a blue funk (fam.) [pasar miedo], to be cowardly (ser miedoso). || *Tener miedo a* or *de*, to be afraid *o* scared of, to fear: *tener miedo a la oscuridad*, to be afraid of the dark. || *Tener miedo (de) que*, to be afraid that: *tengo miedo que haga una tontería*, I am afraid that he will do sth. stupid. || *Tener miedo hasta de la sombra de sí mismo*, to be afraid of one's own shadow. || *Tener un miedo cerval*, to be scared stiff.
miedoso, sa adj. Fearful, timorous. || Cowardly (cobarde).
miel f. Honey: *dulce como la miel*, as sweet as honey. || — FIG. *Dejar a uno con la miel en los labios*, to leave s.o. unsatisfied, to cut short s.o.'s enjoyment. | *Hacerse de miel*, to be too kind. || *Luna de miel*, honeymoon. || *Miel de caña*, molasses. || FAM. *Miel sobre hojuelas*, better still, so much the better. || FIG. *No hay miel sin hiel*, no rose without a thorn. | *Palabras de miel*, honeyed words. || *Panal de miel*, honeycomb. || FIG. *Ser todo miel*, to be all [sugar and] honey.
mielga f. BOT. Lucerne [U.S., alfalfa].
mielgo, ga adj. Twin.
mielina f. ANAT. Myelin, myeline.
mielitis f. MED. Myelitis.
miembro m. ANAT. Member, limb (brazo, pierna, etc.). | Member (miembro viril). || MAT. Member (de una ecuación). || FIG. Member (de una comunidad): *miembro vitalicio*, life member; *miembro con plenos poderes*, fully-fledged member. || ANAT. *Miembro viril*, virile *o* male member.
— Adj. Member: *Estado miembro*, member State.
miente f. (Ant.). Mind, thought. || — *Caer en* or *en las mientes*, to come to mind. || *Ni por mientes*, never. || *Parar* or *poner mientes en*, to think of, to consider. || *Traer a las mientes*, to recall, to bring to mind (recordar). || *Venirse a las mientes*, to occur to, to come to [s.o.'s] mind.
mientras adv./conj. While, whilst: *mientras yo trabajo, él juega*, while I work, he plays. || [For] as long as, so long as: *mientras viva, pensaré en usted*, I shall think of you as long as I live. || Meanwhile (mientras tanto). || — *Mientras más*, the more: *mientras más tiene, más desea*, the more he has, the more he wants. || *Mientras que*, whereas (oposición): *él lo confesó, mientras que tú no dijiste nada*, he owned up to it, whereas you said nothing. || *Mientras no se pruebe lo contrario*, until proven otherwise. || *Mientras tanto*, meanwhile, in the meantime.
miera f. Juniper oil.
miércoles m. Wednesday: *el miércoles pasado, que viene*, last, next Wednesday; *vendré el miércoles*, I shall come on Wednesday; *viene los miércoles, cada miércoles*, he comes on Wednesdays, every Wednesday. || — *Miércoles de ceniza*, Ash Wednesday. || *Miércoles Santo*, Holy Wednesday [of Holy Week].
mierda f. POP. Shit. || FAM. Muck, filth (suciedad). || — POP. *Es una mierda*, it is crap. | *Es un Don Mierda*, he's a nobody. | *¡Váyase a la mierda!*, go to hell!

mies f. Corn [U.S., grain] (cereales ya maduros): *segar la mies*, to reap the corn. || Harvest time (tiempo de la siega). || — Pl. Corn, *sing.*: *las mieses están a punto para ser segadas*, the corn is ready for reaping. || Cornfields (campos).
miga f. Crumb (migaja, parte interior del pan). || Bit, crumb (pedacito en general). || FIG. y FAM. Substance, marrow, pith, core (meollo). | Snag (dificultad). || (Ant.). Pap (papilla). || — Pl. CULIN. Fried breadcrumbs. || — FIG. y FAM. *Hacer buenas migas*, to get on well (*con*, with), to hit it off (*con*, with). | *Hacer malas migas*, to get on badly (*con*, with), not to hit it off *o* not to get on (*con*, with). || *Hacer migas*, to crumb (el pan), to smash to bits *o* pieces (hacer trizas), to shatter (cansar), to ruin (proyectos, etc.), to get [s.o.] down (fastidiar a una persona), to make mincemeat of (dejar muy maltrecho), to floor (confundir, derrotar en una discusión), to make [s.o.] go to pieces (deshacer moralmente). || *Hacerse migas*, to be smashed to pieces. || *Migas ilustradas*, breadcrumbs fried with pieces of larding bacon. || FIG. *Tener mucha miga*, to be marrowy *o* full of substance (tener sustancia), to be full of interest (ser interesante), to give sth. to think about, to be no straightforward matter (ser complicado). || *Tierra de miga*, heavy *o* clayey soil.
migaja f. Crumb (de pan). || Bit, crumb, scrap (pedacito). || FIG. Scrap, bit (de ciencia, etc.). || — Pl. Leftovers, leavings, scraps (sobras). || *Migaja de pan*, breadcrumb.
migajón m. Crumb. || FIG. y FAM. Marrow, pith, substance.
migala f. Mygale (araña).
migar v. tr. To crumble (partir en trozos). || To put lumps of bread in [a liquid]: *migar la leche*, to put lumps of bread in milk.
migración f. Migration.
migratorio, ria adj. Migratory, migrating (las aves). || Migratory: *movimiento migratorio*, migratory movement. || *Cultivo migratorio*, shifting cultivation.
Miguel n. pr. m. Michael (nombre de pila). || *Miguel Ángel*, Michelangelo.
mihrab m. Mihrab (de una mezquita).
mijo m. BOT. Millet.
mil adj. A thousand, one thousand: *mil hombres, mil años*, one thousand men, a thousand years. || Thousandth (milésimo). || — *El año mil*, the year one thousand. || *El año mil novecientos setenta y cinco*, the year nineteen [hundred and] seventy-five. || *Las Mil y Una Noches*, the Thousand and One Nights. || *Mil millones*, one *o* a milliard, a thousand million [U.S., a *o* one billion]: *cinco mil millones de pesetas*, five milliard pesetas. || FIG. *Mil veces*, thousands of times, a thousand times.
— M. [One *o* a] thousand (número). || — Pl. Thousands: *muchos miles de libras*, many thousands of pounds. || — FIG. *A las mil y quinientas*, at an unearthly hour. || *Miles de veces*, thousands of times. || *Miles y miles*, thousands and thousands.
miladi o **milady** f. Milady.
milagrería f. Fantastic tale, tale of miracles (narración). || Superstitious belief in miracles (tendencia a creer en milagros).
milagrero, ra adj. FAM. [Who is] always imagining miracles (que imagina milagros). | Miracle-working, miraculous (milagroso).
milagro m. Miracle. || Wonder: *los milagros de la naturaleza*, the wonders of Nature. || Miracle, wonder: *es un milagro que hayas salido vivo del accidente*, it is a miracle you came out of the accident alive. || TEATR. Miracle play (en la Edad Media). || Votive offering (exvoto). || — *Cuéntenos su vida y milagros*, tell us all about yourself, tell us your life history. || *De* or *por milagro*, miraculously, by a miracle. || FIG. *Hacer milagros*, to work wonders. | *Vive de milagro*, it is a miracle he is still alive (persona enferma), it is amazing how he manages (persona pobre).
milagroso, sa adj. Miraculous. || Miraculous, wonderful, extraordinary (maravilloso).
milamores m. BOT. Red valerian.
Milán n. pr. GEOGR. Milan.
milanés, esa adj./s. Milanese.
Milanesado n. pr. m. GEOGR. Milanese.
milano m. Kite (ave). || Flying gurnard (pez). || TECN. *Cola de milano*, dovetail [joint].
mildeu o **mildiu** m. AGR. Mildew.
milenario, ria adj. Millenary, millennial.
— M. Millennium (período, aniversario).
milenio m. Millennium [one thousand years].
milenrama f. BOT. Milfoil, yarrow.
milésimo, ma adj. Thousandth, millesimal.
— M. y f. Thousandth. || — F. *Amer.* Thousandth (de peso).
milhojas f. BOT. Milfoil, yarrow. || — M. Millefeuille, flaky pastry (pastel).
mili f. FAM. Military service. || *Estar en la mili*, to be in the army. || *Hacer la mili*, to do one's military service.
miliamperímetro m. Milliammeter.
miliamperio m. ELECTR. Milliampere.
miliar adj. Milliary (columna). || MED. Miliary: *fiebre miliar*, miliary fever.
milibar m. FÍS. Millibar.
milicia f. Militia (tropa): *milicias concejiles*, municipal militia. || Military service (servicio militar). || Soldiery, soldiering (profesión de soldado). || Art of war (arte de hacer la guerra). || Choir (de ángeles). || *Milicias universitarias*, students' military service, *sing.*
miliciano, na adj. [Of the] militia, military.
— M. Militiaman [pl. *militiamen*].
milicurie m. FÍS. Millicurie.
miligramo m. Milligram, milligramme.
mililitro m. Millilitre [U.S., milliliter].
milimétrico, ca adj. Millimetric.
milímetro m. Millimetre [U.S., millimeter].
milimicra f. Millimicron.
militante adj./s. Militant.
militar adj. Military: *academia militar*, military academy. || Militia (de la milicia). || — *Arte militar*, art of war. || *Cartilla militar*, military record. || *Código militar*, military law. || *Gobierno militar*, military government. || *Tribunal militar*, court-martial.
— M. Soldier, military man. || — *Los militares*, the military. || *Militar de infantería*, infantryman, foot-soldier.
militar v. intr. To serve in the army, to soldier (en el ejército). || To fight in the war, to militate (ant.) [en la guerra]. || FIG. To militate: *militan muchas pruebas en su favor*, much evidence militates in his favour. || — *Milita en el partido comunista*, he is a militant Communist-party member. || *Militar a favor de* or *en defensa de*, to plead for, to speak for (defender).
militarismo m. Militarism.
militarista adj. Militarist, militaristic.
— M. y f. Militarist.
militarización f. Militarization.
militarizar v. tr. To militarize.
militarote m. FAM. Military man, soldier.
militermia f. FÍS. Millitherm.
milivatio m. FÍS. Milliwatt.
milivoltio m. FÍS. Millivolt.
milmillonésimo, ma adj./s. Thousand-millionth [U.S., billionth].
milocha f. Kite (cometa).
milonga f. *Amer.* Popular Argentinian song and dance. || Andalusian song.
milonguero, ra m. y f. Singer *o* dancer of "milongas".
milord m. My Lord (tratamiento), lord (nombre). || Light barouche (carruaje).
— OBSERV. Pl. *milores*.
milpa f. *Amer.* Maize field [U.S., cornfield].
milpear v. intr. *Amer.* To till (labrar). | To sprout (el maíz).
milpiés m. ZOOL. Wood louse (cochinilla). | Millipede (miriápodo).
milrayas m. inv. Striped cloth (tejido).
milla f. Nautical *o* geographical mile, mile (medida marina). || Mile (medida inglesa).
millar m. Thousand: *un millar de libras*, a thousand pounds. || — Pl. Thousands (gran cantidad): *millares y millares de personas*, thousands and thousands of people. || *A millares*, by the thousand, in thousands.
— OBSERV. A milliard [U.S., billion] in Spanish is *mil millones*.
millarada f. About a thousand: *gastó una millarada de pesos*, he spent about a thousand pesos. || Thousands, *pl.* (muchos).
millón m. Million: *un millón de personas*, a million people; *millones de habitantes*, millions of inhabitants. || — *A millones*, by the million, in millions. || *Mil millones*, one *o* a milliard, a thousand million [U.S., one *o* a billion]. || *Se lo he dicho millones de veces*, I've told him thousands of times *o* time and time again. || *Un millón de gracias*, thanks a million.
millonada f. About a million. || FIG. Small fortune, packet: *su traje costó una millonada*, his suit cost a small fortune.
millonario, ria adj./s. Millionaire.
millonésimo, ma adj./s. Millionth.
mimar v. tr. To pet, to coddle (acariciar). || To pamper (tratar con muchas atenciones). || To spoil, to overindulge (a los niños): *niño mimado*, spoilt child. || To flatter (halagar). || To mime (teatro).
mimbral m. Osiery, osier bed.
mimbre m. y f. Osier (arbusto). || Wicker, withe (varita). || *Cesta de mimbre*, osier *o* wicker basket.
mimbrear v. intr. To sway (moverse).
— V. pr. To sway.
mimbreño, ña adj. Osier-like, willowy.
mimbrera f. Osier (arbusto). || Osier bed, osiery (mimbreral). || Willow (sauce).
mimbreral m. Osiery, osier bed.
mimbroso, sa adj. Osier, wicker (cosa). || Full of *o* covered in osiers (sitio).
mimeografía f. *Amer.* Mimeographing.
mimeografiar v. tr. *Amer.* To mimeograph.
mimeógrafo m. *Amer.* Mimeograph.
mimético, ca adj. Mimetic.
mimetismo m. Mimicry.
mímico, ca adj. Mimic.
— F. Mimic art, mimicry.
mimo m. Mime (teatro, actor). || Coddling, petting (caricias, cariño). || Pampering (atenciones). || Spoiling,

overindulgence (con los niños). || *Hacerle mimos a uno*, to coddle *o* to pamper s.o., to make a fuss of s.o.
mimógrafo m. Mimographer, writer of mimes.
mimosa f. Mimosa (flor).
mimoso, sa adj. Finicky, fussy (melindroso). || Coddling, petting (muy afectuoso). || Pampering, full of attentions (excesivamente atento). || Spoilt, spoiled, pampered (mimado). || Flattering (halagador). || Delicate (delicado).
mina f. Mine (yacimiento, excavación): *mina de plata*, silver mine. || Underground conduit (para conducir aguas, etc.), underground passage, tunnel (comunicación). || MIL. Mine (galería, explosivo): *mina anticarro, de acción retardada, contra personal, flotante, submarina*, antitank, delayed-action, antipersonnel, floating, submarine mine. || Lead: *mina de lápiz*, pencil lead. || FIG. Mine, storehouse: *mina de información*, mine of information. | Sinecure, cushy *o* soft job (fam.) [empleo]. || Mina (moneda griega). || — *Cámara* or *hornillo de mina*, mine chamber, blasthole. || *Campo de minas*, minefield. || *Escuela de Ingenieros de Minas*, mining college *o* school. || *Fondear minas*, to lay mines. || *Mina de carbón*, coal mine. || FIG. *Mina de oro*, gold mine. || *Rastrear minas*, to sweep mines.
minado m. Mining, mine-laying (colocación de minas).
minador, ra adj. Mining.
— M. Sapper (que abre minas), miner (que las instala) [soldado]. || Mining engineer (ingeniero). || MAR. Minelayer (buque).
minar v. tr. To mine, to bore *o* to tunnel through: *minar una montaña*, to mine a mountain. || MIL. To mine (colocar minas): *minar un puerto*, to mine a harbour. || To undermine, to wear away (cavar lentamente): *acantilados minados por las olas*, cliffs undermined by the waves. || FIG. To undermine (la autoridad, la salud, etc.). || — FIG. *Las drogas le han minado*, drugs have undermined his health. | *Minarle a uno el terreno*, to cut the ground from under s.o.'s feet.
minarete m. Minaret.

— OBSERV. *Minarete* is a Gallicism for *alminar*.

mineral adj. Mineral: *reino mineral*, mineral kingdom; *aguas minerales*, mineral waters.
— M. Mineral. || Ore: *mineral de hierro*, iron ore. || Fountainhead (origen).
mineralización f. Mineralization.
mineralizador, ra adj. Mineralizing.
mineralizar v. tr. To mineralize.
mineralogía f. Mineralogy.
mineralógico, ca adj. Mineralogical.
mineralogista m. Mineralogist.
minería f. Mining (laboreo, trabajo). || Mining industry (industria). || Mines, *pl.* (minas de un país o de una comarca). || Miners, *pl.* (los mineros).
minero, ra adj. Mining: *zona minera*, mining zone.
— M. Miner (obrero). || Mineowner (propietario), mineoperator (explotador). || *Amer.* Mouse (ratón).
Minerva n. pr. f. Minerva.
mingitorio m. Urinal.
mingo m. [Red] object ball (bola de billar). || FAM. *Poner el mingo*, to excel (sobresalir), to attract attention (llamar la atención), to cause a scandal (ser escandaloso).
miniar v. tr. To paint in miniature.
miniatura f. Miniature: *en miniatura*, in miniature. | *Coche miniatura*, miniature car.
miniaturista m. y f. Miniaturist, miniature painter.
miniaturización f. Miniaturization.
miniaturizar v. tr. To miniaturize.
minifalda f. Miniskirt.
minifundio m. Small property *o* farm.
mínima f. MÚS. Minim [U.S., half note] (nota). || Minimum temperature (temperatura). || FIG. Smallest *o* slightest thing (cosa muy pequeña).
minimizar v. tr. To minimize (quitar importancia a).
mínimo, ma adj. Minute, tiny (pequeño). || Minute, detailed (minucioso). || Minimum, lowest: *temperatura mínima*, minimum temperature. || Minimum, smallest, least: *la mínima cantidad*, the smallest amount. || — *Con el mínimo esfuerzo*, with the minimum amount of effort. || *En lo más mínimo*, in the least, in the slightest, at all. || *Mínimo común múltiplo*, lowest common multiple. || *Sin hacer el más mínimo esfuerzo*, without the slightest effort.
— M. Minim (religioso). || Minimum: *gana un mínimo de*, he earns a minimum of. || — *Al mínimo* or *a lo más mínimo*, to a minimum. || *Como mínimo*, at least, at the very least.
minimum m. Minimun.
minino, na m. y f. FAM. Puss, pussy, kitty (gato). | Child (niño).
minio m. Minium, red lead oxide.
ministerial adj. Ministerial.
ministerio m. Ministry. || — *Ministerio de Comercio*, Board of Trade [U.S., Department of Commerce]. || *Ministerio de Comunicaciones*, G.P.O., General Post office [U.S., Post Office Department]. || *Ministerio de Educación Nacional* or *de Instrucción Pública*, Ministry of Education [U.S., Department of Education] (en España ahora Ministerio de Educación y Ciencia). || *Ministerio de Estado* (ant.) or *de Asuntos Exteriores* or *de Relaciones Exteriores*, Foreign Office [U.S., State Department]. || *Ministerio de Gobernación*, v. GOBERNACIÓN. || *Ministerio de Hacienda*, v. HACIENDA. || *Ministerio de Información y Turismo*, Ministry [U.S., Department] of Information and Tourism. || *Ministerio de la Vivienda*, Ministry [U.S., Department] of Housing. || *Ministerio del Ejército* or *de la Guerra*, War Office [U.S., Defense Department]. || *Ministerio del Interior*, Ministry of the Interior. || *Ministerio de Marina*, Admiralty [U.S., Department of the Navy]. || *Ministerio de Obras Públicas*, Ministry [U.S., Department] of Public Works. || *Ministerio de Trabajo*, Ministry of Labour [U.S., Department of Labor]. || *Ministerio público* or *fiscal*, Department of the Public Prosecutor.
ministra f. Woman minister. || Minister's wife (esposa de un ministro).
ministrable adj. FAM. Likely to become a Minister of State.
ministro m. Minister: *ministro sin cartera*, minister without portfolio; *ministro de la Iglesia*, minister of Religion. || — *Ministro de Comunicaciones*, Postmaster General. || *Ministro de Educación*, Minister of Education [U.S., Secretary of Education.] || *Ministro de Estado* (ant) or *de Asuntos Exteriores* or *de Relaciones Exteriores*, Secretary of State for Foreign Affairs, Foreign Secretary [U.S., Secretary of State]. || *Ministro de Gobernación* or *del Interior*, v. GOBERNACIÓN. || *Ministro de Hacienda*, v. HACIENDA. || *Ministro de Trabajo*, Minister of Labour [U.S., Secretary of Labor]. || *Ministro plenipotenciario*, minister plenipotentiary. || *Primer Ministro*, Prime Minister, Premier (jefe del Gobierno).
minnesinger m. Minnesinger, minnesänger (juglar alemán).
minoración f. Diminution, lessening, reduction.
minorar v. tr. To diminish, to lessen, to reduce.
minoría f. Minority. || *Minoría de edad*, minority, infancy, nonage.
minoridad f. (P.us.). Minority, nonage, infancy.
minorista m. Retailer, retail dealer (comerciante al por menor). || REL. Clergyman holding minor orders.
— Adj. Retail (comercio).
minoritario, ria adj. Minority.
Minotauro n. pr. m. MIT. Minotaur.
minucia f. Trifle (menudencia). || — Pl. (Ant.). Tithe (*sing.*) on fruit (diezmo). || Minutiae, minor details.
minuciosidad f. Meticulousness, thoroughness (de persona). || Minuteness (de inspección, estudio, etc.).
minucioso, sa adj. Meticulous, thorough, scrupulous (persona). || Minute, detailed, thorough (inspección, estudio, etc.).
minué m. Minuet (baile).
minuendo m. MAT. Minuend.
minúsculo, la adj. Minuscule, minute, diminutive (diminuto). || Minuscule, petty (insignificante). || Small (letra).
— F. Small letter.
minuta f. Menu (comida). || Draft (borrador). || Minute, memorandum (apunte). || List of employees, payroll (lista). || [Lawyer's] bill (cuenta de un abogado).
minutar v. tr. To draft [a contract].
minutario m. Minute book.
minutería f. Automatic time switch (interruptor).
minutero m. Minute hand (del reloj).
minuto m. Minute (tiempo): *vuelvo dentro de un minuto*, I shall be back in a minute. || Minute (de círculo). || — *Al minuto*, a moment later: *y al minuto estaba de vuelta*, and a moment later he was back; this very minute, at once; *tráigamelo al minuto*, bring it to me this very minute. || *Minuto a minuto*, minute by minute.
Miño n. pr. m. GEOGR. Minho (río).
miñona f. IMPR. Minion.
mío, mía adj. y pron. poses. de la 1.ª pers. Mine: *este libro es el mío*, this book is mine; *esto es mío*, this is mine. || Of mine, my (después del sustantivo): *un amigo mío*, a friend of mine, one of my friends; *amigo mío*, my friend; *queridos hijos míos*, my dear children. || FIG. My dear (cariño): *padre mío*, my dear father. || — *¡Dios mío!*, my God!, good heavens! || *En derredor mío*, around me. || FIG. y FAM. *Ésta es la mía*, this is the moment I've been waiting for. | *Esto es cosa mía*, this is my affair *o* business. || FAM. *Hijo mío*, my son (dicho por un cura), son, young fellow (en general). || *Lo mío*, my affairs, what belongs to *o* concerns me: *no se meta en lo mío*, don't interfere in my affairs. || *Lo mío, mío y lo tuyo de entrambos*, what's yours is mine and what's mine is my own. || *Los míos*, my folks, my people (familia).

— OBSERV. The construction of the type la *casa mía* is frequent in Spanish and reinforces the idea of possession.

miocardio m. ANAT. Myocardium: *infarto del miocardio*, infarct of the myocardium.
miocarditis f. MED. Myocarditis.
mioceno adj./s.m. GEOL. Miocene.
miógrafo m. Myograph.
mioma m. MED. Myoma.
miope adj. Myopic, shortsighted, nearsighted.
— M. y f. Shortsighted *o* nearsighted person.
miopía f. MED. Myopia, shortsightedness, nearsightedness.

miosota f. o **miosotis** m. BOT. German madwort, forget-me-not.
mir m. Mir (comunidad agrícola en la Rusia zarista).
mira f. Sight (de un instrumento, un arma). || Levelling rod *o* staff (topografía). || Watchtower (torre). || FIG. Intention, design (intención): *con miras poco honradas*, with dishonourable intentions. | Objective, goal, aim (objetivo). || — Pl. MAR. Prow guns. || — *Amplitud de miras*, broad-mindedness. || *Con miras a*, with a view to. || *De miras estrechas*, narrow-minded. || *Estar a la mira de*, to be on the lookout for, to be watching out for. || *Estrechez de miras*, narrow-mindedness. || *Línea de mira*, line of sight. || *Mira taquimétrica*, stadia rod. || FIG. *Poner la mira* or *las miras en*, to cast one's eyes upon (mirar), to aspire to, to aim at (tener como objectivo): *poner la mira en el ascenso*, to aim at promotion; to fix one's sights on, to have one's eyes on (echar el ojo a). || *Punto de mira*, front sight (de una escopeta), target (blanco). || FIG. *Tener sus miras en*, to have one's sights fixed on, to have designs on (codiciar).
mirabel m. Mock cypress, summer cypress. || Sunflower (girasol). || — *Ciruela mirabel*, mirabelle [plum] (fruto). || *Ciruelo mirabel*, mirabelle [plum tree] (árbol).
mirada f. Look: *una mirada severa*, a stern look. || Eyes, *pl.*, look: *leer en la mirada*, to read in s.o.'s eyes, to tell by s.o.'s look. || Glance (ojeada): *abarcar con una sola mirada*, to take in with a single glance. || Gaze, stare, regard (p.us.) [prolongada]. || Look, expression (expresión): *una mirada melancólica*, a melancholy look. || Knowing look (guiño). || — *Apartar la mirada de*, to look away from. || *Clavar* or *fijar la mirada en*, to fix one's eyes on, to stare at. || *Detuvo la mirada en*, his eyes fell upon. || *Echar una mirada a*, to glance at, to run one's eye over (mirar), to keep an eye on (cuidar, vigilar). || *Fulminar con la mirada*, to look daggers at. || *Huir de las miradas de uno*, to avoid looking s.o. in the eye (no mirar en los ojos), to avoid being seen by s.o., to hide from s.o.'s sight (evitar ser visto). || *Lanzar una mirada a*, to glance at. || *Levantar la mirada*, to raise one's eyes, to look up. || *Mirada de soslayo*, sidelong glance. || *Mirada fija*, stare. || *Seguir con la mirada*, to follow with one's eyes (algo, alguien que se mueve), to watch [sth. *o* s.o.] move *o* go away (algo, alguien que se aleja). || *Ser el blanco de las miradas*, to be the centre of attention. || *Tener la mirada perdida*, to have a faraway *o* distant look in one's eyes. || *Volver la mirada*, V. VOLVER.
miradero m. Centre of attention *o* attraction, cynosure (punto de mira). || Vantage point, lookout, observatory (lugar de observación).
miradita f. Knowing look (guiño). || Peek, quick glance (mirada).
mirado, da adj. Cautious, circumspect (receloso). || Looked upon *o* on, thought of: *bien* or *mal mirado*, well *o* badly looked on. || Considerate (considerado). || Careful (cuidadoso): *es muy mirado con sus cosas personales*, he is very careful with his personal belongings. || *Bien mirado, el asunto no tiene importancia*, all things considered *o* all in all, the matter is of no importance.
mirador m. Mirador, windowed balcony, bay window (balcón). || Mirador, observatory, vantage point, lookout (lugar de observación).
miraguano m. BOT. Silver thatch, thatch palm.
miramiento m. Look, looking (acción de mirar). || Caution, circumspection, prudence, care (circunspección). || Considerateness, consideration, regard (comedimiento). || Misgiving (timidez). || — Pl. Respect, *sing.*, regard, *sing.*, consideration, *sing.*: *tener miramientos con las personas de edad*, to show respect towards elderly people. || — *Andar con miramientos*, to go *o* to tread carefully. || *Sin miramientos*, inconsiderately, disrespectfully, without consideration, without regard (sin respeto), without ceremony (sin cumplidos).
mirar v. tr. e intr. To look. || To look at: *mirar un cuadro*, to look at a painting. || To look in: *mirar un escaparate*, to look in a shopwindow. || To watch: *mirar un espectáculo*, to watch a show. || FIG. To think [about], to consider (pensar): *sin mirar las consecuencias*, without considering the consequences. || To watch, to be careful, to mind, to look [to] (tener cuidado): *mire usted dónde pone los pies*, watch where you're putting your feet. || To go and see, to go and look, to see (informarse): *mira si ha llegado una carta*, go and see if a letter has arrived. || To see, to make sure (cuidar): *mire a que no le falte nada*, see that you're not short of anything. || To keep an eye on, to watch (vigilar). || FIG. To look to, to take account of, to tend to (tender, cuidar): *mirar por sus intereses*, to look to one's interests. || To look at *o* in, to search, to examine (registrar). || To look up to, to look highly upon (mostrar estimación a). || — *Bien mirado todo* or *mirándolo bien* or *si se mira bien*, all in all, upon reflexion, all things considered. || FAM. *De mírame y no me toques*, very fragile (cosa frágil), unapproachable, like a bear with a sore head (de carácter áspero). || *¡Mira!*, look! (llamando la atención), look here! (protestando), why!, well I never! (sorpresa), listen! (¡oye!), look out! (cuidado). || *¡Mira a quién se lo cuentas* or *se lo vas a contar!*, you're telling me!, you can say that again!, you don't say! || *¡Mira lo que haces!*, watch what you're doing. || *¡Mira qué casa más hermosa!, ¡mira qué hermosa es!*, what a beautiful house!, how beautiful it is! || *¡Mira que no tiene suerte!*, he really is unlucky! || *¡Mira que si...!*, imagine if...!, just think if...!: *¡mira que si no hubiera venido!*, imagine if he hadn't come! || *¡Mira que si es verdad!*, if ever it is true! || *¡Mira quien habla!*, look *o* hark who's talking!, you can talk! || *Mirar a*, to look to, to think about: *sólo mira a su provecho*, he only looks to his own gain; to watch, to look at, to gaze at: *mirar a la gente que pasa*, to watch the people go by; to overlook, to look out on, to look on to, to open on to: *mi ventana mira a la calle*, my window overlooks the street; to face, to look towards: *la casa mira al sur*, the house faces the south; to look in: *mirar a la cara*, to look in the face *o* eye. || *Mirar al trasluz*, to hold up to the light (por transparencia), to candle (un huevo). || *Mirar atrás*, to look back. || FIG. *Mirar bien, mal a uno*, to like, to dislike s.o. | *Mirar con buenos, con malos ojos*, V. OJO. || *Mirar con los ojos abiertos como platos*, to look at goggle-eyed *o* wide-eyed, to goggle at. || *Mirar con mala cara*, to scowl at. || *Mirar de arriba abajo*, to look up and down, to eye from head to foot. || *Mirar de hito en hito*, to stare at. || *Mirar de reojo* or *de soslayo* or *con el rabillo del ojo*, to look at out of the corner of one's eye. || *Mirar de través*, to look sideways at. || *Mirar fijamente a uno*, to stare at s.o. || *Mirar frente a frente* or *cara a cara*, to look straight in the face *o* in the eye. || *Mirar por*, to look out of: *mirar por la ventana*, to look out of the window; to look through: *mirar por un agujero*, to look through a hole: *mirar algo por el microscopio*, to look at sth. through a microscope; to look after, to take care of, to tend to: *mirar por su salud*, to look to one's health; *mirar por los niños*, to look after the children; to think of: *mira por tu reputación*, think of your reputation. || *Mirar por encima*, to glance briefly at, to glance over, to skim. || FIG. y FAM. *Mirar por encima del hombro*, to look down on, to look down one's nose at. | *Mirar por los cuatro costados*, to eye up *o* over, to eye from head to foot (una persona), to look at from every angle (un problema). || *No se dignó mirarme*, he would not *o* he did not deign to look at me. || *Se mire como se mire* or *por donde se mire*, whichever way you look at it. || *Sin mirar en gastos*, regardless of expense.
— V. pr. To look at o.s.: *mirarse al* or *en el espejo*, to look at o.s. in the mirror. || To look at one another *o* each other (dos o más personas). || To think carefully, to think twice: *se mirará muy bien de* or *antes de vender su casa*, you had better think twice about *o* before selling your house. || To look to one's dignity *o* decorum (comportarse con decoro), to look to one's modesty *o* decency (comportarse con recato). || FIG. *Mirarse en alguno*, to be completely wrapped up in s.o. (querer mucho), to model o.s. upon (tomar como ejemplo).
mirasol m. Sunflower (girasol).
miríada f. Myriad. || *Miríadas de estrellas*, myriads of stars, a myriad of stars.
miriagramo m. Myriagramme, myriagram.
miriámetro m. Myriametre [U.S., myriameter].
miriápodo adj./s.m. ZOOL. Myriapod, myriopod.
mirífico, ca adj. Wonderful, marvellous.
mirilla f. Peephole, spyhole (para observar). || Target, sight (para dirigir visuales). || MIL. Vision slit (de carros de combate).
miriñaque m. Crinoline (de falda). || Trinket, bauble (alhaja). || *Amer.* Pilot, rail guard, cowcatcher (de locomotora).
mirlo m. Blackbird (ave). || FIG. y FAM. Affected gravity *o* solemnity. || — *Buscar un mirlo blanco*, to look for the impossible. || FIG. *Un mirlo blanco*, a rare bird, one in a million.
mirmidón m. Dwarf, very small man.
mirón, ona adj. Nosey [U.S. nosy], inquisitive (curioso). || Onlooking (mientras trabajan otros, etc.). — M. y f. Nosey-parker (curioso). || Onlooker, spectator (espectador). || Kibitzer (jugando a las cartas). || *Estar de mirón*, to stand by (quedarse sin hacer nada).
mirra f. BOT. Myrrh.
mirtáceas f. pl. BOT. Myrtaceae.
mirtillo m. BOT. Bilberry (arándano).
mirto m. BOT. Myrtle (arrayán).
misa f. Mass. || — *Ayudar a misa*, to serve at Mass. || *Cantar misa*, to sing *o* to say one's first Mass [a newly-ordained priest]. || *Decir misa*, to say Mass. || FIG. *Estar como en misa*, to be deathly silent, to be as quiet as a mouse (una persona) *o* as mice (varias personas) [fam.]. || *Ir a misa*, to go to Mass, to attend Mass. || *Misa cantada*, Sung Mass. || *Misa de campaña*, outdoor Mass. || *Misa de cuerpo presente*, requiem *o* funeral Mass. || *Misa de difuntos*, Mass for the dead, requiem. || *Misa del alba*, morning Mass. || *Misa del gallo*, midnight Mass [on Christmas Eve]. || *Misa mayor*, High Mass. || *Misa negra*, black mass. || *Misa pontifical*, Pontifical Mass. || *Misa rezada*, Low Mass. || FAM. *No saber de la misa la media*, not to know what one is talking about. || *Oír misa*, to hear Mass. || FAM. *Ser de misa y olla*, to be ignorant. || *Tocar a misa*, to ring for mass.

misacantano m. Priest saying his first Mass (por primera vez). || Fully ordained priest [entitled to say Mass] (que puede celebrar misa).
misal m. Missal (libro).
misantropía f. Misanthropy.
misantrópico, ca adj. Misanthropic.
misántropo adj. m. Misanthropic.
— M. Misanthrope, misanthropist.
miscelánea f. Miscellany, medley (mezcla). || Miscellany, miscellanea, *pl.* (colección): *miscelánea literaria,* literary miscellany.
misceláneo, a adj. Miscellaneous.
miscible adj. Miscible (mezclable).
miserable adj. Wretched (muy pobre): *una habitación, una familia miserable,* a wretched room, family. || Miserable (ínfimo, escaso, lastimoso): *un sueldo miserable,* a miserable wage; *estaba en un estado miserable,* he was in a miserable condition. || Shameful, despicable, contemptible, vile (malvado): *conducta miserable,* shameful conduct. || Miserly, mean, stingy (tacaño). || *¡Miserable de mí!,* woe is me!
— M. y f. Scoundrel, wretch (canalla). || Miser, skinflint (tacaño).
miserere m. Miserere. || MED. *Cólico miserere,* ileus.
miseria f. Wretchedness, misery (de condiciones). || Misery, destitution, extreme poverty: *vivir en la miseria,* to live in misery. || Misery, misfortune, calamity (desgracia). || Miserliness, meanness, stinginess (avaricia). || Lice, *pl.,* vermin, *pl.* (piojos). || FIG. y FAM. Pittance, next to nothing: *trabajar por una miseria,* to work for a pittance *o* for next to nothing. || — *Estar en la miseria,* to be poverty-striken *o* down-and-out. || *Miseria negra,* dire poverty.
misericordia f. Mercy, compassion: *pedir misericordia,* to beg for mercy. || Misericord, misericorde (puñal, pieza en los coros de las iglesias).
misericordioso, sa adj. Merciful, compassionate: *misericordioso con los desvalidos,* merciful to the destitute.
misero, ra adj. FAM. Churchy, who attends Mass frequently. || Who receives a stipend only for saying Mass (sacerdote).
mísero, ra adj./s. V. MISERABLE.
misérrimo, ma adj. Very wretched (muy pobre). || Very miserly (tacaño).
misia o **misiá** f. *Amer.* FAM. Missus, Missis (señora).
misil m. Missile (cohete).
misión f. Mission (cometido). || REL. Mission.
misional adj. Missionary.
misionero, ra adj./s. Missionary.
misionero, ra adj. [Of *o* from] Misiones (en Argentina y Paraguay).
— M. y f. Native *o* inhabitant of Misiones.
Misisipí n. pr. m. GEOGR. Mississippi.
misiva f. Missive (carta).
mismamente adv. FAM. Just, precisely, exactly.
mismísimo, ma adj. FAM. Himself, herself, themselves: *vi al mismísimo presidente,* I saw the president himself. || Very same, selfsame: *en ese mismísimo momento,* at that very same moment. || — *En el mismísimo centro,* in the very centre, right in the centre. || *Es el mismísimo demonio,* he is the devil himself *o* the devil in person.
mismo, ma adj. Same (antes del sustantivo): *del mismo color,* of the same colour; *en la misma época,* at the same time. || Myself, yourself, himself, herself, ourselves, yourselves, themselves, etc. (después de pronombres personales): *yo mismo,* I myself; *él mismo,* he himself; *ellos mismos,* they themselves. || Itself (pl. *themselves*): *ocurrió en la ciudad misma,* it happened in the city itself; *es la vanidad misma,* he is vanity itself. || Himself, herself, themselves (para corroborar la identidad de la persona): *el mismo presidente se levantó,* the president himself stood up. || Own, very, even (hasta): *sus mismos hermanos le odiaban,* his own *o* very brothers hated him, even his brothers hated him. || Just (igual): *esto mismo decías tú,* that's just what you said. || Right (después de los adverbios de lugar): *aquí mismo,* right here. || — *Ahora mismo,* right now, right away. || *Al mismo tiempo* or *a un mismo tiempo,* at the same time. || *Así mismo,* likewise, in the same way (de la misma manera), also (también), that's it, that's right (así es). || *Ayer mismo,* just yesterday, only yesterday. || *Del mismo modo,* in the same way (de la misma manera), likewise, also (también). || FIG. *El mismo que viste y calza,* the very same, none other. || *En el mismo suelo,* on the bare floor. || *En sí mismo,* in itself. || *Es lo mismo,* it's all the same, it's the same thing, it makes no difference. || *Eso viene a ser lo mismo,* that amounts to *o* comes to the same thing. || *Estar en las mismas,* to be back where one started. || *Este chico y el que vi ayer son el mismo,* this boy and the one I saw yesterday are one and the same. || *Hoy mismo,* today, this very day. || *Lo mismo,* the same [thing]. || *Lo mismo con,* just like, the same goes for. || *Lo mismo da,* it doesn't matter, it's all the same, it makes no difference. || *Lo mismo que,* the same as, just like. || *Lo mismo si... que si...,* it makes no difference whether... or whether... || *Lo mismo uno que otro,* both of them. || *Mañana mismo,* [as early as] tomorrow: *saldré mañana mismo,* I shall leave [as early as] tomorrow. || *Por lo mismo,* for that reason, that is why. || *Por lo mismo que,* for the very reason that. || *Por sí mismo,* [by] o.s. || *Quedar en las mismas,* to be back where one started. || *Volver a las mismas,* to get back to where one started.
misogamia f. Misogamy.
misoginia f. Misogyny.
misógino, na adj. Misogynous.
— M. Misogynist.
miss f. Miss.
mistar v. tr. FAM. *No mistar,* to keep quiet *o* hush.
misterio m. Mystery. || TEATR. Mystery (auto). || — *Andar con misterios* or *hacer misterios,* to act in a mysterious manner. || *Hablar con misterio,* to speak mysteriously. || *Hacer algo con misterio,* to do sth. secretly *o* in secret.
misterioso, sa adj. Mysterious.
mística f. Mystical theology. || Mysticism.
misticismo m. Mysticism.
místico, ca adj. Mystical.
— M. y f. Mystic.
mistificación f. Falsification || Trick (engaño).
mistificar v. tr. To falsify (falsificar). || To trick, to deceive (engañar).
mistral m. Mistral (viento).
Misuri n. pr. m. GEOGR. Missouri.
mita f. *Amer.* Mita. | Ancient tribute. | Cattle shipped by train.

— OBSERV. *La mita* was an institution of indigenous origin which, adopted by the Spanish colonists, regulated the work of the Indians. The latter were contracted by drawing lots to work in the mines and on public works.

mitaca f. *Amer.* Harvest (cosecha).
mitad f. Half: *a mitad de precio,* at half price. || Middle (centro): *en la mitad de la novela,* in the middle of the novel. || FAM. Half (esposa): *mi cara mitad,* my better half. || — *En* or *a la mitad del camino,* halfway, halfway there (yendo a un sitio). || *En mitad de,* in the middle of. || *Mitad y mitad,* half and half. || FAM. *Partir a uno por la mitad,* to ruin s.o.'s plans. || *Partir por la mitad,* to cut in half, to cut into two (cortar).
— Adv. Half: *mitad hombre, mitad animal,* half man, half beast.
mitayo m. Indian employed in the mines and on public works (v. MITA).
mítico, ca adj. Mythical.
mitigación f. Mitigation.
mitigador, ra adj. Mitigating, mitigative, mitigatory.
— M. y f. Mitigator.
mitigante adj. Mitigating, mitigative, mitigatory.
mitigar v. tr. To mitigate: *mitigar una pena,* to mitigate a penalty. || To alleviate, to relieve (un dolor, la soledad). || To quench (la sed). || To satisfy (el hambre). || To relieve: *mitigar el paro,* to relieve unemployment. || To palliate (paliar). || To allay (preocupaciones). || To reduce (el calor).
mitin m. Meeting, rally.

— OBSERV. Pl. *mítines.*

mito m. Myth.
mitología f. Mythology.
mitológico, ca adj. Mythological.
mitólogo m. Mythologist.
mitomanía f. Mythomania.
mitómano, na adj./s. Mythomaniac.
mitón m. Mitt (guante).
mitosis f. BIOL. Mitosis.
mitote m. Dance of the Aztec Indians (baile).
mitra f. Mitre [U.S., miter]: *recibir la mitra,* to receive the mitre.
mitrado, da adj. Mitred [U.S., mitered]: *abad mitrado,* mitred abbot.
— M. Archbishop (arzobispo), bishop (obispo), prelate (prelado).
Mitrídates n. pr. HIST. Mithridates.
mitridatismo m. Mithridatism.
miura m. Fierce breed of fighting bull (toro). || FIG. Wild one (indomable). | Devil (malintencionado).
mixomatosis f. VET. Myxomatosis.
mixomicetos m. pl. BOT. Myxomycetes.
mixtificación f. V. MISTIFICACIÓN.
mixtificar v. tr. V. MISTIFICAR.

— OBSERV. This verb and its substantive, although in current use, are not admitted by the Academy.

mixto, ta adj. Mixed: *escuela mixta,* mixed school; *comisión mixta,* mixed committee. || Half-bred (mestizo). || — *Tren mixto,* passenger and goods train. || *Tribunal mixto,* mixed tribunal.
— M. Match (fósforo). || Inflammable compound (sustancia inflamable).
mixtura f. Mixture (mezcla). || Compound (medicamento). || *Amer.* Flowers (*pl.*) given as a gift (flores).
mixturar v. tr. To mix.
mízcalo m. Edible milk mushroom (hongo).
mnemónico, ca adj. Mnemonic.
— M. y f. Mnemonic person.
mnemotecnia o **mnemotécnica** f. Mnemonics.
mnemotécnico, ca adj. Mnemonic.
moabita adj./s. Moabite.
moaré m. Moire (tela).
mobiliario m. Furniture. || JUR. [Household] furniture.
moblaje m. Furnishings, *pl.,* furniture.

moblar* v. tr. To furnish.
moca m. Mocha.
mocar v. tr. To blow *o* to wipe [s.o.'s] nose.
— V. pr. To blow *o* to wipe one's nose.
mocarrera f. Runny nose: *tener mocarrera*, to have a runny nose.
mocarro m. FAM. Snot [which runs from the nose].
mocasín m. Moccasin (calzado).
mocear v. intr. FAM. To sow one's wild oats (correr aventuras). | To act like a youngster (comportarse como un mozo).
mocedad f. Youth (juventud). || Prank (travesura). || — Pl. Youth, *sing.*: *en mis mocedades*, in my youth.
mocerío m. [Group of] young people.
mocetón, ona m. y f. Strapping lad (chico), strapping *o* buxom lass (chica).
moción f. Motion (proposición): *moción de censura*, censure motion; *adoptar una moción*, to carry a motion; *votar una moción*, to vote on a motion; *presentar una moción*, to bring forward *o* to table a motion; *se rechaza la moción*, the motion is rejected *o* lost; *queda aprobada la moción por veinte votos a favor, siete en contra y dos abstenciones*, the motion is carried by 20 votes to 7 with 2 abstentions; *apoyar una moción*, to second a motion; *declarar una moción admisible*, to declare a motion receivable; *aplazar una moción sine die*, to table a motion; *¿se puede aceptar esta moción?*, would this motion be in order? || Motion, movement (movimiento). || Inclination (inclinación). || Divine inspiration.
mocito, ta adj. Very young.
— M. y f. Youngster, lad (chico), young girl, youngster, lass (chica).
moco m. Mucus, mucosity (término científico), snot (fam.). || Snuff (cabo de la mecha). || Drippings, *pl.* (de una vela). || Caruncle (del pavo). || Red-hot scoria *o* slag (del hierro). || MAR. Martingale. || — FIG. y FAM. *Caérsele el moco*, to be a dunce. || *Limpiar los mocos a alguien*, to wipe *o* to blow s.o.'s nose. || *Limpiarse los mocos*, to blow one's nose. || FIG. y FAM. *Llorar a moco tendido*, V. LLORAR. | *No es moco de pavo*, it's no trifle; *este trabajo no es moco de pavo*, this job is no trifle. | *Seis mil dólares no son moco de pavo*, six thousand dollars are not to be sniffed at. || *Se me caen los mocos*, my nose is running.
mocoso, sa adj. Snotty-nosed. || Bad mannered (maleducado).
— M. y f. Snotty-nosed child. || FIG. y FAM. Brat (niño mal educado).
mocosuelo, la adj. Snotty-nosed.
— M. y f. Snotty-nosed child *o* youngster.
mocosuena adv. FAM. *Traducir "mocosuena, mocosuene"*, to translate word for word.
mochales adj. inv. FAM. *Estar mochales*, to be crazy *o* cracked (loco). | *Estar mochales por*, to be crazy about, to be head over heels in love with (enamorado).
moche m. *A troche y moche*, helter-skelter, pell-mell (rápida y confusamente), haphazardly (al azar).
mochila f. Pack (del soldado). || Rucksack, pack, knapsack (de excursionista, etc.). || Provisions, *pl.* (víveres).
mocho, cha adj. Blunt (sin punta). || Hornless, dehorned (sin cuernos). || Pruned (mondado de ramas). || Topped (mondado de copa). || FIG. y FAM. Shorn (pelado). || *Amer.* Mutilated (mutilado). | Conservative (conservador). | Reactionary (reaccionario). || *Escopeta mocha*, hammerless rifle.
— M. Handle (de un instrumento). || Stock, butt (culata).
mochuelo m. ZOOL. Litte owl (ave). || FIG. y FAM. Bore, burdensome task. || IMPR. Omission (omisión). || — FIG. *Cada mochuelo a su olivo*, everyone about his own business, everyone to his own home. || FAM. *Cargar con el mochuelo*, to get stuck *o* lumbered with the worst job (hacer el trabajo más fastidioso), to be left holding the baby [U.S., to carry the can] (cargar con la responsabilidad).
moda f. Fashion, style: *la moda del año 1975*, the 1975 fashion, the fashion in 1975. || — *A la moda*, fashionable, in fashion, in (fam.) [adjetivo], fashionably, in fashion (adverbio): *vestir a la moda*, to dress fashionably. || *A la moda de París*, in the Paris fashion, in the Paris style. || *De moda*, in fashion, fashionable, in (fam.): *estar de moda*, to be in fashion, to be fashionable. || *Estar muy de moda*, to be highly fashionable, to be all the rage (fam.). || *Fuera de moda*, out of fashion. || *Pasado de moda*, old-fashioned, out of date. || *Pasarse de moda*, to go out of fashion. || *Ponerse de moda*, to come into fashion, to become fashionable. || *Revista de modas*, fashion magazine. || *Seguir la moda*, to follow fashion. || *Ser la última moda*, to be the latest fashion *o* the latest style. || *Tienda de modas*, fashion shop.
modal adj. Modal.
— M. pl. Manners: *modales distinguidos*, distinguished manners; *modales finos*, refined manners. || — *Con buenos modales*, politely, courteously. || *Tener buenos, malos modales*, to be well-mannered, ill-mannered. || FAM. *¡Vaya modales!*, what manners!
modalidad f. Modality. || Form, kind, type (clase). || Category (categoría). || Way, manner (modo).
modelado m. Modelling [U.S., modeling]: *el modelado de una escultura*, the modelling of a sculpture. || Shape (forma).
modelador, ra adj. Modelling [U.S., modeling].
— M. Modeller [U.S., modeler].
modelar v. tr. To model. || FIG. To model, to pattern: *modelar su conducta según*, to model one's behaviour on. | To form, to shape: *modelar el alma de alguien*, to form s.o.'s mind.
modelista m. y f. Modeller [U.S., modeler] (modelador). || Dress designer (de costura).
modelo adj. inv. Model: *es una niña modelo*, she is a model child; *empresa modelo*, model company.
— M. Model (patrón): *tomar por modelo*, to take as a model. || FIG. Model. || *Modelo reducido*, scale model.
— F. Model, fashion model (de modas). || *Desfile de modelos*, fashion show, fashion parade.
moderación f. Moderation: *obrar con moderación*, to act in *o* with moderation.
moderado, da adj./s. Moderate.
— Adv. MÚS. Messo forte, moderato.
moderador, ra adj. Moderating.
— M. y f. Moderator. || — M. FÍS. Moderator.
moderar v. tr. To moderate: *moderar sus deseos*, to moderate one's desires. || To control, to restrain (restringir). || To reduce (la velocidad).
— V. pr. To control o.s. || *Moderarse en las palabras*, to be careful what one says, to measure one's words (hablar con comedimiento).
modernamente adv. Recently (recientemente). || At the present [time], at the moment, nowadays (actualmente).
modernidad f. Modernity.
modernismo m. Modernism.
modernista adj./s. Modernist.
modernización f. Modernization.
modernizar v. tr. To modernize.
— V. pr. To be modernized.
moderno, na adj. Modern: *la edad moderna*, the modern age. || *A la moderna*, in the modern way.
— M. y f. Modern (persona). || *Lo moderno*, modern things (cosas modernas), the modern thing.
modestia f. Modesty. || *Vestido con modestia*, simply dressed (con sencillez), modestly dressed (con decoro).
modesto, ta adj. Modest.
— M. y f. Modest person.
modicidad f. Moderateness, reasonableness.
módico, ca adj. Moderate, reasonable: *pagar una suma módica*, to pay a moderate amount.
modificable adj. Modifiable.
modificación f. Modification.
modificador, ra o **modificante** adj. Modifying.
— M. y f. Modifier.
modificar v. tr. To modify (transformar).
modificativo, va adj. Modifying.
modificatorio, ria adj. Modifying.
modillón m. ARQ. Modillion.
modismo m. GRAM. Idiom.
modista m. y f. Dressmaker, couturier, modiste.
modistería f. *Amer.* Fashion shop.
modistilla f. Dressmaker's assistant (aprendiza). || Dressmaker (modista importante).
modisto m. Dressmaker, couturier, modiste.

— OBSERV. This word is a barbarism often used in place of *modista*.

modo m. Manner, way, mode (manera): *a su modo*, in one's own way; *modo de pensar*, way of thinking. || GRAM. Mood. || MÚS. Mode. || — Pl. Manners (modales): *buenos, malos modos*, good, bad manners. || — *Adverbio de modo*, adverb of manner. || *Modo adverbial*, adverbial phrase. || *Modo de empleo*, instructions (*pl.*) for use. || *Modo subjuntivo*, subjunctive mood.

— OBSERV. *Modo* and *manera* are often interchangeable. For the expressions in which *modo* is used see MANERA which can be substituted by *modo*.

modorro, rra adj. Drowsy, heavy (adormecido). || Infected by staggers (el ganado). || Overripe, soft (una fruta). || FIG. Ignorant (ignorante).
— M. y f. Ignorant person. || — M. Miner poisoned by mercury (minero). || — F. Drowsiness, heaviness (sueño pesado). || Dullness, torpor (sopor). || VET. Staggers, *pl.* (del ganado lanar).
modosidad f. Quietness, good behaviour [U.S., good behavior].
modoso, sa adj. Quiet, well-behaved. || Modest, demure (recatado).
modulación f. Modulation. || *Modulación de frecuencia*, frequency modulation.
modulador, ra adj. Modulating.
— M. y f. Modulator.
modular v. intr. y tr. To modulate.
módulo m. MAT. y FÍS. Modulus. || Module (en arquitectura). || Anthropometric measurement (antropometría). || MÚS. Modulation. || Module (lunar).
modus vivendi m. Modus vivendi.
mofa f. Mockery (burla). || *Hacer mofa de*, to mock, to make fun of, to scoff at, to jeer at.
mofador, ra adj. Mocking, scoffing, sneering, jeering.
— M. y f. Mocker, scoffer.
mofadura f. Mockery, scoffing.
mofar v. intr. To mock, to scoff.
— V. pr. To mock, to make fun of, to scoff at.

mofeta f. ZOOL. Skunk (mamífero). || Mofette, moffette (fisura, gas). || Firedamp (grisú).
moflete m. FAM. Chubby cheek.
mofletudo, da adj. Chubby-cheeked. || *Una chica mofletuda*, a girl with chubby cheeks.
mogol, la adj./s. Mongolian, mongol. || *El Gran Mogol*, the Great Mogul.
mogolismo m. Mongolism.
mogollón m. Meddling (entremetimiento). || FAM. Sponger (gorrón). || FAM. *De mogollón*, for nothing, free (gratis), without paying (sin pagar), effortlessly, without effort (sin esfuerzo), by chance, by accident (por casualidad).
mogón, ona adj. One-horned, broken-horned (res).
mogote m. Knoll, mound (montículo). || Stack (hacina). || Antler (del ciervo).
mohair m. Mohair.
moharra f. Spear head.
mohicano, na adj./s. Mohican (indio).
mohín m. Grimace, face: *hacer un mohín*, to make a face.
mohíno, na adj. Sulky (melancólico). || Gloomy, sad (abatido). || Annoyed (disgustado). || Black (caballo negro). || *Mulo mohíno*, hinny (burdégano).
— F. Annoyance, anger (enojo).
moho m. Mould [U.S., mold], mildew (hongos). || Rust (del hierro). || Verdigris (del cobre). || Mould (en peras y manzanas). || — *Criar moho*, to go *o* to become mouldy (cubrirse de moho), to stagnate, to turn into a cabbage (vegetar). || FIG. *No criar moho*, to be always on the go. || *Oler a moho*, to smell mouldy. || *Saber a moho*, to taste mouldy.
mohoso, sa adj. Mouldy [U.S., moldy] (cosa orgánica). || Rusty (hierro). || *Ponerse mohoso*, to go *o* to become mouldy (cosa orgánica), to rust (hierro).
moisés m. Cradle (cuna). || Carrycot (para transportar al niño).
Moisés n. pr. m. Moses.
mojado, da adj. Wet, damp, moist (una cosa). || Wet (mejillas, labios, ojos). || FIG. *Llueve sobre mojado*, V. LLOVER.
mojador m. Damper (humectador). || Water pot (para la ropa).
mojama f. Salted tuna.
mojar v. tr. To wet, to damp, to moisten (humedecer). || To dip: *mojar la pluma en el tintero, el pan en el chocolate*, to dip one's pen in the inkwell, one's bread in one's chocolate. || To soak (la lluvia, etc.). || To dampen (la ropa para lavar). || To sprinkle (rociar). || To palatalize (en fonética). || FIG. y FAM. To celebrate: *mojar una victoria*, to celebrate a victory. | POP. *Mojar el gaznate*, to wet one's whistle.
— V. intr. FIG. To get involved (*en*, in)[en un negocio].
— V. pr. To get wet (por la lluvia, etc.).
mojicón m. FAM. Blow (golpe): *pegarle un mojicón a uno*, to give s.o. a blow [in the face]. | Punch (puñetazo). || Sponge cake (bizcocho). || Bun (bollo).
mojiganga f. Masquerade, masked ball (fiesta de máscaras). || Farce (en teatro). || FIG. Mockery.
mojigatería f. Hypocrisy. || Prudishness (pudor exagerado). || Sanctimoniousness, religious bigotry (beatería).
mojigatez f. Hypocrisy.
mojigato, ta adj. Hypocritical (hipócrita). || Prudish (excesivamente púdico). || Sanctimonious (santurrón).
— M. y f. Hypocrite (hipócrita). || Religious bigot, sanctimonious person (beato). || Prude.
mojinete m. Coping of a wall (caballete). || Crest (del tejado). || *Amer*. Fronton (de fachada).
mojón m. Landmark (en el camino). || Pile (montón). || Dung (excremento). || *Mojón kilométrico*, milestone.
moka m. Mocha (café).
mol m. QUÍM. Mole.
molar adj. ANAT. Molar.
— M. Molar, molar tooth.
molde m. TECN. Mould [U.S., mold], cast. || Knitting needle (para hacer punto). || CULIN. Mould. || FIG. Model, pattern (modelo). || IMPR. Form. || — *Letras de molde*, printed letters. || *Pan de molde*, soft, thin-crusted bread. || *Venirle a uno de molde*, to be just what one needs, to be just right for one.
moldeable adj. Mouldable [U.S., moldable]. || Manageable (persona).
moldeado m. Moulding [U.S., molding], casting (acción). || Cast (resultado).
moldeador, ra adj. Moulding [U.S., molding].
— M. y f. Moulder [U.S., molder], caster.
moldeamiento m. Moulding [U.S., molding], casting.
moldear v. tr. To cast (vaciar en yeso). || To make a casting (en un molde). || To mould [U.S., to mold], to shape (dar forma). || FIG. To shape, to mould, to form: *la vida moldea a los hombres*, life shapes men.
moldura f. Moulding [U.S., molding]. || — *Moldura cromada*, chromium strip. || ARQ. *Moldura ovalada*, gadroon.
moldurar v. tr. To put a moulding on.
mole adj. Soft (muelle). || *Huevos moles*, V. HUEVO.
— M. *Amer*. Fricassee of meat with chili sauce. || — F. Mass, bulk (cosa voluminosa).
molécula f. FÍS. Molecule. || *Molécula gramo*, gram molecule.
molecular adj. FÍS. Molecular.
moledor, ra adj. Grinding, crushing (que muele). || FAM. Exhausting, tiring, wearisome (agotador). | Boring, wearisome (aburrido).
— M. y f. FIG. y FAM. Bore (persona). || — M. Grinder, crusher (de caña de azúcar).
moledura f. Grinding, milling (del trigo). || FIG. Fatigue, exhaustion, weariness (cansancio).
moler* v. tr. To grind (en general). || To grind, to mill: *moler trigo*, to grind wheat. || To pound (machacar). || To pulverize (pulverizar). || To press (aceituna). || FIG. To tire out, to wear out (cansar). [V. MOLIDO]. | To bore (fastidiar). || *Amer*. To press, to express [sugar cane]. || FAM. *Moler a golpes* or *a palos*, to beat up, to beat black and blue.
moleskín o **molesquín** m. Moleskin.
molestar v. tr. To annoy (enfadar, irritar): *me molesta su falta de educación*, his bad manners annoy me. || To get on s.o.'s nerves, to annoy (poner nervioso): *me molestan esos martillazos*, that hammering is getting on my nerves *o* gets on my nerves. || To bother (incomodar): *¿le molesta el humo?*, does the smoke bother you? || To mind (importarle a uno): *no me molesta esperar*, I don't mind waiting; *¿le molesta venir?*, do you mind coming?; *¿le molestaría prestarme cien libras?*, would you mind lending me a hundred pounds? || To inconvenience, to mind (causar inconveniente): *¿le molestaría dejarlo para el viernes?*, would it inconvenience you to leave it until Friday?, would you mind leaving it until Friday? || To disturb, to bother, to trouble (importunar, interrumpir): *perdone que le moleste*, I'm sorry to bother you; *que no me moleste nadie*, I don't want to be disturbed, don't let anybody disturb me. || To worry (preocupar). || To pester (importunar insistentemente): *siempre me molestan con la misma queja*, they are always pestering me with the same complaint; *¡deja de molestarme ya!*, stop pestering me! || To hate, not to like (no gustarle a uno): *me molestaría llegar tarde*, I should hate to arrive late, I shouldn't like to arrive late; *me molesta tener que repetirlo*, I hate to *o* I don't like to have to repeat it. || To offend, to hurt (herir). || To hurt (hacer daño): *estos zapatos me molestan*, these shoes hurt me. || To trouble, to bother (un dolor). || — *Este asunto empieza a molestarme*, this business is beginning to get on my nerves; I am beginning to get tired of this business. || *Me molestaría verlo otra vez*, I should hate to *o* I shouldn't like to meet him again, it would be awkward for me to meet him again.
— V. intr. To be a nuisance (ser fastidioso). || To be unpleasant (ser desagradable).
— V. pr. To worry, to bother (preocuparse): *no se moleste por mí*, don't worry about me. || To take the trouble, to bother: *no se molestó en ayudarme*, he didn't take the trouble to help me. || To take offence (ofenderse): *molestarse por*, to take offence at. || To get angry *o* annoyed *o* cross (enfadarse). || *No se moleste*, don't bother.
molestia f. Annoyance, bother, trouble: *esto le acarreó muchas molestias*, this caused him a lot of bother. || Nuisance (fastidio): *dar* or *causar molestia a uno*, to be a nuisance to s.o. || Inconvenience (inconveniente). || Discomfort (incomodidad). || Unpleasantness (cosa desagradable). || FIG. Trouble (trabajo): *se tomó la molestia de ir*, he took the trouble to go. || Indisposition (de la salud). || — *Acusar* or *tener molestia en una pierna*, to have a pain in the leg. || *¡Qué molestia!*, what a nuisance! || *Ser una molestia*, to be a nuisance: *es una molestia ir a ese sitio ahora*, it's a nuisance to go to this place now. || *Si no es molestia* or *si no le sirve de molestia*, if it's not too much trouble for you, if it doesn't bother *o* trouble you.
molesto, ta adj. Boring, tiresome (aburrido): *¡qué molesto es hacer cada día la misma cosa!*, how boring it is doing the same thing every day! || Annoying, troublesome (fastidioso): *las faldas largas son molestas*, long skirts are troublesome. || Inconvenient: *ser molesto para uno*, to be inconvenient for s.o. || Trying (pesado): *es un hombre muy molesto*, he is a very trying man. || Uncomfortable (incómodo): *viaje molesto*, uncomfortable trip; *estar molesto en un sillón*, to be uncomfortable in an armchair. || Awkward (que estorba): *un paquete molesto*, an awkward parcel. || Unpleasant, nasty (sabor, olor). || Embarrassing, awkward: *una pregunta molesta*, an embarrassing question. || Irritating (irritante). || Embarrassed (confuso). || Cross (enfadado). || Offended (ofendido). || Discontented (descontento). || — *Lo molesto*, the trouble: *lo molesto es tener que subir a pie*, the trouble is having to go up on foot. || *Si no es molesto para ti*, if it is no trouble to you.
molestoso, sa adj. *Amer*. V. MOLESTO.
moleta f. Muller (piedra para moler). || Glass polisher (para pulir el vidrio).
molibdeno m. Molybdenum (metal).
molicie f. Softness. || Fondness for luxury. || *Vivir en la molicie*, to have an easy *o* a soft life.
molido, da adj. Ground (en general). || Ground, milled: *trigo molido*, milled wheat. || Pulverized, powdered (triturado). || Granulated (azúcar). || FIG. y FAM. Beat, worn-out, all in (cansado).

molienda f. Grinding (en general). || Grinding, milling (del trigo). || Pulverizing, crushing (trituración). || Pressing, crushing (de las aceitunas). || Processing season (aceitunas, trigo, etc.). || Batch being ground (cantidad). || FIG. y FAM. Exhaustion (cansancio). | Tiresome task (tarea pesada). | Nuisance (cosa molesta).
moliente adj. Grinding, milling. || *Corriente y moliente*, common or garden, run-of-the-mill, ordinary.
molinera f. Miller's wife (mujer del molinero). || Miller (que se ocupa de un molino).
molinería f. Milling industry (industria). || Mills, *pl.* (molinos).
molinero, ra adj. Milling.
— M. Miller.
molinete m. Ventilator (de ventana). || Whirligig, windmill [U.S., pinwheel] (juguete). || Circular swing *o* sweep (movimiento). || MAR. Windlass. || *Amer.* Catherine wheel, girandole (de cohete).
molinillo m. Grinder, mill: *molinillo de café, de pimienta*, coffee, pepper grinder. || Mincer (de carne). || Whisk (de chocolatera). || Whirligig, windmill [U.S., pinwheel] (juguete).
molino m. Mill: *molino de agua*, water mill; *molino de papel*, paper mill. || FIG. Tornado (persona bulliciosa). | Nuisance, pest (persona molesta). || — FIG. *Luchar contra los molinos de viento*, to tilt at windmills. || *Molino de sangre*, animal-driven mill (de animales), hand-operated mill (de mano). || *Molino de viento*, windmill. || FIG. *Molinos de viento*, imaginary enemies.
molturación f. V. MOLIENDA.
molturado, da adj. V. MOLIDO.
molturar v. tr. To grind, to mill.
molusco m. ZOOL. Mollusc.
molla f. Lean [meat] (de la carne). || Crumb (miga). || — Pl. FAM. Flab, *sing.* (gordura de una persona).
mollar adj. Tender, soft (blando). || FIG. Cushy, easy and lucrative. || — *Carne mollar*, boneless lean meat. || *Tierra mollar*, soft ground.
mollate m. FAM. Red wine (vino).
molleja f. Gizzard (de las aves). || Sweetbread (de ternera, de cordero). || ANAT. Thymus gland (timo).
mollera f. ANAT. Crown of the head. | Fontanel, fontanelle (fontanela). || FIG. Brains, *pl.*, common sense (seso). || — FIG. y FAM. *Cerrado de mollera*, V. CERRADO. | *Ser duro de mollera*, to be hardheaded *o* obstinate (obstinado), to be thick *o* dense (torpe). | *Tener ya dura la mollera*, to be too old to change.
mollete m. Fleshy part, flab (del brazo). || Chubby cheek (moflete). || Roll (panecillo).
mollina o **mollizna** f. Drizzle, fine rain.
molliznar o **molliznear** v. impers. To drizzle.
momentáneamente adv. Momentarily (durante un momento). || Right now, at the moment (ahora mismo).
momentáneo, a adj. Momentary (breve).
momento m. Moment (tiempo muy corto): *lo haré dentro de un momento*, I'll do it in a moment. || Moment (ocasión): *escoger el momento favorable*, to choose a favourable moment; *momento oportuno*, opportune moment. || Time: *ha llegado el momento de irse*, the time has come to leave. || Instant (instante). || FIG. Moment (importancia). || FÍS. Moment: *momento de inercia*, moment of inertia. | Momentum (producto de la masa y la velocidad). || — *A cada momento*, all the time. || *A cualquier momento*, at any moment *o* time. || *Al momento*, at once, immediately. || *Del momento*, of the day, current (actual): *la moda del momento*, the fashion of the day, the current fashion. || *De momento*, at the moment, at present (ahora), at first (primeramente). || *Dentro de un momento*, in a moment. || *Desde el momento en que*, from the moment when, from the time when. || *Desde ese momento* or *a partir de ese momento*, from that moment. || *De un momento a otro*, at any moment *o* time. || *En aquel momento*, at that moment. || *En buen momento*, at a good time, at the right time. || *En el mejor momento*, at the best time. || *En el momento actual*, at the present time. || *En el momento (en) que*, at the very moment when, just when. || *En el momento menos pensado*, when least expected. || *En el primer momento*, in the beginning, at the start. || *En este momento*, just now, at this moment. || *En estos momentos*, at the moment, at present, at the present time *o* moment. || *En los momentos actuales*, at present, at the present time. || *En mal momento*, at a bad time. || *En todo momento*, at any moment *o* time. || *Hace un momento*, not a moment ago. || *Ha pasado su momento*, he's had his day. || *Momento crucial*, crucial moment. || *Momento fatídico*, fatal moment. || *Momento psicológico*, psychological moment. || *Momentos después*, a few moments later, moments later. || *No tener un momento libre*, not to have a minute free. || *Por el momento*, for the moment. || *Por momentos*, every moment, fast. || *Ser el hombre del momento*, to be the man of the moment. || *Tener buenos momentos*, to have one's [good] moments. || *Últimos momentos*, last minutes, last moments. || *¡Un momento!*, just a minute!, just a moment!
momia f. Mummy. || FIG. *Estar hecho una momia*, to be all skin and bones.
momificación f. Mummification.
momificar v. tr. To mummify.
— V. pr. To become mummified, to mummify.

momio, mia adj. Lean (carne).
— M. Bargain (ganga). || Cushy job (trabajo fácil y rentable). || Extra, bonus (suplemento). || FAM. *De momio*, free, for nothing (de balde).
mona f. Female monkey (hembra del mono). || FAM. Copycat, ape (persona que imita). | Drunkenness [U.S., drunk] (borrachera). || Old maid (juego de cartas). || TAUR. Metal leg guard. || *Amer.* Mannequin (maniquí). || — FAM. *Aunque la mona se vista de seda, mona se queda*, you can't make a silk purse out of a sow's ear. | *Coger* or *pillar una mona*, to get sozzled *o* sloshed *o* stoned *o* plastered. | *Corrido como una mona* or *hecho una mona*, ashamed. | *Dormir la mona*, to sleep it off. | *Estar mona*, to be stoned. | *Mandar a freír monas*, to tell [s.o.] to jump in the lake. | *Quedarse corrido como una mona* or *hecho una mona*, not to know where to put o.s., to be so embarrassed.
monacal adj. Monastic.
monacato m. Monkhood, monasticism.
monacillo m. V. MONAGUILLO.
monada f. Kindness (amabilidad). || Pretty thing, lovely thing: *en esta tienda hay verdaderas monadas*, in this shop there are some really pretty things. || Pretty girl (chica bonita). || Flattery (halago). || Caress (carantoña). || Charming little way (acción graciosa de un niño). || Silliness (tontería). || Nasty trick, dirty trick (mala jugada). || — Pl. Simpering ways (melindres). || Grimaces, faces (gestos). || — FIG. *¡Qué hay monada!*, hullo, beautiful! | *¡Qué monada!*, isn't it lovely?, how lovely! | *¡Qué monada de pulsera!*, what a lovely *o* a pretty bracelet! | *Ser una monada*, to be pretty, to be lovely: *esta niña es una verdadera monada*, this girl is really pretty.
mónada m. FIL. Monad.
monadismo m. FIL. Monadism.
monago m. o **monaguillo** m. Acolyte, altar boy, child who assists the priest.
monarca m. Monarch.
monarquía f. Monarchy: *monarquía absoluta*, absolute monarchy.
monárquico, ca adj. Monarchical, monarchic.
— M. y f. Monarchist.
monarquismo m. Monarchism.
monasterio m. Monastery.
monástico, ca adj. Monastic.
monda f. Pruning, trimming (de los árboles). || — Pl. Peelings (desperdicios): *mondas de patatas*, potato peelings. || Cleaning (limpieza). || Cleaning out (de los pozos). || Exhumation (de los restos humanos). || — FAM. *Es la monda*, it's great, it's terrific (magnífico), it's sheer hell (muy malo), it's killing, it's hilarious (es muy divertido). | *Este tipo es la monda*, this fellow is the limit *o* takes the cake (es el colmo), this chap is hilarious (muy gracioso), this fellow is great (estupendo).
mondadientes m. inv. Toothpick.
mondador, ra m. y f. Pruner (de árboles). || Peeler (de frutas y legumbres). || Cleaner (que limpia).
mondadura f. V. MONDA.
mondante adj. FAM. Hilarious, killing.
mondaoídos m. inv. Earpick.
mondar v. tr. To clean (quitar lo inútil). || To hull: *cebada mondada*, hulled barley. || To trim, to prune (podar). || To strip (el tronco de un árbol). || To peel, to skin (patatas, tomates, fruta). || To shell (guisantes, nueces, etc.). || To dredge, to clean out (un río). || To cut, to clip (cortar). || FIG. y FAM. To clean out, to fleece (en el juego). || — FAM. *¡Anda y que te monden!*, get away! | *Mondar a palos*, to give a thrashing, to thrash.
— V. pr. FAM. *Mondarse de risa*, to split one's sides laughing, to laugh one's head off. || *Mondarse los dientes*, to pick one's teeth.
mondo, da adj. Pure, clean. || Plain: *el hecho mondo es*, the plain fact is. || Bare: *mi sueldo mondo es*, my bare salary is. || — FIG. y FAM. *Mondo y lirondo*, pure and simple. || *Es la verdad monda y lironda*, it's the plain truth.
mondongo m. Innards, *pl.* (tripas). || Tripe (guiso). || FAM. Intestines, *pl.* (intestinos). || *Amer.* FIG. Ridiculous get-up (adefesio).
mondonguería f. Tripe shop. || Pork butcher's [shop] (charcutería).
mondonguero, ra m. y f. Tripe shopkeeper. || Pork butcher (charcutero).
moneda f. Money, currency: *la moneda española*, the Spanish currency. || Coin (pieza). || — *Acuñar* or *labrar* or *batir moneda*, to mint money. || *Casa de la Moneda*, mint. || *Moneda contante y sonante*, hard cash. || *Moneda de cuenta*, money of account. || *Moneda de papel*, paper money. || *Moneda falsa*, counterfeit money. || *Moneda fiduciaria*, fiduciary money. || *Moneda imaginaria*, money of account. || *Moneda suelta* or *fraccionaria*, small change. || FIG. *Pagar a uno en* or *con la misma moneda*, to give s.o. a taste of his own medicine, to pay s.o. back in his own coin. || *Papel moneda*, paper money. || FIG. *Ser moneda corriente*, to be everyday stuff *o* run-of-the-mill stuff. || *Se ruega moneda fraccionaria*, please tender the exact fare (rótulo en transportes públicos).
monedero m. Minter (que hace moneda). || Purse (portamonedas). || *Monedero falso*, counterfeiter.
monegasco, ca adj./s. Monegasque, Monacan.

monería f. V. MONADA.
monetario, ria adj. Monetary.
— M. Collection of coins and medals.
monetización f. Monetization.
monetizar v. tr. To monetize. || To mint (acuñar).
mongol, la adj. Mongol, Mongolian, Mongolic (de Mongolia). || Mongolic (idioma).
— M. y f. Mongol, Mongolian (persona de Mongolia). || — M. Mongolic (idioma).
Mongolia n. pr. f. Mongolia: *Mongolia Interior, Exterior*, Inner, Outer Mongolia.
mongólico, ca adj./s. V. MONGOL. || MED. Mongol, mongolian.
mongolismo m. MED. Mongolism.
moni m. FAM. Dough (dinero).
monicaco m. FAM. Shrimp (hombrecillo).
monigote m. Lay brother (de un convento). || Rag doll, paper doll (muñeco ridículo). || Ridiculous figure [painted usually by children] (dibujo mal hecho). || FIG. y FAM. Puppet (persona sin personalidad). || Humorous sketch (dibujo humorístico). || Bad painting (pintura mal hecha). || *Monigote de nieve*, snowman.
monín, ina o **monino, na** adj. FAM. V. MONO.
monipodio m. Unlawful meeting (conciliábulo). || *El patio de Monipodio*, a den of thieves.
monís f. Trinket.
monises m. pl. FAM. Dough, *sing*, money, *sing*. (dinero): *tener monises*, to have dough.
monísimo, ma adj. Very pretty, very lovely, etc. (V. MONO).
monismo m. FIL. Monism.
monitor, ra m. y f. Monitor.
monja f. Nun. || *Meterse a monja*, to become a nun, to take the veil.
monje m. Monk (fraile). || Anchorite (anacoreta). || Coal tit (ave).
monjil adj. Nun's, of nuns (de monjas). || FIG. Excessively demure (excesivamente recatado).
— M. Nun's habit. || Mourning dress (traje de luto).
mono, na adj. FAM. Pretty, good-looking (bonito): *¡qué chica más mona!*, what a pretty girl! | Lovely, nice (amable). | Cute, lovely, pretty, nice: *¡qué abrigo más mono!*, what a cute coat! | Darling (gracioso): *un niño muy mono*, a darling child.
— M. Monkey, ape (animal). || Joker (en los naipes). || FIG. Ape (burlón). | Silhouette, drawing (de animal u hombre). | Ridiculous figure (monigote): *pintar monos en la pared*, to draw ridiculous figures on the wall. | Ape (hombre muy feo). | Pansy (afeminado). || Overalls, *pl.*, dungarees, *pl.* (traje de una sola pieza). || Rompers, *pl.* (de niño). || — FIG. *El último mono*, the least important, the pip-squeak, the lowest of the low. | *Estar de monos*, to be cross *o* angry. || *Mono aullador*, howler monkey. || *Mono capuchino*, capuchin monkey. || FIG. *Mono de imitación*, ape, copycat, imitator, mimic. || *Mono sabio*, trained ape (en el circo), "monosabio", bullring attendant (en tauromaquia). || FIG. y FAM. *¿Qué me miras?, ¿tengo monos en la cara?*, what are you looking at?, do you want a signed photograph?
monoácido, da adj./s.m. QUÍM. Monoacid.
monobásico, ca adj. QUÍM. Monobasic.
monobloque adj. Monobloc.
monocamerismo m. Unicameralism.
monocarril adj./s.m. Monorail.
monocasco adj. Monocoque (barco, avión).
monocilíndrico, ca adj. Single-cylinder.
monocorde adj. MÚS. Single-string (instrumento). || Monotonous (monótono).
monocordio m. MÚS. Monochord.
monocotiledóneo, a adj. BOT. Monocotyledonous.
— F. Monocotyledon.
monocromático, ca adj. Monochromatic.
monocromía f. Monochromy.
monocromo, ma adj./s.m. Monochrome.
monóculo, la adj. Monocular.
— M. Monocle (lente). || Eye patch (vendaje).
monocultivo m. Monoculture.
monodia f. MÚS. Monody.
monofásico, ca adj. Monophase, singlephase.
monofisismo m. Monophysitism (herejía).
monofisita adj. Monophysitic.
— M. Monophysite (hereje).
monogamia f. Monogamy.
monógamo, ma adj. Monogamous.
— M. y f. Monogamist.
monografía f. Monograph.
monográfico, ca adj. Monographic.
monograma m. Monogram.
monolingüe adj. Monolingual.
monolítico, ca adj. Monolithic.
monolito m. Monolith.
monologar v. intr. To soliloquize.
monólogo m. Monologue.
monomanía f. Monomania, fixed idea.
monomaniaco, ca o **monomaníaco, ca** o **monomaniático, ca** adj. Monomaniacal.
— M. y f. Monomaniac.
monometalismo m. Monometallism.
monometalista adj. Monometallic.
— M. y f. Monometallist.
monomio m. MAT. Monomial.
monomotor adj. AVIAC. Single-engine.
— M. Single-engine aeroplane.
mononuclear adj. Mononuclear.
mononucleosis f. MED. Mononucleosis.
monoplano adj./s.m. Monoplane.
monoplaza adj./s.m. Single-seater.
monopolio m. Monopoly.
monopolización f. Monopolization.
monopolizador, ra adj. Monopolizing, monopolistic.
— M. y f. Monopolizer.
monopolizar v. tr. To monopolize.
monorrail o **monorriel** adj./s.m. Monorail.
monosabio m. TAUR. "Monosabio", bullring attendant.
monosacárido m. QUÍM. Monosaccharide.
monosilábico, ca adj. GRAM. Monosyllabic: *lengua monosilábica*, monosyllabic language.
monosílabo, ba adj. GRAM. Monosyllabic.
— M. Monosyllable.
monoteísmo m. REL. Monotheism.
monoteísta adj. REL. Monotheistic.
— M. y f. Monotheist.
monotipia f. IMPR. Monotype (procedimiento).
monotipo m. IMPR. Monotype (máquina).
monotonía f. Monotony.
monótono, na adj. Monotonous.
monotremas m. pl. ZOOL. Monotremata.
monovalente adj./s.m. Monovalent.
monseñor m. Monseigneur. || Monsignor (prelado italiano).
monserga f. FAM. Boring *o* tiresome speech: *nos colocó la monserga de siempre*, he gave us the same old boring speech. | Lecture, sermon: *no me vengas con monsergas*, don't give me a lecture. | Story, tale, lie: *todo eso no son más que monsergas*, it is all one big story. || — FAM. *Dar la monserga a uno*, to annoy *o* to pester s.o. | *¡Qué monserga!*, what a nuisance!
monstruo adj. inv. Fantastic: *una cena monstruo*, a fantastic dinner.
— M. Monster.
monstruosidad f. Monstrosity.
monstruoso, sa adj. Monstrous.
monta f. Mount (accion de montar). || Mating season (apareamiento de caballo y yegua). || Sum, total (suma). || Value, account, importance: *negocio de poca monta*, business of little importance; *libro, persona de poca monta*, book, person of little value.
montacargas m. inv. Hoist, goods lift, service lift [U.S., freight elevator]
montado, da adj. Mounted (soldado, artillería). || Saddled (caballo). || Riding: *montado en un autobús, en bicicleta, en un asno*, riding in a bus, riding a bicycle, riding an ass. || Organized, set up (organizado). || TECN. Set (diamante, etc.). | Assembled (máquina). || TEATR. Staged (una obra). || *Un hombre montado a caballo*, a man on horseback.
— M. Mounted soldier (soldado).
montador, ra m. y f. Fitter (el que monta). || Assembler (operario). || Setter (joyero). || TEATR. Stager, producer. || Mounter (fotógrafo). || CINEM. Film cutter. || — M. Horse block, mounting block (para montar a caballo). || *Montador mecánico electricista*, electrical assembler.
montadura f. Mounting. || Harness, trappings, *pl.* (del caballo). || Mounting, setting (engaste).
montaje m. Assembly, setting up, assembling, mounting (de una máquina). || Fitting out (de un taller). || Putting together, assembling, mounting (de un reloj). || Setup, staging (en el teatro). || Cutting, editing, mounting (de una película). || Setting (de una joya). || Building, putting together (de un aparato de radio). || *Cadena* or *línea de montaje*, assembly line.
montanera f. Acorn pasture [for hogs].
montanero m. Forest ranger.
montante m. Upright (de una armazón). || Leg (de una máquina). || Prop, post (de una mina). || Stanchion (soporte). || Total sum, amount (importe, total). || ARQ. Mullion (de una ventana). | Post (de una puerta). | Small window over a door (ventana). || Espadon, two-handed sword (arma). || DEP. Goal post (de una portería).
— F. High tide (marea).
montaña f. Mountain: *cadena de montañas*, chain of mountains, mountain chain. || FIG. Mountain: *una montaña de libros*, a mountain of books. || *Amer.* Undergrowth (monte bajo), brush, scrub (maleza). || — FIG. *Hacer de todo una montaña*, to make a mountain out of a molehill. || *La Montaña*, region of Santander [Spain]. || *Montaña rusa*, switchback, scenic railway [U.S., roller coaster] (de un parque de atracciones).
montañero, ra m. y f. Mountaineer, climber. || *Escuela de montañeros*, mountaineering school.
montañés, esa adj. Mountain, highland. || Of *La Montaña* [region of Santander].
— M. y f. Mountain dweller, highlander. || Inhabitant of *La Montaña*.
montañismo m. Mountaineering, climbing. || *Escuela de montañismo*, mountaineering school.
montañoso, sa adj. Mountainous.
montaplatos m. inv. Food lift, service lift [U.S., dumbwaiter].

montar v. intr. To ride: *montar a caballo, en bicicleta, en burro, en coche*, to ride a horse, a bicycle, on a donkey, in a car. || To mount, to get on (subir): *montar a caballo* or *en un caballo*, to mount one's horse. || To go up: *no me gusta montar en avión, en globo*, I don't like going up in an aeroplane, in a balloon. || To get on, to board (pasajeros): *montar en un avión, en un tren, en un barco*, to get on an aeroplane, on a train, on a boat. || To get into: *montar en un coche*, to get into a car. || To be of importance: *este negocio monta poco*, this business is of little importance. || To amount to, to come to: *la cuenta montó a cien pesetas*, the bill amounted to a hundred pesetas. || — *Montar a* or *en la grupa*, to ride pillion [U.S., to ride on the pillion pad]. || *Montar a pelo*, to ride bareback. || FIG. *Montar en cólera*, to flare up, to fly into a temper. || *Silla de montar*, saddle. || FIG. *Tanto monta*, it's all the same. || *Tanto monta, monta tanto Isabel como Fernando*, the motto of the Spanish Catholic rulers, Isabel and Fernando, indicating equal division of authority between the two.
— V. tr. To mount, to get on (subirse a un caballo). || To ride (conducir). || To lift (subir). || To fit out (organizar). || To set up (una fábrica). || To mount, to set (una joya). || To assemble, to put together, to set up (una máquina). || To hang (una puerta). || To make (un vestido). || AUT. To fit (un neumático). || To furnish, to set up (amueblar una casa). || To wind (un muelle). || To mount (la guardia). || To beat, to whip (los huevos). || To overlap (una cosa sobre otra). || To cover (a la hembra). || To cock (un arma). || TEATR. To set, to mount (un decorado). | To stage (una obra dramática). || CINEM. To edit, to mount (una película). || MIL. To mount (una ofensiva).

montaraz adj. Savage, wild (animales). || Rough, coarse (de modales toscos). || Unsociable (arisco, insociable). || Mountain, highland (de la sierra).

montazgo m. Tribute paid for the passage of cattle.

monte m. Mountain (montaña): *montes altos*, high mountains; *Montes Cantábricos*, Cantabrian Mountains. || Mount (aislado o con nombre propio): *Monte de los Olivos*, Mount of Olives. || Forest, woodland (bosque): *monte espeso*, thick forest. || Stack, pile (naipes que quedan por robar). || Monte (juego). || *Amer.* Country (campo). || FIG. y FAM. Mop (cabellera). || — *Administración de montes*, Forestry Commission [U.S., Department of Forestry]. || *Conejo de monte*, wild rabbit. || *Echarse* or *hacerse al monte*, to take to the hills. || *Escuela de montes*, forestry school. || *Monte alto*, forest, trees, *pl.* || *Monte bajo*, scrub, underbrush, undergrowth. || *Monte de piedad*, pawnshop. || ANAT. *Monte de Venus*, mons veneris (pubis), Mount of Venus (de la mano). || *Monte pío*, v. MONTEPÍO. || FIG. *No todo el monte es orégano*, it is not all plain sailing, life is not just a bowl of cherries.

montepío m. Assistance fund. || *Amer.* Pawnshop (monte de piedad). | Widow's pension fund (viudedad).

montera f. Cloth cap (para la cabeza). || Bullfighter's hat (de los toreros). || Huntress, hunter (que caza). || Skylight, glass roofing (cubierta de cristales). || Cover (de alambique). || MAR. Triangular sail (vela). || FAM. *Ponerse el mundo por montera*, not to care what people think *o* what people say.

montería f. Venery (arte de cazar). || Hunting (caza mayor).

monterilla f. MAR. Triangular sail.
— M. Mayor [of a town] (alcalde).

montero m. Huntsman, hunter (cazador). || Beater (ojeador). || *Montero mayor*, master of the hounds.

montés, esa adj. Wild. || *Gato montés*, wildcat.

Montescos n. pr. m. pl. Montagues.

montevideano, na adj./s. Montevidean.

Montevideo n. pr. GEOGR. Montevideo.

montículo m. Hillock, monticule.

montilla m. Montilla (vino).

monto m. Total, sum (total).

montón m. Heap, pile. || FIG. y FAM. Heap, pile, heaps, *pl.*, piles, *pl.*: *un montón de cosas*, a heap of things; *un montón de papeles*, a pile of papers. | Good many: *un montón de años, de días*, a good many years, days. | Piles, *pl.*, bags, *pl.*, stacks, *pl.*: *tener montones de dinero*, to have bags of money. || — FIG. *A montones*, lots of (mucho): *pasteles a montones*, lots of cakes. | *Del montón*, ordinary, commonplace, average: *ser del montón*, to be ordinary. | *Salirse del montón*, to stand out from the crowd. | *Un montón de gente*, lots (*pl.*) of people,

montonera f. *Amer.* Group of mounted rebels (de rebeldes). | Stack, pile (almiar).

montonero m. *Amer.* Guerrilla, fighter (guerrillero).

montuno, na adj. Mountain. || *Amer.* Country, rustic (rústico). | Wild (montaraz).

montuoso, sa adj. Mountainous (montañoso). || Wooded (con bosque).

montura f. Mount (cabalgadura). || Saddle (silla). || Setting (de una joya). || Frame (de gafas). || Assembly, mounting (de una máquina).

monumental adj. Monumental. || FIG. y FAM. Well built (una mujer). | Terrible, horrible, awful: *tener un catarro monumental*, to have a terrible cold. | Enormous, huge (enorme). | Terrific (estupendo).

monumento m. Monument, memorial: *monumento a los Caídos*, war memorial. || Monument, building: *monumentos históricos*, ancient monuments. || Temporary altar (el Jueves Santo). || FIG. Monument: *un monumento de erudición*, a monument of learning. || FIG. y FAM. *Esta chica es un monumento*, this girl is a beauty.

monzón m. y f. Monsoon (viento).

moña f. Hair ribbon (lazo). || Chignon, bun (moño). || TAUR. Coloured ribbons, *pl.* [worn by the bull for identification]. | Ornament of ribbons worn on the back of the head of the bullfighter. || Doll (muñeca). || FAM. Booze-up (borrachera).

moño m. Chignon, bun (de pelo). || Bow [of ribbons] (lazo de cintas). || Tuft, crest (de algunos pájaros). || — FIG. y FAM. *Agarrarse del moño*, to tear each other's hair out, to pull each other's hair. | *Estar hasta el moño*, to be fed up. | *Ponerse moños*, to brag, to boast (jactarse), to put on airs (presumir).

moñudo, da adj. Tufted, crested (ave).

moquear v. intr. To run [the nose].

moqueo m. FAM. Runny nose.

moquero m. Handkerchief (pañuelo).

moqueta f. Moquette (alfombra).

moquete m. FAM. Punch on the nose *o* in the face.

moquetear v. tr. FAM. To punch on the nose *o* in the face.
— V. intr. To run (the nose].

moquillo m. Distemper (catarro de los perros). || Pip (de las aves). || FAM. *Pasar el moquillo*, to have a rough time of it.

moquita f. Mucus (moco fluido).

mor de (por) loc. adv. Because of.

mora f. BOT. Mulberry (fruto). || Blackberry (zarzamora). || JUR. Delay, mora (demora). || Moorish woman (mujer árabe).

morabito m. Marabout.

morada f. House, abode, dwelling [place] (casa o habitación). || Stay, sojourn (estancia). || *La última morada*, the last resting place.

morado, da adj. Purple, violet. || — FIG. y FAM. *Estar morado*, to be sozzled *o* sloshed (borracho). | *Pasarlas moradas*, to have a rough time, to go through hell *o* murder. | *Ponerse morado*, to stuff o.s.: *me puse morado de comer, de higos*, I stuffed myself with food, with figs. | *Se puso morado de vino*, he drank gallons of wine.

morador, ra adj. Dwelling, living, residing.
— M. y f. Inhabitant, dweller, resident.

moral adj. Moral: *principios morales*, moral principles.
— M. Mulberry tree (árbol). || — F. Morals, *pl.* (ética). || Morale (ánimo): *la moral de las tropas, de un equipo*, the morale of the troops, of a team; *levantar* or *elevar la moral*, to raise the morale. || *Tener la moral baja* or *estar bajo de moral*, to be in poor spirits, to be low spirited.

moraleja f. Moral (de una fábula).

moralidad f. Morality, morals, *pl.*

moralismo m. Moralism.

moralista adj. Moralistic.
— M. y f. Moralist.

moralización f. Moralization.

moralizador, ra adj. Moralizing.
— M. y f. Moralizer, moralist.

moralizar v. tr. e intr. To moralize.

morapio m. FAM. Red wine, plonk (vino).

morar v. intr. To reside, to dwell.

moratoria f. JUR. Moratorium.

moratorio, ria adj. Moratory.

morbidez f. Softness, tenderness.

morbididad f. V. MORBILIDAD.

mórbido, da adj. Morbid (no sano): *estado mórbido* morbid state; *literatura mórbida*, morbid literature || Delicate, soft, tender (delicado).

morbilidad f. MED. Morbidity, sick rate (estadística).

morbo f. Disease, illness (enfermedad).

morbosidad f. Morbidity.

morboso, sa adj. Morbid, unhealthy (no sano). || Morbific (que causa enfermedad). || Sick, diseased (enfermo).

morcilla f. CULIN. Black pudding, blood sausage. || Poisoned sausage [for killing dogs]. || TEATR. Ad lib, improvised part (del actor). || FAM. *¡Que te den morcilla!*, go to hell!, get lost!

morcillero, ra m. y f. Pork butcher. || Ad-libber, improviser, extemporizer (actor).

mordacidad f. Mordacity, pungency, sting.

mordaga f. FAM. Booze-up [U.S., drunk] (borrachera). || FAM. *Coger una mordaga*, to get sozzled *o* canned.

mordaz adj. Corrosive, mordant (corrosivo). || Stinging, biting, pungent (al paladar). || FIG. Biting, caustic, pungent, burning: *críticas mordaces*, biting criticism.

mordaza f. Gag (en la boca). || MAR. Compressor (del ancla). || VET. Pincers, *pl.* (para castrar). || TECN. Clamps, *pl.*, jaws, *pl.* (del torno). | Fishplate (de carriles).

mordazmente adv. Bitingly, sarcastically, acrimoniously.

mordedor, ra adj. Vicious, which bites, fierce (perro). || FIG. Sarcastic (persona).

mordedura f. Bite.

morder* v. tr. To bite: *le ha mordido una serpiente*, a snake has bitten him. || FIG. To gossip about, to

run down (murmurar). | To nibble away at, to wear down (quitar por porciones). || IMPR. To etch (una plancha). || TECN. To bite (la lima). || FIG. *Morder el polvo*, to bite the dust.
— V. intr. To bite. || To catch (un engranaje). || FIG. *Está que muerde*, he is in a nasty temper.
— V. pr. To bite: *morderse las uñas*, to bite one's nails. || FIG. *Morderse la lengua*, V. LENGUA. | *Morderse los labios*, to bite one's lip (para no hablar o no reirse). | *Morderse los puños*, to kick o.s. | *No morderse la lengua*, V. LENGUA.
mordicar v. tr. To sting.
mordido, da adj. Bitten.
— F. Bite (en la pesca). || *Amer.* Bribe (soborno).
mordiente adj. Mordant, biting (que corroe).
— M. Mordant (sustancia corrosiva). || FIG. Bite, punch: *la delantera falta de mordiente*, the forwardline lacks bite.
mordiscar o **mordisquear** v. tr. To nibble [at].
mordisco m. Bite. || — *Dar* or *pegar* or *tirar un mordisco*, to bite, to bite at, to take a bite at. || *El perro me tiró un mordisco*, the dog went for me.
mordisqueo m. Nibbling.
morena f. Muraena, moray (pez). || Sheaf, bundle (de cereal segado). || Moraine (de un glaciar).
moreno, na adj. Brown. || Tanned, brown (por el sol). || Dark, black (pelo). || Dark, swarthy, dark-skinned (de piel oscura). || *Amer.* Coloured, negro (de raza negra).
— M. y f. FIG. y FAM. Negro (hombre), negress (mujer) [de raza negra]. || *Amer.* Mulatto. || Dark man (hombre), brunette (chica). || — *Pan moreno*, brown bread. || *Ponerse moreno*, to get tanned, to get a suntan.
morenote, ta adj. Very brown, dark.
morera f. BOT. White mulberry (árbol).
moreral m. White mulberry field.
morería f. Moorish district *o* neighbourhood (barrio). || Moorish country (país).
moretón m. FAM. Bruise (equimosis).
morfema m. GRAM. Morpheme.
Morfeo n. pr. m. MIT. Morpheus.
morfina f. Morphine, morphia.
morfinismo m. Morphinism.
morfinomanía f. Addiction to morphine.
morfinómano, na adj. Morphine.
— M. y f. Morphine addict, morphinomaniac.
morfología f. Morphology.
morfológico, ca adj. Morphologic, morphological.
morfosis f. Morphosis.
morganático, ca adj. Morganatic.
morgue f. Morgue.
— OBSERV. Gallicism for *depósito de cadáveres*.
moribundo, da adj./s. Moribund.
morigeración f. Moderation, temperance.
morigerado, da adj. Well-mannered (de buenos modales). || Moderate, temperate (moderado).
morigerar v. tr. To moderate (templar).
morilla f. BOT. Morel (cagarria).
morillo m. Andiron, firedog.
morir* v. intr. To die: *morir muy joven*, to die very young; *morir de vejez*, to die of old age. || To end (una línea de transporte, etc.). || To die, to go out (el fuego). || To come out (una calle). || To fade, to droop (una flor). || To die out *o* away (un sonido). || FIG. To die, to end: *mi amor por ella murió aquel mismo día*, my love for her died that very day. || — FIG. y FAM. *¡Así se muera!*, good riddance to him! || *Haber muerto*, to be dead. || *Moría la tarde*, the afternoon was coming to a close *o* was almost over. || *Morir ahogado*, to drown. || *Morir ahorcado*, to be hanged. || *Morir al pie del cañon*, V. PIE. || *Morirás antes de que muera el día*, you will die before the day is out *o* before the end of the day. || *Morir con las botas puestas* or *vestido*, to die with one's boots on. || *Morir de frío* or *helado*, to freeze to death. || *Morir de muerte natural*, to die a natural death. || *Morir de repente*, to die suddenly. || *Morir fusilado*, to be shot. || *¡Muera el dictador!*, down with *o* death to the dictator! || *Muerto a tiros*, shot [dead].
— V. tr. To kill (matar).
— V. pr. To die: *morirse de cáncer*, to die of cancer; *¡me muero!*, I'm dying. || — FIG. *Es para morirse de risa*, it's absolutely killing *o* hilarious. | *Morirse de aburrimiento*, to be bored stiff *o* bored to death. | *Morirse de envidia*, to be green with envy. | *Morirse de frío*, to freeze to death. | *Morirse de ganas de*, to be dying to. || *Morirse de hambre*, to starve to death, to die of starvation (sentido propio), to starve (figurado). || FIG. *Morirse de inquietud*, to be worried to death *o* worried sick. | *Morirse de miedo*, V. MIEDO. | *Morirse de risa*, to die laughing, to be tickled to death. || FIG. y FAM. *Morirse por el cine, por una chica, por el fútbol*, to be crazy about the cinema, about a girl, about football (gustarle a uno muchísimo). | *Morirse por ir al cine, por salir con ella*, to be dying to go to the cinema, to go out with her. | *Morirse sin decir Jesús*, to die very suddenly. | *¡Que me muera sí!*, may I be struck down if.
morisco, ca adj. Moorish.
— M. y f. Morisco (moro bautizado).
— OBSERV. The term *morisco* is applied to the Spanish Moors who, during the Reconquest (711 to 1492), accepted Christianity.
morisma f. Moors, *pl.* || Multitude of Moors.
morisqueta f. Grimace (mueca). || Dirty trick (engaño).
morlaco, ca adj. Sly, cunning (taimado).
— M. y f. Sly fox (fam.), cunning person. || — M. FAM. Bull (toro). || *Amer.* Peso (peso). | Money (dinero).
mormón, ona m. y f. Mormon.
mormónico, ca adj. Mormon.
mormonismo m. Mormonism (doctrina religiosa).
moro, ra adj. Moorish. || Mohammedan (mahometano). || Unbaptized (no bautizado). || White-stockinged (caballo).
— M. y f. Moor (árabe). || Mohammedan (mahometano). || Moro [Mohammedan native of Mindanao and other Malaysian islands]. || — FIG. y FAM. *Hay moros en la costa*, the coast is not clear, watch out. | *Hubo moros y cristianos*, there was trouble *o* a big brawl. | *Prometer el oro y el moro*, V. ORO.
morocho, cha adj. FIG. y FAM. *Amer.* Robust, strong (fuerte). | Swarthy, dark-skinned (moreno de piel). | Dark, brunette (de pelo).
— M. *Amer.* Type of maize (maíz).
morosamente adj. Slowly (con lentitud). || Late (con dilación).
morosidad f. Slowness, dilatoriness (lentitud). || Lateness, delay (tardanza). || Inactivity (falta de actividad). || JUR. Arrears (*pl.*) of payment.
moroso, sa adj. Dilatory: *deudor moroso*, dilatory debtor. || Slow, unhurried (lento). || Lazy, sluggish (perezoso). || Late, tardy (que se detiene). || *Declaración morosa*, morose declaration.
— M. y f. Slow payer, defaulter (retrasado en el pago).
morrada f. Butt (golpe). || Slap (guantada).
morral m. Gamebag (del cazador). || MIL. Knapsack, pack.
morralla f. Rubbish, trash (cosas sin valor). || Small fish (pescadillos). || FIG. Rabble (gente despreciable).
morrena f. GEOGR. Moraine (de glaciar).
morrillo m. Fleshy part of the neck (de animal). || TAUR. Muscular protrusion on the bull's neck. || FAM. Thick neck. || Pebble, round stone (canto rodado). || Rubblework (mampostería).
morriña f. Homesickness, nostalgia (nostalgia). || Sadness, despondency, gloom (tristeza). || VET. Dropsy.
morrión m. Morion (casco antiguo). || Shako (gorro militar).
morro m. Snout, nose (hocico de animal). || FAM. Thick lips, *pl.* (labios abultados). || FIG. y FAM. Lips, *pl.* (labios). || Knoll, hill (monte). || Pebble (guijarro). || MAR. Pier, jetty (malecón). || Butt, grip (de pistola). || Nose (de un avión). || Nose cone (de un cohete). || Nose, hood (de un coche). || Head (la parte redonda). || — *Beber a morro*, to drink from the bottle, to drink straight from the bottle. || *Caer de morros*, to nose-dive. || FIG. y FAM. *Estar de morros*, to be in a bad mood (estar enfadado). | *Estar de morros con*, to be cross with. || FAM. *Poner morros*, to purse one's lips, to look cross. | *Romperle a alguien los morros*, to punch s.o. in the nose.
morrocotudo, da adj. FAM. Tremendous, terrible (imponente): *un susto, un batacazo morrocotudo*, a tremendous scare, fall. | Huge, enormous (enorme). || Magnificent, terrific (magnífico).
morrón m. FAM. Blow, bang (golpe).
morrongo, ga m. y f. FAM. Cat (gato).
morsa f. ZOOL. Walrus (mamífero).
morse m. Morse (alfabeto).
mortadela f. Mortadella, bologna sausage.
mortaja f. Shroud (sudario). || TECN. Mortise (muesca). || *Amer.* Cigarette paper.
mortal adj. Mortal: *los seres mortales*, mortal beings. || Mortal, fatal: *herida mortal*, mortal wound. || Lethal, deadly: *una dosis mortal*, a lethal dose. || FIG. Mortal: *pecado mortal*, mortal sin. | Mortal, deadly: *odio, dolor mortal*, mortal hatred, pain. | Dreadful, awful: *aburrimiento, trabajo mortal*, dreadful boredom, work. | Unbearable, unending (espera). || — *Restos mortales*, mortal remains. || *Salto mortal*, somersault.
— M. y f. Mortal: *un mortal feliz*, a happy mortal.
mortalidad f. Mortality (condición de mortal). || Mortality: *la mortalidad infantil*, infant mortality. || Death rate, mortality (índice).
mortalmente adv. Mortally, fatally: *mortalmente herido*, mortally wounded. || FIG. Mortally: *odiar a uno mortalmente*, to hate s.o. mortally. | Dreadfully, deadly, deathly: *una película, una fiesta mortalmente aburrida*, a dreadfully boring film, party. || — FIG. *Aburrirse mortalmente*, to be bored stiff *o* to death. || *Pecar mortalmente*, to commit a mortal sin.
mortandad f. Mortality, loss of life: *el bombardeo, la epidemia produjo* or *causó gran mortandad*, the bombing, the epidemic caused heavy mortality. || Death toll (número de muertos).
mortecino, na adj. Dying, fading (que se apaga): *la luz mortecina del crepúsculo*, the fading glow of twilight. || Dim, pale (débil): *la luz mortecina de una vela*, the dim light of a candle. || Dull, faded (color). || Moribund (moribundo).
morterada f. MIL. Shot from a mortar. || FIG. Volley (andanada).
morterete m. Small mortar (artillería). || Gun for firing salutes (para salvas). || Lampion (de iluminación). || Brick (ladrillo).

mortero m. Mortar (almirez, argamasa). || MIL. Mortar (cañón).
mortífero, ra adj. Deadly, fatal: *una epidemia mortífera*, a deadly epidemic. || Deadly, lethal: *un arma mortífera*, a lethal weapon.
mortificación f. Mortification (privación). || Torment.
mortificador, ra o **mortificante** adj. Mortifying. || Wounding, cutting (hiriente).
mortificar v. tr. To mortify (dañar, humillar): *mortificar la carne*, to mortify the flesh. || To torment, to plague (atormentar). || To wound, to cut, to hurt (herir). || To mortify, to deaden (una parte del cuerpo).
mortinatalidad f. Infant mortality.
mortinato, ta adj. Stillborn.
— M. y f. Stillborn child.
mortuorio, ria adj. Mortuary. || Of mourning, of the deceased: *casa mortuoria*, house of mourning *o* of the deceased. || — *Lecho mortuorio*, deathbed. || *Paño mortuorio*, funeral pall.
morueco m. Ram (carnero).
moruno, na adj. Moorish (moro).
morusa f. FAM. Dough, money (dinero).
Mosa n. pr. m. GEOGR. Meuse (río).
mosaico m. Mosaic (azulejo).
mosaico, ca adj. Mosaic, of Moses (de Moisés).
mosaísmo m. Mosaism.
mosca f. Fly (insecto). || Fly (cebo para pescar): *caña de mosca*, fly rod. || Tuft of hair (en la barbilla). || FIG. y FAM. Dough, cash (dinero). | Pest, nuisance (persona molesta). | Nuisance, annoyance, bother (molestia). || — Pl. Sparks (chispas). || Spots before the eyes (en los ojos). || — FIG. y FAM. *Aflojar* or *soltar la mosca*, to fork out, to cough up, to pay up. | *Caer como moscas*, to drop *o* to fall like flies. | *Cazar* or *papar moscas*, to gape, to catch flies, to daydream. | *Es incapaz de matar* or *hacer daño a una mosca*, he wouldn't *o* he couldn't harm *o* hurt a fly. | *Estar mosca*, to be suspicious. | *Más moscas se cogen con miel que con hiel*, you catch more flies with honey than with vinegar. | *Mosca muerta*, V. MOSQUITA. | *No se oía ni una mosca*, you could have heard a pin drop. || *Peso mosca*, flyweight (boxeo). || FIG. y FAM. *Por si las moscas*, just in case. | *¿Qué mosca le ha picado?*, what's eating you? | *Tener la mosca* or *estar con la mosca detrás de* or *en la oreja*, V. OREJA.
moscada adj. f. *Nuez moscada*, nutmeg.
moscarda f. Blowfly, meat fly, bluebottle (moscón). || Eggs, *pl.* (de las abejas).
moscardear v. intr. To lay [eggs] (las abejas). || To rise (los peces). || FIG. y FAM. To nose around, to stick *o* to poke one's nose into everything.
moscardón m. ZOOL. Botfly (parásito). | Blowfly (moscón). | Hornet (abejón). || FIG. y FAM. Bore, nuisance, pest (persona pesada).
moscardoneo m. Buzz, buzzing.
moscareta f. Flycatcher (pájaro).
moscarrón m. Botfly (insecto).
moscatel adj. Muscat (uva).
— M. Muscatel, muscadel (vino). || — F. Muscat (uva).
moscón m. Blowfly, meat fly, bluebottle (insecto). || FIG. y FAM. Bore, nuisance, pest (persona pesada).
mosconear v. tr. To annoy, to bother, to pester (molestar).
— V. intr. To be a nuisance, to make a nuisance of o.s. (molestar). || To buzz (zumbar).
mosconeo m. Buzz, buzzing (zumbido). || FIG. Pestering (insistencia).
Moscovia n. pr. f. GEOGR. Muscovy.
moscovita adj./s. Muscovite.
Moscú n. pr. GEOGR. Moscow.
mosén m. Sir (título antiguo).
— OBSERV. Today this title is reserved for priests in certain regions of Spain (Catalonia, Aragon).
mosquear v. tr. To shoo away (espantar las moscas). || To swat (matar las moscas). || FIG. y FAM. To smell fishy: *este asunto me mosquea*, this business smells fishy to me.
— V. pr. To shoo flies away || FIG. To get annoyed *o* irritated (picarse). | To take offence (ofenderse). | To become suspicious (sospechar algo).
mosqueo m. Shooing *o* swatting of flies. || FIG. Resentment (pique). | Suspicion (sospecha).
mosquetazo m. Musket shot (tiro). || Musket wound (herida).
mosquete m. Musket (arma).
mosquetería f. Troop of musketeers, musketry. || TEATR. Groundlings, *pl.* [spectators who stood at back of the theatre].
mosquetero m. Musketeer. || TEATR. Groundling.
mosquetón m. Musketoon (arma).
mosquita f. Warbler (ave). || — FIG. y FAM. *Hacerse la mosquita muerta*, to look as if butter would not melt in one's mouth. | *Mosquita muerta*, hypocrite.
mosquitero m. Mosquito net.
mosquito m. Mosquito (insecto). || Gnat, midge (mosca pequeña).
mostacilla f. Mustard-seed shot, dust shot (perdigón). || Glass bead (abalorio).
mostacho m. Moustache, mustache (bigote). || FIG. y FAM. Spot on the face (mancha). || MAR. Bowsprit.
mostachón m. Macaroon (bollo).
mostaza f. Mustard. || Mustard seed (semilla). || Mustard-seed shot, dust shot (perdigones de caza).
mostense adj./s. Premonstratensian (religioso).
mosto m. Must.
mostrable adj. Showable. || Demonstrable.
mostrador, ra adj. Demonstrating, showing.
— M. y f. Demonstrator, exhibitor. || — M. Counter (en una tienda). || Bar (en un café). || Face (de reloj).
mostrar* v. tr. To show (enseñar). || To show, to indicate (indicar). || To display, to exhibit, to show, to manifest (manifestar): *mostrar interés*, to show interest. || To demonstrate, to show (dar muestras de): *mostrar gran paciencia*, to demonstrate great patience. || To point out, to show (señalar). || FIG. *Mostrar las uñas*, V. UÑA.
— V. pr. To show o.s. || To appear: *mostrarse en público*, to appear in public. || To be: *se mostró muy amable conmigo*, he was very kind to me. || To prove, to make: *se mostró un excelente jefe*, he made *o* he proved an excellent leader.
mostrenco, ca adj. JUR. Ownerless (sin propietario): *bienes mostrencos*, ownerless property. || FAM. Homeless (sin casa). | Stray (animal). | Coarse (rudo). | Dense, slow (ignorante). | Fat, heavy (pesado, gordo).
mota f. Spot, speck, mote (mancha pequeña). || FIG. Slight flaw (defecto insignificante). || Speck (en el ojo). || Burl, knot (en el paño). || Hillock (elevación del terreno).
mote m. Nickname (apodo): *poner mote*, to give a nickname. || Device, motto (divisa). || *Le pusieron como mote...*, they nicknamed him...
moteado m. Speckling, flecking (de un tejido).
motear v. tr. To fleck, to speckle, to dapple.
motejador, ra adj. Nicknaming.
— M. y f. Nicknamer.
motejar v. tr. To tag, to label, to call: *le han motejado de avaro*, they have labeled him a miser.
motel m. Motel (hotel).
motete m. MÚS. Motet.
motilón, ona adj. Hairless (pelón).
— M. FAM. Lay brother (lego).
motín m. Riot, uprising, insurrection (del pueblo). || Mutiny (de tropas).
motivación f. Motivation.
motivador, ra adj. Motivating.
— M. y f. Causer (causante).
motivar v. tr. To motivate, to cause (causar). || To justify (justificar). || To explain (explicar).
motivo m. Motive, reason, cause: *motivo de disputa*, cause of dispute. || Grounds, *pl.*: *motivos de divorcio*, grounds for divorce. || Motif (en música, en pintura, etc.). || — *Bajo ningún motivo*, under no circumstances, on no account. || *Con este motivo*, for this reason. || *Con mayor* or *con más motivo*, even more so. || *Con motivo de*, because of, owing to (debido a), on the occasion of. || *Dar motivo a*, to give rise to, to provoke. || *Darle a uno motivo* or *motivos para*, to give s.o. reason to (con verbo) *o* for (con sustantivo). || *De mi, tu, su motivo propio*, on my, your, his [her] own initiative. || *Exposición de motivos*, motivation. || *Motivo decorativo* or *ornamental*, decorative *o* ornamental motif. || *No ser motivo para*, to be no reason to *o* for. || *Por cuyo motivo*, on account of which. || *Por motivos de salud*, for reasons of health, for health reasons, on health grounds. || *Sin motivo alguno*, without any reason, for no reason at all.
moto f. Motor bike, motorcycle.
motoarado m. AGR. Motor tractor.
motobomba f. Motor pump.
motocarro m. Three-wheeler.
motocicleta f. Motorbike, motorcycle: *montar en motocicleta*, to ride a motorcycle.
motociclismo m. Motorcycling.
motociclista m. y f. Motorcyclist.
motociclo m. Motorcycle.
motocompresor m. Compressor.
motocross m. Moto-cross, cross-country motorcycle racing.
motocultivo m. Mechanized agriculture.
motoguadañadora f. AGR. Motor scythe.
motón m. MAR. Block, pulley: *motón de rabiza*, tail block.
motonave f. Motorboat, motor ship.
motonería f. MAR. Set of blocks or pulleys.
motoniveladora f. Leveller, bulldozer.
motopropulsor m. Motor propellor.
motor, ra adj. Motor: *músculos motores*, motor muscles. || Moving (moviente). || *Lancha motora*, motorboat.
— M. Engine, motor: *motor de explosión, de reacción*, internal combustion engine, jet engine. || — *Motor de arranque*, starting motor. || *Motor fuera borda*, outboard motor.
motora f. Motorboat.
motorismo m. Motorcycling (motociclismo).
motorista m. y f. Motorcyclist.
motorización f. Motorization.
motorizado, da adj. Motorized: *división motorizada*, motorized division.
motorizar v. tr. To motorize.
motorreactor m. Jet engine.
motosegadora f. AGR. Motor scythe.
mototractor m. AGR. [Motor] tractor.

motovelero m. Motor sailer.
motovolquete m. TECN. Mechanical tipping device.
motricidad f. Motivity.
motriz adj. f. Motive, driving: *fuerza motriz*, motive force.
movedizo, za adj. Moving, shifting (no firme). || Loose (fácil de mover). || FIG. Inconsistent, fickle (persona). | Unsettled, changeable (situación). || *Arenas movedizas*, quicksand, *sing*.
movedor, ra adj. Moving.
— M. y f. Mover.
mover* v. tr. To move: *mover el brazo*, to move one's arm. || To shake (la cabeza para negar). || To nod (la cabeza para asentir). || To stir: *mover el café*, to stir one's coffee. || To wag (el rabo). || FIG. To incite (incitar): *mover a la rebelión*, to incite to rebellion. | To stir up (a las masas). | To drive, to move: *movido por la curiosidad*, driven by curiosity. | To provoke, to cause (provocar): *mover discordia*, to cause discord. | To move, to stir (conmover). || To move (las piezas del ajedrez). || TECN. To drive (impulsar). | To power (impeler). | To work (hacer funcionar). | To pull (arrastrar). || — FIG. *Mover a*, to move to: *mover a compasión*, to move to pity. | *Mover a uno a risa*, to make s.o. laugh. | *Mover cielo y tierra*, to move heaven and earth. || *Mover la cabeza de arriba abajo*, to nod. || *Mover la cabeza de un lado a otro*, to shake one's head. || FIG. *Mover la curiosidad*, to arouse s.o.'s curiosity. | *Mover los hilos*, to pull [the] strings. | *Ser movido por el interés*, to be motivated by personal gain.
— V. intr. ARQ. To spring (un arco).
— V. pr. To move: *¡no se mueva!*, don't move!; *moverse alrededor del Sol*, to move round the sun; *se mueve con dificultad*, he moves with difficulty. || To wriggle, to fidget: *este niño no deja de moverse*, this child never stops wriggling. || FIG. To move around: *para conseguir una buena colocación hay que moverse*, in order to get a good job you have to move around. | To make a move, to act (obrar). || To be rough (el mar). || FIG. y FAM. To get a move on: *¡muévete!*, get a move on! || FIG. y FAM. *Moverse más que el rabo de una lagartija* or *que un saco de ratones*, to be fidgety, to have ants in one's pants.
movible adj. Movable, moveable.
movido, da adj. Moved: *movido de* or *por la piedad*, moved by pity. || Blurred, fuzzy (fotografía). || Motivated: *movido por el interés*, motivated by personal gain. || FIG. Active (persona). | Lively (animado). || Restless (que no deja de moverse). || *Amer.* Thin, skinny, rachitic (delgaducho). | Rough, choppy (mar).
moviente adj. Moving, mobile.
móvil adj. Movable, moveable: *fiesta móvil*, movable feast. || FIG. Unstable, changeable (inestable). || — TECN. *Material móvil*, rolling stock (ferrocarril). || *Timbre móvil*, fiscal *o* revenue stamp.
— M. Motive: *el móvil de un crimen*, the motive of a crime. || FÍS. Moving body (cuerpo en movimiento). || ARTES. Mobile.
movilidad f. Mobility.
movilizable adj. Mobilizable.
movilización f. Mobilization.
movilizar v. tr. To mobilize.
movimiento m. Movement, motion: *el movimiento de las olas*, the movement of the waves. || FÍS. Motion: *movimiento perpetuo*, perpetual motion. || Upheaval, uprising (revuelta). || Movement: *movimiento revolucionario*, revolutionary movement. || Shake (de cabeza, de un lado a otro), nod (de cabeza, de arriba abajo). || Movement, activity (actividad). || Traffic (de automóviles). || Action (de un libro). || COM. Fluctuations, *pl.* (del mercado). | Trend (de los precios). | Change, movement (cambio). || FIG. Stir, change, evolution, movement (de ideas). | Fit, outburst (de celos, de risa, etc.). || Move (en los juegos). || GEOL. Tremor: *movimiento sísmico*, earth tremor. || MIL. Movement, move. || ASTR. Movement. || MÚS. y MED. Movement. || — *Dar movimiento a* or *poner en movimiento*, to put *o* to set in motion. || *El movimiento del péndulo*, the swing *o* the swinging of the pendulum. || FIG. *El movimiento se demuestra andando*, one should always set a good example. || *Estar en movimiento*, to be in motion, to be moving. || COM. *Movimiento de existencias*, rotation of stock. || *Movimiento de tierras*, earthwork. || MAR. *Movimiento de un puerto*, shipping entries and clearances. || MIL. *Movimiento envolvente*, outflanking movement. || *Tienda* or *comercio de mucho movimiento*, busy shop.
moxte V. OXTE.
moyuelo m. Grits, *pl.* (salvado). || Bran (afrecho).
moza f. Girl, young girl, lass (muchacha joven). || Bachelor girl (soltera). || Servant, maid (criada). || Washerwoman's paddle (de las lavanderas). || Last hand (última mano en los juegos). || — *Buena moza*, good-looking woman (mujer), good-looking girl (muchacha). || *Es una real moza*, she is a pretty girl *o* a good looker. || *Moza de fortuna* or *del partido*, daughter of pleasure, prostitute.
mozalbete m. Young lad, young fellow.
mozárabe adj. Mozarabic.
— M. y f. Mozarab.
— OBSERV. The term *Mozarab* applies to the Spanish Christians living in Moslem Spain, and their art and literature which flourished especially in the kingdom of León in the 10th and early 11th centuries.
mozarrón, ona m. y f. Hearty lad (muchacho), hearty lass (muchacha).
mozo, za adj. Young (joven). || Single, unmarried (soltero). || *En sus años mozos*, when he was young, in his youth.
— M. y f. Young boy, lad (muchacho), young girl, lass (muchacha). || Bachelor (soltero), bachelor girl (soltera). || — M. Waiter (camarero). || Servant (criado). || Porter [U.S., porter, redcap] (de estación). || Conscript (soldado). || Coat hanger, clothes hanger (percha). || — *Mozo de caballos, de cuadra*, stableboy, groom. || *Mozo de café*, waiter. || *Mozo de carnicero*, butcher's boy. || *Mozo de comedor*, waiter. || *Mozo de cordel* or *de cuerda*, porter. || *Mozo de espuelas*, footman. || *Mozo de estación*, porter. || TAUR. *Mozo de estoques*, sword boy, bullfighter's aid. || *Mozo de habitación*, valet (en un hotel). || *Mozo de labranza*, farmhand. || *Ser un buen mozo*, to be a fine figure of a man.
mozuelo, la m. y f. Youngster.
muaré m. Moiré (tela).
mucamo, ma m. y f. *Amer.* Servant (hombre o mujer), maid (mujer).
muceta f. Mozetta, mozzetta (vestidura eclesiástica). || Hood (en la universidad).
mucilaginoso, sa adj. Mucilaginous.
mucílago m. BOT. Mucilage.
mucosidad f. Mucosity, mucus.
mucoso, sa adj. Mucous.
— F. Mucosa, mucous membrane.
múcura o **mucura** f. *Amer.* Pitcher, earthenware jar (vasija).
mucus m. Mucus.
muchachada f. Kids, *pl.*, boys and girls, *pl.*, group of kids (pandilla). || Prank (acción propia de niño).
muchachear v. intr. To act childishly.
muchachería f. V. MUCHACHADA.
muchacho, cha m. y f. Youngster, youth (joven). || — M. Servant (criado). || Lad, boy, youth (chico). || — F. Maid (criada). || Young girl, lass (chica).
muchachuelo, la m. y f. Kid.
muchedumbre f. Crowd, flock (de gente). || Flock (de pájaros).
muchísimo, ma adj. Very much, a lot of.
— Adv. A great deal, a lot.
mucho, cha adj. A lot of (gran cantidad): *mucha agua*, a lot of water. || Many, a lot of (numerosos): *muchos niños*, many children, a lot of children. || Many (con *los*, *sus*, etc.): *a causa de sus muchas tareas no puede salir*, because of his many tasks he can't go out. || Much, a lot of: *¿tienes mucho trabajo?*, have you much work?; *no tengo mucho trabajo*, I have not much work. || Great, very great (grande): *es mucha tu responsabilidad en este asunto*, your responsibility in this matter is very great. || — *Aquí hay mucho estudiante*, there are lots of students here. || *¡Es mucha mujer!*, what a woman she is! || *Éste es mucho coche para ustedes*, this car is far too big for you. || *Hace mucho calor, frío*, it is very hot *o* warm, cold. || *Muchas gracias*, thank you very much. || *Muchas veces*, very often, many times. || FIG. *Mucho ruido y pocas nueces*, much ado about nothing. || *Muchos pocos hacen un mucho*, every little [bit] helps, many a little makes a mickle. || *Mucho tiempo*, a long time.
— Pron. Many [people], a lot [of people]: *muchos piensan que*, many people think that, a lot of people think that. || Many, a lot: *muchos de mis amigos son extranjeros*, many of my friends are foreigners. || A lot: *me queda mucho por hacer*, I still have a lot to do. || Much, a lot: *¿te queda mucho todavía?*, do you still have much left? || — *Los muchos que*, everyone who, all those who. || *Son muchos los que* or *muchas las que*, there are many [people] who.
— Adv. Much: *mucho más joven que*, much younger than. || A lot: *ha viajado mucho*, he has travelled a lot. || A lot, very much: *¿te has divertido? — Sí, mucho*, have you enjoyed yourself? *o* did you enjoy yourself? — Yes, very much. || A long time: *hace mucho que no le veo*, I have not seen him for a long time. || — *Como mucho*, at the most, at the outside: *ganarás como mucho diez mil pesetas*, you will earn ten thousand pesetas at the most. || *Con mucho*, by far, far and away, easily: *es con mucho el más simpático*, he is by far the nicest. || *Correr mucho*, to run fast. || *Ir mucho*, to go often. || *Me alegro mucho*, I am very glad. || *Mucho antes*, a long time before, long before. || *Mucho después*, a long time after, long after. || *Mucho más*, much more, a lot more. || *Mucho mejor*, much better, a lot better. || *Mucho menos*, much less, a lot less. || *Mucho peor*, much worse, a lot worse. || *Muy mucho*, very much. || *Ni con mucho*, not nearly, nothing like: *no es con mucho tan simpático como su hermano*, he is not nearly as nice as his brother. || *Ni mucho menos*, not by any means, by no means: *no es tonto, ni mucho menos*, he is by no means stupid, he is not stupid by any means. || *No es para mucho*, it's not up to much. || *Pesar mucho*, to be heavy, to weigh a lot. || *Por mucho que*, no matter how much, however much: *por mucho que trabaje, no consigue nada*, no matter how much he works, he never gets

anywhere; *por mucho que insistas, no lo haré*, however much you insist, I shall not do it; however fast, however hard, etc.: *por mucho que corra*, however fast it goes; *por mucho que trabaje*, however hard he works. || *Quedarse mucho*, to stay long *o* a long time. || *Ser mucho para*, to mean a lot to. || *Si no es mucho pedir*, if it's not asking too much. || *Tener en mucho*, to think a lot of, to think highly of, to hold in high esteem (apreciar mucho). || *Trabajar mucho*, to work hard.
— Interj. Quite, quite right.

— OBSERV. Aunque *much* corresponda a *mucho* conviene señalar que no se suele usar en frases afirmativas. Por otra parte es preciso subrayar que *much* sólo puede ir acompañado de una palabra singular y *many* de un término en plural.

muda f. Change of underwear (ropa). || Moult; moulting [U.S., molt, molting] (cambio de la piel en los animales). || Moulting season [U.S., molting season] (estación en que se realiza). || Slough (de las serpientes). || Breaking (de la voz). || Moving house, move, removal (traslado de domicilio).
mudable adj. Changeable (cambiable). || Inconstant, fickle (cambiadizo).
mudada f. *Amer*. Change of underwear.
mudanza f. Change (cambio). || Removal, move (de domicilio). || Moving into a house (instalación de una casa). || Figure, movement (de baile). || MÚS. Shift. || — *Camión de mudanzas*, removal van. || *Estar de mudanza*, to be moving. || *Hacer la mudanza*, to move house, to move. || *Hacer la mudanza de los muebles*, to have one's furniture removed.
mudar v. tr. e intr. To change (cambiar): *mudar el agua en vino*, to change water into wine; *han mudado de oficina*, they have changed office; *mudar de ropa*, to change one's clothes. || To change (a un niño). || To moult [U.S., to molt] (un animal). || To break (la voz): *el chico está mudando la voz*, the boy's voice is breaking. || To move (cambiar de destino): *le han mudado de oficina*, they have moved him to another office. || To move (instalarse): *mudar de piso*, to move to a new flat; *mudar de casa*, to move house. || FIG. To change (variar): *mudar de idea* or *de parecer*, to change one's mind; *mudar de color*, to change colour. || — FIG. *Muda el lobo los dientes mas no las mientes*, a leopard cannot change its spots. || *Mudar de piel*, to shed its skin, to moult [U.S., to molt]. || *Mudar de pluma*, to moult [U.S., to molt].
— V. pr. To change, to get changed (cambiarse de ropa). || To change *mudarse de falda*, to change one's skirt. || To move house, to move (cambiar de domicilio). || *Se te está mudando la voz*, your voice is breaking.
mudéjar adj./s. Mudejar.

— OBSERV. The word applies to those Moslems who remained in Castile after the Reconquest and to their art, which dates from the 12th to the 16th century and is characterized by Islamic influence (minarets, multicoloured decorations, etc.).

mudez f. Dumbness, muteness. || Silence (silencio).
mudo, da adj. Dumb: *es mudo de nacimiento*, he was born dumb. || FIG. Mute, silent (callado): *se quedó mudo durante toda la reunión*, he remained silent throughout the whole meeting. | Speechless, dumb (sin poder hablar). || Silent, mute (letra). || GEOGR. Blank, skeleton (mapa). || — *Cine mudo, película muda*, silent cinema *o* films, silent film. || FIG. y FAM. *Mudo como un muerto* or *como una tumba*, as close as a clam. || *Mudo de admiración*, speechless with admiration. || *Quedarse mudo de asombro*, to be dumbfounded *o* awestruck.
— M. y f. Dumb *o* mute person. || Deaf-mute (sordomudo). || *Los mudos*, the dumb, the mute.
mueblaje m. Furniture.
mueble m. Piece of furniture. || Cabinet (armario). || — Pl. Furniture, *sing*. || — *Con muebles*, furnished. || *Mueble bar*, cocktail cabinet. || *Mueble cama*, foldaway bed unit. || *Tienda de muebles*, furniture shop.
— Adj. *Bienes muebles*, personal property, *sing*., personalty, *sing*., movables.
mueblería f. Furniture shop.
mueblista m. Furniture maker (que fabrica). || Furniture dealer (que vende).
mueca f. Face (burlesca). || Grimace (de dolor, de disgusto). || *Hacer muecas a*, to make faces at, to pull faces at.
muecín m. Muezzin (almuédano).
muela f. Millstone (de molino). || Grindstone, whetstone (de afilar). || Molar (diente molar). || Tooth (diente): *el niño está echando las muelas*, the baby is cutting his teeth; *empastar una muela*, to fill a tooth. || Hillock (cerro). || BOT. Vetch (planta). || — *Dolor de muelas*, toothache. || *Muela cordal* or *del juicio*, wisdom tooth. || *Muela picada*, decayed tooth. || *Muela postiza*, false tooth. || FIG. y FAM. *No hay ni para una muela*, there is not enough to feed a sparrow.
muellaje m. MAR. Dockage, wharfage.
muelle adj. Soft (blando). || Luxurious, soft, easy: *llevar una vida muelle*, to lead a luxurious life.
— M. MAR. Wharf, dock (de un puerto). || Pier (malecón). || Embankment (a lo largo de un río). || Freight platform (de ferrocarril). || Spring (de un mecanismo): *colchón de muelles*, spring mattress. || — TECN. *Muelle antagonista* or *de retorno*, pullback spring. || *Muelle en espiral*, coil spring, spiral spring.
muellemente adv. Delicately, gently. || Softly (blandamente). || Comfortably (cómodamente).
muera f. Salt (sal).
muérdago BOT. Mistletoe.
muermo m. Glanders, *pl*. (del caballo).
muerte f. Death: *condenado a muerte*, condemned to death; *fiel hasta la muerte*, faithful unto death. || Murder (homicidio). || FIG. Death (desaparición). || TAUR. The kill. || — *A muerte*, to the death: *luchar a muerte*, to fight to the death. || *A vida o muerte*, life-and-death, life-or-death: *una operación a vida o muerte*, a life-and-death operation. || FIG. *Con la muerte en el alma*, sick at heart. || *Dar muerte a*, to kill, to put to death. || FIG. y FAM. *De mala muerte*, crummy, lousy, rotten: *un coche de mala muerte*, a lousy car; *una película de mala muerte*, a crummy film; *pueblo de mala muerte*, V. PUEBLO. || *De muerte*, big, enormous: *un susto de muerte*, a big fright. || *Encontrar la muerte*, to meet one's death. || *En el artículo de la muerte*, in the article of death, at the point of death. || *Estar a dos pasos de la muerte*, to be at death's door. || *Estar a la muerte*, to be dying. || *Estar a las puertas de la muerte*, to be at death's door. || *Estar en su lecho de muerte*, to be on one's deathbed. || *Guerra a muerte*, war to the knife, war to the bitter end. || *Hasta la muerte*, to the death. || *Morir de muerte natural*, to die a natural death. || JUR. *Muerte civil*, civil death, attainder. || FIG. y FAM. *Muerte chiquita*, nervous shudder. || *Muerte repentina*, sudden death. || *Odiar a muerte*, to loathe. || *Pasar de vida a muerte*, to pass away. || *Retar a muerte*, to challenge to a fight to the death. || FIG. *Ser la muerte*, to be deadly. | *Sufrir mil muertes*, to die a thousand deaths.
muerto, ta adj. Dead. || FAM. Killed (matado): *muerto en la guerra*, killed in the war, killed in action. | Dead (muy cansado). || FIG. Dead, flat, dull (colores). | Dead, lifeless (sin actividad). || DEP. Dead. || JUR. Dead (letra). || — *Caer muerto*, to drop down dead. || *Cal muerta*, slaked lime. || *Dar por muerto a uno*, to assume s.o. dead. || FIG. *Estar más que muerto*, to be dead and buried. | *Estar muerto de cansancio*, to be dead tired. | *Estar muerto de frío*, to be freezing *o* frozen to death. | *Estar muerto de hambre*, to be starving to death. | *Estar muerto de miedo*, to be scared to death. || *Horas muertas*, dead hours. || *Lengua muerta*, dead language. || *Más muerto que vivo*, more dead than alive, half-dead. || *Medio muerto*, half-dead. || FIG. y FAM. *Muerto el perro se acabó la rabia*, dead dogs don't bite. || *Nacido muerto*, stillborn. || ARTES. *Naturaleza muerta*, still life (bodegón). || FIG. y FAM. *No tener dónde caerse muerto*, not to have a penny to one's name. || MAR. *Obra muerta*, upperworks, *pl*. || *Punto muerto*, neutral (en un coche), dead centre (en mecánica), stalemate, deadlock, impasse (en negociaciones, etc.). || *Se busca vivo o muerto*, wanted dead or alive. || FIG. y FAM. *Ser letra muerta*, to become a dead letter.
— M. y f. Dead person, dead man (hombre), dead woman (mujer). || Corpse, body (cadáver). || — M. Dummy (en los naipes). || — Pl. Casualties: *en ese accidente hubo diez muertos*, there were ten casualties in that accident. || Dead: *los vivos y los muertos*, the quick and the dead; *resucitar de entre los muertos*, to rise from the dead. || — FIG. *Caer como un muerto*, to fall in a heap. | *Callarse como un muerto*, to keep quiet, not to say a word. | *Cargar con el muerto*, to be left holding the baby *o* the bag [U.S., to carry the can]. || *Doblar* or *tocar a muerto*, to toll, to toll the knell. || FIG. y FAM. *Echarle a uno el muerto*, to pass the buck to s.o. | *Hacer el muerto*, to float on one's back (natación). | *Hacerse el muerto*, to play possum *o* dead. | *Más pálido que un muerto*, as pale as death, as white as a sheet. || *Ser un muerto de hambre*, to be a starveling.

— OBSERV. *Muerto* is the past participle of *morir*.

muesca f. Notch, nick (corte). || TECN. Mortise, mortice (entalladura). | Mortising, morticing (operación). || Earmark, nick in the ear (en el ganado). || TECN. *Hacer muesca en*, to mortise, to mortice.
muestra f. Sample (de una tela o mercancía). || Show, display (exposición de mercancías). || Specimen (de un libro). || Sign, signboard (de una tienda). || Model (modelo). || Face, dial (esfera de reloj). || Sample (en estadística). || MIL. Review (revista). || Turnup (naipes). || FIG. Sample: *nos dio una muestra de su saber*, he gave us a sample of his knowledge. | Proof (prueba): *esto es muestra de que no me quiere*, this is proof that he does not love me; *ser buena muestra de algo*, to be good proof of sth. | Sign: *muestra de cansancio*, sign of fatigue. | Show, token: *muestra de aprecio*, token of esteem. || — *Botón de muestra*, sample. || *Como botón de muestra*, as a sample. || *Dar muestras de*, to show signs of. || *Feria de muestras*, trade fair. || *Hacer muestras de*, to show, to display. || TECN. *Muestra de perforación*, core sample (en un pozo de petróleo) || FIG. *Para muestra basta un botón*, one example is enough. || *Perro de muestra*, pointer. || FIG. *Por la muestra se conoce el paño*, you can judge a man by his work. || *Vivienda* or *piso de muestra*, model home *o* apartment.

muestrario m. Collection of samples.
muestreo m. Sampling (estadística).
mufla f. TECN. Muffle (hornillo).
mufti m. Mufti (jurisconsulto musulmán).
mugido m. Moo, mooing, low, lowing (de la vaca). || Bellow, bellowing (del toro). || FIG. Howl, moan (del viento).
mugidor, ra o **mugiente** adj. Mooing, lowing. || Bellowing.
mugir v. intr. To low, to moo (las vacas). || To bellow (el toro). || FIG. To bellow, to roar (de ira). | To moan, to howl (el viento).
mugre f. Filth, dirt, grime (suciedad).
mugriento, ta adj. Filthy, grimy, dirty.
mugrón m. AGR. Layer (tallo de la vid). | Sucker, shoot, sprig (brote de una planta).
muguete m. BOT. Lily of the valley (planta). || MED. Thrush (enfermedad).
mujer f. Woman: *diez mujeres*, ten women. || Wife (esposa): *le presento a mi mujer*, may I introduce you to my wife. || — FAM. *Es una mujer de bandera* or *de tronío*, she is a knockout *o* a bombshell *o* an eye-opener. || *Mi futura mujer*, my bride-to-be. || *¡Mujer!*, woman: *¡mujer, no llores tanto!*, don't cry so, woman! || *Mujer de gobierno*, housekeeper. || *Mujer de la limpieza*, charwoman. || *Mujer de su casa*, housewife, homemaker. || *Mujer de vida airada, de mal vivir, mundana* or *perdida*, loose *o* scarlet woman. || *Mujer fatal*, femme fatale, vamp. || *Mujer pública*, prostitute, streetwalker. || *Ser mujer*, to be a grown woman. || *Ser muy mujer*, to be very feminine. || *Tomar mujer*, to take a wife, to marry. || *Tomar por mujer*, to take to wife *o* for one's wife.
mujercilla f. Little *o* small woman. || Worthless woman, woman of no account (mujer poco estimable). || Strumpet, tart (prostituta).
mujerero adj. m. *Amer.* Fond of the girls, womanizing (mujeriego).
mujeriego, ga adj. Feminine, womanly (propio de mujeres). || — *Montar a la mujeriega* or *a mujeriegas*, to ride sidesaddle. || *Ser mujeriego*, to be fond of the girls, to be a woman chaser, to be one for the girls.
— M. Wolf, womanizer, woman chaser.
mujeril adj. Feminine, womanly, woman's (propio de mujeres). || Womanish, effeminate (afeminado).
mujerío m. [Crowd of] women.
mujerona f. Big *o* strapping woman.
mujeruca f. Old woman.
mujerzuela f. Small *o* little woman (mujer chiquita). || Loose woman, hussy, prostitute (prostituta). || Fishwife (maleducada).
mujik m. Moujik (campesino ruso).
mújol m. ZOOL. Mullet (pez).
mula f. ZOOL. Mule, she-mule (animal). || Mule, slipper (calzado). || Shoe worn by the Pope (calzado del Papa). || FIG. Mule: *testarudo como una mula*, as stubborn as a mule. | Brute, animal, beast (bruto). | Ass, idiot (idiota). || *Amer.* Shoulder pad (de los cargadores).
mulada f. Drove of mules (recua). || FIG. y FAM. Stupid *o* foolish thing (tontería).
muladar m. Rubbish dump, tip, shoot (vertedero de basuras). || Dungheap (estiércol). || FIG. Dump (sitio sucio o corrompido).
muladí adj./s. Renegade [Spaniard who accepted Mohammedanism during the Reconquest].
mular adj. Mule, of a mule *o* mules. || *Ganado mular*, mules, *pl.*
mulato, ta adj. Mulatto. || FIG. Dark, dark-skinned, dark-complexioned (moreno). || *Amer.* Dark silver ore.
— M. y f. Mulatto (hombre), mulattress (mujer).
mulé (dar) loc. FAM. To bump off (matar).
mulero, ra adj. Mule (mular). || Mule-breeding (relativo a la producción).
— M. Muleteer (mozo).
muleta f. Crutch (para andar). || TAUR. "Muleta": *torear de muleta*, to fight [the bull] with the "muleta". || Support, prop (sostén).
muletear v. tr. TAUR. To fight [the bull] with the "muleta"
muletero m. Muleteer. || TAUR. Bullfighter who uses the "muleta", matador.
muletilla f. TAUR. "Muleta". || Button (botón). || Cross-handle cane (bastón). || FIG. Pet word *o* phrase (estribillo). | Padding, fill-in (palabra inútil).
muletón m. Melton (tela). || Undertablecloth (mantel).
mulillas f. pl. TAUR. Mules that drag the dead bull from the ring.
mulo m. Mule. || FIG. y FAM. Ass, idiot (idiota). | Mule (testarudo). | Brute, animal, beast (bruto). || — FIG. *Estar hecho un mulo*, to be as strong as an ox (muy fuerte). | *Hacer el mulo*, to be a brute. | *Trabajar como un mulo*, to work like a dog *o* a horse.
multa f. Fine. || Ticket (por estar mal aparcado, etc.). || — *Imponer* or *poner* or *echar una multa a uno*, to fine s.o., to impose a fine on s.o. (en general), to give s.o. a ticket (por estar mal aparcado). || *Me pusieron una multa de mil pesetas*, I was fined a thousand pesetas.
multar v. tr. To fine: *multar a uno en mil pesetas*, to fine s.o. one thousand pesetas.
multicanal adj. Multichannel (en televisión).
multicelular adj. Multicellular.
multicolor adj. Multicoloured [U.S., multicolored].
multicopia f. Duplicating.
multicopiar v. tr. To duplicate.
multicopista f. Duplicator, mimeograph, duplicating machine. || *Tirar* or *hacer con multicopista*, to duplicate.
multiforme adj. Multiform.
multilateral adj. Multilateral.
multimillonario, ria adj./s. Multimillionaire.
multinacional adj. Multinational.
multíparo, ra adj. Multiparous (mujer o animal).
— F. Multipara.
multiplano m. AVIAC. Multiplane.
múltiple adj. Multiple: *sistema múltiple*, multiple system. || Many, manifold (numerosos).
— M. Manifold.
múltiplex adj. Multiplex (telégrafo).
multiplexor m. Multiplexer
multiplicable adj. Multipliable.
multiplicación f. Multiplication.
multiplicado, da adj. Multiplied. || TECN. *Directa multiplicada*, overgeared fourth, overdrive.
multiplicador, ra adj. Multiplying.
— M. Multiplier.
multiplicando m. MAT. Multiplicand.
multiplicar v. tr. To multiply. || TECN. To gear up. || FIG. To multiply, to increase. || *Tabla de multiplicar*, multiplication table.
— V. pr. To multiply. || FIG. To go out of one's way, to exert o.s. to the utmost, to be everywhere (hacer el máximo): *se multiplicaba para hacernos la estancia más agradable*, she went out of her way to make our stay more enjoyable. || *Creced y multiplicaos*, go forth and multiply.
multiplicativo, va adj. Multiplicative.
multiplicidad f. Multiplicity.
múltiplo, pla adj. MAT. Multiple.
— M. MAT. Multiple.
multisecular adj. Centuries-old.
multitud f. Multitude: *una multitud de detalles*, a multitude of details. || Multitude, crowd (muchedumbre). || *Tener multitud de ocupaciones*, to have lots of things to do.
multitudinario, ria adj. Multitudinous.
mullido, da adj. Fluffy, soft, downy (blando y cómodo): *cama mullida*, soft bed.
— M. Flock, stuffing (para rellenar).
mullir* v. tr. To beat, to soften (la lana). || To fluff up (un colchón). || To loosen, to break up, to hoe (la tierra).
muncho, cha adj./adv. (Ant.) FAM. V. MUCHO.
mundanal adj. Worldly, of the world, mundane (p.us.). || *Huir del mundanal ruido*, to flee the hubbub of worldly life.
mundanalidad f. Worldliness.
mundanear v. intr. To be wordly-minded.
mundanería f. Worldliness, wordly-mindedness (apego a lo terrestre). || Social-mindedness (afición a la vida social). || Worldly behaviour (acción mundana).
mundano, na adj. Worldly, of the world, earthly, mundane (p.us.): *placeres mundanos*, worldly pleasures. || Social-minded: *persona mundana*, social-minded person. || Society: *reunión mundana*, society gathering. || — *La vida mundana*, social life. || *Llevar una vida muy mundana*, to lead a very active social life. || *Mujer mundana*, loose *o* light *o* scarlet woman (prostituta).
— M. y f. Worldly person, socialite.
mundial adj. World: *la primera guerra mundial*, the First World War; *a escala mundial*, on a world scale. || Worldwide, universal: *una organización mundial*, a worldwide organization.
— M. World championship.
mundillo m. World, circles, *pl.*: *el mundillo financiero*, the financial world; *el mundillo literario*, the literary world. || Clotheshorse (secadero). || Pillow for making lace (para hacer encaje). || Bedwarmer (calentador para la cama). || BOT. Snowball.
mundo m. World: *dar la vuelta al mundo*, to go around the world. || FIG. World, realm: *el mundo de los negocios*, the business world; *el mundo literario*, the literary world. | World of difference: *hay un mundo entre las dos versiones*, there is a world of difference between the two versions. | Experience. || Saratoga trunk (baúl). || REL. World, secular life. || BOT. Snowball. || — FIG. *Al fin del mundo*, at the back of beyond (sitio), at the end of time (tiempo). | *Anda* or *está el mundo al revés*, it's a topsy-turvy world. | *Así va el mundo*, so it goes, that's the way it goes. | *Aunque se hunda el mundo*, come what may. | *Como todo el mundo*, like everyone else, like other people. || *Conocido por* or *en el mundo entero*, known the world over, world-famous. || FIG. *Correr mundo*, to roam the world over, to travel far and wide, to see the world. | *Dar un mundo por*, to give the world for. | *De mundo*, of the world: *hombre de mundo*, man of the world; *mujer de mundo*, woman of the world. | *Desde que el mundo es mundo*, since the world began, from *o* since the beginning of time. | *Echar al mundo*, to bring into the world, to give birth to, to bring forth. | *Echarse al mundo*, to become a prostitute. | *El gran mundo*, high society, high life. | *El mundo es de los audaces*, fortune helps those who help them-

selves. | *El mundo es un pañuelo* or *¡qué pequeño es el mundo!*, it's a small world. | *El mundo no se hundirá por eso*, it's not the end of the world. || *El Nuevo, el Antiguo* or *Viejo Mundo*, the New, the Old World. || *En el mundo entero*, all over the world, the world over, throughout the whole world. || FIG. *En el otro mundo*, in the next World, in the hereafter. | *En este mundo de Dios* or *en este bajo mundo*, here below. | *En todo el mundo*, everywhere. | *Entrar en el mundo*, to come out, to make one's début in society. | *Estar todavía en el mundo de los vivos*, to be still living, to be in land of the living. | *Hacerse un mundo de algo*, to make a big thing of sth. | *Hasta el fin del mundo*, to the edges of the earth. | *Irse al otro mundo*, to pass away. | *Mandar* or *enviar al otro mundo*, to bump s.o. off, to do s.o. in. | *Medio mundo*, loads of people, no end of people. | *No es cosa* or *nada del otro mundo*, V. COSA. | *No ser de este mundo*, to live in a world of one's own. | *Ponerse el mundo por montera*, V. MONTERA. | *Por esos mundos de Dios*, here and there (en varios sitios), God Knows where (no se sabe dónde). | *Por nada del mundo, por todo el oro del mundo*, not for all the world, not for [anything in] the world, not for all the tea in China, not for all the money in the world. | *Prometer este mundo y el otro*, to promise the earth, to promise the moon and stars. | *Recorrer* or *rodar mundo*, to roam the world over, to see the world. | *Salir de* or *dejar este mundo*, to depart this world, to pass away (morir). | *Se le hundió el mundo*, his world tumbled down around him, his world caved in. | *Tener mundo*, to have savoir vivre, to be a man of the world, to know how to act in society, to know one's way around. | *Todo el mundo*, everyone, everybody. | *Traer al mundo*, to bring into the world. | *Valer un mundo*, to be worth one's weight in gold, to be worth one's salt (persona), to be worth its weight in gold (cosa). | *Venir al mundo*, to come into the world. | *Ver mundo*, to see the world, to see things, to see life. | *Vivir en el otro mundo*, to live at the back of beyond (vivir muy lejos). | *Vivir en otro mundo*, to live in another world.

mundología f. Worldliness, worldly wisdom (experiencia). || Savoir vivre (reglas mundanas).

mundonuevo m. Peep show (cosmorama).

mundovisión m. Transoceanic television broadcasting, broadcasting by satellite (televisión).

munición f. MIL. Ammunition, munition. || Shot (perdigones): *munición menuda*, small shot. || Load, charge (carga). || — *Disparar con munición de fogueo*, to fire blanks. || *Municiones de boca*, provisions, rations. || *Pan de munición*, ration bread.

municionamiento m. MIL. Supplies, *pl.*

municionero, ra m. y f. Supply officer.

municipal adj. Municipal.
— M. Policeman.

municipalidad f. Municipality.

municipalización f. Municipalization.

municipalizar v. tr. To municipalize.

munícipe m. Inhabitant of a district.

municipio m. Municipality (término municipal). || District (conjunto de vecinos). || Town council (concejo). || Town hall (alcaldía).

munificencia f. Munificence.

munífico, ca adj. Munificent.

muniqués, esa adj. [Of *o* from] Munich.
— M. y f. Native *o* inhabitant of Munich.

muñeca f. Wrist (del brazo). || Doll (juguete): *muñeca de trapo*, rag doll. || Dummy, mannequin (maniquí). || Polishing bag, pouncing bag, pad (para barnizar o estarcir). || FIG. y FAM. Doll (muchacha guapa). || *Amer.* Dummy (maqueta de un libro).

muñeco m. Boy doll (juguete). || Puppet (marioneta). || Funny figure (figura tosca, dibujo, etc.). || FIG. y FAM. Puppet, pawn (persona dominada por otra). | Popinjay (jovenzuelo presumido). || *Muñeco de nieve*, snowman.

muñeira f. Popular Galician dance.

muñequera f. Wristlet, wristband (de los gimnastas). || (P.us.). Watch strap, watchband (de reloj de pulsera).

muñequilla f. Polishing bag, pad (para barnizar). || *Amer.* Small ear of maize [U.S., of corn]. || *Dar con la muñequilla*, to French-polish (un mueble).

muñidor m. Beadle (de una cofradía).

muñón m. Stump (en una amputación). || Trunnion, gudgeon (del cañón).

muñonera f. MIL. Trunnion hole, gudgeon socket.

murajes m. BOT. Pimpernel.

mural adj. Mural: *pintura mural*, mural painting. || Wall: *mapa mural*, wall map.
— M. Mural, fresco (fresco).

muralla f. Wall, rampart (muro muy grueso): *las murallas de Ávila*, the ramparts of Ávila. || Wall: *la Gran Muralla de China*, the Great Wall of China.

murar v. tr. To wall, to surround with a wall.

murciélago m. ZOOL. Bat.

murena f. ZOOL. Moray, muraena (pez).

múrex m. ZOOL. Murex.

murga f. Band of street musicians (compañía de músicos). || Foul-smelling liquid which runs from piled-up olives (alpechín). || — FIG. y FAM. *Dar la murga* or *ser una murga*, to be a drag *o* a bind *o* a bore. | *¡Qué murga!*, what a drag *o* a bind *o* a bore!
— M. FAM. Drag, bind, bore (lata, pesadez).

murguista m. Street musician.

múrice m. ZOOL. Murex. || POÉT. Murex, purple.

murmullo m. Murmur, murmuring (ruido sordo). || Murmur, whispering (de las voces). || Babbling, rippling, murmuring (de un arroyo). || Sigh, sighing, murmur, whisper (del viento). || Buzzing (zumbido).

murmuración f. Gossip, backbiting.

murmurador, ra adj. Murmuring (ruido sordo). || Gossiping (maldiciente).
— M. y f. Gossip.

murmurante adj. Murmuring. || Gossiping (maldiciente).

murmurar v. tr. e intr. To murmur: *el viento murmura*, the wind murmurs. || To whisper (hablar en voz baja). || FIG. To mutter: *¿qué está usted murmurando?*, what are you muttering about? | To mutter, to grumble (con hostilidad). || To gossip (criticar): *murmurar de alguien*, to gossip about s.o.

muro m. Wall: *muro de contención*, retaining wall. || Rampart (muralla). || *Muro del sonido*, sound barrier.

murria f. FAM. Sadness, blues, *pl.* (tristeza). || FAM. *Tener murria*, to have the blues, to be down in the dumps, to feel low.

murrio, rria adj. FAM. Sad, blue.

mus m. Card game.

musa f. Muse.

musaraña f. Shrew, shrewmouse (ratón del campo). || FIG. Small creature (animalejo). || FIG. y FAM. *Mirar a las musarañas* or *pensar en las musarañas*, to be in the clouds, to be miles away, to be daydreaming.

muscular adj. Muscular.

musculatura f. Musculature (conjunto de los músculos). || Muscularity (grado de fortaleza). || *Tener musculatura*, to have muscles, to be muscular.

músculo m. Muscle. || — *Hombre de músculos*, muscleman. || *Tener músculos*, to have muscles.

musculoso, sa adj. Muscular (que tiene músculos). || Brawny, beefy (robusto).

muselina f. Muslin (tela).

museo m. Museum: *museo de historia natural*, natural history museum. || — *Museo de (figuras de) cera*, waxworks, wax museum. || *Museo de pintura*, art gallery.

muserola f. Noseband (correa).

musgaño m. Shrew.

musgo m. BOT. Moss. || *Cubierto de musgo*, mossy, moss-grown, moss-covered.

musgoso, sa adj. Mossy, moss-grown, moss-covered.

música f. Music: *música de cámara, instrumental, sacra, vocal*, chamber, instrumental, sacred, vocal music; *poner música a un poema*, to set a poem to music. || Band (banda). || — *Caja de música*, musical box [U.S., music box]. || *Escuela de música sacra*, choir school. || FIG. y FAM. *Irse con la música a otra parte*, to clear out, to sling one's hook. | *Mandar con la música a otra parte*, to send s.o. packing *o* to blazes. | *Música celestial*, drivel, hot air. || *Música de fondo*, background music. || *Música y letra*, words and music, music and lyrics. || FIG. y FAM. *Música ratonera*, caterwauling. | *Venir con músicas*, to talk bunkum *o* baloney.

musical adj. Musical: *comedia musical*, musical comedy.

musicalidad f. Musicality, musicalness.

músico, ca adj. Musical.
— M. y f. Musician.

musicógrafo, fa m. y f. Musicographer.

musicología f. Musicology.

musicólogo, ga m. y f. Musicologist.

musicómano, na m. y f. Melomane.

musiquero m. Music cabinet.

musiquilla f. FAM. Cheap *o* paltry music.

musitación f. Whispering.

musitar v. intr. To whisper (susurrar). || To mumble, to mutter (hablar entre dientes).

muslime adj./s. Moslem, Muslim, Mussulman.

muslímico, ca adj. Moslemic, Mussulmanic.

muslo m. ANAT. Thigh. || Drumstick, leg (de pollo).

musmón m. ZOOL. Mouflon.

mustang o **mustango** m. Mustang (caballo).

mustela f. ZOOL. Dogfish (pez). | Weasel (comadreja).

musteriense adj. Mousterian.
— M. Mousterian period (prehistoria).

mustiarse v. pr. To wither, to wilt.

mustio, tia adj. Withered, wilted (planta). || Gloomy, sad (persona).

musulmán, ana adj./s. Moslem, Mussulman, Muslim.

mutabilidad f. Mutability, changeableness.

mutable adj. Mutable.

mutación f. Change, mutation [cambio]. || BIOL. Mutation. || TEATR. Change of scene, scene change. || Change of weather (del tiempo).

mutante adj./s. BIOL. Mutant.

mutilación f. Mutilation. || Disablement.

mutilado, da adj. Crippled, disabled (persona). || Mutilated.
— M. y f. Cripple, disabled person.

mutilador, ra adj. Mutilating. || Crippling, maiming.
— M. y f. Mutilator.

mutilar v. tr. To mutilate, to mangle (destrozar). || To cripple, to maim (dejar inválido). || To deface (una estatua). || FIG. To mutilate (un texto).

MÚSICA, *f.* — MUSIC

I. Términos (*m.*) generales. — General terms.

sostenido *m.*, diesi *f.*	sharp
bemol *m.*	flat
becuadro *m.*	natural [sign]
pentagrama *m.*	staff, stave
la *m.*, si *m.*, do *m.*, re *m.*, mi. *m.*, fa *m.*, sol, *m.*	A, B, C, D, E, F, G
clave (*f.*) de sol	G *o* treble clef
clave (*f.*) de fa	F *o* bass clef
clave (*f.*) de do	C *o* tenor *o* alto clef
redonda *f.*, semibreve *f.*	semibreve [U.S., whole note]
blanca *f.*, mínima *f.*	minim [U.S., half note]
negra (*f.*) con puntillo	dotted crotchet [U.S., dotted *o* quarter note]
corchea *f.*	quaver [U.S., eighth note]
semicorchea *f.*	semiquaver [U.S., sixteenth note]
fusa *f.*	demisemiquaver [U.S., thirty-second note]
semifusa *f.*	hemidemisemiquaver [U.S., sixty-fourth note]
pausa *f.*	rest
suspiro *m.*	crotchet rest [U.S., quarter rest]
semitono *m.*	semitone
calderón *m.*	pause
compás *m.*	time: bar (división), rhythm (ritmo)
compás (*m.*) de tres por cuatro	three-four time
ritmo *m.*	rhythm
síncopa *f.*	syncope, syncopation
tono *m.*	tone (intervalo), pitch (altura)
tono (*m.*) mayor, menor	major, minor key
escala *f.*, gama *f.*	scale
arpegio *m.*	arpeggio
solfeo *m.*	solfeggio, solmization
diapasón *m.*	diapason, range (conjunto de notas), tuning fork (para afinar)
metrónomo *m.*	metronome
acorde *m.*	chord
cadencia *f.*	cadence
contrapunto *m.*	counterpoint
letra *f.*	lyrics, *pl.*, words, *pl.*
partitura *f.*	score
orquesta *f.*	orchestra
director (*m.*) de orquesta	conductor
batuta *f.*	baton
banda *f.*	band
solo *m.*: dúo *m.*	solo; duet, duo
terceto *m.*	trio
cuarteto *m.*	quartet, quartette
coral *f.*	choir, choral society

II. Géneros (*m.*) musicales. — Musical forms.

música (*f.*) instrumental, vocal, de cámara	instrumental, vocal, chamber music
música (*f.*) religiosa *or* sacra	sacred music
música (*f.*) llana	plainsong
oratorio *m.*	oratorio
motete *m.*	motet
cantata *f.*	cantata
cántico *m.*	canticle
salmo *m.*	psalm
villancico *m.*	[Christmas] carol
sonata *f.*	sonata
sinfonía *f.*	symphony
concierto *m.*	concerto
preludio *m.*	prelude
obertura *f.*	overture
fuga *f.*	fugue
intermedio *m.*	interlude
ópera *f.*	opera
ópera (*f.*) cómica	opéra comique
ópera (*f.*) bufa	comic opera
zarzuela *f.*, opereta *f*	operetta
comedia (*f.*) musical	musical [comedy]
melodía *f.*	melody
canción *f.*, canto *m.*	song
cante (*m.*) flamenco	flamenco [song]
estribillo *m.*	chorus
balada *f.*	ballad
canción (*f.*) de cuna, nana *f.*	lullaby
himno *m.*	hymn; anthem (nacional)

III. Instrumentos (*m.*) de teclado. — Keyboard instruments.

piano (*m.*) de cola	grand piano
teclado *m.*	keyboard
tecla *f.*	key
pedal *m.*	pedal
cuerda *f.*	string
macillo *m.*	hammer
pianola *f.*	pianola
clave *m.*, clavecín *m.*	harpsichord
órgano *m.*	organ
registro *m.*	register, organ stop
armonio *m.*	harmonium
organillo *m.*, pianillo *m.*	barrel organ

IV. Instrumentos (*m.*) de cuerda. — String instruments.

instrumentos (*m. pl.*) de arco	bowed instruments
violín *m.*; viola *f.*	violin; viola
violoncelo *m.*	cello, violoncello
contrabajo *m.*	contrabass, double bass
prima *f.*: bordón *m.*	first string; bass string
ese *f.*	sound hole
caja (*f.*) de resonancia	sound box
sordina *f.*	mute, sourdine
arco *m.*	bow
arpa *f.*; cítara *f.*	harp; zither
lira *f.*	lyre
guitarra *f.*; laúd *m.*	guitar; lute
banjo *m.*	banjo
púa *f.*, plectro *m.*	plectrum
traste *m.*	fret
mástil *m.*	neck
ceja *f.*	nut
caballete *m.*, puente *m.*	bridge

V. Instrumentos (*m*) de viento. — Wind instruments.

instrumento (*m.*) de madera	woodwind [instrument]
flauta *f.*	flute
caramillo *m.*	pipe, shawm
armónica *f.*	harmonica, mouth organ
oboe *m.*	oboe
gaita *f.*	bagpipes *pl.*
acordeón *m.*	accordion
corno (*m.*) inglés	English horn, tenor oboe, cor anglais
clarinete *m.*	clarinet
fagot *m.*	bassoon
contrafagot *m.*	double bassoon, contrabassoon
instrumentos (*m. pl.*) de metal, cobres *m. pl.*	brass instruments
trompa *f.*; trompeta *f.*	horn; trumpet
cornetín *m.*, corneta *f.*	cornet
trombón *m.*	trombone
saxofón *m.*	saxophone
boquilla *f.*, embocadura *f.*	mouthpiece
lengüeta *f.*	reed
llave *f.*	key
pistón *m.*	piston

VI. Instrumentos (*m.*) de percusión. — Percussion instruments.

tambor *m.*; timbal *m.*	drum; kettledrum
pandero *m.*	tambourine
pandereta *f.*	small tambourine
bombo *m.*	bass drum
palillo *m.*	drumstick
platillos *m. pl.*	cymbals
címbalo *m.*	cymbal
xilófono *m.*	xylophone
vibráfono *m.*	vibraphone
castañuelas *f. pl.*	castanets

mutis m. TEATR. Exit. || *Hacer mutis*, to keep quiet, to say nothing (callarse), to go away (irse), to exit (en teatro).

mutismo m. Silence, mutism (p.us.).

mutual adj. Mutual (mutuo).
— F. Mutual benefit society.

mutualidad f. Mutuality. || Mutual benefit society (asociación).

mutualismo m. Mutualism.

mutualista adj. Mutualistic. || Mutual-benefit-society (de la asociación).
— M. y f. Mutualist. || Member of a mutual benefit society.

mutuamente adv. Mutually.

mútulo m. ARQ. Mutule.

mutuo, tua adj. Mutual, joint: *por mutuo consentimiento*, by mutual consent. || Reciprocal, mutual: *odio mutuo*, mutual hatred. || *Seguro mutuo*, mutual insurance (seguro), mutual insurance agency (agencia de seguros).
— F. Mutual benefit society (mutualidad).

muy adv. Very, quite: *muy inteligente*, very intelligent; *muy lejos*, very far; *eso es muy inglés*, that's very English; *se fue muy satisfecho*, he left quite happy. || Very, extremely (más ponderativo): *estoy muy satisfecho*, I'm extremely satisfied. || Very, quite (con adverbio de manera): *iba muy despacito*, he went very slowly. || Too (demasiado). || Much: *muy estimado*, much esteemed. || Widely, much: *muy leído*, widely read. || — FAM. *El muy mentiroso de Juan*, that great liar of a John. || *Fue muy de lamentar*, it was much to be regretted. || *La realidad es muy otra*, it's very different in reality, the truth is quite different. || *Muy conocido*, very well-known. || *Muy de noche*, very late at night. || *Muy de nuestro tiempo*, very much a part of our times. || *Muy hombre*, very much of a man, a real man. || FAM. *Muy mucho*, very much. || *Muy señor mío*, Dear Sir, [beginning of a letter]. || *Por muy ... que*, however ..., no matter how: *por muy idiota que sea*, however stupid he may be; *por muy de prisa que vayas*, it doesn't matter how fast you go. || *Ser muy de*, to be just like, to be very [much] like: *eso es muy de él*, that is just like him. || *Tener muy en cuenta*, to bear very much in mind.

my f. Mu (letra griega).

N

n f. N (letra del alfabeto). || MAT. N (potencia): *diez a la potencia n*, ten to the power of n. || X (fulano): *la condesa N.*, Countess X.

— OBSERV. The Spanish *n* is pronounced like the English *n*.

nabab m. Nabob.
nabiforme adj. Napiform, turnip-shaped.
nabo m. BOT. Turnip (planta). | Root vegetable (raíz cualquiera). || Dock (de la cola de un animal). || ARQ. Central pillar (eje). | Newel (de escalera de caracol). || MAR. Mast (palo). || FIG. *Cada cosa en su tiempo y los nabos en adviento*, there is a time and place for everything, all in good time.
naborí m. *Amer.* Indian freeman who worked as a servant.
naboría f. *Amer.* Distribution of Indians to serve under the conquistadores.
Nabucodonosor n. pr. m. Nebuchadnezzar.
nácar m. Nacre, mother-of-pearl.
nacarado, da adj. Nacreous, pearly.
nacarar v. tr. To give a pearly lustre to.
nacáreo, a o **nacarino, na** adj. Mother-of-pearl, nacreous (de nácar o que lo parece).
nacela f. ARQ. Scotia (moldura cóncava).
nacer* v. intr. To be born (hombre o animal): *le nació un hijo*, a son was born to her; *cuando nazca mi primer hijo*, when my first baby is born. || To hatch (de un huevo). || To begin to grow, to sprout (vegetal). || To rise (el Sol, la Luna). || To start, to begin (carreteras). || To break, to dawn (el día). || To rise, to have its source (río). || To spring up (agua). || FIG. To be born *o* conceived (ideas). | To form (una sospecha). | To originate (originarse). | To stem, to spring (surgir). || — *Al nacer*, at birth. || *Entre ellos ha nacido el odio*, hatred has grown between them. || *Nacer al amor*, to awaken to love. || *Nacer con buena estrella*, to be born under a lucky star. || FIG. y FAM. *Nacer de pie*, v. PIE. || *Nacer para*, to be born to (con verbo): *nació para sufrir*, she was born to suffer; to be a born (con sustantivo): *nació para soldado*, he is a born soldier. || *Nadie nace enseñado*, we all have to learn. || FIG. y FAM. *No nací ayer*, I wasn't born yesterday. | *Volver a nacer*, to have a narrow escape *o* a close shave (salvarse).
— V. pr. To split (abrirse la tela).

— OBSERV. The verb *nacer* has two past participles, one regular, *nacido*, and the other irregular, *nato*.

nacido, da adj. Born: *nacido de padres humildes*, born of humble parents. || Né, née: *la señora de Thomas, nacida Johnson*, Mrs. Thomas, née Johnson. || — *Bien nacido*, of noble birth (linaje), well-bred (bien educado). || *Mal nacido*, mean (vil), ill-bred (mal educado). || *Recién nacido*, newborn.
— M. *Los nacidos*, human beings (seres humanos). || *Los nacidos en España*, those born in Spain. || *Ningún nacido*, nobody. || *Todos los nacidos*, everybody. || *Un recién nacido*, a newborn baby.
naciente adj. Nascent. || Rising: *el Sol naciente*, the rising sun. || Dawning: *el día naciente*, the dawning day. || Growing: *el naciente interés por la política*, the growing interest in politics. || FIG. New (reciente). | Budding, nascent (amor, amistad). || HERÁLD. Issuant.
— M. East (oriente).
nacimiento m. Birth: *partida de nacimiento*, birth certificate; *de nacimiento noble*, of noble birth. || Hatching (de huevos). || Source (de un río). || Spring (agua). || REL. Nativity scene, crib. || FIG. Birth: *nacimiento de una nación*, birth of a nation. | Source, origin, root (origen). | Beginning, start (principio). || — FIG. *Dar nacimiento a*, to give rise to. || *De nacimiento*, born, from birth: *es ciego de nacimiento*, he was born blind, he has been blind from birth; by birth: *español de nacimiento*, Spanish by birth. || *Lugar de nacimiento*, place of birth, birthplace. || *Regulación de nacimientos*, birth control.
nación f. Nation: *las Naciones Unidas*, the United Nations. || Country, state (país, estado). || People (pueblo). || — FAM. *Ser español de nación*, to be Spanish by birth. | *Un inglés de nación*, a native Englishman, an Englishman by birth.
nacional adj. National: *la prensa nacional*, the national press; *himno nacional*, national anthem; *renta nacional*, national income; *producto nacional bruto*, gross national product. || Domestic: *vuelo, mercado nacional*, domestic flight, market. || *Carretera nacional*, A road, arterial road [U.S., arterial highway].
— M. National. || — Pl. National militia, *sing.* [in the Spanish Civil War].
nacionalidad f. Nationality. || *Doble nacionalidad*, dual nationality *o* citizenship.
nacionalismo m. Nationalism.
nacionalista adj. Nationalist, nationalistic.
— M. y f. Nationalist.
nacionalización f. Nationalization. || Naturalization (de una persona).
nacionalizar v. tr. To nationalize (industria, ferrocarriles, etc.). || To naturalize (naturalizar).
— V. pr. To become naturalized (naturalizarse).
nacionalsindicalismo m. National Syndicalism.
nacionalsindicalista adj./s. National Syndicalist.
nacionalsocialismo m. National Socialism.
nacionalsocialista adj./s. National Socialist.
nada f. Nothingness (el no ser). || Nothing: *hombre salido de la nada*, man risen from nothing.
— M. The slightest thing, anything at all (la menor cosa): *un nada le asusta*, the slightest thing frightens him.
— Pron. Nothing, not ... anything: *no ha hecho nada nuevo*, he has done nothing new, he has not done anything new. || Anything (algo): *¿has visto nada igual?*, have you ever seen anything like it?
— Adv. Not at all; *no es nada guapa*, she is not at all pretty; *no nos ayudó nada*, he did not help us at all.
— Interj. Not at all, you're welcome (de nada, no es nada). || No! (¡no!): *¡nada, nada!*, no, no! || Nothing much (poca cosa): *¿qué hay de nuevo? — Nada. Fuimos a...*, what's new? — Nothing much. We went to ... || Well, ... (pues): *nada, que fuimos al cine y ...*, well, we went to the cinema and ...
— *Amer. A cada nada*, continually, every five minutes. || *¡Ahí es nada!*, just fancy! || *Antes de nada*, first of all. || *Casi nada*, hardly: *no habla casi nada*, he hardly speaks; hardly ... any: *no hace falta casi nada de dinero*, you hardly need any money; next to nothing, hardly ... anything: *no me costó casi nada*, it cost me next to nothing, it hardly cost me anything. || *Como si nada*, as though it were nothing at all. || *Con intentarlo no se pierde nada*, there's no harm in trying. || *Con nada se caerá este cuadro, está muy poco seguro*, it will not take much to make this picture fall, it is very unsafe. || *De nada*, don't mention it, you're welcome. || *Dentro de nada*, in a moment. || *En nada estuvo que cayera*, he very nearly fell. || *Hace nada*, just a moment ago. || *Lo haré en nada de tiempo*, I'll do it in no time at all. || *Nada*, right: *nada, hay que proseguir*, right, let's go on. || *Nada de*, no: *nada de excusas*, no excuses; *nada de jugar aquí*, no playing here; nothing (con adj.): *nada de extraordinario*, nothing unusual; no... at all (con sustantivo): *no tiene nada de paciencia*, he has no patience at all. || *Nada de eso*, nothing of the sort. || *Nada de nada*, nothing at all: *no sabe nada de nada*, he knows nothing at all; not at all (de ningún modo). || *Nada de salir ahora*, [you can] forget about going out now.

|| *Nada más*, that's all (eso es todo), no sooner (en cuanto): *nada más verla corrió a saludarla*, no sooner did he see her than he ran to meet her; nothing more: (*no hay*) *nada más difícil que...*, [there is] nothing more difficult than... || *Nada más y nada menos*, no more, no less. || *Nada más y nada menos que*, no more, no less: *me pidió nada más y nada menos que mil pesetas*, he asked me for a thousand pesetas, no more, no less. || *Nada menos*, no less: *es el alcalde, nada menos*, he is the mayor, no less. || *Nada menos que*, no less than: *ha heredado nada menos que diez millones de pesetas*, he has inherited no less than ten million pesetas. || FAM. *Ni nada*, or anything: *no quiere estudiar ni nada*, he won't study or anything. || *No es nada*, it's nothing. || *No hace nada que salió*, he left just a moment ago. || (*No hay*) *nada como un vaso de buen vino*, [there's] nothing like a glass of good wine. || *No hay nada de eso, de eso nada*, nothing of the sort. || *No los nombró para nada*, he never mentioned them at all. || *No me dice nada*, I don't think much of it. || *No reparar en nada*, to stop at nothing. || *No ser nada*, to be a nobody (personas), to be nothing (accidentes, heridas, etc.). || *No servir para nada*, to be of no use at all, to be completely useless. || *No tener nada que ver con*, to have nothing to do with. || *No tiene nada de particular*, there is nothing special about it (es corriente), there is not much in it (no es complicado). || *No tocarle nada a uno*, to be no relation of. s.o., not to be related at all to s.o.: *esta chica no me toca nada*, this girl is no relation of mine. || *Peor es nada*, it's better than nothing. || *Por menos de nada*, at the slightest thing, for no reason at all: *por menos de nada se enfada*, he gets angry at the slightest thing. || *Por nada*, for no reason (por la menor razón), for next to nothing: *lo compré por nada*, I got it for next to nothing. || *Por nada del mundo*, not for anything [in the world], not for all the tea in China: *por nada del mundo haría eso*, I wouldn't do that for anything *o* for all the tea in China. || *Pues nada*, right [then], O.K. [then]. || *Quedarse en nada*, to come to nothing. || *Tener en nada*, to think very little of, to take no notice of (no hacer caso a).

nadador, ra m. y f. Swimmer.
— Adj. Swimming.

nadar v. intr. To swim: *nadar de espalda*, to swim backstroke *o* on one's back. || FIG. To be rolling, to wallow: *nadar en dinero*, to be rolling in money. | To swim (en un vestido demasiado amplio). || — FIG. y FAM. *Nadar en sudor*, to be bathed *o* soaked in sweat. | *Nadar entre dos aguas*, to run with the hare and hunt with the hounds. | *Nadar y guardar la ropa*, V. ROPA.
— V. tr. To swim, to do: *nadar el crawl*, to do the crawl.

nadería f. Mere trifle, mere nothing.

nadie pron. indef. Nobody, no-one, no one, not anybody: *no había nadie*, there was nobody; *no lo sabe nadie*, no one knows. || — *A nadie se le ocurre hacer tal cosa*, nobody would think of doing such a thing. || *Nadie es profeta en su tierra*, V. PROFETA. || *Nadie más*, nobody else. || *No he hablado con nadie*, I haven't spoken to anybody.
— M. FIG. Nobody, insignificant person. || — *No ser nadie*, to be a nobody (no ser importante), to be not just anybody (ser alguien). || *No somos nadie*, how insignificant we all are. || *Un don nadie*, a nobody. || *Usted no es nadie para decirme eso*, you have no right to say that to me, who are you to say that?
— OBSERV. When *nadie* precedes the verb, the negative particle *no* is omitted.

nadir m. ASTR. Nadir.

nado (a) adv. *Cruzaremos el río a nado*, we shall swim across the river. || *Se salvó a nado*, he swam to safety.

nafta f. Naphtha. || *Amer.* Petrol [U.S., gasoline].

naftalina f. Naphthalene.

nafteno m. QUÍM. Naphthene.

naftol m. QUÍM. Naphthol.

nailon m. Nylon.

naipe m. Card, playing card: *barajar los naipes*, to shuffle the cards; *una baraja de naipes*, a pack of cards. || — FIG. *Castillo de naipes*, house of cards. || *Tener buen* or *mal naipe*, to be lucky *o* unlucky (en el juego).

naja f. ZOOL. Naja (serpiente). || POP. *Salir de naja* or *de najas*, to push off, to get out of it (irse).

najarse v. pr. POP. To push off, to get out of it, to clear off (irse).

nalga f. Buttock. || — Pl. Bottom, *sing.*, buttocks (trasero).

nalgar adj. Gluteal.

nalgatorio m. FAM. Rear end, bottom, seat, backside.

nana f. FAM. Gran, granny, grandma, nan, nanna, nanny (abuela). | Lullaby (canción de cuna). || *Amer.* Nanny (niñera). | Wet nurse (nodriza). || FAM. *En el año de la nana*, in the year dot.

¡nanay! interj. POP. Nothing doing! (¡ni hablar!).

nanita o **nanaya** f. *Amer.* Grandmother (abuela). | Lullaby (canción de cuna).

nano,na m. y f. Imp (insulto cariñoso).

nanosegundo m. Nanosecond.

nanquín m. Nankeen (tela).

nao f. Ship, vessel (barco).

naonato, ta adj. Born at sea.

napa m. Glacé lamb (piel).

napalm m. Napalm: *bomba de napalm*, napalm bomb.

napias f. pl. POP. Conk, *sing.*, snout, *sing.* (narices).

napoleón m. Napoleon [former French gold coin].

Napoleón n. pr. m. Napoleon.

napoleónico, ca adj. Napoleonic.

Nápoles n. pr. GEOGR. Naples.

napolitano, na adj./s. Neapolitan.

naranja f. Orange (fruto): *zumo de naranja*, orange juice. || — FIG. *Media naranja*, dome, cupola (cúpula), better half (esposa o marido). || *Naranja navel*, navel orange. || POP. *¡Naranjas!* or *¡naranjas de la China!*, nothing doing! (¡ni hablar!). || *Naranja sanguina*, blood orange. || *Naranja tangerina*, tangerine.
— Adj. inv./s.m. Orange: *un vestido naranja*, an orange dress; *naranja claro*, light orange.

naranjada f. Orangeade.

naranjado, da adj. Orange, orange-coloured (naranja). || Orangish (tirando a naranja).

naranjal m. Orange grove.

naranjazo m. Blow with an orange.

naranjero, ra adj. Orange, of oranges. || Having a diameter of eight to ten centimetres (cañón, tubo).
— M. y f. Orange seller (vendedor). || Orange grower (cultivador). || — M. Blunderbuss (trabuco).

naranjo m. Orange tree.

narcisismo m. Narcissism.

narcisista m. y f. Narcissist.
— Adj. Narcissistic.

narciso m. BOT. Narcissus (flor). || FIG. Narcissus, narcissist (hombre enamorado de sí mismo).

Narciso n. pr. m. Narcissus.

narcoanálisis m. MED. Narcoanalysis.

narcosis f. MED. Narcosis.

narcótico, ca adj./s.m. MED. Narcotic: *el opio es un narcótico*, opium is a narcotic.

narcotina f. QUÍM. Narcotine.

narcotismo m. MED. Narcotism, narcosis.

narcotizante adj./s.m. MED. Narcotic.

narcotizar v. tr. To narcotize.

nardo m. BOT. Nard, spikenard.

narguile m. Narghile, hookah (pipa turca).

narigón, ona adj. Long-nosed, big-nosed.
— M. y f. Long-nosed person. || — M. Long *o* big nose.

narigudo, da adj. Long-nosed, big-nosed.

nariguera f. Nose ring.

nariz f. Nose: *nariz aguileña* or *aquilina*, aquiline nose. || Nostril (orificio nasal). || FIG. Sense of smell, nose (olfato). | Bouquet (del vino). || TECN. Nose (de una herramienta). | Nozzle (de un tubo). | Catch (del picaporte). || — Pl. Nose, *sing.*
— FIG. y FAM. *Caerse de narices*, to nose-dive (un avión), to fall flat on one's face (una persona). | *Darle a uno con la puerta en las narices* or *cerrar la puerta en las narices de alguien*, to shut *o* to slam the door in s.o.'s face. | *Darle a uno en la nariz*, to have a feeling: *me da en la nariz que no vendrá*, I have a feeling he will not come. || *Darle a uno en las narices*, to show s.o. what for: *el actor bordó su papel para darles en las narices a sus detractores*, the actor gave a brilliant perfomance to show his critics what for. | *Darse de narices con*, to bump into. | *Darse de narices en*, to come up against (un obstáculo). | *Dejarle a uno con un palmo* or *con dos palmos de narices*, V. PALMO. || FIG. *En mis mismas narices*, right under my very nose. || FIG. y FAM. *Estar hasta las narices de*, to be fed up to teeth with *o* of, to have had enough of. || FIG. *Hablar con* or *por la nariz*, to speak through one's nose. || FIG. y FAM. *Hacer algo por narices*, to do something because one feels like it. | *Hinchársele las narices a uno*, to flare up. || *Limpiarse las narices*, to wipe one's nose. || FIG. y FAM. *Meter la nariz* or *las narices en todo*, to poke *o* to stick one's nose in everywhere, to be a busybody. || FAM. *¡Narices!*, rubbish!, rot! || *Nariz chata*, snub nose. || *Nariz perfilada*, perfect *o* regular *o* well-shaped nose. || *Nariz respingada* or *respingona* or *remangada*, turned-up nose. || FIG. y FAM. *¡Ni narices!*, or anything: *¡ni postre ni narices!*, no sweet or anything! | *No ver más allá de sus narices*, not to be able to see further than the end of one's nose. | *Quedarse con un palmo de narices*, V. PALMO. | *¡Qué narices!*, my foot!, my eye! | *Refregar* or *refrotar algo a alguien por las narices*, to rub sth. in. | *Romperse las narices* or *darse de narices*, to fall flat on one's face. || *Sangrar* or *echar sangre por las narices*, to have a nose-bleed, to bleed from the nose. || FIG. *Sólo hace lo que le sale de las narices*, he only does what he feels like doing. || *Sonarse las narices*, to blow one's nose. || FIG. y FAM. *Tener a alguien agarrado por las narices*, to lead s.o. by the nose. | *Tener a alguien montado en las narices*, not to be able to stand *o* to stomach s.o.: *la tengo montada en las narices*, I can't stand her. || *Tienes el libro delante de tus narices*, the book is right under your nose.

narizón, ona adj. FAM. Big-nosed, long-nosed.

narizota f. FAM. Big nose, conk. || — Pl. M. y f. FAM. Long-nosed man *o* woman.

narrable adj. Narratable.

narración f. Narrating, narration (acto de narrar). || Narrative, narration, account (relato). || Narrative (parte de un discurso).

narrador, ra adj. Narrative.
— M. y f. Narrator.

narrar v. tr. To relate, to tell, to narrate.
narrativa f. Narrative, account (relato). || Narrative (arte de narrar).
narrativo, va adj. Narrative.
narria f. Trolley, dolly (vehículo).
nártex m. ARQ. Narthex.
narval m. Narwhal, narwal, narwhale (pez).
nasa f. Fish trap (para el pescado). || Basket (cesta). || Bin (para el pan).
nasal adj./s.f. Nasal. || — *Consonante nasal*, nasal consonant. || ANAT. *Fosas nasales*, nasal fossae.
nasalidad f. Nasality.
nasalización f. Nasalization: *nasalización de un sonido*, nasalization of a sound. || Speaking through one's nose (gangueo).
nasalizar v. tr. To nasalize.
— V. intr. To speak through one's nose (defecto).
nata f. Fresh cream, cream (de la leche). || Skin (encima de la leche cocida). || FIG. Cream, pick, best (lo mejor). || *Amer.* Slag (escoria). || — FIG. *La flor y nata*, v. FLOR. || *Nata batida*, whipped cream.
natación f. Swimming.
natal adj. Natal (relativo al nacimiento). || Native: *mi país natal*, my native country. || Home: *mi ciudad natal*, my home town.
— M. Birth (nacimiento). || Birthday (cumpleaños).
natalicio, cia adj. Birthday.
— M. Birth (nacimiento). || Birthday (cumpleaños). || — Pl. Births column, *sing.* (en un periódico).
natalidad f. Natality, birthrate. || *Índice de natalidad*, birthrate, natality.
natatorio, ria adj. Swimming, natatorial, natatory. || *Vejiga natatoria*, air *o* swimming bladder.
natillas f. pl. Custard, *sing.* (dulce).
natividad f. Nativity.
Natividad f. Christmas (Navidad).
nativismo m. Nativism.
nativista adj./s. Nativist.
nativo, va adj. Native (natural): *oro nativo*, native gold; *profesor nativo*, native teacher. || Natural, innate, inborn, native (innato). || — *Lengua nativa*, native language, mother tongue. || *Suelo nativo*, native soil, homeland, motherland.
— M. y f. Native: *los nativos*, the natives. || *Inglés por nativos*, English classes given by native teachers.
nato, ta adj. Born: *enemigo nato*, born enemy; *es un artista nato*, he is a born artist.
natrón m. MIN. Natron.
natura f. Nature (naturaleza). || *Contra natura*, unnatural.
natural adj. Natural: *recursos naturales*, natural resources; *gas natural*, natural gas. || Native (de un país). || Fresh (fruta). || Straight, neat (whisky, etc.). || Natural (sencillo, sin afectación): *una persona muy natural*, a very natural person. || MÚS. Natural. || — *Agua natural*, tapwater. || *Ciencias naturales*, natural sciences. || *De tamaño natural*, life-sized: *retrato de tamaño natural*, life-sized portrait. || *Es muy natural que*, it is perfectly natural that. || *Hijo natural*, illegitimate *o* natural child. || *Historia natural*, natural history, nature study. || *Ley natural*, natural law. || MAT. *Logaritmo natural*, natural logarithm. || *Muerte natural*, natural death. || *Ser natural de*, to come from: *es natural de Sevilla*, he comes from Seville.
— Adv. Naturally, of course (por supesto).
— M. Nature (carácter): *de un natural celoso*, of a jealous nature. || Native: *los naturales de un país*, the natives of a country. || TAUR. Natural pass [made with the muleta in the left hand]. || — *Al natural*, natural, in its own juice (productos de conserva), realistic (descripción). || *De buen, mal natural*, good-natured, bad-natured. || *Parecer muy natural*, to seem quite natural. || *Pintar del natural*, to paint from nature. || *Ser guapa al natural*, to be pretty without make-up on. || *Ser lo más natural del mundo*, to be the most natural thing in the world.
naturaleza f. Nature: *la Madre Naturaleza*, Mother Nature; *amante de la naturaleza*, nature lover. || Nature (natural, clase). || Nationality (nacionalidad). || Naturalization: *carta de naturaleza*, naturalization papers. || — *Ciencias de la naturaleza*, natural sciences. || *Contra la naturaleza*, against nature, unnatural. || *Dejar obrar a la naturaleza*, to let nature take its course. || *Las leyes de la naturaleza*, the laws of nature. || *Naturaleza divina, humana*, divine, human nature. || ARTES. *Naturaleza muerta*, still life. || *Por naturaleza*, by nature, naturally: *los jóvenes son generosos por naturaleza*, the young are generous by nature *o* naturally generous. || *Vuelta a la naturaleza*, return to nature.
naturalidad f. Naturalness, native ease. || Citizenship, nationality (pertenencia a un pueblo). || — *Aquí te roban con la mayor naturalidad*, they rob you here and think nothing of it. || *Con la mayor naturalidad*, as if it were the most natural thing in the world. || *Díselo con toda naturalidad*, tell him quite simply *o* frankly *o* straightforwardly. || *Leyó la noticia con toda naturalidad*, he read the news in a natural voice. || *Oyó la noticia con la mayor naturalidad*, he took the news quite calmly.
naturalismo m. Naturalism (doctrina, literatura).
naturalista adj. Naturalistic.
— M. y f. Naturalist.
naturalización f. Naturalization.
naturalizado, da adj. Naturalized.
— M. y f. Naturalized person.
naturalizar v. tr. To naturalize.
— V. pr. To become naturalized.
naturismo m. Naturism.
naturista adj. Naturistic.
— M. y f. Naturist.
naufragar v. intr. To sink, to be wrecked (barcos). || To be shipwrecked (personas). || FIG. To fall through, to fail (un negocio).
naufragio m. Shipwreck, wreck (barco). || FIG. Failure, disaster.
náufrago, ga adj. Shipwrecked (personas).
— M. y f. Shipwreck, wreck (barco). || Shipwrecked person, castaway (persona). || — M. Shark (tiburón). || *Sociedad de salvamento de náufragos*, lifeboat institution.
náusea f. Nausea, sickness (ganas de vomitar). || Seasickness (en un barco). || FIG. Disgust, repulsion (asco). || — *Dar náuseas a uno*, to make s.o. sick, to sicken s.o., to nauseate s.o. || *Sentir* or *tener náuseas*, to feel sick.
nauseabundo, da adj. Sickening, nauseating, nauseous.
nauta m. POÉT. Mariner.
náutico, ca adj. Nautical. || — *Club náutico*, yacht club. || *Deportes náuticos*, water *o* aquatic sports. || *Rosa náutica*, compass card.
— F. Navigation, seamanship.
nautilo m. Nautilus (molusco).
navaja f. Penknife, pocketknife (de bolsillo). || Razor (de afeitar). || Razor clam (molusco). || Tusk (de un jabalí). || Sting (de insecto). || — *Navaja barbera*, cutthroat razor [U.S., straight razor]. || *Navaja de injertar*, grafting knife. || *Navaja de muelle*, flickknife [U.S., switchblade knife].
navajada f. o **navajazo** m. Stab (profunda). || Gash (superficial). || Slash, stab (golpe).
naval adj. Naval: *agregado naval*, naval attaché. || — *Base naval*, naval base. || *Combate naval*, naval *o* sea battle. || *Escuela Naval*, Naval College.
Navarra n. pr. f. GEOGR. Navarre.
navarro, rra adj./s. Navarrese.
nave f. Ship, vessel (barco). || Nave (de una iglesia). || Shop (parte de una fábrica). || — REL. *La Nave de San Pedro*, the Roman Catholic Church. || *Nave lateral*, aisle (de iglesia). || FIG. *Quemar las naves*, to burn one's boats [U.S., to burn one's bridges]. || *Se alquila nave industrial*, industrial premises (*pl.*) *o* factory to let.
navecilla f. Censer (para incienso).
navegabilidad f. Navigability (de río, etc.). || Seaworthiness (de barco). || Airworthiness (de avión).
navegable adj. Navigable (río, etc.). || Seaworthy (barco). || Airworthy (avión).
navegación f. Navigation: *navegación submarina, aérea*, submarine, aerial navigation. || Shipping: *abierto a la navegación*, open to shipping. || — *Certificado de navegación*, seaworthiness certificate. || *Líneas de navegación*, shipping lines. || *Navegación a vela*, yachting. || *Navegación costera* or *de cabotaje*, coastal navigation. || *Navegación de altura*, ocean navigation. || *Navegación fluvial*, river navigation.
navegador, ra adj./s.m. V. NAVEGANTE.
navegante adj. Sailing, navigating.
— M. MAR. y AVIAC. Navigator.
navegar v. intr. To navigate, to sail (barcos). || To navigate, to fly (aviones). || — *Navegar a la vela*, to sail. || *Navegar en conserva*, to sail in convoy *o* together. || FIG. *Saber navegar*, to know what one is doing.
— V. tr. To sail, to navigate (barcos): *navegar los mares*, to sail the seas.
naveta f. Small ship (barco). || Censer (para el incienso). || Drawer (gaveta). || ARQ. Prehistoric tomb in the Balearic Islands.
navicert m. Navicert, navigation certificate (licencia de navegación en tiempo de guerra).
Navidad f. REL. Nativity (nacimiento de Jesucristo). || Christmas (fiesta cristiana). || — Pl. Christmas, *sing.*: *en Navidades*, at Christmas; *felices Navidades*, merry *o* happy Christmas; *felicitar las Navidades*, to wish s.o. a happy Christmas. || — *Árbol de Navidad*, Christmas tree. || *Canción de Navidad*, Christmas carol (villancico). || *Pascua de Navidad*, Christmas. || *Por Navidad*, at Christmas. || *Tarjeta de felicitación de Navidad*, Christmas card.
navideño, ña adj. Christmas.
naviero, ra adj. Shipping.
— M. Shipowner (armador). || — F. Shipping company (compañía).
navío m. Ship, vessel (barco). || *Capitán de navío*, sea captain.
náyade f. MIT. Naiad, water nymph. || BOT. Naiad.
nazareno, na adj./s. Nazarene. || — M. Penitent [in Holy Week processions]. || *El Nazareno*, Jesus of Nazareth, The Nazarene.
Nazaret n. pr. GEOGR. Nazareth.
nazi adj./s. Nazi (nacionalsocialista).
nazismo m. Nazism (nacionalsocialismo).
nebladura f. Smut (tizón del trigo).
neblina f. Mist (niebla).
neblinoso, sa f. Misty.

nebulosidad f. Nebulosity, cloudiness (cualidad de nebuloso). || Obscurity, haziness (de ideas, etc.).
nebuloso, sa adj. Nebulous. || Cloudy, hazy, misty (cielo). || FIG. Hazy, vague, obscure (ideas).
— F. Nebula.
necear v. intr. To talk nonsense (decir tonterías). || To play the fool (hacer tonterías).
necedad f. Foolishness, silliness, stupidity, nonsense (tontería). || — *Decir necedades*, to talk nonsense. || *Hacer una necedad*, to do sth. stupid. || *Soltar una necedad*, to say sth. stupid, to come out with a silly remark.
necesariamente adv. Necessarily, of necessity. || Really: *tenemos que ir necesariamente*, we really must go.
necesario, ria adj. Necessary: *cumple las condiciones necesarias*, he has the necessary qualifications, he fulfils the necessary requirements. || — *No ser necesario*, not to be necessary, there to be no need, not to have to, not to need to: *no es necesario que vengas si no quieres*, it is not necessary for you to come *o* there is no need for you to come if you do not want to, you need not come *o* you do not need to come *o* you do not have to come if you do not want to. || *Ser necesario*, must, to have to (obligación): *es necesario que abonen este terreno*, you must fertilize *o* you have to fertilize this land; must, to have to, to need to (necesidad): *es necesario que lleguemos a las siete para coger el tren*, we must arrive *o* we have to arrive *o* we need to arrive at seven o'clock to catch the train; to need, to be needed (con sustantivo): *es necesario un millón de pesetas para llevarlo a cabo*, we need a million pesetas to complete it, a million pesetas are needed to complete it. || *Si es necesario*, if necessary, if need be.
— M. *Lo necesario*, what is necessary. || *Lo estrictamente necesario*, the bare necessities: *sólo he comprado lo estrictamente necesario*, I only bought the bare necessities; what is *o* was strictly necessary: *sólo le he dicho lo estrictamente necesario*, I only told him what was strictly necessary.
neceser m. Toilet case (bolsa de aseo). || Kit (estuche con utensilios): *neceser de afeitar*, shaving kit. || *Neceser de costura*, workbox, sewing box.
necesidad f. Necessity: *hoy en día el coche es una necesidad*, these days a car is a necessity. || Need: *la necesidad de una reforma agraria*, the need for agricultural reform. || Need, want, poverty, necessity, straits, *pl.* (pobreza): *al morir su padre quedaron en la mayor necesidad*, when their father died they were left in dire need. || Starvation, hunger (hambre): *morir de necesidad*, to die of starvation *o* hunger. || — Pl. Needs: *gana bastante para satisfacer sus necesidades*, he earns enough to satisfy his needs. || FAM. Needs: *necesidades corporales*, bodily needs. || Hardships (dificultades): *pasar necesidades*, to suffer hardships. || — *Artículos de primera necesidad*, basic necessities. || *En caso de necesidad*, if necessary, if need be, in case of need. || *Hacer de necesidad virtud*, to make a virtue of necessity. || FAM. *Hacer sus necesidades*, to answer nature's call, to relieve o.s. || *La necesidad aguza el ingenio*, necessity is the mother of invention. || *La necesidad carece de ley*, necessity knows no law. || *Por necesidad*, out of necessity. || *Tener necesidad de*, to need. || *Verse en la necesidad de*, to feel it necessary to, to feel obliged to.
necesitado, da adj. In need: *estoy necesitado de consejo*, I am in need of advice. || Needy (pobre): *es una familia muy necesitada*, they are a very needy family. || — *Andar necesitado de, estar necesitado de*, to need. || *Andar un poco necesitado de dinero*, to be a little short of money. || *Verse necesitado a*, to feel it necessary to, to feel the need to, to feel obliged to (con verbo). || *Verse necesitado de*, to need (con sustantivo).
— M. y f. Needy *o* poor person (pobre). || — Pl. *Los necesitados*, the needy, the poor.
necesitar v. tr. To need, to require, to necessitate (exigir). || To need: *necesito tu ayuda, dinero*, I need your help, money *o* some money. || To want: *se necesita mecanógrafa*, typist wanted. || Must, to need to, to have to (ser preciso): *necesito hablarte mañana*, I must speak to you tomorrow.
— V. intr. To need: *necesito de usted*, I need you.
— V. pr. To be needed, to be wanted.
necio, cia adj. Silly, foolish.
— M. y f. Fool, idiot (idiota).
necrófago, ga adj. Necrophagous.
necrofilia f. Necrophilia.
necrofobia f. Necrophobia.
necróforo m. Burying beetle (insecto).
necrología f. Necrology. || Obituary column (en un periódico).
necrológico, ca adj. Necrological. || *Nota necrológica*, obituary notice.
necrólogo m. Necrologist.
necromancia f. Necromancy.
necrópolis f. Necropolis.
necropsia f. Necropsy, autopsy.
necrosis f. MED. Necrosis.
néctar m. Nectar.
nectáreo, a adj. Nectareous, nectarous.
neerlandés, esa adj. Dutch, [of *o* from the] Netherlands.
— M. y f. Dutchman (hombre), Dutchwoman (mujer), Netherlander (persona). || — M. Dutch (lengua). || — Pl. *Los neerlandeses*, the Dutch.
nefando, da adj. Abominable, hateful, odious. || *Un crimen nefando*, a heinous crime.
nefasto, ta adj. Unlucky, ill-fated, fateful.
nefelión m. MED. Nubecula.
nefralgia f. MED. Nephralgia.
nefrítico, ca adj. Nephritic, renal.
nefritis f. MED. Nephritis.
negable adj. Deniable. || Refusable.
negación f. Negation, denial (de un hecho). || Refusal (negativa). || GRAM. Negative. || — *Dos negaciones equivalen a una afirmación*, two negatives make an affirmative *o* a positive. || FIG. *Es la negación de la belleza*, she is anything but beautiful.
negado, da adj. FIG. Incapable, incompetent (incapaz). || FIG. y FAM. Useless: *alguien negado para las matemáticas*, s.o. useless at mathematics.
— M. y f. FIG. y FAM. Dead loss (nulidad).
negador, ra adj. Denying.
— M. y f. Denier.
negar* v. tr. To deny: *negar un hecho*, to deny a fact; *no niego que sea cierto*, I do not deny that it might be true. || To refuse, to reject, to deny (rechazar): *negar una acusación*, to deny a charge. || To refuse (rehusar): *negar un permiso*, to refuse permission; *negar la mano a uno*, to refuse to shake hands with s.o.; *le negaron la entrada*, they refused him entry. || To disclaim (responsabilidad). || To deny (a Cristo).
— V. pr. To refuse: *se niega a pagar*, he refuses to pay. || To decline (una invitación). || *Negarse a una visita*, to refuse to see a visitor.
negativa f. Negative: *contestar con la negativa*, to reply in the negative. || Denial (de un hecho). || Refusal: *su negativa le trajo muchas dificultades*, his refusal caused him a lot of difficulties; *negativa rotunda*, flat refusal.
negativamente adv. Negatively. || *Responder negativamente*, to answer in the negative.
negativismo m. Negativism.
negativo, va adj. Negative. || MAT. Minus: *signo negativo*, minus sign.
— M. FOT. Negative.
negatón m. FÍS. Negatron, negaton.
negligé m. Négligé, negligee (bata).
negligencia f. Neglect (abandono, dejadez). || Negligence, carelessness (en el vestir, la conducta, etc.).
negligente adj. Negligent, neglectful: *negligente en* or *para sus deberes*, negligent in carrying out his duties, neglectful of his duties. || Careless: *es un conductor negligente*, he is a careless driver.
— M. y f. Careless person.
negociabilidad f. Negotiability.
negociable adj. Negotiable.
negociación f. Negotiation: *en negociación*, under negotiation; *entablar negociaciones*, to enter into *o* to open negotiations. || Clearance (de un cheque).
negociado m. Section, department (en una oficina). || *Jefe de negociado*, head of department.
negociador, ra adj. Negotiating.
— M. y f. Negotiator.
negociante m. y f. Merchant: *negociante al por mayor*, wholesale merchant. || Dealer: *negociante en coches*, car dealer. || — M. Businessman (hombre de negocios).
negociar v. tr. e intr. To negotiate: *negociar un tratado de paz*, to negotiate a peace treaty. || To negotiate, to trade (comerciar): *negociar con Francia*, to negotiate *o* to trade with France. || To trade, to deal: *negociar en cereales*, to trade in cereals. || *Negociar al por mayor, al por menor*, to trade wholesale, retail.
negocio m. Business: *dedicarse a los negocios*, to be in business. || Business, trade (comercio): *el negocio de los vinos*, the wine trade. || Business, concern (empresa): *tiene un negocio de vinos*, he has a wine business. || Affair, concern, business (asunto): *eso no es negocio suyo*, that is not his affair. || Deal, transaction (transacción comercial). || Bargain (compra ventajosa). || Shop, store (tienda). || — Pl. Business, *sing.* || — *Encargado de negocios*, chargé d'affaires (diplomático). || FIG. *Hablar de negocios*, to talk shop. || *Hacer negocio*, to do good business. || *Hacer un buen, mal negocio*, to make a good, bad deal. || *Hombre de negocios*, businessman. || FIG. y FAM. *¡Mal negocio!*, it looks bad!, nasty business! | *¡Menudo negocio has hecho!*, you've done well for yourself, haven't you? || *Negocio redondo*, profitable deal (transacción), profitable business (comercio). || *Negocio sucio* or *turbio*, dirty business, shady deal. || *Poner un negocio*, to set up *o* to start up a business.
negra f. V. NEGRO.
negrada f. *Amer.* Black slaves, *pl.* (esclavos negros). | Negroes, *pl.* (conjunto de negros).
negrear v. intr. To look black (parecer negro). || To darken, to blacken (ponerse oscuro).
negrería f. *Amer.* V. NEGRADA.
negrero, ra adj. Black slave: *barco negrero*, black slave ship.
— M. y f. Slave trader (persona que se dedica al

comercio de esclavos). || FIG. Slave driver (jefe exigente). | Tyrant (tirano).
negrilla f. IMPR. Boldface.
negrillo m. Elm (olmo). || *Amer.* Silver ore (mineral).
negrita f. IMPR. Boldface (negrilla).
negrito, ta m. y f. Little negro boy (chico), little negro girl (chica), piccaninny [U.S., pickaninny]. || Negrillo (pigmeo de África). || Negrito (pigmeo de Asia y Oceanía).
negro, gra adj. Black: *un coche negro*, a black car; *tus manos están negras*, your hands are black. || Dark, black (oscuro): *pelo negro, ojos negros*, dark *o* black hair, dark *o* black eyes; *tabaco negro*, black tobacco. || Negro (de raza negra): *tribu, raza negra*, negro tribe, race. || Coloured, black (de color). || FIG. Black, gloomy (sombrío): *¡qué perspectiva más negra!*, what a gloomy outlook! || FIG. y FAM. Furious, hopping mad (enfadado). || — HIST. *Camisa negra*, blackshirt. || *Cerveza negra*, brown ale; stout. || DEP. *Cinturón negro*, black belt. || FIG. y FAM. *Estar negro con*, to be livid with *o* mad at (una persona), to be desperate about (una cosa). | *Estar negro de envidia*, to be green with envy. || *Lista negra*, black list. || *Magia negra*, black magic, black art. || *Mercado negro*, black market. || *Misa negra*, black mass. || *Negro como el azabache*, jetblack (pelo). || *Negro como el carbón* or *como un tizón*, as black as coal, as black as soot. || *Negro como la pez*, pitch-black, as black as pitch, pitch-dark. || *Negro como la boca del lobo*, as black as pitch, like the black hole of Calcutta (sin luz). || FIG. *Oveja negra* or *garbanzo negro*, black sheep. || *Pan negro*, brown bread. || FIG. y FAM. *Pasarlas negras*, to have a rough time. || *Peste negra*, black death. || *Pimienta negra*, black pepper. || FIG. y FAM. *Poner a uno negro*, to make s.o. mad (enfadar), to beat s.o. black and blue (de golpes). | *Ponerse negro*, to get mad, to lose one's temper (ponerse furioso), to get a suntan (broncearse), to look bad (un asunto). || HIST. *Príncipe Negro*, Black Prince. || *Selva Negra*, Black Forest. || FIG. y FAM. *Suerte negra*, tough *o* rotten luck. | *Tener ideas negras*, to be down in the dumps. | *Verlo todo negro*, to be very pessimistic. | *Verse negro para* or *vérselas negras para*, to have a lot of trouble to. || MED. *Vómito negro*, black vomit.
— M. y f. Negro (hombre), negress (mujer). || FIG. y FAM. *Trabajar como un negro*, to work like a black *o* like a slave. || — M. Black (color). || Tan (bronceado). || Black *o* dark tobacco (tabaco): *no me gusta el negro*, I don't like black tobacco. || — FOT. *En blanco y negro*, in black and white. || QUÍM. *Negro animal*, animal charcoal. || *Negro de humo, de marfil*, lampblack, ivory black. || — F. MÚS. Crotchet [U.S., quarter note]. || Buttonned foil (espada). || Bad luck (mala suerte). || FIG. y FAM. *Hacer pasar las negras a alguien*, to give s.o. a rough time.
negroide adj. Negroid.
negror m. o **negrura** f. Blackness, darkness.
negruzco, ca adj. Blackish, darkish.
neguilla f. BOT. Corn cockle (planta abundante en los sembrados). | Nigella (arañuela).
negus m. Negus.
nematelmintos m. pl. ZOOL. Nemathelminthes.
nematodos m. pl. ZOOL. Nematodes.
nemoroso, sa adj. POÉT. Sylvan.
nemotecnia f. Mnemonics, mnemotechny.
nemotécnico, ca adj. Mnemotechnic.
nene, na m. y f. Baby (niño pequeño). || — F. Love, dear, darling (expresión cariñosa).
nenúfar m. BOT. Water lily.
neocaledonio, nia adj./s. New Caledonian.
neocatolicismo m. Neo-Catholicism.
neocatólico, ca adj. Neo-Catholic.
neocelandés, esa adj. [Of *o* from] New Zealand.
— M. y f. New Zealander.
neoclasicismo m. Neoclassicism.
neoclásico, ca adj. Neoclassic, neoclassical.
— M. y f. Neoclassicist.
neocolonialismo m. Neocolonialism.
neocolonialista adj./s. Neocolonialist.
neocristianismo m. Neo-Christianity.
neocristiano, na adj./s. Neo-Christian.
neoescolástico, ca adj. Neo-Scholastic.
— F. Neo-Scholasticism.
neofascismo m. Neofascism.
neófito, ta m. y f. Neophyte, novice.
neógeno m. GEOL. Neocene.
neogótico, ca adj. Neo-Gothic.
neogriego, ga adj. Neo-Greek.
neoimpresionismo m. Neo-Impressionism.
neolatino, na adj. Neo-Latin. || *Lenguas neolatinas*, Romance languages.
neolítico, ca adj. Neolithic.
— M. Neolith.
neologismo m. Neologism.
neólogo, ga m. y f. Neologist.
neomaltusianismo m. Neo-Malthusianism.
neón m. Neon (gas): *alumbrado de neón*, neon lighting.
neoplatonismo m. o **neoplatonicismo** m. Neoplatonism.
neoplatónico, ca adj. Neoplatonic.
— M. y f. Neoplatonist.
neopositivismo m. Neopositivism.
neorrealismo m. Neorealism.
neorrealista adj./s. Neorealist.
neorromanticismo m. Neoromanticism.
neorromántico, ca adj./s. Neoromantic.
neotomismo m. Neo-Thomism.
neoyorquino, na adj. [Of *o* from] New York.
— M. y f. New Yorker.
neozelandés, esa adj./s. V. NEOCELANDÉS.
neozoico, ca adj. GEOL. Neozoic.
Nepal n. pr. m. Nepal.
nepalés, esa adj./s. Nepalese.
neperiano, na adj. MAT. Napierian.
nepote m. Nepote.
nepotismo m. Nepotism.
neptúneo, a o **neptúnico, ca** adj. Neptunian.
neptunio m. QUÍM. Neptunium.
Neptuno n. pr. m. MIT. Neptune.
nequáquam adv. FAM. Certainly not.
nereida f. MIT. Nereid, sea nymph. || ZOOL. Nereid.
Nerón n. pr. m. Nero. || FIG. Tyrant (tirano).
neroniano, na adj. Neronian.
nervadura f. ARQ. Ribs, *pl.* || BOT. Venation, nervation. || ZOOL. Veins, *pl.* (de insectos).
nerviado, da adj. BOT. Nervate.
nervio m. ANAT. Nerve: *nervio óptico*, optic nerve. || Rib, vein, nerve (de una hoja). || Sinew (de la carne). || ARQ. Rib, nerve. || MÚS. String. || TECN. Band (de un libro). || ZOOL. Vein (en insectos). || FIG. Sinews, *pl.*: *el nervio de la guerra*, the sinews of war. | Nerve (valor). | Energy, strength, vigour, mettle (energía). || — *Ataque de nervios*, fit of hysterics, hysterics: *hizo que le diera un ataque de nervios*, he sent her into hysterics. || *Crisparle los nervios a uno*, to get on s.o.'s nerves. || *Estar enfermo de los nervios*, to suffer from a nervous complaint. || FIG. *Estar hecho un manojo de nervios*, to be a bundle of nerves. || *Guerra de nervios*, war of nerves. || *Nervio de buey*, bull's pizzle. || *Nervios de acero*, nerves of steel. || *Poner los nervios de punta*, to set one's nerves on edge, to get on s.o.'s nerves. || *Tener los nervios de punta*, to be [all] on edge. || *Tener los nervios bien templados*, to have steady nerves. || *Tener nervio*, to have nerve.
nerviosidad f. o **nerviosismo** m. Nervousness, nerves, *pl.* || Irritability, excitability (excitación). || Agitation (agitación). || Impatience (impaciencia). || *Quitar a uno el nerviosismo* or *la nerviosidad*, to soothe s.o.'s nerves.
nervioso, sa adj. Nervous: *sistema nervioso*, nervous system; *depresión nerviosa*, nervous breakdown. || Nerve (célula, centro). || Sinewy, wiry (cuerpo, miembro). || AUT. Responsive, lively (motor). || BOT. Nervate (hoja). || FIG. Fidgety, nervy (impaciente). | Excitable, highly-strung (impresionable). | Irritable. || — *¡No te pongas nervioso!*, don't get excited!, take it easy!, calm down! || *Poner nervioso a alguien*, to get on s.o.'s nerves. || *Ponerse nervioso*, to get excited, to get worked up. || *Tiene una depresión nerviosa*, he has had a nervous breakdown.
nervosidad f. o **nervosismo** m. V. NERVIOSIDAD.
nervudo, da adj. Vigorous, strong (fuerte). || FAM. Sinewy, wiry (miembro).
nervura f. Ribbing (de un libro).
nesga f. Bias (en un vestido). || Gore (pieza triangular).
nesgado, da adj. Cut on the bias.
nesgar v. tr. To cut on the bias (cortar al bies). || To gore (poner una pieza triangular).
nestorianismo m. Nestorianism.
nestoriano, na adj./s. Nestorian.
neto, ta adj. Pure, simple (una verdad). || Clear (ideas, estilo, conciencia). || Net: *peso, precio, beneficio neto*, net weight, price, profit.
neuma m. MÚS. Neume.
neumático, ca adj. Pneumatic.
— M. Tyre [U.S., tire]. || — *Juego de neumáticos*, set of tyres. || *Neumáticos contra pinchazos, sin cámara de aire*, puncture-proof, tubeless tyres.
neumococo m. Pneumococcus.
neumogástrico adj./s.m. Pneumogastric (nervio).
neumonía f. MED. Pneumonia.
neumónico, ca adj. Pneumonic.
neumotórax m. MED. Pneumothorax.
neuralgia f. MED. Neuralgia.
neurálgico, ca adj. MED. Neuralgic. || FIG. *Punto neurálgico*, weak spot, weakness.
neurastenia f. MED. Neurasthenia.
neurasténico, ca adj. MED. Neurasthenic.
neurisma m. MED. Aneurism.
neurítico, ca adj. MED. Neuritic.
neuritis f. MED. Neuritis.
neuroblasto m. BIOL. Neuroblast.
neurocirugía f. MED. Neurosurgery.
neuroesqueleto m. ZOOL. Neuroskeleton.
neurología f. MED. Neurology.
neurológico, ca adj. MED. Neurological.
neurólogo m. MED. Neurologist.
neuroma m. MED. Neuroma.
neurona f. ANAT. Neuron.
neurópata m. y f. MED. Neuropath.
neuropatía f. MED. Neuropathy.
neuropatología f. MED. Neuropathology.
neuróptero adj. m./s.m. ZOOL. Neuropteran. || — M. pl. Neuroptera.
neurosis f. MED. Neurosis.
neurótico, ca adj./s. MED. Neurotic.

neurotomía f. MED. Neurotomy.
neurovegetativo, va adj. ANAT. Neurovegetative.
neutoniano, na adj. FÍS. Newtonian.
neutonio m. FÍS. Newton.
neutral adj./s. Neutral.
neutralidad f. Neutrality. || *Mantener la neutralidad*, to remain neutral.
neutralismo m. Neutralism.
neutralista adj./s. Neutralist.
neutralización f. Neutralization.
neutralizador, ra adj. QUÍM. Neutralizing.
— M. Neutralizer, neutralizing agent.
neutralizante adj./s.m. V. NEUTRALIZADOR.
neutralizar v. tr. To neutralize.
neutrino m. FÍS. Neutrino.
neutro, tra adj. GRAM. Neuter. || JUR., ELECTR., MIL. y QUÍM. Neutral. || BIOL. Sexless, neuter.
— M. GRAM. Neuter.
neutrón m. FÍS. Neutron.
nevada f. Snowfall: *fuerte nevada*, heavy snowfall.
nevadilla f. BOT. Whitlowwort (planta).
nevado, da adj. Snow-covered: *montañas nevadas*, snow-covered mountains. || Covered with snow: *la carretera está nevada*, the road is covered with snow. || POÉT. y FIG. Snowy, snow-white (blanco).
— M. *Amer.* Snow-capped mountain, mountain with perpetual snow. || *Amer. El nevado de Sajama*, Mount Sajama.
nevar* v. impers. To snow: *nevar mucho*, to snow heavily.
— V. tr. To cover with snow (cubrir de nieve). || FIG. To whiten (poner blanco).
nevasca f. Snowfall (nevada). || Blizzard (ventisca).
nevatilla f. Wagtail (ave).
nevera f. Refrigerator, fridge (fam.) [refrigerador]. || FIG. Icebox (sitio muy frío): *esta habitación es una nevera*, this room is like an icebox.
nevero m. Perennial snowcap *o* snowfield.
nevisca f. Light snowfall.
neviscar v. impers. To snow lightly *o* a little.
nevo m. Naevus, birthmark (mancha en la piel). || Mole (lunar).
nevoso, sa adj. Snowy.
newton m. FÍS. Newton.
newtoniano, na adj. FÍS. Newtonian.
nexo m. Link, bond, tie, nexus (vínculo). || Connection (relación). || *Palabras sin nexo*, unrelated *o* unconnected words.
ni conj. Neither, nor: *él no lo hizo, ni ella*, he did not do it, neither did she. || Not even (ni siquiera): *ni lo dijo a sus amigos*, he did not even tell his friends; *no tenía ni donde pasar la noche*, he did not even have anywhere to spend the night; *ni que fueras su padre*, not even if you were his father. || — *Ni más ni menos*, no more, no less. || *Ni nada*, or anything, nor anything: *no sabe leer ni nada*, he cannot read or anything, he can neither read nor anything; *no le gusta ni el arroz, ni la carne, ni el pescado, ni nada*, he does not like rice, or meat, or fish, or anything *o* he likes neither rice, nor meat, nor fish, nor anything. || *Ni... ni*, neither... nor: *ni tú ni yo le podemos ayudar ahora*, neither you nor I can help him now; *no tengo ni té ni café*, I have neither tea nor coffee; *no tiene ni bolígrafo ni lápiz*, he has neither a pen nor a pencil; *ni come ni duerme*, he neither eats nor sleeps. || *Ni que fuesen niños, ni que fueses un niño*, they are worse than children, you are worse than a child. || *Ni que fuera suyo*, anyone would think it were yours *o* his *o* hers. || *Ni que fuera tonto*, what do you take me [*o* him *o* her] for? || *Ni siquiera*, not even: *no quedó ni siquiera una silla vacía*, there was not even one free seat left; *ni siquiera me lo dijo*, he did not even tell me. || *Ni un, ni una*, not... a...: *no me quedaré ni un minuto más aquí*, I shall not stay here a minute more. || *Ni uno, ni una*, not one: *ni uno se quedó*, not one remained. || *Ni uno ni otro*, neither, neither the one nor the other (sujeto): *ni uno ni otro nos parece bien*, neither seems right to us; not... either [of them] (complemento): *no pienso comprar ni uno ni otro*, I do not intend to buy either [of them]. || *Ni unos ni otros*, none of them (sujeto): *no vinieron ni unos ni otros*, none of them came; not... any of them (complemento): *no compres ni unos ni otros*, do not buy any [of them]. || *No... ni*, not... or, neither... nor: *no come ni duerme*, he does not eat or sleep, he neither eats nor sleeps. || *No... ni... ni*, not... either... or: *no quiero ni agua ni vino*, I do not want either water or wine. || *Sin... ni*, without... or: *salió sin beber ni comer*, he went out without drinking or eating.
Niágara n. pr. m. GEOGR. Niagara: *las cataratas del Niágara*, Niagara Falls.
nibelungos m. pl. MIT. Nibelungen.
nicaragua f. BOT. Balsam apple.
Nicaragua n. pr. f. GEOGR. Nicaragua.
nicaragüense adj./s. Nicaraguan.
nicotina f. QUÍM. Nicotine.
nicotínico, ca adj. Nicotinic.
nicotinismo o **nicotismo** m. MED. Nicotinism, nicotine poisoning.
nictación f. Nictation (parpadeo).
nictalopia f. MED. Day blindness (visión mejor de noche). Nyctalopia (visión mejor de día).
nictitante adj. ZOOL. Nictitating.
nicho m. Niche, recess (hornacina).
nidación f. MED. Nidation.
nidada f. Brood (de pollos). || Clutch (de huevos).
nidal m. Nest (ponedero de las gallinas). || Nest egg (huevo). || FIG. Haunt, hangout (lugar frecuentado por una persona). | Hiding place (escondrijo).
nidificación f. Nidification, nest building.
nidificar v. intr. To nest, to nidify, to build a nest.
nido m. Nest. || FIG. Den, nest: *nido de bandidos*, den of thieves. | Hiding place (escondrijo). | Nest (hogar). | Hotbed (criadero). | Source (fuente, origen). | — FIG. *Caer del nido*, to come down to earth with a bump. || *Camas de nido*, pullout beds. || FIG. *Encontrar el pájaro en el nido*, to find the person for whom one was searching. | *En los nidos de antaño, no hay pájaros hogaño*, where are the snows of yesteryear? || *Mesas de nido*, nest (*sing.*) of tables. || *Nido de abejas*, smocking (costura), honeycomb (de un radiador, etc.). || MIL. *Nido de ametralladoras*, machine gun nest. | *Nido de urraca*, outwork (trinchera). || FIG. *Nido de víboras*, nest of vipers. | *Parece que se ha caído del nido*, he is still wet behind the ears.
niebla f. Fog (densa). || Mist (neblina). || BOT. Mildew (hongo parásito). || MED. Nubecula (en el ojo, en la orina). || FIG. Mental confusion, fogginess (confusión). || — *Hay niebla*, it is foggy. || FAM. *Niebla meona*, drizzle. || *Tarde de niebla*, foggy afternoon.
niel m. TECN. Niello (del metal).
nielado m. TECN. Niello (procedimiento).
nieto, ta m. y f. Grandson (chico), granddaughter (chica). || — M. pl. Grandchildren.
nieve f. Snow: *blanco como la nieve*, as white as snow. || — Pl. Snow, *sing.*, snows: *son las primeras nieves*, it is the first snow. || — CULIN. *A punto de nieve*, stiff: *claras batidas a punto de nieve*, egg whites beaten till stiff. || *Copo de nieve*, snowflake.
nife m. GEOL. Core [of the Earth].
Nigeria n. pr. f. Nigeria.
nigeriano, na adj./s. Nigerian.
nigromancia f. Necromancy.
nigromante o **nigromántico, ca** m. y f. Necromancer.
— Adj. Necromantic.
nigua f. ZOOL. Chigoe (parásito).
nihilismo m. Nihilism.
nihilista adj. Nihilistic.
— M. y f. Nihilist.
nikel m. Nickel (metal).
Nilo n. pr. m. GEOGR. Nile: *Alto Nilo*, Upper Nile.
nilón m. Nylon (textil).
nimbar v. tr. To encircle with a halo.
nimbo m. Nimbus (nube). || Halo (en la cabeza, etc.).
nimboestrato m. Nimbostratus (nube).
nimiedad f. Triviality (pequeñez). || Trifle (fruslería). || Excess (demasía). || Verbosity (prolijidad). || Meticulousness (meticulosidad).
nimio, mia adj. Insignificant, petty, unimportant, minor, trivial (de poca importancia): *detalles nimios*, petty details. || Overmeticulous (muy meticuloso). || Excessive (excesivo). || Verbose (prolijo). || Stingy (mezquino). || *De nimia importancia*, quite unimportant, minor.
ninfa f. MIT. y ZOOL. Nymph. || ANAT. Nympha. || FIG. *Ninfa Egeria*, Egeria.
ninfea m. BOT. Nymphaea, water lily (nenúfar).
ninfómana o **ninfomaníaca** f. Nymphomaniac.
ninfomanía f. MED. Nymphomania.
ningún adj. indef. V. NINGUNO.
— OBSERV. *Ningún* is the apocopated form of *ninguno*. It is used before a masculine singular noun.
ninguno, na adj. indef. No: *ninguna casa me conviene*, no house suits me. || No, not any (con negación): *no voy a ninguna escuela*, I do not go to any school, I go to no school; *no tiene valor ninguno*, it has no value, it hasn't any value. || — *De ninguna manera* or *de ningún modo*, not at all, by no means, in no way. || *En ninguna parte*, nowhere. || *Ninguna cosa*, nothing. || *No es ningún imbécil*, he is no fool.
— Pron. indef. None, not one, not any: *ninguno entre ellos*, none of them. || Neither, not... either (de dos): *no tomo ninguno de estos dos libros*, I will take neither of these two books, I will not take either of these two books. || No one, nobody (nadie): *ninguno lo sabrá*, no one will know. || *Como ninguno*, like no one else [does *o* did].
— OBSERV. When *ninguno* precedes the verb, the adverb *no* disappears: *ninguno sabe*, but *no sabe ninguno*, nobody knows.
niña f. Girl, little girl: *una niña encantadora*, a charming girl. || ANAT. Pupil (del ojo). || FAM. Dear, my dear (término de cariño). || FIG. *Es la niña de mis ojos* or *le quiero como a la niña de mis ojos*, she is my pride and joy *o* the apple of my eye.
niñada f. Childishness, childish thing.
niñear v. intr. To act like a child, to act childishly.
niñería f. Childish act *o* thing, childishness (acción propia de niño). || FIG. Trifle, trifling matter, triviality (cosa sin importancia).
niñero, ra adj. Fond of children (aficionado a los niños).
— F. Nursemaid, nanny.

niñez f. Childhood, infancy. || FIG. Infancy. || — Pl. Childishness, *sing.* (niñerías). || *Volver a la niñez*, to be in one's second childhood.

niño, na adj. Young, small: *es aún muy niña para ir de compras*, she is still very young to go shopping. || Childish (infantil). || FIG. Immature, inexperienced (sin experiencia).
— M. Boy: *un niño muy simpático*, a very nice boy. || Baby: *voy a tener un niño*, I am expecting a baby. || FAM. Dear, my dear (voz de cariño). || — F. V. NIÑA. || — Pl. Children: *tengo dos niños, un hijo y una hija*, I have two children: a boy and a girl. || — *De niño*, as a child. || *Desde niño*, from childhood. || *Es el niño mimado de su madre*, he is his mother's pet *o* his mother's blue-eyed boy. || FIG. y FAM. *Estar como un niño con zapatos nuevos*, to be like a dog with two tails. || *Hacer un niño a una chica*, to get a girl in the family way, to get a girl pregnant. || *Niño bitongo* young upstart (repipi). || *Niño bonito*, pet (persona preferida), show-off (presumido). || *Niño de la Bola*, Baby Jesus. || *Niño de pecho* or *de teta*, babe-in-arms. || *Niño expósito* or *de la piedra*, foundling. || *Niño gótico*, show-off. || *Niño Jesús*, Baby Jesus. || *Niño mimado*, spoilt child. || *Niño prodigio*, child prodigy. || *Niño zangolotino*, big baby. || *¡No seas niño!*, don't be such a baby! || FIG. y FAM. *¡Qué poeta ni qué niño muerto!*, he is about as much a poet as I am.

niobio m. QUÍM. Niobium.

nipón, ona adj./s. Japanese, Nipponese.

níquel m. Nickel (metal).

niquelado m. o **niqueladura** f. Nickel-plating, nickelling.

niquelar v. tr. To nickel-plate, to nickel.

niqui m. Tee-shirt (camisa).

Nirvana m. REL. Nirvana.

níspero m. BOT. Medlar (árbol y fruto).

nitidez f. Brightness, clarity, clearness (brillo). || Clearness, clarity: *la nitidez del agua*, the clearness of the water. || Sharpness, clarity, clearness (de una foto). || FIG. Unblemished nature, purity.

nítido, da adj. Clear, sharp: *foto nítida*, sharp photograph. || Bright, clean (limpio). || Clear (agua).

nitración f. QUÍM. Nitration.

nitrado, da adj. Nitrated.

nitral m. Nitre *o* saltpetre works *o* bed [U.S., niter *o* saltpeter works *o* bed].

nitratación f. QUÍM. Nitration.

nitratar v. tr. QUÍM. To nitrate.

nitrato m. QUÍM. Nitrate: *nitrato sódico*, sodium nitrate. || *Nitrato de Chile*, Chile saltpetre [U.S., Chile saltpeter].

nitrería f. Nitre bed [U.S., niter bed].

nítrico, ca adj. QUÍM. Nitric.

nitrificación f. QUÍM. Nitrification.

nitrificador, ra adj. QUÍM. Nitrifying.

nitrificar v. tr. QUÍM. To nitrify.

nitrilo m. QUÍM. Nitrile.

nitrito m. QUÍM. Nitrite.

nitro m. QUÍM. Nitre [U.S., niter], saltpetre [U.S., saltpeter].

nitrobenceno m. QUÍM. Nitrobenzene.

nitrocelulosa f. QUÍM. Nitrocellulose.

nitrogenado, da adj. QUÍM. Nitrogenous.

nitrógeno m. QUÍM. Nitrogen (gas).

nitroglicerina f. QUÍM. Nitroglycerine.

nitroso, sa adj. QUÍM. Nitrous.

nitrotolueno m. QUÍM. Nitrotoluene.

nitruración f. TECN. Nitrogenation, nitriding.

nitruro m. QUÍM. Nitride.

nivel m. Level. || Level, height (altura). || FIG. Level: *al nivel nacional, ministerial*, at a national, ministerial level; *nivel económico*, economic level. | Standard: *esta universidad tiene un nivel más alto que la otra*, the standard in this university is higher than in the other one. || TECN. Level (instrumento): *nivel de burbuja*, spirit level. || MIN. Level (en minas). || — *Al mismo nivel*, at the same level, level. || *Al nivel de*, at the same level as, on a level with, level with. || *Al nivel del mar*, at sea level. || *A nivel*, level. || *Conferencia de alto nivel*, top-level *o* high-level conference. || *Estar al nivel de las circunstancias*, to rise to the occasion. || *La ciudad está a 500 metros sobre el nivel del mar*, the city is 500 metres above sea level. || *Nivel de agua*, water level. || *Nivel de vida*, standard of living. || *Paso a nivel*, level crossing [U.S., railroad *o* grade crossing].

nivelación f. Levelling [U.S., leveling].

nivelador, ra adj. Levelling [U.S., leveling].
— M. y f. Leveller [U.S., leveler].

nivelamiento m. FIG. Levelling [U.S., leveling].

nivelar v. tr. To level (poner al mismo nivel). || To level, to make even (allanar el terreno). || To survey (en topografía). || FIG. To even out, to make even *o* equal (igualar). | To balance: *nivelar el presupuesto*, to balance the budget.
— V. pr. To become level, to level out.

níveo, a adj. POÉT. Niveous, snowy.

nivoso, sa adj. Snowy.

no adv. No (en respuestas): *no, señor*, no, Sir. || Not (delante de un verbo): *no deberías*, you should not, you shouldn't; *no vinieron*, they did not come, they didn't come; *no lo hagas*, do not do it, don't do it; *no comer*, not to eat. || Not any, no (ningún): *no tiene dinero*, he has not any money, he has no money. || Not (en frases sin verbo): *todavía no*, not yet; *¿por qué no?*, why not?; *¡yo no!*, not I.
— M. No: *contestó con un no categórico*, he replied with a definite no.
— *¡A que no!*, I bet you don't! || *¿A que no?*, do you want to bet? || *¡Carlos no, Felipe sí!*, Charles out, Philip in!, down with Charles, up with Philip! || *¡Cómo no!*, of course. || *¡Cómo que no!*, no ?, what do you mean, no? || *Creo que no*, I don't think so. || *Cuidado que no se escape*, be careful [that] he does not escape. || *Decir que no*, to say no. || *Ernesto vino ayer, ¿no?*, Ernest came yesterday, didn't he? || *Es inglés, ¿no?*, he is English, isn't he? || *¡Eso sí que no!*, certainly not!, of course not! || *No aceptación*, nonacceptance. || *No agresión*, nonaggression: *firmar un pacto de no agresión*, to sign a nonaggression pact. || *No alineación*, nonalignement. || *No alineado*, nonaligned. || *No beligerencia*, nonbelligerency. || *No bien*, no sooner: *no bien llegué, me llamaron*, I had no sooner arrived than they called me. || *No ... casi*, hardly: *no habla casi*, he hardly speaks. || *No combatiente*, noncombatant. || *No comprometido*, noncommittal. || *No conformidad* or *no conformismo*, nonconformity. || *No cooperación*, noncooperation. || *No digo que no*, I won't say no. || *No es que*, it is not that. || *No existencia*, nonexistence. || *No existente*, nonexistent. || *No ferroso*, nonferrous. || *No hay de qué*, don't mention it, not at all, you are welcome. || *No hay para qué* or *por qué*, there is no reason to. || *No intervención*, nonintervention. || *No más*, v. MÁS. || *No menos de*, no less than. || *No mucho*, not much. || *No ... nada*, not at all: *no te entiendo nada*, I do not understand you at all. || *No negociable*, nonnegotiable. || *No por cierto*, certainly not, indeed not. || *No sea que*, in case. || *No sectario*, nonsectarian. || *No ... sino*, not ... but: *no es militar sino abogado*, he is not a soldier but a lawyer; nothing but: *no hace sino criticar*, he does nothing but criticize; just, only (sólo). || *No sólo ... sino también* or *sino que*, not only ... but also. || *No tal*, no such thing. || *No violencia*, nonviolence. || *No ya*, not only. || FIL. *No yo*, nonego. || *¡Que no!*, no!, certainly not! || *Ya no*, no longer, not ... any more: *ya no leo*, I no longer read, I do not read any more.
— OBSERV. In Latin America, *no más* occurs in a number of idioms, such as: *aquí no más*, right here; *así no más*, middling; *ayer no más*, only *o* just yesterday; *tome no más*, do take it.
— Las contracciones *don't, can't, won't*, etc. son ligeramente familiares. Por lo tanto es preferible evitarlas en la lengua escrita.

nobelio m. QUÍM. Nobelium.

nobiliario, ria adj. Nobiliary, noble.

nobilísimo, ma adj. Very noble, most noble.

noble adj. Noble (aristócrata). || Noble, honest, upright (honrado). || *Noble en su porte*, distinguished looking.
— M. Noble, nobleman (aristócrata). || — Pl. Nobles, nobility, *sing.*

nobleza f. Nobility, aristocracy (nobles, aristocracia). || Nobility (cualidad de noble). || Honesty, uprightness, nobleness (honradez). || — *Nobleza obliga*, "noblesse oblige". || *Tener sus títulos de nobleza*, to be of the nobility.

nocible adj. Noxious, harmful.

noción f. Notion, idea: *no tiene noción de francés*, he has no idea of French. || — Pl. Slight knowledge, *sing.*: *tiene nociones de matemáticas*, he has a slight knowledge of mathematics. || Smattering, *sing.*: *tener nociones de inglés*, to have a smattering of English.

nocividad f. Noxiousness, harmfulness.

nocivo, va adj. Noxious: *gas nocivo*, noxious gas. || Harmful, injurious: *nocivo a* or *para la salud*, harmful to the health.

noctambulismo m. Noctivagation, noctambulism.

noctámbulo, la adj. Noctivagant, noctambulant.
— M. y f. Noctivagant, noctambule.

noctívago, ga adj. POÉT. Noctivagant.

nocturnidad f. JUR. Nocturnal character [of a crime].

nocturno, na adj. Nocturnal: *aparición nocturna*, nocturnal apparition. || Evening: *clases nocturnas*, evening classes. || Night: *avión, tren, vuelo nocturno*, night plane, train, flight; *vida nocturna*, night life. || BOT. y ZOOL. Nocturnal, night: *aves nocturnas*, night birds.
— N. MÚS. Nocturne.

noche f. Night: *la noche anterior*, the previous night, the night before; *ayer por la noche*, last night. || Late evening, night: *ven por la noche después de cenar*, come round late in the evening *o* come round at night after dinner. || Nighttime, night: *cuando vino la noche*, when nighttime came, when night fell. || FIG. Dark (oscuridad): *le asusta la noche*, he is scared of the dark. | Night: *las noches oscuras del alma*, the dark nights of the soul. || — *A boca de noche*, at dusk, at twilight. || *Al caer la noche*, at nightfall. || *Buenas noches*, good evening (al atardecer), good night (al despedirse): *dar las buenas noches*, to say good evening *o* good night. || *Cerrada la noche* or *ya entrada la noche*, after nightfall. || *De la noche a la mañana*, v. MAÑANA. || *De noche*, at night. || FIG. *De noche todos los gatos son pardos*, everything looks the same in the dark. || *Durante la noche*, in the night. || *En las altas horas de la noche*, in the small hours, late at night. || *Es de noche*, it is dark *o* nighttime. || *Esta*

noche, tonight. || *Función de noche*, late performance. || *Hacer de la noche día*, to turn night into day. || *Hacer noche*, to spend the night (pasar la noche). || *Hacerse de noche*, to grow dark (anochecer). || *¡Hasta la noche!*, see you tonight. || *Hasta muy entrada la noche*, until late at night. || *Las mil y una noches*, the Arabian Nights. || *Mañana por la noche*, tomorrow night. || *Media noche*, midnight. || *Noche Buena*, Christmas Eve. || *Noche cerrada*, dark night. || *Noche de bodas*, wedding night. || *Noche de estreno*, first night. || *Noche en claro* or *en blanco* or *en vela* or *toledana*, sleepless night. || *Noche Vieja*, New Year's Eve. || *Noche y día*, night and day. || *Pasar la noche de juerga*, to make a night of it. || *Por la noche*, at night, at nighttime, by night, in the night. || *Se está haciendo de noche*, night is falling *o* coming on, it is growing dark. || FIG. *Ser la noche y el día*, to be as different as night and day. || *Toda la noche*, all night, the whole night. || *Trabajar de noche* or *por la noche*, to work at night (cualquier persona), to work nights (un trabajador). || *Traje de noche*, evening dress, evening gown.
Nochebuena f. Christmas Eve.
nochero m. *Amer.* Night watchman (guarda). | Bedside table (mesilla de noche).
Nochevieja f. New Year's Eve. || — *Cena de Nochevieja*, New Year's Eve dinner. || *Día de Nochevieja*, New Year's Eve.
nodal adj. Nodal: *punto nodal*, nodal point.
nodo m. Node.
No-Do m. CINEM. Newsreel.

— OBSERV. *No-Do* is an abbreviation of *noticiario documental* in Spain.

nodriza f. Wet nurse (ama de cría). || Nanny (niñera). || TECN. Vacuum tank (depósito). || *Avión, buque nodriza*, mother aircraft, ship.
nodular adj. Nodular (relativo a los nódulos). || Nodulose, nodulous (que tiene nódulos).
nódulo m. Nodule, node.
Noé n. pr. m. Noah. || *El arca de Noé*, Noah's ark.
nogal m. Walnut (árbol, madera).
nogalina f. Walnut stain.
noguera f. BOT. Walnut tree.
nogueral m. Walnut grove, wood of walnut trees.
nómada adj. Nomadic.
— M. y f. Nomad.
nomadismo m. Nomadism.
nombradía f. Renown, fame (fama).
nombrado, da adj. Famous, renowned, well-known (célebre). || Aforementioned (susodicho). || *Nombrado más adelante*, hereinafter mentioned.
nombramiento m. Appointment (designación para un cargo). || Confirmation of appointment (título).
nombrar v. tr. To appoint: *nombrar a alguien para un cargo*, to appoint s.o. to a post; *nombrar a alguien alcalde*, to appoint s.o. [as] mayor. || To name, to mention (mencionar). || JUR. To name, to appoint (un heredero). || MIL. To commission.
nombre m. GRAM. Noun (sustantivo): *nombre común, propio*, common, proper noun. || Name, Christian name, first name (nombre de pila). || Name (apellido y nombre de pila): *su nombre es John Smith*, his name is John Smith. || FIG. Name (fama): *hacerse un nombre*, to make a name for o.s. || — *Caer en el nombre de una persona*, to remember s.o.'s name. || *Dar un nombre a*, to give a name to, to call. || *Decir el nombre de*, to name, to say the name of: *decir el nombre de sus cómplices*, to name one's accomplices. || *De nombre*, in name only: *rey de nombre*, king in name only; called, named: *un chico, Pedro de nombre*, a boy called Peter; by name: *le conozco sólo de nombre*, I know him only by name. || *En nombre de*, in the name of: *en nombre de la ley*, in the name of the law; on behalf of: *dar las gracias en nombre del presidente*, to give thanks on behalf of the president. || *En nombre mío, tuyo, etc.*, in my name, in your name, etc. || *Le pusieron el nombre de su padre*, they named him after his father. || *Llamar las cosas por su nombre*, to call a spade a spade. || *Nombre artístico, comercial*, stage, trade name. || *Nombre de pila*, Christian *o* first name. || *Nombre gentilicio*, gentilic name. || *Nombre postizo*, assumed name. || *Nombre y apellidos*, full name, name in full. || FIG. *No tener nombre*, to be unspeakable (ser incalificable). || *Poner de nombre*, to call: *mis padres me pusieron de nombre Úrsula*, my parents called me Ursula. || *Por el nombre*, by name: *llamar a alguien por el nombre*, to call s.o. by name. || *Responder al nombre de*, to answer to the name of. || *Sin nombre*, unspeakable, nameless (incalificable).
nomenclador o **nomenclátor** m. Catalogue of names. || *Nomenclátor de calles*, list of streets, street index.
nomenclatura f. Nomenclature.
nomeolvides m. inv. BOT. Forget-me-not (planta).
nómina f. List (lista). || COM. Payroll (lista de personal). || — *Cobrar la nómina*, to be paid. || *Estar en nómina*, to be on the staff. || *Nómina de salarios*, payroll.
nominación f. Appointment, nomination.
nominador, ra adj. Appointing, nominating.
— M. y f. Appointer, nominator.
nominal adj. Nominal: *valor nominal*, nominal value. || Nominal, in name only: *el jefe nominal*, the nominal leader. || GRAM. Nominal, substantival.
nominalismo m. FIL. Nominalism.
nominalista adj. Nominalist, nominalistic.
— M. y f. Nominalist.
nominar v. tr. To name, to call (nombrar).
nominativo, va adj. GRAM. Nominative. || COM. Nominal (título). | Bearing a person's name (cheque).
— M. GRAM. Nominative: *nominativo absoluto*, nominative absolute.
nominilla f. Pay warrant, voucher.
non adj. (P.us.). Odd, uneven (impar).
— M. pl. Odds: *jugar a pares y nones*, to play odds and evens. || — FIG. y FAM. *Decir nones*, to refuse point blank. | *Quedar de non*, to be odd man out, to be left out, to be left without a partner.
nona f. Nones, *pl.* (hora canónica). || Nones, *pl.* (del calendario romano).
nonada f. Trifle, trifling *o* unimportant thing.
nonagenario, ria adj./s. Nonagenarian, ninety-year-old.
nonagésimo, ma adj./s. Ninetieth. || *Nonagésimo primero, segundo*, ninety-first, ninety-second.
nonato, ta adj. Born by Caesarian section. || FIG. Unborn, nonexistant (que aún no existe).
noningentésimo, ma adj./s. Ninehundredth.
nonio m. TECN. Nonius, vernier.
nono, na adj. Ninth. || *Décimo nono*, nineteenth.
non plus ultra loc. lat. Ne plus ultra.
nopal m. BOT. Nopal, prickly pear.
noquear v. tr. DEP. To knock out (boxeo).
norabuena f. Congratulations, *pl.*
— Adv. Fortunately.
noramala adv. Unfortunately.
noray o **norai** m. MAR. Bollard.
nordeste adj. Northeast, northeastern (parte). || Northeasterly (dirección, viento).
— M. Northeast. || Northeasterly (viento). || — *Nordeste cuarta al este*, northeast by east. || *Nordeste cuarta al norte*, northeast by north.
nórdico, ca adj. Northern (del Norte). || Nordic (escandinavo, etc.).
— M. y f. Northerner. || Nordic (escandinavo, etc.). || — M. Norse (idioma).
nordista adj. Northern, unionist.
— M. y f. Northerner, Unionist (en la guerra de Secesión norteamericana).
noreste m. V. NORDESTE.
noria f. Noria, waterwheel (para sacar agua). || Big wheel [U.S., ferris wheel] (en una feria).
norma f. Rule, norm, standard: *hay que respetar ciertas normas de conducta*, certain norms of behaviour must be observed. || Principle, norm, rule (principio). || *Normas de ortografía*, spelling rules.
normal adj. Normal: *estado normal*, normal state; *es normal que se disculpe*, it is normal that he should apologize. || QUÍM. y MAT. Normal. || — *Escuela Normal*, Teachers' Training College [U.S., Normal School]. || *Lo normal*, the normal thing. || *Superior a lo normal*, above normal, above average.
— F. MAT. Normal (perpendicular). || Teachers' Training College [U.S., Normal School] (escuela).
normalidad f. Normality. || — *Con normalidad* normally. || *Con toda normalidad*, quite normally. || *La situación en el país ha vuelto a la normalidad*, the situation in the country has returned to normal, calm has been completely restored in the country.
normalista m. y f. Student teacher (alumno).
normalización f. Normalization. || Standardization (en la industria).
normalizar v. tr. To normalize, to restore to normal. || To standardize (en la industria).
— V. pr. To return to normal.
Normandía n. pr. f. GEOGR. Normandy.
normando, da adj./s. Norman. || — M. Norman French (lengua). || HIST. Norseman (vikingo).
normativo, va adj. Normative.
nornordeste adj./s.m. North-northeast.
nornoroeste o **nornorueste** adj./ adv./s.m. North-northwest.
noroeste adj. Northwest, northwesterly, north-western. || — *Noroeste cuarta al norte*, northwest by north. || *Noroeste cuarta al oeste*, northwest by west. || *Viento noroeste*, northwest *o* northwesterly wind.
— M. Northwest.
norte m. North. || North wind, northerly wind (viento). || FIG. Aim, goal (objetivo): *la prosperidad del país debe ser nuestro norte*, the prosperity of the country must be our aim. | Guide (orientación, guía). || — *Del norte*, northern: *las provincias del norte*, the northern provinces; north: *África del Norte*, North Africa; north, northerly: *viento del norte*, northerly wind. || MAR. *Norte cuarta al nordeste, al noroeste*, north by northeast, by northwest. | *Norte de brújula*, magnetic north. || FIG. *Perder el norte*, to lose one's bearings.
— Adj. North, northern: *el ala norte de la casa*, the north wing of the house. || Northerly: *rumbo norte*, northerly direction. || North, northerly (viento).
norteafricano, na adj./s. North African.
Norteamérica n. pr. f. GEOGR. North America.
norteamericano, na adj./s. American, North American (estadounidense).
nortear v. intr. MAR. To sail northwards (el buque). || To veer towards the north (el viento).

NOMBRES (*m.*) DE PILA — CHRISTIAN NAMES

(*Su forma familiar está entre paréntesis*)

I. Nombres (*m.*) masculinos. — Masculine names.

Abrahán	Abraham (*Abe*)
Adolfo	Adolph
Adriano	Adrian
Alano	Alan
Agustín	Austin, Augustin
Alberto	Albert
Alejandro	Alexander (*Alex, Alec, Al*)
Alfonso	Alphonso
Alfredo	Alfred (*Alf, Alfie*)
Andrés	Andrew (*Andy*)
Antonio (*Toni, Tonete*)	Anthony (*Tony*)
Arturo	Arthur (*Art*)
Augusto	Augustus (*Gus, Gussie*)
Bartolomé (*Bartolo*)	Bartholomew (*Bart*)
Benito	Benedict (*Bennet, Bennett*)
Benjamín	Benjamin (*Ben, Bennie*)
Bernardo	Bernard (*Bernie, Bern*)
Carlos	Charles (*Chas, Charlie*)
Clemente	Clement (*Clem*)
Cristóbal	Christopher (*Chris*)
Daniel	Daniel (*Dan, Danny*)
David	David (*Dave, Davy*)
Dionisio	Dennis
Eduardo	Edward (*Ted, Teddie, Ed, Eddie*)
Elías	Elijah, Ellis, Eliot, Elliot
Emilio	Emil
Enrique	Henry (*Harry, Hank*)
Ernesto	Ernest
Estanislao	Stanislaus, Stanly (*Stan*)
Esteban	Stephen, Steven (*Steve*)
Federico	Frederick (*Fred, Freddy*)
Felipe	Philip (*Phil*)
Fernando (*Nano*)	Ferdinand
Francisco (*Paco, Paquito, Pancho, Curro, Frasquito*)	Francis (*Frank, Franky*)
Gabriel	Gabriel (*Gaby, Gabe*)
Gerardo	Gerald (*Jerry, Gary*)
Gregorio	Gregory (*Greg*)
Gualterio	Walter
Guillermo	William (*Will, Willy, Bill, Billy*)
Gustavo	Gustavus (*Gus*)
Haroldo	Harold (*Hal*)
Hugo	Hugh
Ignacio (*Nacho*)	Ignatius
Isaac	Isaac
Jaime, Jacobo, Santiago, Diego	James (*Jim, Jimmy*)
Javier	Xavier
Joaquín	Joachim
Jorge	George (*Georgie*)
José (*Pepe*)	Joseph (*Joe, Joey*)
Juan	John (*Johnny, Jack*)
Julián	Julian
Julio	Julius (*Jule*)
Leonardo	Leonard (*Len, Lenny*)
Leopoldo (*Polo*)	Leopold
Lorenzo (*Loren*)	Lawrence, Laurence (*Larry, Lawry*)
Luis	Lewis (*Lew*)
Manuel (*Manolo*)	Emmanuel (*Manny*)
Marcos	Mark, Marcus
Martín	Martin (*Marty*)
Mateo	Matthew (*Matt, Mat*)
Matías	Matthias
Mauricio	Morris, Maurice (*Morrie, Morry*)
Miguel	Michael (*Mike, Micky*)
Nicolás	Nicholas (*Nick*)
Oliverio	Oliver (*Noll*)
Pablo	Paul
Patricio	Patrick (*Pat, Paddy*)
Pedro (*Perico*)	Peter (*Pete*)
Rafael (*Rafa*)	Raphael
Raimundo	Raymond (*Ray*)
Ramón (*Moncho*)	Raymond (*Ray*)
Raúl	Ralph
Ricardo	Richard (*Dick, Dicky*)
Roberto	Robert (*Bob, Rob, Robby*)
Rodolfo	Rudolph
Samuel	Samuel (*Sam, Sammy*)
Simón	Simon
Teodoro (*Teo*)	Theodore (*Ted, Teddy*)
Timoteo	Timothy (*Tim*)
Tomás	Thomas (*Tom, Tommy*)
Vicente	Vincent (*Vince*)
Víctor	Victor (*Vic*)

II. Nombres (*m.*) femeninos. — Feminine names.

Adela	Adela, Ethel (*Della*)
Alejandra	Alexandra (*Sandra*)
Alicia	Alice
Ana	Anne, Ann, Anna, Hannah (*Nan, Nancy*)
Bárbara	Barbara
Beatriz	Beatrice, Beatrix (*Trixie*)
Brígida	Bridgit
Carlota	Charlotte
Carolina	Caroline, Carol
Catalina	Catherine, Kathleen (*Cathy, Kate, Kitty, Kay*)
Clara	Clara, Clare
Cristina	Christine (*Chris, Chrissie, Tina*)
Diana	Diana
Dorotea	Dorothy (*Dora, Dolly, Dot*)
Edita	Edith
Elena	Ellen, Helen (*Nell, Nelly*)
Enriqueta	Henrietta, Harriet (*Hattie*)
Ester	Esther, Hesther, Hester (*Hetty*)
Eva	Eve
Florencia	Florence (*Flo, Flossie*)
Francisca (*Paca, Paquita, Frasquita*)	Frances (*Fran, Fanny, France*)
Inés	Agnes (*Aggie*)
Irene	Irene
Isabel	Elizabeth, Elisabeth, Isabella (*Liz, Lizzie, Beth, Betty, Bess, Bessie*)
Juana	Joan, Jane, Jean (*Janie, Jeanie, Jenny*)
Josefa (*Pepa, Pepita*)	Josephine (*Jo*)
Julia (*Juli*)	Julia (*Juliet*)
Juliana	Juliana, Gillian (*Gill, Jill*)
Leonor	Eleanor, Leonore, Leonora (*Nell, Nora*)
Lucía	Lucy
Luisa	Louise
Magdalena	Madeline, Magdalene (*Madge*)
María (*Mari*)	Mary (*Molly, Moll, Polly, May, Mae*)
Margarita (*Margara*)	Margaret, Marjorie (*Maggie, Madge, Maisy, Meg, Mog, Peggy, Marge*)
Matilde	Matilda, Mathilda (*Maud, Tilly, Tilda*)
Rosa	Rosemary (*Rose, Rosy*)
Rosalinda	Rosalind
Sara	Sarah (*Sally*)
Sofía (*Sofi*)	Sophie, Sophia (*Sophy*)
Susana	Susan, Susannah (*Sue, Susie*)
Teresa (*Tere*)	Teresa, Theresa (*Terry, Tess*)
Victoria	Victoria (*Vickie*)
Virginia	Virginia (*Ginnie*)

III. Nombres españoles sin equivalentes en inglés.

Álvaro *m.*, Amparo *f.*, Ángel *m.*, Angustias *f.*, Asunción (*Asun*) *f.*, Aurelia *f.*, Carmen (*Menchu*) *f.*, Concepción (*Concha, Conchita*) *f.*, Consuelo *f.*, Dolores (*Lola, Lolita*) *f.*, Domingo *m.*, Encarnación (*Encarna*) *f.*, Gonzalo *m.*, Guadalupe *f.*, Jesús (*Chucho*) *m.*, Lurdes *f.*, Mercedes (*Merche*) *f.*, Nieves *f.*, Paloma *f.*, Pilar *f.*, Purificación (*Pura*) *f.*, Rosario (*Charo*) *f.*, Salvador *m.* Sergio *m.*, Sol *f.*, Soledad *f.*, Tecla *f.*, Trinidad (*Trini*) *f.*

IV. English Christian names without equivalents in Spanish.

Masculine — Brian, Cedric, Colin, Clive, Clyde, Derrick, Desmond, Donald, Douglas, Gordon, Howard, Humphrey, Kelvin, Malcolm, Niel, Noel, Ronald, Roy, Stewart *o* Stuart, Terrence

Feminine — Edna, Gladys, Hilda, June, Linda.

norteño, ña adj. Northern.
— M. y f. Northerner.

nórtico, ca adj. Nordic. || Northern.

Noruega n. pr. f. GEOGR. Norway.

noruego, ga adj./s. Norwegian.

norueste adj./s.m. V. NOROESTE.

norvietnamita m. y f. North Vietnamese.

nos pron. pers. de 1.ª pers. del pl. m. y f. Us (complemento directo): *nos están llamando*, they are calling us. || Us, to us (complemento indirecto): *nos dio caramelos*, he gave us sweets, he gave sweets to us. || Us (forma reflexiva en imperativo): *sentémonos*, let us sit down. || Ourselves (forma reflexiva en los demás tiempos): *nos estamos lavando*, we are washing ourselves. || [To] one another, [to] each other (forma pronominal): *nos queremos mucho*, we love each other dearly; *nos escribimos a menudo durante el verano*, we wrote to one another often during the summer. || We (forma mayestática): *Nos, Carlos de Inglaterra*, We, Charles of England. || — *Nos acostamos a las diez*, we go to bed at ten. || *Nos lo compró*, he bought it from us (de nosotros), he bought it for us (para nosotros). || *Ruega por nos*, pray for us. || *Venga a nos en tu reino*, Thy kingdom come (en el padrenuestro).

nosotros, tras pron. pers. de 1.ª pers. del pl. m. y f. We (sujeto): *nosotros somos ingleses*, we are English. || Us (complemento): *vino con nosotros*, he came with us. || — *Entre nosotros*, between ourselves, between the two of us, between you and me (confidencialmente). || *Para nosotros*, for us: *lo hizo para nosotros*, he did it for us; ourselves (reflexivo): *no compramos nada para nosotros*, we didn't buy anything for ourselves. || *Somos nosotros* or *nosotras*, it is we, it is us. || *Somos nosotros* or *nosotras quienes* or *los que* or *las que*, we are the ones who, it is we who.

— OBSERV. Since in Spanish the verb can be used without a subject pronoun (*iremos*, we shall go), the use of *nosotros* as the subject implies a certain emphasis.

nostalgia f. Nostalgia.

nostálgico, ca adj. Nostalgic.

nóstico, ca adj./s. Gnostic.

nota f. Note (anotación). || Footnote (al pie de una página). || Marginal note (al margen). || Note (apunte): *tomar notas*, to take notes. || Mark (en un ejercicio): *dar, sacar una mala nota*, to give, to get a bad mark.

|| Grade (en el bachillerato). || Class (en licenciatura). || Remark (observación). || Note (comunicación escrita): *nota diplomática*, diplomatic note. || Notice (reseña). || MÚS. Note: *nota falsa*, wrong note. || FIG. Note, touch: *dar una nota de elegancia*, to add a touch of elegance. || — FIG. y FAM. *Dar la nota*, to make o.s. conspicuous (singularizarse), to lead the way, to set the fashion (dar el tono). || FIG. *De mala nota*, of ill repute, with a bad reputation. | *De nota*, famous (célebre). || FIG. y FAM. *Forzar la nota*, to go too far, to exaggerate. || *Notas de sociedad*, society column. || *Tomar nota de un pedido*, to note down an order, to make a note of an order.
nota bene f. Note, nota bene, N.B.
notabilidad f. Noteworthiness, remarkableness. || Notable (persona).
notabilísimo, ma adj. Very notable.
notable adj. Notable, remarkable, noteworthy: *una obra notable*, a notable piece of work; *un abogado notable*, a remarkable lawyer. || Notable, appreciable (apreciable). || Considerable.
— M. Notable, worthy: *asamblea de notables*, assembly of notables. || Merit (en exámenes): *sacó un notable*, he passed with merit.
notación f. MAT. y MÚS. Notation (signos). || Annotation (nota).
notar v. tr. To notice, to note: *notar algo a primera vista*, to notice sth. at first sight; *notar la diferencia*, to note the difference; *notar una falta*, to note a mistake. || To indicate, to point out (señalar). || To mark (un escrito): *notar los errores al margen*, to mark the mistakes in the margin. || To jot down, to take down (apuntar). || To find: *te noto muy cambiado*, I find you have changed a lot. || To feel: *noto que hay algo que no funciona bien*, I feel that there is sth. wrong. || To criticize (criticar). || — *Hacer notar*, to point out. || *Hacerse notar*, to stand out, to draw attention to o.s.
— V. pr. To feel: *me noto un poco extraño*, I feel rather strange. || To show: *no se nota la mancha*, the stain does not show. || To be apparent, to be able to be seen: *se nota cierto progreso económico*, a certain amount of economic progress can be seen. || *No se nota*, it does not show, you cannot tell, you would never know.
notaría f. Notarial profession. || Notary's office (oficina).
notariado, da adj. Authenticated by a notary [U.S., notarized].
— M. Body of notaries (corporación).
notarial adj. Notarial: *actas notariales*, notarial deeds.
notario m. Commissioner for oaths (en Inglaterra): *ante notario*, before a commissioner for oaths. || Notary, solicitor (en los demás países excepto en los Estados Unidos). || Notary public (en Estados Unidos). || — *Notario de diligencias*, process server. || *Pasante de notario*, notary's clerk.
noticia f. News, piece of news: *una mala noticia*, bad news. || News item (en un periódico). || — Pl. News, *sing.*: *traer noticias*, to bring news. || News, *sing.* (en la radio y la televisión). || Information, *sing.*: *según nuestras noticias*, according to our information. || — *Circula la noticia de que*, it is rumoured that, rumour has it that. || *Dar una noticia a alguien*, to give s.o. some news *o* a piece of news (cualquier noticia), to break the news to s.o. (noticia importante). || || *Enviar a alguien a buscar noticias*, to send s.o. for news. || *Es la primera noticia que tengo*, it is the first I have heard of it. || *Estar atrasado de noticias*, to be out of date. || FIG. *¡Esto es noticia!*, there's a turnup for the books. || *Las malas noticias llegan las primeras*, no news is good news. || FIG. *No tener noticia de*, to have had no news from *o* of, not to have heard anything of, not to know anything about. | *No tengo noticia*, I've heard nothing about it, I have no idea. || FAM. *Noticia bomba* big news, sensational news. || *Noticia necrológica*, obituary [notice]. || *Noticia remota*, vague memory. || *Tener noticias de uno*, to hear from s.o.: *no tengo noticias suyas desde hace cinco años*, I haven't heard from his for five years. || *Últimas noticias*, latest news.
noticiar v. tr. To inform of, to notify.
noticiario m. Newscast, news bulletin (radio, televisión). || Newsreel (cine).
noticiero, ra adj. News (periodico).
— M. y f. Journalist, reporter (reportero). || — M. Newspaper (periódico).
notición m. FAM. Sensational news, big news.
noticioso, sa adj. Well-informed. || Learned (erudito). || *Noticioso de ello, corrió a contárselo a su padre*, on hearing that *o* when he found out about that he ran to tell his father.
notificación f. Notification.
notificar v. tr. To notify, to inform of.
notificativo, va adj. Notifying, informative.
notoriamente adv. Plainly, evidently (evidentemente).
notoriedad f. Fame (fama). || Notoriety (mala reputación).
notorio, ria adj. Famous, well-known (conocido). || Notorious: *un criminal notorio*, a notorious criminal. || Obvious (claro). || — *Notorio a todos*, known by everyone. || *Ser público y notorio*, to be common knowledge.
noumeno m. FIL. Noumenon.
nova f. ASTR. Nova.
novación f. JUR. Novation.
novador, ra adj. Innovating.
— M. y f. Innovator.
novar v. tr. JUR. To novate.
novatada f. Rough joke, ragging [U.S., hazing] (broma pesada). || Beginner's blunder (acción de un novato). || — *Dar una novatada*, to rag [U.S., to haze]. || *Pagar la novatada*, to make a beginner's blunder.
novato, ta adj. New, inexperienced: *novato en los negocios*, new to *o* inexperienced in business.
— M. y f. Novice, beginner. || — M. Recruit (en el ejército). || Fresher [U.S., freshman] (en los colegios).
novecientos, tas adj./s. Nine hundred. || *Mil novecientos*, one thousand nine hundred, nineteen hundred (cifra), nineteen hundred (año).
novedad f. Newness, novelty: *la novedad de un producto*, the newness of a product. || News (noticia). || Change (cambio): *sigue sin novedad*, there is no change. || — Pl. Latest fashions: *sólo vendemos novedades*, we sell only the latest fashions. || — *¿Hay novedad?*, have you heard anything?, anything new?, any news? || *No es ninguna novedad*, that is nothing new. || *Sin novedad*, no change, no news, nothing new (nada nuevo), safely, without incident: *aterrizó sin novedad*, he landed without incident; nothing to report (militar): *sin novedad en el frente*, nothing to report from the front. || FIG. y FAM. *Tener novedad*, to be expecting a happy event (una mujer). || *Tengo novedad*, I have some news.
novedoso, sa adj. *Amer*. Novel.
novel adj. New (nuevo).
— M. Beginner, novice, newcomer.
novela f. Novel: *novela por entregas*, serialized novel. || FIG. Story (mentira). || — *Novela corta*, short story. || *Novela de capa y espada*, cloak-and-dagger novel. || *Novela de tesis*, novel with a message. || *Novela policiaca*, detective story. || *Novela radiofónica*, radio serial. || *Novela rosa*, romance.
novelador, ra m. y f. Novelist.
novelar v. tr. To convert into novel form, to novelize.
— V. intr. To write novels. || FIG. To tell stories *o* fibs (mentir).
novelear v. intr. FIG. y FAM. To exaggerate, to dramatize.
novelería f. Liking for all that is new (afición a novedades). || Liking for novels (afición a las novelas). || Romantic ideas.
novelero, ra adj. Curious about all that is new (amigo de novedades). || Fond of reading novels (aficionado a las novelas). || Highly imaginative (que tiene mucha imaginación).
novelesco, ca adj. Fictional (de la ficción). || Novelistic (referente a las novelas). || Novelesque: *situación novelesca*, novelesque situation. || *Género novelesco*, fiction.
novelista m. y f. Novelist.
novelística f. Fiction (género novelesco). || Art of writing novels. || Novel (conjunto de novelas). || Treatise on the novel (tratado).
novelístico, ca adj. Fictional (de la ficción). || Novelistic (de la novela).
novelizar v. tr. To novelize, to convert into novel form.
novelón m. Saga.
novena f. Novena.
novenario m. First nine days of mourning (tiempo de luto). || Funeral service celebrated on the ninth day after a person's death. || Novena, novenary (novena).
noveno, na adj./s. Ninth. || *La novena parte*, a ninth.
noventa adj./s.m. Ninety. || Ninetieth (nonagésimo).
noventavo, va adj./s Ninetieth (nonagésimo).
noventayochista adj. Of *o* relating to the generation of 1898 (de la generación del 98).

— OBSERV. The *generación del* 98 was a group of Spanish writers which formed after the loss of Cuba, Puerto Rico and the Philippines. 1898 marked the end of Spanish colonial power, and the writers were conscious of the isolation of their country, the failure of its policies and, at the same time, of its social, economic and artistic problems. The forerunners of the movement were Larra, Ganivet, Joaquín Costa and Macías Picavea and the most important figures in the *generación del* 98 proper Unamuno, Azorín, Valle Inclán, Baroja, Antonio Machado, Ramiro de Maeztu and Benavente.

noventón, ona adj. Ninety-year-old, in one's nineties.
— M. y f. Ninety-year-old, person in his [*o* her] nineties.
novia f. Girlfriend (amiga). || Fiancée (prometida). || Bride (en el día de la boda). || — *Pedir a la novia*, to ask for a girl's hand [in marriage]. || *Traje de novia*, wedding dress.
noviazgo m. Courtship, engagement. || *Han tenido un noviazgo de siete años*, they have been going out together for seven years.
noviciado, da m. REL. Noviciate. || FIG. Apprenticeship (aprendizaje).
novicio, cia adj. FIG. New: *novicio en los negocios*, new to business.
— M. y f. REL. Novice. || FIG. Novice, apprentice, beginner (principiante).

noviembre m. November: *el 11 de noviembre de 1918*, the eleventh of November, 1918.
novilunio m. New moon.
novilla f. Heifer.
novillada f. TAUR. Bullfight with young bulls. || Herd of young bulls (rebaño).

— OBSERV. In the *novillada* only young bulls and those unsuitable for the real *corridas* are used.

novillero m. Herdsman who cares for young bulls (vaquero). || TAUR. Apprentice matador [one who has not yet received the *alternativa*]. || FAM. Truant.
novillo m. Young bull, bullock (animal). || FIG. y FAM. *Hacer novillos*, to play truant [U.S., to play hooky] (no ir a clase).
novio m. Boyfriend (amigo). || Fiancé (prometido). || Groom, bridegroom (en el día de la boda). || — *Los novios*, the newlyweds (recién casados), the bride and groom (antes de la ceremonia). || FIG. *Quedarse compuesta y sin novio*, to be left in the lurch *o* high and dry (quedarse sin algo después de tenerlo preparado), to be jilted (los novios). || *Ser novios formales*, to be engaged. || *Viaje de novios*, honeymoon.

— OBSERV. La palabra *fiancé* se aplica solamente cuando existe un compromiso matrimonial.

novísimo, ma adj. Very new, brand new. || Latest (último). || *Novísima Recopilación*, revised code of Spanish law, completed in 1845.
— M. pl. REL. End (*sing.*) of one's life [death, judgment, hell, heaven].
novocaína f. QUÍM. Novocaine.
nubada o **nubarrada** f. Sudden shower, downpour (chaparrón). || FIG. Crowd, abundance (multitud).
nubarrado, da adj. Watered, moiré (tela): *seda nubarrada*, watered silk.
nubarrón m. Large storm cloud.
nube f. Cloud. || Cloud (de polvo, de humo, etc.). || FIG. Swarm, cloud: *nube de langostas*, cloud of locusts. | Swarm, crowd: *una nube de chiquillos*, a swarm of little boys. | Cloud: *no hay una nube en mi felicidad*, there is not a single cloud on my horizon. || Cloud (en una piedra preciosa). || MED. Cloud, film (en la córnea de los ojos). || — FIG. *Caer de las nubes*, to wake up. | *Como caído de las nubes*, out of the blue. | *Descargar la nube*, to rain (llover), to hail (granizar), to explode with anger (desahogar la cólera). | *Estar en las nubes*, to be daydreaming. | *Estar por las nubes*, to be sky-high (precios). | *Nube de verano*, passing cloud (disgusto pasajero). | *Pasar como una nube de verano*, to be short-lived. | *Poner en* or *por las nubes*, to praise to the skies (ensalzar), to make [prices] soar *o* rocket (los precios). | *Ponerse por las nubes*, to praise o.s. to the skies (ensalzarse), to soar, to rocket (los precios).
núbil adj. Nubile.
nubilidad f. Nubility.
nublado, da adj. Cloudy (con algunas nubes): *un cielo nublado*, a cloudy sky. || Overcast (cubierto de nubes).
— M. Cloud. || FIG. Menace, threat (amenaza). | Crowd (multitud). | Anger (enfado).
nublar v. tr. To cloud. || FIG. To cloud, to mar: *la discusión nubló la alegría reinante*, the argument marred everyone's happiness.
— V. pr. To cloud over (el cielo). || FIG. To cloud over: *se me ha nublado la vista*, my eyes have clouded over.
nubloso, sa adj. Cloudy (nublado). || FIG. Unlucky.
nubosidad f. Cloudiness.
nuboso, sa adj. Cloudy.
nuca f. Nape. || *Golpe en la nuca*, rabbit punch.
nucleado, da adj. Nucleate.
nuclear adj. Nuclear: *armas nucleares*, nuclear weapons.
nucleico, ca adj. Nucleic: *ácido nucleico*, nucleic acid.
nucleína f. Nuclein.
núcleo m. Kernel, stone [U.S., pit] (hueso de una fruta). || FÍS. Nucleus: *núcleo atómico*, atomic nucleus. || ASTR., BIOL. y QUÍM. Nucleus. || ELECTR. Core (de una bobina). || FIG. Nucleus, hard core (elemento central). | Central point (punto central). || — *Núcleo de población*, centre of population. || *Núcleo residencial*, residential area, housing estate.
nucléolo m. BIOL. Nucleolus.
nucleón m. FÍS. Nucleon.
nucleónico, ca adj. FÍS. Nucleonic.
— F. FÍS. Nucleonics.
nucleoplasma m. BIOL. Nucleoplasm.
nucleoproteína f. BIOL. Nucleoprotein.
nudillo m. Knuckle (articulación de los dedos). || TECN. Plug. || FIG. *Comerse* or *morderse los nudillos*, to bite one's nails [with impatience, etc.].
nudismo m. Nudism.
nudista adj./s. Nudist.
nudo, da adj. JUR. *Nuda propiedad*, ownership without usufruct, bare ownership. | *Nudo propietario*, owner without usufruct, bare owner.
nudo m. Knot (de cuerda, de corbata, de árbol). || French knot (costura). || Centre: *nudo de comunicación*, communications centre. || Junction: *nudo ferroviario*, railway junction. || FIG. Bond, tie, link (vínculo). | Crux: *el nudo de la cuestión*, the crux of the problem; *el nudo de la novela*, the crux of the novel. || ANAT. Knot. || MAR. Knot (unidad de velocidad): *navegar a quince nudos*, to sail at fifteen knots. || — *Nudo corredizo*, slipknot. || *Nudo de carreteras*, intersection. || *Nudo gordiano*, Gordian knot. || *Nudo plano* or *llano*, reef knot. || *Tener un nudo en la garganta*, to have a lump in one's throat.
nudosidad f. MED. Nodosity.
nudoso, sa adj. Knotted, knotty (madera). || Gnarled (tronco, bastón). || Gnarled (mano).
nuera f. Daughter-in-law.
nuestro, tra adj. poses. m. y f. Our: *nuestro país*, our country; *nuestra casa*, our house; *nuestros amigos*, our friends. || Of ours, our: *un coche nuestro*, a car of ours, one of our cars. || — *En nuestro país, en nuestra casa*, in our country, at home. || *Nuestra Señora*, Our Lady. || *Padre nuestro que estás en los cielos*, our Father which art in Heaven (en el padrenuestro). || *¡Ya es nuestro!*, we have got him *o* it.
— Pron. poses. Ours: *vuestra casa es mayor que la nuestra*, your house is bigger than ours; *esta casa es nuestra*, this house is ours.
— M. *Lo nuestro*, [what is] ours. || *Pondremos de lo nuestro*, we shall do our best, we shall put our best foot forward. || *Vayamos a lo nuestro*, let us get back to the point *o* to the matter in hand. || — Pl. *Los nuestros*, our side, our friends, ours (nuestros amigos): *¿es usted de los nuestros?*, are you one of our friends?, are you one of ours?, are you on our side?; our family, our people (nuestra familia).
nueva f. Piece of news. || — Pl. News, *sing.*, tidings (noticias). || — FIG. *Hacerse de nuevas*, to feign surprise. || *La Buena Nueva*, the Good News.
nuevamente adv. Newly, recently (recientemente). || Again, anew (de nuevo).
Nueva Escocia n. pr. f. GEOGR. Nova Scotia.
Nueva York n. pr. GEOGR. New York.
nueve adj./s.m. Nine: *en este cuarto hay nueve personas*, there are nine people in this room. || Ninth: *el nueve de agosto*, the ninth of August. || — *A las nueve*, at nine o'clock. || *Son las nueve de la noche*, it is nine p. m.
nuevo, va adj. New: *casa nueva*, new house; *luna nueva*, new moon; *alumno nuevo*, new pupil. || — *Año Nuevo*, New Year. || *De nuevo*, again (otra vez), new: *estar vestido de nuevo*, to be wearing new clothes; *¿qué hay de nuevo?*, what's new? || *El coche está nuevo*, the car is as good as new. || *¿Es nueva esta técnica para ti?*, are you new to this technique? || *No hay nada nuevo bajo el Sol*, there's nothing new under the sun. || *Nueva Caledonia, Guinea, Inglaterra, Orleáns, Zelanda*, New Caledonia, Guinea, England, Orleans, Zealand. || *Ser nuevo en el oficio*, to be new to the job.
— M. *Lo nuevo*, new things, *pl.*: *lo nuevo gusta siempre*, people always like new things; the new: *tirar lo viejo y quedarse con lo nuevo*, to throw out the old and keep the new.
nuez f. Walnut (del nogal). || Nut (en general): *cascar nueces*, to crack nuts; *nuez de corojo*, corozo nut. || ANAT. Adam's apple (en la garganta). || MÚS. Nut (de violín). || Sear (de ballesta, de fusil). || — FAM. *Apretar a uno la nuez*, to wring s.o.'s neck. | *Mucho ruido y pocas nueces*, much ado about nothing. || *Nuez moscada*, nutmeg. || *Nuez vómica*, nux vomica.
nulamente adv. In vain, with no effect, to no avail.
nulidad f. JUR. Nullity. || Incompetence, incapacity. || FAM. *Ser una nulidad*, to be a nonentity, to be useless (ser un incapaz).
nulípara adj. MED. Nulliparous.
— F. MED. Nullipara.
nulo, la adj. Useless: *hombre nulo*, useless man. || Void, null and void (sin valor). || Zero, nonexistent (no existente). || — Pl. Misère, *sing.* (en bridge). || — DEP. *Combate nulo*, draw (boxeo, lucha). || JUR. *Nulo y sin valor*, null and void.
numantino, na adj./s. Numantian.
numen m. Divinity, numen (dios). || Inspiration, muse: *numen poético*, poetic inspiration.
numerable adj. Numerable.
numeración f. Numeration. || Numbering (acción de poner números). || Numbers, *pl.*: *han cambiado la numeración de la calle*, the house numbers have been changed. || Numerals, *pl.* (sistema): *numeración arábiga, romana*, Arabic, Roman numerals. || IMPR. Pagination.
numerador m. MAT. Numerator. || TECN. Numbering machine (aparato).
numeral adj. Numeral.
numerar v. tr. To count (contar). || To number (poner un número). || IMPR. To paginate.
numerario, ria adj. Numerary.
— N. Hard cash, cash, money (dinero).
numérico, ca adj. Numerical.
número m. Number (cantidad): *un número crecido de alumnos*, an increased number of pupils; *número de votos*, number of votes. || Figure, numeral (cifra): *número romano*, Roman numeral. || Number (en una serie): *número premiado*, winning number. || Number, copy, issue (ejemplar de una publicación): *número atrasado*, back number. || TEATR. Number, act: *hacer un número cómico*, to do a comedy act. || FIG. Piece of outrageous behaviour, thing done to attract attention. || Size (medida de los zapatos, cuellos, guantes, etc.). || GRAM. Number: *número singular, plural*, singular, plural number. || — *Académico de número*, member of the Academy. || *Áureo número*,

golden number. || *De número*, regular, titular. || *El mayor número de*, the majority of, the greatest number of. || *En gran número*, in large numbers. || *En números redondos*, in round numbers *o* figures. || *Hacer número*, to make up the number. || FAM. *Hacer números*, to reckon up. || FIG. *Hacer un número*, to do sth. outrageous [to attract attention]. || *Ley de los grandes números*, law of large numbers. || *Libro de los Números*, Book of Numbers (del Pentateuco). || FÍS. *Número atómico*, atomic number. || *Número cardinal*, *ordinal*, cardinal, ordinal number. || *Número de matrícula*, registration number (de un coche). || *Número de referencia*, reference number. || GRAM. *Número dual*, dual number. || *Número entero*, whole number. || *Número extraordinario*, special edition (de una publicación). || *Número impar*, odd number. || *Número mixto*, fraction. || *Número par*, even number. || *Número primo*, prime number. || *Número quebrado* or *fraccionario*, fraction. || *Número redondo*, round number *o* figure. || *Número suelto*, number, edition (periódico). || FIG. *Número uno*, the best, [the] number one (el mejor). | *Sin número*, countless. || FAM. *¡Vaya número!*, what a carry on!

numerosamente adv. Numerously.

numerosidad f. Numerosity.

numeroso, sa adj. Numerous, many: *hay numerosos pueblos por el estilo*, there are numerous villages like that. || *Familia numerosa*, large family.

numismático, ca adj. Numismatic.
— M. y f. Numismatist (perito en numismática). || — F. Numismatics.

numulita f. Nummulite (fósil).

nunca adv. Never: *no volveré nunca* or *nunca volveré*, I shall never come back. || Ever: *¿has conocido nunca a tal hombre?*, have you ever known such a man? || — *Casi nunca*, hardly ever. || *¡Hasta nunca!*, farewell for ever! || *Más que nunca*, more than ever. || *Nunca jamás*, never ever, never [emphatic form of *nunca*]. || *Nunca más*, never again, no more, nevermore.

nunciatura f. Nunciature.

nuncio m. Nuncio: *nuncio apostólico*, papal nuncio. || FIG. Omen, portent, forerunner (presagio): *este viento es nuncio de lluvia*, this wind is an omen of rain. || Bearer: *ha sido el nuncio de la buena nueva*, he was the bearer of the good tidings. || — FAM. *¡Cuéntaselo al nuncio!*, tell that to the marines! | *¡Que te lo diga el nuncio!*, don't ask me! || *Que te lo haga el nuncio*, don't ask me to do it.

nupcial adj. Nuptial, wedding. || — *Banquete nupcial*, wedding breakfast. || *Galas nupciales*, wedding dress, *sing.* || *Marcha nupcial*, wedding march.

nupcialidad f. Marriage rate.

nupcias f. pl. Nuptials, wedding, *sing.* || — *Contraer segundas nupcias*, to remarry, to marry for the second time. || *Hijos de segundas nupcias*, children of a second marriage.

nurse f. Nurse (niñera).

nutación f. ASTR. y BOT. Nutation.

nutria o **nutra** f. ZOOL. Otter (mamífero).

nutricio, cia adj. Nutritious. || Foster (padre).

nutrición f. Nutrition.

nutrido, da adj. Nourished, fed (alimentado). || FIG. Large, abundant: *nutrida asistencia*, large attendance. | Loud: *aplausos nutridos*, loud applause. || — MIL. *Fuego nutrido*, heavy fire (graneado). || *Mal nutrido*, undernourished. || FIG. *Nutrido de*, full of.

nutrimento o **nutrimiento** m. Nourishment, nutriment.

nutrir v. tr. To nourish, to feed. || FIG. To feed: *los recuerdos nutren su odio*, his memories feed his hatred.
— V. pr. To feed, to live: *nutrirse de*, to live on.

nutritivo, va adj. Nutritious. || *El valor nutritivo de un alimento*, a food's nutritional value, the food value of a product.

ny f. Nu (letra griega).

nylon m. Nylon (tejido): *camisa de nylon*, nylon shirt.

ñ f. Ñ (esta letra no existe en el alfabeto inglés).
— OBSERV. The sound is that of the *ni* in onion.

ña f. FAM. *Amer.* V. DOÑA.

ñacanina f. *Amer.* Large poisonous snake.

ñaco m. *Amer.* Porridge (gachas).

ñacurutú m. *Amer.* Owl (lechuza).

ñame m. BOT. Yam (planta). || *Amer.* FIG. y FAM. Hoof, foot (pie).

ñandú m. ZOOL. Rhea, nandu.

ñandubay m. *Amer.* Nandubay.

ñandutí m. *Amer.* Nanduti [lace made mainly in Paraguay].

ñango, ga adj. *Amer.* Ungraceful, ungainly. | Weak (débil).

ñaña f. *Amer.* Elder sister. | Nursemaid (niñera).

ñapa f. *Amer.* V. LLAPA.

ñapango, ga adj. Mulatto.
— M. y f. Mulatto, mestizo.

ñapindá m. BOT. Mimosa.

ñato, ta adj. *Amer.* Snub-nosed (chato). || *Amer.* FIG. Ugly (feo).

ñeque adj. *Amer.* Strong, vigorous.
— M. Strength, vigour. || *Hombre de ñeque*, brave man.

ñiquiñaque m. FAM. Piece of junk (cosa). | Good-for-nothing (persona).

ñisñil m. *Amer.* BOT. Cattail (anea).

ño m. *Amer.* FAM. Mister (señor).

ñoclo m. CULIN. Macaroon.

ñoñería o **ñoñez** f. Insipidity (sosería). || Prudery (mojigatería). || Fussiness, whining (melindrería).

ñoño, ña adj. Insipid (soso). || Prudish, straight-laced (mojigato). || Finnicky, fussy, whining (melindroso).
— M. y f. Whiner, drip (fam.), insipid character.

ñoqui m. CULIN. Gnocchi.

ñorbo m. *Amer.* BOT. Passionflower.

ñu m. ZOOL. Gnu (antílope).

ñudo m. (Ant.). Knot (nudo).

O

o f. O (letra): *una o mayúscula, minúscula*, a capital, small o. || *No saber hacer la o con un canuto*, not to know a thing.
— OBSERV. The Spanish *o* is pronounced like the *o* in the English word *hot*.

o conj. Or. || — *O... o*, either ... or: *iremos o al teatro o al cine*, we shall go either to the theatre or to the cinema. || *O sea*, in other words, that is to say, that is. || *O sea que*, in other words, so, that is to say (en conclusión).

— Observ. When used between two numbers, *o* takes a written accent in order to avoid any possible confusion with zero: *10 ó 12*, ten or twelve. *U* is used in place of *o* when the word following begins with *o* or *ho*: *siete u ocho*, seven or eight; *uno u otro*, one or the other; *ayer u hoy*, yesterday or today.

oasis m. inv. Oasis.
obcecación f. Blindness.
obcecadamente adv. Blindly.
obcecado, da adj. Blinded: *obcecado por la pasión*, blinded by passion. || Obstinate.
obcecar v. tr. To blind (ofuscar).
— V. pr. To be blinded.
obedecedor, ra adj. Obedient.
obedecer* v. tr. To obey: *obedecer las órdenes*, to obey [the] orders; *obedecer al superior*, to obey one's superior; *obedecer las leyes*, to obey the law.
— V. intr. To do as one is told, to obey: *calla y obedece*, be quiet and do as you are told. || To respond: *la enfermedad obedeció a los medicamentos*, the illness responded to the medicine. || — *Esta reunión obedece a varias razones*, this meeting has been called for a number of reasons. || *Hacerse obedecer*, to obtain *o* to command obedience. || *Mi visita obedece a una razón*, there is a reason for my visit. || *Obedecer al hecho de que*, to be due to.
obedecimiento m. o **obediencia** f. Obedience.
obediente adj. Obedient.
obelisco m. Obelisk. || Impr. Dagger, obelisk.
obencadura f. Mar. Shrouds, *pl.*, set of shrouds.
obenque m. Mar. Shroud.
obertura f. Mús. Overture.
obesidad f. Obesity.
obeso, sa adj. Obese.
— M. y f. Obese person.
óbice m. Obstacle, impediment. || *Eso no fue óbice para que siguiese mi camino*, that did not prevent me from continuing on my way.
obispado m. Bishopric.
obispal adj. Episcopal.
obispalía f. Bishopric (obispado). || Episcopal palace.
obispo m. Bishop. || — *Obispo auxiliar*, auxiliary bishop. || Fam. *Trabajar para el obispo*, to work for nothing.
óbito m. Decease, demise.
obituario m. Obituary (en un periódico).
objeción f. Objection: *levantar* or *poner una objeción*, to raise an objection.
objetante adj. Objecting.
— M. Objector.
objetar v. tr. e intr. To object: *le objeté que no lo podríamos hacer*, I objected that we should not be able to do it. || To object to (oponerse a). || *No tengo nada que objetar*, I have no objection *o* no objections.
objetivación f. Objectification.
objetivar v. tr. To objectify.
objetividad f. Objectivity. || *Con objetividad*, objectively, with objectivity.
objetivismo m. Objectivism.
objetivo, va adj. Objective.
— M. Objective, aim, goal, end (finalidad): *perseguir un objetivo*, to pursue a goal. || Mil. Target, objective. || Fís. Objective. || Fot. Lens: *objetivo gran angular*, wide-angle lens; *objetivo zoom*, zoom lens.
objeto m. Object: *un objeto voluminoso*, a large *o* cumbersome object. || Object, aim, purpose, end (finalidad). || Theme, subject (tema). || Gram. Object. || — *Carecer de* or *no tener objeto*, to be useless *o* of no purpose. || *Con* or *al objeto de*, in order to, to, with the aim of. || *¿Con qué objeto?*, to what end?, for what purpose? || *Con* or *a tal objeto*, to this end, for this purpose. || *Depósito de objetos perdidos*, lost property office [U.S., lost and found office]. || *Hacerle a alguien objeto de*, to make s.o. the object of. || *Objetos de escritorio*, writing materials. || *Objetos de regalo*, gifts, presents. || *Ser objeto de*, to be the object of. || *Sin objeto*, uselessly, pointlessly (adverbio), useless, pointless (adjetivo). || *Tiene por objeto*, his aim is (persona), its purpose is, its aim is (cosa).
objetor m. Objector: *objetor de conciencia*, conscientious objector.
oblación f. Oblation.
oblato, ta adj./s. Rel. Oblate. || — F. Rel. Oblation.
oblea f. Culin. y Rel. Wafer. || Med. Capsule (sello).
oblicuángulo, la adj. Oblique-angled.
oblicuar v. intr. To slant. || Mil. To incline (*hacia*, to).
— V. tr. To slant, to put into an oblique position.
oblicuidad f. Obliquity.
oblicuo, cua adj. Oblique, slanting. || Mat. Oblique. || *Mirada oblicua*, sidelong glance.
— M. Anat. Oblique (músculo). || — F. Mat. Oblique (línea).
obligación f. Obligation (deber). || Duty, obligation: *conocer sus obligaciones*, to know one's duties; *cumplir con sus obligaciones*, to fulfil one's obligations. || Obligation: *obligaciones matrimoniales*, marital obligations. || Constraint, obligation: *obligaciones sociales*, social constraints. || Com. Bond. || — *Antes es la obligación que la devoción*, business before pleasure. || *Faltar a sus obligaciones*, to fail in one's duty. || *Tener obligación de*, to have to, to be under an obligation to.
obligacionista m. y f. Com. Bondholder.
obligado, da adj. Obliged: *estar* or *verse obligado a trabajar*, to be obliged to work. || Compulsory, obligatory (obligatorio): *la asistencia no es obligada*, attendance is not obligatory. || — *Es obligado decir*, it is necessary to say. || *Estar obligado a alguien*, to be obliged to s.o.
— M. Supplier (abastecedor).
obligar v. tr. To oblige, to compel, to force: *obligar a alguien a entregarse*, to oblige s.o. to give himself up. || To force (empujar): *hay que obligarlo para que entre*, one must force it to get it in.
— V. pr. To put o.s. under an obligation, to bind o.s. (comprometerse).
obligativo, va adj. Obligatory, compulsory.
obligatoriedad f. Obligatoriness, compulsoriness.
obligatorio, ria adj. Obligatory, compulsory.
obliteración f. Med. Obliteration.
obliterador, ra adj. Med. Obliterating.
obliterar v. tr. Med. To obliterate (obstruir).
oblongo, ga adj. Oblong.
obnubilación f. Obnubilation.
oboe m. Mús. Oboe (instrumento). | Oboist (oboísta).
oboísta m. y f. Mús. Oboist (músico).
óbolo m. Mite: *dar su óbolo*, to give one's mite.
obra f. Work (trabajo): *poner manos a la obra*, to get down to work. || Piece of work: *la mesa que ha hecho es una obra preciosa*, the table he has made is a beautiful piece of work. || Work (libro, pieza musical, cuadro, etc.): *una obra de Calderón*, a work by Calderón. || Works, *pl.*, œuvre (producción total): *su obra es muy extensa*, he has a very large œuvre, he has written many works. || Work (buena acción): *obras de beneficencia*, charitable works; *buenas obras*, good works. || Work (poder): *por obra de la Divina Providencia*, by work of Divine Providence. || Act (acto). || Workmanship (ejecución): *en esta pulsera tiene más valor la obra que los materiales*, the value of this bracelet lies more in the workmanship than in the materials used. || Work: *obra de mampostería*, masonry work. || Work: *obras públicas*, public works. || Building site, construction site: *hay una obra frente a mi casa*, there is a building site opposite my house. || Tecn. Hearth [of a kiln furnace]. || — *Al pie de la obra*, delivered on site. || *Atención, obras*, danger, men at work (construcción de un edificio), roadworks ahead (en la carretera). || *Cerrado por obras*, closed for repairs. || *Contratista de obras*, v. CONTRATISTA. || *De obra*, in deed: *maltratar de obra*, to mistreat in deed. || *Estar de obras*, to have workmen in: *los vecinos están de obras*, the neighbours have got workmen in. || *Estar en obras*, to be under construction (en construcción), to be undergoing modifications (renovación), to be under repair (reparación). || *Maestro de obras*, v. MAESTRO. || *¡Manos a la obra!*, let's get down to work! || *Meterse en obras*, to undertake a job. || *Ministerio de Obras Públicas*, v. MINISTERIO. || *Obra de arte*, work of art. || *Obra de caridad*, charitable deed *o* work. || *Obra de construcción*, construction *o* building site. || *Obra de encargo*, commissioned work. || *Obra de hierro*, ironwork. || Fig. *Obra de romanos*, Herculean task. || *Obra de teatro*, [stage] play. || *Obra exterior*, outwork (fortificación). || *Obra maestra*, masterpiece. || Mar. *Obra muerta*, upperworks, *pl.* || *Obra pía*, religious foundation (fundación religiosa), charity, charitable institution (institución de beneficencia). || *Obras completas*, complete works, collected works. || *Obras pías*, charity, *sing.* || *Obras son amores, que no buenas razones*, actions speak louder than words. || Mar. *Obra viva*, quickwork. || *Poner algo en* or *por obra*, to carry out sth. || *Por obra de*, thanks to. || *Por obra y gracia del Espíritu Santo*, by the grace of God.
obrador, ra adj. Working (que obra).
— M. Workshop (taller).
obraje m. Manufacture (fabricación). || Workshop (taller).
obrar v. tr. To do (hacer): *obrar el bien*, to do good. || To work (la madera). || To have an effect on (una medicina). || To build, to construct (construir). || To work, to bring about (milagros, etc.).
— V. intr. To act (actuar): *obrar libremente*, to act freely; *obrar como una persona honrada*, to act honourably. || To behave (comportarse). || To act, to do: *obrar bien, mal*, to act well, badly. || To proceed: *obré según lo previsto*, I proceeded as planned. || To work, to have an effect: *el remedio comienza a obrar*, the remedy is beginning to have an effect. || Fam. To do one's duty (exonerar el vientre). || To be: *el papel obra en sus manos*, the paper is in his hands. || *Obra en mi poder su atenta carta del 19*, I acknowledge receipt of *o* I have received your letter of the 19th.
obrerada f. Fam. Workmen, *pl.*, workers, *pl.*
obrería f. Funds (*pl.*) [for the upkeep of a church].
obrerismo m. Labour movement [U.S., labor movement] (movimiento obrero). || Workmen, *pl.*, workers, *pl.* (conjunto de obreros).
obrero, ra adj. Working: *clase obrera*, working class. || Labour [U.S., labor]: *sindicato obrero*, labour union. || Worker (insecto).
— M. y f. Worker (en una fábrica). || — M. Workman, labourer [U.S., laborer] (fuera de una fábrica). || Labourer [U.S., laborer] (en el campo). || Churchwarden (de iglesia). || — F. Zool. Worker (abeja,

etc.). || — *Obrero especializado*, skilled workman. || *Obrero estacional* or *temporero*, seasonal *o* temporary worker. || *Obrero portuario*, dock worker, docker.
obscenidad f. Obscenity.
obsceno, na adj. Obscene.
obscuramente adv. V. OSCURAMENTE.
obscurantismo m. V. OSCURANTISMO.
obscurantista adj./s. V. OSCURANTISTA.
obscurecer v. tr. V. OSCURECER.
obscurecimiento m. V. OSCURECIMIENTO.
obscuridad f. V. OSCURIDAD.
obscuro, ra adj. V. OSCURO.
obseder v. tr. To obsess.
obsequiado, da adj. Who receives a gift. || In whose honour a reception is held.
— M. y f. Receiver of a gift. || Guest of honour.
obsequiador, ra u **obsequiante** adj. Attentive, obliging (obsequioso). || Who gives (que regala).
— M. y f. Host. || Giver (que regala).
obsequiar v. tr. To give, to offer, to bestow upon: *obsequiar a un amigo con libros*, to give books to *o* to bestow books upon a friend. || To offer: *obsequiar con una copa de vino español*, to offer a glass of Spanish wine to. || To hold [sth.] in s.o.'s honour: *obsequiar a alguien con un banquete*, to hold a banquet in s.o.'s honour. || To lavish attention on (agasajar). || To court (galantear).
obsequio m. Gift, present (regalo). || Honour: *en obsequio del artista*, in honour of the artist. || Attention, kindness (agasajo). || — *Deshacerse en obsequios con uno*, to lavish attention on s.o. || *Obsequio del autor*, complimentary copy.
obsequiosamente adv. Obligingly. || Obsequiously (con exceso).
obsequiosidad f. Obligingness. || Obsequiousness (cumplidos excesivos).
obsequioso, sa adj. Obliging, attentive: *obsequioso con las damas*, obliging with *o* attentive to the ladies. || Obsequious (excesivamente atento).
observable adj. Observable.
observación f. Observation (de un fenómeno). || Observation, remark, comment (indicación). || Note, observation (nota aclaratoria). || Objection. || — *Enfermo en observación*, patient under observation. || *Hacer una observación*, to make a remark.
observador, ra adj. Observant.
— M. y f. Observer.
observancia f. Observance (de las reglas). || *Regular observancia*, strict observance.
observante adj. Observing (que observa). || Observant (que cumple preceptos).
— M. y f. Observer. || — M. Observant (de la orden de San Francisco).
observar v. tr. To observe (mirar). || To observe (cumplir). || To notice, to observe: *he observado que ha cambiado mucho últimamente*, I have noticed that he has changed a lot lately. || To observe, to remark (comentar).
— V. pr. To be noted.
observatorio m. Observatory.
obsesión f. Obsession. || *Tener la obsesión de la muerte*, to be obsessed with death.
obsesionante adj. Obsessive.
obsesionar v. tr. To obsess: *obsesionado por los recuerdos*, obsessed with *o* by memories.
obsesivo, va adj. Obsessive (que obsesiona). || Obsessional: *psicosis obsesiva*, obsessional psychosis.
obseso, sa adj. Obsessed.
— M. y f. Obsessed person.
obsidiana f. MIN. Obsidian.
obsoleto, ta adj. Obsolete (anticuado).
obstaculizar v. tr. To hinder, to hamper: *obstaculizar el movimiento*, to hinder [s.o.'s] movement. || To obstruct, to block: *obstaculizar el paso*, to obstruct the way.
obstáculo m. Obstacle: *superar* or *vencer un obstáculo*, to overcome an obstacle. || — DEP. *Carrera de obstáculos*, obstacle race (atletas), steeplechase (caballos). | *Carrera sin obstáculos*, flat race. || *Poner obstáculos a*, to obstruct, to hinder, to put obstacles in the way of.
obstante (no) adv. Nevertheless, however, notwithstanding (sin embargo). || All the same (de todos modos).
— Prep. In spite of, despite (a pesar de): *no obstante mis consejos hace lo que le da la gana*, in spite of my advice he does as he pleases.
obstar v. intr. To hinder, to obstruct (estorbar). || To prevent (impedir): *eso no obsta para que continúe*, that does not prevent my continuing.
obstetricia f. MED. Obstetrics.
obstétrico, ca adj. MED. Obstetric, obstetrical (relativo a la obstetricia).
obstinación f. Obstinacy, stubbornness (terquedad). || Steadfastness (tenacidad).
obstinado, da adj. Obstinate, stubborn (terco). || Steadfast (tenaz).
obstinarse v. pr. To become obstinate. || To persist: *se obstina en negarlo*, he persists in denying it. || To stick to: *obstinarse en una decisión*, to stick to a decision.
obstrucción f. Obstruction. || *Tácticas de obstrucción*, obstruction tactics.
obstruccionismo m. Obstructionism.
obstruccionista adj./s. Obstructionist.
obstructor adj. MED. Obstruent.
— M. y f. Obstructor.
obstruir* v. tr. To obstruct, to block (cerrar). || FIG. To obstruct, to hinder, to impede, to interfere with (estorbar).
— V. pr. To get blocked [up]: *se obstruyó el lavabo*, the washbasin got blocked up.
obtemperar v. tr. To obey, to comply with: *obtemperar una orden*, to obey an order.
obtención f. Obtaining, obtention.
obtener* v. tr. To obtain, to get: *obtener buenos resultados*, to obtain good results.
obturación f. Obturation, plugging (de un conducto). || Closing, sealing off (de una cavidad). || Filling (de una muela). || FOT. *Velocidad de obturación*, shutter speed.
obturador, ra adj. Obturating, closing.
— M. Plug, stopper (para tapar). || FOT. Shutter: *obturador de cortina*, roller-blind shutter. || ANAT. y TECN. Obturator.
obturante adj. Obturating, closing.
obturar v. tr. To obturate, to plug. || To close (una cavidad). || To fill (una muela).
obtusángulo adj. m. MAT. Obtuse-angled: *triángulo obtusángulo*, obtuse-angled triangle.
obtuso, sa adj. MAT. Obtuse. || FIG. Dull, obtuse. || *Obtuso de entendimiento*, dense, slow, obtuse.
obús m. Shell, obus (proyectil). || Howitzer (cañón corto).
obviar v. tr. To obviate, to remove: *obviar un inconveniente*, to obviate a drawback. || To impede, to hinder (impedir).
obvio, via adj. Clear, evident, obvious (evidente). || *Obvio es decir*, needless to say, obviously.
oc m. *Lengua de oc*, langue d'oc.
oca f. Goose (ánsar). || *Juego de la oca*, snakes and ladders.
ocarina f. MÚS. Ocarina.
ocasión f. Occasion, time: *en aquella ocasión estaba lloviendo*, it was raining that time *o* on that occasion. || Opportunity, chance: *se nos presentó la ocasión de ganar mucho dinero*, we had the opportunity to make a lot of money; *perder una ocasión*, to miss a chance; *aprovechar una ocasión*, to take an opportunity, to make the most of an opportunity; *esta reunión me da la ocasión de saludarle*, this meeting gives me an opportunity to greet you. || Bargain (mercancía de lance). || Reason, cause, occasion, motive: *no dar ocasión de quejarse*, not to give cause for complaint. || (Ant.). Hazardous situation. || — *A la ocasión la pintan calva*, make hay while the sun shines, strike while the iron is hot. || *Asir* or *coger* or *agarrar la ocasión por los cabellos* or *por los pelos*, to seize the opportunity by the scruff of the neck. || *Con ocasión de*, on the occasion of. || *Dar ocasión a*, to give rise to. || *Dejar escapar una ocasión*, to miss one's chance, to let an opportunity go by. || *De ocasión*, secondhand (de segunda mano), bargain (de precio reducido), reduced [in price] (de precio rebajado). || *En cierta ocasión*, on a certain occasion. || *En la primera ocasión*, at the first opportunity. || *En ocasiones*, at times, sometimes. || *En varias ocasiones*, on several occasions. || *La ocasión hace al ladrón*, opportunity makes the thief.
ocasionador, ra adj. Causing, responsible, occasioning (que ocasiona).
— M. Causer, person responsible.
ocasional adj. Occasional (que ocurre de vez en cuando). || Chance, accidental (fortuito): *un encuentro ocasional*, a chance meeting.
ocasionalismo m. Occasionalism.
ocasionalista adj. Occasionalistic.
— M. y f. Occasionalist.
ocasionalmente adv. By chance, accidentally (por casualidad). || Occasionally (de vez en cuando).
ocasionar v. tr. To occasion, to cause (causar). || (P.us.) To jeopardize, to endanger (poner en peligro).
ocaso m. Sunset (momento del día). || Setting (de un astro): *el ocaso del Sol*, the setting of the sun. || Occident, west (occidente). || FIG. Decline (decadencia): *el ocaso de un imperio*, the decline of an empire. | End: *su ocaso se acerca*, his end is nigh. || FIG. *En el ocaso de la vida*, in the twilight of life, in one's later years.
occidental adj. Western: *el mundo occidental*, the western world. || West: *Berlín Occidental*, West Berlin.
— M. y f. Westerner, person from the West. || — Pl. People of the western world, the western world, *sing.*
occidentalismo m. Westernism, Occidentalism.
occidentalista m. y f. Occidentalist.
occidentalización f. Westernization, Occidentalization.
occidentalizar v. tr. To westernize, to Occidentalize.
occidente m. West, occident: *al occidente*, towards the west. || *El Occidente*, the West.
occipital adj./s.m. ANAT. Occipital (hueso).
occipucio m. ANAT. Occiput.
occisión f. Violent death, murder.
occiso, sa adj. Murdered.
— M. y f. Deceased, murder victim, victim (persona matada violentamente).

Oceanía n. pr. f. GEOGR. Oceania.
oceánico, ca adj. Oceanic (del océano). || Oceanian Oceanic (de Oceanía).
Oceánida f. Oceanid (ninfa).
océano m. Ocean: *el Océano Índico*, the Indian Ocean. || FIG. Ocean, sea: *un océano de amargura*, a sea of bitterness.
oceanografía f. Oceanography.
oceanográfico, ca adj. Oceanographic, oceanographical.
oceanógrafo, fa m. y f. Oceanographer.
ocelo m. Ocellus (mancha, ojo).
ocelote m. Ocelot (mamífero).
ocio m. Idleness (inactividad). || Leisure time, leisure, spare time (tiempo libre): *la ocupación del ocio*, the occupation of leisure time. || Pastime (diversión). || *Ratos de ocio*, leisure, spare *o* leisure time.
ociosamente adv. Idly.
ociosear v. intr. *Amer.* To idle (holgazanear).
ociosidad f. Idleness. || *La ociosidad es madre de todos los vicios*, idleness is the root of all evil.
ocioso, sa adj. Idle: *vida ociosa*, idle life; *palabras ociosas*, idle words. || Lazy (holgazán). || Pointless, useless (inútil).
— M. y f. Idler.
ocluir v. tr. To occlude.
— V. pr. To become occluded.
oclusión f. Occlusion. || Stop (en fonética).
oclusivo, va adj./s. f. Occlusive: *consonante oclusiva*, occlusive consonant.
ocre m. Ochre [U.S., ocher]: *ocre amarillo*, yellow ochre; *ocre rojo*, red ochre.
— Adj. inv. Ochreous.
octaédrico, ca adj. MAT. Octahedral.
octaedro m. MAT. Octahedron.
octagonal adj. MAT. Octagonal.
octágono, na adj. MAT. Octagonal.
— M. Octagon.
octano m. QUÍM. Octane. || *Índice de octano*, octane number.
octante m. MAR. y MAT. Octant.
octava f. REL., POÉT. y MÚS. Octave.
octaviano, na adj. HIST. Octavian: *paz octaviana*, Octavian peace.
octavilla f. Octavo (octava parte de un pliego de papel). || Pamphlet, leaflet (hoja de propaganda). || Octet (estrofa).
Octavio n. pr. m. Octavian.
octavo, va adj./s. Eighth. || — *En octavo*, octavo (libro). || *Enrique VIII (octavo)*, Henry VIII [the eighth]. || *La octava parte*, an eighth.
octeto m. MÚS. Octet.
octingentésimo, ma adj./s. Eight hundredth. || *Octingentésimo aniversario*, octigentenary.
octogenario, ria adj./s. Octogenarian, eighty-year-old.
octogésimo, ma adj./s. Eightieth. || *Octogésimo primero, segundo*, eighty-first, eighty-second.
octogonal adj. MAT. Octagonal.
octógono, na adj. MAT. Octagonal.
— M. Octagon.
octópodo, da adj./s.m. ZOOL. Octopod, octopodan.
octosilábico, ca adj. Octosyllabic.
octosílabo, ba adj. Octosyllabic.
— M. Octosyllable.
octubre m. October: *Madrid, 6* or *a 6 de octubre de 1972*, Madrid, 6th October, 1972.
ocular adj. Ocular. || *Testigo ocular*, eyewitness.
— M. Eyepiece, ocular.
oculista adj. *Médico oculista*, oculist.
— M. y f. Oculist.
ocultación f. Dissimulation. || ASTR. Occultation. || Concealment (encubrimiento). || JUR. *Ocultación de parto*, concealment of a child.
ocultador, ra adj. Concealing.
— M. y f. Concealer. || — M. FOT. Mask.
ocultamente adv. Occultly (misteriosamente). || Stealthily (a hurtadillas). || Secretly (secretamente).
ocultar v. tr. To hide, to conceal: *ocultar un objeto*, to hide an object; *ocultar su juego*, to conceal one's game. || ASTR. To occult. || To conceal (encubrir). || *Ocultar a* or *de la vista de alguien*, to hide *o* to conceal from s.o., to put out of s.o.'s sight.
— V. pr. To hide: *ocultarse de sus padres*, to hide from one's parents. || ASTR. To occult.
ocultis (de) loc. FAM. On the sly (a hurtadillas).
ocultismo m. Occultism.
ocultista adj./s. Occultist.
oculto, ta adj. Secret (secreto): *influencia oculta*, secret influence. || Hidden, concealed (escondido). || Ulterior: *motivo oculto*, ulterior motive. || — *Ciencias ocultas*, occult sciences *o* arts. || *De oculto*, stealthily.
ocume m. Okoume, okume (árbol).
ocupación f. Occupation, profession (empleo). || Occupation (de un lugar). || MIL. Occupation: *la ocupación de una ciudad*, the occupation of a city. || *Tener muchas ocupaciones*, to have many activities.
ocupado, da adj. Occupied (casa, ciudad, etc.). || Taken: *¿está ocupado el asiento?*, is this seat taken? || Busy (que tiene mucho que hacer). || Engaged (el retrete).
ocupante m. y f. Occupant, occupier. || Occupant (de un vehículo). || MIL. Occupier.
ocupar v. tr. To take up, to occupy: *la lectura ocupa mis ratos de ocio*, reading takes up my spare time. || To keep [s.o.] occupied *o* busy, to give [s.o.] sth. to do (dar que hacer). || To occupy (un país, una fábrica, un piso). || To employ (emplear obreros). || To take over (apoderarse de). || To occupy, to hold (un puesto). || — *El armario ocupa demasiado espacio*, the wardrobe takes up too much space. || *Ocupar la presidencia*, to occupy the chair (en una reunión).
— V. pr. To look after (cuidar): *ocuparse de un niño*, to look after a child. || To do (hacer): *¿de qué se ocupa este señor?*, what does this man do? || To be in charge of: *se ocupa de la seguridad*, he is in charge of security. || To deal with, to do sth. about, to see to: *tenemos que ocuparnos de esta cuestión*, we have to deal with this question. || To engage: *ocuparse en obras útiles*, to engage in useful works. || To see to, to attend to (atender): *ocuparse de un cliente, de un enfermo*, to see to a client, to a patient. || To pay attention to (hacer caso). || *¡Ocúpate de tus cosas!*, mind your own business!
ocurrencia f. Occurrence, event (acontecimiento). || FIG. Witticism (chiste). || Idea: *¡tienes cada ocurrencia!*, what funny ideas you get!; *¡vaya ocurrencia!*, what a funny idea! || *Tener ocurrencia*, to be witty.
ocurrente adj. FIG. Witty (chistoso, gracioso). | Imaginative, full of ideas.
ocurrir v. intr. To occur, to happen (acontecer): *eso ocurre todos los años*, that occurs every year. || — *Ocurra lo que ocurra*, happen what may. || *¿Qué ocurre?*, what's the matter?, what's going on? || *¿Qué ocurrió?*, what happened? || *¿Qué te ocurre?*, what's the matter [with you]?
— V. pr. To occur, to come: *la idea se me ocurrió ayer*, the idea occurred to me yesterday; *es lo único que se me ocurre*, it is the only thing that occurs to me. || To take it into one's head to: *de repente se le ocurrió irse*, all of a sudden he took it into his head to go. || — *A nadie se le ocurre hacer esto*, nobody would think of doing this. || *Que no se te ocurra repetirlo*, don't let it happen again. || *¡Se le ocurre cada cosa!*, he gets some odd ideas. || *Se me ocurre que*, it occurs to me that.
ochavo m. Brass coin, farthing (moneda). || — *No tener ni un ochavo*, not to have a brass farthing [U.S., not to have a red cent]. || *No valer un ochavo*, not to be worth a brass farthing *o* a damn.
ochavón, ona adj./s. Octoroon.
ochenta adj./s. Eighty. || Eightieth (octogésimo).
ochentavo, va adj./s. Eightieth.
ochentón, ona adj. FAM. Eighty-year-old, in one's eighties.
— M. y f. FAM. Eighty-year-old, person in his [*o* her] eighties.
ocho adj. Eight: *ocho personas*, eight people. || Eighth (octavo): *en el año ocho de su reinado*, in the eighth year of his reign. || Eighthly (en el octavo lugar). || — *A las ocho*, at eight o'clock, at eight. || *Aplazar para dentro de ocho días*, to put off for a week. || *Unos ocho niños*, some eight children, eight or so children, about eight children. || *Volver a los ochos días*, to return in a week *o* in a week's time *o* after a week.
— M. Eight. || FIG. *Más chulo que un ocho*, as proud as a peacock.
ochocientos, tas adj./s.m. Eight hundred: *cuatro mil ochocientos*, four thousand eight hundred. || *Mil ochocientos*, eighteen hundred.
oda f. Ode.
odalisca f. Odalisque.
odeón m. Odeon, odeum.
odiar v. tr. To hate, to detest, to loathe: *te odio*, I hate you; *odio las multitudes*, I hate crowds.
odio m. Hatred, hate. || — *Mirada de odio*, look of hate *o* of hatred, hateful look. || *Por odio a*, out of hatred for. || *Tener odio a uno*, to hate s.o., to feel hatred towards s.o. || *Tomar* or *cobrar odio a*, to take an extreme dislike to, to begin to hate.
odiosamente adv. Hatefully, odiously (con odio). || Disgracefully, shamefully: *estás tratando odiosamente a tu amigo*, you are treating your friend shamefully.
odiosidad f. Hatefulness, odiousness. || Disgracefulness, shamefulness (carácter vergonzoso).
odioso, sa adj. Hateful, odious, detestable. || *Hacerse odioso*, to become objectionable.
Odisea n. pr. f. Odyssey.
odontología f. MED. Dentistry, odontology. || *Escuela de odontología*, school of dentistry.
odontólogo m. Dentist, odontologist, dental surgeon.
odorante adj. Odorous.
odorífero, ra o **odorífico, ca** adj. Odoriferous, odorous.
odre m. Wineskin (pellejo). || FIG. y FAM. Drunkard, boozer, old soak (borracho).
oersted o **oerstedio** m. FÍS. Oersted (unidad).
oesnoroeste o **oesnorueste** m. West-northwest.
oessudoeste o **oessudueste** m. West-southwest.
oeste m. West. || — *Del oeste*, western: *las regiones del oeste*, the western regions; west, westerly: *viento del oeste*, west wind. || *Una película del Oeste*, a western.
— Adj. West: *el ala oeste de la casa*, the west wing of the house. || West, westerly: *viento oeste*, west wind. || Westerly: *rumbo oeste*, westerly direction.

Ofelia n. pr. f. Ophelia.
ofendedor, ra adj. Offending.
— M. y f. Offender.
ofender v. tr. To offend, to insult.
— V. pr. To take offence [U.S., to take offense]: *ofenderse por todo*, to take offence at anything. || To fall out (reñir): *ofenderse con un amigo*, to fall out with a friend.
ofendido, da adj. Offended. || *Darse por ofendido*, to take offence [U.S., to take offense].
— M. y f. Offended person.
ofensa f. Offence [U.S., offense].
ofensivo, va adj. Offensive, rude, nasty (persona, palabras). || Offensive, nasty, bad (molesto). || MIL. Offensive.
— F. Offensive: *pasar a la ofensiva*, to take the offensive; *estar a la ofensiva*, to be on the offensive.
ofensor, ra adj. Offending.
— M. y f. Offender.
oferente adj. Offering.
— M. y f. Offerer.
oferta f. Offer (propuesta): *oferta en firme*, firm offer. || Tender (para realizar una obra): *hacer una oferta*, to put in a tender. || Bid, offer (para comprar algo): *me han hecho una oferta de un millón de pesetas por la casa*, I have been made an offer of a million pesetas for the house. || Gift, present (regalo). || COM. Special offer: *oferta del día*, today's special offer. || COM. *Ley de la oferta y la demanda*, law of supply and demand.
ofertorio m. Offertory (parte de la misa). || Humeral (humeral).
off (en) loc. adv. Offstage.
office m. Pantry (antecocina).
offset m. IMPR. Offset.
oficial adj. Official: *documento, hora oficial*, official document, time.
— M. Skilled workman (en una fábrica). || Skilled labourer (en albañilería). || Office worker, employee, clerk (oficinista). || Civil servant (funcionario). || Official (juez eclesiástico). || MIL. Officer: *oficial retirado, de complemento*, retired, reserve officer; *oficial de la escala activa*, officer on the active list. || — *Oficial de peluquería*, barber's assistant. || MAR. *Oficial de guardia*, officer of the watch. || *Oficial de sanidad*, sanitary officer. || MIL. *Oficial subalterno*, subaltern. || *Primer oficial*, head clerk (de un notario), mate (de la marina).
oficiala f. [Female] worker (obrera). || Female office worker *o* employee *o* clerk (de oficina). || Officer (del Ejército de Salvación). || *Oficiala de modistería*, dressmaker's assistant.
oficialidad f. MIL. Officers, *pl.* || Officiality (carácter oficial).
oficialización f. Officialization.
oficializar v. tr. To make official.
oficiante m. REL. Officiant.
oficiar v. tr. To celebrate (la misa). || To communicate officially (una noticia).
— V. intr. To officiate (el sacerdote). || FIG. *Oficiar de*, to act as, to officiate as.
oficina f. Office (despacho). || Agency: *oficina de colocación*, employment agency. || Laboratory (de farmacia). || — *Horas de oficina*, business hours, office hours. || *Oficina de objetos perdidos*, lost property office [U.S., lost and found office]. || *Oficina de turismo*, tourist information office. || *Oficina Internacional del Trabajo*, International Labour Office.
oficinal adj. MED. Officinal: *planta oficinal*, officinal plant.
oficinesco, ca adj. FAM. Bureaucratic.
oficinista m. y f. Office worker, clerk. || — Pl. White-collar workers.
oficio m. Occupation, profession (profesión). || Job (trabajo). || Post, position, office (puesto). || Trade: *aprender un oficio*, to learn a trade; *hacer su oficio*, to go about one's trade. || Role, function (función). || Communiqué, official note (comunicación). || Pantry (antecocina). || REL. Service. | Mass (misa). || — *Artes y oficios*, arts and crafts. || *Buenos oficios*, good offices. || *De oficio*, ex officio: *miembro de oficio*, ex officio member; by trade: *ser albañil de oficio*, to be a mason by trade; officially (oficialmente), automatically (automáticamente). || FIG. *Esos son los gajes del oficio*, those are the occupational hazards *o* the drawbacks. || *No hay oficio malo*, no job is too menial. || *No tener oficio ni beneficio*, to have no job, to be out of a job. || REL. *Oficio de difuntos*, office for the dead. | *Oficio divino* or *mayor*, Divine Service. || *Oficio manual*, handicraft. || *Saber su oficio*, to know one's job. || *Santo Oficio*, Holy Office. || *Ser del oficio*, to be in the trade. || *Tener mucho oficio*, to be very skilful.
oficiosamente adv. Diligently (con diligencia). || Obligingly (con complacencia). || Officiously (con entrometimiento). || Unofficially (no oficialmente). || Semiofficially (semioficialmente). || *Decir algo oficiosamente*, to say sth. off the record.
oficiosidad f. Diligence, industriousness (laboriosidad). || Complaisance, obligingness (solicitud). || Officiousness (importunidad). || Officiousness (no oficialidad).
oficioso, sa adj. Diligent, industrious (diligente). || Obliging (solícito). || Officious, meddlesome (importuno). || Unofficial (no oficial). || Semiofficial (semioficial). || *De fuente oficiosa*, unofficially, from an unofficial source.
ofidio, dia adj./s.m. ZOOL. Ophidian.
ofrecer* v. tr. To offer: *ofrecer a uno un cigarrillo*, to offer s.o. a cigarette; *le ofrecí mi amistad, mi ayuda*, I offered him my friendship, my help. || To give (regalar). || To give, to hold, to throw (un banquete, una fiesta). || To bid, to offer: *ofreció cien libras por el cuadro*, he bid a hundred pounds for the picture. || To offer [up] (un sacrificio). || To present, to offer, to have: *ofrece muchas ventajas*, it offers many advantages; *ofrecer un aspecto lúgubre*, to present a dismal aspect; *ofrecer pocas posibilidades de éxito*, to have little chance of success. || To offer, to give: *ofreció poca resistencia*, it offered little resistance. || *Ofrecer el brazo*, to offer one's arm.
— V. pr. To offer o.s.: *ofrecerse en sacrificio*, to offer o.s. in sacrifice. || To offer one's services as, to offer to be: *ofrecerse de ayudante*, to offer one's services as an assistant, to offer to be an assistant. || To offer: *ofrecerse para hacer un trabajo*, to offer to do a job; *se ofreció para llevarnos a la sierra*, he offered to take us to the mountains. || FIG. To occur to s.o., to come to s.o.'s mind (pensar). || — *Ofrecerse a la vista de alguien*, to appear before s.o.'s eyes. || *¿Qué se le ofrece a usted?*, what can I do for you?, may I help you?
ofrecimiento m. Offer (oferta). || Offering (de un sacrificio).
ofrenda f. Offering.
ofrendar v. tr. To offer, to make an offering of: *ofrendar su alma a Dios*, to offer one's soul to God. || To offer, to give: *ofrendó su vida por la patria*, he gave his life for his country.
oftalmía f. MED. Ophthalmia.
oftálmico, ca adj. MED. Ophthalmic: *arteria oftálmica*, ophtalmic artery.
oftalmología f. MED. Ophthalmology.
oftalmológico, ca adj. MED. Ophthalmologic, ophthalmological.
oftalmólogo m. Ophthalmologist.
oftalmoscopia f. MED. Ophthalmoscopy.
oftalmoscopio m. Ophthalmoscope.
ofuscación f. u **ofuscamiento** m. Blindness (ceguera). || Blinding, dazzling (acción de cegar). || Confusion (mental).
ofuscar v. tr. To blind, to dazzle: *el sol me ofuscó*, the sun blinded me. || FIG. To dazzle (deslumbrar). | To blind: *ofuscado por la pasión*, blinded by passion. | To confuse (confundir).
— V. pr. To be blinded *o* dazzled (por la luz). || FIG. To be dazzled: *no te dejes ofuscar por las apariencias*, don't let yourself be dazzled by appearances. | To be blinded. | To be confused.
ogresa f. Ogress.
ogro m. Ogre.
oh! interj. Oh!
ohm u **ohmio** m. ELECTR. Ohm.
óhmico, ca adj. ELECTR. Ohmic.
oíble adj. Audible.
oída f. Hearing. || *De* or *por oídas*, by hearsay.
oídio m. BOT. Oidium.
oído m. Ear (órgano): *taparse los oídos*, to cover one's ears; *oído interno*, inner ear. || Hearing (sentido): *tener el oído fino*, to have sharp hearing. || Vent (de un arma de fuego). || — FIG. *Abrir los oídos*, to open one's ears. | *Aguzar el oído*, to prick up one's ears. || *Al oído*, in one's ear: *hablar al oído*, to whisper in s.o.'s ear; by ear (oyendo), to *o* on the ear: *agradable al oído*, pleasant on the ear. || *A pregunta necia, oídos sordos*, V. PREGUNTA. || *Caer en oídos sordos*, to fall on deaf ears. || *Dar oídos a*, to lend an ear to (prestar atención), to give credit to (creer). || MÚS. *De oído*, by ear. || *Dolerle a uno los oídos*, to have earache. || *Duro de oído*, hard of hearing. || FIG. *Entrar por un oído y salir por el otro*, to go in one ear and out the other. || *Estar mal del oído*, to be hard of hearing. || FIG. *Hacer oídos de mercader* or *oídos sordos*, to turn a deaf ear. || *Ha llegado a mis oídos*, it has come to my notice *o* attention. || FIG. *Lastimar el oído* or *los oídos*, to hurt *o* to split one's ears. | *Le estarán zumbando los oídos*, his ears must be burning. | *Machacar los oídos*, to say [the same thing] over and over again. | *No dar crédito a sus oídos*, not to [be able to] believe one's ears. || FAM. *¡Oído al parche!*, V. PARCHE. || *Pegarse al oído*, to be catchy (música, etc.). || *Prestar oído* or *oídos a*, to lend an ear to. || FIG. *Regalarle el oído a uno*, to flatter s.o. || *Ser todo oídos*, to be all ears. || *Tener (buen) oído*, to have a good ear.
oidor, ra adj. Hearing.
— M. y f. Hearer. || — M. JUR. Judge (juez).
oidoría f. Judgeship.
oíl m. Oïl: *lengua de oíl*, langue d'oïl.
oír* v. tr. To hear: *oír un ruido*, to hear a noise. || To listen to, to hear [out] (atender, escuchar): *oír un ruego*, to listen to a request. || JUR. To hear (un caso). || — *Al oírle hablar así*, to listen to him, || *Aquí donde usted me oye*, as sure as I'm standing here. || *Como lo oyes*, just as I've said. || *Dejarse oír*, to be heard. || *¡Dios le oiga!*, may your prayers be answered. || *Dios oyó mi ruego*, God answered my prayer. || FAM. *Es como quien oye llover*, V. LLOVER. | *Estar harto de oír*, to be sick of hearing. || *He oído decir que*, I have

heard that. || FIG. *Las paredes oyen*, walls have ears. || *Lo oí caer*, I heard it fall. || FAM. *¡Lo que hay que oír!*, what next! || FIG. *Ni visto ni oído*, in a flash. | *No hay peor sordo que el que no quiere oír*, none so deaf as those who don't want to hear. || *¡Oiga!*, I say!, hey! (para llamar la atención), hello! (teléfono). || *Oír hablar de*, to hear of: *en mi vida he oído hablar de eso*, I have never heard of that in my life. || *Oír al revés*, to misunderstand. || *Oír mal*, to be hard of hearing, to be a little deaf (algo sordo), to misunderstand (entender mal). || *Oír misa*, to hear Mass. || *Oír, ver y callar*, to keep one's lips sealed. || FAM. *¡Oye!*, hey!: *oye, ¿qué te has creído?*, hey! what do you think this is?; now look here! (como reprensión). || FIG. *Usted ha oído campanas (y no sabe dónde)*, V. CAMPANA.
— V. pr. To be heard: *se oyó un grito estremecedor a lo lejos*, a frightful cry was heard in the distance.

ojal m. Buttonhole (para abrochar un botón): *con una flor en el ojal*, with a flower in one's buttonhole. || Eye (agujero). || FAM. Hole, wound (herida): *abrirle a uno un ojal*, to make a hole in s.o.

¡ojalá! interj. I hope so!, let's hope so!, I wish it were true!, if only he [it, they, etc.] would [could, did, etc.]!, would to God! (p.us.): *puede ser verdad ... — ¡Ojalá!*, it may be true ... — I hope so! || I [only] hope *o* wish [that], let's hope [that], would to God that (p.us.): *¡ojalá apruebe!*, I hope he passes!, would to God that he pass! || If only: *¡ojalá viviera aún!*, if only he were still alive!

ojeada f. Glance. || FIG. Brief survey, glance: *echaron una ojeada a la situación actual*, they made a brief survey of *o* they cast a glance at the present situation. || — *Echar* or *dar una ojeada a*, to glance at, to run one's eye over, to take a quick look at. || *Echa una ojeada al niño*, have a look at the baby.

ojeador m. Beater (en la caza).

ojear v. tr. To eye (mirar). || To stare at (mirar fijamente). || To beat up [game] (en la caza). || FIG. To scare off *o* away (espantar). | To cast the evil eye on (aojar).

ojén m. Anisette (bebida).

ojeo m. Beating (en la caza).

ojera f. Ring (de los ojos). || Eyebath (lavaojos). || *Tener ojeras*, to have rings under one's eyes.

ojeriza f. Spite, ill will, grudge, dislike. || — *Tenerle ojeriza a uno*, to have *o* to bear a grudge against s.o. || *Tomarle ojeriza a uno*, to take a dislike to s.o.

ojeroso, sa adj. With rings under one's eyes (persona). || *Estar ojeroso*, to have rings under one's eyes.

ojete m. Eyelet, grummet (para pasar un cordón). || POP. Arse (ano).

ojiva f. ARQ. Ogive. || MIL. Warhead (de proyectil). || Nose cone (de un cohete espacial).

ojival adj. Ogival. || *Estilo ojival*, Ogival *o* Gothic style.

ojo m. Eye: *tener ante los ojos*, to have before one's eyes; *saltarle un ojo a alguien*, to put out s.o.'s eye. || Hole (agujero). || Opening (abertura). || Speck of oil *o* of fat (en el caldo). || Eye, hole (de pan, queso). || Eye (de aguja). || Bow (de llave). || Keyhole (de cerradura). || Span (de puente). || Spring (manantial). || Eye (de la cola del pavo). || Soaping, lathering (jabonadura). || Mesh (de red). || Eye (de huracán). || IMPR. Face (de una letra). || TECN. Eye, helve ring (de una herramienta). || POP. Hole (ano). || FIG. Perspicacity. | Care, caution (cuidado). || — Pl. Bows, rings (de tijeras). || — FIG. *Abrir el ojo*, to keep one's eyes open. | *Abrirle los ojos a uno*, to open s.o.'s eyes. | *Abrir los ojos*, to keep one's eyes open (vigilante), to open one's eyes (*ante*, to) [percatarse de algo]. | *Alegrársele a uno los ojos*, to shine *o* to sparkle with joy [the eyes]: *se le alegraron los ojos*, his eyes shone with joy. || *A (los) ojos de*, in the eyes of (según). || *Alzar los ojos al cielo*, to raise *o* to lift one's eyes to heaven. || FIG. *Andar con cien ojos*, to keep one's eyes open, to be on one's guard. || *Andar ojo alerta*, to keep one's eyes open. || *A ojo*, by eye. || *A ojo [de buen cubero]*, by guesswork, by rule of thumb (sin medir), in a rough and ready way (sin precisión). || *A ojo de buen cubero debe de pesar diez kilos*, at a rough estimate it must weigh about ten kilos. || *A ojos cerrados*, with one's eyes closed, blindfold. || *A ojos vistas*, visibly (claramente): *crecer a ojos vistas*, to become visibly larger. || FIG. *Bailarle a uno los ojos de alegría*, to sparkle *o* to dance with joy [the eyes]: *le bailaban los ojos de alegría*, his eyes sparkled with joy. || *Cerrar los ojos*, to close one's eyes, to go to sleep (dormirse), to pass away (morir). | *Cerrar los ojos a*, to close *o* to shut one's eyes to. | *Comerse con los ojos*, to gloat over, to look greedily at (codiciar), to devour with one's eyes (con amor), to look daggers at (con ira). | *Como los ojos de la cara*, like the apple of one's eye. | *Con los ojos cerrados*, blindly, with one's eyes closed (sin reflexionar), with one's eyes shut, with complete confidence (con completa confianza). | *Costar* or *valer un ojo de la cara*, to cost *o* to be worth a fortune. | *Cuatro ojos*, four-eyes (que lleva gafas). | *Cuatro ojos ven más que dos*, two heads are better than one. | *Dar en los ojos a uno*, to be *o* to get in one's eyes (el Sol). || FIG. *Daría un ojo de la cara por*, I'd give my right arm *o* anything for. | *Dar un ojo a*, to soap (la ropa). | *Delante de los ojos*, right before one's eyes, before one's very eyes, under one's very nose. || *¡Dichosos los ojos que te ven!*, how glad I am to see you!, you're a sight for sore eyes! || FIG. *Donde pone el ojo pone la bala* or *la piedra*, he is a dead shot. | *Dormir con los ojos abiertos* or *con un ojo abierto como las liebres*, to sleep with one eye open. | *Echar el ojo a*, to set one's eye on, to have one's eyes on. | *El ojo del amo engorda al caballo*, the master's eye makes the mill go. | *Entrar por los ojos a uno*, to catch s.o.'s eye, to take s.o.'s fancy. | *En un abrir y cerrar de ojos*, in the twinkling of an eye, in a wink. | *Estar ojo avizor*, to keep a sharp lookout. || *Guiñar el ojo*, to wink. || FIG. *Hacer caer la venda de los ojos*, to open s.o.'s eyes. | *Hacer ojo*, to lather (el jabón). | *Hasta los ojos*, up to the eyes, up to one's neck. | *Ir con mucho ojo*, to tread very carefully. | *Írsele a uno los ojos por* or *tras una cosa*, to eye sth. greedily (desear), to goggle at sth. (mirar). | *Llena antes el ojo que la barriga* or *la tripa*, his eyes are bigger than his belly. | *Llorar con un ojo*, to cry crocodile tears. | *Meterle al público un producto por los ojos*, to shove a product down the public's throat (elogiar). | *Meterse por el ojo de una aguja*, to have a finger in every pie. || *Mirar a* or *en los ojos*, to look into s.o.'s eyes, to look s.o. in the eye. || FIG. *Mirar con buenos ojos*, to look favourably upon. | *Mirar con el rabillo del ojo*, to look out of the corner of one's eye [at]. | *Mirar con malos ojos*, to frown on. | *Mirar con ojos de carnero degollado*, to make sheep's eyes at. | *Mirar con ojos terribles*, to look sternly at, to stare fiercely at, to glare at. | *Mirar con otros ojos*, to see in a different light. | *No dar crédito a sus ojos*, not to believe one's eyes. | *No pegar el ojo* or *ojo*, not to sleep a wink, not to get a wink of sleep (no poder dormir). | *No quitar los ojos de encima* or *no quitar ojo a*, not to take one's eyes off, to keep watching (no dejar de mirar), not to let out of one's sight, to keep an *o* one's eye on (vigilar). | *No tener a quien volver los ojos*, to have no one to look to *o* to turn to. | *No tener a dónde volver los ojos*, not to know which way to turn. | *No tener ojos más que para*, to have eyes only for. | *No tener telarañas en los ojos*, not to be blind, to have one's eyes about one. || *¡Ojo!*, look out!, careful!, watch out!, watch it! || FIG. y FAM. *Ojo a la funerala*, black eye, shiner. || *Ojo con*, watch, be careful about *o* of *o* with, beware of. || *Ojo de besugo*, bulging eye. || *Ojo de buey*, bull's-eye window (ventana), porthole (en un barco). || *Ojo de cristal*, glass eye. || *Ojo de gallo*, corn [on the foot] (callo). || *Ojo de gato*, cat's eye, tigereye (ágata). || *Ojo de la llave*, keyhole. || *Ojo eléctrico*, electric eye. || FAM. *Ojo en compota*, black eye. || RAD. *Ojo mágico*, magic eye. || FIG. *Ojo por ojo, diente por diente*, an eye for an eye, a tooth for a tooth. || *Ojos achinados*, almond eyes. || *Ojos hundidos*, sunken eyes. || *Ojos oblicuos*, slant eyes. || *Ojos pícaros*, saucy eyes. || FIG. *Ojos que no ven, corazón que no siente*, out of sight, out of mind. || *Ojos rasgados*, almond eyes. || *Ojos saltones*, bulging eyes. || *Ojos tiernos*, tender eyes. || *Pasar a los ojos de uno como un tonto*, to look a fool in s.o.'s eyes. || *Pasar los ojos por*, to run one's eye over. || FAM. *Ponerle a uno un ojo a la funerala*, to give s.o. a black eye, to black s.o.'s eye. || FIG. *Poner los ojos* or *el ojo en*, to set one's eye on, to fix one's sights on. | *Poner los ojos en blanco*, to swoon (*delante de*, over) [mostrar una admiración exagerada por]. | *Por sus lindos ojos*, for nothing, gratis. || *Revolver los ojos*, to roll one's eyes. || FIG. *Sacar los ojos a uno*, to bleed s.o. white (pedir mucho dinero). | *Salta a los ojos*, it is obvious, it is as plain as a pikestaff. || *Se le arrasaron los ojos en lágrimas*, his eyes filled with tears. || *Se le humedecieron los ojos*, tears came to his eyes. || FIG. *Ser el ojo* or *el ojito derecho de alguien*, to be s.o.'s [little] blue-eyed boy *o* girl. | *Ser todo ojos*, to be all eyes. | *Tener buen ojo* or *ojo clínico para*, to have a good *o* sure eye for. || FIG. y FAM. *Tener cuatro ojos*, to be a four-eyes (llevar gafas). | *Tener entre ojos a uno*, to have a grudge against s.o., to have it in for s.o. || FIG. *Tener los ojos puestos en*, to have set one's heart on. | *Tener los ojos vendados* or *tener una venda en los ojos*, to go around blindfolded *o* with one's eyes closed, to be blind. | *Tener mal de ojo*, to be jinxed. | *Tener muy buen ojo para*, to have a very good eye *o* a real flair for (ser perspicaz). | *Tener ojo de buen cubero*, to have a sure *o* an accurate eye. | *Tener ojos de lince*, to have eyes like a hawk *o* sharp eyes. || FAM. *Tener un ojo aquí y el otro en Pekín*, to be cross-eyed (ser bizco). || *Torcer los ojos*, to squint. || FIG. *Traer entre ojos*, to keep one's eye on. | *Ver con buenos ojos*, to look favourably upon. | *Ver con malos ojos* to look unfavourably upon, to frown on. | *Ver algo con los mismos ojos*, to see eye to eye over sth.

ojota f. *Amer.* Sandal (sandalia).

okapí m. ZOOL. Okapi (mamífero).

okumé m. BOT. Okoume, okume (árbol africano).

ola f. MAR. Wave. || FIG. Wave: *ola inflacionista, de protestas*, wave of inflation, of protest. || — FIG. *La nueva ola*, the new wave. || *Ola de calor, de frío*, heat wave, cold spell.

¡ole! u **¡olé!** interj. Bravo!, well done!

oleáceas f. pl. BOT. Oleaceae.

oleada f. Large wave, surge, billow (ola). || FIG.

Surge, wave (de gente). | Wave: *oleada de suicidios*, wave of suicides.
oleaginosidad f. Oleaginousness.
oleaginoso, sa adj. Oleaginous. || *Semilla oleaginosa*, oilseed.
— M. Oilseed.
oleaje m. Swell (marejada). || Surf (olas espumosas).
olecráneo o **olécranon** m. ANAT. Olecranon.
oleícola adj. Olive-growing (del cultivo del olivo). || Of the olive oil industry, olive oil.
oleicultor m. Olive grower (cultivador). || Olive oil manufacturer (productor).
oleicultura f. Olive growing (cultivo del olivo). || Olive oil industry (producción de aceite).
oleífero, ra adj. Oleiferous, oil-producing: *planta oleífera*, oleiferous plant.
oleína f. QUÍM. Olein.
óleo m. Oil, olive oil (aceite de oliva). || REL. Chrism, oil. || Oil (pintura). || — *Los Santos Óleos*, Holy Oil. || *Pintar al óleo*, to paint in oils. || *Pintura al óleo*, oil painting.
oleoducto m. Pipeline.
oleografía f. Oleography.
oleómetro m. Oleometer.
oleosidad f. Oiliness.
oleoso, sa adj. Oily.
óleum m. QUÍM. Oleum.
oler* v. tr. To smell. || FIG. To smell, to scent (sospechar). | To nose into, to pry into (curiosear). | To smell out, to sniff out (descubrir).
— V. intr. To smell: *oler a tabaco*, to smell of tobacco; *oler bien, mal*, to smell good *o* nice, bad *o* nasty. || FIG. To smell, to smack: *sus palabras huelen a traición*, his talk smacks of treason. | To sound: *huele a mentira, a traducción*, it sounds like a lie, like a translation. || — FIG. *Ese señor huele a policía*, that gentleman has got policeman written all over him. | *Este asunto no me huele bien*, this business smells fishy to me. | *Oler a chamusquina*, V. CHAMUSQUINA. || *Oler a difunto*, V. DIFUNTO.
— V. pr. FIG. To feel, to sense: *me huelo que va a llover*, I feel that it is going to rain. | To smell, to sense, to scent: *olerse un peligro, una intriga*, to smell danger, a plot. || — FIG. *Me lo olía*, I sensed it, I thought as much. | *Olerse la tortilla*, to see it coming.
olfatear v. tr. To sniff, to smell. || FIG. y FAM. To smell, to scent (sospechar). | To smell out, to sniff out (descubrir). | To nose into, to pry into (curiosear). || To smell *o* to nose out, to scent out [game] (los perros).
olfateo m. Sniffing, smelling. || FIG. Snooping (curioseo).
olfato m. Smell, sense of smell. || FIG. Intuition, instinct, flair (instinto). || FIG. *Tener olfato para los negocios*, to have a flair *o* a nose for business.
olíbano m. Olibanum, frankincense.
oliente adj. Smelling, odorous. || — *Bien oliente*, pleasant-smelling. || *Mal oliente*, bad-smelling, malodorous.
oligarca m. Oligarch.
oligarquía f. Oligarchy.
oligárquico, ca adj. Oligarchic, oligarchical.
oligisto adj./s.m. MIN. Oligist. || *Oligisto rojo*, haematite, hematite, red iron ore.
oligoceno, na adj./s.m. GEOL. Oligocene.
oligoelemento m. Trace element.
oligofrenia f. Oligophrenia.
Olimpia n. pr. f. HIST. Olympia.
olimpiada u **olimpíada** f. Olympic games, *pl.*, Olympics, *pl.* (juegos). || Olympiad (período).
olímpicamente adv. Olympianly, loftily: *despreciar olímpicamente*, to despise Olympianly.
olímpico, ca adj. Olympian (del Olimpo): *Júpiter olímpico*, Olympian Jupiter. || Olympic (de Olimpia): *juegos olímpicos*, Olympic games. || FIG. Olympian, haughty, lofty (altivo): *desdén olímpico*, Olympian contempt. || *Ciudad olímpica*, Olympic village.
Olimpo n. pr. m. MIT. Olympus: *Monte Olimpo*, Mount Olympus.
oliscar u **olisquear** v. tr. FAM. To sniff, to smell (oler). || FIG. To nose *o* to pry into (curiosear).
— V. intr. To smell [bad].
oliva f. Olive (aceituna): *aceite de oliva*, olive oil. || Olive, olive tree (olivo). || ZOOL. Owl (lechuza). || ANAT. Olivary body. || *Color verde oliva*, olive, olive-green.
oliváceo, a adj. Olive, olive-green.
olivar m. Olive plantation, olive grove.
olivar v. tr. AGR. To cut off the lower branches of.
olivarero, ra adj. Olive-growing: *región olivarera*, olive-growing region. || Olive: *industria olivarera*, olive industry.
Oliveto n. pr. m. *Monte Oliveto*, Mount of Olives.
olivícola adj. Olive-growing.
olivicultor m. Olive grower.
olivicultura f. Olive growing.
olivífero, ra adj. Covered with olive trees, oliviferous, rich in olives.
olivina f. u **olivino** m. MIN. Olivine.
olivo m. Olive tree, olive (árbol). || — *Huerto de los Olivos*, Garden of Olives. || *Monte de los Olivos*, Mount of Olives. || FIG. *Olivo y aceituno todo es uno*, it's much of a muchness, it's as broad as it is long. || FIG. *Tomar el olivo*, to take shelter behind the barrier (el torero), to take to one's heels (huir).
olmeda f. u **olmedo** m. Elm grove.
olmo m. BOT. Elm, elm tree.
ológrafo, fa adj./s.m. Holograph.
olor m. Smell, odour [U.S., odor]: *un olor a rosa*, a smell of roses. || Scent (de la caza). || Scent, fragrance, perfume (buen olor). || FIG. Smell, smack. || — *Agua de olor*, toilet water. || *Morir en olor de santidad*, to die in the odour of sanctity. || *Tener olor a*, to smell of, to have a smell of.
oloroso, sa adj. Odorous, sweet-smelling, fragrant.
olvidable adj. Forgettable.
olvidadizo, za adj. Forgetful. || FIG. Ungrateful, with a short memory (desagradecido). || *Hacerse el olvidadizo*, to pretend to forget, to pretend not to remember.
olvidado, da adj. Forgotten. || Forgetful (olvidadizo). || FIG. Ungrateful (desagradecido).
— M. y f. Forgetful person (olvidadizo). || FIG. Ungrateful person.
olvidar v. tr. To forget: *olvidar una fecha, la hora*, to forget a date, the time; *olvidemos el pasado*, let us forget the past. || To leave behind, to forget: *olvidar el bolso*, to leave one's bag behind. || To forget, to omit, to leave out (omitir): *olvidar un nombre en una lista*, to omit a name from a list.
— V. pr. To be forgotten (estar olvidado): *un favor no debe olvidarse*, a good turn should not be forgotten. || To forget: *no se te olvide*, don't forget; *se me olvidó decírtelo* or *me olvidé de decírtelo*, I forgot to tell you; *se le olvidaron todas nuestras atenciones*, he forgot all the attention we lavished on him. || FIG. *Olvidarse de sí mismo*, not to think of o.s., to have no thought for o.s.
olvido m. Forgetting (acción de olvidar). || Forgetfulness (descuido): *en un momento de olvido*, in a moment's forgetfulness. || Omission, oversight (omisión). || Oblivion (estado de lo olvidado): *caer en el olvido*, to fall *o* to sink into oblivion. || — *Dar* or *echar al* or *en el olvido*, to cast into oblivion, to forget. || *Dejar en el olvido*, to leave in oblivion. || *Enterrar en el olvido*, to cast into oblivion. || *Estar en el olvido*, to lie in oblivion. || *Sacar del olvido*, to rescue from oblivion.
olla f. Pot (vasija). || Kettle (para hervir agua). || Stew, hotpot (guisado). || Eddy, whirlpool (remolino). || FIG. Hotchpotch. || — FIG. *Olla de grillos*, madhouse, bedlam, bear garden. || *Olla de presión* u *olla exprés*, pressure cooker. || *Olla podrida*, highly-seasoned hotpot.
ollar m. Nostril (de las caballerías).
ollero, ra m. y f. Potter. || FIG. *Cada ollero alaba su puchero*, each of us blows his own trumpet at some time or other.
ombligo m. ANAT. Navel, umbilicus. || FIG. Centre. || — FIG. y FAM. *Encogérsele a uno el ombligo*, to get cold feet. || BOT. *Ombligo de Venus*, Venus's-navelwort.
ombú m. Ombu (árbol de América).
omega f. Omega (letra griega).
omento m. ANAT. y ZOOL. Omentum (redaño).
Omeyas m. pl. HIST. Ommiads, Ommiad dynasty.
ómicron f. Omicron (letra griega).
ominoso, sa adj. Abominable, execrable (abominable). || Ominous, foreboding (de mal agüero).
omisión f. Omission (abstención): *pecado de omisión*, sin of omission. || Omission, neglect (descuido). || Forgetfulness (olvido). || Oversight (distracción).
omiso, sa adj. Neglectful, careless (descuidado). || *Hacer caso omiso de*, V. CASO.
omitir v. tr. To omit, to neglect: *omitió decírmelo*, he omitted to tell me. || To omit, to leave out, to miss out (excluir). || To omit, to pass over, to skip (pasar en silencio).
ómnibus m. Omnibus, bus (carruaje público). || *Tren ómnibus*, slow *o* stopping train.
omnidireccional adj. RAD. Omnidirectional, all direction.
omnímodamente adv. Absolutely, totally.
omnímodo, da adj. All-embracing, absolute, total.
omnipotencia f. Omnipotence.
omnipotente adj. Omnipotent, almighty, all-powerful.
omnipresencia f. Omnipresence.
omnipresente adj. Omnipresent.
omnisapiente adj. Omniscient, all-knowing.
omnisciencia f. Omniscience.
omnisciente adj. Omniscient, all-knowing.
ómnium m. COM. General trading company. || Open race (carrera).
omnívoro, ra adj. ZOOL. Omnivorous.
— M. y f. ZOOL. Omnivore.
omóplato u **omoplato** m. ANAT. Shoulder blade, scapula.
onagro m. Onager (asno salvaje).
onanismo m. Onanism.
onanista adj. Onanist.
once adj. Eleven: *once personas*, eleven people. || Eleventh (undécimo): *el siglo XI (once)*, the eleventh century; *Pío XI (once)*, Pius XI [the eleventh].
— M. Eleven (equipo de fútbol). || Eleven (número). || Eleventh (fechas): *el once de mayo*, the eleventh of May, May [the] eleventh. || — *A las once*, at eleven

o'clock. || *Las once*, elevenses (refrigerio). || *Son las once de la noche*, it is eleven p. m.
onceno, na adj./s. Eleventh.
onda f. Wave (en el agua). || FÍS. Wave: *ondas acústicas, hertzianas, amortiguadas, portadoras*, sound, Hertzian, damped, carrier waves. || Wave (en el pelo). || Scallop (costura). || FIG. Flicker (de la llama). || — RAD. *De onda corta*, shortwave. | *Longitud de onda*, wavelength. | *Onda corta*, short wave. || *Onda de choque* or *onda expansiva*, shock wave (explosión). || RAD. *Onda extracorta*, ultrashort wave. | *Onda larga*, long wave. | *Onda media*, medium wave.
ondeado, da adj. Waving, undulating, waved, wavy. || Wavy, waved (pelo).
ondeante adj. Undulating. || Fluttering, waving, flapping (bandera).
ondear v. intr. To undulate, to rise and fall in waves (mar). || To ripple (el agua). || To wave, to stream: *sus cabellos ondeaban al viento*, her hair streamed in the wind. || To flutter, to wave (una bandera). || To flicker, to waver (una llama). || To scallop (costura).
— V. pr. To swing, to sway.
ondeo m. Undulation, rippling (del agua). || Waving (del pelo). || Fluttering, waving, flapping (de una bandera). || Flickering, waving (de una llama).
ondina f. MIT. Undine.
ondulación f. Undulation. || Wave (del pelo). || Wave, ripple (del agua). || Winding (sinuosidad). | *Ondulación permanente*, permanent wave.
ondulado, da adj. Rolling (paisaje). || Undulating (superficie). || Uneven (carretera). || Wavy (pelo). || Corrugated (hierro, cartón).
— M. Wave (del pelo).
ondulante adj. Undulating. || Wavy (pelo). || Rippling, undulating (agua). || Flickering, waving (llama).
ondular v. tr. e intr. To wave (pelo). || To undulate, to wave, to ripple (trigo). || To slither (culebra). || To corrugate (hierro).
ondulatorio, ria adj. Undulatory. || — *Mecánica ondulatoria*, wave mechanics. || *Movimiento ondulatorio*, wave motion, undulatory movement.
oneroso, sa adj. Onerous.
ónice m. y f. MIN. Onyx (ágata).
onírico, ca adj. Oneiric (de los sueños).
ónix m. MIN. Onyx (ágata).
onomástico, ca adj. Onomastic. || — *Día onomástico*, saint's day. || *Índice onomástico*, index of names.
— F. Onomastics. || Saint's day (día del santo).
onomatopeya f. Onomatopoeia.
onomatopéyico, ca adj. Onomatopoeic.
ontología f. FÍL. Ontology.
ontológico, ca adj. FIL. Ontological.
ontólogo m. FIL. Ontologist.
O.N.U. f. U.N. (Organización de las Naciones Unidas).
onubense adj. [Of *o* from] Huelva [formerly *Ónuba*].
— M. y f. Native *o* inhabitant of Huelva.
onza f. Ounce (medida de peso). || ZOOL. Ounce.
onzavo, va adj./s. Eleventh.
oosfera f. Oosphere.
oospora f. BOT. Oospore (huevo).
opa adj. *Amer.* Stupid, idiotic (idiota). || *¡Opa!*, hullo!
opacidad f. Opacity, opaqueness.
opaco, ca adj. Opaque. || Dull, dim (ruido, luz). || FIG. Gloomy (triste).
opalescencia f. Opalescence.
opalescente adj. Opalescent.
opalino, na adj. Opal (del ópalo). || Opaline (color).
— F. Opaline.
ópalo m. MIN. Opal. || *Color de ópalo*, opal.
opción f. Option, choice. || Right (derecho). || COM. Option.
ópera f. Opera. || Opera, opera house (edificio). || — *Ópera bufa*, opéra bouffe, comic opera. || *Ópera cómica*, opéra comique.
operable adj. Operable.
operación f. Operation: *operación aritmética, quirúrgica*, arithmetical, surgical operation. || MIL. Operation. || COM. Transaction, deal. || — COM. *Fondo de operaciones*, working capital. || *Operación cesárea*, Caesarian *o* Caesarean section. || MIL. *Operación de limpieza*, mopping-up operation.
operacional adj. Operational.
operado, da adj. Who has been operated on.
— M. y f. Surgical patient.
operador, ra m. y f. Operator. || Surgeon (cirujano). || CINEM. Cameraman (de rodaje). | Projectionist (de proyección). || — M. MAT. Operator.
operante adj. Operating, working, operative. || Effective (que produce el efecto deseado).
operar v. tr. To operate on *o* upon: *operar a uno de una pierna, de apendicitis*, to operate on s.o.'s leg, on s.o. for appendicitis. || To work (un milagro). || To bring about (una transformación, cierto efecto, etc.). || To effect, to bring about (una curación).
— V. intr. To operate (actuar, obrar). || To operate, to work, to take effect: *la medicina empieza a operar*, the medicine is beginning to work. || COM. To do business, to deal.
— V. pr. To occur, to come about (efectuarse). || MED. To have an operation.
operario, ria m. y f. Operative, worker, operator. || — *Operario de máquina*, machinist, machine operator. || *Operario electricista*, electrician. || — M. Monk who tends and confesses the sick (religioso).
operativo, va adj. Operative.
operatorio, ria adj. Operative. || *Choque operatorio*, postoperative shock.
opérculo m. Operculum.
opereta f. Operetta.
operístico, ca adj. Operatic.
opimo, ma adj. Rich (rico). || Abundant, plentiful (abundante).
opinable adj. Debatable, moot.
opinante m. y f. Opiner.
opinar v. intr. To think: *¿qué opinas de esto?*, what do you think of this? || To express *o* to give one's opinion: *opinar de* or *sobre política*, to express one's opinion of politics. || To have an opinion, to think: *opinar bien de uno*, to have a good opinion of s.o., to think well of s.o.
opinión f. Opinion: *la opinión pública*, public opinion; *dar su opinión*, to give one's opinion. || View, opinion: *tenemos las mismas opiniones*, we have the same views. || — *Andar en opiniones*, to be talked about, to make tongues wag. || *Cambiar de opinión*, to change one's mind. || FIG. *Casarse uno con su opinión*, to stick to one's opinion. || *Compartir la opinión de* or *abundar en la opinión de*, to share the same opinion as. || *En mi opinión*, in my opinion. || *Es cuestión de opinión*, that is a matter of opinion. || *Ese muchacho no me merece buena opinión*, I have a poor opinion of that boy. || *Salvo mejor opinión*, failing a better idea *o* suggestion. || *Según opinión de*, in the opinion of. || *Ser de opinión que*, to be of the opinion that. || *Sondeo de la opinión pública*, public opinion poll.
opio m. Opium.
opiomanía f. Opium addiction.
opiómano, na adj. Addicted to opium, opium-addicted.
— M. y f. Opium addict.
opíparamente adv. In splendid style, sumptuously, lavishly.
opíparo, ra adj. Sumptuous, splendid, lavish: *banquete opíparo*, sumptuous feast.
oponente adj. Opposing. || ANAT. Opponent (músculo).
— M. y f. Opponent.
oponer* v. tr. To oppose: *oponer una fuerza militar a otra*, to oppose one military force against another; *oponer dos equipos*, to oppose two teams. || To offer, to put up (resistencia). || To raise (objeción). || To use (armas).
— V. pr. To oppose each other (dos personas). || To oppose, to be opposed to, to be against: *oponerse a un proyecto*, to oppose a plan. || To object to (poner reparos a). || To oppose, to go against, to be in opposition to, to contradict (contradecir). || To resist (resistir). || To be opposite, to face (estar enfrente). || *Oponerse a una moción*, to oppose a motion.
oponible adj. Opposable.
oporto m. Port, port wine.
Oporto n. pr. GEOGR. Oporto.
oportunidad f. Opportunity, chance: *tuve la oportunidad de ir a Australia*, I had the opportunity of going to *o* to go to Australia; *en la primera oportunidad*, at the first opportunity. || Opportuneness, timeliness: *la oportunidad de su llegada*, the timeliness of his arrival. || Appropriateness, suitability, advisability (de una medida, etc.). || — *Aprovechar, no aprovechar una oportunidad*, to seize, to miss an opportunity. || *No dejar escapar la oportunidad*, not to let the opportunity slip by.
oportunismo m. Opportunism.
oportunista adj. Opportunist, opportunistic.
— M. y f. Opportunist.
oportuno, na adj. Suitable, appropriate: *tomar las medidas oportunas*, to take the appropriate measures. || Opportune, timely, seasonable: *una llegada oportuna*, a timely arrival. || Suitable, fitting, apposite: *respuesta oportuna*, suitable reply. || Advisable (aconsejable). || Witty (persona). || — *En el momento oportuno*, at the right moment. || *Oportuno en las réplicas*, quick at repartee.
oposición f. Opposition: *se mantuvo firme en su oposición*, he did not let up in his opposition. || Competitive examination, competition (examen): *hacer una oposición a la cátedra de estudios hispánicos*, to sit a competitive examination for the chair of Hispanic studies. || Opposition (en política): *el líder de la oposición*, the leader of the opposition. || ASTR. Opposition. || — *Catedrático por oposición*, professor selected by means of a competitive examination. || *En oposición con*, in opposition to, opposed to. || *Ganar las oposiciones a una cátedra*, to win a chair in a competitive examination.
oposicionista m. y f. Member of the opposition, opposition member, oppositionist.
opositar v. intr. To sit a competitive examination.
opositor, ra m. y f. Opponent (adversario). || Candidate (candidato).
oposum m. ZOOL. Opossum.
opresión f. Oppression (de un pueblo). || *Opresión en el* or *de pecho*, tightness of the chest, difficulty in breathing.
opresivo, va adj. Oppresive: *ley opresiva*, oppressive law; *clima opresivo*, oppressive climate.

opreso, sa adj. Oppressed.
opresor, ra adj. Oppressing, oppressive.
— M. y f. Oppressor.
oprimente adj. Oppressing, oppressive.
oprimido, da adj. Oppressed: *los pueblos oprimidos*, oppressed peoples. || *Tener el corazón oprimido*, to be sick at heart.
— M. y f. Oppressed person. || *Los oprimidos*, the oppressed.
oprimir v. tr. To press: *oprimir un botón*, to press a button. || To squeeze, to press (apretar). || To be too tight: *me oprimen los zapatos*, my shoes are too tight for me. || To compress (gas). || To grasp (picaporte). || FIG. To oppress (tiranizar). | To weigh down (agobiar). | To seize, to overcome (afligir): *la emoción oprimía a los espectadores*, the spectators were seized with emotion. | To wring: *oprimir el corazón*, to wring one's heart.
oprobiar v. tr. To defame, to revile, to disgrace.
oprobio m. Opprobrium, ignominy, disgrace, shame: *cubrir de oprobio*, to cover with opprobrium. || *Ser el oprobio de su familia*, to be a disgrace to one's family. || *Y para mayor oprobio*, and to my (your, his, etc.) great shame.
oprobioso, sa adj. Opprobrious, ignominious, shameful, disgraceful.
optar v. intr. To opt, to choose: *optar por una línea de conducta*, to opt for *o* to choose a line of conduct; *optó por quedarse*, he opted *o* he chose to stay. || To choose: *optar entre dos candidatos*, to choose between two candidates. || To apply (*a*, for) [un puesto].
optativo, va adj. GRAM. Optative. || Optional (facultativo).
— M. GRAM. Optative.
óptico, ca adj. Optic, optical (del ojo, de la visión): *nervio, ángulo óptico*, optic nerve, angle. || Optical (de la luz, de los lentes, etc.): *instrumentos ópticos*, optical instruments. || — *Ilusión óptica*, optical illusion. || *Telégrafo óptico*, signal *o* optical telegraph.
— F. FÍS. Optics. || Optical system, optics [of camera, etc.] (aparato). || FIG. Viewpoint, approach (enfoque). || Opticians's shop (tienda). || — M. Optician (comerciante).
óptimamente adv. In the best possible way, perfectly.
optimismo m. Optimism.
optimista adj. Optimistic.
— M. y f. Optimist.
óptimo, ma adj. Optimum, very best, most favourable. || *Porvenir óptimo*, brilliant future.
— M. Optimum.
— Interj. Capital!, first rate!
opuestamente adv. Contrarily.
opuesto, ta adj. Opposed: *opuesto a una medida*, opposed to a measure. || Opposed, opposite, conflicting, contrary: *dos versiones opuestas*, two opposed versions. || Opposite: *en sentido opuesto*, in the opposite direction. || Conflicting (intereses). || BOT. y MAT. Opposite. || DEP. Opposing (equipo).
opugnación f. Opposition, oppugnation (oposición). || Attack, oppugnation (ataque).
opugnador m. (P.us.). Oppugner, opponent (adversario). || Attacker.
opugnar v. tr. (P.us.). To oppose, to oppugn (oponerse). || To oppugn, to controvert, to oppose (impugnar). || To attack, to assail, to oppugn (asaltar).
opulencia f. Opulence.
opulento, ta adj. Opulent.
opus m. MÚS. Opus.
opúsculo m. Opuscule, booklet (folleto).
oquedad f. Hole (hoyo). || Cavity, hollow (cavidad).
oquedal m. Wood [without undergrowth].
ora conj. Now: *ora sabio ora ignorante*, now wise, now ignorant. || Whether: *ora de día, ora de noche*, whether by day, whether by night.
oración f. REL. Prayer, orison (p.us.): *estar en oración*, to be at prayer. || Oration, speech (discurso). || Sentence (frase). || GRAM. Speech: *parte de la oración*, part of speech. | Clause: *oración relativa*, relative clause. || — Pl. First part (*sing.*) of the catechism, prayers. || Angelus, *sing.* (toque de campanas). || — FIG. *Oración de ciego*, monotonous drone, singsong. || *Oración dominical*, Lord's Prayer. || *Oración fúnebre*, funeral oration. || *Oración mental, vocal*, mental, vocal prayer. || *Rezar sus oraciones*, to say one's prayers.
oracional adj. GRAM. Sentential.
— M. Prayer book.
oráculo m. Oracle.
orador, ra m. y f. Speaker, orator (que habla en público). || *Orador sagrado*, preacher. || — M. Preacher (predicador).
oral adj. Oral: *aprobar los exámenes orales*, to pass the oral exams.
— M. Oral, viva voce (examen).
Orange n. pr. HIST. Orange.
orangután m. ZOOL. Orangutan, orangoutang.
orante adj. Praying, in prayer. || *Estatua orante*, orant, statue in the posture of prayer.
orar v. intr. To pray (*a*, to; *por*, for) [hacer oración]: *orar por los difuntos*, to pray for the dead. || To make a speech, to speak (hablar).
orate m. y f. Madman (hombre), madwoman (mujer), lunatic. || *Casa de orates*, lunatic asylum.
oratoriano m. Oratorian (religioso).
oratorio, ria adj. Oratorical.
— M. Oratory, chapel (capilla). || MÚS. Oratorio. || — F. Oratory, oratorical art.
orbe m. Orb, circle (círculo). || Orb, sphere (esfera). || FIG. World (mundo): *en todo el orbe*, throughout the world. || ASTR. Orb.
orbícola adj. Found all over the world, worldwide.
órbita f. ASTR. Orbit. || ANAT. Orbit, eye socket. || FIG. Sphere, field [of activity]. || — ASTR. *En órbita*, in orbit. | *Poner en órbita*, to put into orbit. | *Puesta en órbita*, putting into orbit.
orbital adj. Orbital: *vuelo orbital*, orbital flight.
orbitario, ria adj. Orbital.
orca f. ZOOL. Orc, grampus, killer whale (cetáceo).
Orcadas n. pr. f. pl. GEOGR. Orkneys, Orkney Islands (islas).
órdago m. Staking of all one's money (en juegos). || — FAM. *De órdago*, great, fantastic [U.S., swell]: *una película de órdago*, a fantastic film; tidy, right old, terrific, hell of a [U.S., helluva]: *un jaleo de órdago*, a right old racket; complete, prize: *un idiota de órdago*, a prize idiot; hell of a: *una tontería de órdago*, a hell of a daft thing to do.
ordalías f. pl. Ordeal, *sing.* (en la Edad Media).
orden m. y f. Order, command: *obedecer una orden*, to obey an order; *dar la orden de hacer algo*, to give the order to do sth. || Order (disposición metódica, armoniosa): *por orden cronológico*, in chronological order; *por orden de antigüedad*, in order of seniority; *la habitación está en orden*, the room is in order. || Nature, character, order (categoría): *éstos son problemas de orden financiero*, these are problems of a financial nature. || Field (sector): *en el orden económico se plantean ciertos problemas*, certain problems arise in the economic field. || ARQ., BOT. y ZOOL. Order: *orden dórico, corintio, jónico*, Doric, Corinthian, Ionic order; *orden de los coleópteros*, order of coleoptera. || Order: *una orden de caballería*, an order of knighthood. || JUR. Writ (mandato). | Warrant: *una orden de detención* or *de arresto, de registro*, a warrant for arrest, search warrant. | Order, decision, decree (decisión). | Order (paz): *restablecer el orden*, to restore order. || MIL. Order: *orden cerrado, de batalla*, close, battle order. || REL. Order. || COM. Order. || — *A la orden de*, to the order of (cheque). || *Alterar el orden público*, to disturb the peace. || *A sus órdenes*, at your service. || MIL. *¡A sus órdenes!*, or *¡a la orden!*, Sir! | *Citar en el orden del día*, to mention in despatches. || *Del orden de*, of the order of. || *De orden de*, by order of, on the orders of. || *De primer orden*, first-class, first-rate. || *En el orden natural de las cosas*, in the nature of things. || *En orden a*, with regard to (en relación con), for (para). || *Fuerzas del orden*, forces of law and order. || *Hasta nueva orden*, until further orders *o* notice. || *Llamada al orden*, call *o* calling to order. || *Llamar al orden*, to call to order. || *Mantener el orden*, to keep order. || MIL. *Marchar en orden disperso*, to march in extended order. || *Orden de antigüedad*, seniority, length of service. || MIL. *Orden de combate*, combat order. || JUR. *Orden de comparecencia*, summons. || *Orden de expedición*, delivery order. || *Orden del día*, agenda (reunión, asamblea, etc.), order of the day (militar). || *Orden de sucesión*, order of succession. || COM. *Orden de pago*, order of payment (libramiento). || REL. *Órdenes mayores, menores, mendicantes*, major, minor, mendicant orders. || *Órdenes sagradas*, holy orders. || JUR. *Orden formal* or *terminante*, injunction. || *Orden público*, law and order, public order. || *¡Orden y compostura!*, behave yourself! || COM. *Páguese a la orden de*, pay to the order of. || *Poner en orden*, to put in order. || *Por orden de*, on the orders of, by order of. || *Por orden de aparición* or *de salida a escena*, in order of appearance. || *Por su orden*, in its turn, in its proper order. || *Real orden*, Order in Council. || *Sin orden ni concierto*, without rhyme or reason: *hablar sin orden ni concierto*, to talk without rhyme or reason; any old how (desordenado).
— OBSERV. The word *orden* is feminine when it means "command" and in its military and ecclesiastic senses.
ordenación f. Order, arrangement (disposición). || Ordering, arranging (acto de disponer). || Row (en el punto). || ARQ. Arrangement [of rooms, etc.]. || Grouping, arrangement (de las figuras en un cuadro). || REL. Ordination (de un sacerdote). || Development: *ordenación rural*, rural development. || — *Ordenación de los recursos de un país*, regional planning. || *Ordenación de pagos*, controller's office [in certain ministries].
ordenada f. MAT. Ordinate.
ordenadamente adv. In an orderly way, neatly.
ordenado, da adj. Ordered, in order, tidy (cosas). || Orderly, tidy (persona). || REL. Ordained, in holy orders.
ordenador, ra adj. Ordering. || REL. Ordaining.
— M. REL. Ordainer. || Computer (calculadora electrónica). || *Ordenador de pagos*, controller, payments officer [in certain ministries].
ordenamiento m. Ordinance (ordenanza). || Ordering, putting in order (de papeles, asuntos, etc.). || Tidying up: *el ordenamiento de una biblioteca*, the tidying up of a bookcase.

ordenancista adj. Strict, rigourous.
— M. y f. Disciplinarian, martinet.
ordenanza f. Ordinance (disposición). || Order, method (orden, método). || Order, command (mandato). || *Ordenanzas municipales*, bylaws, byelaws.
— M. MIL. Orderly (asistente). || Office boy (en oficinas).
ordenar v. tr. To order (mandar). || To put in order, to set in order: *ordenar unos papeles, sus asuntos*, to put some papers, one's affairs in order. || To tidy up, to set in order: *ordenar un armario*, to tidy up a cupboard. || To direct (encaminar): *ordenar los esfuerzos a*, to direct one's efforts towards. || REL. To ordain, to confer holy orders on. || — *Ordenar de diácono*, to ordain deacon. || *Ordenar en filas*, to line up, to marshal.
— V. pr. REL. To be *o* to become ordained, to take *o* to enter holy orders, to receive ordination.
ordeñador m. Milker.
ordeñadora f. Milkmaid (mujer). || Milking machine, milker (máquina).
ordeñar v. tr. To milk: *ordeñar una vaca*, to milk a cow. || To pick (las aceitunas).
ordeño m. Milking (de las vacas). || Picking [of olives].
¡órdiga! interj. FAM. *¡Anda la órdiga!*, blimey! [U.S., well, I'll be damned!]
ordinal adj. Ordinal: *adjetivos numerales ordinales*, ordinal numeral adjectives.
— M. Ordinal (number). || REL. Ordinal.
ordinariamente adv. Ordinarily, usually, as a rule (normalmente). || Rudely, coarsely (groseramente).
ordinariez f. Coarseness, vulgarity, rudeness (cualidad de grosero, vulgar). || Coarse *o* vulgar *o* rude thing (dicho grosero). || — *Decir ordinarieces*, to be rude. || *Es de una ordinariez*, he [*o* she] is awfully coarse. || *¡Qué ordinariez!*, how vulgar!
ordinario, ria adj. Ordinary, usual, common, normal (corriente). || Ordinary, mediocre (mediocre): *un trabajo muy ordinario*, a very ordinary piece of work. || Daily (diario). || Coarse, rude, vulgar (grosero): *una mujer ordinaria*, a coarse woman; *un chiste ordinario*, a coarse joke.
— M. Daily household expenses, *pl.* (gastos de casa). || Messenger (recadero). || Ordinary (obispo). || FIG. Coarse *o* uncouth *o* vulgar person. || — *De ordinario*, usually, ordinarily. || *Ordinario de la misa*, ordinary of the mass.
ordinariote, ta adj. FAM. Very common.
oréada o **oréade** f. MIT. Oread (ninfa).
orear v. tr. To air: *orear una camisa, un cuarto*, to air a shirt, a room.
— V. pr. To air, to be aired. || FIG. To get a breath of fresh air (airearse).
orégano m. BOT. Origan, oregano, marjoram. || FIG. *No todo el monte es orégano*, v. MONTE.
oreja f. Ear: *tener grandes orejas*, to have big ears; *orejas tiesas, gachas*, erect, drooping ears. || Flap (de zapato). || Tab (para meter una bota). || Handle (de vasija). || Wing (de sillón). || Palm, fluke (de ancla). || Mouldboard [U.S., moldboard] (del arado). || Claw (de martillo). || TECN. Lug. || — *Aguzar las orejas*, to prick up its ears (animal), to prick up one's ears (persona). || FIG. y FAM. *Apearse* or *salir por las orejas*, v. APEAR. || FIG. *Asomar* or *enseñar* or *descubrir la oreja*, to show one's true colours. | *Calentarle a uno las orejas*, v. CALENTAR. || FIG. *Con las orejas gachas*, crestfallen. || TAUR. *Cortar una oreja, dos orejas*, to win *o* to be awarded an ear, two ears [as a reward for a good performance]. || FIG. *Estar con* or *tener la mosca* or *la pulga detrás de la oreja*, to be suspicious *o* uneasy. | *Haberle visto las orejas al lobo*, to have had a narrow escape *o* a close shave. | *Hacer orejas de mercader*, to turn a deaf ear. | *Mojarle a uno la oreja*, to pick a quarrel with s.o., to provoke s.o. || *Oreja de abad*, pancake (tortita), Venus's navelwort (planta). || ZOOL. *Oreja marina* or *de mar*, sea ear, abalone. || FIG. *Ponerle a uno la mosca* or *la pulga detrás de la oreja*, to arouse s.o.'s suspicions, to make s.o. suspicious. | *Tirar de la oreja a Jorge*, to gamble. || *Tirar de las orejas a uno*, to pull s.o.'s ears. || FIG. y FAM. *Untar la oreja con saliva a uno*, to pick a quarrel with s.o. | *Verle a uno la oreja*, to see through s.o., to see s.o.'s true colours.
orejera f. Earflap (de gorra). || Earpiece, cheek piece (de casco de guerra). || Mouldboard [U.S., moldboard] (de arado). || Wing (de sillón). || Disc worn in the ear by certain Indians.
orejón m. Dried peach *o* apricot (melocotón o albaricoque). || HIST. Inca nobleman. || FAM. Big-ears (persona). || *Darle a uno un orejón*, to pull s.o.'s ear.
orejudo, da adj. Long-eared, lop-eared (animal). || Big-eared (persona).
— M. ZOOL. Long-eared bat (murciélago).
orejuela f. Handle (asa).
oreo m. Breeze, breath of wind (aire). || Airing (ventilación).
orfanato m. Orphanage (asilo de huérfanos).
orfandad f. Orphanhood, orphanage (estado de huérfano). || Orphan's allowance (pensión). || FIG. Forlornness, isolation.
orfebre m. Goldsmith, silversmith.
orfebrería f. Goldsmithery, silversmithing.
orfelinato m. Orphanage (orfanato).
— OBSERV. This is a Gallicism for *orfanato*.
Orfeo n. pr. m. Orpheus.
orfeón m. MÚS. Choral society.
orfeónico, ca adj. [Of a] choral society.
orfeonista m. Member of a choral society.
órfico, ca adj. Orphean, Orphic (de Orfeo). || Orphic (poesías, dogmas, etc.).
— F. pl. Orphic festivities.
organdí m. Organdie [U.S., organdy] (tela).
— OBSERV. The Spanish word *organdí* has two plural forms, *organdís* and *organdíes*.
orgánico, ca adj. Organic.
organigrama m. Chart.
organillero m. Organ-grinder.
organillo m. Barrel organ, hurdy-gurdy.
organismo m. Organism: *el organismo humano*, the human organism. || Organization (organización). || Body (institución). || *Los organismos especializados de la O.N.U.*, the specialized agencies of the U.N.
organista m. y f. MÚS. Organist.
organización f. Organization. || *Organización de las Naciones Unidas (O.N.U.)*, United Nations Organization [U.N.O., U.N.]
organizable adj. Organizable.
organizado, da adj. Organized.
organizador, ra adj. Organizing.
— M. y f. Organizer. || — M. BIOL. Organizer.
organizar v. tr. To organize.
— V. pr. To be organized: *se organizó una fiesta*, a party was organized. || To get organized (arreglarse). || — FIG. *Menudo escándalo se organizó*, there was a tidy rumpus. | *Se organizó una pelea*, a fight broke out.
órgano m. Organ: *los órganos de la digestión*, the digestive organs. || Body: *órgano legislativo*, legislative body. || MÚS. Organ (instrumento). || TECN. Part, member: *órgano de transmisión*, driving part; *órgano motor*, driving member. || FIG. Organ (medio o agente). || *Órgano de manubrio*, barrel organ.
organum m. MÚS. Organum.
orgasmo m. Orgasm.
orgía f. Orgy.
orgiástico, ca adj. Orgiastic.
orgullo m. Conceit, arrogance, haughtiness (arrogancia). || Pride (sentimiento legítimo). || FIG. Pride: *es el orgullo de la familia*, he is the pride of the family. || *No caber en sí de orgullo* or *reventar de orgullo*, to be bursting with pride.
orgulloso, sa adj. Proud, arrogant, haughty: *orgulloso de* or *por su riqueza*, proud of *o* arrogant *o* haughty about one's wealth. || Conceited (engreído). || Proud (legítimamente satisfecho): *estar orgulloso de su padre*, to be proud of one's father. || FIG. *Más orgulloso que don Rodrigo en la horca*, as proud as a peacock.
orientable adj. Turning (que gira). || Adjustable.
orientación f. Aspect, prospect, exposure (de un edificio). || Orientation, guidance, direction (dirección): *orientación por las estrellas*, orientation by the stars. || Pointing (de una aguja magnética, veleta, etc.). || Positioning (de un cañón, una antena, etc.). || FIG. Tendency (tendencia). || MAR. Trimming (acción), trim (efecto) [of sails]. || — *Con orientación al mediodía*, facing south, with a southern aspect. || *No me gusta la orientación que están tomando las cosas*, I don't like the way things are going. || *Orientación profesional*, vocational guidance.
orientador, ra m. y f. Adviser, counsellor (consejero). || Careers adviser (orientación profesional).
oriental adj. Oriental, eastern.
— M. y f. Oriental.
orientalismo m. Orientalism.
orientalista adj./s. Orientalist.
orientalizar v. tr. To orientalize.
— V. pr. To orientalize.
orientar v. tr. To orient, to orientate (un edificio). || To guide, to give directions to (a una persona). || To direct (dirigir). || To position: *orientar una antena, un cañón*, to position an aerial, a cannon. || FIG. To guide (guiar). || MAR. To trim [sails]. || *Casa orientada al sur*, house facing *o* looking south.
— V. pr. To orient o.s., to get *o* to find one's bearings: *orientarse con una brújula*, to orient o.s. with a compass. || To point: *la aguja de la brújula se orienta hacia el norte*, the compass needle points north. || To head, to make (*hacia*, for) [hacia un lugar]. || *Se orienta hacia la contabilidad*, he is going in for accountancy.
oriente m. East (punto cardinal). || East, Orient (países asiáticos). || East wind (viento). || Orient (de una perla). || FIG. Origin (origen). || — *Cercano* or *Próximo Oriente*, Near East. || *Extremo* or *Lejano Oriente*, Far East. || *Gran Oriente*, Grand Lodge (de la masonería). || *Oriente Medio*, Middle East.
orificación f. MED. Filling [of a tooth] with gold, aurification.
orificar v. tr. MED. To fill [a tooth] with gold.
orífice m. Goldsmith.
orificio m. Orifice. || TECN. Orifice, hole, opening. || — TECN. *Orificio de admisión*, inlet. | *Orificio de colada*, taphole, tapping hole, draw hole. | *Orificio de salida*, outlet.

oriflama f. HIST. Oriflamme. || Banner, standard, banderole (bandera).
origen m. Origin, beginning, start (principio). || Origin (procedencia): *una canción de origen español*, a song of Spanish origin. || Origin, extraction, birth (familia): *de humilde origen*, of humble origin. || Origin, cause, starting point (causa): *el origen de una disputa*, the origin of a dispute. || Origin, source, derivation (de una palabra, una costumbre, etc.). || — *Dar origen a*, to give rise to. || *Desde su origen*, from the beginning. || *En su origen*, originally, in the beginning. || *Tener su origen en*, to originate in *o* with *o* from.
original adj. Original (cuadro, texto, etc.). || Original, inventive, creative (escritor, etc.). || Original, novel (argumento de un libro, idea, etc.). || Odd, queer, singular (extraño). || Of origin: *país original*, country of origin. || — *Pecado original*, original sin. || CINEM. *Versión original*, original version.
— M. y f. Odd *o* singular character: *es un original*, he's an odd character. || — M. Original (texto, modelo, cuadro): *leer a Shakespeare en el original*, to read Shakespeare in the original. || IMPR. Manuscript.
originalidad f. Originality. || Oddness, strangeness, singularity (carácter excéntrico).
originalmente adv. Originally, from the beginning (originariamente). || Originally, with originality (de modo original). || Oddly, strangely, singularly (extrañamente).
originar v. tr. To originate, to give rise to, to cause, to start (causar).
— V. pr. To originate, to have its origin *o* source, to spring (proceder).
originariamente adv. Originally.
originario, ria adj. Original. || Originating, coming, native (que tiene su origen). || — *La costumbre es originaria de Escocia*, the custom originated in Scotland. || *Soy originario de Gales*, I come from Wales.
orilla f. Shore (del mar). || Bank (de un río): *en las orillas del Támesis*, on the banks of the Thames. || Side, edge, shore (de un lago). || Edge, side (de un camino, un bosque, un campo). || Rim (de un vaso). || Edge (de una mesa, etc.). || Selvedge, selvage, list (de una tela). || Fresh breeze (vientecillo). || — *A orillas de*, beside (al lado de). || *A orillas del mar*, at the seaside (lugar de veraneo), on the seashore *o* coast: *el faro está a orillas del mar*, the lighthouse is on the coast. || *La casita a orillas del lago*, the little lakeside house, the little house by the lake. || *Zaragoza está situado a orillas del Ebro*, Saragossa is on the Ebro.
orillar v. tr. To edge, to trim: *orillar con galón*, to edge with braid. || To selvedge (formar orillo en la tela). || To skirt, to go round (un bosque, un lago, etc.). || FIG. To get round, to surmount (una dificultad). | To wind up, to settle (un asunto). | To settle: *orillar una diferencia*, to settle a difference.
— V. intr. y pr. To reach the bank (de un río) *o* the shore (del mar).
orillo m. Selvedge, selvage, list [of cloth].
orín m. Rust. || — Pl. Urine, *sing.*
orina f. Urine.
orinal m. Chamber pot. || Bedpan (para enfermos).
orinar v. tr. e intr. To urinate.
— V. pr. To wet o.s.
Orinoco n. pr. m. GEOGR. Orinoco.
Orión m. ASTR. Orion.
oriundez f. Origin.
oriundo, da adj. Native, indigenous: *una planta oriunda de México*, a plant native to Mexico, a plant indigenous in Mexico. || From, native, originating: *persona oriunda de Escocia*, person from Scotland, person native of *o* originating from Scotland.
— M. y f. Native.
orla f. Border, edging, fringe (de una tela). || Ornamental border (de una página). || HERÁLD. Orle.
orladura f. Border, edging, fringe (de la tela). || Ornamental border (de una página).
orlar v. tr. To border, to edge, to trim. || To frame with an ornamental border (una página). || HERÁLD. To provide with an orle. || *Orlar con* or *de árboles*, to line with trees.
orlón m. Orlon (tela).
ornamentación f. Ornamentation, adornment.
ornamental adj. Ornamental.
ornamentar v. tr. To adorn, to ornament.
ornamento m. Ornament, adornment, embellishment (adorno). || ARQ. Ornament, ornamentation (conjunto de adornos). || FIG. Moral qualities, *pl.* || — Pl. REL. Ornaments.
ornar v. tr. To adorn, to embellish, to ornament. || *Ornado en sus más bellas galas*, decked out in all one's finery.
ornato m. ARQ. Ornament. || Ornamentation (arte *o* manera de adornar). || Adornment (adorno).
ornitología f. Ornithology.
ornitológico, ca adj. Ornithological.
ornitólogo m. Ornithologist.
ornitorrinco m. ZOOL. Ornithorhynchus, duckbill, platypus.
oro m. Gold: *un reloj de oro*, a gold watch; *dólar oro*, gold dollar. || — Pl. Spanish card suit bearing a representation of one or more gold coins [equivalent to diamonds]. || — FIG. *Apalear oro*, to be rolling in money. | *Comprar algo a peso de oro*, to pay a fortune for sth., to pay the earth for sth. | *Corazón de oro*, heart of gold. || *Chapado de oro*, gold-plated. || *De oro*, gold, golden. || *Fiebre del oro*, gold rush, gold fever. || FIG. *Guardar como oro en paño*, to treasure. | *Hacerse de oro*, to make a fortune. || *La Edad de Oro*, the Golden Age. || *Lavado del oro*, gold washing. || *Libro de oro*, visitor's book. || *Lingote de oro*, gold ingot *o* bar. || *Mina de oro*, gold mine. || FIG. *No es oro todo lo que reluce*, all that glitters is not gold. || *Oro batido*, beaten gold. || *Oro blanco*, white gold. || *Oro de ley*, fine gold. || *Oro en barras*, gold bars, bullion. || *Oro en hojas* or *en panes*, gold leaf. || *Oro en polvo*, gold dust. || *Oro molido*, ground gold. || FIG. *Oros son triunfos*, it's money that counts. || *Pan de oro*, gold leaf. || FIG. *Pedir el oro y el moro*, to ask the earth. | *Por todo el oro del mundo*, for all the money in the world. | *Prometer el oro y el moro*, to promise the earth, to promise the moon and stars. || *Regla de oro*, golden rule. || *Reserva de oro*, gold reserve. || FIG. *Ser una mina de oro*, to be a gold mine. | *Tener voz de oro*, to have a beautiful voice. || *Vajilla de oro*, gold plate. | *Valer su peso en oro* or *tanto oro como pesa*, V. PESO.
orogénesis f. GEOL. Orogenesis.
orogenia f. GEOL. Orogeny.
orogénico, ca adj. GEOL. Orogenic.
orografía f. Orography.
orográfico, ca adj. Orographic, orographical.
orometría f. Orometry.
orondo, da adj. Rounded (vasija). || FIG. y FAM. Puffed up with pride, self-satisfied (orgulloso). | Potbellied (gordo).
oropel m. Tinsel. || FIG. Tinsel, frippery (falsa apariencia). || *De oropel*, flashy.
oropéndola f. Oriole (ave).
oroya f. *Amer.* Cable basket.
orozuz m. Liquorice, licorice.
orquesta f. MÚS. Orchestra: *orquesta de cámara*, chamber orchestra. | Band: *orquesta de baile*, dance band. || *Director de orquesta*, conductor.
orquestación f. MÚS. Orchestration, scoring. || FIG. Orchestration.
orquestal adj. MÚS. Orchestral.
orquestar v. tr. To orchestrate, to score: *orquestar una composición*, to orchestrate a composition. || FIG. To orchestrate.
orquidáceas f. pl. BOT. Orchidaceae.
orquídeo, a adj. BOT. Orchidaceous.
— F. BOT. Orchid.
ortega f. Sandgrouse (ave).
ortiga f. Nettle (planta).
ortigal m. Nettle patch *o* field.
orto m. Rising [of sun or star].
ortocentro m. MAT. Orthocentre [U.S., orthocenter].
ortocromático, ca adj. Orthocromatic.
ortodoxia f. Orthodoxy.
ortodoxo, xa adj./s. Orthodox.
ortogénesis f. BIOL. Orthogenesis.
ortogenético, ca adj. BIOL. Orthogenetic.
ortognatismo m. Orthognathism.
ortogonal adj. MAT. Orthogonal.
ortografía f. Spelling, orthography: *cometer una falta de ortografía*, to make a spelling mistake. || ARQ. Orthography, orthographic projection.
ortografiar v. tr. To spell: *no saber ortografiar una palabra*, not to know how to spell a word.
ortográfico, ca adj. Spelling, orthographic, orthographical.
ortología f. Orthoepy.
ortopedia f. MED. Orthopaedics, orthopedics.
ortopédico, ca adj. Orthopaedic, orthopedic.
— M. y f. Orthopaedist, orthopedist.
ortopedista m. y f. Orthopaedist, orthopedist.
ortóptero, ra adj. ZOOL. Orthopterous.
— M. ZOOL. Orthopteran, orthopteron. || — Pl. ZOOL. Orthoptera.
ortótropo, pa adj. BOT. Orthotropic, orthotropous.
oruga f. ZOOL. Caterpillar. || BOT. Rocket (jaramago). || TECN. Caterpillar (de vehículo). || *Auto oruga*, caterpillar tractor, tracked vehicle.
orujo m. Marc [of grapes or olives].
orvallar v. impers. To drizzle.
orvallo m. Drizzle (llovizna).
orza f. Glazed earthenware jar (vasija). || MAR. Luffing (acción de orzar). | Centreboard [U.S., centerboard], sliding keel (pieza).
orzar v. intr. MAR. To luff.
orzuelo m. MED. Stye, sty. || Trap (trampa).
os pron. pers. 2.ª pers. pl. You, to you (dativo): *os digo*, I tell you, I say to you. || You (acusativo): *os vi ayer*, I saw you yesterday. || Yourselves, to yourselves (reflexivo): *vosotros os vestís*, you dress yourselves. || Each other, to each other (recíproco): *vosotros os escribís*, you write to each other. || *Os lo compré*, I bought it for you (para vosotros), I bought it from you (de vosotros).
— OBSERV. The enclitic use of this pronoun in the imperative causes the verb's final *d* to be dropped (*deteneos*, stop) except with the verb *ir* (*idos*, go away, leave).

osa f. She-bear. || — FAM. *¡Anda la osa!*, what a carry on! || ASTR. *Osa Mayor*, Great Bear, Ursa Major. | *Osa Menor*, Little Bear, Ursa Minor.
osadamente adv. Daringly, boldly, fearlessly. || Boldly, impudently, shamelessly (descaradamente).
osadía f. Daring, boldness, fearlessness. || Boldness, audacity, impudence, shamelessness (descaro).
osado, da adj. Daring, bold, fearless (valeroso). || Bold, impudent, shameless (atrevido, descarado).
osamenta f. Skeleton (esqueleto). || Bones, *pl.* (conjunto de huesos).
osar v. intr. To dare, to venture (atreverse).
osario m. Ossuary.
oscar m. Oscar (premio).
oscense adj./s. Huescan [Huesca, town in Spain, formerly *Osca*].
oscilación f. Oscillation. || Swinging (de péndulo). || Fluctuation (de precios). || FIG. Hesitation, wavering (vacilación).
oscilador m. FÍS. Oscillator.
oscilante adj. Oscillating.
oscilar v. intr. To oscillate. || To swing (el péndulo). || FIG. To oscillate, to fluctuate, to vary: *los precios oscilan*, prices fluctuate. || To oscillate, to waver, to hesitate (vacilar).
oscilatorio, ria adj. Oscillatory.
oscilógrafo m. FÍS. Oscillograph.
oscilograma m. Oscillogram.
osciloscopio m. FÍS. Oscilloscope.
ósculo m. Kiss: *ósculo de paz*, kiss of peace. || Osculum (en una esponja).
oscuramente adv. Obscurely.
oscurantismo m. Obscurantism.
oscurantista adj. Obscurantist.
— M. y f. Obscurantist, obscurant.
oscurecer* v. tr. To darken, to obscure, to dim. || To darken, to deepen (un color). || FIG. To obscure, to fog, to cloud, to obfuscate (volver poco inteligible). | To confuse (la mente). | To put in the shade, to overshadow (deslucir): *él oscurece a sus hermanos*, he puts his brothers in the shade. | To obscure, to conceal: *oscurecer la verdad*, to obscure the truth. || To tarnish (la reputación). || ARTES. To shade.
— V. intr. To get dark, to grow dark.
— V. pr. To darken, to grow dark, to cloud over (el cielo). || To grow dim (la vista). || FIG. To wane (la gloria, etc.).
oscurecimiento m. Darkening, clouding (del cielo). || Darkening, deepening (de un color). || Dimming (de la vista, la luz).
oscuridad f. Darkness (del cielo, de la noche). || FIG. Obscurity, lack of clarity (falta de claridad). | Obscurity: *vivir en la oscuridad*, to live in obscurity. || *Tener miedo a la oscuridad*, to be afraid of the dark.
oscuro, ra adj. Dark: *cueva oscura*, dark cave. || Dark (color): *llevar un traje oscuro*, to wear a dark suit; *gris oscuro*, dark grey [U.S., dark gray]. || Dark, gloomy, overcast (nublado). || Obscure, inconspicuous (poco conocido). || Obscure: *de origen oscuro*, of obscure origin. || FIG. Obscure, abstruse (difícil de comprender). | Gloomy, black: *el porvenir es muy oscuro*, the future is very gloomy. | Shady (sospechoso): *un asunto oscuro*, a shady business. || — *A oscuras*, in the dark. || FIG. *Llevar una vida oscura*, to be *o* to keep in the background. | *Oscuro como boca de lobo*, pitch-dark. | *Quedarse a oscuras*, to be left in the dark.
oseína f. ANAT. Ossein.
óseo, a adj. Osseous, bony: *tejido óseo*, osseous tissue. || Bone, of the bone (del hueso).
osera f. Bear's den.
osezno m. ZOOL. Bear cub.
osificación f. Ossification.
osificar v. tr. To ossify.
— V. pr. To ossify, to become ossified.
Osiris n. pr. m. MIT. Osiris.
osmanlí adj./s. Osmanli.
ósmico, ca adj. QUÍM. Osmic.
osmio m. Osmium (metal).
osmómetro m. FÍS. Osmometer.
ósmosis u **osmosis** f. FÍS. Osmosis.
osmótico, ca adj. Osmotic.
oso m. ZOOL. Bear: *oso blanco, negro, pardo*, polar, black, brown bear. || FIG. Ape, gorilla (hombre peludo o feo). | Lone wolf (persona insociable). || — FAM. *Hacer el oso*, to act the goat (hacer reír), to court (cortejar). || *Oso de felpa*, teddy bear (muñeco). || *Oso gris*, grizzly, grizzly bear. || *Oso hormiguero*, anteater. || *Oso lavador*, racoon [U.S., raccoon]. || *Oso marino*, fur seal. || *Oso marsupial*, koala, koala bear.
¡oste! interj. V. OXTE.
osteína f. QUÍM. Ostein, ossein.
osteítis f. MED. Osteitis.
ostensible adj. Obvious, patent, ostensible.
ostensivo, va adj. Ostensive, evident.
ostentación f. Ostentation, show, [vain] display. || — *Con ostentación*, ostentatiously. || *Hacer ostentación de*, to show off, to parade, to flaunt, to air: *hacer ostentación de sus riquezas*, to show off one's wealth; *hacer ostentación de su antimilitarismo*, to flaunt one's antimilitarism.
ostentador, ra adj. Ostentatious.
— M. y f. Ostentatious person, show-off.
ostentar v. tr. To show (mostrar). || To show off, to parade, to flaunt, to air: *ostentar sus riquezas, sus ideas revolucionarias*, to flaunt one's riches, one's revolutionary ideas. || To sport: *ostentar un sombrero nuevo*, to sport a new hat. || To show: *ostenta un gran talento de escritor*, he shows a great talent for writing. || To have, to hold (poseer): *ostentar un título de licenciado en ciencias*, to have a Bachelor of Science degree.
ostentativo, va adj. Ostentatious.
ostentatorio, ria adj. Ostentatious.
ostentoso, sa adj. Ostentatious.
osteoartritis f. MED. Osteoarthritis.
osteoblasto m. Osteoblast.
osteología f. Osteology.
osteológico, ca adj. Osteologic, osteological.
osteólogo, ga m. y f. Osteologist.
osteoma m. MED. Osteoma (tumor).
osteomielitis f. MED. Osteomyelitis.
osteópata m. y f. Osteopath.
osteopatía f. Osteopathy.
osteopático, ca adj. Osteopathic.
osteoplastia f. MED. Osteoplasty.
osteotomía f. MED. Osteotomy.
ostiario m. Ostiary, doorkeeper (clérigo).
ostión m. Large oyster (ostrón).
ostra f. Oyster (molusco).
ostracismo m. Ostracism. || *Condenar al ostracismo*, to ostracize.
ostral m. Oyster bed.
ostrero, ra adj. Oyster.
— M. y f. Oyster seller (vendedor). || — M. Oyster bed (ostral). || Oyster catcher (ave).
ostrícola adj. [Of] oyster culture. || *La industria ostrícola*, the oyster industry.
ostricultor m. Oyster producer.
ostricultura f. Oyster culture, ostreiculture.
ostrogodo, da adj. Ostrogothic.
— M. y f. Ostrogoth.
ostrón m. Large oyster.
osuno, na adj. Bear-like.
otalgia f. MED. Otalgia, earache.
otálgico, ca adj. Otalgic.
O.T.A.N. f. N.A.T.O. (Organización del Tratado del Atlántico Norte).
otaria f. ZOOL. Otary.
otario, ria adj. *Amer.* Silly, stupid, foolish (tonto).
oteador, ra m. y f. Lookout, watcher.
otear v. tr. To scan, to search: *otear el horizonte*, to scan the horizon. || To survey, to observe: *desde este monte oteo toda la llanura*, from this hill I can survey the whole plain. || To watch, to observe, to scrutinize (escudriñar).
Otelo n. pr. m. Othello.
otero m. Hillock, knoll (collado).
otitis f. MED. Otitis, inflammation of the ear.
otolaringología f. MED. Otolaryngology.
otología f. MED. Otology.
otólogo m. Otologist.
otomano, na adj./s. Ottoman.
— F. Ottoman (sofá).
otoñada f. Autumn.
otoñal adj. Autumnal, autumn, of autumn [U.S., fall, of *o* in the fall]: *la temporada otoñal*, the autumnal season; *una mañana otoñal*, one autumn morning.
otoñar v. intr. To spend the autumn. || To grow in autumn (la hierba).
otoñizo, za adj. V. OTOÑAL.
otoño m. Autumn [U.S., fall]: *en el otoño*, in autumn, in the fall. || Autumn aftermath (hierba). || FIG. Autumn: *en el otoño de la vida*, in the autumn of one's life.
otorgamiento m. Granting, concession: *el otorgamiento de un privilegio*, the granting of a privilege. || Authorization, consent, permission (permiso). || Awarding (de un premio). || Conferring (de poderes). || JUR. Deed of agreement, agreement, contract [drawn up before and authenticated by a notary].
otorgante adj. Granting (de privilegios, etc.). || Awarding (de un premio). || Conferring (de poderes).
otorgar v. tr. To grant, to give: *otorgar un indulto, la mano de su hija*, to grant pardon, one's daughter's hand. || To award (un premio). || To confer (poderes, honores, etc.). || JUR. To execute, to draw up [a deed in the presence of a notary]. | To make, to draw up (a will). || — *Nos ha otorgado su ayuda*, he has graced us with his assistance. || *Quien calla otorga*, V. CALLAR.
otorragia f. MED. Haemorrhage of the ear.
otorrinolaringología f. MED. Otorhinolaryngology.
otorrinolaringólogo m. MED. Otorhinolaryngologist.
otoscopio m. Otoscope.
otro, tra adj. Other: *¿leíste la otra novela?*, did you read the other novel?; *¿no comiste los otros pasteles?*, haven't you eaten the other cakes? || Another: *tengo otra hermana*, I have another sister; *lo haremos otro día*, we shall do it another day. || — *Al otro día*, [the *o* on the] next day, the following day, the day after. || *Con otras palabras*, in other words. || *Del otro lado de la calle*, on the other side of the street, across the street. || *El otro día*, the other day. || *De otro modo, de otra manera*, [in] another way; otherwise. || *En otra época*, in former times, in a bygone era. || *En otra ocasión*, on another occasion. || *En*

otra parte, somewhere else, elsewhere. || *En otro tiempo*, in former times, formerly. || *¿En qué otro sitio?*, where else? || *Entre otras cosas*, among *o* amongst other things. || *Es otro yo*, he is a second self *o* my alter ego. || *Esperamos tener una vida mejor en el otro mundo*, we hope that we will live better in the next world. || Fig. *Esto es otro cantar*, v. CANTAR. || *Los tiempos son otros*, times have changed. || *Ninguna otra cosa*, nothing else. || *Ninguna otra persona*, nobody else. || *No ha podido ir a otro sitio*, he could not go to any other place *o* anywhere else. || *Nos dieron otras dos mil pesetas*, they gave us another two thousand pesetas. || *Otra cosa*, something else (algo diferente), another thing (algo más). || *Otra persona*, somebody else. || *Otra vez*, again: *vendrá otra vez*, he will come again; *¡otra vez usted!*, you again! || *¡Otra vez!*, encore! (espectáculos). || *Otros tantos*, just as many, as many more. || *Por otra parte, por otro lado*, on the other hand. || *Vinieron otras muchas mujeres*, many other women came.
— Pron. Another [one]: *ésta es otra de mis hermanas*, this is another of my sisters; *ayer vino otro*, another one came yesterday; *hay uno para mí y otro para ti*, there is one for me and another for you. || Someone else, somebody else: *que lo haga otro*, let someone else do it. || — Pl. Others: *unos no sabían, otros no querían*, some did not know, others did not want to. || — *Algunos otros*, some others, a few others. || *Algún otro*, somebody else. || *Cualquier otro que*, anyone [else] but: *cualquier otro que tú lo hubiese aceptado*, anyone but you would have accepted it. || Fam. *¡Cuénteselo a otro!*, come off it!, pull the other leg!, tell it to the marines! || *El otro, la otra*, the other [one]: *este libro y el otro*, this book and the other. || *Entre otras*, among *o* amongst other things. || *Es una idea como otra cualquiera*, it is an idea. || *Hablar de esto y de lo otro*, to talk about this, that and the other, to talk about this and that. || *¡Hasta otra!*, see you again!, see you soon!, so long! || *Lo otro*, the other thing (cosa distinta), the rest (lo demás): *lo otro me da igual*, I don't care about the rest. || *Los otros, las otras*, the others, the other ones. || *Ningún otro*, nobody else. || *No fue otro que el director*, it was none other than the headmaster. || *¡Otra!*, encore! (espectáculos). || *Otro más*, one more, another one. || *Otro que tal*, another one. || *Otros dos*, another two, two more, two others. || *Otros muchos*, many others. || *Otros pocos*, a few others. || *Otros tantos*, just as many, as many more: *se marcharon veinte y otros tantos llegaron*, twenty left and just as many arrived. || *Otro tanto*, the same (lo mismo), as much again (el doble). || *Uno a otro, uno con otro, uno y otro*, v. UNO.
otrora adv. Formerly.
otrosí adv. Furthermore.
— M. Jur. Petition [made after the principal petition] (apartado de una exposición).
ova f. Alga.
ovación f. Ovation.
ovacionar v. tr. To give [s.o.] an ovation, to acclaim.
oval u **ovalado, da** adj. Oval, egg-shaped, oviform.
ovalar v. tr. To make oval, to oval.
ovalización f. Ovalization.
ovalizar v. tr. To ovalize, to oval, to make oval.
óvalo m. Oval.
ovar v. intr. To lay, to lay eggs (las aves).
ovárico, ca adj. Ovarian.
ovariectomía f. Med. Ovariectomy.
ovario m. Anat. y Bot. Ovary. || Arq. Moulding decorated with ova.
ovariotomía f. Med. Ovariotomy.
ovas f. pl. Spawn, *sing.*, roe, *sing.*, fish eggs (hueva).
oveja f. Ewe (hembra del carnero). || Sheep (carnero): *un rebaño de ovejas*, a flock of sheep. || *Amer.* Llama. || — Pl. Fig. Sheep. || — Fig. *Cada oveja con su pareja*, every Jack has his Jill. | *Contar ovejas*, to count sheep (para dormirse). | *Encomendar las ovejas al lobo*, to set the cat among the pigeons. | *Oveja descarriada*, lost sheep. | *Oveja negra*, black sheep.
ovejero, ra m. y f. Shepherd, shepherdess.
— Adj. *Perro ovejero*, sheepdog.
ovejuno, na adj. Sheep, sheep's. || *Ganado ovejuno*, sheep, *pl.*
overo, ra adj. Peach-coloured (caballo).
overtura f. Mús. Overture.
ovetense adj. [Of *o* from] Oviedo [town in Asturias].
— M. y f. Inhabitant *o* native of Oviedo.
Ovidio n. pr. m. Ovid.
óvidos m. pl. Zool. Ovidae.
oviducto m. Zool. Oviduct.
oviforme adj. Oviform.
ovillar v. tr. To roll *o* to wind into a ball.
— V. pr. To roll up into a ball, to curl up.
ovillejo m. Small ball (ovillo).
ovillo m. Ball (de hilo, de lana). || Pile, heap (montón). || — *Hacerse un ovillo*, to crouch down, to curl up (acurrucarse), to get all tangled up *o* muddled up (confundirse). || *Por el hilo se saca el ovillo*, by putting two and two together [one gets four].
ovino, na adj. Ovine. || *Ganado ovino*, sheep, *pl.*
— M. Sheep.
oviparidad f. Oviparity.
ovíparo, ra adj. Zool. Oviparous.
oviscapto m. Zool. Ovipositor.
ovni m. UFO, unidentified flying object.
ovo m. Arq. Ovum.
ovocito m. Biol. Oocyte.
ovoide adj./s.m. Ovoid.
óvolo m. Arq. Ovolo.
ovovivíparo adj. Zool. Ovoviviparous.
ovulación f. Ovulation.
ovular adj. Ovular.
ovular v. intr. To ovulate.
óvulo m. Bot. y Biol. Ovule.
oxácido m. Quím. Oxyacid.
oxálico, ca adj. Quím. Oxalic.
oxalidáceas f. pl. Bot. Oxalidaceae.
oxear v. tr. To shoo away.
oxford f. Oxford (tejido).
oxhídrico, ca adj. Quím. Oxyhydrogen: *soplete oxhídrico*, oxyhydrogen torch.
oxhidrilo m. Quím. Hydroxyl.
oxiacetilénico, ca adj. Oxyacetylene: *soplete oxiacetilénico*, oxyacetylene torch.
oxidable adj. Oxidizable, oxidable.
oxidación f. Oxidation. || Rusting (moho).
oxidado, da adj. Rusty (mohoso). || Oxidized.
oxidante adj. Oxidizing.
— M. Oxidizing agent, oxidant, oxidizer.
oxidar v. tr. To oxidize. || To rust (enmohecer).
— V. pr. To become oxidized, to oxidize. || To rust, to get rusty: *el cerrojo se ha oxidado*, the bolt has rusted.
óxido m. Quím. Oxide. || Rust (orín).
oxigenación f. Quím. Oxygenation.
oxigenado, da adj. Oxygenated. || Bleached, peroxided: *pelo oxigenado*, bleached hair. || *Agua oxigenada*, hydrogen peroxide, oxygenated water.
oxigenar v. tr. Quím. To oxigenate.
— V. pr. Fam. To get a breath of fresh air.
oxígeno m. Oxygen: *cámara de oxígeno*, oxigen tent.
oxigenoterapia f. Med. Oxygen treatment.
oxihemoglobina f. Biol. Oxyhemoglobin, oxyhaemoglobin.
oxítono, na adj./s.m. Gram. Oxytone.
oxiuro m. Oxyuris (lombriz).
oxoniense adj. Oxford, Oxonian, Oxfordian.
— M. y f. Oxonian, Oxfordian.
¡oxte! interj. Clear off!, shoo!, scat! || *Sin decir oxte ni moxte*, without [saying] a word.
oyente adj. Listening.
— M. y f. Hearer, listener. || Auditor (estudiante). || — Pl. Listeners (radio). || Audience, *sing.* (público).
ozonador u **ozonizador** m. Ozonizer, ozonator.
ozonar u **ozonificar** u **ozonizar** v. tr. To ozonize, to ozonate.
ozonización u **ozonificación** f. Ozonization, ozonation.
ozonizado, da adj. Ozonic.
ozono m. Quím. Ozone.
ozonómetro m. Quím. Ozonometer.
ozonosfera f. Ozonosphere.

P

p f. P: *una p minúscula*, a small p.
— OBSERV. The Spanish *p* is pronounced like the English *p*.

pabellón m. Pavilion (edificio): *el pabellón español en la feria de X*, the Spanish pavilion in the X fair. || Summerhouse (en el jardín). || Block [U.S., pavilion] (de un hospital, etc.). || Bell tent (tienda de campaña). || Flag, banner (bandera): *izar el pabellón nacional*, to hoist the national flag. || MAR. Flag, nationality. || Canopy (cortina de cama). || Hangings, *pl*, drapings, *pl.* (de trono, de altar, etc.). || MÚS. Bell (de un instrumento). || Horn (de fonógrafo). || HÉRALD. Pavilion. || MIL. Stack (de fusiles). || ANAT. External ear, outer ear, pavilion (de la oreja). || Pavilion (de una piedra preciosa). || — *Arriar pabellón*, to lower the flag. || *Pabellón de caza*, shooting box.

pabilo m. Wick (de vela).

Pablo n. pr. m. Paul.

pábulo m. Pabulum, food. || — FIG. *Dar pábulo a*, to encourage, to feed. | *Dar pábulo a las críticas*, to lay o.s. open to criticism, to expose o.s. to criticism.

paca f. ZOOL. Paca (roedor). || Bale (fardo): *una paca de algodón*, a bale of cotton.

pacana f. Pecan (árbol, fruto).

pacatería f. Prudery, prudishness (ñoñería). || Calmness, quietness (tranquilidad).

pacato, ta adj. Gentle, calm, quiet (tranquilo). | Prudish (ñoño).

pacay m. *Amer.* Pacay tree (árbol).
— OBSERV. Pl. *pacayes* or *pacaes.*

pacayar m. *Amer.* Plantation of pacay trees.

pacense adj. [Of *o* from] Béja [Portugal]. || [Of *o* from] Badajoz [Spain].
— M. y f. Inhabitant *o* native of Béja *o* of Badajoz.

paceño, ña adj. [Of *o* from] La Paz [Bolivia, Honduras and Salvador].
— M. y f. Inhabitant *o* native of La Paz.

pacer* v. intr. To pasture, to graze.
— V. tr. To pasture, to graze (apacentar). || To eat (comer). || To gnaw (roer).

paces f. pl. Peace, *sing.* (V. PAZ.)

paciencia f. Patience: *armarse de paciencia*, to muster one's patience; *todo se alcanza con paciencia*, everything is possible with [a little] patience. || Slowness (lentitud). || Almond cake (bollo). || — *Acabarle* or *consumirle a uno la paciencia*, to make s.o. lose patience, to try one's patience. || *Acabársele* or *agotársele a uno la paciencia*, to lose patience. || *Con paciencia se gana el cielo*, all things come to him who waits, slow and steady wins the race. || *Esperar con paciencia*, to wait patiently. || *Llevar* or *tomar algo con paciencia*, to take sth. calmly. || *Perder la paciencia*, to lose patience, to lose one's temper. || *Probarle a alguien la paciencia*, to try s.o.'s patience. || *Tener paciencia*, to have patience, to be patient (ser paciente), to wait patiently, to be patient (esperar). || *Tener perdida la paciencia* or *habérsele agotado a uno la paciencia*, to be at the end of one's tether.

paciente adj./s. Patient.

pacientemente adv. Patiently.

pacienzudo, da adj. Very patient.

pacificación f. Pacification. || FIG. Appeasement, pacification (apaciguamiento).

pacificador, ra adj. Pacifying.
— M. y f. Peacemaker.

pacificar v. tr. To pacify (un país). || FIG. To pacify, to calm (los ánimos). | To reconcile (las personas).
— V. pr. FIG. To calm down, to grow calm (calmarse).

pacífico, ca adj. Calm, peaceful. || Peaceful: *coexistencia pacífica*, peaceful coexistence. || Peaceable, peaceful, pacific (carácter).

Pacífico n. pr. m. Pacific. || *El océano Pacífico*, the Pacific Ocean.

pacifismo m. Pacifism.

pacifista adj./s. Pacifist.

pack m. Ice floe (banco de hielo). || Pack (rugby).

paco m. ZOOL. Alpaca, paco. || Sniper (guerrillero en Marruecos). || *Amer.* Paco (mineral de plata).

pacotilla f. Shoddy goods, *pl.*, trash (de poca calidad). || Goods (*pl.*) carried by seamen free of freight charges. || *De pacotilla*, shoddy, gimcrack, shoddily made (de poca calidad), gimcrack (joyas).

pacotillero m. Seller of shoddy goods. || *Amer.* Hawker, pedlar [U.S., peddler] (buhonero).

pactar v. intr. To make a pact, to come to an agreement. || FIG. *Pactar con el diablo*, to sell one's soul to the devil, to make a pact with the devil.
— V. tr. To agree upon *o* on *o* to.

pacto m. Pact, agreement: *pacto de no agresión*, nonaggresion pact.

pactolo m. FIG. Gold mine (fuente de riquezas).

pachá m. Pasha (bajá). || FIG. *Vivir como un pachá*, to live like a king.
— OBSERV. This word is a widely used Gallicism.

pachamama f. *Amer.* Earth.

pachamanca f. *Amer.* Meat roasted between hot stones. | FIG. Disorder.

pachanga f. *Amer.* Rowdy celebration (fiesta). | Mexican dance (baile).

pacholí m. Patchouli (planta y perfume).

pachón, ona adj. Basset (perro). || *Amer.* Hairy (peludo), woolly (lanudo).
— M. y f. Basset hound (perro). || — M. FAM. Phlegmatic fellow.

pachorra f. FAM. Sluggishness, indolence, slowness (indolencia). | Calmness (tranquilidad).

pachorrudo, da adj. FAM. Sluggish, slow, indolent (indolente). | Phlegmatic, calm (tranquilo).

pachucho, cha adj. Overripe (fruta). || FIG. Weak (débil). | Unwell, sickly, shaky (malucho). || FIG. *Estar pachucho*, to feel unwell, to be unwell.

pachulí m. Patchouli (planta y perfume).

paddock m. Paddock.

padecer* v. tr. To suffer, to suffer from: *padecer dolores de estómago*, to suffer from stomachache; *padecer hambre, frío*, to suffer from hunger, from cold; *los males que padecen*, the evils which they suffer. || To endure (aguantar): *padecer privaciones*, to endure privations. || To have, to suffer from (enfermedades): *padecer viruela*, to have smallpox. || FIG. To bear (soportar): *padecer castigo*, to bear a punishment; *padecer las impertinencias de uno*, to bear s.o.'s impertinence. | To suffer, to know (pasar): *padecer grandes desgracias*, to know great troubles. | To suffer (agravios o insultos). || *Padecer error*, to be mistaken, to be a victim of error.
— V. intr. To suffer: *padecimos mucho durante la epidemia*, we suffered greatly during the epidemic. || FIG. To suffer, to be hurt: *padecer en la honra*, to suffer in one's dignity. || — *Padecer de*, to suffer from: *padecer de los nervios*, to suffer from nerves. || *Padecer del corazón*, to suffer from heart trouble, to suffer with one's heart, to have a heart condition.

padecido, da adj. Suffered.

padecimiento m. Suffering (sufrimiento). || Ailment (enfermedad).

padrastro m. Stepfather (marido de la madre). || FIG. y FAM. Harsh father (padre severo). || FIG. Obstacle, impediment (estorbo). || MED. Hangnail (en las uñas).

padrazo m. FAM. Indulgent *o* easygoing father.

padre m. Father: *de padre a hijo*, from father to son. || Priest (sacerdote). || Father (religioso): *el padre Bartolomé de las Casas*, Father Bartolomé de las Casas; *sí, Padre*, yes, Father. || Male (macho). || FIG. Origin, mother. | Father, creator. || — Pl. Parents, father and mother: *sus padres son muy simpáticos*, his parents are very nice. || — FIG. *A padre ganador, hijo gastador*, a miserly father makes a lavish son. || FIG. y FAM. *Darle a uno una paliza de padre y muy señor mío*, to give s.o. a hell of a beating (pegarle fuerte). || *Dios Padre*, God the Father. || *El Padre Santo* or *El Santo Padre*, the Holy Father, the Pope. || *Los Santos Padres* or *los Padres de la Iglesia*, the Fathers of the Christian Church. || FIG. y FAM. *No lo entiende ni su padre*, it is absolutely incomprehensible. || *Padre conscripto*, conscript father (senador de Roma). || *Padre de almas*, priest. || *Padre de familia*, father. || *Padre de la patria*, Father of his country, founding father. || *Padre espiritual*, spiritual father. || *Padre Eterno*, Heavenly Father. || *Padre Nuestro*, Our Father, Lord's Prayer (oración). || *Padre nutricio*, foster father. || *Padre político*, father-in-law. || FIG. y FAM. *¡Que lo haga su padre!*, get someone else to do it! | *Saberlo como el Padre Nuestro*, v. SABER. | *Ser un padre para*, to be a father to.
— Adj. FAM. Terrific, huge, tremendous. || FIG. y FAM. *Llevarse un susto padre*, to be frightened out of one's wits, to get the fright of one's life. | *Pegarse* or *darse la vida padre*, to live like a king, to live it up. | *Tener un éxito padre*, to be a big hit.

padrear v. intr. To breed (engendrar).

padrenuestro m. Lord's Prayer, Our Father (oración). || FIG. y FAM. *En un padrenuestro*, in a wink of an eye, in no time at all.

padrinazgo m. Godfathership. || FIG. Protection, patronage, sponsorship.

padrino m. Godfather (de un niño). || Second (en un desafío). || Sponsor (que patrocina). || — Pl. Godparents. || — FIG. *El que no tiene padrinos, no se bautiza*, you cannot get anywhere without connections. || *Padrino de boda*, best man.

padrón m. Census (censo): *hacer el padrón*, to take a census. || Model, pattern (dechado). || Memorial, memorial pillar (columna conmemorativa). || FIG. Infamy, dishonour [U.S., dishonor]. || FAM. Indulgent *o* easy-going father (padrazo). || *Amer.* Stallion (semental).

paella f. Paella (dish made with rice, meat, seafood and several vegetables).

paflón m. ARQ. Soffit (sofita).

paga f. Pay, wages, *pl.* (sueldo): *cobrar la paga*, to receive one's wages; *hoja de paga*, pay slip. || Payment (pago). || Payer (pagador). || — *Día de paga*, payday. || *Paga extraordinaria*, extra pay.

pagable adj. Payable.

pagadero, ra adj. Payable: *pagadero a la vista, a plazos, al portador*, payable on *o* at sight, in instalments, to bearer.

pagado, da adj. Paid: *pagado por adelantado*, paid in advance. || Returned (sentimiento). || — *Asesino pagado*, hired assassin. || FIG. *Estamos pagados*, we are quits. || *Pagado de sí mismo*, self-satisfied.

pagador, ra adj. Paying.
— M. y f. Payer.

pagaduría f. Pay office. || *Depositaría-pagaduría*, disbursement office.

pagamiento m. Payment.

paganismo m. Paganism, heathenism.

paganizar v. tr. To paganize.
— V. intr. To become a pagan.

pagano, na adj./s. Pagan, heathen. || — M. FAM. Scapegoat, victim (víctima). | Payer (pagador). | One who pays: *siempre soy yo el pagano*, I'm always the one who pays.

pagar v. tr. To pay (una cantidad): *pagar al contado, por meses, a plazos, por adelantado*, to pay cash, monthly, in instalments, in advance. || To pay for: *¿cuánto pagaste tu vestido?*, how much did you pay for your dress? || FIG. To pay: *pagar las consecuencias*, to pay the consequences. | To pay for: *pagar cara una victoria*, to pay dearly for a victory; *pagar un crimen*, to pay for a crime. | To return (afecto): *pagar a uno su cariño*, to return s.o.'s affection. | To repay: *pagar con ingratitud*, to repay with ingratitude. || — *A pagar a la recepción*, cash on delivery. || *¡Dios se lo pague!*, God bless you! || FIG. y FAM. *El que la hace la paga*, one must face the music, one must face the consequences. || *Pagar a toca teja*, to pay cash down *o* cash. || *Pagar con su vida*, to pay with one's life. || FIG. *Pagar el daño* or *el pato* or *los vidrios rotos*, to carry the can. || *Pagar en especie*, to pay in kind. || FIG. *Pagar en* or *con la misma moneda*, to pay s.o. back in his own coin, to give s.o. a taste of his own medicine. || *Pagar en metálico* or *en efectivo*, to pay [in] cash. || *Pagar las culpas ajenas*, to pay for the sins of others. || *Un amor mal pagado*, unrequited love. || FAM. *¡Ya me las pagarás!* or *¡me las has de pagar!*, you shall pay for it!
— V. intr. To pay: *¿has pagado ya?*, have you paid yet?
— V. pr. To be paid. || To cost (costar): *la leche se paga a once pesetas el litro*, milk costs eleven pesetas a litre. || — FIG. *Pagarse de*, to be proud of (ufanarse). | *Pagarse de sí mismo*, to be full of o.s., to be conceited.

pagaré m. Promissory note, I.O.U.

pagaya f. Paddle (remo).

pagel m. Red sea bream (pez).

página f. Page: *en la página anterior*, on the previous page.

paginación f. Pagination, paging.

paginar v. tr. To page, to paginate.

pago m. Payment: *pago al contado*, cash payment; *hacer* or *efectuar un pago*, to make a payment. || Estate, property, lands, *pl.* (finca). || FIG. Retribution: *recibir el pago de sus malas acciones*, to receive retribution for ones evil deeds. | Return, payment: *en pago de*, in return for. | Price: *el pago de la gloria*, the price of fame. || *Amer.* Country (país), village (pueblo), area, region (zona). || — *En pago*, in payment (para pagar), in return (como recompensa). || *Mediante el pago de mil pesetas*, on payment of one thousand pesetas. || *Pago a cuenta*, payment on account. || *Pago adelantado* or *anticipado*, payment in advance, advance payment. || *Pago a plazos*, payment in instalments, deferred payment. || *Pago contra entrega*, cash on delivery. || *Pago de viñas*, region of vineyards. || *Amer. Pago en cuotas*, payment in instalments, deferred payment. || *Pago en especie*, payment in kind. || *Pago en metálico*, payment in [hard] cash. || *Pago inicial*, down payment.

pagoda f. Pagoda.

pagro m. Porgy (pez).

paguro m. Hermit crab (crustáceo). || Sea spider (araña de mar).

paila f. Frying pan (sartén).

paipai m. Fan (abanico).

pairar v. intr. MAR. To lie to.

pairo m. MAR. *Estar al pairo*, to be lying to.

país m. Country (nación): *país satélite*, satellite country. || Land, country: *país natal*, native land. || Cloth *o* paper backing (del abanico). || FIG. *En el país de los ciegos, el tuerto es rey*, v. CIEGO.

paisaje m. Countryside, landscape. || Cloth *o* paper backing (de abanico).

paisajista adj./s. Landscape painter.

paisana f. Country dance. || V. PAISANO.

paisanada f. *Amer.* Country people *o* folk, *pl.*, peasants, *pl.*

paisanaje m. Civilians, *pl.*, civil population (población civil). || State of being a compatriot *o* a fellow citizen.

paisano, na adj. Of the same region *o* country.
— M. y f. Compatriot, fellow countryman (hombre), fellow countrywoman (mujer) [del mismo país]: *un paisano mío*, a compatriot of mine. || *Amer.* Countryman (hombre), countrywoman (mujer), peasant (campesino). || *Es un paisano mío*, he is from my home *o* from my region (de la misma región). || — M. Civilian (por oposición a militar). || — *Ir de paisano*, to be wearing civilian clothes. || *Traje de paisano*, civilian clothes, *pl.*

Países Bajos n. pr. m. pl. GEOGR. Netherlands (Holanda).

— OBSERV. The name *Países Bajos* was given to the territories which were under Spain's dominion in the "Siglo de Oro" (Holland, Belgium and part of northern France). Nowadays it is the official Spanish name for the Netherlands.

PAÍSES, *m.* — COUNTRIES		HABITANTES, *m.* — INHABITANTS	
Abisinia *f.*	Abyssinia	*abisinios*	Abyssinians
Afganistán *m.*	Afghanistan	*afganos*	Afghans
África *f.*	Africa	*africanos*	Africans
África (*f.*) del Sur (Rep.)	South Africa (Rep.)	*sudafricanos*	South Africans
Albania *f.*	Albania	*albaneses*	Albanians
Alemania *f.*	Germany	*alemanes*	Germans
Alto Volta *m.*	Upper Volta	*altovoltaicos*	
América *f.*	America	*americanos*	Americans
Andorra *f.*	Andorra	*andorranos*	Andorrans
Antillas *f. pl.*	Antilles	*antillanos*	Antilleans
Arabia (*f.*) Saudita *or* Saudí	Saudi Arabia	*sauditas*	Saudi Arabians
Argentina *f.*	Argentina, the Argentine	*argentinos*	Argentines
Asia *f.*	Asia	*asiáticos*	Asians
Australia *f.*	Australia	*australianos*	Australians
Austria *f.*	Austria	*austriacos*	Austrians
Basutolandia *f.*	Basutoland		Basutos
Bélgica *f.*	Belgium	*belgas*	Belgians
Birmania *f.*	Burma	*birmanos*	Burmans, Burmese
Bolivia *f.*	Bolivia	*bolivianos*	Bolivians
Botswana *m.*	Botswana	*botswaneses*	
Brasil *m.*	Brazil	*brasileños, brasileros*	Brazilians
Bulgaria *f.*	Bulgaria	*búlgaros*	Bulgarians
Cambodia *f.*, Camboya *f.*	Cambodia	*camboyanos*	Cambodians
Camerún *m.*	Cameroun	*cameruneses*	Camerouns
Canadá *m.*	Canada	*canadienses*	Canadians
Ceilán *m.*	Ceylon	*cingaleses*	Ceylonese
Centroafricana (Rep.)	Central African Rep.	*centroafricanos*	Central Africans
Ciudad (*f.*) del Vaticano	Vatican City		
Colombia *f.*	Colombia	*colombianos*	Colombians
Congo *m.*	Congo	*congoleños*	Congolese
Corea *f.*	Korea	*coreanos*	Koreans
Costa (*f.*) de Marfil	Ivory Coast	*marfileños*	
Costa Rica *m.*	Costa Rica	*costarricenses*	Costa Ricans
Cuba *f.*	Cuba	*cubanos*	Cubans
Chad *m.*	Chad	*chadianos*	
Checoslovaquia *f.*	Czechoslovakia	*checoslovacos*	Czechs, Czechoslovaks
Chile *m.*	Chile	*chilenos*	Chileans
China *f.*	China	*chinos*	Chinese
Chipre *m.*	Cyprus	*chipriotas*	Cypriots
Dahomey *m.*	Dahomey	*dahomeyanos*	Dahomeans

Dinamarca *f.*	Denmark	*daneses, dinamarqueses*	Danes
Dominicana (Rep.)	Dominican Rep.	*dominicanos*	Dominicans
Ecuador *m.*	Ecuador	*ecuatorianos*	Ecuadorians
Egipto *m.*	Egypt	*egipcios*	Egyptians
El Salvador *m.*	El Salvador	*salvadoreños*	Salvadorans, Salvadorians
Escocia *f.*	Scotland	*escoceses*	Scotts, Scottish
España *f.*	Spain	*españoles*	Spanish, Spaniards
Estados (*m. pl.*) Unidos de América	United States of America	*norteamericanos, estadounidenses*	Americans
Etiopía *f.*	Ethiopia	*etíopes*	Ethiopians
Filipinas *f. pl.*	Philippines	*filipinos*	Filipinos
Finlandia *f.*	Finland	*finlandeses, fineses*	Finns
Francia *f.*	France	*franceses*	French
Gabón *m.*	Gabon	*gaboneses*	Gabonese
Gales (País [*m.*] de)	Wales	*galeses*	Welsh
Gambia *f.*	Gambia	*gambienses, gambianos*	Gambians
Ghana *f.*	Ghana	*ghaneses*	Ghanaians, Ghanians
Gran Bretaña *f.*	Great Britain	*británicos*	British
Grecia *f.*	Greece	*griegos*	Greeks
Guatemala *f.*	Guatemala	*guatemaltecos*	Guatemalans
Guinea *f.*	Guinea	*guineos*	Guineans
Haití *m.*	Haiti	*haitianos*	Haitians
Holanda *f.*	the Netherlands	*holandeses*	Dutch
Honduras *m.*	Honduras	*hondureños*	Hondurans
Hungría *f.*	Hungary	*húngaros*	Hungarians
India *f.*	India	*indios*	Indians
Indonesia *f.*	Indonesia	*indonesios*	Indonesians
Inglaterra *f.*	England	*ingleses*	English
Irán *m.*	Iran	*iraníes*	Iranians, Iranis
Irak *or* Iraq *m.*	Irak *o* Iraq	*iraqueses, iraquíes*	Irakians, Irakis
Irlanda *f.*	Ireland	*irlandeses*	Irish
Islandia *f.*	Iceland	*islandeses*	Icelanders
Israel *m.*	Israel	*israelíes*	Israelis
Italia *f.*	Italy	*italianos*	Italians
Jamaica *f.*	Jamaica	*jamaicanos*	Jamaicans
Japón *m.*	Japan	*japoneses*	Japanese
Jordania *f.*	Jordan	*jordanos*	Jordanians
Kenya *m.*, Kenia *m.*	Kenya	*kenianos*	Kenyans
Khmer *or* Kmer (Rep.)	Khmer Rep.	*kmer*	Khmer, Khmers
Kuwait *m.*, Koweit *m.*	Kuwait	*kuwaitíes*	Kuwaitis
Laos *m.*	Laos	*laosianos*	Laotians
Lesotho *m.*	Lesotho		
Líbano *m.*	Lebanon	*libaneses*	Lebanese
Liberia *f.*	Liberia	*liberianos*	Liberians
Libia *f.*	Libya	*libios*	Libyans
Luxemburgo *m.*	Luxembourg, Luxemburg	*luxemburgueses*	Luxembourgers, Luxemburgers
Madagascar *m.*	Madagascar	*malgaches*	Madagascans
Malasia *f.*	Malaya	*malayos*	Malayans
Malí *m.*	Mali	*malienses*	Malians
Malta *f.*	Malta	*malteses*	Maltese
Marruecos *m.*	Morocco	*marroquíes*	Moroccans
Mauritania *f.*	Mauritania	*mauritanos*	Mauritanians
Méjico *m.*, México *m.*	Mexico	*mejicanos, mexicanos*	Mexicans
Mónaco *m.*	Monaco	*monegascos*	Monegasques
Nepal *m.*	Nepal	*nepaleses*	Nepalis, Nepalese
Nicaragua *f.*	Nicaragua	*nicaragüenses*	Nicaraguans
Níger *m.*	Niger	*nigerinos*	
Nigeria *f.*	Nigeria	*nigerianos*	Nigerians
Noruega *f.*	Norway	*noruegos*	Norwegians
Nueva Zelanda *f.*	New Zealand	*neocelandeses*	New Zealanders
Oceanía *f.*	Oceania		Oceanian
Países (*m. pl.*) Bajos	Netherlands	*holandeses*	Dutch
Panamá *m.*	Panama	*panameños*	Panamanians
Paquistán *m.*, Pakistán *m.*	Pakistan	*paquistaníes*	Pakistanies
Paraguay *m.*	Paraguay	*paraguayos*	Paraguayans
Persia *f.*	Persia	*persas*	Persians
Perú *m.*	Peru	*peruanos*	Peruvians
Polonia *f.*	Poland	*polacos*	Poles, Polish
Portugal *m.*	Portugal	*portugueses*	Portuguese
Puerto Rico *m.*	Puerto Rico	*puertorriqueños*	Porto Ricans
Reino (*m.*) Unido de Gran Bretaña	United Kingdom of Great Britain	*británicos*	British
Rodesia *f.*, Rhodesia *f.*	Rhodesia	*rodesios*	Rhodesians
Ruanda *m.*	Rwanda	*ruandeses*	Rwandese
Rumania *f.*	Rumania, Roumania	*rumanos*	Rumanians, Roumanians
Rusia *f.*	Russia	*rusos*	Russians
San Marino (Rep. de)	San Marino	*sanmarinenses*	San Marinese
Senegal *m.*	Senegal	*senegaleses*	Senegalese
Siam *m.*	Siam	*siameses*	Siamese
Siria *f.*	Syria	*sirios*	Syrians
Somalia *f.*	Somalia	*somalíes*	Somalians
Sudán *m.*	Sudan	*sudaneses*	Sudanese
Suecia *f.*	Sweden	*suecos*	Swedes, Swedish
Suiza *f.*	Switzerland	*suizos*	Swiss
Tailandia *f.*	Thailand	*tailandeses*	Thais, Thailanders
Tanzania *f.*	Tanzania	*tanzanianos*	Tanzanians
Togo *m.*	Togo	*togoleses*	Togolese
Túnez *m.*	Tunisia	*tunecinos*	Tunisians
Turquía *f.*	Turkey	*turcos*	Turks, Turkish
Uganda *m.*	Uganda	*ugandeses*	Ugandans
Unión (*f.*) de Repúblicas Socialistas Soviéticas	Union of Soviet Socialist Republics	*soviéticos*	Soviets
Uruguay *m.*	Uruguay	*uruguayos*	Uruguayans
Venezuela *m.*	Venezuela	*venezolanos*	Venezuelans
Vietnam *m.*	Viet-Nam	*vietnamitas*	Vietnamese
Yemen *m.*	Yemen	*yemeníes*	Yemenis, Yemenites
Yugoslavia *f.*	Yugoslavia	*yugoslavos*	Yugoslavs, Yugoslavians
Zaire *m.*	Zaire	*zairenses*	Zairians
Zambia *f.*	Zambia	*zambianos*	Zambians

paja f. Straw: *paja centenaza*, rye straw. ‖ FIG. Rubbish, trash (nadería). | Padding, waffle (en un artículo). ‖ POP. Masturbation. ‖ *Amer.* Tap (grifo). ‖ — FIG. *A humo de pajas*, V. HUMO. ‖ *Choza de paja*, straw hut. ‖ *Echar pajas*, to draw straws (juego). ‖ FIG. *En un quítame allá esas pajas*, in the wink of an eye, in a jiffy. ‖ POP. *Hacerse una paja*, to masturbate. ‖ FIG. *Hombre de paja*, man of straw. | *Meter paja*, to fill out, to pad (en un artículo). ‖ *Patatas paja*, potato straws. ‖ FIG. *Por un quítame allá esas pajas*, for nothing, for no reason at all. ‖ *Techo de paja*, thatched roof. ‖ FIG. *Ver la paja en el ojo ajeno y no la viga en el propio*, to see the mote in another's eye and not the beam in one's own.

pajar m. Straw loft.

pájara f. (P.us.) Hen bird (pájaro). ‖ Kite (cometa). ‖ Paper bird (de papel). ‖ FIG. Sly woman (mujer astuta). | Wicked woman (mujer mala). ‖ FAM. *Pájara nocturna*, tart (ramera).

pajarera f. Bird cage, aviary (jaula).

pajarería f. Bird shop (tienda). ‖ Flock of birds (bandada).

pajarero, ra adj. Bird, of *o* pertaining to birds. ‖ FAM. Chirpy, merry, gay, happy (alegre). ‖ Gaudy (telas). ‖ Loud, gaudy (colores). ‖ Shy, skittish (caballo).

— M. Bird dealer (vendedor de pájaros). ‖ Bird catcher *o* hunter, fowler (cazador). ‖ *Enrique I el Pajarero*, Henry I the Fowler.

pajarilla f. Small bird. || Kite (cometa). || — FAM. *Abrasársele a uno las pajarillas*, to be boiling hot. | *Alegrársele a uno las pajarillas*, to be overjoyed.

pajarita f. Paper bird (de papel). || Kite (cometa). || — *Corbata de pajarita*, dickie bow, bow tie. || *Pajarita de las nieves*, wagtail (aguzanieves).

pajarito m. Small bird, nestling (ave). || — FIG. y FAM. *Comer como un pajarito*, not to eat enough to feed a sparrow. | *Me lo ha dicho el pajarito verde* or *me lo dijo un pajarito*, a little bird told me. | *Quedarse muerto como un pajarito*, to die peacefully.

pájaro m. Bird: *coger pájaros*, to catch birds. || FIG. Sly old fox, cunning bird, crafty devil (astuto). || — FIG. *A vista de pájaro*, from a bird's eye view. || FIG. *El pájaro voló*, the bird has flown. | *Más vale pájaro en mano que ciento volando*, a bird in the hand is worth two in the bush. | *Matar dos pájaros de un tiro*, to kill two birds with one stone. || *Pájaro bobo*, penguin (pingüino). || *Pájaro carpintero*, woodpecker. || FIG. y FAM. *Pájaro de cuenta* or *de cuidado*, nasty customer, nasty piece of work. || FIG. *Pájaro de mal agüero*, bird of ill omen. || FAM. *Pájaro gordo*, bigwig, big shot (pez gordo). || *Pájaro mosca*, hummingbird. || FIG. *Tener pájaros en la cabeza* or *tener la cabeza llena de pájaros* or *tener la cabeza a pájaros*, to have bats in the belfry (ser tonto), to be a scatterbrain (distraído).

— OBSERV. The word *pájaro* is applied to small birds; for larger birds the word *ave* is used.

pajarota o **pajarotada** f. FAM. Hoax, canard (noticia falsa).

pajarraco m. FAM. Ugly bird (pájaro grande y feo). || FIG. y FAM. Rogue, villain (persona).

pajaza f. Leftover straw.

paje m. Page. || MAR. Ship's boy, deck boy, cabin boy (grumete).

pajillero, ra m. y f. POP. Masturbator.

pajizo, za adj. Straw-coloured (color de paja). || Straw, of straw (de paja).

pajolero, ra adj. FAM. Damn, blasted, bloody (pop.), damned: *estoy harto de esta pajolera casa*, I'm fed up with this damn house. | Punctilious, fastidious (puntilloso).

pajón m. Coarse straw.

pajuela f. Sulphur match (para encender).

Pakistán n. pr. m. GEOGR. Pakistan.

pakistaní adj./s. Pakistani.

pala f. Shovel (instrumento). || Shovelful (contenido de la pala). || Bat [U.S., paddle] (del juego de ping-pong). || Bat (pelota y béisbol). || Racket (tenis). || Blade (de remo, de hélice, de la azada, etc.). || Paddle (de noria, para lavar, etc.). || Slice (de cocina). || Setting (de una sortija). || Spade (de jardinero, de niño). || Fleshing knife (de curtidores). || Vamp (del calzado). || Point (del cuello de una camisa). || BOT. Leaf (de chumbera). || Flat surface [of a tooth] (de un diente). || Incisor (incisivo del caballo). || Straight part [of epaulette] (de charretera). || [Hinge] blade (de bisagra). || — FAM. *A punta de pala* or *a punta pala*, in large quantity, a lot. || *Pala cargadora*, mechanical digger. || *Pala de zapador*, short-handled shovel. || *Pala mecánica*, power shovel.

palabra f. Word (vocablo): *una palabra española*, a Spanish word; *no decir palabra*, not to say a word. || Word: *me repitieron sus palabras*, they repeated his words to me. || Word (promesa): *hombre de palabra*, man of his word; *tener palabra* or *cumplir su palabra*, to keep one's word. || Speech, faculty of speech (don de hablar). || Right to speak (derecho de hablar en una asamblea). || Word (teología).

— Interj. On my honour!, I give you my word! (se lo aseguro), my word! (sorpresa).

— *Ahorrar palabras*, not to waste words. || *A buen entendedor, pocas palabras bastan*, a word to the wise is enough. || *Al decir, al oír estas palabras*, with *o* saying these words, [on] hearing these words. || *A palabras necias, oídos sordos*, I'll treat that remark with the contempt it deserves. || *Bajo palabra*, on one's honour. || *Cogerle a uno la palabra*, to take s.o. at his word. || *Comerse las palabras*, to swallow one's words, not to articulate (articular mal), to eat one's words (retirar lo dicho). || FIG. *Comprender* or *entender a medias palabras*, to read between the lines. || *Conceder la palabra a* or *dar la palabra a*, to call upon, to give the floor to (en una asamblea). || *Con medias palabras*, cryptically: *decir con medias palabras*, to say cryptically. || *Cortar la palabra*, to interrupt. || *Cumplir con su palabra*, to keep one's word. || *Dar palabra*, to give one's word. || *Decir la última palabra*, to have the last word. || *Decirle a uno cuatro palabras bien dichas*, to tell s.o. a thing or two. || *Decir una palabra al oído*, to whisper in s.o.'s ear. || *Dejar a uno con la palabra en la boca*, not to let s.o. speak. || *De palabra*, by word of mouth, orally. || *Dichas estas palabras* or *con estas palabras*, with these words. || *Dirigir la palabra a*, to address, to speak to. || *El delegado español tiene la palabra*, the Spanish delegate has the floor. || *Empeñar la palabra*, to give one's word. || *En cuatro palabras*, in [a] few words. || *En otras palabras*, in other words. || *En pocas palabras*, in brief (en un discurso). || *En toda la acepción* or *extensión de la palabra*, in every sense of the word. || *Entretener con buenas palabras*, to keep s.o.'s hopes up. || *En una palabra*, in a word, in short. || *Estar pendiente de las palabras de uno*, to be hanging on s.o.'s every word. || *Faltar a su palabra*, to break one's word, to go back on one's word. || *Gastar palabras*, to waste words. || *Gastar pocas palabras*, to speak concisely (ser conciso), not to be very talkative (ser poco hablador). || *Hablar a medias palabras*, to speak cryptically. || *Hacer uso de la palabra*, to speak, to take the floor, to address the meeting. || *Juego de palabras*, play on words, pun. || *Las palabras se las lleva el viento*, words are not binding [it is better to have a promise in writing]. || *Llevar la palabra*, to be the spokesman (ser el portavoz), to bear the word (de Cristo). || *Me basta con su palabra*, your word is good enough for me. || *Medir* or *sopesar las palabras*, to weigh one's words. || *Ni una palabra*, not a word. || *Ni una palabra más*, not another word. || *No entender palabra*, not to understand a single word. || *No saber ni una palabra de*, to know nothing whatsoever about (un asunto), not to know a single word of (un idioma). || *No tener palabra*, to be unreliable. || *Palabra clave*, key word. || *Palabra de doble sentido*, word with a double meaning. || *Palabra de honor*, word of honour. || *Palabra de matrimonio*, promise of marriage. || *Palabra por palabra*, word for word. || *Palabras al aire* or *al viento*, hot air. || *Palabras altisonantes* or *rimbombantes*, pompous *o* high-flown words. || *Palabras cruzadas*, crossword (crucigrama). || FIG. *Palabras del Evangelio*, Grospel truth. | *Palabras encubiertas*, cryptic words (medias palabras). || *Palabras históricas*, historical words. || *Palabras mayores*, strong words. || *Pedir la palabra*, to ask for the floor, to ask to speak. || *Pocas palabras pero buenas*, let us be brief but to the point. || *Quitarle a uno la palabra de la boca*, to take the words right out of s.o.'s mouth. || *Retiro mi palabra*, I withdraw what I said. || *Según las palabras de Cristo*, according to Christ's words. || *Ser de pocas palabras*, not to be very talkative. || *Sin decir una palabra*, without a word. || *Tener la palabra*, to speak (hablar), to have the floor (en una conferencia). || *Tener la última palabra*, to have the last word. || FIG. *Tener unas palabras con alguien*, to have a few words with s.o. || *Tomar la palabra*, to take the floor, to address the meeting. || *Tomarle a uno la palabra*, to take s.o. at his word. || *Tratar mal de palabra a uno*, to insult s.o.

palabrear v. intr. FAM. To chat.

palabreja f. Strange word.

palabreo m. Chatter.

palabrería f. o **palabrerío** m. FAM. Wordiness. || *Es pura palabrería*, it's just words.

palabrero, ra adj. Talkative (hablador). || Unreliable (poco formal).

— M. y f. Talkative person, chatterbox (charlatán). || Unreliable person (persona poco seria).

palabrita f. Pointed word. || *Le dije cuatro palabritas*, I told him a thing or two.

palabrota f. FAM. Swearword. || *Decir palabrotas*, to swear.

palacete m. Mansion, manor (casa particular). || Small palace.

palaciego, ga adj. Court: *vida palaciega*, court life. || Palatial (magnífico).

— M. y f. Courtier.

palacio m. Palace: *Palacio Real*, Royal Palace; *palacio episcopal*, episcopal palace. || Large mansion, palace (casa suntuosa). || — *El Palacio de Justicia*, the Law Courts, *pl.* || FIG. *Las cosas de palacio van despacio*, v. COSA. | *Palacio encantado*, enchanted castle.

palada f. Shovelful. || Stroke of an oar (golpe de remo).

paladar m. ANAT. Palate. || Taste (sabor). || FIG. Palate, taste (gusto). || FIG. *Tener el paladar delicado*, to have a delicate palate.

paladear v. tr. To taste, to relish, to savour.

paladeo m. Tasting, relishing, savouring (saboreo).

paladial adj./s.f. Palatal.

paladín m. Paladin. || FIG. Champion (defensor): *ser el paladín de la libertad*, to be the champion of freedom.

paladinamente adv. Openly, clearly.

paladino, na adj. Clear, obvious.

paladio m. Palladium (metal).

paladión m. Palladium (estatua de Palas). || FIG. Palladium (salvaguardia).

palafito m. Palafitte, lake dwelling.

palafrén m. Palfrey. || Servant's horse.

palafrenero m. Groom (mozo de caballos). || Equerry (de la casa real).

palanca f. Lever, crowbar. || TECN. Lever. || Handle (manecilla). || Hand brake (del freno). || Stockade (fortificación). || Springboard (trampolín). || FIG. Pull, influence (influencia). || — *Palanca de cambio*, gear stick, gear change [U.S., gearshift]. || *Palanca de mando*, control lever, control column. || *Palanca de mando del timón*, rudder bar. || *Salto de palanca*, high diving (deporte), high dive (cada salto).

palangana f. Washbasin (jofaina). || — M. *Amer.* FAM. Show-off, braggart (fanfarrón). | Cheeky devil (descarado).

palanganada f. *Amer.* FAM. Bragging (fanfarronada).

palanganear f. *Amer.* FAM. To brag (fanfarronear).

palanganero m. Washstand.
palangre m. MAR. Boulter.
palanquear v. tr. *Amer.* To lever.
palanquera f. Stockade (empalizada).
palanqueta f. Crowbar, small lever (palanca pequeña). || Jemmy [U.S., jimmy], crowbar (para forzar puertas). || MAR. Bar shot.
Palas n. pr. f. Pallas.
palastro m. Sheet iron (chapa de hierro). || Steel plate (de acero). || Plate (de cerradura).
palatal adj./s.f. GRAM. Palatal.
palatalización f. GRAM. Palatalization.
palatalizar v. tr. GRAM. To palatalize.
Palatinado n. pr. m. GEOGR. Palatinate.
palatino, na adj. Court (de palacio). || Palatine (del Palatinado). || ANAT. Of the palate, palatal, palatine. || ANAT. *Bóveda palatina*, roof of the mouth, palate.
— M. y f. Palatine.
palco m. Box (espectáculo): *palco principal*, first-tier box. || — TEATR. *Palco de platea*, ground-floor box. | *Palco de proscenio*, stage *o* proscenium box.
palear v. tr. To shovel.
palenque m. Arena (recinto). || Palisade, fence (empalizada). || *Amer.* Hitching post (para atar animales). || — FIG. *Palenque político*, political arena. | *Salir al palenque*, to enter the arena *o* the fray.
paleo m. Shovelling.
paleogeografía f. Paleogeography.
paleografía f. Paleography.
paleográfico, ca adj. Paleographic.
paleógrafo m. Paleographer.
paleolítico, ca adj. Paleolithic.
paleólogo m. Paleologist.
Paleólogo n. pr. Paleologus.
paleontología f. Paleontology.
paleontológico, ca adj. Paleontologic.
paleontólogo m. Paleontologist.
paleozoico, ca adj./s.m. Paleozoic.
palermitano, na adj./n. Palermitan.
Palestina n. pr. f. GEOGR. Palestine.
palestino, na adj./s. Palestinian.
palestra f. FIG. Arena: *la palestra parlamentaria*, the parliamentary arena. || FIG. *Salir* or *saltar a la palestra*, to enter the fray *o* the arena.
paleta f. Small shovel. || Pastry slice (para dulces). || Palette (de pintor). || Trowel (palustre). || Front tooth (diente). || Slice (de cocina). || Bat (de criquet). || Pallet (de reloj). || Paddle (de noria). || Blade (de ventilador, de hélice, etc.). || Blade (de remo). || Coal shovel (badila). || ANAT. Shoulder blade. || Bat [U.S., paddle] (de ping-pong). || MAR. Blade. || TECN. Pallet (de carretilla). || FIG. Scale of colours, palette.
paletada f. Shovelful (contenido de la pala). || Trowelful (contenido de la llana). || Blow with a shovel *o* a trowel (golpe). || FAM. Blunder (necedad). || — FIG. y FAM. *A paletadas*, heaps of, loads of: *había pasteles a paletadas*, there were heaps of cakes. | *En dos paletadas*, in a wink of an eye, in two ticks, in a thrice.
paletazo m. Glancing blow (del toro): *el toro le dio un paletazo*, the bull's horn caught him a glancing blow.
paletear v. intr. To thrash about with the oars, to row ineffectively.
paleteo m. Thrashing of the oars.
paletilla f. ANAT. Shoulder blade (omoplato). | Sternum cartilage. || Shoulder (en carnicería): *paletilla de cordero*, shoulder of mutton. || Shoulder blade (del ganado). || Candlestick (palmatoria).
paleto, ta adj. FAM. Peasant, boorish.
— M. y f. FAM. Country bumpkin, peasant, yokel.
paletó m. (P.us.). Coat, greatcoat.
paletón m. Bit (de llave). || Front tooth (diente).
paliación f. Palliation.
paliadamente adv. Secretly, in secret.
paliar v. tr. To palliate.
paliativo, va adj./s.m. Palliative.
palidecer* v. intr. To turn pale, to pale: *hacer palidecer a alguien*, to cause s.o. to turn pale. || To fade, to grow pale (colores). || To wane (el día). || To grow dim (la luz). || FIG. To be on the wane: *la fama de este artista está palideciendo*, this artist's fame is on the wane.
— V. tr. To make pale.
palidez f. Paleness, pallidness (de una persona). || Paleness, pallor (de la tez). || Wanness (de la luna).
pálido, da adj. Pale: *ponerse muy pálido*, to turn very pale. || Pale, light (color). || — *Estilo pálido*, colourless style. || FIG. *Rostro pálido*, paleface.
paliducho, cha adj. FAM. Palish, pale.
palier m. TECN. Bearing.
palillero m. Penholder (portaplumas).
palillo m. Small stick. || Toothpick (mondadientes). || Spindle (de encajera). || Needle holder (para las agujas). || Drumstick (de tambor). || Thin loaf (de pan). || Stem (de tabaco). || Stalk (de uva). || Spoon tool (de los escultores). || — Pl. Chopsticks: *los chinos comen con palillos*, the Chinese eat with chopsticks. || Pins (del billar). || FAM. Banderillas. || Castanets (castañuelas). || — FAM. *Estar hecho un palillo*, to be as thin as a rake. | *Tocar todos los palillos*, to try all possible avenues. | *Unas piernas como palillos*, legs like matchsticks.

palimpsesto m. Palimpsest.
palíndromo, ma adj. Palindromic.
— M. Palindrome.
palingenesia f. Palingenesis.
palinodia f. Palinode. || FIG. y FAM. *Cantar la palinodia*, to recant, to retract.
palio m. Pallium (manto griego). || Pallium (pontifical). || Canopy, baldachin (dosel). || HERÁLD. Pall (perla). || — *Bajo palio*, under a canopy. || FIG. *Recibir con palio* or *bajo palio*, to receive with great pomp.
palique m. FAM. Chat. || — FAM. *Dar palique a*, to chat to *o* with. | *Estar de palique*, to be chatting.
paliquear v. intr. FAM. To chat.
palisandro m. Rosewood (árbol, madera).
palista m. Pelota player (pelota vasca).
palito m. Small stick. || *Amer.* FAM. *Pisar el palito*, to fall into the trap.
palitoque o **palitroque** m. Stick (palo). || Banderilla (de toros). || Stroke (escritura).
paliza f. Beating, hiding, thrashing: *darle a uno una paliza*, to give s.o. a hiding. || — FIG. y FAM. *La excursión fue una paliza*, the trip was exhausting. | *Le espera una paliza en casa*, he's for it when he gets home. | *Les pegamos una paliza*, we thrashed them, we beat them hollow (un equipo a otro).
palizada f. Palisade, fence (valla). || Enclosure (sitio cercado).
palma f. Palm tree, palm (árbol). || Palm leaf (hoja). || Date palm, date tree (datilera). || Palm (de la mano). || Sole (de la pata del caballo). || Palm [piece] (de un guante). || FIG. Palm (símbolo de triunfo). || — Pl. Applause, *sing.* (aplausos), clapping, *sing.* (para marcar el ritmo), slow handclapping, *sing.* (como desaprobación). || — *Batir* or *dar palmas*, to clap [one's hands], to applaud. || *Conocer como la palma de la mano*, to know like the back *o* the palm of one's hand. || FIG. y FAM. *Llevarse la palma*, to carry off the palm (triunfar), to take the cake (en sentido irónico). || *Palma datilera*, date palm, date tree. || *Palma de abanico*, palmyra. || *Palma indiana*, coconut palm. || *Palmas de tango*, rhythmic clapping, *sing.* || FIG. y FAM. *Ser liso como la palma de la mano*, to be as flat as a pankake. | *Traer en palmas a uno*, to pamper s.o.
palmada f. Slap (golpe con la palma de la mano). || Clapping (para llamar). || — Pl. Applause, *sing.* (aplauso), clapping, *sing.* (para marcar el ritmo). || — *Dar palmadas*, to clap [one's hands]. || *Darse una palmada en la frente*, to tap one's forehead.
palmadita f. Tap. || *Dar una palmadita en el hombro*, to tap on the shoulder.
palmar adj. ANAT. Palmar: *músculo palmar*, palmar muscle. || FIG. Obvious, clear, evident (evidente). || One span long (longitud).
— M. Palm grove (sitio). || TECN. Card, teasel (cardencha). || FAM. *Más viejo que un palmar*, as old as Methuselah, as old as the hills.
palmar v. intr. FAM. To kick the bucket, to snuff it (morir).
palmarés m. Service record (historial).
palmario, ria adj. Obvious: *error palmario*, obvious mistake.
palmatoria f. Cane, palmer (de maestro). || Candlestick (de una vela).
palmeado, da adj. Palmate, palm shaped (de forma de palma). || Palmate, webbed (ligado por una membrana). || *Pata palmeada*, webfoot, webbed foot.
palmear v. intr. To applaud, to clap [one's hands].
palmeo m. Measuring by palms *o* spans.
palmer m. Micrometer calliper *o* caliper.
palmera f. Palm tree (árbol). || Palm leaf (hoja). || Date palm, date tree (datilera). || Palm cake (galleta). || *Palmera datilera*, date palm, date tree.
palmeral m. Palm grove.
palmero m. *Amer.* Palm tree (árbol).
palmeta f. Cane (de los maestros). || Caning (castigo).
palmetazo m. Caning (golpe con la palmeta). || Slap (bofetada).
palmiche o **palmicho** m. Royal palm (árbol). || || Fruit of the royal palm (fruto).
palmípedo, da adj. Palmiped, web-footed.
— M. Palmiped, web-footed animal.
palmista f. *Amer.* Palmist (quiromántica).
palmita f. Palm marrow (médula). || FIG. *Llevar* or *traer* or *tener en palmitas a alguien*, to pamper s.o., to wait on s.o. hand and foot.
palmito m. BOT. Palmetto (árbol). || Palm heart (tallo comestible). || FIG. y FAM. Little face (cara): *buen palmito*, pretty little face. | Good looks, *pl.* (aspecto). || FIG. y FAM. *Tener un buen palmito*, to be good-looking.
palmo m. Span, palm (medida). || — FIG. y FAM. *Con un palmo de lengua (fuera)*, panting. || FIG. *Conocer palmo a palmo*, to know like the back of one's hand. | *Cristóbal crece a palmos*, you can almost see Christopher growing. | *Dejar con un palmo de narices*, to let s.o. down. | *Hacer un palmo de narices*, to thumb one's nose, to cock a snook. || *Palmo a palmo*, step by step, inch by inch. || FIG. *Palmo de tierra*, small plot of land (espacio pequeño). | *Quedarse con un palmo* or *dos palmos de narices*, to be out of luck.

palmotear v. intr. To clap [one's hands], to applaud (aplaudir).
palmoteo m. Applause, clapping (aplauso).
palo m. Stick: *esgrimía un palo*, he was brandishing a stick. || Stick (trozo de madera). || Staff, pole (grande, para andar o defenderse). || Wood (madera). || Blow with a stick (golpe). || Handle (mango): *palo de una escoba*, handle of a broom. || FAM. Banderilla (toros). || MAR. Mast (mástil). || Pole (vara). || Pin (para jugar al billar). || Shot (jugada en el billar). || Gallows, *pl.* (suplicio). || Suit [in cards]: *jugar del mismo palo*, to follow suit. || Stroke (de una letra). || HERÁLD. Pale. || Stalk (del fruto). || Perch (en un gallinero). || Club (para jugar al golf). || Stake (estaca). || *Amer.* Tree (árbol). | Gulp (trago). || — *Amer. A medio palo*, half-finished. || FIG. *Andar a palos*, to be always quarrelling. || *A palos*, with a stick (con un palo). || FIG. *A palo seco*, v. SECO. | *Cáersele a uno los palos del sombrajo*, to be discouraged. | *Dar (de) palos*, to beat. | *Dar palos de ciego*, to lash out wildly (golpear sin cuidado), to grope about in the dark (tantear). || FIG. y FAM. *Dar un palo*, to pull to pieces, to slate (criticar), to charge the earth: *en este restaurante te dan un palo*, in this restaurant they charge the earth; to be a blow to: *esta reforma ha dado un palo a la agricultura*, this reform has been a blow to agriculture. || *De palo*, wooden: *pierna de palo*, wooden leg; *cuchara de palo*, wooden spoon. || FIG. *De tal palo tal astilla*, v. ASTILLA. | *Estar hecho un palo*, to be as thin as a rake. || FIG. y FAM. *Moler a palos*, to beat black and blue, to beat up. || *Palo brasil*, brazilwood. || *Palo campeche*, camwood. || *Amer. Palo de agua*, downpour (chaparrón). || *Palo de escoba*, broomstick, broom handle. || *Palo de jabón*, quillai, soapbark. || MAR. *Palo de mesana*, mizzenmast. || *Palo de Pernambuco*, Pernambuco wood. || *Palo de rosa*, rosewood. || MAR. *Palo de trinquete*, foremast. || *Palo dulce*, liquorice root. || *Amer. Palo ensebado*, greasy pole (cucaña). || MAR. *Palo mayor*, mainmast. || *Palo santo*, lignum vitae (*palo santo* es barbarismo en el sentido de *palisandro*). || FIG. y FAM. *Ser más tieso que el palo de una escoba*, to be as stiff as a board. || *Amer.* FIG. *Ser un palo*, to be remarkable.
paloduz m. Liquorice root.
paloma f. Pigeon, dove. || Dove: *la paloma de la paz*, the dove of peace. || FIG. Lamb (persona bondadosa). | Pure woman (mujer pura). || FAM. Anisette with water (bebida). || MAR. Sling of a yard. || — Pl. Whitecaps, white horses (olas pequeñas). || — *Paloma buchona*, pouter. || *Paloma casera*, domestic pigeon. || *Paloma de moño*, crested pigeon. || *Paloma mensajera*, carrier pigeon, homing pigeon, homer. || *Paloma silvestre*, wild pigeon. || *Paloma torcaz*, ringdove, wood pigeon. || *Paloma zurita*, rock pigeon, rock dove (de color apizarrado), ringdove, wood pigeon (torcaz).
palomar m. Dovecote, pigeon house, pigeon loft.
palometa f. Butterfly nut, wing nut (tuerca).
palomilla f. Grain moth (polilla). || Small butterfly (mariposa). || ZOOL. Nymph, chrysalis. || Back (del caballo). || Wing nut, butterfly nut (tuerca). || *Amer.* FAM. Rabble, mob (gente). || — Pl. Whitecaps, white horses (del mar).
palomino m. Young pigeon *o* dove (pájaro). || Stain on a shirttail (mancha). || *Amer.* White horse (caballo). || FIG. *Un palomino atontado*, a silly fool.
palomita f. Popcorn (roseta). || Anisette and water (anís con agua). || *Amer.* Darling, love (amor). || *Cuello de palomita*, wing collar.
palomo m. [Cock] pigeon. || FAM. Fool, idiot (necio).
palotazo m. TAUR. Glancing blow (paletazo).
palote m. Small stick. || Pothook (para aprender a escribir). || *Amer.* Rolling pin (de cocina).
palpabilidad f. Palpability.
palpable adj. Palpable.
palpablemente adv. Palpably: *la producción ha aumentado palpablemente*, production has increased palpably.
palpación f. Palpation, touching, feeling.
palpador m. TECN. Testing spike.
palpadura f. o **palpamiento** m. Palpation, touching, feeling.
palpar v. tr. To palpate, to feel, to touch (tocar). || FIG. To feel, to appreciate: *ahora palpa los efectos de su pereza*, he is now feeling the effects of his laziness.
— V. pr. To grope (a oscuras). || FIG. To be felt (percibirse): *se palpaba el malestar en toda la oficina*, unease was felt throughout the office.
palpitación f. Palpitation, throbbing, throb (del corazón): *tener palpitaciones*, to suffer from palpitations.
palpitante adj. Throbbing, palpitating: *con el corazón palpitante*, with a throbbing heart. || FIG. Trembling: *palpitante de júbilo*, trembling with joy. | Burning (candente).
palpitar v. intr. To palpitate, to throb. || To palpitate, to beat (latir).
pálpito m. *Amer.* Presentiment, hunch, feeling, foreboding (corazonada).
palta f. *Amer.* Avocado pear (aguacate).
palto m. *Amer.* Avocado (árbol).
palúdico, ca adj. MED. Malarial. || Marshy, swampy (pantanoso). || *Fiebre palúdica*, malaria.
— M. y f. Person suffering from malaria.
paludismo m. MED. Malaria.
palurdo, da adj. FAM. Boorish, peasant.
— M. y f. FAM. Boor, peasant, yokel, country bumpkin.
palustre m. Trowel (llana de albañil).
— Adj. Boggy, marshy (de un pantano).
pallador m. *Amer.* V. PAYADOR.
pallar m. *Amer.* Haricot bean (judía).
pallar v. tr. MIN. To sort [ore].
pamela f. Broad-brimmed hat (sombrero).
pamema f. FAM. Fuss (aspaviento). | Rubbish, nonsense (tontería). | Trifle (cosa insignificante). | Flattery (halago). || FAM. *Déjate de pamemas*, stop your fussing.
pampa f. Pampas, *pl.* (llanura). || — M. y f. Pampean Indian (indio).
— Adj. *Amer.* Of *o* from the pampas, pampean: *indio pampa*, Indian from the pampas. | With a white head (animal). | Dishonest (negocio). || — *Amer. A la pampa*, in the open air, under the stars. | *Estar en sus pampas*, to be at one's ease. | *Quedar en pampa*, to be disappointed.
pámpana f. Vine leaf (hoja de viña).
pámpano m. Tendril, vine shoot (zarcillo de la vid). || Vine leaf (pámpana). || Salp (pez).
pampanoso, sa adj. With many tendrils.
pampeano, na adj. *Amer.* Of *o* from the pampas, pampean.
— M. y f. Inhabitant *o* native of the pampas, pampean.
pampear v. intr. *Amer.* To travel across *o* through the pampas.
pamperada f. *Amer.* Season when the west wind blows.
pampero, ra adj. Of *o* from the pampas, pampean.
— M. y f. Inhabitant *o* native of the pampas, pampean. || — M. Strong west wind blowing across the pampas.
pampino, na adj. *Amer.* V. PAMPERO.
pampirolada f. Sauce made from bread and garlic. || FIG. y FAM. Nonsense, rubbish (necedad).
pamplina f. Chickweed (planta). || FIG. y FAM. Rubbish, nonsense, piffle (necedad): *déjeme de pamplinas*, stop talking nonsense; *¡basta de pamplinas!*, that's enough rubbish! | Trifle (cosa sin importancia). || *Pamplina de agua*, brookweed.
pamplinada o **pamplinería** f. FAM. Rubbish, nonsense.
pamplinero, ra o **pamplinoso, sa** adj. Stupid, foolish, silly.
Pamplona n. pr. GEOGR. Pamplona (Navarra).
pamplonés, esa o **pamplonica** adj. [Of *o* from] Pamplona.
— M. y f. Inhabitant *o* native of Pamplona.
pamporcino m. BOT. Cyclamen, sowbread.
pan m. Bread: *pedazo de pan*, piece of bread; *pan con mantequilla*, bread and butter. || Loaf [of bread] (barra). || Bar, cake (de jabón, de sal). || Dough (para empanadas). || FIG. Wheat [U.S., corn] (trigo). || Loaf (masa): *pan de higo*, fig loaf. || Leaf [of hammered gold or silver]. || FIG. Living, bread: *ganarse el pan*, to earn one's living. || — FIG. *A falta de pan buenas son tortas*, half a loaf is better than none. || *Árbol del pan*, breadfruit tree. || FIG. *Cara de pan mascado*, wan *o* pasty face. || FAM. *Con su pan se lo coma*, good luck to him. || FIG. *Contigo pan y cebolla*, we can *o* we shall live on love. || *El pan nuestro de cada día*, our daily bread. || FIG. *Es pan comido*, it's as easy as pie *o* as A B C, it's a piece of cake (es muy fácil). | *Estar a pan y agua*, to be on bread and water. | *Llamar al pan pan y al vino vino*, to call a spade a spade. | *No sólo de pan vive el hombre*, man does not live on bread alone. || *Pan ácimo*, unleavened bread. || *Pan bazo* or *moreno*, brown bread. || *Pan bendito*, Communion bread. || *Pan blanco* or *candeal*, white bread. || *Pan casero* homemade bread. || *Pan de azúcar*, sugar loaf. || *Pan de centeno*, rye bread. || *Pan de flor*, fine wheaten bread. || *Pan de molde*, soft, thin-crusted bread. || *Pan de munición*, ration bread. || *Pan de Viena*, milk bread. || *Pan duro*, stale bread. || *Amer.* FIG. *Pan francés*, uproar, hubbub [made by discontented audience] (espectáculo). || *Pan genovés*, Genoese cake. || *Pan integral*, wholemeal bread. || *Pan rallado*, breadcrumbs, *pl.* || *Pan tierno*, fresh bread. || *Pan toast*, rusk. || *Pan tostado*, toast. || FIG. *Por un mendrugo de pan*, for a bite to eat, for a crust of bread. | *Quitarle a uno el pan de la boca*, to take the bread out of somebody's mouth. | *Repartirse como pan bendito*, to be distributed in driblets *o* sparingly. | *Ser un pan* or *ser bueno como un pedazo de pan* or *ser más bueno que el pan*, to be kindness itself. || *Sopa de pan*, soup in which bread is dunked. || *Tierra de pan llevar*, wheatland. || FIG. *Venderse como pan bendito*, to sell like hot cakes (venderse en grandes cantidades).
Pan n. pr. m. MIT. Pan.
pana f. Corduroy, cord (tela). || *Amer.* Breakdown (avería). || *Pana lisa*, velvet (terciopelo).
panacea f. Panacea (remedio).
panadería f. Baker's, bakery, bread shop. || Breadmaking, baking (oficio del panadero).
panadero, ra m. y f. Baker.
panadizo m. MED. Felon, whitlow.

panafricanismo m. Pan-Africanism.
panafricano, na adj. Pan-African.
panal m. Honeycomb (de colmena). || Honeycomb (dulce). || *En forma de panal*, honeycombed.
panamá m. Panama [hat] (jipijapa).
Panamá n. pr. m. GEOGR. Panama.
panameño, ña adj./s. Panamanian.
panamericanismo m. Pan-Americanism.
panamericanista adj./s. Pan-Americanist.
panamericano, na adj. Pan-American. || *Carretera panamericana*, Pan-American Highway.
panarabismo m. Pan-Arabism.
panarizo m. Felon, whitlow (panadizo).
pancarta f. Poster, placard.
— OBSERV. This word is a Gallicism for *cartel*.
pancista adj./s. FAM. Opportunist.
páncreas m. ANAT. Pancreas.
pancreático, ca adj. Pancreatic: *jugo pancreático*, pancreatic juice.
pancromático, ca adj. Panchromatic.
pancho, cha adj. FAM. *Quedarse tan pancho*, to be *o* to remain unmoved.
panda m. Panda (mamífero del Himalaya). || — F. Gallery of a cloister. || FAM. Band, gang (pandilla).
pandear v. intr. y pr. To warp, to bend (la madera). || To bulge, to sag (una pared).
pandectas f. pl. JUR. Pandect, *sing.* (código). || HIST. The Pandects (de Justiniano). || Index book, *sing.* (cuaderno).
pandemia f. MED. Pandemic.
pandémico, ca adj. MED. Pandemic.
pandemonio o **pandemónium** m. Pandemonium.
pandeo m. Warping (acción de combarse la madera). || Warp, buckle (efecto). || Bulging, sagging (de las paredes). || Bulge (forma combada).
pandereta f. Tambourine. || — *La España de pandereta*, the tourist's Spain, typical Spain. || FIG. y FAM. *Zumbar la pandereta a uno*, to thrash s.o.
panderetazo m. Bang on a tambourine.
panderete m. *Tabique de panderete*, brick partition.
panderetero, ra m. y f. Tambourine player. || Tambourine maker *o* seller.
pandero m. MÚS. Tambourine. || Kite (cometa).
pandilla f. Band, gang: *una pandilla de niños*, a gang of children. || Team: *¡vaya pandilla!*, what a team! || Clique, coterie (camarilla).
pandino, na adj. [Of *o* from] Pando [town in Bolivia]. — M. y f. Native *o* inhabitant of Pando.
pandit m. Pandit (brahmán).
pando, da adj. Curved, bulging, sagging (pared). || Warped, curved, bent (madera). || Slow, slow-moving (lento). || FIG. Slow, deliberate, unhurried (pausado).
— M. Plateau (entre montañas).
Pandora n. pr. f. MIT. Pandora: *caja de Pandora*, Pandora's box.
panear v. intr. *Amer.* To boast, to brag (fanfarronear).
panecillo m. [Bread] roll. || FIG. *Venderse como panecillos*, to sell like hot cakes.
panegírico, ca adj. Panegyrical.
— M. Panegyric.
panegirista m. Panegyrist.
panegirizar v. tr. To panegyrize, to eulogize.
panel m. Panel (de una puerta). || — Pl. ARQ. Panelling.
panera f. Breadbasket (cesta del pan).
panero m. Breadbasket.
paneslavismo m. Pan-Slavism.
paneslavista adj./s. Pan-Slavist.
paneuropeo, a adj./s. Pan-European.
panfilismo m. Extreme kindness.
pánfilo, la adj. FAM. Sluggish, slow (desidioso). | Indolent (remolón). | Stupid, foolish (tonto).
panfletista m. Pamphleteer, lampoonist.
panfleto m. Pamphlet, lampoon.
— OBSERV. *Panfleto* and *panfletista* are Gallicisms for *libelo* and *libelista*.
pangermanismo m. Pan-Germanism.
pangermanista adj./s. Pan-Germanist.
pangolín m. Pangolin (mamífero).
panhelenismo m. Panhellenism.
paniaguado m. (P.us.). Servant. || FAM. Protégé: *los paniaguados del ministro*, the minister's protégés.
pánico, ca adj./s.m. Panic: *sembrar el pánico*, to cause panic. || — *De pánico*, wonderful, marvellous (magnífico), awful, ghastly (horroroso).
paniego, ga adj. Wheat: *tierra paniega*, wheatland. || Who eats a lot of bread, bread-loving (persona).
panificación f. Bread making, baking.
panificar v. tr. To make bread with (harina).
panislamismo m. Pan-Islamism.
panizo m. BOT. Millet (planta). | Maize [U.S., corn] (maíz).
panocha o **panoja** f. Ear (de maíz).
panoli o **panolis** adj. FAM. Stupid, foolish.
— M. y f. Fool.
panoplia f. Panoply (armadura). || Arms *o* weapon collection.
panorama m. Panorama. || FIG. Panorama: *el panorama de la situación económica*, the panorama of the economic situation. | Scene, view (vista). || FIG. *Cambio de panorama*, change of scenery.

panorámico, ca adj. Panoramic. || *Pantalla panorámica*, panoramic screen.
— F. Panorama, view (en un cine).
panqué o **panqueque** m. *Amer.* Pancake (hojuela).
pantagruélico, ca adj. Pantagruelian.
pantagruelismo m. Pantagruelism.
pantaleta f. o **pantaletas** f. pl. *Amer.* Knickers, *pl.*, panties, *pl.*
pantalón m. o **pantalones** m. pl. Trousers, *pl.* (de hombre). || Panties, *pl.*, knickers, *pl.* (interiores de mujer). || Trousers, *pl.*, slacks, *pl.* (de mujer). || — *Falda pantalón*, culotte-skirt. || FIG. y FAM. *Llevar* or *ponerse los pantalones*, to wear the trousers (mandar la mujer). || *Pantalón bombacho*, V. BOMBACHO. || *Pantalón corto*, shorts, *pl.* (de deporte), short trousers, *pl.* (de niño). || *Pantalón tubo*, slacks, *pl.* || *Pantalón vaquero*, jeans, *pl.*
pantalonero, ra m. y f. Trouser maker.
pantalla f. Shade, lampshade (de lámpara). || Screen (cine): *en la pantalla*, on the screen. || Fireguard (de chimenea). || TECN. Screen: *pantalla de radar*, radar screen. | Screen, shield, guard (para proteger). || FIG. Front, cover, blind: *servir de pantalla*, to serve as *o* to be a front (una persona). || *Amer.* Fan (abanico). || — *Hacer pantalla con la mano*, to shade one's eyes with one's hand. || *La pequeña pantalla*, the small screen, the television (la televisión). || *Llevar a la pantalla*, to screen, to film. || *Pantalla acústica*, baffle.
pantanal m. Marsh, bog, marshland.
pantano m. Marsh, bog (natural). || Reservoir, dam (embalse).
pantanoso, sa adj. Marshy, boggy. || FIG. Difficult, thorny (negocio).
panteísmo m. Pantheism.
panteísta adj. Pantheistic.
— M. y f. Pantheist.
panteístico, ca adj. Pantheistic.
panteón m. Pantheon. || Mausoleum (sepultura). || *Panteón de familia*, family vault.
pantera f. ZOOL. Panther.
pantógrafo m. Pantograph.
pantomima f. Pantomime.
pantomimo m. Mime.
pantoque m. MAR. Bilge.
pantorrilla f. Calf [of the leg].
pantorrillera f. Padded stocking.
pantufla f. o **pantuflo** m. Slipper.
panza f. FAM. Belly (barriga). || Rumen (de rumiante). || Belly (de vasija). || FAM. *Aterrizar sobre la panza*, to make a belly landing.
panzada f. Blow in the belly (golpe). || FAM. Bellyful (hartazgo). || — FAM. *Darse una panzada*, to eat *o* to have one's fill (saciarse), to be fed up (*de*, with), to have had a bellyful (*de*, of) [estar harto], to do a bellyflop (al tirarse al agua). | *Darse una panzada de reír*, to collapse laughing *o* with laughter. | *Una panzada de*, a lot of.
panzazo m. FAM. *Darse un panzazo*, to do a belly-flop, to bellyflop (en el agua).
panzón, ona o **panzudo, da** adj. Paunchy, potbellied, big-bellied, fat (hombre), round (cosa).
pañal m. Nappy [U.S., diaper] (de recién nacido). || Shirttail (de camisa). || — Pl. Nappies [U.S., diapers]: *niño en pañales*, baby in nappies. || — FIG. *Criarse en buenos pañales*, to be born with a silver spoon in one's mouth, to have a good start in life. | *Dejar en pañales a uno*, to leave s.o. standing. || *Estar en pañales*, to be in nappies (niño), to be wet behind the ears, to be green (ser novato), to be still in one's infancy: *la aviación estaba entonces en pañales*, aviation was still in its infancy; *una industria en pañales*, an industry which is still in its infancy.
pañería f. Draper's shop [U.S., dry-goods store] (tienda). || Drapery [U.S., dry goods, *pl.*] (paños).
pañero, ra adj. Textile, cloth: *industria pañera*, textile industry.
— M. y f. Draper [U.S., dry-goods dealer].
pañito m. V. PAÑO.
paño m. Wool, woollen cloth [U.S., woolen cloth] (tela de lana). || Cloth, material (tela). || Dishcloth (trapo de cocina). || Duster (trapo para quitar el polvo). || Cloth (para limpiar). || Width (ancho de una tela). || Drapery, hanging (colgadura). || MED. Towel: *paño higiénico*, sanitary towel. || Dullness (falta de brillo). || Mist, cloud (en un cristal). || Flaw (de un diamante). || Pebble dash (enlucido). || Wall, panel (pared). || MAR. Sails, *pl.* (velas). || — Pl. Hangings. || ARTES. Drapery, *sing.* || — *Al paño*, aside. || FIG. *Conocer el paño*, to know one's stuff. | *El buen paño en el arca se vende*, good merchandise needs no publicity. | *Estar en paños menores*, to be in one's undies *o* underclothes. | *Jugar a dos paños*, to play a double game, to run with the hare and hunt with the hounds. | *No andarse con paños calientes*, not to use half measures. || *Paño de altar*, altar cloth. || *Paño de billar*, billiard cloth. || *Paño de manos*, hand towel (toalla). || *Paño fúnebre* or *mortuorio* or *de tumba*, pall. || *Paños calientes*, packing, *sing.* (remedio), half measures (paliativo). || *Paños menores*, underwear, *sing.*, underclothes, undies. || FIG. y FAM. *Ser del mismo paño*, to be tarred with the same brush, to be two of a kind. | *Ser el paño de lágrimas de alguien*, V. LÁGRIMA. || *Traje de paño negro*, black woollen suit.

pañol m. MAR. Storeroom, store. || *Pañol de municiones*, ammunition room.
pañoleta f. Fichu (para los hombros). || Necktie, tie (del torero).
pañolón m. Shawl. || Large handkerchief (pañuelo).
pañosa m. TAUR. "Muleta" [cloth cape].
pañuelo m. Handkerchief (para las narices). || Scarf (en la cabeza), fichu (en los hombros). || — *Pañuelo de bolsillo*, pocket handkerchief. || FIG. *Ser grande como un pañuelo*, to be as small as can be, to be tiny *o* minute.
papa m. Pope (sumo pontífice).
papa f. Potato (patata). || FAM. Hoax (noticia falsa). || — FIG. *No saber ni papa de*, not to have a clue about, to know nothing whatsoever about: *de esto no sé ni papa*, I haven't a clue about this. || *Amer. Papa del aire*, yam. | *Papa dulce*, sweet potato (batata).
papá m. FAM. Daddy, papa, dad (padre). || *Papá Noel*, Father Christmas.
papable adj. Papable (un cardenal).
papada f. Double chin (de una persona). || Dewlap (del buey).
papado m. Papacy.
papafigo m. Figpecker (ave). || Golden oriole (oropéndola).
papagayo m. Parrot (ave). || *Amer.* Kite (cometa). || FIG. y FAM. Parrot, magpie, chatterbox (parlanchín). || FIG. y FAM. *Repetir como un papagayo*, to repeat parrot-fashion, to parrot.
papahígo m. Figpecker (ave).
papaína f. QUÍM. Papain.
papaíto m. FAM. Daddy, dad.
papal adj. Papal: *decretos papales*, papal decrees.
— M. *Amer.* Potato field.
papalina f. Cap which covers the ears (gorra). || Bonnet (cofia). || FAM. *Coger una papalina*, to get sozzled *o* canned (emborracharse).
papamoscas m. inv. Flycatcher (ave). || FIG. Simpleton, fool (tonto).
papanatas m. inv. FAM. Simpleton, fool (tonto). | Gaper (mirón).
papanatería f. o **papanatismo** m. FAM. Simplicity, silliness (idiotez). | Gaping (mirada).
papar v. tr. To swallow (tragar). || FIG. y FAM. *Papar moscas*, to catch flies, to gape, to daydream.
paparrucha o **paparruchada** f. FAM. Hoax (mentira). | Worthless thing (cosa inútil). | Piece of nonsense, silly thing (tontería).
papaveráceas f. pl. BOT. Papaveraceae.
papaverina f. QUÍM. Papaverine.
papaya f. Papaya fruit (fruto).
papayo m. Papaya tree (árbol).
papel m. Paper: *papel corriente*, ordinary paper. || Paper (escrito). || Piece of paper, sheet of paper (hoja). || Piece of paper (pedazo): *dame un papel para apuntar esto*, give me a piece of paper to write this down. || TEATR. Role, part: *primer papel*, first role, leading part; *segundo papel*, second role, minor part. || FIG. Role: *tu papel es obedecer*, your role is to obey. || COM. Paper money, banknotes, *pl.* || — Pl. Papers (documentación). || Newspapers, papers (periódicos). || — FIG. *Blanco como el papel*, as white as a sheet. || *Desempeñar* or *representar un papel*, to play a role *o* a part. || FIG. *Emborronar papel*, to scribble. | *Encajar muy bien en un papel*, to fit the part. || *Fábrica de papel*, paper mill. || FIG. *Hacer buen, mal papel*, to do well, badly; to cut a good figure, a bad figure. || *Hacer el papel de*, to play, to play the part of. || FIG. *Hacer papel de*, to act as (servir de). || *Hacer un pobre papel*, to give a poor show. || *Papel atrapamoscas*, flypaper. || *Papel autográfico*, autographic paper. || *Papel biblia*, bible paper, India paper. || *Papel carbón*, carbon paper. || *Papel cebolla*, pelure paper. || *Papel cuadriculado*, squared paper, graph paper. || *Papel cuché*, coated paper. || *Papel de barba*, untrimmed paper. || *Papel de calcar*, tracing paper. || *Papel de cartas*, writing paper, notepaper. || *Papel de dibujo*, drawing paper. || *Papel de embalar* or *de envolver*, wrapping paper. || *Papel de empapelar*, wallpaper. || *Papel de escribir*, notepaper, writing paper. || *Papel de estaño*, tinfoil. || *Papel de estraza* or *de añafea*, wrapping *o* brown paper. || *Papel de filtro*, filter paper. || *Papel de fumar*, cigarette paper. || *Papel del Estado*, government bonds, *pl.* || *Papel de lija* or *de vidrio*, sandpaper. || *Papel de marca*, foolscap paper. || *Papel de música* or *pautado*, music paper. || *Papel de pagos*, stamp, stamped paper. || *Papel de pegar*, sticky *o* gummed paper. || *Papel de periódico*, newsprint (papel de baja calidad), newspaper: *envuelto en papel de periódico*, wrapped in newspaper. || *Papel de plata*, silver paper. || *Papel de pruebas*, paper used for proofs. || *Papel de seda* or *de culebrilla*, tissue paper. || *Papel de tornasol*, litmus paper. || *Papel en blanco*, clean *o* fresh sheet of paper. || *Papel engomado*, sticky *o* gummed paper. || *Papeles de a bordo*, ship's papers. || *Papel esmerilado*, emery paper. || *Papel glaseado* or *de brillo*, glossy paper. || *Papel higiénico* or *sánico*, toilet paper. || *Papel kraft*, kraft. || FIG. *Papel mojado*, worthless piece of paper (documento). || *Papel moneda*, paper money, banknotes, *pl.* || *Papel pintado*, wallpaper. || *Papel secante*, blotting paper. || *Papel sellado*, stamp, stamped paper. || *Papel sin sellar*, unstamped paper. || *Papel tela*, cloth finish writing paper (para carta). || *Papel vegetal*, grease-proof paper. || *Papel vergé* or *verjurado*, laid paper. || *Papel vitela*, vellum paper. || *Papel volante*, leaflet. || FIG. *Se cambiaron los papeles*, the roles have been reversed. | *Ser papel mojado*, to be worthless. | *Sobre el papel*, on paper. | *Venir a uno con papeles*, to tease *o* to torment s.o.
papelear v. intr. To rummage through papers. || FIG. y FAM. To show off (querer aparentar).
papeleo m. Rummaging through papers. || *El papeleo administrativo*, red tape, paper work.
papelera f. Wastepaper basket (cesto). || Paper mill (fábrica). || Writing desk (mueble).
papelería f. Stationer's (tienda). || Pile *o* mess of papers (papeles en desorden).
papelero, ra adj. Paper. || FIG. Pretentious, showy (ostentoso).
— M. y f. Stationer, paper manufacturer *o* seller. || FIG. Show-off (ostentoso). || — M. *Amer.* Newspaper seller.
papeleta f. Ticket: *papeleta de rifa*, draw ticket. || File card (ficha). || Ballot paper, voting paper: *papeleta en blanco*, blank ballot paper. || Pawn ticket (de monte de piedad). || Question paper (papel que lleva una pregunta en un examen). || Question (pregunta). || Report (calificación de un examen). || FIG. Problem, poser (problema). | Tough *o* unpleasant job (incordio). | Drag (pesadez): *¡menuda papeleta!*, what a drag! || — FIG. *Le ha tocado una mala papeleta*, yours is a tough job. | *Plantear una papeleta difícil*, to pose a problem.
papelillo o **papelito** m. Sachet (de medicina). || Confetti. || Cigarette (cigarro). || Piece of paper (trozo de papel).
papelón, ona adj. FAM. Pretentious, showy (presumido).
— M. y f. FAM. Show-off, pretentious *o* showy person. || — M. Scrap of paper (papelucho). || Bristol board (cartulina). || Cornet (cucurucho). || *Amer.* Brown sugar | Ridiculous role. | Blunder (plancha).
papelote o **papelucho** m. FAM. Scrap of paper.
papera f. MED. Goitre [U.S., goiter] (bocio). || — Pl. Mumps, *sing.* (enfermedad).
papero, ra adj. *Amer.* Potato.
papi m. FAM. Daddy, dad (papá).
papiamento m. Dialect spoken in Curaçao.
papila f. ANAT. Papilla.
papilar adj. ANAT. Papillary.
papilionáceo, a adj. Papilionaceous.
— F. pl. Papilonaceae.
papiloma m. MED. Papilloma.
papilla f. Pap (para niños). || — FIG. y FAM. *Echar la primera papilla*, to be as sick as a dog, to be violently sick. | *Hacer papilla a uno*, to make mincemeat of s.o. | *Hecho papilla*, fagged out, shattered (muy cansado), a mess, a write-off (destrozado).
papillote m. Curl paper (para el pelo).
Papiniano n. pr. m. Papinian.
papiro m. Papyrus.
pápiro m. FAM. Banknote.
papirología f. Study of papyri.
papirólogo, ga m. y f. Person who studies papyri.
papirotada o **papirotazo** m. Fillip (golpe). || *Amer.* Stupid thing (sandez).
papirote m. Fillip (golpe).
papirusa f. FAM. *Amer.* Good looker [U.S., doll] (muchacha).
papisa f. *La papisa Juana*, Pope Joan.
papismo m. Papistry, popery.
papista adj. Papist, popish. || FIG. *Ser más papista que el papa*, to out-Herod Herod.
— M. y f. Papist.
papo m. Dewlap (de los animales). || Double chin, jowl (sotabarba). || Craw, maw (buche de las aves). || MED. Goitre [U.S., goiter] (bocio).
paprika f. Paprika.
papú o **papúa** adj./s. Papuan.
Papuasia n. pr. f. GEOGR. Papua.
paquear v. intr. To snipe (un soldado aislado).
— V. tr. To snipe at.
paquebote m. MAR. Packet boat, packet.
paquete m. Packet (caja): *un paquete de cigarrillos*, a packet of cigarettes. || Package (lío), parcel (de mayor bulto). || Packet boat (buque). || Passenger in a sidecar (moto). || FAM. Dandy. | Joke, trick (embuste): *dar un paquete*, to play a trick. || POP. Task, job (cosa pesada): *¡vaya un paquete!*, what a job! || — MIL. y FAM. *Meter un paquete*, to bawl out. || *Paquete postal*, parcel.
paquete, ta adj. *Amer.* Elegant, spruce, smart.
paquetería f. Small business. || *Amer.* Affectation.
paquidermo adj. m. ZOOL. Pachydermatous.
— M. ZOOL. Pachyderm.
Paquistán n. pr. m. GEOGR. Pakistan.
paquistaní adj./s. Pakistani.
par adj. Even: *número par*, even number. || Equal, like (semejante).
— M. Pair (dos unidades): *un par de zapatos*, a pair of shoes. || Peer (dignidad). || Pair, couple: *un par de huevos*, a couple of eggs. || Couple: *por un par de pesetas*, for a couple of pesetas. || Equal (igual). || ARQ. Rafter. || MAT. Even number. || FÍS. Couple (electricidad). || TECN. Couple (de fuerzas). || — F.

COM. Par. || — F. pl. MED. Placenta, *sing.* || — *Abierto de par en par,* wide open. || *Abrir de par en par,* to open wide. || *A la par* or *al par,* at par (monedas): *cambio a la par,* exchange at par. || *A la par,* together (conjuntamente), at the same time (igualmente): *es alto y gordo a la par,* he is tall and at the same time fat. || *A la par que,* at the same time as, as, while: *cantaba a la par que bailaba,* he sang as he danced; and, cum: *es sabio a la par que artista,* he is a wise man and an artist *o* a wise man cum artist; both, at the same time: *éste es un vestido moderno a la par que elegante,* this dress is both modern and elegant. || *Al par de,* on an equal footing with. || *A pares,* in pairs, in twos, two by two. || *Ir a la par de,* to go with, to match. || *Jugar a pares y nones,* to play odds and evens. || FAM. *Le dio un par de bofetadas,* she slapped his face. || *No tener par,* to have no parallel, to be unique. || *Sin par,* without equal *o* par, matchless, peerless. || *Voy a decirle un par de palabras,* I am going to tell him a thing or two.

para prep.

> **1.** Destino. — **2.** Sitio, dirección. — **3.** Tiempo. — **4.** Relación, comparación. — **5.** Locuciones.

1. DESTINO. — For: *este libro es para ti,* this book is for you; *es importante para la salud,* it is important for the health; *ha sido muy desagradable para nosotros,* it was very unpleasant for us; *bueno para la garganta,* good for the throat. || To, in order to: *para cantar bien,* in order to sing well. || To: *nombrar para un cargo,* to appoint to a post; *no tengo tiempo para comer,* I have no time to eat; *no tengo permiso para salir,* I am not allowed to go out; *eso no tiene utilidad para mí,* that is of no use to me; *es primordial para la industria,* it is vital to industry. || As: *le han contratado para secretario,* they have engaged him as secretary.
2. SITIO, DIRECCIÓN. — Towards (hacia): *caminó para el árbol, para el coche,* he walked towards the tree, towards the car. || To: *voy para el pueblo,* I am going to the village.
3. TIEMPO. — For: *tiene pan para dos días,* he has enough bread for two days; *me voy para una semana,* I am going away for a week. || By, at: *volverá para Navidad,* he will come back by Christmas. || — *Faltaban diez días para Navidad,* there were ten days till Christmas. || *Para Navidades hará dos años,* it will be two years ago this Christmas. || *Va para dos años que,* it is nearly two years since.
4. RELACIÓN, COMPARACIÓN. — As for, as regards, in regard to (por lo que toca). || For (comparación): *hace buen tiempo para la estación,* the weather is good for the season; *para un hombre normalmente tan antipático se ha portado muy amablemente,* for a man who is normally so unpleasant he has been very nice. || Compared with, to: *eso es mucho para lo que él suele dar,* that is a lot compared with what he usually gives.
5. LOCUCIONES. — *Dar para,* to give enough money for: *dar para pan,* to give enough money for bread; *dar para vestirse,* to give enough money to dress o.s.; to be enough for (ser bastante para). || *Decir para sí,* to say to o.s. || *Estar para,* V. ESTAR. || *Este hombre es para matarle,* this man ought to be put away. || *Haber nacido para pintar,* to have been born to paint. || *Haber nacido para ser pintor,* to be a born painter. || *Ir para los cuarenta años,* to be about forty [age]. || *Ir para casa,* to go home. || *Ir para la taberna,* to go to *o* towards the tavern. || *Ir para viejo,* to grow old. || *Lo leyó para él,* he read it to himself. || *No es para tanto,* there is no need to make such a fuss. || *Para abajo,* downward, downwards, down. || *Para arriba,* upward, upwards, up. || *Para atrás,* behind (detrás), backwards (hacia atrás). || *Para con,* to, towards: *ingrato para con sus padres,* ungrateful to one's parents. || *Para concluir,* in conclusion, to conclude. || *Para eso,* for that. || *Para mí,* in my opinion, as far as I am concerned (a mi parecer). || *Para que,* so that, in order that: *para que venga,* so that he should come. || *¿Para qué?,* why?: *¿para qué vienes?,* why are you coming?; what... for?: *¿para qué sirve esto?,* what is this for?; what for? (¿y de qué me serviría?). || *¿Para qué te voy a contar?,* there is no need to tell you. || *Para siempre,* for ever. || *Ser para nada,* to be good for nothing, to be useless. || *Ser para todo,* to be good for everything. || *Ser para volverse loco,* to be enough to drive one mad. || *Tener para sí que,* to think that, to believe that.

parabellum m. Automatic pistol (pistola).
parabién m. Congratulations, *pl.* || Greeting. || *Dar el parabién,* to congratulate.
parábola f. Parable (de Cristo). || MAT. Parabola.
parabólico, ca adj. Parabolic.
parabolizar v. tr. To parabolize.
parabrisas m. inv. Windscreen [U.S., windshield].
paraca f. *Amer.* Wind [blowing from the Pacific].
paracaídas m. inv. Parachute. || — *Lanzamiento en paracaídas,* parachuting. || *Lanzar en paracaídas,* to parachute. || *Tirarse* or *lanzarse en paracaídas,* to parachute.
paracaidismo m. Parachuting, parachute jumping: *practicar el paracaidismo,* to go in for parachuting.
paracaidista adj. *Tropas paracaidistas,* paratroopers. — M. y f. Parachutist. || MIL. Paratrooper.
parachispas m. inv. Spark arrester.
parachoques m. inv. Bumper [U.S., fender] (de coche). || Buffer (de vagón).
parada f. Stop (sitio): *parada discrecional,* request stop; *parada del autobús,* bus stop. || Stopping (acción). || Stop, halt (en el camino): *una parada de cinco minutos,* a five-minute stop. || Rank, stand (de taxis). || Pause, break (detención). || Pen (para rebaños). || Stud farm (acaballadero). || Relay, relay post (para caballos de reemplazo). || Relay (caballos de reemplazo). || Parade (espectáculo). || Stake (en el juego). || Parry (esgrima). || MIL. Parade. || MÚS. Pause. || Dam (presa de un río). || DEP. Save, stop (en fútbol). || *Amer.* Boasting. || — *Hacer parada,* to stop. || *Parada en firme,* dead stop *o* halt (equitación). || *Parada en seco,* dead stop *o* halt. || *Parada y fonda,* stop-restaurant facilities (en una estación).
paradera f. Sluice gate (de molino). || Seine net (red).
paradero m. Whereabouts, *pl.* (sitio). || Destination (destino). || Home, residence (morada). || FIG. End (término): *tendrá mal paradero,* she'll come to a bad end. || *Amer.* Station (apeadero). || — *Averiguar el paradero de,* to ascertain the whereabouts of, to locate. || *No conozco su paradero,* I do not know where he is *o* where he lives.
paradigma m. GRAM. Paradigm (modelo).
paradigmático, ca adj. GRAM. Paradigmatic.
paradisiaco, ca o **paradisíaco, ca** adj. Paradisiac, paradisiacal, heavenly: *un sitio paradisiaco,* a heavenly place.
parado, da adj. Stationary: *estaba parado en medio de la calle,* he was stopped in the middle of the road. || Still, motionless (quieto). || Idle, at rest (cosa, máquina). || Unemployed, out of work (sin trabajo). || Closed, at a standstill (una fábrica). || FIG. Slow, indolent (poco activo). | Idle, unoccupied (desocupado). | Lazy (perezoso). || *Amer.* Standing (de pie). || — FIG. *Dejar mal parado,* V. MALPARAR. | *Quedarse parado,* to be dumbfounded *o* struck dumb. | *Salir bien, mal parado,* to manage *o* to come off well, badly (una persona), to turn out well, badly (un asunto).
— M. Unemployed person. || *El número de parados ha incrementado mucho,* the number of unemployed has greatly increased.
paradoja f. Paradox.
paradójico, ca adj. Paradoxical.
parador, ra adj. Stopping. || Heavy-betting (en los juegos).
— M. y f. Heavy better *o* bettor (en los juegos). || — M. Inn (mesón). || "Parador" [State hotel].
paraestatal adj. Which cooperates with the State, semi-official.
parafernal adj. JUR. Paraphernal. || *Bienes parafernales,* paraphernalia, wife's personal property as distinct from her dowry.
parafina f. Paraffin. || *Aceite de parafina,* mineral oil.
parafinado m. Paraffining, oiling with paraffin.
parafinar v. tr. To paraffin.
parafraseador, ra m. y f. Paraphraser.
parafrasear v. tr. To paraphrase.
paráfrasis f. inv. Paraphrase.
parafrástico, ca adj. Paraphrastic.
paragoge f. GRAM. Paragoge.
paragógico, ca adj. Paragogic.
paragolpes m. inv. *Amer.* Bumper [U.S., fender] (parachoques).
parágrafo m. (P.us.). Paragraph (párrafo).
paragranizo adj. m. Antihail (cañón).
paraguas m. inv. Umbrella.
Paraguay n. pr. m. GEOGR. Paraguay (país y río).
paraguaya f. Kind of peach.
paraguayo, ya adj./s. Paraguayan.
paraguazo m. Blow from *o* with an umbrella.
paragüería f. Umbrella shop.
paragüero, ra m. y f. Umbrella dealer (vendedor). || — M. Umbrella stand (para poner paraguas). || — F. *Amer.* Umbrella stand.
parahúso m. Drill.
paraíso m. Paradise. || FIG. Paradise, heaven. || TEATR. Gods, gallery [U.S., peanut gallery]. || — *Ave del paraíso,* bird of paradise. || *Paraíso terrenal,* earthly paradise.
paraje m. Place, spot: *paraje desconocido,* unknown place *o* spot. || Area, region: *paraje salvaje,* wild area *o* region. || State (estado). || — Pl. MAR. Waters. || *¿Qué haces por estos parajes?,* what are you doing in these parts?
paralaje f. ASTR. Parallax.
paralelamente adv. Parallel, in a parallel direction.
paralela f. Parallel (línea). || Trench, parallel (foso). || — Pl. Parallel bars (gimnasia).
paralelepípedo m. MAT. Parallelepiped
paralelismo m. Parallelism.
paralelo, la adj. Parallel: *paralelo a* or *con,* parallel to; *correr paralelo a,* to run parallel to. || — DEP. *Barras paralelas,* parallel bars (en gimnasia). || *Las "Vidas paralelas" de Plutarco,* Plutarch's "Parallel lives".
— M. Parallel: *el paralelo treinta y tres,* the thirty-

third parallel. || *Establecer un paralelo entre*, to compare, to parallel, to draw a parallel between.
paralelogramo m. MAT. Parallelogram.
parálisis f. MED. Paralysis: *parálisis infantil, parcial*, infantile, partial paralysis; *parálisis progresiva*, creeping paralysis. || FIG. Paralysis.
paralítico, ca adj./s. Paralytic.
paralización f. MED. Paralysis. || FIG. Paralysis.
paralizador, ra o **paralizante** adj. Paralysing.
— M. y f. Paralyser.
paralizar v. tr. To paralyse, to paralyze: *paralizado de una pierna, de terror*, paralysed in one leg, with fright.
— V. pr. To become paralysed. || FIG. To be paralysed, to come to a standstill.
paralogismo m. Paralogism, fallacy.
paramagnético, ca adj. ELECTR. Paramagnetic.
paramagnetismo m. ELECTR. Paramagnetism.
paramento m. Adorning, decoration (acción). || Adornment, ornamental covering. || Facing (de una pared). || Caparison (de caballo). || — Pl. Paraments, vestments (del altar).
paramera f. Barren region.
paramétrico, ca adj. Parametric.
parámetro m. MAT. Parameter.
paramilitar adj. Paramilitary, semi-military.
paramnesia f. Paramnesia.
páramo m. Wide barren plain.
parangón m. Pattern, model (dechado). || Comparison. || *Sin parangón*, incomparable, matchless.
parangonable adj. Comparable (*con*, to).
parangonar m. To compare (*con*, to) [comparar]. || IMPR. To justify.
paraninfo m. Auditorium, assembly hall (en una universidad). || Best man (en una boda).
paranoia f. MED. Paranoia.
paranoico, ca adj./s Paranoiac.
paranomasia f. Paranomasia.
parapetarse v. pr. To take shelter, to take cover. || FIG. To barricade o.s.: *se ha parapetado en su habitación*, he has barricaded himself in his room. | To take refuge: *parapetarse tras el silencio*, to take refuge in silence.
parapeto m. Parapet, railing, railings, *pl.* (de un puente). || MIL. Breastwork, parapet. || FIG. Wall, barricade.
paraplejía f. MED. Paraplegia.
parapléjico, ca adj./s. Paraplegic.
parar v. intr. To stop: *ha parado la lluvia, ha parado de llover*, the rain has stopped, it has stopped raining. || To stop, to halt: *pararon en medio de la calle*, they stopped in the middle of the street. || To end, to lead: *este camino va a parar al bosque*, this road ends at *o* leads to the wood. || To end up (llegar a). || To get: *parar en las manos de*, to get into the hands of. || To give up (abandonar): *no pararé hasta lograrlo*, I won't give up until I succeed. || To stay: *pararé en casa de mi tío*, I shall stay at my uncle's. || To stay, to stop, to put up: *actualmente paro en el hotel X*, at the moment I am staying at the X hotel. || FIG. To decide: *pararon en que se marcharían al día siguiente*, they decided to leave the next day. || To point (el perro). || — *¿Adónde vamos a parar?*, where are we going? || FIG. *Ir a parar*, V. IR. || *Mis esfuerzos pararon en nada*, my efforts came to nothing. || *No paró hasta que obtuvo lo que quería*, he did not stop until he had got what he wanted. || *Parar en seco*, to stop dead *o* suddenly. || *Sin parar*, without stopping, nonstop, continuously. || *Trabajaba, hablaba sin parar*, he never stopped working, talking. || *Trabajamos sin parar*, we worked nonstop. || *Venir a parar*, V. VENIR. || *Y pare usted de contar*, and that is as far as it goes.
— V. tr. To stop: *pare el coche aquí*, stop the car here. || To point (perro de caza). || To parry, to ward off [a blow, a thrust] (boxeo, esgrima). || To stop (un balón). || To fix (la atención). || — FIG. *Parar los pies* or *el carro a uno*, to put s.o. in his place. | *Parar mientes en*, to think of, to consider: *sin parar mientes en las consecuencias*, without thinking of *o* considering the consequences.
— V. pr. To stop: *aquí no nos podemos parar*, we cannot stop here. || *Amer.* To stand up (ponerse de pie). | To get up (de la cama). || — *No pararse en barras*, to stop at nothing. || *Pararse a pensar*, to stop to think. || *Pararse en algo*, to pay attention to something. || *Pararse en seco*, to stop dead *o* in one's tracks. || *Pararse en tonterías*, to mess about. || *Sin pararse en detalles*, without going into details.
pararrayo m. o **pararrayos** m. inv. Lightning conductor [U.S., lightning rod] (en edificios). || Lightning arrester (en aparatos eléctricos).
paraselene f. ASTR. Paraselene.
parasicología f. Parapsychology.
parasimpático, ca adj. Parasympathetic.
— M. Parasympathetic nervous system.
parasitario, ria adj. Parasitic, parasitical.
parasiticida adj./s.m. Parasiticide.
parasítico, ca adj. Parasitic, parasitical.
parasitismo m. Parasitism.
parásito, ta adj. Parasitic, parasitical (*de*, on).
— M. Parasite. || FIG. Parasite. || — Pl. Interference, *sing.*, atmospherics, static, *sing.* (en la radio).
parasol m. Parasol, sunshade (quitasol). || FOT. Sunshade.
paratífico, ca adj. MED. Paratyphoid.
paratifoidea adj.f./s.f. Paratyphoid.
paratiroides adj. Parathyroid.
— F. pl. Parathyroids.
paratopes m. inv. *Amer.* Buffer (de tren).
paratuberculosis f. MED. Paratuberculosis.
paratuberculoso, sa adj. MED. Paratuberculous.
Parcas n. pr. f. pl. MIT. Fates, Parcae.
parcela f. Plot, piece of ground, parcel (de tierra). || Particle (átomo). || *División en parcelas*, division into plots, parcelling out.
parcelable adj. Divisible into plots.
parcelación f. Division into plots, parcelling out (de un terreno).
parcelar v. tr. To divide into plots, to parcel out: *parcelar un bosque*, to parcel out a forest.
parcelario, ria adj. Divided into plots *o* parcels (parcelado). || *Concentración parcelaria*, land consolidation [regrouping of lands].
parcial adj. Partial (incompleto): *vista parcial*, partial view. || Partial (injusto): *juicio parcial*, partial judgment. || — Adj./s. Partisan.
parcialidad f. Partiality, prejudice, bias (prejuicio). || Clique, faction, party (grupo).
parcialmente adv. Partially, partly, part (en parte). || Partially (injustamente).
parcimonia f. Parsimony (parsimonia).
parcísimo, ma adj. Very sparing (alabanzas, detalles, palabras). || Very frugal, very scanty (comida). || Very moderate (gastos).
parco, ca adj. Sparing: *parco en el hablar* or *en palabras*, sparing in words. || Mean (mezquino). || Moderate, scanty: *parco en el comer*, a moderate *o* a scanty eater. || Frugal, scanty (comida, etc.). || — *Parco en cumplidos*, sparing in compliments. || *Parco en gastar*, economical (que gasta poco), mean, tightfisted (fam.) [avaro].
parcómetro m. Parking meter.
parche m. Patch (en un neumático). || Plaster (emplasto). || Patch (para remendar). || Patch (colorete). || Botch, daub (pintura). || FIG. Person *o* thing which is out of place. || TAUR. Cockade, knot of ribbons stuck onto the bull's forehead. || Drumhead (de un tambor). || FIG. Drum (tambor). || MED. Specially coated plaster used to detect tuberculosis, skin test. || — *Bolsillo de parche*, patch pocket. || FIG. y FAM. *¡Oído al parche!*, be careful!, look out!, watch your step! | *Pegar un parche a uno*, to put one over on s.o. (engañar).
parchís o **parchesi** m. Parcheesi.
pardear v. intr. To be *o* to stand out *o* to look brown.
¡pardiez! interj. FAM. Goodness me!, good Lord!
pardillo, lla adj./s. Peasant, yokel (palurdo). || — M. Linnet (pájaro).
pardo, da adj. Brown: *oso pardo*, brown bear. || Dark, grey (tiempo, cielo, etc.). || Flat, dull (voz). || *Amer.* Mulatto. || FIG. *Tener gramática parda*, to have plenty of gumption.
pardusco, ca adj. Brownish, greyish.
pareado, da adj. Matching (emparejado). || *Versos pareados*, rhyming couplets.
— M. pl. Rhyming couplets.
parear v. tr. To match, to pair, to put together (formar pares). || To mate, to pair (animales). || TAUR. To place *o* to stick the banderillas in [a bull].
parecer m. Opinion, view: *a mi parecer*, in my opinion *o* view; *tomar parecer de uno*, to ask for s.o.'s opinion *o* view. || Appearance, looks, *pl.* (aspecto): *buen parecer*, pleasant appearance. || JUR. Expert opinion *o* advice (dictamen). || — *Al parecer*, to all appearances, apparently. || *Arrimarse al parecer de uno*, to adopt s.o.'s opinion. || *De buen parecer*, good-looking, nice-looking. || *De mal parecer*, ugly, plain. || *Mudar de parecer*, to change one's mind. || *Parecer de peritos*, expert opinion. || *Por el buen parecer*, to keep up appearances, for form's sake. || *Según el parecer de*, according to. || *Ser del parecer que*, to be of the opinion that.
parecer* v. intr. e impers. To seem, to look, to appear: *parece cansado*, he seems *o* he looks tired; *parece que va a llover*, it seems that *o* it looks as if it is going to rain. || To seem: *parece imposible a su edad*, it seems impossible at his age. || To be like, to look like, to seem like: *parece seda*, it is like silk. || To appear (aparecer). || To think (juzgar): *¿qué te parece?*, what do you think? || To be all right with (consentir): *iremos ahora si te parece*, we shall go now if it is all right with you. || To be convenient (ser conveniente): *podemos trabajar en mi casa si te parece*, we can work in my house if it is convenient for you. || To like (querer): *si te parece te lo llevo a tu casa*, if you like I shall take it home for you. || — *A lo que parece*, to all appearances, apparently. || *Así parece*, so it seems. || *Aunque no lo parezca*, incredible as it may seem. || *Como le parezca*, as you like. || *Me ha parecido verle*, I thought I saw him. || *Me parece que*, I think [that], it seems to me that. || *Me parece que sí, que no*, I think so, I don't think so. || *No parece tener la edad que tiene*, he doesn't look his age. || *Parece como si desease...*, it looks as if he wanted to... || *Parece mentira que*, it hardly seems possible that, who would

have thought that? || *Parece ser que*, it seems that. || *Según lo que parece*, to all appearances. || *Si le parece bien*, if it is all right with you, if you like. || *Si le parece mal*, if you disagree, if you don't like the idea.
— V. pr. To look like, to resemble: *se parece mucho a su padre*, he looks a lot like his father, he resembles his father a great deal. || To be alike, to look like *o* to resemble each other (aspecto): *los dos hermanos no se parecen nada*, the two brothers are not at all alike, the two brothers do not look at all like each other. || To be alike, to resemble each other: *se parecen en el carácter, en las facciones*, they are alike in character, in their features. || *Ni nada que se le parezca*, nor anything of the sort, far from it.
parecido, da adj. Alike: *los dos hermanos son muy parecidos*, the two brothers are very alike. || Like: *es muy parecido a su hermano*, he is a lot like his brother. || Of the kind, one like it: *éste o uno parecido*, this one or one of the kind *o* or one like it. || Similar (semejante). || Lifelike: *un retrato muy parecido*, a very lifelike portrait. || — *Algo parecido*, sth. of the kind *o* of the sort, sth. like that. || FAM. *Bien parecido*, good-looking, nice-looking, not bad (una persona). || *Ser parecido a*, to be like.
— M. Resemblance, likeness: *parecido de familia*, family likeness *o* resemblance. || Similarity (semejanza). || *Tener parecido con uno*, to bear a resemblance to s.o.
pared f. Wall (de casa, etc.): *pared de ladrillos*, brick wall. || ANAT. Wall. || — FIG. *Blanco como la pared*, white as a sheet *o* as a ghost. || FIG. y FAM. *Como si hablara a una pared*, like talking to a [brick] wall. | *Darse contra las paredes*, to tear one's hair out. || *Dejar pegado a la pared*, to nonplus (dejar confuso), to ruin (arruinar). || *Entre cuatro paredes*, between four walls. || FIG. *Entre la espada y la pared*, V. ESPADA. || FIG. y FAM. *Está que se sube por las paredes*, he is hopping mad. | *Estar pegado a la pared*, to be flat broke (sin un cuarto). || FIG. *Las paredes oyen*, walls have ears. || *Lienzo de pared*, stretch of wall. || *Pared divisoria* or *intermedia*, internal *o* dividing wall. || *Pared maestra*, main wall. || *Pared medianera*, party wall. || FIG. y FAM. *Subirse por las paredes*, to go up the wall, to hit the roof (enfadarse), to be hopping mad (estar furioso). || *Vivir pared por medio*, to live in adjoining rooms *o* houses.
paredón m. Thick wall. || Piece of wall (en ruinas). || Place of execution. || — *¡Al paredón!*, to the firing squad! || *Llevar al paredón*, to send before the firing squad.
pareja f. Pair (par). || Couple (hombre y mujer): *ser una buena pareja*, to make a good couple. || Pair, couple: *una pareja de amigos*, a pair *o* a couple of friends; *una pareja de palomas*, a pair *o* a couple of pigeons. || Boy and girl (hijo e hija). || Pair of Civil Guards (guardias). || Partner (de baile y juego). || Brace (caza). || Pair (de naipes). || — Pl. Two pairs, doublet, *sing.* (dados). || — *Doble pareja*, two pairs (póker). || FIG. *Hacer pareja con*, to be two of a kind: *hace pareja con su amiga*, she and her friend are two of a kind. || *Por parejas*, two by two, in pairs.
parejo adv. *Amer.* At the same time, together.
parejo, ja adj. Similar, the same, alike. || Even, smooth, flush (regular). || — *Correr parejo con*, to be on an equal footing with, to be on a par with, to be paralleled by. || *Ir parejos*, to be equal. || DEP. *Van parejos*, they are neck and neck.
parénquima m. ANAT. y BOT. Parenchyma.
parentela f. Relations, *pl.*, relatives, *pl.* (conjunto de parientes).
parentesco m. Relationship, kinship. || — FIG. *Parentesco espiritual*, spiritual bond. || *Parentesco político*, relationship by marriage.
paréntesis m. inv. Parenthesis (frase). || Brackets, *pl.* (signo). || FIG. Interruption, break. || — *Abrir, cerrar el paréntesis*, to open, to close brackets. || *Entre paréntesis*, in parentheses, in brackets. || *Sea dicho entre paréntesis*, incidentally, be it said parenthetically.
pareo m. Pairing off, matching (unión). || Loincloth (taparrabos). || Mating (de las aves).
paresa f. Peeress.
pargo m. Porgy (pez).
parhelia f. o **parhelio** m. ASTR. Parhelion, mock sun.
parhilera f. ARQ. Ridgepole.
paria m. Pariah. || FIG. Outcast, pariah.
parida adj. f. Who, which has given birth. || *Recién parida*, woman who has just given birth.
paridad f. Equality, parity (igualdad). || Parity (de las monedas). || Comparison (comparación).
paridígito adj. Whose toes form pairs (animal).
pariente, ta m. y f. Relative, relation (miembro de la familia): *pariente cercano*, close relative. || — *Medio pariente*, distant cousin. || *Pariente político*, in-law, relative by marriage. || — M. FAM. Old man (esposo). || — F. FAM. Missus (esposa).
— OBSERV. Parents [mother and father] is translated in Spanish by *padres*.
parietal adj. Parietal.
— M. Parietal bone.
parietaria f. BOT. Pellitory.
parihuelas f. pl. Stretcher, *sing.*
paripé m. FAM. *Dar el paripé*, to trick, to fool (engañar). | *Hacer el paripé*, to put on airs (presumir), to put on an act: *se detestan, pero en público hacen el paripé*, they detest each other, but in public they put on an act; to pretend: *no entiende ni palabra de inglés, pero hace el paripé*, he doesn't understand a word of English, but he pretends to.
parir v. intr. To give birth (mujer y animales). || To calve (la vaca). || To foal (los solípedos). || FIG. y FAM. *Por si fuéramos pocos parió la abuela*, that's all we needed, that's the last straw.
— V. tr. To bear (mujer), to give birth to (mujer y animales). || FIG. y FAM. To produce, to cause.
Paris n. pr. m. MIT. Paris.
París n. pr. GEOGR. Paris.
parisién o **parisino, na** o **parisiense** adj./s. Parisian.
parisilábico, ca o **parisílabo, ba** adj. Parisyllabic.
paritario, ria adj. Joint: *comisión paritaria*, joint committee.
parkerización f. TECN. Parkerization.
parking m. Car park [U.S., parking lot].
parlador, ra adj. Talkative.
— M. y f. Chatterbox.
parlamentar v. intr. To parley, to hold a parley (dos enemigos). || FAM. To chatter, to gossip (conversar).
parlamentario, ria adj. Parliamentary: *sistema parlamentario*, parliamentary system.
— M. Member of parliament [U.S., congressman] (miembro). || Parliamentarian. || Negotiator (que parlamenta).
parlamentarismo m. Parliamentarianism (doctrina). || Parliamentary government (gobierno parlamentario).
parlamento m. Parliament (asamblea). || Parley, negotiation (negociación). || Speech (discurso). || TEATR. Tirade. || FAM. Chatter (charla).
parlanchín, ina adj. Chatty, talkative.
— M. y f. Chatterbox.
parlante adj. HERÁLD. Canting, allusive: *armas parlantes*, canting *o* allusive arms. || Talking (sonoro).
parlar v. intr. To chat, to gossip (charlar). || To talk, to speak (hablar).
parlotear v. intr. FAM. To chatter, to prattle.
parloteo m. FAM. Gossip, small talk, chatter, prattle.
parmesano, na adj./s. Parmesan. || *Queso parmesano*, Parmesan cheese.
parnasianismo m. Parnassian School (literatura).
parnasiano, na adj./s. Parnassian.
Parnaso n. pr. m. Parnassus (montaña).
parné o **parnés** m. POP. Cash, loot, dough (dinero).
paro m. Tit (ave). || Stoppage, standstill (suspensión en el trabajo). || Unemployment (desempleo): *paro estacional*, seasonal unemployment. || — *Estar en paro forzoso*, to be unemployed. || ZOOL. *Paro carbonero*, coal tit, coletit. || *Paro encubierto*, underemployment. || *Paro forzoso*, unemployment.
parodia f. Parody.
parodiar v. tr. To parody.
paródico, ca adj. Parodic, parodical.
parodista m. Parodist.
parón m. EQUIT. Refusal. || Sudden *o* dead stop (parada en seco).
paronimia f. Paronymy.
paronímico, ca adj. Paronymous.
parónimo, ma adj. Paronymous.
— M. Paronym (vocablo).
paronomasia f. Paronomasia (en retórica).
parótida f. ANAT. Parotid.
parotiditis m. MED. Parotitis.
paroxismo m. Paroxysm. || FIG. Paroxysm, climax.
paroxítono, na adj./s.m. GRAM. Paroxytone.
parpadear v. intr. To blink, to wink (los ojos). || To flicker, to blink (la luz). || To twinkle (las estrellas).
parpadeo m. Blinking, winking, blink, wink (ojos). || Flickering, blinking, flicker (luz). || Twinkling, twinkle (estrellas).
párpado m. ANAT. Eyelid.
parque n. Park, gardens, *pl.* || Garden: *parque zoológico*, zoological garden. || Playground (de niños). || — *Parque automóvil*, number of cars on the road (en un país). || *Parque de artillería*, artillery park. || *Parque de atracciones*, fairground, fun fair. || *Parque de bomberos*, fire station. || *Parque de coches or de estacionamiento*, car park [U.S., parking lot]. || *Parque nacional*, national park.
parqué m. Parquet.
parqueadero m. *Amer.* Car park [U.S., parking lot].
parquear v. tr. *Amer.* To park (aparcar).
parquedad f. Parsimony, frugality (sobriedad). || Moderation, temperance (templanza). || Scantiness, paucity: *la parquedad de las raciones*, the scantiness of the rations.
parqueo m. *Amer.* Parking (acción). | Car park [U.S., parking lot] (para estacionar).
parquet m. Parquet.
parquímetro m. Parking meter.
parra f. Grapevine (vid). || — *Hoja de parra*, fig leaf (en esculturas, etc.). || *Parra virgen*, Virginia creeper. || FIG. y FAM. *Subirse a la parra*, to blow one's top, to hit the roof (enfadarse).
parrafada f. o **parrafeo** m. FAM. Chat (charla). | Speech (perorata). || FAM. *Echar una parrafada*, to have a chat.

parrafear v. intr. To chat, to have a chat.

párrafo m. Paragraph. || — FAM. *Echar un párrafo*, to have a chat. || *Hacer párrafo aparte*, to start a new paragraph (escribiendo). || *Párrafo aparte*, new paragraph (punto y aparte), to change the subject (cambio de conversación).

parral m. Grapevine (vid). || Vine arbour [U.S., vine arbor] (parra en una armazón).

parranda f. FAM. Party, spree (juerga). || Band of musicians *o* singers (cuadrilla). || — FAM. *Andar* or *estar de parranda*, to be out on a binge *o* for a good time. | *Irse de parranda*, to go out on a binge *o* for a good time.

parrandear v. intr. FAM. To go out on a binge *o* for a good time (irse de parranda).

parrandeo m. FAM. Fling, party, binge (juerga).

parrandista m. FAM. Reveller (juerguista).

parricida m. y f. Parricide, patricide (criminal). — Adj. Parricidal, patricidal.

parricidio m. Parricide, patricide (crimen).

parrilla f. Grill, gridiron. || Grate, grating (de locomotora, de horno). || Grillroom (en un restaurante). || Earthenware jug (recipiente). || — *Bistec a la parrilla*, grilled steak. || *Carne asada en la parrilla*, grilled meat. || *Parrilla eléctrica*, electric grill.

parrillada f. Barbecue.

párroco m. Parish priest. || *Cura párroco*, parish priest.

parroquia f. REL. Parish church (iglesia). | Parish, parishioners, *pl.* (gente). | Parish (territorio). || Customers, *pl.*, clients, *pl.*, clientele (de comerciante). || Supporters, *pl.* (de equipo deportivo).

parroquial adj. Parish, parochial: *iglesia parroquial*, parish church.

parroquiano, na m. y f. [Regular] customer, client (de un comerciante). || Regular [customer] (de un bar). || REL. Parishioner.

parsec m. ASTR. Parsec.

parsimonia f. Parsimony (parquedad). || Moderation, temperance (templanza). || Calmness (calma). || *Con parsimonia*, calmly, unhurriedly.

parsimonioso, sa adj. Parsimonious. || Calm, unhurried (tranquilo).

parte f. Part: *como parte del pago*, in part payment; *parte de la oración*, part of speech; *parte del ejército quedó allí*, part of the army remained there. || Section (sección). || Share, part, portion (de un reparto). || Share, interest (comercio). || MAT. Part (v. OBSERV). || Spot, point: *parte sensible*, sensitive spot. || Side (lado). || Place, spot (lugar): *en aquella parte*, in that place. || Way (camino): *echar por otra parte*, to go a different way. || Faction, party (parcialidad, bando). || Side (rama de parentesco): *primos de* or *por parte de mi madre*, cousins on my mother's side. || TEATR. Part, role (papel): *hacer su parte*, to play one's part. | Actor, actress (actor). || Side (en una contienda): *¿por qué parte estás?*, which side are you on? || JUR. Party, part (contratante, litigante). | Portion (de herencia). || MÚS. Part. || — Pl. Private parts, privates (órganos genitales). || — *A* or *en otra parte*, somewhere else, elsewhere. || *A partes iguales*, into equal parts *o* shares. || *A una y otra parte*, on both sides. || *Constituirse parte en contra de alguien*, to bring a civil action against s.o. || *Cuarta parte*, quarter, fourth part. || *Dar parte en*, to give a share in. || *De algún, poco, mucho tiempo a esta parte no le hemos visto*, we haven't seen him for some, a short, a long time. || *De mi parte*, on my behalf, for me (en nombre mío). || *De parte a parte*, back and forth, from one side to the other (de un lado a otrc), from top to bottom, completely (sin omitir nada), right through (atravesar). || *De parte de*, from, on behalf of (en nombre de), on the side of (a favor de). || *¿De parte de quién?*, who is calling? (teléfono), your name, please? (hablando). || *De una parte a otra*, back and forth, to and fro. || *De una y otra parte*, from both sides (movimiento), on both sides (en, de los dos lados), on *o* from all sides (por todas partes). || *Echar algo a buena parte, a mala parte*, to take sth. the right way, the wrong way. || *En alguna* or *en cierta parte de España*, somewhere in Spain. || *En cualquier otra parte*, anywhere else. || *En cualquier parte donde*, anywhere. || *En dos partes iguales*, in half, into two equal parts. || *En esta parte*, here, around here, hereabouts. || *En gran parte*, to a large extent, in large measure. || *En ninguna parte*, nowhere. || *En otra parte*, somewhere else. || *En parte*, partly, in part. || *¿En qué parte de?*, in which part of?, where in? || FAM. *En salva sea la parte*, where it hurts most, you know where (las posaderas). || *En todas las partes del mundo*, in the four corners of the earth. || *En todas partes*, everywhere, all over the place (fam.). || FIG. y FAM. *En todas partes cuecen habas*, it's the same the whole world over. || *Entrar a formar parte de*, to be a part of, to form a part of. || *Entrar* or *ir a la parte en*, to take a share in, to go shares in. || *Ir a otra parte*, to go somewhere else. || *La mayor parte*, the majority, most (con el verbo en plural). || *La mayor parte de*, most, the majority of (cuando hay varios): *la mayor parte de los españoles*, most Spaniards, the majority of Spaniards; most of, the greater part of (de un entero): *la mayor parte de España*, most of Spain. || FIG. *La parte del león*, the lion's share. | *La parte en la que la espalda pierde su casto nombre*, the you know what. || *Llevar la mejor parte*, to have the advantage. || *Llevarse la mejor parte*, to come off best, to get the best of it, to get the best of the bargain. || *Mirar a otra parte*, to look the other way *o* in another direction. || FIG. *No ir a ninguna parte*, to have no importance, to be nothing (no tener importancia). || *No llevar a ninguna parte*, not to get one anywhere, to get one nowhere. || *No ser* or *no tener parte en*, to have nothing to do with. || *Parte alícuota*, aliquot part. || JUR. *Parte civil*, plaintiff claiming damages [in a criminal case]. || *Parte contraria*, opposing party (en pleito), opposing team (equipo). || *Parte del mundo*, continent. || *Parte por parte*, piece by piece, step by step, systematically. || *Partes pudendas* or *vergonzosas*, private parts, privates. || *Poner* or *hacer de su parte*, to do one's bit. || *Ponerse de parte de*, to side with. || *Por ambas partes*, on both sides. || *Por cualquier parte que lo vea*, from whichever side he looks at it. || *Por mi parte*, for my part, as for me, as far as I am concerned (en cuanto a mí), on my side (por mi lado). || *Por otra parte*, [and] on the other hand, moreover (además). || *Por parte de*, on the part of. || *Por partes*, bit by bit, stage by stage. || *Por todas partes*, everywhere, from all sides. || FIG. *Por todas partes se va a Roma*, all roads lead to Rome. || *Por una parte y por otra*, on the one hand and on the other. || *Saber de buena parte*, to have heard from a reliable source. || *Ser juez y parte*, to be judge in one's own case. || *Ser parte en*, to take part in (participar), to be a party to (en un juicio). || *Tener a uno de su parte*, to have s.o. on one's side. || *Tener* or *tomar parte en*, to take part in, to participate in, to have a part in (colaborar), to receive a share of (compartir). || *Tercera parte*, third: *disminuir algo en una tercera parte*, to reduce sth. by a third. || *Tomar en mala parte*, to take in bad part *o* badly. || *¡Vayamos por partes!*, first things first.

— M. Report (informe): *parte facultativo, meteorológico*, progress, weather report. || Despatch (telegrama oficial). || Communiqué (comunicado). || News report (diario hablado). || — *Dar parte*, to give notice. || *Dar parte de algo*, to announce sth., to let know of sth., to inform of sth. || *Dar parte de uno*, to report s.o. || MIL. *Ir al parte*, to be reported. || *Parte de boda*, wedding card.

OBSERV. *Parte* is also used to express fractions: *las dos terceras partes de nueve son seis*, six is two thirds of nine; *la tercera parte de nueve*, a third of nine.

parteluz m. Mullion (de ventana).

partenogénesis f. inv. Parthenogenesis.

Partenón n. pr. m. Parthenon.

partenueces m. inv. Nutcracker.

partera f. Midwife.

partero m. Male midwife, obstetrician.

parterre m. Flower bed (de jardín). || Stalls, *pl.*, orchestra stalls, *pl.* [U.S., orchestra] (de cine, teatro).

partición f. Sharing out, division, distribution (reparto). || Partition, division (de un territorio). || Partition (de una herencia). || MAT. Division (división). || HERÁLD. Quarter, partition.

participación f. Participation (parte): *participación en un crimen*, participation in a crime. || Contribution (contribución): *su participación en los sucesos*, his contribution to the events. || COM. Interest: *su participación en la empresa*, his interest in the firm. | Share (acción). | Investment (inversión). || Notice (aviso): *dar participación de sus propósitos*, to give notice of one's intentions. || Part of a lottery ticket (en la lotería). || DEP. Entry (en un torneo). || — *Participación de boda*, wedding card. || *Participación en los beneficios*, profit sharing.

participante adj. Participating, participant (que toma parte).

— M. y f. Informant, informer, notifier (que comunica). || Participant, participator (que toma parte). || Competitor, participant (en un concurso).

participar v. tr. To announce (una noticia): *participar la buena noticia*, to announce the good news. || To inform of (con sustantivo): *nos participó los sucesos de aquel día*, he informed us of the events of that day. || To inform, to notify (con locución verbal): *nos participa nuestro corresponsal que se ha casado X*, our correspondent informs us that X has married.

— V. intr. To participate, to take part: *participar en el trabajo*, to take part in the work. || To enter, to go in (un concurso): *participar en un concurso*, to enter [for] *o* to go in for a competition. || To partake: *el mulo participa del burro y del caballo*, the mule partakes of the ass and the horse. || To have a share: *participar en los beneficios*, to have a share in *o* of the profits. || To invest (invertir). || To share (compartir): *participar de la misma opinión*, to share the same opinion; *participar en una herencia*, to share in an inheritance.

partícipe adj. Participating, participant (que colabora). || Interested (que tiene interés).

— M. y f. Participant (que colabora). || Interested party (que tiene interés). || Beneficiary (beneficiario). || — *Hacer partícipe a uno de una cosa*, to give s.o. a share in sth. (compartir), to inform s.o. of sth. (informar), to make s.o. a party to sth. (implicar). || *Ser partícipe en*, to take part in. || *Ser partícipes en*, to be partners in (un negocio, un crimen).

participio f. GRAM. Participle. || — *Participio activo* or *de presente*, present participle. || *Participio pasivo* or *de pretérito*, past participle.
partícula f. Particle.
particular adj. Particular: *en ciertos casos particulares*, in some particular cases. || Peculiar (propio): *particular a* or *de un país*, peculiar to a country. || Peculiar (raro): *un sabor particular*, a peculiar taste. || Individual: *el interés particular debe ser sacrificado en aras del interés colectivo*, individual interest must be sacrificed to the common interest. || Personal, private: *asuntos particulares*, personal *o* private affairs; *correspondencia particular*, personal *o* private correspondence. || — *Alojarse en una casa particular*, to live with a family. || *Casa particular*, private house *o* home. || *Clase particular*, private lesson. || *En particular*, in particular. || *Nada de particular*, nothing special. || *No venga a mi despacho sino a mi casa particular*, do not come to my office but to my home *o* to my house.
— M. Matter, subject, point (asunto): *no sé nada de este particular*, I know nothing about this matter. || Member of the public (persona cualquiera). || Private individual, individual (individuo). || Civilian: *vestido de particular*, dressed as a civilian, in civilian dress.
particularidad f. Peculiarity, particularity.
particularismo m. Particularism.
particularista adj. Particularistic.
— M. y f. Particularist.
particularización f. Particularization.
particularizar v. tr. To specify, to particularize (especificar). || To prefer, to favour [U.S., to favor] (preferir). || To distinguish (diferenciar). || To give details about (detallar).
— V. pr. To stand out, to be distinguishable (destacar): *se particulariza por su color*, it stands out because of *o* it is distinguishable by its colour. || To distinguish o.s.: *se particularizó en la batalla de...*, he distinguished himself in the battle of...
particularmente adv. Particularly, in particular.
partida f. Departure (salida). || Band, gang (cuadrilla): *partida de ladrones*, band of thieves. || Certificate (de nacimiento, de matrimonio, de defunción). || COM. Entry, item (asiento en una cuenta). | Item, heading, entry (de un presupuesto)): *partida arancelaria*, tariff item; *el comercio de exportación tiene como principales partidas*, the principal items under exports are. || Consignment, batch (remesa): *una partida de muebles*, a consignment of furniture. || Party: *partida de caza*, hunting party. || MIL. Party: *partida de reconocimiento*, reconnaissance party. || Game, hand (juego): *echar una partida de naipes*, to have a game of cards. || Hand (manos de juego). || — *Contabilidad por partida doble*, double-entry bookkeeping. || *Dar la partida por ganada*, to think it is all over. || *Jugar una mala partida*, to have a bad game (jugar mal), to play a dirty trick on (hacer una mala jugada). || *Las Siete Partidas*, laws compiled by Alfonso X the Wise [13th century]. || *Partida de campo*, picnic. || *Partida de gente*, a crowd of people. || COM. *Partida doble*, double entry. || FAM. *Partida serrana*, dirty trick. || COM. *Partida simple*, single entry.
partidario, ria adj. Partisan. || Partisan, guerrilla.
— M. y f. Follower, supporter, partisan (seguidor). || Advocate (defensor). || Guerrilla, partisan (en la guerra). || *Amer.* Sharecropper (aparcero).
partidismo m. Favouritism [U.S., favoritism] (por uno). || Party spirit (en opiniones).
partidista adj. Partisan.
partido, da adj. Divided, split. || HERÁLD. Party.
— M. Party (político): *régimen de partido único*, single-party system. || Side (lado). || Camp (posición ideológica): *abandonar el partido de la oposición*, to leave the opposition camp. || Backing, support (apoyo). || Support, supporters, *pl.*, followers, *pl.* (partidarios). || Advantage, profit, benefit (ventaja). || Course [of action] (proceder). || Measure, step (medida). || Team (equipo): *el partido contrario*, the opposing team. || Game: *partido amistoso*, friendly game; *partido de pelota*, game of pelota. || Match (encuentro organizado): *partido de desempate*, deciding match; *partido de vuelta*, return match. || District (distrito). || Match (de matrimonio): *un buen partido*, a good match. || *Amer.* Small farm (finca). | Parting [U.S., part] (crencha). || — *Darse a partido*, to give in. || *Partido judicial*, judicial district. || *Sacar partido de*, to benefit by, to profit from, to take advantage of. || FIG. *Ser un partido*, to be eligible (un soltero). || *Tener partido*, to have supporters (partidarios), to be successful (tener éxito). || *Tomar el partido de*, to decide on (una cosa), to decide to (con verbo). || *Tomar partido por*, to side with. || *Venirse a partido*, to give in.
partidor m. Distributor (repartidor).
partidura f. Parting [U.S., part] (raya del pelo).
partir v. tr. To divide, to split (dividir): *partir algo en dos*, to divide sth. in two. || To share (compartir): *partir entre cuatro*, to share between four; *partir como hermanos*, to share like brothers. || To distribute (distribuir). || To crack: *partir nueces*, to crack nuts. || To cut, to chop: *partir leña*, to cut wood. || To cut (con un cuchillo): *partir una manzana por la mitad*, to cut an apple in two. || To break (con las manos): *partir el pan*, to break the bread. || FIG. To break (el corazón). || MAT. To divide. || To cut (cortar las cartas). || — FIG. *Estar a partir un piñón*, to be hand in glove. | *Partir a uno por el eje* or *por en medio* or *por la mitad*, to mess things up for s.o. (fastidiar). | FAM. *Partir la cara a uno*, to break s.o.'s neck, to smash s.o.'s face in. || *Partir la diferencia*, to split the difference (dividir), to compromise (transigir). || FIG. *¡Que le parta un rayo!*, to hell with him!
— V. intr. To set off *o* out, to leave (marcharse): *partir para Laponia*, to set off for Lapland; *partir con rumbo a*, to set out in the direction of. || FIG. To begin, to start: *partir de un supuesto falso*, to begin with a false supposition. || — *A partir de*, starting from. || *A partir de hoy*, as of today, from today on, starting today. || *Es el quinto a partir de la derecha*, he is the fifth one from the right. || *Partiendo de la base de que*, assuming that. || FIG. *Quien parte y reparte se lleva la mejor parte*, he who cuts the cake takes the biggest slice.
— V. pr. To set off *o* out, to leave (irse). || To break (romperse). || To split (dividirse). || — FIG. *Partirse de risa*, to split one's sides laughing, to die laughing. | *Partirse el pecho*, to break one's back, to slave away. | *Partirse el pecho por uno*, to go out of one's way for s.o., to do one's utmost for s.o.
partitivo, va adj./s.m. GRAM. Partitive.
partitura f. MÚS. Score.
parto m. Delivery, childbirth (de una mujer): *parto sin dolor*, painless delivery; *parto prematuro*, premature delivery. || Parturition (de un animal). || FIG. Giving birth (producción). | Brainchild, creation (obra de ingenio, resultado). || — *Asistir en un parto*, to deliver a baby. || *Estar de parto*, to be in labour (una mujer), to be parturient (animales). || *Mal parto*, miscarriage. || *Morir de parto* or *quedarse en el parto*, to die in childbirth (la madre), to be stillborn (el niño). || *Parto de la oveja*, lambing. || *Parto de la yegua*, foaling. || FIG. *Ser el parto de los montes*, to be an anticlimax.
parto, ta adj./s. Parthian: *la flecha del parto*, the Parthian shaft.
parturienta adj. f./s.f. Parturient.
parva f. AGR. Unthreshed corn.
parvedad f. Smallness, minuteness, tiny size (pequeñez). || *Hacer algo con parvedad de medios*, to barely have the means to do sth. (una acción), to barely have the means to make sth. (fabricar algo).
parvo, va adj. Small, little.
parvulario m. Infant school.
párvulo, la adj. Small, little (pequeño). || Simple, naïve, innocent (ingenuo).
— M. y f. Child, infant (niño). || *Escuela* or *colegio de párvulos*, infant school.
pasa f. Raisin (uva seca). || MAR. Channel, pass (canal estrecho). || Pass (en los juegos). || — FIG. y FAM. *Estar hecho una pasa*, to be completely wizened. || *Pasas de Corinto*, currants.
pasable adj. Passable.
pasacalle m. MÚS. Passacaglia.
pasacintas m. inv. Bodkin.
pasada f. Passage, passing (acción de pasar). || Flight (de aves). || TECN. Operation (de máquina herramienta). || Row [of stitches] (línea de puntos). || Tacking stitch (hilvanado). || EQUIT. Passade. || — *A la primera pasada no lo vi*, the first time I went past I did not see it. || *Dar una pasada con la plancha a un pantalón*, to run *o* to pass the iron over a pair of trousers. || *De pasada*, in passing: *dicho sea de pasada*, let it be said in passing. || FAM. *Hacer una mala pasada a*, to play a nasty *o* dirty trick on.
pasadero, ra adj. Passable (mediano). || Bearable (aguantable). || Fair (salud). || Passable (transitable).
— M. y f. Stepping stone.
pasadizo m. Corridor, passage (pasillo). || Alley (en las calles, etc.).
pasado, da adj. Past: *tiempos pasados*, past times. || Last: *el viernes pasado*, last Friday. || Old-fashioned, outmoded (anticuado). || Faded (descolorido). || Worn (usado). || Rotten, overripe, bad (fruta). || Off, bad (carne). || Overdone (comida guisada). || Stale (una noticia, etc.). || GRAM. Past. || — *El pasado día 3*, the third of last month (hablando), the 3rd ult. (en cartas comerciales). || *En los años pasados*, in years gone by, in years past. || *Huevo pasado por agua*, boiled egg. || *Pasadas las 12*, after twelve. || *Pasado de moda*, old-fashioned, out of date. || *Pasado mañana*, the day after tomorrow.
— M. Past: *olvidar el pasado* or *lo pasado*, to forget the past. || GRAM. Past (tiempo). || — *Lo pasado, pasado está*, let bygones be bygones (hay que olvidarlo), what is done is done (no hay que lamentarse).
pasador, ra m. y f. Smuggler (contrabandista). || — M. Colander (colador para alimentos grandes), strainer (para té, café, etc.). || Filter (filtro). || Espagnolette (de ventana). || Bolt (pestillo). || Bodkin (pasacintas). || Slide (para el pelo). || Tie clip, tie pin (de corbata). || Brochette (para condecoraciones). || Clasp (broche). || Stud (para el cuello de la camisa). || TECN. Pin. || MAR. Marlinspike, marlinespike (especie de punzón). || — Pl. Cuff links (gemelos). || *Pasador de seguridad*, safety lock.

pasaje m. Passage (paso). || Passage (de un libro). || Passage (derecho). || Fare, passage (precio del viaje). || Ticket, passage (billete de avión o barco). || Passengers, *pl.* (pasajeros). || MAR. Voyage, crossing, passage (viaje). || Alleyway, passageway (calle). || MAR. Channel, strait, pass (estrecho). || MÚS. Change of key.

pasajero, ra adj. Passing, fleeting, transient, temporary (que dura poco). || Busy (sitio frecuentado). || — Adj./s. Passenger (viajero). || — *Ave pasajera,* V. AVE. || *Capricho pasajero,* passing fancy.

pasamanería f. Passementerie. || Passementerie factory (fábrica). || Passementerie shop (tienda).

pasamanero, ra m. y f. Passementerie maker (fabricante). || Passementerie seller (vendedor).

pasamano m. o **pasamanos** m. inv. Handrail, rail (de una escalera exterior, etc.). || Banister, banisters, *pl.* (de la escalera de una casa). || Strap (para agarrarse). || MAR. Gangway.

pasamontañas m. inv. Balaclava.

pasante adj. Passing. || HERÁLD. Passant.
— M. Assistant (de abogado, de médico, etc.). || Clerk (de notario): *primer pasante,* head clerk.

pasantía f. Assistantship (función de pasante). || Probationary period (tiempo que dura).

pasapasa m. Sleight of hand (prestidigitación).

pasaportar v. tr. FAM. To deal with, to dispatch, to account for (matar). | To rush off (despachar): *pasaportar un trabajo,* to rush off a job. | To pack off (mandar): *pasaportó a su hijo a Francia,* he packed his son off to France.

pasaporte m. Passport: *expedir un pasaporte,* to issue a passport. || MIL. Travel documents, *pl.* || FIG. Free hand, carte blanche: *dar pasaporte para,* to give s.o. a free hand to. | Passport: *pasaporte a la fama,* passport to fame. || FIG. *Dar pasaporte a uno,* to give s.o. his marching orders (despedir).

pasapurés m. inv. Potato masher.

pasar v. tr. To pass (en sentido general). || To move (trasladar). || To take (llevar). || To give, to hand, to pass (dar): *pásame el azúcar,* pass me the sugar. || To pass on, to give (un mensaje). || To hand over: *pasar los poderes a,* to hand over one's powers to. || To send (una cuenta). || To take, to lead (llevar a una persona). || To give: *le he pasado mi constipado,* I have given him my cold. || To get over (curarse de una enfermedad). || To run: *pasar la mano por el pelo,* to run one's fingers through one's hair. || To sit, to take, to pass (un examen). || To cross, to pass, to go over (un río, una calle). || To pass through (atravesar). || To go over, to cross (la sierra). || To strain, to pass through (colar). || To slip, to pass: *pasar un papel por debajo de la puerta,* to slip a piece of paper under the door. || To put (poner): *pasar el brazo por la ventana,* to put one's arm out of the window. || To smuggle, to pass (de contrabando). || To pass off (falsa moneda). || To go through (traspasar). || To swallow (tragar). || To overtake, to pass (un coche). || FIG. To go beyond, to overstep (los límites). | To outdo, to be better than (superar). | To last (durar). | To suffer, to go through, to endure (desgracias, dolor físico): *¡lo que he pasado!,* the things I have been through! | To bear (tolerar, soportar). | To be (seguido de un adjetivo): *pasar mucho frío,* to be very cold. | To suffer from, to know: *pasar hambre,* to suffer from hunger. | To put up with: *no hay que pasarle todas sus tonterías,* we must not put up with all his nonsense. | To overlook, to let go *o* pass (una falta). || To spend, to pass (el tiempo): *pasar la noche fuera,* to spend the night outside; *pasa el tiempo divirtiéndose,* he spends his time enjoying himself. || To leave out, to pass over, to bypass (omitir). || To turn over: *pasar la página,* to turn over the page. || COM. To charge (en cuenta).
— *¿Cómo lo pasas?,* how are you getting on? || *Pasar a alguien a cuchillo,* to put s.o. to the sword. || *Pasar algo en limpio,* to make a fair copy of sth. || *Pasar al toro con la muleta,* to make a pass with the muleta. || *Pasar el balón a,* to pass the ball to, to pass to. || *Pasar el rato,* to while away the time, to kill time. || *Pasar en blanco,* to leave out, to miss out (omitir). || *Pasar en silencio,* to make no mention of, to keep quiet about. || *Pasar la noche en blanco,* to have a sleepless night. || FAM. *Pasarlas canutas* or *negras* or *moradas, pasar las de Caín* or *las negras,* to go through hell *o* murder, to have a rough time. || *Pasar las cuentas del rosario,* to tell one's beads. || *Pasar lista,* V. LISTA. || *Pasarlo bien,* to have a good time. || FAM. *Pasarlo bomba,* to have a great time *o* a ball *o* a whale of a time. || *Pasarlo mal,* not to enjoy o.s. (aburrirse), to have a hard time *o* a bad time (tener dificultades). || FIG. *Pasar por alto* to leave out, to skip, to miss out, to omit (omitir), to miss out, to forget about (olvidar). || *Pasar por encima,* to look *o* to glance through (un escrito), to overlook, to turn a blind eye to (hacer la vista gorda). || FIG. *Pasar por la piedra a uno,* to leave s.o. standing (vencer). || *Pasar por las armas a,* to shoot, to execute. || *Pasar revista a,* to inspect (en el cuartel), to review (en un desfile), to review (problemas, etc.). || *Pasar un mal rato,* to have a bad time of it. || *¡Que lo pase bien!,* have a good time! || *¿Qué tal lo pasó en la fiesta?,* how did you enjoy the party? || *Ya te he pasado muchas,* I have already put up with enough from you.
— V. intr. To pass (en sentido general). || To go, to pass, to move: *pasar de un sitio a otro,* to go from one place to another. || To pass, to get through *o* past *o* by: *déjame pasar,* let me pass, let me get past. || To pass: *los enemigos no pasarán,* the enemy shall not pass. || To call *o* to drop in, to come round: *pasaré por tu casa,* I shall call in at your house, I shall come round to your house. || To go through: *pasar con el disco cerrado,* to go through a red light. || To go, to pass: *este tren pasa por Londres,* this train goes through London. || To pass, to go past: *el tren pasó muy rápidamente,* the train went pass at a great speed; *el autobús pasa por tu casa,* the but goes past your house. || To come in, to go in: *¡pase!,* come in!; *dígale que pase,* tell him to come in. || To go: *ha pasado de empleado a director,* he has gone from employee to director. || To be legal tender, to pass (moneda). || To go [off] (transcurrir): *¿cómo pasó la sesión?,* how did the session go? || To happen (ocurrir): *y el accidente ¿cómo pasó?,* how did the accident happen?; *¿qué pasa?,* what's happening? || To be the matter: *¿qué te pasa?,* what's the matter with you? || To go by, to pass: *a medida que pasan los años,* as the years go by; *¡cómo pasa el tiempo!,* how time passes! || To come to an end, to be over (acabarse): *ya pasarán los malos momentos,* the bad times will soon come to an end. || To go *o* to be out [of fashion] (no estar de moda). || To wash, to do: *esta excusa no pasa,* this excuse will not wash. || To pass (ser aprobado). || To be passed *o* carried (una moción). || To be accepted (una propuesta). || To pass (cartas, juegos).
— *Aquí no pasó nada,* it is nothing to worry about, it is alright. || *De ahí no pasa,* that's all (esto es todo), that's as far as he can go (es lo más que puede hacer). || *De ésta no pasa,* this is the very last time. || *De hoy no pasa que lo haga,* I'll do it this very day. || *Hacerse pasar por,* to pass o.s. off as. || *Ir pasando,* to get by, to make out, to manage. || *Lo mismo pasa con él,* it's the same with him. || *Lo que pasa es que,* the thing is that. || *Pasar a,* to proceed: *pasemos al punto 3 del orden del día,* let us proceed to item 3 on the agenda; to come to: *paso ahora a su pregunta,* I now come to your question; to start to (con infinitivo), to start (con gerundio): *pasó a recitar otra poesía,* he started reciting another poem. || *Pasar a decir algo,* to go on to say sth. || *Pasar adelante,* to go on, to proceed. || *Pasar a mejor vida,* to pass away, to pass on to better things. || *Pasar a ser,* to become, to come to be. || *Pasar con,* to make do with, to get by with, to manage with (arreglarse), to be under instruction with (abogado, médico). || *Pasar con poco,* to get along with very little, to manage on very little, to make do with very little. || *Pasar de* (cierto número), to be more than, to be over: *pasan de los veinte,* there are more than twenty; *no pasa de los cuarenta años,* he is not more than *o* no more than forty; *pasa de los cuarenta años,* he is over forty years old. || FIG. *Pasar de castaño oscuro,* to be going too far, to be a bit much. | *Pasar de la raya* or *de los límites,* to go too far. || *Pasar de largo,* V. LARGO. || *Pasar* (*de las palabras*) *a las manos,* to come to blows. || *Pasar de moda,* to be out of fashion: *ha pasado, pasará de moda,* it is, it will be out of fashion; to go out of fashion: *el sombrero pasa de moda cada tres años,* hats go out of fashion every three years. || *Pasar de vida a muerte,* to pass away, to give up the ghost. || *Pasar por,* to be considered: *pasa por el científico más importante,* he is considered the most important scientist; to be taken for, to pass for: *pasó por invitado,* he passed for a guest. || *Pasar por casa de uno,* to call in at *o* to drop in at *o* to come round to s.o.'s house. || *Pasar por ello,* to know what it is like (saber lo duro que es), to put up with it (aguantarlo), to go through with it (hacerlo). || *Pasar por la imaginación* or *por la cabeza,* to occur to one, to cross one's mind: *ni siquiera me pasó por la cabeza,* it did not even occur to me *o* cross my mind. || *Pasar por todo con tal que,* to put up with anything as long as. || *Pasar por un puente,* to go over *o* to cross a bridge. || *Pasar sin,* to do *o* to go without (prescindir). || *Pase lo que pase,* whatever happens, happen what may, come what may. || *Pase* (*por una vez*), just don't let it happen again. || *Paso,* I pass (naipes). || *Y que pase lo que pase,* and we shall see what happens (ya veremos).
— V. impers. To happen (ocurrir).
— V. pr. To pass, to pass off (en general). || To be over: *se ha pasado la primavera,* Spring is over. || To miss: *se me pasó el turno,* I missed my turn. || To go over: *pasarse al enemigo, al otro cuarto,* to go over to the enemy, to the other room. || To go too far (excederse). || To get over: *ya se me pasará,* I'll get over it. || To forget: *se me ha pasado lo que me dijiste,* I have forgotten what you said. || To do *o* to go without (prescindir). || To fade, to wither (flores). || To fade (la belleza). || To wear out (tela). || To go bad *o* off (frutas, legumbres, etc.). || To be overdone (guisado). || To leak (recipiente). || To be porous (ser poroso). || To spend, to pass (tiempo): *se pasó seis meses allí,* he spent six months there. || To be loose (tener juego, estar holgado). || — *Pasarse de,* to be too: *pasarse de bueno,* to be too good. || FIG. *Pasarse de la raya* or *de los límites,* to go too far. | *Pasarse de listo* or *de vivo,* to be too clever by half. | *Pasarse*

de rosca, v. ROSCA. || *Pasarse el peine*, to run a comb through one's hair. || *Pasarse el tiempo cantando*, to be always singing. || *Pasárselo en grande*, to have a whale of a time, to have a fabulous time. || *Pasarse por*, to call in at, to pass by: *pasarse por la oficina*, to call in at the office.

pasarela f. Footbridge (puentecillo). || MAR. Gangway, gangplank (de embarcación). || Catwalk (en los teatros).

pasatiempo m. Pastime, hobby, amusement.

pascal m. Pascal (unidad de presión).

pascua f. Passover (fiesta judía). || Christmas (Navidad): *¡felices Pascuas y próspero Año Nuevo!*, merry Christmas and a happy New Year! || Easter (pascua de Resurrección). || Epiphany (los Reyes). || Pentecost (Pentecostés). || — FIG. y FAM. *Cara de pascua*, v. CARA. || *Comulgar por Pascua florida*, to do one's Easter duty, to take the Sacrament at Easter. || *Dar las pascuas*, to wish s.o. a merry Christmas. || FIG. *Estar como unas pascuas*, to be as happy as a lark, to be as pleased as Punch. || FAM. *Hacer la pascua a alguien*, to mess things up for s.o. (fastidiar). || FIG. *Ocurrir de Pascuas a Ramos*, to happen once in a blue moon. || *Pasar las Pascuas en familia*, to spend Christmas with one's family *o* at home. || *Pascua del Espíritu Santo*, Whitsunday, Pentecost. || *Pascua de Navidad*, Christmas. || *Pascua de Resurrección*, Easter. || *Pascua florida*, Easter. || FAM. *Y santas pascuas*, and that's all there is to it, and that's that.

pascual adj. Paschal.

pase m. Pass (autorización). || Permission (permiso). || Invitation. || Showing (de una película). || DEP. y TAUR. Pass. || Feint (en esgrima). || COM. Permit. || Pass (de prestidigitador, etc.). || *Amer.* Passport (pasaporte). || — DEP. *Pase adelantado* or *adelante*, forward pass. || *Pase de favor*, safe-conduct (salvoconducto). || DEP. *Pase hacia atrás*, backward pass, back pass.

paseante adj. Passing, going past (transeúnte).
— M. y f. Passer-by (pl. *passers-by*), walker, stroller (transeúnte). || — Pl. People out for a walk, strollers. || FIG. *Paseante en corte*, loafer.

pasear v. tr. To take for a walk (dar un paseo). || FIG. To parade, to show off (exhibir, fanfarronear).
— V. intr. y pr. To go for a walk: *pasearse por el campo*, to go for a walk in the country. || To take a walk (dar un paseo). || To go for a ride (en bicicleta, coche, caballo). || To go for a trip (en barco). || To run: *las chinches se paseaban por todas partes*, bugs were running all over the place. || FIG. To idle, to loaf about (holgazanear).

paseíllo m. Opening parade (de toreros).

paseo m. Walk (a pie), drive, ride (en coche), ride (en bicicleta, a caballo), trip, row, sail (en barco): *dar un paseo*, to go for a walk *o* ride, etc. || Excursion. || Walking (acción). || Promenade, walk, public walk, avenue (avenida). || Parade (de toreros). || — FIG. *Dar el paseo*, to take s.o. out to be shot (fusilar). | *Mandar* or *enviar a uno a paseo*, to send s.o. away, to send s.o. packing, to tell s.o. to go to blazes. | *Mandarlo todo a paseo*, v. MANDAR. | *¡Váyase a paseo!*, go to blazes! go to hell!

pasicorto, ra adj. Who *o* which takes short steps.

pasiego, ga adj./s. [Of *o* from the] Pas Valley [in the Spanish province of Santander]. || — FAM. F. Nurse (ama de cría).

pasiflora f. BOT. Passionflower.

pasillo m. Corridor, passage (corredor). || TEATR. Promenade (en la sala). | Short play, sketch (obra corta). || FIG. Lobby. || *Amer.* Mat (estera). || — *Pasillo aéreo*, air corridor. || *Pasillo rodante*, public walkway [U.S., moving sidewalk].

pasión f. Passion: *dejarse llevar por la pasión*, to give way to passion, to let passion take over; *tener pasión por la música*, to have a passion for music. || REL. Passion: *la Pasión según San Mateo*, the Passion according to St. Matthew. || *Tener pasión por alguien*, to be passionately fond of s.o., to have a passion for s.o.

pasional adj. Passional. || *Crimen pasional*, crime of passion, crime passionel.

pasionaria f. BOT. Passionflower.

pasito adv. Gently, softly.

pasitrote m. Short trot.

pasividad f. Passivity, passiveness.

pasivo, va adj. Passive. || — *Clases pasivas*, pensioners. || *Pensión pasiva*, State pension, pension. || GRAM. *Voz pasiva*, passive voice, passive.
— M. COM. Liabilities, *pl.* || *En el pasivo*, on the debit side.

pasmado, da adj. Flabbergasted, astounded, amazed, completely astonished (de asombro). || Frozen stiff, perished (de frío). || Stupefied, openmouthed (atontado). || Frozen (plantas). || — *Mirar con cara de pasmado*, to look in astonishment at, to look flabbergasted at. || *Pasmado de admiración*, overwhelmed with wonder, flabbergasted, astounded, amazed.

pasmar v. tr. To leave flabbergasted, to flabbergast, to astound, to amaze, to astonish (asombrar): *su respuesta me ha pasmado*, his answer left me flabbergasted. || To freeze to death (enfriar mucho a uno). || To freeze, to blight (helar las plantas). || To make [s.o.] faint (causer desmayo).
— V. pr. To be flabbergasted *o* astounded *o* amazed *o* astonished (quedarse asombrado). || To be frozen stiff, to be perished (estar helado). || To be frozen (las plantas). || To faint (desmayarse). || MED. To get lockjaw. || To tarnish, to fade (colores, barniz).

pasmarota f. FAM. Fuss.

pasmarote m. FAM. Dope, dunce (necio).

pasmo m. Chill (enfriamiento). || MED. Lockjaw. || FIG. Amazement, astonishment, shock (asombro). | Marvel, wonder (lo que produce asombro).

pasmoso, sa adj. Amazing, astounding, astonishing.

paso m. Step, pace: *dar tres pasos*, to take three steps. || Walk, gait (modo de andar). || Gait (del caballo). || Pace (ritmo): *aminorar el paso*, to slow down one's pace. || Step, pace (distancia): *a tres pasos*, three steps away. || Passing, passage (acción): *al paso del tren*, on the train's passing; *el paso del tiempo*, the passage of time. || Crossing, passage (cruce): *el paso del mar Rojo por los judíos*, the crossing of the Red Sea by the Jews. || Path, way, way through, passage: *el paso está libre*, the path is clear. || Passage (derecho). || Clearing, surmounting (de un obstáculo). || Step, stair (de escalera). || Footprint, track (huella). || Footstep (ruido del paso). || Track, trail (rastro de la caza). || Pass (naipes). || Step (de baile). || Deed (aventura). || FIG. Advance, advances, *pl.*, progress: *la industria aeronáutica ha dado un gran paso últimamente*, the aircraft industry has made great progress *o* great advances lately. | Transition (transición). | Step, move (trámite): *dar pasos para*, to take steps *o* to make moves towards. || Passage, migration (de las aves). || Stitch (en costura). || GEOGR. Pass (entre montañas). | Strait, straits, *pl.* (estrecho): *Paso de Calais*, Straits of Dover. || "Paso", stage [each important stage in the Passion of Christ, and the platforms bearing sculptured scenes from the Passion, carried through the streets in Holy Week]. || TEATR. Sketch, short play. || Pitch (de hélice, de tornillo).
— *Abrir paso a*, to make way for. || *Abrirse* or *hacerse paso entre*, to force *o* to fight one's way through (en una muchedumbre, etc.), to break through (las tropas). || *Abrirse paso a codazos, a tiros*, to elbow, to shoot one's way through. || *Abrirse paso en la vida*, to make one's way in life (triunfar). || *A buen paso*, at a good pace, smartly, quickly. || FIG. *A cada paso*, at every step *o* turn. || *Adelantar cuatro pasos*, to take four steps forward, to go forward *o* to advance four steps. || FIG. *A dos pasos*, a few steps away, a short way away. || FIG. *A ese paso*, at this *o* that rate. || FIG. *A grandes pasos*, by leaps and bounds (avanzar). || *Alargar el paso*, to lengthen one's stride, to step out. || *Al paso*, in passing, on the way, when one passes by (al pasar), at a walking pace: *ir al paso*, to go at a walking pace; slowly (lentamente). || *Al paso que*, at the same time as, while (al mismo tiempo), as (como). || *Al paso que va*, at this rate. || *A mi paso*, as I went by *o* passed, in passing. || *A mi paso por Londres*, when I pass through London. || *Andar al mismo paso que*, to keep pace with. || FIG. *Andar a paso de buey* or *de carreta*, to go at a snail's pace. || *Andar a paso largo*, to stride. || FIG. *Andar con pasos contados*, to tread warily, to watch one's step. | *Andar en malos pasos*, to go astray, to get into bad ways. || MIL. *A paso de ataque* or *de carga* or *gimnástico* or *ligero*, at the double. | *A paso de maniobra*, at ease. || FIG. *A paso de tortuga*, at a snail's pace. || *A paso lento*, at a slow pace. || *A pasos agigantados*, with giant strides (con paso largo), by leaps and bounds (muy rápidamente). || *A pocos pasos*, a few steps away. || *Apretar* or *acelerar* or *aligerar el paso*, to quicken one's pace. || *Ave de paso*, v. AVE. || *Ceda el paso*, give way (señal de tráfico). || *Ceder el paso a*, to make way for, to let [s.o.] pass (dejar pasar), to give way to, to give place to (dar lugar a). || *Cerrar el paso*, to block the way (interceptar el camino), to put a stop to (impedir). || *Coger algo al paso*, to collect sth. on one's way *o* in passing. || *Coger el paso*, to get *o* to fall into step (sentido propio), to get into the swing of things, to get the hang of it (adaptarse). || *Coger un peón al paso*, to take a pawn in passing (ajedrez). || *Con paso alegre*, gaily, happily. || *Cortar el paso a uno*, to block s.o.'s path, to cut s.o. off, to intercept s.o., to bar s.o.'s way. || *Dar (el) paso a uno*, to let s.o. pass. || FIG. *Dar los primeros pasos*, to take the first steps, to make the first moves. | *Dar* or *dejar paso a*, to open the way to. | *Dar un buen paso*, to take a great step. | *Dar un mal paso*, to make a wrong move, to take a false step. || *Dar un paso adelante*, to step forward, to take a step forward (al andar), to make progress, to gain ground: *ha dado un paso adelante en su vida*, he has made progress in life; *las negociaciones han dado un paso adelante*, progress has been made in the negotiations. || *Dar un paso atrás*, to step back, to take a step backwards (al andar), to lose ground (retroceder). || *Dar un paso en falso*, to stumble, to trip (andando), to make a wrong move, to take a false step (obrar desacertadamente). || *Dejar paso libre*, v. DEJAR. || *De paso*, in passing, on the way: *de paso iré a ver a mi tía*, on the way I shall call in and see my aunt; passing through, stopping off: *estaba de paso en Madrid*, I was just passing through Madrid *o* stopping off

in Madrid; in passing: *de paso habló del Cid*, in passing he talked about El Cid. || *Dicho sea de paso*, incidentally, by the way. || *Enderezar sus pasos a*, to direct one's steps towards, to make one's way towards. || *Entrar de paso*, to drop in, to call in. || FIG. *Estar a dos pasos de la muerte*, to be at death's door. || MIL. *Ir al paso*, to keep *o* to march in step. || *Lo difícil es el primer paso*, the first step is the most difficult. || FIG. *Ir por sus pasos contados*, to go one's own sweet way, to jog along at one's own pace. | *Llevar a buen paso*, to speed along. || MIL. *Llevar el paso* or *ir con paso acompasado*, to keep *o* to march in step. || *Mal paso*, fix, tight spot: *sacarle a uno de un mal paso*, to get s.o. out of a fix. || MIL. *Marcar el paso*, to mark time. || *Medir a pasos*, to pace (a room), to pace *o* to pace off *o* to pace out (a distance). || FIG. *Medir sus pasos*, to watch one's step. | *No podemos dar un paso sin*, we cannot do anything *o* we cannot make a move without. || *¡Paso!* or *¡paso libre!*, gangway!, make way! || FIG. *Paso adelante*, breakthrough, step forward, step in the right direction: *este descubrimiento ha sido un gran paso adelante*, this discovery was a great breakthrough. || *Paso a nivel*, level crossing [U.S., railroad *o* grade crossing]. || *Paso a paso*, step by step. || *Paso atrás*, step backwards (andando), backward step (retroceso). || EQUIT. *Paso de ambladura* or *de andadura*, amble. | *Paso de costado*, passage. || *Paso de cuatro*, pas de quatre (danza). || MIL. *Paso de la oca*, goose step. || *Paso del ecuador*, crossing the line (línea ecuatorial), half-way point [in a course of study] (mitad de la carrera). || *Paso de peatones*, pedestrian crossing [U.S., crosswalk]. || MAR. *Paso de popa a proa*, fore-and-aft gangway. || MÚS. *Paso doble*, paso doble. || *Paso elevado*, flyover. || *Paso firme*, sure step. || *Paso franco* or *libre*, free passage *o* access. || *Paso protegido*, right-of-way (señal de tráfico). || *Paso subterráneo*, subway (para peatones), underpass (para coches). || *Primeros pasos*, first steps (de un niño, de una ciencia), début: *dar sus primeros pasos en la diplomacia*, to make one's début as a diplomat. || *Prohibido el paso*, no entry, no trespassing (para personas), no entry, no thoroughfare (para los automóviles). || *Quitar algo del paso*, to move sth. out of the way. || *Romper el paso*, to break step. || FIG. *Salir al paso de*, to forestall: *salir al paso de las críticas*, to forestall one's critics; to waylay: *hoy Pablo me salió al paso*, Paul waylayed me today; to go to meet (salir al encuentro de). | *Salir del paso*, to get out of trouble *o* out of the fix. || *Seguir los pasos a uno*, to watch s.o.'s every move (observar). || *Seguir los pasos de uno*, to follow *o* to trail s.o. (seguir), to follow in s.o.'s footsteps (imitar). || JUR. *Servidumbre de paso*, right-of-way. || MIL. *¡Un paso al frente, ar!*, one step forward, march! || *Volver sobre sus pasos*, to retrace one's steps, to go back (desandar lo andado), to retract *o* to withdraw *o* to take back a statement (desdecirse).
— Adv. Gently, softly: *hable paso*, speak softly.

paso, sa adj. Dried (fruta). || — *Ciruela pasa*, prune. || *Uvas pasas*, raisins.

pasodoble m. Paso doble.

pasoso, sa adj. *Amer.* Porous.

pasquín m. (Ant.). Pasquinade, lampoon (epigrama). || Poster (cartel). || Tract (octavilla).

passing-shot m. Passing shot (tenis).

pasta f. CULIN Paste, dough (masa sin cocer). | Pastry (masa cocida): *pasta de hojaldre*, puff pastry. || Paste: *pasta de gambas*, shrimp paste. || Full binding (de un libro). || ARTES. Impasto (empaste). || FIG. Makings, *pl.* (madera): *tiene pasta de torero*, he has the makings of a bullfighter. || FAM. Dough, cash, loot (dinero). || — Pl. Pasta, *sing.* (tallarines, etc.). || Petits fours, small cakes [U.S., cookies] (pastelillos). || — *Libro en pasta*, bound book. || *Media pasta* or *pasta holandesa*, quarter binding. || *Pasta de dientes* or *dentífrica*, toothpaste. || *Pasta de hígado*, pâté de foie, liver paste. || *Pasta de madera*, wood pulp. || *Pasta de papel*, paper pulp. || FIG. y FAM. *Ser de buena pasta*, to be a good soul, to be good-natured. | *Tiene muy buena pasta*, he's got what it takes, there is good stuff in him.

pastaca f. *Amer.* Pork stew (guiso).

pastaflora f. Sponge cake. || FIG. y FAM. *Ser de pastaflora*, to be a good soul.

pastaje o **pastal** m. *Amer.* Pasture.

pastar v. tr. e intr. To pasture, to graze.

pasteca f. MAR. Snatch block.

pastel m. Cake: *pastel de crema, de almendras*, cream, almond cake. || Pie: *pastel de carne*, meat pie; *pastel de frutas*, fruit pie. || Pastel (color, dibujo, lápiz). || FIG. y FAM. Crooked *o* sharp dealing (trampa). | Mess (lío). || IMPR. Pie (letras confundidas). || — Pl. Pastry, *sing.* || — *Azul pastel*, pastel blue. || FIG. y FAM. *Descubrir el pastel*, to get wise, to cotton on (adivinar), to spill the beans, to squeal (chivarse). || *Dibujo al pastel*, pastel, pastel drawing. || *Hierba pastel*, woad (planta). || *Pintar* or *dibujar al pastel*, to do pastel drawings, to draw in pastels.

pastelear v. intr. FIG. y FAM. To play for time, to stall (temporizar). | To be a bootlicker (adular).

pasteleo m. FIG. y FAM. Stalling, playing for time (temporización). | Licking, bootlicking (adulación).

pastelería f. Cakes, *pl.*, pastries, *pl.* (pasteles). || Confectionery (dulces). || Confectioner's, cake shop (tienda).

pastelero, ra m. y f. Pastrycook (repostero). || Person who sells cakes (vendedor). || FIG. y FAM. Staller (que temporiza). | Bootlicker, licker (adulador).

pastelista m. y f. Pastellist (pintor).

pastense adj. [Of *o* from] Pasto.
— M. y f. Inhabitant *o* native of Pasto (ciudad de Colombia).

pasterización o **pasteurización** f. Pasteurization.

pasterizado, da o **pasteurizado, da** adj. Pasteurized.

pasterizar o **pasteurizar** v. tr. To pasteurize (esterilizar por pasterización).

pastiche m. Pastiche, imitation (de una obra).

pastilla f. Bar, cake, tablet (de jabón). || Piece, square (de chocolate). || Pastille, lozenge (de menta, etc.). || MED. Tablet (tableta). || — *Pastilla de café con leche*, toffee. || *Pastilla para la tos, para la garganta*, cough drop, throat lozenge.

pastinaca f. Whip-tailed sting ray (pez). || BOT. Parsnip.

pastizal m. Pasture *o* grazing land, pasture.

pasto m. Pasture, pasture *o* grazing land, pasturage (sitio). || Grazing (acción). || Pasture, pasturage (hierba). || Food, fodder, feed (pienso para el ganado). || FIG. Food, nourishment (alimento). || *Amer.* Grass, lawn (césped). || — FIG. y FAM. *A pasto*, in plenty. | *A todo pasto*, without limit, freely, in great quantity. || *Dar algo de pasto a los cerdos*, to feed sth. to the pigs. || FIG. *Dar pasto a*, to give cause for (causar). || *De pasto*, table (vino). || *Derecho de pasto*, grazing rights. || FIG. *El incidente sirvió de pasto a los periódicos*, the newspapers thrived on the incident. | *Las novelas son su pasto*, he thrives on novels. || *Pasto comunal*, common pasturage, common pasture. || FIG. *Pasto espiritual*, spiritual food *o* sustenance *o* nourishment. || *Pasto seco*, fodder. || FIG. *Ser pasto de la actualidad*, to be a headline story. | *Ser pasto del fuego* or *de las llamas* or *del incendio*, to be fuel for the flames, to be consumed by the fire *o* the flames. | *Su nombre sirve de pasto al chismorreo*, his name is food for gossip.

pastor, ra m. y f. Shepherd (hombre), shepherdess (mujer) [que cuida el ganado]. || — M. Protestant minister, clergyman, pastor (sacerdote). || — *El Buen Pastor*, the Good Shepherd. || *Perro pastor*, sheepdog.

pastoral adj. Pastoral. || *Anillo pastoral*, pastoral ring.
— F. Pastoral (poema, del obispo). || MÚS. Pastorale.

pastorear v. tr. To graze, to pasture, to put out to pasture (apacentar). || FIG. To lead, to guide (el sacerdote).
— V. intr. To graze, to pasture.

pastorela f. Pastourelle.

pastoreo m. Shepherding.

pastoril adj. Pastoral.

pastosidad f. Pastiness. || Furring, furriness (de la lengua). || Pastosity, thickness (de pintura).

pastoso, sa adj. Pasty, doughy (blando, suave). || Pastose, thick, impasto (pintura). || — *Boca, lengua pastosa*, coated *o* furry mouth, tongue. || *Voz pastosa*, rich *o* mellow voice.

pasturaje m. Pasture, pasture *o* grazing land. || Grazing rights, *pl.* (derecho).

pata f. Leg (pierna de animal). || Foot (pie de animales bípedos). || Paw (pie de animales cuadrúpedos con garras). || Hoof (pie de caballo, vaca, cerdo, oveja, etc.): *pata hendida*, cloven hoof. || FAM. Leg (pierna del hombre). || Leg (de mueble): *una mesa de cuatro patas*, a table with four legs. || Tab, strap (de vestidos). || Duck (hembra del pato). || — FAM. *¡Abajo las patas!*, hands off! (hablando a una persona), down!, get down! (a un animal). | *A cuatro patas*, on all fours (a gatas). || FIG. *A la pata coja*, blindfold (muy fácilmente). || FIG. *A la pata la llana*, simply, without ceremony *o* formalities. || *Andar a la pata coja*, to hop [along]. || FAM. *A pata*, on foot (a pie). || *De pata hendida*, cloven-hoofed. || FIG. y FAM. *Echar las patas por alto*, to blow one's top, to go mad (con enfado). | *¡En cada pata!*, and the rest! [said of a person who claims to be younger than he or she is]. | *Enseñar la pata*, to show the cloven hoof, to reveal one's true self. | *Estirar la pata*, to kick the bucket (morir). | *Mala pata*, tough *o* bad luck. | *Metedura de pata*, bloomer, blunder. | *Meter la pata*, to put one's foot in it. | *Pata de banco*, clanger: *salir con una pata de banco*, to drop a clanger. || *Pata de cabra*, heel-glazing iron (herramienta de zapatero). || *Pata de gallina*, starshake (enfermedad de los árboles). || *Pata de gallo*, goose foot (planta), broken check material (tela), clanger (fam.) [despropósito]. || MAR. *Pata de ganso*, crowfoot. || *Pata de mosca*, scrawl (garabatos). || *Pata de palo*, wooden leg, peg leg. || FAM. *Patas arriba*, flat on one's back (caer), upside down, topsy turvy (desordenado). || *Patas de gallo*, crow's feet (arrugas). || FIG. y FAM. *Poner a uno de patas en la calle*, V. PATITA. | *Tener mala pata*, to be unlucky.

pataca f. BOT. Jerusalem artichoke.

patada f. Kick (puntapié). || Stamp (en el suelo). || — FIG. y FAM. *A patadas*, loads of, thousands of: *hay pasteles a patadas*, there are loads of cakes. | *Dar la patada a alguien*, to give s.o. the boot. | *Darle* *cien patadas a uno*, to get on one's nerves (molestar). || *Dar patadas en el suelo*, to stamp one's feet. || FIG. y FAM. *Darse (de) patadas*, to clash: *el verde se da de patadas con el azul*, green clashes with blue. || *Dar una patada a*, to kick. || FIG. y FAM. *Echar a alguien a patadas*, to kick s.o. out. | *Hacer algo a patadas*, to make a botch of sth., to botch sth. | *Hacer algo en dos patadas*, to do sth. in two ticks *o* in two shakes. | *Largar una patada en el trasero*, to kick s.o. in the pants *o* up the behind *o* up the backside. | *Le costará muchas patadas lograrlo*, you will have to push for it. | *Tratar a patadas*, to kick *o* to push around.

patagón, ona adj./s. Patagonian.

Patagonia n. pr. f. GEOGR. Patagonia.

patagónico, ca adj. Patagonian.

patalear v. intr. To hop about with rage, to stamp one's feet with rage (de rabia). || To kick (el niño en la cuna).

pataleo m. Stamping (en el suelo). || Kicking (en el aire). || FIG. y FAM. *El derecho de* or *al pataleo*, the right to kick *o* to protest.

pataleta f. Tantrum, fit: *a Pedro le dio una pataleta*, Peter went into *o* threw a tantrum, Peter had a fit.

patán m. FAM. Country bumpkin, yokel (rústico). | Duffer, lout, boor (tonto).

patanería f. FAM. Churlishness, boorishness.

¡pataplún! interj. Crash!, bang!

patarráez m. MAR. Preventer shroud.

Patas n. pr. m. FAM. Old Nick (el demonio).

patata f. Potato: *patata temprana*, early *o* new potato; *puré de patatas*, mashed potatoes. || Potato (batata): *patatas dulces*, sweet potatoes. || — *Patata de caña*, Jerusalem artichoke (pataca). || *Patatas al vapor*, boiled potatoes. || *Patatas fritas*, chips [U.S., French fries]. || *Patatas fritas a la inglesa*, crisps [U.S., potato chips]. || *Patatas paja*, potato straws.

patatal o **patatar** m. Potato field.

patatero, ra adj. Potato, of the potato. || FAM. Risen from the ranks (oficial del ejército).
— M. y f. Potato grower (cultivador), potato seller (vendedor).

patatín patatán (que) FAM. And so on and so forth.

patatús m. inv. FAM. Faint, fainting fit (desmayo). || FAM. *Le dio un patatús*, he went out like a light.

pateador, ra adj. *Amer.* Which kicks, vicious (animal). || *Ser pateador*, to kick, to be a kicker.

pateadura f. o **pateamiento** m. FAM. Stamping. | Scolding (represión). | Jeers, *pl.* (de una obra de teatro).

patear v. tr. FAM. To kick (dar patadas a), to stamp on (pisar). || FIG. To tread on, to trample on (pisotear). | To boo, to jeer, to give the bird (una obra de teatro).
— V. intr. FAM. To stamp one's feet (en el suelo). | To bustle about, to chase about all over the place (para conseguir algo). || DEP. To kick, to punt (en rugby). || To kick (animal). || To kick (arma).

patena f. REL. Paten. || FIG. *Limpio como una patena*, as clean as a whistle *o* as a new pin.

patentado, da adj. Patent, patented.
— M. y f. Patentee.

patentar v. tr. To patent (invento). || To register, to patent: *marca patentada*, registered trade mark.

patente adj. Patent, obvious (evidente). || *Letras patentes*, letters patent.
— F. Licence [U.S., license] (autorización). || Patent (de invención). || MAR. Sea letter. || *Amer.* Licence plate (de automóvil). || — *Hacer patente*, to show clearly, to make evident. || MAR. *Patente de corso*, letter *o* letters of marque. || MAR. *Patente de navegación*, ship's certificate of registration. | *Patente de sanidad*, bill of health. | *Patente limpia, sucia*, clean, foul bill of health.

patentemente adv. Patently, obviously.

patentizar v. tr. To make evident *o* obvious, to show.

pateo m. FAM. Stamping (de impaciencia, rabia). || Trampling (pisoteo). || Jeers, *pl.* (en el teatro).

paterfamilias m. inv. Paterfamilias.

paternal adj. Paternal: *autoridad paternal*, paternal authority. || Fatherly: *amor paternal*, fatherly love.

paternalismo m. Paternalism.

paternalista adj. Paternalistic.

paternidad f. Paternity, fatherhood: *la paternidad acarrea muchas responsabilidades*, paternity entails many responsibilities. || FIG. Paternity (de una idea). || — *Atribuir la paternidad de un libro a*, to father a book on. || *Investigación de la paternidad*, affiliation suit.

paterno, na adj. Paternal (autoridad). || Fatherly (cariño). || Paternal, on one's father's side: *mi abuelo paterno*, my paternal grandfather, my grandfather on my father's side.

paternóster m. Lord's Prayer, Paternoster (oración).

Pateta n. pr. m. FAM. Old Nick (demonio).

patético, ca adj. Pathetic, moving, touching, poignant (conmovedor).

patetismo m. Pathos.

patiabierto, ta adj. FAM. Bandy, bowlegged.

patibulario, ria adj. Sinister, harrowing: *rostro patibulario*, sinister expression.

patíbulo m. Scaffold, gallows, *pl.* (cadalso). || FIG. *Carne de patíbulo*, gallows bird.

paticojo, ja adj. FAM. Gammy-legged, lame.
— M. y f. FAM. Cripple, lame person.

paticorto, ta adj. Short-legged.

patidifuso, sa adj. FAM. Flabbergasted, dumbfounded, nonplussed: *quedarse patidifuso*, to be flabbergasted.

patilargo, ga adj. Long-legged.

patilla f. Scar (de un arma de fuego). || Arm, side (de gafas). || MÚS. Position of the left hand on guitar-like instruments. || — Pl. Sideburns, sideboards, sidewhiskers (pelo en las sienes). || Kiss curls (peinado femenino).

Patillas n. pr. FAM. Old Nick (el demonio).

patilludo, da adj. With long thick sideburns.

patín m. Skate (para patinar): *patín de hielo* or *de cuchilla*, ice skate; *patín de ruedas*, roller skate. || Shoe (calzado de niños pequeños). || Scooter (patineta). || Paddle boat (hidropedal). || Runner (de un trineo). || AVIAC. Skid (de aterrizaje): *patín de cola*, tail skid. || TECN. Shoe, block (del freno).

pátina f. Patina. || — *Dar pátina a*, to patinate, to coat with a patina. || *La pátina del tiempo*, weathering.

patinadero m. Skating rink.

patinador, ra m. y f. Skater.

patinaje m. Skating: *patinaje sobre ruedas*, roller skating; *patinaje artístico*, figure skating; *patinaje sobre hielo*, ice skating. || Skidding (de un coche).

patinar v. intr. To skate (un patinador). || To skid (un vehículo). || To slide (resbalar voluntariamente). || To slip, to slide (resbalar sin querer). || FIG. To slip up, to make a blunder *o* a slip (meter la pata).
— V. tr. To patinate, to coat with a patina, to give a patina to (dar pátina).

patinazo m. Skid (de un vehículo). || FIG. y FAM. Slip, boob, blunder (planchazo). || *Dar un* or *pegar un patinazo*, to skid, to go into a skid (resbalar), to make a slip *o* a boob *o* a blunder, to slip up (meter la pata).

patineta f. o **patinete** m. Scooter.

patinillo m. Small yard (de una casa).

patio m. Yard (de una casa). || Patio (en una casa española). || — TEATR. *Butaca de patio*, seat in the stalls [U.S., seat in the orchestra]. | *Patio de butacas*, stalls, *pl.* [U.S., orchestra]. || *Patio de escuela* or *de recreo*, schoolyard, playground. || *Patio de Monipodio*, den of thieves.

patiquebrar v. tr. To break the leg of [an animal].

patita f. FIG. y FAM. *Poner a uno de patitas en la calle*, to kick s.o. out, to throw s.o. out on his ear (echar).

patitieso, sa adj. Stiff-legged (con las piernas paralizadas). || FIG. y FAM. Paralysed [with cold, fear, etc.]. | Stiff, starchy, stuck-up (estirado). || — FIG. y FAM. *Dejar patitieso*, to dumbfound, to astound, to astonish (asombrar). | *Quedarse patitieso*, to be bowled over *o* astounded *o* astonished *o* flabbergasted (asombrarse).

patituerto, ta adj. Crooked-legged. || FIG. y FAM. Crooked, lopsided, misshapen (torcido).

patizambo, ba adj. Knock-kneed. || Cow-hocked (caballo).

pato m. Duck: *pato salvaje* or *silvestre*, wild duck || Drake (pato macho). || FAM. Drip, bore, dull person (persona sosa y tonta). || — FIG. y FAM. *La edad del pato*, an awkward age. | *Pagar el pato*, to carry the can, to foot the bill. || *Pato de flojel*, eider (ave).

patochada f. Blunder, bloomer (disparate). || — *Decir patochadas*, to talk nonsense. || *Hacer patochadas*, to play the fool.

patogenia o **patogenesia** f. MED. Pathogenesis.

patogénico, ca adj. MED. Pathogenetic, pathogenic.

patógeno, na adj. MED. Pathogenic.

patología f. MED. Pathology.

patológico, ca adj. MED. Pathologic, pathological.

patólogo, ga m. y f. Pathologist.

patoso, sa adj. FAM. Clumsy, awkard (torpe). Tiresome, wearisome (cargante).
— M. y f. Bore.

patraña f. FAM. Hoax, fabrication (mentira).

patrañero, ra m. y f. FAM. Hoaxer, joker, trickster.

patria f. Mother country, homeland, fatherland, native land: *volver a la patria*, to return to one's mother country. || — *La madre patria*, mother country, motherland. || *La patria chica*, home, one's home town *o* area. || *Merecer bien de la patria*, to have served one's country well. || *Patria adoptiva*, country of adoption. || *Patria celestial*, heaven, paradise.

patriarca m. Patriarch.

patriarcado m. Patriarchate. || Patriarchate, patriarchy (régimen).

patriarcal adj. Patriarchal.
— F. Patriarchal church. || Patriarchate (territorio).

patriciado m. Patriciate.

Patricio n. pr. m. Patrick.

patricio, cia adj. Patrician. || Aristocratic, noble.
— M. y f. Patrician. || Aristocrat, noble.

patrimonial adj. Patrimonial, hereditary.

patrimonio m. Patrimony, heritage. || — *Patrimonio forestal del Estado*, crown forests (en Inglaterra), State forests (en otros países). || *Patrimonio real*, crown land.

patrio, tria adj. Native, home: *suelo patrio*, native soil. || Paternal (del padre): *patria potestad*, paternal authority. || *Amer.* Army, belonging to the army (caballo).

patriota adj. Patriotic.
— M. y f. Patriot.
patriotería f. Chauvinism, jingoism.
patriotero, ra adj. Chauvinistic, jingoistic.
— M. y f. Chauvinist, jingoist.
patriótico, ca adj. Patriotic.
patriotismo m. Patriotism.
patrístico, ca adj. Patristic.
— F. Patristics.
patrocinador, ra adj. Sponsoring.
— M. y f. Sponsor, patron (hombre), patroness (mujer).
patrocinar v. tr. To sponsor, to patronize: *campaña patrocinada por*, campaign sponsored by.
patrocinio m. Patronage, sponsorship (amparo).
patrón m. Patron. || Captain, skipper, master (de un barco). || Landlord (de pensión). || Master (de esclavos). || Pattern (en costura). || Standard (modelo): *patrón oro*, gold standard. || REL. Patron. || FIG. Master, boss (jefe). || — FIG. *Cortado por el mismo patrón*, cast in the same mould, tarred with the same brush. | *Donde hay patrón no manda marinero*, the boss is the boss. || BOT. *Patrón de injerto*, stock. || REL. *Santo patrón*, patron saint.
patrona f. Patroness (protectora). || Landlady (de casa de huéspedes). || Employer (jefe). || Owner (dueña). || REL. Patron saint, patroness,
patronal adj. Employers', of employers: *sindicato patronal*, employers' association *o* union. || REL. Patronal. || *Cierre patronal*, lockout.
patronato m. Patronage, sponsorship (protección): *bajo el patronato de*, under the patronage of. || Board of trustees (de una obra benéfica). || Board, organization (organización): *patronato de turismo*, tourist board. || Employers, *pl.* (patronos). || Trust, foundation (fundación). || Centre (centro). || Society: *patronato de los Amigos de...*, society of the Friends of... || — *Patronato de apuestas mutuas*, pari-mutuel. || *Patronato real*, royal patronage.
patronazgo m. Patronage: *bajo el patronazgo de*, under the patronage of. || *A Santa Bárbara corresponde el patronazgo de la artillería*, Saint Barbara is the patron saint *o* the patroness of artillerymen.
patronímico, ca adj./s.m. Patronymic.
patrono, na m. y f. Boss (jefe). || Patron saint, patron (santo), patron saint, patroness (santa). || Patron (hombre), patroness (mujer) [de una obra benéfica]. || Owner, employer (empresario).
patrulla f. Patrol: *estar de patrulla*, to be on patrol. || FIG. Band, group (cuadrilla). || — *Coche patrulla*, patrol car. || *Estar de patrulla en* or *por*, to patrol: *unos soldados estan de patrulla en la frontera*, soldiers patrol the border. || *Jefe de patrulla*, patrol leader.
patrullar v. intr. To patrol, to go on patrol.
patrullero, ra adj. Patrol (avión, buque).
— M. Patrol boat (barco). || Patrol car (coche). || Patrol plane (avión).
patulea f. FAM. Bunch of kids (chiquillos). | Disorderly soldiers, *pl.* (soldadesca). | Mob (muchedumbre).
Paúl adj./s. REL. Vincentian (de San Vicente de Paúl).
paular v. intr. FAM. To chat, to talk (hablar). || — FAM. *Ni paula ni maula*, he doesn't even open his mouth. | *Sin paular ni maular*, without saying a word.
paulatinamente adj. Slowly, little by little, gradually.
paulatino, na adj. Slow, gradual. || *De un modo paulatino*, gradually.
paulina f. Decree of excommunication. || FIG. y FAM. Scolding, reprimand (reprensión).
paulista adj. [Of *o* from] São Paulo [Brazil].
— M. y f. Native *o* inhabitant of São Paulo. || — M. Paulinist (miembro de una congregación).
Paulo n. pr. m. Paul.
pauperismo m. Pauperism.
pauperización f. Pauperization.
paupérrimo, ma adj. Very poor, poverty-stricken.
pausa f. Pause, break (interrupción). || Slowness (lentitud). || MÚS. Rest. || — *A pausas*, at intervals. || *Con pausa*, calmly, unhurriedly.
pausado, da adj. Slow, calm. || *Pausado en el hablar*, deliberate in one's speech.
— Adv. Slowly, calmly, unhurriedly.
pauta f. Rule, guide (regla). || Line, lines, *pl.* (rayas). || FIG. Model, example (dechado): *servir de pauta a*, to act as a model for. || MÚS. Staff (del papel). || *Amer.* Writing guide (falsilla). || FIG. *Dar* or *marcar la pauta*, to set the example, to lay down the norm *o* the guideline.
pautar v. tr. To rule. || FIG. To regulate: *vida pautada*, regulated life. || MÚS. To rule (pentagrama). || *Papel pautado*, ruled paper (para escribir), music paper.
pava f. Turkey-hen (ave). || FIG. Bore, dull woman (mujer sosa). || Furnace bellows, *pl.* (fuelle). || FAM. Butt (colilla). || *Amer.* Kettle (para el mate). || — *Pava real*, peahen. || FIG. y FAM. *Pelar la pava*, to court, to woo.
pavada f. Flock of turkeys. || FIG. y FAM. Silliness, foolishness, stupidity (tontería).
pavana f. Pavan (danza).
pavés m. Large shield (escudo grande).
pavesa f. Spark, ember (chispa). || Cinder (ceniza). || — FIG. y FAM. *Estar hecho una pavesa*, to be a shadow of one's former self. | *Pavesa humana*, human torch.
pavía f. Clingstone peach (fruto).
Pavía n. pr. GEOGR. Pavia.
pávido, da adj. Terrified.
pavimentación f. Paving [of a street *o* road] (revestimiento). || Tiling, flooring (con losas, losetas).
pavimentar v. tr. To pave (con adoquines, asfalto, etc.). || To tile, to floor (con losas, losetas).
pavimento m. Paving, pavement (de adoquines, asfalto, etc.). || Tiling, flooring (de losas o losetas).
pavipollo m. Young turkey. || FAM. Dunce, fool (bobo).
pavisoso, sa o **pavitonto, ta** adj. Silly, stupid, foolish (mentecato).
— M. y f. Ninny, nincompoop, fool: *este chico es un pavitonto*, this boy is a fool.
pavo m. Turkey (ave). || FIG. y FAM. Ninny, drip (necio). | Five pesetas (un duro). || *Amer.* Stowaway (polizón). || — FIG. y FAM. *Comer pavo*, to be a wallflower (en un baile). | *Edad del pavo*, awkward age. | *Encendido como un pavo*, as red as a beetroot. | *Hincharse como un pavo real* or *ser más orgulloso que un pavo*, to be as proud as a peacock. | *No es moco de pavo*, V. MOCO. || *Pavo real*, peacock. || FIG. y FAM. *Subírsele a uno el pavo*, to blush, to go as red as a beetroot. | *Tener pavo*, to be shy *o* timid.
pavón m. Peacock (pavo real). || Peacock butterfly (mariposa). || TECN. Bluing, bronzing (del acero).
pavonado, da adj. Dark blue. || Blued, bronzed (acero).
— M. Bluing, bronzing (del acero).
pavonar v. tr. To blue, to bronze (acero).
pavonear v. tr. To deceive, to delude (engañar).
— V. intr. y pr. To strut, to peacock, to show off (presumir).
pavoneo m. Strutting, showing off.
pavor m. Fear, terror, panic, dread.
pavorosamente adj. Fearfully, frightfully (de una manera espantosa). || Trembling with fear (con pavor).
pavoroso, sa adj. Fearful, frightful, dreadful, terrifying (espantoso).
paya f. *Amer.* Improvised song of a travelling minstrel.
payada f. *Amer.* Improvised song of a travelling minstrel (canción). | Party at which travelling minstrels perform and compete with each other (fiesta).
payador m. *Amer.* Travelling minstrel.

— OBSERV. The word *payador* was used in the 19th century, notably in the countries of the River Plate, to designate the travelling minstrels who improvised songs to the accompaniment of their guitars. Santos Vega is the outstanding example of the Argentinan *payador*.

payadura f. *Amer.* Improvised song.
payar v. intr. To improvise songs accompanying o.s. on the guitar.
payasada f. Clownery, buffoonery, clowning. || *Hacer payasadas*, to clown about, to act the clown.
payasear v. intr. To clown, to clown about.
payaso m. Clown (del circo). || FIG. Clown, buffoon, joker (persona poco seria). || *Hacer el payaso*, to act the clown.
payés, esa m. y f. Peasant [in Catalonia and the Balearic Islands]. || *Payeses de remensa*, serfs bound to the soil (en la Cataluña medieval).
payo, ya adj. Peasant, rustic. || Who is not a Gypsy (en el lenguaje de los gitanos). || — M. y f. Peasant (campesino). || FAM. Fool, dunce (mentecato). || *Amer.* Albino.
paz f. Peace: *pedir la paz*, to sue for peace; *mantener la paz*, to keep the peace. || Peacefulness, tranquillity, peace and quiet (tranquilidad). || REL. Pax (imagen que besaban los fieles). || — Pl. Peace, *sing.*: *firmar las paces*, to make peace (individuos). || — *¡A la paz de Dios!*, God be with you! || *Dejar en paz*, to leave alone, to leave be: *déjame en paz*, leave me alone; *deja en paz esa silla, a tu hermano*, leave that chair, your brother alone. || *Descansar en paz*, to rest in peace. || *Estar en paz*, to be at peace (no estar en guerra), to be even, to be quits (no deberse nada). || *Firmar la paz*, to sign a peace treaty (Estados). || *Hacer las paces*, to make [it] up, to make peace. || *Mantenimiento de la paz*, peace-keeping. || *No dar paz a la lengua*, not to stop talking, not to shut up (fam.). || *No dejar en paz a uno*, to give s.o. no peace, to plague s.o. || *¡Paz a sus cenizas!*, peace to his ashes! || *Paz octaviana*, Octavian peace. || *Pipa de la paz*, V. PIPA. || *Poner paz*, to make peace, to reconcile: *poner paz entre varias personas*, to make peace, between *o* to reconcile several people. || *Quedar en paz*, to make peace (no estar más en guerra), to get even (saldar la deuda). || *Que en paz descanse*, may he rest in peace: *mi marido, que en paz descanse, era militar*, my husband, may he rest in peace, was a serviceman. || *Tener la conciencia en paz*, to have a clear conscience. || *¡Vaya en paz!*, go in peace! || *¡Y aquí paz y después gloria!* or *¡y en paz!*, it's as simple as that!, that's all there is to it!, and that's final!
pazguatería f. Silliness, simplicity, doltishness (simpleza). || Prudishness (mojigatería).
pazguato, ta adj. Silly, simple, doltish (simple). || Old-maidish, prudish (mojigato).
— M. y f. Simpleton, dolt (tonto). || Prude (gazmoño).
pazo m. Country manor (en Galicia).
¡pche! o **¡pchs!** interj. Pshaw!, bah!
pe f. P [name of the letter p]. || *De pe a pa*, from beginning to end, from A to Z.

pea f. POP. Drunkenness (borrachera). || — POP. *Agarrar una pea*, to get blind drunk, to get pissed. | *Tener una pea encima*, to be blind drunk *o* pissed.
peaje m. Toll (derecho de paso).
peajero, ra m. y f. Toll collector.
peal m. *Amer.* Lasso, *m.* (lazo).
pealar v. tr. *Amer.* To lasso (el caballo).
peana f. Stand, pedestal (zócalo). || Platform (del altar). || Window sill (de una ventana). || FIG. *Adorar el santo por la peana*, to court the mother in order to marry the daughter.
peatón m. Pedestrian (transeúnte): *paso de peatones*, pedestrian crossing [U.S., crosswalk].
pebe m. *Amer.* Kid, youngster (niño).
pebeta f. *Amer.* Young girl.
pebete m. Joss stick (sustancia aromática). || FIG. y FAM. Stink (mal olor). || Fuse, touch paper (de cohete). || *Amer.* Kid, youngster (niño).
pebetero m. Incense burner.
peca f. Freckle (en la piel).
pecadillo m. Peccadillo.
pecado m. Sin: *pecado mortal, venial, original*, mortal *o* deadly, venial, original sin. || Defect (defecto en una cosa). || FIG. y FAM. Shame, crying shame (lástima): *¡qué pecado!*, what a shame!, it's a crying shame! || — FIG. y FAM. *De mis pecados*, of mine: *esta niña de mis pecados*, this child of mine. || FIG. *En el pecado va la penitencia*, every sin carries its own punishment. || *Estar en pecado*, to be in sin. || *Los siete pecados capitales*, the seven deadly sins. || FIG. y FAM. *Más feo que un pecado*, as ugly as sin. || *Morir en pecado*, to die unrepentant. || *No hay pecado sin remisión*, there is no sin without remission. || *Pecado confesado es medio perdonado*, a fault confessed is half redressed. || *Pecado nefando*, sodomy. || *Por mis pecados*, for my sins. || *Todo pecado merece perdón*, there is forgiveness for every sin.
pecador, ra adj. Sinful, sinning.
— M. y f. Sinner, transgressor. || *Pecador de mí*, sinner that I am.
pecaminoso, sa adj. Sinful.
pecar v. intr. To sin. || FIG. To be at fault (razonamiento). | To do *o* to be wrong (una persona). || — *No pecar de generoso*, not to be guilty of generosity, not to be exactly overgenerous. || *Pecar con la intención* or *de intención*, to have sinful *o* evil thoughts. || *Pecar de palabra, de obra*, to sin by word, by deed. || *Pecar de severo, de confiado*, to be too *o* overly severe, confident. || *Pecar por defecto*, to fall short of the mark. || *Pecar por exceso*, to overdo it, to go too far. || *Pecar por omisión*, to sin by omission.
pecarí o **pécari** m. Peccary (mamífero).
pecblenda f. MIN. Pitchblende.
peccata minuta loc. lat. FAM. Peccadillo.
pecera f. Fishbowl (redonda), aquarium (acuario).
pecio m. Flotsam, wreckage (de un naufragio).
pecíolo o **peciolo** m. BOT. Petiole.
pécora f. Head of sheep (res lanar). || FIG. *Mala pécora*, wicked woman (mujer mala), tramp (prostituta).
pecoso, sa adj. Freckled, freckly: *cara pecosa*, freckled face. || *Niña pecosa*, freckle-faced girl.
— M. y f. Freckle-faced person.
pectíneo, a adj. ANAT. Pectineal (músculo).
pectoral adj. Pectoral: *músculos pectorales*, pectoral muscles. || Cough: *pastillas pectorales*, cough drops.
— M. Pectoral cross (de obispo). || Pectoral, cough medicine. || Breastplate (de sacerdote judío). || Pectoral (adorno).
pecuario, ria adj. [Of] livestock.
peculado m. JUR. Peculation, embezzlement.
peculiar adj. Peculiar, particular, characteristic: *traje peculiar de una región*, costume peculiar to *o* characteristic of a region.
peculiaridad f. Peculiarity.
peculio m. Peculium. || FIG. Own *o* private *o* personal money: *lo tuve que pagar de mi peculio*, I had to pay it out of my own money.
pecuniariamente adv. Pecuniarily, financially (económicamente). || Cash (en metálico).
pecuniario, ria adj. Pecuniary. || *Pena pecuniaria*, fine.
pechada f. *Amer.* Push [with the chest] (empujón). | Touch for a loan (sablazo). || FAM. *Darse una pechada de trabajar*, to work a lot.
pechar v. tr. To pay as a tax (pagar). || *Amer.* FAM. To push [with the chest] (empujar). | To sponge off [s.o.], to touch [s.o.] for a loan (pedir dinero).
— V. intr. FAM. *Pechar con*, to shoulder, to take on, to bear: *pechar con el trabajo más difícil*, to shoulder the most difficult job. || FAM. *Siempre tengo que pechar con la más gorda*, I always get stuck with the fattest girl.
pechblenda f. MIN. Pitchblende.
pechera f. Shirtfront (de camisa de hombre). || Front (de otras prendas de vestir). || Jabot (chorrera). || Breast collar (arnés del caballo). || FAM. Breast, bosom (de la mujer). || *Amer.* Apron (mandil). || *Pechera postiza*, dicky.
pechero, ra adj. Taxable. || Plebeian (plebeyo).
— M. Bib (babero). || Plebeian, commoner (plebeyo). || Taxpayer (que paga tributo).
pechina f. Shell (venera). || ARQ. Pendentive (de bóveda).
pecho m. ANAT. Chest: *en el pecho*, on the chest. | Breast, bosom, bust (de la mujer). || Breast (de un animal). || Slope, gradient (repecho). || Tax, tribute (tributo). || FIG. Heart (ánimo). | Courage, spirit (valor, esfuerzo). | Voice (calidad de la voz). || — FIG. *Abrir su pecho a alguien*, to unbosom o.s. *o* to open one's heart to s.o. | *A lo hecho, pecho*, it is no use crying over spilt milk. || MED. *Angina de pecho*, angina pectoris. || FIG. *A pecho descubierto*, unprotected, defenceless (sin protección), with an open heart (con franqueza). || *Apretar contra su pecho*, to hug to one's breast. || FIG. *Criar a sus pechos*, to take s.o. under one's wing. || *Dar el pecho*, to breast-feed, to nurse, to suckle (a un niño), to face [up to], to confront (a un peligro). || FIG. *Descubrir el pecho*, to open one's heart. || FIG. y FAM. *Echarse entre pecho y espalda*, to put *o* to tuck away. || *Enfermo del pecho*, consumptive. || FIG. *No caberle a alguien la alegría, el orgullo en el pecho*, to be bursting with happiness, pride. | *Partirse el pecho*, V. PARTIR. || *Sacar el pecho*, to stick out one's chest. || *Tomar el pecho*, to nurse, to suck (un niño). || *Tomar* or *tomarse una cosa a pecho*, to take sth. to heart.
pechuga f. Breast [of fowl] (pecho de ave): *una pechuga de pollo*, a breast of chicken. || FIG. y FAM. Slope, gradient (cuesta). | Bosom (de mujer). || *Amer.* Sangfroid, nerve.
pechugona adj. FAM. Big-breasted, big-bosomed, buxom.
— F. FAM. Big-breasted girl *o* woman, buxom lass.
pedagogía f. Pedagogy.
pedagógico, ca adj. Pedagogic, pedagogical, teaching.
pedagogo m. Pedagogue [U.S., pedagog]. || Teacher, educator (educador). || Tutor (ayo). || Schoolmaster (maestro de escuela). || FAM. Pedant.
pedal m. Pedal: *los pedales de una bicicleta*, the pedals of a bicycle; *pedal de embrague, de freno*, clutch, brake pedal. || MÚS. Pedal (de piano, órgano): *pedal fuerte*, loud pedal. || *Dar a los pedales*, to pedal.
pedalear v. intr. To pedal.
pedaleo m. Pedalling.
pedáneo adj. m. JUR. *Juez pedáneo*, justice of the peace.
pedanía f. *Amer.* District.
pedante adj. Pedantic.
— M. y f. Pedant.
pedantear v. intr. To be pedantic.
pedantería f. Pedantry.
pedantesco, ca adj. Pedantic.
pedantismo m. Pedantism, pedanticism, pedantry.
pedazo m. Piece: *un pedazo de pan*, a piece of bread. || — *A pedazos*, in pieces, in bits. || *Caerse a pedazos*, to fall to pieces *o* to bits. || FIG. *Caerse uno a pedazos* or *estar hecho pedazos*, to be worn out, to be all in, to be dead beat. | *Ganarse un pedazo de pan*, to earn one's living. || *Hacer pedazos*, to break *o* to smash to pieces (romper), to tear to pieces (desgarrar), to tear to pieces (a una persona). || *Hacerse pedazos*, to fall to pieces. || FIG. y FAM. *Morirse* or *estar (muerto) por los pedazos de alguien*, to be madly in love with s.o. | *Pedazo de alcornoque, de animal, de bruto*, you dope, you beast, you brute. | *Pedazo del alma* or *del corazón*, apple of one's eye. || *Saltar algo en pedazos*, to blow to pieces. || FIG. *Ser un pedazo de pan*, to be kindness itself. | *Tener el corazón hecho pedazos*, to be heartbroken.
pederasta m. Paederast [U.S., pederast].
pederastia f. Paederasty [U.S., pederasty].
pedernal m. Silex. || Flint (piedra de chispa). || FIG. *Duro como el* or *como un pedernal*, as hard as a rock.
pederse v. pr. POP. To fart.
pedestal m. Pedestal (de estatua): *pedestales de mármol*, marble pedestals. || Stand, pedestal (peana). || FIG. Stepping-stone (apoyo). || *A su madre la tiene (puesta) en un pedestal*, he has placed his mother on a pedestal.
pedestre adj. Pedestrian. || FIG. Pedestrian, commonplace. | Vulgar. || *Carrera pedestre*, footrace.
pedestrismo m. Footrace (deportes).
pediatra o **pedíatra** m. MED. Paediatrician, paediatrist [U.S., pediatrician, pediatrist].
pediatría f. MED. Paediatrics [U.S., pediatrics].
pedicular adj. Pedicular.
pedículo m. BOT. Peduncle (pedúnculo).
pedicuro, ra m. y f. Chiropodist (callista). || — F. Chiropody (cuidado de los pies).
pedido m. COM. Order: *entregar, hacer un pedido*, to fill, to make an order; *los pedidos pendientes*, [the] pending orders. || Request (petición): *hacer, atender un pedido*, to make, to grant a request. || — *A pedido de*, at the request of. || *Hoja de pedido*, order form.
pedidor, ra adj. Demanding (exigente). || Who is always asking for sth.
— M. y f. Petitioner. || Client, customer (cliente).
pedigree o **pedigrí** m. Pedigree.
pedigüeño, ña adj. FAM. Persistent.
— M. y f. FAM. Pest, nuisance.
pediluvio m. MED. Foot bath.
pedimento m. Petition, request. || JUR. Suit, petition. | Claim of ownership (en derecho inmobiliario). || JUR. *Pedimento del fiscal*, indictment of the public prosecutor.
pedir* v. tr. To ask for, to request (seguido de sustantivo): *pedir dinero, un libro*, to ask for money, for

a book. || To ask (seguido de un verbo): *me pidió que le pagase la deuda*, he asked me to pay off the debt. || To ask for, to order (encargar): *pedir un café*, to order a cup of coffee. || To beg (pedir limosna). || COM. To order (hacer un pedido). || To require, to demand (requerir): *tal oficio pide paciencia*, such a job requires patience. || To ask (poner precio): *pide demasiado por el piso*, he is asking too much for the flat. || To ask for s.o.'s hand in marriage (a una mujer). || — *A pedir de boca*, V. BOCA. || *No hay más que pedir*, what more do you want? || *No se puede pedir más*, one couldn't ask for more. || *Pedir disculpas*, to apologize. || JUR. *Pedir en justicia*, to sue. || *Pedir la luna*, V. LUNA. || *Pedir la paz*, to sue for peace. || *Pedir limosna*, to ask for alms, to beg. || FIG. *Pedir peras al olmo*, to ask for the impossible. || *Pedir prestado*, to borrow: *tuve que pedir prestado diez libras*, I had to borrow ten pounds; to ask [s.o.] to lend, to ask for a loan of, to ask to borrow: *me pidió prestado el coche*, he asked me to lend him my car, he asked to borrow my car. || *Pedir socorro* or *auxilio*, to ask for help.

pedo m. POP. Fart (ventosidad). | Drunkenness (borrachera). || — POP. *Estar pedo*, to be canned, to be pissed (estar borracho). || *Pedo de lobo*, puffball (hongo). || POP. *Pegarse* or *tirarse un pedo*, to fart, to break wind.

pedología f. Pedology.

pedorrera f. POP. String of farts.

pedorrero, ra adj. POP. Farting.
— M. y f. POP. Farter.

pedrada f. Blow with *o* from a stone (golpe). || — *A pedradas*, by stoning. || *Matar a pedradas*, to stone to death. || *Pegar una pedrada a uno*, to throw a stone at s.o. || FIG. y FAM. *Venir* or *caer como pedrada en ojo de boticario*, to come in the nick of time, to come just right.

pedrea f. Stoning (con piedras). || Fight with stones, stone-throwing fight (combate). || Hail (granizo). || FIG. y FAM. Small prizes, *pl.* (en la lotería).

pedregal m. Stony *o* rocky ground.

pedregoso, sa adj. Stony, rocky.

pedrería f. Precious stones, *pl.*, jewels, *pl.*

pedrisca m. Hail (granizo). || Hailstorm (granizada).

pedriscal m. Stony *o* rocky ground.

pedrisco m. Hail (granizo). || Hailstorm (granizada). || Stony ground (pedregal).

pedrizo, za adj. Stony, rocky.
— F. Stony *o* rocky ground (pedregal). || Stone wall (valla).

Pedro n. pr. m. Peter. || FIG. *Como Pedro por su casa*, as if he owned the place.

pedrusco m. Rough stone.

pedunculado, da adj. BOT. Pedunculate, pedunculated.

peduncular adj. BOT. Peduncular.

pedúnculo m. BOT. y ANAT. Peduncle.

peerse v. pr. POP. To fart, to break wind.

pega f. ZOOL. Magpie (urraca). | Remora (pez). || Sticking (acción de pegar con cola). || Pitch, coating (baño de pez). || FAM. Hoax, trick (chasco). | Difficulty: *aclarar una pega a un alumno*, to clear up a difficulty for a student. | But, snag: *hay una pega*, there is a but (hay un pero). | Snag (engorro): *asunto lleno de pegas*, job full of snags. | Difficulty, problem: *hoy no hay ninguna pega para conseguir un pasaporte*, today there is no problem in getting a passport. | Inconvenience (inconveniente). | Beating, thrashing (zurra). || MIN. Firing of a blast (de barreno). || — FAM. *De pega*, sham, fake. | *Ésa es la pega*, that's the catch *o* snag. | *Poner pegas a*, to find fault with (criticar), to put up obstacles to, to raise objections to (poner dificultades).

pegada f. DEP. Stroke, hit (en pelota, tenis, etc.). | Punch, blow (en boxeo).

pegadizo, za adj. Sticky (pegajoso). || FIG. Sponging (gorrón). | Contagious, catching: *tener una risa pegadiza*, to have a contagious laugh. | Catchy (música, etc.). | False, imitation (falso).

pegado, da adj. Stuck (con cola). || Burnt: *la leche está pegada*, the milk is burnt. || FAM. Bad, hopeless, useless: *estar pegado en matemáticas*, to be hopeless at mathematics. || *Oler a pegado*, to smell of burning.
— M. Patch, sticking plaster.

pegador m. MIN. Blaster. || Puncher (boxeador).

pegadura f. Sticking, gluing, glueing (acción de pegar). || Joint (unión).

pegajosidad f. Stickiness. || Viscosity (viscosidad).

pegajoso, sa adj. Sticky (que se pega). || Viscous, sticky (viscoso). || Contagious, catching (contagioso). || FIG. y FAM. Mellow (meloso). | Tiresome, boring (cargante).

pegamento m. Glue (para pegar). || Rubber solution (para los parches).

pegar v. tr. To stick (término más general): *pegar un sello en un sobre*, to stick a stamp on an envelope. || To glue, to paste (con cola). || To put up, to post (carteles). || To sew on (coser): *pegar un botón*, to sew on a button. || To fire: *pegar un tiro*, to fire a shot. || To put flush against *o* right up against: *pegar el piano a la pared*, to put the piano flush against the wall. || To give, to strike (golpes): *pegar un palo*, to strike a blow with a stick. || To hit, to strike: *pegar a un niño*, to hit a child. || To let out: *pegar un grito*, to let out a yell. || To hit (al balón). || To give: *le he pegado mi enfermedad*, I have given him my illness. || — MIL. *Codos pegados al cuerpo*, elbows in. || *Goma de pegar*, glue. || *Iban pegados uno a otro*, they walked along side by side *o* arm in arm. || *No pegar ojo*, not to sleep a wink. || *Papel de pegar*, sticking paper. || FAM. *Pegarle cuatro gritos a alguien*, to give s.o. a piece of one's mind, to haul s.o. over the coals. || *Pegar fuego a algo*, to set fire to sth. || *Pegar saltos de alegría*, to jump for joy. || *Pegar un salto*, to jump. || *Pegar un susto a uno*, to give s.o. a fright, to frighten s.o. || *Pelo pegado*, plastered-down hair. || *Sin pegar un tiro*, without firing a shot.
— V. intr. To stick (adherir). || To go, to match (sentar bien o mal): *dos colores que no pegan uno con otro*, two colours which don't go together. || To fit, to go [well], to look right: *este cuadro no pega aquí*, this picture doesn't go here *o* doesn't look right here. || To touch, to adjoin (estar contiguo). || To hit (dar un golpe). || To beat (dar una paliza). || To strike, to hit (dar en un punto, en el blanco, etc.). || To trip, to stumble (tropezar). || To beat down, to be hot (el sol). || — *No me pega que haya sido él*, I don't think *o* believe that it was he. || *No pega*, it's not right (no conviene), it won't hold, it won't wash (no venga con cuentos). || *Pegar duro* or *fuerte*, to hit hard. || *Quien pega primero pega dos veces*, the first blow is half the battle.
— V. pr. To stick (fijarse, adherir en general). || To get close to, to press o.s. against: *pegarse a la pared*, to get close to the wall. || To burn, to stick to the pan (un guiso): *el arroz se ha pegado*, the rice has burnt. || To lie down on: *pegarse al suelo*, to lie down on the ground. || To hit each other *o* one another, to fight (pelearse varias personas). || FIG. To hang around s.o., to stick to s.o. (estar siempre con una persona). | To be catching *o* catchy: *el acento del Sur se pega fácilmente*, the Southern accent is very catching. | To be contagious, to be catching (una enfermedad). | To pass on (una costumbre). || FAM. To lead (llevar): *¡hay que ver la vida que se pega!*, you should see the life he leads! | To get through (una comilona, un trabajo). | To go on (hacer un viaje, dar un paseo). | To have (tener, pasar). | To become fond of, to take a liking to (aficionarse). || — FIG. *Coche que se pega muy bien a la carretera*, car which holds the road well. || *El coche se pegó a la acera*, the car pulled over to the curb. || FIG. *¡Es para pegarse un tiro!*, it's enough to make you scream! | *Esta canción se me ha pegado al oído*, I can't get this song out of my mind. || FIG. y FAM. *Pegarse como una lapa*, V. LAPA. | *Pegársela a uno*, to take s.o. in, to put one over on s.o. (engañar): *se la pegó a su socio*, he took his partner in; to deceive: *se la pegaba a su marido*, she was deceiving her husband; to fool, to trick, to catch (hacer picar con una broma o engaño). | *Pegársele a uno las sábanas*, V. SÁBANA. || *Pegarse un tiro*, to shoot o.s.

pegaso m. Pegasus (pez).

Pegaso n. pr. m. MIT. Pegasus.

pegatina f. Sticker.

pego m. FAM. *Dar el pego*, to fool, to take in (engañar).

pegote m. Plaster, sticking plaster (emplasto). || FIG. y FAM. Sticky mess, stodgy mess (guiso apelmazado). | Compact mass (cosa espesa). | Sponger (gorrón). | Patch, botch (parche). | Tasteless addition (en una obra de arte). || FAM. *¡Qué pegote!*, what a pest *o* a nuisance! (persona), what a sight! (cosa).

pegual m. *Amer.* Cinch, girth (sobrecincha).

peguntoso, sa adj. Sticky, gluey.

peinada f. FAM. Combing.

peinado, da adj. Combed.
— M. Hairstyle (del pelo). || Combing, carding (de textiles).

peinador, ra m. y f. Hairdresser (el que peina).
— M. Peignoir, bathrobe (bata). || *Amer.* Dressing table (tocador). || — F. Wool-combing machine.

peinadura f. Combing [the hair] (acción). || — Pl. Combings.

peinar v. tr. To comb s.o.'s hair: *peinar a un niño*, to comb a child's hair. || To comb: *peino mi peluca a diario*, I comb my wig daily. || To do s.o.'s hair: *¿quién peina a la reina?*, who does the Queen's hair? || To comb out (desenredar). || To brush, to touch (rozar ligeramente). || To comb, to card (la lana). || — FIG. y FAM. *Peinar canas*, to be getting old, to be going grey. | *Peinar los naipes*, to stack the cards.
— V. pr. To comb one's hair. || To have one's hair done (hacerse peinar).

peinazo m. Lintel (de puerta o ventana).

peine m. Comb (para el pelo). || Comb, card (para la lana). || Reed (de telar). || FIG. y FAM. Sly fellow (hombre astuto), sly minx (mujer astuta). || TEATR. Gridiron (telar). || — *Pasarse el peine*, to comb one's hair. || *Peine de balas*, cartridge clip. || *Peine espeso*, toothcomb [U.S., fine-tooth comb].

peineta f. Back comb [large ornamental comb]. || *Amer.* Toothcomb [U.S., fine-tooth comb] (lendrera). || FIG. y FAM. *¡Mira qué peineta!*, you must be joking!
— OBSERV. The *peineta* is a large curved comb usually made of shell. It is worn in the chignon and serves to hold the mantilla in place.

peje m. Fish (pez). || FIG y FAM. Crafty devil (astuto). || — *Peje araña*, stingfish (pez). || *Peje diablo*, scorpion fish (pez).

pejepalo m. Stockfish, dried cod.
pejesapo m. Toadfish, angler.
pejiguera f. FAM. Nuisance, bind, drag (fastidio).
Pekín n. pr. GEOGR. Peking.
pekinés, esa adj./s. Pekingese, *inv.*, Pekinese, *inv.* — M. Pekingese, pekinese (perro).
pela f. Peeling (de frutas o legumbres). || FAM. Peseta: *dame cinco pelas*, give me five pesetas.
pelada f. *Amer.* Haircut (corte de pelo). | Bald head (calva). | Blunder (tontería). || *Amer.* FAM. *La pelada*, death (muerte).
peladar m. *Amer.* Bare land (páramo).
peladera f. MED. Alopecia, baldness. || *Amer.* Gossip (crítica).
peladilla f. Sugared almond (almendra confitada). || FIG. Pebble (guijarro). || FAM. Bullet (proyectil).
pelado, da adj. Bald, hairless (cabeza). || Peeled (la piel). || Bare, barren (terreno). || Peeled, pared (mondado). || Fleshless, clean (hueso). || Plain (estilo). || Round (número): *un número pelado*, a round number. || FIG. Bare: *nos pagaron el sueldo pelado*, they paid us the bare salary. || Smooth (guijarro). || *Amer.* Insolent (insolente). | Coarse (grosero). || — FAM. *Dejar a uno pelado, estar pelado*, to leave s.o. broke, to be broke. | *Tengo cien pesetas peladas*, I've only got a hundred pesetas.
— M. Bare patch (terreno). || Haircut (corte de pelo). || FAM. Pauper, poor man (pobre). | Poor devil (pobre diablo). || *Amer.* Fellow, guy (individuo). | Child (niño).
pelador m. Barker (que descorteza).
peladura f. Barking (de árboles). || Peeling (de frutas). || Peelings, *pl.* (mondaduras).
pelafustán m. FAM. Idler, ne'er-do-well (perezoso). | Poor devil (pobre hombre).
pelagatos m. inv. FAM. Poor devil, ragamuffin (pobre hombre). || FAM. *Había cuatro pelagatos*, there was hardly anybody.
pelagianismo m. Pelagianism (herejía).
pelagiano, na adj./s. Pelagian.
pelágico, ca adj. Pelagic (de alta mar): *fauna pelágica*, pelagic fauna.
Pelagio n. pr. m. Pelagius (hereje).
pelagra f. MED. Pellagra.
pelaje m. Coat, fur (de un animal). || FIG. y FAM. Appearance, looks, *pl.* (apariencia). || FAM. *Y otros del mismo pelaje*, and others like him.
pelambre m. Hair, fur, coat (pelo del animal). || Lime pit (baño de cal). || MED. Alopecia, baldness (caída del pelo). || — F. FAM. Mop (cabellera), long hair (pelo largo), thick hair (pelo espeso).
— OBSERV. This word is often used in the feminine.
pelambrera f. Mob (cabellera), long hair (pelo largo), thick hair (pelo espeso). || Baldness (calvicie).
pelamen m. FAM. Hair (pelambre).
pelana m. o **pelanas** m. inv. FAM. Poor devil, ragamuffin (pelagatos).
pelandusca f. FAM. Prostitute, whore (ramera).
pelapatatas m. inv. Potato peeler.
pelar v. tr. To cut (el pelo). || To peel: *pelar patatas, un melocotón*, to peel potatoes, a peach. || To shell (mariscos, guisantes, habas). || To pluck (ave). || To strip (un árbol, un hueso, etc.). || FIG. y FAM. To clean out, to fleece (ganar a otro todo el dinero). | To strip, to despoil (despojar). | To pull to pieces, to slate (criticar). || *Amer.* To beat. || — FIG. y FAM. *Duro de pelar*, a hard nut. | *Hace un frío que pela*, it is freezing cold, it is icy. || FIG. *Pelar la pava*, to court, to woo. || *Amer. Pelar los ojos*, to open one's eyes wide, to goggle, to stare wide-eyed.
— V. pr. FAM. To get one's hair cut. || To peel (la piel). || *Amer.* To become confused (confundirse). || — FAM. *Correr que se las pela*, to run like mad. || FAM. *Pelárselas*, to do sth. speedily. | *Pelárselas por una cosa*, to be dying for sth. (desear), to do one's utmost to get sth. (hacer todo lo posible).
pelásgico, ca adj. Pelasgic, pelasgian.
pelasgo, ga adj./s. Pelasgian.
peldaño m. Step (de escalera). || Rung (de escalera de mano).
pelea f. Battle, fight, combat, scuffle (fam.) [contienda]. || Fight (de animales, en deportes). || Quarrel, row, fight (riña). || FIG. Struggle (por conseguir una cosa). || — FAM. *Buscar pelea*, to be looking for a fight. || *Gallo de pelea*, gamecock, fighting cock. || *Pelea de gallos*, cockfight.
peleado, da adj. *Estar peleado con alguien*, to have fallen out with s.o., not to be on speaking terms with s.o.
peleador, ra adj. Quarrelsome, pugnacious (aficionado a pelear). || *Gallo peleador*, gamecock, fighting cock.
— M. Fighter.
pelear v. intr. To fight (luchar). || To battle (batallar). || To quarrel (con palabras). || To war, to battle, to fight: *el Cid peleó contra los moros*, the Cid warred against the Moors. || FIG. To war (elementos, cosas). | To struggle: *peleaba por vencer su pasión*, he struggled to control his passion. || FIG. *Pelear por*, to struggle for (afanarse por algo).
— V. pr. To fight: *pelearse a puñetazos*, to fight with one's fists. || FAM. To quarrel, to fall out (*con*, with) [enemistarse].
pelechar v. intr. To moult (mudar el pelo o la pluma). || To grow hair (echar pelos), to grow feathers (echar plumas). || FIG. y FAM. To begin to prosper (prosperar). | To take a turn for the better (salud).
pelele m. Rag doll, puppet (muñeco). || Rompers, *pl.* (de un niño). || FIG. y FAM. Puppet, tool: *era un pelele en sus manos*, he was a puppet in his hands.
pelendengue m. V. PERENDENGUE.
peleón, ona adj. Quarrelsome, pugnacious. || *Vino peleón*, cheap wine, plonk (pirriaque).
— M. y f. Troublemaker.
pelerina f. Pelerine (capa femenina).
peletería f. Furriery (oficio y comercio). || Furrier's shop, fur shop (tienda). || Furs, *pl.*, peltry (pieles).
peletero, ra adj. Fur: *la industria peletera*, the fur industry.
— M. Furrier (vendedor de pieles).
peliagudo, da adj. FIG. y FAM. Arduous: *un trabajo peliagudo*, an arduous task. | Thorny, tricky, ticklish: *un asunto peliagudo*, a thorny affair.
pelícano o **pelicano** m. Pelican (ave). || Forceps (de dentista).
pelicorto, ta adj. Short-haired.
película f. Pellicle (piel). || TECN. Film (de fotos). | Pellicle (hoja de gelatina sensible). || CINEM. Film, picture [U.S., movie, motion picture] (cine): *película muda, de miedo*, silent, horror film. || — FAM. *De película*, extraordinary, sensational. || *Echar o poner una película*, to show a film. || *Película del Oeste*, Western. || *Película en colores*, colour film (para sacar fotos), film in colour (en el cine). || *Película en jornadas or de episodios*, serial.
peliculado m. FOT. Stripping.
pelicular adj. Pellicular.
peliculero, ra adj. FAM. Film (de cine). | Keen on films, keen on the cinema (aficionado). || FIG. y FAM. Dreamy and highly imaginative (fantasioso).
— M. y f. FAM. Film fan, film enthusiast (aficionado). | Film maker (director), film actor (actor). || FIG. y FAM. Dreamer, dreamy and highly imaginative person. || — M. pl. Film people (gente de cine).
peliculoso, sa adj. Pellicular.
peligrar v. intr. To be in danger: *usted peligra en una región tan apartada*, you are in danger in such an isolated region. || To be in danger, to be threatened: *actualmente peligran gravemente los valores eternos de la persona humana*, at present the eternal values of the human being are gravely threatened *o* are in grave danger. || *Hacer peligrar*, to menace, to threaten: *las tensiones internas hacen peligrar el equilibrio del país*, [the] internal tensions menace the stability of the country.
peligro m. Danger, peril: *huir del peligro*, to flee from danger; *arrostrar el peligro*, to face the peril. || Risk, danger (riesgo). || — *Con peligro de su vida*, at the risk of one's life. || *Corramos el peligro*, let's risk it. || *Correr (el) peligro de*, to run the risk of: *corremos (el) peligro de perder el tren*, we run the risk of missing the train. || *Correr peligro* or *estar en peligro*, to be in danger. || *Correr un peligro*, to run *o* to take a risk. || *En peligro*, in danger. || MAR. *En peligro de naufragio*, in distress, in danger of shipwreck. || *Estar enfermo de peligro*, to be critically ill. || *Fuera de peligro*, out of danger. || *Peligro de muerte*, deadly danger. || *Poner en peligro*, to endanger. || FIG. *Quien busca el peligro, en él perece*, if you play with fire you will be burnt. || *Vivir entre peligros*, to live dangerously.
peligrosidad f. Dangerousness, danger.
peligroso, sa adj. Dangerous: *peligroso de manejar*, dangerous to handle; *es peligroso jugar con armas*, it is dangerous to play with weapons. || Dangerous, risky, hazardous, perilous: *empresa peligrosa*, perilous enterprise. || *Es peligroso asomarse al exterior*, do not lean out of the window (letrero).
pelilargo, ga adj. Long-haired.
pelillo m. Short hair (pelo corto). || Down (vello). || FIG. y FAM. Trifle, a mere nothing (nadería). || — FIG. y FAM. *Echar pelillos a la mar*, V. MAR. | *No reparar en pelillos*, not to bother with details (no reparar en detalles), to stop at nothing (no tener escrúpulos). | *No tener pelillos en la lengua*, not to mince one's words, to be outspoken. | *Pararse en pelillos*, to be easily offended (enfadarse), to worry about trifles (pararse en pequeñeces).
pelirrojo, ja adj. Ginger, red-haired, red-headed.
— M. y f. Redhead.
pelirrubio, bia adj. Blond, fair-haired.
— M. Blond, fair-haired man *o* boy. || — F. Blonde, fair-haired girl *o* woman.
pelitre m. BOT. Pyrethrum.
pelma o **pelmazo** adj. FIG. y FAM. Boring.
— M. y f. FIG. y FAM. Bore (persona pesada): *¡no seas pelma!*, don't be such a bore! || — M. Stodgy mass.
pelo m. Hair (de hombre o animal). || Hair (un cabello). || Hair (cabellos): *cortarle el pelo a uno*, to cut s.o.'s hair. || Whisker (del bigote o barba). || Fur, hair, coat (pelos o color de un animal). || Down (de ave). || Hair, down, bristle (de planta). || Bristle (del cepillo). || Strand, thread (hebra de una tela). || Pile, nap (de un tejido). || Flaw, defect (en un diamante). || Raw silk (seda cruda). || TECN. Flaw (defecto). | Fretsaw (sierra fina). || DEP. Kiss (en el billar).

— *A contra pelo*, the wrong way, against the nap. || FIG. *Agarrarse* or *asirse de un pelo*, to clutch at a straw *o* at straws. || *Al pelo*, to a tee, perfectly (perfectamente), with the nap, the right way (en las telas), just at the right moment (en el momento oportuno). || FIG. *A pelo*, bareheaded, hatless (sin sombrero), bareback (equitación). | *Buscar pelos en la sopa*, to find fault with everything. | *Coger la ocasión por los pelos*, V. OCASIÓN. | *Con pelos y señales*, in the minutest detail. || *Cortarse el pelo*, to have one's hair cut (por otro), to cut one's hair (uno mismo). || FIG. *Cortar un pelo en el aire*, to be as sharp as a razor (cuchillo, persona perspicaz). | *Cuando las ranas críen pelos*, V. RANA. | *Dar para el pelo a uno*, to leave s.o. in a sorry state (pegar). | *Estuvieron a un pelo de ganarnos el partido, faltó un pelo para que nos ganasen el partido*, they came within an inch *o* within a hairbreadth of beating us. | *Estar hasta la punta del pelo de* or *estar hasta los pelos de*, to be fed up with, to be sick and tired of. | *Faltó un pelo para que se cayese*, he very nearly fell. | *Hombre de pelo en pecho*, real man. | *Lucirle a uno el pelo*, to be as fit as a fiddle (bien de salud). || *Montar a pelo*, to ride bareback (a caballo). || FIG. *No tener pelo de tonto*, to be no fool. | *No tener pelos en la lengua*, not to mince one's words, to be outspoken. | *No verle el pelo a uno*, not to see hide nor hair of s.o. || *Pelo de camello*, camel hair (tela). || FIG. y FAM. *Pelo de la dehesa*, uncouth ways, rusticity. | *Por el pelo de una hormiga*, by a hairbreadth. | *Por los pelos*, by the skin of one's teeth: *se libró por los pelos*, he escaped by the skin of his teeth. | *Quitar el pelo de la dehesa a alguien*, to rub the corners off s.o. | *Relucirle a uno el pelo*, to be glowing with health. | *Se le pusieron los pelos de punta*, his hair stood on end. || FIG. *Se le ve el pelo de la dehesa*, V. DEHESA. || *Sin pelos en la barba*, beardless, smooth-faced. || FIG. *Soltar el pelo de la dehesa*, V. DEHESA. | *Soltarse el pelo*, to take one's hair down (despeinarse), to let one's hair down (hacer su santa voluntad). | *Tirarse de los pelos*, to tear one's hair (de desesperación), to tear each other's hair out (pelearse). | *Tomarle el pelo a uno*, to pull s.o.'s leg (burlarse). | *Traído por los pelos*, farfetched. | *Venir al pelo*, to come in very handy (ser muy útil), to suit [s.o.] to a tee, to suit [s.o.] down to the ground (convenirle), to come just at the right moment (ser oportuno).

pelón, ona adj. With a crew cut *o* a brush cut (con el pelo al rape): *un chico pelón*, a boy with a crew cut. || Hairless (sin pelo o con poco pelo). || Bald (calvo). || FIG. y FAM. Empty-headed, stupid (de escaso entendimiento). | Broke, skint (sin dinero).
— M. FAM. Poor devil (desgraciado). || *Amer.* Child (niño). || — F. MED. Alopecia (alopecia). || FAM. *La pelona*, Death (la Muerte).

peloponense adj./s. Peloponnesian.

Peloponeso n. pr. m. GEOGR. Peloponnese.

pelota f. Ball: *jugar a la pelota*, to play ball. || Ball (de manteca, etc.). || Pelota (juego vasco). || FIG. y FAM. Bonce, nut (cabeza). || *Amer.* Cowhide raft. || — Pl. POP. Balls (testículos). || — FIG. y FAM. *Dejar a uno en pelota*, to clean s.o. out (quitar todo el dinero), to leave s.o. stark naked (dejar desnudo). | *En pelota*, starkers. | *Estar en pelota*, to be in one's birthday suit. || POP. *Estar hasta las pelotas de*, to be sick to death of. || FIG. y FAM. *Jugar a la pelota con uno*, to play around with s.o., to use s.o. | *La pelota está aún en el tejado*, it is still in the air. || *Pelota base*, baseball. || *Pelota bombeada*, lob (fútbol). || *Pelota corta*, short ball (tenis). || *Pelota rasante*, drive (tenis). || FIG. y FAM. *Rechazar* or *devolver la pelota a alguien*, to give s.o. a taste of his own medicine, to give s.o. tit for tat.
— M. FAM. Creeper, toady (adulador).

pelotari m. y f. Pelota player.

pelotazo m. Blow with a ball. || *Le dio un pelotazo en la cara*, the ball hit him in the face.

pelotear v. tr. To audit, to check (una cuenta).
— V. intr. To knock up (tenis). || To kick a ball around (en fútbol, etc.). || To throw *o* to toss about (lanzar). || FIG. To argue, to quarrel (reñir). || *Amer.* To cross [a river] in a cowhide raft.

peloteo m. Knock-up (tenis). || Warm-up (en fútbol, etc.). || FIG. Exchange: *peloteo de notas diplomáticas*, exchange of diplomatic notes.

pelotera f. FAM. Quarrel, squabble, row (pelea). || FAM. *Armar una pelotera*, to kick up a rumpus. | *Armar una pelotera a uno*, to have a go at s.o.

pelotilla f. Pellet (pelota pequeña). || FIG. y FAM. Soft soap (adulación). || FIG. y FAM. *Hacerle a alguien la pelotilla*, to soft-soap s.o., to butter s.o. up (adular).

pelotilleo m. FAM. Soft soap.

pelotillero, ra m. y f. FAM. Creeper, toady, fawner (adulador).
— Adj. FAM. Fawning.

pelotón m. Big ball. || Bundle (de pelos o hilos). || Mil. Squad: *pelotón de ejecución*, firing squad. | Picket (de guardia). || Crowd (muchedumbre).

peluca f. Wig (cabellera postiza): *llevar (una) peluca*, to wear a wig. || FIG. y FAM. Scolding, dressing down (reprensión).

pelucón, ona m. y f. Conservative (en Chile).

pelucona f. FAM. Doubloon (moneda).

peluche f. Plush.
— OBSERV. This word is a Gallicism for *felpa*.

peludo, da adj. Hairy (de mucho pelo). || Long-haired (de pelo largo).

peluquería f. Hairdresser's shop (para señoras), barber's shop (para caballeros): *comprar una peluquería*, to buy a hairdresser's shop. || Hairdresser's (para señoras), barber's (para caballeros): *ir a la peluquería*, to go to the hairdresser's.

peluquero, ra m. y f. Hairdresser (para señoras), barber (para caballeros).

peluquín m. Toupee (peluca pequeña). || — FIG. y FAM. *Ni hablar del peluquín*, out of the question. | *Tomarle el peluquín a uno*, to pull s.o.'s leg.

pelusa f. Down (de planta). || Choke (de alcachofa). || Fluff (de telas). || Fluff, dust (suciedad). || FAM. Jealousy (entre niños). || — *Soltar pelusa*, to shed fluff (una tela). || FAM. *Tener pelusa*, to be jealous.

pelusilla f. Mouse-ear (planta). || FAM. Jealousy (envidia).

pelviano, na o **pélvico, ca** adj. ANAT. Pelvic.

pelvis f. ANAT. Pelvis.

pella f. Round mass (masa redonda). || Lump, trowelful (de yeso, etc.). || Blob (de merengue). || Block: *pella de mantequilla*, block of butter. || Raw lard (manteca de cerdo). || Head (de coliflor). || — FIG. y FAM. *Hacer pella*, to play truant [U.S., to play hooky] (no asistir a clase). | *Tener una pella de dinero*, to have a pile of money.

pelleja f. Skin (pellejo). || FAM. Bag of bones (persona flaca). | Whore (ramera). || — FIG. y FAM. *Jugarse la pelleja*, to risk one's neck. | *Salvar la pelleja*, to save one's skin.

pellejería f. Tannery (curtiduría). || Skins, *pl.* (pieles). || — Pl. *Amer.* Trouble, *sing.* (dificultad).

pellejero m. Tanner, leather dresser. || Leather dealer.

pellejo m. Skin (piel). || Skin, hide (de animal). || Skin, peel (de fruta). || Wineskin (odre). || FIG. y FAM. Drunkard, boozer (borracho). || — FIG. y FAM. *Dar, dejar* or *perder el pellejo*, to give *o* to lose one's life. | *Defender el pellejo*, to defend one's life. | *Jugarse el pellejo, arriesgar el pellejo*, to risk one's neck. | *No caber en el pellejo*, to be good and fat (estar muy gordo). | *No caber en el pellejo de gozo, de orgullo*, to be overflowing with joy, to be bursting with pride. | *No quisiera estar* or *hallarme en su pellejo*, I wouldn't want to be in his shoes. | *No tener más que el pellejo*, to be all skin and bones. | *Quitar a uno el pellejo*, to bump s.o. off (matar), to gossip about s.o. (murmurar), to fleece s.o., to clean s.o. out (dejar sin dinero). | *Salvar el pellejo*, to save one's skin.

pellejudo, da adj. Loose-skinned, flabby-skinned.

pelliza f. Pelisse (de pieles). || MIL. Dolman.

pellizcar v. tr. To pinch: *pellizcarle a uno en la mejilla*, to pinch s.o. on the cheek, to pinch s.o.'s cheek. || To take a pinch of (tomar un poco de). || To nibble [at] (comer sin apetito).

pellizco m. Pinch (acción de pellizcar). || Bruise (hematoma). || Pinch, bit (pequeña porción). || FIG. Sharp pain: *pellizco en el corazón*, sharp pain in the heart. || — *Dar* or *tirar un pellizco a uno*, to give s.o. a pinch. || *Darse* or *cogerse un pellizco*, to get pinched. || *Pellizco de monja*, hard twisting pinch (con las uñas), macaroon (dulce).

pena f. Sorrow, grief (pesadumbre): *la muerte de su amigo le causó mucha pena*, the death of his friend caused him great sorrow. || Difficulty: *lo he hecho con mucha pena*, I did it with great difficulty. || Penalty, pain, punishment (castigo): *pena de muerte*, death penalty. || FAM. Pain (dolor físico). || Penna (pluma de ave). || MAR. Peak. || (Ant.). Necklace, ribbon (cinta). || *Amer.* Uneasiness, discomfort (malestar). || — Pl. Hardships, toils (dificultades). || Torments (del infierno). || — *A duras penas*, with great difficulty. || *Ahorrarse la pena de*, to save o.s. the trouble *o* the bother of. || *Alma en pena*, soul in torment. || *¡Allá penas!*, that's not my worry! || *A penas*, hardly, barely, scarcely. || *Bajo* or *so pena de*, under penalty of, under pain of. || *Da pena que*, it's a shame *o* a pity that. || *Estar que da pena*, to be in a sorry state *o* in a pitiful state. || *Estos pobrecitos huérfanos me dan tanta pena*, I feel so sorry for these poor little orphans. || *¡Es una pena!* or *¡qué pena!*, it's a shame!, it's a pity!, what a shame!, what a pity!; *¡qué pena que no hayas venido antes!*, what a shame you didn't arrive sooner; *es una pena que esté tan enferma*, it's a pity that she is so ill. || *Me da pena que no pueda venir a cenar con nosotros*, I'm sorry that you can't come to dinner with us. || *Me da pena verte tan triste*, I'm sorry to see you so sad, it grieves me to see you so sad. || *Merecer* or *valer la pena*, to be worthwhile, to be worth it: *merece la pena*, it is worth it; to be worth, to be worth the trouble: *merece la pena visitar la catedral*, the cathedral is worth visiting *o* worth a visit, it is worth the trouble to pay a visit to the cathedral. || *Morir de pena*, to die of a brokenheart. || *No merece la pena molestarse*, it's not worth bothering, it's not worth it. || FAM. *Pasar la pena negra*, to go through hell. || *Pena capital*, capital punishment. || *Pena infamante*, penalty involving loss of civil rights. || *Se lo di porque me dio pena*, I gave it to him because I felt sorry for him. || *Ser de pena*, to be lamentable *o* pitiful. || *Sería una pena dejarlo*, it seems a shame to leave it. || *Vale la pena verlo*, it is worth seeing. || *Vivir sin pena ni gloria*, to live an uneventful life.

penable adj. Punishable.

penacho m. Tuft, crest (de aves). || Plume [de un morrión]. || FIG. Trail, plume (de humo). | Arrogance, haughtiness (soberbia). || MIL. *Penacho de plumas*, plume.

penado, da m. y f. Convict (delincuente).
— Adj. Grieved, sad, sorrowful (triste). || Difficult (difícil).

penal adj. Penal: *código penal*, penal code.
— M. Penitentiary, prison (penitenciaría).

penalidad f. Suffering, hardship (trabajos): *pasar muchas penalidades*, to go through much hardship. || DEP. Penalty. || JUR. Penalty, punishment.

penalista m. y f. Criminal lawyer (abogado). || Expert in criminal law (especialista en derecho penal).

penalización f. Sanction (castigo). || Penalty (deporte).

penalizar v. tr. To penalize.

penalty m. DEP. Penalty. | Penalty kick (rugby). || *Punto de penalty*, penalty spot.

penar v. tr. To punish, to chastise.
— V. intr. To suffer, to toil (padecer). || — FIG. *Penar de amores*, to be unhappy in love. | *Penar por una cosa*, to long *o* to pine *o* to yearn for sth.

penates m. pl. Penates (dioses). || FAM. *Volver a los penates*, to return home.

penca f. BOT. Fleshy leaf. | Joint (hoja del nopal). || Whip (azote). || *Amer.* Prickly pear (chumbera). | Agave (pita).

penco m. FAM. Hack, nag (jamelgo). || Agave (pita). || FAM. Dope, ass (tonto).

pencón, ona adj./s. [Of *o* from] Concepción [Chile].
— M. y f. Native *o* inhabitant of Concepción.

pendejada f. FAM. *Amer.* Foolishness, stupidity (tontería). || Cowardliness (cobardía).

pendejear v. intr. To act the fool, to fool around.

pendejo m. Pubic hair. || *Amer.* FIG. y FAM. Coward (cobarde). | Idiot, fool (imbécil).

pendencia f. Fight, quarrel, trouble (contienda): *armar una pendencia*, to start a fight, to stir up trouble. || *Se armó una pendencia*, a fight broke out.

pendenciero, ra adj. Quarrelsome, pugnacious.
— M. y f. Troublemaker.

pender v. intr. To hang: *los frutos penden de las ramas*, the fruit hangs from the branches. || To depend: *esto pende de su decisión*, this depends on *o* upon his decision. || FIG. To be pending (pleito, negocio). || FIG. *Pender de un hilo* or *de un pelo*, to be hanging by a thread.

pendiente adj. Hanging: *pendiente de una rama*, hanging from a branch. || FIG. Pending: *problemas pendientes*, pending problems; *pedidos pendientes*, pending orders. || Outstanding: *asuntos pendientes*, outstanding business; *deudas pendientes*, outstanding debts; *asignaturas pendientes*, outstanding subjects. || Sloping (inclinado). || — FIG. *Dejar pendiente a uno*, to fail s.o. (en un examen). | *Estar pendiente*, to be pending (no estar resuelto). | *Estar pendiente de*, to depend on (depender), to be waiting for: *estoy pendiente de su decisión*, I am waiting for your decision; to be always glued to: *estar pendiente de la televisón*, to be always glued to the television; to be on the watch for: *estar pendiente de los errores de uno*, to be on the watch for s.o.'s mistakes. | *Estar pendiente de los labios de alguien*, to hang on s.o.'s every word. | *Estar pendiente de un cabello*, to be hanging by a thread.
— F. Slope, gradient (cuesta): *pendiente suave, pronunciada* or *empinada*, gentle *o* slight, steep slope. || Slope (de un monte). || Pitch (de un tejado). || — *En pendiente*, sloping. || FIG. *Estar en la pendiente del vicio*, to be sinking into vice. || FIG. y FAM. *Remontar la pendiente*, to get back on one's feet.
— M. Earring (joya para las orejas). || Pendant (colgante). || MIN. Top.

péndola f. Pendulum (péndulo). || Pendulum clock (reloj). || ARQ. Queen post (de un tejado). | Suspension cable (de un puente colgante). || Quill, pen (pluma).

pendolón m. ARQ. King post.

pendón m. Banner, standard (insignia militar o de cofradía). || Pennon (insignia feudal). || Tiller, shoot (de un árbol). || FIG. y FAM. Whore, tart (mujer de mala vida). | Lanky woman (mujer desgarbada). | Rat, rotter (sinvergüenza).

pendona f. FIG. y FAM. Whore, tart.

pendonear v. intr. FAM. To gallivant, to gad about.

pendular adj. Pendular.

péndulo, la adj. Hanging (colgante).
— M. Pendulum (cuerpo oscilante, de reloj).

pene m. ANAT. Penis.

peneque adj. FAM. Drunk (borracho).

penetrabilidad f. Penetrability.

penetrable adj. Penetrable. || FIG. Understandable (fácil de entender).

penetración f. Penetration. || MIL. Breakthrough. || FIG. Insight (sagacidad).

penetrador, ra adj. V. PENETRANTE.

penetrante adj. Penetrating. || Deep (herida). || FIG. Piercing, shrill (voz). | Sharp, keen, acute (inteligencia). | Biting, piercing (frío). | Searching, penetrating (mirada). | Sharp (arma).

penetrar v. tr. To penetrate, to pierce. || FIG. To pierce: *la respuesta penetró su corazón*, the answer pierced him to the heart. | To find out, to penetrate: *penetrar un secreto*, to find out a secret. | To fathom, to penetrate (un misterio). || FIG. *Estar penetrado de las ideas de*, to be imbued with the ideas of.
— V. intr. To penetrate, to go into: *penetrar en la selva*, to penetrate into the forest. || To enter, to go in: *penetrar en un cuarto*, to enter a room. || FIG. *El frío penetra en los huesos*, the cold gets right into one's bones.
— V. pr. To become aware: *penetrarse de la realidad de un hecho*, to become aware of the reality of a fact. || To steep o.s. (*de*, in) [un tema]. || To imbibe (de unas ideas).

penicilina f. MED. Penicillin.

penicillium m. Penicillium (moho).

penillanura f. GEOGR. Peneplain, peneplane.

Peninos n. pr. m. pl. GEOGR. Pennines. || *Montes Peninos*, Pennine Chain, Pennines.

península f. GEOGR. Peninsula: *la Península Ibérica*, the Iberian Peninsula. || Isthmus (istmo).

peninsular adj./s. Peninsular.

penique m. Penny (moneda inglesa, que desde 1971 representa la centésima parte de la libra esterlina en vez de la doscientas cuarentava parte anteriormente).

— OBSERV. *Penny* hace en plural *pence* cuando se trata del valor de la moneda y *pennies* si se refiere a la misma moneda. Dos peniques se traduce por *two pennies, twopence* o *tuppence* según el caso; tres peniques por *three pennies, threepence* o *thruppence;* medio penique se dice *half penny* o *ha'penny* y medios peniques *half-pennies, ha'pennies, halfpence* o *ha'pence.* Por otra parte, la palabra *pence* va siempre unida con las cifras de la decena: *fivepence, ninepence*, etc. Ejemplo: *there are four pennies on the table* (cuatro monedas de un penique), *there is fourpence on the table* (monedas por un valor de cuatro peniques).

penitencia f. Penitence (sentimiento). || Penance (castigo). || — *Como penitencia*, as penance. || *Cumplir la penitencia*, to do penance. || *En penitencia*, as a penance. || *Hacer penitencia*, to do penance (un pecador), to share a modest meal: *venga a casa a hacer penitencia*, come over to my place to share a modest meal. || *Imponer una penitencia a uno*, to give s.o. a penance.

penitenciado, da adj. Condemned by the Inquisition. || *Amer.* Imprisoned (encarcelado).

penitencial adj. Penitential.

penitenciar v. tr. To impose penance on.

penitenciaría f. Penitentiary (tribunal eclesiástico en Roma, cárcel). || Office of penitentiary (cargo de penitenciario).

penitenciario, ria adj. Penitentiary: *régimen penitenciario*, penitentiary system.
— M. REL. Penitentiary, confessor.

penitente adj./s. Penitent.

Penjab n. pr. m. Punjab.

penol m. MAR. Yardarm (de verga). | Peak (de antena).

penoso, sa adj. Laborious, toilsome, arduous, hard: *un trabajo penoso*, a laborious job. || Distressing, sorry, lamentable (lamentable). || Burdensome (pesado). || Grieved, distressed (afligido).

penquisto, ta adj. [Of o from] Concepción [Chile].
— M. y f. Native *o* inhabitant of Concepción.

pensado, da adj. Thought. || Thought-out (reflexionado). || — *Bien pensado*, well-intentioned (persona), considered, well thought-out (cosa). || *Bien pensado, no vale la pena*, after thinking it over *o* all things considered it's not worth it. || *De pensado*, on purpose (de intento). || *El día menos pensado*, when least expected, any day. || *En el momento menos pensado*, when least expected. || *¡No sea mal pensado!*, don't be so evil-minded. || *Tener pensado algo*, to have sth. in mind, to be planning sth., to be thinking of sth. || *Una solución mal pensada*, a poorly thought-out solution, an unthinking solution.

pensador, ra adj. Thinking.
— M. y f. Thinker. || *Libre pensador*, freethinker.

pensamiento m. Thought (facultad). || Thought (ideas): *el pensamiento de Platón*, Plato's thought. || Mind (mente). || Maxim, saying (sentencia). || FIG. Suspicion (sospecha). || BOT. Pansy (flor). || — *Adivinar los pensamientos de uno*, to read s.o.'s thoughts. || FIG. *Como el pensamiento*, in a flash. || *Con el pensamiento puesto en*, with the idea of. || *Libertad de pensamiento*, freedom of thought. || *Libre pensamiento*, free thought. || *Ni por pensamiento*, I wouldn't think of it. || *No pasarle a uno por el pensamiento*, not to cross one's mind, not to occur to one. || *Venirle a uno al pensamiento*, to come to mind.

pensante adj. Thinking.

pensar* v. tr. e intr. To think: *¿pensarán los animales?*, are animals able to think?; *pensar mucho*, to think hard; *pensar en todo*, to think of everything. || To think [over], to think [about]: *piensa bien este problema*, think this problem over well, think carefully about this problem; *piénsalo*, think it over, think about it. || To think [about]: *¿en qué piensas?*, what are you thinking about? || To intend, to think (tener intención): *pienso salir mañana*, I intend to go out *o* I am thinking of going out tomorrow. || To devise, to design, to plan (concebir): *pensado para durar mucho*, planned to last a long time. || — *Dar (a uno) que pensar*, to make one think. || *Llegó cuando menos se pensaba*, he arrived when least expected. || *¡Ni lo piense!*, forget it, don't dream of it. || *¡Ni pensarlo!*, not by any means!, not a bit of it! || *Pensándolo mejor* or *bien*, on second thoughts, on reflection. || *Pensar bien, mal de*, to think well, badly of. || FIG. y FAM. *Pensar con los pies*, to talk through one's hat. || *Pensar en lo peor*, to think the worst. || *Pensarlo mucho*, to think it over. || *Pensar que*, to think that. || *Piense lo que piense*, whatever you think. || *Pienso, luego existo*, I think, therefore I am. || *Sin pensar* or *sin pensarlo*, without thinking, without stopping to think. || *Sólo con pensarlo*, just thinking about it. || *Tendría que pensarlo dos veces antes de hacerlo*, you should think twice before doing that.

pensativo, va adj. Pensive, thoughtful.

Pensilvania n. pr. f. GEOGR. Pennsylvania.

pensilvano, na adj./s. Pennsylvanian.

pensión f. Pension: *pensión de retiro*, retirement pension. || Board and lodging (en un hotel), charge for board and lodging (precio). || Boardinghouse (casa de huéspedes). || Boarding school (colegio). || FIG. y FAM. Burden (gravamen). || — *Cobrar la pensión*, to draw one's pension (persona jubilada). || *Media pensión*, partial board. || *Pensión alimenticia*, alimony, allowance for necessities. || *Pensión completa*, full board. || *Pensión pasiva*, v. PASIVA. || *Pensión vitalicia*, life annuity.

pensionado, da adj. Pensioned.
— M. y f. Pensioner. || — M. Boarding school (colegio).

pensionar v. tr. To pension, to give a pension.

pensionista m. y f. Boarder (de colegio). || Pensioner (del Estado). || *Medio pensionista*, v. MEDIOPENSIONISTA.

pentaedro m. Pentahedron.

pentagonal adj. Pentagonal.

pentágono, na adj. MAT. Pentagonal.
— M. Pentagon.

pentagrama o **pentágrama** m. MÚS. Stave, staff.

pentarquía f. Pentarchy.

pentasílabo, ba adj. Pentasyllabic.
— M. Pentasyllable.

Pentateuco m. Pentateuch (libro sagrado).

pentatlón m. DEP. Pentathlon.

Pentecostés m. Whitsun, Whitsuntide: *en* or *por Pentecostés*, at Whitsun. || Pentecost (fiesta hebraica). || *Domingo de Pentecostés*, Whitsunday, Pentecost.

pentedecágono m. MAT. Pentadecagon.

pentodo m. FÍS. Pentode.

pentotal m. MED. Pentothal.

penúltimo, ma adj./s. Penultimate, last but one, next to last.

penumbra f. ASTR. Penumbra. || Semi-obscurity, shadow, semi-darkness, half light.

penuria f. Penury, shortage, scarcity (escasez). || Poverty, need (miseria).

peña f. Rock (roca). || Circle, group (de amigos). || FIG. *Ser una peña*, to have a heart of stone.

peñaranda (en) loc. FAM. In pawn [U.S., in hock] (empeñado).

peñascal m. Rocky ground.

peñasco m. Large rock, crag (roca). || ANAT. Petrosal bone (del oído). || ZOOL. Murex (molusco).

peñascoso, sa adj. Rocky, craggy.

péñola f. Quill, pen.

peñón m. Rock: *el Peñón de Gibraltar*, the Rock of Gibraltar.

peo m. POP. Fart (pedo).

peón m. Unskilled labourer [U.S., unskilled laborer] (obrero no especializado). || Farm labourer, farmhand (en una granja o hacienda). || Pawn (ajedrez). || Piece, man (damas). || TECN. Spindle (árbol). || MIL. Foot soldier (infante). || TAUR. Assistant. || (P.us.). Pedestrian (peatón). || — *Peón caminero*, navvy, roadman. || *Peón de albañil*, hod carrier, hodman, building labourer.

peonada f. Day's work [of a labourer] (trabajo). || *Amer.* Gang of workers *o* labourers (obreros).

peonaje m. MIL. Foot soldiers, *pl.* || Gang of workers (obreros).

peonar v. intr. *Amer.* To be a labourer.

peonería f. Day's ploughing (tierra labrada).

peonía f. Peony (planta).

peonza f. Top (trompo). || — FIG. y FAM. *Bailar como una peonza*, to spin like a top. | *Ser una peonza*, to be always on the move, to be fidgety, not to be able to keep still.

peor adj. Worse (comparativo): *tu ejercicio es peor que el suyo*, your exercise is worse than his. || Worst (superlativo): *llevarse la peor parte*, to get the worst part.
— Adv. Worse: *peor que nunca*, worse than ever. || — *Cada vez peor*, worse and worse, from bad to worse. || *En el peor de los casos* or *poniéndose en el peor de los casos*, at worst, if the worst comes to the worst. || *Lo peor*, the worst thing. || *Peor para ti, para él*, that's too bad, that's your, his lookout. || *Peor que peor*, worse still, so much the worse, worse and worse. || *Tanto peor*, too bad, so much the worse. || *Y lo que es peor*, and what is more *o* worse.

peoría f. Worsening, deterioration (empeoramiento). || Worseness (cualidad de peor).

Pepa n. pr. f. (dim. de *Josefa*, Josephine). Josie. || *¡Viva la Pepa!*, hurrah! (expresa alegría), I'll be damned! (expresa desaprobación).

Pepe n. pr. m. (dim. de *José*, Joseph). Joe.

pepinar m. Cucumber patch.

pepinazo m. FIG. y FAM. Explosion, blast (explosión). | Shell (obús). | Cannonball shot (en fútbol).

pepinillo m. Gherkin (planta y fruto).

pepino m. BOT. Cucumber. || FAM. Shell (obús). || — FIG. y FAM. *No importar un pepino*, not to matter. | *(No) me importa un pepino* or *tres pepinos*, I couldn't care less, I don't give a hang. | *No valer un pepino*, not to be worth a brass farthing *o* a damn. || BOT. *Pepino del diablo*, squirting cucumber.

pepita f. Seed, pip (de fruto). || Nugget (de oro). || Pip (enfermedad de las gallinas). || *Amer.* Seed (de cacao).

Pepita n. pr. f. (dim. de *Pepa*). Josie.

pepito m. Small meat sandwich (bocadillo).

Pepito n. pr. m. (dim. de *Pepe*). Joey.

pepitoria f. Fricassee [prepared with egg yoke]: *pollo en pepitoria*, chicken fricassee. || FIG. Jumble (desorden).

pepla f. FAM. Nuisance: *¡qué pepla tener que salir ahora!*, what a nuisance having to go out now!

peplo m. Peplum (túnica antigua).

pepona f. Large paper doll (muñeca). || FIG. *Se pinta como una pepona*, she paints herself like a doll.

pepsina f. QUÍM. Pepsin.

peque m. y f. FAM. Child.

pequeñajo, ja adj. FAM. Small.
— M. y f. Small person: *es una pequeñaja*, she's a small girl. || Child (niño).

pequeñez f. Smallness, littleness, small size (tamaño). || Infancy (infancia). || Tender age (corta edad). || FIG. Meanness (mezquindad). | Slightest thing (cosa insignificante): *una pequeñez le asusta*, the slightest thing frightens him. | Trifle: *no pararse* or *no reparar en pequeñeces*, not to stop at trifles. || *Pequeñez de miras*, narrow-mindedness.

pequeñín, ina adj. Very small, very little, tiny.
— M. y f. Child, tot.

pequeño, ña adj. Small, little (persona, cosa). || Young (de poca edad). || Short (bajo, corto).
— M. y f. Child (niño). || Youngest: *en casa soy el pequeño*, in my family I am the youngest. || Small person (persona pequeña). || — *De pequeño*, as a child, when one was small. || FIG. *Dejar pequeño*, to put in the shade. || *El hijo más pequeño*, the youngest son. || *Los infinitamente pequeños*, the infinitely small. || *Pequeño burgués*, petit bourgeois, lower middle-class. || *Reproducción en pequeño*, scale model.

— OBSERV. *Pequeño* generally follows the noun: *un libro pequeño*, a small book.

pequeñuelo, la adj./s. V. PEQUEÑÍN.

Pequín n. pr. GEOGR. Peking.

pequinés, esa adj./s. Pekinese, pekingese.

per prep. *Per cápita*, per capita.

pera f. Pear (fruto): *pera de agua*, juicy pear. || Goatee (barba). || Pear-shaped switch (interruptor eléctrico). || FIG. Sinecure, cushy job (empleo). || — FIG. y FAM. *Estar como pera* or *como perita en dulce*, to be pampered like a baby. | *No partir peras con nadie*, not to become over-friendly with anybody. | *Partir peras con uno*, to be very friendly with s.o. | *Pedir peras al olmo*, to ask for the impossible. | *Ponerle a uno las peras al cuarto*, to clamp down on s.o.
— Adj. Smartly dressed (elegante).

peral m. Pear tree (árbol).

peraleda f. Pear orchard.

peraltar v. tr. ARQ. To stilt (un arco). || TECN. To bank (carreteras): *curva peraltada*, banked curve.

peralte m. ARQ. Superelevation. || Superelevation, banking (en las carreteras).

perborato m. QUÍM. Perborate.

perca f. ZOOL. Perch (pez).

percal m. Percale, calico (tejido). || FIG. *Conocer bien el percal*, to know one's stuff.

percalina f. Percaline (tela).

percance m. Mishap, setback, misfortune (contratiempo). || Perquisite, profit (provecho). || *Los percances del oficio*, the drawbacks of the job.

percatarse v. pr. To notice, to perceive: *me he percatado del peligro*, I have noticed the danger. || To realize (comprender): *se percató de la importancia del asunto*, he realized the importance of the matter.

percebe m. Goose barnacle (molusco). || FIG. y FAM. Fool, dope (necio).

percepción f. Perception (sensación). || Idea, notion (idea). || Collection (de dinero).

percepcionismo m. Perceptionism.

perceptibilidad f. Perceptibility (sensación).

perceptible adj. Perceptible, perceivable, noticeable (que se siente o que es visible). || Payable, receivable, collectable (que se cobra).

perceptivo, va adj. Perceptive: *facultades perceptivas*, perceptive faculties.

perceptor, ra adj. Percipient (que percibe o distingue). || Receiving (de impuestos).
— M. y f. Percipient, perceiver. || Collector, receiver (de impuestos).

percibible adj. Payable, collectable (cobrable).

percibir v. tr. To perceive, to notice, to sense (sentir): *percibió un ruido leve*, he perceived a faint sound. || To collect, to receive (cobrar dinero).
perclorato m. QUÍM. Perchlorate.
percloruro m. QUÍM. Perchloride.
percolador m. Percolator.
percusión f. Percussion: *instrumentos de percusión*, percussion instruments; *arma de percusión*, percussion gun. || MED. Percussion.
percusor m. Hammer, firing pin (de un arma). || MED. Plexor. || Striker, hammer (en general).
percutir v. tr. To strike, to hit. || MED. To percuss.
percutor m. V. PERCUSOR.
percha f. Hanger, clothes hanger, coat hanger (para colgar ropa, etc.). || Clothes rack (colgador fijo en la pared). || Perch (de las aves). || Rack (para utensilios). || Perch (perca, pez). || FIG. y FAM. *Tener buena percha*, to have a good physique, to be well-built.
perchero m. Clothes rack (percha).
percherón, ona adj./s. Percheron (caballo de tiro).
perdedor, ra adj. Losing.
— M. y f. Loser: *buen, mal perdedor*, good, bad loser.
perder* v. tr. To lose (un libro, una fortuna, la vida, un combate, etc.): *perdió mucho dinero en el juego*, he lost a lot of money gambling; *perder a su padre*, to lose one's father; *he perdido mi monedero*, I have lost my purse. || To waste (malgastar, desperdiciar, no aprovechar): *perder el tiempo en detalles*, to waste time on details; *sin perder un momento*, without wasting a moment; *no pierdas energía con esto*, don't waste your energy on that. || To miss (el tren, el avión, etc.): *si no nos damos prisa perderemos el barco*, if we do not hurry we shall miss the boat. || To miss, to waste (una oportunidad): *perdí la ocasión*, I missed my chance; *no debes perder una oportunidad tan buena*, you mustn't waste such a good opportunity. || To lose (el respeto). || To forget (la cortesía). || To get out of, to get rid of, to shake, to break (una costumbre). || To damage, to harm (dañar). || To spoil (estropear). || To ruin (arruinar). || — FIG. y FAM. *Andar* or *estar perdido por uno*, to be crazy about s.o., to be head over heels in love with s.o. || *Dar algo por perdido*, to give sth. up as lost. || *El que todo lo quiere, todo lo pierde*, the more you want, the less you get. || *Hasta perder la respiración*, until one is out of breath: *corrió hasta perder la respiración*, he ran until he was out of breath. || *No hay tiempo que perder*, there is *o* we have no time to lose. || *No perder de vista a alguien*, not to lose sight of s.o., not to let s.o. out of one's sight, not to take one's eyes off s.o. || *No tener nada que perder*, to have nothing to lose. || FIG. *Perder el color*, to turn pale, to grow pale (una persona). | *Perder el juicio* or *la razón*, to take leave of one's senses, to go out of one's mind, to lose one's mind. || *Perder la esperanza*, to lose hope. || FIG. *Perder la cabeza*, to lose one's head. | *Perder los estribos* or *el dominio de sí mismo*, v. ESTRIBO. || *Perder pie*, v. PIE. || *Perder terreno*, to lose ground. || *Perder unos kilos*, to lose a little weight (una persona). || JUR. *Perder un pleito*, to lose a case.
— V. intr. To lose (no ganar): *perdimos*, we lost. || To leak (un recipiente). || To depreciate, to lose its value (el dinero). || *Salir perdiendo*, to lose, to lose out, to be the loser, to come off worst.
— V. pr. To get lost, to lose one's way (una persona). || To be lost (una cosa). || To lose, to mislay: *se le pierde todo*, he loses everything. || To be lost (no oírse, no verse). || To disappear, to die out (desaparecer). || To be wasted, to go to waste (desperdiciarse). || To get lost *o* confused (enmarañarse). || To be ruined *o* spoiled (estropearse). || To go to the bad (corromperse una persona). || — *El barco se alejó hasta perderse de vista*, the boat [moved off and] disappeared into the distance. || *Es capaz de perderse por el dinero*, there is nothing he wouldn't do for money. || *Los tulipanes se extendían hasta perderse de vista*, tulips stretched as far as the eye could see. || *¡No te lo pierdas!*, don't miss it! || FIG. *Perderse por alguien*, to be crazy about s.o. | *¡Tú te lo pierdes!*, that's your lookout, that's your hard luck.
perdición f. Loss. || FIG. Ruin, undoing: *ir uno a su perdición*, to go to one's ruin. | Ruin, undoing, ruination: *será tu perdición*, it will be the ruin of you, it will be your undoing *o* your ruination. | Dissipation (disipación). || REL. Perdition, damnation.
pérdida f. Loss: *la pérdida del paraguas*, the loss of the umbrella; *sentir la pérdida de alguien*, to regret the loss of s.o. || Waste (de tiempo, de esfuerzos). || Leak, leakage (de un líquido, del aire). || Ruin, destruction (ruina). || Damage, harm (daño). || — Pl. MIL. Losses, casualties (bajas). || — *No tiene pérdida*, you can't miss it (al indicar una dirección). || *Pérdida del sentido* or *del conocimiento*, loss of consciousness. || COM. *Pérdidas y ganancias*, profit and loss. | *Vender con pérdida*, to sell at a loss.
perdidamente adv. Madly, desperately, hopelessly (con exceso): *perdidamente enamorado (de)*, madly in love [with]. || Uselessly (inútilmente).
perdidizo, za adj. FAM. Deliberately *o* purposely mislaid (cosa). || Who gets lost easily (persona). || — *Hacerse el perdidizo*, to make o.s. scarce, to hide. || *Hacerse perdidizo*, to lose on purpose (cartas).
perdido, da adj. Lost. || Stray (una bala). || Idle, spare, odd (momentos, ratos). || Isolated (lugar). || Wasted (esfuerzo, tiempo). || Lost, ruined (cosecha). || Loose (mujer). || Wrapped up, lost, absorbed (en los pensamientos). || Hopelessly ill (enfermo). || FAM. Filthy (muy sucio). || Covered: *estar perdido de barro*, to be covered with mud. || Confirmed, inveterate, incorrigible: *un borracho perdido*, a confirmed drunkard. || — *A fondo perdido*, at one's own expense, with no hope of retrieving it. || *A ratos perdidos*, in one's spare moments. || *Depósito* or *oficina de objetos perdidos*, v. OBJETO. || FIG. *Estar perdido por*, to be crazy about. || FIG. y FAM. *Estar más perdido que Carracuca*, v. CARRACUCA. || *Loco perdido*, raving mad. || *Trabajo perdido*, wasted effort *o* work.
— M. FAM. Scamp, rake (golfo). || IMPR. Overplus printing. || *Hacerse el perdido*, to hide.
perdigón m. Young partridge (pollo de perdiz). || Decoy (perdiz que sirve de reclamo). || Small shot (munición). || FAM. Spendthrift, wastrel, waster (derrochador). | Loser (en juegos). | Saliva (saliva). | Bit of snot (moco). | Failure, failed student (suspendido). || FAM. *Echar perdigones*, to splutter, to spray saliva.
perdigonada f. Discharge of small shot, shot (tiro de perdigones). || Shot wound (herida).
perdigonera f. Ammunition *o* shot pouch.
perdiguero, ra adj. Partridge-hunting. || *Perro perdiguero*, setter.
— M. Game dealer (el que vende caza).
perdimiento m. V. PERDICIÓN y PÉRDIDA.
perdis m. FAM. Rake (calavera).
perdiz f. Partridge. || — *Perdiz blanca*, rock ptarmigan. || FIG. *Y vivieron felices, comieron perdices y a mí no me dieron*, and they lived happily ever after (al final de un cuento).
perdón m. Pardon, forgiveness: *pedir perdón de*, to beg pardon for. || REL. Pardon. || — *Con perdón* or *con perdón de los presentes*, by your leave, if you don't mind. || *Con perdón sea dicho*, no offense meant, if you will pardon my saying so. || *Pedir perdón a uno*, to apologize to s.o. || *¡Perdón!*, sorry!, I beg your pardon!
perdonable adj. Pardonable, forgivable.
perdonador, ra adj. Pardoning, forgiving.
— M. y f. Pardoner.
perdonar v. tr. e intr. To excuse, to pardon, to forgive (dispensar, disculpar): *perdone la molestia*, excuse me for bothering you; *perdone, pero creo que no es así*, excuse me but I think you are mistaken. || To miss (perder, dejar): *no perdonar un baile, una ocasión*, not to miss a dance, a chance. || To overlook (omitir): *no perdonar un detalle*, not to overlook a detail. || To spare (un esfuerzo). || To shirk from, to let go by (no aprovechar): *no perdonar medio de enriquecerse*, not to shirk from any means of getting rich. || To forgo, to renounce (renunciar). || To exempt, to excuse (exceptuar). || — *Perdonarle la vida a uno*, to spare s.o.'s life. || *¡Perdone usted!*, pardon me!, I beg your pardon!, sorry! || *Que Dios lo haya perdonado*, may God have mercy on him.
perdonavidas m. inv. FIG. y FAM. Bully, braggart (valentón).
perdulario, ria adj. Careless, negligent (descuidado). || Forgetful (olvidadizo). || Vicious (vicioso).
— M. y f. Sloven (descuidado). || Rogue (pillo). || Rake (disoluto).
perdurabilidad f. Eternal nature, unending nature, everlasting nature (de lo eterno). || Perdurability, durability (de lo duradero).
perdurable adj. Eternal, everlasting, unending, imperishable (eterno). || Lasting, perdurable (duradero). || Incessant, endless (incesante).
perdurablemente adj. Eternally.
perdurar v. intr. To last a long time, to last (durar). || To subsist (subsistir).
perecedero, ra adj. Perishable: *bienes perecederos*, perishable goods. || Mortal (mortal). || Temporal, transient, transitory (que ha de acabarse).
perecer* v. intr. To perish. || To die (morir).
— V. pr. *Perecerse por*, to be dying to (seguido de infinitivo), to be dying for (seguido de sustantivo).
perecimiento m. Disappearance (desaparición). || Death (muerte). || End (fin).
perecuación f. Proportional distribution (de las cargas).
peregrinación f. Pilgrimage (viaje). || Pilgrimage (a un santuario): *ir en peregrinación a Santiago de Compostela*, to go on a pilgrimage to Santiago de Compostela.
peregrinaje m. (P.us.). Pilgrimage.
peregrinamente adv. Peculiarly, strangely (de un modo raro).
peregrinante adj. Travelling [U.S., traveling].
— M. Pilgrim (peregrino).
peregrinar v. intr. To go on a pilgrimage. || To travel, to journey, to peregrinate (por tierras extrañas). || FIG. To go to and fro.
peregrino, na adj. Travelling [U.S., traveling] (que viaja). || Migrating (aves). || Exotic, strange (exótico). || FIG. Peculiar, singular, odd, strange (extraño): *una idea peregrina*, a peculiar idea.
— M. y f. Pilgrim (que va a un santuario).
perejil m. BOT. Parsley.

perendengue m. Cheap ornament, trinket (adorno). || Earring (arete).

Perengano, na m. y f. So-and-so. || *Mengano y Perengano*, so-and-so and what's-his-name.

— OBSERV. The word *Perengano* is only used after the nouns *Fulano* and *Mengano* to indicate a name which one has forgotten.

perenne adj. BOT. Perennial (planta). | Evergreen (hojas). || Perennial (manantial). || FIG. Perennial, everlasting: *belleza perenne*, perennial beauty.

perennemente adv. Perennially, perpetually. || Forever, for ever (siempre, constantemente).

perennidad f. Perenniality, perpetuity.

perentoriamente adv. Peremptorily (terminantemente). || Urgently, pressingly (urgentemente).

perentoriedad f. Peremptoriness. || Urgency.

perentorio, ria adj. Peremptory (terminante): *con tono perentorio*, in a peremptory tone. || Peremptory, pressing, urgent (apremiante). || — JUR. *Excepción perentoria*, peremptory plea, demurrer. || *Plazo perentorio*, strict time limit.

pereza f. Laziness, sloth, indolence, idleness (holgazanería). || ZOOL. Sloth (perezoso). || — *Me da pereza ir a...*, I can't be bothered *o* it's too much trouble going to... || *Pereza mental*, mental laziness, sluggishness of mind. || *Sacudir la pereza*, to shake off one's laziness. || *Tener pereza*, to feel *o* to be lazy.

perezosamente adv. Lazily. || Sluggishly, slowly, without hurrying, unhurriedly (lentamente).

perezoso, sa adj. Lazy, slothful, indolent, idle (holgazán). || FIG. Sluggish, slow-moving, slow (lento): *arroyo perezoso*, sluggish stream.
— M. y f. Lazybones, loafer, idler, sluggard, lazy person (holgazán). || — M. ZOOL. Sloth (desdentado). || FIG. *Ni corto ni perezoso*, v. CORTO.

perfección f. Perfection: *canta a la perfección*, she sings to perfection. || *A la perfección*, to perfection, perfectly.

perfeccionador, ra adj. Perfectioning. || Improving (que mejora).

perfeccionamiento m. Perfection, perfecting. || Improvement, betterment (mejora). || Further training (estudios).

perfeccionar v. tr. To perfect, to bring to perfection (hacer perfecto). || To improve, to [make] better (mejorar). || To brush up (sus conocimientos). || To finish off (acabar).

perfeccionista m. y f. Perfectionist.

perfectamente adv. Perfectly.
— Interj. Right!, quite!, agreed!, of course!

perfectibilidad f. Perfectibility. || Improvability.

perfectible adj. Perfectible. || Improvable, betterable (mejorable).

perfecto, ta adj. Perfect (excelente). || FIG. Perfect (absoluto): *un perfecto imbécil*, a perfect idiot. || — GRAM. *Futuro perfecto*, future perfect. | *Pretérito perfecto*, perfect, present perfect.

perfidia f. Perfidy, treachery.

pérfido, da adj. Perfidious, treacherous.

perfil m. Profile (parte lateral): *perfil izquierdo*, left profile; *ver a uno de perfil*, to see s.o. in profile. || Profile, contour, outline, silhouette (contorno): *el perfil de un caballo*, the outline of a horse. || Upstroke, thin stroke (de las letras). || FIG. Profile, portrait (retrato moral). || Section, cross section (de un plano). || Profile, vertical section (geología). || TECN. Profile. || — Pl. FIG. Attentions, courtesies (miramientos). | Refinement, *sing.* (delicadeza). | Finishing touches (retoques). | Features, characteristics (aspectos). || — *De perfil*, in profile, from the side. || *Retrato de medio perfil*, three-quater-face *o* semi-profile portrait. || *Tomar perfiles*, to trace. || *Vista de perfil*, side view, profile.

perfilado, da adj. In profile (de perfil). || Outlined (dibujado). | Long and thin (rostro). || Perfect, well-shaped, regular (nariz, boca, etc.). || TECN. Streamlined (coche, etc.).
— M. Profile (perfil). | TECN. Streamlining.

perfilar v. tr. To profile, to draw in profile. || To outline (contorno). || FIG. To shape (dar forma). | To polish, to apply the finishing touches to (rematar). || TECN. To streamline (coche, avión, etc.).
— V. pr. To present one's profile, to turn sideways. || FIG. To take shape *o* definite form: *los proyectos se perfilan*, the plans are taking shape. | To be outlined, to stand out: *el campanario se perfilaba en el cielo*, the belfry was outlined *o* stood out against the sky. | To titivate o.s. (aderezarse). || TAUR. To prepare for the kill.

perfoliado, da adj. BOT. Perfoliate.

perforación f. Perforation, piercing. || TECN. Punch hole, perforation (taladro en tarjetas, etc.). | Boring, drilling (de barrenos, pozos de petróleo, etc.). || MED. Perforation.

perforado m. Perforation. || TECN. Punching, perforating (de tarjetas). | Boring, drilling (minería).

perforador, ra adj. Perforating. || TECN. Punching, perforating (de tarjetas). | Boring, drilling (minería).
— M. y f. Perforator. || TECN Puncher (de tarjetas). | Borer, driller (minería). || — F. Borer, drill, drilling machine (minería). || Punch, punching machine (de tarjetas, etc.).

perforante adj. Perforating.

perforar v. tr. To perforate, to pierce. || To go *o* to pass *o* to run through, to pierce: *un túnel que perfora una montaña*, a tunnel which runs through a mountain. || TECN. To punch, to perforate (tarjetas, etc.). | To bore, to drill: *perforar un agujero en la pared, un túnel en el monte*, to bore a hole in the wall, a tunnel through the mountain. || MED. *Úlcera perforada*, perforating ulcer.

performance f. Performance (resultado notable).

perfumadero m. Perfume pan, cassolette (pebetero).

perfumador m. Perfume pan (pebetero). || Perfume atomizer (pulverizador).

perfumar v. tr. To perfume, to scent.
— V. intr. To be fragrant, to perfume.
— V. pr. To perfume o.s., to scent o.s. || *Se perfuma demasiado*, she uses too much perfume.

perfume m. Perfume, scent (de tocador). || Perfume, fragrance, aroma, scent (aroma).

perfumería f. Perfumery (fabricación, tienda). || Perfumery, perfume (productos).

perfumero, ra o **perfumista** m. y f. Perfumer.

perfusión f. MED. Perfusion.

pergamino m. Parchment. || — Pl. FIG. y FAM. Titles of nobility, title deeds (títulos de nobleza). | Diploma, *sing.* [U.S., sheepskin, *sing.*] (diploma).

pergeñar v. tr. To rough out, to sketch out (diseñar). || To prepare (un texto). || To arrange (arreglar).

pergeño m. Look, appearance (apariencia).

pérgola f. Pergola (emparrado). || Rooftop garden (sobre la techumbre).

periantio m. BOT. Perianth.

pericardio m. ANAT. Pericardium.

pericarpio m. BOT. Pericarp.

pericia f. Expertness, expertise (saber). || Skill, expertise, dexterity (práctica).

pericial adj. Expert, expert's, experts': *dictamen, tasación pericial*, expert's advice, appraisal; *informe pericial*, expert report.

periclitar v. intr. To be in danger *o* in jeopardy (peligrar). || To decline (decaer).

perico m. Parakeet, parrakeet (ave). || Toupee (peluca). || Chamberpot, jerry (fam.) [orinal]. || MAR. Mizzen topgallant mast (palo) *o* sail (vela).

Perico n. pr. m. (dim. de *Pedro*). FAM. Pete. || — FIG. y FAM. *Más duro que la pata de Perico*, as hard as iron (en general), as tough as leather (carne). || FAM. *Perico el de los palotes*, John Smith [U.S., Joe Doe], any Tom, Dick or Harry. | *Perico entre ellas*, lady's man, ladies' man.

pericón m. Popular Argentinian dance (baile).

pericráneo m. ANAT. Pericranium.

peridoto m. MIN. Peridot.

periferia f. MAT. Periphery. || Periphery, outkirts, *pl.* (de una población).

periférico, ca adj. Peripheric, peripheral. || Outlying (barrio).

perifollo m. BOT. Chervil. || — Pl. FIG. y FAM. Frills, trimmings, frippery, *sing.* (adorno).

perifrasear v. intr. To periphrase.

perífrasis f. inv. Periphrasis (circunloquio).

perifrástico, ca adj. Periphrastic.

perigeo m. ASTR. Perigee.

perilla f. Goatee [beard] (barbilla). || [Pear-shaped] switch (interruptor eléctrico). || Pear-shaped ornament (adorno). || Lobe (de oreja). || Pommel (de silla de montar). || — FIG. y FAM. *¡De perilla!* or *¡de perillas!*, great!, splendid! | *Venirle a uno de perilla* or *de perillas*, to come in very handy (ser muy útil), to suit s.o. to a tee, to suit s.o. down to the ground (convenirle), to come just at the right moment for s.o. (en el momento oportuno).

perillán m. FAM. Rascal, little monkey, rogue.

perimétrico, ca adj. Perimetric.

perímetro m. MAT. Perimeter. || *Perímetro de caderas*, hip measurement.

perineo m. ANAT. Perineum.

perinola f. Teetotum (juguete).

periodicidad f. Periodicity.

periódico, ca adj. Periodic, periodical: *el movimiento periódico de los planetas*, the periodic motion of the planets. || Recurrent (fiebre). || Periodical (publicación). || MAT. *Fracción periódica*, recurring decimal.
— M. Newspaper (diario): *puesto de periódicos*, newspaper stand; *periódico de la tarde*, evening newspaper. || Periodical (revista, etc.).

periodicucho m. FAM. Rag (periódico malo).

periodismo m. Journalism.

periodista m. y f. Journalist, newspaperman (hombre), journalist, newspaperwoman (mujer), reporter, pressman (hombre), reporter, presswoman (mujer).

periodístico, ca adj. Journalistic (estilo, etc.). || *Artículo periodístico*, newspaper article.

período o **periodo** m. Period, time: *el período de (las) vacaciones*, the holiday period. || Period, era, age (época). || ASTR. Period: *periodo lunar*, lunar period. || GEOL. Period, cycle. || MED. Period (menstruación, fase de una enfermedad). || MAT. Period. || MUS. y GRAM. Period. || FÍS. Period. || — *Periodo de arrendamiento*, duration *o* term of a lease. || *Período de prácticas*, probationary period, period of instruction, training. || *Período de sesiones*, session, sitting (de una asamblea).

periostio m. ANAT. Periosteum.

peripatético, ca adj. FIL. Peripatetic. || FIG. y FAM. Ridiculous [in one's opinions or assertions].
— M. y f. FIL. Peripatetic. || — F. FAM. Streetwalker (ramera).

peripatetismo m. Peripateticism.

peripecia f. Peripeteia, peripetia, vicissitude (cambio de fortuna). || Incident (incidente). || Adventure (aventura). || Drama.

periplo m. Periplus (p.us.), tour.

peripuesto, ta adj. FAM. Spruced up, dressed up, dolled up (ataviado). || FIG. *Estar muy peripuesto*, to be dressed up to the nines, to be all dolled up.

periquete m. FAM. *En un periquete*, in a tick, in a jiffy, in no time.

periquito m. Parakeet, parrakeet (ave).

periscópico, ca adj. Periscopic.

periscopio m. Periscope.

perisístole f. MED. Perisystole.

peristáltico, ca adj. ANAT. Peristaltic.

peristilo m. ARQ. Peristyle.

peritación f. o **peritaje** m. Expert *o* expert's opinion *o* report *o* work (informe). || Expert's fee (honorarios). || Engineering studies, *pl.* [aeronautical, industrial, etc.] (carrera).

perito, ta adj. Expert (especialista). || Expert, skilled, skilful (hábil). || Experienced (experimentado). || Qualified, proficient (calificado). || *Ser perito en la materia*, to be an expert on the subject.
— M. Expert. || — *A juicio de peritos*, according to expert opinion. || *Perito aeronáutico, agrónomo*, aeronautical, agricultural engineer [qualified from an *Escuela de Peritos*, school of aeronautics, agricultural college]. || *Perito electricista*, qualified electrician. || *Perito en contabilidad* or *perito mercantil*, chartered *o* qualified accountant [U.S., certified civil accountant]. || *Perito tasador*, expert appraiser.

peritoneo m. ANAT. Peritoneum.

peritonitis f. MED. Peritonitis.

perjudicado, da adj. Damaged. || Injured, harmed (persona, fama, etc.). || Wronged (moralmente).

perjudicador, ra o **perjudicante** adj. Prejudicial, harmful, injurious, detrimental.

perjudicar v. tr. To damage (causar daño material). || To harm, to injure, to cause detriment to (la salud, la fama, etc.). || To wrong (en lo moral). || To detract from the looks of, to spoil the appearance of, not to suit (desfavorecer). || *Perjudicar los intereses de uno*, to prejudice *o* to be prejudicial to s.o.'s interests.

perjudicial adj. Prejudicial, harmful, injurious, detrimental.

perjuicio m. Damage (daño). || Harm, injury, detriment (en la salud). || Wrong, moral injury, prejudice (daño moral): *reparar el perjuicio que se ha hecho*, to redress the wrong one has done. || [Financial] loss (económico). || — *Causar perjuicio a*, to damage, to cause damage to (causar daño material), to harm, to injure, to cause detriment to (la salud, la fama, etc.), to wrong, to do [s.o.] wrong (en lo moral). || *Con* or *en perjuicio de*, to the prejudice of, to the detriment of. || *En perjuicio suyo*, to his detriment. || *Sin perjuicio de* or *de que* or *que*, even though, without dismissing the possibility that. || *Sin perjuicio de sus derechos*, without prejudice to *o* without detriment to *o* without prejudicing his rights.

perjurar v. intr. To perjure o.s., to forswear o.s., to commit perjury (jurar con falsedad). || To swear, to curse (jurar mucho).
— V. pr. To perjure o.s.

perjurio m. Perjury (juramento en falso).

perjuro, ra adj. Perjured, forsworn.
— M. y f. Perjurer.

perla f. Pearl: *perla cultivada*, cultured pearl; *perla fina*, real pearl. || IMPR. Pearl, four-point type (carácter). || HERÁLD. Pall (palio). || FIG. Pearl, gem, jewel, treasure (persona *o* cosa excelente). || — FIG. y FAM. *Baila, canta de perlas*, she dances, she sings a treat *o* like a dream. | *De perlas*, perfectly (adverbio), excellent, marvellous (adjetivo). | *Hablar de perlas*, to speak words of gold. | *Me parece de perlas*, it seems fine to me. || *Pesca de perlas*, pearl fishing. || *Pescador de perlas*, pearl diver *o* fisher. || FIG. *Venirle a uno de perlas*, to come in very handy (ser muy útil), to suit s.o. to a tee, to suit s.o. down to the ground (convenirle), to come just at the right moment (ser oportuno).
— Adj. inv. Pearl: *gris perla*, pearl grey.

perlado, da adj. Pearl-shaped, pearly (en forma de perla). || Pearly, pearl-coloured (de color de perla). || *Cebada perlada*, pearl barley.

perlé adj. m. *Algodón perlé*, crochet *o* corded cotton.

perlería f. Pearls, *pl.*, collection of pearls.

perlero, ra adj. Pearl: *industria perlera*, pearl industry.

perlesía f. MED. Paralysis, palsy. | Muscular atony [especially in the aged].

perlífero, ra adj. Pearl-producing. || *Ostra perlífera*, pearl oyster.

permanecer* v. intr. To remain: *permanecer inmóvil*, to remain motionless; *la situación permanece grave*, the situation remains serious. || To stay (residir): *Juan permaneció dos años en Londres*, John stayed two years in London.

permanencia f. Permanence (duración constante): *la permanencia de las leyes*, the permanence of laws. || Stay (estancia): *durante mi permanencia en el extranjero*, during my stay abroad; *los cosmonautas han batido el récord de permanencia en el espacio*, the cosmonauts have broken the record for the longest stay in space. || Constancy, perseverance (perseverancia).

permanente adj. Permanent, lasting. || Standing (ejército, comisión, etc.). || *Servicio permanente*, all-day service.
— F. Permanent wave, perm (fam.) [de los cabellos]. || *Hacerse la permanente*, to have one's hair permed.

permanentemente adv. Permanently.

permanganato m. QUÍM. Permanganate.

permeabilidad f. Permeability, perviousness: *permeabilidad del terreno*, permeability of the land.

permeable adj. Permeable, pervious. || FIG. Pervious (influenciable).

permi m. FAM. Leave (permiso militar): *tener un permi de quince días*, to have fifteen day's leave.

pérmico, ca o **permiano, na** adj./s.m. GEOL. Permian.

permisible adj. Permissible.

permisión f. V. PERMISO.

permisivo, va adj. Permissive.

permiso m. Permission (autorización): *pedir, dar, tener permiso*, to ask, to give, to have permission. || Permit, licence [U.S., license] (documento): *permiso para* or *de caza, de construir*, hunting licence, building permit. || Leave, furlough (del soldado): *estar de* or *con permiso*, to be on leave. || Tolerance [in coinage] (moneda). || — *Con permiso* or *con su permiso* or *con permiso de usted*, if I may, with your permission, if you don't mind, by *o* with your leave. || MIL. *Licencia con permiso ilimitado*, long leave. || *Permiso al país de origen*, home leave (diplomático). || *Permiso de conducir* or *de conducción*, driving licence [U.S., driver's license]. || *Permiso de residencia*, residence permit.

permitido, da adj. Permitted, allowed.

permitidor, ra adj. Permitting, allowing.
— M. y f. Permitter, allower.

permitir v. tr. To permit, to allow (dejar): *permitir que desembarque un pasajero*, to permit a passenger to disembark. || To permit, to put up with, to tolerate (tolerar). || To permit, to enable, to allow (hacer posible): *su fortuna le permite viajar mucho*, his wealth permits him to do a lot of travelling. || — *Mis recursos no me lo permiten*, I can't afford it. || *¡Permítame!*, excuse me! (perdone), allow me! (para ayudar a uno). || *Permítame que le diga*, allow me to tell you *o* to say. || *Si el tiempo lo permite*, weather permitting. || *¿Usted permite?*, may I?
— V. pr. To be permitted *o* allowed (estar permitido): *no se permite fumar aquí*, smoking is not allowed in here. || To permit o.s., to allow o.s.: *permitirse el lujo de*, to permit o.s. the luxury of. || To take the liberty of *o* to (tomarse la libertad de): *me permito escribirle*, I am taking the liberty of writing to you. || — *Me permito recordarle que*, allow me to remind you that. || *Me permito rogarle que*, may I make so bold as to ask you to. || *Si se me permite la expresión*, if you will forgive the expression.

permuta f. Exchange. || MAT. Permutation.

permutabilidad f. Exchangeability. || MAT. Permutability.

permutable adj. Exchangeable. || MAT. Permutable.

permutación f. Exchange. || MAT. Permutation.

permutador m. Changeover switch (conmutador).

permutar v. tr. To exchange, to barter, to swap (cambiar). || To exchange, to switch (empleos). || MAT. To permute.

pernada f. Kick (golpe). || Kicking *o* thrashing about [with one's legs] (movimiento violento). || — *Dar pernadas*, to kick, to thrash about [with one's legs]. || JUR. *Derecho de pernada*, droit du seigneur, jus primae noctis.

pernear v. intr. To kick, to kick one's legs, to thrash about [with one's legs].

pernera f. Trouser leg (pernil).

perniabierto, ta adj. Open-legged (con las piernas abiertas). || Bandy-legged (defecto físico).

pernicioso, sa adj. Pernicious.

pernil m. Ham, haunch and thigh (de un animal). || Ham (de cerdo). || Leg (de pantalón). || Haunch (de caza mayor).

pernio m. Strap hinge (de gozne).

perniquebrar* v. tr. To break [s.o.'s] leg *o* legs.
— V. pr. To break a *o* one's leg.

pernituerto, ta adj. Crooked-legged.

perno m. Bolt (tornillo).

pernoctar v. intr. To sleep out, to stay out all night (pasar la noche fuera de su propio domicilio). || To spend *o* to stay the night: *pernoctaremos en Burgos*, we shall stay the night in Burgos.

pero m. Apple tree [producing elongated fruit] (árbol). || [Elongated variety of] apple (fruto). || *Amer.* Pear tree (peral).

pero conj. But: *pero no quiero ir*, but I don't want to go; *es bonito pero caro*, it is nice, but expensive; *¿pero no ibas a ver a tu abuelo?*, but weren't you going to see your grandfather? || But, yet (sin em-

bargo): *la casa era pequeña pero cómoda*, the house was small yet comfortable. || Then, now (objeción, desaprobación): *¿pero que hace usted aquí?*, what are you doing here, then?, now what are you doing here? || — *¡Pero bueno!*, why!, now look! || *Pero dígame...*, come on, tell me... || *¡Pero qué chica más simpática!*, why, what a friendly girl!, isn't she a friendly girl! || *¡Pero que muy bien hecho!*, very well done indeed! || *¿Pero quieres dejarme en paz?*, leave me alone, will you! || *¡Pero si está más guapa que nunca!*, why *o* well, if she isn't prettier than ever! || *¿Pero te vas a callar?*, are you going to be quiet or aren't you? || *Pero vamos a ver*, let's see now.
— M. FAM. Fault (defecto): *poner* or *encontrar peros a*, to find fault with. | Snag (dificultad): *tener muchos peros*, to have a lot of snags. | Objection (reparo): *poner peros a*, to raise objections to. || — *No hay pero que valga*, no buts, there are no buts about it. || *Sin un pero*, faultless.

perogrullada f. FAM. Platitude, truism.

Perogrullo n. pr. m. *Verdad de Perogrullo*, platitude, truism.

perol m. Pot (vasija de metal). || Saucepan (cacerola).

peroné m. ANAT. Fibula (hueso).

peroneo, a adj. ANAT. Peroneal, fibular.

peroración f. Peroration, speech.

perorador, ra m. y f. Perorator.

perorar v. intr. To perorate, to make *o* to deliver a speech.

perorata f. Long-winded speech, tiresome speech. || *Echar una perorata*, to hold forth, to spout.

peróxido m. QUÍM. Peroxide.

perpendicular adj. Perpendicular, at right angles (*a*, to).
— F. Perpendicular.

perpendicularidad f. Perpendicularity.

perpetración f. Perpetration.

perpetrador, ra adj. Perpetrating.
— M. y f. Perpetrator.

perpetrar v. tr. To perpetrate (un delito).

perpetua f. BOT. Everlasting, everlasting flower.

perpetuación f. Perpetuation.

perpetuar v. tr. To perpetuate: *las pirámides perpetúan el recuerdo de los faraones*, the pyramids perpetuate the memory of the pharaohs.
— V. pr. To be perpetuated.

perpetuidad f. Perpetuity: *a perpetuidad*, in perpetuity. || *Trabajos forzados a perpetuidad*, penal servitude for life.

perpetuo, tua adj. Perpetual, everlasting. || Life, for life (que dura toda la vida): *exilio perpetuo*, exile for life; *cadena perpetua*, life imprisonment. || *Nieves perpetuas*, perpetual snow.

perpiaño adj. m. ARQ. *Arco perpiaño*, ribbed arch.
— M. ARQ. Bondstone, parpen [U.S., perpend] (piedra).

perplejamente adv. Perplexedly (confusamente), hesitantly (con irresolución).

perplejidad f. Perplexity (confusión), hesitancy (indecisión).

perplejo, ja adj. Perplexed, puzzled (confuso), hesitant (vacilante). || *Dejar perplejo*, to perplex.

perquirir* v. tr. To investigate, to inquire into.

perquisición f. Inquiry, investigation (pesquisa).

perquisidor, ra adj. Inquiring, investigating.
— M. Investigator.

perra f. Bitch (animal). || FAM. Penny [U.S., cent *o* dime] (dinero): *no tengo ni una perra* or *estoy sin una perra*, I haven't a penny to my name. | Tantrum (rabieta): *coger una perra*, to go into a tantrum. | Pigheadedness (obstinación). || — Pl. FAM. Cash, *sing*, lolly, *sing*. (dinero): *tiene muchas perras*, he's got lots of cash. || — FAM. *Ha cogido* or *está con* or *tiene la perra de un coche deportivo*, he's got this thing *o* an obsession about a sports car. || *Perra chica*, [copper] five-cent piece. || *Perra gorda*, [copper] ten-cent coin.

perrada f. Pack of dogs (jauría). || FIG. y FAM. Dirty trick (mala jugada).

perramente adv. FIG. y FAM. Very badly.

perrera f. Kennel, doghouse (casita del perro). || Pound, kennels, *pl*. (de perros sin dueño). || Dogcatcher's wagon (camión). || Dog box [on a train] (de tren). || FAM. Grind, fag, drag (trabajo). | Bad payer (mal pagador). | Tantrum (rabieta).

perrería f. Pack of dogs (jauría). || Gang [of thieves, villains, etc.]. || FIG. y FAM. Dirty trick (mala acción): *hacerle una perrería a uno*, to play a dirty trick on s.o. || FAM. *Decir perrerías de uno*, to talk dirt about s.o., to say nasty things about s.o.

perrero m. Dogcatcher (que recoge perros vagabundos). || Houndman, keeper of hounds (que cuida los perros de caza). || Dog lover (a quien le gustan los perros).

perrilla f. FAM. Penny, farthing, copper [U.S., cent, dime]. || *Amer.* Sty, stye (orzuelo). || FAM. *No tener una perrilla*, not to have a penny to one's name [U.S., not to have a cent], to be stony-broke, to be flat broke.

perrillo m. Little dog, pup, puppy (perro).

perro m. Dog (animal). || FAM. Penny, copper, farthing [U.S., cent, dime] (moneda). | Dog, cur (hombre despreciable). || — FIG. *Allí no atan los perros con longanizas*, money does not grow on trees there. | *Andar* or *llevarse como el perro y el gato* or *como perros y gatos*, V. LLEVAR. | *¡A otro perro con ese hueso!*, pull the other one!, don't give me that!, tell it to the Marines! (no me lo creo), no chance, you'll be lucky!, come off it! (para rechazar una proposición desagradable). | *A perro flaco todo son pulgas*, misfortunes rain upon the wretched. || *Cuidado con el perro*, beware of the dog. || FIG. y FAM. *Dar perro a uno*, to keep s.o. waiting (dar un plantón). | *Darse a perros*, to get mad, to go up the wall, to blow one's top (irritarse). | *De perros*, lousy, filthy: *tiempo de perros*, filthy weather; *estar de un humor de perros*, to be in a filthy mood; lousy, hell of a: *hemos tenido un día de perros*, we've had a hell of a day. | *Echar a perros*, to waste, to idle away [time]. | *El perro del hortelano* (*que ni come ni deja comer*), the dog in the manger. | *Estar como los perros*, to be very salty [food]. | *Estar más malo que los perros*, to be as sick as a dog. | *Llevar una vida de perros*, to lead a dog's life. | *Morir como un perro*, to die without receiving Extreme Unction (sin los auxilios de la religión), to die a lonely *o* a forgotten man (solo o abandonado). | *Muerto el perro se acabó la rabia*, dead dogs don't bite. || *Perro alano*, mastiff. || *Perro caliente*, hot dog. || *Perro callejero*, stray dog. || *Perro cobrador*, retriever. || *Perro corredor*, hound. || *Perro danés*, Great Dane. || *Perro de aguas* or *de lanas*, water spaniel. || *Perro de casta*, pedigree dog. || *Perro de muestra*, pointer. || *Perro de presa* or *perro dogo*, bulldog. || *Perro de Terranova*, Newfoundland dog. || *Perro faldero*, lapdog. || *Perro galgo* or *lebrel*, greyhound. || *Perro ganadero*, sheepdog. || FIG. *Perro ladrador poco mordedor*, his bark is worse than his bite. || *Perro lobo*, Alsatian. || *Perro marino*, dogfish (cazón). || *Perro mastín*, mastiff. || *Perro pachón* or *perro tranvía* (fam.), basset hound, basset. || *Perro pastor*, sheepdog. || *Perro pekinés*, pekinese, pekingese. || *Perro perdiguero*, setter. || *Perro podenco*, spaniel. || *Perro raposero*, foxhound. || *Perro rastrero*, tracker. || FIG. *Perro sarnoso*, mangy cur. || *Perro sin dueño*, stray *o* ownerless dog. || *Perro sabueso*, bloodhound. | FIG. *Perro viejo*, old hand, sly old fox, wily bird (hombre astuto). | *Por dinero baila el perro*, there is nothing money cannot buy (con dinero se consigue todo), you never get sth. for nothing. | *Tratar a alguien como a un perro*, to treat s.o. like dirt *o* like a dog.

perro, rra adj. FAM. Hell of a, rotten, lousy: *pasé una noche perra*, I had a hell of a night. || — FAM. *Esta vida perra*, this wretched life. | *¡Qué suerte más perra!*, what rotten luck!

perroquete m. MAR. Topgallant mast (juanete).

perruno, na adj. Dog, dog's, canine.
— F. Dog biscuit (pan).

persa adj./s. Persian (de la Persia antigua y moderna).

persecución f. Persecution (tormento). || Pursuit (acoso, seguimiento): *ir en persecución de uno*, to set off in pursuit of s.o. || *Carrera de persecución*, pursuit (en ciclismo).

persecutorio, ria adj. Pursuing (que acosa o sigue). || Persecutory, persecuting (que atormenta). || *Manía persecutoria*, persecution mania, persecution complex.

perseguidor, ra adj. Pursuing (que acosa o sigue). || Persecuting (que atormenta). || JUR. Prosecuting.
— M. Pursuer (que acosa o sigue). || Persecutor (que atormenta). || JUR. Prosecutor, plaintiff. || Pursuit rider (en ciclismo).

perseguimiento m. Persecution (tormento). || Pursuit (acoso, seguimiento).

perseguir* v. tr. To pursue, to chase, to be *o* to go *o* to run after (seguir). || To persecute: *Diocleciano persiguió a los cristianos*, Diocletian persecuted the Christians. || JUR. To prosecute. || FIG. To pursue, to hound (acosar): *perseguir a sus deudores*, to pursue one's debtors. | To pursue, to aim at, to go after, to strive after (intentar conseguir): *perseguir el bienestar del pueblo, un puesto en el ministerio*, to pursue the well-being of the people, a post in the ministry. | To pester, to harass (importunar): *perseguir con sus demandas*, to pester with one's demands. | To persecute, to torment (los remordimientos, etc.). || *Me persigue la mala suerte*, I am dogged by ill luck.

perseverancia f. Perseverance: *perseverancia en el trabajo, en estudiar*, perseverance in one's work, in studying.

perseverante adj. Persevering.

perseverantemente adv. Perseveringly.

perseverar v. intr. To persevere: *perseverar en una empresa*, to persevere in an enterprise. || To persist (*en*, in), to continue (*en*, to) [con infinitivo]: *persevera en callarse*, he persists in saying nothing.

Persia n. pr. f. GEOGR. Iran, Persia (hoy), Persia (en la Antigüedad).

persiana f. Persienne, slatted shutter (postigo). || Blind (enrollable): *persiana veneciana*, Venetian blind. || Persienne (tela).

pérsico m. Peach [tree] (árbol). || Peach (fruto).

Pérsico adj. GEOGR. *Golfo Pérsico*, Persian gulf.

persignar v. tr. To cross, to make the sign of the cross over.
— V. pr. To cross o.s.

persistencia f. Persistence: *persistencia en el error, en rehusar*, persistence in error, in refusing.

persistente adj. Persistent.
persistir v. intr. To persist: *persistir en creer*, to persist in believing.
persona f. Person (hombre o mujer). || Personage, personality, figure (hombre importante). || Character, personage (en una obra literaria). || GRAM. Person: *la tercera persona del singular*, the third person singular. || Person (en teología). || — Pl. People: *convidar a ocho personas*, to invite eight people; *varias personas*, several people. || — *Dárselas de persona importante*, to act important, to put on airs. || *De persona a persona*, man to man (de hombre a hombre), between ourselves (entre nosotros). || *Enciclopedia en persona*, walking encyclopaedia. || *En la persona de*, in the person of. || *En persona*, in person: *es el diablo en persona*, he is the devil in person. || JUR. *Persona jurídica* or *social* or *civil*, artificial person, body corporate, legal entity. || *Persona mayor*, adult, grown-up. || JUR. *Persona natural*, natural person. || *Por persona*, each, per person, per head. || *Ser muy buena persona*, to be very nice *o* kind. || *Sin acepción de personas*, without respect of persons. || JUR. *Tercera persona*, third person, third party.
personaje m. Personage, person of mark, important person (persona importante). || Character, personage (en una obra literaria).
personal adj. Personal: *un asunto personal*, a personal affair. || Private, personal: *habitación, entrevista personal*, private room, interview. || GRAM. Personal (pronombre). || *Los intereses general y personal*, public and private interest.
— M. Personnel, staff, employees, *pl.* (empleados). || FAM. Bods, *pl.*, people (gente). || Ancient tax (tributo). || — *El personal dirigente*, the managerial staff. || *El personal docente*, the teaching staff. || *Personal de tierra*, ground crew *o* staff.
personalidad f. Personality: *culto a la personalidad*, personality cult; *desdoblamiento de la personalidad*, split personality. || — JUR. *Personalidad jurídica*, legal status. || *Tener personalidad*, to have personality *o* character.
personalismo m. Personalism. || Personal remark (observación). || Preference, partiality (parcialidad).
personalista adj. Personalist, personalistic.
— M. y f. Personalist.
personalización f. Personalization.
personalizar v. tr. To personalize. || To personify, to embody (personificar). || GRAM. To make personal (un verbo).
— V. intr. To make a personal reference *o* remark.
personarse v. pr. To come *o* to appear in person (presentarse): *se personó en mi casa*, he came in person to my house, he appeared in person at my house. || To go to *o* to visit [the scene of the occurrence]: *la policía se personó rápidamente en el lugar del crimen*, the police quickly went to the scene of the crime. || To meet (reunirse). || JUR. To appear.
personería f. Procuration. || JUR. Personality.
personero m. Procurator.
personificación f. Personification.
personificar v. tr. To personify: *Nerón personificaba la crueldad*, Nero personified cruelty; *personificar los animales*, to personify animals. || *Es la avaricia personificada*, he is avarice personified.
perspectiva f. Perspective: *perspectiva aérea, lineal*, aerial, linear perspective. || Perspective, scene, view (vista). || FIG. Perspective, prospect, outlook: *buenas perspectivas económicas*, good economic perspectives. | Perspective (distancia): *no tenemos suficiente perspectiva para juzgar estos acontecimientos*, we do not have sufficient perspective to judge these events, we cannot yet judge these events in the proper perspective. || *En perspectiva*, in perspective (dibujo), in perspective, in prospect, in view (proyecto).
perspectivo, va adj. Perspective.
perspicacia o **perspicacidad** f. Keen eyesight, keenness of sight (agudeza de vista). || FIG. Perspicacity, perspicaciousness, insight (penetración).
perspicaz adj. Keen, sharp (vista). || FIG. Perspicacious, sharp, shrewd (sagaz).
perspicuo, cua adj. Clear, transparent. || FIG. Perspicuous (estilo, orador).
persuadidor, ra adj. Persuasive.
— M. y f. Persuasive person.
persuadir v. tr. To persuade: *le persuadí de mi sinceridad, de que no mentía*, I persuaded him of my sincerity, that I was not lying. || — *Dejarse persuadir*, to allow o.s. to be persuaded *o* prevailed upon. || *Persuadido que*, convinced that.
— V. pr. To persuade o.s., to become persuaded *o* convinced.
persuasible adj. Plausible, credible (creíble).
persuasión f. Persuasion. || Firm belief (convicción).
persuasiva f. Persuasive power, persuasiveness.
persuasivo, va adj. Persuasive, convincing.
— M. y f. Persuasive person.
persuasor, ra adj. Persuasive.
— M. y f. Persuasive person.
persulfato m. QUÍM. Persulphate [U.S., persulfate].
pertenecer* v. intr. To belong, to be: *estas casas pertenecen a mi padre*, these houses belong to my father *o* are my father's. || To belong: *el pino pertenece a la familia de las coníferas*, the pine belongs to the family of conifers. || — *A mí no me pertenece decidir*, it is not for me *o* it is not up to me to decide. || *Eso pertenece al pasado*, that is a thing of the past.
perteneciente adj. Belonging, which belongs: *una finca perteneciente al Estado*, a property belonging to the State. || JUR. Belonging.
pertenencia f. Possession, ownership, property (propiedad): *reivindicar la pertenencia de algo*, to lay claim to the possession of sth. || Possession (territorio). || Outbuilding, annex (de una finca, de un palacio, etc.). || Membership (*a*, of) [a un partido, etc.]. || MIN. Claim [of one square acre].
pértiga f. Pole (vara). || DEP. *Salto de pértiga*, pole vault.
pértigo m. Shaft (de carro).
pertiguero m. Verger (de iglesia).
pertinacia f. Pertinacity, obstinacy (terquedad). || FIG. Persistence (larga duración).
pertinaz adj. Pertinacious, obstinate (obstinado). || FIG. Persistent.
pertinazmente adv. Pertinaciously, obstinately. || FIG. Persistently.
pertinencia f. Pertinence, relevance. || Opportuneness (oportunidad).
pertinente adj. Pertinent, relevant (que viene al caso). || Opportune, apt, appropriate (oportuno).
pertinentemente adv. Pertinently, relevantly. || Opportunely (oportunamente).
pertrechar v. tr. MIL. To supply with stores and ammunition, to equip, to munition. || FIG. To prepare, to arrange (disponer). | To supply (proveer).
— V. pr. To equip *o* to provide o.s. (*de, con*, with).
pertrechos m. pl. MIL. Stores and ammunition, munitions. || Equipment, *sing.*, implements: *pertrechos de labranza*, farming equipment, farm implements. || *Pertrechos de pesca*, fishing tackle, *sing.*
perturbación f. Perturbation, disturbance (disturbio): *perturbaciones sociales*, social perturbations. || Disorder, unsettlement (desorden). || Perturbation (de la mente). || Perturbation (de un astro, de una aguja magnética). || MED. Upset, disorder, disturbance. || *Perturbación del orden público*, disturbance *o* breach of the peace.
perturbado, da m. y f. Mentally unbalanced person.
perturbador, ra adj. Disturbing (alborotador). || Perturbing (que desasosiega).
— M. y f. Disturber.
perturbar v. tr. To disturb (trastornar): *perturbar el orden público*, to disturb the peace. || To perturb (desasosegar a uno). || To unsettle, to upset (el tiempo). || To upset (un proyecto). || MED. To upset, to unsettle, to disturb (el organismo). | To disturb (la mente).
Perú n. pr. m. GEOGR. Peru. || — FIG. *Valer un Perú*, to be worth a fortune (cosa), to be a treasure, to be worth one's weight in gold (persona).
peruanismo m. Peruvianism, Peruvian word (vocablo) *o* expression (giro).
peruano, na adj./s. Peruvian.
perulero, ra adj./s. (P.us.). Peruvian (peruano). || — M. y f. Emigrant returned from Peru with a fortune. || — M. Earthenware jar (vasija).
perversidad f. Perversity.
perversión f. Perversion, corruption, depravation.
perverso, sa adj. Perverse, depraved. || Evil (malo).
— M. y f. Pervert. || Evil doer (persona mala).
pervertido, da adj. Perverted.
— M. y f. Pervert.
pervertidor, ra adj. Perversive, perverting.
— M. y f. Perverter.
pervertimiento m. Perversion, perverting.
pervertir* v. tr. To pervert, to deprave, to corrupt (corromper). || To distort (un texto). || To corrupt (el gusto).
— V. pr. To be *o* to become perverted.
pervinca f. Periwinkle.
pervivencia f. Survival (supervivencia).
pervivir v. intr. To survive (supervivir).
pesa f. Weight: *una balanza y sus pesas*, a balance and its weights. || Weight (de un reloj). || Handset (microteléfono). || — Pl. Weights, dumbbells (gimnasia). || — DEP. *Levantamiento de pesas*, weight-lifting. || *Pesas y medidas*, weights and measures.
pesabebés m. inv. Baby-weighing scales, *pl.*
pesacartas m. inv. Letter-weighing scales, *pl.*
pesada f. Weighing.
pesadamente adv. Heavily. || Slowly (lentamente). || FIG. Tiresomely, annoyingly.
pesadez f. Heaviness, weight (peso): *la pesadez de un bulto*, the heaviness of a bundle. || FIG. Heaviness (del estómago, de la cabeza, etc.). | Sluggishness, slowness (lentitud): *la pesadez de sus movimientos*, the sluggishness of his movements. | Pigheadedness (terquedad). | Bind, bore (persona molesta): *¡qué pesadez!*, what a bore! | Nuisance, bore, bind, drag (fastidio): *es una pesadez tener que ir a ese sitio ahora*, it is a drag having to go there now. || (P.us.). FÍS. Gravity (gravedad). || — FIG. y FAM. *Este hombre ¡qué pesadez!*, what a bore that man is! || *Sentir pesadez de cabeza, de estómago*, to feel heavy-headed, to have a heavy feeling in one's stomach.
pesadilla f. Nightmare. || FIG. Nightmare, bugbear, pet aversion: *es mi pesadilla*, it is my bugbear. || *De pesadilla*, nightmarish.

pesado, da adj. Heavy, weighty: *una maleta pesada*, a heavy suitcase. || Heavy: *metal pesado*, heavy metal. || FIG. Sluggish, slow (movimiento). | Heavy (paso). | Heavy, ungainly (torpe). | Heavy, deep (sueño). | Heavy (cabeza, ojos, etc.). | Sultry, heavy (tiempo). | Heavy (terreno, comida). | Tough, hard (trabajo). | Heavy, wearisome (penoso). | Boring, tedious, tiresome, dull (molesto). | In bad taste (broma). || Stiff (mecanismo). || QUÍM. Heavy (aceite, hidrógeno). || MIL. Heavy (artillería). || — *Agua pesada*, heavy water. || FIG. y FAM. *Más pesado que un saco de plomo*, deadly boring, as dull as ditchwater. | — M. y f. FIG. y FAM. Bore, drag, bind, pest: *ser un pesado*, to be a bore.

pesador, ra adj. [Used for] weighing.
— M. y f. Weigher, weighman (hombre), weighwoman (mujer).

pesadumbre f. Heaviness (pesadez). || FIG. Bind, bother (molestia). | Sorrow, grief (sentimiento): *tener mucha pesadumbre*, to be in great sorrow, to be filled with grief. | Disagreement, upset (riña).

pesaje m. DEP. Weighing-in: *el pesaje de los dos boxeadores*, the weighing-in of the two boxers.
— OBSERV. This is a Gallicism for *peso*.

pesaleche m. Milk hydrometer.

pesalicores m. inv. FÍS. Alcoholometer (alcohómetro). | Aerometer (aerómetro).

pésame m. Condolences, *pl.*, sympathy: *dar el pésame*, to express one's condolences, to send one's sympathy. || *Mi más sentido pésame*, my deepest sympathy.

pesante adj. Weighty (que pesa). || Sad (triste).

pesantez f. Gravity (gravedad).

pesar m. Sorrow, grief (pena). || Regret (remordimiento). || — *A pesar de*, in spite of, despite: *a pesar de sus padres*, in spite of one's parents. || *A pesar de los pesares*, in spite of everything. || *A pesar de que*, in spite of *o* despite [the fact that], although: *a pesar de estar malo* or *de que estaba malo*, despite being ill, despite the fact that he was ill, although he was ill. || *A pesar de todo*, in spite of *o* despite everything, for all that (a pesar de los pesares), all the same: *me lo han prohibido, pero lo haré a pesar de todo*, they have forbidden me to do it, but I shall all the same. || *A pesar de todos*, in spite of everyone. || *A pesar mío, suyo*, against my will, against his will; despite me, despite him. || *Con gran pesar mío*, much to my sorrow. || *Sentir* or *tener pesar por haber...*, to regret having..., to feel *o* to be sorry for having...

pesar v. tr. To weigh. || To weigh in (a jockeys, a boxeadores). || To weigh down: *me pesan los zapatos*, my shoes weigh me down. || FIG. To weigh (examinar): *pesar el pro y el contra*, to weigh the pros and the cons. || FIG. *Pesar sus palabras*, to weigh one's words.
— V. intr. To weigh: *un paquete que pesa tres kilos*, a parcel weighing three kilos. || To be heavy *o* weighty, to weigh a lot (tener mucho peso). || FIG. To weigh heavily (*a*, on, upon), to be a burden (*a*, on, upon) [ser una carga]. | To fall (recaer): *muchas obligaciones pesan sobre él*, many obligations fall upon him. | To be sorry, to regret (sentir): *me pesa que no haya venido*, I regret *o* I am sorry that he has not come. | To grieve (entristecer). | To carry a lot of weight, to play an important part, to count for a lot (influir): *mis argumentos pesaron mucho en su decisión*, my arguments played an important part in his decision. || — FIG. *Mal que te pese*, whether you like it or not. || *Pesar corrido*, to give good measure. || FIG. *Pesarle a uno en el alma*, to weigh on *o* upon s.o.'s mind. | *Pesarle a uno los años*, to be weighed down by the years. || *Pesar menos que*, to be lighter than. || *Pesar poco*, to be light. || *Pese a*, despite, in spite of: *pese a sus muchas tareas vino*, he came in spite of his many duties. || *Pese a que*, in spite of, despite (a pesar de que). || *Pese a quien pese*, come what may. || *¡Ya te pesará!*, you'll be sorry!, you'll regret it!

pesario m. MED. Pessary.

pesaroso, sa adj. Sorry, regretful (que se arrepiente). || Sorrowful, sad (triste, afligido).

pesca f. Fishing, angling: *ir, estar de pesca*, to go, to be fishing; *la pesca del salmón*, salmon fishing. || Fish, *pl.* (peces): *aquí hay mucha pesca*, there are a lot of fish in these parts. || Catch (lo pescado): *buena pesca*, a good catch. || — FIG. *Andar a la pesca de cumplidos*, to fish for compliments. || *Pesca con caña, con red*, angling, netting. || *Pesca de bajura* or *de litoral, de altura*, coastal *o* inshore fishing, deep-sea fishing. || *Pesca de la ballena*, whaling. || *Pesca de perlas*, pearl diving *o* fishing. || *Pesca submarina*, underwater fishing. || FIG. y FAM. *Y toda la pesca*, and Uncle Tom Cobley and all, and all the rest of the crew (personas), and what not, and what have you (y todo lo demás).

pescada f. Hake (pez, manjar).

pescadería f. Fish shop, fishmonger's.

pescadero, ra m. y f. Fishmonger.

pescadilla f. Whiting (pez). || FIG. *Es la pescadilla mordiéndose la cola*, I am (you are, he is, etc.) right back where I (you, he, etc.) started.

pescado m. Fish. || *Día de pescado*, day of abstinence, fish day.
— OBSERV. *Pescado* is a fish that has been caught, considered as food; *pez* is a live fish still in water.

pescador, ra adj. Fishing.
— M. y f. Fisher, fisherman (hombre), fisherwoman (mujer). || — *Pescador de caña*, angler. || *Pescador de perlas*, pearl diver *o* fisher. || — M. ZOOL. Angler. || — F. Sailor blouse (camisa).

pescante m. Coachman's seat, driver's seat (en los carruajes). || Shelf, support (tabla), hanger (palo, barra) [en la pared]. || TEATR. Hoist [for apparitions] (tramoya). || MAR. Davit. || Jib, boom (construcción).

pescar v. tr. To fish, to fish for (tratar de coger). || To catch (coger). || FIG. y FAM. To land, to get (lograr): *pescar un buen puesto, un marido*, to land a good job, a husband. | To pick up, to get, to get hold of (encontrar): *¿dónde has pescado esta noticia?*, where did you pick up this piece of news? | To grasp, to get (comprender). | To catch, to get (coger): *pescar un resfriado*, to catch a cold. | To catch, to nab, to cop (a un desprevenido). | To catch out: *estudiante difícil de pescar en historia*, student hard to catch out in history. | To fish for, to tout for (clientes).
— V. intr. To fish. || — *Ir a pescar*, to go fishing. || FIG. *Pescar a* or *en río revuelto*, to fish in troubled waters. || *Pescar con caña*, to angle.

pescozada f. o **pescozón** m. Cuff round the scruff of the neck.

pescuezo m. Neck (de un animal). || FAM. Scruff of the neck (de las personas). || FIG. Pride, haughtiness (soberbia). || — FIG. y FAM. *Apretar* or *estirar* or *torcer* or *retorcer a uno el pescuezo*, to wring s.o.'s neck. | *Ser más malo que la carne de pescuezo*, to be a load of rubbish, to be worse than bad (en general), not to be fit for the pigs (comida), to be as rotten as they come (persona), to be a horrid little beast (niño). | *Torcer el pescuezo*, to break one's neck (morir).

pesebre m. Rack, manger, crib (de una cuadra).

pesebrera f. Row of racks *o* mangers.

pesero m. *Amer.* Fixed-fare taxi.

peseta f. Peseta (moneda española). || *Amer.* Twenty-five centavos [in Mexico]. || FIG. y FAM. *Cambiar la peseta*, to throw up, to be sick (vomitar).

pesetero, ra adj. FAM. Peseta, one peseta (que cuesta una peseta). | Penny-pinching, stingy (avaro).
— M. y f. Skinflint (avaro).

pésimamente adv. Very badly, abominably, terribly.

pesimismo m. Pessimism.

pesimista adj. Pessimistic.
— M. y f. Pessimist.

pésimo, ma adj. Very bad, abominable, terrible.

peso m. Weight (fuerza de gravitación y su medida): *el peso del aire*, the weight of air; *un peso de diez kilos*, a weight of ten kilos. || FÍS. Weight: *peso atómico*, atomic weight. || Weight (cosa pesada, de una balanza). || Weight (carga): *el suelo no puede resistir el peso de tantos muebles*, the floor cannot bear the weight of so much furniture. || Balance, scales, *pl.* (balanza). || Weighing (acción de pesar). || Weighing-in (de los jockeys, de los boxeadores). || Peso (moneda). || DEP. Shot, weight: *lanzamiento del peso*, shot put; *lanzar el peso*, to put the shot. || FIG. Weight (importancia o influencia): *argumentos de peso*, arguments that carry weight. | Weight, burden (carga): *el peso de los años, de la responsabilidad*, the weight of years, of responsibility.
— *Al peso*, by the weight. || FIG. *A peso de oro*, for its weight in gold, at a ransom price (a precio muy subido): *vender algo a peso de oro*, to sell sth. for its weight in gold. | *Caerse de* or *por su peso*, to go without saying, to be self-evident, to stand to reason. || *Coger* or *tomar una cosa en peso*, to feel the weight of sth., to try sth. for weight (sopesar). || *Dar buen peso*, to give good weight. || FIG. *De peso*, influential: *gente, persona de peso*, influential people, person. | *De poco peso*, lightweight. || *Hacer peso*, to give *o* to add weight, to make heavy. || DEP. *Levantamiento de pesos*, weight-lifting. || *Levantar en peso*, to lift bodily || *Lleva la dirección de la empresa en peso*, he runs the firm entirely on his own, the running of the firm rests entirely upon his shoulders. || FIG. *No tener mucho peso* or *ser cosa de poco peso*, to carry little weight. || *Peso atómico, molecular*, atomic, molecular weight. || *Peso bruto*, gross weight. || *Peso de baño*, bathroom scales, *pl.* || *Peso en vivo*, live weight (carnicería). || *Peso específico*, specific weight. || *Peso mosca, gallo, pluma, ligero, mediano ligero, medio, semipesado, pesado*, flyweight, bantamweight, featherweight, lightweight, welterweight, middleweight, light heavy-weight *o* cruiser, heavyweight (boxeo). || *Peso muerto*, deadweight. || *Peso neto*, net weight. || FIG. *Quitarle a uno un peso de encima*, to take a load off s.o.'s mind. | *Valer su peso en oro*, to be worth its *o* one's weight in gold. || *Vender al peso*, to sell by weight.

pespuntar v. tr. To backstitch.

pespunte m. Backstitch. || *Medio pespunte*, running stitch.

pespuntear v. tr. To backstitch.

pesquera f. Fishery, fishing ground.

pesquería f. Fishing, fishery (actividad). || Fishery, fishing ground (sitio).

pesquero, ra adj. Fishing: *buque, puerto pesquero*, fishing boat, port.
— M. Fishing boat.

pesquis m. FIG. y FAM. Insight (perspicacia). | Sense, gumption (inteligencia).

pesquisa f. Inquiry: *hacer una pesquisa judicial sobre*, to conduct a judicial inquiry into. || [House] search (en casa de uno). || — M. *Amer.* Detective.
pesquisador m. *Amer.* Detective.
pesquisar v. tr. To inquire into, to investigate. || To search (en casa de uno).
pesquisidor, ra adj. Inquiring, investigating. || Searching.
— M. y f. Inquirer, investigator. || Searcher. || Examining magistrate (juez).
pestaña f. Eyelash, lash (del ojo). || Fringe, edging (adorno de una tela). || Hem (en una costura). || Rim, edge (borde saliente). || TECN. Flange (de rueda, etc), rim (de llanta). || Tongue (de una lata de sardinas). || Joint (ceja de un libro). || — Pl. BOT. Cilia. || — FIG. *No mover pestaña*, not to bat an eyelid. | *No pegar pestaña*, not to sleep a wink, not to get a wink of sleep. | *Quemarse las pestañas*, to swot hard (estudiar mucho), to burn the midnight oil (por la noche).
pestañear v. intr. To blink, to wink. || FIG. *Sin pestañear*, without batting an eyelid, without turning a hair.
pestañeo m. Blinking, winking.
pestazo m. FAM. Stink, stench (hedor).
peste f. Plague: *peste bubónica*, bubonic plague. || FIG. y FAM. Stink, stench (mal olor). | Pestilence, evil (cosa mala). | Corruption, rottenness (depravación). | Poison (persona malvada): *esta mujer es una peste*, this woman is poison. | Plague, pest (niño): *¡estos niños son la peste!*, what a plague *o* what pests these children are! | Plague (plaga, exceso): *una peste de ratas*, a plague of rats. || — Pl. Curses, words of execration. || — FIG. y FAM. *Decir* or *echar pestes de uno*, to drag s.o. through the mud, to heap abuse upon s.o., to run s.o. down. | *Huir de uno como de la peste*, to avoid *o* to shun s.o. like the plague. | *¡Mala peste se lo lleve!*, a plague on him! || *Peste aviar*, fowl pest. || *Peste negra*, Black Death.
pesticida m. Pesticide.
pestífero, ra adj. Pestiferous. || Foul, fetid, stinking, foul-smelling (que tiene mal olor). || Plague-stricken (enfermo de la peste).
— M. y f. Plague victim (enfermo).
pestilencia f. Pestilence (epidemia). || Stink, fetid smell, stench (hedor).
pestilencial f. Pestilential, pestilent. || Fetid, stinking, foul-smelling (que tiene mal olor).
pestilente adj. Pestilent, pestilential (pestífero). || Fetid, stinking, foul-smelling (que huele mal).
pestillo m. Bolt (cerrojo). || Bolt (de la cerradura): *pestillo de golpe*, spring bolt.
pestiño m. Honey-coated pancake.
pestorejo m. Nape of the neck.
pestoso, sa adj. Foul-smelling, stinking, foul.
pesuña f. Hoof.
petaca f. Tobacco pouch (de cuero), tobacco tin (de metal) [para el tabaco]. || Cigar case (para cigarros puros). || Cigarette case (para cigarrillos). || Leather covered chest (baúl). || *Amer.* Suitcase (maleta). || — M. y f. *Amer.* Lazy person. || — Adj. inv. *Amer.* Idle, lazy (perezoso).
pétalo m. BOT. Petal.
petanca f. French bowls, *pl.* (juego).
petardear v. tr. MIL. To blow down [a door] with a petard *o* with petards (derribar con petardos). | To hurl a petard *o* petards at (disparar petardos).
— V. intr. To backfire (un automóvil).
petardista m. y f. FAM. Sponger, cadger (sablista). | Swindler (estafador).
petardo m. Cracker, firecracker: *tirar petardos*, to fire crackers. || MIL. Petard (explosivo). || FIG. y FAM. Swindle (estafa). | Horror, crow, ugly old bag (mujer fea): *¡qué petardo!*, what a horror! || FIG. y FAM. *Pegarle a uno un petardo*, to touch s.o. for a loan, to cadge a loan off s.o.
petate m. Palm matting (estera). || Bed roll (de ropa de la cama). || FAM. Luggage (de pasajero). | Crook, swindler (embustero). | Runt, squirt (hombre insignificante). || *Amer.* Sleeping mat. || FIG. y FAM. *Liar el petate*, to pack up [and go] (marcharse), to kick the bucket (morir).
petatearse v. pr. *Amer.* FAM. To peg out (morir).
petatería f. *Amer.* Mat making (fábrica), mat shop (tienda).
petenera f. Andalusian popular song. || FIG. *Salirse* or *salir por peteneras*, to go off at a tangent, to say sth. completely irrelevant.
petición f. Request, demand (acción de pedir): *hacer una petición*, to make a request. || Petition (a una autoridad): *elevar una petición al Gobierno*, to get up a petition to the Government. || JUR. Petition, claim (pedimento). || Petition (oración). || — *A petición*, by request. || *A petición de*, at the request of. || *Consulta previa petición de hora*, consultation by appointment. || *Petición de divorcio*, petition for divorce. || *Petición de indulto*, appeal for a reprieve. || *Petición de mano*, proposal. || *Petición de más*, plus petitio, demand for more than is due. || *Petición de principio*, petitio principii, begging the question.
peticionar v. tr. *Amer.* To petition.
peticionario, ria adj. *Amer.* Petitioning (solicitante).
— M. y f. Petitioner.
petifoque m. MAR. Flying jib.
petigrís m. Squirrel [fur].
petimetre m. Dandy, fop, dude.
petirrojo m. Redbreast, robin (pájaro).
petiso, sa adj. *Amer.* Short, squat.
— M. *Amer.* Small horse (caballo).
petisú m. Cream puff (pastelillo).
petitoria f. Request, petition.
petitorio, ria adj. Petitionary.
— M. Fam. Insistent and tiresome demand *o* request. || Medicine catalogue (en una farmacia). || *Medicamento incluido en el petitorio del Seguro de Enfermedad*, medicine paid for by the health service.
petizo, za adj./s.m. *Amer.* V. PETISO.
peto m. Breastplate, plastron (de armadura). || Plastron, ornamental front [of bodice] (de vestido). || Bib (babero, de un delantal). || TAUR. [Horse's] protective padding (de caballo de los picadores). || Plastron (de tortuga). || *Peto de trabajo*, work apron.
petral m. Breastplate (correa).
Petrarca n. pr. m. Petrarch.
petrarquismo m. Petrarchism.
petrarquista adj. Petrarchan.
— M. y f. Petrarchist.
petrel m. Petrel (ave).
pétreo, a adj. Stone, of stone (de piedra). || Stony (pedregoso). || Rocky, stone-like, petrous (p.us.): *dureza pétrea*, rocky hardness. || *Arabia Pétrea*, Arabia Petraea.
petrificación f. Petrification, petrifaction.
petrificante adj. Petrifying.
petrificar v. tr. To petrify, to turn into stone. || FIG. To petrify, to root to the spot.
— V. pr. To petrify, to be petrified.
petrífico, ca adj. Petrifying.
petrografía f. Petrography.
petroleado m. AUT. Spraying [of underchassis] with oil.
petrolear v. tr. AUT. To spray with oil.
petróleo m. Petroleum, oil, mineral oil: *petróleo crudo* or *en bruto*, crude *o* base oil. || — *Petróleo lampante*, paraffin, paraffin oil, kerosene. || *Pozo de petróleo*, oil well.
petrolero, ra adj. Oil, petroleum, mineral-oil: *la industria petrolera*, the oil industry. || *Amer.* Petroliferous, oil-bearing.
— M. Oil tanker (buque). || — M. y f. Incendiary. || Petroleum retailer (vendedor).
petrolífero, ra adj. Oil-bearing, petroliferous, petroleum-bearing, petroleum-producing.
petrología f. Petrology.
petroquímica f. Petrochemistry.
petroquímico, ca adj. Petrochemical. || *Producto petroquímico*, petrochemical.
petulancia f. Arrogance (presunción).

— OBSERV. *Petulance* en inglés significa "mal humor", "irritabilidad".

petulante adj. Arrogant (presumido).

— OBSERV. *Petulant* en inglés significa "malhumorado", "irritable".

petulantemente adv. Arrogantly, pertly.
petunia f. Petunia (flor).
peyorativo, va adj. Pejorative, deprecatory.
peyote m. Peyote, peyotl (cacto).
pez m. Fish: *pez de agua dulce*, freshwater fish; *pez marino*, salt-water fish. || — FIG. *Buen pez*, wily bird, foxy person. || FIG. y FAM. *El pez grande se come al chico*, the big fish swallow up the little ones. | *Estar como el pez en el agua*, to be in one's element, to feel completely at home. | *Estar pez*, to be a dunce (*en*, at, in), not to have a clue (*en*, about) [ignorar todo]. || *Peces de colores*, goldfish. || FIG. y FAM. *Pez de cuidado*, nasty customer. || *Pez de san Pedro*, John dory. || *Pez espada*, swordfish. || FIG. y FAM. *Pez gordo*, big shot, bigwig (persona importante). || *Pez luna*, moonfish, sunfish. || *Pez martillo*, hammerhead. || *Pez mujer*, manatee, sea cow (manatí). || *Pez piloto*, pilot fish. || *Pez sierra*, sawfish. || *Pez volador* or *volante*, flying fish. || FIG. y FAM. *Por la boca muere el pez*, V. BOCA.

— OBSERV. *Pez* is a live fish; *pescado* is a fish that has been caught, considered as food.

pez f. Pitch, tar (para pegar). || MED. Meconium. || *Pez griega*, colophony, rosin (colofonia).
pezón m. BOT. Stalk, stem (de flores, frutos), stem (de hojas). || Nipple (de la teta). || Knob (protuberancia). || TECN. Tip (de ejes).
pezonera f. Linchpin (de eje). || Nipple shield (de rueda).
pezpita f. o **pezpítalo** m. Wagtail (aguzanieves).
pezuña f. Hoof.

— OBSERV. *Pezuña* is a cloven hoof (cows, sheep, etc.). *Casco* is the hoof of a horse.

phi f. Phi (letra griega).
pi f. Pi (letra griega). || MAT. Pi (número).
piache (tarde) loc. FAM. Too late [for the fair].
piada f. Cheep, chirp (de pájaro). || FIG. y FAM. Expression, saying [borrowed from someone else].
piador, ra adj. Cheeping, chirping.
piadosamente adv. Compassionately (con lástima). || Piously (con devoción).
piadoso, sa adj. Compassionate, pitiful (que compadece). || Pious, devout (devoto): *alma piadosa*, pious soul. || *Mentira piadosa*, white lie.

piafador, ra adj. Pawing, stamping (caballo).
— M. Pawer, stamper.

piafar v. intr. To paw the ground (rascar el suelo), to stamp (dar patadas).

pialar v. tr. *Amer.* To lasso [an animal] by its feet.

piamadre o **piamáter** f. ANAT. Pia mater.

piamente adv. Piously (con devoción).

Piamonte n. pr. m. GEOGR. Piedmont.

piamontés, esa adj./s. Piedmontese.

pian, pian o **pian, piano** loc. adv. FAM. Ever so slowly, little by little, nice and easy.

pianillo m. Barrel organ (organillo).

pianísimo adv. MÚS. Pianissimo.

pianista m. y f. Pianist (músico). || Piano maker, piano manufacturer (fabricante), piano dealer (vendedor).

pianístico, ca adj. Pianistic.

piano m. MÚS. Piano: *tocar el piano*, to play the piano. || — *Afinador de pianos*, piano tuner. || *Piano de cola*, grand piano. || *Piano de manubrio*, street piano, hurdy gurdy. || *Piano de media cola*, baby grand piano. || *Piano recto* or *vertical*, upright piano. || *Taburete de piano*, piano stool.
— Adv. MÚS. Piano.

pianoforte m. Pianoforte.

pianola f. Pianola.

piante m. y f. FAM. Grouser.

piar m. Cheeping, chirping, peeping (de las aves).

piar v. intr. To cheep, to chirp, to peep (las aves). || FIG. y FAM. To grouse (protestar). || FAM. *Piar por*, to cry for.

piara f. Herd (de cerdos, ovejas, caballos).

piastra f. Piastre, piaster (moneda).

pibe, ba m. y f. *Amer.* FAM. Kid.

piberío m. *Amer.* Kids, *pl.*, bunch of kids (chiquillos).

pica f. Pike (arma). || Pick (herramienta). || Pikeman (soldado). || TAUR. Goad, picador's lance *o* pike. || MED. Pica. || ZOOL. Magpie (urraca). || Stonemason's hammer (escoda). || *Amer.* Tapping (de hevea). | Pique, resentment (pique). | Narrow path (sendero). || FIG. y FAM. *Poner una pica en Flandes*, to pull off sth. very difficult.

picacera f. *Amer.* Pique, resentment.

picacho m. Peak (de una montaña).

picada f. V. PICADURA.

picadero m. Riding school, manège (para aprender a montar). || Ring [for training wild horses] (para caballos salvajes). || MAR. Stock, block (madero). || FAM. Bachelor pad (cuarto). || *Amer* Slaughterhouse (matadero).

picadillo m. Minced meat, mince (de carne). || Chopped onion (de cebolla). || Sort of hash (guiso). || FIG. *Hacer picadillo*, to cut to pieces, to make mincemeat of (a un ejército, una persona), to smash to pieces (algo).

picado m. Mincing (de la carne). || Pricking-out (de una cartulina de encaje). || Diving (acción), dive (resultado) [de un avión, pájaro]. || Knocking, pinking [U.S., pinging] (de un motor). || Punching, clipping (de un billete). || Cutting (de las piedras). || MÚS. Staccato. || Mince (picadillo).

picado, da adj. Sour (bebida). || Bad, off (fruta, alimento). || High (carne mala). || Bitten (por araña, pulga, serpiente). || Stung (por una avispa). || CULIN. Minced (carne). | Chopped (cebolla). || Cut (tabaco). || Choppy (mar). || FIG. Piqued, nettled, narked (fam.) [ofendido]. || *Amer.* FAM. Picked, sozzled (achispado). || — *Diente picado*, decayed *o* bad tooth. || MÚS. *Nota picada*, staccato note. || *Picado de viruelas*, pockmarked.

picador m. TAUR. "Picador". || Horsebreaker (de caballos). || Miner (minero). || CULIN. Chopping board.

picadora f. Mincer, mincing machine (para picar).

picadura f. Bite (de araña, pulga, serpiente). || Sting (de avispa). || Peck (de pájaro). || Spot (en las frutas). || Cut tobacco, loose tobacco (tabaco). || Pockmark (de viruela). || Moth hole (de polilla). || Decay, caries (en las muelas). || *Tener una picadura en un diente*, to have a bad tooth *o* a decayed tooth.

picafigo m. Figpecker (ave).

picaflor m. Hummingbird (ave). || *Amer.* FIG. Romeo, flirt (mariposón).

picajón, ona o **picajoso, sa** adj. FAM. Touchy, peevish.

picamaderos m. inv. Woodpecker (ave).

picana f. *Amer.* Goad (del boyero).

picanear v. tr. *Amer.* To goad.

picante adj. Hot, piquant, pungent: *salsa picante*, piquant sauce. || Spicy, highly seasoned (comida). || Sour, tart (vino). || FIG. Spicy, racy, risqué: *chiste picante*, spicy joke. | Pungent, pointed, biting, cutting, stinging: *palabras picantes*, pungent words. | Sharp, biting (contestación).
— M. Piquancy (de la pimienta, de una salsa, etc.), spiciness (de un manjar). || FIG. Pungency, pointedness (mordacidad). | Spice, zest (de un relato, un chiste). || Pepper (pimienta). || *Amer.* Piquancy, highly-seasoned dish.

picapedrero m. Stonecutter.

picapica f. *Amer.* Plant with itch-producing leaves or stalk. || *Polvillos de picapica*, itching powder.

picapleitos m. inv. FAM. Litigious fellow (pleitista). | Caseless *o* briefless lawyer (abogado sin pleitos).

picaporte m. Doorhandle (tirador de la puerta). || Latch (barrita). || Latchkey (llave). || Doorknocker (aldaba).

picar v. tr. To prick, to pierce (con instrumento punzante). || To peck, to peck at (morder o comer las aves). || To bite (araña, pulga, serpiente). || To sting (avispa). || To eat into (los gusanos). || To prickle (barba, espinas). || TAUR. To prick, to goad [the bull]. || To bite (el pez): *picar el anzuelo*, to bite the hook. || To burn, to sting, to be hot on (ser picante): *la pimienta pica la lengua*, pepper burns the tongue, pepper is hot on the tongue. || To pick at, to nibble at (comer poco). || To mince, to chop up, to hash (hacer picadillo con la carne). || To chop up (la cebolla). || To cut up (el tabaco). || To spur on (espolear un caballo), to break [in] (adiestrar). || To punch, to clip (los billetes). || To perforate (perforar). || To cut (piedras). || To roughen (una pared, una piedra de molino). || To crush, to pound (hacer pedazos). || FIG. To pique, to nettle, to nark (fam.) [enojar]. | To wound (el amor propio). | To pique, to arouse (la curiosidad). | To prick: *le pica la conciencia*, his conscience pricks him. | To spur on, to goad on (estimular). || To spin (una bola de billar, un balón). || MIL. To harass (acosar). || MAR. To cut: *picar un cable*, to cut a cable. | To speed up [the rowing] (remar más deprisa). || MÚS. To strike [a note] briefly and sharply. || To add the finishing touches to, to touch off [a painting] (pintura). || To pink (perforar para adorno), to prick out (el dibujo de un encaje). || — FIG. y FAM. *A quien le pique que se rasque*, if the cap fits, wear it. || *Me pica la espalda, la herida*, my arm, the wound itches (escuece). || *Me pica mucho la boca*, my mouth is on fire. || *Me pican los ojos con el humo*, the smoke is making my eyes smart *o* sting. || FIG. y FAM. *¿Qué mosca le ha picado?*, what's eating him?, what's biting him?
— V. intr. To prick (agujerear). || To peck (morder las aves). || To bite (araña, pulga, serpiente). || To sting (la avispa). || To prickle (la barba, espinas). || To bite (un pez). || To bite (el frío). || To bite, to cut (el viento). || To nibble, to have a nibble (comer muy poco). || To burn, to be hot [on the tongue o palate] (ajo, pimienta, etc.). || To be sharp *o* tart (el vino). || To itch, to sting (la piel). || To smart, to sting (una herida). || To dive, to nosedive (un avión). || To blaze down, to scorch (el Sol). || To pick (con un pico). || To knock, to rap [at the door] (llamar a la puerta). || To pick a page at random (abrir un libro al azar). || To knock, to pink [U.S., to ping] (un motor). || To cut (cortar piedra). || FIG. To swallow it (dejarse atraer o engañar). | To slip up, to let the cat out of the bag (dejar escapar un secreto). | To bite, to nibble (dejarse atraer los compradores, etc.). || — FIG. *Picar en*, to dabble in (aprender nociones superficiales), to be something of a: *picar en poeta*, to be something of a poet; to border on: *picar en insolencia*, to border on insolence; to be quite: *picar en gracioso*, to be quite witty; to swallow, to fall for, to be taken in by (creerse una cosa). || FIG. y FAM. *Picar (muy) alto*, to aim [very] high.
— V. pr. To become moth-eaten (por la polilla). || To get worm-eaten (la madera por la carcoma). || To spot, to mildew (la ropa por la humedad). || To rust (un metal). || To spot, to go rotten (una fruta). || To turn sour (el vino, la leche). || To go bad, to decay (dientes). || To get choppy (el mar). || To be in rut (los animales machos). || FIG. To get piqued *o* nettled *o* narked (fam.) [ofenderse]. | To get cross (enfadarse). || *Amer.* FAM. To get pickled *o* sozzled. || — FIG. *El que se pica* or *quien se pica ajos come*, V. AJO. | *Picarse con*, to be piqued by, to be set on one's mettle by (sentirse estimulado), to be dead set on sth. (desear). | *Picarse de*, to think o.s., to think one is: *se pica de gracioso*, he thinks himself funny; *se pica de poeta*, he thinks he is a poet. | *Picarse en el juego*, to get the gambling itch.

picaramente adv. Slyly, wilily (con astucia). || Mischievously (de manera traviesa). || Despicably (con vileza). || *Mirar picaramente a uno*, to give s.o. a mischievous *o* a coy look.

picaraza f. ZOOL. Magpie (urraca).

picarazado, da adj. *Amer.* Pockmarked (picado de viruela).

picardear v. tr. To corrupt, to teach bad ways.
— V. intr. To be a rogue. || To play up, to get up to mischief (niño). || To say rude things (decir).
— V. pr. To go to the bad, to become corrupted.

picardía f. Despicable action, dirty trick, vile deed (acción baja). || Crookedness, roguishness (bribonería). || Craftiness, slyness (astucia). || Naughty *o* mischievous trick, prank, mischief (travesura). || Rude thing, naughty thing (palabra o acción licenciosa). || Gang of rogues (grupo). || — Pl. (P.us.). Insults (insultos). || FIG. *Tener mucha picardía*, to be a real scamp, to be full of mischief (niño), to have many a trick up one's sleeve (hombre).

picaresca f. Gang of rogues (pandilla). || Roguery, roguish life (vida). || Picaresque novel: *la picaresca es una creación literaria española*, the picaresque novel is a Spanish literary creation.

picarescamente adv. Roguishly.

picaresco, ca adj. Picaresque: *novela picaresca*, picaresque novel. || Roguish, arch, mischievous: *una mirada picaresca*, an arch look. || Picaresque (literatura).

pícaro, ra adj. Despicable, base (vil). || Rascally, roguish, crooked (bribón). || Crafty, sly, wily (astuto). || Evil-minded (malicioso). || Naughty, mischievous (niño). || FIG. Scampish, rascally, saucy (calificativo cariñoso). || *Este pícaro mundo*, this damned world.
— M. y f. Rascal, crook, rogue (bribón). || Crafty *o* sly person (astuto). || Villain (malicioso). || FIG. Scamp, rascal (pillo, sinvergüenza). || — M. "Pícaro", rogue (tipo de la literatura española). || — *A pícaro, pícaro y medio*, diamond cut diamond. || *Pícaro de cocina*, kitchen boy, scullion (ant.) [pinche].

picarón, ona adj. FAM. Roguish, rascally, mischievous.
— M. y f. Rogue, rascal.

picatoste m. Round of fried bread (pan frito). || Round of toast (pan tostado).

picaza f. Magpie (urraca).

picazón f. Tingling, itch, itching (leve), stinging, sting, smarting (escozor fuerte). || FIG. y FAM. Annoyance, pique (enfado). | Anxiety, uneasy feeling (desazón moral).

picea f. Spruce (abeto).

Picio n. pr. m. FAM. *Más feo que Picio*, as ugly as sin.

pickpocket m. Pickpocket (ratero).

pick-up m. Record player (tocadiscos). || TECN. Pickup (fonocaptor).

picnic m. Picnic (comida campestre).

pícnico, ca adj. Pyknic.

picnómetro m. Pycnometer, pyknometer.

pico m. Beak, bill (de ave). || Beak (de insecto). || Beak, sharp point (parte saliente). || Corner (de un mueble): *golpearse contra el pico de la mesa*, to bump into the corner of the table. || Corner (de sombrero, pañuelo, cuello). || Pick, pickaxe (herramienta). || Lip (de cazuela), spout, beak (de tetera, etc.). || Peak (cima, montaña). || Piece [of a skirt hem] that dips (de una falda). || Nappy (de niño). || FIG. Crust (extremo del pan). | Bread stick (panecillo de forma alargada). | Odd money (suma). || FIG. y FAM. Gift of the gab (habladuría). | Mouth, lips, *pl.*, trap (boca). || Socket (de candil). || MAR. Gaff. || *Amer.* Acorn barnacle (bálano). | Kiss (beso). || — Pl. Spades (en los naipes). || — FIG. y FAM. *Andar* or *irse de picos pardos*, to go on a binge [U.S., to go have a blast] (irse de juerga), to gad about, to lead a gay life (ser amigo de juergas). | *Callar* or *cerrar* el *pico*, to shut one's trap, to belt up (callarse), to shut [s.o.] up (hacer callar). | *Costar un pico*, to cost a pretty penny, to cost quite a bit. | *Darse el pico*, to kiss (besarse), to get on very well (llevarse muy bien). | *Hincar el pico*, to peg out, to kick the bucket (morirse), to throw in the sponge, to give in (darse por vencido). | *Irse del pico*, to shoot one's mouth off, to talk too much. | *Perderse por el pico*, to talk too much, to talk o.s. into trouble. || *Pico carpintero*, woodpecker. || *Pico de cigüeña*, geranium. || TECN. *Pico de colada*, nose [of Bessemer converter]. | *Pico de cuervo*, bird's beak (instrumento). || *Amer. Pico de frasco* or *de canoa*, toucan (tucán). || *Pico verde*, green woodpecker (ave). || *Sombrero de dos picos*, two-cornered hat, cocked hat. || *Sombrero de tres picos*, three-cornered hat, tricorn. || FIG. y FAM. *Ser* or *tener un pico de oro*, to have the gift of the gab. | *Trabajar de pico y pala*, to work like a slave, to work with pick and shovel. || *Y pico*, -odd: *cien pesetas y pico*, a hundred-odd pesetas; just after, a little after: *son las tres y pico*, it is just after three.

picón, ona adj. With protruding upper teeth (animal). || FAM. Touchy, peevish (susceptible).
— M. Small coal (carbón). || Stickleback (pez).

piconero m. Coalman, small-coal merchant.

picor m. Itch, itching, prickling (escozor), smarting, stinging (en los ojos). || *Dar picor*, to itch, to smart.

picota f. Pillory (suplicio). || Spire (de torre). || Peak (de montaña). || Boy's game (juego). || MAR. Support rod (de guimbalete). || Bigarreau cherry (cereza). || FIG. *Poner a uno en la picota*, to hold s.o. up to obloquy, to pillory s.o.

picotada f. o **picotazo** m. V. PICADURA.

picoteado, da adj. Pecked.

picotear v. tr. To peck, to peck at (morder o comer las aves). || FIG. To pick at, to nibble at (comer un poco).
— V. intr. To toss it's head (el caballo). || FIG. To pick at one's food (comer poco). || FIG. y FAM. To patter, to prattle (hablar).
— V. pr. FIG. To squabble, to bicker (reñir).

picoteo m. Pecking (de pájaros). || FIG. Nibble, nibbling (acción de comer).

picotón m. *Amer.* V. PICADURA.

pícrico adj. m. QUÍM. Picric (ácido).

picto, ta adj. Pictish, Pict.
— M. y f. Pict (de Escocia). || — M. Pictish (lengua).

pictografía f. Pictography, picture writing (escritura). || Pictograph (imagen aislada).

pictográfico, ca adj. Pictographic.

pictórico, ca adj. Pictorial: *interés, motivo pictórico*, pictorial interest, motif. || Painting (para pintar).

picudilla f. Rail (ave).

picudo, da adj. Pointed, with a point (puntiagudo). || Lipped: *cazuela picuda*, lipped pan. || Spouted, beaked (tetera, etc.). || Long-beaked, long-billed (ave). || Long-snouted, long-nosed (hocicudo). || Peaked (montaña).

pichilingo m. *Amer.* Kid.

pichincha f. *Amer.* Bargain, good deal (ganga).

pichón m. Young pigeon (pollo de paloma). || Pigeon: *tiro de pichón*, pigeon shooting. || FIG. y FAM. Dove, pet (término cariñoso): *ven acá pichón*, come here, my dove. || *Amer.* Novice (novicio).

pichona f. Hen pigeon (ave). || FAM. Dove, pet (término cariñoso).

pichonear v. tr. *Amer.* To swindle (estafar).

pidgin-english m. Pidgin English, pidgin.

pídola f. Leapfrog (juego). || *Saltar a pídola*, to leapfrog.

pidón, ona adj. FAM. Always asking for things.
— M. y f. FAM. *Es un pidón*, he's always asking for things.

pie m. Foot (pl. *feet*) [de hombre, de animal]. || Foot (de mueble, escalera, montaña): *al pie de la colina*, at the foot of the hill. || Foot (de las medias). || Stand (de una máquina de fotografiar, de un telescopio, etc.). || Base, foot (de una columna). || Stem (de una copa). || BOT. Stalk, stem (tallo). | Plant (planta entera): *mil pies de lechugas*, a thousand lettuce plants. | Stock (de viña). || Sediment (poso). || Foot (de un escrito): *al pie de la página*, at the foot of the page. || Legend, caption (de foto o dibujo). || Ending (de un documento). || Name of signatory (firma). || Foot (medida): *de dos pies de altura*, two feet high, two foot high. || Foot (de verso). || FIG. Foundation, basis (fundamento). || MAT. Foot, base (de una recta). || Residue of pressed grapes (de uvas).
— *A cuatro pies*, on all fours (a gatas). || FIG. *A los pies de alguien*, at s.o.'s service (al servicio de), at s.o.'s beck and call (bajo el dominio de). || *A los pies de la cama*, at the foot of the bed. || *Al pie de*, at the foot of: *al pie de un árbol*, at the foot of a tree; next to (junto), almost (casi). || *Al pie de fábrica*, at factory price (precio). || *Al pie de la escalera*, at the foot of the stairs. || *Al pie de la letra*, V. LETRA. || *Al pie de la obra*, delivered on site. || *A pie*, on foot (andando). || *A pie enjuto*, dryshod, without getting one's feet wet. || *A pie firme*, steadfastly. || *A pie juntillas* or *juntillo* or *con los pies juntos*, with one's feet together: *saltar a pie juntillas*, to jump with one's feet together; firmly: *cree a pie juntillas todo lo que le dicen*, he firmly believes everything they tell him. || FIG. *Atado de pies y manos*, bound hand and foot. | FIG. *Besar los pies*, V. OBSERV. | *Buscar cinco* or *tres pies al gato*, to split hairs (hilar muy fino), to make life more difficult than it is, to complicate matters (complicarse la vida). | *Caer de pie como los gatos*, to fall *o* to land on one's feet. | *Cojear del mismo pie*, to have the same faults. | *Con el pie en el estribo*, about to *o* ready to leave. | *Con pies de plomo*, carefully, warily. || *Dar con el pie*, to tap one's foot [on the ground] (en el suelo), to kick (tropezar, dar una patada). || FIG. *Dar pie a*, to give cause for. || *De pie*, standing: *estar de pie*, to be standing; full-length (retrato, foto). || *De pies a cabeza*, from head to foot (enteramente), to the hilt (armado). || *Echar pie a tierra*, to dismount (caballería), to get out, to alight (coche). || *En pie*, standing: *estaba en pie*, he was standing; up and about, on one's feet (curado), standing (las cosechas), on the hoof (ganado). || *En pie de guerra*, on a war footing. || FIG. *Entrar con el pie derecho* or *con buen pie*, to start off on the right foot *o* footing, to make a good start. | *En un pie de igualdad*, on an equal footing. | *Esperar a pie firme*, to wait resolutely. | *Esta frase no tiene ni pies ni cabeza*, I can't make head or tail of this sentence (no la entiendo). | *Estar con un pie en el aire*, to be a rolling stone. | *Estar en pie*, to be still there (problema). | *Fallarle a uno los pies*, to lose one's balance, to overbalance. || *Gente de a pie*, foot soldiers, *pl.*, infantry (soldados). || *Golpear el suelo con el pie*, to stamp *o* to tap one's foot on the ground. || *Hacer pie*, to be in one's depth (en el agua). || FIG. *Hacerle un pie agua a uno*, to mess things up for s.o. || FIG. *Hacer una cosa con los pies*, to botch *o* to bungle sth., to do sth. in a slapdash way (hacerla muy mal). || *Ir a pie*, to walk, to go on foot. || FIG. *Írsele los pies a uno*, to slip: *se le fueron los pies*, he slipped. | *Levantarse con el pie izquierdo*, to get up on the wrong side of the bed. || *Ligero de pies*, light-footed. || FIG. *Meter un pie en algún sitio*, to get a foothold somewhere. | *Morir al pie del cañón*, to die with one's boots on, to die in harness. | *Nacer de pie*, to be born under a lucky star. | *No da pie con bola*, he can't do a thing right. | *No levanta dos pies del suelo*, he is tiny. | *No poner los pies más en un sitio*, not to set foot in a place again. | *No tener ni pies ni cabeza*, to be ridiculous *o* absurd, to be nonsense. || *No tenerse de pie*, not to be able to stand up: *desde su enfermedad no se tiene de pie*, since his illness he cannot stand up; not to hold water: *la historia no se tiene de pie*, your story does not hold water. || FIG. *Pararle a uno los pies*, to put s.o. in his place (poner a alguien en su sitio). | *Pensar con los pies*, to talk through one's hat. || *Perder pie*, to lose one's footing, to slip (caerse), to go out of one's depth (en el agua), to lose one's way (confundirse). || *Pie a pie*, little by little. || MIL. *Pie a tierra*, dismount (orden). || *Pie de altar*, surplice fees (emolumentos). || *Pie de amigo*, support, prop (estaca). || MED. *Pie de atleta*, athlete's foot (dolencia).

|| FIG. y FAM. *Pie de banco*, stupid thing (necedad). || BOT. *Pie de becerro*, cuckoo pint (aro). || *Pie de burro*, acorn barnacle. || *Pie de cabra*, crowbar (palanca), goose barnacle (crustáceo). || *Pie de imprenta*, publisher's imprint, imprint. || *Pie de liebre*, kind of clover (trébol). || ARQ. *Pie derecho*, upright. || *Pie de rey*, slide calliper. || POÉT. *Pie forzado*, forced rhyme. || *Pie plano*, flatfoot: *tener los pies planos*, to have flatfeet. || *Pie prensatelas*, foot (costura). || POÉT. *Pie quebrado*, a line of four or five syllables [alternating with other longer lines]. || *Pie zambo*, clubfoot. || *Pies contra cabeza*, head to tail. || *Poner el pie en tierra firme*, to set foot on dry land. || FIG. *Poner en pie*, to set up, to establish. || *Poner los pies en*, to set foot in. || *Poner pie en*, to set foot on (desembarcar). || FIG. *Poner pies en polvorosa*, to take to one's heels [U.S., to take a powder]. || *Ponerse en* or *de pie*, to stand up, to rise to one's feet. || FIG. *Quedar en pie*, to be still there, to remain (una dificultad), to remain standing, to be left standing (un edificio). | *Saber de qué pie cojea uno*, to know s.o.'s weak spots. | *Sacar los pies del plato*, to overstep the mark (ir demasiado lejos), to come out of one's shell (dejar de ser tímido). | *Ser más viejo que el andar a pie*, to be as old as the hills. | *Ser pies y mano de uno*, to be s.o.'s right hand. | *Soldado de a pie*, foot soldier. | *Tener buenos* or *muchos pies*, to be a good walker. | *Tener el estómago en los pies*, v. ESTÓMAGO. || *Tener los pies hacia fuera*, to have splay feet. || FIG. *Tener* or *estar con un pie en el sepulcro* or *en la sepultura* or *en el hoyo*, to have one foot in the grave. | *Trabajar con los pies*, to be all thumbs, to work clumsily. | *Tratar a alguien con la punta del pie*, to kick s.o. around. || *Volver pie atrás*, to turn back, to go back (desandar lo andado), to go back on *o* to take back what one has said (desdecirse), to back down (ceder).

— OBSERV. The Spanish expression "*besar los pies*", like "*besar las manos*", is a formal expression of respect used in letters, and may be translated by "Yours respectfully"

piececito m. Little foot, tootsie (fam.).

piedad f. Pity, compassion (compasión): *mover a uno a piedad*, to move s.o. to pity; *hombre sin piedad*, man without pity. || Piety, piousness (religiosa). || Respect (filial). || ARTES. Pietà (la Virgen). || — *Con piedad*, with pity, pityingly (sentimiento): *mirar a alguien con piedad*, to look at s.o. with pity. || *Dar piedad*, to be pitiful. || *Me dan piedad*, I feel sorry for them. || *Por piedad*, out of pity. || *¡Por piedad!*, for pity's sake! || *Tener piedad de*, to take pity on. || *¡Tenga un poco de piedad!*, show some sympathy!

piedra f. Stone. || Hailstone (granizo). || MED. Stone (en el riñón). || Flint (de encendedor). || Millstone (de molino). || Place where foundlings were left (de inclusa). || FIG. Stone: *corazón de piedra*, heart of stone. || — FIG. *Ablandar las piedras*, to melt a heart of stone. | *A tiro de piedra*, a stone's throw away. | *Cerrar a piedra y lodo*, to shut tight. | *Es un día señalado con piedra blanca*, it is a red-letter day. | *Hasta las piedras lo saben*, the whole world knows it. | *Menos da una piedra*, it is better than nothing. | *No dejar piedra por mover*, to leave no stone unturned. | *No dejar piedra sobre piedra*, to raze to the ground, not to leave a stone standing. | *Pasar a uno por la piedra*, to leave s.o. standing (vencer). || *Piedra amoladera* or *de amolar*, grindstone. || *Piedra angular* or *fundamental*, cornerstone. || *Piedra arenisca*, sandstone. || *Piedra berroqueña*, granite. || *Piedra de afilar*, hone, whetstone. || *Piedra de cal* or *caliza*, limestone. || *Piedra de construcción*, stone [used in building]. || *Piedra de chispa*, flint (pedernal). || *Piedra de encendedor* or *de mechero*, flint. || FIG. *Piedra de* or *del escándalo*, cause *o* source of scandal. || *Piedra del altar*, altar stone. || *Piedra de molino*, millstone. || *Piedra de sillería* or *sillar*, ashlar. || *Piedra de toque*, touchstone. || *Piedra filosofal*, philosopher's stone. || *Piedra fina*, semi-precious stone. || *Piedra imán*, lodestone. || *Piedra infernal*, lunar caustic. || *Piedra meteórica*, meteoric stone. || *Piedra molar*, millstone grit. || FIG. *Piedra movediza, nunca moho la cobija*, a rolling stone gathers no moss. || *Piedra pómez*, pumice stone. || *Piedra preciosa*, precious stone. || *Poner la primera piedra*, to lay the cornerstone, to lay the foundation stone. || FIG. *Quedarse de piedra*, to be thunderstruck. | *Tirar la piedra y esconder la mano*, to hit and run. | *Tirar la primera piedra*, to cast the first stone. | *Tirar piedras al tejado ajeno*, to blame s.o. else. || *Tirar piedras contra uno*, to throw stones at s.o., to stone s.o. (apedrear), to criticize s.o. (censurar).

piedrecita f. Pebble.

piel f. Skin (del cuerpo). || Leather, skin (cuero): *piel de Rusia*, Russian leather. || Fur, skin, pelt (de animal con pelo largo). || Fur (para prenda de vestir). || Skin, peel (de las frutas). || — Pl. Fur, *sing.*: *un abrigo de pieles*, a fur coat. || — *Artículos de piel*, leather goods. || FIG. y FAM. *Dar la piel para obtener algo*, to give one's right arm for sth. || *Piel de gallina*, goose pimples, *pl.*, gooseflesh. || *Piel de zapa*, shagreen. || FIG. y FAM. *Ser de la piel del diablo*, to be a little devil (niño). || *Suavizar las pieles*, to stake skins. || FIG. *Un piel roja*, a redskin. | *Vender la piel del oso antes de haberlo matado*, to count one's chickens before they are hatched.

piélago m. POÉT. Sea, ocean. || High sea (alta mar). || FIG. Sea (abundancia).

pielitis f. MED. Pyelitis.

pienso m. Fodder, feed: *piensos compuestos*, mixed feed. || FIG. y FAM. *¡Ni por pienso!*, I wouldn't dream of it!

pierna f. Leg: *pierna de madera*, wooden leg. || Leg, drumstick (de ave). || Leg (de compás). || Downstroke (de letra). || Lobe (de nuez). || — FIG. y FAM. *Cortarle a uno las piernas*, to stop s.o. in his tracks. | *Dormir a pierna suelta* or *tendida*, v. DORMIR. | *Estirar las piernas*, to stretch one's legs.

pierrot m. Pierrot (payaso).

pietismo m. REL. Pietism (doctrina).

pietista m. y f. REL. Pietist.

pieza f. Part, piece: *las piezas de un motor*, the parts of a motor. || Play (de teatro). || Piece (de música). || Patch (remiendo). || Roll, piece (de tejido). || Piece, head (de caza). || Piece, coin (moneda). || Man, piece (ajedrez). || Room (habitación). || Piece (de vajilla). || Unit of pressure (unidad de presión). || Ordinary heraldic bearing (heráldica). || FIG. Specimen (ejemplar): *ha cazado una buena pieza*, he has bagged a fine specimen. || — FIG. y FAM. *Dejar de una pieza*, to leave speechless: *esta noticia me dejó de una pieza*, this news left me speechless. || *De una pieza*, in one piece (cosa), upright (persona). || FIG. *¡Es una buena* or *linda pieza!*, a fine one he is!, he is a right one! | *Me he quedado de una pieza*, I was speechless *o* flabbergasted. || *Pieza corta*, sketch (de teatro). || *Pieza de artillería*, piece of artillery. || *Pieza de autos*, file on a case. || *Pieza de convicción*, vital evidence. || *Pieza de museo*, museum exhibit, show piece, museum piece. || *Pieza de recambio* or *de repuesto*, spare part. || *Pieza oratoria*, speech. || *Poner una pieza*, to patch (remendar). || *Por piezas*, in pieces, piece by piece. || *Un dos piezas* a suit (traje de mujer), a bikini (bikini).

piezoelectricidad f. FÍS. Piezoelectricity.

piezoeléctrico, ca adj. FÍS. Piezoelectric.

piezometría f. Piezometry.

piezométrico, ca adj. Piezometric.

piezómetro m. FÍS. Piezometer.

pífano m. MÚS. Fife.

pifia f. Miscue (en el billar). || FIG. y FAM. Blunder, bloomer (descuido): *cometer una pifia*, to make a bloomer. || *Amer.* Mockery, joke (burla).

pifiar v. intr. To miscue (en el billar). || FIG. y FAM. To blunder, to make a bloomer (meter la pata). || *Amer.* To mock (burlarse).

pigargo m. Osprey, fish hawk (ave).

Pigmalión n. pr. m. Pygmalion.

pigmentación f. Pigmentation.

pigmentar v. tr. To pigment.

pigmentario, ria adj. Pigmentary.

pigmento m. Pigment.

pigmeo, a m. y f. Pygmy.

— Adj. Pygmean, Pygmy.

pignoración f. Pledge (en el monte de piedad).

pignorar v. tr. To pawn, to pledge.

pignoraticio, cia adj. JUR. Pignoratious, of *o* pertaining to a pledge.

pigricia f. Laziness (pereza). || *Amer.* Trifle (trivialidad).

pija f. POP. Prick (miembro viril).

pijama m. Pyjamas, *pl.* [U.S., pajamas, *pl.*].

pije adj. *Amer.* FAM. Ridiculous. || Pretentious, haughty (cursi).

pijo, ja adj. FAM. Daft (tonto).

— M. y f. FAM. Fool (tonto). || — M. POP. Prick.

pijota f. Codling (pescadilla). || *Hacer pijotas*, to play ducks and drakes, to skim stones across the water.

pijotada f. V. PIJOTERÍA.

pijotería f. FAM. Bother, nuisance (molestia). | Silly thing (cosa estúpida). | Trifle (menudencia). || *Amer.* Meanness (tacañería). || FAM. *No me vengas con pijoterías*, don't bother me.

pijotero, ra adj. FAM. Bothersome, tiresome (pesado). | Damned, damn: *este pijotero niño*, this damned child. || *Amer.* FAM. Mean, stingy (tacaño).

— M. y f. FAM. Bore, pest, nuisance, drag (pesado). || *Amer.* FAM. Skinflint, miser (tacaño).

pila f. Heap (rimero), pile (montón): *una pila de leña*, a pile of wood. || FIG. Loads, *pl.* (serie): *tiene una pila de niños*, he has loads of children. | Loads, *pl.*, heaps, *pl.*, stacks, *pl.*, piles, *pl.* (gran cantidad). || Basin (de fuente). || Sink (de cocina). || Stoup (de agua bendita). || Font (para bautizar). || Trough (bebedero). || ARQ. Pier (machón de un puente). || FÍS. Battery, cell: *pila seca*, dry battery. || *Amer* Fountain (fuente). || — *Nombre de pila*, Christian name, first name. || *Pila atómica*, atomic pile. || *Sacar de pila*, to be a godparent.

pilar m. ARQ. Pillar (columna). | Pier (de un puente). || Milestone (mojón). || Basin, bowl (de fuente). || FIG. Pillar, prop (apoyo). || Prop [forward] (rugby).

pilar v. tr. To pound [grain].

pilastra f. ARQ. Pilaster.

Pilato (Poncio) n. pr. m. Pontius Pilate.

pilcha f. *Amer.* FAM. [Peasant's] clothes, *pl.*

píldora f. Pill. || FIG. y FAM. Bad news. || — FIG. y FAM. *Dorar la píldora*, to gild the pill. | *Se tragó la píldora*, he swallowed it, he fell for it (se lo creyó), he swallowed the bitter pill (tuvo que aguantarlo).

pileta f. Small stoup (de agua bendita). || Small basin (fuente). || Sink (de cocina). || *Amer.* Swimming pool (piscina).
pilífero, ra adj. Piliferous.
piliforme adj. Piliform.
pilón m. Basin (de fuente). || Trough (bebedero). || Mortar (mortero). || Sugarloaf (azúcar). || ARQ. Pylon (puerta monumental). | Pillar, post (columna). || *Martillo pilón*, drop hammer.
pilongo, ga adj. Thin (flaco). || *Castaña pilonga*, dried chestnut.
pilórico, ca adj. Pyloric.
píloro m. ANAT. Pylorus.
pilorriza f. BOT. Calyptra.
pilosidad f. Pilosity.
piloso, sa adj. Pilose: *sistema piloso*, pilose system.
pilotaje m. MAR. y AVIAC. Pilotage, piloting. || ARQ. Piles, *pl.* (conjunto de pilotes). || *Pilotaje sin visibilidad*, blind flying.
pilotar v. tr. MAR. To pilot, to steer, to navigate. || AVIAC. To pilot, to fly. || To drive (un coche). || FIG. To guide, to lead, to show the way to (guiar).
pilote m. Pile, stake (estaca). || — Pl. Piles: *construido sobre pilotes*, built on piles.
pilotear v. tr. V. PILOTAR.
piloto m. MAR. Pilot: *piloto práctico*, coastal *o* harbour pilot. | Pilot, mate, second in command (de un buque). || Pilot (de un avión). || Driver (conductor de un coche). || AUT. Rear light (luz posterior), sidelight, parking light (luz de posición). || Pilot lamp (para indicar el funcionamiento de un aparato). || Pilot light (en los aparatos de gas). || FIG. Guide (guía). || — *Avión sin piloto*, pilotless plane. || *Piloto de altura*, high-sea pilot. || *Piloto de línea* or *civil*, airline pilot. || *Piloto de pruebas*, test pilot.
— Adj. Pilot (que sirve de modelo): *fábrica piloto*, pilot plant.
piltra f. FAM. Bed, pit, sack (cama).
piltrafa f. FAM. Gristly meat (carne mala). || FAM. Wretch, poor specimen (persona). || *Amer.* Bargain (ganga). || — Pl. Scraps (residuos). || FIG. y FAM. *Hacer piltrafas*, to make mincemeat of (destrozar).
pillaje m. Plunder, pillage (saqueo).
pillapilla m. *Jugar al pillapilla*, to play tag, to play tick, to play it.
pillar v. tr. To pillage, to plunder, to loot (saquear). || FAM. To catch: *pillar a un ladrón*, to catch a thief; *pillar el tren*, to catch the train; *pillar un resfriado*, to catch a cold. | To run over: *cuidado que no te pille un coche*, be careful that a car does not run you over. | To get (obtener). || — FAM. *Me pilla bastante lejos*, it's quite a way. | *Me pilla de camino*, it's on my way. | *Me pilló un dedo la puerta del coche*, I caught my finger *o* I got my finger caught in the car door. | *No me pilla de camino*, it's out of my way.
pillastre o **pillastrón** m. FAM. Scoundrel, rogue, rascal (bribón). | Rascal (niño).
pillear v. intr. FAM. To lead the life of a scoundrel, to get up to roguery. | To play tricks, to be mischievous (los niños).
pillería f. FAM. Gang of scoundrels. | Trick (engaño). | Rascality, knavery (carácter de pillo).
pillete o **pillín** m. FAM. Little rascal, little scamp (pilluelo).
pillo, lla m. y f. FAM. Rogue, scoundrel (persona mayor). | Rascal, scamp (niño). || — FIG. *A pillo, pillo y medio*, set a thief to catch a thief. || *Dárselas de pillo*, to try to be smart *o* big, to think o.s. big.
— Adj. Naughty (malo).
pilluelo, la m. y f. FAM. Scallywag, little rascal, urchin, little scamp (chico malo).
¡pim! interj. Bang!, boom! || *Pim, pam pum*, Aunt Sally (pimpampún).
pimental m. Pepper patch.
pimentar v. tr. FIG. To season (sazonar).
pimentero m. Pepper plant (arbusto).
pimentón m. CULIN. Paprika (polvo).
pimienta f. Pepper. || FIG. y FAM. Spice. || — *Echar pimienta*, to pepper. || FIG. y FAM. *Sal y pimienta*, charm.
pimiento m. Pimiento (planta). || Pimiento, pepper (fruto). || Paprika (pimentón). || Pepper plant || — FIG. y FAM. *Me importa un pimiento*, I couldn't care less, I don't give a hoot. || *Pimiento chile*, chilli. || *Pimiento morrón*, sweet pepper.
pimpampúm m. Aunt Sally (en las ferias).
pimpante adj. Smart, trim, spruce (peripuesto). || Self-assured, pleased with o.s. (seguro de sí mismo).
pimpi m. FAM. Fool, idiot (bobo). | Bighead, snob (presumido).
pimpinela f. BOT. Burnet (rosácea), pimpernel (umbelífera) [planta].
pimplar v. tr. FAM. To down (beber).
— V. intr. FAM. To booze, to tipple.
— V. pr. FAM. To down.
pimpollo m. Shoot (vástago). || Young tree (árbol nuevo). || Rosebud (capullo). || FIG. y FAM. Angel, cherub (niño). | Handsome boy (joven), good-looker, pretty girl (chica).
pinabete m. Fir [tree] (abeto).
pinacoteca f. Art *o* picture gallery, pinacotheca.
pináculo m. Pinnacle. || FIG. Pinnacle, acme, peak: *estar en el pináculo de la gloria*, to be at the peak of one's glory. || FIG. *Poner a alguien en el pináculo*, to extol s.o., to praise s.o. to the skies.
pinado, da adj. Pinnate, pinnated (hoja).
pinar m. Pine grove, pinewood.
pinaza f. Pinnace (embarcación).
pincel m. Paintbrush, brush. || FIG. Style [of painting] (modo de pintar). | Painter, artist (pintor). | Work, painting (obra).
pincelada f. Stroke of a brush, brushstroke. || MED. Painting (en la garganta). || FIG. Touch (rasgo): *pincelada fuerte*, firm touch. || FIG. *Dar la última pincelada*, to put the finishing *o* final touch.
pinciano, na adj. [Of *o* from] Valladolid.
— M. y f. Native *o* inhabitant of Valladolid.
pinchadiscos m. inv. Disc jockey.
pinchadura f. Prick (con una espina, etc.).
pinchar v. tr. To prick: *las espinas pinchan*, thorns prick. || To puncture (neumático). || FIG. To tease, to goad, to annoy (irritar). | To goad, to push, to prod (incitar). | To wound (mortificar). | To stir up (provocar). | To annoy, to rile (enojar). || MED. To inject.
— V. intr. To get punctured, to puncture (neumático). || FIG. y FAM. *Ni pincha ni corta*, he cuts no ice.
— V. pr. To prick o.s. (con un alfiler). || To get punctured, to puncture (neumático). || FIG. y FAM. To tease *o* to taunt one another (meterse uno con otro).
pinchaúvas m. inv. FAM. Good-for-nothing.
pinchazo m. Prick. || Puncture, blowout (de neumático). || FIG. Scathing remark (dicho malicioso).
pinche m. Kitchen boy, scullion (de cocina). || FIG. y FAM. *Haber sido pinche antes de cocinero*, to be nobody's fool, to know all the tricks.
pinchito m. CULIN. Small skewer, brochette (para asar). | Skewer (de carne). || *Pinchitos morunos*, shish kebab.
pincho m. Point. || Prickle, thorn (de planta). || Spine (de animal). || CULIN. Skewer (asador). || *Amer.* Hatpin. || *Pincho moruno*, shish kebab.
Píndaro n. pr. m. Pindar.
pindonga f. FAM. Gadabout (mujer).
pindonguear v. intr. FAM. To gallivant, to gad [about].
pindongueo m. FAM. Gallivanting, gadding [about].
pineal adj. ANAT. Pineal: *cuerpo pineal*, pineal body.
pineda f. Pine grove, pinewood (pinar).
pínfano m. MÚS. Dulcimer.
pingajo m. FAM. Rag, tatter.
pinganilla f. *Amer.* Dandy (currutaco). || *Amer. En pinganillas*, crouching (en cuclillas), on tiptoe (de puntillas), on tenterhooks (en situación incierta).
pingo m. FAM. Rag, tatter (pingajo). | Gadabout (mujer). || *Amer.* Horse (caballo). | Devil (diablo). || — Pl. FAM. Togs, gear, *sing.* [clothes] (trapos viejos).
pingonear v. intr. FAM. To gallivant, to gad [about].
ping-pong m. Table tennis, ping-pong.
pingüe adj. Fatty (graso). || FIG. Fat, big, large: *obtener pingües beneficios*, to make fat profits. | Profitable, fat (negocio). | Abundant, plentiful (abundante).
pingüino m. ZOOL. Penguin.
pinitos m. pl. FAM. First steps [of a convalescent, a child, etc.]: *hacer pinitos*, to take one's first steps.
pinnado, da adj. BOT. Pinnate.
pinnípedo, da adj./s. ZOOL. Pinniped.
pino, na adj. Steep (pendiente).
— M. BOT. Pine (árbol). || FIG. y POÉT. Bark, vessel, craft, boat (nave). || First step: *hacer pinos*, to take one's first steps. || — FIG. y FAM. *En el quinto pino*, at the back of beyond, in the middle of nowhere (muy lejos). || *Hacer el pino*, to stand on one s head. || *Pino albar* or *royo* or *silvestre*, Scotch pine. || *Pino alerce*, larch. || *Pino carrasco*, Aleppo pine. *Pino piñonero* or *real*, stone pine, umbrella pine. || *Pino rodeno* or *marítimo*, pinaster, cluster pine.
pinol o **pinole** o **pínole** m. *Amer.* Roasted maize flour, pinole.
pinolero, ra m. y f. *Amer.* FAM. Nicaraguan.
pinreles m. pl. POP. Hooves [U.S., dogs] (pies).
pinsapar m. Grove of Spanish firs.
pinsapo m. Spanish fir [tree] (árbol).
pinta f. Stain, mark, spot (mancha). || Spot (lunar). || Drop (gota). || Mark [on playing cards]. || Pint (medida). || Trump (triunfo en cartas). || FIG. Appearance, aspect, look (aspecto). || *Amer.* Colour [of an animal] (color). | Race, pedigree, stock (casta). || — Pl. Typhoid, *sing.* (tabardillo). || — M. Scoundrel, rogue (golfo). || — FIG. *Con esa pinta no le recibirán en ningún sitio*, the way he looks they will not accept him anywhere. | *Tener buena pinta*, to look good. | *Tener mala pinta*, to look bad (la situación), to look off-colour, to look under the weather (parecer enfermo). | *Tener pinta de*, to look like: *tener pinta de pícaro*, to look like a rogue.
pintada f. Guinea fowl (ave). || Graffito.
pintado, da adj. Painted: *pintado de azul*, painted blue. || Painted, made-up [face] (rostro). || Speckled (la piel de los animales). || — FIG. y FAM. *Eso le puede pasar al más pintado*, that could happen to the best of us. | *Es su padre pintado*, he's the spitting image of his father. | *Ir* or *sentar que ni pintado*, to suit to a tee. | *No puedo verle ni pintado*, I can't bear *o*

stand *o* stick him, I can't bear the sight of him, I hate the very sight of him. || *Papel pintado*, wallpaper. || FIG. y FAM. *Venir como pintado* or *que ni pintado*, to suit to a tee, to suit down to the ground.
— M. Painting (acción de pintar).
pintamonas m. inv. FAM. Dauber (mal pintor).
pintar v. tr. To paint (con pintura): *pintar un retrato*, to paint a portrait; *pintar de rojo una habitación*, to paint a room red. || To draw, to sketch (dibujar): *píntame un caballo*, draw me a horse. || FIG. To describe, to depict, to paint (describir). || — FIG. *No pintar nada*, not to fit in, to be out of place (estar fuera de su ámbito), not to have a say, to cut no ice (no tener influencia). || *Pintar al fresco, al óleo*, to paint in fresco, in oils. || *Pintar al temple*, V. TEMPLE. || *Pintar con pistola*, to spray. || FIG. y FAM. *Pintarla*, to put it on, to put on airs and graces.
— V. intr. To paint. || To ripen (las frutas). || FIG. To come out, to show (mostrarse).
— V. pr. To put one's makeup on, to make up (el rostro). || To put one's lipstick on (los labios). || To make one's eyes up (los ojos). || FIG. To appear, to show [o.s.]: *la felicidad se pintaba en su rostro*, his happiness showed in his face. || — FIG. y FAM. *Para esto me las pinto solo*, this is right up my street. | *Se las pinta solo*, there's no one like him.
pintarrajar o **pintarrajear** v. tr. FAM. To daub, to bedaub.
— V. pr. FAM. To put on layers of makeup.
pintarroja f. ZOOL. Dogfish (lija).
pintiparado, da adj. Exactly the same, identical (semejante). || Just right, just at the right time: *llegar pintiparado*, to arrive just at the right time. || Perfectly [well]: *esta corbata viene pintiparada con este traje*, this tie goes perfectly with this suit. || — *Es pintiparado a su hermano*, he is the spitting image of his brother. || *Venir pintiparado*, to come just right (ser oportuno), to suit [s.o.] to a tee (convenirle a uno).
pintiparar v. tr. FAM. To compare (comparar). | To make alike (asemejar).
Pinto n. pr. FAM. *Estar entre Pinto y Valdemoro*, to be tipsy (medio borracho), to be undecided, to sit on the fence (estar indeciso).
pinto, ta adj *Caballo pinto*, pinto. || *Judía pinta*, pinto bean.
pintor, ra m. y f. Painter. || *Amer.* Haughty *o* conceited *o* boastful person (fachendoso). || — *Pintor de brocha gorda*, [house] painter (de puertas, ventanas, etc.), dauber, bad painter (mal pintor). || *Pintor de cuadros*, painter, artist. || *Pintor decorador*, decorator. || TEATR. *Pintor escenógrafo*, painter of scenery, scenery painter.
pintoresco, ca adj. Picturesque. || Colourful [U.S., colorful] (estilo).
pintoresquismo m. Picturesqueness. || Colour [U.S., color] (del estilo).
pintorrear v. tr. FAM. To daub: *pintorrear de azul y rojo*, to daub in blue and red.
pintura f. Paint (color): *cuidado con la pintura*, wet paint (letrero). || Painting: *pintura rupestre*, cave painting; *la pintura de la casa*, the painting of the house. || Picture, painting (cuadro). || FIG. Description, picture, portrayal (descripción). || — FIG. y FAM. *No poder ver a uno ni en pintura*, not to be able to stand *o* to bear *o* to stick s.o., no to be able to bear the sight of s.o. || *Pintura a la acuarela*, watercolour. || *Pintura a la aguada*, gouache. || *Pintura al fresco*, fresco. | *Pintura al temple*, tempera painting. || *Pintura con pistola*, spray painting.
pinturero, ra dja. FAM. Dressy, showy. | Haughty, conceited (presumido).
— M. Dandy (elegante). | Haughty man (presumido). || — F. Showy woman. | Haughty woman.
pinza f. Pincer, nipper, claw (de cangrejo, etc.). || Dart (costura). || TECN. Pincers, *pl.* || Peg, pin (para colgar la ropa lavada). || — Pl. Tweezers: *pinzas para* or *de depilar*, eyebrow tweezers. || — *Pinzas de dentista*, forceps. || *Pinzas para el azúcar*, sugar tongs (tenacillas). || *Pinza sujetapapeles*, paper clip. || FIG. y FAM. *Sacársele a uno con pinzas*, to drag it out of s.o.
pinzón m. Chaffinch (ave). || *Pinzón real*, bullfinch.
piña f. [Pine] cone (del pino). || Fruit, cone (de otros árboles). || Pineapple (ananás). || FAM. Blow (puñetazo). || FIG. Clan, clique (grupo cerrado). | Cluster, group (de personas). | Cluster, bunch (de cosas).
piñata f. *Domingo de piñata*, the first Sunday of Lent.
— OBSERV. The *piñata* is a pot full of sweets which is broken with sticks during a masked ball on the first Sunday of Lent.
piñón m. Pine seed *o* nut (simiente del pino). || Pinion (rueda): *piñón de cambio*, bevel pinion. || Ass at the rear of the herd (burro). || Rear sprocket wheel (de bicicleta). || — FIG. y FAM. *Estar a partir un piñón con uno*, to be hand in glove with s.o. || TECN. *Piñón fijo*, fixed wheel. | *Piñón libre*, freewheel. | *Piñón mayor*, sprocket wheel (de bicicleta). | *Piñón planetario*, planet gear.
piñonata f. o **piñonate** m. Candied pine nut.
piñonero adj. m. *Pino piñonero*, stone pine, umbrella pine (árbol).
— M. ZOOL. Bullfinch (pinzón real).
pío m. Chirping, cheeping (de las aves). || Clucking (del pollo). || FAM. Desire, yearning (deseo). || FIG. y FAM. *No decir ni pío*, not to say a word.
Pío n. pr. m. Pius: *Pío nono* (IX), Pius IX [the ninth].
pío, a adj. Pious (devoto). || Charitable (compasivo). || Piebald (caballo). || *Obra pía*, V. OBRA.
piocha f. Pickaxe [U.S., pickax] (zapapico).
piojo m. Louse. || — *Piojo de mar*, whale louse (crustáceo). || FIG. y FAM. *Piojo resucitado*, upstart.
piojoso, sa adj. Lousy (lleno de piojos). || FIG. Stingy, mean (mezquino). | Dirty (sucio).
piola f. MAR. Houseline. || Leapfrog (juego): *jugar a la piola*, to play leapfrog. || *Amer.* String (bramante).
piolar v. intr. To cheep, to chirp (pájaro).
piolet m. Ice axe, piolet (alpinismo).
pión, ona adj. Cheeping, chirping. || FIG. Peevish, crabbed (protestón).
pionero m. Pioneer (precursor, adelantado).
piorrea f. MED. Pyorrhoea [U.S., pyorrhea].
pipa f. Pipe: *fumar en pipa*, to smoke a pipe. || Barrel, cask (tonel). || Pipe (medida). || Pip (pepita). || Seed (de girasol, melón, etc.). || MÚS. Pipe (flauta). | Reed (lengüeta). || — FIG. y FAM. *Eso es el cuento de la buena pipa*, it goes on and on. || *Pipa de la paz*, pipe of peace, peace pipe. || TECN. *Pipa del distribuidor*, distributor arm (automóvil).
pipe-line m. Pipe line (oleoducto).
piperáceas f. pl. BOT. Piperaceae.
pipería f. Barrels, *pl.*
pipermín m. Peppermint.
pipeta f. Pipette.
pipi m. POP. Ass, clot (tonto). | Squaddy, soldier (soldado).
pipí m. FAM. Wee-wee. || *Hacer pipí*, to wee-wee, to wee.
pipiar v. intr. To cheep, to chirp (piar).
pípila f. *Amer.* Turkey.
pipiolo m. FAM. Novice, newcomer [U.S., greenhorn] (inexperto), new boy (de una escuela). | Little boy (niño). | Youngster (joven).
pipirigallo m. BOT. Sainfoin.
pipiritaña f. Flute, pipe (caramillo).
pipirrana f. Cucumber and tomato salad (en Andalucía).
pipistrelo m. Pipistrelle, small bat (murciélago).
pipudo, da adj. FAM. Fantastic, terrific, wonderful, great (espléndido).
pique m. Pique, resentment (resentimiento). || Self-esteem (amor propio). || MAR. Crotch. || *Amer.* Chigoe (nigua). | Pepper (ají). | Path (senda). || — *A pique*, sheer [cliff] (a plomo). || *A pique de*, on the point of (a punto de). || *Echar a pique*, to sink (un barco, un negocio), to ruin (los proyectos, una empresa). || *Estar a pique de hacer algo*, to almost do sth., to be about to do sth.: *he estado a pique de caerme*, I almost fell. || *Irse a pique*, to sink (un barco), to fail (fracasar), to be ruined (arruinarse, frustrarse). || *Tener un pique con alguien*, to have a grudge against s.o.
piqué m. Piqué (tela).
piquera f. Entrance hole [in beehive] (de colmenas). || Bunghole (de tonel). || TECN. Taphole (altos hornos). | Barrel (de lámpara).
piquero m. Pikeman (soldier). || Miner (minero).
piqueta f. Pickaxe [U.S., pickax]. || Ice axe, piolet (de montañero). || *Amer.* Weak wine (aguapié).
piquete m. Picket: *piquete de huelga*, strike picket. || Squad: *piquete de ejecución*, firing squad. || Sting (pinchazo). || Small hole (agujero). || Stake, post (jalón). || *Amer.* Yard (corral).
pira f. Pyre (hoguera). || FIG. y FAM. *Irse de pira*, to play truant [U.S., to play hooky] (no ir a clase).
piragua f. Pirogue (embarcación). || Canoe (de madera). || Kayak (de tela).
piragüismo m. Canoeing.
piragüista m. y f. Canoeist.
piramidal adj. Pyramidal.
pirámide f. Pyramid: *pirámide truncada*, truncated pyramid. || — *Pirámide de las edades*, pyramid-shaped graph showing the age of the population. || *Tronco de pirámide*, trunk of a pyramid.
piramidión m. ARQ. Pyramidion.
piraña f. *Amer.* Piranha (pez).
pirarse v. pr. FAM. To buzz off, to hop it, to clear off (marcharse): *estoy deseando pirarme*, I'd like to buzz off.
pirata m. Pirate. || FIG. Hard-hearted man, brute (hombre despiadado). || *Pirata aéreo*, highjacker.
— Adj. FIG. Pirate (clandestino): *edición, emisión pirata*, pirate edition, broadcast.
piratear v. intr. To pirate, to practise piracy. || FIG. To pirate (copiar). | To steal (robar).
piratería f. Piracy. || *Piratería aérea*, high-jacking.
pirático, ca adj. Pirate, piratical.
piraya f. *Amer.* Piranha (pez).
pirca f. *Amer.* Dry-stone wall.
pirenaico, ca adj./s. Pyrenean.
Pireo (El) n. pr. m. GEOGR. Piraeus.
pirético, ca adj. Pyretic.
pirex m. Pyrex (vidrio).
pirexia f. MED. Pyrexia.
piri m. POP. *Darse el piri*, to buzz off, to hop it.
pirindola f. [Spinning] top (perinola).
pirindolo m. FAM. Thing, thingummyjig.
pirineo, a adj. Pyrenean (pirenaico).
Pirineos n. pr. m. pl. GEOGR. Pyrenees.

piripi adj. FAM. Merry, tipsy (un poco ebrio).
pirita f. MIN. Pyrites. | Pyrite, iron pyrites (de hierro).
pirofosfato m. QUÍM. Pyrophosphate.
pirofosfórico adj. m. QUÍM. Pyrophosphoric: *ácido pirofosfórico*, pyrophosphoric acid.
pirograbado m. Pyrogravure, pyrography.
pirolisis f. Pyrolisis.
piromancia f. Pyromancy.
pirómano, na adj. Pyromaniacal.
— M. y f. Pyromaniac.
pirometría f. Pyrometry.
pirómetro m. Pyrometer (termómetro).
piropear v. tr. FAM. To compliment, to pay flirtatious compliments to.
piropo m. FAM. Compliment, amorous compliment, flirtatious remark [especially in the street]. || FAM. *Decir* or *echar piropos a*, to compliment, to pay flirtatious compliments to.
piróscafo m. Steamship (barco de vapor).
pirosfera f. Pyrosphere.
pirosis f. MED. Pyrosis.
pirotecnia f. Pyrotechnics.
pirotécnico, ca adj. Pyrotechnical, pyrotechnic, firework.
— M. Pyrotechnist (obrero).
piroxeno m. MIN. Pyroxene.
pirrarse v. pr. FAM. *Pirrarse por*, to rave about, to be crazy about (estar loco por).
pirriaque m. POP. Plonk (vino).
pírrico, ca adj./s. Pyrrhic (danza). || *Victoria pírrica*, Pyrrhic victory.
pirriquio m. POÉT. Pyrrhic.
Pirro n. pr. m. Pyrrhus.
pirueta f. Pirouette. || *Con una hábil pirueta evitó la pregunta*, he neatly sidestepped the question, he cleverly dodged the question.
piruetear v. intr. To pirouette.
pirulí m. Lollipop (caramelo).
pirulo m. Earthenware pitcher (botijo). || *Amer.* Slim child.
pis m. FAM. Wee-wee (orina). || FAM. *Hacer pis*, to wee.
pisa f. Fulling (del paño). || Pressing, treading (aceituna o uva). || Mating (de los animales). || FAM. Hiding (zurra).
pisada f. Track, trace, footprint, trail [of steps] (huella). || Step, footstep: *se oían sus pisadas*, his steps were heard. || Pressing, treading (de la fruta). || Trampling (aplastamiento). || Fulling (de paños). || *Seguir las pisadas de uno*, v. SEGUIR.
pisadura f. V. PISADA.
pisapapeles m. inv. Paperweight.
pisar v. tr. To stand on, to tread on: *pisarle el pie a uno*, to stand on s.o.'s foot. || To step on (poner el pie casualmente). || To full: *pisar paños*, to full cloth. || To tread, to press: *pisar uvas*, to press grapes. || To tread down (tierra). || MÚS. To pluck (las cuerdas). | To strike [the keys] (las teclas). || To cover (el macho). || FIG. To trample on, to abuse, to humiliate (pisotear). | To take away (quitar): *pisarle el puesto a uno*, to take away s.o.'s job, to take s.o.'s job away from him. | To pinch, to steal (robar). || — FIG. *Ir* or *andar pisando huevos*, to walk carefully. | *No se deja pisar por nadie*, he does not let anyone tread on him. || *No vuelvo a pisar más esa casa*, I shall not set foot in that house again. || *Pisar el acelerador*, to put one's foot on *o* to step on *o* to press the accelerator, to put one's foot down. || *Pisar el escenario* or *las tablas*, to be on the stage, to tread the boards: *es la primera vez que este actor pisa el escenario*, it is the first time that this actor has been on the stage. || *Pisar las huellas de alguien*, to follow s.o.'s track *o* trail. || FIG. *Pisarle a uno el terreno*, to beat s.o. to it. || *Prohibido pisar el césped*, keep off the grass.
— V. intr. To tread, to step. || To be one above the other [storeys of a building].
pisaúvas m. inv. Grape treader.
pisaverde m. FAM. Dandy (joven presumido).
piscícola adj. Piscicultural.
piscicultor m. Piscicultivator.
piscicultura f. Pisciculture.
piscifactoría f. Fish hatchery.
pisciforme adj. Pisciform.
piscina f. Swimming pool (para bañarse). || Fishpond (estanque). || Piscina (de iglesia).
Piscis n. pr. m. ASTR. Pisces.
piscívoro, ra adj. Piscivorous.
— M. y f. Piscivorous animal.
pisco m. *Amer.* Pisco brandy (aguardiente). | Earthenware picher (botijo).
piscolabis m. inv. FAM. Snack: *tomar un piscolabis*, to have a snack.
pisiforme adj. ANAT. Pisiform (hueso).
piso m. Floor, storey (de una casa): *casa de seis pisos*, six-floor building. || Floor: *vive en el sexto piso*, he lives on the sixth floor. || Flat [U.S., apartment] (vivienda): *piso de tres habitaciones*, three-roomed flat. || Deck (de un autobús). || Stage (de un cohete). || Tread (de un neumático). || Sole (suela de un zapato). || Layer (capa). || Ground (suelo). || Floor (de madera). || Surface (de la calle). || Seam, layer (capa geológica). || MIN. Level. || — *Autobús de dos pisos*, double-decker bus. || *Casa de pisos*, v. CASA. || *Piso bajo*, ground floor [U.S., first floor]. || *Piso principal*, v. PRINCIPAL.
pisón m. Beetle (de cantero).
pisotear v. tr. To trample on, to trample underfoot (aplastar). || To stamp on (dar pisotones a). || FIG. To trample on (desconsiderar).
pisoteo m. Trampling.
pisotón m. FAM. Stamp on the foot. || *Darle a uno un pisotón*, to tread *o* to stamp on s.o.'s foot.
pispar v. tr. POP. To pinch, to nick [U.S., to hook] (robar). || *Amer.* To watch (acechar).
pisqueño, ña adj. [Of *o* from] Pisco (Perú).
— M. y f. Native o inhabitant of Pisco.
pista f. Trail, track (huella). || Track (de carreras). || Runway (de aviones). || Court (de tenis). || Run, slope (de esquí). || Rink (de hielo, de patinaje). || Ring (de circo). || Trail: *pista falsa*, false trail. || — *Corredor en pista*, cyclist who races only on indoor tracks. || *Estar sobre la pista*, to be on the scent, to be on the track. || *Pista de aterrizaje*, runway, landing strip. || *Pista de baile*, dance floor. || *Pista de ceniza*, dirt track. || *Pista para ciclistas*, cycle path. || *Seguir la pista*, to follow the trail *o* track, to be on the trail *o* track, to trail, to track.
pistachero m. Pistachio (alfóncigo).
pistacho m. Pistachio [nut] (fruto).
pistilo m. BOT. Pistil.
pisto m. Dish of fried vegetables (fritada). || FIG. y FAM. *Darse pisto*, to put on airs.
pistola f. Pistol (arma): *tiro de pistola*, pistol shot. || Spray gun, sprayer (para pintar). || *Pistola ametralladora*, submachine gun.
pistolera f. Holster.
pistolero m. Gangster, gunman (bandolero). || Hired killer (asesino pagado).
pistoletazo m. Pistol shot.
pistón m. Piston (émbolo): *el recorrido del pistón*, the stroke of the piston. || Percussion cap, cartridge cap (de arma de fuego). || MÚS. Piston [valve] (de instrumento). | Cornet (corneta de llaves).
pistonudo, da adj. POP. Great, fantastic, terrific.
pita f. BOT. Agave (planta). || Pita [thread] (hilo). || Whistling, hissing (en el teatro). || [Glass] marble (canica). || *Recibir una pita*, to be hissed.
pitada f. Whistle. || Whistling, hissing (en el teatro). || *Amer.* Puff (de cigarro). || FIG. y FAM. *Dar una pitada*, to hiss, to boo (en el teatro).
Pitágoras n. pr. m. Pythagoras: *tabla de Pitágoras*, Pythagorean table.
pitagórico, ca adj./s. Pythagorean.
pitanza f. [Daily] ration, dole (ración de comida). || FAM. Daily bread (alimento cotidiano).
pitar v. intr. To whistle, to blow a whistle. || FIG. y FAM. To work, to go well (marchar). || To hoot (un coche). || *Amer.* To smoke. || FIG. y FAM. *Salir pitando*, v. SALIR.
— V. tr. To whistle at, to hiss, to boo: *pitar una obra de teatro*, to whistle at a play. || To whistle: *el árbitro pitó al jugador*, the referee whistled the player. || (P.us.) To pay (pagar). || *Amer.* To smoke (fumar).
pitarra f. Sleep, rheum (p.us.) [legaña].
pitarroso, sa adj. With sleep *o* rheum in one's eyes.
pitecántropo m. ZOOL. Pithecanthropus.
pitejo m. FAM. Undertaker.
pitia f. Pythoness (de Delfos).
Pitias n. pr. m. Pythias.
pítico, ca adj. Pythian (de Delfos): *juegos píticos*, Pythian games.
pitido m. Whistling (ruido producido por el aire, etc.). || Whistle (con el pito): *le llamó con un pitido*, he called him with a whistle. || Hooting (del klaxon).
pitillera f. Cigarette case (petaca).
pitillo m. FAM. Cigarette: *liar, echar un pitillo*, to roll, to smoke a cigarette.
pítima f. MED. Poultice. || FAM. Drunkenness (borrachera). || FAM. *Coger una pítima*, to get plastered *o* sozzled.
pitiminí m. Fairy rose bush (rosal). || *Rosa de pitiminí*, fairy rose.
pitio, tia adj. Pythian.
pitío m. V. PITIDO.
pito m. Whistle (instrumento). || Hooter (de un automóvil). || Whistle (del tren). || Spout (de vasija). || FAM. Fag, ciggy (cigarrillo). || Jack, jackstone (taba). || ZOOL. Tick (insecto). | Woodpecker (pájaro). || POP. Prick (miembro viril). || *Amer.* Pipe. || — FAM. *Cuando pitos, flautas, cuando flautas, pitos*, if it's not one thing it's another. | *Entre pitos y flautas hemos perdido la mañana*, what with one thing and another we have wasted the morning. | *Me oyes como quien oye el pito del sereno*, it's like talking to a brick wall. | *No me importa un pito, no se me da un pito*, I couldn't care less, I don't give a damn *o* a hang. | *No valer un pito* or *tres pitos*, not to be worth a tinker's cuss. | *Pitos flautos*, foolery, fooling. | *Por pitos o flautas*, for some reason [or another]. | *Ser el pito del sereno*, to be a nobody.
pitoche m. FAM. Whistle (pito).
pitón m. Python (serpiente). || Horn (de toros, etc.). || Spout (de botijos). || Shoot (de árbol). || *Amer.* Hose pipe (de riego). || *Pitón de escalada*, piton, peg (alpinismo).
pitonazo m. Butt (golpe). || Gore (herida).
pitonisa f. Pythoness.
pitorrearse v. pr. FAM. To make fun of, to scoff at.

pitorreo m. FAM. Joke (broma). | Farce (farsa). | Fuss, to-do (alboroto). || — FAM. *Tomarlo todo a pitorreo*, to take everything as a big joke. | *Traerse un pitorreo con*, to make fun of.
pitorro m. Spout (de vasija).
pitpit m. Pipit (ave).
pituita f. ANAT. Pituita.
pituitario, ria adj. ANAT. Pituitary: *membrana pituitaria*, pituitary membrane.
pituso, sa adj. FAM. Sweet, cute, lovely (niños). — M. y f. FAM. Kid, child.
pivotante adj. BOT. Tap-rooted (raíz).
pivote m. TECN. Pivot (gorrón). || Pivot (baloncesto).
píxide f. Pyx (copón).
piyama m. Pyjamas, *pl.* [U.S., pajamas, *pl.*].
pizarra f. Slate (piedra y tablilla para escribir). || Blackboard. (encerado): *salir a la pizarra*, to go up *o* out to the blackboard.
pizarral m. Slate quarry.
pizarreño, ña adj. Slaty, slatey.
pizarrería f. Slate quarry.
pizarrero m. Slater.
pizarrín m. Slate pencil.
pizarrón m. *Amer.* Blackboard (encerado). | Scoreboard (marcador en deportes).
pizarroso, sa adj. Slated, slaty, slatey.
pizca f. FAM. Tiny piece (trozo pequeño): *yo sólo como una pizca de pan*, I eat only a tiny piece of bread. | Pinch (de sal, etc.). | Drop (cosa líquida). | Just a little bit: *con una pizca de suerte hubiera ganado yo*, with just a little bit of luck I should have won; *se parece una pizca a su padre*, he looks just a little bit like his father. || — FAM. *Ni pizca*, not at all, not in the least, not a bit: *eso no me gusta ni pizca*, I don't like that at all; *no tiene ni pizca de autoridad*, he has no authority at all. | *No hay pizca de vino*, there is no wine at all.
pizpereta o **pizpireta** adj. f. FAM. Bright, lively, cheerful (alegre).
pizpita o **pizpitilla** f. ZOOL. Wagtail.
pizza f. CULIN. Pizza.
pizzicato m. MÚS. Pizzicato.
placa f. Plate: *placa de matrícula*, number plate [U.S., license plate]. || Badge [of an order] (insignia). || Plaque (medalla conmemorativa). | Sign (para señalar). || FOT. Plate. || Plate (rótulo). || Record (de gramófono). || *Placa giratoria*, turntable (de ferrocarriles).
placaje m. Tackle (rugby). || *Hacer un placaje*, to tackle, to bring down (rugby).
placear v. tr. To market (vender).
pláceme m. Congratulations, *pl.* || *Dar el pláceme a uno*, to congratulate s.o.
placenta f. ANAT. y BOT. Placenta.
placentario, ria adj. Placental.
placentero, ra adj. Charming, pleasant (agradable): *es un jardín placentero*, it is a charming garden. || Amusing (entretenido).
placer* m. Pleasure (diversión, gusto): *los placeres de la vida*, the pleasures of life; *tengo el placer de anunciar*, I have pleasure in announcing; *será un placer para mí*, it will be a pleasure for me. || Will (voluntad): *tal es mi placer*, such is my will. || Amusement, enjoyment (entretenimiento). || Delight: *placeres de la carne*, carnal delights. || MAR. Sandbank (arena). || MIN. Placer. || *Amer.* Pearl fishing ground. || — *A placer*, as much as one wants (en la cantidad que uno quiere), at one's leisure (lentamente). || *Mentir a placer*, to lie for the sake of lying. || *Un viaje de placer*, a holiday trip.
placer v. intr. To like: *me place estudiar*, I like studying. || *Si me place*, if I like, if I want to.

— OBSERV. The Spanish verb *placer* is little used and usually appears in an impersonal form.

placero, ra adj. Of *o* on the square *o* marketplace. — M. y f. Tradesman, stallholder (en la plaza).
plácet m. Placet (diplomático).
placidez f. Placidity.
plácido, da adj. Calm, still, peaceful (quieto). || Placid, tranquil (tranquilo). || Pleasant (grato).
placiente adj. Pleasant, agreeable.
plácito m. Opinion (parecer).
plafón m. ARQ. Soffit (sofito).
plaga f. Scourge (de un pueblo). || Plague, calamity, catastrophe (infortunio). || Disaster, catastrophe (daño). || BOT. Pest, blight. || Plague (de langostas). || Plague, epidemic (abundancia de cosas malas). || Glut, surfeit (de cosas buenas): *hay plaga de frutas*, there is a surfeit of fruit. || *Las diez plagas de Egipto*, the ten plagues of Egypt.
plagal adj. MÚS. Plagal.
plagar v. tr. To cover (cubrir): *plagar de heridas*, to cover with wounds. || To fill: *carta plagada de faltas*, letter full of mistakes. || — *Estar plagado de*, to be overburdened *o* plagued with: *plagado de hijos*, overburdened with children; *plagado de deudas*, plagued with debts. || *Plagado de ratas*, rat-infested.
— V. pr. To become covered in.
plagiar v. tr. To plagiarize (copiar).
plagiario, ria adj. Plagiaristic.
— M. y f. Plagiarist. || *Amer.* Kidnapper (raptor).
plagio m. Plagiarism. || Pastiche (imitación). || *Amer.* Kidnapping (rapto).
plagióstomos m. pl. ZOOL. Plagiostomi.
plan m. Plan, project (proyecto): *hacer planes*, to make plans. || Scheme, skeleton, framework, plan (esquema): *el plan de un libro*, the plan of a book. || Plan: *plan quinquenal*, five-year plan; *plan de construcción*, building plan. || Idea, intention (propósito). || Programme (programa). || Date (cita). || Way (modo). || Attitude (actitud). || Level (nivel). || Height (altura). || FIG. y FAM. Boyfriend (novio), girlfriend (novia). || MAR. Bilge. || MED. Diet: *estar a plan para adelgazar*, to be on a slimming diet. | Course of treatment: *seguir un plan para engordar*, to be on a course of treatment to put on weight. || MIN. Floor (piso). || *Amer.* Plain (planicie). || — *A todo plan*, on a grand scale. || *En plan de*, as: *en plan de vencedor*, as the winner. || *En plan de broma*, as a joke, for a laugh *o* a joke: *meterse con alguien en plan de broma*, to tease s.o. for a laugh. || *En plan grande*, on a grand scale. || *En plan político*, from the political point of view. || *En un plan de intimidad*, on an intimate footing. || *Plan de ataque*, plan of attack. || *Plan de estudios*, course of study, curriculum, syllabus. || *¿Tienes plan para mañana?*, are you booked for tomorrow?, are you doing anything tomorrow?
plana f. Page (página). || Side, page of paper (en la escuela). || Plain (llanura). || TECN. Drawknife (de carpintero). | Trowel (llana). — *A plana y renglón*, line for line the same (imprenta), perfectly, exactly (perfectamente). || *A toda plana*, full spread (titular), full page (página entera). || FIG. *Corregir* or *enmendar la plana*, to criticize (criticar), to surpass, to outdo (superar). || *En primera plana*, on the front page (en los periódicos). || *Estar en la primera plana de la actualidad*, to be in the headlines *o* in the news. || MIL. *Plana mayor*, staff.
planador m. TECN. Planisher.
plancton m. Plankton.
plancha f. Plate (de metal). || Iron (utensilio): *plancha eléctrica*, electric iron. || Ironing (ropa planchada, acción de planchar). || IMPR. Plate. || FIG. y FAM. Boob, bloomer, blunder (error). || Dangerous play (fútbol). || MAR. Gangplank (pasarela). || — *Hacer la plancha*, to float [on one's back]. || *Plancha de blindaje*, armour plate. || FIG. y FAM. *Tirarse una plancha*, to boob, to put one's foot in it.
planchada f. MAR. Gangplank (puentecillo). || *Amer.* FAM. Boob, bloomer, blunder.
planchado m. Ironing, pressing. || *Camisa que no necesita planchado*, non-iron *o* drip-dry shirt.
planchado, da adj. Ironed. || FAM. Broke (sin dinero). || *Amer.* FAM. Very smart.
planchador, ra m. y f. Ironer. || *Máquina planchadora*, ironing machine.
planchar v. tr. To iron, to press. || *Amer.* To flatter (adular). || *Mesa de planchar*, ironing board.
— V. intr. To iron, to do the ironing.
planchazo m. FAM. Boob, bloomer, blunder (metedura de pata). || Dangerous play (en fútbol). || FAM. *Tirarse un planchazo*, to boob, to put one's foot in it.
planchón m. Large plate. || FAM. Boob, bloomer, blunder (planchazo).
planeador m. Glider (avión).
planeadora f. Leveller (máquina de nivelar).
planear v. tr. To plan: *planear un viaje*, to plan a journey; *planear una reforma*, to plan a reform. || To draw up a plan of (hacer un plano de).
— V. intr. To glide (avión). || *Vuelo planeado*, gliding.
planeo m. Gliding (aviación).
planeta m. ASTR. Planet.
planetario, ria adj. Planetary. || TECN. *Piñón planetario*, planet gear.
— M. Planetarium. || TECN. Planet gear.
planetarium m. Planetarium.
planetoide m. Planetoid.
planicie f. Plain (llanura). || Plateau (meseta).
planificación f. Planning.
planificador, ra adj. Planning.
— M. y f. Planner.
planificar v. tr. To plan.
planilla f. *Amer.* List (lista). | Table (cuadro). | Ticket (billete). | Form, application form, blank (formulario). | Ballot paper (papeleta de voto).
planimetría f. Planimetry, surveying.
planímetro m. Planimeter.
planisferio m. Planisphere.
planning m. Planning.
plano, na adj. Flat, level, even, smooth: *terreno plano*, flat land; *superficie plana*, flat surface. || Flat: *zapatos planos*, flat shoes. || MAT. Plane (geometría). | Straight: *ángulo plano*, straight angle.
— M. Map, plan (mapa): *he comprado un plano de la ciudad*, I have bought a map of the city. || ARQ. Plan, draught [U.S., draft] (de construcción). || MAT. Plane. || Shot (cine, foto). || Plane (de avión). || Flat (de la espada). || — *Caer de plano*, to fall flat [on one's face], to fall full length. || *Dar de plano*, to strike with the flat of a sword (con el sable), to shine straight: *el sol daba de plano en la habitación*, the sun was shining straight into the room. || *De plano*, straightforwardly, directly. || *De primer plano*, of the first rank, of the utmost importance. || *En el primer, en el segundo, en el último plano*, in the foreground, in the middle distance, in the background: *en el primer*

plano del cuadro, in the foreground of the picture. || FIG. *Estar en primer plano*, to be in the limelight. || *Hacer* or *alzar* or *levantar un plano*, to make a survey (topografía). || *Plano acotado*, contour map. || *Plano americano*, three-quarter view *o* shot, view *o* shot from the knees up (cine). || *Plano de cola*, tailplane (de avión). || *Plano de fondo*, background (en pintura). || *Plano de incidencia*, plane of incidence. || *Plano de tiro*, line *o* plane of sight *o* fire. || *Plano general* or *largo* or *de conjunto*, overall plan *o* survey. || *Plano inclinado*, chute. || FIG. *Poner en primer plano*, to bring to the fore. | *Ponerse en primer plano*, to come to the fore. || CINEM. *Primer plano*, close-up, close shot. || *Segundo plano*, middle distance.

planocóncavo, va adj. Plano-concave.

planoconvexo, xa adj. Plano-convex.

planta f. Plant (vegetal): *planta de adorno, forrajerra, carnosa, trepadora*, decorative, forage, fleshy, climbing plant. || Ground plan (plano): *planta de la casa*, ground plan of the house. || Floor, storey: *vivo en la primera planta*, I live on the first floor. || Sole (del pie). || Factory, plant (fábrica): *planta siderúrgica*, iron and steel plant. || Plant: *planta eléctrica*, electricity plant. || Field (plantío). || MAT. Foot (de una perpendicular). || FIG. Plan (plan). || Stance, position of the feet (danza, esgrima). || — FIG. y FAM. *Buena planta*, good appearance. || *Construir una casa de nueva planta*, to build a new building. || *Planta baja*, ground floor [U.S., first floor]. || FIG. *Ser una planta de estufa*, to be a hothouse person. | *Tener buena planta*, to look good, to be good-looking (ser apuesto).

plantación f. Plantation: *plantación de plátanos*, banana plantation. || Planting (acción).

plantado, da adj. Planted. || — FIG. y FAM. *Bien plantado*, good-looking, well turned out. | *Dejar a uno plantado*, to stand s.o. up, not to turn up (no acudir a una cita), to leave s.o. standing there (dejar solo), to walk out on s.o. (abandonar), to finish with s.o. (entre novios), to let s.o. down (no prestar ayuda). | *Dejarlo todo plantado*, to drop everything, to leave everything where it is. | *Quedarse plantado*, to stand (permanecer), to be left standing there (quedarse solo).

plantador, ra adj. Who plants, planting.
— M. Planter (el que planta). || Dibble, dibber (instrumento agrícola). || — F. AGR. Planter (máquina).

plantaina f. BOT. Plantain (llantén).

plantar adj. ANAT. Plantar.

plantar v. tr. AGR. To plant (plantas, un terreno). || FIG. To found, to set up, to establish (establecer). || To set, to put, to place (poner). || To put in (un poste, una estaca). || FIG. y FAM. To land, to plant (un golpe), to give, to land (una bofetada). | To throw: *plantar en la calle*, to throw out; *plantar en la cárcel*, to throw into prison. | To give up, to finish with, to chuck (abandonar). | To shut up (dejar callado).
— V. pr. FIG. y FAM. To stand o.s.: *se plantó ante la puerta, en la calle*, he stood himself in the doorway, in the street. | To stand firm (aguantarse). | To get, to be: *en dos horas me plantaré en su casa*, I'll get to *o* I'll be at your house in two hours. | To stop (pararse). | To settle, to install o.s.: *plantarse en Cádiz*, to settle in Cádiz. | *Amer*. To dress up (ataviarse). || *Me planto*, I stick (cartas).

plante m. Strike, stoppage (huelga). || Mutiny (motín). || *Dar un plante a alguien*, to put s.o. in his place.

planteamiento m. Exposition (exposición). || Raising (de un problema). || Institution, introduction (de sistemas, reformas, etc.). || MAT. Laying out, layout, setting out (enfoque de un problema), phrasing (formulación de un problema).

plantear v. tr. To expound, to set forth, to state (exponer). || To create, to raise (causar): *la reforma planteó muchas dificultades*, the reform created many difficulties. || To raise, to bring up, to introduce (introducir un tema, un pleito, etc.). || To plan, to plan out, to think out (planear). || To institute, to introduce (sistemas, reformas, instituciones). || To start (empezar). || MAT. To lay out, to set out (enfocar un problema), to phrase (formular un problema). || *Plantear la cuestión de confianza*, to ask for a vote of confidence.
— V. pr. To arise: *se nos plantea el problema de la devaluación*, there arises the question of devaluation, the question of devaluation arises.

plantel m. Nursery, seedbed (de plantas). || FIG. Nursery, training establishment (institución).

planteo m. MAT. Laying out, setting out, layout (de un problema).

plantificación f. Institution, introduction, establishment (de instituciones, sistemas, reformas).

plantificar v. tr. To institute, to introduce, to establish (establecer). || FIG. y FAM. To put, to stick (plantar algo o a uno en cierto sitio). | To land, to plant (un golpe).
— V. pr. FAM. To install o.s., to plant o.s.: *se plantificó en la casa sin avisarnos*, he installed himself in the house without warning us. | To get: *con el coche nos plantificamos allí en dos minutos*, in the car we got there in no time.

plantígrado, da adj./s. ZOOL. Plantigrade.

plantilla f. Insole (suela interior). || Sole (de calcetín). || Payroll, staff, personnel, employees, *pl.* (empleados): *estar en plantilla en una empresa*, to be on the payroll of a firm. || Payroll, list of staff *o* personnel *o* employees (lista del personal). || Model, pattern (modelo). || Plan, design (plano). || French curve (de los dibujantes). || — *Empleado de plantilla*, member of the permanent staff. || *Plantilla de estarcir*, stencil.

plantío, a adj. Cultivable (labrantío). || Cultivated, planted (labrado).
— M. Field (campo): *plantío de patatas*, field of potatoes. || Patch (labrantío pequeño): *plantío de lechugas*, lettuce patch. || Planting (acción).

plantón m. Seedling (planta joven para trasplantar). || — FIG. y FAM. *Dar (un) plantón a uno*, to stand s.o. up (si se trata de la novia), not to turn up (no acudir), to keep s.o. waiting (tardar mucho). || *Estar de plantón*, to be on extra guard duty (centinela), to cool one's heels, to stand waiting (estar esperando).

plañidero, ra adj. Plaintive, mournful: *voz plañidera*, plaintive voice.
— F. Hired mourner.

plañido o **plañimiento** m. Moan, lamentation.

plañir* v. intr. (P.us.). To wail, to moan, to lament.

plaqué m. Gold *o* silver plate.

plaqueta f. Plaquette (placa pequeña). || BIOL. Blood platelet (de sangre).

plasma m. BIOL. Plasma.

plasmar v. tr. To shape, to mould [U.S., to mold]. || FIG. To capture: *el artista plasmó su pena*, the artist captured her grief.
— V. pr. FIG. To materialize: *el descontento popular se plasmó en una huelga general*, popular discontent materialized into a general strike.

plasta f. Thick paste. || FAM. Botch (cosa mal hecha). || — *Al llegar al suelo se hizo una plasta*, when it hit the ground it was completely flattened. || FIG. y FAM. *El arroz está hecho una plasta*, the rice has gone all sticky *o* gooey.

plasticidad f. Plasticity.

plástico, ca adj. Plastic: *materias plásticas*, plastic materials.
— M. Plastic: *plásticos industriales*, industrial plastics. || Plastic explosive (explosivo). || — *Bomba de plástico*, plastic bomb. || *Voladura con plástico*, demolition with plastic explosives. || — F. Plastic art.

plastificación f. Plasticization.

plastificado, da adj. Plasticized
— M. Plasticization.

plastificante adj. Plasticizing, plastifying.

plastificar v. tr. To plasticize, to plastify.

plastrón m. Breastplate (pechera). || Plastron (en esgrima). || Dicky, shirtfront (de camisa). || Wide tie, kipper (corbata). || Plastron (de quelonios).

plata f. Silver (metal): *estatua de plata*, silver statue. || Silver, silverware (vajilla u objetos de plata): *limpiar la plata*, to clean the silver. || FIG. Money (dinero): *tener mucha plata*, to have a lot of money. || — FIG. *Hablar en plata*, to put it plainly. | *Hacer plata*, to make a mint *o* a fortune. | *La Tacita de Plata*, Cádiz. || *Limpio como la plata*, shining bright, as clean as a whistle *o* as a new pin. || *Plata alemana*, German *o* nickel silver. || *Plata sobredorada*, silver gilt. || *Amer. Sin plata*, broke (sin dinero). || FIG. *Tender* or *hacer un puente de plata*, V. PUENTE.

platabanda f. BOT. Flower bed. || ARQ. Flat moulding.

platada f. *Amer.* Dish, plateful.

plataforma f. Platform. || Open goods wagon, flatcar (vagón de mercancías). || FIG. Stepping-stone: *le va a servir de plataforma para la fama*, it will serve him as a stepping-stone to fame. || — *Plataforma continental*, continental shelf. || *Plataforma de lanzamiento*, launching pad. || *Plataforma de perforación*, drilling rig. || *Plataforma de salida*, starting block (natación). || *Plataforma giratoria*, turntable (ferrocarril). || *Plataforma móvil*, moving pavement *o* carpet [U.S., moving sidewalk] (pasillo rodante). || *Plataforma rodante*, dolly (cine).

platal m. *Amer.* FAM. Fortune (dineral).

platanal o **platanar** m. Banana plantation.

platanazo m. *Amer.* FAM. Fall (caída). | Downfall, collapse, fall (caída de un gobierno).

platanera f. Banana plantation (plantación). || Banana seller (vendedora).

platanero m. Banana tree (plátano). || Banana seller (vendedor).

plátano m. Banana tree (árbol frutal). || Banana (fruta). || Plane tree (árbol).

platea f. TEATR. Stalls, *pl.* [U.S., orchestra] (patio). | Parterre box (palco de platea).

plateado, da adj. Silvered, silver-plated (cubierto de plata). || Silver, silvery (de color de plata). || *Amer.* Wealthy (adinerado).
— M. Silver plate, silver plating (baño de plata).

plateador m. Silver plater.

plateadura f. Silver plate, silver plating (plateado).

platear v. tr. To silver, to silver-plate.

plateau m. CINEM. Set, film set (plató).

platelmintos m. pl. ZOOL. Platyhelminthes.

platense adj. Of the Plate River (río), [of *o* from] La Plata [town in Argentina].
— M. Native *o* inhabitant of La Plata *o* of the Plate River.

plateresco, ca adj. ARQ. Plateresque (estilo).
platería f. Silversmithing (oficio de platero). || Silversmith's workshop (taller). || Silversmith's, jeweller's (tienda). || *Artículos de platería*, silverware, *sing.*
platero m. Silversmith (artista). || Jeweller (joyero).
plática f. Talk, chat (charla). || Sermon (religioso). || — *Estar de plática*, to be chatting. || MAR. *Libre plática*, pratique. || *Se pasaron la tarde de plática*, they spent the afternoon chatting.
platicar v. intr. To talk, to chat, to converse (conversar). || *Amer.* To talk, to speak (hablar). | To say, to tell (decir).
platija f. Flounder, plaice (pez).
platillo m. Saucer (de una taza). || Small plate (plato). || Disc (pieza). || Pan, tray, scale (de balanza). || Plate (de mendigos). || MÚS. Cymbal (instrumento). || *Amer.* Course, dish (plato). || — *Pasar el platillo*, to pass round the hat, to take a collection. || *Platillo volante*, flying saucer.
platina f. TECN. Stage, slide (de microscopio). | Worktable (de máquina herramienta). || IMPR. Platen (de la máquina de imprimir).
platinado m. TECN. Platinizing.
platinar v. tr. To platinize.
platinífero, ra adj. Platiniferous.
platino m. Platinum (metal): *esponja de platino*, platinum sponge. || — Pl. AUT. Points, contact points (motor). || — *Rubia platino*, platinum blonde. || *Teñir de rubio platino*, to dye platinum blond.
platirrino m. ZOOL. Platyrrhine (mono).
plato m. Plate (plato llano). || Dish (plato hondo): *plato sopero*, soup dish; *plato frutero*, fruit dish. || Dish (guiso): *plato exquisito*, exquisite dish; *plato del día*, dish of the day. || Course (parte de una comida): *comida de tres platos*, three course meal. || Plateful, plate, dish (contenido de un plato). || Pan, scale, tray (de balanza). || Plate (del embrague). || FIG. Butt (objeto de críticas). | Talking point, subject for gossip (tema de hablillas). || ARQ. Metope (metopa). || DEP. Clay pigeon (tiro). || — FIG. *Comer en el mismo plato*, to be very close friends. | *¿Desde cuándo hemos comido en el mismo plato?* or *¿en qué plato hemos comido juntos?*, please remember whom you are talking to [reproof of familiarity]. || *Huevos al plato*, fried eggs. || *Lavar* or *fregar los platos*, to wash the dishes, to wash up. || FIG. *Pagar los platos rotos*, to carry the can, to pay the consequences. | *Parece que no ha roto un plato en su vida*, butter wouldn't melt in his mouth. || *Plato de segunda mesa*, warmed-up leftovers, *pl.* (restos de comida), second best, stand-in (persona designada para sustituir a otra), old hat (lo ya conocido), second hand (ya usado). || *Plato fuerte* or *de resistencia*, main course. || *Plato giratorio*, turntable (de tocadiscos). || *Plato montado*, tiered cake. || *Primer plato*, first course. || *Ser plato del gusto de uno*, to be the spice of life for s.o. || *Tiro al plato*, trapshooting. || FIG. *Vender por un plato de lentejas*, to sell for a mess of pottage.
plató m. CINEM. Set, film set.
Platón n. pr. m. Plato.
platónicamente adv. Platonically.
platónico, ca adj. Platonic.
— M. y f. Platonist.
platonismo m. Platonism.
platudo, da adj. *Amer.* FAM. Rich, wealthy (rico).
plausibilidad f. Plausibility. || Praiseworthiness.
plausible adj. Plausible, acceptable (admisible). || Praiseworthy, commendable (laudable).
playa f. Beach: *en la playa*, on the beach. || Seaside resort (estación balnearia).
play back m. CINEM. Playback.
playboy m. Playboy.
playera f. T-shirt (camisa). || Popular Andalusian song (canto). || — Pl. Plimsolls [U.S., sneakers] (zapatos de lona).
playero, ra adj. Beach (de playa).
plaza f. Square: *plaza mayor*, main square. || Parvis, square (de una iglesia). || Market, market place (mercado): *ir a la plaza* to go to [the] market. || COM. Place, town, market. || Town (población). || Place, seat (asiento): *reservar una plaza*, to reserve a seat. || Place, space: *estacionamiento de quinientas plazas*, car park with five hundred places. || Post, position, job (empleo): *cubrir una plaza*, to fill a post. || MIL. Fortified town, stronghold, fortress (ciudad fortificada). || Bullring (de toros). || TECN. Hearth (de un horno). || — *Hacer plaza*, to make room. || *¡Plaza!*, make way! || *Plaza de abastos*, market. || *Plaza de armas*, parade ground (campo de instrucción). || *Plaza de toros*, bullring. || *Plaza fuerte*, fortified town, stronghold, fortress. || *Plaza vacante*, situation vacant, vacancy. || FIG. *Sacar a la plaza*, to tell the world about, to shout from the rooftops. || MIL. *Sentar plaza*, to enlist, to join up. || FIG. *Sentar plaza de*, to confirm o.s. to be.
plazo m. Period (periodo): *tenemos un plazo de tres meses para pagar la cuenta*, we have a period of three months to pay the bill. || Date (fecha): *letra pagadera a plazo fijo*, bill payable at a fixed date. || Time (tiempo). || Instalment [U.S., installment] (parte de un pago): *lo pagamos en doce plazos*, we payed for it in twelve instalments. || Term (de una letra). || Time limit (límite de tiempo).
— *A corto plazo*, forthwith, within a short time, as soon as possible (pronto), short-dated (efectos comerciales), short-term: *un préstamo a corto plazo, una inversión a corto plazo*, a short-term loan, a short-term investment; *esta medicina hace efecto a corto plazo*, this medicine has a short-term effect. || *A largo plazo*, long-dated (efectos comerciales), long-term (préstamo, inversión, etc.), in the long run (más tarde). || *Antes del vencimiento del plazo*, before maturity, prior maturity. || *A plazo vencido*, on maturity, on the expiry date. || *Comprar, vender a plazos*, to buy, to sell on hire-purchase *o* on credit [U.S., on the installment plan]. || *Dar a uno un mes de plazo para pagar*, to give s.o. a month to pay. || *El plazo vence mañana*, the payment is due tomorrow. || *En breve plazo*, within a short time, at short notice (dentro de poco). || *En el plazo de un año*, within a year. || *En un plazo de quince días*, at a fortnight's notice. || *Operación a plazo*, credit transaction, transaction for the account (en la Bolsa). || *Plazo de despedida*, notice. || *Plazo de respiro*, grace, respite. || *Plazo suplementario*, extension. || *Vencimiento del plazo*, maturity date.
plazoleta o **plazuela** f. Small square.
pleamar f. MAR. High tide, high water.
plebe f. Common people, *pl.*, masses, *pl.*, plebeians, *pl.* || FAM. Plebs, *pl.* (despectivo).
plebeyez f. Plebeianism, plebianism. || FIG. Plebianism, vulgarity, commonness.
plebeyo, ya adj./s. Plebeian, plebian.
plebiscitar v. tr. To submit to a plebiscite (someter a plebiscito). || To approve by plebiscite (aprobar).
plebiscitario, ria adj. Plebiscitary.
plebiscito m. Plebiscite.
plectognatos m. pl. ZOOL. Plectognaths.
plectro m. Plectrum, pick (púa).
plegable o **plegadizo, za** adj. Pliable (flexible). || Folding, collapsible: *silla plegable*, folding chair.
plegadera f. Paper knife (para cortar). || Folder, bone blade (para plegar).
plegado m. o **plegadura** f. Folding (acción de plegar). || Pleating (tableado de una tela). || Pleats, *pl.*, folds, *pl.* (conjunto de pliegues). || Bending (encorvamiento).
plegador, ra adj. Folding.
— M. Bone blade (para plegar papel). || F. IMPR. Folding machine.
plegadura f. V. PLEGADO.
plegamiento m. GEOL. Folding.
plegar* v. tr. To fold (hacer un doblez). || To bend (doblar). || To pleat (tablear una tela). || GEOL. To fold.
— V. pr. To bend (doblarse). || FIG. To bow, to give way, to submit (someterse).
plegaria f. Prayer.
pleistoceno, na adj./s.m. GEOL. Pleistocene.
pleita f. Plaited strand of esparto grass.
pleiteador, ra o **pleiteante** adj. Pleading. || *Las partes pleiteantes*, the litigants.
— M. y f. Litigant.
pleitear v. intr. To litigate, to plead. || FIG. To argue (discutir).
pleitesía f. Hommage, tribute (homenaje): *rendir pleitesía a*, to pay hommage to, to pay a tribute to.
pleitista adj. Litigious (litigioso). || Pettifogging (aficionado a pleitos). || Quarrelsome (peleón).
— M. y f. Litigious person. || Pettifogger.
pleito m. JUR. Lawsuit, case: *ganar un pleito*, to win a lawsuit. || Case (caso): *el pleito de X contra Y*, the case of X against Y. || Feud, dispute (disputa). || — Pl. FAM. Pettifogging, *sing.*: *ser aficionado a pleitos*, to be fond of pettifogging. || — JUR. *Armar pleito*, to go to law. | *Entablar pleito*, to bring an action, to bring suit. | *Poner pleito a uno*, to bring an action against s.o., to sue s.o. | *Tener un pleito con alguien*, to be at law with s.o.
plenamar f. High tide, high water (pleamar).
plenario, ria adj. Plenary: *indulgencia, sesión plenaria*, plenary indulgence, session.
plenilunio m. Full moon (luna llena).
plenipotencia f. Full *o* unlimited powers, *pl.*
plenipotenciario, ria adj./s. Plenipotentiary.
plenitud f. Plenitude, fullness: *en la plenitud de*, in the fullness of. || FIG. Prime (de una persona): *alcanzar la plenitud*, to reach one's prime.
pleno, na adj. Full: *en plena actividad*, in full activity; *en plena posesión de sus facultades*, in full possession of his faculties. || — *A plena vista*, in full view. || *A pleno sol*, in the sunshine, under the sun. || *En plena calle*, in the middle of the street. || *En plena cámara de los lores*, in the House of Lords itself. || *En plena cara*, straight in the face, right in the face. || *En plena rebeldía*, in open revolt. || *En pleno día*, in broad daylight. || *En pleno invierno, plena selva*, in the heart of [the] winter, of the jungle. || *Hacer algo con pleno derecho*, to have every right to do sth. || *La asamblea en pleno*, the entire assembly. || *Pleno empleo*, full employment. || *Plenos poderes*, full powers.
— M. Plenary meeting, plenum (reunión).

— OBSERV. The adjective *pleno* is used mainly in the abstract.

pleonasmo m. GRAM. Pleonasm (repetición).
pleonástico, ca adj. Pleonastic.
plepa f. FAM. Nuisance.

plesiosauro m. Plesiosaur (fósil).
pletina f. Iron plate (metalurgia).
plétora f. Plethora, abundance.
pletórico, ca adj. Plethoric, abundant. || *Pletórico de*, full of.
pleura f. ANAT. Pleura.
pleural adj. ANAT. Pleural.
pleuresía f. MED. Pleuresy.
pleurítico, ca adj./s. MED. Pleuritic. || — Adj. Pleural: *derrame pleurítico*, pleural effusion.
pleuritis f. inv. MED. Pleuritis.
plexiglás m. Perspex, plexiglass, plexiglas.
plexo m. ANAT. Plexus: *plexo solar*, solar plexus.
pléyade f. Pléiade (poetas franceses). || Pleiad, group, number (conjunto). || — Pl. ASTR. y MIT. Pleiades.
plica f. Sealed envelope (sobre cerrado). || Escrow (documento legal).
pliego m. Sheet *o* piece *o* leaf of paper (hoja de papel). || Sealed letter (documento cerrado). || Sealed orders, *pl.* (documento militar). || IMPR. Signature, gathering. || — *Pliego de cargos*, list of charges. || *Pliego de condiciones*, specifications, *pl.*
pliegue m. Fold (doblez). || Pleat (tabla): *los pliegues de una falda*, the pleats of a skirt. || GEOL. Fold (ondulación del terreno).
Plinio n. pr. m. Pliny: *Plinio el Viejo, el Joven*, Pliny the Elder, the Younger.
plinto m. ARQ. Plinth (de columna). || Horse (en gimnasia).
plioceno m. GEOL. Pliocene.
plisado m. Pleating (acción y efecto de plisar). || Pleats, *pl.*, pleating (tablas, tableado).
plisar v. tr. To pleat: *plisar una falda*, to pleat a skirt.
plomada f. Plumb line (de albañil). || Sinker (de red). || MAR. Sounding line (sonda). || Lead pencil (lápiz).
plomar v. tr. To seal with lead.
plomazo m. Lead shot wound.
plombagina f. MAR. Plumbago, graphite.
plombaginácea f. BOT. V. PLUMBAGINÁCEA.
plomear v. intr. To score a bull's-eye *o* a hit.
plomería f. Plumbing (oficio de plomero). || Lead roofing (de tejado).
plomero m. Plumber.
plomífero, ra adj. MIN. Plumbiferous. || FIG. y FAM. Boring, dull (pesado).
plomizo, za adj. Leaden.
plomo m. Lead (metal). || Lead weight (peso). || Plumb line (plomada). || Slug, lead shot (de fusil). || Sinker (de red). || Fuse (electricidad). || FAM. Super (gasolina). | Drag, bore, pest (pesado). || — FIG. *Andar con pies de plomo*, to tread warily. || *A plomo*, straight down, vertically, plumb (verticalmente). || FIG. y FAM. *Caer a plomo*, to fall flat (una persona). || *Caer como un plomo*, to fall *o* to drop like a stone. || ELECTR. *Se fundieron los plomos*, the fuses have gone, the fuses have blown. || FIG. y FAM. *Ser un plomo*, to be a bore *o* a drag. || *Soldadito de plomo*, tin soldier. || FIG. *Tener un sueño de plomo*, to be dog-tired.
plomo, ma adj. Leaden, lead-coloured.
pluma f. Feather, plume (p.us.): *pluma de ganso*, goose feather; *colchón de plumas*, feather bed. || Plume, feather (de adorno). || MAR. y TECN. Derrick. || Pen (para escribir, de metal). || Quill (para escribir, de ave). || FIG. Writer (escritor). | Pen, style (estilo). | Pen: *el periodista vive de su pluma*, a journalist lives by his pen. || *Amer.* Tap (grifo). || — Pl. Flight, *sing.* (de una flecha). || — *Escribir al correr de la pluma* or *a vuela pluma*, to let one's pen run on. || *Peso pluma*, featherweight (boxeador). || *Pluma estilográfica*, fountain pen. || *Tomar la pluma*, to put pen to paper. || FIG. y FAM. *Vestirse* or *engalanarse con plumas ajenas*, to strut in borrowed plumes *o* feathers.
plumada f. Stroke of a pen, flourish.
plumafuente f. *Amer.* Foutain pen (estilográfica).
plumaje m. Plumage, feathers, *pl.* (de aves). || Plume, crest (de casco).
plumajería f. Plumage.
plumajero, ra m. y f. Plumassier.
plumaria adj. f. *Arte plumaria*, art of decorating with ornamental plumes.
plumazo m. Stroke of one's pen: *lo tachó de un plumazo*, he crossed it out with a stroke of his pen.
plumazón f. Plumage (plumaje).
plumbagina f. MIN. Plumbago, graphite.
plumbaginácea f. BOT. Plumbago. || — Pl. BOT. Plumbaginaceae.
plúmbeo, a adj. Leaden, heavy as lead. || FIG. Deep (sueño). | Boring, dull (aburrido).
plumeado m. Hatching (en pintura).
plumear v. tr. To hatch, to hatch in (en pintura). || *Amer.* To write (escribir).
plumería f. o **plumerío** m. Bunch *o* pile of feathers.
plumero m. Feather duster (para quitar el polvo). || Pencil box *o* case (estuche). || MIL. Plume (penacho). || *Amer.* Penholder (portaplumas). || FIG. y FAM. *Vérsele a uno el plumero*, to see through s.o., to be able to see through s.o.
plumetís m. Plumetis (tela).
plumier m. Pencil box *o* case.

— OBSERV. This word is a Gallicism for *plumero*.

plumífero, ra adj. Plumed, feathered.
— M. FAM. Pen-pusher (chupatintas).
plumilla f. o **plumín** m. Small feather. || Nib (de estilográfica). || BOT. Plumule.
plumista m. Clerk (empleado).
plumón m. Down (de las aves). || Eiderdown (edredón).
plumoso, sa adj. Feathery.
plúmula f. BOT. Plumule.
plural adj./s.m. Plural: *poner una palabra en plural*, to put a word into the plural.
pluralidad f. Plurality. || — *A pluralidad de votos*, by a majority of votes. || *Una pluralidad de personas*, a great number of people.
pluralismo m. Pluralism.
pluralista m. Pluralist.
pluralizar v. tr. GRAM. To pluralize, to put into the plural. || FIG. To use the plural, to generalize.
pluricelular adj. Pluricellular.
pluriempleo m. Moonlighting.
plurilingüe adj./s. Polyglot. || — Adj. Multilingual.
pluripartidismo m. Multi-partyism.
pluripartidista adj. Multi-party.
plurivalencia f. QUÍM. Polyvalence. || Versatility.
plurivalente adj./s.m. QUÍM. Polyvalent. || Versatile.
plus m. Bonus (gratificación). || — *Plus de carestía de vida*, cost-of-living bonus. || *Plus petición*, plus petitio.
pluscafé m. *Amer.* Liqueur [taken after coffee].
pluscuamperfecto m. GRAM. Pluperfect.
plusmarca f. Record: *batir la plusmarca*, to break the record.
plusmarquista m. y f. Record holder.
plusvalía f. Appreciation, increased value, gain in value.
plúteo m. Shelf (anaquel).
Plutarco n. pr. m. Plutarch.
plutocracia f. Plutocracy.
plutócrata m. y f. Plutocrat.
plutocrático, ca adj. Plutocratic.
Plutón n. pr. m. ASTR. Pluto.
plutonio m. MIN. Plutonium (metal).
pluvial adj. Pluvial, rain: *erosión pluvial*, pluvial erosion. || REL. *Capa pluvial*, pluvial, cope.
pluviógrafo m. Pluviograph.
pluviometría f. Pluviometry.
pluviómetro m. Pluviometer, rain gauge.
pluviométrico, ca adj. Pluviometric.
pluviosidad f. Pluviosity.
pluvioso, sa adj. Pluvious, rainy (lluvioso).
p.m. (abreviatura de *post-meridiem*). P.m.: *a las tres p.m.*, at three p.m.
pneumococo m. MED. Pneumococcus.
poa f. Poa (hierba). || MAR. Bridle.
población f. Population (acción de poblar, habitantes): *población activa*, working population. || Town, city (ciudad). || Village (pueblo). || Centre of population (núcleo urbano). || Built-up area (en el código de la circulación). || BIOL. Population.
poblacho m. FAM. Hole, dump (pueblo).
poblada f. *Amer.* Rebellion, revolt, riot, uprising (sedición). | Crowd (gentío).
poblado, da adj. Populated, inhabited (con gente o animales). || Wooded (con árboles): *paisaje poblado*, wooded countryside. || Thick (la barba). || Bushy (cejas). || FIG. Full of: *composición poblada de faltas*, composition full of mistakes. || *Poblado de*, peopled with, populated with.
— M. Built-up area (lugar): *atravesar un poblado*, to go through a built-up area. || Town, city (ciudad). || Centre of population (núcleo urbano).
poblador, ra adj. Resident, inhabitant (que reside).
— M. y f. Settler, inhabitant (habitante). || Colonist, settler, founder (fundador de una colonia).
poblano, na m. y f. Villager (aldeano). || — Adj. [Of *o* from] Puebla [town in Mexico]. || — M. y f. Inhabitant *o* native of Puebla.
poblar* v. tr. To populate, to people (con gente). || To populate (con animales). || To plant (con plantas). || To stock: *poblar un río de peces*, to stock a river with fish. || To inhabit (habitar). || To colonize, to found, to settle (fundar). || FIG. To people, to stock, to fill.
— V. pr. To become peopled. || To become crowded, to fill [*de*, with] (llenarse). || To bud, to leaf (plantas).
pobre adj. Poor: *una familia pobre*, a poor family; *pobre en minerales*, poor in minerals. || FIG. Poor: *el pobre de tu padre*, your poor father. | Little, no: *pobre consuelo*, little consolation. || — FIG. *Hacer un pobre papel*, to give a poor perfomance. | *¡Pobre de él!*, poor fellow!, the poor thing! | *¡Pobre de mí!*, poor old me!, poor me! | *¡Pobre desgraciado!*, poor devil!, poor thing! | *¡Pobre de ti!*, you poor thing! | *¡Pobre de ti si...!*, you'll be sorry if...! | *Ser más pobre que Carracuca* or *que una rata* or *que las ratas*, to be as poor as a church mouse.
— M. y f. Poor person *o* man *o* woman: *un pobre*, a poor man. || — Pl. Poor people, poor: *hay demasiados pobres en el mundo*, there are too many poor people in the world; *los pobres*, the poor. || JUR. *Abogacía de pobres*, legal aid.
pobrecito, ta m. y f. Poor little thing.
— Adj. Poor little.
pobrería f. o **pobrerío** m. V. POBRETERÍA.
pobrete, ta m. y f. Poor devil, poor thing.
pobretear v. intr. To play the poor man, to put on the agony.

pobretería f. Poverty (escasez). || FAM. Poor people, *pl.* (pobres). | Beggars, *pl.* (mendigos).

pobretón, ona adj. Wretched, very poor.
— M. y f. Poor wretch, poor thing.

pobreza f. Poverty, indigence, need (falta de dinero). || Penury (penuria). || Poorness: *pobreza de espíritu*, poorness of spirit. || Scarcity (escasez): *pobreza de metales*, scarcity of metals. || Lack (falta): *pobreza de recursos*, lack of resources. || Barrenness, sterility (de la tierra). || FIG. Meanness (falta de magnanimidad). || — JUR. *Beneficio de pobreza*, legal aid. || FIG. *Pobreza no es vileza*, poverty is no crime, it is no crime to be poor.

pocero m. Well digger (el que hace pozos). || Sewerman (alcantarillero).

pocilga f. Pigsty, piggery (de cerdos). || FIG. y FAM. Pigsty.

pocillo m. Sump (para recoger líquidos). || Cup (jícara).

pócima o **poción** f. Potion. || FIG. Concoction, brew.

poción f. Potion. || FIG. Concoction, brew.

poco, ca adj. sing. Not much, little (no mucho) [v. OBSERV.]: *tiene poco dinero*, he has not much money; *queda poca leche*, there is not much milk left; *con poco respeto*, with little respect. || Little, small: *de poco interés*, of small interest.
— Adj. pl. Not many, few: *pocos árboles*, not many trees; *aquí son pocas las casas antiguas*, there are not many old houses here. || — *Hay pocos que*, there are not many who. || *Lo poco*, how little: *y ya sabes lo poco que me gusta leer*, and you know how little I like reading. || *Muchos pocos hacen un mucho*, v. MUCHO. || *Poca cosa*, nothing much: *¿qué hicisteis? — Poca cosa*, what did you do? — Nothing much. || *Pocas palabras pero buenas*, v. PALABRA. || *Pocas veces*, not very often. || *Poco tiempo*, just a short time, just a little while: *salió hace poco tiempo*, he went out *o* he left just a short time ago. || *Tiene poca inteligencia*, he is not very intelligent. || *Tiene poca memoria*, he has not a very good memory. || *Unos pocos*, a few, some: *unas pocas casas*, a few houses; *unos pocos de los que quedan*, a few of those which remain.
— Adv. Not very much, little: *bebo poco*, I do not drink very much, I drink little. || Not very (con adjetivo): *es poco inteligente*, he is not very intelligent. || Not long (poco tiempo): *se quedó poco allí*, he did not stay there long. || — *A poco de*, shortly after, a short time after: *a poco de llegar aquí murió*, shortly after he arrived here he died. || *A poco que*, if ... at all (por poco que). || *Dentro de poco*, shortly, soon. || FAM. *De poco más o menos*, of little *o* no account. || *Equivocarse por muy poco*, not to be far out *o* wrong: *me equivoqué por muy poco*, I was not far out. || *Es poco*, it's not much. || *Estar en poco*, to almost do sth., to very nearly do sth.: *estuvo en poco que le pegase*, he very nearly hit him. || *Hace poco*, a short time ago, not long ago. || *Muy poco*, very little (no bastante). || *No es poco*, that's not bad. || *No poco*, a lot (con verbo), a lot of (con sustantivo), very (con adjetivo). || *O poco menos*, or something like that. || *Poco antes, después*, shortly before, after. || *Poco a poco*, little by little, gradually. || *¡Poco a poco!*, easy does it!, gently now! || *Poco falta para*, it is not long before (indica tiempo), a little more and (indica cantidad): *poco falta para llenarlo*, a little more and it will be full. || *Poco ha faltado* or *poco faltó para que perdiese el tren*, he nearly missed *o* he almost missed the train. || *Poco más, poco menos*, not much more, not much less: *tiene poco más de treinta años*, he is not much more than thirty years old; *poco más viejo que yo*, not much older than I. || *Poco más o menos*, more or less. || *Poco o nada*, little or nothing. || *Por poco*, nearly, almost: *por poco me caigo*, I nearly fell over. || *Por poco que*, if... at all: *por poco que te muevas romperás la silla*, if you move at all you will break the chair; *por poco inteligente que sea lo entenderá*, if he is at all intelligent he will understand. || *Por poco que sea*, little as it is, little as it might seem. || *Tener en poco*, to think little of, not to think much of. || *Un poco más*, a little more, not much more: *un poco más caro que el tuyo*, not much more expensive than yours. || *Un poco más joven que yo*, a little younger *o* not much younger than I. || *Un poco menos*, a little less. || *Vivir con muy poco*, to live on very little. || *Y por si fuera poco*, and to top it all.
— M. *Un poco*, a little. || *Un poco de*, a little: *un poco de pan*, a little bread; *un poco más de vino*, a little more wine.

— OBSERV. Cuando el adjetivo *poco* acompaña un sustantivo abstracto el inglés suele sustituir *not much* (seguido del sustantivo) por *not very* (seguido del adjetivo correspondiente): *tiene poca importancia*, it is not very important.

pocho, cha adj. Faded, discoloured (flores, colores). || Pale, off-colour (personas). || Overripe, soft (fruta).

pochocho, cha adj. *Amer.* Chubby, plump (gordo).

pochola f. FAM. Nice girl.

poda f. AGR. Pruning (acción). || Pruning season (temporada).

podadera f. AGR. Pruning shears, *pl.* (tijeras), pruning knife (cuchillo).

podador m. Pruner.

podagra f. MED. Podagra, gout.

podar v. tr. To prune, to trim (árboles). || FIG. To prune, to trim (quitar lo inútil).

podenco, ca adj./s.m. Spaniel (perro).

poder m. Power (dominio, autoridad). || Possession (posesión): *pasar a poder de*, to pass into the possession of. || Capacity (capacidad): *tiene un gran poder de trabajo*, he has a great capacity for work. || Strength (fuerza física). || Power, ability (facultad). || JUR. Power. || TECN. Power. || — Pl. Powers, power, *sing.*: *con plenos poderes*, with full powers. || — *Bajo el poder de*, under the power of, in the hands of (caer, estar, etc.). || *Casarse por poderes*, to marry by proxy. || *Dar a uno poder para*, to authorize *o* to allow s.o. to, to give s.o. the power to. || *Dar poderes*, to give proxy. || *De poder a poder*, man to man (discutir, hablar, etc.). || *División* or *separación de poderes*, separation of powers. || *Entrega* or *transmisión de poderes*, handing over of power. || *Entregar los poderes*, to hand over power. || *Estar en el poder*, to be in power (un gobierno). || *Estar en poder de alguien*, to be in the power *o* in the hands of s.o. (una persona), to be in s.o.'s hands *o* possession (una cosa). || FIG. *Hacer un poder*, to make an effort (un esfuerzo). || *Llegar a poder de uno*, to reach s.o. || *Obrar en poder de uno*, to be in s.o.'s hands *o* possession. || *Obrar por poderes*, to act by proxy. || *Ocupar el poder*, to be in power. || *Plenos poderes*, full powers, full power. || *Poder absoluto, ejecutivo, judicial, legislativo*, absolute, executive, judicial, legislative power. || *Poder adquisitivo*, purchasing power. || MIL. *Poder disuasivo*, deterrent. || *Por poderes*, by proxy. || *Tener en su poder*, to have, to have in one's possession (una cosa), to have it in one's power to (tener la posibilidad de).

poder* v. tr. To be able to, can (presente), could (pretérito) [capacidad física] [v. OBSERV.]: *este animal no puede nadar*, this animal cannot *o* can't swim; *le dolía tanto que no podía andar*, it hurt him so much that he could not *o* couldn't walk *o* that he was unable to walk; *hubiéramos podido ir si*, we could have gone if, we should have been able to go if. || May, might (pidiendo o dando permiso): *¿puedo salir esta noche?*, may I go out tonight?; *su padre dijo que podía ir al baile*, her father said that she might go to the dance. (V. OBSERV.) || To be allowed to (permiso ya dado): *no puede salir después de las diez*, she is not allowed to go out after ten o'clock; *no pudo ir*, he was not allowed to go (no le dejaron ir). || May, might (posibilidad): *ha podido pasar sin ser visto*, he may have passed without being seen; *puede venir en cualquier momento*, he may come at any moment. || Might (sugerencia): *por lo menos podría saludarnos*, he might at least say hello [to us]. || — *A más no poder*, v. MÁS. || *A poder ser*, if possible. || *Aquellos que pueden*, those who can, those who are able. || *El que puede lo más puede lo menos*, once difficult things are mastered easy things are all the easier. || *Hasta más no poder* or *hasta no poder más*, as much [hard, long, etc.] as one can: *corrimos hasta más no poder*, we ran as fast *o* as far as we could. || *No poder con*, not to be able to do anything with, not to be able to cope with (no poder dominar): *no puedo con este niño*, I cannot do anything with this child; not to be able to stand (no aguantar): *no puedo con la hipocresía*, I cannot stand hypocrisy. || *No poder más*, to be exhausted, to be all in (agotado), not to be able to stand any more: *¡no puedo más!*, I cannot stand any more! || *No poder más que*, can only: *no puedo más que decírselo a mis superiores*, I can only tell my superiors. || *No poder menos que* or *de*, *no poder sino*, not to be able to help: *no pude menos que invitarle a cenar*, I could not help asking him to dinner. || *No puede ser*, it *o* that is impossible. || *Por lo que pudiera ocurrir*, because of what might happen. || *Puede ser*, maybe, perhaps. || *Puede ser que*, it may be that, it is possible that, perhaps, maybe. || *¿Se puede?*, may I [*o* we]?

— OBSERV. El verbo *can* no tiene infinitivo ni participios ni tiempo futuro. Para expresar estas ideas hay que emplear el verbo *to be able*: *no podremos ir*, we shall not be able to go; *no pudiendo correr*, being unable to run, not being able to run.
El pasado del verbo *may* es *might*. No obstante *might* es de por sí un verbo auxiliar que se emplea para pedir permiso y también para expresar una posibilidad.
Aunque el único sentido normal de *can* sea el de tener la capacidad física de hacer algo, se emplea cada día más este verbo para todos los significados de *poder*.

poderdante m. y f. Principal.

poderhabiente m. y f. Manager, managing director, signing clerk (que firma). || Agent (que representa). || Proxy (que tiene el poder de otro).

poderío m. Power.

poderosamente adv. Powerfully.

poderoso, sa adj. Powerful. || Good, effective (remedio). || Strong, powerful (motivo, razón). || Rich, wealthly (rico).

podio m. Podium.

podología MED. Podology.

podómetro m. Pedometer.

podre f. Pus (humor).

podredumbre f. Putrefaction, rottenness. || Pus (humor). || FIG. Corruption, rot, rottenness. | Uneasiness (desasosiego).

podridero m. Compost heap.

podrido, da adj. Rotten. || — *Oler a podrido*, to smell rotten. || FIG. y FAM. *Estar podrido de dinero*, to be filthy rich *o* stinking rich.
podrir* v. tr. V. PUDRIR.
podzol m. Podzol.
poema m. Poem. || MÚS. Poem: *poema sinfónico*, symphonic poem. || — FIG. *Es un poema*, it is quite something. || *Poema en prosa*, prose poem.
poemario m. Book of poems *o* of verse.
poemático, ca adj. Poematic, poetic.
— F. Theme.
poesía f. Poetry (género literario). || Poem (poema).
poeta m. Poet.
poetastro m. FAM. Poetaster, would-be poet.
poético, ca adj. Poetic, poetical.
— F. Poetics (arte).
poetisa f. Poetess.
poetizar v. tr. To poetize, to poeticize.
pogrom o **pogromo** m. Pogrom.
poise m. Poise (unidad de viscosidad).
póker m. Poker (juego). || Poker (dados): *póker de ases*, poker of aces. || Four of a kind (naipes): *tengo un póker*, I have four of a kind. || *Póker de ases*, four aces (naipes).
polaco, ca adj. Polish.
— M. y f. Pole (habitante). || — M. Polish (lengua).
polaina f. Gaiter (en las pantorrillas).
polar adj. Polar: *círculo polar*, polar circle. || — *Casquete polar*, polar cap. || *Clima polar*, polar climate. || *Estrella polar*, polestar. || *Oso polar*, polar bear.
polaridad f. Polarity.
polarímetro m. FÍS. Polarimeter.
polariscopio m. FÍS. Polariscope.
polarización f. Polarization.
polarizador, ra adj. Polarizing.
— M. Polarizer.
polarizar v. tr. FÍS. To polarize. || FIG. To concentrate on (concentrar).
— V. pr. To polarize.
polaroid m. Polaroid.
polca f. Polka (música y baile).
pólder m. Polder.
polea f. Pulley.
poleadas f. pl. Porridge, *sing.* (gachas).
polémico, ca adj. Polemic, polemical.
— F. Polemic, controversy (controversia). || Polemics (arte de la discusión).
polemista m. y f. Polemist, polemicist.
polemizar v. intr. To indulge in a polemic, to argue.
polen m. BOT. Pollen.
polenta f. CULIN. Polenta.
poli m. FAM. Cop (policía). || — F. FAM. Police, cops, *pl.* (cuerpo de policía).
poliandra adj. Polyandrous.
poliandria f. Polyandry.
policéfalo, la adj. Polycephalous.
policía f. Police, police force: *policía urbana*, urban police. || Courtesy (cortesía). || — *Policía judicial*, Criminal Investigation Department. || MIL. *Revista de policía*, kit check *o* inspection. || *Viene la policía*, the police are coming.
— M. Policeman (agente).
policiaco, ca o **policíaco, ca** o **policial** adj. Police. || Detective: *película, novela policiaca*, detective film, story.
policlínica f. MED. Polyclinic.
policroísmo m. FÍS. Polychroism.
policromado, da adj. Polychrome.
policromía f. Polychromy.
policromo, ma o **polícromo, ma** adj. Polychromatic.
policultivo m. Mixed farming.
Polichinela n. pr. m. Punchinello, Punch.
polidactilo, la adj./s. Polydactyl.
poliédrico, ca adj. Polyhedral, polyhedric, polyhedrical.
poliedro adj. m. MAT. Polyhedral.
— M. MAT. Polyhedron.
poliéster m. QUÍM. Polyester.
poliestireno m. QUÍM. Polystyrene.
polietileno m. QUÍM. Polyethylene, polythene.
polifacético, ca adj. Many-sided, versatile.
polifásico, ca adj. FÍS. Polyphase.
polifonía f. MÚS. Polyphony.
polifónico, ca adj. Polyphonic.
poligamia f. Polygamy.
polígamo, ma adj. Polygamous.
— M. Polygamist.
poliginia f. Polygyny.
poliglotía f. Polyglotism.
polígloto, ta o **poligloto, ta** adj./s. Polyglot.
poligonáceas adj. BOT. Polygonaceous.
— F. pl. BOT. Polygonaceae.
poligonal adj. MAT. Polygonal.
polígono m. MAT. Polygon. || MIL. Rifle range. || — *Polígono de desarrollo*, development area. || *Polígono industrial*, industrial estate.
poligrafía f. Polygraphy.
polígrafo m. Polygraph.
polilla f. Moth (insecto).
polimería f. QUÍM. Polymerism.
polimérico, ca adj. Polymeric.
polimerización f. Polymerization.
polimerizar v. tr. QUÍM. To polymerize.
polímero, ra adj. QUÍM. Polymeric.
— M. QUÍM. Polymer.
polimórfico, ca adj. Polymorphic.
polimorfismo m. Polymorphism.
polimorfo, fa adj. Polymorphic, polymorphous.
Polinesia n. pr. f. GEOGR. Polynesia.
polinesio, sia adj./s. Polynesian.
polinífero, ra adj. Polliniferous.
polinización f. BOT. Pollination.
polinizar v. tr. To pollinate.
polinómico, ca adj. MAT. Polynomial.
polinomio m. MAT. Polynomial.
polio f. MED. Polio.
poliomielitis f. MED. Poliomyelitis.
poliomielítico, ca adj. Poliomyelitic.
— M. y f. Person affected with poliomyelitis.
polipasto m. [Hoisting] tackle, rigging (poleas).
polipéptido m. QUÍM. Polypeptide.
polípero m. ZOOL. Polypary.
polipétalo, la adj. Polypetalous.
pólipo m. ZOOL. Polyp. || MED. Polypus, polyp.
polisacárido m. QUÍM. Polysaccharide.
polisílabo, ba o **polisilábico, ca** adj. GRAM. Polysyllabic, polysyllabical.
— M. Polysyllable.
polisón m. Crinoline (de faldas).
polispasto m. [Hoisting] tackle, rigging (poleas).
polissoir m. Nail polisher (para las uñas).
polista m. Polo player.
polisurco adj. AGR. Having many furrows.
politburó m. Politburo.
politécnico, ca adj. Polytechnic, polytechnical. || *Escuela politécnica*, polytechnic [school].
— M. Polytechnician.
politeísmo m. Polytheism.
politeísta adj. Polytheistic.
— M. y f. Polytheist.
política f. Politics (arte de gobernar): *dedicarse a la política*, to devote o.s. to politics; *la política partidista*, party politics; *meterse en política*, to get mixed up in politics. || Policy (manera de obrar): *política exterior, agraria*, foreign, agricultural policy; *política hábil*, skilful policy; *política de buena vecindad*, good neighbour policy.
politicastro, tra m. y f. Petty politician, politicaster.
político, ca adj. Political: *partido político*, political party. || Courteous, polite (cortés). || Politic, tactful, wary (prudente). || -in-law (pariente): *padre político*, father-in-law; *hermana política*, sister-in-law; *hija política*, daughter-in-law. || By marriage (para tíos, primos y sobrinos): *es pariente político suyo*, he is a relative of his by marriage. || — *Economía política*, economics. || *Por parte política*, by marriage.
— M. Politician, statesman.
politicón, ona adj. Keenly interested in politics. || Ceremonious, obsequious (ceremonioso).
— M. y f. Person who is keenly interested in politics. || Ceremonious person.
politiquear v. intr. FAM. To play at politics, to dabble in politics (interesarse superficialmente). | To job (con fines deshonestos).
politiqueo m. o **politiquería** f. FAM. Dabbling in politics (interés superficial). | Political jobbery (corrupción).
politización f. Politization.
politizar v. tr. To politicize.
polivalencia f. QUÍM. Polyvalence. || FIG. Versatility.
polivalente adj. QUÍM. Polyvalent, multivalent. || FIG. Multivalent, versatile.
polivinilo m. Polyvinyl.
póliza f. Policy (de seguros): *suscribir, rescindir una póliza*, to take out, to cancel a policy. || Contract (contrato). || Stamp (sello de impuesto). || Papers, *pl.* (de mercancías). || *Póliza adicional*, additional clause (seguro).
polizón m. Stowaway (en un buque).
polizonte m. FAM. Cop, bobby (policía).
poljé m. GEOL. Polje (depresión).
polo m. Pole: *polo Norte, Sur*, North, South Pole. || ELECTR. Pole: *polo negativo, positivo*, negative, positive pole. || Popular Andalusian tune (canto). || Iced lolly [U.S., eskimo pie] (helado). || Sportshirt (camisa). || Polo (juego). || FIG. Pole (término opuesto). | Pole, focus (centro). | Zone, area: *polo de desarrollo*, development area. || — *Polo acuático*, water polo. || FIG. *Ser el polo opuesto de*, to be the complete opposite of. | *Ser polos opuestos*, to be poles apart.
polola f. *Amer.* FAM. Flirt (muchacha coqueta).
pololear v. tr. *Amer.* To annoy (molestar). | To court (requebrar).
— V. intr. To flirt.
pololos m. pl. Bloomers.
polonés, esa adj. (P.us.). Polish.
— M. y f. (P.us.). Pole. || — F. MÚS. Polonaise.
Polonia n. pr. f. GEOGR. Poland.
polonio m. QUÍM. Polonium.
poltrón, ona adj. Lazy, idle.
— F. Easy chair (silla poltrona).
poltronear v. intr. FAM. To slack, to idle.
poltronería f. Laziness, idleness.
polución f. Pollution.

poluto, ta adj. Stained, soiled (manchado).
Pólux n. pr. m. MIT. Pollux.
polvareda f. Dust cloud, cloud of dust: *levantar una polvareda*, to raise a dust cloud. || FIG. Storm, to-do (escándalo).
polvera f. [Powder] compact, powder box.
polvero m. *Amer.* Dust cloud, cloud of dust (polvareda). | Handkerchief (pañuelo).
polvo m. Dust (de la tierra). || Dust (suciedad): *hacer* or *levantar polvo*, to raise dust. || Powder (medicina, química, cocina). || Pinch (porción pequeña). || FIG. Remains, *pl.* (cenizas de los muertos). || POP. Screw. || — Pl. Powder, *sing.* (cosmético): *polvos de talco*, talcum powder; *polvos de arroz*, rice *o* face powder. || — *Café en polvo*, instant coffee. || *Convertirse en polvo*, to turn to dust. || *En polvo*, powdered: *chocolate en polvo*, powdered chocolate; *leche en polvo*, powdered milk. || FIG. y FAM. *Estar hecho polvo*, to be worn out, to be exhausted (cansado), to be depressed (deprimido). | *Hacer polvo*, to annihilate (vencer), to pulverize, to beat to a pulp (pegar), to smash to smithereens (hacer añicos), to reduce to dust (destruir), to wear out, to exhaust (dejar sin fuerzas), to depress (deprimir), to ruin: *tu decisión ha hecho polvo todos mis proyectos*, your decision has ruined all my plans. | *Hacerse polvo*, to be ruined (estropearse), to smash to smithereens (hacerse añicos). | *Hacerse polvo la vista*, to ruin one's sight: *con tanto trabajo la vista se le ha hecho polvo*, so much work has ruined his sight. | *Limpio de polvo y paja*, clear, net (precio y sueldo). || *Nieve en polvo*, powdery snow. || *Oro en polvo*, gold dust. || FIG. *Morder el polvo*, to bite the dust. || *Polvo cósmico*, cosmic dust. || *Polvo de carbón*, coal dust. || FIG. y FAM. *Polvos de la Madre Celestina*, magical cure-all. || *Ponerse polvos*, to powder one's face. || *Quitar el polvo*, to dust. || FIG. *Reducir a polvo*, to reduce to dust. | *Sacudir el polvo a uno*, V. SACUDIR. || *Tabaco en polvo*, snuff.
pólvora f. Gunpowder, powder (explosivo). || Fireworks, *pl.* (pirotecnia). || FIG. Bad temper (mal genio). | Vivacity, liveliness (vivacidad). || — *Algodón pólvora*, guncotton. || *Correr la pólvora*, to perform a fantasia. || *Fábrica de pólvora y explosivos*, gunpowder factory. || FIG. y FAM. *Gastar la pólvora en salvas*, to waste one's efforts *o* one's ammunition. | *Has descubierto la pólvora*, and Queen Ann's dead. | *No ha inventado la pólvora*, he didn't invent gunpowder, he's as thick as two short planks [U.S., he doesn't know enough to come in out of the rain]. | *Propagarse como un reguero de pólvora*, to spread like wildfire.
polvoriento, ta adj. Dusty: *cuarto polvoriento*, dusty room; *carretera polvorienta*, dusty road.
polvorilla m. y f. FAM. *Ser un* or *una polvorilla*, to be touchy *o* quick-tempered.
polvorín m. Very fine gunpowder (explosivo). || Powder flask (frasco). || Powder magazine, gunpowder arsenal (almacén de pólvora). || FIG. Spitfire (persona de genio vivo). | Powder keg: *este país es un polvorín*, this country is like a powder keg. || *Amer.* Tic (garrapata).
polvorista m. Firework maker (de fuegos artificiales). || Gunpowder maker (de explosivos).
polvorón m. Very dry Spanish sweet of a floury consistency (pastelillo).
polvoroso, sa adj. (P.us.). Dusty.
polvoso, sa adj. *Amer.* Dusty.
polla f. Pullet, young hen (gallina joven). || Stake (juegos). || Bet (en las carreras). || FIG. y FAM. Girl, lass (muchacha). || POP. Prick (miembro viril). || *Amer.* Horse race (carrera de caballos). || — ZOOL. *Polla cebada*, fattened chicken. | *Polla de agua*, marsh hen, water hen, moorhen.
pollada f. Brood (de una gallina).
pollastre m. Chick, chicken (pollo). || FIG. y FAM. Kid, youngster (joven).
pollastro, tra m. y f. Young cock (macho), young hen (hembra). || FIG. y FAM. Kid, youngster (joven). || — M. FIG. y FAM. Sly old fox (persona astuta).
pollear v. intr. FAM. To become *o* to get interested in girls *o* in the opposite sex: *mi hijo empieza ya a pollear*, my son is already beginning to get interested in girls. | To act like a youngster (una persona mayor).
pollera f. Baby walker (para niños). || Henhouse (gallinero). || Chicken coop (caja de pollos). || Petticoat (falda interior). || *Amer.* Skirt (falda).
pollería f. Poultry shop, poulterer's (tienda).
pollero, ra m. y f. Poulterer, poultry seller.
pollerón m. *Amer.* Riding skirt.
pollino, na m. y f. Young ass, young donkey.
pollito, ta m. y f. FIG. y FAM. Kid, youngster. || Chick (pollo), young pullet (polla).
pollo m. Chick (cría de la gallina al nacer). || Chicken (ya más crecido): *pollo asado*, roast chicken. || Young (de las aves). || POP. Spit (gargajo). | Frog [in the throat]. || FIG. y FAM. Boy, kid, youngster (hasta los 15 años), boy, young man (después). | Chap, fellow (individuo). || — Pl. FIG. y FAM. Young men. || — FAM. *Pollo pera*, dandy, spiv [U.S., dude] (lechuguino). || *Pollo tomatero*, tender young fryer.
polluelo m. Chicken, chick.
pomáceo, a adj. BOT. Pomaceous.
pomada f. Ointment (medicina). || Pomade (cosmético).
pomar m. Orchard (de árboles frutales). || Apple orchard (manzanar).
pomelo m. BOT. Grapefruit (fruta). | Grapefruit tree (árbol).
pómez adj. f. *Piedra pómez*, pumice stone.
pomo m. Pommel (de espada, de bastón). || Knob (de puerta). || Flagon (licores). || Bottle of perfume, scent bottle (frasco).
pompa f. Pomp (esplendor): *con gran pompa*, with great pomp. || Display (ostentación). || Bubble: *pompa de jabón*, soap bubble. || Billow, puff (en la ropa). || Spread of a peacock's tail (del pavo real). || MAR. Pump (bomba). || — Pl. FIG. Pomps (vanidades). || — FIG. *Hacer pompa de*, to make a show of (ostentar). || *Pompas fúnebres*, funeral (ceremonia), undertaker's, funeral director's (funeraria).
Pompeya n. pr. GEOGR. Pompeii.
pompeyano, na adj./s. Pompeian.
Pompeyo n. pr. m. Pompey (el Magno). || Pompeius (Sexto).
pompi m. FAM. Bottom, backside.
pomposamente adv. Pompously (con arrogancia). || With great pomp, splendidly.
pomposidad f. Pomp, display, splendour. || Pomposity (de una persona).
pomposo, sa adj. Pompous (persona). || Splendid, magnificent, sumptuous.
pómulo m. ANAT. Cheekbone (hueso). | Cheek (mejilla).
poncha f. *Amer.* Blanket (manta).
ponchada f. *Amer.* Pile, great quantity, lot.
ponche m. Punch [drink].
ponchera f. Punch bowl.
poncho m. *Amer.* Poncho (prenda de vestir). || *Amer.* FAM. *Estar a poncho*, to be in the dark (estar pez).
ponderable adj. Praiseworthy (elogiable). || Ponderable (que se puede pesar).
ponderación f. Weighing, pondering, deliberation (consideración). || Deliberation, calm: *habla con ponderación*, he speaks with deliberation. || Exaggerated *o* excessive praise, eulogy (encarecimiento). || Balance (equilibrio). || Weighing (acción de pesar). || *Estar por encima de toda ponderación*, to be above praise, to be inestimable, to be too good for words.
ponderadamente adv. Measuredly, judiciously.
ponderado, da adj. Measured (cosa). || Prudent, tactful (persona). || Calm, steady, well-balanced (mentalidad).
ponderar v. tr. To weigh up, to ponder over, to deliberate on, to consider (examinar). || To balance (equilibrar). || To speak highly of, to praise highly (elogiar): *ponderar un libro*, to speak highly of a book. || To weigh (sopesar).
ponderativo, va adj. Excessive (que encarece). || Thoughtful, meditative (reflexivo). || Deliberative. || Eulogistic, highly favourable (elogioso).
ponedero m. Nest box.
ponedora adj. f. Egg-laying, laying (gallina).
ponencia f. Position of reporter *o* of rapporteur (cargo). || Report (informe). || Rapporteur (ponente). || JUR. Reporter.
ponente adj. Reporting.
— M. JUR. Reporter. || Rapporteur (en una conferencia).
poner* v. tr. To put: *pon este libro en la mesa*, put this book on the table; *estaría mejor poner este cuadro aquí*, it would be better to put this painting here. || To place (colocar). || To set: *pon derecha la lámpara*, set the lamp straight. || To put in, to drive in (un clavo). || To set, to lay (disponer): *poner la mesa*, to set the table. || To put on (ropa): *poner un abrigo a un niño*, to put a coat on a child, to put a child's coat on. || To put: *poner dinero en la caja de ahorros*, to put money in the savings bank. || To put, to invest (invertir dinero). || To contribute, to give, to put (dar dinero). || To stake, to bet, to put (en el juego). || To bet (apostar): *pongo diez pesetas a que lo hago*, I bet ten pesetas that I do it. || MAT. To put down (una cifra). || To put (inscribir): *poner un nombre en una lista*, to put a name on a list. || To translate, to put (escribir): *puse la frase en francés*, I translated the sentence into French. || To send (enviar): *le puse un telegrama, una carta*, I sent him a telegram, a letter. || To send, to put: *poner a un niño interno*, to send a child to a boarding school, to put a child in a boarding school. || To make (con adjetivos): *poner triste, rojo*, to make sad, red. || To state (enunciar): *poner sus condiciones*, to state one's conditions. || To raise (objeciones). || To cause, to provoke (causar, provocar). || To put, to place, to leave, to get: *eso me puso en un apuro*, it put me in a difficult situation, it got me into a fix. || To impose (un impuesto). || To give (una multa). || To give, to assign (señalar un trabajo). || To pose, to raise, to set (un problema). || To suppose, to say (suponer): *pongamos que no dije nada*, let us suppose that I said nothing. || To take (tardar): *puso dos horas en venir*, he took two hours coming, it took him two hours to come. || To take, to exercise: *poner gran cuidado en*, to take great care to. || To appoint, to make (nombrar para un puesto): *a Juan lo han puesto de secretario*, they have appointed John secretary. || To give, to call (un nombre, un mote). || To call (calificar): *poner a alguien de embustero*, to call s.o.

a liar. || To put, to expose: *poner en peligro*, to put in danger, to expose to danger. || To get, to take (llevar): *el avión te pone en Madrid en una hora*, the plane will get you to Madrid in an hour. || To fit up, to equip (amueblar una casa). || To open, to set up (abrir una tienda, etc.). || To install: *poner el gas*, to install gas. || To switch on, to turn on, to put on (la radio, la televisión). || To show, to put on (una película): *ponen esta película en el cine Médicis*, they are showing this film in the Médicis cinema. || To put on (en el teatro). || To connect, to put through (*con*, to) [poner al habla por teléfono]. || To set, to adjust (un reloj en hora). || To lay (las gallinas). || — *Ir muy bien puesto*, to be very well dressed. || *Llevar puesto*, to wear. || *¿Me puede usted poner con X?*, may I speak to X, please?, can you put me through to X, please? || *Poner a asar la carne*, to put the meat on to roast. || *Poner a buen recaudo*, to put in safekeeping (a salvo). || *Poner a fuego y a sangre*, to put to fire and sword. || *Poner al día*, to bring up to date. || *Poner a mal tiempo buena cara*, to keep a stiff upper lip, to keep one's chin up. || *Poner a prueba*, v. PRUEBA. || *Poner a punto*, v. PUNTO. || *Poner a* or *de un lado*, to put on one side. || *Poner a secar la ropa*, to put the washing out to dry. || *Poner a uno a contribución*, to make s.o. contribute. || FIG. *Poner a uno como un trapo*, v. TRAPO. | *Poner a uno de vuelta y media*, to call s.o. all the names under the sun. || *Poner a votación*, to put to the *o* a vote. || *Poner bien a uno*, to praise s.o. || FIG. *Poner buena cara a*, v. CARA. || *Poner cara de*, v. CARA. || *Poner casa*, to move [into a house] (para uno mismo), to give a house to (para otra persona). || *Poner ceño*, to frown. || *Poner colorado a uno*, to make s.o. blush. || FIG. y FAM. *Poner como nuevo*, to make as good as new. || *Poner cuidado en*, to be careful *o* to take care in. || *Poner de comer*, to feed. || *Poner de mal humor*, to put in a bad mood. || *Poner de nombre*, to name, to call: *mis padres me pusieron de nombre Miguel*, my parents named me Michael. || *Poner de su bolsillo*, to put in [money] out of one's own pocket. || *Poner de su lado a uno*, to put s.o. on one's side, to win s.o. over. || *Poner de su parte* or *de su lado*, to do one's bit. || *Poner en claro*, to clarify, to make clear: *poner en claro un asunto*, to clarify a matter. || *Poner en condiciones de*, to put in a position to, to enable to. || *Poner en duda*, to doubt, to question (dudar), to put in doubt (poner en tela de juicio). || *Poner en ejecución* or *en práctica*, to put into practice. || *Poner en guardia a uno*, to put s.o. on his guard. || *Poner en la calle*, to throw out. || *Poner en limpio*, to make a fair copy of (un escrito), to clarify, to clear up (un asunto). || *Poner en pie*, to set up. || *Poner en tela de juicio*, to put in doubt, to put in question. || *Poner entre la espada y la pared*, to put between the devil and the deep blue sea (lío). || *Poner en venta*, to put up for sale. || *Poner los ojos en*, to set eyes on. || *Poner los pelos de punta*, to make s.o.'s hair stand on end. || *Poner mal a uno*, to illtreat s.o. (maltratar), to speak ill of s.o. (hablar mal). || *Poner mala cara*, to be sulky (*a uno*, with s.o.), to sulk (*a una cosa*, about sth.). || *Poner malo a uno*, to make s.o. ill. || *Poner manos a la obra*, to set to work, to start work. || *Poner música a*, to set to music: *poner música a versos*, to set verse to music. || FIG. *Poner por las nubes*, to praise to the skies. || *Poner por testigo a*, to call to witness, to take to witness. || *Poner término a*, to put an end to. || *Poner tierra por medio*, to make o.s. scarce. || *Poniendo que*, supposing that. || *¿Qué ponen en el cine hoy?* what's on at the pictures today.
— V. pr. To place o.s., to put o.s. (colocarse). || To become, to get (volverse): *ponerse furioso*, to become furious. || To turn (colores): *ponerse colorado*, to turn red. || To dress, to wear (vestirse): *ponerse de azul*, to dress in blue, to wear blue. || To put on (para abrigarse): *¡ponte un abrigo!*, put on a coat! || To put on (cosméticos). || To set (los astros). || To get down to: *no es que sea un trabajo difícil, pero hay que ponerse*, it is not that it is difficult work, it is just a case of getting down to it. || To bet (apostar): *me pongo contigo a que termino este trabajo*, I bet you I finish this work. || To be, to arrive (llegar): *en media hora nos ponemos en tu casa*, we shall be at your house in half an hour. || To take a job: *ponerse de chófer*, to take a job as a chauffeur. || To point (un perro). || To land (avión), to light, to alight (aves). || — *¡No se ponga así!*, don't be like that! || *Ponerse a*, to start: *se puso a llorar*, he started to cry. || *Ponerse a bien con alguien*, to get on good terms with s.o. || *Ponerse a cubierto*, to get under cover. || *Ponerse a dieta*, to put o.s. on a diet. || *Ponerse al corriente*, to find out (enterarse), to keep up to date (mantenerse al día). || *Ponerse al teléfono*, to answer the telephone (al descolgar el aparato), to come to the phone (después de descolgado). || *Ponerse a régimen*, to put o.s. on a diet. || *Ponerse a servir*, to get a job as a servant, to go into service. || *Ponerse bueno*, to recover. || *Ponerse cómodo* or *a sus anchas*, to make o.s. at home *o* comfortable. || FAM. *Ponerse como el quico*, v. QUICO. || *Ponerse de acuerdo*, to come to an agreement, to agree. || *Ponerse de grasa, de lodo hasta los pelos*, to get grease, mud all over o.s. || *Ponerse delante*, to get in the way (estorbar). || *Ponerse de largo*, v. LARGO. || *Ponerse de luto*, to go into mourning. || *Ponerse de mal en peor*, to go from bad to worse. || *Ponerse de pie*, to stand [up]. || FAM. *Ponerse de tiros largos*, to put on one's Sunday best, to dress up. || *Ponerse en camino*, to set out, to start out. || *Ponerse en contacto* or *en relación con*, to get in touch with, to contact. || *Ponerse en contra de*, to oppose. || *Ponerse en el lugar de uno*, to put o.s. in s.o.'s place. || *Ponerse enfermo*, to fall ill. || *Ponerse en filas*, to line up to form ranks (alinearse). || *Ponerse guapo*, to smarten o.s. up. || *Amer.* FAM. *Ponérsela*, to get stoned *o* sloshed (emborracharse). || *Ponerse malo*, to fall ill, to be ill. || *Ponerse trágico*, to get melodramatic (una persona), to become a tragedy (una cosa).

poney m. Pony (caballo).

poniente m. West (oeste). || West wind (viento).

pontaje o **pontazgo** m. Bridge toll.

pontear v. tr. To make a bridge over.

pontificado m. Pontificate.

pontifical adj. Pontifical.
— M. Pontifical (libro). || Pontificals, *pl.* (ornamentos). || FIG. *De pontifical*, in pontifical dress (con ornamentos litúrgicos de obispo), in one's Sunday best (bien vestido).

pontificar v. intr. To pontificate.

pontífice m. REL. Pontiff. || HIST. Pontifex (en Roma). || *El Sumo Pontífice*, the Sovereign Pontiff.

pontificio, cia adj. Pontifical.

pontón m. MAR. Lighter, pontoon (buque). | Pontoon (puente). || Float (de un avión).

pontonero m. MIL. Pontoneer, pontonier.

ponzoña f. Venom, poison (de los animales). || Poison (de los vegetales o minerales). || FIG. Poison: *la ponzoña de una doctrina mala*, the poison of an evil doctrine. | Venom (malevolencia).

ponzoñoso, sa adj. Poisonous.

pool m. COM. Pool.

popa f. MAR. Stern. || — *A popa*, astern, abaft. || FIG. *De popa a proa*, from top to bottom, through and through. | *Todo va viento en popa*, everything is going smoothly, everything is going well. | *Vamos viento en popa*, we are in luck, it is all systems go, the wind is with us.

popayaneso, sa o **popayanense** adj. [Of *o* from] Popayán (Colombia).
— M. y f. Native *o* inhabitant of Popayán.

pope m. Pope (sacerdote ruso).

popelín m. o **popelina** f. Poplin (tela).

popí m. *Amer.* Manioc (mandioca).

poplíteo, a adj. ANAT. Popliteal.

popote m. *Amer.* Straw (paja). || FIG. *Estar hecho un popote*, to be as thin as a rake.

populachería f. Cheap popularity.

populachero, ra adj. Cheap (barato). || Vulgar, common (vulgar). || Popular: *drama populachero*, popular drama.

populacho m. Populace, masses, *pl.*, plebs, *pl.*

popular adj. Popular: *un artista popular*, a popular artist. || Of the people: *la educación popular*, the education of the people. || Folk, popular (música, etc.). || Colloquial (lenguaje). || *República Popular*, People's Republic.

popularidad f. Popularity.

popularización f. Popularization.

popularizar v. intr. To popularize.
— V. pr. To become popular.

populazo m. Populace, masses, *pl.*, plebs, *pl.*

populista m. y f. Populist.

populoso, sa adj. Populous.

popurrí m. MÚS. Potpourri.

poquedad f. Smallness, meagreness, paucity: *la poquedad de sus recursos*, the meagreness of his resources. || Timidity (timidez). || Trifle (nadería).

póquer m. V. PÓKER.

poquitín m. FAM. A tiny little bit.

poquito, ta adj. A little bit of. || — Pl. A few.
— Adv. A little, a bit.
— M. A little bit. || — *A poquito(s)*, little by little, bit by bit. || *Poquito a poco*, little by little.

por prep.

> **1.** Causa, medio, agente. — **2.** Destino, designio. — **3.** Sitio. — **4.** Tiempo. — **5.** Con un infinitivo. — **6.** Modo. — **7.** Distributiva. — **8.** Sentidos diversos. — **9.** Locuciones.

1. CAUSA, MEDIO, AGENTE. — By (agente): *la carta fue escrita por él*, the letter was written by him. || Because of (motivo): *por su mucha edad no trabaja*, he does not work because of his old age. || From, out of, because of: *por necesidad*, out of necessity. || For: *por miedo a*, for fear of. || For, because of: *lo han despedido por perezoso*, he was dismissed for laziness *o* because of his laziness. || About: *inquieto por*, worried about. || Because (seguido de un participio pasado): *cayó por herido*, he fell because he was wounded. || — *Por causa tuya*, because of you, thanks to you. || *Por tu culpa he perdido el tren*, I missed the train because of you *o* thanks to you, you made me miss the train.

2. DESTINO, DESIGNIO. — For: *lo hice por ti*, I did it for you; *iré por ti*, I'll go for you. || To: *lo hice por ayudarte*, I did it to help you. || For, as: *tomar por jefe, por esposa*, to take for one's chief, for one's wife. || In: *interesarse por alguien*, to be interested in s.o. || *Lo digo por ti*, I'm telling you for your own sake, I'm only thinking of you.
3. SITIO. — Via, by: *ir a Madrid por Burgos*, to go to Madrid via Burgos. || Through: *al pasar por Madrid*, passing through Madrid; *pasamos por el túnel*, we went through the tunnel. || On, along: *por el lado derecho*, on the right side. || At: *atravesó la frontera por Irún*, he crossed the frontier at Irún. || Towards, around (cerca de): *eso está por Pamplona*, that is towards Pamplona. || Throughout: *por toda la ciudad*, throughout the whole town. || In, along, through: *pasearse por la calle*, to walk in the street. || In: *por mi barrio*, in my district.
4. TIEMPO. — About, towards (fecha aproximada): *vendré por el 5 de marzo*, I shall come about the 5th of March. || At (fecha): *llegó por Navidad*, he arrived at Christmas. || On: *llegó por San Juan*, he arrived on St John's Day. || In, during: *por el verano, por la mañana*, in *o* during the summer, the morning. || For (plazo): *vendré por tres días*, I shall come for three days. || — *Por ahora*, for the time being, for the moment. || *Por la noche*, in *o* during the night, at night.
5. CON UN INFINITIVO. — In order to, so as to (con vistas a): *por no equivocarse*, in order not to make a mistake. || For, because (a causa de): *le han castigado por haber mentido*, they punished him for having lied *o* for lying *o* because he had lied. || Because, as, since: *no vine por tener mucho trabajo*, I did not come because I had a lot of work; *por no saber qué hacer, me fui*, as I did not know what to do, I went away. || In: *por hacer una fortuna, perdió su dignidad*, in making a fortune he lost his dignity. || To be [with past participle] (sin): *todo está aún por hacer*, everything is still to be done.
6. MODO. — By: *por señas*, by signs; *viajar por tren*, to travel by train. || By, because of: *la conocí por el sombrero*, I recognized her by her hat. || By, according to (conforme): *juzgar por*, to judge by. || By: *amable por naturaleza*, kind by nature. || In: *por escrito*, in writing; *por orden alfabético*, in alphabetical order; *cortado por la mitad*, cut in half.
7. DISTRIBUTIVA. — Per, for each: *a diez pesetas por persona*, ten pesetas per person. || By the: *comprar por metros, por docenas, por cientos*, to buy by the metre, by the dozen, by the hundred. || A, per: *una libra por hora*, a pound an hour; *cien kilómetros por hora*, a hundred kilometres per hour *o* an hour.
8. SENTIDOS DIVERSOS. — For, in exchange for: *trocar una cosa por otra*, to swap one thing for another. || For, instead of (en vez de): *pagar por otro*, to pay for s.o. else. || On behalf of (en nombre de). || For: *tener un tugurio por casa*, to have a slum for a house. || Out of, through, for (a favor de). || For (precio): *por cien pesetas*, for a hundred pesetas. || For (con ir, mandar, etc.): *vino por fósforos*, he came for matches; *lo mandé por vino*, I sent him for wine. || As for, for (en cuanto a): *por lo que dijiste ya veremos*, as for what you said, we shall see about that later. || As for, for, as far as: *por mí*, as for me, for my part, as far as I am concerned. || Times (multiplicación): *tres por cuatro, doce*, three times four, twelve. || By (superficie): *dos metros por cuatro*, two metres by four. || For: *diez ciudadanos por cada labrador*, ten city dwellers for each agricultural worker.
9. LOCUCIONES. — *Agradecer por*, to thank for. || *Empezar por*, to start by (con verbo): *empezó por reírse*, he started by laughing; to start with (persona): *empezaron por su padre*, they started with his father. || *Estar por*, V. ESTAR. || *Ir por*, to go and fetch, to go for. || *Juzgar a uno por las apariencias*, to judge s.o. by appearances. || *Por allá*, over there, that way. || *Por ciento*, percent: *un interés del tres por ciento*, three percent interest. || *Por cierto*, V. CIERTO. || *Por cuanto*, since, in as much as. || *¡Por Dios!*, V. DIOS. ||. *Por donde*, by where; wherever: *por donde voy los encuentro*, wherever I go I meet them; from which (de lo cual). || *Por ejemplo*, for instance, for example (verbigracia), as an example: *tomar a uno por ejemplo*, to take s.o. as an example. || *Por el honor*, on one's honour. || *Por el mundo*, all over the world. || *Por entre*, through, between. || *Por eso* or *por eso mismo*, that is why, for that reason: *por eso lo hago* or *lo hago por eso*, that is why I do it, I do it for that reason; exactly: *pero él no viene* — *¡Por eso!*, but he is not coming. — Exactly! || *Por eso es por lo que*, that is why. || *Por esta vez*, this time. || *Por favor*, please. || *Por fuera*, V. FUERA. || *Por lo cual*, [and] so, [and] that is why, [and] that is the reason. || *Por lo largo y por lo ancho*, to and fro. || *Por lo menos*, at least. || *Por lo... que*, so (con adjetivo): *no pude moverlo por lo pesado que era*, he was so heavy that I could not move him. || *Por mandato de*, on the orders of. || *Por más, por mucho, por muy que*, however much, no matter how much (V. OBSERV.) || *Por medio de*, V. MEDIO. || *Por menos que...*, however little... || *Por ... que*, however ...: *por buena que sea*, however good she is *o* she may be; *por mucha prisa que tenga*, however much of a hurry he is in *o* he may be in; *por poco que sea*, however little it is *o* it may be. || *Por que*, because [*que*, in this sense, has no written accent]. || *Por qué*, why: *no sé por qué viene tan a menudo*, I don't know why he comes so often. || *Por si acaso*, just in case, in case: *por si acaso vienes*, just in case you come. || *Por sí mismo*, by himself. || *Por sí solo*, all by himself, all on his own. || *Por tanto*, [and] so. || *Por uno que calla, diez gritan*, for every one who keeps quiet there are ten who shout. || *Por un sí o por un no*, for nothing, over nothing. || *Preguntar por*, V. PREGUNTAR.

— OBSERV. Hay que distinguir tres casos en la traducción de *por más, por mucho, por muy que:*
1. — *Con un adjetivo: por más* or *por muy guapa que es* or *sea*, however pretty *o* no matter how pretty she is.
2. — *Con un verbo: por más* or *por mucho que trabaje*, however much *o* no matter how much he works.
3. — *Con un sustantivo: por más libros que tenga, no sabe nada*, however many *o* no matter how many books he has, he knows nothing: *por mucho dinero que tenga*, however much *o* no matter how much money he has.

porcachón, ona o **porcallón, ona** adj. FAM. Filthy, dirty.
— M. y f. FAM. Pig.
porcelana f. Porcelain, china. || Chinaware, china (vajilla).
porcentaje m. Percentage: *le dan cierto porcentaje sobre las ventas*, he is given a certain percentage of what he sells. || Rate (índice): *porcentaje de modulación*, modulation rate. || Ratio (proporción, relación).
porcentual adj. Percentage.
porcino, na adj. Porcine, pig, of *o* relating to pigs. || *Pan porcino*, sowbread (planta).
— M. Small pig (cochinillo). || — Pl. Swine, pigs (ganado porcino).
porción f. Share, part, portion: *la porción de cada uno*, each person's share. || Part, portion: *le dio una porción de lo que tenía*, he gave him part of what he had. || Piece, portion: *dame una porción de este pastel*, give me a piece of this cake. || Portion (en una comunidad). || Sum (de dinero). || FIG. Quantity: *una porción reducida de frutas*, a small quantity of fruit. | Lot, crowd, number: *llegó una porción de gente*, a crowd of people arrived.
porcionero, ra o **porcionista** adj./s. Participant.
porcuno, na adj. Porcine, pig.
— M. pl. Pigs.
porche m. Arcade (soportal). || Porch (de una casa). || Porch (atrio).
pordiosear v. intr. To beg.
pordioseo m. o **pordiosería** f. Begging.
pordiosero, ra adj. Begging.
— M. y f. Beggar.
porfía f. Persistence (persistencia). || Obstinacy, stubbornness (obstinación). || Dispute, struggle (lucha). || *A porfía*, emulously, in competition.
porfiado, da o **porfiador, ra** adj. Persistent (persistente). || Obstinate, stubborn (obstinado): *un representante porfiado*, a stubborn salesman. || Keen: *una discusión porfiada*, a keen argument. || Fierce, bitter (enemigo).
— M. y f. Obstinate person.
porfiar v. intr. To persist (continuar): *porfiar en negar*, to persist in denying. || To persist in trying (intentar porfiadamente). || To argue stubbornly (discutir obstinadamente). || To wrangle (disputarse). || To vie (rivalizar). || — *Porfiar en que*, to insist on (querer), to insist that (afirmar). || *Porfiar sobre* or *acerca de*, to wrangle over.
pórfido m. MIN. Porphyry.
porfírico, ca o **porfídico, ca** adj. MIN. Porphyritic.
pórfiro m. MIN. Porphyry.
pormenor m. Detail [not to be confused with *por menor*, in detail]: *los pormenores de un asunto*, the details of a subject.
pormenorizar v. tr. To give a detailed account of, to detail, to go into the details of.
— V. intr. To go into detail.
pornografía f. Pornography.
pornográfico, ca adj. Pornographic.
pornógrafo m. Pornographer.
poro m. Pore (en la piel). || *Amer.* Maté gourd.
porongo m. *Amer.* Gourd (calabaza).
pororó m. *Amer.* Popcorn (roseta de maíz).
porosidad f. Porosity, porousness.
poroso, sa adj. Porous.
porotada f. *Amer.* CULIN. Dish of beans.
porotal m. *Amer.* Beanfield (plantación). || *Amer.* FIG. *Un porotal de*, a lot of.
poroto m. *Amer.* Bean (judía, frijol). | Food (comida).
porque conj. Because (motivo): *no vino porque no quiso*, he did not come because he did not want to. || So that (para que): *porque viniese*, so that he came. || *Porque no* or *porque sí*, just because (para negar o afirmar tajantemente).
porqué m. Reason, the whys and the wherefores, *pl.* (motivo): *saber el porqué de cada cosa*, to know the whys and the wherefores of *o* the reason for everything.
porquería f. FAM. Filth (suciedad). | Rubbish (basura, cosa de poco valor): *quítame esta porquería*, take this rubbish away; *este reloj es una porquería*, this watch is rubbish. | Dirty story *o* joke: *siempre cuenta porquerías*, he's always telling dirty stories. | Nastiness (indecencia). | Dirty trick (jugarreta). | Nasty *o* awful

food (comida mala). | Trifle, worthless thing (cosa de poco valor). || — *Esta calle es una porquería*, this street is foul *o* filthy (muy sucia). || *Tu cuarto está hecho una porquería*, your room is like a pigsty.
porqueriza f. Pigsty (pocilga).
porquerizo, za o **porquero, ra** m. y f. Swineherd.
porra f. Club, cudgel, bludgeon (arma). || Baton (de guardia de circulación). || Truncheon (arma de caucho). || TECN. Sledgehammer (de fragua). || Bank (en los juegos de naipes). || Last player (en los juegos de muchachos). || TEATR. Claque. || Fritter (churro de Madrid). || FIG. y FAM. Bore, pest (persona pesada). | Vanity (presunción). || — FAM. *Guardia de la porra*, traffic cop. || FIG. y FAM. *Irse a la porra*, to fall flat (un proyecto), to be ruined (estropearse). | *Mandar a la porra*, to send packing. | *¡Qué porra!*, what a drag *o* a bore! | *¡Vete a la porra!*, go to the devil!, go to blazes!, go to hell!
— Interj. FAM. Damn!
porrada f. Blow (golpe). || Blow with a club (con la porra). || FIG. y FAM. Nonsense, twaddle (necedad). | Pile, heap, loads, *pl.*: *una porrada de cosas*, a pile of *o* loads of things. || FAM. *Una porrada de dinero*, lots *o* loads of money.
porrazo m. Blow. || Bump (golpe, choque). || *Amer.* Pile, heap, loads, *pl.* (montón). || — *De golpe y porrazo*, V. GOLPE. || *Obligar a uno a porrazos a hacer algo*, to bludgeon s.o. into doing sth. || *Pegarse un porrazo contra*, to bump into, to bang into, to crash into: *se pegó un porrazo contra un árbol*, he bumped into a tree.
porrillo m. Mason's hammer (maza de cantero). || FAM. *A porrillo*, by the ton, galore.
porrita f. Bank (en los juegos de naipes).
porro, rra adj. FAM. Dull, stupid, thick (torpe).
— M. FAM. Idiot, dope, fool. | Joint (marihuana).
porrón, ona adj. FAM. Dull, stupid (torpe). || FAM. *A porrones*, by the ton, galore, in abundance.
— M. Wineskin with a long spout. || Earthenware jug (botijo). || Garlic sauce (salsa).
porrudo, da adj. FAM. Dull, stupid.
porta m. MAR. Port, porthole. || TAUR. *A porta gayola*, pass made when the bull enters the ring.
— Adj. f. ANAT. Portal: *vena porta*, portal vein.
portaagujas m. inv. Needle holder.
portaaviones m. inv. Aircraft carrier.
portabandera f. Flag holder (cosa). || Standard bearer, banner bearer, colour bearer (persona).
portabombas m. inv. Bomb carrier.
portabotellas m. inv. Bottle rack.
portacartas m. inv. Briefcase (cartera).
portacruz m. Cross bearer.
portachuelo m. Gorge (entre montañas).
portada f. Façade, front (de casa, de iglesia). || Porch (puerta). || IMPR. Title page (de un libro). | Cover (de una revista). || FIG. Façade (fachada).
portadilla f. IMPR. Half *o* bastard title (anteportada).
portadocumentos m. inv. Briefcase (cartera).
portador, ra adj. Carrying, bearing.
— M. y f. Carrier: *portador de gérmenes*, germ carrier. || — M. COM. Bearer: *pagar al portador*, to pay the bearer; *el portador de la carta*, the bearer of the letter.
portaequipajes m. inv. Boot [U.S., trunk] (en un coche). || Carrier (de bicicleta). || Luggage rack (de tren).
portaestandarte m. Standard bearer (oficial).
portafolio m. *Amer.* Briefcase.
portafusil m. Sling [for a rifle].
portaguión m. MIL. Standard bearer.
portaherramientas m. inv. TECN. Toolholder.
portaje m. Toll (portazgo).
portal m. Entrance hall (zaguán). || Porch (de edificio). || Arcade (soportal). || Crèche, crib (de Navidad).
portalámparas m. inv. Socket [for a bulb].
portalápiz m. Pencil holder.
portalibros m. inv. Book straps, *pl.*
portaligas m. inv. Suspender belt.
portalón m. Monumental gate *o* door (puerta). || MAR. Gangway.
portamaletas m. inv. Boot [*Amer.*, trunk] (de un coche).
portamantas m. inv. Straps (*pl.*) for carrying travelling rugs.
portaminas m. inv. Propelling pencil.
portamonedas m. inv. Purse.
portante m. Amble (del caballo). || FIG. y FAM. *Tomar el portante*, to go, to leave, to make o.s. scarce.
portanuevas m. y f. inv. Bearer of news.
portañica o **portañuela** f. Fly (de los pantalones).
portañola f. MAR. Porthole (porta).
portaobjetos m. inv. Slide (de microscopio).
portaplumas m. inv. Penholder.
portar v. intr. MAR. To stand up to bad weather.
— V. tr. To carry, to bear (llevar).
— V. pr. To behave: *portarse bien*, to behave well, to behave o.s.
portarretrato m. Photograph frame.
portatacos m. inv. Cue rack (en el billar).
portátil adj. Portable.
portaviandas m. inv. Food can [U.S., dinner pail, dinner bucket] (fiambrera).
portaviones m. inv. Aircraft carrier.
portavoz m. Megaphone (bocina). || Spokesman (persona autorizada).
portazgo m. Toll (impuesto).
portazguero m. Tollkeeper.
portazo m. Bang, slam of a door. || — FIG. *Dar a uno un portazo*, to slam the door in s.o.'s face. || *Dar un portazo*, to slam the door. || *Oír un portazo*, to hear a door slam.
porte m. Transport, carriage (transporte). || Carriage transport charges, *pl.* (precio). || Conduct, behaviour [U.S., behavior] (comportamiento). || Bearing (compostura). || Air, appearance (aspecto). || — *Franco de porte*, carriage paid (transporte), post-free, postpaid (correos). || *Porte debido*, carriage forward. || *Porte pagado*, carriage paid (en comercio), postage paid (en correos).
porteador, ra adj./s. Carrier.
portear v. tr. To carry (llevar). || To slam (la puerta).
— V. intr. To slam (una puerta). || *Amer.* To go away (marcharse).
portento m. Marvel, wonder. || *Es un portento de inteligencia*, he is exceptionally intelligent.
portentoso, sa adj. Prodigious, marvellous.
porteño, ña adj. [Of *o* from] Puerto de Santa María [Spain] *o* Buenos Aires [Argentina] *o* Puerto Cortés [Honduras] *o* Valparaíso [Chile] *o* Puerto Barrios [Guatemala].
— M. y f. Native *o* inhabitant of Puerto de Santa María, of Buenos Aires, etc.
porteo m. Transport, carriage.
portería f. Caretaker's lodge, doorman's lodge (habitación). || Caretaker's job, doorman's job (empleo). || REL. Gate house (conventos). || Goal [line] (fútbol).
portero, ra m. y f. Caretaker, janitor (de casa de vivienda). || Doorman, doorkeeper (que vigila). || Concierge (en Francia, España). || — M. DEP. Goalkeeper (guardameta). || — *Portero de estrados*, court usher (de tribunal). || *Portero eléctrico*, interphone, intercom.
— Adj. REL. *Hermano portero*, monk who acts as doorkeeper.
portezuela f. Small door. || Door (de coche).
pórtico m. Portico: *un pórtico griego*, a Greek portico. || Porch: *el pórtico de la Gloria en Santiago de Compostela*, the porch of the Gloria in Santiago de Compostela. || Portal: *los pórticos de la catedral de Chartres*, the portals of Chartres cathedral. || Arcade (soportales). || FIG. Gateway.
portilla f. MAR. Porthole. || Gate [in a field].
portillo m. Opening, gap (de muro). || Chip (de plato). || Small door (puerta pequeña). || Gate (en una muralla). || Wicket (postigo). || Pass (entre montañas). || FIG. Weak spot (punto vulnerable). | Opening (posibilidad).
portland m. Portland cement (cemento).
portón m. Large door. || Hall door (del vestíbulo).
portorriqueño, ña adj./s. Puerto Rican.
portuario, ria adj. Harbour, port, of *o* pertaining to a port. || *Trabajador portuario*, docker.
portuense adj. [Of *o* from] Puerto de Santa María [Spain]. || [Of *o* from] Ostia [Italy].
— M. y f. Native *o* inhabitant of Puerto de Santa María [Spain], native *o* inhabitant of Ostia [Italy].
Portugal n. pr. m. GEOGR. Portugal.
portugués, esa adj./s. Portuguese. || — M. Portuguese (lengua).
portuguesismo m. Portuguese word *o* phrase.
portulano m. MAR. Portolano, portulan (mapa).
porvenir m. Future: *un joven con porvenir*, a young man with a future; *un porvenir espléndido*, a fine future. || — *En el* or *en lo porvenir*, in future (de hoy en adelante), in the future (en el futuro). || *Sin porvenir*, with no future, with no prospects.
pos (en) adj. *En pos de*, behind, after (detrás). || *Ir en pos de*, to be looking for, to pursue.
posada f. Inn (mesón). || Guest house, boarding house (casa de huéspedes), || Home, dwelling (morada). || Hospitality, shelter: *dar posada*, to offer hospitality, to give shelter.
posadeño, ña adj. [Of *o* from] Posadas [Argentina].
— M. y f. Native o inhabitant of Posadas.
posaderas f. pl. FAM. Backside, *sing.*, behind, *sing.*, buttocks (trasero).
posadero, ra m. y f. Landlord, landlady (de casa de huéspedes). || Innkeeper (de mesón).
posar v. intr. To alight, to settle (un pájaro). || To pose, to sit (para foto o pintura). || To put on airs (darse importancia). || To lodge (alojarse).
— V. tr. To put, to lay: *posó su mano sobre mi cabeza*, he put his hand on my head. || To put down (dejar en el suelo, etc.).
— V. pr. To settle (depositarse). || To alight, to settle (un pájaro). || To land (un avión).
— OBSERV. *Posar* is a Gallicism in the sense of *servir de* or *como modelo a un pintor* and of *darse importancia.*
poscomunión f. REL. Post-Communion.
posdata f. Postscript.
pose f. FOT. Exposure (exposición). || Airs, *pl.*, pose, affectation (afectación). || Pose (de un modelo).
— OBSERV. *Pose* is a Gallicism.
poseedor, ra adj. Who possesses.
— M. y f. Owner, possessor: *elia es la poseedora*, she is the possessor. || Holder: *el poseedor de un récord*, the holder of a record.

poseer v. tr. To possess, to have, to own. || To have, to enjoy (disfrutar). || To hold (un récord). || To master, to know perfectly (un idioma, un tema). || To possess (una mujer). || To haunt (obsesionar). — V. pr. To keep o.s. under control, to control o.s.
poseído, da adj. Possessed. || Possessed, overcome (por un afecto, etc.). || Full of o.s. (engreído). || *Está muy poseída de sus conocimientos*, she is very conscious of her knowledge.
— M. y f. Possessed person (por el demonio). || *Gritaba como un poseído*, he was screaming like one possessed.
Poseidón n. pr. m. MIT. Poseidon.
posesión f. Possession, property, ownership (propiedad). || Possession (colonia de un Estado). || Possession (del demonio). || *Amer.* Property, estate (finca rústica). || — Pl. Property, *sing.*, estate, *sing.* || — *Dar posesión de un cargo a uno*, to hand over a post to s.o. || *Estar en posesión de*, to hold: *está en posesión del récord de los 110 metros vallas*, he holds the record for the 110 metres hurdles. || *Toma de posesión*, taking over (en un cargo), investiture (investidura). || *Tomar posesión de*, to take over, to take possession of (una casa), to take up (un cargo).
posesionar v. tr. To hand over, to give possession of. — V. pr. To take possession, to take over. || To seize (apoderarse).
posesivo, va adj./s.m. Possessive.
poseso, sa adj. Possessed: *poseso del demonio*, possessed by the devil.
— M. y f. Possessed person (poseído).
posesor, ra adj./s. V. POSEEDOR.
posesorio, ria adj. JUR. Possessory.
posfecha f. Postdate.
posfechar v. tr. To postdate.
posguerra f. Postwar years, *pl.*, postwar period.
posibilidad f. Possibility. || Opportunity, chance, possibility (oportunidad). || — Pl. Chances, possibilities: *calcular las posibilidades de éxito*, to calculate the chances of success. || *Quizás no tenga la posibilidad de verle*, it may not be possible for me to see him, I may not be able to see him, I may not get a chance to see him.
posibilitar v. tr. To make possible, to facilitate (hacer posible). || To allow, to permit (permitir).
posible adj. Possible: *es posible que venga*, it's possible that he will come; *hacer posible*, to make possible. || — *De ser posible*, if possible. || *En* or *dentro de lo posible*, as far as possible, as much as possible. || *En la medida de lo possible*, as far as possible, insofar as it is possible. || *Hacer todo lo posible para*, to do everything within one's power *o* everything possible to, to do one's best *o* one's utmost to. || *¡No es posible!*, really! (exclamación de disgusto), well I never! (de incredulidad). || *¿Será posible que no te lo haya dicho?*, is it possible that he didn't tell you? || *Si es posible*, if possible, if it is possible. || *Si me es posible*, if I possibly can. || *Tan pronto como sea posible*, as soon as possible.
— M. pl. FAM. Means, resources (fortuna).
posiblemente adv. Possibly. || Probably (probablemente).
posición f. Position, place (sitio). || Position, attitude, posture (postura). || Position, standing, status: *posición social*, social position. || Position: *ocupar una posición honorable*, to occupy an honourable position. || MIL. Position. || — *Entrar en posición*, to position, to line up (cañón). || FIG. *Hallarse en una mala posición*, to be in a bad way.
positivado m. FOT. Printing.
positivismo m. FIL. Positivism. || Realism (realismo).
positivista adj. FIL. Positivist. || Realistic (realista). — M. y f. FIL. Positivist. || Realist.
positivo, va adj./s.m. Positive. || — F. FOT. Positive, [positive] print.
pósito m. Communal granary (granero). || Cooperative.
positón o **positrón** m. Positron (electrón positivo).
posma adj. FAM. Dull, sluggish (lento). | Bothersome, tiresome (latoso). | Nonchalant (sin entusiasmo).
— M. y f. FAM. Dullard, dull person. | Nonchalant person. | Pest, nuisance, bore (persona latosa). || — F. FAM. Dullness (lentitud). | Nuisance (lata).
poso m. Sediment, lees, *pl.*, dregs, *pl.* (de vino u otro líquido). || Grounds, *pl.* (de café). || FIG. Vestige, trace (huella). || *Formar poso*, to settle (líquido).
posología f. Dosage (dosis). || Posology (en terapéutica).
posponer* v. tr. To put in second place, to put behind *o* below, to value less (estimar menos). || To postpone, to put off (diferir). || GRAM. To postpone, to place after. || *Posponer el interés personal al general*, to put the public interest before one's personal interest.
posposición f. Subordination, putting after. || Postponement. || GRAM. Postposition.
posta f. Relay of post horses (de caballos). || Piece (pedazo). || Pellet of buckshot (perdigón). || Stake (envite). || ARQ. Volute. || — Pl. ARQ. Scroll, *sing.* (adorno). || — *A posta*, on purpose, intentionally (adrede). || *Caballo de posta*, relay horse, post horse. || *Silla de posta*, post chaise.
postal adj. Postal. || — *Giro postal*, money order, postal order. || *Paquete postal*, parcel [sent by post]. || *Tarjeta postal*, postcard.
— F. Postcard (tarjeta).
postbalance m. *Venta postbalance*, stocktaking sale [U.S., post-inventory sale].
postcombustión f. TECN. Reheating, afterburning.
postdata f. Postscript.
postdiluviano, na adj. Postdiluvian.
poste m. Pole: *poste telegráfico*, telegraph pole. || Pillar (columna). || Post (estaca). || Picket (para caballos). || TECN. Pylon. || DEP. Post (de una portería). || — FAM. *Más tieso que un poste*, as stiff as a board. || *Poste indicador*, signpost. || FAM. *Quedarse parado como un poste*, to stand dead still.
postema f. MED. Abscess (absceso).
poste restante f. *Amer.* Poste restante [U.S., General delivery] (lista de correos).
postergación f. Postponement, delay (retraso). || Adjournment (aplazamiento oficial). || Passing over (relegación). || Omission (olvido).
postergar v. tr. To postpone, to put off (aplazar). || To adjourn (caso oficial). || To pass over (a un empleado). || To leave on one side (dejar de lado).
posteridad f. Posterity (descendencia).
posterior adj. Posterior, rear, back (trasero). || Subsequent (ulterior). || Later: *su cumpleaños fue posterior al mío*, his birthday was later than mine.
posteriori (a) loc. A posteriori.
posterioridad f. Posteriority. || *Con posterioridad*, later, subsequently.
posteriormente adv. Subsequently, later [on].
postescolar adj. After school (después de la escuela), postgraduate (después de la universidad).
postfijo m. Suffix, postfix (sufijo).
postglacial adj. Postglacial.
postguerra f. Postwar years, *pl.*, postwar period.
postigo m. Shutter (de ventana). || Secret *o* hidden door (puerta falsa). || Door (puerta). || Wicket (puerta abierta en otra mayor). || Gate (de ciudad).
postilla f. MED. Scab (en la piel). || Annotation, note (aclaración).
postillón m. Postilion, postillion (conductor).
postilloso, sa adj. MED. Scabby.
postimpresionismo m. Postimpressionism.
postimpresionista adj./s. Postimpressionist.
postín m. FAM. Airs, *pl.* (presunción). | Elegance. || — FAM. *Darse postín*, to put on airs, to show off, to swank. | *Un traje de mucho postín*, a very chic *o* elegant dress.
postinear v. intr. V. POSTÍN (*darse*).
postinero, ra adj. FAM. Snooty, swanky (presumido). | Chic, elegant, posh (elegante).
postizo, za adj. False: *cabellos postizos*, false hair; *diente postizo*, false tooth. || Artificial: *pierna postiza*, artificial leg. || Detachable (cuello). || Assumed (nombre).
— M. Hairpiece, switch (de pelo).
postmeridiano, na adj. Postmeridian, afternoon.
postnatal adj. Postnatal.
postoperatorio, ria adj. Postoperative.
postor m. Bidder (en una subasta). || *Al mayor* or *mejor postor*, to the highest bidder.
postpalatal adj. Postpalatal.
postración f. Prostration.
postrado, da adj. Prostrate.
postrar v. tr. To prostrate, to overcome: *postrado por la calentura*, prostrated by fever; *postrado por la desgracia*, overcome by unhappiness. || To prostrate, to humiliate (humillar).
— V. pr. To prostrate o.s., to kneel down (arrodillarse). || To weaken (debilitarse). || To be overcome (por las desgracias).
postre adj. Last (postrero).
— M. Dessert, sweet: *tomar de postre fruta*, to have fruit for dessert. || *A los postres*, at the dessert. || — F. *A la postre*, in the end, at last, finally.
postremo, ma adj. Last, ultimate.
postrer adj. m. Last (postrero): *el postrer suspiro*, the last sigh.

— OBSERV. This word is the apocopated form of *postrero*, and is used before masculine singular nouns.

postrero, ra adj. Last: *el día postrero*, the last day.
postrimer adj. Last [apocopated form of *postrimero*].
postrimería f. End [of life, etc.]. || REL. Death. || *En las postrimerías del siglo*, towards *o* at the end of the century.

— OBSERV. This word is mainly used in the plural form.

postrimero, ra adj. Last.
post scriptum m. inv. Postscript (posdata).
postsincronización f. CINEM. Postsynchronization.
postsincronizar v. tr. CINEM. To postsynchronize.
postulación f. Collection [in the streets, for a charity] (colecta). || REL. Postulation.
postulado m. Postulate.
postulador m. REL. Postulator.
postulante, ta m. y f. Postulant, applicant (candidato). || Collector [for a charity] (el que hace una colecta).
postular v. tr. To postulate. || To request, to ask for, to demand: *postular medidas*, to ask for measures. || To apply for (un cargo). || To be a candidate for (ser candidato).
— V. intr. To collect [for charity] (hacer una colecta).
póstumo, ma adj. Posthumous.

postura f. Position, posture, attitude (situación): *una postura incómoda*, an uncomfortable position. || FIG. Attitude, position: *no saber qué postura tomar*, not to know what attitude to take. | Position, stand: *su postura no es muy clara*, his position is not very clear. || Laying (de los huevos). || Egg (huevo). || Sapling (arbolillo). || Price fixed by the authorities (de mercancías). || Bid (en una almoneda). || Pact, agreement (convenio). || Bet, wager (apuesta). || Stake (en los juegos).
postventa o **posventa** adj. After-sale: *servicio postventa*, after-sale service.
potable adj. Drinkable, potable. || FAM. Palatable, decent, acceptable (aceptable). || *Agua potable*, drinking water.
potaje m. Dish of dried vegetables. || FIG. Jumble, muddle (mezcla confusa).
potasa f. QUÍM. Potash.
potásico, ca adj. QUÍM. Potassic.
potasio m. Potassium (metal).
pote m. Pot (tarro). || Pan, pot (para cocer). || Jar (de farmacia). || Stew (cocido en Galicia). || FIG. y FAM. Pout (gesto). || *Amer.* Tin, can (lata). | Flowerpot (maceta). || — FIG. y FAM. *A pote*, in abundance (mucho). | *Darse pote*, to put on airs, to swank.
potencia f. FÍS. y MAT. Power: *la potencia de un motor*, the power of an engine. || Power (nación): *las grandes potencias*, the Great Powers. || Potency, virility (de un hombre). || — Pl. Faculties [of memory, understanding and will] (del alma). || — MAT. *Elevar un número a la cuarta potencia*, to raise a number to the fourth power. || *En potencia*, potential, in the making, potentially. || *Potencia al freno*, brake horsepower. || *Potencia nuclear*, nuclear power. || MAT. *Tres elevado a la segunda potencia, a la tercera potencia, a la cuarta potencia*, three squared, cubed, to the power of four.
potenciación f. MAT. Involution.
potencial adj. Potential. || — GRAM. *Modo potencial*, conditional [tense]. | *Potencial simple*, present conditional [tense].
— M. Potentiality, potential. || *Potencial humano*, manpower.
potencialidad f. Potentiality, potential.
potenciar v. tr. To give power to. || To increase the power of. || To make possible, to allow (facultar). || To increase the possibilities of.
potenciómetro m. FÍS. Potentiometer.
potentado m. Potentate.
potente adj. Powerful: *una máquina potente*, a powerful machine. || Virile (capaz de engendrar). || Powerful, strong, mighty (persona, voluntad). || Leading (empresa).
potenza f. HERÁLD. Potent cross.
potenzado, da adj. *Cruz potenzada*, potent cross.
poterna f. Postern (en las fortificaciones).
potestad f. Power (poder). || Podesta (gobernador en Italia). || — Pl. REL. Powers, sixth order (*sing.*) of Angels. || JUR. *Patria potestad* or *potestad paternal*, paternal authority, patria potestas.
potestativo, va adj. JUR. Facultative. || Optional.
potingue m. FAM. Concoction.
Potosí m. FIG. *No vale un Potosí*, it [he, she, etc.] is not worth a thing. | *Ser un Potosí* or *valer un Potosí*, to be worth one's weight in gold *o* its weight in gold.
— OBSERV. From the town of Potosí, in Bolivia, which is famous for its silver mines.
potosino, na adj. [Of *o* from] Potosí [in Bolivia].
— M. y f. Native *o* inhabitant of Potosí.
potra f. Filly (caballo). || FAM. Hernia (hernia). || FIG. y FAM. Luck (suerte). || FIG. y FAM. *Tener potra*, to be lucky.
potrada f. Herd of colts.
potranca f. Young filly.
potranco m. Colt (potro).
potrillo m. Young colt.
potro m. Colt (caballo). || Rack, instrument of torture (de tormento). || Stanchion [for branding] (para veterinarios o herradores). || [Vaulting] horse (gimnasia). || *Potro con arzón*, pommelled horse, side horse.
potroso, sa adj. MED. Ruptured. || FAM. Lucky (afortunado).
— M. y f. MED. Person suffering from a hernia. || FAM. Lucky person.
poyete m. Small stone bench. || FIG. y FAM. *Quedarse en el poyete*, to be left on the shelf, to be an old maid (solterona), to be a wallflower (en el baile).
poyo m. Stone bench (banco).
poza f. Large puddle (charca).
pozal m. Bucket, pail (cubo). || Rim of a well (brocal). || Jar (tinaja).
pozo m. Well (de agua, de petróleo). || Shaft (de mina). || Hole, deep part (en un río). || Pit (hoyo seco). || Bank (en los naipes). || MAR. Hold (bodega). | Bilge (sentina). | Fish tank [on a boat] (de peces). || FIG. Well, fountain (fuente). || *Amer.* Spring (manantial). | Large puddle (charca). || — FAM. *Mi gozo en un pozo*, that's just my luck. || *Pozo artesiano*, artesian well. || FIG. *Pozo de ciencia*, well *o* fountain of knowledge. || *Pozo negro*, cesspool.
pracrito o **prácrito** m. Prakrit (idioma de la India).
práctica f. Practice: *aprender con la práctica*, to learn by practice. || Experience, knowledge. || Method. || — Pl. Practical studies (clases). || Training, *sing.* (preparación). || Devotions (devociones). || — *Es práctica establecida*, it is the custom, it is standard practice. || *Período de prácticas*, practical training period. || *Poner en práctica*, to put into practice.
practicabilidad f. Practicability.
practicable adj. Practicable. || Passable [road, etc.] (transitable).
— M. Practicable (en el teatro).
practicaje m. Pilotage [in a port].
practicante adj. Practising (en religión).
— M. y f. Nurse (auxiliar de medicina). || Assistant chemist (de botica). || Practitioner, person who practises his *o* her religion (en religión).
practicar v. tr. To practise [U.S., to practice]: *practicar un idioma*, to practise a language. || To practise, to make a practice of: *practicar la virtud*, to practise virtue. || To go in for: *practicar los deportes*, to go in for sport. || To play: *practicar el fútbol*, to play football. || To make (un agujero). || To perform, to do (hacer). || *Practicar la esgrima*, to fence.
— V. intr. REL. To practise, to be practising.
práctico, ca adj. Practical (cómodo). || Handy (cosa). || Useful, convenient (medida, medio). || Expert, experienced (ejercitado). || *Clases prácticas*, practical lessons, practicals.
— M. Coastal pilot. || *Barco del práctico*, pilot boat.
pradera f. Meadow (pequeña). || Prairie (grande, especialmente en Estados Unidos).
prado m. Meadow. || Promenade (paseo).
Praga n. pr. GEOGR. Prague.
pragmático, ca adj. Pragmatic.
— M. y f. Pragmatist.
pragmatismo m. Pragmatism.
pragmatista adj. Pragmatic.
— M. y f. Pragmatist.
praseodimio m. Praseodymium (metal).
preamplificador m. RAD. Preamplifier.
prebenda f. Prebend (de canónigo). || FIG. y FAM. Sinecure (oficio lucrativo).
prebendado m. Prebend, prebendary.
prebendar v. tr. To bestow a prebend on.
— V. intr. To obtain a prebend.
prebostazgo m. (Ant.). Provostship.
preboste m. Provost.
precalentador m. TECN. Preheater.
precalentamiento m. TECN. Preheating.
precalentar v. tr. To preheat.
precambriano, na o **precámbrico, ca** adj. GEOL. Precambrian.
— M. Precambrian era.
precariedad f. Precariousness.
precario, ria adj. Precarious.
precaución f. Precaution (medida). || Precaution, foresight, caution (prudencia). || — *Con precaución*, cautiously, carefully, warily. || *Por precaución*, as a precaution, as a safety measure.
precaucionarse v. pr. To take precautions.
precaver v. tr. To guard against, to take precautions against (tomar precauciones). || To prevent (impedir).
— V. pr. To be on one's guard, to take precautions: *precaverse de un peligro*, to be on one's guard against danger. | To forestall: *precaverse contra la miseria*, to forestall poverty.
precavidamente adv. Cautiously, warily.
precavido, da adj. Cautious, prudent, wary, careful (prudente). || Provident (previsor). || Cunning (astuto).
precedencia f. Precedence, priority (de fecha, de importancia).
precedente adj. Preceding: *los años precedentes a éste*, the preceding years, the years preceding this one. || Previous (previo). || Earlier (anterior).
— M. Precedent (antecedente): *sentar un precedente*, to establish *o* to set a precedent. || *Sin precedentes*, unprecedented.
preceder v. tr. e intr. To precede, to go before.
preceptista adj. Preceptive.
— M. y f. Preceptist, theorist.
preceptivo, va adj. Mandatory.
— F. Precepts, *pl.*, rules, *pl.* (literaria).
precepto m. Precept (de un arte, etc.). || Order, rule (orden). || — *Cumplir con el precepto*, to fulfill one's obligations. || *Fiestas de precepto*, days of obligation.
preceptor, ra m. [Private] tutor. || — F. Governess.
preceptorado m. Tutorship, post of tutor. || Post of governess.
preceptoril adj. Tutorial, of *o* pertaining to a tutor *o* governess.
preces f. pl. Prayers.
precesión f. ASTR. Precession: *precesión de los equinoccios*, precession of the equinoxes. || Reticence.
preciado, da adj. Valuable, precious (de valor). || Esteemed, appreciated (estimado): *una obra muy preciada*, a highly esteemed work.
preciar v. tr. To appreciate, to esteem (apreciar). || To value, to appraise (tasar).
— V. pr. To be conceited, to be vain (estar engreído). || To boast (jactarse). || To think o.s.: *se precia de inteligente*, he thinks himself clever. || — *Como cualquier español que se precie*, like any self-respecting Spaniard. || *Preciarse de orador*, to boast of being an orator, to consider o.s. a great orator.
precinta f. Official seal (en las aduanas).

precintado, da adj. Sealed.
— M. Sealing (de un paquete).
precintar v. tr. To seal, to place a seal on (un paquete). || JUR. To seal, to seal off.
precinto m. Placing of seals. || Lead seal (marchamo). || JUR. Official seal. || Seal (de una botella). || — JUR. *Colocación de precinto*, sealing off. | *Violación* or *quebrantamiento de precinto*, breaking of seals.
precio m. Price: *precio ofrecido, al contado, de coste, de lista, neto*, asking, cash, cost, list, net price. || Fare (de un viaje). || Rate, charge (de un hotel). || Value, worth (valor). || — *A cualquier precio*, whatever the price *o* the cost (cualquiera que sea el precio), at any cost (cualesquiera que sean las circunstancias). || FIG. *Al precio de*, at the cost of. || *Control de precios*, price control. || *De gran* or *de mucho precio*, expensive, dear, costly (cosa), valuable (persona). || *Fijación de precio* or *de precios*, price fixing. || *Fuera de precio*, priceless, beyond price. || *Lista de precios*, price list. || *Lo compraría a precio de oro*, I would pay a fortune for it. || *Mantenimiento de los precios*, price support. || *No tener precio*, to be priceless. || *Poner a precio la cabeza de uno*, to put a price on s.o.'s head. || *Poner precio a*, to put a price on. || *Precio alambicado* or *estudiado*, rock-bottom price, cheapest possible price. || *Precio al por mayor*, wholesale price. || *Precio barato* or *bajo*, low price. || *Precio corriente* or *de mercado*, market price. || *Precio de compra*, purchase price. || *Precio de fábrica*, factory price, ex-works price. || *Precio de tasa*, fixed price. || *Precio de venta*, sale price. || *Precio fijo*, fixed price. || *Precio fuerte*, full price. || *Precio por unidad*, unit price. || *Precio tope*, top price, ceiling price. || *Subida de precio*, price rise. || *Subida de precios*, rise in prices, rising prices. || *Tener en gran precio*, to esteem highly.
preciosidad f. Great value (valor). || Charm, beauty (encanto): *la preciosidad de esta joya*, the charm of this jewel. || Beauty, marvel (cosa preciosa): *esta pulsera es una preciosidad*, this bracelet is a beauty. || Jewel, beauty, darling (mujer, niño). || Preciosity (culteranismo). || *¡Qué preciosidad de niña!*, what a delightful *o* a darling *o* a lovely *o* a gorgeous child!
preciosismo m. Preciosity (afectación).
preciosista adj. Precious, affected (afectado). || Precious, of *o* pertaining to the "précieux".
— M. "Précieux", precious writer. || — F. "Précieuse" (literata).
precioso, sa adj. Precious, valuable (de gran precio). || FIG. Delightful, beautiful, lovely, wonderful (hermoso): *una mujer preciosa*, a beautiful woman. | Wonderful, beautiful: *un coche precioso*, a wonderful car. | Witty (chistoso, festivo). || *Piedra preciosa*, precious stone.
preciosura f. V. PRECIOSIDAD.
precipicio m. Precipice (corte). || Abyss: *caer al precipicio*, to fall into the abyss. || FIG. Ruin, downfall (ruina).
precipitación f. Precipitation, rainfall (lluvia). || Haste, precipitation (prisa). || QUÍM. Precipitation. || *Con precipitación*, hastily, hurriedly; precipitately.
precipitadamente adv. Hastily, hurriedly (muy rápidamente). || Precipitately (con demasiada prisa).
precipitadero m. Precipice (corte). || Abyss (abismo).
precipitado, da adj. Hasty, hurried, rapid (rápido). || Rash, reckless, precipitate (imprudente). || Headlong (huida).
— M. QUÍM. Precipitate, deposit (sedimento).
precipitar v. tr. To hurl down, to throw, to cast down (algo, alguien). || To push headlong, to hurl *o* to throw headlong (a una persona empujándola). || To hasten, to rush, to hurry on, to speed along, to accelerate (apresurar). || QUÍM. To precipitate.
— V. pr. To throw *o* to hurl o.s.: *precipitarse contra el enemigo*, to hurl o.s. against the enemy. || To pounce (*sobre*, on) [sobre una presa]. || To rush [headlong]: *precipitarse hacia la salida*, to rush towards the exit. || To hurry, to hasten (darse prisa). || FIG. To gather momentum (acontecimientos, etc.). | To be hasty (actuar apresuradamente). || QUÍM. To precipitate. || *No precipitarse*, to take one's time, not to hurry.
precipitosamente adv. V. PRECIPITADAMENTE.
precipitoso, sa adj. V. PRECIPITADO.
precisamente adv. Precisely, exactly, just (justamente): *por esto precisamente*, precisely because of that. || Really (realmente). || Specially: *vino precisamente para verte*, he came specially to see you. || *¡Precisamente!*, exactly!, precisely!
precisar v. tr. To specify, to state exactly (indicar). || To define exactly (definir). || To state clearly: *precisa tu idea*, state your idea clearly. || To need (necesitar): *preciso datos*, I need information. || To force (forzar). || — *Se precisa un contable*, accountant needed *o* required. || *Verse precisado a*, to be forced to, to be obliged to.
— V. impers. To be necessary (ser necesario).
precisión f. Precision: *instrumento de precisión*, precision instrument. || Accuracy, exactness (exactitud). || Need (necesidad): *tengo precisión de tu ayuda*, I have need of your help. || — Pl. Details, particulars. || *Tirar con precisión*, to hit the *o* one's target (dar en el blanco), to aim accurately *o* well (apuntar bien).
preciso, sa adj. Precise, clear, concise (claro). || Necessary, essential (necesario): *las cualidades precisas*, the essential qualities; *es preciso tener coche*, it is essential to have a car. || Precise, very, exact: *el día preciso de nuestra marcha*, the precise day of our departure. || Accurate, exact (exacto). || — *Cuando sea preciso*, when necessary. || *Ser preciso*, to be necessary, must: *es preciso que vengas*, it is necessary for you to come, you must come. || *Tener tiempo preciso para ir*, to have just enough time to go.
precitado, da adj. Aforementioned, above-mentioned, aforesaid.
preclaro, ra adj. Outstanding, illustrious.
precocidad f. Precocity, precociousness. || Earliness (de una planta).
precognición f. Precognition, foreknowledge.
precolombino, na adj. Pre-Columbian, before Columbus (anterior a Colón).
precombustión f. Precombustion (de motor diesel).
precompresión f. Precompression.
preconcebir* v. tr. To preconceive.
preconización f. Recommendation (recomendación). || Suggestion, proposal (sugerencia). || Advice (consejo). || Praising (alabanza). || REL. Preconization (de un prelato).
preconizador, ra adj. Advising, advisory.
— M. y f. Adviser (consejero). || Advocate, partisan (partidario). || Praiser (que alaba).
preconizar v. tr. To praise (alabar). || To recommend, to advise (recomendar). || To advise (aconsejar). || To suggest, to propose (proponer). || To advocate (ser partidario de). || REL. To preconize.
precoz adj. Precocious (persona). || Early (fruta).
precursor, ra adj. Precursory, premonitory. || *Los signos precursores de la desgracia*, the forerunners of misfortune.
— M. Precursor, forerunner.
predecesor, ra m. y f. Predecessor.
predecir* v. tr. To predict, to forecast, to foretell.
predestinación f. Predestination.
predestinado, da adj. Predestined.
— M. y f. Predestinate.
predestinar v. tr. To predestine, to predestinate.
predeterminación f. Predetermination.
predeterminante adj. Predetermining.
predeterminar v. tr. To predetermine.
predial adj. Predial, praedial.
prédica f. Sermon (sermón protestante). || — Pl. FIG. Preaching, *sing*.
predicable adj. Which can be preached, predicable.
— M. GRAM. Predicable.
predicación f. Preaching. || Sermon.
predicaderas f. pl. FAM. Eloquence, *sing*.
predicado m. GRAM. Predicate.
predicador, ra m. y f. Preacher. || — M. ZOOL. Praying mantis (insecto).
predicamento m. FIL. Predicament. || FIG. Influence, weight (influencia). | Prestige (prestigio).
predicante m. Predicant.
predicar v. tr. e intr. To preach: *el cura predicaba la virtud*, the vicar preached virtue. || FIG. To sermonize, to preach to, to lecture (amonestar o reprender). || — *Predicar con el ejemplo*, to set an example. || *Predicar en el desierto*, to preach in the wilderness. || *Una cosa es predicar y otra es dar trigo*, it is easy to talk, actions speak louder than words.
predicativo, va adj. GRAM. Predicative.
predicción f. Prediction, forecast. || Forecast (del tiempo).
predicho, cha adj. Aforesaid, aforementioned.
predigerido, da adj. Predigested.
predigestión f. Predigestion.
predilección f. Predilection.
predilecto, ta adj. Favourite: *mi hijo predilecto*, my favourite son. || Favourite, preferred: *ciudad predilecta de los pintores*, favourite town of painters, town preferred by painters.
predio m. Estate, property (heredad). || — *Predio rústico*, country estate *o* property. || *Predio urbano*, town property.
predisponer* v. tr. To predispose. || *Predisponer contra*, to prejudice against.
predisposición f. Predisposition. || *Predisposición contra*, prejudice against.
predispuesto, ta adj. Predisposed. || *Predispuesto contra*, prejudiced against.
predominación o **predominancia** f. Predominance, predominancy, predomination.
predominante adj. Predominant, predominating, prevailing.
predominar v. tr. To predominate over. || FIG. To overlook (una casa, etc.).
— V. intr. To predominate, to prevail.
predominio m. Predominance, predominancy, prevalence.
preelegir* v. tr. To choose *o* to select beforehand *o* in advance, to preselect (escoger). || To elect beforehand (por elección). || *Preelegido*, preselected, previously chosen *o* selected; previously elected.
preeminencia f. Preeminence.
preeminente adj. Preeminent.
preempción f. Preemption.
preestablecer v. tr. To preestablish.

preestablecido, da adj. Preestablished.
preexcelencia f. Preeminence.
preexistencia f. Preexistence.
preexistente adj. Preexistent, preexisting.
preexistir v. intr. To preexist.
prefabricación f. Prefabrication.
prefabricar v. tr. To prefabricate.
prefacio m. Preface, foreword. || *Hacer un prefacio a un libro*, to preface a book.
prefecto m. Prefect.
prefectura f. Prefecture.
preferencia f. Preference. || Predilection. || Terraces (*pl.*) in front of the stands (localidad en un campo de fútbol). || — *Con preferencia a*, with preference to. || *De preferencia*, preferably. || *Preferencia de paso*, right of way, priority (en una carretera).
preferente adj. Prefering (que prefiere). || Preferential: *trato preferente*, preferential treatment. || Preference, preferential (acción de una sociedad). || Preferable (que se prefiere). || Excellent: *ocupar un lugar preferente*, to occupy an excellent place. || Superior, better (superior).
preferentemente adv. Preferably (de preferencia). || Preferentially.
preferible adj. Preferable.
preferiblemente adv. Preferably.
preferido, da adj. Preferred, favourite.
— M. y f. Favourite.
preferir* v. tr. To prefer: *prefiero con mucho* or *mucho más*, I much prefer. || To like: *el que menos prefiero*, the one I like the least. || *Prefiere quedarse dos días*, he prefers to stay two days, he would rather stay two days.
prefiguración f. Prefiguration.
prefigurar v. tr. To prefigure, to foreshadow.
prefijar v. tr. GRAM. To prefix. || To arrange beforehand, to prearrange, to fix in advance (fijar de antemano).
prefijo, ja adj. Prefixed.
— M. GRAM. Prefix. || Area code (teléfonos).
prefloración f. BOT. Vernation, aestivation [U.S., estivation].
preformación f. Preformation.
preformar v. tr. To preform.
preglaciar adj. GEOL. Preglacial.
pregón m. Public announcement (noticia). || Street vendor's cry *o* shout *o* call (de vendedor). || Bann (para un matrimonio).
pregonar v. tr. To proclaim, to shout *o* to cry out (publicar en voz alta). || To hawk [one's wares] (un vendedor). || FIG. To reveal, to tell, to make public (revelar): *pregonar una noticia*, to reveal a piece of news. | To praise (alabar). || (P.us.). To proscribe, to outlaw (proscribir). || FIG. *Pregonar a bombo y platillos* or *a voz en grito*, to shout from the rooftops.
pregonero, ra adj. Proclaiming, divulging.
— M. y f. Proclaimer (que proclama). || Divulger (que revela). || Street vendor (que vende). || — M. Town crier (empleado municipal).
preguerra f. Prewar period.
pregunta f. Question (interrogación): *pregunta indiscreta, capciosa*, indiscreet, catch question; *hacer preguntas*, to ask questions; *no contestó a mi pregunta*, he didn't answer my question. || — *A pregunta necia, oídos sordos* or *oídos de mercader*, ask a silly question, [and you will] get a silly answer. || FIG. y FAM. *Estar* or *andar a la cuarta pregunta*, to be flat broke. | *Estrechar a preguntas*, to ply with questions. || *Hacer una pregunta a alguien*, to ask s.o. a question, to put a question to s.o. || FIG. y FAM. *Quedarse a la cuarta pregunta*, to be cleaned out, to be left penniless.
preguntador, ra adj. Inquisitive.
— M. y f. Questioner (el que hace una pregunta). || Inquisitive person (curioso).
preguntar v. tr. To ask: *pregúntaselo a él*, ask him. || To question: *preguntar a un candidato*, to question a candidate. || *Preguntar por*, to ask about *o* after, to ask for news of: *preguntar por alguien*, to ask after s.o.; to ask for (querer ver *o* hablar): *preguntan por usted en el teléfono*, s.o. is asking for you on the telephone.
— V. pr. To wonder: *me pregunto qué hora es*, I wonder what time it is. || To ask o.s.

— OBSERV. Do not confuse *preguntar* with *pedir*, which means *to ask for* in the sense of *to request*.

preguntón, ona adj. FAM. Inquisitive, nosey: *un niño preguntón*, an inquisitive child.
— M. y f. FAM. Nosey parker, inquisitive person.
prehistoria f. Prehistory.
prehistoriador, ra m. y f. Prehistorian.
prehistórico, ca adj. Prehistoric.
preincaico, ca adj. HIST. Pre-Incan.
prejudicial adj. JUR. Interlocutory (cuestión, etc.). || Pre-judicial (acción).
prejuicio m. Prejudice: *prejuicio racial*, racial prejudice. || Bias (falta de objetividad). || Prejudgment (acción de prejuzgar). || — *Crearle a uno un prejuicio*, to prejudice s.o. || *Tener prejuicios*, to be prejudiced: *tiene prejuicios raciales*, he is racially prejudiced; to be biassed: *no lo encuentras inteligente porque tienes prejuicios*, you do not think he is intelligent because your are biassed.
prejuzgar v. tr. To prejudge.
prelacía f. Prelature, prelacy.
prelación f. Preference, priority, precedence: *orden de prelación*, order of preference. || *Tener prelación sobre*, to take preference over, to come before: *haría falta que la generosidad tuviese prelación sobre el egoísmo*, generosity should come before egoism.
prelado m. Prelate.
prelatura f. Prelature, prelacy.
preliminar adj./s.m. Preliminary.
preludiar v. intr. y tr. MÚS. To prelude. || FIG. To prelude, to lead up to.
preludio m. Prelude.
premarital adj. Premarital.
prematuramente adv. Prematurely.
prematuro, ra adj. Premature.
— M. y f. Premature baby.
premeditación f. Premeditation. || JUR. *Con premeditación*, with malice aforethought, with premeditation.
premeditadamente adv. With premeditation, deliberately.
premeditado, da adj. Premeditated, deliberate.
premeditar v. tr. To premeditate.
premiado, da adj. Winning, prize-winning: *número premiado*, winning number. || Rewarded: *premiado por su heroísmo*, rewarded for his heroism. || Prize: *novela premiada*, prize novel.
— M. y f. Winner, prizewinner.
premiar v. tr. To reward: *premiar a uno por su heroísmo*, to reward s.o. for his heroism. || To give *o* to award a prize to (en un certamen). || *Salir premiado*, to win a prize.
premilitar adj. Premilitary.
premio m. Reward, recompense (recompensa). || Prize, award: *llevarse el premio*, to win the prize; *premio de consolación*, consolation prize. || COM. Premium. || — *Como premio a*, as a reward for. || *Premio en metálico*, cash prize, prize money. || *Premio gordo*, first prize, grand prize. || *Reparto* or *distribución de premios*, prizegiving.
premiosidad f. Tightness (estrechez). || Awkwardness (molestia, dificultad). || Awkwardness, clumsiness (torpeza).
premioso, sa adj. Tight (ajustado). || Urgent (urgente). || Heavy: *una carga premiosa*, a heavy burden. || Awkward (movimientos, habla, etc.). || Strict (estricto). || Awkward, clumsy (estilo, lenguaje, etc.).
premisa f. Premise (en lógica).
premolar m. Premolar (diente).
premonición f. Premonition.
premonitorio, ria adj. MED. Premonitory. || Indicative, warning.
premura f. Urgency (urgencia). || Haste (prisa). || Lack [of time, of space] (falta de tiempo, espacio).
prenatal adj. Prenatal, antenatal.
prenda f. Pledge, security, guarantee (garantía). || Token, pledge (prueba de amistad). || Deposit (señal). || Article of clothing, garment (ropa). || Linen (de mesa y de cama). || Darling (apelativo cariñoso). || COM. Security. || — Pl. Forfeits (juego). || Qualities, gifts, talents (buenas cualidades). || — *Dar en prenda*, to pledge. || *En prenda de*, as a token of, as a pledge of. || *No dolerle prendas a uno*, not to mind admitting one's faults (admitir sus errores), to spare no expense *o* effort (no escatimar gastos o esfuerzos). || FIG. y FAM. *No soltar prenda*, not to commit o.s., to be noncommittal. || *Prenda interior*, undergarment. || FIG. y FAM. *Soltar prenda*, to commit o.s.
prendarse v. pr. To fall in love (*de*, with) [una persona]. || To take a fancy (*de*, to] [un objeto]. || To be captivated (*de*, by), to be enchanted (*de*, with) [estar cautivado por].
prendedor m. Pin, clasp, brooch (broche). || Clip (de una estilográfica).
prender v. tr. To seize, to grasp (asir). || To arrest, to apprehend (detener a uno). || To put in prison, to imprison (encarcelar). || To catch, to capture, to take prisoner (capturar). || To fasten (sujetar algo). || To set (fuego): *han prendido fuego a la casa*, they have set fire to the house. || *Amer.* To light (encender). | To switch on (la luz). || *Prender con alfileres*, to pin.
— V. intr. To take root (arraigar). || To take (un injerto, una vacuna). || To take, to catch (fuego): *el fuego no prende*, the fire is not taking *o* will not take. || FIG. To catch.
— V. pr. To dress up (engalanarse una mujer). || To catch fire (encenderse). || To mate (los animales). || *Amer.* To get drunk (embriagarse).

— OBSERV. The verb *prender* has two past participles: *prendido* and *preso*. *Prendido* usually means "fastened", and *preso* "arrested", "imprisoned".

prendería f. Secondhand shop.
prendero, ra m. y f. Secondhand dealer (comerciante), || — M. Skirt hanger (percha).
prendido, da adj. Enchanted, captivated (encantado).
prendimiento m. Capture, arrest, seizure.
prenombrado, da adj. *Amer.* Aforementioned, aforesaid.
prenombre m. Christian name, first name.

— OBSERV. "Christian name" is usually translated by *nombre* or *nombre de pila*.

prensa f. Press, printing press (máquina para imprimir). || TECN. Press: *prensa hidráulica*, hydraulic

press. || Press (publicaciones, periódicos): *libertad de prensa*, freedom of the press. || *— Dar a la prensa*, to publish, to print. || *Entrar en prensa*, to go to press. || FIG. *Tener buena, mala prensa*, to have a good, a bad press.
prensado m. Calendering, lustre (de los tejidos). || Pressing (acción de prensar).
prensador, ra adj. Pressing.
— M. y f. Press operator, presser.
prensaestopas m. inv. TECN. Stuffing box.
prensar v. tr. To press.
prensatelas adj. inv. *Pie prensatelas*, foot.
prensil adj. Prehensile: *cola prensil*, prehensile tail.
prensilla f. Presser foot (de máquina de coser).
prensor adj. m. ZOOL. Zygodactyl (aves).
prenupcial adj. Antenuptial, prenuptial.
preñado, da adj. Pregnant. || Bulging, sagging (pared). || Full, charged (lleno): *palabras preñadas de amenazas*, words full of *o* charged with menace.
preñar v. tr. To get pregnant (mujer). || To impregnate (animal).
preñez f. Pregnancy.
preocupación f. Preoccupation, worry, care, concern. || *Tiene la preocupación de que le va a pasar algo*, he is worried that sth. is going to happen to him.
preocupado, da adj. Worried, concerned, preoccupied.
preocupar v. tr. To worry, to preoccupy (inquietar). || To bother (molestar). || To bias, to prejudice (predisponer). || To previously occupy (ocupar antes). || *Es lo que menos me preocupa*, that is the least of my worries.
— V. pr. To worry, to get worried: *preocuparse por su salud*, to worry about one's health. || To be worried *o* concerned (estar preocupado). || *— No se preocupa por nada*, he doesn't worry about anything, nothing worries him. || *¡No se preocupe!*, don't worry! || *Se preocupó de que todo estuviera acabado a tiempo*, he saw to it that everything was finished in time.
prepalatal adj. Prepalatal (en fonética).
preparación f. Preparation. || Training (entrenamiento). || Preparation (en farmacia). || Cooking, preparation (en cocina).
preparado, da adj. Prepared, ready. || CULIN. Ready cooked.
— M. Preparation (en farmacia).
preparador, ra m. y f. Assistant (en laboratorio, etc.). || Trainer, coach (en deportes).
preparamiento m. Preparation. || Training (entrenamiento).
preparar v. tr. To prepare: *está bien preparado para la vida*, he is well prepared for life; *le estamos preparando una sorpresa*, we are preparing a surprise for him. || To prepare, to get ready: *estoy preparando la cena*, I am getting dinner ready. || To prepare for: *preparar un examen*, to prepare for an examination. || DEP. To train, to coach.
— V. pr. To get ready, to prepare [o.s.]: *nos estamos preparando para las vacaciones*, we are getting ready for the holidays, we are preparing [ourselves] for the holidays.
preparativo, va adj. Preparatory, preliminary.
— M. Preparation (preparación).
preparatorio, ria adj. Preparatory, preliminary.
— M. Preparatory studies, *pl.*
preponderancia f. Preponderance.
preponderante adj. Preponderant. || *Voto preponderante*, casting vote.
preponderar v. intr. To preponderate, to predominate. || To prevail (una opinión).
preponer* v. tr. To put before (anteponer).
preposición f. GRAM. Preposition. || *Preposición inseparable*, prefix.
prepositivo, va adj. GRAM. Prepositive.
prepotencia f. Prepotency.
prepotente adj. Prepotent, very powerful.
prepucio m. ANAT. Prepuce, foreskin.
prerrafaelismo m. Pre-Raphaelitism.
prerrafaelista o **prerrafaelita** adj./s. Pre-Raphaelite.
prerrogativa f. Prerogative (privilegio).
prerromanticismo m. Preromanticism.
presa f. Capture, seizure (acción de prender). || Catch, prize (cosa apresada): *una buena presa*, a good catch. || Quarry (animal o persona que se caza). || Prey, catch (animal cazado): *el zorro se llevó su presa*, the fox carried off its prey. || FIG. Victim (víctima): *presa de los calumniadores*, victim of slanderers. || Prey: *ser presa de pesadillas*, to be a prey to nightmares. || Hold, grip (lucha, alpinismo). || Dam (embalse). || Millrace [U.S., flume] (de molino). || MAR. Prize (barco capturado). || *Amer.* Slice (tajada), piece (pedazo). || — Pl. Fangs (colmillos). || Talons, claws (de ave de rapiña). || *— Ave de presa*, bird of prey. || *Hacer presa en una cosa*, to seize sth. || *Presa de contención*, reservoir.
presagiar v. tr. To presage, to portend, to forebode, to betoken.
presagio m. Omen, portent (señal de suerte o desgracia): *buen, mal presagio*, good, bad omen. || Premonition, foreboding (premonición).
presagioso, sa adj. Foreboding.
presbicia f. MED. Longsightedness, farsightedness, presbyopia.
présbita o **présbite** adj. Longsighted, farsighted, presbyopic.
presbiterado o **presbiterato** m. Priesthood.
presbiteral adj. Presbyteral, presbyterial, priestly.
presbiterianismo m. Presbyterianism.
presbiteriano, na adj./s. Presbyterian.
presbiterio m. Presbytery.
presbítero m. Presbyter, priest (clérigo).
presciencia f. Prescience, foreknowledge.
presciente adj. Prescient.
prescindible adj. Dispensable.
prescindir v. intr. To ignore, to disregard (hacer caso omiso). || To do without: *ya no puedo prescindir de su ayuda*, I can no longer do without his help. || To omit, to leave out (omitir). || To forget (olvidar). || To get rid (*de*, of) [desembarazarse]. || To manage *o* to do without (arreglárselas sin algo).
prescribir v. tr. To prescribe, to lay down (ordenar). || MED. To prescribe (recetar). || JUR. To prescribe.
— V. intr. JUR. To prescribe. || FIG. To expire, to lapse.
prescripción f. Prescription. || MED. *Prescripción facultativa*, medical prescription.
prescriptible adj. Prescriptible.
prescripto, ta o **prescrito, ta** adj. Prescribed (señalado). || JUR. Annulled, null and void (juicio).
preselección f. RAD. Preselection. || DEP. Seeding.
preseleccionar v. tr. DEP. To seed.
preselector m. RAD. Preselector.
presencia f. Presence. || Bearing, presence (porte): *mujer de buena presencia*, a woman of good bearing. || *— En presencia del rey*, in the presence of the king, in the king's presence. || *Hacer acto de presencia*, to be present, to put in an appearance. || *Presencia de ánimo*, presence of mind.
presencial adj. *Testigo presencial*, eyewitness.
presenciar v. tr. To witness, to see, to watch: *presenciar un accidente*, to witness an accident. || To attend, to be present at: *el presidente presenció una corrida*, the president attended a bullfight.
presentable adj. Presentable.
presentación f. Presentation. || Appearance (aspecto): *su presentación es siempre impecable*, his appearance is always impeccable. || Presentation, appearance (aspecto de una mercancía). || Display (exposición). || Parade, show (de moda). || Introduction (de dos personas por una tercera): *carta de presentación*, letter of introduction. || *— Presentación en sociedad*, coming out. || *Todavía no has hecho las presentaciones*, you still have not introduced us.
presentador, ra m. y f. Compère [U.S., master of ceremonies] (en el teatro, la televisión, etc.).
presentante adj. Presenting.
presentar v. tr. To present. || To present, to give, to offer (ofrecer). || To put forward, to submit (un proyecto, una propuesta, etc.). || To present (un informe). || To file (una queja, denuncia). || To introduce (una persona a otra). || To propose, to nominate, to present: *presentar a uno para un puesto*, to propose s.o. for a post. || To have (tener). || To show, to display (mostrar). || To tender: *presentar la dimisión*, to tender one's resignation. || To put on (una obra de teatro). || To show (una película). || JUR. To produce (testigos). | To submit (pruebas). || *— Le presento a mi madre*, may I introduce you to my mother, I would like you to meet my mother. || *Le presento el testimonio de mi consideración*, I remain yours faithfully (al final de una carta). || *Presentar armas*, to present arms. || *Presentar la cuestión de confianza*, to ask for a vote of confidence. || *Presentar los respetos*, to pay one's respects. || JUR. *Presentar una demanda contra uno*, to bring an action against s.o., to sue s.o. || *Ser presentado en sociedad*, to come out.
— V. pr. To present o.s. || To arise, to come up (una dificultad, una cuestión). || To turn up, to come up, to arise (una oportunidad). || To report (ante una autoridad, para empezar a trabajar): *tengo que presentarme ante el jefe a las tres*, I have to report to the boss at three o'clock. || To appear, to look (un negocio). || To go (ir). || To come (venir). || To appear, to turn up (aparecer): *se presentó en mi casa a las doce de la noche*, he appeared at my house at midnight. || To turn up (acudir a una cita). || To introduce o.s. (darse a conocer): *permita que me presente*, allow me to introduce myself. || To stand, to run (como candidato): *presentarse a presidente*, to stand for president. || To sit, to take [a un examen]. || To apply (*a*, for) [para conseguir un empleo]. || *Presentarse en sociedad*, to come out.
presente adj. Present. || *— Estar presente en*, to be present at. || *Hacer presente*, to notify, to inform, to tell, to let know (avisar), to impart, to disclose, to announce (dar a conocer), to state (declarar). || *Las personas presentes*, those present. || *Tener presente*, to bear in mind, to remember, not to forget: *hay que tener presente esta posibilidad*, we must bear this possibility in mind.
— M. Present (regalo). || GRAM. Present. || *— En el presente*, at present, at the present time. || *Hasta el presente*, up to the present. || *La presente* (*carta*), this letter. || *Lo presente*, the present. || *Los presentes*, those present. || *Mejorando lo presente*, present company excepted. || GRAM. *Participio de presente*, present participle.

presentemente adv. At present, now.
presentimiento m. Presentiment, foreboding, premonition.
presentir* v. tr. To have a presentiment of, to have a foreboding of.
preservación f. Preservation. || Protection.
preservador, ra adj. Preservative, preserving. || Protective.
preservar v. tr. To preserve (*contra*, from). || To protect (proteger).
preservativo, va adj. Preservative.
— M. Contraceptive sheath, condom.
presidario m. Convict (presidiario).
presidencia f. Presidency (de una nación). || Chairmanship (de una reunión). || *Ocupar la presidencia*, to take *o* to occupy the chair (en una reunión).
presidencial adj. Presidential.
presidenta f. President. || Chairwoman (de una asamblea). || President's wife (esposa del presidente).
presidente m. President (de la nación). || Chairman, president (de una asamblea). || Speaker (del Parlamento). || Premier (del Consejo de Ministros). || JUR. Presiding magistrate (de un tribunal).
presidiario m. Convict (prisionero).
presidio m. Prison (prisión). || Convicts, *pl.* (prisioneros). || Hard labour: *diez años de presidio*, ten years' hard labour. || Fortress, stronghold (fortaleza). || Garrison (guarnición). || Praesidium (en la U.R.S.S.).
presidir v. tr. To preside over *o* at. || To chair, to be chairman of (debate, reunión). || FIG. To reign over: *la tristeza presidió la reunión*, sadness reigned over the party. | To dominate, to prevail in (dominar). || *Presidir el duelo*, to be chief mourner.
— V. intr. To preside. || To take *o* to occupy the chair (en una reunión).
presidium m. Praesidium, presidium (presidencia del Consejo Supremo de los Soviets).
presilla f. Loop (en el borde de una prenda). || Fastener (para cerrar). || Loop (vuelta hecha en una cuerda, hilo o alambre). || Loop (del cinturón). || Buttonhole stitch (punto de ojal).
presión f. Pressure: *ejercer presión*, to exert pressure. || — *A presión*, under pressure. || *Ejercer* or *hacer presión*, to press. || *Grupo de presión*, pressure group. || *Olla de presión*, pressure cooker. || MED. *Presión arterial* or *sanguínea*, blood pressure. || *Presión atmosférica*, atmospheric pressure.
presionar v. tr. To press, to push (apretar). || FIG. To put pressure on, to press.
— V. intr. To press.
preso, sa adj. Imprisoned, under arrest (detenido). || Stricken (bajo los efectos de). || *Preso de pánico*, panic-stricken.
— M. y f. Prisoner.
prestación f. Contribution (aportación). || Help (ayuda). || Services, *pl.* (servicios). || Benefit: *prestación por maternidad*, maternity benefit; *prestaciones sociales*, social benefits. || JUR. Prestation. || — JUR. *Prestación de juramento*, swearing in. || *Prestación personal*, compulsory communal work.
prestado, da adj. Lent (a alguien). || Borrowed (de alguien): *una chaqueta prestada*, a borrowed jacket. || Lent, loaned (dinero). || — *Dar prestado*, to lend, to loan. || *El único ejemplar que tenemos está prestado*, the only copy we have is on loan. || *Pedir* or *tomar prestado*, to borrow. || *Vivir de prestado*, to live on what one can borrow.
prestador, ra adj. Lending.
— M. y f. Lender.
prestamente adv. Quickly, rapidly.
prestamista m. y f. Moneylender.
préstamo m. Lending (acción de prestar). || Borrowing (acción de pedir prestado). || Loan (cantidad o cosa que se presta). || — COM. *Ley de préstamo y arriendo*, lend-lease act. || *Pedirle a uno un préstamo*, to ask s.o. for a loan, to borrow sth. from s.o. || JUR. y MAR. *Préstamo a la gruesa*, bottomry loan.
prestancia f. Excellence. || Distinction, elegance.
prestar v. tr. To lend: *prestar dinero*, to lend money. || To lend, to give (ayuda, etc.). || To do, to render (un favor). || To pay, to lend: *prestar atención*, to pay attention, to lend one's attention. || — *Prestar auxilio* or *socorro* or *ayuda*, to give help *o* aid *o* assistance. || *Prestar juramento*, to take the oath. || *Prestar oídos*, to lend one's ear. || *Prestar servicio*, to be of service *o* assistance. || *Prestar testimonio*, to bear witness. || *Prestar una declaración jurada*, to make a statement *o* a declaration under oath. || *Tomar prestado*, to borrow.
— V. intr. To lend: *prestar con interés*, to lend at interest. || To stretch (estirarse). || To serve (servir).
— V. pr. To consent (consentir). || To lend o.s. (persona), to lend itself (cosa). || To be suitable *o* favourable (*a*, for) [ser adecuado para]. || *Prestarse a discusión*, to be debatable.
prestatario, ria m. y f. Borrower.
preste m. (Ant.). Priest. || *Preste Juan*, Prester John (personaje fabuloso de la Edad Media).
presteza f. Promptness. || *Con presteza*, promptly, quickly.
prestidigitación f. Conjuring, prestidigitation, sleight of hand, magic.
prestidigitador m. Conjurer, conjuror, prestidigitator, magician.
prestigiado, da adj. Prestigious, famous.
prestigiar v. tr. To give prestige to (dar prestigio a).
prestigio m. Prestige. || Sleight of hand (magia). || Trick (engaño).
prestigioso, sa adj. Prestigious, famous.
presto, ta adj. Prompt, quick (pronto): *presto en las respuestas*, prompt to answer. || Ready, prepared (dispuesto). || MÚS. Presto.
— Adv. Promptly, quickly. || MÚS. Presto.
presumible adj. Presumable, probable, likely. || *Era presumible*, it was to be presumed.
presumido, da adj. Presumptuous. || Pretentious, conceited.
presumir v. tr. To presume, to assume, to suppose (conjeturar). || *Amer.* To court (cortejar).
— V. intr. To be vain *o* conceited (ser vanidoso). || To swank, to show off (jactarse). || To be presumptuous (ser presumido). || To think o.s., to think one is (creerse): *presume de poeta*, he thinks he is a poet; *presume de listo, de valiente*, he thinks himself clever, brave. || — *Es de presumir que*, it is to be supposed that, presumably, supposedly. || *Presumir demasiado de su fuerza*, to overestimate one's strength. || *Según cabe presumir*, presumably, as may be presumed.
presunción f. Conceit, vanity, presumptuousness (vanidad). || Presumption, supposition (suposición). || JUR. Presumption: *presunción legal*, legal presumption.
presuntamente adv. Presumably, supposedly, presumedly.
presuntivo, va adj. Presumed, supposed.
presunto, ta adj. Presumed, supposed: *es el presunto autor del crimen*, he is the presumed author of the crime. || Presumptive: *heredero presunto*, presumptive heir. || Would-be, so-called, supposed: *el presunto poeta*, the would-be poet.
presuntuosidad f. Vanity, presumptuousness, conceit.
presuntuoso, sa adj. Presumptuous, conceited, vain.
presuponer* v. tr. To presuppose. || V. PRESUPUESTAR.
presuposición f. Presupposition.
presupuestar v. tr. To work out (calcular). || To work out the cost of, to cost (calcular el precio de). || To draw up the budget for, to budget (elaborar el presupuesto de).
presupuestario, ria adj. Budgetary, budget.
presupuestívoro, ra m. y f. FAM. Person living off the State.
presupuesto, ta adj. Presupposed. || Estimated (calculado). || *Presupuesto que*, assuming *o* supposing that.
— M. Budget (de ingresos y gastos): *equilibrar el presupuesto*, to balance the budget. || Estimate (estimación): *hacer un presupuesto*, to make an estimate. || Motive, reason (motivo). || Assumption, supposition.
presurización f. Pressurization.
presurizar v. tr. To pressurize.
presuroso, sa adj. In a hurry, anxious (que tiene prisa): *presuroso de marcharse*, in a hurry to leave. || Prompt, speedy (rápido). || Quick, light (pasos).
pretal m. Breast strap (de caballo).
pretencioso, sa adj. Pretentious, presumptuous, conceited (persona). || Pretentious (estilo, cosas).
pretender v. tr. To seek, to try for, to be after (intentar conseguir). || To apply for (solicitar). || To aspire to (honores). || To want (querer): *pretende llegar a la cima*, he wants to reach the top. || To intend to (tener la intención de). || To try to, to seek to (intentar). || To aim at (una meta, objetivo). || To claim (afirmar): *pretender poder hacer algo*, to claim to be able to do sth.; *pretende haber conocido al presidente*, he claims to have known the president. || To claim, to pretend to (el trono). || To court (cortejar). || To pretend (fingir). || *¿Qué pretende decir con eso?*, what does he mean by that?
pretendido, da adj. So-called (llamado). || Would-be, so-called, supposed (presunto). || Pretended, supposed (simulado): *pretendida amabilidad*, pretended kindness.
pretendiente adj. Pretending, aspiring.
— M. Pretender (al trono). || Suitor (a una mujer). || Applicant, candidate (*a*, for) [un puesto]. || Claimant (de una herencia).
pretensado, da adj. Prestressed.
pretensar v. tr. TECN. To prestress.
pretensión f. Pretension, claim (reivindicación): *tener pretensiones de*, to lay claim to. || Aim, object (finalidad, propósito). || Aspiration. || Pretentiousness (vanidad). || Pretence (para engañar). || — *Sin pretensiones*, unpretentious. || *Tiene la pretensión de casarse conmigo*, he expects *o* he thinks he is going to marry me.
pretensioso, sa adj. V. PRETENCIOSO.
preterición f. Preterition, omission. || JUR. Preterition.
preterir* v. tr. To leave out, to miss out, to pass over. || JUR. Not to mention, to pretermit [an heir in a will].
pretérito, ta adj. Past. || FIG. Past, former.
— M. Past. || GRAM. Past. || — GRAM. *Pretérito anterior*, past anterior. | *Pretérito imperfecto*, imperfect. || *Pretérito indefinido*, past historic, preterite, preterit. | *Pretérito perfecto*, perfect, present perfect. || *Pretérito pluscuamperfecto*, pluperfect.

— OBSERV. The Spanish *pretérito* is not to be confused with the English *preterite*, which is translated by *pretérito indefinido*.

pretexta f. Praetexta, pretexta (toga).
pretextar v. tr. To pretext, to allege, to put forward as a pretext, to plead, to claim.
pretexto m. Pretext. || — *Con el* or *so pretexto de*, under the pretext of. || *Con el pretexto de que*, under the pretext that, with the excuse that, pretending that, on the pretence that.
pretil m. Parapet (de puente, de balcón).
pretina f. Belt, waistband (correa).
pretor m. Praetor, pretor (magistrado romano).
pretoría f. Praetorship.
pretorial adj. Praetorial, pretorial.
pretorianismo m. Praetorianism.
pretoriano, na adj./s. Praetorian.
pretorio, ria adj. Praetorian.
— M. Praetorium.
pretura f. Praetorship.
preu m. FAM. V. PREUNIVERSITARIO.
preuniversitario m. An advanced level course of study lasting one year, and the ensuing examination. Those who pass the examination may go on to study at university.

— OBSERV. En Inglaterra no existe este curso. El Bachillerato Medio consta de 5 años y el Superior de 7, es decir 2 más. El examen final, llamado G.C.E. Advanced Level, permite el ingreso en la universidad.

prevalecer* v. intr. To prevail (*sobre*, against, over) [dominar, sobresalir]. || To take root (arraigar plantas). || FIG. To thrive (prosperar).
— V. pr. To take advantage of, to use (aprovechar).
prevaleciente adj. Prevailing, prevalent.
prevaler* v. intr. To prevail.
— V. pr. To take advantage (*de*, of), to use (aprovecharse de).
prevaricación f. Abuse of trust, breach of trust, prevarication.
prevaricador, ra adj. Dishonest.
— M. y f. Prevaricator.
prevaricar v. intr. To betray one's trust.
prevención f. Prevention (para impedir): *prevención del crimen*, crime prevention. || Precaution (precaución). || Preparation, provision (preparativo): *las prevenciones para el viaje*, preparations for the journey. || Warning (aviso). || Prejudice (prejuicio). || Police station (de policía): *llevar a alguien a la prevención*, to take s.o. to the police station. || MIL. Guard (soldado). | Guardhouse (cuerpo de guardia). || JUR. Preventive detention (detención preventiva). || *Tener prevención contra uno*, to be prejudiced against s.o.
prevenido, da adj. Prepared, ready (dispuesto). || Precautious, cautious, prudent (precavido). || Warned, forewarned (advertido). || *Hombre prevenido vale por dos*, forewarned is forearmed.
prevenir* v. tr. To prepare, to make ready (preparar). || To prevent, to forestall (impedir). || To foresee, to anticipate, to provide for (prever). || To avoid (evitar). || To warn, to forewarn (avisar, advertir). || To prejudice, to bias, to predispose (predisponer). || *Más vale prevenir que curar*, prevention is better than cure.
— V. pr. To make ready, to get ready, to prepare o.s. (prepararse). || To take precautions [against sth.] (tomar precauciones). || To provide for: *prevenirse contra toda eventualidad*, to provide for every eventuality.
preventivo, va adj. Preventive: *medicina preventiva*, preventive medicine. || JUR. *Detención preventiva*, protective custody, remand in custody.
preventorio m. MED. Preventorium (sanatorio).
prever* v. tr. To foresee, to forecast. || To anticipate, to provide for (prevenirse). || To expect (esperar).
previamente adv. Previously, beforehand.
previo, a adj. Previous: *cuestión previa*, previous question. || Preliminary (preparatorio). || — *Previa consulta a los interesados*, the interested parties having been consulted. || *Previa enmienda al texto*, an amendment having been made to the text, the text having been amended. || *Previo acuerdo de los demás*, subject to the agreement of the others. || *Previo aviso*, notice, prior notice: *previo aviso de un mes*, a month's notice. || *Previo pago*, after payment.
previsible adj. Foreseeable, predictable.
previsión f. Forecast (lo que se prevé). || Estimate (evaluación). || Foresight (clarividencia). || Prudence, precaution (prudencia). || — *Caja de previsión*, social security. || *En previsión de*, as a precaution against. || *Previsión del tiempo*, weather forecast. || *Previsión social*, social security.
previsivo, va adj. Farsighted, thoughtful, provident.
previsor, ra adj. Provident, thoughtful, farsighted. || *Poco previsor*, improvident, imprudent.
previsto, ta adj. Foreseen, predicted: *tenía previsto su fracaso*, I had foreseen his failure. || Provided: *previsto por los estatutos*, provided by the statutes. || — *Como previsto*, as anticipated *o* planned. || *Estaba previsto su fracaso*, his failure was predictable *o* foreseeable, it was evident that he would fail. || *No es un caso previsto por la ley*, there is no provision in the law for a case such as this.
prez m. Honour [U.S., honor], glory.
prieto, ta adj. Firm (carne). || Tight (apretado). || Very dark, black (color). || Stingy (tacaño).
prima f. Prime (hora canónica). || MÚS. First string (cuerda). || Cousin: *prima carnal*, first cousin. || COM. Premium: *prima de seguro*, insurance premium. | Bonus, bounty (gratificación): *prima de rendimiento*, output bonus. | Subsidy (subvención). || MIL. First quarter of the night. || MAR. *Prima de flete*, primage.
primacía f. Primacy (superioridad, dignidad de primado).
primada f. FAM. *Es una primada pagar tanto*, it is stupid to pay so much.
primado m. REL. Primate.
primar v. intr. To have *o* to take priority.
primario, ria adj. Primary: *escuela, enseñanza primaria*, primary school, education; *instintos primarios*, primary instincts. || — POÉT. *Acento primario*, primary accent. || GEOL. *Era primaria*, primary era.
— M. ELECTR. Primary. || — F. Primary school.
primate m. ZOOL. Primate. || FIG. Important figure *o* person (prócer).
primavera f. Spring (estación). || Spring, springtime (época). || BOT. Primrose. || Silk cloth printed with a flower pattern (tela). || FIG. Prime, springtime: *en la primavera de su vida*, in the prime of [his] life. || — M. y f. FIG. y FAM. Drip (despistado).
primaveral adj. Spring: *un vestido primaveral*, a spring dress. || Springlike.
primazgo m. Cousinhood, cousinship (parentesco). || Primacy (primacía).
primer adj. First: *primer piso*, first floor. || *Primer ministro*, Prime Minister, Premier.

— OBSERV. *Primer* is the apocopation of *primero*, used before a masculine singular noun.

primera f. AUT. First, first gear, low gear (velocidad). || First class: *viajar en primera*, to travel first class. || — *A la primera*, first time: *conseguirlo a la primera*, to succeed first time. || FIG. *A las primeras de cambio*, at the first opportunity. | *De primera*, first-class, first-rate (muy bueno), first-rate (muy bien), really well (muy bien hecho). | *Venirle a uno de primera*, to come in very handy (ser muy útil), to suit s.o. to a tee, to suit s.o. down to the ground (convenir), to come just at the right moment (ser oportuno).
primeramente adv. Firstly, first (en primer lugar).
primerizo, za adj. Novice (principiante). || MED. Primiparous.
— M. y f. Novice, beginner (novicio). || — F. Primipara.
primero, ra adj. First: *el primer hombre*, the first man; *la primera empleada*, the first employee. || Front, first (página). || Primary: *primera enseñanza*, primary education. || Former (anterior). || Best (mejor). || Leading, principal (más importante). || — *Artículos de primera necesidad*, basic necessities. || *Página primera*, page one. || *Primera actriz*, leading lady, star. || *Primera línea*, front line. || *Primeras materias*, raw materials. || *Vino por la mañana a primera hora*, he came early in the *o* first thing in the morning.
— M. y f. First: *es la primera de su clase*, she is first in her class. || Number one (el número uno). || Best (mejor). || — *A primeros de mes*, at the beginning of the month. || *Lo primero es lo primero*, first things first. || *Primero de año*, New Year's day. || *Primero de cordada*, leader, first on the rope (alpinismo). || *Primero entre sus pares*, the best man in his field. || *Ser el primero en*, to be the first to (con verbo). || — F. V. PRIMERA.
— Adv. First: *haz esto primero*, do this first. || Firstly (en una enumeración). || Before: *llegaré primero que tú*, I shall arrive before you. || Better, sooner (mejor): *primero morir que vivir en la esclavitud*, it is better to die than to live in slavery, I would sooner die than live in slavery.
primicias f. pl. First fruits: *las primicias del campo*, the first fruits of the countryside. || FIG. First fruits. || *Tener las primicias de una noticia*, to be the first to hear a piece of news.
primigenio, nia adj. Primitive, original.
primípara adj. f. MED. Primiparous.
— F. Primipara.
primitivismo m. Primitivism.
primitivo, va adj. Primitive. || Original: *a su estado primitivo*, to its original state.
— M. Primitive.
primo, ma adj. MAT. Prime: *número primo*, prime number. || *Materia prima*, raw material.
— M. y f. Cousin: *primo hermano* or *carnal*, first cousin; *primo segundo*, second cousin. || FIG. y FAM. Drip, dunce, dope: *este pobre chico es un primo*, this poor lad is a drip. || — FIG. y FAM. *Hacer el primo*, to be taken for a ride (dejarse engañar). | *Tiene cara de primo*, he looks a right drip.
primogénito, ta adj. First-born, eldest.
— M. y f. First-born.
primogenitura f. Primogeniture, birthright. || *Vender su primogenitura por un plato de lentejas*, to sell one's birthright *o* heritage for a mess of pottage.
primor m. Delicacy (finura). || Fine thing, lovely thing (cosa bonita). || Skill (destreza). || — *Esta chica, este bordado es un primor*, this girl, this embroidery is exquisite *o* beautiful. || *Hacer con primor*, to do

most skilfully. || *Que es un primor*, marvellously, wonderfully: *canta que es un primor*, she sings wonderfully.

primordial adj. Fundamental, essential, basic, primordial (fundamental). || Prime, primary (interés, importancia): *es de importancia primordial*, it is of prime importance.

primorosamente adv. Skilfully, exquisitely.

primoroso, sa adj. Exquisite, beautiful, fine (hermoso). || Skilful [U. S., skillful] (diestro).

prímula f. BOT. Primula.

primuláceas f. pl. BOT. Primulaceae.

princeps adj. First, original; *edición princeps*, first edition.

princesa f. Princess.

principado m. Principality, princedom (territorio y título). || Primacy (primacía). || — Pl. Principalities (séptimo coro de los ángeles).

principal adj. Principal, main (más importante). || Illustrious (noble). || Very important: *un asunto principal*, a very important matter. || — *Carretera principal*, main road. || GRAM. *Oración principal*, main clause. || *Piso principal*, main floor, first floor [U.S., second floor] (de una casa), dress circle (de teatro). || *Puerta principal*, front *o* main door.

— M. Principal (capital). || Chief, head boss (jefe de una fábrica, etc.). || Main floor, first floor [U.S., second floor] (de una casa). || Dress circle (de teatro, cine). || COM. y JUR. Principal. || *Lo principal*, the main thing *o* point.

príncipe adj. First, original: *edición príncipe*, first edition.

— M. Prince: *príncipe consorte*, prince consort; *príncipe heredero*, crown prince; *príncipe real*, prince royal. || — *El Príncipe Azul*, Prince Charming. || *Príncipe de Asturias*, crown prince of Spain. || *Vivir como un príncipe*, to live like a king, to live it up.

principesco, ca adj. Princely.

principianta f. Beginner, novice, learner.

principiante adj. Novice. || Who is beginning.

— M. y f. Beginner, novice, learner.

principiar v. tr. e intr. To start, to begin.

principio m. Start, beginning: *el principio de las negociaciones*, the start of [the] negotiations. || Origin, source (origen). || Principle, idea (idea). || Principle (teorema): *el principio de Arquímedes*, Archimedes' principle. || Principle (moral): *mis principios no me permiten hacerlo*, my principles will not allow me to do it. || Entrée (comidas). || Principle, rudiment, first notion: *principios de metafísica*, principles of metaphysics. || — *Al principio*, at first: *al principio no sabía qué decir*, at first he did not know what to say; *al principio no sabía nada, pero ahora trabaja bien*, at first he knew nothing, but now he works well; at the start, at the beginning: *al principio de la obra*, at the start of the play. || *A principios de* or *del mes*, at the beginning of the month. || *Dar principio a*, to start off. || *Del principio al fin* or *desde el principio hasta el fin*, from beginning to end, from start to finish. || *Desde el principio*, from the first, from the outset. || *El principio de conservación*, the instinct of self-preservation. || *En principio*, in *o* on principle. || *En un principio*, at first, to start with. || *Es el principio del fin*, it is the beginning of the end. || *Por principio* or *por principios*, on principle. || *Principio quieren las cosas*, it is a start. || *Sin principios*, unprincipled. || *Tener por principio*, to make a point of. || *Tener principio*, to start, to begin.

pringada f. Bread dipped in gravy *o* dripping.

pringar v. tr. To get grease on, to stain with fat (ensuciar). || To dip in the dripping (pan). || FAM. To wound (herir). | To drag, to involve: *pringarle a uno en un asunto*, to drag s.o. into an affair. | To slander, to run down (deshonrar). || FIG. y FAM. *¡Ya la has pringado!*, now you've done it!, that's torn it!

— V. intr. FAM. To work, to get stuck in (trabajar). | To make a packet (sacar tajada). | To get mixed up (mezclarse). || *Amer.* To drizzle (lloviznar).

— V. pr. To get grease on, to stain with fat (mancharse). || FIG. To get mixed up (en un asunto feo).

pringoso, sa adj. Greasy.

pringue m. y f. Dripping (que suelta el tocino al freírlo). || Grease stain (mancha).

prior, ra m. y f. REL. Prior (hombre), prioress (mujer).

priorato m. Priory (comunidad). || Priorate (cargo).

priori (a) loc. lat. A priori.

prioridad f. Priority.

prioritario, ria adj. Priority, having priority. || *Ser prioritario* to take *o* to have priority.

prisa f. Haste, hurry (apresuramiento). || Urgency (urgencia). || Speed (velocidad). || Rush (afluencia de gente o trabajo). || — *A prisa* or *de prisa*, quickly, swiftly, fast (rápidamente), hastily, hurriedly, in a hurry (apresuradamente). || *A toda prisa*, as quickly as possible, posthaste. || *Correr prisa*, to be urgent. || *Darse prisa*, to hurry, to hurry up. || *¡Date prisa!*, hurry up! || *¡De prisa!*, hurry up! || *De prisa y corriendo*, V. CORRER. || *Estar* or *andar con prisas*, to be in a hurry, to be pressed for time. || *Hay prisas*, we are in a hurry, we are pressed for time, it is urgent. || *Meter* or *dar prisa a uno*, to hurry s.o., to rush s.o. || *¿Por qué tantas prisas?*, why all the hurry?, what's the big hurry *o* rush? || *Tener prisa*, to be in a hurry. || *Tener prisa por* or *en*, to be in a hurry to.

prisión f. Prison (cárcel). || Imprisonment (encarcelamiento). || Capture, arrest, seizure (acción de prender). || Bond (atadura moral). || — Pl. Irons, shackles, chains (grilletes). || — JUR. *Prisión por deudas*, imprisonment for debts. | *Prisión preventiva*, remand in custody. | *Reducir a uno a prisión*, to imprison s.o., to put s.o. in prison.

prisionero, ra m. y f. Prisoner: *hacer prisionero a uno*, to take s.o. prisoner; *prisionero de guerra*, prisoner of war.

prisma m. MAT. Prism.

prismático, ca adj. MAT. Prismatic.

— M. pl. Binoculars.

prístino, na adj. Pristine, original.

privación f. Deprivation, deprival (acción). || Loss (pérdida). || Privation (falta). || *Pasar privaciones*, to suffer privation.

privadamente adv. Privately, in private: *discutir privadamente de algo*, to discuss sth. in private.

privado, da adj. Private: *clase privada*, private lesson. || Personal. || Confidential. || — *Privado de*, bereft of, without. || *Vida privada*, privacy: *no tener vida privada*, to have no privacy; private life: *no tiene por qué meterse en mi vida privada*, my private life is no concern of his.

— M. Favourite [U.S., favorite] (del rey). || Private: *en público y en privado*, in public and in private.

privanza f. Favour [U.S., favor].

privar v. tr. To deprive: *privar a uno de algo*, to deprive s.o. of sth. || To forbid (prohibir). || To prevent: *esto me privó de verte*, this prevented me from seeing you. || *El médico le privó de tabaco*, the doctor told him to stop smoking.

— V. intr. To be in favour [U.S., favor] (tener privanza): *privar con uno*, to be in s.o.'s favour. || To be popular, to be in fashion (tener aceptación). || To be present, to prevail (prevalecer).

— V. pr. To deprive o.s., to go without: *privarse de tabaco*, to deprive o.s. of cigarettes, to go without cigarettes. || To abstain from (abstenerse). || *No privarse de nada*, to lack nothing.

privativo, va adj. GRAM. Privative. || Particular (propio). || *Ser privativo de*, to be exclusive to.

privilegiado, da adj. Privileged. || — *Memoria privilegiada*, exceptionally good memory. || *Unos pocos privilegiados*, a privileged few.

— M. y f. Privileged person.

privilegiar v. tr. To grant a privilege to, to privilege, to favour [U.S., to favor].

privilegio m. Privilege.

pro m. Profit, advantage, benefit (ventaja). || — *En pro de*, for, on behalf of, for the benefit of: *campaña en pro de los subnormales*, campaign for the mentally handicapped. || *Hombre de pro*, upright *o* honest man. || *Los pros y los contras*, the pros and cons. || *No estar ni en pro ni en contra*, to be neither for nor against.

— Prep. In favour of [U.S., in favor of], on behalf of, for.

proa f. MAR. Prow, bows, *pl.*, bow. || — *Mascarón de proa*, figurehead. || FIG. *Poner la proa a algo*, to aim at sth., to set one's sights on sth. | *Poner la proa a alguien*, to turn against s.o. || MAR. *Poner proa a*, to set sail for, to make for, to head for.

probabilidad f. Probability, likelihood: *según toda probabilidad*, in all probability. || Chance, hope, prospect: *tener poca probabilidad de ganar*, to have little chance of winning. || *Probabilidades de vida*, life expectancy, *sing.*

probabilismo m. Probabilism.

probabilista adj./s. Probabilist.

probable adj. Probable, likely (casi cierto): *apenas probable*, hardly likely; *es poco probable que venga*, he is not likely to come. || Provable (demostrable).

probablemente adv. Probably, in all likelihood.

probación f. Proof (prueba). || Probation (noviciado).

probado, da adj. Proven, proved (demostrado). || Proven (acreditado): *es remedio probado*, it is a proven remedy.

probador, ra adj. Testing, test. || Proving.

— M. Fitting room (en una tienda).

probanza f. JUR. Proof.

probar* v. tr. To test, to put to the test (poner a prueba): *probar su fuerza*, to test one's strength. || To try (experimentar). || To prove (demostrar). || To try on: *probar un vestido*, to try on a dress. || To taste, to try: *probar el vino*, to taste the wine. || To try, to attempt (intentar): *probó levantarse*, he tried to get up. || — *No probar ni bocado*, not to eat a bite. || *Probar de todo*, to try a little of everything. || *Probar ventura*, to try one's luck.

— V. intr. To try (intentar). || To suit (sentar). || — *Probar a*, to try to, to attempt to. || *Probar bien*, to suit: *vivir en el campo me prueba bien*, living in the country suits me. || *Probar no cuesta nada*, there is no harm in trying.

— V. pr. To try on: *me probé un abrigo*, I tried on a coat; *ya me lo probé*, I have already tried it on.

probatorio, ria adj. Probative, probatory.

probeta f. QUÍM. Graduated test tube *o* flask, graduate. || MIL. Eprouvette (para la pólvora).

probidad f. Probity, integrity (honradez).
problema m. Problem: *resolver* or *solucionar un problema* to solve a problem.
problemático, ca adj. Problematic, problematical.
— F. Problems, *pl.*
probo, ba adj. Honest, upright.
probóscide f. ANAT. Proboscis.
proboscidios m. pl. ZOOL. Proboscideans, proboscidians.
procacidad f. Insolence, impudence (insolencia). || Indecency (indecencia).
procaína f. QUÍM. Procaine.
procaz adj. Insolent, impudent (insolente). || Shameless (sinvergüenza). || Indecent (indecente).
procedencia f. Origin, source. || Port of origin (de un barco). || JUR. Merits, *pl.* (de una petición, una demanda, etc.). || Cogency (de una idea).
procedente adj. Reasonable, sensible (sensato). || Fitting, proper (adecuado). || JUR. Admissible. || — *El tren procedente de Madrid*, the train from Madrid. || *Palabras procedentes del latín*, words which come from Latin, words derived from Latin. || *Procedente de*, coming from, proceeding from.
proceder m. Conduct, behaviour [U. S., behavior].
proceder v. intr. To come, to proceed: *esta palabra procede del latín*, this word comes from Latin. || To behave, to act (portarse). || To proceed, to go ahead, to get on (*a*, with) [pasar a]: *proceder a la elección*, to proceed with the election. || To be advisable (ser conveniente): *procede hacerlo con método*, it is advisable to do it methodically. || To be fitting, to be right (ser apto o justo). || To be sensible (ser sensato). || JUR. To be admissible *o* relevant *o* pertinent. || — JUR. *Proceder contra uno*, to institute *o* to take proceedings against s.o. || *Proceder de consuno*, to work in concert. || JUR. *Según proceda*, as befitting.
procedimiento m. Method, procedure, process (método). || Procedure (en asambleas). || JUR. Procedure (serie de trámites), proceedings, *pl.* (acción judicial).
proceloso, sa adj. Tempestuous, stormy.
prócer adj. Eminent, noble, illustrious. || FIG. Majestic, noble, lofty (árboles, etc.).
— M. Member of the Upper Chamber (en el parlamento). || Eminent person (persona importante).
procesado, da adj. JUR. Procedural, of the proceedings (del proceso). | Accused (acusado).
— M. y f. Accused, defendant.
procesal adj. JUR. Procedural, of the proceedings. || — *Costas procesales*, legal costs. || *Derecho procesal*, procedural law.
procesamiento m. JUR. Prosecution. || — *Auto de procesamiento*, indictment. || *Procesamiento de datos*, data processing (informática).
procesar v. tr. JUR. To prosecute (*por*, for).
procesión f. Procession. || — FIG. *La procesión va por dentro*, still waters run deep. | *No se puede repicar y andar en la procesión*, one cannot do two things at once.
procesional adj. Processional.
procesionalmente adv. In procession.
procesionaria adj. f. Processionary.
procesionario m. Processional (libro).
proceso m. Process (método): *proceso químico, industrial*, chemical, industrial process. || JUR. Trial, lawsuit, action (pleito). | Procedure (serie de trámites). || Process: *proceso mental*, thought *o* mental process. || Course (transcurso): *en el proceso de una vida*, in the course of a lifetime. || MED. Course, progress (de una enfermedad). || ANAT. Process. || *Proceso de datos*, data processing (informática).
proclama f. Proclamation. || — Pl. Banns (amonestaciones): *correr las proclamas*, to publish the banns.
proclamación f. Proclamation (notificación pública). || Acclamation (alabanza pública).
proclamador, ra m. y f. Proclaimer.
proclamar v. tr. To proclaim (anunciar). || To acclaim (aclamar).
— V. pr. To proclaim o.s.
proclítico, ca adj./s.m. GRAM. Proclitic.
proclive adj. Inclined, disposed (inclinado).
proclividad f. Proclivity (propensión).
procomún o **procomunal** m. Public service *o* utility.
procónsul m. Proconsul.
proconsulado m. Proconsulate (cargo). || Proconsulship (tiempo).
proconsular adj. Proconsular.
procreación f. Procreation.
procreador, ra adj. Procreant, procreative.
— M. y f. Procreator, begetter.
procrear v. tr. To procreate.
procumbente adj. BOT. Procumbent.
procura f. Power of attorney, proxy, procuration (poder dado). || *Amer.* Search (busca). | Obtaining (obtención).
procuración f. Power of attorney, proxy. || Office of a lawyer or procurator (oficio). || *Por procuración*, by procuration, by proxy.
procurador, ra m. y f. Procurator, lawyer (abogado). || REL. Procurator (hombre), procuratrix (mujer). || Procurator (magistrado romano). || — *Procurador a* or *de* or *en Cortes*, Member of Parliament. || FIG. y FAM. *Procurador de pobres*, busybody.
procuraduría f. Procurator's *o* lawyer's office.
procurar v. tr. To try (intentar): *procura venir temprano*, try to arrive early. || To get (obtener). || To procure, to manage to get: *le procuré un piso*, I procured a flat for him. || To give, to bring: *este niño sólo me procura satisfacciones*, this child gives me nothing but satisfaction. || *Procurar que*, to make sure that.
— V. pr. To procure o.s.
prodigalidad f. Prodigality.
pródigamente adv. Prodigally.
prodigar v. tr. To lavish (dar mucho). || To squander (malgastar). || FIG. To lavish: *prodigar cuidados*, to lavish care. || *No prodigar*, to be mean with.
— V. pr. To do one's best to please *o* to help (intentar agradar). || To be generous (*en*, with) [ser generoso]. || To make an exhibition of o.s., to show off (presumir).
prodigio m. Prodigy. || Prodigy, miracle, wonder: *hacer prodigios*, to work wonders. || *Niño prodigio*, child prodigy.
prodigiosidad f. Prodigiousness.
prodigioso, sa adj. Prodigious, wonderful (maravilloso). || FAM. Fabulous, enormous.
pródigo, ga adj. Prodigal, wasteful (despilfarrador). || Generous, lavish: *pródigo de* or *en alabanzas*, generous with praise; *pródigo con todos*, generous to *o* with everyone. || *El Hijo Pródigo*, the Prodigal Son.
pródromo m. Prodrome (síntoma).
producción f. Production: *producción en serie*, mass production.
producente adj. Productive. || Lucrative, profitable (negocio). || Producing, causing (que causa).
producible adj. Producible.
producir* v. tr. To produce. || To produce, to bear (frutos). || COM. To produce. | To bear, to yield (interés). || *Producir beneficios*, to yield profits, to be profitable.
— V. pr. To appear (aparecer): *producirse en público*, to appear in public. || To come about, to take place, to happen, to occur (un suceso).
productibilidad f. Productibility.
productividad f. Productivity.
productivo, va adj. Productive. || Lucrative, profitable (negocio).
producto, ta adj. (P.us.). Produced.
— M. Product: *productos manufacturados*, manufactured products. || AGR. Produce: *productos agrícolas*, farm produce (V. OBSERV.) || Proceeds, *pl.*: *el producto de una venta*, the proceeds of a sale. || COM. Yield, profit. | Product: *producto nacional bruto*, gross national product. || MAT. Product. || — *Producto derivado* by-product. || *Productos alimenticios*, foodstuffs. || *Productos de belleza*, cosmetics. || *Productos de consumo*, consumer goods. || *Productos químicos*, chemicals.

— OBSERV. La palabra inglesa *produce* se refiere a los productos agrícolas y hortícolas en general (*los productos agrícolas de Irlanda*, Ireland's farm produce). Cuando se trata de un solo producto se emplea *product* (*un producto hortícola*, a horticultural product).

productor, ra adj. Producing.
— M. y f. Producer. || Worker (trabajador). || — M. CINEM. Producer.
proemio m. Preface, introduction, proem.
proeza f. Exploit, heroic deed, feat (hazaña).
profanación f. Profanation, desecration.
profanador, ra adj. Profanatory. || Irreverent.
— M. y f. Profaner. || Irreverent person.
profanar v. tr. To profane, to desecrate (un lugar sagrado). || To show insufficient respect for (tener poco respeto). || To violate (una tumba). || To defile, to pollute (la inocencia). || To blacken (el recuerdo de alguien).
profano, na adj. Profane, worldly (no sagrado). || Profane, irreverent (que no respeta lo sagrado). || Uninitiated, lay, ignorant (ignorante). || (P.us.). Irreverent. || Indecent (indecente).
— M. y f. Uninitiated *o* ignorant person, layman. || (P.us.). Irreverent person. || *Los profanos*, the profane, the uninitiated.
profase f. BIOL. Prophase.
profecía f. Prophecy.
proferir* v. tr. To utter, to speak (palabras). || To hurl (insultos).
profesar v. tr. To profess (una doctrina, religión). || To teach (enseñar): *profesar la medicina*, to teach medicine. || To profess, to practise (ejercer una profesión). || To profess, to declare, to put forth (una opinión). || To have, to profess, to feel: *profesar un amor profundo a*, to have a deep love for.
— V. intr. To profess [vows] (religión). || To profess, to teach (enseñar).
profesión f. Profession. || REL. Taking of vows (de votos). | Profession, declaration (de fe). || — *De profesión escritor*, a writer by profession. || *Hacer profesión de*, to profess, to make a profession of.
profesional adj./s. Professional. || *Un profesional del crimen*, a professional criminal.
profesionalismo m. Professionalism.

profesionalizar v. tr. To professionalize.
profeso, sa adj. Professed.
— M. Professed monk. || — F. Professed nun.
profesor, ra m. y f. Teacher (en la escuela). || Lecturer (en la universidad). || — *Profesor auxiliar*, assistant [teacher]. || *Profesor de canto, de esgrima*, singing, fencing teacher *o* master. || *Profesor de gimnasia*, gym instructor *o* teacher.
profesorado m. Teaching profession (profesión). || [Teaching] staff, teachers, *pl.* (escuela), staff, lecturers, *pl.* (universidad) [cuerpo docente]. || Post of teacher (escuela), post of lecturer (universidad) [cargo].
profesoral adj. Teaching (escuela), lecturing (universidad): *trabajos profesorales*, teaching work.
profeta m. Prophet. || *Nadie es profeta en su tierra*, a prophet is without honour in his own country.
profético, ca adj. Prophetic.
profetisa f. Prophetess.
profetizador, ra adj. Prophesying.
— M. y f. Prophesier.
profetizar v. tr. e intr. To prophesy.
profiláctico, ca adj. MED. Prophylactic.
— F. MED. Prophylaxis.
profilaxis o **profilaxia** f. MED. Prophylaxis.
prófugo, ga adj./s. Fugitive (fugitivo). || — M. Deserter (del servicio militar). || JUR. Refractory person.
profundamente adv. Deeply. || FIG. Profoundly, deeply. | Soundly (dormir).
profundidad f. Depth: *trescientos pies de profundidad*, three hundred feet in depth. || FIG. Profundity (del pensamiento). | Soundness (del sueño). | Profoundness, deepness (de un misterio). | Profundity, depth, extent (del saber). || — *Poca profundidad*, shallowness. || FOT. *Profundidad de campo*, depth of field.
profundizar v. tr. To deepen, to make deeper. || FIG. To study in depth, to go *o* to delve deeply into, to examine thoroughly. || *Profundizar las cosas*, to get to the bottom of things.
— V. intr. To deepen. || FIG. To deepen (volverse más profundo). | To go deeply into a subject, to study a subject in depth. | *Tenemos que profundizar más*, we must go into it more deeply.
profundo, da adj. Deep: *un pozo profundo*, a deep well. || FIG. Profound: *pensamientos profundos*, profound thoughts; *miseria profunda*, profound poverty. | Utter (ignorancia). | Deep, heartfelt (respeto). | Deep, sound (sueño). | Pitch, inky, thick (oscuridad). || — *En la desesperación más profunda*, in the depths of despair. || *En lo más profundo de mi ser*, in the bottom of my heart, in my heart of hearts.
profusamente adv. Profusely.
profusión f. Profusion. || *Con profusión*, profusely.
profuso, sa adj. Profuse.
progenie f. Line, lineage, family (generación). || Progeniture, progeny, offspring (descendientes).
progenitor m. Progenitor. || — Pl. Ancestors (antepasados). || Parents (padres).
progenitura f. Progeniture, offspring (progenie).
progesterona f. Progesterone.
progestina f. Progestin.
prognatismo m. Prognathism.
prognato, ta adj. Prognathous, prognathic.
— M. y f. Prognathous person.
programa f. Programme [U.S., program] (de espectáculos, en la televisión, etc.). || Schedule, programme (de actividades). || Programme (en la informática). || Programme, platform (de un partido político). || Curriculum, programme (de estudios). || *Programa de vuelo*, flight programme.
programación f. Programming.
programador, ra adj. Programming.
— M. y f. Programmer. || — M. Programmer (electrónica).
programar v. tr. To programme [U.S., to program]. || To programme, to plan: *programar una reforma*, to programme a reform.
progresar v. intr. To progress, to make progress.
progresión f. Progression (adelanto). || MÚS. Progression. || MAT. *Progresión aritmética, geométrica*, arithmetic, geometric progression.
progresismo m. Progressivism (doctrina política). || Progressionism (creencia en el progreso).
progresista adj./s. Progressive: *periódico progresista*, progressive newspaper.
progresividad f. Progressiveness.
progresivo, va adj. Progressive.
progreso m. Progress, *inv.* || *Hacer progresos*, to make progress, to progress.
prohibición f. Prohibition. || Prohibition (de bebidas alcohólicas en los Estados Unidos). || *Levantar la prohibición de*, to lift the ban on.
prohibicionismo m. Prohibitionism.
prohibicionista adj./s. Prohibitionist.
prohibido, da adj. Forbidden, prohibited: *terminantemente prohibido*, strictly forbidden. || — *Dirección prohibida*, no entry (calle). || *Prohibido aparcar*, no parking. || *Prohibido el paso*, v. PASO. || *Prohibido fijar carteles*, stick no bills. || *Prohibido fumar*, no smoking, smoking prohibited.
prohibir v. tr. To forbid, to prohibit (vedar): *te prohibo que salgas*, I forbid you to go out; *prohibir a uno que haga algo*, to prohibit s.o. from doing sth. || — *Se prohibe fumar*, no smoking. || *Se prohibe la entrada*, no entry.
prohibitivo, va adj. Prohibitive: *ley prohibitiva*, prohibitive law; *precio prohibitivo*, prohibitive price.
prohibitorio, ria adj. Prohibitory.
prohijamiento m. Adoption.
prohijar v. tr. To adopt (a un niño, opiniones).
prohombre m. Great figure *o* man, outstanding man (persona notable). || Leader (dirigente).
proindivisión f. JUR. Joint possession.
pro indiviso loc. lat. JUR. Pro indiviso.
proís o **proíz** m. MAR. Mooring post (noray).
prójima f. FAM. Woman (mujer). | Tart (mujer libertina). | Better half (esposa).
prójimo m. One's fellow man, neighbour [U.S., neighbor]. || FAM. Bloke (sujeto). || — *Amar al prójimo como a sí mismo*, to love one's neighbour as o.s. || *Ser bueno con su prójimo*, to be good to others *o* to one's fellow man.
prolapso m. MED. Prolapse, prolapsus.
prole f. Offspring, progeny.
prolegómenos m. pl. Prolegomena (introducción).
prolepsis f. Prolepsis (anticipación).
proletariado m. Proletariat.
proletario, ria adj./s. Proletarian.
proletarización f. Proletarianization.
proletarizar v. tr. To proletarianize.
proliferación f. Proliferation.
proliferar v. intr. To proliferate.
prolífero, ra adj. Proliferous.
prolífico, ca adj. Prolific.
prolijidad f. Prolixity, tediousness, verbosity, longwindedness (pesadez). || Meticulousness, thoroughness (meticulosidad). || Extensiveness.
prolijo, ja adj. Prolix, long-winded, tedious, verbose: *estilo prolijo*, prolix style. || Exhaustive, thorough (exhaustivo). || Meticulous (meticuloso).
prologar v. tr. To prologue, to preface, to write a preface *o* prologue to.
prólogo m. Prologue, preface, introduction, foreword. || FIG. Prelude.
prologuista m. Writer *o* author of a prologue *o* preface.
prolonga f. MIL. Prolonge.
prolongación f. Prolongation. || Extension (de una ciudad, calle).
prolongadamente adv. Lengthily, at great length: *hablar prolongadamente*, to speak lengthily.
prolongado, da adj. Prolonged. || Oblong, long (apaisado). || Lengthy (de mucho tiempo).
prolongador, ra adj. Prolonging, who *o* which prolongs.
— M. y f. Prolonger, person who prolongs.
prolongamiento m. Prolongation.
prolongar v. tr. To prolong, to extend.
— V. pr. To be prolonged. || To extend (extenderse). || To last longer: *la sesión se prolongó más de lo previsto*, the meeting lasted longer than expected. || *La reunión se ha prolongado*, the meeting ended late *o* went on late *o* lasted longer than expected.
promediar v. tr. To divide in two. || To average out (sacar el promedio).
— V. intr. To mediate. || *Al promediar el mes de junio*, in the middle of June.
promedio m. Middle (punto de división en dos). || Average: *el promedio es de mil toneladas*, the average is one thousand tons. || — *Calcular el promedio de las exportaciones*, to calculate average exports. || *El promedio de las exportaciones fue de X libras*, exports averaged X pounds. || *El promedio de sus ingresos es de*, their average income is. || *En* or *como promedio*, on average. || *Ganan un promedio de cien libras*, they earn one hundred pounds on average.
promesa f. Promise: *cumplir su* or *con su promesa*, to keep one's promise; *faltar a una promesa*, to break a promise. || Vow (religioso). || FIG. Hope: *este joven bailarín es la promesa de la compañía*, this young dancer is the hope of the company.
prometedor, ra adj. Promising, full of promise.
— M. y f. Promiser.
prometeo m. QUÍM. Promethium.
Prometeo n. pr. m. MIT. Prometheus.
prometer v. tr. To promise: *prometer hacer algo*, to promise to do sth. || FIG. *Prometer el oro y el moro*, to promise the earth, to promise the moon and stars.
— V. intr. To promise. || — *Este niño promete*, this child shows promise *o* promises much. || *Es un tenista que promete*, he is a promising tennis player.
— V. pr. To promise o.s. || To expect (esperarse). || To get engaged (*con*, to) [desposarse]. || FAM. *Prometérselas felices*, to have high hopes.
prometido, da adj. Promised (futuro). || Engaged (novios): *prometido con*, engaged to.
— M. Fiancé (novio). || — F. Fiancée (novia). || — *Cumplir con lo prometido*, to keep one's promise. || *Lo prometido es deuda*, a promise is a promise.
prominencia f. Protuberance, projection, bulge. || Rise (del terreno). || FIG. Prominence, prominency.
prominente adj. Prominent, projecting, protruding (saliente). || FIG. Prominent.
promiscuidad f. Promiscuity, promiscuousness.
promiscuo, cua adj. Promiscuous.

promisión f. Promise. || *Tierra de Promisión*, Promised Land.
promisorio, ria adj. JUR. Promissory: *juramento promisorio*, promissory oath. || Promising (alentador).
promoción f. Promotion. || — *Partido de promoción*, promotion match (deportes). || *Promoción de ventas*, sales promotion. || *Ser de la misma promoción universitaria*, to graduate in the same year, to be in the same year.
promocionar v. tr. COM. To promote.
promontorio m. Promontory, headland (punta). || Small hill (colina). || ANAT. Promontory.
promotor, ra o **promovedor, ra** adj. Promotive.
— M. y f. Promoter, originator, cause (origen). || COM. Promoter. || Instigator (instigador).
promover* v. tr. To promote (elevar): *promover a uno a capitán*, to promote s.o. to captain. || To promote (promocionar). || To foster, to favour (fomentar). || To provoke, to cause (provocar). || To start (empezar). || To instigate, to stir up (sublevaciones, etc.). || To cause, to give rise to (dar lugar a).
promovido, da adj. Promoted.
promulgación f. Promulgation, enactment. || FIG. Announcement.
promulgador, ra adj. Promulgating.
— M. y f. Promulgator.
promulgar v. tr. To promulgate to enact (una ley, etc.). || FIG. To promulgate, to proclaim, to make public (divulgar una cosa).
pronación f. ANAT. Pronation.
pronador, ra adj. ANAT. Pronating.
— M. ANAT. Pronator.
pronaos m. Pronaos (de templo griego).
prono, na adj. Prone [to]. || Prone (echado sobre el vientre). || *Decúbito prono*, prone decubitus.
pronombre m. GRAM. Pronoun: *pronombre personal*, personal pronoun.
pronominado, da o **pronominal** adj. GRAM. Pronominal.
pronosticación f. Prognostication, forecasting.
pronosticador, ra m. y f. Prognosticator, forecaster.
pronosticar v. tr. To forecast, to foretell, to predict, to prognosticate. || MED. To give the prognosis of.
pronóstico m. Prognostication, prediction, forecast (predicción). || Forecast (del tiempo). || MED. Prognosis. || — MED. *De pronóstico leve*, not serious. | *Pronóstico reservado*, prognosis that has not yet been disclosed.
prontamente adv. Quickly.
prontito adv. FAM. At once, right now (en seguida). | Very quickly, on the double (muy rápido).
prontitud f. Speed, promptness, quickness (rapidez). || Quickness, sharpness (de la inteligencia).
pronto, ta adj. Quick, fast, rapid (rápido): *pronto a enfadarse*, quick to anger. || Ready (dispuesto): *pronto para salir*, ready to go out. || — *Ser pronto de genio*, to be quick-tempered. || *Una pronta curación*, a speedy recovery.
— M. Sudden movement, start: *le dio un pronto*, he gave a start, he made a sudden movement. || Sudden impulse, urge (arrebato repentino). || Sudden feeling (sentimiento inesperado).
— Adv. Fast, quickly (de prisa). || Early (temprano): *llegó muy pronto*, he arrived very early. || *Amer.* Suddenly (de pronto). || — *Al pronto*, at first. || *Cuanto más pronto mejor*, the sooner the better. || *De pronto*, suddenly, all at once (de repente), hastily, hurriedly, quickly (apresuradamente). || *¡Hasta pronto!*, see you soon! || *Lo más pronto (posible)*, as soon as possible, as fast as possible. || *Por de* or *por lo pronto*, for the moment, for the time being (por ahora), at least, anyway (al menos), meanwhile (mientras tanto). || *Tan pronto ... como*, as soon as (en cuanto), no sooner ... than: *tan pronto ríe como llora*, he no sooner laughs than he cries.
prontuario m. Summary. || Handbook (compendio). || Notebook (libro de apuntes).
pronunciable adj. Pronounceable.
pronunciación f. Pronunciation. || JUR. Passing (de una sentencia). || *Pronunciación figurada*, phonetic transcription.
pronunciado, da adj. Pronounced. || FIG. Pronounced (marcado). | Sharp (curva). | Marked, noticeable (acentuado).
pronunciamiento m. Rising, insurrection (alzamiento). || JUR. Pronouncement, pronouncing [of sentence].
pronunciar v. tr. To pronounce: *pronunciar bien una palabra*, to pronounce a word well. || To pronounce, to speak: *pronunció dos palabras*, he pronounced two words. || To deliver: *pronunciar un discurso*, to deliver a speech. || JUR. To pronounce, to pass: *pronunciar un fallo*, to pronounce sentence.
— V. pr. To be pronounced. || To rise up (sublevarse). || To pronounce o.s., to declare o.s. (declararse).

— OBSERV. *Pronunciarse* is a Gallicism when used as a synonym of *declararse, manifestarse.*

propagación f. Propagation, spreading.
propagador, ra adj. Propagating, propagative.
— M. y f. Propagator, spreader: *propagador de noticias falsas*, propagator of false rumours.
propaganda f. Propaganda (a favor de una idea, opinión, etc.). || Advertising, publicity (comercial). || COM. *Hacer propaganda*, to advertise.
propagandista adj./s. Propagandist.
propagandístico, ca adj. [Of *o* pertaining to] propaganda. || COM. Advertising, publicity.
propagar v. tr. To propagate. || FIG. To spread, to propagate: *propagar una noticia*, to spread a piece of news. | To divulge (algo secreto). || FÍS. To propagate, to convey (la luz, el sonido).
— V. pr. To propagate, to spread (noticias). || FÍS. To be conveyed (la luz, el sonido). || To spread (una epidemia).
propagativo, va adj. Propagative.
propalación f. Spreading, propagation.
propalador, ra adj. Propagating, propagative.
— M. y f. Propagator, spreader. || Divulger (divulgador).
propalar v. tr. To spread, to propagate: *propalar una noticia*, to spread a piece of news. || To divulge (divulgar).
propano m. QUÍM. Propane (gas).
proparoxítono, na adj. Proparoxytone.
propasar v. tr. To go beyond, to overstep.
— V. pr. To go too far, to overstep the limits (excederse).
propender v. intr. To tend, to be inclined (inclinarse): *propende a la tristeza*, he tends towards sadness, he is inclined to sadness || To have a leaning towards (estar aficionado).

— OBSERV. The regular past participle of this verb is *propendido*. The irregular past participle *propenso* is used only as an adjective.

propensión f. Propensity (*a*, for), tendency (*a*, to, towards), inclination (*a*, to). || MED. Predisposition, susceptibility.
propenso, sa adj. Inclined, prone: *ser propenso a la ira*, to be inclined to anger.
propergol m. Propellant.
propi f. FAM. Tip (propina).
propiamente adv. Exactly, really. || — *El centro propiamente dicho*, the centre proper, the centre itself. || *No es un oficial propiamente dicho*, strictly speaking he is not an officer, he is not really an officer, he is not an officer in the true sense of the word.
propiciación f. Propitiation.
propiciador, ra adj. Propitious.
— M. y f. Propitiator.
propiciar v. tr. To placate, to appease: *propiciar la ira divina*, to placate the anger of the gods. || To propitiate (hacer propicio). || *Amer.* To patronize, to favour [U. S., to favor] (auspiciar).
propiciatorio, ria adj. Propitiatory.
propicio, cia adj. Propitious, favourable: *ocasión propicia*, propitious moment. || Suitable: *es la persona más propicia para este trabajo*, he is the most suitable person for this job. || *Ser propicio a*, to be inclined *o* prone to.
propiedad f. Property (lo que posee uno). || Property, estate (terreno, casa). || Ownership, proprietorship (hecho de poseer). || Property, quality (característica). || Perfect likeness (semejanza). || FÍS. y QUÍM. Property. || — *De la propiedad de*, belonging to. || *Emplear una palabra con propiedad*, to use a word correctly. || JUR. *Nuda propiedad*, bare ownership, ownership without usufruct. || *Pertenecer en propiedad*, to rightfully belong. || *Propiedad horizontal* or *de casa por pisos*, joint-ownership of a block of flats. || *Propiedad industrial*, patent rights, *pl.* || *Propiedad inmobiliaria*, real estate. || *Propiedad literaria*, copyright.
propietario, ria adj. Proprietary.
— M. Owner (de cualquier cosa). || Proprietor, owner (de casa, fábrica, etc.). || AGR. Landowner, landlord, property owner (de tierras). || — JUR. *Nudo propietario*, bare owner, owner without usufruct. | *Propietario de bienes inmuebles*, property owner. || *Ser propietario de*, to own. || — F. Owner, proprietress, landlady.
propileo m. ARQ. Propylaeum.
propina f. Tip, gratuity (gratificación). || — *Dar una propina a un camarero*, to tip a waiter. || *Dejar una propina*, to leave a tip. || FAM. *De propina*, as a tip (como propina), in addition, extra (por añadidura).
propinar v. tr. To give (dar): *propinar una paliza*, to give a hiding.
propincuidad f. Proximity, propinquity.
propincuo, cua adj. Near.
propio, pia adj. Own (que pertenece): *su propio hijo*, his own son. || Own (característico): *su carácter propio*, his own character; *en su propio interés*, in your own interest. || Particular, peculiar (particular). || Natural: *propio de su edad*, natural for his age. || GRAM. Proper: *nombre propio*, proper noun. | Proper, strict, real: *sentido propio*, strict meaning. || Suitable, correct (conveniente). || Own, real: *su pelo propio*, his own hair. || Himself, herself, etc.: *el propio interesado debe firmar*, the interested party himself must sign. || Same: *hacer lo propio*, to do the same. || — *Amer. Al propio*, on purpose (expresamente). || *Al propio tiempo*, at the same time. || *De propio*, on purpose. || *En propias manos*, personally, in person. || FAM. *Es muy propio de él*, it's very typical of him, it's just like him. || *Lo propio*,

the same [thing] (lo mismo): *haré lo propio que tú*, I shall do the same as you. || *Lo propio sucede con*, it is the same with, the same thing happens with. || *Ser propio de*, to be characteristic of *o* peculiar to: *la irreflexión es propia de los niños*, thoughtlessness is characteristic of children; *la llovizna es propia de esta región*, drizzle is characteristic of this region.
— M. Messenger (mensajero): *despachar un propio*, to send a messenger. || REL. Proper. || — Pl. Communal *o* public property, *sing.*
propóleos m. Propolis (sustancia cérea).
proponedor, ra o **proponente** adj. Proposing.
— M. y f. Proposer.
proponer* v. tr. To propose, to put forward, to suggest: *proponer un parecer*, to propose an idea. || To propound (una teoría). || To move, to propose (en una reunión): *propongo que se levante la sesión*, I move that the meeting be adjourned.
— V. pr. To propose: *se propone salir mañana para Madrid*, he proposes to leave for Madrid tomorrow. || To mean, to intend, to propose (tener intención de). || *Tú te has propuesto que lleguemos tarde*, you are determined to make us arrive late.
proporción f. Proportion: *guardar las proporciones*, to keep a sense of proportion; *en proporción con*, in proportion to; *las proporciones del cuerpo humano*, the proportions of the human body; *guardar proporción con*, to be in proportion with; *fuera de proporción*, out of proportion. || Chance, opportunity (oportunidad). || Opportunity (coyuntura): *esperar una buena proporción*, to wait for the right opportunity. || MAT. Proportion, ratio (razón). || — Pl. Size, *sing.* (tamaño). || Extent, *sing.* (extensión). || — *A proporción de*, according to (según). || *En grandes proporciones*, greatly, to a great extent, on a large scale. || *No hay ninguna proporción*, there is no comparison. || *No sabemos en qué proporción intervino él*, we do not know to what extent he was involved. || MAT. *Proporción aritmética, geométrica*, arithmetic, geometric proportion.
proporcionable adj. Proportionable.
proporcionado, da adj. Proportionate, in proportion. || Suitable (adecuado). || *Bien proporcionado*, well proportioned.
proporcional adj. Proportional.
proporcionalidad f. Proportionality. || Proportion.
proporcionalmente adv. Proportionally.
proporcionar v. tr. To proportion: *proporcionar sus gastos a sus recursos*, to proportion one's expenditure to one's means. || To furnish, to provide (facilitar): *proporcionar trabajo a alguien*, to provide s.o. with work. || To give (dar). || To lend (prestar). || To procure, to bring (procurar): *proporcionar provecho*, to procure a benefit. || To adapt: *proporcionar los medios al objeto*, to adapt the means to the end.
— V. pr. To procure, to obtain, to get: *proporcionarse dinero*, to procure money.
proposición f. Proposition, proposal (sugerencia). || Proposal, offer (oferta). || MAT. Proposition. || GRAM. Clause (oración).
propósito m. Intention (intención): *buenos propósitos*, good intentions. || Purpose, aim, object (objetivo). || Subject [matter] (tema). || — *A propósito*, by the way (por cierto) opportunely, at the right time (oportunamente), useful, handy (útil): *el dinero que me enviaste me vino muy a propósito*, the money that you sent me came in very handy; on purpose, intentionally (a posta): *perdona, no lo hice a propósito*, excuse me, I didn't do it on purpose; suitable, fitting, appropriate (adecuado): *ese vestido no es a propósito para ir de excursión*, that dress is not very suitable for an excursion. || *A propósito de*, with regard to, on the subject of, speaking of: *a propósito de dinero ¿cuándo me vas a pagar?*, speaking of money, when are you going to pay me?; because of (con motivo de). || *Con el propósito de*, in order to. || *Con este propósito*, to this end. || *De propósito*, on purpose, intentionally, deliberately (a posta). || *Fuera de propósito*, irrelevant, beside the point. || *Poco a propósito*, rather unsuitable, rather inadequate. || *Tener el propósito de aprender*, to intend to *o* to propose to *o* to mean to learn.
propretor m. Propraetor, propretor.
propretura f. Propraetorship, propretorship.
propuesta f. Proposal, proposition, suggestion: *a propuesta de*, at the proposal of. || Offer, proposal (oferta). || Tender (de obras públicas).
propugnación f. Defence [U.S., defense], advocacy.
propugnar v. tr. To defend, to advocate.
propulsar v. tr. To propel, to drive (impeler). || To reject, to refuse (rechazar). || FIG. To foster, to promote (fomentar).
propulsión f. Propulsión: *propulsión a chorro* or *por reacción*, jet propulsion. || *Con propulsión a chorro*, jet-propelled.
propulsivo, va adj. Propulsive.
propulsor, ra adj. Propulsive. || *Cohete propulsor*, rocket propulsor.
— M. Propulsor.
prorrata f. Quota, share [U.S., prorate]. || *A prorrata*, pro rata, proportionally.
prorratear v. tr. To apportion [U.S., to prorate], to share out *o* to divide proportionally.
prorrateo m. Apportionment [U.S., proration], sharing. || *A prorrateo*, pro rata, proportionally.
prórroga f. Prorogation, prolongation, extension. || COM. Extension. || MIL. Deferment. || DEP. Extra time [U.S., overtime] (de un partido). || *Prórroga tácita*, tacit extension (de un acuerdo, etc.).
prorrogable adj. That can be prolonged *o* extended.
prorrogación f. Prorogation, extension.
prorrogar v. tr. To prorogue, to prolong. || To extend (ampliar). || MIL. To defer.
prorrumpir v. intr. To shoot forth, to spring up (brotar). || FIG. To burst out, to burst: *prorrumpir en llanto, en sollozos, en carcajadas*, to burst out crying, sobbing, laughing, to burst into tears, sobs, laughter. || To break out: *prorrumpían las críticas por todos los lados*, criticism broke out on all sides. || — *Los espectadores prorrumpieron en aplausos*, the spectators burst into applause. || *Prorrumpir en gritos de alegría, de dolor*, to shout for *o* with joy, to scream *o* to yell with pain. || *Prorrumpir en insultos*, to unleash a shower of insults, to hurl abuse. || *Prorrumpir en lágrimas*, to burst into tears.
prosa f. Prose. || FIG. Prosaicness, prosaic nature, prose (aspecto vulgar de las cosas). | Hot air (palabrería). || FIG. y FAM. *Gastar mucha prosa*, to talk and talk, to go on and on.
prosador, ra m. y f. Prosaist, prose writer. || FIG. y FAM. Chatterbox, talker, windbag (hablador).
prosaico, ca adj. Prosaic.
prosaísmo m. Prosaism. || FIG. Prosaicness, prosaic nature: *el prosaísmo de las tareas cotidianas*, the prosaicness of everyday tasks.
prosapia f. Ancestry, lineage (alcurnia).
proscenio m. TEATR. Proscenium. || *Palco de proscenio*, proscenium box, stage box.
proscribir v. tr. To proscribe, to banish (echar). || FIG. To proscribe, to prohibit (prohibir). || To outlaw (a un criminal).
proscripción f. Proscription, banishment (destierro). || FIG. Proscription, prohibition (prohibición). || Outlawing (de criminales).
proscriptor, ra adj. Proscriptive.
— M. Proscriber.
proscrito, ta adj. Proscribed, banished. || Outlawed (criminal).
— M. y f. Exile. || Outlaw (criminal).
prosecución f. Pursuit, pursuance: *la prosecución de un negocio, de un ideal*, the pursuit of a business deal, of an ideal. || Continuation (continuación).
proseguimiento m. V. PROSECUCIÓN.
proseguir* v. tr. To pursue: *proseguir sus estudios*, to pursue one's studies. || To proceed, to carry on with, to continue with: *proseguiremos el trabajo mañana*, we shall carry on with the work tomorrow. || To continue, to go on, to carry on: *prosiguió hablando*, he went on talking. || *Proseguir su camino*, to continue on one's way.
— V. intr. To continue, to go on, to proceed (seguir): *proseguir con* or *en su tarea*, to go on with one's task. || To continue, to persist (el mal tiempo).
— OBSERV. One should not confuse *proseguir* with *perseguir*.
proselitismo m. Proselytism.
proselitista adj. Proselytizing.
prosélito m. Proselyte, convert.
prosénquima m. BOT. Prosenchyma.
prosificar v. tr. To put into prose.
prosimios m. pl. ZOOL. Prosimii.
prosista m. Prosist, prose writer.
prosístico, ca adj. Prosaic, of *o* pertaining to prose.
prosodia f. GRAM. Prosody.
prosódico, ca adj. GRAM. Prosodic.
prosopopeya f. Prosopopoeia. || FIG. Pomposity.
prospección f. Prospecting, prospection (del subsuelo). || Canvassing, survey, prospection (del mercado).
prospectar v. tr. To prospect.
prospectivo, va adj. Prospective.
prospecto m. Prospectus.
prospector m. Prospector.
prósperamente adv. Prosperously.
prosperar v. tr. To prosper, to make prosperous.
— V. intr. To prosper, to thrive, to flourish: *los negocios prosperan*, business is prospering. || To thrive (un país). || To prosper, to be successful (una persona).
prosperidad f. Prosperity. || Success (éxito).
próspero, ra adj. Prosperous, thriving, flourishing: *comercio próspero*, prosperous business. || Prosperous, wealthy, well-to-do, well-off (persona). || *Feliz y próspero Año Nuevo*, happy and prosperous New Year.
próstata f. ANAT. Prostate [gland].
prostático, ca adj. MED. Prostate, prostatic.
— M. Prostate sufferer.
prostatitis f. MED. Prostatitis.
prosternación f. Prostration.
prosternarse v. pr. To prostrate o.s.
próstesis f. GRAM. Prosthesis.
prostíbulo m. Brothel (lupanar).
próstilo m. ARQ. Prostyle.
prostitución f. Prostitution.
prostituir* v. tr. To prostitute. || FIG. To prostitute: *prostituir su talento*, to prostitute one's talent.
— V. pr. To prostitute o.s.
prostituta f. Prostitute.

protactinio m. QUÍM. Protactinium.
protagonista m. y f. Protagonist, main character, hero (hombre), heroine (mujer) [de novela, drama, película, etc.]. || TEATR. y CINEM. *Ser el protagonista*, to play the lead, to star (un actor).
protagonizar v. tr. To play the lead in, to star in: *¿quién protagoniza la película?*, who plays the lead in the film?, who stars in the film?
protargol m. QUÍM. Protargol.
protección f. Protection. || *Sistema de protección*, protective *o* safety system.
proteccionismo m. Protectionism.
proteccionista adj./s. Protectionist.
protector, ra o **protectriz** adj. Protective, protecting. || FIG. Patronizing (actitud). || *Sociedad protectora de animales*, Society for the Prevention of Cruelty to Animals.
— M. Protector, defender (defensor). || Patron (de las artes, etc.). || Mouthpiece (boxeo). || Stocking protector (de las medias). || HIST. Protector (de Inglaterra). || — F. Protectress. || Patroness.
protectorado m. Protectorate.
proteger v. tr. To protect: *¡que Dios le proteja!*, may God protect you!
protegido, da adj. Protected, favoured. || TECN. Guarded.
— M. y f. Protégé (hombre), protégée (mujer). || *Paso protegido*, right-of-way.
proteico, ca adj. Protean (cambiante). || QUÍM. Proteinic, proteic, proteinaceous.
proteido m. QUÍM. Proteid.
proteína f. QUÍM. Protein.
proteínico, ca adj. QUÍM. Proteinic.
proteles m. ZOOL. Proteles.
Proteo n. pr. m. MIT. Proteus.
protervidad f. Perversity, wickedness.
protervo, va adj. Perverse, wicked.
— M. y f. Pervert.
protésico, ca adj. MED. Prosthetic.
prótesis f. GRAM. Prosthesis, prothesis. || MED. Prosthesis: *prótesis dental*, dental prosthesis. || REL. Prothesis.
protesta f. Protest: *hacer una protesta*, to raise a protest. || Protestation (de inocencia). || COM. Protest (de letras). || JUR. *Bajo protesta*, under protest.
protestación f. Protestation.
protestador, ra adj. Protesting, protestant.
— M. y f. Protester.
protestante adj. Protesting, protestant (que protesta). || REL. Protestant.
— M. y f. Protester. || REL. Protestant.
protestantismo m. Protestantism.
protestar v. intr. To protest (reclamar). || FAM. To grumble (refunfuñar): *siempre está protestando*, he is always grumbling. || *Protestar de su inocencia*, to protest one's innocence.
— V. tr. COM. To protest, to give notice of a protest (una letra).
protesto m. Protestation (protesta). || COM. Protest.
protestón, ona m. y f. FAM. Moaner, grumbler.
prótidos m. pl. QUÍM. Protides.
protocolar v. tr. To protocol, to protocolize.
protocolar o **protocolario, ria** adj. Established by protocol. || FIG. Formal: *invitación protocolaria*, formal invitation.
protocolización f. JUR. Probate (de un testamento).
protocolizar v. tr. To protocol, to protocolize. || JUR. To probate.
protocolo m. Protocol. || Medical record. || FIG. Etiquette, formalities, *pl.* || *Jefe de protocolo*, Chief of Protocol.
protohistoria f. Protohistory.
protohistórico, ca adj. Protohistoric.
protomártir m. Protomartyr.
protón m. FÍS. Proton.
protónico, ca adj. FÍS. Protonic.
protonotario m. REL. Protonotary, prothonotary. || *Protonotario apostólico*, protonotary apostolic.
protoplasma m. BIOL. Protoplasm.
protoplasmático, ca o **protoplásmico, ca** adj. BIOL. Protoplasmic.
protoplasto m. BIOL. Protoplast.
protórax m. ZOOL. Prothorax.
prototipo m. Prototype.
protóxido m. QUÍM. Protoxide.
protozoario o **protozoo** m. ZOOL. Protozoon.

— OBSERV. El pl. inglés de esta palabra es *protozoa*.

protráctil adj. Protractile: *lengua protráctil*, protractile tongue.
protractor, ra adj. ANAT. *Músculo protractor*, protractor.
protrombina f. QUÍM. Prothrombin.
protuberancia f. Protuberance.
protuberante adj. Protuberant.
protutor, ra m. y f. JUR. Protutor.
provecto, ta adj. Old (antiguo). || Advanced: *edad provecta*, advanced age.
provecho m. Profit, benefit: *sin provecho alguno*, without any profit. || Progress (adelanto). || Advantage (ventaja). || — FAM. *¡Buen provecho!*, enjoy your meal! || *De provecho*, useful (útil), profitable (provechoso). || *En provecho de*, in favour of, to the advantage of, to the profit of. || *No le será de ningún provecho*, it will be of no use to him. || *Para su provecho*, for one's own good, to one's own advantage. || *Sacar provecho de*, to benefit from, to profit by (beneficiarse de), to take advantage of (aprovecharse de), to make the most of (aprovechar al máximo).
provechosamente adv. Profitably, beneficially. || Advantageously.
provechoso, sa adj. Beneficial, good: *provechoso a* or *para la salud*, beneficial to *o* good for one's health. || Profitable: *venta, experiencia provechosa*, profitable sale, experience. || Useful (útil). || Advantageous (ventajoso).
proveedor, ra adj. Purveying, supplying.
— M. y f. Supplier, purveyor (abastecedor). || *Proveedor de fondos*, financial backer.
proveer v. tr. To supply, to provide, to furnish: *proveer a uno de ropa, de alimentos*, to provide s.o. with clothes, with food. || To attend: *ella proveía a sus necesidades*, she attended to his needs. || To decide, to resolve (disponer). || To fill (una vacante).
— V. intr. JUR. To make a ruling, to rule (decidir). || JUR. *Para mejor proveer*, until further enquiries have been made.
— V. pr. To provision o.s. (aprovisionarse). || To provide o.s. (*de*, with) [proporcionarse].
proveniente adj. Arising, originating, resulting (procedente).
provenir* v. intr. To come from, to arise from, to issue from, to originate in (proceder).
Provenza n. pr. f. GEOGR. Provence (Francia).
provenzal adj./s. Provençal.
proverbial adj. Proverbial.
proverbio m. Proverb (refrán). || Saying (dicho). || — Pl. Proverbs (libro de la Biblia).
providencia f. Providence: *la Divina Providencia*, Divine Providence. || Measure, step (disposición): *tomar las providencias necesarias para*, to take the necessary measures in order to. || FIG. Providence. || JUR. Ruling, judgment (resolución). || *Tomar una providencia*, to make a decision.
providencial adj. Providential.
providencialismo m. Providential philosophy.
providencialista m. y f. Providential philosopher.
providencialmente adj. Providentially.
providenciar v. tr. To take [steps]. || JUR. To decide on, to rule on.
providente adj. Provident (próvido). || Prudent (previsor).
próvido, da adj. Provident (prevenido). || Propitious, favourable (propicio).
provincia f. Province. || — *Capital de provincia*, county town [U.S., county seat]. || *Vivir en la provincia*, to live in the provinces.
provincial adj. Provincial. || *Diputación provincial*, county council.
— M. REL. Provincial.
provinciala f. REL. Provincial.
provincialato m. REL. Provincialate.
provincialismo o **provincianismo** m. Provincialism.
provinciano, na adj./s. Provincial.
provisión f. Provision (acción). || Provision, supply: *hacer provisión de azúcar*, to get in a supply of sugar. || Measure (medida). || Cover, deposit, funds, *pl.* (en banco). || — Pl. Provisions, food, *sing.* (comida). || — *Provisión de fondos*, reserve funds, *pl.*, financial cover. || *Provisiones de boca*, provisions, victuals, food, *sing.*
provisional adj. Provisional. || *Gerente provisional*, acting manager.
provisionalidad f. Provisional state.
provisionalmente adv. Provisionally.
provisor m. y f. Purveyor, supplier, caterer (proveedor). || REL. Vicar-general.
provisora f. Cellaress [of a convent].
provisorio, ria adj. *Amer.* Provisional, provisory.
provisto, ta adj. Supplied, provided: *provisto de*, provided with.
provocación f. Provocation, incitement, instigation.
provocador, ra adj. Provocative, provoking. || *Una mirada provocadora*, a provocative glance.
— M. y f. Provoker.
provocante adj. Provocative, provoking.
provocar v. tr. To provoke: *provocar a uno*, to provoke s.o. || To rouse (despertar). || To cause: *provocar la risa* or *a risa*, to cause laughter. || To cause, to start: *una chispa provocó el incendio*, a spark started the fire; *el incidente que provocó la guerra*, the incident which started the war. || To cause, to bring about (ocasionar). || To make one feel sick (dar ganas de vomitar). || *Amer.* To feel like (apetecer): *no me provoca ir hoy*, I don't feel like going today.
provocativo, va adj. Provocative.
proxeneta m. Procurer, pimp, pander. || — F. Procuress.
proxenetismo m. Procuring, pandering.
próximamente adv. Soon, shortly, before long (dentro de poco). || Approximately, more or less (aproximadamente).
proximidad f. Nearness, closeness, proximity (cercanía). || *En las proximidades de*, close to, near, in the vicinity of.

próximo, ma adj. Near, close (cerca): *próximos unos a otros*, near [to] *o* close to one another. || Nearby, neighbouring [U.S., neighboring] (vecino). || Next: *el año próximo*, next year; *el mes próximo*, next month; *la próxima vez*, the next time; *el próximo 31 de agosto*, on the 31st August next. || — *En fecha próxima*, shortly, at an early date. || *Estar próximo a*, to be near, to be close to (al lado de), to be about to, to be on the point of (a punto de). || *Mes próximo pasado*, last month.

proyección f. Projection. || Showing (de una película). || Projection (de diapositivas). || FIG. Diffusion: *la proyección de la cultura*, the diffusion of culture. || *Proyección cónica*, conic projection.

proyectar v. tr. To project. || To plan, to be thinking of: *proyecto salir para los Estados Unidos*, I plan to leave *o* I am thinking of leaving for the United States. || To project, to hurl, to throw (lanzar). || To cast, to shed, to project (una luz). || To project, to cast (una sombra). || To emit, to pour, to gush (un líquido). || To show, to project (una película). || To project (fotos). || MAT. y FÍS. To project. || ARQ. To plan. || TECN. To design.

proyectil m. Projectile, missile. || Missile: *proyectil teledirigido* or *teleguiado*, guided missile; *proyectil balístico*, ballistic missile.

proyectista m. y f. Planner, schemer (planificador). || Designer, planner (diseñador).

proyecto m. Project, plan, scheme: *no es más que un proyecto*, it is just a project; *proyectos ambiciosos*, ambitious plans. || TECN. Plan, design. || Draft: *proyecto de acuerdo*, draft agreement; *proyecto de resolución*, draft resolution. || — *Estar en proyecto*, to be in the planning stage. || *Proyecto de ley*, bill: *presentar un proyecto de ley*, to introduce a bill. || *Tener en proyecto*, to be planning. || *Tener proyectos*, to have plans. || *Tengo un viaje en proyecto*, I am planning a trip.

proyector, ra adj. Projecting.
— M. Projector (para proyectar imágenes). || Condenser (óptico). || Searchlight (reflector). || Spotlight (en teatro, cine).

prudencia f. Prudence, caution (cuidado). || Moderation (templanza). || Wisdom (sagacidad). || Discretion (cordura). || *Con prudencia*, cautiously, prudently.

prudencial adj. Prudential. || FAM. Moderate: *una cantidad prudencial*, a moderate amount. | Approximate, rough (cálculo).

prudenciarse v. pr. *Amer.* To control o.s.

prudente adj. Prudent, wise: *un consejero prudente*, a wise adviser. || Cautious, wary, prudent (circunspecto). || Reasonable: *acostarse a una hora prudente*, to go to bed at a reasonable hour. || Careful (conductor, etc.). || *Lo más prudente sería*, it would be advisable to, it would be wisest *o* best to.

prudentemente adv. Prudently, wisely. || Carefully (cuidadosamente).

prueba f. Proof: *dar una prueba de lo que se afirma*, to give proof of what one says; *salvo prueba en contrario* or *en contra*, if there is no proof to the contrary; *con las pruebas en la mano*, with the proof in hand. || Proof, sign, token (señal): *dar pruebas de devoción*, to give a proof of one's devotion. || Test, examination (parte de un examen): *mañana tenemos la prueba de inglés*, tomorrow we have the English test. || Event (en deportes). || Tasting (de bebidas). || Fitting (de prenda de vestir): *sala de pruebas*, fitting room. || TECN. Test, trial. | Test (ensayo): *pruebas nucleares*, nuclear tests; *piloto de prueba*, test pilot. || MAT. Proof. || QUÍM. Experiment, test. || JUR. Evidence, proof. || IMPR. Proof. || FOT. Proof, print. || FIG. Trial, hardship, ordeal: *ha tenido que pasar duras pruebas en su vida*, he has lived through a lot of hardship *o* trials. || — Pl. Acrobatics (ejercicios acrobáticos). || — *A guisa de prueba*, by way of proof. || *A prueba*, on trial: *llevarse una radio a prueba*, to take a radio home on trial. || *A prueba de*, proof against. || *A prueba de agua, de bomba, de bala, de choques*, etc., waterproof, bombproof, bulletproof, shockproof, etc. || *A toda prueba*, unyielding, unwearying. || *Banco de pruebas*, testing bench. || IMPR. *Corregir pruebas*, to proofread. || *Dar prueba de*, to give *o* to produce proof of. || *Dar pruebas de inteligencia*, to show intelligence. || *Dar pruebas de su aptitud*, to prove one's ability. || *En prueba de*, in proof of, to prove. || MAT. *Hacer prueba de*, to prove the accuracy of (un cálculo). || *Hacer la prueba del nueve*, to cast out the nines. || CINEM. *Hacer una prueba*, to screen-test (a una persona), to shoot a trial take (hacer un ensayo). || *Los empleados están dando pruebas de descontento*, the employees are showing signs of discontent. || *Poner* or *someter a prueba*, to put to the test, to test, to try out (la amistad, un empleado, un avión, etc.). || *Prueba absoluta*, proof positive. || *Prueba de ello es que*, the proof of it is that. || *Prueba de inteligencia*, intelligence test. || *Prueba mixta*, mixed trials, *pl.* (esquí). || FOT. *Prueba negativa*, negative proof. | *Prueba positiva*, positive, print. || FAM. *Pruebas al canto*, with evidence to prove it. || *Someter a uno a una prueba de aptitud*, to give s.o. an aptitude test. || *Tomar a prueba*, to take on trial.

prurigo m. MED. Prurigo.

prurito m. MED. Pruritus, itch (comezón). || FIG. Itch, eagerness, urge (deseo excesivo).

Prusia n. pr. f. GEOGR. Prussia.

prusiano, na adj./s. Prussian. || *Azul de Prusia*, Prussian blue.

prusiato m. QUÍM. Prussiate.

prúsico, ca adj. QUÍM. *Ácido prúsico*, prussic acid.

psi f. Psi (letra griega).

psicastenia f. MED. Psychasthenia.

psicasténico, ca adj. MED. Psychasthenic.

psicoanálisis m. inv. Psychoanalysis.

psicoanalista m. y f. Psychoanalyst.

psicoanalítico, ca adj. Psychoanalytic, psychoanalytical.

psicoanalizar v. tr. To psychoanalyse, to psychoanalyze.

psicodélico, ca adj. Psychedelic.

psicodrama m. Psychodrama.

psicología f. Psychology.

psicológico, ca adj. Psychological: *momento psicológico*, psychological moment. || *Guerra psicológica*, psychological warfare.

psicologismo m. Psychologism.

psicólogo, ga adj. Psychological.
— M. y f. Psychologist.

psicometría f. Psychometry.

psicomotor, ra adj. Psychomotor.

psiconeurosis f. inv. MED. Psychoneurosis.

psicópata m. y f. MED. Psychopath.

psicopatía f. MED. Psychopathy.

psicopático, ca adj. MED. Psychopathic.

psicopatología f. MED. Psychopathology.

psicosis f. inv. MED. Psychosis. || FIG. Psychosis: *psicosis de guerra*, war psychosis.

psicosomático, ca adj. Psychosomatic.

psicotecnia f. Psychotechnology.

psicotécnico, ca adj. Psychotechnological.

psicoterapia f. MED. Psychotherapy.

psique o **psiquis** f. Psyche.

Psique o **Psiquis** n. pr. f. MIT. Psyche.

psiquiatra m. y f. MED. Psychiatrist.

psiquiatría f. MED. Psychiatry.

psiquiátrico, ca adj. MED. Psychiatric.

psíquico, ca adj. Psychic, psychical.

psiquismo m. Psychism.

psitacosis f. inv. MED. Psittacosis.

psoas m. inv. Psoas (músculo).

psoriasis f. inv. MED. Psoriasis.

pteridofita f. BOT. Pteridophyte.

pterodáctilo m. ZOOL. Pterodactyl.

pterópodo m. ZOOL. Pteropod.

pterosaurio m. ZOOL. Pterosaur.

ptialina f. Ptyalin.

ptialismo m. Ptyalism.

ptolemaico, ca adj. Ptolemaic.

Ptolomeo n. pr. m. Ptolemy.

ptomaína f. BOT. Ptomaine.

ptosis f. inv. MED. Ptosis.

púa f. Sharp point (punta aguda). || Quill (de erizo o puerco espín). || Tooth (de peine). || Prong, tine (del tenedor). || Barb (de alambrada). || Thorn (de rosa, etc.). || AGR. Graft, scion (de injerto). || MÚS. Plectrum (plectro). || Needle (de gramófono). || *Amer.* Spur (espolón de ave).

púber, ra adj. Pubescent, adolescent, who has reached puberty.
— M. y f. Pubescent youth, adolescent.

pubertad f. Puberty.

pubescencia f. Pubescence.

pubescente adj. Pubescent.

pubiano, na o **púbico, ca** adj. ANAT. Pubic.

pubis m. ANAT. Pubes (parte inferior del vientre). || ANAT. *Hueso pubis*, pubis.

publicable adj. Publishable.

publicación f. Publication (obra publicada, acción de publicar). || *Se ruega la publicación*, for the favour of publication in your columns.

publicador, ra adj. Publishing.
— M. y f. Publisher.

publicano m. HIST. Publican.

publicar v. tr. To publish: *publicar un libro*, to publish a book. || To announce, to proclaim (proclamar). || To publicize, to make public, to divulge (hacer público). || To publish (los bandos). || MED. To issue (un parte facultativo).
— V. pr. To be published (libro): *acaba de publicarse*, it has just been published.

publicidad f. Publicity (en general). || COM. Advertising: *agencia de publicidad*, advertising agency. || CINEM. y RAD. Advertisement, advert (anuncio publicitario). || — *Dar publicidad a*, to give publicity to. || *Hacer publicidad por*, to advertise. || FAM. *Publicidad a bombo y platillos*, noisy *o* loud publicity.

publicista m. y f. Publicist. || *Amer.* COM. Publicity agent.

publicitario, ria adj. Advertising, publicity: *empresa publicitaria*, advertising firm.

público, ca adj. Public: *opinión pública*, public opinion. || — *Deuda pública*, national debt, public debt. || *Es público que*, it is common knowledge that, it is well known that, everybody knows that. || *Hacer pública una cosa*, to publicize *o* to make public *o* to publish sth. || *Ser público y notorio*, to be common knowledge.

— M. Public: *aviso al público*, notice to the public; *se ruega al público*, the public are requested; *hablar en público*, to speak in public. || FIG. People, *pl.*: *la sala estaba llena de público*, the room was full of people. || Audience (en un espectáculo, en una sala). || Spectators, *pl.* (en deportes). || Viewers, *pl.* (de la televisión). || Readers, followers, *pl.*: *cada escritor tiene su público*, every writer has his followers. || — FIG. *Dar al público*, to publish (una novela, etc.), to present (obra de teatro). || *Público en general* or *gran público*, general public. || *Sacar al público*, to publicize, to make public, to publish.
pucallpeño, ña adj. [From] Pucallpa (Perú).
— M. y f. Native *o* inhabitant of Pucallpa.
pucará m. *Amer.* Small fort (fortaleza incaica). | Archaeological site.
pucherazo m. Blow with a pot. || FIG. y FAM. *Dar pucherazos*, to rig the elections, to count votes that were not cast.
puchero m. Pot, cooking pot (vasija). || Stew (guisado). || FIG. y FAM. Daily bread (alimento diario). || — FIG. y FAM. *Calentar* or *hacer cocer el puchero*, to keep the pot boiling. | *Ganarse el puchero*, to earn one's daily bread, to earn a living. | *Hacer pucheros*, to pout (un niño).
puches m. o f. pl. Gruel, *sing.*, porridge, *sing.* (gachas).
puchito, ta m. y f. *Amer.* Child.
pucho m. Cigar *o* cigarette butt (colilla). || *Amer.* Leftover (resto de algo). | Baby, youngest (hijo más joven).
pudding m. Pudding.
pudelado m. Puddling.
pudelar v. tr. TECN. To puddle.
pudendo, da adj. Shameful (vergonzoso). || *Partes pudendas*, pudenda, private parts.
pudibundez f. Affected modesty, prudishness, prudery.
pudibundo, da adj. Bashful, modest (pudoroso). || Prudish (mojigato).
pudicicia f. Pudicity, modesty, chastity.
púdico, ca adj. Chaste, modest.
pudiente adj. Rich, wealthy, well-to-do (rico).
— M. y f. Wealthy person. || *Los pudientes*, the wealthy.
pudín m. Pudding.
pudor m. Modesty. || Shame (vergüenza). || Decency (decencia). || Chastity (castidad). || — *Atentado contra el pudor*, indecent assault. || *Sin pudor*, shameless. || *Ultraje contra el pudor*, indecent exposure.
pudoroso, sa adj. Bashful, modest. || Prudish (mojigato). || Chaste, virtuous (casto).
pudrición m. Putrefaction, rotting.
pudridero m. Rubbish dump (vertedero). || Temporary vault (para cadáveres).
pudrimiento m. Rotting, putrefaction (acción). || Rottenness, rot (efecto).
pudrir* v. tr. To rot, to putrefy, to decay.
— V. pr. To rot, to putrefy. || FIG. To be spoilt. || — FIG. y FAM. *¡Ahí te pudras!*, to hell with you! | *Pudrirse de aburrimiento*, to be bored stiff. | *Pudrírsele la sangre a uno*, to get worked up. | *Un por ahí te pudras*, a dicky [U.S., a rumble seat] (de coche).
puebla f. Town (población).
pueblacho m. FAM. V. POBLACHO.
pueblada f. *Amer.* Uprising, riot (motín).
pueblerino, na adj. Village. || FIG. Rustic: *gustos pueblerinos*, rustic tastes.
— M. y f. Villager.
pueblero, ra m. y f. Villager.
pueblo m. Town (población). || Village (población pequeña). || People (nación): *todos los pueblos de Europa*, all the peoples of Europe; *el pueblo español*, the Spanish people. || People, *pl.*, common people, *pl.*, masses, *pl.* (el vulgo): *hacer un llamamiento al pueblo*, to call on the people. || — *De pueblos*, from the country. || *Hombre del pueblo*, man of the people. || *Pueblo bajo*, lower class people. || FAM. *Pueblo de mala muerte*, dump, hole [U.S., hick town].
puente m. Bridge (sobre un río). || FIG. Long weekend (entre dos fiestas): *hacer puente*, to take *o* to have a long weekend. | Gap (espacio de tiempo). || ELECTR. Bridge: *puente de Wheatstone*, Wheatstone bridge. || MÚS. Bridge (de violín). || MAR. Bridge (plataforma sobre la cubierta). | Deck (cubierta). || MED. Bridge (en las muelas). || — *Cabeza de puente*, bridgehead. || FIG. *Hacer* or *tender un puente de plata a uno*, to present s.o. with a golden opportunity. || *Puente aéreo*, airlift (para abastecimiento), air shuttle (para viajeros). || *Puente basculante*, bascule bridge. || *Puente colgante*, suspension bridge. || *Puente de aterrizaje* or *de despegue*, flight deck (en los portaaviones). || *Puente de barcas* or *de pontones*, pontoon bridge. || FIG. *Puente de los asnos*, pons asinorum. || MAR. *Puente de mando*, bridge. || *Puente en esviaje*, skew bridge. || *Puente ferroviario*, railway bridge. || *Puente giratorio*, swing bridge. || *Puente grúa*, bridge crane. || *Puente levadizo*, drawbridge. || *Puente para peatones*, footbridge. || *Puente transbordador*, transporter bridge. || AUT. *Puente trasero*, rear axle. || *Tender un puente sobre*, to throw a bridge over.
puercamente adv. Dirtily, filthily (con suciedad). || FIG. Nastily, disgustingly (asquerosamente).
puerco, ca adj. Dirty, filthy (sucio). || FIG. Nasty, disgusting (asqueroso). | Smutty, bawdy (obsceno).
— M. Pig, swine (cerdo). || — F. Sow (cerda). || — M. y f. FIG. y FAM. Pig, sloven (persona sucia). | Swine, rogue (sinvergüenza). || — FIG. y FAM. *A cada puerco le llega su San Martín*, every dog has his day. | *Echar margaritas a los puercos*, to cast pearls before swine. || *Puerco espín*, porcupine.
puericia f. Childhood.
puericultor, ra m. y f. Specialist in puericulture.
puericultura f. Puericulture.
pueril adj. Puerile, childish.
puerilidad f. Puerility, childishness.
puerilismo m. Puerilism, childishness.
puerperal adj. MED. Puerperal.
puerperio m. Puerperium (sobreparto).
puerro m. Leek (planta).
puerta f. Door: *abrir una puerta*, to open a door; *escuchar detrás de las puertas*, to listen behind doors. || Door (de coche, vagón, mueble, etc.). || Gate (de una ciudad). || Gate (del Infierno). || FIG. Gateway, doorway (medio de acceso): *la puerta de la fama*, the gateway to fame. || DEP. Goal (en fútbol, hockey, etc.). || — FIG. *Abrir la puerta a*, to open the door to. | *A las puertas de*, on the verge of: *estar a las puertas de un conflicto*, to be on the verge of a conflict. | *A las puertas de la muerte*, at death's door. || *A puerta cerrada*, in camera (jurisprudencia), behind closed doors. || FIG. *Cerrar la puerta a*, to close the door on. || *Coche de dos puertas*, 2-door car. || FIG. *Coger* or *tomar la puerta*, to leave, to go. | *Cuando una puerta se cierra, cien se abren*, when one door closes another always opens. | *Dar a uno con* or *cerrar la puerta en las narices*, to slam *o* to shut the door in s.o.'s face. | *Dejar* or *reservarse una puerta abierta*, to leave a door open. || *De puerta en puerta*, from door to door. || *De puertas adentro*, at home. || *Echar la puerta abajo*, to break the door down. || FIG. *Encontrar todas las puertas cerradas*, to find all doors closed. | *En puertas*, just around the corner. | *Llamar a la puerta de alguien*, to call on s.o. for help (pedir ayuda). | *Poner a uno en la puerta de la calle*, to throw *o* to turn s.o. out (expulsar), to sack s.o., to fire s.o., to turn s.o. out (a un empleado). | *Poner puertas al campo*, to try to stem the tide. || *Puerta accesoria*, side door. || *Puerta a puerta*, door-to-door transport (transporte), house-to-house canvassing (venta, reparto). || *Puerta automática*, automatic door (en el metro). || *Puerta cochera*, carriage *o* car entrance. || *Puerta de corredera*, sliding door. || *Puerta de entrada*, front door. || *Puerta de servicio*, tradesmen's entrance. || *Puerta excusada o falsa*, concealed door. || *Puerta giratoria*, revolving door. || *Puerta principal*, main entrance. || *Puerta secreta*, secret door. || *Puerta trasera*, back door. || *Puerta vidriera*, glass door (puerta), French window (que da al balcón). || FIG. *Tener puerta abierta*, to have an open door.
puertaventana f. French window.
puerto m. Port, harbour [U.S., harbor] (abrigo para la navegación). || Port: *puerto pesquero*, fishing port. || Seaport (marítimo): *Cádiz es un puerto*, Cádiz is a seaport. || Mountain pass, col (paso entre montañas). || FIG. Haven, refuge, shelter (amparo). || — *Llegar a buen puerto*, to reach port, to get safely into port. || *Puerto aéreo*, airport. || MAR. *Puerto comercial*, commercial *o* trading port. | *Puerto de amarre* or *de matrícula*, port of registry. || FIG. y FAM. *Puerto de arrebatacapas*, den of thieves. || *Puerto de arribada* or *de escala*, port of call. || *Puerto de carga*, commercial port. || *Puerto deportivo*, pleasure harbour. || *Puerto de salvación*, haven of refuge. || *Puerto franco* or *libre*, free port. || *Tomar puerto*, to reach *o* to make port.
Puerto Príncipe n. pr. GEOGR. Port-au-Prince (Haití).
Puerto Rico n. pr. m. GEOGR. Puerto Rico.
puertorriqueño, ña adj./s. Puerto Rican.
pues adv. conj. Since, as (ya que): *póntelo tú, pues lo compraste*, since you bought it, you wear it. || Because: *no pude salir, pues vino mi abuela*, I couldn't go out because my grandmother came. || So (así). || Then (entonces). || Well (consecuencia): *pues te arrepentirás*, well you'll regret it. || Yes (afirmación). || Well, of course (interjección familiar). || Hum! (duda). || What? (interrogación). || — *Así, pues*, therefore, so therefore. || *Pues bien*, thus (por lo tanto), good, OK, right then (bueno). || *¡Pues claro!*, of course! || *Pues que*, being that, since (puesto que). || *¿Pues qué?*, so what? || *¿Y pues?*, so?, so what?

— OBSERV. This particle used at the beginning of a sentence reinforces the idea which one wishes to express (*¡pues no faltaba más!*, now that's all we needed!). It may also have various meanings depending on the intonation: *pues peor*, even worse; *pues mejor*, so much the better; *¡pues no!*, certainly not!

puesta f. Setting (de un astro). || Bet (cantidad que se apuesta). || Laying (de huevos). || Putting: *puesta en cultivo, en órbita, en servicio*, putting into cultivation, into orbit, into service. || — *Puesta al día*, bringing up to date. || *Puesta a punto*, tuning (de un motor), adjusting (arreglo). || *Puesta de espaldas*, fall *o* pinfall (en una lucha). || *Puesta de largo*, début, coming out. || *Puesta de Sol* or *puesta del Sol*, sunset. || *Puesta en escena*, staging. || *Puesta en marcha*, starting (de una máquina), beginning (de un proyecto).
puestear v. intr. To set up a stall.
puestero m. *Amer.* Salesman, stallholder, vendor (el que tiene o atiende un puesto). || Ranch hand, herdsman (en las estancias).

puesto, ta adj. Placed, set put (colocado). || Worn (la ropa). || Dressed (persona): *bien, mal puesto*, well, badly dressed. || Laid (la mesa). || *Tener puesto*, to have on, to be wearing: *tenía puesta una chaqueta nueva*, he had a new jacket on, he was wearing a new jacket; *tenía el sombrero puesto*, he had his hat on, he was wearing his hat.
— M. Small shop (tiendecita): *puesto de flores*, small flower shop. || Stall (en el mercado). || Stand (en una exposición). || Post, job, position (empleo): *tener un buen puesto*, to have a good job. || Seat (sitio): *el puesto del piloto*, the pilot's seat. || Place (lugar): *déjame tu puesto*, let me have your place. || Place, position (de un alumno). || Hide [U.S., blind] (en la caza). || MIL. Post: *puesto avanzado*, advanced post; *puesto de mando*, command post. || — MIL. *¡A sus puestos!*, action stations! || *Copar los dos primeros puestos*, to win the first two places (en deportes). || *Incorporarse a su puesto de trabajo*, to take up one's duties. || *Puesto de abastecimiento*, supply station. || *Puesto de periódicos*, newsstand, newspaper stand. || *Puesto de socorro*, first-aid station *o* post.
— Conj. *Puesto que*, since, as (ya que).
puf m. Pouf (taburete bajo).
— OBSERV. This word is a Gallicism.
pufo m. FAM. Trick (engaño). || Debt (deuda): *dejar de pufo mil pesetas*, to leave a debt of thousand pesetas. || FAM. *Dar el pufo*, to trick.
púgil o **pugilista** m. Pugilist (gladiador que combatía a puñetazos). || Boxer, pugilist, fighter (boxeador).
pugilato m. Pugilism, boxing (boxeo). || Brawl (pelea). || Dispute (discusión).
pugilismo m. Pugilism.
pugilístico, ca adj. Pugilistic.
pugna f. Fight, battle, struggle (lucha). || *Entrar, estar en pugna con*, to clash with.
pugnacidad f. Pugnacity, aggressiveness (belicosidad).
pugnar v. intr. To fight, to struggle (luchar). || FIG. To insist. || *Pugnar por entrar*, to struggle to get in.
pugnaz adj. Pugnacious, aggressive.
puja f. Bid (en una subasta). || Struggle, fight (lucha). || — *Hacer una puja*, to make a bid (en una subasta), to make an effort (esforzarse). || *Se hicieron pujas fuertes*, the bidding was high.
pujador, ra m. y f. Bidder.
pujamen m. MAR. Foot of a sail.
pujante adj. Strong, vigorous (vigoroso). || Powerful (poderoso).
pujanza f. Strength (fuerza), vigour [U.S., vigor] (robustez), power (poder).
pujar v. tr. To bid up, to raise.
— V. intr. To bid higher (en una subasta). || To bid (en las cartas). || To struggle (luchar). || FIG. y FAM. To pout (hacer pucheros). || To grope for words (expresarse con dificultad). | To hesitate (vacilar). || FAM. To strain (al hacer de vientre).
pujavante m. Butteris (de herrador).
pujido m. Scream (lamento).
pujo m. MED. Tenesmus. || FIG. Longing, yearning (ansia). | Irresistible urge (gana incontenible). | Aspiration: *tenía pujos de ser pintor*, he had aspirations to be a painter. | Attempt, try (intento).
pulcramente adv. Neatly, tidily.
pulcritud f. Neatness, tidiness, cleanliness (esmero). || Care (cuidado). || *Vestir con pulcritud*, to dress neatly.
pulcro, cra adj. Neat, tidy, clean. || Exquisite (estilo).
pulga f. ZOOL. Flea (insecto). || Tiddlywink (peón para jugar). || — FIG. y FAM. *A perro flaco todo son pulgas*, v. PERRO. | *Buscarle a uno las pulgas*, to taunt s.o., to pick a fight with s.o. | *Estar con* or *tener la pulga detrás de la oreja*, v. OREJA. | *Hacer de una pulga un elefante*, to make a mountain out of a molehill. | *No aguantar pulgas*, to stand for no nonsense. | *Sacudirse uno las pulgas*, to stand for no nonsense | *Tener malas pulgas*, to be touchy *o* bad-tempered.
pulgada f. Inch (medida).
pulgar m. Thumb (dedo). || Shoot (viña). || *Dedo pulgar*, thumb.
pulgarada f. Fillip, flick (papirote). || Pinch (pizca): *una pulgarada de tabaco*, a pinch of tobacco. || Inch (pulgada).
Pulgarcito n. pr. m. Tom Thumb.
pulgón m. ZOOL. Plant louse.
pulguillas m. y f. inv. FAM. Touchy person.
pulidamente adv. Neatly, carefully. || Politely (cortésmente).
pulidez f. Refinement, polish, elegance (refinamiento). || Neatness (pulcritud). || Shine, polish (brillo).
pulido, da adj. Polished: *metal pulido*, polished metal. || Smooth (liso). || Refined, polished, elegant (refinado). || Neat, smart, trim (pulcro).
— M. Polishing (pulimento). || Shine, polish (brillo).
pulidor, ra adj. Polishing.
— M. Polisher (instrumento). || TECN. Polishing machine (máquina).
pulimentar v. tr. To polish (pulir).
pulimento m. Polishing (acción). || Polish, shine (brillo).
pulir v. tr. To polish: *pulir el mármol, el vidrio, un metal*, to polish marble, glass, metal. || To smooth (alisar). || To put the final touch to, to finish off (perfeccionar una cosa). || FIG. To polish, to refine: *pulir el estilo*, to polish one's style. | To refine, to give polish to, to civilize: *pulir a un lugareño*, to refine a peasant. || FAM. To sell off (vender). | To steal, to pinch (hurtar). || To adorn, to embellish (adornar).
— V. pr. To become polished. || FIG. To acquire polish (una persona).
pulmón m. Lung: *gritar con todas las fuerzas de los pulmones*, to scream at the top of one's lungs; *pulmón de acero*, iron lung.
pulmonado, da adj./s.m. ZOOL. Pulmonate.
pulmonar adj. Pulmonary, lung.
pulmonía f. MED. Pneumonia.
pulmoniaco, ca o **pulmoníaco, ca** adj. Pneumonic.
pulóver m. Jumper, pullover (jersey).
pulpa f. Pulp (tejidos animales o vegetales): *pulpa dental* or *dentaria*, dental pulp; *pulpa de un fruto*, pulp of a fruit. || *Pulpa de madera*, wood pulp.
pulpejo m. Soft flesh. || Soft part of the hoof (del caballo).
pulpería f. *Amer.* Grocer's shop [U.S., grocery store] (tienda). | Tavern (taberna).
pulpero m. *Amer.* Grocer, owner of a "pulpería" (de una tienda). | Tavern keeper (de una taberna).
pulpitis f. MED. Pulpitis.
púlpito m. Pulpit (de un predicador).
pulpo m. Octopus (cefalópodo). || Octopus luggage elastic (para fijar paquetes).
pulposo, sa adj. Pulpy, fleshy.
pulque m. *Amer.* "Pulque" [Mexican drink].
pulquería f. *Amer.* Pulque bar, "pulquería".
pulquero, ra m. y f. *Amer.* Keeper of a "pulquería".
pulquérrimo, ma adj. Immaculate, impeccable.
pulsación f. Pulsation (acción). || Beat, throb (del corazón). || Stroke, tap, touch (mecanografía).
— OBSERV. In Spanish the expression *pulsaciones por minuto* is used to determine the efficiency rate of a typist. In English the equivalent would be "words per minute".
pulsador, ra adj. Pulsating.
— M. Button (de timbre eléctrico): *pulsador del timbre*, bell button.
pulsar v. tr. To play (tocar): *pulsar un instrumento músico*, to play a musical instrument. || To press, to push: *pulsar un botón*, to press a button. || To take *o* to feel the pulse of (tomar el pulso). || FIG. To sound out (tantear un asunto): *pulsar la opinión pública*, to sound out public opinion.
— V. intr. To beat, to throb (latir el pulso).
pulsátil adj. Pulsating, beating, pulsatile.
pulsativo, va adj. Pulsatory.
pulsear v. intr. To Indian-wrestle.
pulsera f. Bracelet (joya). || Watch strap (de reloj). || — *Pulsera de pedida*, engagement bracelet (v. OBSERV.). || *Reloj de pulsera*, wristwatch.
— OBSERV. In Spanish-speaking countries the equivalent to the «engagement ring» is the *pulsera de pedida*.
— En los países de habla inglesa se suele ofrecer una « sortija de pedida » (engagement ring).
pulsímetro m. Pulsimeter.
pulso m. ANAT. Pulse. | Wrist (muñeca). || Strength in one's wrist (fuerza). || Steady hand (para hacer trabajos delicados). || FIG. Prudence, care, caution: *obrar con pulso*, to proceed with caution. || *Amer.* Bracelet (pulsera). || — *A pulso*, with one's own bare hands, all alone. || *Dibujo a pulso*, freehand drawing. || *Echar un pulso*, to Indian-wrestle. || *Ganarse, conseguir algo a pulso*, to earn sth. (haciendo esfuerzos). || *Pulso arrítmico* or *irregular*, irregular pulse. || *Pulso sentado* or *normal*, regular pulse. || *Tomar el pulso a la opinión*, to sound out opinion. || *Tomarle el pulso a alguien*, to take *o* to feel s.o.'s pulse.
pulsómetro m. TECN. Pulsometer.
pulsorreactor m. AVIAC. Pulse-jet engine.
pululación f. Pullulation.
pulular v. intr. To pullulate, to swarm, to teem.
pulverizable adj. Pulverizable.
pulverización f. Pulverization (de sólidos). || Atomization (de líquidos).
pulverizador m. Pulverizer. || Jet (del carburador). || Spray gun (para pintar). || Atomizer, spray (de perfume).
pulverizar v. tr. To pulverize. || To atomize, to spray (un líquido). || FIG. To shatter, to smash: *pulverizar un vaso*, to shatter a glass. | To pulverize, to smash: *pulverizar al enemigo, un récord*, to smash the enemy, a record. | To tear to pieces: *pulverizar una teoría*, to tear a theory to pieces. | To dissipate, to waste: *pulverizó su fortuna*, he dissipated his fortune.
— V. pr. To pulverize.
pulverulencia f. Pulverulence.
pulverulento, ta adj. Pulverulent.
pulla f. Taunt, gibe (expresión aguda y picante). || Dig, cutting remark (observación mordaz). || Obscenity, obscene word (palabra grosera). || FAM. Insinuation: *tirar pullas a uno*, to make insinuations about s.o. || *Amer.* Machete.
pullman m. Pullman.
pull-over m. Pullover.
¡pum! interj. Boom!, bang!
puma m. ZOOL. Puma.
puna f. *Amer.* "Puna" (páramo). | "Puna", mountain sickness (soroche).

punción f. MED. Puncture: *punción lumbar*, lumbar puncture. || Sharp pain (punzada).
puncionar v. tr. To puncture.
punching ball m. Punchball [U.S., punching bag].
pundonor m. Honour, dignity.
pundonoroso, sa adj. Honourable, honest (honrado). || Conscientious (concienzudo).
puneño, ña adj. [Of *o* from] Puno (Perú). — M. y f. Native *o* inhabitant of Puno.
pungente adj. Sharp, stabbing (dolor).
pungimiento m. Prick (punzada).
pungir v. tr. To prick, to punch (punzar).
punible adj. Punishable (castigable).
punición f. Punishment.
púnico, ca adj. Punic (cartaginés): *las Guerras Púnicas*, the Punic wars. || FIG. *Fe púnica*, bad faith.
punir v. tr. (P.us.). To punish.
punitivo, va adj. Punitive.
punitorio, ria adj. *Amer.* Punitive.
Punjab n. pr. m. GEOGR. Punjab.
punta f. Point (extremo agudo). || Tip (extremo): *punta del pie*, tip of the toe. || Head, point (de una flecha). || End (final). || Horn (asta del toro). || Point (lengua de tierra). || Sourness (sabor agrio del vino). || Pointing, point (del perro de caza). || Butt (colilla). || Nib (de una herramienta). || Nail (clavo). || FIG. Bit, streak: *tener una punta de loco*, to have a streak of madness, to be a bit crazy. || MIL. Point. || Small bunch (de ganado). || *Amer.* Group (de personas). | Bunch (de cosas). | Source (cabecera de río). || — Pl. Point lace, *sing.*, needlepoint, *sing.* (encaje). || — *Amer. A punta de*, by means of. || FAM. *A punta de pala*, V. PALA. || *Bailar de puntas*, to dance on tiptoe. || *Con el escote en punta*, V-neck. || *De punta*, on end. || *De punta a cabo* or *de punta a punta*, from one end to the other, from A to Z. || *De punta en blanco*, dressed up to the nines (muy bien vestido), in full armour (con la armadura completa). || FIG. *Estar de punta con*, to be at odds with (enfadados). | *Estar hasta la punta de los pelos de*, to be fed up with. || *Horas punta*, rush hours, peak hours. || FIG. *Poner los nervios de punta*, to set one's nerves on edge, to get on one's nerves. | *Poner los pelos de punta a uno*, to make one's hair stand on end. | *Ponerse de punta*, to stand on end (el pelo). | *Ponerse de punta con uno*, to get angry with s.o. || *Sacar punta a*, so sharpen (afilar), to find fault with (interpretar maliciosamente): *sacan punta a todo lo que digo*, they find fault with everything I say. || FIG. *Tener algo en la punta de la lengua*, to have sth. on the tip of one's tongue. | *Tener los nervios de punta*, to be [all] on edge. || FIG. *Tratar a alguien con la punta del pie*, to kick s.o. around. || *Velocidad punta*, top speed.
puntada f. Stitch: *coser a puntadas largas*, to sew with long stitches. || FIG. Note (apunte). | Sharp pain (punzada). | Insinuation (indirecta). || FIG. y FAM. *No dar puntada*, not to do a thing.
puntal m. Prop, shore, strut (madero). || FIG. Support (sostén). | Foundation, base (elemento principal). | Pillar: *este chico es el puntal del equipo*, this boy is the pillar of the team. || MAR. Depth (altura del barco). | Stanchion.
puntano, na adj. [Of *o* from] San Luis [Argentina]. — M. y f. Native *o* inhabitant of San Luis.
puntapié m. Kick. || *Echar a puntapiés*, to kick out.
puntarenense adj. [Of *o* from] Punta Arenas [Chile], [of *o* from] Puntarenas [Costa Rica]. — M. y f. Native *o* inhabitant of Punta Arenas [Chile] *o* Puntarenas [Costa Rica].
puntazo m. Slight gore (cornada).
punteado m. MÚS. Plucking (de guitarra). || Dotted line (serie de puntos). || Dotting, stippling (acción).
puntear v. tr. MÚS. To pluck (las cuerdas). | To dot (una nota). || To check (en una lista). || To dot, to mark with dots (trazar puntos). || To check (una cuenta). || To dot (hacer puntos). || *Amer.* To lead, to walk at the front of.
puntel m. Punty (en fábricas de vidrio).
punteo m. Plucking (de guitarra). || COM. Checking (de una cuenta).
puntera f. Toe (de media). || Toecap (de calzado). || Cap, top (para lápices). || FAM. Kick (puntapié). || *De puntera*, with the tip of the toe (fútbol).
puntería f. Aiming, aim (de un arma). || Aim: *enmendar la puntería*, to change one's aim. || FIG. Marksmanship (destreza). || — *Dirigir la puntería*, to aim (*hacia*, at) [sin disparar], to shoot at (disparando). || *Tener buena, mala puntería*, to be a good, bad shot, to be a good, bad marksman.
puntero, ra adj. Outstanding: *un médico, un equipo puntero*, an outstanding physician, team. — M. Pointer (para señalar). || TECN. Puncheon (de herrero). | Chisel (de cantero).
punterola f. MIN. Small pick.
puntiagudo, da adj. Pointed, sharp.
puntilla f. Fine lace, picot (encaje). || Nib (de una pluma). || Tack (tachuela). || TAUR. "Puntilla", dagger [for finishing off the bull]. || FIG. The final blow, the last straw (remate). || TECN. Tracing point. || *Amer.* Penknife (cortaplumas). || — *Andar de puntillas*, to walk on tiptoe, to tiptoe. || *Dar la puntilla a*, to kill, to finish off (un toro), to finish (una persona). || *De puntillas*, on tiptoe.
puntillazo m. Kick (puntapié). || Coup de grâce (al toro).
puntillero m. TAUR. Bullfighter who deals the coup de grâce.
puntillismo m. Pointillism (pintura).
puntillista adj./s. Pointillist (pintor).
puntillo m. Punctilio, unimportant point (nimiedad). || MÚS. Dot. || Honour (pundonor).
puntilloso, sa adj. Ticklish, punctilious (quisquilloso). || Finical, punctilious (detallista y exigente).
punto m. Dot, point (señal). || Sight (del fusil). || Place, spot, point (lugar). || Stitch (costura): *punto por encima, de cadeneta, de cruz, de dobladillo*, overcast, chain, cross, hem stitch; *escapársele a uno un punto*, to drop a stitch. || Mark (de las notas escolares). || Taxi rank *o* stand. || Point (que se gana en toda clase de juegos). || Point (de una pluma). || Point (en una discusión): *en ese punto no estamos de acuerdo*, we differ on that point. || Subject, matter (asunto). || Item (del orden del día). || Honour, dignity (pundonor). || Punter (que juega contra la banca en los juegos de azar). || Moment (momento). || Hole (agujero). || Dot (de la *i* y la *j*). || Full stop [U.S., period] (al final de la frase). || MED. Stitch (en cirugía). || IMPR. Point (medida tipográfica). || FÍS. Point: *punto de fusión, de congelación*, melting, freezing point. || FIG. y FAM. Rascal, rogue (sinvergüenza). || MAR. Reckoning, position: *echar* or *señalar* or *hacer el punto*, to plot the reckoning. || GEOGR. Point: *puntos cardinales*, cardinal points. || MÚS. Dot, point (señal). | Pitch (tono). || — *Al llegar a este punto*, at this point, having come thus far. || *Al punto*, at once, immediately. || *Al punto que*, at the very moment that. || *A punto*, ready (preparado), on time (a la hora): *llegar a punto*, to arrive on time; just right, just at the right time, just in time (en el momento oportuno). || FIG. *A* or *en punto de caramelo*, at a perfect moment, just at the right time. || *A punto fijo*, exactly, for sure, precisely. || ARQ. *Arco de medio punto*, semicircular arch. || *Bajar de punto*, to decline, to decrease. || *Coger los puntos*, to mend, to pick up the stitches. || FIG. *Con puntos y comas*, in detail, in minute detail, in every detail. | *Conocer los puntos que calza uno*, to know what s.o. is capable of, to know where one stands with s.o. || *Dar el punto a algo*, to do sth. to a turn, to do sth. just right. | FIG. *Dar en el punto*, to hit the nail on the head. || *Dar veinte puntos de ventaja*, to give a twenty point advantage. || *De punto*, knitted. || *De todo punto*, absolutely: *es de todo punto imposible*, it's absolutely impossible. || *Dos puntos*, colon. || *En punto*, sharp, on the dot: *son las dos en punto*, it's two on the dot; *ven a las dos en punto*, come at 2 sharp. || *En su punto*, done to a turn, just right, perfect, ready: *el arroz está en su punto ahora*, the rice is done to a turn. || *Estar a punto de*, to be about to, to be on the point of: *estoy a punto de salir*, I am about to go out; to be on the verge of: *estar a punto de caerse*, to be on the verge of falling. || *Hacer punto*, to knit. || *Hasta cierto punto*, up to a point, to a certain extent. || *Hasta el punto de*, to the point of, to the extent of. || *Hasta tal punto*, to such a point *o* an extent. || *Labores de punto*, knitting. || *Línea de puntos*, dotted line, stippled line. || FIG. *No perder punto*, not to miss a thing. || *Poner a punto*, to tune up (un motor, una máquina, etc.), to finish off, to round off, to put the finishing touch to (dar el último toque). || FIG. *Poner en su punto*, to get into shape. | *Poner los puntos a alguien* or *algo*, to have got one's eye on s.o. *o* sth. | *Poner los puntos sobre las íes*, to dot the i's and cross the t's | *Poner punto en boca*, to shut up. || *Poner punto final a*, to put a stop to (suprimir), to finish (acabar). || *Por puntos*, on points: *victoria por puntos*, a win on points (en boxeo). || *Amer. Punto acápite*, full stop, new paragraph [U.S., period, new paragraph]. || *Punto crítico*, critical point. || *Punto culminante*, climax, high point (culminación), highest peak *o* mountain (de un país). || *Punto de apoyo*, V. APOYO. || *Punto de arranque*, starting point. || FIG. *Punto débil*, weak spot *o* point. || MED. *Punto débil*, weak spot *o* point. || MED. *Punto de costado*, stitch (dolor). || *Punto de ebullición*, boiling point. || *Punto de honor*, point of honour. || *Punto de interrogación, de admiración*, question, exclamation mark. || *Punto de mira*, front sight (de arma), target (objetivo). || *Punto de partida*, starting point. || *Punto de penalty*, penalty spot (en fútbol). || *Punto de referencia*, point of reference. || *Punto de vista*, point of view, viewpoint: *desde este punto de vista*, from this point of view. || FIG. *¡Punto en boca!*, mum's the word!, don't say a word! || *Punto filipino*, V. FILIPINO. || *Punto final*, full stop. || *Punto flaco*, weak spot *o* point. || *Punto menos que*, a shade less than, not quite. || *Punto muerto*, neutral (automóvil), dead centre (en mecánica), deadlock, stalemate, impasse: *las negociaciones han llegado a un punto muerto*, the negotiations have reached a deadlock. || *Punto por punto*, point by point. || *Puntos de sutura*, stitches. || *Puntos suspensivos*, suspension marks *o* points. || *Punto y aparte*, full stop, new paragraph [U.S., period, new paragraph] (escritura), another story: *eso ya es punto y aparte*, that's another story. || *Punto y coma*, semicolon.
puntuable adj. Counting.

puntuación f. Punctuation (escribiendo). || Scoring (acción de marcar puntos). || Score, number of points (en deportes, recuentos, etc.). || Mark [U.S., grade] (calificación). || *Signos de puntuación*, punctuation marks.
puntual adj. Punctual: *es muy puntual*, he is very punctual. || Precise, accurate, reliable, punctual: *un puntual relato*, an accurate account. || Exact. — Adv. On time, punctually: *llegó puntual a la cita*, he arrived on time for the appointment.
puntualidad f. Punctuality. || Exactness, preciseness, accuracy (precisión).
puntualizar v. tr. To arrange, to fix (concretar): *puntualicemos el lugar de la cita*, let us arrange a meeting place. || To fix in mind (grabar en la memoria). || To settle, to determine (determinar). || To describe in detail, to give a detailed account of (referir detalladamente). || To perfect, to put the finishing touches to (perfeccionar).
puntualmente adv. Punctually (con puntualidad). || On time, punctually: *llegó puntualmente*, he arrived on time. || In detail (punto por punto): *me contó puntualmente lo sucedido*, he told me what happened in detail.
puntuar v. tr. To punctuate (al escribir). || To mark [U.S., to grade] (poner notas).
— V. intr. To score [points] (en deportes).
punzada f. Prick (herida). || FIG. Sharp pain (dolor agudo). | Pang (de conciencia). || — *Me da punzadas el pie*, I have sharp pains in my foot. || *Punzada en el costado*, stitch, sharp pain in the side.
punzador, ra adj. Pricking.
punzante adj. Prickly, pricking (que pincha). || Sharp, shooting (dolor físico). || Sharp (agudo, en punta). || FIG. Cutting, biting (mordaz). | Caustic, biting (mortificante).
punzar v. tr. To prick. || TECN. To punch. || FIG. To give shooting pains (un dolor). | To prick (la conciencia). | To torment (atormentar).
punzó adj. Flame-red, ponceau (rojo muy vivo).
punzón m. TECN. Needle (de válvula de aguja). | Burin (buril). | Punch (para marcar monedas). | Pricker (dibujo).
punzonar v. tr. TECN. To punch.
puñada f. Punch (puñetazo). || *Dar de puñadas*, to punch.
puñado m. Handful (porción): *un puñado de arena*, a handful of sand. || FIG. Handful: *un puñado de gente*, a handful of people. || FIG. *A puñados*, by the handful, lots of: *gasta dinero a puñados*, he spends lots of money, he spends money by the handful.
puñal m. Dagger. || FIG. *Poner el puñal en el pecho*, to hold a knife at s.o.'s throat.
puñalada f. Stab [of a dagger]. || FIG. Blow, shock: *la pérdida de su hijo fue para ella una puñalada*, the loss of her son was a blow to her. | Sudden stab of pain (dolor). || — FIG. y FAM. *Coser a puñaladas a uno*, to cut s.o. to pieces. | *Dar una puñalada trapera*, to stab [s.o.] in the back. || *Murió de una puñalada*, he was stabbed to death, he died of a stab wound. || FIG. y FAM. *¡No es puñalada de pícaro!*, there is no great rush.
puñeta f. POP. *Hacer la puñeta*, to get on [s.o.'s] nerves, to pester, to annoy (molestar), to mess things up [for s.o.] (estropearlo todo), to masturbate (*Amer.*). | *¡Qué puñeta!*, hell! | *Ser la puñeta*, to be a drag *o* a bind *o* a bore. | *¡Vete a hacer puñetas!*, get lost!, go to hell!
puñetazo m. Punch. || — *A puñetazos*, with one's fist *o* fists. || *Dar a uno de puñetazos*, to punch s.o. || *Dar puñetazos en*, to hammer on, to pound on (la mesa, etc.).
puñetero, ra adj. POP. Rotten, lousy, stinking: *un trabajo puñetero*, a rotten job. | Bloody: *no cuenta más que el puñetero dinero*, money is the only bloody thing that counts. || POP. *Vida puñetera*, dog's life.
puño m. Fist (mano cerrada). || Handful (puñado). || Cuff (de una camisa). || Handle (mango). || Handlebar (de bicicleta). || MAR. Tack (de una vela): *puño de la amura*, tack of a sail. || Hilt (de una espada). || — *Amenazar a alguien con el puño*, to threaten s.o. with one's fist, to shake one's fist at s.o. || FIG. *Apretar los puños*, to try one's best. || *A puño cerrado*, with one's fists. || FIG. y FAM. *Caber en un puño*, to fit in the palm of one's hand. | *Comerse los puños*, to be starving, to be famished. | *Como puños*, great big, whopping great (enorme). | *Como un puño*, as big as your fist: *un huevo como un puño*, an egg as big as your fist; tiny, very small: *una habitación como un puño*, a very small room. || *De su puño y letra*, by [his, her, etc.] own hand. || FIG. y FAM. *Es una verdad como un puño*, it's as plain as a pikestaff. | *Hombre de puños*, strong man. | *Meter a uno en un puño*, to get s.o. in the palm of one's hand. | *Morderse los puños*, to kick o.s. | *Por puños*, on one's own. | *Tener a alguien en un puño*, to have s.o. under one's thumb, to have s.o. eating out of one's hand.
pupa f. Pustule, pimple. || Cold sore (en los labios). || Scab (postilla). || Hurt, sore (en lenguaje infantil). || FIG. y FAM. *Hacer pupa a uno*, to hurt s.o.
pupila f. Pupil (del ojo). || Prostitute (de una casa de trato). || V. PUPILO. || FAM. *Tener pupila*, to be sharp.
pupilaje m. JUR. Pupilage, pupillage (condición de pupilo). || Tutelage, guardianship (tutela). || Boarding-house (casa de huéspedes). || Fee, board (precio).
pupilar adj. Pupillar.
pupilo, la m. y f. Ward, pupil, orphan (huérfano). || Boarder (huésped). || FIG. Ward (protegido). || *Casa de pupilos*, boardinghouse (casa de huéspedes).
pupitre m. Desk (mueble de madera).
pupo m. *Amer.* Navel (ombligo).
puquial o **puquio** m. *Amer.* Spring, source.
puramente adv. Purely, simply (simplemente).
puré m. Purée: *puré de tomates*, tomato purée. || — FIG. y FAM. *Estar hecho puré*, to be shattered (hecho añicos, muy cansado, muy abatido). || FIG. *Puré de guisantes*, pea-souper [U.S., pea soup], thick fog (niebla). || *Puré de patatas*, mashed potatoes.
pureza f. Purity, pureness (calidad de puro). || Virginity (doncellez). || FIG. Innocence.
purga f. Purgative, purge (medicina). || FIG. Purge (eliminación). || TECN. Residue (restos).
purgación f. MED. Purgation (acción de purgarse). || Period (menstruación). || REL. Purgation. || — Pl. MED. FAM. Gonorrhoea, *sing.*, the clap, *sing.* (fam.)
purgador, ra adj. TECN. Purging.
— M. TECN. Purge cock.
purgamiento m. Purgation, purging.
purgante adj. Purgative. || *Iglesia purgante*, church suffering.
— M. Purgative, purge.
purgar v. tr. To purge (a un enfermo). || To cleanse, to clean (limpiar). || FIG. To purify (purificar). | To purge, to liquidate (eliminar). | To expiate, to purge, to atone for: *purgar una culpa*, to expiate an error. || TECN. To drain, to vent. || *Purgar los caracoles*, to clean snails.
— V. pr. To take a purgative.
purgativo, va adj. Purgative (que purga).
purgatorio m. Purgatory: *ánima* or *alma del purgatorio*, soul in purgatory. || FIG. Purgatory.
puridad f. Purity (pureza).
purificación f. Purification. || *La fiesta de la Purificación*, the Purification.
purificador, ra adj. Purifying, cleansing.
— M. y f. Purifier (persona que purifica). || M. REL. Purificator (para el cáliz y para los dedos).
purificar v. tr. To purify. || To cleanse (limpiar).
— V. pr. To become purified, to purify.
purificatorio, ria adj. Purificatory.
Purísima n. pr. f. REL. The Immaculate Conception.
purismo m. Purism.
purista adj. Puristical, puristic.
— M. y f. Purist.
puritanismo m. Puritanism.
puritano, na adj. Puritan, puritanical.
— M. y f. Puritan.
puro, ra adj. Pure (sin mezcla): *oro puro, ciencias puras*, pure gold, pure sciences. || Sheer: *la vi por pura casualidad*, I saw her by sheer chance; *por puro aburrimiento*, out of sheer boredom. || Simple, plain: *la pura verdad*, the plain truth. || Pure: *puro castellano*, pure Castilian. || Chaste, pure (casto). || Neat, straight (bebida alcohólica). || Clear (el cielo). || *Amer.* Only, just (solamente). || — *A puro*, by means of, by dint of. || *De puro cansado se desmayó*, he collapsed from sheer tiredness, he was so tired that he just collapsed. || *De puro gordo no cabe por la puerta*, he is so fat that he can't get through the door. || *Un pura sangre*, a thoroughbred (caballo).
puro m. Cigar (cigarro puro).
púrpura f. Purple (molusco). || Purple (colorante, tela). || Purple (color). || POÉT. Blood (sangre). || FIG. Purple (dignidad). || MED. Purpura. || HERÁLD. Purpure.
purpurado m. Cardinal (prelado).
purpurar v. tr. To dye purple (teñir de púrpura). || To dress in purple.
purpurear v. intr. To have a purple hue.
purpúreo, a adj. Purple.
purpurina f. Purpurin (sustancia colorante roja). || Metallic paint (pintura).
purpurino, na adj. Purple (purpúreo).
purulencia f. MED. Purulence.
purulento, ta adj. Purulent.
pus m. MED. Pus, matter.
pusilánime adj. Pusillanimous, fainthearted (tímido).
pusilanimidad f. Pusillanimity, faintheartedness, cowardliness (cobardía).
pústula f. MED. Pustule, pimple.
pustuloso, sa adj. MED. Pustular: *erupción pustulosa*, pustular eruption. || Pustulous, pustulate, pimply: *cara pustulosa*, pimply face.
puta f. POP. Whore.
putada f. POP. Dirty trick (faena).
putativo, va adj. Putative, supposed.
putear v. intr. POP. To go whoring (andar de putas). | To solicit (una prostituta).
puto n. POP. Bugger (cabrón).
putrefacción f. Putrefaction, rotting, decay.
putrefacto, ta adj. Putrefied, rotten.
putrescencia f. (P.us.) Putrescence.
putrescente adj. Putrescent, rotting.
putrescible adj. Putrescible.
putridez f. Putrefaction, rotting.
pútrido, da adj. Putrid, putrified, rotten.

putsch m. Putsch (alzamiento).
puya f. TAUR. Steel point, goad [of the lance]. | Jab *o* blow with the lance. || FIG. Dig, gibe, cutting remark (pulla).
puyazo m. Blow *o* jab with the lance. || FIG. Dig, gibe, cutting remark.
puzolana f. Pozzolana (roca volcánica).

Q

q f. Q.
— OBSERV. This letter in Spanish is always followed by a silent *u* and has the sound of the *c* in the English word *cave*.
quantum m. FÍS. Quantum. || *Teoría de los quanta*, quantum theory.
— OBSERV. Pl. *quanta*.
que pron. rel. Who, that (sujeto para personas): *el hombre que vive aquí*, the man who lives here. || Whom, who, that (complemento para personas): *el hombre que vi*, the man [whom] I saw. (V. OBSERV.) || That, which (sujeto y complemento para cosas): *el libro que está sobre la mesa*, the book that is on the table; *el libro que estoy leyendo*, the book [that] I am reading. || Which (se puede omitir cambiando el orden de la frase): *el cuchillo con (el) que corto el pan*, the knife with which I cut the bread, the knife I cut the bread with; *la silla en (la) que estoy sentado*, the chair in which I am sitting, the chair I am sitting in. || What: *es en lo que pensaba*, that is what I was thinking of. || — *Al que, a la que*, to [whom]: *la mujer a la que me dirigí*, the woman to whom I spoke, the woman I spoke to; to [which]: *el libro al que me refiero*, the book to which I am referring, the book I am referring to. || *Dar que pensar*, to make one think. || *De que, del que, de la que, de los que, de las que*, of whom: *el hombre del que hablo*, the man of whom I am speaking; of which (para cosas): *estas revistas, de las que varias son nuestras*, these magazines, several of which are ours. || *De que se trata*, in question: *el asunto de que se trata*, the matter in question. || *El día que llegaste*, the day you arrived *o* of your arrival. || *En el momento en que*, the moment [that] (en cuanto): *en el momento en que llegue*, the moment he arrives; just as (justo cuando). || *Es por lo que*, that is why. || *Es su padre el que manda*, it is his father who commands. || *Lo que*, v. LO. || *Lo que es peor*, what is more *o* worse. || FAM. *¡Lo que faltaba!*, that's all we needed! || *Lo que quieras*, anything you like. || *Yo que tú*, if I were you.
— Conj. No se traduce: *quiero que vengas*, I want you to come; *te dije que volvieras más tarde*, I told you to come back later; *le ruego que venga*, I beg you to come. || That (se omite con frecuencia): *me temo que lo haya echado todo a perder*, I'm afraid [that] he may have ruined everything; *¿sabes que me caso mañana?*, do you know [that] I'm getting married tomorrow? || Because (se omite con frecuencia): *hable más fuerte, que oigo mal*, speak louder [because] I can't hear you; *no podemos, que no tenemos dinero*, we can't, we have no money. || Or: *queramos que no*, whether we like it or not; *dámelo que te pego*, give it to me or I'll hit you. || If: *que viene, bien, que no viene, nos arreglamos sin él*, if he comes, fine, if he doesn't, we'll manage without him. || — *Antes que*, before: *no iré antes que todo esté listo*, I'll not leave before everything is ready; *antes que yo*, before me. || *A que*, I bet that: *¡a que llego primero! — ¡A que no!*, I bet [that] I get there first. — I bet you don't! || *¡Claro que no!*, of course not! || *¡Claro que sí!*, of course! || *Corre que te corre*, in a hurry, fast. || || *Cualquier otro que no fuese él*, anyone but him. || *Decir que no, que sí*, to say no, yes. || *El que*, the fact that, that: *me extraña el que no me hayan dicho nada*, I am surprised [that] they haven't said anything, the fact that they haven't said anything surprises me. || *Está que parece otro*, he seems another person. || *Más, menos que*, more, less than. || *No hay más que apretar el botón*, you only have to press the button. || *No hay más que hablar*, there's nothing more to be said. || *Por más que*, v. MÁS. || *Que da asco*, disgusting (adj.), disgustingly (adv.). || *Que da gloria* or *gusto*, marvellously, beautifully (adv.), lovely, wonderful (adj.). || *Que da miedo*, v. MIEDO. || *¡Que lo echen!*, throw him out! || *¡Que me dejen en paz* or *tranquilo!*, leave me alone!, stop pestering me! (Vds), tell them to leave me alone (ellos). || *Que no*, no: *dijo que no*, he said no; of course not (claro que no), no, no (enérgicamente), not: *era su tía que no su madre*, it was his aunt not his mother; without: *no hay día que no me acuerde de ella*, not a day goes by without my thinking of her. || *¡Que se divierta!*, enjoy yourself!, have fun! || *Que sí*, yes (sí), of course (claro que sí). || *¡Que sí era él!*, yes it was him. || *Que tengan ustedes mucha suerte*, I wish you [good] luck. || *Tan ... que*, so ... that. || *Tanto más cuanto que*, all the more so since. || *Ya que*, since.
— OBSERV. En inglés, el pronombre relativo con función de complemento se omite muy frecuentemente (*el libro que estoy leyendo*, the book I am reading; *el chico que vi*, the boy I saw).
Cuando *que* se refiere a personas y tiene función de complemento directo, la forma *who* sustituye con frecuencia *whom*, en la lengua hablada, aunque sea incorrecto desde un punto de vista puramente gramatical.
qué adj. interr. y exclamat. What (con sustantivo): *¿qué hora es?*, what time is it?; *¡qué suerte!*, what luck!; *¡qué chico más simpático!*, what a nice boy!; *¡qué idea tan rara!*, what a strange idea! || Which (entre varios): *¿qué color prefieres?*, which colour do you prefer? || How (con adj. o adv.): *¡qué despacio va este tren!*, how slow this train is going!; *¿qué edad tienes?*, how old are you?; *¡qué calor hace!*, how hot it is!; *¡qué guapa estás!*, how pretty you look! || — *¿De qué tamaño?*, what size?, how big? || *¡Qué bien!*, how marvellous! || *¡Qué de!*, what a lot of: *¡qué de gente!*, what a lot of people! || *¡Qué divertido!*, what fun! || *¡Qué miedo!*, what a fright! (¡qué susto!), how scary!, how frightening! (¡qué espantoso!).
— Pron. interr. What: *¿qué pasa?*, what's happening?; *¿qué dijiste?*, what did you say?; *¿qué es esto?*, what is this?; *¿en qué piensa usted?*, what are you thinking about?; *¿para qué sirve esto?*, what is this for? || — *¿De qué le sirve tener un coche si no sabe conducir?*, what good is a car to you if you don't know how to drive? || *¿De qué se trata?*, what's it all about? || *El qué dirán*, what people say. || *¿Qué dice?*, what did you say? || *¿Qué es de Pedro?*, how is Peter? || *¿Qué es de su vida?*, how are you? || *¿Qué es lo que ocurre?*, what is the matter? || *¿Qué hay?*, v. HABER. || *¿Qué le parece?*, what do you think of it? || *¿Qué más da?*, what difference does it make? || *¿Qué sé yo?*, how should I know? || *¿Qué tal?*, how: *¿qué tal le pareció la película?*, how did you like the film?; *¿qué tal el viaje?*, how was the trip? || FAM. *¿Qué tal?*, how are you? | *¡Qué va!*, come off it!, nonsense!, rubbish! || *Un no sé qué*, a certain something. || *¿Y a mí qué?*, what about me? (¿y para mí?), what's that got to do with me? (¿qué tiene que ver conmigo?). || *¿Y qué?*, so what?
quebracho m. Quebracho (árbol). || Breakaxe [U.S., breakax] (madera).
quebrada f. Narrow pass (paso entre montañas). || Ravine, gorge (hondonada). || *Amer.* Stream.
quebradero m. FIG. y FAM. *Quebradero de cabeza*, headache: *ya tengo suficientes quebraderos de cabeza*, I've got enough headaches already.
quebradizo, za adj. Fragile, brittle: *el cristal es quebradizo*, crystal is fragile. || FIG. Fragile, frail, delicate: *salud quebradiza*, fragile health. | Feeble, weak (voz).
quebrado, da adj. Broken (roto). || Broken, rough, uneven (terreno). || MED. Herniary. || FIG. Dull, dim (color). | Hoarse, faltering: *voz quebrada por la emoción*, voice hoarse with emotion. || COM. Bankrupt. || — *Línea quebrada*, broken line. || *Número quebrado*, fraction.
— M. MAT. Fraction: *quebrado decimal*, decimal fraction. || MED. Hernia. || COM. Bankrupt.
quebradura f. Fracture, break (fractura). || Crack, fissure, split (grieta). || MED. Hernia, rupture.
quebrajoso, sa adj. Fragile.
quebrantable adj. Fragile (frágil). || FIG. Delicate.
quebrantador, ra adj. Contravening (de la ley). || Crushing (que machaca).
— M. y f. Offender, violator, transgressor (de la ley).

quebrantahuesos m. inv. ZOOL. Lammergeyer [U.S., lammergeier] (ave que vive en regiones montañosas). | Osprey, fish hawk (pigargo). || FIG. y FAM. Bore (pesado).
quebrantamiento m. Breaking, breaking up. || FIG. Violation, contravention, infringement: *quebrantamiento de la ley*, violation of the law. | Breaking, breach (de un compromiso, del ayuno). | Weakening, deterioration (de la salud). | Broken health (salud quebrantada). | Exhaustion (agotamiento). || — *Quebrantamiento de destierro*, violation of exile. || JUR. *Quebrantamiento de forma*, faulty drafting. | *Quebrantamiento de sellos*, breaking of seals.
quebrantaolas m. inv. MAR. Breakwater.
quebrantar v. tr. To break: *quebrantar un vaso*, to break a glass. || To crush (machacar): *quebrantar aceitunas*, to crush olives. || To split (hender). || To crack (resquebrajar). || FIG. To break, to violate, to transgress: *quebrantar la ley*, to break the law. | To break (promesa, sello, ayuno). | To lower, to break: *quebrantar el ánimo, la moral (a uno)*, to lower [s.o.'s] spirits, morale. | To weaken (debilitar). | To shake: *quebrantar una convicción*, to shake s.o.'s conviction. | To harm, to injure (salud). | To warm (templar un líquido). | To tone down, to soften (color). | To force open (abrir forzando). | To break into (entrar sin derecho). || *Quebrantar el destierro*, to violate one's exile.
— V. pr. To break, to crack, to split (romperse). || FIG. To crack up (una persona).
quebranto m. Weakening, deterioration (deterioro). || Exhaustion (agotamiento). || Broken health (salud quebrantada). || Discouragement (del ánimo). || Loss (pérdida). || Damage, harm (daño). || Affliction, distress (dolor profundo). || *Quebranto de fortuna*, severe financial setback.
quebrar* v. tr. To break: *quebrar un vaso*, to break a glass. || To bend, to twist (doblar, torcer): *quebrar el cuerpo*, to bend one's body. || FIG. To put an end to (acabar con). | To tone down, to soften (templar un color).
— V. intr. To break (romperse). || COM. To go bankrupt.
— V. pr. To break, to be broken (romperse). || MED. To rupture o.s. (herniarse). || FIG. To break, to become hoarse: *se le quebró la voz con la emoción*, her voice became hoarse with emotion. || — FAM. *No quebrarse*, not to overdo it. | *Quebrarse la cabeza*, to rack one's brains.
queche m. MAR. Ketch.
quechemarín m. *Amer.* Coasting lugger (lugre).
quechua adj. Quechuan.
— M. y f. Quechua.
quechuismo m. Quechuan word *o* expression.
queda f. Curfew: *tocar a queda*, to sound the curfew. || *Toque de queda*, curfew [bell].
quedar v. intr. To remain, to stay (permanecer): *la chica quedó en casa*, the girl stayed at home. || To remain: *al final quedaron muy amigos*, in the end they remained good friends. || To arrange to meet: *quedé con ellos a las ocho*, I arranged to meet them at eight o'clock. || To be: *queda lejos*, it is a long way away; *la junta quedó constituida tras la segunda votación*, the board was constituted after the second vote; *su segunda novela queda muy por debajo de la primera*, his second novel is quite inferior to his first; *quedé extrañadísimo*, I was astonished; *quedar fuera de peligro*, to be out of danger. || To stand: *así queda la cosa*, that's how it stands. || To end, to stop, to leave off: *ahí quedó la conversación*, the conversation ended there. || To be left: *quedan cinco minutos*, there are five minutes left. || — *¿Dónde habíamos quedado?*, where were we? (¿qué decíamos?). || *¿En qué quedamos?*, what is it to be?, what shall we do? (¿qué hacemos?), so: *¿en qué quedamos?, ¿vienes o no vienes?*, so, are you coming or not? || *Eso queda a mi cuidado*, I'll take care of that. || *He quedado con ella a las ocho*, I have a date with her at eight. || *La carta quedó sin contestar*, the letter remained unanswered *o* was left unanswered. || *La chaqueta le queda corta*, the jacket is too short for him. || *Me quedan sólo cinco pesetas*, I've only got five pesetas left. || *Por mí que no quede*, do as you please, don't let me stop you. || *Queda de usted atentamente*, I remain, yours faithfully, Yours faithfully (en una carta). || *Queda de usted su affmo. y s.s.*, Yours faithfully (en una carta). || *Quedan cinco días para los exámenes*, there are five days to go before the exams. || *¿Queda pan?*, is there any bread left? || *Queda por saber si*, it remains to be seen whether. || *Quedar algo que ni pintado*, to fit like a glove: *el traje le queda que ni pintado*, the suit fits him like a glove; to be *o* to look perfect: *este cuadro queda aquí que ni pintado*, this painting looks perfect here. || *Quedar bien*, to look good: *el cuarto queda muy bien con su nuevo empapelado*, the room looks very good with the new wallpaper; to go well: *quedan bien tus nuevos zapatos con tu traje gris*, your new shoes go well with your grey suit; to go down well, to perform well: *el cantante ha quedado bien*, the singer performed well; to make a good impression: *regalando flores siempre quedas bien*, you always make a good impression with flowers. || *Quedar ciego*, to go blind (por viejo, etc.), to be blinded (por un accidente). || *Quedar cojo*, to be lamed *o* crippled. || *Quedar con vida*, to survive. || *Quedar de acuerdo*, to agree, to reach an agreement. || *Quedar en*, to agree to, to decide to: *quedamos en salir mañana*, we have agreed to go out tomorrow; *quedaron en ir todos de negro*, they all agreed to go dressed in black; to agree, to say [that]: *quedó en venir a las siete*, he agreed to come at seven, he said he was coming at seven. || *Quedar mal*, to come out badly, to look bad: *la foto quedó muy mal*, the photo came out very badly; to perform badly: *el cantante quedó tan mal que le pitaron*, the singer performed so badly that he was booed; to make a bad impression: *he quedado muy mal con sus padres*, I made a very bad impression on her parents. || *Quedar para*, to arrange to meet: *hemos quedado para mañana*, we have arranged to meet tomorrow. || *Quedar por*, to remain to be, to have still to be: *queda mucho por hacer*, much remains to be done; *queda por pagar el teléfono*, the telephone bill has still to be paid. || *Quedar todo en casa*, to remain in the family: *metiendo al niño en el negocio, todo quedará en casa*, if we put our son in the business it will remain in the family. || FAM. *Ya le queda poco*, he doesn't have much longer, he doesn't have much time left.
— V. pr. To stay, to remain: *se quedó un año en Lima*, he stayed a year in Lima; *quedarse en la cama, en casa*, to stay in bed, at home; *quedarse silencioso*, to remain silent. || To stay (en un hotel, etc.). || To go, to become: *quedarse cojo, ciego, sordo*, to go lame, blind, deaf. || To remain, to stay: *quedarse soltero*, to stay single. || To be left: *quedarse huérfano*, to be left an orphan. || — FAM. *Me quedé de una pieza*, I was speechless *o* flabbergasted. || *No saber con qué quedarse*, not to know what to choose. || FIG. *Quedarse ahí*, to die (morir). || *Quedarse anticuado*, to go out of fashion *o* style. || FIG. *Quedarse a oscuras* or *in albis*, to remain *o* to be left in the dark. || *Quedarse atrás*, to stay behind (queriendo), to be left behind (sin querer). || *Quedarse boquiabierto* or *con la boca abierta*, v. BOQUIABIERTO. || *Quedarse como quien ve visiones*, v. VISIÓN. || *Quedarse (con)*, to keep: *se quedó con mi libro*, he kept my book; *si te gusta tanto quédatelo*, if you like it so much, keep it; to take (tomar): *me quedo con éste*, I'll take this one; to have left: *después de haber comprado este vestido me quedé con cien pesetas*, after buying this dress I had a hundred pesetas left; to be left with (cargar con). || FIG. *Quedarse con dos palmos de narices*, v. PALMO. || *Quedarse con hambre*, to still be hungry. || FIG. *Quedarse con las ganas*, to have to do without, to have to go without, to have to forget the idea, not to get what one wanted. | *Quedarse con uno*, to fool s.o. (engañar). | *Quedarse cortado*, not to know what to say. || *Quedarse corto*, v. CORTO. | *Quedarse de piedra*, to be thunderstruck. | *Quedarse encima*, to have the last word. | *Quedarse en el poyete* or *poyetón*, to be a wallflower (en un baile), to be left on the shelf (quedar solterona). | *Quedarse en la calle*, v. CALLE. | *Quedarse helado*, v. HELADO. | *Quedarse limpio*, to be cleaned out. || *Quedarse pálido*, to turn pale. || FIG. *Quedarse para vestir santos*, to be left on the shelf. | *Quedarse plantado*, v. PLANTADO. || *Quédate quieto*, keep quiet (cállate), keep still (no te muevas). || *Quedarse sin*, to run out of (acabársele a uno): *me he quedado sin tinta*, I have run out of ink; to be left [without]: *quedarse sin habla*, to be left speechless; *quedarse sin esperanzas*, to be left in despair *o* without hope; *quedarse sin trabajo*, to be left jobless *o* without work; *quedarse sin una gorda*, to be left penniless *o* without a penny; not to, to go without (con verbo): *quedarse sin comer*, not to eat. || *Se me quedó mirando*, he just stared at me.
quedo, da adj. Calm, tranquil, still. || Quiet (silencioso): *el niño está muy quedo*, the child is very quiet. || Low, soft (voz): *en voz queda*, in a low voice. || Soft, gentle (ruido).
— Adv. Softly, quietly: *hablar muy quedo*, to speak very quietly.
quehacer m. Duty, task: *nuestro quehacer cotidiano*, our daily duty. || — Pl. Tasks, chores, duties: *los quehaceres domésticos*, the household chores. | Business, *sing.*: *ir a sus quehaceres*, to go about one's business.
queja f. Moan, groan (de dolor): *las quejas de un enfermo*, the moans of a sick person. || Complaint: *las quejas de los vecinos*, the complaints of the neighbours; *las quejas de un acreedor*, the complaints of a creditor. || JUR. Complaint: *presentar una queja*, to lodge a complaint. || — *Dar motivo de queja*, to give reason for complaint. || *Dar quejas* or *queja de uno, de algo*, to complain about s.o., about sth. || *Tener queja de*, to have a complaint about.
quejarse v. pr. To moan, to groan (gemir): *quejarse lastimosamente*, to moan pitifully. || To complain: *quejarse de uno*, to complain about s.o. || — *No me puedo quejar*, I can't complain. || *Quejarse de algo a uno*, to complain to s.o. about sth. || *Quejarse de hambre*, to complain that one is hungry. || *Quejarse de vicio*, to complain for the sake of it.
quejica o **quejicoso, sa** adj. Grumpy, querulous, hard to please. || *No seas tan quejica*, stop moaning, don't be such a grouse.
— M. y f. Grouse, moaner.

quejido m. Moan, groan: *los quejidos de un herido*, the moans of a wounded person. || *Dar* or *lanzar quejidos*, to moan, to groan.
quejigal m. Gall oak grove.
quejigo m. BOT. Gall oak (roble).
quejón, ona adj./s. V. QUEJICA.
quejoso, sa adj. Displeased, angry, annoyed (enfadado): *estoy quejoso de tu comportamiento*, I am annoyed at your behaviour.
quejumbre f. Moaning, groaning (gemidos). || Grumbling, complaining, moaning (de descontento).
quejumbrón, ona adj. Whining, plaintive.
— M. y f. Moaner.
quejumbroso, sa adj. Whining, plaintive, complaining.
— M. y f. Moaner.
quelonios m. pl. ZOOL. Chelonians.
quema f. Burning (acción de quemar): *la quema de los herejes, de los conventos*, the burning of heretics, of the convents. || Death by fire, the stake: *condenado a la quema*, condemned to death by fire. || COM. Clearance sale (liquidación de géneros). || *Amer.* Burning of fields. || FIG. *Huir de la quema*, to flee from danger.
quemadero m. Stake (para los sentenciados). || Incinerator (para basuras).
quemado, da adj. Burnt (U.S., burned]. || FIG. Burnt-out [U.S., burned-out]: *un futbolista, un equipo quemado*, a burnt-out footballer, team. | Embittered, resentful (amargado, resentido).
— M. Burning: *huele a quemado*, I can smell burning. || Patch of burnt land (chamicera).
quemador, ra adj. Burning.
— M. Burner: *quemador de gas*, gas burner.
quemadura f. Burn (herida): *quemadura de tercer grado*, third-degree burn. || Scald (causado por un líquido caliente). || AGR. Smut (tizón). | Cold blight (de las plantas heladas). || *Quemadura de sol*, sunburn.
quemar v. tr. To burn: *quemar papeles*, to burn papers. || To burn down *o* out (destruir con fuego). || To set fire to (prender fuego a). || FAM. To burn: *el sol nos quemó*, the sun burnt us. | To burn (el dinero). || To sell at a reduction, to sell cheap (malbaratar). || AGR. To nip, to blight (desecar las plantas heladas). || FIG. To overtrain: *un entrenador que quema a sus jugadores*, a trainer who overtrains his players. | To wear out: *un exceso de actuaciones quema a los actores*, too many performances wear out the actors. || — *A quema ropa*, at point-blank range, point-blank. || FIG. *Para mí es un político quemado*, as far as I am concerned he is a has-been. | *Quemar cartuchos*, to fire shots. | *Quemar etapas*, to get on in leaps and bounds. | *Quemar la sangre*, to make one's blood boil: *su cachaza me quema la sangre*, his calmness makes my blood boil. | *Quemar las naves*, to burn one's boats [U.S., to burn one's bridges]. || *Quemar una colección de fuegos artificiales*, to let off fireworks.
— V. intr. To burn. || To be burning hot *o* boiling hot (estar muy caliente).
— V. pr. To burn o.s.: *quemarse con una cerilla*, to burn o.s. with a match. || To burn [up] (papeles, etc.). || To burn [down], to be burnt down (una casa, etc.). || To burn (un asado). || — FIG. *Quemarse la sangre*, to fret (preocuparse mucho). | *Quemarse las cejas* or *las pestañas* (*estudiando*), to burn the midnight oil. | *¡Que te quemas!*, you're boiling (en juegos).
quemarropa (a) loc. adv. Point-blank, at point-blank range (disparo y contestación).
quemazón f. Burning (acción de quemar). || Burn (quemadura). | Intense heat (calor excesivo). | FIG. Sore, sting (dolor). | Itch (comezón). || FIG. *Sentía una gran quemazón por haber sido tan mal tratado*, I felt annoyed *o* resentful at having been treated so badly.
quena f. *Amer.* Quena, Indian flute.
— OBSERV. The *quena* is a reed flute generally with five finger holes. It is used mainly by the Indians of Peru and Bolivia.
quenopodiáceas f. pl. BOT. Chenopodiaceae.
quepis m. Kepi (gorro).
queque m. *Amer.* Cake.
queratina m. BIOL. Keratin.
querella f. (Ant.). Moan, groan (queja). || JUR. Complaint. || Quarrel, dispute (riña).
querellante adj. Complaining.
— M. y f. JUR. Complainant, plaintiff.
querellarse v. pr. JUR. To lodge a complaint [against].
querelloso, sa adj. Querulous (quejica).
querencia f. Homing instinct (instinto de los animales). || Favourite place (sitio preferido). || FAM. Home (hogar). || (P.us.). Affection, attachment (cariño). || TAUR. Tendency of the bull to go towards a certain part of the ring.
querencioso, sa adj. Homing, which tends to return to the same spot.
querendón, ona m. y f. FAM. Lover (amante).
querer* v. tr. To want (desear): *quiero un helado*, I want an ice cream; *¿cuánto quiere por el cuadro?*, how much does he want for the picture?; *se lo ofrecí pero no lo quiso*, I offered it to him, but he didn't want it; *le dije que viniese, pero no quiso*, I told him to come but he didn't want to; *quiero ir al cine*, I want to go to the pictures; *quiero que lo hagas tú*, I want you to do it; *quería que lo hicieses tú*, I wanted you to do it. || To want, to like: *¿quiere un cigarrillo?*, would you like a cigarette?, do you want a cigarette? || To wish, to like, to want: *haga lo que quiera*, do as you wish, do what you like; *si usted quiere*, if you like *o* wish *o* want. || To love (con amor): *me quiere, no me quiere*, she loves me, she loves me not; *te quiero con todo mi corazón*, I love you with all my heart; *quiere mucho a sus hijos*, she loves her children dearly. || To be fond of (tener cariño a). || To like (encontrar simpático). || To hope (esperar): *quisiera que no lloviese mañana*, I hope it doesn't rain tomorrow. || To wish, to like: *quisiera que estuviera aquí*, I wish he were here, I would like him to be here. || To try (intentar): *me quiso matar*, he tried to kill me. || To be about to (estar a punto de): *quería amanecer*, dawn was about to break. || To need (necesitar): *esta planta quiere agua*, this plant needs water. || To require, to demand (requerir): *la urbanidad quiere que se ceda el asiento a las señoras*, politeness requires that one should give up one's seat to a lady. || To be looking for *o* asking for (buscar): *se le ve que quiere pelea*, he is obviously looking for trouble. || To claim (pretender): *su teoría quiere que*, his theory claims that. || — *Como quien no quiere la cosa*, quite nonchalantly *o* offhandedly, just like that. || *Como quiera*, as you like. || *Como quiera que*, since, inasmuch as (dado que). || *Cuando quiera*, whenever you like, any time. || *Cuando quiera que*, whenever. || *Donde quiera*, v. DONDEQUIERA. || FAM. *Gente de quiero y no puedo*, people who live above their means. || *¡No lo quiera Dios!*, Heaven forbid!, God forbid! || *No quiero sus excusas*, I don't want your excuses. || *¡Por lo que más quieras!*, for Heaven's sake! || *¿Qué más quieres?*, what more do you want? || FAM. *¡Qué más quisieras tú!*, you'd like that, wouldn't you? || *Que quiera que no quiera* or *quiera o no quiera*, [whether you] like it or not. || *¿Qué quiere decir con eso?*, what do you mean by that? || *¿Qué quiere decir esto?*, what does this mean?, what is the meaning of this? || *¿Qué quieres?*, what do you want? || *¿Qué quieres que yo le haga?*, what do you want me to do [about it]? || *Que si quieres (arroz, Catalina)*, it is [was] useless. || *Querer bien a uno*, to like s.o., to be fond of s.o. (tenerle afecto). || *Querer decir*, to mean. || *Querer es poder*, where there's a will there's a way. || *Querer mal a uno*, not to like s.o., to have it in for s.o. (fam.). || *Querer más*, to prefer. || *Quería saber si*, I wanted to know if. || *Queriendo*, on purpose, deliberately, intentionally. || *Quien bien te quiere te hará llorar*, you have to be cruel to be kind, spare the rod and spoil the child. || *Quiérase o no*, like it or not. || *Quieras que no*, like it or not (a la fuerza). || *¿Quiere darme las tijeras, por favor?*, would you give me the scissors, please? || *Quiere llover*, it's trying to rain, it looks like rain. || *Quisiera ir contigo*, I'd like to go with you. || *Sin querer*, unintentionally, without meaning to: *lo hice sin querer*, I did it unintentionally, I didn't mean to do it. || *Sí, quiero*, I will (en la boda).
— V. pr. To love each other. || FAM. *Quererse como tórtolos*, to be like turtledoves.
querer m. Affection, love, fondness.
queretano, na adj. [Of *o* from] Querétaro [Mexico].
— M. y f. Native *o* inhabitant of Querétaro.
querido, da adj. Loved: *querido por sus hijos*, loved by his children. || Dear: *querido tío*, dear uncle; *mi querida prima*, my dear cousin. || Darling, dear: *sí, querida*, yes, darling. || — *Fórmula tan querida por*, favourite formula of, formula so much liked by. || *Mi querido amigo*, my dear *o* beloved friend.
— M. Lover (amante). || — F. Lover, mistress: *echarse una querida*, to take a mistress.
querindongo, ga m. y f. FAM. Lover.
quermes m. Kermes (insecto).
quermese f. Kermis.
queroseno m. Kerosene.
querubín m. Cherubim.
quesadilla f. *Amer.* Cheesecake (pastel).
quesera f. Cheese factory (fábrica). || Cheese dish (plato). || Cheese mould [U.S., cheese mold].
quesería f. Cheese shop (tienda).
quesero, ra adj. Cheese: *industria quesera*, cheese industry.
— M. y f. Cheese maker *o* seller. || Lover of cheese (aficionado).
queso m. Cheese. || — FIG. y FAM. *Dársela con queso a uno*, to take s.o. in, to put one over on s.o. (engañar). || *Queso de bola*, Edam cheese. || *Queso de cabra*, goat cheese. || *Queso de cerdo* or *de cabeza*, headcheese. || *Queso de Chester*, Cheshire cheese.
quetzal m. Quetzal (ave). || Quetzal (moneda).
quevedesco, ca adj. [Of] Quevedo.
quevedos m. pl. Pince-nez, *sing.*
¡quiá! interj. FAM. Come off it!, nonsense!, rubbish!, never!
quiasma m. ANAT. Chiasma (cruce).
quicial m. TECN. Hinging post (de puerta o ventana).
quicio m. TECN. Pivot hole (gozne). | Frame (marco de puerta o ventana). || — FIG. *Fuera de quicio*, beside o.s. (persona), out of order (cosa). | *Sacar de quicio a uno*, to make s.o. wild, to infuriate s.o. (enfurecer). | *Sacar de quicio una cosa*, to carry sth. to extremes. | *Salir de quicio*, to fly off the handle.

Quico m. FAM. *Ponerse como el Quico*, to stuff o.s. (hincharse de comer).
quiché adj./s. Quiche [Indian of Guatemala].
quichua adj. Quechuan.
— M. Quechua, Quechuan.
quichuismo m. V. QUECHUISMO.
quid m. Gist, crux, main point: *¡ahí está el quid!*, there is the gist. || — *Dar en el quid*, to hit the nail on the head. || *Quid pro quo*, misunderstanding (malentendido), mistake (error).
quídam m. FAM. Somebody or other (fulano). | Nobody (don nadie).
quiebra f. Break (rotura). || Crack, fissure (grieta). || COM. Bankruptcy (bancarrota). | Crash (crac). || FIG. Collapse: *la quiebra de los valores humanos*, the collapse of human values. || — COM. *Declararse en quiebra*, to declare bankruptcy. | *Estar en quiebra*, to be bankrupt.
quiebro m. Dodge (ademán). || Dribbling (fútbol). || MÚS. Grace notes, *pl.* || TAUR. Dodge. || *Dar un quiebro*, to dribble (fútbol), to dodge (el torero).
quien pron. rel. (de sujeto) Who: *fue su padre quien lo dijo*, it was his father who said it; *su madre, quien estaba escuchando, dijo*, his mother, who was listening, said. || Anyone who, whoever: *quien no sabe eso es tonto*, anyone who doesn't know that is stupid; *quien acabe el último paga*, whoever finishes last pays. || Someone [who]: *ya encontraré quien me haga este trabajo*, I shall find s.o. who will do this job *o* s.o. to do this job for me. || — *A quien*, whom, that (complemento directo): *la persona a quien quiero*, the person whom I love (v. OBSERV.), to whom (complemento indirecto): *las personas a quienes* or *a quien hablo*, the people to whom I am speaking. || *A quien se tiene que dirigir usted es a ese señor*, that is the man you must speak to. || *Como quien*, like he who [she who, etc.], like the one who: *se porta como quienes le han educado*, he acts like those who raised him; as if: *hace como quien no oye*, he acts as if he doesn't hear. || *Como quien dice*, as it were, so to speak. || *Como quien no quiere la cosa*, V. QUERER. || *De quien*, of anyone who, of whoever, of he who [she who, etc.]: *el alma de quien muere sin bautismo va al limbo*, the soul of he who dies unbaptized goes to limbo; whose (cuyo): *en casa de quien*, in whose house. || *Es ... quien*, it is ... who: *es su madre quien manda*, it is his mother who rules. || *Habrá quien lo sepa*, there will surely be s.o. who knows. || *Hay quien dice*, there are people who say, there are those who say, some say. || *La gente con quien vive*, the people he lives with. || *No es quien para hacer esto*, he is not one to do this, it is not his place to do this. || *No hay quien se ocupe de él*, there is no one to take care of him. || *Quien más quien menos*, everybody.

— OBSERV. En el lenguaje hablado *whom* se suprime a menudo (*the person I love; the people I am speaking to*).

quién pron. interr. o exclam. Who (sujeto): *¿quién es?*, who is it?; *¿quiénes son estos dos chicos?*, who are these two boys?; *dime quién es*, tell me who it is. || Whom, who (con preposición): *¿para quién trabajas?*, for whom do you work?, who do you work for?; *¿con quién ibas ayer?*, who were you with *o* with whom were you yesterday? (V. OBSERV.). || — *¿De quién?*, whose?: *¿de quién es este abrigo?*, whose is this coat?, whose coat is this?; *no sé de quién es*, I don't know whose it is. || *Dime con quién andas y te diré quién eres*, a man is known by the company he keeps. || *¡Quién pudiera!*, if only I could! || *Quién ... quién*, some ... some. || *¿Quién sabe?*, who knows? || *¿Quién vive?*, who goes there?

— OBSERV. En la lengua hablada *who* sustituye con frecuencia a *whom* cuando va acompañado por una preposición o cuando es complemento directo del verbo, aunque, desde un punto de vista puramente gramatical, *whom* sea la única forma correcta.

quienquiera pron. indef. Whoever, anyone, anybody: *quienquiera que lo vea*, whoever sees him, anyone *o* anybody who sees him. || *Quienquiera que sea*, whoever it may be, whoever it is.

— OBSERV. The plural *quienesquiera* is rare.

quietismo m. FIL. Quietism (doctrina). || FIG. Immobilism.
quietista adj./s. Quietist.
quieto, ta adj. Still (sin ruido). || Motionless, still (inmóvil). || Calm, quiet (persona, vida, mar, etc.): *por el momento todo está quieto*, everything is quiet at the moment. || — *¡Déjame quieto!*, leave me alone! || *¡Estate quieto!*, keep still! || *No sabe estarse quieto*, he can't keep still. || *¡Quieto!*, don't move!, keep still! (no te muevas), down, boy! (a un perro), whoa, boy! (a un caballo). || *¡Todo el mundo quieto!*, nobody move! (en un asalto, etc.).
quietud f. Stillness, calm, quietude.
quijada f. ANAT. Jawbone.
quijera f. Cheek strap (de los arriendos).
quijotada f. Quixotic deed, quixotism.
quijote m. Cuisse (de la armadura). || Rump, croup (del caballo). || FIG. y FAM. *Un quijote*, a quixote.
Quijote (Don) n. pr. m. Don Quixote. || *El Quijote*, Don Quixote (obra de Cervantes).
quijotería f. Quixotism.
quijotesco, ca o **quijotil** adj. Quixotic.
quijotismo m. Quixotism.
quilatador m. Assayer (de oro).
quilate m. Carat [U.S., carat, karat]: *oro de 18 quilates*, 18 carat gold. || Ancient coin. || — FIG. y FAM. *De muchos quilates*, of great value. | *No tiene dos quilates de juicio*, he's got no sense at all, he hasn't got an ounce of sense.
quilo m. BIOL. Chyle. || FIG. y FAM. *Sudar el quilo*, to sweat blood.
quilo m. Kilogram, kilogramme, kilo.
quilombo m. *Amer.* Brothel (lupanar). | Hut (choza).
quilla f. MAR. Keel: *quilla de balance*, bilge keel. || Breastbone, keel (de las aves). || *Dar de quilla a un barco*, to keel a boat, to keel a boat over.
quillay m. *Amer.* Quillaja (palo de jabón).
quillotra f. FAM. Concubine (manceba).
quillotrar v. tr. (P.us.). FAM. To stir up, to rouse, to excite, to stimulate (excitar). | To woo, to court (galantear). | To meditate, to ponder (meditar). | To adorn, to embellish (engalanar).
— V. pr. To grumble (quejarse).
quillotro m. (P.us.). FAM. Stimulus (estímulo). | Sign (señal). | Love affair (amorío). | Headache, worry (quebradero de cabeza). | Wooing, courting (requiebro) | Adornment (gala). | Friend (amigo).
quimera f. MIT. Chimera. || FIG. Quarrel, argument (contienda): *buscar quimera*, to be looking for a quarrel. || Daydream, pipe dream (sueño): *vivir de quimeras*, to live on daydreams. || Chimera, wild idea (idea absurda).
quimérico, ca adj. Chimerical, unrealistic.
quimerista adj. Dreaming. || Quarrelsome.
— M. y f. Dreamer (soñador). || Troublemaker (pendenciero).
química f. Chemistry: *química general*, *mineral* or *inorgánica*, *orgánica*, general, inorganic, organic chemistry.
químico, ca adj. Chemical: *productos químicos*, chemical products.
— M. y f. Chemist.
quimioterapia f. MED. Chemotherapy.
quimista m. Alchemist (alquimista).
quimo m. BIOL. Chyme.
quimono m. Kimono.
quina f. Cinchona bark (corteza). || MED. Quinine. || Galbanum (gálbano). || — FIG. y FAM. *Más malo que la quina*, revolting, disgusting (una cosa), horrible, nasty (una persona). | *Tragar quina*, to put up with murder (aguantarse).
quinario ria adj. Quinary, consisting of five elements.
— M. Five-day devotion (cultos durante cinco días).
quincalla f. Hardware, ironmongery (objetos).
quincallería f. Hardware shop, ironmongery.
quincallero, ra m. y f. Hardware dealer, ironmonger.
quince adj. num. Fifteen: *quince chicos*, fifteen boys. || — *Quince días*, a fortnight: *hace quince días*, a fortnight ago. || *Unos quince libros*, about fifteen books.
— Adj. ord. *Luis XV (quince)*, Louis XV [the fifteenth]; *el día quince*, the fifteenth; *el siglo XV (quince)*, the 15th [fifteenth] century.
— M. Fifteen (número). || Fifteen, team [in Rugby Union] (equipo de rugby). || — FIG. y FAM. *Dar quince y raya a*, V. RAYA. || *El quince no sale nunca*, [number] fifteen never comes up.
quincena f. Fortnight. || MÚS. Fifteenth. || *Recibir su quincena*, to receive one's fortnightly pay.
quincenal adj. Fortnightly, twice monthly (que se hace cada quincena). || Fortnight-long (que dura una quincena).
quincenalmente adv. Every fortnight, fortnightly.
quinceno, na adj. Fifteenth.
— M. y f. Fifteen-month-old mule.
quincuagenario, ria adj. Made up of fifty units *o* parts. || Fifty-year-old, quinquagenarian, in one's fifties (cincuentón).
— M. y f. Fifty-year-old [person], quinquagenarian, man [*o* woman] in his [*o* her] fifties (cincuentón).
quincuagésimo, ma adj./s.m. Fiftieth. || — F. REL. Quincuagesima.
quincha f. *Amer.* Reed binding (para techos, muros).
quinchar v. tr. *Amer.* To build [mud or cane walls, etc.] using reeds to strengthen them.
quingentésimo, ma adj./s. Five hundredth.
quinielas f. pl. Football pools (fútbol).
quinielista m. y f. Person who does the pools (fútbol).
quinientos, tas adj. Five hundred: *quinientos hombres*, five hundred men; *quinientos veinte*, five hundred and twenty; *el año quinientos*, the year five hundred. || *Mil quinientos*, one thousand five hundred, fifteen hundred (número), fifteen hundred (año).
quinina f. Quinine.
quino m. BOT. Cinchona (árbol).
quinoa f. BOT. Quinoa (planta).
quínola f. Card game in which the best hand is a four-card flush (juego de naipes).
quinona f. QUÍM. Quinone.
quinqué m. Oil lamp (lámpara). || FAM. *Tener mucho quinqué*, to be very sharp *o* bright.
quinquefolio m. BOT. y ARQ. Cinquefoil.
quinquenal adj. Quinquennial, five-year. || *Plan quinquenal*, five-year plan.
quinquenio m. Quinquennium, five-year period.

QUÍMICA, *f.* — CHEMISTRY

I. Laboratorio, *m.* — Laboratory.

mechero (*m.*) Bunsen	Bunsen burner
producto *m.*	product
frasco *m.*	flask
aparato *m.*	apparatus
indicador (*m.*) pH	pH indicator
matraz *m.*	matrass
tornasol *m.*	litmus
papel (*m.*) de tornasol	litmus paper
probeta (*f.*) graduada	graduate, graduated flask
reactivo *m.*	reagent
tubo (*m.*) de ensayo	test tube
bureta *f.*	burette
retorta *f.*	retort
alambique *m.*	still
copela *f.*	cupel
crisol *m.*	crucible, melting pot
pipeta *f.*	pipette
filtro *m.*	filter
agitador *m.*	stirring rod

II. Composición, *f.* — Composition.

elemento *m.*	element
cuerpo *m.*	body
compuesto *m.*	compound
átomo *m.*	atom
átomo-gramo *m.*	gram atom
molécula *f.*	molecule
electrólito *m.*	electrolyte
ión *m.*	ion
anión *m.*	anion
catión *m.*	cation
electrón *m.*	electron
isótopo *m.*	isotope
isómero *m.*	isomer
polímero *m.*	polymer
símbolo *m.*	symbol
radical *m.*	radical
fórmula (*f.*) desarrollada	structural formula
valencia *f.*	valence, valency
monovalente, bivalente	monovalent, bivalent
halógeno *m.*	halogen
enlace *m.*	bond
mezcla *f.*	mixture
combinación *f.*	combination (operación); compound (compuesto)
aleación *f.*	alloy
peso (*m.*) atómico	atomic weight
número (*m.*) atómico	atomic number
masa (*f.*) atómica	atomic mass

III. Elementos, *m.* — Elements.

metal *m.*	metal
metaloide *m.*	metalloid
plomo *m.* (Pb)	lead
hierro *m.* (Fe)	iron
oro *m.* (Au)	gold
plata *f.* (Ag)	silver
platino *m.* (Pt)	platinum
cobre *m.* (Cu)	copper
níquel *m.* (Ni)	nickel
aluminio *m.* (Al)	aluminium
cinc *m.* (Zn)	zinc
estaño *m.* (Sn)	tin
mercurio *m.* (Hg)	mercury
oxígeno *m.* (O)	oxygen
nitrógeno *m.* (N)	nitrogen
helio *m.* (He)	helium
hidrógeno *m.* (H)	hydrogen
criptón *m.* (Kr)	krypton
carbono *m.* (C)	carbon
potasio *m.* (K)	potassium
sodio *m.* (Na)	sodium
azufre *m.* (S)	sulphur
fósforo *m.* (P)	phosphorus
yodo *m.* (I)	iodine
calcio *m.* (Ca)	calcium
bario *m.* (Ba)	barium
manganeso *m.* (Mn)	manganese
flúor *m.* (F)	fluorine
cloro *m.* (Cl)	chlorine
boro *m.* (B)	boron
bromo *m.* (Br)	bromine
magnesio *m.* (Mg)	magnesium
antimonio *m.* (Sb)	antimony
cobalto *m.* (Co)	cobalt
curio *m.* (Cm)	curium
uranio *m.* (U)	uranium
radio *m.* (Ra)	radium
plutonio *m.* (Pu)	plutonium
radón *m.* (Rn)	radon

IV. Compuestos, *m.* — Compounds.

química (*f.*) orgánica	organic chemistry
química (*f.*) inorgánica	inorganic chemistry
derivado *m.*	derivative
serie *f.*	series
ácido *m.*	acid
ácido (*m.*) clorhídrico, sulfúrico, nítrico	hydrochloric, sulphuric, nitric acid
agua (*f.*) fuerte	nitric acid, aqua fortis
ácido (*m.*) graso	fatty acid
ácido (*m.*) orgánico	organic acid
ácido (*m.*) sulfhídrico; sulfuro (*m.*) de hidrógeno	hydrosulphuric acid; hydrogen sulfide
álcali *m.*	alkali
amoniaco *m.*	ammonia
base *f.*	base
hidrato *m.*; hidróxido *m.*	hydrate; hydroxide
hidrácido *m.*	hydracid
hidrocarburo *m.*	hydrocarbon
anhídrido *m.*	anhydride
alcaloide *m.*	alkaloid
aldehído *m.*	aldehyde
óxido *m.*	oxide
fosfato *m.*	phosphate
acetato *m.*	acetate
metano *m.*	methane
butano *m.*	butane
sal *f.*	salt
sufijos:	*suffixes*:
-uro	-ide
-ato	-ate
-ito	-ite
-oso	-ous
-ico	-ic
carbonato (*m.*) de potasio *or* potásico	potassium carbonate
sosa *f.*; carbonato (*m.*) sódico	soda; sodium carbonate
potasa (*f.*) cáustica	caustic potash
sosa (*f.*) cáustica	caustic soda
éster *m.*	ester
gel *m.*	gel

V. Reacción (*f.*) química. — Chemical reaction.

análisis *m.*	analysis
fraccionamiento *m.*	fractionation
reacción (*f.*) endotérmica	endothermic reaction
reacción (*f.*) exotérmica	exothermic reaction
precipitación *f.*	precipitation
precipitado *m.*	precipitate
destilar	to distil, to distill
destilación *f.*	distillation
calcinar	to calcine
oxidar	to oxidize
alcalinización *f.*	alkalinization
oxigenar	to oxigenate, to oxidize
neutralizar	to neutralize
hidrogenar	to hydrogenate
hidratar	to hydrate
deshidratar	to dehydrate
fermentación *f.*	fermentation
solución *f.*	solution
combustión *f.*	combustion
fusión *f.*	fusion, melting
alcalinidad *f.*	alkalinity
isomería *f.*	isomerism, isomery
hidrólisis *f.*	hydrolysis
electrólisis *f.*	electrolysis
electrodo *m.*	electrode
ánodo *m.*	anode
cátodo *m.*	cathode
catalizador *m.*	catalyst
catálisis *f.*	catalysis
oxidación *f.*	oxidization, oxidation
reducción *f.*	reduction
reductor *m.*	reducer
disolución *f.*	dissolution, solution
síntesis *f.*	synthesis
reversible	reversible

quinqui m. Fam. Hardware dealer, ironmonger. (vendedor de quincalla). | Fam. Villain, rogue.

quinquina f. Cinchona (quina).

quinta f. Villa, country house, manor (casa). || Mil. Call-up, conscription (reclutamiento). | Contingent of troops called up in one year (reemplazo). || Quinte (esgrima). || Mús. Fifth. || — Mil. *Entrar en quintas*, to reach call-up age. | *Es de la misma quinta que yo*, we were called up in the same year. | *Librarse de quintas*, to be exempted from military service.

quintaesencia f. Quintessence.

quintaesenciado, da adj. Quintessenced, quintessential.

quintaesenciar v. tr. To quintessence, to quintessentialize.

quintal m. Quintal (peso). || *Quintal métrico*, a hundred kilogrammes, quintal (peso de cien kilos).

— Observ. The former Spanish *quintal* weighed one hundred pounds.

quintana f. Villa, country house.

quintar v. tr. To take one in five (uno de cada cinco). || Mil. To call up, to conscript, to draft. || Agr. To plough for the fifth time.

— V. intr. To reach its fifth day [the moon] (la luna). || To bid a fifth higher, to raise the bid by a fifth.

quinteo m. Drawing of lots [*de*, for].

quintería f. Farm, property (finca).

quintero m. Farmer (arrendatario). || Farm labourer, farmhand (mozo de labranza).

quinteto m. Mús. Quintet, quintette.

quintilla f. Five-line stanza (estrofa de cinco versos).

quintillizos, zas m. y f. pl. Quintuplets, quins (fam.).

quintillón m. Quintillion.

Quintín n. pr. m. Quentin. || V. San Quintín.

quinto, ta adj. Fifth. || — *En quinto lugar*, fifthly, in fifth place. || *La quinta columna*, the fifth column. || *La quinta parte*, a fifth. || *Quinto*, fifthly (en una enumeración).

— M. Fifth. || Mil. Conscript, recruit.

quintuplicación f. Quintupling.

quintuplicar v. tr. To quintuple.

— V. pr. To quintuple.

quíntuplo, pla adj./s.m. Quintuple.

quinua f. Bot. Quinoa (planta).

quinzavo, va adj./s.m. Fifteenth.

quiñón m. Piece *o* plot of land.

quiosco m. Kiosk (en general). || Summerhouse (en el jardín). || — *Quiosco de música*, bandstand. || *Quiosco de periódicos*, newspaper stand *o* stall, newsstand.
quipos o **quipus** m. pl. Quipus.
— OBSERV. The *quipus* are knotted threads used by the Incas for recording information. The meaning was interpreted according to the colour of the threads, the number of knots, etc.
quiquiriquí m. Cock-a-doodle-doo (canto del gallo).
quirófano m. Operating theatre [U.S., operating room].
quiromancia f. Chiromancy, palmistry.
quiromántico, ca adj. Chiromantic, palmist.
— M. y f. Chiromancer, palmist.
quiropodia f. Chiropody.
quiropráctica f. MED. Chiropractic.
quiropráctico m. MED. Chiropractor.
quiróptero, ra adj./s.m. ZOOL. Chiropteran.
quirquincho m. [Kind of] armadillo (armadillo).
quirúrgico, ca adj. Surgical.
quiscal m. Grackle (ave).
quisicosa f. FAM. Puzzle, riddle.
quisque pron. FAM. *Cada* or *todo quisque*, everyone, absolutely everybody *o* everyone.
quisquilla f. Trifle, triviality (pequeñez). || Shrimp (camarón).
— Adj./s. V. QUISQUILLOSO. || *Color quisquilla*, light pink.
quisquilloso, sa adj. Finical [U.S., finicky], fastidious, punctilious, fussy: *jefe quisquilloso*, fastidious boss. || Touchy, sensitive (susceptible).
— M. y f. Fastidious person. || Touchy person.
quiste m. MED. Cyst.
quisto, ta adj. V. BIENQUISTO, MALQUISTO.
quistoso, sa adj. Cystic.
quita f. Release from a debt (de una deuda). || *De quita y pon*, detachable, removeable.
quitación f. Income, salary, wage.
quitaesmalte m. Nail varnish *o* nail polish remover.
quitaipón m. V. QUITAPÓN.
quitamanchas adj. inv. Stain removing.
— M. inv. Stain remover.
quitanieves m. inv. Snowplough [U.S., snowplow].
quitapesares m. inv. FAM. Consolation (consuelo). | Distraction (que distrae).
quitapiedras m. inv. Cowcatcher (de locomotora).
quitapón m. Headstall ornament for mules (adorno). || *De quitapón*, detachable, removeable.
quitar v. tr. To take off, to remove: *quitar el abrigo a alguien*, to take s.o.'s coat off; *quitar la tapa, la piel*, to remove *o* to take off the lid, the peel. || To take, to take away: *quítale ese cuchillo al niño*, take that knife [away] from the baby; *le quitaron el pasaporte*, they took his passport away [from him]. || To take: *quitar la vida a alguien*, to take s.o.'s life. || MAT. To take [away], to subtract (restar): *quitar uno de tres*, to take one from three. || To free, to relieve: *quitar a uno una preocupación*, to free s.o. of a worry. || To relieve, to stop, to take away (un dolor). || To get rid of, to remove (una mancha). || To extract, to remove, to separate: *quitar las impurezas a un mineral*, to extract the impurities from a mineral. || To remove, to take off (una pieza). || To snatch (con violencia): *le quitó el bolso de las manos*, he snatched the bag from her hands. || To take, to steal (robar): *me han quitado el bolso*, s.o. has taken my bag. || To stop, to prevent (impedir): *eso no quita que sea un holgazán*, that does not stop his being lazy. || FIG. To detract: *su fracaso no le quita nada de sus cualidades*, his failure does not detract from his qualities. || To reduce, to detract from: *quitarle valor a una cosa*, to reduce the value of sth. || — *De quita y pon*, detachable, removeable: *impermeable con capucha de quita y pon*, raincoat with a detachable hood. || FIG. y FAM. *En un quítame allá esas pajas*, V. PAJA. || FIG. *Me has quitado las palabras de la boca*, you took the words right out of my mouth. || FIG. y FAM. *Ni quito ni pongo rey*, it's none of my business, it's nothing to do with me. | *Por un quítame allá esas pajas*, for no reason at all. | *¡Que me quiten lo bailado!*, nothing can take away the good times I've had. | *¡Quita!*, get off!, get away! | *¡Quita, hombre!*, come, now!, come off it! || *Quitando el primero me gustan todos*, apart from *o* except for the first one I like them all. || *Quitar de encima* or *de en medio*, to get rid of, to get out of the way: *me lo han quitado de en medio*, they have got rid of it *o* him for me. || FIG. y FAM. *Quitar el hipo*, to take one's breath away. || *Quitar la idea de*, to dissuade, to persuade not to: *le he quitado la idea de irse*, I have dissuaded him from going, I have persuaded him not to go. || *Quitar la mesa*, to clear the table. || FIG. y FAM. *Quitar la vida*, to be the death of: *este niño me quita la vida*, this child will be the death of me. || *Quitarle el sueño a uno*, to prevent *o* to stop one's sleeping. || *Quitarle la razón a alguien*, to show that s.o. is wrong (culpar a uno de error), to drive s.o. mad (volverle a uno loco). || *Quitarle mucho tiempo a uno*, to take up a lot of one's time. || FIG. *Quitar ojo* or *quitar los ojos de encima*, V. OJO. | *Quitar un peso de encima*, to take a load off one's mind.
— V. pr. To be removed: *el molde se quita a los dos días*, the mould is removed after two days. || To come out *o* off (una mancha): *esa mancha no se quita con agua*, that stain won't come out with water. || To take off, to remove: *quitarse la boina*, to take off one's beret; *quitarse los zapatos*, to take off one's shoes. || To get rid of (deshacerse de). || — *Consiguió quitarse de la bebida*, he managed to give up drinking. || *Eso quíteselo usted de la cabeza*, you can get that idea out of your head. || *Quitarse años*, to lie about one's age. || FAM. *Quitarse de encima*, V. ENCIMA. || *Quitarse de en medio*, V. MEDIO. || *Quitarse el sombrero*, to tip one's hat (para saludar). || FAM. *Quitarse el sombrero ante*, to take one's hat off to (de admiración). | *¡Quítate de bobadas¡*, stop messing about!, enough of this nonsense! | *¡Quítate de en medio!*, get out of the way! | *¡Quítate de mi vista!*, get out of my sight! | *¡Quítese de ahí!*, get away with you!
quitasol m. Parasol, sunshade.
quitasueño m. FAM. Nightmare, worry.
quite m. Removal (acción de quitar). || Parry (esgrima). || Dodge (movimiento evasivo). || TAUR. "Quite", movement to attract the bull's attention away from a man in danger. || — TAUR. *Dar el quite*, to draw the bull away. || *Estar al quite*, to be ready to draw the bull away (tauromaquia), to be ready to come to s.o.'s aid (en defensa de uno).
quiteño, ña adj. [Of *o* from] Quito [Ecuador].
— M. y f. Native *o* inhabitant of Quito.
quitina f. QUÍM. Chitin.
quitinoso, sa adj. Chitinous.
quitrín m. *Amer.* Two-wheeled open carriage.
quizá o **quizás** adv. Perhaps, maybe: *quizá venga*, perhaps he will come.
quórum m. Quorum (de una asamblea).

R

r f. R.
— OBSERV. The Spanish *r* must be rolled. Initial *r*, *r* after the letters *l, n, s*, and the double *r* (*rr*) are the strongest and several trills must be produced in pronouncing them. In writing, the double *r* must not be split at the end of a line.
ra m. inv. Roll, drum roll (redoble del tambor).
Ra n. pr. Ra (dios egipcio).
rabadilla f. FAM. Rump, parson's nose (de pollo). | Back (de conejo, de liebre). || ANAT. Coccyx.
rabanal m. Radish bed, radish patch.
rabanera f. Radish seller (vendedora). || FIG. y FAM. Coarse woman, fishwife (mujer grosera).
rabanero, ra adj. FIG. y FAM. Short (vestidos). | Coarse (grosero, descarado).
rabanillo m. Wild radish (planta crucífera). || Small radish.
rabanito m. Radish.
rabaniza f. Radish seed (simiente). || Wall rocket (planta).
rábano m. Radish (planta). || — FAM. *Me importa un rábano*, I couldn't care less. || *Rábano blanco*, horseradish. || *Rábano silvestre*, wild horseradish. || FAM. *Tomar el rábano por las hojas*, to get hold of the wrong end of the stick.
rabear v. intr. To wag its tail (un perro). || MAR. To swing her stern (un barco).

rabel m. Rebec (instrumento de música).
rabí m. Rabbi (título). || Rabbi, rabbin (rabino).
rabia f. MED. Rabies (enfermedad). || FIG. Rage, fury, anger. || — FIG. *Dar rabia*, to make furious, to infuriate, to make one's blood boil: *me da rabia leer tales mentiras*, it makes me furious to read such lies. | *Muerto el perro se acabó la rabia*, dead dogs don't bite. | *Que da rabia*, maddening, infuriating (adjetivo), maddeningly, infuriatingly (adverbio). | *Rabia, rabieta* or *rabia, rabiña*, yah!, yah! | *Reventar de rabia*, to foam at the mouth. | *Tener rabia a uno*, to have it in for s.o., not to be able to stand [the sight of] s.o. | *Tomarle rabia a uno*, to take a dislike to s.o.
rabiar v. intr. MED. To have rabies (padecer rabia). || FIG. To be furious, to rage, to rave. || — FIG. *A rabiar*, rabid: *republicano a rabiar*, rabid republican; wildly, without restraint (sin parar): *aplaudir a rabiar*, to applaud wildly. | *Está que rabia*, he is furious, he is seething, he is hopping mad. | *Estar a rabiar con uno*, to be at daggers drawn with s.o. | *Hacer rabiar a uno*, to make s.o. see red, to make s.o. furious, to make s.o.'s blood boil. | *Me gusta a rabiar*, I am mad about it, I adore it. | *Pica que rabia*, it is as hot as the devil. | *Rabiar de dolor*, to writhe in agony *o* in pain. | *Rabiar de hambre, de sed*, to be dying of hunger, of thirst. | *Rabiar por*, to long to, to be dying to: *está rabiando por irse*, he is dying to go. | *Rabiar por algo*, to long for sth., to be dying for sth. | *Soy más alto que tú, ¡rabia!*, I am taller than you, so there!
rabiatar v. tr. To tie by the tail.
rábico, ca adj. MED. Rabid.
rabicorto, ta adj. With a short tail, short-tailed. || FIG. y FAM. Wearing a short skirt *o* a miniskirt, in a short skirt *o* a miniskirt: *una chiquilla rabicorta*, a girl in a short skirt.
rabieta f. FAM. Tantrum, paddy (de un niño). || FAM. *Coger una rabieta*, to fly into a tantrum.
rabietas m. y f. inv. FAM. Little terror.
rabihorcado m. Frigate bird (ave).
rabilargo, ga adj. With a long tail, long-tailed.
— M. Kind of magpie (ave).
rabillo m. Small tail (cola corta). || Stalk, stem (de una hoja o fruto). || Tab, strap (de pantalón o de chaleco). || BOT. Darnel (cizaña). || Mildew spot [on cereals] (mancha en los cereales). || Corner (del ojo). || FAM. *Mirar con el rabillo del ojo*, to look out of the corner of one's eye [at].
rabinato m. Rabbinate (dignidad de rabino).
rabinismo m. Rabbinism (doctrina de los rabinos).
rabino m. Rabbi, rabbin. || *Gran rabino*, chief rabbi.
rabión m. Rapids, *pl.*
rabiosamente adj. Furiously.
rabioso, sa adj. Rabid: *perro rabioso*, rabid dog. || FIG. Furious (enojado): *estar rabioso con alguien*, to be furious with s.o. | Rabid (fanático). | Gaudy, shocking, loud (color). | Very strong *o* hot (sabor). || — *Dolor rabioso*, agony, torment. || *Rabioso de ira*, furious, livid, foaming at the mouth, seething.
rabisalsera adj. f. FAM. Shameless, brazen (mujer).
rabiza f. Tip (de la caña de pescar). || MAR. Short lashing rope (de cordaje).
rabo m. Tail: *el rabo del perro*, the dog's tail. || Stalk, stem (de una hoja o fruto). || Corner (del ojo). || Tail (de una letra). || FIG. Tail, train (cosa que cuelga). || — FIG. y FAM. *Aún está el rabo por desollar*, the worst is yet to come. | *Irse, volver con el rabo entre las piernas*, to go away, to come back with one's tail between one's legs.
rabón, ona adj. Bobtail, tailless.
— F. *Amer.* Camp follower. || FAM. *Hacer rabona*, to play truant, to skive [U. S., to play hooky *o* hookey].
racamenta f. o **racamento** m. MAR. Parrel.
racanear v. intr. FAM. To slack (no trabajar). | To be stingy (ser tacaño).
rácano, na adj. FAM. Idle (holgazán). | Stingy (tacaño).
racial adj. Racial: *problemas raciales*, racial problems. || Race, racial: *odio racial*, race hatred.
racimo m. BOT. Raceme. || Bunch, cluster: *racimo de uvas*, bunch of grapes. || FIG. Bunch, cluster (conjunto).
raciocinación f. Ratiocination, reasoning.
raciocinar v. intr. To ratiocinate, to reason.
raciocinio m. Reason (razón): *carecer de raciocinio*, to lack reason. || Reasoning (razonamiento).
ración f. Ration, share (parte). || Helping, portion (en una fonda, en un bar): *una ración de gambas*, a helping of shrimps. || MIL. Ration. || REL. Prebend (prebenda). || — FIG. *A ración*, meanly, stingily. | *Poner a media ración*, to put on short rations. | *Tener su ración de*, to get one's share *o* one's fill of.
racionabilidad f. Judgment, reason.
racional adj. Rational: *método racional*, rational method; *un ser racional*, a rational being.
— M. Rational being.
racionalidad f. Rationality.
racionalismo m. Rationalism.
racionalista adj. Rationalist, rationalistic.
— M. y f. Rationalist.
racionalización f. Rationalization.
racionalizar v. tr. To rationalize.
racionamiento m. Rationing. || MIL. Rationing out. || *Cartilla de racionamiento*, ration card, ration book.
racionar v. tr. To ration: *racionar el pan*, to ration bread. || MIL. To ration out.
racionista m. y f. Person who lives on an allowance. || Person who is rationed (racionado). || TEATR. Bit-part actor (actor).
racismo m. Racialism.
racista adj. Racialistic, racialist.
— M. y f. Racialist.
racket m. Racket.
racor m. Connecter, adapter. || AUT. Hose.
racha f. Gust of wind (ráfaga de viento). || Spell: *una racha de frío*, a cold spell. || FIG. Series, run, wave: *una racha de triunfos*, a series of successes. || — FIG. *A rachas*, by fits and starts. || FIG. y FAM. *Estar de racha* or *tener una buena racha*, to have a run of good luck. | *Tener una mala racha*, to be out of luck, to have a run of bad luck.
rada f. MAR. Roadstead, bay.
radar m. Radar. || *Pantalla de radar*, radar screen.
radarista m. Radar operator.
radiación f. FÍS. Radiation. || Broadcasting (en la radio).
radiactividad f. Radioactivity.
radiactivo, va adj. Radioactive.
radiado, da adj. BOT. y ZOOL. Radiate. || RAD. Broadcast, transmitted. || *Un programa radiado*, a radio programme.
— M. BOT. Radiate plant. || ZOOL. Radiate animal.
radiador m. Radiator: *radiador de gas*, gas radiator.
radial adj. Radial: *neumáticos radiales*, radial tyres; *carretera radial*, radial road.
radián m. MAT. Radian (unidad angular).
radiante adj. FÍS. Radiant: *calor radiante*, radiant heat. || FIG. Radiant, shining, bright: *rostro radiante*, radiant face. || — FIG. *Radiante de alegría*, radiant with joy. || *Superficie radiante*, radiating surface, surface of radiation.
radiar v. intr. To radiate.
— V. tr. To irradiate, to radiate. || RAD. To broadcast, to transmit. || MED. To treat with X rays.
radicación f. MAT. Evolution [extraction of roots from an expression]. || FIG. Establishment, taking root, setting in [of a custom, vice, etc.].
radical adj./s. Radical: *medios radicales*, radical measures. || — M. GRAM. y MAT. Radical, root. || CHEM. Radical, radicle.
radicalismo m. Radicalism (política radical).
radicalsocialismo m. Radical Socialism.
radicalsocialista adj./s. Radical Socialist.
radicante adj. Rooted, taking root. || FIG. Emanating, issuing.
radicar v. intr. To reside, to live: *radicado en Madrid*, residing in Madrid. || To be, to be situated: *una finca que radica en la provincia de Guadalajara*, a farm which is situated in the province of Guadalajara. || BOT. To take root. || FIG. *Radicar en*, to lie in, to stem from.
— V. pr. To settle [down] (domiciliarse). || To take root (arraigarse).
radícula f. BOT. Radicle.
radiestesia f. Water divining.
radiestesista m. y f. Water diviner.
radio m. Radius: *radio de curvatura*, radius of curvature. || Spoke (de una rueda). || RAD. Wireless *o* radio operator. || FIG. Radius: *en un radio de cien kilómetros*, within a radius of a hundred kilometres. || MIL. Range (alcance): *de largo radio de acción*, long-range. || ANAT. Radius (hueso). || QUÍM. Radium (metal). || — *Radio de acción*, jurisdiction, sphere, field (sector). || *Radio de giro*, turning circle (de un vehículo). || BOT. *Radio medular*, medullary ray.
— F. Radio, wireless. || Radio [set], wireless [set] (aparato). || — *Dirección por radio*, radio control. || *Por radio*, by radio, on *o* over the radio. || *Radio galena*, crystal detector set.
radioactividad f. Radioactivity.
radioactivo, va adj. Radioactive.
radioaficionado, da m. y f. Radio ham, radio amateur.
radioaltímetro m. Radio altimeter.
radioastronomía f. Radio astronomy.
radiobiología f. Radiobiology.
radiocobalto m. Radiocobalt.
radiocompás m. Radio compass.
radiocomunicación f. Radio communication.
radioconductor m. Radioconductor.
radiodiagnosis f. o **radiodiagnóstico** m. X-ray diagnosis.
radiodifundir v. tr. To broadcast.
radiodifusión f. Broadcasting. || *Estación de radiodifusión*, radio station, transmitter.
radiodifusor, ra adj. Broadcasting. || *Estación radiodifusora*, radio station, transmitter.
radioelectricidad f. Radioelectricity.
radioeléctrico, ca adj. Radioelectrical.
radioelemento m. Radioelement.
radioemisora f. Radio station, transmitter.
radioescucha m. y f. Listener [U.S., auditor].
radiofaro m. Radio beacon.
radiofonía f. Radiotelephony, radio.
radiofónico, ca adj. Radio, wireless.
radiófono m. Radiophone.
radiofotografía f. Radiophotograph, radiophoto.

radiofrecuencia f. Radio frequency.
radiogoniometría f. Radiogoniometry.
radiogoniométrico, ca adj. Radiogoniometric.
radiogoniómetro m. Radiogoniometer, direction finder.
radiografía f. Radiography (técnica). || Radiograph, X-ray [photograph] (imagen). || *Hacerse una radiografía,* to have an X-ray, to be X-rayed.
radiografiar v. tr. To X-ray, to radiograph (con rayos X).
radiográfico, ca adj. Radiographic, X-ray.
radiógrafo m. Radiographer.
radiograma m. Radiogram.
radioisótopo m. FÍS. Radioisotope.
radiolarios m. pl. ZOOL. Radiolaria.
radiolocalización f. Radiolocation.
radiología f. Radiology.
radiólogo m. Radiologist.
radiometría f. Radiometry.
radiométrico, ca adj. Radiometric.
radiómetro m. ASTR. y FÍS. Radiometer.
radiomicrómetro m. Radiomicrometer.
radionavegación f. Radio navigation.
radionavegante m. Radio officer.
radioquímica f. Radiochemistry.
radiorreceptor m. Radio receiver, wireless [set], radio [set].
radioscopia f. Radioscopy.
radioscópico, ca adj. Radioscopic.
radiosensibilidad f. Radiosensitivity.
radiosonda f. Radiosonde.
radiotécnica f. Radiotechnology.
radiotécnico, ca adj. Radiotechnological.
— M. Radio engineer.
radiotelefonía f. Radiotelephony.
radiotelefónico, ca adj. Radiotelephonic.
radiotelefonista m. y f. Radio operator.
radioteléfono m. Radiotelephone.
radiotelegrafía f. Radiotelegraphy.
radiotelegrafiar v. tr. To radiotelegraph.
radiotelegráfico, ca adj. Radiotelegraphic. || *Despacho radiotelegráfico,* radiotelegram.
radiotelegrafista m. y f. Radio *o* wireless operator.
radiotelegrama m. Radiotelegram.
radiotelescopio m. Radio telescope.
radioterapia f. Radiotherapy.
radioterápico, ca adj. Radiotherapeutic.
radiotorio m. Radiothorium.
radiotransmisión f. Radiotransmission, broadcasting.
radiotransmisor m. Radio transmitter.
radioyente m. y f. Listener.
radiumterapia f. Radiotherapy.
radón m. QUÍM. Radon (gas).
raedera f. Scraper. || Trowel (llana). || Shovel (azada).
raedor, ra adj. Scraping.
— M. y f. Scraper. || — M. Strickle, leveller (rasero).
raedura f. Scraping (acción de raer). || Scrapings, *pl.* (parte raída). || Worn part *o* patch (de un traje).
raer* v. tr. To scrape (raspar). || To scrape off (quitar raspando). || FAM. To wear out (traje). || To level (nivelar). || To extirpate, to eradicate (extirpar).
Rafael n. pr. m. Raphael.
rafaelesco, ca adj. Raphaelesque.
ráfaga f. Gust (de viento). || Flash (de luz). || Burst [of machine-gun fire] (de ametralladora).
rafia f. BOT. Raffia.
raglán adj./s.m. Raglan: *mangas raglán,* raglan sleeves.
ragú m. CULIN. Ragout.
raid m. Raid (incursión). || AVIAC. Long-distance flight.
raído, da adj. Worn, threadbare, frayed: *traje raído,* threadbare suit. || Shameless (desvergonzado).
raigambre f. Roots, *pl.* (de una planta). || FIG. Deep-rootedness. | Tradition: *familia de raigambre republicana,* family of Republican tradition. || FIG. *Costumbre de honda raigambre en Castilla,* deep-rooted Castilian custom.
raigón m. Thick root (tocón). || Root (de un diente). || FAM. Stump (de un diente cariado).
raíl o **rail** m. Rail. || *Rail guía,* runner, curtain rail.
raimiento m. Scraping (acción). || Scraping, scrapings, *pl.* (resultado).
Raimundo n. pr. m. Raymond.
raíz f. BOT. Root. || ANAT. Root (de un diente). || GRAM. Root. || MAT. Root: *raíz cuadrada, cúbica,* square, cube root. || Origin, source (origen). || — FIG. *A raíz de,* straight after, immediately after, as a result of. || *Arrancar* or *cortar de raíz,* to uproot (árbol), to wipe out, to eradicate, to uproot (suprimir completamente), to nip in the bud (hacer abortar). || *Echar raíces,* to take root (una planta, costumbre, etc.), to settle [down] (instalarse). || BOT. *Raíz adventicia, pivotante* or *columnar* or *napiforme,* adventitious, napiform root. || *Sacar de raíz,* to pull up by the roots (plantas), to wipe out, to eradicate, to uproot (acabar con). || FIG. *Tener raíces,* to be deep-rooted: *la virtud tiene raíces profundas en su corazón,* virtue is deep-rooted in his heart.
raja f. Slice (de melón, sandía, etc.): *hacer rajas,* to cut slices. || Cut (cortadura). || Crack, split (hendidura). || Slit (en costura). || Vent (de chaqueta). || Crack (en un plato).
rajá m. Rajah (soberano de la India).
rajado, da adj. Split, cracked (hendido). || FIG. y FAM. Yellow.
— M. y f. FIG. y FAM. Chicken, funk, coward, person who backs out. || FAM. *Te lo mereciste por rajado,* it's your own fault for backing out.
rajadura f. Split, crack (hendidura).
rajamiento m. FAM. Backing out.
rajar v. tr. To slice, to cut into slices: *rajar un melón,* to cut a melon into slices. || To split, to crack (hender). || To slit (hacer una raja en). || To chop, to split (leña).
— V. intr. FAM. To boast, to brag (jactarse). | To chatter (parlotear). | To moan, to grumble (refunfuñar).
— V. pr. To crack, to split. || FAM. To back out, to quit, to chicken out (desistir).
rajatabla (a) adv. Vigorously, strictly. || *Cumplir una orden a rajatabla,* to carry out an order to the letter.
rajeta f. Coarse coloured cloth (tela). || — M. y f. FAM. Chicken (miedoso).
rajón m. Rip, tear (rasguño). || Chicken (cobarde). || Braggart (jactancioso).
ralea f. Type, sort (raza). || Prey (de aves de cetrería). || — *Es un hombre de baja ralea,* he is a low sort. || *Gente de la misma ralea,* birds of a feather.
ralentí m. CINEM. Slow motion (cámara lenta): *escena al ralentí,* slow motion sequence, sequence in slow motion. || *Funcionar al ralentí,* to tick over (motor).
ralo, la adj. Sparse, thin (pelo, árboles). || With gaps between them (dientes). || Thin, fine (tela fina). || Threadbare (tela desgastada). || Loosely woven (de tejido muy separado). || Scattered (diseminado). || Rare (aire).
rallado, da adj. Grated: *queso rallado,* grated cheese.
— M. Grating.
rallador m. Grater (utensilio de cocina).
ralladura f. Gratings, *pl.* || *Ralladuras de queso,* grated cheese.
rallar v. tr. To grate: *rallar zanahorias,* to grate carrots. || FIG. y FAM. To grate on (molestar).
rallo m. Grater (rallador). || Earthenware jug (vasija).
rallye m. AUT. Rally.
rama f. Branch, bough (de árbol). || FIG. Branch: *las diferentes ramas del saber,* the different branches of knowledge. | Branch (de una familia). || IMPR. Chase. || — FIG. y FAM. *Andarse por las ramas,* to beat about the bush. || *En rama,* raw: *algodón en rama,* raw cotton. || FIG. y FAM. *No andarse por las ramas,* not to beat about the bush, to get *o* to go straight to the point.
ramada f. Branches, *pl.* (ramaje).
ramadán m. Ramadan (noveno mes musulmán).
ramaje m. Branches, *pl.* (ramas). || Floral pattern *o* design (de una tela).
ramal m. Branch (parte secundaria). || Branch line, branch (de ferrocarril). || Foothill (de una cordillera). || Branch (tramo). || Flight (de escalera). || Strand (de una cuerda). || Halter (ronzal). || Secondary gallery (de mina). || RAD. Wire. || — *De la carretera principal arranca un ramal hacia Burgos,* a branch of the main road goes off to Burgos. || MIL. *Ramal de trinchera,* secondary trench, side trench.
ramalazo m. Lash (golpe). || FIG. Weal, mark (señal dejada). | Sharp pain (dolor). | Fit (de locura, de depresión). | Gust (de viento). | Lash (de lluvia). || FIG. *Tener un ramalazo de loco,* to be a little mad, to have a streak of madness in one.
rambla f. Gully (cauce). || Torrent (torrente). || Avenue, boulevard (paseo). || TECN. Tenter (para los paños). || *Amer.* Dock (muelle).
rameado, da adj. Flowery, with a floral pattern *o* design (tejido).
ramera f. Prostitute, whore.
rami m. Rummy (juego de naipes).
ramificación f. Ramification. || FIG. Consequence, repercussion (consecuencia). | Branch, subdivision (rama).
ramificarse v. pr. To ramify, to branch. || FIG. To branch out *o* off, to ramify.
ramilla f. Twig.
ramillete m. Bunch (ramo de flores), bouquet (artísticamente hecho), posy (más pequeño). || FIG. Collection: *ramillete de máximas,* collection of maxims. | Bunch, group: *ramillete de muchachas,* bunch of girls.
ramilletero, ra m. y f. Florist. || — M. Vase.
ramiza f. Branches, *pl.*
ramnáceas f. pl. BOT. Rhamnaceae.
ramo m. [Small] branch (rama pequeña). || Bouquet, posy, bunch (ramillete): *ramo de flores,* bouquet of flowers. || COM. Branch, department, line (sección). | Field (sector). || Sheaf (manojo de hierbas). || FIG. Branch (subdivisión). || — *Domingo de Ramos,* Palm Sunday. || FIG. *Tener un ramo de locura,* to be a little mad, to have a streak of madness in one.
ramojo m. Loose branches, *pl.*
ramón m. Twigs (*pl.*) cut for use as fodder.
Ramón n. pr. m. Raymond.
ramonear v. tr. To prune (los árboles). || To browse on (los animales).
ramoneo m. Pruning (poda). || Pruning season (época).
ramoso, sa adj. Ramose, with many branches.
rampa f. MED. Cramp (calambre). || Ramp (plano inclinado). || *Rampa de lanzamiento,* launching pad.

rampante adj. HERÁLD. Rampant.
ramplón, ona adj. Common, vulgar: *artículo ramplón,* vulgar article; *tío ramplón,* common type. | Dull, heavy: *versos ramplones,* dull poetry.
— M. Calk (de herradura).
ramplonería f. Vulgarity (vulgaridad). || Poor taste (falta de gusto).
rampojo m. Grape stem (escobajo).
rampollo m. Cutting [of a tree].
rana f. Frog: *ancas de rana,* frogs' legs. || Game resembling Aunt Sally [consisting of throwing coins into the mouth of a model frog] (juego). || — FIG. y FAM. *Cuando las ranas críen* or *tengan pelos,* when pigs fly *o* have wings. | *No ser rana,* to be no fool. || *Rana de zarzal,* tree frog. || *Rana marina* or *pescadora,* angler (pejesapo). || *Rana mugidora,* bullfrog. || FIG. y FAM. *Salir rana,* fo fall through, to misfire, to go wrong *o* amiss: *mi proyecto ha salido rana,* my plan has fallen through; to be a disappointment (un hijo, etc.), to let [s.o.] down (una persona a otra).
rancajo m. Splinter (espina, astilla).
ranciar v. tr. To make rancid.
— V. pr. To become rancid *o* stale.
rancidez o **ranciedad** f. Rancidity, rancidness, rankness, staleness.
rancio, cia adj. Rancid, stale (la comida, etc.). || Rancio (licor). || FIG. Old-fashioned, antiquated: *una solterona un poco rancia,* an old-fashioned spinster. | Ancient: *de rancio abolengo,* from an ancient family.
— M. Rancidity, rancidness, rankness. || Grease (del paño). || Rancio wine (vino). || *Oler a rancio,* to smell rancid.
rancheadero m. Settlement.
ranchear v. intr. y pr. To form a settlement, to make a camp, to camp.
— V. tr. *Amer.* To pillage, to loot.
rancheo m. *Amer.* Pillage, pillaging, sacking.
ranchera f. *Amer.* Popular song.
ranchería f. Settlement, camp (conjunto de ranchos).
ranchero m. Cook, camp cook (el que guisa el rancho). || Leader of a settlement (de un campamento). || *Amer.* Farmer, rancher (dueño de un rancho).
rancho m. Mess, communal meal (comida). || FAM. Bad food, swill (comida mala). || Farm (finca). || Ranch (finca en Norteamérica). || Camp, settlement (campamento): *rancho de gitanos,* gipsy camp. || *Amer.* Hut (choza). || MAR. Crew's quarters, *pl.* (alojamiento). || FIG. *Hacer rancho aparte,* to keep to o.s., to go one's own way.
randa f. Lace, lace trimming.
— M. FAM. Pickpocket.
randera f. Lacemaker.
rangífero m. Reindeer (reno).
rango m. Rank (categoría). || *Amer.* Luxury (lujo). | Pomp (pompa). | Generosity (generosidad). | Nag (rocín). || — *Conservar* or *mantener su rango,* to maintain one's standing. || *De alto* or *mucho rango,* high-ranking. || *Tener rango de,* to have the position of.
ránidos m. pl. ZOOL. Ranidae.
ranilla f. Frog (del caballo).
ranunculáceas f. pl. BOT. Ranunculaceae.
ranúnculo m. BOT. Ranunculus, buttercup.
ranura f. Groove. || Slot (de un teléfono público, de una máquina tragaperras). || — *Hacer una ranura en,* to make a groove in, to groove. || TECN. *Ranura de engrase,* lubrication groove.
rapabarbas m. inv. FAM. Barber (barbero).
rapacejo m. Band of a fringe (alma de fleco). || Fringe (fleco). || Lad, youngster (muchacho).
rapacería f. Rapacity. || Childish prank (muchachada).
rapacidad f. Rapacity.
rapador m. FAM. Barber (barbero).
rapadura f. o **rapamiento** m. Shave, shaving (de la barba). || Crop, cropping (del pelo). || *Amer.* Brown sugar.
rapapiés m. inv. Jumping jack (petardo).
rapapolvo m. FAM. Dressing down, telling off: *echar un rapapolvo a alguien,* to give s.o. a dressing down.
rapar v. tr. To shave (afeitar). || To crop, to give a close haircut (cortar el pelo al rape). || FIG. y FAM. To pinch, to lift, to nick (hurtar).
— V. pr. To shave, to have a shave (afeitarse). || To have a close haircut (cortarse el pelo).
rapaz adj. Rapacious. || ZOOL. Predatory. || *Ave rapaz,* bird of prey.
— M. y f. Rapacious person. || — M. pl. ZOOL. Predators. | Birds of prey (aves).
rapaz o **rapazuelo** m. Lad, boy, youngster.
rapaza o **rapazuela** f. Lass, girl, youngster.
rape m. ZOOL. Angler (pez). || Quick shave (afeitado). || — *Al rape,* close: *pelo cortado al rape,* close-cropped hair. || FIG. y FAM. *Dar un rape,* to give a dressing down *o* a telling off (reprender).
rapé m. Snuff, rappee (tabaco en polvo).
rapidez f. Rapidity, speed.
rápido, da adj. Rapid, fast, swift, quick, speedy. || Express, fast (tren).
— M. Express (tren). || — Pl. Rapids (río).
— Adv. Quickly. || FAM. *¡Venga, rápido!,* make it snappy!, hurry up!, look lively!
rapiña f. Robbery, stealing, theft (hurto). || *Ave de rapiña,* bird of prey.
rapiñador, ra m. y f. Sneak thief, robber.
rapiñar v. tr. e intr. FAM. To pinch, to steal,to thieve.
rapónchigo m. Rampion (planta).
raposa f. Fox (zorro). || Vixen, female fox, she-fox (zorra). || FIG. y FAM. Sly fox.
raposear v. intr. To be sly *o* cunning.
raposeo m. Cunning, artfulness, guile.
raposera f. Foxhole.
raposería o **raposía** f. [Sly] trick (ardid). || Cunning, artfulness, guile (astucia).
raposo m. Fox (zorro). || FIG. Fox (astuto).
rapsoda m. Rhapsodist.
rapsodia f. Rhapsody.
rapsódico, ca adj. Rhapsodic, rhapsodical.
raptar v. tr. To abduct, to kidnap (una persona).
rapto m. Abduction, kidnapping (de personas). || Ecstasy, rapture (éxtasis). || Impulse (impulso). | Burst, fit, upsurge [of anger, etc.] (de cólera). || MED. Swoon, faint. || *El rapto de las Sabinas,* the rape of the Sabine women.
raptor, ra m. y f. Abductor, kidnapper.
raque m. Beachcombing.
raquear v. intr. To beachcomb.
Raquel n. pr. f. Rachel.
raquero, ra adj./s. Pirate (pirata). || — M. Beachcomber. || Thief [who operates in ports] (ratero).
raqueta f. Racket (de tenis, etc.). || [Croupier's] rake (de croupier). || Snowshoe (para andar por la nieve). || Hedge mustard (jaramago).
raquialgia f. MED. Rachialgia.
raquídeo, a adj. Rachidian: *bulbo raquídeo,* rachidian bulb.
raquis m. ANAT. y BOT. Rachis.
raquítico, ca adj. MED. Rachitic, rickety (persona). || Stunted (plantas). || Weak (débil). || FIG. Rickety (destartalado).
— M. y f. Rachitic person.
raquitismo m. MED. Rachitis, rickets.
raramente adj. Rarely, seldom (rara vez). || Strangely, oddly (extrañamente).
rarefacción f. Rarefaction.
rarefacer* v. tr. To rarefy (enrarecer).
— V. pr. To rarefy.
rarefacto, ta adj. Rarefied.
rareza f. Rarity, scarcity (poca frecuencia). || FIG. Oddity (peculiaridad). || FIG. *Tiene sus rarezas,* he is a bit odd.
rarificar v. tr. To rarefy.
rarificativo, va o **rarificante** adj. Rarefactive.
raro, ra adj. Rare (poco frecuente). || Rare, scarce (escaso). || FIG. Strange, odd, bizarre, weird (extraño): *una manera muy rara de expresarse,* a very strange way of expressing o.s.; *¡qué raro!,* how odd! || QUÍM. Rare, rarefied (gas). || — FIG. *Me miró como a un bicho raro,* he looked at me as if I came from outer space. | *¡Qué cosa más rara!,* how very strange! || *Rara vez,* rarely, seldom. || FIG. *Sentirse raro,* to feel out of sorts, to feel a bit odd. || *Son raros los estudiantes que terminan la carrera,* very few students finish their course.
ras m. *A ras de,* [on a] level with. || *A ras de tierra,* on ground level. || *Lleno* or *llena al ras,* full to the brim (recipiente), level (cucharada). || *Ras con ras,* level. || *Volar a ras de tierra,* to skim the ground, to fly low, to hedgehop.
rasa f. Threadbare *o* thin patch (en una tela).
rasadura f. Levelling.
rasamente adj. Clearly, openly.
rasante adj. Grazing, close: *tiro rasante,* grazing shot. || Low, skimming (vuelo).
— F. Slope (de un camino). || *Cambio de rasante,* brow of a hill.
rasar v. tr. To graze, to skim: *rasar el suelo,* to graze the ground. || To level (pasar el rasero). || To raze, to rase (arrasar). || AVIAC. *Rasando el suelo,* flying low, skimming the ground, hedgehopping.
rasca f. *Amer.* Drunkenness (borrachera).
rascacielos m. inv. Skyscraper (edificio).
rascacio m. Scorpion fish (pez).
rascada f. *Amer.* Scraping, scratching.
rascadera f. Scraper. || FAM. Currycomb (almohaza).
rascado, da adj. Scraped, scratched (rajado). || Irascible, irritable. || FAM. Drunk (borracho).
rascador m. Scraper (raedera). || Ornamental hair slide (en el pelo). || Strip on a matchbox for striking matches, striking surface (para los fósforos). || Sheller, husker (para desgranar). || MIL. Sheller (de una granada). || AUT. *Rascador de aceite,* scraper ring.
rascadura f. Scratch (en la piel). || Scratching (acción). || Scraping, scrubbing (para quitar algo).
rascamiento m. Scratching (en la piel). || Scraping, scrubbing (para quitar algo).
rascar v. tr. To scratch (con la uña). || To scrape (raspar). || FAM. To scratch away at (la guitarra). || — FIG. *El comer y el rascar, todo es empezar,* v. COMER. || FIG. y FAM. *Vámonos, que aquí no hay nada que rascar,* let's go, there's nothing doing around here.
— V. pr. To scratch [o.s.]. || *Amer.* To get drunk (emborracharse). || FIG. *A quien le pique que se rasque,* if the cap fits, wear it.
rascatripas m. inv. FAM. Third-rate fiddle player (violinista malo).
rascón, ona adj. Sour, sharp, rough, tart (vino).
— M. Water rail (polla de agua).
rasera f. Spatula, fish slice.

rasero m. Leveller. || Strickle (para el grano). || FIG. *Medir por el mismo rasero*, to treat impartially, to give the same treatment.
rasete m. Satinet, satinette (tela).
rasgado, da adj. Torn. || FIG. Wide (boca). | Almond (ojos).
— M. Tear, rip, rent (rasgadura).
rasgadura f. Tear, rip, rent.
rasgar v. tr. To tear, to rip, to rent (romper).
— V. pr. *Amer.* To die.
rasgo m. Characteristic, feature, trait. || Stroke (pintando). || Feat, act (de heroísmo, etc.). || — Pl. Features [of the face]. || Characteristics (de la escritura). || — *Explicar a grandes rasgos*, to outline, to explain briefly. || *Rasgo de ingenio*, stroke of genius, flash of wit.
rasgón m. Tear, rip, rent.
rasgueado m. Strumming.
rasguear v. tr. To strum. || FIG. To write (escribir).
— V. intr. To make flourishes [with a pen].
rasgueo m. Strumming (de la guitarra).
rasguñar v. tr. To scratch (arañar). || To sketch (un boceto).
rasguño m. Scratch (arañazo). || Sketch (boceto).
rasilla f. Kind of serge (tela). || Tile (ladrillo).
raso, sa adj. Smooth (liso). || Flat, level (llano). || Level: *una cucharada rasa*, a level spoonful. || Clear, cloudless: *cielo raso*, clear sky. || Backless (sin respaldo). || Low (pelota, vuelo). || — *Al raso*, in the open air (al aire libre), cropped (muy corto). || *Cielo raso*, ceiling (techo). || *En campo raso*, in the open country. || *Hacer tabla rasa de*, v. TABLA. || MIL. *Soldado raso*, private.
— M. Satin (tela).
raspa f. Backbone, bone (de un pescado). || BOT. Beard (eje). | Stalk (de un racimo de uvas).
raspado m. MED. Scrape, scraping. || Scraping (raedura). || Scratching out (para borrar).
raspador m. Erasing knife, scraper (para raspar lo escrito). || TECN. Scraper, scraping knife.
raspadura f. Scratching. || Scraping (raspado). || Grating (rallado). || Scratching out (para borrar). || Scrapings, *pl.* (residuo del raspado). || Scratch (huella). || *Amer.* Brown sugar.
raspamiento m. V. RASPADURA.
raspante adj. Scraping, which scrapes. || Sharp, rough, tart (vino).
raspar v. tr. To scrape. || To scratch (arañar). || To graze (la piel). || To scrape off (pintura). || To be sharp *o* rough on: *vino que raspa la boca*, wine which is sharp on the palate. || To steal (hurtar). || To scratch out (algo escrito). || TECN. To scrape. || To graze, to skim (rasar). || *Amer.* To tell off (reprender). || FIG. *Raspando*, just, by the skin of one's teeth: *aprobar raspando*, to pass by the skin of one's teeth.
— V. intr. To be rough (la piel). || To be sharp *o* rough (vino).
raspear v. intr. To scratch (la pluma).
raspetón (de) loc. *Amer.* Sideways (de lado). | Askance (mirar). | In passing (de pasada).
raspilla f. BOT. Forget-me-not.
raspón m. *Amer.* Telling off, scolding, dressing down (reconvención). | Graze, scratch (desolladura).
rasposo, sa adj. Rough, sharp (áspero).
rasqueta f. MAR. Scraper. || *Amer.* Currycomb (almohaza).
rasquetear v. tr. *Amer.* To currycomb, to brush down (almohazar).
rastacuero m. Upstart, parvenu (advenedizo).
rastra f. Trail, track (huella). || Cart (carro). || Harrow (grada). || String [of onions, garlic, etc.] (ristra). || Trawl [net] (para pescar). || *Amer.* Decorative buckle of a gaucho's belt. || — *A la rastra* or *a rastras*, dragging, trailing (arrastrando), grudgingly, unwillingly (de mal grado). || FAM. *Andar a rastras*, to have a hard time of it. | *Ir a rastras de uno*, to depend on s.o. | *Llevar a rastras*, to drag [along]: *llevar a alguien a rastras al médico*, to drag s.o. along to the doctor's; to have still to do: *llevo dos asignaturas a rastras*, I still have two subjects to do.
rastreador, ra adj. Tracker, tracking. || — MAR. *Barco rastreador*, trawler. || *Rastreador de minas*, minesweeper.
rastrear v. tr. To track, to trail, to trace (seguir las huellas). || To trawl (en la pesca). || To sweep (minas). || To drag (un río para buscar algo). || To sell [meat] in the market.
— V. intr. To fly low, to skim the ground (un avión). || AGR. To rake. || To trawl (pescar). || FIG. To make inquiries.
rastreo m. Dragging. || Tracking (seguimiento). || AGR. Raking (con el rastrillo). | Harrowing (con la grada). || Trawling (en la pesca). || Sweeping (minas).
rastrera f. MAR. Lower studding sail.
rastreramente adv. Basely.
rastrero, ra adj. Creeping, crawling: *animal rastrero*, creeping animal. || BOT. Creeping (tallo). || Low (vuelo). || Trailing (vestido, etc.). || FIG. Cringing (persona). | Creeping (conducta). | Base, vile: *ambiciones rastreras*, base ambitions. || *Perro rastrero*, tracker.
rastrillada f. Rake (con el rastrillo). || *Amer.* Track, trail (pista). || — Pl. Rakings.
rastrillado m. Raking. || Combing, dressing, hackling (de textiles).
rastrillador, ra m. y f. Raker. || Comber (de textiles). || — F. AGR. Harrow.
rastrillaje m. AGR. Raking.
rastrillar v. tr. To rake: *rastrillar las avenidas de un jardín*, to rake the paths of a garden. || AGR. To harrow (con la grada). || TECN. To hackle, to dress, to comb (cáñamo, lino). || *Amer.* To fire (disparar). | To strike (un fósforo).
rastrillo m. AGR. Rake (rastro). || Hackle, comb (para el cáñamo, el lino). || MIL. Portcullis (de fortificación). || TEATR. Light batten. || TECN. Ward (de cerradura).
rastro m. AGR. Rake (para recoger hierba, paja, etc.). | Harrow (grada). | Layer (mugrón). || Abattoir, slaughterhouse (matadero). || FIG. Trace, sign: *ni rastro de*, no trace of; *no encontrar rastro de*, to find no trace of. | Trail, tracks, *pl.*, track: *seguir el rastro*, to follow the trail. | Scent (olor). | Path (de una tormenta). || — *El Rastro*, the flea market in Madrid. || *Perder el rastro de alguien*, to lose track of s.o., to lose s.o.'s scent.
rastrojar v. tr. AGR. To clear of stubble, to glean.
rastrojera f. Stubble field (tierras). || Season during which cattle graze on stubble (temporada).
rastrojo m. Stubble (paja). || Stubble field (campo segado). || *Amer.* Waste, remains, *pl.*
rasurador m. Electric razor.
rasurar v. tr. (P.us.) To shave (afeitar).
— V. pr. To shave (afeitarse).
rata f. Rat (mamífero roedor): *rata de alcantarilla*, brown rat. || — FIG. y FAM. *Más pobre que las ratas* or *que una rata*, as poor as a church mouse. | *No había ni una rata*, there was not a living soul. | *No mataría ni a una rata*, he wouldn't hurt a fly. | *No se salvó ni una rata*, no one escaped, the same happened to everyone. || *Rata blanca*, white mouse. || *Rata de agua*, water rat. || FIG. y FAM. *Rata de hotel*, hotel thief. | *Rata de sacristía*, bigoted churchwoman.
— M. FAM. Thief (ratero).
ratafía f. Ratafia (licor).
ratania f. Rhatany (planta).
rata parte loc. lat. Pro rata (prorrata).
rataplán m. Rub-a-dub, ra-ta-ta (del tambor).
rata por cantidad loc. adv. Pro rata.
rateado, da adj. Pro rata.
ratear v. intr. To crawl, to creep (arrastrarse).
— V. tr. To steal (robar). || To give out pro rata, to share out proportionally (repartir).
rateo m. Pro rata distribution.
ratería f. Petty theft, pilfering.
raterismo m. Petty thieving, petty thefts, *pl.*
ratero, ra adj. Creeping (rastrero). || FIG. Cringing, creeping (despreciable). || Thieving (ladrón). || — *Perro ratero*, tracker. || *Un tío ratero*, a thief.
— M. y f. Thief, petty thief (ladrón). || Pickpocket (carterista). || *Ratero de hotel*, hotel thief.
raticida m. Raticide, rat poison.
ratificación f. Ratification.
ratificar v. tr. To ratify.
— V. pr. To be ratified.
ratificatorio, ria adj. Ratifying, confirmatory.
ratina f. Ratteen (tela).
rato adj. m. *Matrimonio rato*, unconsummated marriage.
rato m. While, time, moment: *salió hace un rato*, he went out a while ago. || — *A cada rato*, all the time, every couple of minutes. || *Al poco rato*, a short time after, shortly after. || *A ratos*, from time to time, at times. || *A ratos perdidos* or *en los ratos perdidos*, in odd moments. || *A ratos ... y a ratos*, one moment ... the next: *a ratos está sonriente y a ratos serio*, one moment he is smiling, the next he is serious. || *De rato en rato*, from time to time. || *Hace mucho rato que*, it is a long time since. || *Hacerle pasar un mal rato a alguien*, to give s.o. a rough time. || *Amer.* *¡Hasta cada rato!*, see you soon!, see you later! [U.S., so long!] (hasta luego). || FAM. *¡Hasta otro rato!*, cheerio!, I'll be seeing you! [U.S., so long!] (hasta la vista). | *Hay para rato*, it'll take quite a while. || *Llevarse un mal rato*, to have a bad time. || *Para pasar el rato*, to pass the time, to kill time, to while away the time. || *Pasar un buen rato*, to have a good time. || *Pasar un mal rato*, to have a rough *o* a bad time of it. || *Ratos libres* or *de ocio*, free *o* spare time. || FAM. *Saber un rato de*, to know quite a bit *o* a lot about. | *Tener ratos*, to have one's moments (persona). || *Un buen rato*, a good time (momento agradable), a good while, some time, quite a while (mucho tiempo). || FIG. y FAM. *Un rato*, really (muy): *esta película es un rato buena*, this film is really good; loads, *pl.*, heaps, *pl.*, piles *pl.* (gran cantidad).
ratón m. Mouse (animal). || — *El ratón Mickey* or *Miguelito*, Mickey Mouse. || FAM. *Es un ratón de biblioteca*, he is a bookworm. || *Más vale ser cabeza de ratón que cola de león*, it is better to reign in hell than to serve in heaven. || *Ratón almizclero*, muskrat. || *Ratón campesino*, field mouse.
— OBSERV. El plural de *mouse* es *mice*.
ratona f. Mouse (hembra del ratón).

ratoncillo m. Little mouse (ratón pequeño).
ratoncito m. *Amer.* Blind-man's buff (juego). || FAM. *El ratoncito Pérez,* the good fairy (personaje infantil).
ratonera f. Mousetrap (trampa para ratones). || Mousehole (madriguera del ratón). || *Amer.* Hovel (casucha). || FIG. y FAM. *Caer en la ratonera,* to fall into the trap.
ratonero, ra o **ratonesco, ca** o **ratonil** adj. Mousy. || — *La raza ratonil,* the mouse tribe. || *Música ratonera,* caterwauling.
rauco, ca adj. POÉT. Raucous, harsh.
raudal m. Torrent (corriente de agua). || FIG. Floods, *pl.: un raudal de lágrimas,* floods of tears; *raudales de luz,* floods of light. || — *A raudales,* in torrents. || *Entrar a raudales,* to stream in, to flood in.
raudo, da adj. Rapid, swift (veloz).
ravioles o **raviolis** m. pl. Ravioli.
raya f. Line (línea). || Parting [U.S., part] (del peinado). || Stripe (lista). || Crease (del pantalón). || Rifling (de un arma de fuego). || Dash (en un escrito, en el alfabeto morse). || Limit (límite). || Line (de la mano). || Scratch (trozo raspado). || ZOOL. Ray (pez). || *Amer.* Wages, *pl.,* pay (sueldo). | Pitching pennies (juego). || — *Camisa a rayas,* striped shirt. || FIG. y FAM. *Cruz y raya,* v. CRUZ. | *Dar ciento y raya* or *quince y raya a,* to run rings round s.o., to knock spots off s.o. || *Hacerse la raya,* to part one's hair. || FIG. y FAM. *Mantener a raya a un inferior,* to keep an inferior in his place. || *Pasar la raya,* to go over the line (atletismo). || FIG. *Pasarse de la raya,* to go too far, to overstep the mark. || *Raya de puntos,* dotted line. || *Tener a raya,* to keep at bay *o* in check.
rayadillo m. Striped cotton (tela).
rayado, da adj. Striped: *tela rayada,* striped cloth. || Ruled, lined: *papel rayado,* ruled paper. || Rifled: *cañón rayado,* rifled barrel.
— M. Stripes, *pl.,* stripe (rayadura). || Lines, *pl.,* ruled lines, *pl.* (pauta). || Rifling (de un cañón).
rayano, na adj. Bordering, adjacent. || On the border (frontera). || *Rayano en,* bordering on.
rayar v. tr. To rule, to line, to draw lines on (el papel). || To stripe (la tela). || To cross *o* to strike out (borrar). || To rifle (un arma de fuego). || To underline (subrayar). || To scratch, to score (una superficie dura).
— V. intr. To border on: *su jardín raya con el mío,* his garden borders on mine. || FIG. To border on, to verge on: *este acto raya en la locura,* this action borders on madness. | To be nearly, to be going on for, to be pushing (fam.): *rayar en los cuarenta,* to be nearly forty. || To dawn (el día, el alba). || — *Al rayar el alba,* at dawn, at daybreak. || FIG. *Rayar a gran altura,* to shine, to distinguish o.s., to excel.
rayero m. *Amer.* Judge [at a horse-race meeting].
rayo m. Ray: *los rayos del Sol,* the sun's rays. || Ray, beam: *un rayo de luz,* a ray of light. || Lightning (en una tormenta): *ser alcanzado por el rayo,* to be struck by lightning. || Spoke (de una rueda). || FÍS. Ray: *rayos catódicos,* cathode rays. || Thunderbolt: *los rayos de Júpiter,* Jupiter's thunderbolts. || FIG. Live wire: *esta niña es un rayo,* this child is a live wire. || — FIG. *Caer como un rayo,* to be a bombshell (noticias). || *Caer fulminado por un rayo,* to be struck by lightning. || FIG. *Con la velocidad del rayo,* as quick as a flash, in a flash, like lightning. | *Echaba rayos por los ojos,* his eyes flashed with rage. | *Echar rayos y centellas,* to be furious. | *Mal rayo me parta si...,* may I be struck down if ... | *Más vivo que un rayo,* as quick as lightning. | *¡Que le parta un rayo!,* to hell with him!, damn him! || *Rayo de luna,* moonbeam. || *Rayo de sol,* sunbeam. || *Rayos cósmicos,* cosmic rays. || *Rayos gamma,* gamma rays. || *Rayos X,* X rays. || FIG. *Salir como un rayo,* to fly out, to shoot out. | *Temer a uno como al rayo,* to fear s.o. like the devil. | *¡Y a mí que me parta un rayo!,* and what about me?
rayón m. o **rayona** f. Rayon (tejido).
rayuela f. Pitch and toss (juego). || *Amer.* Hopscotch (tejo).
raza f. Race: *raza negra,* Negro race; *raza humana,* human race. || Breed, strain (de animales). || FAM. Tribe: *la raza ratonil,* the mouse tribe. || Ray, beam (de luz). || VET. Sand crack. || *De raza,* thoroughbred (caballo), pedigree (perro).
razón f. Reason. || Reason, cause (motivo): *tener razón para,* to have cause to. || Message (recado): *llevar una razón,* to take a message. || MAT. Ratio (proporción). || — *A razón de,* at the rate of. || *Asistirle a uno la razón,* to have right on one's side, to be in the right. || *Atenerse* or *avenirse a razones,* to give way *o* to listen *o* to bow to reason. || *Cerrado por vacaciones. Razón: café la Perla,* closed for holidays. Inquiries to La Perla. || *Con mayor razón,* with all the more reason. || *Con razón,* quite rightly, with good reason: *se ha quejado con razón,* he quite rightly complained. || *Con razón o sin ella,* rightly or wrongly. || *Con razón que le sobra* or *con toda la razón* or *con mucha razón,* quite *o* very rightly. || *Dar la razón a uno,* to say that s.o. is right, to agree with s.o. || *Dar razón de,* to inform about, to give information about, to tell about. || *Dar razón de sí,* to show signs of life. || *En razón a* or *de,* because of. || *Entrar en razón,* to listen to reason, to see sense. || *¡Eso es ponerse en razón!,* now you're being reasonable! || *Estar cargado de razón,* to be completely right (persona, argumento). || *Lo hizo con mucha razón,* he was very right to do it. || *Meter* or *poner* or *hacer entrar en razón,* to make listen to reason, to make see sense. || *No hay razón que valga,* there is no excuse *o* no valid reason. || *No tener razón,* to be wrong, not to be right. || *Obras son amores, que no buenas razones,* actions speak louder than words. || *Perder la razón,* to take leave of one's senses, to go out of one's mind. || *Ponerse en razón,* to be reasonable, to listen to reason. || *Por una razón o por otra,* for some reason, for some reason or another. || *Quitar la razón a alguien,* to say that s.o. is wrong, to disagree with s.o. (no estar de acuerdo), to prove s.o. wrong (demostrar que se equivoca). || *Razón de estado,* reason of state. || *Razón de más para,* all the more reason for [doing sth.], another reason for, one more reason for. || FAM. *Razón de pie de banco,* preposterous talk. || *Razón de ser,* raison d'être. || MAT. *Razón directa, inversa,* direct, inverse ratio. || *Razón social,* trade name. || *Reducirse a la razón,* to listen to reason. || *Sin razón,* wrongly. || *Tener razón,* to be right: *usted tiene toda la razón,* you are quite *o* so right. || *Tener razón en hacer algo,* to be right to do sth. || *Uso de razón,* power of reasoning.
razonable adj. Reasonable: *pretensión razonable,* reasonable claim; *precio razonable,* reasonable price.
razonadamente adv. Reasonably, rationally.
razonado, da adj. Reasoned, well-reasoned, considered.
razonador, ra adj. Reasoning.
— M. y f. Reasoner, person who reasons.
razonamiento m. Reasoning.
razonar v. intr. To reason: *razonar bien,* to reason well. || To talk (hablar).
— V. tr. To reason out (problema).
razzia f. Razzia, foray, raid.
re m. MÚS. Re, ray.
rea f. (P.us.) Accused [woman], defendant.
Rea n. pr. f. MIT. Rhea.
reabastecer v. tr. To revictual.
reabrir v. tr. To reopen.
reabsorbente adj. Reabsorbent.
reabsorber v. tr. To reabsorb.
reabsorpción f. Reabsorption.
reacción f. Reaction: *reacción en cadena,* chain reaction. || — *Avión de reacción,* jet [plane], jet-propelled aeroplane. || *Propulsión por reacción,* jet propulsion.
reaccionar v. intr. To react. || QUÍM. To react.
reaccionario, ria adj./s. Reactionary.
reacio, cia adj. Stubborn (obstinado). || Reticent: *se mostró reacio a mi propuesta,* he was reticent about my proposal. || *Estar reacio a hacer algo,* to be reluctant to do sth.
reacondicionar v. tr. To recondition.
reactancia f. ELECTR. Reactance.
reactivación f. Reactivation (de un suero). || Recrudescence, reactivation (recrudescencia). || Recovery (de la Bolsa, de la economía).
reactivar v. tr. To reactivate (la economía, etc.).
reactivo, va adj. Reactive.
— M. QUÍM. Reagent.
reactor m. FÍS. Reactor: *reactor nuclear,* nuclear reactor. || Jet, jet plane, jet-propelled aircraft (avión).
reactorista m. AVIAC. Jet pilot.
reacuñación f. Recoinage, remintage.
readaptación f. Readaptation. || Retraining: *readaptación profesional,* industrial retraining. || Rehabilitation (de un enfermo).
readaptar v. tr. To readapt. || To retrain (trabajadores). || To rehabilitate (a un enfermo).
readmisión f. Readmission.
readmitir v. tr. To readmit. || To reemploy (a un empleado).
reafirmar v. tr. To reaffirm, to reassert.
reagravarse v. pr. To get worse again.
reagrupación f. o **reagrupamiento** m. Regrouping.
reagrupar v. tr. To regroup.
— V. pr. To regroup.
reajustar v. tr. To readjust.
— V. pr. To readjust.
reajuste m. Readjustment: *reajuste de los salarios,* readjustment of salaries. || Change, reshuffle: *reajuste de un gobierno,* government reshuffle.
real adj. Real (efectivo): *necesidades reales,* real necessities. || Royal (del rey): *palacio real,* royal palace; *estandartes reales,* royal standards. || Royal: *águila real,* royal eagle. || FIG. Splendid, fine (regio). | Handsome, fine (hermoso): *un real mozo,* a handsome boy. || — *Camino real,* v. CAMINO. || FAM. *No me da la real gana,* I don't feel like it, I don't want to. || *Una real moza,* a lovely girl.
— M. One quarter of a peseta (moneda de 25 céntimos): *diez reales,* two and a half pesetas. || Fairground (ferial). || MIL. Camp: *alzar* or *levantar el real* or *los reales,* to break camp. || — *Lo real,* reality. || FAM. *No tener un real,* not to have a penny to one's name. | *No vale un real,* it is not worth a red cent. | *Sentar sus reales,* to settle down, to establish o.s.
realce m. Relief: *bordar a realce,* to embroider in relief. || FIG. Sparkle, [touch of] splendour (esplendor): *dar realce a una fiesta,* to give a sparkle *o* a touch of splendour to an occasion. | Importance. || — FIG.

Dar realce a su estilo, to enhance one's style. | *Poner de realce*, to bring out, to highlight.

realejo m. MÚS. Small organ (órgano).

realengo, ga adj. Royal, regal. || *Bienes de realengo*, possessions of the crown (real), possessions of the State (del Estado).

realeza f. Royalty.

realidad f. Reality. || Truth (verdad). || — *En realidad*, in fact, actually. || *La realidad es que*, the fact of the matter is that. || *Tenemos que atenernos a la realidad*, we must face the facts.

realismo m. Realism (doctrina filosófica y artística). || Royalism (fidelidad a la monarquía).

realista adj. Realistic (en arte, filosofía). || Royalist (partidario de la monarquía).
— M. y f. Realist (en arte, filosofía). || Royalist (partidario de la monarquía).

realizable adj. Attainable (meta). || Feasible, practical (factible). || COM. Saleable, realizable (activo).

realización f. Realization. || Fulfilment, execution, carrying out (ejecución). || Fulfilment (de las esperanzas). || COM. Selling, sale (venta). | Realization (del activo). || Production (cine, televisión). || Broadcast (radio).

realizar v. tr. To carry out, to accomplish, to effect: *realizar un proyecto*, to carry out a plan. || To accomplish, to attain, to achieve (la meta). || To fulfil: *realizar sus esperanzas*, to fulfil one's hopes. || To make: *realizar un viaje*, to make a journey. || COM. To realize, to sell: *realizar sus bienes*, to sell one's belongings. | To make, to realize (beneficio, contrato). || *Realizar gestiones*, to negotiate.
— V. pr. To be fulfilled: *sus esperanzas se realizaron*, his hopes were fulfilled. || To come true (los sueños, deseos). || To be carried out, to be accomplished (un plan). || To take place (tener lugar).

realmente adv. Really, truly (de verdad). || Really, actually, in fact (en realidad).

realquilar v. tr. To sublet (subarrendar). || To relet (alquilar de nuevo).

realzado, da adj. Raised.

realzar v. tr. To raise, to lift (levantar). || To highlight (en pintura). || FIG. To give sparkle *o* colour to (una fiesta). | To enhance, to heighten, to bring out (belleza).

reanimable adj. Revivable.

reanimación f. Revival.

reanimar v. tr. To revive. || To relight (la llama olímpica). || FIG. To revive (vigorizar). || *Reanimar la conversación*, to bring back a bit of life into the conversation, to liven up the conversation.
— V. pr. To revive (personas). || To liven up again (fiesta, conversación, etc.).

reanudación f. o **reanudamiento** m. Renewal, resumption, reestablishment: *reanudación de las relaciones diplomáticas*, reestablishment of diplomatic relations. || Resumption (de conversaciones). || Renewal (de una amistad). || Reopening (del Parlamento). || Return: *reanudación de las clases*, return to school.

reanudar v. tr. To renew: *reanudar una amistad*, to renew a friendship. || To resume: *reanudar conversaciones*, to resume talks; *reanudar un debate*, to resume a debate; *reanudar un servicio de autobuses*, to resume a bus service. || — *Reanudar el paso* or *la marcha*, to set off again. || *Reanudar las clases*, to go back to school (los alumnos).
— V. pr. To start again, to resume: *se reanudaron las conversaciones*, the talks started again.

reaparecer* v. intr. To reappear (volver a aparecer). || To make a comeback (un artista, un político). || To recur (un fenómeno).

reaparición f. Reappearance. || Comeback (de actor, político). || Recurrence (de un fenómeno).

reapertura f. Reopening.

rearmar v. tr. To rearm.
— V. pr. To rearm.

rearme m. Rearmament.

reasegurar v. tr. To reinsure.

reaseguro m. Reinsurance.

reasentamiento m. Move, transfer (de colonos, refugiados).

reasumir v. tr. To reassume, to resume.

reasunción f. Reassumption, resumption.

reata f. Rope *o* strap used to keep animals in single file (correa). || Packtrain (de caballos, mulas, etc.). || Lead mule (que va en cabeza). || — *De reata*, in single file. || *Enganche de reata*, tying [of mules] in single file.

reatar v. tr. To reattach, to retie (volver a atar). || To tie tightly (atar firmemente). || To tie in single file [horses or mules].

reavivar v. tr. To revive (reanimar). || To rekindle, to revive (sentimientos, etc.).

rebaba f. Rough edge. || Burr (de un metal fundido).

rebaja f. Discount, reduction (descuento). || Lowering (del nivel). || — *Grandes rebajas*, big reductions (saldos). || *Vender con rebaja*, to sell at a discount.

rebajado, da adj. Lowered. || Reduced (precios). || FIG. Humiliated. || ARQ. Depressed (arco en general). | Basket-handle (arco apainelado). || Softened, toned down (color).
— M. Person exempted from military service.

rebajador m. FOT. Reducer.

rebajamiento m. Lowering. || FIG. Humiliation. || ARQ. Depressing. || Softening, toning down (de los colores). || FOT. Reduction.

rebajar v. tr. To lower (bajar). || To deduct, to make a reduction of: *rebajar mil pesetas*, to make a reduction of one thousand pesetas. || To cut, to reduce (precios). || To reduce (mercancías, etc.). || To reduce, to diminish, to cut: *rebajarle a uno el sueldo*, to reduce s.o.'s wages. || To diminish (intensidad). || FIG. To humiliate, to deflate. || ARQ. To depress. || To tone down, to soften (colores). || FOT. To reduce. || *Estar rebajado de gimnasia*, to be excused *o* let off gym.
— V. pr. To be lowered. || To go off sick (un empleado). || MIL. To be let off: *Pérez se rebajó de la faena de cocina*, Perez was let off mess duty. || FIG. *Rebajarse a*, to stoop to, to descend to.

rebaje m. MIL. Exemption.

rebajo m. TECN. Groove, rabbet. || ARQ. Batter (derrame del basamento).

rebalsa f. Pool, pond, puddle. || MED. Engorgement.

rebalsar v. tr. To dam, to dam up.
— V. pr. To become dammed, to collect in a pool.

rebalse m. Dam (presa). || Pool of stagnant water (agua estancada).

rebanada f. Slice: *rebanada de pan*, slice of bread.

rebanar o **rebanear** v. tr. To slice, to cut into slices (cortar en rebanadas). || To slice off, to cut off (cortar).

rebañadera f. Grapnel.

rebañadura f. Remains, *pl.*, leftovers, *pl.* [of food in a saucepan, etc.].

rebañar v. tr. To finish off (comida). || FIG. To clean out. || To glean (el trigo). || *Rebañar el plato con pan*, to wipe one's plate clean with bread.

rebaño m. Flock (de ovejas). || Herd (de otros animales). || FIG. Flock (congregación de fieles).

rebasadero m. MAR. Safe place [for passing].

rebasar v. tr. To exceed, to pass: *rebasar una cantidad*, to exceed an amount. || To go beyond (una marca). || To surpass: *el éxito rebasó nuestros pronósticos*, the success surpassed our forecasts. || MAR. To pass (un cabo). || To overtake (adelantar). || *Rebasar los límites*, to overstep the mark, to go too far (exagerar).
— V. intr. To overflow (un líquido).

rebatible adj. Refutable.

rebatimiento m. Refutation.

rebatiña f. Fight, scramble (pelea).

rebatir v. tr. To refute (un argumento, etc.): *rebatir una teoría*, to refute a theory. || To reject, to rebuff (rechazar propuestas, etc.). || To repel, to ward off, to drive back (un ataque). || To stop (un golpe). || To parry (en esgrima). || To resist (una tentación). || To reduce, to lower (rebajar). || To deduct (descontar).

rebato m. Alarm: *tocar a rebato*, to sound the alarm. || MIL. Surprise attack (ataque repentino).

rebautizar v. tr. To rebaptize, to rechristen.

rebeca f. Cardigan (jersey).

Rebeca n. pr. f. Rebecca.

rebeco m. Chamois (gamuza).

rebelarse v. pr. To rebel, to revolt: *rebelarse contra el gobierno*, to rebel against the government.

rebelde adj. Rebellious. || JUR. Defaulting. || Rebellious, unruly, unmanageable (indócil). || *Ser rebelde a*, to be in revolt against (rebelarse contra), to resist.
— M. y f. Rebel. || JUR. Defaulter.

rebeldía f. Rebelliousness. || JUR. Default. || — JUR. *Condenado en rebeldía*, judged by default. || *Declararse en rebeldía*, to rebel, to revolt (sublevarse), to default (en un juicio). || *Estar en rebeldía*, to be in revolt. || *Sentencia en rebeldía*, judgment by default *o* in contumacy.

rebelión f. Rebellion, revolt. || *La rebelión de las masas*, The Revolt of the Masses (obra de Ortega y Gasset).

rebencazo m. Lash [of a whip] (golpe). || Crack [of a whip] (chasquido).

rebenque m. Whip (látigo). || MAR. Lashing. || MAR. *Sujetar con rebenques*, to lash.

rebenqueada f. V. REBENCAZO.

rebenquear v. tr. *Amer.* To whip.

rebién adv. Very well indeed.

rebina f. AGR. Third dressing [of land].

rebinar v. tr. AGR. To give the third dressing.

rebisabuelo, la m. y f. Great-great-grandfather (hombre), great-great-grandmother (mujer).

rebisnieto, ta m. y f. Great-great-grandson (chico), great-great-granddaughter (chica).

reblandecer* v. tr. To soften (ablandar).
— V. pr. To soften, to become soft.

reblandecimiento m. Softening. || MED. Softening: *reblandecimiento cerebral*, softening of the brain.

rebobinado m. Rewinding.

rebobinar v. tr. To rewind.

rebonito, ta adj. FAM. Lovely, gorgeous.

reborde m. Edge, flange: *en el reborde*, on the edge.

rebordeador m. TECN. Flanger.

rebordear v. tr. To flange.

rebosadero m. Overflow. || Spillway (de embalse).

rebosadura f. o **rebosamiento** m. Overflowing, overflow (de un líquido).

rebosante adj. Brimming, overflowing, bursting: *estar rebosante de vitalidad*, to be overflowing with vitality.

rebosar v. intr. To overflow, to brim over (un recipiente). || FIG. To be overflowing *o* brimming *o* bursting: *rebosar de entusiasmo*, to be overflowing with enthusiasm. | To abound (ser abundante). || — FIG. *Rebosar de riquezas*, to be rolling in money. | *Rebosar de salud, de alegría*, to be brimming *o* glowing with health, with joy.
rebotador, ra adj. Bouncing.
rebotadura f. Bounce (rebote). || Napping (de las telas).
rebotar v. intr. To bounce, to rebound: *la pelota rebotó en el suelo*, the ball bounced on the ground. || To ricochet (bala). || *Hacer rebotar una pelota contra la pared*, to bounce a ball against the wall.
— V. tr. To clinch (un clavo). || To nap (los paños). || To drive *o* to push back, to repel (rechazar). || FAM. To annoy, to get on s.o.'s nerves.
— V. pr. To worry, to get upset (turbarse). || To get angry (irritarse).
rebote m. Bounce, rebound (de la pelota). || Ricochet (balas o piedras). || *De rebote*, on the rebound.
rebotica f. Back room of a chemist's shop.
rebozadamente adv. Secretly, in secret.
rebozar v. tr. To muffle with *o* to wrap in a cloak. || CULIN. To cover with batter *o* breadcrumbs, to fry in batter *o* breadcrumbs (pescado, frituras).
— V. pr. To muffle o.s. with one's cloak.
rebozo m. Wrap, shawl, cloak (prenda de vestir). || Mantilla (mantilla). || FIG. Dissimulation. || — *De rebozo*, secretly, in secret. || *Sin rebozo*, openly, frankly.
rebrotar v. intr. To shoot, to sprout (retoñar).
rebrote m. Shoot. || FIG. Renewal.
rebueno, na adj. FAM. Very good, marvellous.
rebufar v. intr. To snort loudly (un animal).
rebujar v. tr. V. ARREBUJAR.
rebujina o **rebujiña** f. FAM. Bustle (alboroto). | Crowd (muchedumbre).
rebullicio m. Bustle (movimiento). || Hubbub, commotion, stir (ruido y movimiento).
rebullir* v. intr. To stir, to come to life.
— V. pr. To stir.
rebusca f. Search (búsqueda). || Gleaning (de uvas, de cereales). || Gleanings, *pl.* (espigueo). || FIG. Leavings, *pl.*, leftovers, *pl.* (desecho).
rebuscado, da adj. Recherché, pedantic, affected, elaborate (estilo, palabra, etc.).
rebuscador, ra adj. Searching. || Gleaning (de uvas, cereales).
— M. y f. Searcher. || Gleaner (de uvas, cereales etc.).
rebuscamiento m. Affectation (afectación).
rebuscar v. tr. To search thoroughly (un sitio). || To search for (una cosa). || AGR. To glean (uvas, cereales).
rebusco m. Search (rebusca).
rebuznador, ra adj. Braying.
rebuznar v. intr. To bray.
rebuzno m. Braying, bray.
recabar v. tr. To obtain [by entreaty]: *recabar fondos para*, to obtain funds for. || To ask for (solicitar). || To claim (reclamar). || *Recabar toda la atención*, to require all one's attention.
recadero, ra m. y f. Messenger. || — M. Errand boy (niño que lleva los recados). || Deliveryman (hombre que lleva los pedidos).
recado m. Errand: *le haré el recado*, I shall run the errand for him; *le mandé a un recado*, I sent him on an errand. || Message (mensaje): *¿quiere dejarle un recado?*, would you like to leave him a message? || Materials, *pl.*, gear, tackle: *recado de escribir*, writing materials. || *Amer.* Saddle and trappings, *pl.* || — Pl. Shopping, *sing.*, errands (compras): *voy a hacer los recados*, I'm going to do the shopping.
recaer* v. intr. To fall again, to fall back (caer de nuevo). || To backslide, to relapse (en vicios, errores, etc.). || To have a relapse, to relapse (un enfermo). || FIG. To fall: *la culpa recae sobre él*, the blame falls on him; *el premio recayó en el más digno*, the prize fell to the worthiest. | To hit (afectar). | To come back *o* round: *la conversación recae siempre sobre el mismo tema*, the conversation always comes back to the same topic.
recaída f. Backsliding, relapse (en vicios, errores, etc.). || Relapse (de un enfermo).
recalada f. MAR. Landfall, sighting of land.
recalar v. tr. To soak, to saturate.
— V. intr. To swim underwater (bucear). || MAR. To sight land. || *Amer.* To end up, to arrive (llegar).
recalcadamente adv. Emphatically, insistently.
recalcadura f. Pressing, squeezing, packing. || FIG. Repetition.
recalcar v. tr. To press, to squeeze (apretar). || To pack, to cram (rellenar). || FIG. To stress, to underline, to emphasize: *recalcar la importancia*, to stress the importance. | To stress, to accent, to emphasize: *recalcar una frase, una sílaba*, to accent a sentence, a syllable. | To agree: *siempre he pensado lo mismo, recalcó su primo*, that is what I have always thought, agreed his cousin. | To insist on (insistir). || *Siempre está recalcando lo mismo*, he is always coming out with the same thing, he is always saying the same thing.
— V. intr. MAR. To list, to heel.
— V. pr. To sit back (arrellanarse).
recalcificación f. Recalcification.
recalcitrante adj. Recalcitrant.
recalcitrar v. intr. To back away *o* up, to step back (retroceder). || FIG. To be recalcitrant, to resist.
recalentador m. Boiler (calentador de agua). || TECN. Superheater.
recalentamiento m. Superheating. || Overheating (calentamiento excesivo). || Reheating (recocido).
recalentar* v. tr. To superheat. || To reheat, to warm up (comida). || To overheat (calentar demasiado). || FIG. To excite (excitar).
— V. pr. To be superheated. || To overheat (calentarse demasiado). || To be on heat (estar en celo). || To spoil (ciertas sustancias). || To rot (maderas). || FIG. To get excited (excitarse).
recalmón m. MAR. Lull.
recalzar v. tr. AGR. To ridge, to bank up earth around [U.S., to hill] (plantas). || ARQ. To underpin, to reinforce.
recalzo m. Extra felloe (de la llanta). || ARQ. Reinforcement, underpinning. || AGR. Ridging, banking up of earth around plants [U.S., hilling].
recamado m. [Relief] embroidery.
recamador, ra m. y f. Embroiderer.
recamar v. tr. To embroider in relief (bordar).
recámara f. Dressing room (vestuario). || Chamber (de arma de fuego). || Blast hole (de mina). || Reserve (timidez). || *Amer.* Bedroom (alcoba). || FIG. *Antonio tiene mucha recámara*, Anthony is very reserved.
recambiable adj. Refillable, able to be refilled.
recambiar v. tr. To change again (cambiar de nuevo). || To change, to change over (una pieza). || COM. To draw [a redraft].
recambio m. Change (acción de cambiar). || Refill (de estilográfica). || Spare, spare part (pieza). || *De recambio*, spare: *rueda de recambio*, spare wheel.
recancamusa f. FAM. Ruse, trick.
recancanilla f. Kind of hopping game (juego de niños). || FIG. y FAM. Emphasis, stress. || *Hablar con recancanilla*, to emphasize one's words, to speak emphatically.
recapacitar v. tr. e intr. To think over, to consider: *recapacitar sobre una cosa*, to think sth. over, to consider sth.
— V. intr. To think things over, to reflect (reflexionar).
recapitulación f. Recapitulation, summing up, summary.
recapitulador, ra m. y f. Recapitulator.
recapitular v. tr. To recapitulate, to sum up.
recapitulativo, va adj. Recapitulative, recapitulating.
recarga f. Refill.
recargable adj. Refillable, able to be refilled.
recargar v. tr. To reload (cargar de nuevo). || To overload (sobrecargar). || To increase, to raise: *recargar los impuestos*, to increase taxes; *recargar del diez por ciento*, to increase by ten percent. || To put a strain on: *esto recarga mi presupuesto*, that is putting a strain on my budget. || To recharge (una batería). || To lengthen [a sentence] (una condena). || FIG. To overburden, to load down: *recargar de obligaciones*, to load down with duties. || — *Estilo recargado*, overelaborate style. || *Recargado de adornos*, overornate, over-adorned. || FIG. *Recargar el cuadro* or *las tintas*, to exaggerate, to overdo it.
recargo m. New load *o* burden, additional load *o* burden (nuevo cargo). || Increase (de impuestos, de precios). || Refill (recarga). || Additional payment, surcharge (sobretasa): *un recargo del diez por ciento*, a ten percent surcharge, an additional payment of ten percent. || JUR. Increase, lengthening (de pena). || MED. Temperature rise. || MIL. Extra period [of service] (tiempo suplementario).
recatadamente adv. Prudently, cautiously (con prudencia). || Becomingly, modestly, fittingly (decentemente). || Humbly (humildemente).
recatado, da adj. Prudent, cautious (prudente). || Reserved (reservado). || Modest, demure, decent (mujer).
recatar v. tr. To hide, to cover up (encubrir).
— V. pr. To take care, to be careful (andar con cuidado). || To act discreetly (actuar sin ostentación). || To hesitate (vacilar). || — *Recatarse de la gente*, to hide o.s. away. || *Sin recatarse*, openly.
recato m. Prudence, caution (prudencia). || Modesty (pudor). || Reserve.
recauchutado m. Retreading (de un neumático).
recauchutar v. tr. To retread (un neumático).
recaudación f. Takings, *pl.*, take (cobro): *la recaudación ascendió a 2000 pesetas*, the takings amounted to 2,000 pesetas; *hacer una buena recaudación*, to have good takings. || Collection, collecting (acción de recaudar). || Receipts, *pl.*, returns, *pl.* (contribuciones, tasas, impuestos). || Tax collector's office (sitio): *ir a la Recaudación*, to go to the tax collector's office.
recaudador m. Tax collector: *oficina del recaudador*, tax collector's office. || *Recaudador de contribuciones*, tax collector.
recaudamiento m. V. RECAUDACIÓN.
recaudar v. tr. To take, to collect (recibir). || To collect (contribuciones). || To put in a safe place (asegurar). || To recover (una deuda).

recaudo m. Precaution (precaución). || Collection (recaudación). || Care (cuidado). || JUR. Deposit (fianza). || *Estar a buen recaudo*, to be in safekeeping *o* in a safe place.

recazo m. Guard (de espada). || Back (del cuchillo).

recelar v. tr. e intr. To suspect (barruntar): *recelo que va a venir hoy*, I suspect he is going to come today. || To fear, to be afraid (temer): *recelo que me suceda alguna desgracia*, I fear that some misfortune may befall me. || To be suspicious (desconfiar): *recelar de todo*, to be suspicious of everything. || To excite (a una yegua).

recelo m. Distrust, mistrust (desconfianza): *acoger con cierto recelo*, to greet with a certain amount of distrust. || Suspicion (suspicacia). || Fear (temor). || — *Mirar con recelo*, to look suspiciously at. || *Tener recelo de*, to distrust.

receloso, sa adj. Distrustful, suspicious: *receloso con sus amigos*, suspicious of his friends. || Fearful, apprehensive (temeroso).

recensión f. Review, write-up (fam.) [reseña de una obra]. || Recension (obra revisada).

recental adj. Sucking, unweaned: *ternero recental*, sucking calf.
— M. Suckling.

recentar* v. tr. To leaven.
— V. pr. To be renewed (renovarse).

recentísimo, ma adj. Very recent.

recepción f. Receipt (de un paquete, etc.). || Reception, reception desk (en un hotel). || Reception (fiesta). || Admission. || JUR. Examination [of witnesses].

recepcionista m. y f. Receptionist.

receptáculo m. Receptacle.

receptividad f. Receptivity, receptiveness.

receptivo, va adj. Receptive.

receptor, ra adj. Receiving. || *Aparato receptor*, receiver, receiving set.
— M. Receiver, recipient (persona). || Receiver, receiving set (radio, televisión). || ANAT. y BIOL. Receptor. || — *Receptor de control*, monitor. || *Receptor de televisión*, television set *o* receiver. || *Receptor universal*, person who can be given any blood group during transfusion. || — F. Receiver (máquina).

receptoría f. Tax collector's office.

recesión f. Recession (en economía).

recésit m. Holiday (recle).

recesivo, va adj. Recessive (en biología).

receso m. (P.us.). Recession. || *Amer.* Recess (vacaciones). || *Amer. Entrar en receso*, to recess (una asamblea).

receta f. CULIN. Recipe. || MED. Prescription, recipe (p.us.). || FIG. Recipe (fórmula): *tener una receta para hacer fortuna*, to have a recipe for making a fortune. || FIG. y FAM. *Receta de vieja*, old wives' tale.

recetador m. Practising doctor (médico).

recetante adj. Prescribing.
— M. Practising doctor (médico).

recetar v. tr. MED. To prescribe.

recetario m. Prescription (del médico). || Prescription book *o* record (en un hospital). || Pharmacopoeia (farmacopea).

reciamente adv. Strongly, vigourously.

recibí m. *Poner el recibí a* or *en una factura*, to sign a receipt.

recibidor, ra adj. Receiving.
— M. Receiver, recipient (persona). || Entrance hall (entrada). || Antechamber (antesala).

recibimiento m. Reception. || Welcome, reception (acogida): *tuvo muy mal recibimiento*, he got a very bad welcome. || Reception (fiesta). || Entrance hall (vestíbulo). || Antichamber (antesala).

recibir v. tr. e intr. To receive, to entertain: *siendo mujer de ministro tiene que recibir a menudo*, being a Minister's wife she often has to entertain. || To receive, to welcome: *el ministro fue recibido con gran pompa*, the minister was received with great pomp. || To receive: *el Presidente no pudo recibirme*, the President couldn't receive me. || To receive, to welcome, to take: *no recibieron muy bien su propuesta*, his proposal was not very well received. || To accept: *reciba mi sincera enhorabuena*, accept my sincere congratulations. || TAUR. V. OBSERV. || — *Reciba un atento saludo de*, Yours sincerely. || COM. *Recibí* or *recibimos*, received with thanks. || *Recibir con los brazos abiertos*, to welcome with open arms. || *Recibir una negativa*, to be refused, to meet with a refusal. || *Ser recibido como los perros en misa*, to be as welcome as a bull in a china shop.
— V. pr. To graduate. || *Recibirse de doctor*, to receive one's doctor's degree, to qualify as a doctor.
— OBSERV. In bullfighting terminology this verb is used mainly in the expression *matar recibiendo;* this entails the bullfighter thrusting as the bull charges. The alternative is *matar a volapié*, the bullfighter moving towards the stationary bull to kill it.

recibo m. Receipt (documento). || Reception, receiving (recibimiento). || Small living room (sala). || Antechamber (antesala). || — *Acusar recibo*, to acknowledge receipt. || *Estar de recibo*, to be acceptable (un traje, etc.), to be decent *o* presentable (una persona).

reciclado m. Retraining.

reciclar v. tr. To retrain.

recidiva f. MED. Relapse.

reciedumbre f. Strength.

recién adv. Recently, newly: *casa recién construida*, recently built house; *una flor recién abierta*, a newly opened flower. || — *Estar recién*, to have just: *estar recién llegado*, to have just arrived; *está recién hecho*, it has just been done; *estaba recién comido*, he had just eaten. || *Los recién casados*, the newlyweds. || *Los recién llegados*, the newcomers. || *Los turistas recién llegados*, the tourists who have just arrived. || *Recién salido del colegio*, just out of school, fresh from school. || *Un niño recién nacido*, a newborn baby.
— OBSERV. In Spain, *recién*, which is the apocopation of *recientemente*, is used only before past participles. In Latin America it is very common with the active mood of the verb, in the sense of "not long ago" (*recién hemos llegado*, we have just arrived; *recién en 1886*, as early as 1886).

reciente adj. Recent: *una noticia reciente*, recent news. || Fresh: *queso reciente*, fresh cheese. || *Construida en fecha reciente*, newly *o* recently built.

recientemente adv. Recently, of late, lately.

recinto m. Enclosure. || Precinct, precincts, *pl.*, grounds, *pl.* (zona delimitada): *el recinto de la escuela*, the school precinct. || Area (área).

recio, cia adj. Strong, vigorous, robust (vigoroso). || Sturdy, strong (grueso). || Loud (voz). || Rigorous, harsh, severe (frío, temperatura). || Heavy (lluvia). || Wild, violent (tempestad, corriente de agua, etc.). || *En lo más recio del combate, del invierno, del verano*, in the thick of the battle, in the dead of [the] winter, at the height of [the] summer.
— Adv. Loudly, loud: *hablar recio*, to speak loudly. || Heavily, hard: *llover recio*, to rain hard. || *De recio*, strongly, vigorously, violently.

récipe m. FAM. Prescription (receta). | Scolding, telling off (reprimenda).

recipiendario m. Newly elected member.

recipiente adj. Receiving, recipient.
— M. Recipient (persona). || Vessel, receptacle, container (vasija, etc.). || TECN. Bell glass. || QUÍM. Receiver.

reciprocación f. GRAM. Reciprocity. || Reciprocation.

reciprocarse v. pr. To reciprocate.

reciprocidad f. Reciprocity.

recíproco, ca adj./s.f. Reciprocal. || *A la recíproca*, vice versa.

recitación f. Recitation, recital.

recitado m. MÚS. Recitative. || Recitation (recitación).

recitador, ra adj. Reciting.
— M. y f. Reciter.

recital m. Recital: *músico que ha dado recitales por todo el mundo*, musician who has given recitals throughout the world. || Reading (de poesías).

recitar v. tr. To recite.

recitativo m. MÚS. Recitative.

reclamación f. Claim, demand (petición). || Protest, complaint (queja): *hacer una reclamación*, to lodge *o* to make a complaint.

reclamador, ra m. y f. JUR. Claimant.

reclamar v. tr. To claim, to demand (pedir): *reclamar lo que se le debe a uno*, to claim what is due to one. || To require, to demand, to need (exigir). || To call (las aves). || *La multitud reclamaba que saliese el Presidente al balcón*, the crowd clamoured for the President [to appear].
— V. intr. JUR. To appeal (protestar): *reclamar contra un fallo*, to appeal against a sentence. || To protest, to complain: *reclamar contra una decisión*, to protest against a decision. || — MAR. *Izar a reclamar*, to hoist home. || JUR. *Reclamar en juicio*, to appeal.

reclamo m. Decoy bird (ave amaestrada). || Birdcall (pito). || Call (llamada). || COM. Advertisement (anuncio). | Advertising slogan (frase publicitaria). || JUR. Claim. || IMPR. Catchword. || FIG. Inducement. || *Acudir al reclamo*, to answer the call.

recle m. Holiday (en los conventos).

reclinación f. Leaning.

reclinar v. tr. To lean.
— V. pr. To lean: *reclinarse en* or *sobre*, to lean on.

reclinatorio m. Prie-dieu (para arrodillarse).

recluido, da adj. Shut *o* locked in (encerrado).

recluir* v. tr. To imprison (encarcelar). || To confine (en un manicomio). || To shut *o* to lock in (encerrar). || To shut away (apartar).
— V. pr. To shut o.s. off *o* away.

reclusión f. Seclusion. || Prison, imprisonment, confinement (prisión). || Retreat (lugar de retiro).

recluso, sa adj. Imprisoned. || *Población reclusa*, prison population.
— M. y f. Prisoner (en una prisión).

recluta m. MIL. Recruit. | Conscript (quinto).
— F. Conscription, recruitment (reclutamiento). [V. RECLUTAR (Observ.)].

reclutador m. MIL. Recruiting officer (V. RECLUTAR [Observ.]).

reclutamiento m. Recruitment, conscription. | Recruits, *pl.*, conscripts, *pl.* (conjunto de reclutas). [V. RECLUTAR (Observ.)].

reclutar v. tr. MIL. To recruit, to conscript. || To recruit (trabajadores). || *Amer.* To round up (reunir el ganado).
— OBSERV. Las palabras inglesas *recruit* y *conscript* no son sinónimas. *To recruit* es alistar reclutas voluntarios, *to conscript* es obligarlos a alistarse.

recobrable adj. Recoverable.
recobrar v. tr. To recover: *recobrar la salud, el buen humor, la confianza*, to recover one's health, one's good humour, one's confidence. || To recapture (una ciudad). || To make up [for] (tiempo perdido). || To get back: *recobrar aliento, sus derechos*, to get one's breath back, one's rights back. || To regain: *recobrar la esperanza, las fuerzas*, to regain hope, strength. || — *Recobrar el espíritu* or *el sentido*, to come round, to regain consciousness, to come to. || *Recobrar su dinero*, to find one's money (encontrar), to get one's money back (cubrir gastos).
— V. pr. To get one's money back (desquitarse). || To come round *o* to (volver en sí). || To recover, to recuperate, to get better (recuperarse).
recobro m. Recovery. || Convalescence.
recocer* v. tr. To recook, to warm up (volver a cocer). || To cook for a long time (cocer mucho tiempo). || To overcook (cocer demasiado). || TECN. To anneal (el acero, el vidrio).
— V. pr. To cook for a long time (cocer mucho). || FIG. To be consumed (*de*, with).
recocido, da adj. Recooked (vuelto a cocer). || Overcooked, overdone (demasiado cocido). || Cooked for a long time (muy cocido).
— M. Annealing (vidrio, acero).
recocina f. Scullery.
recochinearse v. pr. FAM. To make fun of, to mock (burlarse). | To ogle (viendo un espectáculo licencioso). | To have fun *o* a good time (divertirse).
recochineo m. FAM. Mocking, mockery (burla). | Fun, lark: *¡qué recochineo!*, what a lark!, what fun! || FAM. *Y encima con recochineo*, and not only that, he laughed about it.
recodadero m. Elbow rest.
recodar v. intr. To wind, to twist, to turn (un río).
— V. intr. y pr. To lean [one's elbows] (*en*, on).
recodo m. Twist, turn (de río). || Bend (de carretera). || Angle (ángulo). || Nook, recess: *casa con muchos recodos*, house with many nooks.
recogedero m. Place where things are collected (sitio). || Dustpan (pala para la basura).
recogedor, ra adj. Collecting.
— M. y f. Collector. || AGR. Harvester (de la cosecha). | Picker (de frutas, patatas, etc.). || — M. Dustpan (para la basura). || AGR. Kind of rake (instrumento).
recogemigas m. inv. Crumb scoop [for sweeping up crumbs].
recogepelotas m. inv. Ball boy.
recoger v. tr. To take again, to take back (coger de nuevo). || To collect, to gather: *recoger datos, leña*, to collect information, wood. || To save, to collect: *recoger sellos de correo*, to save postage stamps. || To collect (dinero). || To gather (el polvo). || To wipe up (agua, etc. en el suelo). || To pick up: *recoge el libro que se ha caído*, pick up the book which has fallen; *recoger dos entradas de teatro*, to pick up two theatre tickets. || To gather, to stop (la pelota). || To pick up, to fetch, to go for (a uno): *le recogeré a las ocho*, I shall pick you up at eight o'clock. || AGR. To gather in, to bring in (poner al abrigo): *recoger las mieses*, to gather in the harvest. | To harvest (cosechar). || To pick (fruta, flores). || To put away (poner en su sitio). || To take in, to shelter, to welcome (dar asilo). || To seize (retirar de la circulación): *recoger un periódico*, to seize a newspaper. || To lift *o* to pick up (la falda). || To roll up (las mangas). || To take in, to shorten (en costura). || MAR. To take in (las velas). || FIG. To reap: *recoger el fruto de su trabajo*, to reap the fruit of one's work. | To get (obtener). || — *Quien siembra vientos recoge tempestades*, he who sows the wind shall reap the whirlwind. || *Recoger el caballo*, to draw up one's horse. || FIG. *Recoger el guante*, to take up the gauntlet *o* the challenge. | *Recoger laureles*, to reap *o* to win laurels. || *Recoger los platos de la mesa*, to clear the table, to clear the dishes away.
— V. pr. To withdraw within o.s. (ensimismarse). || REL. To recollect o.s. || To go home (retirarse a su casa): *se recoge temprano*, he goes home early. || To go to bed (irse a la cama). || To gather together (los animales). || To pick *o* to lift up (la falda). || — *Recogerse el pelo*, to put one's hair up. || *Recogerse en sí mismo*, to withdraw within o.s.
recogida f. Collection (del correo, de la basura, etc.). || AGR. Harvest, harvesting (cosecha). || Seizure (de un periódico). || (Ant.). Withdrawal (retirada).
recogidamente adv. Retiringly (apartado). || Solitarily, alone (en soledad). || Quietly (tranquilamente). || Devoutly (con devoción).
recogido, da adj. Short (animal). || Small (pequeño). || Withdrawn (apartado del mundo). || Secluded: *vida recogida*, secluded life. || Quiet (tranquilo). || Pinned *o* tied back (pelo).
recogimiento m. Withdrawal (del espíritu). || AGR. Roundup (del ganado). || REL. Recollection. || *Vivir con gran recogimiento*, to lead a very withdrawn *o* secluded life.
recolar* v. tr. To refilter, to filter *o* to strain again.
recolección f. AGR. Harvest, harvesting, picking (acción). | Harvest time (temporada). || Collection, gathering: *recolección de informaciones estadísticas*, collection of statistical information. || REL. Retreat (retiro). | Strict observance (de la regla en los conventos).
recolectar v. tr. To harvest, to gather in (cosechar). || To collect (colectar).
recolector m. Collector.
recoleto, ta adj. Quiet, peaceful (calle, plaza). || Withdrawn, retiring (una persona).
— M. y f. Recollet (religioso).
recomendable adj. Recommendable. || Commendable (laudable). || *No ser recomendable*, to be unwise, to be inadvisable.
recomendación f. Recommendation (consejo, etc.). || References, *pl.*, testimonial (referencias). || — *Carta de recomendación*, recommendation, letter of introduction. || *Recomendación del alma*, prayers for the dying. || *Valerse de la recomendación de alguien*, to give s.o. as a reference.
recomendado, da adj. Recommended.
— M. y f. Protégé, protégée.
recomendador, ra adj. Recommendatory.
recomendante m. Person who recommends, recommender.
recomendar* v. tr. To recommend, to advise (aconsejar). || To commend (alabar). || To confide (confiar). || *Te lo recomiendo*, I recommend it to you.
recomendatorio, ria adj. Recommendatory.
recomenzar v. tr. To recommence, to begin *o* to start again.
recomerse v. pr. FIG. To be consumed (*de*, with, by).
recompensa f. Recompense, reward. || *En recompensa de*, in return for, as a reward for.
recompensable adj. Rewardable, recompensable.
recompensar v. tr. To recompense, to reward: *recompensar por un trabajo*, to recompense for a job. || To compensate (compensar).
recomponer* v. tr. To recompose. || To repair (arreglar). || To dress up, to doll up (fam.) [acicalar].
— V. pr. To dress up, to doll o.s. up (fam.) [acicalarse].
recomposición f. Recomposition.
recompuesto, ta adj. Recomposed. || Repaired (arreglado). || Dressed up, dolled up (acicalado).
reconcentración f. o **reconcentramiento** m. Concentration.
reconcentrar v. tr. To concentrate. || To conceal (el odio, etc.). || To bring together (reunir).
— V. pr. To concentrate (abstraerse). || To withdraw into o.s. (ensimismarse). || To build up (el odio, etc.).
reconciliable adj. Reconcilable.
reconciliación f. Reconciliation.
reconciliador, ra adj. Reconciling, reconciliatory.
— M. y f. Reconciler.
reconciliar v. tr. To reconcile.
— V. pr. To be reconciled.
reconcomerse v. pr. FIG. V. RECOMERSE.
reconcomio m. FIG. Longing, urge, itch (deseo). | Grudge (rencor). | Remorse (remordimiento). | Doubt, suspicion, misgiving (sospecha).
recondenado, da adj. FAM. Damn, damned: *¡recondenada vida!*, this damn life!
reconditez f. Heart of hearts. || Bottom: *la reconditez del alma*, the bottom of the soul.
recóndito, ta adj. Secret, hidden. || — *En lo más recóndito de*, in the depths of. || *En lo más recóndito del alma*, deep inside. || *Lo más recóndito del asunto*, the heart of the matter. || *Lo más recóndito del corazón*, one's heart of hearts, the bottom of one's heart.
reconducción f. JUR. Renewal, extension (prórroga).
reconducir* v. tr. JUR. To renew, to extend (prorrogar).
reconfirmar v. tr. To reconfirm.
reconfortación f. Comfort.
reconfortante adj. Comforting.
— M. MED. Tonic.
reconfortar v. tr. To comfort (confortar). || To cheer up (animar). || MED. To strengthen, to fortify.
reconocer* v. tr. To recognize: *no te reconocí a primera vista*, I didn't recognize you at first sight. || To distinguish, to identify (distinguir). || To admit, to acknowledge: *reconocer sus faltas*, to admit one's mistakes; *lo reconozco*, I admit it. || To recognize (un gobierno). || To recognize: *reconocer por hijo*, to recognize as one's son. || To face: *reconozcamos los hechos*, let's face the facts. || To survey (el terreno). || MED. To examine. || MIL. To reconnoitre [U.S., to reconnoiter], to make a reconnaissance. || To check, to go through (registrar). || To be grateful for (mostrarse agradecido). || — FIG. *Reconocer el terreno*, to see how the land lies. || *Reconocer la evidencia*, to bow to the evidence.
— V. pr. To be recognized *o* known. || To admit: *reconocerse culpable*, to admit one's guilt.
reconocible adj. Recognizable.
reconocidamente adv. Gratefully, with gratitude (con gratitud). || Obviously, clearly (evidentemente). || Avowedly (por confesión propia).
reconocido, da ad. Grateful (agradecido). || Recognized. || Confessed, acknowledged (confesado).
reconocimiento m. Recognition: *el reconocimiento de un error, de un amigo*, the recognition of a mistake, of a friend; *el reconocimiento de un niño*, the recognition of a child. || Recognition (de un gobierno). || Confession, acknowledgement, admission (confesión). || Check, inspection (registro). || Gratitude (gratitud). || MIL. Reconnaissance: *avión de recono-*

cimiento, reconnaissance plane. || — *En reconocimiento a los servicios prestados*, in appreciation of services rendered, for services rendered. || *Reconocimiento de deuda*, acknowledgement of debt. || MED. *Reconocimiento médico*, medical examination, checkup.
reconquista f. Reconquest.
— OBSERV. The name *Reconquista* applies especially to the period from 718 (battle of Covadonga) to 1492 (the taking of Granada by Ferdinand and Isabel), during which the Spanish people fought the Moslem invaders who had occupied a large part of the Peninsula.
reconquistar v. tr. To reconquer (un país). || To reconquer, to recapture (una ciudad). || FIG. To recover, to win back.
reconsiderar v. tr. To reconsider.
reconstitución f. Reconstitution. || JUR. Reconstruction.
reconstituir* v. tr. To reconstitute. || JUR. To reconstruct (un crimen).
reconstituyente adj./s.m. Reconstituent.
reconstrucción f. Reconstruction, rebuilding.
reconstructivo, va adj. Reconstructive.
reconstruir* v. tr. To reconstruct, to rebuild.
recontar* v. tr. To recount, to count again (una cuenta). || To retell, to tell again (una historia).
recontento, ta adj. Delighted, overjoyed.
— M. Delight, joy.
¡recontra! interj. Damn!, blast!
reconvención f. Reproach, reprimand (censura). || JUR. Counterclaim, cross action.
reconvenir* v. tr. To reproach, to reprimand, to rebuke: *reconvenir a uno por alguna cosa*, to reproach s.o. with sth. || JUR. To counterclaim.
reconversión f. Reconversion. || Retraining (nueva formación).
reconvertir* v. tr. To reconvert. || To retrain (dar nueva formación).
— V. pr. To be reconverted *o* retrained.
recopilación f. Summary, résumé, compendium (compendio). || Compilation: *recopilación de poemas*, compilation of poems. || Code: *recopilación de leyes*, code of laws.
— OBSERV. The name *Recopilación* is given to the official code of Spanish laws which was established in 1567. The *Nueva Recopilación* and the *Novísima Recopilación* are two more modern versions, which were compiled in 1775 and 1805 respectively.
recopilador m. Compiler.
recopilar v. tr. To compile (reunir). || To summarize (resumir). || To codify, to compile (leyes).
récord m. Record (marca): *batir, tener, establecer un récord*, to break *o* to beat, to hold, to set up a record; *el poseedor del récord*, the record holder.
— Adj. Record: *en un tiempo récord*, in record time.
recordable adj. Memorable.
recordación f. Memory (recuerdo). || Remembering (accion de recordar). || *Un presidente de feliz recordación*, a president who left a happy memory.
recordador, ra o **recordante** adj. Reminiscent [of].
recordar* v. tr. To remind of: *recordar un hecho a uno*, to remind s.o. of a fact; *esta muchacha me recuerda a su madre*, this girl reminds me of her mother. || To remember, to recall (acordarse de): *recuerdo tu visita*, I remember your visit; *recuerdo que llegó muy tarde*, I remember that he arrived very late. || To recall, to bring to mind, to be reminiscent of (hacer pensar en): *este paisaje recuerda un cuadro de Turner*, this scenery is reminiscent of a painting by Turner. || To commemorate: *hacer algo para recordar un acontecimiento*, to do sth. to commemorate an event. || (Ant.). *Amer.* To wake up (despertar). || *Para recordar*, in memory *o* remembrance of (una persona), to commemorate (un acontecimiento).
— V. intr. To wake up (despertarse). || To reminisce (pensar en o hablar de los viejos tiempos). || To remember (acordarse). || — *Que yo recuerde*, as far as I can recall *o* remember. || *Si bien recuerdo*, if I remember rightly. || *Si mal no recuerdo*, if my memory serves me well, if I remember rightly, as far as I can remember.
— V. pr. To wake up (despertarse).
recordativo, va adj. Reminiscent.
recordatorio m. Notice of death (estampa en recuerdo de los difuntos). || Reminder (medio para hacer recordar). || Reminder (advertencia). || Lesson: *para que te sirva de recordatorio*, as a lesson to you.
recordman, recordwoman m. y f. Record holder.
— OBSERV. Although these words are often used, there does exist the Spanish equivalent *plusmarquista.*
recorrer v. tr. To go *o* to travel through *o* over, to cross: *recorrer una ciudad*, to go through a city. || To tour, to travel round *o* through (un país). || To cover, to scour (buscando algo). || To cover, to go, to come, to travel (una distancia): *llegaron aquí después de haber recorrido miles de kilómetros*, they arrived here having covered *o* travelled thousands of kilometres; *hemos recorrido una gran distancia*, we have come *o* covered a great distance. || To look over, to run through (un escrito). || To inspect, to examine, to check, to go through (registrar). || IMPR. To overrun. || *Recorrer mundo*, to see the world.
recorrida f. *Amer.* V. RECORRIDO.
recorrido m. Journey: *es un recorrido precioso*, it is a beautiful journey; *un recorrido por España*, a journey through Spain. || Journey, run: *es un recorrido muy largo*, it is a long journey. || Distance covered (distancia recorrida). || Route (trayecto): *el recorrido del autobús, de una procesión*, the bus route, the route of a procession. || Path, flight path (trayectoria de proyectil). || Round: *el recorrido del cartero*, the postman's round. || DEP. Run (en esquí). | Round (en golf, equitación, etc.): *un recorrido sin faltas*, a clear round. || IMPR. Overrun. || TECN. Stroke (del émbolo). | Overhaul (repaso, arreglo general). || FAM. Good talking-to (reprensión larga): *darle un recorrido a alguien*, to give s.o. a good talking-to.
recortable m. Cutout.
recortado, da adj. Cut out. || Jagged (un borde). || Uneven, irregular (una superficie).
recortadura f. Cutting. || — Pl. Cuttings.
recortar v. tr. To cut (imágenes, etc.). || To recut, to cut again (volver a cortar). || To trim, to cut *o* to even off (el borde de una pieza). || To outline (pintura). || To trim (el pelo).
— V. pr. To stand out, to be outlined: *la torre se recortaba en el cielo*, the tower stood out against the sky.
recorte m. Cutting [out] (acción). || Trim (de pelo). || Cutting (fragmento cortado): *recorte de prensa*, press cutting. || Cutout (para los niños). || Piece [that has been cut] (metales, telas). || TAUR. Dodge (del torero). || — Pl. Cuttings (de metal, cuero, papel). || FIG. *Estar hecho de recortes*, to be a scissors-and-paste job.
recoser v. tr. To resew, to sew again (volver a coser). || To darn, to mend (zurcir).
recosido m. Darning, mending (acción de recoser). || Mend, darn (zurcido).
recostado, da adj. Recumbent, reclining (en un sofá, etc.). || Leaning (en la mesa, etc.).
recostar* v. tr. To lean (apoyar). || To lean, to bend (inclinar).
— V. pr. To lean: *recostarse en* or *sobre*, to lean on. || To lean back, to recline (hacia atrás). || To lie down (tumbarse).
recova f. Poultry business (comercio). || Poultry market (mercado). || Pack [of dogs] (jauría). || *Amer.* Market.
recovar v. intr. To trade in poultry and eggs.
recoveco m. Bend, turn, twist (vuelta). || Nook, odd corner (en casas). || FIG. Cunning (artificio). | Recess: *los recovecos del alma, del corazón*, the recesses of the mind, of the heart. || — *Sin recovecos*, frank (franco), frankly (sinceramente). || *Un asunto con muchos recovecos*, a complicated business.
recovero, ra m. y f. Poultry merchant.
recre m. Holiday (recle).
recreable adj. Recreational.
recreación f. Recreation.
recrear v. tr. To amuse, to entertain (divertir). || To recreate (crear de nuevo). || *Recrear la vista*, to be a joy to behold.
— V. pr. To amuse o.s., to enjoy o.s. (entretenerse). || To relax (solazarse): *recrearse en leer*, to relax with a book *o* by reading. || FAM. To enjoy, to delight, to take pleasure: *recrearse con un hermoso espectáculo*, to enjoy a magnificent show; *recrearse con el mal ajeno*, to delight in *o* to take pleasure in the misfortune of others.
recreativo, va adj. Recreational: *velada recreativa*, recreational evening. || Entertaining (que distrae).
recrecer* v. intr. To rise (el río). || To increase (aumentar).
— V. pr. To recover one's spirits, to cheer up (reanimarse).
recrecimiento m. Increase (aumento). || Rise (de un río). || FIG. New zeal.
recremento m. Recrement.
recreo m. Break, playtime [U.S., recess] (en el colegio). || Recreation, amusement (entretenimiento). — *Casa de recreo*, country house. || *De recreo*, pleasure: *barco de recreo*, pleasure boat; *viaje de recreo*, pleasure trip. || *Ser un recreo para la vista*, to be a joy to behold. || *Tren de recreo*, miniature railway (en parques, zoos, etc.).
recría f. Breeding.
recriador m. Breeder.
recriar v. tr. To breed (animales).
recriminación f. Recrimination, reproach.
recriminador, ra adj. Recriminative.
recriminar v. tr. To recriminate, to make a recrimination against: *recriminar a uno*, to make a recrimination against s.o. || To reproach: *recriminar a uno su conducta*, to reproach s.o. with his conduct.
— V. pr. To recriminate each other *o* one another.
recriminatorio, ria adj. Recriminatory.
recrudecer* v. intr. To be rising *o* increasing again, to be on the rise *o* increase again: *recrudece la criminalidad*, the crime rate is on the rise again. || To worsen, to deteriorate (empeorar). || *El frío recrudece*, it is getting colder again.
— V. tr. To cause to break out again. || To worsen (empeorar).
— V. pr. To break out again, to recrudesce.
recrudecimiento m. o **recrudescencia** f. Worsening: *recrudecimiento del frío*, worsening of the

cold. || Rise: *recrudecimiento de la criminalidad*, rise of the crime rate. || Recrudescence, new outbreak: *recrudecimiento de una enfermedad*, recrudescence of an illness.
recrudescente adj. Worsening, deteriorating (tiempo). || Rising (criminalidad). || Recrudescent, worsening (enfermedad).
recta f. V. RECTO.
rectal adj. ANAT. Rectal.
rectamente adv. In a straight line. || FIG. Rightly, justly (con justicia). | Wisely (con juicio). | Correctly, rightly (con exactitud).
rectangular adj. MAT. Rectangular.
rectángulo adj. MAT. Rectangular. || MAT. *Triángulo rectángulo*, right-angled *o* rectangular triangle.
— M. Rectangle.
rectificable adj. Rectifiable.
rectificación f. Rectification. || Correction.
rectificado m. TECN. Rebore.
rectificador, ra adj. Rectifying.
— M. ELECTR. Rectifier (de corriente). || QUÍM. Rectifier. || — F. Grinder (máquina).
rectificar v. tr. To rectify, to right (un error, un mal). || To change (su voto). || To correct (corregir). || ELECTR. To rectify. || TECN. To rebore (un cilindro).
— V. intr. To correct o.s.
rectificativo, va adj. Rectifying.
— M. Rectifying document.
rectilíneo, a adj. Rectilinear.
rectitis f. MED. Proctitis.
rectitud f. Straightness. || FIG. Rectitude, uprightness (justicia).
recto, ta adj. Straight: *línea recta*, straight line. || FIG. Just, fair: *juez recto*, just judge. | Sound (juicio). | Upright, honest, honourable (honrado): *hombre recto*, upright man. | Lawful, proper (intención). || True, proper, literal (sentido). || *Ángulo recto*, right angle.
— Adv. Straight on: *siga recto*, go straight on.
— M. ANAT. Rectum (del intestino). | Rectus (músculo): *recto del abdomen*, rectus abdominis. || Recto (de una página).
— F. MAT. Straight line (línea). || Straight stretch, straight (de una carretera, etc.). || DEP. Straight.
rector, ra adj. Principal, main: *idea rectora*, principal idea. || Guiding (principio, etc.). || Driving, leading: *fuerza rectora*, driving force. || Leading (persona). || *País rector del mundo occidental*, leading Western country.
— M. Rector (de universidad, de colegios religiosos). || FIG. Leader, head, chief (dirigente). | Line: *rector del pensamiento*, line of thought.
— OBSERV. In Spain the rector of a University receives the title of *Magnífico* (Rector magnífico de la Universidad de Salamanca).
rectorado m. Rectorate, rectorship (cargo).
rectoral adj. Rectorial.
— F. REL. Rectory.
rectoría f. Rectorate, rectorship (cargo). || REL. Rectory (casa del rector).
rectoscopia f. MED. Proctoscopy.
rectoscopio m. MED. Proctoscope.
recua f. Drove (de caballos o mulas). || FIG. y FAM. Gang, band.
recuadrar v. tr. To frame (enmarcar). || To grid, to divide into squares (cuadricular).
recuadro m. Frame (marco). || Box (en un periódico). || Square (cuadro).
recubrir v. tr. To cover. || To coat (con pintura).
recuelo m. Strong bleach (lejía). || FAM. *Café de recuelo*, weak coffee.
recuento m. Recount. || Count (enumeración). || — *Hacer el recuento de los libros*, to count [up] the books. || *Hacer el recuento de votos*, to recount the votes.
recuerdo m. Memory, recollection: *un recuerdo confuso*, a vague recollection; *un recuerdo desagradable*, an unpleasant memory. || Memory, remembrance: *en recuerdo de*, in memory of. || Booster (vacuna). || Souvenir: *tienda de recuerdos*, souvenir shop. || Keepsake (objeto para recordar algo o a alguien): *guarda esto como recuerdo*, take this as a keepsake. || — *Dele recuerdos a*, remember me to, give my regards *o* best wishes to. || MED. *Dosis de recuerdo*, booster injection. || *Guardar un feliz recuerdo de*, to have happy memories of. || *Muchos recuerdos*, kindest regards.
reculada f. Backing, reversing (de un vehículo). || Backward movement (retroceso). || Recoil, recoiling (de un arma). || FIG. Backdown.
recular v. intr. To back, to reverse (un vehículo). || To go back, to back (un animal). || To move back (moverse hacia atrás). || To retreat (un ejército). || To recoil (un arma). || FIG. To back down (rajarse).
reculones (a) loc. FAM. Backwards.
recuperable adj. Recuperable, recoverable, retrievable.
recuperación f. Recuperation, recovery. || Making up (de un retraso). || Recovery, picking up (de un astronauta). || Recovery (de un país).
recuperador, ra adj. Recuperative.
— M. Recuperator.
recuperar v. tr. To recuperate, to retrieve, to recover (un objeto). || To recuperate, to recover (la salud). || To recover (la vista, etc.). || To get back (un puesto). || To regain: *recuperar el conocimiento*, to regain consciousness. || To win back, to get back: *recuperar la confianza, el cariño de uno*, to win back s.o.'s confidence, s.o.'s affection. || To make up for (compensar): *recuperar el tiempo perdido*, to make up for lost time. || To make up (ganar): *recuperar una hora de trabajo*, to make up an hour's work. || TECN. To reclaim (los subproductos). | To salvage (metales). || — *Hallarse totalmente recuperado*, to have made a complete recovery, to be completely well again. || *Recuperar el sentido*, to come round, to regain consciousness.
— V. pr. To recuperate, to recover: *recuperarse de una enfermedad*, to recuperate from an illness. || To feel better: *después de haber dormido tanto me he recuperado*, I feel better after such a long sleep. || To get over (de una emoción): *recuperarse de su tristeza*, to get over one's sadness. || To recover, to pick up (los negocios). || *Recuperarse de una pérdida*, to recoup a loss.
recuperativo, va adj. Recuperative.
recurrencia f. MED. Recurrence.
recurrente adj. Recurrent. || Adj./s. JUR. Appellant.
recurrir v. intr. To turn, to appeal: *recurrir a alguien*, to turn to s.o. || To have recourse, to resort: *recurrir a la astucia*, to resort to cunning. || To appeal: *recurro a su generosidad*, I appeal to your generosity. || JUR. To appeal.
recurso m. Recourse, resort (acción de recurrir). || Recourse (medio). || Resource: *recursos económicos, naturales*, economic, natural resources. || JUR. Appeal. || — *Carecer de recursos económicos*, to lack funds, to be short of funds. || *Como* or *en último recurso*, as a last resort. || *Haber agotado todos los recursos*, to be at the end of one's resources. || *Hombre de recursos*, resourceful man. || *No hay otro recurso*, it is the only way, there is no alternative. || JUR. *Recurso de casación*, high-court appeal.
recusable adj. Objectionable.
recusación f. Rejection. || JUR. Recusation, challenge.
recusante adj./s. Recusant.
recusar v. tr. To reject, to refuse. || JUR. To recuse, to challenge.
rechazable adj. Refusable.
rechazador, ra adj. Refusing, who refuses.
rechazamiento m. Refusal, repulse: *rechazamiento de una oferta*, refusal of an offer. || Rejection: *rechazamiento de una petición*, rejection of a petition. || Repelling, beating off (del enemigo). || Denial (negación).
rechazar v. tr. To refuse, to reject, to turn down: *rechazar una oferta*, to refuse an offer. || To repulse, to repel, to drive back: *rechazar un ataque, al enemigo*, to repel an attack, the enemy. || To push back, to push away (empujar hacia atrás). || To reject: *rechazar una petición, un pretendiente*, to reject a petition, a suitor. || To refute (refutar). || To deny (negar). || To refuse (rehusar): *rechazar un regalo*, to refuse a present. || To resist (una tentación). || To reflect (la luz).
rechazo m. Rebound (rebote). || Recoil (de un arma). || FIG. Refusal, rejection (de una oferta). | Denial (negación). || MED. Rejection (de un trasplante). || *De rechazo*, indirectly, consequently (como consecuencia), as it richocheted (una bala), on the rebound (una pelota).
rechifla f. Long whistle (sonido). || FIG. Derision, mockery (burla). | Booing, jeering (abucheo). || FIG. *Se retiró en medio de una rechifla*, he withdrew amidst booing and jeering.
rechiflar v. tr. To whistle hard (silbar). || To hiss, to boo (abuchear).
— V. intr. To whistle, to hiss.
— V. pr. To make fun, to mock (burlarse).
rechinador, ra adj. Squeaky (rueda de carro, etc.). || Creaky (puerta, escalera, etc.). || Clanking, grinding, grating (máquina). || Grating, grinding, gnashing (dientes).
rechinamiento m. Squeaking (de una rueda, etc.). || Creak, creaking (de puerta, escalera, etc.). || Clanking, grinding (de máquina). || Grating, grinding, gnashing (de dientes).
rechinante adj. V. RECHINADOR.
rechinar v. intr. To squeak (chirriar). || To creak (una puerta, etc.). || To clank, to grate, to grind (máquinas). || To grind, to grate, to gnash (los dientes). || FIG. To do *o* to accept sth. reluctantly.
rechistar v. intr. To whisper (chistar). || *Sin rechistar*, without replying, without saying a word (sin contestar), without a murmur, without saying a word (sin protestar).
rechoncho, cha adj. FAM. Tubby, chubby, plump.
rechupado, da adj. FAM. Skinny (muy flaco).
rechupete (de) loc. FAM. Delicious, scrumptious (comida). | Marvellous, fabulous (muy bueno).
— Adv. *Le salió de rechupete*, he got on just fine, everything went really well for him. || *Pasarlo de rechupete*, to have a whale of a time.
red f. Net (para pescar, cazar). || Net: *red de tenis*, tennis net. || Network (ferroviaria, de carreteras, de

radio, de teléfono, de distribución). || ELECTR. Mains, *pl.* [U.S., house current]. || Network, netting, mesh (de hilos entrelazados). || Hairnet (redecilla). || Rack (de tren). || Chain (de almacenes). || Graph: *red de estadísticas*, graph of statistics. || FIG. Trap (trampa): *caer en la red*, to fall into the trap; *caer en las propias redes*, to be caught in one's own trap; *tender una red a uno*, to set a trap for s.o. | Ring, network: *red de espionaje*, spy ring. || — *Echar* or *tender las redes*, to cast one's net. || *Red barredera*, trawl. || *Red de alambre*, wire mesh *o* netting. || *Red de carreteras*, road network *o* system. || ANAT. *Red vascular*, vascular system.
redacción f. Writing (acción de escribir). || Wording (palabras empleadas). || Editing, redaction (preparación para publicar). || Drafting, drawing up (de un tratado, etc.). || Editorial staff (conjunto de redactores). || Editorial office (oficina). || Essay, composition (ejercicio).
redactar v. tr. To write (escribir). || To word (formular): *un texto mal redactado*, a badly-worded text. || To edit, to redact (preparar para publicar). || To draft, to draw up (un tratado, etc.). || To write, to compose (un ejercicio).
redactor, ra m. y f. Writer (escritor). || Editor (que prepara algo para publicación). || Subeditor (de periódico). || *Redactor jefe*, editor in chief (de cualquier publicación), editor (de periódico).
redada f. MAR. Casting [of nets]. | Catch, haul (pescado). || FIG. Raid, roundup (de la policía). | Gang, band (de ladrones). || FIG. *Hacer una redada en un sitio*, to raid a place.
redaño m. ANAT. Mesentery. || — Pl. FAM. Guts (valor).
redecilla f. Net, mesh, netting (tejido). || Hairnet (para el pelo). || String bag (para la compra). || Luggage rack (para el equipaje). || ZOOL. Reticulum (de rumiantes).
redecir v. tr. To repeat, to say again.
rededor m. Surroundings, *pl.* (contorno). || *Al* or *en rededor*, v. ALREDEDOR.
redención f. Redemption.
redentor, ra adj. Redeeming.
— M. y f. Redeemer. || — *El Redentor*, the Redeemer. || FIG. *Meterse a redentor*, to intervene (entrometerse).
redentorista m. Redemptorist.
redescuento m. COM. Rediscount.
redhibición f. JUR. Redhibition.
redhibir v. tr. To cancel the sale of [merchandise].
redhibitorio, ria adj. JUR. Redhibitory.
redicho, cha adj. Repeated. || Hackneyed (trillado). || FAM. Affected, pretentious, stilted (pedante).
rediente m. Redan (en fortificaciones).
¡rediez! interj. Good heavens!, Good God!
redil m. Fold, sheepfold. || FIG. Fold: *hacer volver al redil a una oveja descarriada*, to bring a lost sheep back to the fold.
redilear v. tr. To round up (el ganado).
redimible adj. Redeemable.
redimidor, ra m. y f. Redeemer.
redimir v. tr. To redeem: *redimir cautivos*, to redeem captives. || FIG. y JUR. To redeem.
— V. pr. To buy one's liberty. || FIG. To redeem o.s.
redingote m. Redingote.
rédito m. Interest, yield. || *Prestar dinero a rédito*, to lend money at interest.
redituable adj. Interest yielding, which yields interest.
redituar v. tr. To yield, to produce (una renta).
redivivo, va adj. Resuscitated, revived.
redoblado, da adj. Intensified, redoubled. || TECN. Reinforced. || MIL. *Paso redoblado*, double-quick march.
redobladura f. o **redoblamiento** m. Intensification, redoubling. || TECN. Reinforcing. | Clinching (de un clavo).
redoblante m. Side drum (tambor).
redoblar v. tr. To intensify, to redouble (reiterar): *redoblar sus esfuerzos*, to redouble one's efforts. || To clinch (un clavo). || To bend back, to fold (doblar). || To double: *redoblar una consonante*, to double a consonant. || To redouble (bridge). || *Redoblar sus gritos*, to scream even louder.
— V. intr. To roll, to beat (los tambores). || To play a roll on the drum (persona).
redoble m. Intensification, redoubling (redoblamiento). || Roll (del tambor). || Redouble (bridge). || *Hacer redoble*, to redouble (bridge).
redoblón m. Rivet.
redoma f. Flask (de química).
redomado, da adj. Sly, artful (astuto). || Utter, out-and-out, proper: *pícaro redomado*, utter scoundrel.
redomón, ona adj. *Amer.* Half broken-in, half-tamed.
— M. *Amer.* Horse which is half broken-in *o* half-tamed.
redonda f. (P.us.). Region (comarca). || Pasture (dehesa). || Round hand (letra manuscrita). || Roman type (letra de imprenta). || MAR. Square sail (vela). || MÚS. Semibreve. || — *A la redonda*, around: *diez leguas a la redonda*, ten leagues around. || FIG. *Se oía a un kilómetro a la redonda*, you could hear it a mile off.
redondamente adv. In a circle. || FIG. Categorically, flatly (rotundamente).
redondear v. tr. To round [off], to make round. || FIG. To round off, to make up to a round number: *redondear una cantidad*, to make a sum up to a round number. || *Redondear los bajos*, to level off the hem (de un traje).
— V. pr. To be *o* to become round (ser redondo). || FIG. To start living comfortably (enriquecerse).
redondel m. Circle (círculo). || Short cape (capa). || Arena, ring (en la plaza de toros).
redondez f. Roundness. || *En toda la redondez de la tierra*, on the face of the Earth, in the whole wide world.
redondilla f. Quatrain (poesía). || Round hand (letra).
— OBSERV. The *redondilla* is made up of four octosyllabics, rhyming in the pattern a b b a.
redondo, da adj. Round: *una mesa redonda*, a round table; *letra redonda*, round letter. || FIG. Whose four grandparents are of noble families. | Clear, straightforward (sin rodeos). | Flat (negativa). | Complete, all-round: *triunfo redondo*, complete success. || — FIG. y FAM. *Caerse redondo* or *en redondo*, to collapse, to fall in a heap (caerse de repente), to drop dead (morir). || *Cuenta redonda*, round sum. || *Dar una vuelta en redondo*, to turn right round. || *En redondo*, around (a la redonda). || *Negarse en redondo*, to refuse point-blank, to flatly refuse. || *Negocio redondo*, excellent deal *o* piece of business. || *Número redondo*, round number *o* figure. || *Tener cinco metros en redondo*, to be five metres round. || FIG. *Virar en redondo*, v. VIRAR.
— M. Circle.
redopelo m. Brushing against the nap. || *A* or *al redopelo*, against the nap.
redorar v. tr. To gild again, to regild.
reducción f. Reduction (aminoración). || MED. Setting (de un hueso). || *Amer.* Village of Indians converted to Christianity.
— OBSERV. The "reducciones" were Indian villages created by the Spanish missionaries during the colonization. The most famous were those of the *Misiones jesuíticas del Paraguay*.
reducibilidad f. Reducibility.
reducible adj. Reducible.
reducido, da adj. Reduced. || Limited (limitado). || Small (pequeño). || Limited, small, poor: *un rendimiento muy reducido*, a very poor yield. || Confined (espacio). || Low (precio). || Narrow (estrecho). || MIL. *Quinta de efectivos reducidos*, year in which there are few conscripts.
reducimiento m. Reduction.
reducir* v. tr. To reduce: *reducir en una cuarta parte*, to reduce by a quarter; *reducir a polvo*, to reduce to dust; *reducir al silencio*, to reduce to silence. || To reduce, to cut down (cantidad, duración, etc.). || To abridge (un texto). || To reduce, to bring down: *la tasa ha sido reducida del 10 al 5 por ciento*, the rate has been reduced from 10 to 5 percent. || To subdue (al enemigo, etc.). || QUÍM. y MAT. To reduce. || To convert (convertir). || MED. To set. || — *Reducir a la razón*, to make see reason. || *Reducir a prisión*, to send to prison. || *Reducir a su más mínima expresión*, to reduce to its lowest terms *o* simplest expression (matemáticas), to reduce to almost nothing.
— V. pr. To be reduced: *reducirse a lo más preciso*, to be reduced to the bare essentials. || To come [down] to, to boil down to, to amount to: *todo esto se reduce a nada*, all this comes down to nothing. || FIG. To limit *o* to confine o.s.: *tú te reduces a cumplir tu obligación*, you limit yourself to carrying out your duty. || FIG. *Esto se reduce a decir*, that is like saying, that boils down to saying.
reductibilidad f. Reducibility.
reductible adj. Reducible.
reducto m. Redoubt.
reductor, ra adj. TECN. y QUÍM. Reducing.
— M. QUÍM. Reducer, reducing agent. || Reducer (de velocidad).
redundancia f. Redundancy.
redundante adj. Redundant.
redundar v. intr. (P.us.). To overflow (rebosar). || To abound: *redundar en citas*, to abound with quotations. || — *Esto redundará en perjuicio de usted*, that will turn against you. || *Esto redundará en provecho de usted*, that will be *o* redound to your advantage. || *Redundar en*, to redound to.
reduplicación f. Intensification, redoubling (acción de reduplicar). || BOT. y GRAM. Reduplication.
reduplicado, da adj. Reduplicated. || BOT. y GRAM. Reduplicate.
reduplicar v. tr. To intensify, to redouble (redoblar). || To reduplicate.
reduplicativo, va adj. Reduplicative.
reedición f. Reissue.
reedificación f. Reconstruction, rebuilding.
reedificador, ra adj. Reconstructing, rebuilding.
reedificar v. tr. To reconstruct, to rebuild.
reeditar v. tr. To reprint, to reissue.
reeducación f. Reeducation.
reeducar v. tr. To reeducate.
reelección f. Reelection.
reelecto, ta adj. Reelected.
— M. y f. Reelected person.
reelegibilidad f. Reeligibility.

reeligible adj. Reeligible.
reelegido, da adj. Reelected.
— M. y f. Reelected person.
reelegir* v. tr. To reelect.
reembarcar v. tr. To reembark.
— V. pr. To reembark.
reembarco m. Reembarkation (de personas).
reembargar v. tr. JUR. To seize again.
reembarque m. Reshipment (de cosas).
reembolsable adj. Reimbursable, repayable. || Returnable (depósito).
reembolsar v. tr. To reimburse, to repay (a una persona). || To repay (dinero). || To refund, to return (depósito).
— V. pr. To recover (recuperar).
reembolso m. Repayment, reimbursement. || Refund (de un depósito). || *Enviar algo contra reembolso*, to send sth. cash on delivery *o* C.O.D.
reemplazable adj. Replaceable.
reemplazante m. y f. Replacement, substitute.
reemplazar v. tr. To replace, to substitute.
reemplazo m. Replacement. || Annual draft of recruits (quinta). || Replacement (en la milicia). || MIL. *De reemplazo*, reserve, from the reserve.
reemprender v. tr. To start again.
reencarnación f. Reincarnation.
reencarnarse v. pr. To be reincarnated.
reencuadernación f. Rebinding.
reencuadernar v. tr. To rebind (un libro).
reencuentro m. Collision (de cosas). || MIL. Clash, skirmish.
reenganchado m. MIL. Reenlisted soldier.
reenganchar v. tr. MIL. To reenlist.
— V. pr. MIL. To reenlist.
reenganche m. MIL. Reenlistment. | Reenlistment bonus (gratificación).
reengendrar v. tr. To regenerate.
reensayar v. tr. To test again, to retest, to try out again. || TEATR. To re-rehearse, to rehearse again.
reensayo m. Retesting (de máquina). || TEATR. Rehearsal, second rehearsal.
reenviar v. tr. To send back, to return (al sitio de procedencia). || To forward (reexpedir).
reenvidar v. tr. To raise [the bid] (juegos).
reenvío m. Forwarding (reexpedición). || Return (al sitio de procedencia).
reenvite m. Raised bid.
reestrenar v. tr. To revive, to put on again (teatro, cine).
reestreno m. Revival (teatro, cine).
reestructuración f. Reorganization.
reestructurar v. tr. To reorganize.
reexaminación f. Reexamination.
reexaminar v. tr. To reexamine.
reexpedición f. Forwarding. || *Se ruega la reexpedición*, please forward.
reexpedir* v. tr. To forward, to send on. || *Se ruega reexpedir al destinatario*, please forward.
reexportación f. Reexport.
reexportar v. tr. To reexport.
refacción f. Refection, snack (comida ligera). || Repair, repairs, *pl.* (reparación). || Extra, bonus (gratificación). || COM. Allowance.
refajo m. Petticoat, underskirt, slip (enagua). || Skirt (falda).
refección f. Refection (comida ligera). || Repair, repairs, *pl.* (reparación).
refectorio m. Refectory, dining hall.
referencia f. Reference. || Account, report (de un suceso). || — Pl. References (informes). || — *Con referencia a*, with reference to, concerning. || *Hacer referencia a*, to refer to, to make a reference to. || *Por referencias*, by hearsay.
referendario m. Countersigner.
referéndum m. Referendum.
referente adj. *Referente a*, concerning, regarding.
referible adj. Referable.
referir* v. tr. To recount, to tell of: *referir hechos interesantes*, to tell of interesting facts. || To refer (remitir). || To refer, to relate (relacionar). || To place, to refer: *refiere el suceso al primer mes de la guerra*, he places the event in the first month of the war.
— V. pr. To refer (remitirse): *esto se refiere a lo que te dije ayer*, this refers to what I told you yesterday. || To refer to, to mean, to be speaking about (aludir): *no me refiero a usted*, I am not referring to you. || GRAM. To agree. || *Por lo que se refiere a eso*, as for that, as regards that.
refilado m. IMPR. Trimming (con la guillotina).
refilar v. tr. IMPR. To trim.
refilón (de) loc. Briefly (de pasada): *ver algo de refilón*, to see sth. briefly. || Obliquely, sideways (de soslayo). || — *Chocar de refilón contra un coche*, to graze a car. || *Mirar de refilón*, to look at out of the corner of one's eye, to look askance at.
refinación f. Refining (refinado).
refinadera f. Stone roller for refining chocolate.
refinado, da adj. Refined: *azúcar refinado*, refined sugar. || FIG. Refined (distinguido).
— M. TECN. Refining: *el refinado del petróleo*, oil refining.
refinador, ra adj. Refining.
— M. y f. Refiner.
refinadura f. Refining.
refinamiento m. Refinement (esmero).
refinar v. tr. TECN. To refine (metal, azúcar, etc.). || FIG. To refine, to polish (el estilo).
— V. pr. To become refined. || TECN. To be refined.
refinería f. Refinery: *refinería petrolífera*, oil refinery.
refino, na adj. Very fine, extra fine (muy fino).
— M. Refining (refinado). || Grocer's (tienda de comestibles).
reflectancia f. FÍS. Reflectance.
reflectante adj. Reflecting: *superficie reflectante*, reflecting surface.
reflectar v. tr. FÍS. To reflect (reflejar).
reflector, ra adj. FÍS. Reflecting, reflective.
— M. Reflector. || Projector (proyector). || ELECTR. Spotlight. || MIL. y AVIAT. Searchlight.
reflectorizado, da adj. Reflecting, reflective (placa).
reflejado, da adj. Reflected: *rayo reflejado*, reflected ray.
reflejante adj. Reflecting, reflective: *superficie reflejante*, reflecting surface.
reflejar v. tr. To reflect: *el espejo refleja la luz*, the mirror reflects light. || FIG. To reflect, to reveal: *nuestros ojos reflejan nuestros sentimientos*, our eyes reflect our feelings. | To show, to reveal: *una cara que refleja bondad*, a face which shows goodness.
— V. pr. To be reflected. || FIG. To be reflected: *la felicidad se reflejaba en su rostro*, his happiness was reflected in his face; *el precio de la materia prima se refleja en el del producto acabado*, the price of the raw material is reflected in that of the finished product.
reflejo, ja adj. Reflected: *rayo reflejo*, reflected ray. || Reflexive (verbo). || Reflex (movimiento).
— M. Reflection: *reflejos en el agua*, reflections in the water. || Reflex: *reflejo condicionado*, conditioned reflex. || FIG. Reflection (imagen). || Gleam, glint (brillo). || Rinse: *darse un reflejo rojizo*, to give one's hair a red rinse. || Streak (efecto del sol en el pelo).
reflexibilidad f. Reflexibility.
reflexible adj. Reflexible.
reflexión f. FÍS. Reflection. || FIG. Reflection (acción de reflexionar). || — *Con reflexión*, on reflection. || *Sin reflexión*, without thinking, unthinkingly.
reflexionar v. intr. To reflect, to think: *reflexionar sobre un asunto*, to reflect on *o* to think about a matter; *reflexionar antes de actuar*, to think before acting.
reflexivamente adv. GRAM. In the reflexive form, reflexively. || Reflectively, thoughtfully (reflexionando).
reflexivo, va adj. Reflective, reflecting (que refleja). || Reflective, thoughtful: *un niño reflexivo*, a reflective child. || Considered (acción). || GRAM. Reflexive.
reflorecer* v. intr. To flower *o* to blossom *o* to bloom again. || FIG. To flourish again, to reflourish.
reflorecimiento m. Second flowering *o* blossoming *o* blooming. || FIG. Renaissance.
refluir* v. intr. To flow back (un líquido). || To redund (*en*, in), to lead (*en*, to) [dar lugar a].
reflujo m. Ebb (marea).
refocilación f. Enjoyment, delight.
refocilar v. tr. To amuse, to delight.
— V. pr. To enjoy o.s., to delight (alegrarse). || *Refocilarse con*, to enjoy, to delight in.
refocilo m. V. REFOCILACIÓN.
reforma f. Reform: *reforma agraria*, land reform. || REL. Reformation. || ARQ. Modification, change, alteration (modificación). || *Cerrado por reformas*, closed for repairs *o* improvements.
reformable adj. Reformable.
reformación f. Reform, reformation.
reformado, da adj. Reformed. || Modified, altered (cambiado). || Improved (mejorado).
reformador, ra adj. Reforming.
— M. y f. Reformer.
reformar v. tr. To reform. || To improve, to carry out improvements in, to renovate: *reformar una cocina*, to improve a kitchen. || To modify, to alter, to change (modificar). || To reorganize (una empresa, etc.). || To modify (un texto). || To alter (en costura).
— V. pr. To reform, to mend one's ways.
reformativo, va adj. Reformative.
reformatorio, ria adj./s.m. Reformatory. || *Reformatorio de menores*, remand home.
reformismo m. Reformism.
reformista adj./s. Reformist.
reforzado, da adj. Reinforced, strengthened.
— M. Tape, binding, ribbon.
reforzador, ra adj. Reinforcing, strengthening.
— M. FOT. Intensifier, intensifying agent. || ELECTR. Booster.
reforzar* v. tr. To reinforce, to strengthen: *reforzar un tubo, una pared*, to reinforce a tube, a wall. || FOT. To intensify. || MIL. To reinforce. || ELECTR. To boost. || *Reforzar el ánimo a*, to comfort, to encourage.
— V. pr. To be reinforced, to be strengthened.
refracción f. FÍS. Refraction: *ángulo de refracción*, angle of refraction. || *Índice de refracción*, refractive index.
refractar v. tr. FÍS. To refract.
refractario, ria adj. Refractory, heat-resistant (mal conductor del calor). || Fireproof (resistente al fuego). || FIG. Refractory. || — *Ser refractario a los cambios*, to be opposed *o* unamenable to change, to resist

change. || *Ser refractario a los idiomas,* to be a hopeless case where languages are concerned.
refractivo, va adj. Refractive.
refractómetro m. Refractometer.
refractor m. Refractor.
refrán m. Saying, proverb. || — FIG. *Según reza el refrán,* as the saying goes, as the proverb says. | *Tener refranes para todo,* to have an answer for everything.
refranero m. Collection of sayings *o* proverbs.
refranesco, ca adj. Proverbial.
refrangibilidad f. Refrangibility.
refrangible adj. Refrangible.
refranista m. y f. Person who is fond of quoting proverbs.
refregadura f. o **refregamiento** m. V. REFREGÓN.
refregar* v. tr. To rub (frotar). || FIG. y FAM. To throw back at (un reproche). || FIG. *Refregar algo a alguien,* to go on at s.o. about sth., to rub sth. in.
refregón m. FAM. Rubbing, rub. | Mark (señal).
refreír* v. tr. To refry, to fry again (freír de nuevo). || To overfry (patatas, etc.), to overcook (carne).
refrenable adj. Suppressible, controllable.
refrenado, da adj. In check, restrained (un caballo, las pasiones).
refrenamiento m. Suppression, restraint, repression.
refrenar v. tr. To rein [in], to check (a un caballo). || FIG. To restrain, to keep in check, to curb, to suppress, to repress (las pasiones).
— V. pr. To restrain o.s.
refrendación f. Visa (de un pasaporte). || Countersigning (acción). || Countersignature (firma).
refrendador, ra adj. Countersigning.
refrendar v. tr. To visa, to stamp (un pasaporte). || To countersign, to endorse (legalizar). || To approve (una ley).
refrendario m. Countersigner.
refrendata f. Countersignature.
refrendo m. Visa (de un pasaporte). || Countersigning (acción de firmar). || Countersignature (firma). || Approval: *ley sometida al refrendo popular,* law submitted to popular approval.
refrescante adj. Refreshing.
refrescar v. tr. To refresh, to cool (líquidos, etc.). || FIG. To revive (recuerdos). | To brush up: *refrescar el inglés,* to brush up one's English. || FIG. *Refrescar la memoria,* to refresh one's memory.
— V. intr. To turn fresh: *el tiempo refresca,* the weather is turning fresh. || To freshen (el viento). || To be refreshing (un líquido). || *Esta tarde ha refrescado un poco,* the afternoon has turned a bit fresh.
— V. pr. To take some refreshment, to refresh o.s., to take a refreshing drink (beber algo fresco). || To get some fresh air, to take the air (tomar el fresco).
refresco m. Soft drink, cool drink (bebida). || Refreshment, snack (refrigerio). || — Pl. Refreshments. || — FIG. *De refresco,* fresh. || *Refresco de limón,* lemonade.
refresquería f. *Amer.* Refreshment room (bar).
refriega f. Clash, skirmish, fray (combate). || Scuffle (riña).
refrigeración f. Refrigeration. || Air conditioning (aire acondicionado). || Snack (comida). || Cooling (de un motor). || Chilling (de la carne). || *Refrigeración por aire,* air-cooling.
refrigerador, ra adj. Refrigerating.
— M. Refrigerator.
refrigerante m. QUÍM. Refrigerant (sustancia). | Cooler (recipiente). | Condenser (condensador).
— Adj. Refreshing (refrescante). || Refrigerating, cooling (que enfría).
refrigerar v. tr. To cool, to refrigerate (enfriar). || To refresh (refrescar). || To chill: *carne refrigerada,* chilled meat. || To air-condition (habitación, casa, etc.). || TECN. To cool (motor). | To refrigerate.
— V. intr. y pr. To refresh o.s. (una persona).
refrigerio m. Refreshing drink (bebida). || Snack, refreshment (comida). || FIG. Rest: *lugar de refrigerio,* place of rest. | Rest, peace: *refrigerio eterno,* eternal peace. | Relief (alivio). || *Se servirá un refrigerio durante el descanso,* refreshments will be served in the interval.
refringencia f. FÍS. Refringence.
refringente adj. FÍS. Refringent.
refringir v. tr. FÍS. To refract.
refrito, ta adj. Refried (frito de nuevo). || Over-fried (demasiado frito).
— M. FIG. y FAM. Rehash: *esta obra de teatro es un refrito,* this play is a rehash.
refrotar v. tr. V. REFREGAR.
refuerzo m. Reinforcement, strengthening. || Welt (en costura). || FOT. Intensifying (proceso). | Intensification (resultado). || TECN. Brace, support. || MIL. Reinforcement: *enviar refuerzos,* to send reinforcements.
refugiado, da adj./s. Refugee.
refugiar v. tr. To give refuge to.
— V. pr. To take refuge (de una tormenta, un peligro). || To take shelter (a causa de la lluvia).
refugio m. Refuge, shelter. || Refuge (de montaña). || Traffic island (en la calle). || FIG. Refuge. || — *Refugio antiaéreo,* air-raid shelter. || *Refugio atómico,* fallout shelter. || MIL. *Refugio de invierno,* winter quarters, *pl.*
refulgencia f. Refulgence, brightness, brilliance.
refulgente adj. Refulgent, shining, bright, brilliant.
refulgir v. intr. To shine, to glitter.
refundición f. Recasting. || FIG. Adaptation.
refundidor, ra m. y f. Adaptor, revisor (de libro, ley).
refundir v. tr. To recast: *refundir un cañón,* to recast a cannon. || FIG. To adapt, to rewrite: *refundir una obra,* to adapt a work.
refunfuñador, ra adj. Grumbling, grumpy, moaning.
— M. y f. Grumbler, moaner.
refunfuñadura f. Grumbling, moaning.
refunfuñar v. intr. FIG. y FAM. To grumble, to moan.
refunfuño m. Grumble, moan. || — Pl. Grumbling, *sing.,* moaning, *sing.* || *Déjate de refunfuños,* stop moaning, stop your moaning.
refunfuñón, ona adj. FAM. Grumbling, grumpy, moaning.
— M. y f. FAM. Grumbler, moaner, grouch.
refutable adj. Refutable.
refutación f. Refutation.
refutar v. tr. To refute: *refutar un argumento,* to refute an argument.
regadera f. Watering can: *alcachofa de regadera,* rose of a watering can. || Irrigation ditch (reguera). || FAM. *Está como una regadera,* he's as mad as a hatter.
regadero m. Irrigation ditch.
regadío, a adj. Irrigable: *tierras regadías,* irrigable lands.
— M. Irrigated land (campo). || Irrigation (de un terreno). || — *Cultivo de regadío,* irrigation farming. || *De regadío,* irrigable, irrigated.
regadizo, za adj. Irrigable.
regador, ra m. y f. Waterer.
regadura f. Watering, sprinkling.
regala f. MAR. Gunwale.
regaladamente adv. Comfortably: *estar regaladamente instalado en un sillón,* to be sitting comfortably in an armchair. || Extremely well (muy bien): *comer regaladamente,* to eat extremely well. || In luxury (vivir).
regalado, da adj. Given as a present. || Soft, delicate, dainty (suave). || Comfortable (con comodidades). || FIG. y FAM. Delicious, delightful (delicioso). | Dirt cheap (barato): *estos zapatos están regalados,* these shoes are dirt cheap. || — FIG. *No la quieren ni regalada,* they don't want it at any price, they don't want to know. | *No lo quiero ni regalado,* I wouldn't want it even as a gift. | *Tener* or *llevar vida regalada,* to lead a pleasant life (agradable), to live a life of luxury (lujosa).
regalar v. tr. To give: *¿qué le podemos regalar para su cumpleaños?,* what can we give him for his birthday?; *me regaló su reloj,* he gave me his watch. || To give away: *ya que no lo quería lo regalé,* I gave it away since I didn't want it any more. || To present, to present with: *le regalaron un cuadro al rey,* they presented the king with a painting, they presented a painting to the king. || To give, to give away: *con cada paquete regalan un vaso,* with each packet they are giving a free glass *o* they are giving away a glass. || To flatter (halagar). || To treat royally (tratar muy bien). || — *¿Qué te regalaron para tu cumpleaños?,* what did you get *o* what presents did you get for your birthday? || *Regalar a alguien con atenciones,* to lavish attentions on s.o. || *Regalar a alguien con un banquete,* to entertain s.o. with *o* to treat s.o. to a banquet. || *Regalar el oído,* to flatter: *cumplidos que regalan el oído,* flattering compliments; to be a pleasure to hear, to be a joy to the ear (música, etc.). || *Regalar la vista,* to be a pleasure to see, to be a joy to behold.
— V. pr. To regale o.s., to feast on: *regalarse con pasteles,* to regale o.s. with cakes, to feast on cakes. || To regale o.s., to indulge o.s., to look after o.s. (cuidarse bien). || *Regálate la vista con eso,* feast your eyes on that.
regalía f. Royal prerogative (prerrogativa real). || FIG. Privilege, prerogative. | Bonus (sueldo). || *Amer.* Present, gift (regalo).
regalismo m. Regalism.
regalista m. Regalist.
regaliz m. o **regaliza** f. Liquorice, licorice: *barra de regaliz,* licorice stick.
regalo m. Present, gift (obsequio): *dar de regalo,* to give as a present. || Pleasure, joy (placer): *esta música es un regalo para el oído,* this music is a joy to the ear. || Feast (festín). || Treat (alimento exquisito). || Comfort, ease (comodidad). || *Vivir con gran regalo,* to live a life of ease *o* of luxury.
regalón, ona adj. FAM. Comfort-loving (cómodo). | Delicate (delicado). || Spoilt, pampered (mimado). || *Vida regalona,* easy life, life of ease *o* of luxury.
regante m. Farmer who has the right to irrigate his fields from a certain ditch (dueño). || Labourer who waters the fields, waterer (empleado).
regañadientes (a) loc. Reluctantly, grudgingly, against one's will: *obedecer a regañadientes,* to obey reluctantly.
regañar v. intr. To argue, to quarrel (enfadarse). || To finish (entre novios): *he regañado con mi novio,* I have finished with my boyfriend. || To fall out

(entre amigos). || To moan, to complain, to grumble (quejarse). || To split [open] (frutas). || *Estar regañados*, to have fallen out (dos personas).
— V. tr. To tell off, to scold (reprender): *regañar a un niño*, to tell a child off. || To nag, to go on at (insistentemente).
regañina f. Scolding, telling off.
regaño m. Scolding, telling off.
regañón, ona adj. FAM. Grumpy, grouchy (que se queja). | Nagging (criticón). | Touchy, irritable (enfadadizo).
— M. y f. FAM. Moaner, grouch, grumbler.
regañuza f. Scolding, telling off (reprensión). || Quarrel (pelea).
regar* v. tr. To water (las plantas): *regar las flores*, to water the flowers. || To water, to irrigate (un campo). || To water (un río). || To wash (bañar la costa). || To hose down, to wash down, to water (la calle, etc., para limpiar). || To bathe: *regar una herida*, to bathe a wound; *regar con lágrimas*, to bathe with tears. || FIG. To pour (desparramar). | To sprinkle (rociar).
regata f. MAR. y DEP. Regatta, boat race. | Sailing: *aficionado a la regata*, fond of sailing. || Irrigation ditch (reguera).
regate m. Dodge, duck (del cuerpo). || DEP. Dribbling (con el balón), dodging (del cuerpo). || FIG. y FAM. Dodge.
regateador, ra adj. Haggling.
— M. y f. Haggler.
regatear v. tr. To haggle over (el precio). || To be mean *o* sparing with (dar con parsimonia): *regatear el vino*, to be sparing with the wine. || FIG. To deny: *no le regateo inteligencia*, I don't deny he is intelligent. || — *No les regatea ningún disgusto*, he gives them no end of trouble. || *No regatear esfuerzos*, to spare no effort.
— V. intr. To be awkward (poner dificultades). || To haggle (*sobre*, over) [el precio]. || DEP. To dribble (con el balón), to dodge, to duck (con el cuerpo). || MAR. To race.
regateo m. Haggling, bargaining (entre comprador y vendedor). || DEP. Dribbling (balón), dodging (del cuerpo). || FIG. y FAM. Awkwardness (dificultad). | Dodge (escapatoria).
regato m. Pool (charco). || Stream (arroyo).
regatón m. Tip (contera). || Ferrule (de un bastón, de un tubo).
regatón, ona adj./s. V. REGATEADOR.
regazo m. Lap: *el regazo materno*, the mother's lap. || FIG. Lap (refugio).
regencia f. Regency.
— Adj. inv. Regency: *estilo Regencia*, Regency style.
regeneración f. Regeneration (transformación). || TECN. Regeneration (del caucho). | Reclaiming, processing for re-use (de desechos).
regenerador, ra adj. Regenerative.
— M. y f. Regenerator.
regenerar v. tr. To regenerate (transformar). || TECN. To regenerate (caucho). | To reclaim, to process for re-use (desechos).
regenta f. Manager's wife. || Regent's wife. || Judge's wife. || Teacher (profesora).
regentar v. tr. To manage (dirigir). || To hold (cátedra). || To hold temporarily (un cargo). || FIG. To guide, to preside over (destino). || FAM. To boss.
regente adj. Ruling, governing. || — *Príncipe regente*, Prince Regent. || *Reina regente*, regent.
— M. y f. Regent (de un estado). || — M. Manager (director). || IMPR. Foreman. || Magistrate (magistrado).
regentear v. tr. To rule (con autoridad).
regiamente adv. Regally, royally.
regicida adj. Regicidal.
— M. y f. Regicide (asesino).
regicidio m. Regicide (crimen).
regidor, ra adj. Governing, ruling (gobernante). || Managing (dirigente).
— M. Manager (director). || Town councillor (concejal). || Stage manager (teatro). || Assistant director (en cine). || — F. Manageress. || Town councillor's wife (concejala).
regidoría o **regiduría** f. Town councillorship. || CINEM. Assistant directorship.
régimen m. Rules, *pl.*, regulations, *pl.* (reglas). || System (sistema). || MED. Diet, regimen (p. us.): *ponerse a régimen*, to go on a diet. || Régime, regime, system; *régimen político*, political régime. || Rule (gobierno). || GEOGR. Régime. || GRAM. Government. || TECN. Speed (velocidad): *régimen máximo*, top *o* full speed. | Normal running rate (marcha normal). || — MED. *Poner a alguien a régimen*, to put s.o. on a diet. || TECN. *Régimen de crucero*, optimum running speed (de máquina), cruising speed (de vehículo). || *Régimen de vida*, way of life.
— OBSERV. The plural of the word *régimen* is *regímenes*.

regimentar* v. tr. To regiment.
regimiento m. MIL. Regiment. || Town council (concejo). || Town councillorship (oficio). || Management (dirección). || Government (gobierno).
regio, gia adj. Royal, regal. || FIG. Royal, splendid.
región f. GEOGR. Region. || District, area, zone (zona). || ANAT. Region.
regional adj. Regional.
regionalismo m. Regionalism.
regionalista adj. Regionalistic, regionalist.
— M. y f. Regionalist.
regionalización f. Regionalization.
regionalizar v. tr. To regionalize.
regir* v. tr. To govern, to rule (una nación). || To direct, to manage, to control (una empresa). || To run, to be in charge of (un colegio). || To govern: *la ley de la oferta y la demanda rige el mercado*, the law of supply and demand governs the market. || JUR. To govern. || GRAM. To govern. || *Este verbo rige el acusativo*, this verb takes the accusative.
— V. intr. To be in force, to apply: *aún rige este decreto*, this decree is still in force. || MAR. To steer. || TECN. To work (funcionar). || — *El mes que rige*, the present month. || FIG. y FAM. *No regir*, to be crackers, not to be right in the head (estar loco): *este tipo no rige*, this bloke is crackers *o* is not right in the head; not to work (no funcionar): *mi reloj no rige*, my watch doesn't work. || *Que rigen*, prevailing (condiciones, precios, etc.).
— V. pr. To navigate, to be guided: *regirse por las estrellas*, to navigate by the stars. || FIG. To follow, to be guided: *se rige por su buen sentido*, he follows his common sense, he is guided by common sense.
registrado, da adj. Registered: *marca registrada*, registered trade mark.
registrador, ra adj. Registering. || Inspecting, examining, checking (que inspecciona). || *Caja registradora*, cash register.
— M. y f. Inspector, checker (que inspecciona). || — M. TECN. Recorder. || Registrar (fielato). || *Registrador de la propiedad*, person in charge of the registration of land.
registrar v. tr. To search: *registrar a un ladrón*, to search a thief; *me registraron todo el equipaje*, they searched all my luggage. || To search, to go through (cajón, bolsillos). || To inspect, to examine, to check (inspeccionar). || To register, to enter, to record (anotar en un registro). || To enter, to note, to write down (inscribir). || To register (matricular). || To record (grabar). || FIG. To note, to notice: *hemos registrado un aumento de la criminalidad*, we have noted a rise in the crime rate. || *La policía registró el barrio a fondo*, the police carried out a complete search of the area.
— V. intr. To search: *registró en el armario*, he searched in the wardrobe.
— V. pr. To search, to go through: *registrarse los bolsillos*, to go through one's pockets. || To be reported: *se han registrado disturbios*, disturbances have been reported. || To happen (ocurrir). || To enrol (matricularse). || To register (hacerse anotar).
registro m. Registration, registry, recording (transcripción). || Entry (en un libro). || Register (libro): *registro de hotel*, hotel register. || Roll, list (lista). || Record office (oficina). || Inspection, examination, checking (inspección). || Search, searching (en la aduana, de un lugar). || Bookmark (para señalar las páginas). || MÚS. Register (extensión de la voz o de un instrumento). | Stop (de órgano), pedal (de piano). || TECN. Inspection *o* observation hole (trampilla). | Manhole (abertura en el suelo). | Regulator (de reloj). || — *Registro central*, main register. || *Registro central de penados y rebeldes*, [police] records, *pl.* (servicio). || *Registro civil*, births, marriages and deaths register (libro), registry office, registry [U.S., register office] (oficina). || *Registro de antecedentes penales*, police record (boletín). || *Registro de erratas*, list of errata. || *Registro de la propiedad*, land register *o* records, *pl.* (libro). || *Registro del sonido*, sound recording. || *Registro de patentes y marcas*, patents office. || *Registro electoral*, voting register. || *Registro genealógico*, pedigree (animales). || *Registro mercantil*, business register. || *Registro parroquial*, parish record *o* register. || MÚS. *Registros de lengüeta*, reed stops. || FIG. *Tocar todos los registros*, to pull out all the stops, to try everything *o* every possibility (intentarlo todo).
regla f. Ruler, rule (utensilio). || Rule, regulation (reglamento, norma). || MAT. Rule: *regla de tres*, rule of three. || [Set] pattern, rule (modelo): *responder a una regla*, to follow a [set] pattern. || REL. Rule, order. || Instruction: *reglas para utilizar una máquina de escribir*, instructions for using a typewriter. || MED. Period (menstruación). || (P.us.). Moderation (moderación). || — *Con todas las reglas del arte*, according to the book. || *En regla*, according to the book: *batalla en regla*, battle fought according to the book; in order: *tener sus papeles en regla*, to have one's papers in order; *todo está en regla*, everything is in order. || *Estar en regla con las autoridades*, to be on the right side of the law *o* the authorities. || *Hacerse una regla de ser puntual*, to make a point of being punctual. || *La excepción confirma la regla*, the exception proves the rule. || *Obrar según las reglas*, to play by the rules. || *Por regla general*, generally, usually, as a rule. || *Regla de aligación*, alligation [rule]. || *Regla de cálculo*, slide rule. || *Reglas de la circulación*, traffic regulations. || *Reglas del juego*, rules of the game, laws of the game. || FIG. *Salir de regla*, to go too far, to go beyond the limits. || *Trazar*

una línea con la regla, to rule a line. || *Una excepción a la regla*, an exception to the rule.
reglado, da adj. Temperate, moderate. || *Papel reglado*, ruled *o* lined paper.
reglaje m. TECN. Checking (comprobación). | Overhaul (revisión). | Adjustment, adjusting (ajuste). || MIL. Correction (de la puntería).
reglamentación f. Regulation. || Regulations, *pl.*, rules, *pl.* (reglas).
reglamentar v. tr. To regulate.
reglamentario, ria adj. Required, prescribed, regulation. || Obligatory, compulsory (obligatorio).
reglamento m. Rules, *pl.*, regulations, *pl.* (en general). || Standing orders, *pl.* (de comisión, etc.). || Bylaw (estatuto).
reglar adj. Regular (religioso).
reglar v. tr. To rule [lines] (pautar). || To rule, to rule lines on (papel). || To regulate (someter a reglas). || TECN. To adjust, to regulate (ajustar). | To overhaul (revisar). | To check (comprobar). || MIL. To correct (puntería).
— V. pr. To be guided (*por*, by), to follow (dejarse guiar por). || To conform (*a*, to) [acomodarse].
regleta f. IMPR. Lead. || [Small] ruler (regla).
regletear v. tr. IMPR. To lead.
reglón m. Mason's rule (de albañil).
regocijado, da adj. Joyful, delighted, merry, happy.
regocijar v. tr. To delight, to gladden, to cheer (dar alegría). || To amuse (divertir).
— V. pr. To be happy *o* delighted, to rejoice (ante una noticia, etc.). || To laugh (reír). || To make merry, to enjoy o.s. (divertirse). || To delight, to take pleasure (*de*, in) [de las desgracias ajenas].
regocijo m. Happiness, joy, delight (felicidad). || Merriment, rejoicing (alegría general). || — Pl. Festivities, celebrations. || *Con gran regocijo mío*, much to my delight.
regodearse v. r. FAM. To get immense enjoyment *o* pleasure (*con*, out of), to delight (*con*, in): *regodearse con la lectura*, to get immense enjoyment out of reading. || To ogle [at] (con un espectáculo licencioso). || FIG. To delight, to get great satisfaction: *regodearse en* or *con la desgracia ajena*, to delight in other people's misfortunes, to get great satisfaction out of other people's misfortunes.
regodeo m. FAM. Delight, pleasure, joy: *comerse una perdiz con gran regodeo*, to eat a partridge with great delight. || FIG. Cruel delight (satisfacción maligna).
regoldar v. intr. FAM. To belch, to burp.
regoldo m. Wild chestnut.
regordete, ta adj. FAM. Tubby, plump.
regresar v. intr. To return, to come *o* to go back.
— V. tr. *Amer.* To return, to give back (devolver).
— V. pr. *Amer.* To return, to come *o* to go back.
regresión f. Regression, decline: *epidemia en regresión*, epidemic on the decline *o* in regression. || Drop (disminución): *regresión de las exportaciones*, drop in exports. || Return: *regresión a procedimientos antiguos*, return to former ways. || BIOL. y GEOL. Regression.
regresivo, va adj. Regressive (propenso a la regresión). || Backward (que hace retroceder).
regreso m. Return journey (viaje de vuelta): *un regreso fácil*, an easy return journey. || Return (vuelta). || *Estar de regreso*, to be back, to be home, to have come home (*de*, from).
regüeldo m. FAM. Belch, burp.
reguera f. Irrigation ditch. || MAR. Cable, mooring rope.
reguero m. Trail, trickle (señal): *un reguero de sangre*, a trail of blood. || Irrigation ditch (reguera). || *La noticia se propagó como un reguero de pólvora*, the news spread like wildfire.
regulación f. Regulation. || Adjustment. || Control: *regulación de los precios, de los nacimientos*, price, birth control; *regulación del volumen, del tráfico*, volume, traffic control. || *Regulación de un curso de agua*, regulation of a water course.
regulado, da adj. Arranged, orderly, in order (ordenado). || Regular (regular). || Regulated, adjusted (un aparato). || Controlled (precios, etc.)
regulador, ra adj. Regulating.
— M. Regulator. || TECN. Regulator, governor. | Throttle (de locomotora). | Control, control knob (de una radio o televisión): *regulador de volumen*, volume control.
regular adj. Regular: *movimiento, ritmo regular*, regular movement, rhythm; *clero regular*, regular clergy. || FAM. Not bad, reasonable, average (no tan malo): *es una película regular*, it is not a bad film; *¿qué tal está? — Regular*, what's it like? — Not bad. | In between (entre los dos): *¿te gusta el chocolate espeso o líquido? — Regular*, do you like your chocolate thick or runny? — In between. | Not too: *el agua estaba regular de fría*, the water was not too cold. | Average, run-of-the-mill: *un alumno regular*, an average student. || — FAM. *Estar regular*, to be so-so (ni bien ni mal). || *Por lo regular*, as a rule, generally. || FAM. *¿Y ella, qué tal es? — Regular*, and what is she like? — So-so *o* — Nothing special.
regular v. tr. TECN. To regulate, to adjust (un mecanismo). || To regulate (caudal, flujo). || To regulate (reglamentar). || To control (precios, el mercado). || To regulate, to control (cambios, etc.). || *Regular la circulación*, to control *o* to direct traffic.
regularidad f. Regularity. || *Con regularidad*, regularly.
regularización f. Regularization.
regularizar v. tr. To regularize.
regularmente adv. Regularly. || Not too badly (medianamente). || Usually, generally, as a rule: *regularmente voy al cine dos veces por semana*, I usually go to the cinema twice a week.
regulativo, va adj. Regulative.
régulo m. Regulus, kinglet, petty king (reyezuelo). || Basilisk (basilisco). || QUÍM. Regulus.
regurgitación f. Regurgitation.
regurgitar v. intr. To regurgitate.
regusto m. Aftertaste.
rehabilitable adj. Deserving of rehabilitation (que lo merece), capable of being rehabilitated (a quien se puede rehabilitar).
rehabilitación f. Rehabilitation. || Reinstatement (en un puesto).
rehabilitador, ra adj. Rehabilitative.
rehabilitar v. tr. To rehabilitate. || To reinstate (en un puesto).
rehacer* v. tr. To redo, to do again, to do over (volver a hacer). || To repeat (repetir). || To remake, to rebuild (reconstruir). || To repair, to mend (reparar). || To renew, to do up (renovar).
— V. pr. MED. To recover. || MIL. To rally.
rehacimiento m. Remaking, rebuilding (reconstrucción). || Repairing, mending (reparación). || Recovery.
rehala f. Herd *o* flock belonging to various owners.
rehecho, cha adj. Thickset (persona). || FIG. Rested (descansado). | Recovered (de una enfermedad o desgracia).
rehén m. Hostage: *lo tienen como rehén*, they are holding him hostage.
rehilandera f. Whirligig [U.S., pinwheel] (juguete).
rehilar v. intr. To shake, to quiver (temblar). || To whizz, to whiz (flecha).
— V. tr. To twist (retorcer).
rehilete m. Dart (flechilla). || Shuttlecock (juguete y juego). || Banderilla (banderilla). || FIG. Gibe, dig (dicho malicioso).
rehiletero m. TAUR. Banderillero.
rehogar v. tr. CULIN. To brown (dorar).
rehuir* v. tr. To avoid, to shun, to shy away from, to shrink from (evitar, esquivar).
— OBSERV. When the *u* in *rehuir* is stressed it has a written accent (rehúyo, rehúyes, rehúye, rehúyen).
rehumedecer* v. tr. To soak.
rehusable adj. Refusable.
rehusar v. tr. To decline, to refuse, to turn down (no aceptar). || To refuse (negarse): *rehusar trabajar*, to refuse to work. || To deny (negar).
— V. intr. To refuse.
reidor, ra adj. Jolly, merry (persona). || Laughing, happy (ojos, cara, etc.).
reimportación f. Reimportation.
reimportar v. tr. To reimport.
reimposición f. COM. Reimposition (de impuestos).
reimpresión f. Reprinting (operación). || Reprint (resultado).
reimpreso, sa adj. Reprinted.
reimprimir v. tr. To reprint.
reina f. Queen: *reina madre*, queen mother; *reina viuda*, dowager queen. || Queen [bee] (abeja reina). || Queen (dama en el ajedrez). || — *Reina claudia*, greengage (ciruela). || *Reina de belleza*, beauty queen. || *Reina de los prados*, meadowsweet (flor).
reinado m. Reign: *bajo el reinado de Enrique VIII*, in the reign of Henry VIII. || FIG. Reign.
reinante adj. Reigning, ruling. || FIG. Prevailing, reigning.
reinar v. intr. To reign, to rule: *reinar en* or *sobre España*, to reign over Spain. || FIG. To reign, to prevail. || — *Dividir para reinar*, to divide to rule. || *El rey reina pero no gobierna*, the king reigns, but does not rule. || *Reinaba un desorden total*, complete confusion reigned, the place was in utter chaos.
reincidencia f. Relapse.
reincidente adj./s. Recidivist.
reincidir v. intr. To relapse, to fall back (*en*, into).
reincorporación f. Reincorporation.
reincorporar v. tr. To reincorporate.
— V. pr. *Reincorporarse a*, to rejoin.
reineta f. Pippin (manzana).
reingresar v. intr. To return, to reenter.
reingreso m. Return, reentry.
reino m. Kingdom (de un rey). || Kingdom: *el reino de los animales*, the animal kingdom. || — *El reino de los cielos*, the kingdom of heaven. || GEOGR. *Reino Unido*, United Kingdom.
reinstalación f. Reinstatement (en un puesto). || Reinstallation (en un lugar).
reinstalar v. tr. To reinstate (en un puesto). || To reinstall.
reintegrable adj. Able to be reintegrated. || COM. Refundable, reimbursable, repayable.
reintegración f. Reintegration. || Reimbursement, refund, repayment (de dinero, etc.).
reintegrar v. tr. To reintegrate. || To reimburse, to refund, to pay back (dinero que se ha gastado):

reintegrar una suma a uno, to reimburse s.o. with a sum of money, to refund *o* to pay back a sum of money to s.o. || To reinstate, to reincorporate (reincorporar).
— V. pr. To rejoin (volver a formar parte de). || To return: *reintegrarse a su trabajo, a la patria*, to return to one's job, to one's native country. || To be paid back, to recover: *te reintegrarás de lo que me adelantaste*, you will be paid back what you lent me.

reintegro m. Reintegration. || Refund, repayment, reimbursement (de dinero). || Official stamps, *pl.* (pólizas). || Return of one's stake (lotería). || *Cobrar el reintegro*, to have the price of one's lottery ticket refunded.

reír* v. intr. To laugh: *echarse a reír*, to start laughing, to burst out laughing. || FIG. To laugh, to sparkle (los ojos). || — *Al freír será el reír* or *quien ríe el último, ríe mejor*, he who laughs last laughs longest. || *Dar que reír*, to be laughable *o* ridiculous. || *Reír a carcajadas* or *como un descosido*, to split one's sides laughing. || *Reír a mandíbula batiente*, V. MANDÍBULA. || *Reír con ganas*, to laugh heartily. || *Reír con risa de conejo* or *reír de dientes afuera*, to force a laugh *o* a smile. || *Reír para su capote* or *para su sayo* or *para su coleto* or *para sus adentros* or *a solas*, to laugh *o* to chuckle to o.s., to laugh *o* to chuckle up one's sleeve.
— V. tr. To laugh at: *reírle a uno las gracias*, to laugh at s.o.'s jokes.
— V. pr. To laugh: *no hay de que reírse*, there is nothing to laugh about. || To have a good laugh: *anoche me reí mucho con él*, I had a good laugh with him last night. || To laugh, to make fun (burlarse): *reírse de uno*, to laugh at s.o., to make fun of s.o. || FIG. To split (abrirse). || — *¡Déjeme que me ría!*, that's a good one! || FIG. *Me río yo de los peces de colores*, I'm alright, I'm laughing, I don't give a damn. || *Reírse de uno en su cara* or *en sus barbas*, to laugh in s.o.'s face.

reiteración f. Reiteration.

reiteradamente adv. Repeatedly.

reiterar v. tr. To reiterate, to repeat. || *Reiteradas veces*, repeatedly.

reiterativo, va adj. Reiterative. || Repetitive, repetitious. || GRAM. Frequentative.

reivindicación f. Claim (reclamación). || Vindication.

reivindicar v. tr. To claim (reclamar). || To vindicate (vindicar). || To restore (restablecer). || To recover (recuperar).

reivindicatorio, ria o **reivindicativo, va** adj. Vindicative.

reja f. Grating (alambrera). || Grill, grille (de ventana). || AGR. Ploughshare [U.S., plowshare] (del arado). || — AGR. *Dar una reja*, to plough [U.S., to plow]. || FAM. *Entre rejas*, behind bars (en la cárcel).

rejalgar m. MIN. Realgar.

rejilla f. Latticework (de ventana). || Screen (contra los insectos, etc.). || Grating (de una abertura, de la chimenea). || Grill, gridiron (de un horno). || Wickerwork (de una silla). || Brazier (para calentarse). || Grill (de ventilador). || Grid (de radio). || Luggage rack (para equipaje). || — *De rejilla*, wickerwork: *una silla de rejilla*, a wickerwork chair. || *Rejilla del radiador*, radiator grille (de un coche).

rejón m. TAUR. Lance. || Goad (garrocha).

rejonazo m. Thrust *o* jab of a lance.

rejoncillo m. Lance (rejón).

rejoneador m. Bullfighter on horseback.

rejonear v. tr. To fight on horseback (torear a caballo). || To wound with the lance (clavar el rejón al toro).
— V. intr. To fight [the bull] on horseback.

rejoneo m. Bullfight on horseback (corrida).

rejuvenecedor, ra adj. Rejuvenating.

rejuvenecer* v. tr. e intr. To rejuvenate.
— V. pr. To be rejuvenated, to rejuvenate.

rejuvenecimiento m. Rejuvenation.

relación f. Relation, relationship, connection (conexión): *guardar relación con*, to bear relation to. || Relation: *mantener relaciones amistosas*, to maintain friendly relations; *romper las relaciones diplomáticas*, to break off diplomatic relations. || List (lista). || Record (oficial). || Account, statement, report, relation (narración, relato). || Tale (de dificultades): *les hizo una relación de sus desgracias*, he told them his tale of woe. || Report (ponencia). || JUR. Summing-up, summary (de un juez). || MAT. Ratio (razón), proportion (proporción). || FIG. Relationship: *la relación entre la causa y el efecto*, the relationship between cause and effect. || GRAM. Relation. || — Pl. Acquaintances (personas conocidas). || Connections, contacts, powerful friends (personas influyentes). || — *Con relación a*, in *o* with regard *o* relation to (por lo que se refiere a), in relation to (en comparación con). || *Estar en buenas relaciones con*, to be on good terms with. || *Estar en relación con*, to be in contact with, to have dealings with (tener tratos con). || *Hacer relación a algo*, to refer to *o* to make reference to sth. || *No guardar relación alguna con*, to be out of all proportion to. || *Ponerse en relación*, to get in touch (entrar en contacto). || *Ponerse en relaciones*, to start courting (los novios): *se pusieron en relaciones hace un año*, they started courting a year ago; *se puso en relaciones con ella*, he started courting her. || TECN. *Relación de compresión*, pressure ratio. || *Relaciones comerciales*, trade relations. || *Relaciones de parentesco*, relationship, kinship, blood relationship. || *Relaciones públicas*, public relations. || *Sacar a relación*, to make reference to. || *Tener buenas relaciones*, to be well connected, to have powerful friends. || *Tener relaciones con*, to be in contact with, to have dealings with. || *Tener relaciones (con)*, to be courting, to be going out [with] (ser novio de, ser novios).

relacionable adj. Relatable.

relacionado, da adj. Concerning, regarding (que se refiere). || Related (*con*, to), connected (*con*, with) [que está ligado]. || — *Estar bien relacionado*, to have good connections, to be well connected. || *Todo lo relacionado a*, everything concerning *o* which concerns.

relacionar v. tr. To relate, to connect: *relacionar un hecho con otro*, to relate one fact to another, to connect one fact with another. || To put in touch: *relacionar a uno con otro*, to put s.o. in touch with s.o. else. || To relate, to give an account of, to report (hacer relación de un hecho).
— V. pr. To be related *o* connected (tener conexión). || To refer (referirse). || To get in touch (ponerse en contacto). || *En lo que se relaciona con*, with regard to.

relajación f. FIG. Laxity, looseness, slackness (efecto de relajar costumbres, disciplina, moral, etc.). | Relaxation (diversión). || Slackening, loosening (aflojamiento). || MED. Relaxing (de músculo). | Hernia (hernia). || Easing, relaxation: *relajación de la tensión internacional*, easing of international tension. || *Relajación de la autoridad*, slackening of authority.

relajado, da adj. Loose.

relajador, ra adj. Relaxing. || MED. Laxative.

relajamiento m. V. RELAJACIÓN.

relajante adj. Relaxing. || MED. Laxative.
— M. MED. Laxative.

relajar v. tr. To relax, to loosen: *relajar los músculos*, to relax one's muscles. || To slacken (una cuerda). || FIG. To relax, to slacken (autoridad, disciplina). | To weaken (moralidad). | To ease, to relieve (la tensión). | To be relaxing: *esta música relaja*, this music is relaxing.
— V. pr. To become lax, to weaken, to wane (la moralidad, disciplina, etc.). || To let o.s. go (viciarse). || To relax (descansar). || To slacken, to loosen (aflojarse). || MED. To sprain: *relajarse un tobillo*, to sprain one's ankle.

relajo m. *Amer.* Depravity, debauchery (depravación).

relamer v. tr. To lick.
— V. pr. To lick one's lips (una persona). || To lick its chops (un animal). || FIG. To put on one's warpaint, to paint one's face (pintarse las mujeres). | To smack one's lips (de júbilo). | To gloat, to brag (jactarse).

relamido, da adj. Prim and proper, affected (persona). || Affected (manera, estilo, etc.). || Finical, finicky (cuadro).

relámpago m. Lightning (fenómeno). || Flash of lightning (relámpago aislado). || Eclair (pastel). || VET. Leucoma (en el ojo). || — FIG. *Como un relámpago*, as quick as a flash, like greased lightning. || FOT. *Luz relámpago*, flash. || FIG. *Pasar como un relámpago por*, to flash through, to shoot through.
— Adj. Lightning: *visita relámpago*, lightning visit. || *Guerra relámpago*, blitzkrieg.

relampagueante adj. Sparkling, flashing, gleaming.

relampaguear v. intr. FIG. To sparkle, to flash, to gleam (brillar).
— V. impers. To thunder. || *Cuando relampaguea*, when there is lightning *o* a thunderstorm.

— OBSERV. Para traducir el verbo *relampaguear*, que no existe en inglés, se suelen emplear locuciones con los sustantivos *lightning* (relámpago) y *thunderstorm* (tormenta).

relampagueo m. Lightning (relámpagos). || Flash, glint, spark (centelleo).

relance m. Accident, coincidence (suceso casual). || Second round *o* hand (en los juegos de envite). || *De relance*, by chance.

relapso, sa adj. Who relapses [into crime, etc.]. || REL. Relapsed.
— M. y f. Backslider. || REL. Relapsed heretic.

relatador, ra m. y f. Narrator, teller.

relatar v. tr. To report, to relate, to recount (un suceso). || To tell, to narrate, to recount (un cuento).

relatividad f. Relativity: *teoría de la relatividad*, theory of relativity.

relativismo m. FIL. Relativism.

relativista adj./s. FIL. Relativist.

relativo, va adj. Relative. || — *En lo relativo a*, in *o* with regard to, as regards, as for, with relation to. || *Relativo a*, relative to.
— M. GRAM. Relative.

relato m. Story, tale (cuento). || Report, account (informe). || Narration, relating (acción de narrar).

relator m. y f. Narrator, teller (de un cuento). || — M. Rapporteur (ponente). || Reporter (en los tribunales).

relatoría f. Reportership (cargo de relator). || Reporter's office (oficina).

relé m. ELECTR. y RAD. Relay.

relectura f. Second reading, rereading.

releer v. tr. To reread, to read again.
relegación f. Relegation.
relegar v. tr. To relegate. || *Relegar al olvido una cosa,* to consign sth. to oblivion, to banish sth. from one's mind, to forget all about sth.
relente m. Evening dew (humedad). || Chill of the night air (frescura).
relevación f. JUR. Exoneration, exemption (de una obligación). | Release (de un contrato). || MIL. Relief.
relevador m. ELECTR. Relay.
relevante adj. Outstanding.
relevar v. tr. To paint in relief (pintar). || To carve in relief, to emboss (tallar). || To substitute for, to take the place of, to replace (sustituir a uno). || To relieve, to take over from (tomar el relevo de). || To exempt, to exonerate: *relevar a uno de una obligación,* to exonerate s.o. from an obligation. || MIL. To relieve (un centinela). || *Ser relevado de su mando,* to be relieved of one's command.
— V. pr. To take turns (turnarse).
relevo m. MIL. Relief, change. || Relay (deportes): *carrera de relevos,* relay race. || — *Caballos de relevo,* relay horses. || *100 metros relevos,* 100 metres relay. || *Relevo estilos,* medley relay (natación). || *Tomar el relevo de,* to relieve, to take over from.
relicario m. Reliquary, shrine (caja con reliquias). || Locket (medallón).
relieve m. Relief. || Embossing (estampado). || FIG. Prominence (importancia). | Social standing (categoría social). || — Pl. Leavings, leftovers, scraps (de comida). || — *Alto relieve,* high relief. || *Bajo relieve,* low relief, bas-relief. || FIG. *De relieve,* prominent, important. || *En relieve,* in relief. || *Formar relieve,* to stand out. || *Mapa en relieve,* relief map, map in relief. || *Medio relieve,* half relief, mezzo-rilievo. || *Película en relieve,* three-dimensional film. || *Poner de relieve,* to emphasize, to underline.
religión f. Religion. || Religiousness, piety (cualidad de religioso). || FIG. Religion, cult. || *Entrar en religión,* to take vows.
religiosamente adv. Religiously. || FIG. Religiously, scrupulously.
religiosidad f. Religiousness, religiosity, piety. || FIG. Religiousness, thoroughness, punctiliousness.
religioso, sa adj. Religious. || Religious, pious (piadoso): *hombre religioso,* religious man. || FIG.

RELIGIÓN, *f.* — RELIGION

I. Religiones, *f.* — Religions.

cristianismo *m.*	Christianity
cristiandad *f.*	Christendom
catolicismo *m.*	Catholicism
protestantismo *m.*	Protestantism
reforma *f.*	Reformation
luteranismo *m.*	Lutheranism
calvinismo *m.*	Calvinism
anglicanismo *m.*	Anglicanism
anabaptismo *m.*	Anabaptism
metodismo *m.*	Methodism
puritanismo *m.*	Puritanism
cuaquerismo *m.*	Quakerism
judaísmo *m.*	Judaism
islamismo *m.*	Islamism
brahmanismo *m.*	Brahmanism, Brahminism
budismo *m.*	Buddhism
paganismo *m.*	paganism
fetichismo *m.*	fetishism

II. El sentimiento (*m.*) religioso. — Religious feeling.

fe *f.*	faith
adoración *f.*	worship, adoration
devoción *f.*	devotion, devoutness
piedad *f.*	piety
oración *f.*, plegaria *f.*	prayer
invocación *f.*, advocación *f.*	invocation
ofrenda *f.*	offering
fervor *m.*	fervour [U.S., fervor]
misticismo *m.*	mysticism
contemplación *f.*	contemplation
bienaventuranza *f.*	blessedness
éxtasis *m.*	ecstasy
tentación *f.*	temptation
blasfemia *f.*	blasphemy
sacrilegio *m.*	sacrilege
anatema *m.*	anathema
profanación *f.*	profanation
impiedad *f.*	impiety
incredulidad *f.*	lack of faith
ateísmo *m.*	atheism
conversión *f.*	conversion

III. El mundo (*m.*) sobrenatural. — The supernatural.

Dios *m.*	God
el Salvador	The Saviour [U.S., The Savior]
el Espíritu Santo	The Holy Ghost, The Holy Spirit
ángel *m.*	angel
arcángel *m.*	archangel
querubín *m.*	cherubim, cherub
serafín *m.*	seraph
legiones (*f. pl.*) celestes	heavenly host
diablo *m.*, demonio *m.*	devil
el más allá	the beyond
paraíso *m.*	paradise
cielo *m.*	heaven
purgatorio *m.*	purgatory
infierno *m.*	hell
limbo *m.*	limbo
los elegidos *m. pl.*	the elect
los condenados *m. pl.*, los réprobos *m. pl.*	the reprobate
gracia *f.*	grace
alma *f.*	soul
visión *f.*	vision
aparición *f.*	apparition
misterio *m.*	mystery
milagro *m.*	miracle

IV. Libros (*m.*) sagrados. — Sacred Books.

la Biblia	the Bible
el Antiguo Testamento	the Old Testament
el Nuevo Testamento	the New Testament
el Evangelio	the Gospel
el Talmud	the Talmud
el Corán, el Alcorán	the Koran

V. Clero, *m.* — Clergy.

clero (*m.*) secular	secular clergy
clero (*m.*) regular	regular clergy
papa *m.*	pope
cardenal *m.*	cardinal
arzobispo *m.*	archbishop
obispo *m.*	bishop
canónigo *m.*	canon
sacerdote *m.*	priest
cura *m.*; cura (*m.*) párroco	vicar; parish priest
padre *m.*	father
vicario *m.*	vicar
monje *m.*	monk
religiosa *f.*, monja *f.*	nun
hermana *f.*	sister
pastor *m.*	protestant minister, pastor, clergyman
rabino *m.*	rabbi, rabbin
pope *m.*	pope
mitra *f.*	miter, mitre
báculo (*m.*) pastoral	crosier, crozier, staff
anillo (*m.*) pastoral	bishop's ring
casulla *f.*	chasuble
capa *f.*	cape
sotana *f.*	cassock

VI. Lugares (*m.*) del culto. — Places of worship.

abadía *f.*	abbey
santuario *m.*	sanctuary
catedral *f.*	cathedral
iglesia *f.*	church
templo *m.*	temple
basílica *f.*	basilica
capilla *f.*	chapel
convento *m.*	convent
monasterio *m.*	monastery
claustro *m.*	cloister
ermita *f.*	hermitage
colegiata *f.*	collegiate church
nave *f.*	nave
crucero *m.*	transept
altar (*m.*) mayor	high altar
coro *m.*	choir
cruz *f.*	cross
custodia *f.*, ostensorio *m.*	monstrance
sagrario *m.*	tabernacle
copón *m.*	ciborium, pyx
cáliz *m.*	chalice
incensario *m.*	censer, thurible
pila (*f.*) bautismal	font
pila (*f.*) de agua bendita	holy-water basin
hisopo *m.*	aspergillum
púlpito *m.*	pulpit
vidriera *f.*	stained glass window
rosetón *m.*	rose window
fresco *m.*	fresco
icono *m.*	icon
sinagoga *f.*	synagogue
mezquita *f.*	mosque
pagoda *f.*	pagoda

VII. Sacramentos, *m.* — Sacraments.

bautismo *m.*	baptism, christening
confesión *f.*	confession
comunión *f.*	Communion
confirmación *f.*	confirmation
orden *f.*	order
matrimonio *m.*	marriage
extremaunción *f.*	extreme unction

VIII. Oficios, *m.* — Offices, services.

misa *f.*	mass
misa (*f.*) mayor *or* cantada	High Mass, sung mass
misa (*f.*) rezada	Low Mass
vísperas *f. pl.*	vespers
sermón *m.*, plática *f.*	sermon
salmo *m.*	psalm
letanía *f.*	litany
cántico *m.*	canticle
Vía Crucis *m.*	Via Crucis, Way of the Cross
procesión *f.*	procession
rosario *m.*	Rosary

Conscientious, scrupulous, punctilious, religious (concienzudo, escrupuloso). || — *Cumplir con sus deberes religiosos*, to fulfil one's religious duties. || *Hacerse religioso, religiosa*, to become a monk, a nun, to take vows.
— M. Monk, religious (monje). || — F. Nun, religious (monja).

relimpio, pia adj. Spick-and-span, as clean as a new pin.

relinchador, ra adj. Neighing, whinnying.

relinchante adj. Neighing, whinnying.

relinchar v. intr. To neigh, to whinny.

relincho m. Neigh, whinny. || FIG. y FAM. Whoop [of joy] (grito de alegría). || *Dar relinchos*, to neigh, to whinny (el caballo).

relindo, da adj. Very pretty, lovely.

relinga f. MAR. Boltrope (de las velas). | Balk, baulk, headline (de una red de pescar).

relingar v. tr. MAR. To rope (una vela).
— V. intr. MAR. To flap (las velas).

reliquia f. Relic. || MED. Aftereffect, result (de una enfermedad). || — Pl. FIG. Remains, relics (restos, vestigios). || *Reliquia de familia*, family heirloom.

reloj m. Clock: *el reloj de la estación*, the station clock; *el reloj de la torre*, the clock on the tower; *dar cuerda a un reloj*, to wind up a clock. || Watch (reloj de pulsera). || — DEP. *Carrera contra reloj*, race against the clock. || FIG. *Marchar como un reloj*, to run *o* to work like clockwork (una cosa). || *Poner en hora un reloj*, to put a clock right. || *Reloj automático*, timer. || *Reloj de agua*, water clock. || *Reloj de arena*, sandglass, hourglass. || *Reloj de bolsillo*, pocket watch. || *Reloj de caja*, grandfather clock. || *Reloj de campana*, chiming clock. || *Reloj de cuco*, cuckoo clock. || *Reloj de péndulo*, pendulum clock. || *Reloj de pulsera*, wristwatch, watch. || *Reloj de sol* or *solar*, sundial. || *Reloj despertador*, alarm clock. || *Reloj parlante*, talking clock. || *Reloj registrador*, time clock.

relojería f. Watchmaking, clockmaking (arte). || Watchmaker's, clockmaker's, jeweller's (tienda). || — *Bomba con mecanismo de relojería*, time bomb. || *Mecanismo de relojería*, clockwork.

relojero, ra m. y f. Watchmaker, clockmaker.

reluciente adj. Shining, glittering, sparkling, gleaming (brillante). || Bonny, healthy-looking (sano).

relucir* v. intr. To shine: *el sol reluce*, the sun is shining. || To glitter, to gleam, to sparkle: *el agua reluce bajo el sol*, the water glitters in the sunlight. || FIG. To shine (destacarse). || — FIG. *No es oro todo lo que reluce*, all that glitters is not gold. || *Sacar a relucir*, to bring out (poner en relieve), to bring up (mencionar): *siempre saca a relucir todos los favores que me ha hecho*, he always brings up all the favours he has done me. || *Salir a relucir*, to come to light.

reluctancia f. ELECTR. Reluctance.

reluctante adj. Reluctant, unwilling (reacio).

relumbrante adj. Dazzling, resplendent, brilliant.

relumbrar v. intr. To shine, to sparkle, to gleam, to glitter. || To shine (el sol). || To dazzle (deslumbrar).

relumbrón m. Flash, glare (golpe de luz). || FIG. Flashiness, ostentation. || — FIG. *De relumbrón*, flashy. || *Vestirse de relumbrón*, to wear flashy clothes, to dress flashily.

rellanar v. tr. To level again.
— V. pr. To sit back (en un sillón).

rellano m. Landing (de escalera). || Shelf (en una vertiente).

rellenar v. tr. To fill in *o* out: *rellenar un formulario*, to fill in a form. || To fill (un pastel). || To stuff: *rellenar un pollo*, to stuff a chicken; *rellenar un sillón*, to stuff an armchair. || To pack, to stuff, to cram (un armario, una maleta, etc.). || To pad (en costura). || To fill in (un hueco). || To fill up (llenar completamente). || To refill, to replenish (llenar de nuevo). || To top up (algo parcialmente vacío). || AVIAC. To refuel. || FAM. To feed [s.o.] up (hartar de comida). | To pad out (un discurso, escrito, etc.): *¿por qué no cuentas unos chistes para rellenar?*, why don't you tell some jokes to pad it out?
— V. pr. To be filled in *o* up. || FAM. To stuff o.s.

relleno, na adj. Packed, stuffed, crammed, full up (completamente lleno). || Full: *cara rellena*, full face. || CULIN. Stuffed: *aceitunas rellenas*, stuffed olives. || Soft-centered (caramelos). || Cream (pasteles).
— M. Stuffing, filling (cocina). || Filling (acción de llenar). || Padding, stuffing, wadding (de un asiento). || Padding, wadding (en costura). || Filling-in (de un hueco). || Filler (material para rellenar). || Ullage (de los toneles). || FIG. Padding (parte superflua). || *Material de relleno*, filler.

remachado m. Riveting (acción).

remachador m. Riveter.

remachadora f. Riveting machine *o* hammer, riveter.

remachar v. tr. To rivet (un metal). || To clinch (un clavo). || FIG. To stress, to drive home: *remachar sus palabras*, to stress one's words. | To crown: *remachar su victoria*, to crown one's victory.

remache m. Riveting (del metal). || Clinching (de un clavo). || Rivet (roblón).

remador, ra m. y f. Rower.

remallar v. tr. To mend.

remanencia f. FÍS. Remanence.

remanente adj. FÍS. Residual, remanent (corriente, etc.). || Leftover, remaining, residual (que queda). || COM. Surplus.
— M. Remainder, remnants, *pl.*, remains, *pl.*, rest. || Balance (saldo). || Surplus (de la producción).

remangar v. tr. To turn *o* to roll up (el pantalón o las mangas). || To pull *o* to tuck up, to bunch (las faldas, etc.). || *Con la camisa remangada*, with one's shirt sleeves rolled up, in one's shirt sleeves.
— V. pr. To roll up one's sleeves (las mangas). || To tuck up: *se remangó las faldas*, she tucked up her skirt.

remansarse v. pr. To slow right down, to flow very slowly (río).

remanso m. Pool of still water (charca). || Backwater (agua estancada). || FIG. Sluggishness (lentitud). || FIG. *Un remanso de paz*, a haven of peace.

remar v. intr. To row: *remar contra la corriente*, to row against the current. || FIG. *Remar en la misma galera*, to be in the same boat.

remarcable adj. Remarkable.
— OBSERV. This word is a Gallicism for *muy notable*.

remarcar v. tr. To mark again (marcar otra vez).
— OBSERV. En inglés *to remark* significa sobre todo "observar".

rematadamente adv. Absolutely, utterly: *rematadamente malo*, absolutely awful.

rematado, da adj. Out-and-out, absolute, utter: *un pillo rematado*, an out-and-out rascal. || JUR. Convicted. || *Loco rematado*, v. LOCO.

rematador m. Goal scorer (en fútbol).

rematamiento m. V. REMATE.

rematante m. Highest bidder.

rematar v. tr. To put out of its misery (para que no sufra más): *rematar un caballo herido*, to put a wounded horse out of its misery. || To kill (matar). || To use up (agotar). || To finish off (en costura). || COM. To knock down (subasta). | To sell off cheap (venta). || FIG. To add the finishing touches to (perfeccionar): *rematar una labor*, to add the finishing touches to a piece of work. | To finish off (terminar): *remató su discurso con una anécdota*, he finished off his speech with an anecdote. | To crown: *el éxito remató sus esfuerzos*, his efforts were crowned by success. | To finish off (a alguien). || *Amer*. To pull up sharply (el caballo). || ARQ. To be at the top of, to top, to crown.
— V. intr. To end up: *el campanario remataba en punta*, the bell tower ended up in a point. || DEP. To shoot [at goal], to take *o* to have a shot [at goal] (en fútbol). || DEP. *Rematar de cabeza*, to head a goal. || FIG. *Rematar en*, to end in.

remate m. End (término). || Finishing touch (toque final). || ARQ. Finial, top. || DEP. Shot (fútbol). || Last stitch (en costura). || FIG. Crowning: *el remate de su carrera política*, the crowning of his political career. || JUR. Highest bid (puja). || *Amer*. Auction (subasta). || — *Como remate*, to top it all: *y como remate perdí mis papeles*, and to top it all I lost my papers. || *Como remate de*, to round off: *como remate de su actuación*, to round off his act. || FIG. *Dar remate a*, to round off: *dio remate a su viaje con la visita al centro de investigaciones nucleares*, he rounded off his journey with a visit to the nuclear research centre. || *De remate*, utterly (completamente), utter (completo). || *Loco de remate*, v. LOCO. || *Para remate*, to top it all. || *Por remate*, finally.

rematista m. *Amer*. Auctioneer.

rembolsar v. tr. V. REEMBOLSAR.

rembolso m. V. REEMBOLSO.

remedable adj. Imitable, mimicable.

remedador, ra adj. Imitating, mimicking.
— M. y f. Imitator, mimic.

remedar v. tr. To imitate, to copy (imitar): *remedar la voz de uno*, to imitate s.o.'s voice. || To mimic, to ape (para burlarse).

remediable adj. Remediable. || *Fácilmente remediable*, easily remedied.

remediador, ra adj. Remedial.

remediar v. tr. To remedy, to put right, to repair (daño, perjuicio). || FIG. To solve (resolver): *gritando no remedias nada*, you will not solve anything by shouting; *tu venida no remediará nada*, your coming will not solve anything. | To put a stop to, to do sth. about (evitar que continúe): *el gobierno debe remediar este estado de anarquía*, the government must put a stop to this state of anarchy. | To help (ayudar): *siento no poder remediarte*, I am sorry I cannot help you. || *No poder remediar*, not to be able to help: *no pude remediar el echarme a reír*, I could not help laughing out loud; *no lo puedo remediar*, I can't help it.

remedio m. Remedy, cure (contra la enfermedad): *remedio casero*, household remedy. || FIG. Remedy, solution. | Help, consolation, relief (ayuda, consuelo). || JUR. Recourse, remedy (recurso). || — *A grandes males, grandes remedios*, desperate ills call for desperate measures. || *Como último remedio*, as a last resort. || *El remedio es peor que la enfermedad*, the remedy is worse than the disease. || *Ella no tiene remedio*, she's a hopeless case. || FIG. *Ni para un remedio*, none at all: *no se encontraba una habitación ni para un remedio*, no rooms were to be found at all. || *No hay más remedio que*, all we (you, etc.) can do is, there is nothing left to do but. || *No hay remedio*, there is nothing we (you, etc.) can do about it. || *No tener más remedio*, to have no alternative *o* choice. || *No tiene remedio*, it's unavoidable (es inevitable), there's nothing we (you, etc.) can do about it (no tiene solucion). || *Poner remedio a*, to put a stop to, to do sth. about. || *¿Qué remedio me queda?*, what else can I do? || FIG. *Remedio heroico*, drastic measure. || *Sin remedio*, without fail (sin falta).

remedo m. Imitation (acción). || Imitation, copy. || Travesty, parody (plagio).

remembranza f. Memory, remembrance.

rememoración f. Recollection, remembrance.

rememorar v. tr. To recall, to remember.

rememorativo, va adj. Commemorative.

remendable adj. Mendable, repairable.

remendado, da adj. Patched: *pantalones remendados*, patched trousers. || Patchy (animales).

remendar* v. tr. To mend, to repair (arreglar). || To patch (echando remiendos). || To mend (zurcir). || To darn (calcetines). || To mend (una red). || FIG. To correct.

remendón, ona adj. Mending. || *Zapatero remendón*, cobbler, shoemender.
— M. y f. Mender. || Cobbler, shoemender (zapatero).

remensa f. V. PAYÉS.

remera f. Remex, quill feather.
— OBSERV. El plural de *remex* es *remiges*.

remero, ra m. y f. Rower.

remesa f. COM. Shipment, consignment (de mercancías). || Remittance (de dinero).

remesar v. tr. COM. To ship, to send, to consign (mercancías). | To remit (dinero). || (P.us.). To tear out, to pull out (la barba, el pelo).

remeter v. tr. To put back (volver a meter). || To tuck in: *remeter las sábanas, la camisa*, to tuck in the sheets, one's shirt.

remiendo m. Mending, repairing (acción de remendar). || Mend (parte remendada). || Patching (con un pedazo nuevo). || Patch: *echar un remiendo a un pantalón*, to put a patch on a pair of trousers. || IMPR. Job, piece of work. || FIG. Improvement (mejora). || — *A remiendos*, piecemeal. || FAM. *Echar un remiendo a una cosa*, to patch sth. up. || *No hay mejor remiendo que el del mismo paño*, if you want a thing done well do it yourself.

remige f. Remex (pluma).
— OBSERV. El plural es *remiges* en ambos idiomas.

remilgado, da adj. Fussy, finicky (con la comida). || Fastidious (exigente). || Affected (en el hablar, el vestir). || Prudish (moralmente). || *Hacer el remilgado*, to make a great fuss.

remilgarse v. pr. To be fussy *o* affected *o* prudish *o* fastidious (ser remilgado). || To put on an act (hacer gestos afectados).

remilgo m. Fastidiousness (exigencia). || Affectation. || *Andar con* or *hacer remilgos*, to make a fuss, to be fussy (ser melindroso), to be fastidious (ser exigente).

remilgoso, sa adj. *Amer.* V. REMILGADO.

remilitarización f. Remilitarization.

remilitarizar v. tr. To remilitarize.

reminiscencia f. Reminiscence.

remirado, da adj. Cautious, careful (prudente). || Prudish (moralmente). || Affected (afectado). || Fussy (con la comida).

remirar v. tr. To look over, to look at again, to have another look at (mirar de nuevo). || To look again and again at (mirar repetidas veces). || To take a close look at, to examine (mirar detenidamente).
— V. pr. To take great pains (*en*, over).

remisamente adv. Remissly, carelessly (negligentemente). || Begrudgingly (con poca voluntad).

remisibilidad f. Remissibility.

remisible adj. Remissible.

remisión f. Sending (envío). || Delivery (entrega): *la remisión de un paquete*, the delivery of a parcel. || REL. Remission, forgiveness: *la remisión de los pecados*, the remission of sins. || MED. Remission (de una enfermedad). || JUR. Remission (de una pena). || Reference: *texto lleno de remisiones*, text full of references. || Postponement (diferimiento). || — *No hay pecado sin remisión*, v. PECADO. || FIG. *Sin remisión*, without fail (sin remedio).

remisivo, va adj. Reference: *nota remisiva*, reference mark. || Remissive (que perdona).

remiso, sa adj. Remiss, slack (negligente). || Reluctant, unenthusiastic (reacio): *muchedumbre remisa a la hora de aplaudir*, a reluctant crowd when it comes to applauding. || *No ser remiso en*, to be ready and willing to.

remisor, ra m. y f. *Amer.* Sender.

remisorias f. pl. JUR. Transfer of a case to another court.

remisorio, ria adj. Remissive.

remite m. Sender's name and address.

remitencia f. MED. Remission.

remitente adj. Who sends. || MED. Remittent.
— M. y f. Sender: *devuélvase al remitente*, return to sender.

remitido m. Advertisement, announcement (en el periódico).

remitir v. tr. To send, to ship, to consign (enviar mercancías). || To remit (dinero). || To deliver (entregar). || To postpone (aplazar). || To remit, to forgive: *remitir los pecados*, to remit sins. || To refer: *el autor nos remite a la primera parte*, the author refers us to the first part. || JUR. To transfer (un caso). | To remit (una pena).
— V. intr. To subside: *ha remitido el temporal*, the storm has subsided. || To remit, to subside (fiebre). || To refer: *remitir a la página diez*, to refer to page ten.
— V. pr. To abandon o.s.: *remitirse a la Providencia*, to abandon o.s. to Providence. || To leave it: *remitirse a la decisión de otro*, to leave it to s.o. else's decision. || To refer: *me remito a las pruebas existentes*, I refer to the existing evidence; *remítanse a la primera página*, refer to the first page.

remo m. Oar (grande). || Paddle (pequeño). || Rowing (deporte). || (Ant.) Galley. || — Pl. FIG. Limbs (del hombre). | Legs (de los cuadrúpedos). | Wings (de aves). | Hardships (dificultades). || — *Barca de remo*, rowing boat [U.S., rowboat]. || *Ir a remo*, to row.

Remo n. pr. m. Remus.

remoción f. Removal. || Shake-up, reshuffle (cambio de personal). || *Remoción de tierras*, earthworks, *pl.*

remojar v. tr. To soak, to steep: *remojar garbanzos en agua*, so soak chickpeas in water. || To soak (la colada, el cáñamo). || To dip, to dunk: *remojar una galleta en el té*, to dip a biscuit in one's tea. || To soak again (volver a mojar). || To soak, to drench (involuntariamente). || FIG. y FAM. To celebrate, to drink to: *remojar un éxito*, to celebrate a success. || *Amer.* To tip (dar una propina). || FIG. y FAM. *Esto hay que remojarlo*, this calls for a celebration *o* for a drink.
— V. pr. To soak: *garbanzos que se remojan en el agua*, chickpeas soaking in water. || FIG. To get soaked *o* drenched.

remojo m. Soaking. || FIG. y FAM. Dip (baño): *darse un remojo*, to take a dip. || *Amer.* Tip (propina). || *Echar* or *dejar* or *poner a* or *en remojo*, to soak, to leave to soak (garbanzos, ropa, etc.), to let ride (un asunto).

remojón m. FAM. Soaking (acción de mojar mucho). | Cloudburst (lluvia): *¡qué remojón!*, what a cloudburst! || CULIN. Sop, piece of bread [soaked in milk, gravy, etc.].

remolacha f. Beet: *remolacha azucarera*, sugar beet. || Beetroot [U.S., beet] (encarnada y comestible). || *Remolacha forrajera*, mangel-wurzel.

remolachero, ra adj. Beet: *la industria remolachera*, the beet industry.
— M. y f. Beet grower (cultivador). || Worker in a beet factory (obrero).

remolcador m. MAR. Tug, tugboat. || AUT. Breakdown lorry.

remolcar v. tr. To tow, to take in tow. || FIG. To rope in: *remolcar a uno*, to rope s.o. in. || MAR. *Remolcar abarloado*, to tow alongside.

remoler* v. tr. To grind up.

remolinar o **remolinear** v. intr. y pr. To swirl, to eddy (agua). || To whirl, to spin (en el aire). || To mill around (la gente). || To crowd together, to throng (amontonarse).

remolino m. Swirl, eddy, whirlpool (del agua). || Whirl, whirlwind (del aire). || Whirl, cloud (de polvo, etc.). || Cowlick (de pelo). || Throng (masa de gente). || Milling (movimiento de la muchedumbre).

remolón, ona adj. Lazy, slack.
— M. Upper tusk (del jabalí). || — M. y f. Shirker, idler, slacker. || *Hacerse el remolón*, to shirk, to slack (eludir el trabajo), to refuse to budge (no moverse).

remolonear v. intr. To shirk, to slack.

remoloneo m. Shirking, slacking.

remolque m. Towing (acción de remolcar). || Towline, towrope (cabo). || Trailer (detrás de un coche). || Caravan [U.S., trailer] (de turismo). || — *A remolque*, on tow. || *Dar remolque a*, to tow. || *Grúa remolque*, breakdown truck. || *Ir a remolque de*, to be towed by (ser remolcado por), to be roped in by (ir forzado). || *Llevar a uno a remolque*, to take s.o. in tow (sentido propio), to rope s.o. in (obligar a seguir).

remonín, ina o **remonísimo, ma** o **remono, na** adj. FAM. Beautiful, gorgeous, adorable.

remonta f. Repair (reparación). || Leather patch (del pantalón de montar). || MIL. Remount.

remontar v. tr. To mend, to repair (remendar). || To overcome, to beat, to master (un obstáculo). || To beat up (la caza). || MIL. To remount (proveer de caballos). || *Remontar el vuelo*, to soar.
— V. pr. To go back: *remontarse hasta la época prehistórica*, to go back to prehistoric times. || To soar (pájaro). || HIST. To take to the hills (esclavos). || FIG. To soar (espíritu). || COM. To amount to (cantidad). || *El castillo se remonta al siglo XIV*, the castle dates back to *o* dates from the 14 th century.

remontista m. MIL. Remount serviceman.

remoquete m. FIG. Nickname (apodo). | Cutting remark, dig (dicho punzante). || Punch (puñetazo).

rémora f. ZOOL. Remora (pez). || FIG. Hindrance: *las viejas estructuras constituyen una rémora para el progreso*, old structures are a hindrance to progress.

remorder* v. tr. To gnaw (morder insistentemente). || FIG. To trouble, to worry, to give cause for remorse. || *El recuerdo de su crimen le remuerde la conciencia*,

his crime preys on his mind, he has a guilty conscience *o* he is full of remorse when he remembers the crime he committed.
— V. pr. To suffer remorse (sentir remordimiento). || To fret (preocuparse).
remordimiento m. Remorse: *estar torturado por el remordimiento*, to be tortured by remorse. || *Tener remordimientos*, to feel remorse.
remosquearse v. pr. FAM. To be wary (escamarse). || IMPR. To mackle.
remotamente adv. Remotely, vaguely: *lo recuerdo remotamente*, I can remotely remember it.
remoto, ta adj. Remote: *países remotos*, remote lands; *peligro remoto*, remote danger. || Vague (vago). || — *La remota Antigüedad*, the far-distant past. || *Ni la más remota posibilidad*, not the remotest chance.
remover* v. tr. To move (mover). || To remove (quitar). || To stir (el café, etc.). || To shake up (agitar). || To turn over, to dig up (la tierra). || FIG. To revive, to rake up: *remover recuerdos*, to revive memories. | To remove (a uno de su empleo). | To stir up (un asunto).
remozamiento m. Rejuvenation. || FIG. Brightening-up (de un vestido, etc.). | Bringing up to date, modernization (de las instituciones).
remozar v. tr. To rejuvenate. || FIG. To brighten up (una fachada, un vestido, etc.). | To bring up to date, to modernize (actualizar).
— V. pr. To be rejuvenated. || To look much younger (parecer más joven). || FIG. To be brightened up: *se ha remozado toda la ciudad para las fiestas*, the whole town has been brightened up for the celebrations.
remplazable adj. Replaceable.
remplazante m. y f. Substitute.
remplazar v. tr. V. REEMPLAZAR.
remplazo m. V. REEMPLAZO.
rempujar v. tr. FAM. To shove, to push.
rempujón m. FAM. Shove, push.
remunerable adj. Remunerable.
remuneración f. Remuneration.
remunerador, ra adj. Remunerating (que remunera). || Remunerative (rentable). || Rewarding (que da satisfacción).
— M. y f. Remunerator.
remunerar v. tr. To remunerate, to pay (pagar).
— V. intr. To be remunerative (ser rentable). || To be rewarding (ser satisfactorio).
remunerativo, va adj. Remunerative.
remuneratorio, ria adj. Remuneratory.
renacentista adj. inv. Renaissance: *estilo renacentista*, Renaissance style.
renacer* v. intr. To be reborn (nacer de nuevo). || BOT. To grow again (las plantas). | To bloom again (flores). || FIG. To revive (recobrar fuerzas). | To reappear (reaparecer). || FIG. *El día renace*, a new day is dawning.
renaciente adj. Renascent: *paganismo renaciente*, renascent paganism. || *El día renaciente*, the dawn of a new day.
renacimiento m. HIST. Renaissance. || Rebirth, revival (acción de renacer). || FIG. Recovery, rebirth (recuperación): *el renacimiento de una nación*, the recovery of a nation. | Revival (reaparición).
— Adj. inv. Renaissance (estilo).
renacuajo m. ZOOL. Tadpole. || FIG. y FAM. Shrimp (persona pequeña).
renal adj. Renal, kidney.
Renania n. pr. f. GEOGR. Rhineland.
renano, na adj. Rhenish, [of *o* from the] Rhineland, [of *o* from] the Rhine.
— M. y f. Rhinelander.
rencilla f. Quarrel (riña). || — Pl. Arguing, *sing.*, bickering, *sing.*, arguments (discusiones).
rencilloso, sa adj. Quarrelsome, peevish. || Resentful (rencoroso).
renco, ca adj. Lame (cojo).
rencor m. Rancour [U.S., rancor]. || Resentment (resentimiento). || *Guardar rencor a uno por algo*, to hold a grudge against s.o. *o* to bear s.o. malice because of sth.
rencoroso, sa adj. Rancourous [U.S., rancorous] (propenso a sentir rencor). || Resentful (dominado por el rencor).
rendajo m. ZOOL. Jay (arrendajo).
rendibú m. *Hacer el rendibú a uno*, to flatter s.o. (lisonjear), to treat s.o. well (obsequiar).
rendición f. Surrender: *la rendición de Breda*, the surrender of Breda. || Yield (rendimiento).
rendidamente adv. Submissively, obsequiously, humbly.
rendido, da adj. Surrendered (ciudad, pueblo, etc.). || Submissive (que se somete voluntariamente). || Obsequious, humble, submissive (obsequioso). || Worn-out, exhausted (muy cansado). || — *Admirador rendido*, devoted admirer. || *Rendido de amor por*, madly in love with.
rendija f. Crack: *mirar por la rendija de la puerta*, to look through the crack in the door.
rendimiento m. Yield: *este terreno tiene un rendimiento bajo*, this land has a low yield. || COM. Yield, return. || Output (lo que produce una máquina, un obrero, una fábrica). || TECN. Efficiency. | Performance (de un motor). || FIG. Obsequiousness (obsequiosidad). | Submission, submissiveness (sumisión). | Fatigue, exhaustion (gran cansancio).
rendir* v. tr. To defeat, to subdue, to conquer (derrotar). || To take (una fortaleza). || To surrender (entregar): *rendir la ciudad*, to surrender the town. || To dip (la bandera). || To produce, to yield (producir). || To yield (ganancia). || To yield, to bear (interest). || To bear (fruto). || To give, to render (las gracias). || To pay, to do (homenaje). || To give (una cuenta). || To hand over (la guardia). || To wear out, to exhaust (agotar): *este paseo me ha rendido*, this walk has worn me out. || To dominate (dominar). || To overcome (superar). || To vomit, to throw up (fam.) || — FIG. *Rendir cuentas*, to account for one's actions. || *Rendir culto a*, v. CULTO. || *Rendir el alma*, to give up the ghost. || *Rendir pleitesía a*, to pay tribute *o* hommage to.
— V. intr. To pay: *este trabajo no rinde*, this work does not pay. || To produce: *el negocio rinde para mantener una familia*, the business produces enough to support a family.
— V. pr. To surrender, to submit, to give in: *rendirse al enemigo*, to surrender to the enemy. || To give in, to submit (darse por vencido). || To wear o.s. out (cansarse). || MAR. To snap, to break (la verga). || — *Rendirse a la evidencia*, to bow to the evidence. || *Rendirse a la razón*, to listen to reason.
renegado, da adj. Renegade. || FAM. Gruff, bad-tempered (de mal carácter).
— M. y f. Renegade. || FAM. Nasty piece of work (de mal carácter).
renegador, ra adj. Blasphemous, profane.
— M. y f. Blasphemer.
renegar* v. intr. To renounce, to deny, to abjure: *renegar de su fe*, to renounce one's faith. || To disown: *renegar de su familia*, to disown one's family; *todos tus amigos renegarían de ti*, all your friends would disown you. || To blaspheme (blasfemar). || FAM. To swear (decir groserías). | To grumble (refunfuñar). | To complain (quejarse).
— V. tr. To deny strongly.
renegón, ona adj. FAM. Grumpy, grumbling (refunfuñón).
— M. y f. FAM. Moaner.
renegrido, da adj. Black (negro). || Blackened (ennegrecido).
rengífero m. ZOOL. Reindeer (reno).
renglón m. Line (escrito). || Item, heading (de una cuenta). || — FIG. *A renglón seguido*, straight away, immediately afterwards. | *Leer entre renglones*, to read between the lines. || *Poner unos renglones a alguien*, to drop s.o. a line.
renglonadura f. Ruled lines, *pl.*, ruling.
rengo, ga adj. Lame (cojo).
— M. y f. Cripple.
renguear v. intr. *Amer.* To limp (renquear).
renguera f. *Amer.* Limp (cojeo). | Lameness (cojera).
reniego m. Curse, oath (dicho injurioso). || Moaning, *inv.* (protestas).
renio m. Rhenium (metal).
reno m. ZOOL. Reindeer.
renombrado, da adj. Renowned, famous (famoso).
renombre m. Renown, fame (fama). || Nickname (sobrenombre). || *De renombre*, of renown, renowned, famous.
renovable adj. Renewable.
renovación f. Renewal (de un pasaporte, un contrato, un arriendo, votos, etc.). || Renovation (de una cosa en mal estado). || Decorating, redecoration (de una habitación). || Reorganization, shake-up (de personal).
renovar* v. tr. To renew: *renovar un pasaporte, votos, un contrato*, to renew a passport, vows, a contract. || To renew, to replace (el personal de una casa, el mobiliario, etc.). || To renovate (una cosa en mal estado). || To redecorate (volver a decorar): *renovar una habitación*, to redecorate a room. || To reorganize (una organización, etc.). || FIG. *Renovar la herida*, to open up an old wound.
— V. pr. To be renewed.
renquear v. intr. To limp, to hobble. || FIG. y FAM. To dither (vacilar).
renqueo m. Limp.
renta f. Income: *impuesto sobre la renta*, income tax; *renta per cápita*, per capita income. || Rent: *la renta del piso*, the rent for the flat; *renta de bienes raíces* or *de la tierra* or *del suelo*, ground rent. || National debt (deuda pública). || Interest, return (beneficio). || — *A renta*, on lease. || *Distribución de la renta*, distribution of wealth. || *Renta bruta*, gross income. || *Renta de una finca urbana*, rental value. || *Renta nacional*, national income. || *Renta pagada por el Estado*, interest on Government bonds. || *Renta pública*, national revenue. || *Renta vitalicia*, life annuity. || *Vivir de sus rentas*, to live on one's private income.
rentabilidad f. Profitability.
rentabilizar v. tr. To make profitable.
rentable adj. Profitable: *un negocio rentable*, a profitable business. || *Ya no es rentable*, it is no longer economic.
rentado, da adj. Of independent means.
rentar v. tr. To yield, to produce (rendir). || *Amer.* To let (alquilar).

rentero, ra m. y f. Tenant farmer (colono).
rentista m. y f. Bondholder, holder of Government bonds (accionista). || Person of independent means (que vive de sus rentas).
rentístico, ca adj. Financial: *reforma rentística*, financial reform.
renuevo m. Bot. Shoot, sprout. || Renewal (renovación). || Bot. *Echar renuevos*, to sprout.
renuncia f. Renunciation (*a*, of). || Jur. Waiver, renunciation (a un derecho, una queja, etc.). || Resignation (a un puesto). || *Hacer renuncia de*, to renounce.
renunciable adj. Renounceable.
renunciación f. o **renunciamiento** m. Renunciation.
renunciante adj. Renunciant, renunciative.
— M. y f. Renunciant.
renunciar v. intr. To give up, to abandon: *renunciar a un proyecto*, to give up a project; *renunciar a la lucha*, to give up the struggle. || Jur. To renounce (a una herencia, a la corona etc.). | To waive, to drop (una demanda). || To resign: *renunciar a su puesto*, to resign one's post. || To renounce, not to follow suit (en los naipes). || To withdraw (*a*, from) [en una competición].
— V. tr. To relinquish, to give up: *renunciar sus derechos en otro*, to give up one's rights in favour of s.o. else.
— V. pr. To deny o.s.
renuncio m. Renounce, failure to follow suit (naipes). || — Fig. y fam. *Coger en renuncio*, to catch out. || *Hacer renuncio*, to renounce, not to follow suit (naipes).
renvalsar v. tr. Tecn. To rabbet.
renvalso m. Tecn. Rabbet (en carpintería).
reñidamente adv. Bitterly (luchar).
reñidero m. Cockpit, cockfighting pit, pit.
reñido, da adj. On bad terms, at odds: *estar reñido con un amigo*, to be on bad terms with a friend. || Bitter, hard-fought (lucha, batalla). || Tough, hard-fought: *un partido muy reñido*, a very tough match. || Incompatible: *lo útil no está reñido con lo bello*, usefulness and beauty are not incompatible. || *En lo más reñido de la lucha*, in the thick of the struggle.
reñidor, ra adj. Quarrelsome. || Irritable (regañón).
reñidura f. Fam. Scolding, telling off, dressing down.
reñir* v. intr. To quarrel, to argue (disputar). || To fight (pelearse). || To fall out (enemistarse): *he reñido con mi novio, con mi familia*, I have fallen out with my boyfriend, with my family. || *Reñir por*, to fight for *o* over.
— V. tr. To tell off, to scold (reprender): *reñir a un niño*, to tell a child off. || To fight, to wage (una batalla).
reo m. y f. Jur. Defendant, accused (acusado): *absolver a un reo*, to acquit a defendant. | Culprit (persona culpable). | Criminal. || *Reo de Estado*, person accused of treason.
— M. Sea trout (pez).

— Observ. Note that the feminine form is *la reo* and not *la rea*.

reoca f. Fam. *Es la reoca*, that's the limit *o* the last straw (es el colmo), that's priceless (es muy gracioso).
reóforo m. Fís. Rheophore.
reojo (mirar de) loc. To look [at s.o. *o* at sth.] out of the corner of one's eye. || Fig. To look askance at (con enfado).
reómetro m. Rheometer.
reordenar v. tr. To rearrange.
reorganización f. Reorganization. || *Reorganización ministerial*, Cabinet reshuffle.
reorganizador, ra adj. Reorganizing.
— M. y f. Reorganizer.
reorganizar v. tr. To reorganize. || To reshuffle (el gobierno).
reostático, ca adj. Fís. Rheostatic.
reóstato o **reostato** m. Fís. Rheostat.
repanchingarse o **repantigarse** v. pr. To loll, to sprawl out: *repantigarse en un sillón*, to loll in an armchair.
repanocha f. Fam. V. reoca.
reparable adj. Repairable: *daño reparable*, repairable damage. || Noteworthy (digno de atención).
reparación f. Repair: *taller de reparaciones*, repair shop. || Repairing, mending (acción). || Fig. Reparation (compensación, satisfacción). || — *En reparación*, being repaired, undergoing repair. || *Hacer una reparación a*, to repair, to do a repair job on.
reparador, ra adj. Fig. Reparative (de una ofensa). | Refreshing: *sueño reparador*, refreshing sleep. | Fortifying (alimento, medicina). | Faultfinding (criticón).
— M. Repairman. || — M. y f. Fig. Faultfinder.
reparamiento m. Repair. || Fig. Reparation.
reparar v. tr. To repair, to mend, to fix (arreglar): *reparar un reloj*, to repair a clock. || Fig. To make amends for (una ofensa). | To make up for (remediar una falta). | To correct (corregir una falta). | To renew, to restore (las fuerzas). || To notice (notar): *reparar un error*, to notice a mistake. || To parry (un golpe).
— V. intr. To notice (ver): *no reparé en su presencia*, I did not notice his presence. || To pay attention [*en*, to], to take notice [*en*, of] (hacer caso): *nadie reparó en lo que decía*, nobody took any notice of what he was saying. || To think (reflexionar). || To realize (darse cuenta). || — *No repara en nada*, he stops at nothing. || *No reparar en gastos*, to spare no expense. || *Reparar en detalles*, to pay attention to details. || *Reparar en pelillos* or *en pormenores*, to be a stickler for details.
reparativo, va adj. Reparative.
reparo m. Repair. || Fault (falta): *Noel está siempre poniendo reparos a la cocina de Jill*, Noel is always finding fault with Jill's cooking. || Objection (objeción). || Parry (en esgrima). || Reservation, reserve: *aprobar una decisión con cierto reparo*, to approve a decision with some reservation. || Med. Remedy. || — *No andes con reparos*, no buts (no vaciles). || *No tener reparo en*, not to be afraid to, not to hesitate to: *no tenga nunca reparo en decir lo que usted piensa*, never be afraid to say what you think; *no tiene reparo en hacer cualquier cosa*, he is not afraid to do anything. || *Poner reparos a todo*, to raise objections to everything, to find fault with everything. || *Sin reparo*, without consideration.
reparón, ona adj. Faultfinding (criticón).
— M. y f. Faultfinder.
repartición f. Sharing out (reparto). || Division. || Parcelling out (de un terreno). || Distribution.
repartidor, ra m. y f. Distributor (el que reparte). || — M. Delivery man *o* boy (de compras). || — *Repartidor de la leche*, milkman. || *Repartidor de periódicos*, paperboy.
repartimiento m. Sharing out (reparto). || Distribution (distribución). || Jur. Assessment (del impuesto).
repartir v. tr. To share out, to apportion: *repartir una suma entre tres hombres*, to share out a sum of money between three men. || To partition (un país). || To give out, to hand out, to distribute: *repartir los premios*, to give out the prizes. || To deliver: *el cartero reparte el correo*, the postman delivers the mail; *repartir la leche*, to deliver the milk. || To serve out (comida). || To hand out, to deal out: *repartir golpes*, to hand out blows. || To deal (naipes). || To space out, to spread out (colocar en varios sitios). || To parcel out (un terreno). || Teatr. To cast. || Fig. y fam. *Repartir leña*, v. leña.
reparto m. Sharing out: *el reparto del dinero*, the sharing out of the money. || Division. || Parcelling out (de terrenos). || Distribution (distribución). || Partition, partitioning: *el reparto de Polonia*, the partition of Poland. || Delivery: *reparto del correo, de la leche*, delivery of the mail, milk delivery. || Teatr. y Cinem. Cast (actores). | Casting (distribución de papeles). || Deal (naipes). || — *Coche de reparto*, delivery van. || *Hacer el reparto del dinero*, to share out the money. || *Le tocó poco en el reparto*, he did not get a very big share. || *Reparto de premios*, prize-giving.
repasar v. tr. To go over [again], to reexamine (examinar de nuevo). || To revise, to go over (lección). || To go *o* to look over: *el actor repasó su papel*, the actor went over his part. || To check, to look over (para corregir). || To polish up (dar los últimos toques). || To glance over *o* through (leer superficialmente). || To mend (la ropa). || To check, to overhaul (una máquina). || To go over (pasar de nuevo): *repasar el cepillo por la madera*, to go over the wood with the plane.
— V. intr. To go back: *repasar por una calle*, to go back through a street.
repasata f. Fam. Scolding, telling off (reprimenda): *dar una repasata a uno*, to give s.o. a scolding.
repaso m. Revision (de una lección). || Check (de un aparato). || Mending (de la ropa). || Fam. Scolding, telling off (repasata). || — *Curso de repaso*, refresher course. || *Dar un repaso a*, to look over *o* through: *el actor dio un repaso a su papel*, the actor looked over his part; to mend (la ropa), to glance over *o* through (leer superficialmente), to add the finishing touches to (dar la última mano), to check, to overhaul (una máquina).
repatriación f. Repatriation.
repatriar v. tr. To repatriate.
— V. pr. To be repatriated. || To return to one's country (volver a su patria).
repechar v. intr. To go uphill.
repecho m. Steep slope (cuesta). || *A repecho*, uphill.
repelente adj. Repulsive, repellent, disgusting. || *Niño repelente*, little know-all.
repeler v. tr. To repulse, to repel (rechazar). || To reject (un argumento). || To repel (un ataque). || To throw out: *repeler a intrusos de su domicilio*, to throw intruders out of one's home. || To reflect: *el color blanco repele el calor*, white reflects heat. || To repel: *esta pintura repele el agua*, this paint repels water. || Fig. To repel (disgustar). | To disgust, to repel (asquear): *las arañas me repelen*, spiders disgust me.
— V. pr. To be incompatible.
repelo m. The wrong way [opposite direction to the nap] (de una tela). || Fibre [U.S., fiber] (de la madera). || Anat. Hangnail. || Fig. Repugnance, disgust (repugnancia). || *Darle repelo a uno*, to make one sick.
repeluco o **repelús** o **repeluzno** m. Shiver. || *Darle a uno repeluzno*, to give s.o. the shivers.

repellado m. Plastering-up.
repellar v. tr. To plaster up.
repensar v. tr. To reconsider, to think over.
repente m. FAM. Start (movimiento). | Fit: *un repente de ira*, a fit of rage *o* temper. | Sudden feeling: *me dio el repente que iba a suicidarse*, I had the sudden feeling that he was going to commit suicide. || *De repente*, suddenly.
repentinamente adv. Suddenly.
repentino, na adj. Sudden: *muerte repentina*, sudden death.
repentizar v. intr. MÚS. To sight-read, to play at sight. || To ad-lib, to improvise, to extemporize (improvisar).
repercutida f. V. REPERCUSIÓN.
repercusión f. Repercussion. || — *De amplia repercusión*, far-reaching. || *Un discurso que ha tenido mucha repercusión en el país*, a speech which had great repercussions in the country (consecuencias), a speech which caused a great stir in the country (reacciones).
repercutir v. intr. To resound, to re-echo, to reverberate (el sonido). || To rebound (rebotar). || *Repercutir en*, to have repercussions on, to affect (tener repercusiones).
— V. tr. To reflect.
— V. pr. To reverberate (el sonido).
repertorio m. Index, repertory (list). || TEATR. Repertoire, repertory: *poner en el repertorio*, to include in the repertoire.
repesar v. tr. To reweigh.
repesca f. Second chance to qualify [given to those eliminated in a competition].
repescar v. tr. To give a second chance to qualify.
repetición f. Repetition. || MÚS. Repeat. || — *Fusil de repetición*, repeater, repeating rifle. || *Reloj de repetición*, repeater, repeating watch.
repetido, da adj. Repeated: *repetidas ausencias*, repeated absences *o* absence. || — *En repetidas ocasiones*, on many occasions, many times. || *Repetidas veces*, many times, repeatedly, again and again.
repetidor, ra adj. Repeating. || *Alumno repetidor*, student who is repeating a year.
— M. y f. Lecturer (en la universidad). || Private tutor, coach (en privado). || TECN. Relay, booster station: *repetidor de televisión*, television relay. | Repeater (de teléfono).
repetir* v. tr. To repeat: *repetir una frase*, to repeat a sentence; *repetir un curso*, to repeat a year. || To recite: *repetir la lección*, to recite the lesson. || To do again (hacer de nuevo). || To start again (comenzar de nuevo). || To have a second helping of (un plato). || TEATR. To revive (reestrenar). || To re-echo (las palabras de otro).
— V. intr. To take a second helping (de un plato). || To repeat [on one]: *la sardina repite*, sardines repeat [on one]. || *Estar repetido*, to be duplicated (estar hecho dos veces), to be a double: *este sello está repetido*, this stamp is a double.
— V. pr. To repeat o.s. || To recur: *la epidemia se ha repetido tres veces este año*, the epidemic has recurred three times this year. || To come, to fall: *fiesta que se repite siempre en la misma fecha*, celebration which always comes on the same date. || To repeat [on one] (un sabor). || — *No ha habido que repetírselo dos veces*, he did not need to be told twice. || *¡Que no se repita!*, don't let it happen again! || *¡Que se repita!*, encore!, more!
repicar v. tr. To ring, to peal, to sound (las campanas). || To prick *o* to sting again (picar de nuevo). || To repique (en los naipes). || To mince finely (cortar).
— V. intr. To peal, to ring out, to chime (las campanas). || To beat (el tambor).
repintar v. tr. To repaint.
— V. pr. To make up, to lay on the makeup (maquillarse excesivamente). || IMPR. To mackle.
repipi adj. FAM. La-di-dah. || *Niño repipi*, precocious little horror.
repique m. Peal, ringing, chiming (de las campanas). || Repique (en los naipes).
repiquete m. Lively peal (de campanas).
repiquetear v. intr. To peal out (campanas). || To beat (tambor). || FIG. To pitter-patter: *la lluvia repiqueteaba en el tejado*, the rain pitter-pattered on the roof. | To drum (con los dedos en la mesa).
repiqueteo m. Lively peal (de campanas). || Beating (de tambor). || FIG. Pitter-patter (de la lluvia). || Rattle, clatter (de ametralladora, etc.).
repisa f. ARQ. Corbel. || Shelf (estante). || *Repisa de chimenea*, mantelpiece.
replantación f. Replanting.
replantar v. tr. AGR. To replant. | To transplant (trasplantar).
replantear v. tr. To lay out a ground plan of (un edificio). || To restate (un problema).
repleción f. Repletion.
replegable adj. Folding. || AVIAC. Retractable (tren de aterrizaje).
replegado, da adj. Replicate (doblado).
replegar* v. tr. To fold up (doblar). || AVIAC. To retract (el tren de aterrizaje).
— V. pr. MIL. To fall back.
repleto, ta adj. Crammed full, packed: *calle repleta de gente*, street crammed full of *o* packed with people. || Plump, chubby (rechoncho). || Full, full up, replete (ahíto). || *Bolsa repleta*, well-lined purse.
réplica f. Retort, rejoinder (contestación). || Replica (copia). || JUR. Replication. || *Sin réplica*, unquestionably (indiscutiblemente), speechless (cortado): *se quedó sin réplica*, he was left speechless.
replicar v. tr. To answer (contestar).
— V. intr. To retort, to answer, to rejoin (p.us.). || To argue, to answer back: *los niños deben obedecer sin replicar*, children should do as they are told without answering back.
replicón, ona adj. Argumentative (respondón).
repliegue m. Fold, crease. || MIL. Withdrawal. || FIG. Recess: *los repliegues del alma humana*, the recesses of the human mind.
repoblación f. Repopulation (de un país). || Restocking (de un río, un estanque). || *Repoblación forestal*, reafforestation [U.S., reforestation].
repoblar* v. tr. To repopulate (un país). || To restock (un río, un estanque). || To reafforest [U.S., to reforest] (con árboles).
repollo m. Cabbage (col). || Head (de lechuga).
repolludo, da adj. Round-headed (plantas). || FIG. Tubby (rechoncho).
reponer* v. tr. To put back, to replace (poner de nuevo). || To replace (sustituir). || To revive, to bring back, to put on again (obra de teatro). || To restore (salud). || To reply, to retort (replicar). || To replenish: *reponer las existencias*, to replenish one's stocks. || To restore (en un cargo).
— V. pr. To recover (salud). || *Reponerse de*, to recover from, to get over.
reportaje m. Report, article (en el periódico): *reportaje gráfico*, illustrated report. || RAD. Report, item.
reportamiento m. Restraint, control.
reportar v. tr. To transfer (en litografía). || To bring (proporcionar): *su participación sólo le ha reportado desgracias*, his taking part has only brought him misfortune. || *Reportarle beneficio a uno*, to benefit s.o.
— V. pr. To calm down (serenarse). || To restrain *o* to control o.s. (moderarse).
reporte m. News report *o* item. || [Piece of] gossip (chisme). || Transfer (litografía).
repórter m. Reporter.
reporteril adj. Reportorial.
reporterismo m. Reporting, journalism, news reporting.
reportero, ra m. y f. Reporter, news reporter.
reportista m. IMPR. Lithographer.
reposadamente adj. Calmly.
reposadero m. Ladle (en los hornos).
reposado, da adj. Rested, relaxed (descansado). || Calm (el mar). || Calm, peaceful (tranquilo). || Unhurried, steady (pausado).
reposapiés m. inv. Footrest (de moto, etc.).
reposar v. intr. To lie, to rest, to be buried (yacer). || To rest, to take a rest, to repose (p.us.): *después de comer suele reposar un rato*, after lunch he usually rests a while *o* he usually takes a little rest. || To relax (solazándose).
— V. intr. y pr. To settle (un líquido).
reposición f. Replacement. || Revival (teatro, cine). || Replenishment: *reposición de existencias*, replenishment of stocks. || MED. Recovery.
reposo m. Rest: *gozar de un bien merecido reposo*, to enjoy a well-earned rest; *un mes de reposo absoluto*, a month's complete rest. || — *Cuerpo en reposo*, body at rest. || *Tierra en reposo*, fallow land.
repostar v. intr. y pr. To stock up (reponer provisiones). || To refuel (buque, avión, etc.). || To fill up (coche).
repostería f. Confectioner's, cake shop (tienda). || Pantry (despensa). || Pastrymaking (arte u oficio).
repostero m. Pastrycook (pastelero). || Butler to the king (cargo palaciego). || Cloth ornamented with a coat of arms (paño).
repotente adj. FAM. *Me da la repotente gana de salir*, I realy feel like going out. | *No me da la repotente gana*, I just don't feel like it.
reprender v. tr. To reprehend, to reprimand: *le reprendió su mala conducta*, he reprehended him for his bad behaviour.
reprensible adj. Reprehensible.
reprensión f. Reprimand, reprehension.
reprensivo, va o **reprensor, ra** adj. Reproachful, reprehensive.
represa f. Dam (en un río). || Millpond (para un molino).
represalia f. Reprisal, retaliation. || *Tomar* or *ejercer represalias contra*, to take reprisals *o* to retaliate against.
represar v. tr. To dam (un río). || To hold back (las aguas). || FIG. To contain, to repress (reprimir).
representable adj. Representable. || Performable (obra de teatro).
representación f. Representation. || JUR. Representation. || TEATR. Performance.
— *En representación de*, as a representative of, representing. || JUR. *Heredero por representación*,

representative heir. || *Hombre de representación,* man of some importance *o* some standing.
representador, ra adj. Representing.
representante adj./s. Representative: *representante comercial, diplomático,* commercial, diplomatic representative.
— M. y f. Actor, actress (comediante).
representar v. tr. To present again (volver a presentar). || To represent: *este dibujo representa una casa,* this drawing represents a house; *representar un país,* to represent a country. || To stand for, to represent: *este símbolo representa el infinito,* this symbol stands for infinity. || TEATR. To play, to act (un papel): *representó muy bien su papel,* he played his part very well. | To perform, to play (una obra de teatro). || To look (aparentar): *no representa la edad que tiene,* he does not look his age; *representa unos cuarenta años,* he looks about forty [years old]. || To represent (equivaler): *libro que representa diez años de trabajo,* book which represents ten years' work. || To look worth: *este mueble no representa lo que te ha costado,* this piece of furniture does not look worth what you paid for it.
— V. pr. To imagine, to picture (imaginarse).
representativo, va adj. Representative.
represión f. Suppression. || Repression (psicológica).
represivo, va adj. Repressive.
reprimenda f. Reprimand, reprehension.
reprimible adj. Repressible, suppressible.
reprimir v. tr. To repress, to suppress. || To suppress, to quell (un levantamiento). || To hold back, to repress, to suppress (risa, llanto, etc.). || To repress (en psicología).
— V. pr. *Reprimirse de hacer algo,* to stop o.s. *o* to refrain from doing sth.
reprise f. AUT. Acceleration (poder de aceleración).
reprobable adj. Reproachable, reprehensible, reprovable.
reprobación f. Reprobation, reproof, reproval.
reprobado, da adj. Reprobate, damned (réprobo).
reprobador, ra adj. Reproachful, reproving, reprehensive.
reprobar* v. tr. To condemn, to reprobate (una acción): *repruebo toda clase de violencia,* I condemn violence of any kind. || To reproach, to reprove, to rebuke (a una persona): *reprobar a uno su comportamiento,* to reproach s.o. with his behaviour. || To disapprove [of] (desaprobar). || REL. To damn, to reprobate.
reprobatorio, ria adj. Reprobative, reprobatory.
réprobo, ba adj./s. Reprobate, damned.
reprochable adj. Reproachable.
reprochador, ra m. y f. Reproachful person.
reprochar v. tr. To reproach: *reprochar algo a alguien,* to reproach s.o. for *o* with sth.
— V. pr. To reproach o.s.
reproche m. Reproach, reproof: *aguantar reproches injustos,* to suffer unjust reproach.
— OBSERV. *Reproach* y *reproof* suelen emplearse en singular.
reproducción f. Reproduction. || MED. Recurrence (de una enfermedad). || *Derechos de reproducción,* copyright.
reproducible adj. Reproducible.
reproducir* v. tr. To reproduce: *reproducir un cuadro,* to reproduce a painting. || To reproduce, to breed (criar animales).
— V. pr. To reproduce. || MED. To recur (una enfermedad). || To reoccur, to happen again (ocurrir de nuevo).
reproductibilidad f. Reproducibility.
reproductividad f. Reproductivity.
reproductor, ra adj. ANAT. Reproductive. || Breeding (animal). || Reproducing: *máquina reproductora,* reproducing machine.
— M. y f. Breeder (animal).
reprografía f. Reproduction (de documentos, etc.).
repropio, pia adj. Balky, stubborn, restive (caballo).
reps m. Rep, repp (tela).
reptación f. Slither, crawl.
reptante adj. Slithering, crawling. || BOT. Creeping.
reptar v. intr. To slither, to snake, to crawl.
reptil adj. Reptilian, reptile.
— M. Reptile.
república f. Republic. || — *La República Argentina,* the Argentine Republic. || *La República Dominicana,* the Dominican Republic. || *República de las letras,* republic of letters.
republicanismo m. Republicanism.
republicanizar v. tr. To republicanize.
— V. pr. To be republicanized.
republicano, na adj./s. Republican.
repudiable adj. Repudiable.
repudiación f. Repudiation. || JUR. *Repudiación de la herencia,* renunciation *o* relinquishment of one's inheritance.
repudiar v. tr. To repudiate (a una mujer, una doctrina, etc.). || JUR. To renounce, to relinquish.
repudio m. Repudiation.
repudrir v. tr. To rot completely.
— V. pr. To rot away. || FIG. y FAM. To eat one's heart out, to pine away.

repuesto, ta adj. Replaced, put back (puesto de nuevo). || Restored (en un cargo). || Recovered (de salud).
— M. Provisions, *pl.,* food supplies, *pl.* (comestibles). || Supply: *tenemos buen repuesto de gasolina,* we have a good supply of petrol. || Spare part, spare (pieza). || Sideboard (mueble). || *De repuesto,* in reserve (en reserva), spare (de recambio): *rueda de repuesto,* spare wheel.
repugnancia f. Repugnance, aversion, disgust: *sentir repugnancia a* or *hacia,* to feel repugnance towards; *sentir repugnancia por,* to feel repugnance at. || Contradiction, opposition, incompatibility: *repugnancia entre dos teorías,* contradiction between two theories. || Reluctance (desgana). || *Las arañas me dan repugnancia,* I loathe *o* detest spiders.
repugnante adj. Disgusting, repugnant, repulsive, revolting.
repugnar v. intr. Not to be able to stand, to loathe, to detest: *los sapos me repugnan,* I cannot stand *o* I loathe toads. || To disgust: *me repugnó su comportamiento,* his behaviour disgusted me. || To hate: *me repugna tener que hacerlo,* I hate having to do it.
— V. tr. To hate (tener aversión).
— V. pr. To contradict each other.
— OBSERV. Nótese que para traducir el verbo intransitivo hace falta invertir la construcción en inglés.
repujado, da adj. TECN. Repoussé, embossed.
— M. TECN. Repoussé [work], embossing.
repujar v. tr. TECN. To emboss.
repulir v. tr. To repolish, to polish up (pulir de nuevo). || FIG. To spruce up, to dress up to the nines (acicalar).
— V. pr. FIG. To dress up to the nines, to spruce o.s. up.
repulsa f. Refusal, rejection (negativa). || Rebuff (a una persona).
repulsar v. tr. To reject (una pretensión). || To rebuff (a una persona).
repulsión f. Repulsion, repugnance (aversión). || Rejection (repulsa).
repulsivo, va adj. Repulsive (repelente).
repullo m. Jump, start (sobresalto). || *Dar un repullo,* to jump, to start.
repunta f. Headland, cape, point (cabo). || FIG. Slight sign, inkling (indicio).
repuntar v. intr. To turn (la marea).
— V. tr. *Amer.* To round up (el ganado).
— V. pr. To turn sour (el vino). || FIG. y FAM. To fall out (enfadarse).
repunte m. Turn (de la marea). || *Amer.* Roundup, rounding up (del ganado).
reputación f. Reputation.
reputado, da adj. Reputed: *bien reputado,* highly reputed. || *Mal reputado,* of ill repute.
reputar v. tr. To deem, to consider, to repute, to think (considerar): *le reputan de experto,* he is considered *o* deemed an expert, he is reputed *o* thought to be an expert.
requebrar* v. tr. To court (cortejar). || To flatter (lisonjear). || To break in tiny pieces (quebrar mucho).
requemado, da adj. Scorched, burnt, charred (quemado). || Tanned, brown, bronzed (la tez).
requemar v. tr. To scorch, to burn, to char (quemar). || To scorch, to parch (las plantas). || To burn (la lengua, el paladar). || MED. To inflame. || To tan, to bronze (la tez).
— V. pr. To scorch. || To scorch, to parch (las plantas). || FIG. To harbour resentment (reconcomerse).
requerible adj. Requisite.
requerido, da adj. Required, requisite. || JUR. Summoned, summonsed.
requeridor, ra o **requeriente** adj. Requiring.
— M. y f. Requirer. || JUR. Summoner.
requerimiento m. JUR. Injunction, summons (intimación). | Request (demanda).
requerir* v. tr. To urge, to beg, to call on, to ask, to request: *requerir a alguien para que haga algo,* to ask s.o. to do sth. || To need, to require, to call for (necesitar): *esto requiere mucha atención,* this needs a lot of attention. || To require, to call for: *las circunstancias lo requieren,* the circumstances require it; *esta conducta requiere castigo,* this behaviour calls for punishment. || To order (ordenar). || JUR. To summon (intimar). | To notify (avisar). || *Requerir de amores,* to court, to woo.
requesón m. Cottage cheese (queso). || Curd (cuajada).
requete pref. FAM. This prefix is often added to an adjective in Spanish to intensify it : *requetebueno,* really good; *es un requetetonto,* he is a complete fool; *requetelleno,* brimful, full to the top.
requeté m. "Requeté", Carlist volunteer. || Carlist forces, *pl.* (organización militar carlista).
requetebién adv. Marvellously, wonderfully.
requiebro m. Flattering *o* flirtatious remark, compliment (a mujeres). || MIN. Stamped *o* crushed ore. || *Decir requiebros a,* to flatter (lisonjear), to court (cortejar).
réquiem m. Requiem.
requirente adj. Requiring.
— M. y f. Requirer. || JUR. Summoner.
requisa f. Requisition (requisición). || Inspection.
requisar v. tr. To requisition.
requisición f. Requisition.

requisito, ta adj. Required, requisite. || JUR. Summoned.
— M. Requirement, requisite: *este documento satisface todos los requisitos*, this document fulfils all the requirements. || *Requisito previo*, prerequisite. || *Ser requisito indispensable*, to be absolutely essential.
requisitoria f. JUR. Requisition, demand.
res f. Beast, animal: *reses de matadero*, animals for slaughter. || Head, *inv.*: *rebaño de veinte reses*, flock of twenty head. || — *Amer. Carne de res*, beef. || *Res vacuna*, head of cattle.
— OBSERV. *Res* is applied only to large animals.
resabiado, da adj. Vicious (animales). || TAUR. Experienced (por haber sido toreado).
resabiarse v. pr. To become vicious (animales). || To fall into bad habits (personas).
resabido, da adj. Well-known (perfectamente sabido). || Pedantic (que se precia de sabio). || *Es sabido y resabido que*, it is a perfectly well-known fact that.
resabio m. Bad habit (vicio). || Unpleasant aftertaste (sabor desagradable).
resaca f. MAR. Undertow, undercurrent. || COM. Redraft. || FAM. Hangover: *tener resaca*, to have a hangover.
resalado, da adj. FIG. y FAM. Witty, charming.
resalir* v. intr. To protrude, to jut out.
resaltar v. intr. To stand out (destacarse): *las flores rojas resaltaban sobre el césped*, the red flowers stood out against the lawn. || To jut out (un balcón). || To rebound, to bounce (rebotar). || *Hacer resaltar*, to emphasize, to stress (subrayar hablando), to bring out, to set off: *el marco hacía resaltar la belleza del cuadro*, the frame set off the beauty of the picture.
resalte m. Ledge, projection (en la pared).
resalto m. Bounce, rebound (rebote). || Projection, protrusion (parte que sobresale).
resalvo m. BOT. Sapling.
resarcible adj. Indemnifiable. || Repayable (reembolsable).
resarcimiento m. Indemnification, compensation. || Repayment (reembolso).
resarcir v. tr. To indemnify, to compensate (indemnizar): *resarcir a alguien de una pérdida*, to indemnify s.o. for a loss. || To repay (reembolsar): *resarcir a uno de sus gastos*, to repay s.o.'s expenses.
— V. pr. To make up for: *resarcirse de una pérdida*, to make up for a loss.
resbalada f. *Amer.* Slide (resbalón).
resbaladero, ra adj. Slippery (resbaladizo).
— M. Skating rink, slippery spot (sitio resbaladizo). || Chute, slide (para la madera).
resbaladizo, za adj. Slippery. || FIG. Ticklish, delicate (delicado).
resbalador, ra adj. Sliding.
resbaladura f. Skid *o* slide mark.
resbalamiento m. V. RESBALÓN.
resbalante adj. Slippery.
resbalar v. intr. y pr. To slide (deslizarse): *resbalar en el hielo*, to slide on the ice. || To slip [over] (involuntariamente): *resbaló y se cayó*, he slipped and fell. || AUT. To skid (un coche). | To slip (el embrague). || To trickle (caer lentamente un líquido): *las gotas de lluvia resbalaban por los cristales*, the raindrops trickled down the windows. || FIG. To slip up (incurrir en un desliz).
resbalón m. Slide (voluntario). || Slip, slide (involuntario). || Skid (de un coche). || FIG. Slip, slipup (desliz). || *Dar un resbalón*, to slide, to slip.
resbaloso, sa adj. Slippery (resbaladizo).
rescaldar v. tr. To scald.
rescatable adj. Redeemable.
rescatador, ra m. y f. Redeemer. || Rescuer.
rescatar v. tr. To recapture, to recover: *rescatar una ciudad*, to recapture a town. || To recover, to rescue (a prisioneros). || To ransom (pagar por la libertad). || To save, to rescue (algo o alguien que está en peligro). || To pick up (astronautas). || To recover (recuperar). || To make up [for] (el tiempo perdido). || FIG. To rescue: *rescatar del olvido*, to rescue from oblivion.
rescate m. Recapture, recovery (de una ciudad). || Recovery, rescue (de prisioneros). || Ransom (dinero). || Picking up (de los astronautas). || Rescue (de gente en peligro). || Recovery (recuperación). || COM. Redemption. || *Exigir* or *imponer rescate por alguien*, to hold s.o. to ransom [U.S., to hold s.o. in ransom], to ransom s.o.
rescaza f. ZOOL. Scorpion fish, hogfish (pez).
rescindible adj. Rescindable, rescissible.
rescindir v. tr. To cancel, to rescind, to annul (un contrato).
rescisión f. Rescission, cancellation.
rescisorio, ria adj. Rescissory (que rescinde).
rescoldo m. Embers, *pl.* || FIG. Misgiving, lingering doubt (recelo).
rescripto o **rescrito** m. Rescript.
resecación f. Thorough drying, drying up, drying out.
resecar v. tr. MED. To resect (un órgano). || To dry up *o* out (secar mucho). || To parch, to scorch (las plantas).
— V. pr. To dry up, to parch. || *Se me reseca la boca*, my mouth is dry *o* parched.
resección f. MED. Resection.
reseco, ca adj. Very dry, parched. || FIG. Skinny (flaco).
reseda f. BOT. Reseda, mignonette (planta).
resedáceas f. pl. BOT. Resedaceae.
resentido, da adj. Resentful. || — *Estar resentido contra uno*, to bear resentment towards s.o., to be annoyed with s.o. || *Estar resentido por*, to resent, to be resentful of.
— M. y f. Resentful person.
resentimiento m. Resentment.
resentirse* v. pr. To feel the effects: *resentirse de una antigua herida*, to feel the effects of an old wound. || To be weakened (debilitarse): *la casa se resintió con la explosión*, the building was weakened by the explosion. || — *Resentirse con* or *contra uno*, to bear s.o. resentment, to be annoyed with. s.o. || *Resentirse de* or *por algo*, to take offence at sth., to resent sth. || *Resentirse de la pierna*, to still have a bad leg, to still have trouble with one's leg.
reseña f. Description (descripción). || Account (relación): *reseña histórica*, historical account. || Review, report, account (de periódico): *reseña de los libros recientemente publicados*, review of recently published books.
reseñar v. tr. To give a description of, to describe (describir). || To give an account of, to report on (dar informaciones sobre). || To review (una obra).
reserva f. Reservation, booking (en un hotel, tren, etc.): *reserva de habitaciones*, room reservation, reservation of rooms. || Reserve, stock (cosa reservada): *reservas de comida*, food reserves, stock of food. || COM. Reserves, *pl.*: *reserva de divisas*, foreign currency reserves. || Reservation: *reserva de indios*, Indian reservation. || Reserve (de animales). || REL. Reservation. || MIL. Reserve, reserves, *pl.* || Reservedness, reserve (de carácter): *nos acogió con su reserva habitual*, he received us with his usual reserve. || Reservation (salvedad): *acepto con ciertas reservas*, I accept, but with certain reservations. || — Pl. Reserves. || — *A reserva de*, except for. || *A reserva de que*, unless. | *Con la mayor reserva*, in the strictest confidence (confidencialmente). || *Con reserva*, reservedly. || *De* or *en reserva*, reserve, in reserve: *tropas de reserva*, reserve troops, troops in reserve; reserve: *provisiones de reserva*, reserve food supply. || *Guardar* or *tener en reserva*, to keep in reserve. || *Guardar reserva*, not to commit o.s. || *Reserva mental*, mental reservation. || *Sin reserva*, unreservedly, without reservation.
— M. y f. Reserve (deportes).
reservable adj. Reservable.
reservación f. Reservation.
reservadamente adv. Confidentially, in confidence.
reservado, da adj. Reserved: *tener plazas reservadas*, to have reserved seats. || Confidential (asunto). || Reserved (carácter).
— M. Reserved *o* private room (en un restaurante, etc.). || Reserved compartment (en un tren). || REL. Host kept in the ciborium.
reservar v. tr. To reserve: *reservar una parte de los beneficios para obras pías*, to reserve part of the profits for charity. || To reserve, to save, to keep: *reservó la mejor noticia para el final*, he saved the best news until last; *reserva tus consejos para ti*, keep your advice to yourself. || To reserve, to book (una habitación, un asiento en un tren, en el teatro, etc.). || To withhold, to reserve: *reservar su opinión*, to withhold one's opinion. || REL. To reserve.
— V. pr. To save o.s.: *me reservo para mañana*, I am saving myself for tomorrow. || To take it easy (cuidarse). || To reserve, to withhold: *reservarse el juicio acerca de algo*, to reserve one's judgment on sth.
reservativo, va adj. Reserve.
reservista m. MIL. Reserve, reservist.
reservón, ona adj. FAM. Very quiet *o* reserved. || TAUR. Hesitant, reluctant (el toro).
resfriado, da adj. Cooled, cold. || *Estar resfriado*, to have a cold (estar constipado).
— M. Cold (catarro): *coger un resfriado*, to catch a cold. | Chill (enfriamiento).
resfriadura f. VET. Cold.
resfriamiento m. Cooling (acción de enfriar). || MED. Chill (enfriamiento).
resfriante m. Cooler [of a still].
resfriar v. tr. To cool (enfriar). || FIG. To cool (moderar). || MED. To give [s.o.] a cold.
— V. intr. To cool [down].
— V. pr. MED. To catch *o* to get a cold (acatarrarse). | To catch *o* to get a chill (enfriarse). || FIG. To cool off (la amistad, las relaciones, etc.).
resfrío m. V. RESFRIADO.
resguardar v. tr. To protect, to shelter: *esta mampara nos resguarda del viento*, this screen shelters us from the wind. || To protect (amparar). || To safeguard (salvaguardar).
— V. pr. To protect o.s. || FIG. To be careful, to be wary, to take precautions (obrar con cautela).
resguardo m. Protection. || Safeguard, guarantee: *este documento le servirá de resguardo*, this document will be your safeguard. || Guarantee (bancario). || Counterfoil [U.S., stub] (de un talonario). || Receipt

(recibo). || Voucher (vale). || Frontier guard (aduana). || MAR. Sea room.
residencia f. Residence: *residencia veraniega*, summer residence. || Hall of residence [U.S., dormitory]: *residencia de estudiantes*, students' hall of residence. || Residential hotel (hotel). || Home (asilo): *residencia de ancianos*, old people's home. || Headquarters, *pl.* (de una organización). || Head office (de una compañía). || JUR. Impeachment (de un funcionario). || — *Interdicción de residencia*, prohibition from entering an area. || *Permiso de residencia*, residence permit. || *Tener su residencia*, to reside.
residencial adj. Residential.
residenciar v. tr. To impeach, to hold an enquiry into [s.o.'s] conduct (a un funcionario). || To call to account (a un particular).
residente adj. Resident, residing: *residente en París*, residing in Paris. || Resident: *médico residente*, resident doctor. || — *Ministro residente*, minister resident. || *No residente*, non-resident.
— M. y f. Resident.
residir v. intr. To reside, to live: *residir en Londres, en el campo*, to reside in London, in the country. || FIG. To lie, to reside: *ahí es donde reside la dificultad*, that is where the difficulty lies. || FIG. *Residir en*, to reside in, to rest with, to be vested in: *el poder legislativo reside en el Parlamento*, legislative power resides in Parliament.
residual adj. Residual, residuary. || — *Aguas residuales*, sewage, *sing.* || *Aire residual*, residual air.
residuo m. Residue (desecho, sobra). || QUÍM. Residuum. || MAT. Remainder. || — Pl. Waste, *sing.*, refuse, *sing.* (materiales inservibles). || Remains (restos).
resiembra f. Replanting, resowing.
resignación f. Resignation.
resignadamente adv. With resignation, resignedly.
resignado, da adj. Resigned.
resignar v. tr. To resign (un cargo). || To hand over (el mando).
— V. pr. To resign o.s.: *resignarse a vivir modestamente*, to resign o.s. to a modest life.
resignatario m. Resignee.
resiliencia f. FÍS. Resilience, resiliency.
resina f. Resin.
resinar v. tr. To tap [a tree] for resin (un árbol).
resinero, ra adj. Resin.
— M. Resiner (obrero).
resinoso, sa adj. Resinous.
resistencia f. Resistance: *resistencia pasiva*, passive resistance; *resistencia a la infección*, resistance to infection. || ELECTR. Resistance. || Endurance, stamina (aguante). || Strength (de los materiales). || Resistance, opposition (hostilidad): *el proyecto encontró mucha resistencia*, the plan met with a lot of resistance. || — *La Resistencia*, the Resistance (política). || *Oponer resistencia*, to offer resistance, to resist.
resistente adj. Resistant, resistent (que resiste). || Strong (material). || Hard-wearing (tela, superficie, etc.). || BOT. Hardy. || Indefatigable (incansable). || *Resistente a la presión*, resistant to pressure, pressure-resistant.
— M. Resistance fighter, member of the Resistance.
resistir v. intr. To resist: *resistir al ataque*, to resist the attack. || To have endurance *o* stamina: *¿ya estás cansado? Tú no resistes nada*, tired already? You have no stamina. || To last, to wear well (durar). || *El secador resiste todavía*, the hairdryer is still working.
— V. tr. To resist: *resistir la tentación*, to resist temptation. || To resist: *este producto no resiste el calor*, this product does not resist heat. || To bear, to endure, to stand (soportar): *no resisto el calor*, I cannot bear the heat. || To stand up to: *este libro no resistirá la crítica*, this book will not stand up to the critics. || To withstand (peso, presión, etc.). || To defy: *precio que resiste toda competencia*, price which defies all competition.
— V. pr. To struggle, to resist, to offer resistance (forcejear). || To refuse (negarse): *me resisto a hacer una cosa tan desagradable*, I refuse to do such an unpleasant thing. || — *Me resisto a creerlo*, I find it hard to believe. || *Se le resiste el inglés*, English gives him trouble.
resistividad f. ELECTR. Resistivity.
resma f. Ream (de papel).
resmilla f. One fifth of a ream, four quires (de papel).
resobado, da adj. Hackneyed, trite (trillado).
resol m. Glare *o* reflection of the sun.
resoluble adj. Soluble, solvable.
resolución f. Solution (de un problema). || Resolution (en una asamblea): *adoptar una resolución*, to adopt a resolution; *un proyecto de resolución*, a draft resolution. || Resolution, resolve, determination (determinación). || Decision. || — *En resolución*, in short, in summary, to sum up. || *Hombre de resolución*, man of decision.
resolutivamente adv. Resolutely, with determination.
resolutivo, va adj./s.m. Resolvent. || *Parte resolutiva*, operative part (de una resolución, de una ley).
resoluto, ta adj. Resolute (determinado).
resolutorio, ria adj. JUR. Resolutive, resolutory.
resolvente adj./s.m. Resolvent.
resolver* v. tr. e intr. To solve, to resolve: *resolver un problema*, to solve a problem. || To resolve, to settle (conflicto). || To overcome (dificultad). || To resolve, to decide: *resolvió marcharse*, he resolved to leave. || To resolve (descomponer). || MED. To resolve. || QUÍM. To dissolve. || JUR. To decide: *resolver a favor de uno*, to decide in s.o.'s favour. || *Resolver por unanimidad*, to resolve unanimously.
— V. pr. To be solved: *el problema se resolvió sin mucha dificultad*, the problem was solved without much difficulty. || To work out: *todo se resolverá con el tiempo*, everything will work out in time. || To end up: *las negociaciones se resolvieron en un compromiso*, the talks ended up in a compromise. || To resolve, to make up one's mind, to decide: *resolverse a salir*, to resolve to go out. || MED. To resolve.
resollar* v. intr. To breathe heavily, to breathe noisily (respirar con ruido). || To puff and blow (jadear). || FIG. y FAM. To show signs of life: *hace mucho tiempo que no resuella*, it's a long time since he showed any signs of life. || FIG. y FAM. *Sin resollar*, without a word (sin hablar).
resonador, ra adj. Resounding, resonant.
— M. Resonator.
resonancia f. Resonance. || Echo (eco). || MÚS. Harmony. || FIG. Importance. | Renown (fama). | Repercussions, *pl.* (consecuencias). || FIG. *Tener resonancia*, to cause a stir (un suceso).
resonante adj. Resounding, resonant (sonoro). || FIG. Resounding: *una victoria resonante*, a resounding victory.
resonar v. intr. To resound, to re-echo, to ring. || To resound (un cuarto vacío).
resoplar v. intr. To puff and blow, to breathe heavily (respirar con ruido). || To pant (por cansancio). || To snort, to puff and blow (por enfado).
resoplido o **resoplo** m. Heavy breathing (respiración fuerte). || Panting (jadeo). || Snort (de un caballo). || Snort (de enfado). || FIG. Sharp retort (contestación brusca). || — *El coche iba dando resoplidos*, the car chugged along. || *Llegamos a la cima dando resoplidos*, we arrived panting at the top.
resorber v. tr. To reabsorb.
— V. pr. To be reabsorbed.
resorción f. Reabsorption, resorption.
resorte m. Spring (muelle): *resorte espiral*, coil spring. || Springiness, elasticity (elasticidad). || — Pl. FIG. Strings: *tocar todos los resortes*, to pull all the strings one can. || FIG. *Conocer todos los resortes de algo*, to know all the ins and outs of sth.
respaldar m. Back (respaldo).
respaldar v. tr. To endorse, to indorse (escribir en el respaldo de). || FIG. To support, to back [up] (apoyar). | To back, to cover: *depósitos respaldados por el oro*, deposits backed by gold.
— V. pr. To lean [back]: *respaldarse contra un árbol*, to lean against a tree. || FIG. *Respaldarse en*, to base o.s. on.
respaldo m. Back (de silla). || Back, reverse side, verso (de un papel). || Endorsement, indorsement (lo escrito en el dorso). || FIG. Backing, endorsement, support (apoyo). | Backing (financiero).
respectar v. intr. To concern, to regard: *por lo que respecta a tu hermano, nos arreglaremos*, we shall sort sth. out as regards your brother *o* as far as your brother is concerned.
— OBSERV. Not to be confused with *respetar*, to respect.
respectivamente o **respective** adv. Respectively.
respectivo, va adj. Respective. || *En lo respectivo a*, as regards, with regard to.
respecto m. Respect. || — *Al respecto* or *a este respecto*, about *o* on the matter, in this respect: *me pidieron aclaraciones al respecto*, they asked me to shed some light on the matter. || *Con respecto a* or *respecto a* or *respecto de*, with regard to, as regards (en cuanto a), in relation to (con relación a). || *Respecto a mí*, as for me, as far as I am concerned.
résped m. [Forked] tongue (de las serpientes). || Sting (de la abeja).
respetabilidad f. Respectability.
respetable adj. Respectable. || *A respetable distancia*, from *o* at a respectable distance.
— M. FAM. Audience (público).
respetador, ra adj. Respectful.
respetar v. tr. To respect: *respetar a los superiores, la ley*, to respect one's superiors, the law. || To spare (conservar). || — *Hacerse respetar*, to command respect. || AUT. *Respetar la prioridad*, to give way.
— V. pr. To respect o.s., to have self-respect. || To be respected (la ley, etc.).
respeto m. Respect (*a*, for): *infundir respeto*, to inspire respect; *respeto a la ley*, respect for the law. || Consideration. || — Pl. Respects: *presentar sus respetos a uno*, to pay one's respects to s.o. || — *Campar por sus respetos*, to do as one pleases. || *De respeto*, respectable (respetable), spare (reservado). || *Faltar al respeto a uno*, to lack respect for s.o., to be disrespectful towards s.o. || *Por respeto a*, out of consideration for. || *Respeto de sí mismo*, self-respect.
respetuosidad f. Respect, respectfulness.
respetuoso, sa adj. Respectful. || *Dirigir sus saludos respetuosos a*, to pay one's respects to.

respingado, da adj. Turned-up: *nariz respingada*, turned-up nose.
respingar v. intr. To shy, to start (un animal). || To kick (persona). || To be higher on one side, to be lopsided (la falda, el abrigo).
respingo m. Start, jump: *pegar* or *dar un respingo*, to give a start.
respingón, ona adj. FAM. *Nariz respingona*, turned-up nose.
respirable adj. Breathable, respirable.
respiración f. Breathing, respiration: *respiración ruidosa*, noisy *o* loud breathing. || Breath (aliento): *perder la respiración*, to lose one's breath. || Ventilation (ventilación). || — *Cortarle a uno la respiración*, to take s.o.'s breath away, to leave s.o. breathless (un susto, una noticia, etc.), to wind s.o., to knock the breath out of s.o. (un golpe). || *Faltarle a uno la respiración*, to be breathless *o* out of breath: *al llegar al séptimo piso me faltaba la respiración*, when I got to the seventh floor I was out of breath. || *Respiración artificial*, artificial respiration. || *Respiración boca a boca*, mouth-to-mouth respiration, the kiss of life. || *Sin respiración*, breathless.
respiradero m. Ventilator. || Air vent *o* valve (orificio de aeración). || Snorkel (para pesca submarina). || Ventilation shaft (en una mina). || FIG. Breather, respite, rest (descanso).
respirador, ra adj. Breathing. || Respiratory: *músculos respiradores*, respiratory muscles.
— M. Respiratory muscle.
respirar v. intr. To breathe, to respire (p.us.): *todavía respira*, he is still breathing. || To breathe a sigh of relief, to breathe again (con alivio). || To get one's breath back: *dejar respirar a los caballos*, to let the horses get their breath back. || — FIG. *No dejar respirar a alguien*, not to give s.o. a moment's peace. | *No poder respirar*, to be up to one's neck (de trabajo). | *No respirar*, not to breathe a word. | *Sin respirar*, without stopping for breath, non-stop (sin descansar), without a word (sin hablar).
— V. tr. To breathe [in], to respire (p.us.). || To inhale. || FIG. To exude (olor). || FIG. *Respirar felicidad*, to ooze happiness.
respiratorio, ria adj. Respiratory. || *Aparato respiratorio*, respiratory system.
respiro m. Breathing (respiración). || FIG. Rest, breather, break (descanso): *tomarse un respiro*, to take a breather. | Break (tregua). | Peace, respite: *no dar respiro*, to give no peace. || — *Plazo de respiro de tres días*, three days' grace. || *Respiro de alivio*, sigh of relief.
resplandecer* v. intr. To shine: *el sol resplandece*, the sun shines. || To blaze, to glow (un fuego). || To glitter, to gleam (plata, etc.). || FIG. To shine, to glow: *su rostro resplandecía de felicidad*, her face shone with joy. | To shine, to stand out (sobresalir).
resplandeciente adj. Shining, resplendent. || FIG. Outstanding (sobresaliente). | Glowing, radiant, shining: *resplandeciente de salud*, glowing with health.
resplandecimiento m. Brilliance, brightness, resplendence.
resplandor m. Brightness, brilliance, resplendence: *el resplandor del sol*, the brightness of the sun. || Flash (momentáneo). || Blaze, glow (de llamas). || Glitter, gleam (de vidrieras, etc.). || FIG. Splendour.
responder v. tr. To answer.
— V. intr. To reply, to answer: *responder a una carta, una pregunta*, to reply to *o* to answer a letter, a question. || To answer, to respond to (a un llamamiento). || To answer: *responder a la amistad con grosería*, to answer friendliness with rudeness. || To answer back (replicar). || To answer (el eco). || To respond: *responder a un tratamiento*, to respond to a treatment; *no responde a mis súplicas*, he does not respond to my pleas. || To answer: *esta medida responde a una necesidad*, this measure answers a need. || To correspond [*a*, with] (corresponder). || To be responsible (ser responsable): *son los padres los que deben responder de la conducta de sus hijos*, the parents are responsible for their children's behaviour. || To take the responsibility (aceptar la responsabilidad). || To vouch (apoyar, confirmar): *yo puedo responder de lo que dice*, I can vouch for what he says. || — *Los mandos no responden*, the controls don't respond. || *Responder a las especificaciones, las necesidades*, to meet the specifications, the needs. || *Responder al nombre de*, to go by the name of, to be called. || *Responder a una descripción*, to fit a description. || *Responder a una obligación*, to honour an obligation. || *Responder por*, to vouch for, to guarantee (garantizar).
respondón, ona adj. Argumentative, cheeky, saucy.
responsabilidad f. Responsibility. || — *Cargar a uno con la responsabilidad de*, to make s.o. responsible for. || *Cargar con la responsabilidad de*, to take the responsibility for, to answer for. || *Responsabilidad limitada*, limited liability. || *Sociedad de responsabilidad limitada*, private company.
responsabilizarse v. pr. To take the responsibility.
responsable adj. Responsible (*de*, for). || JUR. Liable (*de*, for). | Responsible (de su conducta). || — *Hacerse responsable de algo*, to assume responsibility for sth. || *La persona responsable*, the person in charge (el encargado).
responso m. REL. Prayer for the dead.
responsorio m. REL. Responsory, response.
respuesta f. Answer, reply (contestación). || Response (reacción). || — *Dar la callada por respuesta*, not to deign to answer, to say nothing in reply. | *Tener siempre respuesta*, to have an answer for everything.
resquebradura f. Crack (grieta).
resquebrajadizo, za adj. Easily cracked, fragile, brittle.
resquebrajadura f. o **resquebrajamiento** m. Crack (grieta).
resquebrajar v. tr. To crack (barro, loza, etc.).
— V. pr. To crack.
resquebrar v. tr. To crack (resquebrajar).
resquemor m. Sting (en la boca). || FIG. Inner torment, uneasiness (desasosiego). | Remorse (remordimiento). | Resentment (resentimiento).
resquicio m. Chink, crack (abertura). || FIG. Opening, chance (ocasión). | Slight chance (posibilidad pequeña). || FIG. *Un resquicio de esperanza*, a glimmer of hope.
resta f. MAT. Subtraction (operación aritmética). | Remainder (resto).
restablecer* v. tr. To reestablish. || To restore (orden, monarquía).
— V. pr. To recover (de una enfermedad). || To be reestablished (una institución). || To be restored (orden, monarquía).
restablecimiento m. Reestablishment. || Restoration (del orden, de la monarquía). || Recovery (de salud).
restallar v. intr. To crack (el látigo). || To crack (crujir). || To crackle (el fuego). || To click (la lengua).
restallido m. Crack (de látigo). || Crackle (del fuego). || Click (de la lengua).
restante adj. Remaining. || *Lo restante*, the remainder, the rest.
restañadero m. Estuary (estuario).
restañadura f. o **restañamiento** m. Retinning (con estaño). || Stanching (de la sangre).
restañar v. tr. To retin (volver a estañar). || To resilver (espejo). || To stanch (sangre, herida).
— V. intr. To crack (restallar).
— V. intr. y pr. To stop bleeding (una herida).
restaño m. Stanching (de herida).
restar v. tr. MAT. To subtract, to take [away]: *restar dos de cinco*, to take two [away] from five, to subtract two from five. || To deduct, to take away (deducir). || FIG. To reduce, to lessen (autoridad, importancia, etc.). || To return (la pelota en el tenis).
— V. intr. To subtract, to do subtraction. || To remain, to be left: *es todo lo que resta de su capital*, it is all that is left of his capital; *no nos resta más que marcharnos*, it only remains for us to leave.
restauración f. Restoration.
restaurador, ra adj. Restorative, restoring.
— M. y f. Restorer.
restaurante o **restaurant** m. Restaurant. || *Coche restaurante*, restaurant car (de tren).
restaurar v. tr. To restore.
restinga f. MAR. Bank, shoal.
restingar m. MAR. Shoals, *pl.*
restitución f. Restitution, return.
restituible adj. Restorable, returnable.
restituidor, ra adj. Restoring.
— M. y f. Restorer.
restituir* v. tr. To restitute. || To return, to restore, to give back (devolver). || To restore (restaurar).
restitutorio, ria adj. Restitutory.
resto m. Rest, remainder: *el resto de su fortuna*, the rest of his fortune. || Remainder, balance (saldo de una cuenta). || Stake (cantidad que se juega.) || All one has (todo lo que se tiene): *apostar el resto*, to bet all one has. || DEP. Return (devolución). | Receiver (jugador). || MAT. Remainder. || — Pl. Ruins (de un monumento). || Remains: *restos mortales*, mortal remains. || Leftovers (de comida). || FIG. *Echar el resto*, to put all one has into it, to give it all one has got (trabajar mucho), to stake everything one has got, to put one's shirt on it (naipes).
restón m. DEP. Receiver (tenis).
restorán m. Restaurant.
restregadura f. o **restregamiento** m. Rubbing (refregamiento). || Rub mark (señal).
restregar* v. tr. To rub hard (frotar). || To scrub (el suelo).
restregón m. Rub (acción de frotar). || Scrub (del suelo). || Rub mark (señal).
restricción f. Restriction: *restricciones a las importaciones*, import restrictions.
restrictivo, va adj. Restrictive.
restricto, ta adj. Restricted (limitado).
restringente adj. Restrictive.
restringible adj. Restrainable.
restringir v. tr. To restrict, to limit. || MED. To contract.
— V. pr. To reduce, to cut down on: *restringirse en los gastos*, to reduce [one's] spending.
restriñidor, ra m. MED. Astringent.
restriñimiento m. MED. Astringency.
restriñir* v. tr. To astringe, to constrict (astringir). || To constipate (estreñir).

resucitación f. MED. Resuscitation.
resucitado, da adj. Resuscitated.
— M. y f. Resuscitated person. || FIG. Person who suddenly appears after a long absence.
resucitar v. intr. MED. To resuscitate. || REL. To rise from the dead.
— V. tr. MED. To resuscitate, to bring back to life. || To raise (a los muertos). || To revive: *el vino me resucitó*, the wine revived me. || To revive, to bring back: *resucitar un recuerdo*, to bring back a memory.
resudar v. intr. To perspire *o* to sweat slightly. || To exude (los árboles).
resueltamente adv. Resolutely, determinedly, with determination.
resuelto, ta adj. Resolute, determined. || Firm: *tono resuelto*, firm tone.
resuello m. Breathing (acción de resollar). || — *Perder el resuello* or *quedarse sin resuello*, to get out of breath, to be out of breath. || FIG. *Quitarle a uno el resuello*, to take one's breath away.
resulta f. Result, effect, consequence (efecto). || Decision, outcome (de una deliberación). || *De resultas*, as a result: *se quedó ciego de resultas de una enfermedad*, he went blind as a result of an illness.
resultado m. Result: *se colocarán los resultados en el tablón de anuncios*, the results will be posted on the notice board. || Result, outcome: *el resultado del examen*, the result of the examination; *el resultado de un pleito*, the result of a lawsuit; *la operación tuvo resultado satisfactorio* the operation had a satisfactory outcome. || Answer: *el resultado de una multiplicación*, the answer to a multiplication. || — *Dar buen resultado*, to work (una maniobra). || *Tener por resultado*, to have the effect of, to lead to.
resultando m. JUR. *Los resultandos*, the whereases.
resultante adj./s.f. Resultant.
resultar v. intr. To result: *de tantas medidas discriminatorias resultó un descontento general*, general discontent resulted from so many discriminatory measures; *resultar en*, to result in. || To turn out, to come out, to work out: *el experimento no ha resultado como esperábamos*, the experiment didn't turn out as we expected. || To be: *aquí la vida resulta muy barata*, the cost of living here is very low, living here is very cheap; *resultó herido en el accidente*, he was injured in the accident; *resulta difícil comprenderlo*, it is difficult to understand; *sus esfuerzos resultaron vanos*, his efforts were in vain. || To happen, to occur: *resulta que no tenemos dinero*, it so happens that we don't have any money. || To turn out to be (ser finalmente): *las negociaciones resultaron un fracaso*, the negotiations turned out to be a failure. || To seem: *ella me resulta muy simpática*, she seems very nice to me. || To go: *este collar resulta muy bien con este vestido*, this necklace goes very well with this dress. || To be worth (ser conveniente): *no resulta comer a la carta*, it is not worth eating à la carte. || To come to (costar): *el traje completo resulta por unas tres mil pesetas*, the complete suit comes to about three thousand pesetas. || — *De esto resulta que*, from this we can deduce *o* infer that, it follows from this that. || *Esta broma me está resultando ya un poco pesada*, this joke is beginning to annoy me. || *La habitación nos resulta pequeña*, we find the room small. || *No resultó*, it didn't work. || *Parecía que iba a quedarse soltera pero resulta que al final se casó*, it looked like she was going to remain single, but in fact she finally got married. || *Resulta que cuando llegamos a la estación el tren había salido*, it turned out that when we arrived at the station the train had already left. || *Resulta que no tengo dinero*, the thing *o* the fact is that I haven't got any money. || *Resultar ser*, to happen to be, to turn out to be: *resultó ser el hijo de un amigo mío*, he turned out to be the son of a friend of mine. || *Si resulta ser verdadero*, if it proves to be true. || *Viene a resultar lo mismo*, it amounts to the same thing.
resumen m. Summary, résumé. || Abstract (sumario). || — *En resumen*, in short. || *Hacer un resumen de*, to make a summary of, to summarize.
resumidamente adv. In summary form (de manera resumida). || Briefly (en pocas palabras).
resumidero m. *Amer.* Drain, sewer (alcantarilla).
resumido, da adj. Summarized. || *En resumidas cuentas*, in short, in a word.
resumir v. tr. To summarize: *resumir un libro*, to summarize a book. || To sum up (recapitular). || To abbreviate (abreviar). || To abridge, to shorten (cortar).
— V. pr. To be summarized, to be summed up: *esto se puede resumir en cuatro palabras*, this can be summed up in four words. || To amount to, to boil down to (venir a ser).
resurgencia f. Reappearance (de un curso de agua).
resurgimiento m. Reappearance (de un curso de agua). || FIG. Resurgence, revival (reaparición). | Recovery: *el resurgimiento de la economía nacional*, the recovery of the national economy. || *El resurgimiento de Italia*, the Risorgimento of Italy.
resurgir v. intr. To reappear (un río, etc.). || FIG. To rise up again, to reappear (aparecer de nuevo).
resurrección f. Resurrection. || — *Domingo de Resurrección*, Easter Sunday. || *Pascua de Resurrección*, Easter.

retablo m. Retable, altarpiece.
retacar v. tr. To hit [the ball] twice (en billar).
retacería f. Remnants, *pl.* (de tejidos).
retaco m. Short shotgun (arma). || FIG. y FAM. Shorty (persona). || Short cue (en billar).
retador, ra adj. Challenging.
— M. y f. Challenger.
retaguardia f. Rearguard. || *Quedarse a retaguardia*, to bring up the rear.
retahíla f. String: *una retahíla de niños*, a string of children; *una retahíla de triunfos, de desgracias*, a string of victories, of misfortunes. || Stream, string (de insultos).
retal m. Remnant, left-over piece, scrap.
retama f. BOT. Broom.
retamal o **retamar** m. BOT. Broom field.
retar v. tr. To challenge. || To accuse (acusar). || FIG. To reproach. | To scold (reprender). || *Retar en duelo*, to challenge to a duel.
retardación f. Delay, retardation.
retardado, da adj. Retarded, delayed (retrasado). || *Bomba de efecto retardado*, delayed-action bomb, time bomb.
retardar v. tr. To slow down: *retardar el avance de una enfermedad*, to slow down the advance of a disease. || To delay, to hold up (retrasar).
retardatriz adj. f. *Fuerza retardatriz*, retardative force.
retardo m. Delay. || *Bomba de retardo*, delayed-action bomb, time bomb.
retasa o **retasación** f. Reappraisal.
retasar v. tr. To reappraise.
retazo m. Remnant, piece, scrap (tela). || FIG. Fragment, portion, piece.
retejar v. tr. To retile, to repair the tiling of.
retejer v. tr. To weave closely.
retemblar* v. intr. To shake, to tremble: *el piso retembló*, the flat shook.
retemplar v. tr. *Amer.* To enliven (dar vigor).
retén m. Reserves (*pl.*), reserve corps (de bomberos, de soldados en el cuartel). || Reinforcements, *pl.* (refuerzo). || TECN. Stop. || *De retén*, in reserve.
retención f. Retention (acción de retener). || Stoppage, deduction (parte deducida). || MED. Retention: *retención de orina*, urine retention. || *Capacidad de retención*, power of retention (memoria).
retenedor adj. Retaining.
— M. *Retenedor de puerta*, safety chain (para que no se abra enteramente), door catch (para mantenerla abierta).
retener* v. tr. To hold (impedir que se vaya): *retén este caballo para que no se escape*, hold this horse so that he doesn't escape. || To keep (guardar): *siempre retiene los libros prestados más de lo debido*, he always keeps books he has borrowed longer than he should. || To hold back, to keep back: *quería emigrar pero su familia le retuvo*, he wanted to emigrate but his family kept him back. || To hold: *la esponja retiene el agua*, sponge holds water. || To retain, to remember (en la memoria). || COM. To deduct, to withhold: *retienen veinte dólares semanales de mi sueldo*, they deduct twenty dollars a week from my salary. || — *Retener el aliento*, to hold one's breath. || *Retener la atención de alguien*, to hold s.o.'s attention. || *Retener la lengua*, to hold one's tongue.
— V. pr. To hold o.s. back, to restrain o.s.
retenida f. MAR. Guy (cable).
retenimiento m. V. RETENCIÓN.
retentiva f. Memory (memoria).
retentivo, va adj. Retentive.
reticencia f. Insinuation, innuendo: *un discurso lleno de reticencias*, a speech full of insinuation *o* of innuendos.
reticente adj. Insinuating.
rético, ca adj./s. Rhaetian. || — M. Rhaeto-Romanic (lengua).
reticulado, da adj. Reticulated.
retícula f. Reticle (óptica). || ARTES. Tint.
reticular adj. Reticular.
retículo m. Reticle (óptica). || ZOOL. Reticulum. || Net, network (tejido en forma de red).
retina f. ANAT. Retina.
retinal o **retiniano, na** adj. ANAT. Retinal.
retinitis f. MED. Retinitis (enfermedad).
retintín m. Ringing (en los oídos). || FIG. y FAM. Sarcastic tone: *preguntar algo con retintín*, to ask sth. in a sarcastic tone.
retiración f. IMPR. Form for backing.
retirada f. MIL. Withdrawal: *la retirada de las tropas de un país*, the withdrawal of troops from a country. | Retreat: *tocar retirada*, to sound the retreat; *batir en retirada*, to beat a retreat. || Withdrawal: *retirada del carnet de conducir*, withdrawal of one's driving licence. || Ebbing: *la retirada de las aguas*, the ebbing of the tide. || Retirement: *la retirada de un actor*, an actor's retirement. || Removal, clearing [away]: *retirada de la nieve*, snow clearing. || Recall (de un embajador). || Retreat, refuge (lugar seguro). || — *Cubrir la retirada*, to cover the retreat (tropas). || MIL. *Emprender la retirada*, to retreat.
retiradamente adv. In seclusion: *vivir retiradamente*, to live in seclusion. || FIG. Secretly, in secret.

retirado, da adj. Remote (lejano): *barrio retirado*, remote neighbourhood. || Secluded: *vida retirada*, secluded life. || Retired (jubilado).
— M. Retired person.
retiramiento m. V. RETIRO.
retirar v. tr. To remove: *retirar los platos de la mesa*, to remove the plates from the table. || To move away (un mueble). || To draw back (la mano, las sábanas, etc.). || To withdraw: *retirar dinero del banco*, to withdraw money from the bank; *retirar un proyecto de ley*, to withdraw a bill from Parliament. || To take away: *retirar el carnet de conducir a alguien*, to take away s.o.'s driving licence. || To take back, to retract: *retirar su palabra*, to take back one's promise; *retirar lo dicho*, to retract what one has said. || IMPR. To print the back of a sheet. || To recall, to withdraw: *retirar a un embajador*, to recall an ambassador. || To withdraw (una moneda). || To pension off, to retire (a un empleado). || DEP. To withdraw.
— V. pr. To draw back, to move back, to withdraw: *retirarse de la ventana*, to draw back from the window. || To retire, to go into retirement (jubilarse). || MIL. To withdraw, to retreat (tropas). || DEP. To withdraw, to retire. || To retire: *retirarse a su cuarto*, to retire to one's room. || To ebb (la marea). || To go into seclusion (apartarse del mundo). || — *No se retire*, hold on [U.S., don't hang up] (al teléfono). || *Puede usted retirarse*, you may leave. || *Retirarse a dormir*, to go to bed, to retire to one's bedroom.
retiro m. Retirement: *llegar a la edad del retiro*, to reach retirement age. || [Retirement] pension (pensión); *cobrar el retiro*, to receive one's pension. || Retreat (lugar tranquilo): *un retiro campestre*, a country retreat. || Withdrawal (retirada). || REL. Retreat.
reto m. Challenge (desafío): *aceptar el reto*, to accept the challenge. || Threat (amenaza): *echar retos*, to make threats. || *Lanzar un reto*, to challenge, to throw a challenge.
retobado, da adj. *Amer.* Saucy, impudent (respondón). | Stubborn, obstinate (obstinado). | Sly, crafty (astuto).
retobar v. tr. *Amer.* To cover with leather (forrar con cuero). | To cover with sackcloth (con arpillera).
retobo m. *Amer.* Refuse, junk (deshecho). | Sackcloth (arpillera).
retocador, ra m. y f. FOT. Retoucher.
retocar v. tr. To touch up, to retouch: *retocar una fotografía* to retouch a photograph. || To alter (la ropa).
retoñar o **retoñecer*** v. intr. BOT. To shoot, to sprout (una planta). || FIG. To reappear.
retoño m. BOT. Sprout, shoot (de planta). || FAM. Kid (niño).
retoque m. Retouching, touching up (de fotografía, maquillaje, etc.). || Alteration (de la ropa).
retor m. Twisted cotton fabric (tela).
retorcedor m. Twister.
retorcedura f. V. RETORCIMIENTO.
retorcer* v. tr. To twist: *retorcer un alambre*, to twist a wire. || To twine (cabos). || To wring: *retorcer la ropa*, to wring the clothes; *retorcer el pescuezo a uno*, to wring s.o.'s neck. || To twirl (el bigote). || FIG. To twist: *retorcer un argumento*, to twist an argument. | To alter, to twist, to distort (un sentido).
— V. pr. To writhe: *retorcerse de dolor*, to writhe in pain. || To double up: *retorcerse de risa*, to double up with laughter.
retorcido, da adj. Twisted. || FIG. Twisted: *tenía la mente retorcida*, he had a twisted mind. | Involved: *lenguaje retorcido*, involved style. | Devious (taimado).
— M. Twisting.
retorcimiento m. Twisting (del hilo). || Twining (de cabos). || Wringing (de la colada). || FIG. Involved nature (del estilo). | Twistedness (de la mente). | Deviousness (de una persona).
retórica f. Rhetoric. || — Pl. FAM. Talk, *sing.*, verbiage, *sing.* (palabrería). || FAM. *No me vengas con retóricas*, do me a favour (déjame tranquilo).
retórico, ca adj. Rhetorical.
— M. Rhetorician (especialista en retórica).
retornamiento m. Return.
retornar v. tr. To return, to give back (devolver).
— V. intr. y pr. To return, to go back: *retornaron a su patria*, they returned to their country. || *Retornar en sí*, to regain consciousness.
retornelo m. MÚS. Ritornello.
retorno m. Return: *retorno al campo*, return to the country. || Exchange (cambio). || *Retorno de llama*, backfire.
retorromano, na adj./s. Rhaetian (rético). || — M. Rhaeto-Romanic (lengua).
retorsión f. V. RETORCIMIENTO.
retorta f. Retort.
retortero m. Turn (vuelta). || — FAM. *Andar al retortero*, to be extremely busy, to have a million things to do. | *Traer a uno al retortero*, to keep s.o. busy *o* on the move *o* on the go (baquetear), to be on one's mind (preocupar).
retortijón m. Twist. || Stomach cramp (de tripas).
retostar* v. tr. To toast again (volver a tostar). || To toast too much. || To tan (broncear).
retozador, ra adj. Frolicsome, playful (juguetón).
retozar v. intr. To frolic, to romp (juguetear).
retozo m. Frolic, romp (jugueteo). || Playfulness. || — Pl. Frolicking, *sing.*
retozón, ona adj. Frolicsome, playful.
retracción f. Retraction.
retractable adj. Retractable.
retractación f. Retraction, recantation, retractation. || Withdrawal (en la Bolsa). || *Retractación pública*, public retraction.
retractar v. tr. To recant, to retract, to withdraw: *retractar una opinión*, to recant an opinion.
— V. pr. To retract, to recant: *retractarse de una declaración*, to retract a statement. || *Me retracto*, I take that back.
retráctil adj. Retractile. || Retractable (tren de aterrizaje).
retractilidad f. Retractility.
retractivo, va adj. Retractive.
retracto m. Retraction, withdrawal: *retracto de autorización*, withdrawal of authorization. || JUR. *Derecho de retracto*, right of repurchase.
retractor adj. Retractive.
— M. Retractor.
retraer* v. tr. To bring back, to bring again (volver a traer). ||.To dissuade (disuadir). || JUR. To repurchase.
— V. pr. To withdraw (retirarse). || To take refuge (*a*, in) [refugiarse].
retraído, da adj. Solitary. || FIG. Reserved, shy (tímido). | Unsociable (insociable).
retraimiento m. Retirement, withdrawal (acción). || Seclusion (vida aislada). || FIG. Reserve, shyness (timidez).
retranca f. Breeching (del arnés). || *Amer.* Brake (de coche). || — *Correa de retranca*, breeching strap. || FIG. *Tener mucha retranca*, to have a lot of experience.
retranquear v. tr. To sight [with one eye].
retransmisión f. Passing on (de un mensaje). || RAD. [Live] broadcast. | Repeat (segunda difusión).
retransmisor m. TECN. Transmitter.
retransmitir v. tr. To pass on (un mensaje). || RAD. To broadcast [live]. | To repeat (dar una emisión por segunda vez). | To relay (servir de repetidor).
retrasado, da adj. Late: *un tren retrasado*, a late train. || Slow: *reloj retrasado*, slow clock. || Backward, underdeveloped: *países retrasados*, backward countries. || Late, behind: *estoy retrasado en el pago del alquiler*, I'm behind with the rent. || Retarded, backward: *un niño retrasado*, a retarded child. || Behind: *estar retrasado en gramática*, to be behind in grammar; *tener trabajo retrasado*, to be behind in one's work. || *Voy cinco minutos retrasado*, my watch is five minutes slow.
— M. y f. Mentally retarded person.
retrasar v. tr. To delay: *la lluvia nos ha retrasado*, the rain has delayed us; *he retrasado mi viaje*, I have delayed my trip. || To postpone, to put off (aplazar). || To put back (un reloj). || To retard, to slow down (progreso). || To hold up: *la producción fue retrasada por la huelga*, production was held up by the strike.
— V. intr. To be slow: *mi reloj retrasa*, my clock is slow. || To fall behind (en el trabajo, etc.).
— V. pr. To be late, to arrive late, to be delayed: *perdón por haberme retrasado*, excuse me for being late; *el avión se retrasó*, the aeroplane was late. || To fall behind (en el trabajo, los estudios, el pago). || To lose (un reloj). || To be put off (ser aplazado).
retraso m. Delay: *el retraso del tren*, the delay of the train. || Underdevelopment, backwardness (poco desarrollo). || Slowness (de un reloj). || Deficiency, retardation: *retraso mental*, mental retardation. || — *El tren llegó con retraso*, the train arrived late. || *Llegué con diez minutos de retraso*, I arrived ten minutes late. || *Llevamos un retraso de un mes en el trabajo*, we are a month behind in our work.
retratador, ra m. y f. Portrait painter.
retratar v. tr. To paint a portrait of, to portray (un pintor). || To photograph, to take a photograph of (fotografiar). || FIG. To portray, to depict: *un escritor que retrata fielmente las costumbres de la época*, a writer who faithfully portrays the customs of the era. || *Hacerse retratar*, to have one's portrait painted.
— V. pr. To have one's photograph taken (fotografiarse). || To have one's picture painted (por un pintor). || To be reflected: *la imagen de Narciso se retrataba en el agua*, the image of Narcissus was reflected in the water. || FAM. To cough up (pagar).
retratista m. y f. Portrait painter (pintor). || FOT. Photographer.
retrato m. Portrait: *hacer un retrato de cuerpo entero*, to do a full-length portrait; *retrato de tamaño natural*, life-size portrait. || Photograph. || FIG. Portrayal, portrait, description (descripción). || FIG. *Es el vivo retrato de su padre*, he is the living image of his father.
retrechar v. intr. To back (el caballo).
retrechería f. FAM. Attractiveness, charm (encanto). | Slyness, cunning (astucia). | Crafty trick (subterfugio).
retrechero, ra adj. FAM. Attractive, charming: *cara retrechera*, attractive face. | Crafty, artful (astuto). | Slippery (hábil para escurrir el bulto).

retrepado, da adj. Lounging: *cómodamente retrepado en su mecedora*, comfortably lounging in his rocking chair.
retreparse v. pr. To lean back: *retreparse en una silla*, to lean back in a chair. | To lounge back (ponerse cómodo).
retreta f. MIL. Retreat: *tocar retreta*, to sound the retreat. || *Amer.* Open-air band concert. | Series (retahíla).
retrete m. Lavatory, toilet.
retribución f. Retribution, payment (remuneración). || Fee (de un artista). || Reward (recompensa).
retribuir* v. tr. To pay (pagar): *un empleo bien retribuido*, a well-paid job. || To recompense, to reward (recompensar). || *Amer.* To return, to repay (corresponder a un favor).
retributivo, va o **retribuyente** adj. Repaying, rewarding.
retro JUR. *Venta con pacto de retro*, sale subject to right of vendor to repurchase.
retroacción f. Retroaction. || Retrocession (retroceso).
retroactividad f. Retroactivity.
retroactivo, va adj. Retroactive: *una ley con efecto retroactivo*, a retroactive law.
retrocarga (de) adv. Breech-loading (arma).
retroceder v. intr. To go back, to move back: *retroceder un paso*, to go back a step. || To go back, to turn back: *como la calle estaba cortada tuvimos que retroceder*, as the street was blocked we had to go back. || To go down, to drop (el nivel de agua). || FIG. To go back, to look back: *para comprender los acontecimientos de hoy, hay que retroceder al siglo pasado*, in order to understand the events of today, one must look back to last century. | To back down (echarse atrás). || MIL. To give ground, to fall back, to retreat. || To recoil (arma de fuego). || AUT. To change down [U.S., to gear down] (velocidades). || — *Hacer retroceder*, to force back. || FIG. *No retroceder*, to stand firm.
retrocesión f. JUR. Retrocession. || *Hacer retrocesión de*, to retrocede.
retroceso m. Retrocession, backward movement. || Recoil: *el retroceso de un arma de fuego*, the recoil of a firearm. || FIG. Recession: *un retroceso en la economía*, a recession in the economy. || MED. Aggravation (de una enfermedad). || TECN. Back stroke (de pistón). || Screwback (en el billar). || MIL. Withdrawal, retreat. || Return (de una máquina de escribir).
retrocohete m. Retrorocket.
retroflexión f. MED. Retroflexion.
retrogradación f. ASTR. Retrogradation, regression (de un planeta).
retrogradar v. intr. To retrograde.
retrógrado, da adj. Retrograde: *movimiento retrógrado*, retrograde movement. || FIG. Reactionary.
— M. y f. Reactionary (reaccionario).
retrogresión f. Retrogression.
retropropulsión f. AVIAC. Jet propulsion.
retrospección f. Retrospection.
retrospectivo, va adj. Retrospective: *una exposición retrospectiva*, a retrospective exhibition. || *Mirada retrospectiva*, look back.
retrotraer* v. tr. To antedate, to predate. || To take *o* to carry back: *recuerdo que nos retrotrae a nuestra infancia*, memory that takes us back to our childhood.
retrovender v. tr. To sell back [to the original vendor].
retrovendición o **retroventa** f. JUR. Selling back to the vendor.
retroversión f. MED. Retroversion.
retrovisor m. AUT. Rearview mirror, driving mirror (interior). | Wing mirror, rearview mirror (exterior).
retrucar v. intr. To kiss (bolas de billar).
— V. tr. To throw back at s.o. (un argumento).
retruco m. Kiss (en el billar).
retruécano m. Pun, play on words.
retruque m. Kiss (billar).
retumbante adj. Resonant, resounding. || Bombastic, pompous (estilo).
retumbar v. intr. To resound, to echo: *la sala retumbaba con los aplausos*, the hall resounded with applause. || To thunder, to boom (el cañón, el trueno).
retumbo m. Resounding, echoing (acción). || Echo (sonido). || Thunder, boom (cañón, trueno).
reúma o **reuma** m. MED. Rheumatism.
reumático, ca adj./s. Rheumatic: *anciano reumático*, rheumatic old man; *dolor reumático*, rheumatic pain.
reumatismo m. MED. Rheumatism.
reumatoideo, a adj. MED. Rheumatoid.
reunión f. Reunion (de gente que se había separado). || Gathering: *reunión social*, social gathering. | Assembly, gathering, crowd (de mucha gente). | Meeting (conversación): *el director tuvo una reunión con sus empleados*, the director had a meeting with his employees; *celebrar una reunión*, to hold a meeting. || Meeting: *punto de reunión*, meeting place. || Session [U.S., meeting] (período de sesiones).
reunir v. tr. To assemble: *reunir las tropas*, to assemble the troops. || To join together: *reunir dos pisos*, to join two flats together. || To put together: *podríamos reunir nuestros ahorros*, we could put our savings together. || To fulfil: *los que reúnen estos requisitos pueden venir*, those who fulfil these requirements may come. || To assemble, to collect, to gather (datos). || To make (una colección). || To collect (fondos). || To assemble, to get together: *reunir unos amigos*, to assemble some friends. || *Reunir sus fuerzas*, to summon one's strength (una persona), to join forces (dos personas, dos países, etc.).
— V. pr. To join together. || To meet: *me reuniré con vosotros a las ocho*, I'll meet you at 8. || To meet (una asamblea).
revacunación f. MED. Revaccination.
revacunar v. tr. To revaccinate.
reválida f. Final examination (examen de fin de estudios). || Revalidation (revalidación). || *Reválida de bachillerato*, General Certificate of Education [U.S., high school diploma].
revalidación f. JUR. Revalidation.
revalidar v. tr. JUR. To revalidate. || To take a final examination in (unos estudios).
revalorar v. tr. To revalue.
revalorización f. Revaluation. || Revaluation, revalorization (de una moneda).
revalorizar v. tr. To revalue. || To revalue, to revalorize (una moneda).
revaluación f. Revaluation, revalorization.
revancha f. Revenge. || *Tomar* or *tomarse la revancha*, to take revenge, to get one's own back.
— OBSERV. *Revancha* is a Gallicism often used instead of *desquite*.
revanchista adj. Revengeful.
— M. y f. Revenger, avenger.
revelación f. Revelation. || FIG. Revelation, surprise (equipo, deportista, cantante, etc.). || *Esa noticia fue una revelación para todos nosotros*, that news was an eye-opener for *o* a revelation to all of us.
revelado m. FOT. Developing.
revelador, ra adj. Revealing.
— M. y f. Revealer. || — M. FOT. Developer.
revelar v. tr. To reveal, to disclose (secreto). || To reveal: *Dios reveló su deseo a los israelitas*, God revealed His will to the Israelites. || To show (enseñar). || FOT. To develop.
— V. pr. To reveal o.s.
revellín m. Ravelin (fortificación). || Mantelpiece (de chimenea).
revendedor, ra adj. Reselling.
— M. y f. Reseller (persona que revende). || Retailer (detallista). || *Revendedor de entradas*, ticket tout.
revender v. tr. To resell. || To retail (el detallista). || To tout (billetes).
revenimiento m. Cave-in (de una mina). || Shrinkage (encogimiento).
reventa f. Resale. || Retail (venta al por menor). || *Comprar una entrada en la reventa*, to buy a ticket off a tout.
reventadero m. Rugged *o* rough ground. || FIG. y FAM. Grind (trabajo penoso).
reventador m. TEATR. Catcaller.
reventante adj. Exhausting, tiring.
reventar* v. intr. To burst: *las burbujas reventaban en la superficie del agua*, the bubbles burst on the surface of the water; *el neumático reventó*, the tyre burst. || To give way, to burst: *la presa ha reventado*, the dam has given way. || To break (romperse). || FIG. y FAM. To be dying to: *está que revienta por ir al cine*, he's dying to go to the cinema. | To burst: *reventar de orgullo*, to be bursting with pride. | To hate: *me revienta tener que pedirle perdón*, I hate having to ask his pardon. | To disgust, to make sick: *ese tío me revienta*, that fellow disgusts me *o* makes me sick. | To kick the bucket, to peg out (morirse). || — FIG. y FAM. *Comer hasta reventar*, to eat until one bursts. | *Reventar de cansancio*, to be dead tired. | *Reventar de gordo*, to be as fat as a pig. | *Reventar de rabia*, to hit the roof (saltar), to be fighting mad (estar furioso). | *Reventar de risa*, V. RISA.
— V. tr. To burst (un globo, un neumático, etc.). | To crush, to smash (aplastar). || To break (romper). || FIG. y FAM. To tire [s.o.] out, to kill [s.o.] (fatigar). | To ride hard (un caballo).
— V. pr. To burst. || To burst, to burst open (absceso). || To crush (aplastarse). || To burst, to blow (neumático). || FIG. To tire o.s. out, to kill o.s. (de cansancio).
reventón adj. m. *Clavel reventón*, large carnation.
— M. Burst. || Blowout, flat tyre (de un neumático). || FIG. y FAM. Jam, difficulty (apuro, dificultad). || *Amer.* Outcrop (de mineral). || — *Darse un reventón de trabajar*, to kill o.s. working. || *Darse* or *pegarse un reventón para hacer algo*, to make an all-out effort to get sth. done.
reverberación f. Reflection, reverberation.
reverberante adj. Reflecting, reverberating.
reverberar v. intr. To be reflected, to reverberate (reflejarse). || To glint (destellar).
reverbero m. Reflection, reverberation (reverberación). | Reflector. | Reflecting lamp (farol). || *Amer.* Cooking stove. || *Horno de reverbero*, reverberatory furnace.
reverdecer* v. intr. To grow green again. || FIG. To revive, to acquire new vigour (remozarse).
reverdecimiento m. Growing green again, turning green again.

reverencia f. Reverence. || Bow (de hombre), curtsy (de mujer). || — *Hacer una reverencia*, to bow (hombre), to curtsy (mujer). || *Su Reverencia*, Your Reverence.
reverenciable adj. Venerable.
reverencial adj. Reverential.
reverenciar v. tr. To revere, to venerate.
reverendísimo, ma adj. REL. Most Reverend.
reverendo, da adj./s. REL. Reverend. || — Adj. FAM. Huge, enormous: *una reverenda tontería*, an enormous blunder.
reverente adj. Reverent, respectful.
reversibilidad f. Reversibility.
reversible adj. Reversible.
reversión f. Reversion.
reversivo, va adj. Reversive.
reverso m. Reverse. || FIG. *El reverso de la medalla*, V. MEDALLA.
revertir* v. intr. To revert, to return (volver). || JUR. To revert. || To result, to turn out (resolverse en). || — *Poner una conferencia a cobro revertido*, to make a reverse-charge call. || *Revertir en beneficio de*, to be to the advantage of. || *Revertir en perjuicio de*, to be to the detriment of.
revés m. Wrong side: *el revés de un tejido*, the wrong side of a cloth. || Back: *el revés de la mano*, the back of the hand. || Backhander, blow with the back of the hand (golpe). || Slap (bofetada). || Backhand [stroke] (en tenis). || FIG. Misfortune: *los reveses de la vida*, the misfortunes of life. | Setback, reverse (fracaso). || — *Al revés*, inside out (con lo de dentro fuera), back to front (con lo de delante detrás): *ponerse el jersey al revés*, to put one's pullover on inside out *o* back to front; backwards (invertido el orden), the other way round (en sentido inverso), the wrong way (mal): *comprender, ir al revés*, to understand, to go the wrong way; vice versa. || *Al revés de*, contrary to: *al revés de lo que se dice*, contrary to what is said. || *Del revés*, upside down (con lo de arriba abajo), inside out (con lo de dentro fuera), back to front (con lo de delante detrás). || *Es el mundo al revés*, it's a topsy-turvy world. || *Reveses de fortuna*, setbacks, reverses of fortune. || *Todo le sale al revés*, everything he does turns out wrong. || *Volver algo del revés*, to turn sth. round (cambiar de posición), to turn sth. inside out (sacar lo de dentro fuera).
revesado, da adj. Complex, intricate, complicated (un asunto). || Unruly, mischievous (niños).
revestido o **revestimiento** m. Covering (del suelo, etc.). || TECN. Coating (con un metal). | Lining (de un tubo). | Sheathing (de un cable).
revestir* v. tr. To cover, to surface: *revestir el suelo con linóleo*, to cover the floor with lino. || TECN. To line (una tubería). | To sheathe (un cable). | To coat (con metal). || To put on (poner un vestido). || To wear (llevar un vestido). || FIG. To take on, to acquire: *revestir nuevas dimensiones*, to take on new dimensions. || — FIG. *El acto revistió gran solemnidad*, it was a solemn occasion. | *La ceremonia revistió gran brillantez*, the ceremony went off splendidly, it was a splendid ceremony.
— V. pr. To put on (la ropa). || To put on one's vestments (el sacerdote). || — FIG. *Revestirse de energía*, to summon up one's energy. | *Revestirse de paciencia*, to be patient.
revigorizar v. tr. To revigorate, to reinvigorate.
revirada f. MAR. Tacking.
revisación o **revisada** f. *Amer*. V. REVISIÓN.
revisar v. tr. To revise, to go through: *revisar un texto*, to revise a text. || To check, to revise: *revisar una traducción*, to check a translation. || To overhaul [U.S., to check]: *hacer revisar el coche*, to have the car overhauled. || To review (volver a ver). || To inspect (billetes). || To check, to audit (cuentas).
revisión f. Revision, review. || Checking, revision (de una traducción, etc.). || Inspection (de billetes). || TECN. Overhaul, check. || *Revisión de cuentas*, audit, auditing.
revisionismo m. Revisionism.
revisionista adj./s. Revisionist.
revisor, ra adj. Revisory.
— M. Reviser, revisor. || Inspector. || Ticket inspector, inspector [U.S., conductor] (de billetes). || *Revisor de cuentas*, auditor.
revisoría f. Post of inspector. || Post of auditor (de cuentas).
revista f. Magazine, review, journal: *revista científica*, scientific magazine. || Inspection. || MIL. Review. || Revue (espectáculo). || Review (artículo): *revista teatral*, stage review. || — *Pasar revista a*, v. PASAR. || *Revista comercial*, trade paper. || *Revista de modas*, fashion magazine.
revistar v. tr. To review.
revistero m. Reviewer, critic (de un periódico). || Magazine rack (para colocar revistas).
revivificación f. Revivification.
revivificar v. tr. To revivify.
revivir v. intr. To revive. || To be renewed, to break out again: *revivió la discordia*, discord broke out again. || *Hacer revivir*, to bring back to life.
— V. tr. To bring back to life (evocar).
revocabilidad f. Revocability.
revocable adj. Revocable.
revocación f. Revocation. || Recall (de un embajador).
revocador m. Plasterer (albañil).
revocadura f. V. REVOQUE.
revocar v. tr. To revoke: *revocar una orden, una ley, un decreto*, to revoke an order, a law, a decree. || To cancel (anular). || To dismiss, to remove from office (destituir a un funcionario). || To dissuade (disuadir). || ARQ. To resurface (poner nueva fachada). | To plaster, to stucco (enlucir). | To whitewash (encalar). || To blow back: *el viento revoca el humo*, the wind blows the smoke back.
revocativo, va adj. Revocative.
revocatorio, ria adj. Revocatory.
revoco m. V. REVOQUE.
revolcadero m. Wallow (de animales).
revolcar* v. tr. To knock down, to knock over (tirar al suelo). || FIG. To defeat, to floor (derrotar). || FAM. To fail (en un examen).
— V. pr. To roll: *revolcarse en el suelo*, to roll on the ground. || To wallow (animales): *revolcarse en el fango*, to wallow in the mud. || FAM. *Revolcarse de dolor, de risa*, to double up with pain, with laughter.
revolcón m. Fall: *sufrir un revolcón sin consecuencias*, to have a minor fall. || TAUR. Tumble. || FIG. y FAM. *Dar un revolcón a uno*, to wipe the floor with s.o. (en una discusión).
revolear o **revolotear** v. intr. To fly about, to flutter about.
revoloteo m. Fluttering (de pájaros). || FIG. Stir, commotion (revuelo).
revoltijo o **revoltillo** m. Mess, jumble, clutter: *un revoltijo de papeles*, a jumble of papers. || Heap, pile (montón). || *Revoltillo de huevos*, scrambled eggs, *pl.*
revoltoso, sa adj. Mischievous (travieso): *niño revoltoso*, mischievous child. || Unruly (difícil de gobernar). || Restless (turbulento). || Seditious, rebellious (sedicioso).
— M. y f. Mischievous child, scamp. || Rebel (rebelde). || Troublemaker (alborotador).
revolución f. Revolution: *la revolución industrial*, the Industrial Revolution; *la Revolución Francesa*, the French Revolution. || ASTR. y TECN. Revolution: *40 revoluciones por minuto*, 40 revolutions per minute.
revolucionar v. tr. To revolutionize.
revolucionario, ria adj./s. Revolutionary.
revolver* v. tr. To mix (mezclar). || To toss: *revolver la ensalada*, to toss the salad. || To stir (un líquido). || To rummage through: *revolver sus papeles*, to rummage through one's papers. || To rummage in (un cajón, etc.). || To turn upside down, to disarrange: *revolver la casa*, to turn the house upside down. || To entangle, to confuse (confundir, mezclar). || To stir up: *revolver los ánimos*, to stir up the people. || To irritate, to annoy (irritar). || To upset, to turn: *esto me revuelve el estómago*, this upsets my stomach. || To roll (los ojos). || To turn (la cabeza). || — *Revolver algo en la cabeza*, to turn sth. over in one's mind. || *Revolver la sangre*, to make one's blood boil.
— V. pr. To toss and turn: *revolverse en la cama*, to toss and turn in bed. || To turn round (dar la vuelta). || To turn: *el toro se revolvió contra el torero*, the bull turned on the bullfighter. || To roll: *revolverse en la hierba*, to roll in the grass. || To turn stormy (el tiempo). || To get rough (el mar). || To turn cloudy (un líquido). || *Revolverse contra alguien*, to turn against s.o.
revólver m. Revolver.
revoque m. ARQ. Resurfacing (limpieza, reparación, etc.). | Plastering (enlucido). | Whitewashing (encalado). | Plaster, stucco (material).
revuelco m. Fall (caída). || TAUR. Tumble. || Roll (en la hierba). || Wallow (en el fango).
revuelo m. Second flight. || Fluttering (revoloteo). || FIG. Stir, commotion: *la noticia produjo gran revuelo en los medios taurinos*, the news caused a great stir in bullfighting circles. || *Amer*. Blow that a fighting cock gives with its spur. || FIG. *De revuelo*, in passing.
revuelta f. Revolt, rebellion (motín). || Disturbance (alteración del orden). || Quarrel (riña). || Turn, bend (vuelta). || Corner (esquina). || *Dar vueltas y revueltas*, to go round and round.
revueltamente adv. In a disorderly way, higgledy-piggledy, pell-mell.
revuelto, ta adj. Jumbled, in a mess, in disorder, in disarray (papeles, etc.). || Tangled (enredado). || Cloudy (líquidos). || Rough, stormy (mar). || Variable, unsettled, changeable (tiempo). || Excited, agitated, worked up (fam.), annoyed: *la gente está revuelta a causa de la subida de precios*, people are annoyed at the rise in prices. || Turbulent, stormy: *vivimos en tiempos revueltos*, we are living in turbulent times. || Mischievous (travieso). || Restless (turbulento). || Docile, easy to handle (caballo). || — *Huevos revueltos*, scrambled eggs. || *Pelo revuelto*, dishevelled hair.
revulsión f. MED. Revulsion.
revulsivo, va adj./s.m. MED. Revulsive.
rey m. King (monarca). || King (en juegos). || FIG. King: *el león es el rey de la selva*, the lion is the king of the jungle. || — Pl. King and Queen (rey y reina). || — FIG. *A cuerpo de rey*, like a king: *tratar a uno a cuerpo de rey*, to treat s.o. like a king; *vivir a cuerpo de rey*, to live like a king. | *A rey muerto, rey puesto*,

off with the old, on with the new. | *Cada uno es rey en su casa*, a man's home is his castle. | *Del tiempo del rey que rabió*, as old as the hills. || *Día de Reyes*, Epiphany, Twelfth-Day. || *Hablando del rey de Roma, por la puerta asoma*, v. HABLAR. || *Libro de los Reyes*, Book of Kings. || *Los Reyes Católicos*, the Catholic Monarchs [Ferdinand and Isabella]. || *Los Reyes Magos*, v. MAGO. || FIG. *Ni quito ni pongo rey*, v. QUITAR. | *No temer ni rey ni roque*, to fear nothing and nobody. || *Rey de armas*, king of arms. || *Rey de codornices*, corncrake (ave). || *Rey de gallos*, mock king in a carnival. || *Rey de reyes*, King of Kings. || *Rey Sol*, Sun King.

reyerta f. Quarrel, wrangle (disputa).

reyezuelo m. Kinglet (rey, ave).

rezado, da adj. Said, spoken. || *Misa rezada*, Low Mass.

rezagado, da m. y f. MIL. Straggler. || Latecomer (que llega tarde). || — *Ir rezagado*, to lag behind. || *Quedar rezagado*, to be left behind.

rezagar v. tr. To leave behind (dejar atrás). || To delay, to postpone, to put off (retrasar).
— V. pr. To fall behind (retrasarse). || To lag behind (quedarse atrás).

rezar v. intr. To pray: *rezar a Dios*, to pray to God. || To say, to go: *según reza el refrán*, as the saying goes. || To say (un escrito). || To apply: *esta ley no reza para los ex combatientes*, this law does not apply to ex-servicemen || *Esto no reza conmigo*, that does not concern me.
— V. tr. To say: *rezar una oración*, to say a prayer. || To say (misa, el rosario). || To say, to read: *el escrito reza lo siguiente*, the document says the following *o* reads as follows. || FIG. y FAM. *Ser más fácil que rezar un credo*, to be as easy as pie.

rezno m. Bot, bott (larva). || BOT. Castor-oil plant.

rezo m. Praying (acción de rezar). || Prayer (oración). || Office (oficio litúrgico).

rezón m. MAR. Grapnel, grappling iron.

rezongador, ra adj. FAM. Grumbling, grouchy, grumpy.
— M. y f. Grumbler, moaner, grouch.

rezongar v. intr. FIG. y FAM. To grumble, to moan, to complain.

rezongo o **rezongueo** m. Grumbling, moaning.

rezongón, ona o **rezonguero, ra** o **rezonglón, ona** adj./s. V. REZONGADOR.

rezumar v. tr. To ooze, to exude: *la pared rezuma humedad*, the wall oozes moisture. || FIG. To ooze: *canción que rezuma tristeza*, song which oozes sadness.
— V. intr. To seep, to ooze (el contenido): *el aceite rezuma a través de la loza*, the oil seeps through the pot. || To leak (una vasija). || To bead: *el sudor le rezumaba por la frente*, the sweat beaded on his forehead. || *Le rezuma el orgullo*, he oozes pride.
— V. pr. To leak: *el botijo se rezuma*, the pitcher leaks. || To ooze, to seep (el contenido).

rezumo m. Sweating.

Rhesus m. MED. *Factor Rhesus*, rhesus factor.

Rhodesia n. pr. f. GEOGR. Rhodesia (Rodesia).

ría f. Estuary, river mouth (desembocadura). || GEOGR. Ria (valle invadido por el mar).

riachuelo o **riacho** m. Brook, stream.

riada f. Flood (crecida). || Flood, inundation (inundación). || FIG. Flood: *riada de visitantes*, flood of visitors.

ribazo m. Embankment, slope.

ribera f. Bank (de un río). || Shore, seashore (del mar).

riberano, na adj./s. *Amer.* V. RIBEREÑO.

ribereño, ña adj. Riparian (p.us.), on the bank, along the bank (en general). || Riverside (al lado de un río). || Waterfront (que da al mar). || *Los países ribereños del Danubio*, the countries which lie along the Danube.
— M. y f. Riverside dweller (al lado de un río). || Waterfront dweller (junto al mar).

ribete m. Border, edging, trimming (orla). || — FIG. *Tener ribetes cómicos*, to have a comical side. | *Tener ribetes de poeta*, to be sth. of a poet.

ribeteado, da adj. Bordered, edged. || *Tener los ojos ribeteados de rojo*, to have red-ringed eyes.

ribetear v. tr. To border, to edge, to trim (una tela). || FIG. To border.

ribonucleico, ca adj. Ribonucleic (ácido).

ricacho, cha o **ricachón, ona** m. y f. FAM. Moneybags.

ricadueña o **ricahembra** f. Wife *o* daughter of a nobleman, noblewoman.

ricahombría f. (Ant.). Nobility.

ricamente adv. Richly (con opulencia). || Marvellously, wonderfully (muy bien).

Ricardo n. pr. m. Richard.

ricino m. BOT. Castor-oil plant. || *Aceite de ricino*, castor oil.

rico, ca adj. Rich, wealthy: *un rico propietario*, a rich property owner. || Rich: *persona rica de virtudes*, person rich in virtues. || Fertile, rich: *tierra rica*, fertile land. || Full: *un viaje rico en aventuras*, a trip full of adventures. || Rich, magnificent: *adornado con ricos bordados*, adorned with rich embroidery. || Delicious: *pastel muy rico*, delicious cake. || Adorable, lovely: *¡qué niño más rico!*, what an adorable child! || — FAM. *Estar muy rica*, to be a nice bit of stuff, to be a gorgeous piece (una chica). || *Hacerse rico*, to get rich. || FAM. *Oye rico, ¿qué te has creído?* hey!, what's the big idea? || *¡Rico!*, love, dear. | *¡Un momento, rico!*, just a minute, mate!
— M. y f. Rich person. || — Pl. The rich. || *Nuevo rico*, nouveau riche.

rictus m. Grin. || *Rictus de dolor*, wince [of pain].

ricura f. Deliciousness. || *¡Qué ricura de niño!*, what a darling child!, what an adorable child!

ridiculez f. Ridiculousness, absurdity (cualidad de absurdo). || Ridiculous thing (cosa ridícula o insignificante). || Nothing, triviality: *se han peleado por una ridiculez*, they fought over nothing. || *Es una ridiculez hacer eso*, it's ridiculous to do that.

ridiculizar v. tr. To ridicule, to deride (burlarse). || To make a fool of, to ridicule (dejar en ridículo).

ridículo m. Reticule (bolso de señora).

ridículo, la adj. Ridiculous, ludicrous, absurd: *decir cosas ridículas*, to say ridiculous things. || Ridiculously small, minute: *una ganancia ridícula*, a ridiculously small profit.
— M. Ridiculous. || — *Caer en el ridículo*, to become ridiculous. || *Hacer el ridículo* or *quedar en ridículo*, to make a fool of o.s. || *Poner en ridículo*, to make a fool of, to ridicule.

riego m. Irrigation (irrigación). || Watering (en el jardín). || — *Boca de riego*, hydrant. || *Canal de riego*, irrigation canal. || *Riego asfáltico*, cutback. || *Riego por aspersión*, sprinkling. || ANAT. *Riego sanguíneo*, circulation of the blood.

riel m. Rail, track: *los rieles del tranvía*, the tram rails; *riel de cortina*, curtain rail. || Ingot, bar (de metal).

rielar v. intr. POÉT. To glitter: *la Luna en el mar riela*, the moon glitters on the sea. || To twinkle (las estrellas).

rielera f. Ingot mould [U.S., ingot mold].

rienda f. Rein (correa). || — Pl. FIG. Reins, control, *sing: las riendas del gobierno*, the reins of government. || — FIG. *Aflojar las riendas*, to slacken the rein, to ease up. | *A rienda suelta*, with a free rein (sin freno), at full speed (muy rápidamente). | *Coger* or *tomar las riendas de*, to take in hand. | *Dar rienda suelta a*, to give free rein to. | *Empuñar las riendas*, to take the reins, to take control. | *Llevar las riendas*, to hold the reins, to be in control. | *Tirar de la rienda a*, to tighten the reins on.

riente adj. Laughing. || FIG. Bright, cheerful: *riente jardín*, cheerful garden.

riesgo m. Risk, danger: *correr un riesgo*, to run a risk. || — *A* or *con riesgo de*, at the risk of. || *Correr (el) riesgo de*, to run the risk of. || *Por su cuenta y riesgo*, at one's own risk. || *Seguro a todo riesgo*, fully comprehensive insurance.

riesgoso, sa adj. *Amer.* Risky, dangerous.

Rif n. pr. m. GEOGR. Rif.

rifa f. Raffle (tómbola). || Quarrel (riña).

rifado, da adj. Raffled. || FIG. *Este chico está rifado*, this young man is highly sought-after.

rifar v. tr. To raffle, to raffle off. || To draw lots for (echar a suertes).
— V. pr. MAR. To split (una vela). || FIG. y FAM. *Todo el mundo se rifa su compañía*, everyone vies for her company.

rifirrafe m. FAM. Row, scuffle (riña).

rifle m. Rifle (arma).

riflero m. *Amer.* Rifleman.

rigidez f. Rigidity, stiffness. || FIG. Strictness (severidad). | Inflexibility. || *Rigidez cadavérica*, rigor mortis.

rígido, da adj. Rigid, stiff: *una barra de acero rígida*, a rigid steel bar. || Stiff: *pierna rígida*, stiff leg. || FIG. Strict, rigorous: *disciplina rígida*, strict discipline; *moral rígida*, strict morals. | Inflexible. | Expressionless (inexpresivo). || *Quedarse rígido*, to get stiff (de frío), to go rigid (un cadáver).

rigodón m. Rigadoon.

rigor m. Severity, strictness, rigour [U.S., rigor] (severidad): *el rigor de un juez*, the severity of a judge. || Exactness, precision, rigorousness (exactitud). || Rigour, severity, harshness: *el rigor del clima polar*, the harshness of the polar climate. || — *De rigor*, de rigueur. || *Después del discurso de rigor*, after the inevitable speech. || *En el rigor del verano*, in the height of [the] summer. || *En rigor*, strictly speaking. || FIG. *Ser el rigor de las desdichas*, to be born under an unlucky star.

rigorismo m. Rigorism, strictness. || Austerity: *el rigorismo de los puritanos*, the austerity of the Puritans.

rigorista adj./s. Rigorist.

rigurosamente adv. Severely (con severidad). || Rigorously, accurately (con exactitud). || Meticulously (minuciosamente). || Strictly, absolutely: *rigurosamente exacto*, absolutely exact.

riguroso, sa adj. Rigorous, accurate, exact (exacto). || Harsh (actitud). || Severe, tough (severo). || Strict (estricto). || Harsh, severe (tiempo). || Meticulous (minucioso).

rijoso, sa adj. Quarrelsome (camorrista). || Sensitive, touchy (susceptible). || Sensual, lustful (sensual). || In rut: *caballo rijoso*, horse in rut.

rilar v. intr. To tremble, to shake, to shudder (de miedo). || To shiver, to shudder (de frío).
rima f. Rhyme. || — Pl. Poems, poetry, *sing.*
rimador, ra adj. Rhyming.
— M. y f. Rhymer, rhymester.
rimar v. intr. y tr. To rhyme.
rimbombancia f. Grandiloquence, pomposity, bombast (del estilo).
rimbombante adj. Resounding, ringing. || Grandiloquent, pompous, bombastic, high-flown: *estilo rimbombante*, grandiloquent style. || Showy, ostentatious: *vestido rimbombante*, showy dress.
rímel m. Mascara (para los ojos).
rimero m. Heap, pile (montón).
Rin n. pr. m. Rhine: *valle del Rin*, Rhine valley.
rincón m. Corner: *en un rincón de la habitación*, in a corner of the room. || FIG. Corner, nook, remote place (lugar apartado). || *Poner* or *castigar en el rincón*, to put in the corner (a un niño castigado).
— OBSERV. *Rincón* applies exclusively to reentrant angles, as opposed to *esquina* which indicates a salient angle.
rinconada f. Corner.
rinconera f. Corner table (mueble). || ARQ. Wall between a corner and the nearest recess.
ring m. DEP. Ring (de boxeo y lucha).
ringlera f. Row, line.
ringorrango m. Curlicue, flourish (en la escritura). || Frill, adornment (adorno).
rinitis f. MED. Rhinitis.
rinoceronte m. ZOOL. Rhinoceros.
rinofaringe f. ANAT. Rhinopharynx.
rinofaringitis f. MED. Rhinopharyngitis.
rinología f. MED. Rhinology.
rinólogo m. MED. Rhinologist.
rinoplastia f. MED. Rhinoplasty.
riña f. Brawl, fight (pelea): *una riña sangrienta*, a bloody brawl. || Quarrel, argument (discusión): *riña de niños*, childish quarrel. || *Riña de gallos*, cockfight.
riñón m. ANAT. Kidney. || CULIN. Kidney: *riñones al jerez*, kidney in sherry sauce. || FIG. Heart, centre: *vivo en el mismo riñón de Madrid*, I live right in the heart of Madrid; *el riñón del asunto*, the heart of the matter. || MIN. Nodule, kidney ore. || ARQ. Spandrel. || — Pl. Loins (lomos). || — FIG. *Costar un riñón*, V. COSTAR. | *Cubrirse el riñón*, to feather one's nest. | *Pegarse al riñón*, to be very nutritious (un alimento). | *Tener el riñón bien cubierto*, to be well off *o* well heeled. | *Tener riñones*, to have guts, to have nerve.
riñonada f. ANAT. Cortical tissue of the kidney (tejido). || Loin (de res): *chuleta de riñonada*, loin chop. || CULIN. Kidney stew (guiso). || FIG. y FAM. *Costar una riñonada*, to cost the earth.
río m. River: *el río Misisipí*, the River Mississippi, the Mississippi River. || FIG. River, stream (de lágrimas, sangre). || — FIG. *A río revuelto ganancia de pescadores*, it's an ill wind that blows nobody good. | *Cuando el río suena agua lleva*, there's no smoke without fire. | *Pescar en* or *a río revuelto*, to fish in troubled waters. || *Río abajo*, downstream. || *Río arriba*, upstream. || *Río de lava*, stream of lava. || FIG. *Todavía ha de correr mucha agua por el río*, a lot of water has still to flow under the bridge.
riobambeño, ña adj. [Of *o* from] Riobamba (Ecuador).
— M. y f. Native *o* inhabitant of Riobamba.
riojano, na adj. [Of *o* from] La Rioja (Argentina y España).
— M. y f. Native *o* inhabitant of La Rioja.
rioplatense adj. Of *o* from the River Plate region.
— M. y f. Native *o* inhabitant of the River Plate region.
riostra f. ARQ. Brace, strut.
ripia f. Lath, batten (tabla delgada). || Rough surface (de un madero aserrado).
ripio m. Rubble filling, broken stone (relleno de albañilería). || Residue (residuo). || Refuse (escombros). || FIG. Padding (palabrería inútil): *meter ripio*, to do a lot of padding. | Word used to fill in a verse (palabra superflua). || FIG. *No perder ripio*, not to miss a trick.
ripioso, sa adj. Filled with unnecessary words (versos).
riqueza f. Riches, *pl.*, wealth. || — Pl. Riches: *amontonar riquezas*, to pile up riches.
riquísimo, ma adj. Extremely rich. || FIG. Absolutely delicious (comida).
risa f. Laugh. || Laughter: *la risa del público*, the laughter of the audience. || Laughingstock (hazmerreír): *ser la risa de todo el mundo*, to be the laughingstock of everyone. || — *Caerse* or *desternillarse* or *mondarse* or *morirse* or *reventar* or *troncharse de risa*, to split one's sides laughing, to die laughing. || *Contener la risa*, to keep a straight face. || *Dar risa*, to make one laugh. || *Es* (*cosa*) *de risa*, it's laughable, it's enough to make one laugh. || *Llorar de risa*, to cry laughing. || *Me entró* or *me dio la risa*, I began to laugh, I couldn't help laughing. || *¡Qué risa!*, how very funny!, what a laugh! (fam.) || *Risa burlona* or *socarrona*, mocking laugh, horselaugh. || *Risa de conejo*, forced laugh *o* smile. || *Risa nerviosa* or *loca*, hysterical laughter. || *Ser motivo de risa*, to be sth. to laugh about. || *Soltar la risa*, to burst out laughing. || *Tener un ataque de risa*, to have a fit of laughter. || *Tomar una cosa a risa*, to take sth. as a joke, to laugh sth. off.
risada f. V. RISOTADA.
risco m. Crag, cliff.
risible adj. Laughable.
risilla o **risita** f. Giggle, titter. || False laugh (risa falsa).
risión f. Derision, mockery (mofa). || Laughingstock (hazmerreír). || *Objeto de risión*, laughingstock.
risorio m. ANAT. Risorius (músculo).
risotada f. Guffaw, boisterous laugh. || — *Dar risotadas*, to guffaw. || *Soltar una risotada*, to burst out laughing.
rispidez f. Harshness.
ristra f. String: *una ristra de ajos, de cebollas*, a string of garlic, of onions. || FIG. y FAM. String, pack: *una ristra de mentiras*, a string of lies. || *En ristra*, in single file.
ristre m. *En ristre*, at the ready (lanza).
ristrel m. Wooden moulding.
risueño, ña adj. Smiling: *cara risueña*, smiling face. || FIG. Happy, gay (contento). | Pleasant, cheerful: *pradera risueña*, pleasant meadow. | Bright (prometedor): *un porvenir risueño*, a bright future.
Rita n. pr. f. Rita. || — FIG. y FAM. *¡Cuéntaselo a Rita!*, tell it to the marines! | *¡Que lo haga Rita!*, I'm not going to do it!, let s.o. else do it!
ritmar v. tr. To put rhythm into (dar ritmo).
rítmico, ca adj. Rhythmic, rhythmical.
ritmo m. Rhythm. || FIG. Pace, rate: *el ritmo de trabajo*, the rate of work. || *Dar ritmo*, to put rhythm (*a*, into).
rito m. Rite. || FIG. Ritual (costumbre): *los ritos de la vida familiar*, the rituals of family life.
ritornelo m. MÚS. Ritornello.
ritual adj. Ritual. || *Libro ritual*, ritual.
—. M. Ritual. || FIG. *Ser de ritual*, to be a ritual *o* a custom, to be customary.
ritualidad f. Ritualism, rituality.
ritualismo m. Ritualism.
ritualista adj. Ritualistic.
— M. y f. Ritualist.
rival adj./s. Rival.
rivalidad f. Rivalry.
rivalizar v. intr. To rival: *rivalizar en simpatía, en belleza*, to rival in kindness, in beauty.
rivera f. Brook (arroyo).
rizado, da adj. Curly: *tener el pelo rizado*, to have curly hair. || Curled (artificialmente). || Ripply (la superficie del agua). || Choppy, wavy: *mar rizada*, choppy sea.
— M. Curling (acción).
rizador m. Curling iron.
rizar v. tr. To curl (el pelo). || To ripple (la superficie del agua). || To make choppy (el mar). || To crease, to crumple (tela, papel).
— V. pr. To curl. || To go curly, to curl: *se me rizó el pelo con la lluvia*, my hair has gone curly with the rain. || To ripple (la superficie del agua). || To become *o* to get choppy (el mar).
rizo, za adj. Curly: *pelo rizo*, curly hair.
— M. Curl, lock (de cabellos). || Ripple (del agua). || Terry velvet (terciopelo). || AVIAC. Loop: *rizar el rizo*, to loop the loop. || MAR. Reef point. || — *Nudo de rizo*, reef knot. || MAR. *Tomar rizos*, to take in sail, to reef.
rizófago, ga adj. Rhizophagous (animal).
rizoma m. BOT. Rhizome.
rizópodo m. ZOOL. Rhizopod. || — Pl. Rhizopoda.
— Adj. Rhizopodous.
rizoso, sa adj. [Naturally] curly (el pelo).
ro interj. Rock-a-by, hushaby.
roa f. MAR. Stem.
roano, na adj./s.m. Roan.
robador, ra adj. Robbing, thieving.
— M. y f. Robber, thief.
róbalo o **robalo** m. ZOOL. Bass (pez).
robar v. tr. To steal, to rob (algo): *robar mil pesetas*, to steal a thousand pesetas; *le han robado el reloj*, s.o. robbed him of his watch, s.o. stole his watch from him. || To rob (a una persona): *me han robado*, I've been robbed. || To break into, to burgle (una casa). || To kidnap, to abduct (raptar). || To eat away (el mar). || To carry away (los ríos). || To draw (juego de cartas). || FIG. To rob: *en esta tienda te roban*, in this shop they rob you. | To steal, to capture (la atención). | To steal [away]: *robar el corazón*, to steal one's heart [away]. | To take (la vida). || *Robar con fractura* or *efracción*, to burgle, to commit burglary.
robín m. Rust (orín).
robinia f. BOT. Robinia, acacia.
robladura f. Clinching (de un clavo).
roblar v. tr. To clinch (un clavo).
roble n. Oak, oak tree (árbol). || FIG. y FAM. Robust *o* strong person (persona). || — *De roble*, oak. || FIG. *Más fuerte que un roble*, as strong as an ox (fuerte), as solid as a rock (resistente).
robledal m. o **robleda** f. o **robledo** m. Oak grove.
roblón m. Rivet: *roblón de cabeza plana, fresada, redonda*, flathead, countersunk, buttonhead rivet.
roblonar v. tr. To rivet.
robo m. Robbery, theft: *cometer un robo*, to commit a robbery; *robo a mano armada*, armed robbery.

|| Stolen article (cosa robada). || Draw (en los juegos de cartas). || FIG. Robbery (estafa). || — *Robo con agravante*, aggravated theft. || *Robo con fractura* or *efracción*, burglary.
roborar v. tr. To fortify, to strengthen (reforzar). || FIG. To corroborate (corroborar).
robot m. Robot. || FIG. Puppet (pelele).

— OBSERV. The plural of *robot* in Spanish is *robots*, as in English.

robustecer* v. tr. To strengthen, to make strong *o* robust.
— V. pr. To become strong, to gain strength.
robustecimiento m. Strengthening, fortifying.
robustez f. Robustness, strength (de personas). || Strength: *la robustez de un puente*, the strength of a bridge. || Sturdiness, solidness: *la robustez de un coche*, the sturdiness of a car.
robusto, ta adj. Robust, strong (persona). || Strong, sturdy, solid (una construcción, etc.).
roca f. Rock: *roca sedimentaria*, sedimentary rock; *escalar una roca*, to climb a rock. || FIG. Stone: *corazón de roca*, heart of stone. || — *Cristal de roca*, rock crystal. || FIG. *Firme como una roca*, as solid as a rock. || *Roca viva*, bare rock.
rocadero m. Distaff head (de la rueca).
rocalla f. Stone chippings, *pl.* (al tallar la piedra). || Rubble (desprendida de la roca). || Large glass bead (abalorio grueso).
Rocallosas n. pr. f. pl. GEOGR. *Montañas Rocallosas*, Rocky Mountains.
rocalloso, sa adj. Rocky, rubbly (lleno de trozos de roca). || Stony (lleno de piedras).
roce m. Rubbing, chafing: *roce de los zapatos, del cuello*, rubbing of one's shoes, of one's collar. || Touch (ligero): *el roce de su mano le dio escalofríos*, the touch of her hand made him shiver. || Rub, mark, scuff (en la pared, un mueble, etc.). || Chafe mark (en la piel). || FIG. Contact (trato entre personas). | Friction: *roces entre dos naciones vecinas*, friction between two neighbouring countries. || TECN. Friction.
rociada f. Sprinkling, spraying (acción y efecto de rociar). || Dew (rocío). || FIG. Shower, hail: *una rociada de golpes, de insultos*, a shower of blows, of insults.
rociadera f. Watering can (regadera).
rociador m. Sprayer, clothes sprinkler.
rociadura f. Sprinkling, spraying.
rociar v. tr. To sprinkle, to spray: *rociar con agua*, to sprinkle with water. || To water, to sprinkle: *rociar las flores*, to water the flowers. || FIG. To wash down: *una comida rociada con una botella de clarete*, a meal washed down with a bottle of claret. | To scatter, to strew (arrojar cosas dispersas). || To moisten (humedecer).
— V. intr. *Ha rociado durante la noche*, dew has formed *o* has fallen during the night.
rocín m. Hack, nag (caballo). || FIG. Stupid fellow, clodhopper.
rocinante m. Worn-out nag.
rocino m. Hack, nag (caballo).
rocío m. Dew. || Drizzle (llovizna).
rococó m. Rococo (estilo).
rocoso, sa adj. V. ROCALLOSO.
roda f. MAR. Stem.
rodaballo m. ZOOL. Turbot (pez). || FIG. y FAM. Sly dog, crafty devil (hombre taimado).
rodado, da adj. Dappled (caballo). || Smooth (piedra). || FIG. Experienced (experimentado). || Run-in (automóvil). || — *Canto rodado*, boulder (grande), pebble (pequeño). || *Tránsito rodado* or *circulación rodada*, vehicular *o* road traffic. || FIG. *Venir rodado*, V. VENIR.
— M. *Amer.* Vehicle. || — F. Imprint, tyre mark.
rodadura f. Rolling.
rodaja f. Disc (de metal u otra materia). || Slice (de limón, salchichón). || Rowel (estrellita de la espuela). || Small wheel (ruedecilla). || Roll, fold (de grasa). || TECN. Cutting *o* perforating wheel. || *En rodajas*, sliced, in slices.
rodaje m. Wheels, *pl.* (conjunto de ruedas). || Filming, shooting (de una película). || Running in (de un motor, de un coche). || — *En rodaje*, running in (coche). || *Secretaria de rodaje*, continuity girl, script girl (cine).
rodamiento m. Bearing: *rodamiento de bolas, de rodillos*, ball, roller bearing.
Ródano n. pr. m. GEOGR. Rhone.
rodante adj. Rolling.
rodapelo m. Brushing against the nap.
rodapié m. Skirting board [U.S., baseboard] (zócalo de una pared). || Dust ruffle (de cama, de mesa).
rodaplancha f. Ward (de la llave).
rodar* v. intr. To roll: *la pelota rueda*, the ball rolls. || To turn (una rueda). || To run: *coche que rueda bien*, car that runs well. || To travel, to go: *rodar a cien kilómetros por hora*, to go at a hundred kilometres per hour. || To roll (accidentalmente): *el coche rodó cuesta abajo*, the car rolled downhill. || To fall: *rodar escaleras abajo*, to fall down the stairs. || CINEM. To shoot, to film. || FIG. To roam: *rodar por las calles, por el mundo*, to roam the streets, the world. | To move about (ir de acá para allá). | To go around: *mil proyectos rodaban en su cabeza*, a thousand ideas were going around in his head. || *Amer.* To stumble, to fall (un caballo). || — FIG. y FAM. *Andar rodando*, to be scattered around: *no quiero que mis libros anden rodando por la casa*, I don't want my books to be scattered around the house. | *Echarlo todo a rodar*, V. ECHAR. || *Rodar por el mundo*, to roam the world over (viajar), to exist (existir).
— V. tr. To film, to shoot: *rodar una película*, to film a picture. || To run in (un motor, un coche). || To roll (un objeto redondo). || To travel: *haber rodado todo el mundo*, to have travelled all over the world.
Rodas n. pr. GEOGR. Rhodes.
rodear v. tr. To enclose, to inclose: *rodear un huerto con una cerca*, to enclose a garden with a fence. || To wrap: *rodear la cabeza con una venda*, to wrap one's head in a bandage. || To surround: *la policía rodeó la casa*, the police surrounded the house. || To go around: *el camino rodea la montaña*, the road goes around the mountain. || *Amer.* To round up (el ganado). || *Le rodeé el cuello con mis brazos*, I threw my arms round his neck.
— V. pr. To surround o.s.: *rodearse de los mejores consejeros*, to surround o.s. with the best advisors. || *Rodearse de lujo*, to lavish luxury on o.s.
rodela f. Buckler, round shield. || *Amer.* Pad (rodete).
rodeno, na adj. Red, reddish (rojo, rojizo). || BOT. *Pino rodeno*, cluster, pinaster.
rodeo m. Detour, roundabout way: *dar un rodeo*, to make a detour, to go by a roundabout way. || Roundup (del ganado). || Rodeo (fiesta de rancheros). || Corral (lugar donde se celebra). || *Amer.* Mexican bullfight. || — Pl. FIG. Evasiveness, *sing.* (al hablar). || — FIG. *Andar* or *andarse con rodeos*, to beat about the bush. | *Dejémonos de rodeos*, let's get to the point. | *No andarse con rodeos*, to get straight to the point, not to beat about the bush.
rodera f. Rut, track (carril).
Rodesia n. pr. f. GEOGR. Rhodesia.
rodesiano, na adj./s. Rhodesian.
rodete m. Bun, chignon (de pelo). || Pad, cushion, padded ring (para cargar algo sobre la cabeza). || Ward (de cerradura). || Roll [of fat] (de grasa en una persona). || Fifth wheel (de carruaje).
rodilla f. ANAT. Knee. || Pad (para llevar algo sobre la cabeza). || Floorcloth, cloth (para fregar suelos). || — *Caer de rodillas*, to fall on one's knees. || *De rodillas*, kneeling (de hinojos), on bended knees (humildemente): *pedir algo de rodillas*, to ask for sth. on bended knees. || *Doblar la rodilla*, to go down on one knee (arrodillarse), to humble o.s. (humillarse). || *Estar de rodillas*, to be kneeling, to kneel. || *Hincar la rodilla*, to go down on one knee, to kneel. || *Hincarse de rodillas*, to go down on one's knees, to kneel [down].
rodillada f. o **rodillazo** m. Blow given with the knee. || Blow on the knee. || *Dar un rodillazo a alguien*, to knee s.o.
rodillazo m. TAUR. Kneeling pass.
rodillera f. Knee guard (protección). || Knee patch (refuerzo en los pantalones). || Pad (para llevar pesos sobre la cabeza). || *Hacer rodilleras*, to go baggy *o* to bag at the knees (un pantalón).
rodillo m. Roller. || Platen, roller (de la máquina de escribir). || Rolling pin (de cocina). || Mangle (de lavadora). || IMPR. *Rodillo entintador*, inking roller.
rodio m. QUÍM. Rhodium.
rododendro m. BOT. Rhododendron.
rodomiel m. Rose honey.
rodrigar v. tr. To prop up, to stake (una planta).
rodrigazón f. Season when plants are propped up.
rodrigón m. Prop, stake (para las plantas). || FIG. y FAM. Chaperon.
roedor, ra adj. Rodent, gnawing.
— M. Rodent.
roedura f. Gnawing (acción). || Gnaw mark (marca dejada al roer). || Gnawed part (porción roída).
roel m. HERÁLD. Roundel.
roela f. Blank, planchet (en numismática).
roentgen m. FÍS. Roentgen, röntgen.
roentgenoterapia f. MED. Roentgenotherapy.
roer* v. tr. To nibble [at]: *roer una galleta*, to nibble [at] a biscuit. || To gnaw: *el perro está royendo un hueso*, the dog is gnawing a bone. || FIG. To gnaw, to nag (atormentar): *su conciencia le roe*, he is gnawed by pangs of conscience, his conscience nags him. | To nibble away at, to eat away (quitar poco a poco). || — FIG. y FAM. *Dar que roer a uno*, to give s.o. a tough time. | *Un problema duro de roer*, a hard problem to solve, a hard nut to crack.
— V. pr. To bite: *roerse las uñas*, to bite one's fingernails.
rogación f. Request (petición). || — Pl. REL. Rogations (letanías).
rogador, ra o **rogante** adj. Supplicatory.
rogar* v. tr. e intr. To request, to ask (pedir): *le rogué que viniera en seguida*, I requested him to come at once. || To beg, to plead (con humildad): *le ruego un poco de compasión*, I beg you *o* I beg of you *o* I plead with you to take pity on me. || To implore (implorar). || To pray: *rogar a Dios*, to pray to God. || — *Hacerse de rogar*, to take a lot of asking, to play hard to get, to have to be coaxed. || *No se hace de rogar*, he doesn't have to be asked twice. || *Ruega por nos*, pray for us. || *Se ruega no fumar*, no smoking

please, you are requested to refrain from smoking. || *Se ruega la publicación*, v. PUBLICACIÓN.
rogativa f. Rogation. || *Hacer rogativas para que llueva*, to pray for rain.
rogativo, va adj. Supplicatory.
rogatorio, ria adj. JUR. Rogatory: *comisión rogatoria*, rogatory commission.
roído, da adj. Gnawed, eaten (carcomido). || Miserable.
rojete m. Rouge (colorete).
rojez f. Redness.
rojizo, za adj. Reddish.
rojo, ja adj. Red: *pelo rojo*, red hair. || Ruddy (las mejillas). || — FAM. *Estar más rojo que un cangrejo*, to be as red as a beetroot. || VET. *Mal rojo*, swine fever. || *Ponerse rojo*, to blush, to go red (ruborizarse), to turn red (cualquier cosa). || *Ponerse rojo de ira*, to get fighting mad.
— Adj./s.m. FAM. Red, communist (comunista). || Republican. || — M. Red. || — *El disco está en rojo*, the lights are red, the traffic light is on red. || FIG. *La discusión se puso al rojo vivo*, the discussion became heated. | *La situación está al rojo vivo*, the situation is electric *o* is very tense. || *Poner al rojo*, to heat until red hot, to make red hot. || *Rojo blanco*, white hot. || *Rojo cereza*, cherry red. || *Rojo de labios*, lipstick.
Rojo (Mar) n. pr. m. GEOGR. Red Sea.
rol m. Roll (lista). || MAR. Muster roll.
roldana f. Pulley wheel.
rollizo, za adj. Round (cilíndrico). || Chubby, plump: *niño rollizo*, chubby child.
— M. Round log (madero).
rollo m. Roll: *rollo de papel*, roll of paper. || Rolling pin (de pastelero). || Coil (de cuerda). || Roll (carrete de película). || Round log (de madera). || Scroll (de pergamino). || FAM. Roll, layer (carne). | Bore, drag: *ese tío, la conferencia es un rollo*, that fellow, the lecture is a bore. || (Ant.). Stone pillar. || — FAM. *¡Largue el rollo!*, speech! | *Perdón por todo este rollo*, forgive me for boring you to death. | *Soltó su rollo clásico*, he came out with his usual boring tale, he said what he always says. | *¡Vaya rollo!*, what a bore!
Roma n. pr. GEOGR. Rome. || — FIG. y FAM. *Cuando a Roma fueres, haz lo que vieres*, when in Rome do as the Romans do. | *Por todas partes se va a Roma* or *todos los caminos van a Roma*, all roads lead to Rome. | *Revolver Roma con Santiago*, to leave no stone unturned, to move heaven and earth.
romadizo m. MED. Head cold.
romana f. Steelyard (balanza).
romance adj. Romance: *las lenguas romances*, Romance languages.
— M. Romance (lengua). || Spanish, Castilian (castellano). || Romance (composición poética con versos octosílabos). || — FIG. *En buen romance*, clearly, plainly. || *Romance de ciego*, ballad sung on the street by a blind man.
romancero, ra m. y f. Author or singer of Spanish romances. || — M. Collection of Spanish romances.
romanear v. tr. To weigh on a steelyard.
romanesco, ca adj. Roman (de los romanos). || Novelesque.
románico, ca adj./s.m. ARQ. y ARTES. Romanesque. || *Lenguas románicas*, Romance languages.
romanilla adj. Round.
— F. Round hand (letra).
romanismo m. Romanism.
romanista m. y f. Romanist.
romanizar v. tr. To Romanize.
romano, na adj./s. Roman. || — *El Imperio Romano*, the Roman Empire. || *Lechuga romana*, cos lettuce [U.S., romaine lettuce]. || *Números romanos*, Roman numerals. || FIG. *Obra de romanos*, Herculean task.
romanticismo m. Romanticism.
romántico, ca adj./s. Romantic.
romanticón, ona adj. Romantic: *espíritu romanticón*, romantic spirit.
romanza f. MÚS. Romance.
rombal adj. Rhombic.
rómbico, ca adj. Rhombic.
rombo m. MAT. Rhombus. || Turbot (rodaballo).
romboédrico, ca adj. Rhombohedral.
romboedro m. Rhombohedron.
romboidal adj. Rhomboidal.
romboide m. MAT. Rhomboid.
romboideo, a adj. Rhomboid.
Romeo n. pr. m. Romeo.
romería f. Pilgrimage (peregrinación): *ir de romería*, to go on a pilgrimage. || Festival at a local shrine (fiesta popular).
romero, ra adj. Who goes on a pilgrimage, pilgrim.
— M. y f. Pilgrim (peregrino). || — M. Rosemary (arbusto). || Pilot fish (pez).
romo, ma adj. Blunt, dull: *punta roma*, blunt point. || Snub (nariz). || Snub-nosed (persona). || FIG. Dull (torpe).
rompecabezas m. inv. Puzzle (juego). || Jigsaw [puzzle] (de tacos de madera). || FIG. Puzzle, riddle (problema complicado).
rompedera f. TECN. Punch.
rompedero, ra adj. Breakable, fragile.
rompedor, ra adj. Destructive. || Hard on one's clothes.
— M. y f. Destructive person, breaker.
rompedura f. Breaking.
rompehielos m. inv. Icebreaker (barco).
rompehuelgas m. inv. FAM. Strikebreaker, blackleg, scab (esquirol).
rompelotodo m. inv. Destructive person.
rompenueces m. inv. Nutcracker (cascanueces).
rompeolas m. inv. Breakwater, jetty.
romper v. tr. To break: *romper una silla*, to break a chair. || To smash, to shatter, to break: *romper la vajilla*, to smash the dishes. || To break down (una valla). || To snap, to break (una cuerda). || To tear (papel, tela). || To wear out: *romper el calzado*, to wear out one's shoes. || FIG. To interrupt, to break: *romper la monotonía*, to break the monotony. | To break off (las relaciones, la amistad). | To initiate, to begin (empezar): *romper las hostilidades*, to initiate hostilities. | To cut through, to cleave: *el barco rompe las aguas*, the boat cuts through the water. | To violate, to break (una ley). || — MIL. To open: *romper el fuego*, to open fire. | To break through (el frente enemigo). || DEP. To break [service] (tenis). || FIG. y FAM. To smash in: *romperle la cara* or *las narices a uno*, to smash s.o.'s face in. || — MIL. *¡Rompan filas!*, fall out!, dismiss! || *Romper el ayuno*, to break one's fast. || FIG. *Romper el hielo*, to break the ice. || MIL. *Romper filas*, to break ranks, to fall out. || *Romper la marcha*, to lead the way. || FIG. y FAM. *Romper una lanza por*, to fight for, to defend.
— V. intr. To break (las olas). || FIG. To break off relations, to break off, to break up: *ha roto con su novia*, he has broken up with his girlfriend. | To break: *romper con el pasado*, to break with the past. | To burst out, to burst into: *rompió a hablar*, he burst out talking; *romper en llanto*, to burst out crying, to burst into tears. || To bloom, to blossom (las flores). || — *Al romper el alba* or *el día*, at dawn, at daybreak. || FIG. *De rompe y rasga*, determined, resolute. | *Quien rompe paga*, one must pay the consequences [of one's actions].
— V. pr. To break: *se rompió la silla*, the chair broke. || To break, to smash (una vasija). || To snap (una cuerda). || To tear (un papel, una tela). || To break, to fracture: *romperse una pierna*, to break one's leg. || To break down: *se me rompió el coche*, my car broke down. || To wear out (zapatos). || — FIG. y FAM. *Romperse las narices*, v. NARIZ. | *Romperse los cascos* or *la cabeza*, to rack one's brains.
rompible adj. Breakable, fragile.
rompiente m. Reef, shoal (escollo).
rompimiento m. V. RUPTURA.
Rómulo n. pr. m. Romulus.
ron m. Rum.
ronca f. Bellow [of a buck deer in rut] (bramido). || Rutting season (época). || Halberd (arma).
roncador, ra adj. Snoring (que ronca).
— M. y f. Snorer.
roncamente adv. Hoarsely. || Coarsely, roughly (toscamente).
roncar v. intr. To snore (durmiendo). || To bellow [a buck deer in the rutting season]. || FIG. To roar (el mar). | To roar, to howl (el viento).
roncear v. intr. To dawdle (remolonear). || FAM. To flatter, to soft-soap (halagar).
roncería f. Dawdling, slowness (lentitud). || FAM. Flattery, soft soap (halago).
roncero, ra adj. Dawdling (remolón). || Grouchy (regañón). || Flattering, soft-soaping (halagador). || MAR. Slow (embarcación).
ronco, ca adj. Hoarse, raucous (áspero): *voz ronca*, hoarse voice. || Hoarse (que tiene ronquera): *estar ronco*, to be hoarse. || Raucous, harsh (sonido).
roncha f. Swelling, lump, bump (en la piel). || Slice (rodaja).
ronda f. Round (vuelta dada para vigilar). || Watch (vigilancia). || Patrol (patrulla). || Round (del cartero). || Beat (de la policía). || Group of young minstrels (conjunto musical). || Hand (en juegos de cartas). || Ring road (camino de circunvalación). || FAM. Round (convidada): *pagar una ronda*, to stand a round. || FIG. Round (de negociaciones). || *Amer.* Circle (corro). || *Camino de ronda*, v. CAMINO.
rondador, ra adj. Making rounds. || Serenading.
— M. y f. Patrolman, night watchman (vigilante). || Serenader. || *Amer.* Ecuadorian panpipe (flauta).
rondalla f. Group of serenaders *o* minstrels. || Tale, story (patraña).
rondar v. intr. To patrol, to go the rounds (para vigilar). || To prowl (merodear).
— V. tr. To go around (dar vueltas). || FIG. To threaten: *la gripe le está rondando*, the flu is threatening him. | To be about: *rondar la cincuentena*, to be about fifty. | To pursue (andar en pos de). | To court (a una mujer). | To walk up and down: *rondar la calle*, to walk up and down the street. | To serenade. || FIG. *Me está rondando el sueño*, I am feeling very sleepy.
rondel m. Rondel (poema).
rondeño, ña adj. [Of *o* from] Ronda [town in Spain].
— M. y f. Native *o* inhabitant of Ronda. || — F. Fandango of Ronda.
rondó m. MÚS. Rondo.

rondón (de) loc. Unannounced, without warning (sin avisar): *entrar de rondón*, to enter without warning. || Unexpectedly (inesperadamente).
ronquear v. intr. To be hoarse.
ronquedad f. Hoarseness (de la voz). || Raucousness (de un ruido).
ronquera f. Hoarseness. || *Tener* or *padecer ronquera*, to be hoarse.
ronquido m. Snore. || Snoring. || FIG. Howling: *el ronquido del viento*, the howling of the wind.
ronronear v. intr. To purr (un gato).
ronroneo m. Purring (del gato).
ronzal m. Halter.
ronzar v. tr. To crunch (al comer). || MAR. To lever.
roña f. VET. Mange (del ganado). || Dirt, filth (mugre). || Rust (orín). || FAM. Stinginess (tacañería).
— Adj. FAM. Stingy, tight (roñoso).
— M. y f. FAM. Skinflint, scrooge.
roñería f. V. ROÑOSERÍA.
roñica adj. FAM. Stingy, tight.
— M. y f. FAM. Skinflint, scrooge.
roñosería f. FAM. Stinginess.
roñoso, sa adj. VET. Mangy: *carnero roñoso*, mangy sheep. || Dirty, filthy (mugriento). || Rusty (oxidado). || FAM. Stingy, tight (avaro). || *Amer.* Rancorous (rencoroso).
ropa f. Clothes, *pl.*, clothing, dress, garments, *pl.* || — *A quema ropa*, V. QUEMAR. || *Con la ropa hecha jirones*, in tatters, with one's clothes in tatters. || FIG. *Hay ropa tendida*, be careful what you say. | *La ropa sucia se lava en casa*, one should not wash one's dirty linen in public. | *Nadar y guardar la ropa*, to have the best of both worlds. || *Ropa blanca*, linen, drapery (sábanas, etc.), lingerie (de mujer), underwear (de hombre). || *Ropa de cama*, bed linen. || *Ropa hecha*, ready-made *o* ready-to-wear clothes. || *Ropa interior*, underclothes, *pl.*, underwear. || *Ropa lavada* or *por lavar*, washing. || *Ropa planchada*, ironing. || CULIN. *Ropa vieja*, meat stew (guiso). || FIG. *Tentarse la ropa*, to think about it, to hesitate.
ropaje m. Robes, *pl.*, vestments, *pl.* (ropa suntuosa). || Heavy clothes, *pl.* (ropa excesiva). || ARTES. Drapery. || FIG. *Traicionar a uno bajo el ropaje de la amistad*, to betray s.o. under the banner of friendship.

ROPA, *f.* — CLOTHING

vestido *m.*	clothes *pl.*, garments *pl.* (ropa), dress (de mujer)	pijama *m.* [*Amer.*, piyama *m.*]	pyjamas *pl.* [U.S., pajamas *pl.*]
vestimenta *f.*	clothes *pl.*, garments *pl.*	polo *m.*; niqui *m.*	polo shirt; T-shirt
vestuario *m.*	wardrobe, clothes *pl.*	marinera *f.*	middy blouse
vestidura *f.*, indumentaria *f.*, indumento *m.*, atavío *m.*, atuendo *m.*	clothing, clothes *pl.*, garments *pl.*	bolero *m.*	bolero
		jersey *m.*	sweater
		jersey (*m.*) de mangas cortas	short-sleeved sweater
hábito *m.*	habit	jersey (*m.*) de cuello vuelto	roll-neck sweater
prenda (*f.*) de vestir	garment		
ropa (*f.*) hecha	ready-made *o* ready-to-wear clothes *pl.*	jersey (*m.*) con escote redondo	round-neck sweater
traje *m.*	suit (de hombre), dress (de mujer)	conjunto *m.*	suit, outfit, ensemble (vestido), twinset (de jerseys)
traje (*m.*) cruzado	double-breasted suit		
traje (*m.*) sastre *or* de chaqueta	tailored suit	rebeca *f.*	cardigan
		pantalón *m.*	trousers *pl.*
traje (*m.*) de calle	town clothes *pl.*	pantalón (*m.*) vaquero	jeans *pl.*
traje (*m.*) de diario	everyday clothes *pl.*	pantalones (*m. pl.*) cortos	short trousers
traje (*m.*) de noche, de etiqueta	evening, formal dress	pantalón (*m.*) bombacho	knickers *pl.* (de niño), knickerbockers *pl.* (de hombre)
chaqué *m.*	tailcoat, morning coat		
frac *m.*	dress coat, tails *pl.*	pantalón (*m.*) de golf	plus fours *pl.*
smoking *m.*	dinner jacket [U.S., tuxedo]	tirantes *m. pl.*	braces [U.S., suspenders]
		vuelta *f.*	turnup
terno *m.*	three-piece suit	calzas *f. pl.*	breeches
ajuar *m.*	trousseau (de novia), layette (de niño)	calzones *m. pl.*	trousers
		cinturón *m.*	belt
uniforme *m.*	uniform	falda *f.* [*Amer.*, pollera *f.*]	skirt
uniforme (*m.*) de gala	full dress uniform	falda (*f.*) pantalón	divided skirt, split skirt
mono *m.*; pelele *m.*	overalls *pl.*; rompers *pl.*	ropa (*f.*) blanca	underwear, underclothes *pl.*
toga *f.*	gown, robe (de magistrado)		
		calzoncillos *m. pl.*	underpants, pants [U.S., shorts]
túnica *f.*	tunic		
abrigo *m.* [*Amer.*, tapado *m.*]	overcoat (de hombre), coat (de mujer)	slip *m.*	briefs *pl.* (de hombre), panties *pl.* (de mujer)
gabán *m.*	overcoat, topcoat	bragas *f. pl.*, cucos *m. pl.*	panties, knickers
abrigo (*m.*) de pieles	fur coat	sostén *m.*	brassière, bra
sobretodo *m.*	overcoat	ajustador *m.*	corselet
capa *f.*	cape, cloak	faja *f.*; corsé *m.*	girdle; stays *pl.*, corset
manto *m.*	mantle, cloak	combinación *f.*	slip, petticoat
chilaba *f.*	jellaba, djellaba, jelab	enaguas *f. pl.*	petticoat *sing.*, underskirt *sing.*
chaquetón *m.*	three-quarter coat		
zamarra *f.*	sheepskin jacket	medias *f. pl.*	stockings
pelliza *f.*	pelisse	ligas *f. pl.*	suspenders [U.S., garters]
impermeable *m.*, gabardina *m.*	mac, mackintosh, raincoat	liguero *m.*	suspender belt [U.S., garter belt]
anorak *m.*; trenca *f.*	anorak; duffle coat	calcetines *m. pl.*	socks
poncho *m.*	poncho	leotardo *m.*	tights *pl.*, leotard
capucha *f.*; bufanda *f.*	hood; scarf, muffler	pañuelo *m.*	handkerchief
mantón *m.*, chal *m.*	shawl	taparrabo *m.*	bathing trunks *pl.*
toquilla *f.*	knitted shawl	bañador *m.*, traje (*m.*) de baño	bathing costume, swimsuit, bathing suit
estola (*f.*) de pieles	fur stole		
manguito *m.*	muff	bikini	bikini
chaqueta *f.*, americana *f.* [*Amer.*, saco *m.*]	jacket	delantal *m.*	apron (sin peto), pinafore (con peto)
bolsillo *m.*	pocket	mandil *m.*	apron
solapa *f.*	lapel	calzado *m.*, zapato *m.*	shoe
casaca *f.*; levita *f.*	dress coat; frock coat	suela *f.*; tacón *m.*	sole; heel
cazadora *f.*	jerkin	cordón *m.*	lace
chaleco *m.*	waistcoat	zapatos (*m. pl.*) de charol	patent leather shoes
guardapolvo *m.*	dust coat (prenda de vestir), housecoat [U.S., duster] (bata), overall (de niño, dependiente)	mocasín *m.*	moccasin
		bota *f.*	boot
		zapatillas *f. pl.*, chinelas *f. pl.*	slippers
		sandalia *f.*	sandal
bata *f.*	dressing gown (salto de cama), housecoat [U.S., duster] (traje de casa)	alpargatas *f. pl.*	canvas shoes, rope-soled shoes
		chanclo *m.*	clog (de madera), galosh, overshoe (de goma)
batín *m.*	short dressing gown		
salto (*m.*) de cama	dressing gown	zueco *m.*	clog, sabot, wooden shoe
albornoz *m.*	bathrobe	guante *m.*	glove
ruso *m.*	ulster	corbata *f.*	tie [U.S., necktie]
quimono *m.*	kimono	corbata (*f.*) de pajarita *or* de lazo	bow tie
camisa *f.*	shirt		
cuello (*m.*) postizo	detachable collar	chalina *f.*	cravat
cuello (*m.*) de pajarita *or* de palomita	wing collar	sombrero *m.*	hat
		sombrero (*m.*) hongo *or* melón *or* bombín	bowler hat
cuello (*m.*) vuelto	roll *o* polo neck		
cuello (*m.*) de pico	V-neck	sombrero (*m.*) de copa	top hat
manga *f.*; puño *m.*	sleeve; cuff	jipijapa *f.*	Panama hat
ojal *m.*	buttonhole	boina *f.*	beret
blusa *f.*	blouse	gorra *f.*	peaked cap, cap with a visor
camiseta *f.*	T-shirt (camisa corta), vest [U.S., undershirt] (de ropa interior)		
		gorro *m.*	cap
		tocado *m.*	hat, headdress
camisón *m.*, camisa (*f.*) de dormir	nightgown, nightdress (de mujer), nightshirt (de hombre)	turbante *m.*	turban
		pamela *f.*	broad-brimmed straw hat
		velo *m.*	veil

ropavejería f. Old-clothes shop.
ropavejero, ra m. y f. Second-hand dealer (de baratijas). || Old-clothesman (de ropa vieja).
ropería f. Clothes shop, clothing store (tienda). || Clothier's trade (industria). || Old-clothes shop (ropavejería). || Linen room (en comunidades).
ropero m. Wardrobe [U.S., clothes closet] (para guardar la ropa). || Charitable organization that distributes clothes to the poor (institución de caridad).
ropero, ra m. y f. Clothier.
roque m. Rook (ajedrez). || FIG. y FAM. *Estar, quedarse roque*, to be, to fall asleep.
roqueda f. o **roquedal** m. Rocky place.
roquedo m. Crag, rock (peñasco).
roquefort m. Roquefort (queso).
roqueño, ña adj. Rocky. || Hard as a rock (duro).
roqueta f. Turret (fortificación).
roquete m. Rochet (vestidura eclesiástica).
rorcual m. ZOOL. Rorqual, finback (ballena).
rorro m. Baby (niño pequeñito). || *Amer.* Doll (muñeca).
ros m. MIL. Cap.
rosa f. Rose: *ramo de rosas*, bouquet of roses. || Red spot [on the body] (mancha). || Rosette (hecha con cintas de colores). || ARQ. Rose window (rosetón). || Pink, rose (color): *un rosa claro*, a pale pink. || — *Agua de rosas*, rose water. || FIG. *Color de rosa*, pink, rose, rose-coloured. || FIG. y FAM. *Estar como las propias rosas*, to feel as fit as a fiddle. || FIG. *La vida no es un lecho de rosas*, life is not a bed of roses. | *No hay rosa sin espinas*, every rose has its thorn. | *Novela rosa*, novelette, romantic novel. | *Pintar las cosas de color de rosa*, to paint everything in the garden rosy. || *Rosa de Jericó*, rose of Jericho. || *Rosa de los vientos* or *náutica*, compass card. || *Rosa de pitiminí*, v. PITIMINÍ. || *Rosa de té*, tea rose. || *Rosa silvestre*, dog rose. || FIG. *Verlo todo de color de rosa*, to see everything through rose-coloured glasses.
— Adj. inv. Pink: *un traje rosa*, a pink dress.
rosáceo, a adj. Rosy. || MED. *Acné rosácea*, acne rosacea.
rosado, da adj. Pink, rosy, rose-coloured (color de rosa). || Rose-flavoured: *miel rosada*, rose-flavoured honey. || *Amer.* Red-roan (caballo). || *Color rosado*, pink.
— Adj./s.m. Rosé (vino).
rosal m. Rosebush. || — *Rosal silvestre*, dog rose. || *Rosal trepador*, rambling rose.
rosaleda o **rosalera** f. Rose garden.
rosarino, na adj. [Of *o* from] Rosario (Argentina).
— M. y f. Native *o* inhabitant of Rosario.
rosario m. Rosary, beads, *pl.*: *rezar el rosario*, to tell one's beads, to say the rosary. || FIG. Series, string: *un rosario de imprecaciones, de desdichas*, a series of imprecations, of misfortunes. || FIG. y FAM. Backbone (columna vertebral). || TECN. Chain [of buckets]. || — FIG. *Acabar como el rosario de la aurora*, to end abruptly (una reunión). || TECN. *Rosario hidráulico*, chain pump.
rosbif m. Roast beef.
rosca f. Thread (de un tornillo). || Roll (pan). || Doughnut (bollo). || Roll of fat (de gordura). || Ring (de humo). || *Amer.* Pad, round pad (rodete para llevar pesos en la cabeza). || — FIG. y FAM. *Hacer la rosca a uno*, to suck up to s.o. || *Hacerse una rosca*, to curl up [in a ball]. || *Pasarse de rosca*, to go too far (pasarse de los límites), to lose its thread (un tornillo). || *Paso de rosca*, pitch. || *Rosca de Arquímedes*, Archimedes' screw. || *Tapón de rosca*, screw-on cap.
roscado, da adj. Spiral-shaped. || Threaded (tornillo).
— M. TECN. Threading.
roscar v. tr. To thread.
rosco m. Ring-shaped cake (roscón). || Doughnut (bollo). || Roll (pan). || Ring (flotador). || FIG. y FAM. Zero: *me han puesto un rosco en física*, I got zero in physics.
roscón m. Ring-shaped cake. || *Roscón de Reyes*, twelfth-cake, twelfth-night cake.
Rosellón n. pr. m. GEOGR. Roussillon.
róseo, a adj. Rosy, roseate.
roséola f. MED. Roseola.
roseta f. Small rose (rosa pequeña). || Flush (en las mejillas). || Rosette (de cintas de colores). || *Amer.* Rowel (de espuela). || — Pl. Popcorn, *sing.* (maíz).
rosetón m. ARQ. Rose window. | Rosette (adorno).
rosicler m. Rosy hue of dawn.
rosillo, lla adj. Pink, rosy (rosado). || Reddish (rojizo). || Roan (caballo).
rosquilla f. Doughnut. || Grub, caterpillar (larva). || FIG. y FAM. *Venderse como rosquillas*, to sell like hot cakes (fácilmente).
rosquillero, ra m. y f. Doughnut maker (fabricante). || Doughnut seller (vendedor).
rostrado, da o **rostral** adj. Rostral: *columna, corona rostral*, rostral column, crown.
rostro m. Face, countenance: *un rostro alegre, sonriente*, a happy, smiling face. || Beak (pico del ave). || MAR. Rostrum, beak. || — FIG. *Hacer rostro a*, to face. || FIG. y FAM. *Tener mucho rostro*, to have a lot of cheek *o* nerve. | *Torcer el rostro*, to pull a face, to grimace. || *Volver el rostro*, to turn one's head aside.
rota f. Rout, defeat (derrota). || BOT. Rattan. || REL. Rota (tribunal).
rotáceo, a adj. BOT. Rotate.
rotación f. Rotation. || — COM. *Fondo de rotación*, revolving fund. || AGR. *Por rotación*, in rotation. | *Rotación de cultivos*, crop rotation.
rotacismo m. Rhotacism (fonética).
rotatorio, ria adj. Rotatory.
rotario, ria m. y f. Rotarian.
rotativo, va adj. Rotary, revolving (giratorio).
— F. IMPR. Rotary press. || — M. Newspaper (periódico): *rotativo matutino*, morning newspaper.
roten m. Rattan, ratan (planta). || Rattan cane (bastón).
rotería f. *Amer.* Poor, *pl.*, rabble (pobres).
rotífero m. ZOOL. Rotifer.
roto, ta adj. Broken: *juguete roto*, broken toy; *cuerda rota*, broken string. || Shattered, broken: *cristal roto*, broken glass. || Torn (tela, papel). || FIG. Broken (hombre). | Shattered, ruined: *una vida rota por los desengaños*, a life shattered by bitter experiences.
— M. Hole (en tela). || *Amer.* Common man, poor man. | FAM. Chilean (chileno). || FIG. *Nunca falta un roto para un descosido*, birds of a feather flock together.
rotograbado m. IMPR. Rotogravure.
rotonda f. ARQ. Rotunda.
rotor m. AVIAC. y TECN. Rotor.
rótula f. ANAT. Kneecap, patella, rotula. || TECN. Ball-and-socket joint.
rotulación f. Lettering.
rotulador m. Felt-tipped pen (lápiz). || Letterer (pintor).
rotular v. tr. To letter. || To mark in the names on, to label, to letter: *rotular un plano*, to mark in the names on a map.
rotular o **rotuliano, na** adj. ANAT. Rotulian.
rótulo m. Sign: *rótulo luminoso*, electric sign. || Poster, sign, notice (letrero). || Label (etiqueta). | Title (título). || Lettering (de un mapa). || — Pl. CINEM. Subtitles.
rotundamente adv. Flatly, categorically: *se negó rotundamente*, he flatly refused. || Emphatically: *dijo rotundamente que sí*, he emphatically agreed.
rotundidad f. Firmness: *la rotundidad de su negativa me descorazonó*, the firmness of his refusal disheartened me. || Rotundity (redondez). || Polish (del lenguaje).
rotundo, da adj. Flat, categorical, resounding, firm (negativa): *un no rotundo*, a resounding no. || Emphatic, categorical (afirmación). || Round (redondo). || Well-rounded (frase). || Resounding (éxito).
rotura f. Breaking, breakage (acción de romper). || Break (parte quebrada). || Fracture, break (de un hueso). || Tear, rip, rent (de un tejido).
roturación f. AGR. Ploughing [U.S., plowing], breaking up [of untilled ground].
roturador, ra adj. Ploughing [U.S., plowing].
— F. AGR. Plough [U.S., plow].
roturar v. tr. AGR. To plough [U.S., to plow], to break up.
round m. DEP. Round (asalto de boxeo).
roya f. BOT. Mildew, rust, blight.
royalty f. Royalty.
roza f. Groove, hollow (en la pared). || Cleared ground (tierra rozada).
rozadora f. MIN. Coal-cutting machine (máquina).
rozadura f. Scratch: *la bala le hizo una rozadura en el casco*, the bullet made a scratch on his helmet. || Abrasion, sore (desolladura). || Chafe (caballos).
rozagante adj. Showy (persona, vestido). || Spirited, lively (caballo). || Splendid, magnificent.
rozamiento m. Rubbing (roce). || TECN. Friction. || AGR. Clearing [of the ground] (desbroce). || FIG. Friction.
rozar v. tr. To graze: *la rueda rozó el bordillo de la acera*, the wheel grazed the curb. || To rub against: *la silla roza la pared*, the chair rubs against the wall. || To touch, to brush against: *mi mano le rozó la cara*, my hand touched her face. || To skim (una superficie). || To scratch (causando un arañazo). || To dirty (ensuciar). || AGR. To clear (un terreno). | To graze (el ganado): *rozar la hierba*, to graze the grass. || FIG. To be bordering on: *rozar la cuarentena*, to be bordering on forty; *su actitud roza el descaro*, his attitude borders on impudence. | To touch on: *es un asunto que roza la religión*, it's a subject which touches on religion. || FIG. *Rozamos el accidente*, we nearly had an accident.
— V. intr. To rub. || *Rozar con*, to border on, to touch on.
— V. pr. To rub, to brush: *se rozó con el alambre*, he rubbed against the wire. || FIG. To rub shoulders: *rozarse con artistas*, to rub shoulders with artists. || MAR. To chafe (desgastarse).
rúa f. Street (calle).
ruano, na adj. Roan (caballo).
rubefacción f. MED. Rubefaction.
rubefaciente adj./s.m. MED. Rubefacient.
rúbeo, a adj. Reddish.
rubéola f. MED. German measles, rubella.
rubescente adj. Rubescent.
rubeta f. Tree frog (rana de zarzal).
rubí m. Ruby. || Jewel (de un reloj). || — *Rubí balaje*, balas ruby. || *Rubí de Bohemia*, rose quartz.

— OBSERV. Pl. *rubíes*.

rubia f. Bot. Madder (granza). || Estate car, shooting brake [U.S., station wagon] (coche). || Blonde (mujer de pelo rubio). || Fam. Peseta (moneda). || Fam. *Rubia de frasco*, peroxide blonde.
rubiáceas f. pl. Bot. Rubiaceae.
rubial m. Madder field (campo de granzas).
rubiales m. y f. inv. Fam. Blond (hombre rubio). | Blonde (mujer rubia).
rubicán adj. Roan.
rubicela f. Min. Rubicelle.
Rubicón n. pr. m. Geogr. Rubicon. || *Atravesar* or *pasar el Rubicón*, to cross the Rubicon.
rubicundez f. Rubicundity. || Reddishness (del pelo). || Med. Rubefaction.
rubicundo, da adj. Rubicund. || Reddish (pelo). || Ruddy (rebosante de salud).
rubidio m. Rubidium (metal).
rubificar v. tr. To redden. || Med. To rubefy.
rubio, bia adj. Blond, blonde, fair: *tiene el pelo rubio*, she has blond hair. || *Tabaco rubio*, Virginia tobacco.
— M. Blond, blonde (color). || Blond (hombre con pelo rubio). || Zool. Red gurnard (pez). || — F. V. rubia.
rublo m. Rouble (moneda rusa).
rubor m. Bright red (color). || Blush, flush (en las mejillas). || Fig. Shame (vergüenza). | Abashment, bashfulness (pudor). || — Fig. *Causar* or *producir rubor*, to make blush. | *Sentir rubor*, to be ashamed (avergonzarse).
ruborizado, da adj. Blushing: *cara ruborizada*, blushing face. || Fig. Ashamed (avergonzado). | Abashed (por el pudor).
ruborizar v. tr. To make blush.
— V. pr. To blush, to turn red. || Fig. To feel ashamed *o* bashful *o* abashed (avergonzarse).
ruboroso, sa adj. Blushing, bashful.
rúbrica f. Rubric, section (sección de periódico). || Heading, title (título). || Flourish, paraph (trazo añadido a la firma). || Initials, *pl.* (del nombre). || Red mark (señal roja). || *Ser de rúbrica*, to be customary.
rubricante adj. Signatory, who signs.
rubricar v. tr. To initial (un documento, etc.). || Fig. To round off: *el torero rubricó su faena con una gran estocada*, the bullfighter rounded off his display with an impressive sword thrust. || *Firmado y rubricado*, signed and sealed.
rubro, bra adj. Red (encarnado).
— M. *Amer.* Heading, title (rúbrica). | Item, entry (en contabilidad).
rucio, cia adj. Grey (animal). || Grey-haired (persona).
— M. Donkey (asno).
ruco, ca adj. *Amer.* Worn-out.
ruche (estar) loc. Fam. To be flat broke *o* stony broke.
rucho m. Donkey, jackass (borrico).
ruda f. Bot. Rue (planta). || Fig. y fam. *Es más conocido que la ruda*, everybody knows him.
rudeza f. Roughness, coarseness, rudeness.
rudimental o **rudimentario, ria** adj. Rudimentary.
rudimento m. Rudiment.
rudo, da adj. Coarse, rough, unpolished (tosco). || Hard, difficult (difícil): *trabajo rudo*, hard job. || Rude, crude: *franqueza ruda*, rude frankness.
rueca f. Distaff (para hilar).
rueda f. Wheel. || Castor (de un mueble). || Circle, ring (de personas). || Spread (de un pavo). || Slice: *rueda de merluza*, slice of hake. || Rack (suplicio). || — *Barco de ruedas*, paddle steamer. || Fig. y fam. *Comulgar con ruedas de molino*, to swallow *o* to believe anything, to be very gullible. || *De* or *con dos ruedas*, two-wheeled. || Fig. y fam. *Hacer comulgar con ruedas de molino*, to pull the wool over s.o.'s eyes, to take s.o. in. || *Hacer la rueda*, to spread its tail (pavo), to court (cortejar), to cajole (lisonjear). || Fig. *Ir sobre ruedas*, to go *o* to run smoothly. || *La rueda de la fortuna*, the wheel of fortune. || *Patinaje sobre ruedas*, roller-skating. || *Patines de ruedas*, roller skates. || *Rueda catalina*, Catherine wheel (relojería). || *Rueda delantera*, *trasera*, front, rear wheel. || *Rueda de molino*, millstone. || *Rueda dentada*, cog, cogwheel. || *Rueda de paletas* or *álabes*, paddle wheel. || *Rueda de prensa*, press conference. || *Rueda de recambio* or *de repuesto*, spare wheel. || *Rueda de trinquete*, ratchet wheel. || *Rueda hidráulica*, waterwheel; mill wheel (de molino). || *Rueda libre*, freewheel. || *Ruedas gemelas*, dual wheels.
ruedo m. Round mat (esterilla). || Edge, border (borde). || Hem (de la falda). || Taur. Bullring (redondel). || — *Dar la vuelta al ruedo*, to go round the ring receiving applause [the matador]. || Fig. *Echarse al ruedo*, to enter the fray.
ruego m. Request (petición): *a ruego mío*, at my request. || Entreaty, plea (súplica). || *Le envío estos datos con el ruego de que los publique*, I am sending you this information in the hope that you will publish it.
rufián f. Pimp (chulo). || Villain, rogue (granuja).
rufianear v. intr. To pander.
rufianesco, ca adj. Villainous.
— F. Underworld (hampa).
rufo, fa adj. Blond (rubio). || Red-haired (pelirrojo). || Curly (rizado). || Self-satisfied, smug (ufano).
rugby m. Rugby (deporte). || *Rugby a trece*, Rugby League.
rugido m. Roar. || Fig. Shout, bellow (grito). | Howl, howling (de dolor, del viento).
rugidor, ra o **rugiente** adj. Roaring, bellowing.
ruginoso, sa adj. Rusty (mohoso).
rugir v. intr. To roar, to bellow. || Fig. To shout, to bellow (dar gritos). | To howl (el viento).
rugosidad f. Rugosity.
rugoso, sa adj. Wrinkled, rugose. || Rough (áspero).
ruibarbo m. Bot. Rhubarb.
ruido m. Noise: *los ruidos de la calle*, the noises of the street. || Sound (sonido). || Din, row (alboroto): *hacer* or *meter ruido*, to make a din. || Fig. Stir: *esta noticia va a hacer mucho ruido*, this news is going to cause a big stir. | Row, rumpus (escándalo). || — *Mucho ruido y pocas nueces* or *mucho ruido por nada*, much ado about nothing. || *Ruido ambiental*, noise. || *Ruido de fondo*, background noise. || *Sin ruido*, without making a noise, noiselessly, silently.
ruidosamente adv. Noisily. || Loudly: *aplaudir ruidosamente*, to applaud loudly.
ruidoso, sa adj. Noisy, loud. || Fig. Sensational: *noticia ruidosa*, sensational piece of news.
ruin adj. Vile, base, foul, despicable: *gente, acción ruin*, base people, deed. || Mean, stingy (avaro). || Miserable: *persona de ruin aspecto*, miserable-looking person. || Puny (raquítico). || Vicious, mean (caballo). || *En nombrando al ruin de Roma, asoma*, talk of the devil.
ruina f. Ruin, collapse (acción de hundirse). || Fig. Wrack and ruin: *vamos a la ruina*, we are going to wrack and ruin. | Ruin, downfall: *va a ser su ruina*, it will be the ruin of him *o* his downfall. | Fall: *la ruina del Imperio Romano*, the fall of the Roman Empire. | Destruction (de las ilusiones). || — Pl. Ruins: *una casa en ruinas*, a house in ruins; *las ruinas de una ciudad*, the ruins of a city. || — *El negocio le llevó a la ruina*, the business ruined him. || *Lo encontré hecho una ruina*, I found him a shadow of his former self *o* a wreck. || *Un edifico que amenaza ruina*, a building on the verge of collapse.
ruindad f. Vileness, meanness (vileza). || Mean act, piece of villainy (acción ruin). || Meanness, stinginess (tacañería).
ruinoso, sa adj. Ruinous: *un negocio ruinoso*, a ruinous business. || Tumbledown, in ruins: *castillo ruinoso*, castle in ruins. || Dilapidated: *casas ruinosas*, dilapidated houses. || *En estado ruinoso*, ramshackle, run-down, dilapidated.
ruiponce m. Bot. Rampion.
ruiseñor m. Nightingale (pájaro).
ruleta f. Roulette (juego de azar). || *Ruleta rusa*, Russian roulette.
rulo m. Roller, land leveller. || Roller (para el pelo). || Rolling pin (para la cocina).
Rumania n. pr. f. Geogr. Rumania, Roumania, Romania.
rumano, na adj./s. Rumanian, Roumanian.
rumazón f. Mar. Overcast horizon.
rumba f. Rumba (baile).
rumbeador o **rumbero** m. *Amer.* Pathfinder, guide.
rumbear v. intr. *Amer.* To head (*hacia*, for). | To get one's bearings (orientarse).
rumbo m. Direction (dirección). || Aviac. y Mar. Course: *corregir el rumbo*, to correct the course. || Fig. Course: *tomar otro rumbo*, to take another course; *marcar el rumbo*, to set the course. | Lavishness (generosidad). | Pomp. || — Mar. *Abatir el rumbo*, to fall to leeward. | *Cambiar de rumbo*, to change course. || Fig. *Celebrar una boda con mucho rumbo*, to have a very lavish wedding. || *Hacer rumbo a un sitio*, to head for a place. || Mar. *Navegar rumbo a*, to be bound for, to be on course for. || Fig. *Perder el rumbo*, to lose one's bearings. || *Poner rumbo a*, to head for. || *Rumbo a*, heading for, bound for. || Fig. *Tomar buen rumbo*, to take a turn for the better (un asunto).
rumboso, sa adj. Generous, lavish (generoso). || Lavish, splendid (magnífico): *una fiesta rumbosa*, a lavish party.
rumi m. Roumi, Christian.
— Observ. Term used by Moslems to refer to Christians.
rumia f. Rumination.
rumiante adj./s.m. Ruminant.
rumiar v. tr. To ruminate, to chew (masticar). || Fig. To ruminate, to think over: *rumiar un proyecto*, to think a plan over. | To grumble, to growl (refunfuñar).
— V. intr. To ruminate, to chew the cud (un animal).
rumor m. Rumour [U.S., rumor]. || Murmur: *se oía un rumor de voces*, a murmur of conversation could be heard; *el rumor de las aguas*, the murmur of the water. || Rustle, whisper (de los árboles). || — *El rumor general*, popular rumour. || *Según los rumores*, rumour has it that.
rumorear v. tr. e intr. To rumour [U.S., to rumor].
— V. pr. To be rumoured: *se rumorea que*, it is rumoured that.
rumoroso, sa adj. Murmuring, babbling: *arroyo rumoroso*, murmuring stream, babbling brook.

runa f. Rune (antiguo carácter escandinavo).
rúnico, ca adj. Runic.
runrún m. Rumour [U.S., rumor] (hablilla): *corre el runrún*, the rumour is going around. || Murmur, buzz (de voces).
runrunearse v. pr. To be rumoured [U.S., to be rumored], to be said: *se runrunea que van a subir los precios*, it is said that prices are going to rise.
rupestre adj. Rupestrian, rupestral. || Rock: *planta rupestre*, rock plant. || *Pintura rupestre*, cave *o* rupestrian painting.
rupia f. Rupee (moneda).
rupicabra o **rupicapra** f. Chamois (gamuza).
ruptor m. ELECTR. Contact breaker.
ruptura f. Breaking (acción de romper). || Break (parte rota). || Fracture (fractura). || Breaking-off (de relaciones). || Breakup (de dos personas). || Breaking (de un contrato). || MIL. Breakthrough. || ELECTR. *Corriente de ruptura*, breaking current.
rural adj. Rural: *los problemas rurales*, rural problems. || Country, rural: *cura, médico rural*, country priest, doctor. || — *Éxodo rural*, depopulation of rural areas. || *Finca rural*, country estate.
Rusia n. pr. f. GEOGR. Russia.
rusificación f. Russianization, Russification.
rusificar v. tr. To Russianize, to Russify.
ruso, sa adj./s. Russian. || — M. Russian (idioma).
rusófilo, la adj./s. Russophile.
rusticidad f. Rusticity. || Uncouthness (patanería).
rústico, ca adj. Rustic, rural, country. || Uncouth (tosco).
— F. *En rústica*, paperback, paperbound: *edición en rústica*, paperbound edition. || — M. Countryman, peasant (campesino). || Rustic, yokel (palurdo).
rustiquez f. Rusticity.
Rut n. pr. f. Ruth.
ruta f. Route, itinerary (itinerario): *la ruta de Don Quijote*, the route of Don Quixote. || Road, way (camino): *señalar la ruta de la victoria*, to point out the road to victory. || MAR. Course. || — *Hoja de ruta*, waybill. || *Ruta aérea*, air lane.
rutáceas f. pl. BOT. Rutaceae.
rutenio m. QUÍM. Ruthenium.
rutilante adj. Shining, brilliant, rutilant.
rutilar v. intr. To shine.
rutilo m. MIN. Rutile.
rútilo, la adj. (P.us.). Rutilant, shining.
rutina f. Routine: *apartarse de la rutina diaria*, to get away from the daily routine; *por mera rutina*, as a matter of mere routine.
rutinario, ria o **rutinero, ra** adj. Routine: *procedimiento rutinario*, routine procedure. || Unimaginative (persona).
ruzafa f. Garden (jardín de recreo).

S

s f. S (letra): *una s mayúscula, minúscula*, a capital, a small s.
Saba n. pr. GEOGR. Sheba: *la reina de Saba*, the Queen of Sheba.
sábado m. Saturday: *vendré el sábado*, I shall come on Saturday; *el sábado pasado*, last Saturday; *el sábado que viene*, next Saturday. || REL. Sabbath (de los judíos). || — FIG. *Hacer sábado*, to do the weekly cleaning. || *Sábado de Gloria* or *Santo*, Easter Saturday. || *Tener sábado inglés*, to work only half a day on Saturday.
sabalera f. Fire grate (de un horno). || Shad net (red).
sábalo m. Shad (pez).
sabana f. Savannah, savanna (llanura).
sábana f. Sheet (de cama): *sábana bajera, encimera*, bottom, top sheet. || Altar cloth (del altar). || FIG. Sheet (de nieve, etc.). || FIG. y FAM. Thousand-peseta note. || FIG. y FAM. *Pegársele a uno las sábanas*, to oversleep: *ha llegado tarde esta mañana porque se le pegaron las sábanas*, he arrived late this morning because he overslept.
sabandija f. Bug (bicho). || FIG. Louse, slob (persona despreciable).
sabanear v. intr. *Amer.* To round up *o* to herd cattle [on the savannah].
sabanilla f. Altar cloth (del altar).
sabañón m. Chilblain. || FIG. y FAM. *Comer como un sabañón*, to eat like a horse.
sabático, ca adj. Sabbatical.
sabatino, na adj. Saturday. || REL. Sabbatine: *bula sabatina*, sabbatine bull.
— F. REL. Saturday religious service. || Saturday lesson (lección).
sabedor, ra adj. Informed, aware. || *Ser sabedor de algo*, to be aware of sth., to know sth.
sabelotodo m. y f. inv. FAM. Know-all [U.S., know-it-all].
sabeo, a adj./s. Sabaean, Sabean.
saber m. Knowledge, learning: *persona de gran saber*, person of great learning. || — *El saber no ocupa lugar*, one never knows too much. || *Según mi leal saber y entender*, to the best of my knowledge.
saber* v.tr. To know: *saber griego, la lección*, to know Greek, the lesson; *no querer saber nada*, not to want to know. || To know how to, to be able to: *saber leer y escribir*, to know how to read and write; *no sabe nadar*, he cannot swim. || To be good at: *sabe muchas matemáticas*, he is very good at mathematics. || To learn, to find out (enterarse): *supe que habías venido*, I found out that you had come. || To know (conocer): *yo sé muy bien la historia de Francia*, I know French history very well. || — *A saber si lo que dice es verdad*, I wonder if what he says is true. || *Cada uno sabe dónde le aprieta el zapato*, everyone knows his own weaknesses, everyone knows where the shoe pinches. || *¡Conque ya lo sabes!*, so now you know! || *¡Cualquiera sabe!*, it's anybody's guess. || *¡De haberlo sabido antes!*, if only I'd known! || *Dejar a alguien sin saber qué decir*, to leave s.o. speechless. || *Hacer saber*, to inform, to let know. || *¡Lo sabré yo!*, I ought to know!, I know better than anyone! || *Lo sé*, I know. || *Me dio no sé qué pastel*, he gave me some cake or other. || *No saber alguien lo que se pesca* or *dónde se mete*, not to know what one is letting o.s. in for. || *No saber a qué atenerse*, v. ATENERSE. || *No saber a qué carta quedarse*, to be all at sea, to be in a dilemma. || *No saber a qué santo encomendarse*, v. SANTO. || *No saber dónde meterse*, not to know what to do with o.s., to wish o.s. a hundred miles away. || *No saber nada de nada*, not to know anything about anything. || FAM. *No saber ni jota* or *ni papa* or *ni pío de algo*, not to know the first thing about sth., not to have a clue about sth. | *No saber por dónde se anda*, not to know what one is doing. | *No saber uno dónde tiene las narices*, not to know left from right. | *No sé cuántos*, sth. or other. || *Para que lo sepas*, let me tell you, for your information. || *¿Qué sé yo?*, how do I know?, how should I know? || *Que yo sepa*, as far as I know, to my knowledge. || *Sabe Dios*, God only knows. || *Sabe Dios si*, God knows if. || FIG. *Saber al dedillo* or *de corrido* or *de carrerilla*, to have at one's fingertips, to know by heart, to know backwards. | *Saber algo como el Padre Nuestro*, to know sth. backwards *o* by heart *o* backwards and forwards. | *Saber algo de buena tinta*, to have sth. on good authority, to get sth. straight from the horse's mouth. || FAM. *Saber arreglárselas*, v. ARREGLAR. | *Saber cuántas son cinco*, to know what's what. || *Saber de fijo* or *a punto fijo*, to know for sure *o* for certain. || *Saber de memoria*, to know by heart. || *Saber de sobra que*, to know only too well that. || *Saber ir a un sitio*, to know the way to a place, to know how to get to a place. || *Saber lo que se quiere*, to know one's own mind. || FAM. *Saber más de la cuenta*, to know too much. | *Saber más que Lepe*, v. LEPE. || *Saber mucho* or *un rato de*, to know a lot about. || FAM. *Se las sabe todas*, he is nobody's fool, he knows all the tricks. || *¡Si lo sabré!*, I should know!, I ought to know! || *Sin saberlo yo (tú, etc.)*, without my (your, etc.) knowledge, without my (your, etc.) knowing it. || *Te lo haré saber cuanto antes*, I'll let you know as soon as possible. || *¿Tú qué sabes?*, what do you know? || *Un no sé qué*, a certain sth. || FAM. *Van a saber quién soy yo*, they're going to hear from me. | *¡Vete a saber!*, who knows!, your guess is as good as mine. || *¡Vete a saber lo que ha hecho!*, goodness knows what he has done! || *¡Ya lo sabía yo!*, that's what I thought!, I thought as much! || *¿Yo qué sé?*, how

am I supposed to know?, how should I know? || *!Y qué sé yo!*, and how should I know!
— V. intr. To know. || To taste (tener sabor). || — *A saber*, namely, that is, that is to say. || *Queda por saber*, it remains to be seen: *queda por saber si vendrá o no*, it remains to be seen whether he will come or not. || *¿Quién sabe?*, who knows?, who can tell? || FAM. *¿Sabe?*, you know? || *Saber a*, to taste of *o* like: *esto sabe a miel*, this tastes of honey; to smack of, to be like: *los consuelos le saben a injurias*, consolation is like an insult to him. || *Saber a gloria*, to taste divine, to be delicious. || *Saber de*, to hear from, to have news from: *hace un mes que no sé de mis padres*, I haven't heard from my parents in a month; to know [of]: *sé de sitios que son muy tranquilos*, I know of some very quiet places. || *Saber mal*, to taste bad: *esta sopa sabe mal*, this soup tastes bad; to be embarrassing: *me sabe muy mal ir a verle después de lo que ha pasado*, it is very embarrassing to go and see him after what happened; not to appreciate: *lo que has hecho me sabe muy mal*, I don't appreciate what you did at all; to upset, to annoy (molestar).
— V. pr. To be discovered (ser descubierto). || To know (por haber estudiado), to have learned (por experiencia): *yo me sé la lección*, I know the lesson, I have learnt my lesson. || — *No se sabe*, nobody knows. || *Se lo sabe todo*, he knows everything. || *¡Sépase cuántas veces fui!*, I went goodness knows how many times. || *Sépase que*, let it be known that. || *Se puede saber si*, can you tell me if *o* whether. || *Se sabe que*, it is known that, it is a known fact that. || *Todo llega a saberse*, everything comes to light in the end. || *¿Y se puede saber por qué?*, might one ask why?

sabiamente adv. Expertly (con ciencia). || Wisely, sensibly, sagely (sensatamente).

sabidillo, lla m. y f. FAM. Know-all [U.S., know-it-all].

sabido, da adj. Known: *sabido es que*, it is known that. || Learned, knowledgeable (que sabe mucho). || — *Como es sabido*, as is well known, as everyone knows (como todos lo saben), that goes without saying (no hace falta decirlo). || *De sabido*, of course (por supesto). || *Es cosa sabida que*, it is well known that. || *Tener sabido que*, to know [that].

sabiduría f. Wisdom (prudencia). || Knowledge, wisdom, learning (instrucción). || REL. Wisdom. || — *La sabiduría eterna* or *increada*, eternal wisdom. || *Libro de la Sabiduría*, Book of Wisdom.

sabiendas (a) loc. adv. Knowingly, on purpose (a propósito). || Knowingly, consciously (con conocimiento de causa). || *A sabiendas de que*, knowing full well that, fully aware that.

sabihondez f. FAM. Pedantry, pedantism.

sabihondo, da adj. Pedantic, know-all [U.S., know-it-all].
— M. y f. Know-all [U.S., know-it-all], pedant.

sabino, na adj./s. HIST. Sabine. || *El rapto de las sabinas*, the rape of the Sabine women.

sabio, bia adj. Learned (que posee sabiduría). || Wise, sensible (prudente). || Trained (animal): *perro sabio*, trained dog. || FIG. y FAM. Know-all [U.S., know-it-all] (pedante).
— M. y f. Learned man, learned woman, learned person (que posee sabiduría). || Scholar (que tiene conocimientos profundos de una disciplina). || Sage (prudente). || FIG. y FAM. Know-all [U.S., know-it-all]. || — *De sabios es mudar de opinión*, only fools never change their minds. || *Los Siete Sabios de Grecia*, the Seven Sages *o* Wise Men of Greece.

sabiondo, da adj. V. SABIHONDO.

sablazo m. Blow with a sabre (golpe). || Sabre wound (herida). || FIG. y FAM. Sponging, cadging, scrounging. || FIG. y FAM. *Dar un sablazo a uno*, to cadge *o* to scrounge money off s.o., to tap s.o. (pedir dinero).

sable m. Sabre [U.S., saber] (arma): *desenvainar el sable*, to draw *o* to unsheathe one's sabre. || HERÁLD. Sable (negro). || FIG. Sponging, cadging, scrounging (arte de sacar dinero). || *Tirar el sable*, to fence (esgrima).

sableador, ra m. y f. FAM. Sponger, cadger, scrounger.

sablear v. intr. FAM. To sponge, to cadge, to scrounge (pedir dinero prestado).

sablista adj. FAM. Sponging, cadging, scrounging.
— M. y f. FAM. Sponger, cadger, scrounger.

saboneta f. Hunter [watch].

sabor m. Taste, flavour [U.S., flavor], savour [U.S., savor] (p.us.): *un sabor a naranja*, an orange flavour. || FIG. Flavour: *un poema de sabor clásico*, a poem with a classical flavour. || — Pl. Beads (del bocado del caballo). || — *Con sabor a naranja*, orange-flavoured. || *Mal sabor de boca*, bad taste in one's mouth (alimento, mala impresión). || FIG. *Sabor local*, local colour. | *Sin sabor*, flat, dull, insipid, tasteless.

saborcillo m. Slight taste.

saborear v. tr. To taste (percibir el sabor). || To flavour (dar sabor). || FIG. To savour, to relish (apreciar).
— V. pr. To relish, to savour (deleitarse). || FIG. To relish, to savour.

saboreo m. Savouring [U.S., savoring].

sabotaje m. Sabotage.

saboteador, ra m. y f. Saboteur.

sabotear v. tr. To sabotage.

Saboya n. pr. f. GEOGR. Savoy.

saboyano, na adj./s. Savoyard.

sabroso, sa adj. Delicious, tasty, savoury. || FIG. Pleasant, delightful. | Meaty (libro). | Racy: *una broma sabrosa*, a racy joke.

sabuco m. BOT. Elder (saúco).

sabueso, sa adj./s. *Perro sabueso*, bloodhound. || — M. FIG. Detective, sleuth (investigador).

saburra f. Fur (en la lengua).

saburral o **saburroso, sa** adj. MED. Coated, furry (lengua).

saca f. Taking out, withdrawal, removal (efecto de sacar). || Big sack (costal). || Mailbag (del correo). || COM. Export. | Supply, stock (de efectos estancados). || Authorized copy *o* duplicate (de un documento). || Group of prisoners executed in reprisal.

sacabala f. Bullet-extracting forceps.

sacabalas m. inv. Worm (para armas de fuego).

sacabocados m. inv. Punch.

sacabotas m. inv. Bootjack.

sacabrocas m. inv. Nail puller, pincers, *pl.* (de zapatero).

sacabuche m. MÚS. Sackbut.

sacaclavos m. inv. Nail puller, pincers, *pl.*

sacacorchos m. inv. Corkscrew.

sacacuartos m. inv. V. SACADINERO.

sacadinero m. o **sacadineros** m. inv. Bauble (bisutería). || Swindle, fiddle (espectáculo sin valor). || — M. y f. FAM. Sponger, cadger, scrounger (sablista). | Swindler (estafador).

sacador, ra adj. Pulling, extracting (que saca).
— M. y f. Person who pulls *o* extracts, remover (que saca). || Server (tenis).

sacáis m. pl. POP. Peepers, eyes (ojos).

sacaliña f. Pointed stick, goad (garrocha). || FIG. Cunning (socaliña).

sacamanchas m. inv. Stain remover, spot remover (quitamanchas).

sacamantecas m. inv. FAM. Ripper, criminal who cuts open his victims.

sacamuelas m. y f. inv. FAM. Dentist (dentista). || — M. inv. Charlatan (vendedor). || Chatterbox (hablador). || *Mentir más que un sacamuelas*, to lie through one's teeth.

sacaperras m. inv. V. SACADINERO.

sacapuntas m. inv. Pencil sharpener.

sacar v. tr. e intr. To stick out (la lengua, el pecho, etc.). || To get out, to take out: *sacar un pañuelo del bolsillo*, to take a handkerchief out of one's pocket. || To pull out, to extract, to take out: *sacar un diente*, to pull a tooth out. || To draw: *sacó la pistola*, he drew his gun; *sacar la espada*, to draw one's sword; *sacar agua*, to draw water. || To draw [out]: *sacar una papeleta*, to draw [out] a slip of paper. || To remove, to take out: *sacar un armario de un cuarto*, to remove a wardrobe from a room. || To remove, to get out *o* off: *sacar una mancha*, to remove a stain. || To put out (un ojo). || To remove, to take off (suprimir): *saqué dos nombres de la lista*, I took two names off the list. || To get, to obtain: *ha sacado mucho dinero de sus cuadros*, he has got a lot of money from his paintings; *ha sacado el pasaporte en Madrid*, he got his passport in Madrid; *sacar un buen número en la lotería*, to get a winning number in the lottery. || To get, to win (un premio). || To get (una entrada, un billete). || To take out: *le han sacado del colegio para las vacaciones*, they have taken him out of school for the holidays. || To bring out (nuevo modelo). || To take (muestras). || To make (hacer): *sacar fichas*, to make file cards. || To set, to start (una moda). || To win, to obtain, to get: *sacar la mayoría en las elecciones*, to win a majority in the elections. || To take: *una película sacada de una novela*, a film taken from a novel. || To deduce, to conclude (deducir). || To extract (extraer): *el azúcar se saca de la remolacha*, sugar is extracted from sugar beet. || To show (enseñar): *sacar los dientes*, to show one's teeth; *¿me puede sacar ese abrigo negro?*, would you show me that black coat? || To give (un apodo). || To find (encontrar): *el profesor sacó tres faltas en el dictado*, the teacher found three mistakes in the dictation. || To reach, to find, to get (respuesta, solución). || To solve (un problema). || To take out, to withdraw, to draw: *sacar dinero del banco*, to withdraw money from the bank. || To get out: *sacar de prisión*, to get out of prison. || FOT. To take: *me sacó una foto*, he took a photograph of me; *sacar fotografías*, to take photographs. | To have made, to make (una copia). || MAT. To extract, to find (una raíz cuadrada). || To take out: *tienes que sacar a tu hermana más, la pobrecita se aburre*, you should take your sister out more, the poor girl gets bored. || COM. To produce, to turn out (producir). || FIG. To get out: *no se le puede sacar una palabra*, you can't get a word out of him. | To come out with: *siempre nos saca la historia de su vida*, he always comes out with the story of his life. | To mention, to bring up (mencionar). | To draw: *saqué fuerzas de flaqueza*, I drew strength from nowhere. | To let out (en costura). | To make, to form: *del grupo de chicos sacaron dos equipos*, they formed two teams from the group of boys. || MIN. y QUÍM. To extract (extraer). || DEP. To serve (tenis). | To throw in [to play] (desde la banda), to kick off (desde el centro), to take a goal kick (de la puerta), to clear (despejar), to take (un córner) [fútbol]. || — FAM. *A mí me saca medio metro*, he's half a metre taller than me. || *Sacar a bailar*, to ask to dance. || *Sacar a colación*, to bring up, to mention. || *Sacar adelante*, V. ADELANTE. || *Sacar a flote*, V. FLOTE. || *Sacar a la vergüenza pública*, to put to public shame. || *Sacar a la venta*, to put on sale *o* up for sale. || *Sacar algo a* or *por suerte*, to draw [lots] for sth. || *Sacar a luz*, to publish (publicar), to bring to light (descubrir), to throw light on (dar aclaraciones sobre). || *Sacar a pasear a uno*, to take s.o. for a walk. || *Sacar apuntes* or *datos*, to take notes. || *Sacar a relucir*, V. RELUCIR. || *Sacar a subasta*, to put up for auction. || *Sacar a uno de sus costumbres*, to make s.o. change his ways, to change s.o.'s ways. || *Sacar brillo a los zapatos*, to polish *o* to shine one's shoes. || *Sacar cuartos*, to make money: *sólo le interesa sacar cuartos*, he is only interested in making money; to get money (*a*, out of) [obtener dinero]. || *Sacar de banda*, to throw in, to take a throw-in (fútbol). || *Sacar defectos a todos*, to find fault with *o* faults in everyone. || FIG. *Sacar del arroyo a uno*, to drag s.o. from the gutter. || *Sacar del olvido*, to rescue from oblivion. || *Sacar de mentira verdad*, to lie in order to get at the truth. || *Sacar de pila a uno*, to be s.o.'s godparent. || *Sacar de pobre*, to save from poverty. || *Sacar de puerta*, to take a goal kick (fútbol). || FIG. *Sacar de quicio* or *de tino* or *de sus casillas a uno*, V. QUICIO, TINO, CASILLA. | *Sacar de raíz*, V. RAÍZ. | *Sacar de sí a uno*, to infuriate s.o., to make s.o. mad *o* furious. | *Sacar de un mal paso a uno*, to get s.o. out of a fix, to help s.o. out. || *Sacar el cuello*, to stretch one's neck. || *Sacar el dobladillo*, to let the hem down *o* out. || FIG. *Sacar el jugo a uno*, to bleed s.o. dry *o* white. || *Sacar en claro* or *en limpio de*, to get out of, to solve: *hablé con él pero no saqué nada en claro*, I talked with him but got nothing out of him *o* but solved nothing; to clear up (aclarar). || *Sacar en* or *a hombros a uno*, to carry s.o. shoulder-high *o* on one's shoulders. || *Sacar la conclusión de que*, to come to the conclusion that (llegar a la conclusión), to draw the conclusion that (inferir). || *Sacar la mano*, to put one's hand out. || *Sacar la verdad a uno*, to get the truth from *o* out of s.o. || *Sacarle a uno una idea de la cabeza* or *del magín*, to get an idea out of s.o.'s head. || FIG. *Sacar los colores a la cara de alguien*, to make s.o. blush. | *Sacar los pies del plato*, V. PIE. || *Sacar pajas*, to draw straws. || FIG. *Sacar punta a*, to find fault with (criticar). || *Sacar punta a un lápiz*, to sharpen a pencil. || MED. *Sacar sangre*, to take *o* to draw blood. || *Sacar una buena media*, to have a good average. || *Sacar una buena* or *mala nota*, to get a good *o* bad mark. || *Sacar una conclusión*, to draw a conclusion. || *Sacar un beneficio de*, to profit by. *Sacar veinte metros de ventaja*, to be twenty metres ahead (un corredor). || *Sacar ventaja a, sacar ventaja de*, V. VENTAJA.

— V. pr. To take off: *sácate los zapatos*, take off your shoes. || To have taken: *me he sacado una foto en casa del fotógrafo*, I had a photograph of myself taken at the photographer's.

sacarífero, ra adj. Sacchariferous.
sacarificación f. QUÍM. Saccharification.
sacarificar v. tr. QUÍM. To saccharify.
sacarímetro m. QUÍM. Saccharimeter, saccharometer.
sacarino, na adj. Saccharine.
— F. QUÍM. Saccharin.
sacaroideo, a adj. Saccharoid.
sacaromicetos m. pl. Saccharomyces.
sacarosa f. QUÍM. Saccharose, sucrose.
sacatacos m. inv. Worm (de una escopeta).
sacatapón m. Corkscrew.
sacatrapos m. inv. MIL. Worm.
sacerdocio m. Priesthood.
sacerdotal adj. Sacerdotal, priestly.
sacerdote m. Priest: *sumo sacerdote*, high priest.
sacerdotisa f. Priestess.
saciable adj. Satiable.
saciar v. tr. To satiate, to sate, to satisfy (hartar). || FIG. To satiate, to satisfy one's desire for: *saciar su venganza*, to satisfy one's desire for vengeance. || *Saciar la sed*, to quench *o* to slake one's thirst.
— V. pr. To satiate o.s. (hartarse). || FIG. To be satisfied: *saciarse con poco*, to be satisfied with little. || *Saciarse de sangre*, to slake one's thirst for blood.
saciedad f. Satiety, satiation. || — *Comer* or *beber hasta la saciedad*, to eat *o* to drink one's fill. || *Repetir algo hasta la saciedad*, to say sth. over and over again.
saco m. Sack, bag (costal). || Sack, bag, sackful, bagful (contenido). || Smock, coarse dress (vestidura). || Sack, plunder, pillage (saqueo). || ANAT. Sac. || MAR. Bight (ensenada). || *Amer.* Jacket (chaqueta). | Handbag, bag [U.S., pocketbook] (bolso). || — FIG. *Caer en saco roto*, to go in one ear and out the other, to fall upon deaf ears. || *Carrera de sacos*, sack race. || *Entrar a saco*, to pillage, to plunder, to sack. || *La avaricia rompe el saco*, V. AVARICIA. || FIG. *No echar una cosa en saco roto*, to take good note of sth. || *Saco de dormir*, sleeping bag. || FIG. *Saco de huesos*, bag of bones. | *Saco de malicias* or *de prestidigitador*, bag of tricks. | *Saco de mentiras*, pack of lies. || *Saco de noche* or *de viaje*, overnight bag. || FIG. *Saco roto*, spendthrift (manirroto). || MIL. *Saco terrero* or *de arena*, sandbag. || FIG. *Tenía dinero a sacos*, he had bags of money *o* stacks of money. | *Vaciaron el saco*, they got it out of their system.
sacramentado, da adj. Having received the Extreme Unction *o* the last sacraments (con el viático). || Consecrated (la hostia). || — *Jesús sacramentado*, the Host. || *Ser sacramentado*, to receive the Extreme Unction *o* the last sacraments.
sacramental adj. Sacramental. || — *Auto sacramental*, V. AUTO. || *Especies sacramentales*, Eucharistic species. || *Palabras sacramentales*, ritual words.
— M. Sacramental. || — F. Brotherhood devoted to the worship of the Sacrament. || *La Sacramental de San Isidro*, the Cemetery of the Brotherhood of Saint Isidorus [in Madrid].
sacramentar v. tr. To administer the last sacraments *o* the Extreme Unction to. || To consecrate (la hostia).
sacramentario m. REL. Sacramentarian.
sacramente adv. Sacredly (sagradamente).
sacramento m. REL. Sacrament: *administrar los últimos sacramentos*, to administer the last sacraments. || — *El sacramento del altar*, the Eucharist. || *El Santísimo Sacramento*, the Blessed Sacrament. || *Recibir los sacramentos*, to receive the last sacraments.
sacrificable adj. Sacrificeable.
sacrificadero m. Sacrificial altar.
sacrificado, da adj. Sacrificed. || Self-sacrificing: *es una persona muy sacrificada*, he is a very self-sacrificing person. || COM. *Vender a un precio sacrificado*, to sacrifice, to sell at a sacrificial price.
sacrificador, ra m. y f. Sacrificer.
sacrificar v. tr. To sacrifice. || To slaughter (una res para el consumo).
— V. pr. To sacrifice o.s.: *sacrificarse por uno*, to sacrifice o.s. for s.o.
sacrificatorio, ria adj. Sacrificial.
sacrificio m. Sacrifice. || Slaughter (de una res). || *Ofrecer un sacrificio*, to offer *o* to make a sacrifice, to sacrifice: *ofrecer un sacrificio a los dioses*, to make a sacrifice to the gods.
sacrilegio m. Sacrilege.
sacrílego, ga adj. Sacrilegious.
— M. y f. Sacrilegious person, sacrilegist (ant.).
sacrismoche o **sacrismocho** m. FAM. Poor man dressed in black (hombre vestido de negro).
sacristán m. Sacristan, verger, sexton.
sacristana f. Sacristan's *o* verger's *o* sexton's wife (mujer del sacristán). || Vestry nun (religiosa).
sacristanía f. Office of sexton *o* verger *o* sacristan.
sacristía f. Sacristy, vestry (en las iglesias). || Office of sacristan *o* verger *o* sexton (sacristanía).
sacro, cra adj. Sacred: *la vía sacra*, the Sacred Way. || Holy: *Sacra Familia*, Holy Family. || ANAT. Sacral (del sacro). || — REL. *El Sacro Colegio*, the Sacred College, the College of Cardinals. || *El Sacro Imperio Romano*, the Holy Roman Empire. || *Fuego sacro*, sacred fire. || *Historia sacra*, sacred history, Bible history. || ANAT. *Hueso sacro*, sacrum. || *Música sacra*, sacred music.
—M. ANAT. Sacrum.
sacroilíaco, ca adj. ANAT. Sacroiliac.
sacrosanto, ta adj. Sacrosanct.
sacudida f. Shake, shaking (agitación). || Shake, jolt, jerk (movimiento brusco). || Jolt, jerk (de un vehículo). || Shock, tremor (de un terremoto). || Jerk, toss (de la cabeza). || FIG. Shock (emoción fuerte). | Upheaval (en la política). || FIG. y FAM. Good hiding, beating (paliza): *darle una sacudida a su hijo*, to give one's son a good hiding. || — *Avanzar dando sacudidas*, to jolt *o* to bump *o* to jerk along. || *Dar una sacudida a una alfombra*, to beat a carpet. || *Sacudida eléctrica*, electric shock.
sacudido, da adj. Shaken (movido). || FIG. Surly, ill-disposed: *un muchacho sacudido*, a surly boy. | Self-assured (desenvuelto). || FIG. *Está más sacudido que una estera*, he is completely shameless.
sacudidor, ra adj. Shaking, beating.
— M. Whisk, beater (instrumento para sacudir las alfombras, etc.).
sacudidura f. o **sacudimiento** m. Shaking, shake, jolt (sacudida). || MED. Succussion.
sacudir v. tr. To shake (agitando). || To beat (dando golpes): *sacudir una alfombra*, to beat a carpet. || To jerk, to tug (una cuerda). || To toss, to shake (la cabeza). || To wag (la cola). || To jolt (coche, tren). || To chase away (ahuyentar). || FIG. To give: *sacudir una bofetada, una paliza*, to give a slap in the face, a beating. | To beat, to spank (a un niño). | To beat up (dar una paliza). | To scold (reñir). | To shake (conmocionar). || — *Sacudir el polvo*, to shake off the dust, to dust (traje), to dust (muebles), to tan s.o.'s hide, to give s.o. a beating (dar una paliza). || FIG. *Sacudir el yugo*, to throw off the yoke. || FAM. *Sacudir la mosca*, to fork out, to cough up, to pay up (pagar). || FIG. *Sacudir los nervios*, to shatter s.o.'s nerves.
— V. pr. To shake, to shake o.s. || FIG. To shake off, to get rid of: *se sacudió de su amigo fácilmente*, he shook off his friend easily. || FAM. To fork out, to cough up, to pay up (dinero): *¡sacúdase!*, cough up!
sachar v. tr. To weed.
sachem m. Sachem.

sádico, ca adj. Sadistic.
— M. y f. Sadist.
sadismo m. Sadism.
saduceo, a adj. Sadducean.
— M. y f. Sadducee.
saeta f. Arrow (grande), dart (pequeña) [arma]. || Hand [of a watch] (manecilla). || Magnetic needle (brújula). || Religious song, "saeta" (copla).
— OBSERV. The *saeta* is a short and fervent prayer of popular origin that is sung at the passing of a procession, especially in Andalusia, during Holy Week.
saetada f. o **saetazo** m. Shot from a bow, arrow shot (disparo). || Arrow wound (herida).
saetear v. tr. To shoot an arrow at (asaetear).
saetera f. Loophole (aspillera). || FIG. Narrow window (ventanilla).
saetero m. Archer, bowman (soldado).
saetilla f. Dart, small arrow (saeta pequeña). || Hand [of a watch] (manecilla). || BOT. Sagittaria, arrowhead.
saetín m. Millcourse, millrace (de molino). || Brad, tack (clavito).
safari m. Safari (cacería): *está de safari*, he is on safari.
safena adj. f. ANAT. Saphenous: *vena safena*, saphenous vein.
— F. ANAT. Saphena.
sáfico, ca adj./s.m. Sapphic: *verso sáfico*, sapphic verse. || *Poesía sáfica*, sapphics, *pl.*, sapphic verse.
safismo m. Sapphism.
Safo n. pr. f. Sappho.
saga f. Sorceress, witch (bruja). || Saga (leyenda escandinava).
sagacidad f. Sagacity (perspicacia). || Astuteness, shrewdness (astucia).
sagaz adj. Sagacious (perspicaz). || Astute, shrewd (astuto).
sagitario m. Archer, bowman (saetero). || ASTR. Sagittarius (constelación y signo del zodiaco).
sagrado, da adj. Sacred, holy, consecrated (dedicado a Dios). || Holy: *Sagrada Familia*, Holy Family; *Sagrada Comunión*, Holy Communion. || — *Fuego sagrado*, sacred fire. || *Historia sagrada*, sacred history, Bible history. || *Sagrada Escritura*, Holy Scripture. || *Sagrado Corazón*, Sacred Heart.
— M. Asylum, sanctuary, place of refuge (asilo). || — *Acogerse a sagrado*, to take holy sanctuary. || *Estar acogido a sagrado*, to be given sanctuary *o* asylum.
sagrario m. Shrine, sanctuary (parte del templo). || Tabernacle (para el Santísimo). || Chapel that serves as a parish church in some cathedrals.
saguntino, na adj./s. Saguntine.
Sagunto n. pr. GEOGR. Sagunto.
Sáhara o **Sahara** n. pr. m. GEOGR. Sahara.
saharauí adj./n. Saharan.
sahariana f. Bush shirt *o* jacket.
sahariano, na o **sahárico, ca** adj./s. Saharan, Saharian.
sahino m. ZOOL. Peccary, Mexican hog.
sahornarse v. pr. To get chafed *o* sore.
sahumadura f. Perfuming with incense. || Aromatic smoke (humo). || Aromatic substance (sustancia aromática).
sahumar v. tr. To perfume with incense.
sahumerio m. V. SAHUMADURA.
saimirí m. ZOOL. Squirrel monkey (mono).
saín m. Animal fat, fat (grasa).
sainete m. TEATR. Short comedy, one-act farce (pieza jocosa y corta). | Curtain raiser (que se representa al principio de las funciones teatrales). || Titbit, choice morsel (bocadito sabroso).
sainetear v. intr. To act in farces.
sainetero o **sainetista** m. Writer of farces.
sainetesco, ca adj. Farcical, burlesque.
saíno m. ZOOL. Peccary, Mexican hog.
sajadura f. MED. Incision.
sajar v. tr. MED. To lance (un absceso, etc.). | To make an incision in, to cut open (abrir).
sajón, ona adj./s. Saxon.
Sajonia n. pr. f. GEOGR. Saxony. || *Baja Sajonia*, Lower Saxony.
sajú m. ZOOL. Sapajou (mono).
sajuriana f. *Amer.* Traditional Peruvian dance.
sakí m. ZOOL. Saki (mono). || Sake, saki (bebida).
sal f. Salt: *una pizca de sal*, a pinch of salt; *sal marina*, sea salt; *sal gema* or *pedrés*, rock salt. || FIG. Wit, spice (gracia). | Charm, liveliness (encanto). || — Pl. Smelling salts (para reanimar). || Salts: *sales de baño*, bath salts. || — FIG. *Con su sal y pimienta*, with a lot of wit. || FIG. y FAM. *Echar en sal una cosa*, to put sth. on ice. | *Echarle sal en la mollera a uno*, to quieten s.o. down. || *Echar sal a*, to salt. || FIG. *La sal de la tierra*, the salt of the earth. | *La sal de la vida*, the spice of life. || QUÍM. *Sal amoniaco* or *amoniaca*, sal-ammoniac. || *Sal común*, common salt. || *Sal de frutas*, fruit salts. || *Sal de la Higuera*, Epsom salts, liver salts. || *Sal de mesa*, table salt. || *Sal de plomo* or *de Saturno*, lead acetate. || *Sal morena* or *de cocina*, kitchen salt, cooking salt. || FIG. *Tener mucha sal*, to be great fun (persona), to be very funny (chiste).
sala f. Room (cuarto): *sala de comisiones*, committee room. || Large room (cuarto grande). || Living room, sitting room, lounge (sala de estar). || House (de un teatro). || Ward (en un hospital). || JUR. Court (tribunal): *sala de lo criminal*, criminal court. || — *Deporte en sala*, indoor sport. || *Sala capitular*, chapter house. || JUR. *Sala de apelación, de justicia*, court of appeal, of justice. || *Sala de batalla*, sorting room (en correos). || *Sala de clase*, classroom. || *Sala de conferencias*, lecture theatre *o* room, lecture hall (en una universidad), conference room, conference hall (para reuniones). || *Sala de espectáculos*, theatre [U.S., theater]; cinema. || *Sala de espera*, waiting room. || *Sala de estar*, living room, sitting room, lounge. || *Sala de estreno*, first-run cinema [U.S., first-run picture theater] (cine). || *Sala de exposición*, showroom. || *Sala de fiestas*, ballroom, dance hall (de baile), reception hall (en un ayuntamiento), nightclub, cabaret (con espectáculo). || *Sala del consejo* or *de la junta*, boardroom. || *Sala de lectura*, reading room. || *Sala del trono*, throne room. || *Sala de máquinas*, engine room. || *Sala de prevención*, guardroom. || *Sala de recibir*, drawing room. || *Sala de subastas*, auction room.
salacidad f. Salaciousness, prurience.
salacot m. Topee, topi (casco).
saladar m. Salt marsh (marismas). || Salt meadow (terreno).
saladería f. Meat-salting industry.
saladero m. Salting tub (lugar para salar). || Salting factory (casa para salar). || "Salting tub", former prison in Madrid (cárcel). || *Amer.* Slaughterhouse that salts its meat.
saladillo adj. m. *Tocino saladillo*, half-salted bacon.
salado, da adj. CULIN. Salt, salted, salty (carne, etc.). | Salty: *demasiado salado*, too salty. || Salt (agua). || FIG. Witty, funny (gracioso). | Spirited, sharp (ingenioso). | Darling, cute, lovely: *tiene dos niños muy salados*, she has two lovely children. | Winsome, attractive, charming (atractivo). || *Amer.* Unfortunate (desgraciado).
salador, ra m. y f. Salter. || — M. Salting tub (sitio).
saladura f. Salting.
salamanca f. ZOOL. Salamander (salamandra). | Small lizard (lagartija).
Salamanca n. pr. GEOGR. Salamanca.
salamandra f. ZOOL. Salamander. || Salamander stove (calorífero). || *Salamandra acuática*, newt, triton.
salamanqués, esa adj. [Of *o* from] Salamanca.
— M. y f. Native *o* inhabitant of Salamanca.
salamanquesa f. Gecko (lagarto).
salamanquino, na adj. [Of *o* from] Salamanca.
— M. y f. Native *o* inhabitant of Salamanca. || — F. *Amer.* Lizard (lagartija).
salame m. *Amer.* Salami (salchichón).
salar m. *Amer.* Salt marsh.
salar v. tr. CULIN. To salt (para sazonar o conservar). || *Amer.* To dishonour (deshonrar). | To spoil (echar a perder). | To bring bad luck to (causar mala suerte a).
salarial adj. Wage, salary: *incremento salarial*, wage increase.
salariar v. tr. To pay a wage *o* a salary to (asalariar).
salario m. Wages, *pl.*, wage, pay, salary: *deducir del salario*, to deduct from one's wages. || — *Fijación de salarios máximos*, fixing of maximum wage. || *Salario a destajo*, piece rate. || *Salario base* or *básico*, basic wage. || *Salario colectivo*, collective wage. || *Salario de convenio colectivo*, conventional wage. || *Salario de hambre*, starvation wages. || *Salario por hora*, hourly rate. || *Salario por unidad de tiempo*, wage *o* rate per unit of time. || *Salario tope* or *máximo*, top *o* maximum wage.
salaz adj. Salacious, prurient.
salazón f. Salting (acción). || Salting industry (industria). || — Pl. Salted meat, *sing.* (carne salada). || Salted fish, *sing.* (pescado salado).
salceda f. o **salcedo** m. Willow grove.
salcochar v. tr. To boil in salt water.
salchicha f. Pork sausage.
salchichería f. Pork butcher's [shop].
salchichero, ra m. y f. Pork butcher.
salchichón m. Highly-seasoned sausage (embutido).
saldar v. tr. To liquidate, to pay, to settle (una (cuenta). || To sell off (vender a bajo precio). || FIG. To settle (divergencias). || FIG. *Saldar una cuenta*, to pay s.o. back, to get even with s.o.
saldista m. Dealer in clearance lines.
saldo m. COM. Balance: *saldo acreedor, deudor*, credit, debit balance; *saldo a favor* or *positivo*, favourable balance; *saldo en contra* or *negativo*, adverse balance. || [Bargain] sale (liquidación de mercancías). || Liquidation, settlement, payment (pago): *saldo de una cuenta*, settlement of an account. || FIG. Remnant, leftover (cosa de poco valor).
saledizo, za adj. Projecting.
— M. ARQ. Projection (parte que sobresale). | Ledge (en un muro). | Corbelling, overhang (balcón, etc.). || *En saledizo*, projecting.
salero m. Saltcellar (para echar sal). || Salt warehouse (almacén). || TECN. Salt mine. || FIG. y FAM. Charm, allure (en una mujer): *esa chica tiene mucho salero*, that girl has a lot of charm. | Elegance (elegancia). | Wit (ingenio). || *Un actor con mucho salero*, a very funny *o* witty actor.
saleroso, sa adj. FIG. y FAM. Charming, winsome: *chica salerosa*, charming girl. | Funny, amusing, witty (divertido).

salesa f. Nun of the Order of the Visitation. || *Las Salesas*, the Law Courts [in Madrid].
salesiano, na adj./s. REL. Salesian.
saleta f. Court of appeal (sala de apelación). || Royal antechamber (antecámara).
salicilato m. QUÍM. Salicylate.
salicílico, ca adj. QUÍM. Salicylic.
sálico, ca adj. Salic: *ley sálica*, Salic law.
salicor m. BOT. Saltwort.
salida f. Departure, leaving (partida): *a su salida de Madrid*, on his leaving Madrid, on his departure from Madrid. || Departure: *la salida del tren*, the departure of the train, the train's departure. || Exit, way out (puerta). || Leak (de gas, de líquido). || Projection (parte saliente). || Rising (de un astro). || Publication (de un libro, una revista). || Appearance (de un periódico). || Lead (en juegos de cartas). || FIG. Way out (medio). | Excuse (pretexto). | Loophole (escapatoria). | Opening: *los licenciados en ciencias tienen muchas salidas*, there are many openings for science graduates. | Way out, solution (solución): *no veo salida a este problema*, I can't see any way out of *o* any solution to this problem. | Outcome, result (resultado). || FAM. Witticism, witty remark (ocurrencia). | Comeback, repartee (réplica). || AVIAC. Recovery (después de un picado). || COM. Production, output (producción). | Sale (venta). | Outlet, market (posibilidad de venta): *encontrar salida para un producto*, to find an outlet *o* a market for a product. | Shipment (transporte de mercancías). | Debit (de una cuenta). | Outlay (dinero gastado). || DEP. Start: *salida lanzada, parada*, flying, standing start. || TECN. Outlet, vent (orificio de salida). || MIL. Sortie, sally. || TEATR. Entrance [of an actor]: *salida a escena*, entrance on stage. || — *A la salida del cine*, coming out of the cinema. || *Calle sin salida*, cul-de-sac, dead-end street. || *Dar la salida*, to give the starting signal. || COM. *Dar salida a*, to sell, to find an outlet *o* a market for: *hemos dado salida a todas nuestras existencias*, we have sold all our stocks. || *De salida*, from the start, to begin with. || *Dio salida a su cólera*, he gave vent to his anger. || DEP. *Línea de salida*, starting line. || FIG. *No tengo otra salida que aceptar su propuesta*, I have no option but to accept his proposal. | *Prepararse una salida*, to arrange a way out for o.s. || *Salida de artistas*, stage door. || *Salida de baño*, bathrobe (para casa), beach robe (para la playa). || *Salida de caja*, debit. || *Salida de divisas*, outflow of currency. || *Salida de emergencia* or *de incendio*, emergency *o* fire exit. || *Salida del cascarón* or *del huevo*, hatching. || *Salida del Sol*, sunrise. || FAM. *Salida de pata de banco*, clanger. || *Salida de tono*, improper remark (observación inoportuna), silly remark (tontería). || DEP. *Salida nula*, false start. || *Tener salida*, to come out (acabar): *una calle que tiene salida a*, a street that comes out on to; to open: *la casa tiene salida al bulevar*, the house opens on to the boulevard; to have an outlet: *un país que no tiene salida al mar*, a country which has no outlet to the sea; to sell well (mercancías). || FIG. *Tener salida para todo*, to have an answer to everything.
salidero, ra adj. Fond of going out.
— M. Exit, way out (salida).
salidizo m. ARQ. V. SALEDIZO.
salido, da adj. Bulging (ojos). || Prominent (frente, mentón, etc.). || Projecting (que sobresale). || On heat (animales).
saliente adj. ARQ. Projecting, overhanging. || Rising (Sol). || Retiring, outgoing (que abandona sus funciones). || FIG. Salient (importante). | Outstanding (persona). || — *Ángulo saliente*, salient angle. || MIL. *Guardia saliente*, retiring *o* outgoing guard.
— M. (P.us.). East (oriente). || Projection, overhang, ledge (parte que sobresale). || Peak (pico). || MIL. Salient.
salífero, ra adj. GEOL. Saliferous.
salificación f. QUÍM. Salification.
salificar v. tr. QUÍM. To salify.
— V. pr. QUÍM. To salify.
salina f. Salt mine. || — Pl. Saltworks, saltern, *sing*.
salinero m. Salter, salt merchant.
salinero, ra adj. Salt: *industria salinera*, salt industry. || With red and white spots (un toro).
salinidad f. Salinity.
salino, na adj. Saline.
salio, lia adj./s. HIST. Salian.
salir* v. intr. To leave: *para llegar a tiempo tendremos que salir a las cinco*, to get there on time we will have to leave at five o'clock; *el tren salió de la estación*, the train left the station; *el rápido sale a las dos*, the express leaves at two. || To depart, to leave: *el tren para París sale de la estación de Chamartín*, the Paris train departs from Chamartin station *o* leaves from Chamartin station. || To go out: *salir de casa*, to go out of the house; *salir a la calle*, to go out into the street; *salir con amigos*, to go out with friends. || To come out: *si no sales en seguida entro yo*, if you don't come out at once I'm coming in. || To be out (no estar): *la señora ha salido*, madam is out. || To go: *salir de viaje*, to go on a trip. || To get out: *el pájaro no puede salir de su jaula*, the bird can't get out of its cage. || To appear: *le gusta mucho salir en los periódicos, en la televisión*, he likes to appear in the newspapers, on television. || To rise, to come up *o* out (un astro). || To come up (vegetales). || To come out (flores). || To grow (crecer el pelo). || To stick out, to project, to jut out (relieve). || To come out, to be published (publicarse): *¿cuándo salió su última novela?*, when did his last novel come out? || To come in: *acaba de salir una nueva moda*, a new fashion has just come in. || To be raised, to speak *o* to come out: *una voz salió en su defensa*, a voice spoke out in his defence. || To spring (aparecer inesperadamente): *¿de dónde sales?*, where have you sprung from? || To start, to make the first move (juegos). || To open (al principio de un juego de cartas), to lead (después de una baza). || To come up, to be drawn (en la lotería). || To be elected (ser elegido). || To come out *o* off (una mancha). || DEP. To start (corredores). || TEATR. To enter, to come on (un actor). || MAR. To sail. || FIG. To get over, to get out of: *por fin hemos salido de ésta*, we have finally got out of that. | To turn out [to be]: *salió muy inteligente*, he turned out [to be] very intelligent; *el melón salió muy sabroso*, the melon turned out very tasty. | To go, to turn out: *¿cómo le salió el examen?*, how did his exam go? | To spring to mind (ocurrírsele a uno de repente). | To be able to think of: *no me sale su apellido*, I can't think of his surname. | To come to light, to come out (descubrirse). | To turn up, to come up (una oportunidad): *me ha salido una colocación muy buena*, a very good job has turned up for me. || — *Al niño le salió un diente*, the baby cut a tooth. || FIG. *A lo que salga* or *a lo que saliere*, trusting to luck (al buen tuntún). || *Ha salido cara, cruz*, it's heads, tails (echando suertes). || *Me ha salido una cana*, I have got a grey hair. || *No conseguiré nunca salir de pobre*, I'll always be poor. || *No me sale este problema*, I can't work this problem out. || *Pedro salió airoso de la prueba*, Peter passed the test with flying colours. || *Recién salido de la universidad*, just out of university, fresh from university. || *Salga lo que saliere* or *salga lo que salga*, come what may. || *Salir a*, to take after: *el niño ha salido a su madre*, the boy takes after his mother; to come to, to cost: *la comida me salió a cuarenta pesetas*, the meal came to forty pesetas, the meal cost me forty pesetas; to come out into, to lead to: *la calle sale a la plaza*, the street comes out into the square. || FIG. *Salir adelante*, to get on *o* by, to make out. || *Salir a flote*, V. FLOTE. || FIG. *Salir a la calle*, to come out (publicarse). || *Salir a la pizarra*, to go to the blackboard. || *Salir a la superficie*, to come *o* to float to the surface (objeto), to surface (submarino). || *Salir al encuentro de alguien*, V. ENCUENTRO. || *Salir al escenario* or *a escena*, to come on stage, to enter. || *Salir al paso de*, V. PASO. || *Salir a pasear* or *de paseo*, to go [out] for a walk. || *Salir barato, caro*, to be *o* to work out cheap, expensive. || *Salir bien*, to work, to turn out well: *la estratagema le salió bien*, his stratagem worked *o* turned out well; to turn out *o* to come out well: *este dibujo me ha salido bien*, this picture I drew came out well; to come out well (en una foto, retrato, etc.), to come *o* to pull through well: *la operación era grave, pero el enfermo ha salido bien*, the operation was serious but the patient has come through well; to come out all right (de un mal paso), to pass (de un examen), to go off well (fiesta, reunión, etc.): *la primera representación salió muy bien*, the first performance went off very well. || *Salir bien librado*, to come out unscathed, to get off lightly. || *Salir con*, to come out with (decir): *ahora sales tú con eso*, and now you come out with this; to get (obtener): *ha salido con lo que quería*, he has got what he wanted; to go out with [U.S., to date] (los novios), to lead, to play (en juegos de cartas): *salir con el rey de espadas*, to lead the king of spades; to get done (hacer): *es capaz de salir con todo el trabajo*, he will probably get all the work done. || FIG. y FAM. *Salir con las orejas gachas*, to come out with one's tail between one's legs. || *Salir de*, to leave (un sitio): *al salir del trabajo lo haré*, I'll do it when I leave work; to cease to be (dejar de ser): *ha salido de ministro*, he has ceased to be minister; to come out as: *sale de teniente*, he comes out as a lieutenant; to dispose of, to sell (vender), to come from: *el azúcar sale de la remolacha*, sugar comes from sugar beet. || *Salir de apuros*, V. APURO. || *Salir de cuidado*, V. CUIDADO. || *Salir de dudas*, to shed one's doubts. || *Salir de la habitación*, to be up and about (un enfermo). || *Salir del cascarón* or *del huevo*, to hatch. || *Salir del coma*, to come out of *o* to emerge from a coma. || *Salir del paso*, V. PASO. || *Salir de madre*, to overflow (un río). || FIG. *Salir de Málaga para entrar en Malagón*, to jump out of the frying pan into the fire. || *Salir de sus casillas*, V. CASILLA. || *Salir de una enfermedad*, to get over *o* to pull through an illness. || *Salir de un compromiso*, to break an engagement. || *Salir empatados*, to tie, to draw. || *Salir en defensa de alguien* or *algo*, to come out in defence of s.o. *o* sth. || *Salir fiador de*, V. FIADOR. || *Salir mal*, not to do very well, to do badly, to come unstuck (una persona): *me salió mal el examen*, I did badly in the exam; not to work, to go wrong, to misfire: *la estratagema le salió mal*, his stratagem did not work; not to be very good, not to come out very well (fotografía, dibujo, retrato, etc.), to come out badly (de un mal

paso), to be a failure (ser un fracaso). || *Salir mal parado*, to come out the worse for wear. || *Salir perdiendo*, to lose out, to come off worst. || FAM. *Salir pitando* or *de estampía*, to go *o* to be off like a shot *o* like a rocket. || *Salir para*, to leave for (dirigirse a). || FIG. *Salir por alguien*, to come to s.o.'s defence (en una contienda), to vouch for s.o. (salir fiador de). || FAM. *Salir por peteneras*, v. PETENERA. | *Salir que ni pintado*, to come out beautifully. || *¡Tiene a quien salir!*, like father, like son! || *Todavía no le ha salido novio*, she still hasn't got a boyfriend.

— V. pr. To leak [out] (líquido): *el agua se sale por el agujero*, the water is leaking out of the hole. || To leak (un recipiente). || To leak, to escape: *el gas se sale*, the gas is leaking. || To overflow: *río que se ha salido de su cauce*, river that has overflowed its banks. || To leave: *salirse de un club*, to leave a club. || To get out: *el pájaro se salió de la jaula*, the bird got out of the cage. || To escape (evadirse). || To go off: *salirse de la carretera*, to go off the road (un coche). || To boil over, to spill over, to overflow (rebosar): *la leche se ha salido*, the milk has boiled over. || To come off, to become disconnected (desconectarse). || — *No salirse de la legalidad*, to keep within the law. || *No se saldrá de pobre*, he will always be poor. || FIG. *Salirse con la suya*, to get *o* to have one's own way: *Tomás siempre se sale con la suya*, Thomas always gets his own way. || *Salirse de las reglas*, to break the rules. || *Salirse de la vía*, to go off *o* to leave the rails. || *Salirse de lo corriente*, to be out of the ordinary. || *Salirse de los límites*, to go beyond the limits. || *Salirse del tema*, to get off the subject, to digress. || *Salirse de madre*, to overflow (río), to lose one's self-control (enfadarse). || *Salirse de tono*, to make an improper remark. || *Salirse por la tangente*, v. TANGENTE. || *Se le salieron los colores a la cara*, his face turned red, he blushed.

salitrado, da adj. Saltpetrous.

salitral adj. Saltpetrous.

— M. Salpetre works, *pl.*, nitre works, *pl.* (explotación). || Salpetre deposit *o* bed (yacimiento).

salitre m. Saltpetre [U.S., salpeter], nitre [U.S., niter].

salitrería f. Saltpetre works, *pl.*, nitre works, *pl.*

salitrero, ra adj. Saltpetrous.

— M. Saltpetre worker. || — F. Saltpetre deposit *o* bed (yacimiento).

salitroso, sa adj. Saltpetrous.

saliva f. Saliva. || — FIG. *Estoy gastando saliva en balde*, I'm wasting my breath. | *Tragar saliva*, to swallow one's feelings, to hold one's peace.

salivación f. Salivation.

salivadera f. *Amer.* Spittoon.

salivajo m. Spit, spittle.

salival o **salivar** adj. Salivary: *glándulas salivales*, salivary glands.

salivar v. intr. To salivate. || *Amer.* To spit (escupir).

salivazo m. Spit. || *Echar un salivazo*, to spit.

salivoso, sa adj. Salivous.

salmanticense *o* **salmantino, na** adj. [Of *o* from] Salamanca.

— M. y f. Native *o* inhabitant of Salamanca.

salmer m. ARQ. Skewback.

salmista m. Psalmist (autor de salmos).

salmo m. Psalm: *el Libro de los Salmos*, the Book of Psalms.

salmodia f. Psalmody. || FAM. Drone (ruido monótono).

salmodiar v. intr. To sing psalms. || FAM. To drone.

salmón m. Salmon (pez). || *Cría de salmones*, salmon breeding.

salmonado, da adj. Salmon-like. || *Trucha salmonada*, salmon trout.

salmoncillo m. Samlet (pez).

salmonero, ra adj. Salmon: *escala salmonera*, salmon ladder.

salmonete m. Red mullet, surmullet (pez).

salmónidos m. pl. ZOOL. Salmonidae.

salmuera f. Brine. || *Salazón en salmuera*, brining.

salobral adj. Saline (terreno).

salobre adj. Brackish (ligeramente salado). || Briny (muy salado). || Salty (salado).

salobreño, ña adj. Saline (tierra).

salobridad f. Saltiness, brackishness.

Salomón n. pr. m. Solomon.

salomónico, ca adj. Solomonic. || ARQ. *Columna salomónica*, wreathed column.

salón m. Lounge, sitting room. || Drawing room (para recibir visitas). || Hall: *salón de actos* or *de reuniones*, assembly hall. || Show, exhibition (exposición): *salón del automóvil*, Motor Show. || Salon, coterie (literario, etc.). || Common room (de colegio, etc.). || — *Salón de baile*, ballroom, dance hall. || *Salón de belleza*, beauty parlour. || *Salón de conferencias*, lecture room. || *Salón de demostraciones*, showroom. || *Salón de fiestas*, dance hall. || *Salón de peluquería*, hairdressing salon. || *Salón de pintura*, art gallery. || *Salón de té*, tearoom, teashop.

saloncillo m. Private room.

salpicadero m. Dashboard, fascia, facia (de un coche).

salpicadura f. Splashing, spattering (acción). || Splash (de algo líquido): *salpicaduras de pintura*, splashes of paint. || Spatter (de barro).

salpicar v. tr. To splash (con un líquido). || To spatter (con barro). || To sprinkle (rociar). || To dot (con puntos). || To scatter: *mesa salpicada de flores*, table scattered with flowers. || FIG. To sprinkle, to intersperse: *una conversación salpicada de chistes*, a conversation sprinkled with jokes; *texto salpicado de citas*, text sprinkled with quotations. || — *Salpicado de estrellas*, star-spangled. || *Traje salpicado de motas*, spotted dress.

salpicón m. CULIN. Salmagundi. || (Ant.). Leftover beef with onion sauce. || Splash, spatter (salpicadura). || *Amer.* Fruit juice (bebida). || *Salpicón de mariscos*, seafood cocktail.

salpimentar* v. tr. To season (sazonar). || FIG. To spice, to season (amenizar).

salpresar v. tr. To salt down.

salpullido m. Rash (erupción). || Fleabite (de la pulga).

salsa f. Sauce: *salsa blanca*, white sauce; *salsa tártara*, tartare sauce, tartar sauce. || Gravy (de la carne). || Dressing (para la lechuga). || FIG. Sauce, appetizer: *no hay mejor salsa que el apetito*, hunger is the best sauce. || FAM. Sauce, zest (salero). || — FIG. *Cocerse en su propia salsa*, to stew in one's own juice. | *En su (propia) salsa*, in one's element. | *La salsa de la vida*, the spice of life. || *Media salsa*, court bouillon. || *Salsa bechamel* or *besamel*, béchamel *o* white sauce. || *Salsa de tomate*, tomato sauce. || *Salsa mahonesa* or *mayonesa*, mayonnaise. || *Trabar una salsa*, to thicken a sauce.

salsera f. Sauceboat, gravy boat (para salsa). || Small saucer (salsercilla).

salsereta o **salserilla** f. Small saucer (de pintor).

salsifí m. BOT. Salsify.

salsoláceas f. pl. BOT. Salsolaceae.

saltabanco m. y f. o **saltabancos** m. y f. inv. FIG. y FAM. Mountebank, charlatan (que vende medicinas). || Tumbler, acrobat (saltimbanqui). || Punch and Judy showman (titiritero).

saltabardales o **saltabarrancos** m. y f. inv. FIG. y FAM. Harum-scarum, scatterbrain, happy-go-lucky.

saltable adj. Jumpable.

saltadero m. Jumping place. || Jet of water (surtidor).

saltadizo, za adj. Fragile, brittle (quebradizo).

saltador, ra adj. Jumping.

— M. y f. Jumper. || *Saltador de pértiga*, pole vaulter. || — M. Skipping rope (comba).

saltadura f. Chip.

saltamontes m. inv. ZOOL. Grasshopper.

saltaojos m. inv. BOT. Peony.

saltar v. intr. To jump, to leap: *saltó desde la azotea*, he jumped from the terrace; *saltó en el caballo*, he leapt on to the horse; *saltó en la silla*, he jumped up on [to] the chair. || To jump (en paracaídas). || To fidget (brincar): *saltaba de impaciencia*, he fidgeted impatiently. || To hop, to skip (dar saltitos). || To bounce (pelota). || To break (romperse). || To burst (estallar). || To burst, to explode (explotar). || To come off, to come loose, to come out (desprenderse). || To come off (un botón). || To spring *o* to dash *o* to bound *o* to leap forward (salir con ímpetu). || To spring, to spurt, to gush (brotar). || To pop out *o* off: *el tapón ha saltado*, the cork has popped out. || To break off, to come off (deshacerse una pieza). || To fly [off] (virutas, trozos de madera). || FIG. To jump, to skip: *saltar de un tema a otro*, to jump from one subject to another; *alumno que ha saltado de una clase a otra*, pupil who jumped from one year to another. | To blow up (enfadarse): *saltó al oír tales insultos*, he blew up on hearing such insults. || — FIG. *Cuando* or *donde menos se piensa salta la liebre*, things always happen when you least expect them to. | *Estar a la que salta*, to be ready for the first thing that pops up. || *Hacer saltar*, to blow up (destruir), to jump (un caballo). || *Hacer saltar la banca*, to break the bank. || *Hacer saltar las lágrimas a uno*, to bring tears to one's eyes, to make one cry. || *Saltar a la comba*, to skip. || FIG. *Saltar a la palestra*, v. PALESTRA. | *Saltar a la vista* or *a los ojos*, to be obvious, to be as plain as a pikestaff. || *Saltar al agua*, to jump into the water. || *Saltar a tierra*, to leap ashore (de un barco). || *Saltar con pértiga*, to pole-vault. || FIG. *Saltar con una impertinencia*, to come out with an impertinent remark. | *Saltar de alegría*, to jump for *o* with joy. || *Saltar de la cama*, to leap out of bed. || *Saltar sobre*, to pounce on. || *Saltó y dijo*, he suddenly said, he upped and said. || FIG. y FAM. *Y ahora saltas tú con eso*, and now you come out with that.

— V. tr. To jump [over], to leap [over]: *saltar un arroyo*, to jump over a brook. || To jump [over], to leap [over], to vault (over): *saltar una tapia*, to jump over a wall. || To blow up (con un explosivo). || To put out (un ojo). || To knock out (dientes, etc.). || To pull off (arrancar). || To break (romper). || To jump (en el juego de damas). || To cover (el macho a la hembra). || FIG. To jump, to skip (omitir). || — FIG. y FAM. *Saltar la tapia*, to go over the wall. | *Saltarle la tapa de los sesos a uno*, to blow s.o.'s brains out.

— V. pr. To skip, to jump (en un escrito, un escalafón): *me he saltado una página*, I have skipped a page. || To miss, to skip (una comida). || — FIG. y FAM. *Saltarse algo a la torera*, to completely ignore sth. | *Saltarse la tapa de los sesos*, v. TAPA. | *Saltarse un semáforo*, to jump the lights. || *Se le saltaron las*

lágrimas, tears welled up in his eyes, tears came to his eyes.
saltarín, ina adj. Jumping, skipping (que salta). || Dancing (que baila). || Restless (agitado). || FIG. Scatterbrained, harum-scarum (atolondrado).
— M. y f. Dancer.
salteado m. CULIN. Sauté.
salteador m. Highwayman, holdup man.
salteamiento m. Holdup, highway robbery (robo). || Assault, surprise attack (asalto).
saltear v. tr. To hold up, to rob, to waylay (robar). || To pounce on (atacar por sorpresa). || To make less frequent, to space out (espaciar): *saltear las visitas*, to make one's visits less frequent. || To do [sth.] in fits and starts, to skip through *o* over [sth.] (hacer algo saltándose partes). || CULIN. To sauté. || FIG. To take by surprise. || *Hilera de chopos y sauces salteados*, row of alternating black poplars and willows.
salteño, ña adj. [Of *o* from] Salto (Uruguay). || [Of *o* from] Salta (Argentina).
— M. y f. Native *o* inhabitant of Salto (Uruguay). || Native *o* inhabitant of Salta (Argentina).
salterio m. REL. Psalter, psalmbook (libro). || MÚS. Psaltery (instrumento).
saltimbanqui m. Member of a travelling circus. || Acrobat, tumbler (acróbata).
saltito o **saltillo** m. Little jump *o* hop. || *Dar saltitos* or *andar a saltitos*, to hop, to skip [along].
salto m. Jump, leap, bound: *de un salto*, in a bound. || Falls, *pl.*, waterfall, cascade (de agua). || Precipice (despeñadero). || Unevenness (desnivel). || Omission (omisión). || DEP. Jump: *salto de altura, de longitud*, high, long jump. | Vault: *salto de* or *con pértiga* [*Amer.*, *garrocha*], pole vault. | Dive: *salto del ángel*, swan dive. || FIG. Springboard: *la televisión ha sido para él un salto a la fama*, television has been his springboard to fame. || TECN. Chute. || — *A salto de mata*, from hand to mouth, from one day to the next (vivir al día), like a shot (con mucha velocidad), as it bolts from cover (liebre), haphazardly (de cualquier manera). || *A saltos*, by leaps and bounds, in leaps and bounds. || *Bajar de un salto*, to jump down. || *Cruzar de un salto*, to leap over, to jump over. || *Dar saltos de alegría*, to jump for *o* with joy. || *Dar* or *pegar un salto*, to jump, to leap, to bound. || FAM. *Dar* or *pegar un salto por casa de alguien*, to drop by s.o.'s house, to pop over to s.o.'s house. || *Dar un salto atrás*, to jump back *o* backwards. || FIG. *Dar un salto en el vacío*, to take a shot in the dark, to do sth. blindly. || *De un salto*, with one bound, with one jump. || FIG. *El corazón me dio un salto*, my heart skipped a beat. | *En un salto*, in a jiffy, in a flash (rápidamente). || *Ir* or *avanzar a saltos*, to jump along. || FIG. *Ir en un salto a* or *plantarse en un salto en*, to pop *o* to nip over to. || *Salto de cama*, négligé [U.S., negligee]. || FIG. *Salto de carnero*, buck (de un caballo). || DEP. *Salto de la carpa*, jackknife. || *Salto de lobo*, sunk fence. || DEP. *Salto de trampolín*, springboard dive. || MAR. *Salto de viento*, shift *o* change of wind. || DEP. *Salto mortal*, somersault. || *Subir de un salto*, to jump up. || DEP. *Triple salto*, hop, step and jump.
saltón, ona adj. Jumping, hopping (que anda a saltos). || Bulging (ojos).
— M. ZOOL. Grasshopper (saltamontes).
salubérrimo, ma adj. Very healthy *o* salubrious.
salubre adj. Salubrious, healthy.
salubridad f. Salubrity, healthiness.
salud f. Health (del cuerpo): *salud delicada*, delicate health. || REL. Salvation: *la salud eterna*, eternal salvation. || Welfare (bienestar). || — *Beber a la salud de uno*, to drink to s.o.'s health. || *Comité de Salud Pública*, Public Safety Committee. || FIG. *Curarse en salud*, to take precautions (precaverse). || *Estar bien, mal de salud*, to be in good, in bad health. || *Estar rebosante de salud* or *vender salud*, to be brimming *o* glowing with health. || *Gastar salud*, to be in *o* to enjoy good health, to be healthy. || *Gozar de buena salud*, to be in *o* to enjoy good health. || *Jurar por la salud de alguien*, v. JURAR. || *Mirar por su salud*, to look after *o* to take care of one's health. || *Recobrar la salud*, to recover one's health. || *Salud de hierro*, iron constitution. || *Tener poca salud*, not to be very healthy.
— Interj. FAM. Greetings! || *¡A su salud!* or *¡salud y pesetas!* or *¡salud!*, cheers!, good health!
saludable adj. Healthy (sano). || Good, healthy (provechoso, benéfico). || Salutary, wholesome: *un castigo saludable*, a salutary punishment.
saludador m. Quack (curandero).
saludar v. tr. To greet (muestra de cortesía). || To acknowledge, to say hello to: *no me saluda nunca por la calle*, he never acknowledges me in the street. || MIL. To salute. || FIG. To salute, to hail: *saludar el advenimiento de la libertad*, to hail the arrival of freedom. || FAM. To look at: *este alumno no ha saludado siquiera la lección*, this pupil hasn't even looked at the lesson. || FIG. To cure by magic (curar por ensalmo). || — *Ir a saludar a alguien*, to call in and see s.o., to go and say hello to s.o. || *Le saluda atentamente* (*su seguro servidor*), Yours faithfully, Yours truly (cartas). || *Salude de mi parte a*, give my regards to *o* my best to.
— V. intr. MIL. To salute.
saludo m. MIL. Salute. || Bow (inclinación). || Greeting, salutation. || — Pl. Regards, best wishes. || — *Atentos saludos* or *saludos cordiales de*, best wishes [from]. || *Reciba un atento saludo de*, Yours sincerely. || *Saludos respetuosos*, respectfully yours, Yours faithfully. || *¡Un saludo a María!*, give my regards *o* my best to Mary!, say hello to Mary for me!
Salustio n. pr. Sallust.
salutación f. Salutation, greeting. || REL. *La Salutación angélica*, the Hail Mary.
salutífero, ra adj. Salutary, wholesome.
salustista m. y f. Salvationist, member of the Salvation Army (miembro del Ejército de Salvación).
salva f. MIL. Salvo, volley: *tirar una salva*, to fire a volley. | Salute (en honor de alguien). || Thunder, storm: *salva de aplausos*, thunder of applause. || Tasting (prueba de la comida). || Ordeal (de un acusado). || Tray, salver (bandeja). || Oath, vow, solemn promise (juramento). || — *Cartucho para salvas*, blank cartridge. || FIG. *Gastar la pólvora en salvas*, to waste one's efforts *o* one's ammunition.
salvación f. Rescue, delivery, salvation. || REL. Salvation: *la salvación eterna*, eternal salvation. || — *Ejército de Salvación*, Salvation Army. || *Este enfermo no tiene salvación*, there is no hope for this patient. || FIG. *Tabla de salvación*, v. TABLA.
salvadera f. Sandbox (para secar la tinta).
salvado m. Bran (afrecho).
Salvador (El) n. pr. m. GEOGR. El Salvador.
salvador, ra adj. Saving.
— M. y f. Saviour [U.S., savior], rescuer. || MAR. Salvager, salvor. || *El Salvador*, the Saviour [U.S., the Savior], Jesus Christ.
salvadoreño, ña adj./s. Salvadoran.
salvaguarda f. V. SALVAGUARDIA.
salvaguardar v. tr. To safeguard.
salvaguardia f. Safeguard. || FIG. Guardian: *la O.N.U. es la salvaguardia de la paz*, the U.N. is the guardian of peace.
salvajada f. Savage *o* brutal act *o* deed, savagery (acto). || Horror, atrocity: *las salvajadas de la guerra*, the horrors of war.
salvaje adj. Savage (feroz). || Wild (no domesticado): *animal salvaje*, wild animal. || Wild (plantas, paisaje). || Savage (sin cultura). || Uncivilized, primitive (primitivo).
— M. y f. Savage (persona en estado primitivo). || FIG. Savage, boor (bruto).
salvajería f. V. SALVAJADA.
salvajino, na adj. Wild, savage. || *Carne salvajina*, game, meat from wild animals.
— M. y f. Savage. || — F. Furs, *pl.*, skins, *pl.*, pelts, *pl.* (pieles). || Wild animals, *pl.* (fieras montesas). || Game (carne).
salvajismo m. Savagery.
salvamanteles m. inv. Tablemat.
salvamento m. Rescue, saving (acción de salvar). || REL. Salvation (salvación). || Salvage (de naufragios). || FIG. Refuge (refugio). || — *Bote de salvamento*, lifeboat. || *Equipo de salvamento*, rescue party. || *Operaciones de salvamento*, rescue operations. || *Sociedad de salvamento de náufragos*, Lifeboat Association.
salvar v. tr. To save, to rescue (de un peligro): *salvar a un náufrago*, to save a shipwrecked person. || To salvage (un barco). || To save: *salvar su honor*, to save one's honour; *salvó a su hijo de la ruina*, he saved his son from ruin. || To jump over: *salvar un arroyo*, to jump over a stream. || To clear (un obstáculo). || To negotiate: *los montañeros salvaron la cadena de montañas en dos días*, the mountaineers negotiated the mountain range in two days. || To cover (una distancia). || To span, to cross: *el puente salva el río*, the bridge spans the river. || To get round (evitar): *salvar una dificultad*, to get round a difficulty. || To overcome (resolver) || To exclude, to except (excluir): *salvando la posibilidad de*, excepting the possibility of. || To notarize (autorizar un documento). || FIG. To make up for, to compensate for: *su simpatía lo salva todo*, her kindness makes up for everything. || *El honor está salvado*, honour is saved.
— V. pr. REL. To save one's soul, to be saved. || To survive, to escape: *salvarse de un accidente terrible*, to survive a nasty accident. || To recover (un enfermo). || — FAM. *Salvarse por los pelos*, to escape by the skin of one's teeth. || *¡Sálvese quien pueda!*, every man for himself!
salvavidas m. inv. Life preserver (cualquier dispositivo). || Life buoy (boya). || Life belt (cinturón). || Lifeboat (bote, lancha). || Fender, guard (en tranvías).
— Adj. Life-saving. || — *Bote salvavidas*, lifeboat. || *Chaleco salvavidas*, life jacket.
salvedad f. Condition, proviso (condición). || Exception (excepción). || Reservation, qualification (reserva). || Distinction (distinción).
salvia f. BOT. Salvia, sage.
salvilla f. Salver, tray (bandeja).
salvo, va adj. Safe. || FAM. *Le dio en salva sea la parte*, it hit him you know where *o* in the you-know-what, it hit him where it hurts most.
— Adv./prep. Except [for], save: *todos vinieron salvo él*, everyone came except for him. || — *A salvo*,

safe and sound (ileso), safe, out of danger (fuera de peligro): *a salvo de*, safe from; safe: *su reputación está a salvo*, her reputation is safe. || *Dejar a salvo*, to safeguard (salvaguardar), to spare: *la revolución no dejó a salvo ningún convento*, the revolution didn't spare a single convent. || *Poner a salvo*, to put in a safe place. || *Ponerse a salvo*, to reach safety. || *Salvo casos en que*, except for cases where *o* in which. || *Salvo el parecer de usted*, unless I hear to the contrary, unless otherwise notified. || *Salvo que*, unless (a no ser que).

salvoconducto m. Safe-conduct.

samario m. Samarium (metal).

samario, ria adj. [Of *o* from] Santa Marta [Colombia].
— M. y f. Native *o* inhabitant of Santa Marta.

samaritano, na adj./s. Samaritan.

samba f. Samba (baile).

sambenito m. Sanbenito [cloak worn by those condemned by the Inquisition] (capotillo). || FIG. Disgrace, dishonour (mala fama). | Taboo (tabú). || — FIG. *A mí me han colgado ese sambenito*, they have given me a bad name. | *Le han colgado el sambenito de embustero*, they have branded him a liar.

samnita adj./s. HIST. Samnite.

Samotracia n. pr. GEOGR. Samothrace.

samovar m. Samovar (tetera rusa).

sampaguita *f.* Kind of jasmine.

sampán m. MAR. Sampan (embarcación china).

samurai m. Samurai (guerrero japonés).

samuro m. *Amer.* Turkey buzzard (ave).

san adj. (apocopated form of *santo*) Saint, St: *San Pedro*, Saint Peter. || *¿A qué hora dicen la misa en San Pedro?*, at what time is mass at St Peter's.
— OBSERV. *San* is used before all masculine names of saints except Tomás, Tomé, Toribio and Domingo.

sanable adj. Curable.

sanador, ra adj. Healing, curing.
— M. y f. Healer, person who cures.

sanalotodo m. Cure-all (emplasto). || FIG. Panacea (remedio útil para todo).

sanamente adv. Healthily. || FIG. Sincerely.

sanar v. tr. To heal, to cure.
— V. intr. To recover (un enfermo). || To heal (una herida).

sanatorio m. Sanatorium, sanitarium (para tuberculosis). || Clinic, nursing home: *mi mujer ha dado a luz en el sanatorio*, my wife has just given birth in the clinic. || Hospital (hospital). || *Sanatorio psiquiátrico*, psychiatric clinic.

San Bernardo (perro de) m. Saint Bernard.

sanción f. Sanction.

sancionable adj. Sanctionable.

sancionador, ra adj. Sanctioning.
— M. y f. Sanctioner.

sancionar v. tr. To sanction: *sancionar una ley*, to sanction a law. || To sanction, to penalize: *este comerciante ha sido sancionado por venta ilícita de mercancías*, this merchant has been penalized for the illegal sale of merchandise.

sanco m. *Amer.* Gruel (gachas). | Thick mud (barro).

sancochar v. tr. CULIN. To parboil.

sancocho m. *Amer.* Stew made with meat, yucca and bananas.

sancta m. REL. Forepart of the tabernacle.

sanctasanctórum m. Sanctum sanctorum, holy of holies. || FIG. Sanctum, sanctum sanctorum.

sancho m. *Amer.* Ram (carnero). | Domestic animal.

Sancho n. pr. m. Sancho. || *Al buen callar llaman Sancho*, V. CALLAR.

sanchopancesco, ca adj. Like Sancho Panza, down-to-earth.

sandalia f. Sandal.

sándalo m. BOT. Sandal, sandalwood (árbol y madera).

sandáraca f. Sandarac (resina, mineral).

sandez f. Nonsense (palabra). || Silly thing (acto). || Silliness (cualidad). || — *Decir sandeces*, to talk nonsense. || *Es una sandez*, it's silly.

sandía f. BOT. Watermelon.

sandio, dia adj. Silly, nonsensical.
— M. y f. Fool, dolt.

sanducero, ra adj. [Of *o* from] Paysandú [Uruguay].
— M. y f. Native *o* inhabitant of Paysandú.

sandunga f. FAM. Charm (encanto). | Wit (gracia). || *Amer.* Party (parranda). | Typical Mexican dance.

sandunguero, ra adj. FAM. Charming (encantador). | Witty (gracioso).

sandwich m. Sandwich (emparedado).
— OBSERV. In Spanish the plural is *sandwiches* or *sandwichs*.

saneado, da adj. Drained (el terreno). || Stabilized (la moneda). || Reorganized (las finanzas). || Sound: *tiene una posición muy saneada*, he has a very sound position.

saneamiento m. Drainage (desecación de un terreno). || Stabilization (de la moneda). || Reorganization (de las finanzas). || JUR. Guarantee. | Indemnification. || *Artículos de saneamiento*, sanitary ware, bathroom goods *o* fixtures.

sanear v. tr. To drain, to dry out (el terreno). || To rid of damp (una casa). || To put right, to mend (reparar). || To stabilize (la moneda). || To reorganize (las finanzas). || JUR. To guarantee (garantizar). | To indemnify (indemnizar).

sanedrín m. HIST. Sanhedrin, Sanhedrim.

sanfasón m. *Amer.* Cheek (fam.), nerve, (fam.), insolence (desfachatez). || *Amer. A la sanfasón*, nonchalantly (despreocupadamente), carelessly (descuidadamente).

sanforizado, da adj. Sanforized (textiles).

sangradera f. MED. Lancet (lanceta). | Basin for blood (vasija para la sangre). || Sluice, sluiceway, irrigation ditch (caz). || Sluice, sluice gate, floodgate (compuerta).

sangrador m. Bloodletter (el que sangra). || Sluice gate, outlet (compuerta).

sangradura f. ANAT. Inner part of the elbow (sangría). || MED. Incision into a vein (corte). || FIG. Drain, outlet (en un canal).

sangrante adj. Bleeding (herida). || FIG. Flagrant (injusticia, etc.).

sangrar v. tr. To bleed: *sangrar a un enfermo*, to bleed a sick person. || To drain (un terreno). || To tap, to draw resin from (un pino). || IMPR. To indent. || FIG. y FAM. To bleed dry *o* white (sacar todo el dinero). | To filch (robar). || TECN. To tap (una tubería).
— V. intr. To bleed. || — FIG. *Estar sangrando*, to be still fresh (ser reciente). || *Estás sangrando por la nariz*, your nose is bleeding. || FAM. *Sangrar como un cochino* or *un toro*, to bleed profusely, to gush blood, to bleed like a pig.
— V. pr. MED. To have o.s. bled.

sangraza f. Contaminated blood.

sangre f. Blood. || FIG. Blood (linaje, parentesco): *sangre azul*, blue blood; *tener sangre de reyes*, to have royal blood. || — *A sangre fría*, in cold blood. || *A sangre y fuego*, mercilessly. || *Azotar a alguien hasta hacerle sangre*, to beat s.o. black and blue. || FIG. y FAM. *Calentarle la sangre a uno*, V. CALENTAR. || FIG. *Chorrear sangre*, to cry out to heaven (una acción monstruosa). | *Chupar la sangre a uno*, to bleed s.o. white *o* dry. | *Dar la sangre* or *la sangre de las venas por algo* or *alguien*, to give one's right arm for sth. *o* s.o. || MED. *Dar sangre*, to give blood. || *Derramar sangre*, to shed blood. || ZOOL. *De sangre caliente*, *fría*, warm-blooded, cold-blooded. || *Donante de sangre*, blood donor. || *Echar sangre*, to bleed. || FAM. *Echar sangre como un cochino* or *un toro*, to bleed like a pig *o* profusely. || *Echar sangre por las narices*, to have a nosebleed, to bleed from the nose. || FIG. *Estar bañado en sangre*, to be bathed in blood. || *Estar chorreando sangre*, to be gushing blood. || *Hacer sangre*, to draw blood. || FIG. *Helarle la sangre a uno*, to make s.o.'s blood run cold. | *La letra con sangre entra*, V. LETRA. | *Lavar con sangre*, to avenge with blood (un agravio, una afrenta). | *La voz de la sangre*, the call of blood. | *Le bulle* or *hierve la sangre*, he is hot-blooded. | *Lo lleva en la sangre*, it is *o* it runs in his blood. | *Llevar* or *tener en la sangre*, *llevar en la masa de la sangre*, to have in one's blood (algo), to have got in one's blood (alguien). || *Naranja de sangre*, blood orange. || FIG. *No llegó la sangre al río*, it wasn't too serious. | *No quedar sangre en el cuerpo* or *en las venas*, to be scared stiff. || *Pura sangre*, thoroughbred (caballo). || FIG. *Quemarle* or *freírle a uno la sangre*, to make s.o.'s blood boil. | *Sangre fría*, coolness, sangfroid. | *Se le quemó la sangre*, his blood boiled, it made his blood boil. | *Subírsele a uno la sangre a la cabeza*, to see red. | *Sudar sangre*, to sweat blood. | *Tener la sangre gorda*, to be sluggish. | *Tener las manos manchadas de sangre*, to have blood on one's hands. | *Tener mala sangre*, to be evil-minded. | *Tener sangre de artistas*, to come from a line of artists. | *Tener sangre de horchata* or *no tener sangre en las venas*, to have water in one's veins, to have no blood in one's veins. || *Tracción de* or *a sangre*, animal traction.

sangregorda m. y f. FAM. Sluggard, oaf.

sangría f. ANAT. Inner part of the elbow. || MED. Bleeding, bloodletting. || Draining outlet (en un canal). || Tap (en un árbol). || "Sangría", sangaree (p.us.) [refreshing sweet drink made from red wine, oranges and lemons]. || FIG. Drain, outflow: *una sangría en el capital*, a drain on capital, an outflow of capital. || IMPR. Indentation. || TECN. Tapping [of molten metal] (en los altos hornos). || FIG. *Sangría monetaria*, monetary drain.

sangrientamente adv. Bloodily.

sangriento, ta adj. Bloody, bloodstained, covered with blood: *manos sangrientas*, bloody hands. || Bleeding (herida). || FIG. Bloody: *batalla sangrienta*, bloody battle. | Cruel: *una broma sangrienta*, a cruel joke. || Crying, outrageous (injusticia). || Cruel, cutting, deadly (injuria).

sanguaraña f. Popular Peruvian dance (baile).

sanguijuela f. ZOOL. Leech, bloodsucker. || FIG. Leech, sponger, bloodsucker.

sanguina f. Sanguine (lápiz y dibujo). || Blood orange, sanguine orange (naranja).

sanguinario, ria adj. Bloodthirsty.
— F. Bloodstone (piedra preciosa). || BOT. Bloodroot.

sanguíneo, a adj. Sanguineous. || Blood: *grupo sanguíneo*, blood group; *vasos sanguíneos*, blood vessels.

sanguino, na adj. Sanguineous. || Bloodthirsty (sanguinario). || *Naranja sanguina*, blood orange, sanguine orange.

— M. BOT. Red dogwood (cornejo). || — F. Blood orange, sanguine orange (naranja).
sanguinolencia f. Bloodiness, sanguinolence (p.us.).
sanguinolento, ta adj. Bloody, bleeding (que echa sangre). || Bloodstained, sanguinolent (p.us.) [manchado de sangre]. || FIG. Blood-red (color). || *Ojos sanguinolentos*, bloodshot eyes.
sánico adj. m. *Papel sánico*, toilet paper.
sanidad f. Health (salud): *sanidad pública*, public health. || Sanitation: *problemas de sanidad*, sanitation problems. || — *Certificado* or *patente de sanidad*, health certificate. || MIL. *Cuerpo de Sanidad Militar*, medical corps. || *Dirección General de Sanidad*, Ministry of Health. || *Inspector de Sanidad*, sanitary inspector. || *Medidas de sanidad*, sanitary measures.
sanie o **sanies** f. MED. Sanies.
sanitario, ria adj. Sanitary: *cordón sanitario*, sanitary cordon; *medidas sanitarias*, sanitary measures.
— M. MIL. Military health officer.
sanjuanada f. Festival of Saint John's Day.
sanjuanero, ra adj. Ripe by Saint John's Day (frutas). || [Of] Saint John's Day. || [Of *o* from] San Juan [Cuba].
— M. y f. Native *o* inhabitant of San Juan.
sanjuanista adj. Of the Order of Saint John of Jerusalem.
— M. Knight of the Order of Saint John of Jerusalem.
sanluisero, ra adj. [Of *o* from] San Luis.
— M. y f. Native *o* inhabitant of San Luis [Argentina].
sanmartiniano, na adj. Of *o* like San Martín [Argentine general].
sano, na adj. Healthy: *persona sana*, healthy person; *clima sano*, healthy climate. || Healthy, wholesome: *un alimento sano*, a wholesome food. || FIG. Sound: *una filosofía sana*, a sound philosophy. || Good: *no queda un plato sano en toda la casa*, there is not one good plate left in the entire house. || Good, sound: *una manzana sana*, a good apple. || Sound (saneado): *un negocio sano*, a sound business. || FIG. Healthy, wholesome (sin vicios): *tiene ideas muy sanas*, he has very healthy ideas. || — FIG. *Cortar por lo sano*, v. CORTAR. || *Estar en su sano juicio*, to be in one's right mind. || *Estar más sano que una manzana* or *una pera*, to be as fit as a fiddle. || *Sano de cuerpo y alma*, sound in mind and body. || *Sano y salvo*, safe and sound.
San Quintín n. pr. GEOGR. Saint Quentin. || FIG. y FAM. *Se armó la de San Quintín*, all hell broke loose. | *Se va a armar la de San Quintín*, there's going to be real trouble *o* a hell of a row.
sánscrito, ta adj./s.m. Sanskrit.
sanseacabó loc. FAM. *Y sanseacabó*, and that's the end of it, and that's all there is to it.
sansimoniano, na adj. FIL. Saint-Simonian.
— M. y f. Saint-Simonian, Saint-Simonist.
sansimonismo m. FIL. Saint-Simonism.
sansirolé m. FAM. Nincompoop, simpleton (bobo).
Sansón n. pr. m. Samson. || FIG. *Ser un Sansón*, to be as strong as an ox.
santabárbara f. MAR. Magazine.
santacruzeño, ña adj. [Of *o* from] Santa Cruz [Argentina].
— M. y f. Native *o* inhabitant of Santa Cruz.
santafecino, na adj. [Of *o* from] Santa Fe [Argentina].
— M. y f. Native *o* inhabitant of Santa Fe.
santafereño, ña adj. [Of *o* from] Santa Fe [Colombia].
— M. y f. Native *o* inhabitant of Santa Fe.
santamente adv. *Vivir santamente*, to live like a saint, to live a saintly life.
santandereano, na adj. [Of *o* from] Santander [Colombia].
— M. y f. Native *o* inhabitant of Santander.
santanderino, na o **santanderiense** adj. [Of *o* from] Santander [Spain].
— M. y f. Native *o* inhabitant of Santander.
santateresa f. ZOOL. Praying mantis.
santero, ra adj. Sanctimonious (beato).
— M. y f. Caretaker of a sanctuary (que cuida un santuario). || Alms collector [who carries the image of a saint] (que pide limosna).
Santiago n. pr. Santiago [city in Chile, Cuba, etc.].
Santiago n. pr. m. James (persona). || Saint James (orden). || — *Camino de Santiago*, Milky Way (vía láctea), the road to Santiago de Compostela (peregrinación). || *¡Santiago!* or *¡Santiago y cierra España!* or *¡Santiago y a ellos!*, ancient Spanish war cry. || *Santiago de Compostela*, Santiago de Compostela (ciudad), St. James the Greater (apóstol).
santiagueño, ña adj. Ripe by Saint James' Day (frutas). || [Of *o* from] Santiago del Estero [Argentina].
— M. y f. Native *o* inhabitant of Santiago del Estero.
santiaguero, ra adj. [Of *o* from] Santiago de Cuba.
— M. y f. Native *o* inhabitant of Santiago de Cuba.
santiagués, esa adj. [Of *o* from] Santiago de Compostela [Spain].
— M. y f. Native *o* inhabitant of Santiago de Compostela.
santiaguino, na adj. [Of *o* from] Santiago de Chile.
— M. y f. Native *o* inhabitant of Santiago de Chile.
santiaguista adj. Of the Order of Saint James.
— M. y f. Knight of the Order of Saint James.
santiamén m. Instant. || FAM. *En un santiamén*, in a jiffy, in an instant, in no time at all: *hizo su trabajo en un santiamén*, he did his work in a jiffy; *llegué a Madrid en un santiamén*, I arrived in Madrid in no time at all.
santidad f. Saintliness, holiness. || — *Olor de santidad*, odour of sanctity. || *Su Santidad*, His Holiness.
santificable adj. Sanctifiable.
santificación f. Sanctification.
santificador, ra adj. Sanctifying.
— M. y f. Sanctifier.
santificante adj. Sanctifying.
santificar v. tr. To sanctify. || To consecrate (un lugar). || To keep, to observe (los domingos y fiestas). || FIG. To excuse, to forgive (disculpar). || REL. *Santificado sea Tu Nombre*, hallowed be Thy Name.
santiguada f. Sign of the cross.
santiguamiento m. Making the sign of the cross (acción de santiguar). || Crossing o.s., making the sign of the cross (acción de santiguarse).
santiguar v. tr. To bless, to make the sign of the cross over (bendecir). || To make the sign of the cross over (los curanderos). || FIG. To slap (abofetar).
— V. pr. To cross o.s., to make the sign of the cross (persignarse).
santísimo, ma adj. Very *o* most holy. || — FAM. *Hacerle a uno la santísima pascua*, to mess things up for s.o. (fastidiar), to play a dirty trick on s.o. (hacer una mala jugada). || *La Virgen Santísima*, the Holy Virgin. || *Santísimo Sacramento*, Holy Sacrament. || FAM. *Todo el santísimo día*, all the livelong day, all day long.
— M. The Holy Sacrament.
santo, ta adj. Holy: *Semana Santa*, Holy Week; *la santa Iglesia católica*, the holy Catholic Church. || Saintly, holy: *una persona santa*, a saintly person. || Holy: *la Tierra Santa*, the Holy Land. || Consecrated, holy (consagrado): *tierra santa*, holy ground. || FAM. Blessed: *me tuvo esperando toda la santa tarde*, he kept me waiting all the blessed afternoon; *tuve que dormir en el santo suelo*, I had to sleep on the blessed floor. || Saint: *Santo Tomás*, Saint Thomas; *Santa Ana*, Saint Ann. || — *Ciudad Santa*, Holy City. || *Espíritu Santo*, Holy Spirit *o* Ghost. || *Guerra santa*, holy war. || FAM. *Hacer su santa voluntad* or *su santo gusto*, to do as one jolly well *o* damn well pleases. || *Jueves Santo*, Holy Thursday, Maundy Thursday. || *La Santa Sede*, the Holy See. || *Padre Santo* or *Santo Padre*, Holy Father. || *Sábado Santo*, Holy Saturday. || HIST. *Santa Alianza*, Holy Alliance. || *Santa Biblia*, Holy Bible. || *Santa Faz*, Holy Face. || *Santo Grial*, Holy Grail. || *Santo Oficio*, Holy Office, Inquisition. || *Santo óleo*, holy oil. || FIG. *Santo y bueno*, all well and good. || FAM. *Todo el santo día*, all the livelong day, all day long. || *Un santo varón*, a saint. || *Viernes Santo*, Good Friday. || FIG. *¡Y santas Pascuas!*, and that's that!, and that's all there is to it!
— M. y f. Saint (v. OBSERV.). || FAM. Image of a saint (grabado). || FIG. Saint (persona muy buena). || — M. Name day: *hoy es mi santo*, today is my name day; *felicitar a uno (por) su santo*, to congratulate s.o. on his name day. || — FAM. *Adorar el santo por la peana*, v. PEANA. | *Alabar a su santo*, to look after one's own interests. | *Alzarse* or *cargar con el santo y la limosna*, to clear off with everything. | *Aquello fue llegar y besar el santo*, it was as easy as pie, it was a piece of cake, it was like taking candy from a baby. | *¿A santo de qué...?*, why on earth...?, why the devil...? || FIG. *Comerse los santos*, to be sanctimonious. || FAM. *Desnudar a un santo para vestir a otro*, to rob Peter to pay Paul. || *El día* or *la fiesta de Todos los Santos*, All Saints' Day. || FAM. *Hacerse el santo*, to play the little saint. | *Írsele a uno el santo al cielo*, to lose one's train of thought (en una conversación), to clean forget, to completely forget: *ayer fue tu cumpleaños y se me fue el santo al cielo*, yesterday was your birthday and I completely forgot. | *No es santo de mi devoción*, I'm not exactly fond of him. | *No saber a qué santo encomendarse*, to be at one's wits' end, not to know where to turn. || *Por todos los santos (del cielo)*, by the gods (juramento), for goodness sake (exclamación). || FAM. *Quedarse para vestir santos*, to be left on the shelf, to remain an old maid. || *Santo patrón* or *titular*, patron saint. || *Santo y seña*, password. || FAM. *Ser bueno como un santo*, to be as good as gold. | *Tener el santo de espaldas*, to have hard luck, to be unlucky. | *Todos los santos tienen novena*, my [your, our, etc.] time will come.

— OBSERV. *Saint* se suele abreviar en *St* delante de un nombre propio: *Santo Tomás*, St Thomas

Santo Domingo n. pr. GEOGR. Santo Domingo. || REL. Saint Dominic.
santón m. Mohammedan monk (mahometano). || FIG. y FAM. Sanctimonious hypocrite, bigot (hipócrita). | Big shot, big wheel (persona influyente).
santoral m. Book of life stories of the Saints (vidas de santos). || Sanctorale (libro de coro). || Sanctoral calendar (lista). || *Santoral del día*, saint of the day.
santuario m. Sanctuary, shrine. || *Amer.* Buried treasure (tesoro).
santurrón, ona adj. Sanctimonious (beato). || Hypocritical (hipócrita).
— M. y f. Sanctimonious person (beato). || Hypocrite.

santurronería f. Sanctimoniousness. || Hypocrisy.
saña f. Rage, fury (furor). || Cruelty (porfía). || *Con saña*, cruelly, viciously.
sañoso, sa o **sañudo, da** adj. Furious, enraged (enfurecido). || Cruel, vicious (encarnizado).
sapajú m. ZOOL. Sapajou (mono).
sapan m. BOT. Sapanwood.
sapidez f. Sapidity, taste, savouriness [U.S., savoriness].
sápido, da adj. Sapid, savoury.
sapiencia f. Wisdom, sapience (sabiduría). || Book of Wisdom [in the Apocrypha] (de la Biblia). || Knowledge (conocimientos): *la sapiencia de este chico me admira*, this boy's knowledge amazes me.
sapiencial adj. Sapiential. || *Libros sapienciales*, sapiential books.
sapiente adj. Wise, sapient (sabio).
sapo m. ZOOL. Toad (batracio). || FIG. Beast, animal (animalito). || *Amer.* Game resembling Aunt Sally [consisting in throwing coins into the mouth of a model frog] (juego). || FIG. y FAM. *Echar sapos y culebras* or *gusarapos*, to rant and rave.
saponáceo, a adj. Saponaceous.
saponaria f. BOT. Soapwort.
saponificación f. QUÍM. Saponification.
saponificar v. tr. QUÍM. To saponify.
— V. pr. To saponify.
saponita f. MIN. Saponite.
sapote m. BOT. Sapodilla (zapote).
saprófito, ta adj. BOT. Saprophytic.
— M. Saprophyte.
saque m. Serve, service (tenis). || Kickoff (fútbol). || Server (jugador). || *Amer.* Distillery (de aguardiente). || — *Hacer* or *tener el saque*, to kick off (fútbol), to serve (tenis). || *Hacer el saque de puerta*, to take a goal kick (fútbol). || *Línea de saque*, service line (tenis). || *Romper el saque*, to break [the] serve *o* service (tenis). || *Saque de banda*, throw-in (fútbol), line-out (rugby). || *Saque de castigo*, free kick. || *Saque de centro*, kickoff. || *Saque de esquina*, corner kick, corner. || *Saque de puerta*, goal kick. || FIG. y FAM. *Tener un buen saque*, to be a big eater (comer mucho).
saqueador, ra adj. Plundering, pillaging, looting, sacking.
— M. y f. Plunderer, pillager, looter, sacker.
saqueamiento m. Plunder, looting, pillage, sacking.
saquear v. tr. To plunder, to loot, to pillage, to sack. || FIG. To loot, to plunder.
saqueo m. Plunder, looting, pillage, sacking: *el saqueo de Roma*, the sacking of Rome.
saquería f. Manufacture of sacks (fabricación). || Sacks, *pl.* (sacos).
saquero, ra m. y f. Person who makes or sells sacks.
saquete m. Small bag *o* sack. || Cartridge bag (del cañón).
saquito m. Small bag *o* sack.
Sara n. pr. f. Sarah.
saraguate o **saraguato** m. *Amer.* Species of ape.
sarampión m. MED. Measles. || FIG. Cancer, malady: *el amor es un sarampión de todas las edades*, love is a cancer of all ages.
sarandí m. *Amer.* BOT. Waterside bush of the family Euphorbiaceae.
sarao m. Soirée (reunión).
sarape m. *Amer.* Serape, sarape (capote de monte).
sarapico m. ZOOL. Curlew (zarapico).
sarasa m. FAM. Queer, fairy (marica).
sarazo adj. m. *Amer.* Ripening, half-ripe (maíz). | Tipsy (achispado). | Rancid (agua de coco, coco).
sarcasmo m. Sarcasm.
sarcásticamente adv. Sarcastically.
sarcástico, ca adj. Sarcastic.
sarcófago m. Sarcophagus.
sarcoma m. MED. Sarcoma (tumor).
sarcomatoso, sa adj. MED. Sarcomatous.
sardana f. Sardana (danza catalana).
sardanapalesco, ca adj. Sardanapalian. || FIG. *Llevar una vida sardanapalesca*, to live it up.
Sardanápalo n. pr. m. Sardanapalus.
sardanés, esa adj. [Of *o* from the] Cerdagne Valley (Cataluña).
— M. y f. Native *o* inhabitant of the Cerdagne Valley.
sardina f. ZOOL. Sardine: *sardinas en espetones*, sardines on a spit *o* skewer. || FIG. *Estar como sardinas en banasta* or *en lata*, to be [packed] like sardines.
sardinal m. Sardine net (red).
sardinel m. ARQ. Rowlock (obra de ladrillos).
sardinero, ra adj. Sardine: *barco sardinero*, sardine boat.
— M. y f. Sardine seller.
sardineta f. Small sardine. || MIL. Pointed chevron (galón).
sardo, da adj. Spotted (el ganado). || — Adj./s. Sardinian (de Cerdeña). || — M. Sardinian (lengua).
sardónico, ca adj. Sardonic: *risa sardónica*, sardonic laugh.
sarga f. Serge, twill (tela).
sargazo m. BOT. Sargasso, gulfweed. || GEOGR. *Mar de los Sargazos*, Sargasso Sea.
sargenta f. Halberd, halbert (alabarda). || Sergeant's wife (mujer). || FIG. y FAM. Tyrant, dragon, grouch: *su mujer es una sargenta*, his wife is a tyrant.
sargentear v. tr. FIG. y FAM. To boss about.
— V. intr. FIG. y FAM. To be bossy.
sargentería f. Sergeantship.
sargentía f. Sergeancy, sergeantship, rank of sergeant.
sargento m. MIL. Sergeant. || FIG. y FAM. Tyrant, grouch: *su director es un sargento*, his director is a tyrant. || *Sargento mayor*, quartermaster-sergeant, sergeant major.
sargentona f. FAM. Tyrant, dragon.
sargo m. Sargo (pez).
sari m. Sari (traje femenino en la India).
sariga f. *Amer.* Opossum (zarigüeya).
sarmentoso, sa adj. Sarmentose (relativo o parecido a un sarmiento). || Climbing, twining (árbol, planta). || FIG. Bony, scrawny (miembros).
sarmiento m. Vine shoot. || FIG. *El pobre está ya hecho un sarmiento*, the poor man is already a bag of bones.
sarna f. MED. Itch, scabies. || VET. Mange. || FIG. y FAM. *Más viejo que la sarna*, as old as the hills.
sarniento, ta adj. *Amer.* V. SARNOSO.
sarnoso, sa adj. Itchy, scabby. || VET. Mangy.
— M. y f. Person suffering from the itch *o* scabies.
sarpullido m. Rash.
sarraceno, na adj./s. HIST. Saracen. || *Trigo sarraceno*, buckwheat, saracen corn.
Sarre n. pr. m. GEOGR. Saar (región industrial). | Saarland (territorio).
— OBSERV. The words *Sarre* in Spanish and *Saar* in English take the definite article.
sarrillo m. Death rattle (estertor). || Tartar (sarro). || BOT. Arum (aro).
sarro m. Deposit, incrustation, crust (en una vasija). || Scale, fur (de una caldera). || Tartar (de los dientes). || BOT. Rust, mildew, blight (roya). || MED. Fur, coating (de la lengua).
sarroso, sa adj. Incrusted (vasija). || Scaly, furry (caldera). || Covered with tartar, tartarous (dientes). || Coated, furry, saburral (lengua). || BOT. Rusted, mildewed, blighted (planta).
sarta f. String: *sarta de cebollas*, string of onions. || FIG. String, line (de personas). | String: *en medio de su discurso soltó toda una sarta de citas*, in the middle of his speech he came out with a whole string of quotations; *soltó una sarta de mentiras*, he came out with a string of lies. || FIG. *Esta carta es una sarta de embustes*, this letter is a tissue *o* a web of lies.
sartén f. Frying pan. || FIG. Oven, furnace: *este cuarto es una sartén*, it is like an oven in here. || FIG. y FAM. *Tener la sartén por el mango*, to have the whip hand, to run the show.
sartenada f. Panful, pan.
sartenazo m. Blow with a frying pan. || FIG. y FAM. Belting, beating (paliza).
sarteneja f. Small frying pan. || *Amer.* Dried-out hollow (depresión). | Crack (grieta).
sartenejal m. *Amer.* Dry cracked land.
sartorio adj. m. ANAT. Sartorial (músculo).
— M. ANAT. Sartorius.
sasafrás m. BOT. Sassafras.
sasánida adj./s. HIST. Sassanian.
sastra f. Woman tailor, tailoress (que hace trajes de hombre). || Mender (que arregla los trajes). || Seamstress (costurera). || Tailor's wife (mujer del sastre).
sastre m. Tailor. || Costumier (de teatro). || — FIG. y FAM. *Cajón de sastre*, v. CAJÓN. | *Entre sastres no se pagan hechuras*, v. HECHURA. || *Sastre* or *traje sastre*, tailored suit (de mujer). || *Sastre de señoras*, dressmaker. || *Sastre de viejo*, mending tailor. || FIG. y FAM. *Ver algo desde el tendido de los sastres*, to have a full view *o* a bird's eye view of sth.
sastrería f. Tailoring (oficio). || Tailor's [shop] (tienda): *ir a la sastrería*, to go to the tailor's.
Satán o **Satanás** n. pr. m. Satan.
satánico, ca adj. Satanic, diabolical.
satanismo m. Satanism.
satélite adj. Satellite: *país satélite*, satellite country; *ciudad satélite*, satellite town.
— M. ASTR. Satellite: *satélite artificial*, artificial satellite. || TECN. Planet wheel, loose pinion (piñón). || FIG. Satellite (persona). | Satellite (país, ciudad). || *Satélite de Satán*, fiend.
satelización f. Putting into orbit.
satelizar v. tr. To put into orbit.
satén m. Sateen (raso).
satín m. Satinwood.
satinado, da adj. Satiny, satin-like, shiny. || *Papel satinado*, glossy paper.
— M. Gloss, shine.
satinar v. tr. To satin, to satinize. || To gloss (el papel).
sátira f. Satire.
satírico, ca adj. Satirical, satiric (de la sátira). || Satyrical, satyric (del sátiro).
— M. Satirist.
satirizar v. tr. e intr. To satirize.
sátiro m. MIT. Satyr. || ZOOL. Satyr butterfly. || FIG. Satyr, lecher (hombre lascivo).
satisdación f. JUR. Bail (fianza).
satisfacción f. Satisfaction: *dar entera satisfacción*, to give complete satisfaction. || Satisfying, sating (del apetito). || Satisfaction, fulfilment (de un deseo). || — *A satisfacción de*, to the satisfaction of. || *Pedir*

satisfacción de una ofensa, to demand satisfaction for an offence. || *Satisfacción de sí mismo*, self-satisfaction. || *Tener mucha satisfacción de sí mismo*, to be very self-satisfied.

satisfacer* v. tr. To satisfy. || To pay (pagar): *satisfacer una deuda*, to pay a debt. || To give satisfaction, to make amends: *satisfacer de* or *por una ofensa*, to give satisfaction for an offence. || To compensate (compensar). || To meet, to satisfy: *satisfacer (a) la demanda*, to meet the demand; *satisfacer todos los requisitos*, to meet all the requirements. || To meet (gastos). || MAT. To satisfy. || COM. To honour (letra de cambio). || To expiate (expiar). || JUR. *Satisfacer una demanda*, to accede to a request.
— V. pr. To be satisfied, to satisfy o.s. (contentarse). || To avenge o.s., to take vengeance (vengarse). || To obtain satisfaction (considerarse desagraviado).

satisfaciente adj. Satisfying, satisfactory.

satisfactoriamente adv. Satisfactorily.

satisfactorio, ria adj. Satisfactory: *contestación satisfactoria*, satisfactory answer. || REL. Satisfactory.

satisfecho, cha adj. Satisfied, content. || Smug, self-satisfied. || — *Darse por satisfecho con*, to be satisfied with. || *Dejar satisfecho a*, to satisfy. || FAM. *Me he quedado satisfecho*, I'm full, I've had enough (comida).

sátrapa m. HIST. Satrap.

satrapía f. HIST. Satrapy.

saturabilidad f. QUÍM. Saturability.

saturable adj. Saturable.

saturación f. Saturation.

saturado, da adj. Satured. || FIG. Tired, sick, saturated (harto): *estoy saturado de derecho civil*, I'm sick *o* tired of civil law, I'm saturated with civil law.

saturador m. Saturator, saturater.

saturar v. tr. To saturate.

saturnal adj. Saturnian.

saturnales f. pl. HIST. Saturnalia.

saturnino, na adj. Saturnine (triste). || Saturnine (del plomo). || *Cólico saturnino*, lead *o* painter's colic.

saturnio, nia adj. Saturnian.

saturnismo m. MED. Lead poisoning, saturnism.

Saturno n. pr. m. ASTR. y MIT. Saturn.

sauce m. BOT. Willow (árbol). || — BOT. *Sauce cabruno*, goat willow. | *Sauce llorón*, weeping willow.

sauceda f. o **saucedal** m. o **saucera** f. BOT. Willow grove.

saúco m. BOT. Elder (arbusto).

saudade f. Nostalgia (añoranza).

saudí o **saudita** adj. f. Saudi: *Arabia Saudita*, Saudi Arabia.

saudoso, sa adj. Nostalgic.

sauna f. Sauna.

saurio, ria adj./s.m. ZOOL. Saurian. || — Pl. Sauria.

savia f. BOT. Sap. || FIG. Sap, vitality. || FIG. *Infundir nueva savia en una empresa*, to infuse new blood in an undertaking.

saxífraga f. BOT. Saxifrage.

saxofón o **saxófono** m. MÚS. Saxophone, sax (fam.).

saya f. Skirt (falda). || Petticoat (enaguas).

sayal m. Sackcloth (tela).

sayo m. Cassock, cloak (casaca). || Smock, loose garment (vestido amplio). || Tunic (abrigo de los soldados romanos). || — FIG. y FAM. *Cortarle a uno un sayo*, to run s.o. down (criticar). | *Decir para su sayo*, to say to o.s. | *Hacer de su capa un sayo*, V. CAPA. | *Hasta el cuarenta de mayo no te quites el sayo*, V. MAYO.

sazón f. Ripeness, maturity (madurez). || Flavour [U.S., flavor] (sabor). || Seasoning (aderezo). || FIG. Time (momento). || — *A la sazón*, at that time, then. || *En sazón*, in season, ripe (fruta), at the right moment, opportunely (oportunamente). || *Fuera de sazón*, inopportunely (inoportunamente), out of season (fruta).
— Adj. *Amer.* Ripe, mature: *plátano sazón*, ripe banana.

sazonado, da adj. Ripe (maduro). || Seasoned (aderezado). || Tasty (sabroso). || FIG. Witty (gracioso).

sazonar v. tr. To season, to flavour (manjares). || To ripen, to mature (madurar). || FIG. To add spice *o* relish to (amenizar): *sazonar un relato con salidas ingeniosas*, to add spice to a tale with witty remarks.
— V. pr. To ripen, to mature (madurar).

scooter m. Scooter (motocicleta).

scout m. Scout (explorador).

script girl f. CINEM. Continuity girl, script girl (secretaria de rodaje).

scherzo m. MÚS. Scherzo.

schnorchel m. MAR. Snorkel.

se pron. pers. 1. — Oneself, himself, herself, itself, yourself, yourselves, themselves (acción reflexiva): *vengarse*, to avenge oneself; *se cuidan bien*, they take good care of themselves; *ella se alaba*, she flatters herself. || Each other, one another (el uno al otro): *ellos se odian*, they hate one another; *se están hablando*, they are talking to each other. || Muchos verbos pierden su forma reflexiva en inglés: *sentarse*, to sit down; *acostarse*, to go to bed; *levantarse*, to rise, to get up; *quejarse*, to complain; *casarse*, to get married; *pasearse*, to take a walk, etc. || Algunos verbos pueden tomar la forma reflexiva en inglés o no tomarla: *lavarse*, to wash, to wash oneself; *se compró un perro*, he bought himself a dog, he bought a dog.
2. — Subject + to be + past participle (voz pasiva): *se siega el trigo en agosto*, the wheat is cut in August; *se me entregaron dos cartas*, two letters were given to me; *se piden voluntarios*, volunteers are called for. [In this case, the construction in Spanish is reflexive although its meaning is not].
3. — It + to be + past participle (uso impersonal): *se sabe que*, it is known that; *se dice que*, it is said that.
4. — One, s.o., you, people, we, they (indefinido): *nunca se sabe*, one never knows; *el domingo no se trabaja*, we do not work on Sunday; *se dice que*, people say that; *Señor, se le llama*, Sir, s.o. is calling you. || — *Aquí se habla demasiado*, there is too much talking here. || *Se bailaba y se cantaba*, there was dancing and singing, people danced and sang.
5. — To him, to her, to it, to you, to them (dativo, dirigiéndose a): *se lo diré (a él)*, I will tell him; *se lo diremos (a usted or a ustedes)*, we will tell you; *se las mandaré (a ellos)*, I will send them to them [in Spanish the indirect object precedes the direct object]. || For him, for her, for it, for you, for them (para él, etc.): *se lo compraré (a ella)*, I'll buy it for her. || From him, from her, from it, from you, from them (de él, etc.): *se lo arrancó bruscamente*, he tore it from him. || *Se ha roto una muela*, he broke his tooth.
— OBSERV. The pronoun *se* is enclitic when it is the object of an infinitive (callarse), of a gerund (quejándose), or of an imperative (siéntese).
— One should note that in Spanish the reflexive frequently replaces the passive voice (*se resolvió el problema*, the problem was solved; *se felicitó a los vencedores*, the winners were congratulated).
— La forma reflexiva de cada uno de los verbos se ha tratado por separado en el artículo del verbo correspondiente (v. pasearse en PASEAR).

sebáceo, a adj. Sebaceous: *glándulas sebáceas*, sebaceous glands.

sebo m. Tallow (para velas, jabón). || Suet (para guisar). || Grease, fat (grasa). || Fat (gordura). || Grease, grime, filth (suciedad grasienta). || ANAT. Sebum. || FAM. Drunkenness (borrachera). || — FAM. *Amer. Hacer sebo*, to idle, to loaf (holgazanear). || FAM. *¡Vaya sebo que cogió anoche!*, the state he was in last night! (¡qué borrachera!).

seborrea f. MED. Seborrhea.

seboso, sa adj. Tallowy (untado de sebo). || Suety (guiso). || Greasy, fatty (grasiento). || Greasy, grimy, filthy (sucio).

seca f. Drought (sequía). || Dry season (época). || Sandbank, sandbar (secano). || MED. Swollen gland (hinchazón de las glándulas).

secadal m. Dry land (tierra seca). || Non-irrigable land (no irrigable).

secadero, ra adj. That can be dried (frutas).
— M. Drying room *o* place (lugar).

secado m. Drying. || Seasoning (de maderas).

secador m. Dryer, drier. || Hair dryer (de pelo). || *Amer.* Towel (toalla). || *Secador centrífugo*, spin dryer (centrifugadora).

secadora f. Clothes dryer, dryer, drier (máquina para secar la ropa).

secamente adv. Dryly, drily.

secamiento m. Drying (secado).

secano m. Unirrigated land (no regado). || Dry land, dry region (por escasez de lluvia). || Sandbank, sandbar (banco de arena). || — *Campo de secano*, land used for dry farming. || *Cultivo de secano*, dry farming.

secante adj. Drying (que seca). || Blotting (para tinta). || Siccative, quick-drying: *pintura secante*, quick-drying paint. || MAT. Secant.
— M. Blotting paper, blotter (papel). | Siccative (sustancia). || DEP. Marker, player who marks an opponent (jugador). || — F. MAT. Secant.

secar v. tr. To dry (la ropa, etc.). || To dry, to wipe (enjugar): *secar los platos*, to dry the dishes. || To blot (con papel secante). || To mop, to wipe dry (el suelo). || To wipe (la mesa, etc.). || To wipe up, to mop up (un líquido derramado). || To dry up (la tierra, las frutas, una úlcera, una fuente, un pozo). || To dry up, to wither (las plantas). || To season (la madera). || FIG. To wipe away, to dry (las lágrimas). | To harden [one's heart] (el alma). | To annoy, to bore (aburrir). || DEP. To mark.
— V. pr. To dry: *espera que se seque*, wait until it dries. || To dry o.s.: *secarse al sol después de un baño*, to dry o.s. in the sun after a swim. || To dry up (suelo, líquido, úlcera). || To run dry, to dry up (río, fuente, pozo). || To dry up, to wither, to wilt (planta). || FIG. To waste away (persona o animal). | To become hardhearted (el alma). | To dry, to wipe away: *sécate las lágrimas*, dry your tears. || *Secarse el sudor de la frente*, to mop one's brow.

secarrón, ona adj. FAM. Very dry (carácter).

sección f. Section, cutting (cortadura): *la sección de un hueso*, the cutting of a bone. || Section (parte o grupo). || Section (dibujo). || Department (de un almacén): *sección de caballeros*, men's department. || MAT. y MIL. Section. || IMPR. Page, section (en un periódico): *la sección deportiva*, the sports page. || — *Sección de anuncios* or *de publicidad*, advertising

section. || *Sección de trabajo*, labour department. || *Sección transversal*, cross section.
seccionador m. ELECTR. [Disconnecting] switch.
seccionamiento m. Sectioning.
seccionar v. tr. To divide into sections, to section.
secesión f. Secession (de un Estado).
secesionista adj./s. Secessionist.
seco, ca adj. Dry (sin humedad): *la ropa está seca*, the clothes are dry; *terreno, tiempo seco*, dry land, weather. || Dry (sin agua): *río seco*, dry river. || Dried up, withered (flores ajadas). || Dried (flores de herbario, frutas). || Dry (pan, leña). || FIG. Skinny (flaco). | Dry (no dulce): *champaña seca*, dry champagne. | Pure (puro). | Sharp (ruido, golpe): *un ruido seco*, a sharp sound. | Dry, hacking (tos). | Curt, sharp, dry (contestación). | Dry (genio, estilo, etc.). | Hard (corazón). | Plain (explicación). || Dead (árbol). || — *Ama seca*, dry nurse. || *A palo seco*, under bare poles (barco), simply, on its own, just, nothing else (sin acompañamiento): *comimos pan a palo seco*, we ate bread on its own, we just ate bread. || *A secas*, simply, just: *se llama Pedro a secas*, he is just called Peter; by itself, on its own: *emplear una palabra a secas*, to use a word by itself. || FIG. y FAM. *Dejar seco*, to bump off (matar), to leave speechless (sin saber qué decir). || *En seco*, dry: *limpieza en seco*, dry cleaning; dead, suddenly: *parar en seco*, to stop dead; sharply: *frenar en seco*, to pull up sharply; high and dry (fuera del agua). || FIG. *Estar seco*, to be parched *o* thirsty (tener sed). || *Hojas secas*, dead leaves. || FIG. *Más seco que una pasa* or *un higo* or *un ripio*, as thin as a rake, completely wizened. | *Parar a uno en seco*, to cut s.o. short.
secoya f. BOT. Sequoia (árbol).
secreción f. Secretion.
secreta f. JUR. Secret investigation. || REL. Secret (oración). || Water closet (excusado). || FAM. Secret police.
secretar v. tr. To secrete.
secretaría f. Secretaryship (cargo de un secretario). || Secretary's office (oficina de un secretario). || Secretariat, secretariate (oficina administrativa). || Government department (del gobierno). || *Secretaría de Estado*, State Department (en el Vaticano y en los Estados Unidos).
secretariado m. Secretariat, secretariate (oficina). || Secretaryship (cargo).
secretario, ria adj. (Ant.). Entrusted with secrets, confidential (persona).
— M. y f. Secretary: *secretaria particular*, private secretary; *secretario general*, secretary general. || — *Secretaria de rodaje*, continuity girl; script girl. || *Secretario de Estado*, Secretary of State. || *Secretario municipal*, town clerk. || — M. Secretary bird (ave).
secretear v. intr. FAM. To talk confidentially, to whisper.
secreteo m. FAM. Whispering. || *Andar con secreteos*, to whisper to each other.
secreter m. Secretaire, writing desk, escritoire (mueble).
secretina f. Secretin (hormona).
secreto, ta adj. Secret, hidden (oculto). || Secret (información, agente, sociedad). || Secret, confidential (confidencial). || Secretive (persona). || *Votación secreta*, secret ballot.
— M. Secret: *revelar un secreto*, to reveal *o* to tell a secret. || Secrecy (condición): *hecho en secreto*, done in secrecy. || MÚS. Soundboard. || Combination (de una cerradura). || — *Bajo secreto de confesión*, under the seal of confession *o* of the confessional. || *De* or *en secreto*, in secret, in secrecy, secretly. || *Estar en el secreto*, to be in on the secret. || *Guardar un secreto*, to keep a secret. || FAM. *Secreto a voces*, open secret. || *Secreto de Estado*, state secret. || *Secreto de fabricación*, trade secret. || *Secreto profesional*, professional secrecy.
secretor, ra o **secretorio, ria** adj. ANAT. Secretory.
secta f. Sect.
sectador, ra adj./s. Sectarian.
sectario, ria adj./s. Sectarian.
sectarismo m. Sectarianism.
sector m. MAT. COM. Sector: *sector esférico*, spherical sector; *sector económico*, economic sector; *sector público, privado*, public, private sector. || MIL. Sector. || FIG. Area (zona). | Section (parte).
sectorial adj. MAT. COM. Sectorial.
secuaz m. Underling, henchman: *Al Capone y sus secuaces*, Al Capone and his henchmen. || Follower, partisan (partidario).
— OBSERV. This word usually has a pejorative meaning.
secuela f. Consequence, sequel, result (consecuencia). || MED. Sequela.
secuencia f. Sequence (en la misa). || CINEM. Sequence.
secuestración f. Sequestration.
secuestrador, ra adj. JUR. Sequestrating. || Kidnapping. || Hijacking, high-jacking.
— M. y f. JUR. Sequestrator. || Kidnapper (de una persona). || Hijacker, high-jacker (de aviones).
secuestrar v. tr. JUR. To confiscate, to seize, to sequester (embargar bienes, retirar un periódico, etc.). || To kidnap, to abduct (una persona). || To high-jack, to hijack (un avión). || FIG. To sequester, to sequestrate (aislar a alguien).
secuestro m. Confiscation, seizure, sequestration (de bienes, periódicos, etc.). || Kidnapping, abduction: *el secuestro de una persona*, the kidnapping of a person. || High-jacking, hijacking (de un avión). || MED. Sequestrum.
secular adj. Secular (seglar): *clero secular*, secular clergy; *brazo secular*, secular arm. || Century-old (de cien años o más): *árbol secular*, century-old tree. || Secular (que se repite cada siglo o que dura un siglo). || FIG. Age-old, century-old: *un prejuicio secular*, an age-old prejudice.
— M. REL. Secular.
secularización f. Secularization.
secularizar v. tr. To secularize.
secundar v. tr. To second, to support (apoyar). || To assist (ayudar).
secundario, ria adj. Secondary.
— M. Secondary.
secundinas f. pl. MED. Afterbirth, *sing.*
sed f. Thirst: *sed insaciable*, unquenchable thirst. || FIG. Thirst, hunger: *la sed del oro*, the thirst for gold. || AGR. Drought (de las tierras). || — *Apagar* or *quitar la sed*, to quench one's thirst: *una bebida que quita la sed*, a drink that quenches one's thirst. || *Dar sed*, to make thirsty. || *Rabiar de sed*, to be dying of thirst. || *Tener sed*, to be thirsty. || FIG. *Tener sed de*, to be thirsty for, to thirst for, to long for.
seda f. Silk (textil): *seda cruda, floja*, raw, floss silk. || Bristle (cerda de puerco o jabalí). || — FIG. *Aunque la mona se vista de seda, mona se queda*, V. MONA. || *De seda*, silk: *un traje de seda*, a silk dress; silken, silky (como la seda). || FIG. *Entrar como una seda*, to enter *o* to go in quite easily. || *Gusano de seda*, silkworm. || FIG. *Hecho una seda*, like a lamb, as meek as a lamb (persona). | *Ir* or *marchar como una seda*, to go *o* to run like clockwork, to go smoothly, to go like a charm. || *Seda artificial*, artificial silk. || *Ser como una seda*, to be as meek as a lamb (dócil), to be as smooth as silk (suave).
sedación f. MED. Sedation. || Soothing, calming (mitigación).
sedal m. Fishing line (para la pesca). || MED. Seton.
sedán m. Sedan (automóvil de carrocería cerrada).
sedante adj. MED. Sedative. || FIG. Soothing.
— M. MED. Sedative.
sedar v. tr. (P.us.). To sedate, to quiet, to soothe.
sedativo, va adj./s.m. MED. Sedative.
sede f. See (episcopal). || Seat (de un gobierno). || Headquarters, *pl.* (de una organización): *la sede de la O.N.U.*, the headquarters of the U. N. || — *Santa Sede*, Holy See. || *Sede social*, head office (sociedad).
sedear v. tr. To brush (joyas).
sedentario, ria adj. Sedentary.
sedentarismo m. Sedentariness.
sedente adj. (P.us.). Seated, sitting, sedentary (estatua).
sedeño, ña adj. Silken, silky (sedoso). || Bristly (animal).
sedera f. Bristle brush (del joyero).
sedería f. Silk trade (cría, elaboración y comercio). || Silk shop (tienda donde se vende seda). || Drapery, draper's (tienda de tejidos).
sedero, ra adj. Silk: *industria sedera*, silk industry.
— M. Silk dealer (negociante en seda). || Draper (negociante en tejidos).
sedicente o **sediciente** adj. So-called, would-be.
— OBSERV. Este adjetivo es un barbarismo en español empleado en lugar de su equivalente *supuesto*.
sedición f. Sedition (rebelión).
sedicioso, sa adj. Seditious.
— M. y f. Rebel (rebelde). || Mutineer (amotinado). || Troublemaker (que provoca disturbios).
sediente adj. JUR. *Bienes sedientes*, real estate, *sing.*
sediento, ta adj. Thirsty. || FIG. Dry, parched (campos). | Thirsty, hungry: *sediento de poder*, power hungry, power thirsty.
sedimentación f. Sedimentation.
sedimentar v. tr. To deposit, to settle (un sedimento). || FIG. To settle (calmar).
— V. pr. To settle (depositarse). || FIG. To settle down, to calm down (sosegarse).
sedimentario, ria adj. Sedimentary.
sedimento m. Sediment, deposit.
sedoso, sa adj. Silky, silken.
seducción f. Seduction. || Seductiveness, charm, fascination, allure (atractivo).
seducir* v. tr. To seduce, to tempt: *seducir con hermosas promesas*, to seduce with attractive promises. || To seduce (a una mujer). || To captivate, to fascinate. || To attract, to seduce: *esta idea me seduce*, this idea attracts me.
seductivo, va adj. Seductive (que seduce). || Seductive, tempting (cosa). || Captivating, fascinating (sonrisa).
seductor, ra adj. Seductive (que seduce). || Seductive, tempting (cosa). || Captivating, fascinating (fascinante).
— M. y f. Seducer (que seduce). || Charmer (que encanta).
sefardí o **sefardita** adj. Sephardic.
— M. y f. Sephardi.
— OBSERV. El plural de la palabra inglesa es *Sephardim*.
— *Sefardí* is the name given to the Spanish and Portuguese Jews in the Balkans and North Africa

who have conserved their manner of speech from the XV century when they were expelled from the Peninsula.

segadera f. Sickle (hoz). || Scythe (guadaña).

segador m. Harvester, reaper (trabajador). || ZOOL. Harvestman.

segadora adj. f. Mowing, reaping (máquina).
— F. Mower, reaper, mowing machine, reaping machine (máquina). || Lawnmower (para el césped). || Harvester, reaper (mujer). || — *Segadora atadora*, binder. || *Segadora trilladora*, combine harvester.

segar* v. tr. To reap, to cut (la mies). || To mow, to cut (la hierba). || FIG. To cut off (cortar). | To cut down, to mow down: *segados en plena juventud*, cut down in their prime. | To ruin (frustrar).

seglar adj. Secular, lay (laico): *el apostolado seglar*, the secular apostolate.
— M. y f. Layman (hombre), laywoman (mujer).

segmentación f. Segmentation.

segmentar v. tr. To segment.
— V. pr. To segment.

segmentario, ria adj. Segmentary, segmental.

segmento m. MAT. Segment. || TECN. Ring: *segmento del émbolo*, piston ring. || ZOOL. Segment.

segoviano, na o **segoviense** adj./s. Segovian.

segregación f. Segregation: *segregación racial*, racial segregation. || BIOL. Secretion.

segregacionismo m. Segregationism.

segregacionista adj./s. Segregationist.

segregar v. tr. To segregate (apartar). || BIOL. To secrete (secretar).

segregativo, va adj. Segregative.

segueta f. Fretsaw.

seguida f. Rhythm. || (P.us.). Continuation. || — *Coger la seguida*, to get into the swing of things. || *De seguida*, without a break, continuously (seguidamente), at once, right away (inmediatamente). || *En seguida*, at once, straight away, immediately, right away (sin esperar): *lo llamé y vino en seguida*, I called him and he came right away; *lo haré en seguida*, I'll do it at once. || *En seguida termino*, I'm nearly finished *o* through. || *Voy en seguida*, I'm just coming, I'll be right there.

seguidamente adv. Continuously, without a break (sin interrupción). || Straight away, straight afterwards, next (inmediatamente después).

seguidilla f. MÚS. "Seguidilla".

seguido, da adj. Continuous. || Successive, consecutive: *nuestro equipo ha ganado seis partidos seguidos*, our team has won six successive games. || In succession, in a row, running: *seis días seguidos*, six days in a row, six days running. || In a row: *ha tenido dos niños seguidos*, she has had two boys in a row. || One straight after the other: *ha tenido tres niños muy seguidos*, she has had three children one straight after the other. || Straight, direct (camino, carretera). || *Acto seguido* V. ACTO.
— Adv. Straight on *o* ahead: *vaya seguido*, go straight on. || Behind, after (detrás). || *Amer.* Often (a menudo). || *Todo seguido*, straight ahead: *siga usted, es todo seguido*, keep on going, it is straight ahead.

seguidor, ra adj. Following (que sigue).
— M. y f. Follower. || — M. DEP. Supporter, fan, follower (aficionado). | Follower (en ciclismo). || Guide lines, *pl.* [for writing] (pauta). || Suitor (pretendiente).

seguimiento m. Continuation (continuación). || Pursuit (perseguimiento). || TECN. Tracking (de un satélite): *estación de seguimiento*, tracking station. || *Ir en seguimiento de*, to go in pursuit of.

seguir* v. tr. To follow (ir detrás o después). || To chase, to pursue (perseguir). || To continue, to pursue, to carry on: *sigamos nuestras investigaciones*, let's continue our investigations. || To follow (un consejo, una doctrina). || To do, to take: *estuve siguiendo un cursillo de tres semanas*, I did a three-week training course. || To follow: *es difícil seguir sus explicaciones*, it is difficult to follow his explanations. || To take (marcha, curso, etc.): *la enfermedad sigue su curso*, the illness is taking its course. || To hound (acosar). || To follow (la pista). || To follow up (un indicio). || To court (cortejar). || To track (un satélite). || — FIG. *El que la sigue la mata*, perseverance gives results. || *Seguir con los ojos a uno*, to follow s.o. with one's eyes. || *Seguir de cerca a uno*, to follow s.o. closely. || *Seguir la carrera de*, to study: *seguir la carrera de médico*, to study medicine. || FIG. *Seguir la corriente*, V. CORRIENTE. || *Seguir las huellas* or *las pisadas de alguien*, to follow s.o.'s tracks *o* trail, to trail s.o. (seguir el rastro), to follow in s.o.'s footsteps (hacer igual que otro). || *Seguir su camino*, to continue on one's way (continuar adelante), to carry on, to get on with it (continuar con lo que se está haciendo): *tú sigue tu camino y no te preocupes de lo que dicen*, you carry on and don't worry about what they say.
— V. intr. To follow, to come after, to come next (venir después). || To follow on, to continue: *este artículo sigue en la página 7*, this article follows on on page 7. || To carry on, to go on, to continue: *¡sigue!*, carry on!, go on!; *¡sigamos!*, let's continue! || To go on (con una idea). || To remain (permanecer): *siguió de pie*, he remained standing. || To be still (estar todavía): *sigue en París*, he is still in Paris; *mi tío sigue enfermo*, my uncle is still sick; *sigue trabajando*, he is still working. || To still + verb: *sigo sin comprender*, I still don't understand; *sigo sin recibir noticias*, I still haven't received any news. || — *Como sigue*, as follows. || *¿Cómo sigue?*, how is he?, how is he doing?, how is he getting on? (¿qué tal está?), what comes next?, how does it go on? (intentando recordar algo). || *¡Que siga bien!*, keep well. || *Seguir* (con verbo en gerundio), to keep on (gerundio), to go on (gerundio), to continue (gerundio): *seguir leyendo*, to keep on reading. || *Seguir adelante*, V. ADELANTE. || *Seguir con su trabajo*, to carry on working, to carry on with one's work. || *Seguir en su error*, to persist *o* to continue in one's error. || FIG. y FAM. *Seguir en sus trece*, to stick to one's guns. || *Seguir en su trabajo*, to be still in the same job. || *Seguir por una carretera*, to go along a road. || *Seguir siendo*, to be still, to continue to be: *a pesar de su edad sigue siendo guapa*, in spite of her age she is still good-looking. || *¡Sigamos!*, on with the show! (en el teatro). || *Sigue*, continued (folletín), P.T.O., please turn over (carta, documento).
— V. pr. To follow (ir a continuación). || To ensue, to follow (ocurrir como consecuencia). || To deduce, to infer (inferirse). || To spring, to issue, to be derived (derivarse). || *De esto se sigue que*, it follows that.

seguiriya f. MÚS. "Seguidilla" (seguidilla flamenca).

según prep. According to, depending on: *según la edad que tienes*, according to how old you are, according to your age; *según las circunstancias*, depending on the circumstances. || In accordance with, according to (de conformidad con): *te pagaré según tu trabajo*, I will pay you in accordance with your work; *según el Tratado de Roma*, according to the Treaty of Rome. || Depending on: *según te encuentres mañana*, depending on how you feel tomorrow; *según el tiempo*, depending on the weather. || According to: *según lo que me dijo*, according to what he told me; *según ellos*, according to them; *Evangelio según San Lucas*, Gospel according to Saint Luke; *según las últimas noticias*, according to the latest news.
— Adv. So: *no podía moverse, según estaba de cansado*, he couldn't move he was so tired. || It all depends, it depends: *vendrá o no, según*, he may or may not come, it depends. || Depending on: *según me diga que sí o que no*, depending on whether he says yes or no. || According to: *según me dijo*, according to what he told me. || Just as (igual que): *sigue todo según estaba*, everything is just as it was. || As (a medida que): *según nos acercábamos el ruido aumentaba*, as we approached the noise grew louder. || — *Es según*, it all depends, it depends. || *Según cómo vayamos*, depending on how we go. || *Según están las cosas*, the way things are at present. || *Según estén las cosas*, depending on *o* according to how things stand. || *Según que haga frío o calor*, depending on whether it is hot or cold. || *Según se frotaba las manos debía de estar contento*, he must have been pleased judging by the way be rubbed his hands together. || *Según y como* or *según y conforme*, just as, exactly as (igual que): *te lo diré según y como me lo dijeron*, I will tell you it just as it was told to me. | *Según y cómo* or *según y conforme*, depending on how: *vendré según y cómo me encuentre*, I'll come depending on how I feel; it all depends, it depends (depende).

segunda f. Double turn of a lock (cerradura). || Second class: *viajar en segunda*, to travel in second class. || Second (velocidad). || Seconde (de esgrima). || FIG. Double *o* veiled *o* hidden meaning: *hablar con segundas*, to talk with double meanings. || MÚS. Second.

segundar v. tr. To repeat (repetir). || To help, to second (ayudar).
— V. intr. To come second, to be second.

segundario, ria adj. Secondary.

segundero, ra adj. Of the second crop of the year (fruto).
— M. Second hand (en un reloj).

segundo, da adj. Second. || — *De segunda mano*, V. MANO. || *En segundo lugar*, secondly (en conversación), in second place (en una competición). || *Segunda enseñanza*, secondary education. || *Segunda intención*, double meaning: *hablar con segundas intenciones*, to talk with double meanings. || *Segundas nupcias*, second marriage. || *Segundo jefe*, assistant chief. || *Segundo piso*, second floor [U.S., third floor]. || *Sobrino segundo*, first cousin once removed.
— Adv. Second (en segundo lugar).
— M. y f. Second [one] (segunda persona). || — M. Second (del reloj). || Second in command *o* in authority (en una jerarquía). || Second floor [U.S., third floor] (piso). || MAT. Second. || DEP. Second (en boxeo). || — MAR. *El segundo de a bordo*, the first mate. || FIG. *Sin segundo*, peerless, unrivalled.

segundogénito, ta adj./s. Second-born.

segundón m. Second son (segundo hijo). || Younger son (hijo que no es el primogénito).

segur f. Axe (hacha). || Sickle (hoz).

seguramente adv. For sure, for certain (con certidumbre). || Probably (probablemente). || Surely (muy probablemente). || Securely, safely (sujetar, etc.).

seguridad f. Security, safety: *la seguridad del país está en peligro*, the security of the country is in danger. || Security: *las mujeres buscan la seguridad*, women long for security; *las pensiones dan la seguridad para la vejez*, pensions give security in old age; *medidas de seguridad para proteger un arma secreta*, security measures to protect a secret weapon. || Safety: *la seguridad en carretera depende del estado de la calzada*, road safety depends upon the state of the road surface. || Reliability: *la seguridad del frenado*, the reliability of the brakes. || Safety, safeness: *la seguridad de un puente*, the safety of a bridge. || Surety, certainty (certidumbre). || Conviction: *hablar con seguridad*, to speak with conviction. || Sureness (destreza, firmeza). || — *Con seguridad*, securely (con fijeza), for sure, for certain (seguramente). || *Consejo de Seguridad*, Security Council (de la O.N.U.). || *Con toda seguridad*, with complete *o* absolute certainty (sin riesgo), for sure, for certain (seguramente). || *De seguridad*, safety: *cerradura de seguridad*, safety lock; *cinturón de seguridad*, safety belt. || *Dirección General de Seguridad*, police headquarters. || *En la seguridad de que*, knowing that, with the surety that. || *En seguridad*, in safety. || *Para mayor seguridad*, for safety's sake, to be on the safe side. || *Seguridad en sí mismo*, self-confidence. || *Seguridad Social*, Social Security. || *Tener la seguridad de que*, to be sure *o* certain that. || *Tengan la seguridad de que*, rest assured that.

seguro, ra adj. Sure, certain (cierto): *estoy seguro de que ha venido*, I am sure that he has come. || Secure: *nuestra victoria es segura*, our victory is secure. || Safe: *un sitio seguro*, a safe place; *inversión segura*, safe investment. || Solid, firm, secure (firme). || Secure, steady, stable (estable). || Firm, definite (fecha). || Reliable, dependable, trustworthy (de fiar). || Reliable: *fuentes seguras*, reliable sources. || Reliable, trustworthy: *informaciones seguras*, reliable information. || — *Dar por seguro*, to take for granted. || *Lo más seguro es irse*, the safest thing *o* the best thing is to go.

— Adv. For sure, for certain.

— M. Insurance: *seguro a todo riesgo*, fully comprehensive insurance; *seguro contra accidentes*, accident insurance; *seguro contra robo*, insurance against theft, theft insurance; *seguro contra terceros*, third-party insurance; *seguro contra incendios*, fire insurance; *seguro sobre la vida* or *seguro de vida*, life insurance; *compañía de seguros*, insurance company; *prima de seguro*, insurance premium. || Safety device (dispositivo de seguridad). || Safety catch (de armas). || — *A buen seguro*, surely, without a doubt *o* any doubt. || *De seguro*, surely, without a doubt *o* any doubt. || *En seguro*, in safekeeping, in a safe place (a salvo). || *Ir sobre seguro*, to be on safe ground. || *Póliza de seguro*, insurance policy. || *Saber a buen seguro*, to know for certain. || *Seguros sociales*, social *o* national insurance, *sing.*, social security, *sing.* || *Sobre seguro*, without any risk, safely.

seibo m. *Amer.* BOT. Ceibo.

seis adj./s. Six: *el seis de corazones*, the six of hearts. || — *El reloj dio las seis*, the clock struck six. || *Son las seis*, it is six o'clock. || — M. Sixth (fecha): *el seis de enero*, the 6th [sixth] of January, January 6th [the sixth].

seisavo, va adj./s. Sixth. || — M. Hexagon.

seiscientos, tas adj./s. Six hundred: *dos mil seiscientos*, two thousand six hundred; *el año seiscientos*, the year six hundred. || *Seiscientos veinte*, six hundred and twenty.

seise m. One of six choir boys who sing and dance in the cathedral of Seville during certain festivals.

seisillo m. MÚS. Sextuplet.

seísmo m. Earthquake, seism (p. us.) [terremoto].

selacio m. ZOOL. Selachian.

selección f. Selection: *selección natural*, natural selection. || Selection (conjunto de cosas seleccionadas): *una selección de libros*, a selection of books.

seleccionado, da adj. DEP. Selected.

— M. y f. Player selected for a team.

seleccionador, ra m. y f. DEP. Selector.

seleccionar v. tr. To select, to choose, to pick [out] (elegir). || DEP. To select.

selectividad f. RAD. Selectivity.

selectivo, va adj. Selective. || (*Curso*) *selectivo*, selective course taken before one begins technical studies at university.

selecto, ta adj. Selected: *poesías selectas*, selected poems. || FIG. Choice, select (superior): *vinos selectos*, select wines. | Select: *sociedad selecta*, select society. || *Ser de lo más selecto*, to be of the very best.

selector m. Selector.

selenio m. QUÍM. Selenium.

selenita f. Selenite. || — M. y f. Moon dweller.

selenografía f. ASTR. Selenography.

selenográfico, ca adj. Selenographic.

selenógrafo m. ASTR. Selenographer.

seleúcidas n. pr. m. y f. pl. HIST. Seleucids.

self f. ELECTR. Self-induction coil.

selfinducción f. Self-induction.

Seltz pr. n. *Agua de Seltz*, seltzer [water].

selva f. Forest: *selva virgen*, virgin forest. || Jungle (jungla). || — *La ley de la selva*, the law of the jungle. || GEOGR. *Selva Negra*, Black Forest. | *Selva tropical*, tropical forest.

selvático, ca adj. Forest, woodland (de las selvas): *árboles selváticos*, woodland trees. || FIG. Crude, uncouth (inculto).

selvoso, sa adj. Forest, forested, wooded. || Jungle (con jungla).

sellado, da adj. Sealed. || Stamped: *carta, papel sellado*, stamped letter, paper. || AUT. *Circuito sellado*, sealed circuit.

— M. Sealing, affixing of seals. || Stamping (de una carta).

sellador, ra adj. Stamping (que franquea). || Sealing.

— M. y f. Stamper (franqueador). || Sealer (de documentos oficiales, etc.).

selladura f. Sealing (de un documento oficial). || Stamping (de una carta). || Sealing (lacrado).

sellar v. tr. To seal (un documento oficial). || To stamp (estampar el sello): *me sellaron este papel en el consulado*, they stamped this paper for me in the consulate. || To seal (cerrar): *sellar con lacre*, to seal with wax. || To stamp (timbrar). || To hallmark, to stamp (joyas, monedas). || FIG. To brand, to stamp (marcar). | To seal (la amistad). | To seal (cerrar): *sellar los labios*, to seal one's lips. | To close, to end (concluir).

sello m. Stamp (viñeta de papel): *sello fiscal*, revenue stamp; *poner un sello en un sobre*, to put a stamp on an envelope. || Seal (de documento oficial). || Seal (de metal). || Stamp, seal (seña! impresa). || Rubber stamp, rubber seal (de caucho). || Signet ring (sortija). || Stamp office (oficina). || MED. Capsule. || Hallmark, stamp (de joyas y monedas). || FIG. Mark: *sus obras llevan su sello*, his works carry his mark. | Stamp, mark: *el sello del genio*, the mark of genius. | Hallmark, seal: *sello de distinción*, hallmark of distinction. || — Pl. Seals: *quebrantamiento* or *violación de sellos*, breaking of seals, || — FIG. *Echar el sello a una cosa*, to put the finishing touches to sth., to finish sth. off. || *Estampar* or *poner el sello*, to stamp, to seal. || FIG. *Marcar a alguien con el sello de*, to brand s.o.: *le han marcado con el sello de mentiroso*, they have branded him a liar. || *Sello de correo*, postage stamp. || *Sello de Salomón*, Solomon's seal.

semáforo m. Semaphore (marítimo). || Traffic lights, *pl.* (de tráfico urbano). || Signal (de ferrocarril).

semana f. Week: *Semana grande* or *mayor* or *Santa*, Holy Week; *dos veces a la semana*, twice a week. || Week's wages, *pl.* (salario semanal). || Game similar to hopscotch (juego). || — *Días entre semana*, weekdays. || *Entre semana*, during the week. || *Fin de semana*, weekend (sábado y domingo), weekend case (maletín). || *La semana pasada, que viene*, last, next week. || FAM. *La semana que no tenga viernes*, never in a month of Sundays, when pigs have wings *o* begin to fly. || *Semana inglesa*, five and a half day week. || *Semana laboral*, working week.

semanal adj. Weekly: *salario semanal*, weekly wage. || *Descanso semanal*, weekly closing day (de una tienda).

semanalmente adv. Weekly.

semanario, ria adj. Weekly.

— M. Weekly (periódico). || Set of seven razors (navajas de afeitar). || Set of seven bracelets (pulseras).

semanero, ra m. y f. Person employed by the week.

semántico, ca adj. Semantic.

— F. Semantics.

semasiología f. Semantics, semasiology.

semblante m. Countenance, visage, face: *semblante risueño*, smiling face. || FIG. Look (aspecto). || — *Componer el semblante*, to regain one's composure. || *En su semblante*, in one's face. || *Mudar de semblante*, to change colour (personas), to take on a different aspect (cosas). || *Tener buen, mal semblante*, to look well, bad (salud), to be in a good, a bad mood, to be in good, bad humour (humor).

semblanza f. Portrait, biographical sketch.

sembradera f. Drill, seed drill (máquina).

sembradío, a adj. Cultivable, cultivatable.

sembrado m. Sown field *o* land.

sembrador, ra adj. Sowing, seeding.

— M. y f. Sower. || — F. Drill, seed drill (sembradera).

sembradura f. Sowing, seeding. || Sown land (sembrado).

sembrar* v. tr. AGR. To sow, to seed (un campo): *un terreno sembrado de patatas*, a piece of land sown with potatoes. | To sow (las semillas). || FIG. To sow, to spread: *sembrar el pánico*, to sow panic. | To spread, to diffuse (una doctrina). | To scatter, to strew (un camino con flores, palmas). || — FIG. *Quien siembra recoge*, one reaps what one has sown. | *Quien siembra vientos recoge tempestades*, v. RECOGER. | *Sembrar la discordia*, to sow discord.

sembrío m. *Amer.* Sown land.

semejante adj. Similar, alike: *dos objetos semejantes*, two similar objects. || Similar, such: *en semejante caso*, in a similar case, in such a case. || Such, like that: *nunca he visto a semejante tonto*, I have never seen such a fool; *cuando oigo cosas semejantes*, when I hear things like that. || MAT. Similar. || — *Es muy semejante a ti*, he is quite like you. || *Son muy semejantes*, they are very much alike *o* very similar. || *Una cosa semejante*, sth. of the sort, sth. like that.

— M. Fellow man (prójimo). || *No tiene semejante*, it has no equal.

semejanza f. Resemblance, likeness (parecido). || Similarity: *la semejanza de los métodos*, the similarity of methods. || Simile (símil). || MAT. Similarity. || — *A semejanza de*, after, in the manner of, like. || *Tener semejanza con*, to bear a resemblance to, to resemble.
semejar v. intr. To seem to be, to seem (parecer). || To look like (parecerse a).
— V. pr. To resemble each other, to be similar, to be *o* to look alike. || *Semejarse a*, to be like, to resemble.
semen m. BIOL. Semen, sperm. || BOT. Seed (semilla).
semental adj. m. Breeding, stud (animal macho). || Seed (de la semilla). || Sowing (de la siembra).
— M. Sire, stud animal (caballo).
sementera f. Sowing, seeding (acción). || Sowing time, seedtime (temporada). || Sown land (tierra). || FIG. Hotbed (*de*, of), breeding ground (*de*, for).
sementero m. Seedbag (saco). || Seeding, sowing (sementera).
semestral adj. Half-yearly, biannual.
semestre m. Period of six months. || Semester (en una Universidad americana). || COM. Half-yearly payment (pago).
semianual adj. Semiannual.
semiárido, da adj. Semiarid.
semiautomático, ca adj. Semiautomatic.
semibreve f. MÚS. Semibreve [U.S., whole note].
semicilíndrico, ca adj. Semicylindrical.
semicilindro m. Semicylinder.
semicircular adj. Semicircular.
semicírculo m. MAT. Semicircle.
semicircunferencia f. MAT. Semicircumference.
semiconductor m. ELECTR. Semiconductor.
semiconsciente adj. Semiconscious, half-conscious.
semiconsonante adj. GRAM. Semiconsonantal.
— F. GRAM. Semiconsonant.
semicorchea f. MÚS. Semiquaver [U.S., sixteenth note].
semicromático, ca adj. MÚS. Semichromatic.
semicualificado, da adj. Semiskilled.
semiculto, ta adj. Half-learned (palabra).
semidesierto, ta adj. Half-deserted.
semidesnudo, da adj. Half-naked.
semidiámetro m. MAT. Semidiameter.
semidifunto adj. Half-dead.
semidiós m. Demigod.
semidirecto, ta adj. Semidirect.
semidoble adj. BOT. y REL. Semi-double.
semidormido, da adj. Half-asleep.
semieje m. Semiaxis.
semiesfera f. Hemisphere.
semiesférico adj. Hemispherical.
semifallo m. Singleton (bridge).
semifinal f. Semifinal.
semifinalista adj. Semifinal.
— M. y f. Semifinalist.
semifino, na adj. Semifine.
semifusa f. MUS. Hemidemisemiquaver [U.S., sixty-fourth note].
semilunar adj. ANAT. Semilunar.
semilla f. BOT. Seed. || FIG. Source, cause, seed, seeds, *pl.* (origen). || FIG. *Echar la semilla de la discordia*, to sow the seeds of discord.
semillero m. Nursery, seedbed. || FIG. Seedbed (cantera): *esta universidad es un semillero de estadistas*, this university is a seedbed of statesmen. | Hotbed, breeding ground (de criminales, etc.). | Source: *esto ha sido un semillero de disturbios*, this has been a source of disturbances.
semimanufacturado, da adj. Semi-manufactured.
semimedio m. DEP. Welterweight (en boxeo).
seminal adj. BIOL. Seminal: *líquido seminal*, seminal fluid.
seminario m. Seminary (colegio eclesiástico). || Nursery, seedbed (semillero). || Seminar (de investigaciones). || — *Seminario de teología*, theological seminary *o* college. || *Seminario mayor*, Roman Catholic seminary, training college [for priesthood]. || *Seminario menor*, secondary school [staffed by priests].
seminarista m. Seminarist.
seminífero, ra adj. ANAT. y BOT. Seminiferous.
seminómada adj. Seminomadic.
— M. y f. Seminomad.
seminuevo, va adj. Almost new.
semioculto, ta adj. Half-hidden.
semioficial adj. Semiofficial.
semiología f. MED. Semeiology, semiology.
semiológico, ca adj. MED. Semeiologic, semiologic.
semiólogo m. MED. Semeiologist, semiologist.
semiótico, ca adj. Semeiotic, semiotic.
— F. Semeiotics, semiotics.
semipesado adj. m./s.m. Light heavyweight (boxeo).
semipleno, na adj. JUR. Incomplete, imperfect.
semiprecioso, sa adj. Semiprecious.
semiproducto m. By-product.
semirrecto adj. m. Forty-five degree (ángulo).
semirrefinado, da adj. Semi-refined.
semirremolque m. Semitrailer.
semirrígido, da adj. Semirigid.
semisalvaje adj. Half-savage.
semisólido, da adj./s.m. Semisolid.
semita adj. Semitic.
— M. y f. Semite.
semítico, ca adj. Semitic.
semitismo m. Semitism.
semitista m. y f. Semitist.
semitono m. MÚS. Semitone, halftone.
semitransparente adj. Semitransparent.
semivivo, va adj. Half-alive.
semivocal adj. GRAM. Semivocalic.
— F. GRAM. Semivowel.
sémola f. Semolina.
semoviente adj. *Bienes semovientes*, livestock, *sing.*
sempiterno, na adj. Sempiternal, everlasting, eternal (eterno). || FIG. Everlasting, unending (fastidioso).
— F. BOT. Everlasting flower, immortelle.
Sena n. pr. m. GEOGR. Seine.
senado m. Senate. || FIG. Assembly.
senador m. Senator.
senaduría f. Senatorship.
senatorio, ria o **senatorial** adj. Senatorial.
sencillamente adv. Simply.
sencillez f. Simplicity: *hablar con mucha sencillez*, to speak with great simplicity. || Unaffectedness, simplicity, naturalness (falta de afectación). || — *Con sencillez*, simply. || *Un mecanismo de una gran sencillez*, a very simple mechanism.
sencillo, lla adj. Simple, easy (fácil): *no hay cosa sencilla en este mundo*, nothing is easy in this world. || Single: *una escopeta de un cañón sencillo*, a single barrel shotgun; *billete sencillo*, single ticket. || BOT. Single. || Plain (sin adorno): *una fachada sencilla*, a plain façade. || Simple, unpretentious: *una comida sencilla*, a simple meal. || Plain, simple: *un vestido sencillo*, a plain dress. || Simple, harmless, guileless (sin malicia). || Natural, unaffected, unsophisticated (natural). || Gullible, naïve (ingenuo). || — *No hay cosa más sencilla*, there is nothing simpler. || *Sencillo a la par que elegante*, simple but elegant.
— M. *Amer.* Small change (suelto).
sencillote, ta adj. FAM. Simple.
senda f. Path, track, footpath. || FIG. Road, way, path: *tomar la mala senda*, to take the wrong road, to go the wrong way.
sendero m. Path, track, footpath (senda).
sendos, das adj. pl. Each: *los niños recibieron sendos regalos*, the children each received a present; *los tres hombres llevaban sendos sombreros*, the three men were each wearing a hat.
Séneca n. pr. m. Seneca. || FIG. Man of wisdom.
senectud f. Old age.
Senegal n. pr. m. GEOGR. Senegal.
senegalés, esa adj./s. Senegalese.
senescal m. Seneschal.
senescencia f. Aging, ageing, senescence.
senescente adj. Aging, ageing, senescent.
senestrado, da adj. HERÁLD. Sinister.
senil adj. Senile (de la vejez).
senilidad f. Senility.
senior m. Senior.
seno m. ANAT. Breast (pecho). | Womb (matriz). | Sinus (de un hueso): *seno frontal*, frontal sinus. || Bosom: *guardó la carta en el seno*, she put the letter in her bosom. || FIG. Bosom: *en el seno del mar*, in the bosom of the sea; *el seno de la iglesia*, the bosom of the church. || MAR. Bay, gulf (bahía pequeña). | Belly (de una vela). | Trough (entre las olas). || MAT. Sine. || ARQ. Spandrel. || Cavity, recess (cavidad). || *El seno de Abrahán*, the bosom of Abraham.
sensación f. Sensation: *causar sensación*, to cause a sensation; *este número ha sido la sensación de la noche*, this act was the sensation of the evening. || Feeling, sensation: *sensación de calor*, feeling of warmth.
sensacional adj. Sensational.
sensacionalismo m. Sensationalism.
sensacionalista adj. Sensationalistic, sensational.
— M. y f. Sensationalist.
sensatez f. Good sense, sensibleness (buen sentido). || Sensibleness, wisdom: *la sensatez de una respuesta*, the sensibleness of an answer.
sensato, ta adj. Sensible.
sensibilidad f. Sensibility. || Sensitivity, feeling (perceptibilidad de sensaciones): *tiene muy poca sensibilidad en el brazo*, he has very little feeling in his arm; *pinta con sensibilidad*, he paints with feeling. || Sensitivity (de aparatos, etc.). || *Tiene mucha sensibilidad*, he is very sensitive (impresionable), he is very softhearted *o* compassionate (compasivo).
sensibilización f. FOT. y MED. Sensitization.
sensibilizar v. tr. FOT. y MED. To sensitize.
sensible adj. Sentient, feeling (capaz de tener sensaciones): *un ser sensible*, a sentient being. || Sensitive (impresionable): *una mujer sensible*, a sensitive woman. || Tenderhearted (compasivo). || Sensible, perceptible (perceptible). || Tangible: *el mundo sensible*, the tangible world. || Noticeable, appreciable: *sensibles adelantos*, noticeable advances. || Sensitive: *un aparato sensible*, a sensitive device; *sensible a la luz*, sensitive to light. || FOT. Sensitive. || Lamentable, deplorable (lamentable). || — FIG. *Corazón sensible*, tender heart. || *Sensible al tacto*, tender, sensitive to the touch (que duele todavía), which can be felt, perceptible to the touch, tangible (que se nota tocando). || *Sitio sensible*, tender *o* sore spot. || *Un oído sensible*, a sensitive ear.
sensiblemente adv. Appreciably, noticeably.

sensiblería f. Sentimentality, sentimentalism. || Schmaltz (fam.), sloppiness (fam.) [peyorativo].
sensiblero, ra adj. Schmaltzy (fam.), over-sentimental, sloppy (fam.).
sensitiva f. Bot. Sensitive plant, mimosa.
sensitivo, va adj. Sensitive, susceptible (sensible). || Sense: *órgano sensitivo*, sense organ. || Sentient (que tiene facultades sensoriales).
sensorial o **sensorio, ria** adj. Sensorial, sensory.
sensual adj. Sensual; sensuous.
sensualidad f. Sensuality.
sensualismo m. Sensualism.
sensualista adj. Sensualistic.
— M. y f. Sensualist.
sentada f. Sitting (asentada). || Sit-in (huelga de estudiantes). || Sit-down strike (huelga de empleados). || *Amer.* Reining in [of a horse in full gallop]. || *De una sentada*, in one sitting.
sentado, da adj. Seated, sitting [down]: *estar sentado*, to be seated *o* sitting [down]. || Established, settled (asentado). || Stable (estable). || Fig. Sensible, steady (sesudo, reflexivo). | Sedate (sosegado). || Bot. Sessile. || — Fig. *Dar algo por sentado*, to take sth. for granted, to assume sth. | *Haber sentado la cabeza*, to have settled down. || *Pan sentado*, stale bread. || *Quiero dejar sentado que*, I want to make it clear that. || *Sentado esto*, having established this.
sentadura f. Sore (en la piel).
sentamiento m. Arq. Settling.
sentar* v. tr. To seat, to sit [a alguien]. || To set (poner firme). || To press (una costura). || To establish, to set up, to lay [down] (establecer algo). || To state, to affirm (una conclusión). || To pitch (una tienda). || *Amer.* To rein in sharply (un caballo). || — Fig. *Sentar cabeza*, to settle down, to calm down (volverse razonable). | *Sentar las bases de*, to lay the foundations of. || *Sentar plaza*, to enlist, to join up (un soldado). || *Sentar por escrito*, to put [down] in writing. || Fig. *Sentar sus reales*, v. REAL. || *Sentar un precedente*, v. PRECEDENTE.
— V. intr. To suit, to become (favorecer): *no te sienta nada bien el amarillo*, yellow doesn't suit you at all; *te sienta muy bien este peinado*, this hairstyle really suits you; *esa actitud no te sienta nada bien*, that attitude doesn't become you at all. || To fit (las medidas de la ropa, etc.): *me sienta bastante bien la chaqueta, pero el pantalón me está pequeño*, the jacket fits me quite well, but the trousers are too small. || To agree with (digerirse bien o mal): *los caracoles me sientan fatal*, snails don't agree with me at all. || To suit (convenir). || — *Sentar bien*, to do good, to be good for (hacer buen efecto): *bébete este té, que te sentará bien para el dolor de vientre*, drink this tea, it will be good for your tummy ache *o* it will do your tummy good; to like, to appreciate (gustar a uno): *los cumplidos siempre sientan bien*, people always like to be flattered; to take well (tomar a bien): *le sentó bien lo que le dije*, he took what I said well. || *Sentar como anillo al dedo*, to fit like a glove (estar bien ajustado), to suit down to the ground (convenir o favorecer mucho). || *Sentar como un tiro*, v. TIRO. || *Sentar mal*, not to appreciate: *la broma le sentó muy mal*, he didn't appreciate the joke; to take badly (tomar a mal). || *Te habrá sentado mal algo que comiste*, sth. you ate must have disagreed with you.
— V. pr. To sit [down]: *se sentó en una silla*, he sat down in a chair; *siempre me siento aquí*, I always sit here. || To settle: *el poso del café se ha sentado en el fondo de la taza*, the coffee dregs have settled in the bottom of the cup. || To settle down, to clear up (el tiempo, etc.). || Arq. To settle. || To rub (los zapatos). || Fig. *Sentársele a uno el juicio*, to come to one's senses.
sentencia f. Maxim (máxima). || Fig. Ruling, decision (decisión). || Jur. Sentence: *pronunciar la sentencia*, to pronounce *o* to pass sentence; *cumplir la sentencia*, to serve one's sentence. || — Jur. *Sentencia en rebeldía*, judgment by default *o* in contumacy. | *Sentencia firme*, final judgment. | *Visto para sentencia*, ready for judgment.
sentenciar v. tr. To judge (juzgar). || To sentence (condenar): *sentenciar al exilio*, to sentence to exile.
sentencioso, sa adj. Sententious.
sentidamente adv. Regretfully (con pesar). || Sincerely (sinceramente).
sentido m. Meaning, sense (significado): *esta frase tiene varios sentidos*, this sentence has various meanings. || Sense: *sentido común*, common sense; *buen sentido*, good sense; *el sentido de la vista, del olfato*, the sense of sight, of smell. || Consciousness (conocimiento). || Direction: *en sentido contrario*, in the opposite direction. || Sense: *los negros tienen un buen sentido del ritmo*, Negroes have a good sense of rhythm; *sentido del humor*, sense of humour. || Feeling (sentimiento): *lo leyó con mucho sentido*, he read it with a lot of feeling. || — *Aguzar el sentido*, to prick up one's ears, to listen attentively. || *Calle de sentido único*, one-way street. || *Con los cinco sentidos*, for all one is worth: *escuché con los cinco sentidos*, I listened for all I was worth. || Fam. *Costar un sentido*, to cost the earth *o* a fortune. || *Dar mal sentido a algo*, to take sth. the wrong way. || *Dar sentido torcido a*, to twist the meaning of. || *De doble sentido*, with double meaning. || Fig. *Dejar sin sentido*, to stun. || *Embargar los sentidos*, to take one's breath away (de admiración). || *En cierto sentido*, in a sense. || *En contra del sentido común*, against common sense, in defiance of common sense. || *En el buen sentido de la palabra*, in the best sense of the word. || *En el sentido amplio de la palabra*, in the broad sense of the word. || *En tal sentido*, to this effect. || *En todos los sentidos*, in every sense (una palabra), in all directions (en todas direcciones), in every way (en todos los aspectos). || *Esto no tiene sentido*, this doesn't make sense. || Fig. *Hacerle perder el sentido a uno*, to drive s.o. insane. || Fam. *Llevar* or *pedir un sentido*, to ask the earth. || *No le encuentro sentido alguno*, I can't make any sense [out] of it. || *Perder el sentido*, to faint, to lose consciousness (desmayarse), to go out of one's mind, to lose one's senses (volverse loco). || Fam. *Poner sus cinco sentidos en una cosa*, to give one's undivided attention to sth., to put everything one has into sth. || Fam. *Quitar el sentido*, to take one's breath away, to knock s.o. out: *esta mujer me quita el sentido*, this woman knocks me out. || *Recobrar el sentido*, v. RECOBRAR. || *Sentido de la orientación*, sense of direction. || *Sentido figurado*, figurative sense. || *Sin sentido*, meaningless (palabra, etc.), senseless, unconscious (inconsciente). || *Tener sentido*, to make sense. || *Tomar una cosa en buen, en mal sentido*, to take sth. the right, the wrong way.
sentido, da adj. Deeply felt, deepest, heartfelt, sincere: *sentido pésame*, sincere condolences, deepest sympathy. || Deeply felt: *una muerte muy sentida*, a very deeply felt death. || Moving, touching (conmovedor). || Tender: *un sentido recuerdo*, a tender memory. || Fig. Sensitive, touchy (sensible).
sentimental adj. Sentimental. || — *Aventura sentimental*, love affair. || *Vida sentimental*, love life.
— M. y f. Sentimentalist.
sentimentalismo m. Sentimentalism, sentimentality.
sentimentaloide adj. Fam. Schmaltzy, over-sentimental.
sentimiento m. Feeling: *tener sentimientos cariñosos*, to have affectionate feelings; *un sentimiento de alegría*, a feeling of joy. || Sentiment: *sentimientos nobles, liberales*, noble, liberal sentiments. || Regret, sorrow (pesar). || Grief, sorrow (aflicción). || Sense (sentido): *sentimiento del deber*, sense of duty. || — *Con mi mayor sentimiento*, with my deepest regret. || *Herir los sentimientos de alguien*, to hurt s.o.'s feelings. || *Le acompaño en el sentimiento*, my deepest sympathy, I sympathize with you.
sentina f. Mar. Bilge. || Fig. Sewer, cesspool (albañal). | Den of iniquity (donde hay vicio).
sentir m. Sentiment, feeling: *el sentir de la nación*, national sentiment. || Judgment, opinion, view (parecer). || *En mi sentir*, in my opinion.
sentir* v. tr. e intr. To feel: *¿no sientes frío, hambre?*, don't you feel cold, hungry?; *yo nunca siento el frío*, I never feel the cold. || To hear (oír): *sentimos una fuerte explosión*, we heard a loud explosion. || To sense, to feel, to have the feeling that (barruntar): *sentí que alguien me seguía*, I sensed s.o. was following me. || To have a feeling for: *sentir la poesía*, to have a feeling for poetry. || To feel (en lo moral): *sintió mucha pena*, he felt a great deal of sorrow. || To regret, to feel *o* to be sorry (afligirse): *siento que se vaya*, I am sorry that you're going; *siento no haberle visto*, I regret not having seen him, I'm sorry I didn't see him. || To feel (opinar). || To feel the effect of (una enfermedad, etc.). || To be affected by, to feel the effect of: *muchas flores sienten la falta de lluvia*, many flowers are affected by the lack of rain. || — *Dar que sentir*, to give cause for regret. || *Dejarse sentir*, to begin to make itself felt. || *Dejarse sentir el calor, el frío*, to begin to get hot, cold (el tiempo). || *Lo siento*, I'm sorry. || *Lo siento mucho*, I'm very sorry, I'm so sorry. || *Marcharse sin sentir*, to leave unnoticed, to slip out. || *Sentir en el alma*, to be deeply sorry, to regret deeply. || *Sin sentir*, just like that, without noticing: *se nos pasó la mañana sin sentir*, the morning went by just like that *o* without our noticing it; just like that: *se tragó la pastilla sin sentir*, he swallowed the pill just like that.
— V. pr. To feel: *sentirse enfermo, obligado a*, to feel ill, obliged to. || To suffer (*de*, from) [de una enfermedad]. || — *Comienza a sentirse el frío en noviembre*, it starts to get cold in November. || *Me siento mal*, I feel ill *o* sick. || Fig. *No se siente una mosca*, it is dead silent, you could hear a pin drop. || *Sentirse como en su casa*, to feel at home. || Fig. *Sentirse como un pez en el agua*, to be in one's element, to feel completely at home. || *Sentirse con ánimos para hacer algo*, to feel like doing sth., to feel up to doing sth.
sentón m. *Amer.* Reining in. || *Dar un sentón*, to rein in sharply.
seña f. Sign, signal: *hacer señas*, to make signs. || Mark (marca). || Mil. Password. || — Pl. Address, *sing.*: *le di mis señas*, I gave him my address. || Description, *sing.* (filiación). || — *Dar señas de satisfacción*, to show signs of satisfaction. || *Hablar por señas*, to talk in sign language. || *Las señas son mortales*, it's perfectly clear. || *Me hizo señas para que empezara*, he signalled to me to start. || *Por más*

señas, more specifically. || *Santo y seña*, password. || *Señas personales*, description, *sing.*

señal f. Mark (marca). || Signal: *al ver su señal nos paramos*, when we saw his signal, we stopped; *señal de alarma*, alarm signal; *dar la señal*, to give the signal. || Sign, indication (signo, indicio): *buena, mala señal*, good, bad sign. || Sign (letrero). || Mark, scar (cicatriz). || Proof, sign (prueba). || Bookmark (en un libro). || Landmark (mojón). || COM. Deposit, token payment (dinero): *dejar una señal*, to leave a deposit. || Dialling tone (teléfono). || Token, indication: *dar una señal de su talento*, to give an indication of one's talent. || Trace, track (rastro). || Reminder (recordatorio). || Mark of distinction (de distinción). || — *Código de señales*, signal code. || *¿Da la señal de llamada?*, is it ringing? (el teléfono). || *En señal de*, as a token of (como muestra de), as proof of (como prueba de). || *Explicar con pelos y señales*, V. EXPLICAR. || *Me hacía señales*, he was signalling to me. || *Ni señal*, not a trace. || *No dar señales de vida*, not to show any signs of life. || *Señal de ataque*, signal to attack. || REL. *Señal de la Cruz*, the sign of the cross. || *Señal del casco*, bottle receipt (de las botellas). || *Señal de ocupado*, engaged tone [U.S., busy signal]. || *Señal de peligro*, danger signal. || *Señal de prohibición de estacionamiento*, no parking sign. || *Señal de tráfico*, traffic *o* road sign (placa). || *Señales de socorro*, distress signals. || *Señales urbanas*, urban traffic signs *o* signals. || *Señal para marcar*, dialling tone [U. S., dial tone]. || *Sin dejar señal*, without a trace, without leaving a trace. || AUT. *Utilizar las señales acústicas*, to sound one's horn.

señaladamente adv. Expressly, especially, specifically (especialmente). || Distinctly (claramente).

señalado, da adj. Outstanding, distinguished (insigne). || Exceptional: *un señalado favor*, an exceptional favour. || Appointed, set, fixed, arranged: *en el día señalado*, on the appointed day. || Noticeable, marked: *una ausencia señalada*, a noticeable absence. || Confirmed: *un señalado anarquista*, a confirmed anarchist. || Marked, scarred: *el accidente le ha dejado señalado para toda la vida*, the accident left him marked for life. || FIG. *Un día señalado*, a special day, a red-letter day.

señalamiento m. Signalling (acción de señalar). || JUR. Designation.

señalar v. tr. To mark (poner una señal): *señalar las faltas con lápiz*, to mark the mistakes with a pencil. || To point to: *las manecillas del reloj señalan las tres y media*, the hands of the clock are pointing to half past three. || To point out, to call *o* to draw s.o.'s attention to (hacer observar): *me señaló un error*, he pointed out a mistake to me, he drew my attention to a mistake. || To point out: *señalar algo a la atención del público*, to point sth. out to the public. || To arrange, to make (una cita). || To set, to fix (una fecha, un precio). || To set (un trabajo). || To give, to show: *el reloj señala la hora*, the clock gives the time. || To mark: *eso señaló el fin del imperio romano*, this marked the end of the Roman Empire. || To indicate (indicar). || To scar, to mark (dejar cicatriz). || To announce (anunciar). || To signpost (carretera, trayecto). || To mark down (puntos en un juego de naipes). || To mark (baraja). || To sign and seal (rubricar). || To appoint, to designate: *señalar a alguien para hacer algo*, to appoint s.o. to do sth. || *Señalar algo con el dedo*, to point at *o* to sth.
— V. pr. FIG. To stand out (perfilarse). | To stand out: *señalarse por su elegancia*, to stand out by one's elegance. | To distinguish o.s. (distinguirse).

señalización f. Signposting (colocación de señales). || Road signs, *pl.* (señales de tráfico). || Railway signals, *pl.* (de ferrocarriles).

señalizar v. tr. To signpost.

señero, ra adj. Alone, solitary (solo). || Unique, unequalled, unrivalled (sin par). || FIG. *Figura señera*, outstanding figure.

señor, ra adj. Distinguished, noble (distinguido). || FIG. Some, fine: *una señora herida*, a fine wound, some wound; *¡es una señora calabaza!* that's some pumpkin!
— M. Man, gentleman: *un señor mayor*, an elderly gentleman. || Mister, Mr.: *el señor Pérez*, Mr. Perez; *Señor Presidente*, Mr. Chairman, Mr. President (en una asamblea). || Sir: *buenos días, señor*, good morning, Sir. || Lord: *señor feudal*, feudal lord. || Master (amo): *el siervo mató a su señor*, the serf killed his master. || Owner (propietario). || Sir (título real). || My Lord (dirigiéndose a lores, jueces, etc.). || — *A lo gran señor*, in grand style. || *A tal señor, tal honor*, honour to whom honour is due. || *Dárselas* or *echárselas de señor*, to put on airs, to give o.s. airs. || *De padre y muy señor mío*, V. PADRE. || *El Señor, Nuestro Señor*, The Lord, Our Lord. || *El señor conde, marqués*, my lord, your lordship (dirigiéndose a la persona), my lord, his lordship (hablando a un tercero). || *El señor de la casa*, the master of the household. || *El señor no está*, the master is not in. || *El señor obispo*, my Lord Bishop. || *Es mi dueño y señor*, he is my lord and master. || *Estimado señor*, Dear Sir. || *Los señores de Tarazona*, Mr. and Mrs. Tarazona, the Tarazonas. || *Muy señores nuestros*, gentlemen. || *Muy señor mío*, Dear Sir. || FIG. *¡No señor!*, definitely not! || *Pues sí señor*, yes indeed. || *¡Señor!*, good Lord. || *Señor de horca y cuchillo*, V. HORCA. || REL. *Señor de Los Ejércitos*, Lord of Hosts. || *Señor Don Miguel de Unamuno*, Mr. M. de Unamuno, M. de Unamuno, Esq. (en un sobre). || *¡Señores!*, gentlemen! || *Ser siempre señor de sus actos*, to be master of one's actions. || *Ser todo un señor*, to be a real *o* a perfect gentleman. || *¡Sí señor!*, yes, Sir! (es así), bravo! (en el cante flamenco). || *Su señor padre*, your [dear] father.
— F. Lady, woman: *una señora mayor*, an elderly lady. || Mrs.: *la Señora de Pérez*, Mrs. Perez; *Señora Doña Isabel Martín de Ibarra*, Mrs. Isabel Martin Ibarra. || Madam (tratamiento de cortesía): *buenos días, señora*, good morning, Madam. || FAM. Wife (esposa): *recuerdos a su señora*, my regards to your wife. || — *La señora condesa, marquesa*, my *o* your ladyship. || *La señora de Tal*, Mrs. So-and-So. || *La señora no está*, Madam is out. || *Muy señora mía*, Dear Madam. || *Nuestra Señora*, Our Lady. || *Peluquería de señoras*, ladies' hairdresser. || *Señora de compañía*, lady's companion. || *Señoras y señores*, ladies and gentlemen. || *Ser toda una señora*, to be a real *o* a perfect lady. || *Sí señora*, yes, Madam. || *Su señora madre*, your [dear] mother.

— OBSERV. Obsérvese que cuando la palabra « señor » antecede un título profesional no suele traducirse en inglés en la mayoría de los casos (*el señor alcalde*, the mayor, *el señor cura*, the priest).

señorear v. tr. e intr. To dominate, to control, to rule (mandar). || FIG. To tower over, to dominate (desde lo alto). | To master, to control (las pasiones). || FAM. To lord it (dárselas de señorito). | To keep calling [s.o.] Sir, to sir.
— V. pr. To seize, to seize control of, to take over (apoderarse de).

señoría f. Lordship (hombre), ladyship (mujer) [título]. || Lordship (terreno). || Rule, sway, dominion (gobierno). || Seigniory, seignory (en Italia). || *Su Señoría*, your *o* his lordship, my lord (a un señor), your *o* her ladyship, my lady (a una señora).

señorial adj. Lordly (relativo a un señorío). || FIG. Stately (imponente): *una casa señorial*, a stately home. | Aristocratic (aristocrático). | Elegant: *un barrio señorial*, an elegant district. || Gentlemanly (comportamiento).

señoril adj. V. SEÑORIAL.

señorilmente adv. In a lordly *o* gentlemanly fashion.

señorío m. Dominion, rule, sway (mando). || Seigniory (derecho y territorio del señor). || Manor, estate (propiedad). || Nobility, lordliness (calidad de señor). || FIG. Dignity (dignidad). | Distinction (distinción). | Stateliness (majestuosidad). | Mastery, control (de las pasiones). | Distinguished people, *pl.* (gente distinguida). || *Señorío feudal*, suzerainty, lordship.

señorita f. Young lady. || Miss (tratamiento de cortesía): *Señorita Pelayo*, Miss Pelayo. || FAM. Miss (nombre que dan los criados a sus amas): *Señorita, le llaman*, Miss, you're wanted. || *La señorita Isabel me lo dio*, Miss Isabel gave it to me.

— OBSERV. Spanish servants frequently call their mistress *señorita* even if she is married
— En inglés la palabra *Miss* va seguida del apellido de la persona a quien uno se refiere, p. ej. *¿está la señorita en casa?*, is Miss Jones at home?

señoritingo, ga m. y f. FAM. Rich little daddy's boy, rich little daddy's girl.

señoritismo m. Privileges (*pl.*) of the rich.

señorito m. Young gentleman. || FAM. Master [of the house] (nombre que dan los criados a sus amos): *el señorito ha salido*, the master has gone out. || Rich little daddy's boy (hijo de un padre influyente y rico).

señorón, ona adj. Distinguished, lordly (muy señor). || FAM. *No seas tan señorón*, don't be so lordly *o* so high and mighty.
— M. y f. FAM. Big shot.

señuelo m. Lure (para halcones). || Decoy (reclamo). || Lark mirror (para alondras). || FIG. Bait (espejuelo). | Trap (trampa): *caer en el señuelo*, to fall into the trap. || *Amer.* Lead steer (buey guía). | Group of tame young bulls that lead wild cattle (mansos). | Lead mare (madrina de la tropilla). || FIG. *La juventud se marcha a otros países tras el señuelo de los salarios altos*, young people are lured abroad by the prospect of high wages.

seo f. Cathedral (en Aragón).

sépalo m. BOT. Sepal.

separable adj. Separable. || TECN. Detachable, removable.

separación f. Separation (acción, duración, etc.). || Space, gap (distancia). || TECN. Removal (de una pieza). || JUR. *Separación matrimonial*, legal separation.

separadamente adv. Separately.

separado, da adj. Separated, separate. || Separated: *está separada de su marido*, she is separated from her husband. || — *Por separado*, separately; under separate cover (correos). || *Tiene los dientes separados*, he has gaps between his teeth, he has gappy teeth.

separador, ra adj. Separative.
— M. Separator.

separar v. tr. To separate (una cosa o persona de otra). || To move away (apartar): *separa la silla del*

radiador, move the chair away from the radiator. || To keep away: *su trabajo le separa de la familia*, his work keeps him away from his family. || FIG. To put *o* to set aside, to keep (guardar): *separa una tajada de sandía para mí*, put a slice of watermelon aside for me. || To divide, to break up, to split (palabras, sílabas). || To separate, to sort [out]: *separar los cuchillos de los tenedores*, to separate the knives from the forks. || To dismiss, to remove: *separar a un funcionario de su puesto*, to dismiss a civil servant from his job. || TECN. To detach. || — *Bajo las piernas separadas de Gulliver pasó todo el pueblo*, the whole town passed between Gulliver's open legs. || *No se le puede separar de sus libros*, he and his books are inseparable, nothing will drag him away from his books.
— V. pr. To separate (un matrimonio). || To part company, to separate (dos o más personas). || To part with: *nunca me separaré de esta joya*, I'll never part with this jewel. || To move away from: *el barco se iba separando cada vez más de la costa*, the ship moved farther and farther away from the coast. || To cut o.s. off (romper las relaciones): *se ha separado de toda la familia*, he has cut himself off from all his family. || To retire: *se ha separado de su negocio*, he has retired from his business. || To leave: *Pedro se ha separado de la pandilla*, Peter has left the gang. || JUR. To waive [a right]. || TECN. To come off *o* away. || *Se ha separado de su mujer*, he and his wife have separated.

separata f. IMPR. Offprint, separate.
separatismo m. Separatism.
separatista adj./s. Separatist.
separativo, va adj. Separative.
sepedón n. ZOOL. Seps (lagarto).
sepelio m. Interment, burial.
sepia f. ARTES. Sepia (tinta). || ZOOL. Cuttlefish.
seps m. ZOOL. Seps (lagarto).
septembrino, na adj. September, of September.
septenado o **septenato** m. Septennate.
septenal adj. Septennial.
septenario, ria adj./s.m. Septenary.
septenio m. Septennium, septennate.
septentrión m. North (norte). || ASTR. Great Bear (Osa Mayor).
septentrional adj. Northern, north.
septenviro m. Septemvir.
septeto m. MÚS. Septet, septette.
septicemia f. MED. Septicaemia.
septicémico, ca adj. MED. Septicaemic.
septicidad f. Septicity.
séptico, ca adj. Septic.
septiembre m. September: *nació el 4 de septiembre*, he was born on the 4th of September.

— OBSERV. The dictionary of the Spanish Academy of the language admits the spelling *setiembre*, which is used by the majority of South American authors and even by certain Spanish authors (Unamuno, Cela) who alternate between the two spellings. One should note that in the pronunciation the *p* is scarcely sounded.

septillo m. MÚS. Septimole.
séptima f. MÚS. Seventh: *séptima menor, aumentada*, minor, augmented seventh. || Septime (esgrima). || MÚS. *Séptima de dominante*, dominant seventh.
séptimo, ma adj./s. Seventh: *el séptimo cielo*, the seventh heaven. || The Seventh: *Carlos VII* (*séptimo*), Charles VII [the Seventh]. || — *En séptimo lugar*, in seventh place, seventh. || *La séptima parte*, one seventh, a seventh.
septingentésimo, ma adj./s. Seven hundredth.
septuagenario, ria adj. Septuagenarian, seventy-year-old.
— M. y f. Septuagenarian, man [*o* woman] in his [*o* her] seventies, seventy-year-old.
septuagésima f. REL. Septuagesima (fiesta).
septuagésimo, ma adj./s. Seventieth.
septuplicar v. tr. To septuple.
séptuplo, pla adj. Septuple, sevenfold.
— M. Septuple.
sepulcral adj. Sepulchral. || — *Lápida sepulcral*, gravestone, tombstone. || FIG. *Silencio sepulcral*, deathly silence. || *Voz sepulcral*, sepulchral voice.
sepulcro m. Sepulchre [U.S., sepulcher], grave, tomb. || — *El Santo Sepulcro*, the Holy Sepulchre. || *Sepulcro blanqueado*, whited sepulchre. || FIG. *Ser un sepulcro*, to be as silent as the grave. | *Tener un pie en el sepulcro*, to have one foot in the grave.
sepultador, ra m. y f. Gravedigger.
sepultamiento m. Burial, entombment.
sepultar v. tr. To bury, to entomb (enterrar). || To trap: *mineros sepultados*, trapped miners. || FIG. To bury (olvidar): *recuerdos sepultados*, buried memories. | To conceal, to bury (ocultar): *una caja sepultada bajo varios objetos*, a box concealed under several objects. | To bury: *sepultado en sus pensamientos*, buried in thought; *pueblo sepultado bajo las rocas*, town buried under the rocks.
sepulto, ta adj. Buried.
sepultura f. Burial, sepulture (acto). || Grave, tomb, sepulchre [U.S., sepulcher] (tumba). || — *Dar sepultura*, to bury. || *Dar sepultura cristiana*, to give a Christian burial. || FAM. *Estar con un pie aquí y otro en la sepultura*, to have one foot in the grave. | *Genio y figura hasta la sepultura*, V. GENIO.
sepulturero m. Gravedigger.
sequedad f. Dryness (cualidad de seco). || FIG. Curtness, abruptness (en el trato). | Dryness (del estilo).
sequedal o **sequeral** m. Dry land.
sequía f. Drought.
séquito m. Entourage, retinue (de personas). || FIG. Aftermath, train (consecuencias): *la guerra y su séquito de horrores*, war and its aftermath of horror.
ser m. Being: *los seres humanos*, human beings. || Existence, life (vida). | Essence, substance (esencia). — *Dar el ser*, to give life, to bring into the world. *En lo más íntimo de su ser*, deep down, deep inside himself, in his heart of hearts. || *Ser Supremo*, Supreme Being.
ser* v. intr.

1. Sentidos generales. — **2.** Ser de. — **3.** Ser para. — **4.** Usos diversos.

1. SENTIDOS GENERALES. — To be: *ser o no ser*, to be or not to be; *soy español*, I am Spanish; *somos dos*, there are two of us; *son las ocho*, it is eight o'clock; *serán las diez*, it will be about ten o'clock; *serían las diez cuando nos fuimos*, it would be ten o'clock when we left; *es fácil*, it is easy; *soy yo*, it's me, it is I. || To be, to happen (suceder): *¿qué ha sido?*, what was it?; *¿cómo fue eso?*, how did that happen?, how was that? || To be, to take place: *la toma de Granada fue en 1492*, the conquest of Granada was in 1492. || To be (costar): *¿cuánto es la carne?*, how much is the meat? || To be, to belong to (pertenecer): *este libro es mío*, this book is mine, this book belongs to me. || To be, to make: *dos y dos son cuatro*, two and two is four. || To be: *soy yo el que lo hice* or *quien lo hizo*, I am the one who did it, it was I who did it.
2. SER DE. — To be made of, to be of (materia): *la mesa es de madera*, the table is made of wood. || To be from, to come from: *¿de dónde eres?*, where are you from?, where do you come from? || To be, to belong to (pertenecer): *es de Juan*, it is John's, it belongs to John; *¿de quién es?*, whose is it?, who does it belong to? || To be by, to be written by (un autor). || To be like (ser característico): *es muy de él*, that is just like him. || To be with *o* for, to be on s.o.'s side (ser partidario): *soy de Juan*, I am with John *o* on John's side. || To be: *¡hay que ver como es de goloso!*, what a glutton he is!, how greedy he is! || To be, to be worth (deber): *es de ver*, it should be seen, it is worth seeing. || To become of, to happen to: *¿qué habría sido de mí?*, what would have become of me?; *¿qué ha sido de tu novia?*, what has happened to your girlfriend? || *Es de creer, esperar que*, it is to be believed, hoped that. || *Este comportamiento no es de un caballero*, that is not a gentlemanly way to behave, such behaviour does not become a gentleman.
3. SER PARA. — To be for: *esta carta es para ti*, this letter is for you. || To be fitting for, to suit (apto para). || — *Es para morirse de risa*, it is hilarious, it is enough to make you die laughing. || *Esta clase de vida no es para mí*, this kind of life isn't for me. || *Ser para poco*, to be of next to no use, to be of little account.
4. USOS DIVERSOS. — *Ahora soy todo suyo*, right, I'm all yours. || *A no ser por*, had it not been for, if it were not for, but for. || *A no ser que*, unless: *a no ser que él llegue antes*, unless he arrives *o* should arrive first. || *¡Así sea!*, so be it! || *Aun cuando fuera*, even if one *o* it were. || *Aunque fuese*, even if one *o* it were: *aunque fuese verdad*, even if it were true. || *¿Cómo es eso?*, how's that? || *Cómo es que...?*, how is it that...?, how come...?: *¿cómo es que no me lo has dicho antes?*, how come you didn't tell me sooner? || *¡Cómo ha de ser!*, what can you expect? || *¿Cómo puede ser?*, how come? || *Como sea*, any way at all, one way or another (de cualquier manera), anyway (de todas maneras). || *Con ser*, in spite of being (a pesar de ser). || *De no ser así*, if not, otherwise. || *De no ser por*, had it not been for, but for, if it were not for. || *Érase que se era* or *érase una vez*, once upon a time [there was] (en cuentos). || *Es decir*, that is to say, in other words. || *Es más*, what is more. || *Eso es*, that's it, that's right. || *Esto es*, that is to say (es decir). || *Lo que sea*, anything, anything at all. || FAM. *¡No es para menos!*, and rightly so!, I should think so, too! || *No puede ser*, that can't be, that's impossible. || *No sea que* or *no vaya a ser que*, unless (a menos que), in case, lest (ant.) [por si acaso]. || *No somos nada* or *nadie*, it just goes to show how insignificant we are. *O sea, en otros términos*, in other words, that is to say, that is. || *O sea que*, in other words, so, that is to say (en conclusión). || *O somos o no somos*, let's get on with it, what are you waiting for? || *Por si fuera poco*, and on top of that, and to top it all (para colmo). || *Que no sea*, except, but (salvo): *cualquiera que no sea Juan*, anyone but John. || *¿Quién es?*, who is it?; who is speaking? (en el teléfono). || *Sea*, right, agreed (de acuerdo). || *Sea como sea*, one way or another (de todas maneras). || *Sea lo que Dios quiera*, V. DIOS. || *Sea lo que fuere* or *lo que sea*, be that as it may. || *Sea o no sea*, anyway. || *Sea ... sea*, either ... or. || *Ser de lo que no hay*, to be unique. || *Ser muy suyo*, to keep very much to o.s., to be very independent (ser independiente), to be very selfish (ser muy egoísta),

to be different (ser especial). || *Siendo así que*, since. || *Si no es por*, if it were not for, if it hadn't been for, but for: *si no es por mí se mata*, if it were not for me he would have killed himself. || *Si no es que*, unless. || *Si yo fuera usted*, if I were you. || FAM. *Un si es no es*, a bit, somewhat. || *Ya sea... ya sea...*, either ... or ... || *Yo soy la madre*, I'll be mother (en juegos de niños).

— OBSERV. *Ser*, in contrast to *estar*, indicates an essential or permanent quality of the subject: *es una mujer*, she is a woman: *es joven, española, simpática, secretaria*, she is young, Spanish, nice, a secretary. *Ser* is also used as an auxiliary verb in the passive voice: *el carbón es extraído por los mineros*, the coal is extracted by the miners; *fue asesinado*, he was murdered.

sera f. Pannier, basket, frail (espuerta).
sérac m. GEOL. Serac (en un glaciar).
seráfico, ca adj. Seraphic, angelic. || Fransiscan (orden). || — *Doctor Seráfico*, Seraphic Doctor [St Bonaventura]. || *Sueño seráfico*, peaceful sleep *o* slumber.
serafín m. REL. Seraph. || FAM. Angel (ángel). || FIG. Angel, beauty (persona hermosa). || — Pl. REL. Seraphim.
serbal m. Service tree (árbol).
Serbia n. pr. f. GEOGR. Serbia.
serbio, bia adj./s. Serb, Serbian.
serbocroata adj./s Serbo-Croatian.
serena f. Serenade.
serenar v. tr. To calm (el mar, etc.). || FIG. To calm down, to pacify (a uno). || To settle, to clear (un líquido).
— V. pr. To calm o.s., to calm down (persona). || To grow calm (mar). || To settle, to clear (líquido).
serenata f. MÚS. Serenade. || FIG. y FAM. *Dar la serenata*, to pester (molestar).
serenero m. *Amer.* Headscarf (pañuelo).
serenidad f. Serenity (sosiego). || Calm, calmness, tranquillity (tranquilidad). || Peacefulness (quietud). || Clearness (del cielo). || Serenity (título). || *Conservó la serenidad*, he remained calm *o* unruffled.
serenísimo, ma adj. *Su Alteza Serenísima*, His Serene Highness.
sereno, na adj. Cloudless, clear (cielo). || Fine: *tiempo sereno*, fine weather. || FIG. Calm, serene, tranquil (apacible): *no sé cómo puede permanecer tan sereno*, I don't know how you can stay so calm. | Serene (sosegado). | Calm, peaceful, quiet: *el ambiente en la oficina está muy sereno ahora*, the atmosphere in the office is very peaceful now. | Sober (no borracho). || — FIG. *Ponerse sereno*, to sober up. || *Se mantuvo sereno*, he remained calm.
— M. Night watchman (vigilante). || Cool night air (humedad nocturna). || *Al sereno*, in the open air, out in the open.

— OBSERV. The *sereno* is a man who keeps watch during the night after the street doors of the blocks of flats have been locked. He has the keys to these doors and opens them to people who return home late.

sereta f. o **serete** m. Small basket *o* frail.
sergas f. pl. Deeds, exploits (hazañas): *Las Sergas de Esplandián*, The Exploits of Esplandian.
serial m. Serial (en radio o televisión).
seriamente adv. Seriously.
seriar v. tr. To arrange in series, to seriate.
sericícola adj. Sericultural.
sericicultor o **sericultor** m. Sericulturist.
sericicultura o **sericultura** f. Sericulture.
serie f. Series. || Instalment (de un empréstito). || Break (en el billar). || MAT. Series. || FIG. Series, string: *toda una serie de acontecimientos*, a whole series of events. | Succession. || — *Artículo fuera de serie*, oddment. || *Coches fabricados en serie*, mass-produced cars. || ELECTR. *En serie*, in series. || FIG. *Fuera de serie*, out of the ordinary, unusual. || *Novela por serie*, novel in serial form. || *Producción en serie*, mass production. || FIG. *Se ha publicado una serie de artículos sobre este tema*, a series of articles has been published on this subject.
seriedad f. Seriousness: *me lo dijo con toda seriedad*, he told me in all seriousness. || Gravity (gravedad). || Staidness (gravedad excesiva). || Reliability, trustworthiness, dependability (comportamiento digno de confianza). || Honesty, uprightness (honradez). || Sense of propriety (decencia). || Sense of responsibility (formalidad). || Seriousness, gravity: *la seriedad de una enfermedad*, the seriousness of an illness. || — *Falta de seriedad*, lack of seriousness, irresponsibility, levity. || *¡Qué poca seriedad tienes!*, how frivolous you are! || *Un hombre de gran seriedad*, a very serious man. || *¡Un poco de seriedad!*, let's be serious now!
serigrafía f. Serigraphy, silk-screen process.
serijo o **serillo** m. Small basket *o* frail.
seringa f. *Amer.* BOT. Seringa.
serio, ria adj. Serious: *lo dijo en tono serio*, he said it in a serious voice. || Grave (grave). || Staid (excesivamente grave). || Reliable, trustworthy, dependable (confiable). || Honest, upright (honrado). || Proper (decente). || Responsible (formal). || Sober (sobrio): *color serio*, sober colour. || Formal: *traje serio*, formal suit. || Grave, serious (enfermedad, etc.). || — *Mantenerse serio*, to stay serious, to keep a straight face. || *Ponerse serio*, to become serious, to look serious.
— Adv. *En serio*, seriously. || *¿En serio?*, seriously?, really? || *Hablar en serio*, to be serious, to speak seriously: *¿hablas en serio?*, are you serious? || *No hablar en serio*, not to be serious, to be joking, not to mean it. || *Tomar en serio*, to take seriously. || *Va en serio*, it's looking *o* becoming *o* getting serious (es grave), it's true, seriously (es verdad).
sermón m. REL. Sermon: *Sermón de la Montaña*, Sermon on the Mount. || FIG. y FAM. Sermon, lecture (reprimenda): *echarle un sermón a uno*, to give s.o. a lecture.
sermoneador, ra adj. Fault-finding.
— M. y f. Fault-finder (criticón). || Sermonizer (que reprende).
sermonear v. tr. FAM. To lecture, to sermonize (reprender insistentemente). || To sermonize, to preach (predicar).
— V. intr. To sermonize.
sermoneo m. FAM. Sermon, lecture.
serología f. Serology.
serón m. Large basket *o* frail. || FAM. *Es más basto que un serón*, he's as crude as they come.
serosidad f. Serosity.
seroso, sa adj. Serous.
seroterapia f. MED. Serotherapy.
serpa f. AGR. Sterile shoot (de la vid).
serpentaria f. BOT. Green dragon.
serpentario m. ZOOL. Serpent eater, secretary bird.
Serpentario n. pr. m. ASTR. Serpens.
serpenteante adj. Winding, twisting (camino). || Meandering, winding (río).
serpentear v. intr. To slither, to crawl, to wriggle (culebrear). || To wind, to twist and turn (un camino). || To wind, to meander (un río).
serpenteo m. Slithering, crawling, wriggling (culebreo). || Winding, twisting (de un camino). || Winding, meandering (de un río).
serpentín m. Worm (de alambique). || Coil (espiral). || MIL. Serpentine (parte del arcabuz, pieza de artillería). | Cock [of gun].
serpentina f. [Paper] streamer (de papel). || MIN. Serpentine. || MIL. V. SERPENTÍN.
serpentino, na adj. Serpentine, snaky (relativo a las serpientes). || Winding, serpentine (camino, río).
serpiente f. ZOOL. Snake, serpent. || FIG. y FAM. Snake, snake in the grass (persona pérfida). || — *Serpiente de anteojo*, cobra. || *Serpiente de cascabel*, rattlesnake. || FIG. *Serpiente de verano*, make-believe news [used to fill newspapers in the summer].
serpol m. BOT. Wild thyme, mother of thyme (tomillo).
serpollar v. intr. To shoot, to sprout (un árbol).
serpollo m. BOT. Shoot, sprout.
serradizo, za adj. *Madera serradiza*, timber.
serrado, da adj. Sawed. || Serrate, serrated, toothed (dentado).
serrador, ra adj. Sawing.
— M. Sawyer.
serraduras f. pl. Sawdust, *sing.* (serrín).
serrallo m. Seraglio (harén). || FIG. Brothel.
serranía f. Mountain range, mountains, *pl.*
serraniego, ga adj. Mountain, highland.
serranil m. Knife.
serranilla f. Lyric composition generally on a romantic theme.
serrano, na adj. Mountain, highland. || — *Jamón serrano*, cured ham. || FAM. *Mi cuerpo serrano*, yours truly, myself. | *Partida serrana*, rotten *o* dirty trick (mala jugada).
— M. y f. Highlander. || — F. Lyric composition generally on a romantic theme (serranilla).
serrar* v. tr. To saw (aserrar). || To saw off (quitar con la sierra). || To saw up (en pedazos).
serrátil adj. ANAT. Irregular (pulso). || *Juntura serrátil*, serrated suture.
serrato adj. Serrated (serrado).
— M. Serratus (músculo).
serrería f. Sawmill.
serreta f. Small saw (sierra pequeña).
serrijón m. Secondary chain (de montañas).
serrín m. Sawdust (partículas de madera).
serrucho m. Handsaw, saw.
Servia n. pr. f. GEOGR. Serbia.
servible adj. Serviceable, usable.
servicial adj. Obliging, accommodating, helpful.
— M. *Amer.* Servant (criado).
servicio m. Service: *estar al servicio de uno*, to be in the service of s.o. || Servants, *pl.*: *es cada día más difícil encontrar servicio*, it gets harder every day to find servants. || Domestic help (asistenta). || Favour [U.S., favor], service (favor). || Service: *servicio de reparaciones*, repair service. || Service, set (juego): *servicio de té*, tea service. || Service: *sercicio de mesa*, dinner service. || Service (en los restaurantes, hoteles). || Service charge: *servicio incluido*, service charge included. || Maid's room, servant's quarters: *un piso de cuatro habitaciones y servicio*, a four-roomed flat with servant's quarters. || Serve, service (en el tenis). || REL. Service. || Chamber pot (orinal). || Enema (lavativa). || — Pl. Services. || Toilet, *sing.*, lavatory, *sing.* [U.S., rest room, *sing.*]. || — MAR. *Barco de servicio*, harbour craft, tender. || *El lunes será puesto en servicio* or *entrará en servicio el nuevo teleférico*, the new cable car will be put into operation on Monday *o* will go into operation on Monday.

|| *En acto de servicio*, in the service of one's country, in action (morir). || *En condiciones de servicio*, operational. || *Estar al servicio del gobierno*, to be on government service. || *Estar de* or *en servicio*, to be on duty. || *Galería de servicio*, underground gallery *o* works (obras públicas). || MIL. *Galón de servicio*, service stripe. || *Hacer un flaco servicio*, to be of little use (ser de poco uso), to play a dirty trick on (hacer una mala jugada). || *Hoja de servicios*, service record (de los militares), record (de los deportistas). || *Prestar servicio*, to serve (criado, funcionario). || *Prestar un servicio*, to do a favour, to do a service (persona), to do a service (cosa). || MIL. *Servicio activo*, active service. || *Servicio a domicilio*, home delivery service. || *Servicio de café*, coffee set. || *Servicio de comunicación*, communications service. || *Servicio militar*, military service. || *Servicio permanente*, 24-hour service. || *Servicio postventa*, after-sales service. || *Servicio público*, public service (autobuses, etc.), civil service (funcionarios). || *Servicio secreto*, secret service. || *Servicio social*, social service (v. OBSERV.)

— OBSERV. The *servicio social* is a Spanish institution, similar to military service for men, which is required of unmarried Spanish women. During three months of full-time duty or six months of part-time duty they take courses in politics, religion, sociology, art, etc.

servidor, ra m. y f. Servant. || — M. MIL. Gunner. || — *Servidor de usted*, at your service, your servant. || *Su seguro servidor*, Yours faithfully *o* truly (en una carta), your humble servant. || FAM. *Un servidor*, yours truly (yo). || *¡Un servidor!*, your servant, Sir! — Interj. Present! (cuando se pasa lista).

servidumbre f. Servitude. || Staff of servants, servants, *pl.* (conjunto de criados): *tomar una nueva servidumbre*, to take on a new staff of servants. || Obligation (obligación). || — *Servidumbre de paso*, right-of-way. || *Servidumbre de vistas*, right to open windows overlooking another person's property.

servil adj. Servile. || FIG. Subservient. | Grovelling, abject, base (rastrero). || Menial (oficio). || Slavish (imitación). || — Adj. m./s.m. HIST. Absolutist [name given by the liberals to the conservatives in Spain at the beginning of the 19th century.]

servilismo m. Servility. || FIG. Subservience. || HIST. Absolutism.

servilón, ona adj. m./s.m. HIST. Absolutist.

servilleta f. Table napkin, serviette (de mesa). || FAM. *Doblar la servilleta*, to kick the bucket (morir).

servilletero m. Napkin ring.

servio, via adj./s Serbian, Serb.

serviola f. MAR. Cathead.

servir* v. tr. To serve, to wait on: *servir a su amo*, to serve one's master. || To serve [with]: *servir vino a alguien*, to serve s.o. [with] wine. || To serve: *servir a la patria*, to serve one's country. || MIL. To man (artillería). || To tend, to mind (una máquina). || DEP. y COM. To serve. || REL. To serve. || To follow suit (naipes). || To help, to assist, to be of service (ayudar). || — *¿En qué puedo servirle?*, what can I do for you?, may *o* can I help you? || *Me sirven, gracias*, I am being served, thank you. || *No se puede servir a Dios y al diablo*, you can't serve God and the devil at the same time. || *Para servirle*, at your service. || FAM. *¡Pues sí que le sirve de mucho!*, that will do him a lot of good! || *Servir en la mesa*, to serve *o* to wait at table. || *Servir una causa*, to serve a cause. || *Un whisky bien servido*, a well-poured whisky.

— V. intr. To be a servant, to be in service (criado). || To serve, to wait (camarero). || To be of use, to be useful (ser útil). || MIL. To do one's military service (hacer el servicio militar). | To serve (en el ejército). || DEP. To serve. || To work (funcionar). || To follow suit (naipes). || — *Eso no sirve*, that's no good. || *No servir para nada*, to be of no use at all, to be no good at all, to be useless: *esto no me sirve para nada*, this is of no use at all to me; to be no use: *llorar no sirve para nada*, it is no use crying. || *¿Para qué sirve llorar, ganar tanto dinero?*, what is the use *o* the good of crying, of earning so much money? || *Servir de*, to serve as. || *Servir de estorbo*, to get in the way: *este piano sólo sirve de estorbo*, this piano just gets in the way; to be too much trouble: *si no le sirve de estorbo*, if it is not too much trouble. || *Servir de intérprete*, to act as interpreter. || *Servir para*, to be used for: *un bolígrafo sirve para escribir*, a biro is used for writing; to be for: *¿para qué podría servir esto?*, what could this be for? || *Yo no sirvo para esta clase de cosas*, I am no good at this sort of thing.

— V. pr. To serve *o* to help o.s.: *sírvase usted mismo*, help yourself. || To help o.s.: *sírvete queso*, help yourself to cheese. || To use: *servirse de un diccionario*, to use a dictionary. || To be kind enough to: *sírvase usted decirme su nombre*, would you be kind enough to tell me your name. || *Sírvase sentarse*, do take a seat, do sit down, please take a seat, would you like to take a seat?

servita m. REL. Servite.

servocroata adj./s. Serbo-Croatian.

servofreno m. Servo brake.

servomando m. TECN. Servo control.

servomecanismo m. TECN. Servomechanism.

servomotor m. TECN. Servomotor.

sesada f. Brains, *pl.* (de animal). || CULIN. Fried brains.

sésamo m. BOT. Sesame (alegría). || *¡Sésamo ábrete!*, open sesame!

sesamoideo, a adj. ANAT. Sesamoid (hueso).

sesear v. intr. To pronounce the Spanish *c* (before *e* or *i*) and *z* as an *s* (v. SESEO.).

sesenta adj./s.m.inv. Sixty. || Sixtieth (sexagésimo). || — *Sesenta y uno, y dos, etc.*, sixty-one, sixty-two, etc. || *Tiene unos sesenta años*, he is about sixty years old. || *Unos sesenta*, about sixty.

sesentavo, va adj./s. Sixtieth.

sesentón, ona adj. Sixty-year-old, in one's sixties. — M. y f. Sixty-year-old, person in his [*o* her] sixties.

seseo m. Pronunciation of the Spanish *c* (before *e* or *i*) and *z* as *s*.

— OBSERV. The *seseo* is common in Andalusia, the Canary Islands and in the Spanish-speaking countries of Latin America.

sesera f. Brainpan (de animal). || FAM. Grey matter, brains, *pl.* (inteligencia): *este chico no tiene mucha sesera*, that boy hasn't got much grey matter.

sesgadamente adv. On a slant, on the bias, on the skew.

sesgado, da adj. Slanting, slanted (inclinado). || Cut on the bias, cut on the skew (cortado).

sesgadura f. Cutting on the bias *o* on the skew (acción). || Cut on the bias *o* on the skew (corte al sesgo).

sesgar v. tr. To cut on the bias *o* on the skew (cortar). || To slant, to skew, to put askew (colocar).

sesgo, ga adj. Slanting, slanted (inclinado).
— M. Slant (inclinación). || Bias (en costura). || FIG. Subterfuge (quiebro). | Turn (rumbo): *tomar un mal sesgo*, to take a turn for the worse. || *Al sesgo*, on the bias (cortar), askew, awry, slanting (no en la posición debida).

sesión f. Session, sitting (de un tribunal, etc.). || Meeting, session (reunión): *sesión a puerta cerrada*, closed session; *sesión de apertura, plenaria*, opening, plenary session; *en sesión pública*, in public meeting; *reanudar la sesión*, to resume the meeting. || Session (de concilio). || Show, performance (de teatro). || Showing, session (de cine). || Sitting (pintor o escultor). || — *Abrir, levantar la sesión*, to open, to adjourn the meeting (una asamblea). || *Celebrar una sesión*, to hold a meeting. || *Período de sesiones*, session (de una asamblea). || *Se abre la sesión*, the meeting is open, the meeting is declared open. || CINEM. *Sesión continua*, continuous showing. || *Sesión de clausura*, closing *o* final meeting, closing *o* final session. || *Sesión de espiritismo*, séance.

seso m. ANAT. Brain. || FIG. Brains, *pl.*, grey matter, sense (juicio): *tienes muy poco seso*, you have very little sense. || — Pl. CULIN. Brains: *sesos de carnero*, lamb brains. || — FIG. y FAM. *Beberle los sesos a uno*, to have s.o. bewitched *o* under one's spell. | *Calentarse* or *devanarse* or *estrujarse los sesos*, to rack one's brains. | *Perder el seso*, to lose one's head, to go out of one's mind. | *Tomás le sorbe el seso a María*, Mary is head over heels in love with Thomas, Mary is mad about Thomas.

sesquicentenario, ria adj./s.m. Sesquicentennial.

sesquióxido m. QUÍM. Sesquioxide.

sesteadero m. Shady resting place for cattle.

sestear v. intr. To have a nap, to take a siesta (descansar). || To rest in the shade (el ganado).

sesteo m. *Amer.* Nap, siesta. | V. SESTEADERO.

sestercio m. Sesterce (moneda romana).

sesudamente adv. Wisely, sensibly (sensatamente). || Intelligently, cleverly (inteligentemente).

sesudo, da adj. Brainy (inteligente). || Wise, sensible (sensato).

set m. Set (en tenis, cine).

seta f. BOT. Mushroom (hongo).

setal m. Mushroom patch.

setecientos, tas adj./s.m. Seven hundred: *dos mil setecientos veinte*, two thousand seven hundred and twenty; *el año setecientos*, the year seven hundred. || *Mil setecientos*, one thousand seven hundred, seventeen hundred.

setenta adj./s.m. Seventy. || Seventieth (septuagésimo). || *Setenta y uno, setenta y dos*, seventy-one, seventy-two.

setentavo, va adj./s. Seventieth.

setentón, ona adj. Seventy-year-old, in one's seventies.
— M. y f. Seventy-year-old, person in his [*o* her, etc.] seventies.

setiembre m. September (v. SEPTIEMBRE [*Observ.*]).

seto m. Fence (cercado). || Hedge (seto vivo). || *Seto vivo*, hedge, quickset hedge.

setter m. Setter (perro).

seudo adj. inv. y pref. Pseudo.

seudónimo, ma adj. Pseudonymous.
— M. y f. Pseudonym, pen name: *escribir con un seudónimo*, to write under a pen name.

seudópodo m. ZOOL. Pseudopod, pseudopodium.

severidad f. Severity, strictness (en el trato). || Sternness (de aspecto). || Severity (de un estilo, etc.). || — *Castigar con severidad*, to punish severely. || *Obrar con severidad*, to be severe *o* strict.

severo, ra adj. Strict: *una disciplina severa*, strict discipline; *un profesor muy severo*, a very strict teacher. || Harsh, severe: *un castigo severo*, a harsh punishment.

|| Severe, harsh (críticas). || FIG. Harsh, bleak, severe (invierno). | Harsh, stern (cara). | Stark, severe, harsh (estilo, traje): *la severa fachada del monasterio,* the stark façade of the monastery.
sevicia f. Cruelty, brutality.
Sevilla n. pr. GEOGR. Seville. || *Quien fue* or *va a Sevilla perdió* or *pierde su silla,* he who goes to the fair loses his chair.
sevillano, na adj./s. Sevillian. || — F. pl. Sevillian music and dance.
sexagenario, ria adj./s. Sexagenarian.
Sexagésima f. REL. Sexagesima.
sexagesimal adj. Sexagesimal.
sexagésimo, ma adj./s. Sixtieth. || *Sexagésimo primero, segundo,* sixty-first, sixty-second.
sex appeal m. Sex appeal.
sexcentésimo, ma adj./s. Six hundredth.
sexenio m. [Period of] six years.
sexo m. Sex. || — *Bello sexo,* fair sex. || *Sexo débil, fuerte,* gentle *o* weaker, stronger sex. || *Sin sexo,* sexless.
sexología f. Sexology.
sexólogo m. Sexologist.
sexta f. REL. Sext (hora). || MÚS. Sixth.
sextante m. MAR. Sextant. || Sextans (moneda romana).
sexteto m. MÚS. Sextet, sextette.
sextillo m. MÚS. Sextuplet (seisillo).
sextina f. Sestina (en poesía).
sexto, ta adj. Sixth. || The Sixth: *Alfonso VI* (sexto), Alphonse VI [the Sixth]. || — *En sexto lugar,* in sixth place, sixth. || *La sexta parte,* one sixth, a sixth.
— M. Sixth. || FAM. The sixth commandment (del Decálogo).
sextuplicar v. tr. To sextuple, to increase sixfold, to multiply by six.
— V. pr. To sextuple, to increase sixfold.
séxtuplo, pla adj. Sextuple, sixfold.
— M. Sextuple.
sexuado, da adj. Sexed.
sexual adj. Sexual (relaciones). || Sex: *vida sexual,* sex life; *órganos sexuales,* sex organs.
sexualidad f. Sexuality.
sexualmente adv. Sexually.
sexy adj. Sexy.
shah m. Shah (soberano persa).
shakespeariano, na adj. Shakespearian, Shakespearean.
shantung m. Shantung (tela).
sheriff m. Sheriff.
sherry m. Sherry (vino de Jerez).
shimmy m. Shimmy (danza). || AUT. Shimmy.
shock m. MED. Shock.
shorts m. pl. Shorts (pantalón corto).
shrapnel m. MIL. Shrapnel (granada).
shunt m. ELECTR. Shunt (derivación).
si m. MÚS. Ti, si, B.
si conj. If: *si viene mañana, avísame,* if he comes tomorrow, let me know; *si no lloviera saldríamos a pasear,* if it weren't raining we would go for a walk. || Whether, if: *dime si vendrás mañana,* tell me whether you are coming tomorrow; *no sé si iré o no,* I don't know whether I'll go or not. || When, if: *¿por qué lo aceptas ahora si ayer lo rechazaste?,* why do you accept now when yesterday you refused. || What if, supposing, suppose, I wonder if (con duda): *¿si me habrá mentido?,* what if he lied to me?, supposing he lied to me? || But: *¡si en esta habitación no hay nadie!,* but there's no one in this room!; *¡si te digo que no lo quiero!,* but I tell you I don't want it! || How much (cuánto): *¡sabes si lo estimo!,* you know how much I think of him! || — *Como si,* as if: *quiero a este niño como si fuera mi hijo,* I love this boy as if he were my own son. || *Como si nada,* as if it were nothing at all. || *Incluso si,* even if: *incluso si me amenazaran, no lo haría,* even if they threatened me I wouldn't do it. || *Por si* or *por si acaso,* just in case, in case. || FAM. *Que si esto que si lo otro,* this that and the other. || *Si acaso,* if [by chance *o* by any chance]. || *Si bien,* even though: *si bien no sabía nada,* even though he didn't know anything. || *¡Si fuera verdad!,* if only it were true. || *Si no,* if not, otherwise. || *¡Si será posible!,* it's not possible! || *¿Si será verdad?,* what if it's true? || *Si... si,* whether... or: *no supo decir si ocurrió de noche si de día,* he couldn't say whether it happened at night or during the day. || *Si supieran,* if [only] they knew.
sí pron. pers. refl. 3ª persona. Himself, herself, itself [pl. themselves]: *sólo piensa en sí,* he only thinks of himself (él), she only thinks of herself (ella); *la luz se apagó por sí misma,* the light went out by itself. || Yourself [pl. yourselves] (refiriéndose a usted): *Ud. sólo piensa en sí mismo,* you only think of yourself. || Oneself (impersonal): *hay cosas que uno tiene que hacer por sí mismo,* there are certain things one has to do by oneself; *hablar de sí,* to talk of *o* about oneself. || Each other (el uno con el otro): *hablaban entre sí,* they were talking to each other. || Themselves (cuando hay más de dos personas): *hablaban entre sí,* they were talking among themselves. || — *Decir para sí,* to say to o.s. || *De por sí, en sí,* in itself, per se: *un libro bueno de por sí,* a good book in itself. || *Entre sí,* to himself, to herself, to o.s., etc. (para sí): *dijo entre sí,* he said to himself. || *Estar en sí,* to be in one's right mind, to be quite rational. || *Estar fuera de sí,* to be beside o.s. (de furia o de alegría). || *Estar sobre sí,* to be on one's guard, to keep one's wits about one (estar alerta), to control o.s. (dominarse). || *Mirar para sí mismo,* to look after o.s. || *Poner a uno fuera de sí,* to make s.o. mad *o* wild (de furia), to make s.o. jump for joy (de alegría). || *Por sí y ante sí,* oneself, of one's own accord. || *Sí misma,* herself; itself; yourself. || *Sí mismo,* himself; itself; yourself. || *Volver en sí,* to come to, to come round, to regain consciousness.
sí adv. Yes: *¿vienes conmigo? — Sí,* are you coming with me? — Yes. || — *Claro que sí* or *sí por cierto,* of course; yes, of course; certainly. || *Contestar sí o no,* to answer yes or no. || *Creo que sí,* I think so. || *Decir que sí,* to say yes: *no decir ni que sí ni que no,* to say neither yes nor no. || *Ella no irá pero yo sí,* she won't go but I shall. || *Ella no lee pero yo sí,* she doesn't read but I do. || FAM. *¡Eso sí que no!,* certainly not! || *Hablar porque sí,* to talk for the sake of it. || *Pero sí,* but (después de una frase negativa): *no tiene hermanos pero sí cuatro hermanas,* he has no brothers, but he has four sisters. || *Porque sí,* because, because I [he, she, etc.] feel *o* felt like it (porque me da *o* me dio la gana), because that's the way it is (porque es así). || *Por sí o por no,* just in case. || *¡Pues sí!,* well, yes!, of course!, by all means! || *¡Que sí, hombre!,* yes, I tell you!, I tell you it is! || *Sí que,* really, certainly [for emphasis]: *ahora sí que nos vamos a reír,* we are really going to laugh now; *ése sí que sabe lo que quiere,* that fellow certainly knows what he wants. || *¡Sí lo es!,* it certainly is!, I'll say it is! || *Un día sí y otro no,* every other day, on alternate days. || *Yo sí vendré,* I'll certainly come.
— M. Yes: *un sí categórico,* a definite yes. || Consent, approval, agreement (consentimiento). || — *Dar el sí,* to say yes, to accept (para casarse), to agree, to give one's consent *o* approval, to say yes (asentir). || *Los síes y los noes,* v. SÍES. || *Sin que falte ni un sí ni un no,* in minute detail.
sial m. GEOL. Sial.
Siam n. pr. m. GEOGR. Siam.
siamés, esa adj./s. Siamese. || *Hermanos siameses,* Siamese twins.
sibarita adj. Sybaritic.
— M. y f. Sybarite.
sibarítico, ca adj. Sybaritic.
sibaritismo m. Sybaritism.
Siberia n. pr. f. GEOGR. Siberia.
siberiano, na adj./s. Siberian.
sibila f. Sibyl.
sibilante adj./s. f. Sibilant.
sibilino, na adj. Sibylline.
sic adv. Sic.
sicalíptico, ca adj. Suggestive, erotic (escabroso).
sicamor m. Judas tree (ciclamor).
sicario m. Hired assassin.
sicastenia f. Psychasthenia.
sicasténico, ca adj. Psychasthenic.
sicigia f. ASTR. Syzygy.
Sicilia n. pr. f. GEOGR. Sicily.
siciliano, na adj./s. Sicilian.
siclo m. Shekel.
sicoanálisis m. Psychoanalysis.
sicoanalista m. y f. Psychoanalyst.
sicoanalítico, ca adj. Psychoanalytic, psychoanalytical.
sicoanalizar v. tr. To psychoanalyze, to psychoanalyse.
sicodélico, ca adj. Psychedelic.
sicodrama m. Psychodrama.
sicofanta o **sicofante** m. (Ant.). Sycophant.
sicología f. Psychology.
sicológico, ca adj. Psychological.
sicólogo, ga m. y f. Psychologist.
sicometría f. Psychometry.
sicómoro o **sicomoro** m. BOT. Egyptian sycamore (árbol exótico). | Sycamore, maple (plátano falso).
siconeurosis f. MED. Psychoneurosis.
sicópata m. y f. MED. Psychopath.
sicopatía f. MED. Psychopathy.
sicopático, ca adj. MED. Psychopathic.
sicopatología f. MED. Psychopathology.
sicosis f. Psychosis.
sicoterapia f. MED. Psychotherapy.
sidecar m. Sidecar.

— OBSERV. In Spanish the plural of *sidecar* is *sidecares.*

sideral o **sidéreo, a** adj. ASTR. Sidereal, astral.
siderita f. MIN. Siderite.
siderosa f. MIN. Siderite.
siderosis f. MED. Siderosis.
siderurgia f. Iron and steel industry, siderurgy.
siderúrgico, ca adj. Iron and steel: *industria siderúrgica,* iron and steel industry; *fábrica siderúrgica,* iron and steel works.
sidra f. Cider (bebida).
siega f. Reaping (acción de segar). || Harvesting (acción de segar y recoger). | Harvest (temporada). || Harvest (mies segada).
siembra f. Sowing (acción de sembrar). || Sowing time (temporada). || Sowed *o* sown field (sembrado).
siempre adv. Always: *siempre tendrá dinero,* he will always have money. || All the time, always, forever

(sin descanso): *siempre habla*, he talks all the time, he is always talking. || Certainly (seguramente). || — *Como siempre*, as usual, as always. || *De siempre*, same old, usual: *es el cuento de siempre*, it is the same old story; usual: *a la hora de siempre*, at the usual time; old: *un amigo de siempre*, an old friend. || *Eso se viene haciendo desde siempre*, this has always been done. || *Estar siempre con*, to be always with (ir con). || FAM. *Está siempre con la misma monserga*, he's always singing the same tune. || *Lo de siempre*, the same old thing, the same old story. || *Para* or *por siempre*, for ever [U.S., forever]. || *Para* or *por siempre jamás*, for ever and ever [U.S., forever and ever]. || *Siempre pasa lo mismo*, it's always the same. || *Siempre que* or *siempre y cuando*, provided that, as long as (con que), every time that, whenever (cada vez que).

siempretieso m. Tumbler, roly-poly (juguete).

siempreviva f. BOT. Everlasting flower, immortelle.

sien f. Temple: *con las sienes entrecanas*, with greying temples.

sierpe f. Serpent (serpiente).

sierra f. TECN. Saw: *sierra abrazadera, de arco, de cinta, de contornar*, rip saw *o* pit saw, bow saw, band saw *o* belt saw *o* ribbon saw, compass saw *o* scroll saw. || Sierra, mountain range (cordillera). || Mountains, *pl.*, sierra: *pasar las vacaciones en la sierra*, to spend one's holidays in the mountains. || ZOOL. Sawfish (pez). || — *En forma de sierra*, sawlike, saw-shaped. || TECN. *Sierra para metales*, hacksaw.

siervo, va m. y f. Slave (esclavo). || Serf (en la Edad Media). || Servant: *siervo de Dios*, servant of God.

síes m. pl. Ayes, yeas: *contar los síes y los noes*, to count the ayes and the nays.

sieso m. ANAT. Rectum.

siesta f. Siesta, [afternoon] nap: *dormir* or *echar una siesta*, to have a siesta, to have one's afternoon nap. || Hottest part of the day (calor del mediodía). || *Siesta del carnero* or *del fraile*, nap before lunch.

siete adj. Seven.
— M. Seven: *el siete de corazones*, the seven of hearts. || Seventh: *el siete de abril*, the seventh of April. || FAM. L-shaped tear (rasgón). || TECN. Dog (de un banco de carpintero). || *Amer.* Anus (ano). || — FIG. y FAM. *Comer más que siete*, to eat like a horse. | *Hablar más que siete*, v. HABLAR. | *Saber más que siete*, to know a lot. | *Ser más embustero que siete*, to be a big liar. || *Son las siete*, it is seven o'clock.

sietemesino, na adj. Seven-month.
— M. Seven-month baby. || FIG. y FAM. Little squirt.

sieteñal adj. Seven-year-old.

sífilis f. MED. Syphilis.

sifilítico, ca adj./s. Syphilitic.

sifón m. Siphon (para trasvasar líquidos). || U-bend, trap (tubería). || Siphon (de agua gaseosa). || FAM. Soda water, soda: *échame un poco de sifón en el vaso*, pour a little soda water in my glass.

sigilar v. tr. To seal, to stamp (sellar). || To conceal (ocultar).

sigilo m. Seal, stamp (sello). || FIG. Secret (secreto). | Discretion (discreción). || Stealthiness (cautela). || — *Con gran sigilo*, with *o* in great secrecy. || *Sigilo sacramental*, secrecy of the confessional.

sigilografía f. Sigillography.

sigiloso, sa adj. Secret (secreto). || Discreet (discreto). || Stealthy (cauteloso).

sigla f. Abbreviation, initials, *pl.* (inicial): *O.N.U. es la sigla de la Organización de las Naciones Unidas*, U.N.O. is the abbreviation of the United Nations Organization.

siglo m. Century: *ser del siglo* X (*diez*), to date from *o* to be from *o* to belong to the 10 th [tenth] century. || FIG. World: *fuera del siglo*, apart from the world; *retirarse del siglo*, to withdraw from the world. | Ages, *pl.*: *hace un siglo que no le he visto*, I haven't seen him for ages. | Time, century: *al correr de los siglos*, with the passing of time *o* of the centuries. || — *Dentro de un siglo*, in a hundred years' time, in a century. || REL. *En el siglo*, in the world: *Santa Teresa de Jesús, en el siglo Teresa de Cepeda y Ahumada*, Saint Theresa of Avila, in the world Theresa de Cepeda y Ahumada. || *Por los siglos de los siglos*, for ever and ever [U.S., forever and ever] (para siempre), world without end (en oraciones). || *Siglo de las luces*, Age of Enlightenment. || *Siglo de Oro*, Golden Age.

sigma f. Sigma (letra griega).

sigmoideo, a adj. Sigmoid.

signar v. tr. To sign (firmar). || To mark, to put a seal on (sellar). || To make the sign of the cross over, to sign (persignar).
— V. pr. To cross o.s. (persignarse).
— OBSERV. In Spanish the usual word for *to sign* (a letter, etc.) is *firmar*.

signatario, ria adj./s. Signatory (firmante).

signatura f. Stamp, mark, sign (señal). || Signature (firma). || IMPR. y MÚS. Signature. || Catalogue number (para clasificar un libro).

significación f. Meaning (significado). || FIG. Significance (importancia): *un hecho de gran significación*, a fact of great significance.

significado, da adj. Signified, indicated (señalado). || FIG. Well-known (conocido).
— M. Meaning (sentido): *no conozco el significado de esta palabra*, I don't know the meaning of this word. || Significance (de un acontecimiento).

significante adj. Significant.

significar v. tr. To mean, to signify: *en latín "magister" significa maestro*, in Latin "magister" means teacher. || To indicate, to make known: *significar a uno sus intenciones*, to make one's intentions known to s.o. || To express, to make known (hacer presente). || FIG. To mean: *esto significa mucho para mí*, this means a lot to me. | To be important: *él significa mucho en el ayuntamiento*, he is very important at the town hall.
— V. pr. To stand out (destacar). || To distinguish o.s. (distinguirse). || To declare o.s., to come out as (declararse): *se significó como monárquico*, he declared himself a monarchist.

significativo, va adj. Significative (*de*, of) [indicativo]. || FIG. Significant (importante): *es significativo que*, it is significant that. | Meaningful, meaning (mirada, etc.).

signo m. Sign: *las golondrinas son el signo de la llegada de la primavera*, swallows are the sign of the arrival of spring. || IMPR. y MÚS. Sign. || Mark: *signo de puntuación, de admiración, de interrogación*, punctuation, exclamation, question mark. || Symbol: *signo fonético*, phonetic symbol. || ASTR. Sign (del zodiaco). || MAT. Sign: *signo igual, más, menos*, equals, plus, minus sign. || Tendency (tendencia): *signo político*, political tendency. || Flourish, mark (de los notarios). || Fate, destiny (destino). || — *Bajo el signo de*, under the sign of. || *Signo de la cruz*, sign of the Cross. || *Signos monetarios*, monetary units. || *Signos Morse*, Morse code, *sing*.

siguemepollo m. Ribbon [on a dress] (en el vestido). || Choker, neckband (collar).

siguiente adj. Following, after, next: *el año siguiente*, the following year, the year after. || Following: *nos ayudaron las personas siguientes*, the following people helped us. || — *Anunció lo siguiente*, he announced the following. || *¡Que pase el siguiente!*, next please!

sil m. Yellow ochre (ocre).

sílaba f. Syllable: *sílaba abierta, aguda* or *tónica*, *cerrada* or *trabada*, open, accentuated *o* stressed *o* accented, closed syllable.

silabar v. intr. To syllable.

silabear v. tr. e intr. To syllable, to pronounce syllable by syllable (pronunciar). || To syllabicate, to divide into syllables.

silabario m. Spelling book, syllabary.

silabeo m. Syllabication, division into syllables.

silábico, ca adj. Syllabic.

silba f. Hissing, catcalls, *pl.* (rechifla). || *Dar una silba*, to hiss, to whistle.

silbador, ra adj. Whistling (que silba). || Hissing, catcalling, jeering (que desaprueba).

silbante adj. Whistling (que silba). || Sibilant (sibilante). || MED. Sibilant, wheezing. || FIG. Catcalling, jeering, hissing (que desaprueba).

silbar v. tr. To whistle (una melodía). || To whistle to: *silbar al perro*, to whistle to the dog. || To blow (un pito). || FIG. To hiss, to boo (en el teatro, etc.).
— V. intr. To whistle. || To whistle (el viento). || To whine, to whistle, to whizz (una bala). || To whizz (una flecha). || MED. To wheeze. || FIG. To hiss, to catcall, to boo (en el teatro, etc.). | To ring, to buzz (los oídos).

silbatina f. *Amer.* Catcalls, *pl.*, hissing (silba).

silbato m. Whistle (pito).

silbido m. Whistle, whistling. || Hissing, catcalls, *pl.* (abucheo). || Whistle (del viento). || Whizz (de bala, flecha). || MED. Wheeze. || *Dar un silbido*, to whistle.

silbo m. Whistle, whistling. || FIG. y FAM. *Estar más flaco que un silbo*, to be as skinny as a rake.

silbón m. ZOOL. Widgeon (ave).

silenciador m. TECN. Silencer (de arma). || AUT. Silencer, muffler.

silenciar v. tr. To muffle, to silence (ahogar un ruido). || To hush up (ocultar un acontecimiento). || To keep quiet about, to make no mention of (no hablar de un acontecimiento). || To silence (callar).

silencio m. Silence: *silencio sepulcral*, deathly silence; *sufrir en silencio*, to suffer in silence. || MÚS. Rest (pausa). || — *En silencio*, in silence. || FIG. *Entregar al silencio*, to cast into oblivion. || *Guardar silencio*, to keep silent *o* quiet. || *Imponer silencio a uno*, to keep s.o. quiet, to order s.o. to be silent, to call for silence. || *Pasar algo en silencio*, to keep quiet about sth., to make no mention of sth. || *Reducir al silencio*, to silence. || *Romper el silencio*, to break the silence. || MÚS. *Silencio de corchea*, quaver rest.

silencioso, sa adj. Quiet: *persona, casa silenciosa*, quiet person, house. || Silent, quiet, noiseless (máquina).
— M. Silencer, muffler (en un automóvil).

silepsis f. GRAM. Syllepsis.

sílex m. Silex, flint (pedernal).

sílfide f. Sylph.

silfo m. MIT. Sylph.

silicato m. QUÍM. Silicate.

sílice f. QUÍM. Silica (roca).

silíceo, a adj. Siliceous.

silícico, ca adj. QUÍM. Silicic.

silicio m. QUÍM. Silicon.

silicona f. QUÍM. Silicone.
silicosis f. MED. Silicosis.
silo m. Silo (almacén de grano).
silogismo m. Syllogism.
silogístico, ca adj. Syllogistic, syllogistical.
silogizar v. intr. To syllogize.
silueta f. Silhouette. || Figure (figura). || Outline (contorno). || ARTES. Outline sketch, silhouette.
siluetear v. tr. To silhouette.
siluriano, na o **silúrico, ca** adj./s.m. GEOL. Silurian.
siluro m. Catfish (pez). || MAR. Self-propelling torpedo.
silva f. Miscellany (colección).
silvanita f. MIN. Sylvanite.
silvano m. Sylvan, silvan (divinidad de la selva).
silvático, ca adj. V. SELVÁTICO.
silvestre adj. Wild: *plantas silvestres*, wild plants; *fruta silvestre*, wild fruit. || FIG. Rustic (rústico).
silvicultor m. Forestry expert, silviculturist.
silvicultura f. Sylviculture, silviculture, forestry.
silvoso, sa adj. Forested, wooded.
silla f. Chair: *sentarse en una silla*, to sit down in a chair. || Saddle (de jinete). || REL. See (sede). || FIG. Dignity (dignidad). || — *Caballo de silla*, saddle horse. || *Juez de silla*, umpire (tenis). || FIG. y FAM. *Pegársele a uno la silla*, to overstay one's welcome. || *Silla arzobispal*, archbishopric, archdiocese, archsee. || *Silla curul*, curule. || *Silla de coro*, choir stall. || *Silla de la reina*, chair (entre niños). || *Silla de manos*, sedan chair. || *Silla de montar*, riding saddle. || *Silla de posta*, post chaise. || *Silla de rejilla*, cane chair. || *Silla de ring*, ringside seat. || *Silla de ruedas*, wheelchair. || *Silla de tijera* or *plegable*, folding chair. || *Silla eléctrica*, electric chair. || REL. *Silla episcopal* or *obispal*, see. || *Silla gestatoria*, gestatorial chair (del papa). || *Silla giratoria*, swivel chair. || *Silla inglesa*, English saddle, hunting saddle. || *Silla poltrona*, easy chair.
sillar m. Ashlar (piedra). || Horse's back (lomo).
sillería f. Chairs, *pl.*, set of chairs (asientos). || Seating, seats, *pl.* (en los auditorios, etc.). || Choir stalls, *pl.* (del coro). || Chairmaker's workshop, chair factory (taller). || ARQ. Ashlar.
sillero, ra m. y f. Chairmaker (fabricante de sillas). || Chair seller (vendedor). || Chair mender (reparador). || Saddler (que hace sillas de montar).
silleta f. Small chair (silla).
silletazo m. Blow with a chair.
sillín m. Saddle, seat (de bicicleta o motocicleta). || Light riding saddle (silla de montar).
sillón m. Armchair (butaca). || Sidesaddle (de montar). || — *Sillón de orejas*, wing chair. || *Sillón de ring*, ringside seat. || *Sillón de ruedas*, wheelchair (para un inválido). || *Sillón giratorio*, swivel chair.
sima f. Chasm, abyss. || FIG. Depths, *pl.* (abismo).
— OBSERV. Do not confuse *sima*, chasm, with *cima*, top.
simbiosis f. BIOL. Symbiosis.
simbiótico, ca adj. BIOL. Symbiotic.
simbólico, ca adj. Symbolic, symbolical.
simbolismo m. Symbolism.
simbolización f. Symbolization.
simbolizar v. tr. To symbolize.
símbolo m. Symbol: *el símbolo del hierro es Fe*, Fe is the symbol for iron. || *El símbolo de los apóstoles* or *de la Fe*, the Apostles' Creed, the Creed.
simetría f. Symmetry.
simétrico, ca adj. Symmetrical, symmetric.
símico, ca adj. ZOOL. Simian, apish, apelike.
simiente f. AGR. Seed (semilla).
simiesco, ca adj. Simian, apish, apelike.
símil adj. Similar, alike.
— M. Similarity, resemblance (semejanza). || Comparison: *hacer un símil entre dos países*, to make a comparison between two countries. || Simile (figura retórica).
similar adj. Similar.
similicuero m. Imitation leather.
similigrabado m. Process-engraving, half-tone engraving.
similitud f. Similitude, similarity.
similitudinario, ria adj. (P.us.). Similar.
simio m. ZOOL. Simian (mono).
simón m. Horse-drawn *o* hackney carriage.
simonía f. Simony.
simoniaco, ca o **simoniático, ca** adj. Simoniac.
— M. y f. Simoniac, simonist.
simpa f. *Amer.* Plait (trenza de pelo).
simpatía f. Liking: *le tengo mucha simpatía*, I have a great liking for him; *le he cogido simpatía*, I have taken a liking to him. || Affection, fondness (cariño). || Friendship (amistad). || Friendliness, congeniality (amabilidad). || Charm (encanto). || Friend (amigo): *no tiene simpatías en la oficina*, he has no friends in the office. || Sympathy, solidarity (solidaridad). || MED. Sympathy. || — *Dolores de simpatía*, sympathy pains. || *No me tiene simpatía*, he doesn't like me. || *Simpatías y antipatías*, likes and dislikes. || *Una persona que tiene mucha simpatía*, a very likeable *o* pleasant *o* nice person.
— OBSERV. One should not confuse *simpatía* with *sympathy* (compasión).
simpático, ca adj. Nice, likeable (amable): *es muy simpático*, he is very nice. || Pleasant (agradable). || Kind, nice, friendly: *fue muy simpático conmigo*, he was very kind to me. || Charming (encantador). || — *Él no me ha caído simpático*, I didn't take to him, I didn't like him much. || *Intentar hacerse simpático*, to try to ingratiate o.s. || *Me es simpática esta chica*, I like that girl. || *Tinta simpática*, invisible ink, sympathetic ink.
— M. ANAT. *Gran simpático*, sympathetic nervous system.
simpatizante adj. Sympathizing.
— M. y f. Sympathizer.
simpatizar v. intr. To get on: *no sé si van a simpatizar*, I don't know if they are going to get on. || To hit it off: *simpatizaron en seguida*, they hit it off at once. || To take to, to hit it off: *simpaticé con ella en seguida*, I took to her at once, we hit it off at once. || To sympathize (*con algo*, with sth.).
simple adj. Simple (no compuesto, sin adorno). || Single (sencillo, único): *una simple capa de pintura*, a single coat of paint. || Simple, easy (fácil). || Just one, one single (que basta por sí solo): *con una simple palabra*, with just one word. || GRAM. Simple: *tiempo simple*, simple tense. || Simple, plain, unpretentious (no afectado). || Simple, guileless (incauto). || Simple, half-witted (tonto). || Mere (mero): *esto es un simple trámite*, this is a mere formality. || BOT. Single. || — QUÍM. *Cuerpo simple*, simple body. || *Es un simple carpintero*, he is just a carpenter *o* a simple carpenter. || *Por simple descuido*, out of sheer *o* through sheer carelessness, through pure carelessness.
— M. Simpleton, half-wit (bobo). || Singles, *inv.* (en tenis): *un simple caballeros*, a men's singles. || MED. Simple [planta medicinal].
simplemente adv. Simply. || *Pura y simplemente*, purely and simply.
simpleza f. Simpleness, simplicity (cualidad de simple). || Naïvety (ingenuidad). || Stupid thing (tontería). || Trifle (cosa de poco valor). || — Pl. Nonsense, *sing.* (tonterías).
simplicidad f. Simplicity, simpleness (de una cosa). || Naïvety (candor).
simplificable adj. Simplifiable.
simplificación f. Simplification.
simplificador, ra adj. Simplifying.
— M. y f. Simplifier.
simplificar v. tr. To simplify.
simplismo m. Oversimplification, simplism.
simplista adj. Simplistic, over-simple.
simplón, ona adj. Gullible, simple, naïve.
— M. y f. Simpleton, half-wit.
simposio o **simpósium** m. Symposium.
simulación f. Simulation. || Sham (fingimiento). || Malingering (fingiendo enfermedad).
simulacro m. Simulacrum (representación). || Mockery (farsa): *el pleito no fue más que un simulacro*, the trial was no more than a mockery. || Idol, image (imagen). || Show, sham, pretence [U.S., pretense] (fingimiento). || Semblance (apariencia). || — *Hacer el simulacro de*, to pretend to. || *Un simulacro de ataque*, a simulated *o* sham attack.
simulado, da adj. Feigned: *tristeza simulada*, feigned sorrow. || Simulated: *miedo simulado*, simulated fear; *vuelo simulado*, simulated flight; *fue un accidente simulado*, it was a simulated accident.
simulador, ra adj. Simulative.
— M. y f. Shammer, pretender. || Malingerer (que finge estar enfermo). || *Es un hábil simulador*, he is a good shammer *o* pretender.
simular v. tr. To feign: *simula sentimientos que no tiene*, he feigns feelings he doesn't have. || To simulate, to feign, to pretend: *simula que tiene miedo*, he simulates *o* feigns fear, he pretends to be afraid. || To pretend: *simula que trabaja*, he pretends that he is working. || To sham, to rig: *simularon el accidente*, they rigged the accident. || *Pasarse la vida simulando*, to spend one's life pretending *o* in pretence, to live a life of pretence.
— V. intr. To malinger, to feign illness.
simultáneamente adv. Simultaneously.
simultanear v. tr. To do simultaneously *o* at the same time (dos cosas). || To combine: *simultanea el trabajo con la diversión*, he combines work and pleasure. || — *Simultanea la carrera de derecho y la de ciencias*, he is studying law and science at the same time. || *Simultanear la risa con las lágrimas*, to smile through one's tears.
simultaneidad f. Simultaneity.
simultáneo, a adj. Simultaneous.
simún m. Simoom, simoon (viento).
sin prep. Without: *sin él no podría hacer nada*, without him I couldn't do anything; *sin hacerlo tú*, without your doing it. || Without, with no: *me quedé sin carbón*, I was left with no coal. || Not counting (sin contar). || — *Dejar algo sin terminar*, to leave sth. unfinished. || *Estar sin* (*con un infinitivo*), not to have been: *el cuarto está sin hacer*, the room has not been made. || *Estoy sin desayunar*, I haven't had any breakfast. || *Hijas sin casar*, unmarried daughters. || *Quedarse sin cenar*, to go without dinner. || *Quedarse sin provisiones*, to run out of provisions. || FIG. *Sigue sin levantar cabeza*, he hasn't got his head above water yet. || *Sin ambages ni rodeos*, without any beating about the bush. || FAM. *Sin blanca* or *cinco* or *gorda*

or *linda* or *un céntimo* or *un cuarto* or *una perra*, stony *o* flat broke. || *Sin cesar*, v. CESAR. || *Sin compromiso*, without obligation (sin obligación), unattached (sin obligaciones matrimoniales). || FAM. *Sin decir esta boca es mía* or *ni pío*, without saying a word, without opening one's mouth. | *Sin decir oxte ni moxte*, without a word, without warning. || *Sin demora* or *dilación*, without delay. || *Sin Dios*, Godless. || *Sin embargo*, nevertheless, however. || *Sin entrada*, no down payment. || *Sin escala*, non-stop: *vuelo sin escala*, non-stop flight. || *Sin eso* or *sin lo cual*, otherwise. || *Sin falta*, without fail. || *Sin hogar*, homeless. || *Sin inconvenientes*, without inconvenience. || FIG. *Sin levantar cabeza*, without looking up *o* stopping (sin dejar de trabajar). || *Sin más ni más*, without more ado, without further ado. || *Sin pies ni cabeza*, ridiculous, absurd, nonsensical, without rhyme or reason. || *Sin que*, without: *los niños se comieron el pastel sin que los viera*, the children ate the cake without my seeing them. || JUR. *Sin recurso*, unappealable. || *Sin sellar*, unsealed.

— OBSERV. En muchos casos la preposición *sin* seguida por un sustantivo se puede traducir al inglés sea mediante el sufijo *-less*, cuando se trata de una locución adjetival (*sin piedad*, merciless; *sin casa*, homeless; *sin vergüenza*, shameless), sea con el sufijo *-lessly*, en los casos en que corresponde a una locución adverbial (*castigar sin compasión*, to punish mercilessly).

— Cuando *sin* va seguido por un infinitivo se puede traducir al inglés con el prefijo *un-* colocado delante del participio pasivo del verbo (*trabajo sin acabar*, unfinished work).

sinagoga f. Synagogue.

Sinaí n. pr. m. GEOGR. Sinai.

sinalagmático, ca adj. JUR. Synallagmatic.

sinalefa f. GRAM. Synaloepha [U.S., synalepha].

sinántropo m. Sinanthropus, Peking man.

sinapismo m. MED. Mustard plaster. || FIG. y FAM. Bore, drag, nuisance (persona o cosa pesada).

sinartrosis f. ANAT. Synarthrosis.

sincerar v. tr. To exonerate.

— V. pr. To exonerate o.s., to vindicate o.s. (justificarse). || To open one's heart: *sincerarse con sus amigos*, to open one's heart to one's friends. || To tell the truth, to come out into the open (decir la verdad).

sinceridad f. Sincerity: *decir algo con toda sinceridad*, to say sth. in all sincerity.

sincero, ra adj. Sincere.

sinclinal adj. GEOL. Synclinal.

— M. GEOL. Syncline.

síncopa f. MÚS. Syncopation, syncope. || GRAM. Syncope.

sincopar v. tr. GRAM. y MÚS. To syncopate. || FIG. To abridge (abreviar).

síncope m. MED. y GRAM. Syncope.

sincrético adj. Syncretic.

sincretismo m. Syncretism.

sincretista m. y f. Syncretist.

sincrociclotrón m. FÍS. Synchrocyclotron.

sincrónico, ca adj. Synchronous, synchronic, synchronistic. || Simultaneous: *dos hechos sincrónicos*, two simultaneous events. || Synchronic (linguística).

sincronismo m. Synchronism. || Simultaneity.

sincronización f. Synchronization.

sincronizado, da adj. Synchronized. || AUT. Syncromesh.

sincronizador m. CINEM. Synchronizer. || AUT. Synchromesh.

sincronizar v. tr. To synchronize.

— V. intr. RAD. To tune in (*con*, to).

síncrono, na adj. Synchronous.

sincrotrón m. FÍS. Synchrotron.

sindáctilo, la adj./s.m. ZOOL. Syndactyl, syndactyle.

sindéresis f. Good judgment.

sindicable adj. Eligible to join a trade union.

sindicado, da adj. Who belongs to a trade union.

— M. Syndicate, body of trustees (junta de síndicos).

sindical adj. Union, trade-union [U.S., labor union]: *problemas sindicales*, trade-union problems. || Syndical.

sindicalismo f. Trade unionism, unionism (sistema). || Syndicalism (teoría política).

sindicalista adj. Union, trade-union [U.S., labor union]. || Syndicalist (partidario del sindicalismo).

— M. y f. Trade unionist, unionist. || Syndicalist.

sindicar v. tr. To unionize.

— V. pr. To join a union (afiliarse a un sindicato). || To form a trade union [U.S., a labor union] (formar un sindicato).

sindicato m. Trade union [U.S., labor union] (de trabajadores). || Syndicate (grupo).

síndico m. Syndic, trustee.

sindineritis f. FAM. *Tener sindineritis*, to be broke.

síndrome m. MED. Syndrome.

sinécdoque f. Synecdoche.

sinecura f. Sinecure.

sine die loc. adv. Sine die (sin fijar fecha ni día).

sine qua non loc. adv. *Condición sine qua non*, prerequisite, essential condition.

sinéresis f. GRAM. Synaeresis, syneresis.

sinergia f. Synergy.

sinérgico, ca adj. Synergic.

sinestesia f. Synaesthesia [U.S., synesthesia].

sinfín m. No end, an endless number. || *Citó un sinfín de nombres*, he quoted countless names *o* an endless number of names *o* no end of names.

sinfinidad f. FAM. Multitude, endless number. || *Una sinfinidad de*, countless, no end of.

sínfisis f. ANAT. Symphysis.

sinfonía f. Symphony: *sinfonía incompleta*, unfinished symphony.

sinfónico, ca adj. Symphonic.

— F. Symphony orchestra.

sinfonista m. Symphonist.

singladura f. MAR. Day's run (recorrido). | Day (día).

singlar v. intr. MAR. To steer, to navigate.

single m. Singles, *inv.* (tenis). || Single (coche cama).

singleton m. Singleton (semifallo en el bridge).

singracia adj. Dull, insipid (soso).

— F. Dullness.

singular adj. Singular, unique (único). || Outstanding (excepcional). || FIG. Odd, peculiar, singular: *una persona singular*, a peculiar person. || *Combate singular*, single combat.

— M. GRAM. Singular: *en singular*, in the singular. || FIG. *En singular*, in particular.

singularidad f. Singularity.

singularizar v. tr. To single out, to distinguish, to singularize (distinguir). || GRAM. To use in the singular.

— V. intr. To speak in the singular.

— V. pr. To stand out, to distinguish o.s. (distinguirse).

sinhueso f. FAM. Tongue (lengua). || FAM. *Darle a la sinhueso*, to chin-wag.

siniestra f. Left hand (mano izquierda).

siniestrado, da adj. Damaged. || HERÁLD. Sinister.

— M. y f. Victim [of an accident, etc.].

siniestro, tra adj. Left: *mano siniestra*, left hand. || Left, left-hand: *lado siniestro*, left-hand side. || FIG. Sinister, ominous: *mirada siniestra*, sinister look. | Fateful, disastrous (funesto). | Evil (malo). || *A diestro y siniestro*, v. DIESTRO.

— M. Catastrophe, disaster (catástrofe). || Accident (accidente). || Fire (incendio).

sinnúmero m. Endless number, no end. || *Hubo un sinnúmero de víctimas*, there were countless victims *o* no end of victims.

sino m. Fate, destiny (hado, destino).

sino conj. But (para contraponer un concepto afirmativo a uno negativo): *no era él sino su hermano*, it wasn't him but his brother. || But, except: *nadie ha venido sino su hermano*, no one has come but your brother. || — *No parece sino que es idiota*, he looks a complete idiot. || *No... sino*, v. NO. || *No sólo... sino*, not only... but. || *No sólo... sino que* or *sino que también*, not only... but [also]: *no sólo pide, sino que exige*, he not only asks but demands. || *Sino que*, but (pero): *no lo leí sino que lo hojeé*, I didn't read it but flicked through it; except that, but (salvo): *fue todo muy bien sino que llovió un poco*, everything went well except that it rained a little.

— OBSERV. A veces la expresión *sino que* no se traduce al inglés (*no basta que usted lo diga, sino que quiero verlo*, it isn't enough that you say so, I want to see it).

sinodal adj. Synodal.

sinódico, ca adj. Synodical, synodal. || ASTR. Synodic, synodical.

sínodo m. Synod (junta). || *El Santo Sínodo*, the Holy Synod (en Rusia).

sinojaponés, esa adj. Sino-Japanese.

sinología f. Sinology.

sinólogo, ga m. y f. Sinologist, sinologue.

sinonimia f. Synonymity, synonymy.

sinonímico, ca adj. Synonymic.

sinónimo, ma adj. Synonymous.

— M. Synonym.

sinopsis f. inv. Synopsis. || — Pl. Synopses.

sinóptico, ca adj. Synoptic, synoptical. || *Cuadro sinóptico*, chart, diagram.

sinovia f. ANAT. Synovia.

sinovial adj. ANAT. Synovial. || *Cápsula sinovial*, synovial capsule.

sinovitis f. MED. Synovitis.

sinrazón f. Wrong, injustice: *las sinrazones de la política*, the injustices of politics. || Absurdity, foolish thing, nonsense (disparate).

sinsabor m. Displeasure, unpleasantness (disgusto). || FIG. Trouble, worry: *este trabajo me ha causado muchos sinsabores*, this job has brought me a lot of troubles. | Sorrow (pena).

sinsombrerismo m. FAM. Hatlessness, going hatless, not wearing a hat.

sinsonte m. Mockingbird.

sinsustancia m. y f. FAM. Nonentity.

sintáctico, ca adj. GRAM. Syntactic, syntactical.

sintaxis f. GRAM. Syntax.

sinterización f. TECN. Sintering.

sinterizar v. tr. TECN. To sinter.

síntesis f. Synthesis.

sintético, ca adj. Synthetic: *caucho sintético*, synthetic rubber.

sintetizar v. tr. To synthesize, to synthetize.

sintoísmo m. Shintoism, shinto (religión).

sintoísta m. y f. Shintoist.

síntoma m. Symptom.

sintomático, ca adj. Symptomatic. || FIG. Significant (que revela algo).
sintomatología f. MED. Symptomatology.
sintonía f. ELECTR. Syntony. || RAD. Signature tune (de una emisión). || FIG. Harmony. || RAD. *Bobina de sintonía*, tuning coil.
sintónico, ca adj. Syntonic.
sintonismo m. Syntony.
sintonización f. Syntonization, tuning. || *Mando de sintonización*, tuner, tuning knob.
sintonizador m. RAD. Tuner, tuning knob.
sintonizar v. tr. To syntonize, to tune. || RAD. To tune in. || *Sintonizan ustedes con Radio San Sebastián*, you are tuned to *o* tuned in to Radio San Sebastián.
sinuosidad f. Sinuosity. || Bend, curve (curva). || FIG. Tortuosity (rodeo): *las sinuosidades de la diplomacia*, the tortuosities of diplomacy.
sinuoso, sa adj. Sinuous, winding: *una carretera sinuosa*, a winding road. || Wavy: *línea sinuosa*, wavy line. || FIG. Devious (retorcido).
sinusitis f. MED. Sinusitis.
sinusoidal adj. MAT. Sinusoidal.
sinusoide f. MAT. Sine curve, sinusoid.
sinvergonzón, ona adj./s. V. SINVERGÜENZA.
sinvergüencería f. Shamelessness (desvergüenza). || Dirty trick (fam.), rotten thing to do (fam.) [acto].
sinvergüenza adj. Brazen, shameless (granuja). || Cheeky (descarado).
— M. y f. Scoundrel (granuja). || Rotter (canalla). || Brat (gamberro). || Cheeky devil (descarado). || — *¡Qué sinvergüenza eres!*, you've got a nerve! || FAM. *Un tío sinvergüenza*, a real rotter.
sinvergüenzada f. *Amer.* FAM. Dirty trick, rotten thing to do.
sinvivir m. Unbearable situation.
Sión n. pr. Zion.
sionismo m. Zionism.
sionista adj./s. Zionist.
siquíatra o **siquiatra** m. MED. Psychiatrist.
siquiatría f. MED. Psychiatry.
síquico, ca adj. Psychic.
siquiera conj. Even if *o* though (aunque): *préstame el coche, siquiera sea por unos días*, lend me the car, even if only for a few days. || *Siquiera... siquiera*, whether... or whether: *siquiera venga, siquiera no venga*, whether he comes or whether he doesn't.
— Adv. At least (por lo menos): *dame siquiera las gracias*, you might at least thank me; *déjame siquiera acabar*, at least let me finish. || Just: *¡si ganáramos siquiera para comer!*, if we just earned enough to eat! || Even, just: *si pudiera irme siquiera una semana*, if I could just go for a week, if I could go even for a week. || Even: *sin enterarse siquiera de lo que pasaba*, without even realizing what was happening. || — *Ni siquiera* or *no... siquiera*, not even: *no tiene siquiera zapatos*, he hasn't even got any shoes; *ni siquiera me lo dijo*, he didn't even tell me. || *¿Y te ayudó?* — *Ni siquiera*, and did he help you? — Not at all *o* — By no means.
siquismo m. Psychism.
Siracusa n. pr. GEOGR. Syracuse.
siracusano, na adj./s. Syracusan.
sirena f. MIT. Siren (ninfa). || Mermaid (de los cuentos de hadas). || Siren (señal acústica).
sirénido o **sirenio** m. ZOOL. Sirenian. || — Pl. Sirenia.
sirga f. MAR. Towrope. || *Camino de sirga*, towpath.
sirgar v. tr. MAR. To tow.
Siria n. pr. f. GEOGR. Syria.
siriaco, ca adj. Syrian.
— M. Syriac (idioma antiguo).
sirimbo, ba adj. *Amer.* Stupid, silly.
— F. *Amer.* Fainting fit.
sirimiri m. Drizzle (llovizna).
siringa f. *Amer.* Rubber tree. || MÚS. Syrinx, flute.
siringe m. Syrinx (de las aves).
sirio, ria adj./s. Syrian.
siroco m. Sirocco (viento).
sirope m. *Amer.* Syrup (jarabe).
sirvienta f. Maid, servant (criada).
sirviente adj. Serving.
— M. Servant (criado). || Waiter (camarero). || MIL. Gunner (de artillería).
sisa f. FAM. Pilfering, petty theft (hurto). || Dart (en un vestido). || Armhole (de la manga).
sisador, ra adj. Pilfering.
— M. y f. Pilferer, petty thief.
sisal m. BOT. Sisal (pita).
sisar v. tr. To pilfer, to filch (en las compras). || To take in, to dart (un vestido).
— V. intr. To pilfer.
sisear v. tr. e intr. To hiss.
siseo m. Hiss, hissing.
sísmico, ca adj. Seismic.
sismo m. Earthquake, seism (seísmo).
sismógrafo m. Seismograph.
sismograma m. Seismogram.
sismología f. Seismology.
sismológico, ca adj. Seismologic, seismological.
sismómetro m. Seismometer.
sisón m. ZOOL. Little bustard.
sisón, ona adj. FAM. Pilfering, filching.
— M. y f. FAM. Pilferer, petty thief.
sistema m. System: *sistema político*, political system. || Method (método). || — *Por sistema*, as a rule. || *Proceder con sistema*, to proceed systematically. || *Sistema cegesimal*, centimetre-gram-second system. || *Sistema cristalino* or *cristalográfico*, crystalline system. || *Sistema de altavoces*, public address system. || *Sistema de numeración*, number system. || *Sistema decimal*, decimal system. || MAT. *Sistema de ecuaciones*, simultaneous equations, *pl.* || *Sistema métrico*, metric system. || *Sistema montañoso*, mountain chain. || *Sistema nervioso*, nervous system. || *Sistema planetario*, planetary system. || *Sistema solar*, solar system. || *Sistema tributario*, tax system.
sistemar v. tr. *Amer.* To systematize.
sistemáticamente adv. Systematically.
sistemático, ca adj. Systematic.
— F. Systematics.
sistematización f. Systematization.
sistematizar v. tr. To systematize, to systemize.
sístole f. ANAT. Systole.
sitiado, da adj. Besieged.
— M. y f. Besieged.
sitiador, ra adj. Besieging.
M. y f. Besieger
sitial m. Seat of honour. || Seat (asiento).
sitiar v. tr. MIL. To besiege, to lay siege to: *sitiar una ciudad*, to lay siege to a town, to besiege a town. || FIG. To surround, to hem in: *sitiaron al ladrón*, they surrounded the thief.
sitio m. Place: *vete a tu sitio*, go to your place. || Spot, place: *es un sitio precioso*, it's a lovely spot. || Space, room (espacio): *ocupar mucho sitio*, to take up *o* to occupy a lot of space; *hay sitio de sobra*, there's plenty of room. || MIL. Siege (cerco). || Location, site (para un edificio). || *Amer.* Lot, building site (solar para edificar). | Small farm (granja pequeña). || — FIG. y FAM. *Cada cosa en su sitio y un sitio para cada cosa*, there is a time and a place for everything. || *Cambiar de sitio*, to move. || *Cambiar de sitio con*, to change places with. || *Cualquier sitio*, anywhere. || FIG. y FAM. *Dejar a alguien en el sitio*, to kill s.o. on the spot. || *Dejar or ceder el sitio*, to give up one's place. || *En cualquier sitio*, anywhere. || MIL. *En estado de sitio*, in a state of siege. || *En todos los sitios*, everywhere. || *Hacer sitio*, to make room. || MIL. *Levantar el sitio*, to raise the siege. || FIG. y FAM. *Ponerle a alguien en su sitio*, to put s.o. in his place. || MIL. *Poner sitio a*, to lay siege to, to besiege. || FIG. *Quedarse en el sitio*, to die [on the spot]. || *Real sitio*, royal residence.
sitios adj. pl. JUR. *Bienes sitios*, real estate, *sing.*
sito, ta adj. Located (colocado). || Situated: *una casa sita en Madrid*, a house situated in Madrid. || JUR. *Bienes sitos*, real estate, *sing.*
situación f. Situation: *una situación peligrosa*, a dangerous situation. || Location, site (sitio): *la situación de una casa*, the location of a house. || Condition, state: *no está en situación de hacer un viaje*, he is in no condition to travel. || Position, standing (posición social). || — *Estar en situación de*, to be in a position to: *está en situación de conseguir un puesto en el ministerio*, he is in a position to get a job in the ministry. || *Amer. Precios de situación*, reduced prices. || *Ser dueño de la situación*, to be in control of the situation, to have the situation under control. || *Situación acomodada*, sound financial position. || *Situación activa*, active service. || *Situación social*, social position.
situado, da adj. Situated. || FIG. *Estar bien situado*, to be in a comfortable position, to be comfortably off.
situar v. tr. To place, to put (poner). || To situate, to site, to locate: *una ciudad situada a orillas del mar*, a town located on the coast. || COM. To place, to invest (invertir). | To earmark (asignar fondos).
— V. pr. To be successful, to do well for o.s., to make o.s. a good position (alcanzar una buena posición). || To be situated (estar). || To take [a stand], to adopt [a position] (adoptar una posición).
siútico, ca adj. *Amer.* FAM. Terribly posh, affected (cursi).
siutiquería o **siutiquez** f. FAM. *Amer.* Pretentiousness, poshness, affectedness (cursilería).
siux adj./s. Sioux (indio norteamericano).
sixtino, na adj. Sistine. || *La Capilla Sixtina*, the Sistine Chapel.
Sixto n. pr. m. Sixtus.
sketch m. Sketch (en cine y teatro).
slalom m. DEP. Slalom (prueba de habilidad).
slam m. Slam (en bridge).
slip m. Pants, *pl.*, underpants, *pl.*, briefs, *pl.*
slogan m. Slogan (lema publicitario).
sloop m. MAR. Sloop (balandro).
smash m. DEP. Smash (mate en tenis).
smoking m. Dinner jacket [U.S., tuxedo].
snack-bar m. Snack bar (cafetería).
snipe m. MAR. Snipe (barco).
snob adj. Snobbish.
— M. y f. Snob.
snobismo m. Snobbery, snobbishness.
so m. FAM. You: *¡so tonto!*, you idiot!
so prep. Under: *so pena de*, under penalty of.
¡so! interj. Whoa! [to stop a horse].
soasar v. tr. To roast lightly.
soba f. Kneading (del pan). || FAM. Thrashing, hiding (paliza): *le dieron una soba*, they gave him a thrashing. || FIG. Fulling (pieles). || POP. Fondling, pawing (manoseo).

sobacal adj. ANAT. Axillary.
sobaco m. ANAT. Armpit.
sobadero m. Fulling mill (de pieles).
sobado, da adj. Kneaded (pan). || FIG. Worn, shabby: *el cuello de la camisa está muy sobado*, the collar of the shirt is very worn. | Shabby, dog-eared: *un libro muy sobado*, a very shabby book. || FIG. y FAM. Well-worn, hackneyed (tema, asunto). || CULIN. Short (torta).
sobadura f. Kneading (pan). || Fulling (de las pieles). || POP. Fondling, pawing (manoseo).
sobaquera f. Armhole (del vestido). || Dress shield (para no manchar el vestido de sudor). || Underarm *o* body odour (olor).
sobaquillo (de) adv. TAUR. On the side.
sobaquina f. Body *o* underarm odour.
sobar v. tr. To knead (pan). || To full (pieles). || FIG. To thrash, to give a hiding, to wallop (zurrar). | To handle, to finger (manosear). | To pester (molestar). || POP. To caress, to fondle (acariciar). | To paw (acariciar pesadamente).
— V. pr. POP. To pet, to cuddle (acariciarse).
sobarba f. Noseband (de la brida). || Double chin (papada).
sobeo m. Strap used to attach the yoke to the pole of the cart (de un carro). || POP. Fondling, pawing.
soberanamente adv. Extremely, supremely (muy).
soberanía f. Sovereignty. || *Plaza de soberanía*, territory under the sovereignty of another country (Ceuta, Melilla).
soberano, na adj. Sovereign: *poder, estado soberano*, sovereign power, state. || FIG. Sovereign, supreme: *la belleza soberana*, the supreme beauty; *soberano desprecio*, sovereign contempt. | Excellent. || FIG. y FAM. *Dar una soberana paliza*, to give a real good hiding.
— M. y f. Sovereign. || *Los soberanos*, the King and Queen.
soberbia f. Pride (orgullo, pecado capital). || Arrogance, haughtiness, excessive pride (altivez). || FIG. Anger (ira).
soberbiamente adv. Arrogantly. || FIG. Superbly, magnificently.
soberbio, bia adj. Proud (orgulloso). | Arrogant, haughty (altivo). || FIG. Magnificent, superb, splendid (magnífico). | Spirited (caballo). | Angry, furious (colérico). || FIG. y FAM. *Le dieron una soberbia paliza*, they gave him a real good hiding.
sobo m. V. SOBA.
sobón, ona adj. POP. Randy, fresh (chico). | Randy, fruity (chica). || FIG. Skiving, idle (remolón). || POP. *Es muy sobón*, he's all hands, he's ever so randy.
— M. POP. Randy bloke. | Skiver, slacker (remolón). || — F. POP. Randy girl. | Skiver, slacker (remolona).
sobordo m. MAR. Inspection (de la carga). | Manifest (relación de cargamento).
sobornable adj. Bribable, venal.
sobornación f. Bribery, bribing.
sobornador, ra adj. Bribing.
— M. y f. Briber.
sobornal m. Overload.
sobornar v. tr. To bribe.
soborno m. Bribery, bribing (acción). || Bribe (dinero dado). || *Amer.* Overload (sobrecarga). || *Amer. De soborno*, in addition, additional.
sobra f. Surplus, excess. || — Pl. Leftovers (de comida). || Trash, *sing.* (desperdicios). || — *De sobra*, more than enough, to spare, plenty of (mucho): *tengo dinero de sobra*, I have more than enough money; spare, extra: *¿tienes algún lápiz de sobra?*, have you got a spare pencil? || FIG. *Estás de sobra*, you are not wanted, you are in the way. || *Saber de sobra*, to know only too well.
sobradamente adv. Extremely (muy). || *Estar sobradamente satisfecho*, to be more than happy.
sobradero m. Overflow pipe (desagüe).
sobradillo m. Penthouse (sobre ventana o puerta).
sobrado, da adj. More than enough, plenty of: *tiene sobrados motivos de queja*, he has more than enough reason to complain. || Plenty of: *estoy sobrado de amistades*, I have plenty of friends. || — *Tener sobrada razón*, to be quite right. || *Y con sobrada razón*, and quite rightly so.
— Adv. Too (demasiado).
— M. ARQ. Attic, garret (desván). || *Amer.* Kitchen shelf (vasar). || — Pl. *Amer.* Leftovers (sobras).
sobrante adj. Remaining (que queda). || Leftover, spare (que sobra). || Surplus (excedente).
— M. Surplus.
sobrar v. intr. To have left over, to be left over: *me sobran cien pesetas*, I have one hundred pesetas left over; *sobra vino*, there is some wine left over. || To have more than enough, to be more than enough: *me sobra dinero*, I have more than enough money; *aquí sobra pan*, there is more than enough bread here. || To have plenty of: *te sobra tiempo*, you have plenty of time. || To be one [two, three, etc.] too many: *sobran cuatro libros*, there are four books too many. || To be too much (haber demasiado). || To be in the way (estorbar): *tú sobras*, you are in the way. || Not to be necessary, to be unnecessary (ser inútil): *sobran los detalles*, the details are not necessary. || — *Basta y sobra*, that's more than enough. || *No estar sobrado de*, to be a little short of. || *Sobrarle a uno la gracia*, to be ever so funny.
sobrasada f. Majorcan sausage (embutido).
sobre m. Envelope (de carta): *poner en un sobre*, to put in an envelope. || Packet: *sobre de sopa*, packet of soup. || — *Bajo sobre*, under cover. || *Por sobre separado*, under separate cover.
sobre prep. On, upon (v. OBSERV.): *sobre la mesa*, on the table. || On top of (encima de): *poner un libro sobre otro*, to put one book on top of another. || On: *imponer un gravamen sobre*, to levy a tax on. || On, about: *hablar sobre un tema*, to talk about a subject; *un libro sobre el arte*, a book on art. || Around, round about, about: *tengo sobre mil pesetas*, I have around 1000 pesetas; *vendré sobre las ocho*, I will come about eight o'clock. || Upon: *dice insulto sobre insulto*, he says insult upon insult. || Above (por encima de): *sobre nosotros veíamos un cielo tempestuoso*, above us we saw a stormy sky. || Over: *el avión pasó sobre nosotros*, the plane passed over our heads. || Onto: *las ventanas dan sobre la plaza*, the windows look onto the square. || Down on *o* upon: *el ejército vino sobre los campesinos*, the army came down upon the farmers. || In addition to, on top of (además de): *le dio tres mil pesetas sobre lo estipulado*, he gave him three thousand pesetas in addition to the agreed sum; *sobre los problemas que ya tenía, ahora tiene otros*, he has got other problems now in addition to the ones he already had. || Over, above (en una jerarquía): *sobre él sólo tiene un jefe*, he has only got one boss over him. || Above: *tres grados sobre cero*, three degrees above zero. || Near (cerca de): *está sobre la calle de Goya*, it is near Goya Street. || — FIG. y FAM. *Sobre ascuas*, on tenterhooks. || *Sobre aviso*, on one's guard, forewarned. || *Sobre gustos no hay nada escrito*, V. GUSTO. || *Sobre manera* or *modo*, exceedingly. || *Sobre poco más o menos*, more or less, just about. || *Sobre ser rica es hermosa*, not only is she rich, but she is also beautiful; she is beautiful as well as rich. || *Sobre todo*, especially, above all: *me gusta España, sobre todo Andalucía*, I like Spain, especially Andalusia; chiefly (principalmente).
— OBSERV. Aunque *upon* tiene el mismo sentido que *on* su uso es menos frecuente.
sobreabundancia f. Superabundance, overabundance.
sobreabundante adj. Superabundant, overabundant.
sobreabundar v. intr. To superabound (*en*, with).
sobreagudo, da adj. MÚS. High-pitched.
sobrealimentación f. Overfeeding.
sobrealimentar v. tr. To overfeed. || TECN. To supercharge.
sobrealzar v. tr. To raise up.
sobreañadir v. tr. To superadd, to add on.
sobreasada f. Majorcan sausage (embutido).
sobrebota f. *Amer.* Legging.
sobrecalentar v. tr. To overheat.
sobrecama f. Bedspread.
sobrecaña f. VET. Splint.
sobrecarga f. Overload (exceso de carga). || Packing strap (cuerda or soga). || COM. Surcharge (en un sello). || FIG. Additional burden.
sobrecargar v. tr. To overload. || To weigh down, to overburden (una persona). || To fell (una costura). || To surcharge (un sello).
sobrecargo m. MAR. Supercargo.
sobreceja f. Brow.
sobrecejo o **sobreceño** m. Frown.
sobrecincha f. Surcingle, girth (del caballo).
sobrecoger v. tr. To startle (miedo). || To take by surprise (frío). || To frighten (asustar).
— V. pr. To startle, to give a start (asustarse). || To give a start (de horror). || *Sobrecogerse de miedo*, to be seized with fear.
sobrecomprimir v. tr. AVIAC. To pressurize.
sobrecubierta f. Dust cover, jacket (de libro). || Extra cover.
sobredicho, cha adj. Aforesaid, aforementioned, above-mentioned.
sobredorar v. tr. To gild (los metales). || FIG. To gloss over (disimular).
sobreedificar v. tr. To build over *o* on.
sobreentender* v. tr. To understand (comprender). || To guess, to deduce (deducir).
— V. pr. To be understood, to be implied.
sobreentendido, da adj. Implied, implicit.
sobreentrenamiento m. DEP. Overtraining.
sobreentrenar v. tr. DEP. To overtrain.
sobreesdrújulo, la adj. V. SOBRESDRÚJULO.
sobreestadía f. V. SOBRESTADÍA.
sobreexceder v. tr. To exceed.
sobreexcitación f. Overexcitement.
sobreexcitar v. tr. To overexcite.
— V. pr. To get overexcited.
sobreexponer v. tr. To overexpose.
sobreexposición f. Overexposure.
sobrefalda f. Overskirt.
sobrefaz f. Surface.
sobrefusión f. QUÍM. Supercooling.
sobrehaz f. Surface.
sobrehilado m. Whipstitching.
sobrehilar v. tr. To whipstitch.
sobrehílo m. Whipstitch.

sobrehumano, na adj. Superhuman.
sobreimpresión f. FOT. y CINEM. Superimposition.
sobrejuanete m. MAR. Royal mast.
sobrelecho m. ARQ. Underside of a stone.
sobrellenar v. tr. To overfill.
sobrellevar v. tr. FIG. To bear, to endure (aguantar). | To help to bear, to share (ayudar a otro).
sobremanera f. Exceedingly, excessively.
sobremesa f. Table cover, table covering (tapete). || Dessert (postre). || Chat *o* conversation after dinner: *tuvimos una agradable sobremesa ayer*, we had a nice chat after dinner yesterday. || — *De sobremesa*, after-dinner: *charla de sobremesa*, after-dinner chat. || *Estar de sobremesa*, to be sitting round the table after dinner.
sobremesana f. MAR. Mizzen topsail.
sobrenadar v. intr. To float.
sobrenatural adj. Supernatural. || REL. *Vida sobrenatural*, life after death.
sobrenaturalismo m. Supernaturalism.
sobrenombre m. Nickname. || *Dar a uno el sobrenombre de*, to nickname s.o.
sobrentender* v. tr. V. SOBREENTENDER.
sobrepaga f. Bonus.
sobreparto m. Postnatal confinement. || — *Dolores de sobreparto*, afterpains. || *Morir de sobreparto*, to die in childbirth.
sobrepasar v. tr. To surpass, to exceed. || To exceed (unos límites). || AVIAC. To overshoot [the runway] (la pista). || DEP. To beat (vencer).
— V. pr. *Sobrepasarse a sí mismo*, to surpass o.s.
sobrepelo m. *Amer.* Saddlecloth.
sobrepelliz f. REL. Surplice.
sobrepeso m. Overload (exceso de carga). || *Sobrepeso de equipaje*, excess baggage.
sobreponer* v. tr. To superimpose (*en*, on), to put on top (*en*, of). || To put before (anteponer).
— V. pr. To overcome: *sobreponerse a su dolor*, to overcome one's pain. || To pull o.s. together: *te tienes que sobreponer*, you must pull yourself together. || To triumph (*a*, over) [vencer].
sobreporte m. Extra postage.
sobreprecio m. Surcharge.
sobreprima f. Extra premium (seguros).
sobreproducción f. Overproduction, excess production.
sobrepuerta f. Pelmet [over a door].
sobrepuesto, ta adj. Superimposed.
— M. Appliqué work (ornamentación). || Basket *o* clay covering for a beehive.
sobrepuja f. Overbid, overbidding (en las subastas).
sobrepujar v. tr. To surpass: *ella sobrepuja a todas sus hermanas en belleza*, she surpasses all her sisters in beauty. || To overbid, to outbid (subasta).
sobrequilla f. MAR. Keelson.
sobrero adj. Extra, spare (sobrante). || TAUR. Spare [bull] (toro).
— M. TAUR. Spare bull (toro).
sobresalienta f. TEATR. Understudy.
sobresaliente adj. Projecting, overhanging. || Outstanding : *una de las personas más sobresalientes de su época*, one of the most outstanding figures of his time.
— M. High mark, excellent mark (nota superior). || First class honours, *pl.* (en un examen de licenciatura). || TAUR. Substitute bullfighter. || Understudy (actor que reemplaza a otro).
sobresalir* v. intr. To project, to jut out, to stick out (resaltar). || To stick out, to jut out: *hay un adoquín que sobresale de la acera*, there is a paving stone sticking out of the pavement. || FIG. To excel, to stand out: *él sobresale entre todos sus amigos*, he stands out from all his friends. | To stand out, to be conspicuous (diferenciarse).
sobresaltar v. tr. To startle, to give a fright, to make [s.o.] jump.
— V. pr. To be startled (*con*, *por*, by), to start (*con*, *por*, at).
sobresalto m. Start (movimiento). || Fright, scare (susto): *me dio un sobresalto*, he gave me a fright.
sobresaturación f. Supersaturation.
sobresaturar v. tr. To supersaturate.
sobresdrújulo, la adj. GRAM. Accented on the syllable preceding the antepenultimate one [as in *devuélvemelo*, give it back to me].
sobreseer v. tr. JUR. To stay: *sobreseer la causa*, to stay proceedings.
sobreseimiento m. JUR. Stay (provisional): *el sobreseimiento de una causa*, the stay of proceedings. || JUR. *Sobreseimiento libre*, nonsuit.
sobresello m. Second seal, double seal.
sobrestadía f. MAR. Demurrage (días de prórroga e indemnización).
sobrestante m. Foreman (capataz).
sobrestimación f. Overestimate.
sobrestimar v. tr. To overestimate.
sobresueldo m. Bonus.
sobretasa f. Surcharge.
sobretensión f. ELECTR. Surge.
sobretodo m. Overcoat (abrigo). || Overall (para proteger un traje).
sobrevenir* v. intr. To happen, to occur, to take place (ocurrir). || *Les sobrevino una catástrofe*, disaster befell them, disaster struck [them].
sobrevidriera f. Screen (tela metálica). || Second window (segunda vidriera).
sobreviviente adj. Surviving.
— M. y f. Survivor.
sobrevivir v. intr. To survive. || *Sobrevivir a*, to outlive, to survive (una persona), to survive (una epidemia).
sobrevolar* v. tr. AVIAC. To fly over, to overfly.
sobrexcedente adj. Excess.
sobrexceder v. tr. To exceed.
sobrexcitación f. Overexcitement.
sobrexcitar v. tr. To overexcite.
— V. pr. To overexcite o.s., to become *o* to get overexcited.
sobriedad f. Soberness, restraint, sobriety.
sobrino, na m. y f. Nephew (hombre), niece (mujer). || — *Sobrino carnal*, nephew. || *Sobrino político*, nephew by marriage. || *Sobrino segundo*, first cousin once removed.
sobrio, bria adj. Sober: *es muy sobrio en sus costumbres*, he has very sober habits; *color, estilo, discurso sobrio*, sober colour, style, speech. || Light (comida). || — *Ser sobrio de palabras*, to speak with restraint. || *Sobrio en la bebida*, temperate in one's drinking habits.
socaire m. MAR. Lee. || — MAR. *Al socaire*, leeward. || FIG. *Al socaire de*, protected by.
socaliña f. Cunning (ardid).
socaliñar v. tr. To get [sth.] through cunning (conseguir con maña).
socaliñero, ra adj. Cunning, crafty.
— M. y f. Cunning *o* crafty person, sly dog.
socapa f. Pretext, pretence [U.S., pretense]. || *A socapa*, surreptitiously.
socarrar v. tr. To scorch, to singe (chamuscar).
socarrón, ona adj. Sarcastic, ironical. || Sly (taimado). || *Una sonrisa socarrona*, a sly smile.
socarronería f. Sarcasm, irony. || Slyness (carácter taimado).
socavación f. Undermining.
socavar v. tr. To undermine, to dig under. || FIG. To undermine.
socavón m. Excavation. || Gallery (galería). || Subsidence (hundimiento). || Hollow (hueco).
sociabilidad f. Sociability.
sociable adj. Sociable.
social adj. Social. || COM. *Razón social*, trade name.
socialdemócrata adj. Social-Democratic.
— M. y f. Social Democrat.
socialdemocracia f. Social Democracy.
socialismo m. Socialism.
socialista adj./s. Socialist.
socialización f. Nationalization. || Socialization.
socializar v. tr. To nationalize. || To socialize.
socialmente adv. Socially.
sociedad f. Society: *la sociedad en que vivimos*, the society in which we live; *sociedad protectora de animales*, society for the prevention of cruelty to animals. || Company, society (comercial). || — *Alta* or *buena sociedad*, high society. || *Ecos de sociedad*, v. ECO. || *Entrar* or *presentarse en la sociedad*, to make one's début, to come out. || *Sociedad anónima*, joint-stock company [U.S., corporation]. || *Sociedad comanditaria* or *en comandita*, limited partnership. || *Sociedad cooperativa*, cooperative, cooperative society. || *Sociedad conyugal*, marriage partnership. || *Sociedad de Naciones*, League of Nations. || *Sociedad (de responsabilidad) limitada*, limited-liability company. || *Sociedad mercantil*, trading company. || *Sociedad secreta*, secret society.
socio, cia m. y f. Member (de una asociación): *socio de un club*, member of a club. || Partner, associate (de una sociedad comercial): *¿cuántos socios hay en el negocio?*, how many partners are there in the business? || FAM. Chap, fellow, guy. || — *Hacerse socio*, to become a member. || *Socio comanditario*, sleeping partner [U.S., silent partner]. || *Socio de número*, full member.
socioeconómico, ca adj. Socioeconomic.
sociología f. Sociology.
sociológico, ca adj. Sociological.
sociólogo, ga m. y f. Sociologist.
socolor m. Pretext, pretence [U.S., pretense]. || *Socolor de*, under the pretext of.
socorredor, ra adj. Helping.
— M. y f. Helper.
socorrer v. tr. To help, to assist, to relieve: *socorrer a los pobres*, to help the poor. || To relieve (una ciudad).
socorrido, da adj. Helpful (dispuesto a socorrer). || Well stocked (abastecido). || FAM. Handy, useful: *es un traje muy socorrido*, it is a very handy dress.
socorrismo m. First aid. || Life saving (en una piscina, una playa).
socorrista m. y f. Person trained in first aid. || Lifesaver (en piscina, playa).
socorro m. Help, aid, assistance: *prestar socorro*, to give aid. || MIL. Relief (soldados). | Supplies, *pl.*, provisions, *pl*, (provisiones). || — *Agua de socorro*, v. AGUA. || *Casa de socorro*, v. CASA. || *Fuerzas de socorro*, reinforcements. || *Ir en socorro de alguien*, to go to s.o.'s aid. || *Puesto de socorro*, first-aid post. || *Señal de socorro*, distress signal.
— Interj. Help!
Sócrates n. pr. m. Socrates.

socrático, ca adj. Socratic.
sochantre m. REL. Succentor.
soda f. QUÍM. Soda (sosa). || Soda water (bebida).
sódico, ca adj. QUÍM. [Of] sodium: *carbonato, bicarbonato sódico*, sodium carbonate, bicarbonate.
sodio m. QUÍM. Sodium: *cloruro de sodio*, sodium chloride.
Sodoma n. pr. HIST. Sodom.
sodomía f. Sodomy.
sodomita adj./s. Sodomite.
sodomítico, ca adj. Sodomite.
soez adj. Rude, vulgar, dirty.
sofá m. Sofa. || *Sofá cama*, studio couch.
Sofía n. pr. f. Sophia (nombre de pila). || GEOGR. Sofia.
sofión m. Snort, bellow (bufido). || Rebuff (negación). || Scolding (reprensión). || Blunderbuss (trabuco).
sofisma m. Sophism.
sofista adj. Sophistic.
— M. y f. Sophist.
sofistería f. Sophistry.
sofisticación f. Use of sophistry (de un razonamiento). || Sophistication (afectación). || Adulteration.
sofisticado, da adj. Sophisticated (afectado). || Adulterated (falsificado).
sofisticar v. tr. To adulterate (falsificar). || To sophisticate (quitar naturalidad).
sofístico, ca adj. Sophistical, sophistic.
sofito m. ARQ. Soffit.
soflama f. Flicker (del fuego). || FIG. Blush (en el rostro). | Harangue (discurso ardoroso). | Deceit (engaño). | Cajolery (zalamería).
soflamar v. tr. To scorch, to singe (quemar ligeramente). || FIG. To make blush (abochornar). | To deceive (engañar). | To cajole (zalamear).
— V. pr. To burn (quemarse).
sofocación f. Suffocation (pérdida del aliento). || Choking sensation (ahogo). || FIG. Suppression (de una revolución). | Hushing up (de un escándalo). | Blushing (rubor). | Embarrasing situation (situación molesta).
sofocador, ra o **sofocante** adj. Suffocating (humo, gas). || Stifling, suffocating (calor, clima). || Stuffy (atmósfera).
sofocar v. tr. To suffocate, to stifle (hacer perder la respiración). || To put out, to smother (un incendio). || FIG. To suppress, to put down, to stifle (una revolución). | To stop (una epidemia). | To make [s.o.] blush (avergonzar). | To anger, to upset (irritar).
— V. pr. To suffocate, to stifle (de calor). || To get out of breath (al hacer un esfuerzo). || To choke (atragantarse). || FIG. To blush (ruborizarse). | To get angry, to get upset (irritarse).
Sófocles n. pr. m. Sophocles.
sofoco m. Suffocation. || Choking sensation (ahogo). || FIG. Shame (vergüenza). | Embarrassing situation (vergüenza). || FIG. y FAM. *Le dio un sofoco*, it gave him quite a turn.
sofocón m. FAM. Shock (gran disgusto). || FAM. *Me llevé un gran sofocón*, I was beside myself.
sofoquina f. FAM. Shock (sofocón). | Suffocating heat (calor sofocante). || FAM. *¡Vaya sofoquina que hace aquí!*, it's stifling here!
sofreír* v. tr. To fry lightly.
sofrenada f. Sharp jerk on the reins (caballo). || FIG. Talking-to, dressing down (reprimenda).
sofrenar v. tr. To rein in sharply (al caballo). || FIG. To give a good talking-to *o* a good dressing down (reprender). | To restrain (las pasiones).
software m. Software (de una computadora).
soga f. Rope, cord (cuerda). || *Amer.* Leather strap (tira de cuero). || — FIG. *Dar soga a uno*, to get s.o. to speak (darle cuerda), to make fun of s.o. (burlarse). | *Echar la soga tras el caldero*, to throw helve after hatchet. | *Estar con la soga al cuello*, to have one's neck in a noose, to have a knife at one's throat. | *Siempre se quiebra la soga por lo más delgado*, the weakest goes to the wall.
soja f. BOT. Soya bean, soja bean [U.S., soybean].
sojuzgador, ra adj. Subjugating, subduing.
— M. y f. Subjugator, subduer.
sojuzgar v. tr. To subjugate, to subdue (someter). || To rule tyrannically (tratar tiránicamente).
sol m. Sun: *sol poniente, naciente, de medianoche*, setting, rising, midnight sun. || Sun, sunlight, sunshine (luz solar): *el sol descolora la pintura*, the sunlight takes the colour out of the paintwork. || Sol (unidad monetaria del Perú). || FIG. Darling: *¡qué sol de niño!*, what a darling child! || TAUR. Seats (*pl.*) in the sun (en la plaza de toros). || QUÍM. Sol (coloide). || MÚS. Sol (nota). || — *Al ponerse el sol*, at sunset. || *Al salir el sol*, at sunrise. || *Al sol*, in the sun. || FIG. y FAM. *Arrimarse al sol que más calienta*, V. ARRIMARSE. || *Bajo el sol*, in the sun: *estoy a gusto bajo el sol*, I like being in the sun; under the sun: *no hay nada nuevo bajo el sol*, there is nothing new under the sun. || FIG. y FAM. *Como el sol que nos alumbra*, as clear as the light of day. || *Da el sol de pleno*, the sun beats down directly. || *De sol*, sunny: *una tarde de sol*, a sunny afternoon. || *De sol a sol*, from sunrise to sunset. || *El Rey Sol*, the Sun King. || *El sol aprieta*, the sun is hot *o* strong. || *Hace sol*, it is sunny, the sun is shining. || FIG. y FAM. *Más hermoso que un sol*, V. HERMOSO. | *No dejar a uno ni a sol ni a sombra*, not to leave s.o. alone *o* in peace, to pester *o* to hound s.o. || FIG. *Pegársele el sol a alguien*, to get suntanned. || *Quemadura de sol*, sunburn. || *Rayo de sol*, V. RAYO. || *Reloj de sol*, sundial. || FIG. y FAM. *¡Salga el sol por Antequera!*, come what may! || BOT. *Sol de las Indias*, sunflower. || *Sol y sombra*, stands in the bullring which are first in the sun and then in the shade (plaza de toros), drink of brandy and anisette (bebida). || *Tendido de sol*, stands (*pl.*) in the sun (plaza de toros). || *Tomar el sol*, to sunbathe, to bask in the sun (tumbado), to take the sun (paseándose, etc.).
solado m. Flooring.
solador m. Floorer.
soladura f. Flooring.
solamente adv. Only: *no solamente*, not only. || — *Con solamente que* or *solamente con que no me moleste*, provided [that] he does not bother me, as long as he does not bother me. || *Estoy muy agradecido, solamente que no sé expresarlo*, I am very grateful, but I do not know how to show it. || *Solamente que fuese un poco menos caro, lo compraría*, if only it were a little cheaper I would buy it.
solana f. Sunny place *o* spot. || Sunshine: *ahora hay mucha solana*, there is a lot of sunshine now. || Veranda (de una casa).
solanácea f. BOT. Solanum. || — Pl. Solanaceae.
solanera f. Sunstroke, sunburn (insolación). || Scorching sun (sol fuerte).
solano m. East wind (viento). || BOT. Nightshade.
solapa f. Lapel (de una chaqueta). || Flap (de bolsillo, de libro, de sobre). || FIG. Pretext.
solapadamente adv. Slyly, in an underhand way.
solapado, da adj. Sly, underhand.
solapar v. tr. To overlap (cubrir parcialmente). || To put lapels on (una chaqueta). || FIG. To hide, to cover up (ocultar).
solar adj. Solar, of the sun. || — *Año solar*, solar year. || ANAT. *Plexo solar*, solar plexus. || *Rayos solares*, sun's rays, rays of sunlight. || *Sistema solar*, solar system.
— M. Lot, plot (terreno): *acaban de comprar un solar para hacerse una casa*, they have just bought a lot to build a house on. || Building site (terreno donde se está construyendo). || Family, lineage, line (linaje). || Family seat, country seat, ancestral home (casa solariega).
solar* v. tr. To resole (calzado). || To floor (suelo).
solariego, ga adj. Family (del patrimonio). || Noble. || *Casa solariega*, V. CASA.
solario m. Solarium.
solaz m. Recreation, entertainment (diversión). || Solace, consolation, relief (alivio). || Relaxation (descanso). || *A solaz*, with pleasure.
solazar v. tr. To divert, to amuse, to entertain (divertir). || To solace, to console (aliviar).
— V. pr. To amuse o.s., to enjoy o.s.
solazo m. FAM. Scorching sun.
soldable adj. Weldable, that can be soldered.
soldada f. Salary (sueldo). || Pay (de soldado, de marinero).
soldadesca f. Military profession, soldiering. || Soldiery (grupo de soldados). || Undisciplined troops, *pl.* (soldados indisciplinados).
soldadesco, ca adj. Soldier-like, soldierly. || Barrack-room (lenguaje, etc.).
soldadito m. Soldier: *soldadito de plomo*, tin *o* toy soldier.
soldado m. Soldier. || — *Soldado bisoño*, raw recruit. || *Soldado cumplido*, discharged soldier. || *Soldado de artillería*, artilleryman. || *Soldado de caballería*, trooper, cavalryman. || *Soldado de infantería*, infantryman. || *Soldado de infantería de marina*, marine. || *Soldado de primera, de segunda clase*, private first class, private. || *Soldado desconocido*, unknown warrior *o* soldier. || *Soldado montado*, cavalryman. || *Soldado raso*, private, private soldier. || *Soldado romano*, Roman soldier [in the Holy Week processions]. || *Soldado voluntario*, volunteer.
soldador m. Welder (obrero). || Soldering iron (instrumento).
soldadora f. Welder, welding machine.
soldadote m. FAM. Soldier, military man.
soldadura f. Welding, soldering (acción). || Soldered joint, weld. || — *Soldadura a tope*, butt welding. || *Soldadura autógena*, [oxyacetylene] welding. || *Soldadura blanda*, soft soldering. || *Soldadura fuerte*, hard soldering. || *Soldadura oxiacetilénica*, oxyacetylene welding. || *Soldadura por puntos*, spot welding.
soldar* v. tr. To weld, to solder. || FIG. To mend (una falta). || *Soldar por puntos*, to spot-weld.
— V. pr. FIG. To join together (unirse). | To knit (huesos).
soleá f. Melancholy Andalusian song and dance.
— OBSERV. Pl. *soleares*.
soleado, da adj. Sunny.
soleamiento m. Exposure to the sun.
solear v. tr. To expose to the sun, to put in the sun.
soleares f. pl. V. SOLEÁ.
solecismo m. GRAM. Solecism.
soledad f. Solitude (estar solo). || Loneliness (sentirse solo). || Grieving (nostalgia). || Lonely place (sitio). || V. SOLEÁ.

solemne adj. Solemn. || FIG. Downright: *es una solemne tontería*, it is downright madness. | Terrible: *un solemne error*, a terrible mistake.
solemnidad f. Solemnity (seriedad). || Ceremony (acto). || Formality (trámite). || FAM. *Pobre de solemnidad*, penniless.
solemnizar v. tr. To solemnize, to celebrate (celebrar). || To commemorate (conmemorar).
solenoide m. FÍS. Solenoid.
sóleo m. ANAT. Soleus (músculo).
soler* v. intr. To usually [do, etc.], to be in the habit of (acostumbrar): *suele venir el lunes*, he usually comes on Mondays, he is in the habit of coming on Mondays. || To [be, do, etc.] usually *o* frequently *o* often *o* generally (ser frecuente): *los españoles suelen ser morenos*, the Spanish are usually dark; *suele equivocarse*, he is frequently mistaken; *aquí suele hacer mucho frío*, it is generally very cold here. || To use to (sólo empleado en pasado): *solía leer por la tarde*, he used to read in the afternoon. || *Suele llover mucho aquí*, it usually *o* frequently *o* often *o* generally rains a lot here, it tends to rain a lot here.
solera f. Prop (soporte). || Lower millstone (de molino). || Bottom (de un canal). || TECN. Floor (de horno). | Stone pavement (de un puente o alcantarilla). || Lees, *pl.* (heces del vino). || Reserve (reserva de vino). || Flat stone base (para postes, etc.). || FIG. Tradition (tradición). | Lineage (linaje). || — *Familia de mucha solera*, old-established family. || *Marca de solera*, old-established brand, prestige brand. || *Vino de solera*, vintage wine.
solería f. Leather for soles. || Flooring (suelo).
soleta f. Patch (remiendo). || FIG. y FAM. *Picar* or *tomar soleta*, to beat it (irse).
solevantar v. tr. To lift. || FIG. To stir up.
solfa f. MÚS. Solfeggio, sol-fa (solfeo). || FIG. y FAM. Thrashing (paliza). || — FIG. y FAM. *Echar una solfa a uno*, to give s.o. a good talking-to. | *Poner en solfa*, to ridicule. | *Tomar a solfa*, not to take seriously.
solfatara f. GEOL. Solfatara.
solfear v. tr. To sol-fa. || FIG. y FAM. To give a good thrashing (zurrar). | To give a good talking-to (reprender).
solfeo m. MÚS. Solfeggio (arte). || FIG. y FAM. Thrashing (paliza). | Talking-to (acción de reprender).
solicitación f. Requesting (acción de pedir). || Request (petición). || Invitation (para salir). || Canvassing (de votos). || Temptation (tentación). || *Solicitación de fondos*, call for funds.
solicitador, ra o **solicitante** m. y f. Petitioner (el que pide). || Applicant (el que hace una solicitud).
solicitar v. tr. To request: *solicitar una entrevista*, to request an interview. || To ask for, to seek (un permiso). || To apply for: *solicitar un empleo*, to apply for a job. || To attract (llamar la atención). || To pursue, to chase after (fam.) [a una persona]. || To court (una mujer). || To canvass for (votos). || FÍS. To attract. || *Es una chica muy solicitada*, she is very much in demand, she is a very popular girl.
solícito, ta adj. Solicitous, obliging (amable): *es muy solícito conmigo*, he is very solicitous with me. || — *El camarero se acercó solícito*, the waiter came over attentively. || *Mostrarse solícito con*, to be obliging with. || *Un hijo solícito*, an affectionate son.
solicitud f. Solicitude, care (cuidado). || Application (para un puesto). || Request (petición): *dirigir una solicitud*, to make a request. || Petition (instancia). || *A solicitud*, on request.
solidar v. tr. To consolidate, to strengthen, to reinforce (reforzar). || To prove (demostrar).
solidaridad f. Solidarity. || *Por solidaridad con*, out of solidarity with, in simpathy with.
solidario, ria adj. Solidary. || JUR. Jointly responsible *o* liable (persona). | Mutually binding (obligación). | Common (responsabilidad). || TECN. Integral (pieza).
solidarizar v. tr. JUR. To render jointly liable *o* responsible.
— V. pr. To make common cause, to line up: *solidarizarse con los huelguistas*, to make common cause with the strikers. || To support (apoyar).
solideo m. Skullcap (de eclesiástico).
solidez f. Strength, firmness, solidity (resistencia). || Solidity (naturaleza sólida). || FIG. Soundness (de un argumento). || Fastness (de un color).
solidificación f. Solidification.
solidificar, solidificarse v. tr. y pr. To solidify.
sólido, da adj. Solid: *cuerpo, alimento sólido*, solid body, food. || Strong (resistente). || Firm (firme). || Solid, secure (seguro, estable). || FIG. Sound (argumento, principio, base). || Fast (color).
— M. MAT. y FÍS. Solid. || Solidus (moneda romana).
soliloquiar v. intr. To soliloquize, to talk to o.s.
soliloquio m. Soliloquy, monologue.
solio m. [Canopied] throne (trono).
solípedo, da adj./s.m. ZOOL. Soliped.
solista m. y f. MÚS. Soloist.
solitaria f. Tapeworm: *tener la solitaria*, to have a tapeworm. || Post chaise (carruaje).
solitario, ria adj. Solitary (persona). || Solitary, lonely, deserted, secluded (lugar).
— M. y f. Hermit, recluse (ermitaño). || Solitary person (persona que busca la soledad). || — M. Solitaire (juego de naipes). || Solitaire (diamante).
solito, ta adj. FAM. All alone.
sólito, ta adj. Usual, customary.
soliviantar v. tr. To rouse, to stir up (excitar a una actitud rebelde). || To irritate (irritar). || To worry (preocupar). || *Soliviantado por los celos*, eaten up *o* consumed with envy.
solo, la adj. Alone, by o.s.: *hacer algo solo*, to do sth. by o.s.; *vivir solo*, to live alone. || Lonely: *sentirse solo*, to feel lonely. || Only, sole (único): *su sola preocupación*, his only worry. || Single: *ni una sola crítica*, not a single criticism. || Unique (sin par). || MÚS. Solo: *violín solo*, solo violin. || — *A solas*, alone, by o.s.: *él come a solas*, he eats alone. || *Café solo*, black coffee. || *Como él solo*, as only he can. || FIG. *De solo a solo*, alone. || *Eso marcha solo*, that's no trouble at all. || *Quedarse solo*, to have no equal (no tener rival), to be left alone in the world (quedarse huérfano, viudo, etc.). || *Se presenta una sola dificultad*, there is just one *o* only one difficulty.
— M. Solitaire, solo (naipes). || Solo: *un solo de tambor*, a drum solo; *un solo para soprano*, a soprano solo.
sólo adv. Only, solely, merely, just: *sólo quiero que vengas*, I only want you to come. || — *Aunque sólo sea por un día*, even if it is only for one day. || *Con sólo* or *sólo con* (con infinitivo), just by (con gerundio): *con sólo decir esta palabra*, just by saying this word. || *Con sólo que* or *sólo con que*, provided that, as long as (con tal que). || *Con sólo que, sólo con que falte una persona, no podemos hacer nada*, it just needs one person to be missing and we cannot do anything; if just one person is missing, we cannot do anything. || *No sólo ... sino*, not only ... but: *no sólo en este pueblo sino en toda la provincia*, not only in this village, but in all the province; *no sólo canta sino que también baila*, she not only sings, but she also dances. || *Sólo que*, only, but: *me gustó la blusa, sólo que era demasiado pequeña*, I liked the blouse, only it was too small; *yo iré, sólo que no me divierte nada*, I'll go, but I won't enjoy it at all. || *Sólo un momento*, just a minute, just a moment. || *Tan sólo*, only, merely, just: *tan sólo quiero que me dejen en paz*, I only want them to leave me alone. || *Tan sólo con* (con infinitivo), just by (con gerundio): *tan sólo con decirme la verdad*, just by telling me the truth. || *Tan sólo con que* (con subjuntivo), if only: *tan sólo con que vayas a verle*, if only you go to see him. || *Tan sólo te pido que me dejes tranquilo*, all I want is to be left alone, the only thing I ask of you is that you leave me alone.
solomillo m. Sirloin.
solomo m. Sirloin (solomillo). || Loin of pork (de cerdo).
solsticio m. ASTR. Solstice: *solsticio de invierno, de verano*, winter, summer solstice.
soltar* v. tr. To release. || To let go of, to drop: *soltó un plato*, he dropped a plate. || To free, to set free, to release (un preso). || To let loose (los animales). || To unleash (un perro). || To untie, to undo: *soltar un nudo*, to untie a knot. || To loosen, to slacken, to ease (aflojar). || To pay out: *soltar un poco de cuerda*, to pay out a little rope. || To drop (puntos). || To give off (desprender): *esto suelta mucho humo*, this gives off a lot of smoke. || To loosen (el vientre). || FIG. To resolve: *soltar una dificultad*, to resolve a difficulty. | To give up (ceder, abandonar). || MAR. To cast off: *suelta las amarras*, cast off the ropes. || AUT. To release (el freno). || AVIAC. To release, to drop: *soltar una bomba*, to release a bomb. || FAM. To tell, to come out with (contar). | To say, to come out with, to hurl: *me soltó una grosería*, he hurled a nasty remark at me. | To give: *nos soltó un discurso pesadísimo*, he gave us a very boring speech. | To blurt out, to let out (un secreto). | To break: *soltar la noticia*, to break the news. | To heave (un suspiro). | To utter, to let out (un grito). | To give, to land, to deal: *soltar un puñetazo*, to land a punch. | To cough up: *soltar diez dólares*, to cough up ten dollars. || To shed: *la culebra suelta la piel*, the snake sheds its skin. || — FAM. *No soltar prenda*, V. PRENDA. | *Sin soltar un cuarto*, without spending a penny. || FIG. y FAM. *Soltar coces*, to lash out. || *Soltar la lengua*, to loosen s.o.'s tongue. || FAM. *Soltar la pasta*, to fork up, to cough up. || *Soltar la risa*, to burst out laughing. || *Soltar una andanada*, to fire a broadside (marítimo), to lash out (injurias). || *Soltar una carcajada* or *una risotada*, to burst out laughing. || FAM. *¡Suelta!*, out with it! (dilo). || *¡Suéltame!*, let me go!
— V. pr. To come unfastened, to come untied (desanudarse). || To get loose, to break loose: *el perro se soltó de la correa*, the dog got loose from the leash. || To break, to come undone (puntos). || To come off (desprenderse). || To come out, to come unscrewed (tornillo). || To loosen (vientre). || FIG. To get the knack: *soltarse en el trabajo*, to get the knack of the job. | To lose one's shyness, to become more self-confident (desenvolverse una persona): *ya era hora de que se soltara este chico*, it is about time this boy lost his shyness. | To start (un niño): *hasta hace unos días no andaba, acaba de soltarse ahora*, a few days ago he could not walk, he has just started now. | To become *o* to get fluent o proficient: *ya empiezo*

a soltarme en francés, I am just beginning to get fluent in French. || — FAM. *Soltarse a su gusto*, to let off steam. || MAR. *Soltarse de las amarras*, to cast off. || *Soltarse de manos*, to take one's hands off the handlebars (de un manillar de bicicleta). || *Soltarse el pelo*, v. PELO. || *Soltársele a uno la lengua*, to become very talkative.
— OBSERV. The past participle of *soltar* is irregular *(suelto, suelta)*.
soltería f. Celibacy.
soltero, ra adj. Unmarried, single: *él está soltero*, he is unmarried; *quedarse soltero*, to stay single.
— M. Bachelor, unmarried man. || — F. Single woman, spinster. || — *Apellido de soltera*, maiden name. || *Despedida de soltera*, hen party. || *Despedida de soltero*, stag party. || *La Sra. López, de soltera Gómez*, Mrs. López, née *o* nee Gómez.
solterón m. Old bachelor.
solterona f. Spinster, old maid.
soltura f. Looseness, slackness. || Agility (agilidad). || FIG. Ease, fluency (al hablar): *hablar con mucha soltura*, to speak with great ease. || Confidence, assurance (seguridad). || JUR. Release (de un preso). || Shamelessness (descaro). || — FIG. *Con soltura*, fluently, with ease: *hablar un idioma con soltura*, to speak a language fluently; with ease, gracefully (moverse). | *Soltura de palabras*, fluency. | *Soltura de vientre*, looseness of the bowels.
solubilidad f. Solubility.
soluble adj. Soluble (que se disuelve). || Solvable, soluble (que se resuelve).
solución f. Solution: *la solución de un problema*, the solution to a problem. || QUÍM. Solution. || Ending, dénouement: *la solución del drama*, the dénouement of the drama. || *Solución de continuidad*, interruption, solution of continuity.
solucionar v. tr. To solve, to resolve: *solucionar un problema*, to solve a problem. || *Solucionar una huelga*, to settle a strike.
solvencia f. Solvency (capacidad para pagar deudas). || Settlement (pago).
solventar v. tr. To settle (una deuda). || To solve, to resolve (una dificultad). || To settle (un asunto).
solvente adj. Solvent.
— M. QUÍM. Solvent.
solla f. Plaice (pez).
sollado m. MAR. Orlop.
sollamar v. tr. To scorch, to singe.
sollastre m. Scullion, kitchen boy (pinche). || FIG. Rascal, rogue.
sollo m. ZOOL. Sturgeon (pez). || FIG. y FAM. *Estar gordo como un sollo*, to be as fat as a pig.
sollozante adj. Sobbing.
sollozar v. intr. To sob.
sollozo m. Sob: *estallar* or *prorrompir en sollozos*, to burst into sobs. || *Decir algo entre sollozos*, to say sth. sobbing, to sob sth.
soma m. Soma.
somalí adj./s. Somali.
Somalia n. pr. f. GEOGR. Somalia.
somanta f. FAM. Beating, licking (tunda). | Spanking (a los niños). || FAM. *Le dio una somanta de palos*, he gave him a real thrashing.
somatén m. Militia [in Catalonia] (milicia). || Tocsin, alarm (rebato): *tocar a somatén*, to sound the alarm. || FIG. y FAM. Disorder, uproar (alboroto).
— Interj. Catalan war cry.
somático, ca adj. MED. Somatic.
somatología f. MED. Somatology.
sombra f. Shade: *está sentado en la sombra del árbol*, he is sitting in the shade of the tree; *luz y sombra*, light and shade. || Shadow: *la sombra del árbol se proyecta en la pared*, the shadow of the tree is cast on the wall. || FIG. Ghost, shade (fantasma): *las sombras de los muertos*, the ghosts of the dead. | Wit (agudeza). | Luck (suerte). || Shadow (en televisión). || TAUR. Shady section of the bullring. || ASTR. Umbra. || FIG. Darkness: *bruscamente las sombras de la noche cayeron sobre el castillo*, suddenly the darkness of night fell upon the castle; *no veo nada más que sombras a mi alrededor*, all I see is darkness around me. | Shadow (acompañante). | Spot, stain (mancha). | Bit, trace, shade (un poco). || *Amer.* Sunshade (quitasol). | Awning (toldo). | Underlines, *pl.* (falsilla). || — *A la sombra*, in the shade: *los viejos se sentaron a la sombra*, the old men sat in the shade; in jail (en chirona); undercover, secretly: *los contrabandistas trabajan a la sombra*, smugglers work undercover. || FIG. *Burlarse* or *reírse de su sombra*, to laugh at everything. || *Dar sombra*, to give shade (un árbol). || *Dar sombra a*, to shade. || FIG. *Desconfía hasta de su sombra, no se fía ni de su sombra*, he does not even trust his own shadow. || *Hacer sombra*, to cast a shadow (dar sombra), to put in the shade (exceder en calidad). || FIG. *Mala sombra*, bad luck. | *Ni por sombra*, in the least (lo más mínimo): *no sospecharon de él ni por sombra*, they didn't suspect him in the least; by no means (de ninguna manera). | *No dejar a uno ni a sol ni a sombra*, v. SOL. | *No ser más que la sombra* or *ni sombra de lo que era*, to be a mere shadow of one's former self. | *No tiene ni sombra de gracia*, that's not the slightest bit funny. | *Sombra de duda*, shadow of a doubt. || MAT. *Sombra proyectada*, cast shadow. || *Sombras chinescas*, shadow theatre. || FIG. y FAM. *Tener buena sombra*, to be witty (ser ocurrente), to be lucky (tener suerte). | *Tener mala sombra*, to be unpleasant (ser antipático), to be unlucky (no tener suerte), to bring bad luck, to be a jinx (traer mala suerte). | *Tener miedo hasta de su sombra*, to be afraid of one's own shadow. | *Tener una sombra de parecido con*, to bear a faint resemblance to.
sombraje o **sombrajo** m. Shelter from the sun, sunshade. || FIG. *Se le cayeron los palos del sombrajo*, he was discouraged.
sombrar v. tr. To shade.
sombreado m. Shading (gradación del color).
sombreador m. Eyeshadow.
sombrear v. tr. To cast a shadow upon (dar sombra). || To shade (árboles). || To strengthen (un color). || To shade (un dibujo).
sombrerazo m. Doff of one's hat.
sombrerera f. Milliner, hatter. || Hatbox (caja para sombreros).
sombrerería f. Hatter's (tienda para caballeros). || Milliner's (tienda para señoras). || Hat factory (fábrica).
sombrerero m. Hatter (de sombreros para caballeros). || Milliner (de sombreros para señoras).
sombrerete m. Small hat. || BOT. Pileus, cap (de los hongos). || Cowl (de chimenea). || TECN. Cap (de carburador, etc.). | Bonnet (de válvula).
sombrerillo m. BOT. Pileus, cap (de los hongos). | Venus's-navelwort (ombligo de Venus).
sombrero m. Hat: *ponerse el sombrero*, to put on one's hat. || Sounding board (del púlpito). || (Ant.). Spanish grandee's privilege [of keeping his hat on in the presence of the king]. || Cowl, hood (de chimenea). || BOT. Pileus, cap (de los hongos). || MAR. Head (del cabrestante). || TECN. Cap. || — *Calarse el sombrero*, to jam *o* to put one's hat firmly on one's head. || *Con el sombrero puesto* or *en la cabeza*, with one's hat on. || *Quitarse el sombrero ante*, to take one's hat off to (para saludar o admirar). || *Sin sombrero*, hatless, bareheaded. || *Sombrero calañés*, v. CALAÑÉS. || *Sombrero canotier*, straw hat, boater. || *Sombrero cordobés* or *de ala ancha*, wide-brimmed Andalusian hat. || *Sombrero chambergo*, soft hat with a wide brim upturned on one side. || *Sombrero de campana*, cloche hat. || *Sombrero de canal* or *de canoa* or *de teja*, priest's hat. || *Sombrero de copa*, top hat. || *Sombrero de jipijapa*, Panama hat. || *Sombrero de muelles*, opera hat, crush hat. || *Sombrero de paja*, straw hat. || *Sombrero de tres picos* or *sombrero de candil* or *sombrero de tres candiles*, three-cornered hat, cocked hat. || *Sombrero flexible*, soft felt hat, trilby. || *Sombrero hongo*, bowler hat (bombín). || *Sombrero jíbaro*, peasant hat.
sombrilla f. Sunshade, parasol (quitasol).
sombrío, a adj. Sombre [U.S., somber], gloomy (lóbrego). || Dark (oscuro). || Shaded (sombreado). || FIG. Sullen, gloomy (melancólico).
someramente adv. Briefly, superficially.
somero, ra adj. Shallow (de poca profundidad). || FIG. Brief (corto). | Shallow, superficial: *un estudio somero*, a shallow study.
someter v. tr. To subdue, to put down: *someter a los rebeldes*, to subdue the rebels. || To subject: *someter a los rebeldes a cinco años de cárcel*, to subject the rebels to five years in prison; *someter el producto a análisis*, to subject the product to analysis. || To master, to overcome, to subdue (las pasiones). || To subordinate (subordinar). || To submit, to present (entregar). || — *Someter algo a la aprobación de alguien*, to submit sth. for s.o.'s approval. || *Someter a prueba*, to test, to put to the test. || *Someter a tratamiento*, to put under treatment (a un enfermo). || *Someter a una autoridad*, to refer to an authority for a decision. || *Someter a votación*, to put to the vote.
— V. pr. To surrender, to yield (en una lucha). || To undergo: *someterse a una operación*, to undergo an operation. || *Someterse a la opinión de la mayoría*, to bow to the opinion of the majority.
sometimiento m. Submission, submissiveness, subjection (de una persona). || Submission, presentation (de una propuesta, etc.).
somier m. Spring mattress (de cama).
somnambulismo m. Somnambulism, sleepwalking.
somnámbulo, la adj. Somnambulistic, somnambulant.
— M. y f. Somnambulist, sleepwalker.
somnífero, ra adj. Somniferous, soporific, sleep-inducing.
— M. Sleeping pill.
somnolencia f. Somnolence, sleepiness, drowsiness.
somnolento, ta o **somnoliento, ta** adj. Somnolent, sleepy, drowsy (soñoliento).
somorgujar v. tr. To plunge, to submerge, to duck.
— V. intr. y pr. To dive, to plunge (bucear).
somorgujo m. Loon, diver, grebe (ave).
somormujar v. tr. V. SOMORGUJAR.
son m. Sound (sonido): *al son del acordeón*, to the sound of the accordion. || FIG. News, word, rumour [U.S., rumor] (noticia): *corre el son de que le han matado*, the news is going around that they have killed him. | Manner, mode, way (modo): *en este son*, in this manner. || MÚS. Name of an Afro-Antillean dance. || — FIG. *¿A qué son?, ¿a son de qué?*, why?,

for what reason?, for what motive? | *¿A qué son viene esa pregunta?*, what is the reason for that question? || FIG. *Bailar al son que tocan*, to toe the line, to run with the pack. | *En son de*, in a ... tone *o* way *o* manner *o* mood: *en son de burla*, in a humorous tone. | *En son de broma*, jokingly. | *No saber a qué son bailar*, not to know what road to take, to be in a quandary. | *Sin ton ni son*, without rhyme or reason. | *Venir en son de paz*, to come in peace, to come in the spirit of peace.
sonadero m. Handkerchief (pañuelo).
sonado, da adj. Famous (famoso). || Talked-about: *un escándalo muy sonado*, a much talked-about scandal. || — FAM. *Hacer una que sea sonada*, to cause a scandal *o* a sensation *o* a great stir. || *Los días sonados*, holidays.
sonador, ra adj. Noisemaking, sound-producing (que suena o hace ruido).
— M. y f. Noisemaker. || — M. Handkerchief (pañuelo).
sonaja f. Rattle (de niño). || — Pl. Jingling metal disks. || [Type of] tambourine, *sing.* (pandereta).
sonajero m. Rattle.
sonambulismo m. Somnambulism, sleepwalking.
sonámbulo, la adj. Somnambulistic, somnambulant.
— M. y f. Somnambulist, sleepwalker.
sonante adj. Sonant (que suena). || Resounding (que resuena). || Sonorous (sonoro).
sonar m. MAR. Sonar (aparato de detección por el sonido).
sonar* v. intr. To sound: *sonar a hueco*, to sound hollow; *esta trompeta suena raro*, this trumpet sounds funny. || To ring: *la campana suena*, the bell rings. || To strike (reloj): *acaban de sonar las dos*, it has just struck two. || To ring (teléfono). || To be pronounced, to be sounded (una letra): *en la palabra "que" la "u" no suena*, in the word "que" the "u" is not pronounced. || FIG. y FAM. To sound familiar, to ring a bell: *no me suena ese nombre*, that name does not sound familiar [to me]. | To look familiar, to ring a bell: *me suena su cara*, his face rings a bell. || To be mentioned (mencionarse): *su nombre suena entre los de los posibles ministros*, his name is mentioned among those of the possible ministers. || — *Como suena*, as it is pronounced (como se pronuncia), just as I am telling you (literalmente). || FIG. *Cuando el río suena agua lleva*, V. RÍO. | *Sonar a*, to sound like: *eso me suena a burla*, that sounds like a joke to me. | *Sonar bien, mal*, to sound right, wrong (parecer correcto, incorrecto).
— V. tr. To blow (las narices): *no me deja que le suene las narices*, he won't let me blow his nose. || To sound (el claxon, etc.). || To ring (el timbre, una campana). || To sound, to tap, to bang: *sonó la moneda en el mostrador*, he sounded the coin on the counter. || MÚS. To sound, to play (un instrumento).
— V. pr. To blow one's nose (las narices). || *Sonarse las narices*, to blow one's nose.
sonata f. MÚS. Sonata.
sonatina f. MÚS. Sonatina.
sonda f. MAR. Sounding (acción). | Sounding line *o* lead. || MED. Sound, probe. || MIN. Drill, bore. || TECN. Sounding balloon (en meteorología). | Probe (en aeronáutica): *sonda espacial*, space probe. || MAR. *Sonda acústica*, sonic depth finder, echo sounder.
Sonda f. GEOGR. *Islas de la Sonda*, Sunda Islands.
sondable adj. Fathomable.
sondador m. MAR. Sonic depth finder, echo sounder.
sondaje m. V. SONDEO.
sondaleza f. MAR. Sounding line *o* lead.
sondar v. tr. V. SONDEAR.
sondear v. tr. MAR. To sound, to take soundings in. || MED. To probe, to sound. || MIN. To drill, to bore. || FIG. To investigate, to explore (el terreno). | To probe, to sound: *sondear la opinión pública*, to probe public opinion. | To sound out (a una persona).
sondeo m. MAR. Sounding. || MED. Probing, sounding. || MIN. Boring, drilling. || TECN. Wind observation (meteorología). || FIG. Poll, inquiry. || — TECN. *Muestra de sondeo*, drilling sample. || *Sondeo de la opinión pública*, public opinion poll, gallup poll. || MIN. *Sondeo del petróleo*, drilling for oil.
sonetista m. Sonneteer.
soneto m. Sonnet.
songa f. *Amer.* Sarcasm, irony. || *A la songa*, slyly.
sónico, ca adj. Sonic, sound.
sonido m. Sound: *sonido estereofónico*, stereophonic sound; *el sonido de un disparo*, the sound of a shot. || MED. Murmur. || Sound (fonético). || — *Luz y sonido*, son et lumière. || *Velocidad del sonido*, speed of sound.
soniquete m. V. SONSONETE.
sonómetro m. Sonometer.
sonoridad f. Sonority, sonorousness.
sonorización f. Recording the sound track of a film. || Voicing (en fonética). || Installation of amplifying equipment.
sonorizar v. tr. To record the sound track of [a film]. || To voice (en fonética). || To install amplifying equipment in.
sonoro, ra adj. Sonorous. || Sonorous, loud, resounding: *una voz sonora*, a resounding voice. || Sonant, voiced (en fonética). || — *Banda sonora*, sound track. || *Efectos sonoros*, sound effects. || *Onda sonora*, sound wave. || *Película sonora*, talking picture, talkie (fam.).
sonreír v. intr. To smile: *ella sonríe siempre*, she is always smiling; *me sonrió*, she smiled at me. || FIG. To smile on: *la vida le sonríe*, life smiles on him.
— V. pr. To smile.
sonriente adj. Smiling.
sonrisa f. Smile: *tiene una sonrisa bonita*, she has a pretty smile. || — *No perder la sonrisa*, to keep smiling. || *Sonrisa abierta*, broad smile.
sonrojar v. tr. To make blush (avergonzar).
— V. pr. To blush (avergonzarse).
sonrojo m. Blush, blushing (rubor). || Shame (vergüenza).
sonrosado, da adj. Rosy, pink.
sonrosar o **sonrosear** v. tr. To colour *o* to turn pink.
— V. pr. To blush, to turn pink.
sonsacador, ra adj. Wheedling, coaxing, cajoling.
— M. y f. Wheedler, coaxer, cajoler.
sonsacamiento m. Wheedling, coaxing, cajoling.
sonsacar v. tr. To wheedle, to coax, to cajole (sacar algo con palabras amables): *sonsacarle algo a alguien*, to wheedle sth. out of s.o. || To worm out (un secreto). || To entice away (atraer engatusando).
sonsear v. intr. *Amer.* To behave stupidly, to act the fool.
sonsera o **sonsería** f. *Amer.* Silliness (estupidez). | Mere trifle (nadería).
sonso, sa adj. *Amer.* Silly, stupid, inane.
— M. y f. *Amer.* Silly person, fool, bore.
sonsonete m. Rhythmic tapping (golpecitos). || FIG. Song, tune (cantinela). | Monotonous tone, singsong (voz monótona). | Mocking tone (tono de burla).
soñación f. FAM. *¡Ni por soñación!*, not on your life!, not likely!
soñado, da adj. Dream, of one's dreams: *su casa soñada*, the house of her dreams, her dream house. || *Que ni soñado*, marvellous, wonderful: *fue un espectáculo que ni soñado*, it was a marvellous show.
soñador, ra adj. Dreamy, given to dreaming.
— M. y f. Dreamer.
soñar* v. tr. e intr. To dream: *soñó que era rico*, he dreamed he was rich. || To daydream, to dream (despierto): *ella siempre está soñando*, she is always daydreaming; *¿en qué estás soñando?*, what are you dreaming about? || — *¡Ni lo sueñes!* or *¡ni soñarlo!*, not on your life!, not likely! || *Soñar con*, to dream of *o* about: *sueño con ir a Grecia*, I dream of going to Greece. || FAM. *Soñar con los angelitos*, to have sweet dreams. || *Soñar con quimeras*, to build castles in the air. || *Soñar despierto*, to daydream, to dream. || *Soñar en un mundo mejor*, to dream of a better world. || *Soñar en voz alta*, to talk in one's sleep.
soñarrera o **soñera** f. Deep sleep (sueño profundo). || Sleepiness, drowsiness (ganas de dormir).
soñolencia f. Somnolence, sleepiness, drowsiness.
soñolientamente adv. Sleepily, drowsily.
soñoliento, ta adj. Somnolent, sleepy, drowsy.
sopa f. Soup (plato): *sopa de fideos, de cebolla*, noodle, onion soup. || Food served to the poor (comida repartida entre los pobres). || Sop (trozo de pan mojado). || — Pl. Dish consisting of pieces of bread soaked in a liquid (pan mojado en líquido). || — FIG. *Dar sopas con honda a alguien*, to leave s.o. standing, to outshine s.o. | *De la mano a la boca se pierde la sopa*, there is many a slip 'twixt the cup and the lip. | *Estar hecho una sopa*, to be soaked through, to be sopping wet. | *Está hasta en la sopa*, there's no getting away from him (al estar harto de alguien), I am tired of hearing about him (harto de oír hablar de alguien). || *Sopa de ajo*, garlic soup. || *Sopa de cangrejos*, crab bisque. || *Sopa de sobre*, packet soup. || *Sopa de tomate*, tomato soup. || *Sopa de verduras*, vegetable soup. || *Sopa juliana*, julienne soup. || FIG. *Tenerle a uno hasta en la sopa*, to be fed up with s.o. (estar harto de uno), to be tired of hearing about s.o. (harto de oír hablar de uno). || FIG. *Vivir* or *comer de la sopa boba*, to live off others, to be a parasite.
sopapear v. tr. FAM. To slap (dar una bofetada).
sopapo m. Slap (bofetada). || Chuck under the chin.
sopar o **sopear** v. tr. To dip, to sop, to dunk (el pan).
sopero, ra adj. Soup: *plato sopero*, soup dish; *cuchara sopera*, soup spoon.
— M. Soup dish (plato). || — F. Soup tureen (fuente).
sopesar v. tr. To try the weight of (pesar). || FIG. To weigh up (examinar): *sopesar las posibles dificultades*, to weigh up the possible difficulties.
sopetón m. Toast soaked in oil (pan tostado). || FAM. Slap (golpe). || *De sopetón*, unexpectedly, suddenly.
sopicaldo m. Thin soup.
sopita f. Light soup (sopa ligera). || Finger, sop (trozo de pan).
sopitipando m. FAM. Fainting spell (desmayo). || *Le dio un sopitipando*, he fainted.
¡sopla! interj. Good gracious!, good heavens!
sopladero m. Vent.
soplado, da adj. FIG. y FAM. Drunk, tight (borracho). | Overdressed (acicalado). | Conceited (vanidoso).
— M. Glassblowing (del vidrio). || MIN. Deep fissure.
soplador, ra m. y f. Blower. || Troublemaker (incitador). || — M. Glassblower (de vidrio). || Fan (aventador). || *Amer.* Prompter (teatro).
sopladura f. Blowing (acción). || Glassblowing (del vidrio). || Air hole *o* bubble (defecto).

soplamocos m. inv. FAM. Slap, punch.
soplapollas adj. inv. POP. V. JILIPOLLA.
soplar v. intr. To blow: *soplar con la boca*, to blow with the mouth; *el viento sopla*, the wind blows. || FAM. To squeal (denunciar). | To whisper the answer (apuntar). | To booze (beber).
— V. tr. To blow out (apagar): *soplar una vela*, to blow out a candle. || To blow off: *soplar los polvos de encima del libro*, to blow the dust off the book. || To blow up: *soplar un globo*, to blow up a balloon. || To blow on: *soplar la sopa para que se enfríe*, to blow on the soup to cool it. || To fan (el fuego). || FIG. To inspire (la musa). | To whisper: *soplar la respuesta a uno*, to whisper the answer to s.o. || TECN. To blow (vidrio). || FIG. To huff (juego de damas). || FIG. y FAM. To split on, to squeal on (delatar). | To tell on, to tell tales on, to tattle on (entre niños). | To deal, to fetch (golpes). | To steal, to snitch, to pinch (birlar). | To rush (cobrar): *¿cuánto te soplaron por eso?*, what did they rush you for that? || — FIG. y FAM. *El negocio ya no sopla como antes*, business is not as good as it used to be. | *Saber de qué lado sopla el viento*, to know which way the wind blows. | *Soplar una torta a alguien*, to slap s.o.
— V. pr. To blow on: *soplarse los dedos para calentárselos*, to blow on one's fingers to warm them. || FAM. To down (comida): *soplarse una botella de vino*, to down a bottle of wine. | To spend (tiempo).
soplete m. Blowlamp [U.S., blowtorch] (de soldador). || Blowtube (de vidrieros).
soplido m. Blow, puff. || Blast (muy fuerte).
soplillo m. Fan (aventador).
soplo m. Blow, puff (con la boca). || Gust (de viento). || FIG. Second, minute, moment: *llego en un soplo*, I'll be with you in a moment. || FIG. y FAM. Sneak, telltale (niño soplón). | Informer (de la policía). | Tip-off (delación). || — FIG. y FAM. *Dar el soplo*, to squeal, to split (denunciar), to inform (informar). || FIG. *La vida es un soplo*, life is short. || MED. *Soplo cardiaco*, heart murmur.
soplón, ona adj. FAM. Tattletale, telltale, sneaky (entre niños).
— M. y f. FAM. Tattletale, telltale, sneak (entre niños). | Informer, squealer (de la policía). || *Amer.* Prompter (apuntador). | Policeman (policía).
soplonear v. intr. FAM. To squeal, to split.
soplonería f. FAM. Taletelling, sneaking.
soponcio m. FAM. Faint, swoon. || FAM. *Me dio un soponcio*, I fainted.
sopor m. Sleepiness, drowsiness.
soporífero, ra o **soporífico, ca** adj. Soporiferous, soporific, sleep-inducing.
— M. y f. Soporific, sleeping pill.
soportable adj. Bearable.
soportador, ra adj. Supporting.
— M. y f. Supporter.
soportal m. Portico, porch (de una casa). || — Pl. Arcade, colonnade (de una calle).
soportar v. tr. To support, to bear, to carry, to hold up: *las columnas soportan el arco*, the columns support the arch. || FIG. To bear, to endure, to stand: *no puedo soportar a mi primo*, I can't stand my cousin; *soportó bien la operación*, he bore the operation well. | To weather (una tormenta, un huracán).
soporte m. Support. || HERÁLD. Supporter (de blasón). || Base, stand (de una figura). || Holder (de maceta, de lápiz, etc.). || Stand (atril de libro, partituras musicales). || Hanger, bracket (de repisa). || Prop (para muros). || Rest (para herramientas, escopetas, tacos de billar). || FIG. Support, pillar (apoyo).
soprano m. y f. MÚS. Soprano.
sor f. Sister (religiosa): *Sor María*, Sister Mary.
sorber v. tr. To suck (un huevo, la sangre, etc.). || To sip (un líquido). || FIG. To soak up, to absorb (absorber). | To swallow up (el mar). | To breath in, to inhale (por la nariz). || — FIG. y FAM. *Sorber el seso a uno*, V. SESO. | *Sorberse los vientos por alguien*, to be crazy about s.o.
— V. pr. To soak up, to absorb.
sorbete m. Sherbet, water ice: *sorbete de limón*, lemon sherbet. || *Amer.* Top hat (chistera).
sorbetera f. Freezer (heladora).
sorbetón m. Gulp (de líquido).
sorbito m. Little sip.
sorbo m. Sip: *sólo tomé un sorbo de leche*, I only took a sip of milk. || Gulp (trago). || — *Beber a sorbos*, to drink in small sips, to sip one's drink. || *De un sorbo*, in one swallow.
sorche o **sorchi** m. FAM. Soldier (soldado), recruit (recluta).
sordamente adv. Silently. || Secretly.
sordera f. Deafness.
sordidez f. Squalor (suciedad). || Meanness (avaricia).
sórdido, da adj. Sordid, squalid (sucio). || Mean, miserable (avaro).
sordina f. MÚS. Damper (piano). | Mute (instrumentos de viento). || *En sordina*, muted (música), secretly, on the quiet (en secreto).
sordino m. MÚS. Fiddle.
sordo, da adj. Deaf: *sordo de nacimiento*, deaf from birth; *quedarse sordo*, to go deaf. || Voiceless, unvoiced (en fonética). || FIG. Dull (dolor). | Muffled, dull (voz, ruido). | Pent-up, held back: *una cólera sorda*, pent-up anger. | Deaf, indifferent, unmoved: *permaneció sordo a mis ruegos*, he remained unmoved by o deaf to my pleas. | Secret, undeclared (guerra). | Dim, dull (linterna). || — FIG. y FAM. *A la sorda, a lo sordo, a sordas*, silently, on the quiet. || *A palabras necias, oídos sordos*, V. PALABRA.
— M. y f. Deaf person. || — *Hacerse el sordo*, to turn a deaf ear, to pretend not to hear. || *Los sordos*, deaf people, the deaf.
sordomudez f. Deaf-muteness.
sordomudo, da adj. Deaf-and-dumb, deaf-mute.
— M. y f. Deaf-mute.
sorgo m. BOT. Sorghum.
sorianense adj. [Of *o* from] Soriano (Uruguay).
— M. y f. Native *o* inhabitant of Soriano (Uruguay).
soriano, na adj. [Of *o* from] Soria (Old Castile).
— M. y f. Native *o* inhabitant of Soria.
soriasis f. MED. Psoriasis.
sorites m. Sorites (raciocinio).
sorna f. Sarcasm (mofa). || Calmness, coolness, deliberation (calma). || — *Hablar con sorna*, to talk sarcastically. || *Mirar con sorna*, to look mockingly *o* slyly at.
sorocharse v. pr. *Amer.* To get mountain sickness. | To blush (avergonzarse).
soroche m. *Amer.* Mountain sickness. | Blush (rubor). | Galena (piedra).
sorocho, cha *Amer.* Unripe (fruta).
sorprendente adj. Surprising, amazing, astonishing.
sorprender v. tr. To surprise, to amaze, to astonish (causar sorpresa): *¿le sorprende la noticia?*, does the news surprise you? || To catch unawares, to surprise, to take by surprise (coger desprevenido): *sorprendió al ladrón*, he caught the thief unawares. || To discover (descubrir): *sorprendimos su secreto*, we discovered his secret. || To abuse, to deceive (engañar): *sorprender su buena fe*, to abuse one's good faith. || To overhear (una conversación).
— V. pr. To be surprised, to be amazed: *se sorprendió al verme*, he was surprised to see me.
sorprendido, da adj. Surprised, amazed, astonished: *quedarse sorprendido ante*, to be surprised at *o* by. || Caught (cogido). || Discovered (descubierto). || Abused (engañado).
sorpresa f. Surprise: *¡vaya sorpresa!*, what a surprise! || Surprise (del roscón de Reyes). || Surprise (regalo inesperado). || Astonishment, surprise, amazement: *se le notó la sorpresa en la cara*, you could see the astonishment in his face. || — *Ataque por sorpresa*, surprise attack. || *Coger de sorpresa*, to catch unawares, to take by surprise. || *Con gran sorpresa suya*, much to his surprise, to his great surprise. || *Dar* or *causar* or *producir una sorpresa a alguien*, to surprise s.o., to give s.o. a surprise.
sorpresivo, va adj. *Amer.* Unexpected (inesperado). | Surprising (que sorprende).
sorrostrada f. Insolence.
sorteable adj. Able to be drafted (recluta). || Which can be raffled (rifa).
sorteador, ra adj. Raffling.
— M. y f. Raffler.
sorteamiento m. Raffle, casting *o* drawing of lots.
sortear v. tr. To draw *o* to cast lots for (echar a suertes): *no sabían a quién darlo, y lo sortearon*, they did not know who to give it to, so they drew lots for it. || To allot (asignar o repartir puestos, trabajos, etc.). || To decide by lot (decidir). || To choose by lot (escoger). || To draft (los quintos). || To toss up for (echar a cara o cruz). || To raffle (rifar). || FIG. To avoid (evitar). | To overcome, to get round (un obstáculo, una dificultad). | To elude (eludir). | To dodge (esquivar). | To evade, to get round (las preguntas). || DEP. To dribble (driblar). | To dodge (esquivar). || *Hoy sortean los premios de la lotería*, they are drawing the winning numbers in the lottery today.
— V. intr. To draw lots (echar a suertes). || To toss up (echar a cara o cruz).
sorteo m. Draw: *el ganador del sorteo*, the winner of the draw. || Allotment (de puestos). || Toss (a cara o cruz). || Draw (de la lotería): *sorteo extraordinario de Navidad*, special Christmas draw. || Raffle (rifa). || FIG. Dodging, evading (acción de evitar o esquivar). || *Por sorteo*, by lot: *elegido por sorteo*, chosen by lot.
sortija f. Ring (anillo). || Curl, ringlet (de pelo). || Hunt the thimble (juego). || *Sortija de sello*, signet ring.
sortilegio m. Sorcery, witchcraft, witchery (hechicería). || Spell: *echar un sortilegio a*, to cast a spell on. || Charm (encanto).
sortílego, ga m. y f. Sorcerer, wizard (hechicero). || Soothsayer (adivino).
S.O.S. m. S.O.S. (señal de socorro): *lanzar un S.O.S.*, to send out an S.O.S.
sosa f. BOT. Saltwort. || QUÍM. Soda: *sosa cáustica*, caustic soda.
sosaina m. y f. Dull person, bore.
sosamente adv. In a dull *o* uninteresting way, boringly.
sosegadamente adv. Calmly, quietly.
sosegado, da adj. Calm, quiet.
sosegador, ra adj. Calming, quieting, tranquilizing.
— M. y f. Pacifier.

sosegar* v. tr. To calm, to quieten, to tranquilize (calmar). || To reassure: *la noticia me ha sosegado*, the news has reassured me.
— V. intr. To rest (descansar).
— V. pr. To calm down (tranquilizarse).
sosera f. Boring thing (cosa sosa).
sosería f. Insipidity, insipidness. || FIG. Insipidity, insipidness, dullness. || *Ser una sosería*, to be dull *o* boring.
sosia m. Double.
sosiego m. Tranquility, calmness, quietness. || *Con sosiego*, calmly.
soslayar v. tr. To put sideways, to tip on its side, to put on a slant (inclinar). || FIG. To avoid, to dodge, to evade (eludir). | To get round (una dificultad, un obstáculo).
soslayo (al o **de)** loc. Sideways, aslant, on a slant. || FIG. *Mirar de soslayo*, to look sideways [at], to look out of the corner of one's eye [at] (mirar de lado), to look askance [at] (con desaprobación).
soso, sa adj. Tasteless, insipid (de poco sabor). || Saltless, unsalted (sin sal). || FIG. Dull, boring, uninteresting (sin gracia). | Silly (tonto). | Dull, flat : *chiste soso*, dull joke; *estilo soso*, flat style.
sospecha f. Suspicion: *despertar las sospechas*, to arouse suspicion; *la policía tiene sospechas de él*, the police have suspicions about him. || — *Fuera* or *por encima de toda sospecha*, above suspicion. || JUR. *Tener en sospecha*, to hold under suspicion. || *Tener la sospecha de que*, to have a suspicion that. || *Tener sospechas de que*, to have one's suspicions that, to suspect that. || *Vehementes* or *vivas sospechas*, a strong suspicion.
sospechable adj. Suspicious, open to suspicion, suspect.
sospechar v. tr. e intr. To suspect: *sospecho que Pedro miente*, I suspect that Pedro is lying. || To think, to imagine, to suppose: *lo sospechaba*, I imagined as much. || *Sospechar de*, to suspect, to be suspicious of.
sospechosamente adv. Suspiciously.
sospechoso, sa adj. Suspicious: *un tipo sospechoso*, a suspicious character. || Suspect (dudoso).
— M. y f. Suspicious person, suspect: *han detenido a varios sospechosos*, several suspects have been detained.
sostén m. Support (soporte). || ARQ. Support, prop. || MAR. Steadiness (de un barco). || Bra, brassière (prenda de mujer). || FIG. Support, pillar (apoyo). | Sustenance (sustento). || — *Sostén de* or *con cuerpo*, *sostén largo*, long-line brassière. || FIG. *Sostén de familia*, breadwinner.
sostenedor, ra adj. Supporting, sustaining.
— M. y f. Supporter, upholder (defensor).
sostener* v. tr. To support, to hold up: *sostener con una viga*, to support with a beam; *columnas que sostienen una bóveda*, columns that support a vault. || To hold (sujetar). || To hold up: *el agua de mar nos sostiene más que el agua dulce*, salt water holds us up more than fresh water; *estabas tan borracho que te tuvimos que sostener*, you were so drunk that we had to hold you up. || To bear (ataque, peso). || To carry, to bear (carga). || To keep up, to maintain (la velocidad, la categoría, los precios). || FIG. To defend, to uphold (defender): *sostener la causa*, to defend the cause. | To endure, to tolerate, to stand, to bear: *sostener una situación muy desagradable*, to tolerate a very disagreeable situation. | To carry on, to hold, to keep up (conversación). | To support, to keep, to maintain, to provide for (una familia). | To maintain, to carry on, to keep up: *sostener una correspondencia con alguien*, to maintain correspondence with s.o.; *sostener buenas relaciones*, to maintain good relations. | To hold (entrevista). | To maintain, to affirm: *él sostiene que el gobierno va a caer*, he maintains that the government is going to fall. | To support, to back (apoyar). | To keep going (dar fuerza): *al final lo único que le sostenía era el deseo de vivir*, in the end it was just his will to live which kept him going. || *Sostener la mirada de alguien*, to stare s.o. out, to look s.o. unflinchingly in the eye.
— V. pr. To hold o.s. up, to support o.s. (agarrándose a algo). || To stand up (mantenerse de pie): *no podía sostenerme de cansado que estaba*, I was so tired I could not stand up. || FIG. To remain (continuar). | To stay, to remain: *sostenerse en el poder*, to stay in power. | To support o.s., to earn a living: *me sostengo dando clases*, I earn a living giving lessons. | To keep going, to live: *se sostiene a base de inyecciones*, he lives on injections. || — FIG. *Sostenerse en*, to stand firm in: *se sostiene en su actitud liberal*, he stands firm in his liberal attitude. | *Sostenerse mutuamente*, to support one another *o* each other.
sostenidamente adv. Steadily.
sostenido, da adj. MÚS. Sharp: *fa sostenido*, f sharp. || Sustained: *esfuerzo sostenido*, sustained effort. || Continuous || Steady (en la Bolsa).
— M. MÚS. Sharp: *doble sostenido*, double sharp.
sostenimiento m. Support (apoyo). || Maintenance (mantenimiento). || Sustenance: *el padre se encarga del sostenimiento de la familia*, the father is responsible for the sustenance of the family. || Keeping, maintaining (de relaciones). || Defence (de una tesis).
sota f. Jack, knave (naipe).
sotabanco m. Attic, garret (buhardilla). || ARQ. Springer (de arco).
sotabarba f. Newgate frill (barba). || Double chin (papada).
sotana f. Soutane, cassock.
sótano m. Basement. || Cellar (bodega).
sotavento m. MAR. Leeward.
sotechado m. Shed.
soterrado, da adj. Buried, underground (enterrado). || FIG. Hidden, concealed (oculto).
soterramiento m. Burying.
soterraño, ña adj. Subterranean, underground.
soterrar* v. tr. To bury.
sotileza f. (Ant.). Subtlety (sutileza).
soto m. Grove (arboleda). || Thicket (matorral).
soufflé m. CULIN. Soufflé.
soviet m. Soviet.
soviético, ca adj. Soviet.
— M. y f. Soviet, Russian.
sovietización f. Sovietization.
sovietizar v. tr. To sovietize.
sovjoz m. State farm in the U.S.S.R.
spaghettis m. pl. Spaghetti, *sing.*
spleen m. Spleen.
sport m. Sports: *chaqueta de sport*, sports jacket; *coche de sport*, sports car. || *Ir vestido de sport*, to be dressed casually.
— OBSERV. In Spanish, *sport* is used only to qualify certain cars or pieces of clothing. « Sport » (football, etc.) is translated by *deporte* (*I like sport*, me gusta el deporte).
sprint m. DEP. Sprint.
sprintar v. intr. DEP. To sprint.
sprinter m. DEP. Sprinter (velocista).
sputnik m. Sputnik (satélite artificial).
staccato adj./s.m. MÚS. Staccato.
stajanovismo m. Stakhanovism.
stajanovista m. y f. Stakhanovite.
staliniano, na adj./s. Stalinist.
stalinismo m. Stalinism.
stalinista adj./s. Stalinist.
stand m. Stand (caseta).
standard adj. Standard: *modelo standard*, standard model.
standardización f. Standardization.
standardizar v. tr. To standardize.
standing m. Standing (posición social). || DEP. Balancing [on a stationary bicycle].
starter m. AUT. Choke. || DEP. Starter (juez de salida).
statu quo m. Status quo.
steeplechase m. Steeplechase (carrera de obstáculos).
sténcil m. Stencil (cliché de multicopista).
steward m. Steward (auxiliar de vuelo).
stick m. DEP. Stick (hockey).
stock m. Stock (existencias).
stock-car m. Stock car (para competiciones).
stop m. Stop sign (señal de tráfico). || Stop (en un telegrama).
strip-tease m. Striptease.
su (pl. *sus*) adj. pos. de la 3ª persona. His [de él]: *su padre*, his father. || Her [de ella]: *su padre*, her father. || Its [neutro]: *su color* (*del cuadro*), its colour. || One's [de uno]. || Your [de usted, de ustedes]: *su hermano*, your brother. || Their [de ellas, de ellos, neutro]: *su padre*, their father; *sus ejércitos*, their armies.
suabo, ba adj./s. Swabian.
suasorio, ria adj. Persuasive.
suave adj. Soft, smooth: *cutis suave*, soft skin. || Smooth, even: *carretera suave*, smooth road. || FIG. Mild, clement (el tiempo). | Gentle, soft (el viento). | Mild, lenient (castigo, regla, ley). | Mild, smooth (sabor, tabaco). | Gentle, mild, sweet (de carácter). | Soft, gentle, subdued (luz, color). | Gentle, soft, smooth (voz, música, sonido, movimiento). | Easy, smooth: *paso suave*, easy pace. | Gentle (pendiente, curva). || — FIG. *Más suave que un guante*, as meek as a lamb. | *Suave como el terciopelo* or *la piel de un niño* or *la piel de una manzana*, [as] smooth as silk *o* as a baby's skin.
suavidad f. Smoothness, softness, suavity (p.us.): *la suavidad de su cutis*, the softness of her skin. || Smoothness, evenness: *la suavidad de la carretera*, the smoothness of the road. || FIG. Mildness (del tiempo). | Leniency (de castigo, regla, ley). | Mildness, smoothness (de sabor). | Gentleness, mildness, sweetness (del carácter). | Softness (de color, luz). | Gentleness, softness, smoothness (de voz, música, sonido, movimiento). | Ease, smoothness: *la suavidad de su paso*, the smoothness of his gait. | Gentleness (de pendiente, curva).
suavizador, ra adj. Smoothing, softening.
— M. Razor strop.
suavizar v. tr. To soften: *suaviza la piel*, it softens the skin. || To make smoother (una pasta). || To smooth [out]: *suavizar la superficie*, to smooth the surface. | To strop (navaja de afeitar). || FIG. To soften, to temper, to sweeten (carácter). | To temper, to ease (castigo, regla, ley). | To temper (caballo). | To soften, to tone down, to subdue (luz, color). | To soften (sonido, voz). | To ease: *suavizar el paso*, to ease the pace. | To make more gentle (curva, pendiente). || FIG. *Suavizar asperezas*, to smooth things over.

subacuático, ca adj. Subaqueous, underwater.
subafluente m. Tributary.
subalimentación f. Undernourishment, underfeeding (desnutrición).
subalimentado, da adj. Undernourished, underfed.
subalimentar v. tr. To undernourish, to underfeed.
subalterno, na adj. Subordinate, subaltern. || Auxiliary (personal). || Secondary (secundario).
— M. Subordinate, subaltern.
subálveo, a adj. Subfluvial.
subarrendador, ra m. y f. Subtenant (subarrendatario). || Subletter (que da en arrendamiento).
subarrendamiento m. Sublease.
subarrendar* v. tr. To sublet, to sublease.
subarrendatario, ria m. y f. Subtenant.
subarriendo m. Sublease.
subártico, ca adj. Subartic.
subasta f. JUR. Auction (venta). | Tender (para la ejecución de una obra). || — *Sacar a subasta*, to auction. || *Salir a subasta*, to be on auction. || *Vender en pública subasta*, to put up for auction, to sell at auction, to auction, to auction off.
subastador, ra m. y f. Auctioneer.
subastar v. tr. To auction [off], to sell at auction.
subcampeón m. Runner-up.
subcarpeta f. Folder (para documentos).
subclase f. BOT. y ZOOL. Subclass.
subclavio, via adj. ANAT. Subclavian.
subcomisión f. o **subcomité** m. Subcommittee.
subconsciencia f. Subconscious.
subconsciente adj./s.m. Subconscious.
subcontinente m. Subcontinent.
subcontratista m. Subcontractor.
subcontrato m. Subcontract. || *Ceder, tomar en subcontrato*, to subcontract.
subcutáneo, a adj. Subcutaneous: *inyección subcutánea*, subcutaneous injection.
subdelegación f. Subdelegation.
subdelegado, da adj./s. Subdelegate.
subdelegar v. tr. To subdelegate.
subdesarrollado, da adj. Underdeveloped.
subdesarrollo m. Underdevelopment.
subdiaconado o **subdiaconato** m. REL. Subdiaconate.
subdiácono m. REL. Subdeacon.
subdirección f. Assistant *o* deputy managership (cargo). || Assistant *o* deputy manager's office (oficina).
subdirector m. Assistant manager, deputy manager.
súbdito, ta adj. Subject (de un monarca).
— M. y f. Citizen (de un país). || Subject (de un monarca).
subdividir, subdividirse v. tr. y pr. To subdivide.
subdivisión f. Subdivision.
subdominante f. MÚS. Subdominant.
subempleo m. Underemployment.
suberoso, sa adj. Suberous, suberose.
subespecie f. BOT. y ZOOL. Subspecies.
subestación f. ELECTR. Substation.
subestimación f. Underestimation.
subestimar v. tr. To underestimate.
subexponer v. tr. FOT. To underexpose.
subexposición f. FOT. Underexposure.
subexpuesto, ta adj. FOT. Underexposed.
subfamilia f. BOT. y ZOOL. Subfamily.
subfluvial adj. Subfluvial.
subgénero m. BOT. y ZOOL. Subgenus.
subgobernador m. Lieutenant *o* deputy governor.
subibaja m. Seesaw (columpio).
subida f. Ascent: *la subida de la montaña*, the ascent of the mountain. || Climb: *una subida peligrosa*, a dangerous climb. || Slope, hill (pendiente). || FIG. Rise, increase (precios). | Rise (temperatura). | Increase (aumento). || *Luchar contra la subida de precios*, to combat rising prices.
subido, da adj. FIG. High: *precios subidos*, high prices. | Intense, bright, strong (color). | Strong (olor). || — FIG. *Subido de color* or *de color subido*, V. COLOR. | *Subido de precio*, high-priced, expensive. | *Subido de tono*, daring, risqué.
subíndice m. MAT. Subindex.
subinquilino, na m. y f. Subtenant.
subir v. tr. To go up, to climb (una calle, una cuesta). || To go up to climb, to climb up, to ascend (escalera). || To put (poner): *subir el equipaje al tren*, to put the luggage on the train. || To carry up, to bring up, to take up: *sube la maleta al piso*, carry the suitcase up to the apartment. || To raise (una pared). || To lift, to raise (cabeza). || FIG. To turn up (radio, televisión). | To increase (sonido). | To strengthen, to tone up (color). | To increase, to put up, to raise (sueldo, precio). | To increase *o* to put up *o* to raise the price of (una mercancía). | To promote (promocionar). || MÚS. To raise (tono).
— V. intr. To go up, to come up: *subir al quinto piso*, to go up to the fifth floor; *subir en ascensor*, to go up in a lift. || To get into: *subir a un coche*, to get into a car. || To get in: *¡anda, sube!*, come on!, get in! || To get on, to board (barco, tren, avión): *subir al avión*, to get on the plane. || To mount, to get on (animales, bicicleta): *subir a caballo*, to mount one's horse. || To rise, to climb, to go up: *el avión sube*, the plane climbs. || To rise (río, marea, sol). || To slope up (terreno). || FIG. To increase: *la curiosidad de todo el mundo sube*, everyone's curiosity is increasing. | To rise, to go up: *suben los precios*, prices are rising; *sube la temperatura*, the temperature rises. | To get worse (la fiebre). | To get on, to get ahead, to advance: *ha subido mucho en su profesión*, he has got on well in his profession. || To rise, to grow [higher] (una pared al construirse). || To climb (trepar): *subir a un árbol*, to climb up a tree. || COM. To total, to come to, to amount to: *la cuenta sube a 1000 pesetas*, the bill comes to 1000 pesetas. || MÚS. To go up, to rise (tono). || — *Es más fácil bajar que subir*, it's easier coming down than going up. || *Subir a bordo*, to go *o* to come aboard, to board. || FIG. *Subir a las tablas*, to go on the stage. | *Subir al trono*, to come to *o* to ascend [to] the throne. | *Subir de categoría*, to better one's position (una persona), to become more select (un barrio, etc.). | *Subir de tono*, V. TONO.
— V. pr. To climb up (implica dificultad o esfuerzo): *subirse a un árbol*, to climb up a tree; *subirse al muro, al tejado*, to climb up on the wall, up on the roof. || To go up (por una escalera, etc.): *subirse a su cuarto*, to go up to one's room. || To rise (los precios). || To get into (a un coche). || To get on, to board (barco, avión). || To mount, to get on (a caballo). || To pull up: *súbete los calcetines*, pull your socks up. || — FIG. *Subirse a la parra*, V. PARRA. | *Subirse a las barbas de*, to treat disrespectfully. | *Subirse a* or *por las paredes*, V. PARED. | *Subírsele a la cabeza a uno*, to go to one's head (vino honores, cargos): *el vino se le subió a la cabeza*, the wine went to his head. | *Subírsele el pavo a uno* or *subírsele los colores a la cara a uno*, to blush, to go as red as a beetroot. | *Subírsele la sangre a la cabeza a uno*, to see red. | *Subírsele los humos a la cabeza a alguien*, V. HUMO.
súbitamente adv. Suddenly, all of a sudden, unexpectedly.
súbito, ta adj. Sudden, unexpected: *cambio súbito de temperatura*, sudden change in temperature; *una súbita llamada*, an unexpected call. || *De súbito*, suddenly, unexpectedly, all of a sudden.
— Adv. Suddenly.
subjefe m. Assistant chief.
subjetividad f. Subjectivity.
subjetivismo m. FIL. Subjectivism.
subjetivo, va adj. Subjective.
subjuntivo, va adj./s.m. GRAM. Subjunctive.
sublevación f. Revolt, rebellion, rising.
sublevar v. tr. To incite *o* to rouse to rebellion (excitar). || FIG. To infuriate, to upset: *tanta injusticia me subleva*, all this injustice infuriates me.
— V. pr. To revolt, to rebel, to rise [up] (rebelarse).
sublimación f. Sublimation.
sublimado m. QUÍM. Sublimate.
sublimar v. tr. To sublimate, to sublime. || To sublime, to praise, to exalt (ensalzar a alguien).
— V. pr. To sublime.
sublime adj. Sublime. || Noble, lofty (noble, elevado). || *Lo sublime*, the sublime.
sublimidad f. Sublimity.
sublunar adj. Sublunary, sublunar, earthly.
submarinista m. Submarine crew member.
submarino adj. Submarine, underwater.
— M. Submarine (buque).
submaxilar adj. ANAT. Submaxillary: *glándula submaxilar*, submaxillary gland.
submúltiplo, pla adj./s.m. MAT. Submultiple.
subnormal adj. MED. Subnormal (anormal): *niños subnormales*, subnormal children. || — M. MAT. Subnormal (de una curva).
suboficial m. MIL. Non-commissioned officer, warrant officer. || MAR. Petty officer.
suborbitario, ria adj. ANAT. Suborbital.
suborden m. BOT. y ZOOL. Suborder.
subordinación f. Subordination.
subordinado, da adj. Subordinate. || GRAM. *Oración subordinada*, subordinate clause.
— M. y f. Subordinate.
subordinar v. tr. To subordinate: *subordinar la razón a la fe*, to subordinate reason to faith.
— V. pr. To subordinate o.s.
subproducción f. Underproduction.
subproducto m. By-product.
subrayable adj. Noteworthy, worth emphasizing.
subrayado, da adj. Underlined. || In italics (en bastardilla).
— M. Underlining (con una línea). || Italics, *pl.*
subrayar v. tr. To underline, to underscore. || FIG. To emphasize, to underline (poner énfasis): *subrayar cada palabra con un ademán*, to emphasize each word with a gesture.
subreino m. ZOOL. Subkingdom.
subrepción f. Subreption.
subrepticio, cia adj. Surreptitious.
subrigadier m. MIL. Lance corporal.
subrogación f. JUR. Subrogation.
subrogar v. tr. JUR. To subrogate, to substitute.
— V. pr. To be subrogated *o* substituted.
subsanable adj. Excusable (disculpable). || Reparable, repairable, mendable (reparable).
subsanar v. tr. To excuse, to overlook (disculpar). || To repair, to mend (reparar). || FIG. To rectify, to put right, to remedy, to correct, to mend (remediar): *subsanar un error*, to correct an error. | To get round,

to overcome (una dificultad, un obstáculo). | To make up for (compensar).
subscribir v. tr. V. SUSCRIBIR.
subscripción f. V. SUSCRIPCIÓN.
subscripto, ta adj. V. SUSCRITO.
subscriptor, ra m. y f. V. SUSCRIPTOR.
subsecretaría f. Undersecretaryship (cargo). || Undersecretary's office (oficina).
subsecretario, ria m. y f. Undersecretary. || *Subsecretario de Estado*, undersecretary of State.
subsecuente adj. Subsequent.
subseguir*, subseguirse v. intr. y pr. To follow.
subsidiario, ria adj. Subsidiary. || JUR. Ancillary.
subsidio m. Subsidy, grant, aid. || — *Subsidio de enfermedad*, sick pay *o* benefit. || *Subsidio de paro*, unemployment benefit. || *Subsidio de vejez*, old age pension. || *Subsidio de vivienda*, housing allowance. || *Subsidios familiares*, family allowance.
subsiguiente adj. Subsequent.
subsistencia f. Subsistence (vida). || Sustenance (lo necesario para vivir).
subsistente adj. Surviving, lasting, subsisting, [still] existing.
subsistir v. intr. To subsist, to survive, to last, to remain, to still exist (perdurar): *subsiste la costumbre*, the custom survives. || To subsist, to live (vivir).
subsónico, ca adj. Subsonic.
substancia f. V. SUSTANCIA.
— OBSERV. The spelling *sustancia* (without *b*) is at present the more common. This applies to all Spanish words beginning with *subst*, except *substrato*.
substanciación f. V. SUSTANCIACIÓN.
substancial adj. V. SUSTANCIAL.
substancialismo m. V. SUSTANCIALISMO.
substanciar v. tr. V. SUSTANCIAR.
substancioso, sa adj. V. SUSTANCIOSO.
substantivar v. tr. V. SUSTANTIVAR.
substantividad f. V. SUSTANTIVIDAD.
substantivo, va adj./s.m. V. SUSTANTIVO.
substitución f. V. SUSTITUCIÓN.
substituible adj. V. SUSTITUIBLE.
substituidor, ra adj. V. SUSTITUIDOR.
substituir* v. tr. V. SUSTITUIR.
substitutivo, va adj./s.m. V. SUSTITUTIVO.
substituto, ta m. y f. V. SUSTITUTO.
substracción f. V. SUSTRACCIÓN.
substraendo m. V. SUSTRAENDO.
substraer* v. tr. V. SUSTRAER.
substrato m. GEOL. y FIL. Substratum. || FIG. Substratum.
subsuelo m. Subsoil.
subtangente f. MAT. Subtangent.
subte m. *Amer.* Underground, tube [U.S., subway] (metro).
subtender v. tr. MAT. To subtend.
subteniente m. MIL. Second lieutenant.
subterfugio m. Subterfuge.
subterráneo, a adj. Subterranean, underground.
— M. Cellar (bodega). || Underground passage *o* tunnel (conducto). || *Amer.* Underground [U.S., subway] (metro).
subtipo m. Subtype.
subtitular v. tr. To subtitle.
subtítulo m. Subtitle.
subtotal m. COM. Subtotal.
subtropical adj. Subtropical.
suburbano, na adj. Suburban.
— M. y f. Suburbanite. || — M. Suburban train.
suburbio m. Suburb (arrabal). || Slums, *pl.* (barrio pobre).
subvalorar v. tr. To underrate, to underestimate.
subvención f. Subsidy, subvention, grant.
subvencionar v. tr. To subsidize.
subvenir* v. tr. To help, to assist (*a*, with *o* in) [ayudar]. || To meet, to defray (los gastos). || To pay for, to defray the cost of (proveer).
subversión f. Subversion. || Revolution (revolución).
subversivo, va adj. Subversive: *literatura subversiva*, subversive literature.
subvertir* v. tr. To subvert. || To disturb (el orden).
subyacente adj. Subjacent, underlying.
subyugación f. Subjugation.
subyugador, ra adj. FIG. Captivating (cautivador).
subyugar v. tr. To subjugate. || FIG. To master, to subdue (sus pasiones). | To captivate, to charm (encantar).
succínico, ca adj. Succinic (ácido).
succión f. Suction.
succionar v. tr. To suck, to suck in.
sucedáneo, a adj. Substitute, succedaneous.
— M. Substitute, succedaneum.
suceder v. intr. To succeed, to follow: *Juan sucede a Carlos en el puesto*, John succeeds Charles in the job; *la noche sucede al día*, night follows day. || To succeed (a un rey). || To be the heir of (ser el heredero de): *los hijos suceden a sus padres*, the sons are the heirs of their fathers. || To happen, to occur (ocurrir): *sucedió que*, it happened that; *eso sucede a menudo*, that often happens. || — *Lo más que puede suceder*, the worst that can happen. || *Lo que sucede es que*, the fact is that. || *Por lo que pueda suceder*, just in case. || *¿Qué sucede?*, what is the matter?, what is going on? || *Suceda lo que suceda*, come what may, whatever happens. || *Sucede con el fútbol lo mismo que con el baloncesto*, it is the same with football as it is with basketball.
— V. pr. To follow each other *o* one another.
sucedido m. FAM. Happening, event (suceso). || *Lo sucedido*, what happened; what has happened; what had happened.
sucesión f. Succession, series (serie): *una sucesión de desgracias*, a succession of misfortunes. || JUR. Issue, heirs, *pl.*: *se murió sin sucesión*, he died without issue. | Inheritance (herencia): *sucesión intestada, testada*, intestate, testate inheritance. | Succession: *en la línea de sucesión al trono*, in the line of succession to the throne. || — JUR. *Derecho de sucesión*, inheritance rights. | *Derechos de sucesión*, probate duties (al legalizar un testamento), death duty, death tax (al heredar). | *Sucesión forzosa*, forced inheritance, inheritance-at-law. | *Sucesión universal*, universal succession (la del heredero universal).
sucesivamente adv. Successively. || *Y así sucesivamente*, and so forth, and so on.
sucesivo, va adj. Successive, following. || Consecutive: *ha tenido tres operaciones sucesivas*, he had three consecutive operations. || Running: *cinco días sucesivos*, five days running. || — *En días sucesivos*, in days to come. || *En lo sucesivo*, henceforth (de ahora en adelante), thenceforth (a partir de entonces).
suceso m. Event, happening, occurrence (acontecimiento). || Incident (incidente). || Outcome, issue (resultado). || *El lugar del suceso*, the scene of the accident (accidente), the scene of the crime (crimen), the site of the disaster (siniestro). || *Sección de sucesos*, accident and crime reports, *pl.* (en los periódicos).
sucesor, ra adj. Succeeding.
— M. y f. Successor (el que viene después). || Heir (heredero).
sucesorio, ria adj. JUR. Successory. || *Comunidad sucesoria*, community of heirs.
suciamente adv. Dirtily, filthily. || DEP. Unfairly. || FIG. Vilely.
suciedad f. Dirt, filth (cosa que ensucia). || Dirtiness, filthiness: *la suciedad de un cuarto*, the dirtiness of a room. || FIG. Obscenity. | Foul deed (acción innoble). | Vileness (ruindad). || DEP. Unfairness.
sucintamente adv. Briefly, succintly, concisely.
sucinto, ta adj. Brief, concise, succint. || FIG. Brief (muy corto).
sucio, cia adj. Dirty: *trapo sucio*, dirty rag. || Filthy (muy sucio). || DEP. Dirty, foul, unfair: *juego sucio*, foul play. || Unfair (poco honrado). || FIG. Dirty, filthy, nasty: *siempre me dan el trabajo sucio*, they always give me the dirty work. | Dirty, shady (negocio). | Dirty, filthy: *lenguaje sucio*, dirty language. | Despicable, vile (ruin). || Which dirties easily: *el blanco es un color sucio*, white is a colour which dirties easily. || FIG. Off, dirty: *un rojo sucio*, an off red. | Smudged: *un dibujo sucio*, a smudged drawing. || — FIG. *Conciencia sucia*, guilty conscience. || FIG. *En sucio*, in rough, in rough draft. || FIG. y FAM. *Estar más sucio que el palo de un gallinero*, to be filthy dirty. || FIG. *Jugar sucio*, to play dirty *o* foul. || FIG. y FAM. *Lengua sucia*, coated *o* furred tongue (de indigestión). | *Tener una lengua sucia*, to be foul-mouthed.
sucre m. Sucre (unidad monetaria del Ecuador).
sucrense adj. [Of *o* from] Sucre (Venezuela, Bolivia).
— M. y f. Native *o* inhabitant of Sucre (Venezuela, Bolivia).
sucreño, ña adj. [Of *o* from] Sucre [Bolivia].
— M. y f. Native *o* inhabitant of Sucre.
sucrosa f. QUÍM. Sucrose.
suculencia f. Succulence.
suculento, ta adj. Succulent.
sucumbir v. intr. To succumb, to yield: *el castillo sucumbió a los ataques*, the castle succumbed to the attacks. || To succumb, to die (morir). || FIG. To succumb, to yield: *sucumbir a la tentación*, to yield to temptation. | To be defeated: *sucumbió en las elecciones*, he was defeated in the elections. | To fall (imperio, país). || JUR. To lose a suit.
sucursal adj. Branch.
— F. Branch office, branch: *la sucursal de un banco*, the branch of a bank. || Subsidiary: *la sucursal de una empresa*, the subsidiary of a company.
sud m. *Amer.* South.
sudación f. Sweating.
sudadera f. Sweat. || V. SUDADERO. || FAM. *Pegarse una sudadera*, to sweat buckets, to get covered with sweat.
sudadero m. Handkerchief, sweating cloth (paño). || Saddlecloth (debajo de la silla de montar). || Sweating room (sitio para baños de sudor). || Damp patch (sitio húmedo).
Sudáfrica n. pr. f. GEOGR. South Africa.
sudafricano, na adj./s. South African.
Sudamérica n. pr. f. GEOGR. South America.
sudamericano, na adj./s. South American.
Sudán n. pr. m. GEOGR. Sudan.
sudanés, esa adj./s. Sudanese (del Sudán). || *Los sudaneses*, the Sudanese.
sudar v. intr. To perspire, to sweat: *sudo mucho*, I perspire a lot. || To sweat: *las paredes sudan*, the walls sweat. || FIG. To work hard (trabajar mucho).

|| FIG. y FAM. *Sudar a chorros* or *a mares*, to drip with sweat.
— V. tr. To make sweaty (mojar): *sudó la ropa de la cama*, he made the bed linens sweaty. || FIG. y FAM. To make a great effort for, to work hard for: *he sudado el premio*, I worked hard for the prize. | To make a great effort to, to work hard to: *sudó el aprobado del examen*, he worked hard to pass the exam. || FIG. To exude, to ooze, to give off: *los pinos sudan resina*, pine trees exude sap. || — FIG. y FAM. *Sudar la gota gorda* or *el quilo* or *tinta*, to be dripping with sweat (transpirar mucho), to sweat blood (para hacer un trabajo). | *Sudar sangre*, to sweat blood.

sudario m. Shroud (para cadáveres). || REL. *El Santo sudario*, the Holy Shroud.

sudestada f. Southeasterly wind.

sudeste adj. Southeast, southeastern (parte). || Southeasterly (dirección). || Southeast (viento).
— M. Southeast. || Southeast wind (viento).

Sudetes n. pr. m. pl. Sudeten Mountains.

sudista adj. HIST. Southern.
— M. y f. HIST. Southerner.

sudoeste adj. Southwest, southwestern (parte). || Southwesterly (dirección). || Southwest (viento).
— M. Southwest. || Southwest wind (viento).

sudor m. Sweat, perspiration. || FIG. Moisture, sweat (en una pared, etc.). || — Pl. Hard work, *sing.*, sweat, *sing.* (trabajo). || — FIG. *Con el sudor de su frente*, by the sweat of one's brow. || FIG. y FAM. *Costarle a uno muchos sudores*, to cause s.o. a lot of sweat. | *Chorrear de sudor* or *estar bañado en* or *empapado en sudor*, to be dripping with sweat *o* bathed in sweat, to be in a sweat. || *Tener la frente cubierta* or *perlada de sudor*, to have perspiration on one's brow. || FIG. *Tener sudores fríos*, to be in a cold sweat.

sudorífero, ra adj. Sudoriferous.

sudorífico, ca adj./s.m. Sudorific.

sudoríparo, ra adj. ANAT. Sudoriferous, sudoriparous. || *Glándula sudorípara*, sweat gland.

sudoroso, sa adj. Sweaty, sweating.

sudsudeste m. South-southeast. || South-southeast wind (viento).

sudsudoeste m. South-southwest. || South-southwest wind (viento).

Suecia n. pr. f. GEOGR. Sweden.

sueco, ca adj. Swedish.
— M. Swedish (idioma). || — M. y f. Swede. || FIG. y FAM. *Hacerse el sueco*, to pretend not to understand, to play dumb, to turn a deaf ear.

suegra f. Mother-in-law.

suegro m. Father-in-law. || *Los suegros*, one's parents-in-law, one's in-laws.

suela f. Sole. || Strong leather (cuero). || Leather tip (del taco de billar). || Washer (del grifo). || ZOOL. Sole (lenguado). || ARQ. Socle (zócalo de un muro). | Skirting board (madero en la parte inferior de la pared). || — Pl. Sandals (sandalias). || — FIG. y FAM. *Duro como la suela de un zapato*, tough as leather. || *Medias suelas*, half soles. || FIG. y FAM. *No llegarle a uno a la suela del zapato*, not to hold a candle to s.o. | *Un pícaro de siete suelas*, an out-and-out villain.

sueldo m. Salary, pay (retribución): *sueldo mensual*, monthly salary. || — *A sueldo*, paid: *un espía a sueldo*, a paid spy; hired: *asesino a sueldo*, hired assassin. || *Estar a sueldo*, to be on a salary. || *Estar a sueldo (de)*, to be employed [by] (un empleado), to be in the pay [of] (espías, asesinos, etc.). || *Sueldo atrasado*, back pay. || *Sueldo base*, basic pay. || *Sueldo de hambre*, starvation pay.

suelo f. Ground: *los niños estaban jugando en el suelo*, the children were playing on the ground; *se cayó al suelo*, he fell to the ground. || Soil, land: *suelo fértil*, fertile soil; *en suelo extranjero*, on foreign soil. || Floor, flooring (interior): *el suelo de esta habitación*, the floor of this room. || FIG. Bottom (de un recipiente). || Surface: *el suelo de la carretera está resbaladizo*, the road surface is slippery. || — FIG. *Arrastrar a uno por el suelo* or *por los suelos*, to drag s.o. through the mud, to run s.o. down. | *Arrastrarse* or *echarse por los suelos*, to grovel, to humble o.s., to crawl. | *Besar el suelo*, to fall flat on one's face. | *Dar consigo* or *con los huesos en el suelo*, to fall, to come a cropper. || FIG. *¡Del suelo no pasa!*, it won't hurt (cuando se cae algo). | *Echar al suelo*, to demolish. | *Echar por los suelos*, to ruin (hacer fracasar un plan, etc.). | *En el santo suelo*, on the [blessed] floor *o* ground. | *Estar por los suelos*, to be held in low esteem (cosas, personas), to be rock-bottom (precios), to be very low (moral). | *Irse al suelo*, to fall through: *todas mis esperanzas se han ido al suelo*, all my hopes have fallen through. | *Medir el suelo*, to fall full-length. | *Poner por los suelos*, to run down. || *Suelo patrio* or *natal*, native land, homeland. || *Venirse al suelo*, to fall down (derrumbarse), to fail (fracasar).

suelta f. Release (de palomas, de presos). || Fetter (de los animales). || Reserve team of oxen (bueyes). || Place where oxen are released to graze. || *Dar suelta*, to give time off (dar tiempo libre).

suelto, ta adj. Loose: *los caballos están sueltos en el prado*, the horses are loose in the meadow; *el tornillo está suelto*, the screw is loose; *venden el arroz suelto*, they sell rice loose. || Loose, down (pelo): *ella lleva el pelo suelto*, she wears her hair down. || Undone (cordones). || Untied (sin atar). || Odd: *tengo dos tomos sueltos de la enciclopedia*, I have two odd volumes of the encyclopedia; *un zapato suelto*, an odd shoe. || Free, released, out: *ha estado en la cárcel, pero ya está suelto*, he was in jail, but he has been released *o* he is out now. || Loose, at large: *el asesino anda suelto todavía*, the killer is still at large. || Loose (el vientre). || Fluid, thin (líquido). || Loose, loose-fitting (prendas de vestir). || FIG. Isolated: *esos son hechos sueltos*, those are isolated facts. | Fluent, easy-flowing (conversación, estilo). | Free: *movimientos sueltos*, free movements. | Agile, nimble (ágil). | Daring (atrevido). | Free and easy (desembarazado): *una mujer suelta*, a free and easy woman. | Blank (verso). || — FIG. *Cabo suelto*, loose end: *no dejes ningún cabo suelto en este asunto*, don't leave any loose ends in this affair. | *Dar rienda suelta (a)*, to give free rein [to]. || *Dinero suelto*, loose change. || FIG. *Estar muy suelto en*, to be good *o* quite fluent in: *ya está muy suelto en inglés*, he is good at English now. || *Estos artículos no se venden sueltos*, these articles are not sold separately *o* singly *o* loose. || *Hojas sueltas*, loose sheets [of paper] (de papel). || *Piezas sueltas*, parts. || FIG. *Ser suelto de manos*, to be free with one's hands.
— M. Change, small *o* loose change: *no tengo suelto*, I haven't any small change. || Item (de periódico).

sueño m. Sleep: *sueño pesado*, heavy sleep. || Drowsiness, sleepiness (cansancio, ganas de dormir). || Dream: *anoche tuve un sueño horrible*, last night I had a horrible dream. || FIG. Dream, illusion (ilusión): *esos son sueños de juventud*, those are the dreams of youth. | Dream (encanto): *es un sueño*, he's a dream; *he visto un niño que es un sueño*, I saw a dream of a baby. || — FIG. *Caerse de sueño*, to be falling asleep on one's feet. || *Coger* or *conciliar el sueño*, to get to sleep. || *Dar sueño*, to make sleepy: *este discurso me da sueño*, this speech is making me sleepy. || FIG. y FAM. *Descabezar un sueño*, to take forty winks, to have a nap. || FIG. *Dormir el sueño de los justos*, to sleep the sleep of the just. | *Dulce sueño* beloved (amado). || *Echar un sueño*, to take a nap. || MED. *Enfermedad del sueño*, sleeping sickness. || FIG. *En sueños*, in one's dreams. || *Entregarse al sueño*, to abandon o.s. to sleep, to sink into sleep. || *Entre sueños*, half asleep. || FIG. *Eso lo has visto en sueños*, you must have been dreaming. | *Espantar el sueño*, to ward off sleep. || *La clave de los sueños*, the key to dream interpretation. || FIG. *La vida es sueño*, life is a dream. | *Mundo de sueños*, dream world. | *¡Ni en* or *por sueños!*, not on your life! || *Perder el sueño por algo*, to lose sleep over sth. || *Quitar el sueño*, to keep awake: *el café te quitará el sueño*, the coffee will keep you awake; *los problemas de la oficina me quitan el sueño*, office problems keep me awake. || FIG. *Sueño de una noche de verano*, midsummer night's dream. | *Sueño dorado*, life's dream, greatest dream: *mi sueño dorado es vivir en el campo*, my greatest dream *o* my life's dream is to live in the country. | *Sueño eterno*, eternal rest *or* sleep. | *Sueño hecho realidad*, dream come true. || *Sueño hipnótico*, hypnotic sleep. || *Tener el sueño ligero*, to be a light sleeper. || *Tener sueño*, to be *o* to feel tired *o* sleepy. || *Tengo un sueño que no veo*, I am falling asleep on my feet.

suero m. Whey (de la leche). || Serum (de la sangre). || MED. *Suero fisiológico*, physiological salt solution, physiological saline solution.

sueroterapia f. MED. Serotherapy, serum therapy.

suerte f. Fate, destiny: *así lo quiso la suerte*, fate willed it so. || Luck, fortune (buena or mala fortuna): *tener mala suerte*, to have bad luck. || Destiny, fate, lot (porvenir): *tu suerte está decidida*, your destiny is decided. || Lot, situation, conditions, *pl.* (condiciones): *mejorar la suerte de los campesinos*, to improve the lot of the rural population. || Lot (elección): *elegir por* or *a suerte*, to decide by lot. || Kind, sort: *conoce a toda suerte de personas*, he knows all kinds of people. || Quality, class (calidad): *primera suerte*, first class. || Manner, way (manera). || Trick (de prestidigitador). || Lot (parcela). || TAUR. Stage, "suerte" [one of the divisions of the bullfight]. || *Amer.* Lottery ticket (billete de lotería). | — *¡Buena suerte!* or *¡suerte!*, good luck! || *Caerle* or *tocarle a uno en suerte*, to fall to s.o.'s lot: *me ha caído en suerte nacer rico*, it fell to my lot to be born rich. || *Confiar en la suerte*, to trust to luck. || *Con un poco de suerte ganaremos*, with a bit of luck we'll win. || *Dar* or *traer buena, mala suerte*, to bring good, bad luck, to be lucky, unlucky. || *De otra suerte*, otherwise. || *De suerte que*, so [that]: *te hemos tratado muy bien de suerte que no tienes por qué quejarte*, we have treated you very well, so you have no reason to complain. || *De tal suerte que*, in such a way that. || *Echar suertes* or *echar a suertes*, to draw lots: *echar algo a suertes*, to draw lots for sth.; to toss [for sth.] (a cara o cruz). || *Estar de mala suerte*, to be out of luck. || *Estar de suerte*, to be in luck. || *Golpe de suerte*, stroke of luck. || *Hombre de suerte*, lucky man. || FIG. *La suerte es ciega*, luck is blind. || *La suerte está echada*, the die is cast. || *Leerle la suerte a uno*, to tell s.o.'s fortune. || *¡Mala suerte!*, hard luck!, bad luck! || || TAUR. *Poner en suerte (el toro)*, to place [the bull]. || *Por suerte*, luckily, fortunately: *por suerte vino*, fortunately he came. || *Probar (la) suerte*, to try one's

luck. || *¡Qué suerte más negra* or *más perra!*, what rotten luck! || *¡Que tengas (mucha) suerte!*, good luck!, the best of luck! || *Quiso la suerte que*, as fate would have it, as luck would have it. || *Salir a suerte*, to be drawn. || *Tener buena, mala suerte*, to be lucky, unlucky, to have good, bad luck. || *Tener la suerte de*, to be lucky enough to. || *Tener suerte*, to be lucky. || *Tener una suerte loca* or *de mil demonios*, to have the luck of the devil. || *Tentar la suerte*, to push one's luck, to tempt fate. || *Traer buena, mala suerte*, to be lucky, unlucky, to bring good luck, bad luck: *el número que me trae buena suerte*, my lucky number.
suertero, ra adj. *Amer.* Lucky.
— M. *Amer.* Seller of lottery tickets.
suertudo, da adj. Lucky, jammy (fam.).
sueste m. Southeast. || MAR. Sou'wester, southwester (sombrero).
suéter m. Sweater.
Suez m. pr. GEOGR. Suez: *canal de Suez*, Suez canal.
suficiencia f. Sufficiency (capacidad). || Adequacy (conveniencia). || FIG. Competence, capability. | Self-importance, smugness, complacency (presunción). || FIG. *Tener aire de suficiencia*, to look smug, to look cocksure.
suficiente adj. Sufficient, enough (bastante). || Suitable (apto). || FIG. Self-important, cocksure, self-satisfied, smug, complacent (engreído). || — *Lo suficiente*, sufficient, enough: *tengo lo suficiente para vivir*, I have enough to live on. || *No tiene suficiente anchura*, it is not wide enough.
suficientemente adv. Sufficiently, enough: *suficientemente grande*, sufficiently big, big enough.
sufijo, ja adj. GRAM. Suffixal.
— M. GRAM. Suffix.
sufra f. Backband (del harnés).
sufragáneo, a adj./s.m. Suffragan.
sufragar v. tr. To help, to support (ayudar). || To pay, to defray, to cover: *sufragar los gastos de un pleito*, to pay the cost of a suit. || To finance, to pay for: *sufragar un proyecto*, to finance a project.
— V. intr. *Sufragar por*, to vote for.
sufragio m. Suffrage: *sufragio universal*, universal suffrage. || Vote (voto): *recuento de sufragios*, counting of the votes. || Help, aid (ayuda). || REL. Service for the redemption of souls from purgatory.
sufragismo m. Suffragettism.
sufragista m. Suffragist (adicto al sufragismo). || — F. Suffragette.
sufrido, da adj. Long-suffering, patient (paciente). || FIG. y FAM. Complaisant (marido). || FIG. Serviceable, hard-wearing (tela). || FIG. *Un color poco sufrido*, an easily soiled colour.
— M. Complaisant husband.
sufridor, ra adj. Suffering.
sufrimiento m. Suffering (dolor). || Misery (miseria). || FIG. Tolerance (tolerancia). | Patience (paciencia). | Sufferance (capacidad para sufrir).
sufrir v. tr. To suffer: *sufrir persecuciones*, to suffer persecutions. || To have, to suffer (experimentar): *ha sufrido un grave accidente*, he has had a bad accident; *sufrir un ataque de corazón*, to have a heart attack. || To undergo: *sufrir una operación, un cambio*, to undergo an operation, a change. || To do, to sit, to take (un examen). || To suffer: *sufrir una derrota, las consecuencias*, to suffer defeat, the consequences; *sufrir reveses de fortuna, un fracaso*, to suffer setbacks, a failure. || To tolerate: *no sufriré tus insultos*, I will not tolerate your insults. || FAM. To bear, to stand, to put up with (tolerar a una persona): *no puedo sufrir a Juan*, I can't stand John. || FIG. *Sufrir su* or *un calvario*, to carry one's cross.
— V. intr. To suffer: *durante su vida sufrió mucho*, during his life he suffered a lot. || — FIG. *Sufrir como un condenado*, to go through hell. || *Sufrir de*, to suffer from *o* with: *sufro de dolores de cabeza*, I suffer from headaches; *sufrir del corazón*, to suffer with one's heart, to suffer from heart trouble.
sugerencia f. Suggestion.
sugerente o **sugeridor, ra** adj. Suggestive.
sugerir* v. tr. To suggest.
sugestión f. Suggestion (sugerencia). || Autosuggestion. || Hypnotic power (poder hipnótico).
sugestionable adj. Suggestible, impressionable, easily influenced.
sugestionador, ra adj. Suggesting.
sugestionar v. tr. To influence. || To have a hypnotic power over (dominar, fascinar).
sugestivo, va adj. Suggestive, stimulating. || Attractive.
suicida adj. Suicidal.
— M. y f. Suicide (persona). || FIG. Daredevil, madcap (intrépido).
suicidarse v. pr. To commit suicide, to take one's life.
suicidio m. Suicide: *intento de suicidio*, attempted suicide.
sui géneris adj. Sui generis.
suite f. Suite (en un hotel). || MÚS. Suite.
Suiza n. pr. f. GEOGR. Switzerland.
suizo, za adj./s. Swiss: *suizo alemán*, Swiss German. || — M. (Ant.). Foot soldier. || Bun (bollo).
— OBSERV. El plural de *Swiss* es *Swiss*.
sujeción f. Subjection (acción de sujetar). || Subjection, subordination: *sujeción a las leyes*, subordination to the law. || Fastening (ligadura). || Obligation: *no me gustan las sujeciones*, I don't like obligations.
sujetador, ra adj. Fastening, binding.
— M. Brassière, bra (prenda femenina). || Fastener (objeto para sujetar). || Clip (para el pelo, papeles).
sujetalibros m. inv. Bookend.
sujetapapeles m. inv. Paper clip.
sujetar v. tr. To secure, to fasten, to hold, to fix, to attach (fijar): *este cuadro está sujetado* or *sujeto por un clavo*, this picture is held by a nail. || To hold (sostener): *sujeta el libro un momento*, hold the book a moment. || To keep hold of, to hold down (a la fuerza): *los guardias lo sujetaron para que no se escapase*, the guards held him down so that he wouldn't escape. || To seize (agarrar). || To hold up: *unos tirantes le sujetan el delantal*, straps hold up her apron. || To tie tightly (atar): *sujeta bien el nudo*, tie the knot tightly. || To hold in place, to keep in place (el pelo). || To fasten together (papeles). || To subdue (someter). || To subordinate (subordinar). || FIG. To restrain, to control, to keep in check, to hold down *o* back: *este chico necesita a alguien que le sujete*, this boy needs s.o. to restrain him; *hay que sujetar al pueblo para evitar la revolución*, the people must be held down *o* kept in check to avoid revolution. | To tie down: *los quehaceres de la casa la sujetan mucho*, the housework ties her down a lot. || DEP. To tackle (rugby). || *Sujetar con grapas, con clavos*, to staple, to nail.
— V. pr. To hold on, to hang on: *para no caer me sujeté a las ramas*, so as not to fall I hung on to the branches; *¡sujétate bien!*, hold on tight! || To stay up: *sin tirantes este pantalón no se sujeta*, without braces these trousers won't stay up. || To subject o.s. [*a*, to] (someterse). || FIG. To abide by, to respect, to stick to: *hay que sujetarse a la constitución*, one must abide by the constitution. | To act in accordance with (ajustarse a).
sujeto, ta adj. Subject, liable (susceptible): *este proyecto está sujeto a cambios*, this plan is subject to changes. || Fastened, secure: *la cuerda está bien sujeta*, the rope is securely fastened *o* quite secure. || Attached, fixed: *¿está el cuadro bien sujeto?*, is the painting firmly fixed? || FIG. Subject (sometido): *sujeto a derechos arancelarios*, subject to customs duties. | Tied down (ocupado): *está muy sujeto al trabajo de la oficina*, he is very tied down by office work. || — *Sujeto a la aprobación de*, subject to the approval of. || FIG. *Tener a alguien muy sujeto*, to keep s.o. well in check, to keep s.o. under close control.
— M. Fellow, individual (persona): *la policía detuvo a un sujeto sospechoso*, the police detained a suspicious fellow. || GRAM. y FIL. Subject.
sulfamida MED. Sulphonamide [U.S., sulfonamide].
sulfatación f. QUÍM. Sulphating [U.S., sulfating].
sulfatado m. QUÍM. Sulphating [U.S., sulfating].
sulfatador, ra adj. Which sulphates, sulphating [U.S., sulfating].
— F. Sulphating machine [U.S., sulfating machine].
sulfatar v. tr. QUÍM. To sulphate [U.S., to sulfate].
sulfato m. QUÍM. Sulphate [U.S., sulfate): *sulfato de hierro*, iron sulphate.
sulfhídrico, ca adj. QUÍM. Sulphuretted [U.S., sulfuretted]. || *Ácido sulfhídrico*, hydrosulphuric acid, hydrogen sulphide.
sulfito m. QUÍM. Sulphite [U.S., sulfite].
sulfurado, da adj. QUÍM. Sulphuretted [U.S., sulfuretted]. || FIG. Infuriated.
— M. AGR. Sulphuration, sulphurization [U.S., sulfuration, sulfurization].
sulfurar v. tr. QUÍM. To sulphurate, to sulphurize [U.S., to sulfurate, to sulfurize]. || FIG. To infuriate (irritar).
— V. pr. FIG. To lose one's temper: *¡no te sulfures!*, don't lose your temper!
sulfúrico, ca adj. QUÍM. Sulphuric [U.S., sulfuric]: *ácido sulfúrico*, sulphuric acid.
sulfuro m. QUÍM. Sulphide [U.S., sulfide].
sulfuroso, sa adj. QUÍM. Sulphurous, sulphureous [U.S., sulfurous, sulfureous]. || *Agua sulfurosa*, sulphur water [U.S., sulfur water].
sultán m. Sultan.
sultana f. Sultana.
sultanato m. o **sultanía** f. Sultanate.
suma f. Sum: *la suma de tres y cuatro es siete*, the sum of three and four is seven. || Sum, total: *la factura llegó a la suma de cinco mil pesetas*, the bill came to a sum *o* a total of five thousand pesetas. || Sum, amount (de dinero). || MAT. Addition: *hacer una suma*, to do *o* to make an addition. || FIG. Summary (recopilación). | Substance, essence (lo más sustancial de una cosa). || — *En suma*, in short. || MAT. *Hacer sumas*, to do sums, to add up.
sumador, ra adj. Adding.
— F. Adding machine.
sumamente adv. Extremely, highly.
sumando m. MAT. Addend.
sumar v. tr. To add, to add up: *sumar dos números*, to add two numbers. || To amount to, to total: *sus ingresos suman diez mil pesetas*, his income amounts to ten thousand pesetas. || To total: *tres países que suman cien millones de habitantes*, three countries

which total one hundred million inhabitants. || FIG. To gather (recopilar). | To summarize, to sum up (compendiar). || *Máquina de sumar*, adding machine.
— V. intr. MAT. To add up. || *Suma y sigue*, carried forward (en contabilidad), and that's not all (y hay más).
— V. pr. To join [in]: *me sumé a la conversación*, I joined in the conversation; *sumarse a un partido*, to join a party. || *Otras ventajas que se suman a la rapidez son*, advantages other than speed which come into play *o* which must be taken into account are.
sumaria f. JUR. Indictment.
sumarial adj. JUR. Pertaining to an indictment.
sumariamente adv. Summarily.
sumariar v. tr. JUR. To indict.
sumario, ria adj. Summary, brief (breve). || JUR. Summary: *proceso sumario*, summary proceedings.
— M. Summary (resumen). || JUR. Indictment. || FIG. *Pertenece al secreto del sumario*, it should be kept secret.
sumarísimo, ma adj. JUR. Swift, expeditious.
sumergible adj. Submersible.
— M. Submarine (embarcación).
sumergimiento m. Submersion, submergence.
sumergir v. tr. To submerge. || FIG. To overwhelm [*en*, with] (agobiar). | To plunge (hundir).
— V. pr. To sink, to submerge. || FIG. *Sumergirse en*, to become immersed in.
sumerio, ria adj./s. Sumerian.
sumersión f. Submersion, submergence.
sumidero m. Drain, sewer (alcantarilla). || Cesspool (pozo negro).
sumiller m. (Ant.) Chamberlain.
suministración f. V. SUMINISTRO.
suministrador, ra adj. Which supplies, supplying.
— M. y f. Supplier (proveedor).
suministrar v. tr. To supply, to provide, to furnish (proveer): *suministrar algo a alguien*, to supply s.o. with sth., to supply sth. to s.o.
suministro m. Supply. || Supply, supplying, provision (acción de suministrar). || — Pl. Supplies (víveres). || Supply, *sing.*: *nuestros suministros de municiones*, our ammunition supply. || *Suministro a domicilio*, home delivery.
sumir v. tr. To sink, to submerge (hundir). || REL. To receive (consumir). || FIG. To plunge: *sumir a alguien en la duda*, to plunge s.o. into doubt; *sumir a alguien en la miseria*, to plunge s.o. into misery.
— V. pr. To sink (hundirse). || To run away (las agüas residuales, etc.). || FIG. To immerse o.s., to become immersed: *se sumió en los estudios*, he immersed himself in his studies. || To be sunken (las mejillas, el pecho). || FIG. *Sumirse en el sueño*, to sink into a deep sleep.
sumisión f. Submission. || Submissiveness (carácter sumiso).
sumiso, sa adj. Submissive.
súmmum m. Summit: *el súmmum de la sabiduría*, the summit of knowledge. || Height: *el súmmum de la desvergüenza*, the height of shamelessness. || *Ser el súmmum*, to be the limit (ser el colmo).
sumo, ma adj. Greatest, highest: *la suma felicidad*, the greatest happiness. || Supreme, highest: *suma autoridad*, supreme authority. || Extreme : *con sumo cuidado*, with extreme care. || — *A lo sumo*, at [the] most. || *De sumo*, completely. || *El Sumo Sacerdote*, the High Priest. || *En sumo grado*, v. GRADO. || *Sumo Pontífice*, Sovereign Pontiff.
sunlight m. CINEM. Sunlight.
sunna f. Sunna, Sunnah (ortodoxia musulmana).
sunnita m. Sunnite (musulmán ortodoxo).
suntuario, ria adj. Sumptuary.
suntuosidad f. Sumptuosity (lujo). || Sumptuousness (magnificencia).
suntuoso, sa adj. Sumptuous: *una casa suntuosa*, a sumptuous house.
supeditación f. Subjection, subordination.
supeditar v. tr. To subdue (avasallar). || To subordinate (subordinar). || FIG. To subject: *supedito mi viaje a la decisión de mis padres*, I subject my trip to my parents' decision. || *Estar supeditado a*, to be subject to, to depend on: *todo está supeditado a la venta de la casa*, everything is subject to the sale of the house.
— V. pr. To subject o.s. to, to bow to: *no estoy dispuesta a supeditarme a sus caprichos*, I will not subject myself to his whims.
súper adj. FAM. Super.
— F. Super (gasolina).
superable adj. Superable, surmountable.
superabundancia f. Superabundance.
superabundante adj. Superabundant.
superabundar v. intr. To superabound.
superación f. Overcoming: *la superación de dificultades*, the overcoming of difficulties, overcoming difficulties. || Excelling (de uno mismo). || *Afán de superación*, urge to improve o.s. *o* to better o.s.
superactividad f. Superactivity.
superalimentación f. Overfeeding.
superalimentar v. tr. To overfeed.
superar v. tr. To surpass (ser superior): *este producto supera a todos*, this product surpasses all others. || To outshine, to beat, to outdo (a una persona). || To overcome (al adversario). || To overcome: *he superado todas las dificultades*, I have overcome all the difficulties. || To break, to beat (una plusmarca). || — *Estar superado*, to be over: *la época del colonialismo está superada*, the age of colonialism is over. || *Hemos superado lo más difícil*, we are over the most difficult part, the worst is behind us now.
— V. pr. To surpass o.s., to excel o.s.: *se ha superado en el examen*, he excelled himself in the exam. || To better o.s., to do better: *en la vida hay que intentar superarse*, one must always try to better o.s.
superávit m. COM. Surplus, superavit.
— OBSERV. According to the Spanish Academy the word *superávit* is invariable. In practice, however, the plural forms *superávit* and *superávits* are both used.
supercapitalización f. Overcapitalization.
supercapitalizar v. tr. COM. To overcapitalize.
supercarburante m. High-octane fuel.
superciliar adj. ANAT. Superciliary: *arco superciliar*, superciliary arch *o* ridge.
supercompresión f. TECN. Supercharging.
supercomprimir v. tr. TECN. To supercharge.
superchería f. Fraud, trick.
superdesarrollado, da adj. Overdeveloped.
superdesarrollo m. Overdevelopment.
superdirecta f. AUT. Overdrive.
superdominante f. MÚS. Superdominant.
supereminencia f. Supereminence.
supereminente adj. Supereminent.
superempleo m. Overemployment.
supererogación f. Supererogation.
superestructura f. Superstructure.
superfetación f. Superfetation, superfoetation.
superficial adj. Superficial. || — *Aguas superficiales*, surface waters. || *Herida superficial*, flesh wound, superficial injury.
superficialidad f. Superficiality.
superficialmente adv. Superficially.
superficie f. Surface: *la superficie del agua*, the surface of the water. || Area (extensión): *la superficie de una ciudad*, the area of a city. || MAT. Area (área). || — *De superficie*, surface: *transporte de superficie*, surface transport. || MAR. *Salir a la superficie*, to surface (un submarino, buceador), to come *o* to float to the surface (un objeto). || AGR. *Superficie aprovechable*, cultivable land. || AUT. *Superficie de rodadura*, tread (del neumático). || *Superficie de rozamiento*, friction surface. || AVIAC. *Superficie sustentadora*, lifting surface. || *Superficie terrestre*, land surface.
superfino, na adj. Superfine.
superfluidad f. Superfluity, superfluousness.
superfluo, a adj. Superfluous.
superfortaleza f. AVIAC. Superfortress (avión).
superfosfato m. QUÍM. Superphosphate.
superheterodino m. Superheterodyne (radio).
superhombre m. Superman.
superhumeral m. REL. Superhumeral.
superintendencia f. Superintendence.
superintendente m. Superintendent.
superior adj. Superior, high: *de calidad superior*, high quality. || Upper: *mandíbula superior*, upper jaw; *los pisos superiores*, the upper floors. || Upper, top: *la parte superior de la biblioteca*, the upper part of the bookcase. || Higher, above: *todos los números superiores a diez*, all numbers above ten *o* higher than ten. || Superior: *es superior a todos*, he is superior to everybody. || Better (mejor). || *Enseñanza superior*, higher education.
superior m. Superior: *tienes que obedecer a tu superior*, you must obey your superior. || REL. Superior (de convento o monasterio).
superiora f. REL. Mother superior.
superioridad f. Superiority. || Advantage: *el púgil tuvo una clara superioridad sobre su adversario*, the boxer had a clear advantage over his opponent. || *La superioridad*, a higher authority.
superlativo, va adj. Superlative (excelente). || GRAM. Superlative.
— M. GRAM. Superlative.
supermercado m. Supermarket.
supernumerario, ria adj. Supernumerary. || MIL. On leave without pay.
— M. y f. Supernumerary.
superpoblación f. Overpopulation (del mundo, de un país). || Overcrowding, overpopulation (de las ciudades).
superpoblado, da adj. Overpopulated (mundo, país). || Overcrowded, overpopulated (ciudad).
superponer* v. tr. To superpose, to superimpose. || FIG. To put before: *él superpone la ambición a la tranquilidad*, he puts ambition before tranquility.
— V. pr. FIG. To come before (anteponerse): *al miedo se superpone el sentido del deber*, the sense of duty comes before fear.
superposición f. Superposition.
superpotencia f. Superpower, great power.
superpresión f. TECN. Overpressure.
superproducción f. Overproduction. || CINEM. Mammoth production (película).
superpuesto, ta adj. Superimposed, superposed.
superrealismo m. Surrealism.
supersaturación f. QUÍM. Supersaturation.
supersaturar v. tr. To supersaturate.
supersecreto, ta adj. Top secret.

supersónico, ca adj. AVIAC. Supersonic: *avión supersónico*, supersonic aircraft.
superstición f. Superstition.
supersticioso, sa adj. Superstitious.
supérstite adj. JUR. Surviving.
— M. y f. JUR. Survivor.
supervaloración f. Overvaluing, overrating.
supervalorar v. tr. To overvalue, to overrate.
supervisar v. tr. To supervise.
supervisión f. Supervision.
supervisor, ra m. y f. Supervisor.
supervivencia f. Survival. || JUR. Survivorship.
superviviente adj. Surviving.
— M. y f. Survivor.
supervivir v. intr. To survive.
supervoltaje m. ELECTR. Boosting (de la corriente). | Overruning (de una lámpara).
supinación f. Supination.
supinador adj. ANAT. Supinating.
— M. ANAT. Supinator.
supino, na adj. Supine, face up (boca arriba). || — *En posición supina*, in a supine position, face up, on one's back. || *Ignorancia supina*, supine *o* crass ignorance.
— M. GRAM. Supine.
súpito, ta adj. *Amer.* Flabbergasted, dumbfounded (perplejo).
suplantación f. Supplantation, supplanting (reemplazo). || Supposition, forgery (falsificación).
suplantar v. tr. To supplant, to take the place of (reemplazar). || To forge, to falsify (falsificar).
suplementario, ria adj. Supplementary, additional. || Supplementary (ángulos). || Relief, extra (tren). || — *Crédito suplementario*, extension of credit. || *Empleo suplementario*, sideline.
suplemento m. Supplement, additional supply: *necesitamos un suplemento de papel*, we need an additional supply of paper. || Supplement (a una revista, libro, periódico). || Extra charge (cantidad de dinero): *sin suplemento*, without extra charge. || Supplement, excess fare (de un billete de ferrocarril). || MAT. Supplement.
suplencia f. Substitution, replacement.
suplente adj. Substitute, deputy. || DEP. Reserve (jugador).
— M. y f. Substitute. || DEP. Reserve. || TEATR. Understudy.
supletorio, ria adj. Additional, supplementary, extra.
súplica f. Supplication, entreaty (ruego). || Request (petición). || JUR. Petition. || *A súplica de*, at the request of, by request of.
suplicación f. Supplication. || Rolled wafer (barquillo). || JUR. Appeal.
suplicante adj. Beseeching, supplicating, imploring, entreating.
— M. y f. Supplicant.
suplicar v. tr. To supplicate, to implore, to beseech, to beg (rogar): *le suplico que venga*, I beg you to come. || JUR. To appeal to. || *Carta suplicada (a)*, to be forwarded [to]. || *Se suplica no hacer ruido*, please be quiet.
suplicatoria f. JUR. Letters (*pl.*) rogatory.
suplicio m. Torture (tortura). || FIG. Torment, torture: *llevar zapatos estrechos es un suplicio*, tight shoes are a torment *o* are torture. | Anguish (padecimiento moral). || — *El suplicio eterno*, eternal torment. || *Suplicio de Tántalo*, torment of Tantalus. || *Último suplicio*, death penalty (pena de muerte), death: *someter a alguien al último suplicio*, to put s.o. to death.
suplir v. tr. To replace, to substitute (reemplazar): *suplir a un profesor*, to replace a teacher. || To make up for (compensar): *tenemos que suplir la falta de este jugador*, we have to make up for the absence of this player. || To cover up [for] (ocultar): *supliremos su error*, we will cover up for his error. || To make up (poner): *yo supliré lo demás*, I'll make up the rest. || To add (añadir). || To remedy (remediar). || To fill in: *súplanse los espacios en blanco con las respuestas*, fill in the blank spaces with the answers.
suponer m. FAM. Supposition.
suponer* v. tr. To suppose, to assume: *supongamos que lo que dice es mentira*, let's suppose that what he says is false. || To believe (creer): *puedes suponer lo que quieras*, you can believe what you want. || To imagine (imaginar). || To guess (adivinar). || To mean, to involve, to entail: *este proyecto supone grandes gastos*, this plan means *o* entails a considerable outlay. || To mean (significar): *su negativa no supone nada*, his refusal does not mean anything. || — *Como es de suponer*, as is to be expected. || *Le supongo cincuenta años*, I suppose *o* I would say he must be about fifty years old. || *Ser de suponer*, to be possible *o* likely. || *Supongo que sí*, I suppose so. || *Suponiendo que*, assuming *o* supposing that. || *Valor se le supone*, he is supposed to be brave, he is credited with courage.
— V. intr. To count for: *su padre supone mucho en la familia*, his father counts for a great deal in the family.
suposición f. Supposition, assumption. || Slander (calumnia). || JUR. *Suposición de parto, de infante*, setting up a child [to displace the real heir].
supositorio m. Suppository.
supranacional adj. Supranational.
suprarrealismo m. Surrealism.
suprarrenal adj. Suprarenal: *glándula suprarrenal*, suprarenal gland.
suprasensible adj. Supersensible, supersensory, supersensitive.
supremacía f. Supremacy.
supremo, ma adj. Supreme: *la autoridad suprema*, the supreme authority. || Decisive: *tu hora suprema ha llegado*, the decisive moment has come for you. || — *Ser Supremo*, Supreme Being. || *Hora suprema, momento supremo*, dying moments, *pl.* || *Sacrificio supremo*, supreme sacrifice. || *Tribunal supremo*, supreme court.
supresión f. Suppression, elimination: *la supresión de un artículo*, the suppression of an article. || Deletion (de una palabra). || Lifting (de una restricción).
suprimir v. tr. To suppress: *suprimir la libertad de expresión*, to suppress freedom of speech. || To abolish, to suppress (abolir). || To omit, to leave out, to skip (fam.) [omitir]: *suprima los detalles*, skip the details. || To eliminate, to remove (eliminar). || To delete (una palabra). || To lift (una restricción).
supuesto, ta adj. So-called, self-styled, would-be: *un supuesto pintor*, a so-called painter. || Supposed (que se supone): *su supuesto suicidio*, his supposed suicide. || Imaginary: *una supuesta enfermedad*, an imaginary illness. || Hypothetical (hipotético). || — *Dar por supesta una cosa*, to take sth. for granted. || *¡Por supuesto!*, of course!, naturally! || *Por supuesto que*, of course. || *Supuesto que*, since (ya que), if (si). || *Un nombre supuesto*, an assumed name.
— M. Hypothesis, supposition, assumption (hipótesis). || — Pl. Data: *carecemos de los supuestos más elementales*, we are lacking the most elementary data. || — *En el supuesto de que*, supposing that. || MIL. *Supuesto táctico*, military manœuvre.
supuración f. MED. Suppuration.
supurante adj. MED. Suppurating.
supurar v. intr. MED. To suppurate.
supurativo, va adj. Suppurative.
sur m. South: *más al sur*, further south. || South wind (viento).
— Adj. South, southern (parte). || South, southerly (viento). || Southerly (dirección).
sura f. Sura (del Corán).
surá m. Surah (tela).
surafricano, na adj./s. South African.
suramericano, na adj./s. South American.
surata f. Sura (del Corán).
surcar v. tr. AGR. To plough, to furrow (con el arado). || FIG. To plough, to cleave (el agua). | To fly through (el aire). || — FIG. *Frente surcada de arrugas*, furrowed brow. | *Surcar los mares*, to ply the seas.
surco m. AGR. Furrow. || FIG. Wrinkle: *una frente llena de surcos*, a forehead full of wrinkles. | Rut: *las ruedas del carro dejan surcos en la tierra*, the wheels of the cart leave ruts in the ground. | Groove (de disco). | Wake (estela del barco).
surcoreano, na adj./s. South Korean.
sureño, ña o **surero, ra** adj. *Amer.* Southern.
— M. y f. *Amer.* Southerner.
surero m. *Amer.* Cold south wind.
surestada f. *Amer.* Southeasterly wind.
sureste adj./s. m. V. SUDESTE.
surgir v. intr. To spurt up, to spout up, to come out, to spring up (agua). || MAR. To anchor (fondear). || To appear, to tower, to loom up, to rise: *la torre de la catedral surge entre las casas*, the cathedral tower looms up above the houses. || To appear unexpectedly (aparecer de repente). || To emerge (de la sombra). || FIG. To appear, to emerge, to appear on the scene: *ha surgido una nueva actriz*, a new actress has appeared on the scene. | To arise, to crop up, to come up: *han surgido muchas dificultades*, many difficulties have arisen.
suripanta f. FAM. Chorus girl. || POP. Slut (mujer de mal vivir).
surmenaje m. Overwork (físico). || Mental strain *o* fatigue (mental).
suroeste adj./s.m. V. SUDOESTE.
surrealismo m. Surrealism.
surrealista adj. Surrealist, surrealistic.
— M. y f. Surrealist.
sursudoeste m. South-southwest. || South-southwest wind (viento).
sursuncorda m. FAM. The Pope, the king (imaginary authority). || FAM. *No lo hago aunque me lo mande el sursuncorda*, I wouldn't do it for all the tea in China.
surtidero m. Outlet (de un estanque). || Jet (chorro de agua).
surtido, da adj. Assorted: *caramelos surtidos*, assorted sweets. || Well stocked: *estamos surtidos en géneros para esta temporada*, we are well stocked with goods for this season.
— M. Assortment: *un surtido de galletas*, an assortment of biscuits. || Selection: *tener un gran surtido de corbatas*, to have a large selection of ties. || Stock, supply (provisión).
surtidor, ra adj. Supplying, providing.
— M. Jet, spout (chorro de agua). || Fountain (fuente). || Petrol pump [U.S., gas pump], petrol station [U.S., gas station] (de gasolina). || Carburettor jet (del carburador).

surtir v. tr. To supply, to provide, to stock (proveer): *surtir de carbón*, to supply with coal. || — *Surtir efecto*, to have an effect (medicina), to work, to have the desired effect (una estratagema), to come into force, to take effect (ley). || *Surtir el mercado*, to supply the market. || *Surtir un pedido*, to fill an order.
— V. intr. To spout, to spurt, to gush (brotar).
— V. pr. To provide *o* to supply o.s. (*de*, with), to get in: *surtirse de carbón*, to get some coal in. || To be supplied by, to get one's supplies from (en cierto sitio).
surto, ta adj. MAR. Anchored.
survietnamita adj./s. South Vietnamese.
surumpe o **surupí** m. *Amer.* Inflammation of the eyes [caused by the reflection of the sun on the snow].
¡sus! interj. Cheer up! (para animar). || Shoo!, go away! (para ahuyentar). || Come on!, go on! (para excitar).
susceptibilidad f. Susceptibility. || Sensitivity (sensibilidad). || Touchiness (propensión a ofenderse).
susceptible adj. Susceptible. || Sensitive (sensible). || Touchy (propenso a sentirse ofendido). || — *Susceptible de educación*, educable, capable of being educated. || *Susceptible de fluctuaciones*, liable to fluctuate, subject *o* liable to fluctuation. || *Susceptible de mejora*, improvable.
suscitar v. tr. To provoke, to cause: *su discurso suscitó una rebelión*, his speech caused a revolt. || To stir up: *hizo todo lo posible para suscitar una rebelión*, he did his utmost to stir up a rebellion. || To raise, to cause: *esta medida puede suscitar muchos problemas*, this measure is liable to raise a lot of problems. || To arouse (interés). || To provoke, to cause, to start (una discusión).
suscribir v. tr. To sign (firmar): *suscribir la petición*, to sign the petition. || To take out an option on (acciones y valores de bolsa). || To take out a subscription for: *suscribir a alguien a una revista*, to take out a subscription to a magazine for s.o. || FIG. To endorse, to subscribe to: *no suscribo su conducta*, I don't endorse his conduct. || *El que suscribe*, the undersigned.
— V. pr. To subscribe: *suscribirse a una revista*, to subscribe to a magazine.
suscripción f. Subscription: *abrir una suscripción*, to take out a subscription.
suscriptor, ra m. y f. Subscriber.
suscrito, ta adj. Subscribed. || Undersigned (infrascrito).
— M. y f. Undersigned.
susodicho, cha adj. Above-mentioned, aforesaid.
suspender v. tr. To suspend, to hang: *suspender del techo*, to hang from the ceiling. || FIG. To adjourn: *suspender la sesión*, to adjourn the meeting. | To delay, to postpone (aplazar): *han suspendido el trabajo hasta nueva orden*, they have delayed work until new orders. | To discontinue, to suspend: *el servicio de trenes ha sido suspendido*, the train service has been discontinued. | To interrupt (interrumpir). | To fail: *le han suspendido en tres asignaturas*, they have failed him in three subjects. | To astonish, to astound, to amaze (admirar). || *Suspender a uno de empleo y sueldo*, to suspend s.o. without pay.
— V. pr. FIG. To stop (parar). || To rear (un caballo).
suspense m. CINEM. Suspense.
suspensión f. Suspension, hanging. || Suspension: *la suspensión de las pruebas nucleares*, suspension of nuclear tests. || AUT., MÚS. y QUÍM. Suspension. || Interruption (interrupción). || Adjournment (de una reunión). || Postponement (aplazamiento). || Amazement, astonishment (asombro). || JUR. Stay. || — *Suspensión de garantías constitucionales*, suspension of constitutional rights. || *Suspensión de hostilidades*, cease-fire. || *Suspensión de pagos*, suspension of payments.
suspensivo, va adj. Suspensive. || *Puntos suspensivos*, suspension points *o* marks.
suspenso, sa adj. Hanging, suspended: *suspenso en el aire*, hanging in the air. || FIG. Baffled, bewildered (confuso). | Amazed, astonished (pasmado). || Failed (alumno).
— M. Fail, failure (en un examen). || — *Dar un suspenso a alguien*, to fail s.o. (en un examen). || *En suspenso*, pending, outstanding (cuestiones), outstanding (trabajo), in abeyance (pleito). || *Tener el corazón en suspenso*, to be in suspense. || *Tener un suspenso*, to fail, to be failed.
suspensores m. pl. *Amer.* Braces [U.S., suspenders] (tirantes).
suspensorio, ria adj. Suspensory.
— M. Suspensory bandage (vendaje). || Jockstrap (para deportistas).
suspicacia f. Distrust, mistrust, suspicion.
suspicaz adj. Suspicious, distrustful, untrusting.
suspirado, da adj. FIG. Longed-for.
suspirar v. intr. To sigh. || FIG. *Suspirar por*, to long for, to sigh for: *suspira por un abrigo de visón*, she longs for a mink coat.
suspiro m. Sigh: *dar un suspiro*, to heave *o* to give a sigh. || Breath (respiro). || MÚS. Crotchet rest [U.S., quarter rest]. || BOT. Pansy. || FIG. Sigh (del viento). || Glass whistle (pito). || — FIG. *Deshacerse en suspiros*, to heave deep sighs. | *Exhalar* or *dar el último suspiro*, to breathe one's last. | *Lo que no va en lágrimas va en suspiros*, V. LÁGRIMA.
sustancia f. Substance (materia): *¿de qué sustancia están hechos?*, what substance are they made of. || Extract: *sustancia de carne*, meat extract. || FIL. Substance. || FIG. Substance, value: *sus argumentos tienen poca sustancia*, his arguments have little value. | Substance, essence (lo esencial). || Importance (importancia). || — FIG. *En sustancia*, in substance. | *Hombre sin sustancia* or *de poca sustancia*, uninteresting *o* dull person. | *Sin sustancia*, lacking in substance. || ANAT. *Sustancia blanca*, white matter. | *Sustancia gris*, grey matter.
sustanciación f. JUR. Substantiation.
sustancial adj. Substantial (grande, nutritivo, etc.). || Substantial, important: *no dijo nada substancial*, he didn't say anything important. || Fundamental, essential, vital: *es el punto sustancial del discurso*, it is the fundamental point of the speech.
sustancialismo m. FIL. Substantialism.
sustanciar v. tr. To abridge, to condense (compendiar). || JUR. To substantiate.
sustancioso, sa adj. Substantial, wholesome (comida, etc.). || FIG. Meaty (de mucha enjundia).
sustantivar v. tr. GRAM. To use as a noun, to substantivate, to substantivize.
sustantividad f. GRAM. Substantiveness.
sustantivo, va adj. Substantive. || GRAM. Substantive, substantival, noun.
— M. GRAM. Noun, substantive.
sustentable adj. Tenable (teoría). || Sustainable.
sustentación f. Sustenance. || Support (base). || Suspension (retórica). || AVIAC. Lift.
sustentáculo m. Support, prop, stay.
sustentador, ra adj. Sustaining. || AVIAC. *Superficie sustentadora*, lifting surface.
sustentamiento m. V. SUSTENTACIÓN.
sustentante adj. Sustaining. || Supporting (que apoya).
— M. Defender (de una tesis). || Support (apoyo). || ARQ. Support, prop.
sustentar v. tr. To support, to hold up (sostener). || To sustain, to nourish (alimentar). || To sustain, to support, to maintain, to feed (mantener): *sustentar una familia*, to maintain a family. || To maintain (afirmar). || To defend (teoría). || To feed, to foster (esperanzas).
— V. pr. To sustain o.s., to nourish o.s. (alimentarse). || To feed (*con*, on), to live (*con*, on) [comer]. || To subsist (subsistir). || To be held up, to be supported (*con*, by) [apoyarse en]. || *Sustentarse del aire*, to live on air.
sustento m. Sustenance, food (alimento). || Support (apoyo). || FIG. Livelihood, living (medios de subsistencia). || — *Ganarse el sustento*, to earn one's living. || FIG. *Sustento principal*, mainstay.
sustitución f. Substitution.
sustituible adj. Replaceable.
sustituidor, ra adj./s. Substitute.
sustituir* v. tr. e intr. To substitute, to replace: *sustituyeron la bicicleta por la moto*, they substituted the motorcycle for the bicycle, they replaced the bicycle with *o* by the motorcycle. || To replace: *la República sustituyó a la Monarquía*, the Republic replaced the Monarchy. || To change, to replace (cambiar). || To stand in for, to take over from, to replace: *el vicepresidente sustituye al presidente cuando éste está de viaje*, the vicepresident stands in for the president in his absence.
sustitutivo, va adj. Substitutive, substitute.
— M. Substitute (*de*, for).
sustituto, ta m. y f. Substitute. || TEATR. Understudy.
susto m. Fright, scare, shock: *me dio un susto horrible*, it (he, etc.) gave me such a fright, I got such a fright. || — FIG. *Caerse del susto*, to be frightened to death, to get the fright of one's life. || FIG. y FAM. *Darle un susto al miedo*, to be as ugly as sin, to be frightfully ugly, to be hideous. || *Dar un susto a alguien*, to give s.o. a fright, to frighten *o* to scare s.o. || *Darse* or *llevarse* or *pegarse un susto*, to get a fright. || FAM. *Llevarse un susto padre*, to get the fright of one's life. || FIG. *No pasó del susto*, I was more frightened than hurt. || *¡Qué susto me has dado!*, you frightened the life out of me!
sustracción f. Theft (robo). || Removal (extracción). || Deduction. || MAT. Subtraction (resta).
sustraendo m. MAT. Subtrahend (en una sustracción).
sustraer* v. tr. To steal (robar). || To remove (quitar). || To remove, to extract (extraer). || MAT. To subtract. || To deduct (deducir).
— V. pr. To elude, to evade: *se sustrajo a las preguntas indiscretas*, he evaded the indiscreet questions. || To resist: *sustraerse a la tentación*, to resist temptation. || To get out of *o* away from (compromisos, etc.).
susurrante adj. Whispering, murmuring. || Rustling (hojas).
susurrar v. intr. To whisper, to murmur (hablar bajo): *susurrar al oído*, to whisper in s.o.'s ear. || FIG. To murmur (el agua). | To rustle (hojas).
— V. pr. To be rumoured [U.S., to be rumored], to be whispered: *se susurra que está casado*, it is rumoured that he is married.
susurro m. Whisper, murmur. || FIG. Murmur (del agua). | Rustle (de las hojas).

susurrón, ona adj. Whispering, murmuring.
— M. y f. Whisperer.
sutil adj. Thin, fine, light: *una sutil gasa*, a thin gauze. || Gentle (viento). || FIG. Subtle: *una diferencia sutil*, a subtle difference. | Keen, sharp (ingenioso).
sutileza o **sutilidad** f. Fineness, thinness (finura). || FIG. Subtlety (penetración). | Sharpness, keenness (ingenio). | Subtlety (dicho penetrante). | Instinct (de los animales). || *Sutileza de manos*, dexterity (agilidad), light-fingeredness, deftness (del carterista).
sutilizar v. tr. To make fine, to thin down (adelgazar). || FIG. To polish, to refine (pulir). | To subtilize (hacer distinciones sutiles). | To quibble about (discutir). | To sharpen (agudizar).
— V. intr. FIG. To subtilize (actuar con sutileza). | To quibble, to split hairs (hilar fino).
sutra m. Sutra.
sutura f. Seam (unión). || MED. Suture. || MED. *Punto de sutura*, stitch.
suturar v. tr. MED. To suture, to stitch up.
suyo, suya adj. y pron. pos. His (de él), hers (de ella), its (de cosas, animales, etc.), yours (de usted, de ustedes), theirs (de ellos, de ellas) [cuando va acompañado por el artículo o el verbo "ser"]: *suyo no puede ser*, it can't be his (hers, etc.); *él tiene el suyo en la mano*, he's got his in his hand; *éste es el suyo*, this is yours; *no encontraba los suyos*, she couldn't find hers. || His, of his (de él), her, of hers (de ella), its (de cosas, animales, etc.), your, of yours (de usted, de ustedes), their, of theirs (de ellos, de ellas) [con un sustantivo]: *varios amigos suyos*, several friends of theirs, several of their friends; *no vino ningún amigo suyo*, none of his friends came, no friends of his came; *no es culpa suya*, it is not your fault, it is no fault of yours. || Of his, of hers, of yours, of theirs (con un adjetivo demostrativo): *aquella idea suya*, that idea of his; *ese amigo suyo*, that friend of yours. || One's own (de uno mismo). || — *Aguantar lo suyo*, to put up with a lot. || *Cada cual* or *cada uno a lo suyo*, it is best to mind one's own business. || *De suyo*, in itself, by its very nature, intrinsically: *el asunto es de suyo complicado*, the affair is complicated in itself. || *Amer. Eso cae de suyo*, that goes without saying. || FIG. *Estar haciendo de las suyas*, to be up to one's tricks. | *Hacer suyo*, to echo (una opinión, etc.). | *Ir a lo suyo*, to go one's own way (ser independiente), to take care of one's own interests, to look after number one (preocuparse por uno mismo). || *La culpa es suya*, it's his (your, etc.) fault. || *Los suyos*, his (her, etc.) family *o* friends *o* people *o* men *o* supporters *o* side: *los suyos vienen a pasar el fin de semana*, his people are coming over for the weekend. || *Lo suyo*, one's share (su parte), what one deserves: *recibirá lo suyo*, he will get what he deserves. || *Muy suyo*, typical of one: *una broma muy suya*, a typical joke of his; very much his (hers, etc.), very like him (her, etc.): *el estilo es muy suyo*, the style is very much his; aloof, reserved (reservado): *es muy suyo*, he is very aloof. || FIG. y FAM. *Salirse con la suya*, v. SALIR. || *Suyo afectísimo*, Yours faithfully *o* sincerely. || FIG. y FAM. *Una de las suyas*, one of his (her, etc.) tricks. | *Ver la suya*, to get one's chance.
svástica o **swástica** f. Swastika.
swing m. Swing (boxeo y jazz).

T

t f. T (letra): *una t minúscula*, a small t.
taba f. ANAT. Astragalus, anklebone. || — Pl. Knucklebones (juego).
tabacal m. Tobacco plantation.
tabacalero, ra adj. Tobacco: *la industria tabacalera*, the tobacco industry.
— M. y f. Tobacco grower (plantador). || Tobacconist (vendedor de tabaco). || — F. Spanish state tobacco monopoly.
tabaco m. Tobacco. || BOT. Tobacco plant. || Cigar (puro). || Cigarettes, *pl.* (cigarrillos): *¿tienes tabaco?*, have you any cigarettes? || Snuff (rapé): *tomar tabaco*, to take snuff. || Tobacco (color). || Black rot (enfermedad de algunos árboles). || — *Amer.* FIG. y FAM. *Acabársele el tabaco a uno*, to run out of money. || *Tabaco de hebra*, long-cut tobacco. || *Tabaco de hoja*, leaf tobacco. || *Tabaco de mascar*, chewing tobacco. || *Tabaco en polvo* or *rapé*, snuff. || *Tabaco habano*, Havana tobacco. || *Tabaco negro*, black *o* dark tobacco. || *Tabaco picado*, cut tobacco. || *Tabaco rubio*, Virginia tobacco.
tabalear v. tr. To swing (balancear). || To rock (mecer).
— V. intr. To drum (con los dedos).
tabanco m. Stand, stall, booth (puesto de venta). || *Amer.* Loft, attic (desván).
tábano m. Horsefly, gadfly (insecto).
tabaqueada f. *Amer.* Fight, brawl (riña).
tabaquera f. Snuffbox (caja para rapé). || Tobacco box, tobacco jar (caja para tabaco). || Pipe bowl (de la pipa). || *Amer.* Tobacco pouch (bolsa para tabaco).
tabaquería f. Tobacconist's, tobacco shop (tienda).
tabaquero, ra adj. Tobacco.
— M. y f. Cigar maker (fabricante). || Tobacconist (vendedor).
tabaquismo m. Nicotinism.
tabardillo m. Typhoid fever (enfermedad). || Sunstroke (insolación). || FIG. y FAM. Pain in the neck (persona pesada).
tabardo m. Tabard.
tabarra f. FAM. Pain in the neck. || *Dar la tabarra*, to be a pain in the neck.
tabarro m. Wasp (avispa). || Horsefly, gadfly (tábano).
tabasco m. Tabasco [sauce].
tabasqueño, ña adj. [Of *o* from] Tabasco (México).
— M. y f. Native *o* inhabitant of Tabasco
taberna f. Tavern (antiguamente), pub, bar (hoy).
tabernáculo m. Tabernacle.
tabernario, ria adj. Tavern. || FIG. *Lenguaje tabernario*, taproom language.
tabernera f. Tavernkeeper (antiguamente). || Barmaid (camarera). || Landlady, publican (la que lleva la taberna).
tabernero m. Tavernkeeper (antiguamente). || Bartender, barman (barman). || Landlord, publican (el que lleva la taberna).
tabernucho m. o **tabernucha** f. FAM. Dive.
tabes f. MED. Consumption, tabes.
tabica f. Rise, riser (de escalera).
tabicar v. tr. To partition off (cerrar con tabique). || To wall up, to brick up (una puerta, ventana).
— V. pr. To get stopped up, to get bunged up (las narices).
tabique m. Partition, [thin] wall. || *Tabique nasal*, nasal bone.
tabla f. Plank, board (de madera). || Slab (de piedra, mármol). || Sheet (de metal). || Shelf (anaquel). || ARTES. Panel. || Pleat, box pleat (de un vestido). || Notice board [U.S., bulletin board] (para anuncios). || Drawing board (de dibujante). || Index (de un libro). || MAT. Table: *tabla de logaritmos*, logarithm table; *tabla de multiplicar*, multiplication table. || Flat (de una parte del cuerpo). || Calm part [of a river]. || Table, list (lista, catálogo). || Scale (de salarios). | Meat counter (mostrador de carnicero). || AGR. Strip of land, plot, bed. || (Ant.) Geographical map (mapa). | Customs house. || — Pl. TEATR. Stage, *sing.*, boards: *pisar las tablas*, to go on the stage. || TAUR. Barrier, *sing.* (barrera). | Part (*sing.*) of the bullring closest to the barrier. || — FIG. y FAM. *A raja tabla*, v. RAJATABLA. || *Caballeros de la Tabla Redonda*, Knights of the Round Table. || FIG. y FAM. *Escaparse por tablas*, to have a narrow escape *o* a close shave, to escape by the skin of one's teeth. | *Hacer tabla rasa de*, to make a clean sweep of. || TEATR. *Pisar bien las tablas*, to act well. || *Quedar en tablas* or *hacer tablas*, to draw (en ajedrez), to tie (empatar). || FIG. *Salvarse por tablas* or *en una tabla*, to have a narrow escape, to escape by a hairsbreadth *o* by the skin of one's teeth. || *Tabla de dibujo*, drawing board. || *Tabla de juego*, gambling den (casa de juego). || *Tabla de lavar*, washboard. || *Tabla de planchar*, ironing board. || FIG. *Tabla de salvación*, last hope (último recurso), salvation (salvación). || *Tablas alfonsinas*, astronomical tables prepared by order of Alfonso X of Castile. || REL. *Tablas de la Ley*, Tables of the Law. || *Tablas reales*, backgammon (juego). || FIG. *Tener muchas tablas*, to have a lot of presence (actor), to be an old hand (sabérselas todas).
tablada f. AGR. *Amer.* Stockyard.

tablado m. Platform (suelo de tablas). || Stage (para representaciones teatrales). || Flooring (suelo de carro). || Scaffold (cadalso). || Bed frame (de cama). || Flamenco show. || — *Sacar al tablado*, to bring out (actor). || *Salir* or *subir al tablado*, to go on the stage.
tablaje m. Planks, *pl.*, boards, *pl.* (conjunto de tablas). || Gambling den (garito).
tablajería f. Butcher's (carnicería). || Gambling (vicio de jugar).
tablajero m. Butcher (carnicero).
tablao m. Flamenco show.
— OBSERV. *Tablao* is an Andalusian deformation of *tablado*.
tablazón m. Planking. || MAR. Decking (de la cubierta). | Planking (del casco).
tableado, da adj. Pleated (falda, etc.).
— M. Pleats, *pl.* || V. TABLEO.
tablear v. tr. To saw into planks (un madero). || To divide into plots (un huerto). || To level (el suelo). || To pleat (la ropa). || To laminate, to roll (hierro).
tableo m. Sawing into planks (de un madero). || Division into plots (de un huerto). || Levelling (del suelo). || Lamination, rolling (del hierro).
tablero, ra adj. Suitable for cutting into planks. || *Madero tablero*, timber.
— M. Panel, board. || Blackboard (encerado). || Notice board [U.S., bulletin board] (para anuncios). || Dashboard (de coche). || Instrument panel (de avión). || Chessboard (para jugar al ajedrez). || Draughtboard [U.S., checkerboard] (para las damas). || Backgammon board (de tablas reales). || Floor, road (de puente). || Table top (de una mesa). || Gambling den (garito). || Beds, *pl.*, plots, *pl.* (de huerto). || Panel (de puerta). || Cutting table (del sastre). || MAR. Partition, bulkhead (mamparo). || ARQ. Panel. || ELECTR. Switchboard. || — *Tablero de dibujo*, drawing board. || FIG. *Tablero político*, political scene.
tableta f. Block (de madera). || Tablet (pastilla): *una tableta para dolor de cabeza*, a headache tablet. || — *Tableta de chocolate*, bar *o* tablet *o* slab of chocolate. || *Tabletas de San Lázaro*, v. TABLILLA.
tableteado m. Rattling, rattle (sonido).
tabletear v. intr. To rattle (con tablillas). || FIG. To rattle: *las ametralladoras tabletearon*, the machine guns rattled.
tableteo m. Rattling, rattle.
tablilla f. Small board (tabla pequeña). || Small notice board [U.S., bulletin board]. || Cushion between pockets (billar). || MED. Splint. || HIST. Tablet. || *Tablillas de San Lázaro*, rattle [used by lepers].
tablón m. Plank. || Notice board [U.S., bulletin board]. || Springboard (trampolín). || — FAM. *Agarrar* or *coger un tablón*, to get drunk (emborracharse). || *Tablón de anuncios*, notice board [U.S., bulletin board].
tabor m. MIL. Spanish army unit of regular Moroccan troops.
tabú m. Taboo.
tabuco m. Hovel (tugurio).
tábula rasa f. FIL. Tabula rasa.
tabulador m. Tabulator (de máquina de escribir).
tabuladora f. Tabulator, tabulating machine.
tabular adj. Tabular.
tabular v. tr. To tabulate.
taburete m. Stool.
tac m. Tick (onomatopeya).
tacada f. Stroke (billar). || Break (carambolas en el billar). || MAR. Wedges, *pl.*
tacañear v. intr. FAM. To be stingy *o* mean *o* miserly (obrar con avaricia).
tacañería f. Stinginess, miserliness, meanness (avaricia). || Cunning (astucia).
tacaño, ña adj. Mean, stingy, miserly (avaro). || Cunning, sly, crafty (engañoso).
— M. y f. Miser, skinflint (fam.) [avaro]. || Sly fox, crafty devil (engañoso).
tacatá o **tacataca** m. Baby walker.
tacita f. Small cup. || — FAM. *La tacita de plata*, the city of Cádiz. || FIG. *Ser una tacita de plata*, to be as bright as a new pin.
tácito, ta adj. Tacit.
Tácito n. pr. m. Tacitus.
taciturnidad f. Taciturnity.
taciturno, na adj. Taciturn, silent (callado). || Melancholy, sullen (triste).
taco m. Plug, stopper (tarugo). || Wedge (cuña). || Plug (para sujetar algo en la pared). || Cue (de billar). || Rámrod (baqueta). || Plug, wad (cartucho, mina). || Writing pad (para escribir). || Book [of tickets]: *taco de billetes de metro*, book of underground tickets. || Wad [of notes]: *un taco de billetes de cinco libras*, a wad of five-pound notes. || Stub (parte que queda de un billete, etc.). || Snack, bite to eat (refrigerio). || Piece, cube (trocito): *un taco de jamón*, a piece of ham. || Drink of wine (de vino). || Peashooter (juguete de niños). || Stud (de la bota de fútbol). || FIG. y FAM. Swearword (palabrota). | Mess, mix-up (lío). || Fritter (churro). || *Amer.* Heel (del zapato). | "Taco", rolled-up tortilla with filling. || — *Calendario de taco*, tear-off calendar. || FIG. y FAM. *Estar hecho un taco*, to be all mixed up. | *Hacerse un taco*, to get all mixed up. | *Soltar tacos*, to curse, to swear.
tacómetro m. Tachometer.
tacón m. Heel: *tacones altos*, high heels; *tacón aguja*, stiletto heel.
taconazo m. Kick with the heel. || *Dar un taconazo*, to click one's heels.
taconear v. intr. To tap one's heels.
taconeo m. Heel tapping.
táctico, ca adj. Tactical: *el uso táctico de los aviones*, the tactical use of aircraft.
— M. Tactician. || — F. MIL. Tactics (arte). | Tactic (maniobra). || FIG. Tactic.
táctil adj. Tactile.
tactismo m. Taxis (tropismo).
tacto m. Touch (sentido). || Touching, touch (acción de tocar). || FIG. Tact (delicadeza): *falta de tacto*, lack of tact. || — *Al tacto*, to the touch. || *Mecanografía al tacto*, touch-typing. || FIG. *No tener tacto*, to be tactless. || MIL. *Tacto de codos*, elbows touching. || FIG. *Tener tacto*, to be tactful.
tacuara f. *Amer.* Bamboo.
tacurú m. *Amer.* Small ant (hormiga). | Anthill (hormiguero).
tacha f. Flaw, blemish, fault (defecto). || Blemish (descrédito). || — *Poner tachas a*, to find fault with. || *Sin tacha*, flawless (cosa), unblemished (persona).
tachadura f. Erasure, crossing out (acción). || Crossing out: *esta página está llena de tachaduras*, this page is full of crossings out.
tachar v. tr. To erase (borrar): *tacha esta palabra*, erase this word. || To cross out (con una raya). || JUR. To challenge. || To censure, to find fault with (censurar). || FIG. *Tachar de*, to accuse of: *le tachan de cobardía*, they accuse him of cowardliness; to accuse of being: *le tachan de cobarde*, they accuse him of being a coward.
tachero m. *Amer.* Sugar factory worker (en una fábrica de azúcar). | Tinsmith (hojalatero).
tacho m. *Amer.* Boiler (caldero). | Pan (paila). || *Amer. Irse al tacho*, to fail (fracasar).
tachón m. Crossing out, erasure (tachadura). || Large stud (clavo).
tachonar v. tr. To stud, to decorate with studs (adornar con clavos). || To trim (con cintas). || FIG. To dot, to stud: *el cielo estaba tachonado de estrellas*, the sky was dotted with stars.
tachuela f. Tack, stud (clavo). || *Amer.* Metal pan (cacerola).
tafetán m. Taffeta (tela). || Sticking plaster (para heridas). || — Pl. FIG. Colours, flags, standards (bandera). | Finery, *sing.*, frills (galas de mujer). || *Tafetán inglés*, sticking plaster.
tafia f. Tafia, rum (aguardiente).
tafilete m. Morocco leather (cuero).
tafiletear v. tr. To cover *o* to decorate with Morocco leather.
tafiletería f. Morocco leatherwork (arte de curtir). || Morocco leather tannery (taller). || Morocco leather shop (tienda).
tafiletero, ra m. y f. Morocco leather seller.
tagalo, la adj./s. Tagalog (indígena de las Filipinas). || — M. Tagalog (lengua de los tagalos).
tagarnina f. BOT. Golden thistle. || FIG. Poor quality cigar. || FIG. y FAM. *Amer.* Drunkenness (borrachera).
tagarote m. Sparrow hawk (halcón). || FIG. y FAM. Longlegs (hombre alto). | Scribe, clerk, pen-pusher (escribiente). | Gentleman sponger (hidalgo que vive a expensas de los demás).
tagua f. *Amer.* Coot (ave). | Ivory palm, corozo palm (palmera). | Corozo nut (semilla).
tahalí m. Baldric.
Tahití n. pr. GEOGR. Tahiti
tahitiano, na adj./s. Tahitian. || — M. Tahitian (idioma).
tahona f. Bakery (panadería). || Flour mill (molino).
tahonero, ra m. y f. Baker.
tahúlla f. Land measurement in southeast Spain of 11.18 ares [= 0.28 acres].
tahúr m. Cardsharper (fullero).
tahurería f. Gambling den (garito). || Cardsharping (fullería).
taicún m. Shogun, tycoon (título japonés).
taifa f. Faction, party (facción). || FIG. y FAM. Gang of ruffians (gente despreciable). || *Reyes de taifa*, Moorish kings who ruled Spain after the breaking up of the caliphate of Cordova in 1031.
taiga f. Taiga (selva).
tailandés, esa adj./s. Thai.
Tailandia n. pr. f. GEOGR. Thailand.
taimado, da adj. Sly, shrewd, astute (disimulado). || Sullen, bad-humoured (malhumorado). || *Amer.* Lazy (perezoso).
taimería f. Slyness, cunning, shrewdness, astuteness.
taino, na adj./s. Taino (indio). || — M. Taino (idioma).
taita m. Daddy (en lenguaje infantil).
— OBSERV. In Argentina and Chile *taita* is used to address not only one's father but also other people worthy of respect; in the Caribbean it is used to address elderly negro men, whilst among the gauchos of Argentina it means *matón* (bully).
tajada f. Cut, slice (porción): *tajada de melón*, slice of melon. || — FIG. y FAM. *Agarrar* or *coger una tajada*, to get plastered (borracho). | *Hacer tajadas*, to cut to pieces. | *Llevarse la tajada del león* or *llevarse la mejor tajada*, to take the lion's share *o* the largest

part. | *Sacar tajada*, to get one's share (sacar provecho). | *Sacar tajada de todas partes*, to do o.s. proud, to look after number one (aprovecharse de todo).
tajadera f. Chopper (cuchillo). || Cold chisel (cortafrío).
tajadero m. Chopping block (de carnicero).
tajado, da adj. FIG. y FAM. Canned, stewed, plastered (borracho).
tajador, ra adj. Cutting, chopping.
— M. Chopping block (para cortar carne).
tajadura f. Cutting, slicing, chopping (acción). || Cut, slice (porción).
tajamar m. Cutwater (de puente, barco). || *Amer.* Dike, seawall (malecón). | Dam (presa).
tajante adj. Cutting (que corta). || FIG. Sharp, emphatic, categorical: *me dio un "no" tajante*, he gave me a categorical "no".
— M. Butcher.
tajaplumas m. inv. Penknife (cortaplumas).
tajar v. tr. To cut, to chop, to slice (cortar). || To trim, to sharpen (pluma de ave).
tajo m. Cut, incision (corte). || Slash (con espada, cuchillo). || Cutting edge (filo). || Chopping block (para picar la carne). || Job, work (tarea y sitio de la tarea): *vamos al tajo*, let's get on with the job. || Steep cliff (escarpa alta). || Gorge (valle profundo): *el tajo de Ronda*, the gorge of Ronda. || Three-legged stool (taburete). || Executioner's block (del verdugo). || *Amer.* Small path (caminito). || — *Mina a tajo abierto*, opencast mine [U.S., opencut mine]. || *Tirar tajos y estocadas*, to cut and thrust.
Tajo n. pr. m. GEOGR. Tagus (río).
tal adj. Such: *tal es mi punto de vista*, such is my point of view. || Such, so great, so large (tan grande): *tal es su poder que todo el mundo le obedece*, so great is his power that everyone obeys him. || Such a, this, that: *no conozco a tal hombre*, I don't know such a man. || A similar, such a (semejante): *en mi vida he visto tal espectáculo*, I have never in my life seen such a thing. || Such and such: *la calle tal*, such and such a street. || — *Como si tal cosa*, v. COSA. || *De tal manera que*, in such a way that, so that. || *El tal*, that, that fellow: *el tal Juan*, that fellow John. || *Nunca te dije tal cosa*, I never said any such thing, I said no such thing. || *Tal como*, such as (como por ejemplo). || *Tal cual*, an occasional, one or two, a few: *la policía paró tal cual coche*, the police stopped an occasional car; fair, so-so: *he comprado una tela tal cual*, I have bought some fair material. || *Tal vez*, perhaps. || *Tal y tal*, one or two, a few (alguno que otro). || *Un tal*, a certain, a man called: *un tal Rodríguez*, a certain Rodríguez.
— Pron. Such a thing (cosa): *no haré tal*, I will do no such thing. || Someone, someone or other (persona): *tal habrá que ya lo sepa*, someone is bound to know. || — *Como tal*, as such. || *Con tal que* or *con tal de que*, provided that, as long as: *con tal de que vengas, todo irá bien*, provided that you come all will go well. || *El tal*, that one, that fellow, he: *el tal es muy astuto*, that fellow is very cunning. || *Fulano de tal*, v. FULANO. || *¡No hay tal!*, no such thing! (es falso). || *No hay tal como*, there is nothing like: *no hay tal como pasar el día en el campo*, there is nothing like spending a day in the country. || *Otro que tal*, another one. || *Si tal hubiera*, if that were true (si fuera verdad). || *Tal hay que*, some people: *tal hay que opina igual*, some people hold the same opinion. || *Tal o cual*, someone or other (personas indeterminadas). || *Tal para cual*, two of a kind, birds of a feather. || FAM. *Una tal*, a prostitute, a whore. | *¡Voto a tal!*, damn it!, confound it! || *Y tal y cual*, and so on and so forth, and so on (etcétera).
— Adv. So: *tal estaba de emocionado que no me vio*, he was so excited that he didn't see me. || In such a way, as though: *tal hablaba que parecía que lo había visto*, he talked in such a way that it seemed he had seen it, he talked as though he had seen it. || — *¿Qué tal?*, v. QUÉ. || *Tal como* or *tal cual*, the way: *tal como me lo dijo me pareció un insulto*, the way he said it I took it as an insult; just as: *lo encontré tal como lo había dejado*, I found it just as I had left it. || *Tal cual*, just as it is *o* as it was: *lo dejé todo tal cual*, I left everything just as it was. || *Tal ... cual*, like ... like. || *Tal y como están las cosas*, the way things are at present.
tala f. Felling (de árboles). || Pruning (poda). || Destruction, desolation, ruin (destrucción). || MIL. Abatis, defence made with tree trunks (defensa).
talabarte m. Sword belt (cinturón).
talabartería f. Saddlery (taller, tienda).
talabartero m. Saddler.
talache o **talacho** m. *Amer.* Hoe (azada).
talador, ra adj. Cutting, felling (que tala). || Pruning (que poda).
— M. y f. Cutter, feller (que tala). || Pruner (que poda).
taladrador, ra adj. Drilling, boring. || Piercing.
— M. y f. Driller, borer. || — F. Drill (máquina).
taladrar v. tr. To bore, to drill (horadar). || To pierce (perforar). || To punch (billete). || FIG. To pierce (herir los oídos).
taladro m. Drill (taladradora). || Drill, bit (punta). || Gimlet (barrena). || Drill hole (agujero).
talamete m. MAR. Foredeck.
tálamo m. Nuptial bed (lecho conyugal). || Nuptial chamber (alcoba conyugal). || BOT. Thalamus (receptáculo de una flor). || ANAT. Thalamus: *tálamos ópticos*, optic thalami.
talán m. Clang, dingdong (de campana).
talanquera f. Fence (valla). || Barrier, barricade (de defensa). || FIG. Refuge, shelter (refugio).
talante m. Humour, mood, disposition, temper (humor): *estar de buen, de mal talante*, to be in a good, in a bad mood. || Will (voluntad). || — *Hacer algo de buen talante*, to do sth. willingly, to do sth. with good grace. || *Hacer algo de mal talante*, to do sth. unwillingly, to do sth. reluctantly, to do sth. with ill grace.
talar adj. Full-length, long (largo).
— M. pl. MIT. Talaria (alas de Mercurio).
talar v. tr. To fell, to cut (cortar). || To prune (podar). || FIG. To destroy, to ruin, to lay waste (destruir).
talareño, ña adj. [Of *o* from] Talara (Perú).
— M. y f. Native *o* inhabitant of Talara (Perú).
talasocracia f. Thalassocracy.
talasoterapia f. MED. Thalassotherapy, salt water *o* sea air cure.
talavera m. Talavera pottery (cerámica).
talayote m. Talayot, prehistoric stone tower [in the Balearics].
talco m. Talc (mineral). || Tinsel (lámina metálica). || *Polvos de talco*, talcum powder.
talcoso, sa adj. Talcose, talcous.
talcualillo adj. FAM. Fair, so-so (regular). | So-so, not so bad (de salud).
taled m. Tallith (velo judío).
talega f. Bag, sack: *talega de ropa sucia*, laundry bag. || Bagful, sackful, bag, sack (contenido): *una talega de arroz*, a bagful of rice. || Nappy [U.S., diaper] (pañal). || Hairnet (para proteger el peinado). || FIG. y FAM. Wealth, money (dinero). | Sins, *pl.* (pecados).
talegada f. Bagful, sackful (contenido).
talegazo m. Fall (caída). || Blow (golpe).
talego m. Bag, sack (saco).
taleguilla f. Small sack *o* bag (talega pequeña). || TAUR. Bullfighter's breeches, *pl.* (calzón).
talento m. Talent: *un hombre de mucho talento*, a man of great talent. || Talent, gift: *tiene talento para pintar*, he has a gift for painting. || Aptitude (capacidad). || Intelligence, cleverness (inteligencia). || Talent (moneda, peso).
talentoso, sa o **talentudo, da** adj. Talented, gifted.
talero m. *Amer.* Short whip.
Tales n. pr. m. Thales.
talgo m. (nombre registrado). Talgo [articulated train of Spanish invention].
Talía n. pr. f. MIT. Thalia.
talio m. Thallium (metal).
talión m. Talion, retaliation.
talismán m. Talisman, amulet, [lucky] charm.
talmente adv. FAM. Exactly like (exactamente como). | So (tan).
Talmud n. pr. m. Talmud.
talmúdico, ca adj. Talmudic, Talmudical.
talo m. BOT. Thallus.
talófitas f. pl. BOT. Thallophytes.
talón m. Heel (de pie, calzado, media). || MÚS. Heel (del arco del violín). || Heel (de las caballerías). || MAR. Heel (de la quilla). || Flange (del neumático). || ARQ. Talon, ogee moulding (moldura). || Voucher, receipt, coupon (bono, recibo, etc.). || Cheque [U.S., check] (cheque). || Monetary standard (patrón monetario). || — FIG. y FAM. *Apretar los talones*, to take to one's heels, to show a clean pair of heels. | *Ir pegado a* or *pisarle a uno los talones*, to be on s.o.'s heels, to follow close on s.o.'s heels, to tread on s.o.'s heels (seguir, competir). || *Talón de Aquiles*, Achilles' heel.
talonada f. Kick with the heel [to spur one's horse].
talonador m. DEP. Hooker (rugby).
talonaje m. DEP. Heeling, heeling out (rugby).
talonar v. tr. DEP. To heel out (rugby).
talonario, ria adj. With stubs. || *Libro talonario*, stub book.
— M. Book of vouchers, book of coupons, book of receipts, stub book (de vales, recibos). || Chequebook [U.S., checkbook] (de cheques).
talonazo m. Kick with the heel.
talonera f. Heel piece (de medias, calcetines). || Binding (de pantalones).
talquera f. Powder box (para polvos de talco).
talud m. Talus, slope.
talla f. Carving (en madera). || Engraving (del metal). || Cutting (de piedras preciosas). || Height, stature (estatura): *hombre de poca talla*, man of small stature. || Size (de ropa). || Tally, measuring stick (palo para medir). || Hand (juego de baraja). || Tallage (tributo antiguo). || MED. Lithotomy, removal of gallstones (operación de vejiga). || Reward (premio). || MAR. Purchase block. || *Amer.* Chat (charla). || — FIG. *De talla*, prominent, outstanding. | *Ser de talla para* or *tener talla para*, to be cut out for (ser capaz de).
tallado, da adj. Carved (madera). || Cut (piedra). || Engraved (metal). || Shaped, formed.
— M. Carving (en madera). || Engraving (en metal). || Cutting (de piedras preciosas).

tallador m. Engraver (grabador). || MIL. Man who measures recruits.
talladura f. Notch (corte).
tallar adj. Ready for cutting: *leña tallar*, wood ready for cutting.
— M. Forest ready for cutting (bosque).
tallar v. tr. To carve (madera). || To engrave (metal). || To cut (piedras preciosas). || To measure the height of (medir). || To deal (en los juegos de azar). || To tax (imponer tributos). || To appraise (tasar).
— V. intr. *Amer.* To chat (charlar). | To court (cortejar).
tallarín m. Noodle.
talle m. Waist (cintura): *talle de avispa*, wasp waist. || Figure, shape (de mujer): *talle esbelto*, svelte figure. || Physique, build (de hombre). || Measurement from shoulder to waist (en costura).
tallecer* v. intr. BOT. To sprout, to shoot (entallecer).
taller m. Workshop, shop: *taller de cerámica*, ceramic workshop. || Studio, atelier (de pintor, escultor). || Garage, repair shop (de reparaciones de coche). || Factory, plant (fábrica).
tallista m. Sculptor, wood carver (escultor). || Engraver (que graba).
tallo m. BOT. Stem, stalk (de la planta). | Sprout, shoot (renuevo). || *Amer.* BOT. Cabbage (col).
tamal m. *Amer.* Tamale, minced meat and red peppers wrapped in corn husk or banana leaves. | Package (bulto). || *Amer.* FAM. Intrigue (intriga).
tamalería f. *Amer.* Tamale shop.
tamalero, ra m. y f. *Amer.* Tamale maker (que hace tamales). | Tamale seller (vendedor).
tamandúa m. Tamandua, tree-dwelling anteater.
tamango m. *Amer.* [Gaucho's] boot (calzado).
tamañito, ta adj. FIG. y FAM. Confused (confundido). || *Dejarle a uno tamañito*, to make s.o. feel small.
tamaño, ña adj. Such a big, so big a (tan grande): *no se puede superar tamaña dificultad*, we cannot overcome so big an obstacle. || Such a small, so small a (tan pequeño). || — FAM. *Abrir tamaños ojos*, to open one's eyes wide. || *Tamaño como*, as large as (tan grande como), as small as (tan pequeño como).
— M. Size: *¿de qué tamaño son los zapatos?*, what size are the shoes? || Dimensions, *pl.* (dimensión). || Volume, capacity (volumen). || FIG. Importance (importancia). || — *Del tamaño de*, as large as. || *Tamaño natural*, life size.
támara f. Date palm (palmera). || Date palm grove (terreno poblado de palmeras). || — Pl. Cluster (*sing.*) of dates.
tamarao m. Tamarau, Philippine buffalo.
tamarindo m. BOT. Tamarind (árbol, fruta).
tamarisco o **tamariz** m. BOT. Tamarisk (taray).
tamarugal m. *Amer.* Grove of carob trees.
tamarugo m. *Amer.* Carob tree.
tamba f. *Amer.* Indian wrap-around skirt.
tambaleante adj. Staggering, tottering, reeling. || Wobbly (mueble). || FIG. Unstable, shaky: *instituciones tambaleantes*, shaky institutions.
tambalear v. pr. To stagger, to totter, to reel. || To wobble (mueble). || FIG. To be unstable *o* shaky: *las estructuras de esta organización se tambalean*, the foundations of this organization are shaky.
tambaleo m. Staggering, tottering, unsteadiness, reeling (de persona). || Wobbliness (de mueble).
tambarria f. *Amer.* Rave, good time [U.S., blast, ball] (jolgorio).
tambero, ra adj. *Amer.* Tame (manso). | Dairy (ganado).
— M. y f. *Amer.* Innkeeper (ventero). | Dairy farmer (granjero).
también adv. Also, too, as well likewise (igualmente). || — *¿También?*, that as well? || *Yo también*, me too, so am I [so do I, so was I, etc.]
tambo m. *Amer.* Inn (parador). | Dairy farm (vaquería).
tambor m. Drum (instrumento). || Drummer (persona). || ANAT. Eardrum (tímpano del oído). || Sieve, sifter (para el azúcar). || Revolving drum (de rifa o lotería). || Tambour, embroidery frame (para bordar). || Roaster (para tostar café). || ARQ. Drum, tambour (de cúpula o columna). | Small room, cubicle (aposento). || Cylinder (de revólver). || TECN. Cylinder, barrel (cilindro). | Drum (de lavadora). | Brake drum (del freno). || MAR. Paddle box (en los vapores). | Capstan (para enrollar un cable). || FIG. *A tambor batiente*, in triumph, triumphantly (triunfalmente).
tamborear v. intr. V. TAMBORILEAR.
tamboreo m. Drumming, beating.
tamboril m. MÚS. Small drum, tabor.
tamborilear v. intr. To drum (con los dedos). || To beat (el tamboril). || FIG. To patter, to pitter-patter (la lluvia).
— V. tr. To praise, to extol (alabar). || IMPR. To plane [down].
tamborileo m. Drumming, beating.
tamborilero m. Drummer.
tamborilete m. IMPR. Planer. || MÚS. Small drum.
tamborín o **tamborino** m. MÚS. Tabor.
Támesis n. pr. m. GEOGR. Thames.
tamiz m. Sieve, sifter. || — FIG. *Pasar por el tamiz*, to screen, to sift. || *Tamiz vibratorio*, vibrating screen.
tamizar v. tr. To sieve, to sift, to pass through a sieve: *tamizar harina*, to sift flour. || To filter (luz). || FIG. To screen (seleccionar).

tampoco adv. Not either, nor, neither: *tampoco va Juan*, John is not going either, nor is John going, neither is John going; *mi madre no contestó y yo tampoco*, my mother didn't answer and I didn't either *o* neither did I.
tampón m. Ink pad (para entintar).
tam-tam m. MÚS. Tom-tom.
tamujal m. Buckthorn patch.
tamujo m. BOT. Buckthorn.
tamul adj./s. Tamil. || — M. Tamil (idioma).
tan m. Rat-a-tat-tat, rub-a-dub (del tambor). || Clang, dong (de la campana).
tan (apócope de *tanto*) adv. So: *no seas tan necio*, don't be so stupid. || Such, so: *no necesito un piso tan grande*, I do not need such a large flat, I do not need so large a flat. || — *Cuan... tan*, as ... as: *cuan bueno el padre, tan malo el hijo*, the father is as good as the son is bad. || *De tan bueno, acaba por parecer tonto*, he is so good-natured that he appears stupid. || *De tan ... como*, because ... so, so ... that: *no podía dormir de tan preocupado como estaba*, I was so worried that I could not sleep, I could not sleep because I was so worried. || *Ni tan siquiera*, even. || *¡Qué ... tan!*, what a: *¡qué chica tan guapa!*, what a pretty girl! || *Tan ... como*, as ... as: *tan malo como su hermano*, as bad as his brother; *tan fácilmente como usted dice*, as easily as you say. || *Tan es así que*, so much so that. || *Tan pronto como*, as soon as. || *Tan ... que*, so ... [that]: *el viento es tan fuerte que rompe las ramas*, the wind is so trong [that] it breaks the branches. || *Tan siquiera*, just, only: *si tuviera tan siquiera mil pesetas*, if I had just *o* if only I had a thousand pesetas. || *Tan sólo*, v. SÓLO.
— OBSERV. The form *tan* can only precede adjectives, adverbs and nouns used as adjectives: *me encuentro tan a gusto aquí*, I feel so comfortable here: *soy tan poeta como tú*, I am just as much a poet as you. When *tan* and an adjective precede a noun, the indefinite article is not used in Spanish: *tan importante negocio*, such an important business.
tanagra f. Tanagra (estatuita). || ZOOL. Tanager, tanagra (ave).
tanate m. *Amer.* Leather bag (zurrón de cuero). || FIG. y FAM. *Amer. Cargar con los tanates*, to pack one's bags.
tanda f. Group (grupo). || Layer (capa): *una tanda de ladrillos*, a layer of bricks. || Series, *inv.* (serie). || Shower (de golpes). || Batch (cantidad): *¿cuándo sale la próxima tanda de pan?*, when will the next batch of bread be ready? || Job (tarea). || Shift (grupo de obreros, período de trabajo): *tiene la tanda de diez a seis*, he is on the ten till six shift. || Turn (turno). || AGR. Turn to use the water (disfrute del agua). || Game (partida): *una tanda de billar*, a game of billiards. || *Amer.* Performance (representación). | Bad habit (resabio).
tándem m. Tandem.
tandeo m. Distribution of irrigation water by turns.
tanganillas (en) adj. Shaky, insecure, unsteady, unsafe.
tanganillo m. Support, prop.
tángano, na adj. *Amer.* Short, squat (bajito).
tangará m. ZOOL. Tanager, tanagra (ave).
tangencia f. Tangency.
tangencial adj. Tangential.
tangente adj./s.f. Tangent. || FIG. y FAM. *Salirse por la tangente*, to fly off *o* to go off at a tangent (hacer una digresión), to evade the issue, to dodge the question (esquivar una pregunta).
Tánger n. pr. GEOGR. Tangier.
tangerino, na adj. [Of *o* from] Tangier, Tangerine.
— M. y f. Native *o* inhabitant of Tangier, Tangerine.
tangible adj. Tangible, palpable.
tango m. MÚS. Tango.
tangón m. MAR. Boom (botalón).
tanguear v. intr. To tango.
tanguista f. Cabaret girl [U.S., taxi girl].
tánico, ca adj. QUÍM. Tannic.
tanino m. QUÍM. Tannin.
tanque m. Tank, resevoir (depósito). || MIL. Tank (carro de combate). || Tanker (barco cisterna). || Road tanker (camión cisterna).
tanquista m. MIL. Tanker.
tanrec m. ZOOL. Tenrec, tanrec.
tanta f. *Amer.* Cornbread.
tantalio m. QUÍM. Tantalum.
tántalo m. QUÍM. Tantalum. || ZOOL. Wood stork.
Tántalo n. pr. m. MIT. Tantalus.
tantán m. Tom-tom (tambor). || Gong (batintín).
tantarán o **tantarantán** m. Rat-a-tat-tat, rub-a-dub (sonido del tambor). || FIG. y FAM. Bang (golpe).
tanteador m. Scorekeeper, scorer (persona). || Scoreboard (marcador). || Scorer (goleador).
tantear v. tr. To work out roughly, to estimate, to guess (calcular aproximadamente). || To size up, to gauge (medir): *estoy tanteando la tela a ver si hay bastante para una blusa*, I am sizing up the material to see if there is enough for a blouse. || FIG. To try out, to test (ensayar, probar). | To sound out (la actitud de una persona). | To examine, to study (un proyecto). || To keep the score of (el juego). || To sketch, to outline (un dibujo). || FIG. *Tantear el terreno*, to see how the land lies.

— V. intr. To grope, to feel one's way (titubear). || DEP. To keep score, to score.

tanteo m. Rough estimate, approximate calculation (cálculo aproximado). || Sizing up (medida). || Test (prueba). || Study, examination (examen). || Sounding (sondeo). || Groping, feeling one's way (titubeo). || DEP. Score. || ARTES. Outline, sketch.

tanto, ta

1. Adjetivo. — **2.** Adverbio. — **3.** Sustantivo. — **4.** Pronombre.

1. ADJETIVO. — So much (singular), so many (plural): *no bebas tanto vino*, don't drink so much wine; *¡tengo tantos amigos!*, I have so many friends! || As much (singular), as many (plural) [comparación]: *tengo tanto dinero como él*, I have as much money as he; *tengo tantos amigos como ella*, I have as many friends as she. || — *De* or *con tanto*, through so much, with so much, because of so much: *me he vuelto ronco de tanto hablar*, I have become hoarse with talking so much. || *No ser tanto como para*, to be not enough *o* not as many to: *la diferencia no fue tanta como para hacer variar el resultado*, the difference was not enough to alter the result. || *Otros tantos* or *otras tantas*, so many more, as many more: *las estrellas son otros tantos soles*, the stars are so many more suns. || *Tanto tiempo*, such a long time, so long. || *Y tantos* or *y tantas*, just over, odd: *mil pesetas y tantas*, just over a thousand pesetas, a thousand pesetas odd, a thousand-odd pesetas; something: *el año mil novecientos setenta y tantos*, the year nineteen seventy something.

2. ADVERBIO. — So much: *no hables tanto*, don't talk so much; *trabaja tanto que nunca tiene tiempo para descansar*, he works so much that he never has time to rest. || Such a long time, so long: *para venir aquí no tardará tanto*, he won't take such a long time to get here; *hace tanto que no lo veo*, it has been so long since I last saw him. || So often: *tanto me has dicho su nombre que ya me acuerdo*, you have told me his name so often that it has stuck. || — *A tanto*, to such an extent, to such a degree: *a tanto había llegado la decadencia*, things had deteriorated to such a degree. || *Cuanto más ... tanto más*, the more... the more: *cuanto más sufro tanto más me hacen sufrir*, the more I suffer, the more they make me suffer. || *En tanto*, *entre tanto* or *mientras tanto*, in the meantime, meanwhile. || *En tanto que*, as long as, while, whilst (mientras que), until (hasta que). || *Eso es tanto como*, that is like, that is as good as: *eso es tanto como decir que es estúpido*, that is like saying he's stupid. || *Hasta tanto que*, as long as. || *Ni tanto así*, not even this much. || *Ni tanto ni tan calvo* or *ni tanto ni tan poco*, neither one extreme nor the other. || *No es tanto como para*, it is nothing to *o* not enough to, it is not worth: *no es tanto como para enfadarte*, it is nothing to get angry about, it is not worth losing your temper over. || *No tanto ... como*, not so much ... as: *su fracaso no se debe tanto a su ignorancia como a su pereza*, his failure is due not so much to his ignorance as to his laziness. || *No ... tanto como para*, not ... enough to: *no ha bebido tanto como para ponerse enfermo*, he didn't drink enough to make him ill. || *Por lo tanto* or *por tanto*, so, therefore. || *Tanto así*, just like that. || *Tanto bueno* or *tanto bueno por aquí*, so good to see you. || *Tanto... como*, both, as well as: *tanto aquí como allí*, here as well as there, both here and there; as much ... as: *de eso sé tanto como él*, I know as much about this as he. || *¡Tanto como eso!*, as much as that! || *Tanto como una belleza no es, pero mona sí*, I wouldn't go so far as to say she's beautiful, but she's certainly pretty. || *Tanto cuanto*, as much as: *tiene tanto cuanto dinero necesita*, he has as much money as he needs. || *Tanto más*, the more, all the more. || *Tanto más ... cuanto más*, the more ... the more. || *Tanto más ... cuanto que*, all the more ... since *o* because. || *Tanto mejor*, all the better, so much the better. || *Tanto menos*, all the less, so much the less. || *Tanto peor*, so much the worse, too bad. || *Tanto si ... como si*, whether ... or: *tanto si come como si no come, se va a morir*, he will die whether he eats or not. || FIG. y FAM. *Tanto vales cuanto tienes*, a man is worth as much as he owns. || *Tanto y más*, as much and more. || *¡Y tanto!*, and how!, you can say that again!

3. SUSTANTIVO. — Point (en un juego). || DEP. Goal (en el fútbol): *marcar un tanto*, to score a goal. || Counter (ficha). || Chip (en el póker). || Certain sum *o* amount (suma): *se paga un tanto al contado y el resto a plazos*, a certain amount is paid in cash and the rest in instalments. || Percentage, part: *me darás un tanto de la ganancia*, you will give me a percentage of the profit. || — *Algún tanto*, somewhat, a bit: *el calor ha cedido algún tanto*, the heat has let up somewhat. || *Apuntar* or *señalar los tantos*, to keep score. || *Apuntarse un tanto*, to score a point. || COM. *A tanto alzado*, on a lump sum basis. || *Estar al tanto*, to be up to date (estar al día): *estoy al tanto de las noticias*, I am up to date on the news; to be on the alert (estar a la expectativa). || *¿Estás al tanto?*, do you know anything about it?, do you know the latest?, have you heard? || *Las tantas*, late: *son las tantas*, it is late; *vino a las tantas de la noche*, he came late at night. || *Poner al tanto*, to bring up to date (poner al corriente), to let know, to inform: *le pondré al tanto de lo que hayamos decidido*, I'll let you know what we decide. || COM. *Tanto alzado*, overall price, lump sum. || *Tanto por ciento*, percentage. || *Tener al tanto*, to keep up to date. || FIG. *Un tanto*, somewhat, a little, rather: *es un tanto perezoso*, he is somewhat lazy. | *Un tanto a favor de alguien*, a point in s.o.'s favour. | *Un tanto en contra de alguien*, a point against s.o., a black mark.

4. PRONOMBRE. — So much (singular), so many (plural): *cada uno tiene que pagar tanto*, each has to pay so much; *vinieron tantos que no sabíamos cómo alojarlos*, so many people came that we did not know where to put them all. || This, that: *a tanto conduce el vicio*, that is where vice gets you. || — *A tantos de*, one day in, sometime in: *llegaron a tantos de agosto*, they arrived sometime in August. || *No es para tanto*, there is no need to make such a fuss. || *Otro tanto*, v. OTRO. || *Uno de tantos*, nothing special, one of many: *él es uno de tantos*, he is nothing special.

tanza f. Line (pesca).

tañedor, ra m. y f. Player: *tañedor de guitarra*, guitar player.

tañer* v. tr. To play: *tañer un instrumento*, to play an instrument.
— V. intr. To toll (las campanas). || To drum (tabalear).

tañido m. Sound (de un instrumento). || Tolling (de las campanas).

tao m. Tau [badge of the orders of St Anthony and St John].

taoísmo m. Taoism.

taoísta adj./s. Taoist.

tapa f. Lid: *la tapa de un baúl*, the lid of a trunk; *la tapa de un pupitre*, the lid of a desk. || Top: *la tapa de una botella*, a bottle top. || Cover (de libro). || AUT. Head (de cilindro). || Lift (capa del tacón). || Savoury tidbit, appetizer (para tomar con bebidas). || Gate (compuerta de canal). || Horny part (casco del caballo). || Round [of beef] (de las reses). || — FIG. y FAM. *Levantar* or *saltar la tapa de los sesos a alguien*, to blow s.o.'s brains out. | *Levantarse* or *saltarse la tapa de los sesos*, to blow one's brains out (suicidarse).
— OBSERV. *Tapas* are savoury tidbits (olives, salted nuts, pieces of cheese or sausage, etc.) served in Spanish bars to accompany a drink.

tapaboca f. Scarf, muffler (bufanda).

tapabocas m. inv. Scarf, muffler (bufanda). || MIL. Tampion (del cañón).

tapacubos m. inv. AUT. Hubcap.

tapaculo m. ZOOL. Fish resembling sole (pez). || BOT. Hip (escaramujo).

tapada f. Veiled woman. || *Amer.* Denial (mentís).

tapadera f. Cover, lid, top: *la tapadera de un cazo*, the lid of a pot. || Plug, stopper (para un agujero). || FIG. Cover, front (encubridor).

tapadillo m. Covering one's face with a veil *o* scarf. || MÚS. Flute stop (del órgano). || FAM. *De tapadillo*, secretly.

tapado, da adj. Covered (cubierto). || Wrapped (envuelto). || *Amer.* All the same colour (caballo, yegua).
— M. *Amer.* Coat (abrigo). | Buried treasure (tesoro enterrado).

tapador, ra adj. Covering.
— M. Cover, lid, top (tapa). || Plug, stopper (para agujeros). || FIG. Cover.

tapadura f. Covering (cobertura). || Plugging, stopping up (de un agujero).

tapafunda f. Flap (de pistolera).

tapagujeros m. inv. FIG. y FAM. Botcher, bad bricklayer *o* mason. | Stand-in (sustituto).

tapajuntas m. inv. ARQ. Fillet [sealing door or window joints].

tápalo m. *Amer.* Shawl, cloak (chal o mantón).

tapanco m. *Amer.* Loft (desván). | Bamboo awning (toldo).

tapar v. tr. To cover: *la colcha tapa las mantas*, the bedspread covers the blankets. || To wrap up (con ropa). || To cover (en la cama). || To hide, to cover [up]: *las nubes tapaban el sol*, clouds hid the sun. || To plug, to stop, to stop up (un agujero). || To put the top on (una botella). || To put the lid on (una lata, cacerola, etc.). || FIG. To conceal, to hide (un criminal). | To cover up (una falta). | To obstruct, to block (la vista). || *Amer.* To fill (empastar). || MIL. To stop up (una brecha). || *Tener la nariz tapada*, to have a blocked-up nose.
— V. pr. To cover up, to wrap up (abrigarse). || To cover [up]: *taparse los oídos*, to cover [up] one's ears.

tapara f. *Amer.* Gourd.

taparo m. *Amer.* Gourd tree.

taparrabo m. Loincloth (de salvaje). || Bathing trunks, *pl.* (bañador).

tape m. *Amer.* Guarani Indian.

tapera f. *Amer.* Ruined village (pueblo). | Hovel, shack (vivienda).

tapete m. Runner (de mesa). || Rug (alfombra). || — FIG. *Estar sobre el tapete*, to be under consideration, to be on the carpet. | *Poner sobre el tapete*, to put on the carpet, to bring up. || *Tapete verde*, gambling table.
tapia f. Adobe *or* mud wall (de adobe). || Wall (muro de cerca). || — FIG. y FAM. *Más sordo que una tapia*, as deaf as a post. | *Saltar la tapia*, V. SALTAR.
tapiar v. tr. To wall in, to enclose (cerrar con tapias). || FIG. To brick up, to wall up, to close up: *tapiar una ventana*, to wall up a window.
tapicería f. Tapestry making (arte o industria de hacer tapices). || Tapestries, *pl.* (tapices). || Upholstery material (tela para tapizar). || Upholsterer's (tienda de tela para muebles). || Draper's (tienda de cortinajes). || Upholstery (de coche, de muebles).
tapicero, ra m. y f. Tapestry maker (que hace tapices). || Upholsterer (que tapiza muebles, etc.).
tapioca f. Tapioca.
tapir m. ZOOL. Tapir.
tapisca f. *Amer.* Corn harvest.
tapiscar v. tr. *Amer.* To harvest [corn].
tapiz m. Tapestry.
tapizar v. tr. To tapestry, to hang with tapestries (una pared). || To upholster (muebles, coche). || To carpet (el suelo).
tapón m. Stopper, cork (de las botellas). || Bung (de tonel). || Top (tapa). || MED. Tampon. || FIG. y FAM. Shorty, shorthouse (persona). || FIG. Obstruction (obstrucción). || — FIG. y FAM. *Al primer tapón, zurrapa*, unlucky from the beginning. || FIG. *Estado tapón*, buffer state. || *Tapón corona*, cap, top. || FIG. y FAM. *Tapón de alberca* or *de cuba*, shorty, shorthouse (persona). || *Tapón de cerumen*, wax in the ear. || *Tapón de desagüe*, drain plug. || *Tapón de espita*, spigot. || *Tapón de rosca* or *de tuerca*, screw-on cap.
taponamiento m. MED. Tamponage, tamponade. || Traffic jam (de coches). || Closing (de una brecha). || Plugging, stopping up (de un agujero).
taponar v. tr. To plug, to stop up (un orificio). || To close up: *taponar la brecha*, to close up the gap. || To cork, to stopper (una botella). || MED. To tampon.
taponazo m. Pop (ruido). || FAM. Shot (fútbol). || *Recibir un taponazo en el ojo*, to be hit in the eye by a flying cork.
taponería f. Corks, *pl.*, stoppers, *pl.* (tapones). || Cork *o* stopper factory (fábrica). || Cork *o* stopper store (tienda). || Cork *o* stopper industry (industria).
taponero, ra adj. Cork, stopper: *industria taponera*, stopper industry.
— M. y f. Cork *o* stopper maker *o* seller.
tapujo m. Muffler (para la cara). || FIG. Deceit (engaño). | Secrecy (secreto).
taqué m. TECN. Stopper, stop.
taquear v. tr. *Amer.* To ram (un arma). | To fill (llenar).
— V. intr. *Amer.* To tap one's heels (taconear).
taquera f. Rack for billiard cues.
taquería f. *Amer.* "Taco" shop.
taquero, ra m. y f. *Amer.* "Taco" seller.
taquicardia f. MED. Tachycardia.
taquigrafía f. Shorthand, stenography.
taquigrafiar v. tr. To write in shorthand, to stenograph.
taquigráficamente adv. In shorthand.
taquigráfico, ca adj. Shorthand. || *Actas taquigráficas*, verbatim record (de una reunión).
taquígrafo, fa m. y f. Stenographer, shorthand writer. || Verbatim reporter (de una conferencia).
taquilla f. Filing cabinet (archivador). || Set of pigeonholes (mueble de casillas). || Booking office, ticket office (en las estaciones, etc.). || TEATR. Box office. || Locker (armario). || FIG. Takings, *pl.*, returns, *pl.*, box office (dinero cobrado). || FIG. *Hacer taquilla* or *tener buena taquilla* or *ser un éxito de taquilla*, to be good box office (una película, un artista, etc.).
taquillero, ra adj. Good box office (película, actor). || *Éxito taquillero*, box-office success.
— M. y f. Ticket clerk, booking clerk.
taquimeca f. FAM. Shorthand typist.
taquimecanógrafa f. Shorthand typist.
taquimetría f. Tachymetry.
taquímetro m. Tachymeter.
tara f. Tare (peso). || Defect (defecto). || Tally, tally stick (tarja).
tarabilla f. Millclapper (de molino). || Catch, latch (de ventana, puerta). || Wooden peg [used to tighten the cord of a frame saw] (de sierra). || FIG. y FAM. Chatterbox (persona). | Jabber, chatter (retahíla de palabras desordenadas). || *Amer.* Bull roarer (juguete).
tarabita f. Tongue (de la cincha). || *Amer.* Rope [of a cableway].
taracea f. Marquetry, intarsia.
taracear v. tr. To inlay: *taraceado con marfil*, inlaid with ivory.
tarado, da adj. Defective, damaged (mercancía). || Handicapped (persona).
tarambana adj. Mad, wild (alocado).
— M. y f. Crackpot, madcap.
taranta f. Type of flamenco song (canto). || *Amer.* Fit (locura pasajera). | Whim (idea pasajera). | Fainting spell (desmayo). | Drunkenness (borrachera).
tarantela f. Tarantella (baile y música).
tarántula f. Tarantula (araña). || FIG. *Picado de la tarántula*, nervous, jumpy.
tarar v. tr. To tare.
tarará f. Tantara, tantarara [trumpet blast].
tararear v. tr. To hum.
tarareo m. Humming.
tarasca f. Monster (monstruo). || FIG. y FAM. Hag, battle-axe (mujer de carácter violento). || *Amer.* Big mouth.
tarascada f. Bite (mordedura). || Scratch (arañazo). || FIG. y FAM. Sharp retort (contestación).
tarascar v. tr. To bite.
tarascón m. o **tarascona** f. Monster (monstruo). || *Amer.* Bite (mordedura).
taray m. BOT. Salt cedar, tamarisk.
tarazana f. o **tarazanal** m. Dockyard (atarazana).
tardador, ra adj. Slow, delaying, tarrying.
— M. y f. Delayer, tarrier.
tardanza f. Delay (retraso). || Slowness (lentitud).
tardar v. intr. To take: *este trabajo tardará una hora*, this work will take an hour; *¿cuánto tarda el tren de Paris a Madrid?*, how long does the train from Paris to Madrid take? || To take *o* to be a long time: *el tren tarda en llegar*, the train is taking a long time to arrive; *¡cuánto tardas en vestirte!*, what a long time you take to get dressed! || To delay, to linger: *no tardo ni un minuto*, I won't delay a minute. || — *A más tardar*, at the latest. || *No tardaré mucho*, I won't be long, I won't take long, it won't take me long. || *No tardé nada en terminarlo*, I finished it in no time. || *No tardes en decírmelo*, tell me at once.
tarde f. Afternoon (desde mediodía hasta las cinco o las seis). || Evening (después). || — *A la caída de la tarde*, at dusk, at nightfall. || *A las cuatro de la tarde*, at four o'clock in the afternoon, at four p.m. || *Buenas tardes*, good afternoon (hasta las seis), good evening (después de las seis). || *Dar las buenas tardes*, to say good afternoon *o* good evening. || *De tarde en tarde*, now and then, from time to time. || *Función de la tarde*, matinée. || *Por la tarde*, in the afternoon, in the evening. || *Tarde de toros*, bullfight: *hoy es tarde de toros*, today there is a bullfight.
— Adv. Late: *levantarse tarde*, to get up late; *llegó tarde a la oficina*, he arrived late at the office. || Too late (demasiado tarde): *ya es tarde para marcharse*, it is too late now to leave. || — *Hacerse tarde* or *hacérsele tarde a uno*, to grow *o* to get late: *se me hizo tarde y no pude ir al teatro*, it grew late and I couldn't go to the theatre. || *Lo más tarde*, at the latest. || *Luego es tarde*, later on is too late. || *Más tarde o más temprano*, sooner or later. || *Más vale tarde que nunca* or *nunca es tarde si la dicha es buena*, better late than never. || *Tarde o temprano*, sooner or later. || FAM. *Tarde piache*, too late [for the fair].
tardecer* v. intr. To get *o* to grow dark.
tardíamente adv. Too late, tardily, belatedly.
tardígrado, da adj./s.m. ZOOL. Tardigrade. || — M. pl. Tardigrada.
tardío, a adj. Late, overdue, belated, tardy: *llegada tardía*, belated arrival. || Slow: *tardío en decidirse*, slow to decide. || *Fruto tardío*, late fruit.
tardísimo adv. Very late.
tardo, da adj. Slow (lento). || Late (retrasado). || Slow: *tardo en comprender*, slow to understand. || Slow, dull, dense (torpe).
tardón, ona adj. FAM. Very slow (que tarda mucho). | Slow, dull (torpe).
— M. y f. FAM. Slowcoach.
tarea f. Task, job, piece of work: *dar una tarea a alguien*, to assign s.o. a piece of work, to give s.o. a job to do. || Work: *agobiado de tarea*, overburdened with work. || — *Eso no es tarea de unos días*, it's no small job. || *Tareas escolares*, schoolwork, homework. || FIG. *Tarea le mando*, you'll have your work cut out there.
tarifa f. Tariff, rate: *tarifa reducida*, reduced rate; *tarifa completa*, full tariff; *tarifa de fuera de temporada*, off-season tariff. || Fare (transportes). || Price list (tabla de precios).
tarifar v. tr. To tariff, to fix a tariff for.
— V. intr. FIG. To quarrel (enfadarse).
tarima f. Platform, stand (tablado). || Stool, footstool (para los pies). || Bench (banquillo).
tarja f. Shield, buckler (escudo). || Tally, tally stick (palo). || FAM. Belt, blow (golpe). || *Amer.* [Visiting] card [U.S., calling card].
tarjar v. tr. To tally. || *Amer.* To cross out (tachar).
tarjeta f. Card: *el abogado me dio su tarjeta*, the lawyer gave me his card. || ARQ. Cartouche, tablet with inscription. || Title and imprint (mapas). || — *Tarjeta de crédito*, credit card. || *Tarjeta de identidad*, identity card. || *Tarjeta de Navidad*, Christmas card. || *Tarjeta de visita*, visiting card [U.S., calling card]. || *Tarjeta perforada*, punch card. || *Tarjeta postal*, postcard.
tarjeteo m. Exchange of visiting cards.
tarjetera f. *Amer.* V. TARJETERO.
tarjetero m. Card case, small wallet for carrying cards.
tarlatana f. Tarlatan (tela).
Tarpeya n. pr. f. Tarpeia. || *Roca Tarpeya*, Tarpeian Rock.

tarquín m. Slime, ooze (cieno).
Tarquino n. pr. m. HIST. Tarquin.
tarquino, na adj. *Amer.* Thoroughbred (animal vacuno).
— M. y f. Thoroughbred animal.
tarraconense adj. [Of *o* from] Tarragona.
— M. y f. Native *o* inhabitant of Tarragona.
Tarraconense n. pr. HIST. Tarraconensis [province of Roman-occupied Spain].
tárraga f. 17th century Spanish dance.
tarraja f. Diestock (para tornillos). || Modelling board [U.S., modeling board] (para yeso). || *Amer.* Leather tally.
tarreña f. Clay castanet (castañuela).
tarro m. Jar: *un tarro de mermelada*, a jam jar. || *Amer.* Horn (cuerno). | Top hat (sombrero de copa).
tarsiano, na adj. ANAT. Tarsal.
tarso m. ANAT. Tarsus.
tarta f. Cake, tart (pastel). || Baking pan (tartera). || *Tarta de boda*, wedding cake.
tártago m. BOT. Spurge.
tartajear v. intr. To stutter, to stammer.
tartajeo m. Stuttering, stammering (acción). || Stutter, stammer (defecto).
tartajoso, sa adj. Stuttering, stammering.
— M. y f. Stutterer, stammerer.
tartamudear v. intr. To stutter, to stammer.
tartamudeo m. Stuttering, stammering (acción). || Stutter, stammer (defecto).
tartamudez f. Stuttering, stammering.
tartamudo, da adj. Stuttering, stammering. || *Es tartamudo*, he stutters.
— M. y f. Stutterer, stammerer.
tartán m. Tartan, Scotch plaid (tela).
tartana f. MAR. Tartan (barco). || Trap, light carriage (carro).
tartáreo, a adj. POÉT. Tartarean.
Tartaria n. pr. f. GEOGR. Tartary.
tartárico, ca adj. QUÍM. Tartaric.
tártaro, ra adj. Tartar (de Tartaria).
— M. QUÍM. Tartar. || Tartar (sarro). || POÉT. Tartarus, hell.
tartera f. Baking pan (para hacer tartas). || Lunch box [U.S., dinner pail *o* bucket] (fiambrera).
tartesio, sia adj./s. HIST. Tartessian.
tartrato m. QUÍM. Tartrate.
tártrico, ca adj. QUÍM. Tartaric.
tartufería f. Hypocrisy.
tartufo m. Hypocrite (mojigato).
tarugo m. Chunk, piece (de madera, etc.). || Piece of stale bread (pan duro). || Wooden peg *o* plug (clavija). || Wooden paving block (para pavimentar calles). || FIG. y FAM. Blockhead, dolt (zoquete).
tarumba adj. FAM. Confused (confuso). || — FAM. *Volver tarumba*, to drive mad (volver loco), tò confuse, to rattle (aturdir). | *Volverse tarumba*, to go mad (volverse loco), to get confused (confundirse).
tas m. Anvil (yunque pequeño).
tasa f. Appraisal, valuation (valoración). || Tax (impuesto): *tasa de importación*, import tax. || Limit (límite): *poner una tasa a los gastos mensuales*, to put a limit on one's monthly outlay. || Measure, standard (medida, regla). || Rate (tipo, índice): *tasa de natalidad*, birth rate. || *Sin tasa* or *sin tasa ni medida*, without limit, limitless (sin límites), without any moderation (sin moderación).
tasación f. Appraisal, valuation (valoración). || Calculation (cálculo).
tasadamente adv. With moderation. || Scantily (escasamente).
tasador, ra adj. Appraising.
— M. y f. Valuator, valuer [U.S., appraiser].
tasajear v. tr. *Amer.* To jerk (la carne).
tasajo m. Jerked meat (carne seca y salada). || Piece of meat (trozo de carne).
tasajudo, da adj. *Amer.* Tall and thin.
tasar v. tr. To appraise, to value (valorar): *tasar un cuadro*, to appraise a painting. || To fix *o* to set the price of (fijar el precio de). || To regulate (los precios). || To tax (gravar). || FIG. To limit, to ration: *tasar la comida a un enfermo*, to limit a patient's food; *en la pensión tasan hasta el agua*, in the boardinghouse they even ration the water.
tasca f. Bar, pub (taberna). || Gambling den (timba). || *Amer.* MAR. Crosscurrent. || FAM. *Ir de tascas*, to go on a pub crawl [U.S., to go barhopping].
tascar v. tr. To scutch, to swingle (cáñamo). || FIG. To munch, to champ (la hierba). || FIG. y FAM. *Tascar el freno*, to champ at the bit.
tasugo m. ZOOL. Badger.
tata m. FAM. *Amer.* Daddy (papá). || — F. Nurse, nanny (niñera). || FAM. Maid (criada).
tataibá m. *Amer.* Mulberry.
tatarabuela f. Great-great-grandmother.
tatarabuelo m. Great-great-grandfather. || — Pl. Great-great-grandparents.
tataranieta f. Great-great-granddaughter.
tataranieto m. Great-great-grandson. || — Pl. Great-great-grandchildren.
tátaro, ra adj./s. Tatar.
tatas f. pl. *Andar a tatas*, to begin to walk, to take one's first steps (empezar a andar), to crawl [on all fours] (andar a gatas).
¡tate! interj. Be careful!, take care!, look out! (cuidado). || Slowly!, steady! (para detener). || I see!, so that's it! (ya comprendo).
tatetí m. *Amer.* Naughts-and-crosses [U.S., tick-tacktoe].
tatito m. FAM. *Amer.* Daddy, papa (papá).
tato, ta adj. Lisping [who pronounces *c* and *s* like *t*].
— M. FAM. Little brother, kid brother (hermano pequeño).
tatú m. ZOOL. Tatouay, giant armadillo.
tatuaje m. Tattooing (acción). || Tattoo (dibujo).
tatuar v. tr. To tattoo.
tatusa f. *Amer.* Little woman (mujercilla).
tau m. Tau cross, tau (cruz). || — F. Tau, nineteenth letter in the Greek alphabet.
taumaturgia f. Thaumaturgy.
taumatúrgico, ca adj. Thaumaturgic, thaumaturgical.
taumaturgo m. Thaumaturge.
Taúride n. pr. GEOGR. Tauris.
taurino, na adj. Taurine (del toro). || Bullfighting (de la corrida).
— F. QUÍM. Taurine, taurin.
Tauro n. pr. m. GEOGR. Taurus. || ASTR. Taurus.
taurófilo, la adj. Fond of bullfighting.
— M. y f. Bullfighting fan.
tauromaco, ca adj. Bullfighting, tauromachian. || Knowledgeable about bullfighting.
— M. y f. Bullfighting connoisseur *o* expert.
tauromaquia f. Bullfighting, tauromachy.
tauromáquico, ca adj. Bullfighting, tauromachian: *término tauromáquico*, bullfighting term.
tautología f. GRAM. Tautology (pleonasmo).
tautológico, ca adj. GRAM. Tautological.
taxativamente adv. Limitatively. || Precisely.
taxativo, va adj. Limitative, restrictive. || Precise.
taxi m. Taxi, taxicab, cab.
taxia f. BIOL. Taxis.
taxidermia f. Taxidermy.
taxidérmico, ca adj. Taxidermic, taxidermal.
taxidermista m. y f. Taxidermist.
taxímetro m. Taximeter (contador). || Taxi, taxicab (coche).
taxis f. BIOL. y MED. Taxis.
taxista m. y f. Taxi driver, cab driver, cabby.
taxonomía f. Taxonomy.
taxonómico, ca adj. Taxonomic, taxonomical.
taylorismo m. Taylorism, scientific management.
taylorización f. Introduction of scientific management techniques.
tayuyá BOT. *Amer.* Type of watermelon.
taza f. Cup: *una taza de porcelana*, a porcelain cup. || Bowl (de retrete). || Cup, cupful: *ha tomado tres tazas de café*, he has had three cups of coffee. || Basin (de una fuente). || Basket hilt (de la espada). || *Amer.* Basin. || *Taza de té*, cup of tea (llena de té), teacup (que sirve para el té).
tazón m. Bowl, large cup (taza grande).
te pron. pers. You, to you: *te veo*, I can see you; *te hablo*, I speak to you; *te lo di*, I gave it to you. || You, for you: *te he traído unas flores*, I have brought you some flowers, I have brought some flowers for you. || REL. Thee, to Thee.
— Pron. refl. Yourself: *lávate*, wash yourself. || REL. Thyself. || *Te lo puedes quedar*, you can keep it [for yourself].
te f. T (letra t). || T square (escuadra).
té m. Tea (planta, bebida): *té con limón*, lemon tea. || Tea (reunión): *convidar a alguien para el té*, to invite s.o. to tea; *té baile*, tea dance. || — FAM. *Dar el té*, to bore, to bother. || *Salón de té*, tearoom. || *Té de Méjico*, Mexican tea. || *Té de los jesuitas* or *del Paraguay*, maté, Paraguay tea.
tea f. Torch (antorcha). || FIG. y FAM. *Coger una tea*, to get plastered (emborracharse).
teatino, na m. y f. REL. Theatine.
teatral adj. Theatre, drama: *grupo teatral*, drama group. || Theatrical, melodramatic (exagerado): *en tono teatral*, in a theatrical tone. || *Obra teatral*, play, dramatic work.
teatralidad f. Theatricality.
teatro m. Theatre [U.S., theater] (sitio): *vamos al teatro esta noche*, we're going to the theatre tonight. || Theatre, drama, dramatic works, *pl.* (literatura dramática): *el teatro de Lope de Vega*, the theatre of Lope de Vega. || Theatre, acting, theatrical profession (profesión): *dedicarse al teatro*, to go into the theatre. || Stage: *dejar el teatro*, to give up the stage; *escribe para el teatro*, he writes for the stage. || FIG. Theatre: *el teatro de la batalla*, the theatre of the battle. | Scene (lugar de un acontecimiento). || — FIG. *Echarle teatro*, to playact, to exaggerate. | *Hacer teatro*, to playact, to be dramatic. || *Obra de teatro*, play, theatrical work. || *Teatro de la ópera*, opera house. || MIL. *Teatro de operaciones*, battlefield. || FIG. *Tener mucho teatro*, to be theatrical *o* melodramatic.
tebaico, ca adj. Theban (de Tebas).
Tebaida n. pr. f. Thebaid.
tebano, na adj./s. Theban (de Tebas).
Tebas n. pr. GEOGR. Thebes.
tebeo m. Comic [U.S., comic book].
teca f. Teak (árbol). || ANAT. y BOT. Theca. || Relicary (relicario).
tecali m. Mexican alabaster, tecali.

tecla f. Key (de instrumento de música, máquina de escribir). || — FIG. y FAM. *Dar en la tecla*, to strike the right note (acertar). || *Tecla de retroceso*, back-spacer, back space key. || FIG. *Tocar la tecla sensible*, to find s.o.'s soft *o* weak spot. | *Tocar una tecla* or *teclas*, to pull strings.
teclado m. Keyboard.
tecleado m. Fingering.
teclear v. intr. To finger the keyboard. || To type (escribir a máquina). || To play the piano (tocar el piano). || FIG. y FAM. To drum [one's fingers].
— V. tr. FIG. To sound out, to feel out.
tecleo m. Fingering (de instrumento). || Drumming (con los dedos). || *Se oía el tecleo de las máquinas de escribir*, you could hear the clatter of the typewriters.
tecnecio m. QUÍM. Technetium.
técnica f. Technique (método): *técnica de fabricación*, manufacturing technique. || Technique (habilidad). || Technology (tecnología). || Engineering: *técnica hidráulica*, hydraulic engineering. || *Los progresos de la técnica*, the technological advances.
técnicamente adv. Technically.
tecnicidad f. Technicality.
tecnicismo m. Technicality (carácter técnico). || Technical word *o* term (palabra).
técnico, ca adj. Technical: *diccionario técnico*, technical dictionary; *terminología técnica*, technical terms. || Technological (tecnológico).
— M. y f. Technician.
tecnicolor m. Technicolor: *en tecnicolor*, in technicolor.
tecnocracia f. Technocracy.
tecnócrata m. y f. Technocrat.
— Adj. Technocratic.
tecnología f. Technology.
tecnológico, ca adj. Technological.
tecnólogo, ga m. y f. Technologist.
tecol m. *Amer.* Maguey worm.
tecolines m. pl. FAM. *Amer.* Dough, *sing.*, money, *sing.*
tecolote m. *Amer.* Owl.
tecomate m. *Amer.* Gourd (calabaza). | Earthenware cup (vasija de barro).
tectónico, ca adj. Tectonic.
— F. Tectonics.
tectrices f. pl. ZOOL. Tectrices.
techado m. Roof, roofing (techo). || Shed (cobertizo). || *Bajo techado*, under cover, indoors.
techador m. Roofer.
techar v. tr. To roof.
techo m. Ceiling (parte interior). || Roof (tejado): *techo de paja*, straw *o* thatched roof. || AUT. Roof. || AVIAC. Ceiling. || FIG. Roof, house: *acoger a uno bajo su techo*, to take s.o. under one's roof, to take s.o. into one's house. || — *Techo corredizo*, sliding *o* sun roof. || *Vivir bajo el mismo techo*, to live under the same roof.
techumbre m. Roof, roofing (cubierta).
tedéum o **Te Deum** m. REL. Te Deum.
tediar v. tr. To loathe (odiar).
tedio m. Boredom, tedium (aburrimiento). || Annoyance (fastidio). || Loathing (repugnancia).
tedioso, sa adj. Tedious, boring (fastidioso). || Bothersome, annoying (molesto).
tegmen m. BOT. Tegmen.
tegucigalpense adj. [Of *o* from] Tegucigalpa (Honduras).
— M. y f. Native *o* inhabitant of Tegucigalpa.
tegumentario, ria adj. Tegumentary.
tegumento m. Tegument.
Teherán n. pr. GEOGR. Teheran, Tehran.
teína f. QUÍM. Theine.
teísmo m. Theism.
teísta adj. Theistic.
— M. y f. Theist.
teja f. Tile: *teja plana*, plain *o* flat tile; *teja de cumbrera*, ridge tile. || FAM. Priest's shovel hat (sombrero de cura). || Steel facing (de la espada). || MAR. Notch (muesca). || — FIG. y FAM. *A toca teja*, cash. | *De tejas abajo*, in this world (en la tierra). | *De tejas arriba*, in heaven (en el cielo). || *Teja flamenca*, pantile.
tejadillo m. Small roof (tejado). || Top, roof, cover (de un carruaje).
tejado m. Roof, tile roof. || — FIG. *Hasta el tejado*, full, packed. | *La pelota está aún en el tejado*, it is still in the air. | *Tiene el tejado de vidrio*, he is no one to talk, people who live in glass houses shouldn't throw stones.
tejamaní o **tejamanil** m. *Amer.* Shingle.
tejano, na adj./s. Texan.
tejar m. Tile works.
tejar v. tr. To tile.
Tejas n. pr. m. GEOGR. Texas.
tejavana f. Shed (cobertizo). || Building with a plain tile roof.
tejedera f. Weaver (tejedora). || Water strider (insecto).
tejedor, ra adj. Weaving (que teje). || *Amer.* FIG. y FAM. Intriguing, scheming (intrigante).
— M. y f. Weaver (que teje). || — M. Water strider (araña). || Weaverbird (ave).
tejedura m. Weaving (acción de tejer). || Texture (textura).
tejeduría f. Art of weaving, weaving (arte de tejer). || Weaving mill (taller).
tejemaneje m. FAM. To-do, fuss (actividad). | Trickery, scheming, goings-on, *pl.* (intriga). || FAM. *¿Qué tejemaneje te traes?*, what are you up to?, what are you cooking up?
tejer v. tr. To weave (entrelazar). || To spin: *la araña teje su tela*, the spider spins its web. || To knit (hacer punto). || FIG. To weave, to prepare: *está tejiendo su futuro*, he is preparing his future. | To plot, to weave, to concoct: *le están tejiendo una trampa*, they are concocting a trap for him. || *Amer.* To scheme (intrigar). || FIG. *Tejer y destejer*, to chop and change.
tejería f. Tile works (tejar).
tejeringo m. Fritter (churro).
tejero m. Tile maker.
tejido m. Weave: *un tejido muy apretado*, a very tight weave. || Weaving (acción). || Material, fabric (tela). || Textile. || ANAT. Tissue: *tejido muscular*, muscle tissue. || FIG. Tissue, web: *un tejido de embustes*, a tissue of lies. || — *Fábrica de tejidos*, textile factory. || *Tejido de punto*, jersey.
tejo m. Disk, quoit (plancha metálica circular). || Quoits, *pl.* (juego). || TECN. Step bearing (tejuelo). || Gold ingot (lingote de oro). || Blank (para hacer una moneda). || Hopscotch (juego de niñas). || Yew (árbol).
tejocote m. *Amer.* Hawthorn (planta).
tejoleta f. Piece of tile (pedazo de teja). || Clay castanet (tarreña).
tejón m. ZOOL. Badger.
tejonera f. Badger burrow.
tejuelo m. Small disk *o* quoit (plancha circular metálica). || TECN. Step bearing. || Label (en el lomo de un libro).
tela f. Material, cloth, fabric: *he comprado la tela para el vestido*, I have bought the material for the dress. || Web, cobweb (de araña). || Film, skin (de nata). || Skin, membrane (de las frutas). || ANAT. Membrane. | Film (en el ojo). || ARTES. Canvas (lienzo). | Painting (cuadro). || FIG. y FAM. Dough (dinero). || FIG. Conversation material, sth. to talk about: *tienen tela para rato*, they have plenty to talk about. || — *Encuadernación en tela*, cloth binding. || FIG. *Estar en tela de juicio*, to be in doubt. | *Hay tela de que cortar*, there is an awful lot to be done. | *Poner en tela de juicio*, to question, to put in doubt. || *Tela de araña*, spider's web, cobweb. || *Tela de cebolla*, onion skin. || *Tela de saco*, burlap. || *Tela metálica*, wire netting.
telamón m. ARQ. Telamon.
telar m. Loom (máquina). || Sewing press (de los encuadernadores). || ARQ. Frame (de puerta o ventana). || — Pl. Textile mill, *sing.* (fábrica). || TEATR. Flies. || FIG. *Tener algo en el telar*, to have sth. in the making.
telaraña f. Web, spider's web, cobweb. || FIG. Trifle, bagatelle, nothing (cosa de poca importancia). || — FIG. *Mirar las telarañas*, to stargaze. | *Tener telarañas en los ojos*, to be blind.
telarañoso, sa adj. Cobwebby, cobwebbed.
tele f. FAM. Telly, T.V. (televisión).
telecine o **telecinematógrafo** m. Telecine.
telecomunicación f. Telecommunication.
telediario m. Television news bulletin, news: *el telediario de las nueve*, the nine o' clock news.
teledifusión f. Telecast, television broadcast.
teledinámico, ca adj. Telodynamic.
teledirección f. Remote control.
teledirigido, da adj. Remote-controlled. || *Proyectil teledirigido*, guided missile.
teledirigir v. tr. To operate *o* to guide by remote control.
teleferaje m. Telpherage.
teleférico m. Cable car *o* railway.
telefilm m. Telefilm.
telefonazo m. FAM. Ring, telephone call. || *Dar un telefonazo a alguien*, to ring s.o. up, to give s.o. a ring, to call s.o.
telefonear v. tr. e intr. To telephone, to phone.
telefonema m. Telephoned telegram.
telefonía f. Telephony: *telefonía sin hilos*, wireless telephony.
telefónicamente adv. By telephone.
telefónico, ca adj. Telephone, phone, telephonic. || — *Cabina telefónica*, telephone box *o* booth. || *Central telefónica*, telephone exchange. || *Compañía telefónica*, telephone company. || *Llamada telefónica*, telephone call, phone call.
telefonista m. y f. Telephone operator.
teléfono m. Telephone, phone. || — *Guía de teléfonos*, telephone directory *o* book. || *Le llaman por teléfono*, you're wanted on the telephone. || *Llamar a alguien por teléfono*, to telephone s.o., to phone s.o., to ring s.o. up, to call s.o. || FIG. *Teléfono rojo*, hot line.
telefoto m. Phototelegraph, telephotograph, telephoto.
telefotografía f. Telephotography.
telefotográfico, ca adj. Telephoto, telephotographic.
telegrafía f. Telegraphy: *telegrafía sin hilos*, wireless telegraphy.
telegrafiar v. tr. e intr. To telegraph, to wire.
telegráficamente adv. By telegraph, by telegram, telegraphically.
telegráfico, ca adj. Telegraphic. || *Giro telegráfico*, money order.

TELECOMUNICACIONES, *f.* — TELECOMMUNICATIONS

I. Correos, *m. pl.* — Post office, *sing.*

oficina (*f.*) de correos	post office
estafeta (*f.*) de correos	sub-post office [U.S., branch post office]
ventanilla *f.*	window
apartado (*m.*) de correos	post-office box
lista (*f.*) de correos	poste restante [U.S., General Delivery]
casillero *m.*	pigeonholes *pl.*
pesacartas *m. inv.*	letter-scales *pl.*
saca (*f.*) postal	mailbag
mesa (*f.*) de batalla	sorting table
clasificador (*m.*) de cartas	mail sorter
buzón *m.*	letter box [U.S., mailbox]
cartero *m.*	postman [U.S., mailman]
cartería *f.*, sala (*f.*) de batalla	sorting office
recogida (*f.*) de cartas	collection
reparto (*m.*) del correo	delivery
correo (*m.*) aéreo	air mail, airmail
por avión	[by] air mail
paquete (*m.*) postal [*Amer.*, encomienda *f.*]	parcel
valija (*f.*) diplomática	diplomatic pouch, diplomatic bag
envío (*m.*) contra reembolso	cash on delivery
carta (*f.*) urgente	express *o* special delivery letter
carta (*f.*) certificada	registered letter
carta (*f.*) adjunta	covering letter
certificar	to register
echar una carta	to post a letter
papel (*m.*) de escribir	writing paper
correspondencia *f.*	correspondence
despachar la correspondencia	to deal with the mail
cartec *m.*	exchange of letters
acuse (*m.*) de recibo	acknowledgement of receipt
a vuelta de correo	by return of post
sobre *m.*	envelope
destinatario *m.*	addressee (de carta), consignee (de paquete), payee (de giro)
remitente *m.* y *f.*	sender
dirección *f.*	address
distrito (*m.*) postal	postal district
interior	local
referencia *f.*	reference
membrete *m.*	letterhead
encabezamiento *m.*	heading
fecha *f.*; fechador *m.*	date; date stamp
postdata *f.*, posdata *f.*, post scriptum *m. inv.*	postscript
se ruega la reexpedición, remítase al destinatario *or* a las nuevas señas	please forward
tarjeta (*f.*) postal	postcard
circular *f.*	circular [letter]
impresos *m. pl.*	printed matter *sing.*
giro (*m.*) postal	money *o* postal order
giro (*m.*) telegráfico	telegraphic money order
sello *m.* [*Amer.*, estampilla *f.*]	stamp
franqueo *m.*	franking, stamping
franqueo (*m.*) concertado	postage paid
franquicia (*m.*) postal	exemption from postal charges
matasellos *m. inv.*	postmark
sobretasa *f.*	extra postage

II. Telegrafía, *f.* — Telegraphy.

telégrafo *m.*	telegraph
telégrafos *m. pl.*, oficina (*f.*) central de telégrafos	telegraph office
telégrafo (*m.*) Morse	Morse code
punto *m.*; raya *f.*	dot; dash
telegrafía (*f*) sin hilos	wireless telegraphy
código (*m.*) telegráfico	telegraphic address
receptor *m.*	receiver
manipulador *m.*	telegraph key
teleimpresor *m.*, teletipo *m.*	teleprinter, teletype, teletypewriter
telegrafía *f.*	telegraphy
telegrafiar	to telegraph, to wire
telegrafista *m.* y *f.*	telegrapher, telegraph operator, telegraphist
radiotelegrafía *f.*	radiotelegraphy, wireless
radiotelegrafiar	to radiotelegraph, to wireless
radiotelegrafista *m.* y *f.*	wireless operator
telegrama *m.*	telegram, wire (fam.)
poner *or* enviar un telegrama	to send a telegram
telegrama (*m.*) cifrado	coded telegram, telegram in code
respuesta (*f.*) pagada	reply paid
télex *m.*	telex
cable *m.*, cablegrama *m.*	cable, cablegram
cablegrafiar	to cable, to send a cable
comunicaciones (*f. pl.*) vía satélite	satellite communications

III. Teléfonos, *m.* — Telephones.

central (*f.*) telefónica	telephone exchange
teléfono *m.*	telephone, phone
teléfono (*m.*) manual	manual telephone
teléfono (*m.*) automático	automatic telephone
aparato *m.*	telephone, phone
microteléfono *m.*	combined set
teléfono (*m.*) interior	interphone
receptor *m.*	receiver
auricular *m.*	earpiece, receiver
disco (*m.*) selector *or* de llamada	dial
horquilla *f.*	hook
macillo *m.*, martillo *m.*	hammer
interruptor *m.*	switch
clavija *f.*	plug
contador *m.*	counter, meter
circuito *m.*	circuit
frecuencia *f.*	frequency
conexión *f.*	connection, connexion
desconexión *f.*	disconnection, disconnexion
selector *m.*	selector
tablero (*m.*) de conexión	switchboard
red (*f.*) de teléfonos	telephone network
centralita (*f.*) de teléfonos	switchboard
extensión *f.*	extension
línea *f.*; cable *m.*	line; cable
telefonista *m.* y *f.*	telephone operator
operadora *f.*	operator
ficha (*f.*) de teléfono	token
cabina (*f.*) *or* locutorio (*m.*) de teléfonos	telephone box *o* kiosk [U.S., telephone booth]
abonado (*m.*) de teléfonos	telephone subscriber
llamada (*f.*) telefónica, telefonazo *m.*	telephone call, ring
conferencia (*f.*) interurbana	long-distance call, trunk call
conferencia (*f.*) urbana	local call
conferencia (*f.*) con cobro revertido	reverse-charge call [U.S., collect telephone call]
informaciones *f. pl.*	directory inquiries
marcar un número	to dial a number
prefijo *m.*, código (*m.*) territorial	area code, code number
timbre (*m.*) de llamada	ring
señal (*f.*) para marcar	dialling tone
señal (*f.*) de comunicando	engaged tone
está comunicando	it's engaged
llamar por teléfono, telefonear	to telephone, to call [up], to ring up
descolgar el teléfono	to lift *o* to pick up the telephone
¡oiga!, ¡dígame!	hello!
¡hable!	you're through
¡al habla!	speaking!
quisiera hablar con...	could you put me through to...
¿con quién hablo?	who is speaking?
el Sr. Pérez al aparato	Mr. Pérez speaking
¿de parte de quién?	who is calling?
no se retire	please hold on
colgar el teléfono	to hang up
guía (*f.*) de teléfonos, anuario (*m.*) telefónico, listín (*m.*) de teléfonos	telephone directory *o* book
telefonía *f.*	telephony
telefonema *m.*	telephoned telegram

telegrafista m. y f. Telegrapher, telegraph operator, telegraphist.
telégrafo m. Telegraph.
telegrama m. Telegram, wire (fam.).
teleguiar v. tr. To operate *o* to guide by remote control.
teleimpresor m. Teleprinter, teletype, teletypewriter.
telele m. Fainting spell (desmayo).
Telémaco n. pr. m. Telemachus.
telemando m. Remote control.
telemecánico, ca adj. Telemechanic. — F. Telemechanics.
telemetría f. Telemetry.
telemétrico, ca adj. Telemetric.
telémetro m. Range finder, telemeter.
telencéfalo m. ANAT. Telencephalon.
telenque adj. *Amer.* Silly, foolish (bobo).
teleobjetivo m. FOT. Telephoto lens, telelens.
teleología f. Teleology.
teleológico, ca adj. Teleological, teleologic.
teleósteo adj. ZOOL. Teleostean, teleost. — M. Teleost.
telépata m. y f. Telepathist.
telepatía f. Telepathy.
telepático, ca adj. Telepathic.
telequinesia f. Telekinesis.
telera f. Plough pin (del arado). || Transom, cross-piece (del carro). || MIL. Transom (de cureña). || Jaw (de prensa). || MAR. Rack block. || Sheep pen (redil). || *Amer.* Rectangular biscuit. | Oval loaf of bread.
telerón m. Transom.
telescópico, ca adj. Telescopic.
telescopio m. Telescope.
telesilla f. Chair lift.
telespectador, ra m. y f. Televiewer, viewer.
telesquí m. Ski lift.
telestesia f. Telesthesia.
teletipo m. Teletype, teleprinter, teletypewriter.
televidente m. y f. Viewer, televiewer.
televisar v. tr. To televise.
televisión f. Television: *ver la televisión*, to watch television. || FAM. Television set (televisor). || — *Televisión en colores*, colour television. || *Transmitir por televisión*, to televise.

televisivo, va adj. Telegenic (apto para ser televisado). || Television (de televisión).
televisor m. Television, television set.
télex m. Telex.
telilla f. Light camlet (tela). || Film, skin (en líquidos).
telón m. Curtain, drop curtain. || — FIG. *Telón de acero*, iron curtain. || TEATR. *Telón de boca*, house *o* drop curtain. | *Telón de fondo* or *de foro*, backdrop, backcloth. | *Telón metálico*, safety curtain.
telonero, ra adj. First on (artista). || *Combate telonero*, preliminary bout (boxeo).
— M. y f. First act (en los espectáculos).
telúrico, ca adj. Telluric.
telurio m. QUÍM. Tellurium (metal).
telurismo m. Influence of the earth [on the inhabitants of a region].
tema m. Topic, subject, theme (asunto): *el tema de la conversación*, the subject of the conversation. || Theme, subject (de un libro, de un discurso). || GRAM. Stem. || MÚS. Theme. || Translation into a foreign language (traducción inversa). || Obsession, mania (manía). || Grudge, ill will (antipatía). || Question (en un examen). || Subject (en oposiciones). || — *Atenerse al tema*, to keep to the point. || FAM. *Cada loco con su tema*, everyone has his hobbyhorse. || *Salirse del tema*, v. SALIR. || *Tener tema para un rato*, to have plenty to talk about.
temario m. Programme [U.S., program] (lista de temas). || Agenda (de una conferencia).
temático, ca adj. Thematic. || GRAM. Stem.
— F. Theme, subject (conjunto de temas). || Doctrine (doctrina). || Ideology (ideología). || Philosophy (filosofía).
tembetá m. *Amer.* Stick worn by some Indians in the lower lip.
tembladal m. Quaking bog, quagmire (tremedal).
tembladera f. Shaking fit (temblor). || Thin two-handled bowl (vasija). || Jewel mounted on a spiral (joya). || *Amer.* Quaking bog, quagmire (tremedal). || ZOOL. Torpedo, electric ray (pez). || BOT. Quaking grass.
tembladeral m. *Amer.* Quaking bog, quagmire.
tembladero, ra adj. Trembling, shaking.
— M. Quaking bog, quagmire.
temblador, ra adj. Trembling, shaking.
— M. y f. REL. Quaker.
temblar* v. intr. To shake, to tremble, to shudder, to quiver: *el miedo le hizo temblar*, he trembled with fear; *durante el terremoto todas las casas temblaban*, during the earthquake all the houses were shaking. || To shiver (de frío). || To tremble (la voz). || FIG. To tremble *o* to shake with fear (tener miedo). || FIG. y FAM. *Dejó temblando la botella*, he nearly finished off the whole bottle.
tembleque m. Shaking fit (temblor intenso): *le dio un tembleque*, he had a shaking fit. || Trembler (persona). || Jewel mounted on a spiral (joya).
temblequear v. intr. To shake, to tremble, to quiver (temblar). || FIG. y FAM. To pretend to tremble.
temblequeteo m. FAM. Shivers, *pl.*, shakes, *pl.*
tembletear v. intr. To shake, to tremble, to quiver.
temblón, ona adj. Shaking, trembling, quivering, tremulous (que tiembla).
temblor m. Tremor, shudder. || Shivering, shivers, *pl.* (de frío). || Trembling (de la voz). || FIG. Shiver: *me da temblores pensar en lo que va a pasar*, it gives me the shivers to think what is going to happen. || *Amer.* Earthquake. || *Temblor de tierra*, earthquake, earth tremor.
tembloroso, sa adj. Shaking, trembling, quivering, tremulous (que tiembla). || Trembling, tremulous (voz).
temedor, ra adj. Fearful, afraid.
temer v. tr. To be afraid of, to fear: *teme a su padre*, he is afraid of his father. || To be afraid, to fear (sospechar con inquietud): *temo que no me lo devuelva*, I am afraid he won't give it back to me. || REL. To fear: *temer a Dios*, to fear God. || *No temer ni a Dios ni al diablo*, v. DIOS.
— V. intr. To be afraid. || — *Ser de temer*, to be dangerous. || *Temer por*, to fear for, to be afraid for: *temo por su vida*, I fear for his life.
— V. pr. To be afraid: *me temo que no venga*, I am afraid he won't come; *me lo temo*, I am afraid so.
temerario, ria adj. Rash, reckless, bold, foolhardy, temerarious: *un joven temerario*, a reckless youth; *un acto temerario*, a rash act. || *Un juicio temerario*, a rash judgment.
temeridad f. Temerity, recklessness.
temerosamente adv. Fearfully.
temeroso, sa adj. Frightful, fearful (que causa terror). || Fearful, timorous, timid (medroso). || — *Temeroso de*, afraid of: *temeroso de sus superiores*, afraid of his superiors. || *Temeroso de Dios*, God-fearing.
temible adj. Fearsome, fearful, dreadful, frightful: *un arma temible*, a fearful weapon.
Temis n. pr. f. MIT. Themis.
Temístocles m. pr. m. Themistocles.
temor m. Fear: *el temor al castigo*, fear of punishment. || Dread, apprehension (recelo). || — *Por temor a* or *de*, for fear of: *por temor de herirle, no le dije la verdad*, I didn't tell him the truth for fear of hurting him. || *Temor de Dios*, fear of God. || *Tener mucho temor a*, to be terrified of.
témpano m. Floe (de hielo). || FIG. *Ser un témpano*, to be as cold as ice *o* as an iceberg.
temperamental adj. Temperamental.
temperamento m. Temperament, disposition, nature (manera de ser): *tiene un temperamento tranquilo*, he has a quiet temperament. || Weather (temperie). || MÚS. Temperament. || *Tener temperamento*, to be temperamental, to have a temperament.
temperancia f. Temperance, moderation.
temperante adj. Calming (que tempera). || MED. Sedative. || *Amer.* Teetotal.
— M. y f. Teetotaller [U.S., teetotaler].
temperar v. tr. To temper, to moderate (moderar). || To mitigate. || MED. To calm (calmar). || MÚS. To temper.
— V. intr. *Amer.* To have a change of air.
— V. pr. To warm up (el tiempo).
temperatura f. Temperature: *temperatura máxima*, maximum temperature. || MED. Temperature, fever (fiebre, calentura): *tener temperatura*, to have a temperature. || *Temperatura absoluta, crítica*, absolute, critical temperature.
temperie f. Weather [conditions].
tempero m. Favourable condition of the land [for sowing].
tempestad f. Storm, tempest (tormenta). || FIG. Storm: *una tempestad de aplausos, de insultos*, a storm of applause, of insults; *levantó una tempestad de protestas*, it raised a storm of protest. || — FIG. *Levantar tempestades*, to produce turmoil. || *Tempestad de arena, de nieve*, sandstorm, snowstorm. || FIG. *Una tempestad en un vaso de agua*, a storm in a teacup.
tempestear v. intr. To storm. || FIG. y FAM. To rant and rave (estar furioso).
tempestividad f. Timeliness.
tempestivo, va adj. Opportune, timely (oportuno).
tempestuoso, sa adj. Turbulent, stormy, tempestuous: *tiempo tempestuoso*, stormy weather. || FIG. Stormy: *el ambiente tempestuoso de la asamblea*, the stormy atmosphere at the assembly.
tempisque m. *Amer.* BOT. Ironwood.
templa f. Distemper (pintura).
templado, da adj. Temperate, moderate (sobrio). || Lukewarm, warm (tibio): *agua templada*, lukewarm water. || Temperate, mild (clima, tiempo). || Temperate (región). || MÚS. Tuned, in tune. || FIG. Restrained (estilo). | Moderate (moderado). | Brave, courageous (valiente). | Bright (listo). || TECN. Tempered (cristal, metal). || *Amer.* Drunk (borracho). | Tipsy (achispado). || — FIG. y FAM. *Estar bien, mal templado*, to be in a good, in a bad mood. | *Nervios bien templados*, nerves of steel, steady nerves.
templador, ra adj. Tempering. || MÚS. Tuning.
— M. MÚS. Tuning fork (diapasón). | Tuner (el que templa). || TECN. Temperer (obrero). | Turnbuckle (tensor).
templadura f. Tempering (metal). || MÚS. Tuning.
templanza f. Temperance (virtud). || Moderation. || Mildness, temperateness (del clima). || Harmony [of colours] (en pintura).
templar v. tr. To temper, to moderate (moderar). || To make temperate (volver templado). || To warm up (agua fría). || To cool down (agua caliente). || To restrain, to control (reprimir). || To calm down (apaciguar). || To appease (la cólera). || MÚS. To tune, to temper. || TECN. To temper (acero, vidrio). || To blend (armonizar los colores). || To soften (color, luz). || To tighten (atirantar, apretar).
— V. intr. To warm up (el tiempo).
— V. pr. To be moderate, to control o.s. (moderarse). || To warm up (ponerse templado). || *Amer.* To fall in love (enamorarse). | To get tipsy (bebiendo).
templario m. Knight Templar, Templar.
temple m. Temper (metal, vidrio). || Atmospheric conditions, *pl.*, weather (tiempo). || Temperature (temperatura). || FIG. Temper, humour, mood: *estar de buen, de mal temple*, to be in a good, in a bad mood. | Spirit, energy (energía). | Resoluteness (entereza). || ARTES. Tempera, tempera paint (pintura). || MÚS. Tuning, tempering. || FIG. Average, mean. || — *Dar temple*, to temper. || ARTES. *Pintar al temple*, to paint in tempera.
Temple m. REL. Order of the knights Templar.
templete m. Small temple (templo pequeño). || Niche (para imágenes). || Kiosk (pabellón).
templo m. Temple. || Church (iglesia). || FIG. Temple (de sabiduría, justicia, etc.). || — FIG. y FAM. *Como un templo*, huge, enormous: *una mentira como un templo*, a huge lie; real: *una mujer como un templo*, a real woman. | *Es una verdad como un templo*, it is the patent truth.
tempo m. MÚS. Tempo (movimiento).
temporada f. Season: *temporada de verano*, summer season; *temporada teatral*, theatre season; *temporada de toros*, bullfighting season. || Period of time, spell: *pasamos una temporada en Málaga*, we spent a period of time in Malaga. || Period, time: *la mejor temporada de mi vida*, the best time of my life. || — *De fuera de temporada*, off-season: *tarifas de fuera de temporada*, off-season rates. || *En plena temporada*, at the height of the season. || *Estar de temporada*, to be on holiday. || *Hace una temporada que no trabaja*, he has been

out of work for a while. || *Por temporadas*, on and off. || *Temporada baja*, off season. || *Temporada de calma* or *de poca venta* or *de venta reducida*, slack season.

temporal adj. Temporal (contrapuesto a espiritual o eterno): *el poder temporal de los papas*, the temporal power of the Popes. || Temporary, provisional (de poca duración): *un empleo temporal*, a temporary job. || Worldly (material): *los bienes temporales*, worldly goods. || ANAT. Temporal (de la sien). || GRAM. Temporal.
— M. Storm, tempest (tempestad). || Rainy spell (lluvia). || Seasonal worker (obrero). || ANAT. Temporal bone. || — *Capear el temporal*, to weather the storm. || *Correr un temporal*, to go through a storm (en el mar).

temporalidad f. Temporality. || — Pl. Temporalities (beneficios eclesiásticos).

temporalizar v. tr. To make temporal.

temporáneo, a o **temporario, ria** adj. Temporary, provisional.

Témporas f. pl. REL. Ember days.

temporero, ra adj. Seasonal, temporary.
— M. Seasonal *o* temporary worker (obrero).

temporizar v. intr. To temporize (contemporizar). || To pass the time, to kill time (matar el tiempo).

tempranal adj. Early-yielding (tierra, plantío).

tempranamente adv. Early (temprano). || Too early (prematuramente).

tempranero, ra adj. Early-rising (persona). || AGR. Early. || *Ser tempranero*, to be an early riser (persona).

tempranito adv. FAM. Very early, nice and early.

temprano, na adj. Early (plantas).
— M. Early crop: *recoger los tempranos*, to gather in the early crops.
— Adv. Early: *levantarse temprano*, to get up early. || *Más temprano*, earlier.

ten m. FAM. *Tener mucho ten con ten*, to be very careful.

tenacidad f. Tenacity. || Perseverance. || TECN. Tensile strength.

tenacillas f. pl. Small pliers *o* tongs (tenazas pequeñas). || Sugar tongs (para el azúcar). || Curling iron, *sing.* (para rizar el pelo). || Tweezers (de depilar). || Cigarette holder, *sing.* (para tener cogido el cigarrillo). || Snuffers (despabiladeras).

tenallón m. MIL. Tenail, tenaille (fortificación).

tenante m. Supporter (de un escudo).

tenar adj./s.m. ANAT. Thenar.

tenaz adj. Tenacious (persona). || Persistent (dolor). || Hard to remove (mancha). || Adhesive, sticky (pegajoso): *la pez es muy tenaz*, pitch is very sticky. || Stubborn (resistencia).

tenaza f. o **tenazas** f. pl. Pliers, pincers (herramienta). || Tongs (para el fuego). || Claws, pincers (de crustáceos). || Tenail, tenaille (fortificación). || Tongs (para hielo, pasteles). || MED. Forceps. || TECN. Jaws (del torno). || Tenace (juego de baraja). || — FIG. y FAM. *Eso no se puede coger ni con tenazas*, I wouldn't touch it with a barge pole. || DEP. *Hacer tenaza*, to get *o* to put a scissors hold on (lucha libre). || FIG. y FAM. *No hay manera de* or *no se puede sacárselo ni con tenazas*, wild horses couldn't drag it out of him.

tenazada f. Gripping *o* holding [with pliers or tongs] (con tenazas). || Clink (ruido). || FIG. Hard bite (mordisco fuerte).

tenazón (a o **de)** loc. adv. Without taking aim, blindly.

tenca f. ZOOL. Tench (pez).

tendal m. Awning (toldo). || Canvas used to catch olives (para recoger aceitunas). || Drying place (tendedero). || *Amer.* Shearing shed (para esquilar los animales). | Drying floor (para secar café, cacao). | Lot, heap (gran cantidad).

tendedero m. Drying place (sitio para tender ropa).

tendejón m. Little shop.

tendel m. Levelling line (cuerda). || Layer of mortar (capa de mortero).

tendencia f. Tendency, trend: *la tendencia al aumento de precios*, the tendency for prices to rise, the trend towards rising prices. || — *Tendencia política*, political tendency. || *Tener tendencia a hacer algo*, to tend to do sth., to have a tendency to do sth.

tendencioso, sa adj. Tendentious [U.S., tendencious].

tendente adj. Directed, aimed: *medidas tendentes a una mejora económica*, measures directed towards economic improvement.

ténder m. Tender (de la locomotora).

tender* v. tr. To spread, to spread out, to lay out: *tender el mantel sobre la mesa*, to spread the tablecloth over the table; *tender la ropa en el suelo para que se seque*, to spread clothes on the ground to dry. || To lay (poner en posición horizontal). || To put out, to stretch out (la mano). || To hang out (ropa en una cuerda). || To stretch (cuerda). || To lay (vía, cable). || To cast (redes). || To build, to throw (puente). || To set, to lay (emboscada). || To draw (un arco). || To plaster (revestir las paredes con una capa de cal). || MAR. To spread (velas).
— V. intr. To tend, to have a tendency: *tiende a ser perezoso*, he tends towards laziness, he tends to be lazy, he has a tendency to be lazy.
— V. pr. To stretch out, to lie down: *tenderse en* or *por el suelo*, to stretch out on the floor. || To lay down, to throw one's cards on the table (naipes). || To run at full gallop (caballo). || To droop (las mieses).

tenderete m. Stall, stand (puesto de venta). || Display (exposición de mercancías). || Pile, heap (montón desordenado).

tendero, ra m. y f. Shopkeeper. || — M. Tent maker (que fabrica tiendas de campaña).

tendido, da adj. Spread out, laid out (extendido). || Hung out (ropa). || Lying down (persona). || — *A galope tendido*, V. GALOPE. || FIG. y FAM. *Dejar tendido a uno*, to floor s.o. | *Dormir a pierna tendida*, to sleep soundly, to sleep like a log. | *Hablar largo y tendido*, V. LARGO. | *Llorar a moco tendido*, V. LLORAR.
— M. Construction, building (de un puente). || Laying (de un cable). || Wash, washing (ropa puesta a secarse). || Batch of bread (tanda de pan). || Coat of plaster (capa de yeso). || TAUR. Lower tiers (*pl.*) of seats excluding the first row. || Slope [of a roof from ridge to eaves] (del tejado). || Run (de encaje). || *Amer.* Bed linen. || FIG. *Para el tendido*, for the masses.

tendiente adj. Tending (*a*, to).

tendinoso, sa adj. Tendinous, sinewy.

tendón m. Tendon. || *Tendón de Aquiles*, Achilles' tendon.

tenducha f. o **tenducho** m. FAM. Small run-down shop.

tenebrosidad f. Darkness, gloom. || FIG. Shadiness.

tenebroso, sa adj. Dark, gloomy, tenebrous (oscuro). || FIG. Dark, gloomy: *un porvenir muy tenebroso*, a very dark future. | Shady, sinister: *maquinaciones tenebrosas*, shady dealings.

tenedor m. Fork (utensilio de mesa): *un tenedor de plata*, a silver fork. || COM. Bearer, holder. || Owner (el que posee). || — *Tenedor de acciones*, stockholder. || *Tenedor de libros*, bookkeeper.

teneduría f. Bookkeeping. || *Teneduría de libros*, bookkeeping.

tenencia f. Possession: *tenencia ilícita de armas*, illicit possession of arms. || MIL. Lieutenancy (cargo de teniente). || *Tenencia de alcaldía*, position of deputy mayor.

tener* v. tr. To have, to have got: *tener dinero*, to have money; *tener buenas cualidades*, to have good qualities; *el ministro tiene una entrevista esta tarde*, the minister has an interview this afternoon. || To have, to have got, to own, to possess (ser propietario de): *tiene dos casas en Madrid*, he owns two houses in Madrid. || To hold, to have: *tenía el sombrero en la mano*, he was holding his hat in his hand. || To hold, to contain (contener). || To weigh (pesar). || To be, to measure (medir): *la habitación tiene seis metros por diez*, the room is six metres by ten. || To keep (mantener): *el ruido me ha tenido despierto toda la noche*, the noise kept me awake all night. || To hold (celebrar): *tener una asamblea*, to hold an assembly. || To take (coger): *ten tu billete*, take your ticket; *tenga Vd. la vuelta*, take the change. || To keep, to be in charge of (ocuparse de): *tener los libros*, to keep the books. || To have, to spend (pasar): *hemos tenido un día muy bueno*, we have had a very good day. || To have, to receive (recibir). || To keep, to maintain (conservar): *tener en buen estado*, to keep in good shape. || To have (dar a luz): *acaba de tener un niño*, she has just had a baby. || — *¡Ahí lo tienes!*, you see!, so there you are! (ya ves), there it is (allí está). || *Allí tiene...*, there is..., there are ... || *Aquí tiene...*, here is... || *¿Conque ésas tenemos?*, is that so?, so that's the way it is. || *¿Cuántos años tienes?*, how old are you? || *¡Él tenía que ser!*, it would be him!, it had to be him! || *Eso no tiene nada que ver*, that has nothing to do with it, that is irrelevant. || FIG. *No sabe lo que tiene*, he doesn't realize how lucky he is. || *No tendremos ni para empezar con esto*, we won't go far with this. || FAM. *No tenerlas todas consigo*, V. CONSIGO. || *No tener más que*, to have only to: *no tienes más que llamar para que vaya en seguida*, you have only to call and I shall be there at once. || FIG. *No tener más que lo puesto*, to have only the shirt on one's back. || *No tener nada de particular*, to be nothing extraordinary *o* unusual. || *No tener nada que ver con*, to have nothing to do with: *yo no tengo nada que ver con eso*, I have nothing to do with that. || *No tener razón*, to be wrong. || *¿Qué tiene de particular?*, what is so unusual about that? || *¿Qué tienes?*, what's the matter [with you]?, what's wrong [with you]? || *Quien más tiene más quiere*, the more one has the more one wants. || *Quien tuvo retuvo*, one always retains something of one's past glory *o* splendour *o* fortune. || *Tener a bien*, to see fit, to think it better: *tuve a bien quedarme más tiempo*, I saw fit to stay longer; to be so good *o* so kind as to (tener la amabilidad de). || *Tener a la vista* or *ante los ojos*, to have before one's eyes. || *Tener al corriente*, to keep informed. || *Tener al día*, to keep up to date. || *Tener algo de beber, de comer*, to have [got] sth. to drink, to eat. || *Tener a mano*, to have at *o* to hand, to have handy. || *Tener a menos*, to consider it beneath o.s.: *tiene a menos trabajar*, he considers it beneath himself to work. || *Tener ante sí*, to have before one: *el comité tiene ante sí un informe*, the committee has before it a report. || *Tener ... años*, to be ... [years old]: *tiene cuarenta años*, he is fourty [years old]. || FIG. y FAM. *Tener atravesado*, V. ATRAVESADO. || *Tener calor*, to be hot. || *Tener cinco pies de*

alto y tres de ancho, to be five feet high and three feet wide. || *Tener con que* or *para vivir*, to have enough to live on. || *Tener ... de retraso*, to be ... late: *tenemos una hora de retraso*, we are an hour late. || FIG. *Tener encima*, to be loaded down with, to have on: *tengo una cantidad enorme de trabajo encima*, I have an enormous amount of work on. || *Tener en cuenta*, V. CUENTA. || *Tener en mucho, en poco*, V. MUCHO, POCO. || *Tener envidia*, to be envious. || *Tener fama*, to be famous, to be well known. || *Tener frío*, to be cold. || *Tener ganas de*, V. GANA. || *Tener hambre*, to be hungry. || *Tenerla tomada con uno*, to have it in for s.o. || *Tener lugar*, V. LUGAR. || *Tener paciencia*, to be patient. || *Tener para sí*, to think, to believe: *tengo para mí que ya ha llegado*, I think he has arrived. || *Tener parte en*, V. PARTE. || *Tener por*, to consider, to regard as (considerar): *le tengo por inteligente*, I consider him intelligent. || *Tener por seguro*, to rest assured: *ten por seguro que te llamará*, rest assured he will call you. || *Tener puesto*, to wear, to have on. || *Tener que*, to have to, must: *tengo que irme*, I have to go, I must go. || *Tener que ver con*, V. VER. || *Tener razón*, to be right. || *Tener sed*, to be thirsty. || *Tener sobre sí*, to be in charge of. || *Tener sueño*, V. SUEÑO. || *Tener suerte*, V. SUERTE. || FIG. y FAM. *Tener una encima*, to be drunk *o* canned *o* plastered. || *Tiene mucho de su padre*, he takes after his father. || *Tienen el jardín hecho un barrizal*, their garden is like a swamp. || *Ya tiene años* or *ya tiene sus añitos*, he's no spring chicken.
— V. intr. To have money (tener dinero). || *Yo no tengo*, I haven't got any.
— V. pr. To stop, to halt (detenerse): *¡tente!*, stop! || To catch o.s. (al caerse). || To stay, to keep (mantenerse): *tente quieto*, keep still. || To stand up: *el niño se tiene solo*, the child stands up alone. || — FIG. y FAM. *Estar uno que no se tiene*, to be so tired that one cannot stand up (de cansado), to be so drunk that one cannot walk straight (de borracho). || *Tenerse de* or *en pie*, to stand up. || *Tenerse en mucho*, to think highly of o.s. || *Tenerse en poco*, to underrate o.s., to underestimate o.s. || FIG. *Tenerse firme*, to stand firm, to stand one's ground. || FIG. y FAM. *Tenérselas tiesas*, V. TIESO. || *Tenerse por*, to consider o.s.

— OBSERV. Como existen muchas expresiones con el verbo *tener* se han tratado generalmente en el artículo correspondiente al sustantivo de la frase considerada.
— The auxiliary verb «to have» is usually translated by *haber*. If, however, one wishes to stress the result obtained, the verb *tener* may replace *haber* as the auxiliary. In this case the past participle agrees in number and gender with the object of the verb: *tengo ahorradas unas veinte mil pesetas*, I have [got] some twenty thousand pesetas saved up (*he ahorrado veinte mil pesetas*, I have saved twenty thousand pesetas). This usage of *tener* as an auxiliary verb does not necessarily affect the English translation: *no tengo acabado el trabajo*, I haven't finished the work.
— V. HAVE. (*Observ.*).

tenería f. Tannery (curtiduría).
tenguerengue (en) loc. adv. Unstable: *estar en tenguerengue*, to be unstable.
tenia f. Tapeworm, taenia (gusano). || ARQ. Taenia (moldura).
tenida f. Meeting (reunión).
tenienta f. Lieutenant's wife (mujer del teniente).
tenientazgo m. Lieutenancy.
teniente adj. Holding, owning, possessing, having (que tiene). || Unripe (fruta). || FIG. y FAM. Hard of hearing. | Stingy, tightfisted, tight (tacaño).
— M. Lieutenant. || — *Segundo teniente*, second lieutenant. || *Teniente coronel*, lieutenant colonel. || *Teniente de alcalde*, deputy mayor. || *Teniente general*, lieutenant general.
tenífugo, ga adj./s.m. Taeniafuge, teniafuge.
tenis m. Tennis (juego). || Tennis court (campo de tenis). || *Tenis de mesa*, ping-pong, table tennis.
tenista m. y f. Tennis player.
tenor m. Tenor: *a juzgar por el tenor de su discurso*, judging by the tenor of his speech. || MÚS. Tenor. || — FIG. *A este tenor*, at this rate, if this continues. || *A tenor*, likewise, in the same fashion: *comimos mucho y bebimos a tenor*, we ate a lot and drank likewise. || *A tenor de*, in accordance with.
tenorio m. Don Juan, lady-killer.
tenrec m. ZOOL. Tenrec, tanrec.
tensar v. tr. To tauten (un cable). || To draw (un arco). || *Tensado*, taut, tense, tautened (cable), drawn (arco).
tensión f. Tension. || Tautness, tightness (de una cuerda). || TECN. Stress. || ELECTR. Tension, voltage: *alta tensión*, high tension *o* voltage. || FIG. Tension, strained relations, *pl.*: *tensión entre dos países*, strained relations between two countries. | Tenseness (de la situación). | Tension, stress, strain: *mi madre está bajo una tensión enorme*, my mother is under enormous strain. || — *Cable de alta tensión*, high-tension cable. || *Tener la tensión alta*, to suffer from high blood pressure. || *Tensión arterial*, blood pressure. || *Tensión nerviosa*, nervous tension *o* stress. || *Tensión superficial*, surface tension.
tenso, sa adj. Tense, tight, taut (tirante). || FIG. Tense, strained: *relaciones tensas entre las dos familias*, tense relations between the two families.
tensor, ra adj. Tightening, tensile (que tensa).
— M. ANAT. Tensor. || Tightener (dispositivo que sirve para tensar). || TECN. Turnbuckle (aparato). | Tension (de máquina de coser). | Stiffener (de camisa). || MAT. Tensor.
tentación f. Temptation: *ceder a la tentación*, to yield to temptation; *no nos dejes caer en la tentación*, lead us not into temptation.
tentaculado, da adj. Tentacled.
tentacular adj. Tentacular.
tentáculo m. ZOOL. Tentacle.
tentadero m. Pen where the bravery of young bulls is tested.
tentador, ra adj. Tempting, enticing: *proposición tentadora*, tempting proposal.
— M. Tempter. || *El Tentador*, the Devil. || — F. Temptress.
tentadura f. Mercury test of silver ore.
tentalear v. tr. To feel.
tentar* v. tr. To touch, to feel (examinar por medio del tacto). || To tempt, to entice: *la serpiente tentó a Eva*, the serpent tempted Eve. || To tempt, to attract (atraer). || To attempt, to try (intentar). || To try, to test (someter a prueba). || MED. To probe. || — FIG. *Tentar a Dios*, to tempt Providence (intentar algo muy peligroso). | *Tentar al diablo*, to tempt the devil, to look for trouble.
— V. pr. To feel o.s. || FIG. *Tentarse la ropa*, V. ROPA.
tentativa f. Attempt, try: *tentativa infructuosa*, unsuccessful attempt. || (Ant.) Entrance examination (en la universidad). || JUR. *Tentativa de asesinato*, attempted murder.
tentemozo m. Prop (puntal). || Pole prop (del carro). || Tumbler, roly-poly (juguete). || Cheek strap (quijera del caballo).
tentempié m. Bite to eat, snack (refrigerio). || Tumbler, roly-poly (dominguillo).
tentenelaire m. y f. Child of a quadroon and a mulatto.
— M. *Amer.* Hummingbird (colibrí).
tentetieso m. Tumbler, roly-poly (juguete).
tenue adj. Thin, tenuous, delicate: *los hilos tenues del gusano de seda*, the tenuous threads of the silkworm. || Thin, light (niebla). || Weak, subdued, faint (voz, luz). || Flimsy (tela). || Simple, natural (estilo). || Insignificant (de poca importancia).
tenuidad f. Tenuity, delicacy, thinness (poco grosor). || Thinness (de la niebla). || Weakness, faintness (de luz, voz). || Flimsiness (de la tela). || Simplicity (estilo). || Trifle (cosa de poca entidad).
tenuirrostro m. ZOOL. Tenuiroster. || — Pl. ZOOL. Tenuirostres.
teñible adj. Dyeable.
teñido, da adj. Dyed: *un abrigo teñido de azul*, a coat dyed blue. || Tinted, dyed (pelo). || FIG. Tinged.
— M. Dyeing (acción). || Dye (color).
teñir* v. tr. To dye: *teñir un abrigo de verde*, to dye a coat green. || To stain (manchar). || To tone down (un color). || FIG. To tinge.
— V. pr. To dye one's hair: *se ha teñido de rubio*, she has dyed her hair blond.
teocali m. Teocalli (templo mejicano).
teocracia f. Theocracy.
teocrático, ca adj. Theocratic.
Teócrito n. pr. m. Theocritus.
teodicea f. Theodicy.
teodolito m. Theodolite.
Teodorico n. pr. m. Theodoric.
teodosiano, na adj. Theodosian: *el código teodosiano*, the Theodosian Code.
Teodosio n. pr. m. Theodosius.
teogonía f. Theogony.
teologal adj. Theological, theologic. || *Virtudes teologales*, theological virtues.
teología f. Theology: *la teología católica*, Catholic theology. || FIG. y FAM. *No meterse en teologías*, not to get into deep water.
teológico, ca adj. Theological, theologic.
teologizar v. intr. To theologize.
teólogo, ga adj. Theological (teologal).
— M. y f. Theologian.
teorema m. Theorem: *teorema de Pitágoras*, Pythagoras theorem.
teoría f. Theory. || — *En teoría*, theoretically, in theory. || *Teoría de los quanta*, quantum theory.
teóricamente adv. Theoretically.
teórico, ca adj. Theoretical.
— M. y f. Theoretician. || — F. Theoretics, theory.
teorizar v. intr. To theorize.
— V. tr. To theorize on.
teosofía f. Theosophy.
teosófico, ca adj. Theosophical, theosophic.
teósofo m. Theosophist.
tepache m. *Amer.* Mexican drink made from pulque, water, pineapple and cloves.
tepe m. Sod.
tepeizcuinte m. *Amer.* ZOOL. Spotted cavy, paca (roedor).
tepetate m. *Amer.* Rock used in construction.
teponascle m. *Amer.* Teponaxtle, Mexican slit-drum.
tequila m. Tequila (bebida).
tequio m. *Amer.* Nuisance.
terapeuta m. y f. MED. Therapist.

terapéutica f. Therapeutics, therapy.
terapéutico, ca adj. Therapeutic, therapeutical.
terapia f. MED. Therapy.
teratología f. Teratology.
terbio m. QUÍM. Terbium (metal).
tercamente adv. Obstinately, stubbornly.
tercelete adj. ARQ. *Arco tercelete*, tierceron.
tercena f. Government tobacco warehouse. || *Amer.* Butcher's shop (carnicería).
tercer adj. (apócope de *tercero*). Third: *vivo en el tercer piso*, I live on the third floor. || *Tercer Mundo*, Third World.
— OBSERV. *Tercero* is always apocopated before a masculine singular noun even if another adjective comes between it and the noun. It is occasionally apocopated before a feminine noun: *la tercer noche.*
tercera f. Tierce, sequence of three cards (juegos de naipes). || Procuress (alcahueta). || MÚS. Third. || AUT. Third (velocidad). || Third class (en el tren). || Tierce (en esgrima).
terceramente adv. Thirdly, in the third place.
tercería f. Mediation, arbitration (de un tercero). || Procuring (de los alcahuetes). || JUR. Right of third party.
tercerilla f. Triplet (poesía).
tercero, ra adj. Third: *la tercera calle a la derecha*, the third street on the right. || — *Carlos III* (*tercero*), Charles III [the third]. || REL. *Orden tercera*, third order. || *Por tercera persona*, by a third party. || *Seguro contra tercera persona*, third party insurance. || *Ser tercero*, to be the odd man out (en una reunión). || *Tercera parte*, third (división): *cinco es la tercera parte de quince*, five is a third of fifteen.
— M. y f. Third, third one. || — M. Third party, third person: *causar daño a un tercero*, to harm a third party. || REL. Tertiary. || Third floor: *vivo en el tercero*, I live on the third floor. || Third year (tercer curso). || Pimp, procurer (alcahuete). || Go-between (intermediario). || Mediator, arbitrator (que zanja una cuestión). || *Ser el tercero en discordia*, to be the arbitrator *o* the mediator.
— OBSERV. V. TERCER.
tercerol m. MAR. Third [any object situated in third position].
tercerola f. Musketoon (arma). || Small flute (flauta). || Medium-sized barrel (barril). || FAM. Third class (en los trenes).
terceto m. Tercet (estrofa). || MÚS. Trio.
tercia f. Third (tercio). || Third of a "vara" (medida). || REL. Tierce. || Tierce (en los juegos de naipes). || AGR. Third digging.
terciado, da adj. Crosswise (atravesado). || Medium-sized (toro). || *Azúcar terciado*, brown sugar.
— M. Broadsword (espada). || Wide ribbon (cinta).
terciador, ra adj. Mediating, arbitrating.
— M. y f. Mediator, arbitrator.
terciana f. o **tercianas** f. pl. MED. Tertian fever, tertian.
terciar v. tr. To divide into three parts (dividir). || To place diagonally *o* crosswise (poner en diagonal). || To wear across one's chest (una prenda de ropa). || AGR. To plough for the third time. | To cut [a plant] near the roots. || To balance [the weight] (sobre la acémila). || *Amer.* To water down (aguar).
— V. intr. To arbitrate, to mediate (mediar). || To make up the number (completar el número). || To participate, to take part (participar). || To reach the third day (la luna).
— V. pr. To occur, to arise, to present itself (una posibilidad). || *Si se tercia*, should the occasion arise.
terciario, ria adj. Third (tercero en orden). || — Adj./s. m. GEOL. Tertiary. || — M. y f. REL. Tertiary.
tercio, cia adj. Third (tercero).
— M. Third (tercera parte). || Each of the three parts of a rosary. || MIL. Infantry regiment [in the 16th and 17th centuries]. | Legion: *tercio extranjero*, foreign legion. || Division (de la guardia civil). || TAUR. Stage, phase, part [of the bullfight]: *tercio de varas*, opening stage, picador stage; *tercio de banderillas*, banderilla stage. | Each of the three concentric zones of the bullring. || Each of the three stages of the horse race (en equitación). || Pack (de una acémila). || MAR. Harbour guild. || — TAUR. *El tercio de muerte*, the kill. || JUR. *Tercio de libre disposición*, disposable portion [of estate].
terciopelado, da adj. Velvety.
terciopelo m. Velvet: *cortinas de terciopelo*, velvet curtains.
terco, ca adj. Stubborn, obstinate (obstinado).
terebenteno m. QUÍM. Terebenthene.
terebintáceas f. pl. BOT. Terebinthaceae.
terebinto m. BOT. Terebinth, turpentine tree.
Terencio n. pr. m. Terence.
Teresa n. pr. f. Theresa.
teresiano, na adj. Of Saint Theresa of Ávila.
— F. MIL. Cap. || REL. Teresian.
tergal m. (nombre registrado). French polyester fabric (tejido).
tergiversable adj. Which can be misrepresented *o* twisted *o* distorted.
tergiversación f. Distortion, twisting, misrepresentation.
tergiversador, ra adj. Distorting.
— M. v f. Person who distorts *o* misrepresents the facts.
tergiversar v. tr. To distort, to twist, to misrepresent (palabras, sentido).
terliz m. Ticking (tela).
termal adj. Thermal.
termas f. pl. Thermae, hot baths, hot springs.
termes m. ZOOL. Termite.
termia f. FÍS. Therm.
térmico, ca adj. Thermal, thermic, heat: *energía térmica*, thermal power.
terminación f. Termination, ending (acción de acabarse). || Completion: *la terminación de la obra duró dos meses*, the completion of the work took two months. || Finish (acabado). || End, final part (parte final). || GRAM. Ending.
terminacho m. FAM. Vulgar expression, rude word (palabra indecente o poco culta). | Barbarism (término bárbaro).
terminal adj. Terminal, final, ultimate. || BOT. Terminal. || *Estación terminal*, terminus (de transportes).
— M. ELECTR. Terminal. || — F. *Terminal* or *terminal aérea*, air terminal.
terminante adj. Categorical: *una negativa terminante*, a categorical refusal. || Peremptory: *una orden terminante*, a peremptory command. || Conclusive, definite: *resultados terminantes*, conclusive results. || Strict (prohibición).
terminantemente adv. Categorically. || Peremptorily. || Conclusively, definitely. || Strictly: *queda terminantemente prohibido*, it is strictly forbidden.
terminar v. tr. To finish, to complete: *terminar la carrera*, to finish one's studies. || To end (poner fin a). || To conclude (concluir). || *Dar algo por terminado*, to finish sth. (acabar), to consider sth. finished (considerar acabado).
— V. intr. To finish, to end: *el espectáculo termina a las once*, the show finishes at eleven. || To end, to finish, to close: *la reunión terminó a medianoche*, the meeting ended at midnight. || To draw to a close, to end, to finish (llegar a su fin): *la conferencia se está terminando*, the conference is drawing to a close. || To conclude (concluir). || To finish: *no he terminado de comer*, I haven't finished eating. || To have just (acabar de): *termino de llegar*, I have just arrived. || To end up: *terminó yéndose a América* or *terminó por irse a América*, he ended up going to America; *terminé rendido*, I ended up exhausted. || FIG. To break up (reñir): *mi hermana y su novio han terminado*, my sister and her boyfriend have broken up. || MED. To come to the final stage (una enfermedad). || — *Éramos muy amigos pero terminamos mal*, we were good friends but we ended up on bad terms. || *Este chico terminará mal*, this boy will come to a sticky end *o* will come to no good. || *No termino de comprender*, I still cannot understand. || *Terminar loco*, to go mad. || *¡Termina ya!*, get it finished.
— V. pr. To end (llegar a su fin). || To run out (agotarse): *se ha terminado el vino*, the wine has run out. || *Se terminó la reunión*, the meeting is over.
término m. End, finish, conclusion: *llegamos al término del viaje*, we reached the end of the trip; *poner término a*, to put an end to. || Term, word (palabra): *término técnico*, technical term. || GRAM. MAT. y FIL. Term. || Terminus (de una línea de transporte). || Boundary (frontera). || Boundary marker (mojón). || Period, term (plazo): *dentro de un término de ocho días*, within a period of eight days. || District, area: *término municipal*, municipal district. || Place (lugar señalado). || Object, aim, goal (objetivo). || Condition, state (estado de una persona o cosa). || Place (en una enumeración): *en primer término*, in the first place. || ARQ. Term. || — Pl. Conditions, terms: *los términos del tratado*, the terms of the treaty. | Terms (relaciones): *está en malos términos con sus padres*, he is on bad terms with his parents. || — *Dar término a*, to finish off. || *En términos de*, in terms of. || *En términos generales*, in general, generally speaking. || *En términos propios*, clearly. || *En último término*, as a last resort. || FIG. *Invertir los términos*, to get it the wrong way round. || *Llevar a buen término*, to see through *o* to carry out successfully. || *Llevar a término*, to see [sth.] through, to carry out. || *Mantenerse en el término medio*, to be moderate. || *Medios términos*, evasions. || ARTES. *Primer término*, foreground. | *Segundo término*, middle distance. || *Término medio*, average: *por término medio*, on the average; in-between: *no hay término medio*, there is no in-between; compromise (compromiso). || *Términos del intercambio*, terms of trade, terms of exchange.
terminología f. Terminology.
terminológico, ca adj. Terminological.
términus m. Terminus (estación terminal).
termita o **termite** m. ZOOL. Termite (comején).
termitero m. Termite nest.
termo m. Thermos flask *o* bottle, thermos. || Boiler, water heater (termosifón).
termocauterio m. MED. Thermocautery.
termodinámico, ca adj. Thermodynamic.
— F. Thermodynamics.
termoelectricidad f. Thermoelectricity.

termoeléctrico, ca adj. Thermoelectric. || *Par termoeléctrico*, thermocouple, thermoelectric couple.
termoelemento m. Thermoelement.
termoendurecible o **termoestable** adj. Thermosetting.
termógeno, na adj. Thermogenous, thermogenic.
termógrafo m. Thermograph.
termoiónico, ca adj. Thermionic.
termología f. Thermology.
termometría f. Thermometry.
termométrico, ca adj. Thermometric, thermometrical.
termómetro m. Thermometer: *termómetro clínico*, clinical thermometer; *termómetro de máxima y mínima*, maximum and minimum thermometer.
termonuclear adj. Thermonuclear.
termopar m. FÍS. Thermocouple.
termopila f. ELECTR. Thermopile.
Termópilas n. pr. f. pl. Thermopylae.
termoplástico, ca adj. Thermoplastic.
termoquímica f. Thermochemistry.
termoquímico, ca adj. Thermochemical.
termorregulación f. Thermoregulation.
termorregulador m. Thermoregulator, thermostat.
termos m. Thermos flask, thermos bottle, thermos.
termosifón m. Boiler, water heater (calentador de agua). || FÍS. Thermosiphon.
termostato m. Thermostat.
termoterapia f. MED. Thermotherapy.
terna f. List of three candidates for a post. || Pair of threes (en los dados). || Set of dice (juego de dados).
ternario, ria adj. Ternary. || MÚS. *Compás ternario*, ternary form.
— M. Three days' devotion.
terne adj. m. FAM. Bullying.
ternera f. Calf (animal). || Veal (carne): *chuleta de ternera*, veal chop.
ternero m. Calf: *ternero recental*, sucking calf.
ternerón, na adj. FAM. Softhearted, easily moved, sentimental.
— M. y f. FAM. Softy, softhearted person.
terneza f. Tenderness. || — Pl. FAM. Sweet nothings.
ternilla f. Gristle, cartilage.
ternilloso, sa adj. Gristly, cartilaginous.
ternísimo, ma adj. Very tender.
terno m. Set of three (tres cosas). || Three-piece suit (traje). || FAM. Curse, swearword (voto). || IMPR. Three sheets folded together. || Tern (en la lotería). || *Amer.* Set of jewellery [consisting of earrings, necklace, and brooch] (joyas). || *Echar ternos*, to curse, to swear.
ternura f. Tenderness. || Sweet nothing (palabra cariñosa).
tero m. *Amer.* ZOOL. South American lapwing.
terpeno m. QUÍM. Terpene.
Terpsícore n. pr. f. MIT. Terpsichore.
terquedad f. Stubbornness, obstinacy.
terracota f. Terra-cotta.
terrado m. Flat roof, roof terrace (azotea).
terraja f. Diestock (para tornillos). || Modelling board (para molduras).
terraje m. Rent [paid on arable land].
terrajero m. Tenant farmer.
terral adj. m. Land: *viento terral*, land wind.
— M. Land wind.
terramicina f. MED. Terramycin.
terranova m. Newfoundland dog (perro).
Terranova n. pr. GEOGR. Newfoundland.
terraplén m. Embankment (de la carretera y de la vía de ferrocarril). || MIL. Terreplein, earthwork, embankment. || Slope (pendiente).
terraplenar v. tr. To level off (nivelar). || To embank, to bank up (hacer terraplén).
terráqueo, a adj. Terraqueous. || *Globo terráqueo*, globe, earth.
terrateniente m. y f. Landowner, landholder.
terraza f. Terrace, roof terrace (azotea). || Terrace, balcony (balcón). || Terrace: *sentarse en la terraza de un café*, to sit down on a café terrace. || AGR. Terrace (bancal). || AGR. *Cultivo en terrazas*, terracing.
terrazgo m. Arable land, field (tierra). || Land rent (arrendamiento).
terrazguero m. Tenant farmer.
terrazo m. Ground (en pintura). || Terrazzo (revestimiento para el suelo).
terremoto m. Earthquake.
terrenal adj. Worldly: *bienes terrenales*, worldly goods. || *Paraíso terrenal*, earthly paradise.
terreno, na adj. Earthly, worldly: *vida terrena*, earthly life.
— M. Ground, land, terrain: *terreno desigual*, rough land. || Piece of land: *comprar un terreno en el campo*, to buy a piece of land in the country. || Plot, site (solar): *se venden terrenos para la construcción*, building plots for sale. || FIG. Field, sphere (esfera): *en el terreno de la medicina*, in the field of medicine. || GEOL. Terrain, terrane. || Soil, ground, earth (suelo): *terreno pedregoso*, stony ground. || DEP. Field, ground: *terreno de fútbol*, football ground. || — FIG. *Ceder terreno*, to give way. || *Coche todo terreno*, jeep. || FIG. *El país es terreno abonado para tal ideología*, the country is ready for such an ideology. | *Ganar, perder terreno*, to gain, to lose ground. | *Meterse en el terreno de otro*, to interfere. | *Minarle a uno el terreno*, V. MINAR. | *Preparar el terreno*, to pave the way. || MIL. *Reconocer el terreno*, to reconnoitre. || FIG. *Saber alguien el terreno que pisa*, to know what's what. | *Sobre el terreno*, on the spot. | *Tantear el terreno*, to see how the land lies. | *Terreno abonado*, breeding ground, hotbed. | *Terreno conocido*, familiar ground (tema). || *Terreno de camping*, camping site, camping ground. || *Terreno de honor*, duelling ground. || FIG. *Terreno vedado*, taboo.
térreo, a adj. Earthy. || *De color térreo*, earth-coloured.
terrero, ra adj. Earth (de tierra). || Low, skimming (vuelo de algunas aves). || FIG. Humble (humilde). || *Amer.* One-storey (casa).
— M. Pile of earth, mound (montón de tierra). || Terrace (terraza). || Public square (plaza pública). || Target, mark (blanco de tiro). || Alluvium (tierra de aluvión). || MIN. Spoil heap.
terrestre adj. Terrestrial, earthly.
terrible adj. Terrible, awful, dreadful (atroz). || *Hace un calor terrible*, it's terribly hot.
terrícola m. y f. Earth dweller (habitante de la Tierra). || Earthling (en ciencia ficción).
— Adj. Terricolous.
terrier m. Terrier (perro).
terrífico, ca adj. Terrifying, dreadful, awful, frightful.
terrígeno, na adj. Terrigenous.
territorial adj. Territorial: *límites territoriales*, territorial limits; *aguas territoriales*, territorial waters. || — *Código territorial*, area code, code number (teléfonos). || *Impuesto territorial*, land tax.
territorialidad f. Territoriality.
territorio m. Territory. || *Amer.* Region, district.
terrizo, za adj. Earthenware (hecho de tierra).
— M. y f. Bowl (barreño.)
terrón m. Clod (de tierra). || Lump (de sal, azúcar, harina). || Marc (residuo de aceitunas). || — Pl. Farmland, *sing.*
terror m. Terror. || HIST. Terror.
terrorífico, ca adj. Terrifying, dreadful, awful, frightful.
terrorismo m. Terrorism.
terrorista m. y f. Terrorist.
terrosidad f. Earthiness.
terroso, sa adj. Earthy. || Brown, earth-coloured.
terruño m. Country, native land, native soil (país, patria). || Clod (terrón). || Piece of land (parcela de tierra). || Land (tierra que se trabaja).
terso, sa adj. Clear, clean (claro). || Smooth (liso): *piel tersa*, smooth skin. || Polished, glossy, shiny (brillante). || FIG. Smooth, flowing, easy (estilo).
tersura o **tersidad** f. Smoothness: *la tersura de la piel*, the smoothness of one's skin. || Shininess, glossiness (brillo). || FIG. Smoothness, easiness, polish (del estilo).
tertulia f. Gathering of friends, get-together (reunión). || Circle, group (peña). || Back room (de un café). || Upper gallery (del antiguo teatro). || — *Tener tertulia*, to have a get-together, to meet. || *Tertulia literaria*, literary circle, coterie (grupo), literary gathering (reunión).
Tertuliano n. pr. m. Tertullian.
tertuliano, na o **tertuliante** m. y f. Participant in a social or literary gathering. || *Uno de los tertulianos*, one of the people present.
tertuliar v. intr. *Amer.* To have a get-together, to meet.
tertulio, lia m. y f. V. TERTULIANO.
terutero o **teruteru** m. *Amer.* ZOOL. South American lapwing.
terylene m. Terylene.
Tesalia n. pr. f. GEOGR. Thessaly.
tesaliense o **tesalio, lia** adj./s. Thessalian.
Tesalónica n. pr. f. GEOGR. Thessalonica.
tesar v. tr. MAR. To tauten, to tighten.
— V. intr. To back, to back up, to pull back (bueyes).
tesina f. Project.
tesis f. Thesis (de Universidad). || Theory, idea (opinión): *él y yo sostenemos la misma tesis*, he and I hold the same theory. || Theory (opinión). || FIL. Thesis. || — *Novela de tesis*, novel with a message. || *Tesis doctoral*, doctoral thesis.
tesitura f. MÚS. Tessitura. || Frame of mind, mood (estado de ánimo). || Situation, circumstances, *pl.* (circunstancia): *en esta tesitura*, in this situation.
tesón m. Firmness, inflexibility (firmeza). || Tenacity, perseverance (perseverancia). || *Sostener con tesón una opinión*, to firmly maintain an opinion.
tesonería f. Perseverance, tenacity (perseverancia). || Obstinacy, stubbornness (obstinación).
tesonero, ra adj. Persevering, tenacious (perseverante).
tesorería f. Treasury, treasurer's office (oficina). || Treasurership (cargo).
tesorero, ra m. y f. Treasurer. || REL. Custodian [of a church's valuables].
tesoro m. Treasure: *tesoro escondido*, buried treasure. || Treasury, exchequer (del Estado). || REL. Valuables, *pl.*, collection of relics and ornaments (de una iglesia). || Thesaurus (libro). || FIG. Treasure, gem, jewel: *la muchacha es un verdadero tesoro*, the maid is really a treasure. || FIG. y FAM. Dear, treasure, precious: *mi tesoro*, my treasure. || — *Bono del Tesoro*, Treasury bond. || *Tesoro público*, Treasury.
Tespis n. pr. m. Thespis.
test m. Test.

testa f. Front (frente). || Head (cabeza). || BOT. Testa. || *Testa coronada*, crowned head.
testáceo, a adj. ZOOL. Testacean, testaceous.
testado, da adj. Testate.
testador m. Testator, testate.
testadora f. Testatrix, testate.
testaferro m. Front man, man of straw.
testamentaría f. Testamentary execution (gestiones). || Estate, inheritance (herencia). || Meeting of executors (junta).
testamentario, ria adj. Testamentary.
— M. Executor. || — F. Executrix.
testamento m. Will, testament: *hacer* or *otorgar testamento*, to make one's will. || — REL. *Antiguo* or *Viejo Testamento*, Old Testament. | *Arca del Testamento*, Ark of the Covenant. | *Nuevo Testamento*, New Testament. || JUR. *Testamento abierto*, nuncupative will. | *Testamento auténtico*, legal will. | *Testamento cerrado*, sealed will. | *Testamento ológrafo*, holograph will. | *Testamento público*, public will.
testar v. intr. To make one's will *o* one's testament.
— V. tr. To erase (tachar).
testarada f. Knock on the head. || FAM. Obstinacy, stubbornness (terquedad).
testarazo m. Knock on the head (golpe en la cabeza). || Butt (golpe dado con la cabeza). || Header, head (en fútbol).
testarudez f. Obstinacy, stubbornness.
testarudo, da adj. Stubborn, obstinate.
— M. y f. Stubborn *o* obstinate person.
teste m. ANAT. Testis.
testera f. Front, front part (parte delantera). || Forehead (de un animal). || Frontstall (de la armadura de un caballo). || Forward-facing seat (en un carruaje). || Wall (de horno de fundición).
testerada f. o **testerazo** m. V. TESTARADA y TESTARAZO.
testero m. Front, front part (testera). || Wall (pared). || MIN. Stope.
testicular adj. ANAT. Testicular.
testículo m. ANAT. Testicle.
testificación f. Testification. || Testimony (testimonio).
testifical adj. JUR. Witness.
testificante adj. Testifying.
testificar v. tr. e intr. To testify.
testigo m. y f. JUR. Witness: *esta mujer es la primera testigo*, this woman is the first witness. || — M. Evidence, witness, proof (prueba): *las catedrales antiguas son testigos de la fe de nuestros antepasados*, our old cathedrals are evidence of *o* bear witness to the faith of our ancestors. || DEP. Stick, baton (en carrera de relevos). || TECN. Core (de sondeo). || — *Lámpara testigo*, pilot light, warning light. | *Poner* or *tomar por testigo a uno*, to call *o* to take s.o. to witness. || *Pongo por testigo al cielo*, I swear to God, as God is my witness. || JUR. *Testigo de cargo*, witness for the prosecution. | *Testigo de descargo*, witness for the defence. | *Testigo de vista* or *testigo ocular*, eyewitness. || REL. *Testigos de Jehová*, Jehovah's Witnesses.
testimonial adj. JUR. Testimonial.
— F. pl. JUR. Documentary evidence, *sing*. || REL. Testimonial, *sing*.
testimoniar v. tr. To be evidence *o* proof of, to testify to, to bear witness to: *estas ruinas testimonian la existencia de una civilización*, these ruins testify to the existence of a civilization.
testimonio m. JUR. Testimony, evidence. | Attestation, affidavit (hecho por escribano). || Mark, token: *testimonio de amistad*, token of friendship. || — *Falso testimonio*, perjury, false evidence. || *Levantar falsos testimonios*, to bear false witness, to commit perjury; to slander (calumniar). || FIG. *Según el testimonio de*, according to. || *Testimonio de pésame*, condolences, *pl.*
testosterona f. BIOL. Testosterone.
testuz m. Forehead (frente). || Nape (nuca del toro, de la vaca).
tesura f. Rigidity, stiffness (rigidez).
teta f. Teat, nipple (pezón). || Breast, tit (fam.), boob (fam.) [pecho]. || Udder, teat (de animales). || FIG. Hillock, knoll (montículo). || — *Dar la teta a*, to suckle, to breast-feed, to nurse. || *Niño de teta*, babe-in-arms. || *Quitar la teta a*, to wean. || FIG. *Teta de vaca*, meringue (merengue), viper's grass (escorzonera).
tetania f. MED. Tetany.
tetánico, ca adj. MED. Tetanic.
tetanizar v. tr. To tetanize.
tétano o **tétanos** m. MED. Tetanus.
tetera f. Teapot. || *Amer.* Nipple (del biberón).
tetero m. *Amer.* Baby's bottle, feeding bottle (biberón).
tetilla f. Nipple (de los mamíferos machos). || Nipple (del biberón).
Tetis n. pr. f. MIT. Thetis.
tetón m. Stub (de una rama).
tetona adj. FAM. Busty, buxom, large-breasted.
— F. POP. Busty *o* buxom wench.
tetraédrico, ca adj. MAT. Tetrahedral.
tetraedro m. MAT. Tetrahedron.
tetragonal adj. MAT. Tetragonal.
tetralogía f. Tetralogy.
tetrámero, ra adj. Tetrameral, tetramerous.
tetramotor adj. Four-engined.
— M. Four-engined aircraft.
tetrápodo, da adj./s.m. ZOOL. Tetrapod.
tetrarca m. Tetrarch.
tetrarquía f. Tetrarchy, tetrarchate.
tetrasílabo, ba adj. Tetrasyllabic.
— M. Tetrasyllable.
tetrástrofo adj. Having four lines, four-line.
— M. Quatrain.
tetravalente adj. Tetravalent.
tétrico, ca adj. Gloomy, sullen (sombrío).
tetrodo m. ELECTR. Tetrode.
Tetuán n. pr. GEOGR. Tetuan.
tetuda adj./s. FAM. V. TETONA.
teucali m. Teocalli (templo mexicano).
teúrgia f. Theurgy.
teúrgico, ca adj. Theurgic, theurgical.
teutón, ona adj. Teutonic.
— M. y f. Teuton.
teutónico, ca adj. Teutonic.
— M. Teutonic (idioma).
textil adj./s.m. Textile: *industria textil*, textile industry.
texto m. Text. || *Libro de texto*, textbook.
textual adj. Textual.
textualmente adv. Textually. || *Lo que dijo textualmente fue lo siguiente*, his exact words were, this is exactly what he said.
textura f. Texture (trama de un tejido). || Weaving (acción de tejer). || Structure (de un mineral).
teyú m. *Amer.* ZOOL. Iguana.
tez f. Complexion (cutis).
tezontle m. *Amer.* Volcanic rock [used for building].
thai adj./s. Thai, Tai.
theta f. Theta (letra griega).
ti pron. pers. You: *a ti*, to you; *para* or *por ti*, for you. | Yourself: *¿lo has hecho para ti?*, did you make it for yourself? || REL. Thee, Thyself (dirigiéndose a Dios). || — FAM. *De ti para mí*, between you and me. | *Hoy por ti, mañana por mí*, you can do the same for me sometime. || *Para ti mismo*, for yourself.
tía f. Aunt. || FAM. Old: *la tía María*, old Mary. | Bird [U.S., gal, dame] (mujer cualquiera). | Tart, whore (prostituta). || — FAM. *A tu tía* or *cuéntaselo a tu tía*, tell it to the marines. | *No hay tu tía*, there's nothing doing. || *Tía abuela*, great-aunt, grandaunt. || *Tía carnal*, aunt. || *Tía segunda*, first cousin once removed.
tialina f. BIOL. Ptyalin.
tiamina f. Thiamine, thiamin.
tiangue o **tiánguez** o **tianguis** m. *Amer.* Market.
tiara f. Tiara.
Tíber n. pr. m. GEOGR. Tiber.
Tiberíades n. pr. GEOGR. Tiberias.
tiberio m. FAM. Row, uproar, shindy: *armar un tiberio*, to kick up a shindy *o* a row, to make an uproar.
Tiberio n. pr. m. Tiberius.
Tibet (El) n. pr. m. GEOGR. Tibet.
tibetano, na adj./s. Tibetan.
tibia f. ANAT. Tibia, shinbone.
tibial adj. Tibial (de la tibia).
tibiamente adv. FIG. Unenthusiastically, tepidly.
tibieza f. Lukewarmness, tepidity. || FIG. Lack of enthusiasm, coolness, tepidity.
tibio, bia adj. Lukewarm, tepid: *agua tibia*, lukewarm water. || FIG. Lukewarm, unenthusiastic, cool, tepid (poco fervoroso): *recibimiento tibio*, lukewarm reception. || FIG. y FAM. *Ponerle tibio a alguien*, to call s.o. all the names under the sun.
Tibulo n. pr. m. Tibullus.
tiburón m. ZOOL. Shark. || FIG. Shark. || *Amer.* Egotist, self-seeker (egoísta).
tic m. Tic, twitch: *tiene un tic nervioso*, he has a nervous tic. || FIG. Habit, mannerism (manía).
Ticiano n. pr. m. Titian.
ticket m. Ticket.
tico, ca adj./s. *Amer.* Costa Rican (costarriqueño).
tictac m. Ticktock, tick, ticking (de reloj). || Tapping (de máquina de escribir).
tiemblo m. BOT. Aspen (álamo temblón).
tiempo m. Time: *no tengo tiempo para hacerlo*, I have no time to do it; *tardó mucho tiempo en hacerlo*, it took him a long time to do it. || Time, times, *pl.*, age, epoch, days, *pl.*, era: *en tiempo de César*, in the time of Caesar. || Season, time (estación): *no es tiempo de naranjas*, it is not the orange season. || Weather: *hace buen tiempo*, the weather is fine; *¿qué tiempo hace?*, what's the weather like?; *tiempo cargado*, overcast weather. || FAM. Age (edad): *tu hijo y el mío son del mismo tiempo*, your son and mine are of the same age. || Moment, time (momento): *no era tiempo de llorar*, it was no time for crying; *se acerca el tiempo*, the moment is drawing near; *cuando sea tiempo*, when the time is right. || MAR. Stormy weather. || GRAM. Tense: *tiempo simple, compuesto*, simple, compound tense. || MÚS. Movement (parte). | Time (compás). || DEP. Half (periodo): *primer, segundo tiempo*, first, second half. || Stage (fase). || TECN. Stroke: *motor de cuatro tiempos*, four-stroke engine. || — *Aclararse* or *alzarse el tiempo*, to clear: *cuando se alza el tiempo*, when the weather clears. || FIG. *Acomodarse* or *adaptarse al tiempo*, to adapt o.s. to the circumstances. || *Ahora no es tiempo*, it's too late. || *Algún tiempo atrás*, some time ago. || *Al*

mismo tiempo, at the same time. || *Al poco tiempo*, a short time after, soon after. || *¡Al tiempo!* or *y, si no, al tiempo*, time will tell! || *Andando el tiempo*, in the course of time, as time goes by *o* passes. || *Andar con el tiempo*, to keep up with the times. || *Antes de tiempo*, early, before time (con anticipación), at the wrong time *o* moment (inoportunamente), prematurely (parto). || *A su debido tiempo*, in due course, in due time. || *A su tiempo*, at the right moment: *hazlo a su tiempo*, do it at the right moment; in due time, in due course: *todo vendrá a su tiempo*, everything will come in due time. || *A tiempo*, in time, just in time (en el momento oportuno): *has llegado a tiempo*, you have arrived just in time; on time: *nunca llega a su casa a tiempo*, he never gets home on time. || *A través de los tiempos*, through the ages. || *A un tiempo*, at the same time. || *Breve* or *corto tiempo*, short while. || *Cierto tiempo*, a while, a certain time. || *¡Cómo pasa* or *vuela el tiempo!*, how time flies! || *Con el tiempo*, in the course of time, in time, with time: *con el tiempo lo conseguiremos*, we shall succeed in time. || *Confiar* or *dejar algo al tiempo*, to let things take their course. || *Con tiempo*, in advance (por adelantado): *hay que sacar las entradas con tiempo*, you have to get the tickets in advance; unhurriedly (sin prisa), in plenty of time (con tiempo de sobra), in time (en el momento oportuno). || *¿Cuánto tiempo?*, how long? || *Darle a uno tiempo de* or *para*, to have enough time to: *no me da tiempo de ir allí*, I don't have enough time to go there; to give s.o. time to: *nunca me das tiempo para hacer las cosas como es debido*, you never give me time to do things properly. || *Dar tiempo al tiempo*, to give it time. || *De algún tiempo a esta parte* or *de un tiempo a esta parte*, for some time now. || FIG. *Del tiempo de Maricastaña* or *del rey que rabió*, as old as the hills. || *Demasiado tiempo*, too long. || *Desde hace (mucho) tiempo*, for a long time: *no le he visto desde hace tiempo*, I haven't seen him for a long time. || *De tiempo en tiempo*, from time to time. || *De tiempo inmemorial*, from time immemorial. || *El tiempo corre*, time flies, time passes quickly. || *El tiempo dirá*, time will tell. || FIG. *El tiempo es oro*, time is money. || *El tiempo se me hace largo*, time seems to drag by *o* to pass very slowly. || *En el tiempo en que*, when, in the days when. || FIG. *Engañar el tiempo*, to kill time. || *En la noche de los tiempos*, in the mists of time. || *En los buenos tiempos*, in the good old days. || *En los tiempos que corren* or *en estos tiempos*, nowadays. || *En mis tiempos*, in my time, in my day. || *En otros tiempos* or *en un tiempo*, in the past, in former times. || *En tiempos de*, at the time of, in the days of. || FIG. *En tiempos del rey que rabió* or *en tiempos de Maricastaña*, in the days of good Queen Bess, in days of yore. || *En tiempos remotos*, in the distant past. || *Estar a tiempo de*, to still have time to. || *Fuera de tiempo*, out of season (fuera de su estación), untimely, inopportune, at the wrong moment (inoportuno). || *Ganar tiempo*, to save time (para adelantar), to gain time: *introducir toda clase de dificultades para ganar tiempo*, to create all sorts of difficulties so as to gain time. || *Gastar el tiempo*, to waste time. || *Hace bastante tiempo que nos conocemos*, we have known each other for quite a while. || *Hace (mucho) tiempo*, a long time ago: *me lo pediste hace tiempo*, you asked me for it a long time ago. || *Hace (mucho) tiempo que no pasas por aquí*, you haven't been round for a long time, it has been a long time since you last came round. || *Hacer tiempo*, to kill time. || *Haga buen o mal tiempo*, come rain or shine. || FIG. *Le faltó tiempo para decirlo*, it didn't take him long to say it. || *Malgastar el tiempo*, to waste [one's] time. || *Más tiempo*, longer (frase afirmativa), any longer (frase negativa o interrogativa). || FAM. *Más vale llegar a tiempo que rondar un año*, it's best to be in the right place at the right time. || *Matar el tiempo*, to kill time. || *No hay tiempo que perder*, there is no time to lose. || *Pasar el tiempo*, to pass the time. || *Pasarse el tiempo leyendo*, to spend one's time reading. || *Perder el tiempo*, to waste time. || FIG. *Poner a mal tiempo buena cara*, V. CARA. || *Por aquel tiempo*, at that time. || *¡Qué tiempos los actuales!*, what times we live in! || *¿Qué tiempo tiene este niño?*, how old is this boy? || *Requerir* or *tomar tiempo*, to take time. || *Ser de su tiempo*, to be in step with the times: *él es de su tiempo*, he is in step with the times; to be one's age: *Juan era de mi tiempo*, John was my age. || *Sin perder tiempo*, at once. || *Tener tiempo para todo*, to find time for everything. || *Tiempo atrás*, some time ago: *tiempo atrás solíamos ir allí*, we used to go there some time ago. || FOT. *Tiempo de exposición*, exposure, exposure time. || *Tiempo de Pasión*, Passion Week. || FAM. *Tiempo de perros*, lousy *o* filthy weather. || *Tiempo ha*, a long time ago. || *Tiempo libre*, spare *o* free time. || ASTR. *Tiempo medio*, mean time. || *Tiempos actuales* or *modernos*, modern times. || ASTR. *Tiempo verdadero*, true time. || *Todo el tiempo*, all the time, always (siempre), all the time: *todo el tiempo que estuvimos allí*, all the time we were there. || *Tomarse tiempo* or *tomarlo con tiempo* to take one's time. || *Ya es tiempo de* or *para*, it is time to.

tienda f. Shop [U.S., store]: *tienda de antigüedades*, antique shop; *abrir tienda*, to set up shop, to open a shop. || Grocer's [U.S., grocery store] (de comestibles). || Tent (de campaña): *dormir en la tienda*, to sleep in the tent. || Awning, canvas cover (de un barco). || Cover (de carro). || *Amer.* Draper's (de telas). || — MIL. *Batir tiendas*, to strike camp. || *Ir de tiendas*, to go shopping, to go round the shops. || *Tienda de comestibles*, grocer's [U.S., grocery store]. || *Tienda de campaña*, tent: *armar una tienda de campaña*, to pitch a tent. || *Tienda de modas*, boutique. || MED. *Tienda de oxígeno*, oxygen tent. || *Tienda de ultramarinos*, grocer's, grocer's shop, grocery [U.S., grocery store].

tienta m. MED. Probe. || TAUR. Test of bravery of young bulls. || FIG. Artfulness, sagacity, cleverness. || — *Andar a tientas*, to grope along. || *A tientas*, feeling one's way, gropingly.

tientaguja f. Sounding rod.

tiento m. Touch (sentido del tacto). || Blind man's cane *o* stick (de los ciegos). || Ropewalker's pole (contrapeso). || FIG. Tact, prudence (miramiento). | Caution, care (prudencia). || ARTES. Maulstick. || Steady hand, sureness of hand (pulso). || FIG. y FAM. Blow, punch (golpe). | Swig (trago). | Bite (bocado). || MÚS. Preliminary notes, *pl.* [before playing]. || ZOOL. Tentacle, feeler. || *Amer.* Strip of leather (tira de cuero). || — FIG. *Andar con tiento*, to tread carefully, to watch one's step. || *A tiento*, gropingly, feeling one's way. || FAM. *Coger el tiento*, to get the knack. | *Dar un tiento a*, to test, to try (intentar), to take a swig from: *dar un tiento a la botella*, to take a swig from the bottle.

tientos m. pl. Flamenco dance and song.

tiernamente adv. Tenderly.

tierno, na adj. Tender: *carne tierna*, tender meat. || Soft (blando). || FIG. Young: *un tierno niño*, a young child. || Tender, affectionate, loving: *corazón tierno*, tender heart; *esposa tierna*, affectionate wife. || FIG. Sensitive, tender (sensible). | Soft, delicate: *un color tierno*, a soft colour. || *Amer.* Green, unripe (frutos). || — FIG. *Edad tierna*, tender age. || *Pan tierno*, fresh bread.

tierra f. Earth (planeta). || Land (superficie no cubierta por el mar): *ver tierra*, to see land. || Earth, soil: *un saco de tierra*, a bagful of soil. || Ground (suelo): *durmió en la tierra*, he slept on the ground. || AGR. Land: *cultivar la tierra*, to cultivate the land. || Native country (país) *o* region (región): *mi tierra*, my native country; *nunca salió de su tierra*, he never left his native region. || Soil (comarca): *tierra española*, Spanish soil. || ELECTR. Earth [U.S., ground]. || — Pl. Land, *sing.*: *tiene tierras en el norte*, he has land in the north. || — FIG. y FAM. *Besar la tierra*, to fall flat on one's face. || FIG. *Besar uno la tierra que otro pisa*, to worship the ground s.o. walks on. | *Caer por tierra*, to crumble (las ilusiones, etc.). || *Dar en tierra* or *dar consigo en tierra*, to fall [down]. | *Dar en tierra con*, to drop *o* to throw on the ground. || *Echar a tierra*, to knock down, to demolish (un edificio). || FIG. *Echar por tierra*, to wreck, to dash to the ground, to crush, to destroy: *una objeción que echa por tierra un razonamiento*, an objection which destroys an argument. || FIG. *Echarse por tierra*, to humiliate o.s. | *Echar tierra a*, to hush up (ocultar). | *En tierra de ciegos el tuerto es rey*, V. CIEGO. | *En toda tierra de garbanzos*, everywhere, all over the world. | *Estar comiendo* or *mascando tierra*, to be pushing up daisies. || FAM. *La tierra de María Santísima*, Andalusia. || *Poner pie en tierra*, to dismount (de caballo), to get out *o* off, to disembark (de un vehículo). || FIG. y FAM. *Poner tierra por medio*, to make o.s. scarce. || *Por estas tierras*, in these parts. || *Por tierra*, overland, by land. || *Tierra adentro*, inland. || *Tierra de batán*, fuller's earth. || *Tierra de cultivo* or *de labor* or *de labranza*, farmland, arable land, agricultural land. || *Tierra de Jauja*, V. JAUJA. || *Tierra de nadie*, no man's land. || *Tierra de pan llevar* or *paniega*, wheatland. || *Tierra de Promisión* or *Prometida*, Promised Land. || *Tierra firme*, terra firma. || *Tierra rara*, rare earth. || *Tierra Santa*, Holy Land. || *Tierra vegetal*, humus, mold, topsoil. || AVIAC. *Tocar tierra*, to touch down. || *Tomar tierra*, to land (avión, barco, pasajeros). || FIG. *Tragársele a uno la tierra*, to disappear into nowhere: *a Juan se le ha tragado la tierra*, John has disappeared into nowhere. || *Venirse a tierra*, to collapse (hundirse), to collapse, to crumble (ilusiones), to fall through (planes). || *Ver tierras*, to travel, to see the world (viajar mucho).

tierruca f. Country, native land (terruño). || FAM. *La Tierruca*, the province of Santander.

tieso, sa adj. Stiff, rigid (rígido): *pierna tiesa*, stiff leg. || Erect, straight, upright (erguido). || Firm (firme). || Taut, tight (tenso). || FIG. Proud, arrogant, stuck-up (engreído). | Stiff, starchy (envarado). | Brave, courageous (valiente). | Stubborn, unbending (terco). | Well, in good shape: *está muy tieso a pesar de sus años*, he is in good shape in spite of his years. || FIG. y FAM. Dead, stiff (muerto). || — FIG. y FAM. *Dejar tieso*, to leave penniless (sin dinero). | *Estar tieso*, to be stony-broke [U.S., to be stone-broke]. | *Estar* or *ser más tieso que un ajo* or *que un huso* or *que el palo de una escoba*, to be as stiff as a board *o* as a poker. || *Poner las orejas tiesas*, to prick up its ears (perro). || *Tener las orejas tiesas*, to be prick-

eared (perro). || FIG. y FAM. *Tenérselas tiesas a* or *con alguien*, to stand up to s.o., not to budge, to hold firm.
— Adv. Hard, strongly.
tiesto m. Flowerpot (maceta). || Potsherd, broken piece of earthenware (pedazo de vasija). || *Amer.* Pot, bowl (vasija).
tiesura f. Rigidity, stiffness (rigidez). || FIG. Stiffness, starchiness (gravedad exagerada).
tífico, ca adj. MED. Typhous.
— M. y f. Person suffering from typhus.
tiflitis f. MED. Typhlitis.
tifo m. V. TIFUS.
tifogénico, ca adj. MED. Typhogenic.
tifoideo, a adj. Typhoid: *fiebre tifoidea*, typhoid fever.
tifón m. Typhoon.
tifus m. MED. Typhus. || FIG. y FAM. Claque, people (*pl.*) with free seats.
— MED. *Tifus asiático*, cholera, Asiatic cholera. | *Tifus de América*, yellow fever. || *Tifus de Oriente*, bubonic plague.
tigra f. Tigress (tigre hembra). || *Amer.* Female jaguar (jaguar hembra).
tigre m. Tiger. || *Amer.* Jaguar. || FIG. Tiger, bloodthirsty person (persona cruel). || *Tigre hembra*, tigress.
tigrero, ra adj. *Amer.* Brave.
— M. *Amer.* Jaguar hunter.
tigresa f. Tigress.

— OBSERV. *Tigresa* is a Gallicism for *tigra*.

tigrillo m. *Amer.* Ocelot.
tija f. Stem (de la llave).
tijera f. Scissors, *pl.* (para cortar). || Sawbuck, sawhorse (para aserrar madera). || First feather of a hawk's wing (pluma). || DEP. Scissors, scissors hold (en la lucha libre). | Scissors (salto). || Drainage ditch (para desagüe). || Sheepshearer (esquilador). || Brace (de carro). || — Pl. Scissors: *tijeras para las uñas*, nail scissors. || Shears (de jardín, etc.) || FIG. y FAM. Backbiter, *sing.*, gossip, *sing.* (murmurador). || — *Asiento* or *silla de tijera*, folding chair. || *Cama de tijera*, folding bed. || FIG. *Cortado con la misma tijera*, tarred with the same brush, cast in the same mould. || *Echar* or *meter la tijera en*, to start cutting (cortar). || *Escalera de tijera*, stepladder. || DEP. *Salto de tijera*, scissors.
tijereta f. Small scissors, *pl.*, pair of small scissors. || BOT. Tendril (de la viña). || ZOOL. Earwig (insecto). || DEP. *Salto de tijereta*, scissors.
tijeretada f. o **tijeretazo** m. Snip.
tijeretear v. tr. To cut, to snip (dar tijeretazos). || FIG. y FAM. To meddle in.
tijereteo m. Cutting, snipping (acción de tijeretear). || Click, snip, snip-snipping (ruido).
tijerilla o **tijeruela** f. BOT. Tendril (de la viña).
tila f. Lime, linden (árbol). || Linden blossom, lime blossom (flor). || Linden-blossom tea, lime-blossom tea (infusión).
tílburi m. Tilbury.
tildado, da adj. With an accent (con acento). || With a tilde (ñ).
tildar v. tr. To put an accent on (poner acento). || To put a tilde on (la ñ). || To cross out (tachar). || FIG. To call, to brand, to label: *le tildan de avaro*, they call him a miser.
tilde m. Tilde (sobre la ñ). || Accent (acento). || Fault, flaw, blemish (tacha). || Iota, dot, tittle (cosa insignificante). || FIG. *Poner tilde a*, to criticize.
tiliáceas f. pl. BOT. Tiliaceae.
tiliche m. *Amer.* Trinket.
tilichero m. *Amer.* Pedlar [U.S., peddler].
tilín m. Ting-a-ling (de la campanilla). || — FIG. y FAM. *Amer. En un tilín*, in a flash. || FAM. *Hacer tilín*, to appeal. | *Le hizo tilín*, he liked it [*o* her, etc.].
tilingo, ga adj. *Amer.* Silly (tonto).
tilma f. *Amer.* Blanket, poncho.
tilo m. BOT. Lime, linden (árbol).
tilla f. MAR. Deck.
tillado m. MAR. Planking, boarding.
timador, ra m. y f. FAM. Swindler, cheat.
tímalo m. Grayling (pez).
timar v. tr. FAM. To swindle, to cheat (estafar): *le timaron mil pesetas*, they swindled him out of a thousand pesetas. | To cheat, to trick (engañar): *en esa tienda me timaron*, they cheated me in that shop.
— V. pr. FAM. To make eyes at each other. || FAM. *Timarse con*, to make eyes at.
timba f. FAM. Hand [of cards] (partida de juego). | Gambling den (garito).
timbal m. MÚS. Kettledrum, timbal. | Small drum (pequeño). || Meat pie, timbale (empanada). || — Pl. MÚS. Timpani.
timbalero m. Kettledrummer.
timbiriche m. *Amer.* Alcoholic drink (bebida). | Small shop (tiendecilla).
timbrado, da adj. Stamped. || *Papel timbrado*, stamped paper (sellado), letterhead stationery (con membrete).
timbrar v. tr. To stamp (poner un sello). || To seal (sellar). || HERÁLD. To crest (un escudo de armas). || *Máquina de timbrar*, stamper, stamping machine.
timbrazo m. Loud *o* long ring (ruido). || *Dar un timbrazo*, to ring the bell.
timbre m. Stamp, seal (sello). || COM. Fiscal *o* revenue stamp (fiscal). || Bell, electric bell (de la puerta): *tocar el timbre*, to ring the bell. || Timbre, ring (sonido característico): *timbre metálico*, metallic ring. || MÚS. Timbre. || HERÁLD. Crest, timbre: *timbre de nobleza*, crest of nobility. || — FIG. *Timbre de gloria*, title *o* claim to fame. || *Timbre móvil*, fiscal *o* revenue stamp.
timeleáceo, a adj. Thymelaeaceous.
timidez f. Shyness, timidity, bashfulness.
tímido, da adj. Timid, shy, bashful. || *Venga, no seas tan tímido*, come on, don't be shy.
timo m. Grayling (pez). || FAM. Swindle, confidence trick (estafa): *un timo de mil pesetas*, a one thousand peseta swindle. | Trick (engaño). | ANAT. Thymus. || — FIG. y FAM. *Dar un timo a*, to swindle. | *Esta película es un timo*, this film is a swindle *o* a waste of money. | *Timo del sobre*, envelope trick.
timón m. MAR. y AVIAC. Rudder. || Beam (del arado). || Pole (de carro). || FIG. Helm: *manejar el timón*, to be at the helm. || *Amer.* AUT. Steering wheel (volante). || — AVIAC. *Timón de dirección*, rudder. | *Timón de profundidad*, elevator.
timonear v. intr. To steer, to be at the helm.
timonel m. MAR. Steersman, helmsman.
timonera f. ZOOL. Rectrix, tail feather. || MAR. Wheelhouse.
timonero adj. Beam: *arado timonero*, beam plough.
— M. MAR. Steersman, helmsman.
timorato, ta adj. Timid, shy (tímido). || Godfearing (que teme a Dios). || Prudish, priggish (mojigato).
timpánico, ca adj. Tympanic.
timpanismo m. o **timpanitis** f. o **timpanización** f. MED. Tympanites.
timpanizarse v. pr. MED. To become distended with gases.
tímpano m. MÚS. Kettledrum (timbal). | Type of dulcimer. || ANAT. Tympanum, eardrum. || ARQ. Tympanum. || IMPR. Tympan. || Top, bottom (tapa de tonel). || — Pl. MÚS. Tympani.
tina f. Large earthen vat (tinaja). || Vat, tub, tank, copper (recipiente): *tina de tintorero*, cleaner's vat. || Bathtub (para bañarse).
tinaja f. Large earthen vat (recipiente). || Vat (cantidad).
tinajero m. Potter [who makes and sells large earthen vats] (fabricante o vendedor). || Stand for large earthen jars (donde se colocan).
tinamú m. ZOOL. Tinamou (ave).
tindalización f. FÍS. Tyndall effect.
Tíndaro n. pr. m. MIT. Tyndareus.
tinerfeño, ña adj. [Of *o* from] Tenerife.
— M. y f. Native *o* inhabitant of Tenerife.
tingitano, na adj. [Of *o* from] Tangier, Tangerine.
— M. y f. Native *o* inhabitant of Tangier, Tangerine.
tinglado m. Shed (cobertizo). || Platform, raised floor (tablado). || FIG. Intrigue, plot, mystery (intriga). | Mix-up, muddle (embrollo). || *Amer.* Sea turtle. || — FIG. y FAM. *Conocer el tinglado*, to see through it, to know exactly what is going on. | *Manejar el tinglado*, to pull the strings. | *¡Menudo tinglado se ha formado!*, what a fuss!, what a to-do!
tinieblas f. pl. Darkness, *sing.*, obscurity, *sing.*: *las tinieblas de la noche*, the darkness of night. || REL. Tenebrae. || FIG. Confusion, darkness, ignorance. || — FIG. *Ángel de tinieblas*, prince of darkness. | *Estoy en tinieblas sobre sus verdaderas intenciones*, I am in the dark about his true intentions, I am ignorant of his true intentions.
tino m. FIG. Skill, dexterity (habilidad). | Good judgment (juicio). | Common sense, sense (buen sentido). | Moderation (moderación). || Good aim (puntería con un arma). || Metal *o* stone vat (tina). || Wine *o* olive press (lagar). || — *A tino*, gropingly, feeling one's way. || FIG. *Obrar con tino*, to act wisely. | *Perder el tino*, to take leave of one's senses. | *Sacar de tino a uno*, to make s.o. lose his temper, to infuriate s.o., to make s.o. mad.| *Sin tino*, stupidly (insensatamente), immoderately (sin moderación), madly, headlong, recklessly (correr, etc.).
tinta f. Ink (de la pluma): *escribir con tinta*, to write in ink. || Tint, hue (color). || Ink (de los calamares, etc.). || — Pl. Colours, hues: *pintar con tintas azules*, to paint with blue hues. || FIG. Shades: *pintar el futuro con tintas negras*, to paint the future in shades of black. || — FIG. *De buena tinta*, on good authority, from a reliable source, straight from the horse's mouth. || *Media tinta*, half tone, half tint (que une los claros con los oscuros), first coat of a fresco painting (de fresco). || FIG. y FAM. *Medias tintas*, vague words, generalities (soluciones o respuestas indeterminadas), half measures (medidas inadecuadas). | *Recargar las tintas*, to exaggerate, to lay it on, to overdo it. || *Saber de buena tinta*, to have it on good authority *o* from a reliable source, to get it straight from the horse's mouth. || FIG. y FAM. *Sudar tinta*, to sweat blood. || *Tinta china*, Indian ink [U.S., India ink]. || *Tinta de imprenta*, printer's ink. || *Tinta simpática*, invisible *o* sympathetic ink.
tintar v. tr. To tint, to dye (teñir).
tinte m. Dye (colorante). || Dyeing, dyeing process (operación de teñir). || Dyer's [shop] (tienda donde se tiñe). || Dry cleaner's (tienda donde se limpia en seco). || Stain (para la madera). || FIG. Shade, colouring,

overtones, *pl.*: *tener un tinte político*, to have political overtones. | Veneer, gloss (barniz).
tinterillo m. FIG. y FAM. Pen-pusher (chupatintas). || *Amer.* Pettifogger.
tintero m. Inkwell, inkstand (recipiente). || Age mark in horse's tooth (del caballo). || IMPR. Ink fountain. || FIG. y FAM. *Se lo dejó en el tintero* or *se le quedó en el tintero*, it completely slipped his mind, he clean forgot about it.
tintillo adj. Light red (vino).
— M. Light red wine.
tintín m. Clink, clinking, chink (vasos). || Jingle, jingling, tinkle, tinkling, ting-a-ling (campanilla).
tintinar o **tintinear** v. intr. To clink (vasos). || To jingle, to tinkle, to ting-a-ling (campanilla).
tintineo m. Clink, clinking (vasos). || Jingle, jingling, tinkle, tinkling, ting-a-ling (campanilla).
tinto, ta adj. Dyed, stained (teñido). || Red: *vino tinto*, red wine. || *Amer.* Dark red. | Black (café). || FIG. Tinged.
— M. Red wine: *una botella de tinto*, a bottle of red wine. || *Amer.* Black coffee.
tintóreo, a adj. Tinctorial.
tintorería f. Dyeing (acción de teñir). || Dry cleaning (limpieza en seco). || Dyer's [shop] (taller donde se tiñe). || Dry cleaner's (taller donde se limpia en seco).
tintorero, ra m. y f. Dyer (que tiñe). || Dry cleaner (que limpia en seco).
— F. *Amer.* Female shark.
Tintoreto n. pr. m. Tintoretto.
tintorro m. FAM. Plonk, rough red wine.
tintura f. Dye, tint. || FIG. Notion, slight knowledge, smattering: *tengo una tintura de historia literaria*, I have a smattering *o* some notion of literature. || MED. Tincture: *tintura de yodo*, tincture of iodine.
tiña f. ZOOL. Honeycomb moth. || MED. Tinea, ringworm. || FIG. y FAM. Misery, poverty (pobreza). | Meanness, stinginess (tacañería).
tiñería f. FAM. Meanness, stinginess (tacañería).
tiñoso, sa adj. Scabby. || FAM. Mean, stingy (tacaño).
tío m. Uncle. || FAM. Old, uncle: *el tío Juan*, old John. | Fellow, bloke, chap, guy: *un tío estupendo*, a fantastic fellow. | So-and-so (peyorativo): *¡qué tío más idiota!*, the silly so-and-so! || *Amer.* Uncle, old [before the name of an elderly Negro] (negro viejo). || — Pl. Uncle and aunt. || — FIG. y FAM. *El tío del saco*, the bogyman. | *El Tío Sam*, Uncle Sam. | *Tener un tío en las Indias*, to have a rich uncle. || *Tío abuelo*, great-uncle. || *Tío segundo*, first cousin once removed.
tiovivo m. Roundabout, merry-go-round [U.S., merry-go-round, carousel, carrousel].
tipa f. *Amer.* Wicker basket (cesta). | Trollop (mujer despreciable).
tiparraco, ca o **tipejo, ja** m. y f. FAM. Wretch, twerp, blighter, heel (persona despreciable).
típico, ca adj. Typical. || Characteristic. || Traditional. || Picturesque (pintoresco).
tipificación f. Classification (clasificación). || Standardization (uniformización).
tipificar v. tr. To standardize (uniformizar). || To typify (caracterizar).
tipismo m. Local colour: *lleno de tipismo*, full of local colour. || Traditional *o* characteristic nature (carácter típico). || *El tipismo andaluz*, all the things characteristic of Andalusia, everything one associates with Andalusia.
tiple m. MÚS. Soprano [voice] (voz). | Treble guitar (guitarrita). || — M. y f. MÚS. Soprano, soprano singer.
tipo m. Type (modelo). || Type, kind, class (clase): *¿qué tipo de coche tiene?*, what kind of car does he have? || Rate: *tipo de cambio, de interés*, rate of exchange, of interest. || Percentage (descuento). || Type, type of person: *es un tipo deportivo*, he is the sporting type. || Figure, shape (de mujer), physique, build (de hombre): *esta chica tiene un tipo bonito*, that girl has a pretty figure. || Appearance (facha). || FAM. Fellow, chap, character: *¡qué tipo más extraordinario!*, what an extraordinary fellow!; *es un tipo malo*, he is a nasty character. || IMPR. Type. || Type: *tipo ario*, Aryan type. || — FIG. y FAM. *Jugarse el tipo*, to risk one's neck. | *Me juego el tipo a que*, I bet anything you like that.
tipografía f. Typography, printing (arte). || Printing works *o* press (lugar).
tipográfico, ca adj. Typographical, typographic, printing.
tipógrafo, fa m. y f. Typographer.
tipología f. Typology.
tipómetro m. Type gauge.
tipoy m. Tunic [worn by South American Indians].
típula f. Crane fly, daddy longlegs.
tíquet o **tiquete** m. Ticket.
tiquismiquis m. pl. FAM. Silly scruples (reparos nimios). | Bowing and scraping, affected manners (cortesías afectadas). | Bickering, silly little fights, quarrelling (peleas). || FAM. *Andarse con tiquismiquis*, to be fussy.
tira f. Strip (de tela, papel, etc.). || Strap: *las tiras de los zapatos*, the straps of the shoes. || Comic strip, strip cartoon (del periódico). || MAR. Fall. || — FIG. y FAM. *Esperé la tira para coger el autobús*, I waited ages *o* an eternity for the bus. | *Quitar la piel a tiras* or *sacar las tiras del pellejo*, to tear [s.o.] to pieces (criticar).
tirabala m. Blowpipe, peashooter.
tirabeque m. Tender pea (guisante mollar). || Catapult [U.S., slingshot] (tiragomas).
tirabotas m. inv. Boot hook.
tirabuzón m. Corkscrew (sacacorchos). || FIG. Ringlet, curl (rizo de cabello). || AVIAC. Spin. || DEP. Twist (del trampolín). || FIG. y FAM. *Sacarle a uno las palabras con tirabuzón*, to drag *o* to twist the words out of s.o.
tirada f. Long distance, stretch (distancia). || Series: *nos leyó una tirada de versos*, he read us a series of verses. || IMPR. Printing (acción). | Edition: *segunda tirada*, second edition; *una tirada de veinte mil ejemplares*, a twenty thousand copy edition. || FAM. Tart (fulana). || — *De* or *en una tirada*, in one go. || IMPR. *Tirada aparte*, offprint.
tirado, da adj. FAM. Dead easy, as easy as pie: *este trabajo está tirado*, this work is dead easy. | Dirt cheap (barato): *este reloj está tirado*, this watch is dirt cheap. || Streamlined (embarcación). || TECN. Drawn.
— M. TECN. Wiredrawing (de los metales). || Printing.
tirador, ra m. y f. Shooter, marksman (hombre), markswoman (mujer). || Drawer (de metales). || — *Es buen tirador*, he is a good shot *o* a good marksman. || *Tirador de arco*, archer, bowman. || *Tirador de fusil*, rifleman. || — M. Handle, knob (de puerta, de cajón). || Bellpull, rope (de campanilla). || Catapult [U.S., slingshot] (tiragomas). || IMPR. Pressman. || TECN. Drawplate (para los metales). || *Amer.* Gaucho's belt [frequently decorated with silver coins]. || *Tirador de oro*, gold wiredrawer.
tirafondo m. MED. Forceps, surgical pincers, *pl.* || Screw (tornillo).
tiragomas m. inv. Catapult [U.S., slingshot].
tiralevitas m. inv. FAM. Bootlicker, crawler.
tiralíneas m. inv. Drawing pen, ruling pen. || FIG. *Con tiralíneas*, with great precision.
tiramollar v. tr. MAR. To slacken.
tiranía f. Tyranny.
tiranicida m. y f. Tyrannicide (asesino).
tiranicidio m. Tyrannicide (crimen).
tiránico, ca adj. Tyrannic, tyrannical.
tiranización f. Tyrannizing.
tiranizar v. tr. To tyrannize.
tirano, na adj. Tyrannic, tyrannical.
— M. y f. Tyrant.
tirante adj. Tight, taut, tense (tenso). || FIG. Tense, strained: *relaciones tirantes*, strained relations. || FIG. *Estar tirante*, to be on bad terms, to be at odds: *estamos tirantes*, we are on bad terms; *Juan está tirante con su hermano*, John is at odds with *o* on bad terms with his brother.
— M. Trace, harness trace (de caballería). || Strap (de falda, delantal, ropa interior). || ARQ. Tie, tie beam. || TECN. Brace, stay, strut. || — Pl. Braces, [U.S., suspenders] (del pantalón).
tirantez f. Tenseness, tautness, tightness. || FIG. Tension, strained relations, *pl.*, tenseness, strain: *tirantez entre el presidente y sus ministros*, tension between the president and his ministers. || FIG. *Tirantez de las relaciones*, strained relations.
tirapié m. Stirrup (del zapatero).
tirar v. tr. To throw, to toss, to sling (fam.): *tirar un libro al suelo*, to throw a book to the ground; *tirar piedras a uno*, to throw stones at s.o. || To drop (dejar caer). || To spill (un líquido): *tirar el agua en la mesa*, to spill the water on *o* over the table. || To knock over (volcar): *tirar un vaso de vino*, to knock over a glass of wine. || To pull down, to knock down (derribar): *tirar un árbol*, to pull down a tree; *tirar una casa*, to pull a house down. || To pull (traer hacia sí): *tirar la puerta*, to pull the door. || To stretch, to draw, to pull (estirar). || To throw away *o* out, to discard (desechar): *este abrigo está ya para tirarlo*, this coat is ready to be thrown away. || To waste, to throw away, to squander (disipar): *tirar dinero*, to squander money. || IMPR. To print, to run off (imprimir). || FOT. To print. | To take (tomar): *tira una foto del niño*, take a photo of the child. | To make (fotocopia). || To reproduce. || TECN. To draw, to draw out (estirar un metal). || To fire (un cañonazo, un cohete). || AVIAC. To drop (paracaidista, bomba). || FAM. To run down (criticar): *me está siempre tirando*, he is always running me down. | To sell for a giveaway price, to give away (vender barato). || DEP. To take: *tirar un saque de esquina*, to take a corner. || MAT. To draw (línea, curva). | To drop (perpendicular). || To give: *le tiró un pellizco*, he gave him a pinch. || *Amer.* To carry, to transport (transportar). || — *Tirar abajo*, to pull down, to knock down, to demolish (un edificio), to break down (una puerta). || FIG. y FAM. *Tirar coces*, V. COZ. | *Tirar indirectas*, V. INDIRECTA. | *Tirar la casa por la ventana*, to spare no expense, to go overboard, to lash out (fam.). | *Tirar la piedra y esconder la mano*, V. PIEDRA. || *Tirar un beso a alguien*, to blow s.o. a kiss. || *Tirar un mordisco a alguien*, to bite s.o., to give s.o. a bite.
— V. intr. To pull, to draw (una chimenea): *esta chimenea tira bien*, this chimney draws well. || To fire, to shoot: *tirar con rifle*, to fire a rifle; *tirar al aire*, to fire *o* to shoot into the air; *¡no tire!*, don't

shoot! || To pull, to tug: *tirar de una cuerda*, to pull [on] a rope; *tirar a alguien de la manga*, to tug at s.o.'s sleeve. || To draw, to attract: *el imán tira del hierro*, the magnet attracts iron. || To pull, to draw: *el caballo tira del carro*, the horse draws the cart. || FAM. To work, to run, to pull (funcionar): *este motor tira bien*, this motor works well. || FIG. To attract, to appeal to (atraer): *no le tira la pintura*, painting does not attract him. | To turn (torcer): *tira a la derecha*, turn right. | To go: *tira adelante*, go straight on. | To take, to go (*por*, by))[coger]: *si tirásemos por este camino llegaríamos antes*, if we took this road we would arrive sooner. | To last (durar): *esta falda tirará todo el invierno*, this skirt will last all winter. | To make do [with], to get by *o* along [on] (mantenerse): *él tira con diez mil pesetas al mes*, he makes do with ten thousand pesetas a month. | To tend towards: *este color tira a rojo*, this colour tends towards red. | To be rather: *él tira a tacaño*, he is rather miserly. | To be attracted to *o* inclined towards: *tira para cura*, he is attracted to the priesthood. | To take after, to look like (parecerse a): *ella tira más bien a su padre*, she takes more after her father. || To draw, to pull out (sacar un arma): *tiraron de las espadas*, they pulled out their swords. || To pull out, to take out (sacar cualquier cosa). || DEP. To shoot (chutar).

— FIG. *A más tirar* or *a todo tirar* or *tirando por alto*, at the most, at the outside. | *Dejar tirado a uno*, to abandon s.o. (abandonar), to leave s.o. behind, to surpass s.o. (superar), to astonish s.o. (dejar asombrado). || FIG. y FAM. *Ir tirando*, to get along, to get by, to cope, to manage: *vamos tirando*, we are managing. || FIG. *La cabra siempre tira al monte*, V. CABRA. | *La patria siempre tira*, one always feels drawn by one's homeland. || *Naranja que tira a rojo*, reddish orange. || FAM. *Tirando*, so-so. || FIG. *Tirando por bajo*, at least. || *Tirar al blanco*, to shoot at a target. || *Tirar a matar* or *tirar con bala*, to shoot to kill (con un arma de fuego), to pull [s.o.] to pieces (criticar mucho). || FIG. *Tirar de la lengua*, to draw s.o. out. || FIG. y FAM. *Tirar de la levita*, to butter up, to flatter (adular). || FIG. *Tirar largo* or *de largo* or *por largo*, to spend lavishly (dinero), to use [etc.] freely: *si tiras de largo la pintura*, if you put the paint on freely; to estimate high (calcular). | *Tirar por lo alto*, to have high ambitions, to aim high (ser ambicioso), to do things in style *o* in a big way (no escatimar los gastos). || *Tira tú ahora*, it's your turn *o* go now. || FIG. y FAM. *Tira y afloja*, give and take (toma y daca), tact, diplomacy (tacto).

— V. pr. To jump, to throw *o* to hurl o.s. (arrojarse): *se tiró al agua*, he jumped into the water. || To spring, to jump, to rush (abalanzarse): *el perro se tiró sobre el* or *al niño*, the dog jumped on *o* rushed at the child. || To lie down (tumbarse): *se tiró en la cama*, he lay down on the bed. || FIG. To spend: *se tiró un día entero pescando*, he spent a whole day fishing. | To have to put up with (tener que aguantar): *se tiró un viaje muy largo*, he had to put up with a very long trip. || DEP. To dive (a la pelota). || POP. To lay, to have (a una chica). || — FIG. y FAM. *Tirarse al suelo de risa*, to roll about laughing. | *Tirarse a matar*, to pull each other to pieces. || *Tirarse de cabeza a la piscina*, to dive into the swimming pool. || FIG. y FAM. *Tirarse del moño*, to tear each other's hair out. | *Tirarse los trastos a la cabeza*, V. TRASTO. | *Tirarse un planchazo* or *una plancha*, V. PLANCHAZO.

tiricia f. FAM. Jaundice (ictericia).

tirilla f. Strip, band (tira pequeña). || Neckband (de camisa).

tirio, ria adj./s. Tyrian. || FIG. *Tirios y troyanos*, opposing parties.

tirita f. MED. Plaster.

tiritar v. intr. To shiver, to shake, to tremble (*de*, with). || FIG. y FAM. *Dejar un plato tiritando*, to almost completely polish off a dish.

tiritera f. Shivers, *pl.*, shivering, shaking, trembling. || *Le dio la tiritera*, he started shivering.

tiritón m. Shiver. || *Dar tiritones*, to make one shiver: *de pensarlo me dan tiritones*, it makes me shiver to think about it.

tiritona f. FAM. Shivers, *pl.*, shivering, shaking, trembling. || — FAM. *Dar una tiritona*, to make shiver. | *Tener una tiritona*, to have the shivers, to shiver.

tiro m. Throw (lanzamiento). || Shot, discharge (disparo, ruido): *tiro de pistola*, pistol shot; *se oyen tiros*, shots are heard. || Shooting (acción o arte): *tiro al blanco*, target shooting. || Shot (herida, huella). || Shot, bullet (bala). || Load, charge (carga). || Range (sitio): *tiro al blanco*, target *o* rifle range. || MIL. Gun (pieza de artillería). | Firing, fire (manera de disparar): *tiro directo*, direct firing; *tiro oblicuo*, oblique fire. | Range (alcance): *a tiro de escopeta*, within rifle range. || Throw (distancia): *a tiro de piedra*, within a stone's throw; *un tiro de 55 metros*, a 55-metre throw. || Length (de un tejido). || Distance between crotch and waist of trousers (de pantalón). || Shoulder width (de vestido). || Flight (de escalera). || Draught [U.S., draft] (de chimenea). || Team (de animales): *tiro de caballos*, team of horses. || FIG. Blow (golpe duro). | Petty theft (robo). | Joke, prank, trick (chasco). || Pulley *o* hoisting rope, pull chain *o* rope (cuerda de garrucha). || Harness trace (tirante). || DEP. Shot (fútbol, etc.): *tiro a gol*, shot at goal. || MIN. Shaft (pozo). | Depth (profundidad). || VET. Stable vice (de los caballos). || *Amer.* Edition (tirada). || — Pl. Belt, *sing.* (para la espada). || *Amer.* Braces [U.S., suspenders] (tirantes). || — *A tiro*, within range (de arma), within reach (asequible): *se me puso a tiro*, he came within my reach. || FIG. *A tiro de ballesta*, at a glance. || *A tiro hecho*, with precision (apuntando bien), deliberately, purposely, intentionally (adrede). || *A tiro limpio*, firing, guns blazing. || *Animal de tiro*, draught animal. || *Campo de tiro*, shooting range. || *Dar* or *pegar un tiro*, to fire a shot, to shoot. || FAM. *Darse* or *pegarse un tiro*, to shoot o.s., to commit suicide. | *De tiros largos*, all dressed up, dressed to kill. || FIG. *Errar el tiro*, to miss the mark, to fail. || FIG. y FAM. *La noticia le sentó como un tiro*, the news came as a blow to him, he took the news very badly. | *Le salió el tiro por la culata*, it backfired on him. || FAM. *Liarse a tiros*, to start shooting, to have a shoot-out. || *Matar a alguien a tiros*, to shoot s.o. dead. || FIG. y FAM. *Matar dos pájaros de un tiro*, to kill two birds with one stone. | *Ni a tiros*, not for love nor money. || FIG. *Pegar cuatro tiros*, to shoot. | *Poner el tiro muy alto*, to aim high. || *Sin pegar un tiro*, without firing a shot. || DEP. *Tiro al plato*, trapshooting. || *Tiro de* or *con arco*, archery. || *Tiro de gracia*, coup de grâce, death blow. || DEP. *Tiro de pichón*, pigeon shooting.

Tiro n. pr. m. Tyre.

tiroideo, a adj. ANAT. Thyroid.

tiroides m. ANAT. Thyroid, thyroid gland.

— Adj. ANAT. Thyroid.

tiroidina f. MED. Thyroid extract.

tiroiditis f. MED. Thyroiditis.

Tirol n. pr. m. GEOGR. Tyrol.

tirolés, esa adj./s. Tyrolese, Tyrolean.

tirón m. Tug, pull, jerk (en una cuerda, etc.). || Jerk, jolt (sacudida). || Cramp (de estómago, de músculo). || Tyro, novice (aprendiz). || FAM. Good distance, long stretch *o* way (distancia): *hay un tirón de aquí a tu casa*, there's a good distance between your house and here. || FIG. Pull (atracción). || — *A tirones*, jerkily (avanzar, etc.). || *Dar un tirón a*, to tug *o* to pull at, to give a tug. || *Dar un tirón de orejas*, to pull *o* to tweak s.o.'s ear. || *De un tirón*, straight off (al primer intento), all at once, in one go (de una sola vez): *leer una novela de un tirón*, to read a novel in one go; at a stretch, at one stretch, in one go: *hacer cincuenta kilómetros de un tirón*, to do fifty kilometres at a stretch. || *Me lo arrancó de un tirón*, he pulled *o* yanked it away from me. || *Ni a dos tirones*, never in a million years.

tirotear v. tr. To snipe at, to fire at, to take shots at, to shoot at: *le tirotearon desde el tejado*, they shot at him from the roof.

— V. pr. To exchange shots *o* fire, to shoot at each other, to fire at each other.

tiroteo m. Firing, shooting (acción de tirotear). || Shooting, firing, shots, *pl.* (ruido): *se oía un tiroteo a lo lejos*, shooting was heard in the distance. || Skirmish (escaramuza).

tirotricina f. QUÍM. Tyrothricin.

Tirreno n. pr. m. *Mar Tirreno*, Tyrrhenian Sea.

tirria f. FAM. Dislike. || — FAM. *Tener tirria a*, to have a grudge against, to have it in for, to dislike. | *Tomar tirria a uno*, to take a dislike to s.o.

tisana f. Infusion, ptisan, tisane.

tisanuro adj./s.m. ZOOL. Thysanuran. || — Pl. ZOOL. Thysanura.

tísico, ca adj. Phthisical, tubercular, consumptive.

— M. y f. Consumptive.

tisiología f. MED. Phthisiology.

tisiólogo m. MED. Phthisiologist.

tisis f. MED. Phthisis, tuberculosis, consumption.

tisú m. Lamé (tela).

— OBSERV. Pl. *tisúes* o *tisús*.

tita f. FAM. Auntie, aunty.

titán m. Titan.

titánico, ca adj. Titanic. || QUÍM. Titanic. || FIG. *Un trabajo titánico*, a titanic *o* gigantic task *o* job.

titanio m. Titanium (metal).

títere m. Puppet, marionette. || FIG. Weakling, puppet (persona que se deja dominar). || — Pl. Puppet show, *sing.* || — FIG. *No dejar títere con cabeza*, to turn everything upside down, to break everything in sight. | *No queda títere con cabeza*, there's not a plate in the house left unbroken. || *Teatro de títeres*, puppet show.

titerista m. y f. V. TITIRITERO.

tití m. ZOOL. Titi (mono).

titilación f. Quiver, tremble, shaking. || Twinkling, twinkle (de las estrellas). || Flicker (del fuego, etc.).

titilador, ra o **titilante** adj. Quivering. || Twinkling (estrella). || Flickering (fuego).

titilar o **titilear** v. intr. To quiver (temblar). || To twinkle (estrella). || To flicker, to twinkle (luz).

titileo m. Twinkling (de una estrella).

titirimundi m. Cosmorama.

titiritaina f. FAM. Row, din, racket (bulla).

titiritar v. intr. To tremble, to shiver, to shake.

titiritero, ra m. y f. Puppeteer (que maneja los títeres). || Tightrope walker (volatinero). || Acrobat, juggler, mountebank (saltimbanqui).
tito m. FAM. Uncle (tío).
Tito n. pr. m. Titus.
Tito Livio n. pr. m. Livy.
titubeante adj. Shaky, staggering, unsteady, tottering: *un andar titubeante*, a shaky walk. || Stammering (que farfulla). || FIG. Hesitant (que duda).
titubear v. intr. To stagger, to totter (oscilar). || FIG. To hesitate, to waver: *titubea en venir*, he hesitates to come; *titubeaba si lo haría*, he hesitated about doing it. || To falter, to stammer (farfullar).
titubeo m. Staggering, tottering, stagger, unsteadiness (al andar). || Hesitation, hesitancy, wavering (vacilación). || Stammering (acción de farfullar).
titulación f. QUÍM. Titration.
titulado, da adj. Entitled (un libro, etc.). || Qualified; *enfermera titulada*, qualified nurse. || FIG. So-called: *un titulado pintor*, a so-called painter. || *Ser titulado en medicina*, to have a degree in medicine.
titular adj. Titular: *profesor, obispo titular*, titular professor, bishop. || DEP. Regular: *jugador titular*, regular player. || *Juez titular*, regular judge.
— M. y f. Holder (de pasaporte, etc.). || *Hacer titular*, to confirm [s.o.] in his post. || — M. pl. Headlines (de periódico).
titular v. tr. To title, to entitle, to call (poner un título). || QUÍM. To titrate.
— V. intr. To receive a title of nobility.
— V. pr. To be titled, to be called (un libro, etc.). || To call o.s.
titularización f. Confirmation of s.o. in his post.
titularizar v. tr. To confirm [s.o.] in his post.
titulillo m. IMPR. Running head, running title.
título m. Title (de una obra). || Title (dignidad): *título de nobleza*, title of nobility. || Titled person (dignatario). || Degree: *título de licenciado*, bachelor's degree. || Diploma (diploma). || Qualification: *tener los títulos necesarios*, to have the necessary qualifications. || COM. Security, bond (valor): *título al portador*, bearer bond. || FIG. Quality (calidad). | Right (derecho). || JUR. Title: *título de propiedad*, title deed. | Heading (de un texto legal). | Item (de un presupuesto). || IMPR. Title (de libro, etc.). | Headline (en periódicos). || QUÍM. Titre [U.S., titer]. || — *A título de*, in the capacity of, as (en calidad de), by way of (en concepto de). || *Conceder un título*, to give *o* to grant a title. || *Con el mismo título*, with the same title (igual), with the same motive (por el mismo motivo). || *¿Con qué título?*, by what right? || *Títulos cotizables*, listed shares. || *Título de pago*, title of payment. || *Título de renta*, government bond. || *Título de piloto*, pilot's certificate.
tiza f. Chalk: *escribir con tiza*, to write with chalk. || Chalk (de billar). || *Una tiza*, a piece of chalk.
Tiziano n. pr. m. Titian.
tizna f. Grime, dirt.
tiznado, da adj. Dirty, blackened, sooty (manchado). || *Amer.* Drunk (ebrio).
tiznadura f. Blackening, smudging (acción). || Smudge, smut (tiznón).
tiznajo m. Smudge.
tiznar v. tr. To blacken, to smudge with black, to soil with soot (manchar de negro). || To soil, to dirty (manchar, ensuciar). || To blacken [with soot]: *tiznar una pared*, to blacken a wall [with soot]. || FIG. To blacken, to soil, to stain: *tiznar la reputación de alguien*, to blacken s.o.'s reputation.
— V. pr. To get dirty (mancharse). || To blacken: *se tiznaron la cara*, they blackened their faces. || *Amer.* To get drunk (emborracharse).
tizne m. y f. Soot (hollín). || Grime, soot, black, dirt (suciedad). || FIG. Stain.
tiznón m. Smudge, smut.
tizón m. Half-burnt stick, smouldering brand (palo a medio quemar). || Half-burnt log (leño a medio quemar). || FIG. Stain (mancha en la fama). || BOT. Smut (parásito). || ARQ. Header (del sillar). || FAM. *Negro como un tizón*, as black as soot *o* as coal.
tizona f. FAM. Sword.

— OBSERV. *Tizona* was the name of the Cid's sword.

tizonadas f. pl. o **tizonazos** m. pl. FIG. y FAM. Hellfire, *sing.* (infierno).
tizoncillo m. Smut (enfermedad de los vegetales).
tizonear v. intr. To poke, to stir up (el fuego).
tlacoyo m. *Amer.* Omelet made with kidney beans.
tlacuache m. *Amer.* Opossum (zarigüeya).
tlapalería f. *Amer.* Hardware shop.
tlaspi m. Candytuft (planta).
tlazol m. *Amer.* Tops of sugar cane or corn used as fodder.
toa f. *Amer.* Towrope, rope (maroma).
toalla f. Towel: *toalla de baño*, bath towel; *toalla de manos*, hand towel. || *Toalla de felpa*, Turkish towel.
toallero m. Towel rail, towel rack.
toar v. tr. MAR. To tow (remolcar).
toba f. Tufa (piedra). || Tartar (sarro). || BOT. Cotton thistle (cardo borriquero).
tobáceo, a adj. Tufaceous, tuffaceous.
tobar m. Tufa quarry.
tobera f. Nozzle.
tobillera adj. f. FAM. *Niña tobillera*, teenager [U.S., bobby-soxer].
— F. Ankle support.
tobillo m. ANAT. Ankle. || FIG. *No le llega ni al tobillo*, he is no match for him, he can't hold a candle to him.
tobogán m. Slide, chute (para niños, mercancías). || Toboggan (para deslizarse por la nieve).
toca f. Headdress. || Wimple, cornet (de religiosa). || Hat (sombrero).
tocable adj. Touchable. || Playable (obra musical).
tocadiscos m. inv. Record player, gramophone.
tocado adj. Wearing [on one's head]: *tocado con un sombrero negro*, wearing a black hat. || FIG. y FAM. Touched, crazy (loco). || FAM. *Tocado en la cabeza*, touched in the head, not all there.
— M. Hat, headdress (sombrero). || Coiffure, hairdo (peinado). || Touch (esgrima).
tocador, ra m. y f. MÚS. Player. || — *Tocador de arpa*, harpist, harp player. || *Tocador de guitarra*, guitarist, guitar player. || — M. Dressing table (mueble para mujer). || Boudoir, dressing room (cuarto). || Vanity case (neceser). || FAM. Powder room, ladies' room (servicios). || *Artículos de tocador*, cosmetics.
tocadura f. Headdress (tocado). || Hairdo (peinado). || FAM. Crazy thing (locura).
tocamiento m. Touching.
tocante adj. Touching. || — *Dijo unas palabras tocantes a la economía*, he touched on the economy, he briefly mentioned the economy, he said a few words about the economy. || *En lo tocante a*, with reference to. || *Tocante a*, about, concerning, with reference to: *no diré nada tocante a la economía*, I won't say anything about the economy.
tocar v. tr. To touch: *tocar algo con el dedo*, to touch sth. with one's finger; *le tocó el hombro*, he touched him on the shoulder; *las montañas parecían tocar las nubes*, the mountains seemed to touch the clouds. || MÚS. To play: *tocar la guitarra, el piano, los discos*, to play the guitar, the piano, the records. | To play, to beat (el tambor). | To play, to blow (la trompeta). || To touch, to feel, to handle: *se ruega no tocar la mercancía*, please do not handle the goods; *tócalo a ver cómo te parece*, feel it and see what you think. || To chime, to strike (dar la hora el reloj). || To ring: *tocar la campana*, to ring the bell. || MIL. To sound: *tocar diana, la retirada*, to sound reveille, the retreat. || To touch, to hit (esgrima). || To hit (un blanco, etc. con un tiro). || To essay, to test with a touchstone, to touch (metal precioso). || To stop at, to put in at, to call at: *el barco tocará los siguientes puertos*, the boat will stop at the following ports. || To touch up (una pintura). || FIG. To touch on, to mention briefly (mencionar): *tocar un tema*, to touch on a subject. | To touch, to reach (impresionar): *me has tocado el corazón*, you've touched my heart. || — *A toca teja*, cash, cash down (pagar). || FIG. *Toca madera*, touch wood. || *Tocar el timbre*, to ring the bell. || FIG. *Tocar en lo vivo*, to cut to the quick. || *Tocar la bocina* or *el claxon*, to sound *o* to blow the horn. || FIG. *Tocar por encima*, to briefly touch on (un asunto). | *Tocar todos los registros*, v. REGISTRO.
— V. intr. To knock: *tocar a la puerta*, to knock on the door. || To ring (una campana). || To be up to: *me toca decirlo*, it is up to me to say it; *no le toca a usted hacer este trabajo*, it is not up to you to do this job. || To win (en suerte): *le tocó el gordo*, he won first prize. || To fall: *tocar a uno en un reparto*, to fall to one, to fall to one's lot *o* share; *le tocó a él ir a buscarlo*, it fell to him to go and fetch it. || To be one's turn: *a usted le toca tomar la palabra*, it is your turn to speak; *a ti te toca jugar*, it is your turn to play; *¿a quién le toca ahora?*, whose turn is it now? || To be related to, to be a relation of (ser pariente): *Antonio no me toca nada*, Anthony is not related to me at all; *¿qué te toca Clemente?*, how is Clement related to you?, what relation of yours is Clement? || To have to, to be time to; *ahora toca pagar*, now we have to pay, now it is time to pay. || To stop, to put in, to call (barco, avión): *el avión tocará en Palma*, the plane will stop at Palma. || FIG. To touch, to reach: *le tocó Dios en el corazón*, God reached his heart. | To concern: *este asunto me toca de cerca*, this matter concerns me deeply. || — *No es a ti a quien le toca aguantar a los niños*, you're not the one who has to put up with the children. || *Por lo que a mí me toca*, as far as I am concerned. || *Tocar a misa*, to ring the bell for mass. || *Tocar a muerto*, to toll [the knell]. || *Tocar a rebato*, to sound the alarm. || *Tocar a su fin*, to be coming to an end (estar a punto de acabar), to be on the point of death (estar a punto de morir). || *Tocar con*, to be next to: *mi casa toca con la suya*, my house is next to yours. || FIG. *Tocar en*, to verge on (rayar en).
— V. pr. To touch o.s. || To touch [each other] (dos cosas o personas). || To cover one's head (cubrirse la cabeza). || To put on *o* on one's head: *tocarse con un sombrero*, to put a hat on. || To do one's hair (peinarse).
tocata f. MÚS. Toccata. || FAM. Thrashing, spanking (paliza).
tocateja (a) adv. Cash, cash down: *pagar a tocateja*, to pay cash down.
tocay m. Tokay (vino).
tocayo, ya m. y f. Namesake.

tocinería f. Pork butcher's.
tocinero, ra m. y f. Pork butcher.
tocino m. Bacon. || Fat, lard. || — *Tocino de cielo*, sweet made of eggs and syrup. || *Tocino entreverado*, [streaky] bacon. || *Tocino gordo*, fat bacon.
— Interj. Pepper! (en el juego de la comba).
toco m. *Amer.* Niche (hornacina).
tocología f. Tocology, obstetrics.
tocólogo m. Tocologist, obstetrician.
tocomate m. *Amer.* Pumpkin (calabaza).
tocón m. Stump (de un árbol o miembro).
toconal m. Land covered with tree stumps. || Olive grove (olivar).
tocuyo m. *Amer.* Coarse cotton cloth.
tocho m. Iron ingot.
todavía adv. Still: *duerme todavía* or *todavía duerme*, he is still sleeping; *¿trabajas todavía en la misma oficina?*, do you still work in the same office? || Still, yet: *no ha venido todavía*, he still hasn't come, he hasn't come yet. || — *Todavía más*, even more (con adjetivo), even (con adjetivo comparativo): *el rico quiere enriquecerse todavía más*, the rich man wants to become even richer; still more, even more: *éste cuesta todavía más*, this one costs even more. || *Todavía no*, not yet.
todito, ta adj. FAM. All: *ha llorado todita la noche*, he cried all night [long]; *se ha comido toditos los pasteles*, he has eaten all the cakes. || — *Se lo ha bebido todito todo*, he has drunk every single drop of it. || *Se lo ha comido todito todo*, he has eaten it all up, he has eaten every single bit of it.
todo, da adj. y pron. indef. All: *lo saben todos los hombres*, all men know it; *han venido todos*, they have all come. || Every (cada): *todo buen cristiano*, every good Christian; *todos los días, los meses*, every day, month. || Everything: *todo está preparado*, everything is ready; *me gusta todo*, I like everything. || All: *mi falda está toda manchada*, my shirt is all dirty; *este pescado es todo espinas*, this fish is all bones. || Full of (lleno de): *la calle era toda baches*, the street was full of holes. || All of, all, the whole of: *España toda aprueba la decisión*, all Spain *o* all of Spain *o* the whole of Spain approves the decision. || Every inch, every bit, a real (un verdadero): *es todo un hombre*, he's a real man. he's every inch *o* every bit a man. || Exactly like, the image of (igual que): *eres todo tu padre*, you are exactly like your father, you are the image of your father.
— Adv. Completely, entirely, all, totally.
— *Ante todo*, above all, first and foremost, first of all. || *A pesar de todo*, V. PESAR. || *Así y todo*, V. ASÍ. || *A toda velocidad* or *marcha* or *mecha*, *a todo correr*, [at] full speed, [at] top speed. || *A todo esto*, in the meantime (mientras tanto), by the way, speaking of that (hablando de esto). || *A todo riesgo*, fully comprehensive (seguro). || *A todo vapor*, V. VAPOR. || *Considerándolo todo*, all things considered. || *Con toda mi alma* or *de todo corazón*, with all my heart. || *Con todas sus fuerzas*, with all his might *o* strength. || *Con todo* or *con todo y con eso*, in spite of everything, nevertheless, even so. || *Después de todo*, after all. || *De todas formas* or *en todo caso*, anyway. || *De todo hay en la viña del Señor*, it takes all sorts *o* all kinds to make a world. || *En todo el día no lo he visto*, I haven't seen him all day. || *En todo el mundo no hay uno parecido*, there is not another one like it anywhere in the world. || *Eso es todo*, that's all. || *Es todo uno*, it's all the same. || *Fue todo uno*, it all happened at once. || *Hacer todo lo posible*, V. POSIBLE. || *Ha viajado por toda España*, he has travelled all over Spain. || *Hay de todo*, there are all sorts of things (toda clase de cosas), there are all sorts (varios tipos de la misma cosa). || *Lo ... todo*, it all, everything: *lo sabe todo*, he knows it all; *lo he dicho todo*, I have said everything; *lo estás estropeando todo*, you are ruining everything. || *Lo he buscado en* or *por toda la casa*, I have searched for it all over the house. || *O todo o nada*, [it is] all or nothing. || *Ser toda sonrisa*, to be all smiles. || *Ser todo ojos, todo oídos*, to be all eyes, all ears. || *Sobre todo*, above all, especially. || *Todo aquel que*, anyone who, whoever. || FAM. *Todo Cristo* or *todo Dios*, absolutely everybody. || *Todo cuanto, todos cuantos*, V. CUANTO. || *Todo el mundo*, everybody, everyone: *lo sabe todo el mundo*, everybody knows that. || *Todo el que*, anyone who, whoever: *todo el que quiera venir que me siga*, anyone who wants to come *o* whoever wants to come, follow me. || *Todo eran quejas*, it was all complaints, there were nothing but complaints. || *Todo incluido*, everything included, all in. || *Todo lo contrario*, quite the contrary *o* the opposite. || *Todo lo demás*, everything else, all the rest. || *Todo lo más*, at the most (como mucho), at the latest (como muy tarde). || *Todo lo que*, anything *o* everything [which], whatever: *todo lo que te parezca útil*, anything [which] you think might be useful. || *Todo lo ... que* or *todo cuanto*, as ... as: *no estuvo todo lo simpático que yo esperaba*, he wasn't as nice as I hoped. || *Todo o nada*, [it is] all or nothing. || *Todo quisque*, [absolutely] everybody. || *Todos*, everybody, everyone (todo el mundo), all: *somos todos hermanos*, we are all brothers; all of: *todos nosotros*, all of us. || *Todos los días*, every day. || *Todos los que puedan*, all those who can. || *Todos ustedes*, all of you. || *Todos y cada uno*, all and sundry, each and every one. || *Y todo*, and all, and everything: *perdió su perro y todo*, he lost his dog and all; although: *cansado y todo siguió trabajando*, although he was tired he carried on working.
todo m. Whole: *una parte del todo*, a part of the whole; *considerado como un todo*, taken as a whole. || All, everything (cada cosa). || — *Del todo*, entirely, wholly, all: *no es del todo antipático*, he's not entirely unpleasant; quite, absolutely: *estamos decididos del todo*, we are absolutely determined; quite, really, very (muy): *está triste del todo*, he is very sad; right: *arriba del todo, abajo del todo*, right at the top, right at the bottom. || *El todo*, my all, my whole (en las charadas). || *Jugarse el todo por el todo*, V. JUGAR. || *Quien todo lo quiere todo lo pierde*, the more you want the less you get. || *Ser el todo*, to be the most important thing (cosa), to be the mastermind, to run the show (persona).
todopoderoso, sa adj./s. All-powerful, omnipotent, almighty. || *El Todopoderoso*, the Almighty (Dios).
toffee m. Toffee (pastilla de café con leche).
tofo m. MED. Tophus (nodo).
toga f. Toga (de los romanos). || Gown, robe (de magistrado).
togado, da adj. Togaed, togated (romanos). || Robed (magistrados).
— M. Gentleman of the robe, lawyer. || — Pl. *Los togados*, the gentlemen of the robe, the legal profession, the lawyers.
Togo n. pr. m. GEOGR. Togo.
toisón m. Fleece. || *Orden del Toisón de Oro*, Order of the Golden Fleece.
— OBSERV. The Golden Fleece that was captured by Jason and the Argonauts is called *vellocino de oro*.
tojal m. Furze-covered place.
tojo m. BOT. Furze.
tokai m. Tokay (vino).
Tokio n. pr. GEOGR. Tokyo.
tolanos m. pl. Short hairs on the nape of the neck.
toldar v. tr. V. ENTOLDAR.
tolderia f. *Amer.* Indian camp, Indian village.
toldero m. Salt retailer.
toldilla f. MAR. Poop deck.
toldo m. Awning (en un patio, una tienda, una calle, etc.). || Tilt, awning, canvas cover (en un carro o camión). || Sunshade (en la playa). || *Amer.* Tent, tepee (de los indios).
tole m. FIG. Hubbub, uproar, clamour [U.S., clamor]. || — FAM. *Armar un tole*, to cause uproar, to cause a commotion (causar protestas), to kick up a fuss *o* a stink (protestar). | *Tomar el tole*, to beat it (irse).
toledano, na adj./s. Toledan. || FIG. *Pasar una noche toledana*, to have *o* to spend a sleepless night.
Toledo n. pr. GEOGR. Toledo.
tolemaico, ca adj. Ptolemaic.
tolerable adj. Tolerable.
tolerancia f. Tolerance. || Tolerance, toleration: *tolerancia religiosa*, religious tolerance. || TECN. Tolerance.
tolerante adj. Tolerant.
tolerantismo m. Toleration, religious tolerance.
tolerar v. tr. To tolerate (permitir). || — *¿Cree que tolerará el peso?*, do you think it will take *o* stand *o* bear the weight? || *Mi hígado no tolera este tipo de comida*, my liver cannot take this kind of food. || *Película tolerada por la censura*, film approved by the censor. || *Tolerada para menores*, suitable for children, U-certificate (película cinematográfica). || *Tolerar demasiado a alguien*, to be too tolerant *o* lenient with s.o.
tolete m. MAR. Thole, tholepin. || *Amer.* [Short] club *o* stick, cudgel (garrote).
toletole m. FAM. Hubbub, uproar, commotion (jaleo).
tolita f. Tolite (explosivo).
Tolomeo n. pr. m. Ptolemy.
tolondro, dra adj. Scatterbrained.
— M. y f. Scatterbrain. || — M. Bump, lump, swelling (chichón).
tolondrón m. Bump, lump, swelling (chichón). || FIG. *A tolondrones*, by fits and starts.
Tolosa n. pr. GEOGR. Tolosa [Spain]. | Toulouse [France].
tolteca adj./s. Toltec.
tolueno m. QUÍM. Toluene.
tolva f. Hopper, chute.
tolvanera f. Dust storm.
tollina f. FAM. Hiding, thrashing, beating.
toma f. Taking [over], assumption: *toma de control*, assumption of control. || Taking, capture, seizure (conquista): *la toma de Granada*, the capture of Granada. || Dose (medicamentos): *una toma de quinina*, a dose of quinine. || Tap, outlet (de agua). || Inlet, intake (de aire). || Socket, plug, terminal (enchufe). || Lead, wire [U.S., cord] (cable). || CINEM. Take, shot. || *Amer.* Irrigation ditch, channel (acequia). || — *Toma de conciencia*, awareness. || *Toma de corriente*, power point, A.C. outlet, plug. || *Toma de hábito*, taking of vows. || *Toma de mando*, taking [over] *o* assumption of command. || *Toma de muestras*, sampling. || *Toma de posesión*, V. POSESIÓN. || *Toma de rapé*, pinch of snuff. || *Toma de sangre*, blood sample. || *Toma de sonido*, sound recording. || *Toma de tierra*, earth [U.S., ground] (de una antena),

landing, touchdown (de un avión), landing (de un paracaidista). || CINEM. *Toma de vistas*, shooting, filming.

tomada f. Capture, taking, seizure (captura).

tomadero m. Handle (agarradero). || Outlet, tap (de agua).

tomado, da adj. *Amer.* Drunk. || *Voz tomada*, hoarse voice.

tomador, ra adj. Taking (que toma). || Stealing, thieving (que roba). || *Amer.* Drunken (que bebe). || *Perro tomador*, retriever.
— M. y f. Taker (que toma). || Thief (ladrón). || *Amer.* Drinker, drunkard (bebedor). || — M. COM. Drawee (de una letra de cambio). || MAR. Gasket.

tomadura f. Taking (toma). || Dose (de una medicina). || MIL. Taking, capture (de una ciudad). || FAM. *Tomadura de pelo*, joke, big hoax *o* joke (burla): *fue todo una tomadura de pelo*, it was all a big hoax; daylight robbery, rip-off (precio abusivo).

tomahawk m. Tomahawk (hacha de guerra).

tomaína f. QUÍM. Ptomaine.

tomar v. tr. To take (coger con la mano). || To take (un taxi, apuntes, una curva, etc.): *tomar una foto, un baño, un pedido*, to take a photo, a bath, an order. || To catch (el autobús, etc.): *no pude tomar el tren porque llegué tarde*, I couldn't catch the train because I arrived too late. || To go by (ir en). || To take, to go by: *tomamos el camino más corto*, we took the shortest road. || To take, to accept (un regalo, etc.). || To have, to eat: *tomar el desayuno*, to have breakfast. || To have, to drink (beber): *¿qué quieres tomar?*, what would you like to drink? || MIL. To take, to capture (conquistar). || MED. To take (el pulso, la temperatura, una medicina). || To get into, to acquire: *tomar malas costumbres*, to acquire bad habits. || To take, to adopt, to make (adoptar): *tomar decisiones*, to make decisions. || To take (empezar a tener): *tomar forma*, to take shape. || To take on, to adopt (un aspecto). || To take on, to hire (contratar): *tomar un criado*, to take on a servant. || To rent, to take (alquilar): *han tomado una casa en la playa*, they have taken a house by the beach. || To take over (un negocio). || To buy, to get (comprar): *tomar las entradas*, to get the tickets. || To take: *tomar una cita de un autor*, to take a quotation from an author. || To take, to steal (robar). || To get back (recobrar). || To cover (el macho a la hembra). || — *A toma y daca*, on a give and take basis. || FAM. *Haberla tomado con alguien*, to have it in for s.o. || *Lo toma o lo deja*, take it or leave it. || FIG. *Más vale un toma que dos te daré*, a bird in the hand is worth two in the bush. || *¡Toma!*, here!, here you are!: *toma, aquí tienes el lápiz*, here, here's the pencil; fancy that! (asombro o sorpresa), no!, really? (incredulidad), take that! (tómate ésa), huh!, poo! (¡eso no es nada!), well!, so!, aha! (exclamación de entendimiento): *¡toma! ¡ahora lo comprendo!*, well! Now I understand!; you see!, I told you so! (¡ya ves!), it serves you right (tienes tu merecido), here! (para llamar un perro). || *Tomar a broma*, V. BROMA. || *Tomar afecto a*, V. AFECTO. || *Tomar algo a bien, a mal*, to take sth. well, badly. || *Tomar algo sobre sí*, to take sth. upon o.s. || *Tomar aliento*, V. ALIENTO. || *Tomar a medias*, to split, to share. || *Tomar a pecho*, to take to heart. || *Tomar asiento*, to take a seat, to sit down. || *Tomar a una persona por otra*, to take s.o. for s.o. else: *te tomé por tu hermano*, I took you for your brother. || *Tomar como ejemplo*, V. EJEMPLO. || *Tomar de la mano*, to take by the hand. || *Tomar el fresco*, to get some fresh air. || *Tomar el pecho*, to nurse, to suck. || FIG. *Tomar el pelo a uno*, to pull s.o.'s leg. || FAM. *Tomar el portante*, V. PORTANTE. || *Tomar en cuenta*, V. CUENTA. || *Tomar en serio*, to take seriously. || *Tomar estado*, to marry (casarse), to take holy orders (profesar). || *Tomar frío*, to catch a cold. || *Tomar fuerzas*, to get back *o* to recover one's strength. || *Tomar la delantera*, V. DELANTERA. || *Tomar la palabra*, to speak, to take the floor (hablar), to take [s.o.] at his word (creer). || *Tomar las aguas*, to take the waters. || *Tomar las armas*, V. ARMA. || FIG. y FAM. *Tomarlas* or *tomarla con uno*, to pick on s.o., to have a go at s.o. (tomar tirria, criticar). | *Tomar las de Villadiego*, to beat it, to take to one's heels. || *Tomar las lecciones*, to make [s.o.] recite his lessons. || *Tomar medidas*, to take measures *o* steps. || *Tomar nota*, to take note. || *Tomar odio a*, to get to hate. || *Tomar partido por*, to side with, to take sides with. || *Tomar por*, to take for: *¿por quién me tomas?*, who do you take me for? || *Tomar por escrito*, to take down, to write down. || *Tomar prestado*, to borrow. || *Tomar sangre*, to take blood. || *Tomar tiempo*, to take time (requerir tiempo). || AVIAC. *Tomar tierra*, to land. || FAM. *¡Tómate ésa!*, take that!
— V. intr. To turn, to go: *tome a la derecha*, turn right. || To take (una planta, un injerto, etc.). || *Amer.* To drink (beber). || FAM. *Tomar y*, to go and, to up and: *tomó y se fue*, he upped and left, he went and left.
— V. pr. To take: *tomarse unas vacaciones*, to take a holiday; *tomarse la libertad de*, to take the liberty to (con infinitivo) *o* of (con gerundio). || To eat (comer). || To drink (beber). || To take (medicina). || To get rusty (cubrirse de moho). || To go bad (vino). || — *Tomarse el trabajo* o *la molestia de*, to take the trouble to. || *Tomárselo con calma*, to take it easy. || *Tomarse por alguien*, to think one is somebody.

Tomás n. pr. m. Thomas. || — *Santo Tomás de Aquino*, Saint Thomas Aquinas. || *Tomás Moro*, Thomas More.

tomatada f. Fried tomatoes, *pl.*

tomatal m. Tomato patch *o* bed *o* field.

tomatazo m. Blow with a tomato. || *Le recibieron a tomatazos*, the people threw rotten tomatoes at him.

tomate m. Tomato (fruto y planta). || FAM. Hole, spud (en las medias, etc.). || — FIG. *Colorado como un tomate*, as red as a beetroot. || *Salsa de tomate*, tomato sauce (casera), ketchup, catsup (embotellada). || FAM. *Tener tomate*, to be difficult *o* awkward *o* bothersome: *este trabajo tiene mucho tomate*, this job is really difficult.

tomatera f. Tomato (planta). || FAM. *Tener tomatera*, to put on airs.

tomatero, ra m. y f. Tomato seller (vendedor) *o* grower (cultivador). || *Pollo tomatero*, V. POLLO.

tomavistas m. inv. Cinecamera [U.S., movie camera]. || Television camera.

tómbola f. Tombola.

tomillar m. Field of thyme.

tomillo m. Thyme (planta).

tomineja f. o **tominejo** m. Hummingbird.

tomismo m. REL. y FIL. Thomism.

tomista adj. REL. y FIL. Thomistic, Thomist.
— M. y f. REL. y FIL. Thomist.

tomístico, ca adj. Thomistic.

tomiza f. Esparto rope.

tomo m. Volume (de un libro). || FIG. Size (tamaño). | Importance (importancia). || FIG. *De tomo y lomo*, out-and-out, utter, first rate: *es un sinvergüenza de tomo y lomo*, he's an out-and-out cad.

tomógrafo m. MED. Scanner.

ton m. *Sin ton ni son*, without rhyme or reason.

tonada f. Song, tune (canción). || Tune (música). || *Amer.* Accent (dejo).

tonadilla f. Ditty (canción). || "Tonadilla" [short musical piece popular in the 18th century].

tonadillero, ra m. y f. Writer of popular songs. || — F. Songstress, singer [of "tonadillas"].

tonal adj. MÚS. Tonal.

tonalidad f. Tonality. || RAD. *Control de tonalidad*, tone control.

tonante adj. Thundering.

tonar v. intr. To thunder.

tonca adj. f. BOT. *Haba tonca*, tonka bean.

tondino m. ARQ. Astragal.

tondo m. ARQ. Round moulding (mediacaña).

tonel m. Barrel, cask, keg (cuba y contenido). || AVIAC. Barrel roll (acrobacia). || FIG. *Juan está como un tonel*, John is ever so fat.

tonelada f. Ton (peso). || MAR. Ton (medida): *tonelada de arqueo*, register ton. || Barrels, *pl.*, casks, *pl.* (toneles). || *Tonelada larga, métrica, corta*, long, metric, short ton.

tonelaje m. Tonnage (de un navío): *tonelaje bruto*, gross tonnage.

tonelería f. Barrelmaking, cooperage (fabricación). || Barrel shop, cooperage, coopery (taller). || Barrels, *pl.*, casks, *pl.* (toneles).

tonelero, ra adj. Barrel, cask.
— M. Cooper, barrelmaker.

tonelete m. Small barrel, keg, cask (tonel). || Child's short skirt (traje de niño). || Piece of armour protecting the body between the waist and the knees (armadura). || Short silk skirt [worn by men] (vestidura antigua). || Ballet skirt, tutu (faldilla de bailarina).

tonga f. Layer (capa). || *Amer.* Pile, heap. | Task, job, work (tarea).

tongada f. Layer (capa).

tongo m. DEP. Bribery [in sports]. || — DEP. *Aquí hay tongo*, it's been fixed *o* rigged, it's a fix. | *Hubo tongo en el combate*, the fight was fixed *o* rigged.

tongonearse v. pr. *Amer.* V. CONTONEARSE.

tongoneo m. *Amer.* V. CONTONEO.

tonicidad f. Tonicity.

tónico, ca adj. Tonic, accented, stressed: *sílaba tónica*, accented syllable. || MED. y MÚS. Tonic.
— M. Tonic: *la quina es un tónico*, quinine is a tonic. || *Tónico cardiaco*, cardiotonic. || — F. MÚS. Tonic. || FIG. Tendency, trend: *la tónica general*, the general tendency; *la tónica de la Bolsa*, the trend of the Stock Market. || FIG. *Marcar la tónica*, to set the pace *o* the trend.

tonificación f. Toning up, invigoration.

tonificante adj. Invigorating, tonic.

tonificar v. tr. MED. To tone up, to invigorate.

tonillo m. Singsong, monotone (tono monótono). || Accent (dejo). || Sarcastic tone (retintín).

tonina f. Tunny, tuna (atún). || Dolphin (delfín).

Tonkín n. pr. m. GEOGR. Tonkin.

tono m. Tone (de voz, color, etc.): *su tono de voz*, his tone of voice; *el tono de una carta*, the tone of a letter. || MÚS. Tone (de un sonido). | Key: *tono mayor, menor*, major, minor key. | Pitch (altura). | Key (tecla). | Slide (vara). || ANAT. y MED. Tone (de un músculo). || FIG. Class, social standing (de una familia, etc.). | Conceit (presunción). | Tone (carácter). || FAM. Energy (energía). || — *A este tono*, like this, this way. || *A tono con*, in tune *o* harmony with. || FIG. *Bajar el tono*, to lower one's voice, to tone down.

| *Bajarle el tono a uno*, to take s.o. down a peg. | *Cambiar de tono*, to change one's tune *o* one's tone. | *Dar buen tono*, to give tone *o* class *o* prestige (dar prestigio). | *Dar el tono*, to set the tone *o* standard. | *Darse tono*, to put on airs. | *De buen tono*, elegant, fashionable, stylish. | *De mal tono*, common, vulgar. | *Decir en todos los tonos*, to tell [sth. to s.o.] time and again. || *En tono airado*, in an angry tone [of voice]. || FIG. *Estar a tono con*, to be in proportion with: *paga un alquiler que no está a tono con sus ingresos*, the rent he pays is out of proportion with his income; to be on a level with (estar al mismo nivel), to be on the same wavelength as (entenderse muy bien con otra persona). | *Fuera de tono*, inappropriate, out of place. | *Mudar de tono*, to change one's tune *o* one's tone. | *Ponerse a tono con alguien*, to adapt o.s. to s.o. | *Salida de tono*, v. SALIDA. || *Subir* or *subirse de tono*, to warm up (una conversación), to become louder (la voz, etc.), to become arrogant *o* haughty (adoptar un aire arrogante).

Tonquín n. pr. m. GEOGR. Tonkin.

tonquinés, esa adj./s. Tonkinese.

tonsila f. ANAT. Tonsil (amígdala).

tonsilar adj. ANAT. Tonsillar.

tonsilectomía f. MED. Tonsillectomy.

tonsilitis f. MED. Tonsillitis.

tonsura f. Tonsure. || *Prima tonsura*, tonsure (ceremonia).

tonsurado adj. m. Tonsured (clérigo).
— M. Cleric, priest.

tonsurar v. tr. To tonsure (un clérigo). || To cut (el pelo). || To shear (la lana).

tontada f. V. TONTERÍA.

tontaina o **tontainas** adj. FAM. Foolish, silly.
— M. y f. FAM. Fool, idiot.

tontamente adv. Foolishly, stupidly.

tontarrón, ona adj. FAM. Idiotic, stupid.
— M. y f. FAM. Blockhead, numbskull, fool.

tontear v. intr. To act the fool, to fool about (hacer tonterías). || To talk nonsense (decir tonterías). || To flirt (flirtear).

tontedad o **tontera** f. Foolishness, silliness.

tontería f. Foolishness, stupidity, idiocy (cualidad). || Silly thing (acción, dicho). || Stupid remark (dicho). || FIG. Trifle, foolish thing (nadería): *gastarse el dinero en tonterías*, to spend one's money on trifles. || — *Decir tonterías*, to talk nonsense. || *¡Déjate de tonterías!*, don't be stupid! (al hablar), stop messing *o* fooling about! (al actuar). || *Dejémonos de tonterías*, let's be serious. || *Hacer tonterías*, to mess about, to fool about. || *He hecho una tontería*, I've done a stupid thing. || *Lo compré por una tontería*, I got it for next to nothing. || *No es ninguna tontería*, it's serious (va en serio), it's not bad at all (no está nada mal).

tontillo m. Farthingale (de una falda).

tontina f. Tontine (asociación). || FAM. Fool. || FAM. *No seas tontina*, don't be silly.

tontito m. Maternity dress (prenda de maternidad). || Smock (bata corta).

tontivano, na adj. Pretentious, conceited, foppish.
— M. y f. Fop.

tonto, ta adj. Foolish, stupid, silly, dumb, idiotic: *una idea tonta*, a foolish idea. || *Es lo bastante tonto para creerlo*, he's fool enough to believe it.
— M. y f. Fool, dolt, idiot: *¡qué tonto!*, what a fool!; *¡tonto tú!*, you're the fool! || — M. Clown (payaso). || — *A tontas y a locas*, haphazardly, any old how. || *Hablar a tontas y a locas*, to talk without rhyme or reason, to talk foolishly. || *Hacer el tonto*, to act the fool (hacer el idiota), to flirt (tontear). || *Hacerse el tonto*, to play *o* to act dumb. | *Hasta los tontos lo saben*, any fool knows that. || *¡No tan tonto!*, he's not as stupid as you think *o* as he looks. || *Ponerse tonto*, to do [sth.] too much (exagerar), to flirt (tontear), to put on airs (presumir). || *¡Qué tonto es!*, what a fool he is! || *Ser tonto de capirote* or *de remate* or *ser más tonto que Abundio* or *una mata de habas*, to be a prize idiot, to be as mad as a hatter *o* as daft as a brush.

tontuelo, la adj. FAM. Naïve, silly.
— M. y f. FAM. Little fool, silly thing (persona).

tontuna o **tontura** f. Foolishness, silliness (tontería).

toña f. Tipcat (juego). || Tipcat, cat, catty (palo). || FAM. Blow (golpe). || FAM. *Coger una toña*, to get drunk *o* plastered *o* canned.

¡top! interj. Stop!, whoa!

topacio m. Topaz.

topada f. Butt (topetada).

topar v. tr. To butt (los carneros). || To bump against (tropezar). || To run into, to bump into (encontrar a alguien). || To come across, to find (encontrar algo). || To run into, to bump into (chocar). || FIG. To run into, to encounter (dificultades). || MAR. To butt (dos maderos). || *Amer.* To try out (dos gallos).
— V. intr. To butt (los carneros). || To take a bet (en el juego). || FIG. To work (salir bien): *lo dije a ver si topaba*, I said it to see if it would work. || FIG. *La dificultad topa en esto*, this is the difficulty *o* the trouble *o* the problem.
— V. pr. To meet (encontrarse). || To butt [each other] (los carneros). || *Toparse con*, to encounter, to run into, to bump into.

tope m. Butt, end (extremo). || Bump, knock, bang (golpe). || Butt (con la cabeza). || Stop, check, catch (mecanismo). || Buffer (de locomatora). || Buffer stop [U.S., bumping post] (de línea férrea). || Bumper (de tranvía). || Bumper guard, overrider (de coche). || FIG. Difficulty, snag, rub (obstáculo): *ahí está el tope*, there's the rub. | Limit: *poner tope a sus ambiciones*, to put a limit to one's ambitions. | Quarrel (riña). | Scuffle (reyerta). || MAR. Masthead (del mastelero). | Butt-end of a plank (extremo de un tablón). | Topman (marinero de vigía). || *Amer.* Simulated cock fight (pelea de gallos). || — *A* or *al tope*, end to end. || *De tope a tope*, from end to end. || FIG. *Estar hasta los topes*, to be loaded to the gunwales (un barco), to be crammed full (estar muy lleno), to be fed up *o* browned off (estar harto). || *Hasta el tope*, to the brim. || FIG. *Llegar al tope*, to reach one's limit. | *Rebasar el tope*, to go too far *o* beyond the limits. || *Repostar a tope*, to fill up, to fill to the brim (gasolina). || *Tope de puerta*, doorstop. || *Tope de retención*, stop.
— Adj. Top, maximum: *precio tope*, top price. || *Fecha tope*, deadline, closing date.

topear v. tr. *Amer.* To unhorse.

topetada f. Butt (de un carnero). || Butt, bump (con la cabeza).

topetar v. tr. e intr. To butt. || FIG. To bump into.

topetazo m. Butt (de los carneros). || Butt, bump (con la cabeza). || Crash, bump, bang, collision (de dos cosas). || *Darse un topetazo*, to bump *o* to bang *o* to crash into each other (dos cosas).

topetón m. V. TOPETAZO.

tópico, ca adj. MED. Topical, local. || Commonplace, trite.
— M. MED. External local application. || Cliché, commonplace, trite saying (lugar común). || *Amer.* Topic, subject (tema de conversación).

topinambur m. BOT. Jerusalem artichoke.

topo m. ZOOL. Mole (mamífero). || FIG. y FAM. Awkward person, blunderer (torpe). || *Amer.* League and a half (medida). | Large pin (alfiler). || FIG. y FAM. *Ver menos que un topo*, to be as blind as a bat.

topocho, cha adj. FAM. *Amer.* Chubby (rechoncho).

topografía f. Topography (configuración). || Surveying, topography (levantamiento de planos).

topográfico, ca adj. Topographic, topographical.

topógrafo m. Topographer. || Surveyor (agrimensor).

topolino m. y f. Teenager, youngster (joven). || — M. Wedge-heeled shoe (zapato).

topología f. Topology.

toponimia f. Toponymy, study of place-names (ciencia). || Place-names, *pl.* (nombres).

toponímico, ca adj. Toponymic, toponymical.

topónimo m. Toponym, place-name.

toque m. Touch: *toque de varita mágica*, touch of the magic wand; *dale un toque*, give him a touch. || Peal, pealing, ringing (de campanas). || Blare, blaring, sound, sounding (de trompetas, etc.). || Hoot, blast (de sirena, claxon). || Beat, beating (de tambores). || ARTES. Touch (pincelada ligera). || Test (ensayo de metales preciosos). || FIG. Warning (advertencia). | Blow (golpe), tap (golpecito). || DEP. Touch (en esgrima). || MIL. Bugle call. || *Amer.* Turn (turno). || — FIG. *Dar el toque de alarma*, to sound the alarm. | *Dar el último toque a*, to put the finishing touch to. | *Dar otro toque a un cliente*, to have another attempt at convincing a client. | *Darse un toque*, to see to one's makeup. | *Dar un toque a uno*, to put s.o. to the test (probar), to take s.o. to task (llamar al orden), to sound s.o. out (sondear). || MED. *Dar unos toques en la garganta*, to paint one's throat. || *Piedra de toque*, touchstone. || *Toque de alarma*, alarm signal (rebato), warning (aviso). || FIG. *Toque de atención*, warning, warning note. || DEP. *Toque de balón*, ball control. || *Toque de diana*, reveille. || *Toque de difuntos*, knell, passing bell (de campanas), last post (de trompeta). || *Toque del alba*, Angelus bell. || ARTES. *Toque de luz*, highlight. || *Toque de oración*, Angelus bell, call to prayer. || *Toque de queda*, curfew [bell]. || *Toque de timbre*, ring of a bell. || *Último toque*, final *o* finishing touch.

toquetear v. tr. FAM. To fiddle with, to finger, to play about with. || MÚS. FAM. To mess about on (un instrumento). || FAM. To pet, to caress, to fondle (a una persona).
— V. intr. FAM. To rummage.

toqueteo m. FAM. Handling, fiddling, touching (de una cosa). | Petting, fondling (de una persona).

toqui m. *Amer.* Araucan Indian chief.

toquilla f. Knitted shawl (prenda de punto). || Kerchief, headscarf (pañuelo). || Gauze *o* ribbon adornment for a man's hat (adorno antiguo). || *Amer.* Straw hat (sombrero de paja). | Low palm tree (palmera).

tora f. Torah (de los israelitas). || Ancient tax (tributo). || BOT. Nutgall (agalla).

torácico, ca adj. ANAT. Thoracic. || *Caja* or *cavidad torácica*, thoracic *o* chest cavity.

torada f. Drove *o* herd of bulls.

toral adj. Main, principal: *arco toral*, main arch.
— M. TECN. Mould [U.S., mold] (molde). | Copper bar (barra de cobre).

tórax m. ANAT. Thorax.

torbellino m. Whirlwind (viento). || Dust cloud (de polvo). || FIG. Whirl, turmoil, swirl (de cosas). |

Whirlwind (persona). || FIG. *Irrumpir como un torbellino*, to burst in like a whirlwind.
torcaz o **torcazo, za** adj./s.f. *Paloma torcaz*, ringdove, wood pigeon.
torcecuello m. Wryneck (ave).
torcedero, ra adj. Twisted.
— M. Twister (instrumento).
torcedor, ra adj. Twisting.
— M. y f. Twister (que tuerce lana, seda, etc.). || — M. Spindle (huso). || FIG. Torment, torture (tormento). || *Amer*. Tobacco twister.
torcedura f. Twist, twisting. || MED. Sprain, twist, strain. || Bad wine (vino malo).
torcer* v. tr. To twist: *torcer una cuerda, el brazo de uno*, to twist a rope, s.o.'s arm. || To change (desviar): *torcer el rumbo*, to change course; *torcer el curso de un razonamiento*, to change one's line of reasoning. || To turn, to round (dar la vuelta): *le vi al torcer la esquina*, I saw him as I turned the corner. || To bend (doblar). || To warp (alabear). || To move [round], to move slightly (desplazar ligeramente). || To slant (un cuadro). || FIG. To twist, to distort: *torcer el sentido de una frase*, to distort the meaning of a sentence. | To bend (la justicia, la verdad). | To pervert (pervertir). | To corrupt (corromper). | To screw up, to contort (la cara). || MED. To twist, to sprain (un miembro). | To strain, to pull (un músculo). || DEP. To spin (una pelota). || — FIG. y FAM. *Dar su brazo a torcer*, to give in. || *Torcer el gesto* or *el semblante*, to grimace, to pull a face. || *Torcer los ojos*, to squint (bizquear).
— V. intr. To turn: *el camino, el coche tuerce a la derecha*, the road, the car turns [to the] right. || To swerve (desviarse bruscamente).
— V. pr. To twist (una cuerda, etc.). || To bend (doblarse). || To become slanted (ladearse). || To warp (alabearse la madera). || To buckle, to bend (el metal). || To screw up, to contort (la cara). || FIG. To go sour (el vino). | To curdle (la leche). | To take a turn for the worse (la salud). | To go astray, to turn bad: *este muchacho se ha torcido*, this boy has gone astray. | To go awry, to go wrong (frustrarse). | To take a sudden turn (los acontecimientos, la historia). | To be corrupted, to go crooked (un juez). || — FIG. *Se me ha torcido la suerte*, my luck has gone bad, my luck has turned [for the worse]. || *Se me torció el tobillo*, I sprained *o* I twisted my ankle. || *Torcerse un músculo*, to pull a muscle.
torcida f. Wick (mecha). || Fans, *pl.* (partidarios).
torcidamente adv. Crookedly, wryly. || Deviously (con artimaña).
torcido, da adj. Twisted. || Twisting, winding (camino). || Twisted, sprained, strained (un miembro). || Crooked, slanted (oblicuo). || Buckled, bent (metal, rueda). || Warped (madera). || Crossed (ojos). || FIG. Twisted (mente). | Devious, crooked (tramposo). | Hypocritical. || *Llevas la corbata torcida*, your tie is crooked.
— M. Roll of candied fruits (frutas en dulce). || Bad wine (vino malo). || Strong silk thread (hebra de seda).
torcijón m. Twisting (retorcimiento). || MED. Stomach cramp (retortijón). || VET. Gripes, *pl.*
torcimiento m. Twist, twisting. || MED. Sprain, twist, strain.
torcionario m. Torturer.
tórculo m. Screw press.
tordillo, lla adj. Dapple-grey (caballo).
— M. y f. Dapple-grey horse.
tordo, da adj. Grey, gray (gris). || Dapple-grey (caballo).
— M. y f. Dapple-grey horse (caballo). || Thrush (ave). || — M. *Amer.* Starling (estornino).
toreador, ra m. (P.us.) Toreador, bullfighter.

— OBSERV. The usual term in Spanish is *torero*.

torear v. tr. TAUR. To fight (lidiar un toro). || FIG. To avoid, to dodge, to sidestep (evitar algo o a alguien). | To handle well (manejar bien). | To put [s.o.] off, to keep [s.o.] at bay (entretener). | To confuse [with contradictions]. | To banter, to mock, to tease (burlarse). || *Amer.* To goad (azuzar). || — *Llevar el toro toreado*, to have complete control of the bull. || FIG. y FAM. *No se deja torear por nadie*, he doesn't let anyone mess him about. || *Toro toreado*, vicious bull.
— V. intr. TAUR. To fight bulls (lidiar toros). || To fight: *¡qué bien ha toreado hoy!*, he really fought well today. || *Amer.* To bark (ladrar). || *Romero toreaba mejor que nadie*, Romero was the best bullfighter of them all.
toreo m. TAUR. Bullfighting (arte y acción). || FIG. y FAM. Banter (burla). || FIG. y FAM. *¡Se acabó el toreo!*, that's enough!, no more fooling around! (se acabó la burla).
torera f. Bolero (chaquetilla). || FIG. y FAM. *Saltarse algo a la torera*, to completely ignore sth.
torería f. Bullfighters, *pl.*, bullfighting circles, *pl.*
torero, ra adj. TAUR. Bullfighting.
— M. TAUR. Bullfighter.
torete m. Young bull (toro joven).
toribio m. FAM. Simple Simon, simpleton (tonto). || — Pl. Reformatory, *sing.* (para niños indisciplinados).
tórico, ca adj. Toric.
toril m. TAUR. Bullpen [where bulls are kept before a bullfight].
torillo m. Dowel (espiga). || ARQ. Torus (moldura). || Blenny (pez).
torio m. QUÍM. Thorium.
torito m. Small bull.
tormenta f. Storm. || FIG. Storm (riña, discusión, etc.): *la tormenta ha pasado ya*, the storm is over now. | Misfortune (adversidad, desgracia). || — *Hacer frente a la tormenta*, to brave the storm. || FIG. *Una tormenta en un vaso de agua*, a storm in a teacup.
tormento m. Torture, torment (dolor). || Torture (del reo). || FIG. Torment, anguish (angustia). || — *Dar tormento*, to torture, to put to torture (a un reo), to torment (molestar). || *Estas botas son un tormento*, these boots are agony.
tormentoso, sa adj. Stormy.
torna f. Return (vuelta). || Weir (presa). || — *Cuando se vuelvan las tornas*, when the tables turn, when our luck changes. || *Volverle a uno las tornas*, to give s.o. tit for tat (corresponder uno al proceder de otro), to turn the tables on s.o. (hacer sufrir a otro lo que uno ha sufrido).
tornaboda f. Day after the wedding.
tornadizo, za adj. Changeable, fickle (cambiadizo). || Renegade (renegado).
— M. y f. Turncoat.
tornado m. Tornado (huracán).
tornaguía f. Receipt.
tornamiento m. Change, turn.
tornapunta f. Prop, stay (puntal).
tornar v. tr. To return, to give back (devolver). || To turn, to make (volver): *la tinta tornó el agua negra*, the ink made the water black. || To turn, to change, to transform (convertir): *tornar una cosa en otra*, to turn one thing into another.
— V. intr. To return, to go back (regresar). || To begin again: *tornó a hablar*, he began to talk again. || *Tornar en sí*, to come to, to regain consciousness (volver en sí).
— V. pr. To turn, to become (ponerse): *el cielo se tornó azul*, the sky became blue. || To return (regresar). || *Tornarse en*, to turn into *o* to, to become.
tornasol m. BOT. Sunflower. || Litmus (materia colorante): *papel de tornasol*, litmus paper. || Iridescence (viso).
tornasolado, da adj. Iridescent (color). || Shot (tejido): *seda tornasolada*, shot silk.
tornasolar v. tr. To make iridescent.
— V. intr. To become iridescent, to look iridescent.
tornatrás m. y f. Throwback.
tornavía f. Turntable.
tornavoz m. Sounding board.
torneado, da adj. Turned (hecho a torno). || FIG. Shapely, nicely rounded (cuerpo).
— M. TECN. Turning [on the lathe].
torneador m. Turner, lathe operator (tornero). || Jouster (en un torneo).
torneadura f. Shaving (viruta). || TECN. Turning [on the lathe].
tornear v. tr. To turn [on the lathe]: *tornear una pata de mesa*, to turn a table leg.
— V. intr. To revolve, to spin, to go round (dar vueltas). || To tourney, to joust (en un torneo).
torneo m. HIST. Tourney, joust, tournament. || Tournament, competition (competición).
tornera f. Nun in attendance at the revolving window of a convent.
tornería f. Turnery (arte y taller).
tornero m. Turner, lathe operator (que hace obras en el torno). || Errand boy, messenger (recadero de monjas).
tornillo m. Screw (rosca). || Small lathe (torno pequeño). || — FIG. y FAM. *Apretarle a uno los tornillos*, to put the screws *o* the pressure on s.o. || MIL. *Hacer tornillo*, to desert. || FIG. y FAM. *Le falta un tornillo* or *tiene flojos los tornillos*, he has a screw loose. || *Tornillo de banco*, vice [U.S., vise], clamp. || *Tornillo de mordazas*, jaw vice. || *Tornillo de orejas*, thumbscrew. || *Tornillo sin fin*, worm gear, endless screw.
torniquete m. Turnstile (barra giratoria). || MED. Tourniquet.
torniscón m. FAM. Slap (golpe dado en la cara). | Pinch (pellizco).
torno m. Lathe (máquina herramienta): *labrar a torno*, to turn on the lathe. || Winch, windlass, winding drum (para levantar pesos). || Revolving window (en los conventos). || Revolving food stand (de comedor). || Bend, turn (recodo). || Turn, revolution (movimiento circular). || — *En torno a*, around, round, about (alrededor), with regard to, as far as [sth.] is concerned, about (en cuanto a). || *Torno de alfarero*, potter's wheel. || *Torno de banco*, vice [U.S., vise], clamp. || *Torno de hilar*, spinning wheel. || *Torno elevador*, winch.
toro m. ZOOL. Bull: *toro bravo* or *de lidia*, fighting bull. || ARQ. Torus (moldura). || ASTR. Taurus (Tauro). || MAT. Tore, torus. || — Pl. Bullfights, bullfighting, *sing.*: *¿le gustan los toros?*, do you like bullfights? || Bullfight, *sing.* (corrida): *ir a los toros*, to go to a *o* to the bullfight. || Bullfighting, *sing.* (arte, negocio, etc.). || — FIG. *Coger al toro por los*

cuernos, to take the bull by the horns. | *Echarle* or *soltarle a uno el toro*, to give s.o. a piece of one's mind (decir las cuatro verdades). | *Estar hecho un toro*, to be a strong *o* a strapping lad. | *Ir al toro*, to get to the point. | *¡Otro toro!*, let's change the subject. | *Ser fuerte como un toro*, to be as strong as an ox. | *Ser un toro corrido*, to be nobody's fool, to be an old hand, to be no easy mark. || *Toro de fuego*, fireworks on a bull-shaped frame. || FIG. *Ver los toros desde la barrera*, to sit on the fence, to be an onlooker.
toronja f. Seville orange, bitter orange (naranja). || Grapefruit (pomelo).
toronjil m. o **toronjina** f. Lemon balm.
toronjo m. Seville orange tree, bitter orange tree. || Grapefruit tree.
torozón m. VET. Gripes, *pl.*
torpe adj. Awkward, clumsy (falto de habilidad). || Ungainly (desgarbado). || Stupid, dim (necio). || Slow, heavy, sluggish, torpid (movimientos). || Slow (en comprender). || Lewd, indecent: *torpes instintos*, lewd instincts. || Crude, obscene (conducta). || — FIG. y FAM. *Más torpe que un arado*, as thick as two short planks. || *Torpe de oídos*, hard of hearing.
torpedeamiento m. Torpedoing.
torpedear v. tr. To torpedo.
torpedeo m. Torpedoing.
torpedero m. Torpedo boat (barco).
torpedista m. Torpedoist, torpedoman.
torpedo m. MIL. Torpedo. || ZOOL. Electric ray, torpedo (raya).
torpemente adv. Clumsily, awkwardly (sin destreza). || Heavily, sluggishly (pesadamente). || Slowly (lentamente).
torpeza f. Clumsiness, awkwardness (falta de destreza). || Ungainliness (desgarbo). || Slowness, stupidity, dimness (necedad). || Heaviness, torpidity (pesadez). || Crudeness, obscenity (obscenidad). || *Cometer una torpeza*, to make a blunder.
torpón, ona adj. Very clumsy *o* stupid.
torpor m. Torpor.
torques f. Torque (collar antiguo).
torrado m. Toasted chick-pea.
torrar v. tr. To toast (tostar).
torre f. Tower: *la torre Eiffel*, the Eiffel tower; *la Torre de Londres*, the Tower of London. || Castle, rook (ajedrez). || Bell tower (campanario). || Turret (de buque de guerra). || Villa, country house (quinta). || ELECTR. Pylon (poste). || — *Torre albarrana* or *flanqueante*, turret. || *Torre de Babel*, Tower of Babel. || *Torre de control* or *de mando*, control tower (aeropuerto), conning tower (portaviones). || *Torre de extracción*, derrick, oil derrick (de petróleo), headgear (de una mina). || *Torre del homenaje*, donjon, keep. || FIG. *Torre de marfil*, ivory tower (aislamiento). || *Torre de perforación*, derrick. || MAR. *Torre de vigía*, crow's nest.
torrecilla f. Small tower.
torrefacción f. Torrefaction, roasting.
torrefactar v. tr. To torrefy, to torrify (en general). || To roast (el café).
torrefacto, ta adj. Torrefied, roasted.
torrefactor m. Roaster.
torrencial adj. Torrential: *lluvia torrencial*, torrential rain.
torrente m. Torrent (curso de agua). || ANAT. Bloodstream (la sangre). || FIG. Flood, torrent (abundancia): *un torrente de injurias*, a flood of insults. || — *A torrentes*, in torrents. || *Llover a torrentes*, to rain torrents, to rain cats and dogs.
torrentera f. Course of a torrent (cauce).
torrentoso, sa adj. Torrential.
torreón m. Large fortified tower.
torrero m. Lighthouse keeper (de faro). || Keeper of a villa (de una casa).
torreta f. ARQ. Turret. || Conning tower (en los submarinos). || AVIAT. MAR. y MIL. Turret (de un tanque, etc.).
torreznada f. Dish of fried bacon.
torreznero, ra adj. Idle, loafing (holgazán).
— M. y f. Loafer, idler (holgazán).
torrezno m. Fried bacon.
tórrido, da adj. Torrid.
torrija f. Bread soaked in milk and egg and fried [U.S., French toast].
torsión f. Torsion. || TECN. Torsion: *barra de torsión*, torsion bar. || — FÍS. *Balanza de torsión*, torsion balance. | *Momento de torsión*, torque.
torso m. ANAT. Torso. || ARTES. Bust.
torta f. CULIN. Cake, tart. || FIG. Cake (masa aplastada). || FAM. Slap, wallop (bofetada). | Drunkenness (borrachera). || IMPR. Fount, font (paquete de caracteres). | Form kept for distribution. || AGR. Oil cake (tortada). || *Amer.* Sandwich. || — FIG. *La torta costó un pan*, it was more trouble than it was worth. | *Ni torta*, not a thing: *no ve ni torta*, he can't see a thing. | *Pegarse una torta*, to come a cropper (caerse, chocar). | *Son tortas y pan pintado*, that's child's play (no es difícil), that's nothing (no es nada). || FAM. *Tener una torta*, to be drunk *o* sozzled *o* sloshed.
tortada f. Meat *o* chicken pie (pastel). || AGR. Oil cake.
tortazo m. FAM. Hard slap, wallop (bofetada). || — FIG. y FAM. *Pegarse un tortazo*, to come a cropper (caerse), to have a crash (en coche). | *Pegarse un tortazo contra un árbol*, to bash *o* to crash into a tree.
tortedad f. Blindness in one eye.
tortícolis or **torticolis** m. o f. Stiff neck [U.S., wryneck], crick in one's neck, torticollis: *tener tortícolis*, to have a stiff neck.

— OBSERV. This word is generally used in the feminine.

tortilla f. Omelet, omelette: *tortilla de jamón, de patatas*, ham, potato omelet; *tortilla a la francesa*, French omelet. || *Amer.* Tortilla, corn cake. || — FIG. *Hacerse una tortilla*, to be flattened *o* squashed flat. | *Hacer tortilla a*, to flatten. | *Se ha vuelto la tortilla*, the tables have turned, the boot is on the other foot (la situación ha cambiado).
tortillero, ra m. y f. Tortilla maker *o* seller. || — F. POP. Lesbian.
tortita f. Pancake.
tórtola f. Turtledove (pájaro).
tortolito, ta adj. Inexperienced.
tórtolo m. Male turtledove. || — Pl. FIG. Lovebirds (pareja enamorada).
tortuga f. Tortoise (de tierra). || Turtle (de mar). || MIL. Testudo. || FIG. *Andar a paso de tortuga*, to walk at a snail's pace.
tortuosidad f. Tortuosity.
tortuoso, sa adj. Tortuous, winding: *una carretera tortuosa*, a tortuous road. || FIG. Devious, tortuous: *métodos tortuosos*, tortuous means.
tortura f. Torture (tormento). || FIG. Torment, torture, anguish (angustia).
torturar v. tr. To torture.
— V. pr. To torture o.s. (atormentarse).
torus m. ANAT. Torus.
torva f. Snow storm (nieve). || Rain storm *o* squall (lluvia).
torviscal m. Field of spurge flax.
torvisco m. BOT. Spurge flax.
torvo, va adj. Grim, fierce: *mirada torva*, grim look.
tory adj./s.m. Tory (conservador).
torzadillo m. Fine silk twist.
torzal m. Silk twist (hilo de seda). || Twine, twist (de cualquier tipo de hebras). || *Amer.* Leather lasso.
torzón m. VET. Gripes, *pl.*
tos f. Cough: *tener tos*, to have a cough. || Coughing: *su tos no me dejó dormir*, his coughing prevented me from sleeping. || — *Acceso de tos*, coughing fit *o* spell *o* bout. || MED. *Tos ferina*, whooping cough, hooping cough.
tosca f. Tufa, tuff (piedra).
Toscana n. pr. f. GEOGR. Tuscany.
toscano, na adj./s. Tuscan. || — M. Tuscan (dialecto).
tosco, ca adj. Rustic, crude: *una silla tosca*, a rustic chair. || Rough, coarse: *tela tosca*, coarse cloth. || FIG. Uncouth, crude (persona).
tosedor, ra adj. Coughing.
toser v. intr. To cough. || — FIG. y FAM. *A mí nadie me tose*, no one pushes me around, no one tells me what to do. | *No hay quien le tosa*, nobody can compete with him.
tósigo m. Poison. || FIG. Grief, sorrow (pena).
tosigoso, sa adj. Poisoned (envenenado). || Coughing (que padece tos).
tosquedad f. Coarseness, crudeness, roughness.
tostada f. Piece *o* slice of toast. || *Amer.* Nuisance, bore (lata). || — Pl. Toast: *¿cuántas tostadas quieres?*, how much toast do you want? || — FIG. y FAM. *Dar* or *pegar la tostada a uno*, to trick *o* to cheat s.o., to put one over on s.o. | *Olerse la tostada*, to smell a rat.
tostadero m. *Tostadero de café*, coffee roaster.
tostado, da adj. Roasted (el café). || Toasted (el pan). || FIG. Tanned, brown (la tez). | Brown (color).
— M. Roasting (del café). || Toasting (del pan). || FIG. Tan (de la piel). || *Amer.* Toasted maize (maíz).
tostador, ra adj. Roasting (el café, etc.). || Toasting (el pan).
— M. y f. Roaster. || Toaster. || — M. Roaster (de café). || Toaster (de pan).
tostadura f. Roasting (del café). || Toasting (del pan).
tostar* v. tr. To roast (el café, etc.). || To toast (el pan). || CULIN. To brown. || FIG. To roast, to burn (calentar demasiado). | To tan, to brown (la piel). | To beat, to tan, to give a beating *o* a hiding (dar una paliza).
— V. pr. FIG. To tan, to turn brown (ponerse moreno). || To roast (el café, etc.). || To toast (el pan).
tostón m. Toasted chick-pea (torrado). || Crouton (pan frito). || Toast soaked in oil (pan empapado en aceite). || Roast sucking pig (cochinillo). || FAM. Bore, drag, bind (persona o cosa pesada). | Silver coin (moneda). || — FIG. y FAM. *Dar el tostón a uno*, to get on s.o.'s nerves. | *¡Qué tostón!*, what a bore!
total adj. Total, complete: *fue un triunfo total*, it was a total triumph.
— Adv. So: *total, que me marché*, so I left. || After all (al fin y al cabo).
— M. Total, sum (suma). || Whole (totalidad). || — *En total*, in a word (en una palabra), as a whole (en conjunto).
totalidad f. Totality, whole. || — *En su totalidad*, as a whole. || *La totalidad de la obra*, the whole of the work. || *La totalidad de las familias*, all the families.

totalitario, ria adj. Totalitarian.
totalitarismo m. Totalitarianism.
totalización f. Totalization.
totalizador, ra adj. Totalizing.
— M. Totalizer, totalizator (máquina de sumar).
totalizar v. tr. To totalize, to total, to add up (sumar). || To add up to, to total (ascender a).
totalmente adv. Totally, wholly, completely.
totay m. *Amer.* Palm tree.
tótem m. Totem.
— OBSERV. Pl. *tótemes* o *tótems.*
totémico, ca adj. Totemic, totemistic.
totemismo m. Totemism.
totilimundi m. Cosmorama. || FAM. Everybody.
totoneca o **totonaca** adj. Totonac.
— M. y f. Totonac, Totonaco, Totonaca (pueblo indio). || — M. Totonacan (idioma).
totora f. *Amer.* Cattail (planta). || Boat made of cattail (en el lago Titicaca).
totoral m. Place overgrown with cattails.
totuma f. o **totumo** m. *Amer.* Calabash (fruto y vasija).
toxicidad f. Toxicity.
tóxico, ca adj. Toxic, toxicant, poisonous.
— M. Toxicant, poison.
toxicología f. Toxicology.
toxicológico, ca adj. Toxicological.
toxicólogo m. Toxicologist.
toxicomanía f. Drug addiction, toxicomania.
toxicómano, na adj. Addicted to drugs.
— M. y f. Drug addict.
toxicosis f. MED. Toxicosis.
toxina f. Toxin.
tozudez f. Stubbornness, obstinacy.
tozudo, da adj. Stubborn, obstinate.
— M. y f. Stubborn *o* obstinate person.
tozuelo m. [Back of the] neck (cerviz).
traba f. Tie, bond (unión). || Hobble, trammel (para caballos). || FIG. Obstacle, hindrance (estorbo). || JUR. Seizure (embargo). || TECN. Lock. || — Pl. Fetters (de un preso). || FIG. *Poner trabas a,* to hinder, to put obstacles in the way of.
trabacuenta f. Mistake (error). || FIG. Dispute.
trabadero m. Pastern (de caballos).
trabado, da adj. Hobbled (animales). || Fettered (un preso). || With two white stockings (caballo). || Robust (robusto). || Wiry, sinewy (nervudo). || Sound, coherent (discurso).
trabadura f. Joining (unión). || Bond, tie (lazo).
trabajado, da adj. Worked. || FIG. Worn-out (cansado). | Elaborate (estilo).
trabajador, ra adj. Working (que trabaja). || Hard-working, industrious (que trabaja mucho).
— M. y f. Worker, labourer. || *Trabajador estacional,* seasonal worker. || — M. Workman, workingman. || — F. Workwoman, workingwoman.
trabajar v. intr. To work: *trabajar en una obra,* to work on a construction site; *trabajar mucho,* to work hard. || To act (un actor). || To be under stress, to be stressed (una viga). || To warp (la madera). || FIG. To work (obrar). | To work at, to strive to (esforzarse por): *trabajar en imitar a su maestro,* to strive to imitate one's master. || MAR. To work. || — FIG. *Hacer trabajar,* to make work (el dinero). || FIG. y FAM. *Matarse trabajando,* to work o.s. to death. || *Poner a trabajar,* to put to work. || *Trabajar a destajo,* to be on piecework. || FIG. *Trabajar como un condenado* or *una bestia* or *un negro* or *un mulo,* to work like a slave *o* a black *o* a horse *o* a dog. || *Trabajar de,* to be, to work as (oficio): *trabajar de sastre,* to be a tailor; to play the role of, to play (actor): *trabaja de Don Juan,* he plays the role of Don Juan. || *Trabajar de balde,* to work for nothing. || *Trabajar en balde,* to work in vain. || *Trabajar en el teatro,* to work in the theatre. || FIG. y FAM. *Trabajar para el obispo,* to work for nothing. || *Trabajar por horas,* to be paid by the hour.
— V. tr. To work: *trabajar la madera,* to work wood. || CULIN. To knead (la masa). || FIG. To bother, to disturb (molestar). || AGR. To till, to work (la tierra). || To work in, to be in (tener como oficio). || To train, to work out (un caballo). || FIG. To work on, to persuade (intentar convencer a uno). | To work on *o* at (sus lecciones, una novela, una idea, etc.). | To bring out, to play up (acentuar): *necesitamos trabajar más el lado melodramático,* we must play up the melodramatic side.
— V. pr. To work on, to study: *me estoy trabajando el asunto,* I'm working on the matter. || FIG. To work on, to persuade (a una persona).
trabajo m. Work, labour [U.S., labor]: *trabajo manual,* manual labour. || Work (obra). || Effort, labour [U.S., labor] (esfuerzo): *es trabajo perdido,* it's a waste of effort, it's wasted effort. || Job, task (tarea). || Work, job, employment: *trabajo de jornada entera, de media jornada,* full-time, part-time employment. || Job, position, post (puesto). || Labour [U.S., labor], workers, *pl.* (los obreros). || Work, study (estudio). || Work, acting (de un actor). || FÍS. Work. || — Pl. Hardships (penas). || — *Accidente de* or *del trabajo,* industrial accident. || *Ahorrarse el trabajo de,* to spare o.s. the trouble *o* the bother of. || *Con mucho* or *con gran trabajo,* with great difficulty. || *Costar trabajo,* v. COSTAR. || *Darle duro al trabajo,* to work hard at it, to put one's nose to the grindstone. || *Darse el trabajo de,* to take the trouble to. || *Dar trabajo,* to make work, to give work (proporcionar una ocupación), to give trouble (ser difícil). || *Día de trabajo,* workday, working day. || *Estar sin trabajo,* to be out of work *o* unemployed. || *Ir al trabajo,* to go to work. || *Lengua de trabajo,* working language. || *Programa de trabajo,* work schedule. || *Puesto de trabajo,* job. || *Ropa de trabajo,* working clothes. || *Sin trabajo,* easily (sin dificultad), unemployed, out of work (obrero). || *Tomarse el trabajo de,* to take the trouble to. || *Trabajo a destajo,* piecework. || *Trabajo a jornal,* work paid by the day. || *Trabajo clandestino,* illegal work. || *Trabajo de encargo,* work done to order. || FIG. *Trabajo de chinos,* very delicate and tedious work. || *Trabajo de equipo,* teamwork. || *Trabajo en el terreno,* fieldwork. || *Trabajo estacional,* seasonal work. || *Trabajo intelectual,* brainwork. || *Trabajo por horas,* work paid by the hour, timework. || *Trabajo por turno,* shift work. || *Trabajos de Hércules,* Labours of Hercules. || *Trabajos forzados* or *forzosos,* hard labour [U.S., hard labor]. || *Trabajos manuales,* manual work (en general), handicraft (en la escuela). || FIG. *Trabajo te* or *le mando,* it will take some doing, you will have your work cut out.
trabajosamente adv. Laboriously.
trabajoso, sa adj. Hard, laborious (que cuesta trabajo). || Hard, difficult (difícil): *trabajoso de hacer,* hard to do. || Laboured [U.S., labored] (falto de espontaneidad). || *Amer.* Demanding (exigente). | Bothersome (molesto).
trabalenguas m. inv. Tongue twister.
trabamiento m. Joining, uniting.
trabanco m. Yoke (trangallo).
trabar v. tr. To lock, to fasten (sujetar). || To join, to link, to unite (juntar). || To jam (inmovilizar). || To hobble (un animal). || To shackle, to fetter (a una persona). || To thicken (espesar una salsa, un líquido). || FIG. To start (empezar). | To strike up (conversación). | To hinder, to impede, to obstruct (obstaculizar). || To grasp, to seize (asir). || — FIG. *Trabar amistad,* to strike up a friendship, to become friends. || *Trabar batalla,* to join battle, to do battle.
— V. pr. To become entangled, to get tangled (enmarañarse). || To thicken (una salsa, etc.). || To lock, to jam (un mecanismo). || *Se le trabó la lengua,* he got tongue-tied.
trabazón f. Joining, joints, *pl.* (ensambladura). || FIG. Link, bond, connection (enlace entre cosas). | Consistency, coherence (coherencia). || CULIN. Thickness, consistency (de una salsa, etc.).
trabe f. Beam.
trabilla f. Foot strap (del pie de un pantalón). || Half belt (de chaqueta, etc.). || Dropped stitch (punto que queda suelto).
trabucación f. Upset. || FIG. Confusion, jumble, mix-up (confusión). | Mistake (error).
trabucador, ra adj. Blundering (que se equivoca). || Confusing.
— M. y f. Blunderer.
trabucaire adj. m. FAM. Bold, blustering.
— M. HIST. Catalonian rebel.
trabucar v. tr. To disarrange, to jumble, to mess up, to upset (desordenar). || FIG. To mix up, to confuse (confundir). | To mix up (mezclar).
— V. pr. FIG. To get all mixed up (al hablar o al escribir). || *Se me trabucó la lengua,* I got tongue-tied.
trabucazo m. Shot from a blunderbuss (de trabuco). || FIG. Shock.
trabuco m. Catapult (catapulta). || Blunderbuss (arma de fuego). || Peashooter (juguete). || *Trabuco naranjero,* blunderbuss.
traca f. Jumping jack, string of fireworks. || MAR. Strake.
trácala f. *Amer.* Trick (trampa).
tracalada f. *Amer.* Crowd, mob (muchedumbre). | String (sarta).
tracalero, ra adj. *Amer.* Tricky.
— M. y f. *Amer.* Trickster.
tracción f. Traction. || Pulling (de un cable). || *Tracción delantera,* front-wheel drive (de un coche).
Tracia n. pr. f. GEOGR. Thrace.
tracio, cia adj./s. Thracian.
tracoma m. MED. Trachoma.
tractivo, va adj. Tractive.
tracto m. Lapse of time, interval. || REL. Tract (en la misa). || ANAT. Tract: *tracto intestinal,* intestinal tract.
tractor, ra adj./s.m. Tractor: *hélice tractora,* tractor propeller; *tractor oruga,* caterpillar tractor.
tractorista m. y f. AGR. Tractor driver.
tradición f. Tradition. || JUR. Delivery (entrega).
tradicional adj. Traditional.
tradicionalismo m. Traditionalism.
tradicionalista adj. Traditionalistic.
— M. y f. Traditionalist.
tradicionalmente adv. Traditionally.
tradicionista m. y f. Writer *o* collector of stories relating local traditions.
traducción f. Translation. || — *Traducción directa,* translation out of the foreign language. || *Traducción inversa,* translation into the foreign language.

TRABAJO, m. — WORK

I. Generalidades, f. — General terms.

Ministerio (*m.*) de Trabajo	Ministry of Labour [U.S., Department of Labor]
mercado (*m.*) del trabajo	labour market
bolsa (*f.*) de Trabajo	Labour *o* Employment exchange [U.S., Employment Bureau]
economía (*f.*) laboral	labour management
pleno empleo *m.*	full employment
trabajar por horas	to be paid by the hour
trabajo (*m.*) estacional	seasonal work
trabajo (*m.*) a destajo, por horas, en equipo, por turno	piecework, timework, teamwork, shift work
trabajo (*m.*) en cadena	assembly line work [U.S., serial production]
taller *m.*	workshop
artesanía *f.*	handicrafts *pl.*, crafts *pl.*
oficio *m.*	trade, craft
profesión *f.*	profession, occupation
empleo *m.*	employment, job
colocación *f.*	situation, post
puesto (*m.*) de trabajo	job
vacante *f.*	vacancy
permiso (*m.*) de trabajo	work permit
solicitar un empleo	to apply for a job
petición (*f.*) *or* solicitud (*f.*) de empleo	application [for a job]
agencia (*f.*) de colocaciones	employment bureau
contratar	to engage, to employ
contrato (*m.*) de trabajo	work contract
accidente (*m.*) de trabajo	industrial accident
enfermedad (*f.*) profesional	occupational disease
orientación (*f.*) profesional	vocational guidance
formación (*f.*) profesional	vocational training
readaptación (*f.*) profesional, reconversión *f.*	retraining, reorientation, rehabilitation
vacaciones *f. pl.*	holidays, holiday *sing.*, vacation *sing.*

II. Mano (f.) de obra. — Manpower, labour.

coste (*m.*) de la mano de obra	labour costs *pl.*, labour input
fluctuación (*f.*) de la mano de obra	fluctuation of labour [U.S., of labor]
trabajador *m.*, productor *m.*	worker
trabajador (*m.*) de plantilla	permanent worker
personal *m.*	personnel, staff
empleado *m.*	employee
oficinista *m.* y *f.*	clerk, office worker
asalariado *m.*	salary earner
obrero *m.*	workman
obreros (*m. pl.*) sindicados	organized labour *sing.*
obrero (*m.*) cualificado, no cualificado, especializado	skilled, unskilled, specialized worker
obrero (*m.*) agrícola	farm worker *o* labourer
operario *m.*	worker, labourer [U.S., laborer]
oficial *m.*	skilled workman
jornalero *m.*	day labourer
temporero *m.*	seasonal worker
bracero *m.*, peón *m.*	[unskilled] labourer
colaborador *m.*	collaborator
capataz *m.*	foreman
aprendiz *m.*	trainee, apprentice
aprendizaje *m.*	apprenticeship
artesano *m.*	artisan, craftsman
especialista *m.*	specialist
equipo (*m.*) de noche	night shift
escasez (*f.*) de mano de obra	shortage of labour *o* of manpower
clase (*f.*) obrera	working class
proletario *m.*	proletarian
proletariado *m.*	proletariat
sindicato *m.*	trade union [U.S., labor union]
sindicalista *m.*	trade unionist
sindicalismo *m.*	trade unionism
gremio *m.*	guild; association, society, union
emigración *f.*	emigration
empresario *m.*	employer
enlace (*m.*) sindical	shop steward [U.S., union delegate]
delegado *m.*	delegate
representante *m.* y *f.*	representative
jurado (*m.*) de empresa	works council

III. Condiciones (f.) de trabajo. — Working conditions.

derecho (*m.*) laboral	labour law
leyes (*f. pl.*) laborales, legislación (*f.*) laboral	labour laws, labour legislation
día (*m.*) laborable, día (*m.*) de trabajo,	working day, workday
empleo (*m.*) de dedicación exclusiva *or* de plena dedicación.	full-time employment *o* job *o* work
empleo (*m.*) *or* trabajo (*m.*) de media jornada	part-time employment *o* job *o* work
horas (*f. pl.*) de trabajo	working hours
horas (*f. pl.*) extraordinarias	overtime *sing.*
remuneración *f.*	remuneration
salario *m.*, sueldo *m.*	pay, wage, salary
índice (*m.*) de salarios	wage index
salario (*m.*) mínimo	minimum wage
sueldo (*m.*) base	basic wage
salario (*m.*) bruto	gross wages *pl.*
salario (*m.*) neto, real	net, real wages *pl.*
salario (*m.*) por hora	hourly wages *pl.*, wage rate per hour
salario (*m.*) mensual	monthly wages *pl.*
salario (*m.*) semanal	weekly wages *pl.*
salario (*m.*) a destajo	piecework wage
salario (*m.*) tope *or* máximo	maximum wage [U.S., wage ceiling]
escala (*f.*) móvil	sliding scale
pago (*m.*) en especie	payment in kind
jornal *m.*	daily wages *pl.*
prima *f.*	premium, bonus, extra pay
día (*m.*) de paga	payday
hoja (*f.*) de paga	pay slip
nómina *f.* (de sueldos)	payroll
subsidio (*m.*) de paro	unemployment benefit
pensión (*f.*) de vejez,	old-age pension
jubilación *f.*, retiro *m.*	retirement
convenio (*m.*) colectivo	collective agreement

IV. Conflictos (m.) laborales. — Industrial disputes.

reivindicaciones *f. pl.*	claims
huelga *f.*	strike
huelguista *m.* y *f.*	striker
huelga (*f.*) de brazos caídos *or* de brazos cruzados	down tools, sit-down strike
huelga (*f.*) escalonada *or* alternativa *or* por turno	staggered strike
huelga (*f.*) intermitente	go-slow [U.S., slow-down]
subsidio (*m.*) de huelga	strike pay
piquete (*m.*) de huelga	strike picket
rompehuelgas *m. inv.*, esquirol *m.*	strikebreaker, blackleg
manifestación *f.*	demonstration, manifestation
cierre (*m.*) patronal	lockout
Magistratura (*f.*) del Trabajo	conciliation board in industrial disputes
paro *m.*, desempleo *m.*, desocupación *f.*	unemployment
paro (*m.*) estacional	seasonal unemployment
paro (*m.*) encubierto	underemployment
parado *m.*	unemployed man
los parados *m. pl.*	the unemployed
sanción *f.*	sanction
despedir	to discharge, to dismiss
despido *m.*	dismissal
rescindir un contrato	to terminate a contract
negociación *f.*	negotiation
negociaciones (*f. pl.*) colectivas	collective bargaining *sing.*

traducible adj. Translatable.

traducir* v. tr. To translate: *traducir del español al inglés*, to translate from Spanish into English. ‖ To interpret (interpretar). ‖ To express (expresar). ‖ — *Traducir directamente* or *de corrido*, to translate at sight. ‖ *Traducir literalmente*, to translate literally.
— V. pr. To translate: *esta expresión se traduce fácilmente*, this phrase translates easily. ‖ To result in, to bring about (ocasionar). ‖ To mean in practice (significar).

traductor, ra adj. Translating.
— M. y f. Translator: *traductor jurado*, sworn translator.

traedizo, za adj. Portable. ‖ Carried, transported (llevado).

traedor, ra adj. Carrying.
— M. y f. Carrier, porter.

traer* v. tr. To bring: *traer una carta, noticias*, to bring a letter, news; *trajeron a un prisionero*, they brought a prisoner; *¿qué le trae por aquí?*, what brings you here? ‖ To wear (la ropa): *hoy trae un traje nuevo*, today he is wearing a new suit. ‖ To carry about (llevar encima). ‖ To attract, to draw, to pull (atraer). ‖ To bring, to cause (acarrear): *eso le trajo muchos disgustos*, that caused him a lot of misfortune. ‖ To have: *su retraso nos traía muy preocupados*, their delay had us very worried. ‖ To put forward, to adduce (argumento, testimonio). ‖ To have: *el mes de abril trae treinta días*, the month of April has thirty days. ‖ To contain, to carry, to print: *el periódico traía un artículo sobre las elecciones*, the paper carried an article about the elections. ‖ — FAM. *Me trae sin cuidado*, I don't care, I don't give a damn, I couldn't care less. ‖ *¡Trae!* or *¡traiga!*, here!, give it here!, give it to me!, give me it! ‖ *Traer aguas*, to supply with water. ‖ *Traer a las mentes*, to recall, to bring to mind. ‖ *Traer a mal traer*, to treat badly, to maltreat (maltratar), to keep s.o. busy *o* on the go *o* on the move *o* on his toes (dar trabajo), to get [s.o.] down, to pester (molestar). ‖ *Traer aparejado* or *traer consigo*, V. APAREJADO y CONSIGO. ‖ *Traer al retortero*, V. RETORTERO. ‖ *Traer a uno de aquí para allá*, to order s.o. about (baquetear), to keep s.o. busy *o* on the go *o* on the move (mantener ocupado). ‖ *Traer a uno de cabeza*, to worry s.o. (preocupar), to get on s.o.'s nerves (molestar), to be on s.o.'s mind (ocupar los pensamientos), to drive s.o. mad (volver loco). || *Traer buena, mala suerte*, to bring good, bad luck. || FAM. *Traer cola*, to have serious consequences, to bring trouble. || *Traer entre manos*, v. MANO. || FIG. y FAM. *Traer frito a uno*, to get on s.o.'s nerves. || *Traer loco a uno*, to drive one mad. || FIG. *Traer por la calle de la amargura*, to give a hard time. || *Traer puesto*, to be wearing: *trae puesta su chaqueta nueva*, he is wearing his new jacket. || FIG. *Traer y llevar a uno*, to gossip about s.o.

— V. pr. To bring: *tráete el libro que te pedí*, bring the book I asked you for. || To be up to, to be planning (estar tramando). || — *Traerse entre manos*, v. MANO. || FAM. *Traérselas*, to be terrible *o* shocking (persona, cosa), to be really difficult (ser difícil).

trafagar v. intr. To travel around (distintos países). || To bustle about (trajinar) || To traffic.

tráfago m. Traffic, trade (tráfico). || Hustle and bustle, comings and goings, *pl.* (trajín).

traficante adj. Dealing, trading.

— M. y f. Dealer, trader (negociante). || Trafficker (en productos ilegales).

traficar v. intr. To deal, to trade (*con*, with; *en*, in). || To traffic: *traficar en drogas*, to traffic in drugs. || FIG. To deal illegally in, to make money illegally from. | To keep on the move, to travel a lot (viajar).

tráfico m. Traffic, trade: *tráfico de divisas*, traffic of foreign currency. || Traffic (tránsito): *calle de mucho tráfico*, street with a lot of traffic. || Slave trade (de esclavos): *tráfico de negros*, black slave trade. || — *Accidente de tráfico*, road accident. || *Guardia de tráfico*, traffic policeman. || *Policía de tráfico*, traffic police. || *Tráfico rodado*, vehicular *o* road traffic.

tragabolas m. inv. Aunt Sally (juego).

tragacanto m. BOT. Tragacanth.

tragaderas f. pl. FAM. Throat, *sing.*, gullet, *sing.* (esófago). || FIG. *Tener buenas tragaderas*, to swallow *o* to believe anything (ser crédulo): *tiene buenas tragaderas*, he will believe anything; to be very easy-going *o* excessively tolerant (ser muy tolerante), to really put it away (beber o comer mucho).

tragadero m. FAM. Throat, gullet (garganta). | Hole, drain (agujero).

tragador, ra adj. Swallowing. || Gluttonous (tragón).

— M. y f. Swallower. || Glutton (tragón).

tragahombres m. inv. FAM. Bully.

trágala m. Song sung by Liberal opponents of the Spanish absolutists in 1820. || FAM. *Cantar a uno el trágala*, to laugh in s.o.'s face.

tragaldabas m. y f. inv. FAM. Glutton, pig.

tragaleguas m. y f. inv. FAM. Keen walker, good walker.

tragaluz m. Skylight (en el tejado). || Transom (de puerta o ventana).

tragamillas m. y f. inv. FAM. Keen walker, good walker.

tragante adj. Swallowing.

— M. TECN. Mouth, throat (de un alto horno). | Flue (de un horno de reverbero).

tragantón, ona adj. Gluttonous.

— F. FAM. Tuck-in, feast, spread (comilona). || Gulp (trago). || FAM. *Darse una tragantona*, to have a feast, to tuck in (comiendo).

tragaperras adj. *Máquina tragaperras*, v. MÁQUINA.

tragar v. intr. To swallow: *tragar con dificultad*, to swallow with difficulty.

— V. tr. y pr. To swallow (comer o beber). || FIG. To put away, to devour, to down (comer vorazmente). | To swallow up (hacer desaparecer): *tragado por el mar*, swallowed up by the sea. | To swallow (creer): *se traga cuanto le dicen*, he swallows everything they tell him. | To swallow, to take (soportar): *tragarse un insulto*, to swallow *o* to take an insult. | To soak up (absorber). | To swallow up, to eat up (consumir). || — FIG. y FAM. *Duro de tragar*, hard to swallow (difícil de creer), hard to take *o* to swallow (difícil de aceptar). | *No hay quien se lo trague*, no one will swallow that. | *No poder tragar a uno*, not to be able to stand *o* to stomach s.o.: *no le puedo tragar*, I can't stand him. | *Tenerse tragado algo*, to see it coming. | *Tragar la píldora* or *tragársela*, to swallow it (creérselo), to swallow the bitter pill (aguantar). | *Tragar quina*, v. QUINA. | *Tragar saliva*, v. SALIVA.

tragasables m. inv. Swordswallower.

tragasantos m. inv. FAM. Overpious person.

tragedia f. Tragedy. || *Parar* or *terminar en tragedia*, to have a tragic *o* a sad ending.

trágicamente adv. Tragically. || *Tomar algo trágicamente*, to make a tragedy out of sth.

trágico, ca adj. Tragic, tragical (funesto). || — *Actor trágico*, tragedian. || *Actriz trágica*, tragedienne. || *Lo trágico es que*, the tragedy of it is that, the tragic part is that. || *Ponerse trágico*, to become *o* to get tragic *o* serious (situación), to become all serious, to put on the agony (persona). || *Tomar algo por lo trágico*, to make a tragedy *o* a big thing [out] of sth.

— M. Tragedian (autor).

tragicomedia f. Tragicomedy.

tragicómico, ca adj. Tragicomic.

trago m. Drop, swig (porción de líquido): *echar un trago de vino*, to take a swig of wine. || Gulp, swallow: *beber de un trago*, to drink in one gulp. || ANAT. Tragus (de la oreja). || FAM. Bottle, drink (bebida): *ser aficionado al trago*, to be given to drink, to be fond of the bottle. | Drink, drop: *echemos un trago*, let's have a drink. || FIG. y FAM. Hard blow (adversidad), bad time (mal momento). || — FIG. *A tragos*, little by little. || *Beber a tragos*, to sip, to nurse (fam.). || FIG. *De un trago*, in one go. || FAM. *Echarse un trago al coleto*, to take a swig. || FIG. y FAM. *Fue un mal trago*, it was a hard blow, it was hard to take. | *Pasar un trago amargo*, to have a rough *o* a bad time of it, to go through a rough patch.

tragón, ona adj. FAM. Gluttonous, greedy.

— M. y f. FAM. Glutton, big eater.

tragonería f. FAM. Gluttony.

traición f. Treason (delito): *alta traición*, high treason. || Treachery (perfidia). || — *A traición*, treacherously. || *Hacer traición a su patria*, to betray one's country. || *Una traición*, a betrayal, an act of treachery.

traicionar v. tr. To betray: *traicionar su país*, to betray one's country. || FIG. To betray: *su rostro traicionó sus intenciones*, his face betrayed his intentions; *le traicionó su corazón*, his heart betrayed him.

traicionero, ra adj. Treacherous, traitorous, treasonous. || FIG. Treacherous.

— M. y f. Traitor.

traída f. Bringing (acción de traer). || — *Canal de traída*, headrace. || *Traída de aguas*, water supply.

traído, da adj. Brought (v. TRAER). || FIG. Threadbare, worn-out (vestidos). | Hackneyed, trite (repetido). || — FAM. *Bien traído*, clever, witty (chiste). | *Traído por los pelos*, farfetched. | *Traído y llevado*, hackneyed, well-worn.

traidor, ra adj. Treasonous, traitorous (delictuoso). || Treacherous (pérfido). || Restive, tricky, bad-tempered (caballo).

— M. Traitor. || FIG. Betrayer. | Restive *o* tricky *o* bad-tempered horse. || — F. Traitress. || FIG. Betrayer.

traidoramente adv. Treacherously, traitorously.

trailer m. CINEM. Trailer [U.S., preview, prevue] (avance).

traílla f. Leash, lead (para atar los perros). || Team *o* pack of dogs (conjunto de perros trabados). || Lash (del látigo). || TECN. Leveller (para igualar terrenos). | Scraper (de tractor).

traillar v. tr. To level [land].

traína f. Dragnet (red).

trainera f. Trawler (barco).

traiña f. Sardine net (red).

Trajano n. pr. m. Trajan.

trajano, na adj. Trajan. || *Columna Trajana*, Trajan's Column.

traje m. Suit: *traje de hombre*, man's suit; *traje a la medida*, made-to-measure suit, tailor-made suit; *traje de confección*, ready-made *o* ready-to-wear suit, off-the-peg suit. || Dress (vestido de mujer): *traje de seda*, silk dress. || Costume, dress: *traje regional*, regional dress. || — FIG. y FAM. *Cortar trajes*, to gossip, to criticize people, to backbite. | *Cortar un traje a uno*, to slate s.o., to pull s.o. to pieces, to run s.o. down. || *Traje camisero*, shirtwaist dress. || *Traje cruzado*, double-breasted suit. || *Traje de baño*, bathing suit *o* costume, swimsuit. || *Traje de calle*, town clothes, *pl.*; plain clothes, *pl.* (de un policía). || *Traje de campaña*, battledress. || *Traje de casa*, casual clothes. || *Traje de ceremonia*, full dress (de un militar), formal dress. | *Traje de cuartel*, undress. || *Traje de chaqueta*, [woman's] tailored suit. || *Traje de diario*, everyday clothes. || *Traje de domingo*, Sunday clothes *o* dress, Sunday best (fam.). || MIL. *Traje de faena*, fatigue clothes. || *Traje de luces*, bullfighter's costume (de un torero). || *Traje de malla*, tights. || *Traje de montar*, riding habit. || *Traje de noche*, evening dress, *o* gown. || *Traje de novia*, wedding dress, bridal gown. || *Traje de paisano*, civilian clothes, *pl.* || *Traje de primera comunión*, first communion dress *o* suit. || *Traje de vuelo* or *espacial*, spacesuit. || *Traje largo*, evening gown. || *Traje sastre*, [woman's] tailored suit.

trajear v. tr. To dress, to clothe.

trajín m. Transport, haulage, carriage (transporte). || Work, chores, *pl.*: *el trajín de la casa*, household chores. || FAM. Comings and goings, *pl.*, hustle and bustle (ajetreo). | Work (trabajo). | Lover (amiguita). || *El trajín cotidiano*, the daily round.

trajinante adj. Transporting.

— M. Carrier, haulage contractor.

trajinar v. tr. To transport, to carry. || *Amer.* To search (registrar).

— V. intr. To come and go, to bustle about (ajetrearse). || FAM. To slave away, to toil away (trabajar). || FIG. y FAM. *¿Qué está usted trajinando por ahí?*, what are you cooking up over there?

trajinería f. Transport, carriage, haulage.

trajinero m. Carrier.

tralla f. Rope, cord (cuerda). || Whiplash, lash (del látigo).

trallazo m. Lash [of a whip] (golpe). || Crack (restallido). || FIG. Tongue-lashing, telling off (reprensión).

trama f. Weft, woof (de un tejido). || Tram (hilo de seda). || Screen (en fotograbado). || Blossoming (florecimiento del olivo). || FIG. Plot (argumento). | Plot, scheme (enredo, intriga).

tramador, ra m. y f. Weaver.

tramar v. tr. To weave (tejer). || FIG. y FAM. To scheme, to plot, to cook up (maquinar). | To hatch, to weave (un complot). || FIG. y FAM. *¿Qué estás tramando?*, what are you up to?, what are you cooking up?
— V. intr. To blossom (olivos).
— V. pr. To be afoot, to be going on.
tramitación f. Transaction (de un asunto). || Procedure, steps, *pl.* (trámites). || Negotiation.
tramitar v. tr. To take the necessary steps to obtain, to attend to: *tramitar su pasaporte*, to take the necessary steps to obtain one's passport. || To negotiate, to transact (un negocio, un asunto). || To convey, to transmit (facilitar): *respuesta tramitada a través del embajador*, response transmitted through the ambassador. || To make a study of, to study (un expediente).
trámite m. Step (diligencia): *hay que hacer muchos trámites para conseguir el permiso*, many steps must be taken to obtain the licence. || Formality, requirement (requisito): *cumplir con los trámites necesarios*, to go through the necessary formalities. || Passage, transit (paso). || — Pl. Procedure, *sing.*: *los trámites para la obtención del permiso*, the procedure for obtaining the licence. || JUR. Proceedings.
tramo m. Lot, tract, stretch, plot (de terreno). || Flight (de escalera). || ARQ. Span. || Section, stretch (de carretera, ferrocarril, canal).
tramojo m. Stalk used to tie a sheaf. || *Amer.* Yoke (trangallo).
tramontana f. Tramontane, north wind (viento del norte). || North (norte). || Haughtiness, conceit, pride (soberbia).
tramontano, na adj. Tramontane.
tramontar v. intr. To go over the mountains. || To sink behind the mountains (el sol).
— V. tr. To help escape (ayudar a escapar).
tramoya f. TEATR. Piece of stage machinery (máquina). | Stage machinery (conjunto de máquinas). || FIG. y FAM. Scheme, plot (enredo). || FIG. y FAM. *Una fiesta con mucha tramoya*, a very showy party.
tramoyista m. TEATR. Stagehand, sceneshifter. || FIG. y FAM. Schemer, trickster, swindler (que usa engaños).
trampa f. Trap, snare (caza): *poner una trampa*, to set *o* to lay a trap. || Trapdoor, hatch (abertura en el suelo). || Hatch (de mostrador). || Fly (de pantalón). || Cheating (en el juego). || Ambush (celada). || Debt (deuda). || Trick (de prestidigitación). || MAR. y CULIN. Hatch. || FIG. Trap, snare, pitfall. | Trick, fiddle, hoax (engaño). | Trick (estratagema): *era una trampa para ver si me diría la verdad*, it was a trick to get him to tell me the truth. || — FIG. *Caer en la trampa*, to fall *o* to walk into the trap. | *Coger en la trampa*, to catch red-handed. || *Ganar con trampas*, to win by cheating. || *Hacer trampas*, to cheat: *hacer trampas en el juego*, to cheat at cards; to be on the fiddle (cometer fraude). || *Hecha la ley hecha la trampa*, laws are made to be broken. || *No hay trampa ni cartón* or *sin trampa ni cartón*, there is nothing up my sleeve. || FIG. *Tiene trampa*, there's a catch (hay un truco o una pega). || *Trampa adelante*, out of one debt and into another, constantly in debt. || MIL. *Trampa explosiva*, booby trap.
trampeador, ra adj./s. FAM. V. TRAMPOSO.
trampear v. intr. To cheat (en el juego). || To live by one's wits (vivir de su ingenio). || FIG. To get by, to make out, to manage: *va trampeando*, he gets by.
— V. tr. To swindle, to cheat (estafar).
trampería f. Crookedness. || Cheating, swindling (estafa).
trampero, ra adj. *Amer.* Cheating.
— M. Trapper (cazador).
trampilla f. Trapdoor, hatch (puerta al nivel del suelo). || Oven door *o* window (de un horno). || Fly (del pantalón). || — Pl. TEATR. Cuts and slots.
trampista adj./s. V. TRAMPOSO.
trampolín m. Springboard, diving board (en la piscina). || Ski jump (en la pista de nieve). || FIG. Springboard (base para obtener algo). || *Salto de trampolín*, dive.
tramposo, sa adj. Cheating (en el juego). || Lying (embustero). || Swindling, crooked (petardista).
— M. y f. Cheat, cardsharper (en el juego). || Liar (embustero). || Swindler, crook, trickster (petardista).
tranca f. Cudgel (garrote). || Bar (de puerta). || Binge, drunken spree (borrachera). || — *A trancas y barrancas*, in spite of all the obstacles. || FAM. *Coger una tranca*, to get drunk.
trancada f. Stride (tranco): *en dos trancadas*, in two strides.
trancanil m. MAR. Waterway.
trancazo m. Blow with a cudgel (golpe dado con la tranca). || FIG. y FAM. Flu (gripe).
trance m. Moment, juncture: *un trance desagradable*, a disagreeable moment. || Critical moment (dificultad). || Tight corner *o* spot, fix, awkard situation (mal paso): *sacar a uno de un trance*, to get s.o. out of a fix. || Trance (del medium). || JUR. Distraint, seizure. || — *A todo trance*, at all costs, at any cost. || *El último* or *postrer trance* or *trance mortal*, one's last moments (de la vida). || *En trance de desarrollo*, developing. || *En trance de muerte*, on the point of death. || *Estar en trance de*, to be on the point of *o* in the process of. || *Salió del trance*, he pulled through. || *Trance de armas*, feat of arms.
tranco m. Stride (paso largo). || Leap, jump (salto). || Threshold (umbral). || — *Andar a trancos*, to take big steps, to stride along. || *Amer. A tranco*, at a gallop (un caballo). || FIG. *A trancos*, in a slapdash way. || *En dos trancos*, in a jiffy, in the wink of an eye.
trangallo m. Yoke.
tranquera f. Palisade (estacada).
tranquero m. ARQ. Lintel (piedra).
tranquil m. ARQ. Plumb line. || ARQ. *Arco por tranquil*, flying arch.
tranquilidad f. Tranquillity, calmness (quietud, sosiego). || Respite, peace and quiet *o* tranquillity (descanso): *un momento de tranquilidad*, a moment's peace and quiet. || — *Con toda tranquilidad*, with one's mind at ease (sin preocupaciones): *descansar con toda tranquilidad*, to rest with one's mind at ease; at one's leisure: *estudiar algo con toda tranquilidad*, to study sth. at one's leisure; calmly: *contestó con toda tranquilidad*, he answered calmly. || *Dormir con toda tranquilidad*, to sleep peacefully *o* soundly. || *Para mayor tranquilidad*, to put one's mind at ease, to be sure *o* safe: *para mayor tranquilidad llamaremos a un médico*, to put your mind at ease we shall call a doctor. || *Perder la tranquilidad*, to become anxious *o* uneasy *o* restless.
tranquilizador, ra adj. Tranquillizing [U.S., tranquilizing], reassuring. || Soothing (música, etc.).
tranquilizante adj. MED. Tranquillizing [U.S., tranquilizing].
— M. MED. Tranquillizer [U.S., tranquilizer].
tranquilizar v. tr. To tranquillize [U.S., to tranquilize], to calm [down] (sosegar). || To reassure, to put one's mind at ease: *la noticia me ha tranquilizado*, the news has reassured me.
— V. pr. To calm town, to calm o.s. || To be reassured (*con*, by). || To calm down (tormenta, mar, etc.). || *¡Tranquilízate!*, don't worry!, calm down!, calm yourself!
tranquilo, la adj. Tranquil, calm, peaceful. || Reassured (libre de preocupación). || Calm, still, quiet: *mar tranquilo*, calm sea. || Quiet: *tono tranquilo*, quiet tone. || Clear (conciencia). || — *¡Déjame tranquilo!*, leave me alone! || *Estate tranquilo hasta que vuelva*, stay put *o* stay right there until I get back. || *Se quedó tan tranquilo*, he didn't bat an eyelid. || *Tú, tranquilo*, don't [you] worry, calm down, take it easy: *tú, tranquilo, que todo saldrá bien*, don't you worry, everything will be all right; don't worry: *tú, tranquilo, yo me ocuparé de esto*, don't worry, I'll see to it.
tranquilla f. Small peg, pin (pasador). || FAM. Trap, catch, stratagem.
tranquillo m. FAM. Knack: *coger* or *dar con el tranquillo*, to get the knack.
trans pref. Trans.
— OBSERV. *Trans* often changes to *tras* in Spanish: *transcendental* or *trascendental*.
transacción f. COM. Transaction (acción y efecto). | Transaction, deal (negocio). || Settlement, compromise (acuerdo).
transaccional adj. Transactional.
transalpino, na adj. Transalpine.
transandino, na adj. Of *o* from *o* on the other side of the Andes, trans-Andean.
— M. Train that goes from Chile to Argentina, trans-Andean train (tren).
transar v. intr. *Amer.* V. TRANSIGIR.
transatlántico, ca adj. Transatlantic.
— M. MAR. [Atlantic] liner, ocean liner.
transbordador m. Ferry. || — *Puente transbordador*, transporter bridge. || *Transbordador aéreo*, telpher [U.S., telfer]. || *Transbordador de ferrocarril*, train ferry. || *Transbordador funicular*, cable railway, funicular railway.
transbordar v. tr. To transfer. || MAR. To transship. || To ferry across (en un río).
— V. intr. To change [U.S., to transfer].
transbordo m. Ferrying. || Change, transfer (de un tren a otro). || Transshipment (de un tren o barco a otro). || *Hacer transbordo*, to change [U.S., to transfer] (de tren, de barco, etc.).
transcaspiano, na adj. Transcaspian.
Transcaucasia n. pr. f. GEOGR. Transcaucasia.
transcaucásico, ca adj./s.m. Transcaucasian.
transcendencia f. V. TRASCENDENCIA.
transcendental adj. V. TRASCENDENTAL.
transcendentalismo m. Transcendentalism.
transcendente adj. V. TRASCENDENTE.
transcender v. tr. e intr. V. TRASCENDER.
transcontinental adj. Transcontinental.
transcribir v. tr. To transcribe.
transcripción f. Transcription, transcribing (acción). || MÚS. Transcription (acción y resultado). || Transcription, transcript (cosa transcrita).
transcripto, ta adj. Transcribed.
transcriptor m. Transcriber (aparato).
transcrito, ta adj. Transcribed.
transcurrir v. intr. To pass, to elapse (el tiempo): *transcurrieron diez años*, ten years passed. || To be, to pass: *el día transcurrió tranquilo*, the day passed peacefully, the day was peaceful. || To take place, to go off: *la ceremonia transcurrió sin incidente*, the ceremony went off without incident.

transcurso m. Course (del tiempo): *en el transcurso de los años*, in the course of the years. || Period, space: *pinté este cuadro en el transcurso de dos meses*, I painted this picture in *o* over a period *o* the space of two months. || *En el transcurso de un mes*, in the space *o* the course of a month.
transeúnte m. y f. Passer-by (en una calle). || Temporary resident, transient (que reside transitoriamente).
transferencia f. Transfer, transference (de una propiedad). || Transfer (de fondos). || DEP. Transfer. || Transference (en psicología).
transferible adj. Transferable.
transferidor, ra adj. Transferential.
— M. y f. Transferrer.
transferir* v. tr. To transfer. || To postpone (aplazar).
transfiguración f. Transfiguration.
transfigurar v. tr. To transfigure.
— V. pr. To become transfigured.
transfijo, ja adj. Transfixed.
transfixión f. Transfixion.
transformable adj. Transformable, convertible.
transformación f. Transformation. || DEP. *Transformación de ensayo*, conversion of a try (rugby).
transformador, ra adj. Transforming.
— M. y f. Transformer. || — M. ELECTR. Transformer.
transformamiento m. Transformation.
transformar v. tr. To transform, to change. || DEP. *Transformar un ensayo*, to convert a try.
— V. pr. To become transformed, to change.
transformismo m. Transformism, evolution.
transformista adj. Transformist.
— M. y f. Transformist. || TEATR. Quick-change artist.
tránsfuga m. y f. Deserter (desertor). || Turncoat (en política).
transfundir v. tr. To transfuse (líquidos). || To spread (noticias).
— V. pr. To spread (propagarse).
transfusión f. Transfusion: *hacerle a uno una transfusión de sangre*, to give s.o. a blood transfusion.
transfusor, ra adj. Transfusing.
— M. Transfuser.
transgredir* v. tr. To transgress: *transgredir la ley*, to transgress the law.
transgresión f. Transgression (infracción).
transgresivo, va adj. Transgressive.
transgresor, ra adj. Transgressing.
— M. y f. Transgressor (de una ley, etc.).
transiberiano, na adj. Trans-Siberian.
— M. Trans-Siberian railway.
transición f. Transition. || *Gobierno de transición*, transitional government.
transido, da adj. Overcome (*de*, with) [de angustia, pena, etc.]. || — *Transido de dolor*, racked with pain. || *Transido de frío*, freezing cold, chilled to the marrow. || *Transido de hambre*, starving, weak with hunger. || *Transido de miedo*, terrified, seized with fear, panic-stricken.
transigencia f. Compromise (acuerdo). || Spirit of compromise (actitud). || Tolerance.
transigente adj. Accomodating, compromising (acomodaticio). || Tolerant.
transigible adj. Acceptable.
transigir v. intr. To compromise. || To give in (ceder). || — *Transigir con*, to agree to (aceptar), to tolerate. || *Yo no transijo con nadie*, I refuse to accept a compromise.
Transilvania n. pr. f. GEOGR. Transylvania.
transilvano, na adj./s. Transylvanian.
transistor m. ELECTR. y RAD. Transistor: *radio de transistores*, transistor radio. || FAM. Transistor (aparato de radio).
transistorizado, da adj. Transistorized.
transitable adj. Passable: *camino transitable*, passable road.
transitar v. intr. To travel. || To pass. || — *Calle transitada*, busy street. || *Transitar por las calles*, to go along *o* through the streets.
transitivo, va adj./s.m. GRAM. Transitive.
tránsito m. Transit, movement, traffic (paso): *el tránsito de peatones*, pedestrian transit. || Transit (de mercancías, de viajeros). || Stopping place (sitio). || Traffic (tráfico). || Passageway (camino). || Passing (muerte): *tránsito de la Virgen*, passing of the Virgin. || Assumption (Asunción). || — COM. *Agente de tránsito*, transit agent, forwarding agent. || *Cerrado al tránsito*, road closed (por obras, etc.), no thoroughfare (reservado a los peatones). || *De mucho tránsito*, busy (calle). || *De tránsito*, passing through: *estar de tránsito en una ciudad*, to be passing through a city; in transit (viajeros, mercancías). || *Hacer* or *llevar en tránsito*, to convey [goods] in transit. || *País de tránsito*, country of transit. || *Tránsito rodado*, vehicular *o* road traffic.
transitoriedad f. Transience, transitoriness.
transitorio, ria adj. Transitory. || Provisional (provisional). || Transitional (período).
Transjordania n. pr. f. GEOGR. Transjordania.
translación f. V. TRASLACIÓN.
translaticio, cia adj. Figurative.
translativo, va adj. V. TRASLATIVO.
translimitación f. Overstepping, going too far.
translimitar v. tr. To overstep (derechos). || To cross [over] (fronteras).
translucidez f. Translucence.
translúcido, da o **transluciente** adj. Translucent.
translucir v. tr. V. TRASLUCIR.
transmigración f. Transmigration.
transmigrar v. intr. To transmigrate.
transmigratorio, ria adj. Transmigratory.
transmisibilidad f. Transmissibility.
transmisible adj. Transmissible.
transmisión f. Transmission. || JUR. Transfer, transference (de bienes). || TECN. Transmission. || — Pl. MIL. Signals. || — *Correa de transmisión*, driving belt. || MIL. *Cuerpo de transmisiones*, signal corps. || JUR. *Derechos de transmisión de herencia*, succession duty. || *Transmisión delantera, trasera*, front-wheel, rear-wheel drive. || *Transmisión del pensamiento*, telepathy, thought transmission. || *Transmisión del poder*, transfer of power. || RAD. *Transmisión en directo*, live broadcast. || *Transmisión por cadena, por fricción*, chain, friction drive.
transmisor, ra adj. Transmitting (que transmite).
— M. Transmitter (telegráfico o telefónico).
transmitir v. tr. RAD. To transmit, to broadcast. || To transmit (por morse, etc.). || To hand down (bienes). || JUR. To transfer. || MED. To transmit (una enfermedad).
transmudar v. tr. To move, to transfer (trasladar). || To change, to transform (transformar). || To transmute (transmutar).
transmutabilidad f. Transmutability.
transmutable adj. Transmutable.
transmutación f. Transmutation.
transmutar v. tr. To transmute.
transoceánico, ca adj. Transoceanic.
transónico, ca adj. Transsonic, transonic.
transpacífico, ca adj. Transpacific.
transparencia f. Transparency, transparence. || FOT. Slide, transparency.
transparentar v. tr. To reveal (dejar ver): *su cara transparentaba su alegría*, her face revealed her happiness.
— V. pr. To be transparent, to show through (ser transparente): *este vestido se transparenta*, this dress is transparent. || FIG. To show through, to be *o* to become clear (dejarse ver o adivinar): *sus intenciones se tranparentan*, his intentions show through. | To be worn thin, to be threadbare (un vestido viejo). | To be as thin as a rake (ser flaco).
transparente adj. Transparent. || Clear, transparent (agua, etc.). || See-through, transparent (vestido, etc.). || FIG. Transparent, clear, plain (evidente).
— M. Transparency (colocado ante una luz). || Curtain (cortina). || Shade, blind (pantalla). || Stained-glass window (vidriera). || "Transparency" [sculpture by Narciso Tomé in Toledo cathedral].
transpiración f. BOT. Transpiration. || Perspiration (sudor).
transpirar v. intr. BOT. To transpire. || To perspire (sudar).
transpirenaico, ca adj. Trans-Pyrenean, of *o* from *o* on the other side of the Pyrenees. || Trans-Pyrenean, crossing the Pyrenees.
transplantar v. tr. V. TRASPLANTAR.
transponer* v. tr. To move (mudar de sitio). || To cross over (atravesar). || To disappear behind: *el sol transpuso la montaña*, the sun disappeared behind the mountain. || To disappear round (una esquina). || To transplant (trasplantar).
— V. pr. To disappear (desaparecer). || To set, to go down (el sol). || *Quedarse transpuesto*, to doze *o* to nod off (dormitar).
transportable adj. Transportable.
transportación f. Transportation, transport.
transportador, ra adj. Transporting. || MÚS. Transposing. || *Cinta transportadora*, conveyor belt.
— M. Transporter, conveyor. || MAT. Protractor (instrumento). || — *Transportador aéreo*, cableway. || *Transportador mecánico* or *de cinta*, conveyor belt, belt conveyor.
transportamiento m. Transport (transporte).
transportar v. tr. To transport, to carry (llevar): *transportar a lomo*, to carry on one's back. || MAR. To ship (mercancías). | To transport, to carry (pasajeros). || MÚS. To transpose. || MAT. To transfer, to lay off (un ángulo). || ELECTR. To carry, to transmit (corriente).
— V. pr. To be carried away. || *Transportarse de alegría*, to be carried away with joy, to go into transports.
transporte m. Transport. || COM. Transport, freight, freightage. || MÚS. Transposition. || FIG. Transport (éxtasis). || — *Buque de transporte*, transport ship. || *Transporte a flote*, floating (de la madera). || *Transportes colectivos* or *públicos*, public transport.
transportista m. Transporter, carrier.
transposición f. Transposition. || Setting (del sol). || Disappearance (ocultación).
transubstanciación f. REL. Transubstantiation.
transuránico, ca adj. QUÍM. Transuranic.
transvasar v. tr. V. TRASVASAR.
transvase m. Decanting.
transverberación f. V. TRASVERBERACIÓN.
transversal adj. Transversal, transverse. || Collateral (pariente). || Side: *camino transversal*, side road. ||

Una calle transversal de la Gran Vía, a street which crosses the Gran Vía.
— F. MAT. Transversal. || Side road (calle).
transverso, sa adj. Transverse: *músculo transverso*, transverse muscle.
tranvía m. Tramcar, tram [U.S., streetcar]. || Tramway, tram (sistema). || [Stopping] train (tren).
tranviario, ria o **tranviero, ra** adj. Tramway, tram: *red tranviaria*, tramway system.
— M. Tramway employee (empleado). || Tram driver (conductor).
tranzadera f. Braid.
trapa f. MAR. Spilling line (cabo). || — Pl. MAR. Tackle used to fasten lifeboats on ships. || REL. *La Trapa*, the Trappist order.
trapacear v. intr. To swindle (en ventas). || To deceive, to cheat (engañar). || To play tricks.
trapacería f. Swindle, con, fiddle (en ventas, etc.). || Trick, ruse (pillería). || Hoax, trick, fraud (engaño).
trapacero, ra o **trapacista** adj. Swindling, fiddling (en ventas). || Wily, tricky (pillo). || Deceitful (engañoso).
— M. y f. Swindler, fiddler (petardista). || Trickster, rogue (pillo). || Deceiver, liar, cheat (que engaña).
trapajo m. Rag, tatter.
trapajoso, sa adj. Ragged, shabby, tattered (andrajoso).
trápala f. FAM. Racket, uproar, din, hullabaloo (jaleo). | Lie, fib (embuste). | Trick (engaño). || Hoofbeat, clatter of hooves, clip-clop (de caballo). || — M. FAM. Chatterbox (hablador). | Swindler, trickster, cheat (embustero). | Liar (mentiroso).
trapalear v. intr. FAM. To chatter, to jabber (parlotear). | To fib, to lie (mentir). || To clatter, to clip-clop (un caballo). || To clatter along, to walk *o* to run noisily (una persona).
trapalón, ona adj. FAM. Talkative, garrulous (hablador). | Dishonest, cheating, swindling (embustero). | Lying (mentiroso).
— M. y f. FAM. Trickster, cheat (embustero). || Liar (mentiroso).
trapatiesta f. FAM. Racket, hullaballo, din, uproar (jaleo). | Row, fight, rumpus, brawl (pelea). | Mess (desorden). || FAM. *Armar una trapatiesta*, to kick up a rumpus.
trapeador m. *Amer.* Floor mop.
trapear v. tr. *Amer.* To mop (el suelo).
trapecial adj. MAT. Trapezial [U.S., trapezoid, trapezoidal].
trapecio adj. Trapezius: *músculo trapecio*, trapezius muscle. || *Vestido trapecio*, A-line dress.
— M. MAT. Trapezium [U.S., trapezoid]. || MED. Trapezium (hueso). | Trapezius (músculo). || Trapeze (gimnasia).
trapecista m. y f. Trapeze artist.
trapense adj./s. Trappist (religioso).
trapería f. Rags, *pl.* (trapos). || Old-clothes shop (tienda).
trapero, ra adj. FAM. *Puñalada trapera*, stab in the back.
— M. y f. Ragman, ragpicker.
trapezoedro m. Trapezohedron.
trapezoidal adj. MAT. Trapezoidal, trapezoid.
trapezoide m. MAT. Trapezoid [U.S., trapezium].
trapiche m. Sugar mill (de azúcar). || Press (para aceitunas). || *Amer.* Crusher (molino para pulverizar minerales).
trapichear v. intr. FAM. To scheme, to plot (ingeniarse). | To buy and sell on a small scale (comerciar). | To be mixed up in shady dealings, to be on the fiddle (tener actividades poco claras).
trapicheo m. FAM. Jiggery-pokery, *inv.*, shady dealing, trickery: *trapicheos electorales*, electoral jiggery-pokery. || *Andar con trapicheos*, to scheme, to be mixed up in shady dealings, to be on the fiddle (tener actividades poco claras).
trapichero m. Sugar mill worker.
trapillo m. Small rag (trapo). || FIG. Nest egg, savings, *pl.* (ahorrillos). || *De trapillo*, casually dressed (en traje de casa), shabbily dressed (mal vestido).
trapío m. FIG. y FAM. Charm, elegance (garbo). || TAUR. Fighting spirit (gallardía del toro). | Good stance, surefootedness (buena planta del toro). || *Tener buen trapío*, to carry o.s. well, to move elegantly.
trapisonda f. FIG. y FAM. To-do, commotion, uproar, fuss (jaleo): *armar trapisondas*, to cause a to-do. | Swindle, fiddle (estafa). | Scheme, plot, trick (enredo). || Choppy sea (agitación del mar).
trapisondear v. intr. FAM. To cause a to-do, to kick up a fuss (armar jaleo). | To scheme, to plot (enredar).
trapisondista m. y f. FAM. Troublemaker, rowdy person (alborotador). | Trickster (tramposo). | Schemer, plotter (enredador).
trapito m. Small rag. || — Pl. FAM. Clothes (ropa). || — FAM. *Es elegante con cuatro trapitos*, she looks good whatever she wears. | *Los trapitos de cristianar*, one's Sunday best.
trapo m. Rag (pedazo de tela). || Dishcloth (de cocina): *secar los platos con un trapo*, to dry the dishes with a dishcloth. || Duster (del polvo). || M. P. Canvas (velamen). || FAM. Red cape (del torero). | Curtain (del teatro). || — Pl. FAM. Clothes (ropa). | Rags, tatters (ropa vieja). || — *A todo trapo*, [under] full sail (a toda vela). || FIG. *Hablar de trapos*, to talk about clothes. | *Los trapos sucios se lavan en casa*, one should not wash one's dirty linen in public. | *Poner a uno como un trapo*, to haul s.o. over the coals, to give s.o. a dressing down (reprender), to call s.o. all the names under the sun (insultar). | *Sacar los trapos sucios a relucir*, to rake up the past, to throw the past in s.o.'s face. | *Soltar el trapo*, to burst out crying, to burst into tears (echarse a llorar), to burst out laughing (echarse a reír). | *Tener manos de trapo*, to be a butterfingers.
traque m. Bang, crack (estallido). || Fuse (guía de pólvora).
tráquea f. Trachea, windpipe.
traqueal adj. Tracheal.
traquear v. intr. y tr. V. TRAQUETEAR.
traquearteria f. ANAT. Trachea, windpipe.
traqueítis f. MED. Tracheitis.
traqueo m. V. TRAQUETEO.
traqueotomía f. MED. Tracheotomy.
traquetear v. intr. To explode, to go bang, to go off (la traca). || To rattle, to clatter (hacer ruido): *coche que traquetea*, car that rattles. || To bump *o* to jerk *o* to jolt along, to shake (moverse con sacudidas).
— V. tr. To shake (agitar): *traquetear una botella*, to shake a bottle. || To handle, to finger (manosear).
traqueteo m. Bang, crack (ruido de la traca). || Jolting, bumping (movimiento). || Clatter, rattle, banging (ruido).
traquido m. Crack, bang (ruido).
traquita f. Trachyte.
tras pref. Trans.
— OBSERV. V. TRANS.
tras prep. Behind (detrás): *tras la puerta*, behind the door; *caminaban uno tras otro*, they were walking one behind the other. || After, in pursuit of (en pos de): *corrieron tras el ladrón*, they ran after the thief. || After: *una desgracia tras otra*, one misfortune after another; *tras dos meses de ausencia*, after two months of absence. || On the other side of, beyond (más allá): *tras los Pirineos*, on the other side of the Pyrenees. || Behind, on the other side of: *el sol descendió tras la montaña*, the sun sank behind the mountain. || Behind: *dejó un buen recuerdo tras él*, he left a good memory behind him. || Besides, as well as, in addition to (además): *tras ser inteligente, es guapo*, besides being intelligent, he's good-looking. || *Día tras día*, day after day, day in day out.
— M. FAM. Backside (trasero).
trasalcoba f. Dressing room.
trasalpino, na adj. Transalpine.
trasandino, na adj. V. TRANSANDINO.
trasanteanoche adv. Three nights ago.
trasanteayer o **trasantier** adv. Three days ago.
trasañejo, ja adj. Over three years old (vino).
trasatlántico, ca adj. Transatlantic.
— M. [Atlantic] liner, ocean liner.
trasbordar v. tr. V. TRANSBORDAR.
trasbordo m. V. TRANSBORDO.
trasbotica f. Back shop, back room.
trascendencia f. Transcendence, transcendency. || FIG. Importance, significance, consequence: *un asunto de gran trascendencia*, a matter of great importance. || *Sin trascendencia*, unimportant, insignificant.
trascendental adj. FIL. Transcendental. || Far-reaching (de gran alcance). || Transcendent (superior). || FIG. Extremely important *o* significant (sumamente importante).
trascendentalismo m. FIL. Transcendentalism.
trascendente adj. FIL. Transcendent. || Transcendent (superior). || FIG. Extremely important *o* significant (sumamente importante). || MAT. *Número trascendente*, transcendental number.
trascender* v. intr. To smell [*a*, of] (oler): *el jardín trasciende a jazmín*, the garden smells of jasmine. || To float across, to reach: *el olor trascendía hasta nosotros*, the smell floated across to us. || To become known, to come *o* to leak out, to transpire (divulgarse): *ha trascendido la noticia, su secreto*, the news, his secret has leaked out. || To extend, to spread (extenderse): *la huelga ha trascendido a todas las ramas de la industria*, the strike has spread to all branches of the industry. || FIL. To be transcendent. || — *Ha trascendido que*, we have heard *o* learned that, it has transpired that. || *Según ha trascendido*, according to what we have heard.
— V. tr. FIL. To transcend.
trascendido, da adj. Keen, perspicacious (perspicaz).
trascocina f. Scullery, back kitchen.
trascolar* v. tr. To strain, to filter.
trasconejarse v. pr. To squat (la caza). || To get lost *o* mislaid *o* misplaced (perderse). || *Se me ha trasconejado tu carta*, I have mislaid your letter.
trascordarse* v. pr. To forget (olvidar).
trascoro m. Retrochoir (espacio detrás del coro). || Back of the choir (parte posterior del coro).
trascribir v. tr. V. TRANSCRIBIR.
trascripción f. V. TRANSCRIPCIÓN.
trascurrir v. intr. V. TRANSCURRIR.
trasdós m. ARQ. Extrados (bóveda). | Pilaster (pilastra).
trasegador m. Person who decants wine.
trasegadura f. Decanting (trasiego).

trasegar* v. tr. To upset, to mix up (trastornar). || To move (cambiar de sitio). || To decant (cambiar de recipiente). || To draw off, to rack (para eliminar las heces).
— V. intr. FAM. To drink, to booze (beber).
trasero, ra adj. Back, rear. || — *Parte trasera*, back, rear: *en la parte trasera*, on the back. || *Puente trasero*, rear axle (de coche). || *Rueda trasera*, rear wheel.
— M. ANAT. Bottom, buttocks, *pl.* (de persona). || Hindquarters, *pl.*, rump (de animal). || — Pl. FAM. Ancestors (antepasados).
trasferencia f. V. TRANSFERENCIA.
trasferidor, ra adj./s. V. TRANSFERIDOR.
trasferir v. tr. V. TRANSFERIR.
trasfiguración f. Transfiguration.
trasfigurar v. tr. To transfigure.
trasfixión f. Transfixion.
trasfondo m. Background (fondo). || FIG. Undertone (en las intenciones, etc.).
trasformar v. tr. V. TRANSFORMAR.
trásfuga m. y f. V. TRÁNSFUGA.
trasfundir v. tr. V. TRANSFUNDIR.
trasfusión f. V. TRANSFUSIÓN.
trasfusor, ra adj./s.m. V. TRANSFUSOR.
trasgo m. Goblin, imp (duende). || FIG. Imp (niño).
trasgredir* v. tr. To transgress.
trasgresión f. Transgression.
trasgresor, ra adj./s. V. TRANSGRESOR.
trasguear v. intr. To get up to mischief, to play impish tricks.
trasguero, ra m. y f. Mischievous imp, practical joker (persona).
trashoguero, ra adj. Lazy, stay-at-home.
— M. y f. Stay-at-home. || — M. Fireback (de chimenea). || Large log (leña).
trashojar v. tr. To leaf through (hojear).
trashumación o **trashumancia** f. Transhumance, seasonal migration.
trashumante adj. Transhumant.
trashumar v. intr. To move to new pastures.
trasiego m. Decanting (de líquidos). || Drawing off, racking (para eliminar las heces). || Moving (cambio de sitio).
traslación f. Transfer: *traslación de un preso*, transfer of a prisoner. || Moving (desplazamiento). || Translation (traducción). || Metaphor (metáfora). || ASTR. Passage, movement (de un astro). || MAT. y TECN. Translation.
trasladable adj. Movable. || Transferable.
trasladador, ra adj. Moving, carrying.
— M. y f. Carrier, mover.
trasladar v. tr. To move (mudar de sitio). || To carry, to take, to transport (llevar). || To transfer (a un empleado, etc.): *trasladar a un preso*, to transfer a prisoner; *le trasladaron a Barcelona*, they transferred him to Barcelona. || To postpone (aplazar). || To translate (traducir). || To copy, to transcribe (copiar).
— V. pr. To go: *el ministro se trasladó a Madrid*, the minister went to Madrid. || To move (cambiar de residencia): *la organización va a trasladarse a otro país*, the organization is going to move to another country.
traslado m. Copy, transcript (copia). || Transfer, transferring (de un funcionario). || Moving: *el traslado de un enfermo al hospital*, the moving of a patient to the hospital. || Removal (cambio de residencia). || Transfer, transferring (de restos mortales). || JUR. Communication, notification. || *Dar traslado*, to send a copy.
traslapar v. tr. To overlap (cubrir).
traslapo m. Overlap, overlapping.
traslaticio, cia adj. Figurative: *sentido traslaticio*, figurative sense.
traslativo, va adj. Translative.
traslúcido, da o **trasluciente** adj. Translucent.
traslucir* v. tr. To show, to betray, to reveal (revelar). || *Dejar traslucir*, to insinuate, to suggest, to hint.
— V. pr. To be translucent *o* transparent: *la porcelana se trasluce*, porcelain is translucent. || To show through (dejarse ver). || FIG. To show through, to be plain, to be revealed (inferirse): *se trasluce la verdad en sus palabras*, the truth shows through his words. | To be written (en el rostro). | To leak out, to come to light (algo secreto).
traslumbramiento m. Dazzling (acción). || Dazzlement (efecto).
traslumbrar v. tr. To dazzle (deslumbrar).
trasluz m. Diffused light (luz que pasa a través de un cuerpo traslúcido). || Reflected light (luz reflejada). || — *Al trasluz*, against the light. || *Mirar una diapositiva al trasluz*, to hold a slide up to the light.
trasmallo m. Trammel net (red).
trasmano m. Second hand (en ciertos juegos). || *A trasmano*, out of reach (fuera de alcance), out of the way (apartado).
trasmigración f. Transmigration.
trasmigrar v. intr. To transmigrate.
trasminar v. tr. To make a tunnel in (una galería). || To penetrate, to seep through (pasar a través).
trasmisible adj. Transmissible.
trasmisión f. V. TRANSMISIÓN.
trasmitir v. tr. V. TRANSMITIR.
trasmudar v. tr. V. TRANSMUDAR.
trasmutable adj. Transmutable.
trasmutación f. Transmutation.
trasmutar v. tr. To transmute.
trasnochado, da adj. Stale, old (comida). || FIG. Haggard, run-down, pale (macilento). | Stale, hackneyed (antiguo): *chiste trasnochado*, stale joke.
trasnochador, ra adj. Who stays up late, who keeps late hours (que se acuesta tarde). || Who stays up all night (que no se acuesta).
— M. y f. Night bird, night owl (persona).
trasnochar v. intr. To stay up all night (no acostarse). || To spend a sleepless night (pasar la noche sin dormir). || To spend the night (pernoctar). || To stay up late, to keep late hours: *le gusta trasnochar*, he likes to keep late hours.
trasoñar* v. tr. To dream, to imagine.
trasovado, da adj. BOT. *Hoja trasovada*, obovate leaf.
traspapelado, da adj. Mislaid, misplaced.
traspapelar v. tr. To mislay, to misplace [a piece of paper].
— V. pr. To get mislaid *o* misplaced *o* lost.
trasparencia f. V. TRANSPARENCIA.
trasparentarse v. pr. V. TRANSPARENTAR.
trasparente adj. V. TRANSPARENTE.
traspasable adj. Portable, transportable (que se puede llevar). || Crossable, passable (que se puede atravesar). || Transferable (negocio).
traspasación f. Transfer, transference.
traspasador, ra adj. Transgressing.
— M. y f. Transgressor.
traspasamiento m. V. TRASPASO.
traspasar v. tr. To transfix, to run through: *le traspasó con la espada*, he transfixed him *o* he ran him through with his sword. || To pierce, to go through: *la bala le traspasó el brazo*, the bullet went through his arm. || To transfer, to make over (un derecho, un comercio): *traspasar su negocio*, to transfer one's business. || To sell (vender). || To transgress, to break, to violate (una ley, un reglamento). || DEP. To transfer (un jugador profesional a otro equipo). || To go beyond (ciertos límites). || FIG. To transfix (de dolor físico). | To soak through, to go *o* to come through: *la lluvia traspasa su abrigo*, the rain soaks through his coat. || To cross [over]: *traspasar el arroyo*, to cross the stream. || — *Se traspasa tienda*, shop for sale. || FIG. *Traspasar el corazón*, to pierce one's heart. | *Traspasar el oído*, to pierce one's ears.
traspaso m. Transfer, sale (de un local comercial). || Take-over fee (precio de la cesión). || Property transferred (local traspasado). || DEP. Transfer (de un jugador). || JUR. Conveyance (de una propiedad). | Transfer (de un derecho). | Transgression, infringement (de la ley). || FIG. Grief (pena).
traspatio m. *Amer.* Backyard.
traspié m. Trip, stumble, slip (tropezón). || Trip (zancadilla). || FIG. Faux pas, blunder (equivocación, indiscreción). || *Dar un traspié*, to trip, to stumble, to slip (al andar), to slip up, to make a blunder (cometer un error).
traspiración f. V. TRANSPIRACIÓN.
traspirar v. intr. V. TRANSPIRAR.
traspirenaico, ca adj. V. TRANSPIRENAICO, CA.
trasplantable adj. Transplantable.
trasplantación f. Transplantation.
trasplantar v. tr. To transplant. || MED. To transplant.
— V. pr. FIG. To uproot o.s., to move (cambiar de residencia).
trasplante m. Transplanting. || MED. Transplant, transplantation: *trasplante de corazón, de córnea*, heart, corneal transplant.
trasponer v. tr. V. TRANSPONER.
traspontín m. Folding seat [in a taxi, etc.]. || FAM. Backside (trasero).
trasportín m. Folding seat [in a taxi, etc.].
trasposición f. V. TRANSPOSICIÓN.
traspuesta f. Transposition. || Rise (del terreno). || Flight (huida). || Outbuildings, *pl.* (de una casa).
traspunte m. TEATR. Callboy (que llama a los actores). | Prompter (apuntador).
traspuntín m. Folding seat (asiento).
trasquila f. V. TRASQUILADURA.
trasquilado, da adj. Sheared (ovejas). || Cropped (el pelo). || FIG. y FAM. Cut down, curtailed (mermado). || — FIG. *Fue por lana y volvió trasquilado*, V. LANA. || FIG. y FAM. *Salir trasquilado*, to come out a loser.
— M. FAM. Priest (tonsurado).
trasquilador m. Shearer.
trasquiladura f. Shearing (de ovejas). || Cropping (del pelo). || FIG. y FAM. Cutting down, curtailment (merma).
trasquilar v. tr. To shear (esquilar). || To crop (el pelo). || FIG. y FAM. To cut down, to curtail (mermar).
trasquilón m. FAM. Slash, hole (desigualdad en el corte de pelo). || FIG. y FAM. Big hole *o* dent: *dar un trasquilón a su fortuna*, to make a big hole in one's fortune. || — *A trasquilones*, unevenly (el pelo), haphazardly (sin orden ni concierto). || *Hacer trasquilones en el pelo*, to hack one's hair, to cut one's hair very badly.
trastabillar v. intr. V. TITUBEAR.

trastada f. FAM. Dirty trick (jugarreta): *hacerle una trastada a uno*, to play a dirty trick on s.o. | Prank (travesura). | Practical joke (broma pesada).
trastajo m. FAM. Piece of junk.
trastazo m. FAM. Whack, thump, bang (porrazo). || — FAM. *Darse* or *pegarse un trastazo*, to come a cropper. | *Darse un trastazo contra algo*, to bash *o* to crash *o* to bump into sth.
traste m. Fret (de guitarra, etc.). || Wine taster (vaso). || FAM. *Amer.* Bottom, backside (trasero). || — FAM. *Dar al traste con*, to mess up, to spoil (proyectos), to squander (dinero), to put an end to (paciencia, esperanzas). | *Ir al traste*, to fall through, to be ruined, to be messed up.
trasteador, ra adj. FAM. Noisy, boisterous.
— M. y f. Noise maker, person who makes a noise.
trastear v. tr. To rummage in, to turn upside down (revolver). || MÚS. To play (un instrumento). || TAUR. To work *o* to play [the bull] with the muleta. || FIG. y FAM. To twist [s.o.] round one's little finger, to manœuvre (a uno).
— V. intr. To rummage around (hurgar).
trastejar v. tr. To re-tile (retejar).
trasteo m. TAUR. Working *o* playing [the bull] with the muleta. || FIG. y FAM. Manœuvring.
trastería f. Junk (trastos).
trastero, ra adj. Junk (cuarto).
— M. y f. Junk room.
trastienda f. Back room (de una tienda). || FIG. y FAM. Canniness, cunning (astucia). | Reserve (reserva). || FIG. y FAM. *Tiene mucha trastienda*, he's very canny (astuto), he's a dark horse (reservado).
trasto m. Piece of furniture (mueble). || Utensil. || FAM. Piece of junk (cosa inútil). | Good-for-nothing, dead loss (persona inútil). | Thingumajig, thing (chisme). || TEATR. Flat, wing (bastidor). || — Pl. Junk, *sing.* (cosas inútiles). || Weapons (armas). || || Tackle, *sing.*, gear, *sing.*: *los trastos de pescar*, fishing tackle. || Bullfighter's equipment, *sing.* (de torear). || — FIG. y FAM. *Con todos sus trastos*, with the whole caboodle [U.S., with kit and caboodle]. | *Llevarse los trastos*, to pack up and leave. | *Quita ese trasto de en medio*, get that thing out of the way. | *Tirarse los trastos a la cabeza*, to have a flaming row, to throw pots and pans at one another (reñir). | *Trastos viejos*, junk, *sing.*, old lumber *sing.*
trastocar* v. tr. To disarrange, to upset (trastornar). || To change around completely (cambiar completamente).
— V. pr. To go mad (trastornarse).
trastornado, da adj. Unbalanced (persona, mente).
trastornador, ra adj. Upsetting.
— M. y f. Troublemaker.
trastornadura f. o **trastornamiento** m. V. TRASTORNO.
trastornar v. tr. To upset, to disrupt, to ruin (proyectos, etc.). || To drive mad, to unhinge (volver loco). || To upset, to trouble (inquietar). || To make dizzy (dar mareo). || To drive crazy: *una mujer que trastorna a los hombres*, a woman who drives men crazy. || To turn upside down (desordenar): *Pedro lo ha trastornado todo aquí*, Peter has turned everything upside down here. || To disturb (el orden, la paz). || To disrupt (alterar). || To change completely (cambiar). || — *Trastornarle la mente a alguien*, to drive s.o. mad, to unhinge s.o. || *Trastornarle la salud a alguien*, to be bad for one, to be injurious to one's health.
— V. pr. To get *o* to become upset, to upset o.s. (estar conmovido). || FIG. To go mad, to go out of one's mind (turbarse).
trastorno m. Inconvenience (inconveniente). || Trouble (molestia). || Upheaval: *la crisis económica causó un trastorno en el país*, the economic crisis caused an upheaval in the country. || Disorder, disturbance (mental, político). || Trouble, disorder, upset: *padecer trastornos estomacales*, to have stomach troubles. || Upset: *la instalación de la nueva máquina supondrá un gran trastorno en la fábrica*, the installation of the new machine will mean a major upset in the factory. || — *Causar profundos trastornos en la economía*, to severely disrupt the economy. || *Si no le sirve de trastorno*, if it is not too much trouble.
trastrabillar v. intr. *Amer.* To stagger, to totter.
trastrocamiento m. Switch, reversal, change.
trastrocar* v. tr. To change, to transform (transformar). || To switch *o* to change round (cosas). || To reverse, to invert (el orden). || To change (el significado).
trastrueco o **trastrueque** m. Switch, reversal, change.
trasudación f. Transudation. || Perspiration.
trasudar v. tr. e intr. To transude. || To perspire *o* to sweat slightly (sudar). || *Tiene la camisa trasudada*, his shirt is soaked through with sweat.
trasudor m. Perspiration.
trasuntar v. tr. To copy, to transcribe (copiar). || To summarize (compendiar). || FIG. To exude: *su rostro trasuntaba serenidad*, his face exuded serenity.
trasunto m. Copy. || FIG. Carbon copy, replica (cosa idéntica). | Representation.
trasvasar v. tr. To decant, to transvase (vino). || To transfer (agua de un río a otro, etc.).
trasvase m. Decanting (de vino, etc.). || Transfer (de grandes cantidades de agua, etc.).
trasvenarse v. pr. To extravasate. || FIG. To spill (derramarse).
trasver* v. tr. To distinguish, to perceive, to make out (distinguir). || To see through (ver a través). || Not to see properly (ver mal).
trasverberación f. Transverberation, transfixion.
trasversal adj. V. TRANSVERSAL.
trasverso, sa adj. V. TRANSVERSO.
trasverter* v. intr. To run over, to overflow.
trasvolar* v. tr. To fly over.
trata f. Slave trade *o* traffic, slavery: *trata de blancas*, white slave trade, white slavery.
tratable adj. Easy to get along with, amiable, sociable, friendly.
tratadista m. Writer [of treatises].
tratado m. Treatise: *tratado de matemáticas*, treatise on mathematics. || Treaty (convenio): *tratado de paz, de alianza*, peace, alliance treaty.
tratamiento m. Treatment: *malos tratamientos*, bad treatment. || Title: *tratamiento de señoría*, title of nobility. || MED. Treatment. || TECN. Processing, treatment: *el tratamiento de materias primas*, the processing of raw materials. | Treatment: *tratamiento magnético*, magnetic treatment. || — FIG. *Apear el tratamiento*, V. APEAR. || *Dar tratamiento a uno*, to address s.o. by his title. || *Dar tratamiento de tú, de usted*, to address s.o. as "tú", as "usted". || *Tratamiento de la información*, data processing.
tratante m. Dealer: *tratante en automóviles*, car dealer.
tratar v. tr. To deal with, to discuss (un tema). || To handle, to deal with (ocuparse de). || To treat, to handle, to deal with: *tratar un asunto, un problema con delicadeza*, to treat a matter, a problem with delicacy. || To treat, to handle (manejar): *hay que tratar las cosas con más cuidado*, you should handle things more carefully. || MED. To treat. || TECN. To treat, to process (metal, madera, etc.). || To entertain: *nos trató opíparamente*, he entertained us lavishly. || To treat (a una persona): *tratar a los vencidos con clemencia*, to treat the vanquished mercifully. || To address as, to give the title of (dar cierto tratamiento a uno). || — *Tratar a alguien*, to know s.o., to associate with s.o., to have dealings with s.o. (tener trato con, conocer). || FIG. y FAM. *Tratar a alguien a puntapiés* or *con la punta del pie*, to kick s.o. around. || FAM. *Tratar a alguien como a un perro*, V. PERRO. || *Tratar a alguien con guante blanco*, to handle s.o. with kid gloves. || *Tratar a alguien de ladrón*, to call s.o. a thief. || *Tratar a alguien de tú, de usted*, to address s.o. as "tú", as "usted". || FIG. y FAM. *Tratar a alguien de tú a tú*, to be very informal with s.o. (tratar con naturalidad), to prove to be s.o.'s equal (valer tanto como otro). || FIG. y FAM. *Tratar a alguien por encima del hombro*, to look down on s.o || *Tratar a alguien sin contemplaciones*, to be very abrupt with s.o. || *Tratar a alguien sin miramientos*, to be impolite to *o* inconsiderate towards s.o. || *Tratar algo por separado*, to deal with sth. separately, to treat sth. apart.
— V. intr. *Tratar con*, to associate with, to have dealings with, to know (tener trato con personas), to treat with, to negotiate with (negociar con), to deal with (hablar con), to deal with, to work with, to handle (en el trabajo): *el taxidermista trata con animales muertos*, the taxidermist deals with dead animals. || *Tratar de*, to try to, to attempt to (intentar): *tratar de salir de un apuro*, to try to get out of a jam. || *Tratar de* or *sobre*, to be about, to deal with, to talk about: *¿de qué (tema) trata el libro?*, what is the book about?, what subject does the book deal with?; to talk about, to discuss, to deal with (discutir, hablar de). || *Tratar en*, to deal in (en comercio).
— V. pr. To take care of o.s., to look after o.s. (cuidarse): *se trata muy bien*, he takes good care of himself. || To treat each other (dos personas). || To call each other, to address each other: *se tratan de tú*, they address each other as "tú". || To be about: *¿de qué se trata?*, what is it [all] about? || To talk to each other: *a pesar de la riña que tuvieron, todavía se tratan*, in spite of the quarrel they had they still talk to each other. || — *El asunto de que se trata*, the matter in question. || *Luego se trata sencillamente de encenderlo*, then it's just a question of switching it on. || *Si no se trata más que de eso*, if that's all it is. || *Tratarse con alguien*, to have dealings with s.o., to associate with s.o. || *Ya no se tratan*, they don't have anything to do with each other any more.
trato m. Treatment: *trato inhumano*, inhuman treatment. || Manners, *pl.*, behaviour (modales). || Agreement, bargain, deal (en negocios): *cerrar un trato*, to strike a bargain, to make an agreement, to make *o* to close a deal. || Title (título). || — Pl. Dealings. || — *Casa de trato*, brothel. || *Deshacer un trato*, to break an agreement. || *Estar en tratos con*, to be negotiating with. || *Malos tratos*, ill treatment; cruelty: *acusó a su marido de malos tratos*, she accused her husband of cruelty. || *No tener trato con alguien*, not to have anything to do with s.o. || *Romper el trato con alguien*, to break off relations with s.o. || *Tener trato agradable*, to have a pleasant personality, to be easy to get on with. || *Tener trato con*, to associate with, to know, to be friendly with. || *Tener trato de*

gentes, to have a way with people. || *Tengo un trato superficial con Pedro*, Peter is a casual acquaintance of mine. || *Trato carnal*, sexual intercourse. || *¡Trato hecho!*, it's a deal! || *Trato preferente*, preferential treatment.

trauma m. MED. Trauma.

traumático, ca adj. MED. Traumatic.

traumatismo m. MED. Traumatism.

traumatología f. MED. Traumatology.

travelín o **travelling** m. CINEM. Travelling [U.S., traveling], dollying (procedimiento). | Dolly (plataforma).

través m. Inclination, slant (de un cuadro, etc.). || Bias: *la tela está cortada a través*, the material is cut on the bias. || Setback, reverse, upset (contratiempo, revés). || ARQ. Crossbeam (viga). || MAR. Beam. || Traverse (en fortificaciones). || — *Al través*, crossways. || *A través de* or *al través de*, across, over: *había un árbol colocado a través de la carretera*, there was a tree lying across the road; through: *la monja miró a través de la celosía*, the nun looked through the lattice; through, from: *lo sé a través de mi hermano*, I heard about it through my brother. || MAR. *Dar al través*, to hit broadside on. || *De través*, crossways, crosswise (al través), sideways (de lado), askew, crooked (mal colocado). || MAR. *Ir de través*, to drift off course. || *Mirar de través*, to squint (defecto físico), to look askance *o* out of the corner of one's eyes at (mirar de reojo).

travesaño m. Crosspiece. || Crosspiece, crossbeam, strut (de un tejado). || Bolster (almohada). || DEP. Crossbar (en fútbol). || *Amer.* Sleeper [U.S., crosstie] (de ferrocarril).

travesear v. intr. To get up to mischief, to be naughty (los niños). || To lead a dissolute life.

travesero, ra adj. Cross.
— M. Bolster (almohada).

travesía f. Crossing: *la travesía del Pacífico*, the crossing of the Pacific. || Voyage, crossing (viaje marítimo). || Distance (distancia). || Passage (que comunica dos calles). || Crossroad, cross street (entre dos carreteras). || Urban section of a road, section of a road which crosses a town. || MIL. Traverses (de una fortificación). || MAR. Traverse wind, crosswind. || *Amer.* Broad arid plain [between two mountain ranges] (páramo).

travesío, a adj. Traverse (viento).

travestido m. Transvestite.

travestir* v. tr. To dress as a member of the opposite sex.
— V. pr. To be a transvestite.

travestismo m. Transvestism.

travesura f. Mischief (diablura): *el niño ha estado haciendo travesuras todo el día*, the child has been [getting] up to mischief all day long. || Prank (picardía).: *fue una travesura de niño*, it was a childish prank. || *Hacer travesuras*, to get up to mischief, to be up to mischief.

traviesa f. Sleeper [U.S., crosstie] (de ferrocarril). || ARQ. Crossbeam (del tejado). | Wall (muro). || MIN. Transverse gallery. || Bet (apuesta). || Raise on a bet (algo añadido a la puesta).

travieso, sa adj. Mischievous (que hace diabluras). || Naughty (malo). || Sly, cunning, crafty (astuto). || Sharp, witty (ingenioso). || — *A campo traviesa*, across country. || DEP. *Carrera a campo traviesa*, cross-country race.

trayecto m. Distance (distancia). || Stretch (tramo de carretera). || Way: *nos paramos en el trayecto*, we stopped on the way. || Itinerary, route (recorrido): *el trayecto de la procesión*, the procession route. || Trip, journey (viaje): *tenemos un trayecto de cinco horas*, it is a five-hour journey. || Walk (camino hecho a pie). || Hike (en el campo a pie). || Route, run (de un autobús, etc.).

trayectoria f. Trajectory, path. || FIG. Course, line, path, direction, tendency (orientación).

traza f. Plan, design (de una obra). || Looks, *pl.*, appearance (aspecto): *me gusta su traza*, I like his looks; *no me gusta la traza que tiene*, I don't like the looks of him (una persona) *o* of it (una cosa). || Trace, sign (señal). || MAT. Trace (en geometría). || — FIG. *Darse trazas para*, to manage to, to contrive to: *se dio trazas para llegar a tiempo a la estación*, he managed to arrive at the station on time. || FIG. y FAM. *Este trabajo tiene trazas de no acabar nunca*, this work looks as if *o* as though it will never end. | *La chica tiene trazas de no querer estudiar*, the girl doesn't seem to want to study. || *Tener buena traza*, to be good-looking (una persona), to look promising *o* good (un asunto, un proyecto, etc.). || *Tener buena, mala, poca, mucha traza para algo*, to be good, no good, not very good, very good at sth.

trazado adj. Laid out, made, designed: *el camino está mal trazado*, the road is badly laid out. || — *Bien trazado*, good-looking, nice-looking (de buen ver). || *Mal trazado*, unattractive, ungainly.
— M. Layout (disposición). || Plan, design (proyecto de edificio, puente, etc.). || Drawing, sketch (dibujo). || Outline (contorno). || Course (de una carretera).

trazador, ra adj. Tracer, tracing. || Planning, designing. || *Bala trazadora*, tracer [bullet].
— M. y f. Planner, designer.

trazar v. tr. To draw [up] (un plano, dibujo, etc.). || To sketch, to outline (bosquejar). || To plot, to lay out (un jardín, parque, etc.). || To draw, to trace (una línea). || To trace, to plot (el itinerario). || ARQ. To design (puentes, edificios, etc.). || — FIG. *Trazar las líneas generales de un proyecto*, to draw up the broad outlines of a project. | *Trazar una semblanza de alguien*, to draw a picture of s.o., to depict s.o., to describe s.o. (con palabras).

trazo m. Line: *trazo rectilíneo*, straight line. || Stroke, line (de lápiz, pincel). || Stroke (de una letra). || Sketch, outline (bosquejo). || FIG. Feature, line (de la cara): *el capitán tiene trazos enérgicos*, the captain has energetic features. || Fold (del ropaje). || *Dibujar al trazo*, to draw in outline.

trazumarse v. pr. To ooze, to seep, to exude.

trébede f. o **trébedes** f. pl. Trivet, *sing.* (utensilio). || Raised part of a room under which straw is burnt to provide heat (habitación).

trebejo m. Utensil: *los trebejos de la cocina*, [the] kitchen utensils. || Chessman, chess piece (ajedrez). || — Pl. Equipment, *sing.*, gear, *sing.*: *los trebejos de matar*, the matador's equipment.

trébol m. BOT. Clover, trefoil. || Club (naipe). || ARQ. Trefoil (adorno). || Cloverleaf junction (en carreteras). || — Pl. Clubs (palo de la baraja).

trebolado, da adj. Trefoil.

trebolar m. *Amer.* Clover field.

trece adj. Thirteen: *trece libros*, thirteen books. || Thirteenth: *León XIII* (*trece*), Leo XIII [the thirteenth]; *el día 13* (*trece*) *de febrero*, the 13th [thirteenth] of February.
— M. Thirteenth: *el 13* (*trece*) *de septiembre*, the 13th. [thirteenth] of September. || Thirteen, number thirteen: *ganó el trece*, thirteen won; *vivo en el trece*, I live at number thirteen. || — FIG. *Mantenerse en sus trece*, to stick to one's guns. | *Martes y trece*, unlucky day [corresponde a *Friday the thirteenth* en inglés].

treceno, na adj. Thirteenth.

trecentista adj. [Of *o* in the] fourteenth century.

trecésimo, ma adj. Thirtieth.

trecientos, tas adj./s. m, V. TRESCIENTOS.

trecha f. Sommersault (voltereta). || Trick (ardid).

trecho m. Distance, way: *hay un gran trecho entre las dos ciudades*, there is a great distance between the two cities, the two cities are a long way apart; *anduvimos un buen trecho*, we walked a good *o* a long way. || Stretch: *un trecho muy malo en el camino*, a very rough stretch in the road. || Spell, while, time (espacio de tiempo): *esperé largo trecho*, I waited quite a spell. || AGR. Plot, patch. || FAM. Bit, piece (pedazo). || — *A trechos*, in places, in parts, at times (en ciertas partes), now and again (con discontinuidad en el tiempo). || *De trecho a trecho* or *de trecho en trecho*, at intervals, every so often: *árboles plantados de trecho en trecho*, trees planted at intervals.

tredécimo, ma adj. Thirteenth. || *Una tredécima parte*, a thirteenth.

trefilado m. TECN. Wiredrawing.

trefilador m. TECN. Wiredrawer.

trefiladora f. TECN. Wiredrawing machine.

trefilar v. tr. To draw [wire].

trefilería m. Wireworks, wiredrawing factory.

tregua f. MIL. Truce: *acordar una tregua*, to declare a truce. || FIG. Rest, respite (descanso): *sus acreedores no le dan tregua*, his creditors give him no respite. | Lull, letup (período de actividad menos intensa). || HIST. *Tregua de Dios*, truce of God.

treinta adj. Thirty: *treinta hombres*, thirty men. || *Vino el día treinta de mayo*, he came on the thirtieth of May.
— M. Thirty, number thirty: *juego siempre al treinta*, I always bet on the thirty. || Thirtieth: *el treinta de mayo*, the 30th [thirtieth] of May. || — *Los años treinta*, the thirties. || *Treinta y uno*, thirty-one (número), thirty-first (fecha). || *Unos treinta*, about thirty.

treintaidosavo, va adj. Thirty-second. || IMPR. *En treintaidosavo*, in 32mo, in thirty-twomo.

treintañal adj. Thirty-year-old.

treintavo, va adj./s. Thirtieth.

treintena f. Thirty (treinta unidades): *envíeme una treintena*, send me thirty [of them]. || Thirtieth (treintava parte).

treinteno, na adj. Thirtieth (trigésimo).

tremadal m. Quaking bog, quagmire.

trematodo m. ZOOL. Trematode, fluke.

tremebundo, da adj. Terrible, dreadful, frightful.

tremedal m. Quaking bog, quagmire.

tremendo, da adj. Terrible, frightful, dreadful: *un espectáculo, un crimen tremendo*, a terrible sight *o* spectacle, crime; *un porrazo tremendo*, a terrible bang. || Tremendous, terrific (grandísimo, fortísimo, etc.): *una paliza, un golpe, un disparo tremendo*, a tremendous hiding, blow, shot. || Terrific, terrible (muy grande): *un calor tremendo*, terrible heat; *un disparate tremendo*, a terrible blunder. || FAM. Marvellous, fantastic (persona). || FAM. *Tomarlo por la tremenda*, to take it hard.

trementina f. Turpentine: *esencia de trementina*, oil of turpentine.

tremés o **tremesino, na** adj. Three-month-old. || *Trigo tremés* or *tremesino*, summer wheat.

tremielga f. Crampfish, torpedo fish (pez).

tremolante adj. Waving, fluttering (banderas).
tremolar v. intr. To flutter, to wave.
— V. tr. To wave (banderas). || FIG. To flaunt (ostentar).
tremolina f. Gusty wind (viento). || FIG. y FAM. Uproar, rumpus, fuss: *armar la tremolina*, to kick up a rumpus *o* a fuss, to create uproar.
trémolo m. MÚS. Tremolo.
tremor m. Tremor (temblor).
trémulamente adv. Trembling, tremulously (hacer). || In a trembling voice (decir).
tremulante o **trémulo, la** adj. Trembling, tremulous. || Flickering (luz).
tren m. Train: *tren expreso, ómnibus, rápido, correo,* express, stopping *o* slow, fast, mail train; *tren mixto,* passenger and goods train. || Luggage, equipment, gear (bagaje). || FIG. Pace, speed: *ir a buen tren,* to go at a good pace *o* speed. || Convoy, line (convoy): *un tren de camiones,* a convoy of lorries. || MIL. Convoy. || — *Cambiar de tren,* to change [trains]. || FIG. *Ir a un tren endiablado,* to go at breakneck speed. || *Ir en tren,* to go by train. || FIG. *Perder el tren,* to miss the boat (perder la ocasión). || *Poner un tren suplementario,* to put on an extra *o* a relief train. || *Por tren,* by train. || *Tomar el tren,* to catch a train. || *Tren ascendente, descendente,* up train, down train. || FAM. *Tren botijo* or *de recreo,* excursion train. || *Tren de aterrizaje,* undercarriage, landing gear. || *Tren de cercanías,* commuter *o* suburban train. || *Tren de circunvalación,* peripheral train. || *Tren de engranajes,* gear train. || MIL. *Tren de equipajes,* supply train. || TECN. *Tren de laminación* or *laminador,* rolling mill. || AUT. *Tren delantero, trasero,* front wheel, rear wheel assembly. || *Tren de mercancías,* goods *o* freight train. || TECN. *Tren desbastador,* roughing mill. || FIG. *Tren de vida,* way of life. || *Tren directo,* through train. || *Tren nocturno,* night train. || FIG. *Vivir a todo tren* or *llevar un gran tren de vida,* to live in style *o* on a grand scale.
trena f. FAM. Clink (cárcel). || MIL. Sash.
trenca f. Crosspiece [in a beehive] (de colmena). || Main root (de una cepa). || Duffle coat (abrigo).
trencilla f. Braided *o* plaited ribbon, braid.
trencillar v. tr. To braid.
treno m. Threnody. || Lamentation: *los trenos de Jeremías,* the lamentations of Jeremiah.
Trento n. pr. GEOGR. Trent, Trento.
trenza f. Braid (en costura). || Plait (de cabello). || *Trenza postiza,* switch.
trenzado, da adj. Braided (en costura). || Plaited (cabello). || Intertwined (entrelazado).
— M. Braid (trenza, en costura). || Plait (trenza de pelo). || Braiding, plaiting (trenzas, acción de trenzar). || Entrechat (en la danza). || Crossover step (de caballo).
trenzador, ra m. y f. Braider, plaiter. || — F. TECN. Braiding machine.
trenzar v. tr. To braid, to plait. || To plait (el cabello).
— V. intr. To perform entrechats (los bailarines). || To walk with crossover steps (el caballo).
— V. pr. *Amer.* To wrestle (luchar). | To begin to quarrel (reñir).
trepa f. Climb, climbing (subida). || Drilling, boring (acción de taladrar). || Trimming, edging (guarnición). || Grain (de la madera). || Forward roll, somersault (voltereta). || FIG. Trick, ruse (ardid).
trepado, da adj. Leaning back, reclined (retrepado). || Strong (animales).
— M. Perforation (línea de puntos taladrados). || Trimming, edging (adorno). || Drilling, boring (acción de taladrar).
trepador, ra adj. Climbing, rambling: *planta trepadora,* climbing plant. || ZOOL. *Ave trepadora,* creeper.
— F. pl. BOT. Climbers, ramblers. || ZOOL. Creepers. || Climbing irons (garfios para trepar).
trepanación f. MED. Trepanation.
trepanar v. tr. MED. To trephine, to trepan.
trépano m. MED. Trephine (instrumento). || TECN. Trepan, boring bit (perforadora).
trepar v. tr. e intr. To climb: *trepar a un árbol,* to climb [up] a tree. || To scale: *trepar por una roca,* to scale a rock. || To climb, to creep: *la hiedra trepa por las paredes,* ivy creeps up walls. || To drill, to bore (taladrar). || To trim, to edge (adornar).
trepatroncos m. inv. Blue titmouse (pájaro).
trepidación f. Vibration.
trepidante adj. Vibrating, shaking.
trepidar v. intr. To vibrate, to shake (temblar).
treponema m. ZOOL. Treponema.
tres adj. Three: *tiene tres hermanos,* he has three brothers. || Third: *el día tres de junio,* the third of June.
— M. Third: *el tres de junio,* the third of June. || Three, number three (número). || — *Como tres y dos son cinco,* as sure as eggs are eggs (segurísimo), perfectly clear (evidente). || MÚS. *Compás de tres por dos, tres por ocho, tres por cuatro,* three-two, three-eight, three-four time. || FIG. y FAM. *De tres al cuarto,* v. CUARTO. || MIL. *En formación de a tres,* three abreast. || *Las tres de la mañana* or *de la madrugada, de la tarde,* three o'clock in the morning, in the afternoon. || FIG. *Ni a la de tres,* not for the life of me [of him, etc.]: *no consigo que lo haga ni a la de tres,* I cannot get him to do it for the life of me. | *No ver tres en un burro,* v. BURRO. || MAT. *Regla de tres,* rule of three. || *Son las tres y media,* it is half past three. || *Tres en raya,* noughts-and-crosses [U.S., ticktacktoe].
tresañal o **tresañejo, ja** adj. Three-year-old.
tresbolillo (al) adv. In quincunxes: *plantación al tresbolillo,* plantation in quincunxes.
trescientos, tas adj./s.m. Three hundred: *trescientos veinte,* three hundred and twenty; *en el año trescientos,* in the year three hundred. || *Mil trescientos,* thirteen hundred, one thousand three hundred.
tresdoblar v. tr. To treble, to triple.
tresillo m. Ombre (juego de naipes). || MÚS. Triplet. || Three-piece suite (muebles). || Ring with three stones (sortija).
treta f. Trick (ardid): *valerse de una treta,* to use a trick. || Feint (en esgrima).
Tréveris n. pr. GEOGR. Trier.
trezavo, va adj./s.m. Thirteenth.
tría f. Sorting.
triaca f. MED. Theriaca, antidote. || Cure, remedy (cura).
triácido, da adj./s.m. Triacid.
tríada f. Triad.
triangulación f. Triangulation.
triangulado, da adj. Triangulated (dividido en triángulos). || Triangular (en forma de triángulo).
triangular adj. Triangular: *pirámide, músculo triangular,* triangular pyramid, muscle.
triangular v. tr. To triangulate.
triángulo m. Triangle: *triángulo equilátero, isósceles, escaleno,* equilateral, isosceles, scalene triangle. || MÚS. Triangle.
trías m. GEOL. Trias.
triásico, ca adj. GEOL. Triassic.
— M. GEOL. Trias, Triassic.
triatómico, ca adj. Triatomic.
tribal adj. Tribal.
tribásico, ca adj. QUÍM. Tribasic.
tribu f. Tribe.
tribulación f. Tribulation.
tribuna f. Rostrum, platform (de un orador): *subir a la tribuna,* to go up to the rostrum. || Tribune (para un espectáculo). || DEP. Grandstand. || Gallery (en una iglesia). || — JUR. *Tribuna del acusado,* dock. || *Tribuna de la prensa,* press box. || JUR. *Tribuna del jurado,* jury box.
tribunado m. Tribunate, tribuneship.
tribunal m. JUR. Court: *tribunal de apelación, supremo, tutelar de menores,* court of appeal, High Court [U.S., Supreme Court], juvenile court. || Tribunal: *tribunal de Dios,* tribunal of God; *tribunal militar,* military tribunal. || Board: *tribunal de examen,* board of examiners; *tribunal de conciliación laboral,* conciliation board in industrial disputes. || — *Tribunal de Cuentas,* National Audit Office [U.S., Committee on Public Accounts]. || *Tribunal de Justicia Internacional,* International Court of Justice.
tribuno m. Tribune.
tributable adj. Tributary (sujeto a tributo).
tributación f. Tax, tribute (tributo). || Payment of taxes (pago). || Tax system (régimen tributario).
tributante adj. Taxpaying.
— M. y f. Taxpayer.
tributar v. tr. To pay (pagar). || FIG. To pay: *tributar respeto, homenaje,* to pay respect, tribute. | To show: *tributar cariño,* to show affection.
tributario, ria adj. Tax, taxation: *sistema* or *régimen tributario,* tax system. || Tributary (que paga tributo). || Tributary (corriente de agua).
tributo m. Tribute. || Tax (impuesto). || FIG. Price: *el tributo de la gloria,* the price of fame. | Tribute: *el respeto es el tributo debido a la virtud,* respect is the tribute one pays to virtue.
tricéfalo, la adj. Tricephalous.
tricenal adj. Thirty-year.
tricentenario m. Tercentenary, tricentennial.
tricentésimo, ma adj./s. Three hundredth.
tríceps m. ANAT. Triceps.
triciclo m. Tricycle.
tricípite adj. Tricephalous.
triclínico, ca adj. MIN. Triclinic (cristal).
triclinio m. Triclinium.
tricolor adj. Tricolour [U.S., tricolor], three-coloured [U.S., three-colored]. || *Bandera tricolor,* tricolour [U.S., tricolor].
tricorne adj. POÉT. Three-cornered.
tricornio adj. m. Three-cornered.
— M. Tricorn, three-cornered hat.
tricotar v. tr. To knit. || *Máquina de tricotar,* knitting machine.
tricotomía f. Trichotomy.
tricotosa f. Knitting machine.
tricromía f. Three-colour process, trichromatism.
tricromo, ma adj. Three-colour, three-coloured [U.S., three-color, three-colored].
tricúspide adj. ANAT. Tricuspid: *válvula tricúspide,* tricuspid valve.
— M. ANAT. Tricuspid.
tridáctilo, la adj. Tridactyl.
tridente m. Trident.
tridentino, na adj. Of Trent, Tridentine: *el Concilio tridentino,* the Council of Trent.

tridimensional adj. Three-dimensional, tridimensional.
triduo m. REL. Triduo, Triduum.
triedro, dra adj. MAT. Trihedral.
— M. MAT. Trihedron.
trienal adj. Triennial.
trienio m. Triennium.
trifásico, ca adj. Three-phase, triphase (corriente).
trifenilmetano m. QUÍM. Triphenylmethane.
trifoliado, da adj. BOT. Trifoliate, trifoliated.
triforio m. ARQ. Triforium.
trifulca f. System of three levers [for working the bellows]. || FIG. y FAM. Squabble, rumpus, row: *armar una trifulca*, to kick up a rumpus.
trifurcarse v. pr. To divide into three.
trigal m. Wheat field.
trigémino, na adj.m./s.m. ANAT. Trigeminal.
trigésimo, ma adj./s. Thirtieth. || *Trigésimo primero, segundo, etc.*, thirty-first, thirty-second, etc.
triglifo m. ARQ. Triglyph.
trigo m. BOT. Wheat. || — Pl. BOT. Wheat, *sing.* || — FIG. y FAM. *Meterse en trigo ajeno*, to meddle in s.o. else's affairs. | *No es trigo limpio*, he's a shady character (persona), it's a fishy business (asunto). | *Nunca es mal año por mucho trigo*, you can't have too much of a good thing. || *Trigo atizonado* or *con tizón*, blighted wheat. || *Trigo candeal*, white wheat. || *Trigo chamorro* or *mocho*, summer *o* beardless wheat. || *Trigo duro* or *fanfarrón*, hard wheat. || *Trigo en cierne*, wheat in the blade. || *Trigo marzal*, spring wheat. || *Trigo sarraceno*, buckwheat.
trígono, na adj. MAT. Trigonal.
trigonometría f. Trigonometry.
trigonométrico, ca adj. Trigonometric, trigonometrical.
trigueño, ña adj. Olive-skinned (persona, rostro). || Golden, dark blond (pelo).
triguero, ra adj. Wheat: *campos trigueros*, wheat fields.
— M. Wheat merchant. || Wheat sieve (criba).
trilateral o **trilátero, ra** adj. Trilateral, three-sided.
trilingüe adj. Trilingual.
trilita f. Tolite (explosivo).
trilito m. Trilithon, dolmen.
trilobites m. pl. Trilobites.
trilobulado, da adj. Trilobate. || Trefoil (arco).
trilogía f. Trilogy.
trilógico, ca adj. Of *o* pertaining to a trilogy.
trilla f. Threshing (acción). || Threshing time *o* season (temporada). || Thresher (trillo). || ZOOL. Gurnard (pez). || FAM. Thrashing (tunda).
trillado adj. AGR. Threshed. || FIG. Worn-out, hackneyed, played-out: *un tema trillado*, a worn-out subject. | Beaten: *camino trillado*, beaten path.
trillador, ra adj. Threshing.
— F. Threshing machine (máquina). || *Trilladora segadora*, combine harvester.
trilladura f. AGR. Threshing.
trillar v. tr. AGR. To thresh. || FIG. To wear out, to play out (emplear mucho). | To beat (maltratar).
trillizos, zas m. y f. pl. Triplets.
trillo m. Thresher [drawn by a horse, mule, etc.]. || *Amer.* Path, lane.
trillón m. Trillion [U.S., quintillion].
trimestral adj. Quarterly, three-monthly. || *Exámenes trimestrales*, end-of-term exams.
trimestralmente adv. Quarterly, every three months.
trimestre m. Quarter, trimester. || Term (en la universidad). || Quarterly payment (pago).
trimielga f. Torpedo fish (pez).
trimorfismo m. Trimorphism.
trimorfo, fa adj. Trimorphic, trimorphous.
trimotor adj. m. Three-engined.
— M. Three-engined aircraft.
trinado m. Warble (de un pájaro). || Trill (de un cantante).
trinar v. intr. To warble (un pájaro). || MÚS. To trill. || FIG. y FAM. *Está Juan que trina*, John is fuming *o* furious.
trinca f. Trio, group of three, threesome (reunión de tres personas o cosas). || MAR. Lashing.
trincar v. tr. To tie securely, to bind (atar). || MAR. To lash. || To break up, to smash (romper). || FAM. To catch (apresar). | To hold down (inmovilizar). | To steal (robar). | To drink, to put away, to down (beber). || FAM. *Trincar una trompa*, to get plastered *o* tight.
trincha f. Strap.
trinchado m. Carving (de la carne).
trinchador, ra adj. Carving (de carne).
— M. y f. Carver (de carne). || — M. Carving knife (cuchillo).
trinchante adj. Carving.
— M. Servant [who carved meat in olden times]. || Carving knife (cuchillo). || Meat fork (tenedor). || Stonecutter's hammer (escoda). || Serving table, side table, sideboard (mueble).
trinchar v. tr. To carve, to cut (la carne).
trinchera f. Trench (para defenderse). || Cutting (de ferrocarril). || Ditch (para cables, tuberías, etc.). || Trench coat (abrigo impermeable). || *Guerra de trincheras*, trench warfare.
trinchero adj. Carving (plato).
— M. Serving table, side table, sideboard (mueble). || Carving dish (plato).
trinchete m. Shoemaker's knife. || *Amer.* [Table] knife.
trineo m. Sledge [U.S., sled] (pequeño). || Sleigh (grande).
trinidad f. Trinity.
Trinidad y Tobago n. pr. GEOGR. Trinidad and Tobago.
trinitaria f. BOT. Heartsease, wild pansy.
trinitario, ria adj./s. Trinitarian.
trinitrotolueno m. QUÍM. Trinitrotoluene.
trino, na adj. REL. Triune, three in one. || Trine (triple). || ASTR. Trine.
trino m. MÚS. Trill. || Warble, trill (del pájaro).
trinomio m. Trinomial.
trinquetada f. MAR. Sailing under foresail.
trinquete m. MAR. Foremast (palo). | Foresail (vela). || DEP. Pelota court (frontón). || TECN. Pawl, ratchet (de rueda dentada).
trinquetilla f. MAR. Fore-topmast staysail. | Small jib.
trinquis m. FAM. Swig, drink (trago). | Bottle: *le gusta mucho el trinquis*, he is fond of the bottle. | Drink: *echar un trinquis*, to have a drink.
trío m. Trio.
tríodo m. FÍS. Triode.
trióxido m. QUÍM. Trioxide.
tripa f. Gut, intestine (intestino). || FAM. Stomach, tummy, belly (vientre): *dolor de tripa*, stomachache. | Paunch, gut: *echar tripa*, to put on a paunch; *tener tripa*, to have a paunch. | Belly (panza de una vasija). || Filling (de un cigarro puro). || Catgut: *cuerda de tripa*, catgut string. || — Pl. FAM. Innards, works (de una máquina). | Inside, *sing.*, core, *sing.* (de una fruta, etc.). || — FIG. y FAM. *Echar las tripas*, to throw up (vomitar). | *Hacer de tripas corazón*, to keep a stiff upper lip, to pluck up courage. | *Llenar* or *llenarse la tripa*, to eat one's fill. || *Quitar las tripas a un animal*, to gut an animal. || FIG. y FAM. *Revolver las tripas*, to turn one's stomach. | *Tener malas tripas*, to be cruel *o* ruthless.
tripada f. FAM. *Darse una tripada*, to have one's fill (saciarse), to have had a bellyful (*de*, of) [estar harto].
tripanosoma m. MED. Trypanosome.
tripanosomiasis f. MED. Trypanosomiasis.
tripartición f. Tripartition.
tripartir v. tr. To divide into three.
tripartito, ta adj. Tripartite: *acuerdo tripartito*, tripartite agreement.
tripería f. Tripe shop, butcher's shop where offal is sold.
tripero, ra m. y f. Tripe *o* offal butcher. || — M. Flannel waistband.
tripétalo, la adj. BOT. Tripetalous.
tripicallero, ra m. y f. Tripe seller.
tripicallos m. pl. CULIN. Tripe, *sing.*
triplano m. Triplane (avión).
triplaza adj. Three-seater.
triple adj. Triple. || Triple, three times. || Triple thickness (de tres espesuras).
— M. Triple. || — *Ahora cuesta el triple de lo que costaba*, it costs three times as much as it used to. || *Ser el triple de grande que*, to be three times as big as.
triplicación f. Triplication.
triplicado adj. Triplicate.
— M. Triplicate: *por triplicado*, in triplicate.
triplicar v. tr. To triplicate (producir tres copias idénticas). || To triple, to treble.
— V. pr. To triple, to treble: *la población de Los Ángeles se ha triplicado*, the population of Los Angeles has tripled.
tríplice adj. Triple.
triplicidad f. Triplicity.
triplo, pla adj. Triple.
trípode m. Tripod.
tripón, ona adj. FAM. Potbellied.
tríptico m. Triptych.
triptongo m. GRAM. Triphthong.
tripudo, da adj. FAM. Potbellied.
tripulación f. Crew (de un barco, avión).
tripulante m. Crew member. || — Pl. Crew, *sing.*
tripular v. tr. To man: *satélite tripulado*, manned satellite; *vuelo tripulado*, manned flight.
triquina f. Trichina.
triquinosis f. MED. Trichinosis.
triquinoso, sa adj. Trichinous.
triquiñuela f. FAM. Trick, dodge: *las triquiñuelas del oficio*, the tricks of the trade. || *Andar con triquiñuelas*, to be a trickster.
triquitraque m. Clatter, clackety-clack (de un tren). || Bang, crash (ruido fuerte). || Firework similar to a jumping jack (en pirotecnia).
trirrectángulo, la adj. MAT. Trirectangular.
trirreme m. Trireme.
tris m. Crack (estallido). || Rip (de algo al rasgarse). || — FIG. y FAM. *En un tris*, in a jiffy. | *Estuvo en un tris que le pillara el coche*, he was very nearly run over by the car. | *He estado en un tris de llamar a la policía*, I was on the point of calling *o* I very nearly called the police. | *No lo alcanzó por un tris*, it missed him by a hairsbreadth, it very nearly hit him.
trisagio m. REL. Trisagion.

trisca f. Crunch (crujido). || FIG. Uproar, rumpus, racket (bulla, jaleo).
triscador, ra adj. Rowdy, uproarious.
— M. Saw set (sierra).
triscar v. tr. To mingle, to mix (enredar). || To set (una sierra).
— V. intr. To stamp (patear). || To gambol, to frisk (retozar, un animal). || FIG. To romp, to frollick (persona).
trisecar v. tr. MAT. To trisect.
trisección f. MAT. Trisection.
trisemanal adj. Triweekly.
trisemanalmente adv. Thrice weekly, three times a week (tres veces por semana). || Every three weeks (cada tres semanas).
trisílabo, ba adj. Trisyllabic.
— M. Trisyllable.
triste adj. Sad, unhappy, sorrowful: *triste por la muerte de su padre*, sad because of the death of his father. || Sad, melancholy, gloomy: *tiene un carácter triste*, he has a gloomy character. || Dismal, dreary, gloomy: *un día triste*, a gloomy day; *una calle triste*, a dismal street. || Sad, unfortunate, sorry (situación). || Sad (noticia, canción, etc.). || FIG. Sorry, measly, paltry, miserable: *un triste sueldo*, a sorry salary; *sólo me queda un triste cigarrillo*, I've only got one measly cigarette left. || — FIG. *Es la triste verdad*, it's the sad truth *o* the sorry truth. || *Es triste que no haya ganado*, it's a shame *o* a pity he didn't win.
— M. *Amer.* Sad popular song.
tristeza f. Sadness, sorrow (de una persona). || Sadness, desolation, gloominess, dreariness (de un sitio). || *Siempre me viene a contar sus tristezas*, she always comes to me with her problems.
tristón, ona adj. Melancholy, somewhat sad, gloomy.
trisulfuro m. QUÍM. Trisulphide [U.S., trisulfide].
tritio m. QUÍM. Tritium.
tritón m. ZOOL. Newt.
Tritón m. MIT. Triton.
trituración f. Trituration, grinding, crushing.
triturador, ra adj. Triturating, crushing, grinding.
— F. Crusher, triturator (máquina). || — M. Garbage disposal [unit] (de basura).
triturar v. tr. To grind, to triturate, to crush (moler). || To chew (mascar). || FIG. To make suffer (hacer sufrir). | To tear to pieces (criticar severamente). || FIG. y FAM. *Triturar a palos*, to beat [s.o.] up.
triunfador, ra adj. Triumphant, victorious.
— M. y f. Winner, victor, triumpher.
triunfal adj. Triumphal (arco, etc.). || Triumphant.
triunfalmente adv. Triumphantly.
triunfante adj. Triumphant. || *Salir triunfante*, to emerge victorious.
triunfar v. intr. To triumph (*sobre, de*, over). || FIG. To win, to triumph: *triunfar en un certamen*, to win a contest, to triumph in a contest. | To succeed: *triunfar en la vida*, to succeed in life. || DEP. To win. || To play a trump, to trump (en los juegos de cartas).
triunfo m. Triumph, victory (victoria). || Triumph (en la Roma antigua). || FIG. Success: *triunfo teatral*, theatrical success; *triunfo en la vida*, success in life. || Trump (naipes). || DEP. Win, victory. || *Amer.* Popular dance. || — *En triunfo*, in triumph. || FIG. *Tener todos los triunfos en la mano*, to hold all the trumps.
triunviral adj. Triumviral.
triunvirato m. Triumvirate.
triunviro m. Triumvir.
trivalencia f. Trivalence, trivalency.
trivalente adj. QUÍM. Trivalent.
trivial adj. Trivial, trite (insustancial): *conversación trivial*, trivial conversation. || Commonplace, trite (corriente).
trivialidad f. Triviality (cosa trivial). || Triteness, triviality (cualidad). || — Pl. Trivia, trivialities. || *Decir trivialidades*, to talk trivially.
trivio o **trivium** m. Trivium (estudios). || Junction [of three roads].
triza f. Bit, piece (pedazo pequeño): *hacer trizas*, to smash to pieces. || Shred (jirón): *hacer trizas*, to tear to shreads. || MAR. Halyard. || FIG. *Hacer trizas a uno*, to pull s.o. to pieces, to tear s.o. to shreds (criticar severamente).
trocamiento m. Exchange.
trocánter m. ANAT. Trochanter.
trocar m. MED. Trocar.
trocar* v. tr. To exchange, to barter: *trocar un caballo por una mula*, to exchange a horse for a mule. || To change, to convert: *trocar el amor en odio*, to convert love into hate. || FIG. To confuse, to mix up (confundir, mezclar). || To vomit.
— V. pr. To change (*en*, into).
trocear v. tr. To cut up.
troceo m. Cutting up.
trocla f. Pulley (polea).
tróclea f. ANAT. Trochlea.
trocoide adj./s.f. Trochoid.
trócola f. Pulley.
trocha f. Narrow path, trail (sendero). || Shortcut (atajo). || *Amer.* Gauge, gage (del ferrocarril).
trochemoche (a) o **a troche y moche** adv. V. MOCHE.
trochuela f. Narrow path.
trofeo m. Trophy. || Victory, triumph (triunfo).
troglodita adj. Troglodytical, troglodytic, cave-dwelling. || FIG. Coarse, brutish (bárbaro). | Gluttonous (comilón).
— M. y f. Troglodyte, caveman, cave dweller. || FIG. Brute (bruto). | Glutton (comilón). || — M. ZOOL. Troglodyte (pájaro).
troglodítico adj. Troglodytic, troglodytical.
troica f. Troika.
troj o **troje** f. Granary, barn (granero).
trola f. FAM. Lie, fib (mentira).
trole m. Trolley, trolly, trolley pole.
trolebús m. Trolleybus.
trolero, ra adj. FAM. Lying (mentiroso).
— M. y f. FAM. Liar, fibber.
tromba f. Waterspout. || — FIG. *En tromba*, like a whirlwind. | *Una tromba de agua*, a heavy downpour (aguacero).
trombina f. Thrombin.
trombo m. MED. Thrombus.
trombocito m. Thrombocyte.
trombón m. MÚS. Trombone (instrumento). | Trombonist (músico). || — *Trombón de pistones* or *de llaves*, valve trombone. || *Trombón de varas*, slide trombone.
trombosis f. MED. Thrombosis.
trompa f. Horn: *trompa de caza*, hunting horn. || Trunk (del elefante). || Snout (hocico). || Proboscis (de insecto). || Top, spinning top (trompo). || Humming top (trompo que zumba). || ARQ. Squinch, pendentive. || Trompe (de forja). || Scape (de la cebolla). || FAM. Hooter, snout, conk (nariz). | Thump, bash, bang (puñetazo). || — FAM. *Coger una trompa*, to get tight *o* plastered. | *Estar trompa*, to be tight *o* sozzled *o* plastered. || ANAT. *Trompa de Eustaquio*, Eustachian tube. | *Trompa de Falopio*, Fallopian tube.
— M. Horn player.
trompada f. o **trompazo** m. FAM. Bump, bang, bash (choque). | Thump, bash, punch (puñetazo). || — FAM. *Andar a trompazo limpio* or *darse de trompazos*, to be fighting. | *Darse un trompazo con una puerta*, to bash *o* to bump into a door. | *Darse un trompazo con un coche contra*, to crash into.
trompear v. intr. To spin a top.
— V. tr. *Amer.* To punch, to thump.
trompeta f. MÚS. Trumpet. | Bugle (clarín). || *Tocar la trompeta*, to play the trumpet.
— M. MÚS. Trumpet player, trumpeter. | Bugler (del clarín).
trompetada f. FAM. Blunder (necedad).
trompetazo m. Trumpet blast (sonido). || Blow with a trumpet (golpe). || FIG. y FAM. Blunder (trompetada).
trompetear v. intr. FAM. To play the trumpet.
trompeteo m. Trumpet playing.
trompetería f. Trumpets, *pl.*, trumpet section (de una orquesta). || Trumpets, *pl.* (de un órgano).
trompetero m. Trumpet player, trumpeter (el que toca la trompeta). || Trumpet maker (el que hace trompetas). || MIL. Bugler, trumpeter. || Boarfish (pez).
trompetilla f. Ear trumpet (para oír mejor).
trompetista m. y f. Trumpet player, trumpeter.
trompicar v. tr. To trip, to trip up, to make stumble (hacer tropezar).
— V. intr. To trip, to trip up, to stumble: *trompicó al subir la escalera*, he tripped on the stairs.
trompicón m. Stumble, trip. || FIG. y FAM. Punch (golpe). || FIG. *A trompicones*, by fits and starts.
trompillar v. tr. e intr. To trip, to trip up (trompicar).
trompillón m. ARQ. Keystone of a squinch *o* circular vault.
trompito m. FAM. Chick-pea (garbanzo).
trompo m. Top, spinning top (juguete). || FIG. Dolt, oaf (persona torpe). || FIG. y FAM. *Ponerse como un trompo*, to stuff o.s. silly (de comer), to drink like a fish (de beber).
trompudo, da adj. Thick-lipped.
tronada f. Storm.
tronado, da adj. FAM. Broken-down, old, worn-out (viejo). | Broke, flat broke (sin dinero).
tronador, ra adj. Thundering (que truena). || Detonating.
tronante adj. Thundering, thunderous.
tronar* v. impers. To thunder: *tronó toda la noche*, it thundered all night.
— V. intr. To thunder: *el cañón truena*, the cannon thunders. || FIG. To thunder, to boom: *tronó la voz del capitán*, the captain's voice thundered. | To thunder, to fulminate: *tronar contra el vicio*, to thunder against vice. || — FIG. y FAM. *¡Está que truena!*, he is hopping mad *o* fuming. | *Por lo que pueda tronar*, just in case.
— V. tr. *Amer.* To shoot (fusilar).
tronazón f. *Amer.* Thunderstorm.
troncal adj. Trunk.
troncar v. tr. To truncate.
tronco m. Trunk (de árbol, persona, animal). || ARQ. Trunk, drum (de columna). || Team (dos caballerías). || MAT. Frustum (de cono, pirámide, prisma). || FIG. Stock, lineage (de una familia). | Blockhead (zoquete). || — FIG. y FAM. *Dormir como un tronco*, to sleep like a log. || MAT. *Tronco de cono*, truncated cone.
troncocónico, ca adj. Shaped like a truncated cone.

troncha f. *Amer.* Slice. | Cushy job (trabajo bien remunerado).
tronchar v. tr. To bring down, to fell (árboles): *el viento ha tronchado varios árboles*, the wind has brought down several trees. || FIG. To wear out (rendir de cansancio). | To break [up] (romper). | To break off (quitar, arrancar). | To destroy (las esperanzas). | To cut short (la vida).
— V. pr. FIG. y FAM. *Troncharse de risa*, to split one's sides laughing.
troncho m. Stem, stalk.
tronera f. Loophole (de fortificación). || Porthole (de barco). || Small window (ventanilla). || Pocket (billar).
— M. y f. FIG. y FAM. Harum-scarum (persona de poco juicio).
tronido m. Thunderclap. || FIG. Boom, roar (de cañón, etc.). || — Pl. Thunder, *sing.*
trono m. Throne: *el trono real*, the royal throne. || Crown: *heredar el trono*, to inherit the crown; *lealtad al trono*, loyalty to the crown. || REL. Tabernacle (del Santo Sacramento). | Shrine (para un santo). || — Pl. REL. Thrones.
tronzador m. Two-handed saw (sierra).
tronzar v. tr. To cut up (cortar). || To smash, to shatter (quebrar). || To pleat, to put small pleats in (poner pliegues). || FIG. To wear out, to exhaust (cansar).
tropa f. Troop, flock, crowd (reunión de gente). || MIL. Troops, *pl.*: *la tropa necesita nuevos uniformes*, the troops need new uniforms. | Rank and file, ranks, *pl.* (no oficiales). | Assembly (toque). || *Amer.* Herd, drove (de animales). || — Pl. Troops. || — MIL. *Procede de la clase de tropa*, he came up from the ranks. || FAM. *Ser de tropa*, to be in the army. || MIL. *Tropas aerotransportadas*, airborne troops. | *Tropas de asalto*, storm troops. | *Tropas de línea*, line troops.
tropear v. intr. *Amer.* To divide into herds (el ganado).
tropel m. Throng, mob, rush, crush (muchedumbre). || Hurry, rush (prisa). || Jumble, heap, hodgepodge (montón). || *En tropel*, in a mad rush.
tropelía f. (P.us.) Mad rush (prisa confusa). || Outrage (ultraje). || *Actos de tropelía*, acts of violence.
tropero m. *Amer.* Cowboy, cattle driver.
tropezadura f. Stumble.
tropezar* v. intr. To stumble, to trip: *tropecé al entrar en el cuarto*, I tripped coming into the room. || FIG. To slip up, to go wrong (cometer un error). || — *Tropezar con* or *en*, to stumble on, to trip over (una piedra, etc.). || FIG. *Tropezar con*, to run into, to bump into (chocar), to run into, to bump into, to come across (encontrar a una persona), to run into, to come up against (dificultad), to fall out with, to quarrel with (reñir). || FIG. y FAM. *Tropezar con un hueso*, to hit a snag.
— V. pr. To run *o* to bump into one another (encontrarse).
tropezón m. Stumble, trip (traspiés). || FIG. Slipup, slip (desacierto). || — Pl. Small pieces of food. || — FIG. *A tropezones*, by fits and starts. || *Dar un tropezón*, to stumble, to trip (al andar), to slip up, to go wrong (equivocarse).
tropical adj. Tropical.
trópico, ca adj. Tropic, tropical. || FIG. Tropical (de tropo).
— M. Tropic. || — *Trópico de Cáncer*, Tropic of Cancer. || *Trópico de Capricornio*, Tropic of Capricorn.
tropiezo m. Stumble, trip. || FIG. Slip, slipup (desliz). | Setback, mishap (revés). | Obstacle, snag, stumbling block, hitch (impedimento). | Argument, quarrel (discusión). || *Dar un tropiezo*, to stumble, to trip.
tropismo m. Tropism.
tropo m. Trope, figure of speech.
tropología f. Tropology.
troposfera f. Troposphere.
troquel m. TECN. Die. || FIG. *Formados en el mismo troquel*, cast in the same mould.
troqueladora f. TECN. Stamping press.
troquelar v. tr. To stamp out. || To coin, to mint (acuñar moneda).
troquilo m. Trochilus.
trotacalles m. y f. inv. FAM. Gadabout, saunterer (persona callejera).
trotaconventos f. inv. FAM. Procuress, go-between (alcahueta).
trotada f. Distance, way, walk (trayecto). || *Dar una trotada*, to walk a good distance.
trotador, ra adj. Trotting.
trotamundos m. y f. inv. Globetrotter.
trotar v intr. To trot. || FIG. y FAM. To run *o* to chase about, to be on the go. || — *Empezar a trotar*, to break into a trot. || *Hacer trotar un caballo*, to trot a horse.
trote m. Trot (paso): *a trote corto*, at an easy *o* a slow trot. || FIG. y FAM. Chasing about, running backwards and forwards (actividad). || — Pl. FIG. y FAM. Affairs, business, *sing.* (enredo): *no te debes meter en esos trotes*, you shouldn't get mixed up in such affairs. || — *Al trote*, trotting, at a trot (trotando), in a rush, quickly (de prisa). || FIG. *De* or *para todo trote*, for everyday wear *o* use (vestido). || FIG. y FAM. *Ya no estoy yo para estos trotes*, I can't dash about like that any more, I can't keep up the pace any more.
trotón, ona adj. Trotting (caballo). || FIG. Everyday (de uso diario).
— M. Trotter (caballo).
trotskista adj./s. Trotskyist, Trotskyite.
trova f. Verse (verso). || Poem.
trovador, ra adj. Versifying.
— M. Poet. || Troubadour, minstrel (en la Edad Media). || — F. Poetess.
trovadoresco, ca adj. Troubadour: *una canción trovadoresca*, a troubadour song.
trovar v. intr. To write verse.
trovero m. Trouvère.
Troya n. pr. Troy. || — FIG. y FAM. *Allí* or *aquí fue Troya*, then the trouble began, that was when it started (se armó un escándalo). | *Arda Troya*, come what may, whatever the consequences. || *Caballo de Troya*, Trojan horse.
troyano, na adj./s. Trojan.
trozo m. Piece: *un trozo de papel, de madera*, a piece of paper, of wood. || Part (parte). || Passage (obra literaria o musical). || MAR. Detail. || — MIL. *Trozo de retaguardia*, rear guard (de un ejército). | *Trozo de vanguardia* or *de San Felipe*, advance guard (de un ejército). || *Trozos escogidos*, selected passages, selections (de un escritor).
trucaje m. CINEM. Trick photography.
trucar v. intr. To make the first bet (hacer el primer envite). || To pocket the opponent's ball (en el billar).
trucidar v. tr. To kill [cruelly] (matar).
truco m. Knack (habilidad, tranquillo). || Trick (engaño): *truco de naipes*, card trick. || CINEM. Trick shot. || Pocketing of the opponent's ball (en billar). || Card game (juego de naipes). || — Pl. Billiards, *sing.*, pool, *sing.* (billar). || — FAM. *Andarse con trucos*, to resort to trickery. | *Cogerle el truco a algo*, to get the hang of sth., to get the knack. | *Cogerle el truco a alguien*, to see through s.o., to cotton on to s.o. | *Tener mucho truco*, to be tricky.
truculencia f. Horror, cruelty. || FIG. y FAM. *Déjate de truculencias*, stop dramatizing.
truculento, ta adj. Horrifying, terrifying, ghastly.
trucha f. Trout (pez). || — FIG. y FAM. *No se cogen* or *pescan truchas a bragas enjutas*, nothing ventured nothing gained. || *Trucha arco iris*, rainbow trout. || *Trucha asalmonada*, salmon trout. || *Trucha de mar*, scorpion fish.
truchero, ra adj. Trout: *río truchero*, trout river.
— M. Trout fisherman (pescador). || Trout seller (vendedor).
truchimán, ana m. y f. Dragoman, interpreter (trujamán). || FIG. y FAM. Rascal, scoundrel.
truchuela f. Small trout (trucha pequeña). || Smoked codfish (bacalao curado).
trudgeon m. DEP. Trudgeon (natación).
trueno m. Thunder. || Thunderclap, clap of thunder (estampido). || Boom, bang, report (de arma o cohete). || FAM. Young tearaway *o* madcap, reckless young fellow (atolondrado). || — *Trueno gordo*, finale (fuegos artificiales). || *Voz de trueno*, booming *o* thundering voice.
trueque m. Barter, exchange. || *Amer.* Change. || — *A trueque de*, in exchange for. || *Aun a trueque de perder la fama*, even if it costs me my reputation.
trufa f. Truffle (hongo). || FIG. Lie, fib (mentira).
trufar v. tr. CULIN. To stuff with truffles.
— V. intr. FIG. To fib, to lie (decir mentiras).
truhán, ana adj. Roguish, crooked (desvergonzado). || FAM. Clownish, buffoonish (gracioso).
— M. Rogue, crook (granuja). || FAM. Buffoon, clown (gracioso).
truhanada f. V. TRUHANERÍA.
truhanear v. intr. To cheat, to swindle (engañar). || FAM. To play the buffoon, to jest, to clown.
truhanería f. Roguery, crookedness. || FAM. Buffoonery, clowning.
truhanesco, ca adj. Roguish, crooked (desvergonzado). || FAM. Clownish, buffoonish (gracioso).
truismo m. Truism.
trujamán, ana m. y f. Dragoman, interpreter. || — M. Expert adviser.
trujamanear v. intr. To interpret, to be an interpreter, to work as an interpreter.
trulla f. Racket, uproar, noise.
truncado, da adj. MAT. Truncated: *cono truncado*, truncated cone.
truncamiento m. Truncation. || FIG. Destruction (destrucción). | Cutting short (interrupción).
truncar v. tr. To truncate. || To mutilate (estatua). || To cut short, to cut down (un libro). || FIG. To cut short (interrumpir): *carrera truncada por la muerte*, career cut short by death.
trusa f. *Amer.* Bathing trunks, *pl.*
trust m. COM. Trust.
tse-tsé f. Tsetse [fly] (mosca del sueño).
tu, tus adj. pos. Your: *tu sombrero*, your hat; *tus zapatos*, your shoes. || REL. Thy, Thine.
tú pron. pers. You (sujeto): *tú vas*, you go. || REL. Thou. || — *A tú por tú*, disrespectfully. || *Hablar* or *llamar* or *tratar de tú*, to address as "tú", to address familiarly; to be on friendly terms with (ser amigos). || FIG. *Llamar a Dios de tú*, to be disrespectful. || FAM. *Más eres tú*, who are you to talk!, look who's talking! || *¡Tú!*, hey you!, hey! || *Tú y yo*, tea set for two (servicio de té), place mat for two (mantel).

tuareg m. Tuareg.
tuba f. Tuba, Philippine liquor (licor). || MÚS. Tuba (instrumento).
tuberculina f. MED. Tuberculin.
tubérculo m. BOT. Tuber, tubercle. || MED. y ANAT. Tubercle.
tuberculosis f. MED. Tuberculosis.
tuberculoso, sa adj. Tuberous (tuberoso). || MED. Tuberculous, tubercular.
— M. y f. MED. Person who suffers from tuberculosis, tubercular.
tubería f. Piping, pipes, *pl.*, tubing (conjunto de tubos). || Plumbing (instalación). || Pipe, tube (conducto). || Pipe factory *o* store (fábrica, comercio de tubos).
tuberosa f. BOT. Tuberose.
tuberosidad f. Tuberosity, swelling.
tuberoso, sa adj. Tuberous, tuberose: *raíz tuberosa*, tuberous root.
tubo m. Pipe: *el tubo del agua*, the water pipe. || ANAT. Tube: *tubo capilar*, capillary tube. || Tube (recipiente alargado): *tubo de pasta dentífrica*, toothpaste tube. || Chimney (de lámpara). || MÚS. Pipe (de órgano). || FÍS. Tube: *tubo de rayos catódicos*, cathode-ray tube. || — *Falda tubo*, tight skirt. || *Tubo acústico*, speaking tube. || *Tubo de desagüe*, drainpipe (para lluvia), wastepipe (del lavabo). || *Tubo de drenaje*, drainage tube. || *Tubo de ensayo*, test tube. || *Tubo de escape*, exhaust pipe. || *Tubo de órgano*, organ pipe. || *Tubo de vacío*, vacuum tube. || ANAT. *Tubo digestivo*, alimentary canal. | *Tubo intestinal*, intestinal tract. || *Tubo lanzallamas*, flamethrower. || *Tubo lanzacohetes*, rocket launcher. || *Tubo lanzatorpedos*, torpedo tube.
tubulado, da adj. Tubulate.
tubular adj. Tubular. || *Caldera tubular*, fire-tube boiler.
— M. Bicycle tyre [U.S., bicycle tire].
tucán m. ZOOL. Toucan (ave).
tuco, ca adj. *Amer.* One-armed, one-handed (manco de brazo, de mano). || — M. *Amer.* Firefly (insecto). | Stump (muñón).
tucumano, na adj. [Of *o* from] Tucumán.
— M. y f. Native *o* inhabitant of Tucumán (Argentina).
tucutucu m. *Amer.* Tuco-tuco (topo).
tucuyo m. *Amer.* Coarse cotton cloth.
tudesco, ca adj./s. German. || — FIG. y FAM. *Beber como un tudesco*, to drink like a fish. | *Comer como un tudesco*, to eat like a horse. || — M. German cloak (capote).
Tudor n. pr. Tudor.
tuera f. BOT. Colocynth, bitter apple. || FIG. *Más amargo que la tuera*, as bitter as gall.
tuerca f. Nut. || *Tuerca de aletas* or *de orejas* or *de mariposa*, wing nut.
tuerto, ta adj. One-eyed, blind in one eye: *quedarse tuerto*, to become blind in one eye. || Twisted, bent (torcido). || *A tuertas o a derechas*, rightly or wrongly (con razón o sin ella), by hook or by crook (por las buenas o por las malas).
— M. y f. One-eyed person. || — M. Injustice, wrong (ofensa). || — Pl. MED. Afterpains (entuertos).
tueste m. Toasting (tostadura).
tuétano m. ANAT. Marrow (médula). || FIG. Essence, heart, core, substance (sustancia). || — FIG. y FAM. *Calado hasta los tuétanos*, drenched to the bone. | *Enamorado hasta los tuétanos*, head over heels in love. | *Hasta los tuétanos*, through and through. | *Sacar los tuétanos a uno*, to wring s.o.'s neck.
tufarada f. Strong smell (olor). || Waft (racha de olor). || Gust (racha de aire).
tufo m. Fume (emanación). || Foul odour *o* smell, stink: *tufo de una alcantarilla*, foul odour of a sewer. || Fug (en un cuarto lleno de gente). || Curl (mechón de pelo). || Tufa (toba). || — Pl. FIG. Airs: *tener tufos*, to put on airs.
tugurio m. Hovel, slum, shack (casucha): *vivir en un tugurio*, to live in a shack. || Small room (habitación pequeña). || Shepherd's hut (choza).
tuición f. JUR. Custody, protection.
tuitivo, va adj. JUR. Protective, defensive.
tul m. Tulle (tela).
tulio m. QUÍM. Thulium.
tulipa f. [Tulip-shaped] lampshade.
tulipán m. BOT. Tulip.
tulipanero o **tulipero** m. Tulip tree.
tullecer v. tr. To cripple, to maim (incapacitar). || To paralyse (paralizar).
— V. intr. To be crippled *o* maimed *o* paralysed (lisiarse).
tullidez f. Paralysis. || Disability, disablement.
tullido, da adj. Crippled, disabled, maimed. || Paralysed. || FIG. Exhausted, worn-out (cansado).
— M. y f. Cripple, disabled person.
tullimiento m. Paralysis. || Disability, disablement.
tullir* v. tr. To cripple, to maim (incapacitar). || To paralyse (paralizar). || FIG. To exhaust, to wear out (cansar mucho).
— V. pr. To be crippled *o* paralysed.
tumba f. Tomb, grave (sepultura). || Jolt, lurch (sacudida). || Somersault (voltereta). || Arched top (cubierta arqueada). || *Amer.* Tree clearing. || — FIG. *Abrir su tumba*, to dig one's own grave. | *Ser como una tumba*, to be as silent as the grave.
tumbaga f. Tombac, tomback (aleación). || Tombac ring (sortija de tumbaga). || Ring (sortija).
tumbal adj. Tomb. || *Piedra tumbal*, tombstone.
tumbar v. tr. To knock down *o* over (derribar): *lo tumbó de un golpe*, he knocked him down with one blow. || To knock *o* to bend over (inclinar mucho): *el viento ha tumbado el poste*, the wind has knocked the post over. || FIG. y FAM. To fail: *me tumbaron en latín*, they failed me in Latin. | To knock out (un olor fuerte, etc.). | To overwhelm, to stun: *la visión lo dejó tumbado*, the sight overwhelmed him. || MAR. To keel. || *Amer.* To fell, to clear (los árboles). || POP. To lay (a una mujer). || — *Estar tumbado*, to lie, to be lying down. || FIG. y FAM. *Tumbar de espaldas*, to bowl over: *la noticia me tumbó de espaldas*, the news bowled me over.
— V. intr. To tumble, to fall over (desplomarse). || MAR. To keel. || FIG. y FAM. *Que tumba*, overwhelming: *hay un olor a gasolina que tumba*, there is an overwhelming smell of petrol.
— V. pr. To lie down: *tumbarse en la cama*, to lie down on the bed. || To sprawl, to lounge (repantigarse): *tumbarse en una butaca*, to lounge in an armchair. || FIG. y FAM. To let up, to take it easy (dejar de hacer esfuerzos).
tumbo m. Jolt, bump, jerk (sacudida). || FIG. Difficulty. || *Dar tumbos*, to bump, to lurch, to jerk, to jolt: *el coche daba tumbos por el camino*, the car bumped along the road.
tumbón, ona adj. Lazy, idle (perezoso). || Sly (socarrón).
tumbona f. Sofa, lounge (diván). || Deckchair (silla de lona).
tumefacción f. MED. Tumefaction, swelling.
tumefacer* v. tr. MED. To tumefy, to cause to swell.
tumefacto, ta adj. MED. Swollen.
tumescencia f. MED. Tumescence, swelling.
tumescente adj. MED. Tumescent.
túmido, da adj. Tumid. || ARQ. Swollen.
tumor m. Tumour [U.S., tumor]: *tumores malignos*, malignant tumours.
tumulario, ria adj. Tumular, sepulchral: *inscripción tumularia*, sepulchral inscription.
túmulo m. Tumulus, barrow, burial mound (montecillo artificial). || Catafalque (catafalco). || Tomb (sepultura).
tumulto m. Tumult, turmoil, commotion. || FIG. Uproar.
tumultuoso, sa adj. Tumultuous.
tuna f. BOT. Tuna, prickly pear (fruta y árbol). || Group of student minstrels (estudiantina). || Student minstrel (estudiante). || *Correr la tuna*, to lead an idle and vagrant life.
tunal m. Tuna, prickly pear (nopal). || Tuna grove (sitio).
tunantada f. Mean trick.
tunante adj. Crooked, roguish, rascally (granuja).
— M. y f. Rogue, crook, rascal.
tunantear v. intr. To be crooked *o* roguish.
tunantería f. Crookedness, roguishness (cualidad). || Mean trick (acción).
tunantuelo, la m. y f. Little rascal.
tunda f. Shearing. || FAM. Beating, licking, thrashing: *dar una tunda a uno*, to give s.o. a thrashing.
tundición o **tundido** m. Cloth shearing.
tundidor, ra adj. Cloth shearing.
— M. y f. Cloth shearer. || — F. Cloth shearing machine.
tundidura f. Cloth shearing.
tundir v. tr. To shear (cortar). || FAM. To give a licking *o* a beating *o* a thrashing.
tundra f. Tundra.
tunear v. intr. To lead a vagrant life.
tunecí o **tunecino, na** adj./s. Tunisian.
túnel m. Tunnel. || *Túnel aerodinámico*, wind tunnel.
tunería f. Roguishness, rascality.
Túnez n. pr. GEOGR. Tunis (ciudad). | Tunisia (país).
tungstato m. QUÍM. Tungstate.
tungsteno m. QUÍM. Tungsten, wolfram.
túnica f. Tunic. || ANAT. Tunic, tunica.
tunicado, da adj./s.m. Tunicate.
tunicela f. REL. Tunicle.
tuno, na adj. Roguish, wicked.
— M. y f. Rogue, villain, rascal. || — M. Student minstrel (de la tuna).
tuntún (al o al buen) adv. FAM. Haphazardly, any old how.
tupaya f. ZOOL. Tupaia.
tupé m. Toupee. || FIG. y FAM. Cheek, nerve (descaro).
tupí adj. Tupian.
— M. y f. Tupi. || — M. Tupi (idioma).
tupido, da adj. Thick: *un paño tupido*, a thick cloth. || Dense, thick: *niebla tupida*, dense fog. || FIG. Dense, dim, stupid (torpe).
tupinambo m. BOT. Jerusalem artichoke.
tupir v. tr. To pack tightly (apretar).
— V. intr. To thicken (hierba).
— V. pr. FIG. y FAM. To stuff o.s. (comer mucho).
turba f. Peat, turf (combustible). || Mob, crowd (muchedumbre).
turbación f. Confusion. || Disorder (desorden). || Upset, disturbance (trastorno).

turbado, da adj. Upset, disturbed (preocupado, etc.). || Confused (confuso).
turbador, ra adj. Disturbing, upsetting. || Confusing. — M. y f. Disturber.
turbamiento m. V. TURBACIÓN.
turbamulta f. FAM. Mob.
turbante m. Turban.
turbar v. tr. To stir up (enturbiar). || FIG. To disturb: *turbar la paz*, to disturb the peace. | To upset, to disturb, to worry: *la noticia le turbó visiblemente*, the news visibly upset him. | To confuse (confundir). | To embarrass (dejar perplejo).
— V. pr. To be stirred up *o* disturbed (enturbiarse). || FIG. To be upset *o* worried *o* disturbed: *al oír la pregunta se turbó visiblemente*, he was visibly upset by the question. | To get confused *o* embarrassed.
turbelarios m. pl. ZOOL. Turbellaria.
turbera f. Peat bog.
túrbido, da adj. Turbid, cloudy (falto de transparencia). || Turbid, muddy (sucio).
turbiedad f. Cloudiness, turbidity, turbidness (de líquidos). || Opacity (opacidad). || FIG. Confusion.
turbina f. Turbine: *turbina hidráulica*, hydraulic *o* water turbine. || *Turbina de vapor*, steam turbine.
turbinto m. Pepper shrub.
turbio, bia adj. Turbid, cloudy, muddy: *líquido turbio*, cloudy liquid. || FIG. Shady, suspicious, suspect, fishy: *un negocio turbio*, a shady business. | Troubled, turbulent (agitado): *período turbio*, troubled period. | Blurred, dim, cloudy, unclear: *vista turbia*, blurred vision *o* view. | Confused (confuso). | Obscure, unclear (manera de hablar).
— M. pl. Dregs, sediment, *sing.* (sedimentos).
turbión f. Squall, heavy shower. || FIG. Shower, avalanche, torrent (gran cantidad).
turboalternador m. ELECTR. Turboalternator.
turbobomba m. TECN. Turbopump.
turbocompresor m. TECN. Turbocompressor.
turbodinamo m. ELECTR. Turbodynamo.
turbogenerador m. ELECTR. Turbogenerator.
turbohélice m. TECN. Turboprop.
turbomotor m. TECN. Turbomotor.
turbonada f. Squall, downpour (aguacero). || *Amer.* Strong wind (vendaval).
turbopropulsor m. TECN. Turboprop.
turborreactor m. TECN. Turbojet.
turbosoplante f. TECN. Turboblower.
turboventilador m. TECN. Turboventilator.
turbulencia f. Turbulence: *la turbulencia del agua*, the turbulence of the water. || FIG. Turbulence, disorder, disturbance, commotion (disturbio). | Unruliness (rebeldía). || Turbulence (atmosférica).
turbulento, ta adj. Turbulent, troubled (agitado): *aguas turbulentas*, turbulent waters. || FIG. Boisterous, unruly, disorderly (bullicioso): *alumnos turbulentos*, boisterous pupils. | Troubled, turbulent: *en esta época turbulenta*, in these troubled times.
turco, ca adj. Turkish. || — *Baño turco*, Turkish bath. || *Cama turca*, divan.
— M. y f. Turk. || — M. Turkish (idioma). || — *Cabeza de turco*, scapegoat. || *El Gran turco*, the Grand Turk. || FIG. y FAM. *Más celoso que un turco*, consumed with jealousy.
— F. FIG. y FAM. Booze-up [U.S., drunk]. || FIG. y FAM. *Coger una turca*, to get canned *o* plastered.
turcomano, na adj./s. Turcoman, Turkoman (gente o idioma).
turf f. DEP. Racecourse (pista). | Horse racing, turf (deporte).
turfista m. Turfman.
turgencia f. Turgidity, turgescence.
turgente adj. Turgid.
túrgido, da adj. Turgid.
turibulario m. Thurifer.
turiferario m. Thurifer.
turificar v. tr. To incense, to cense.
turismo m. Tourism: *el turismo todavía no ha afectado la isla*, tourism has not yet affected the island. || Tourism, the tourist trade *o* industry: *el turismo es la primera industria*, tourism is the major industry; *desarrollar el turismo en un país*, to develop a country's tourist industry. || Private car (coche). || — *El turismo ha estropeado la costa*, the tourist invasion has ruined the coast. || *Hacer turismo*, to go touring (en un país), to go sightseeing (en una ciudad).
turista m. y f. Tourist.
turístico, ca adj. Tourist: *una atracción turística*, a tourist attraction.
Turkmenistán n. pr. m. GEOGR. Turkmenistan, Turkomen.
turma f. Truffle (hongo). || ANAT. Testicle (testículo).
turmalina f. MIN. Tourmaline.
túrmix f. Mixer.
turnar, turnarse v. intr. y pr. To take turns: *turnarse para hacer algo*, to take turns to do sth.
turno m. Shift: *turno de día*, day shift. || Shift (cuadrilla). || Turn, go: *es tu turno*, it is your turn. || — *¿A quién le toca el turno?*, whose turn *o* whose go is it?, who is next? || *Estar de turno*, to be on duty. || *Lavamos los platos por turno*, we take turns *o* we take it in turn to do the washing up. || *Trabajar por turnos*, to work in shifts, to work shifts. || *Turno de noche*, night shift.
turolense adj. [Of *o* from] Teruel.
— M. y f. Native *o* inhabitant of Teruel.
turón m. Polecat (animal).
turquesa f. Turquoise (piedra preciosa). || Mould [U.S., mold] (molde) || *Azul turquesa*, turquoise blue, turquoise.
turquesco, ca adj. Turkish.
Turquestán n. pr. m. GEOGR. Turkestan.
turquí o **turquino** adj. m. *Azul turquí*, indigo.
Turquía n. pr. f. GEOGR. Turkey.
turrar v. tr. To toast, to roast (tostar).
turrón m. Nougat (dulce). || FIG. y FAM. Cushy number (cargo).

— OBSERV. The *turrón* is eaten especially at Christmas.

turronería f. Nougat shop, confectioner's.
turronero, ra m. y f. Nougat maker *o* seller, confectioner.
turulato, ta adj. FAM. Flabbergasted, dumbfounded (pasmado). | Dazed (aturdido).
turumba f. *Amer.* Calabash, gourd (vasija).
tururú m. Three of a kind, brelan (en las cartas). || — FAM. *Está tururú*, he is touched in the head. | *¡Tururú!*, that's what you think!
tus m. *Sin decir tus ni mus*, without a word.
— Interj. Here, boy! (a un perro).
tusa f. *Amer.* Corncob, cob of maize (carozo). | Husk of maize [U.S., corn husk]. | Cigar rolled in a corn husk (cigarro). | Mane (del caballo). | Pockmark (hoyo de viruela). | Streetwalker, tart (prostituta).
tusar v. tr. *Amer.* To shear.
tusilago f. BOT. Coltsfoot.
tuso, sa adj. *Amer.* Bobtail, tailless, docked (rabón). | Pockmarked (por la viruela).
— Interj. FAM. Here, boy! (para llamar al perro).
tusona f. FAM. Tart.
tusor m. Tussore [U.S., tussah] (tela).
tute m. Card game. || FAM. Beating, licking (paliza). || FIG. y FAM. *Darse un tute*, to work o.s. into the ground (trabajando), to walk *o* to run o.s. into the ground (andando, corriendo), to stuff o.s. (comiendo).
tuteamiento m. Use of the familiar *tú* form of address.
tutear v. tr. To address as *tú*.
— V. pr. To address one another using the familiar *tú* form.
tutela f. JUR. Guardianship (de personas). | Trusteeship (de territorios). || FIG. Protection (protección). | Guidance (dirección). || — *Bajo tutela*, in ward (persona). || *Territorio bajo tutela*, territory in trusteeship, trust territory.
tutelar adj. Tutelary: *acción tutelar*, tutelary action. || Protecting: *divinidad tutelar*, protecting divinity. || *Ángel tutelar*, guardian angel.
tuteo m. Use of the familiar *tú* form of address.
tutilimundi m. Cosmorama.
tutiplén (a) adv. FAM. Galore: *repartían caramelos a tutiplén*, they were giving out sweets galore. | A lot (mucho). || — FAM. *Comer a tutiplén*, to stuff o.s. | *Llovía a tutiplén*, it was raining buckets.
tutor, ra m. y f. JUR. Guardian. || Guardian, protector (protector). || — M. AGR. Stake, prop (rodrigón).
tutoría f. Guardianship.
tutriz f. JUR. Guardian. || Guardian, protector (protectora).
tutú m. South American bird of prey. || Tutu (de bailarina).
tuyo, ya adj. pos. Of yours, one of your: *un hermano tuyo*, a brother of yours, one of your brothers. || — *Lo tuyo*, what is yours, what belongs to you (lo que te pertenece), your business (lo que te concierne). || *Siempre tuyo*, Yours truly (en una carta).
— Pron. pos. Yours, your own: *tú tienes el tuyo en la mano*, you have yours *o* your own in your hand. || REL. Thine. || — FIG. y FAM. *Hiciste de las tuyas*, you got up to your old tricks || *Los tuyos*, your family *o* friends *o* people *o* men *o* supporters *o* side: *los tuyos están aquí*, your family is here.

— OBSERV. The familiar forms *tuyo, tuya* are generally used to address family members or friends.

tuyu m. *Amer.* Nandu, rhea (ñandú).
tuyuyú m. *Amer.* Type of stork (ave).
tweed m. Tweed (tejido).
tyndalización f. Tyndall effect.

U

u f. U: *una u mayúscula*, a capital u. || *La U consonante*, the V.

— OBSERV. The Spanish *u* is a vowel or semiconsonant and is pronounced rather like the English *oo*. In the groups *gue, gui*, and *que, qui*, the *u* is silent: but when it bears a diaeresis, or occurs in the group *gua, guo*, it is pronounced like the English *oo*: *vergüenza, guasa, antiguo*.

u conj. Or.

— OBSERV. *U* is used instead of *o* before words beginning with *o* or *ho*: *diez u once*, ten or eleven: *belga u holandés*, Belgian or Dutch.

Úbeda n. pr. GEOGR. Úbeda [Andalusia]. || FAM. *Irse por los cerros de Úbeda*, v. CERRO.

ubérrimo, ma adj. Very fertile: *tierra ubérrima*, very fertile land. || Abundant, luxuriant: *vegetación ubérrima*, luxuriant vegetation.

ubicación f. Position, situation, location.

ubicar v. intr. To be, to be situated *o* located *o* placed.
— V. tr. *Amer*. To put, to place. | To nominate (a un candidato). | To park (un coche).
— V. pr. To be, to be situated *o* located *o* placed. || To place o.s.

ubicuidad f. Ubiquity. || *No tengo el don de la ubicuidad*, I can't be everywhere at once.

ubicuo, cua adj. Ubiquitous.

ubre f. Udder.

ucase m. Ukase (edicto del zar). || FIG. Dictation (decisión autoritaria).

Ucrania n. pr. f. GEOGR. Ukraine: *Kiev es la capital de Ucrania*, Kiev is the capital of the Ukraine.

ucraniano, na adj./s. Ukrainian.

ucranio, nia adj./s. Ukrainian.

Ud. pron. pers. (abreviatura de *usted*). V. USTED.

Uds. pron. pers. (abreviatura de *ustedes*). V. USTED.

ued m. Wadi.

¡uf! interj. Phew! (alivio, cansancio). || Ugh! (repugnancia).

ufanarse v. pr. To be proud: *ufanarse con* or *de sus riquezas*, to be proud of one's riches. || To boast (*de*, of), to pride o.s. (*de*, on) [jactarse].

ufanía f. Pride.

ufano, na adj. Proud.

ujier m. Usher.

ukase m. V. UCASE.

ukelele o **ukulele** m. MÚS. Ukelele, ukulele.

ulano m. MIL. Uhlan.

úlcera f. MED. Ulcer.

ulceración f. Ulceration.

ulcerado, da adj. Ulcerated.

ulcerante adj. Ulcerative.

ulcerar, ulcerarse v. tr. y pr. To ulcerate.

ulcerativo, va adj. Ulcerative, ulcerating.

ulceroso, sa adj. Ulcerous.

ulema m. Ulema, ulama (sabio musulmán).

Ulises n. pr. m. MIT. Ulysses.

ulmáceas f. pl. BOT. Ulmaceae.

ulterior adj. Ulterior, farther, further (más allá). || Subsequent, later (que ocurre después). || Following (siguiente).

ulteriormente adv. Subsequently, later, later on.

ultimación f. Conclusion, completion.

últimamente adv. Ultimately, finally (por último). || Lately (recientemente).

ultimar v. tr. To conclude, to complete, to finalize, to finish, to end: *ultimar un trato*, to conclude a deal. || To finalize: *ultimar los detalles*, to finalize the details. || *Amer*. To kill (matar).

ultimátum m. Ultimatum: *dirigir un ultimátum*, to give an ultimatum.

último, ma adj. Last, final: *diciembre es el último mes del año*, December is the last month of the year; *la última palabra*, the last word. || Latter (de dos). || Latest (más reciente): *última moda*, latest fashion. || Furthest, farthest, utmost (más lejano). || Back, last (de atrás). || Top, last (de arriba): *en el último piso*, on the top floor. || Bottom, last (de abajo). || Final (definitivo): *su última decisión*, his final decision. || Lowest (precio).
— M. y f. Last one, last. || Latter (de dos).
— *A la última*, up to date. || *A últimos de mes*, at *o* towards the end of the month. || *Como* or *en último recurso* or *en última instancia*, as a last resort. || *Dar el último toque* or *la última mano*, to put the finishing touches to, to finish off. || FIG. *El último grito* or *la última palabra*, the latest thing *o* craze. || *En último lugar*, as a last resort (si no hay otro remedio), finally (para concluir). || FIG. *¡Es lo último!*, that's the best yet!, that really is the limit! | *¡Es lo último que me faltaba por oír!*, now I've heard everything!, that's the best yet! || FAM. *Estar en las últimas*, to be at death's door, to be on one's deathbed (moribundo), to be down to one's last penny (sin dinero). || *Estos últimos meses*, these *o* the last few months. || FAM. *¡Has hecho las diez de últimas!*, you've had it! || *Llegar el último*, to arrive last. || *Por último*, finally. || *Quedarse con la última palabra*, to have the last word. || *Ser el último en llegar*, to be the last one *o* to be the last *o* to be last to arrive.

ultra adj./s. Ultra (extremista).

ultracentrifugadora f. Ultracentrifuge.

ultracorto, ta adj. Ultrashort.

ultraísmo m. "Ultraism".

— OBSERV. "Ultraísmo" (1919-1923) was a literary movement created by Spanish and Spanish-American poets in search of pure poetry. Its principal representatives were Guillermo de Torre, Jorge Luis Borges, Eugenio Montes and Gerardo Diego.

ultrajador, ra adj. Outrageous. || Insulting (insultante). || Offensive (ofensivo).

ultrajante adj. Outrageous. || Offensive.

ultrajar v. tr. To outrage, to do outrage: *ultrajarle a alguien*, to outrage s.o., to do s.o. an outrage. || To insult (insultar). || To offend (ofender).

ultraje m. Outrage. || Outrage, insult (insulto). || Offence (delito). || *Ultraje a las buenas costumbres*, indecent behaviour, moral offence.

ultrajoso, sa adj. Outrageous. || Offensive.

ultramar m. Overseas countries, *pl*. || — *Azul de ultramar*, ultramarine. || *Ir a ultramar*, to go abroad *o* overseas. || *Provincias de ultramar*, overseas provinces.

ultramarino, na adj. Overseas. || *Azul ultramarino*, ultramarine.
— M. pl. Foreign products *o* foodstuffs (géneros de ultramar). || Groceries, foodstuffs (comestibles). || *Ultramarinos* or *tienda de ultramarinos*, grocer's, grocer's shop, grocery [U.S., grocery store].

ultramicroscopio m. Ultramicroscope.

ultramoderno, na adj. Ultramodern.

ultramontanismo m. Ultramontanism.

ultramontano, na adj./s. Ultramontane.

ultramundano, na adj. Ultramundane.

ultranza (a) loc. To the death (a muerte). || Decisively (con decisión). || Extreme, out-and-out, uncompromising: *un pacifista a ultranza*, an extreme pacifist. || At any price, whatever the cost (cueste lo que cueste).

ultrapasar v. tr. To go beyond, to surpass.

ultrarrápido, da adj. Extra-fast.

ultrarrojo, ja adj./s.m. FÍS. Ultrared, infrared.

ultrasensible adj. Hypersensitive.

ultrasónico, ca adj. Ultrasonic.

ultrasonido m. FÍS. Ultrasound, supersound.

ultratumba f. Beyond the grave: *una voz de ultratumba*, a voice from beyond the grave.

ultraviolado, da o **ultravioleta** adj./s.m. Ultraviolet.

ultravirus m. inv. BIOL. Ultravirus.

úlula f. Tawny owl (ave).

ululación f. Howl, howling (del viento, de un animal). || Hoot, hooting (del búho). || Ululation (p.us.).

ulular v. intr. To howl (viento, animal). || To hoot (búho).

ululato m. Howl, howling (del viento, de un animal). || Hoot, hooting (del búho).

ulva f. BOT. Ulva (alga).

ulluco m. *Amer*. Ullucu, ulluco (planta).

umbelífero, ra adj. BOT. Umbelliferous.
— F. BOT. Umbellifer. || — Pl. BOT. Umbelliferae.

umbeliforme adj. BOT. Umbelliform.

umbilicado, da adj. Umbilicate.

umbilical adj. ANAT. Umbilical: *cordón umbilical*, umbilical cord.

umbral m. Threshold: *en el umbral*, on the threshold. || FIG. Threshold: *el umbral de la vida*, the threshold of life; *umbral de audibilidad*, auditory threshold. | Verge (borde). || — *En el umbral de la audibilidad*, just within hearing. || FIG. *En los umbrales de la muerte*, at death's door. | *Estar en los umbrales de una nueva era*, to be on the threshold of a new era. || *Pisar los umbrales*, to cross the threshold.

umbrela f. ZOOL. Umbrella (de medusa).

Umbría n. pr. f. GEOGR. Umbria.

umbrío, a adj. Shady (umbroso).

umbroso, sa adj. Shady.

un art. indef. A: *un hombre*, a man. || A, one: *un amigo mío*, one of my friends, a friend of mine.
— Adj. num. One: *un águila*, one eagle.

— OBSERV. La *a* inglesa se transforma en *an* delante de una vocal *(an egg)*, y de una *h* no aspirada *(an hour)*.
— *Un* is the apocopated form of *uno* used before a masculine noun, and of *una* before a feminine noun beginning with an accented *a* or *ha* (v. UNO).

una art. indef./adj. num. V. UNO.

unánime adj. Unanimous.

unanimidad f. Unanimity. || *Aprobar por unanimidad*, to approve unanimously.

unanimismo m. Unanimism.
unción f. Unction.
uncir v. tr. To yoke: *uncir los bueyes a un carro,* to yoke the oxen to a cart.
undecágono m. MAT. Undecagon.
undécimo, ma adj./s. Eleventh. || *En undécimo lugar,* eleventhly, in eleventh place.
undulación f. Undulation. || Wave (onda).
undulante adj. Undulant, undulating.
undular v. intr. To undulate.
undulatorio, ria adj. Undulatory.
ungido adj. m. Anointed (sacerdote, etc.).
ungimiento m. Unction.
ungir v. tr. To anoint.
ungüento m. Ointment, unguent.
unguiculado, da adj./s.m. ZOOL. Unguiculate.
unguis m. Unguis (hueso de la órbita).
ungulado, da adj./s.m. ZOOL. Ungulate.
ungular adj. Ungular, nail, of the nail (de la uña).
unible adj. Unitable, uniteable.
únicamente adv. Only, solely.
unicameral adj. Unicameral.
unicelular adj. Unicellular, single-cell.
unicidad f. Unicity, uniqueness.
único, ca adj. Only, sole: *el único culpable,* the only guilty person; *la única persona que ha sido simpática conmigo,* the only person who was nice to me. || FIG. Unique: *un acontecimiento único en la historia,* an event unique in history; *único en su género,* unique in *o* of its kind. || — *Hijo único,* only child. || *Sistema de partido único,* one party *o* single-party system.
— M. y f. Only one: *es el único que me queda,* it is the only one I have left. || — *Lo único,* the only thing: *lo único que puedo hacer,* the only thing I can do. || *¡Lo único que faltaba!,* that's all I [he, she, etc.] needed!
unicolor adj. Of one colour, all one colour.
unicornio m. Unicorn (animal fabuloso). || *Unicornio marino,* narwhal, narwal.
unidad f. Unit: *unidad métrica, monetaria,* metric, monetary unit. || Unity (literaria): *unidad de acción, de lugar, de tiempo,* unity of action, of place, of time. || Harmony (armonía). || Branch (de tren, metro). || Unity: *la unidad política,* political unity. || MAT. y MIL. Unit: *columna de las unidades,* units column; *unidad de combate,* combat unit. || COM. *Coste por unidad,* unit cost.
unidireccional adj. RAD. Unidirectional.
unido, da adj. United: *familia muy unida,* very united family. || *Unidos venceremos,* united we stand.
unificación f. Unification.
unificador, ra adj. Unifying.
— M. y f. Unifier.
unificar v. tr. To unify.
uniformación f. Uniformizing. || Standardization.
uniformar v. tr. To make wear a uniform, to give a uniform to: *uniformar a los empleados de la casa,* to make the employees of the firm wear a uniform. || To uniformize, to make uniform (uniformizar). || To standardize (normalizar).
— V. pr. To become uniform.
uniforme adj. Uniform. || Plain: *color uniforme,* plain colour. || Even, level (superficie). || Steady, uniform (velocidad). || *Hacer uniforme,* to uniformize, to make uniform.
uniforme m. Uniform: *el uso del uniforme,* the wearing of the uniform. || *Uniforme de gala,* full-dress uniform, dress uniform, ceremonial dress, full regimentals, *pl.*
uniformidad f. Uniformity. || Smoothness, evenness (de una superficie).
uniformizar v. tr. To uniformize, to make uniform. || To standardize (normalizar).
unigénito, ta adj. Only: *hijo unigénito,* only child. || REL. Only begotten.
— M. The Son of God (Hijo de Dios).
unilateral adj. Unilateral: *contratos unilaterales,* unilateral contracts.
unilocular adj. BOT. Unilocular.
uninominal adj. Uninominal.
unión f. Union: *la unión del alma y del cuerpo,* the union of body and soul; *la unión de Castilla y León,* the union of Castile and León. || Union: *unión de cooperativas,* cooperative union; *unión aduanera,* customs union. || Meeting [up], joining: *la unión de dos ejércitos,* the meeting up of two armies. || Union, wedding (casamiento). || Union, harmony (armonía). || MED. Closing: *la unión de los labios de una herida,* the closing of the lips of a wound. || TECN. Coupling, joining (acción). | Coupler (manguito). | Coupler (electricidad). | Joint (junta). || — *En unión de,* in the company of (en compañía de), together with (con la participación de). || *La unión hace la fuerza,* united we stand. || *La Unión Soviética,* the Soviet Union. || *Manguito de unión,* coupler.
unionismo m. Unionism.

— OBSERV. "Trade unionism" is translated by *sindicalismo.*

unionista adj./s. Unionist.
uníparo, ra adj. Uniparous.
unipersonal adj. GRAM. Unipersonal. || Individual, for one, single.
unipolar adj. Unipolar.
unir v. tr. To unite, to join [together]: *unir dos familias por un matrimonio,* to unite two families by a marriage; *unir un país con otro,* to join one country with another. || To join [together], to combine: *unir dos campos para hacer uno solo,* to join together two fields to make one. || To link [up]: *una carretera que une Madrid con Alcalá,* a road which links Madrid with Alcalá. || FIG. To combine: *unir la bondad con la firmeza,* to combine goodness with firmness. | To attach: *estamos muy unidos uno con otro,* we are very attached to one another. | To bind: *estar unidos por el mismo interés,* to be bound by the same interest. | To unite: *la desdicha une a los que sufren,* unhappiness unites those who suffer. || COM. To merge (compañías). | To pool (los recursos). || MED. To close (los labios de una herida). || TECN. To join, to attach (juntar). || To mix (mezclar líquidos, etc.).
— V. pr. To unite, to join together (reunirse). || To join, to meet (encontrarse). || To marry (casarse). || FIG. To be combined, to combine (aliarse). | To unite, to be united. | To be attached (afecto). | To associate o.s. with, to second: *me uno a las palabras anteriormente pronunciadas,* I second what has already been said. || COM. To merge, to amalgamate, to combine (compañías).
unisexo adj. inv. Unisex.
unisexual adj. Unisexual.
unisón m. MÚS. Unison.
unisonancia f. Unison.
unísono, na adj. Unisonous, in harmony.
— M. Unison. || FIG. Unison, harmony: *al unísono,* in unison.
unitario, ria adj. Unitary. || Unit: *precio unitario,* unit price. || REL. Unitarian.
— M. y f. REL. Unitarian.
unitarismo m. REL. Unitarianism.
universal adj. Universal. || FIG. World, of the world: *historia universal,* world history. | Worldwide (en todo el mundo). || *De fama universal,* world-famous.
— M. FIL. *Los universales,* the universals.
universalidad f. Universality.
universalización f. Universalization.
universalizar v. tr. To universalize.
universalmente adv. Universally. || All over the world (en el mundo entero).
universidad f. University: *la Universidad de Madrid,* the University of Madrid. || Universality (universalidad). || *Universidad laboral,* college of advanced technology.
universitario, ria adj. University, of *o* pertaining to a university: *reforma universitaria,* university reform.
— M. y f. [University] lecturer (profesor). || [University] student (estudiante).
universo m. Universe.
unívoco, ca adj. FIL. Univocal.
uno, na art. indef. A, an [v. UN (*Observ.*)]
— Adj. One. || — Pl. Some: *unos libros,* some books; *unos años después,* some years later; *unas tijeras,* some scissors. || About, some (aproximadamente): *unos cien kilómetros,* some hundred kilometres. || — *A una* or *a un tiempo,* at the same time. || *De una vez,* in one go. || *El día uno de mayo,* the first of May. || *El tomo uno,* volume one, the first volume. || *Es todo uno* or *todo es uno,* it is one and the same, it is all the same. || *No ser más que uno,* to be the same thing, to be one and the same, to be all the same. || *Uno que otro,* the occasional, the odd, a few: *se veía uno que otro árbol,* the occasional *o* the odd tree *o* a few trees could be seen.
— Pron. One: *él tiene dos hermanos y yo uno,* he has two brothers and I have one; *una de mis hermanas,* one of my sisters. || One, you: *uno tiene sus costumbres,* one has one's habits; *aquí uno no tiene derecho a protestar,* here you have no right to protest; *el ruido acaba por aturdirle a uno,* in the end the noise stuns one. || Someone, somebody (alguien): *preguntar a uno,* to ask someone; *vi a uno que se te parecía mucho,* I saw someone who looked just like you. || — *Cada uno a lo suyo,* it is best to mind one's own business. || *Cada uno, cada una,* each one, every one. || MIL. *De uno en fondo,* in single *o* Indian file. || *Los unos ... los otros,* some ... the others. || *Ni uno ni otro,* neither [one], neither the one nor the other, neither of them. || *No me gusta ni uno ni otro,* I don't like either of them. || *¿Quiere dos? — No, quiero uno solo,* do you want two? — No, I just want *o* I only want one. || *Una de dos,* one of the two. || *Una y no más,* once is enough. || *Uno a otro* or *unos a otros,* [to, at, etc.] each other, one another (reciprocidad): *mirarse uno a otro,* to look at one another. || *Uno a uno* or *uno por uno,* one by one. || *Uno con otro,* taking one thing with another, all things considered, all in all. || *Uno ... el otro,* one ... the other. || *Uno más* or *uno de tantos,* just another face in the crowd, one of many. || *Uno mismo,* oneself, yourself: *esto puede hacerlo uno mismo,* one can do this oneself, you can do this yourself. || *Unos cuantos,* a few, some. || *Unos ... otros,* some ... others, some ... some. || *Unos u otros,* somebody: *tienen que quedarse unos u otros,* somebody has to stay. || *Unos y otros,* all: *empezaron a hablar unos y otros,* they all started to speak. || *Uno tras otro,* one after *o* behind the other (en fila), one after the other (todos). || *Uno u otro,* one or the other, either. || *Uno y otro,* both: *uno*

y otro son muy simpáticos, they are both very nice. — M. One: *uno y uno son dos*, one and one is two. || First: *el uno de abril*, the 1st [first] of April. || Number one, one: *apostar al uno*, to bet on number one. || — *Lo uno ... lo otro*, on the one hand... on the other hand. || *Ni lo uno ni lo otro*, neither one thing nor the other. || — F. *Es la una*, it is one o'clock. || *Quedarse más solo que la una*, to be completely alone. || — M. y f. FAM. Some fellow, some woman: *ahora Lola sale con uno*, Lola is going out with some fellow now.

— OBSERV. V. UN (OBSERV.).

untador, ra adj. Greasing, oiling.
— M. y f. Greaser, oiler.
untadura f. Greasing, oiling (con aceite). || Smearing, rubbing (con ungüento). || TECN. Grease, oil (aceite). || MED. Ointment (ungüento).
untar v. tr. To grease, to oil (con aceite). || MED. To smear, to rub, to anoint (con ungüento): *untar con bálsamo*, to anoint with balm. || To smear, to stain (manchar). || To spread: *untar el pan con mantequilla*, to spread butter on one's bread. || FIG. y FAM. *Untar la mano a alguien*, to grease s.o.'s palm (sobornar).
— V. pr. To smear o.s., to smudge o.s. [*con*, with] (mancharse). || FIG. y FAM. To line one's pockets, to feather one's nest (sacar provecho).
unto m. Grease (grasa). || Ointment (ungüento). || *Amer*. Polish (betún). || FIG. y FAM. *Unto de México*, lolly, cash (dinero).
untuosidad f. Greasiness, oiliness.
untuoso, sa adj. Greasy, oily.
untura f. Greasing. || Anointing (a un enfermo). || Ointment (unto).
uña f. Nail (palabra general), fingernail (de la mano), toenail (del pie): *morderse las uñas*, to bite one's nails *o* fingernails; *uña encarnada*, ingrowing nail *o* toenail. || Claw (garra de los animales). || Hoof (casco). || Sting (de alacrán). || MED. Pterygium (del ojo). || TECN. Notch, nick (muesca). | Claw (arrancaclavos). | Clutch, grab (en mecánica). || MAR. Fluke (del ancla). || Pointed hook (saliente). || — *Arreglarse las uñas*, to manicure one's nails (hacerse la manicura). || FIG. *Enseñar* or *mostrar las uñas*, to show one's claws, to bare one's teeth. | *Esconder las uñas*, to hide one's feelings. | *Estar de uñas*, to be at daggers drawn. | *Hacer una cosa a uña de caballo*, to do sth. at full speed (muy rápidamente). | *Ser uña y carne*, to be inseparable, to be hand in glove. | *Tener las uñas largas* or *afiladas*, to be light-fingered. || *Uña de vaca*, cow's trotter (carnicería).
uñero m. MED. Felon, whitlow (panadizo). | Ingrowing nail (uña encarnada). || — Pl. Thumb index, *sing*. (de un libro). || *Con uñeros*, thumb-indexed (libro).
uñeta f. Small nail (uña pequeña). || TECN. Chisel.
¡upa! interj. Up!, up you go!
upar v. tr. To lift [up] (aupar).
Ural n. pr. m. GEOGR. Ural (río). || *Los Montes Urales* or *los Urales*, the Ural Mountains, the Urals.
uraloaltaico, ca adj. Ural-Altaic.
uranato m. QUÍM. Uranate.
uránico, ca adj. Uranic.
uranífero, ra adj. Uraniferous.
uranio m. Uranium (metal).
uranio, nia adj. Uranic (del cielo).
uranita f. Uranite.
urano m. Uranium oxide (óxido de uranio).
Urano n. pr. MIT. y ASTR. Uranus.
uranografía f. Uranography (cosmografía).
urbanamente adv. Politely, courteously, urbanely.
urbanidad f. Politeness, courtesy, urbanity (cortesía).
urbanismo m. Town planning [U.S., city planning], urbanism.
urbanista adj. Urbanistic.
— M. y f. Town planner [U.S., city planner], urbanist.
urbanístico, ca adj. Urban, city, town (de la ciudad). || Town-planning [U.S., city-planning] (del urbanismo). || *Conjunto urbanístico*, development; housing estate.
urbanización f. Town planning [U.S., city planning] (urbanismo). || Development: *obras de urbanización de una ciudad*, development works in a city. || New town (pueblo nuevo). || Urbanization (fenómeno demográfico). || Upbringing (educación).
urbanizar v. tr. To urbanize (dar carácter urbano). || To develop (los terrenos): *urbanizar una ciudad*, to develop a city. || To civilize, to educate: *urbanizar a un paleto*, to civilize a peasant. || — *Zona sin urbanizar*, undeveloped *o* underdeveloped area. || *Zona urbanizada*, built-up area.
urbano, na adj. Urban, city, town: *población urbana*, urban population. || FIG. Polite, courteous, urbane (cortés). || *Guardia urbano*, policeman.
urbe f. Large city.
urca f. MAR. Hooker (embarcación). || ZOOL. Orc (cetáceo).
urchilla f. BOT. Archil.
urdidor, ra adj. Warping.
— M. y f. Warper. || — M. Warping machine, warper.
urdidura f. Warping. || FIG. Plotting, scheming.
urdimbre o **urdiembre** f. Warp (de un tejido). || Warping (urdidura). || FIG. Intrigue, scheme.
urdir v. tr. To warp. || FIG. To plot, to scheme. || FIG. *Urdir una conspiración*, to intrigue, to plot, to scheme.
urea f. Urea.
uremia f. MED. Uraemia, uremia.
urémico, ca adj. Uraemic, uremic.
uréter m. ANAT. Ureter.
ureteral adj. ANAT. Ureteral.
urétera f. ANAT. Urethra.
uretra f. ANAT. Urethra.
uretral adj. ANAT. Urethral.
urgencia f. Urgency: *con toda urgencia*, with the utmost urgency. || Urgent need (necesidad). || — *Con urgencia*, urgently. || *Cura de urgencia*, first aid. || *Curar de urgencia*, to give first aid to. || JUR. *Recurso de urgencia*, summary procedure.
urgente adj. Urgent: *necesidad urgente*, urgent need. || Express [U.S., special delivery]: *correo urgente*, express mail. || — *Poner una carta urgente*, to send a letter express. || *Recibir una carta urgente*, to receive an express letter [U.S., to receive a special delivery].
urgentemente adv. Urgently.
urgir v. intr. To be urgent, to be pressing: *el asunto urge*, the matter is urgent. || — *Me urge tenerlo*, I need it urgently, it is urgent that I have it as soon as possible. || *Nos urge el tiempo*, we are pressed for time, time is short.
— V. impers. To be urgent, to require immediate attention. || *Urge terminar con el chabolismo*, the slum problem *o* slum clearance requires immediate attention.
— V. tr. To urge: *los delegados urgieron al congreso para que tomara esta medida*, the delegates urged the congress to take this measure.
úrico, ca adj. Uric: *ácido úrico*, uric acid.
urinal adj. Urinary (urinario).
urinario, ria adj. Urinary: *vías urinarias*, urinary tract.
— M. Urinal.
urinífero, ra adj. ANAT. Uriniferous.
urna f. Urn (vasija). || Ballot box (electoral). || Glass case (caja de cristal). || *Ir a las urnas*, to go to the polls.
uro m. ZOOL. Urus, aurochs.
urodelos m. pl. ZOOL. Urodela.
urogallo m. Capercaillie.
urogenital adj. Urogenital.
urografía f. Urography.
urología f. MED. Urology.
urólogo, ga m. y f. Urologist.
uroscopia f. MED. Uroscopy.
urraca f. Magpie (ave). || FIG. Chatterbox, magpie (hablador).
U.R.S.S. f. U.S.S.R. (Unión de Repúblicas Socialistas Soviéticas).
ursulina f. Ursuline (monja).
urticáceas f. pl. BOT. Urticaceae.
urticante adj. Urticant.
urticaria f. Urticaria, hives.
urubú m. Black vulture, urubu.
Uruguay n. pr. m. GEOGR. Uruguay.
uruguayo, ya adj./s. Uruguayan.
urunday o **urundey** m. Urunday (árbol).
usado, da adj. Worn-out, worn (deteriorado). || Used (que ha servido ya). || Worn (ropa). || Secondhand (de segunda mano). || Used: *palabra poco usada*, rarely used word. || Used (utilizado). || (P.us.). *Usado a hacer algo*, used to doing sth. (ejercitado).
usagre m. MED. Infantile impetigo.
usanza f. Usage (uso). || Style, fashion: *a la antigua usanza*, in the old style. || *A la usanza de la Corte*, according to Court custom, in the fashion of the Court.
usar v. tr. To use: *uso tinta negra*, I use black ink; *billete que no se puede usar*, ticket that cannot be used. || To wear: *usa camisas de seda*, he wears silk shirts; *usar gafas*, to wear glasses. || *Estar sin usar*, to be unused.
— V. intr. To use, to make use (hacer uso de). || To exercise: *usar de su derecho*, to exercise one's right. || — *Usa dormir después del almuerzo*, he usually sleeps after lunch, he is in the habit of sleeping after lunch. || *Usar mal de*, to misuse.
— V. pr. To be used: *esta palabra ya no se usa*, this word is no longer used. || To be worn, to be in fashion: *ya no se usan miriñaques*, crinolines are no longer worn. || *Esas cosas ya no se usan*, that sort of thing is not done any more.
Usatges n. pr. m. pl. List of Laws and customs made in Catalonia in the 11th century by Ramón Berenguer.
usía pron. pers. Your lordship.
usina f. Factory.

— OBSERV. *Usina* is a Gallicism frequently used in Uruguay.

uso m. Use (empleo): *el uso de la violencia*, the use of violence. || Use: *perdió el uso de una pierna*, he lost the use of one leg. || Custom, usage (costumbre): *es el uso del país*, it is the custom of the country. || Use: *instrucciones para su uso*, instructions for use. || Exercise: *el uso de la autoridad, de un privilegio*, the exercise of authority, of a privilege. || Wearing (de ropa etc.): *uso indebido de condecoraciones*, illegal wearing of decorations. || — *Al uso*, in fashion, in style (que se estila), in the style *o* fashion *o* way of: *al uso aragonés*, in the Aragonese way. || *Con el uso*, with wear: *los zapatos dan de sí con el uso*, shoes stretch with wear. || *De mucho uso*, hard-wearing. || *Deteriorado por el uso*, worn. || *Deterioro por el* *uso*, wear and tear. || *De uso*, in use. || *De uso corriente*, in common use, in everyday use. || *El uso hace al maestro*, practice makes perfect. || *En buen uso*, in good condition. || *En uso*, in use: *palabra en uso*, word in use. || *En uso de*, making use of, using: *en uso de sus prerrogativas*, making use of his prerogatives; by virtue of: *en uso de las facultades que me han sido conferidas*, by virtue of the powers vested in me. || *Hacer buen uso de*, to make good use of, to put to good use, to use well. || *Hacer mal uso de*, to misuse, to use badly. || *Hacer uso de*, to make use of (utilizar), to exercise (autoridad, etc.). || *Hacer uso de la palabra*, to take the floor, to speak, to address the meeting. || *Para uso de*, to be used by. || MED. *Para uso externo*, for external use. || *Según la moda al uso*, as is customary. || *Ser de uso*, to be used (emplearse), to be worn (llevarse). || *Usos y costumbres de un país*, ways and customs of a country.

usted pron. pers. You: *usted y sus hermanos*, you and your brothers. || — Pl. You: *ustedes y su hija*, you and your daughter. || — *¡A usted!*, thank you! (devolviendo las gracias). || *¿Es de usted este sombrero?*, is this hat yours? || *Hablar* or *tratar de usted*, to address as "usted", to use the polite form of address with. || *La casa de usted*, your house. || *La de usted ¿dónde está?*, where is yours?

— OBSERV. The personal pronoun *usted* is the polite form of address used with strangers and with people who deserve one's respect.
Usted is a contraction of *Vuestra merced* (your honour), and all verbs, pronouns or possessive adjectives qualified by it are construed in the third person (*usted es alto, señor doctor, pero su hijo lo es aún más*, you are tall, doctor, but your son is even taller).
Usted can be written in the abbreviated forms *Ud.* or *Vd.*, and *ustedes Uds.* or *Vds.*

ustorio adj. m. *Espejo ustorio*, burning glass.
usual adj. Usual, common: *términos usuales*, usual terms. || Habitual, usual, customary (habitual).
usualmente adv. Usually.
usuario, ria m. y f. User: *los usuarios de la carretera*, road users. || JUR. Usufructuary.
usucapión f. JUR. Usucapion, usucaption.
usucapir v. tr. JUR. To usucapt.
usufructo m. JUR. Usufruct, use.
usufructuar v. tr. To have the usufruct of, to usufruct.
usufructuario, ria adj./s. Usufructuary.
usura f. Interest, usury (ant.) (interés). || Usury, profiteering. || FIG. *Pagar con usura*, to repay a thousandfold.
usurario, ria adj. Usurious: *beneficio usurario*, usurious profit.
usurero, ra adj. Usurious.
— M. y f. Usurer. || FIG. Profiteer.
usurpación f. Usurpation: *usurpación de estado civil*, usurpation of civil status. || Encroachment, usurpation (intrusión).
usurpador, ra adj. Usurping.
— M. y f. Usurper.
usurpar v. tr. To ursurp: *usurpar un título*, to usurp a title. || FIG. To usurp on *o* upon, to encroach upon *usurpar derechos ajenos*, to usurp on the rights of others.
usurpatorio, ria adj. Usurpatory, usurpative.
usuta f. *Amer.* Sandal (ojota).
ut m. inv. MÚS. Do, doh (do).
utensilio m. Utensil: *utensilios de cocina*, kitchen utensils. || Tool (herramienta). || Device, implement (aparato).
uterino, na adj. Uterine: *hermano uterino*, uterine brother. || *Furor uterino*, nymphomania.
útero m. ANAT. Uterus, womb.
útil adj. Useful (*para*, to). || Fit (apto). || Working (día). || — *¿En qué puedo serle útil?*, can I help you? || *Es muy útil saberlo*, it is a useful thing to know.
— M. Tool (herramienta). || Utensil. || — *Unir lo útil con lo agradable*, to combine *o* to mix business with pleasure. || *Útiles de escritorio, de pintor*, writing, painter's materials. || *Útiles de labranza*, agricultural implements. || *Útiles de matar*, matador's equipment, *sing.* || *Útiles de pesca*, fishing tackle, *sing.*
utilidad f. Usefulness, utility. || COM. Profit (beneficio). || *Impuesto de utilidades*, income tax.
utilitario, ria adj. Utilitarian. || Utility (coche, etc.). — M. Utility car.
utilitarismo m. Utilitarianism.
utilitarista adj./s. Utilitarian.
utilizable adj. Utilizable, useable, usable. || Fit for use (que puede servir). || Ready for use (en condiciones de ser utilizado).
utilización f. Use, utilization, using.
utilizador, ra adj. Utilizing, using.
— M. y f. User, utilizer.
utilizar v. tr. To use, to make use of, to utilize (emplear). || TECN. To harness (la energía, etc.).
útilmente adv. Usefully. || Profitably (con provecho).
utillaje m. Tools, *pl.*, equipment.
utopía f. Utopia.
utópico, ca adj./s. Utopian.
utopista adj./s. Utopian.
utrero, ra m. y f. Young bull, young heifer.
uva f. Grape: *racimo de uvas*, bunch of grapes. || — FIG. y FAM. *Entrar por uvas*, to take the risk (arriesgarse). | *Estar de mala uva*, to be in a bad mood. || *Tomar las uvas* or *las uvas de la suerte*, New Year's Eve custom of eating twelve grapes at midnight which is supposed to bring happiness in the new year. || *Uva albilla*, white grape. || *Uva de mesa*, [table] grape. || *Uva moscatel*, muscatel, muscat. || *Uvas pasas*, raisins.
uve f. V (name of the letter V). || *En forma de uve*, V-shaped.
uvero, ra m. y f. Grape seller. || — M. Sea grape (árbol de América).
— Adj. Grape, of *o* pertaining to grapes: *exportación uvera*, grape exportation.
úvula f. ANAT. Uvula (campanilla).
uvular adj. Uvular.
¡uy! interj. Ouch! (dolor), ugh! (repugnancia), oh! (sorpresa).

V

v f. V (uve): *una v mayúscula*, a capital v. || *V doble*, w.

— OBSERV. The *v* is pronounced like the Spanish *b*.

vaca f. Cow: *vaca lechera*, milk cow, milch cow. || Beef (carne): *estofado de vaca*, beef stew. || Cowhide (cuero). || Stake (dinero jugado en las cartas). || — *Carne de vaca*, beef. || FIG. y FAM. *Parece una vaca*, she's like an elephant. | *Vaca de San Antón*, ladybird [U.S., ladybug]. || *Vaca marina*, sea cow (manatí). || FIG. *Vacas flacas*, lean years. | *Vacas gordas*, years of plenty. | *Ya vendrán las vacas gordas*, my (*o* our, etc.) ship will come in.
vacaciones f. pl. Holidays, holiday, *sing.*, vacation, *sing.*: *vacaciones de verano*, summer holidays; *vacaciones escolares*, school holidays; *vacaciones retribuidas* or *pagadas*, paid holidays. || Vacation, *sing.*, recess, *sing.* (de un tribunal). || — *Estar de vacaciones*, to be on holiday. || *Irse de vacaciones*, to go on holiday. || *Pasamos las vacaciones en Ibiza*, we went to Ibiza for our holidays, we spent our holidays *o* we holidayed in Ibiza.
vacada f. Herd of cows.
vacancia f. Vacancy (vacante).
vacante adj. Vacant: *puesto vacante*, vacant post.
— F. Vacancy, vacant post: *en caso de producirse una vacante*, should there be a vacancy; *cubrir las vacantes en una empresa*, to fill the vacancies in a firm.
vacar v. intr. To fall vacant (quedarse vacante un puesto). || To be vacant (estar vacante). || Not to work (no trabajar). || To stop working (dejar de trabajar). || To devote o.s. [*a, en*, to] (dedicarse a). || To be without (carecer de).
vacarí adj. Leather.
vaccíneo, a adj. MED. Vaccinal.
vaccinostilo m. MED. Vaccinator (lanceta).
vaccinoterapia f. MED. Vaccine therapy.
vaciadero m. Dumping ground, rubbish tip (lugar). || Sewer (conducto).
vaciado m. Casting, moulding [U.S., molding] (acción y resultado): *vaciado de yeso*, plaster casting; *vaciado en molde*, casting in a mould. || Hollowing out (formación de un hueco). || Emptying (de un depósito).

|| Sharpening (de un cuchillo). || *Orificio de vaciado*, tapping hole.
vaciador m. TECN. Caster, moulder [U.S., molder] (de figuras en molde). || Foundry worker (obrero fundidor). || Emptier (instrumento para vaciar).
vaciamiento m. Emptying.
vaciante f. Ebb tide (menguante).
vaciar v. tr. To empty [out] (un líquido, un recipiente): *vaciar un tonel*, to empty a barrel. || To cast, to mould [U.S., to mold]: *vaciar una estatua en bronce*, to cast a statue in bronze. || To drain (un líquido). || To clean: *vaciar un pollo*, to clean a chicken. || To hollow out (ahuecar). || To sharpen (un cuchillo). || To expound at length (una teoría). || To copy out (un texto).
— V. intr. To flow: *río que vacía en el mar*, river which flows into the sea.
— V. pr. To empty. || FIG. To unburden o.s.
vaciedad f. Emptiness (estado de vacío). || FIG. Emptiness (de la conversación, etc.). || *Decir vaciedades*, to talk nonsense.
vacilación f. Hesitation, hesitancy, vacillation (duda). || Irresolution (falta de determinación). || Vacillation, swaying (balanceo). || *Sin vacilaciones*, without hesitation, unhesitatingly.
vacilante adj. Unsteady, shaky (paso, mano, etc.). || Faltering, halting: *voz vacilante*, faltering voice. || Flickering: *luz vacilante*, flickering light. || Hesitant (que tarda en decidirse). || Irresolute (falto de determinación).
vacilar v. intr. To vacillate, to rock, to sway, to wobble (moverse por falta de estabilidad). || To flicker (la luz). || To falter (al hablar). || To fail (la memoria). || To totter, to stumble (al andar). || FIG. To hesitate: *vacilar en su resolución*, to hesitate over one's decision; *vacilar en la elección*, to hesitate about one's choice; *no vaciló en contestar*, he did not hesitate to answer. || *Amer.* To go on a spree. || — FIG. *Hacer vacilar*, to shake: *hacer vacilar las convicciones de uno*, to shake one's convictions. | *Memoria que vacila*, shaky memory. | *Sin vacilar*, without hesitation, unhesitatingly. | *Una persona que vacila mucho*, an indecisive *o* irresolute person, a very hesitant person.
vacío, a adj. Empty: *cajón vacío*, empty drawer; *sala vacía*, empty room. || Vacant, unoccupied, empty: *vivienda vacía*, vacant house. || Unfurnished (sin amueblar). || Vacant, unoccupied (puesto de trabajo). || FIG. Empty: *una conversación vacía*, an empty conversation. || Barren (hembra). || — FIG. *Tener el estómago vacío*, to feel hungry. | *Tener la cabeza vacía*, to be empty-headed. | *Volver con las manos vacías*, to come back empty-handed.
— M. Emptiness, void: *su grito resonó en el vacío*, his cry resounded in the void. || Hole, gap (cavidad). || Space, empty space (espacio). || Blank space (espacio en blanco). || FÍS. Vacuum: *hacer el vacío*, to create a vacuum; *en vacío*, in a vacuum. || ANAT. Flank (ijada). || FIG. Emptiness, void (sentimiento): *sintió un vacío en el corazón*, he felt an emptiness in his heart. | Gap (hueco). | Vacancy (vacante). || — FIG. *Caer en el vacío*, to fall on deaf ears (no ser escuchado). || *Estar suspendido en el vacío*, to be suspended *o* hanging in mid air. || FIG. *Hacer el vacío a uno*, to send s.o. to Coventry, to cold-shoulder s.o. | *Ha quedado un vacío en el despacho desde que se fue*, the office seems empty since he left, the office has not been the same since he left. | *Tener un vacío en el estómago*, to feel hungry. || *Volver de vacío*, to come back empty (un vehículo), to come back empty-handed (una persona).
vacuidad f. Vacuity.
vacuna f. MED. Vaccine. || VET. Cowpox, vaccinia (de la vaca).
vacunación f. MED. Vaccination.
vacunador, ra adj. MED. Vaccinating.
— M. y f. MED. Vaccinator.
vacunar v. tr. MED. To vaccinate. || FIG. To inure.
— V. pr. To be vaccinated.
vacuno, na adj. Bovine. || *El ganado vacuno*, cattle.
vacuo, cua adj. Empty (vacío). || Vacant (vacante). || Vacuous, empty (frívolo, insubstancial).
— M. Void.
vacuola f. Vacuole.
vacuolar adj. Vacuolar.
vade m. Folder (para guardar papeles). || [School] satchel (cartera).
vadeable adj. Fordable, which can be forded (río). || FIG. Surmountable (obstáculo).
vadear v. tr. To ford. || FIG. To overcome, to surmount (una dificultad). | To sound out (el ánimo de uno).
vademécum m. inv. Vademecum (libro). || [School] satchel (de colegial).
vado m. Ford (de un río). || FIG. Way out, solution (salida, solución).
vagabundaje m. Vagabondage.
vagabundear v. intr. To wander, to roam, to lead a vagrant life.
vagabundeo m. Vagabondage.
vagabundo, da adj. Vagrant: *vida vagabunda*, vagrant life.
— M. y f. Rover, wanderer (trotamundos). || Vagabond, vagrant (más despectivo). || Tramp (muy despectivo). || JUR. Vagrant.
vagamundear v. intr. V. VAGABUNDEAR.
vagamundo, da adj./s. FAM. V. VAGABUNDO.
vagancia f. Vagrancy (delito). || Laziness, idleness (ociosidad).
vagante adj. Wandering, roaming (errante). || Loose, free (suelto).
vagar v. intr. To wander [about], to roam [about]: *vagar por el pueblo*, to wander through the village; *se pasó todo el día vagando*, he spent all day just wandering about. || To loaf about, to idle (andar ocioso).
vagido m. Cry, wail [of a newborn baby]. || *Dar vagidos*, to cry.
vagina f. ANAT. Vagina.
vaginal adj. ANAT. Vaginal.
vaginitis f. inv. MED. Vaginitis.
vago, ga adj. Vague: *promesas vagas*, vague promises; *perfil vago*, vague outline. || FOT. y ARTES. Blurred, indistinct. || Lazy, idle (perezoso). || FIG. Vague: *idea vaga*, vague idea. || ANAT. *Nervio vago*, vagus nerve, vagus.
— M. y f. Loafer, idler, slacker (perezoso). || Tramp (vagabundo). || JUR. Vagrant. || — *Hacer el vago*, to laze about. || *Ley de vagos y maleantes*, vagrancy act.
vagón m. Carriage, coach, car (para viajeros): *vagón de primera*, first-class carriage. || Truck, wagon: *vagón para ganado*, cattle truck, cattle wagon. || Wagonload (contenido de un vagón). || — *Vagón cerrado*, van, closed *o* covered wagon. || *Vagón cisterna*, tank wagon, tanker. || *Vagón cuba*, tank wagon, tanker. || *Vagón de mercancías*, goods van *o* wagon [U.S., freight car]. || *Vagón restaurante*, dining car. || *Vagón tolva*, hopper wagon.
vagoneta f. Small wagon.
vagotomía f. MED. Vagotomy.
vagotonía f. MED. Vagotonia, vagotony.
vaguada f. Lowest part of a valley.
vagueación f. Wandering.
vaguear v. intr. V. VAGAR.
vaguedad f. Vagueness: *la vaguedad de sus palabras*, the vagueness of his words. || Indistinctness (de una imagen). || — Pl. Vague remarks: *no ha dicho nada preciso sino sólo vaguedades*, he said nothing definite, he only made vague remarks. || — *Andarse con vaguedades*, to be vague, to speak vaguely. || *Decir vaguedades*, to make vague remarks, to be vague. || *Hablar sin vaguedades*, not to beat about the bush, to get straight to the point.
vaguemaestre m. MIL. Baggage master.
vaharada f. Puff, breath.
vahído m. Dizzy *o* giddy spell (mareo). || *Le dio un vahído*, he felt dizzy *o* giddy.
vaho m. Breath. || Steam, vapour (vapor). || — Pl. MED. Inhalation, *sing.* || Fumes (emanaciones). || *Hay vaho en los cristales*, the windows are steamed up.
vaída adj. f. *Bóveda vaída*, truncated dome.
vaina f. Sheath, scabbard (de espada). || Sheath, case (de navaja). || BOT. Pod: *vaina de guisantes*, pod of peas. | Sheath (del tallo). || ANAT. Sheath. || MAR. Tabling (de vela). || Case (de cartucho). || *Amer.* FAM. Thing (cosa). | Nuisance, bother, bore (molestia). | Luck (suerte).
— M. Good-for-nothing, oaf.
vainazas m. inv. FAM. Slob, lout.
vainica f. Hemstitch.
vainilla f. Vanilla: *helado de vainilla*, vanilla ice cream. || Vanilla (planta).
vaivén m. Swinging, swaying (balanceo). || Rocking (de un tren, una mecedora, etc.). || Coming and going, bustle (de la gente, de los coches, etc.). || FIG. Exchange: *un vaivén de ideas nuevas*, an exchange of new ideas. | Fluctuation, change: *los vaivenes de la vida política*, the fluctuations of political life. | Change of fortune (cambio de fortuna). || Back and forth movement: *el vaivén de la lanzadera*, the back and forth movement of the shuttle. || Up and down movement (movimiento vertical). || — Pl. FIG. Ups and downs (altibajos).
vajilla f. Dishes, *pl.*, crockery. || — *Lavar la vajilla*, to wash up. || *Regalar una vajilla*, to give a set of dishes *o* a dinner service. || *Vajilla de plata*, silverware. || *Vajilla de porcelana*, chinaware.
val m. (P.us.). Valley (valle).
valaco, ca adj./s. Walachian.
Valaquia n. pr. f. GEOGR. Walachia.
Valdemoro n. pr. GEOGR. V. PINTO.
valdepeñas m. Valdepeñas wine.
vale m. Voucher: *vale por diez pesetas*, voucher for ten pesetas. || Receipt (recibo). || Promissory note, IOU (pagaré). || Star (en el colegio). || *Amer.* FAM. Mate [U.S., buddy] (compañero).
valedero, ra adj. Valid.
valedor, ra m. y f. Protector (protector). || *Amer.* Mate [U.S., buddy] (compañero).
valencia f. QUÍM. Valency, valence.
Valencia n. pr. GEOGR. Valencia.
valenciano, na adj. [Of *o* from] Valencia, Valencian.
— M. y f. Inhabitant *o* native of Valencia, Valencian.
valentía f. Courage, valour [U.S., valor], bravery (valor): *la valentía de un general*, the valour of a general. || Bragging, boasting (ostentación de valor). || Boldness, dash: *pintor que maneja el pincel con gran*

valentía, artist who paints with great dash. || Brave deed, act of bravery (acción valerosa).

valentísimo, ma adj. Very brave *o* courageous *o* valiant.

valentón, ona adj. Bragging, boastful.
— M. y f. Braggart.

valentona o **valentonada** f. Bragging, boasting, brag, boast.

valer m. Value, worth, merit.

valer* v. tr. To be worth (tener un valor de): *la casa vale más de lo que pagaste*, the house is worth more than you paid for it. || To cost, to be (costar): *valen seis pesetas el kilo*, they cost *o* they are six pesetas a kilo; *¿cuánto vale?*, how much is it?, how much does it cost? || To mean, to be worth: *este recuerdo vale mucho para mí*, this memory means a lot to me. || To win, to gain, to earn (ganar): *la gloria que le han valido sus hazañas*, the glory which his exploits won [for] him. || To cause (causar): *me ha valido muchos disgustos*, it caused me a lot of trouble. || To cost, to result in: *esa táctica les valió la derrota*, that move cost them defeat, that move resulted in their defeat; *su pereza le valió un suspenso en el examen*, his laziness cost him [failure in] the exam, his laziness resulted in his failing the exam. || To get, to earn: *su comportamiento le valió una paliza*, his behaviour earned him a beating. || MAT. To equal. || To protect, to help, to defend (proteger). || — FAM. *No valer nada*, not to be worth a thing, to be worthless (no tener valor), to be useless (ser muy malo). || *Valer la pena*, to be worth it, to be worth the trouble: *no vale la pena hacerlo*, it is not worth doing, it is not worth it, it is not worth the trouble. || *Valer lo que cuesta*, to be worth the money, to be worth it. || FIG. *Valer lo que pesa en oro* or *tanto oro como pesa* or *un Perú* or *un Potosí*, to be worth one's *o* its weight in gold, to be worth a fortune. || *¡Válgame Dios!*, v. DIOS.
— V. intr. e impers. To be worth: *cada ficha vale por una comida*, each disc is worth a meal. || To cost, to be (costar): *valen a seis pesetas el kilo*, they cost six pesetas a kilo. || To be valuable (tener valor). || To be valid: *el billete me vale aún*, my ticket is still valid; *sus argumentos no valen*, his arguments are not valid. || To count (contar): *este partido no vale*, this match does not count. || To be of use, to help: *no le valió esa astucia*, that trick was of no use to him *o* did not help him. || To do (bastar): *este mismo papel me vale*, this paper will do [me]. || To be suitable, to be right (ser conveniente): *este chico no vale para el cargo*, this boy is not suitable for the job. || To serve (servir): *todavía me valen estos zapatos*, these shoes still serve me. || To be of use, to be useful (ser útil). || To be good: *yo no valgo para esta clase de trabajo*, I am no good at this sort of work; *este año no hay ningún alumno que valga*, not one of the students is any good this year; *¿este martillo te vale?*, is this hammer any good to you? || To be legal tender (monedas). || — *Hacerse valer*, to assert o.s. || *Hacer valer sus derechos*, to exercise one's rights (emplearlos), to assert one's rights (hacerlos prevalecer). || *Hacer valer sus razones*, to assert one's opinions. || *La primera impresión es la que vale*, the first impression is the one that counts. || *Lo que mucho vale, mucho cuesta*, you have to pay for quality. || *Más vale*, it is better (es preferible): *más vale hacerlo ahora*, it is better to do it now; *más vale así*, it is better like that. || *Más vale no hacerlo*, it's better not to do it, I [we, etc.] had better not do it. || *Más vale que lo hagas*, you had better do it. || *Más vale tarde que nunca*, better late than never. || *Más vale un toma que dos te daré*, a bird in the hand is worth two in the bush. || *No hay excusa que valga*, no excuses. || *No hay pero que valga*, no buts. || *No vale*, is does not count (no cuenta), you cannot do that (no hay derecho), that is not right, I do not agree (no estoy conforme). || *No vale para nada*, it [he, she] is useless. || *Sin que valgan excepciones*, without exception. || *Su hermana no vale gran cosa*, his sister is not up to much. || *Tanto vale el uno como el otro*, the one is as good as the other, they are as good as each other. || *Tanto vale hacerlo ahora mismo*, I [you, she, etc.] had better *o* best do it right now. || *Tanto vales cuanto tienes*, a man is worth as much as he owns. || *Un médico que vale* (*mucho*), a [very] good doctor. || FAM. *¡Vale!*, O.K., all right (está bien), that's enough (basta). | *¿Vale?*, is that all right?, will that do?, O.K.? || *Vale mucho tener una buena recomendación*, it is very useful to have good references. || *Valer por*, to be worth: *vale por dos kilos de patatas*, it is worth two kilos of potatoes; to be as good as, to equal: *ese gesto vale por un discurso*, that gesture is as good as a speech. || *Valer tanto como*, to be as good as: *Juan vale tanto como su hermano*, John is as good as his brother. || *Válgame la frase*, if I may say so, if you will pardon *o* excuse the expression.
— V. pr. To be as good as one another. || To use: *valerse de un bastón para andar*, to use a stick for walking; *valerse de un diccionario*, to use a dictionary. || To exercise: *valerse de sus derechos*, to exercise one's rights. || To make use of, to use: *valerse de sus relaciones*, to make use of one's connections. || — *No poder valerse*, to be unable to manage on one's own. || *Valerse de todos los medios*, to try everything. || *Valerse por sí mismo*, to manage by o.s.

valeriana f. BOT. Valerian (planta).

valerosidad f. Valiance, courage, bravery.

valeroso, sa adj. Valiant, courageous, brave: *un soldado valeroso*, a valiant soldier. || Valuable, precious (de mucho precio).

valet m. Jack (sota o jota en la baraja francesa).

valetudinario, ria adj./s. Valetudinarian.

valía f. Value, worth: *joya de mucha valía*, jewel of great value. || Merit, worth (de personas). || Favour [U.S., favor] (confianza).

validación f. Validation.

validar v. tr. To validate.

validez f. Validity. || *Dar validez a*, to validate.

valido, da adj./s.m. Favourite [U.S., favorite].

válido, da adj. Robust, strong: *un hombre válido*, a robust man. || FIG. Valid (que satisface los requisitos): *elección válida*, valid election; *recibo válido*, valid receipt.

valiente adj. Valiant, courageous, brave: *un soldado valiente se expone en los combates*, a brave soldier takes risks in battle. || Boastful, bragging (valentón). || FIG. y FAM. A fine, some: *¡valiente amigo eres!*, a fine friend *o* some friend you are! || — *¡Valiente amigo tienes!*, you've a fine friend there! || *¡Valiente frío!*, it's freezing! || *¡Valiente tonto!*, what a fool!, what an idiot!
— M. y f. Brave man (valeroso). || Braggart (bravucón).

valija f. Suitcase, case (maleta). || Mailbag (del cartero). || *Valija diplomática*, diplomatic bag *o* pouch.

valimiento m. Favour [U.S., favor], good graces, *pl.*: *hombre que tiene valimiento con el rey*, man who is in favour with the king *o* in the good graces of the king. || Worth, value, merit (mérito).

valioso, sa adj. Precious, valuable: *una joya valiosa*, a precious jewel; *tesoro valioso*, valuable treasure. || Highly esteemed (estimado). || Useful (útil). || Rich, wealthy (rico). || FIG. Valuable: *un asesoramiento valioso*, a valuable piece of advice. | Excellent: *¡valiosa idea!*, excellent idea.

valisoletano, na adj./s. V. VALLISOLETANO.

Valkiria f. MIT. Valkyrie.

valón, ona adj./s. Walloon.

valona f. Vandyke [collar]. || *Amer.* Cropped mane (de los caballos).

valor m. Value, worth, merit: *artista de gran valor*, artist of great merit. || Courage, bravery, valiance, valour [U.S., valor]: *el valor de un soldado*, the courage of a soldier. || Value, denomination (de monedas, sellos, etc.). || Courage, heart: *no tengo valor para ir a verle*, I have not got the courage to go and see him. || Importance (importancia). || Efficacy (eficacia). || FIG. Credit: *no doy valor a sus palabras*, I do not give credit to his words. || FAM. Nerve, cheek (cara): *tuvo valor para pedir que le pagaran*, he had the nerve to ask them to pay him. || COM. Value: *valor comercial*, market *o* commercial value; *valor en oro*, value in gold; *por el valor de*, to the value of. || MAT. Value: *valor absoluto*, *relativo*, absolute, relative value. || — Pl. COM. Securities. || Values (principios). || — FAM. *¿Cómo va ese valor?*, how are things? || *Dar* or *conceder valor a*, to attach importance to, to take notice of. || *Depósito de valores*, stock deposit. || *De valor*, valuable: *objeto de valor*, valuable object. || *Objetos de valor*, valuables. || FAM. *¡Qué valor!*, what a nerve!, of all the cheek! (qué caradura). || *Quitar valor a algo*, to reduce the value of sth. (reducir el valor), to minimize the importance of, to play down (quitar importancia). || *Sin valor*, worthless. || FIG. *Tener más valor que un torero*, not to be afraid of anything. || *Valor adquisitivo*, purchasing power. || *Valor alimenticio*, food value. || COM. *Valores en cartera* or *habidos*, share portfolio. | *Valores inmuebles*, real estate. || *Valor recibido*, value received.

valoración f. Valuation, appraisal (estimación). || Appreciation (aumento de valor).

valorar v. tr. To value: *valorar una cosa en alto precio*, to value sth. at a high price. || To appreciate, to raise the value of (aumentar el valor). || *Valorar a alguien en mucho*, to value s.o. highly, to hold s.o. in high esteem.

valorización f. Valuation, valuing (valoración). || Appreciation (revalorización).

valorizar v. tr. To value. | To raise the value of (aumentar el valor).

vals m. Waltz. || — *Bailar el vals*, to waltz. || *Bailar un vals*, to dance a waltz.

valsador, ra m. y f. Waltzer.

valsar v. intr. To waltz.

valuación f. Valuation, appraisal.

valuar v. tr. To value.

valva f. BOT. y ZOOL. Valve.

valvolina f. Jelly-like grease.

válvula f. ANAT. Valve (de las venas). || RAD. Valve [U.S., tube]: *válvula rectificadora*, rectifying valve. || TECN. Valve: *válvula de admisión*, inlet valve; *válvula de seguridad*, safety valve; *esmerilado de válvulas*, grinding of valves. || *Válvula de mariposa*, butterfly valve.

valvular adj. Valvular.

valla f. Fence (cerca). || MIL. Barricade, stockade (fortificación). || FIG. Obstacle, hindrance, barrier

(obstáculo). || DEP. Hurdle: *100 metros vallas*, 100 metres hurdles. || *Amer.* Cockpit [for cockfights]. || *Valla publicitaria*, hoarding.
valladar m. Fence (cerca). || FIG. Obstacle, barrier, hindrance.
vallado m. Fence (cerca). || Defensive wall.
vallar v. tr. To fence, to put a fence round.
valle m. Valley. || FIG. *Valle de lágrimas*, vale *o* valley of tears.
vallejo m. Glen.
vallico m. BOT. Ryegrass.
vallisoletano, na adj. [Of *o* from] Valladolid.
— M. y f. Native *o* inhabitant of Valladolid.
vampiresa f. CINEM. Vamp (mujer fatal).
vampirismo m. Vampirism.
vampiro m. Vampire (murciélago y espectro). || FIG. Vampire.
vanadato m. QUÍM. Vanadate.
vanadio m. Vanadium (metal).
vanagloria f. Vainglory.
vanagloriarse v. pr. To boast: *vanagloriarse de sus conocimientos*, to boast of one's knowledge.
vanaglorioso, sa adj. Vainglorious.
vanamente adj. Vainly, in vain, uselessly (en vano). || Without reason (sin razón). || Vainly (con presunción).
vandálico, ca adj. Vandal, vandalic.
vandalismo m. Vandalism.
vándalo adj./s. Vandal.
vanguardia f. Vanguard. || — *De vanguardia*, of the vanguard (soldados), avant-garde (en arte, música, etc.). || FIG. *Ir a la vanguardia del progreso*, to be in the van of *o* at the forefront of progress.
vanguardismo m. Avant-garde movement.
vanguardista adj. Avant-garde: *una película vanguardista*, an avant-garde film.
vanidad f. Vanity: *hacer algo por pura vanidad*, to do sth. out of sheer vanity. || *Vanidad de vanidades y todo es vanidad*, vanity of vanities, all is vanity.
vanidoso, sa adj. Vain, conceited.
— M. y f. Vain person.
vanilocuencia f. Verbosity.
vanílocuo, cua adj. Verbose.
— M. y f. Prattler.
vaniloquio m. Verbosity.
vano, na adj. Vain: *excusas vanas*, vain excuses; *vanas esperanzas*, vain hopes. || Vain, useless (inútil): *esfuerzos vanos*, useless efforts. || Groundless, unfounded, idle (infundado). || Empty, hollow (vacío). || Vain, conceited (vanidoso). || Frivolous (frívolo). || — *En vano*, in vain, vainly. || *Promesas vanas*, empty promises.
— M. ARQ. Opening, bay (hueco). | Span (distancia).
vapor m. Vapour [U.S., vapor]: *vapor de agua*, water vapour. || Steam (vaho). || MAR. Steamer, steamship (barco). || — Pl. MED. Vapours, hysteria, *sing.*, hysterics. || — FIG. *A todo vapor*, at full steam (barco), at great speed. || *Caldera de vapor*, steam boiler. || *Los vapores del vino*, vapour *o* fumes given off by wine. || *Máquina de vapor*, steam engine. || *Patatas al vapor*, steamed potatoes. || *Vapor de ruedas*, paddle steamer.
vaporar v. tr. To evaporate (evaporar).
vaporización f. Vaporization. || Decating, decatizing (de tejidos).
vaporizador m. Vaporizer, atomizer, spray.
vaporizar, vaporizarse v. tr. y pr. To vaporize.
vaporoso, sa adj. Vaporous. || Sheer, diaphanous (tejido).
vapulear v. tr. To give a hiding *o* a thrashing: *vapulear a un niño*, to give a child a hiding. || To beat (una alfombra). || FIG. To slate (criticar).
vapuleo m. Hiding, thrashing. || Beating (de una alfombra). || FIG. Slating (crítica).
vaqueiro m. Cowherd.
vaquería f. Cowshed (sitio). || Dairy (lechería). || Herd of cows (vacada).
vaquerizo, za adj. Cattle, cow: *corral vaquerizo*, cattle enclosure.
— M. y f. Cowherd. || — F. Cowshed.
vaquero, ra adj. Cattle, cow. || Of *o* pertaining to cowherds or cowboys. || *Pantalón vaquero*, jeans, *pl.*, pair of jeans.
— M. y f. Cowherd (pastor). || Cowboy (en Estados Unidos): *película de vaqueros*, cowboy film. || — M. *Amer.* Whip (látigo).
vaqueta f. Cowhide (cuero).
vaquetón, ona adj. *Amer.* Daring.
vaquillona f. *Amer.* Heifer.
vaquita f. Small cow. || Stake (apuesta). || *Vaquita de San Antón*, ladybird [U.S., ladybug].
var m. ELECTR. Var.
vara f. Staff, pole (palo largo). || Pole: *derribar nueces con una vara*, to knock nuts down with a pole. || Staff, wand (insignia de autoridad). || Stick (palo). || Switch (para azotar). || Shaft (varal de un coche). || Yard [approximately] (medida de longitud). || TAUR. Picador's lance (pica). | Thrust, lunge (garrochazo). || MÚS. Slide (de trombón). || — *Poner una vara*, to thrust at [the bull]. || FIG. *Temer como una vara verde*, to be scared stiff of. | *Tener mucha vara alta*, to be very influential. | *Tener vara alta en un negocio*, to have the upper hand in an affair.
varada f. MAR. Running aground. | Beaching (sacando el barco a la playa). || Gang of farm labourers. || MIN. Three months' work (trabajo). | Three months' wages (pago).
varadera f. MAR. Skid.
varadero m. MAR. Dry dock.
varado, da adj. MAR. Beached (en la playa). | Aground, stranded (encallado). | At anchor (anclado).
varadura f. Running aground (encallamiento). | Beaching.
varal m. Staff, pole (vara). || Shaft (de un carruaje). || TEATR. Batten. || FIG. y FAM. Beanpole (persona muy alta). || *Amer.* Wooden structure upon which meat is dried.
varano m. ZOOL. Monitor (lagarto).
varapalo m. Long staff *o* pole (palo). || Blow with a stick (golpe). || FIG. y FAM. Setback, blow (contratiempo).
varar v. tr. MAR. To launch (botar). | To beach (poner en seco). | To run aground (encallar).
— V. intr. MAR. To run aground (encallar). | To drop anchor (anclar). || FIG. To come to a standstill (un asunto).
varazo m. Blow with a stick *o* pole. || TAUR. Thrust.
vareado m. Knocking down [of fruit, etc.].
vareador m. Beater (de árboles).
varear v. tr. To knock down, to beat down: *varear nueces*, to knock nuts down [from the trees]. || To measure in "varas" (medir por varas). || To beat (lana, alfombras, etc.). || COM. To sell by the yard (vender). || TAUR. To jab with the lance (al toro).
varec m. BOT. Kelp, varec (alga).
varenga f. MAR. Floor timber.
vareo m. Knocking down (de nueces). || Measuring in "varas" (medición por varas).
vareta f. Small pole *o* staff (vara pequeña). || Limetwig (para cazar pájaros). || Taunt, gibe (insinuación molesta). || Stripe (lista de color). || FIG. y FAM. *Irse de vareta*, to have diarrhoea.
varetazo m. TAUR. Sideways butt (paletazo).
Vargas n. pr. *Averígüelo Vargas*, goodness knows.
variabilidad f. Variability.
variable adj. Variable, changeable: *tiempo variable*, changeable weather. || MAT. Variable.
— F. MAT. Variable.
variación f. Variation. || *Variación magnética*, magnetic declination.
variamente adv. Differently. || *Variamente coloreado*, of different colours, variegated.
variante f. Version, variant: *una variante de esa canción*, one version of this song. || Difference.
— Adj. V. VARIABLE.
variar v. tr. To vary: *variar el menú*, to vary the menu. || To switch about, to change round (de posición). || *Galletas variadas*, assorted biscuits.
— V. intr. To vary: *sus respuestas varían*, his answers vary. || To change: *variar de opinión*, to change one's mind *o* opinion; *el viento ha variado*, the wind has changed. || To differ, to be different (ser diferente): *su versión varía de la del vecino*, his version differs from *o* is different from his neighbour's. || MAT. To vary. || *Por no variar*, as usual.
— OBSERV. The *i* in variar bears a written accent in the first, second and third person singular and in the third person plural of the present indicative and subjunctive, and also in the second person singular of the imperative.
varice f. MED. Varicose vein, varix.
varicela f. MED. Chicken pox, varicella.
varicocele m. MED. Varicocele.
varicoso, sa adj. Varicose.
— M. y f. Person suffering from varicose veins.
variedad f. Variety, diversity. || BOT. y ZOOL. Variety. || — Pl. [Variety] show, *sing.* (espectáculo). || FIG. *En la variedad está el gusto*, variety is the spice of life.
varilarguero m. TAUR. Picador.
varilla f. Small stick, rod (vara pequeña). || Rail (de cortinas). || Rib (de abanico, paraguas). || Perch (en una jaula). || Stay (de corsé). || ANAT. Jawbone. || TECN. Rod. || — *Varilla de la virtud* or *de las virtudes* or *encantada* or *mágica*, magic wand. || *Varilla de zahorí*, divining rod. || *Varilla indicadora* or *graduada*, gauge.
varillaje m. Ribs, *pl.*, ribbing (de abanico, de paraguas).
vario, ria adj. Different, diverse (distinto): *tela de varios colores*, material of different colours. || Various, several: *tratar de varios asuntos*, to discuss various subjects. || Variable, changeable (cambiadizo). || Varying, varied (que varía). || Several (unos cuantos): *tiene varios amigos*, he has several friends. || *Asuntos varios* or *cuestiones varias*, [any] other business (en el orden del día).
— Pron. indef. pl. Several, some [people]: *varios piensan que*, some [people] think that.
variólico, ca adj. Variolous.
varioloso, sa adj. Variolous.
— M. y f. Person with smallpox, smallpox case.
varita f. Wand: *varita de la virtud* or *de las virtudes* or *mágica* or *encantada*, magic wand. || Small stick, rod (pequeña vara).
varón m. Man: *esclarecidos varones*, great men. || Boy: *familia compuesta de una hija y tres varones*, family of one girl and three boys. || — *Hijo varón*, male child, son, boy. || *Santo varón*, saint. || *Sexo:*

varón, sex: male (en un pasaporte). || *Varón de Dios*, saint.
varonía f. Male issue, male descent.
varonil adj. Virile, manly: *carácter varonil*, virile character. || Mannish: *una mujer varonil*, a mannish woman.
varraco m. Boar (verraco).
Varsovia n. pr. GEOGR. Warsaw.
varsoviano, na adj. [Of *o* from] Warsaw.
— M. y f. Native *o* inhabitant of Warsaw.
vasallaje m. Vassalage. || Subjection, servitude. || *Rendir vasallaje*, to pay homage.
vasallo, lla adj./s. Vassal. || Subject (súbdito).
vasar m. Kitchen shelf.
vasco, ca adj./s. Basque. || *País vasco*, Basque Country (francés y español). || — M. Basque (lengua).
vascófilo m. Bascologist.
vascón adj. m. Of *o* pertaining to the Vascons (pueblo antiguo).
vascongado, da adj./s. Basque. || *Las Provincias vascongadas*, the [Spanish] Basque Country, the Basque Provinces.
— OBSERV. The *provincias vascongadas* are: *Álava, Guipúzcoa* and *Vizcaya;* their capitals are *Vitoria, San Sebastián*, and *Bilbao*.
Vasconia n. pr. f. GEOGR. The Basque Country.
vascónico, ca adj. V. VASCÓN.
vascuence adj./s.m. Basque (lengua).
vascular adj. Vascular: *tejido vascular*, vascular tissue.
vascularidad f. Vascularity.
vascularización f. Vascularization.
vasectomía f. MED. Vasectomy.
vaselina f. Vaseline. || FIG. y FAM. *Dar mucha vaselina a alguien*, to soft-soap s.o.
vasera f. Large tray for glasses (bandeja para vasos). || Kitchen shelf (vasar).
vasija f. Pot: *vasija de barro*, earthenware pot. || Vase: *una vasija precolombina*, a pre-Columbian vase. || Vessel, recipient, container (recipiente).
vaso m. Glass: *vaso de cristal*, crystal glass; *beberse un vaso de agua*, to drink a glass of water. || Glass, glassful (cantidad). || Vase (florero): *vaso de porcelana*, porcelain vase. || ANAT. Vessel: *vasos sanguíneos*, blood vessels. || BOT. Vessel. || — FIG. *Ahogarse en un vaso de agua*, V. AHOGAR. || FÍS. *Vasos comunicantes*, communicating vessels. || REL. *Vasos sagrados*, sacred vessels.
vasoconstricción f. Vasoconstriction.
vasoconstrictor adj. Vasoconstrictive.
— M. Vasoconstrictor.
vasodilatación f. Vasodilatation.
vasodilatador adj./s.m. Vasodilator.
vasomotor, ra adj. Vasomotor (nervios).
vástago m. Shoot (de planta, árbol). || TECN. Rod (del émbolo). || Descendent, scion, offspring: *el último vástago de una ilustre familia*, the last descendent of an illustrious family. || *Vástago de perforación*, drill stem.
vastedad f. Vastness.
vasto, ta adj. Vast, huge.
vate m. Poet (poeta). || Prophet (adivino).
vaticanista adj. Vatican, of the Vatican.
Vaticano n. pr. m. GEOGR. Vatican.
vaticano, na adj. Vatican, of the Vatican.
vaticinador, ra m. y f. Prophet, seer.
vaticinante adj. Foretelling, prophesying.
vaticinar v. tr. e intr. To prophesy, to foretell.
vaticinio m. Prophecy, prediction.
vatímetro m. ELECTR. Wattmeter.
vatio m. ELECTR. Watt (unidad). || *Potencia en vatios*, wattage.
vatio-hora n. ELECTR. Watt-hour.
vaudeville m. Comedy, vaudeville (comedia ligera).
— OBSERV. En inglés la palabra *vaudeville* se aplica más particularmente a un espectáculo de variedades.
vaudevillesco, ca adj. Comedy, vaudeville.
vaudevillista m. Comedy writer, vaudevillist.
vaya f. FAM. Mockery (burla). || *Dar vaya a*, to make fun of, to mock.
Vd. pron. pers. (abrev. de *usted*). V. USTED.
ve f. V (nombre de la letra *v*).
vecero, ra adj. Alternating. || Biennial (planta).
vecinaje m. Neighbourhood [U.S., neighborhood].
vecinal adj. Local, vicinal: *camino vecinal*, local road.
vecindad f. Neighbourhood [U.S., neighborhood], vicinity: *vive en la vecindad*, he lives in the neighbourhood. || Population (de una ciudad). || Neighbourhood, inhabitants, *pl.* (de un barrio). || Neighbours, *pl.* (los vecinos). || Residents, *pl.* || Nearness, proximity (proximidad). || Similarity (semejanza). || — *Casa de vecindad*, block of flats [U.S., apartment building]. || *Política de buena vecindad*, good neighbour policy.
vecindario m. Population, inhabitants, *pl.*: *el vecindario de una ciudad*, the population of a city. || Neighbourhood, neighbours, *pl.* [U.S., neighborhood, neighbors] (los vecinos): *acudió todo el vecindario*, the whole neighbourhood came. || Residents, *pl.*
vecino, na adj. Neighbouring [U.S., neighboring]: *país vecino*, neighbouring country. || Nearby (cerca). || Next door, next: *vive en la casa vecina de la mía*, he lives in the house next door to *o* next to mine. || FIG. Similar (semejante). || *Nuestras casas son vecinas*, our houses are next [door] to each other, we live next [door] to each other.
— M. y f. Neighbour [U.S., neighbor]: *nuestros vecinos son muy ruidosos*, our neighbours are very noisy. || Resident (residente). || Inhabitant: *los vecinos de Madrid*, the inhabitants of Madrid. || — *Cada* or *cualquier hijo de vecino*, everyone, anyone, every mother's son. || *Los vecinos de esta calle*, the residents in *o* the people who live in this street. || *Ser vecino de Soria*, to live in Soria. || *Son vecinos del mismo piso* or *planta*, they live on the same floor.
vector adj./s.m. Vector: *radio vector*, radius vector.
vectorial adj. Vectorial.
veda f. Close season [U.S., closed season] (pesca, caza). || Prohibition (prohibición). || *Levantamiento de la veda*, opening of the season.
Veda m. Veda (libro sagrado de la India).
vedado m. Private preserve. || — *Cazar en vedado*, to poach, to hunt on a private preserve. || *Vedado de caza*, [game] preserve.
vedamiento m. Prohibition (veda).
vedar v. tr. To prohibit, to forbid, to ban: *vedar la entrada en un sitio*, to prohibit people from entering a place, to ban people from entering a place, to forbid people to enter a place. || To prevent (impedir). || *Coto vedado*, [game] preserve.
vedegambre m. White hellebore (planta).
vedeja f. Long hair.
védico, ca adj. REL. Vedic.
vedija f. Tuft of wool (de lana). || Matted lock [of hair] (de pelo).
vedijoso, sa adj. Having matted wool.
veedor m. (Ant.). Supervisor, inspector: *veedor de caminos*, road inspector. || (Ant.). *Veedor de vianda*, royal caterer.
veeduría f. Supervisorship, inspectorship (cargo). || Inspector's *o* supervisor's office (oficina).
vega f. Fertile plain, fertile valley. || *Amer.* Tobacco plantation [in Cuba].
vegetación f. Vegetation.
vegetal adj. Vegetal: *medicamentos vegetales*, vegetal medicines. || Plant, vegetable: *el reino vegetal*, the vegetable kingdom.
— M. Vegetable.
vegetalina f. Vegetable butter.
vegetalismo m. Vegetarianism.
vegetar v. intr. To grow, to vegetate (plantas). || FIG. To vegetate (las personas).
vegetarianismo m. Vegetarianism.
vegetariano, na adj./s. Vegetarian.
vegetativo, va adj. Vegetative.
veguer m. Magistrate [in Aragon, Catalonia and Majorca] (magistrado).
veguería f. o **veguerío** m. Jurisdiction of a "veguer".
veguero, ra adj. Lowland, of the plains.
— M. Farmer (labrador). || FAM. Cigar (puro).
vehemencia f. Vehemence, passion. || Impetuosity (irreflexión).
vehemente adj. Vehement, passionate (apasionado). || Impetuous (irreflexivo).
vehículo m. Vehicle. || FIG. Vehicle (modo de transmisión). || Transmitter, carrier (de microbios): *las monedas son vehículo de microbios*, coins are transmitters of germs. || *Vehículo espacial*, spacecraft.
veintavo, va adj./s.m. Twentieth (vigésimo).
veinte adj. num. Twenty: *veinte personas*, twenty people; *página veinte*, page 20 [twenty]. || Twentieth: *en el siglo veinte*, in the 20th [twentieth] century; *el día veinte*, [on] the 20th [twentieth]. || — *Los años veinte*, the twenties. || FIG. *Son las menos veinte* or *son las y veinte*, silence reigns (silencio en una conversación). || *Unos veinte*, about twenty.
— M. Twenty (número). || Twentieth: *el veinte de mayo*, the twentieth of May. || Twenty, number twenty: *apostar en el veinte*, to bet on number twenty.
veintena f. About twenty, score: *una veintena de personas*, about twenty people, a score of people.
veinteno, na adj./s.m. Twentieth.
veinteñal adj. Twenty-year, of twenty years.
veintésimo, ma adj./s.m. Twentieth.
veinticinco, ca adj. num./s.m. Twenty-five (cardinal). || Twenty-fifth (ordinal): *el veinticinco de mayo*, the twenty-fifth of May.
veinticuatro adj. num./s.m. Twenty-four (cardinal). || Twenty-fourth (ordinal): *el veinticuatro de junio*, the twenty-fourth of June. || — M. (Ant.) Town councillor [in Andalusia].
veintidós adj. num./s.m. Twenty-two (cardinal). || Twenty-second (ordinal): *el veintidós de enero*, the twenty-second of January.
veintinueve adj. num./s.m. Twenty-nine (cardinal). || Twenty-ninth (ordinal): *el veintinueve de julio*, the twenty-ninth of July.
veintiocho adj. num./s.m. Twenty-eight (cardinal). || Twenty-eighth (ordinal): *el veintiocho de abril*, the twenty-eighth of April.
veintiséis adj. num./s.m. Twenty-six (cardinal). || Twenty-sixth (ordinal): *el veintiséis de marzo*, the twenty-sixth of March.
veintisiete adj. num./s.m. Twenty-seven (cardinal). || Twenty-seventh (ordinal): *el veintisiete de diciembre*, the twenty-seventh of December.
veintitantos, tas adj. About twenty, twenty-odd: *veintitantas personas*, about twenty *o* twenty-odd people. || About the twentieth: *sucedió hacia el*

veintitantos de abril, it happened about the twentieth of April.
veintitrés adj. num./s.m. Twenty-three (cardinal). || Twenty-third (ordinal): *el veintitrés de noviembre es mi cumpleaños*, my birthday is on the twenty-third of November.
veintiún adj. num. Twenty-one: *tener veintiún libros*, to have twenty-one books.
— OBSERV. This adjective is the apocopated form of *veintiuno* before masculine nouns.
veintiuno, na adj. num./s.m. Twenty-one (cardinal). || Twenty-first (ordinal): *el veintiuno de octubre*, the twenty-first of October. || — F. Twenty-one, blackjack, vingt-et-un (juego de azar).
vejación f. o **vejamen** m. Vexation (maltratamiento). || Humiliation (humillación).
vejancón, ona adj. Very old, doddery (fam.).
— M. Old man. || — F. Old woman.
vejar v. tr. To vex, to annoy, to hurt (ofender).
vejatorio, ria adj. Humiliating: *condiciones vejatorias*, humiliating conditions. || Hurtful, vexatious, offensive: *palabras vejatorias*, hurtful words.
vejestorio m. FAM. Old crock.
vejete adj. m. Old.
— M. Old man, old boy.
vejez f. Old age.
vejiga f. ANAT. Bladder. || Blister (en la piel). || — *Vejiga de la bilis*, gall bladder. || *Vejiga natatoria*, air *o* swimming bladder (de los peces).
vejigatorio, ria adj./s.m. MED. Vesicatory.
vejigazo m. Blow with an air-filled bladder. || FAM. *Darse un vejigazo*, to fall flat on one's face.
vejigoso, sa adj. Covered in blisters.
vejiguilla f. Blister (en la piel).
vela f. MAR. Sail: *vela latina*, lateen sail. || Candle: *vela de estearina*, tallow candle. || Wakefulness (desvelo). || Vigil, watch (de un muerto). || Vigil, watching over (de un enfermo). || FIG. Horn (del toro). || — Pl. FAM. Snot, *sing.* (mocos). || — MAR. *Alzar velas* or *hacerse a la vela*, to set sail. | *A toda vela, a velas desplegadas* or *tendidas*, under full sail. | *Barco de vela*, sailing ship. | *Cambiar la vela*, to shift sail. | *Dar la vela*, to set sail. || FIG. y FAM. *Encender* or *poner una vela a Dios y otra al diablo*, to run with the hare and hunt with the hounds. | *Estar a dos velas*, to be broke. || MAR. *Largar las velas*, to set sail. || FIG. *No tener vela en un entierro*, to have no say in the matter. || *Pasar la noche en vela*, to have a sleepless night, not to get a wink of sleep all night. || FIG. *¿Quién te dio vela en este entierro?*, who asked you to poke your nose in? | *Recoger velas*, to back down. | *Ser más derecho que una vela*, to be as straight as a die. || MAR. *Vela al tercio*, lugsail. | *Vela de abanico* or *tarquina*, spritsail. | *Vela de estay*, staysail. | *Vela mayor*, mainsail.
velación f. Vigil, watching over (de un enfermo). || Vigil, wake (de un muerto). || — Pl. Ceremony (*sing.*) of the veil [with which the bride and groom are covered during the wedding].
velacho m. MAR. Fore-topsail (vela).
velada f. Evening: *quedarse de velada con unos amigos*, to spend the evening with a few friends; *velada literaria*, literary evening. || Party [held at night] (reunión de personas).
velado, da adj. Veiled (cubierto con un velo). || FIG. Veiled: *alusión velada*, veiled reference; *ojos velados por lágrimas*, eyes veiled in *o* by tears. || BOT. Blurred. || *Voz velada*, muffled voice.
velador, ra adj. Who watches, watching.
— M. Vigil-keeper (que vela). || Watchman (que hace guardia). || Pedestal table (mesita). || Candlestick (candelero). || *Amer.* Bedside table (mesita de noche).
veladura f. Glaze (en pintura). || FOT. Fog.
velamen m. MAR. Canvas, sails, *pl.* || ANAT. Velamen.
velar v. intr. To stay awake, not to sleep (no dormir). || To stay up (no acostarse). || To keep watch (hacer guardia). || REL. To keep vigil. || To work late (trabajar tarde). || FIG. To watch over, to look after: *velar por la salud de un enfermo*, to watch over a sick person. || *Velar por la observancia de las leyes*, to make sure *o* to ensure that the laws are observed.
— V. tr. To watch over, to sit up with: *velar a un enfermo*, to watch over a sick person. || To stand vigil over (a un muerto). || To veil (cubrir con un velo). || FIG. To veil, to hide (disimular). || FOT. To fog, to blur. || To glaze (en pintura). || *Velar las armas*, to carry out the vigil of arms.
— V. pr. FOT. To be fogged *o* blurred.
velar adj./s.f. ANAT. y GRAM. Velar.
velatorio m. Vigil, wake.
velazqueño, ña adj. Of Velazquez, typical of Velazquez.
veleidad f. Caprice, whim (deseo vano). || Fickleness, inconstancy (versatilidad).
veleidoso, sa adj. Inconstant, fickle.
velero, ra adj. Sailing: *barco velero*, sailing ship *o* boat.
— M. MAR. Sailing ship (barco grande). | Sailing boat (pequeño). | Sailmaker (que hace velas para barcos). || Chandler (de velas de cera).
veleta f. Weather vane, weathercock (para el viento). || Float (de caña de pescar). || — M. y f. FIG. Weathercock, inconstant person (persona).
velilla f. Match (cerilla).
velo m. Veil: *velo de novia*, bride's veil. || FIG. Veil, shroud. || Confusion (confusión). || ANAT. Velum, veil. || — FIG. *Correr* or *echar un velo* or *un tupido velo sobre algo*, to hush sth. up, to draw a veil over sth., to keep sth. quiet. | *Descorrer el velo*, to draw back the veil. || REL. *Tomar el velo*, to take the veil. || ANAT. *Velo del paladar*, velum, soft palate. || REL. *Velo humeral*, humeral veil.
velocidad f. Speed, velocity: *la velocidad de la luz*, the speed of light. || TECN. y AUT. Gear: *tiene cuatro velocidades*, it has four gears; *cambiar la velocidad*, to change gear. || MÚS. Speed (rapidez de ejecución). || — *A gran velocidad*, at a high speed. || *A toda velocidad*, [at] full speed. || AUT. *Caja de velocidades*, gearbox. || FIG. *Confundir el tocino con la velocidad*, not to know one's left hand from one's right. || *Con gran velocidad*, very fast, with great speed. || FIG. *Con la velocidad del rayo*, like lightning, as quick as a flash. || *Disminuir la velocidad*, to reduce speed, to slow down. || *En gran velocidad*, by express (ferrocarril). || *En pequeña velocidad*, by goods train [U.S., by freight] (ferrocarril). || *Ganar velocidad*, to pick up speed. to gather speed. || *Meter la segunda velocidad*, to change into second gear (automóvil). || *Multado por exceso de velocidad*, fined for speeding *o* for exceeding the speed limit. || *Perder velocidad*, to lose speed (un avión, un vehículo), to lose its hold (una moda). || *Primera velocidad*, first *o* bottom *o* low gear. || *Velocidad de crucero*, cruising speed. || *Velocidad de liberación*, escape velocity (de un vehículo espacial). || *Velocidad límite*, speed limit. || *Velocidad máxima* or *tope* or *punta*, top speed.
velocímetro m. Speedometer.
velocípedo m. Velocipede.
velocista m. DEP. Sprinter.
velódromo m. Cycle track [U.S., velodrome].
velomotor m. Moped, small motorcycle.
velón m. Oil lamp (lámpara de aceite). || *Amer.* Thick candle (vela grande).
velonero m. Lamp maker.
velorio m. Wake, vigil (velatorio). || Party, celebration (fiesta). || REL. Taking of the veil (de una monja).
veloz adj. Quick, fast, rapid, swift: *veloz como un rayo*, as quick as lightning *o* as a flash.
— Adv. Fast, quickly, rapidly, swiftly: *corre muy veloz*, he runs very fast.
velozmente adv. Fast, quickly, rapidly, swiftly.
veludillo m. Velveteen (tela).
vello m. Down.
vellocino m. Fleece. || MIT. *Vellocino de oro*, Golden Fleece.
vellón m. Fleece (de carnero u oveja). || Tuft of wool (vedija). || Copper coin (monedas).
vellosidad f. Downiness, fluffiness. || Down (vello).
velloso, sa adj. Downy, hairy, fluffy.
velludillo m. Velveteen (tela).
velludo, da adj. Hairy, shaggy.
— M. Plush (felpa).
vena f. ANAT. Vein. || Vein, streak (de piedras, maderas). || BOT. Vein, rib. || GEOL. y MIN. Vein, seam. || — FIG. y FAM. *Coger a alguien en vena*, to catch s.o. in the right mood. | *Estar de vena para*, to be in the mood for. | *Estar en vena*, to be on form. | *Le ha dado la vena de ir al Polo*, he has taken *o* got it into his head to go to the Pole. | *Tener una vena de loco*, to have a streak *o* a vein of madness. | *Tener vena de pintor*, to have a gift for painting. || FIG. y FAM. *Trabajar por venas*, to work in fits and starts. || ANAT. *Vena cava*, vena cava. | *Vena porta*, portal vein.
venablo m. Javelin, dart (arma). || FIG. *Echar venablos*, to roar with anger.
venadero m. Place frequented by deer (del ciervo).
venado m. Deer, stag (ciervo). || CULIN. Venison.
venal adj. Venal: *funcionario venal*, venal official. || ANAT. Venous (venoso). || Venal, purchasable (que se puede comprar).
venalidad f. Venality.
venático, ca adj. Fickle, inconstant.
venatorio, ria adj. Hunting.
vencedero, ra adj. COM. Falling due (pago).
vencedor, ra adj. Conquering, victorious: *el ejército vencedor*, the conquering army. || Winning, victorious (equipo, jugador).
— M. y f. Conqueror, victor. || Winner, victor (ganador).
vencejo m. Bond (atadura). || ZOOL. Swift (pájaro).
vencer v. tr. To conquer, to vanquish, to defeat, to beat: *vencer a los enemigos*, to defeat the enemy. || DEP. To beat. || FIG. To overcome, to surmount: *vencer un obstáculo*, to surmount an obstacle. || To master (pasiones). | To overcome (tentación, sueño). | To outdo, to surpass, to beat: *vencer a uno en generosidad*, to outdo s.o. in generosity. | To cover (recorrer): *vencer una distancia*, to cover a distance. | To conquer: *el Aconcagua fue vencido en 1897*, the Aconcagua was conquered in 1897. | To break (romper): *el peso de los libros ha vencido la mesa*, the books were so heavy that they broke the table. || *Dejarse vencer*, to give up the fight, to give in.
— V. intr. To win, to triumph (ganar, triunfar). || To fall due, to be payable: *la cuenta vence mañana*,

the bill falls due tomorrow. || To expire (plazo). || To fall due, to mature (deuda).
— V. pr. FIG. To control o.s. (controlarse). | To bend, to sag (doblarse). | To break, to collapse (romperse).
vencetósigo m. BOT. White swallowwort.
vencible adj. Conquerable, vanquishable (país, enemigo). || Beatable (adversario). || FIG. Surmountable, which can be overcome (superable).
vencida f. *A la tercera va la vencida*, third time lucky (para animar), let that be the last time.
vencido, da adj. Defeated, beaten. || Losing (que pierde). || Due, payable (un pagaré, etc.). || Mature, falling due (deuda). || Expired (plazo).
— M. y f. Conquered *o* vanquished person. || DEP. Loser. || — *¡Ay* or *guay de los vencidos!*, woe betide the conquered! || *Darse por vencido*, to give up, to admit defeat. || *La tormenta va de vencida*, the worst of the storm is over. || *Los vencidos*, the conquered, the vanquished (en una guerra), the losers (en deportes, etc.).
vencimiento m. Falling due (de un pagaré, etc.). || Maturity (de una deuda). || Expiration, expiry (de un plazo). || FIG. Overcoming, surmounting (de un obstáculo). || Victory (victoria). || Defeat (derrota). || FIG. Bending (torsión). | Collapse (al romperse).
venda f. Bandage: *venda de gasa*, gauze bandage. || Dressing (vendaje). || Band, fillet (de cabeza). || — FIG. *Quitar a uno la venda de los ojos*, to open s.o.'s eyes. | *Se le cayó la venda de los ojos*, his eyes were opened. | *Tener una venda en los ojos*, v. OJO.
vendaje m. MED. Dressing. || *Vendaje enyesado*, plaster cast (para un miembro roto).
vendar v. tr. To bandage (una herida). || — FIG. *La pasión le venda los ojos*, he is blinded by passion. | *Tener los ojos vendados*, v. OJO. || *Vendar los ojos a alguien*, to blindfold s.o.
— V. pr. To bandage: *vendarse el brazo*, to bandage one's arm.
vendaval m. Gale, strong wind. || FIG. Storm.
vendedor, ra adj. Selling.
— M. Salesman (en una tienda de muebles, coches, etc). || Seller: *vendedor de periódicos*, newspaper seller. || Shop assistant (dependiente). || — F. Salesgirl, saleswoman, shop assistant. || — *Vendedor ambulante*, pedlar [U.S., peddler], hawker. || *Vendedor ambulante de periódicos*, newsboy. || *Vendedor callejero*, street hawker.
vendehúmos m. y f. inv. FAM. Braggart, show-off.
vendeja f. Public sale (feria).
vender v. tr. To sell: *vender naranjas*, to sell oranges; *vender un cuadro en* or *por diez mil pesetas*, to sell a painting for ten thousand pesetas. || FIG. To sell: *vender su alma*, to sell one's soul. | To sell [out], to betray (traicionar): *vender a un amigo*, to sell a friend. || — *Artículo sin vender*, unsold article. || FIG. *El enemigo ha vendido cara su derrota*, the enemy put up a good fight. || *Vender al contado*, to sell for cash. || *Vender al descubierto*, to sell short (en la Bolsa). || *Vender al por mayor*, to wholesale, to sell wholesale. || *Vender al por menor*, to retail. || *Vender a plazos* or *a cuota* (Amer.), to sell on credit. || *Vender cara su vida*, to sell one's life dearly, to put up a good fight. || *Vender caro*, to sell at a high price, to be expensive (un comerciante). || *Vender con pérdida*, to sell at a loss. || *Vender de contrabando*, to sell illegally. || *Vender en pública subasta*, to auction. || FIG. *Vender la piel del oso antes de haberlo matado*, to count one's chickens before they are hatched. || *Vender por las casas*, to sell from door to door. || *Vender salud*, to be glowing *o* brimming with health.
— V. pr. To cost: *actualmente el terreno se vende caro*, land costs a lot these days. || FIG. To sell o.s. (dejarse sobornar). | To give o.s. away (traicionarse). || — "*Se vende*", "for sale". || *Se vende en las principales librerías*, it is on sale in the main bookshops. || *Se vende un coche deportivo*, sports car for sale. || *Venderse a* or *por*, to sell for *o* at, to cost, to fetch: *los huevos se venden a veinte pesetas la docena*, eggs are selling at twenty pesetas a dozen. || FIG. *Venderse caro*, to play hard to get. | *Venderse como rosquillas* or *como pan caliente*, to sell like hot cakes.
vendí m. Certificate of sale.
vendible adj. Saleable, sellable.
vendido, da adj. Sold. || FIG. Lost.
vendimia f. Grape harvest, vintage (recolección). || Vintage: *la vendimia de 1944*, the 1944 vintage.
vendimiador, ra m. y f. Vintager, grape harvester.
vendimiar v. tr. To harvest, to gather (las uvas).
vendo m. Selvedge (de la tela).
venduta f. *Amer.* Auction (subasta).
Venecia n. pr. GEOGR. Venice (ciudad). | Venetia (región).
veneciano, na adj./s. Venetian (de Venecia).
venencia f. Tube [for sampling sherry].
veneno m. Poison (químico o vegetal): *la estricnina es un veneno violento*, strychnine is a powerful poison. || Venom, poison (de los animales). || FIG. Poison (que causa daño moral). | Venom, spite (malevolencia). || FIG. *Sus palabras destilan veneno*, his words are venomous *o* full of venom.
venenosidad f. Poisonousness.
venenoso, sa adj. Poisonous, poison: *seta venenosa*, poisonous mushroom. || Venomous, poison, poisonous: *serpiente venenosa*, venomous snake. || FIG. Poisonous (que causa daño moral). | Venomous (malevolente).
venera f. Scallop (concha). || Spring (manantial).
venerabilísimo, ma adj. Very *o* most venerable.
venerable adj./s. Venerable.
veneración f. Veneration. || Worship (adoración).
venerar v. tr. To venerate, to revere: *venerar a uno por santo*, to venerate s.o. as a saint. || To worship (adorar).
venéreo, a adj. MED. Venereal.
— M. MED. Venereal disease.
venero m. Spring (manantial). || MIN. Seam, vein (yacimiento). || FIG. Source (origen). | Mine: *venero de informaciones*, mine of information.
véneto, ta adj./s. Venetian.
venezolanismo m. Venezuelan expression (giro) *o* word (voz).
venezolano, na adj./s. Venezuelan.
Venezuela n. pr. m. GEOGR. Venezuela.
vengador, ra adj. Avenging.
— M. y f. Avenger.
venganza f. Vengeance, revenge: *clamar venganza*, to demand vengeance; *tomar venganza de alguien*, to take revenge on s.o.
vengar v. tr. To avenge.
— V. pr. To avenge o.s., to take revenge: *vengarse de una afrenta en uno*, to avenge o.s. *o* to take revenge on s.o. for an insult.
vengativo, va adj. Vindictive, vengeful.
venia f. Forgiveness, pardon (perdón). || Permission, leave, consent: *con la venia del profesor*, with the teacher's permission. || Greeting (saludo).
venial adj. Venial: *pecado venial*, venial sin.
venialidad f. Veniality.
venida f. Coming (acción de venir): *idas y venidas*, comings and goings. || Arrival, coming (llegada): *la venida de la primavera*, the arrival of spring. || Flooding (de un río). || Attack (esgrima). || *Me alegro de tu venida*, I am delighted [that] you have come.
venidero, ra adj. Future, coming: *los años venideros*, future years. || *En lo venidero*, in the future.
— M. pl. Future generations, descendants.
venilla f. ANAT. Small vein.
venir* v. intr. To come: *él va a venir*, he is going to come; *¡ven aquí!*, come here; *dile que venga*, tell him to come. || To arrive (llegar): *vino muy cansado*, he arrived very tired. || To come (proceder): *este té viene de Ceilán*, this tea comes from Ceylon; *su mala conducta viene de su educación*, his ill conduct comes from his upbringing. || To come (suceder): *la primavera viene después del invierno*, spring comes after winter. || To have been: *lo vengo diciendo desde hace diez años*, I have been saying it for the last ten years. || To happen (ocurrir). || To be, to come: *su foto viene en la primera página*, his photograph is on the first page. || To be, to be written: *el texto viene en inglés*, the text is written in English. || To be: *este piso nos viene ancho*, this flat is too big for us; *me viene un poco estrecho*, it is rather tight for me. || To be: *vengo triste*, I am sad. || — *¿A dónde quieres venir a parar?*, what are you getting at?, what do you mean by that? || *A mal venir*, at the worst. || *¿A qué viene esto?*, what is that doing here? (un objeto), what is the point of that? (una acción). || *¿A qué viene llorar?*, what is the good *o* the point of crying? || *¿A qué vienes?*, what are you doing here?, what do you want here? || *Como le venga en gana*, as you like, as it suits you, just as you wish. || *De ahí viene que*, so it is that, thus it is that. || *Depende de cómo venga la cosa*, that will depend on the circumstances. || *El año que viene*, next year, the coming year. || *En el periódico de hoy viene un reportaje muy interesante*, in today's paper there is a very interesting report. || *En lo por venir*, in future (de aquí en adelante), in the future (en lo futuro). || *Eso no viene a cuento*, that has nothing to do with it, that is irrelevant (no tiene nada que ver), there is no sense in it (no es oportuno). || *Eso vengo diciendo desde hace tiempo*, that's what I've been saying all along. || *Hacer venir a uno*, to summon s.o., to bring s.o., to send for s.o. || *Le vino en gana marcharse al extranjero*, he took it into his head *o* he got the urge to go abroad. || FIG. *Lo veía venir*, I could see it coming, I was expecting it. || *Me vinieron ganas de reír*, I felt like laughing, I could have laughed. || *Me vino un dolor de muelas terrible*, I got terrible toothache. || FAM. *No le va ni le viene*, it has nothing to do with him, it is none of his business (no le importa), he doesn't care one way or the other, he couldn't care less (le da igual). || *No me viene su nombre a la memoria*, I cannot remember his name, his name escapes me. || *Se le vino* or *le vino a la boca un disparate*, he put his foot in it. || *Si a mano viene*, should the occasion arise. || *Vendrá a tener cincuenta años*, he must be about fifty. || *¡Venga!*, come on!: *¡venga!, que vamos a llegar tarde*, come on, we shall be late; go on! (anda), give it to me!, give it here! (dámelo). || *Venga como venga la cosa*, come what may, whatever happens, whatever may happen. || *Venga lo que venga*, come what may. || *Venga o no venga a cuento*, without rhyme or reason (a tontas y a locas), rightly or wrongly (con razón o sin ella). || *Venir a*, to reach, to arrive at (alcanzar): *vinieron a un acuerdo*, they reached

an agreement; to end up [by] (acabar por): *vinieron a firmar las paces*, they ended up signing the treaty. || *Venir a cuento*, to be opportune (ser oportuno), to be relevant (ser pertinente). || *Venir a la cabeza*, v. CABEZA. || *Venirle a la memoria a uno*, to remember, to occur to: *me vino a la memoria que*, I remembered that, it occurred to me that. || *Venir a la mente*, v. MENTE. || *Venir a las manos*, v. MANO. || *Venir al mundo*, to come into the world. || FAM. *Venir a punto*, to come in handy, to come at a good moment, to come just right. || *Venir a menos*, to go downhill (una empresa), to lose status, to come down in the world (personas). || *Venir a parar*, to come to, to end [up]: *sus ilusiones han venido a parar en eso*, his illusions have come to that; to result in, to lead to (dar lugar a), to reach, to arrive at, to come to: *venir a parar a la misma conclusión*, to reach the same conclusion; to end [up], to stop: *la pelota vino a parar a mis pies*, the ball ended up at my feet. || *Venir a ser*, to boil down to, to amount to: *venir a ser lo mismo*, to boil down to the same thing; to turn out (resultar): *viene a ser más molesto de lo que pensábamos*, it is turning out to be more bothersome than we expected; to be, to amount to: *esto viene a ser una mera estafa*, this is a downright swindle. || *Venir con cuentos*, to tell stories. || *Venir en decretar, en nombrar*, to decree, to appoint. || FAM. *Venirle al pelo a uno*, to suit s.o. down to the ground. || *Venirle bien a uno*, to suit s.o.: *el verde te viene bien*, green suits you; to fit: *¿te viene bien el abrigo? — No, es un poco largo*, does the coat fit you? — No, it is a little long; to come in handy (ser útil): *esas diez mil pesetas me vendrían muy bien*, those ten thousand pesetas would come in very handy for me; to suit (convenir): *me vendría bien ir a las siete*, it would suit me to go at seven. || *Venirle mal a uno*, not to suit s.o., not to fit s.o. (traje), to be inconvenient for s.o., to be a nuisance for s.o. (no convenir): *me viene mal ir esta tarde*, it is inconvenient for me to go this afternoon. || *Venir mejor*, to suit *o* to fit better (convenir o ir mejor), to be better (ser mejor). || FAM. *Venir que ni pintado*, to suit down to the ground, to suit to a tee. | *Venir rodado*, to come *o* to arrive just at the right time *o* moment. || FIG. *Verle venir a uno*, to see s.o. coming. || *Vino una inundación a estropear la cosecha*, a flood destroyed *o* came and destroyed the crop. || *Voy y vengo*, I'll be right back.
— V. pr. To come back, to go back (volver). || To ferment (el vino). || — *La sala se venía abajo con los aplausos*, the applause shook the hall. || *Todo se nos vino encima a la vez*, everything came upon us at once, everything went wrong at once. || *Venirse abajo*, v. ABAJO. || *Venirse al suelo* or *a tierra*, v. SUELO. y TIERRA.

venosidad f. ANAT. Venosity.

venoso, sa adj. Venous: *sangre venosa*, venous blood. || Veiny, veined: *manos venosas*, veined hands. || Veined, ribbed: *hoja venosa*, veined leaf.

venta f. Sale, selling: *la venta de la leche*, the sale of milk; *la compra y la venta de muebles*, the buying and selling of furniture, the purchase and sale of furniture. || Sales, *pl.*: *servicio de venta*, sales department. || Sales, *pl.* (artículos vendidos). || Inn (albergue). || — *Contrato de venta*, bill of sale. || *De venta en todas las librerías*, on sale in all bookshops. || *Estar a la venta* or *en venta*, to be on sale. || *Poner en venta*, to put on sale (un producto), to put up for sale: *no tiene más remedio que poner su casa en venta*, he has no choice but to put his house up for sale. || *Precio de venta*, selling price. || *Precio de venta al público*, retail price. || *Ser un artículo de fácil venta*, to sell. || *Venta a crédito*, sale on credit. || *Venta a domicilio*, door-to-door selling. || *Venta al contado*, cash sale. || *Venta al por menor*, retail. || *Venta a plazos* or *por cuotas* (Amer.), hire purchase [U.S., sale on the installment plan]. || *Venta callejera*, street-selling, peddling. || *Venta de localidades de 7 a 9*, the ticket office *o* the booking office is open from 7 to 9. || *Venta en firme*, firm sale. || *Venta postbalance*, stocktaking sale [U.S., post-inventory sale]. || *Venta pública*, public sale.

ventaja f. Advantage: *tiene la ventaja de ser fuerte*, he has the advantage of being strong. || Benefit: *ventajas sociales*, social benefits. || Profit (provecho). || Advantage (en deportes). || Headstart, start (en una carrera). || — *Dar dos metros de ventaja a uno*, to give s.o. a two-metre start. || *Llevar ventaja a*, to have the advantage over *o* the edge on [s.o]. || *Sacar ventaja a*, to be ahead of; *sacó ventaja de 20 metros* or *de 20 segundos a su competidor*, he was 20 metres *o* 20 seconds ahead of his opponent; *sacar gran* or *mucha ventaja*, to be well ahead; to leave behind (ser superior). || *Sacar ventaja de*, to profit *o* to benefit from.

ventajero, ra o **ventajista** m. y f. *Amer.* Advantage-taker, opportunist.
— Adj. Opportunist.

ventajoso, sa adj. Advantageous: *me ofrecieron condiciones muy ventajosas*, they offered me very advantageous conditions. || Profitable (rentable): *fue un negocio muy ventajoso*, it was a very profitable deal.

ventalla f. Valve [of a legume].

ventana f. Window. || Nostril (de la nariz). || — FIG. *Tirar algo por la ventana*, to waste sth., to throw sth. away. | *Tirar la casa por la ventana*, v. CASA. || *Ventana de guillotina*, sash window. || *Ventana vidriera*, picture window.

ventanaje f. Windows, *pl.*

ventanal m. Large window.

ventanilla f. Window (en los trenes, coches, aviones). || Porthole (en los barcos). || Window (taquilla). || ANAT. Nostril (de la nariz).

ventanillo m. Wicket, small window (postigo pequeño). || Peephole (mirilla). || Ventilator (de un sótano). || Window (de un avión).

venteado, da adj. Windy.

ventarrón m. Gale, strong wind (viento fuerte).

ventear v. impers. To be windy.
— V. tr. e intr. To air, to air out (una habitación, un vestido, etc.). || To sniff (olfatear). || FIG. To snoop (investigar). | To smell (sospechar).
— V. pr. To split (agrietarse). || To blister (los ladrillos al cocerse). || To spoil (estropearse). || FAM. To break wind (ventosear).

ventero, ra m. y f. Innkeeper.
— Adj. *Perro ventero*, pointer.

ventilación f. Ventilation: *la ventilación de un túnel*, the ventilation of a tunnel. || — *Conducto de ventilación*, air duct, ventilation shaft. || MAR. *Manguera de ventilación*, windsail (de lona), air intake (de metal). || *Sin ventilación*, unventilated. || *Ventilación pulmonar*, pulmonary ventilation.

ventilador m. Ventilator (para ventilar). || Fan (para refrescar o mover el aire). || Window fan (en una ventana).

ventilar v. tr. To ventilate: *ventilar un túnel*, to ventilate a tunnel. || To air, to ventilate, to air out: *ventilar la habitación abriendo la ventana*, to air the room by opening the window. || FIG. To air (hacer público). | To clear up [U.S., to take care of] (discutir y resolver).
— V. pr. To be aired, to be aired out (un cuarto, etc.). || To be ventilated (túnel, etc.). || FIG. To be cleared up, to be discussed (resolverse). | To be at stake (estar en juego): *se ventila su porvenir*, his future is at stake. || FIG. y FAM. To knock off, to polish off: *este trabajo me lo ventilo en una hora*, I'll knock off this job in an hour. || To get some fresh air (tomar el aire). || — *El resultado del partido se ventiló en los últimos cinco minutos*, the outcome of the match was decided in the last five minutes. || FAM. *Ventilárselas*, to take care of o.s. (arreglárselas).

ventisca f. Blizzard, snowstorm.

ventiscar v. impers. To blow a blizzard: *está ventiscando*, it is blowing a blizzard.
— V. intr. To swirl (la nieve).

ventisco m. Blizzard, snowstorm.

ventiscoso, sa adj. Snowy.

ventisquear v. intr. V. VENTISCAR.

ventisquero m. Glacier (helero). || Snowdrift (nieve acumulada). || Slope *o* part of a mountain most exposed to snowstorms. || Blizzard, snowstorm (ventisca).

ventolera f. Gust of wind, blast (ráfaga). || Whirligig [U.S., pinwheel] (molinillo de juguete). || — FIG. y FAM. *Darle a uno la ventolera de hacer algo*, to take it into one's head to do sth. | *Darle a uno la ventolera por alguien*, to take a fancy to s.o. | *Tener mucha ventolera*, to be bigheaded, to have a big head (ser muy vanidoso).

ventolina f. Light and variable wind.

ventor, ra adj. Tracking.
— M. Pointer (perro).

ventorrillo m. Roadhouse (merendero).

ventorro m. Small inn (venta pequeña).

ventosa f. MED. Cupping glass. || Suction cup (objeto que se adhiere). || Sucker (de los animales). || Vent, air hole (abertura).

ventosear v. intr. To break wind.

ventosidad f. Wind, flatulence.

ventoso, sa adj. Windy: *día ventoso*, windy day.

ventral adj. Ventral.

ventregada f. Litter (camada).

ventrera f. Cinch (cincha). || Abdominal support (faja). || [Skirt of] tasses (de la armadura).

ventricular adj. Ventricular.

ventrículo m. ANAT. Ventricle.

ventrílocuo, cua adj. Ventriloquistic.
— M. y F. Ventriloquist.

ventriloquia f. Ventriloquy, ventriloquism.

ventrudo, da adj. FAM. Potbellied.

ventura f. Happiness (felicidad). || Good fortune: *tienes la ventura de tener a tus hijos contigo*, you have the good fortune of having your children with you. || [Good] luck: *le deseo mucha ventura en su nuevo trabajo*, I wish you lots of [good] luck in your new job. || Fate, fortune (casualidad): *la ventura quiso que me encontrara con ella*, fate led me to meet her. || Hazard (riesgo). || — *A la ventura* or *a la buena ventura*, at random (al azar), without a fixed plan (sin nada previsto). || *Echar la buena ventura a alguien*, to tell s.o.'s fortune. || *Mala ventura*, bad *o* ill luck. || *Por ventura*, by chance (por casualidad), luckily, fortunately (afortunadamente). || *Probar ventura*, to try one's luck.

venturina f. Aventurine (piedra).

venturo, ra adj. Future.

venturosamente adv. Fortunately.

venturoso, sa adj. Happy (feliz). || Fortunate, lucky (afortunado). || Successful (que tiene éxito).
venus f. ZOOL. Venus (género de moluscos). || FIG. Venus (mujer muy bella).
Venus n. pr. f. MIT. Venus (diosa). || *Monte de Venus*, mound of Venus.
Venus n. pr. m. ASTR. Venus.
ver m. Sight, vision (sentido de la vista). || Looks, *pl.*, appearance (de una persona). || Appearance (de una cosa). || Opinion: *a mi ver*, in my opinion. || *Un hombre de buen ver*, a good-looking man.
ver* v. tr. e intr. To see: *lo he visto con mis propios ojos*, I saw it with my own eyes; *no le vi marcharse*, I didn't see him leave; *no le veo*, I can't see him; *no veo muy bien por qué lo hiciste*, I can't really see why you did it; *vea Vd. si le va este traje*, see if this suit fits you; *ir a ver a un amigo*, to go to see a friend; *voy a ver si puedo*, I'm going to see if I can. || To know (saber): *no veo la decisión que he de tomar*, I don't know what decision to make. || To look at (mirar): *está viendo un documento muy importante*, he's looking at a very important document. || To watch (la televisión). || To find: *te veo cansado*, I find you tired. || JUR. To hear, to try (una causa). || — *¡A más ver!* or *¡hasta más ver!*, I'll be seeing you!, so long! || *A mi modo de ver*, in my opinion, to my way of thinking, the way I see it. || *Aquí donde me ve usted*, as sure as I am standing here now, surprising though it may seem. || *A ver*, let's see, let's have a look (con curiosidad): *a ver qué película echan*, let's see what film they're showing; all right, now then (con tono imperioso): *¡a ver! ¿qué pasa aquí?*, all right, what's going on here? || *¡A ver qué pasa!*, so what! (desafío). || *A ver si*, how about: *a ver si estudias un poco más*, how about studying a little more; I hope [that]: *a ver si puedo acabar este trabajo hoy*, I hope I can finish this job today; what if, supposing: *a ver si es que se ha perdido*, what if he got lost? || *Como si lo viera*, as if I were seeing it with my own eyes. || *Darse a ver*, to show o.s. || *Dejarse ver*, to show up, to show one's face (una persona), to show (manifestarse). || *Dejar ver*, to make it clear *o* understood. || *Deje que vea*, let me see. || *Dígame a ver*, tell me. || *Echar de ver*, to realize, to see (darse cuenta). || *Echa un poco de sal a la sopa a ver qué pasa*, put a little salt in the soup to see what happens. || *Estar viendo*, to be beginning to think (sospechar), to see (imaginarse): *te estoy viendo hacer el equipaje*, I can just see you packing your bags. || *Esto está por ver* or *esto habrá que verlo*, that remains to be seen. || *¡Habría que ver que lo hicieses!*, you wouldn't dare [do it]!, I'd like to see you [do it]! || *Hacer ver algo a alguien*, to point sth. out to s.o., to make s.o. see sth. || *Hay que ver*, you should see, it's amazing: *hay que ver lo que ha crecido*, you should see how much he's grown, it's amazing how much he's grown. || *¡Hay que ver!*, it just goes to show! || *Hay que verlo*, it's worth seeing. || *Hay que verlo para creerlo*, it has to be seen to be believed. || *Le haré ver quien soy yo*, I'll show him. || *Lo estaba viendo*, I could see it coming. || *¿Lo ves?*, see!, you see! || *Manera de ver las cosas*, way of looking at things. || *Mire a ver*, have a look. || *Mire a ver si puede hacerlo*, see if you can do it. || *No dejarse ver*, to keep out of sight (esconderse), to make o.s. scarce (desaparecer). || *No hay quien te vea*, you've been making yourself scarce. || *No le veo la gracia*, I don't think that's funny. || *No poder ver a uno* or *no poder ver a uno ni pintado*, V. PINTADO. || *No tener nada que ver con*, to have nothing to do with. || *No ver más allá de sus narices*, not to be able to see further than the end of one's nose. || *No ver ni jota* or *no ver tres en un burro*, to be as blind as a bat (ser miope), not to be able to see a thing (en un sitio oscuro). || *Nunca he visto cosa igual*, I've never seen anything like it, I've never seen such a thing. || *¡Para que veas!*, so there!, you see! || *Por lo que veo* or *por lo que se ve* or *por lo visto*, apparently, it seems that. || FIG. y FAM. *Que no veo*, ever so, terribly: *tengo un hambre que no veo*, I'm ever so hungry; rotten: *tengo un constipado que no veo*, I've got a rotten cold. || *Ser de ver*, to be worth seeing. || FIG. *Si te he visto no me acuerdo*, you (he, etc.) just don't want to know. | *Te lo veo en la cara*, I can see it in your eyes. | *Tener que ver con*, to have to do with, to concern. | *Tener que ver en*, to have a hand in. | *Te veo venir*, I see you coming, I know what you're after. || *Vamos a ver*, let's see. || *Verás*, you'll see. || *Ver de*, to try to (con infinitivo), to see about (con gerundio). || *Veremos*, we'll see. || *Ver es creer*, seeing is believing. || FIG. *Ver las estrellas*, to see stars. | *Verlas venir*, to catch on quickly. || *Ya lo veo* or *ya se ve*, that's obvious, that's easy to see. || *Ya veremos*, we'll see. || *Ya ves*, you see.
— V. pr. To be seen (ser visto). || To be, to find o.s. (estar): *me veo en un apuro*, I am in a jam. || To see each other (visitarse). || To meet (encontrarse): *¿dónde nos vamos a ver?*, where shall we meet? || To imagine o.s.: *esta chica ya se ve estrella de cine*, this girl already imagines herself a film star. || To remember (recordar): *me veo en mi juventud*, I remember when I was young. || To see o.s. (imaginar algo futuro): *ya me veo en la playa*, I can already see myself on the beach. || To look (parecer). || — *Con tantas torres ya no se ve el cielo*, with so many tower blocks you can't even see the sky. || *¿Cuándo se vio cosa igual?*, did you ever see such a thing? || *Es digno de verse* or *merece verse*, it's worth seeing. || *¡Habrase visto!*, did you ever! || FIG. *Se ve a la legua* or *de lejos*, you can see it a mile away. || *Se ve que*, it is obvious that. || *Véase el capítulo siguiente*, see the following chapter. || *Verse con alguien*, to see s.o. || FIG. *Vérselas con uno*, to deal with s.o.
vera f. Edge, side. || — *A la vera de*, beside, next to. || *A mi vera*, beside me, at *o* by my side.
veracidad f. Truthfulness, veracity.
veranada f. AGR. Summer season.
veranadero m. Summer pasture.
veranda f. Veranda.
veraneante m. y f. Holidaymaker [U.S., summer vacationist].
veranear v. intr. To spend one's summer holidays [U.S., to spend one's summer vacation]: *voy a veranear a Miami*, I'm going to spend my summer holidays in Miami. || *¿Dónde veraneas este año?*, where are you holidaying *o* where are you going for your holidays this summer?, where are you spending your summer holidays this year?
veraneo m. Summer holidays, *pl.* [U.S., summer vacation]: *organizar el veraneo*, to make all the arrangements for one's summer holidays. || — *Ir de veraneo*, to go on holiday [U.S., to take one's vacation]. || *Lugar de veraneo*, summer resort.
veranero m. Summer pasture.
veraniego, ga adj. Summer: *temporada veraniega*, summer season; *vestido veraniego*, summer dress. || *Vas muy veraniego hoy*, you look very summery today.
veranillo m. *Veranillo de San Juan*, warm spell in June. || *Veranillo de San Martín* or *de San Miguel* or *del membrillo*, Indian summer.
verano m. Summer: *vacaciones de verano*, summer holidays. || *Vestirse de verano*, to put on one's summer clothes.
veras f. pl. *Ahora va de veras que me marcho*, now I am really going. || *De veras*, really (realmente), seriously (seriamente). || *Esto va de veras* this is serious, this is no joke. || *Lo siento de veras*, I am truly sorry. || *¿Me lo dices de veras?*, do you really mean that?
veraz adj. Truthful, veracious: *relato veraz*, truthful account. || Reliable: *historiador veraz*, reliable historian.
verbal adj. Verbal: *acuerdo verbal*, verbal agreement; *sustantivo verbal*, verbal noun.
verbalismo m. Verbalism.
verbalista adj. Verbalistic.
— M. y f. Verbalist.
verbasco m. BOT. Mullein.
verbena f. BOT. Verbena, vervain. || Fair (fiesta popular). || Dance [held on the eve of a saint's day] (baile).
verbenáceas f. pl. BOT. Verbenaceae.
verbenero, ra adj. Of the fair.
verbigracia o **verbi gratia** loc. For example, for instance, e.g.
verbo m. GRAM. Verb: *verbo auxiliar*, auxiliary verb; *verbo transitivo*, transitive verb. || Language, style (lenguaje, estilo).
Verbo n. pr. m. REL. Word.
verborrea f. Verbosity (verbosidad). || Verbiage, wordiness (palabrería). || *Tener mucha verborrea*, to be verbose.
verbosidad f. Verbosity, wordiness.
verboso, sa adj. Verbose, wordy.
verdad f. Truth: *juró que diría toda la verdad*, he swore that he would tell the whole truth; *acento de verdad*, ring of truth; *verdad matemática*, mathematical truth. || — *A decir verdad* or *la verdad sea dicha*, to tell the truth, actually. || *Bien es verdad que*, it is of course true that. || *Cantarle* or *decirle a uno cuatro verdades* or *las verdades del barquero*, to give s.o. a piece of one's mind, to tell s.o. a few home truths. || *Decir la verdad*, to tell the truth. || *De verdad*, really (adverbio): *entonces me enfadé de verdad*, then I really got angry; real (adjetivo): *un torero de verdad*, a real bullfighter. || *¿De verdad?*, really? || FAM. *De verdad de la buena*, honest to God, honest to goodness. || *De verdad que sí, que no*, honestly, really. || *En honor a la verdad*, V. HONOR. || *En verdad*, verily (en la Biblia): *en verdad os digo*, verily I say unto you. || *Es la pura verdad*, it's the gospel truth. || *Eso es una verdad como un puño* or *como un templo*, it's the patent truth. || *Es verdad*, it is true. || *Faltar a la verdad*, to lie. || *Hora de la verdad*, moment of truth. || *Jurar decir la verdad, sólo la verdad y nada más que la verdad*, to swear to tell the truth, the whole truth, and nothing but the truth. || *La pura verdad*, the plain truth. || *Las verdades amargan*, the truth hurts. || *La verdad*, to tell the truth, actually: *la verdad no lo sé*, actually I don't know. || *La verdad escueta* or *al desnudo*, the naked truth. || *La verdad es que*, the truth is, actually. || *No es verdad*, it is not true. || *¿No es verdad?*, isn't that so? || *No hay más que los niños y los locos que dicen las verdades*, out of the mouths of babes and fools. || *No todas las verdades son para dichas*, it is sometimes better not to tell the truth. || *Se lo digo de verdad*, I really mean it. || *Si bien es verdad que*, although (aunque). || *Sólo la verdad*

ofende, nothing hurts like the truth. || *Tan de verdad* or *tan verdad como que Dios existe*, it's the gospel truth. || *Uno de verdad*, a real one. || *¿Verdad?*, v. OBSERV. || *Verdad a medias*, half-truth. || *Verdad de Perogrullo*, truism, platitude. || *Verdad es que*, it is true that.

— OBSERV. *Verdad* is also used as an invariable adjective to mean "real", "true" : *los aristócratas verdad*, the real aristocrats.

— La expresión "¿verdad?" no tiene una traducción única sino que varía según la forma y la naturaleza del verbo. En cuanto a la forma, si el verbo se encuentra en una frase afirmativa, la expresión equivalente a "¿verdad?" tiene que ponerse en forma negativa (*estás contento, ¿verdad?*, you are happy, aren't you?) y viceversa (*no estás contento, ¿verdad?*, you are not happy, are you?). Por lo que se refiere a la naturaleza, cuando el verbo es un auxiliar, "¿verdad?" se traduce empleando el mismo auxiliar (*sabes nadar, ¿verdad?*, you can swim, can't you?), pero en el caso en que se trate de un verbo transitivo, intransitivo, pronominal o defectivo hay que utilizar el auxiliar "do" (*trabaja muy bien, ¿verdad?*, he works very well, doesn't he?). Hay que señalar además que el verbo, cualquiera que sea, tiene que ir en el tiempo y persona correspondientes a los del verbo de la frase inicial (*trabajaba muy bien, ¿verdad?*, he worked very well, didn't he?).

verdaderamente adj. Truly, really.

verdadero, ra adj. True, real: *historia verdadera*, true story. || Real, genuine: *un diamante verdadero*, a real diamond. || Truthful, veracious (veraz). || Real, true: *un verdadero amigo*, a real friend. || ASTR. True: *mediodía, norte verdadero*, true noon, north. || — *Es el verdadero retrato de su padre*, he is the spit and image *o* spitting image of his father. || *Lo verdadero*, the true, what is true: *distinguir lo verdadero de lo falso*, to distinguish the true from the false.

verdal adj. Green [even when ripe].

verdasca f. Switch, green stick (vara).

verde adj. Green: *un sombrero verde*, a green hat. || Green, unripe (fruta). || Green, unseasoned (leña). || FIG. Dirty, blue (licencioso): *contar chistes verdes*, to tell dirty jokes. | Young, in the early stages: *el negocio está aún verde*, the deal is still in the early stages. || — *Cuero en verde*, green hide. || FIG. *Estar verde de envidia*, to be green with envy. || *Forraje verde*, green fodder. || FIG. y FAM. *Pasar las verdes y las maduras*, to have a really rough time. | FAM. *Poner verde a uno*, to call s.o. all the names under the sun. || *Tapete verde*, gaming table. || FAM. *Un viejo verde*, a dirty old man.

— M. Green (color): *me gusta el verde*, I like green. || Foliage (de las plantas). || Grass (hierba). || FIG. Impropriety: *lo verde de sus palabras*, the impropriety of his remarks. || *Amer.* Maté, Paraguay tea. || *Verde esmeralda*, emerald green.

verdear v. intr. To look green (tirar a verde). || To grow *o* to turn green: *el campo empieza a verdear*, the countryside is beginning to grow green.

verdeceledón m. Celadon (color).

verdecer v. intr. To grow *o* to turn green.

verdecillo m. Greenfich (pájaro).

verdegal m. Green patch (en un campo). || Green field (campo verde).

verdemar adj. Sea-green.

— M. Sea green.

verdeo m. Olive harvest.

verdeoscuro, ra adj. Dark green.

verderón m. Greenfinch (pájaro). || Cockle (molusco).

verdete m. Verdigris.

verdezuelo m. Greenfinch (pájaro).

verdín m. Verdure, fresh green (de las plantas). || Mildew, mould (moho). || Verdigris (verdete, cardenillo). || Moss (musgo). || Green stain, grass stain (mancha en la ropa).

verdinegro, gra adj. Dark green.

verdolaga f. Purslane (planta).

verdor m. Verdure, greenness, verdancy (color). || FIG. Youth (juventud). | Vigour, strength (vigor).

verdoso, sa adj. Greenish.

verdugado m. Hoopskirt, crinoline.

verdugal m. Hill covered with young plants.

verdugazo m. Lash [with a whip].

verdugo m. Executioner, hangman (ejecutor de la justicia). || BOT. Twig, shoot (vástago). || Whip (látigo). || Weal (verdugón). || Bruise (cardenal). || FIG. Tyrant (tirano). | Scourge (tormento): *ser un verdugo para sus alumnos*, to be the scourge of one's pupils. || ARQ. Horizontal layer of bricks. || TAUR. Sword for accomplishing the "descabello".

verdugón m. Weal (hecho por un látigo). || Bruise (cardenal). || Twig, shoot (renuevo).

verduguillo m. Weal-like swelling [on leaves] (en las hojas). || Small razor (navaja de afeitar). || TAUR. Sword for accomplishing the "descabello".

verdulería f. Greengrocer's (tienda): *ir a la verdulería*, to go to the greengrocer's. || FIG. Coarse word *o* expression (dicho grosero). | Coarseness (grosería).

verdulero, ra m. y f. Greengrocer. || — F. FIG. y FAM. Fishwife (mujer desvergonzada). || FAM. *Hablar como una verdulera*, to speak like a fishwife.

verdura f. Verdure, greenery, greenness: *la verdura de los prados*, the verdure of the meadows. || Greenness (color verde). || — Pl. Vegetables, greens (hortalizas): *comer verduras*, to eat greens. || *Verduras tempranas*, early vegetables *o* greens.

verdusco, ca adj. Dirty green, greenish.

verecundia f. Bashfulness, timidity, shyness (vergüenza).

verecundo, da adj. Bashful, timid, shy (vergonzoso).

vereda f. Path, lane (senda). || *Amer.* Pavement [U.S., sidewalk] (acera). || FIG. y FAM. *Meter en vereda a uno*, to bring s.o. into line.

veredicto m. JUR. Verdict: *veredicto de inculpabilidad*, verdict of not guilty.

verga f. ANAT. Penis. || MAR. Yard.

vergajo m. Pizzle whip, pizzle.

vergé adj. *Papel vergé*, laid paper.

vergel m. Orchard (huerto).

vergeteado, da adj. HERÁLD. Paly.

vergonzante adj. Shameful. || *Pobre vergonzante*, poor but too proud to beg.

vergonzoso, sa adj. Shameful, disgraceful: *huida vergonzosa*, shameful flight. || Shy, timid, bashful (tímido). || ANAT. *Partes vergonzosas*, private parts, privates.

— M. y f. Shy *o* timid *o* bashful person. || *El vergonzoso en palacio*, The Timid Youth at Court (de Tirso de Molina). || — M. ZOOL. Variety of armadillo.

verguear v. tr. To beat (varear).

vergüenza f. Shame (humillación, arrepentimiento): *por vergüenza no quiso confesar que estaba embarazada*, shame prevented her from admitting that she was pregnant. || Embarrassment (confusión, bochorno). || Bashfulness, shyness, timidity (timidez). || FIG. Disgrace, shame (oprobio): *eres la vergüenza de tu familia*, you are a disgrace to your family. || Modesty (pudor). || Honour [U.S., honor], dignity (pundonor): *un hombre con vergüenza*, a man of honour. || — Pl. ANAT. Private parts, privates (partes pudendas). || — *Con* or *para gran vergüenza suya*, much to his shame (humillación), much to his embarrassment (confusión). || *¡Es una vergüenza!*, it is disgraceful *o* shameful!, it is a disgrace! || *Me da vergüenza hablar en público*, I don't like speaking *o* I'm shy about speaking in public, it embarrasses me to speak in public. || *Me da vergüenza su conducta*, your behaviour shames me *o* makes me ashamed. || *Me da vergüenza tener que pedírselo*, I am ashamed to have to ask you for it. || *¿No le da a usted vergüenza?*, aren't you ashamed?, have you no shame? || *Pasé mucha vergüenza*, I was so ashamed (humillación), I was so embarrassed (confusión). || *Perder la vergüenza*, to lose all sense of shame. || *¡Qué poca vergüenza tiene!*, the man has no shame!, he is quite shameless! || *Sacar a alguien a la vergüenza pública*, to put s.o. to public shame. || *Se le cayó la cara de vergüenza*, he blushed with shame *o* died of shame. || *Sin vergüenza*, shameless (desvergonzado), shamelessly (de manera desvergonzada). || *Tener vergüenza*, to be ashamed (*de*, to, of), to be shy: *no tengas vergüenza, cántame algo*, don't be shy, sing me a song. || *Vergüenza para quien piense mal*, honni soit qui mal y pense. || *Vergüenza torera*, dignity (dignidad).

vergueta f. Twig, small switch.

vericueto m. Rough *o* rugged path.

verídico, ca adj. Truthful: *hombre verídico*, truthful man. || True (verdadero): *lo que digo es verídico*, what I am saying is true; *relato verídico*, true story.

verificación f. Checking, inspection, testing (de una máquina, etc.). || Verification, checking (de un resultado). || Carrying out, fulfilment (ejecución).

verificador, ra adj. Checking, inspecting, testing (de una máquina). || Verifying, checking (de un resultado).

— M. y f. Tester, inspector.

verificar v. tr. To check, to inspect, to test (máquinas, etc.). || To check, to verify (un resultado). || To carry out, to perform, to effect: *la aviación verificó un bombardeo*, the air force carried out a bombing raid. || — V. pr. To take place, to be held (tener lugar): *la boda se verificará mañana*, the wedding will take place tomorrow. || To come true (una predicción).

verificativo, va adj. Verificatory.

verisímil adj. Probable, likely.

verisimilitud f. V. VEROSIMILITUD.

verismo m. Verism.

verja f. Grating, grille (de puerta, de ventana). || Railings, *pl.* (cerca).

verjurado, da adj. Laid: *papel verjurado*, laid paper.

verme m. MED. Intestinal worm.

vermicida adj. Vermicidal.

— M. Vermicide.

vermiculado, da adj. ARQ. Vermiculate.

vermicular adj. Vermicular.

vermiforme adj. Vermiform.

vermífugo, ga adj./s.m. Vermifuge, anthelmintic.

verminoso, sa adj. MED. Accompanied by intestinal worms.

vermívoro, ra adj. ZOOL. Vermivorous.

vermut o **vermú** m. Vermouth: *vermut con ginebra*, gin and vermouth. || *Amer.* Matinée (de teatro o cine).

— OBSERV. Pl. *vermús.*

vernáculo, la adj. Vernacular. || *Lengua vernácula*, vernacular.

vernier m. TECN. Vernier (nonio).

vero m. (P.us.) Vair (animal). || HERÁLD. Vair (blasón).

verónica f. Veronica, speedwell (planta). || TAUR. Veronica [pass with the cape]

verosímil adj. Probable, likely. || Credible (relato).

verosimilitud f. Probability, likelihood. || Credibility (de un relato).
verosímilmente adv. Probably.
verraco m. Boar, hog (cerdo). || FAM. *Gritar como un verraco*, to squeal like a pig.
verraquear v. intr. FAM. To grumble, to growl, to moan (gruñir). | To wail, to scream, to howl (berrear).
verraquera f. FAM. Tantrum (rabieta): *agarrar una verraquera*, to throw a tantrum.
verriondez f. Heat, rut (de animales).
verriondo, da adj. On heat (los cerdos, etc.).
verrón m. Boar, hog (cerdo).
verruga f. MED. y BOT. Wart. || FIG. y FAM. Pain in the neck (pesadez).
verrugón m. Large wart.
verrugosidad f. Wart-like swelling.
verrugoso, sa adj. Warty.
versado, da adj. Versed: *versado en lenguas*, versed in languages.
versal adj./s. f. IMPR. Capital (letra).
versalilla o **versalita** adj./s. f. IMPR. Small capital (letra).
Versalles n. pr. Versailles.
versallés o **versallesco, ca** adj. In the style of Versailles. || FIG. y FAM. Old-world: *modos muy versallescos*, very old-world manners. | Princely (principesco).
— M. y f. Native *o* inhabitant of Versailles.
versar v. intr. To go *o* to turn round (girar). || FIG. *Versar sobre*, to deal with, to be about (tratar de).
versátil adj. BOT. y ZOOL. Versatile. || FIG. Fickle, inconstant, changeable (inconstante).
versatilidad f. BOT. y ZOOL. Versatility. || FIG. Fickleness, inconstancy, changeableness.
versícula f. Place where hymnbooks are kept.
versiculario m. Person who sings versicles. || Keeper of hymnbooks.
versículo m. Versicle.
versificación f. Versification.
versificador, ra m. y f. Versifier.
versificante adj. Versifying.
versificar v. intr. To versify, to write verse.
— V. tr. To versify, to put into verse.
versión f. Version: *dos versiones de un suceso*, two versions of an event. || Translation, version (traducción).
versista m. y f. Versifier.
verso m. Verse: *verso blanco* or *suelto*, blank verse. || Line: *un poema de veinte versos*, a poem with twenty lines. || Versicle (versículo). || — *Comedia en verso*, comedy in verse [form]. || *Hacer versos*, to write poetry. || *Poner en verso*, to put into verse. || *Verso libre*, free verse.
verso m. Verso (reverso de una hoja). || MIL. Small culverin (pieza de artillería).
vértebra f. ANAT. Vertebra.
vertebrado, da adj./s.m. ZOOL. Vertebrate.
vertebral adj. Vertebral: *discos vertebrales*, vertebral discs. || *Columna vertebral*, v. COLUMNA.
vertedera f. Mouldboard [U.S., moldboard] (de un arado).
vertedero m. Drain (desaguadero). || Spillway, overflow (para que no rebose). || Rubbish dump, rubbish tip (de basuras). || FAM. Pigsty (estercolero). || *Vertedero de basuras*, v. BASURA.
vertedor, ra adj. Pouring.
— M. y f. Pourer. || — M. Spillway, overflow (desagüe). || Drain (para aguas residuales). || MAR. Bailer, bale, bail (achicador). || Scoop (en una tienda).
verter* v. tr. To pour [out]: *verter el trigo en el depósito*, to pour the wheat into the container. || To spill (derramar): *verter vino en el mantel*, to spill wine on the tablecloth. || To empty [out] (vaciar). || To upset (volcar). || To shed: *verter lágrimas*, to shed tears. || To tip, to dump (basuras). || To translate, to put into (traducir): *verter al francés*, to put *o* to translate into French. || FIG. To pronounce (decir). || FAM. *Verter aguas menores*, to relieve o.s.
— V. intr. y pr. To flow (*a*, into) [un líquido]. || To slope, to fall (una vertiente).
vertical adj. Vertical: *líneas verticales*, vertical lines. || Vertical, upright (posición). || *Formato vertical*, lengthwise format (ilustración).
— F. MAT. Vertical (línea). || — M. ASTR. Vertical *o* azimuth circle.
verticalidad f. Verticality.
verticalmente adv. Vertically.
vértice m. MAT. Vertex (de un ángulo). | Apex (de un cono). || ANAT. Vertex.
verticilo m. BOT. Verticil.
vertiente adj. Pouring, which pours. || *Aguas vertientes*, rainwater flowing off a roof (del tejado).
— F. Slope: *en la vertiente sur de la montaña*, on the south slope of the mountain. || Versant (término geográfico). || Slope (de un tejado). || FIG. Aspect.
vertiginosamente adv. Vertiginously, giddily, dizzily. || *Subir vertiginosamente*, to spiral upwards, to soar (precios).
vertiginosidad f. Vertiginousness.
vertiginoso, sa adj. Vertiginous. || FIG. Giddy, vertiginous (velocidad).
vértigo m. MED. Vertigo, giddiness, dizziness. || Giddiness dizziness (mareo). || FIG. Frenzy (arrebato): *le dio un vértigo*, he went into a frenzy; *una actividad de vértigo*, a frenzy of activity. | Whirl: *dejarse envolver en el vértigo de las fiestas*, to get caught up in the whirl of parties. || — *De vértigo*, frenzied (actividad, etc.), stunning (belleza, etc.). || *La altura me da vértigo*, heights make me giddy *o* dizzy. || *Tener vértigo*, to feel dizzy *o* giddy.
vertimiento m. Pouring [out] (derrame).
vesanía f. MED. Insanity (locura). || Rage, fury (cólera).
vesánico, ca adj. MED. Insane, demented. || Furious.
— M. y f. Madman, madwoman, insane *o* demented person.
vesical adj. MED. Vesical.
vesicante adj./s.m. MED. Vesicant.
vesicatorio, ria adj./s.m. MED. Vesicatory.
vesícula f. Vesicle. || *Vesícula biliar*, gall bladder.
vesicular adj. Vesicular.
vesperal m. Vesperal (libro).
vespertino, na adj. Vespertine, evening. || *Estrella vespertina* or *lucero vespertino*, evening star.
Vespucio n. pr. m. Vespucci.
vestal f. Vestal [virgin] (sacerdotisa de Vesta).
— Adj. Vestal.
vestibular adj. ANAT. Vestibular.
vestíbulo m. ARQ. Hall (de una casa particular). | Vestibule, foyer (de un edificio público). || ANAT. Vestibule.
vestido, da adj. Dressed: *estar bien vestido*, to be well dressed. || Dressed, wearing: *vestido de negro*, dressed in *o* wearing black; *vestido con una chaqueta roja*, dressed in *o* wearing a red jacket.
— M. Clothes, *pl.*, garments, *pl.* (ropa): *los primitivos utilizaban la piel de los animales para su vestido*, primitive man used animal skins as clothes. || Costume: *historia del vestido*, history of costume. || Dress (de mujer): *un vestido de seda*, a silk dress. || — FIG. y FAM. *Cortarle a uno un vestido*, to slate s.o., to pull s.o. to pieces, to criticize s.o. | *Cortar vestidos*, to gossip, to criticize people, to backbite, to tittle-tattle. || *Vestido cerrado*, high-necked dress. || *Vestido de noche*, evening dress *o* gown. || *Vestido tubo* or *tubular*, sheath dress.
vestidor m. Dressing room.
vestidura f. Piece of clothing, garment (prenda de vestir). || Clothing, clothes, *pl.* (ropa). || — Pl. REL. Vestments. || FIG. *Rasgarse las vestiduras*, to make a great to-do.
vestigio m. Vestige (resto). || FIG. Trace (huella). || — Pl. Vestiges, remains (restos): *los vestigios de una civilización*, the vestiges of a civilization.
vestimenta f. Clothes, *pl.*, garments, *pl.*: *llevaba una vestimenta extraña*, he was wearing strange clothes. || — Pl. REL. Vestments. || *Vestimenta ridícula*, ridiculous garb.
vestir* v. tr. To dress, to clothe: *vestir a un niño*, to dress a child. || To dress: *este sastre viste a todos mis hermanos*, this tailor dresses all my brothers. || To buy [s.o.'s] clothes, to clothe: *sus padres le visten todavía*, his parents still buy his clothes, his parents still clothe him. || To wear: *la novia vestía un traje blanco*, the bride was wearing a white dress. || To cover: *vestir de cuero un sillón*, to cover a chair with leather. || To hang: *vestir las paredes con tapices*, to hang the walls with tapestries. || FIG. To embellish (un discurso). | To hide, to cover (la realidad). || — FIG. *Vestir al desnudo*, to help the destitute *o* the poor. | *Vísteme despacio que tengo prisa*, more haste less speed. | *Vistió un rostro de severidad*, he took on *o* he adopted a serious air. || *Yo fui vestido de torero*, I went dressed as a bullfighter.
— V. intr. To dress: *viste bien*, he dresses well. || To wear, to dress in (llevar): *vestir de negro, de uniforme*, to dress in *o* to wear black, uniform. || FIG. To be dressy: *la seda viste mucho*, silk is very dressy. || FIG. y FAM. To be classy *o* smart: *tener un coche deportivo viste mucho*, it is very classy to have a sports car. || — FIG. *El mismo que viste y calza*, the very same, none other. || *Un traje de vestir*, a formal suit *o* dress.
— V. pr. To get dressed, to dress: *está tardando mucho en vestirse*, she's taking a long time to get dressed. || To wear, to dress: *vestirse de negro*, to wear black, to dress in black. || To buy one's clothes: *se viste en las mejores tiendas*, she buys her clothes in the best shops. || FIG. To turn: *los campos se visten de verde*, the fields are turning green. || — FIG. *Vestirse con plumas ajenas*, to strut in borrowed feathers *o* in borrowed plumes. || *Vestirse de*, to dress up as (disfrazarse de). || *Vestirse de largo*, v. LARGO. || *Vestirse de máscara*, to disguise o.s., to dress up. || FAM. *Vestirse de tiros largos*, to put on one's Sunday best, to dress up. || *Vestirse de verano*, to put on one's summer clothes.
vestuario m. Wardrobe, clothes, *pl.* (conjunto de trajes): *tengo que renovar mi vestuario*, I must renew my wardrobe. || Dressing room (donde se visten los actores, etc.). || Costumes, *pl.* (trajes de teatro, de cine). || MIL. Uniform. || DEP. Changing room. || Cloakroom (en un teatro, cine, club, etc.). || *Encargado* or *encargada del vestuario*, dresser (de un actor de teatro), cloakroom attendant (para los abrigos del público).
Vesubio n. pr. m. GEOGR. Vesuvius.
veta f. Vein, streak (de piedra, de madera). || Streak, stripe (raya). || MIN. Vein (de oro, etc.). | Seam (de carbón).

vetar v. tr. To veto, to put a veto on.
vetear v. tr. To grain, to streak (madera, piedra). || To streak (con rayas).
veteranía f. Long experience. || Seniority (antigüedad).
veterano, na adj. Veteran: *un periodista, un soldado veterano*, a veteran reporter, soldier.
— M. Veteran. || FIG. Old hand.
veterinaria f. Veterinary medicine *o* science.
veterinario, ria adj. Veterinary: *medicina veterinaria*, veterinary medicine.
— M. Veterinary surgeon, vet, veterinary [U.S., veterinarian].
veto m. Veto: *derecho de veto*, power *o* right of veto. || — *Poner el veto a*, to veto, to put a veto on. || *Veto absoluto, suspensivo*, absolute, suspensory veto.
vetustez f. Great age, antiquity, ancientness.
vetusto, ta adj. Ancient, very old.
vez f. Time: *tres veces al mes*, three times a month; *cuatro veces seguidas*, four times in a row. || Turn (turno): *hablar a su vez*, to speak in one's turn; *perder la vez*, to lose one's turn; *tengo la vez*, it is my turn. || — *A la vez*, at the same time, at once (al mismo tiempo), together (juntos). || *A la vez que*, at the same time as. || *Algunas veces* or *a veces*, at times, sometimes, occasionally. || *Alguna vez*, sometimes (en alguna ocasión), ever (en preguntas): *¿has estado alguna vez en Roma?*, have you ever been to Rome? || *A veces ... y otras veces*, sometimes... sometimes: *a veces está sonriente y otras veces serio*, he is sometimes smiling and sometimes serious. || *Cada vez*, every time, each time. || *Cada vez más*, more and more (v. OBSERV.). || *Cada vez menos*, (seguido de un adjetivo o de un sustantivo en singular) less and less: *es cada vez menos difícil*, it gets less and less difficult; (seguido de un sustantivo en plural) less and less, fewer and fewer: *hay cada vez menos oportunidades*, there are fewer and fewer opportunities. || *Cada vez mejor, peor*, better and better, worse and worse. || *Cada vez que*, whenever, every *o* each time [that]. || *Contadas veces*, seldom, rarely. || *Demasiadas veces*, too often. || *De una (sola) vez*, in one go. || *De una vez* or *de una vez para siempre*, once and for all. || *De vez en cuando*, from time to time, occasionally. || *Dos veces*, twice. || *Dos veces más rico*, twice as rich. || *En vez de*, instead of. || *Érase una vez*, once upon a time [there was]. || *Estar cada vez peor*, to get worse and worse, to go from bad to worse. || *Hacer las veces de*, to act as, to serve as. || *Hacer otra vez algo*, to do sth. again. || *Infinitas veces*, an infinite number of times. || *Las más de las veces* or *la mayoría de las veces*, usually, most times, more often than not. || *Más de una vez*, more than once. || *Miles de veces*, thousands of times, over and over again. || *Muchas veces*, often, many times. || *Otra vez*, once more (una vez más), again (de nuevo), more, encore (espectáculo): *¡otra vez!*, encore! || *Otras veces*, other times. || *Pase por una vez*, it is all right this once *o* this time. || *Pocas* or *raras veces*, seldom, rarely. || *Por enésima vez*, for the umpteenth time. || *Repetidas veces*, repeatedly, again and again, many times. || *Tal cual vez*, rarely, on rare occasions. || *Tal vez*, perhaps, maybe. || *Toda vez que*, since, seeing that (ya que, dado que). || *Una vez*, once. || *Una vez al año no hace daño*, once in a while never hurt anyone. || *Una vez dice que sí y otra que no*, first he says yes and then he says no. || *Una vez más*, once more, again, once again. || *Una vez que lo hubo hecho*, once he had done it. || *Una vez que otra* or *una que otra vez*, from time to time, occasionally, now and then. || *Una vez tras otra*, over and over again (sin parar). || *Una (vez) y otra vez* or *una vez y cien veces*, time and time again. || *Varias veces*, several times.

— OBSERV. Nótese que la forma *more and more* se sustituye por el comparativo en *-er* cuando el adjetivo que sigue la expresión "cada vez más" se traduce al inglés por una palabra corta : *es cada vez más mona*, she gets prettier and prettier.

vía f. Road, way: *vía romana*, Roman road. || Railway line, line, rail, track (ferrocarril). || Route: *vía marítima*, sea route. || Lane (de autopista). || ANAT. Tract, passage: *vías urinarias*, urinary tract. || QUÍM. Way, process: *vía húmeda, seca*, wet, dry process. || TECN. Track (automóvil). || FIG. Way, means. | Channel: *vía ordinaria*, usual channel. || JUR. Procedure. || — *Cuaderna vía*, verse form with four alexandrines (del mester de clerecía). || *De vía estrecha*, narrow-gauge. || *El tren está en la vía primera*, the train is at platform one. || *Estar en vías de*, to be in the process of. || *Países en vías de desarrollo*, developing countries. || *Por vía aérea*, by air (personas, cargamento, etc.), [by] airmail (correo). || *Por vía oral*, orally. || FIG. *Por vía de*, by means of: *por vía de sufragios*, by means of votes; by way of, as: *por vía de ensayo*, as an experiment. || *Por vía de buen gobierno*, as a cautionary measure. || *Por vía interna*, internally. || *Por vía marítima*, by sea. || *Por vía oficial*, through official channels. || *Recurrir a la vía judicial*, to go to law. || *Vía aérea*, by airmail (correo). || MAR. *Vía de agua*, leak: *abrirse una vía de agua*, to spring a leak. || *Vía de comunicación*, communication channel, means of communication. || *Vía de maniobra*, [railway] siding. || *Vía férrea*, railway [U.S., railroad]. || *Vía fluvial*, waterway. || ASTR. *Vía Láctea*, Milky Way. || *Vía muerta*, siding (ferrocarril). || *Vía pública*, public thoroughfare, public way. || JUR. *Vías de hecho*, acts of violence, assault and battery.
vía prep. Via: *Madrid-Londres vía París*, Madrid-London via Paris.
viabilidad f. Viability. || Feasibility, practicableness (posibilidad de realizarse).
viable adj. Viable. || Feasible, practicable (posible).
viacrucis o **vía crucis** m. Way of the Cross, Stations (*pl.*) of the Cross. || FIG. Calvary (tormento).
viaducto m. Viaduct.
viajador, ra m. y f. Traveller [U.S., traveler] (viajero).
viajante adj. Travelling [U.S., traveling].
— M. y f. Traveller [U.S., traveler]. || *Viajante (de comercio)*, commercial traveller [U.S., traveling salesman].
viajar v. intr. To travel: *viajar por España*, to travel through Spain.
viaje m. Journey, trip: *¿habéis tenido buen viaje?*, did you have a nice journey?; *hacer un viaje a Inglaterra*, to go on a trip to England; *los peregrinos hicieron un viaje muy largo*, the pilgrims went on a long journey. || Travel: *durante sus viajes se encontró con su profesor*, on his travels he met his teacher. || Drive, journey (en coche): *el viaje por la autopista fue algo aburrido*, the drive along the motorway was rather boring. || Load (carga): *echar un viaje de leña*, to go for a load of wood. || FAM. Jab, slash (con una navaja, etc.). | Punch (puñetazo). || TAUR. Butt. || — *Agencia de viajes*, travel agency, travel agent's. || *¡Buen viaje!*, bon voyage!, have a good journey! || *Estar de viaje*, to be away, to be away on a journey, to be travelling. || *Hacer un viaje por toda Escocia*, to tour Scotland, to travel all round Scotland. || *Ir* or *irse de viaje*, to go away, to go on a journey *o* trip. || *No me gustan los viajes*, I don't like travelling. || FIG. y FAM. *¡Para este viaje no se necesitan alforjas!*, a fat lot of good that is! || *Se ha ido de viaje*, he is away on a journey, he has gone away. || *Viaje de buena voluntad*, goodwill visit. || *Viaje de ida*, outward journey. || *Viaje de ida y vuelta*, return journey *o* trip, round trip. || *Viaje de novios*, honeymoon: *fueron en viaje de novios a*, they went on their honeymoon to, they spent their honeymoon in, they honeymooned in. || *Viaje de prueba*, trial *o* test run. || *Viaje de recreo*, pleasure trip. || MAR. *Viaje en barco*, boat trip (corto), voyage (largo). || *Viaje todo comprendido*, all-in trip, inclusive *o* package tour.
viajero, ra adj. Travelling [U.S., traveling] (pasajero).
— M. y f. Traveller [U.S., traveler]. || Passenger. || *¡Viajeros al tren!*, all aboard!
vial adj. Road (de la carretera). || Traffic (de la circulación).
— M. (P.us.). Avenue.
vialidad f. Highway administration (servicios de la vía pública).
vianda f. Food (alimento). || — Pl. Food, *sing.*
viandante m. y f. Traveller [U.S., traveler] (viajero). || Passerby (transeúnte). || Vagabond (vagabundo).
viaticar v. tr. To administer the viaticum to.
viático m. HIST. Viaticum. || REL. Viaticum, Eucharist. || Per diem, daily expense allowance (dietas).
víbora f. Viper (reptil). || FAM. Snake (persona maldiciente).
viborezno m. Young viper (víbora pequeña).
vibración f. Vibration. || TECN. Vibration (del cemento).
vibrado m. Vibration (del cemento).
vibrador, ra adj. Vibrant, vibrating.
— M. Vibrator.
vibráfono m. MÚS. Vibraphone.
vibrante adj. Vibrant, vibrating. || GRAM. Vibrant (sonido).
— F. GRAM. Vibrant.
vibrar v. tr. e intr. To vibrate.
vibrátil adj. Vibratile.
vibrato m. MÚS. Vibrato.
vibratorio, ria adj. Vibratory.
vibrión m. Vibrio (bacteria).
vibromasaje m. MED. Vibromassage.
vicaria f. Deputy to the Mother Superior.
vicaría f. Vicariate. || Vicarage (residencia). || FAM. *Pasar por la vicaría*, to get married [in church].
vicarial adj. Vicarial.
vicariato m. Vicariate.
vicario m. Vicar: *el Papa es el vicario de Jesucristo*, the Pope is the Vicar of Christ. || *Vicario general*, vicar-general.
vicealmirantazgo m. Vice-admiralty.
vicealmirante m. Vice-admiral.
vicecanciller m. Vice-chancellor.
vicecancillería f. Vice-chancellorship (cargo). || Vice-chancellor's office (oficina).
vicecónsul m. Vice-consul.
viceconsulado m. Vice-consulate.
vicegobernador m. Vice-governor.
Vicente n. pr. m. Vincent. || *¿Dónde va Vicente?, donde va la gente*, he [she, etc.] just follows the crowd.
vicepresidencia f. Vice-presidency (en un país). || Vice-chairmanship (en comité, reunión, compañía).
vicepresidente, ta m. y f. Vice-president (de un país). || Vice-chairman (de comité, reunión, compañía).

VIAJES, m. pl. — TRAVEL, sing.

I. Generalidades, f. — General terms.

viaje m.	journey, trip
viaje (m.) de negocios	business trip
viaje (m.) de turismo	holiday
viaje (m.) de recreo	pleasure trip
viaje (m.) organizado	organized tour
viaje (m.) circular	circular tour
viaje (m.) todo comprendido	package tour, inclusive tour
viaje (m.) de ida	outward journey
viaje (m.) de ida y vuelta	return journey, round trip
excursión f.	trip, excursion, outing
gira f.; expedición f.	tour; expedition
turismo m.	tourism
autostop m.	hitchhiking, hitching
itinerario m.	itinerary
trayecto m., recorrido m.	itinerary, route
ruta f.	route
escala f.; etapa f.	stopover; stage
salida (f.) a las 10	departure at 10 a.m.
llegada (f.) a las 24	arrival at 12 p.m.
estancia f. [Amer., estadía f.]	stay
regreso m., vuelta f.	return
embarco m.	embarkation, embarcation
desembarco m.	disembarkation
retraso m.	delay
agencia (f.) de viajes	travel agency
compañía (f.) aérea	airline company
cheque (m.) de viaje	traveller's cheque
billete [Amer., boleto m.]	ticket
billete (m.) de ida	single ticket
billete (m.) de ida y vuelta [Amer., de ida y llamada]	return ticket [U.S., round-trip ticket]
billete (m.) circular	round-trip ticket
precio (m.) del billete	fare
medio billete m.	half [fare], half-price ticket
pasaje m.	passage (precio, billete), passengers pl. (pasajeros)
pasaporte m.	passport
visado m. [Amer., visa f.]	visa
documentación f.	papers pl.
tarjeta (f.) de identidad	identity card
salvoconducto m.	safe-conduct, pass
aduana f.	customs pl.
viajero m., viajante m. y f.	traveller [U.S., traveler]
pasajero m.	passenger
viajante (m.) de comercio	commercial traveller [U.S., traveling salesman]
excursionista m. y f.	excursionist, tripper; hiker (a pie)
turista m. y f.	tourist
polizón m.	stowaway

II. Equipaje, m. — Luggage.

equipaje (m.) de mano	hand luggage
exceso (m.) de equipaje	excess baggage
maleta f. [Amer., valija f.]	suitcase
maletín m.	small suitcase, valise
baúl m.	trunk
mundo m.	Saratoga trunk
bolsa (f.) de viaje	travelling bag
paquete m.; bulto m.	parcel; parcel, package
sombrerera f.	hatbox
mochila f.	rucksack, pack, knapsack
macuto m.	knapsack, haversack

III. Medios (m.) de transporte. — Means of transport.

ferrocarril m.	railway [U.S., railroad]
tren m.	train
red (f.) ferroviaria	railway system o network
exprés m., expreso m., tren (m.) expreso	express train
tren (m.) rápido, rápido m.	fast train
tren (m.) directo	through train
tren (m.) ómnibus	stopping o slow train
tren (m.) botijo or de recreo	excursion train
tren (m.) de cercanías	commuter o suburban train
autovía f., ferrobús m.	railcar
coche m., vagón m.	coach, carriage
coche (m.) cama	sleeping car, sleeper
coche (m.) comedor, coche (m.) restaurante	dining o restaurant o luncheon car
coche (m.) litera	sleeper with couchettes
litera f.	berth, bunk
departamento m., compartimiento m.	compartment
estación f.	station
taquilla f.	booking o ticket office
andén m.; vía f.	platform; track
fonda f.	buffet
sala (f.) de espera	waiting room
consigna f.	left-luggage office [U.S., checkroom]
facturación f.	registration
horario m.	timetable
transbordo m.	change, transfer
enlace m., empalme m.	connection
revisor m.	ticket inspector
barco m.	boat, ship
barco (m.) de pasajeros	[passenger] liner
barco (m.) de velas, velero m.	sailing boat o ship
yate m.	yacht
transatlántico m.	[ocean] liner
paquebote m. [Amer., paquete m.]	packet boat
camarote m.	cabin
travesía f.	crossing
crucero m.	cruise
avión m.	plane, aeroplane [U.S., airplane], aircraft
avión (m.) de reacción, supersónico	jet, supersonic plane
avión (m.) de pasajeros or de línea	airliner, passenger aircraft
avión (m.) de distancias medias or continental	medium-haul aircraft
avión (m.) de larga distancia or transcontinental	long-range o long-haul aircraft
por avión	by air, by plane
línea (f.) aérea	airline
cabina (f.) de pasajeros	passenger cabin
clase (f.) turista	tourist class
primera clase f.	first class
aeropuerto m.; terminal f.	airport; air terminal
azafata f.	air hostess, stewardess
auxiliar (m.) de vuelo	steward
lista (f.) de espera	waiting list
paso (m.) de la aduana	customs formalities pl.
vuelo (m.) directo	non-stop flight
con destino a	to
procedente de	[coming] from
en tránsito	in transit
despegue m.; aterrizaje m.	takeoff; landing
bache m.	air pocket

IV. Alojamiento, m. — Accommodation.

hotel m.; motel m.	hotel; motel
hotel (m.) de lujo	luxury hotel
parador m.	State-run hotel
residencia f.	residential hotel
hostal m., hostería f., posada f.	hostelry, inn
albergue m.	hostel
casa (f.) de huéspedes, pensión f.	boardinghouse
recepción f.	reception
ficha (f.) de hotel	registration form
habitación (f.) individual, doble	single, double room
director (m.) de hotel	hotel manager
portero m.	porter
botones m. inv.	buttons, bellboy
camarera f.	chambermaid
camarero m.	valet
ascensorista m. y f.	lift attendant
jefe (m.) de comedor	headwaiter, maître d'hôtel
media pensión f.	half board
pensión (f.) completa	full board
parar en un hotel	to put up at a hotel
reservar una habitación	to book a room

vicerector m. Vice-rector (de Universidad).

vicesecretaría f. Assistant secretaryship.

vicesecretario, ria m. y f. Assistant secretary.

vicetiple f. Chorus girl.

viceversa adv. Vice versa.

vicia f. BOT. Vetch (arveja).

viciable adj. Corruptible.

viciado, da adj. Corrupt (corrompido). || Contaminated, polluted, vitiated, foul (aire). || Stuffy (atmósfera).

viciador, ra adj. Corrupting.

viciar v. tr. To vitiate, to corrupt (corromper). || To adulterate (adulterar). || To falsify (falsificar). || JUR. To vitiate, to nullify: *error que vicia un contrato*, mistake which nullifies a contract. || To contaminate, to pollute, to vitiate (el aire). || To spoil (estropear). || To distort, to twist (el sentido de algo).
— V. pr. To spoil, to become spoiled (estropearse). || To warp (madera). || To become twisted, to go out of shape (cualquier objeto). || To become contaminated *o* polluted *o* vitiated (el aire). || To be corrupted, to take to vice (enviciarse).

vicio m. Vice: *antro de vicio*, den of vice. || Bad habit (mala costumbre). || JUR. Fault: *vicios ocultos*, hidden faults. || Spoiling (mimo). || Warp, buckle (alabeo). || Defect (defecto). || Incorrect usage (en el lenguaje). || — *Contra el vicio de pedir hay la virtud de no dar*, it is sometimes better to say no [to a person who asks too much]. || *De vicio*, for no reason at all, without reason: *llorar de vicio*, to cry for no reason at all. || *Vicio de forma*, faulty drafting.

viciosamente adv. Badly, wrongly, incorrectly. || Viciously.

vicioso, sa adj. Vicious (persona, animal). || Faulty, defective (cosa). || Vicious, incorrect: *una locución viciosa*, a vicious expression. || FAM. Spoiled (mimado). || *Círculo vicioso*, vicious circle.
— M. y f. Vicious person. || Addict.

vicisitud f. Vicissitude.

víctima f. Victim: *ser la víctima de*, to be the victim of. || — *Hubo cuatro víctimas en el accidente*, there were four casualties in the accident. || FIG. *Víctima propiciatoria*, scapegoat.

victimar v. tr. *Amer.* To kill (matar).

victimario m. Person who bound and held the victim during the sacrifice. || *Amer.* Murderer, killer (asesino).
¡víctor! interj. Bravo!, hurrah!
victorear v. tr. To acclaim, to cheer, to applaud.
victoria f. Victoria (coche).
victoria f. Victory. || Win, victory, triumph (en un deporte, concurso). || — *Cantar victoria*, to proclaim a victory. || *Victoria aplastante* or *rotunda*, resounding *o* overwhelming victory. || *Victoria pírrica*, Pyrrhic victory. || BOT. *Victoria regia*, victoria regia, victoria.
victoriano, na adj./s. Victorian.
victorioso, sa adj. Victorious.
— M. y f. Victor, winner (triunfador).
vicuña f. Vicuna, vicugna, vicuña (mamífero).
vichar v. tr. *Amer.* To spy on (espiar). | FIG. To devour with one's eyes.
vichy m. Kind of gingham (tela).
vid f. Vine, grapevine (planta).
vida f. Life: *vida y muerte*, life and death. || Life, lifetime (duración). || Living: *nivel de vida*, standard of living. || Trump (triunfo en los naipes). || — *Cambiar de vida*, to turn over a new leaf, to change one's way of live. || *Costarle la vida a uno* to cost s.o. his life. || *Cuéntenos su vida y milagros*, tell us all about yourself, tell us your life history. || *Dar la vida*, to give one's life. || *Dar mala vida a uno*, to make s.o.'s life a misery, to give s.o. a bad time. || *Darse buena vida*, to have a good life, to live well *o* comfortably. || *Dar vida a*, to give birth to (un hijo), to bring to life (un retrato, etc.). || *De mala vida* or *de vida airada*, loose-living. || *De por vida*, for life, for ever. || *De toda la vida*, lifelong: *un amigo de toda la vida*, a lifelong friend. || *Durante toda la vida*, one's whole life long *o* through. || FIG. y FAM. *Echarse a la vida*, to go on the game (una mujer). || *En esto le va la vida*, his life depends on it, his life is at stake. || FIG. *¡En la vida!*, never!, never in a million years! || *En mi vida*, never in my life. || *Enterrarse en vida en un pueblucho*, to bury o.s. in a tiny village. || *En vida*, alive, living: *estar en vida*, to be alive. || *En vida de*, during the life *o* lifetime of. || *En vida de mi padre*, during the lifetime of my father, when my father was alive. || *Escapar con vida de un accidente*, to come out of an accident alive *o* safe and sound *o* with one's life. || *¡Esto es vida!*, this is living! || *Ganarse la vida*, to earn one's living. || *Hacerle a uno la vida imposible*, to make life impossible for s.o. || FIG. y FAM. *Hacer por la vida*, to eat. || *Hacer vida ascética*, to lead an ascetic life. || *Hacer vida con uno*, to live with s.o. || *Hacer vida nueva*, to turn over a new leaf, to change one's way of life. || *Hija de mi vida*, my **darling daughter. || *Jugarse la vida*, to risk one's life, to take one's life in one's hand. || *La otra vida*, the next life, the life to come. || *¡La vida!*, that's life.** || *La vida es así*, that's life. || *La vida es sueño*, life is a dream. || *Lleno de vida*, lively, full of life. || *Llevar una vida alegre*, to lead *o* to live *o* to have a happy life. || FIG. *Media vida*, right arm, eyeteeth: *daría media vida por*, I should give my right arm for. || *Meterse en vidas ajenas*, to interfere *o* to meddle [in other people's affairs]. || *¡Mi vida!* or *¡vida mía!* or *¡vida!*, my love!, darling! || *Mientras dura, vida y dulzura*, enjoy life while you can, make the most of it while it lasts. || *Mientras hay vida hay esperanza*, while there's life there's hope. || FIG. y FAM. *Mujer de la vida* or *de mala vida*, prostitute, whore. || *No hubo pérdidas de vida*, no lives were lost, there was no loss of life. || *Pagar con su vida*, to pay with one's life. || *Para toda la vida*, for life, for the whole of one's life. || *Pasar a mejor vida*, to pass away. || *Pasar de vida a muerte*, to pass away. || FAM. *Pegarse la vida padre* or *una buena vida*, to live it up, to live like a king. || *Perder la vida*, to lose one's life. || *¡Por mi vida!*, upon my soul! || *¿Qué es de tu vida?*, how are things?, how are you going on?, how is life? || *¡Qué vida ésta!*, what a life! || *Quitarse la vida*, to take one's own life. || *Seguro de vida*, life insurance. || FIG. y FAM. *Ser de la vida*, to be on the game (mujer). || *Si Dios nos da vida*, if God is willing. || *Sin vida*, lifeless. || *Su vida está pendiente de un hilo*, his life is hanging by a thread. || FIG. y FAM. *Tener siete vidas como los gatos*, to have nine lives. || *Vender cara su vida*, to sell one's life dearly, to put up a good fight. || FIG. *Vida de perros*, dog's life. || *Vida de soltero*, bachelor's life. || *Vida familiar*, family life. || *Vida y milagros*, life story *o* history.
vidalita f. *Amer.* Melancholic folk song.
videncia f. Clear-sightedness.
vidente m. y f. Seer (que adivina el porvenir).
video m. RAD. Video.
vidriado, da adj. Glazed (cerámica).
— M. Glazing, glaze (barniz para cerámica). || Glazed earthenware (cerámica).
vidriar v. tr. TECN. To glaze (la cerámica).
— V. pr. To be glazed. || To become glassy, to become glazed, to glaze over (los ojos).
vidriera f. Glass window (ventana). || Glass door (puerta). || Stained-glass window (vitral). || *Amer.* Shopwindow [U.S., show window] (escaparate). || *Puerta vidriera*, V. PUERTA.
vidriería f. Glassworks (taller). || Glass shop (tienda). || *Vidriería de color*, stained-glass making.
vidriero m. Glassworker (obrero). || Glassmaker (fabricante). || Glazier (que fabrica o coloca cristales).
vidrio m. Glass: *vidrio de ventanas*, glass for windows; *vidrio de color*, stained glass. || — *Fibra de vidrio*, glass fibre. || *Lana de vidrio*, glass wool. || FIG. y FAM. *Pagar los vidrios rotos*, to carry the can. || *Vidrio cilindrado*, plate glass. || *Vidrio deslustrado* or *esmerilado*, ground glass, frosted glass.
vidrioso, sa adj. Glazed, glassy: *ojos vidriosos*, glazed eyes. || Brittle (frágil). || Slippery (suelo). || FIG. Delicate, tricky (difícil de tratar): *tema vidrioso*, delicate subject.
vieira f. Scallop (molusco, concha).
vieja adj./s. f. V. VIEJO.
viejales m. inv. FAM. Old boy.
viejo, ja adj. Old: *soy más viejo que tú*, I am older than you; *un hombre viejo*, an old man; *una vieja gabardina*, an old gabardine. || — *Hacerse viejo*, to grow old, to get old. || FIG. y FAM. *Más viejo que andar a gatas* or *a pie*, as old as the hills. | *Más viejo que Matusalén*, as old as Methuselah. || *Morir de viejo*, to die of old age. || FAM. *No llegará a viejo* or *no hará huesos viejos*, he will not make old bones. || *Plinio el Viejo*, Pliny the Elder.
— M. y f. Old man (hombre), old lady, old woman (mujer): *una vieja muy arrugada*, a very wrinkled old woman. || FAM. Old man (padre, marido). | Old lady *o* woman (madre, esposa). || — Pl. Old people, old folks. || FIG. y FAM. Old folks (padres). || — *Cuento de viejas*, old-wive's tale. || FIG. *Hacer la cuenta de la vieja*, to count on one's fingers. | *Poquito a poco* or *poco a poco hila la vieja el copo*, every little bit helps. || FAM. *Una viejita*, a little old lady. | *Un viejo coquetón* or *verde*, a dirty old man. || *Vamos a tirar todo lo viejo*, we are going to throw out all the old things.
viella f. MÚS. Hurdy-gurdy.
Viena n. pr. GEOGR. Vienna (Austria).
vienés, esa adj./s. Viennese.
viento m. Wind: *viento del oeste*, west wind; *vientos alisios*, trade winds; *viento en popa*, stern wind; *corre bastante viento*, there is quite a wind; *ráfaga de viento*, gust of wind. || Scent (olfato). || Guy (tirante de cuerda). || MÚS. Wind: *instrumentos de viento*, wind instruments. || FAM. Wind (ventosidad). || — MAR. *A favor del viento*, before the wind. || *Al capricho del viento*, at the mercy of the wind. || *Azotado por los vientos*, windswept. || FIG. y FAM. *Beber los vientos por*, to be dying to (con verbo), to be dying for (con sustantivo), to be head over heels in love with (una mujer). || MAR. *Contra el viento*, against the wind, in the teeth of the wind, in the wind's eye. || FIG. *Contra viento y marea*, through *o* come hell and high water, against all odds. | *Corren malos vientos*, the time is not right. || *Corre* or *hace viento*, it is windy. || FIG. *Darle a uno el viento de una cosa*, to get wind of sth. (barruntar). | *Despedir* or *echar con viento fresco*, to send packing, to throw out (echar). || *El viento ha cambiado*, the wind has turned *o* changed. || MAR. *Ganar el viento*, to sail with the wind. || FAM. *Gritar a los cuatro vientos*, to shout from the rooftops. | *Hace un viento de mil demonios*, it's blowing a gale. || MAR. *Hurtar el viento*, to sail against the wind. || FIG. *Ir al amparo del viento* or *irse con el viento que corre*, to follow the tide. | *Ir más rápido que el viento*, to go like the wind. || MAR. *Ir viento en popa*, to sail before the wind. || FIG. *Libre como el viento*, as free as the wind. | *Lo que el viento se llevó*, gone with the wind. | *Lleno de viento*, empty (vacío), conceited (vanidoso). | *Mandar a uno con viento fresco*, to send s.o. packing. || *Molino de viento*, windmill. || FIG. *Moverse a todos los vientos*, to change with the wind, to be as fickle as the wind. || FAM. *¿Qué viento te trae?*, what brings you here? || FIG. *Quien siembra vientos recoge tempestades*, V. RECOGER. | *Tener viento en contra*, to be sailing against the wind. | *Tener viento favorable*, to have the wind behind one. | *Todo va viento en popa*, V. POPA. || *Tomar el viento*, to take the scent (caza). || *Viento de cola*, tail wind. || FIG. *Vamos viento en popa*, V. POPA. || *Viento de costado*, crosswind. || *Viento en contra* or *contrario* or *en proa*, headwind, foul wind.
vientre m. ANAT. Belly, abdomen. | Womb: *llevar un niño en el vientre*, to carry a child in one's womb. || Belly (de vasija, barco). || FIG. Bowels, *pl.* || FÍS. Antinode, loop. || — *Bajo vientre*, lower abdomen. || FAM. *Echar vientre*, to put on weight, to get a potbelly. || REL. *El fruto de tu vientre*, the fruit of thy womb. || *Evacuar* or *exonerar el vientre* or *hacer de vientre*, to have a bowel movement.
viernes m. Friday: *el viernes pasado, que viene*, last, next Friday; *Viernes Santo*, Good Friday. || — *Cara de viernes*, gloomy *o* dismal face. || *Comer de viernes*, to fast, to abstain from eating meat. || FAM. *¿Te lo has aprendido en viernes?*, change the record!, you're always on about the same thing!, give it a rest!
Vietnam n. pr. m. GEOGR. Vietnam. || *Vietnam del Norte, del Sur*, North, South Vietnam.
vietnamita adj./s. Vietnamese.
viga f. Beam, rafter: *viga principal*, main beam. || Girder (metálica). || — *Viga de apuntalamiento*, needle. || *Viga maestra*, main beam. || *Viga transversal*, crossbeam.

vigencia f. Validity (cualidad de vigente). || — *Entrar en vigencia*, to come into force. || *Estar en vigencia*, to be in force. || *Tener vigencia*, to be valid.
vigente adj. In force: *la ley vigente*, the law in force; *estar vigente*, to be in force. || Prevailing (existente).
vigesimal adj. Vigesimal.
vigésimo, ma adj./s.m. Twentieth. || *Vigésimo primero, segundo*, twenty-first, twenty-second.
vigía m. Lookout, watchman. || MAR. Watch. || — F. Watchtower, lookout post (atalaya). || Watch, lookout (acción de vigilar). || MAR. Reef.
vigilancia f. Surveillance (acción de vigilar): *sometido a vigilancia*, under surveillance. || Vigilance, watchfulness (cuidado en el vigilar). || Vigilance committee (servicio).
vigilante adj. Vigilant, watchful (que vigila). || Alert (alerta). || Wakeful (que no duerme).
— M. Watchman (en un edificio). || Guard (de documentos secretos, etc.). || *Amer.* Policeman. || Superviser (en el colegio, trabajo, etc.). || *Vigilante de noche* or *nocturno*, night watchman.
vigilantemente adv. Vigilantly.
vigilar v. tr. To watch [over], to look after (cuidar de). || To supervise: *vigilar un trabajo*, to supervise a job. || To keep an eye on: *vigilar la comida para que no se queme*, to keep an eye on the dinner so that it doesn't burn. || To guard (presos, frontera).
— V. intr. To keep watch (el vigía). || To be vigilant, to be watchful (ser vigilante). || *Vigilar por* o *sobre*, to watch over, to look after.
vigilia f. Vigil (de quien no duerme). || Eve (víspera). || Mass for the dead (de difuntos). || Meatless meal (comida). || REL. Vigil. || — *Día de vigilia*, day of abstinence. || *Hacer* or *comer de vigilia*, to abstain from meat. || *Pasar la noche de vigilia*, to stay awake all night.
vigor m. Force, effect: *entrar en vigor*, to come into force, to take effect; *estar en vigor*, to be in force; *poner en vigor*, to put into effect. || Vigour [U.S., vigor], strength, force (fortaleza). || *Estilo lleno de vigor*, vigorous *o* forceful style.
vigorar v. tr. To invigorate, to fortify (vigorizar).
vigorizador, ra adj. Invigorating, fortifying.
vigorizar v. tr. To invigorate, to fortify.
— V. pr. To be invigorated, to be fortified.
vigorosidad f. Vigour [U.S., vigor], strength.
vigoroso, sa adj. Vigorous, strong.
vigota f. MAR. Deadeye (polea).
viguería f. Framework, beams *pl.*
vigueta f. Small beam (viga pequeña de madera). || Small girder (metálica). || Joist (cabio).
vihuela f. MÚS. Kind of guitar.

— OBSERV. The *vihuela* is a small guitar which was very fashionable in the 16th century before it was superseded by the guitar.

vihuelista m. y f. "Vihuela" player.
vikingo m. Viking.
vil adj. Vile, base, despicable.
vilayato m. Vilayet (división territorial en Turquía).
vileza f. Vileness, baseness. || Despicable act, vile deed (acción vil). || *Pobreza no es vileza*, it is no crime to be poor, poverty is no crime.
vilipendiador, ra adj. Vilifying, abusive, contemptuous, vilipending (p.us.).
— M. y f. Vilifier, vilipender.
vilipendiar v. tr. To vilify, to vilipend (p.us.). || To despise, to scorn (despreciar).
vilipendio m. Scorn, contempt (desprecio). || Vilification (acción). || Humiliation (humillación).
vilipendioso, sa adj. Vilifying, abusive, contemptuous.
vilo (en) loc. adv. In the air (suspendido). || FIG. On tenterhooks (intranquilo, impaciente). | In suspense: *esta novela nos tiene en vilo*, this novel keeps us in suspense.
vilordo, da adj. Lazy, idle.
vilorta f. o **vilorto** m. Wooden ring (aro). || Washer (arandela). || Kind of lacrosse (juego). || BOT. Clematis.
vilote, ta m. y f. *Amer.* Coward.
— Adj. *Amer.* Cowardly.
villa f. Town (ciudad). || Villa (casa). || Small town (pueblo). || *La Villa del Oso y el Madroño* or *la Villa y Corte*, Madrid.
Villadiego n. pr. FIG. y FAM. *Tomar las de Villadiego*, to beat it, to take to one's heels.
villanada f. Villainy, villainous *o* despicable act.
villanaje m. HIST. Villeinage (condición). || Peasantry, peasants, *pl.* (gente villana).
villanamente adv. Basely.
villancejo o **villancete** o **villancico** m. [Christmas] carol (canción de Navidad).
villanería f. Villainy, villainous *o* despicable act (villanía). || Villeinage (villanaje).
villanesca f. Country dance accompanied by singing.
villanesco, ca adj. Of the common folk, country.
villanía f. Villainy, villainous *o* despicable act (acción ruin). || Coarse remark *o* expression (dicho). || HIST. Villeinage (estado).
villano, na adj. Lowly, common, peasant, of *o* pertaining to a villein (que no es noble). || FIG. Rustic (rústico). | Coarse (grosero).
— M. y f. HIST. Villein (que no es noble). || FIG. Villain (persona vil). || — M. Country dance.
villar m. Village (pueblo).
villorrio m. Dump, hole (poblacho).
vinagrada f. Drink of vinegar, water and sugar.
vinagre m. Vinegar. || FIG. y FAM. Sour puss (persona malhumorada). || *Cara de vinagre*, sour expression.
vinagrera f. Vinegar bottle (vasija). || Vinegar seller (vendedora). || Sorrel (acedera). || *Amer.* Heartburn, acidity (acedía). || — Pl. Cruet, *sing.* (angarillas).
vinagrero, ra adj. Vinegar, of *o* pertaining to vinegar.
— M. Vinegar maker *o* seller.
vinagreta f. Vinaigrette [sauce] (salsa).
vinagroso, sa adj. Vinegary. || FIG. y FAM. Sour, grouchy.
vinajera f. REL. Altar cruet.
vinario, ria adj. Wine, of *o* pertaining to wine.
vinate m. FAM. Wine.
vinatera f. MAR. Rope joining two cables *o* spars.
vinatería f. Wine shop (tienda). || Wine trade (comercio).
vinatero, ra adj. Wine, of *o* pertaining to wine: *industria vinatera*, wine industry.
— M. Wine merchant, vintner (comerciante).
vinaza f. Poor wine [drawn from the dregs].
vinazo m. FAM. Rough wine.
vincapervinca f. BOT. Large periwinkle.
vinculable adj. JUR. Entailable.
vinculación f. Linking (acción). || Bond, link (lo que vincula). || JUR. Entailment.
vincular v. tr. To link, to bind, to tie: *dos familias vinculadas entre sí*, two families which are linked together. || To bind: *vinculado por el reconocimiento*, bound by gratitude. || To relate, to connect (relacionar). || To tie, to attach: *los campesinos están vinculados a la tierra*, peasants are attached to the land. || JUR. To entail (los bienes). || FIG. To base: *vincular sus esperanzas en*, to base one's hopes on. || *Estar vinculado con*, to be related to *o* connected with.
— V. pr. To be bound, to be tied.
vínculo m. Tie, link, bond: *vínculos matrimoniales*, matrimonial ties. || JUR. Entail (propiedad). | Entailment (acción de vincular). || FIG. Link: *España sirve de vínculo entre Europa y África*, Spain serves as a link between Europe and Africa.
vincha f. *Amer.* Band [for the hair].
vindicación f. Vengeance, revenge (venganza). || Vindication (defensa).
vindicador, ra adj. Avenging, revenging (que venga). || Vindicatory (que defiende).
— M. y f. Avenger.
vindicar v. tr. To avenge, to revenge (vengar). || To vindicate (defender). || JUR. To claim, to vindicate (reivindicar).
vindicativamente adv. Vindictively.
vindicativo, va adj. Vindictive. || Vindicatory.
vindicatorio, ria adj. Vindicatory.
vindicta f. Vengeance, revenge (venganza).
vinería f. *Amer.* Wineshop.
vínico, ca adj. Wine, of *o* pertaining to wine, vinic.
vinícola adj. Wine-producing, wine, wine-growing.
vinicultor, ra m. y f. Wine producer, winegrower.
vinicultura f. Wine growing, wine production, viniculture.
vinificación f. Vinification, fermentation.
vinílico, ca adj. Vinyl, of *o* pertaining to vinyl.
vinilo m. QUÍM. Vinyl.
vinillo m. FAM. Thin wine (demasiado flojo). | Light wine (ligero).
vino m. Wine: *echar vino*, to pour out wine; *vino de la tierra*, rough wine. || — FAM. *Ahogar las penas en vino*, to drown one's sorrows. | *Bautizar el vino*, to water down wine. | *Dormir el vino*, to sleep it off. | *Tiene el vino alegre*, he is happy when he is drunk. | *Tiene el vino triste*, he is sad when he is drunk. | *Tiene mal vino*, he turns nasty when he is drunk. || *Vino a granel*, wine from the barrel. || *Vino aguado*, watered down wine. || *Vino aloque*, rosé wine. || *Vino añejo*, vintage wine. || *Vino blanco*, white wine. || *Vino de coco*, spirit made from fermented coconut milk. || *Vino de consagrar*, communion *o* altar wine. || *Vino de dos orejas*, good wine. || *Vino de garrote*, wine which needs much pressing. || *Vino de honor*, special wine. || *Vino de Jerez*, sherry. || *Vino de lágrima*, juice which comes from the grapes before they are pressed. || *Vino de mesa*, table wine. || *Vino de Oporto*, port [wine]. || *Vino de pasto*, ordinary wine. || *Vino de quina*, wine laced with cinchona. || *Vino dulce*, sweet wine. || *Vino espumoso*, sparkling wine. || *Vino generoso*, full-bodied *o* generous wine. || FAM. *Vino peleón*, cheap wine, plonk. || *Vino seco*, dry wine. || *Vino tinto*, red wine.
vinoso, sa adj. Wine, of *o* pertaining to wine, vinous (p.us.). || *De color vinoso*, wine-coloured, vinaceous.
viña f. Vineyard. || — AGR. *Arropar las viñas*, to bank up the earth around the vines. || FIG. *De todo hay en la viña del Señor*, it takes all sorts *o* all kinds to make a world. || *Viña loca* or *virgen*, Virginia creeper.
viñador m. Viticulturist, vine grower (cultivador).
viñal m. *Amer.* Vineyard (viñedo).
viñatero m. Viticulturist, vine grower (viñador).
viñedo m. Vineyard.
viñero m. Viticulturist, owner of a vineyard (propietario).
viñeta f. IMPR. Vignette.

viñetero m. IMPR. Cupboard in which vignette moulds are kept.
viola f. MÚS. Viola. || *Viola de gamba*, viola da gamba, || — M. y f. Viola player.
violáceo, a adj. Violaceous, violet.
— F. pl. BOT. Violaceae.
violación f. Violation, infringement (de las leyes). || Rape, violation (p.us.) [de una mujer]. || Violation (de un territorio, etc.). || JUR. *Violación de sellos* or *de precinto*, breaking of seals.
violado, da adj./s.m. Violet.
violador, ra m. y f. Violator (de las leyes). || — M. Rapist (de una mujer).
violar v. tr. To violate, to infringe (las leyes). || To rape, ro ravish, to violate (p.us.) [a una mujer]. || To violate (un territorio).
violencia f. Violence. || Rape (violación). || Embarrassment (embarazo). || JUR. Violence. || Force (fuerza). || *No violencia*, nonviolence.
violentar v. tr. To force (forzar). || To break into (el domicilio). || To use force on (obligar por la fuerza). || To distort, to twist (el sentido de un texto).
— V. pr. To force o.s.
violento, ta adj. Violent: *tempestad violenta*, violent storm; *muerte violenta*, violent death; *persona violenta*, violent person. || DEP. Rough. || Embarrassed, awkward, ill at ease (molesto): *me sentía muy violento en su presencia*, I felt very awkward in his presence. || Embarrassing, awkward, difficult: *me es violento decírselo*, it is embarrassing for me to tell you this.
violeta f. Violet (flor). || — M. Violet (color).
— Adj. inv. Violet: *un vestido violeta*, a violet dress; *luces violeta*, violet lights.
violetera f. Violet seller.
violetero m. Vase for violets.
violín m. MÚS. Violin (instrumento): *tocar el violín*, to play the violin. | Violin (violinista de una orquesta): *primer violín*, first violin. | Violinist, violin player (violinista). || — *Amer*. FIG. y FAM. *Embolsar el violín*, to come back with one's tail between one's legs. || FIG. *Violín de Ingres*, hobby, favourite passtime.
violinista m. y f. Violinist, violin player.
violón m. MÚS. Double bass (instrumento). | Double bass player (músico). || FIG. y FAM. *Tocar el violón*, to talk through one's hat (hablar), to do silly things (obrar), to make a fool of o.s. (hacer el ridículo).
violonchelista o **violoncelista** m. y f. MÚS. Cellist, violoncellist.
violonchelo o **violoncelo** m. MÚS. Cello, violoncello.
vipéreo, a adj. Viperous.
viperino, na adj. Viperine. || FIG. Viperish. || *Lengua viperina*, v. LENGUA.
vira f. Dart (saeta). || Welt [of a shoe] (zapatería).
virada f. MAR. Putting about, tack.
virador m. FOT. Toning liquid. || MAR. Toprope. | Messenger [of capstan] (del cabrestante). || FOT. *Baño virador*, toning bath.
virago f. Mannish woman, virago.
viraje m. Turn, bend (curva). || FOT. y FÍS. Toning. || MAR. Putting about, tack. || Turn (en coche, etc.). | Turning point: *la Revolución francesa marca un viraje decisivo en la historia*, the French Revolution marks a decisive turning point in history.
virar v. tr. e intr. MAR. To put about, to tack. || FOT., MED. y QUIM. To tone. || To turn [round] (coche). || — MAR. *Virar a babor*, to turn to port. | *Virar de bordo*, to put about, to tack. || FIG. *Virar en redondo*, to turn round (volverse), to change completely *o* radically (cambiar completamente). || MAR. *Virar en redondo* or *con viento en popa*, to veer.
virgen adj. Virgin. || FIG. Virgin: *selva, cera virgen*, virgin forest, wax.
— F. Virgin. || Guide (en lagares). || — *Islas Vírgenes*, Virgin Isles. || *La Virgen Santísima*, the Blessed Virgin Mary. || FAM. *Un viva la Virgen*, a happy-go-lucky *o* devil-may-care type.
Virgilio n. pr. m. Virgil, Vergil.
virginal adj. Virginal. || REL. Of the Virgin.
virgíneo, a adj. Virginal.
Virginia n. pr. f. GEOGR. Virginia.
virginiano, na adj./s. Virginian.
virginidad f. Virginity.
virgo m. Virginity. || ANAT. Hymen. || ASTR. Virgo (zodiaco).
vírgula f. Small rod (pequeña vara). || Virgule (rayita). || MED. Cholera *o* comma bacillus.
virgulilla f. Small punctuation mark.
viril adj. Virile. || *Miembro viril*, male member, penis.
— M. Small monstrance within a larger one (custodia). || Glass (vidrio).
virilidad f. Virility.
virilizar v. tr. To virilize.
virola f. Ferrule.
virolento, ta adj. Suffering from smallpox. || Pockmarked (picado de viruela).
— M. y f. Person suffering from smallpox.
virote m. Arrow, dart (arma). || Iron rod [attached to a slave]. || Stuffed shirt (fam.) [persona seria].
virotillo m. ARQ. Short upright brace, strut.
virreina f. Viceroy's wife, vicereine (mujer del virrey). || Vicereine (que gobierna).
virreinato m. Viceroyalty.
virrey m. Viceroy.
virtual adj. Virtual. || Potential. || FÍS. *Imagen virtual*, virtual image.
virtualidad f. Potentiality, possibility. || Virtuality.
virtualmente adv. Virtually.
virtud f. Virtue (cualidad de una persona). || Ability (capacidad). || — *En virtud de*, by virtue of. || *Tener la virtud de*, to have the virtue of (con gerundio), to have the power to (con infinitivo).
virtuosidad f. o **virtuosismo** m. Virtuosity.
virtuoso, sa adj. Virtuous: *una conducta virtuosa*, virtuous conduct. || Skilled (artista).
— M. y f. Virtuous person. || Virtuoso (artista).
viruela f. Smallpox (enfermedad). || Pockmark (cicatriz). || — Pl. Smallpox, *sing*. || — *¡A la vejez viruelas!*, there's no fool like an old fool. || *Picado de viruelas*, pockmarked (cara). || *Viruela del ganado vacuno*, cowpox. || MED. *Viruelas locas*, chicken pox.
— OBSERV. In Spanish the plural form is the more frequently used.
virulé (a la) loc. adv. FAM. *A la virulé*, crooked, twisted (torcido). | *Ojo a la virulé*, black eye.
virulencia f. Virulence.
virulento, ta adj. Virulent.
virus m. inv. Virus: *virus filtrable*, filterable virus. || FIG. Poison, venom.
viruta f. Shaving (de madera, metales).
vis f. *Vis cómica*, comic sense, comicality, humour.
visa f. *Amer*. Visa.
visado, da adj. Endorsed with a visa.
— M. Visa (de un pasaporte).
visaje m. Grimace (mueca). || *Hacer visajes*, to pull *o* to make faces, to grimace.
visajero, ra adj. Grimacing (gestero).
visar v. tr. To endorse (un documento). || To visa, to endorse with a visa (un pasaporte).
vísceras f. pl. ANAT. Viscera.
visceral adj. Visceral.
visco m. Birdlime (liga).
viscosa f. QUIM. Viscose.
viscosidad f. Viscosity.
viscoso, sa adj. Viscous.
visera f. Visor. || Peak (de gorra). || Eyeshade (de jokey). || ARQ. Gutter overhang (goterón). || *Calar* or *calarse la visera*, to lower one's visor.
visibilidad f. Visibility: *hay una visibilidad de tres metros*, visibility is down to three metres. || — *Una curva con poca visibilidad*, a blind bend. || *Visibilidad cero*, zero visibility. || *Vuelo sin visibilidad*, blind flying.
visible adj. Visible. || FIG. Decent (presentable): *¿puedo entrar?, ¿estás visible?*, can I come in? Are you decent?
visiblemente adv. Visibly, perceptibly. || *Engorda visiblemente*, you can see him getting fatter.
visigodo, da adj. Visigothic.
— M. y f. Visigoth.
visigótico, ca adj. Visigothic.
visillo m. Curtain (cortinilla).
visión f. Vision. || Sight: *perdió la visión de un ojo*, he lost his sight in one eye. || View: *visión de conjunto*, overall view. || REL. Vision. || FIG. y FAM. Sight, fright (persona fea). || — FIG. y FAM. *Quedarse como quien ve visiones*, to look as if one has seen a ghost. | *Ver visiones*, to see things, to be deluded.
visionadora f. FOT. Viewer.
visionario, ria adj. Visionary. || FIG. Deluded, subject to hallucinations.
— M. y f. Visionary. || FIG. Person who imagines things.
visir m. Vizier, vizir: *gran visir*, grand vizier.
visirato m. Vizierate.
visita f. Visit: *visita de pésame*, visit of condolence. || Visitors, *pl.* (invitados): *mañana tenemos visita*, we are having visitors tomorrow. || Inspection. || — *Devolver a alguien una visita*, to return a visit *o* a call. || *Estar de visita en casa de una tía*, to be visiting one's aunt *o* paying a visit to one's aunt. || *Ir de visita a casa de uno*, to pay s.o. a call *o* a visit. || FAM. *No me hagas la visita*, don't stand on ceremony. || *Tarjeta de visita*, visiting card. || *Visita de cumplido* or *de cortesía*, courtesy visit *o* call. || FAM. *Visita de médico* or *visita relámpago*, short *o* hurried visit *o* call, flying visit.
visitación f. Rel. Visitation.
visitador ra adj. Fond of visiting.
— M. y f. Person fond of visiting. || Visitor (visitante). || — M. Inspector.
Visitandina f. REL. Visitandine (nun).
visitante adj. Visiting.
— M. y f. Visitor.
visitar v. tr. To visit: *visitar un monumento*, to visit a monument. || To visit, to call on, to go and see: *visitar a un amigo*, to visit a friend. || To visit, to inspect (inspeccionar).
visiteo m. Visiting, visits, *pl.*: *le gusta mucho el visiteo*, he enjoys visiting.
vislumbrar m. To glimpse, to catch a glimpse of. || FIG. To begin to see (una solución).
vislumbre f. Glimmer (claridad tenue). || Glimpse, brief view (vista momentánea). || FIG. Glimmer: *una vislumbre de esperanza*, a glimmer of hope. || *Tener vislumbres de*, to have an inkling *o* a suspicion of.

viso m. Shimmer, sheen: *tela de seda azul con visos morados*, blue silk with a violet shimmer. || Slip, underslip [of a transparent dress or skirt] (forro suelto). || FIG. Appearance, aspect (aspecto). | Glimmer: *bajo unos visos de verdad*, beneath a glimmer of truth. || Eminence (eminencia). || — *Dar visos a una tela*, to put a sheen on a material. || *De viso*, important, prominent: *persona de viso*, prominent person. || *Hacer visos*, to shimmer. || *Tener visos de*, to seem, to appear (parecer). || *Viso cambiante*, shimmer.

visón m. ZOOL. Mink.

visor m. Sight. || FOT. Viewfinder.

visorio, ria adj. Visual.
— M. Expert examination *o* inspection (examen pericial).

víspera f. Day before: *el jueves es la víspera del viernes*, Thursday is the day before Friday. || Eve, day before (de una fiesta). || — Pl. Vespers (oficio religioso). || — *Día de mucho víspera de nada*, no two days are alike. || *En vísperas de*, on the eve of. || HIST. *Vísperas sicilianas*, Sicilian Vespers.

vista f. Sight, eyes, *pl.*, vision: *vista aguda* or *penetrante*, sharp sight; *tener buena vista*, to have good sight. || View: *esta habitación tiene una vista espléndida*, this room has a wonderful view; *vista panorámica*, panoramic view. || Glance, look (vistazo). || View (cuadro, foto). || Appearance, aspect (apariencia). || JUR. Trial, hearing. || — Pl. ARQ. Windows and doors (en los edificios). | View, *sing.*: *casa con vistas al mar*, house with a sea view *o* a view onto the sea. || Meeting, *sing.* (reunión). || — *Agradable a la vista*, pleasing to the eye. || *A la vista*, visible (visible), at *o* on sight: *pagadero a la vista*, payable at sight; on show, on display: *poner a la vista*, to put on show; in sight: *un barco a la vista*, a boat in sight; in view (previsto). || *A la vista de*, at the sight of (al ver), within view of, within sight of: *estábamos a la vista del puerto*, we were within view of the port; in view of, because of: *a la vista de las dificultades*, in view of the difficulties; in the light of (a la luz de), in the presence of: *a la vista de mucha gente*, in the presence of many people. || *A la vista de todos*, openly, publicly. || *A la vista, no son ricos*, you wouldn't think they were rich to look at them. || *Alzar la vista*, to look up, to raise one's eyes. || *A ojos vistas*, visibly. || *Apartar la vista de*, to look away from. || *A primera vista*, at first sight. || *A simple vista*, at first sight, at first (primeramente), at a glance, with the naked eye (fácilmente). || COM. *A tantos días vista*, so many days after sight. || *A vista de ojos*, visibly. || *Bajar la vista*, to look down. || *Clavar* or *fijar la vista en*, to gaze *o* to stare at. || FIG. *Comerse con la vista*, to devour with one's eyes. || *Conocer de vista*, to know by sight. || *Con vistas a*, in anticipation of, as a provision for: *con vistas al frío compré una tonelada de carbón*, as a provision for the cold weather I bought a ton of coal; with a view to: *negociaciones con vistas a una alianza*, negotiations with a view to an alliance. || *Dar una vista a*, to have a look at, to glance at. || *Desde el punto de vista de*, from the point of view of. || *Desde mi punto de vista*, from my point of view. || *Dirigir la vista a*, to turn towards, to look towards. || *Echar la vista a una cosa*, to have one's eye on: *ha echado la vista a ese abrigo*, he has his eye on that coat. || *En vista de*, in view of, considering: *en vista de las circunstancias*, in view of the circumstances. || *En vista de que*, in view of the fact that, since. || *Estar a la vista*, to be obvious *o* evident *o* clear (evidente): *los resultados están a la vista*, the results are obvious; to be in the public eye (una personalidad), to keep an eye on things (vigilar). || *Fijar la vista en*, to stare at. || FIG. *Hacer la vista gorda*, to turn a blind eye, to close one's eyes. || *Hasta donde alcanza la vista*, as far as the eye can see. || *¡Hasta la vista!*, good-bye!, see you! || *Hasta perderse de vista*, V. PERDER. || *Írsele a uno la vista tras algo*, to be dying for sth. (desear). || *La vista engaña*, one should not trust appearances, appearances are deceptive. || *Leer con la vista*, to read silently *o* to o.s. || *Medir a uno con la vista*, to look s.o. up and down, to size s.o. up. || *No perder de vista*, not to lose sight of, not to let out of one's sight. || *No quitar la vista de encima*, not to take one's eyes off. || *No ser agradable a la vista*, not to be a pretty sight. || *Observar la ciudad a vista de pájaro*, to get a bird's-eye view of the town. || *Perder de vista*, to lose sight of. || *Perderse de vista*, to go out of sight. || *Se le nubló la vista*, his eyes became glazed, his eyes glazed over. || FIG. *Saltar a la vista*, to be obvious, to be as plain as a pikestaff. || *Ser corto de vista*, to be shortsighted. || FIG. *Ser largo de vista*, to be farseeing. || *Servidumbre de vistas*, V. SERVIDUMBRE. || FIG. *Tener a la vista*, to have in mind, to plan (un proyecto), to have one's eye on (vigilar), to have within sight (ver). || *Tener mucha vista*, to be farsighted (una persona), to look very nice, to be very pretty *o* attractive (una cosa). || *Tener poca vista*, to be shortsighted, to have bad sight *o* eyes (ver poco), to be shortsighted (no ser perspicaz). || *Tener una vista de lince* or *de águila*, to have eyes like a hawk. || *Torcer la vista*, to squint. || *Traducción a la vista*, unseen *o* sight translation. || *Una foto de la ciudad a vista de pájaro*, a bird's-eye view of the town. || FAM. *Uno de la vista baja*, a pig (cerdo). || FIG. *Vista de conjunto*, overall view. || *Vista general*, panorama, panoramic view. || *Volver la vista atrás*, to look back. || *Ya se ha perdido de vista ése que dices*, the one you are talking about has completely disappeared.

vista m. Customs man, customs officer, customs official (aduanero).

vistavisión f. Wide screen (cine).

vistazo m. Glance. || — *Dar* or *echar un vistazo*, to have a [quick] look. || *Dar* or *echar un vistazo a*, to glance at, to take a glance at, to have a [quick] look at.

vistesantos f. inv. Old maid (solterona).

vistillas f. pl. Viewpoint, *sing.*

visto, ta p. p. V. VER.
— Adj. In view of, considering (en vista de). || — *Cosa nunca vista*, sth. quite unheard-of. || *Estaba visto*, it was to be expected, what can you expect? || *Está muy visto*, it is very common (muy corriente), that is old hat (nada original). || *Estar bien visto*, to be well looked on. || *Estar mal visto*, to be frowned on. || *Está visto que*, it is obvious *o* evident *o* clear that. || *Este espectáculo es algo nunca visto*, this show is unique. || *Ladrillo visto*, uncovered brickwork. || *¡Lo nunca visto!*, you've never seen anything like it! || *Ni visto ni oído*, in a flash. || *Por lo visto*, obviously (por lo que se ve), apparently (según parece). || *Visto bueno* or *visto y conforme*, seen and approved *o* passed. || *Visto que*, in view of the fact that, seeing that, being that.
— M. *Visto bueno*, approval, O.K. || *Dar el visto bueno a*, to give one's approval to, to approve, to okay.

vistosamente adv. Colourfully, brightly: *sala vistosamente engalanada*, colourfully decorated room. || Flashily, showily (de modo llamativo).

vistosidad f. Colourfulness [U.S., colorfulness], brightness. || Showiness, flashiness (aspecto llamativo).

vistoso, sa adj. Colourful [U.S., colorful], bright: *llevar un vestido muy vistoso*, to wear a very colourful dress. || Showy, flashy (llamativo).

visual adj. Visual. || *Campo visual*, visual field, field of vision.
— F. Line of sight. || *Tirar visuales*, to take measurements *o* readings, to survey (topografía).

visualidad f. Colourfulness [U.S., colorfulness], brightness.

visualización f. Visualization.

visualizar v. tr. To visualize.

vital adj. Vital: *órganos vitales*, vital organs. || FIG. Vital (fundamental): *de importancia vital*, of vital importance. || — *Espacio vital*, living space. || FIL. *Impulso* or *elan vital*, vital force, élan vital.

vitalicio, cia adj. Life: *pensión vitalicia*, life annuity; *miembro vitalicio*, life member. || — *Cargo vitalicio*, post held for life. || *Renta vitalicia*, life annuity.
— M. Life annuity.

vitalidad f. Vitality.

vitalismo m. Vitalism (doctrina biológica).

vitalista adj. Vitalistic.
— M. y f. Vitalist.

vitalización f. Vitalization.

vitalizar v. tr. To vitalize.

vitamina f. Vitamin.

vitaminado, da adj. Vitaminized, enriched with vitamins, vitamin-enriched.

vitamínico, ca adj. Vitaminic. || Vitamin: *contenido vitamínico*, vitamin content.

vitando, da adj. To be avoided. || FIG. Odious, hateful.

vitela f. Vellum.

vitelino, na adj. BIOL. Vitelline.

vitelo m. Vitellus, yolk (del huevo).

vitícola adj. Viticultural, vine, vine growing.
— M. Viticulturist, vinegrower.

viticultor m. Viticulturist, vinegrower.

viticultura f. Viticulture, vine growing.

vitíligo m. MED. Vitiligo (despigmentación de la piel).

vitivinícola adj. Viticultural [associated with vine growing and the production of wine].

vitivinicultor m. Winegrower, viticulturist.

vitivinicultura f. Wine growing.

vito m. Andalusian dance and song.

Vito n. pr. m. MED. *Baile de San Vito*, St. Vitus' dance.

vitola f. Band, cigar band (de puros). || Calibrator (para calibrar). || FIG. Appearance (aspecto). || MAR. Scantling, model.

vítor m. Cheer. || — *Dar vítores al presidente*, to cheer *o* to acclaim the president. || *¡Vítor!*, bravo!, hurrah!

vitorear v. tr. To acclaim, to cheer, to applaud.

vitral m. Stained-glass window (de iglesia).

vítreo, a adj. Vitreous: *electricidad vítrea*, vitreous electricity; *humor vítreo*, vitreous humour. || Vitreous (de vidrio).

vitrificable adj. Vitrifiable.

vitrificación f. o **vitrificado** m. Vitrification.

vitrificador, ra adj. Vitrifying.

vitrificar, vitrificarse v. tr. y pr. To vitrify.

vitrina f. Showcase, glass case (en tiendas). || Display cabinet (en una casa). || *Amer.* Shopwindow [U.S., show window] (escaparate).

vitriolar v. tr. To vitriol.

vitriólico, ca adj. Vitriolic.

vitriolo m. Vitriol: *aceite de vitriolo*, oil of vitriol.

vituallar v. tr. To provision, to victual (p.us.).
vituallas f. pl. Provisions, victuals.
vituperable adj. Reprehensible, blameworthy.
vituperación f. Vituperation, reprehension, censure.
vituperador, ra adj. Vituperative, reproachful.
vituperante adj. Vituperative, reproachful.
vituperar v. tr. To vituperate, to reprehend, to censure.
vituperio m. Vituperation, reprehension, censure (vituperación). || Shame, disgrace (vergüenza). || — Pl. Insults, abuse, *sing*.
vituperioso, sa adj. Vituperative, reproachful.
viudal adj. Of a widower *o* widow.
viudedad f. Widowerhood (estado de viudo). || Widowhood (de viuda). || Widow's pension (pensión).
viudez f. Widowerhood (estado de viudo). || Widowhood (estado de viuda).
viudita f. Young widow (mujer). || *Amer.* Widow monkey (mono). | Kind of parrot (loro).
viudo, da adj. Widowed.
— M. Widower. || — F. Widow: *viuda alegre*, merry widow. || Widow bird (ave).
viva m. Cheer. || — *Dar vivas*, to cheer. || *¡Viva!*, hurrah! || *¡Viva el rey!*, long live the king!, hurrah for the king!
vivac m. Bivouac.
vivacidad f. Vivacity, liveliness, vivaciousness. || Sharpness (inteligencia).
vivales m. y f. inv. FAM. Crafty devil, sly one.
vivamente adv. Vividly (brillar o destacarse). || Quickly (rápidamente). || Smartly, briskly (moverse). || Sincerely (sinceramente). || Deeply: *lo siento vivamente*, I am deeply sorry. || Vividly (narrar, recordar). || Sharply (protestar).
vivaque m. Bivouac.
vivaquear v. intr. To bivouac.
vivar m. Warren (de conejos). || Fishpond (estanque para los peces). || Fish hatchery (donde se crían peces).
vivaracho, cha adj. Lively, sprightly, vivacious, bouncy.
vivaz adj. Long-lived (que dura). || Quick-witted, sharp (agudo). || Vigorous (vigoroso). || Lively, vivacious (lleno de vida). || BOT. Perennial.
vivencia f. [Personal] experience.
víveres m. pl. Supplies, provisions: *cortarle los víveres a alguien*, to cut off s.o.'s supplies.
vivero m. Nursery (para plantas). || Fishpond (estanque para peces). || Fish hatchery (donde se crían). || Farm: *vivero de ostras*, oyster farm. || Cloth made in Vivero [Galicia]. || FIG. Nursery, breeding ground: *esta ciudad es un vivero de atletas*, this town is a nursery for athletes.
viveza f. Vividness (de colores, narraciones). || Sharpness (de espíritu). || Keenness, acuteness (de un sentimiento). || Sincerity (sinceridad). || Vivacity, liveliness (de una persona). || Quickness (de movimiento). || Sparkle (de ojos). || Passion, feeling (pasion).
vividero, ra adj. Inhabitable.
vivido, da adj. True, true life, which actually happened [to one].
vívido, da adj. Vivid.
vividor, ra adj. Living, live, alive (que vive). || Shrewd, adept, capable (que sabe manejarse).
— M. y f. Person who makes the most of life. || Opportunist (oportunista).
vivienda f. Housing: *escasez de vivienda*, housing shortage; *problema de la vivienda*, housing problem. || Dwelling (morada). || Habitat (de animales). || House (casa). || Flat (piso). || *Viviendas de renta limitada*, council houses *o* flats [U.S., low cost housing].
viviente adj. Living: *seres vivientes*, living beings. || — *Cuadro viviente*, tableau vivant. || *Los vivientes*, the living.
vivificación f. Vivification.
vivificador, ra adj. Vivifying, life-giving.
vivificante adj. Vivifying, life-giving. || Comforting.
vivificar v. tr. To vivify, to give life to. || To comfort.
vivificativo, va adj. Vivifying, life-giving.
viviparidad f. ZOOL. y BOT. Viviparity.
vivíparo, ra adj. ZOOL. y BOT. Viviparous.
vivir m. Life (vida). || Living (sustento). || Way of life (modo de vivir). || — *Gente de mal vivir*, v. GENTE. || *Tener un vivir decente*, to live reasonably well.
vivir v. intr. To live: *los loros viven mucho tiempo*, parrots live a long time; *vivir en el campo*, to live in the country; *vive en Madrid desde hace tres años*, he has been living in Madrid for three years. || To be alive (estar vivo). || FIG. y FAM. To last (durar). || — *Alegría de vivir*, joy of living, joie de vivre. || *Como se vive se muere*, as we live so shall we die. || *Ir viviendo*, to get by, to get along. || *Mientras yo viva*, as long as I live: *mientras yo viva no te faltará nada*, as long as I live you will want for nothing; over my dead body: *mientras yo viva no lo harás*, you'll do it over my dead body. || *No dejar vivir a uno*, not to give s.o. any peace, not to leave s.o. alone (una persona), to be a constant torment to s.o. (problemas, etc.). || *No vive del miedo que tiene*, he is scared to death, he is tormented *o* plagued by fear. || *¿Quién vive?*, who goes there? (centinela). || *Saber vivir*, to enjoy life to the full. || *Se vive bien en este país*, it's a good life *o* life is good in this country. || *Tener con que vivir*, to have enough to live on. || *¡Viva!*, hurrah!, hurray! || *¡Viva España!*, long live Spain! || *¡Vivan los novios!*, hurray for *o* three cheers for the bride and groom! || *¡Vive Dios!*, good God!, good heavens! (sorpresa). || FIG. y FAM. *Vivir a cuerpo de rey*, to live like a king. || *Vivir al día*, to live from hand to mouth *o* from one day to the next. || *Vivir bien*, to live well (teniendo bastante dinero), to lead an honest life (vivir honestamente), to get along well together (vivir en armonía varias personas). || *Vivir con poco*, to live on very little. || *Vivir del aire*, to live on next to nothing. || *Vivir de ilusiones* or *de quimeras*, to live in a dream world. || *Vivir de sus ahorros*, to live off one's savings. || *Vivir de sus rentas*, to live on one's private income. || *Vivir muy justo*, to scrape a bare living. || *Vivir para ver*, to live and learn. || *Vivir por encima de sus posibilidades*, to live beyond one's means. || *Vivir sin pena ni gloria*, to lead an uneventful life. *Y vivieron felices, comieron perdices, y a mí no me dieron*, and they all lived happily ever after (final de los cuentos).
— V. tr. To go *o* to live through: *vivir momentos difíciles*, to go through difficult times.
vivisección f. Vivisection.
vivisector, ra m. y f. Vivisector.
vivismo m. Doctrine of Luis Vives [16th century Spanish philosopher].
vivista m. Follower of Luis Vives.
vivito, ta adj. FAM. *Vivito y coleando*, alive and kicking, going strong (una persona), not over yet: *el asunto queda vivito y coleando*, the matter is not over yet.
vivo, va adj. Living: *seres vivos*, living beings. || Alive: *está todavía vivo*, he is still alive. || Living (lengua). || Vivid (descripción, color, recuerdo, imaginación, etc.). || Sharp, quick (inteligencia). || Sharp, intense (dolor). || Deep, keen, intense (emociones). || Quick (movimiento). || Strong (protesta). || Lively, vivacious (lleno de vida). || Bright, quick-witted (listo). || Alert (perspicaz). || Quick-tempered (que se enfada fácilmente). || FIG. Cunning, sly, shrewd (astuto). | Unscrupulous (aprovechón). || Sharp (arista, ángulo). || — *Agua viva*, springwater. || *Al* or *a lo vivo*, vividly. || *A viva fuerza*, by main force. || *De viva actualidad*, much talked about, much discussed. || *De viva voz*, v. VOZ. || *Dios vivo*, the living God. || *En carnes vivas* o *en cueros vivos*, [stark] naked (desnudo). | *En carne viva*, raw, red raw (la espalda, la piel, etc.), like an unhealed wound: *un recuerdo que está en carne viva*, a memory which is like an unhealed wound. || *En roca viva*, in *o* out of *o* from living *o* solid rock (tallar, etc.). || *En vivo*, on the hoof (ganadería), with live animals: *experimentar en vivo*, to experiment with live animals. || *Fuerzas vivas*, life *o* driving force [of a town's or nation's economy]. || FIG. *Hay una diferencia como de lo vivo a lo pintado*, there is no comparison. || *Herir en carne viva*, v. CARNE. | *Herir* or *tocar en lo vivo*, to cut *o* to touch to the quick. | *Llegar a lo vivo*, to cut to the quick (a una persona), to reach the quick *o* the heart (de un asunto). | *Llorar a lágrima viva*, v. LLORAR. || MAR. *Obra viva*, quickwork. || FIG. *Pasarse de vivo*, to try to be too clever. | *Ser el vivo retrato de alguien*, to be the spitting image *o* the living image of s.o. | *Ser más vivo que un rayo*, to be as quick as lightning. | *Ser vivo de genio*, to be quick-witted. | *Ser vivo de imaginación*, to have a vivid imagination. || *Seto vivo*, quickset hedge. || FIG. *Tener el genio vivo*, to be quick-tempered *o* easily excitable.
— M. Living person. || FIG. y FAM. Crafty devil (astuto). || Trimming (en costura). || — JUR. *Donación entre vivos*, gift inter vivos. || *Los vivos y los muertos*, the quick *o* the living and the dead.
vizcacha f. Viscacha (roedor).
vizcachera f. Viscacha's warren.
vizcainada *f.* Typically Basque expression. || Typically Basque action.
vizcaíno, na adj./s. Biscayan (de la provincia de Vizcaya). || Basque (del País Vasco).
vizcaitarra adj./s. Basque nationalist.
Vizcaya n. pr. f. GEOGR. Biscay: *la bahía de Vizcaya*, the Bay of Biscay.
vizcondado m. Viscountcy, viscounty (dignidad). || Viscounty (jurisdicción).
vizcondal adj. Of *o* pertaining to a viscount.
vizconde m. Viscount.
vizcondesa f. Viscountess.
vocablo m. Word, vocable (p.us.). || FIG. *Jugar del vocablo*, to make a play on words *o* a pun.
vocabulario m. Vocabulary.
vocación f. Vocation, calling: *errar la vocación*, to miss one's vocation.
vocal adj. Vocal: *cuerdas vocales*, vocal chords; *órganos vocales*, vocal organs.
— F. GRAM. Vowel. || — M. y f. Member: *vocal de una comisión*, committee member.
vocálico, ca adj. Vocalic, vowel.
vocalismo m. Vocalism.
vocalista m. y f. Vocalist (en una orquesta).
vocalización f. Vocalization.
vocalizar v. intr. y tr. To vocalize.
vocalmente adv. Vocally. || Verbally (de palabra).
vocativo m. Vocative.
voceador, ra adj. Vociferous, loud-mouthed.

— M. y f. Shouter (que grita). || — M. Town crier (pregonero).
vocear v. intr. To shout *o* to cry *o* to yell [out].
— V. tr. To cry *o* to shout [out] (un vendedor). || To shout from the rooftops, to proclaim (publicar). || To shout to, to hail (llamar). || To acclaim, to hail (aclamar).
vocería f. o **vocerío** m. Shouting, yelling (gritería). || Uproar, clamour [U.S., clamor] (clamor).
vocero m. Spokesman (portavoz).
vociferación f. Vociferation.
vociferador, ra adj. Vociferous, vociferant.
vociferante adj. Vociferant, vociferous.
vociferar v. intr. y tr. To vociferate, to scream, to shout.
vocinglería f. Shouting (gritería). || Hubbub, uproar, clamour [U.S., clamor] (clamor).
vocinglero, ra adj. Loud-mouthed (que habla mucho y en voz alta).
vodevil m. Vaudeville, music hall.
vodevilesco, ca adj. Vaudevillian.
vodevilista m. Vaudevillian, vaudevillist.
vodka m. o f. Vodka.
vodú m. Voodoo.
volada f. Flight, short flight. || *Amer.* V. BOLADA.
voladera f. Paddle, blade (paleta).
voladero, ra adj. Flying. || Able to fly.
voladizo, za adj. ARQ. Projecting, jutting out: *cornisa voladiza*, projecting cornice.
— M. Projection. || *En voladizo*, projecting.
volado, da adj. IMPR. Superior. || Projecting (voladizo). || — FIG. y FAM. *Estar volado*, to be uneasy (inquieto), not to know where to put o.s. (de vergüenza), to be pressed for time (tener prisa). || FIG. *Hacer algo volado*, to do sth. in a hurry.
volador, ra adj. Flying (que vuela): *pez volador*, flying fish; *aparato volador*, flying machine.
— M. Rocket (cohete). || Flying fish (pez). || *Amer.* Symbolic Mexican game in which men swing on ropes round the top of a very high pole.
voladura f. Blowing-up: *la voladura de un puente*, the blowing-up of a bridge. || Blasting (en una cantera, de una mina).
volandas (en) loc. Off the ground, in the air. || FIG. y FAM. *Llevar a uno en volandas al hospital*, to rush s.o. off to hospital.
volandera f. Grindstone, millstone (de molino). || Washer (arandela). || FIG. y FAM. Lie, fib (mentira).
volandero, ra adj. Newly fledged, ready to fly (volantón). || FIG. Unexpected (imprevisto). | Restless, wandering (que no se queda en un lugar). | Loose (que no está sujeto). | Hanging (suspendido).
volandillas (en) loc. V. VOLANDAS (EN).
volante adj. Flying: *escuadrón, pez, platillo volante*, flying squad, fish, saucer. || FIG. Mobile, itinerant (que va de un sitio a otro): *equipo volante*, mobile team *o* crew. | Temporary (temporal): *campamento volante*, temporary camp. || DEP. *Medio volante*, wing half, half back.
— M. Shuttlecock (rehilete). || Badminton (juego). || Flounce (en vestidos). || Frill (adorno). || Note (comunicación no oficial). || Leaflet (hoja suelta). || AUT. [Steering] wheel. || MED. Card. || TECN. Flywheel (para regularizar el movimiento). | Balance wheel (de reloj). | Coin press (para acuñar moneda). || *Amer.* Volante, two-wheeled carriage (vehículo).
volantín m. *Amer.* Kite.
volantón, ona adj. Newly fledged.
— M. y f. Fledgling.
volapié m. TAUR. "Volapié" [method of killing a bull in which the matador runs at the stationary animal and drives the blade between the shoulders].
volapuk m. Volapük (lengua).
volar* v. intr. To fly (aves, aviones): *este avión vuela a diez mil metros*, this aeroplane flies at an altitude of ten thousand metres. || To be blown away (con el viento): *los papeles volaron*, the papers were blown away. || FIG. To fly (correr): *volar en auxilio de uno*, to fly to s.o.'s aid; *¡cómo vuela el tiempo!*, how time flies! || FAM. To disappear (desaparecer). || ARQ. To project, to jut out (balcón). || — *Echarse a volar*, to fly away *o* off, to take wing (los pájaros), to leave home (dejar el hogar). || FIG. *El pájaro ha volado* or *voló*, the bird has flown. | *Hacer algo volando*, to do sth. as quick as a flash. | *Ir volando*, to fly along, to hurtle along, to speed along (coche, etc.), to go at once, to fly (ir en seguida). | *Ir volando a hacer algo*, to run and do sth. | *Las noticias vuelan*, news spreads fast. | *Pasar, salir volando*, to fly past, out. || *¡Volando!*, jump to it!, on the double!, make it snappy! | *Volar con sus propias alas*, to stand on one's own two feet. || *Volar por encima* or *sobre*, to fly over.
— V. tr. To blow up, to demolish (edificios, etc.). || To blast (en una cantera, una mina). || To flush (las aves en la caza). || To fly (el halcón).
— V. pr. To be blown away, to fly away (con el viento): *los papeles se volaron*, the papers were blown away. || *Amer.* To lose one's temper, to blow up (encolerizarse).
volatería f. Falconry (caza). || Birds, *pl.*, fowl, *pl.* (aves de corral).
volátil adj. Volatile. || FIG. Fickle, changeable, inconstant.
volatilidad f. Volatility. || FIG. Inconstancy, fickleness, changeableness.
volatilización f. Volatilization.
volatilizar v. tr. To volatilize. || FIG. To spirit away (hacer desaparecer).
— V. pr. To volatilize. || FIG. To vanish into thin air (desaparecer).
volatín m. o **volatinero, ra** m. y f. Flier [U.S., aerialist].
volcán m. Volcano.
volcanada f. *Amer.* FAM. Puff (bocanada).
volcanicidad f. Volcanicity. || Volcanism (volcanismo).
volcánico, ca adj. Volcanic.
volcanismo m. Volcanism.
volcanista m. Volcanist, vulcanist.
volcanizar v. tr. To volcanize.
volcar* v. tr. To tip over, to knock over, to upset: *volcar un vaso*, to knock a glass over. || To knock down (un adversario). || To empty out, to pour out (vaciar). || FIG. To make [s.o.] dizzy (turbarle la cabeza a uno). | To make [s.o.] change his mind (hacer que uno cambie de opinión). | To upset, to get on [s.o.'s] nerves (irritar).
— V. intr. To turn over, to overturn (vehículo). || To capsize (barco). || *Volqué con el coche*, I turned the car over.
— V. pr. To fall over (vaso, etc.). || To turn over, to overturn (vehículo). || To capsize (barco). || FIG. To do one's utmost, to bend over backwards: *volcarse para conseguir fondos*, to do one's utmost to raise funds.
volea f. Swingletree, whippletree (carruajes). || DEP. Volley (en el juego de pelota). | Lob (en el tenis y el fútbol).
volear v. tr. To volley (pelota). || AGR. To broadcast, to scatter (semillas).
— V. intr. DEP. To volley.
voleibol m. *Amer.* DEP. Volleyball (balonvolea).
voleo m. Volley (en el juego de pelota). || Hard slap (bofetón). || High kick (en la danza). || — *A* or *al voleo*, at random, randomly, haphazardly (arbitrariamente). || *Del primer* or *de un voleo*, first go, first time. || *Sembrar a* or *al voleo*, to broadcast seed, to scatter seed.
volframina f. QUÍM. Wolframine.
volframio m. QUÍM. Wolfram (tungsteno).
volframita f. QUÍM. Wolframite.
volición f. Volition.
volitivo, va adj. Volitive.
volován m. Vol-au-vent.
volquete m. Tipcart (carro). || Tip-up lorry [U.S., dump truck] (camión).
volquetero m. Lorry driver [U.S., truck driver].
volscos m. pl. Volsci.
voltaico, ca adj. ELECTR. Voltaic.
voltaje m. ELECTR. Voltage.
voltámetro m. ELECTR. Voltameter.
voltamperímetro m. ELECTR. Voltammeter.
voltamperio m. ELECTR. Volt-ampere.
voltariedad f. Inconstancy, fickleness, changeableness.
voltario, ria adj. Inconstant, fickle, changeable.
volteada f. *Amer.* Method of isolating chosen animals from a herd by galloping a horse through the herd.
volteador, ra m. y f. Acrobat, tumbler.
voltear v. tr. To swing: *voltear una honda*, to swing a sling. || To turn, to turn over, to toss (la tierra, el heno, una tortilla, etc.). || To turn round (dar una vuelta). || To overturn (volcar). || To ring out loud, to peal out (las campanas). || To toss *o* to throw up in the air: *el toro volteó al torero*, the bull tossed the bullfighter up in the air. || FIG. y FAM. To fail (en un examen). | To topple (un gobierno).
— V. intr. To roll over (caerse redondo). || To do *o* to turn a somersault [*o* a cartwheel, etc.], to somersault (un volteador). || To peal out, to be at full peal (las campanas).
— V. pr. *Amer.* To turn one's coat, to desert one's party (cambiar de chaqueta). | To turn round (dar la vuelta).
volteo m. Trick riding (equitación). || Peal (de las campanas).
voltereta f. Somersault. || Handspring (poniendo las manos en el suelo). || *Dar volteretas*, to do somersaults, to turn somersaults, to somersault.
volterianismo m. Voltairianism.
volteriano, na adj./s. Voltairean, Voltairian.
voltímetro m. Voltmeter.
voltio m. ELECTR. Volt.
volubilidad f. Inconstancy, fickleness, changeableness, volubility (p.us.). || BOT. Volubility.
volúbilis m. BOT. Convolvulus.
voluble adj. Inconstant, changeable, fickle, voluble (p.us.). || BOT. Voluble, twining.
volumen m. Volume (de recipiente, cantidad, sonido). || Size (tamaño). || Bulk, bulkiness (gran tamaño). || Volume, tome (libro). || — *De mucho volumen*, important, sizeable (importante). || *Poner la radio a todo volumen*, to turn the radio up full. || *Volumen de negocios*, turnover.
volumetría f. Volumetry.
volumétrico, ca adj. Volumetric, volumetrical.

volúmetro m. Volumeter.
voluminoso, sa adj. Voluminous. || Bulky, cumbersome (que ocupa mucho sitio): *paquete voluminoso*, bulky parcel.
voluntad f. Will: *los reflejos no dependen de la voluntad*, one's reflexes are independent of one's will; *lo hago contra mi voluntad*, I am doing it against my will; *tiene mucha voluntad*, he has a strong will. || Wishes, *pl.* (deseos): *hacer algo contra la voluntad de otro*, to do sth. against s.o. else's wishes. || Wish (deseo): *su voluntad es meterse a cura*, his wish is to become a priest. || Willpower (fuerza de voluntad): *es muy listo pero le falta voluntad*, he is very clever, but he lacks willpower. || Affection, liking (cariño). || — *A voluntad*, at will, as one wishes. || *Buena voluntad*, goodwill: *visita de buena voluntad*, goodwill visit; good intentions (buenas intenciones): *tiene buena voluntad*, his intentions are good. || *Con poca voluntad*, reluctantly. || *Fuerza de voluntad*, willpower. || *Ganar la voluntad de uno*, to win s.o. over. || FAM. *Hacer su santa voluntad*, to do exactly as one pleases *o* likes. || *Hágase tu voluntad*, Thy will be done (oración). || *Mala voluntad*, ill will, malice. || *Me atengo a su voluntad*, I leave it to your discretion. || *No tener voluntad propia*, to have no will of one's own. || *Por causas ajenas a nuestra voluntad*, for reasons beyond our control. || *Por su propia voluntad*, of one's own free will. || *Tenerle buena, mala voluntad a uno*, to like, not to like s.o. || JUR. *Última voluntad*, last wish (de un condenado a muerte), last will and testament, will (de un moribundo). || *Voluntad divina*, Divine will. || *Voluntad férrea* or *de hierro*, will of iron. || *Zurcir voluntades*, to pander.
voluntariado m. MIL. Voluntary enlistment.
voluntariedad f. Voluntariness. || Wilfulness [U.S., willfulness] (de una persona obstinada).
voluntario, ria adj. Voluntary. || Wilful [U.S., willful] (obstinado).
— M. y f. Volunteer.
voluntarioso, sa adj. Willing (deseoso de hacer las cosas bien). || Wilful [U.S., willful] (testarudo).
voluptuosidad f. Voluptuousness.
voluptuoso, sa adj. Voluptuous: *vida voluptuosa*, voluptuous life.
— M. y f. Voluptuary.
voluta f. ARQ. Volute, spiral, scroll. || Spiral, column (de humo). || ZOOL. Volute.
volver* v. tr. To turn: *volver la cabeza*, to turn one's head; *volver la esquina*, to turn the corner. || To turn, to turn over (poniendo lo de arriba abajo): *volver una tortilla, la tierra*, to turn an omelette, the earth; *volver la página*, to turn [over] the page. || To turn (*a*, on) [un arma de fuego]. || To turn inside out (poniendo lo de dentro afuera): *volver un calcetín*, to turn a sock inside out. || To make: *el éxito le ha vuelto presumido*, success has made him arrogant. || To turn (convertir): *volver el agua en vino*, to turn water into wine; *el tinte lo volvió verde*, the dye turned it green. || To turn back, to return, to restore: *producto que vuelve el pelo a su color natural*, product which turns hair back to its natural colour. || FIG. To turn: *han vuelto contra él sus propios argumentos*, they turned his own arguments against him. || To put: *volver una frase en la forma pasiva*, to put a sentence into the passive. || To turn (en costura). || — *Volver a la vida a uno*, to bring s.o. back to life, to revive s.o. || *Volver algo a su sitio*, to put sth. back. || *Volver boca abajo*, to turn upside down (una cosa), to turn over (a una persona). || *Volver del revés*, to turn [sth.] inside-out. || FIG. *Volver la casaca*, v. CASACA. || *Volver la espalda*, to turn round (volverse). || *Volver la espalda a uno*, to turn one's back on s.o. (sentido propio), to give s.o. the cold shoulder, to turn one's back on s.o. (sentido figurado). || FIG. *Volver la hoja*, v. HOJA. || *Volver la mirada* or *los ojos a*, to look round at, to turn one's eyes towards. || *Volver la vista atrás*, to look back. || *Volver loco a uno*, to drive s.o. mad.
— V. intr. To go back, to return (estando lejos del sitio de que se habla): *volver a su patria*, to go back to one's homeland. || To come back, to return (estando en el sitio de que se habla): *no vuelvas muy tarde*, don't come back too late. || To go back, to go again, to return (ir de nuevo): *este verano volveremos a París*, this summer we shall go back to Paris *o* we shall go to Paris again. || FIG. To return: *la juventud no vuelve nunca*, one's youth never returns. | To return, to revert: *volvamos a nuestro tema*, let us return to the subject in hand. | To revert: *la tribu ha vuelto al paganismo*, the tribe has reverted to paganism. || — *Hacer volver al buen camino*, to put back on the right road. || *No lo vuelva a hacer*, don't do it again. || *No me volverá a pasar*, I'll not let it happen again. || *Volver a*, to start to... again: *volvió a llover*, it started to rain again. (V. OBSERV.) || *Volver a la carga* or *al ataque*, to renew the attack *o* the assault, to charge again (las tropas), to keep at it (insistir). || *Volver a la infancia*, to be in one's second childhood. || *Volver a las andadas*, to fall back into *o* to revert to one's old habits *o* ways. || *Volver al orden* or *a la normalidad*, to return to normal. || *Volver a lo de siempre*, to get back to the same old thing. || *Volver al redil*, to return to the fold. || *Volver a llevar*, to take back. || *Volver a meter*, to put back. || *Volver a ponerse*, to put back on. || *Volver atrás*, to go back, to turn back. || *Volver con las manos vacías*, to come *o* to go back *o* to return empty-handed. || *Volver en sí*, to come to, to come round, to regain consciousness. || *Volver sobre sus pasos*, v. PASO. || *Vuelva a llenar*, the same again (al convidar a otra copa).
— V. pr. To turn round (dar la vuelta). || To turn: *se volvió hacia mí*, he turned to me. || To go back, to come back, to return (regresar). || To turn over: *se ha vuelto la página*, the page has turned over. || To turn inside out (ponerse al revés). || To become, to turn: *el tiempo se vuelve bueno*, the weather is turning fine; *volverse triste*, to become sad. || To turn [sour] (agriarse). || *Volverse contra alguien* or *en contra de alguien*, to turn against s.o. || *Volverse loco*, to go mad.

— OBSERV. La mayoría de las veces la expresión española *volver a* seguida de un infinitivo se traduce al inglés por el verbo acompañado del adverbio *again* cuando se trata de la repetición de una acción (*volver a cantar*, to sing again) y del adverbio *back* si implica la vuelta del objeto mencionado al sitio donde estaba (*volver a poner un libro en la biblioteca*, to put a book back in the bookcase).

vólvulo m. MED. Volvulus.
vómer m. ANAT. Vomer.
vómica f. MED. Vomica.
vómico, ca adj. Vomitive, emetic. || *Nuez vómica*, nux vomica.
vomitador, ra adj. Vomiting.
— M. y f. Person who vomits.
vomitar v. intr. To be sick, to vomit. || *Dar a uno ganas de vomitar*, to make one feel sick.
— V. tr. To vomit, to bring up. || FIG. To belch, to spew out, to spit: *los cañones vomitaban fuego*, the cannons belched fire. | To hurl: *vomitar injurias*, to hurl abuse. || FIG. y FAM. To spit out, to cough up (revelar). || *Vomitar sangre*, to spit blood.
vomitera f. Sickness. || *Le ha dado la vomitera*, she feels sick.
vomitivo, va adj./s. m. MED. Emetic.
vómito m. Vomiting, vomit (acción). || Vomit (resultado). || — *Vómito de sangre*, hemoptysis. || *Vómito negro*, black vomit, yellow fever.
vomitón, ona adj. FAM. Who often vomits [suckling child].
— F. FAM. *Echar una vomitona*, to be violently sick, to throw up.
vomitorio adj./s. m. Emetic (vomitivo). || — M. Vomitory (de los circos romanos).
vorace adj. POÉT. Voracious (voraz).
voracidad f. Voracity, voraciousness.
vorágine f. Vortex, maelstrom, whirlpool.
voraginoso, sa adj. Swirling, vortical, turbulent, full of whirlpools.
voraz adj. Voracious. || FIG. Raging (llamas, etc.).
vórtice m. Vortex, whirlpool. || Centre of a cyclone (centro de un ciclón). || Hurricane (huracán).
vorticela f. ZOOL. Vorticella.
vortiginoso, sa adj. Vortical, swirling.
vos pron. pers. de la 2.ª pers. del sing. y del pl. You. || Thou (dirigiéndose a Dios).

— OBSERV. *Vos* is used instead of *usted* in poetic and oratorical style to address God or an eminent person: *Señor, Vos sois nuestra Providencia*, Lord, Thou art our Providence. In the seventeenth century *vos* was an intermediate form of address between "tú" and "Vuestra Merced". In many parts of Latin America *vos* has replaced *tú* as the formula for addressing one's equals or inferiors. The accusative form *te* has however survived, and is often used with *vos: a vos te parece bien*, that seems all right to you; *vos te comeréis* or *te comerás este pastel*, you will eat this cake.

vosear v. tr. To address as "vos" (v. VOS [*Observ.*]).
voseo m. Use of "vos" to address s.o. (v. VOS [*Observ.*]).
vosotros, tras pron. pers. de la 2.ª pers. del plural. You: *¿cuándo venís vosotros?*, when are you coming?; *lo hice por vosotros*, I did it for you. || Yourselves: *¿lo habéis discutido entre vosotros?*, have you discussed it amongst yourselves? || — *El coche de vosotros*, your car. || *El de vosotros*, yours.

— OBSERV. This pronoun is the plural form of the familiar "tú" form of address: *a vosotros, hijos míos, os diré lo mismo*, I shall say the same thing to you, my sons.
— This second person plural may also be used by a speaker to address his audience, by an author to address his readers, etc.

votación f. Voting (acción de votar): *modo de votación*, method of voting; *votación a mano alzada*, voting by a show of hands. || Vote: *la votación tuvo lugar ayer*, the vote was taken yesterday; *poner* or *someter a votación*, to put to the vote; *votación unánime*, unanimous vote; *votación nula*, unconclusive vote. || Ballot: *votación adicional* or *de desempate*, second ballot. || — *Por votación popular*, by popular vote. || *Proponer la votación por separado*, to move that a separate vote be taken. || *Votación masiva*, heavy voting. || *Votación nominal*, vote *o* voting by roll call. || *Votación por levantados y sentados*, vote by sitting and standing [U.S., rising vote]. || *Votación secreta*, secret ballot *o* vote.
votante adj. Voting.
— M. y f. Voter.

votar v. tr. e intr. To vote: *votar a mano alzada*, to vote by a show of hands; *votar por uno*, to vote for s.o.; *votar la candidatura de*, to vote for. || To pass (aprobar): *una moción votada por unanimidad*, a motion passed unanimously. || To vote: *votar diez mil libras para la investigación*, to vote ten thousand pounds for research. || To vote on (someter a votación). || To curse, to swear (blasfemar). || REL. To vow. || — *Proceder a votar*, to proceed to a vote. || *Votar puestos en pie* or *por levantados y sentados*, to vote by sitting and standing. || *¡Voto a tal!*, damn it!, confound it!

votivo, va adj. Votive: *misa votiva*, votive Mass.

voto m. Vote: *explicar el voto*, to account for *o* to explain one's vote; *moción aprobada por doce votos a favor y nueve en contra*, motion passed by twelve votes to nine; *dar su voto a*, to give one's vote to. || Vow: *voto de castidad*, vow of chastity; *pronunciar sus votos*, to take vows. || Wish (deseo): *formular votos por el éxito de algo*, to express one's sincere wishes for the success of sth. || Curse (reniego). || — Pl. Vote, *sing.*, votes (conjunto de los votos). || — *Acciones de voto plural*, shares with plural voting rights. || *Depositar un voto*, to cast a vote. || *Derecho al voto*, the right to vote, suffrage, franchise. || *Echar votos*, to curse, to swear (blasfemar). || *Hacer votos por* or *por que*, to earnestly hope for *o* that. || FAM. *No tener ni voz ni voto*, to have no say in the matter. || *Por una mayoría de votos*, by a majority vote. || *Tener voto*, to have the right to vote. || *Tener voz y voto*, V. VOZ. || *Voto de calidad*, casting vote. || *Voto de censura*, vote of censure. || *Voto de confianza*, vote of confidence. || *Voto de gracias*, vote of thanks. || *Voto por poderes*, vote by proxy. || *Votos de felicidad*, best wishes. || *Votos emitidos*, votes cast. || *Votos indecisos*, floating votes. || *Voto solemne*, solemn vow.

vox f. *Ser vox pópuli*, to be common knowledge. || *Vox pópuli*, rumour.

voz f. Voice: *voz cavernosa*, hollow voice; *tener buena voz*, to have a good voice. || Shout, cry (grito). || GRAM. Voice: *voz pasiva, activa*, passive, active voice. | Word (vocablo): *voz culta*, learned word. || Rumour (rumor). || Vote, support (voto). || MÚS. Tone (de un instrumento). | Voice (en una fuga). | Voice (cada cantante). | Part, voice: *una canción para dos voces*, a two-part song. || FIG. Voice: *la voz de la conciencia*, the voice of one's conscience. | Sound (sonido). | Noise (ruido). || — Pl. Voices. || Shouting, *sing.* (gritos). || — *Aclararse la voz*, to clear one's throat. || *Alzar* or *levantar la voz*, to raise one's voice. || *A media voz*, in a low voice, softly (en voz baja), under one's breath (con insinuación). || MÚS. *Apagar la voz*, to dampen [the sound] (de un instrumento). || *A una voz*, with one voice, unanimously. || *A voces*, shouting. || *A voz en cuello* or *en grito*, at the top of one's voice. || *Cantar a dos voces*, to sing a duet. || *Con voz pero sin voto*, without a right to vote, non-voting. || *Con voz y voto*, with a right to vote, voting. || *Corre la voz que*, rumour has it that, it is rumoured that. || *Dar la voz de alarma*, to raise the alarm. || *Dar una voz a uno*, to give s.o. a shout *o* a call. || *Dar voces*, to shout. || FIG. *Dar voces al viento*, to be wasting one's breath. || *Decir algo a voces*, to shout sth. out loud. || *Decir algo en voz alta*, to say sth. aloud *o* out loud. || *De viva voz*, personally, in person (personalmente): *decir algo a alguien de viva voz*, to tell s.o. sth. personally; viva voce, orally, by word of mouth. || FIG. y FAM. *Donde Cristo dio las tres voces*, V. CRISTO. || *En voz alta*, aloud, in a loud voice, out loud. || *En voz baja*, in a low voice, softly, quietly. || *En voz queda*, in a soft voice, softly. || *Estar en voz*, to be in good voice. || *Estar pidiendo a voces*, to be crying out for. || *Forzar la voz*, to strain one's voice. || *Hablar en voz baja, en voz alta*, to speak softly, loudly. || *Hacer correr la voz*, to spread the rumour. || FIG. *Llevar la voz cantante*, to rule the roost. | *No tener voz ni voto*, to have no say in the matter. || *Perder la voz*, to lose one's voice. || *Secreto a voces*, open secret. || *Se le está mudando la voz*, his voice is breaking. || *Ser voz pública*, to be common knowledge. || *Tener la voz tomada*, to be hoarse. || *Tener voz consultiva*, to have a voice but no vote. || *Tener voz y voto*, to be a voting member (en una asamblea). || *Voz aguda*, high *o* high-pitched voice (de una persona), word with the stress on the last syllable (palabra). || *Voz apagada*, weak voice. || MÚS. *Voz cantante*, principal *o* main voice. || *Voz de alarma*, alarm, alarm call. || *Voz del cielo*, voice from the sky. || *Voz del pueblo*, voice of the people. || MIL. *Voz de mando*, order, command. || *Voz de trueno*, thunderous *o* thundering voice. || *Voz estentórea*, stentorian voice. || *Voz pública*, public opinion.

vozarrón m. o **vozarrona** f. Powerful *o* booming voice.

vuecelencia o **vuecencia** pron. pers. Your Excellency [term used, especially in former times, to address a superior].

vuelco m. Upset. || FIG. Change, shake-up (cambio). || Capsizing (de una embarcación). || — *Dar un vuelco*, to overturn (coche), to capsize (barco), to change (cambiar), to go to ruin (ir a la ruina). || *Dar un vuelco a una cosa*, to knock sth. over. || FIG. *Le dio un vuelco el corazón*, his heart skipped a beat.

vuelo m. Flying (acción de volar): *vuelo a ciegas* or *ciego* or *sin visibilidad*, blind flying. || Flight (acto de volar una vez, distancia volada, modo de volar): *ha sido un vuelo excelente*, it has been an excellent flight; *vuelo sin escala*, nonstop flight. || Fullness, flare (de un vestido). || Wing (ala). || Flight feathers, *pl.*, flights, *pl.* (plumas). || Wingspan, wingspread (envergadura). || Lace ruffle (volante). || ARQ. Projection. || — *Al vuelo*, in flight (aves, moscas, etc.): *coger moscas al vuelo*, to catch flies in flight; on the wing (aves), very quickly (rápidamente). || *Alzar* or *emprender* or *levantar* or *tomar el vuelo*, to take flight, to take off (aves), to clear off (marcharse). || *A vuelo de pájaro*, as the crow flies (distancia). || FIG. y FAM. *Cogerlas* or *cazarlas al vuelo*, to catch on quickly, to be quick on the uptake. | *Coger* or *cazar una cosa al vuelo*, to catch on to sth. quickly. | *Cortar los vuelos a uno*, to clip s.o.'s wings. || *De mucho vuelo*, ambitious, far-reaching (persona, proyecto, etc.), full (vestido). || FIG. *De* or *en un vuelo*, quickly, in a trice, in a jiffy. || *Echar las campanas a vuelo*, V. CAMPANA. || FIG. *¡No tantos vuelos!*, don't be so ambitious! || *Personal de vuelo*, flight staff. || *Remontar el vuelo*, to soar [up]. || FIG. *Se hubiera podido oír el vuelo de una mosca*, one could have heard a pin drop. | *Tomar vuelo*, to grow (crecer). || *Vuelo a ras de tierra* or *rasante*, hedgehopping, low flying. || *Vuelo a vela* or *sin motor*, gliding. || *Vuelo de prueba*, test flight. || *Vuelo en picado*, dive. || *Vuelo espacial*, space flight. || *Vuelo nocturno*, night flight. || *Vuelo planeado*, gliding.

vuelta f. Walk, stroll (paseo): *dar una vuelta por la ciudad*, to go for a walk round the town; *dar una vuelta por la tarde*, to go for an afternoon walk. || Return (regreso): *celebrar la vuelta de alguien*, to celebrate s.o.'s return. || Return, return journey, journey back (viaje de regreso). || Return (retorno): *la vuelta de la primavera*, the return of spring. || Return (devolución). || Round (turno en un concurso, un torneo, etc.): *elegido a la primera vuelta*, elected in the first round. || Bend, curve, turn (recodo). || Turn-up (de un pantalón). || Ruffle (adorno en el puño, etc.). || Row (de un collar, haciendo punto). || Loop, coil (de una cuerda, un cabo, etc.). || Back (de una tela, de una hoja de papel). || Change (dinero): *dar la vuelta al comprador*, to give the customer his change; *se quedó con la vuelta*, he kept the change. || Revolution, turn (revolución). || Rotation, turn (rotación). || DEP. Lap (en una carrera): *sólo quedan cuatro vueltas*, there are only four laps to go. || ARQ. Vault (bóveda). | Curve (del intradós). || EQUIT. Volte, volt (del caballo). || Revolution (unidad de ángulo). || Hiding (paliza, tunda): *le dio una vuelta*, he gave him a hiding. || FIG. y FAM. Round (ronda de bebidas). || — *A la vuelta de*, once back from: *a la vuelta de España*, once back from Spain. || FIG. *A la vuelta de diez años*, after *o* at the end of ten years. || *A la vuelta de la esquina*, just round the corner. || *A la vuelta de las vacaciones*, after the holidays. || FIG. *Andar a vueltas con un problema*, to try to come to terms with a problem. || *A vuelta de correo*, by return of post. || FIG. y FAM. *Buscarle a uno las vueltas*, to look for faults in everything s.o. does, to find fault with s.o. || *Cerrar con dos vueltas*, to double-lock. || FIG. *Coger las vueltas*, to get the hang *o* the knack of it (el tranquillo). | *Cogerle las vueltas a uno*, to know how to handle s.o. || FAM. *¡Con vuelta!*, I want it back! (cosa prestada). || FIG. *Dar la vuelta*, to change radically (cambiar). || *Dar la vuelta a*, to go round (alrededor): *dar la vuelta al mundo*, to go round the world; to turn: *dar la vuelta a la llave*, to turn the key; to turn round (girar), to turn upside down (poniendo lo de arriba abajo), to turn inside out (poniendo fuera lo de dentro), to turn over (cambiándolo de lado). || *Dar la* or *una vuelta de campana*, to overturn, to turn over (un coche). || FIG. *Darle cien vueltas a uno*, to knock spots off s.o., to run rings round s.o. || *Dar media vuelta*, to walk out (irse), to about turn [U.S., to about-face] (soldado), to turn round (para volverse atrás), to do a U-turn (coche, etc.). || *Dar* or *darse una vuelta*, to go for a walk *o* a stroll (andando), to go for a ride *o* for a drive *o* for a run (en coche), to make a short trip (hacer un viaje corto). || *Dar vueltas*, to turn round, to go round and round, to spin, to rotate (alrededor de un eje), to twist and turn (un camino), to revolve: *la Tierra da vueltas alrededor del Sol*, the Earth revolves around the Sun; to go round in circles (no llegar a ninguna parte). || *Dar vueltas a*, to turn (llave, etc.), to spin (hacer girar), to turn over: *dar vueltas a una idea en la cabeza*, to turn an idea over in one's mind; to thoroughly examine (examinar), to go round: *dimos dos vueltas a la manzana*, we went twice round the block. || FIG. *El mundo da muchas vueltas*, anything might happen. || *Estar de vuelta (de)*, to be back [from]. || FAM. *Estar de vuelta de todo*, to be blasé. || *¡Hasta la vuelta!*, see you when you come back! || FIG. *Las vueltas de la vida*, the ups and downs of life. | *Le estás dando demasiadas vueltas*, you are worrying too much about it. || *Me da vueltas la cabeza*, my head is swimming, I feel dizzy. || *Media vuelta*, about turn [U.S., about-face] (los soldados), short walk (paseo corto). || FIG. y FAM. *No andar con vueltas*, not to beat about the bush.

| *No hay que darle vueltas*, that's all there is to it, there's nothing more to be said about it. | *No le des más vueltas a este asunto*, let the matter lie, don't think about it any more. | *No tiene vuelta de hoja*, there's no doubt about it (está claro), there is no alternative (no hay otra solución). || *Partido de vuelta*, return match (deportes). || FIG. y FAM. *Poner a uno de vuelta y media*, to call s.o. all the names under the sun. | *Tener muchas vueltas*, to be very tricky *o* complicated. || *Tener vuelta*, to be reversible (la ropa). || *Véase a la vuelta*, please turn over, P.T.O. (continúa al dorso), overleaf (vea en la página siguiente). || *Vuelta a escena*, comeback (de un artista). || TAUR. *Vuelta al ruedo*, lap of honour. || *Vuelta atrás*, backward step. || *Vuelta ciclista*, long-distance cycle race. || *Vuelta ciclista a Francia*, Tour de France. || *Vuelta de campana*, somersault (voltereta con el cuerpo). || *Vuelta sobre el ala*, roll (de un avión). || FAM. *¡Y vuelta!*, not again!

vuelto, ta p. p. V. VOLVER. || — *Cuello vuelto*, v. CUELLO. || *Sombrero con las alas vueltas*, hat with the brim turned up *o* with a turned-up brim.
— M. *Amer.* Change (vuelta de dinero).

vueludo, da adj. Full (de mucho vuelo).

vuesamerced pron. pers. You (vuestra merced).

vuestro, tra adj. pos. de la 2.ª pers. del pl. Your: *vuestro hijo y vuestras hijas*, your son and [your] daughters. || Of yours, your: *uno de vuestros amigos*, a friend of yours, one of your friends.
— Pron. pos. Yours: *mis amigos y los vuestros*, my friends and yours. || — *Los vuestros*, yours, your people (vuestra familia). || *Lo vuestro*, what is yours, what belongs to you.

vulcanismo m. GEOL. Volcanism, vulcanism.

vulcanita f. Vulcanite.

vulcanización f. TECN. Vulcanization.

vulcanizado, da adj. TECN. Vulcanized: *caucho vulcanizado*, vulcanized rubber.

vulcanizador m. TECN. Vulcanizer.

vulcanizar v. tr. TECN. To vulcanize.

Vulcano n. pr. m. MIT. Vulcan.

vulcanología f. Volcanology, vulcanology.

vulcanologista o **vulcanólogo** m. Volcanologist, volcanist, vulcanologist, vulcanist.

vulgar adj. Common, general: *opinión vulgar*, common opinion. || Ordinary, common: *el hombre vulgar*, the common man. || Commonplace, trite, banal: *idea vulgar*, commonplace idea. || Ordinary, humdrum (vida). || Vulgar, common (poco refinado): *gustos vulgares*, vulgar tastes. || Lay, layman's (no técnico): *término vulgar*, lay term. || Vulgar (no sabio): *latín vulgar*, vulgar Latin.

vulgaridad f. Triviality, banality (cosa sabida). || Vulgarity (grosería). || *Decir vulgaridades*, to talk small talk (cosas sabidas), to use bad language, to be rude (groserías).

vulgarismo m. Vulgarism (expresión popular).

vulgarización f. Popularization, vulgarization, extension: *la vulgarización de una ciencia*, the vulgarization of a science.

vulgarizador, ra adj. Popularizing, vulgarizing, extension.
— M. y f. Popularizer, vulgarizer.

vulgarizar v. tr. To vulgarize (hacer vulgar). || To popularize, to vulgarize (exponer algo en forma asequible al vulgo). || To extend (difundir).
— V. pr. To be vulgarized *o* popularized. || To become common *o* ordinary. || To become vulgar *o* common (grosero).

Vulgata n. pr. f. Vulgate (Biblia).

vulgo m. Common people, *pl.*, masses, *pl.*, vulgus (p.us.) [pueblo]. || Laymen, *pl.* (profanos).

vulnerabilidad f. Vulnerability.

vulnerable adj. Vulnerable.

vulneración f. Violation: *vulneración de un tratado*, violation of a treaty. || Wounding, injuring (herida).

vulnerar v. tr. To injure, to wound (herir). || To harm, to injure (perjudicar). || To violate (tratado, ley, contrato).

vulnerario, ria adj./s.m. MED. Vulnerary.
— F. BOT. Lady's finger (planta).

vulpeja f. Vixen, she-fox (zorra).

vulpino, na adj. Vulpine.
— M. Foxtail (planta).

vulva f. ANAT. Vulva.

vulvar adj. Vulvar, vulval.

vulvitis f. inv. MED. Vulvitis.

w f. W (uve doble).
— OBSERV. The letter *w* is not proper to the Spanish language and it is used only in words of foreign origin.

wagneriano, na adj./s. Wagnerian.

wahabita adj./s. Wahhabi, Wahabi.

walhalla m. Walhalla.

walkiria f. Walkyrie (divinidad escandinava).

walk-over m. Walkover (abandono).

wapiti m. ZOOL. Wapiti (ciervo).

warrant m. COM. Warrant (recibo de depósito).

water m. FAM. Toilet, lavatory (retrete).

waterballast m. Water ballast (tanque de agua).

watercloset m. Water closet (retrete).

watergang m. Water gang (canal en Holanda).

water-polo m. Water polo (polo acuático).

watt m. ELECTR. Watt (vatio).

weber o **weberio** m. ELECTR. Weber (unidad).

week-end m. Weekend.

welter m. Welterweight (peso semimedio en boxeo).

western m. Western (película del Oeste).

Westfalia n. pr. f. GEOGR. Westphalia.

wharf m. Wharf (muelle).

whig adj./s.m. Whig (liberal).

whisky m. Whisky (bebida).

wigwam m. Wigwam (choza de indios).

winchester m. Winchester (fusil de repetición).

wintergreen m. BOT. Wintergreen.

wolframio m. Wolfram (metal).

x f. X (equis). || MAT. X. || — *El señor X*, Mr. X. || *Rayos X*, X rays.

xantato m. QUÍM. Xanthate.

xanteno m. QUÍM. Xanthene.

xantina f. QUÍM. Xanthin, xanthine.

xantofila f. Xanthophyll.

xantoma m. MED. Xanthoma.

xenofilia f. Xenophilia.

xenófilo, la adj. Xenophilous.
— M. y f. Xenophile.
xenofobia f. Xenophobia.
xenófobo, ba adj. Xenophobic.
— M. y f. Xenophobe.
xenogénesis f. Xenogenesis.
xenón m. QUÍM. Xenon (gas).
xerófilo, la adj. BOT. Xerophilous.
xerografía f. Xerography.
xerosis f. inv. MED. Xerosis.
xi f. Xi (letra griega).
xifoideo, a adj. ANAT. Xiphoid, xiphoidal.
xifoides adj. ANAT. Xiphoid, xiphoidal.
— M. Xiphoid.
xifosuro adj./s.m. ZOOL. Xiphosuran. || — Pl. Xiphosura.
xileno m. QUÍM. Xylene (hidrocarburo).
xilófago, ga adj. ZOOL. Xylophagous.
— M. pl. Xylophaga.
xilofonista m. y f. MÚS. Xylophonist.
xilófono m. MÚS. Xylophone (instrumento).
xilografía f. Xylography, wood engraving (arte). || Xylograph (impresión).
xilográfico, ca adj. Xylographic, xylographical.
xilógrafo, fa m. y f. Xylographer.

Y

y f. Y (i griega).

— OBSERV. *Y* is a semiconsonant. When it stands on its own, i. e. when it is a conjunction, it is pronounced as a Spanish *i*. At the end of a syllable it diphtongizes the preceding vowel : *rey* [rej]. Between two vowels it has the same sound as the English *y*: *raya* [raja]. Moreover, in certain regions of Spain and several Latin American countries, particularly Argentina, it resembles more a weak English *j* as in beige [beiʒ].

y conj. And: *padre y madre*, father and mother. || After (repetición): *cartas y cartas*, letter after letter. || And: *¡y no me lo habías dicho!*, and you didn't even tell me! || — *Y eso que*, although: *no está cansado, y eso que ha trabajado mucho*, he's not tired although he has worked a lot. || *¿Y qué?*, so what?
ya adv.

1. Tiempo. — **2.** Afirmación. — **3.** Locuciones y empleos diversos.

1. TIEMPO. — Already (con una acción en el pasado): *llegó ya*, he has already arrived; *ya he acabado*, I've already finished; *ya lo sabía*, I already knew. || Already, ever (antes): *¿ya has estado en Francia?*, have you already been to France? || Now (ahora): *ya es rico*, he is rich now; *ya los días van siendo más largos*, the days are getting longer now. || Now, nowadays (actualmente, hoy en día). || Later (más adelante): *ya hablaremos de eso*, we'll speak about that later. || Right away, immediately (en seguida). || Soon (pronto): *ya lo encontrarás, no te preocupes*, you'll soon find it, don't worry. || Any more (negativo): *ya no me gustan esas cosas*, I don't like that sort of thing any more.
2. AFIRMACIÓN. — Well (insistencia): *ya lo creo*, I well believe it. || Now (por fin): *ya me acuerdo*, now I remember. || Right, all right (bien, de acuerdo): *¿mañana vendrás a mi casa?* — *Ya*, come over to my house tomorrow. — All right.
3. LOCUCIONES Y EMPLEOS DIVERSOS. — *Ahora ya no hace nada*, now he doesn't do anything. || *Eso ya no se hace*, that is not done any more. || *No ya*, not only. || *Pues ya*, of course, naturally. || *Si ya*, if. || *¡Ya!*, at last! (por fin), that's it (eso es), quite, of course, yes (sí), right! (entendido). || *¡Ya caigo!*, now I remember! (ya recuerdo), now I see (ya comprendo). || *¡Ya está!*, that's it! || *Ya es hora*, it is [high] time. || *Ya mismo*, right away. || *Ya no me queda más que una libra*, [now] I only have one pound left. || *Ya que*, since, as (puesto que), now that (ahora que). || *Ya se ve*, that's obvious, that's easy to see. || *Ya verás, ya*, you just wait and see. || *Ya veremos*, we shall see, we shall see about it. || *Ya ves*, you see, you know. || *¡Ya, ya!*, yes, yes! || *Ya ... ya*, sometimes ... sometimes (a veces). || *Ya ... ya* or *ya sea ... ya sea*, whether ... or: *ya en el campo, ya en casa*, whether in the country or at home.

— OBSERV. Very often *ya* serves only to emphasize the action expressed in the verb and is not translated in English (*ya voy*, I'm coming).

yaacabó m. Insectivorous bird (ave).
yaba f. *Amer.* Cabbage tree (árbol).
yac m. ZOOL. Yak (búfalo).
yacamar m. *Amer.* Jacamar.
yacaré m. *Amer.* Alligator, caiman, cayman.
yacedor m. Lad who takes horses out to graze at night.
yacente adj. Lying. || — *Estatua yacente*, recumbent statue. || *Herencia yacente*, unclaimed estate, estate in abeyance.
— M. MIN. Floor of a vein (cara inferior de un criadero).
yacer* v. intr. To be lying, to be lying down (estar tendido). || To lie (los muertos). || To be located, to be (estar en algún lugar). || To graze at night (los caballos). || — *Aquí yace*, here lies (un muerto). || *Yacer con*, to lie with.
yaciente adj. Lying.
yacija f. Bed, couch (lecho). || Sepulchre, tomb, grave (sepultura). || *Ser de mala yacija*, to be a poor sleeper.
yacimiento m. GEOL. Bed, deposit. || *Yacimiento petrolífero*, oil field.
yaco m. *Amer.* Variety of otter (nutria).
yactura f. Damage, loss.
yacht m. Yacht (yate).
yachting m. Yachting (navegación a vela).
yagual m. *Amer.* Head pad (rodete).
yaguar m. *Amer.* Jaguar (animal).
yaguareté m. *Amer.* Jaguar (jaguar).
yaguarú m. *Amer.* Otter (nutria).
yaguarundi m. *Amer.* Eyra.
yaguasa f. *Amer.* Yaguaza, tree duck.
yaguré m. *Amer.* Skunk (mamífero).
yak m. Yak (búfalo).
Yakarta n. pr. GEOGR. Djakarta, Jakarta.
yámbico, ca adj. Iambic: *verso yámbico*, iambic verse.
yambo m. Iamb (poesía). || Jambo (árbol).
yanacón o **yanacona** m. *Amer.* Indian tenant farmer (colono). | Indian servant (criado indio).
yanqui adj./s. FAM. Yankee, Yank.
yantar m. (Ant.). Food.
yantar v. tr. (Ant.). To eat.
yapa f. *Amer.* Little extra, bonus (adehala). | Mercury [added to silver ore to facilitate extraction] (azogue). | Tip (propina). | Thick end (del lazo).
yapú m. *Amer.* ZOOL. Variety of thrush (tordo).
yarará f. *Amer.* Viper (víbora).
yaraví m. Melancholic Indian song.
yarda f. Yard (medida).
yare m. Poisonous juice extracted from yucca.
yaro m. Arum (planta).
yatagán m. Yataghan (sable).
yatay m. *Amer.* Palm.
yate m. Yacht.
yaya f. *Amer.* Lancewood (planta). || *Amer. Dar yaya*, to beat, to thrash (apalear).
yaz m. Jazz.
ye f. (P.us.). Name of the letter y.
yedra f. Ivy (planta).
yegua f. Mare. || *Amer.* Cigar butt (colilla del puro).
yeguada f. Herd of horses. || *Amer.* Foolish act *o* remark (disparate).
yeguar adj. [Of] mares.
— M. Herd of mares.
yeguarizo, za adj. [Of a] mare.
yegüería f. Herd of horses.
yegüerizo o **yegüero** m. Keeper of a herd of mares.
yeísmo m. Phenomenon which consists in pronouncing the Spanish letter *ll* like the Spanish *y*.

— OBSERV. This phenomenon is widespread in Spain (Madrid and other large towns, Andalusia, the Balearic and Canary Islands) and in much of Latin America. Though increasingly common, this pronunciation is considered colloquial.

yelmo m. Helmet. || *El yelmo de Mambrino*, Mambrino's helmet (en El Quijote).
yema f. BOT. y ZOOL. Bud (renuevo). || Yolk (del huevo). || Tip (del dedo). || Sweet made of sugar and egg yolk. || FIG. The cream, the best (lo mejor). | Middle (medio). || — *Vinagre de yema*, vinegar made with the wine taken from the centre of the barrel. || *Yema del dedo*, fingertip. || *Yema mejida*, eggnog.
Yemen n. pr. m. GEOGR. Yemen.
yemení o **yemenita** adj./s. Yemenite.
yen m. Yen (unidad monetaria del Japón).
yente m. *Los yentes y vinientes*, people coming and going; passersby (en la calle).
yerba f. Grass (hierba). || Herb (medicinal, etc.). || *Amer*. Maté (yerba mate).
yerbajo m. Weed.
yerbal m. *Amer*. Maté field. || Pasture (herbazal).
yerbatero, ra adj. *Amer*. [Of] maté: *industria yerbatera*, maté industry.
— M. y f. *Amer*. Maté plantation worker *o* owner. || — M. *Amer*. Quack doctor (curandero).
yerbear v. intr. *Amer*. To drink maté.
yermo, ma adj. Uninhabited (despoblado). || Uncultivated (sin cultivar). || Barren (sin vegetación).
— M. Wilderness, desert (sitio deshabitado). || Barren land, waste land (sitio inculto).
yerno m. Son-in-law (hijo político).
yero m. Lentil vetch (planta).
yerra f. *Amer*. Branding.
yerro m. Error, mistake: *enmendar* or *deshacer un yerro*, to correct an error. || — Pl. Errors (extravíos).
yerto, ta adj. Rigid (tieso). || Stiff (un cadáver). || — FIG. *Quedarse yerto*, to be petrified. || *Yerto de frío* frozen stiff.
yervo m. Lentil vetch (yero).
yesal o **yesar** m. Gypsum pit (cantera).
yesca f. Tinder [U.S., amadou, punk]. || FIG. Stimulus, fuel (de pasión o afecto). | Dynamite (situación explosiva). || — Pl. Tinderbox, *sing.*, tinder, *sing.* || — FIG. y FAM. *Arrimar yesca*, to give a hiding *o* a licking. || *Echar una yesca*, to strike a light.
yesera f. Gypsum pit (yesal).
yesería f. Gypsum kiln (fábrica de yeso).
yesero, ra adj. Plaster: *industria yesera*, plaster industry.
— M. Plasterer.
yeso m. GEOL. Gypsum. || Chalk (polvo). || Plaster (empleado en construcción y arte). || Plaster cast (escultura). || — *Dar de yeso*, to plaster (una pared). || *Yeso blanco*, superfine white plaster. || *Yeso mate* or *de París*, plaster of Paris. || *Yeso negro*, rough plaster.
yesón m. Chunk of plaster.
yesoso, sa adj. Gypseous. || Chalky: *terreno yesoso*, chalky soil. || *Alabastro yesoso*, translucent gypsum.
yesquero adj. *Hongo yesquero*, tinder fungus.
— M. Tinder vendor *o* maker. || Pouch (bolsa).
yeyuno m. ANAT. Jejunum.
yezgo m. Danewort, dwarf elder (planta).
ylang-ylang m. Ylang-ylang (planta).
yo pron. pers. de la 1.ª pers. del sing. I: *yo soy*, I am. || — *Soy yo*, it is I, it's me (fam.). || *Soy yo el que habla*, I am the one who is speaking. || *Yo mismo*, I myself. || *Yo que usted* or *yo en su lugar* or *si yo fuera usted*, if I were you, if I were in your place.
— M. FIL. *El yo*, the I, the ego.
yod f. Yod (i griega).
yodado, da adj. Iodized.
yodar v. tr. To iodize.
yodato m. QUÍM. Iodate.
yodhídrico adj. m. QUÍM. Hydriodic (ácido).
yódico, ca adj. QUÍM. Iodic.
yodismo m. MED. Iodism (intoxicación por el yodo).
yodo m. QUÍM. Iodine: *tintura de yodo*, tincture of iodine.
yodoformo m. MED. Iodoform.
yoduración f. QUÍM. Iodization.
yodurado, da adj. QUÍM. Iodized.
yoduro m. QUÍM. Iodide.
yoga m. Yoga.
yogui o **yogi** o **yoghi** m. Yogi.
yogur m. Yogurt, yoghurt, yoghourt.
yohimbina f. QUÍM. Yohimbine.
yola f. MAR. Yawl.
yoquey m. DEP. Jockey.
yoyo m. Yo-yo (juguete).
yperita f. Yperite (gas).
ypsilón f. Upsilon (letra griega).
yterbio m. Ytterbium (metal).
yuambú m. *Amer*. Tinamou.
yubarta f. Finback (cetáceo).
yuca f. BOT. Yucca (planta liliácea). || Cassava, manioc (mandioca).
yucal m. Yucca grove *o* plantation. || Cassava *o* manioc field.
Yucatán n. pr. m. GEOGR. Yucatán.
yucateco, ca adj. Yucatecan.
— M. y f. Yucatec. || — M. Yucatec (lengua).
yugada f. Yoke of land (espacio de tierra labrada en un día). || Land measurement of about 32 hectares. || Yoke of oxen (yunta de bueyes).
yugo m. Yoke (de bueyes, de campana). || FIG. Yoke: *sacudir el yugo*, to throw off the yoke. || MAR. Transom. || FIG. *Yugo del matrimonio*, marriage bond, yoke of marriage.
Yugoslavia n. pr. f. GEOGR. Yugoslavia.
yugoslavo, va adj./s. Yugoslavian, Yugoslav.
yuguero m. Ploughman [U.S., plowman].
yugular adj./s. f. ANAT. Jugular: *vena yugular*, jugular vein.
yugular v. tr. FIG. To nip in the bud.
yumbo, ba m. y f. Indian of Ecuador.
yungas f. pl. *Amer*. Name given to the warm valleys of Peru, Bolivia and Ecuador.
yungla f. Jungle.
yunque m. Anvil. || FIG. Stoic, long-suffering person (en las adversidades). | Tireless worker, plodder (en el trabajo). || ANAT. Incus, anvil (del oído).
yunta f. Yoke, team [of oxen]. || Yoke of land (tierra labrada).
yuntería f. Beasts (*pl.*) of burden. || Stable (establo).
yuntero m. Ploughman [U.S., plowman].
yunto, ta adj. Close (junto).
¡yupi! interj. FAM. Yippee!
yurta f. Tent (choza).
yuruma f. *Amer*. Heart of a palm.
yurumí m. *Amer*. Anteater (oso hormiguero).
yusera f. Nether millstone.
yusión f. JUR. Jussive, order.
yuso adv. (Ant.) Below (abajo).
yuta f. *Amer*. Slug (babosa). || *Amer*. FAM. *Hacer la yuta*, to play truant [U.S., to play hooky].
yute m. Jute (materia textil).
yuxtalineal adj. Juxtalinear.
yuxtaponer* v. tr. To juxtapose.
yuxtaposición f. Juxtaposition.
yuxtapuesto, ta adj. Juxtaposed.
yuyal m. *Amer*. Weed-covered ground.
yuyo m. *Amer*. Weed (yerbajo).
yuyú m. MAR. Dinghy (chinchorro).
yuyuba f. BOT. Jujube (azufaifa).

Z

z f. Z (zeda, zeta): *una z mayúscula*, a capital z.
— OBSERV. The *z* is an interdental fricative which is pronounced like the English *th* (as in *thank*) by placing the tip of the tongue between the teeth.
¡za! interj. Shoo! (a un perro).
zabarcera f. Greengrocer, woman who sells fruit and other food.
zaborda f. o **zabordamiento** m. MAR. Running aground.
zabordar v. intr. MAR. To run aground.
zabordo m. MAR. Running aground (zaborda).
zabro m. Zabrus, caraboid beetle (insecto).
zabullir v. tr. V. ZAMBULLIR.
zaca f. Leather bucket for bailing (en minas).
zacatal m. *Amer*. Pasture.
zacate m. *Amer*. Fodder, hay.
zacatón m. *Amer*. Tall pasture grass.
zadorija f. BOT. Scarlet pimpernel.
zafada f. MAR. Unbending.
zafado, da adj. *Amer*. Cheeky, brazen (descarado). | Sharp, alert (vivo). | Dislocated (huesos).
zafadura f. *Amer*. Dislocation (de un hueso).

zafaduría f. *Amer.* Cheek (descaro).
zafar v. tr. To undo, to untie, to unfasten (soltar): *zafar un nudo*, to undo a knot. || MAR. To unbend (cabos, velas, etc.). || (P.us.) To adorn (adornar).
— V. intr. *Amer.* To leave, to go away.
— V. pr. To escape, to get away (escaparse). || FIG. To get out, to evade: *zafarse de un compromiso*, to get out of a commitment, to evade a commitment. | To get away, to shake off: *zafarse de una persona*, to get away from s.o. | To get out: *zafarse de una situación delicada*, to get out of a delicate situation. || To come off (una correa). || *Amer.* To be dislocated (un hueso). || FAM. *Zafarse con*, to run off with.
zafarrancho m. MAR. Clearing for action. || FIG. y FAM. Mess (estropicio). | Row, rumpus (riña). || — FIG. y FAM. *Armar un zafarrancho*, to kick up a rumpus, to cause uproar. || *Zafarrancho de combate*, call to action stations.
zafiedad f. Coarseness, uncouthness.
zafio, fia adj. Coarse, uncouth.
zafirino, na adj. Sapphirine.
zafiro m. Sapphire.
zafo, fa adj. MAR. Free, clear. | Unscathed, unharmed, safe and sound (ileso).
zafra f. Sugar cane harvest (cosecha de caña). || Sugar cane crop (cantidad cosechada). || Sugar making (fabricación). || Sugar cane harvest season (temporada). || Harvest (cosecha, recolección). || Oil jar, oil can (recipiente). || MIN. Rubbish (escombros).
zafre m. MIN. Zaffer, zaffre (óxido de cobalto).
zafrero m. Rubbish carrier (en las minas).
zaga f. Rear (parte posterior). || Load carried in the rear of a vehicle (carga). || DEP. Defence (U.S., backline) [fútbol]. || — *A la zaga* or *en zaga*, behind, in *o* at the rear. || FIG. *No irle a la zaga a nadie*, to be second to none. | *No irle a uno a la zaga* or *en zaga*, to be every bit as good as s.o. | *No quedarse* or *no ir a la zaga*, not to be left behind, not to be outdone.
— M. Last player (en el juego).
zagal m. Boy, youth, young man (adolescente). || Shepherd boy (pastor mozo).
zagala f. Girl, lass. || Shepherdess (pastora).
zagalejo m. Petticoat (refajo). || Shepherd boy (pastor).
zagalón m. Big boy, strapping lad.
zagalona f. Big girl.
zagual m. Paddle (remo pequeño).
zaguán m. Hall.
zaguanete m. Hall (zaguán). || Room for the royal guard (aposento de la guardia). || Royal guard (guardia).
zaguero, ra adj. Rear, back (trasero). || Bottom (último). || Lagging behind (que está atrasado). || Overloaded in the rear (cargado en la parte trasera).
— M. Back (en deportes).
zagüí m. *Amer.* Squirrel monkey (mono).
zahareño, ña adj. Unsociable (arisco). || Wild (intratable). || Haggard (ave de rapiña).
zahén adj. Of fine gold (moneda).
zahena f. Doubloon (moneda).
zaheridor, ra adj. Upbraiding (que reprende). || Scoffing, mocking (mofador).
zaherimiento m. Upbraiding, reprimand (reprimenda). || Reproach (censura). || Mockery (mofa). || Mortification (mortificación). || Sarcastic criticism (crítica).
zaherir* v. tr. To upbraid, to reprimand (reprender). || To reproach (censurar). || To mock (escarnecer). || To mortify, to hurt one's feelings (mortificar). || To criticize sarcastically.
zahína f. Sorghum (planta).
zahinar m. Sorghum field.
zahonado, da adj. Whose front legs differ in colour from the rest of the body (animal).
zahondar v. tr. To deepen (ahondar).
— V. intr. To sink (hundirse).
zahones m. pl. Chaps.
zahorí m. Seer, clairvoyant (adivino). || Water diviner (de manantiales). || FIG. Mind reader (que sabe adivinar los pensamientos). | Very perceptive person (persona perspicaz).
zahorra f. MAR. Ballast (lastre).
zahúrda f. Pigsty [U.S., pigpen] (pocilga). || FIG. Hovel (tugurio). | Pigsty (casa sucia).
zaida f. ZOOL. Demoiselle (ave).
zaino, na adj. Treacherous, false, deceitful (persona). || Vicious (animal). || Pure black (negro): *toro zaino*, pure black bull. || Chestnut (caballo). || *Mirar a lo zaino*, to look sideways.
Zaire n. pr. m. GEOGR. Zaíre.
zairense adj./s. Zairian.
zalagarda f. Ambush, ambuscade (emboscada). || Skirmish (escaramuza). || Trap, snare (trampa). || FIG. y FAM. Rumpus, to-do (alboroto).
zalama f. o **zalamelé** m. o **zalamería** f. Cajolery, coaxing by flattery (engatusamiento). || Flattery, adulation (adulación).
zalamero, ra adj. Flattering, fawning (adulador). || Cajoling (engatusador).
— M. y f. Flatterer (adulador). || Cajoler (engatusador).
zalea f. Sheepskin.
zalear v. tr. To shake (sacudir).
zalema f. FAM. Salaam (saludo oriental). | Cajolery, coaxing by flattery (engatusamiento). | Flattery (adulación). || — Pl. Bowing and scraping (coba).
zaleo m. Sheepskin (piel). || Shaking (acción de zalear).
zalmedina m. Ancient magistrate of Aragon.
zamacuco m. FAM. Dolt (tonto). | Sly one (hombre solapado). || FIG. y FAM. Drunkenness [U.S., drunk] (borrachera).
zamacueca f. Popular Chilian and Peruvian dance.
zamarra f. Sheepskin jacket (vestidura hecha de piel). || Sheepskin (piel de carnero).
zamarrear v. tr. To shake (sacudir). || FIG. y FAM. To push [s.o.] about, to knock [s.o.] about (zarandear). | To corner (en una discusión).
zamarreo m. Shaking, shake (sacudimiento). || FIG. y FAM. Rough treatment (trato malo).
zamarreón m. FAM. Shaking, shake.
zamarrico m. Sheepskin bag.
zamarrilla f. BOT. Mountain germander.
zamarro m. Sheepskin jacket (zamarra). || Sheepskin (piel de carnero). || FIG. y FAM. Peasant [U.S., hick] (hombre tosco). | Bore (hombre pesado). | Cunning fellow (hombre astuto). || — Pl. *Amer.* Leather chaps.
zamarrón m. Thick sheepskin jacket (zamarra). || Leather apron (mandil).
zamba f. Popular South American dance. || Samba (samba).
zambaigo, ga adj./s. *Amer.* Descendant of a Chinese and an Indian. | Zambo (descendiente de negro e india o viceversa).
zambarco m. Broad breast strap (parte de los arreos). || Strap with a buckle (cincha con hebilla).
zambardo m. *Amer.* Chance (casualidad).
Zambeze n. pr. m. GEOGR. Zambezi.
Zambia n. pr. f. GEOGR. Zambia.
zambo, ba adj. Knock-kneed (de piernas torcidas). || — M. y f. *Amer.* Zambo (hijo de negro e india o viceversa).
— M. ZOOL. Spider monkey (mono).
zambomba f. Kind of drum.
— Interj. Gosh!

— OBSERV. The *zambomba* is a cylinder covered at one end by a tightly stretched skin with a stick fastened to the centre. A deep and monotonous sound is produced by moving the stick up and down. This instrument is used generally during the Christmas season.

zambombazo m. FAM. Punch, thump, hard blow (golpe). | Boom, bang (ruido). | Explosion (explosión).
zambombo m. FAM. Boor, brute.
zamborondón, ona o **zamborrotudo, da** adj. FAM. Clumsy (tosco). | Slapdash (chapucero).
— M. y f. Boorish and clumsy person. || Bungler (chapucero).
zambra f. Moorish festival (fiesta). || FAM. Uproar, rumpus (jaleo). || *Zambra gitana*, Andalusian gipsy dance.
zambullida f. Dive, plunge. || Lunge (treta de la esgrima). || — *Darle a uno una zambullida*, to give s.o. a ducking. || *Darse una zambullida*, to dive into the water (tirarse al agua), to go for a swim, to take a dip (bañarse).
zambullidura f. o **zambullimiento** m. Dive, plunge.
zambullir* v. tr. To plunge, to dip (un objeto). || To duck (persona).
— V. pr. To go for a swim, to go for a dip (bañarse). || To dive, to plunge, to take a dive *o* a plunge (tirarse al agua de cabeza). || FIG. To plunge: *zambullirse en el trabajo*, to plunge into one's work. | To hide (esconderse).
zambullo m. *Amer.* Big dustbin [U.S., garbage can].
zambumbia f. *Amer.* Kind of drum.
Zamora n. pr. GEOGR. Zamora. || FIG. *No se ganó Zamora en una hora*, Rome wasn't built in a day.
zamorano, na adj. [Of *o* from] Zamora.
— M. y f. Native *o* inhabitant of Zamora.
zampa f. ARQ. Pile.
zampabodigos o **zampabollos** m. y f. inv. FAM. Glutton, greedy pig.
zampalimosnas m. y f. inv. FIG. y FAM. Beggar.
zampar v. tr. To hide (esconder). || To gobble down, to wolf down (la comida). || To hurl, to throw, to dash (arrojar): *zampó la jarra de vino en el suelo*, he threw the wine pitcher to the floor. || To dip: *zampó el bizcocho en el café*, he dipped the cake into the coffee. || To deal, to give (una bofetada).
— V. pr. To gobble, to wolf: *se zamparon el almuerzo en un santiamén*, they gobbled down their lunch in a trice. || To dash, to dart (*en*, into) [entrar rápidamente]. || To fall (dejarse caer).
zampatortas m. y f. inv. FAM. Glutton, greedy pig (persona glotona). || FIG. y FAM. Thickhead (torpe).
zampeado m. Piling, piles, *pl.*
zampear v. tr. To drive piles into (un terreno).
zampón, ona adj. Greedy (glotón).
— M. y f. Glutton, greedy pig (fam.)
zampoña f. Panpipe (caramillo). || FIG. y FAM. Nonsense (necedad).
zanahoria f. Carrot (planta).
zanca f. Leg (pierna de las aves). || FIG. y FAM. Shank, leg (pierna). || ARQ. Stringpiece of a staircase (de una escalera). | Leg of a scaffold (de un andamio). || Large pin (alfiler).

zancada f. Stride (paso largo): *dar grandes zancadas*, to take long strides. || — FIG. y FAM. *En dos zancadas*, in a jiffy. || *Irse a zancadas*, to stride off, to go off with long strides. || FIG. *Seguir las zancadas de*, to follow in the footsteps of.
zancadilla f. Trip. || FIG. Trap, trick (trampa). || *Echar la zancadilla* or *poner la zancadilla a uno*, to trip s.o. up, to make s.o. trip (hacerle caer), to put the skids under s.o., to trip s.o. up.
zancadillear v. tr. To trip up, to make trip. || FIG. To set a trap for (armar un trampa), to put the skids under [s.o.], to trip [s.o.] up (perjudicar).
zancado adj. Which has spawned (salmón).
zancajear v. intr. To rush about.
zancajera f. Coach step (del estribo del coche).
zancajo m. Heel bone (hueso). || Heel (del pie, del zapato). || FAM. Lean bone (zancarrón). | Runt (persona fea).
zancajoso, sa adj. Bowlegged.
zancarrón m. FAM. Lean bone (hueso). || FIG. y FAM. Skinny old man, old bag of bones (hombre viejo y flaco). | Bad teacher (mal profesor).
zanco m. Stilt (para andar).
zancón, ona adj. FAM. Lanky, long-legged. || *Amer.* Too short (vestido).
zancudo, da adj. Long-legged, lanky. || ZOOL. Wading. || *Aves zancudas*, waders.
— M. *Amer.* Mosquito (mosquito). || — F. pl. ZOOL. Waders.
zanfonía f. Hurdy-gurdy (instrumento).
zángana f. FAM. Lazy woman, lazybones (holgazana).
zanganada f. FAM. Stupid remark (majadería).
zangandongo, ga o **zangandullo, lla** o **zangandungo, ga** m. y f. FAM. Lazybones, idler, loafer.
zanganear v. intr. FAM. To idle, to loaf *o* to laze around (holgazanear). | To make stupid remarks (decir majaderías).
zanganería f. FAM. Idleness, laziness.
zángano m. Drone (insecto). || FIG. y FAM. Lazybones, idler, loafer (holgazán). | Fool (tonto).
zangarilleja f. FAM. Sloven, slut.
zangarrear v. intr. FAM. To strum a guitar.
zangarriana f. VET. Staggers, *pl.* (modorra). || FAM. Slight recurrent ailment (achaque). || FIG. y FAM. Blues, *pl.*, sadness (tristeza).
zangarullón m. FAM. Big lazybones, lanky loafer.
zangolotear v. tr. To jiggle, to fiddle with, to shake.
— V. intr. FAM. To fidget (una persona).
— V. pr. FAM. To rattle (una puerta, etc.).
zangoloteo m. Jiggling, shaking. || FIG. y FAM. Fidgeting, stirring (de una persona). | Rattling, rattle (de una puerta, etc.).
zangolotino, na adj. FAM. Who does not act his age, childish. || *Niño zangolotino, niña zangolotina*, big baby.
zangón m. FAM. Lanky lazybones, lanky loafer.
zangotear v. intr. To fidget.
zanguanga f. FAM. Malingering, feigning illness. || FAM. *Hacer la zanguanga*, to feign illness, to malinger.
zanguango, ga adj. FAM. Idle, slack (gandul).
— M. y f. FAM. Shirker, loafer, slacker.
zanja f. Ditch, channel, trench: *zanja de desagüe*, drainage channel. || Trench (para los cimientos). || *Amer.* Ravine, gully (arroyada). || *Abrir las zanjas*, to lay the foundations.
zanjar v. tr. To dig a ditch *o* a trench in (abrir una zanja). || FIG. To settle, to clear up: *zanjó el asunto*, he settled the matter. || To surmount, to overcome, to obviate (obstáculos): *zanjar una dificultad*, to obviate a difficulty.
zanjear v. tr. *Amer.* To dig a ditch in.
zanjón m. Large ditch *o* trench.
zanquear v. intr. To waddle (andar torciendo las piernas). || To stride along (dar zancadas). || To rush about (de un lado para otro).
zanquilargo, ga adj. FAM. Long-legged, lanky.
— M. y f. FAM. Lanky person, long-legged person, spindleshanks.
zanquituerto, ta adj. FAM. Knock-kneed.
zanquivano, na adj. FAM. Spindle-legged, spindle-shanked.
Zanzíbar n. pr. m. GEOGR. Zanzibar.
zapa f. Spade (pala de zapador). || Sapping, trenching, digging (acción de zapar). || Shagreen, sharkskin (lija). || *Piel de zapa*, shagreen, sharkskin.
zapador m. MIL. Sapper.
zapallo m. *Amer.* Calabash.
zapapico m. Mattock, pickaxe.
zapar v. tr. MIL. To sap.
zaparrastrar v. intr. FAM. To let one's gown trail behind.
zaparrastroso, sa adj. FAM. V. ZARRAPASTRÓN.
zapata f. TECN. Track, shoe (de oruga). | Washer (arandela). || ARQ. Lintel. || MAR. False keel (falsa quilla). | Shoe (del ancla). || *Amer.* Socle (zócalo). || *Zapata de freno*, brake shoe, brake lining.
zapatazo m. Blow [with a shoe] (golpe). || MAR. Flapping (de una vela). || — Pl. Stamping (*sing.*) *o* pounding (*sing.*) of feet (ruido). || — *Dar zapatazos*, to stamp one's feet. || FIG. *Mandar a zapatazos*, to rule with an iron hand. | *Tratar a zapatazos*, to kick around, to treat like a dog.
zapateado m. "Zapateado" [Spanish heel-tapping dance].
zapateador, ra m. y f. "Zapateado" dancer.
zapatear v. tr. To tap with one's feet. || FIG. To tread on (pisotear). || To touch with the button of the foil (en esgrima).
— V. intr. To paw the ground (el caballo). || To thump (el conejo). || To flap (las velas). || To stamp *o* to tap one's feet (en el baile). || To dance the "zapateado."
— V. pr. FIG. y FAM. To get rid of [s.o.] (quitarse de encima). | To polish off (liquidar rápidamente). || FAM. *Saber zapateárselas*, to know how to look after o.s., to be able to take care of o.s.
zapateo m. "Zapateo", stamping *o* tapping with the feet (en el baile). || Tap dance (con música de jazz). || Pawing (del caballo).
zapatera f. Shoemaker. || Shoemaker's *o* cobbler's wife (mujer del zapatero).
zapatería f. Shoe shop (taller). || Shoe shop [U.S., shoe store] (tienda). || Shoemaking (oficio). || *Zapatería de viejo*, cobbler's, shoe shop, shoe repair shop, shoemender's.
zapatero, ra adj. Tough: *bistec zapatero*, tough steak. || Hard, underdone: *patatas zapateras*, hard potatoes.
— M. y f. Shoe seller *o* dealer (vendedor). || — M. Shoemaker (el que hace zapatos). || Shoemender, cobbler (el que los remienda). || — *Dejar zapatero*, to leave s.o. with no tricks (naipes). || *Quedarse zapatero*, to lose all the tricks (naipes). || *Zapatero a la medida*, bootmaker, shoemaker. || FIG. *¡Zapatero a tus zapatos!*, mind your own business!, the cobbler should stick at his last. || *Zapatero de viejo* or *remendón*, cobbler, shoemender.
zapateta f. Jump accompanied by a slap on the shoe.
zapatiesta f. FAM. Rumpus: *armar una zapatiesta*, to kick up a rumpus.
zapatilla f. Slipper (para estar en casa). || Shoe: *zapatilla de baile*, dancing shoe. || Slipper (de torero). || Tip (billar). || Button (del florete). || Hoof (pezuña). || TECN. Washer (arandela).
zapatillero, ra m. y f. Slipper dealer (vendedor). || Slipper manufacturer (fabricante).
zapato m. Shoe: *un par de zapatos*, a pair of shoes; *zapatos de tacón*, high-heeled shoes; *zapatos de color*, brown shoes. || — FIG. *Encontrar la horma de su zapato*, v. HORMA. | *Saber dónde le aprieta el zapato*, to know where the shoe pinches, to know one's own weaknesses.
zapatón m. FAM. Heavy shoe, clodhopper (zapato grande).
zape m. FAM. Gay, queer (afeminado).
— Interj. Shoo!, scat! (para ahuyentar a los gatos). || *¡Zape de aquí!*, get out of here!
zapear v. tr. To shoo away (gatos). || To scare off *o* away (personas).
zapotal m. Grove of sapodilla trees.
zapote m. Sapodilla (árbol). || Sapodilla plum (fruto).
zapoteco, ca adj. Zapotecan.
— M. y f. Zapotec.
zapotero m. V. ZAPOTE.
zapotillo m. BOT. Sapodilla.
zaque m. Small wineskin *o* goatskin. || FIG. y FAM. Old soak, drunk (borracho).
zaquizamí m. Attic, garret (desván). || Poky hole, cubbyhole (cuchitril).
— OBSERV. *Pl. zaquizamíes.*
zar m. Czar, tzar, tsar.
zarabanda f. MÚS. Saraband, sarabande. || FAM. Whirl, turmoil, confused rush (jaleo).
zarabandista m. y f. Person who dances, plays or composes sarabands.
zaragata f. FAM. Rumpus, row, squabble (riña). | Hubbub (confusión, jaleo, ruido).
zaragate m. *Amer.* Rogue.
zaragatero, ra adj. Quarrelsome, rowdy, troublemaking.
— M. y f. Troublemaker, rowdy person (pendenciero).
zaragatona f. BOT. Ribgrass, fleawort.
zaragocí m. Variety of yellow plum.
Zaragoza n. pr. GEOGR. Saragossa [Spain].
zaragozano, na adj./s. Saragossan. || — M. Calendar which gives meteorological forecasts.
zaragüelles m. Wide-legged overalls (calzones). || Wide-legged breeches (pantalones).
zarambeque m. Negro dance.
zaranda f. Sieve, screen (criba). || Small sieve, strainer (colador). || *Amer.* Spinning top (trompo).
zarandador, ra m. y f. Sifter.
zarandajas f. pl. FAM. Trivialities, trifles.
zarandear v. tr. To sieve, to sift (cribar): *zarandear el trigo*, to sieve the wheat. || To strain (colar). || To shake (sacudir). || To knock about, to jostle: *ser zarandeado por la multitud*, to be knocked about by the crowd. || To keep on the go (mandar de un sitio para otro).
— V. pr. To sway the hips (contonearse).
zarandeo m. Sifting, sieving (con la criba). || Straining (con el colador). || Shaking (meneo). || *Amer.* Swaying of the hips.
zarandero, ra m. y f. Sifter.

zarandillo m. Small sieve *o* screen (zaranda). || FIG. y FAM. Fidget. || FIG. y FAM. *LLevar a uno como un zarandillo*, to keep s.o. on the go.
zarape m. Sarape, serape (sarape). || FAM. Gay, queer (afeminado).
zarapito m. Curlew (ave).
zaraza f. Chintz (tela de algodón).
zarazo, za adj. *Amer.* Half-ripe (fruto).
zarcear v. tr. To clean out (las cañerías).
— V. intr. To flush out game from the undergrowth (el perro). || FIG. To rush about (ajetrearse).
zarceño, ña adj. Brambly.
zarcero adj. *Perro zarcero*, terrier.
— M. Terrier (perro).
zarceta f. Garganey (ave).
zarcillo m. Earring (pendiente). || BOT. Tendril. || Hoe (escardillo).
zarco, ca adj. Light blue: *ojos zarcos*, light blue eyes.
zarevitz m. Czarevitch, tsarevitch.
zariano, na adj. Czaristic, tsaristic.
zarigüeya f. ZOOL. Opossum.
zarina f. Czarina, tsarina.
zarismo m. Czarism, tsarism.
zarista adj. Czaristic, tsaristic.
— M. y f. Czarist, tsarist.
zarpa f. Claw, paw (de un animal). || MAR. Weighing anchor. || FIG. *Echar la zarpa a algo*, to claw at sth. (un animal), to grab sth. (una persona), to get hold of sth. (apoderarse).
zarpada f. Lash of a claw *o* a paw. || *Dar una zarpada a*, to claw *o* to lash out with the claws at.
zarpanel adj. ARQ. *Arco zarpanel*, basket-handle arch.
zarpar v. intr. MAR. To weigh anchor. || *Zarpar del puerto*, to sail out of port.
zarpazo m. Lash of a claw *o* paw. || *Dar un zarpazo*, to lash out with the claws, to claw.
zarpear v. tr. *Amer.* To bespatter, to dirty [with mud]
zarposo, sa adj. Bespattered.
zarracatería f. FAM. Insincere flattery.
zarracatín m. FAM. Bargainer, haggler.
zarrapastrón, ona o **zarrapastroso, sa** adj. FAM. Slovenly, shabby, untidy.
— M. y f. FAM. Sloven, ragamuffin, tramp.
zarria f. Leather thong *o* strap (tira de cuero).
zarza f. BOT. Blackberry bush, bramble. || *Zarra ardiente*, burning bush (en la Biblia).
zarzagán m. Cold wind (cierzo).
zarzal m. Blackberry *o* bramble patch, clump of brambles. || Bush, thicket (matorral).
zarzaleño, ña adj. [Of *o* from the] bramble.
zarzamora f. Blackberry (fruto). || Blackberry bush (zarza).
zarzaparrilla f. BOT. Sarsaparilla.
zarzaparrillar m. Sarsaparilla field.
zarzaperruna f. BOT. Dog rose (escaramujo).
zarzarrosa f. BOT. Dog rose.
zarzo m. Wattle.
zarzoso, sa adj. Brambly, covered with blackberry *o* bramble bushes.
zarzuela f. "Zarzuela" (V. OBSERV.) || CULIN. Fish dish prepared with spicy sauce.

— OBSERV. The *zarzuela* is a Spanish operetta having a spoken dialogue and usually a comic theme.

zarzuelero, ra adj. Of *o* from the "zarzuela".
— M. Author of "zarzuelas."
zarzuelista m. Author *o* composer of "zarzuelas."
¡zas! interj. Bang!, whack!, crash!
zascandil m. FAM. Scatterbrain (tarambana). | Busybody, meddler (entrometido).
zascandilear v. intr. FAM. To snoop, to pry, to meddle (curiosear): *andar zascandileando*, to be snooping around. | To idle, to waste time (vagar).
zeda f. Zed [U.S., zee] (letra).
zedilla f. Cedilla (letra antigua). || Cedilla (signo ortográfico).
zéjel m. "Zejel" [a medieval Spanish poetic composition of Mozarabic origin].
Zelanda o **Zelandia** n. pr. f. GEOGR. Zeeland. || *Nueva Zelanda*, New Zealand.
Zelandés, esa adj. Zeeland.
— M. y f. Zeelander.
zendo, da adj. Zend, Zendic.
— M. Zend (lengua).
zenit m. Zenith (cenit).
Zenón n. pr. m. Zeno.
zeolita f. MIN. Zeolite.
zepelín m. Zeppelin (dirigible).
zeta f. Zed (U.S., zee) [letra]. || Zeta (letra griega).
zeugma o **zeuma** f. GRAM. Zeugma.
zigoma m. ANAT. Zygoma (hueso).
zigomático, ca adj. ANAT. Zygomatic.
zigoto m. BIOL. Zygote.
zigzag m. Zigzag.

— OBSERV. The plural of the Spanish word *zigzag* is *zigzags* or *zigzagues*.

zigzaguear v. intr. To zigzag.
zigzagueo m. Zigzagging.
zimasa f. QUÍM. Zymase.
zinc m. Zinc (cinc).
zíngaro, ra adj./s. Gypsy, tzigane.
zipizape m. FAM. Row, scuffle, rumpus, set-to.
zircón m. Zircon.
¡zis zas! interj. Biff! baff!
ziszás m. Zigzag.
zloty m. Zloty (moneda polaca).
zoantarios m. pl. ZOOL. Zoantharia.
zoantropía f. MED. Zoanthropy.
zócalo m. ARQ. Socle (de un edificio). || Plinth, socle (pedestal). || Skirting board (en la parte inferior de una pared). || GEOL. Insular shelf. || *Amer.* Square (plaza).

— OBSERV. In certain towns and cities of Mexico the name *zócalo* denotes the centre of the "plaza" or public square, and by extension the entire square.

zocato, ta adj. Left-handed (zurdo). || Rubbery (frutas, verduras).
— M. y f. Left-handed person.
zoclo m. Clog, wooden shoe (zueco). || Overshoe (chanclo).
zoco, ca adj. Left-handed (zurdo).
— M. y f. Left-handed person (zurdo). || — M. Moroccan market place (mercado marroquí).
zodiacal adj. ASTR. Zodiacal.
zodiaco m. ASTR. Zodiac: *los signos del zodiaco*, the signs of the zodiac.
zolocho, cha adj. FAM. Simple, dozy.
— M. y f. FAM. Simpleton, dope.
zollipar v. intr. FAM. To sob.
zollipo m. FAM. Sob.
zona f. Zone: *zona glacial, templada, tórrida*, glacial, temperate, torrid zone. || Region, area: *zona vinícola*, wine-growing region. || MED. Shingles. || FIG. Area, zone: *zona de influencia*, area of influence. || — *Zona azul*, restricted parking zone. || *Zona de ensanche*, development area. || *Zona del dólar, del franco, de la libra esterlina*, dollar, franc, sterling area. || *Zona de libre cambio* or *de libre comercio*, free trade area. || *Zona edificada*, built-up area. || *Zona fronteriza*, frontier *o* border zone. || *Zonas verdes*, recreational areas, park and garden areas (en una ciudad), greenbelt (alrededor de una ciudad).
zonal adj. Zonal.
zoncear v. intr. *Amer.* To play the fool, to behave stupidly.
zoncera o **zoncería** f. *Amer.* Silliness (idiotez).
zonda f. *Amer.* Zonda.

— OBSERV. The *zonda* is a hot enervating north wind which sweeps down from the Andes over the Argentine pampas.

zonzo, za adj. *Amer.* Stupid, silly, inane (tonto). || Insipid (soso).
— M. y f. *Amer.* Silly person, fool, bore.
zoo m. Zoo (parque zoológico).
zoófago, ga adj. Zoophagous.
— M. y f. Zoophagan. || — M. pl. Zoophaga.
zoófito m. Zoophyte. || — Pl. Zoophyta.
zoofobia f. Zoophobia.
zoóforo m. ARQ. Zoophorus.
zoogeografía f. Zoogeography.
zooide adj. Zooidal.
— M. Zooid.
zoólatra adj. Zoolatrous.
— M. y f. Zoolater.
zoolatría f. Zoolatry.
zoolito m. Petrified animal, animal fossil.
zoología f. Zoology.
zoológico, ca adj. Zoological. || *Parque zoológico*, zoological garden, zoological gardens, *pl.*, zoo.
— M. Zoo.
zoólogo m. Zoologist.
zoom m. CINEM. Zoom.
zoomorfismo m. Zoomorphism.
zoopsia f. MED. Hallucination in which one sees animals.
zoospora f. BOT. Zoospore.
zoosporangio m. BOT. Zoosporangium.
zootecnia f. Zootechny.
zootécnico, ca adj. Zootechnic, zootechnical.
— M. y f. Zootechnician.
zooterapia f. Zootherapy.
zoótropo m. Zootrope.
zopas m. y f. inv. FAM. Lisper.
zope m. ZOOL. Buzzard (zopilote).
zopenco, ca adj. FAM. Daft, dopey.
— M. y f. FAM. Dope, idiot, fool.
zopilote m. ZOOL. Buzzard (ave de rapiña).
zopo, pa adj. Crippled, maimed (persona). || Crooked (mano, pie). || Clumsy (torpe).
zoquete m. Block *o* chunk of wood (de madera). || Piece of stale bread (de pan). || FIG. y FAM. Dope, blockhead (persona estúpida).
zorcico m. Basque song and dance.
zorito, ta adj. Wild. || *Paloma zorita*, V. ZURITO.
zoroástrico, ca adj./s. Zoroastrian.
zoroastrismo m. Zoroastrianism.
Zoroastro n. pr. m. Zoroaster.
zorollo adi m. *Trigo zorollo*, wheat reaped while unripe.
zorongo m. Kerchief [worn on the head]. || Bun (moño). || "Zorongo" [popular Andalusian dance].
zorra f. ZOOL. Vixen, she-fox (hembra). | Fox (macho). || Dray, truck (carro). || FIG. y FAM. Whore (prostituta). || FIG. y FAM. *Coger una zorra*, to get drunk *o* canned.

ZOOLOGÍA, *f.* — ZOOLOGY

I. Mamíferos, *m.* — Mammals.

caballo *m.*	horse
yegua *f.*	mare
mulo *m.*	mule
potro *m.*	colt, foal
asno *m.*, burro *m.*	ass, donkey
hipopótamo *m.*	hippopotamus
búfalo *m.*	buffalo
toro *m.*	bull
buey *m.*	ox
vaca *f.*	cow
ternera *f.*	calf
cerdo *m.*	pig
carnero *m.*	sheep
cabra *f.*	goat
cordero *m.*	lamb
oveja *f.*	ewe
cebra *f.*	zebra
antílope *m.*	antilope
gacela *f.*	gazelle
ciervo *m.*	deer
reno *m.*	reindeer
jirafa *f.*	giraffe
camello *m.*	camel
dromedario *m.*	dromedary
llama *f.*	llama
alpaca *f.*	alpaca
guanaco *m.*	guanaco
vicuña *f.*	vicuna
elefante *m.*	elephant
rinoceronte *m.*	rhinoceros
gato *m.*	cat
león *m.*	lion
tigre *m.*	tiger
pantera *f.*	panther
leopardo *m.*	leopard
hiena *f.*	hyena, hyaena
lince *m.*	lynx
perro *m.*	dog
lobo *m.*	wolf
zorro *m.*	fox
oso *m.*	bear
tejón *m.*	badger
comadreja *f.*	weasel
nutria *f.*	otter
ardilla *f.*	squirrel
lirón *m.*	dormouse
castor *m.*	beaver
marmota *f.*	marmot
hurón *m.*	ferret
cobayo *m.*	Guinea pig
conejo *m.*	rabbit
liebre *f.*	hare
chinchilla *f.*	chinchilla
rata *f.*	rat
ratón *m.*	mouse
mono *m.*	monkey
orangután *m.*	orangutan
chimpancé *m.*	chimpanzee
gorila *m.*	gorilla
perezoso *m.*	sloth
oso (*m.*) hormiguero	anteater
canguro *m.*	kangaroo
erizo *m.*	hedgehog
puerco espín *m.*	porcupine
topo *m.*	mole
murciélago *m.*	bat
armadillo *m.*	armadillo
ballena *f.*	whale
delfín *m.*	dolphin
marsopa *f.*	porpoise
foca *f.*	seal
morsa *f.*	walrus

II. Aves, *f.* — Birds.

gallo *m.*	cock
gallina *f.*	hen
pollo *m.*	chicken
pintada *f.*	guinea fowl
pavo *m.*	turkey
pavo (*m.*) real	peacock
pato *m.*	duck
oca *f.*, ánsar *m.*	goose
cisne *m.*	swan
ganso *m.*	gander
paloma *f.*	dove
tórtola *f.*	turtledove
pichón *m.*	pigeon
faisán *m.*	pheasant
perdiz *f.*	partridge
codorniz *f.*	quail
garza *f.*	heron
cigüeña *f.*	stork
avestruz *f.*	ostrich
chocha *f.*, becada *f.*	woodcock
agachadiza *f.*	snipe
gaviota *f.*	seagull
pelícano *m.*	pelican
martín (*m.*) pescador	kingfisher
cacatúa *f.*	cockatoo
guacamayo *m.*	macaw
ave (*f.*) de paraíso	bird of paradise
quetzal *m.*	quetzal
águila *f.*	eagle
cóndor *m.*	condor
buitre *m.*	vulture
halcón *m.*	hawk, falcon
pájaro (*m.*) carpintero	woodpecker
perico *m.*	parakeet
loro *m.*	parrot
cuclillo *m.*, cuco *m.*	cuckoo
cuervo *m.*	crow
urraca *f.*	magpie
golondrina *f.*	swallow
gorrión *m.*	sparrow
ruiseñor *m.*	nightingale
canario *m.*	canary
jilguero *m.*	goldfinch
pinzón *m.*	chaffinch
mirlo *m.*	blackbird
petirrojo *m.*	robin
chorlito *m.*	plover
estornino *m.*	starling
alondra *f.*	lark
tordo *m.*	thrush
vencejo *m.*	swift
curruca *f.*	whitethroat
colibrí *m.*	hummingbird
pingüino *m.*, pájaro (*m.*) bobo	penguin
corneja *f.*	scops owl
lechuza *f.*, búho *m.*	owl

III. Reptiles (*m.*) y batracios, *m.* — Reptiles and batrachians.

serpiente *f.*	snake
culebra *f.*	grass snake
boa *f.*	boa
pitón *m.*	python
víbora *f.*	viper, adder
naja *f.*, cobra *f.*	cobra
crótalo *m.*, serpiente (*f.*) de cascabel	rattlesnake
lagarto *m.*	lizard
lagartija *f.*	wall lizard
camaleón *m.*	chameleon
salamandra *f.*	salamander
tritón *m.*	triton, newt
cocodrilo *m.*	crocodile
caimán *m.*	caiman, cayman
aligátor *m.*	alligator
tortuga *f.*	tortoise; turtle
carey *m.*	sea turtle
rana *f.*	frog
sapo *m.*	toad

IV. Peces, *m.* — Fish.

carpa *f.*	carp
lucio *m.*	pike
perca *f.*	perch
anguila *f.*	eel
trucha *f.*	trout
salmón *m.*	salmon
boquerón *m.*	anchovy
atún *m.*, bonito *m.*	tunny, tuna
bacalao *m.*	cod
lenguado *m.*	sole
platija *f.*	plaice
merluza *f.*	hake
caballa *f.*	mackerel
pescadilla *f.*	whiting
arenque *m.*	herring
besugo *m.*	sea bream
rodaballo *m.*	turbot
sardina *f.*	sardine
salmonete *m.*	red mullet, surmullet
raya *f.*	ray; skate
tiburón *m.*	shark
esturión *m.*	sturgeon

V. Insectos, *m.* — Insects.

mosca *f.*	fly
tábano *m.*	horsefly, gadfly
pulga *f.*	flea
piojo *m.*	louse
araña *f.*	spider
mosquito *m.*	mosquito
anofeles *m. inv.*	anopheles
mariquita *f.*	ladybird
cigarra *f.*	cicada
grillo *m.*	cricket
langosta *f.*	locust
saltamontes *m. inv.*	grasshopper
manta (*f.*) religiosa	praying mantis
abeja *f.*	bee
avispa *f.*	wasp
abejorro *m.*	bumble bee
escarabajo *m.*	beetle
oruga *f.*	caterpillar
hormiga *f.*	ant
ciempiés *m. inv.*	centipede
mariposa *f.*	butterfly
libélula *f.*	dragonfly
luciérnaga *f.*	glowworm, firefly
polilla *f.*	moth
chinche *f.*	bug
cucaracha *f.*	cockroach
comején *m.*	termite
tarántula *f.*	tarantula
alacrán *m.*, escorpión *m.*	scorpion

VI. Moluscos (*m.*) y crustáceos, *m.* — Molluscs and crustaceans.

caracol *m.*	snail
jibia *f.*	cuttlefish
calamar *m.*	squid
pulpo *m.*	octopus
percebe *m.*	goose barnacle
almeja *f.*	clam
venera *f.*	scallop
mejillón *m.*	mussel
berberecho *m.*	cockle
ostra *f.*	oyster
erizo (*m.*) de mar	sea urchin
langosta *f.*	spiny *o* rock lobster
bogavante *m.*	lobster
cangrejo *m.*	crab
centollo *m.*	spider crab
langostino *m.*	large prawn
cigala *f.*	Norway lobster
gamba *f.*	prawn
camarón *m.*, quisquilla *f.*	shrimp
cangrejo (*m.*) de río	crayfish

VII. Gusanos, *m.* — Worms.

lombriz (*f.*) de tierra	earthworm
sanguijuela *f.*	leech
tenia *f.*	tapeworm
triquina *f.*	trichina

zorrastrón, ona adj. Sly, foxy, cunning (astuto). — M. Sly fox, sly old fox (hombre). || — F. Sly *o* crafty woman (mujer).

zorrear v. intr. FAM. To use guile, to resort to trickery (ser astuto). | To lead a life of debauchery (llevar una vida disoluta).

zorrera f. Fox hole, earth (madriguera). || FIG. Smoke-filled room. | Drowsiness, heaviness (amodorramiento).

zorrería f. FAM. Foxiness, slyness, cunning (astucia). | Dirty trick, sly trick (cochinada).

zorrero, ra adj. Slow-sailing (barco). || Last (que va el último). || FIG. Foxy, sly, cunning (astuto). || *Perro zorrero*, fox terrier.

zorrilla f. Rail inspection car.

zorrillo m. Fox cub.

zorrillo o **zorrino** m. *Amer.* ZOOL. Skunk.

zorro m. Fox, he-fox (raposo). || Fox [fur], foxskin (piel). || FIG. y FAM. Old fox, cunning fellow (hombre astuto). | Idler, lazybones (perezoso). || *Amer.* ZOOL. Skunk (mofeta). || — Pl. Duster (*sing.*) [made of strips of cloth or leather] (sacudidor). || FIG. y FAM. *Hacerse el zorro*, to play dumb.

zorrón m. FAM. Old fox, cunning fellow (hombre astuto). | Drunkenness [U.S., drunk] (borrachera).

zorrona f. FAM. Whore (prostituta).

zorronglón, ona adj. FAM. Grumbling, complaining, grumpy.
— M. y f. FAM. Grumbler, complainer (refunfuñador).

zorruno, na adj. Fox-like, foxy, vulpine. || FIG. y FAM. *Oler a zorruno*, to smell of old socks *o* of sweaty feet.

zorullo m. FAM. Turd.

zorzal m. ZOOL. Thrush (ave). || FIG. Old fox (hombre astuto). || *Zorzal marino*, black wrasse (pez).

zote adj. Doltish, dull, dopey (fam.).
— M. y f. Dolt, dullard, dope (fam.).

zozobra f. Shipwreck, capsizing (naufragio). || Sinking (hundimiento). || Very bad weather (mal tiempo). || FIG. Anxiety, anguish: *vivir en una perpetua zozobra*, to live in constant anxiety.

zozobrar v. intr. MAR. To be shipwrecked, to capsize (naufragar). | To be in danger (estar en peligro). | To sink, to go down (irse a pique). || FIG. To be ruined (unos planes). | To collapse, to be ruined

(negocio). | To be worried *o* anxious, to worry (estar intranquilo).
zuavo m. Zouave.
zueco m. Clog, sabot, wooden shoe (de madera). || Galosh (de cuero con suela de madera).
Zuinglio n. pr. Zwingli (Zwinglio).
zulacar v. tr. TECN. To cover with lute.
zulaque m. TECN. Lute (betún).
zulú adj./s. Zulu.
Zululandia n. pr. f. GEOGR. Zululand.
zulla f. Sulla, French honeysuckle. || Excrement.
zullarse v. pr. FAM. To dirty o.s.
zumacal m. Sumach field.
zumaque m. BOT. Sumach, sumac.
zumaya f. ZOOL. Night heron (ave zancuda). | Tawny owl (autillo). | Nightjar (chotacabras).
zumba f. Bell [worn by the lead mule or ox] (cencerro grande). || FIG. Teasing, joking (broma). || *Amer.* Beating, thrashing (tunda).
zumbador, ra adj. Buzzing, humming.
— M. Buzzer (aparato).
zumbar v. intr. To buzz, to hum, to ring: *me zumban los oídos*, my ears are buzzing. || To buzz, to hum (los insectos). || To purr (un motor). || — FIG. y FAM. *Ir zumbando*, to be streaking *o* whizzing *o* zooming along (un coche, etc.). | *Salir zumbando*, to shoot off, to zoom off. | *¡Zumbando!*, make it snappy! | *Zumbarle a uno*, to give s.o. a beating *o* a thrashing. — V. tr. FAM. To land, to fetch, to give: *zumbarle a uno una bofetada*, to land s.o. a slap *o* a smack. | | To rag, to tease (tomar el pelo). | To make fun of (burlarse de). || *Amer.* To throw, to fling (arrojar). — V. pr. FAM. To hit one another, to lash out, to let fly (pegarse). | To laugh at, to make fun of (burlarse).
zumbido m. Buzzing, humming, ringing: *zumbido de oídos*, buzzing of the ears, ringing in the ears. || Buzz, buzzing, hum, humming (insectos). || Purr, purring (motor). || Hum, humming, whir, whirring (peonza).
zumbo m. V. ZUMBIDO.
zumbón, ona adj. FAM. Joking, teasing (burlón). | Funny (divertido).
— M. y f. FAM. Clown, joker, tease.
zumo m. Juice: *zumo de tomate*, tomato juice. || Juice, squash: *zumo de naranja, de limón*, orange, lemon squash. || FIG. Profit (provecho). || — FIG. *Sacarle el zumo a uno*, to bleed s.o. dry. || *Zumo de cepas* or *de parras*, wine.
zunchar v. tr. To fasten with a metal hoop *o* band.
zuncho m. Metal hoop *o* band (anillo de metal).
zupia f. Dregs, *pl.*, lees, *pl.*, sediment of wine (poso). || Muddy *o* cloudy wine (vino turbio).
zurcido m. Darning, mending (acción de zurcir). || Mend, darn: *un zurcido en la chaqueta*, a mend in the jacket. || FIG. *Un zurcido de mentiras*, a tissue of lies.
zurcidor, ra m. y f. Darner, mender. || Fine-drawer (de zurcido invisible). || — FIG. *Zurcidora de voluntades*, bawd, procuress, go-between. | *Zurcidor de voluntades*, pimp, procurer, go-between.
zurcidura f. V. ZURCIDO.
zurcir v. tr. To darn, to mend: *zurcir calcetines*, to darn socks. || To fine-draw (de modo invisible). || To sew up (lo muy roto). || FIG. To join *o* to put together (unir). | To concoct, to spin (mentiras). || — FIG. y FAM. *¡Anda y que te zurzan!*, go jump in the lake!, go to hell! | FIG. *Zurcir voluntades*, to pander.
zurdería f. Left-handedness.
zurdo, da adj. Left: *mano zurda*, left hand. || Left-handed (persona). || FIG. y FAM. *No ser zurdo*, to have one's head screwed on, to be no fool.
— M. y f. Left-handed person, left-hander, southpaw (fam.) || — F. Left hand (mano).
zurear v. intr. To coo, to bill and coo (paloma).
zureo m. Cooing, billing and cooing (arrullo).
zurito, ta adj. Wild. || *Paloma zurita*, rock pigeon, rock dove (de color apizarrado), wood pigeon, ringdove (torcaz).
zuro, ra adj. Wild (paloma).
— M. Cob (del maíz).
zurra f. TECN. Currying, dressing, tanning (del cuero). | Curriery (arte del zurrador). || FIG. y FAM. Beating, thrashing (paliza). | Brawl, scuffle (contienda).
zurrador, ra m. Currier, tanner, dresser.
zurrapa f. Lees, *pl.*, dregs, *pl.*, sediment (poso). || Grounds, *pl.* (del café). || FIG. y FAM. Trash, rubbish (cosa despreciable).

— OBSERV. This word is frequently used in the plural.

zurrapelo m. FAM. Dressing down: *dar un zurrapelo a uno*, to give s.o. a dressing down.
zurrapiento, ta o **zurraposo, sa** adj. Full of dregs, muddy (que tiene posos). || Turbid (turbio).
zurrar v. tr. To curry, to dress, to tan (el cuero). || FIG. y FAM. To beat up, to give a thrashing *o* a beating, to lay into (dar una paliza). | To whip, to flagellate (con azotes). | To give [s.o.] a tongue-lashing (reprender). || FIG. y FAM. *Zurrarle a uno la badana*, to tan s.o.'s hide (pegar), to give s.o. a dressing down (con palabras).
— V. pr. FAM. To wet o.s. (irse del vientre o tener temor). || FAM. *Zurrarse la badana*, to thump each other, to lay into each other.
zurriaga f. Whip (látigo).
zurriagar v. tr. To whip, to flog, to lash, to flagellate.
zurriagazo m. Lash [of a whip]. || FIG. Stroke of bad luck, blow, mishap (desgracia).
zurriago m. Whip. || *Zurriago oculto* or *escondido*, hunt the thimble (juego).
zurribanda f. FAM. Beating, thrashing (zurra). | Scuffle, brawl, rumpus (pendencia).
zurriburri m. FAM. Despicable type, scum (sujeto vil). | Shady bunch (grupo). | Uproar, turmoil, confusion (jaleo).
zurrido m. Whack [with a stick] (golpe). || Grating noise (sonido).
zurrón m. Shepherd's pouch *o* bag (bolsa de pastor). || Leather bag (bolsa de cuero). || Husk [of certain fruits] (cáscara).
zurullo m. Lump (grumo). || FAM. Turd (excremento).
zurupeto m. FAM. Unregistered broker (corredor de bolsa). || Unauthorized notary (notario intruso).
zutano, na m. y f. FAM. What's-his-name. || *Fulano, Mengano y Zutano*, Tom, Dick and Harry.

— OBSERV. The noun *zutano* is only used after the words *fulano* and *mengano* to designate a third person whose name is unknown.

¡zuzo! interj. Shoo!, scat! (para espantar al perro).
zuzón m. Groundsel.
zwinglianismo m. REL. Zwinglianism.
zwingliano, na adj./s. Zwinglian.
Zwinglio n. pr. m. Zwingli.

SUMMARY OF SPANISH GRAMMAR

THE SPANISH ALPHABET

The Spanish alphabet is made up of the following 28 letters:

a	**b**	**c**	**ch**	**d**	**e**	**f**	**g**	**h**	**i**	**j**	**k**
a	be	ce	che	de	e	efe	ge	hache	i	jota	ka
l	**ll**	**m**	**n**	**ñ**	**o**	**p**	**q**	**r**	**s**	**t**	
ele	elle	eme	ene	eñe	o	pe	cu	erre	ese	te	
u	**v**	**x**	**y**	**z**							
u	uve	equis	i griega	zeta							

Note: The Spanish alphabet contains three letters which are not found in the English alphabet: **ch** (che), **ll** (elle), **ñ** (eñe). The letter **w** (uve doble *or* ve doble) exists in Spanish only in words of foreign origin, and is therefore not considered part of the Spanish alphabet. All Spanish letters are feminine in gender (*una s mayúscula*, a capital s; *la jota*, the "j").

PRONUNCIATION

The Spanish-English half of this dictionary contains no phonetic transcription of the Spanish for the simple reason that Spanish spelling is an exact reflection of the pronunciation of the language. The pronunciation of each individual letter in Spanish is subject to certain strict rules (see below), and a word is pronounced simply by adding together the sounds of the individual letters which make up the word.
Every letter is pronounced in Spanish with the exception of the inaspirate **h** as in *hacha* [ˈatʃa], and the **u** in the groups *-qu-*, *-gue-*, *-qui-*, which is silent unless it bears a diaeresis (*guerra* [ˈgerra], *paragüero* [paraˈgwero]).

CONSONANTS

Consonants are never doubled in Spanish, except **c, r,** and **n** (a**cc**ión, ca**rr**o, i**nn**ovación). **Ll** is considered a letter in its own right.
1. **b** and **v**. — These two letters represent the same sound in Spanish. They are less explosive than the English **b**.
— In an initial position and after certain consonants, especially *m* and *n*, the sound is similar to that of the English **b** (**b**rillo, **v**aca, con**v**oy).
— Elsewhere the sound is softer. It is a bilabial fricative, similar to the English **v** but pronounced between the upper and lower lip rather than between the lower lip and the upper teeth (a**v**e, la**b**or).
2. **c.** — Before *e* or *i* it is pronounced like the **th** in *thirst* (**c**iudad, **c**eguera). In certain regions (See SESEO) this **c** is pronounced as **s**.
— Elsewhere it is like the hard **c** in *cat* (**c**as**c**o, lo**c**ura, a**c**to).
Note that words like *acción*, *reducción* contain both sounds, the **cc** being pronounced *kth* [kθ].
3. **ch.** — Like the English **ch** [tʃ] in *church* (**c**o**ch**e, mu**ch**a**ch**o).
4. **d.** — In an initial position and after *l* or *n* the sound is similar to that of the English **d**, but pronounced with the tip of the tongue touching the back of the upper front teeth (**d**ebo, con**d**e, cal**d**o).
— Elsewhere the sound is similar to that of the **th** [ð] in *though* (ar**d**uo, cua**d**ra, bo**d**a). This sound varies in intensity and is particularly weak in the verb ending *-ado* and at the end of certain words where it is often scarcely perceptible (ciuda**d**, Madri**d**).
5. **f.** — Like the English **f** in *for* (**f**atal, o**f**erta).
6. **g.** — Before *e* or *i* like the guttural **ch** in Scottish *loch* (**g**estión, ele**g**ir).
In an initial position or after a nasal consonant the **g** is like the hard English **g** in *gate* (**g**arbo, pon**g**o). In other positions the pronunciation is basically similar to this hard **g**, with the difference that the back of the tongue does not quite touch the velum, making the sound more fricative than occlusive (a**g**ua, la**g**o, al**g**o).
7. **h.** — Generally a mute letter, except in certain regions such as Andalusia, where it is sometimes aspirate, and in certain exceptional cases such as the words **h**olgorio, **h**ipido, where the sound is similar to that of the Spanish **j**. In the great majority of words, however, the **h** is mute (**h**ombre, **h**eno).
8. **j.** — Like the guttural **ch** in Scottish *loch* (o**j**o, in**j**erto, pa**j**a).
9. **k.** — Pronounced as in English and found only in words of foreign origin (**k**ilo).
10. **l.** — Like the English **l** (**l**obo, o**l**mo, paño**l**, per**l**a).
11. **ll.** — Somewhat similar to the **lli** in *million* or the [-lj-] sound in *failure* [ˈfeiljə*], but with the two elements, *l* and *y*, pronounced so closely as to become one sound (va**ll**e, **ll**orar, **ll**amar). See YEÍSMO.
12. **m.** — Like the English **m** (**m**ár**m**ol, a**m**ar).
13. **n.** — Pronounced as in English, but with the tip of the tongue touching the back of the upper front teeth (**n**o, cá**n**dido, comú**n**).
— Before hard *c* and *g* and before *j* and soft *g* the Spanish **n** tends to nasalize the preceding vowel and is itself pronounced like the **n** in the English words *song* and *thank* (co**n**goja, ca**n**je).
— Before a bilabial consonant (*b, v*) the sound of the **n** approaches that of the **m** (co**n**vidar).
14. **ñ.** — Pronounced like the **ni** in *onion* (**ñ**ame, ni**ñ**o).
15. **p.** — Slightly less explosive than the English **p**, but more explosive than the English **b** (**p**ara, com**p**rar).
16. **q.** — Found only in the groups *-que* and *-qui* in which the two letters *q* and *u* together have the sound of the English **k** (**q**uedar [keˈðar], **q**uitar [kiˈtar]).
17. **r** and **rr.** — The Spanish **r** is always "rolled" or "trilled", the tip of the tongue vibrating against the hard palate.
— Between two vowels or after a consonant other than *l, n, s,* a single **r** is pronounced with only one "trill".
— In an initial position, and after *l, n,* or *s*, the **r** requires two or three "trills", as does the double **r** (**rr**) whatever its position.
Note: The **rr** may never be split at the end of a line in written Spanish.
18. **s.** — Similar to the English **s** in *soap* (pa**s**o, e**s**perar).
Note: Only words borrowed from other languages begin with **s** followed by a consonant in Spanish. Such words are usually pronounced as if there were an *e* before the **s** (starter [esˈtarter]).
19. **t.** — Slightly less aspirate than in English, and with the tip of the tongue against the back of the upper front teeth (**t**on**t**o, con**t**ra).
20. **v.** — See **b**.
21. **w.** — Broadly speaking the **w** is pronounced like the **v** in Spanish. In certain foreign words the sound is that of the Spanish **u** (**W**aterloo, **w**hisky).
22. **x.** — Similar to the **ks** in *thinks*, although the *k* sound is very weak and tends to disappear completely when this letter precedes a consonant (é**x**ito [ˈeksito], e**x**poner [expoˈner]).
23. **y.** — As a consonant is stronger than the English **y** in *yonder*.
24. **z.** — Pronounced like the **th** [θ] in *think*.
Note: This letter is not used before *e* or *i*, except in certain words of foreign origin and in the name of the letter itself (zeta). This implies the substitution of *c* for *z* in certain verb forms and in the plural of words ending in **z** (pe**z**, pe**c**es; empe**z**ar, empe**c**emos).

VOWELS

Spanish vowels are pure sounds, the position of the mouth remaining the same throughout the pronunciation of the vowel. They are pronounced clearly even in unstressed positions, unlike English vowels, and are not subject to diphthongization (e.g. *lumbago* in English [lʌmˈbeigəu], in Spanish [lumˈbago]).
1. **a.** — An open vowel, similar to but shorter than the **a** in the English *father*. The sound is like the Northern English **a** in *hat*.
2. **e.** — Pronounced like the first **e** in *element*.
3. **i.** — A sound shorter than the **ee** in *seen*, and longer than the **i** in *hit*.
4. **o.** — Similar to the **o** in *hot*.
5. **u.** — Similar to the **oo** in *boot*.
Note: The **u** is mute in the groups *-que*, *-qui* (q**u**erer, eq**u**ipo), and also in the groups *-gue*, and *-gui* (g**u**erra, g**u**itarra), unless it bears a diaeresis (ag**ü**ero).
6. **y.** — Pronounced like the Spanish **i** at the end of a word and when it stands alone as a conjunction. In certain Latin American countries, especially Argentina, Chile and Uruguay, this letter is pronounced like the **si** in *decision*.

DIPHTHONGS AND TRIPHTHONGS

A *diphthong* is one syllable made up of two vowels each of which conserves its own sound. In speaking or writing Spanish one must take care never to divide a diphthong. Spanish diphthongs contain either one strong vowel (**a, e, o**) and one weak vowel (**u, i** and final **y**), e.g. **ai, au; ei, eu; oi, ou; ia, ie, io; ua, ue, uo,** or two weak vowels (**iu, ui**). Unless otherwise indicated by a written accent, the stress automatically falls on the strong vowel if there is one, or on the final vowel of the diphthong if both are weak (c**ai**go, g**ua**nte, r**ui**do).
A triphthong (three vowels in the same syllable) is always formed in Spanish by a strong vowel placed between two weak vowels (**iai, iei; uai, uei**). The stress falls on the strong vowel (no os r**iái**s).
Note: Two strong vowels which occur together are considered as two separate syllables and as such conform to the following rules for tonic stress. In order to put the stress on a vowel other than that on which it would naturally fall, it is necessary to mark the stressed vowel with a written accent (país).

TONIC STRESS AND THE WRITTEN ACCENT

The stress falls on the **penultimate syllable** if the word ends in *a vowel*, *-n* or *-s* (escribo, es**cri**bes, es**cri**ben).

The stress falls on the **final syllable** if the word ends in a *consonant* other than -n or -s or in *y* (agili**dad**, man**tel**, a**mor**, Para**guay**).

Any deviation from the above rules is indicated by means of a written accent (**ár**bol, can**ción**, jabalí), even if the stressed letter is a capital (**Á**frica).

A written accent on the *u* or *i* in a diphthong changes the diphthong into two separate syllables (descon**fío**, ata**úd**). When an accent is needed to stress a syllable containing a diphthong or a triphthong, it must be placed over the strong vowel (averi**guáis**, tam**bién**).

In general the stress remains on the same syllable in the plural as in the singular (esta**ción**, esta**cio**nes). It may therefore be necessary to add or remove a written accent according to the above rules. There are three exceptions (**ré**gimen, re**gí**menes; ca**rác**ter, carac**te**res; es**pé**cimen, espe**cí**menes).

Note: The written accent is also used to distinguish between words which are spelt alike but have different grammatical functions, such as the article *el* and the pronoun *él*, the conjunction *si* and the adverb or the reflexive *sí*, the pronoun *tú* and the possessive adjective *tu*, the conjunction *mas* and the adverb *más*, the adjective *solo* and the adverb *sólo*, the demonstrative adjectives *este*, *esta*, etc. and the demonstrative pronouns *éste*, *ésta*, etc., the relative pronouns *que*, *quien*, etc. and the interrogative and exclamative pronouns *qué*, *quién*, etc., *dé*, 1st and 3rd person of the present subjunctive of the verb "dar", and the preposition *de*, *sé*, 1st person present indicative of "saber" and 2nd person singular of the imperative of "ser", and the reflexive pronoun *se*.

The first element of a compound word is written without an accent (*decimosexto*), unless the word is an adverb formed by an adjective and the adverbial suffix **-mente** (*fácilmente*) or two adjectives joined by a hyphen (*histórico-crítico*).

SPELLING RULES ESTABLISHED BY THE SPANISH ACADEMY IN 1952

Words ending in **-oo** have no written accent (*Feijoo*).

The infinitive ending in **-uir** has no written accent (*huir*).

Monosyllabic verb forms have no written accent (*fue*, *fui*, *dio*, *vio*).

Other monosyllables (*ni*) bear no written accent, except to avoid confusion with similar words (*si*, conjunction, *sí* adverb).

Accents are not added to foreign names unless they have passed into the Spanish language under a hispanicized form.

CAPITAL LETTERS

Capitals are very seldom used in Spanish. Nouns and adjectives of nationality, the days of the week, the months, titles and names of society members or doctrine followers are always written with a small initial letter (*un argentino, la bandera mexicana, martes, febrero, el duque de Rivas, los laboristas*).

THE ARTICLE

	DEFINITE ARTICLE		INDEFINITE ARTICLE	
	singular	*plural*	*singular*	*plural*
MASCULINE	el	los	un	unos
FEMININE	la	las	una	unas

The definite article

The prepositions *a* and *de* combine with the masculine singular definite article *el* to give **al** and **del** respectively (*al chico, del hombre* but *a los chicos, de la(s) mujer(es)*). Immediately before a feminine singular noun beginning with stressed *a* or *ha* the definite article *la* is replaced by **el** (*el agua, el hambre*). Descriptive adjectives take the usual feminine endings (*el agua fría*). The article **la** is used before unstressed *a* or *ha*, and also before feminine proper nouns beginning with stressed *a* or *ha* (*la antítesis, la Ángela, La Haya*).

The definite article is used more frequently in Spanish than in English:

— when the noun is qualified (*la Andalucía oriental*, eastern Andalusia; *la España de la posguerra*, postwar Spain; *la Europa del siglo veinte*, twentieth-century Europe).

— with most names of rivers, seas and mountains.

— before titles (*el rey Arturo*, King Arthur; *el doctor Pérez*, Doctor Pérez; *llame al teniente García*, call Lieutenant García; *el Presidente Roosevelt*, President Roosevelt; *el señor Hernández*, Mr. Hernández; *la señora de Hernández*, Mrs. Hernández; *la señora ha salido*, madam is out), except with *don, doña, santo, santa* (*me lo dijo don Ramón*; *Santa Bárbara*), in direct address (*¿Ud. qué opina, doctor Pérez?*; *buenas tardes, señora*), when the title is in apposition (*el señor X, presidente del club*; *el presidente del club, señor X*), before foreign titles such as Herr, Lord, etc.

— with parts of the body and articles of clothing where in English the possessive adjective is frequently used (*levantó la mano*, he raised his hand; *llevaba la chaqueta en el brazo*, he carried his jacket over his arm). The idea of possession is often conveyed by a weak object pronoun (*me lavé la cara*, I washed my face).

Note the use of the singular in Spanish (*se pusieron la chaqueta*, they put on their jackets).

— in certain expressions of time (*eran las cinco*, it was five o'clock; *es la hora de cenar*, it is dinner time; *se fue el jueves y volvió el domingo*, he left on Thursday and came back on Sunday; *los domingos se aburría*, he used to get bored on Sundays; *la semana que viene*, next week; *el mes, el año, el jueves pasado*, last month, year, Thursday).

— with the seasons (*cuando llegó el invierno*, when winter arrived). After *en* the article is not essential (*en [el] invierno*).

— with certain institutions (*la cárcel, la ciudad, el colegio, el instituto, el mercado, la universidad*).

— with nouns used generically (*los profesores están mal pagados*, teachers are underpaid; *el azúcar es dulce*, sugar is sweet).

— before terms of quantity (*una libra la docena*, a pound a dozen).

— before infinitives (*el comer*, eating).

— to express a percentage (*el diez por ciento*, ten percent).

The names of countries are not generally preceded by the definite article. Those which usually require the article are *la Argentina, el Brasil, el Canadá, la China, el Ecuador, la India, el Japón, el Paraguay, el Perú, el Uruguay*. In case of doubt, however, it is advisable to omit the article with the name of a country.

The definite article is omitted:

— before an unqualified name of a country (*España, México*), with the exceptions mentioned above.

— before certain words (*casa, caza, misa, palacio, paseo, pesca, presidio*) when used with verbs of motion.

— between the name and number of a ruler (*Enrique cuatro*).

The indefinite article

Before feminine nouns beginning with stressed *a* or *ha* the singular indefinite article *una* is replaced by **un** (*un hacha, un ala, un alma*, but *una alumna*).

The plural forms *unos* and *unas* mean *some*, although the English *some* is frequently omitted in Spanish (*unos guantes preciosos*, some lovely gloves; *compré pan también*, I bought some bread too).

Unos and *unas* also indicate approximate quantity (*unos diez días*, about ten days; *tendrá unos cuarenta años*, he must be about forty).

The indefinite article, which is used less in Spanish than in English, is omitted:

— with *ciento* (a hundred), *cierto* (a certain), *igual* (such a), *medio* (half a), *mil* (a thousand), *otro* (another), *semejante* (such a), *tal* (such a), *tan* (such a).

— before an unqualified noun indicating rank, occupation or nationality used after the verbs *ser* or *parecer* (*era oficial de marina*, he was a naval officer; *quiere ser doctor*, he wants to be a doctor). If the noun is qualified the article is used (*es un doctor excelente*, he is an excellent doctor).

— before most nouns in apposition (*Paraguay, país que...*)

— before an unqualified noun dependent on a negative (*no tengo coche*, I haven't got a car; *sin chaqueta ni corbata*, without a jacket or tie; *no dijo palabra*, he did not say a word). The use of the indefinite article in such cases adds emphasis (*no tiene un coche sino tres*, he hasn't got one car, but three; *no dijo ni una palabra*, he did not say a single word).

— after *qué* (*¡qué mujer más guapa!*, what a lovely woman!).

Note: The indefinite article is used in Spanish before an abstract noun followed by a qualifying adjective (*reinaba un silencio total*, total silence reigned).

The English construction *a shirt and tie*, omitting the second article, is impossible in Spanish; the article must be repeated (*una camisa y una corbata*).

The neuter article *lo* serves to substantivize adjectives, adverbs and participles (*lo interesante del caso*, the interesting thing; *lo dicho*, what has been said; *lo antes posible*, as soon as possible). It also intensifies adjectives and adverbs in the construction *lo... que* (*por lo inteligente que es*, because he is so intelligent). [See LO.]

THE NOUN

GENDER

Apart from the straightforward masculine and feminine, the following genders are found in the Spanish language: **ambiguo** which denotes a word that can be either masculine or feminine (*el mar, la mar*), **común** which applies to nouns that change gender according to the sex of the being they represent (*el joven, la joven*), **epiceno** which applies to words having only one form and gender for both the male and the female of the species (*el leopardo, la perdiz*). To distinguish between the male and the female in this case one must add "macho" or "hembra" respectively (*el leopardo hembra*).

Masculine nouns:

— Those ending in **-o** (except *la mano, la moto, la foto, la dinamo, la radio, la nao, la seo*).
— Those ending in **-or** (except *la flor, la coliflor, la labor, la sor*).
— Names of men, male animals, jobs and titles concerning men, seas, rivers, mountains, trees, metals, languages, days, months, colours, and infinitives used as nouns.

Feminine nouns:

— Those ending in **-a** (except *el día, el albacea, el mapa, el monarca, el Papa, el patriarca, el planeta, el cometa, el poeta, el tranvía*, words of Greek origin ending in *-ma*, such as *el diploma, el problema, el idioma*, words ending in *-ista*, such as *dentista, turista*, which can be masculine or feminine, and words usually denoting male beings, such as *el guardia, el cura*).
— Those ending in **-ción** (*la canción*), **-sión** (*la profesión*), **-d** (*la verdad, la red, la virtud*), except *el almud, el alud, el ardid, el ataúd, el césped, el laúd, el sud, el talmud*.
— Names of female beings, jobs and titles concerning women, and the letters of the alphabet.

FORMATION OF THE FEMININE

The general rules are as follows:

for masculine nouns ending in **-o**, replace the **-o** by **-a** (*el abuelo, la abuela; el gato, la gata*);
for masculine nouns ending in a consonant, add **-a** (*el director, la directora; el león, la leona*);
for masculine nouns ending in **-ante, -ente, -ote**, replace the final **-e** by **-a** (*el confidente, la confidenta*);
other feminine ending are **-esa** (*el conde, la condesa*), **-isa** (*el poeta, la poetisa*), **-triz** (*el actor, la actriz*);
some nouns have a completely different feminine equivalent (*hombre, mujer*).

FORMATION OF THE PLURAL

The general rules are as follows:

for words ending in an **unstressed vowel** or a **stressed -e** add **-s** (*los niños, los cafés*);
for words ending in a **consonant, -y** or a **stressed vowel** other than *-e*, add **-es** (*las paredes, los reyes, los alelíes*). There are numerous exceptions in this category, such as *mamás, papás, sofás, dominós*. Note also that, in words ending in **-z**, the **-z** changes to **-c** before the ending **-es** (*voz, voces; luz, luces*);
for words ending in **-s**, which are monosyllabic or stressed on the final syllable, add **-es** (*mes, meses: inglés, ingleses*);
words ending in **-s** or **-x**, which are not stressed on the final syllable, have the same form in the plural as in the singular (*las crisis; los fénix*). [See TONIC STRESS AND THE WRITTEN ACCENT above].

DIMINUTIVES AND AUGMENTATIVES

The use of diminutive and augmentative suffixes is widespread in Spanish. More often than not they indicate the favourable or unfavourable disposition of the user. They are added to nouns and adjectives, the same rules applying to both.
The general rules for the formation of DIMINUTIVES are as follows:

WORD ENDINGS	SUFFIXES	EXAMPLES
-a, -o, consonant (except **-n** or **-r**)	-ito, a -illo, a -uelo, a	cas*ita* cartel*illo* moz*uela*
-e, -n, -r	-cito, a -cillo, a -zuelo, a	nube*cita* cancion*cilla* pastor*zuelo*
monosyllables, words containing a diphthong	-ecito, a -ezuelo, a	pan*ecito* rey*ezuelo*
monosyllables ending in a vowel	-cecito, a -cecillo, a -cezuelo, a	pie*cecito*

The forms **-ito, -cito, -ecito** and **-cecito** are by far the most common and usually suggest endearment as well as smallness. The suffixes **-uelo, -zuelo, -ezuelo, -cezuelo** are often used with pejorative connotations (*mujerzuela*).
The suffixes **-ico, -ín, -ino, -iño** also exist and are used to varying degrees in different regions.
AUGMENTATIVE SUFFIXES are used to a lesser extent than diminutive suffixes, and are often pejorative. They often suggest clumsiness or coarseness.
The commonest augmentative suffix is **-ón, -ona** (*solterón, solterona*). Some others are **-azo, a; -acho, a; -achón, ona; -ote, -a** (*manaza, populacho, corpachón, librote*).
Many augmentatives and diminutives derived in this way have become nouns in their own right (*la silla; el sillín; el sillón*).
Other suffixes worth mentioning here are **-azo** (*cañonazo*) and **-ada** (*pedrada*), which mean *blow* or *shot*, and **-al, -aje, -ar, -edo, -eda** which indicate a plantation or an area where a certain plant abounds, and also a place covered with or abundant in a certain thing (*pedregal*, stony ground; *ramaje*, branches; *olivar*, olive grove; *viñedo*, vineyard; *arboleda*, copse).

THE ADJECTIVE

POSITION OF ADJECTIVES

The position of adjectives in Spanish is a complicated subject, but the following outline of basic principles should prove helpful.
1. Adjectives which describe the noun, distinguishing it from others in its class, are usually placed after it (*un libro rojo; una casa enorme; una pregunta indiscreta*). They are called descriptive adjectives.
2. Adjectives which limit rather than describe are placed before the noun. This category includes the cardinal numbers (*once jugadores*), adjectives of quantity such as *mucho, poco, demasiado, tanto, varios, cuanto*, demonstrative and possessive adjectives (*este profesor; mi lápiz*), *cada, demás, mero, otro, tal*.
3. Ordinal numbers usually precede the noun (*el primer punto*, the first point, though *el punto primero* is also possible; *su último hijo*, his youngest son).
4. The following common adjectives frequently precede the noun: *bueno, malo, nuevo, viejo, joven, pequeño, hermoso*, though this is not a steadfast rule. Broadly speaking, if the adjective precedes the noun, the emphasis falls on the noun (*un buen* **libro** as opposed to *una buena* **revista**). If it follows the noun, more emphasis falls on the adjective (*un libro* **bueno** as opposed to *un libro* **malo**).
5. The meanings of certain common adjectives change according to their position before of after the noun (*distintas* or *diferentes personas*, different [sundry, various, several] people, but *personas distintas* or *diferentes*, different [from one another] people; *varias personas*, several people, but *personas varias*, various [sundry] people; *un nuevo coche*, a new [another] car, but *un coche nuevo*, a [brand-] new car; *un pobre hombre*, a poor [pitiful] man, but *un hombre pobre*, a poor [impecunious] man; *un gran hombre*, a great [important] man, but *un hombre grande*, a tall man).
6. Note the following possibilities when more than one adjective qualifies the same noun (*un pequeño coche rojo*, a small, red car; *sus ojos alegres y sonrientes* or *sus alegres y sonrientes ojos*, her happy, smiling eyes; *la situación económica americana*, the American economic situation. Here the adjective *americana* might be said to describe the noun *situación económica*).

FORMATION OF THE FEMININE

For adjectives which end in **-o** in the masculine singular form, change **-o** to **-a** (*cansado, cansada*);
for adjectives ending in **-án, -ín, -ón, -or** and those indicating nationality add **-a** and remove the written accent where necessary (*holgazán, holgazana; cantarín, cantarina; gordinflón, gordinflona; trabajador, trabajadora; portugués, portuguesa*). Note that comparatives ending in **-or** remain the same in the masculine and feminine (*la mejor manera*), as do certain adjectives of nationality such as *árabe, marroquí, etíope* and all those ending in **-a** (*belga, persa*, etc.);
for adjectives ending in **-ete** or **-ote** replace the final **-e** by **-a** (*regordete, regordeta; vulgarote, vulgarota*);
other adjectives have the same form in both genders (*agrícola, azul, cursi, gris, verde, feliz*, etc.).

FORMATION OF THE PLURAL

The same rules apply to the formation of the plural of adjectives as to the formation of the plural of nouns [See LO.]

AGREEMENT OF ADJECTIVES

— The adjective agrees in number and gender with the noun or pronoun it modifies (*dos muchachas encantadoras*).
— When it precedes more than one noun the adjective agrees with the first of them (*en sosegada paz y reposo*).
— When the adjective follows the nouns the following five rules apply: *a*) if the nouns are all singular or all plural and of the same gender, the adjective takes the plural form and agrees in gender with the nouns (*historia y geografía colombianas*); *b*) if the nouns differ in gender but are all in the singular, the adjective either agrees in number and gender with the last of the nouns (*el hombre y la mujer española*) or takes the masculine plural form (*el hombre y la mujer españoles*), which is the better solution; *c*) if the nouns are all plural but different in gender, the adective may agree with the last noun, though it is preferable to use the masculine plural form of the adjective (*bailes y canciones americanas* or *bailes y canciones americanos*); *d*) if the nouns differ in number and gender, the adjective takes the masculine plural form (*la ciudad y los suburbios adormecidos*); *e*) if the noun is singular when taken with each adjective separately, the adjective takes the singular form (*los ministros español y argentino*).

COMPARATIVES

— A comparison of **equality** is expressed by **tan** (with adjectives) or **tanto** (with nouns)... **como** (*ella es tan alta como yo*, she is as tall as I; *tenías tanto tiempo como yo*, you had as much time as I; *tiene tantos hermanos como tú*, he has as many brothers as you).
— A comparison of **inequality** is expressed by **más ... que** and **menos ... que** (*ella es más simpática que su hermana*, she is more friendly [*or* friendlier] than her sister; *es menos inteligente que tú*, he is not so intelligent as you; *menos exigente que*, less demanding than).
Note: More than and *less than* before a number or an expression of quantity are translated by **más de** and **menos de** (*tengo más que tú* but *tengo más de cien*).
More than and *less than* are translated by **más** and **menos de lo que** (or **de los que**, etc.) when the second member of the comparison is a clause (*tienen más empleados de los que necesitan*; *era más fácil de lo que pensaba*).
— For **irregular** comparatives see below.

SUPERLATIVES

— The **absolute** superlative is formed by placing **muy** before the adjective or adding the suffix **-ísimo** to the adjective (*alto, muy alto, altísimo*). The latter method is more difficult to use since not all adjectives can take the suffix **-ísimo**, e.g. *arduo*. **Muy** should not however be used with *mucho*, the superlative of which is *muchísimo*. The suffix **-ísimo** also makes certain spelling changes necessary: adjectives ending in **-co** take the suffix **-quísimo** (*rico, riquísimo*), those ending in **-go** take the suffix **-guísimo** (*largo, larguísimo*), those ending in **-n** or **-z** take the suffix **-císimo** (*joven, jovencísimo*), those containing a diphthong usually lose it in the superlative (*valiente, valentísimo*), although in many cases both forms are possible (*bueno, buenísimo, bonísimo*; *fuerte, fuertísimo, fortísimo*), adjectives ending in **-io** change this ending to **-ísimo** (*limpio, limpísimo*), but **-ío** becomes **-iísimo** [*pío, piísimo*), adjectives ending in **-ble** take **-bilísimo** (*agradable, agradabilísimo*), those ending in **-bre, -cre, -ero**, take **-érrimo** (*celebre, celebérrimo*; *acre, acérrimo*; *áspero, aspérrimo*), **pobre** and **pulcro** have two superlative forms, one regular (*pobrísimo, pulcrísimo*), the other of Latin origin (*paupérrimo, pulquérrimo*).
— The **relative** superlative is formed as follows: *la más simpática de las mujeres*; *la mujer más simpática que conozco*.

IRREGULAR COMPARATIVES AND SUPERLATIVES

POSITIVE	COMPARATIVE	SUPERLATIVE
bueno	*mejor*	óptimo
malo	*peor*	pésimo
grande	*mayor*	máximo
pequeño	*menor*	mínimo
alto	*superior*	supremo
bajo	*inferior*	ínfimo

Note that *más grande, más pequeño, más alto* and *más bajo* and the regular superlatives *buenísimo, malísimo, grandísimo, pequeñísimo, altísimo* and *bajísimo* also exist (*es más grande que el otro* or *es mayor que el otro*).

NUMBER TABLE

	CARDINAL	ORDINAL
0	cero	
1	uno, una	primero, ra
2	dos	segundo, da
3	tres	tercero, ra
4	cuatro	cuarto, ta
5	cinco	quinto, ta
6	seis	sexto, ta
7	siete	séptimo, ma
8	ocho	octavo, va
9	nueve	noveno, na
10	diez	décimo, ma
11	once	undécimo, ma
12	doce	duodécimo, ma
13	trece	decimotercero, ra
14	catorce	decimocuarto, ta
15	quince	decimoquinto, ta
16	dieciséis	decimosexto, ta
17	diecisiete	decimoséptimo, ma
18	dieciocho	decimoctavo, va
19	diecinueve	decimonoveno, na
20	veinte	vigésimo, ma
21	veintiuno, na	vigésimo (-ma) primero, ra
22	veintidós	vigésimo (-ma) segundo, da
30	treinta	trigésimo, ma
31	treinta y uno	trigésimo (ma) primero, ra
40	cuarenta	cuadragésimo, ma
50	cincuenta	quincuagésimo, ma
60	sesenta	sexagésimo, ma
70	setenta	septuagésimo, ma
80	ochenta	octogésimo, ma
90	noventa	nonagésimo, ma
100	cien *or* ciento	centésimo, ma
101	ciento uno	centésimo (-ma) primero, ra
134	ciento treinta y cuatro	centésimo (-ma) trigésimo (-ma) cuarto, ta
200	doscientos, tas	ducentésimo, ma
300	trescientos, tas	tricentésimo, ma
400	cuatrocientos, tas	cuadringentésimo, ma
500	quinientos, tas	quingentésimo, ma
600	seiscientos, tas	sexcentésimo, ma
700	setecientos, tas	septingentésimo, ma
800	ochocientos, tas	octingentésimo, ma
900	novecientos, tas	noningentésimo, ma
1000	mil	milésimo, ma
1001	mil uno	milésimo (-ma) primero, ra
2034	dos mil treinta y cuatro	dos milésimo (-ma) trigésimo (-ma) cuarto, ta
1 000 000	un millón	millonésimo, ma
1 000 000 000	mil millones	mil millonésimo, ma
1 000 000 000 000	un billón	billonésimo, ma

Cardinal numbers

They are invariable except *uno*, the multiples of *ciento*, *ciento* and *mil* in certain cases, *millón* and its multiples. Numbers 16 to 19 and 21 to 29 inclusive may be written as one word or three (*diecinueve*, *diez y nueve*; *veintitrés*, *veinte y tres*). They are usually written as one word with an accent where necessary to conserve the stress (*veintidós*).

The conjunction **y** is only placed between the tens and the units (*mil treinta y dos*, one thousand and thirty-two).

Uno changes to **una** before a feminine singular noun (*una mujer*), and to **un** before a masculine singular noun (*un hombre*).

Ciento changes to **cien** before a common noun or a number it multiplies (*cien mujeres, cien millones de habitantes, cien mil hombres*). It is never preceded by the indefinite article. Multiples of a hundred are written as one word and agree in number and gender with the noun they multiply (*doscientos hombres, doscientas mil mujeres, quinientas treinta y ocho páginas*). *Cientos de* may be used to mean "hundreds of".

Millón is a masculine noun (*un millón de pesetas, dos millones de pesetas, cuatrocientos veintiún millones de pesetas*).

Mil is used without the article (*cuarenta mil kilómetros*). It has a plural form when used to mean "thousands of" (*miles de víctimas*, thousands of victims; *miles y miles de*, thousands and thousands of).

For numbers eleven hundred and above Spanish uses the formula *mil cien* or *mil ciento, mil doscientos*, etc. (*en el año mil setecientos*, in [the year] seventeen hundred).

Ordinal numbers

They agree with the noun they qualify (*las primeras personas*).

Primero and **tercero** become **primer** and **tercer** in the cases described under the heading APOCOPATION (below).

In everyday Spanish the ordinal numbers are used from one to nine inclusive (*Felipe Segundo*). From ten to twelve inclusive the cardinal or the ordinal is used (*la fila duodécima* or *la fila doce*), and for thirteen and above the cardinal number is used (*el siglo veinte*). There are two forms of the ordinal *ninth* in Spanish, *noveno* and *nono*. The latter is generally used only with the name of the Pope *Pío IX* (*nono*).

There are several ways of conveying the idea of approximate quantity in Spanish. The most common uses the plural indefinite article *unos, unas* (*unas treinta personas*, about thirty people; *unos sesenta kilos*, some sixty kilos). The suffix **-ena** may be used in *docena, quincena* and with numbers which are multiples of ten, such as *veintena, cuarentena*, etc. (*compré una docena de huevos, debe de tener una treintena de diccionarios*).

INDEFINITE ADJECTIVES

The main ones are *alguno, ninguno, cierto, varios, cualquiera, poco, bastante, mucho, demasiado, demás, cuanto, todo, cada, tal, otro, uno, tanto*. They are variable in gender except for *bastante, cualquiera, cada, demás* and *tal*, and variable in number except for *cada, demás* and *varios*.

THE INTERROGATIVE ADJECTIVE

Qué is an invariable interrogative adjective (*¿qué día es?*, what day is it?; *¿qué chaqueta te vas a poner?*, which jacket are you going to wear?).

Cuánto varies in number and gender according to the noun it accompanies (*¿cuántas personas vinieron?*, how many people came?; *¿cuánto tiempo nos queda?*, how much time do we have left?).

The above adjectives are used in direct and indirect questions (*no sabía qué decir*, he did not know what to say). They are also used exclamatively (*¡qué calor!*, isn't it hot!; *¡cuánta gente!*, what a lot of people!).

APOCOPATION

Apocopation is the dropping of the final vowel or syllable of a word. The following words lose their final **-o** before a masculine singular noun: *uno, veintiuno, alguno, ninguno, primero, tercero, postrero, bueno* and *malo* (*un buen hombre, de ningún modo, el primer alumno, el tercer libro, ayer hizo mal tiempo*, etc.). In the case of *veintiuno, alguno, ninguno* a written accent is added to the apocopated form (*veintiún*, etc.).

Santo becomes *san* before the name of a canonized saint (*San Miguel*), except before *Tomás, Tomé, Toribio* and *Domingo* (*Santo Tomás, Santo Tomé, Santo Toribio, Santo Domingo*). The name of St James has become a single word in Spanish (*Santiago*).

Ciento becomes *cien* before a common noun or a number which it multiplies (*cien dólares, cien mil casas*).

Grande becomes *gran* before a masculine singular noun beginning with a consonant (*un gran ruido*). This apocopation is optional before a feminine noun or a masculine noun beginning with a vowel (*una gran mujer, un gran automóvil*).

There are other cases of apocopation. The adverbs **tanto** and **cuanto** become *tan* and *cuan* before an adjective or another adverb (*cuan largo, tan pronto ríe como llora*).

Recientemente becomes *recién* before a past participle (*recién llegado*). **Cualquiera** loses its final **-a** before a masculine singular noun (*cualquier hombre*); this apocopation is also possible before a feminine singular noun (*me parece que cualquier mujer es capaz de hacerlo*).

ADJECTIVES AND PRONOUNS

POSSESSIVE ADJECTIVES AND PRONOUNS

		ONE POSSESSOR	
		singular noun	plural noun
1st pers.	*adj.*	**mi; mío, mía** (my)	**mis; míos, mías** (my)
	pron.	**mío, mía** (mine)	**míos, mías** (mine)
2nd pers	*adj.*	**tu; tuyo, a** (your)	**tus; tuyos, as** (your)
	pron.	**tuyo, a** (yours)	**tuyos, as** (yours)
3rd pers.	*adj.*	**su; suyo, a** (his, her, its)	**sus; suyos, as** (his, her, its)
	pron.	**suyo, a** (his, hers)	**suyos, as** (his, hers)

		SEVERAL POSSESSORS	
		singular noun	plural noun
1st pers.	*adj.*	**nuestro, a** (our)	**nuestros, as** (our)
	pron.	**nuestro, a** (ours)	**nuestros, as** (ours)
2nd pers.	*adj.*	**vuestro, a** (your)	**vuestros, as** (your)
	pron.	**vuestro, a** (yours)	**vuestros, as** (yours)
3rd pers.	*adj.*	**su; suyo, a** (their)	**sus; suyos, as** (their)
	pron.	**suyo, a** (theirs)	**suyos, as** (theirs)

They agree in number and gender with the thing or things possessed and not with the possessor.
The adjectives **mi, tu, su** are always placed before the noun they modify (*mi casa*). **Mío, tuyo, suyo,** however, follow the noun (*la casa mía*). Ambiguity may arise from the use of the adjective **su,** which means "your", "his", "her", "its", "their", and of the pronoun **suyo.** This ambiguity may be avoided by replacing them by *el ... de ella*, etc. (*el coche de ellos*, their car), or by adding *de usted, de ella*, etc. (*su libro de usted,* your book).
The possessive is used to a lesser extent in Spanish than in English and is often replaced by the article. In such a case the idea of possession is often conveyed by a verb in the reflexive form (*se quitó el abrigo*, he took off his coat) or by the indirect object pronoun (*me vendaron la herida*, they bandaged my wound).

DEMONSTRATIVE ADJECTIVES AND PRONOUNS

DEGREE OF REMOTENESS (*adverbs of place*)		MASCULINE and FEMININE singular	plural	NEUTER singular
aquí (here)	*adj.*	**este, esta** (this)	**estos, etsas,** (these)	
	pron.	**éste, ésta** (this [one])	**éstos, éstas** (these [ones])	**esto** (this)
ahí (there)	*adj.*	**ese, esa** (that)	**esos, esas** (those)	
	pron.	**ése, ésa** (that [one])	**ésos, ésas** (those [ones])	**eso** (that)
allí, allá (there)	*adj.*	**aquel, aquella** (that)	**aquéllos, aquellas** (those)	
	pron.	**aquél, aquélla** (that [one])	**aquéllos, aquéllas** (those [ones])	**aquello** (that)

The written accent on the demonstrative pronoun distinguishes it from the demonstrative adjective. Since there are no neuter demonstrative adjectives in Spanish, the neuter demonstrative pronouns bear no written accent.
The three forms **este, ese** and **aquel** correspond to different degrees of remoteness in time and space.
Este is the least remote and denotes the same degree of closeness as *this* in English. **Aquel** indicates the greatest degree of remoteness (*aquella mañana hacía mucho frío*, it was very cold that morning). **Ese** describes an intermediate or an undetermined degree of remoteness (*esa tienda está lejos de casa*, that shop is a long way from home). **Ese** can also have pejorative overtones (*no me gusta nada que salgas con esa gente*, I don't like you going around with the likes of them).
When the demonstrative pronouns refer to nouns mentioned in immediately preceding clauses, **éste,** etc. usually means "the latter" and **aquél,** etc. "the former".
Demonstrative pronouns are often replaced by *el de, la de, los de, las de* (that of, those of, the one of, the one with, those with, the one in, those in) or by *el que, la que, los que, las que* (the one that, those that, the one which, those which, the one who, those who).

PRONOUNS

PERSONAL PRONOUNS

SUBJECT	OBJECTS: NO PREPOSITION — *direct*	OBJECTS: NO PREPOSITION — *indirect*	OBJECTS: AFTER PREPOSITION	OBJECTS: REFLEXIVE
yo (I)	**me** (me, to me, etc.)		**mí** (me)	**me** (myself)
tú (you)	**te** (you, to you, etc.)		**ti** (you)	**te** (yourself)
él (he)	**le, lo** (him)	**le** (to him, etc.)	**él** (him)	**se** (himself)
ella (she)	**la** (her)	**le** (to her, etc.)	**ella** (her)	**se** (herself)
ello (neuter: it)	**lo** (it)	**le** (to it, etc.)	**ello** (it)	**se** (itself)
nosotros, as (we)	**nos** (us, to us, etc.)		**nosotros, as** (us)	**nos** (ourselves)
vosotros, as (you)	**os** (you, to you, etc.)		**vosotros, as** (you)	**os** (yourselves)
ellos (they)	**los** (them)	**les** (to them, etc.)	**ellos** (them)	**se** (themselves)
ellas (they)	**las** (them)	**les** (to them, etc.)	**ellas** (them)	**se** (themselves)

Spanish subject pronouns are usually omitted unless a certain emphasis is required (*no vamos*, we're not going; *nosotros no vamos*, we aren't going). The subject pronoun is normally omitted when it is implicit in the verb ending (*canto*, I sing). It is sometimes necessary to include the pronoun to avoid ambiguity (*cuando él llegó yo cantaba*).
The subject pronoun is used in the second half of a comparison (*la conoces mejor que yo*, you know her better than I) and immediately after *según, salvo, excepto* and sometimes *entre* (*según yo*, according to me).
In certain regions of Spain and Latin America there are variations in the usage of the object pronoun *la, le* and *lo:* **laísmo** is the use of *la* and *las* instead of *le* and *les* as the feminine indirect object pronouns; **leísmo** is the use of *le* and never *lo* as the masculine singular direct object pronoun; **loísmo** is the use of *lo* instead of *le* as the masculine singular direct and indirect object pronoun. These variations are frowned upon by the Spanish Academy, which recommends the use of *lo* as the masculine direct object pronoun (*lo veo*, I see him), and *le* as the indirect object pronoun (*le dije*, I told him). Literary style tends to prefer *le* when reference is made to a person, reserving *lo* for objects.
The object pronoun always precedes the verb (*te hablo*, I am speaking to you), except when the verb is in the infinitive, the gerund or the imperative, in which case the pronoun is enclitic (*mirarle, mirándole, mírale*). This enclitic use of the pronoun is also found in literary style when a verb in the indicative or the conditional is initial in a main or independent clause (*diríale la verdad si la ocasión se me presentase*, I should tell him the truth were the opportunity to arise; *mirábanle con admiración*, they contemplated him in admiration).
When there are two pronouns, the indirect object pronoun is placed before the direct object pronoun (*me lo dio*, he gave it to me; *dámelo*, give it to me). When both pronouns are in the third person *le* or *les* (to him, to her, to them) are replaced by **se** (*se lo diré*, I shall tell him; *dáselo*, give it to him).
Usted (*Ud.* or *Vd.*) and **ustedes** (*Uds.* or *Vds.*) are the polite forms of address used with strangers and people to whom one owes a certain amount of respect (as opposed to the familiar forms of address *tú* and *vosotros*). Personal and possessive pronouns and adjectives related to *usted* and *ustedes* respectively assume the form of the third person singular and the third person plural (*si usted me lo pide, le llevaré a su casa*, if you wish, I shall take you home).
Vos is used instead of *usted* in poetic or oratorial style, in addressing God or an eminent person. (See vos).
The reflexive pronoun is used when the action of a verb refers back to the subject (*nos levantamos tarde*, we got up late). The position of reflexive pronouns is the same as that of object pronouns. With *nos* and *os* in the first and second person plural of the imperative the verb loses its final *-s* and *-d* respectively before the pronouns (*sentémonos, sentaos*).
Himself, herself, itself, themselves preceded by a preposition are translated by **sí** when they refer back to the subject of the verb (*esa mujer siempre habla de sí*, that woman is always talking about herself). If the preposition is *con* it joins with *mí, ti, sí* to form *conmigo, contigo, consigo*.

RELATIVE PRONOUNS

The relative pronoun must never be omitted in Spanish (*el perro que vimos*, the dog [which] we saw).
Within its own clause the relative pronoun may be *a*) the subject, *b*) the direct object, *c*) the prepositional object. Its antecedent (the part of the main clause to which it refers) may be *a*) a person, *b*) a thing, *c*) a clause or verb (*la chica que llamó dejó su número*; *el coche que conducía era nuevo*; *no pudo contestar, de lo cual deducí que ...*).
Que, the most common relative pronoun, can be a subject or a direct object pronoun when the antecedent is a person or a thing (*el amigo que me presentó, el coche que pasó*).
Quien (pl. *quienes*) is used only for persons and agrees in number with its antecedent. It can be the subject, the direct object or the prepositional object in its clause (*fue él quien lo dijo*, it was he who said it; *las mujeres a quienes miraba*, the women [whom] he was watching). Used without an antecedent *quien* means "he who", "anyone who", "whoever", etc. (*quien no estudia no aprende*, he who does not study learns nothing). It can also mean "someone who" (*necesita quien le proteja*, she needs someone to protect her; *no hubo quien me ayudase*, there was no one who would help me).
El que (la, los, las que) and **el cual (la cual, los, las cuales)** sometimes replace *que* and *quien* as the subject pronoun, when the antecedent is a person and the relative clause gives added information about the subject (*encontré a sus hermanas, las cuales iban al colegio*). They may also be used as direct object pronouns in the same kind of clause if the antecedent is a person (*ésta es la muchacha a la que mandaron*, this is the girl they sent), and as prepositional object pronouns applying to persons or things (*el hijo para el que lo compré*, the child for whom I bought it; *la sala por la cual pasamos*, the room we passed through). **Lo que** and **lo cual** are used when the antecedent is a verb or clause (*lo que más me molesta es el calor*, what bothers me most is the heat; *no veo lo que haces*, I cannot see what you are doing; *llegó tarde, lo cual* [or *lo que*] *era de esperar*, he was late, which was to be expected; *nos despedimos de él, con lo cual* [or *lo que*] *subió al tren*, we said good-bye to him, whereupon he boarded the train). Note that *lo cual* may only be used to refer back to something already mentioned.
Cuyo (whose, of whom, of which) agrees in number and gender with the *object possessed* (*la casa cuyo tejado es rojo*, the house with the red roof [the roof of which is red]; *el chico cuyas gafas se rompieron*, the boy whose glasses broke).

INTERROGATIVE PRONOUNS

These differ from the relative pronouns only in that they bear a written accent, both in direct and indirect questions. They are: **qué** (what), **quién** (who, whom), and **cuál** (which, which one).
Qué is invariable in number and gender; **quién** and **cuál** add **-es** in the plural without loss of the written accent (*¿qué ocurre?*, what's happening?; *¿quién fue?*, who was it?; *no sé quién habrá sido*, I don't know who it could have been: *¿a cuáles te refieres?*, to which are you referring?)
Note that in Spanish a question is always introduced by an inverted question mark.

INDEFINITE PRONOUNS

These are **alguien** (someone), **nadie** (no one), **quienquiera** and **cualquiera** (anyone), which become *quienesquiera* and *cualesquiera* in the plural, **uno** (one), **alguno** (someone, some), **ninguno** (no one, none), **se** (one), **algo** (something), **nada** (nothing).
Cualquiera, uno, alguno and *ninguno* do not apocopate when used as pronouns.
Remember that all the indefinite adjectives may also be used as pronouns.

THE ADVERB

Adverbs **of manner** are formed by adding the suffix **-mente** to the feminine singular form of the adjective (*blando, blandamente*; *fácil, fácilmente*). Note that if an adjective carries a written accent the corresponding adverb bears the same accent. When several adverbs appear consecutively the suffix *-mente* is added only to the last one, the others taking the form of the feminine singular adjective (*lenta y perezosamente*, slowly and lazily).
Adverbs **of quantity** may be simple words such as *más* (more), *menos* (less), *bastante* (enough), *demasiado* (too much), *poco* (little), *mucho* (a lot), *tanto* (so much), *cuanto* (as much), or adverbial phrases such as *poco más o menos* (about), *al menos* (at least), etc. These words are invariable when used as adverbs.
Common adverbs **of place** are *abajo, acá, adelante, adentro, ahí, alrededor, allá, allí, aquí, arriba, atrás, cerca, debajo, delante, dentro, detrás, donde, dondequiera, encima, enfrente, fuera, lejos*, etc.
Adverbs **of time** include *ahora, anoche, antaño, antes, aún, ayer, ¿cuándo?, después, entonces, hoy, jamás, luego, mañana, nunca, pronto, siempre, tarde, temprano, todavía, ya*, etc.
In the compound tenses in Spanish the adverb must not be placed between the auxiliary and the main verb (*siempre lo hemos hecho así*, we have always done it that way), unless the auxiliary is *ser*.
The main adverbs **of negation** are *ni, no, no ... más, no ... más que, no ... sino, ya no*. **No** on its own translates the English *no* (*¿lo harás? — No*, will you do it? — No). Before a verb it is equivalent to *not* in English (*no vinieron*, they did not come).
If the negatives *nunca, jamás, nada, nadie, ninguno, tampoco*, and expressions such as *en mi vida, en mis días*, etc. precede the verb, the word **no** is omitted (*nunca lo haré*, I shall never do it). If they follow the verb, **no** must be used (*no lo haré nunca*, I shall never do it).
The comparative of adverbs is formed with **tan, más** or **menos** (*tan despacio como puedas*, as slowly as you can; *más rápido que yo*, faster than I). Four adverbs are compared irregularly: *bien* (mejor), *mal* (peor), *mucho* (más), *poco* (menos).
The superlative of adverbs may be formed with the neuter article *lo* followed by a word or phrase expressing possibility (*lo más pronto posible*, as soon as possible).

THE VERB

CLASSIFICATION

The different types of verb are:
transitive, which have a direct object (*comía cerezas*, I was eating cherries);
intransitive, which have an indirect object or none at all (*voy al cine*, I am going to the pictures; *comía*, I was eating);
reflexive, when the subject and the object of the action are the same person. This verb form uses the reflexive pronouns *me, te, se, nos, os, se*, which are usually placed before the verb (*el niño se lavó*, the child washed [himself]; *el niño se durmió*, the child fell asleep). These pronouns are, however, enclitic in the infinitive (*dormirse*), the imperative (*duérmete*) and the gerund (*durmiéndose*). Compound tenses are formed with the auxiliary **haber**, and the past participle remains invariable (*tu madre se ha dormido*, your mother has fallen asleep). Reciprocity is also expressed in Spanish by the reflexive (*no se conocían antes*, they did not know each other before, they did not know one another before);
impersonal, when they are used only in the third person singular with an indeterminate subject (*llueve*, it is raining). Note that the pronoun *it* is not translated into Spanish. In expressions such as *es tarde* (it is late), *es de noche* (it is dark), *es de desear* (it is desirable), the verb **ser** is impersonal and invariable in number. In telling the time, however, **ser** agrees in number with the hour (*es la una*, it is one o'clock; *son las dos*, it is two o'clock). **Haber** is used impersonally to mean "there is", "there are", etc. (*hay sitio para cien coches*, there is room for a hundred cars; *había cien coches*, there were a hundred cars). When used with *que* and an infinitive it denotes obligation or necessity (*hay que comer*, it is necessary to eat). **Hacer** is used impersonally to describe certain weather conditions (*hace frío, calor*, it is cold, hot) and to indicate the lapse of time (*hace un mes que ocurrió*, it happened a month ago; *hace un mes que no lo veo*, I have not seen him for a month; *está en Madrid desde hace una semana*, he has been in Madrid for a week);
defective, which do not exist in all the normal tenses and persons (like the English verb *must*, which has no past tense, no conditional, etc.). Such verbs in Spanish are *abolir, atañer, concernir, soler*, etc.;
auxiliary, when they are used to conjugate certain tenses of other verbs (see AUXILIARY VERBS below).
Note that a transitive verb in Spanish is not necessarily translated by a transitive English verb (*la bala traspasó la pared*, the bullet went right through the wall).
Spanish reflexive verbs are often intransitive verbs in English (*vestirse*, to dress, to get dressed).
Verbs do not necessarily govern the same preposition in the two languages (*depender de*, to depend on). Such differences are indicated in the corresponding entries in the body of the dictionary.

Personal A

An important feature of Spanish syntax is the use of the preposition **a** before a direct object (noun or pronoun) representing a person or a personified object or being (*no conozco a su padre*, I do not know his father; *mató al toro*, he killed the bull; *esperar a la muerte*, to await death).
The preposition **a** is used before names of towns and countries which are not preceded by the definite article (*visité a España*, I visited Spain), though this rule is often disregarded nowadays.

The **a** is placed before the direct object of a verb which usually has a person for its object (*amar a su país*, to love one's country; *temer a la oscuridad*, to be afraid of the dark).
Note that, when a verb has a direct object and an indirect object, both of which are persons, the **a** is usually omitted before the direct object (*dejó su hijo a su madre*, she left her son with her mother).
The preposition **a** avoids possible confusion of the subject with the object (*ayer encontró Pedro a mi padre*, Peter met my father yesterday), and also of the direct object with the complement (*nombraron director a mi padre*, they made my father director). It also clarifies the order of succession or of superiority one wishes to express (*el adjetivo posesivo precede al sustantivo*, the possessive adjective precedes the noun; *a la tempestad siguió la calma*, calm followed the storm; *al padre le supera en mucho el hijo*, the son is far superior to the father).

The presence or absence of **a** causes certain verbs to change their meaning (*querer*, to want; *querer a*, to love).

VOICES, MOODS AND TENSES

The Passive Voice

The passive voice is conjugated with the auxiliary verb **ser** and the past participle of the verb which agrees in number and gender with the subject (*las alumnas fueron expulsadas*, the pupils were expelled). The agent is introduced by **por** (*fueron expulsadas por el director*, they were expelled by the headmaster).
Use of the passive is far more common in English than in Spanish. When the agent is expressed it is often preferable to use an active construction in Spanish (*las expulsó el director*). Where no agent is expressed the most common way to avoid the passive in Spanish is to use the reflexive form of the verb (*se comen crudos*, they are eaten raw) or a verb in the third person plural (*los venden en el mercado*, they are sold *o* they sell them in the market).

The Infinitive

Use of the infinitive differs considerably in English and Spanish (*me permitió salir*, he allowed me to *or* he let me go out; *se puso a cantar*, he started singing *o* to sing; *insiste en venir*, he insists on coming; *siento no haberle visto*, I am sorry I didn't see him; *¿has oído hablar de?*, have you heard of?).
A must precede the infinitive used after verbs of motion (*fueron a trabajar*, they went to work), of exhorting (*animar a*), inviting (*convidar a*), forcing (*obligar a*), impelling (*mover a*), beginning (*empezar a*), deciding and refusing in their reflexive forms (*decidirse a*, *negarse a*).
Al followed by an infinitive expresses simultaneity (*al llegar vino a verme*, when he arrived *o* on arriving he came to see me); **con** followed by an infinitive expresses manner or concession (*con hacer un esfuerzo lo conseguirás*, if you make an effort you will succeed; *con ser tan tonto es el que más éxito ha tenido*, despite his stupidity he is the one who has been most successful); **de** followed by an infinitive expresses condition (*de haberlo pensado lo hubiera hecho*, if I had thought about it I should have done it); **por** followed by an infinitive expresses cause (*no le dejaron entrar por ir mal vestido*, they did not let him in because he was unsuitably dressed); **sin** followed by an infinitive gives a negative idea (*me quedé sin comer*, I didn't eat; *está sin resolver*, it is unsolved); *quedar por* or *estar por hacer*, *terminar*, etc., mean "to remain to be done, finished, etc."
Most Spanish infinitives can be used as nouns (*en un abrir y cerrar de ojos*, in the twinkling of an eye, in a wink). If they play the role of subject in the sentence they may usually be translated by the English gerund (*el andar es muy saludable*, walking is very healthy). When the infinitive used thus is preceded by a word other than the definite article it often means "the way of doing something" (*su andar gracioso*, her graceful gait *or* walk).
The infinitive can also be the object of a preposition (*le escribiré antes de venir*, I shall write to you before I come *o* before coming).
In spoken Spanish *a* followed by the infinitive is often used as a command or an exhortation (*¡a trabajar!*, [get *o* let's get] to work!).

The Gerund

The Spanish gerund is formed by adding **-ando** or **-iendo** to the stem of the verb and is invariable.
Used without a preposition it indicates manner (*le esperaba leyendo*, he read as he waited for him; *fui corriendo*, I ran), duration and cause (*estando con él no tenía miedo*, when [or because] I was with him I was not afraid).
En followed by the gerund indicates an action immediately prior to that of the main verb (*en llegando se lo diré*, I'll tell him as soon as I arrive).
Estar with the gerund gives the idea of action in progress (*está leyendo*, he is reading) and will be dealt with below (see **The Progressive Tenses** below).
Ir with the gerund indicates progression (*iba creciendo*, it grew and grew). **Seguir** with the gerund indicates continued action (*sigue trabajando*, he is still working).
Llevar with the gerund gives the idea of an action which started at some time in the past and continues at the moment under consideration (*lleva* [*llevaba*] *tres horas esperando*, he has [he had] been waiting for three hours).
The Spanish gerund may not refer to the object of a verb, unlike the English present participle (*vi a un muchacho que corría* [not *corriendo*], I saw a boy running). When the English *-ing* has an adjectival function it is usually translated into Spanish by an adjective or an adjectival phrase (*a flickering light*, una luz vacilante *or* que vacilaba).
The *-ing* form in English is often translated by the Spanish infinitive when it follows a preposition or when it has the function of a noun (*after meeting him*, después de haberle encontrado; *upon meeting him*, al encontrarle; *by trying*, con intentarlo; *walking is very healthy*, el andar es muy saludable; *the singing of the birds*, el cantar de los pájaros).

The Progressive Tenses

The Spanish progressive tenses, which correspond to the English *to be ... -ing*, are formed with the appropriate tense of **estar** and the **gerund** of the verb in question (*está leyendo*). The progressive tenses convey an idea of the continuity of an action taking place at any given moment. This idea is also conveyed in Spanish by the simple present tense and the imperfect (*¿adónde vas?*, where are you going?; *caminaba lentamente*, he was walking slowly). Consequently, the progressive tenses are less frequently used in Spanish than in English, and when used tend to emphasize the idea that the action is in the process of being performed at the moment under consideration (*estaba leyendo cuando llegué*, she was [in the act of] reading when I arrived).
In some cases the progressive tense would never be used, namely when there is no real stress on the continuity of the action (*llevaba un vestido rojo*), and with verbs of motion (*vamos al colegio*, we are going to school).
In certain cases the two forms are more or less interchangeable (*está lloviendo* or *llueve*). In other cases each form would convey a slightly different emphasis (*cuando la encontraron cantaba en un bar*, when they found her she was singing [i.e. she was a singer] in a bar *or* when they found her she was [in the act of] singing in a bar; *cuando la encontraron estaba cantando en un bar*, when they found her she was [in the act of] singing in a bar).
The preterite of *estar* with the gerund conveys an idea which is more difficult to express in English — that of continuing action during a limited time in the past (*estuvieron hablando durante dos horas*, they talked for two [whole] hours, they spent two hours talking).

The Indicative

The **present tense** in Spanish corresponds to the simple present (*dice*, he says), the progressive tense (*llueve*, it is raining) and the form with *do* (*no voy a menudo, pero cuando voy ...*, I don't go very often, but when I do [go] ...).
It is used when asking for instructions (*¿dónde pongo este libro?*, where shall I put this book?), to describe an action beginning in the past and continuing to the present (*llevo aquí un mes* or *hace un mes que estoy aquí*, I have been here for a month; *te están llamando desde hace media hora*, they have been calling you for half an hour), and also with the expressions *por poco* and *casi* (*por poco me caigo*, I almost fell).
The Spanish **imperfect** and **preterite** both correspond to the English preterite, but they are not interchangeable. The **imperfect** describes an action that was going on at some time in the past or when something else happened (*almorzaba* or *estaba almorzando cuando llegaron*, I was having lunch when they arrived) or a customary state or action in the past (*en aquel entonces era muy caro*, it was very expensive in those days; *antes leía mucho pero ya no*, I used to read a lot, but I don't any more). It is also used in telling the time in the past (*eran las ocho de la mañana*, it was 8 a. m.).
The **preterite** stresses the momentariness or the completeness of an action at a definite time in the past (*llovió aquel día*, it rained that day; *a pesar de los esfuerzos que hizo no pudo abrir la puerta*, despite all his efforts he did not manage to open the door).
The **future** is used to describe future action (*iré mañana*, I shall go tomorrow), and also to express probability or supposition (see **Conjecture and Doubt** below). The idea of willingness sometimes present in the English future tense with *will* must be conveyed in Spanish by the present tense of the verb *querer*.

The Subjunctive

This mood is used to present things as possible or doubtful in subordinate and independent clauses. In the first case, the subject in the main clause must be different from the subject of the verb in the subordinate clause (*no quiero que vayas*, I don't want you to go). It is compulsory in a subordinate clause dependent on:

— verbs or other words expressing desire (*quiero que lo hagas*, I want you to do it), request (*me pidió que lo hiciese*, he asked me to do it), command (*me ha mandado que la mate*, he has ordered me to kill her), permission (*no permitieron que saliera*, they did not allow him to go out), prohibition (*les prohibieron que se viesen*, they were forbidden from seeing each other), advice (*te aconsejo que llegues temprano*, I advise you to arrive early), causation (*esto hizo que se perdiesen*, this made them lose their way), necessity (see **Obligation** below), emotions, such as regret, fear or surprise (*siento que no le hayamos podido ayudar*, I am sorry we were unable to help you; *es extraño que no haya llamado*, it is strange that he has not called), uncertainty or negation (*parece dudoso que vaya*, it seems unlikely that he will go; *negó que estuviera casado*, he denied that he was married), preference (*prefiero que tomes la decisión*, I would rather that you took the decision) and evaluation (*es inútil que grites*, it is no good your shouting);

— impersonal expressions of probability (*puede ser que lo consigas*, you might succeed);

— conjunctions which introduce future or hypothetical action (*cuando termines llámame*, call me when you finish; *por mucho que insistas no iré*, I shall not go, however much you insist), including *antes (de) que* (before), *para que* (in order that), *con tal que* (provided that), *a no ser que* (unless), *no porque* (not because), *como si* (as if), etc.;

— a relative pronoun with a negative or indefinite antecedent (*no hay excusa que valga*, no excuses; *haré lo que pueda*, I shall do my best). In the latter case the statement expresses hypothesis because of the future tense;

— conditional clauses (*¿dónde estaría ahora si no te hubiera conocido?*, where should I be now had I never met you?; *si tuviera bastante dinero me compraría una casa*, if I had enough money I should buy a house).

Note: The imperfect of the subjunctive has two endings, **-ra** and **-se**; the former sometimes replaces the conditional (*hubiera* instead of *habría*, *quisiera* instead of *querría*).

There is strict correspondence between the tense of the subjunctive used in the subordinate clause and that of the main verb. The present or perfect subjunctive are used after a verb in the present, future or future perfect (*es inútil que llores*; *es extraño que no haya llamado*). The imperfect or pluperfect subjunctive are used when the main verb is in the imperfect, preterite, conditional, pluperfect or conditional perfect (*habría sido inútil que gritaras*; *era inútil que gritaras*; *fue extraño que no viniese*).

The Imperative

The true imperative is restricted in Spanish to the singular and plural of the second person in affirmative commands (*canta, bebed*). The present subjunctive must be used for the other persons in the affirmative (*cantemos, suban*) as well as for all persons in the negative (*no cantes, no mintamos*).

Object pronouns are enclitic in the affirmative (*cántamelo, subámoslo*). The first and the second person plural of reflexive verbs drop respectively the final *-s* and *-d* before enclitic *nos* and *os* (*levantémonos*; *sentaos*). *Vamos a* followed by an infinitive is another common command form; it is translated by "let us" (*vamos a ver*, let's see).

The Participle

There are two kinds of participle, past and present.
The **past participle** obeys the following rules of agreement:

used *without an auxiliary* it agrees with the noun in the same way as any adjective (*las casas edificadas*, the houses built);

used *with the auxiliary "haber"* it never agrees with the noun (*las he visto*), and the auxiliary and the past participle must not be separated by anything other than an object pronoun (*ha terminado ya*, he has already finished; but *habiéndolo hecho*, having done it);

used *with the auxiliary "ser"* and the *semi-auxiliaries* (andar, encontrarse, estar, hallarse, ir, llevar, quedar, resultar, tener, venir, etc.), it agrees with the noun in number and gender (*fueron tomados por asesinos*, they were taken for murderers; *iban muy bien vestidos*, they were very well dressed; *cuando las tenga hechas*, when you have done them).

The past participle is also used in constructions analogous to the Latin ablative absolute (*acabado el trabajo, saldremos*, when the work is finished we shall go out). In this case it always precedes the noun and agrees with it in number and gender.

Certain verbs have an irregular past participle, such as *abrir* (abierto), *cubrir* (cubierto), *decir* (dicho), *escribir* (escrito), *hacer* (hecho), *imprimir* (impreso), *morir* (muerto), *poner* (puesto), *resolver* (resuelto), *romper* (roto), *ver* (visto), *volver* (vuelto) and their derivatives, such as *descubrir* (descubierto), *entreabrir* (entreabierto), etc. Others have two past participles, one regular, the other irregular: *concluir* (concluido, concluso), *despertar* (despertado, despierto), *elegir* (elegido, electo), *eximir* (eximido, exento), *soltar* (soltado, suelto), *sujetar* (sujetado, sujeto), etc. Most of these irregular past participles have become simple adjectives. The main exceptions are *frito, impreso, preso, provisto* and *roto*, which have either replaced the regular forms or developed a meaning different from theirs (*roto* has replaced *rompido*; *prender* gives *prendido*, which means "fastened", and *preso* which means "taken prisoner".

The **present participle** is formed with the suffixes **-ante, -ente, -iente**.

It exists for a very limited number of verbs and has become an adjective (*referente*) or a noun (*amante*). In its verbal function it has been replaced by the gerund (see **The Progressive Tenses** above).

Conjecture and Doubt

The Spanish future indicative can be used to express conjecture in the present (*tendrá unos cuarenta años*, he must be about forty years old). Conjecture in the past is expressed by the conditional (*tendría unos cuarenta años*, he must have been about forty). The same idea can be conveyed by **deber de** with an infinitive (*debe* or *debía de tener cuarenta años*). For the use of the subjunctive in expressions of uncertainty (see ***The Subjunctive*** above).

Obligation

General obligation is expressed by **hay que** with the infinitive (*hay que trabajar para vivir*, one must work to live) or by the phrases **es preciso, es necesario, es menester** and **hace falta** also followed by the infinitive (*es preciso trabajar, hace falta trabajar*).

Personal obligation is expressed by **tener que** with the infinitive (*tengo que verte*, I must see you; *tuve que disculparme*, I had to apologize) or by **es preciso que, es menester que, es necesario que** and **hace falta que** followed by the subjunctive (*es preciso que cooperemos todos*, we must all cooperate).

AUXILIARY VERBS

Haber. — This auxiliary is used to form the compound tenses of all Spanish verbs, transitive, intransitive and reflexive (*he comido una manzana*, I have eaten an apple; *hemos ido a España*, we have been to Spain; *se habían caído*, they had fallen). The past participle remains invariable.
Note: Haber is also an impersonal verb (*hay*, there is, there are; *había*, there was, there were; *hubo*, there was, there were).
Ser. — Like the English *to be*, **ser** is used to form the passive voice in Spanish (*es apreciada por todos*, she is appreciated by all). The past participle used with the auxiliary **ser** agrees in number and gender with the subject.
Note: Ser is also an intransitive verb which, like the English *to be*, introduces a definition or a description of the subject.
There are other verbs in Spanish which occasionally serve as auxiliaries: *estar, tener, andar, encontrarse, hallarse, ir, llevar, quedar, resultar, venir*, etc.
Ser and **estar**. — For information about the correct use of these verbs consult the English-Spanish half of the dictionary under BE.

HABER

The compound tenses are in italics

Infinitive: haber
Gerund: habiendo
Participle: habido

INDICATIVE

present

Yo he
Tú has
Él ha
Nosotros hemos
Vosotros habéis
Ellos han

imperfect

Yo había
Tú habías
Él había
Nosotros habíamos
Vosotros habíais
Ellos habían

preterite

Yo hube
Tú hubiste
Él hubo
Nosotros hubimos
Vosotros hubisteis
Ellos hubieron

perfect

Yo he habido
Tú has habido
Él ha habido
Nosotros hemos habido
Vosotros habéis habido
Ellos han habido

past anterior

Yo hube habido
Tú hubiste habido
Él hubo habido
Nosotros hubimos habido
Vosotros hubisteis habido
Ellos hubieron habido

pluperfect

Yo había habido
Tú habías habido
Él había habido
Nosotros habíamos habido
Vosotros habíais habido
Ellos habían habido

future

Yo habré
Tú habrás
Él habrá
Nosotros habremos
Vosotros habréis
Ellos habrán

future perfect

Yo habré habido
Tú habrás habido
Él habrá habido
Nosotros habremos habido
Vosotros habréis habido
Ellos habrán habido

CONDITIONAL

simple

Yo habría
Tú habrías
Él habría
Nosotros habríamos
Vosotros habríais
Ellos habrían

perfect

Yo habría habido
Tú habrías habido
Él habría habido
Nosotros habríamos habido
Vosotros habríais habido
Ellos habrían habido

IMPERATIVE

He tú
Habed vosotros
(The remaining forms are borrowed from the present subjunctive).

SUBJUNCTIVE

present

Yo haya
Tú hayas
Él haya
Nosotros hayamos
Vosotros hayáis
Ellos hayan

imperfect

Yo hubiera *o* hubiese
Tú hubieras *o* hubieses
Él hubiera *o* hubiese
Nosotros hubiéramos *o* hubiésemos
Vosotros hubierais *o* hubieseis
Ellos hubieran *o* hubiesen

future

Yo hubiere
Tú hubieres
Él hubiere
Nosotros hubiéremos
Vosotros hubiereis
Ellos hubieren

perfect

Yo haya habido
Tú hayas habido
Él haya habido
Nosotros hayamos habido
Vosotros hayáis habido
Ellos hayan habido

pluperfect

Yo hubiera o *hubiese habido*
Tú hubieras o *hubieses habido*
Él hubiera o *hubiese habido*
Nosotros hubiéramos o *hubiésemos habido*
Vosotros hubierais o *hubieseis habido*
Ellos hubieran o *hubiesen habido*

SER

The compound tenses are in italics

Infinitive: ser
Gerund: siendo
Participle: sido

INDICATIVE

present

Yo soy
Tú eres
Él es
Nosotros somos
Vosotros sois
Ellos son

imperfect

Yo era
Tú eras
Él era
Nosotros éramos
Vosotros erais
Ellos eran

preterite

Yo fui
Tú fuiste
Él fue
Nosotros fuimos
Vosotros fuisteis
Ellos fueron

perfect

Yo he sido
Tú has sido
Él ha sido
Nosotros hemos sido
Vosotros habéis sido
Ellos han sido

past anterior

Yo hube sido
Tú hubiste sido
Él hubo sido
Nosotros hubimos sido
Vosotros hubisteis sido
Ellos hubieron sido

pluperfect

Yo había sido
Tú habías sido
Él había sido
Nosotros habíamos sido
Vosotros habíais sido
Ellos habían sido

future

Yo seré
Tú serás
Él será
Nosotros seremos
Vosotros seréis
Ellos serán

future perfect

Yo habré sido
Tú habrás sido
Él habrá sido
Nosotros habremos sido
Vosotros habréis sido
Ellos habrán sido

CONDITIONAL

simple

Yo sería
Tú serías
Él sería
Nosotros seríamos
Vosotros seríais
Ellos serían

perfect

Yo habría sido
Tú habrías sido
Él habría sido
Nosotros habríamos sido
Vosotros habríais sido
Ellos habrían sido

IMPERATIVE

Sé tú
Sed vosotros
(The remaining forms are borrowed from the present subjunctive).

SUBJUNCTIVE

present

Yo sea
Tú seas
Él sea
Nosotros seamos
Vosotros seáis
Ellos sean

imperfect

Yo fuera *o* fuese
Tú fueras *o* fueses
Él fuera *o* fuese
Nosotros fuéramos *o* fuésemos
Vosotros fuerais *o* fueseis
Ellos fueran *o* fuesen

future

Yo fuere
Tú fueres
Él fuere
Nosotros fuéremos
Vosotros fuereis
Ellos fueren

perfect

Yo haya sido
Tú hayas sido
Él haya sido
Nosotros hayamos sido
Vosotros hayáis sido
Ellos hayan sido

pluperfect

Yo hubiera o *hubiese sido*
Tú hubieras o *hubieses sido*
Él hubiera o *hubiese sido*
Nosotros hubiéramos o *hubiésemos sido*
Vosotros hubierais o *hubieseis sido*
Ellos hubieran o *hubiesen sido*

REGULAR VERBS GROUPS

AMAR (stem *am-*)

The endings are in bold type and the compound tenses in italics

Infinitive: am**ar**
Gerund: am**ando**
Participle: am**ado**

INDICATIVE

present

Yo am**o**
Tú am**as**
Él am**a**
Nosotros am**amos**
Vosotros am**áis**
Ellos am**an**

imperfect

Yo am**aba**
Tú am**abas**
Él am**aba**
Nosotros am**ábamos**
Vosotros am**abais**
Ellos am**aban**

preterite

Yo am**é**
Tú am**aste**
Él am**ó**
Nosotros am**amos**
Vosotros am**asteis**
Ellos am**aron**

perfect

*Yo he am**ado***
*Tú has am**ado***
*Él ha am**ado***
*Nosotros hemos am**ado***
*Vosotros habéis am**ado***
*Ellos han am**ado***

past anterior

*Yo hube am**ado***
*Tú hubiste am**ado***
*Él hubo am**ado***
*Nosotros hubimos am**ado***
*Vosotros hubisteis am**ado***
*Ellos hubieron am**ado***

pluperfect

Yo había amado
Tú habías amado
Él había amado
Nosotros habíamos amado
Vosotros habíais amado
Ellos habían amado

future

Yo amaré
Tú amarás
Él amará
Nosotros amaremos
Vosotros amaréis
Ellos amarán

future perfect

Yo habré amado
Tú habrás amado
Él habrá amado
Nosotros habremos amado
Vosotros habréis amado
Ellos habrán amado

CONDITIONAL

simple

Yo amaría
Tú amarías
Él amaría
Nosotros amaríamos
Vosotros amaríais
Ellos amarían

perfect

Yo habría amado
Tú habrías amado
Él habría amado
Nosotros habríamos amado
Vosotros habríais amado
Ellos habrían amado

IMPERATIVE

Ama tú
Amad vosotros
(The remaining forms are borrowed from the present subjunctive).

SUBJUNCTIVE

present

Yo ame
Tú ames
Él ame
Nosotros amemos
Vosotros améis
Ellos amen

imperfect

Yo amara *o* amase
Tú amaras *o* amases
Él amara *o* amase
Nosotros amáramos *o* amásemos
Vosotros amarais *o* amaseis
Ellos amaran *o* amasen

future

Yo amare
Tú amares
Él amare
Nosotros amáremos
Vosotros amareis
Ellos amaren

perfect

Yo haya amado
Tú hayas amado
Él haya amado
Nosotros hayamos amado
Vosotros hayáis amado
Ellos hayan amado

pluperfect

Yo hubiera o *hubiese amado*
Tú hubieras o *hubieses amado*
Él hubiera o *hubiese amado*
Nosotros hubiéramos o *hubiésemos amado*
Vosotros hubierais o *hubieseis amado*
Ellos hubieran o *hubiesen amado*

TEMER (stem *tem-*)

The endings are in bold type and the compound tenses in italics

Infinitive: temer
Gerund: temiendo
Participle: temido

INDICATIVE

present

Yo temo
Tú temes
Él teme
Nosotros tememos
Vosotros teméis
Ellos temen

imperfect

Yo temía
Tú temías
Él temía
Nosotros temíamos
Vosotros temíais
Ellos temían

preterite

Yo temí
Tú temiste
Él temió
Nosotros temimos
Vosotros temisteis
Ellos temieron

perfect

Yo he temido
Tú has temido
Él ha temido
Nosotros hemos temido
Vosotros habéis temido
Ellos han temido

past anterior

Yo hube temido
Tú hubiste temido
Él hubo temido
Nosotros hubimos temido
Vosotros hubisteis temido
Ellos hubieron temido

pluperfect

Yo había temido
Tú habías temido
Él había temido
Nosotros habíamos temido
Vosotros habíais temido
Ellos habían temido

future

Yo temeré
Tú temerás
Él temerá
Nosotros temeremos
Vosotros temeréis
Ellos temerán

future perfect

Yo habré temido
Tú habrás temido
Él habrá temido
Nosotros habremos temido
Vosotros habréis temido
Ellos habrán temido

CONDITIONAL

simple

Yo temería
Tú temerías
Él temería
Nosotros temeríamos
Vosotros temeríais
Ellos temerían

perfect

Yo habría temido
Tú habrías temido
Él habría temido
Nosotros habríamos temido
Vosotros habríais temido
Ellos habrían temido

IMPERATIVE

Teme tú
Temed vosotros
(The remaining forms are borrowed from the present subjunctive).

SUBJUNCTIVE

present

Yo tema
Tú temas
Él tema
Nosotros temamos
Vosotros temáis
Ellos teman

imperfect

Yo temiera *o* temiese
Tú temieras *o* temieses
Él temiera *o* temiese
Nosotros temiéramos *o* temiésemos
Vosotros temierais *o* temieseis
Ellos temieran *o* temiesen

future

Yo temiere
Tú temieres
Él temiere
Nosotros temiéremos
Vosotros temiereis
Ellos temieren

perfect

Yo haya temido
Tú hayas temido
Él haya temido
Nosotros hayamos temido
Vosotros hayáis temido
Ellos hayan temido

pluperfect

Yo hubiera o *hubiese temido*
Tú hubieras o *hubieses temido*
Él hubiera o *hubiese temido*
Nosotros hubiéramos o *hubiésemos temido*
Vosotros hubierais o *hubieseis temido*
Ellos hubieran o *hubiesen temido*

PARTIR (stem *part-*)

The endings are in bold type and the compound tenses in italics

Infinitive: partir
Gerund: partiendo
Participle: partido

INDICATIVE

present

Yo parto
Tú partes
Él parte
Nosotros partimos
Vosotros partís
Ellos parten

imperfect

Yo partía
Tú partías
Él partía
Nosotros partíamos
Vosotros partíais
Ellos partían

preterite

Yo partí
Tú partiste
Él partió
Nosotros partimos
Vosotros partisteis
Ellos partieron

perfect

Yo he partido
Tú has partido
Él ha partido
Nosotros hemos partido
Vosotros habéis partido
Ellos han partido

past anterior

Yo hube partido
Tú hubiste partido
Él hubo partido
Nosotros hubimos partido
Vosotros hubisteis partido
Ellos hubieron partido

pluperfect

Yo había partido
Tú habías partido
Él había partido
Nosotros habíamos partido
Vosotros habíais partido
Ellos habían partido

future

Yo partiré
Tú partirás
Él partirá
Nosotros partiremos
Vosotros partiréis
Ellos partirán

future perfect

Yo habré partido
Tú habrás partido
Él habrá partido
Nosotros habremos partido
Vosotros habréis partido
Ellos habrán partido

CONDITIONAL

simple

Yo partiría
Tú partirías
Él partiría
Nostros partiríamos
Vosotros partiríais
Ellos partirían

perfect

Yo habría partido
Tu habrías partido
Él habría partido
Nosotros habríamos partido
Vosotros habríais partido
Ellos habrían partido

IMPERATIVE

Parte tú
Partid vosotros
(The remaining forms are borrowed from the present subjunctive).

SUBJUNCTIVE

present

Yo parta
Tú partas
Él parta
Nosotros partamos
Vosotros partáis
Ellos partan

imperfect

Yo partiera *o* partiese
Tú partieras *o* partieses
Él partiera *o* partiese
Nosotros partiéramos *o* partiésemos
Vosotros partierais *o* partieseis
Ellos partieran *o* partiesen

future

Yo partiere
Tú partieres
Él partiere
Nosotros partiéremos
Vosotros partiereis
Ellos partieren

perfect

Yo haya partido
Tú hayas partido
Él haya partido
Nosotros hayamos partido
Vosotros hayáis partido
Ellos hayan partido

pluperfect

Yo hubiera o *hubiese partido*
Tú hubieras o *hubieses partido*
Él hubiera o *hubiese partido*
Nosotros hubiéramos o *hubiésemos partido*
Vosotros hubierais o *hubieseis partido*
Ellos hubieran o *hubiesen partido*

The three different groups of verbs in Spanish can be distinguished by the last two letters of the infinitive.

The *first group* includes verbs ending in **-ar** in the infinitive (am**ar**)

The *second group* includes verbs ending in **-er** in the infinitive (tem**er**).

The third group includes verbs ending in **-ir** in the infinitive (part**ir**).

The only differences between groups two and three lie in the infinitive, the first and second person plural of the present indicative (tem**emos**, tem**éis**; part**imos**, part**ís**) and the imperative second person plural (tem**ed**; part**id**).

The future and conditional are formed by adding the appropriate endings to the infinitive (amar **é**; amar **ía**), and the imperfect subjunctive and the future subjunctive by replacing the third person plural preterite ending *-ron* with the appropriate subjunctive endings (ama **ra**; ama **se**; ama **re**).

SPELLING CHANGES IN CERTAIN VERBS

Spanish rules for spelling and pronunciation (see above) give rise to the following irregularities in the spelling of certain verbs.

VERBS IN -EÍR, -CHIR, -LLIR, -ÑER, -ÑIR

INFINITIVE		GERUND	PRETERITE	IMPERFECT SUBJUNCTIVE	FUTURE SUBJUNCTIVE
-eír	desleír	desliendo	deslió..., deslieron	desliera... desliese...	desliere...
-chir	henchir	hinchendo	hinchó..., hincheron	hinchera... hinchese...	hinchere...
-llir	engullir	engullendo	engulló..., engulleron	engullera... engullese...	engullere...
-ñer	atañer	atañendo	atañó..., atañeron	atañera... atañese...	atañere...
-ñir	astriñir	astriñendo	astriñó..., astriñeron	astriñera... astriñese...	astriñere...

The **unstressed** "**i**" in the verbs disappears between *ch, ll, ñ* and a vowel, i.e. in the gerund, the 3rd person singular and plural of the preterite and tenses derived from these. *Desleír* is included in this category because its stem is to all intents and purposes *desli-*, and the "*i*" is not doubled in the tenses mentioned above as it should be in theory. All these verbs appear in the list of irregular verbs.

VERBS IN -AER, -EER, -OER, -OÍR, -UIR

INFINITIVE		GERUND	PRETERITE	IMPERFECT SUBJUNCTIVE	FUTURE SUBJUNCTIVE
-aer	raer	rayendo	rayó..., rayeron	rayera... rayese...	rayere...
-eer	creer	creyendo	creyó..., creyeron	creyera... creyese...	creyere...
-oer	corroer	corroyendo	corroyó..., corroyeron	corroyera... corroyese...	corroyere...
-oír	oír	oyendo	oyó..., oyeron	oyera... oyese...	oyere...
-uir	concluir	concluyendo	concluyó..., concluyeron	concluyera... concluyese...	concluyere...

The common feature of the above verbs is that the **unstressed** "**i**" between two vowels changes to **y**.
All these verbs appear in the list of irregular verbs.

VERBS IN -CAR, -GAR, -GUAR, -ZAR

	INFINITIVE	PRESENT SUBJUNCTIVE	PRETERITE
-car : c → *qu*	tocar	toque, etc.	toqué
-gar : g → *gu*	pagar	pague, etc.	pagué
-guar : gu → *gü*	amortiguar	amortigüe, etc.	amortigüé
-zar : z → *c*	alcanzar	alcance, etc.	alcancé

Here the final consonant of the stem changes before endings beginning with **-e**, i.e. in the present subjunctive and the first person singular of the preterite of **-ar** verbs.

VERBS IN -CER, -CIR, -GER, GIR, -GUIR, -QUIR

	INFINITIVE	PRESENT INDICATIVE	PRESENT SUBJUNCTIVE
-cer, -cir : c → *z*	mecer	mezo	meza, mezas, etc.
	resarcir	resarzo	resarza, resarzas, etc.
-ger, -gir : g → *j*	proteger	protejo	proteja, protejas, etc.
	dirigir	dirijo	dirija, dirijas, etc.
-guir : gu → *g*	distinguir	distingo	distinga, distingas, etc.
-quir : qu → *c*	delinquir	delinco	delinca, delincas, etc.

Here the final consonant of the stem changes before an ending beginning with **-o** or **-a**, i.e. in the first person singular of the present indicative and in the present subjunctive of **-er** and **-ir** verbs.

TONIC STRESS ON VERBS IN "-IAR" AND "-UAR"

These verbs take a written accent on the **i** or the **u** of the stem in the singular and the 3rd person plural of the present indicative (*confío, confías, confía ..., confían*), of the present subjunctive (*gradúe, gradúes, gradúe ..., gradúen*) and in the 2nd person singular of the imperative (*confía*).

There are exceptions to this rule, notably certain verbs ending in **-iar** (*abreviar, acariciar, apreciar, copiar, estudiar*, etc.) and all verbs ending in **-cuar** and **-guar**.

GROUPS OF IRREGULAR VERBS

The following pages contain a list of irregular Spanish verbs. Since certain irregularities are common to large groups of verbs, here is a summary of the most common changes which affect irregular verbs:

o and **e** in the stem change to **ue** and **ie** respectively. *Volar, helar, poder, perder, concernir* and *discernir* are examples of verbs which undergo this change. The **o** and **e** become diphthongs when in a stressed position, i.e. in the 1st, 2nd and 3rd person singular and the 3rd person plural of the present indicative (*vuelo, vuelas, vuela ..., vuelan*) and of the present subjunctive (*pierda, pierdas, pierda ..., pierdan*), and also in the 2nd person singular of the imperative;

e in the stem changes to **i**. This change affects all **-ir** verbs with an *e* in the stem which is not followed by *r* or *nt*, and also the verb *servir*. The *e* remains only when the ending of the verb begins with *stressed i*. It changes to *i* in all other cases, namely in the 1st, 2nd and 3rd person singular and the 3rd person plural of the present indicative (*pido, pides, pide ..., piden*), in the 3rd person singular and plural of the preterite (*pidió, pidieron*), in the 2nd person singular of the imperative (*pide*), in the present subjunctive (*pida, pidas*, etc.), the imperfect subjunctive (*pidiera* or *pidiese*, etc.), the future subjunctive (*pidiere, pidieres*, etc.), and the gerund (*pidiendo*);

e in the stem becomes **i** in certain cases and **ie** in others. Verbs in **-ir** with an *e* in the stem followed by *r* or *nt* (except *servir*) fall into this category. These verbs undergo the same changes as the preceding group, except in the present indicative, the imperative and the present subjunctive where the diphthong *ie* replaces *i* in stressed positions (*miento, mientes, miente ..., mienten*; *miente*; *mienta, mientas, mienta ..., mientan*);

o in the stem becomes **u** in certain cases and **ue** in others according to the same rules as for the above group. The main verbs in this class are *morir* and *dormir*;

when the stem of a verb ends in vowel followed by **c** this **c** changes to **zc** before endings beginning with *o* or *a*. This category includes verbs ending in **-acer**, **-ecer**, **-ocer**, **-ucir**, except *hacer, cocer, escocer* and *mecer*. This change affects the first person singular of the present indicative (*reconozco*) and the present subjunctive (*reconozca, reconozcas*, etc.).

An added irregularity of verbs ending in **-ducir** is the preterite tense which ends in **-duje**, **-dujiste**, etc. (*conduje*, etc.), and consequently the imperfect and future subjunctive forms which end in **-dujera** or **-dujese**, etc. (*condujera* or *condujese*, etc.) and **-dujere**, etc. (*condujere*, etc.).

verbs ending in **-uir** add a **y** after the *u* before the vowels *a, o, e*, that is in the 1st, 2nd and 3rd person singular and the 3rd person plural of the present indicative (*huyo, huyes, huye ..., huyen*), in the 2nd person singular of the imperative (*huye*), in the 3rd person singular and plural of the preterite (*huyó, huyeron*), and in all forms of the subjunctive (*huya, huyas*, etc.; *huyera, huyeras*, etc.; *huyere, huyeres*, etc.).

Note: Some verbs combine several irregularities (*despliegue, elija, persigo*, etc.).

LIST OF IRREGULAR VERBS

A

abastecer. — Conjugated like *parecer*.
abnegarse. — Like *apretar*.
abolir. — Defective. Conjugated only in those forms which have endings beginning in *i*. *Pres. ind.:* abolimos, abolís; *Imperf.:* abolía, abolías, etc.; *Pret.:* abolí, aboliste, abolió, etc.; *Fut.:* aboliré, abolirás, etc.; *Cond.:* aboliría, abolirías, etc.; *Imper.:* abolid; *Pres. subj.:* (does not exist); *Imperfect subj.:* aboliera, abolieras, etc. (first form); aboliese, abolieses, etc. (second form); *Fut. subj.:* aboliere, abolieres, etc.; *Ger.* aboliendo; *Past. part.:* abolido.
aborrecer. — Like *parecer*.
absolver. — Like *volver*.
abstenerse. — Like *tener*.
abstraer. — Like *traer*.
abuñolar. — Like *contar*.
acaecer. — Like *parecer*. Defective. Conjugated only in 3rd pers. sing.
acertar. — Like *apretar*.
acollar. — Like *contar*.
acontecer. — Like *parecer*. Defective. Conjugated only in 3rd pers. sing. and pl.
acordar. — Like *contar*.
acostar. — Like *contar*.
acrecentar. — Like *apretar*.
acrecer. — Like *parecer*.
adherir. — Like *sentir*.
adir. — Defective. Conjugated only in the infinitive, the gerund and the past participle.
adolecer. — Like *parecer*.
adormecer. — Like *parecer*.
adquirir. — *Pres. ind.:* adquiero, adquieres, etc.; *Pres. subj.:* adquiera, adquiramos, adquiráis, etc.; *Imper.:* adquiere, adquiera, etc. (Regular in the remaining tenses).
aducir. — *Pres. ind.:* aduzco, aduces, aduce, etc.; *Pret.:* adujimos, adujisteis, etc.; *Imper.:* aduce, aduzca, aducid, etc.; *Pres. subj.:* aduzca, aduzcas, aduzcáis, etc.; *Imperf. subj.:* adujera, adujeras, adujerais, etc. (first form); adujese, adujeses, adujeseis, etc. (second form); *Fut. subj.:* adujere, adujeres, etc.; *Ger.:* aduciendo; *Past part.:* aducido.
advenir. — Like *venir*.
advertir. — Like *sentir*.
aferrar. — Like *apretar*.
afluir. — Like *huir*.
afollar. — Like *contar*.
aforar. — Like *contar* (when it means "to grant a privilege").
agorar. — Like *contar* (with diaeresis on diphthong *-üe*).
agradecer. — Like *parecer*.
agredir. — Like *abolir*.
aguerrir. — Like *abolir*. Defective.
alentar. — Like *apretar*.
aliquebrar. — Like *apretar*.
almorzar. — Like *contar*.
amanecer. — Like *parecer*. Impersonal.
amarillecer. — Like *parecer*.
amolar. — Like *contar*.
amorecer. — Like *parecer*.
amortecer. — Like *parecer*.
andar. — *Pret.:* anduve, anduviste, anduvo, anduvimos, anduvisteis, anduvieron: *Imperf. subj.:* anduviera, anduvieras, etc. (first form); anduviese, anduvieses, etc. (second form); *Fut. subj.:* anduviere, anduvieres, etc.
anochecer. — Like *parecer*. Impersonal.
antedecir. — Like *decir*.
anteponer. — Like *poner*.
apacentar. — Like *apretar*.
aparecer. — Like *parecer*.
apercollar. — Like *contar*.
apetecer. — Like *parecer*.
apostar. — Like *contar* (when it means "to bet").
apretar. — *Pres. ind.:* aprieto, aprietas, aprieta, apretamos, etc.; *Pres. subj.:* apriete, aprietes, apretemos, etc.; *Imper.:* aprieta, apriete, apretemos, etc.
aprobar. — Like *contar*.
arborecer. — Like *parecer*.
argüir. — Like *huir*.
aridecer. — Like *parecer*.
arrecirse. — Like *abolir*. Defective.
arrendar. — Like *apretar*.
arrepentirse. — Like *sentir*.
ascender. — Like *hender*.
asentar. — Like *apretar*.
asentir. — Like *sentir*.
aserrar. — Like *apretar*.
asir. — *Pres. ind.:* asgo, ases, asimos, asís, etc.; *Imper.:* ase, asga, asgamos, asid, etc.; *Pres. subj.:* asga, asgáis, etc.
asolar. — Like *contar*.
asonar. — Like *contar*.
astreñir. — Like *teñir*.
astriñir. — Like *mullir*.
atañer. — Like *tañer*. Defective. Conjugated only in 3rd pers. sing. and pl.
atardecer. — Like *parecer*. Impersonal.
atender. — Like *hender*.
atenerse. — Like *tener*.
aterirse. — Like *abolir*. Defective.
aterrar. — Like *apretar* (but regular when it means "to terrify").
atestar. — Like *apretar* (when it means "to fill up").
atraer. — Like *traer*.
atravesar. — Like *apretar*.
atribuir. — Like *huir*.
atronar. — Like *contar*.
avenir. — Like *venir*.
aventar. — Like *apretar*.
avergonzar. — Like *contar*.
azolar. — Like *contar*.

B

balbucir. — Like *abolir*. Defective.
beldar. — Like *apretar*.
bendecir. — Like *decir* (but regular in future indicative, conditional and past participle).
bienquerer. — Like *querer*.
blandir. — Like *abolir*. Defective.
blanquecer. — Like *parecer*.
bruñir. — Like *mullir*.
bullir. — Like *mullir*.

C

caber. — *Pres. ind.:* quepo, cabes, cabe, cabéis, etc.; *Pret.:* cupe, cupiste, cupo, cupimos, cupisteis, cupieron; *Fut.:* cabré, cabrás, cabrá, cabréis, etc.; *Cond.:* cabría, cabrías, etc.; *Imper.:* cabe, quepa, quepamos, etc.; *Pres. subj.:* quepa, quepas, quepáis, etc.; *Imperf. subj.:* cupiera, cupieras, cupierais, etc. (first form); cupiese, cupieses, cupieseis, etc. (second form); *Fut. subj.:* cupiere, cupieres, etc.

caer. — *Pres. ind.:* caigo; *Pres. subj.:* caiga, caigas, caiga, caigamos, caigáis, caigan.
calentar. — Like *apretar*.
carecer. — Like *parecer*.
cegar. — Like *apretar*.
ceñir. — Like *teñir*.
cerner. — Like *hender*.
cernir. — Like *sentir*.
cerrar. — Like *apretar*.
cimentar. — Like *apretar*.
circunferir. — Like *sentir*.
clarecer. — Like *parecer*. Impersonal.
cocer. — *Pres. ind.:* cuezo, cueces, cuece, etc.; *Pres. subj.:* cueza, cuezas, cueza, etc.: *Imper.* cuece, cueza, cozamos, etc.
colar. — Like *contar*.
colegir. — Like *pedir*.
colgar. — Like *contar*.
colorir. — Like *abolir*.
comedirse. — Like *pedir*.
comenzar. — Like *apretar*.
compadecer. — Like *parecer*.
comparecer. — Like *parecer*.
competir. — Like *pedir*.
complacer. — Like *parecer*.
componer. — Like *poner*.
comprobar. — Like *contar*.
concebir. — Like *pedir*.
concernir. — Defective. *Pres. ind.:* concierne, conciernen; *Pres. subj.:* concierna, conciernan; *Imper.:* concierna, conciernan; *Ger.:* concerniendo.
concertar. — Like *apretar*.
concluir. — Like *huir*.
concordar. — Like *contar*.
condescender. — Like *hender*.
condolerse. — Like *volver*.
conducir. — Like *aducir*.
conferir. — Like *sentir*.
confesar. — Like *apretar*.
confluir. — Like *huir*.
conmover. — Like *mover*.
conocer. — Like *parecer*.
conseguir. — Like *pedir*.
consentir. — Like *sentir*.
consolar. — Like *contar*.
consonar. — Like *contar*.
constituir. — Like *huir*.
constreñir. — Like *teñir*.
construir. — Like *huir*.
contar. — *Pres. ind.:* cuento, cuentas, cuenta, contamos, contáis, cuentan; *Pres. subj.:* cuente, cuentes contemos, etc.
contender. — Like *hender*.
contener. — Like *tener*.
contradecir. — Like *decir*.
contraer. — Like *traer*.
contrahacer. — Like *hacer*.
contramanifestar. — Like *apretar*.
contraponer. — Like *poner*.
contravenir. — Like *venir*.
contribuir. — Like *huir*.
controvertir. — Like *sentir*.
convalecer. — Like *parecer*.
convenir. — Like *venir*.
convertir. — Like *sentir*.
corregir. — Like *pedir*.
corroer. — Like *roer*.
costar. — Like *contar*.
crecer. — Like *parecer*.
creer. — *Pret.:* creyó, creyeron; *Imperf. subj.:* creyera, creyeras, etc. (1st form); creyese, creyeses, etc. (2nd form); *Fut. subj.:* creyere, creyeres, etc.; *Ger.:* creyendo.

D

dar. — *Pres. ind.:* doy, das, dais, etc.; *Pret.:* di, diste, dio, disteis, etc.; *Imperf. subj.:* diera, dieras, dierais, etc. (1st form); diese, dieses, dieses, etc. (2nd form); *Fut. subj.:* diere, dieres, etc.
decaer. — Like *caer*.
decentar. — Like *apretar*.
decir. — *Pres. ind.:* digo, dices, decimos, decís, etc.; *Pret.:* dije, dijiste, dijo, etc.; *Fut.:* diré, dirás, diréis, etc.; *Pres. subj.:* diga, digas, digáis, etc.; *Imperf. subj.:* dijera, dijeras, etc. (1st form); dijese, dijeses, etc. (2nd form); *Fut. subj.:* dijere, dijeres, etc.; *Cond.:* diría, dirías, etc.; *Imper.:* di, diga digamos, decid, etc.; *Ger.:* diciendo; *Past part.:* dicho.
decrecer. — Like *parecer*.
deducir. — Like *aducir*.
defender. — Like *hender*.
deferir. — Like *sentir*.
degollar. — Like *contar*.
demoler. — Like *volver*.
demostrar. — Like *contar*.
denegar. — Like *apretar*.
denostar. — Like *contar*.
dentar. — Like *apretar*.
deponer. — Like *poner*.
derretir. — Like *pedir*.
derruir. — Like *huir*.
desacertar. — Like *apretar*.
desacordar. — Like *contar*.
desadvertir. — Like *sentir*.
desaforar. — Like *contar*.
desagradecer. — Like *parecer*.
desalentar. — Like *apretar*.
desandar. Like *andar*.
desaparecer. — Like *parecer*.
desapretar. — Like *apretar*.
desaprobar. — Like *contar*.
desarrendar. Like *apretar*.
desasentar. — Like *apretar*.
desasir. — Like *asir*.
desasosegar. — Like *apretar*.
desatender. — Like *hender*.
desavenir. — Like *venir*.
desbravecer. — Like *parecer*.
descaecer. — Like *parecer*.
descender. — Like *hender*.
desceñir. — Like *teñir*.
descolgar. — Like *contar*.
descollar. — Like *contar*.
descomedirse. Like *pedir*.
descomponer. — Like *poner*.
desconcertar. — Like *apretar*.
desconocer. — Like *parecer*.
desconsolar. — Like *contar*.
descontar. — Like *contar*.
desconvenir. — Like *venir*.
descordar. — Like *contar*.
descornar. — Like *contar*.
desdecir. — Like *decir*.
desdentar. — Like *apretar*.
desembravecer. — Like *parecer*.
desempedrar. — Like *apretar*.
desencordar. — Like *contar*.
desenfurecer. — Like *parecer*.
desengrosar. — Like *contar*.
desenmohecer. — Like *parecer*.
desenmudecer. — Like *parecer*.
desensoberbecer. — Like *parecer*.
desentenderse. — Like *hender*.
desenterrar. — Like *apretar*.
desentorpecer. — Like *parecer*.
desentumecer. — Like *parecer*.
desenvolver. — Like *volver*.
desfallecer. — Like *parecer*.
desfavorecer. — Like *parecer*.
desflorecer. — Like *parecer*.
desgobernar. — Like *apretar*.
desguarnecer. — Like *parecer*.
deshacer. — Like *hacer*.
deshelar. — Like *apretar*.
desherbar. — Like *apretar*.
desherrar. — Like *apretar*.
deshumedecer. — Like *parecer*.
desleír. — Like *reír*.
deslucir. — Like *lucir*.
desmajolar. — Like *contar*.
desmedirse. — Like *pedir*.
desmembrar. — Like *apretar*.
desmentir. — Like *sentir*.
desmerecer. — Like *parecer*.
desobedecer. — Like *parecer*.
desobstruir. — Like *huir*.
desoír. — Like *oír*.
desolar. — Like *contar*.
desoldar. — Like *contar*.
desollar. — Like *contar*.
desosar. — *Pres. ind.:* deshueso, deshuesas, deshuesa, etc.; *Imper.:* deshuesa, deshuese, etc.; *Pres. subj.:* deshuese, deshueses, etc.
despavorirse. — Like *abolir*.
despedir. — Like *pedir*.
desperecer. — Like *parecer*.
despernar. — Like *apretar*.
despertar. — Like *apretar*.
desplacer. — Like *placer*.
desplegar. — Like *apretar*.
despoblar. — Like *contar*.
desteñir. — Like *teñir*.
desterrar. — Like *apretar*.
destituir. — Like *huir*.
destorcer. — Like *torcer*.
destruir. — Like *huir*.
desvanecer. — Like *parecer*.
desvergonzarse. — Like *contar*.
desvestir. — Like *pedir*.
detener. — Like *tener*.
detraer. — Like *traer*.
devenir. — Like *venir*.
devolver. — Like *volver*.
diferir. — Like *sentir*.
difluir. — Like *huir*.
digerir. — Like *sentir*.
diluir. — Like *huir*.
discernir. — *Pres. ind.:* discierno, disciernes, discierne, discernimos, discernís, disciernen; *Pres. subj.:* discierna, disciernas, discernamos, etc.; *Imper.* discierne, discierna, discernid, etc.
disconvenir. — Like *venir*.
discordar. — Like *contar*.
disentir. — Like *sentir*.
disminuir. — Like *huir*.
disolver. — Like *volver*.
disonar. — Like *contar*.

displacer. — Like *placer.*
disponer. — Like *poner.*
distender. — Like *hender.*
distraer. — Like *traer.*
distribuir. — Like *huir.*
divertir. — Like *sentir.*
doler. — Like *mover.*
dormir. — *Pres. ind.:* duermo, duermes, duerme, dormís, etc.; *Pret.* dormí, dormiste, durmió, durmieron; *Imper.* duerme, duerma, durmamos, dormid, etc.; *Pres. subj.:* duerma, duermas, duerma, etc.; *Imperf. subj.:* durmiera, durmieras, etc. (1st form); durmiese, durmieses, etc. (2nd form); *Fut. subj.:* durmiere, durmieres, etc.: *Ger.:* durmiendo.

E

educir. — Like *aducir.*
elegir. — Like *pedir.*
embaír. — Like *abolir.* Defective.
embastecer. — Like *parecer.*
embebecer. — Like *parecer.*
embellaquecerse. — Like *parecer.*
embellecer. — Like *parecer.*
embermejecer. — Like *parecer.*
embestir. — Like *pedir.*
emblandecer. — Like *parecer.*
emblanquecer. — Like *parecer.*
embobecer. — Like *parecer.*
embosquecer. — Like *parecer.*
embravecer. — Like *parecer.*
embrutecer. — Like *parecer.*
emparentar. — Like *aprètar.*
empecer. — Like *parecer.*
empedernir. — Like *abolir.* Defective.
empedrar. — Like *apretar.*
empequeñecer. — Like *parecer.*
empezar. — Like *apretar.*
emplumecer. — Like *parecer.*
empobrecer. — Like *parecer.*
empodrecer. — Like *parecer.*
enaltecer. — Like *parecer.*
enardecer. — Like *parecer.*
encalvecer. — Like *parecer.*
encallecer. — Like *parecer.*
encandecer. — Like *parecer.*
encanecer. — Like *parecer.*
encarecer. — Like *parecer.*
encarnecer. — Like *parecer.*
encender. — Like *hender.*
encentar. — Like *apretar.*
encerrar. — Like *apretar.*
enclocar. — Like *contar.*
encloquecer. — Like *parecer.*
encomendar. — Like *apretar.*
encontrar. — Like *contar.*
encordar. — Like *contar.*
encrudecer. — Like *parecer.*
encruelecer. — Like *parecer.*
endentar. — Like *apretar.*
endentecer. — Like *parecer.*
endurecer. — Like *parecer.*
enflaquecer. — Like *parecer.*
enfurecer. — Like *parecer.*
engrandecer. — Like *parecer.*
engreír. — Like *reír.*
engrosar. — Like *contar.*
engrumecerse. — Like *parecer.*
engullir. — Like *mullir.*
enloquecer. — Like *parecer.*
enlucir. — Like *lucir.*
enmarillecerse. — Like *parecer.*
enmendar. — Like *apretar.*
enmohecer. — Like *parecer.*
enmudecer. — Like *parecer.*
ennegrecer. — Like *parecer.*
ennoblecer. — Like *parecer.*
enorgullecer. — Like *parecer.*
enrarecer. — Like *parecer.*
enriquecer. — Like *parecer.*
enrojecer. — Like *parecer.*
enronquecer. — Like *parecer.*
ensangrentar. — Like *apretar.*
ensoberbecer. — Like *parecer.*
ensombrecer. — Like *parecer.*
ensordecer. — Like *parecer.*
entallecer. — Like *parecer.*
entender. — Like *hender.*
entenebrecer. — Like *parecer.*
enternecer. — Like *parecer.*
enterrar. — Like *apretar.*
entesar. — Like *apretar.*
entontecer. — Like *parecer.*
entorpecer. — Like *parecer.*
entrecerrar. — Like *apretar.*
entreoír. — Like *oír.*
entretener. — Like *tener.*
entrever. — Like *ver.*
entristecer. — Like *parecer.*
entullecer. — Like *parecer.*
entumecer. — Like *parecer.*
envanecer. — Like *parecer.*
envejecer. — Like *parecer.*
envilecer. — Like *parecer.*
envolver. — Like *volver.*
equivaler. — Like *valer.*
erguir. — *Pres. ind.:* irgo *or* yergo, irgues *or* yergues, irgue *or* yergue, erguimos, erguís, irguen *or* yerguen; *Pret.:* erguí, erguiste, irguió, erguimos, erguisteis, irguieron; *Imper.:* irgue *or* yergue, irga *or* yerga, irgamos, etc.; *Pres. subj.:* irga *or* yerga, irgas *or* yergas, irga *or* yerga, irgamos, etc.; *Imperf. subj.:* irguiera, irguieras, etc. (1st form); irguiese, irguieses, etc. (2nd form); *Fut. subj.:* irguiere, irguieres, etc.; *Ger.* irguiendo.
errar. — *Pres. ind.:* yerro, yerras, yerra, erramos, etc.; *Pres. subj.:* yerre, yerres, etc.; *Imper.:* yerra, yerre, erremos, etc.
escabullirse. — Like *mullir.*
escarmentar. — Like *apretar.*
escarnecer. — Like *parecer.*
esclarecer. — Like *parecer.*
escocer. — Like *cocer.*
esforzar. — Like *contar.*
establecer. — Like *parecer.*
estar. — *Pres. ind.:* estoy, estás, etc.; *Pret.:* estuve, estuviste, estuvo, estuvimos, etc.; *Imper.:* está, esté, etc.; *Pres. subj.:* esté, estés, etc.; *Imperf. subj.:* estuviera, estuvieras, etc. (1st form); estuviese, estuvieses, etc. (2nd form); *Fut. subj.:* estuviere, estuvieres, etc.
estatuir. — Like *huir.*
estregar. — Like *apretar.*
estremecer. — Like *parecer.*
estreñir. — Like *teñir.*
excluir. — Like *huir.*
expedir. — Like *pedir.*
exponer. — Like *poner.*
extender. — Like *hender.*
extraer. — Like *traer.*

F

fallecer. — Like *parecer.*
favorecer. — Like *parecer.*
fenecer. — Like *parecer.*
florecer. — Like *parecer.*
fluir. — Like *huir.*
follar. — Like *contar.*
fortalecer. — Like *parecer.*
forzar. — Like *contar.*
fosforecer. — Like *parecer.*
fregar. — Like *apretar.*
freír. — Like *reír*

G

gañir. — Like *mullir.*
garantir. — Like *abolir.* Defective.
gemir. — Like *pedir.*
gobernar. — Like *apretar.*
gruir. — Like *huir.*
gruñir. — Like *mullir.*
guarecer. — Like *parecer.*
guarnecer. — Like *parecer.*
guarnir. — Like *abolir.* Defective.

H

haber. — See AUXILIARY VERBS.
hacendar. — Like *apretar.*
hacer. — *Pres. ind.:* hago, haces, hace, etc.; *Pret.:* hice, hiciste, hizo, etc.; *Fut.:* haré, harás, hará, etc.; *Imper.:* haz, haga, hagamos, etc.; *Cond.:* haría, harías, etc.; *Pres. subj.:* haga, hagas, etc.; *Imperf. subj.:* hiciera, hicieras, etc. (1st form); hiciese, hicieses, etc. (2nd form); *Fut. subj.:* hiciere, hicieres, etc.; *Ger.:* haciendo; *Past part.:* hecho.
heder. — Like *hender.*
helar. — Like *apretar.*
henchir. — Like *pedir.*
hender. — *Pres. ind.:* hiendo, hiendes, hiende, hendemos, hendéis, hienden; *Imper.:* hiende, hienda, hendamos, etc.; *Pres. subj.:* hienda, hiendas etc.
hendir. — Like *sentir.*
herbecer. — Like *parecer.*
herir. — Like *sentir.*
herrar. — Like *apretar.*
hervir. — Like *sentir.*
holgar. — Like *contar.*
hollar. — Like *contar.*
huir. — *Pres. ind.:* huyo, huyes, huye, huimos, huis, huyen; *Pret.:* hui, huiste, huyó, etc.; *Imper.:* huye, huya, huid, etc.; *Pres. subj.:* huya, huyas, huya, etc.
humedecer. — Like *parecer.*

I

imbuir. — Like *huir.*
impedir. — Like *pedir.*
imponer. — Like *poner.*
incensar. — Like *apretar.*
incluir. — Like *huir.*
incoar. — Like *amar,* but defective like *abolir.*
incumbir. — Like *partir.* Defective. Conjugated only in the infinitive, the gerund, the past participle and the 3rd persons sing. and pl. of all tenses.
indisponer. — Like *poner.*
inducir. — Like *aducir.*
inferir. — Like *sentir.*
influir. — Like *huir.*
ingerir. — Like *sentir.*
inquirir. — Like *adquirir.*
instituir. — Like *huir.*
instruir. — Like *huir.*
interferir. — Like *sentir.*
interponer. — Like *poner.*

intervenir. — Like *venir*.
introducir. — Like *aducir*.
intuir. — Like *huir*.
invernar. — Like *apretar*.
invertir. — Like *sentir*.
investir. — Like *pedir*.
ir. — *Pres. ind.*: voy, vas, va, vamos, vais, van; *Pret.*: fui, fuiste, fue, etc.; *Imperf.*: iba, ibas, etc.; *Imper.*: ve, vaya, vayamos, id, vayan; *Pres. subj.*: vaya, vayas, etc.; *Imperf. subj.*: fuera, fueras, etc. (1st form); fuese, fueses, etc. (2nd form); *Fut. subj.*: fuere, fueres, fuere, fuéremos, etc.; *Ger.*: yendo; *Past part.*: ido.

J

jugar. — Like *contar*.

L

languidecer. — Like *parecer*.
lobreguecer. — Like *parecer*. Impersonal.
lucir. — *Pres. ind.*: luzco, luces, luce, etc.; *Imper.*: luce, luzca, luzcamos, lucid, etc.; *Pres. subj.*: luzca, luzcas, etc.

LL

llover. — Like *volver*. Impersonal.

M

maldecir. — Like *decir*.
malherir. — Like *sentir*.
malquerer. — Like *querer*.
maltraer. — Like *traer*.
manifestar. — Like *apretar*.
manir. — Like *abolir*. Defective.
mantener. — Like *tener*.
medir. — Like *pedir*.
mentar. — Like *apretar*.
mentir. — Like *sentir*.
merecer. — Like *parecer*.
merendar. — Like *apretar*.
moblar. — Like *contar*.
moler. — Like *mover*.
morder. — Like *mover*.
morir. — Like *dormir*.
mostrar. — Like *contar*.
mover. — *Pres. ind.*: muevo, mueves, mueve, movemos, movéis, mueven; *Pres. subj.*: mueva, muevas, etc.; *Imper.*: mueve, mueva, movamos, etc.; *Ger.*: moviendo; *Past part.*: movido.
mullir. — *Pret.*: mullí, mulliste, mulló, etc.; *Imperf. subj.*: mullera, mulleras, etc. (1st form); mullese, mulleses, etc. (2nd form); *Fut. subj.*: mullere, mulleres, etc.; *Ger.*: mullendo.

N

nacer. — Like *parecer*.
negar. — Like *apretar*.
nevar. — Like *apretar*. Impersonal.

O

obedecer. — Like *parecer*.
obscurecer. — Like *parecer*.
obstruir. — Like *huir*.
obtener. — Like *tener*.
ofrecer. — Like *parecer*.
oír. — *Pres. ind.*: oigo, oyes, oye, oímos, oís, oyen; *Pres. subj.*: oiga, oigas, etc.; *Imper.*: oye, oiga; *Pret.*: oí, oiste, oyó, etc.; *Ger.*: oyendo; *Past part.*: oído.
oler. — *Pres. ind.*: huelo, hueles, huele, olemos, oléis, huelen; *Pres. subj.*: huela, huelas, etc.; *Imper.*: huele, huela, olamos, oled, huelan.
oponer. — Like *poner*.
oscurecer. — Like *parecer*.

P

pacer. — Like *parecer*.
padecer. — Like *parecer*.
palidecer. — Like *parecer*.
parecer. — *Pres. ind.*: parezco, pareces, etc.; *Imper.*: parece, parezca, etc.; *Pres. subj.*: parezca, parezcas, etc.
pedir. — *Pres. ind.*: pido, pides, pide, pedimos, pedís, piden; *Pret.*: pedí, pediste, pidió, etc.; *Imper.*: pide, pida, pidamos, etc.; *Pres. subj.*: pida, pidas, etc.; *Imperf. subj.*: pidiera, pidieras (1st form); pidiese, pidieses, etc. (2nd form); *Fut. subj.*: pidiere, pidieres, etc.; *Ger.*: pidiendo.
pensar. — Like *apretar*.
perder. — Like *hender*.
perecer. — Like *parecer*.
permanecer. — Like *parecer*.
perniquebrar. — Like *apretar*.
perquirir. — Like *adquirir*.
perseguir. — Like *pedir*.
pertenecer. — Like *parecer*.
pervertir. — Like *sentir*.
placer. — *Pres. ind.*: plazco, places, place, etc.; *Pret.*: plací, placiste, plació *or* plugo, placimos, placisteis, etc.; *Imper.*: place, plazca, placed, etc.; *Pres. subj.*: plazca, plazcas, plazca *or* plegue *or* plega, etc.; *Imperf. subj.*: placiera, placieras, placiera *or* pluguiera, etc. (1st form); placiese, placieses, placiese *or* pluguiese, etc. (2nd form); *Fut. subj.*: placiere, placieres, placiere *or* pluguiere, etc.
plañir. — Like *mullir*.
plegar. — Like *apretar*.
poblar. — Like *contar*.
poder. — *Pres. ind.*: puedo, puedes, puede, podemos, podéis, pueden; *Pret.*: pude, pudiste, pudo, etc.; *Fut.*: podré, podrás, podrá, etc.; *Cond.*: podría, podrías, etc.; *Imper.*: puede, pueda, podamos, et..; *Pres. subj.*: pueda, puedas, pueda, etc.; *Imperf. subj.*: pudiera, pudieras, etc. (1st form); pudiese, pudieses, etc. (2nd form); *Ger.*: pudiendo.
podrir. — Like *pudrir*.
poner. — *Pres. ind.*: pongo, pones, pone, etc.; *Pret.*: puse, pusiste, puso, etc.; *Fut.*: pondré, pondrás, etc.; *Cond.*: pondría, pondrías, etc.; *Imper.*: pon, ponga, pongamos, etc.; *Pres. subj.*: ponga, pongas, etc.; *Imperf. subj.*: pusiera, pusieras, etc. (1st form); pusiese, pusieses, etc. (2nd form); *Fut. subj.*. pusiere, pusieres, etc.; *Ger.*: poniendo; *Past part.*: puesto.
poseer. — Like *creer*.
posponer. — Like *poner*.
preconcebir. — Like *pedir*.
predecir. — Like *decir*.
predisponer. — Like *poner*.
preelegir. — Like *pedir*.
preferir. — Like *sentir*.
preponer. — Like *poner*.
presentir. — Like *sentir*.
presuponer. — Like *poner*.
preterir. — Like *abolir*. Defective.
prevalecer. — Like *parecer*.
prevaler. — Like *valer*.
prevenir. — Like *venir*.
prever. — Like *ver*.
probar. — Like *contar*.
producir. — Like *aducir*.
proferir. — Like *sentir*.
promover. — Like *mover*.
proponer. — Like *poner*.
proseguir. — Like *pedir*.
prostituir. — Like *huir*.
provenir. — Like *venir*.
pudrir. — *Past part.*: podrido.

Q

quebrar. — Like *apretar*.
querer. — *Pres. ind.*: quiero, quieres, quiere, queremos, queréis, quieren; *Pret.*: quise, quisiste, quiso, etc.; *Fut.*: querré, querrás, querrá, etc.; *Imper.*: quiere, quiera, etc.; *Cond.*: querría, querrías, etc.; *Pres. subj.*: quiera, quieras, etc.; *Imperf. subj.*: quisiera, quisieras, etc. (1st form); quisiese, quisieses, etc. (2nd form); *Fut. subj.*: quisiere, quisieres, etc.

R

raer. — *Pres. ind.*: raigo *or* rayo, raes, etc.; *Imper.*: rae, raiga *or* raya, raigamos *or* rayamos, etc.; *Pres. subj.*: raiga *or* raya, raigas *or* rayas, etc.
rarefacer. — Like *parecer*.
reaparecer. — Like *parecer*.
reblandecer. — Like *parecer*.
rebullir. — Like *mullir*.
recaer. — Like *caer*.
recalentar. — Like *apretar*.
recentar. — Like *apretar*.
recluir. — Like *huir*.
recocer. — Like *cocer*.
recolar. — Like *contar*.
recomendar. — Like *apretar*
recomponer. — Like *poner*.
reconducir. — Like *aducir*.
reconocer. — Like *parecer*.
reconstituir. — Like *huir*.
reconstruir. — Like *huir*.
recontar. — Like *contar*.
reconvenir. — Like *venir*.
reconvertir. — Like *sentir*.
recordar. — Like *contar*.
recostar. — Like *contar*.
recrecer. — Like *parecer*.
recrudecer. — Like *parecer*.
reducir. — Like *aducir*.
reelegir. — Like *pedir*.
reexpedir. — Like *pedir*.
referir. — Like *sentir*.
reflorecer. — Like *parecer*.
refluir. — Like *huir*.
reforzar. — Like *contar*.
refregar. — Like *apretar*.
refreír. — Like *reír*.
regar. — Like *apretar*.
regimentar. — Like *apretar*.
regir. — Like *pedir*.
rehacer. — Like *hacer*.
rehuir. — Like *huir*.
rehumedecer. — Like *parecer*.
reír. — *Pres. ind.*: río, ríes, ríe, reímos, reís, ríen; *Pret.*: reí, reíste, rió, etc.; *Imper.*: ríe, ría, reíd, etc.; *Pres. subj.*: ría, rías, ría, riamos, etc.; *Imperf. subj.*: riera, rieras, etc. (1st form); riese, rieses, etc. (2nd form); *Fut. subj.*: riere, rieres, etc.; *Ger.*: riendo.
rejuvenecer. — Like *parecer*.
relucir. — Like *lucir*.
remendar. — Like *apretar*.
remoler. — Like *mover*.
remorder. — Like *mover*.

remover. — Like *mover*.
renacer. — Like *parecer*.
rendir. — Like *pedir*.
renegar. — Like *apretar*.
renovar. — Like *contar*.
reñir. — Like *teñir*.
repetir. — Like *pedir*.
replegar. — Like *apretar*.
repoblar. — Like *contar*.
reponer. — Like *poner*.
reprobar. — Like *contar*.
reproducir. — Like *aducir*.
requebrar. — Like *apretar*.
requerir. — Like *sentir*.
resalir. — Like *salir*.
resentirse. — Like *sentir*.
resolver. — Like *volver*.
resollar. — Like *contar*.
resonar. — Like *contar*.
resplandecer. — Like *parecer*.
restablecer. — Like *parecer*.
restituir. — Like *huir*.
restregar. — Like *apretar*.
restriñir. — Like *mullir*.
retemblar. — Like *apretar*.
retener. — Like *tener*.
retoñecer. — Like *parecer*.
retorcer. — Like *torcer*.
retostar. — Like *contar*.
retraer. — Like *traer*.
retribuir. — Like *huir*.
retrotraer. — Like *traer*.
reventar. — Like *apretar*.
reverdecer. — Like *parecer*.
revertir. — Like *sentir*.
revestir. — Like *pedir*.
revolcar. — Like *contar*.
revolver. — Like *volver*.
robustecer. — Like *parecer*.
rodar. — Like *contar*.
roer. — *Pres. ind.*: roo *or* roigo *or* royo, etc.; *Imper.*: roe, roa *or* roiga *or* roya, etc.; *Pres. subj.*: roa, roas, etc., *or* roiga, roigas, etc., *or* roya, royas, etc.; *Ger.*: royendo.
rogar. — Like *contar*.

S

saber. — *Pres. ind.*: sé, sabes, sabe, etc.; *Pret.*: supe, supiste, supo, etc.; *Fut.* sabré, sabrás, sabrá, etc.; *Imper.*: sabe, sepa, sepamos, etc.; *Cond.*: sabría, sabrías, etc.; *Pres. subj.*: sepa, sepas, etc.; *Imperf. subj.*: supiera, supieras, etc. (1st form); supiese, supieses, etc. (2nd form); *Fut. subj.*: supiere, supieres, etc.; *Ger.*: sabiendo; *Past part.*: sabido.
salir. — *Pres. ind.*: salgo, sales, sale, etc.; *Fut.*: saldré, saldrás, saldrá, etc.; *Imper.*: sal, salga, salgamos, etc.; *Cond.*: saldría, saldrías, etc.; *Pres. subj.*: salga, salgas, etc.; *Ger.*: saliendo; *Past part.*: salido.
salpimentar. — Like *apretar*.
satisfacer. — *Pres. ind.*: satisfago, satisfaces, satisface, etc.; *Pret.*: satisfice, satisficiste, satisfizo, etc.; *Fut.*: satisfaré, satisfarás, satisfará, etc.; *Imper.*: satisfaz *or* satisface, satisfaga, satisfagamos, etc.; *Cond.*: satisfaría, satisfarías, etc.; *Pres. subj.*: satisfaga, satisfagas, etc.; *Imperf. subj.*: satisficiera, satisficieras, etc. (1st form); satisficiese, satisficieses, etc. (2nd form); *Fut. subj.*: satisficiere, satisficieres, etc.; *Past part.*: satisfecho.
seducir. — Like *aducir*.
segar. — Like *apretar*.
seguir. — Like *pedir*.
sembrar. — Like *apretar*.
sentar. — Like *apretar*.
sentir. — *Pres. ind.*: siento, sientes, siente, sentimos, sentís, sienten; *Pret.*: sentí, sentiste, sintió, sentimos, sentisteis, sintieron; *Imper.*: siente, sienta, sintamos, etc.; *Pres. subj.*: sienta, sientas, etc.; *Imperf. subj.*: sintiera, sintieras, etc. (1st form); sintiese, sintieses, etc. (2nd form); *Fut. subj.*: sintiere, sintieres, etc.; *Ger.*: sintiendo.
ser. — See AUXILIARY VERBS.
serrar. — Like *apretar*.
servir. — Like *pedir*.
sobreentender or **sobrentender**. — Like *hender*.
sobreponer. — Like *poner*.
sobresalir. — Like *salir*.
sobrevenir. — Like *venir*.
sobrevolar. — Like *contar*.
sofreír. — Like *reír*.
solar. — Like *contar*.
soldar. — Like *contar*.
soler. — Like *mover*. Defective.
soltar. — Like *contar*.
sonar. — Like *contar*.
sonreír. — Like *reír*.
soñar. — Like *contar*.
sosegar. — Like *apretar*.
sostener. — Like *tener*.
soterrar. — Like *apretar*.
subarrendar. — Like *apretar*.
subseguir. — Like *pedir*.
substituir. — Like *huir*.
substraer. — Like *traer*.
subvenir. — Like *venir*.
subvertir. — Like *sentir*.
sugerir. — Like *sentir*.
superponer. — Like *poner*.
suponer. — Like *poner*.
sustituir. — Like *huir*.
sustraer. — Like *traer*.

T, U

tallecer. — Like *parecer*.
tañer. — *Pret.*: tañí, tañiste, tañó, etc.; *Imperf. subj.*: tañera, tañeras, etc. (1st form); tañese, tañeses, etc. (2nd form); *Fut. subj.*: tañere, tañeres, etc.; *Ger.*: tañendo; *Past part.*: tañido.
tardecer. — Like *parecer*. Impersonal.
temblar. — Like *apretar*.
tender. — Like *hender*.
tener. — *Pres. ind.*: tengo, tienes, tiene, tenemos, tenéis, tienen; *Pret.*: tuve, tuviste, tuvo, etc.; *Fut.*: tendré, tendrás, etc.; *Imper.*: ten, tenga, tengamos, etc.; *Cond.*: tendría, tendrías, etc.; *Pres. subj.*: tenga, tengas, etc.; *Imperf. subj.*: tuviera, tuvieras, etc. (1st form); tuviese, tuvieses, etc. (2nd form); *Fut. subj.*: tuviere, tuvieres, etc.; *Ger.*: teniendo; *Past. part.*: tenido.
tentar. — Like *apretar*.
teñir. — *Pres. ind.*: tiño, tiñes, tiñe, teñimos, teñís, tiñen; *Pret.*: teñí, teñiste, tiñó, etc.; *Imper.*: tiñe, tiña, tiñamos, etc.; *Pres. subj.*: tiña, tiñas, etc.; *Imperf. subj.*: tiñera, tiñeras, etc. (1st form); tiñese, tiñeses, etc. (2nd form); *Fut. subj.*: tiñere, tiñeres, etc.; *Ger.*: tiñendo; *Past part.*: teñido.
torcer. — *Pres. ind.*: tuerzo, tuerces, tuerce, etc.; *Imper.*: tuerce, tuerza, etc.; *Pres. subj.*: tuerza, tuerzas, etc.; *Ger.*: torciendo; *Past part.*: torcido *or* tuerto.
tostar. — Like *contar*.
traducir. — Like *aducir*.
traer. — *Pres. ind.*: traigo, traes, trae, etc.; *Pret.*: traje, trajiste, trajo, etc.; *Imper.*: trae, traiga, traigamos, etc.; *Pres. subj.*: traiga, traigas, etc.; *Imperf. subj.*: trajera, trajeras, etc. (1st form); trajese, trajeses, etc. (2nd form); *Fut. subj.*: trajere, trajeres, etc.; *Ger.*: trayendo; *Past part.*: traído.
transcender. — Like *hender*.
transferir. — Like *sentir*.
transgredir. — Like *abolir*.
transponer. — Like *poner*.
trascender. — Like *hender*.
trascolar. — Like *contar*.
trascordarse. — Like *contar*.
trasegar. — Like *apretar*.
trasgredir. — Like *abolir*.
traslucirse. — Like *lucir*.
trasoñar. — Like *contar*.
trastocar. — Like *contar*.
trastrocar. — Like *contar*.
trasver. — Like *ver*.
trasverter. — Like *hender*.
trasvolar. — Like *contar*.
travestir. — Like *pedir*.
trocar. — Like *contar*.
tronar. — Like *contar*.
tropezar. — Like *apretar*.
tullir. — Like *mullir*.
usucapir. — Defective. Conjugated chiefly in the infinitive.

V

valer. — *Pres. ind.*: valgo, vales, vale, etc.; *Fut.*: valdré, valdrás, valdrá, etc.; *Imper.*: val *or* vale, valga, valgamos, etc.; *Cond.*: valdría, valdrías, etc.; *Pres. subj.*: valga, valgas, etc.; *Ger.*: valiendo; *Past part.*: valido.
venir. — *Pres. ind.*: vengo, vienes, viene, venimos, venís, vienen; *Pret.*: vine, viniste, vino, etc.; *Fut.*: vendré, vendrás, etc.; *Imper.*: ven, venga, vengamos, etc.; *Cond.*: vendría, vendrías, etc.; *Pres. subj.*: venga, vengas, etc.; *Imperf. subj.*: viniera, vinieras, etc. (1st form); viniese, vinieses, etc. (2nd form); *Fut. subj.*: viniere, vinieres, etc.; *Ger.*: viniendo; *Past part.*: venido.
ver. — *Pres. ind.*: veo, ves, ve, etc.; *Imperf.*: veía, veías, etc.; *Imper.*: ve, vea, etc.; *Pres. subj.*: vea, veas, etc.; *Ger.*: viendo; *Past part.*: visto.
verter. — Like *hender*.
vestir. — Like *pedir*.
volar. — Like *contar*.
volcar. — Like *contar*.
volver. — *Pres. ind.*: vuelvo, vuelves, vuelve, etc.; *Pret.*: volví, volviste, etc.; *Imper.*: vuelve, vuelva, etc.; *Pres. subj.*: vuelva, vuelvas, etc.; *Ger.*: volviendo; *Past part.*: vuelto.

Y

yacer. — *Pres. ind.*: yazco *or* yazgo *or* yago, yaces, yace, etc.; *Imper.*: yace *or* yaz, yazca *or* yazga *or* yaga, yazcamos *or* yazgamos *or* yagamos, yaced, etc.; *Pres. subj.*: yazca *or* yazga *or* yaga, yazcas, yazca, etc.; *Ger.*: yaciendo; *Past part.*: yacido.
yuxtaponer. — Like *poner*.

Z

zaherir. — Like *sentir*.
zambullir. — Like *mullir*.

AUTOMÓVIL
MOTORCAR

Fot. Régie Renault.

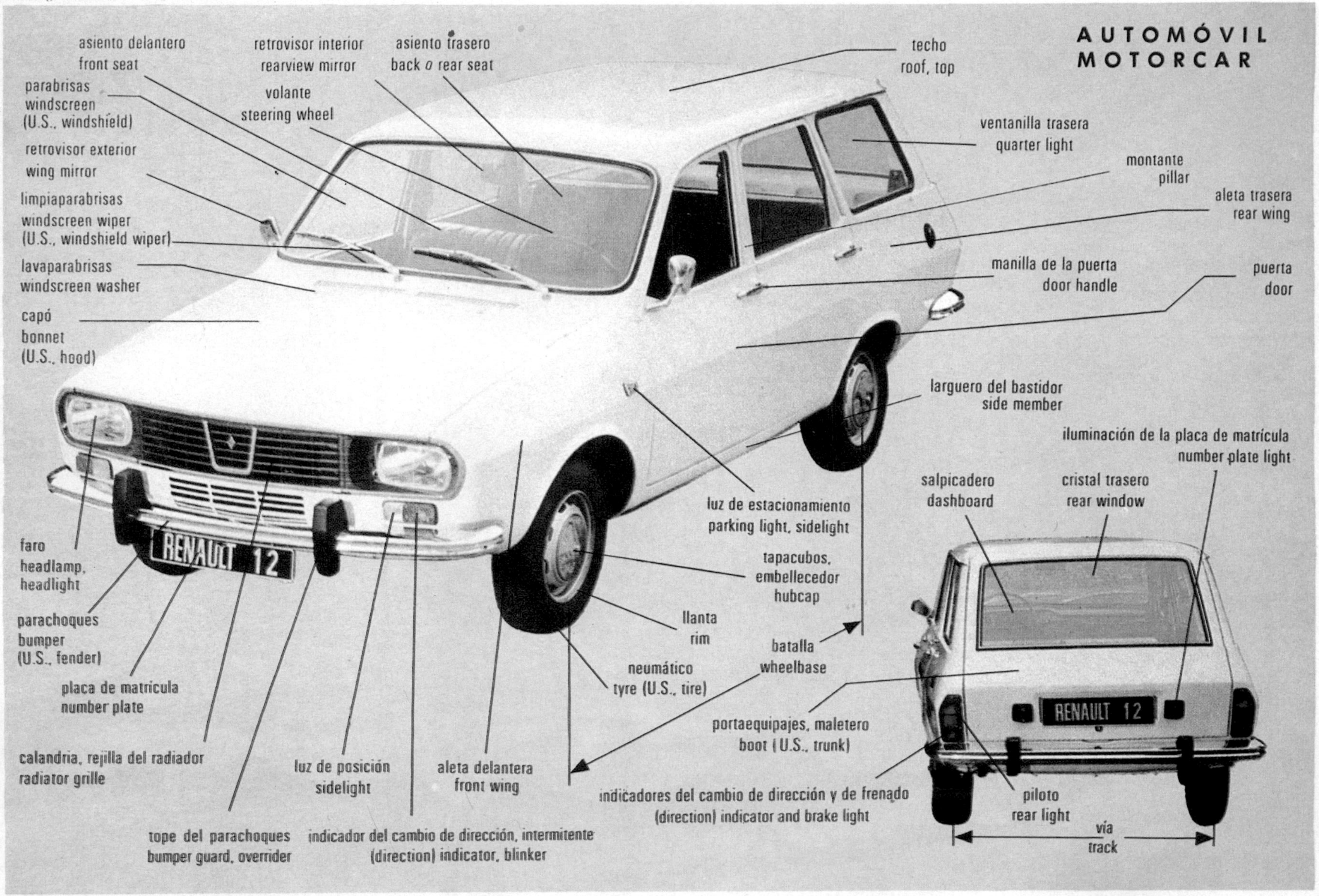

asiento delantero
front seat

parabrisas
windscreen
(U.S., windshield)

retrovisor exterior
wing mirror

limpiaparabrisas
windscreen wiper
(U.S., windshield wiper)

lavaparabrisas
windscreen washer

capó
bonnet
(U.S., hood)

retrovisor interior
rearview mirror

volante
steering wheel

asiento trasero
back *o* rear seat

techo
roof, top

ventanilla trasera
quarter light

montante
pillar

aleta trasera
rear wing

manilla de la puerta
door handle

puerta
door

larguero del bastidor
side member

iluminación de la placa de matrícula
number plate light

salpicadero
dashboard

cristal trasero
rear window

faro
headlamp,
headlight

parachoques
bumper
(U.S., fender)

placa de matrícula
number plate

calandria, rejilla del radiador
radiator grille

tope del parachoques
bumper guard, overrider

luz de posición
sidelight

indicador del cambio de dirección, intermitente
(direction) indicator, blinker

aleta delantera
front wing

luz de estacionamiento
parking light, sidelight

tapacubos,
embellecedor
hubcap

llanta
rim

neumático
tyre (U.S., tire)

batalla
wheelbase

portaequipajes, maletero
boot (U.S., trunk)

indicadores del cambio de dirección y de frenado
(direction) indicator and brake light

piloto
rear light

vía
track

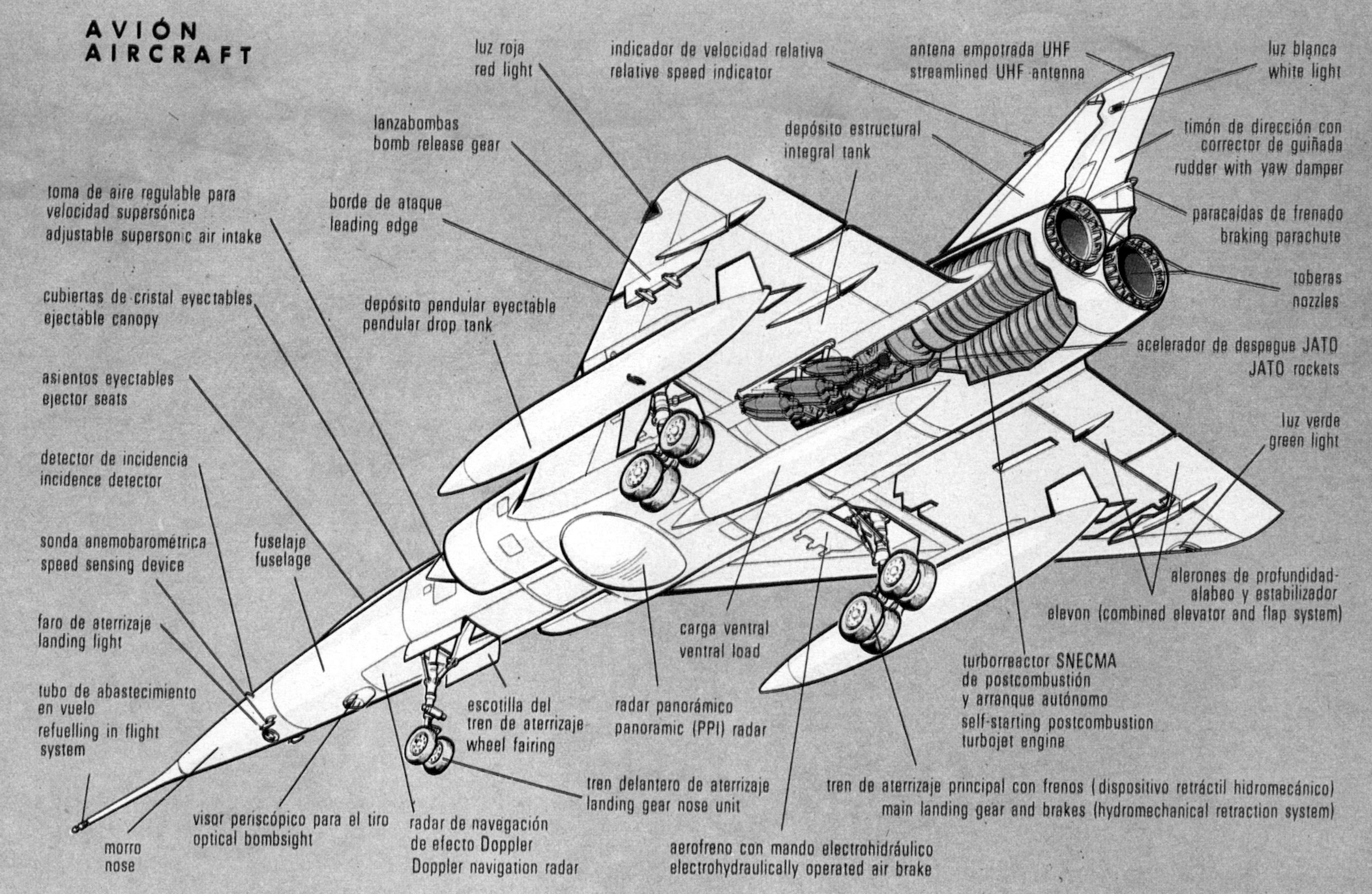
AVIÓN
AIRCRAFT
luz roja
red light
indicador de velocidad relativa
relative speed indicator
antena empotrada UHF
streamlined UHF antenna
luz blanca
white light
lanzabombas
bomb release gear
depósito estructural
integral tank
timón de dirección con
corrector de guiñada
rudder with yaw damper
toma de aire regulable para
velocidad supersónica
adjustable supersonic air intake
borde de ataque
leading edge
paracaídas de frenado
braking parachute
toberas
nozzles
cubiertas de cristal eyectables
ejectable canopy
depósito pendular eyectable
pendular drop tank
acelerador de despegue JATO
JATO rockets
asientos eyectables
ejector seats
luz verde
green light
detector de incidencia
incidence detector
sonda anemobarométrica
speed sensing device
fuselaje
fuselage
alerones de profundidad-
alabeo y estabilizador
elevon (combined elevator and flap system)
faro de aterrizaje
landing light
carga ventral
ventral load
turborreactor SNECMA
de postcombustión
y arranque autónomo
self-starting postcombustion
turbojet engine
tubo de abastecimiento
en vuelo
refuelling in flight
system
escotilla del
tren de aterrizaje
wheel fairing
radar panorámico
panoramic (PPI) radar
tren delantero de aterrizaje
landing gear nose unit
tren de aterrizaje principal con frenos (dispositivo retráctil hidromecánico)
main landing gear and brakes (hydromechanical retraction system)
morro
nose
visor periscópico para el tiro
optical bombsight
radar de navegación
de efecto Doppler
Doppler navigation radar
aerofreno con mando electrohidráulico
electrohydraulically operated air brake

Fot. Snecma.

TURBORREACTOR
TURBOJET ENGINE

quemador
burner

conexión con la tobera de expulsión de los gases
nozzle junction

cámara de combustión
combustion chamber

inyector
injector

compresor axial
axial compressor

paleta
blade

rotor
rotor

estator
stator

arranque por
aire comprimido
compressed air starter

cárter de admisión
admission casing

entrada de aire
air intake

difusor de salida
exhaust diffuser

rectificador de turbina
flow stabilizer

rueda de paletas
bladed wheel

distribuidor de turbina
turbine distributor

bujía de encendido
sparking plug

regulador
regulator

soporte de accesorios
accessories support

inyector de arranque
starting injector

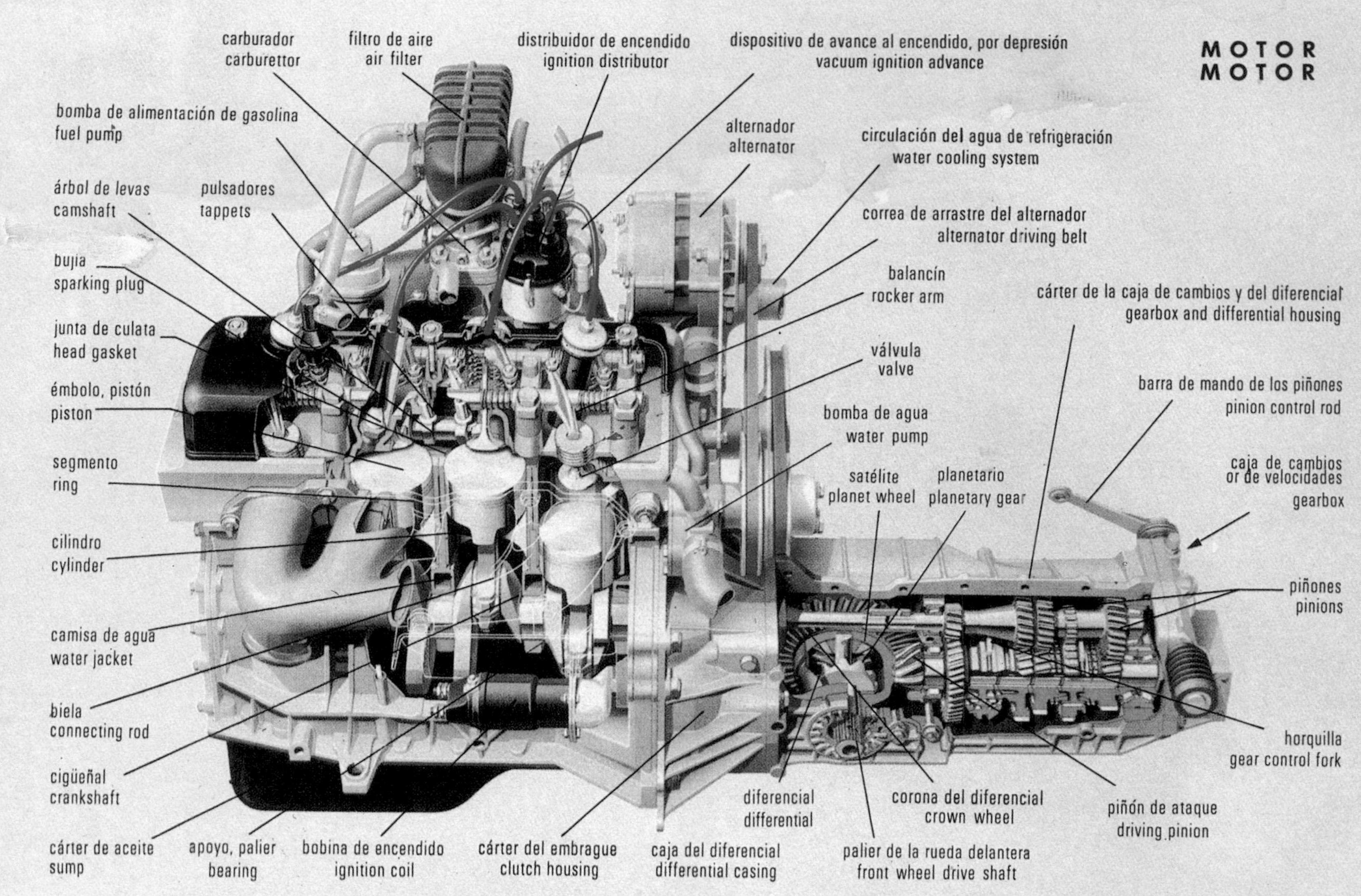
MOTOR
MOTOR
carburador
carburettor
filtro de aire
air filter
distribuidor de encendido
ignition distributor
dispositivo de avance al encendido, por depresión
vacuum ignition advance
bomba de alimentación de gasolina
fuel pump
alternador
alternator
circulación del agua de refrigeración
water cooling system
árbol de levas
camshaft
pulsadores
tappets
correa de arrastre del alternador
alternator driving belt
bujía
sparking plug
balancín
rocker arm
cárter de la caja de cambios y del diferencial
gearbox and differential housing
junta de culata
head gasket
válvula
valve
émbolo, pistón
piston
barra de mando de los piñones
pinion control rod
bomba de agua
water pump
segmento
ring
satélite
planet wheel
planetario
planetary gear
caja de cambios
or de velocidades
gearbox
cilindro
cylinder
piñones
pinions
camisa de agua
water jacket
biela
connecting rod
horquilla
gear control fork
cigüeñal
crankshaft
diferencial
differential
corona del diferencial
crown wheel
piñón de ataque
driving pinion
cárter de aceite
sump
apoyo, palier
bearing
bobina de encendido
ignition coil
cárter del embrague
clutch housing
caja del diferencial
differential casing
palier de la rueda delantera
front wheel drive shaft

Fot. BMW.

MOTOCICLETA
MOTORCYCLE

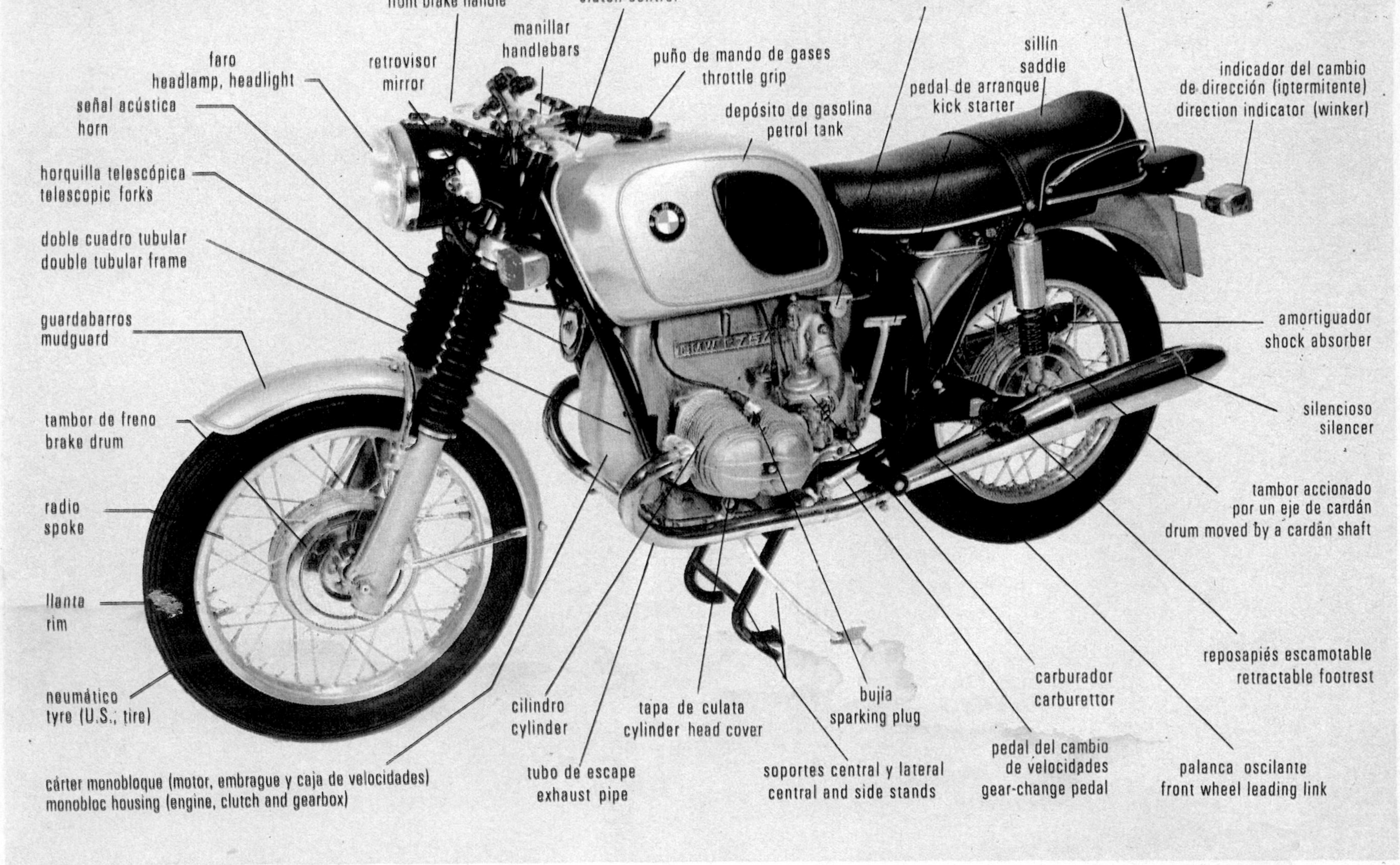

mando del freno delantero
front brake handle

mando del embrague
clutch control

llave de la gasolina
petrol tap

luz posterior
rear light

faro
headlamp, headlight

retrovisor
mirror

manillar
handlebars

puño de mando de gases
throttle grip

sillín
saddle

pedal de arranque
kick starter

indicador del cambio
de dirección (intermitente)
direction indicator (winker)

señal acústica
horn

depósito de gasolina
petrol tank

horquilla telescópica
telescopic forks

doble cuadro tubular
double tubular frame

guardabarros
mudguard

amortiguador
shock absorber

tambor de freno
brake drum

silencioso
silencer

radio
spoke

tambor accionado
por un eje de cardán
drum moved by a cardán shaft

llanta
rim

reposapiés escamotable
retractable footrest

neumático
tyre (U.S., tire)

cilindro
cylinder

tapa de culata
cylinder head cover

bujía
sparking plug

carburador
carburettor

cárter monobloque (motor, embrague y caja de velocidades)
monobloc housing (engine, clutch and gearbox)

tubo de escape
exhaust pipe

soportes central y lateral
central and side stands

pedal del cambio
de velocidades
gear-change pedal

palanca oscilante
front wheel leading link

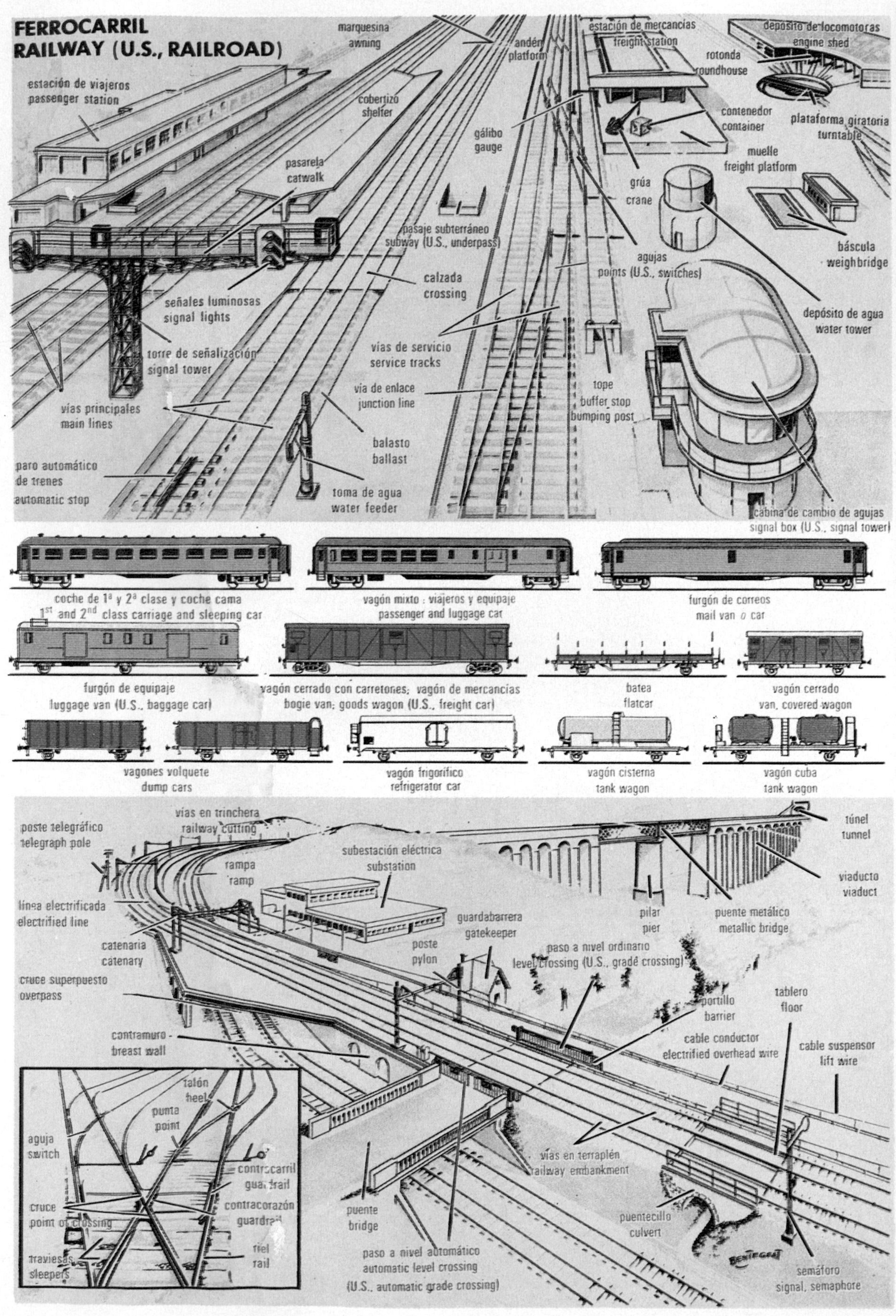
FERROCARRIL
RAILWAY (U.S., RAILROAD)
marquesina
awning
andén
platform
estación de mercancías
freight station
depósito de locomotoras
engine shed
rotonda
roundhouse
estación de viajeros
passenger station
cobertizo
shelter
contenedor
container
plataforma giratoria
turntable
gálibo
gauge
muelle
freight platform
pasarela
catwalk
grúa
crane
pasaje subterráneo
subway (U.S., underpass)
báscula
weighbridge
agujas
points (U.S., switches)
calzada
crossing
señales luminosas
signal lights
depósito de agua
water tower
vías de servicio
service tracks
torre de señalización
signal tower
vía de enlace
junction line
tope
buffer stop
bumping post
vías principales
main lines
balasto
ballast
paro automático
de trenes
automatic stop
toma de agua
water feeder
cabina de cambio de agujas
signal box (U.S., signal tower)
coche de 1ª y 2ª clase y coche cama
1st and 2nd class carriage and sleeping car
vagón mixto : viajeros y equipaje
passenger and luggage car
furgón de correos
mail van o car
furgón de equipaje
luggage van (U.S., baggage car)
vagón cerrado con carretones; vagón de mercancías
bogie van; goods wagon (U.S., freight car)
batea
flatcar
vagón cerrado
van, covered wagon
vagones volquete
dump cars
vagón frigorífico
refrigerator car
vagón cisterna
tank wagon
vagón cuba
tank wagon
poste telegráfico
telegraph pole
vías en trinchera
railway cutting
túnel
tunnel
subestación eléctrica
substation
rampa
ramp
viaducto
viaduct
línea electrificada
electrified line
pilar
pier
puente metálico
metallic bridge
guardabarrera
gatekeeper
catenaria
catenary
poste
pylon
paso a nivel ordinario
level crossing (U.S., grade crossing)
cruce superpuesto
overpass
portillo
barrier
tablero
floor
contramuro
breast wall
cable conductor
electrified overhead wire
cable suspensor
lift wire
talón
heel
punta
point
aguja
switch
contracarril
guardrail
vías en terraplén
railway embankment
cruce
point of crossing
contracorazón
guardrail
puentecillo
culvert
puente
bridge
traviesas
sleepers
riel
rail
paso a nivel automático
automatic level crossing
(U.S., automatic grade crossing)
semáforo
signal, semaphore

Fot. Vie du Rail.

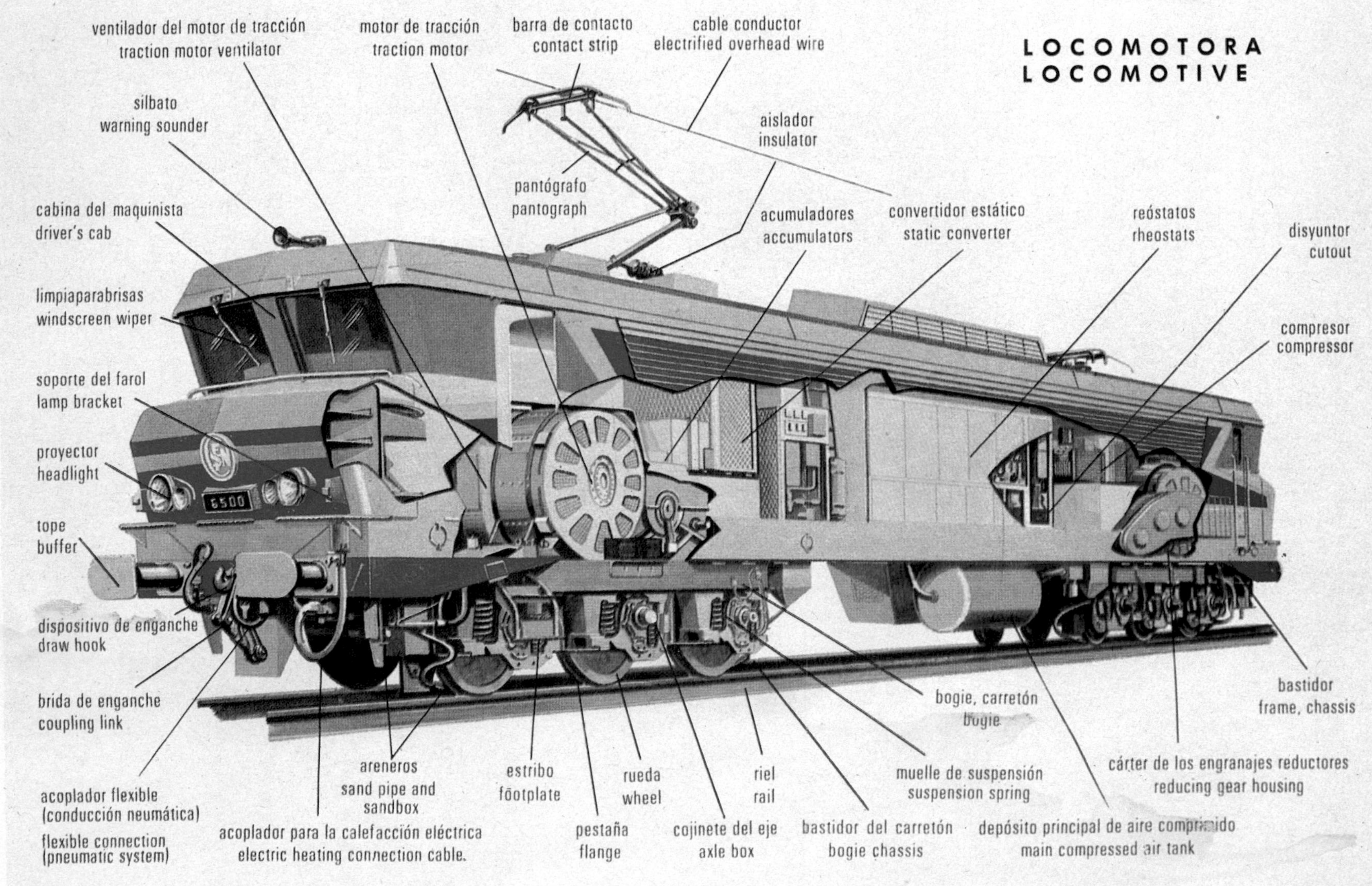

LOCOMOTORA
LOCOMOTIVE
ventilador del motor de tracción
traction motor ventilator
motor de tracción
traction motor
barra de contacto
contact strip
cable conductor
electrified overhead wire
silbato
warning sounder
aislador
insulator
pantógrafo
pantograph
cabina del maquinista
driver's cab
acumuladores
accumulators
convertidor estático
static converter
reóstatos
rheostats
disyuntor
cutout
limpiaparabrisas
windscreen wiper
compresor
compressor
soporte del farol
lamp bracket
proyector
headlight
tope
buffer
dispositivo de enganche
draw hook
brida de enganche
coupling link
bastidor
frame, chassis
bogie, carretón
bogie
cárter de los engranajes reductores
reducing gear housing
areneros
sand pipe and
sandbox
estribo
footplate
rueda
wheel
riel
rail
muelle de suspensión
suspension spring
acoplador flexible
(conducción neumática)
flexible connection
(pneumatic system)
acoplador para la calefacción eléctrica
electric heating connection cable.
pestaña
flange
cojinete del eje
axle box
bastidor del carretón
bogie chassis
depósito principal de aire comprimido
main compressed air tank

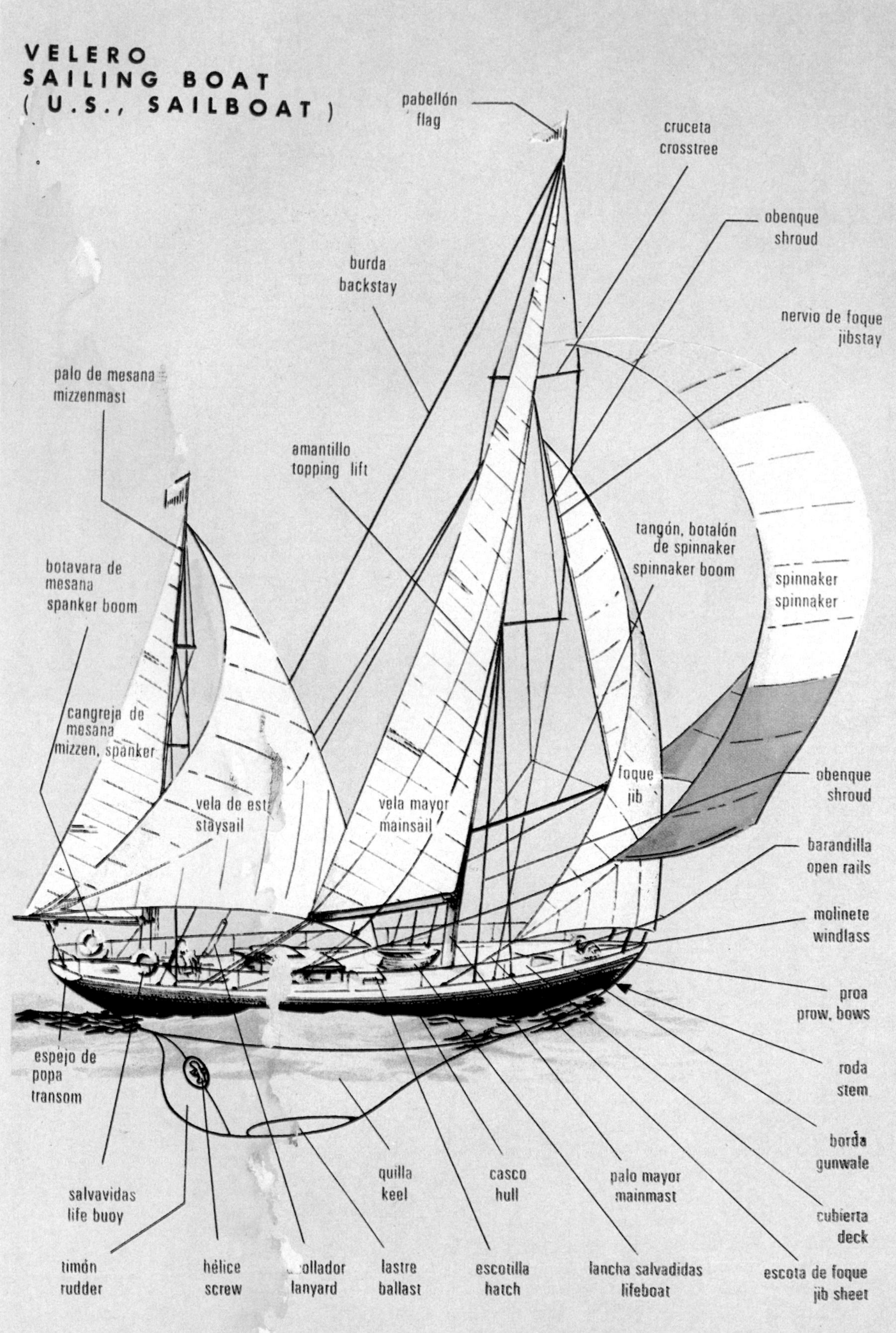
VELERO
SAILING BOAT
(U.S., SAILBOAT)
pabellón
flag
cruceta
crosstree
obenque
shroud
burda
backstay
nervio de foque
jibstay
palo de mesana
mizzenmast
amantillo
topping lift
tangón, botalón
de spinnaker
spinnaker boom
botavara de
mesana
spanker boom
spinnaker
spinnaker
cangreja de
mesana
mizzen, spanker
vela de est
staysail
vela mayor
mainsail
foque
jib
obenque
shroud
barandilla
open rails
molinete
windlass
proa
prow, bows
espejo de
popa
transom
roda
stem
borda
gunwale
quilla
keel
casco
hull
palo mayor
mainmast
salvavidas
life buoy
cubierta
deck
timón
rudder
hélice
screw
ollador
lanyard
lastre
ballast
escotilla
hatch
lancha salvadidas
lifeboat
escota de foque
jib sheet

Fot. Messageries Maritimes.

TRANSATLÁNTICO
LINER

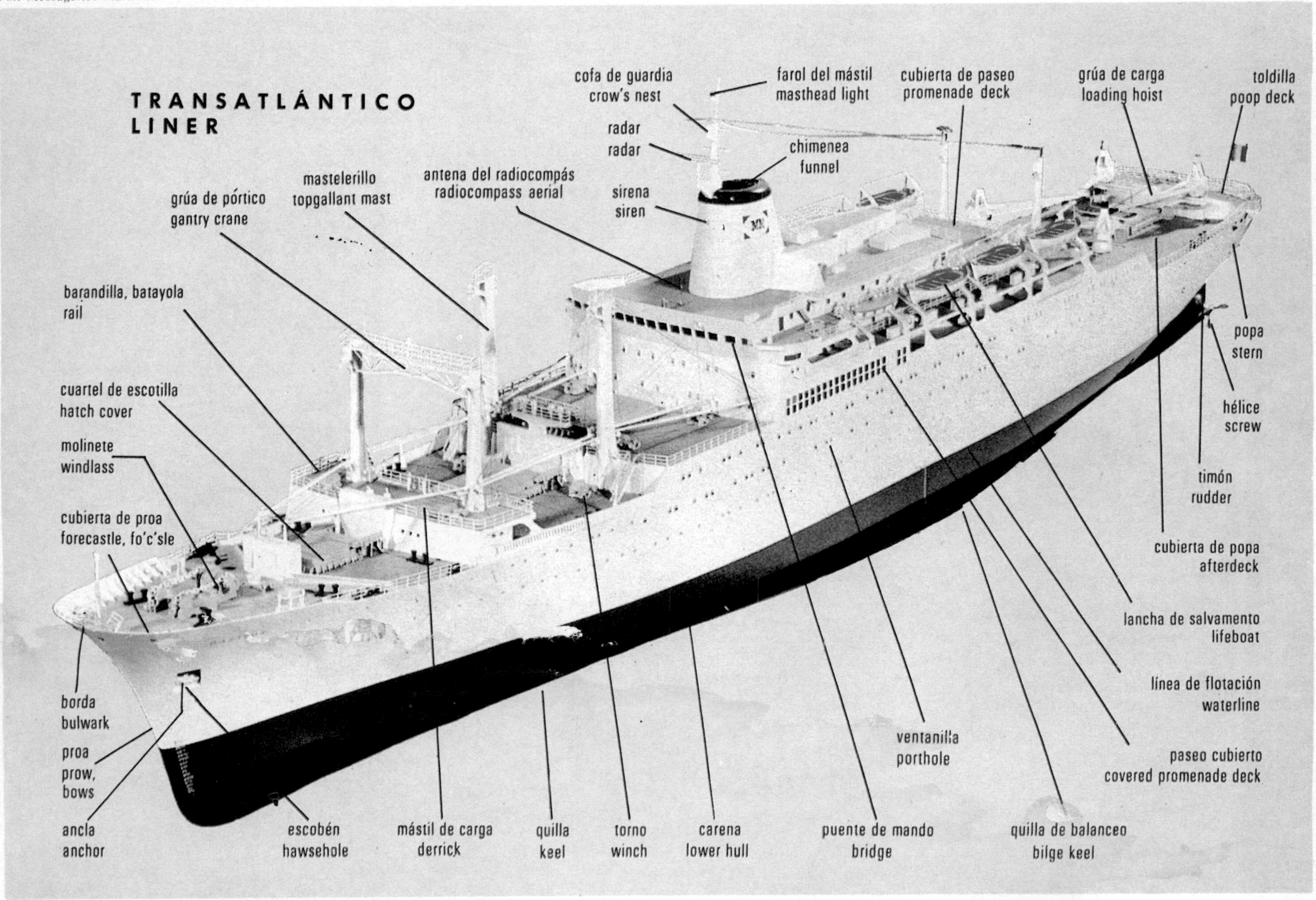

cofa de guardia
crow's nest

farol del mástil
masthead light

cubierta de paseo
promenade deck

grúa de carga
loading hoist

toldilla
poop deck

radar
radar

chimenea
funnel

sirena
siren

mastelerillo
topgallant mast

antena del radiocompás
radiocompass aerial

grúa de pórtico
gantry crane

barandilla, batayola
rail

cuartel de escotilla
hatch cover

molinete
windlass

cubierta de proa
forecastle, fo'c'sle

borda
bulwark

proa
prow,
bows

ancla
anchor

escobén
hawsehole

mástil de carga
derrick

quilla
keel

torno
winch

carena
lower hull

puente de mando
bridge

quilla de balanceo
bilge keel

ventanilla
porthole

paseo cubierto
covered promenade deck

línea de flotación
waterline

lancha de salvamento
lifeboat

cubierta de popa
afterdeck

timón
rudder

hélice
screw

popa
stern

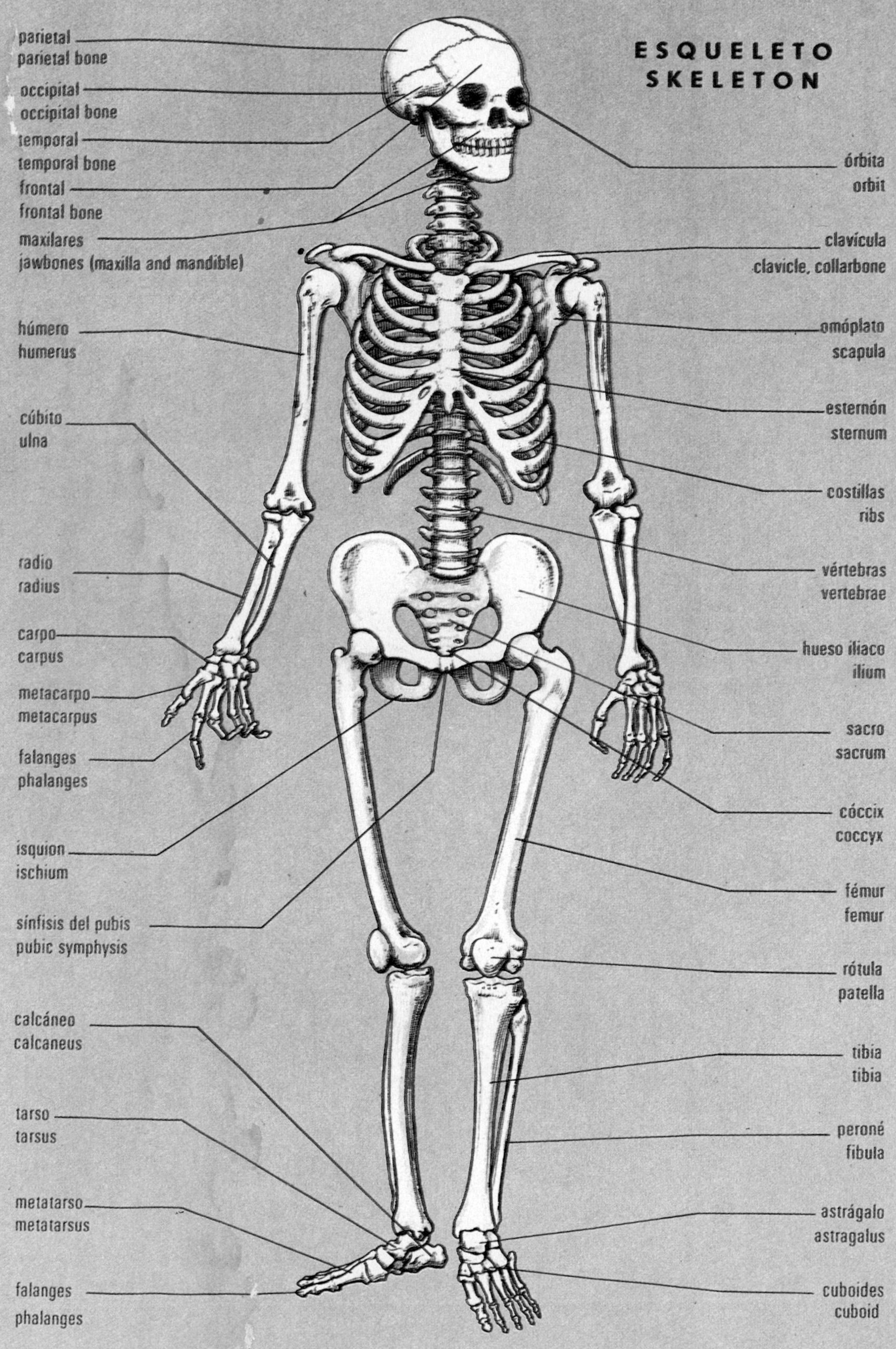
ESQUELETO
SKELETON
parietal
parietal bone
occipital
occipital bone
temporal
temporal bone
frontal
frontal bone
maxilares
jawbones (maxilla and mandible)
órbita
orbit
clavícula
clavicle, collarbone
húmero
humerus
omóplato
scapula
esternón
sternum
cúbito
ulna
costillas
ribs
radio
radius
vértebras
vertebrae
carpo
carpus
hueso iliaco
ilium
metacarpo
metacarpus
sacro
sacrum
falanges
phalanges
cóccix
coccyx
isquion
ischium
fémur
femur
sínfisis del pubis
pubic symphysis
rótula
patella
calcáneo
calcaneus
tibia
tibia
tarso
tarsus
peroné
fíbula
metatarso
metatarsus
astrágalo
astragalus
falanges
phalanges
cuboides
cuboid

ANATOMÍA
ANATOMY

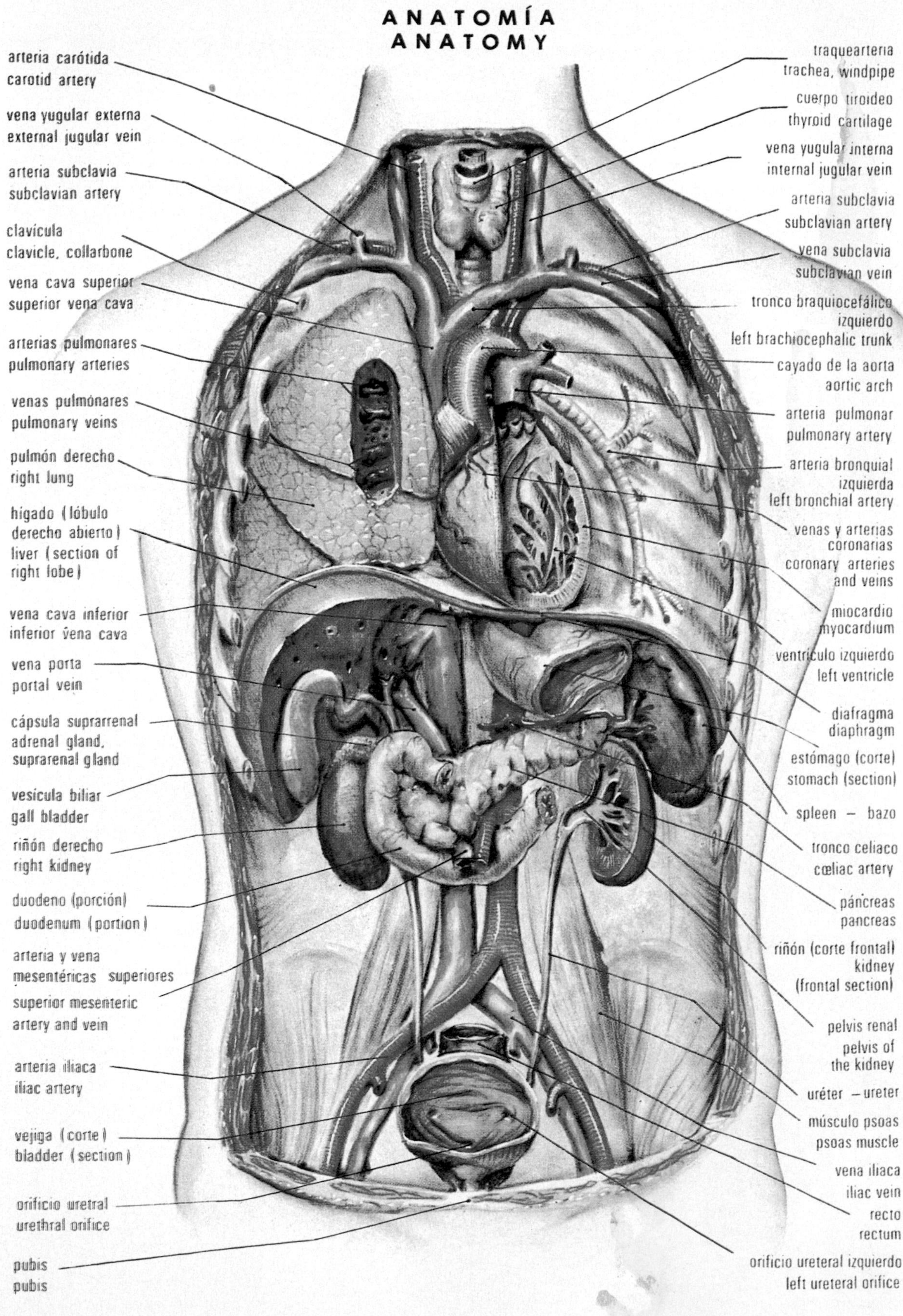
arteria carótida
carotid artery
vena yugular externa
external jugular vein
arteria subclavia
subclavian artery
clavícula
clavicle, collarbone
vena cava superior
superior vena cava
arterias pulmonares
pulmonary arteries
venas pulmónares
pulmonary veins
pulmón derecho
right lung
hígado (lóbulo derecho abierto)
liver (section of right lobe)
vena cava inferior
inferior vena cava
vena porta
portal vein
cápsula suprarrenal
adrenal gland, suprarenal gland
vesícula biliar
gall bladder
riñón derecho
right kidney
duodeno (porción)
duodenum (portion)
arteria y vena mesentéricas superiores
superior mesenteric artery and vein
arteria iliaca
iliac artery
vejiga (corte)
bladder (section)
orificio uretral
urethral orifice
pubis
pubis
traquearteria
trachea, windpipe
cuerpo tiroideo
thyroid cartilage
vena yugular interna
internal jugular vein
arteria subclavia
subclavian artery
vena subclavia
subclavian vein
tronco braquiocefálico izquierdo
left brachiocephalic trunk
cayado de la aorta
aortic arch
arteria pulmonar
pulmonary artery
arteria bronquial izquierda
left bronchial artery
venas y arterias coronarias
coronary arteries and veins
miocardio
myocardium
ventrículo izquierdo
left ventricle
diafragma
diaphragm
estómago (corte)
stomach (section)
spleen – bazo
tronco celiaco
cœliac artery
páncreas
pancreas
riñón (corte frontal)
kidney (frontal section)
pelvis renal
pelvis of the kidney
uréter – ureter
músculo psoas
psoas muscle
vena iliaca
iliac vein
recto
rectum
orificio ureteral izquierdo
left ureteral orifice

TEATRO

THEATRE (U.S., THEATER)

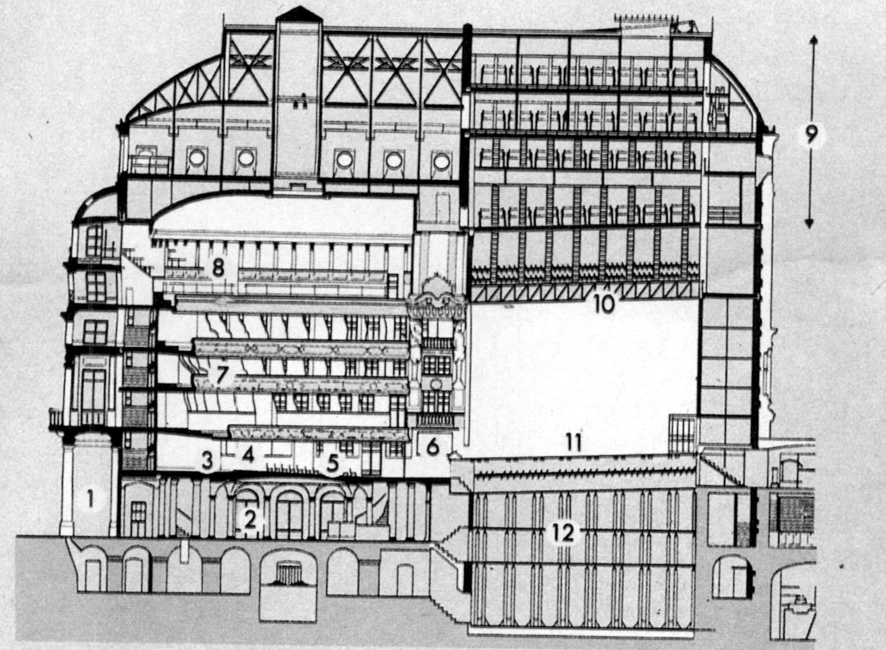

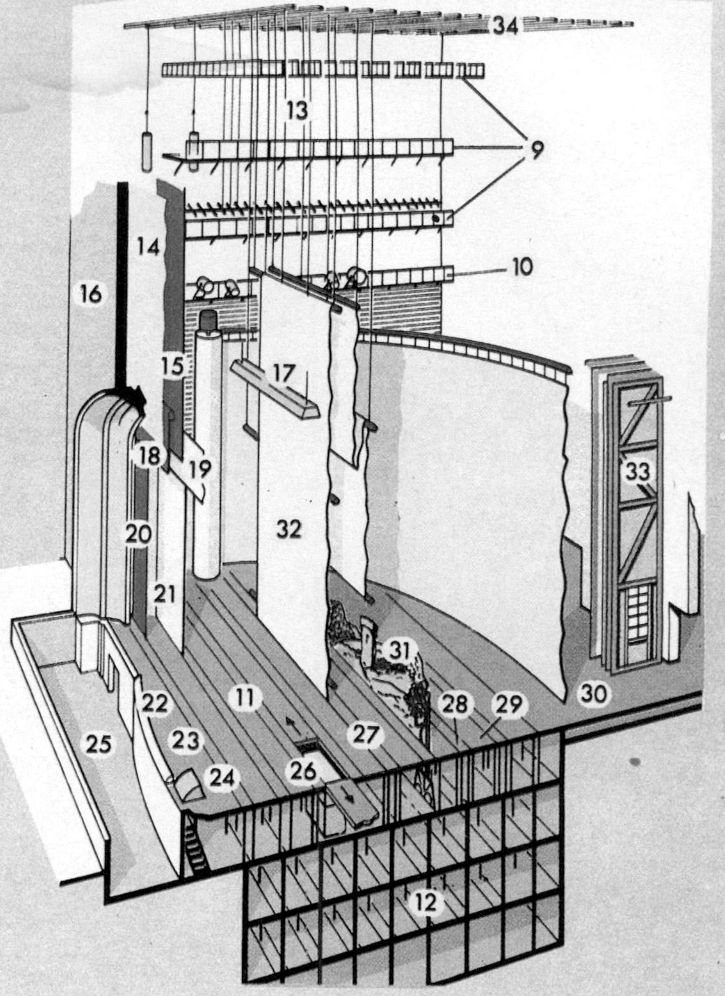

1. Entrada; 2. Vestíbulo; 3. Platea; 4. Palcos; 5. Patio de butacas; 6. Palcos de proscenio; 7. Palcos de entresuelo; 8. Anfiteatro; 9. Telares; 10. Diablas o luces; 11. Escenario; 12. Fosos y contrafosos; 13. Cuerdas de mando; 14. Telón metálico; 15. Telón de boca; 16. Embocadura; 17. Varal para iluminar; 18. Bambalinón; 19. Bambalina de ropa; 20. Alcahuete; 21. Bastidor; 22. Candilejas, batería; 23. Corbata; 24. Concha del apuntador; 25. Foso de orquesta; 26. Escotillón; 27. Trampillas; 28. Carro; 29. Tablero; 30. Tablas del escenario; 31. Trasto, decorado móvil; 32. Telón de foro; 33. Chácena, reserva de decorados; 34. Peine.

1. Entrance; 2. Lobby; 3. Pit; 4. Ground-floor boxes; 5. Stalls [U.S., orchestra]; 6. Stage boxes; 7. Second-tier boxes; 8. Gallery; 9. Flies; 10. Lighting gallery; 11. Stage; 12. Below-stage; 13. Shifting lines; 14. Safety curtain; 15. House curtain; 16. Proscenium arch, face wall; 17. Light batten; 18. Valance; 19. Border; 20. Draw curtain; 21. Tormentor; 22. Footlights; 23. Proscenium; 24. Prompt box; 25. Orchestra pit; 26. Trap, trapdoor; 27. Cuts and slots; 28. Bridge-cut; 29. Stage floor; 30. Slips; 31. Flat; 32. Backdrop, back-cloth; 33. Scenery storage; 34. Gridiron, grid.

Fot. Société Lumifilm.

CINEMATOGRAFÍA : 1. Cámara, *m.*; 2. Cámara, *f.*; 3. Operador; 4. Ayudante de dirección; 5. Ingeniero del sonido con un magnetófono; 6. Jirafista; 7. Jirafa; 8. Foto fija; 9. Claquetista; 10. Claqueta; 11. Maquilladora; 12. Actores; 13. Micrófono; 14. Peine; 15. Spot; 16. Lámpara CREMER; 17. Proyector; 18. Eléctrico; 19. Productor; 20. Plató, estudio; 21. Director; 22. Secretaria de rodaje, script; 23. Ayudante del cámara, foquista; 24. Trípode.

CINEMA : 1. Cameraman; 2. Camera; 3. Director of photography; 4. Assistant director; 5. Sound engineer o monitor man with tape recorder; 6. Boom operator; 7. Boom; 8. Set photographer; 9. Clapper boy; 10. Clapper boards; 11. Makeup girl; 12. Actors; 13. Microphone; 14. Lighting; 15. Parabolic lamp; 16. Spotlight; 17. Spotlight; 18. Electrician; 19. Producer; 20. Set, film set; 21. Director; 22. Continuity girl, script girl; 23. Cameraman's assistant; 24. Tripod, camera stand.

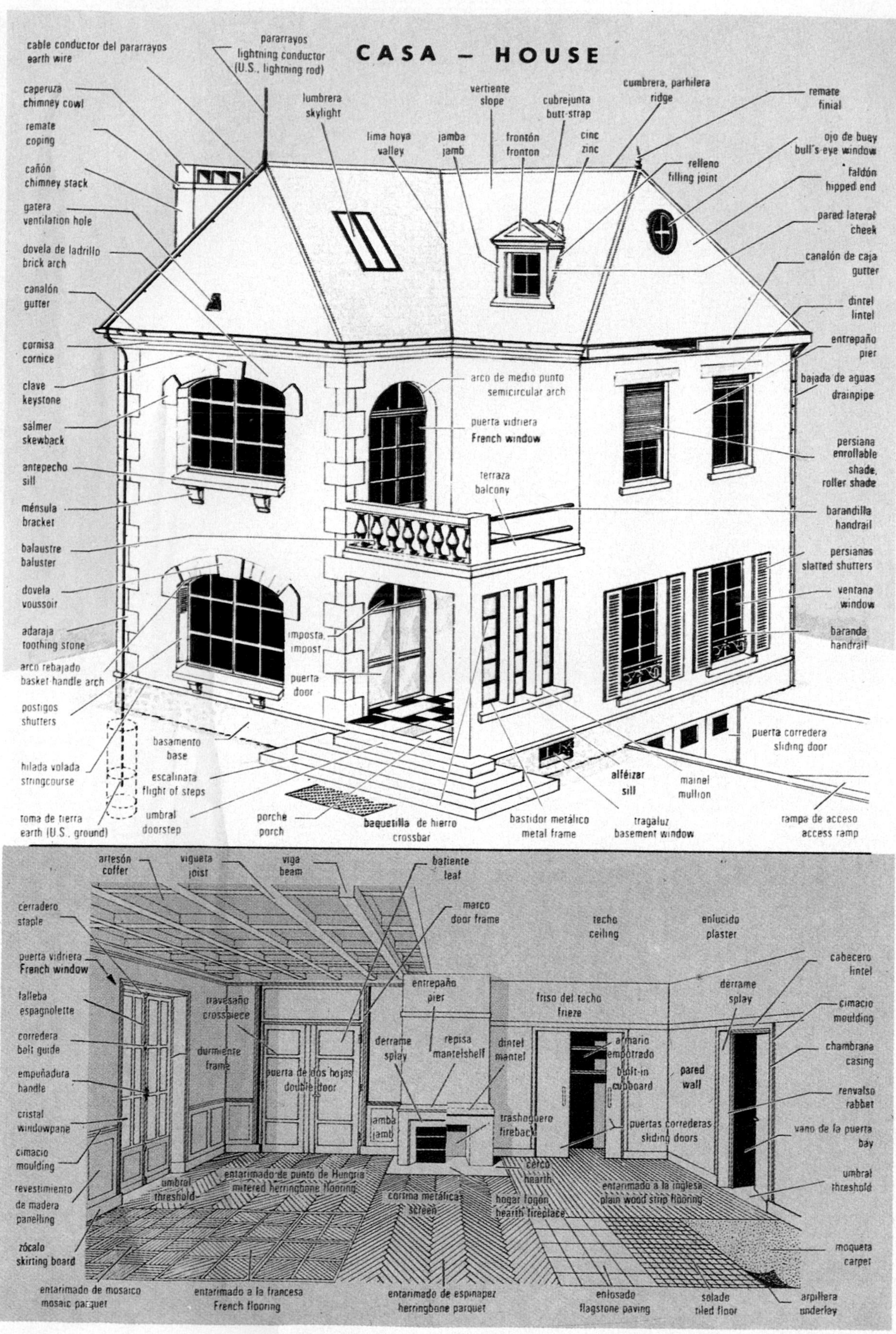
CASA — HOUSE
cable conductor del pararrayos
earth wire
pararrayos
lightning conductor
(U.S., lightning rod)
caperuza
chimney cowl
remate
coping
cañón
chimney stack
gatera
ventilation hole
dovela de ladrillo
brick arch
canalón
gutter
cornisa
cornice
clave
keystone
sálmer
skewback
antepecho
sill
ménsula
bracket
balaustre
baluster
dovela
voussoir
adaraja
toothing stone
arco rebajado
basket handle arch
postigos
shutters
hilada volada
stringcourse
toma de tierra
earth (U.S. ground)
lumbrera
skylight
lima hoya
valley
jamba
jamb
vertiente
slope
frontón
fronton
cubrejunta
butt-strap
cinc
zinc
cumbrera, parhilera
ridge
remate
finial
ojo de buey
bull's eye window
relleno
filling joint
faldón
hipped end
pared lateral
cheek
canalón de caja
gutter
dintel
lintel
entrepaño
pier
bajada de aguas
drainpipe
arco de medio punto
semicircular arch
puerta vidriera
French window
persiana
enrollable
shade,
roller shade
terraza
balcony
barandilla
handrail
persianas
slatted shutters
ventana
window
baranda
handrail
imposta
impost
puerta
door
basamento
base
escalinata
flight of steps
umbral
doorstep
porche
porch
baquetilla de hierro
crossbar
bastidor metálico
metal frame
alféizar
sill
tragaluz
basement window
mainel
mullion
puerta corredera
sliding door
rampa de acceso
access ramp
artesón
coffer
vigueta
joist
viga
beam
batiente
leaf
marco
door frame
techo
ceiling
enlucido
plaster
cerradero
staple
puerta vidriera
French window
falleba
espagnolette
corredera
bolt guide
empuñadura
handle
cristal
windowpane
cimacio
moulding
revestimiento
de madera
panelling
zócalo
skirting board
travesaño
crosspiece
durmiente
frame
puerta de dos hojas
double door
entrepaño
pier
derrame
splay
repisa
mantelshelf
dintel
mantel
jamba
jamb
friso del techo
frieze
armario
empotrado
built-in
cupboard
pared
wall
trashoguero
fireback
puertas correderas
sliding doors
cabecero
lintel
derrame
splay
cimacio
moulding
chambrana
casing
renvalso
rabbet
vano de la puerta
bay
umbral
threshold
umbral
threshold
entarimado de punto de Hungría
mitered herringbone flooring
cortina metálica
screen
cerco
hearth
hogar fogón
hearth fireplace
entarimado a la inglesa
plain wood strip flooring
moqueta
carpet
entarimado de mosaico
mosaic parquet
entarimado a la francesa
French flooring
entarimado de espinapez
herringbone parquet
enlosado
flagstone paving
solado
tiled floor
arpillera
underlay

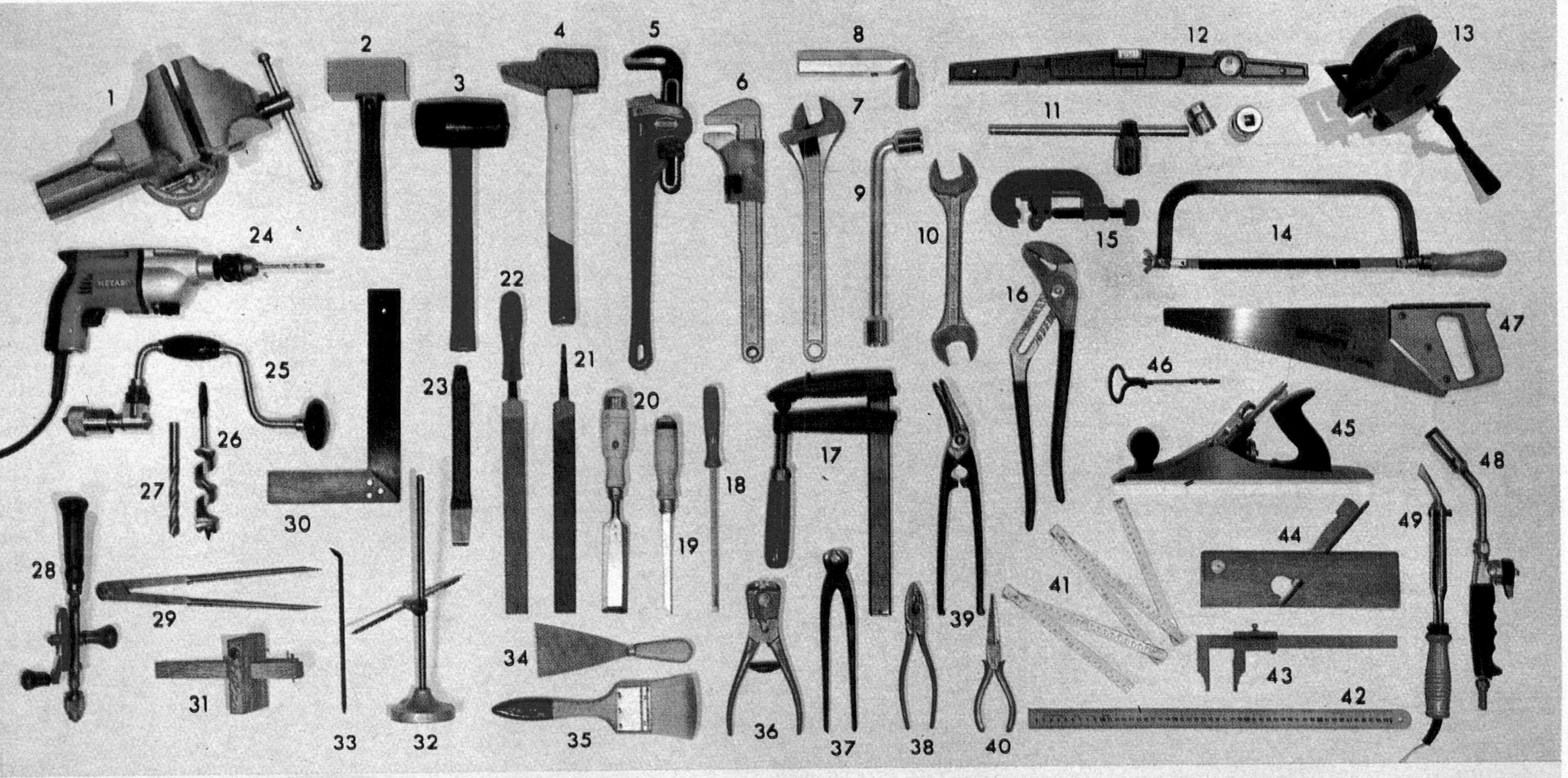

HERRAMIENTAS : 1. Torno de banco paralelo; 2. Maceta; 3. Mazo; 4. Martillo; 5. Llave para tubos; 6. Llave de cremallera; 7. Llave de gusano; 8. Llave de tubo; 9. Llave de pipa para tuercas; 10. Llave plana de doble boca; 11. Llave ajustable; 12. Nivel de agua; 13. Muela abrasiva; 14. Sierra de metales; 15. Cortatubos; 16. Alicates de boca graduable; 17. Cárcel; 18. Destornillador; 19. Escoplo; 20. Formón; 21. Lima; 22. Escofina; 23. Cortafrío; 24. Perforadora eléctrica; 25. Berbiquí; 26. Barrena; 27. Broca; 28. Taladradora; 29. Compás; 30. Escuadra; 31. Gramil de carpintero; 32. Gramil de mecánico; 33. Punta de trazar; 34. Espátula; 35. Brocha; 36. Tenazas de corte; 37. Tenazas; 38. Alicates universales; 39. Cizallas de mano; 40. Alicates de boca plana; 41. Metro; 42. Regleta; 43. Pie de rey; 44. Guillame; 45. Garlopa; 46. Barrena; 47. Serrucho; 48. Soplete; 49. Soldador eléctrico.

TOOLS : 1. Parallel vice; 2. Small square hammer; 3. Mallet; 4. Hammer; 5. Monkey wrench; 6. Rack spanner; 7. Adjustable spanner; 8. Box spanner [U. S., socket wrench]; 9. Elbowed wrench; 10. Double-ended spanner o wrench (U. S.); 11. Shifting spanner; 12. Water level; 13. Grindstone; 14. Hacksaw; 15. Pipe cutter; 16. Adjustable pliers; 17. Clamp; 18. Screwdriver; 19. Crosscut chisel; 20. Firmer chisel; 21. File; 22. Rasp; 23. Cold chisel; 24. Electric drill; 25. Brace; 26. Bit; 27. Drill; 28. Hand drill, wheelbrace; 29. Dividers; 30. Square; 31. Marking gauge; 32. Scribing block; 33. Scriber; 34. Spatula; 35. Paintbrush; 36. Wirecutters; 37. Pincers; 38. Universal pliers; 39. Shears; 40. Flat pliers; 41. Yardstick; 42. Ruler, metal rule; 43. Slide calliper; 44. Rabbet plane; 45. Jack plane; 46. Gimlet; 47. Handsaw; 48. Blowlamp [U. S., blowtorch]; 49. Electric soldering

IGLESIA
CHURCH

corte de una iglesia gótica
cross section of a Gothic church

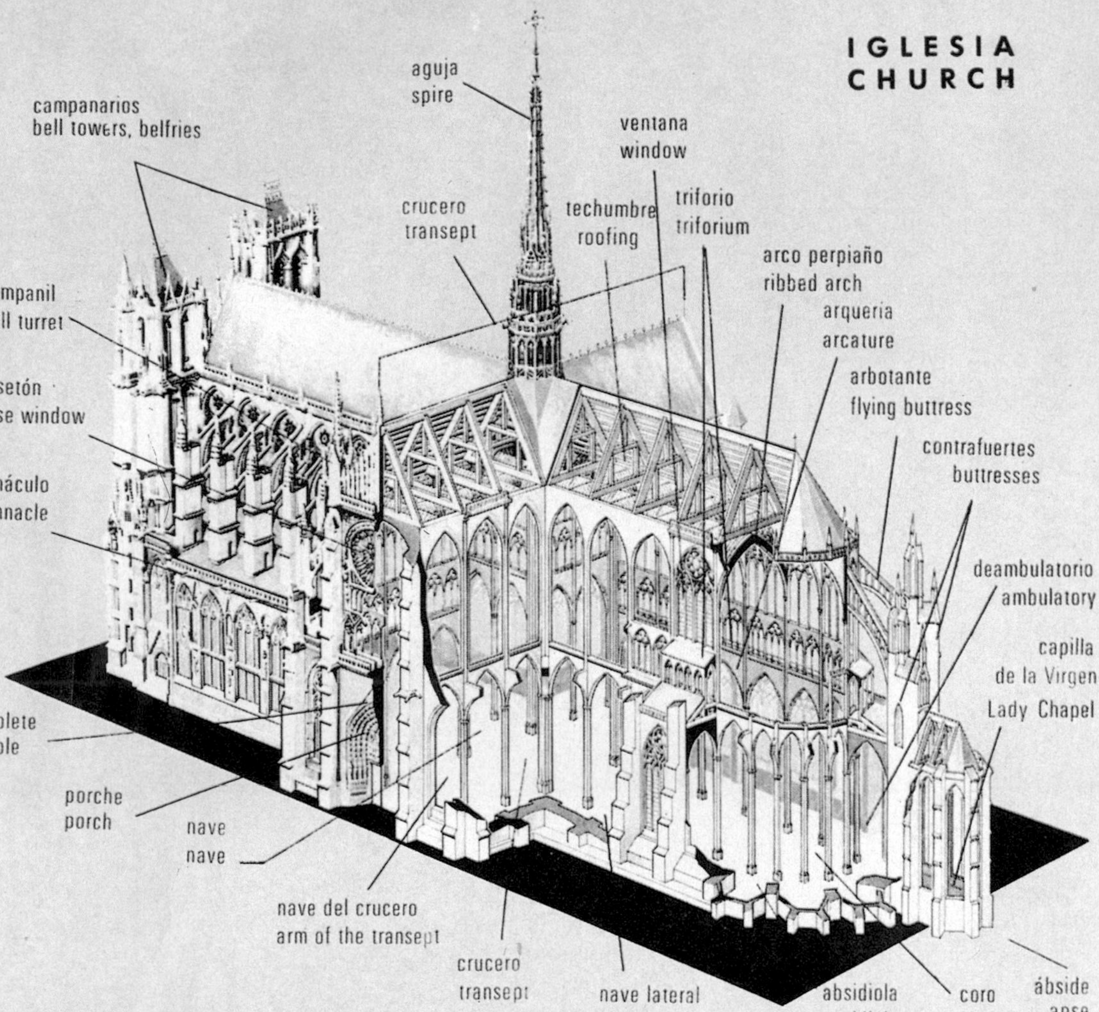

aguja
spire
campanarios
bell towers, belfries
ventana
window
triforio
triforium
crucero
transept
techumbre
roofing
arco perpiaño
ribbed arch
campanil
bell turret
arquería
arcature
arbotante
flying buttress
rosetón
rose window
contrafuertes
buttresses
pináculo
pinnacle
deambulatorio
ambulatory
capilla
de la Virgen
Lady Chapel
gablete
gable
porche
porch
nave
nave
nave del crucero
arm of the transept
crucero
transept
nave lateral
aisle
absidiola
apsidiole
coro
choir
ábside
apse

CRUZ LATINA
LATIN CROSS

CRUZ GRIEGA
GREEK CROSS

deambulatorio
ambulatory
absidiola
apsidiole
coro
choir
nave del crucero
arm of the transept
nave lateral
aisle
ábside
apse
crucero
transept
nave
nave
porche
porch
coro
choir
absidiola
apsidiole
nave del crucero
arm of the transept
ábside
apse
crucero
transept
nave
nave
nártex
narthex

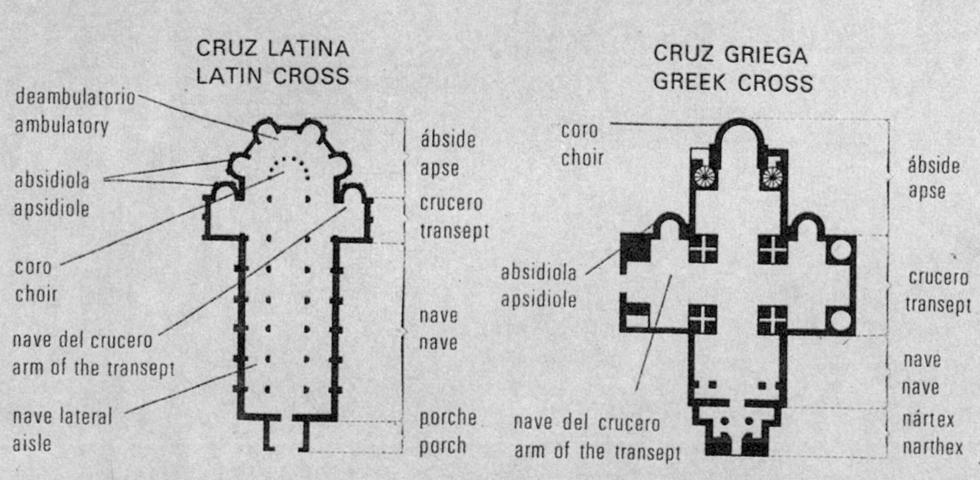

planos de iglesias en forma de cruz latina y cruz griega
plan of Latin cross and Greek cross churches

Larousse

GRAN DICCIONARIO

ESPAÑOL
INGLÉS

ENGLISH
SPANISH

Larousse

GRAN DICCIONARIO

ENGLISH-SPANISH

dirigido y realizado por

Ramón GARCÍA-PELAYO Y GROSS

Profesor de la Universidad de París (Sorbona) y del Instituto de Estudios Políticos
Miembro c. de la Academia Argentina de Letras, de la Academia de San Dionisio de Ciencias,
Artes y Letras, de la Academia Boliviana de la Historia
y de la Real Academia de Bellas Artes de San Telmo

con la colaboración de

Micheline DURAND

Licenciada en Letras, Intérprete de Conferencia
Profesora de la Escuela Superior de Intérpretes y Traductores
de la Universidad de París y del Instituto de Ciencias Políticas

Barry TULETT
Alan Biggins, Carol Cockburn, Barbara Penick,
Della Roberts, Alan Taylor, Gary D. Wright
David E. WARHAM

y de

Fernando GARCÍA-PELAYO
Pilar Andrés Solana, Trinidad Fungairiño,
Elena Real Carbonell, Carmen Warren
José PAU ANDERSEN

MARSELLA 53, MÉXICO 06600, D.F.

Paseo de Gracia 120
Barcelona 08008

17, rue du Montparnasse
75298 París Cedex 06

Valentín Gómez 3530
Buenos Aires R.13

ABBREVIATIONS

abbrev.	abbreviation	abreviatura
adj.	adjective	adjetivo
adv.	adverb	adverbio
adv. phr.	adverbial phrase	locución adverbial
AGR.	Agriculture, rural economy	Agricultura, economía rural
Amer.	Americanism	Americanismo
ANAT.	Anatomy	Anatomía
(Ant.)	Antiquated, obsolete	Anticuado
ARCH.	Architecture, building	Arquitectura, construcción
art.	article	artículo
ARTS.	Arts	Artes
ASTR.	Astronomy	Astronomía
AUT.	Automobile	Automóvil
aux.	auxiliary	auxiliar
AVIAT.	Aviation	Aviación
BIOL.	Biology	Biología
BOT.	Botany	Botánica
CHEM.	Chemistry	Química
CINEM.	Cinematography	Cinematografía
COMM.	Commerce, finance	Comercio, finanzas
comp.	comparative	comparativo
compl.	complement	complemento
conj.	conjunction	conjunción
CULIN.	Culinary, cooking	Culinario, cocina
def.	definite	definido
dem.	demonstrative	demostrativo
dim.	diminutive	diminutivo
ELECTR.	Electricity	Electricidad
exclamat.	exclamatory	exclamativo
f.	feminine	femenino
FAM.	Familiar, colloquial	Familiar
FIG.	Figurative	Figurado
GEOGR.	Geography	Geografía
GEOL.	Geology	Geología
GRAMM.	Grammar	Gramática
HERALD.	Heraldry	Heráldica
HIST.	History	Historia
impers.	impersonal	impersonal
indef.	indefinite	indefinido
Infr.	Infrequent	Poco usado
inter.	interjection	interjección
interr.	interrogative	interrogativo
intr.	intransitive	intransitivo
inv.	invariable	invariable
JUR.	Jurisprudence	Jurisprudencia
Lat. phr.	Latin phrase	locución latina
m.	masculine	masculino
MAR.	Maritime	Marítimo
MATH.	Mathematics	Matemáticas
MED.	Medicine	Medicina
MIL.	Military	Militar
MIN.	Mining, mineralogy	Minería, mineralogía
MUS.	Music	Música
MYTH.	Mythology	Mitología
n.	noun	nombre
num.	numeral	numeral
o.s.	oneself	se
pers.	personal	personal
PHIL.	Philosophy	Filosofía
PHOT.	Photography	Fotografía
PHYS.	Physics	Física
pl.	plural	plural
POET.	Poetry	Poético
POP.	Popular	Popular
poss.	possessive	posesivo
p.p.	past participle	participio pasivo
pr.	pronominal	pronominal
pref.	prefix	prefijo
prep.	preposition	preposición
pret.	preterite	pretérito
PRINT.	Printing	Imprenta
pron.	pronoun	pronombre
pr. n.	proper noun	nombre propio
RAD.	Radio, television	Radio, televisión
rel.	relative	relativo
REL.	Religion	Religión
s.	substantive	sustantivo
s.o.	someone	alguien, uno
SP.	Sports	Deportes
sth.	something	algo
superl.	superlative	superlativo
TAUR.	Tauromachy	Tauromaquia
TECH.	Technology, mechanical engineering, industry	Tecnología, mecánica, industria
THEATR.	Theatre	Teatro
tr.	transitive	transitivo
U.S.	United States	Estados Unidos
v.	verb	verbo
VET.	Veterinary science	Veterinaria
ZOOL.	Zoology	Zoología

ALFABETO FONÉTICO INTERNACIONAL

SONIDOS INGLESES

CONSONANTES

SÍMBOLOS	EJEMPLOS
[b]	bat [bæt]
[d]	dot [dɔt], begged [begd]
[dʒ]	jam [dʒæm], edge [edʒ]
[f]	fat [fæt], phrase [freiz], laugh [lα:f]
[g]	goat [gout], ghastly [ˈgα:stli], guard [gα:d]
[gw]	language [ˈlæŋgwidʒ]
[gz]	exact [igˈzækt]
[ʒ]	measure [ˈmeʒə*], azure [ˈeiʒə*], garage [ˈgærα:ʒ]
[h]	hat [hæt]
[k]	cat [kæt], keen [ki:n], Christmas [ˈkrisməs], antique [ænˈti:k]
[ks]	taxi [ˈtæksi], access [ˈækses], eczema [ˈeksimə]
[kw]	quack [kwæk]
[l]	lap [læp]
[m]	mat [mæt]
[n]	natter [ˈnætə*]
[ŋ]	blank [blæŋk]
[t]	tatter [ˈtætə*], fixed [fikst], thyme [taim]
[tʃ]	chat [tʃæt], match [mætʃ], nature [ˈneitʃə*]
[θ]	thatch [θætʃ]
[ð]	that [ðæt], father [ˈfα:ðə*]
[v]	vat [væt], Stephen [ˈsti:vn]
[z]	haze [heiz], disease [diˈzi:z], scissors [ˈsizəz], xebec [ˈzi:bek]

SEMIVOCALES

SÍMBOLOS	EJEMPLOS
[j]	yet [jet], onion [ˈɔnjən], extraneous [eksˈtreinjəs]
[w]	war [wɔ:*], quite [kwait]; (cf. [kw], [gw])

SEMIVOCALES Y VOCALES

SÍMBOLOS	EJEMPLOS
[ju:]	unit [ˈju:nit], new [nju:], suit [sju:t], adieu [əˈdju:], beauty [ˈbju:ti], yule [ju:l], yew, you [ju:], deuce [dju:s]
[juə]	fewer [ˈfjuə*], pure [ˈpjuə*]
[wʌ]	one, won [wʌn]; (cf. [w], [kw], [gw])

VOCALES

SÍMBOLOS	EJEMPLOS
[æ]	cat [kæt], plait [plæt]
[e]	hen [hen], head [hed], any [eni], bury [ˈberi], leisure [ˈleʒə*], said [sed], leopard [ˈlepəd], friend [frend]
[i]	pig [pig], English [ˈiŋgliʃ], women [ˈwimin], palace [ˈpælis], business [ˈbizinis], pyx [piks], barley [ˈbα:li], sieve [siv], build [bild], carriage [ˈkæridʒ], Greenwich [ˈgrinidʒ], captain [ˈkæptin], Sunday [ˈsʌndi], foreign [ˈfɔrin], forehead [ˈfɔrid]
[ɔ]	cock [kɔk], wash [wɔʃ], because [biˈkɔz], Gloucester [ˈglɔstə*], knowledge [ˈnɔlidʒ]
[u]	bull [bul] book [buk], wolf [wulf], could [kud], worsted [ˈwustid]
[ʌ]	duck [dʌk], come [kʌm], courage [ˈkʌridʒ], blood [blʌd]
[ə]	again [əˈgein], verandah [vəˈrændə], bacon [ˈbeikən], tortoise [ˈtə:təs], famous [ˈfeiməs], suggest [səˈdʒest], collar[ˈkɔlə*], cover [ˈkʌvə*], tapir [ˈteipə*], motor [ˈmoutə*], cupboard [ˈkʌbəd], vigour [ˈvigə*], chauffeur [ˈtʃɔ:fə*], figure [ˈfigə*], litre [ˈlitə*]
[ə:]	bird [bə:d], hermit [ˈhə:mit], earn [ə:n], amateur [ˈæmətə:*], word [wə:d], courteous [ˈkə:tiəs], nurse [nə:s], myrtle [ˈmə:tl], colonel [ˈkə:nl]
[α:]	calf [kα:f], far [fα:*], farm [fα:m], aunt [α:nt], clerk [klα:k], heart [hα:t]
[i:]	sheep [ʃi:p], tea [ti:], scene [si:n], seize [si:z], litre [li:tr], fiend [fi:nd], Caesar [ˈsi:zə*], quay [ki:], people [ˈpi:pl]
[ɔ:]	off [ɔ:f], lawn [lɔ:n], caught [kɔ:t], war [wɔ:*], broad [brɔ:d], born [bɔ:n], thought [θɔ:t], source [sɔ:s], all [ɔ:l], more [mɔ:*], floor [flɔ:*], boar [bɔ:*], your [jɔ:*]
[u:]	goose [gu:s], rule [ru:l], who [hu:], wound [wu:nd], blue [blu:], juice [dʒu:s], screw [skru:], shoe [ʃu:], manœuvre [məˈnu:və*]

DIPTONGOS

SÍMBOLOS	EJEMPLOS
[ai]	ice [ais], fly [flai], aye, eye [ai], height [hait], pie [pai], rye [rai], buy [bai], island [ˈailənd], light [lait]
[ei]	snake [sneik], maid [meid], play [plei], veil [veil], great [greit], phaeton [ˈfeitn], gauge [geidʒ], gaol [dʒeil], grey [grei], weigh [wei]
[ɔi]	coin [kɔin], joy [dʒɔi], buoy [bɔi]
[au]	mouse [maus], cow [kau], plough [plau]
[ou]	go [gou], goat [gout], doe [dou] soul [soul], blow [blou], brooch [broutʃ], mauve [mouv], bureau [bjuəˈrou], yeoman [ˈjoumən], sew [sou], dough [dou], owe [ou]
[ɛə]	bear [bɛə*], care [kɛə*], pair [pɛə*], there [ðɛə*], prayer [ˈprɛə*], mayor [mɛə*], aerial [ˈɛəriəl], heir [hɛə*], vary [ˈvɛəri]
[iə]	deer [diə*], here [hiə*], tier [tiə*], beard [biəd], weird [wiəd], theory [ˈθiəri], idea [ˈaidiə]
[uə]	poor [puə*], sure [suə*], tour [tuə*], pleurisy [ˈpluərisi], cruel [kruəl], Boer [buə*]

TRIPTONGOS

SÍMBOLOS	EJEMPLOS
[aiə]	science [ˈsaiəns], via [ˈvaiə], liar [ˈlaiə*], lion [ˈlaiən], pious [ˈpaiəs], higher [ˈhaiə*], fire [ˈfaiə*], choir [ˈkwaiə*], buyer [ˈbaiə*], dryer [ˈdraiə*], pyre [ˈpaiə*]
[auə]	flower [flauə*], vowel [ˈvauəl], hour [auə*], coward [ˈkauəd]

— OBSERV. El signo (:) colocado después de una vocal indica que ésta es larga. El asterisco (*) señala que la *r* escrita en posición final no se pronuncia en Gran Bretaña, excepto cuando la palabra siguiente empieza por vocal. En los Estados Unidos esta *r* se pronuncia siempre.

Además de los símbolos incluidos en el cuadro se han utilizado otros tres para representar sonidos nasales existentes en palabras tomadas del francés que son ɑ̃ (vol-au-vent [ˈvɔləuˈvɑ̃ŋ]), ɛ̃ (lingerie [ˈlɛ̃ʒəri]) y ɔ̃ (wagon-lit [ˈvægɔ̃nˈli:]).

Para conocer la relación entre los sonidos ingleses y los castellanos es preciso consultar el apartado del "Resumen de gramática inglesa" dedicado a la pronunciación.

Listas de vocabulario

que figuran en la primera parte

Automóvil	Automobile	*Metalurgia*	Metallurgy
Bicicleta	Bicycle	*Música*	Music
Circulación de automóviles	Motoring	*Nombres de pila*	Christian names
Construcción	Construction	*Países*	Countries
Deportes	Sports	*Química*	Chemistry
Enseñanza	Education	*Religión*	Religion
Fiestas religiosas	Feast days	*Ropa*	Clothing
Geografía	Geography	*Telecomunicaciones*	Telecommunications
Herramientas	Tools	*Trabajo*	Work
Jurídico (vocabulario)	Legal terminology	*Viajes*	Travel
Medicina	Medicine	*Zoología*	Zoology

Word lists

included in the second part

Agriculture	*Agricultura*	Maths and physics	*Matemáticas y física*
Arts	*Artes*	Mining	*Minería*
Boats	*Barcos*	Nuclear energy	*Energía nuclear*
Cinematography	*Cinematografía*	Photography	*Fotografía*
Computer	*Computadora*	Politics	*Política*
Conferences	*Conferencias*	Radio and television	*Radio y televisión*
Economic and commercial terms	*Vocabulario de economía y comercio*	Sailing	*Navegación*
Entertainments	*Diversiones*	Town	*Ciudad*
Food and meals	*Alimentos y comidas*	Universe and weather	*Universo y tiempo*
Games	*Juegos*	Vegetables and fruits	*Hortalizas y frutas*
Kinship	*Parentesco*		

Láminas en color fuera de texto — Colour plates

Automóvil	Motorcar	*Transatlántico*	Liner
Avión	Aircraft	*Esqueleto*	Skeleton
Turborreactor	Turbojet engine	*Anatomía*	Anatomy
Motor	Motor	*Teatro*	Theatre
Motocicleta	Motorcycle	*Cinematografía*	Cinema
Ferrocarril	Railway	*Casa*	House
Locomotora	Locomotive	*Herramientas*	Tools
Velero	Sailing boat	*Iglesia*	Church

ENGLISH - SPANISH

A

a [ei] n. A, *f.* (letter): *a small a*, una a minúscula. || MUS. La, *m.*: *A minor*, la menor; *A major*, la mayor; *A flat*, la bemol; *A sharp*, la sostenido. || — FAM. *From A to Z*, de cabo a rabo. || *Number 20 A, Villiers Street*, calle Villiers número 20 duplicado.
— Indef. art. Un, una: *a man*, un hombre; *a woman*, una mujer. || Un tal, una tal, un cierto, una cierta: *a Mr. Jones*, un tal Sr. Jones. || El mismo, la misma: *to be of a size*, tener el mismo tamaño. || Not translated in Spanish: *to make a noise*, hacer ruido; *as a taxpayer*, como contribuyente; *my father is a doctor*, mi padre es médico; *my friend, a teacher of languages*, mi amigo, profesor de idiomas; *what a surprise!*, ¡qué sorpresa!; *a fine answer!*, ¡menuda contestación!; *have you got a flat?*, ¿tienes piso?; *you haven't got a flat*, no tienes piso. || Distributive use: *two shillings a head*, dos chelines por persona; *pears at three shillings a pound*, peras a tres chelines por libra. || Expressing time: *twice a day*, dos veces al día *or* por día; *one hundred miles an hour*, cien millas por hora. || — *A few*, unos pocos, unas pocas, unos, unas: *in a few minutes*, dentro de unos minutos. || *A great many*, muchísimos, muchísimas. || *Half an hour*, media hora. || *So great a man*, un hombre tan grande. || *Such a*, tal: *I don't like such a book*, no me gusta tal libro. || *Too cautious a man*, un hombre demasiado prudente. || *To set an example*, dar ejemplo, dar el ejemplo.

— OBSERV. Se emplea el artículo *a* cuando antecede una palabra que empieza por una consonante (*a boat*, un barco), una "h" aspirada (*a house*, una casa) o una "u" con el sonido de [ju] (*a use*, un empleo). Se sustituye por *an* delante de vocal (*an eye*, un ojo) o "h" muda (*an hour*, una hora).

A-l [ei-wʌn] adj. FAM. De primera categoría. | En plena forma (in good health).
Aachen [ˈɑ:kən] pr. n. GEOGR. Aquisgrán.
abaca [ˈæbəkə] n. Abacá, *m.*
aback [əˈbæk] adv. MAR. En facha. || FIG. *To be taken aback*, quedar sorprendido *or* estupefacto.
abacus [ˈæbəkəs] n. ARCH. MATH. Ábaco, *m.*

— OBSERV. El plural de *abacus* es *abaci* o *abacuses*.

abaft [əˈbɑ:ft] adv. MAR. A popa (towards stern). | En popa (in stern).
— Prep. Detrás de.
abalone [æbəˈləuni] n. ZOOL. Oreja (*f.*) de mar.
abandon [əˈbændən] n. Abandono, *m.* || Desenfado, *m.* (ease).
abandon [əˈbændən] v. tr. Abandonar (to leave). || Renunciar a (to give up). || *To abandon o.s. to*, abandonarse a, entregarse a.
abandoned [—d] adj. Abandonado, da. || Perdido, da (immoral).
abandoning [—iŋ] or **abandonment** [—mənt] n. Abandono, *m.*
abase [əˈbeis] v. tr. Rebajar, degradar.
abasement [—mənt] n. Degradación, *f.*, rebajamiento, *m.*
abash [əˈbæʃ] v. tr. Avergonzar (to make ashamed). || Desconcertar (to disconcert).
abashment [—mənt] n. Vergüenza, *f.*
abate [əˈbeit] v. tr. JUR. Abolir. || Disminuir, reducir (to reduce). || Debilitar (to weaken). || Rebajar, descontar (to deduct).
— V. intr. Reducirse, disminuir. || Calmarse (storm, pain). || Amainar (wind). || Bajar (flood). || Moderarse (violence).
abatement [əˈbeitmənt] n. JUR. Abolición, *f.*, supresión, *f.* || Disminución, *f.* || Alivio, *m.* (of a pain). || Rebaja, *f.*, descuento, *m.* (deduction).
abattoir [ˈæbətwɑ:*] n. Matadero, *m.*
abbacy [ˈæbəsi] n. REL. Abadía, *f.*
Abbasids [ˈæbəsidz] pl. pr. n. HIST. Abasidas, *m.*
abbatial [æˈbeiʃəl] adj. Abacial. || *Abbatial lands*, tierras abadengas.
abbé [ˈæbei] n. REL. Abate, *m.*
abbess [ˈæbis] n. REL. Abadesa, *f.*
abbey [ˈæbi] n. REL. Abadía, *f.*
abbot [ˈæbət] n. REL. Abad, *m.*
abbreviate [əˈbri:vieit] v. tr. Abreviar. || MATH. Simplificar.
abbreviation [əˌbri:viˈeiʃən] n. Abreviación, *f.* (action of abbreviating). || Abreviatura, *f.* (shortened form).: *table of abbreviations*, cuadro de abreviaturas.
A B C [ˈeibi:ˈsi:] n. Abecé, *m.*, alfabeto, *m.*, abecedario, *m.* (alphabet).
abdicate [ˈæbdikeit] v. tr. Abdicar (the throne). || Dimitir de (a function). || Renunciar a (one's rights).
— V. intr. Abdicar: *to abdicate from the throne*, abdicar el trono.
abdication [ˌæbdiˈkeiʃən] n. Abdicación, *f.* || Renuncia, *f.* (of rights). || Dimisión, *f.* (of a function).
abdomen [ˈæbdəmən] n. ANAT. Abdomen, *m.*
abdominal [æbˈdəminl] adj. ANAT. Abdominal: *abdominal muscles*, músculos abdominales.
abducent [æbˈdju:snt] adj. ANAT. Abductor.
abduct [æbˈdʌkt] v. tr. Secuestrar (to kidnap).
abduction [æbˈdʌkʃən] n. Rapto, *m.*, secuestro, *m.* || ANAT. Abducción, *f.*
abductor [æbˈdʌktə*] n. Raptor, ra; secuestrador, ra (kidnapper). || ANAT. Abductor, *m.*
abeam [əˈbi:m] adv. MAR. De través.
abed [əˈbed] adv. En cama.
Abel [ˈeibəl] pr. n. Abel, *m.*
abelmosk [—məusk] n. BOT. Algalia, *f.*
aberrance [æˈberəns] n. Aberración, *f.* || ANAT. Anormalidad, *f.*
aberrant [æˈberənt] adj. Aberrante. || ANAT. Anormal, anómalo, la.
aberration [ˌæbəˈreiʃən] n. Aberración, *f.*
abet [əˈbet] v. tr. Incitar. || JUR. *To aid and abet*, ser cómplice de.
abetment [—mənt] n. Incitación, *f.* || JUR. Complicidad, *f.*
abettor [—ə*] n. JUR. Cómplice, *m.* & *f.* || Instigador, ra.
abeyance [əˈbeiəns] n. Suspensión, *f.* || — *In abeyance*, en suspenso. || *Inheritance in abeyance*, herencia (*f.*) yacente. || *Into abeyance*, en desuso.
abhor [əbˈhɔ:*] v. tr. Aborrecer, odiar, abominar.
abhorrence [əbˈhɔrəns] n. Aborrecimiento, *m.*, odio, *m.* || *To hold in abhorrence*, odiar, aborrecer.
abhorrent [əbˈhɔrənt] adj. Aborrecible, detestable, abominable.
abidance [əˈbaidəns] n. Acatamiento, *m.*, respeto, *m.* (*by*, de) [the law, etc.].
abide* [əˈbaid] v. tr. Tolerar, soportar, aguantar: *I can't abide him*, no le aguanto. || Esperar (to await).
— V. intr. Permanecer (to stay). || Acatar, someterse a, atenerse a: *to abide by the rules*, acatar las reglas. || Cumplir: *to abide by a promise*, cumplir una promesa. || Morar (to dwell).

— OBSERV. Pret. & p.p. ***abode, abided.***

abiding [—iŋ] adj. Duradero, ra. || *Law abiding*, respetuoso de las leyes.
ability [əˈbiliti] n. Habilidad, *f.* (skill). || Capacidad, *f.* || Aptitud, *f.* || — Pl. Talento, *m. sing.* || Inteligencia, *f. sing.*
abject [ˈæbdʒekt] adj. Abyecto, ta; vil, despreciable (despicable). || Miserable (wretched).
abjection [æbˈdʒekʃən] n. Bajeza, *f.*, abyección, *f.*
abjuration [ˌæbdʒuəˈreiʃən] n. Abjuración, *f.*
abjure [əbˈdʒuə*] v. tr. Abjurar [de] (one's faith). || Retractarse de (one's opinion).
ablation [æbˈleiʃən] n. Ablación, *f.*
ablative [ˈæblətiv] n. GRAMM. Ablativo, *m.*: *ablative absolute*, ablativo absoluto.
— Adj. En ablativo. || Ablativo (case).
ablaut [ˈæblaut] n. GRAMM. Apofonía, *f.*
ablaze [əˈbleiz] adj./adv. En llamas, ardiendo (on fire). || Encendido, da (lit up). || FIG. Inflamado, da. | Brillante. || *Ablaze with anger*, furibundo, da.
able [ˈeibl] adj. Listo, ta; inteligente (clever). || Capaz (capable). || Bien hecho (work). || *To be able to*, poder.
able-bodied [—ˈbɔdid] adj. Sano, na; fuerte.
able-bodied seaman [—ˈbɔdidsi:mən] n. MAR. Marinero (*m.*) de primera.
abloom [əˈblu:m] adj./adv. En flor.

ablution [əˈbluːʃən] n. Ablución, *f.*
ably [ˈeibli] adv. Hábilmente.
abnegate [ˈæbnigeit] v. tr. Renunciar a (rights, etc.). || REL. Abjurar.
abnegation [ˌæbniˈgeiʃən] n. Renuncia, *f.* (of rights). || Abnegación, *f.* (self-denial). || REL. Abjuración, *f.*
abnormal [æbˈnɔːməl] adj. Anormal.
abnormality [ˌæbnɔːˈmæliti] n. Anormalidad, *f.*
aboard [əˈbɔːd] adv. A bordo. || — *All aboard!*, ¡viajeros al tren! (on a train), ¡pasajeros a bordo! (on a boat). || *To go aboard*, ir a bordo, embarcarse. || *To take aboard*, llevar a bordo, embarcar.
— Prep. A bordo de.
abode [əˈbəud] n. Residencia, *f.*, domicilio, *m.*: *of no fixed abode*, sin domicilio fijo. || *To take up one's abode*, domiciliarse, fijar domicilio.
abode [əˈbəud] pret. & p.p. See ABIDE.
abolish [əˈbɔliʃ] v. tr. Abolir.
abolishment [—mənt] or **abolition** [ˌæbəˈliʃən] n. Abolición, *f.*
abolitionism [ˌæbə liʃənizəm] n. Abolicionismo, *m.*
abolitionist [ˌæbəˈliʃənist] n. Abolicionista, *m.* & *f.*
abomasum [ˌæbəuˈmeisəm] n. ANAT. Abomaso, *m.*, cuajar, *m.*
— OBSERV. El plural de *abomasum* es *abomasa.*
A-bomb [ˈeibɔm] n. PHYS. Bomba (*f.*) A.
abominable [əˈbɔminəbl] adj. Abominable, detestable. || *The abominable snowman*, el abominable hombre de las nieves.
abominate [əˈbɔmineit] v. tr. Abominar, aborrecer, detestar.
abomination [əˌbɔmiˈneiʃən] n. Aborrecimiento, *m.*, abominación, *f.* (loathing). || FIG. *This wine is an abomination*, este vino es horrible.
aboriginal [ˌæbəˈridʒənl] adj./n. Aborigen, indígena.
aborigines [ˌæbəˈridʒiniːz] pl. n. Aborígenes, *m.* & *f.*
abort [əˈbɔːt] v. intr. MED. Abortar. || FAM. Fracasar (to fail).
— V. tr. Abortar, hacer abortar.
abortifacient [əˈbɔːtiˌfeiʃənt] adj. MED. Abortivo, va.
— N. Abortivo, *m.*
abortion [əˈbɔːʃən] n. Aborto (*m.*) provocado. || FIG. Engendro, *m.*, aborto, *m.* (sth. badly developed). | Fracaso, *m.* (failure).
abortive [əˈbɔːtiv] adj. Abortivo, va. || FIG. Fracasado, da; frustrado, da. || *Abortive medicine*, abortivo, *m.*
abound [əˈbaund] v. intr. Abundar (*in*, *with*, en).
about [əˈbaut] adv. Por aquí y por allá: *he was walking about*, andaba por aquí y por allá. || Por aquí: *there is a lot of flu about*, hay mucha gripe por aquí. || MIL. Media vuelta: *about turn!* [U.S., *about face!*], ¡media vuelta! || A punto de: *I am about to do it*, estoy a punto de hacerlo. || Más o menos: *that's about right*, eso es más o menos exacto. || Casi, unos, alrededor de: *about three thousand men*, alrededor de tres mil hombres; *about two years ago*, hace unos dos años. || Casi, más o menos: *it's just about finished*, está casi acabado. || — *All about*, por todas partes, en todos lados. || *I'm happy to see you up and about*, me alegro de verte de nuevo en pie. || *To be about*, estar a mano. || *To bring about*, see BRING. || *To come about*, see COME.
— Prep. Sobre: *a book about aeroplanes*, un libro sobre aviones. || Acerca de, con respecto a, sobre: *he told me all about him*, me dijo todo acerca de él. || Por: *he worries about his health*, se preocupa por su salud. || En: *he only thinks about him*, piensa sólo en él. || Alrededor de, cerca de (around): *somewhere about Pamplona*, alrededor de Pamplona. || A eso de, hacia: *at about 4 o'clock*, a eso de las cuatro. || Por: *his toys were spread about the garden*, sus juguetes estaban esparcidos por el jardín. || Junto a: *about the fire*, junto al fuego. || — *He has no money about him*, no lleva dinero encima *or* consigo. || *How about me?*, ¿y yo? || *How about that?*, ¿qué te parece? || *What are you about?*, ¿qué hace? || *There is sth. strange about that girl*, esta chica tiene algo [de] extraño. || *What is it about?*, ¿de qué se trata? || *What's that book about?*, ¿de qué trata ese libro?
about-face [—feis] n. U. S. MIL. Media vuelta, *f.* || FIG. Cambio (*m.*) rotundo.
about-face [—feis] v. intr. U.S. MIL. Dar media vuelta.
about-ship [—ʃip] v. intr. MAR. Virar.
about turn [—təːn] n. MIL. Media vuelta, *f.*
about-turn [—təːn] v. intr. MIL. Dar media vuelta.
above [əˈbʌv] adv. Arriba (higher): *it is above*, está arriba. || Anteriormente (before in a printed passage). || De arriba: *the flat above*, el piso de arriba. || Más arriba, más allá (further). || *See above*, véase más arriba.
— Prep. Encima de (higher than): *above your house*, encima de su casa. || Más allá de (beyond): *the road above the village*, la carretera más allá del pueblo. || Más de (more than): *we cannot admit above 25 people*, no se admiten más de 25 personas. || Más arriba de (river). || Sobre: *above sea level*, sobre el nivel del mar; *fifteen degrees above zero*, quince grados sobre cero. || Superior a: *any number above 100*, cualquier número superior a 100. || — *Above all*, sobre todo. || *Above and beyond*, mucho más allá de, por encima de. || *Over and above*, además de. || *People above 18 years of age*, mayores de 18 años. || *To be above all suspicion*, estar por encima de toda sospecha. || *To be above deception*, ser incapaz de engañar.
— Adj. Susodicho, cha; citado anteriormente.
aboveboard [əˈbʌvˈbɔːd] adj. Honrado, da (honest). || Franco, ca; sincero, ra. || Leal.
— Adv. Abiertamente.
above-mentioned [əˈbʌvˈmenʃənd] adj. Anteriormente citado, anteriormente mencionado.
abracadabra [ˌæbrəkəˈdæbrə] n. Abracadabra, *m.*
abrade [əˈbreid] v. tr. Raer, desgastar.
Abraham [ˈeibrəhæm] pr. n. Abrahán, *m.*
abrasion [əˈbreiʒən] n. GEOL. Erosión, *f.* || MED. TECN. Abrasión, *f.*
abrasive [əˈbreisiv] adj. Abrasivo, va.
— N. Abrasivo, *m.*
abreast [əˈbrest] adv. Uno al lado de otro. || MIL. De frente (to march). || — *Four abreast*, en fila de a cuatro. || *To be abreast of the times*, andar con el tiempo. || *To keep abreast of*, mantenerse informado de, estar al tanto *or* al corriente de (news, etc.), estar al día con (all one's work), seguir [el ritmo de] (to keep up with), correr parejo con (in a race).
abridge [əˈbridʒ] v. tr. Condensar, abreviar (a book). || Limitar, reducir (rights). || Privar (to deprive). || Acortar (to shorten).
abridgement or **abridgment** [—mənt] n. Compendio, *m.*, resumen, *m.* || Limitación, *f.*, reducción, *f.* || JUR. Privación, *f.* (of rights).
abroad [əˈbrɔːd] adv. En el extranjero (in a foreign place). || Al extranjero (to a foreign place). || Fuera, fuera de casa (outside). || — *How did the news get abroad?*, ¿cómo se divulgó la noticia? || FIG. *The rumour is abroad that*, corre el rumor de que.
abrogate [ˈæbrəugeit] v. tr. Abrogar.
abrogation [ˌæbrəuˈgeiʃən] n. Abrogación, *f.*
abrupt [əˈbrʌpt] adj. Abrupto, ta; escarpado, da (steep). || Brusco, ca (people). || Brusco, ca (sudden): *an abrupt halt*, una parada brusca. || Entrecortado, da (jerky).
Abruzzi [əˈbrutsiː] pl. pr. n. GEOGR. Abruzos, *m.*
abscess [ˈæbsis] n. MED. Absceso, *m.*
abscissa [æbˈsisə] n. MATH. Abscisa, *f.*
— OBSERV. El plural es *abscissae* o *abscissas.*
abscission [æbˈsiʒən] n. MED. Abscisión, *f.*
abscond [əbˈskɔnd] v. intr. Fugarse, huir.
absence [ˈæbsəns] n. Ausencia, *f.* (of a person). || Falta, *f.* (lack). || JUR. Incomparecencia, *f.* || — *Absence of mind*, distracción, *f.* || *In the absence of*, en ausencia de, a falta de.
absent [ˈæbsənt] adj. Ausente. || Distraído, da (not attentive). || MIL. *To declare s.o. absent without leave*, declararle a uno ausente sin permiso.
absent [æbˈsent] v. tr. *To absent o.s.*, ausentarse.
absentee [ˌæbsənˈtiː] n. Ausente, *m.* & *f.* || Absentista, *m.* & *f.* (landlord, worker).
absenteeism [—izəm] n. Absentismo, *m.*
absentee landlord [—ˈlændlɔːd] n. Absentista, *m.*
absently [ˈæbsəntli] adv. Distraídamente.
absentminded [ˈæbsəntˈmaindid] adj. Distraído, da.
absentmindedness [—nis] n. Distracción, *f.*
absidiole [æbˈsidiəul] n. ARCH. Absidiolo, *m.*
absinth or **absinthe** [ˈæbsinθ] n. Ajenjo, *m.*
absolute [ˈæbsəluːt] adj. Absoluto, ta. || Rotundo, da (denial). || JUR. Irrevocable. || FAM. Completo, ta. | Perfecto, ta (liar, idiot, etc.). || *To obtain an absolute majority*, obtener la mayoría absoluta.
— N. Lo absoluto.
absolute alcohol [—ˈælkəhɔl] n. Alcohol (*m.*) puro.
absolute scale [—skeil] n. PHYS. Escala (*f.*) de Kelvin.
absolution [ˌæbsəˈluːʃən] n. Absolución, *f.*: *to grant absolution*, dar la absolución.
absolutism [ˈæbsəluːtizəm] n. Absolutismo, *m.*
absolutist [ˈæbsəluːtist] adj./n. Absolutista.
absolve [əbˈzɔlv] v. tr. Absolver. || Liberar (from a promise).
absorb [əbˈsɔːb] v. tr. Absorber. || Amortiguar (a shock). || FIG. Absorber. || *To be absorbed in*, estar absorto en.
absorbefacient [əbˌsɔːbiˈfeiʃənt] adj. MED. Absorbente.
— N. Absorbente, *m.*
absorbency [əbˈsɔːbənsi] n. Absorbencia, *f.*
absorbent [əbˈsɔːbənt] adj. Absorbente.
— N. Absorbente *m.*
absorbent cotton [—kɔtn] n. U. S. Algodón (*m.*) hidrófilo.
absorbing [əbˈsɔːbiŋ] adj. Absorbente (work, etc.).
absorption [əbˈsɔːpʃən] n. Absorción, *f.* || FIG. Ensimismamiento, *m.* || AUT. Amortiguamiento, *m.*
absorptive [əbˈsɔːptiv] adj. Absorbente.
absorptivity [əbsɔːpˈtiviti] n. PHYS. Absorción, *f.*
abstain [əbstein] v. intr. Abstenerse: *to abstain from comment*, abstenerse de comentarios.
abstemious [æbˈstiːmjəs] adj. Abstemio, mia.
abstention [æbˈstenʃən] n. Abstención, *f.* (from voting). || Abstinencia, *f.*
abstentionism [—izəm] n. Abstencionismo, *m.*
abstentionist [—ist] n. Abstencionista, *m.* & *f.*
abstinence [ˈæbstinəns] n. Abstinencia, *f.*
abstinent [ˈæbstinənt] adj. Abstinente.
abstract [ˈæbstrækt] adj. Abstracto, ta.
— N. Resumen, *m.* (summary). || Extracto, *m.* (extract). || Abstracción, *f.* || *In the abstract*, en abstracto.
abstract [æbˈstrækt] v. tr. Extraer (to extract). || Resumir (to summarize). || Hacer caso omiso de (an

idea). || Sustraer (to steal). || *To abstract o.s.*, abstraerse, ensimismarse.
abstracted [æb'stræktid] adj. Abstraído, da; ensimismado, da.
abstraction [æb'strækʃən] n. Abstracción, *f.* (generalization). || Extracción, *f.* (extraction). || Distracción, *f.* (of mind). || Sustracción, *f.* (of papers, etc.). || Malversación, *f.* (of funds).
abstruse [æb'stru:s] adj. Abstruso, sa.
abstruseness [—nis] n. Carácter (*m.*) abstruso.
absurd [əb'sə:d] adj. Absurdo, da. || Ridículo, la.
absurdity [—iti] n. Absurdo, *m.*
abulia [ə'bu:liə] n. Abulia, *f.*
abulic [ə'bu:lik] adj. Abúlico, ca.
abundance [ə'bʌndəns] n. Abundancia, *f.*
abundant [ə'bʌndənt] adj. Abundante.
abuse [ə'bju:s] n. Abuso, *m.* (misuse): *abuse of confidence*, abuso de confianza. || Insultos, *m. pl.* (insults).
abuse [ə'bju:z] v. tr. Abusar de (to mistreat, to misuse). || Insultar (to insult). || Denigrar (to disparage). || *He has been abused*, le han engañado.
abusive [ə'bju:siv] adj. Abusivo, va (misusing). || Injurioso, sa (insulting).
abut [ə'bʌt] v. intr. Lindar (*on*, con) [to border]. || Apoyarse (*on*, *against*, en) [to lean against].
abutment [—mənt] n. Límite, *m.* (limit). || ARCH. Contrafuerte, *m.* || Empalme, *m.* (in carpentry).
abutting [—iŋ] adj. Lindante con.
abysm [ə'bizəm] n. Abismo, *m.*
abysmal [ə'bizməl] adj. Abismal, abismático, ca. || FIG. Profundo, da. | Pésimo, ma (very bad).
abyss [ə'bis] n. Abismo, *m.*, sima, *f.*
abyssal [—əl] adj. Abisal.
Abyssinia [,æbi'siniə] pr. n. GEOGR. Abisinia, *f.*
Abyssinian [—n] adj. n. Abisinio, nia.
acacia [ə'keiʃə] n. BOT. Acacia, *f.*
academic [,ækə'demik] adj. Académico, ca (scholarly). || Bizantino, na (too speculative). || Universitario, ria; escolar: *academic year*, curso escolar.
— N. Universitario, *m.*
academical [—əl] adj. Académico, ca (scholarly).
— Pl. n. Vestidura (*f. sing.*) académica.
academic freedom [—'fri:dəm] n. Libertad (*f.*) de cátedra *or* de enseñanza.
academician [ə,kædə'miʃən] n. Académico, ca.
academicism [,ækə'demisizəm] n. Academicismo, *m.*
academism [ə'kædemizəm] n. Academismo, *m.*
academy [ə'kædəmi] n. Academia, *f.* (a specialized institute): *military*, *naval academy*, academia militar, naval. || Intituto (*m.*) de enseñanza media (in Scotland). || U. S. Internado, *m.* || Conservatorio, *m.* (of music).
acaleph [,ækə'li:f] n. ZOOL. Acalefo, *m.*

— OBSERV. El plural de *acaleph* es *acalepha*.

acanthopterygii [,ækænθəptə'ridʒii] pl. n. ZOOL. Acantopterigios, *m.*
acanthus [ə'kænθəs] n. ARCH. BOT. Acanto, *m.*

— OBSERV. El plural de la palabra inglesa *acanthus* es *acanthuses* o *acanthi*.

acaridae [ə'kæridi:] pl. n. ZOOL. Acáridos, *m.*
acarus ['ækərəs] n. ZOOL. Ácaro.

— OBSERV. El plural de *acarus* es *acari*.

acaulescent ['ækɔ:'lesənt] or **acauline** ['ækɔ:lain] adj. BOT. Acaule.
accede [æk'si:d] v. intr. Acceder a (to agree). || Subir a (to the throne). || Tomar posesión de (to a post). || Afiliarse a (to affiliate). || Adherirse a (to a treaty).
accelerant [æk'selərənt] n. CHEM. Acelerador, *m.*, acelerante, *m.*
accelerate [æk'seləreit] v. tr./intr. Acelerar.
accelerating [—iŋ] adj. Acelerador, ra. || *Accelerating force*, fuerza aceleratriz.
acceleration [æk,selə're∫ən] n. Aceleración, *f.* || *Acceleration of* or *due to gravity*, aceleración terrestre.
accelerative [æk'selərətiv] adj. Acelerador, ra.
accelerator [ək,seləreitə*] n. Acelerador, *m.*
accent ['æksənt] n. Acento, *m.*: *written accent*, acento gráfico. || — *In broken accents*, con voz entrecortada. || *To put the accent on*, acentuar, subrayar, hacer hincapié en, recalcar.
accent [æk'sənt] v. tr. Acentuar.
accentuate [æk'sentjueit] v. tr. Acentuar.
accentuation [æk,sentju'eiʃən] n. Acentuación, *f.* (stress).
accept [ək'sept] v. tr. Aceptar: *to accept an invitation, a bill of exchange*, aceptar una invitación, una letra de cambio. || Admitir (to admit).
acceptability [ək,septə'biliti] n. Aceptabilidad, *f.*
acceptable [ək'septəbl] adj. Aceptable. || Adecuado, da; oportuno, na (appropriate). || Admisible.
acceptance [ək'septəns] n. Aceptación, *f.* || Aprobación, *f.* (approval).
acceptation [,æksep'teiʃən] n. Acepción, *f.* (of a word). || Aceptación, *f.* (of an invitation, a bill, etc.).
accepted [ək'septid] adj. Aceptado, da. || Corriente, normal (widely used). || Reconocido, da (s.o. with a quality).
acceptor [ək'septə*] n. Aceptador, ra; aceptante, *m.* & *f.*
access ['ækses] n. Acceso, *m.* || MED. Ataque, *m.*, acceso, *m.* || — *Easy of access*, de fácil acceso (place), muy abordable (person). || *To give access to*, dar entrada a.
accessary [æk'sesəri] adj./n. See ACCESSORY.
accessibility [æk,sesi'biliti] n. Accesibilidad, *f.*
accessible [æk'sesəbl] adj. Accesible, asequible (place). || Abordable (person). || Comprensible (understandable). || *Accessible to pity*, capaz de compasión.
accession [æk'seʃən] n. Acceso, *m.*, entrada, *f.* || Aumento, *m.* (increase). || Accesión, *f.* (to power). || Subida, *f.*, accesión, *f.* (of a king). || Entrada (*f.*) en posesión (to a post). || Adhesión, *f.* (to a party, a treaty). || Asentimiento, *m.*, accesión, *f.* (assent).
accessit [æk'sesit] n. Accésit, *m.*
accessory [æk'sesəri] adj. Accesorio, ria.
— N. Accesorio, *m.* (sth. additional, equipment). || JUR. Cómplice, *m.* & *f.* (accomplice). || *Toilet accessories*, artículos (*m. pl.*) de tocador.
accessory after the fact [— ɑ:ftə*-ðə-fækt] n. JUR. Encubridor, ra; cómplice *m.* & *f.*
accessory before the fact [—bi'fɔ:*-ðə-fækt] n. JUR. Cómplice, *m.* & *f.* [por instigación], instigador, ra.
accidence ['æksidəns] n. GRAMM. Accidente, *m.*
accident ['æksidənt] n. Accidente, *m.* (mishap, catastrophe): *accident insurance*, seguro contra accidentes; *accident to a third party*, accidente contra terceros; *motoring*, *traffic*, *road accident*, accidente de coche, de circulación, de carretera; *aircraft accident*, accidente de aviación; *to meet with an accident*, sufrir un accidente. || Casualidad, *f.*: *we met by accident*, nos encontramos por casualidad. || GEOL. PHIL. REL. Accidente, *m.* || *Industrial accident*, accidente de trabajo.
accidental [,æksi'dentl] adj. Accidental, fortuito, ta. || Accidental (not essential).
— N. MUS. Accidente, *m.*, accidental, *m.*
acclaim [ə'kleim] n. Aclamación, *f.* (enthusiastic praise). || Ovación, *f.* (loud applause).
acclaim [ə'kleim] v. tr. Aclamar: *to acclaim a minister*, aclamar a un ministro; *they acclaimed him leader*, le aclamaron jefe. || Ovacionar (to applaud).
acclamation [,æklə'meiʃən] n. Aclamación, *f.*
acclimate [ə'klaimət] v. tr. U. S. Aclimatar.
acclimation [,æklai'meiʃən] n. U. S. Aclimatación, *f.*
acclimatization [ə,klaimətai'zeiʃən] n. Aclimatación, *f.*
acclimatize [ə'klaimətaiz] v. tr. Aclimatar.
— V. intr. Aclimatarse.
acclivity [ə'kliviti] n. Cuesta, *f.*, subida, *f.*, pendiente, *f.*
accolade ['ækəleid] n. Acolada, *f.*, espaldarazo, *m.* (investment of knighthood). || Panegírico, *m.* (recognition of merit). || MUS. Corchete, *m.*
accommodate [ə'kɔmədeit] v. tr. Acomodar, adaptar (to adjust to circumstances). || Alojar, hospedar (to lodge). || Resolver (a dispute). || Reconciliar (to reconcile). || Caber, haber sitio para: *the car accommodates three people*, en el coche caben tres personas. || Proveer, suministrar (to supply). || Complacer (to do a favour). || ANAT. PHYS. Acomodar.
— V. intr. Acomodarse.
accommodating [—iŋ] adj. Acomodadizo, za. || Servicial (obliging). || Complaciente (husband).
accommodation [ə,kɔmə'deiʃən] n. Alojamiento, *m.* (lodging). || Habitación, *f.* (room). || Cabida, *f.*, capacidad, *f.* (capacity). || Sitio, *m.*, espacio, *m.* (space). || Préstamo, *m.* (loan of money). || Reconciliación, *f.* (reconciliation). || Adaptación, *f.* || Acuerdo, *m.*, convenio, *m.*, arreglo, *m.* (agreement). || ANAT. PHYS. Acomodación, *f.* || Comodidad, *f.* (commodity). || Favor, *m.* (favour). || Ayuda, *f.* (help). || *Book accomodation at the hotel*, reservar habitación en el hotel.
accommodation ladder [—'lædə*] n. MAR. Escala (*f.*) real.
accompaniment [ə'kʌmpanimənt] n. Acompañamiento, *m.*
accompanist [ə'kʌmpənist] n. MUS. Acompañante, *m.* & *f.*
accompany [ə'kʌmpəni] v. tr. Acompañar (*with*, *by*, de).
— V. intr. MUS. Acompañar (*on*, con).
accomplice [ə'kɔmplis] n. Cómplice, *m.* & *f.*
accomplish [ə'kɔmpliʃ] v. tr. Realizar, ejecutar, llevar a cabo (to carry out). || Alcanzar, llegar a, lograr (an end). || Terminar, acabar (to complete). || Recorrer (a distance). || Cumplir (a forecast).
accomplished [—t] adj. Realizado, da; ejecutado, da. || Consumado, da (fact, dancer, etc.). || Competente, experto, ta (skilled).
accomplishment [—mənt] n. Talento, *m.* (talent). || Realización, *f.*, ejecución, *f.* || Logro, *m.* (achievement). || Cumplimiento, *m.* (completion).
accord [ə'kɔ:d] n. Acuerdo, *m.* (agreement): *in accord with*, de acuerdo con. || Armonía, *f.* (harmony). || — *Of one's own accord*, de motu propio, espontáneamente. || *Out of accord with*, en desacuerdo con. || *With one accord*, de común acuerdo.
accord [ə'kɔ:d] v. tr. Conceder, otorgar.
— V. intr. Concordar.
accordance [—əns] n. Conformidad, *f.* || *In accordance with*, de acuerdo con, según, conforme a, con arreglo a, de conformidad con.
accordant [—ənt] adj. Conforme.
according [—iŋ] adv. *According as*, según, a medida que. || *According to*, según.

accordingly [—iŋli] adv. Por consiguiente (therefore). || En consecuencia, como corresponde (correspondingly).
accordion [əˈkɔːdjən] n. Mus. Acordeón, *m.* || *Accordion pleating*, plisado (*m.*) de acordeón.
accordionist [—ist] n. Mus. Acordeonista, *m.* & *f.*
accost [əˈkɔst] v. tr. Abordar, dirigirse a. || Abordar (prostitute).
account [əˈkaunt] n. Cuenta, *f.*: *bank account*, cuenta en el banco. || Cuenta, *f.* (bill). || Estado (*m.*) de cuenta (statement). || Informe, *m.*, relación, *f.* (report). || Importancia, *f.* (importance). || — *By all accounts*, al decir de todos. || *Current account*, cuenta corriente. || *Deposit account*, cuenta a plazo fijo. || *Joint account*, cuenta indistinta. || *Of no account*, de ninguna manera, bajo ningún concepto (not at all), de poca importancia. || *On account*, a cuenta. || *On account of*, a causa de, por motivo de. || *On account of s.o.*, por alguien. || *On every account*, en todos los aspectos. || *On his own account*, por su cuenta. || *On many accounts*, por muchos motivos. || *On no account*, bajo ningún concepto. || *On one's own account*, por su propia cuenta. || *To bring to account*, pedir cuentas a. || *To buy on account*, comprar a plazos *or* a crédito. || *To call to account*, pedir cuentas a. || *To give a good account of o.s.*, causar buena impresión. || *To keep the accounts*, llevar las cuentas. || *To leave out of account*, no tener en cuenta. || *To make little account of*, hacer caso omiso de, tener poco en cuenta. || *To pay into the account of*, abonar en cuenta de. || Fig. *To settle accounts with s.o.*, ajustar las cuentas a uno. || *To settle an account*, liquidar una cuenta. || *To square accounts*, ajustar cuentas. || *To take into account*, *to take account of*, tener en cuenta. || *To turn to account*, sacar provecho de.
account [əˈkaunt] v. tr. Considerar: *I account him handsome*, lo considero guapo. || *To account for*, dar cuenta de, justificar (to justify), explicar (to explain), responder de (to answer for), acabar con, liquidar (to kill).
accountability [əˈkauntəˈbiliti] n. Responsabilidad, *f.*
accountable [əˈkauntəbl] adj. Responsable (*for*, de; *to*, ante). || Explicable.
accountancy [əˈkauntənsi] n. Contabilidad, *f.*
accountant [əˈkauntənt] n. Contable, *m.* & *f.* || *Accountant's office*, contaduría, *f.*
accounting [əˈkauntiŋ] n. Contabilidad, *f.*
accoutre (U. S. **accouter**) [əˈkuːtə*] v. tr. Equipar.
accoutrement (U. S. **accouterment**) [əˈkuːtəmənt] n. Equipo, *m.*
accredit [əˈkredit] v. tr. Acreditar (diplomatically). || Reconocer (to recognize). || Atribuir (to attribute).
accretion [æˈkriːʃən] n. Unión, *f.* (a joining together). || Crecimiento, *m.* (organic growth). || Geol. Acreción, *f.* || Jur. Acrecencia, *f.*, acrecimiento, *m.*
accrue [əˈkruː] v. intr. Derivarse, proceder (to derive). || Acumularse (to accumulate). || *To accrue to*, corresponder a.
accrued interest [—ˈintrist] n. Interés (*m.*) acumulado *or* devengado.
accumulate [əˈkjuːmjuleit] v. tr. Acumular: *to accumulate riches*, acumular riquezas; *to accumulate interest on the capital*, acumular intereses al capital.
— V. intr. Acumularse.
accumulation [əˌkjuːmjuˈleiʃən] n. Acumulación, *f.*
accumulative [əˈkjuːmjulətiv] adj. Acumulativo, va.
accumulator [əˈkjuːmjuleitə*] n. Acumulador, ra. || Electr. Acumulador, *m.*
accuracy [ˈækjurəsi] n. Precisión, *f.*, exactitud, *f.*
accurate [ˈækjurit] adj. Preciso, sa; exacto, ta. || Fiel (memory, translation). || Certero, ra (shot). || Exacto, ta (answer). || De precisión (instrument).
accursed [əˈkəːsid] or **accurst** [əˈkəːst] adj. Condenado, da; maldito, ta. || Odioso, sa (odious).
accusal [əˈkjuːzəl] n. Acusación, *f.*
accusation [ˌækjuˈzeiʃən] n. Acusación, *f.* || *To bring an accusation against*, formular una acusación contra.
accusative [əˈkjuːzətiv] adj. Gramm. Acusativo, va.
— N. Gramm. Acusativo, *m.*
accusatorial [əˈkjuːzəˈtɔriəl] or **accusatory** [əˈkjuːzətəri] adj. Acusatorio, ria.
accuse [əˈkjuːz] v. tr. Acusar: *to accuse of robbery*, acusar de robo.
accused [—d] adj./n. Acusado, da.
accuser [—ə*] n. Acusador, ra.
accustom [əˈkʌstəm] v. tr. Acostumbrar. || *To accustom o.s. to*, *to become accustomed to*, acostumbrarse a.
accustomed [—d] adj. Acostumbrado, da.
ace [eis] n. As, *m.* (in dice, cards, etc.). || Un poco, *m.*: *an ace lower*, un poco más bajo. || "Ace", *m.* (golf, tennis). || — Fig. *As black as the ace of spades*, negro como el carbón. | *He is an ace*, es un as. | *To have an ace up one's sleeve*, tener un triunfo en la mano. | *Within an ace of*, a dos dedos de.
acephalous [əˈsefələs] adj. Acéfalo, la.
acerb [əˈsəːb] adj. Acerbo, ba.
acerbity [əˈsəːbiti] n. Acerbidad, *f.*, acritud, *f.*
acetate [ˈæsitit] n. Chem. Acetato, *m.*
acetic [əˈsiːtik] adj. Chem. Acético, ca.
acetify [əˈsetifai] v. tr. Acetificar.
acetone [ˈæsitəun] n. Chem. Acetona, *f.*
acetyl [ˈæsitil] n. Chem. Acetilo, *m.*
acetylene [əˈsetiliːn] n. Chem. Acetileno, *m.* || *Acetylene torch*, soplete oxiacetilénico.
Achaean [əˈkiən] adj./n. Aqueo, a.
ache [eik] n. Dolor, *m.* || *Aches and pains*, achaques, *m.*
ache [eik] v. intr. Doler (to hurt): *my head aches*, me duele la cabeza. || *To ache for* o *to be aching to*, anhelar, ansiar.
achene [əˈkiːn] n. Bot. Aquenio, *m.*
achievable [əˈtʃiːvəbl] adj. Realizable, factible, hacedero, ra.
achieve [əˈtʃiːv] v. tr. Llevar a cabo, ejecutar, realizar (to carry out). || Conseguir, lograr (to manage to get). || Alcanzar (an aim, a level).
— V. intr. U. S. Alcanzar su objetivo.
achievement [—mənt] n. Realización, *f.*, ejecución, *f.* (carrying out). || Consecución, *f.* (of an aim). || Éxito, *m.*, logro, *m.* (thing achieved). || Hazaña, *f.* (feat). || Herald. Escudo, *m.*
Achilles [əˈkiliːz] pr. n. Aquiles. || — *Achilles heel*, talón (*m.*) de Aquiles. || *Achilles tendon*, tendón (*m.*) de Aquiles.
aching [ˈeikiŋ] adj. Dolorido, da. || Fig. Compungido, da (heart). || Fam. *Aching all over*, molido.
— N. Dolor, *m.*
achromatic [ˌækrəuˈmætik] adj. Acromático, ca.
achromatism [əˈkrəumətizm] n. Acromatismo, *m.*
acid [ˈæsid] adj. Ácido, da (taste, smell, etc.). || Fig. Mordaz, agrio, gria; áspero, ra: *an acid remark*, una observación áspera.
— N. Chem. Ácido, *m.* || Fam. L.S.D., *m.*, alucinógeno, *m.*
acidic [əˈsidik] adj. Chem. Ácido, da. || Fig. Ácido, da; agrio, gria (taste, etc.).
acidification [əˌsidifiˈkeiʃən] n. Acidificación, *f.*
acidify [əˈsidifai] v. tr. Acidificar.
— V. intr. Acidificarse.
acidimeter [ˌæsiˈdimitə*] n. Chem. Acidímetro, *m.*
acidity [əˈsiditi] n. Acidez, *f.*
acidosis [ˌæsiˈdəusis] n. Med. Acidosis, *f.*
acid-proof [ˈæsid-pruːf] or **acid-resisting** [ˈæsid-riˈzistiŋ] adj. A prueba de ácidos.
acid test [ˈæsid-test] n. Chem. Prueba (*f.*) del ácido. || Fig. Prueba (*f.*) decisiva.
acidulate [əˈsidjuleit] v. tr. Acidular.
acidulous [əˈsidjuləs] adj. Acídulo, la; acidulado, da.
acinus [ˈæsinəs] n. Bot. Anat. Ácino, *m.*
— Observ. El plural de *acinus* es *acini*.
ack-ack [ˈækˈæk] n. Defensa (*f.*) antiaérea *or* contra aviones.
acknowledge [əkˈnɔlidʒ] v. tr. Admitir, reconocer (to admit sth. as true). || Reconocer (to recognize officially). || Acusar recibo de (a letter). || Saludar (to greet). || Confesar (to avow). || Agradecer, estar agradecido por (a favour). || *To acknowledge o.s. beaten*, darse por vencido.
acknowledgement or **acknowledgment** [—mənt] n. Admisión, *f.* (admission). || Reconocimiento, *m.* (recognition). || Acuse (*m.*) de recibo (of receipt). || Agradecimiento, *m.*, reconocimiento, *m.* (gratefulness). || Confesión, *f.* (of a misdeed). || Contestación, *f.* (of a greeting). || Recompensa, *f.* (reward). || *In acknowledgement of*, en reconocimiento de.
acme [ˈækmi] n. Cumbre, *f.*, cima, *f.*, apogeo, *m.*: *the acme of glory*, el apogeo de la gloria.
acne [ˈækni] n. Med. Acné, *m.*
acolyte [ˈækəulait] n. Rel. Acólito, *m.*
acolyteship [—ʃip] n. Acolitado, *m.*, acolitazgo, *m.*
aconite [ˈækənait] n. Bot. Acónito, *m.*
aconitine [əˈkɔnitiːn] n. Chem. Aconitina, *f.*
acorn [ˈeikɔːn] n. Bot. Bellota, *f.*
acotyledon [æˌkɔtiˈliːdən] n. Acotiledónea, *f.* (plant without cotyledons).
acotyledonous [—əs] adj. Acotiledóneo, a; acotiledón, ona.
acoustic [əˈkuːstik] adj. Acústico, ca.
acoustics [—s] pl. n. Acústica, *f. sing.*
acquaint [əˈkweint] v. tr. Informar, poner al corriente (*with*, de). || — *To acquaint o.s. with*, informarse sobre (to get information), familiarizarse con (to familiarize o.s.). || *To be acquainted with*, conocer (s.o.), estar al corriente *or* al tanto de, conocer (sth.). || *To be acquainted with the fact that*, saber que. || *To become acquainted with*, conocer a (s.o.), ponerse al corriente de (a fact), aprender (to learn). || *They have long been acquainted*, se conocen desde hace mucho tiempo.
acquaintance [—əns] n. Conocido, da (person). || Conocimiento, *m.* (knowledge): *further acquaintance*, mayor conocimiento. || Relaciones, *f. pl.*, amistades, *f. pl.*: *a wide acquaintance*, muchas relaciones. || — *To improve upon acquaintance*, ganar con el trato. || *To make acquaintance with*, conocer a. || *To make s.o.'s acquaintance*, conocer a uno.
acquaintanceship [əˈkweintənsʃip] n. Conocimiento, *m.* || Relaciones, *f. pl.*
acquiesce [ˌækwiˈes] v. intr. Consentir (*in*, en), asentir (*in*, a) [to assent]. || Conformarse (*in*, con), aceptar (to conform to).
acquiescence [—ns] n. Aquiescencia, *f.*, asentimiento, *m.*, conformidad, *f.* (agreement). || Consentimiento, *m.* (consent).
acquiescent [—nt] adj. Condescendiente, conforme.
acquire [əˈkwaiə*] v. tr. Conseguir (to manage to get). || Adquirir (to get). || Contraer, tomar (a habit).

|| Aprender (a language). || *To acquire a taste for*, tomar gusto a.
acquirement [—mənt] n. Adquisición, *f.* || — Pl. Conocimientos, *m.* (knowledge).
acquiring [—riŋ] adj. Adquisidor, ra; adquiridor, ra.
acquisition [ˌækwiˈziʃən] n. Adquisición, *f.*
acquisitive [əˈkwizitiv] adj. Codicioso, sa.
acquit [əˈkwit] v. tr. JUR. Absolver (an accused). || Liquidar, pagar, satisfacer (a debt). || Cumplir (a promise). || Liberar (of an obligation). || *To acquit o.s.*, defenderse: *he acquitted himself well in the exam*, se defendió bien en el examen.
acquittal [—əl] n. JUR. Absolución, *f.* || Cumplimiento, *m.* (of a duty). || Pago, *m.*, satisfacción, *f.* (of a debt).
acquittance [—əns] n. Liquidación, *f.*, pago, *m.* (of a debt). || Comprobante, *m.*, recibo, *m.* (receipt).
acre [ˈeikə*] n. Acre, *m.* [medida de aproximadamente 4000 metros cuadrados].
acreage [ˈeikəridʒ] n. Superficie (*f.*) en acres.
acrid [ˈækrid] adj. Acre (smell, taste). || FIG. Cáustico, ca.
acridity [æˈkriditi] n. Acritud, *f.* || FIG. Causticidad, *f.*
acrimonious [ˌækriˈməunjəs] adj. Caústico, ca; mordaz.
acrimony [ˈækriməni] n. Acrimonia, *f.*, acritud, *f.*
acrobat [ˈækrəbæt] n. Acróbata, *m.* & *f.*
acrobatic [ˌækrəˈbætik] adj. Acrobático, ca.
acrobatics [—s] n. Acrobacia, *f.*
acrocephalic [ˌækrəseˈfælik] or **acrocephalous** [ˌækrəˈsefələs] adj. Acrocéfalo, la.
acromegalia [ˌækrəuməˈgeiljə] or **acromegaly** [ˌækrəuˈmegəli] n. MED. Acromegalia, *f.*
acronym [ˈækrənim] n. Siglas, *f. pl.*
Acropolis [əˈkrɔpəlis] n. Acrópolis, *f. inv.*
across [əˈkrɔs] adv. A través. || — *To be two feet across*, tener dos pies de ancho. || *To go across*, atravesar, cruzar. || *To swim across*, cruzar a nado.
— Prep. Del otro lado de (on the other side): *the house across the road*, la casa del otro lado de la calle. || A través de (from one side to the other): *across the fields*, a través de los campos.

— OBSERV. El adverbio *across* no se suele traducir literalmente en español; en efecto la mayoría de las veces se expresa por un verbo que contiene la idea implicada por el adverbio.
— Hay casos en los cuales *across*, preposición, no se traduce literalmente, incluyéndose en el verbo: *to walk across the street*, cruzar la calle.

acrostic [əˈkrɔstik] adj. POET. Acróstico, ca.
— N. Acróstico, *m.*
acroter [ˈækrətə*] n. ARCH. Acrotera, *f.*, acrótera, *f.*
acrylic [əˈkrilik] adj. Acrílico, ca.
act [ækt] n. Acto, *m.* (deed, part of a play, etc.). || Acción, *f.*: *act of justice, of war*, acción de justicia, de guerra. || Número, *m.* (artist's routine). || JUR. Acta, *f.* | Ley, *f.*, decreto, *m.* (of Parliament). || Acto, *m.* (of faith). || — Pl. Hechos, *m.* (of the Apostles). || — *Act of bankruptcy*, declaración (*f.*) de quiebra. || *Act of God*, caso (*m.*) de fuerza mayor. || JUR. *Act on petition*, recurso (*m.*) de urgencia. || *Caught in the act*, cogido in fraganti *or* con las manos en la masa *or* en el acto. || *In the act of*, en el momento de. || *They were in the act of stealing*, estaban robando. || *To put on an act*, simular.
act [ækt] v. tr. Desempeñar el papel de (to play the part of). || Desempeñar (a part). || Representar (a play). || Hacer (to act like): *don't act the fool*, no hagas el tonto.
— V. intr. Actuar, obrar (to do a thing). || Comportarse, actuar (to behave). || Obrar, tomar medidas (to take steps). || Actuar (to fulfil a function): *to act as referee*, actuar de árbitro. || Actuar (to intervene, to have an effect): *the police acted quickly* la policía actuó pronto; *acid acts on metal*, el ácido actúa sobre el metal. || Actuar (to perform). || Fingirse (to pretend): *to act dead*, fingirse muerto. || TECH. Funcionar. || — *To act as*, hacer de, actuar de. || *To act for*, obrar en representación de. || *To act on*, guiarse por. || *To act on o upon*, actuar sobre.
acting [—iŋ] adj. Interino, na (provisional). || En funciones, en ejercicio (in office).
— N. Interpretación, *f.*, actuación, *f.* (performance). || Profesión (*f.*) de actor. || Acción, *f.* (act).
actinia [ækˈtinjə] n. ZOOL. Actinia, *f.* (sea anemone).

— OBSERV. El plural de la palabra inglesa es *actinias* o *actiniae*.

actinic [ækˈtinik] adj. Actínico, ca.
actinium [ækˈtiniəm] n. CHEM. Actinio, *m.*
action [ˈækʃən] n. Acción, *f.* (deed, act). || Movimiento, *m.* (movement): *to put in action*, poner en movimiento. || Argumento, *m.*, acción, *f.*, intriga, *f.* (plot of a story or play). || MIL. Acción, *f.* (combat). | Acto (*m.*) de servicio: *he died in action*, murió en acto de servicio. || Medida, *f.*: *disciplinary action*, medida de disciplina. || TECH. Mecanismo, *m.* | Funcionamiento, *m.* || JUR. Acción, *f.*, demanda, *f.*: *to bring an action*, presentar una demanda. | Proceso, *m.* || — *Action!*, ¡acción! (cinematography). || *Actions speak louder than words*, obras son amores, que no buenas razones. || *A man of action*, un hombre de acción. || *Field of action*, esfera (*f.*) de acción. || *Reflex action*, acto reflejo. || *To put into action*, poner en práctica (a plan). || *To put out of action*, estropear, volver inutilizable (sth.). || *To suit the action to the word*, unir la acción a la palabra. || *To take action*, tomar medidas (to intervene), intentar una acción judicial (in justice).
actionable [ˈækʃnəbl] adj. Procesable.
activate [ˈæktiveit] v. tr. Activar. || *Activated carbon, sludge*, carbón, lodo activado.
activation [ˌæktiˈveiʃən] n. Activación, *f.*
activator [ˈæktiveitə*] n. CHEM. Activador, *m.*
active [ˈæktiv] adj. Activo, va. || Vigente (a law). || Vivo, va (interest). || — *Active volcano*, volcán en actividad. || *On active service*, en servicio activo.
active list [—list] n. MIL. Escala (*f.*) activa.
activism [ˈæktivizəm] n. Activismo, *m.*
activist [ˈæktivist] adj./n. Activista.
activity [ækˈtiviti] n. Actividad, *f.*: *field of activity*, esfera de actividad; *activity of a volcano, an acid*, actividad de un volcán, de un ácido.
actor [ˈæktə*] n. Actor, *m.* || JUR. Demandante, *m.* & *f.* || *Leading actor*, primer actor.
actress [ˈæktris] n. Actriz, *f.* || *Leading actress*, primera actriz.
actual [ˈæktjuəl] adj. Verdadero, ra; real (true). || Concreto, ta (case). || Mismo, ma: *I'd like to have the actual figures*, me gustaría tener las cifras mismas. || Actual (present). || *In actual fact*, en realidad.
actuality [ˌæktjuˈæliti] n. Realidad, *f.*

— OBSERV. *Actuality* no significa nunca "actualidad".

actualization [ˌæktjuəlaiˈzeiʃən] n. Realización, *f.* || PHIL. Actualización, *f.*
actualize [ˈæktjuəlaiz] v. tr. Realizar. || Actualizar, describir con realismo. || PHIL. Actualizar.
actually [ˈæktjuəli] adv. En realidad, realmente, verdaderamente (really). || En realidad (as a matter of fact). || Incluso (even). || Actualmente (at present).
— OBSERV. *Actually* no se emplea mucho con el sentido de "actualmente".
actuarial [ˌæktjuˈɛərjəl] or **actuarian** [ˌæktjuˈɛərjən] adj. Actuarial.
actuary [ˈæktjuəri] n. Actuario, *m.*
actuate [ˈæktjueit] v. tr. Accionar, hacer funcionar, poner en movimiento (an engine). || Mover, impulsar (to motivate): *actuated by anger, he killed his friend*, movido por la rabia, mató a su amigo.
acuity [əˈkjuːiti] n. Agudeza, *f.*, acuidad, *f.*
acumen [aˈkjuːmen] n. Perspicacia, f.
acupuncture [ˈækjuˌpʌŋktʃə*] n. Acupuntura, *f.*
acute [əˈkjuːt] adj. Agudo, da (sharp). || MATH. MED. GRAMM. Agudo, da. || FIG. Agudo, da; perspicaz (shrewd). || Grave (crucial, critical).
acute-angled [—ˈæŋgld] adj. Acutángulo, la.
acuteness [əˈkjuːtnis] n. Agudeza, *f.*, perspicacia, *f.* || MED. Carácter (*m.*) agudo. || Agudeza, *f.* (of ear).
acyclic [əˈsaiklik] adj. Acíclico, ca.
ad [æd] n. U. S. FAM. Anuncio, *m.*
adage [ˈædidʒ] n. Adagio, *m.*, refrán, *m.*
adagio [əˈdɑːdʒiəu] adj./adv. MUS. Adagio.
— N. Adagio, *m.*
Adam [ˈædəm] pr. n. Adán, *m.*: *Adam and Eve*, Adán y Eva. || — *I do not know him from Adam*, no le conozco ni por asomo. || FAM. *Adam's ale*, agua, *f.* || *Adam's apple*, nuez, *f.*
adamant [ˈædəmənt] n. Diamante, *m.* (diamond).
— Adj. Inexorable, inflexible (unyielding).
adamantine [ˌædəˈmæntain] adj. Adamantino, na.
adapt [əˈdæpt] v. tr. Adaptar: *to adapt a novel for the theatre*, adaptar una novela al teatro.
adaptability [əˌdæptəˈbiliti] n. Adaptabilidad, *f.*, facultad (*f.*) de adaptación.
adaptable [əˈdæptəbl] adj. Adaptable.
adaptation [ˌædæpˈteiʃən] n. Adaptación, *f.*: *the adaptation of a novel for the theatre*, la adaptación de una novela al teatro.
adapter or **adaptor** [əˈdæptə*] n. ELECTR. Enchufe (*m.*) múltiple (plug). || Adaptador, *m.* (for connecting). || Adaptador, ra (person).
add [æd] v. tr. Añadir. || — *To add in*, incluir. || *To add up*, sumar.
— V. intr. Sumar. || — *To add to*, aumentar. || *To add up*, sumar (to do addition), tener sentido: *his explanation does not add up*, su explicación no tiene sentido. || *To add up to*, alcanzar (to reach), significar (to mean).
addend [ˈædend] n. MATH. Sumando, *m.*
addendum [əˈdendəm] n. Apéndice, *m.*, addenda, *m.*

— OBSERV. El plural de *addendum* es *addenda*.

adder [ˈædə*] n. ZOOL. Víbora *f.* (viper). || U. S. Culebra, *f.* (non-poisonous snake).
addict [ˈædikt] n. Adicto, ta (s.o. addicted to sth. harmful). || Entusiasta, fanático, ca (fanatic). || *Drug addict*, toxicómano, na; drogadicto, ta.
addicted [əˈdiktid] adj. Adicto, ta (*to*, a) [drugs, drink, etc.]. || Fanático, ca (fanatic).
addiction [əˈdikʃən] n. Vicio, *m.* (habitual inclination). || Afición, *f.* (liking).
adding machine [ˈædiŋməˌʃiːn] n. Máquina (*f.*) calculadora.
addition [əˈdiʃən] n. Adición, *f.* (action). || Añadido, *m.*, adición, *f.*, añadidura, *f.* (sth. added). || MATH. Suma, *f.* || *In addition to*, además de.
additional [—l] adj. Adicional. || Suplementario, ria.
additionally [əˈdiʃnəli] adv. Además (furthermore). || Más aún (still more).

addle [ˈædl] adj. Podrido, da (rotten). || Huero, ra (sterile).
addle [ˈædl] v. tr. Pudrir.
— V. intr. Pudrirse.
address [əˈdres] n. Dirección, *f.*, señas, *f. pl.* (place of abode): *home address*, dirección privada. || Súplica, *f.*, petición, *f.* (request). || Habilidad, *f.*, destreza, *f.* (skill). || Discurso, *m.*, alocución, *f.* (speech). || Tratamiento, *m.*, título, *m.* (title). || (Ant.). Modales, *m. pl.* (manners). || *To pay one's addresses to*, cortejar.
address [əˈdres] v. tr. Hablar a (to speak to). || Dirigirse a: *to address the king*, dirigirse al rey. || Dirigir (letter, remarks). || Poner la dirección en (on a letter, parcel, etc.). || Tomar la palabra: *to address the House*, tomar la palabra en el Parlamento. || — *To address o.s. to a job*, ponerse a trabajar. || *To address s.o. as*, dar a uno el tratamiento de.
addressee [ˌædreˈsi:] n. Destinatario, ria.
adduce [əˈdju:s] v. tr. Citar (to quote). || Aducir, alegar (to evoke). || Dar (a proof).
adducent [—nt] adj. ANAT. Aductor.
adduct [əˈdʌkt] v. tr. MED. Efectuar la aducción.
adduction [əˈdʌkʃən] n. MED. Aducción, *f.* || JUR. Alegato, *m.*
adductive [əˈdʌktiv] adj. ANAT. Aductor.
adductor [əˈdʌktə*] n. ANAT. Aductor, *m.*
adenoid [ˈædinɔid] adj. Adenoideo, a.
adept [ˈædept] adj./n. Experto, ta (*at*, en). || Adepto, ta (of a sect).
adequacy [ˈædikwəsi] n. Adecuación, *f.* (suitability). || Suficiencia, *f.* || Exactitud, *f.* (of an idea).
adequate [ˈædikwit] adj. Adecuado, da; suficiente.
adhere [ədˈhiə*] v. intr. Adherirse.
adherence [ədˈhiərəns] n. Adherencia, *f.* || Adhesión, *f.* (to a cause, party).
adherent [ədˈhiərənt] adj. Adhesivo, va (sticky).
— N. Adepto, ta; adherente, *m.* & *f.*, partidario, ria.
adhesion [ədˈhi:ʒən] n. Adhesión, *f.*
adhesive [ədˈhi:siv] adj. Adhesivo, va.
— N. Adhesivo, *m.*
adhesive tape [—teip] n. MED. Esparadrapo, *m.* || Cinta (*f.*) adhesiva.
adiabatic [ˌædiəˈbætik] adj. PHYS. Adiabático, ca.
adieu [əˈdju:] interj. ¡Adiós!
— N. Despedida, *f.*, adiós, *m.* || — *To bid adieu*, decir adiós. || *To take adieu*, despedirse.

— OBSERV. El plural de *adieu* es *adieus* o *adieux*.

Adige [ˈɑ:didʒe] pr. n. GEOGR. Adigio, *m.*
ad infinitum [ˈædinfiˈnaitəm] adv. Sin fin (without end). || Indefinidamente (indefinitely).
adipose [ˈædipəus] adj. Adiposo, sa.
adiposity [ˌædiˈpɔsiti] n. Adiposidad, *f.*
adjacency [əˈdʒeisənsi] n. Proximidad, *f.*
adjacent [əˈdʒeisənt] adj. Adyacente.
adjectival [ˌædʒekˈtaivəl] adj. Adjetival, adjetivo, va.
adjective [ˈædʒiktiv] n. GRAMM. Adjetivo, *m.*
adjoin [əˈdʒɔin] v. tr. Estar contiguo a, lindar con (to be next to). || Unir (to join). || Añadir (to add).
— V. intr. Estar contiguo.
adjoining [—iŋ] adj. Contiguo, gua; limítrofe.
adjourn [əˈdʒə:n] v. tr. Suspender (to suspend). || Aplazar (to postpone). || Suspender, levantar (a meeting).
— V. intr. Suspenderse (a meeting). || Suspender la sesión (the delegates). || *To adjourn to*, pasar a.
adjournment [—mənt] n. Suspensión, *f.* (of a meeting). || Aplazamiento, *m.* (postponement).
adjudge [əˈdʒʌdʒ] v. tr. JUR. Juzgar, decidir (to decide). | Declarar (to find). | Adjudicar (to award). || Otorgar, atribuir, conceder (a prize).
adjudicate [əˈdʒu:dikeit] v. tr. Juzgar (to judge). || Declarar (to declare).
— V. intr. Actuar como juez. || Sentenciar (to sentence).
adjudication [əˌdʒu:diˈkeiʃən] n. JUR. Sentencia, *f.*, fallo, *m.* (judge's decision).
adjunct [ˈædʒʌŋkt] adj. Adjunto, ta.
— N. Adjunto, *m.*
adjunction [æˈdʒʌŋkʃən] n. Adición, *f.*, añadidura, *f.*
adjuration [ˌædʒuəˈreiʃən] n. (Ant.). Adjuración, *f.*
adjure [əˈdʒuə*] v. tr. (Ant.). Adjurar.
adjust [əˈdʒʌst] v. tr. Ajustar (a mechanism, etc.). || Adaptar (to adapt). || Arreglar (to arrange). || Resolver (a difference).
adjustable [—əbl] adj. Ajustable.
adjuster (U. S. **adjustor**) [—ə*] n. Ajustador, *m.*
adjustment [—mənt] n. Ajuste, *m.* (action or means of adjusting). || Adaptación, *f.* || Arreglo, *m.*, solución, *f.*, liquidación, *f.* (settlement). || Modificación, *f.*, cambio, *m.* (change). || Arreglo, *m.* (arrangement). || MIL. Regulación, *f.* (of fire).
adjutancy [ˈædʒutənsi] n. MIL. Ayudantía, *f.*
adjutant [ˈædʒutənt] n. MIL. Ayudante, *m.* || ZOOL. Marabú, *m.* || Ayudante, *m.* (a helper).
adjuvant [ˈædʒuvənt] n. Auxiliar, *m.* & *f.*
ad lib [ˈædˈlib] n. Improvisación, *f.*, morcilla, *f.* (fam.).
ad-lib [ˈædˈlib] v. tr./intr. Improvisar.
ad-lib [ˈædˈlib] adv. A discreción, a voluntad.
administer [ədˈministə*] (U. S. **administrate**) v. tr. Administrar: *to administer justice*, administrar justicia; *to administer medical aid*, administrar ayuda médica. || Aplicar: *to administer a punishment*, aplicar un castigo. || Formular, hacer (questions, etc.). || *To administer an oath to*, tomar juramento a.
— V. intr. Administrar. || *To administer to*, prestar ayuda a (to a person), atender a (to satisfy).
administration [ədˌminisˈtreiʃən] n. Administración, *f.*: *public administration*, administración pública. || U. S. Gobierno, *m.*: *the wartime Administration*, el gobierno de la época de la guerra. || Toma, *f.* (of an oath).
administrative [ədˈministrətiv] adj. Administrativo, va.
administrator [ədˈministreitə*] n. Administrador, ra.
admirable [ˈædmərəbl] adj. Admirable.
admiral [ˈædmərəl] n. MIL. Almirante, *m.*
admiral of the fleet [—ov-ðə-fli:t] n. MIL. Capitán (*m.*) de la Armada.
admiralty [ˈædmərəlti] n. MIL. Almirantazgo, *m.* (the office of admiral). || Ministerio (*m.*) de Marina.
admiration [ˌædməˈreiʃən] n. Admiración, *f.*
admire [ədˈmaiə*] v. tr. Admirar.
admirer [—rə*] n. Admirador, ra. || Enamorado, da (suitor).
admiring [—riŋ] adj. Admirativo, va.
admissibility [ədˌmisəˈbiliti] n. Admisibilidad, *f.*
admissible [ədˈmisəbl] adj. Admisible, aceptable.
admission [ədˈmiʃən] n. Admisión, *f.* (the action of admitting). || Entrada, *f.*: *admission five francs*, entrada cinco francos; *free admission*, entrada gratuita. || Confesión, *f.*: *by his own admission*, por confesión suya. || Reconocimiento, *m.* (acknowledgment). || *The management reserves the right to refuse admission*, reservado el derecho de admisión.
admit [ədˈmit] v. tr. Admitir: *to admit s.o. in a society*, admitir a alguien en una sociedad; *this place admits five hundred people*, este local admite quinientas personas. || Dejar entrar (to allow to enter). || Aceptar, admitir (to accept). || Reconocer, admitir (to recognize): *he admits (to) stealing the car*, reconoce haber robado el coche. || Confesar (to confess). || — *Ticket which admits two*, entrada (*f.*) para dos personas. || *To be admitted to*, ingresar en (an academy).
— V. intr. *To admit of*, admitir, dar lugar, permitir: *his actions admit of no other interpretation*, sus actos no admiten otra interpretación.
admittance [—əns] n. Entrada, *f.* || ELECTR. Admitancia, *f.* || *No admittance*, prohibida la entrada, se prohibe la entrada.
admittedly [—idli] adv. Cierto es que.
admix [ədˈmiks] v. tr. Mezclar.
admixture [—tʃə*] n. Ingrediente, *m.* (ingredient). || Mezcla, *f.* (mixture). || Dosis, *f.* (dose).
admonish [ədˈmɔniʃ] v. tr. Amonestar, reprender (to reprove). || Advertir (to warn). || Exhortar (to exhort). || Aconsejar (to advise).
admonishment [—mənt] or **admonition** [ˌædməuˈniʃən] n. Amonestación, *f.*, reprensión, *f.* (reproof). || Advertencia, *f.*, consejo, *m.* (advice).
admonitory [ədˈmɔnitəri] adj. Admonitorio, ria.
adnexa [ædˈnɛksə] pl. n. Anexos, *m.*
ado [əˈdu:] n. *Much ado about nothing*, mucho ruido y pocas nueces. || *With much ado*, con gran dificultad. || *Without further* o *more ado*, sin más ni más.
adobe [əˈdəubi] n. Adobe, *m.* (a sun-dried brick). || Casa (*f.*) de adobe (building).
adolescence [ˌædəˈlesns] n. Adolescencia, *f.*
adolescent [ˌædəˈlesnt] adj./n. Adolescente.
Adolph [ˈædɔlf] pr. n. Adolfo, *m.*
Adonis [əˈdəunis] pr. n. Adonis, *m.*
adopt [əˈdɔpt] v. tr. Adoptar: *to adopt Western dress*, adoptar la vestimenta occidental; *to adopt a child*, adoptar a un niño. || Aceptar (to accept). || Aprobar (the agenda, etc.). || *Adopted child*, hijo adoptivo.
adoption [əˈdɔpʃən] n. Adopción, *f.* (of a child, custom). || Aprobación, *f.* (approval). || *Country of adoption*, patria adoptiva.
adoptive [əˈdɔptiv] adj. Adoptivo, va.
adorable [əˈdɔ:rəbl] adj. Adorable.
adoration [ˌædɔ:ˈreiʃən] n. Adoración, *f.*
adore [əˈdɔ:*] v. tr. Adorar (to worship).
adorer [—rə*] n. Adorador, ra.
adorn [əˈdɔ:n] v. tr. Adornar.
adornment [—mənt] n. Adorno, *m.*
adrenal [əˈdri:nl] adj. Suprarrenal.
— M. Glándula (*f.*) suprarrenal.
adrenalin [əˈdrenəlin] n. Adrenalina, *f.*
Adrian [ˈeidrjən] pr. n. Adrián, *m.*
Adriatic Sea [ˌeidriˈætik si:] pr. n. Mar (*m.*) Adriático.
adrift [əˈdrift] adj./adv. A la deriva. || — FIG. *To be all adrift*, ir a la deriva, no saber por dónde se anda. || *To break adrift*, romper las amarras. || FIG. *To come adrift*, desprenderse. | *To turn s.o. adrift*, abandonar a uno a su suerte.
adroit [əˈdrɔit] adj. Diestro, tra; hábil.
adroitness [—nis] n. Destreza, *f.*, habilidad, *f.*, maña, *f.*
adsorb [ædˈsɔ:b] v. tr. Adsorber.
adsorbent [—ənt] adj. Adsorbente.
— N. Adsorbente, *m.*
adsorption [—ʃən] n. Adsorción, *f.*
adulate [ˈædjuleit] v. tr. Adular.
adulation [ˌædjuˈleiʃən] n. Adulación, *f.*
adulator [ˈædjuleitə*] n. Adulador, ra.
adulatory [ˈædjuleitəri] adj. Adulador, ra.

adult [ˈædʌlt] adj./n. Adulto, ta (mature). || JUR. Mayor de edad.
adulterate [əˈdʌltərit] adj. Adulterado, da (adulterated). || Adulterino, na (adulterine).
adulterate [əˈdʌltəreit] v. tr. Adulterar.
adulteration [ə,dʌltəˈreiʃən] n. Adulteración, *f.*
adulterator [əˈdʌltəreitə*] n. Adulterador, ra.
adulterer [əˈdʌltərə*] n. Adúltero, *m.*
adulteress [əˈdʌltəris] n. Adúltera, *f.*
adulterine [əˈdʌltərain] adj. Adulterino, na; espurio, ria.
adulterous [əˈdʌltərəs] adj. Adúltero, ra.
adultery [əˈdʌltəri] n. Adulterio, *m.*
adumbrate [ˈædʌmbreit] v. tr. Bosquejar (to give a shadowy account of). || Presagiar (to foreshadow).
advance [ədˈvɑ:ns] n. Adelanto, *m.*, progreso, *m.*: *the advance of civilization*, el progreso de la civilización; *a technical advance*, un adelanto técnico. || Anticipo, *m.*, adelanto, *m.* (payment before it is due). || Subida, *f.*, aumento, *m.* (rise in price or value). || TECH. Avance, *m.* (car): *advance of the ignition* o *spark advance*, avance al encendido. || FIG. Paso: *to make the first advances to*, dar los primeros pasos hacia. || MIL. Avance, *m.* || — Pl. Insinuaciones, *f.* [amorosas]. || — *Advance booking office*, despacho (*m.*) de venta por adelantado. || *In advance*, con anticipación, con antelación; adelantado, da; por anticipado, de antemano. || *The advance guard*, la vanguardia. || *To arrive in advance of*, llegar antes que. || *To be in advance of*, adelantarse a. || *To let s.o. know two days in advance*, avisar a uno con dos días de anticipación. || *To pay in advance*, pagar por adelantado *or* con anticipación. || *Thanks in advance*, gracias anticipadas.
advance [ədˈvɑ:ns] v. tr. Avanzar, adelantar (to move forward). || Adelantar (watch, hour, date): *they advanced the wedding date*, adelantaron la fecha de la boda. || Proponer: *to advance a theory*, proponer una teoría. || Exponer, emitir (an opinion). || Presentar, formular (a claim). || Aumentar: *he advanced his price by fifty per cent*, aumentó el precio en un cincuenta por ciento. || Adelantar, anticipar: *his employer advanced him a month's salary*, el empresario le adelantó el salario de un mes. || Hacer progresar (sciences, etc.). || Ayudar: *his election will advance our cause*, su elección ayudará a nuestra causa. || MIL. Ascender: *they advanced him to general*, le ascendieron a general.
— V. intr. Avanzar, adelantarse (to go forward). || Progresar (to progress). || Avanzar (troops). || Ascender (to go up in rank, status). || Subir, aumentar (prices). || *To advance on*, acercarse a *or* hacia.
advanced [—t] adj. Avanzado, da: *advanced ideas*, ideas avanzadas; *advanced stage of pregnancy*, estado avanzado de gestación. || Adelantado, da; anticipado, da (money). || Adelantado, da: *he is very advanced for his age*, está muy adelantado para su edad. || Adelantado, da (country). || Superior (studies). || *Advanced in years*, entrado en años, de edad avanzada.
advancement [—mənt] n. Adelanto, *m.*, progreso, *m.*: *the advancement of science*, el avance de la ciencia. || Ascenso, *m.* (promotion).
advantage [ədˈvɑ:ntidʒ] n. Ventaja, *f.*: *he has the advantage of me*, me saca ventaja. || Provecho, *m.*, beneficio, *m.*: *for whose advantage?*, ¿en provecho de quién? || Ventaja, *f.* (in tennis). || — *To be in s.o.'s advantage*, ser ventajoso para uno. || *To have the advantage*, jugar con ventaja. || *To have the advantage of numbers*, aventajar en número. || *To take advantage of s.o.*, *of sth.*, aprovecharse *or* sacar partido de alguien de algo. || *To turn sth. to advantage*, sacar provecho de algo.
advantage [ədˈvɑ:ntidʒ] v. tr. Ser ventajoso para, favorecer.
advantageous [,ædvənˈteidʒəs] adj. Ventajoso, sa.
advent [ˈædvənt] n. Advenimiento, *m.*, venida, *f.*
Advent [ˈædvənt] n. REL. Adviento, *m.*
Adventist [ˈædvəntist] n. REL. Adventista, *m.*
adventitious [,ædvenˈtiʃəs] adj. Adventicio, cia.
adventure [ədˈventʃə*] n. Aventura, *f.*
adventure [ədˈventʃə*] v. tr. Aventurar.
— V. intr. Aventurarse.
adventurer [—rə*] n. Aventurero, *m.*
adventuresome [—səm] adj. See ADVENTUROUS.
adventuress [—ris] n. Aventurera, *f.*
adventurous [—rəs] adj. Aventurero, ra (people). || Aventurado, da; arriesgado, da (thing).
adverb [ˈædvə:b] n. GRAMM. Adverbio, *m.*
adverbial [ədˈvə:bjəl] adj. GRAMM. Adverbial: *adverbial phrase*, locución adverbial.
adversary [ˈædvəsəri] n. Adversario, ria.
adversative [ədˈvə:sətiv] adj. GRAMM. Adversativo, va.
adverse [ˈædvə:s] adj. Adverso, sa; opuesto, ta (opposing). || Contrario, ria (wind). || Desfavorable, adverso, sa (unfavourable). || Negativo, va (balance).
adversity [ədˈvə:siti] n. Adversidad, *f.*, infortunio, *m.*
advert [ˈædvə:t] n. FAM. Anuncio, *m.*
advert [ædˈvə:t] v. intr. Referirse, hacer alusión (*to*, a).
advertise (U. S. **advertize**) [ˈædvətaiz] v. tr. Anunciar.
— V. intr. Hacer publicidad *or* propaganda. || Poner un anuncio. || *To advertise for*, buscar por medio de anuncios.
advertisement (U. S. **advertizement**) [ədˈvə:tismənt] n. Anuncio, *m.* || *Classified advertisements*, anuncios (*m.*) por palabras.
advertiser (U. S. **advertizer**) [ˈædvətaizə*] n. Anunciante, *m.* & *f.*
advertising (U. S. **advertizing**) [ˈædvətaiziŋ] n. Publicidad, *f.*, propaganda, *f.*: *television advertising*, la publicidad en televisión. || *Advertising campaign*, campaña publicitaria. || *Advertising company*, empresa de publicidad *or* anunciadora.
advice [ədˈvais] n. Consejo, *m.*: *to seek advice*, pedir consejo. || Asesoramiento, *m.*: *with the technical advice of*, con el asesoramiento técnico de. || COMM. Informe, *m.* (report). || — Pl. Noticias, *f.* || — *A piece of advice*, un consejo. || *As per advice from*, siguiendo el consejo de. || *To take advice*, consultar: *to take medical advice*, consultar al médico; seguir un consejo: *I took his advice*, seguí su consejo. || *To take legal advice*, consultar a un abogado.
advisability [əd,vaizəˈbiliti] n. Conveniencia, *f.*, oportunidad, *f.*
advisable [ədˈvaizəbl] adj. Conveniente, aconsejable. || Juicioso, sa; prudente. || — *If we think it advisable*, si nos parece bien. || *It would be advisable to say so*, sería aconsejable *or* mejor decirlo.
advise [ədˈvaiz] v. tr. Aconsejar (to give advice): *I advise you to travel*, le aconsejo viajar *or* que viaje. || Asesorar (as paid adviser). || Informar (to inform). || COMM. Notificar (to notify).
— V. intr. Aconsejar. || — *To advise on*, ser asesor en. || *To advise with*, consultar.
advised [—d] adj. Aconsejado, da. || Reflexionado, da; pensado, da (considered). || *To keep advised*, tener al tanto *or* al corriente.
advisedly [—idli] adv. Deliberadamente (deliberately). || Con conocimiento de causa (with due consideration).
adviser (U. S. **advisor**) [ədˈvaizə*] n. Consejero, ra; asesor, ra (someone who advises). || U. S. Tutor, *m.* || — *Adviser's office*, asesoría, *f.* || *Legal adviser*, asesor jurídico.
advisory [ədˈvaizəri] adj. Consultivo, va; asesor, ra: *advisory committee*, comisión consultiva. || *In an advisory capacity*, como asesor.
advocacy [ˈædvəkəsi] n. JUR. Defensa, *f.* | Abogacía, *f.* (the work of advocates). || Recomendación, *f.* (recommendation of a line of action). || Apoyo, *m.* (support).
advocate [ˈædvəkit] n. JUR. Abogado, *m.* || Defensor, ra; abogado, da (of a cause). || *The devil's advocate*, el abogado del diablo.
advocate [ˈædvəkeit] v. tr. Defender, abogar por. || Recomendar, preconizar.
advowson [ədˈvauzən] n. JUR. Derecho (*m.*) de patronato. || REL. Colación (*f.*) de un beneficio.
adze or **adz** [ædz] n. Azuela, *f.*
aedile [ˈi:dail] n. Edil, *m.*
Aegean [i:ˈdʒi:ən] adj. Egeo, a: *Aegean Sea*, mar Egeo.
aegis [ˈi:dʒis] n. Égida, *f.* || Patrocinio, *m.*, tutela, *f.* (sponsorship). || *Under the aegis of*, bajo los auspicios de.
Aegisthus [ˈi:dʒisθəs] pr. n. MYTH. Egisto. *m.*
Aeneas [i:ˈni:æs] pr. n. MYTH. Eneas, *m.*
Aeneid [ˈi:niid] pr. n. MYTH. Eneida, *f.*
aeolian [i:ˈəuljən] adj. Eolio, lia. || Eólico, ca (wind).
aeolotropic [ˈi:ələtrəpik] adj. CHEM. Alotrópico, ca.
Aeolus [ˈi:auləs] pr. n. MYTH. Eolo, *m.*
aerate [ˈeiəreit] v. tr. Airear, ventilar (to ventilate). || Gasificar (to charge a liquid with gas). || MED. Oxigenar. || *Aerated water*, agua gaseosa.
aeration [,eiəˈreiʃən] n. Aeración, *f.*, ventilación, *f.* || Gasificación (with gas). || MED. Oxigenación, *f.*
aerial [ˈɛəriəl] adj. Aéreo, a (of or in the air): *aerial photography*, fotografía aérea. || Etéreo, a (ethereal). || *Aerial beacon*, aerofaro, *m.*
— N. Antena, *f.* (radio, TV): *indoor aerial*, antena interior; *transmitting aerial*, antena transmisora.
aerialist [—ist] n. U. S. Equilibrista, *m.* & *f.*, volatinero, ra.
aerie [ˈɛəri] n. Aguilera, *f.* (nest of bird of prey).
aeriform [—fɔ:m] adj. Gaseoso, sa; aeriforme (gaseous). || Inmaterial (unsubstantial).
aerify [—fai] v. tr. Airear (to aerate). || CHEM. Aerificar.
aerobatics [,ɛərəˈbætiks] n. Acrobacia (*f.*) aérea.
aerobe [ˈɛərəub] n. BIOL. Aerobio, *m.*
aerobic [ɛəˈrəubik] adj. BIOL. Aerobio, bia.
aerodrome [ˈɛərədrəum] n. AVIAT. Aeródromo, *m.*
aerodynamic [ˈɛərəudaiˈnæmik] adj. Aerodinámico, ca.
aerodynamics [—s] n. Aerodinámica, *f.*
aerodyne [ˈɛərəudain] n. AVIAT. Aerodino, *m.*
aerofoil [ˈɛərəufɔil] n. AVIAT. Superficie (*f.*) sustentadora.
aerogram [ˈɛərəugræm] n. Aerograma, *m.*, radiograma, *m.*
aerograph [ˈɛərəugrɑ:f] n. Aerógrafo, *m.*
aerolite [ˈɛərəlait] n. Aerolito, *m.*
aeromancy [ˈɛərəmænsi] n. Aeromancia, *f.*
aeromarine [ˈɛərəmæˈri:n] adj. Aeromarítimo, ma.
aeromechanic [ˈɛərəməˈkænik] n. AVIAT. Mecánico (*m.*) de aviación.
aerometer [ɛəˈrɔmitə*] n. Aerómetro, *m.*
aerometry [ɛəˈrɔmetri] n. Aerometría, *f.*
aeromodelling [ˈɛərəˈmɔdliŋ] n. Aeromodelismo, *m.*
aeromotor [ˈɛərəuməutə*] n. Aeromotor, *m.*
aeronaut [ˈɛərənɔ:t] n. Aeronauta, *m.* & *f.*

aeronautic [ˌɛərəˈnɔ:tik] or **aeronautical** [—əl] adj. Aeronáutico, ca.
aeronautics [ˌɛərəˈnɔ:tiks] n. Aeronáutica, *f.*
aeronaval [ˌɛərəˈneivəl] adj. Aeronaval.
aerophagia [ˌɛərəˈfeidʒiə] n. Aerofagia, *f.*
aeroplane [ˈɛərəplein] n. AVIAT. Avión, *m.* || — *Aeroplane modeller*, aeromodelista, *m.* & *f.* || *Aeroplane modelling*, aeromodelismo, *m.* || *Model aeroplane*, aeromodelo, *m.*
aerosol [ˈɛərəsɔl] n. CHEM. Aerosol, *m.* || Pulverizador, *m.* (spray).
aerostat [ˈɛərəstæt] n. Aeróstato, *m.*
aerostatic [ˌɛərəˈstætik] adj. Aerostático, ca.
aerostatics [—s] n. PHYS. Aerostática, *f.*
aerostation [ˌɛərəˈsteiʃən] n. Aerostación, *f.*
aerotechnical [ɛərəˈteknikəl] adj. Aerotécnico, ca.
aerotherapeutics [ˌɛərəuˌθerəˈpjutiks] n. Aeroterapia, *f.*
aerotherapy [ˌɛərəuˈθerəpi] n. Aeroterapia, *f.*
aerothermodynamic [ˈɛərəuˈθə:məudaiˈnæmik] adj. Aerotermodinámico, ca.
aerothermodynamics [—s] n. Aerotermodinámica, *f.*
aery [ˈɛəri] n. Aguilera, *f.*
Aeschylus [ˈi:skiləs] pr. n. Esquilo, *m.*
Aesculapius [ˌi:skjuˈleipjəs] pr. n. Esculapio, *m.*
Aeschines [ˈi:skini:z] pr. n. Esquines, *m.*
Aesop [ˈi:sɔp] pr. n. Esopo, *m.*
aesthete [ˈi:sθi:t] n. Esteta, *m.* & *f.*
aesthetic [i:sˈθetik] adj. Estético, ca.
aesthetical [—əl] adj. Estético, ca.
aesthetician [i:sθəˈtiʃən] n. Estético, *m.*
aestheticism [i:sˈθetisizəm] n. Esteticismo, *m.*
aesthetics [i:sˈθetiks] n. Estética, *f.*
aestival [i:sˈtaivəl] adj. Estival.
aestivate [ˈi:stiveit] v. intr. ZOOL. Pasar el verano en estado de letargo.
aetiological [ˌi:tiəˈlɔdʒikəl] adj. Etiológico, ca.
aetiology [ˌi:tiˈɔlədʒi] n. Etiología, *f.*
Aetna [ˈetnə] pr. n. Etna, *m.*
afar [əˈfɑ:*] adv. Lejos. || *From afar*, desde lejos.
affability [ˌæfəˈbiliti] n. Afabilidad, *f.*
affable [ˈæfəbl] adj. Afable.
affair [əˈfɛə*] n. Asunto, *m.*: *this is no affair of yours*, esto no es [un] asunto tuyo; *affair of state*, asunto de estado. || Asunto, *m.*, cuestión, *f.* (matter): *family affairs*, cuestiones familiares. || Acontecimiento, *m.*: *social affair*, acontecimiento social. || Asunto, *m.*, incidente, *m.* (an incident). || Duelo, *m.* (duel). || Caso, *m.* (case). || Lance, *m.*: *affair of honour*, lance de honor. || Aventura, *f.* (love): *she had an affair with her boss*, tuvo una aventura con su jefe. || — Pl. Negocios, *m.* (business). || — *Current affairs*, actualidad, *f. sing.* || *Foreign Affairs*, Asuntos Exteriores (in Spain), Relaciones Exteriores (in Latin America).
affect [əˈfekt] n. Sentimiento, *m.*
affect [əˈfekt] v. tr. Afectar: *to affect great elegance*, afectar suma elegancia; *this law affects all citizens*, esta ley afecta a todos los ciudadanos; *his mother's death affected him deeply*, la muerte de su madre le afectó profundamente; *the injury affected the whole leg*, la herida afectó a toda la pierna. || Lucir: *to affect a dress*, lucir un traje. || Dárselas de, echárselas de (to pretend to be). || Fingir (to feign).
affectation [ˌæfekˈteiʃən] n. Simulación, *f.* (a pretence). || Afectación, *f.*, amaneramiento, *m.* (artificiality).
affected [əˈfektid] adj. Afectado, da; amanerado, da.
affecting [əˈfektiŋ] adj. Conmovedor, ra (moving).
affection [əˈfekʃən] n. Afecto, *m.*, cariño, *m.* [*for, towards*, por, hacia] (fondness). || MED. Afección, *f.*
affectionate [—it] adj. Afectuoso, sa; cariñoso, sa.
affective [əˈfektiv] adj. Afectivo, va.
affectivity [ˌæfekˈtiviti] n. Afectividad, *f.*
afferent [ˈæfərənt] adj. ANAT. Aferente.
affiance [əˈfaiəns] v. tr. Dar palabra de casamiento.
affidavit [ˌæfiˈdeivit] n. JUR. Declaración (*f.*) jurada. || *Affidavit by process server*, atestiguación (*f.*) forense.
affiliate [əˈfilieit] n. Asociado, da (an associate). || U. S. Filial, *f.* (a subsidiary organization).
affiliate [əˈfilieit] v. intr. Afiliarse. || Asociarse.
— V. tr. Afiliar. || Asociar (to add as an associate). || Legitimar (a child). || Atribuir (a piece of work).
affiliation [əˌfiliˈeiʃən] n. Afiliación, *f.* || Asociación, *f.* || JUR. Legitimación, *f.* (of a child). || *Action for affiliation*, investigación (*f.*) de la paternidad.
affinity [əˈfiniti] n. Afinidad, *f.*
affirm [əˈfə:m] v. tr. Afirmar.
affirmation [ˌæfə:ˈmeiʃən] n. Afirmación, *f.*
affirmative [əˈfə:mətiv] adj. Afirmativo, va.
— N. *An answer in the affirmative*, una respuesta afirmativa.
affirmatory [əˈfə:mətəri] adj. Afirmativo, va.
affix [ˈæfiks] n. GRAMM. Afijo, *m.* || Añadido, *m.*
affix [əˈfiks] v. tr. Sujetar: *he affixed his tie with a pin*, se sujetó la corbata con un alfiler. || Pegar: *to affix an advert to the wall*, pegar un anuncio en la pared. || Poner: *to affix a seal to a document*, poner un sello a un documento; *to affix one's signature to a document*, poner la firma a un documento. || Añadir, agregar (to add). || Echar, atribuir (a blame).
affixed [əˈfikst] adj. GRAMM. Afijo, ja.
afflict [əˈflikt] v. tr. Afligir: *his death afflicted me*, su muerte me afligió. || *To be afflicted with*, estar aquejado de, sufrir de.
affliction [əˈflikʃən] n. Pesar, *m.*, aflicción, *f.* (grief). || Sufrimiento, *m.* (suffering). || Achaque, *m.* (of old age). || MED. Enfermedad, *f.*, aflicción, *f.*
afflictive [əˈfliktiv] adj. Doloroso, sa.
affluence [ˈæfluəns] n. Opulencia, *f.* || Abundancia, *f.*
affluent [ˈæfluənt] adj. Opulento, ta; acaudalado, da (wealthy). || Abundante.
— N. Afluente, *m.* (a tributary stream).
afflux [ˈæflʌks] n. Afluencia, *f.* || MED. Aflujo, *m.*
afford [əˈfɔ:d] v. tr. Permitirse: *can we afford to speak out?*, ¿podemos permitirnos el hablar libremente? || Costearse: *can we afford a new car?*, ¿podemos costearnos un coche nuevo? || Permitirse el lujo: *I can't afford to relax*, no me puedo permitir el lujo de descansar. || Dar, proporcionar: *these trees afford little shelter*, estos árboles dan poca protección. || *The tower affords a nice view*, desde la torre hay una buena vista.
— OBSERV. Excepto cuando significa "dar", el verbo *afford* se emplea precedido de *can* o de *be able*.
afforest [æˈfɔrist] v. tr. Repoblar con árboles.
afforestation [æˌfɔrisˈteiʃən] n. Repoblación (*f.*) forestal.
affranchise [əˈfræntʃaiz] v. tr. Manumitir.
affranchisement [əˈfræntʃizmənt] n. Manumisión, *f.*
affray [əˈfrei] n. JUR. Reyerta, *f.*, refriega, *f.*
affricate [ˈæfrikit] n. Africada, *f.* (consonant).
affricative [æˈfrikətiv] adj. GRAMM. Africado, da.
affront [əˈfrʌnt] n. Afrenta, *f.* || Insulto, *m.* (verbal).
affront [əˈfrʌnt] v. tr. Afrentar. || Insultar (verbally).
affusion [əˈfju:ʒən] n. Afusión, *f.*
afghan [ˈæfgæn] n. U. S. Colcha (*f.*) de punto.
Afghan [ˈæfgæn] adj./n. Afgano, na.
Afghanistan [æfˈgænistæn] pr. n. Afganistán, *m.*
afield [əˈfi:ld] adv. Al campo. || *Far afield*, muy lejos.
afire [əˈfaiə*] adj./adv. Ardiendo, en llamas.
aflame [əˈfleim] adj./adv. En llamas. || — Adj. FIG. Inflamado, da.
afloat [əˈfləut] adj./adv. MAR. Flotando: *the ship was afloat*, el barco estaba flotando. | A flote: *the ship managed to keep afloat after the collision*, el barco consiguió mantenerse a flote tras el choque. | A bordo (on board ship). || Inundado, da (flooded). || FIG. Solvente (free of debt). || *Rumours were afloat that he would resign*, circulaban rumores de que iba a dimitir.
afoot [əˈfut] adj./adv. A pie (walking). || En marcha (beginning to make progress). || FIG. *There is sth. afoot*, se está tramando algo.
afore [əˈfɔ:*] adv./prep. MAR. A proa.
aforementioned [—menʃənd] or **aforesaid** [—sed] adj. Susodicho, cha; antedicho, cha; anteriormente mencionado.
aforethought [—θɔ:t] n. Premeditación, *f.*
— Adj. Premeditado, da. || *With malice aforethought*, con premeditación.
afraid [əˈfreid] adj. Asustado, da: *go with her, because she is afraid*, vete con ella porque está asustada. || — *I am afraid she is out*, lo siento pero ha salido. || *I am afraid I can't come*, me temo que no pueda ir. || *To be afraid for*, temer por. || *To be afraid of*, tener miedo a *or* de (See OBSERV.). || *To feel afraid to speak*, no atreverse a hablar.
— OBSERV. See OBSERV. under FEAR, v. tr.
afresh [əˈfreʃ] adv. De nuevo, otra vez.
Africa [ˈæfrikə] pr. n. África, f. || *South Africa*, África del Sur.
African [ˈæfrikən] adj./n. Africano, na.
Africanist [—ist] n. Africanista.
Africanization [ˌæfrikənaiˈzeiʃən] n. Africanización, *f.*
Africanize [ˈæfrikənaiz] v. tr. Africanizar.
Afrikaans [ˌæfriˈkɑ:ns] n. Afrikaans, *m.*
Afrikaner [ˌæfriˈkɑ:nə*] n. Afrikánder, *m.* & *f.*
Afro-American [ˈæfrəuəˈmerikən] adj./n. Afroamericano, na.
Afro-Asian [ˈæfrəuˈeiʃən] adj./n. Afroasiático, ca.
Afro-Cuban [—ˈkjubən] adj./n. Afrocubano, na.
aft [ɑ:ft] adv. MAR. A popa. | En popa. || *Fore and aft*, de proa a popa.
after [ˈɑ:ftə*] adj. Posterior: *in the after years*, en los años posteriores. || Siguiente (next). || Trasero, ra: *the after parts of a bull*, los cuartos traseros de un toro. || MAR. De popa.
— Prep. Tras (in pursuit of): *she ran after the postman*, corrió tras el cartero; *one after the other*, uno tras otro. || Detrás de (behind): *the police are after her*, la policía está detrás de ella. || Después de: *after a week we went home*, después de una semana nos fuimos a casa. || En busca de (in search of): *she is after a husband*, va en busca de marido. || A la manera de: *paintings after the Dutch masters*, pinturas a la manera de los maestros holandeses. || A imitación de, según el estilo de: *engraving after Poussin*, grabado hecho a imitación de Poussin. || Por, acerca de: *to ask after s.o.*, preguntar por alguien. || — *After all is said and done*, al fin y al cabo. || *After hours*, fuera de horas. || *After you!*, ¡usted primero! || *Day after day*, día tras día. || *He read page after page*, leyó página tras página. || *I am after a red dress*, estoy buscando un traje rojo. || *I have been after that for years*, estoy buscando eso desde hace años. || *It's after five o'clock*, son las cinco pasadas. || U. S. *It's half after four*, son las cuatro y media. || *Named after*, llamado como; llamado en honor a. || *The day after the battle*, el

día siguiente de la batalla. || *The day after tomorrow*, pasado mañana. || *They called me John after my father*, me pusieron Juan por mi padre. || FIG. *To be after s.o.'s blood*, querer matar a alguien. || *To look after*, see LOOK. || *What's he after?*, ¿qué es lo que busca?
— Adv. Después: *before and after*, antes y después; *long after*, mucho tiempo después. || Detrás (behind).
— Conj. Una vez que, después de que: *after he left the room, we started talking*, una vez que salió de la habitación, nos pusimos a hablar.
afterbirth [—bɑ:θ] n. ANAT. Placenta, *f.* || JUR. Nacimiento (*m.*) póstumo.
aftercare [—kɛə*] n. MED. Vigilancia (*f.*) postoperatoria.
afterdamp [—dæmp] n. MIN. Mofeta, *f.*
afterdeck [—dek] n. MAR. Cubierta (*f.*) de popa.
after-dinner [—ˈdinə*] adj. De sobremesa.
aftereffect [—iˈfekt] n. Consecuencia, *f.*, efecto (*m.*) secundario.
afterglow [—gləu] n. Resplandor (*m.*) crepuscular (of sky).
afterlife [—laif] n. Vida (*f.*) futura. || Resto (*m.*) de la vida.
aftermath [—mæθ] n. Repercusiones, *f. pl.*, secuelas, *f. pl.* (consequences). || AGR. Renadío, *m.*, segundo corte, *m.*
aftermost [—məust] adj. MAR. De popa.
afternoon [—ˈnu:n] n. Tarde, *f.* (part of the day). || FIG. Atardecer: *he is in the afternoon of life*, está en el atardecer de la vida. || *Good afternoon*, buenas tardes.
— Adj. De la tarde.
afterpains [—peinz] pl. n. Dolores (*m.*) después del parto, entuertos, *m.* (pain following childbirth).
aftertaste [—teist] n. Regusto, *m.*, mal sabor (*m.*) de boca, resabio, *m.*, gustillo, *m.*
afterthought [—θɔ:t] n. Ocurrencia (*f.*) tardía, idea (*f.*) tardía.
afterward [—wəd] or **afterwards** [—wədz] adv. Después, más tarde (at a later time). || *Long afterward*, mucho después.
afterworld [—wə:ld] n. El más allá, el otro mundo.
again [əˈgen] adv. Otra vez, nuevamente, de nuevo (once more). || Además (in addition). || Por otra parte (on the other hand). || — *Again and again* o *time and again*, una y otra vez. || *As much again*, otro tanto más. || *Never again*, nunca más. || *Now and again*, de vez en cuando. || *Once again*, otra vez. || *To say again and again*, decir una y otra vez. || *What's his name again?*, ¿cómo ha dicho que se llama? || *Would you do it again?*, ¿lo volverías a hacer?
against [əˈgenst] prep. Contra: *to fight against the enemy*, luchar contra el enemigo; *precautions against cold*, precauciones contra el frío; *hailstones against the window*, granizos contra la ventana; *they were warned against the danger*, se les puso en guardia contra el peligro. || En contra de, contra: *I was against him*, estaba en contra de él. || A cambio de: *he gave me his football against my bicycle*, me dio la pelota de fútbol a cambio de la bicicleta. || Para (for). || Al lado de, cerca de (near). || — *As against this*, frente a eso. || *To put it against expenses*, ponerlo en la nota de gastos. || *To run up against*, see RUN.
agami [əˈgæmi] n. ZOOL. Agamí, *m.*
agamic [eiˈgæmik] or **agamous** [ˈægəməs] adj. BIOL. Asexuado, da; asexual. || BOT. Ágamo, ma.
agape [ˈægəpi] n. Ágape, *m.* (Christian banquet). || Amor (*m.*) espiritual.
agape [əˈgeip] adj./adv. Boquiabierto, ta.
agar-agar [ˈeigɑ:eigɑ:] n. Agar agar, *m.*
agaric [ˈægərik] n. BOT. Agárico, *m.*
agate [ˈægət] n. Ágata, *f.* (stone). || Bruñidor, *m.* (bookbinder's tool). || U. S. Tipo (*m.*) de 5,5 puntos (in printing). | Canica *f.* (marble).
Agatha [ˈægəθə] pr. n. Águeda, *f.*
agave [əˈgeivi] n. BOT. Agave, *f.*, pita, *f.*
age [eidʒ] n. Edad, *f.*: *ten years of age*, diez años de edad; *of school age*, en edad escolar; *at the age of ten*, a la edad de diez años; *Middle Ages*, Edad Media; *The Stone Age*, la Edad de Piedra. || Era, *f.*: *the motor car age*, la era del automóvil. || Época, *f.*: *the age of the impressionists*, la época de los impresionistas; *the age I live in*, la época en que vivo. || FIG. Siglo, *m.*, eternidad, *f.*, mucho tiempo, *m.* (long time). || — *Be* o *act your age*, no seas niño. || *Golden Age*, Siglo de Oro (in Spain). || *It's an age since we last met*, hace un siglo que no nos vemos. || *Middle age*, mediana edad. || *Old age*, vejez, *f.* || *The age of consent*, la edad núbil. || *The age of discretion*, see DISCRETION. || *The age of reason*, la edad de la razón or del juicio. || *The awkward age*, la edad del pavo [*Amer.*, la edad del chivateo]. || *To be of age*, ser mayor de edad. || *To be over age*, ser demasiado viejo. || *To be under age*, ser menor de edad (minor), ser demasiado joven (too young). || *To come of age*, alcanzar la mayoría de edad. || *To look one's age*, representar la edad que se tiene. || *What age are you?*, ¿qué edad tiene?
age [eidʒ] v. tr./intr. Envejecer: *she hasn't aged a bit*, no ha envejecido nada.
aged [—id] adj. Anciano, na; viejo, ja; de edad avanzada: *a very aged man*, un hombre muy anciano. || *A boy aged ten*, un niño de diez años de edad.
age group [ˈeidʒgru:p] n. Grupo (*m.*) de personas de la misma edad. || *To be of different age groups*, no tener la misma edad.
ageless [ˈeidʒlis] adj. Eterno, na. || Siempre joven.
agelong [ˈeidʒlɔŋ] adj. Secular.
agency [ˈeidʒənsi] n. Agencia, *f.*: *travel agency*, agencia de viajes; *advertising agency*, agencia de publicidad. || Mediación, *f.*: *through his doctor's agency he received compensation*, por mediación del médico recibió una indemnización. || Acción, *f.* || Agente, *m.*: *natural agency*, agente natural. || — *Free agency*, libre albedrío, *m.* || *Real estate agency*, agencia inmobiliaria. || *Specialized agencies*, organismos especializados (of U.N.).
agenda [əˈdʒendə] n. Orden (*m.*) del día (of a meeting).
agent [ˈeidʒənt] n. Agente, *m.* (a representative): *insurance agent*, agente de seguros. || COMM. Agente, *m.*, representante, *m.* || Apoderado, *m.* (law). || Instrumento, *m.* (instrument). || Agente, *m.* (cause). || CHEM. Agente, *m.*: *cooling agent*, agente refrigerante. || GRAMM. Agente, *m.* || — *Business agent*, agente de negocios. || *Estate agent*, agente inmobiliario.
agent provocateur [ˈæʒɑ̃:prəvɔkəˈtə:*] n. Agente (*m.*) provocador.
age-old [ˈeidʒəuld] adj. Secular (centuries old). || Antiguo, gua (ancient).
agglomerate [əˈglɔmərit] n. Aglomeración, *f.* (a mass or collection). || GEOL. Aglomerado, *m.*
— Adj. Aglomerado, da.
agglomerate [əˈglɔməreit] v. tr. Aglomerar.
— V. intr. Aglomerarse.
agglomeration [əˌglɔməˈreiʃən] n. Aglomeración, *f.*
agglutinant [əˈglu:tinənt] adj. Aglutinante.
— N. Aglutinante, *m.*
agglutinate [əˈglu:tinit] adj. Aglutinado, da.
agglutinate [əˈglu:tineit] v. tr. Aglutinar.
— V. intr. Aglutinarse.
agglutination [əˌglu:tiˈneiʃən] n. Aglutinación, *f.*
agglutinative [əˈglu:tinətiv] adj. Aglutinante (language). || MED. Aglutinativo, va.
aggrandize [əˈgrændaiz] v. tr. Ampliar, agrandar (to make greater in power, rank). || FIG. Exagerar (to exaggerate). | Engrandecer (to magnify).
aggrandizement [əˈgrændizmənt] n. Ampliación, *f.*, agrandamiento, *m.* || FIG. Engrandecimiento, *m.*
aggravate [ˈægrəveit] v. tr. Agravar (to make worse). || FAM. Exasperar, irritar (to exasperate). || JUR. *Aggravated theft*, robo (*m.*) con agravante.
aggravating [—iŋ] adj. Irritante, molesto, ta. || JUR. Agravante
aggravation [ˌægrəˈveiʃən] n. Agravación, *f.* (a making worse). || FAM. Exasperación, *f.*, irritación, *f.* || JUR. Circunstancia (*f.*) agravante.
aggregate [ˈægrigit] n. Agregado, *m.* (mass of different things). || Conjunto, *m.* (whole). || *In the aggregate*, en conjunto, en total, globalmente.
— Adj. Global, colectivo, va; total. || Acumulado, da (amassed). || BOT. GEOL. Agregado, da.
aggregate [ˈægrigeit] v. tr. Agregar, reunir, unir.
— V. intr. Ascender a, totalizar, sumar.
aggregation [ˌægriˈgeiʃən] n. Agregación, *f.* || Reunión, *f.* || Agregado, *m.* (aggregate).
aggression [əˈgreʃən] n. Agresión, *f.*
aggressive [əˈgresiv] adj. Agresivo, va: *an aggressive person*, una persona agresiva. || MIL. De ataque, ofensivo, va: *an aggressive move*, un movimiento de ataque. || Llamativo, va: *an aggressive advertisement*, un anuncio llamativo. || U. S. Emprendedor, ra. | Dinámico, ca; enérgico, ca.
— N. Ofensiva, *f.*
aggressiveness [—nis] n. Agresividad, *f.*, acometividad, *f.*
aggressor [əˈgresə*] n. Agresor, ra.
aggrieved [əˈgri:vd] adj. Agraviado, da.
aghast [əˈgɑ:st] adj. Espantado, da; horrorizado, da (*at*, de) [horrified]. || Pasmado, da (amazed).
agile [ˈædʒail] adj. Ágil.
agility [əˈdʒiliti] n. Agilidad, *f.*
agio [ˈædʒiəu] n. Agio, *m.*
agiotage [ˈædʒətidʒ] n. Agiotaje, *m.*
agitate [ˈædʒiteit] v. tr. Agitar (to shake up, to move). || Discutir, debatir (a question).
— V. intr. *To agitate for*, hacer una campaña en favor de.
agitation [ˌædʒiˈteiʃən] n. Agitación, *f.* || Excitación, *f.*, nerviosismo, *m.* (excitement). || Discusión, *f.*, debate, *m.* || Campaña, *f.* (of an agitator).
agitator [ˈædʒiteitə*] n. Agitador, ra. || Agitador, *m.* (apparatus).
aglet [ˈæglit] n. Herrete, *m.* (of a lace). || MIL. Cordón, *m.* || BOT. Candelilla, *f.*, amento, *m.* (of birch, hazel).
aglow [əˈgləu] adv./adj. Radiante (*with*, de).
agnail [ˈægneil] n. Padrastro, *m.*
agnate [ˈægneit] n. Agnado, *m.*, consanguíneo, *m.*
agnation [æˈneiʃən] n. Agnación, *f.*, consanguinidad, *f.*
Agnes [ˈægnis] pr. n. Inés, *f.*
agnostic [ægˈnɔstik] adj./n. Agnóstico, ca.
agnosticism [ægˈnɔstisizəm] n. Agnosticismo, *m.*
ago [əˈgəu] adj. Hace: *a year ago*, hace un año.
— Adv. *As long ago as 1920*, ya en 1920. || *Long ago*, hace mucho tiempo. || *Not long ago*, hace poco tiempo.
agog [əˈgɔg] adj. Ansioso, sa (eager). || *To set s.o. agog*, infundir curiosidad a uno, intrigar a uno.

agonize [ˈægənaiz] v. tr. Atormentar.
— V. intr. Luchar, hacer esfuerzos desesperados (*after*, por) [to struggle]. || Sufrir horriblemente.
agony [ˈægəni] n. Dolor, *m.* (physical pain). || Angustia, *f.*, congoja, *f.* (mental suffering). || — *The Agony*, La Agonía de Cristo. || *The last agony*, la agonía. || *To go through agonies*, pasarlas moradas. || *To suffer* o *to be in agonies*, sufrir atrozmente.
agony column [—ˈkɔləm] n. FAM. Anuncios (*m. pl.*) personales [relativos a personas u objetos perdidos].
agora [ˈægərə] n. Ágora, *f.*

— OBSERV. El plural de la palabra inglesa es *agorae*.

agoraphobia [ˌægərəˈfəubjə] n. Agorafobia, *f.*
agouti or **agouty** [əˈgu:ti] n. ZOOL. Agutí, *m.*
agraffe [əˈgræf] n. Grapa, *f.*
agrarian [əˈgrɛəriən] adj. Agrario, ria.
agrarianism [—izəm] n. Agrarismo, *m.*
agree [əˈgri:] v. intr. Consentir: *she will never agree to it*, nunca lo consentirá. || Acceder a, aceptar: *to agree to a proposal*, aceptar una propuesta. || Aprobar (to approve). || Ponerse de acuerdo (to come to an agreement). || Estar de acuerdo: *we don't agree about the dog*, no estamos de acuerdo respecto al perro. || Estar de acuerdo, reconocer: *he agreed that it was stupid*, reconoció que aquello era estúpido. || Sentar bien: *this climate agrees with me*, este clima me sienta bien. || Coincidir, concordar: *these two figures don't agree*, estas dos figuras no coinciden. || GRAMM. Concordar. || — *Don't you agree?*, ¿no le parece? || *It is agreed*, de acuerdo. || *To agree on*, convenir en. || *It was agreed that*, se resolvió que, se acordó que. || *To agree upon* o *on*, acordar: *to agree upon a price*, acordar un precio. || *To agree with*, estar de acuerdo con.
— V. tr. Acordar: *both statesmen have agreed to increase cooperation*, ambos estadistas han acordado estrechar la cooperación. || Quedar en: *he agreed to come*, quedó en venir. || Estar de acuerdo con: *do you agree the bill?*, ¿está de acuerdo con la cuenta?
agreeable [əˈgriəbl] adj. Agradable, placentero, ra (pleasant). || Conforme: *to be agreeable to a plan*, estar conforme con un plan. || Conforme, dispuesto: *to be agreeable to doing sth.*, estar conforme en *or* dispuesto a hacer algo. || *Is that agreeable to you?*, ¿está de acuerdo?
agreed! [əˈgri:d] interj. ¡De acuerdo!, ¡conforme!
agreement [əˈgri:mənt] n. Acuerdo, *m.*: *to come to* o *to reach (an) agreement*, llegar a un acuerdo. || Acuerdo, *m.*: *general agreement on tariffs and trade*, acuerdo general sobre tarifas arancelarias y comercio. || JUR. Contrato, *m.* (contract). | Convenio, *m.*: *collective agreements*, convenios colectivos. || Concordancia, *f.*, coincidencia, *f.* (of figures). || GRAMM. Concordancia, *f.* || — *A poor agreement is better than a good court case*, más vale mala avenencia que buena sentencia. || *As per agreement*, según lo convenido. || *By mutual agreement*, de común acuerdo. || *In agreement*, de acuerdo, acorde. || *To conclude an agreement*, concertar un acuerdo.
agricultural [ˌægriˈkʌltʃərəl] adj. Agrícola: *agricultural product, equipment, community*, producto, maquinaria, comunidad agrícola. || — *Agricultural college*, escuela (*f.*) de peritos agrícolas. || *Agricultural engineer*, perito agrícola *or* agrónomo. || *Agricultural expert*, ingeniero agrónomo.
agriculturalist [—ist] n. Agricultor, ra (farmer). || Agrónomo, *m.*, ingeniero (*m.*) agrónomo (expert).
agriculture [ˈægrikʌltʃə*] n. Agricultura, *f.*
agriculturist [ˌægriˈkʌltʃərist] n. See AGRICULTURALIST.
Agrigento [ˌɑ:gridˈʒentəu] pr. n. GEOGR. Agrigento.
agrimony [ˌægriməni] n. BOT. Agrimonia, *f.*, agrimoña, *f.*
Agrippina [ˌægriˈpi:nə] pr. n. Agripina, *f.*
agronomic [ˌægrəˈnɔmik] or **agronomical** [—əl] adj. Agronómico, ca.
agronomist [əˈgrɔnəmist] n. Agrónomo, *m.*
agronomy [əˈgrɔnəmi] n. Agronomía, *f.*
aground [əˈgraund] adj. MAR. Encallado, da (on rock). | Varado, da (in mud, sand).
— Adv. MAR. *To run aground*, encallar, varar.
ague [ˈeigju:] n. MED. Fiebre (*f.*) intermitente (of malaria). | Escalofrío, *m.* (chill, shivering).
ahead [əˈhed] adv. Delante [*of*, de] (in front). || MAR. Avante (direction): *full steam ahead!*, ¡avante a toda máquina! || Antes de: *ahead of schedule*, antes de lo previsto. || Antes que: *to arrive ahead of s.o.*, llegar antes que alguien. || — *Go ahead!*, ¡adelante! || *Straight ahead*, todo seguido, todo derecho. || *To be ahead*, ir ganando, llevar ventaja (in sports). || *To be ahead of*, llevar ventaja a. || *To be ahead of one's time*, anticiparse a su época. || *To get ahead*, adelantar, progresar: *one must work hard to get ahead*, para adelantar uno debe trabajar mucho. || *To get o to go ahead of s.o.*, adelantarse a alguien. || *To go on ahead*, adelantarse. || *To go ahead with*, llevar adelante. || *To look ahead*, mirar el futuro. || *To send on ahead*, mandar por delante.
ahem! [hˈmm] interj. ¡Ejem!
ahoy! [əˈhɔi] interj. MAR. ¡Ah!: *ahoy there!*, ¡ah del barco! || MAR. *Ship ahoy!*, ¡barco a la vista!
ai [ai] n. ZOOL. Aí, *m* (sloth).
aid [eid] n. Ayuda, *f.*: *he was a great aid to me*, fue una gran ayuda para mí; *to give aid*, prestar ayuda. || Auxilio, *m.*, socorro, *m.*, ayuda, *f.*: *to go to the aid of a drowning person*, ir en auxilio de una persona que se ahoga. || Ayudante, *m.* & *f.* (helper). || — *By* o *with the aid of*, con la ayuda de. || *First aid*, primeros auxilios. || *Hearing aid*, aparato (*m.*) para sordos. || *In aid of*, en pro de, a beneficio de. || *Medical aid*, asistencia médica. || *State aid*, ayuda estatal. || *That will be of aid to you*, eso será de utilidad para ti, eso te será útil. || *To come to the aid of*, acudir en ayuda de. || *What's all this in aid of?*, ¿a qué viene todo eso?
aid [eid] v. tr./intr. Ayudar, auxiliar.
aide-de-camp [ˈeiddəˈkɑ̃:] n. MIL. Ayudante (*m.*) de campo, edecán, *m.*

— OBSERV. El plural es *aides-de-camp*.

aide-mémoire [ˈeidmeimˌwɑ:] n. Memorándum, *m.*

— OBSERV. El plural de *aide-mémoire* es *aides-mémoire*.

aidman [ˈeidmən] n. U. S. Enfermero (*m.*) militar.
aid station [ˈeidˌsteiʃən] n. U. S. MIL. Puesto (*m.*) de socorro.
aigrette [ˈeigret] n. ZOOL. Garceta, *f.* || Penacho, *m.* (of feathers). || Diadema, *f.* (of gems).
aiguille [ˈeigwi:l] n. Picacho, *m.* (of rock). || Barrena, *f.* (drill).
aiguillette [ˌeigwiˈlet] n. MIL. Cordón, *m.*
ail [eil] v. tr. Afligir, doler, hacer sufrir.
— V. intr. Estar enfermo, sufrir.
ailanthus [eiˈlænθəs] n. BOT. Ailanto, *m.* (tree).
aileron [ˈeilərən] n. Alerón, *m.* (of aeroplane).
ailing [ˈeiliŋ] adj. Enfermo, ma.
ailment [ˈeilmənt] n. Indisposición, *f.*, malestar, *m.*
aim [eim] n. Puntería, *f.* (when firing a gun): *to take accurate aim*, afinar la puntería; *to have a good aim*, tener buena puntería. || Blanco, *m.*, objetivo, *m.* (target). || Intención, *f.*, propósito, *m.*, objetivo, *m.*, meta, *f.*, fin, *m.* (intention): *what is the aim of these questions?*, ¿cuál es la intención de estas preguntas? || Meta, *f.* (goal): *his aim was to be a doctor*, su meta era ser médico. || — *Missiles which fall short of their aim*, proyectiles que no alcanzan su objetivo. || FIG. *To fall short of one's aim*, no conseguir su propósito. || *To miss one's aim*, errar el tiro. || *To spoil one's aim*, estropearle a uno el tiro. || *To take aim (at s.o.)*, apuntar [a alguien]. || *With the aim of*, con la intención de, con el propósito de, con el objetivo de.
aim [eim] v. tr. Asestar, lanzar (a blow): *he aimed a punch at him*, le asestó un puñetazo. || Apuntar con: *to aim one's gun at s.o.*, apuntar a alguien con la pistola. || FIG. Dirigir (a question, a statement, measures). || *That shot was aimed at you*, ese tiro iba dirigido a ti.
— V. intr. Apuntar: *to aim at s.o.*, apuntar a alguien. || Aspirar, tener el propósito de, pretender: *I aim to become a doctor*, aspiro a ser médico. || *To aim high*, picar muy alto, aspirar a mucho.
aimless [—lis] adj. Sin objeto, sin propósito fijo.
ain't [eint] FAM. contraction of *is not, are not, am not, has not, have not*.
air [ɛə*] n. Aire, *m.* (atmosphere, breeze, the space above us): *to throw a ball up into the air*, echar una pelota al aire; *compressed, liquid air*, aire comprimido, líquido. || Aire, *m.*: *he wore an air of sadness*, tenía un aire de tristeza. || Cara, *f.*, semblante, *m.* (face). || MUS. Aire, *m.*, canción, *f.* (tune): *he sang a merry air*, entonó un aire alegre. || — Pl. Aires, *m.*: *to put on airs*, darse aires. || — *By air*, en avión (to travel), por avión (to send). || FIG. *Conceited air*, aire de suficiencia. || *Foul air*, aire viciado. || *Fresh air*, aire fresco. || FIG. *In the air*, en el aire: *our plans are in the air*, nuestros planes están en el aire; *rumours are in the air that...*, hay rumores en el aire de que... || *In the open air*, al aire libre. || *Into the air*, al aire. || *To be on the air*, hablar por la radio. || *To be put on the air*, radiarse. || *To build castles in the air*, levantar castillos en el aire. || *To get fresh air*, tomar el fresco. || *To have a change of air*, cambiar *or* mudar de aires. || *To have the air of a gentleman*, tener aires de gran señor. || *To leave pending in the air*, dejar en el aire. || FIG. *To live on air*, vivir del aire. | *To put on airs and graces*, darse aires. | *To rend the air*, herir el aire. || FIG. *To vanish into thin air*, evaporarse. | *To walk on air*, no caber en sí de gozo. || *Up in the air*, en el aire.
— Adj. Aéreo, a. || Atmosférico, ca (flow, pressure).
air [ɛə*] v. tr. Airear, ventilar (to expose to the air). || Orear (to hang out to dry). || FIG. Publicar, hacer público (to make known). | Lucir, hacer gala *or* alarde de (one's knowledge).
air attaché [—əˈtæʃei] n. Agregado (*m.*) aéreo.
air base [—beis] n. Base (*f.*) aérea.
air bladder [—ˌblædə*] n. ZOOL. Vejiga (*f.*) natatoria. || BOT. Vesícula, *f.*
airborne [—bɔ:n] adj. Aerotransportado, da (troops). || Transportado *or* llevado por el aire (bacteria, etc.). || En el aire, volando.
air brake [—breik] n. Freno (*m.*) de aire comprimido. | AVIAT. Freno (*m.*) aerodinámico.
airbrush [—brʌʃ] n. Aerógrafo, *m.*
airburst [—bə:st] n. Explosión (*f.*) en el aire.
airbus [—bʌs] n. Aerobús, *m.*
air chamber [—ˌtʃeimbə*] n. Cámara (*f.*) de aire.
air-condition [—kənˌdiʃən] v. tr. Climatizar, instalar aire acondicionado en.
air-conditioned [—kənˈdiʃənd] adj. Con aire acondicionado.

AGRICULTURE — AGRICULTURA, *f.*

I. General terms. — Términos (*m.*) generales.

land, soil	tierra *f.*, suelo *m.*
fertile soil	suelo (*m.*) fértil
lean *o* poor soil	tierra (*f.*) magra
dry soil	tierra (*f.*) de secano
irrigable land	tierra (*f.*) de regadío
humus	mantillo *m.*
wasteland, barren land	yermo *m.*, erial *m.*
arable *o* tilled land	tierra arable *or* de labranza
grass	hierba *f.*
grassland	pastizal *m.*
meadow	prado *m.* (small), pradera *f.* (large)
prairie	pradera *f.*
pasture land	pastos *m. pl.*, pastizal *m.*
to lie fallow	estar en barbecho
fallow	barbecho *m.*
stubble; stubble field	rastrojo *m.*; rastrojal *m.*
straw; hay	paja *f.*; heno *m.*
country, countryside	campo *m.*
countryman	campesino *m.*
countrywoman	campesina *f.*
rural population	población (*f.*) rural
rural exodus	éxodo (*m.*) rural
mechanization of farming	mecanización (*f.*) del campo
mechanized farming	motocultivo *m.*
agronomist	agrónomo *m.*
latifundium, large landed estate	latifundio *m.*
farm	finca *f.*, granja *f.*; explotación (*f.*) rural
cattle farm	explotación (*f.*) ganadera *or* pecuaria
ranch	rancho *m.*
hacienda	hacienda *f.*
holding	propiedad *f.*
plot, parcel, lot	parcela *f.*
cooperative farm	cooperativa *f.*
collective farm	granja (*f.*) colectiva
farmer	agricultor *m.*, cultivador *m.*
producer	productor *m.*
settler	colono *m.*
landowner	terrateniente *m.*
absentee landlord	absentista *m.*
smallholder, small farmer	pequeño agricultor *m.*
rancher	ranchero *m.*
tenant farmer, leaseholder	arrendatario *m.*
sharecropper	aparcero *m.*
ploughman	labrador *m.*
farm labourers [U.S., farm laborers]	obreros (*m.*) agrícolas *or* del campo
farm hand	peón *m.*, mozo (*m.*) de labranza, bracero *m.*
cattle farmer	ganadero *m.*
cowherd, cowboy	vaquero *m.*
shepherd	pastor *m.*
fruit grower	hortelano *m.*
vinegrower	viñador *m.*, viñatero *m.*
vintager	vendimiador *m.*
farming, husbandry	agricultura *f.*
animal husbandry *o* breeding	cría (*f.*) de animales *or* de ganado
dairy farming	cría (*f.*) de ganado lechero
horticulture	horticultura *f.*
market gardening	cultivo (*m.*) de hortalizas
fruit growing	fruticultura *f.*
vinegrowing, viticulture	viticultura *f.*
olive growing	oleicultura *f.*
arboriculture	arboricultura *f.*
silviculture	silvicultura *f.*
agricultural *o* farm products	productos (*m.*) agrícolas *or* agropecuarios
foodstuffs	productos (*m.*) alimenticios
dairy produce *o* products	productos (*m.*) lácteos
dairy industry	industria (*f.*) lechera
crop *o* farming year	campaña (*f.*) agrícola
season	temporada *f.*
agricultural commodities market	mercado (*m.*) agrícola
land *o* agrarian reform	reforma (*f.*) agraria
livestock	ganado *m.*
cattle	ganado (*m.*) vacuno
pruning	poda *f.*
to graft	injertar
to harvest	cosechar
harvest, harvesting	cosecha *f.*
reaping	siega *f.*
to pick	recoger
picking	recolección *f.*
to cut, to mow	cortar, segar
cutting, mowing	corte *m.*, siega *f.*
to thresh	trillar
threshing	trilla *f.*
haymaking	henificación *f.*
to bind (into sheaves)	agavillar
to ensile, to pit	ensilar
soil improvement *o* dressing	abono (*m.*) del suelo
land reclamation	puesta (*f.*) en cultivo de las tierras
irrigation, watering	irrigación *f.*, riego *m.*
to irrigate, to water	irrigar, regar
drainage	drenaje *m.*, avenamiento *m.*
irrigation ditch *o* channel	acequia *f.*, canal (*m.*) de riego
manure	estiércol *m.*
to manure	estercolar
fertilizer	fertilizante *m.*, abono *m.*
to fertilize	abonar, fertilizar
spreading	esparcimiento *m.*
to fumigate	fumigar

II. The farm. — La finca, *f.*

estate	propiedad *f.*
farmhouse	casa *f.*
outbuildings	dependencias *f.*
barn, shed	cobertizo *m.*
granary, grain store	granero *m.*
grain silo	silo (*m.*) para granos
hayloft	henil *m.*
stable	cuadra *f.*, caballeriza *f.*
litter	pajaza *f.*
cowshed	establo *m.*
pigsty [U.S., hog pen]	pocilga *f.*, porqueriza *f.*
sheep pen, fold	redil *m.*, aprisco *m.*, majada *f.*
rabbit hutch	conejera *f.*
hen house, henroost	gallinero *m.*
hen run, chicken run	corral *m.*
incubator, brooder	incubadora *f.*, pollera *f.*
laying house	ponedero *m.*
watering *o* drinking trough	abrevadero *m.*, bebedero *m.*
feeding *o* feed trough	comedero *m.*
feeding rack, manger, crib	pesebre *m.*
greenhouse, glasshouse	invernadero *m.*
nursery	vivero *m.*
seedbed	semillero *m.*
threshing floor	era *f.*
manure *o* dung heap	estercolero *m.*
field	campo *m.*
corn field	trigal *m.*
furrow	surco *m.*
ridge	caballón *m.*
clod	terrón *m.*
terrace	terraza *f.*, bancal *m.*
haystack, hayrick	almiar *m.*, pajar *m.*
shock	fajina *f.*, hacina *f.*
sheaf	gavilla *f.*, haz *f.*
plantation	plantación *f.*
cabbage patch	campo (*m.*) de coles
tomato patch	tomatal *m.*
vineyard	viñedo *m.*
kitchen garden	huerto *m.*
market garden, orchard	huerta *f.* (large), huerto *m.* (small).

III. Land use. — Aprovechamiento (*m.*) del suelo.

land tenure	régimen (*m.*) de la propiedad
tenancy, leasing, lease	arrendamiento *m.*
land settlement policy	política (*f.*) de colonización
land consolidation	concentración (*f.*) parcelaria
to cultivate, to farm	cultivar
to till	cultivar (to cultivate), labrar (to plough)
to manage, to run (a farm)	explotar [una finca]
dry, irrigated farming	cultivo (*m.*) de secano, de regadío
extensive, intensive cultivation	cultivo (*m.*) extensivo, intensivo
crop rotation	rotación (*f.*) de cultivos
mixed farming	policultivo *m.*, cultivo (*m.*) mixto
single-crop farming	monocultivo *m.*
to clear	desbrozar
to weed	escardar
to plough [U.S., to plow]	labrar, arar
ploughing [U.S., plowing]	labranza *f.*, labor *f.*
to fallow, to plough up, to turn	roturar
to loosen	mullir
to dig	layar
to earth up	aporcar
to harrow, to rake	rastrillar
to grow	cultivar
to plant	plantar
to transplant, to plant out	transplantar, replantar
seed	semillas *pl.*
to sow	sembrar
broadcasting, broadcast sowing	siembra (*f.*) al voleo
to stake	rodrigar
stake	rodrigón *m.*, tutor *m.*
to prune	podar, desmochar
threshing machine, thresher	trilladora *f.*
winnower, winnowing machine	aventadora *f.*
binder, sheafer	agavilladora *f.*
grader, sorter	clasificadora *f.*
sieve	criba *f.*
winepress	lagar *m.*
milking machine	ordeñadora (*f.*) mecánica
churn	mantequera *f.*

V. Crops. — Cultivos, *m.*

cereals *pl.*, grain	cereales *m. pl.*
coarse grain	cereales (*m. pl.*) secundarios
rye	centeno *m.*
barley	cebada *f.*
oats	avena *f.*
millet	mijo *m.*
sorghum	sorgo *m.*
bran	salvado *m.*
flour, meal	harina *f.*
wheat [U.S., maize]	trigo *m.*
maize [U.S., corn]	maíz *m.*
maize cob [U.S., corn cob]	mazorca *f.*, panoja *f.*, panocha *f.*
rice	arroz *m.*
buckwheat	alforfón *m.*, trigo (*m.*)

to spray	rociar
insecticide	insecticida *m.*
pesticide	pesticida *m.*
weed killer, herbicide	herbicida *m.*
pest	animal (*m.*) dañino
parasite	parásito *m.*
locust	langosta *f.*
termite	termita *m.*
rodent	roedor *m.*
weeds	malas hierbas *f.*
rust	roya *f.*
smut	tizón *m.*, añublo *m.*
mildew	mildiu *m.*
ergot	cornezuelo *m.*
phylloxera	filoxera *f.*

IV. Agricultural equipment and machinery. — Aperos (*m. pl.*) de labranza y maquinaria (*f.*) agrícola.

shovel	pala *f.*
spade	laya *f.*
hoe	azada *f.*, azadón *m.*
weeding hoe	sacho *m.*, escardadora *f.*
mechanical hoe	binadora *f.*
rake	rastrillo *m.*, rastro *m.*
fork	horquilla *f.*
hayfork, pitchfork	bieldo *m.*, horquilla (*f.*) para el heno
scythe	guadaña *f.*
sickle	hoz *f.*
flail	mayal *m.*
billhook, brushhook	podadera *f.*
(field) roller	rodillo *m.*
plough [U.S., plow]	arado *m.*
ridging plough, ridger	aporcadora *f.*
weeding machine	escardadora *f.*
weeder, weeding hook	escarda *f.*, escardillo *m.*
weeding fork	binador *m.*
disc harrow	rastra (*f.*) *or* grada (*f.*) de discos
clod crusher	desterronadora *f.*
tractor	tractor *m.*
sprinkler	regadera *f.*
manure spreader	esparcidora (*f.*) de estiércol
fertilizer distributor	esparcidora (*f.*) de fertilizantes *or* abonos
planter	plantadora *f.*
seed drill, drilling machine	sembradora *f.*
mower	guadañadora *f.*
(power) mower	motosegadora *f.*
harvester, reaper	segadora *f.* [de cereales]
combine (harvester)	segadora (*f.*) trilladora
binder and reaper	segadora (*f.*) agavilladora
harvesting machinery	cosechadoras *f. pl.*
cotton picker	cosechadora (*f.*) de algodón
potato lifter	arrancadora (*f.*) de patatas

	sarraceno
tea	té *m.*
coffee	café *m.*
cocoa	cacao *m.*
coca	coca *f.*
maté, Paraguay tea	mate *m.*
tobacco	tabaco *m.*
hop	lúpulo *m.*
tuber crops	tubérculos *m.*
sugar cane	caña (*f.*) de azúcar
sugar beet	remolacha (*f.*) azucarera
potato	patata *f.* [*Amer.*, papa *f.*]
sweet potato	batata *f.*, boniato *m.*
vegetables	hortalizas *f.*
carrot	zanahoria *f.*
cassava, manioc	mandioca *f.*, yuca *f.*
turnip	nabo *m.*
yam	ñame *m.*
pulses, leguminous plants	leguminosas *f.*
bean	judía *f.* [*Amer.*, frijol *m.*]
pea	guisante *m.* [*Amer.*, arveja *f.*]
chick-pea	garbanzo *m.*
lentil	lenteja *f.*
soya bean [U.S., soybean]	soja *f.*
forage plants	plantas (*f.*) forrajeras
fodder grain	cereales (*m. pl.*) forrajeros
clover	trébol *m.*
canary grass	alpiste *m.*
lucern, lucerne [U.S., alfalfa]	alfalfa *f.*
textile plants	plantas (*f.*) textiles
cotton	algodón *m.*
flax	lino *m.*
hemp	cáñamo *m.*
American agave	pita *f.*, agave *f.*
henequen	henequén *m.*
sisal	sisal *m.*
kapok tree	kapok *m.*
jute	yute *m.*
Manila hemp	abacá *m.*
raffia	rafia *f.*
yucca	yuca *f.*
oil plants	plantas (*f.*) oleaginosas
sunflower	girasol *m.*
groundnut, peanut	cacahuete *m.* [*Amer.*, maní *m.*]
olive	aceituna *f.*, oliva *f.*
olive tree	olivo *m.*
sesame	sésamo *m.*
castor oil plant	ricino *m.*
rape seed	colza *f.*
rubber tree	caucho *m.*
resin plant	planta (*f.*) resinosa
mangrove	mangle *m.*
fruits	frutas *f.*
fruit tree	árbol (*m.*) frutal
grapevine	vid *f.*
grape	uva *f.*

See also HERRAMIENTAS and VEGETABLES

air conditioner [—kən'diʃənə*] n. Acondicionador (*m.*) de aire.
air conditioning [—kən'diʃəniŋ] n. Aire (*m.*) acondicionado. || Climatización, *f.*, acondicionamiento (*m.*) del aire.
air-cool [—ku:l] v. tr. Refrigerar por aire.
air corridor [—ˌkɔridɔ:*] n. Pasillo (*m.*) aéreo.
aircraft [—krɑ:ft] n. Aeronave, *f.* (any flying machine). || Avión, *m.* (aeroplane): *long-range aircraft*, avión de larga distancia *or* transcontinental; *medium-haul aircraft*, avión de distancias medias *or* continental.

— OBSERV. El plural de *aircraft* es *aircraft*.

aircraft carrier [—krɑ:ft'kæriə*] n. Portaaviones, *m. inv.*, portaviones, *m. inv.*
aircraftman [—krɑ:ftmən] or **aircraftsman** [—krɑ:ftsmən] n. MIL. Cabo (*m.*) segundo.
aircrew [—kru:] n. Tripulación, *f.* [de un avión].
air cushion [—kuʃən] n. Colchón (*m.*) de aire.
airdrome [—drəum] n. AVIAT. Aeródromo, *m.*
air duct [—dʌkt] n. Tubo (*m.*) de ventilación.
airfield [—fi:ld] n. AVIAT. Aeródromo, *m.*, campo (*m.*) de aviación.
airfoil [—fɔil] n. AVIAT. Superficie (*f.*) sustentadora.
air force [—fɔ:s] n. MIL. Fuerzas (*f. pl.*) aéreas, aviación, *f.*
airframe [—freim] n. Estructura (*f.*) de avión.
airfreight [—freit] n. Flete (*m.*) por avión.
airfreighter [—freitə*] n. Avión (*m.*) de carga.
air gap [—gæp] n. ELECTR. Entrehierro, *m.*
air gun [—gʌn] n. Pistola (*f.*) de aire comprimido.
air hammer [—'hæmə*] n. Martillo (*m.*) neumático.
air hole [—həul] n. Respiradero, *m.* || U. S. Bache, *m.*
air hostess [—ˌhəustis] n. Azafata, *f.*
airily [—rili] adv. Alegremente, a la ligera.
airiness [—rinis] n. Ligereza, *f.*
airing [—riŋ] n. Ventilación, *f.* || Oreo, *m.* (for drying). || Paseo (*m.*) para tomar el aire. || FIG. Publicación, *f.* (of views, opinions).
air intake [—inteik] n. Toma (*f.*) de aire.
air lane [—lein] n. Ruta (*f.*) aérea.
airless [—lis] adj. Cargado, da; mal ventilado, da (room). || Sin aire *or* viento.
air letter [—ˌletə*] n. Carta (*f.*) aérea.
airlift [—lift] n. Puente (*m.*) aéreo.
airlift [—lift] v. tr. Transportar por un puente aéreo, aerotransportar.
airline [—lain] n. Línea (*f.*) aérea. || Compañía (*f.*) aérea.
airliner [—lainə*] n. Avión (*m.*) de línea.
airlock [—lɔk] n. Burbuja (*f.*) de aire (in a pipe, etc.). || Compartimiento (*m.*) estanco, esclusa (*f.*) de aire (sealed chamber).
airmail [—meil] n. Correo (*m.*) aéreo. || *By airmail*, por avión, por correo aéreo.
airman [—mən] n. Aviador, *m.*

— OBSERV. El plural es *airmen*.

air marshal [—ˌmɑ:ʃəl] n. MIL. Teniente (*m.*) general.
air mattress [—ˌmætris] n. Colchón (*m.*) neumático.
airplane [—plein] n. U. S. AVIAT. Avión, *m.* || U. S. *Airplane modelling*, aeromodelismo, *m.*
air pocket [—ˌpɔkit] n. Bache, *m.*
airport [—pɔ:t] n. Aeropuerto, *m.*
air pressure [—ˌpreʃə*] n. Presión (*f.*) atmosférica.
airproof [—pru:f] adj. Hermético, ca.
air pump [—pʌmp] n. Bomba (*f.*) de aire.
air raid [—reid] n. MIL. Ataque (*m.*) aéreo. || *Air raid shelter*, refugio antiaéreo.
air route [—ru:t] n. Aerovía, *f.*, ruta (*f.*) aérea.
airscrew [—skru:] n. AVIAT. Hélice, *f.*
air-sea base [—'si:beis] n. Base (*f.*) aeronaval.
air shaft [—ʃɑ:ft] n. MIN. Pozo (*m.*) de ventilación.
airship [—ʃip] n. AVIAT. Dirigible, *m.*, aeronave, *f.*
air shuttle [—ʃʌtl] n. Puente (*m.*) aéreo.
airsick [—sik] adj. Mareado, da [en avión].
airsickness [—nis] n. Mareo, *m.*
airspeed [—spi:d] n. AVIAT. Velocidad (*f.*) aerodinámica.
airspraying [—spreiiŋ] n. Fumigación (*f.*) aérea.
airstream [—stri:m] n. Corriente (*f.*) de aire.
airstrip [—strip] n. AVIAT. Pista (*f.*) de aterrizaje.
airtight [—tait] adj. Hermético, ca. || U. S. FIG. Irrecusable, seguro, ra: *an airtight alibi*, una coartada irrecusable.
air valve [—vælv] or **air vent** [—vent] n. Respiradero, *m.* [orificio de aeración].
airway [—wei] n. Aerovía, *f.*, ruta (*f.*) aérea (route). || Línea (*f.*) aérea (airline). || Conducto (*m.*) de ventilación (in mine).
airwoman [—ˌwumən] n. Aviadora, *f.*

— OBSERV. El plural es *airwomen*.

airworthiness [—ˌwə:ðinis] n. AVIAT. Navegabilidad, *f.*
airworthy [—ˌwə:ði] adj. AVIAT. En condiciones de vuelo.

airy [ˈɛəri] adj. Aireado, da; ventilado, da (open to the air). || Espacioso, sa (large). || Ligero, ra (step). || Alegre (cheerful). || Ligero, ra; frívolo, la (lacking proper seriousness). || Vanidoso, sa (self-complacent). || Airoso, sa (graceful, delicate). || Etéreo, a (immaterial).
aisle [ail] n. ARCH. Nave (*f.*) lateral (of a church). | Pasillo, *m.* (between rows of seats).
aitch [eitʃ] n. Hache, *f.* (letter).
aitchbone [ˈeitʃbəun] n. Cadera, *f.* (of animals). || Cadera, *f.* (cut of beef).
Aix-la-Chapelle [ˈeiksla:ʃæˈpel] pr. n. GEOGR. Aquisgrán.
ajar [əˈdʒa:*] adj./adv. Entreabierto, ta; entornado, da.
akimbo [əˈkimbəu] adv. En jarras, en jarra.
akin [əˈkin] adj. Consanguíneo, a (related by blood). || Semejante (similar).
alabaster [ˈæləba:stə*] n. Alabastro, *m.*
— Adj. Alabastrino, na.
alabastrine [ˌæləˈba:strin] adj. Alabastrino, na.
alack [əˈlæk] interj. ¡Ay de mí!, ¡ay!
alacrity [əˈlækriti] n. Diligencia, *f.*, prontitud, *f.*, alacridad, *f.* (infr.).
Aladdin [əˈlædin] pr. n. Aladino, *m.*
Alan [ˈælən] pr. n. Alano, *m.*
Alans [ˈeilənz] or **Alani** [ˈeiləni] pl. pr. n. Alanos, *m.*
alar [ˈeilə*] adj. Del ala. || MED. Axilar.
Alaric [ˈælərik] pr. n. Alarico, *m.*
alarm [əˈla:m] n. Alarma, *f.* (signal, warning, call to arms): *alarm signal*, señal de alarma. || Susto, *m.*, alarma, *f.* (fear). || Timbre (*m.*) del despertador (in the alarm clock). || — *Alarm call*, voz (*f.*) de alarma. || *Burglar alarm*, dispositivo antirrobo. || *False alarm*, falsa alarma. || *To cry out in alarm*, dar un toque de alarma. || *To raise* o *to give the alarm*, dar la alarma.
alarm [əˈla:m] v. tr. Asustar, alarmar (to frighten). || Dar la alarma, alertar (to warn).
alarm bell [—bel] n. Timbre (*m.*) de alarma.
alarm clock [—klɔk] n. Reloj (*m.*) despertador, despertador, *m.*
alarming [əˈla:miŋ] adj. Alarmante.
alarmist [əˈla:mist] n. Alarmista, *m.* & *f.*
alary [ˈeiləri] adj. Del ala.
alas [əˈlæs] interj. ¡Ay de mí!, ¡ay!
alated [ˈeileitid] adj. Alado, da; con alas.
alb [ælb] n. REL. Alba, *f.*
albacore [ˈælbəkɔ:*] n. ZOOL. Albacora, *f.*
Albania [ælˈbeinjə] n. GEOGR. Albania, *f.*
Albanian [—n] adj. Albanés, esa.
— N. Albanés, esa (people). || Albanés, *m.* (language).
albata [ælˈbeitə] n. Metal (*m.*) blanco, alpaca, *f.*, plata (*f.*) alemana.
albatross [ˈælbətrɔs] n. ZOOL. Albatros, *m.*
albeit [ɔ:lˈbi:it] conj. Bien que, aunque (although): *an intelligent, albeit quiet child*, un niño inteligente, bien que callado.
Albert [ˈælbət] pr. n. Alberto, *m.*
Albigenses [ˌælbiˈgensi:z] pl. pr. n. Albigenses, *m.*
Albigensian [ˌælbiˈgensjən] adj. Albigense. || *Albigensian Crusade*, cruzada de los albigenses.
albinism [ˈælbinizəm] n. Albinismo, *m.*
albino [ælˈbi:nəu] adj./n. Albino, na.
Albion [ˈælbjən] pr. n. Albión, *f.*
albite [ˈælbait] n. MIN. Albita, *f.*
album [ˈælbəm] n. Álbum, *m.*
albumen [ˈælbjumin] n. Albúmina, *f.* (white of an egg). || BOT. Albumen. || BIOL. Albúmina, *f.*
albumin [ˈælbjumin] n. BIOL. Albúmina, *f.*
albuminoid [ælˈbju:minɔid] n. CHEM. Albuminoide, *m.*
— Adj. Albuminoideo, a.
albuminose [ælˈbju:minəus] or **albuminous** [ælˈbju:minəs] adj. Albuminoso sa.
albuminuria [ælˈbju:mi:ˈnjuəriə] n. MED. Albuminuria, *f.*
alburnum [ælˈbə:nəm] n. Alburno, *m.*, alborno, *m.*, albura, *f.* (sapwood).
alcaic [ælˈkeiik] adj. Alcaico, ca.
— N. Alcaico, *m.*
alcazar [ˌælkəˈza:] n. Alcázar, *m.*
alchemist [ˈælkimist] n. Alquimista, *m.*
alchemy [ˈælkimi] n. Alquimia, *f.*
alcohol [ˈælkəhɔl] n. Alcohol, *m.*
alcoholate [—eit] n. Alcoholato, *m.*
alcoholic [ˌælkəˈhɔlik] adj./n. Alcohólico, ca.
alcoholism [ˈælkəhɔlizəm] n. Alcoholismo, *m.*
alcoholization [ˌælkəhɔliˈzeiʃən] n. Alcoholización, *f.*
alcoholize [ˌælkəhɔlaiz] v. tr. Alcoholizar.
alcoholometer [ˌælkəhɔˈlɔmitə*] n. Alcoholímetro, *m.*
alcove [ˈælkəuv] n. Nicho, *m.*, hueco, *m.*
Alcyone [ælˈsaiəni] pr. n. Alción, *f.*
aldehyde [ˈældihaid] n. Aldehído, *m.*
alder [ˈɔ:ldə*] n. BOT. Aliso, *m.* || *Alder grove*, alisar, *m.*, aliseda, *f.*
alderman [ˈɔ:ldəmən] n. Concejal, *m.*
ale [eil] n. Ale, *m.*, cerveza (*f.*) inglesa.
aleatory [ˈæliətəri] adj. Aleatorio, ria.
alembic [əˈlembik] n. Alambique, *m.*
alert [əˈlə:t] adj. Alerta, vigilante (vigilant). || Despierto, ta; despabilado, da (awake). || Activo, va.
— N. Alerta, *f.*, alarma, *f.*: *to give the alert*, dar la alerta. || — *On the alert*, alerta. || *To be on the alert*, estar alerta, estar ojo alerta.
alert [əˈlə:t] v. tr. Alertar.

aleurone [əˈljuərən] n. BOT. Aleurona, *f.*
Alexander [ˌæligˈza:ndə*] pr. n. Alejandro, *m.*: *Alexander the Great*, Alejandro Magno.
Alexandria [ˌæligˈza:ndriə] pr. n. GEOGR. Alejandría.
alexandrine [ˌæligˈzændrain] n. Alejandrino, *m.*
— Adj. Alejandrino, na.
— OBSERV. See ALEJANDRINO.
alexia [æˈleksiə] n. MED. Alexia, *f.*
alexipharmic [əˌleksiˈfa:mik] n. Alexifármaco, *m.*
alfa [ˈælfə] n. Esparto, *m.*
alfalfa [ælˈfælfə] n. BOT. Alfalfa, *f.*
Alfred [ˈælfrid] pr. n. Alfredo, *m.*
alfresco [ælˈfreskəu] adj./adv. Al aire libre.
alga [ˈælgə] n. BOT. Alga, *f.*
— OBSERV. El plural de la palabra inglesa es *algae* o *algas*.
algebra [ˈældʒibrə] n. Álgebra, *f.*
algebraic [ˌældʒiˈbreiik] or **algebraical** [—əl] adj. Algebraico, ca; algébrico, ca.
algebraist [ˌældʒiˈbreiist] n. Algebrista, *m.* & *f.*
Algeria [ælˈdʒiəriə] pr. n. GEOGR. Argelia, *f.*
Algerian [—n] adj./n. Argelino, na.
algid [ˈældʒid] adj. Álgido, da: *algid fever*, fiebre álgida.
algidity [ælˈdʒiditi] n. Algidez, *f.*, frialdad, *f.*
Algiers [ælˈdʒiəz] pr. n. GEOGR. Argel.
alguazil [ˌælgwəˈsil] n. Alguacil, *m.*
alias [ˈeiliæs] adv. Alias.
— N. Alias, *m. inv.*
— OBSERV. El plural de la palabra inglesa es *aliases*.
alibi [ˈælibai] n. JUR. Coartada, *f.*: *to provide an alibi*, presentar una coartada. || FAM. Excusa, *f.*, pretexto, *m.*
Alice [ˈælis] pr. n. Alicia, *f.*: *Alice in Wonderland*, Alicia en el país de las maravillas.
alidad [ˈælidæd] or **alidade** [ˈælideid] n. Alidada, *f.*
alien [ˈeiljən] adj. Extranjero, ra. || — *Alien from*, distinto de (differing in character). || *Alien to*, ajeno a (opposed in nature).
— N. Extranjero, ra (foreigner). || Extraño, ña (outsider).
— OBSERV. *Alien* se aplica sobre todo a los súbditos de otro país que el de uno mismo. *Foreigner* se dice del extranjero por su lengua y su cultura. *Stranger*, forastero o desconocido, se dice del que viene de otro sitio o de la persona a quien no se conocía antes.
alienable [ˈeiljənəbl] adj. Enajenable, alienable.
alienate [ˈeiljəneit] v. tr. Enajenar, alienar (property). || Apartar (from one's friends).
alienation [ˌeiljəˈneiʃən] n. Alienación, *f.*, enajenación, *f.* (transfer, insanity). || Apartamiento, *m.* (from one's friends).
alienist [ˈeiljənist] n. MED. Alienista, *m.* & *f.*
aliform [ˈælifɔ:m] adj. Aliforme.
alight [əˈlait] v. intr. Apearse, bajar (to get down). || Posarse (birds). || Aterrizar, posarse (aircraft).
alight [əˈlait] adj./adv. Ardiendo, da (on fire). || Encendido, da (lit up). || FIG. Encendido, da: *a face alight with happiness*, una cara encendida de alegría. | Encandilado, da: *eyes alight with love*, ojos encandilados de amor. || *To set alight*, incendiar, pegar fuego a.
align [əˈlain] v. tr. Alinear (to line up, to bring into line). || *To align o.s. with*, ponerse del lado de.
— V. intr. Alinearse.
alignment [—mənt] n. Alineación, *f.*, alineamiento, *m.* || — *In alignment*, alineados. || U. S. AUT. *Wheel alignment*, convergencia (*f.*) de las ruedas delanteras.
alike [əˈlaik] adv. De la misma forma *or* manera *or* modo: *we think alike*, pensamos del mismo modo. || *Winter and summer alike*, en invierno como en verano, lo mismo en invierno que en verano.
— Adj. Semejante, parecido, da: *they are all alike*, todos son parecidos. || — *It's all alike to me*, todo me da igual. || *To look alike*, parecerse.
aliment [ˈælimənt] n. Alimento, *m.*
aliment [ˈælimənt] v. tr. Alimentar.
alimental [ˌæliˈmentəl] adj. Alimenticio, cia.
alimentary [ˌæliˈmentəri] adj. Alimenticio, cia. || *Alimentary canal*, tubo digestivo.
alimentation [ˌælimenˈteiʃən] n. Alimentación, *f.*
alimony [ˈæliməni] n. Pensión (*f.*) alimenticia.
aline [əˈlain] v. tr. See ALIGN.
alinement [əˈlainmənt] n. See ALIGNMENT.
aliped [ˈæliped] adj. Quiróptero, ra.
— N. Quiróptero, *m.*
aliquant [ˈælikwənt] adj. Alicuanta.
aliquot [ˈælikwɔt] adj. Alicuota.
— N. Parte (*f.*) alícuota.
alive [əˈlaiv] adj. Vivo, va (living, lively, in existence). || Lleno de, rebosante de (swarming). || Sensible (to an impression). || Atento, ta (to one's interests). || Consciente (conscious). || FIG. Activo, va; enérgico, ca. || Ardiendo (fire). || Del mundo: *the fastest man alive*, el hombre más rápido del mundo. || — *Alive and kicking*, vivito y coleando. || *Any man alive*, cualquier hombre [existente]. || *Dead or alive*, vivo o muerto. || *It's good to be alive!*, ¡qué bueno es vivir! || *Look alive!*, ¡muévete!, ¡menéate! || FAM. *Man alive!*, ¡hombre!, ¡por Dios! || *To be alive to*, darse cuenta de, ser consciente de (to be conscious of). || *To come alive*, cobrar vida. || *To come alive again*, revivir. || *To keep alive*, hacer perdurar (memory), sobrevivir (s.o.).

alkalescence [ˌælkəˈlesns] n. CHEM. Alcalescencia, *f.*
alkalescent [ˌælkəˈlesnt] adj. Alcalescente.
alkali [ˈælkəlai] n. CHEM. Álcali, *m.* || *Alkali metals*, metales alcalinos.

— OBSERV. El plural de *alkali* es *alkalis* o *alkalies*.

alkalify [ˈælkælifai] v. tr. CHEM. Alcalinizar.
alkalimeter [ælkəˈlimitə*] n. CHEM. Alcalímetro, *m.*
alkaline [ˈælkəlain] adj. CHEM. Alcalino, na.
alkaline earth [—ˌəːθ] n. CHEM. Alcalinotérreo, *m.*
alkaline-earth [—ˌəːθ] adj. Alcalinotérreo, a.
alkalinity [ˌælkəˈliniti] n. CHEM. Alcalinidad, *f.*
alkalinization [ˌælkəliniˈzeiʃən] n. CHEM. Alcalización *f.*, alcalinización, *f.*
alkalinize [ˈælkəlinaiz] or **alkalize** [ˈælkəlaiz] v. tr. Alcalizar, alcalinizar.
alkaloid [ˈælkəlɔid] n. CHEM. Alcaloide, *m.*
— Adj. Alcaloideo, a; alcaloide.
alkalosis [ˌælkəˈləusis] n. MED. Alcalosis, *f.*
all [ɔːl] adj. Todo, da: *all the harvest*, toda la cosecha; *all our friends*, todos nuestros amigos; *all the others*, todos los demás; *beyond all doubt*, fuera de toda duda. || Cualquiera (any whatever): *at all hours*, a cualquier hora. || — *All day*, todo el día. || *All men*, todos los hombres. || *All people*, todos. || FIG. *All this and heaven too*, el oro y el moro. || *All told*, todo incluido. || *And all that*, y todo lo demás. || *For all*, con todo, da: *for all his wealth, he was not happy*, con toda su riqueza no era feliz. || *In all sincerity*, con toda sinceridad. || *Of all people*, precisamente: *you, of all people!*, ¡tú precisamente!
— Adv. Completamente, todo, da: *he was all alone*, estaba completamente solo; *she was all covered in mud*, estaba toda cubierta de barro. || — *All along*, see ALONG. || *All along the line*, en toda la línea. || *All at once*, de repente. || *All but*, casi: *he was all but dead*, estaba casi muerto. || *All in*, exhausto, ta; rendido, da. || *All of*, nada menos que: *to cost all of 1 000 pesetas*, costar nada menos que 1 000 pesetas. || *All out*, a toda velocidad (full speed), a fondo, completamente, con todas sus fuerzas: *to go all out*, entregarse a fondo. || *All over*, por todas partes (everywhere), por todo: *all over the house*, por toda la casa; completamente (completely), terminado, da; acabado, da (finished), muy: *that is you all over*, eso es muy tuyo; cien por cien: *he is his father all over*, es su padre cien por cien. || *All set*, listo, ta; dispuesto, ta. || *All the*, mucho: *you'll be all the better for a night's sleep*, estarás mucho mejor después de haber dormido. || *All the more*, más aún. || *All the same*, a pesar de todo. || *All the worse*, tanto peor. || *At all*, algo; *did you know him at all?*, ¿le conocías algo? || SP. *Five all*, cinco a cinco, empatado a 5. || *For good and all*, para siempre, de una vez. || *If he comes at all*, si es que viene. || *It's all but impossible*, es punto menos que imposible. || *Not at all*, nada en absoluto: *did you like it?* — *Not at all*, ¿te gustó? — Nada en absoluto; no hay de qué: *thank you.* — *Not at all*, gracias. — No hay de qué; nada: *it's not at all easy*, no es nada fácil; de ninguna manera, en absoluto (certainly not). || SP. *Score of 15 all*, un tanteo de 15 iguales. || *That's all very well but...*, me parece muy bien pero... || *To be all for*, estar a favor de, parecerle a uno muy bien que. || *To be all the same*, ser igual, dar lo mismo.
— Pron. Todo, da: *when all had been sold*, una vez que se vendió todo; *all decided to go*, todos decidieron ir. || Lo único: *that's all I could do to help him*, es lo único que pude hacer para ayudarle. || — *Above all*, sobre todo. || *After all*, después de todo. || *All in all*, considerándolo todo. || *All of*, todo, da: *all of the books*, todos los libros. || *All of us*, todos nosotros. || *All one*, todo uno. || *All that*, todo lo que: *all that I have*, todo lo que tengo. || *All who*, todos aquellos que. || *And all*, y todo: *there he was hat and all*, allí estaba con sombrero y todo. || *First of all*, ante todo, primero. || *For all*, a pesar de: *for all he may say, I don't believe him*, a pesar de lo que diga no lo creo; en lo que: *for all I care*, en lo que a mí concierne. || *For all I know*, que yo sepa. || *In all*, en total. || *Is that all?*, ¿nada más? || *It's all one*, es igual. || *It was all I could do not to laugh*, faltó poco para que me echase a reír. || *Most of all*, sobre todo, más que nada. || *One and all*, todos y cada uno. || *That's all*, eso es todo. || *When all is said and done*, a fin de cuentas.
— N. Todo *m.*, todos *m. pl.*, todas *f. pl.*: *to stake one's all*, jugárselo todo.
Allah [ˈælə] pr. n. REL. Alá, *m.*
all-American [ˈɔːləˈmerikən] adj. Típicamente americano, na. || *The all-American team*, el mejor equipo americano.
Allan [ˈælən] pr. n. Alano, *m.*
allantois [əˈlæntəuis] n. ANAT. Alantoides, *f.*

— OBSERV. El plural de *allantois* es *allantoides*.

all-around [ˈɔːləˈraund] adj. U. S. Completo, ta.
allay [əˈlei] v. tr. Aliviar (pain). || Calmar (fear, suspicion).
all-clear [ˈɔːlˈkliə*] n. Final (*m.*) de la alarma.
allegation [ˌæleˈgeiʃən] n. JUR. Alegato, *m.*, alegación, *f.*
allege [əˈledʒ] v. tr. JUR. Alegar. || Pretender.
alleged [—d] adj. Prentendido, da; supuesto, ta.
allegiance [əˈliːdʒəns] n. Lealtad, *f.*, devoción, *f.* || Vasallaje, *m.*
allegoric [ˌæleˈgɔrik] adj. Alegórico, ca.
allegorical [—əl] adj. Alegórico, ca.
allegorize [ˈæligəraiz] v. tr. Alegorizar.
allegory [ˈæligəri] n. Alegoría, *f.*
allegretto [ˌæliˈgretəu] adv. MUS. Allegretto, alegreto.
— N. Allegretto, *m.*, alegreto, *m.*
allegro [əˈleigrəu] adv. MUS. Allegro, alegro.
— N. Allegro, *m.*, alegro, *m.*
alleluia [ˌæliˈluːjə] n. REL. Aleluya, *f.*
all-embracing [ɔːlimˈbreisiŋ] adj. Global, que lo abarca todo.
Allen [ˈælin] pr. n. Alano, *m.*
allergic [əˈləːdʒik] adj. MED. Alérgico, ca: *allergic to cats*, alérgico a los gatos.
allergist [ˈælədʒist] n. Médico (*m.*) especialista en alergias.
allergy [ˈælədʒi] n. MED. Alergia, *f.*
alleviate [əˈliːvieit] v. tr. Aliviar, mitigar.
alleviation [əˌliːviˈeiʃən] n. Alivio, *m.*
alleviative [əˈliːviətiv] adj. Aliviador, ra.
— N. Paliativo, *m.*
alleviatory [əˈliːviətəri] adj. Aliviador, ra.
alley [ˈæli] n. Callejón, *m.* (narrow lane). || Paseo, *m.* (in a park). || SP. Bolera, *f.* (for bowling). || Canica (*f.*) de alabastro (marble). || — *Blind alley*, callejón (*m.*) sin salida. || FIG. *That is right up* o *down my alley*, eso es lo mío.
alley cat [—kæt] n. U. S. Gato (*m.*) callejero.
alleyway [—wei] n. Callejón, *m.*
All Fools' Day [ˈɔːlˈfuːlzdei] n. Día (*m.*) de los Inocentes.

— OBSERV. En Inglaterra este día es el uno de abril y no el veintiocho de diciembre como en España.

Allhallows [ˈɔːlˈhæləuz] n. Día (*m.*) de Todos los Santos.
alliance [əˈlaiəns] n. Alianza, *f.*: *alliance treaty*, pacto de alianza. || *The Holy Alliance*, la Santa Alianza.
allied [əˈlaid] adj. Aliado, da (joined in alliance). || Conexo, xa; relacionado, da (related).
Allies (the) [ˈælaiz] pl. n. Los aliados, *m.*
alligation [æliˈgeiʃən] n. Aligación, *f.*, regla (*f.*) de aligación.
alligator [ˈæligeitə*] n. ZOOL. Caimán, *m.*
alligator pear [—pɛə*] n. BOT. Aguacate, *m.*
all-in [ˈɔːl-in] adj. Global. || — *All-in charge*, precio (*m.*) todo incluido. || SP. *All-in wrestling*, lucha (*f.*) libre.
alliterate [əˈlitəreit] v. intr. Escribir *or* hablar usando aliteraciones.
alliteration [əˌlitəˈreiʃən] n. Aliteración, *f.*
alliterative [əˈlitərətiv] adj. Aliterado, da.
all-knowing [ˈɔːlˈnəuiŋ] adj. Omnisciente.
all-night [ˈɔːlˈnait] adj. Abierto toda la noche (bar). || Que dura toda la noche (meeting, etc.).
allocate [ˈæləkeit] v. tr. Asignar. || Repartir (to distribute).
allocation [ˌæləˈkeiʃən] n. Asignación, *f.* || Reparto, *m.* (distribution). || Lo asignado (thing allocated).
allocution [ˌæləuˈkjuːʃən] n. Alocución, *f.*
allodial [əˈləudjəl] adj. JUR. Alodial.
allodium [əˈləudjəm] n. JUR. Alodio, *m.*
allopath [ˈæləupæθ] n. MED. Alópata, *m.* & *f.*
allopathic [ˌæləuˈpæθik] adj. MED. Alopático, ca.
allopathist [əˈlɔpəθist] n. MED. Alópata, *m.* & *f.*
allopathy [əˈlɔpəθi] n. MED. Alopatía, *f.*
allot [əˈlɔt] v. tr. Asignar.
allotment [—mənt] n. Asignación, *f.* (allocation). || Parcela, *f.* (ground). || Reparto, *m.* || Parte, *f.* (share). || U. S. Parte (*f.*) del sueldo de un miembro de las fuerzas armadas, que se envía a una persona designada por él.
allotropic [ˌæləˈtrɔpik] adj. Alotrópico, ca.
allotropy [əˈlɔtrəpi] n. CHEM. Alotropía, *f.*
all-out [ˈɔːlˈaut] adj. Acérrimo, ma; incondicional (unreserved). || Máximo, ma; supremo, ma (effort).
allover [ɔːlˈəuvə*] adj. Repetido por toda la tela [dibujo].
allow [əˈlau] v. tr. Permitir, dejar (to permit). || Autorizar, permitir: *smoking is allowed*, se permite fumar. || Conceder, dar (to grant as a concession, to permit to have). || Dar (time). || Admitir, conceder (to admit). || Admitir, reconocer: *to allow sth. to be true*, reconocer que algo es verdad. || Asignar (to pay regularly). || Dejar: *allow one inch for the margin*, deja una pulgada para el margen. || *To allow o.s.*, permitirse.
— V. intr. *To allow for*, tener en cuenta: *allowing for his stupidity*, teniendo en cuenta su estupidez; dejar un margen para (to leave a margin for): *to allow for unexpected expenses*, dejar un margen para gastos imprevistos. || *To allow of*, admitir.
allowable [əˈlauəbl] adj. Admisible.
allowance [əˈlauəns] n. Pensión, *f.*, renta, *f.* (sum of money paid to a dependant). || COMM. Rebaja, *f.*, descuento, *m.* || Ayuda, *f.*, subsidio, *m.*: *family allowance*, subsidios familiares. || Subvención, *f.* (subsidy). || Concesión, *f.* || Dinero (*m.*) de bolsillo. || Permiso, *m.*, autorización, *f.* || TECH. Tolerancia, *f.* || — *Subsistence allowance*, dietas, *f. pl.* || *To make allowances for*, tener en cuenta (to take into consideration), ser indulgente con (person).
alloy [ˈælɔi] n. CHEM. Aleación, *f.* || FIG. Mezcla, *f.*
alloy [əˈlɔi] v. tr. CHEM. Alear. || FIG. Alterar.

all-powerful [ɔ:lˈpauəful] adj. Omnipotente.
all-purpose [ˈɔ:lˈpə:pəs] adj. Para todo uso, universal.
all right [ˈɔ:lˈrait] adj. See RIGHT.
all-round [ˈɔ:lˈraund] adj. Completo, ta.
All Saints' Day [ˈɔ:lˈseintsdei] n. Día (*m.*) de Todos los Santos.
All Souls' Day [ˈɔ:lˈsəulzdei] n. Día (*m.*) de los Difuntos.
allspice [ˈɔ:lspais] n. Pimienta (*f.*) de Jamaica.
all-star [ˈɔ:lstɑ:*] adj. De primeras figuras.
all-time [ˈɔ:ltaim] adj. Nunca visto, ta: *an all-time success*, un éxito nunca visto. || Nunca alcanzado, da: *an all-time record*, un récord nunca alcanzado.
allude [əˈlu:d] v. intr. Aludir.
allure [əˈljuə*] n. Atractivo, *m.*
allure [əˈljuə*] v. tr. Atraer. || Seducir (to seduce). || Apartar (from one's duty).
allurement [—mənt] n. Atractivo, *m.*
alluring [—iŋ] adj. Atractivo, va; seductor, ra.
allusion [əˈlu:ʒən] n. Alusión, *f.*: *she said in allusion to*, dijo haciendo alusión a.
allusive [əˈlu:siv] adj. Alusivo, va.
alluvial [əˈlu:vjəl] adj. GEOL. Aluvial, de aluvión.
alluvion [əˈlu:vjən] n. GEOL. Aluvión, *m.*
alluvium [əˈlu:vjəm] n. GEOL. Aluvión, *m.*

— OBSERV. El plural de *alluvium* es *alluviums* o *alluvia*.

all-weather [ˈɔ:lˈweðə*] adj. Para todo tiempo.
ally [ˈæli] n. Canica (*f.*) de alabastro (marble).
ally [ˈælai] n. Aliado, da.
ally [əˈlai] v. intr. Aliarse.
— V. tr. Emparentar con. || Hacer alianza con.
almagest [ˈælmədʒest] n. Almagesto, *m.*
alma mater [ˈælməˈmeitə*] n. Alma máter, *f.*
almanac [ˈɔ:lmənæk] n. Almanaque, *m.*
almandine [ˈælməndi:n] n. MIN. Almandina, *f.*
almandite [ˈælməndait] n. MIN. Almandina, *f.*
almemar [ælˈmi:mɑ:*] n. REL. Almimbar, *m.*
almemor [ælˈmi:mɔ:*] n. REL. Almimbar, *m.*
almightiness [ɔlˈmaitinəs] n. Omnipotencia, *f.*
almighty [ɔ:lˈmaiti] adj. Todopoderoso, sa; omnipotente. || FAM. Imponente, enorme. || REL. *The Almighty*, El Todopoderoso, el Altísimo.
almond [ˈɑ:mənd] n. BOT. Almendro, *m.* (tree). | Almendra, *f.* (nut). || — *Burnt almonds*, almendras tostadas. || *Sugar* o *sugared almond*, peladilla, *f.*
almond-eyed [—aid] adj. De ojos rasgados.
almond tree [—tri:] n. Almendro, *m.*
almoner [ˈɑ:mənə*] n. Asistenta (*f.*) social. || Limosnero, *m.* (of church).
Almoravid or **Almoravide** [ˌælməˈrævid] adj./n. Almorávide.
almost [ˈɔ:lməust] adv. Casi.
alms [ɑ:mz] pl. n. Limosna, *f. sing.*
alms box [—bɔks] n. Cepillo (*m.*) para los pobres.
almshouse [—haus] n. Asilo (*m.*) de ancianos.
alodial [əˈləudjəl] adj. JUR. Alodial.
alodium [əˈləudjəm] n. JUR. Alodio, *m.*
aloe [ˈæləu] n. BOT. Áloe, *m.* || — Pl. MED. Áloe, *m. sing.* || *Aloe juice*, acíbar, *m.*
aloft [əˈlɔft] adj./adv. Arriba (up). || En el aire, en alto (up in the air). || MAR. En la arboladura. || En vuelo (plane).
alone [əˈləun] adj. Solo, la: *I was alone*, estaba solo; *all alone*, completamento solo. || Único, ca: *is he alone in speaking so?*, ¿es el único en hablar así? || — *Let alone*, y mucho menos: *I have not twopence, let alone two pounds*, no tengo dos peniques y mucho menos dos libras; sin hablar de. || *To leave* o *to let alone*, dejar en paz (to leave in peace), dejar solo (to leave unaccompanied). || *To stand alone*, ser único (to be unique).
— Adv. Sólo, solamente (exclusively): *that alone can help us*, sólo eso nos puede ayudar.
along [əˈlɔŋ] prep. Por: *I was walking along the street*, iba por la calle. || A lo largo de: *a hedge grows along the path*, hay un seto a lo largo del sendero. || Según (according to).
— Adv. *All along*, constantemente, siempre (all the time), desde el principio (from the beginning). || *Along with*, junto con. || *Bring your guitar along*, tráete la guitarra. || *Come along with me*, venga conmigo. || *Move along, please!*, ¡circulen, por favor! || *To carry along*, llevar consigo. || *To get along*, poder arreglárselas. || *To get along (well) with s.o.*, llevarse bien con alguien. || U. S. *To get along with sth.*, seguir, continuar: *get along with your work!*, ¡sigue trabajando! | *To go along with*, estar de acuerdo con (to agree), acompañar.
alongshore [—ʃɔ:*] adv. A lo largo de la costa.
alongside [—ˈsaid] prep. Junto a, al lado de.
— Adv. Al lado. || MAR. De costado. || *To come alongside*, atracar.
aloof [əˈlu:f] adv. Lejos (apart). || A distancia (at a distance). || *To keep aloof*, mantenerse apartado (*from*, de).
— Adj. Reservado, da.
aloofness [—nis] n. Reserva, *f.*
alopecia [æləˈpi:ʃiə] n. MED. Alopecia, *f.*
aloud [əˈlaud] adv. Alto, en voz alta. || *To cry aloud for*, pedir a gritos: *this situation is crying aloud for a solution*, esta situación está pidiendo a gritos una solución.
alow [əˈləu] adv. MAR. Abajo.
alp [ælp] n. Montaña, *f.* (mountain).
alpaca [ælˈpækə] n. Alpaca, *f.*
alpenstock [ˈælpinstɔk] n. Alpenstock, *m.*, bastón (*m.*) de montañero.
alpha [ˈælfə] n. Alfa, *f.*: *alpha rays*, rayos alfa.
alphabet [ˈælfəbit] n. Alfabeto, *m.*
alphabetic [ˌælfəˈbetik] or **alphabetical** [—əl] adj. Alfabético, ca: *in alphabetical order*, por orden alfabético.
alphabetize [ˈælfəbetaiz] v. tr. Alfabetizar. || Poner en orden alfabético.
alphameric [ælfəˈmerik] or **alphanumeric** [ˌælfənju'-merik] adj. Alfanumérico, ca.
Alphonsine [ælˈfɔnsi:n] adj. *Alphonsine tables*, tablas alfonsinas.
alpine [ˈælpain] adj. Alpino, na; alpestre.
alpinism [ˈælpinizəm] n. Alpinismo, *m.*
alpinist [ˈælpinist] n. Alpinista, *m.* & *f.*
alpist [ˈælpist] n. BOT. Alpiste, *m.* (canary grass).
Alps [ælps] pl. pr. n. GEOGR. Alpes *m.*
already [ɔ:lˈredi] adv. Ya.
alright [ˈɔ:lˈrait] adv. See RIGHT (ALL).
Alsace [ˈælsæs] pr. n. GEOGR. Alsacia, *f.*
Alsatian [ælˈseiʃjən] adj. Alsaciano, na.
— N. Alsaciano, na (inhabitant of Alsace). || Pastor (*m.*) alemán (dog).
also [ˈɔ:lsəu] adv. También (too, as well). || Además (moreover).
also-ran [—ræn] n. Caballo (*m.*) que no se coloca en una carrera (horse racing). || Candidato (*m.*) vencido en una elección (in an election). || FAM. Nulidad, *f.* (nonentity).
Altaic [ælˈteiik] adj. Altaico, ca.
altar [ˈɔ:ltə*] n. REL. Altar, *m.* || — *Altar boy*, monaguillo, *m.* || *Altar cloth*, sabanilla, *f.*, mantel, *m.* || *High altar*, altar mayor. || FIG. *On the altars of*, en aras de.
altarpiece [ˈɔ:ltəpi:s] n. Retablo, *m.*
altar stone [ˈɔ:ltəstəun] n. Ara, *f.*
alter [ˈɔ:ltə*] v. tr. Cambiar, modificar, alterar. || Retocar (a garment). || ARCH. Reformar. || MAR. *To alter course*, cambiar de rumbo.
— V. intr. Cambiar (to change). || *To alter for the worse*, ir cada vez peor, empeorar.
alterability [ˌɔ:ltərəˈbiliti] n. Alterabilidad, *f.*
alteration [ˌɔ:ltəˈreiʃən] n. Cambio, *m.*, modificación, *f.*, transformación, *f.* || ARCH. Reforma, *f.* || Retoque, *m.* (of a garment).
altercate [ˈɔ:ltə:keit] v. intr. Altercar.
altercation [ˌɔ:ltə:ˈkeiʃən] n. Altercado, *m.*
alternant [ɔ:lˈtə:nənt] adj. Alternante.
alternate [ɔ:lˈtə:nit] adj. Alterno, na: *alternate leaves*, hojas alternas; *alternate angles*, ángulos alternos. || *On alternate days*, en días alternos, cada dos días.
— N. Sustituto, *m.*, suplente, *m.* (substitute).
alternate [ˈɔ:ltə:neit] v. tr./intr. Alternar.
alternately [ɔ:lˈtə:nitli] adv. Alternativamente.
alternating [ˈɔ:ltə:neitiŋ] adj. Alternativo, va: *the alternating swing of the pendulum*, el movimiento alternativo del péndulo. || Alterno, na (current).
alternation [ˌɔ:ltə:ˈneiʃən] n. Alternancia, *f.*, alternación, *f.* || *In alternation*, alternativamente.
alternative [ɔ:lˈtə:nətiv] adj. Alternativo, va. || GRAMM. *Alternative conjunction*, conjunción disyuntiva.
— N. Alternativa, *f.* (choice between two things). || *We have no alternative*, no tenemos más remedio.
alternator [ˈɔ:ltə:ˌneitə*] n. ELECTR. Alternador, *m.*
although [ɔ:lˈðəu] conj. Aunque, a pesar de que: *although very old, he is still very active*, aunque muy viejo aún es muy activo; *I'll do it although it cost me my life*, lo haré aunque me cueste la vida; *although it was raining I went out*, salí aunque estaba lloviendo.
— OBSERV. See THOUGH.

altimeter [ˈæltimi:tə*] n. Altímetro, *m.*
altimetry [ælˈtimitri] n. Altimetría, *f.*
altitude [ˈæltitju:d] n. Altitud, *f.* (height above sea level). || MATH. ASTR. Altura, *f.* || — Pl. Alturas, *f.*
alto [ˈæltəu] n. MUS. Contralto, *m.*
altogether [ˌɔ:ltəˈgeðə*] adv. Completamente, del todo (completely). || En total, en conjunto (on the whole). || FAM. *In the altogether*, en cueros vivos.
altruism [ˈæltruizəm] n. Altruismo, *m.*
altruist [ˈæltruist] adj./n. Altruista.
altruistic [ˌæltruˈistik] adj. Altruista.
alum [ˈæləm] n. CHEM. Alumbre, *m.*
alumina [əˈlju:minə] n. CHEM. Alúmina, *f.*
aluminate [əˈlju:mineit] v. tr. TECH. Aluminar.
aluminium [ˌæljuˈminjəm] n. Aluminio, *m.*
aluminothermy [əˈlju:minəˌθə:mi] n. CHEM. Aluminotermia, *f.*
aluminous [əˈlju:minəs] adj. CHEM. Aluminoso, sa.
aluminum [əˈlu:minəm] n. U. S. Aluminio, *m.*
alumna [əˈlʌmnə] n. U. S. Antigua alumna, *f.*

— OBSERV. El plural de la palabra inglesa es *alumnae*.

alumnus [əˈlʌmnəs] n. U. S. Antiguo alumno, *m.*

— OBSERV. El plural de la palabra inglesa es *alumni*.

alunite [ˈæljunait] n. MIN. Alunita, *f.*
alveolar [ælvˈiələ*] adj. Alveolar.
alveolate [ælˈviəlit] adj. Alveolado, da.
alveolus [ælˈviələs] n. Alveolo, *m.*, alvéolo, *m.*

— OBSERV. El plural de *alveolus* es *alveoli*.

always ['ɔ:lweiz] adv. Siempre.
am [æm] pres. See BE.
a.m. ['ei'em] adv. De la mañana.
Amadeus [æmə'di:əs] pr. n. Amadeo, *m.*
amadou ['æmədu:] n. Yesca, *f.*
amalgam [ə'mælgəm] n. Amalgama, *f.*
amalgamate [ə'mælgəmeit] v. tr. Amalgamar.
— V. intr. Amalgamarse.
amalgamation [əˌmælgə'meiʃən] n. Amalgamación, *f.*
amanita [æmə'naitə] n. Amanita, *f.* (fungus).
amanuensis [əˌmænju'ensis] n. Amanuense, *m.*

— OBSERV. El plural de *amanuensis* es *amanuenses*.

amaranth ['æmərænθ] n. BOT. Amaranto, *m.*
amaryllis [ˌæmə'rilis] n. BOT. Amarilis, *f.*
amass [ə'mæs] v. tr. Amontonar, acumular.
amateur ['æmətə*] adj./n. Aficionado, da; amateur.
amateurish ['æmə'tə:riʃ] adj. Aficionado, da; amateur. || De aficionado.
amateurism [æmə'tə:rizəm] n. Calidad (*f.*) de aficionado *or* de no profesional.
amative ['æmətiv] adj. Apasionado, da; amatorio, ria.
amatory ['æmətəri] adj. Amoroso, sa (feelings). || Amatorio, ria (letter). || Erótico, ca (poem).
amaurosis [ˌæmɔ:'rəusis] n. MED. Amaurosis, *f.*
amaze [ə'meiz] v. tr. Asombrar. || *To be amazed at*, estar *or* quedarse asombrado de.
amazement [—mənt] n. Asombro, *m.*
amazing [—iŋ] adj. Asombroso, sa.
amazon ['æməzən] n. Amazona, *f.* || FIG. Marimacho, *m.* (virago).
Amazon ['æməzən] pr. n. GEOGR. Amazonas, *m.*
Amazonian [ˌæmə'zəunjən] adj. Amazónico, ca.
ambages ['æmbidʒi:z] pl. n. Ambages, *m.* (circumlocution).
ambassador [æm'bæsədə*] n. Embajador, *m.*; *ambassador extraordinary, plenipotentiary*, embajador extraordinario, plenipotenciario.
ambassadorship [æm'bæsədəʃip] n. Embajada, *f.*
ambassadress [æm'bæsədris] n. Embajadora, *f.*
amber ['æmbə*] n. BOT. Ámbar, *m.* || Ámbar, *m.* (colour of traffic light).
— Adj. Ambarino, na.
ambergris ['æmbəgris] n. Ámbar (*m.*) gris.
ambidexter [ˌæmbi'dekstə*] adj./n. Ambidextro, tra. || FIG. Falso, sa; hipócrita.
ambidextrous [ˌæmbi'dekstrəs] adj. Ambidextro, tra. || FIG. Doble, falso, sa (two-faced).
ambience ['æmbjəns] n. Ambiente, *m.*
ambient ['æmbjənt] adj. Ambiente.
ambiguity ['æmbi'gju:iti] n. Ambigüedad, *f.*
ambiguous [æm'bigjuəs] adj. Ambiguo, gua.
ambit ['æmbit] n. Ámbito, *m.* || Límites, *m. pl.* (of a land). || Casco, *m.* (of a town).
ambition [æm'biʃən] n. Ambición, *f.*
ambition [æm'biʃən] v. tr. Ambicionar.
ambitious [æm'biʃəs] adj. Ambicioso, sa. || *To be ambitious of*, ambicionar.
ambivalence [æm'bivələns] n. Ambivalencia, *f.*
ambivalent [æm'bivələnt] adj. Ambivalente.
amble ['æmbl] n. Ambladura, *f.* (of a horse).
amble ['æmbl] v. intr. Amblar (a horse). || Andar sin prisa, deambular (a person).
amblyopia [ˌæmbli'əupjə] n. MED. Ambliopía, *f.*
ambo ['æmbəu] n. ARCH. Ambón, *m.* (pulpit).
ambrosia [æm'brəuzjə] n. Ambrosía, *f.*
ambrosial [—l] adj. Ambrosiaco, ca.
Ambrosian [—n] adj. REL. Ambrosiano, na.
ambry ['æmbri] n. Armario, *m.* (cupboard).
ambulance ['æmbjuləns] n. Ambulancia, *f.* || *Ambulance man*, ambulanciero, *m.*
ambulatory ['æmbjulətəri] adj. Ambulatorio, ria. || U.S. MED. No encamado, da.
— N. ARCH. Deambulatorio, *m.*
ambuscade [ˌæmbəs'keid] n. MIL. Emboscada, *f.*
ambush ['æmbuʃ] n. MIL. Emboscada, *f.*: *to lay an ambush*, tender una emboscada. || FIG. Asechanza, *f.*, emboscada, *f.* || *To lie in ambush*, estar emboscado.
ambush ['æmbuʃ] v. tr. Tender una emboscada. || *To be ambushed*, caer en una emboscada.
— V. intr. Emboscarse.
ameba [ə'mi:bə] n. ZOOL. Ameba, *f.*, amiba, *f.*
ameer [e'miə] n. Emir, *m.*
ameliorate [ə'mi:ljəreit] v. tr./intr. Mejorar (to improve).
amelioration [əˌmi:ljə'reiʃən] n. Mejora, *f.*, mejoría, *f.*, mejoramiento, *m.*
amen ['ɑ:'men] interj. Amén.
amenability [əˌmi:nə'biliti] n. Sensibilidad, *f.* (responsiveness). || Responsabilidad, *f.* (responsibility). || Docilidad, *f.* (docility).
amenable [ə'mi:nəbl] adj. Sensible (responsive): *amenable to advice* o *to suggestions*, sensible a los consejos *or* a las sugerencias. || Que se puede someter: *amenable to high temperatures*, que se puede someter a temperaturas elevadas. || Responsable (answerable): *amenable to the law*, responsable ante la ley. || Sujeto, ta: *amenable to a fine*, sujeto a multa. || Dócil, sumiso, sa (obedient). || — *Amenable to argument*, que se deja convencer. || *Amenable to reason*, capaz de avenirse a razones.
amend [ə'mend] v. tr. Enmendar: *to amend the constitution, a law, a text*, enmendar la constitución, una ley, un texto. || Rectificar, corregir (to rectify). || Mejorar (to improve).
— V. intr. Enmendarse (to improve).
amendable [—əbl] adj. Enmendable.
amendment [—mənt] n. Enmienda, *f.*: *to propose an amendment*, proponer una enmienda; *the amendment of a text, a law*, la enmienda de un texto, una ley. || Rectificación, *f.*, corrección, *f.*
amends [—z] pl. n. Reparación, *f. sing.*, compensación, *f. sing.* || — *To make amends for sth.*, compensar algo (to compensate for), reparar (to put right): *to make amends for an offence*, reparar una ofensa. || *To make amends to s.o. for sth.*, compensar a alguien de algo (to compensate), indemnizar a alguien por algo (to indemnify).
amenity [ə'mi:niti] n. Amenidad, *f.* (pleasantness). || Amabilidad, *f.* (of a person). || Comodidad, *f.*: *shower, telephone and other amenities*, ducha, teléfono y otras comodidades. || — Pl. Etiqueta, *f. sing.* (etiquette). || Formalidades, *f.* (formalities). || Normas, *f.* (rules of conduct). || Entretenimientos, *m.* (entertainments). || *The amenities of life*, las cosas agradables de la vida.
amenorrhoea [æˌmenə'ri:ə] n. MED. Amenorrea, *f.*
ament [ə'ment] n. BOT. Amento, *m.* || MED. Débil mental, *m.* & *f.*, subnormal, *m.* & *f.*
amentaceous [ˌæmən'teiʃəs] adj. BOT. Amentáceo, a.
amentia [ei'menʃjə] n. MED. Debilidad (*f.*) mental.
amentiferous [ˌæmən'tifərəs] adj. BOT. Amentífero, ra.
amerce [ə'mə:s] v. tr. Multar (to fine).
amercement [—mənt] n. Multa, *f.* (fine).
America [ə'merikə] pr. n. GEOGR. América, *f.*: *North America*, América del Norte; *South America*, América del Sur; *Central America*, América Central. || [Los] Estados (*m. pl.*) Unidos (the United States).
American [—n] adj./n. Americano, na (in general). || Americano, na; estadounidense, norteamericano, na (of the United States). || — N. Americano, *m.* (language).
Americanism [ə'merikənizəm] n. Americanismo, *m.*
Americanist ['əmerikənist] n. Americanista, *m.* & *f.*
Americanization [əˌmerikənai'zeiʃən] n. Americanización, *f.*
Americanize [ə'merikənaiz] v. tr. Americanizar.
— V. intr. Americanizarse.
americium [ˌæmə'risiəm] n. Americio, *m.*
Amerind ['æmərind] n. Amerindio, dia.
Amerindian [ˌæmər'indjən] adj. Amerindio, dia.
amethyst ['æmiθist] n. Amatista, *f.*
— Adj. Amatista.
ametropia [ˌæme'trəupiə] n. MED. Ametropía, *f.*
amiability [ˌeimjə'biliti] n. Amabilidad, *f.*, afabilidad, *f.*
amiable ['eimjəbl] adj. Amable, afable.
amianthus [æmi'ænθəs] n. Amianto, *m.*
amicability [ˌæmikə'biliti] n. Amabilidad, *f.* || Amistad, *f.* (friendship).
amicable ['æmikəbl] adj. Amistoso, sa; amigable.
amice ['æmis] n. REL. Amito, *m.*
amid [ə'mid] prep. Entre.
amide ['æmaid] n. CHEM. Amida, *f.*
amidol ['æmidɔl] n. CHEM. Amidol, *m.*
amidships (U. S. **amidship**) [ə'midʃips] adv. MAR. En medio del barco.
amidst [ə'midst] prep. Entre.
amine [ə'mi:n] n. CHEM. Amina, *f.*
amino [ə'mi:nəu] adj. Aminado, da.
amino acid [—'æsid] n. CHEM. Aminoácido, *m.*
amir [ə'miə] n. Emir, *m.*
amiss [ə'mis] adj. Inoportuno, na (inopportune). || Malo, la (bad). || — *It would not be amiss for him*, no le vendría mal. || *There is nothing amiss*, no pasa nada. || *There is sth. amiss*, hay algo que no va [bien]. || *What is amiss (with him)?*, ¿qué [le] pasa?, ¿qué hay?
— Adv. Mal (badly, wrongly): *to judge, to play amiss*, juzgar, jugar mal. || Inoportunamente: *to speak amiss*, hablar inoportunamente. || — *To come amiss*, venir mal. || *To go amiss*, salir mal. || *To take amiss*, tomar a mal.
amity ['æmiti] n. Amistad, *f.*
ammeter ['æmitə*] n. Amperímetro, *m.*
ammonia [ə'məunjə] n. CHEM. Amoniaco, *m.*, amoníaco, *m.*
ammoniac [ə'meuniæk] adj. CHEM. Amoniaco, ca; amoníaco, ca: *sal ammoniac*, sal amoniaca.
ammoniacal [ˌæməu'naiəkel] adj. CHEM. Amoniacal.
ammoniated [ə'məunieitid] adj. Amoniacado, da.
ammonite ['æmənait] n. ZOOL. Amonita, *f.* (fossil).
ammonium [ə'meunjəm] n. CHEM. Amonio, *m.*
ammunition [ˌæmju'niʃən] n. Munición, *f.*, municiones, *f. pl.* || FIG. Argumento, *m.*, argumentos, *m. pl.*
amnesia [æm'ni:zjə] n. MED. Amnesia, *f.*
amnesic [æm'ni:zik] adj./n. MED. Amnésico, ca.
amnesty ['æmnesti] n. Amnistía, *f.*
amnesty ['æmnesti] v. tr. Amnistiar.
amnion ['æmniən] n. ANAT. Amnios, *m.*

— OBSERV. El plural de *amnion* es *amnions* o *amnia*.

amniotic [æmni'ɔtik] adj. ANAT. Amniótico, ca.
amoeba [ə'mi:bə] n. ZOOL. Ameba, *f.*, amiba, *f.*

— OBSERV. El plural de *amoeba* es *amoebas* o *amoebae*.

amok [ə'mɔk] adv. FIG. *They ran amok through the town*, atravesaron la ciudad destruyéndolo todo. || *To run amok*, volverse loco (to go mad).

among [əˈmʌŋ] or **amongst** [—st] prep. Entre: *a house among the trees*, una casa entre los árboles; *a king among kings*, un rey entre reyes; *they argued among themselves*, discutían entre ellos. || — *From among*, de entre. || *To be among those who*, ser de los que.
amontillado [əˌmɔntiˈlɑ:dəu] n. Amontillado, *m.* (sherry).
amoral [ˌeiˈmɔrəl] adj. Amoral.
amoralism [—izəm] n. Amoralismo, *m.*
amorality [ˌeiməˈræliti] n. Amoralidad, *f.*
amorist [ˈæmərist] n. Tenorio, *m.*
amorous [ˈæmərəs] adj. Amoroso, sa: *amorous looks*, miradas amorosas. || Enamorado, da (in love). || Enamoradizo, za (who falls in love easily). || Cariñoso, sa (affectionate).
amorphism [əˈmɔ:fizəm] n. Amorfismo, *m.*
amorphous [əˈmɔ:fəs] adj. Amorfo, fa.
amortization [əˌmɔ:tiˈzeiʃən] n. Amortización, *f.*
amortize [əˈmɔ:taiz] v. tr. Amortizar.
amount [əˈmaunt] n. Cantidad, *f.* (quantity): *a large amount of books*, una gran cantidad de libros; *to pay a great amount*, pagar una gran cantidad. || COMM. Importe, *m.* [*Amer.*, monto, *m.*] || *To the amount of*, por valor de, hasta un total de.
amount [əˈmaunt] v. intr. Alcanzar, ascender a, llegar a (to reach): *production amounted to three hundred tons*, la producción ascendió a *or* alcanzó trescientas toneladas. || Sumar, hacer (to add up to): *that amounts to fifteen shillings*, eso suma quince chelines. || Valer: *his argument does not amount to much*, su argumento no vale mucho. || Equivaler a, venir a ser, significar: *his action amounts to treason*, su acción equivale a *or* viene a ser una traición.
amour [əˈmuə*] n. Aventura (*f.*) amorosa, amorío, *m.*
amp [æmp] n. ELECTR. Amperio, *m.*
amperage [ˈæmpəridʒ] n. ELECTR. Amperaje, *m.*
ampere [ˈæmpɛə] n. ELECTR. Amperio, *m.*
ampere-hour [—ˈauə*] n. ELECTR. Amperio hora, *m.*
amperemeter [—ˌmi:tə*] n. Amperímetro, *m.*
ampere-second [—ˈsekənd] n. ELECTR. Amperio segundo, *m.*
ampere-turn [—tɔ:n] n. ELECTR. Amperio vuelta, *m.*
ampersand [—sænd] n. Nombre que se da al signo &.
amphetamine [æmˈfetəmin] n. Anfetamina, *f.*
amphibian [æmˈfibiən] n. Anfibio, *m.*
— Adj. Anfibio, bia.
amphibious [æmˈfibiəs] adj. Anfibio, bia.
amphibole [ˈæmfibəul] n. MIN. Anfíbol, *m.*
amphibolite [æmˈfibəlait] n. MIN. Anfibolita, *f.*
amphibological [ˌæmfibəˈlɔdʒikəl] adj. Anfibológico, ca.
amphibology [ˌæmfiˈbɔlədʒi] n. Anfibología, *f.*
amphictyon [æmˈfiktiən] n. Anfictión, *m.*
amphictyony [æmˌfiktiˈɔni] n. Anfictionía, *f.*
amphioxus [ˌæmfiˈɔksəs] n. ZOOL. Anfioxo, *m.*
amphisbaena [æmfisˈbi:nə] n. ZOOL. Anfisbena, *f.*
amphiscians [æmˈfiʃiənz] pl. n. Anfiscios, *m.*
amphitheatre (U. S. **amphitheater**) [ˈæmfiˌθiətə*] n. Anfiteatro, *m.* (in hospital, university, theatre, Roman games). || GEOL. Circo, *m.*
Amphitrite [ˈæmfitraiti] pr. n. Anfitrita, *f.*
Amphitryon [æmˈfitriən] pr. n. Anfitrión, *m.*
amphora [ˈæmfərə] n. Ánfora, *f.*
— OBSERV. El plural es *amphoras* o *amphorae*.
ample [ˈæmpl] adj. Amplio, plia: *an ample garden*, un jardín amplio; *an ample biography*, una biografía amplia. || Grande: *an ample helping*, una porción grande. || Suficiente, bastante (enough): *it will fit, there's ample room*, cabrá, hay bastante sitio. || Abundante: *an ample meal*, una comida abundante. || De sobra (more than enough): *to have ample time*, tener tiempo de sobra.
ampleness [—nis] n. Amplitud, *f.* || Abundancia, *f.*
amplification [ˌæmplifiˈkeiʃən] n. Amplificación, *f.* (of sound). || Aclaración, *f.*, explicación, *f.* (explanation).
amplifier [ˈæmplifaiə*] n. Amplificador, *m.*
amplify [ˈæmplifai] v. tr. Amplificar (a sound). || Desarrollar (an idea). || Aumentar (one's authority).
amplitude [ˈæmplitju:d] n. Amplitud, *f.*
amply [ˈæmpli] adv. Bien: *amply rewarded*, bien recompensado. || Ampliamente. || Abundantemente.
ampoule [ˈæmpu:l] or **ampule** [ˈæmpju:l] n. Ampolla, *f.*
amputate [ˈæmpjuteit] v. tr. Amputar.
amputation [ˌæmpjuˈteiʃən] n. Amputación, *f.*
Amsterdam [ˌæmstəˈdæm] pr. n. GEOGR. Amsterdam.
amuck [əˈmʌk] adv. See AMOK.
amulet [ˈæmjulit] n. Amuleto, *m.*
amuse [əˈmju:z] v. tr. Entretener: *to amuse one's guests*, entretener a sus invitados. || Divertir: *the joke amused everyone*, el chiste divirtió a todo el mundo. || Distraer, entretener (to occupy the attention of). || — *I am not amused*, no le veo la gracia. || *To amuse o.s.*, distraerse, divertirse. || *To be amused at* o *by*, divertirse con, entretenerse con. || *To keep s.o. amused*, entretener *or* distraer a uno.
amusement [—mənt] n. Distracción, *f.*, diversión, *f.*, entretenimiento, *m.*: *my favorite amusements*, mis distracciones preferidas. || Pasatiempo, *m.* (pastime). || Regocijo, *m.* (laughter): *much to my amusement*, con gran regocijo mío. || — Pl. Atracciones, *f.* (at the fair). || — *Amusement park*, parque (*m.*) de atracciones. || *Look of amusement*, mirada divertida. || *Place of amusement*, lugar (*m.*) de recreo. || *To do sth. for one's amusement*, hacer algo para entretenerse. || *To try to hide one's amusement*, aguantar la risa.
amusing [—iŋ] adj. Divertido, da; gracioso, sa (funny). || Entretenido, da (entertaining). || *To be amusing*, tener gracia, ser divertido.
amygdala [əˈmigdələ] n. ANAT. Amígdala, *f.*
— OBSERV. El plural de *amygdala* es *amygdalae*.
amygdalaceous [əˌmigdəˈleiʃəs] adj. Amigdaláceo, a.
amygdalin [æˈmigdəlin] n. Amigdalina, *f.*
amygdaline [æˈmigdəlain] adj. Amigdalino, na.
amyl [ˈæmil] n. CHEM. Amilo, *m.*: *amyl acetate*, acetato de amilo. || *Amyl alcohol*, alcohol amílico.
amylaceous [ˌæmiˈleiʃəs] adj. Amiláceo, a.
amylase [ˈæmileis] n. Amilasa, *f.*
amylene [ˈæmili:n] n. CHEM. Amileno, *m.*
amylic [əˈmilik] adj. Amílico, ca.
amyloid [ˈæmilɔid] adj. Amiloide.
amyloidosis ˈæmilɔiˈdəusis] n. MED. Amilosis, *f.*
an [æn] indef. art. Un, una.
— OBSERV. See A, indefinite article.
Anabaptism [ˌænəˈbæptizəm] n. Anabaptismo, *m.*
Anabaptist [ˌænəˈbæptist] adj./n. Anabaptista.
anabasis [əˈnæbəsis] n. Anábasis, *f.*
anabolism [əˈnæbəlizəm] n. Anabolismo, *m.*
anachronic [ˌænəˈkrɔnik] adj. Anacrónico, ca.
anachronism [əˈnækrənizəm] n. Anacronismo, *m.*
anachronistic [əˌnækrəˈnistik] adj. Anacrónico, ca,
anacoluthon [ˌænəkəˈlu:θɔn] n. GRAMM. Anacoluto, *m.*
— OBSERV. El plural es *anacolutha* o *anacoluthons*.
anaconda [ˌænəˈkɔndə] n. ZOOL. Anaconda, *f.*
Anacreon [əˈnækriən] pr. n. Anacreonte, *m.*
Anacreontic [əˌnækriˈɔntik] adj. Anacreóntico, ca.
anacrusis [ˌænəˈkru:sis] n. Anacrusis, *f.*
anaemia [əˈni:mjə] n. MED. Anemia, *f.*
anaemic [əˌni:mik] adj. Anémico, ca.
anaerobe [ˈænərəub] n. Anaerobio, *m.*
anaerobic [ænəˈrəubik] adj. Anaerobio, bia.
anaesthesia [ˌænisˈθi:zjə] n. Anestesia, *f.*
anaesthetic [ˌænisˈθetik] adj. Anestésico, ca.
— N. Anestésico, *m.*
anaesthetist [æˈni:sθitist] n. Anestesista, *m.* & *f.*
anaesthetization [æˌni:sθitiˈzeiʃən] n. Anestesia, *f.*
anaesthetize [æˈni:sθitaiz] v. tr. Anestesiar.
anaglyph [ˈænəglif] n. Anáglifo, *m.*
anagoge or **anagogy** [ˈænəgɔdʒi] n. Anagoge, *m.*, anagogía, *f.*
anagram [ˈænəgræm] n. Anagrama, *m.*
anagrammatic [ænəgrəˈmætik] or **anagrammatical** [—əl] adj. Anagramático, ca.
anal [ˈeinəl] adj. ANAT. Anal.
analecta [ˈænəlektə] or **analects** [ˈænəlekts] pl. n. Analectas, *f.*
analeptic [ˌænəˈleptik] adj. Analéptico, ca.
— N. Analéptico, *m.*
analgesia [ˌænælˈdʒi:zjə] n. MED. Analgesia, *f.*
analgesic [ˌænælˈdʒi:zik] adj. Analgésico, ca.
— N. Analgésico, *m.*
analog [ˈænəlɔg] n. See ANALOGUE.
analogic [ænəˈlɔdʒik] or **analogical** [—əl] adj. Analógico, ca.
analogism [əˈnælədʒizəm] n. Analogismo, *m.*
analogize [əˈnælədʒaiz] v. intr. Raciocinar basándose en analogías (to use analogy). || *To analogize with*, presentar analogías con.
— V. tr. Comparar (to compare).
analogous [əˈnæləgəs] adj. Análogo, ga.
analogue [ˈænəlɔg] n. Cosa (*f.*) análoga (thing). || Término (*m.*) análogo (word). || BIOL. Órgano (*m.*) análogo.
analogy [əˈnælədʒi] n. Analogía, *f.* || *On the analogy of*, por analogía con.
analysable or **analyzable** [ˈænəlaizəbl] adj. Analizable.
analysand [əˈnæləˌsænd] n. Persona (*f.*) que sigue un tratamiento de psicoanálisis.
analyse [ˈænəlaiz] v. tr. Analizar. || Psicoanalizar.
analyser [—ə*] n. Analizador, *m.*
analysis [əˈnæləsis] n. Análisis, *m.* || Psicoanálisis, *m.*
— OBSERV. El plural de *analysis* es *analyses*.
analyst [ˈænəlist] n. Analista, *m.* & *f.* || Psicoanalista, *m.* & *f.*
analytic [ˌænəˈlitik] or **analytical** [—əl] adj. Analítico, ca: *analytic language*, lengua analítica; *analytical geometry*, geometría analítica.
analytics [—s] n. Analítica, *f.*
analyzable [ˈænəlaizəbl] adj. Analizable.
analyze [ˈænəlaiz] v. tr. Analizar. || Psicoanalizar.
analyzer [—ə*] n. Analizador, *m.*
anapaest (U. S. **anapest**) [ˈænəpi:st] n. Anapesto, *m* (metrical foot).
anapaestic (U. S. **anapestic**) [ænəˈpi:stik] adj. Anapéstico, ca.
anaphase [ˈænəfeiz] n. Anafase, *f.*
anaphora [əˈnæfərə] n. Anáfora, *f.*
anaphrodisia [ˌænæfrəˈdiziə] n. Anafrodisia, *f.*
anaphrodisiac [ˌænæfrəˈdiziæk] n. Anafrodisiaco, *m.*
— Adj. Anafrodisiaco, ca.
anaphylactic [ˌænəfiˈlæktik] adj. Anafiláctico, ca.
anaphylaxis [ˌænəfiˈlæksis] n. MED. Anafilaxia, *f.*, anafilaxis, *f.*

anarchic [æ'nɑ:kik] or **anarchical** [—əl] adj. Anárquico, ca.
anarchism ['ænəkizəm] n. Anarquismo, *m.*
anarchist ['ænəkist] adj./n. Anarquista.
anarchy ['ænəki] n. Anarquía, *f.*
anastigmatic [,ænəstig'mætik] adj. Anastigmático, ca.
anastomose [ə'næstəməuz] v. intr. BIOL. Anastomosarse.
anastomosis [,ænəstə'məusis] n. BIOL. Anastomosis, *f.*

— OBSERV. El plural de la palabra inglesa es *anastomoses.*

anathema [ə'næθimə] n. REL. Anatema, *m.* || FIG. *It is anathema to him*, le es odioso.
anathematization [ə,næθimətai'zeiʃən] n. Anatematización, *f.*
anathematize [ə'næθimətaiz] v. tr. Anatematizar.
Anatolia [,ænə'təuljə] pr. n. GEOGR. Anatolia, *f.*
anatomic [,ænə'tɔmik] or **anatomical** [—əl] adj. Anatómico, ca.
anatomist [ə'nætəmist] n. Anatomista, *m. & f.*
anatomize [ə'nætəmaiz] v. tr. Anatomizar. || FIG. Analizar.
anatomy [ə'nætəmi] n. Anatomía, *f.*
anatoxin [,ænə'tɔksin] n. MED. Anatoxina, *f.*
anatropal [ə'nætrəpəl] or **anatropous** [ə'nætrəpəs] adj. BOT. Anátropo, pa.
Anaxagoras [,ænæk'sægəræs] pr. n. Anaxágoras, *m.*
ancestor ['ænsistə*] n. Antepasado, *m.*, ascendiente, *m.* || *Ancestor worship*, el culto de los antepasados.
ancestral [æn'sestrəl] adj. Ancestral. || *Ancestral home*, casa solariega.
ancestry ['ænsistri] n. Ascendencia, *f.*, linaje, *m.*
anchor ['æŋkə*] n. MAR. Ancla, *f.* || TECH. Áncora, *f.* (of watch, walls). || FIG. Pilar, *m.* (reliable person). || — MAR. *At anchor*, al ancla, anclado. || FIG. *He had been the anchor of all my hopes*, había puesto todas mis esperanzas en él. | *Sheet anchor*, ancla de salvación. || MAR. *To cast* o *to drop anchor*, echar el ancla, anclar. | *To weigh anchor*, levar anclas, zarpar.
anchor ['æŋkə*] v. tr. MAR. Anclar. || FIG. Sujetar, afianzar (to secure).
— V. intr. MAR. Echar el ancla, fondear, anclar.
anchorage [—ridʒ] n. MAR. Ancladero, *m.*, fondeadero, *m.*, anclaje, *m.* (place). | Derechos (*m. pl.*) de anclaje (fee). | Anclaje, *m.* (action).
anchoress [—ris] n. Anacoreta, *f.*
anchoret [—ret] or **anchorite** [—rait] n. Anacoreta, *m.*
anchovy ['æntʃəvi] n. Boquerón, *m* (fresh or live). || Anchoa, *f.* (salted, in tins).
anchylose ['æŋkiləus] v. tr. Anquilosar.
— V. intr. Anquilosarse.
anchylosis [,æŋki'ləusis] n. MED. Anquilosis, *f.*
ancient ['einʃənt] adj. Antiguo, gua: *Ancient Greece*, Grecia antigua; *ancient customs*, costumbres antiguas; *an ancient copy of a newspaper*, un número antiguo de un periódico. || Anticuado, da (old-fashioned).
— N. Antiguo, *m.*: *the ancients*, los antiguos. || Anciano, na (old person).
ancillary [æn'siləri] adj. Auxiliar: *surgery and ancillary services*, cirugía y servicios auxiliares. || Subordinado, da. || Anexo, xa: *ancillary plants*, fábricas anexas. || Secundario, ria. || Afín (related).
ancon ['æŋkən] n. Ancón, *m.*
ancylostomiasis [,æŋkiləustəu'maiəsis] m. MED. Anquilostomiasis, *f.*
and [ænd] conj. Y, e (see OBSERV.): *men and women*, hombres y mujeres; *thousands and thousands*, miles y miles. || A: *go and look for him*, vete a buscarle. || Omitted in Spanish: *two hundred and thirty*, doscientos treinta; *try and come*, intente venir. || — *And so*, y entonces. || *And so on* o *and so forth*, etcétera. || *And so on, and so forth*, etcétera, etcétera. || *Colder and colder*, cada vez más frío. || *More and more*, cada vez más. || *Now and then*, de vez en cuando. || *To try and do sth.*, tratar de *or* intentar hacer algo. || *You can't come and go without showing the pass*, no puede entrar ni salir sin enseñar el permiso.

— OBSERV. The conjunction *e* replaces *y* before words beginning with *i* or *hi* (vocalic i): *Federico e Isabel*, Frederick and Isabella: *madre e hija*, mother and daughter. However, at the beginning of an interrogative or exclamatory sentence, or before a word beginning with *y* or *hi* followed by a vowel (consonantal *i*), the *y* is retained: *¿y Ignacio?*, and Ignatius?; *vid y hiedra*, vine and ivy; *tú y yo*, you and I.

Andalusia [,ændə'lu:zjə] pr. n. GEOGR. Andalucía, *f.*
Andalusian [—n] adj./n. Andaluz, za.
andante [æn'dænti] adv. MUS. Andante.
— N. MUS. Andante, *m.*
andantino [ændæn'ti:nəu] adv. MUS. Andantino.
— N. MUS. Andantino, *m.*
Andean [æn'di:ən] adj. Andino, na.
Andes ['ændi:z] pl. pr. n. GEOGR. Andes, *m.*
andesite ['ændəzait] n. Andesita, *f.*
andiron ['ændaiən] n. Morillo, *m.*
Andorra [æn'dɔrə] pr. n. GEOGR. Andorra, *f.*
Andorran [—n] adj./n. Andorrano, na.
Andrew ['ændru:] pr. n. Andrés, *m.* || *St Andrew's cross*, cruz (*f.*) de San Andrés, aspa, *f.*
androecium [æn'dri:sjəm] n. BOT. Androceo, *m.*

— OBSERV. El plural de *androecium* es *androecia.*

androgen ['ændrəudʒən] n. BOT. Andrógeno, *m.*
androgyne ['ændrɔdʒin] adj./n. Andrógino, na.
androgynous [æn'drɔdʒinəs] adj. Andrógino, na.
android ['ændrɔid] n. Androide, *m.*
Andromache [æn'drɔməki] pr. n. Andrómaca, *f.*
Andromeda [æn'drɔmidə] pr. n. ASTR. Andrómeda, *f.*
anecdotal [,ænek'dəutl] adj. Anecdótico, ca.
anecdote ['ænikdəut] n. Anécdota, *f.*
anecdotic [,ænek'dɔtik] or **anecdotical** [—əl] adj. Anecdótico, ca.
anecdotist ['ænik,dəutist] n. Anecdotista, *m. & f.*
anemia [ə'ni:mjə] n. U. S. MED. Anemia, *f.*
anemic [ə'ni:mik] adj. U. S. MED. Anémico, ca.
anemograph [ə'neməugrɑ:f] n. PHYS. Anemógrafo, *m.*
anemometer [,æni'mɔmitə*] n. Anemómetro, *m.*
anemometry [,æni'mɔmitri] n. PHYS. Anemometría, *f.*
anemone [ə'neməni] n. BOT. Anémona, *f.*, anémone, *f.* (plant). || *Sea anemone*, anémona de mar.
anemophilous [,ænə'mɔfələs] adj. BOT. Anemófilo, la.
aneroid ['ænərɔid] adj. PHYS. Aneroide: *aneroid barometer*, barómetro aneroide.
anesthesia [,ænis'θi:zjə] n. U. S. MED. Anestesia, *f.*
anesthetic [,ænis'θetik] adj. U. S. Anestésico, ca.
— N. Anestésico, *m.*
anesthetist [æ'ni:sθitist] n. U. S. Anestesista, *m. & f.*
anesthetize [æ'ni:sθitaiz] v. tr. U. S. MED. Anestesiar.
aneurysm or **aneurism** ['ænjuərizəm] n. MED. Aneurisma, *m.*
anew [ə'nju:] adv. Otra vez, de nuevo (again). || De nuevo (afresh).
anfractuosity [,ænfræktju'ɔsiti] n. Anfractuosidad, *f.*
angaria [æn'gæriə] n. Angaria, *f.*
angel ['eindʒəl] n. Ángel, *m.*: *guardian angel*, ángel custudio *or* ángel de la guarda; *fallen angel*, ángel caído. || FIG. Cielo, *m.*: *what an angel you are!*, ¡qué cielo eres! || THEATR. FAM. Productor (*m.*) de una obra. || HIST. Moneda (*f.*) de oro. || *To sing like an angel*, cantar como los ángeles.
angelfish [—fiʃ] n. ZOOL. Angelote, *m.*
angelic [æn'dʒelik] adj. Angelical; angélico, ca.
angelica [æn'dʒelikə] n. BOT. Angélica, *f.*
angelical [—l] adj. Angelical; angélico, ca.
Angelus ['ændʒələs] n. Ángelus, *m.* (prayer, bell).
anger ['æŋgə*] n. Ira, *f.*, cólera, *f.*, enojo, *m.*: *to vent one's anger on s.o.*, desahogar su ira en alguien; *to act in anger*, dejarse llevar por la cólera. || *To speak in anger*, hablar furioso.
anger ['æŋgə*] v. tr. Enojar, enfadar, encolerizar, airar.
— V. intr. Encolerizarse, enfadarse, enojarse.
Angevin or **Angevine** ['ændʒivin] adj./n. Angevino, na; de Anjou.
angina [æn'dʒainə] n. MED. Angina, *f.*: *angina pectoris*, angina de pecho.
anginous [æn'dʒainəs] adj. MED. Anginoso, sa.
angiography [ændʒi'ɔgrəfi] n. Angiografía, *f.*
angiology [ændʒi'ɔlədʒi] n. Angiología, *f.*
angioma [ændʒi'əumə] n. MED. Angioma, *m.*

— OBSERV. El plural de la palabra inglesa es *angiomata* o *angiomas.*

angiosperm ['ændʒiəu,spə:m] n. BOT. Angiosperma, *f.*
angle ['æŋgl] n. Ángulo, *m.*: *alternate angles*, ángulos alternos; *at right angles*, en ángulo recto. || Ángulo, *m.* (of solid). || Punto (*m.*) de vista, aspecto, *m.* (point of view): *that is another angle to the problem*, ése es otro aspecto del problema. || — *At an angle*, al bies (crooked). || *To be at an angle to*, formar ángulo con. || FIG. *To try to look at a problem from another angle*, intentar enfocar el problema de otra manera *or* desde otro punto de vista
angle ['æŋgl] v. intr. Pescar con caña (to fish). || FIG. FAM. *To angle for*, ir a la caza de.
— V. tr. U. S. Formar ángulo con. | FAM. Presentar bajo cierto punto de vista, enfocar (a report).
angled [—d] adj. Angular, angulado, da. || Al bies.
angle iron [—,aiən] n. Angular, *m.*, ángulo, *m.*
angler [—ə*] n. Pescador (*m.*) de caña. || Pejesapo, *m.*, rape, *m.* (fish).
Angles [—z] pl. pr. n. Anglos, *m.*
anglesite [—sait] n. MIN. Anglesita, *f.*
Anglian ['æŋgliən] adj./n. Anglo, gla.
Anglican ['æŋglikən] adj./n. REL. Anglicano, na.
Anglicanism [—izəm] n. REL. Anglicanismo, *m.*
Anglicism ['æŋglisizəm] n. Anglicismo, *m.*
Anglicist ['æŋglisist] n. Anglicista, *m. & f.*
anglicize ['æŋglisaiz] v. tr. Anglicanizar, hacer inglés.
angling ['æŋgliŋ] n. Pesca (*f.*) con caña.
Anglo-American ['æŋgləuə'merikən] adj./n. Angloamericano, na.
Anglo-Arab ['æŋgləu'ærəb] n. Angloárabe, *m. & f.*
Anglo-Arabian ['æŋgləuə'reibjən] adj. Angloárabe.
Anglomania ['æŋgləu'meinjə] n. Anglomanía, *f.*
Anglomaniac ['æŋgləu'meiniæk] n. Anglómano, na.
Anglomaniacal ['æŋgləumə'naiəkəl] adj. Anglómano, na.
Anglo-Norman ['æŋgləu'nɔ:mən] adj./n. Anglonormando, da.
Anglophil or **Anglophile** ['æŋgləufail] adj./n. Anglófilo, la.
Anglophilia [æŋgləu'filiə] n. Anglofilia, *f.*
Anglophobe ['æŋgləufəub] adj./n. Anglófobo, ba.
Anglophobia [,æŋgləu'fəubjə] n. Anglofobia, *f.*
Anglo-Saxon ['æŋgləu'sæksən] adj./n. Anglosajón, ona.
Angolese [æŋgəu'li:z] adj./n. Angolés, esa.
angora [æŋ'gɔ:rə] n. Lana (*f.*) de angora.

Angora [æŋ'gɔ:rə] pr. n. HIST. Angora. || *Angora cat, goat, rabbit*, gato, cabra, conejo de Angora.
angostura [,æŋgɔs'tjuərə] n. BOT. Angostura, *f.*
angrily ['æŋgrili] adv. Con enojo, airadamente.
angry ['æŋgri] adj. Enfadado, da; enojado, da; airado, da: *to be angry at* o *with s.o.*, estar enfadado con alguien; *to be angry at sth.*, estar enfadado por algo. || FIG. Amenazador, ra (menacing). | Tormentoso, sa; borrascoso, sa (sky). | Enfurecido, da; embravecido, da; desencadenado, da (sea). || MED. Inflamado, da (sore). || — *I will be angry*, me enfadaré. || *To get angry*, enfadarse, enojarse, enfurecerse. || *To make angry*, enfadar, enojar, enfurecer, airar.
angstrom ['æŋstrəm] n. PHYS. Angström, *m.*
anguillule [æŋ'gwiljul] n. ZOOL. Anguílula, *f.*
anguish ['æŋgwiʃ] n. Angustia, *f.*, congoja, *f.* || Dolor, *m.* (pain). || MED. Angustia, *f.* || *To be in anguish*, estar angustiado.
anguish ['æŋgwiʃ] v. tr. Angustiar, acongojar.
angular ['æŋgjulə*] adj. Angular (shape, distance, etc.). || Anguloso, sa (features).
angularity [,æŋgju'læriti] n. Forma (*f.*) angular, angularidad, *f.*
angulate ['æŋgjuleit] adj. Angulado, da; anguloso, sa.
anhydride [æn'haidraid] n. CHEM. Anhídrido, *m.*
anhydrite [æn'haidrait] n. MIN. Anhidrita, *f.*
anhydrous [æn'haidrəs] adj. CHEM. Anhidro, dra.
anil ['ænil] n. Añil, *m.*, índigo, *m.*
anile ['einail] adj. Senil. || FAM. Imbécil.
anilin ['ænilin] or **aniline** ['ænili:n] n. CHEM. Anilina, *f.*
animadversion [,ænimæd'və:ʃən] n. Animadversión, *f.* (ill will). || Censura, *f.*, reprobación, *f.* (blame).
animadvert [,ænimæd'və:t] v. intr. *To animadvert on s.o.'s action*, censurar *or* reprobar la acción de alguien.
animal ['æniməl] adj. Animal: *the animal kingdom*, el reino animal. || *Animal charcoal*, carbón (*m.*) animal.
— N. Animal, *m.*: *domestic animal*, animal doméstico; *wild animal*, animal salvaje. || FIG. Animal, *m.* (brute).
animalcule [,æni'mælkju:l] n. ZOOL. Animálculo, *m.*
animal husbandry ['æniməl'hʌzbəndri] n. Ganadería, *f.*, cría (*f.*) de animales.
animalism ['æniməlizəm] n. Animalismo, *m.*
animalist ['æniməlist] adj./n. Animalista.
animality [æni'mæliti] n. Animalidad, *f.* || Reino (*m.*) animal (animal kingdom).
animalize ['æniməlaiz] v. tr. Animalizar.
animal power ['æniməl,pauə*] n. Fuerza (*f.*) de tracción animal.
animal spirits ['æniməl'spirits] pl. n. Vitalidad, *f. sing.*, animación, *f. sing.*, vigor, *m. sing.*
animate ['ænimit] adj. Animado, da; vivo, va: *animate beings*, seres animados.
animate ['ænimeit] v. tr. Animar (to give life to): *the soul animates the body*, el alma anima el cuerpo. || Alentar, animar (to motivate). || Animar (to liven up): *to animate the conversation*, animar la conversación.
animated [—id] adj. Animado, da: *an animated street, person, discussion*, una calle, una persona, una discusión animada. || Vivo, va (lively). || Que tiene vida (painting, sculpture). || *Animated cartoons*, dibujos animados.
animation [,æni'meiʃən] n. Animación, *f.*
animator ['ænimeitə*] n. Animador, ra.
animism ['ænimizəm] n. Animismo, *m.*
animist ['ænimist] n. Animista, *m.* & *f.*
animistic [,æni'mistik] adj. Animista.
animosity [,æni'mɔsiti] n. Animosidad, *f.*
animus ['æniməs] n. Animosidad. *f.* || Ánimo, *m.*, intención, *f.* (will).
anion ['ænaiən] n. PHYS. Anión, *m.*
anise ['ænis] n. BOT. Anís, *m.* || *Star anise*, anís estrellado.
aniseed ['ænisi:d] n. BOT. Anís, *m.*
anisette [,æni'zet] n. Anisete, *m.*, licor (*m.*) de anís.
anisopetalous [ə,naisə'petələs] adj. BOT. Anisopétalo, la.
anisophyllous [ə,naisə'filəs] adj. BOT. Anisófilo, la.
anisotropic [ə,naisə'trɔpik] adj. Anisótropo, pa.
anisotropy [,ænai'sɔtrəpi] n. Anisotropía, *f.*
Ankara ['æŋkərə] pr. n. GEOGR. Ankara.
ankle ['æŋkl] n. ANAT. Tobillo, *m.* || — *Ankle socks*, calcetines, *m.* || *Ankle support*, tobillera, *f.*
anklebone [—bəun] n. Hueso (*m.*) del tobillo.
anklet ['æŋklit] n. Ajorca (*f.*) para el tobillo. || U. S. Calcetín, *m.* (sock).
ankylose ['æŋkiləuz] v. tr. Anquilosar.
— V. intr. Anquilosarse.
ankylosis [æŋki'ləusis] n. MED. Anquilosis, *f.*
ankylostomiasis ['æŋkiləstə'maiəsis] n. MED. Anquilostomiasis, *f.*
Ann [æn] pr. n. Ana, *f.*
annalist ['ænəlist] n. Analista, *m.* & *f.*
annals ['ænlz] pl. n. Anales, *m.*
Annam ['ænæm] pr. n. GEOGR. Anam, *m.*
Annamite ['ænəmait] adj./n. Anamita.
Anne [æn] pr. n. Ana, *f.*
anneal [ə'ni:l] v. tr. TECH. Recocer. || FIG. Endurecer.
annealing [—iŋ] n. TECH. Recocido, *m.*
annelid ['ænəlid] n. ZOOL. Anélido, *m.*
annex [ə'neks] v. tr. Anexionar, anexar (territory). || Añadir, adjuntar (to add). || Adjuntar (to a document).
annex or **annexe** ['æneks] n. Anexo, *m.*, dependencia, *f.* (of a building). || Anexo, *m.*, apéndice, *m.* (of a document). || — Pl. JUR. Anexidades, *f.*
annexation [ænek'seiʃən] n. Anexión, *f.*
annexationism [ænek'seiʃənizəm] n. Anexionismo, *m.*
annexationist [ænek'seiʃənist] adj./n. Anexionista.
annexed [ə'nekst] adj. Anexo, xa; anejo, ja.
annexionism [æ'nekʃənizəm] n. Anexionismo, *m.*
annexionist [æ'nekʃənist] adj./n. Anexionista.
annihilate [ə'naiəleit] v. tr. Aniquilar.
annihilation [ənaiə'leiʃən] n. Aniquilación, *f.*, aniquilamiento, *m.*
anniversary [,æni'və:səri] n. Aniversario, *m.*: *wedding anniversary*, aniversario de boda; *the anniversary of an event*, el aniversario de un suceso. || *Gold, silver anniversary*, bodas (*f. pl*) de oro, de plata.
annona [ə'nəunə] n. BOT. Anona, *f.* (soursop).
annotate ['ænəuteit] v. tr. Anotar (to write explanatory notes in). || Comentar (to comment on).
— V. intr. Poner notas, hacer anotaciones.
annotation [,ænəu'teiʃən] n. Anotación, *f.*, nota, *f.* || Comentario, *m.*
annotator ['ænəuteitə*] n. Anotador, ra.
announce [ə'nauns] v. tr. Anunciar: *to announce a piece of news*, anunciar una noticia; *to announce a guest*, anunciar a un invitado; *he suddenly announced that he was leaving*, de repente anunció que se iba a marchar. || Comunicar, hacer saber (to inform).
— V. intr. Ser locutor (on the radio, television).
announcement [—mənt] n. Anuncio, *m.* || Declaración, *f.* || Aviso, *m.*: *to make an announcement to the public*, dar un aviso al público.
announcer [—ə*] n. Locutor, ra (on the radio, television). || Anunciador, ra.
annoy [ə'nɔi] v. tr. Molestar, fastidiar (to bother). || Enfadar, enojar (to anger). || MIL. Acosar (the enemy). || *To be annoyed about, at*, estar enfadado por, con.
annoyance [ə'nɔiəns] n. Enfado, *m.*, enojo, *m.* (anger). || Molestia, *f.*, fastidio, *m.* (annoying thing). || *What an annoyance!*, ¡qué molesto!, ¡qué fastidio!
annoying [ə'nɔiiŋ] adj. Molesto, ta; fastidioso, sa: *how annoying you are!*, ¡qué molesto eres!; *annoying requirements*, requisitos molestos.
annual ['ænjuəl] adj. Anual: *annual income*, renta anual; *annual ceremony*, ceremonia anual; *annual plant*, planta anual. || BOT. *Annual ring*, capa (*f.*) cortical (of a tree).
— N. Anuario, *m.* (publication). || BOT. Planta (*f.*) anual.
annuitant [ə'njuitənt] n. Rentista, *m.* & *f.*, censualista, *m.* & *f.*
annuity [ə'njuiti] n. Anualidad, *f.* || Renta (*f.*) vitalicia (life annuity).
annul [ə'nʌl] v. tr. Anular (marriages, wills, contracts, etc.). || Cancelar, abrogar (laws). || Denunciar (a treaty).
annular ['ænjulə*] adj. Anular.
annulate ['ænjuleit] adj. Anillado, da.
annulet ['ænjulet] n. Anillito, *m.* (small ring). || ARCH. Collarino, *m.*
annulment [ə'nʌlmənt] n. Anulación, *f.* (of marriages, wills, contracts, etc.). || Cancelación, *f.*, abrogación, *f.* (of laws). || Denuncia, *f.* (of a treaty).
annum ['ænəm] n. Año, *m.* (year). || *Per annum*, por año, al año, anualmente.
annunciate [ə'nʌnʃieit] v. tr. Anunciar.
annunciation [ə,nʌnsi'eiʃən] n. Anuncio, *m.*
Annunciation [ə,nʌnsi'eiʃən] n. REL. Anunciación, *f.*
annunciator [ə'nʌnʃieitə*] n. Anunciador, ra (person). || Cuadro (*m.*) indicador (electric indicator).
anode ['ænəud] n. ELECTR. Ánodo, *m.*
anodic [ə'nɔdik] adj. PHYS. Anódico, ca.
anodon ['ænədɔn] or **anodont** ['ænədɔnt] n. ZOOL. Anodonte, *m.*
anodontia [ænə'dɔnʃə] n. Anodontia, *f.*
anodyne ['ænəudain] adj. MED. Anodino, na. || FIG. Anodino, na.
— N. MED. Anodino, *m.*, calmante, *m.*
anodynia [ænə'diniə] n. MED. Anodinia, *f.*
anoint [ə'nɔint] v. tr. Untar, ungir. || REL. Ungir. || FAM. *To anoint the palm*, untar la mano (to bribe).
anointment [—mənt] n. Ungimiento, *m.*
anomalous [ə'nɔmələs] adj. Anómalo, la.
anomaly [ə'nɔməli] n. Anomalía, *f.*
anon [ə'nɔn] adv. POET. Luego, dentro de poco tiempo. || *Ever and anon*, de vez en cuando.
anona [ə'nəunə] n. BOT. Anona, *f.* (soursop).
anonym ['ænənim] n. Anónimo, *m.* (person). || Seudónimo, *m.* (pseudonym).
anonymity [,ænə'nimiti] n. Anónimo, *m.*, anonimato, *m.*
anonymous [ə'nɔniməs] adj. Anónimo, ma. || *To remain anonymous*, conservar el anónimo.
anopheles [ə'nɔfili:z] n. Anofeles, *m.*
anorak ['ænəræk] n. Anorak, *m.*
anorexia [ænə'reksiə] or **anorexy** ['ænəreksi] n. MED. Anorexia, *f.*
anosmia [ə'nɔzmjə] n. MED. Anosmia, *f.*
another [ə'nʌðə*] adj. Otro, tra: *another cup of coffee*, otra taza de café. || Más (more): *it will take another three years*, tardará tres años más; *another*

ten pounds, diez libras más. || — *Another one*, otro, otra. || *Another time*, otro día (some other day), otra vez (again). || *In another way*, de otra manera. || *Many another*, otros muchos. || *One another*, unos y otros. || *Such another*, otro igual. || *That is another matter*, eso es otra cosa. || *To feel another person*, sentirse distinto, no ser el mismo. || *To help one another*, ayudarse unos a otros. || *Without another word*, sin más palabras, sin decir nada más.
— Pron. Otro, tra: *may I have another?*, ¿puedo tomar otro? || *Another would have done it in a different way*, cualquier otro lo hubiese hecho de manera diferente.
anouran [ə'nurən] adj./n. See ANURAN.
anoxemia [,ænɔk'si:miə] n. MED. Anoxemia, *f.*
anserine ['ænsərain] adj. Ansarino, na. || FIG. Estúpido, da.
answer ['ɑ:nsə*] n. Contestación, *f.*, respuesta, *f.*: *a negative answer*, una contestación negativa. || Réplica, *f.* (to an insult). || Solución, *f.*: *the answer is to study harder*, la solución es estudiar más. || JUR. Réplica, *f.* || MATH. Solución, *f.* (of a problem): *what do you make the answer?*, ¿qué solución tiene? | Resultado, *m.* (of a sum). || Razón, *f.*, explicación, *f.* (reason). || — *In answer to*, en respuesta a, contestando a. || *The answer to one's dreams*, la realización de sus sueños. || *To have an answer for everything*, tener una respuesta para todo, tener siempre respuesta. || *To make no answer*, no contestar. || *To write s.o. an answer*, contestar a uno por escrito.
answer ['ɑ:nsə*] v. tr. Contestar a, responder a (door, etc.). || Contestar [a], responder a (a letter). || Contestar (to one's name). || Contestar a, atender a, responder a (the telephone). || Satisfacer, responder a (one's needs). || Servir para, convenir para (a purpose). || Corresponder a, responder a, cuadrar con: *to answer the description*, corresponder a la descripción. || Escuchar, oír (the prayers). || — JUR. *To answer a charge*, defenderse contra una acusación. || *To answer one's dreams*, realizar los sueños de uno. || *To answer one's expectations*, colmar las esperanzas de uno. || *To answer s.o. back*, replicarle a uno. || MAR. *To answer the helm*, obedecer al timón. || *To answer the requirements*, cumplir *or* satisfacer los requisitos.
— V. intr. Contestar, responder: *to answer correctly*, contestar bien; *to answer to one's name*, contestar al ser llamado; *to answer with a counterattack*, contestar con un contraataque. || Replicar (to retort). || Obedecer: *the car would not answer to the wheel*, el coche no obedecía al volante. || Corresponder: *to answer to a description*, corresponder a una descripción. || Satisfacer: *to answer to one's requirements*, satisfacer los requisitos de uno. || — *Don't answer back!*, ¡no replique!, ¡no sea respondón! || *To answer for*, responder de (sth.), responder por, salir fiador de (s.o.). || *To answer to the name of*, responder al nombre de, tener por nombre.
answerable ['ɑ:nsərəbl] adj. Responsable (*for*, de) [responsible]. || Refutable (objection). || Que admite una respuesta (question). || MATH. Solucionable.
answerer ['ɑ:nsərə*] n. JUR. Fiador, *m.*, garante, *m.*
answering machine ['ɑ:nseriŋmə'ʃi:n] or **answer phone** ['ɑ:nserfəun] n. Contestador (*m.*) automático.
ant [ænt] n. ZOOL. Hormiga, *f.*
anta ['æntə] n. ARCH. Anta, *f.* || ZOOL. Tapir, *m.* [*Amer.*, anta, *f.*].
— OBSERV. El plural de *anta* en inglés es *antae*.
antagonism [æn'tægənizəm] n. Antagonismo, *m.*
antagonist [æn'tægənist] adj./n. Antagonista.
antagonistic [æn,tægə'nistik] adj. Antagónico, ca. || ANAT. Antagonista.
antagonize [æn'tægənaiz] v. tr. Contrariar (to counteract, to annoy). || Suscitar el antagonismo de (to provoke hostility). || Enemistarse con (to become an enemy).
Antarctic [æn'tɑ:ktik] adj. Antártico, ca.
— Pr. n. GEOGR. Antártico, *m.*
Antarctica [æn'tɑ:ktikə] pr. n. GEOGR. Antártida, *f.*
ant bear ['ænt,bɛə*] n. ZOOL. Oso (*m.*) hormiguero.
ante ['ænti] n. Apuesta (*f.*) inicial (poker). || FAM. Cuota, *f.* (the share one pays).
ante ['ænti] v. intr. Apostar. || *To ante up*, contribuir.
anteater ['ænt,i:tə*] n. ZOOL. Oso (*m.*) hormiguero.
antecedence [,ænti'si:dəns] n. Precedencia, *f.*, anterioridad, *f.* || ASTR. Antecedencia, *f.*
antecedent [,ænti'si:dənt] adj. Precedente, anterior, antecedente. || GRAMM. Antecedente.
— N. Antecedente, *m.*: *the antecedents and consequences of the war*, los antecedentes y las consecuencias de la guerra. || GRAMM. MATH. MUS. Antecedente, *m.* || — Pl. Antepasados, *m.*, antecesores, *m.* (ancestors).
antechamber ['ænti,tʃeimbə*] n. Antecámara, *f.*
antechapel ['ænti,tʃæpəl] n. Antecapilla, *f.*
antechoir ['ænti,kwaiə*] n. Antecoro, *m.*
antedate ['ænti'deit] n. Antedata, *f.*
antedate ['ænti'deit] v. tr. Antedatar (to backdate). || Preceder, ser anterior a.
antediluvian ['æntidi'lu:vjən] adj. Antediluviano, na. || FIG. Antediluviano, na; anticuado, da.
— N. FIG. Cavernícola, *m.* (person). | Antigualla, *f.* (thing).
antefix ['æntifiks] n. ARCH. Antefijo, *m.*
antelope ['æntiləup] n. ZOOL. Antílope, *m.*
antemeridian ['æntimə'ridiən] adj. Antemeridiano, na.
ante meridiem ['æntimə'ridiəm] adj. De la mañana, ante meridiem.
— OBSERV. La expresión *ante meridiem* se usa normalmente en la forma abreviada a.m. (*seven a.m.*, las siete de la mañana).
antenatal ['ænti'neitl] adj. Antenatal, prenatal.
antenna [æn'tenə] n. Antena, *f.*
— OBSERV. El plural de *antenna* es *antennae* o *antennas* cuando tiene un sentido zoológico y *antennas* en los demás casos.
antenuptial ['ænti'nʌpʃəl] adj. Prenupcial.
antepenult ['æntipi'nʌlt] n. Antepenúltima, *f.* (antepenultimate syllable).
antepenultimate ['æntipi'nʌltimit] adj. Antepenúltimo, ma.
— N. Antepenúltimo, ma. || Antepenúltima, *f.* (syllable).
anterior [æn'tiəriə*] adj. Anterior (*to*, a).
anteriority [æntiəri'ɔriti] n. Anterioridad, *f.*
anteroom ['æntirum] n. Antecámara, *f.*, antesala, *f.* (antechamber). || Sala (*f.*) de espera (waiting room).
anthelmintic [ænθel'mintik] adj. Vermífugo, ga; antihelmíntico, ca.
— N. Vermífugo, *m.*, antihelmíntico, *m.*
anthem ['ænθəm] n. Himno, *m.*: *national anthem*, himno nacional. || REL. Antífona, *f.*
anther ['ænθə*] n. BOT. Antera, *f.*
antheridium [,ænθə'ridjəm] n. BOT. Anteridia, *f.*
— OBSERV. El plural de *antheridium* es *antheridia*.
anthill ['ænthil] n. Hormiguero, *m.*
anthological [,ænθə'lɔdʒikəl] adj. Antológico, ca.
anthology [æn'θɔlədʒi] n. Antología, *f.*
Anthony ['æntəni] pr. n. Antonio, *m.*
anthozoa ['ænθəu'zəuə] pl. n. ZOOL. Antozoarios, *m.*
anthracene ['ænθrəsi:n] n. Antraceno, *m.*
anthracite ['ænθrəsait] n. Antracita, *f.*
anthrax ['ænθræks] n. MED. Ántrax, *m.*
— OBSERV. El plural de *anthrax* es *anthraces*.
anthrenus [æn'θri:nəs] n. ZOOL. Antreno, *m.* (insect).
anthropocentric [,ænθrəpəu'sentrik] adj. Antropocéntrico, ca.
anthropocentrism [,ænθrəpəu'sentrizəm] n. Antropocentrismo, *m.*
anthropoid ['ænθrəpɔid] adj. Antropoide, antropoideo, a (manlike in appearance).
— N. Antropoide, *m.*
anthropologic [,ænθrəpə'lɔdʒik] or **anthropological** [,ænθrəpə'lɔdʒikəl] adj. Antropológico, ca.
anthropologist [,ænθrə'pɔlədʒist] n. Antropólogo, ga.
anthropology [,ænθrə'pɔlədʒi] n. Antropología, *f.*
anthropometric [,ænθrəpəu'metrik] or **anthropometrical** [—əl] adj. Antropométrico, ca.
anthropometry [,ænθrə'pɔmitri] n. Antropometría, *f.*
anthropomorph ['ænθrəpəu'mɔ:f] n. Antropomorfo, fa.
anthropomorphic [,ænθrəpəu'mɔ:fik] adj. Antropomórfico, ca.
anthropomorphism [,ænθrəpəu'mɔ:fizəm] n. Antropomorfismo, *m.*
anthropomorphite [,ænθrəpəu'mɔ:fait] or **anthropomorphist** [,ænθrəpəu'mɔ:fist] n. Antropomorfita, *m.* & *f.*
anthropomorphous [,ænθrəpəu'mɔ:fəs] adj. Antropomorfo, fa.
anthroponymy [,ænθrə'pɔnimi] n. Antroponimia, *f.*
anthropophagite [,ænθrə'pɔfədʒait] n. Antropófago, ga.
anthropophagous [,ænθrə'pɔfəgəs] adj. Antropófago, ga.
anthropophagy [,ænθrə'pɔfədʒi] n. Antropofagia, *f.*
anthropopithecus [,ænθrəpəupi'θi:kəs] n. Antropopiteco, *m.*
anti ['ænti] pref. Anti [con el sentido de "contra", "contrario a" u "opuesto a"].
— OBSERV. La lista de palabras construidas con este prefijo que damos a continuación no pretende ser exhaustiva. Existen en efecto otras muchas palabras de esta índole tanto en español como en inglés.
antiaircraft ['ænti'ɛəkrɑ:ft] adj. Antiaéreo, a: *antiaircraft gun*, cañón antiaéreo.
antialcoholism ['ænti'ælkəhɔlizəm] n. Antialcoholismo, *m.*
anti-American ['æntiə'merikən] adj. Antiamericano, na.
antibiotic ['æntibai'ɔtik] adj. MED. Antibiótico, ca.
— N. Antibiótico, *m.*
antibody ['ænti,bɔdi] n. BIOL. Anticuerpo, *m.*
anticancerous ['ænti'kænsərəs] adj. Anticanceroso, sa.
anticathode ['ænti'kæθəud] n. PHYS. Anticátodo, *m.*
antichresis [,ænti'kri:sis] n. JUR. Anticresis, *f.*
— OBSERV. El plural de *antichresis* es *antichreses*.
Antichrist ['æntikraist] n. Antecristo, *m.*, anticristo, *m.*
antichristian ['ænti'kristjən] adj. Anticristiano, na.
anticipate [æn'tisipeit] v. tr. Esperar, contar con, prever (to foresee, to expect). || Prometerse (to look forward to). || Anticiparse a, adelantarse a (to forestall): *to anticipate s.o.*, anticiparse a alguien. || Anticiparse a: *he anticipated my wish*, se anticipó a

mi deseo. || Salir al paso de: *to anticipate criticism*, salir al paso de las críticas. || Anticipar, adelantar (payment). || Gastar de antemano (to use or spend in advance).
anticipation [æn,tisi'peiʃən] n. Previsión, *f.* (forecast). || Esperanza, *f.* (hope). || Anticipación, *f.* (of wishes, reactions, etc.). || Gasto (*m.*) anticipado. (spending in advance). || Expectación, *f.* || MUS. Anticipación, *f.* || — *In anticipation*, de antemano. || *In anticipation of the future*, pensando en el futuro. || *To thank s.o. in anticipation*, agradecerle a alguien por anticipado *or* por adelantado.
anticipatory [æn'tisipeitəri] adj. Previsor, ra.
anticlerical ['ænti'klerikl] adj./n. Anticlerical.
anticlericalism [—izəm] n. Anticlericalismo, *m.*
anticlimax ['ænti'klaimæks] n. Decepción, *f.* (disappointment).
anticlinal ['ænti'klainəl] adj. Anticlinal.
anticline ['æntiklain] n. GEOL. Anticlinal, *m.*
anticlockwise [,ænti'klɔkwaiz] adj./adv. En sentido contrario a las agujas del reloj.
anticoagulant ['æntikəu'ægjulənt] adj. Anticoagulante.
— N. Anticoagulante, *m.*
anticolonialism ['æntikə'ləunjəlizəm] n. Anticolonialismo, *m.*
anticolonialist ['æntikə'ləunjəlist] adj./n. Anticolonialista.
anticommunist ['ænti'kɔmjunist] adj./n. Anticomunista.
antics ['æntiks] pl. n. Payasadas, *f.*, bufonadas, *f.* (clowning). || Travesuras, *f.* (tricks). || Cabriolas, *f.* (capers). || *To be up to one's antics*, estar haciendo de las suyas.
anticyclone ['ænti'saikləun] n. Anticiclón, *m.*
anticyclonic ['æntisai'klɔnik] adj. Anticiclonal.
antidazzle ['ænti'dæzl] adj. Antideslumbrante.
antidemocrat ['ænti'deməkræt] n. Antidemócrata, *m.* & *f.*
antidemocratic ['ænti,demə'krætik] adj. Antidemocrático, ca.
antidotal ['æntidəutl] adj. Alexifármaco, ca.
antidote ['æntidəut] n. Antídoto, *m.* (*to*, *for*, *against*, contra).
antiemetic ['æntii'metik] adj. MED. Antiemético, ca.
— N. MED. Antiemético, *m.*
antifascism ['ænti'fæʃizəm] n. Antifascismo, *m.*
antifascist ['ænti'fæʃist] adj./n Antifascista.
antifebrile ['ænti'fi:brail] adj. MED. Antifebrífugo, ga; antifebril.
antifederalist ['ænti'fedərəlist] n. Antifederalista, *m.* & *f.*
antifeminism ['ænti'feminizəm] n. Antifeminismo, *m.*
antifeminist ['ænti'feminist] adj./n. Antifeminista.
antiferment ['ænti'fə:mənt] n. Antifermento, *m.*
antifreeze ['æntifri:z] n. Anticongelante, *m.*
antifriction ['ænti'frikʃən] n. Antifricción, *f.*
antigen ['æntidʒən] n. MED. Antígeno, *m.*
antiglare ['æntiglεə*] adj. Antideslumbrante.
Antigone [æn'tigəni] pr. n. Antígona, *f.*
anti-government ['ænti'gʌvnmənt] adj. Antigubernamental.
antihistamine ['ænti'histəmi:n] adj. Antihistamínico, ca.
— N. Antihistamínico, *m.*
antihysteric ['æntihis'terik] adj. Antihistérico, ca.
antiinflationary ['æntiin'fleiʃnəri] adj. Antiinflacionista.
antiknock ['æntinɔk] adj. Antidetonante.
— N. Antidetonante, *m.*
Antillean [æn'tiliən] adj./n. Antillano, na.
Antilles [æn'tili:z] pl. pr. n. GEOGR. Antillas, *f.*
antilogarithm ['ænti'lɔgəriθəm] n. MATH. Antilogaritmo, *m.*
antilogy [æn'tilədʒi] n. Antilogía, *f.*
antimacassar ['æntimə'kæsə*] n. Antimacasar, *m.*, macasar *m.*
antimagnetic ['æntimæg'netik] adj. Antimagnético, ca.
antimalarial ['æntimə'lεəriəl] adj. Antipalúdico, ca.
anti-masonic ['æntimə'sɔnik] adj. Antimasónico, ca.
antimatter ['ænti,mætə*] n. Antimateria, *f.*
antimilitarism ['ænti'militərizəm] n. Antimilitarismo, *m.*
antimilitarist ['ænti'militərist] adj./n. Antimilitarista.
antimonarchical ['æntimɔ'nɑ:kikəl] adj. Antimonárquico, ca.
antimonial [,ænti'məunjəl] adj. CHEM. Antimonial.
antimoniate [ænti'məunieit] n. CHEM. Antimoniato, *m.*
antimoniated [—id] adj. CHEM. Antimoniado, da.
antimony ['æntiməni] n. CHEM. Antimonio, *m.*
antinational ['ænti'næʃənl] adj. Antinacional.
antineuralgic ['æntinjuə'rældʒik] adj. MED. Antineurálgico, ca.
antinode ['æntinəud] n. Antinodo, *m* (in acoustics).
antinomic [,ænti'nɔmik] or **antinomical** [—əl] adj. Antinómico, ca.
antinomy [æn'tinəmi] n. Antinomia, *f.*
Antioch ['æntiɔk] pr. n. Antioquía.
Antiochus [æn'taiəkəs] pr. n. Antíoco, *m.*
antiparliamentarianism ['ænti,pɑ:ləmen'tεəriənizem] n. Antiparlamentarismo, *m.*
antiparliamentary ['ænti,pɑ:lə'mentəri] adj. Antiparlamentario, ria.
antiparticle ['ænti'pɑ:tikl] n. PHYS. Antipartícula, *f.*
antipathetic ['æntipə'θetik] or **antipathetical** [—əl] adj. Antipático, ca (causing antipathy). || Contrario, ria; opuesto, ta (against).
antipathy [æn'tipəθi] n. Antipatía, *f.*, hostilidad, *f.* || Repugnancia, *f.* (*to*, hacia) [repugnance].
antipatriotic ['ænti,pætri'ɔtik] adj. Antipatriota, antipatriótico, ca.
antipatriotism ['ænti'pætriətizəm] n. Antipatriotismo, *m.*
antiperistaltic ['ænti,peri'stæltik] adj. Antiperistáltico, ca.
antipersonnel ['æntipə:sə'nel] adj. MIL. Antipersonal.
antiphilosophic ['ænti,filə'sɔfik] or **antiphilosophical** [—əl] adj. Antifilosófico, ca.
antiphlogistic ['ætifləu'dʒistik] adj. MED. Antiflogístico, ca.
— N. Antiflogístico, *m.*
antiphon ['æntifən] n. REL. Antífona, *f.*
antiphonal [æn'tifənl] n. Antifonario, *m.*
antiphonary [æn'tifənəri] n. Antifonario, *m.*
antiphrasis [æn'tifrəsis] n. Antífrasis, *f.*
antipodal [æn'tipədl] adj. Antípoda.
antipode [æn'tipəud] n. Antípoda, *m.*
antipodes [æn'tipədi:z] pl. n. GEOGR. Antípodas, *f.*
antipope ['æntipəup] n. Antipapa, *m.*
antiprogressive ['æntiprə'gresiv] adj./n. Antiprogresista.
antiprohibitionist ['ænti,prəui'biʃənist] adj./n. Antiprohibicionista.
antiprotectionist ['æntiprə'tekʃənist] adj./n. Antiproteccionista.
antiproton ['ænti'prəutɔn] n. PHYS. Antiprotón, *m.*
antiputrefactive ['ænti,pju:tri'fæktiv] adj. BIOL. Antipútrido, da.
— N. Antipútrido, *m.*
antipyretic ['æntipai'retik] adj. MED. Antipirético, ca.
— N. Antipirético, *m.*
antipyrine [ænti'pairi:n] n. MED. Antipirina, *f.*
antiquarian [,ænti'kwεəriən] n. Anticuario, *m.*
antiquary ['æntikwəri] n. Anticuario, *m.*
antiquated ['æntikweitid] adj. Anticuado, da.
antique [æn'ti:k] adj. Antiguo, gua; viejo, ja (old). || Anticuado, da (antiquated).
— N. Antigüedad, *f.* || FIG. Antigualla, *f.* (pejorative). || — *Antique dealer*, anticuario, *m.* || *Antiques*, antigüedades. || *Antique shop*, anticuario, *m.*, tienda (*f.*) de antigüedades.
antiquity [æn'tikwiti] n. Antigüedad, *f.* || — Pl. Antigüedades, *f.*
antirabic [ænti'ræbik] adj. Antirrábico, ca.
antirachitic ['æntiræ'kitik] adj. MED. Antirraquítico, ca.
antiradar ['ænti'reidɑ:*] adj. Antirradar.
antireligious ['æntiri'lidʒəs] adj. Antirreligioso, sa.
antirepublican ['æntiri'pʌblikən] adj./n. Antirrepublicano, na.
antirevolutionary ['ænti,revə'lu:ʃnəri] adj./n. Antirrevolucionario, ria.
antirust ['ænti'rʌst] adj. Antioxidante.
antiscians [æn'tisʃənz] pl. n. Antiscios, *m.*
antiscorbutic ['æntiskɔ:'bju:tik] adj. MED. Antiescorbútico, ca.
— N. Antiescorbútico, *m.*
anti-Semite ['ænti'si:mait] n. Antisemita, *m.* & *f.*
anti-Semitic ['æntisi'mitik] adj. Antisemítico, ca.
anti-Semitism ['ænti'semitizəm] n. Antisemitismo, *m.*
antisepsis [,ænti'sepsis] n. MED. Antisepsia, *f.*
antiseptic [,ænti'septik] adj. MED. Antiséptico, ca.
— N. Antiséptico, *m.*
antiskid ['æntiskid] adj. Antideslizante.
antislavery ['ænti'sleivəri] adj. Antiesclavista.
antisocial ['ænti'səuʃəl] adj. Antisocial.
antispasmodic ['æntispæz'mɔdik] adj. MED. Antiespasmódico, ca.
— N. MED. Antiespasmódico, *m.*
antistrophe [æn'tistrəfi] n. Antistrofa, *f.*
antisubmarine ['ænti,sʌbmə'ri:n] adj. Antisubmarino, na.
antitank ['ænti'tæŋk] adj. MIL. Antitanque, contra carros de combate.
antitetanic ['æntite'tænik] adj. MED. Antitetánico, ca.
anti-theft device ['ænti'θeftdi,vais] n. Antirrobo, *m.*
antithesis [æn'tiθisis] n. Antítesis, *f.*
— OBSERV. El plural de *antithesis* es *antitheses*.
antithetic [,ænti'θetik] or **antithetical** [—əl] adj. Antitético, ca.
antitoxic [,ænti'tɔksik] adj. Antitóxico, ca.
antitoxin [,ænti'tɔksin] n. MED. Antitoxina, *f.*
antitrades ['ænti'treidz] pl. n. Contraalisios, *m.* (winds).
antitrust ['ænti'trʌst] adj. Antimonopolista.
antitubercular ['æntitju'bə:kjulə*] adj. MED. Antituberculoso, sa.
antitype ['æntitaip] n. Antitipo, *m.*, prototipo, *m.*
antivenin ['ænti'venin] n. U. S. Antitoxina, *f.*
antivenereal [æntivi'niəriəl] adj. Antivenéreo, a.
antler ['æntlə*] n. Mogote, *m.*, cornamenta, *f.*
antlered [—d] adj. Astado, da.
ant lion ['ænt,laiən] n. Hormiga (*f.*) león (insect).
Antoinette [,æntuɑ'net] pr. n. Antonia, *f.*
Antoninus [,æntəu'nainəs] pr. n. Antonino, *m.*
antonomasia [,æntənə'meiziə] n. Antonomasia, *f.*

Antony [ˈæntəni] pr. n. Antonio, *m.*
antonym [ˈæntənim] n. Antónimo, *m.*
antrum [ˈæntrəm] n. ANAT. Cavidad, *f.*
— OBSERV. El plural de *antrum* es *antra*.
Antwerp [ˈæntwə:p] pr. n. GEOGR. Amberes.
anuran [əˈnjurən] n. ZOOL. Anuro, *m.*
— Adj. Anuro, ra.
anurous [əˈnju:rəs] adj. ZOOL. Anuro, ra.
anury [əˈnju:ri] n. MED. Anuria *f.*
anus [ˈeinəs] n. ANAT. Ano, *m.*
anvil [ˈænvil] n. Yunque, *m.* || ANAT. Yunque, *m.* || FIG. *On the anvil*, sobre el tapete (under discussion), en el telar (in preparation).
anxiety [æŋˈzaiəti] n. Inquietud, *f.*, ansiedad, *f.*, preocupación, *f.* (worry): *anxiety about one's health*, inquietud por su salud; *anxiety for s.o.'s safety*, inquietud por la seguridad de alguien. || Anhelo, *m.*, ansia, *f.* (yearning): *his anxiety to make a good impression*, su ansia de dar una buena impresión. || Ansia, *f.* (intense dread). || MED. Ansiedad, *f.*
anxious [ˈæŋkʃəs] adj. Inquieto, ta; preocupado, da (worried): *an anxious glance*, una mirada inquieta; *anxious about the future*, preocupado por el futuro. || De inquietud: *I spent two very anxious hours*, pasé dos horas de mucha inquietud. || Lleno de preocupaciones: *an anxious job*, un trabajo lleno de preocupaciones. || Deseoso, sa (desirous): *he is anxious to see you*, está deseoso de verte. || Ansioso, sa (yearning): *anxious for riches*, ansioso de riqueza.
anxiously [—li] adv. Con inquietud (worriedly). || Con ansia, ansiosamente: *waiting anxiously for the results*, esperando con ansia los resultados.
anxiousness [—nis] n. Inquietud, *f.*, preocupación, *f.*
any [ˈeni] adj. Alguno, na: *is there any reason?*, ¿hay alguna razón?; *is there any Englishman here?*, ¿hay algún inglés aquí? || Ninguno, na; alguno, na: *there isn't any problem*, no hay ningún problema, no hay problema alguno. || Cualquiera (whatever, whichever): *any book will do*, cualquier libro vale; *any woman will tell you that*, cualquier mujer te lo dirá. || Todo, da; cualquiera (all): *any lack of discipline will be punished*, toda indisciplina será castigada; *to avoid any contact with*, evitar todo contacto con. || Not translated: *have you got any cigarettes?*, ¿tienes cigarrillos?; *is there any bread?*, ¿hay pan?; *don't bring any friends*, no traigas a amigos (see OBSERV. I). || — *Any amount of*, una gran cantidad de. || *Any and every*, todos, todas. || *Any... at all*, algo de: *is there any bread at all?*, ¿hay algo de pan?; cualquiera (no matter which): *any day at all*, un día cualquiera, cualquier día. || *Any day now*, cualquier día de éstos. || *Any minute, any moment, any time now*, de un momento a otro. || *Any old thing*, cualquier cosa. || *At any cost*, a toda costa. || *At any rate*, de todas formas. || *At any time*, en cualquier momento. || *In any case*, en todo caso. || *Not any ... at all*, ninguno, na; alguno, na: *I couldn't find any paper at all*, no podía encontrar papel alguno *or* ningún papel.
— Adv. Algo: *are you any better?*, ¿estás algo mejor?; *did it hurt you any?*, ¿te ha dolido algo? || Nada (in negative constructions): *he isn't any better*, no está nada mejor; *it didn't hurt me any*, no me ha dolido nada. || Not translated: *I can't go any further*, no puedo ir más lejos; *don't do it any more*, no lo hagas más (see OBSERV. II). || — *Any longer*, más tiempo. || *Any the*, algo: *is he any the happier?*, ¿está algo más contento? || *Not any the*, nada: *not any the worse*, nada peor.
— Pron. Alguno, na: *can you see any?*, ¿ves alguno?; *if any of you should arrive late*, si alguno de vosotros llega tarde. || Ninguno, na (in negative sentences): *I don't know any of them*, no conozco a ninguno de ellos. || Cualquiera: *any of them would do it for you*, cualquiera de ellos lo haría por ti. || Not translated: *I can't offer you any wine*; *there isn't any*, no te puedo ofrecer vino, no hay. || — FAM. *Any more for any more?*, ¿alguien quiere algo más? || *If any, I would have chosen the big one*, de haber cogido uno hubiera escogido el grande. || *There are few men, if any, who would be brave enough*, pocos hombres, si los hay, tendrían bastante valor.

— OBSERV. I. Since "any" is a normal feature of negative and interrogative constructions in English, it is often not translated into Spanish.
— OBSERV. II. The adverb "any", when followed by a comparative, is often translated into Spanish by a simple comparative.
— OBSERV. III. *Alguno*, and *ninguno* are apocopated to *algún* and *ningún* in Spanish when they precede a masculine singular noun. Similarly *cualquiera* becomes *cualquier* before a singular masculine or feminine noun.

anybody [—ˌbɔdi] pron. Cualquiera, cualquier persona: *anybody could do it*, lo podría hacer cualquiera, lo podría hacer cualquier persona. || Alguien: *did you see anybody?*, ¿viste a alguien?; *if anybody calls*, si alguien llama. || Nadie (nobody): *I don't know anybody here*, no conozco a nadie aquí. || *Better, worse than anybody*, mejor, peor que nadie.
anyhow [—hau] adv. De cualquier manera, de cualquier modo (carelessly, in any manner). || De todos modos, de todas maneras (in any case).
anymore [—ˈmɔ:*] adv. Nunca más, ya.
anyone [—wʌn] pron. See ANYBODY.
anything [—θiŋ] pron. Algo: *did you say anything?*, ¿has dicho algo? || Nada: *I didn't say anything*, no dije nada; *without saying anything*, sin decir nada. || Cualquier cosa: *he eats anything*, come cualquier cosa; *anything will do*, cualquier cosa valdrá. || Todo: *anything is possible*, todo es posible; *she likes anything classical*, le gusta todo lo clásico. || — *Anything else?*, ¿algo más? || *Have you seen anything of David lately?*, ¿has visto a David últimamente? || *If anything*, de + infin. + algo: *what would you do?* — *If anything I'd take a holiday*, ¿qué harías? — De hacer algo me iría de vacaciones. || *If he were anything of a gentleman*, si fuera realmente un caballero. || *Is there anything I can do for you?*, ¿en qué puedo servirle? (in a shop), ¿puedo hacer algo por ti? || *I would give anything for*, daría cualquier cosa por. || *Like anything*, como nadie: *to work like anything*, trabajar como nadie; como nunca: *it is raining like anything*, llueve como nunca. || *To be anything but stupid*, no ser nada tonto. || *To be as easy as anything*, ser coser y cantar, estar tirado (fam.).
— Adv. Algo: *is he anything like his brother?*, ¿se parece algo a su hermano? || Ni mucho menos, muy lejos de: *it isn't anything like as easy as I thought*, no es, ni mucho menos, tan fácil como pensaba; está muy lejos de ser tan fácil como pensaba. || *Anything but*, todo menos: *he is anything but clever*, es todo menos inteligente.
anyway [—wei] adv. See ANYHOW.
anywhere [—wɛə*] adv. En cualquier sitio, en cualquier parte, donde sea, dondequiera: *put it down anywhere*, ponlo en cualquier sitio. || En algún sitio, en alguna parte: *can you see it anywhere?*, ¿lo ves en algún sitio? || A cualquier sitio, dondequiera, a donde sea (with a verb of motion): *take me anywhere*, llévame a cualquier sitio. || En todas partes (everywhere): *anywhere in the world*, en todas partes del mundo. || — *Anywhere from five to ten pounds*, entre cinco y diez libras. || *Anywhere else*, en cualquier otro sitio. || *Are you anywhere near finished?*, ¿os falta mucho para acabar? || *Miles from anywhere*, muy lejos, en el quinto pino. || *Not anywhere*, en ningún sitio, en ninguna parte; a ninguna parte (motion).
anywise [—waiz] adv. De cualquier manera, de cualquier modo, de cualquier forma (anyhow). || En cierta manera, en cierto modo (in any way). || *Not anywise*, de ninguna manera, de ningún modo (in no way).
aorist [ˈɛərist] n. GRAMM. Aoristo, *m.*
aorta [eiˈɔ:tə] n. ANAT. Aorta, *f.*
aortic [eiˈɔ:tik] adj. Aórtico, ca.
aortitis [eiɔ:ˈtaitis] n. MED. Aortitis, *f.*
apace [əˈpeis] adv. Aprisa, rápidamente.
apache [əˈpæʃ] n. Apache, *m.* (tough).
Apache [əˈpætʃi] n. Apache, *m.*
apanage [ˈæpənidʒ] n. HIST. Infantado, *m.* || Herencia, *f.* (inheritance). || Dependencia, *f.* (territory). || *To be the apanage of*, ser privativo de, ser el patrimonio de.
apart [əˈpɑ:t] adj. Aparte: *he is a man apart*, es un hombre aparte.
— Adv. Aparte: *he stood apart*, se mantuvo aparte; *to put sth. apart*, poner algo aparte; *to treat a matter apart*, tratar un asunto aparte. || Separado por: *ten centimetres apart*, separados por diez centímetros. || Separadamente, por separado: *to consider each topic apart*, examinar cada tema separadamente. || — *Apart from*, aparte de, aparte (except for): *apart from the style I quite like it*, aparte del estilo *or* el estilo aparte, me gusta bastante; aparte de, además de (as well as). || *Joking apart*, bromas aparte. || FIG. *To be miles apart*, estar a kilómetros de distancia. || *To come apart*, desprenderse (to come off), ser desmontable (able to be dismantled), estropearse: *this chair is coming apart*, esta silla se está estropeando. || *To get o to pull two things apart*, separar dos cosas. || *To keep apart*, apartar (to isolate), apartarse (to isolate o.s.), separar (to separate): *to keep the boys apart from the girls*, separar a los chicos de las chicas. || *To live apart*, vivir apartado. || *To move apart to let s.o. pass*, apartarse para dejar pasar a alguien. || *To set apart*, apartar, reservar. || *To stand apart*, mantenerse apartado. || *To stand with one's legs apart*, estar con las piernas separadas. || *To take apart*, desmontar (to dismantle), ser desmontable (able to be dismantled), tomar aparte (a person). || *To tear apart*, destrozar (sth.), hacer trizas (s.o.) || *To tell two things apart*, distinguir dos cosas una de otra.
apartheid [əˈpɑ:theit] n. « Apartheid », *m.*, segregación (*f.*) racial.
apartment [əˈpɑ:tmənt] n. Piso, *m.*, apartamento, *m.* (flat). || Cuarto, *m.*, habitación, *f.* (room). || — Pl. Piso, *m. sing.*, apartamento, *m. sing.* || *Apartment house*, casa (*f.*) de pisos.
apathetic [ˌæpəˈθetik] adj. Apático, ca.
apathy [ˈæpəθi] n. Apatía, *f.* || Indiferencia, *f.*, falta (*f.*) de interés (indifference).
apatite [ˈæpətait] n. MIN. Apatito, *m.*
ape [eip] n. ZOOL. Mono, *m.* || FIG. Imitamonos, *m.* & *f. inv.* || FIG. *To play the ape*, dárselas de gracioso.
ape [eip] v. tr. Imitar, remedar.
apeak [əˈpi:k] adj./adv. MAR. A pique.
apelike [ˈeiplaik] adj. Simiesco, ca.
Apennines [ˈæpinainz] pl. pr. n. GEOGR. Apeninos, *m.*

apepsy [ə'pepsi] n. MED. Apepsia, *f.*
aperient [ə'piəriənt] adj. MED. Laxante.
— N. Laxante, *m.*
aperiodic ['eipiəri'ɔdik] adj. Aperiódico, ca.
apéritif [ə,periti:f] n. Aperitivo, *m.* (drink).
aperitive [ə'peritiv] adj. MED. Laxante.
— N. Laxante, *m.*
aperture ['æpətjuə*] n. Abertura, *f.* || Rendija, *f.*, resquicio, *m.* (crack).
apery ['eipəri] n. Mímica, *f.* (mimicking).
apetalous [ei'petələs] adj. BOT. Apétalo, la; sin pétalos.
apex ['eipeks] n. Ápice, *m.*, cima, *f.* (highest point). || FIG. Cumbre, *f.*, cúspide, *f.* (height). || ASTR. Ápex, *m.* || Vértice, *m.* (of a triangle).
— OBSERV. La palabra inglesa *apex* tiene dos plurales: *apices* y *apexes.*
aphaeresis [æ'fiərisis] n. GRAMM. Aféresis, *f.*
aphasia [æ'feizjə] n. Afasia, *f.*
aphasiac [ə'feisiək] or **aphasic** [ə'feizik] adj./n. MED. Afásico, ca.
aphelion [æ'fi:ljən] n. ASTR. Afelio, *m.*
aphesis ['æfisis] n. GRAMM. Aféresis, *f.*
aphid ['eifid] n. Áfido, *m.* (insect).
aphis ['eifis] n. Áfido, *m.* (insect).
— OBSERV. El plural de *aphis* es *aphides.*
aphonia [æ'fəunjə] n. MED. Afonía, *f.*
aphonic [æ'fɔnik] adj. Afónico, ca; áfono, na.
aphony ['æfəni] n. MED. Afonía, *f.*
aphorism ['æfərizəm] n. Aforismo, *m.*
aphorismic [,æfə'rizmik] o **aphoristic** [,æfə'ristik] adj. Aforístico, ca.
aphrodisiac [,æfrəu'diziæk] adj. Afrodisiaco, ca.
— N. Afrodisiaco, *m.*
Aphrodite [,æfrə'daiti] pr. n. Afrodita, *f.*
aphtha ['æfθə] n. MED. Afta, *f.*
aphthous ['æfθəs] adj. MED. Aftoso, sa: *aphthous fever*, fiebre aftosa.
apiarian [,eipi'ɛəriən] adj. Apícola.
apiarist ['eipjərist] n. Apicultor, ra.
apiary ['eipjəri] n. Colmenar, *m.*, abejera, *f.*
apical ['æpikəl] adj. Apical. || Que está en la cumbre.
apices ['eipisi:z] pl. n. See APEX.
apicultural [,eipi'kʌltʃərəl] adj. Apícola.
apiculture ['eipikʌltʃə*] n. Apicultura, *f.*
apiculturist [—rist] n. Apicultor, ra (beekeeper).
apiece [ə'pi:s] adv. Cada uno: *we had two blankets apiece*, teníamos dos mantas cada uno; *they cost a pound apiece*, cuestan una libra cada uno; *he gave them one apiece*, les dio uno a cada uno. || Por persona, por cabeza (per person).
apish ['eipiʃ] adj. Simiesco, ca (apelike). || FIG. Necio, cia; tonto, ta (stupid). | Imitador, ra; remedador, ra (imitative).
aplanatic [,æplə'nætik] adj. PHYS. Aplanético, ca.
aplenty [ə'plenti] adv. En abundancia.
aplomb [ə'plɔm] n. Aplomo, *m.*, sangre (*f.*) fría.
apnoea or **apnea** ['æpniə] n. MED. Apnea, *f.*
Apocalypse [ə'pɔkəlips] n. Apocalipsis, *m.*
apocalyptic [ə,pɔkə'liptik] or **apocalyptical** [—əl] adj. Apocalíptico, ca.
apocopate [ə'pɔkəpeit] v. tr. GRAMM. Apocopar.
apocopation [ə,pɔkə'peiʃən] n. GRAMM. Apócope, *f.*
apocope [ə'pɔkəpi] n. GRAMM. Apócope, *f.*
Apocrypha [ə'pɔkrifə] pl. n. Libros (*m.*) apócrifos.
apocryphal [—l] adj. Apócrifo, fa.
apod ['æpɔd] n. ZOOL. Ápodo, *m.*
apodal ['æpədəl] adj. ZOOL. Ápodo, da.
apodictic [,æpəu'diktik] adj. Apodíctico, ca (incontestable).
apodosis [ə'pɔdəusis] n. Apódosis, *f.*
— OBSERV. El plural de *apodosis* es *apodoses.*
apogee ['æpəudʒi:] n. ASTR. FIG. Apogeo, *m.*
apolitical [æpɔ'litikəl] adj. Apolítico, ca.
apoliticism [æpɔ'litisizəm] n. Apolitismo.
Apollo [ə'pɔləu] pr. n. MYTH. Apolo, *m.*
Apollonian [,æpə'ləunjən] adj. Apolíneo, a.
apologetic [ə,pɔlə'dʒetik] adj. Apologético, ca: *an apologetic treatise*, un tratado apologético. || *He was very apologetic about the incident*, me ofreció toda clase de disculpas por el incidente.
apologetical [—əl] adj. See APOLOGETIC.
apologetically [—əli] adv. Excusándose, disculpándose.
apologetics [—s] n. Apologética, *f.*
apologia [,æpə'ləudʒjə] n. Apología, *f.*
apologist [ə'pɔlədʒist] n. Apologista, *m.* & *f.*
apologize [ə'pɔlədʒaiz] v. intr. Disculparse (*for*, de, por; *to*, con), pedir perdón (*for*, por; *to*, a).
apologue ['æpəlɔg] n. Apólogo, *m.*
apology [ə'pɔlədʒi] n. Disculpa, *f.*, excusa, *f.*: *my apologies*, mis disculpas. || Apología, *f.*, defensa, *f.* (defence). || FAM. Birria, *f.*: *what an apology for a house!*, ¡vaya birria de casa! || *To make an apology, to offer one's apologies*, disculparse, presentar sus excusas.
aponeurosis [æpənju'rəusis] n. Aponeurosis, *f.*
aponeurotic [æpənju'rɔtik] adj. Aponeurótico, ca.
apophthegm ['æpəuθem] n. Apotegma, *m.*
apophysis [ə'pɔfisis] n. ANAT. Apófisis, *f.*
— OBSERV. El plural de la palabra inglesa *apophysis* es *apophyses.*

apoplectic [,æpəu'plektik] adj./n. Apoplético, ca. || FIG. *To get apoplectic*, ponerse furioso.
apoplexy ['æpəpleksi] n. MED. Apoplejía, *f.*
aporia [ə'pɔ:riə] n. PHIL. Aporía, *f.*
apostasy [ə'pɔstəsi] n. Apostasía, *f.*
apostate [ə'pɔstit] adj./n. Apóstata.
apostatize [ə'pɔstətaiz] v. intr. Apostatar.
apostemate [ə'pɔstəmeit] v. tr. MED. Apostemar.
aposteme [ə'pɔsti:m] n. MED. Apostema, *f.*
a posteriori ['ei-pɔs'teri'ɔ:rai] adj./adv. A posteriori.
apostil [ə'pɔstil] n. Apostilla, *f.*, nota (*f.*) marginal.
apostle [ə'pɔsl] n. Apóstol, *m.*: *the Acts of the Apostles*, los Hechos de los Apóstoles. || FIG. Apóstol, *m.*
apostleship [—ʃip] or **apostolate** [ə'pɔstəlit] n. Apostolado, *m.*
apostolic [,æpəs'tɔlik] or **apostolical** [—əl] adj. Apostólico, ca. || *Apostolic See*, sede apostólica.
apostrophe [ə'pɔstrəfi] n. Apóstrofo, *m.* (punctuation mark). || Apóstrofe, *m.* (in rhetoric).
apostrophize [ə'pɔstrəfaiz] v. tr. Apostrofar.
apothecary [ə'pɔθikəri] n. Boticario, *m.*
apothegm ['æpəθem] n. Apotegma, *m.*
apothem ['æpəθem] n. MATH. Apotema, *f.*
apotheosis [ə,pɔθi'əusis] n. Apoteosis, *f.*
apotheosize [ə'pɔθiəusaiz] v. tr. Deificar (to deify). || Glorificar (to glorify). || Idealizar (to idealize).
appal or **appall** [ə'pɔ:l] v. tr. Horrorizar, espantar (to frighten). || Horrorizar, repugnar (to repulse). || Asombrar (to amaze).
Appalachians [,æpə'leitʃjənz] pr. n. Apalaches, *m. pl.* (mountains).
appalling [ə'pɔ:liŋ] adj. Espantoso, sa; horrible, horroroso, sa (frightening). || Pésimo, ma (very bad). || Asombroso, sa (amazing).
appanage ['æpənidʒ] n. See APANAGE.
apparatus [,æpə'reitəs] n. Aparato, *m.* (system): *digestive apparatus*, aparato digestivo. || Equipo, *m.*: *climbing apparatus*, equipo de montañismo; *breathing apparatus*, equipo de respiración. || Aparatos, *m. pl.* (in gymnastics). || FIG. *The apparatus of government*, el aparato del gobierno.
— OBSERV. El plural de *apparatus* es *apparatuses* o *apparatus.*
apparel [ə'pærəl] n. POET. Atavío, *m.*, indumentaria, *f.* (attire). || Ropa, *f.* (clothes). || MAR. Aparejo, *m.*
apparel [ə'pærəl] v. tr. POET. Ataviar, vestir. || MAR. Aparejar.
apparent [ə'pærənt] adj. Aparente: *his apparent coldness is only shyness*, su aparente frialdad es sólo timidez. || Evidente, claro, ra; manifiesto, ta (obvious): *his sadness was very apparent*, su tristeza era muy evidente. || JUR. *Heir apparent*, presunto heredero.
apparently [—li] adv. Por lo visto, aparentemente, al parecer (seemingly). || Evidentemente, claramente (obviously).
apparition [,æpə'riʃən] n. Aparición, *f.*
apparitor [ə'pæritɔ:*] n. JUR. Ordenanza, *m.*
appeal [ə'pi:l] n. JUR. Apelación, *f.*: *to make an appeal*, presentar *or* interponer una apelación; *without appeal*, sin apelación. || Llamamiento, *m.* (to the masses): *an appeal for rebellion*, un llamamiento a la sublevación; *an appeal on behalf of the blind*, un llamamiento en favor de los ciegos. || Llamada, *f.*: *an appeal for help*, una llamada de socorro. || Súplica, *f.*, ruego, *m.*, petición, *f.* (petition). || Atractivo, *m.*, interés, *m.*: *this has no appeal for the younger generation*, esto no tiene atractivo para los jóvenes. || Solicitación, *f.*: *appeal for funds*, solicitación de fondos. || Cuestación, *f.* (of charity). || — JUR. *Appeal for annulment*, recurso (*m.*) de nulidad. | *Court of appeal*, tribunal (*m.*) de apelación. | *Right of appeal*, derecho (*m.*) de apelación.
appeal [ə'pi:l] v. tr. U. S. JUR. Apelar de. || U. S. JUR. *To appeal a case*, interponer apelación, presentar apelación.
— V. intr. JUR. Apelar (*to*, a; *against*, contra, de): *to appeal against a decision*, apelar de una decisión. || Suplicar, rogar (to beg): *he appealed to the crowd to calm down*, suplicó a la multitud que se calmase. || Recurrir, apelar: *to appeal to s.o.'s kindness*, apelar a la bondad de uno; *to appeal to arms*, recurrir a las armas. || Hacer un llamamiento: *to appeal on behalf of the blind*, hacer un llamamiento en favor de los ciegos. || Gustar (to please): *the idea doesn't appeal to me*, la idea no me gusta. || Interesar, atraer (to interest): *this will appeal to all the readers*, esto interesará a todos los lectores.
appealable [ə'pi:ləbl] adj. JUR. Apelable.
appealing [ə'pi:liŋ] adj. Suplicante (beseeching). || Atrayente, atractivo, va (pleasing). || Conmovedor, ra (touching).
appear [ə'piə*] v. intr. Aparecer (to come into sight): *the town appeared on the horizon*, la ciudad apareció en el horizonte; *he was the last to appear*, fue el último en aparecer; *this custom appears in the tenth century*, esta costumbre aparece en el siglo diez. || Aparecer, publicarse (a book). || Parecer (to seem): *he appears to be very nice*, parece ser muy simpático; *so it appears*, según parece. || THEATR. Actuar (to act). || — JUR. *To appear in court*, comparecer ante un tribunal. || *To appear on the stage*, aparecer en escena.
appearance [—rəns] n. Aparición, *f.* (act of appearing): *the appearance of smoke on the horizon raised*

the sailors' hopes, la aparición de humo en el horizonte dio esperanza a los marineros; *his sudden appearance startled me*, su aparición súbita me sobresaltó. || Aspecto, *m.*, apariencia, *f.* (looks): *his dishevelled appearance*, su aspecto desaliñado. || Aparición, *f.*, publicación, *f.* (of a book). || COMM. Presentación, *f.* || JUR. Comparecencia, *f.* || — Pl. Apariencias, *f.*: *one should not judge by appearances*, no se debe juzgar por las apariencias. || — *Appearances are deceptive*, las apariencias engañan. || *At first appearance*, a primera vista. || THEATR. *First appearance*, primera presentación, début, *m.* || *To all appearances*, según parece, al parecer, por lo visto, aparentemente. || *To keep up appearances*, guardar *or* salvar las apariencias. || *To make an appearance*, aparecer, dejarse ver (at a meeting, party, etc.), tener una actuación, salir (in theatre). || *To put in an appearance*, aparecer, dejarse ver, hacer acto de presencia. || *To put on an appearance of surprise*, simular *or* fingir la sorpresa.

appease [əˈpi:z] v. tr. Apaciguar (to pacify, to calm down). || Aplacar (anger). || Aplacar, mitigar (thirst, hunger).

appeasement [—mənt] n. Apaciguamiento, *m.*

appellant [əˈpelənt] adj./n. JUR. Apelante.

appellate [əˈpelit] adj. JUR. De apelación (court).

appellation [ˌæpəˈleiʃən] n. Título, *m.*, denominación, *f.*, nombre, *m.* (name). || Apodo, *m.* (nickname).

appellative [əˈpelətiv] adj. GRAMM. Apelativo, va.
— N. Apelativo, *m.*

append [əˈpend] v. tr. Añadir, adjuntar (to add, to join). || Adjuntar (sth. to a document). || Poner (one's signature).

appendage [—idʒ] n. ANAT. Apéndice, *m.* || Accesorio, *m.* (accessory, accompaniment). || Añadidura, *f.* (sth. added). || Anexo, *m.* (of building).

appendant [—ənt] adj. Anexo, xa (annexed). || Adjunto, ta (accompanying). || JUR. Accesorio, ria.
— N. Dependencia, *f.* || ANAT. Anexo, *m.* || JUR. Derecho (*m.*) accesorio.

appendectomy [ˌæpinˈdektəmi] or **appendicectomy** [əˌpendiˈsektəmi] n. MED. Apendectomía, *f.*

appendicitis [əˌpendiˈsaitis] n. MED. Apendicitis, *f.*

appendicular [ˌæpenˈdikjulə*] adj. Apendicular.

appendix [əˈpendiks] n. ANAT. Apéndice, *m.* || Apéndice, *m.* (of book).
— OBSERV. El plural de *appendix* es *appendices* o *appendixes*.

apperceive [ˌæpəˈsi:v] v. tr. Percibir, apercibir.

appertain [ˌæpəˈtein] v. intr. Pertenecer (to belong). || Relacionarse (*to*, con) [to be related to]. || Atañer, incumbir (to be incumbent). || Corresponder (to correspond).

appetence [ˈæpitəns] or **appetency** [—i] n. Apetencia, *f.* || Afinidad, f. (between things).

appetent [ˈæpitənt] adj. Ávido, da; codicioso, sa.

appetite [ˈæpitait] n. Apetito, *m.*: *to whet one's appetite*, abrir *or* dar *or* despertar el apetito; *to have a good appetite*, tener mucho apetito. || FIG. Apetito, *m.*, apetencia, *f.* (desire, longing): *appetite for power*, apetito de poder. || — *Sexual appetite*, apetito carnal. || *To eat with an appetite*, comer con mucho apetito.

appetitive [æˈpetitiv] adj. Apetitivo, va.

appetizer [ˈæpitaizə*] n. Aperitivo, *m.* (drink). || Tapa, *f.* (food).

appetizing [ˈæpitaiziŋ] adj. Apetitoso, sa; apetecedor, ra.

Appian Way [ˈæpiənˈwei] pr. n. Vía (*f.*) Apia.

applaud [əˈplɔ:d] v. intr. Aplaudir.
— V. tr. Aplaudir. || FIG. Alabar, celebrar, aplaudir (to praise).

applause [əˈplɔ:z] n. Aplauso, *m.*: *to the applause of*, con el aplauso de. || Aplausos, *m. pl.*: *a thunder of applause*, una salva de aplausos. || FIG. Alabanza, *f.* (praise). | Aprobación, *f.* (approval). || *A round of applause*, una salva de aplausos.

apple [ˈæpl] n. BOT. Manzano, *m.* (tree). | Manzana, *f.* (fruit): *apple pie*, pastel *or* tarta de manzana; *stewed apples*, compota de manzanas. || — *Apple brandy*, aguardiente (*m.*) de manzana. || *Apple green*, verde manzana. || FIG. *The apple of discord*, la manzana de la discordia. | *To be the apple of one's eye*, ser la niña de los ojos de uno.

applecart [—kɑ:t] n. FIG. *To upset s.o.'s applecart*, desbaratar los planes de uno.

applejack [—dʒæk] n. U. S. Aguardiente (*m.*) de manzana.

apple-pie bed [—paiˈbed] n. *To make s.o. an apple-pie bed*, hacer la petaca a uno.

apple-pie order [—paiˈɔ:də*] n. *In apple-pie order*, en perfecto orden.

appliance [əˈplaiəns] n. Aparato, *m.*, dispositivo, *m.*, artefacto, *m.* (apparatus). || Aplicación, *f.* (action). || MIL. Artefacto, *m.* || — Pl. Accesorios, *m.* || *Electrical appliance* o *home appliance*, electrodoméstico, *m.*, aparato electrodoméstico.

applicability [ˌæplikəˈbiliti] n. Aplicabilidad, *f.* || Pertinencia, *f.* (relevance).

applicable [ˈæplikəbl] adj. Aplicable. || Pertinente (relevant).

applicant [ˈæplikənt] n. Aspirante, *m.* & *f.*, pretendiente, *m.*: *applicant for a job*, aspirante *or* pretendiente a un puesto. || Candidato, ta (candidate). || JUR. Demandante, *m.* & *f.*

application [ˌæpliˈkeiʃən] n. Aplicación, *f.*: *the application of a theory*, la aplicación de una teoría; *the application of an ointment*, la aplicación de una pomada; *to show application in one's studies*, mostrar aplicación en los estudios. || Aplicación, *f.* (putting into practice). || Solicitud, *f.* (for a job, etc.): *the closing date for application*, la fecha tope para las solicitudes. || Petición, *f.*, solicitud, *f.* (request, petition). || — *Application form*, formulario, *m.* || MED. *For external application only*, para uso externo. || *To make an application for*, solicitar. || *To make an application to*, dirigirse a. || *To submit an application for membership of an organization*, pedir su ingreso en una organización.

applied [əˈplaid] adj. Aplicado, da. || *Applied for*, solicitado, da.

appliqué [æˈpli:kei] n. Aplicación, *f.* (fabric decoration).

apply [əˈplai] v. tr. Aplicar: *to apply a coat of paint, a theory, a bandage*, aplicar una capa de pintura, una teoría, una venda. || Destinar, afectar, asignar (funds). || JUR. Aplicar (law, rule). || TECH. Accionar. || *To apply o.s. to one's job*, aplicarse en su trabajo.
— V. intr. Aplicarse: *this rule applies to everyone*, esta regla se aplica a todos. || Solicitar: *to apply for a job*, solicitar un trabajo. || — *Apply within*, razón aquí. || *To apply to*, referirse a, ser relativo a (to refer to), dirigirse a, acudir a (to go).

appogiattura [əˌpɔdʒəˈtuərə] n. MUS. Apoyatura, *f.*

appoint [əˈpɔint] v. tr. Señalar, fijar, designar (a time, date, etc.): *at the appointed time*, a la hora fijada. || Nombrar, designar: *to appoint s.o. as mayor*, nombrar a uno alcalde; *to appoint s.o. to a post*, nombrar a uno para un puesto. || Designar (one's heirs). || Aparejar (to fit out). || Amueblar (to furnish).

appointee [əpɔinˈti:] n. Persona (*f.*) designada *or* nombrada.

appointment [əˈpɔintmənt] n. Cita, *f.* (date): *he broke the appointment*, faltó a la cita. || Nombramiento, *m.*, designación, *f.*: *the appointment of a secretary*, el nombramiento de un secretario. || Cargo, *m.*, empleo, *m.* (post). || — Pl. Equipo, *m. sing.* (equipment). || Mobiliario, *m. sing.* (furniture). || — *Appointment book*, agenda (*f.*) de entrevistas. || *By appointment to*, proveedores de. || *To keep an appointment*, acudir a una cita. || *To make an appointment*, pedir hora (at the doctor's, hairdresser's, etc.), quedar, citarse (*with*, con) [a friend].

apportion [əˈpɔ:ʃən] v. tr. Prorratear (a sum). || Asignar, conceder (to assign). || Desglosar (expenses). || Repartir (to share).

apportionment [—mənt] n. Prorrateo, *m.* (of a sum). || Desglose, *m.* (of expenses). || Reparto, *m.* (sharing).

appose [æˈpəuz] v. tr. Añadir.

apposite [ˈæpəzit] adj. Apropiado, da; conveniente.

apposition [ˌæpəˈziʃən] n. Yuxtaposición, *f.* || Añadidura, *f.*, añadido, *m.* (addition). || GRAMM. Aposición, *f*: *in apposition*, en aposición.

appositional [ˌæpəˈziʃənl] or **appositive** [æˈpɔzitiv] adj. Apositivo, va; en aposición.

appraisal [əˈpreizəl] n. Evaluación, *f.*, estimación, *f.*, valoración, *f.*, tasación, *f.*

appraise [əˈpreiz] v. tr. Valorar, evaluar, estimar, tasar.

appraisement [—mənt] n. See APPRAISAL.

appraiser [—ə*] n. U. S. Tasador, *m.* || *Official appraiser*, perito (*m.*) tasador.

appreciable [əˈpri:ʃəbl] adj. Apreciable, estimable: *an appreciable difference*, una diferencia apreciable. || Considerable, grande (considerable).

appreciate [əˈpri:ʃieit] v. tr. Comprender (to understand): *I appreciate your point of view*, comprendo su punto de vista. || Apreciar, estimar: *to appreciate a good film*, apreciar una buena película; *one cannot fully appreciate wealth without having known poverty*, uno no puede apreciar la riqueza sin haber conocido la pobreza. || Agradecer (to be grateful for): *I really appreciate your help*, le agradezco mucho su ayuda. || Apreciar, estimar, tasar, valorar, evaluar (to evaluate). || Aumentar el valor de (to raise the value of). || — *I fully appreciate that...*, me doy perfectamente cuenta de que... || *To appreciate sth. for its true value*, apreciar algo en su justo valor.
— V. intr. Valorizarse, subir.

appreciation [əˌpri:ʃiˈeiʃən] n. Aprecio, *m.*, apreciación, *f.* (understanding, enjoyment). || Agradecimiento, *m.*, reconocimiento, *m.*, gratitud, *f.* (gratitude). || Apreciación, *f.*, valoración, *f.* (appraisal). || Plusvalía, *f.*, subida, *f.*, aumento (*m.*) de valor (rise in value). || Crítica, *f.* (literary).

appreciative [əˈpri:ʃjətiv] or **appreciatory** [əˈpri:ʃjətəri] adj. Apreciativo, va. || Agradecido, da (grateful). || Sensible (sensitive). || Elogioso, sa (flattering). || Atento, ta (audience).

apprehend [ˌæpriˈhend] v. tr. Prender, detener, aprehender (to arrest). || Percibir, comprender (to perceive, to understand). || Temer (to fear).
— V. intr. Comprender.

apprehensible [ˌæpriˈhensəbl] adj. Comprensible. || Perceptible.

apprehension [ˌæpriˈhenʃən] n. Aprensión *f.*, temor, *m.*, recelo, *m.* (fear): *although he is healthy he has the apprehension that he is going to die,* aunque está sano tiene la aprensión de que se va a morir. || Detención, *f.*, prendimiento, *m.*, arresto, *m.* (arrest). || Percepción, *f.* (perception). || Comprensión, *f.* (understanding).

apprehensive [ˌæpriˈhensiv] adj. Aprensivo, va (fearful). || Inquieto, ta (worried): *apprehensive for s.o.'s safety,* inquieto por la seguridad de alguien. || De comprensión: *apprehensive capacity,* capacidad de comprensión. || Inteligente (intelligent). || *To be apprehensive for, that,* temer por, que.

apprehensiveness [—nis] n. Temor, *m.*, recelo, *m.*, aprensión, *f.* (fear). || Comprensión, *f.*

apprentice [əˈprentis] n. Aprendiz, za: *shoemaker's apprentice,* aprendiz de zapatero. || FIG. Principiante, novicio, cia (beginner).

apprentice [əˈprentis] v. tr. Colocar de aprendiz. || *To be apprenticed to,* estar de aprendiz con.

apprenticeship [—ʃip] n. Aprendizaje, *m.*: *to serve one's apprenticeship with,* hacer el aprendizaje con.

apprise or **apprize** [əˈpraiz] v. tr. Informar, avisar.

approach [əˈprəutʃ] n. Acercamiento, *m.*: *the approach of the troops,* el acercamiento de las tropas. || Acceso, *m.*, vía (*f.*) *or* camino (*m.*) de acceso: *the approach to the plateau was perilous,* el camino de acceso a la meseta era peligroso. || Acceso, *m.*: *difficult of approach,* de difícil acceso. || FIG. Manera de abordar *or* de empezar (way of beginning). | Aproximación, *f.* | Planteamiento, *m.*, enfoque, *m.* (way of looking at a problem). | Propuesta, *f.*, proposición, *f.*: *we have made several approaches but he will not sell the picture,* le hemos hecho varias proposiciones pero no quiere vender el cuadro. | Oferta, *f.* (offer). || — Pl. MIL. Aproches, *m.* || *To make approaches to a country,* intentar entrar en contacto con un país.

approach [əˈprəutʃ] v. intr. Acercarse, aproximarse: *the appointed hour was approaching,* se acercaba la hora señalada.

— V. tr. Acercarse a, aproximarse a: *the train was fast approaching the town,* el tren se iba acercando rápidamente a la ciudad. || FIG. Enfocar (to look at): *to approach a problem,* enfocar un problema. | Considerar (to consider). | Parecerse a, ser semejante a (to look like). | Acercarse a, rayar en (to border on): *a passion which approaches madness,* una pasión que se acerca a la locura *or* que raya en locura. | Abordar (to accost a person, to tackle a problem). | Dirigirse a: *to approach s.o. for a loan,* dirigirse a uno para pedirle un préstamo. | Entrar en contacto: *to approach a foreign power in view of a trade agreement,* entrar en contacto con una potencia extranjera con vistas a un acuerdo comercial. || *A man who is easy to approach,* un hombre de fácil acceso *or* abordable.

approachability [əˌprəutʃəˈbiliti] n. Accesibilidad, *f.*

approachable [əˈprəutʃəbl] adj. Accesible (place). || Abordable, accesible (person).

approaching [əˈprəutʃiŋ] adj. Próximo, ma. || Semejante, parecido, da (similar). || Que se acerca.

approachless [əˈprəutʃlis] adj. Inaccesible, inabordable

approbate [ˈæprəubeit] v. tr. U. S. Aprobar.

approbation [ˌæprəuˈbeiʃən] n. Aprobación, *f.*

approbative [ˈæprəubeitiv] adj. Aprobativo, va.

approbatory [ˈæprəubeitəri] adj. Aprobatorio, ria.

appropriate [əˈprəupriit] adj. Apropiado, da; conveniente.

appropriate [əˈprəuprieit] v. tr. Apropiarse de (to (take for o.s.). || Asignar, destinar (to set aside): *to appropriate funds,* asignar fondos.

appropriateness [əˈprəupriitnis] n. Conveniencia, *f.*

appropriation [əˌprəupriˈeiʃən] n. Apropiación, *f.* || Asignación, *f.* (of a sum of money).

appropriator [əˈprəuprieitə*] n. Apropiador, ra. || Usurpador, ra.

approvable [əˈpru:vəbl] adj. Digno de aprobación.

approval [əˈpru:vəl] n. Aprobación, *f.*: *to give one's approval,* dar su aprobación. || *On approval,* a prueba (on trial), previa aceptación (previous acceptance).

approve [əˈpru:v] v. tr. Aprobar: *to approve a plan unanimously,* aprobar un proyecto por unanimidad. || Probar, demostrar (one's quality). || *To be approved by,* tener la aprobación de, ser aprobado por.

— V. intr. Aprobar, dar su aprobación. || *To approve of,* aprobar.

approved school [əˈpru:vdˌsku:l] n. Reformatorio, *m.*, correccional, *m.*

approving [əˈpru:viŋ] adj. Aprobatorio, ria; de aprobación.

approximate [əˈprɔksimit] adj. Aproximado, da.

approximate [əˈprɔksimeit] v. tr. Aproximarse a, acercarse a: *the result approximates the forescast,* el resultado se aproxima al pronóstico.

— V. intr. Aproximarse, acercarse.

approximately [əˈprɔksimitli] adv. Aproximadamente.

approximation [əˌprɔksiˈmeiʃən] n. Aproximación, *f.*

approximative [əˈprɔksimətiv] adj. Aproximado, da.

appurtenance [əˈpə:tinəns] n. Accesorio, *m.* (accessory). || ARCH. Dependencia, *f.* || — Pl. JUR. Anexidades, *f.*

appurtenant [əˈpə:tinənt] adj. Accesorio, ria. || JUR. Anexo, xa.

apricot [ˈeiprikɔt] BOT. Albaricoquero, *m.* (tree). | Albaricoque, *m.* (fruit). || Color (*m.*) albaricoque.

April [ˈeiprəl] n. Abril. || — *April fool,* inocente, *m.* & *f.* (victim of a joke). || *April Fool's Day,* día (*m.*) de los Inocentes. || *April showers bring May flowers,* en abril, aguas mil. || *To make an April fool of,* dar una inocentada a.

— OBSERV. En Inglaterra el día de los Inocentes es el 1 de abril y no el 28 de diciembre como en España.

a priori [ˈeipraiˈɔ:rai] adj./adv. A priori.

apriority [ˌeipraiˈɔriti] n. Apriorismo, *m.*

apron [ˈeiprən] n. Delantal, *m.*, mandil, *m.* (garment). || Salpicadero, *m.* (of a car). || TECH. Placa (*f.*) de distribución. || THEATR. Proscenio, *m.* || AVIAT. Pista (*f.*) delante de los hangares. || FIG. *Tied to his mother's apron strings,* agarrado a las faldas de su madre.

apropos [ˈæprəpəu] adj. Oportuno, na.

— Adv. A propósito, oportunamente. || *Apropos of,* respecto a.

apse [æps] n. ARCH. Ábside, *m.* || ASTR. Ápside, *m.* || *Apse aisle,* deambulatorio, *m.*

apsidal [ˈæpsidl] adj. Absidal.

apsidiole [æpˈsidiəul] n. ARCH. Absidiolo, *m.*

apsis [ˈæpsis] n. Ápside, *m.* (in astronomy).

— OBSERV. El plural de *apsis* es *apsides.*

apt [æpt] adj. Apropiado, da; conveniente (appropriate). || Apto, ta (fitted). || Listo, ta; dotado, da (gifted). || Acertado, da; oportuno, na (remark). || Exacto, ta; atinado, da (description). || Dispuesto, ta (ready). || Susceptible (liable). || Propenso, sa (inclined).

apterous [ˈæptərəs] adj. ZOOL. Áptero, ra.

— N. ZOOL. Áptero, *m.*

apteryx [ˈæptəriks] n. ZOOL. Ápterix, *m.*

aptitude [ˈæptitju:d] n. Aptitud, *f.*: *aptitude test,* prueba de aptitud. || Capacidad, *f.* || Inclinación, *f.*, propensión, *f.* (natural tendency).

aptness [ˈæptnis] n. Lo apropiado. || See APTITUDE.

Apuleius [æpjuˈli:jəs] pr. n. Apuleyo, *m.*

apyretic [ˌæpaiˈretik] adj. MED. Apirético, ca.

apyrexy [æˈpaireksi] n. MED. Apirexia, *f.*

aquafortis [ˈækwəˈfɔ:tis] n. CHEM. Agua (*f.*) fuerte.

aquafortist [—t] n. Acuafortista, *m.* & *f.*

aqualung [ˈækwəlʌŋ] n. Escafandra (*f*) autónoma.

aquamarine [ˌækwəməˈri:n] n. Aguamarina, *f.* (stone). || Color (*m.*) de aguamarina.

— Adj. De color de aguamarina, de color verde mar.

aquaplane [ˈækwəplein] n. Acuaplano, *m.*, hidropatín, *m.*

aqua regia [ˈækwəˈri:dʒjə] n. CHEM. Agua (*f.*) regia.

aquarelle [ˌækwəˈrel] n. ARTS. Acuarela, *f.*

aquarium [əˈkwɛəriəm] n. Acuario, *m.*

— OBSERV. El plural es *aquaria* o *aquariums.*

Aquarius [əˈkwɛəriəs] pr. n. Acuario, *m.*

aquatic [əˈkwætik] adj. Acuático, ca.

— N. BOT. Planta (*f.*) acuática. || ZOOL. Animal (*m.*) acuático. || — Pl. Deportes (*m.*) acuáticos.

aquatint [ˈækwətint] n. ARTS. Acuantinta, *f.*

aqua vitae [ˈækwəˈvaiti:] n. Aguardiente, *m.*

aqueduct [ˈækwidʌkt] n. Acueducto, *m.*

aqueous [ˈeikwiəs] adj. Acuoso, sa; ácueo, a. || GEOL. Sedimentario, ria (rock). || ANAT. *Aqueous humour,* humor acuoso.

aqueousness [—nis] n. Acuosidad, *f.*

aquiferous [əˈkwifərəs] adj. Acuífero, ra.

Aquila [ˈækwilə] pr. n. ASTR. Águila, *f.* (constellation).

aquiline [ˈækwilain] adj. Aquilino, na. || Aguileño, ña; aquilino, na (nose). || De águila.

Aquitaine [ˌækwiˈtein] pr. n. GEOGR. Aquitania, *f.*

Aquitania [ˌækwiˈteinjə] pr. n. HIST. Aquitania, *f.*

ara [ˈærə] n. ZOOL. Guacamayo, *m.*

Ara [ˈærə] n. ASTR. Ara, *m.* (constellation).

Arab [ˈærəb] adj. Árabe.

— N. Árabe, *m.* & *f.* (inhabitant of Arab country). || Árabe, *m.* (language). || FAM. *Street Arab,* golfillo, *m.*, pilluelo, *m.*

arabesque [ˌærəˈbesk] adj. Arabesco, ca.

— N. Arabesco, *m.*

Arabia [əˈreibjə] pr. n. GEOGR. Arabia, *f.*

Arabian [—n] adj. Árabe, arábigo, ga. || De Arabia (desert). || — GEOGR. *Arabian Gulf,* Golfo Arábico. || *Arabian Nights,* Las mil y una noches. || *Arabian Sea,* Mar (*m.*) de Omán.

— N. Árabe, *m.* & *f.*

Arabic [ˈærəbik] adj. Árabe, arábigo, ga. || *Árabic numerals,* numeración arábiga.

— N. Árabe, *m.*

Arabicism [æˈræbisizəm] n. Arabismo, *m.*

Arabist [ˈærəbist] n. Arabista, *m.* & *f.*

arabization [ærəbiˈzeiʃən] n. Arabización, *f.*

arabize [ˈærəbaiz] v. tr. Arabizar.

arable [ˈærəbl] adj. Arable, cultivable.

— N. Tierra (*f.*) cultivable *or* de cultivo.

arachnid or **arachnidan** [əˈræknid] adj. ZOOL. Arácnido, da.

— N. ZOOL. Arácnido, *m.*

arachnoid [əˈræknɔid] adj. ANAT. Aracnoideo, a.

— N. ANAT. Aracnoides, *f. inv.* || ZOOL. Arácnido, *m.*

Aragon [ˈærəgən] pr. n. GEOGR. Aragón, *m.*

Aragonese [ærəgəˈni:z] adj./n. Aragonés, esa.

aragonite [əˈrægənait] n. MIN. Aragonito, *m.*

Aramaean or **Aramean** [ˌærəˈmi:ən] adj./n. Arameo, a.
Aramaic [ˌærəˈmeiik] n. Arameo, *m.* (language).
arapaima [ˌærəˈpaimə] n. ZOOL. Arapaima, *m.*
Araucan [əˈrɔ:kən] or **Araucanian** [ˌærɔ:ˈkeinjən] adj. Araucano, na.
— N. Araucano, na (person). || Araucano, *m.* (language).
araucaria [ˌærɔ:ˈkɛəriə] n. BOT. Araucaria, *f.*
arbalest [ˈɑ:bəlest] or **arbalist** [ˈɑ:bəlist] n. Ballesta, *f.* (crossbow).
arbiter [ˈɑ:bitə*] n. Árbitro, *m.*: *Petronius, arbiter of elegance,* Petronio, árbitro de la elegancia.
arbitrage [ˈɑ:bitridʒ] n. Arbitraje, *m.*
arbitral [ˈɑ:bitrəl] adj. Arbitral.
arbitrament [ɑ:ˈbitrəmənt] n. Arbitraje, *m.*
arbitrarily [ˈɑ:bitrərili] adv. Arbitrariamente.
arbitrariness [ˈɑ:bitrərinis] n. Arbitrariedad, *f.*
arbitrary [ˈɑ:bitrəri] adj. Arbitrario, ria.
arbitrate [ˈɑ:bitreit] v. tr./intr. Arbitrar.
arbitration [ˌɑ:biˈtreiʃən] n. Arbitraje, *m.*: *to go to arbitration,* recurrir al arbitraje. || *Judgment by arbitration,* sentencia (*f.*) arbitral.
arbitrator [ˈɑ:bitreitə*] n. Árbitro, *m.*
arbor [ˈɑ:bə*] n. TECH. Árbol, *m.* || U. S. TECH. Mandril, *m.* || U. S. Emparrado, *m.*, cenador, *m.* || U. S. *Arbor Day,* día (*m.*) del árbol.
arboreal [ɑ:ˈbɔ:riəl] adj. Arbóreo, a.
arborescence [ˌɑ:bəˈresns] n. Arborescencia, *f.*
arborescent [ˌɑ:bəˈresnt] adj. Arborescente.
arboriculture [ˈɑ:bərikʌltʃə*] n. Arboricultura, *f.*
arboriculturist [—rist] n. Arboricultor, *m.*
arborization [ˌɑ:bəriˈzeiʃən] n. Arborización, *f.*
arborvitae [ˈɑ:bəˈvaiti] n. BOT. Árbol (*m.*) de la vida, tuya, *f.* || ANAT. Árbol (*m.*) de la vida.
arbour [ˈɑ:bə*] n. Emparrado, *m.*, cenador, *m.*
arbutus [ɑ:ˈbju:təs] n. BOT. Madroño, *m.*
arc [ɑ:k] n. Arco, *m.*: *arc of a circle,* arco de círculo. || ELECTR. *Electric arc,* arco voltaico.
arcade [ɑ:ˈkeid] n. Arcada, *f.* || Soportales, *m. pl.* (in a square). || *Shopping arcade,* galería (*f.*) comercial.
Arcadia [ɑ:ˈkeidjə] pr. n. Arcadia, *f.*
Arcadian [ɑ:ˈkeidjən] adj./n. Árcade.
arcana [ɑ:ˈkeinə] pl. n. Arcanos, *m.*
arcane [ɑ:ˈkein] adj. Arcano, na; secreto, ta.
arch [ɑ:tʃ] adj. Grande: *his arch rival,* su gran rival. || Malicioso, sa: *an arch look,* una mirada maliciosa.
— N. Arco, *m.* || — ARCH. *Arch behind a lintel,* arco capialzado. || *Arch of heaven,* bóveda (*f.*) celeste. || ARCH. *Basket-handle arch,* arco carpanel *or* apainelado *or* rebajado. || ANAT. *Dental arch,* arco alveolar. || ARCH. *Flat arch,* arco adintelado *or* a nivel. | *Flying arch,* arco por tranquil. | *Gothic arch,* arco de todo punto *or* ojival. | *Horseshoe* o *Moorish arch,* arco de herradura *or* morisco *or* arábigo. | *Inflected arch,* arco de cortina. | *Lancet arch,* arco apuntado *or* lanceolado. | *Ogee arch,* arco conopial. | *Segmental arch,* arco escarzano. | *Semicircular arch,* arco de medio punto. | *Splayed arch,* arco abocinado. | *Stilted arch,* arco peraltado. | *Trefoil arch,* arco trebolado *or* trilobulado. || *Triumphal arch,* arco de triunfo *or* triunfal.
arch [ɑ:tʃ] v. tr. Arquear. || *To arch one's eyebrows,* arquear *or* enarcar las cejas.
— V. intr. Arquearse.
archaeological [ˌɑ:kiəˈlɔdʒikəl] adj. Arqueológico, ca.
archaeologist [ˌɑ:kiˈɔlədʒist] n. Arqueólogo, ga.
archaeology [ˌɑ:kiˈɔlədʒi] n. Arqueología, *f.*
archaeopteryx [ˌɑ:kiˈɔptəriks] n. ZOOL. Arqueopterix, *m.*
archaic [ɑ:ˈkeiik] adj. Arcaico, ca.
archaism [ˈɑ:keiizəm] n. Arcaísmo, *m.*
archaist [ˈɑ:keiist] n. Arcaísta, *m.* & *f.*
archaistic [ɑ:keiˈistik] adj. Arcaizante.
archaize [ˈɑ:keiaiz] v. tr./intr. Arcaizar.
archangel [ˈɑ:kˌeindʒəl] n. Arcángel, *m.*
archangelic [ˈɑ:keinˈdʒelik] adj. Arcangélico, ca.
archbishop [ˈɑ:tʃˈbiʃəp] n. REL. Arzobispo, *m.*
archbishopric [ɑ:tʃˈbiʃəprik] n. REL. Arzobispado, *m.*, archidiócesis, *f.*
archconfraternity [ˈɑ:tʃˌkənfrəˈtə:niti] n. Archicofradía, *f.*
archdeacon [ˈɑ:tʃˈdi:kən] n. REL. Arcediano, *m.*, archidiácono, *m.*
archdeaconate [ˈɑ:tʃˈdi:kənit] n. REL. Arcedianato, *m.*
archdeaconry [ˈɑ:tʃˈdi:kənri] or **archdeaconship** [ˈɑ:tʃˈdi:kənʃip] n. REL. Arcedianato, *m.*
archdiocesan [ˈɑ:tʃdaiˈɔsisən] adj. REL. Archidiocesano, na.
archdiocese [ˈɑ:tʃˈdaiəsis] n. Archidiócesis, *f.*
archducal [ˈɑ:tʃˈdju:kəl] adj. Archiducal.
archduchess [ˈɑ:tʃˈdʌtʃis] n. Archiduquesa, *f.*
archduchy [ˈɑ:tʃˈdʌtʃi] n. Archiducado, *m.*
archduke [ˈɑ:tʃˈdju:k] n. Archiduque, *m.*
archegonium [ˌɑ:kiˈgəunjəm] n. BOT. Arquegonio, *m.*

— OBSERV. El plural de *archegonium* es *archegonia.*

archenemy [ˈɑ:tʃˈenimi] n. Enemigo (*m.*) jurado (the direst enemy). || El diablo, *m.*, Satanás, *m.* (Satan).
archeological [ˌɑ:kiəˈlɔdʒikəl] adj. Arqueológico, ca.
archeologist [ˌɑ:kiˈɔlədʒist] n. Arqueólogo, ga.
archeology [ˌɑ:kiˈɔlədʒi] n. Arqueología, *f.*
archer [ˈɑ:tʃə*] n. Arquero, *m.* || ASTR. *The Archer,* el Sagitario.
archery [ˈɑ:tʃəri] n. Tiro (*m.*) al arco (sport). || Equipo (*m.*) para tiro al arco (equipment).
archetype [ˈɑ:kitaip] n. Arquetipo, *m.*
archfiend [ˈɑ:tʃˈfi:nd] n. See ARCHENEMY.
archidiaconal [ˌɑ:kidaiˈækənl] adj. Del arcediano.
archiepiscopal [ˌɑ:kiiˈpiskəpəl] adj. Arzobispal.
archiepiscopate [ˌɑ:kiiˈpiskəpit] n. REL. Arzobispado, *m.* (archbishopric).
archil [ˈɑ:tʃil] n. BOT. Urchilla, *f.*
archimandrite [ˌɑ:kiˈmændrait] n. REL. Archimandrita, *m.*
Archimedes [ˌɑ:kiˈmi:di:z] pr. n. Arquímedes. || *Archimedes' screw,* tornillo (*m.*) de Arquímedes.
arching [ˈɑ:tʃiŋ] n. Arqueo, *m.* (of the body).
archipelagic [ˌɑ:kipəˈlædʒik] adj. Del archipiélago.
archipelago [ˌɑ:kiˈpeligəu] n. Archipiélago, *m.*
archips [ˈɑ:kips] pl. n. ZOOL. Arquípteros, *m.*
architect [ˈɑ:kitekt] n. Arquitecto, *m.*: *landscape architect,* arquitecto paisajista. || FIG. Artífice, *m.*, autor, *m.*
architectonic [ˌɑ:kitekˈtɔnik] adj. ARCH. Arquitectónico, ca.
— N. Arquitectura, *f.*, arquitectónica, *f.*
architectural [ˌɑ:kiˈtektʃərəl] adj. ARCH. Arquitectónico, ca.
architecture [ˈɑ:kitektʃə*] n. ARCH. Arquitectura, *f.*
architrave [ˈɑ:kitreiv] n. ARCH. Arquitrabe, *m.*
archives [ˈɑ:kaivz] pl. n. Archivo, *m. sing.*: *National Archives,* Archivo Nacional.
archivist [ˈɑ:kivist] n. Archivero, ra; archivista, *m.* & *f.*
archivolt [ˈɑ:kivəult] n. ARCH. Archivolta, *f.*, arquivolta, *f.*
archlute [ɑ:tʃˈlu:t] n. MUS. Archilaúd, *m.*
archly [ˈɑ:tʃli] adv. Maliciosamente.
archness [ˈɑ:tʃnis] n. Malicia, *f.* || Socarronería, *f.*
archon [ˈɑ:kən] n. HIST. Arconte, *m.*
archonship [—ʃip] or **archontate** [—teit] n. Arcontado, *m.*
archpriest [ˈɑ:tʃˈpri:st] n. REL. Arcipreste, *m.*
archpriesthood [—hud] or **archpriestship** [—ʃip] n. Arciprestazgo, *m.*
archway [ˈɑ:tʃwei] n. Arco, *m.*, arcada, *f.*
arc lamp [ˈɑ:k-læmp] n. ELECTR. Lámpara (*f.*) de arco.
Arctic [ˈɑ:ktik] adj. GEOGR. Ártico, ca. || FAM. Helado, da; glacial.
— N. Ártico, *m.* || FAM. El Polo, *m.*: *it's like the Arctic here,* aquí se está como en el Polo. || — *Arctic Circle,* Círculo Polar Ártico. || *Arctic Ocean,* Océano Ártico.
arctics [—s] pl. n. U. S. Botas (*f.*) impermeables.
arcuate [ˈɑ:kjuit] adj. Arqueado, da.
arc welding [ˈɑ:kˈweldiŋ] n. Soldadura (*f.*) por arco.
ardency [ˈɑ:dənsi] n. Ardor, *m.*
ardent [ˈɑ:dənt] adj. Ardiente.
ardour (U. S. **ardor**) [ˈɑ:də*] n. Ardor, *m.*
arduoús [ˈɑ:djuəs] adj. Escarpado, da (slope). || Arduo, dua (strenuous).
arduousness [—nis] n. Dificultad, *f.*
are [ɑ:*] pres. indic. See BE.
are [ɑ:*] n. Área, *f.* [100 square metres].
area [ˈɛəriə] n. Área, *f.*, superficie, *f.* (exact measure). || Superficie, *f.*, extensión, *f.* || Región, *f.* (region). || Zona, *f.* (zone). || Distrito (*m.*) postal (mail). || Campo, *m.*, terreno, *m.*, esfera, *f.* (academic field). || Patio, *m.* (yard). || — SP. *Goal area,* área de gol. || *Metropolitan area,* área metropolitana *or* urbana. || SP. *Penalty area,* área de castigo. || *Sterling area,* zona de la libra esterlina.
area code [—kəud] n. Prefijo, *m.* (telephone).
areaway [ˈɛəriəwei] n. U. S. Patio, *m.*
areca [ˈærikə] n. BOT. Areca, *f.*
arena [əˈri:nə] n. Arena, *f.* || Ruedo, *m.*, redondel, *m.* (of a bullring). || Pista, *f.* (circus). || FIG. Campo, *m.*, esfera, *f.* (field).
arenaceous [ˌæriˈneiʃəs] adj. Arenoso, sa; arenáceo, a.
arenicolous [ˌæriˈnikələs] adj. ZOOL. Arenícola.
aren't [ɑ:nt] contraction of *are not.*
areola [æˈriələ] n. Areola, *f.*, aréola, *f.*

— OBSERV. El plural en inglés es *areolae* o *areolas.*

areole [ˈæriəul] n. Areola, *f.*, aréola, *f.*
areometer [ˌæriˈɔmitə*] n. Areómetro, *m.*
areometry [ˌæriˈɔmitri] n. Areometría, *f.*
areopagite [ˌæriˈɔpəgait] n. Areopagita, *m.*
Areopagus [ˌæriˈɔpəgəs] pr. n. Areópago, *m.*
arête [æˈreit] n. Arista, *f.*
argent [ˈɑ:dʒənt] adj. HERALD. Argénteo, a.
— N. Argén, *m.* (silver).
argentiferous [ˌɑ:dʒənˈtifərəs] adj. Argentífero, ra.
Argentina [ˌɑ:dʒənˈti:nə] pr. n. GEOGR. Argentina, *f.*
argentine [ˈɑ:dʒəntain] adj. Argentino, na.
— N. Metal (*m.*) plateado (metal).
Argentine [ˈɑ:dʒəntain] adj./n. Argentino, na. || *The Argentine,* Argentina, *f.*
Argentinean [ˌɑ:dʒənˈtinjən] adj./n. Argentino, na.
argillaceous [ˌɑ:dʒiˈleiʃəs] adj. Arcilloso, sa.
Argive [ˈɑ:gaiv] adj./n. HIST. Argivo, va.
argon [ˈɑ:gɔn] n. CHEM. Argón, *m.*
argonaut [ˈɑ:gənɔ:t] n. ZOOL. Argonauta, *m.*
Argonaut [ˈɑ:gənɔ:t] n. MYTH. Argonauta, *m.*
argosy [ˈɑ:gəsi] n. MAR. Carraca, *f.*
argot [ˈɑ:gəu] n. Argot, *m.*

arguable [ˈɑ:gju:əbl] adj. Defendible (that can be supported). || Discutible (open to doubt).

argue [ˈɑ:gju:] v. tr. Razonar (to apply reason to). || Discutir (to discuss). || Sostener, mantener, argüir (to maintain). || Persuadir (to persuade). || Demostrar (to indicate).
— V. intr. Discutir (to wrangle): *don't argue!*, ¡no discutas! || Abogar (*for*, por) [to plead]. || Argüir, argumentar (to adduce). || Razonar.

arguer [—ə*] n. Discutidor, ra; argumentador, ra.

argument [ˈɑ:gjumənt] n. Razón, *f.* (reason). || Discusión, *f.*, debate, *m.* (discussion). || Discusión, *f.*, disputa, *f.* (quarrel). || Razonamiento, *m.* (reasoning). || Sumario, *m.* (summary). || JUR. Alegato, *m.* || — *For the sake of argument*, como hipótesis. || *It is beyond argument*, es indiscutible. || *Let's not have any argument*, no discutamos.

argumentation [ˌɑ:gjumenˈteiʃən] n. Argumentación, *f.*, razonamiento, *m.* (reasoning). || Discusión, *f.*, debate, *m.* (discussion).

argumentative [ˌɑ:gjuˈmentətiv] adj. Sujeto a controversia *or* a discusión (matter). || Discutidor, ra; argumentador, ra (person).

argus [ˈɑ:gəs] n. ZOOL. FIG. Argos, *m.*

Argus [ˈɑ:gəs] pr. n. Argos, *m.*

aria [ˈɑ:riə] n. MUS. Aria, *f.*

Ariadne [ˌæriˈædni] pr. n. MYTH. Ariana, *f.*

Arian [ˈɛəriən] adj./n. REL. Arriano, na.

Arianism [—izəm] n. REL. Arrianismo, *m.*

arid [ˈærid] adj. Árido, da.

aridity [æˈriditi] n. Aridez, *f.*

Aries [ˈɛəri:z] n. ASTR. Aries, *m.* (Ram).

aright [əˈrait] adv. (Ant.). Correctamente.

aril [ˈæril] n. BOT. Arilo, *m.*

arise* [əˈraiz] v. intr. Originarse (*from*, en), resultar (*from*, de) [to result]. || Surgir, presentarse, aparecer (to come up). || Plantearse (a problem). || Levantarse (person, sun, storm, building). || Elevarse (cry). || Resucitar (from the dead).
— OBSERV. Pret. ***arose;*** p.p. ***arisen.***

arisen [əˈrizən] p. p. See ARISE.

arista [əˈristə] n. BOT. Arista, *f.*
— OBSERV. El plural de la palabra inglesa es *aristae.*

aristarch [ˈæristɑ:k] n. Aristarco, *m.*

Aristides [ˌærisˈtaidi:z] pr. n. Arístides, *m.*

aristocracy [ˌærisˈtɔkrəsi] n. Aristocracia, *f.*

aristocrat [ˈæristəkræt] n. Aristócrata, *m.* & *f.*

aristocratic [ˌæristəˈkrætik] adj. Aristocrático, ca.

aristolochia [ˌæristəˈləukjə] n. BOT. Aristoloquia, *f.*

Aristophanes [ˌærisˈtɔfəni:z] pr. n. Aristófanes, *m.*

Aritsotelian [ˌæristəˈti:ljən] adj./n. Aristotélico, ca.

Aristotle [ˈæristɔtl] pr. n. Aristóteles, *m.*

arithmetic [əˈriθmətik] n. MATH. Aritmética, *f.* || *Mental arithmetic*, cálculo (*m.*) mental.

arithmetic [ˌæriθˈmetik] adj. Aritmético, ca. || — MATH. *Arithmetic mean*, media aritmética. | *Arithmetic progression*, progresión aritmética.

arithmetical [ˌæriθˈmetikəl] adj. Aritmético, ca.

arithmetician [əˌriθməˈtiʃən] n. Aritmético, ca.

ark [ɑ:k] n. REL. Arca, *f.* || — REL. *Ark of the Covenant*, Arca de la Alianza. || *Noah's Ark*, arca de Noé.

arm [ɑ:m] n. ANAT. Brazo, *m.*: *to give s.o. one's arm*, dar el brazo a uno. || FIG. Brazo, *m.* (of sea, of chair, etc.). || Pata (*f.*) delantera, brazo, *m.* (of animals). || Tentáculo, *m.* (of octopus). || Manga, *f.* (sleeve). || Astil, *m.*, brazo, *m.* (beam of a balance). || Aguilón, *m.*, brazo, *m.* (of a crane). || Radio, *m.* (of a wheel). || Uña, *f.* (of an anchor). || Brazo, *m.* (of record player). || Arma, *f.* (weapon). || MIL. Arma, *f.*: *the infantry arm*, el arma de infantería. || — Pl. HERALD. Escudo, *m. sing.*, armas, *f.* || — *Arms race*, carrera (*f.*) de armamentos. || *Coat of arms*, escudo (*m.*) de armas. || *Feat of arms*, hecho (*m.*) de armas. || *In arms*, en armas. || *Infant in arms*, niño (*m.*) de pecho. || *In one's arms*, en brazos. || *Order arms!*, ¡descansen armas! || *Present arms!*, ¡presenten armas! || *Right arm*, brazo derecho. || *Slope arms!*, ¡sobre el hombro, arma! || *The long arm of the law*, el brazo de la justicia. || *To arms!*, ¡a las armas!, ¡a formar con armas! || *To bear arms*, servir [como soldado]. || *To be up in arms*, haberse levantado en armas (to fight), poner el grito en el cielo, sublevarse (against an abuse). || *To carry arms*, ir armado. || *To carry out the vigil of arms*, velar las armas. || FIG. *To keep s.o. at arm's length*, mantener a uno a distancia. | *To let one's arm be twisted*, dar su brazo a torcer. || *To order arms*, descansar las armas. || *To present arms*, presentar armas. || *To rise up in arms*, alzarse *or* levantarse en armas. || *To surrender one's arms* o *to lay down one's arms*, rendir las armas. || *To take up arms*, tomar las armas. || *To throw one's arms around s.o.'s neck*, echar los brazos al cuello de alguien. || FIG. *To throw one's arms in the air*, levantar los brazos al cielo. || *To walk arm in arm*, ir del brazo *or* cogidos del brazo. || *Under arms*, sobre las armas. || *With one's arms folded*, con los brazos cruzados. || *With open arms*, con los brazos abiertos.

arm [ɑ:m] v. tr. Armar (to provide with arms): *armed forces*, fuerzas armadas. || Proteger (to protect): *armed against the cold*, protegido contra el frío. || Armar (to provide with): *armed with a hammer*, armado de un martillo. || Equipar (to fit with some device). || — *Armed robbery*, robo (*m.*) a mano armada. || *Armed to the teeth*, armado hasta los dientes. || *To arm o.s.*, armarse.
— V. intr. Armarse.

armada [ɑ:ˈmɑ:də] n. MAR. Armada, *f.* || HIST. *The Spanish Armada*, la Armada Invencible.

armadillo [ˌɑ:məˈdiləu] n. ZOOL. Armadillo, *m.*

armament [ˈɑ:məmənt] n. MIL. Armamento, *m.* || — Pl. MIL. Armas, *f.*. armamento, *m. sing.* (military equipment). | Fuerzas, *f.* (military forces).

armature [ˈɑ:mətjuə*] n. TECH. Armadura, *f.* || Armazón, *f.* (metal supporting structure). || ELECTR. Inducido, *m.*

armband [ˈɑ:mˈbænd] n. Brazalete, *m.*

armchair [ˈɑ:mˈtʃɛə*] adj. De sillón. || FIG. *Armchair strategist*, estratega (*m.*) de café.
— N. Sillón, *m.*, butaca, *f.*

Armenia [ɑ:ˈmi:njə] pr. n. Armenia, *f.*

Armenian [—n] adj./n. Armenio, nia. || *Armenian bole*, bol arménico.

armful [ˈɑ:mful] n. Brazada, *f.*

armhole [ˈɑ:mhəul] n. Sisa, *f.* (in sewing).

armillary [ˈɑ:miləri] adj. Armilar: *armillary sphere*, esfera armilar.

Arminian [ɑ:ˈminiən] adj./n. Arminiano, na.

armistice [ˈɑ:mistis] n. Armisticio, *m.*

armlet [ˈɑ:mlit] n. Brazalete, *m.* || Brazo, *m.* (of sea, etc.).

armor [ˈɑ:mə*] n./v. tr. U. S. See ARMOUR.

armorial [ɑ:ˈmɔ:riəl] adj. HERALD. Nobiliario, ria; heráldico, ca. || *Armorial bearings*, blasón, *m.*, escudo (*m.*) de armas.
— N. HERALD. Armorial, *m.*

armorist [ˈɑ:mərist] n. HERALD. Heraldista, *m.* & *f.*

armory [ˈɑ:məri] n. HERALD. Blasón, *m.*, heráldica, *f.* (study). | Armorial, *m.* (book).

armour [ˈɑ:mə*] n. Armadura, *f.* (suit of mail, leather, etc.). || Blindaje, *m.* (on tanks, ships, etc.). || Fuerzas (*f. pl.*) blindadas (armed vehicles). || ZOOL. Armadura, *f.* || HERALD. Blasón, *m.*, escudo (*m.*) de armas.

armour [ˈɑ:mə*] v. tr. Blindar, acorazar. || *Armoured car*, vehículo blindado.

armour-clad (U. S. **armor-clad**) [ˈɑ:mə*ˈklæd] adj. Acorazado, da; blindado, da.

armourer (U. S. **armorer**) [ˈɑ:mərə*] n. Armero, *m.*

armour-plate (U. S. **armor-plate**) [ˈɑ:mə*ˈpleit] n. Blindaje, *m.*

armour-plate (U. S. **armor-plate**) [ˈɑ:mə*ˈpleit] v. tr. Blindar, acorazar.

armour-plating (U. S. **armor-plating**) [—iŋ] n. Blindaje, *m.*, acorazamiento, *m.*

armouring (U. S. **armoring**) [ˈɑ:məriŋ] n. Blindaje, *m.*, acorazamiento, *m.*

armoury (U. S. **armory**) [ˈɑ:məri] n. Arsenal, *m.* (arms store, factory). || U. S. FAM. Armas (*f. pl.*) de fuego (guns).

armpit [ˈɑ:mpit] n. ANAT. Axila, *f.*, sobaco, *m.*

armrest [ˈɑ:mrest] n. Brazo, *m.* (of an armchair).

army [ˈɑ:mi] n. MIL. Ejército, *m.* || FIG. Multitud, *f.* (crowd). || — MIL. *Army chaplain*, capellán (*m.*) castrense. | *Army corps*, cuerpo (*m.*) de ejército. | *Army of occupation*, ejército de ocupación. | *Army register*, escalafón, *m.*

arnica [ˈɑ:nikə] n. BOT. Árnica, *f.* || MED. Tintura (*f.*) de árnica.

aroma [əˈrəumə] n. Aroma, *m.*

aromatic [ˌærəuˈmætik] adj. Aromático, ca.
— N. Planta (*f.*) aromática.

aromatize [əˈrəumətaiz] v. tr. Aromatizar.

arose [əˈrəuz] pret. See ARISE.

around [əˈraund] adv. Por aquí (round here). || Por allá (round there). || Alrededor (in the vicinity). || Por todos lados (on all sides). || Cerca, aproximadamente (near). || — *I don't get around much these days*, no salgo mucho actualmente. || *The other way around*, al revés. || *The word is going around that...*, corre el rumor de que... || *The year around*, durante todo el año. || *To come around*, see COME. || *To get around*, viajar (to travel), salir (to go out), divulgarse, propalarse (a rumour, news). || *To have been around*, haber viajado mucho (to have done much travelling), tener mucha experiencia, haber corrido mundo (to have much experience).
— Prep. Alrededor de (encircling). || A eso de: *around five o'clock*, a eso de las cinco. || Por: *to go around town*, ir por la ciudad. || Cerca de (near).

arousal [əˈrauzəl] n. Despertar, *m.*

arouse [əˈrauz] v. tr. Despertar.
— V. intr. Despertarse.

arpegio [ɑ:ˈpedʒiəu] n. MUS. Arpegio, *m.*

arpeggio [ɑ:ˈpedʒiəu] v. intr. MUS. Arpegiar.

arquebus [ˈɑ:kwibəs] n. Arcabuz, *m.*

arquebusier [ˌɑ:kwibəˈsiə*] n. Arcabucero, *m.*

arraign [əˈrein] v. tr. Acusar (accuse). || Atacar, criticar (an opinion, s.o.). || JUR. Hacer comparecer.

arraignment [—mənt] n. Acusación, *f.* (accusation).

arrange [əˈreindʒ] v. tr. Arreglar, poner en orden (to put in order). || Arreglar (one's hair). || Arreglar (to fix up). || Disponer (to dispose). || Fijar, señalar (to fix upon). || Decidir (to decide). || Planear (to plan). || MUS. Arreglar, adaptar.
— V. intr. Ponerse de acuerdo, acordar (to agree). || Tomar medidas (to see to the details of). || *To arrange to meet s.o.*, quedar *or* citarse con alguien.

arrangement [—mənt] n. Arreglo, *m.* (act of arranging or putting in order). || Orden, *m.* (way in which things are arranged). || Arreglo, *m.* (of a dispute). || Convenio, *m.*, arreglo, *m.*, acuerdo, *m.* (agreement). || Plan, *m.* (plan). || FAM. Combinación, *f.* (combination). || MUS. Arreglo, *m.*, adaptación, *f.* || — Pl. Planes, *m.* || Disposiciones, *f.*, medidas, *f.* (measures).
arrant [ˈærənt] adj. Redomado, da; de marca mayor.
arras [ˈærəs] n. Tapiz, *m.*
array [əˈrei] n. MIL. Formación, *f.*, orden, *m.*: *in battle array*, en orden de batalla. || FIG. Colección, *f.*, serie, *f.* (collection). || Gala, *f.*, atavío, *m.* (ceremonial dress). || Pompa, *f.* (pomp).
array [əˈrei] v. tr. MIL. Formar: *to array the troops*, formar las tropas. || Ataviar (to dress magnificently). || JUR. Formar: *to array the jury*, formar el jurado.
arrears [əˈriəz] pl. n. Atrasos, *m.* || *To be in arrears*, estar atrasado.
arrest [əˈrest] n. Arresto, *m.*, detención, *f.* (seizure by police). || Paro, *m.* (checking of forward movement). || — *Close arrest*, arresto mayor. || *To be under arrest*, estar detenido, estar bajo arresto. || *Under house arrest*, bajo arresto domiciliario. || MIL. *Under open arrest*, bajo arresto simple *or* menor.
arrest [əˈrest] v. tr. Detener, arrestar (to seize legally). || Detener, parar (to check). || Atraer, llamar: *her beauty arrested the attention of all present*, su belleza atrajo la atención de todos los presentes.
arresting [əˈrestiŋ] adj. Que llama la atención, llamativo, va.
arrhythmia [əˈriðmiə] n. Arritmia, *f.*
arrhythmic [əˈriðmik] adj. Arrítmico, ca.
arris [ˈæris] n. ARCH. Arista, *f.* (of a beam). | Lima (*f.*) tesa (of a roof).
arrival [əˈraivəl] n. Llegada, *f.* (act of arriving). || — *New arrival*, recién llegado. || *The first arrivals*, los primeros en llegar *or* llegados.
arrive [əˈraiv] v. intr. Llegar (to reach a destination). || Aparecer (to appear). || Lograr *or* alcanzar éxito, triunfar (to succeed). || *To arrive at*, llegar a (a destination, a conclusion), alcanzar (an objective).
arrivism [ˈærivizəm] n. Arribismo, *m.* (unscrupulous ambition).
arriviste or **arrivist** [ˌæriˈviːst] n. Arribista, *m.* & *f.*
arrogance [ˈærəgəns] or **arrogancy** [—i] n. Arrogancia, *f.*
arrogant [ˈærəgənt] adj. Arrogante.
arrogate [ˈærəugeit] v. tr. *To arrogate to o.s.*, arrogarse, atribuirse.
arrogation [ˌærəuˈgeiʃən] n. Arrogación, *f.*
arrow [ˈærəu] n. Flecha, *f.*
arrowhead [—hed] n. Punta (*f.*) de flecha. || BOT. Saetilla, *f.*
arrowroot [—ruːt] n. Arrurruz, *m.*
arrowy [ˈærəui] adj. Como una flecha.
arroyo [əˈrɔiə] n. U. S. Cauce (*m.*) seco de un río.
arse [ɑːs] n. POP. Culo, *m.*, trasero, *m.*
arsenal [ˈɑːsinəl] n. Arsenal, *m.*
arsenate [ˈɑːsinit] or **arseniate** [ˈɑːsinieit] n. Arseniato, *m.*
arsenic [ˈɑːsnik] n. CHEM. Arsénico, *m.*
— Adj. CHEM. Arsénico, ca.
arsenical [ɑːˈsenikəl] adj. CHEM. Arsenical.
arsenide [ˈɑːsinaid] n. Arseniuro, *m.*
arsenious [ɑːˈsiːnjəs] or **arsenous** [ˈɑːsənəs] adj. CHEM. Arsenioso, sa.
arsine [ˈɑːsiːn] n. Arsina, *f.*
arsis [ˈɑːsis] n. POET. Sílaba (*f.*) acentuada, arsis, *f.*
— OBSERV. El plural de la palabra inglesa es *arses*.
arson [ˈɑːsn] n. JUR. Incendio (*m.*) premeditado.
arsonist [—ist] n. Incendiario, ria.
art [ɑːt] See BE.
— OBSERV. *Art* es la forma antigua de la segunda persona del singular del verbo *to be (are)*.
art [ɑːt] n. Arte, *m.* & *f.*: *a work of art*, una obra de arte; *the art of cooking*, el arte culinario. || — Pl. Letras, *f.*: *bachelor of Arts*, licenciado en letras. || — *Art for art's sake*, el arte por el arte. || *Arts and crafts*, artes y oficios. || *Fine arts*, Bellas Artes.
— OBSERV. In Spanish *arte* is usually feminine in the plural and masculine in the singular, but with certain adjectives it remains feminine (*arte poética, arte cisoria*, etc.)
Artaxerxes [ˌɑːtəgˈzəːksiːz] pr. n. Artajerjes, *m.*
artefact [ˈɑːtifækt] n. Artefacto, *m.*
arterial [ɑːˈtiəriəl] adj. Arterial. || Nacional (road).
arteriole [ɑːˈteriəul] n. Arteriola, *f.*
arteriosclerosis [ɑːˈtiəriəuskliəˈrəusis] n. MED. Arteriosclerosis, *f.*
arteritis [ˌɑːtəˈraitis] n. MED. Arteritis, *f.*
artery [ˈɑːtəri] n. ANAT. Arteria, *f.* || Arteria, *f.* (road, street).
artesian [ɑːˈtiːzjən] adj. Artesiano, na: *artesian well*, pozo artesiano.
artful [ˈɑːtful] adj. Ingenioso, sa.
artfulness [—nis] n. Ingenio, *m.*
arthralgia [ɑːˈθrældʒiə] n. MED. Artralgia, *f.*
arthritic [ɑːˈθritik] adj./n. MED. Artrítico, ca.
arthritis [ɑːˈθraitis] n. MED. Artritis, *f.* || *Rheumatoid arthritis*, reúma (*m.*) articular.
arthritism [ˈɑːθritizəm] n. MED. Artritismo, *m.*
arthropod [ˈɑːθrəpɔd] n. ZOOL. Artrópodo, *m.*
— OBSERV. El plural es *arthropoda* o *arthropods*.

Arthur [ˈɑːθə*] pr. n. Arturo, *m.* || Artús, *m.*, Arturo, *m.* (king).
artichoke [ˈɑːtitʃəuk] n. BOT. Alcachofa, *f.* || *Jerusalem artichoke*, topinambur, *m.*, aguaturma, *f.*, pataca, *f.*
article [ˈɑːtikl] n. Artículo, *m.* (item). || Artículo, *m.* (of newspaper). || Cláusula, *f.* (clause). || REL. Artículo, *m.*: *articles of faith*, artículos de fe. || GRAMM. Artículo, *m.* || ZOOL. Artejo, *m.* || — Pl. Articulado, *m. sing.*, artículos, *m.* (of a law). || — *Articles and conditions*, pliego (*m. sing.*) de condiciones. || *Articles of apprenticeship*, contrato (*m. sing.*) de aprendizaje. || *Article of clothing*, prenda (*f.*) de vestir. || *Articles of incorporation*, estatutos (*m.*) de una sociedad comercial. || *Articles of war*, código (*m. sing.*) de justicia militar. || *Leading article*, artículo de fondo, editorial, *m.* || MAR. *Ship's articles*, rol, *m. sing.* || *Toilet articles*, artículos de tocador, objetos (*m.*) de tocador.
article [ˈɑːtikl] v. tr. Formular. || Colocar de aprendiz. || U. S. JUR. Acusar.
articular [ɑːˈtikjulə*] adj. ANAT. Articular.
articulate [ɑːˈtikjulit] adj. Articulado, da.
articulate [ɑːˈtikjuleit] v. tr./intr. Articular.
articulation [ɑːˌtikjuˈleiʃən] n. Articulación, *f.*
artifact [ˈɑːtifækt] n. Artefacto, *m.*
artifice [ˈɑːtifis] n. Artificio, *m.* (trickery). || Arte, *m.*, ingeniosidad, *f.*, habilidad, *f.* (skill).
artificer [ɑːˈtifisə*] n. Artífice, *m.*
artificial [ˌɑːtiˈfiʃəl] adj. Artificial: *an artificial lake*, un lago artificial. || Sintético, ca; artificial (synthetic). || Químico, ca (manure). || Artificial, afectado, da (affected). || Postizo, za (teeth). || — *Artificial insemination*, inseminación (*f.*) artificial. || *Artificial leg*, pierna (*f.*) artificial. || MED. *Artificial respiration*, respiración (*f.*) artificial.
artificiality [ˌɑːtifiʃiˈæliti] n. Lo artificial, carácter (*m.*) artificial. || Afectación, *f.*
artillery [ɑːˈtiləri] n. MIL. Artillería, *f.*: *heavy artillery*, artillería pesada.
artilleryman [—mən] n. MIL. Artillero, *m.*
artisan [ˌɑːtiˈzæn] n. Artesano, na.
artist [ˈɑːtist] n. Artista, *m.* & *f.*
artiste [ɑːˈtiːst] n. Artista, *m.* & *f.*
artistic [ɑːˈtistik] adj. Artístico, ca.
artistry [ˈɑːtistri] n. Arte, *m.* & *f.*
artless [ˈɑːtlis] adj. Simple, natural (simple). || Cándido, da (guileless). || Torpe, poco habilidoso (unskilful). || Inculto, ta (ignorant).
artlessness [—nis] n. Naturalidad, *f.* || Candidez, *f.*
artsy-craftsy [ˈɑːtsiˈkræfsi] adj. U. S. Que se las da de artista.
arty [ˈɑːti] or **arty-crafty** [ˈɑːtiˈkrɑːfti] adj. Que se las da de artista.
arum [ˈɛərəm] n. BOT. Aro, *m.*
Aryan [ˈɛəriən] adj./n. Ario, ria.
as [æz] conj./adv. Como (like): *do as you like*, haga como guste; *heavy as stone*, pesado como una piedra. || Mientras, cuando (while): *he arrived as you were leaving*, llegó cuando se estaba marchando. || Como, lo que: *do as I tell you*, haz lo que te digo. || Como, lo mismo que: *as you and I*, como tú y yo. || Ya que, puesto que (because): *as he objects I won't read*, no leeré puesto que él se opone. || Como: *as I said yesterday, it is very easy*, como le dije ayer, es muy fácil. || Aunque: *sick as he was, he came to work*, aunque estaba enfermo, vino a trabajar. || — *As... as...*, tan... como...: *as tall as a mountain*, tan alto como una montaña. || *As far as I am concerned*, en lo que a mí se refiere. || *As far as I know*, que yo sepa. || *As for*, en cuanto a, en *or* por lo que se refiere a. || *As from*, a partir de. || *As if*, como si. || *As if to*, como para. || *As it is*, tal [y] como están las cosas. || *As it seems*, según parece. || *As it were*, por decirlo así. || *As long as*, mientras. || *As much as, as many as*, tanto... como, tantos... como: *I have as much money as you*, tengo tanto dinero como tú. || *As many as*, cuantos: *to as many as are present I would say*, a cuantos están presentes afirmo que. || U. S. *As of*, a partir de. || *As regards*, con respecto a. || *As..., so...*, como... también *or* lo mismo... || *As soon as*, tan pronto como. || *As the case may be*, según sea el caso. || *As though*, como si. || *As to*, en cuanto a, en *or* por lo que se refiere a. || *As well*, también. || *As well as*, así como. || *As yet*, hasta ahora. || *So as to*, para: *I did it so as to give him an idea of how hard it is*, lo hice para darle una idea de lo difícil que es. || *Such as*, tal como.
— Prep. En calidad de, como (in the capacity of): *he came as an observer*, vino en calidad de observador. || Como (like). || Por: *as a rule*, por regla general.
asafoetida or **asafetida** [ˌæsəˈfetidə] n. Asa (*f.*) fétida.
asbestos [æzˈbestɔs] n. Amianto, *m.*, asbesto, *m.*
— Adj. De amianto. || — *Asbestos cement*, fibrocemento, *m.* || *Asbestos fiber*, fibra de amianto.
ascend [əˈsend] v. tr. Ascender [a], subir (to climb). || Subir a: *to ascend the throne*, subir al trono. || Subir, remontar (towards the source of a river, etc.).
— V. intr. Subir, ascender. || Elevarse (smoke, balloon).
ascendance or **ascendence** [əˈsendəns] n. Ascendiente, *m.*, ascendencia, *f.*
ascendancy or **ascendency** [—i] n. Ascendiente, *m.*, ascendencia, *f.*
ascendant or **ascendent** [əˈsendənt] adj. Ascendente, ascendiente.
— Pl. n. Ascendientes, *m.*, antepasados, *m.*

ARTS — ARTES, *f.*

I. General terms. — Generalidades, *f.*

work	obra *f.*
work of art	obra (*f.*) de arte
masterpiece	obra (*f.*) maestra
plastic, graphic arts	artes (*f.*) plásticas, gráficas
Fine Arts	Bellas Artes *f.*
art gallery	galería *f.*; museo *m.*
salon	salón *m.*
exhibition; collection	exposición *f.*; colección *f.*
author	autor *m.*
style	estilo *m.*
inspiration	inspiración *f.*
muse	musa *f.*
classicism	clasicismo *m.*
purism	purismo *m.*
conceptism	conceptismo *m.*
gongorism	gongorismo *m.*, culteranismo *m.*
realism	realismo *m.*
surrealism	surrealismo *m.*
romanticism	romanticismo *m.*
naturalism	naturalismo *m.*
symbolism	simbolismo *m.*
impressionism	impresionismo *m.*
expressionism	expresionismo *m.*
existentialism	existencialismo *m.*
futurism	futurismo *m.*
neoclassicism	neoclasicismo *m.*

II. Literature. — Literatura, *f.*

humanities	humanidades *f.*
writer	escritor *m.*
book; volume	libro *m.*; volumen *m.*
theatre [U. S., theater]	teatro *m.*
drama	drama *m.*
comedy	comedia *f.*
tragedy	tragedia *f.*
farce	farsa *f.*
play	obra (*f.*) de teatro
the three unities	las tres unidades *f.*
playwright	dramaturgo *m.*, autor (*m.*) de obras de teatro, comediógrafo *m.*
act; scene	acto *m.*; escena *f.*
plot	argumento *m.*
intrigue	intriga *f.*
story	historia *f.*
episode	episodio *m.*
ending, dénouement	desenlace *m.*
poetry; poet	poesía *f.*; poeta *m.*
poem	poema *m.*
epic poetry	épica *f.*
epopee	epopeya *f.*
ode	oda *f.*
sonnet	soneto *m.*
verse, stanza	estrofa *f.*
line	verso *m.*
rhyme	rima *f.*
metrics	métrica *f.*
prose	prosa *f.*
novel	novela *f.*
biography	biografía *f.*
allegory	alegoría *f.*
science fiction	ciencia (*f.*) ficción
satire	sátira *f.*
essay	ensayo *m.*
composition	composición *f.*
rhetoric	retórica *f.*
oratory	oratoria *f.*
declamation	declamación *f.*
improvisation	improvisación *f.*
criticism; critic	crítica *f.*; crítico *m.*
wit	ingenio *m.*
eloquence	elocuencia *f.*
lyricism	lirismo *m.*

III. Painting. — Pintura, *f.*

artist; painter	artista *m.* y *f.*; pintor *m.*
cave *o* rupestrian painting	pintura (*f.*) rupestre
oil painting	pintura (*f.*) al óleo
painting in fresco	pintura (*f.*) al fresco
tempera painting	pintura (*f.*) al temple
gouache	pintura (*f.*) a la aguada, aguada *f.*
watercolour [U.S., watercolor]	acuarela *f.*
pastel drawing	pintura (*f.*) al pastel
wash; sanguine	lavado *m.*; sanguina *f.*
miniature	miniatura *f.*
engraving	grabado *m.*
drawing	dibujo *m.*
drawing from nature	dibujo (*m.*) del natural
mechanical drawing	dibujo (*m.*) industrial
tracing	calco *m.*
chiaroscuro	claroscuro *m.*
design	diseño *m.*
sketch	esbozo *m.*, bosquejo *m.*, croquis *m.*, boceto *m.*
study	estudio *m.*
triptych, triptich	tríptico *m.*
portrait	retrato *m.*
model	modelo *m.*
caricature	caricatura *f.*
nude	desnudo *m.*
profile	perfil *m.*
foreshortened figure	escorzado *m.*
landscape	paisaje *m.*
seascape	marina *f.*
still life	bodegón *m.*, naturaleza (*f.*) muerta
tapestry	tapiz *m.*
perspective	perspectiva *f.*
colouring [U.S., coloring]	colorido *m.*
shade	sombra *f.*
cubism	cubismo *m.*
abstract	abstracto, ta
figurative	figurativo, va
brush	pincel *m.*
stroke	pincelada *f.*, toque *m.*
finishing touch	último toque *m.*
easel	caballete *m.*
palette	paleta *f.*
palette knife; spatula	espátula *f.*
picture, painting	cuadro *m.*
frame	marco *m.*
chassis	bastidor *m.*
canvas	lienzo *m.*
studio	estudio *m.*
pinacotheca	pinacoteca *f.*

IV. Sculpture. — Escultura, *f.*

sculptor	escultor *m.*
carving	talla *f.*
religious imagery	imaginería *f.*
statue	estatua *f.*
figure	figura *f.*
study	boceto *m.*
bronze	bronce *m.*
terra-cotta	terracota *f.*
wrought iron	hierro (*m.*) forjado
bust	busto *m.*
caryatid	cariátide *f.*
retable, altarpiece	retablo *m.*
stele	estela *f.*
high relief	alto relieve *m.*
low relief, bas-relief	bajorrelieve *m.*
mould [U.S., mold]	molde *m.*
cast; casting	vaciado *m.*
repoussage, repoussé work	repujado *m.*
workshop	taller *m.*

V. Architecture. — Arquitectura, *f.*

architect	arquitecto *m.*
plan	proyecto *m.*
town planning [U.S., city planning]	urbanización *f.*
Doric, Ionic, Corinthian, Composite, Tuscan order	orden (*m.*) dórico, jónico, corintio, compuesto, toscano
Gothic	gótico *m.*
flamboyant Gothic	gótico (*m.*) flamígero
Romanesque	románico *m.*
barroque	barroco *m.*
plateresque	plateresco *m.*
rococo	rococó *m.*
building	edificio *m.*
arch	arco *m.*
vault	bóveda *f.*
ogive	ojiva *f.*
façade	fachada *f.*
frontispiece	frontispicio *m.*
column	columna *f.*
pilaster	pilastra *f.*
pediment, fronton	frontón *m.*

See also CONSTRUCCIÓN

ascension [ə'senʃən] n. Ascensión, *f.* || Rel. *The Ascension,* la Ascensión.

ascent [ə'sent] n. Subida, *f.*, ascensión, *f.*, ascenso, *m.* (act of ascending). || Ascenso, *m.* (promotion). || Cuesta, *f.* (slope). || Subida, *f.* (way up). || *Line of ascent,* ascendencia, *f.*

ascertain [,æsə'tein] v. tr. Comprobar (to verify). || Averiguar (to find out): *I am going to ascertain what happened,* voy a averiguar lo que ha sucedido.

ascertainable [—əbl] adj. Comprobable. || Averiguable.

ascertainment [—mənt] n. Comprobación, *f.* (verification). || Averiguación, *f.*

ascesis [ə'sisəs] n. Ascesis, *f.*

ascetic [ə'setik] adj. Ascético, ca.
— N. Asceta, *m.* & *f.*

ascetical [—əl] adj. Ascético, ca.

asceticism [ə'setisizəm] n. Ascetismo, *m.*, ascética, *f.*

ascomycete [,æskəu'maisi:t] n. Bot. Ascomiceto, *m.*

ascot ['æskət] n. U. S. Fular, *m.*, pañuelo, *m.*

ascribable [əs'kraibəbl] adj. Atribuible, imputable.

ascribe [əs'kraib] v. tr. Atribuir, imputar.

ascription [əs'kripʃən] n. Atribución, *f.*, imputación, *f.*

ascus ['æskəs] n. Bot. Asca, *f.*

— Observ. El plural de *ascus* es *asci.*

asepsis [æ'sepsis] n. Med. Asepsia, *f.*

aseptic [æ'septik] adj. Med. Aséptico, ca.

asepticize [æ'septisaiz] v. tr. Esterilizar, volver aséptico, aseptizar.

asexual [æ'seksjuəl] adj. Asexual, asexuado, da.

ash [æʃ] n. Ceniza, *f.*: *to burn to ashes,* reducir a cenizas. || Bot. Fresno, *m.* (tree). || *Ash Wednesday,* Miércoles (*m.*) de Ceniza.

ashamed [ə'ʃeimd] adj. Avergonzado, da. || *To be ashamed of,* avergonzarse de, estar avergonzado por.

ash bin ['æʃbin] n. Cubo (*m.*) de la basura.

ash can ['æʃkæn] n. U. S. Cubo (*m.*) de la basura.

ashen ['æʃn] adj. Bot. De fresno (of ash tree). || Pálido, da; ceniciento, ta (palid).

ashlar (U. S. **ashler**) ['æʃlə*] n. Sillar, *m.* (building stone). || Sillería, *f.* (stonework).

ashore [ə'ʃɔ:*] adv. Mar. A tierra (towards land). || En tierra (on land). || — *To go ashore,* desembarcar. || *To run ashore,* encallar, varar.

ashtray ['æʃtrei] n. Cenicero, *m.*

ashy [ˈæʃi] adj. Ceniciento, ta.
Asia [ˈeiʃə] pr. n. Asia, *f.*: *Asia Minor*, Asia Menor.
Asian [ˈeiʃən] adj./n. Asiático, ca.
Asiatic [ˌeiʃiˈætik] adj./n. Asiático, ca.
aside [əˈsaid] adv. Al lado (to one side). || Aparte: *joking aside*, bromas aparte. || — *Aside from*, además de (as well as), aparte de (apart from). || *To lay aside*, see LAY. || *To set aside*, anular. || *To step aside*, hacerse a un lado. || *To take aside*, llevar aparte. || *To throw* o *to cast aside*, echar a un lado, desechar.
— N. THEATR. Aparte, *m.* || Digresión, *f.*
asinine [ˈæsinain] adj. Asnal. || FAM. Estúpido, da.
ask [ɑ:sk] v. tr. Preguntar: *ask the way home*, pregunta el camino de casa; *ask him about mealtimes*, pregúntale las horas de las comidas. || Hacer (a question). || Pedir: *may I ask a favour of you?*, ¿te puedo pedir un favor?; *to ask to be allowed to speak*, pedir la palabra; *he asked me to come*, me pidió que viniese. || Invitar (to invite): *I asked them round to dinner*, les invité a cenar. || JUR. Publicar (the banns). || — *Don't ask me!*, ¿yo qué sé? || *Asking price*, precio (*m.*) inicial. || *To ask s.o. in*, decir a alguien que entre.
— V. intr. Preguntar. || — *For the asking*, a pedir de boca. || *This asks for great prudence*, esto requiere mucha prudencia. || *To ask after* o *about* o *for*, preguntar por. || *To ask for it*, buscársela. || *To ask for sth. back*, pedir que se devuelva algo. || FIG. *To ask for the moon*, pedir la luna. || *To ask for trouble*, buscarse problemas.
askance [əsˈkæns] adj. Oblicuamente. || De reojo, de soslayo. || *To look askance at*, mirar con desconfianza *or* recelo *or* con mala cara.
askew [əsˈkju:] adv. De reojo, de soslayo (to look).
— Adj. Torcido, da; ladeado, da.
aslant [əˈslɑ:nt] adv. Oblicuamente.
— Prep. A través de.
asleep [əˈsli:p] adj. Dormido, da (sleeping): *he was fast asleep*, estaba profundamente dormido. || Adormecido, da (numb). || *To fall asleep*, quedarse dormido, dormirse: *he was so tired that he fell asleep*, estaba tan cansado que se quedó dormido.
aslope [əsˈləup] adv./adj. En pendiente.
asp [æsp] n. ZOOL. Áspid, *m.*, áspide, *m.*
asparagus [əsˈpærəgəs] n. BOT. Espárrago, *m.* (vegetable). | Asparagus, *m.* (fern).
aspect [ˈæspekt] n. Aspecto, *m.* (outward appearance). || Punto (*m.*) de vista: *from a personal aspect*, desde un punto de vista personal. || Aspecto, *m.*: *this problem has various aspects*, este problema tiene varios aspectos. || Exposición, *f.*, orientación, *f.* (of a house). || ASTR. Aspecto, *m.* || *Flat with a westerly aspect*, piso orientado al oeste.
aspen [ˈæspən] n. BOT. Álamo (*m.*) temblón.
asperges [əsˈpə:dʒi:z] n. REL. Asperges, *m.*
aspergillum [ˌæspəˈdʒiləm] n. REL. Hisopo, *m.*, aspersorio, *m.*
— OBSERV. El plural de *aspergillum* es *aspergilla*.
aspergillus [ˌæspəˈdʒiləs] n. BOT. Aspergilo, *m.*
— OBSERV. El plural de *aspergillus* es *aspergilli*.
asperity [æsˈperiti] n. Aspereza, *f.*
asperous [ˈæspərəs] adj. Áspero, ra (rough).
asperse [əsˈpə:s] v. tr. Difamar, calumniar (to malign). || Hisopear, asperjar (to sprinkle).
aspersion [əsˈpə:ʃən] n. Difamación, *f.*, calumnia, *f.* (defamation). || Aspersión, *f.* (sprinkling). || *To cast aspersions on s.o.*, difamar *or* calumniar a alguien.
aspersorium [ˌæspəˈsɔ:rjəm] n. REL. Hisopo, *m.*
— OBSERV. El plural es *aspersoria* o *aspersoriums*.
asphalt [ˈæsfælt] n. Asfalto, *m.*
asphalt [ˈæsfælt] v. tr. Asfaltar.
asphalting [—iŋ] n. Asfaltado, *m.*
asphodel [ˈæsfədel] n. BOT. Asfódelo, *m.*, gamón, *m.*
asphyxia [æsˈfiksiə] n. Asfixia, *f.*
asphyxiate [æsˈfiksieit] v. tr. Asfixiar.
— V. intr. Asfixiarse.
asphyxiation [æsˌfiksiˈeiʃən] n. Asfixia, *f.*
aspic [ˈæspik] n. Gelatina (*f.*) de carne *or* de tomate. || ZOOL. Áspid, *m.* || BOT. Espliego, *m.*
aspidistra [ˌæspiˈdistrə] n. BOT. Aspidistra, *f.*
aspirant [əsˈpaiərənt] n. Aspirante, *m.* & *f.*, candidato, ta.
aspirate [ˈæspərit] n. GRAMM. Aspiración, *f.* (sound made by the letter "h"). | Aspirada, *f.* (a consonant).
— Adj. GRAMM. Aspirado, da.
aspirate [ˈæspəreit] v. tr. GRAMM. MED. Aspirar.
aspiration [ˌæspəˈreiʃən] n. Aspiración, *f.*, ambición, *f.* || MED. GRAMM. Aspiración, *f.*
aspirator [ˈæspəreitə*] n. MED. Aspirador, *m.*
aspiratory [—ri] adj. Aspiratorio, ria.
aspire [əsˈpaiə*] v. intr. Aspirar, ambicionar: *to aspire to high positions*, aspirar a *or* ambicionar altos cargos.
aspirin [ˈæspərin] n. MED. Aspirina, *f.*
asquint [əˈskwint] adv./adj. De soslayo, de reojo.
ass [æs] n. ZOOL. Asno, *m.*, burro, *m.* || FAM. Burro, *m.* (a stupid person). || U. S. POP. Culo, *m.* || — FAM. *To be like Buridan's ass*, parecerse al asno de Buridán. | *To make an ass of o.s.*, ponerse en ridículo.
assagai [ˈæsəgai] n. Azagaya, *f.*
assail [əˈseil] v. tr. Asaltar: *the beggars assailed him*, los mendigos le asaltaron. || Atacar, acometer (to attack). || Abrumar (with questions).
assailant [—ənt] n. Agresor, ra; asaltante, *m.* & *f.*
assassin [əˈsæsin] n. Asesino, na: *hired assassin*, asesino pagado.
assassinate [əˈsæsineit] v. tr. Asesinar.
assassination [əˌsæsiˈneiʃən] n. Asesinato, *m.* (murder).
assault [əˈsɔ:lt] n. Ataque, *m.* (vigorous attack): *bayonet assault*, ataque a la bayoneta. || Ultraje, *m.* (violent criticism). || MIL. SP. Asalto, *m.* || JUR. Amenaza, *f.* || — JUR. *Assault and battery*, lesiones, *f. pl.*, vías (*f. pl.*) de hecho. || *Criminal assault*, intento (*m.*) de violación. || *Indecent assault*, atentado (*m.*) contra el pudor. || *To make an assault on*, asaltar a, dar el asalto a.
assault [əˈsɔ:lt] v. tr. Asaltar, atacar: *the thief assaulted him*, el ladrón le asaltó. || JUR. Agredir. | Violar (to rape).
assaulter [—ə*] n. Agresor, *m.*
assay [əˈsei] n. TECH. Aquilatamiento, *m.* (of gold), ensaye, *m.* (of a metal). | Muestra (*f.*) de ensaye (sample of metal).
assay [əˈsei] v. tr. TECH. Ensayar (metals). | Aquilatar (gold). || FIG. Probar, intentar.
assayer [—ə*] n. Ensayador, *m.*
assegai [ˈæsigai] Azagaya, *f.*
assemblage [əˈsemblidʒ] n. Colección, *f.* (of things). || Reunión, *f.* (of persons). || TECH. Montaje, *m.*, ensambladura, *f.*
assemble [əˈsembl] v. tr. Reunir (to bring together). || Armar, montar, ensamblar (to fit together). || JUR. Convocar.
— V. intr. Reunirse, juntarse.
assembler [—ə*] n. Montador, *m.*
assembly [əˈsembli] n. Asamblea, *f.* (parliament). || Reunión, *f.*, asamblea, *f.* (a gathering of people). || TECH. Montaje, *m.* || MIL. Formación, *f.* || — *Assembly hall*, salón (*m.*) de actos. || *Assembly line*, cadena (*f.*) *or* línea (*f.*) de montaje. || *Assembly line production*, producción (*f.*) en cadena. || *Assembly shop*, taller (*m.*) de montaje.
assemblyman [—mən] n. Asambleísta, *m.* || U. S. Miembro (*m.*) de la cámara baja de un Estado.
assent [əˈsent] n. Asentimiento, *m.*, consentimiento, *m.* || Sanción, *f.* (of a law).
assent [əˈsent] v. intr. Asentir, consentir.
assert [əˈsə:t] v. tr. Afirmar (to state as true). || Mantener, sostener (to maintain). || Hacer valer (rights, claims). || *To assert o.s.*, imponerse.
assertion [əˈsə:ʃən] n. Afirmación, *f.*, aserción, *f.* || Reivindicación, *f.* (of a right).
assertive [əˈsə:tiv] adj. Perentorio, ria. || Positivo, va (positive). || Afirmativo, va; asertivo, va (affirmative).
assertor [əˈsə:tə*] n. Asertor, ra. || FIG. Defensor, *m.*, campeón, *m.* (of a cause).
assertory [—ri] adj. Asertorio, ria.
assess [əˈses] v. tr. Evaluar, valorar (*at*, en) [to set an estimated value on]. || Gravar (to impose a tax). || Repartir (expenses). || Juzgar (to consider).
assessment [—mənt] n. Valoración, *f.*, evaluación, *f.*, tasación, *f.*: *the assessment came to twenty pounds*, la valoración fue de veinte libras. || Gravamen, *m.* (tax). || Juicio, *m.* (judgment).
assessor [—ə*] n. Tasador, ra (who estimates values for insurance, taxation, etc.). || Asesor, *m.* (adviser).
asset [ˈæset] n. Ventaja, *f.* (advantage): *having a car is an asset in my profession*, tener coche es una ventaja en mi profesión. || Baza, *f.* (trump). || — Pl. Bienes, *m.*: *personal assets*, bienes muebles; *real assets*, bienes raíces. || COMM. Haber, *m. sing.*, activo, *m. sing.* (positive items on a balance sheet). | Activo, *m. sing.* (total property): *assets in hand*, activo disponible.
asseverate [əˈsevəreit] v. tr. Aseverar, asegurar, afirmar.
asseveration [əˌsevəˈreiʃən] n. Aseveración, *f.*, afirmación, *f.*
assiduity [ˌæsiˈdju:iti] n. Asiduidad, *f.*
assiduous [əˈsidjuəs] adj. Asiduo, dua.
assign [əˈsain] n. JUR. Cesionario, ria.
assign [əˈsain] v. tr. Asignar (to allot). || Designar, nombrar (to nominate). || Ceder (property, right). || Atribuir (to attribute). || Fijar (a date). || Señalar, indicar (a reason).
assignation [ˌæsigˈneiʃən] n. Asignación, *f.* (the act of assigning). || Atribución, *f.* || Designación, *f.*, nombramiento, *m.* || Cita, *f.* (meeting). || JUR. Cesión, *f.*
assignee [ˌæsiˈni:] n. JUR. Cesionario, ria (beneficiary). | Apoderado, da (proxy).
assignment [əˈsainmənt] n. Asignación, *f.* || JUR. Cesión, *f.* (transference of property or rights). | Escritura (*f.*) de cesión (document). || Misión, *f.* (mission). || Tarea, *f.*, trabajo, *m.* (task).
assimilable [əˈsimiləbl] adj. Asimilable.
assimilate [əˈsimileit] v. tr. Asimilar: *to assimilate food*, asimilar la comida; *to assimilate knowledge*, asimilar conocimientos.
— V. intr. Asimilarse.
assimilation [əˌsimiˈleiʃən] n. Asimilación, *f.*
assimilative [əˈsimilətiv] adj. Asimilativo, va.
assimilatory [əˈsimilətəri] adj. Asimilativo, va.
assist [əˈsist] v. tr./intr. Asistir, ayudar (to help): *he assists him in his work*, le asiste en su trabajo. || Asistir, presenciar (to be present). || *To assist in*, tomar parte en.
assist [əˈsist] n. Asistencia, *f.*, ayuda, *f.*

assistance [ə'sistəns] n. Ayuda, *f.*, asistencia, *f.* || *To be of assistance to*, ayudar a.
assistant [ə'sistənt] n. Ayudante, *m.* & *f.*, auxiliar, *m.* & *f.*
— Adj. Ayudante. || — *Assistant cameraman*, ayudante de operador. || *Assistant director*, regidor (*m.*) de escena. || *Assistant teacher*, profesor (*m.*) auxiliar *or* adjunto. || *Assistant secretary*, subsecretario, *m.*, secretario adjunto.
assistantship [—ʃip] n. Ayudantía, *f.*
assize [ə'saiz] n. JUR. Jurado, *m.* (in Scotland). || — Pl. Sesión (*f. sing.*) judicial. || *Assize Court*, Audiencia (*f.*) de lo criminal.
associable [ə'səuʃjəbl] adj. Asociable.
associate [ə'səuʃiit] adj. Asociado, da: *associate publishers*, editores asociados; *associate member*, miembro asociado. || Adjunto, ta (professor). || *War and its associate horrors*, la guerra y los horrores que la acompañan.
— N. Socio, *m.* (partner). || Compañero, ra (friend). || Cómplice, *m.* (in crime).
associate [ə'səuʃieit] v. tr. Asociar. || *To associate o.s. with an idea*, adherirse a una opinión.
— V. intr. Unirse, asociarse (to join together). || Tratarse, tratar: *I refuse to associate with them*, me niego a tratar con ellos.
association [əˌsəusi'eiʃən] n. Asociación, *f.*: *religious association*, asociación religiosa; *European Free Trade Association*, Asociación Europea de Libre Cambio. || COMM. Sociedad, *f.* || Recuerdo, *m.*: *Paris has happy associations for her*, París tiene recuerdos felices para ella. || Relación, *f.* (relationship). || *Association of ideas*, asociación de ideas.
association football [—'futbɔ:l] n. SP. Fútbol, *m.*
associationism [—izəm] n. Asociacionismo, *m.*
associative [ə'səuʃjətiv] adj. De asociación.
assonance ['æsənəns] n. Asonancia, *f.*
assonant ['æsənənt] adj./n. Asonante.
assonate ['æsəuneit] v. intr. Asonantar, asonar.
assonated [—id] adj. Asonantado, da.
assort [ə'sɔ:t] v. tr. Clasificar, ordenar (to classify).
— V. intr. Cuadrar (to fit). || Corresponder, concordar (to agree).
assorted [—id] adj. Clasificado, da (classified). || Variado, da; surtido, da (miscellaneous). || — *Ill-assorted couple*, matrimonio mal avenido. || *Well-assorted couple*, matrimonio bien avenido.
assortment [ə'sɔ:tmənt] n. Surtido, *m.*, variedad, *f.* || Clasificación, *f.*
assuage [ə'sweidʒ] v. tr. Aliviar, mitigar (pain). || Saciar (hunger, thirst). || Satisfacer (desire). || Calmar (anger).
assume [ə'sju:m] v. tr. Asumir: *we assume his guilt*, asumimos su culpabilidad; *he assumed the responsibility*, asumió la responsabilidad. || Tomar, asumir (power). || Tomar, usurpar (to usurp). || Arrogarse (right). || Tomar (an appearance). || Dar por: *we assume him dead*, le damos por muerto. || Adoptar, tomar: *he assumed a foreign accent*, adoptó un acento extranjero; *he assumed a posture of arrogance*, adoptó una postura arrogante. || Manifestarse: *the disease assumes many forms*, la enfermedad se manifiesta de muchas maneras. || Suponer: *I assume you will be there*, supongo que estarás allí. || Tomar, servirse de, utilizar (a name). || Afectar, fingir (a virtue). || Darse (air).
assumed [—d] adj. Supuesto, ta (taken for granted). || Fingido, da; simulado, da (pretended). || Ficticio, cia (fictitious).
assuming [—iŋ] adj. Arrogante, presumido, da. || *Assuming that*, suponiendo que, en el supuesto de que.
assumption [ə'sʌmpʃən] n. Suposición, *f.*, supuesto, *m.* (supposition). || Toma, *f.* (of power). || Apropiación, *f.*, usurpación, *f.* || Pretensión, *f.*, presunción, *f.* (vanity). || — *On the assumption that*, suponiendo que. || REL. *The Assumption*, La Asunción.
assurance [ə'ʃuərəns] n. Seguridad, *f.* (certainty, self-confidence). || COMM. Seguro, *m.* (insurance). || Garantía, *f.* (guarantee). || FIG. Descaro, *m.*, desfachatez, *f.* (impudence). || — *I gave my assurance that I would go*, le di palabra de que iría, le prometí que iría. || *To make assurance doubly sure*, para mayor seguridad.
assure [ə'ʃuə*] v. tr. Asegurar (to insure). || Garantizar, asegurar (to make certain). || Asegurar (to promise).
assured [—d] adj. Asegurado, da (certain, safe). || Seguro, ra (self-confident). || *Rest assured that*, tenga la seguridad de que.
assuredly [—ridli] adv. Ciertamente, seguramente.
assuredness [—ridnis] n. Certeza, *f.* (certainty). || Seguridad, *f.* (self-confidence).
assurer [—ə*] n. Asegurador, ra.
Assyria [ə'siriə] pr. n. GEOGR. Asiria, *f.*
Assyrian [—n] adj./n. Asirio, ria.
Assyriology [əˌsiri'ɔlədʒi] n. Asiriología, *f.*
astatic [ei'stætik] adj. PHYS. Astático, ca.
aster ['æstə*] n. BOT. Aster, *m.*
asterisk ['æstərisk] n. Asterisco, *m.*
asterisk ['æstərisk] v. tr. Poner un asterisco a.
asterism ['æstərizəm] n. ASTR. MIN. Asterismo, *m.*
astern [əs'tə:n] adv. MAR. A popa, de popa, por popa. || Hacia atrás (backwards). || *Astern of*, detrás de.
asteroid ['æstərɔid] n. ASTR. Asteroide, *m.*
— Adj. Asteroide.
asthenia [æs'θi:njə] n. MED. Astenia, *f.*
asthenic [æs'θenik] adj./n. Asténico, ca.
asthma ['æsmə] n. MED. Asma, *f.*
asthmatic [æs'mætik] adj./n. Asmático, ca.
asthmatical [æs'mætikəl] adj. Asmático, ca.
astigmat ['æstigmæt] n. Astigmático, ca.
astigmatic [ˌæstig'mætik] adj. Astigmático, ca.
astigmatism [æs'tigmətizəm] n. Astigmatismo, *m.*
astir [ə'stə:*] adj. Levantado, da (out of bed). || En movimiento (in motion). || En efervescencia (in excitement).
astonish [əs'tɔniʃ] v. tr. Asombrar. || *To be astonished at* o *by*, quedarse asombrado *or* asombrarse de *or* por.
astonishing [—iŋ] adj. Asombroso, sa.
astonishment [—mənt] n. Asombro, *m.*
astound [əs'taund] v. tr. Aterrar (with fear). || Asombrar, pasmar (with wonder, amazement).
astounding [—iŋ] adj. Asombroso, sa; pasmoso, sa.
astrachan [ˌæstrə'kæn] n. Astracán, *m.*
astraddle ['ə'strædl] adv./adj. A horcajadas.
astragal ['æstrəgəl] n. ANAT. ARCH. Astrágalo, *m.*
astragalus [əs'trægələs] n. ANAT. BOT. Astrágalo, *m.*

— OBSERV. El plural de *astragalus* es *astragali*.

astrakhan [ˌæstrə'kæn] n. Astracán, *m.*
astral ['æstrəl] adj. Astral: *astral bodies*, cuerpos astrales.
astray [əs'trei] adv. Por mal camino. || — *To go astray*, extraviarse (to get lost), errar el blanco (bullets, etc.). || *To lead astray*, despistar (to mislead), descarriar, llevar por mal camino.
astrict [ə'strikt] v. tr. Constreñir.
astricted [ə'striktid] adj. Astricto, ta.
astriction [ə'strikʃən] n. Astricción, *f.*
astride [əs'traid] adv./adj. A horcajadas.
— Prep. A horcajadas sobre.
astringe [əs'trindʒ] v. tr. Astreñir.
astringency [əs'trindʒənsi] n. Astringencia, *f.* || FIG. Austeridad, *f.*
astringent [əs'trindʒənt] adj. Astringente. || FIG. Austero, ra (style). | Severo, ra (criticism).
— N. Astringente, *m.*
astrobiology ['æstrəuˌbai'ɔlədʒi] n. Astrobiología, *f.*
astrolabe ['æstrəuleib] n. ASTR. Astrolabio, *m.*
astrologer [əs'trɔlədʒə*] n. Astrólogo, ga.
astrologic [ˌæstrə'lɔdʒik] or **astrological** [—əl] adj. Astrológico, ca.
astrology [əs'trɔlədʒi] n. Astrología, *f.*
astronaut ['æstrənɔ:t] n. Astronauta, *m.* & *f.*
astronautics [ˌæstrə'nɔ:tiks] n. Astronáutica, *f.*
astronavigation ['æstrəuˌnævi'geiʃən] n. Navegación (*f.*) interplanetaria *or* espacial.
astronomer [əs'trɔnəmə*] n. Astrónomo, *m.* || *Astronomer Royal*, director (*m.*) del observatorio astronómico de Greenwich.
astronomic [ˌæstrə'nɔmik] adj. Astronómico, ca: *astronomic unit*, unidad astronómica. || FIG. Astronómico, ca.
astronomical [—əl] adj. Astronómico, ca: *astronomical clock, telescope*, reloj, telescopio astronómico. || FIG. Astronómico, ca.
astronomy [əs'trɔnəmi] n. Astronomía, *f.*
astrophysicist ['æstrəu'fizisist] n. Astrofísico, ca.
astrophysics ['æstrəu'fiziks] n. Astrofísica, *f.*
Asturian [æs'tjuəriən] adj./n. Asturiano, na.
Asturianism [æs'tjuəriænizəm] n. Asturianismo, *m.*
Asturias [æs'tjuəriæs] pl. n. GEOGR. Asturias, *f.*
astute [əs'tju:t] adj. Astuto, ta.
astuteness [—nis] n. Astucia, *f.*
asunder [ə'sʌndə*] adv. En pedazos. || — *To come asunder*, separarse. || *To tear asunder*, hacer pedazos.
asylum [ə'sailəm] n. Refugio, *m.*, asilo, *m.* (place of refuge). || Asilo, *m.*: *to seek political asylum*, pedir asilo político; *to afford asylum to*, dar asilo a. || Asilo, *m.*, hospicio, *m.* (for aged people, etc.). || Manicomio, *m.* (mental house).
asymmetric [ˌæsi'metrik] or **asymmetrical** [—əl] adj. Asimétrico, ca.
asymmetry [æ'simitri] n. Asimetría, *f.*
asymptote ['æsimptəut] n. MATH. Asíntota, *f.*
asymptotic [ˌæsimp'tɔtik] or **asymptotical** [—əl] adj. Asintótico, ca.
asynchronous [ə'siŋkrənəs] adj. Asincrónico, ca.
asyndetic [ˌæsin'detik] adj. Asindético, ca.
asyndeton [æ'sinditən] n. GRAMM. Asíndeton, *m.*

— OBSERV. El plural de *asyndeton* es *asyndetons* o *asyndeta*.

at [æt] prep. En (expressing position, time, manner and condition): *at home*, en casa; *at Peter's*, en casa de Pedro; *at Easter*, en Semana Santa; *good at arithmetic*, bueno en aritmética; *at work*, en el trabajo; *at war*, en guerra. || A (expressing time, position, direction, state and price): *at six o'clock*, a las seis; *at the table*, a la mesa; *at them!*, ¡a ellos!; *sad at leaving*, triste al partir; *at five pesetas a kilogramme*, a cinco pesetas el kilo. || De: *what is he laughing at?*, ¿de qué se ríe?; *attempt at escape*, tentativa de evasión. || Por (through): *to go in at one door and come out at the other*, entrar por una puerta y salir por la otra; *at Christmas*, por Navidades. || — *Angry at*, enfadado con. || *At best*, en el mejor de los casos. || *At first*, al principio. || *At his cries we rushed*, acudimos al oír sus gritos. || *At last*, por fin. || *At least*, al menos, por lo menos. || *At most*, a lo más, a lo sumo, como mucho. || *At once*, en seguida. || *At night*, de noche, por la noche. || *At play*, jugando. || *At present*, actualmente. || *At random*, al azar. || *At sea*, en el mar. || *At that*, además: *he is a footballer and a good one at that*, es futbolista y muy bueno además; sin más: *we have left it a that*, lo hemos dejado sin más; en ese, en esa: *at that moment*, en ese momento; ante eso (because of that): *he laughed and at that they all left*, se rió y ante eso se marcharon todos. || *At your request*, a petición suya. || *To be at*, see BE. || *To look at o.s. in the mirror*, mirarse en el espejo. || *Two at a time*, de dos en dos.

ataraxia [ætəˈræksiə] or **ataraxy** [ˈætəˌræksi] n. Ataraxia, *f.*

atavic [ˈætəvik] adj. Atávico, ca.

atavism [ˈætəvizəm] n. Atavismo, *m.*

atavistic [ˌætəˈvistik] adj. Atávico, ca.

ataxia [əˈtæksiə] or **ataxy** [əˈtæksi] n. MED. Ataxia, *f.*

ate [eit] pret. See EAT.

ateles [ˈætəli:z] n. ZOOL. Ateles, *m.* (monkey).

atellans [əˈtelənz] pl. n. Atelanas, *f.* (Latin comedy).

atelier [ˈætəljei] n. Estudio, *m.* (artist's studio). || Taller, *m.* (workroom).

atheism [ˈeiθiizəm] n. Ateísmo, *m.*

atheist [ˈeiθiist] n. Ateo, a.

atheistic [ˌeiθiˈistik] or **atheistical** [—əl] adj. Ateo, a.

athenaeum [ˌæθiˈni:əm] n. Ateneo, *m.*

Athenian [əˈθi:njən] adj./n. Ateniense.

Athens [ˈæθinz] pr. n. GEOGR. Atenas.

athermanous [æˈθə:mənəs] adj. PHYS. Atérmano, na.

athirst [əˈθə:st] adj. Sediento, ta. || FIG. Ávido, da.

athlete [ˈæθli:t] n. Atleta, *m.*

athletic [æθˈletik] adj. Atlético, ca.

athletics [—s] n. Atletismo, *m.*

at home [ətˈhəum] n. Recepción, *f.*

athwart [əˈθwɔ:t] prep. A través de (across). || Contra (against).
— Adv. De través, transversalmente.

athwartships [—ʃips] adv. MAR. De babor a estribor.

atlantes [ətˈlænti:z] pl. n. ARCH. Atlantes, *m.*

Atlantic [ətˈlæntik] pr. n. GEOGR. Atlántico, *m.*
— Adj. Atlántico, ca: *Atlantic Ocean*, Océano Atlántico.

Atlantis [ətˈlæntis] pr. n. Atlántida, *f.*

atlas [ˈætləs] n. ANAT. Atlas, *m.* || Atlas, *m.* (of maps). || Atlante, *m.* (pillar).
— OBSERV. El plural de *atlas*, cuando significa *atlante*, es *atlantes*.

atmosphere [ˈætməsfiə*] n. Atmósfera, *f.* || FIG. Ambiente, *m.*: *an intellectual atmosphere*, un ambiente intelectual.

atmospheric [ˌætməsˈferik] adj. Atmosférico, ca.

atmospherical [—əl] adj. Atmosférico, ca.

atmospherics [—s] pl. n. RAD. Perturbaciones (*f.*) atmosféricas, parásitos, *m.*, interferencias, *f.*

atoll [ˈætɔl] n. Atolón, *m.*

atom [ˈætəm] n. Átomo, *m.* || FIG. Átomo, *m.* || — *Atom bomb*, bomba atómica. || *Atom smasher*, acelerador (*m.*) de partículas atómicas.

atomic [əˈtɔmik] adj. Atómico, ca: *atomic age*, era atómica. || — *Atomic bomb*, bomba atómica. || *Atomic dust*, polvo radiactivo. || *Atomic energy*, energía atómica. || *Atomic mass*, masa atómica. || *Atomic number*, número atómico. || *Atomic pile*, pila atómica. || *Atomic warhead*, cabeza atómica. || *Atomic weight*, peso atómico.

atomicity [ˌætəˈmisiti] n. CHEM. Atomicidad, *f.*

atomics [əˈtɔmiks] n. Atomística, *f.*

atomism [ˈætəmizəm] n. Atomismo, *m.*

atomist [ˈætəmist] n. Atomista, *m.* & *f.*

atomistic [ˌætəˈmistik] adj. Atomístico, ca.

atomization [ˌætəmaiˈzeiʃən] n. Atomización, *f.*, pulverización, *f.*

atomize [ˈætəmaiz] v. tr. Atomizar, pulverizar.

atomizer [—ə*] n. Atomizador, *m.*, pulverizador, *m.*, vaporizador, *m.*

atonal [eiˈtəunl] adj. MUS. Atonal (toneless).

atonality [ˈeitəuˈnæliti] n. MUS. Atonalidad, *f.*

atone [əˈtəun] v. tr./intr. Expiar, reparar. || *To atone with*, reconciliarse con.

atonement [—mənt] n. Expiación, *f.*, reparación, *f.* || REL. *Day of Atonement*, día (*m.*) de la Expiación.

atonic [æˈtɔnik] adj. Átono, na; atónico, ca (phonetics). || MUS. Atonal. || MED. Atónico, ca (weak).

atony [ˈætəni] n. MED. Atonía, *f.*

atop [əˈtɔp] adv. Encima.
— Prep. Encima de.

atrabiliar [ˌætrəˈbiljə*] adj. Atrabiliario, ria.

atrabilious [ˌætrəˈbiljəs] adj. Atrabiliario, ria.

atrip [əˈtrip] adj. MAR. *With anchor atrip*, con el ancla levada.

atrium [ˈɑ:triəm] n. ARCH. Atrio, *m.* || MED. Aurícula, *f.* (of the heart).
— OBSERV. El plural de *atrium* es *atria*.

atrocious [əˈtrəuʃəs] adj. Atroz.

atrociousness [—nis] n. Atrocidad, *f.*

atrocity [əˈtrɔsiti] n. Atrocidad, *f.*

atrophy [ˈætrəfi] n. MED. Atrofia, *f.*

atrophy [ˈætrəfi] v. tr. Atrofiar.
— V. intr. Atrofiarse.

atropine [ˈætrəpin] n. CHEM. Atropina, *f.*

attach [əˈtætʃ] v. tr. Atar, ligar (to bind, to connect to). || Sujetar (to fasten). || Pegar (to stick). || FIG. Unir, ligar, vincular (to connect). || Unir (to bind by love): *we are very attached to one another*, estamos muy unidos el uno al otro. || Adjuntar (in a letter). || Agregar (to work with): *an expert attached to a delegation*, un experto agregado a una delegación. || MIL. Destinar (to appoint to): *attached to a regiment as a special instructor*, destinado a un regimiento como instructor especial. || JUR. Embargar, incautar. || Imputar (to attribute): *to attach blame*, imputar la responsabilidad. || Dar, atribuir, conceder (to give value to): *to attach importance to*, dar importancia a. || Aplicar, dar (an epithet). || Poner (a seal). || Enganchar (to hook). || — *To be attached to*, corresponder a (to accompany), tener cariño a (to love), estar apegado a, tener apego a: *to be attached to customs*, estar apegado a las costumbres. || *To attach o.s. to*, entrar a formar parte de (to join), coger cariño a (to become fond of).
— V. intr. Colocarse (to be fastened). || Incumbir: *no blame attaches to him*, no le incumbe ninguna responsabilidad. || Corresponder a, pertenecer a (to belong).

attaché [əˈtæʃei] n. Agregado, *m.*

attaché case [əˈtæʃikeis] n. Maletín, *m.*

attachment [əˈtætʃmənt] n. Colocación, *f.*, fijación, *f.* (act of attaching): *the attachment of the door to its frame was not easy*, la colocación de la puerta en el marco no fue fácil. || Sistema (*m.*) de unión (device or method for attaching). || TECH. Acoplamiento, *m.* || Accesorio, *m.* (attached object). || Cariño, *m.*, apego, *m.*, afecto, *m.* (affection): *there is a strong attachment between them*, se tienen mucho apego. || Adhesión, *f.* || Lazo, *m.*, vínculo, *m.* (bond). || JUR. Incautación, *f.*, embargo, *m.* (*on*, de).

attack [əˈtæk] n. Ataque, *m.* (*on*, a, contra): *to launch an attack*, iniciar un ataque; *surprise attack*, ataque por sorpresa. || Agresión, *f.*, ataque, *m.* (on a person). || MED. Ataque, *m.*

attack [əˈtæk] v. tr./intr. Atacar. || Luchar contra, combatir (to fight). || FIG. Asaltar: *attacked by doubts*, asaltado por las dudas. | Acometer, atacar (to undertake). || MED. Aquejar.

attackable [—əbl] adj. Atacable.

attacker [—ə*] n. Atacador, ra.

attacking [—iŋ] adj. Agresor, ra: *attacking army*, ejército agresor.

attain [əˈtein] v. tr. Alcanzar, conseguir. || Alcanzar, llegar a (an age, happiness, knowledge, a rank). || — V. intr. *To attain to*, alcanzar, conseguir: *to attain to perfection*, alcanzar la perfección.

attainability [əˌteinəˈbiliti] n. Accesibilidad, *f.*

attainable [əˈteinəbl] adj. Accesible (*by*, a, para), alcanzable (*by*, por).

attainder [əˈteində*] n. JUR. Muerte (*f.*) civil.

attainment [əˈteinmənt] n. Logro, *m.*, obtención, *f.*, consecución, *f.*, realización, *f.* || — Pl. Conocimientos, *m.* (acquired skill).

attaint [əˈteint] v. tr. Condenar a muerte civil. || MED. Aquejar, afectar.

attar of roses [ˈætə*əvˈrəuziz] n. Esencia (*f.*) de rosas.

attempt [əˈtempt] n. Intento, *m.*, tentativa, *f.* (endeavour, try). || Atentado, *m.* (attack): *attempt upon the security of the State*, atentado contra la seguridad del Estado. || *To make an attempt on s.o.'s life*, atentar contra la vida de *or* a la vida de alguien, cometer un atentado contra alguien.

attempt [əˈtempt] v. tr. Intentar, tratar de (to try to): *he attempted to jump the wall*, intentó saltar el muro. || Intentar, tratar de [hacer] (to try sth.): *he attempted a smile*, intentó sonreír; *they attempted the fortress*, intentaron asaltar la fortaleza; *they attempted a rescue*, intentaron rescatarle. || — *Attempted murder*, tentativa (*f.*) de asesinato. || *To attempt the life of*, atentar contra la vida de *or* a la vida de.

attend [əˈtend] v. tr. Asistir a (to be present at). || Ir a, asistir a (to go regularly to): *he attends evening classes*, asiste a clases nocturnas. || Acompañar (to accompany): *she attended the princess during her tour of the country*, acompañó a la princesa durante su viaje por el país. || Acompañar (to accompany as a result): *success attended his every effort*, el éxito acompañaba todos sus esfuerzos. || Atender (to see to the needs of customers). || Tratar, asistir, atender (to visit and treat): *Mr. X is being attended by his personal physician*, al Sr. X le está tratando su médico particular. || Servir (a maid). || *Well-attended conference*, conferencia muy concurrida.
— V. intr. Atender. || — *To attend at*, asistir a. || *To attend to*, cumplir (one's duties), prestar atención a (to pay attention to), ocuparse de (to apply o.s. to): *I must attend to my work now*, tengo que ocuparme de mi trabajo ahora; atender: *are you being attended to, Sir?*, ¿le atienden, señor?; tener en cuenta (to bear in mind), ejecutar (an order). || *To attend upon*, acompañar.

attendance [—əns] n. Asistencia, *f.*: *attendance is compulsory*, la asistencia es obligatoria. || Compañía, *f.* (company). || MED. Asistencia, *f.*, cuidados, *m. pl.* || — *Cabs in attendance*, taxis (*m.*) en la parada.

|| *To be in attendance*, estar de servicio. || *To dance attendance on*, desvivirse por alguien.
attendant [—ənt] adj. Concomitante (circumstances, etc.). || Asistente, presente (present). || — *Attendant on s.o.*, que sirve *or* acompaña a uno. || *War and its attendant horrors*, la guerra y su secuela de horrores.
— N. Encargado, da (employee in charge). || Acompañante, *m. & f.* (companion). || Asistente, *m. & f.* (person present). || Acomodador, ra (in cinema, theatre). || Sirviente, ta (servant). || Secuela, *f.*: *ignorance and its attendants, fear and prejudice*, la ignorancia y sus secuelas, el miedo y los prejuicios.
attention [ə'tenʃən] n. Atención, *f.*: *to pay attention to*, prestar atención a. || Atención, *f.*: *to attract* o *to draw* o *to call s.o.'s attention*, llamar la atención de uno. || Cuidado, *m.*: *he received medical attention*, recibió cuidados médicos; *attention!*, ¡cuidado! || Servicio, *m.* (service in a shop, restaurant). || — Pl. Atenciones, *f.*: *his constant attentions annoy me*, sus constantes atenciones me molestan. || — MIL. *Attention!*, ¡firmes! || *For the attention of*, a la atención de. || *It has come to my attention that*, me he enterado de que. || *To be all attention*, estar muy atento. || MIL. *To bring to attention*, dar la orden de cuadrarse. || *To call s.o.'s attention to*, llamar la atención de alguien sobre. || MIL. *To come to attention*, ponerse firme, cuadrarse. || *To shower attention on s.o.*, tener mil atenciones con uno. || MIL. *To stand at attention*, estar en posición de firme. | *To stand to attention*, cuadrarse. || *You must pay attention to my advice*, tienes que hacer caso de mi consejo. || *Your attention, please!*, ¡atención!
attentive [ə'tentiv] adj. Atento, ta: *attentive to the slightest sound*, atento al menor ruido. || Aplicado, da; atento, ta (industrious): *an attentive pupil*, un alumno aplicado. || Atento, ta (considerate, thoughtful).
attentiveness [—nis] n. Atención, *f.*
attenuate [ə'tenjueit] v. tr. Atenuar.
— V. intr. Atenuarse.
attenuation [ə,tenju'eiʃən] n. Atenuación, *f.*
attest [ə'test] v. tr. Atestiguar (to affirm, to bear witness to). || Dar fe (to confirm as authentic). || Legalizar (document or signature). || Juramentar (to place on oath).
— V. intr. Dar testimonio (*to*, de).
attestant [ə'testənt] n. Testigo, *m. & f.*
attestation [,ætes'teiʃən] n. Atestación, *f.*, testimonio, *m.* (act of bearing witness). || Testimonio, *m.* (testimony). || Atestación, *f.*, atestado, *m.* (document). || Garantía, *f.*: *that signature is sufficient attestation for us*, esa firma es garantía suficiente para nosotros. || Prestación (*f.*) de juramento (oath).
attic ['ætik] n. Ático, *m.* (top floor). || Desván, *m.* (loft).
Attic ['ætik] adj./n. Ático, ca.
Attica ['ætikə] pr. n. GEOGR. Ática, *f.*
Atticism ['ætisizəm] n. Aticismo, *m.*
Attila ['ætilə] pr. n. Atila, *m.*
attire [ə'taiə*] n. Traje, *m.*, atavío, *m.* || HERALD. Astas (*f. pl.*) de ciervo.
attire [ə'taiə*] v. tr. Vestir, ataviar.
attitude ['ætitju:d] n. Postura, *f.* (position). || Actitud, *f.* (mental state): *attitude of mind*, actitud mental. || AVIAT. Posición, *f.* || *To strike an attitude*, adoptar una postura teatral, tener una actitud estudiada.
attitudinize [,æti'tju:dinaiz] v. intr. Adoptar una postura teatral, tener una actitud estudiada.
attorney [ə'tə:ni] n. JUR. Procurador, *m.* || Apoderado, *m.* (proxy). || U. S. JUR. Abogado, *m.* || — *Attorney general*, fiscal (*m.*) del Tribunal Supremo (in Great Britain), Ministro (*m.*) de Justicia (in U. S.). || *District attorney*, fiscal, *m.*

— OBSERV. El *attorney* es un asesor de derecho consuetudinario y el *attorney general*, miembro del Parlamento, es también presidente del Colegio de Abogados en Inglaterra. Sus funciones son parecidas a las que tiene el fiscal del Tribunal Supremo. En los Estados Unidos el cargo de *attorney general* equivale al de ministro de Justicia.

attract [ə'trækt] v. tr. Atraer.
attraction [ə'trækʃən] n. Atracción, *f.*: *molecular attraction*, atracción molecular; *the main attraction of the fair*, la atracción principal de la feria. || Atractivo, *m.* (of a person).
attractive [ə'træktiv] adj. Atractivo, va: *attractive offer*, oferta atractiva. || Atrayente (interesting). || Atractivo, va (person). || Halagüeño, ña (prospect).
attractiveness [—nis] n. Atracción, *f.*, atractivo, *m.*
attributable [ə'tribjutəbl] adj. Atribuible.
attribute ['ætribju:t] n. Atributo, *m.*: *reason is the attribute of man*, la razón es el atributo del hombre. || GRAMM. Atributo, *m.*
attribute [ə'tribju:t] v. tr. Atribuir.
attribution [,ætri'bju:ʃən] n. Atribución, *f.*
attributive [ə'tribjutiv] adj. Atributivo, va.
attrite [ə'trait] adj. REL. Atrito, ta. || TECH. Desgastado por el roce.
attrition [ə'triʃən] n. Roce, *m.* (rubbing). || Desgaste, *m.* (wearing away, exhausting). || REL. Atrición, *f.*
attune [ə'tju:n] v. tr. MUS. Afinar. || FIG. Adaptar (to adapt). | Armonizar (to bring into harmony).
atypical [,ei'tipikəl] adj. Anormal.
aubade [əu'ba:d] n. MUS. POET. Alborada, *f.*
aubergine ['əubəʒi:n] n. BOT. Berenjena, *f.*
auburn ['ɔ:bən] adj. Castaño, ña.
— N. Color (*m.*) castaño.
auction ['ɔ:kʃən] n. Subasta, *f.* || — *To be on auction*, salir a subasta. || *To put up for auction, to sell at auction*, subastar, poner *or* vender en pública subasta.
auction ['ɔ:kʃən] v. tr. Subastar.
auctioneer [,ɔ:kʃə'niə*] n. Subastador, *m.*
auction room ['ɔ:kʃənrum] n. Sala (*f.*) de subastas.
audacious [ɔ:'deiʃəs] adj. Audaz (daring). || Atrevido, da (too daring).
audaciousness [—nis] or **audacity** [ɔ:'dæsiti] n. Audacia, *f.* (boldness): *to show* o *to display audacity*, demostrar audacia. || Atrevimiento, *m.* (impudence).
audibility [,ɔ:di'biliti] n. Audibilidad, *f.*
audible ['ɔ:dəbl] adj. Audible.
audience ['ɔ:djəns] n. Público, *m.*, auditorio, *m.* (at show, etc.). || Radioyentes, *m. pl.* (of radio). || Telespectadores, *m. pl.* (of television). || Lectores, *m. pl.* (of writer). || Audiencia, *f.* (official reception).
audio frequency ['ɔ:diəu'fri:kwənsi] n. PHYS. Audiofrecuencia, *f.*
audiogram ['ɔ:diəgræm] n. Audiograma, *m.*
audiometer [,ɔ:di'ɔmitə*] n. Audiómetro, *m.*
audio-visual ['ɔ:diəu'vizjuəl] adj. Audiovisual. || *Audio-visual aids*, medios (*m. pl.*) audiovisuales.
audit ['ɔ:dit] n. Revisión (*f.*) *or* intervención (*f.*) de cuentas. || *Audit Office*, Tribunal (*m.*) de Cuentas.
audit ['ɔ:dit] v. tr./intr. Verificar *or* revisar la contabilidad. || U. S. Ser oyente (to a class).
auditing [—iŋ] n. Intervención (*f.*) *or* revisión (*f.*) de cuentas.
audition [ɔ:'diʃən] n. Audición, *f.*
audition [ɔ:'diʃən] v. tr./intr. Dar una audición.
auditive ['ɔ:ditiv] adj. Auditivo, va.
auditor ['ɔ:ditə*] n. Interventor (*m.*) de cuentas (accounts). || U. S. Radioyente, *m. & f.* | Estudiante (*m. & f.*) libre, oyente, *m. & f.*
auditorium [,ɔ:di'tɔ:riəm] n. Sala, *f.* (theatre). || Paraninfo, *m.*, auditorium, *m.* (lecture hall, assembly hall). || Nave, *f.* (of a church). || Locutorio, *m.*, sala (*f.*) de visitas (of a convent).
auditory ['ɔ:ditəri] adj. Auditivo, va.
Augean [ɔ:'dʒiən] adj. De Augias. || FIG. Asqueroso, sa; inmundo, da.
auger ['ɔ:gə*] n. TECH. Barrena, *f.*, taladro, *m.*
aught [ɔ:t] n. Algo (in affirmative sentences). || Nada (in negations). || — *For aught I care*, por mí. || *For aught I know*, que yo sepa.
augite ['ɔ:dʒait] n. MIN. Augita, *f.*
augment ['ɔ:gmənt] v. tr./intr. Aumentar.
augmentation [,ɔ:gmen'teiʃən] n. Aumento, *m.*
augmentative [ɔ:g'mentətiv] adj. Aumentativo, va.
— N. GRAMM. Aumentativo, *m.*
augur ['ɔ:gə*] n. Augur, *m.*
augur ['ɔ:gə*] v. tr./intr. Augurar, pronosticar. || *To augur ill, well*, ser de mal, de buen agüero.
augural ['ɔ:gjurəl] adj. Augural.
augury ['ɔ:gjuri] n. Augurio, *m.*, presagio, *m.*
August ['ɔ:gəst] pr. n. Agosto, *m.*: *on the 15th of August*, el 15 de agosto.
august [ɔ:'gʌst] adj. Augusto, ta.
auguste ['ɔ:gəst] n. Augusto, *m.* (clown).
Augustine [ɔ:'gʌstin] pr. n. Agustín, *m.*
Augustinian [,ɔ:gəs'tiniən] adj. REL. Agustino, na (religious order). || Agustiniano, na (doctrine).
— N. REL. Agustino, na.
Augustinianism [—izəm] or **Augustinism** [ɔ:'gʌstinizəm] n. REL. Agustinianismo, *m.*
Augustus [ɔ:'gʌstəs] pr. n. Augusto, *m.*
aulic ['ɔ:lik] adj. Áulico, ca.
aunt [α:nt] n. Tía, *f.* || *Aunt-in-law*, tía política.
aunty or **auntie** ['α:nti] n. Tía, *f.*
au pair [,əu'pεə*] adj./adv. "Au pair".
— N. Chica (*f.*) "au pair", ayuda (*f.*) familiar.
aura ['ɔ:rə] n. REL. Aureola, *f.* || Aura, *f.*, ambiente, *m.* (atmosphere). || MED. Aura, *f.* || Emanación, *f.* (of flowers, etc.).
aural ['ɔ:rəl] adj. Auricular.
aureate ['ɔ:riit] adj. Dorado, da.
aureola [ɔ:'riələ] or **aureole** ['ɔ:riəul] n. Aureola, *f.*
aureole ['ɔ:riəul] v. tr. Aureolar.
aureomycin [,ɔ:riəu'maisin] n. MED. Aureomicina, *f.*
auric ['ɔ:rik] adj. Áurico, ca.
auricle ['ɔ:rikl] n. Aurícula, *f.*
auricula [ə'rikjulə] n. Aurícula, *f.*

— OBSERV. El plural de la palabra inglesa es *auriculas* o *auriculae*.

auricular [ɔ':rikjulə*] adj. Auricular.
auriculate [ɔ:'rikjulit] adj. Auriculado, da.
auriferous [ɔ:'rifərəs] adj. Aurífero, ra.
Auriga [ɔ:'raigə] n. ASTR. Auriga, *m.* (Waggoner).
aurochs ['ɔ:rɔks] n. ZOOL. Uro, *m.*, auroch, *m.*
aurora [ɔ:'rɔ:rə] n. Aurora, *f.* || — *Aurora australis*, aurora austral. || *Aurora borealis*, aurora boreal.
aurous ['ɔ:rəs] adj. Áurico, ca.
auscultate ['ɔ:skəlteit] v. tr./intr. MED. Auscultar.
auscultation [,ɔ:skəl'teiʃən] n. MED. Auscultación, *f.*
auspice ['ɔ:spis] n. Auspicio, *m.*: *under the auspices of*, bajo los auspicios de.
auspicious [ɔ:s'piʃəs] adj. Propicio, cia; favorable.
auspiciously [—li] adv. Favorablemente, con buenos auspicios.

auspiciousness [—nis] n. Buenos (*m. pl.*) auspicios, carácter (*m.*) propicio.
austere [ɔsˈtiə*] adj. Austero, ra.
austerity [ɔsˈteriti] n. Austeridad, *f.*
Austin Friar [ˈɔstinˈfraiə*] n. REL. Fraile (*m.*) agustino.
austral [ˈɔ:strəl] adj. Austral.
Australasia [ˌɔstrəˈleiʒjə] pr. n. GEOGR. Australasia, *f.*
Australia [ɔsˈtreiljə] pr. n. GEOGR. Australia, *f.*
Australian [—n] adj./n. Australiano, na.
Austrasia [ɔsˈtreiʒjə] pr. n. GEOGR. Austrasia, *f.*
Austria [ˈɔstriə] pr. n. GEOGR. Austria, *f.*
Austrian [—n] adj./n. Austriaco, ca.
autarchic [ɔ:ˈtɑ:kik] or **autarchical** [—əl] adj. Autárquico, ca.
autarchy [ˈɔ:tɑ:ki] n. Autarquía, *f.*, autarcía, *f.*
autarkic [ɔ:ˈtɑ:kik] or **autarkical** [—əl] adj. Autárquico, ca.
autarky [ˈɔ:tɑ:ki] n. Autarcía, *f.*, autarquía, *f.*
authentic [ɔ:ˈθentik] adj. Auténtico, ca.
authenticate [—eit] v. tr. Autenticar, autentificar.
authentication [ɔ:ˌθentiˈkeiʃən] n. Autenticación, *f.*, autentificación, *f.*
authenticity [ˌɔ:θenˈtisiti] n. Autenticidad, *f.*
author [ˈɔ:θə*] n. Autor, ra. || *Author's royalties*, derechos (*m.*) de autor.
authoress [—ris] n. Autora, *f.*
authoritarian [ɔˌθɔriˈtɛərjən] adj./n. Autoritario, ria.
authoritarianism [ɔˌθɔriˈtɛərjənizəm] n. Autoritarismo, *m.*
authoritative [ɔ:ˈθɔritətiv] adj. Autoritario, ria (with an air of command). || Que es una autoridad (book, document). || Autorizado, da (source).
authority [ɔ:ˈθɔriti] n. Autoridad, *f.*: *to have authority over one's employees*, tener autoridad sobre sus empleados. || — *Authority of father*, patria potestad. || *He has no authority to act*, no está autorizado para obrar. || *I have it on good authority*, lo sé de fuente fidedigna. || *On his own authority*, por su propia autoridad. || *On the authority of Cervantes*, con la autoridad de Cervantes. || *To act on the authority of*, obrar por poder de. || *To apply to the proper authority*, dirigirse a la autoridad competente. || *To be an authority*, ser una autoridad. || *To give s.o. authority to*, autorizar a uno para que. || *To have the authority to*, tener autoridad para. || *With complete authority*, con plena autoridad. || *Without authority*, sin autorización.
authorization [ˌɔ:θəraiˈzeiʃən] n. Autorización, *f.*
authorize [ˈɔ:θəraiz] v. tr. Autorizar.
authorless [ˈɔ:θəlis] adj. Anónimo, ma.
authorship [ˈɔ:θəʃip] n. Profesión (*f.*) de escritor. || Paternidad (*f.*) literaria. || — *I claim authorship of this book*, sostengo que soy el autor de este libro. || *Of unknown authorship*, de autor desconocido.
auto [ˈɔ:təu] n. U. S. FAM. Coche, *m.*, auto, *m.* [*Amer.*, carro, *m.*]
autobiographer [ˌɔ:təubaiˈɔgrəfə*] n. Autobiógrafo, *m.*
autobiographic [ˈɔ:təuˌbaiəuˈgræfik] or **autobiographical** [—əl] adj. Autobiográfico, ca.
autobiography [ˌɔ:təubaiˈɔgrəfi] n. Autobiografía, *f.*
autochthon [ɔ:ˈtɔkθən] n. Autóctono, na.

— OBSERV. El plural es *autochthons* o *autochthones*.

autochthonous [ɔ:ˈtɔkθənəs] adj. Autóctono, na.
autoclave [ˈɔ:təkleiv] n. Autoclave, *f.*
autocracy [ɔ:ˈtɔkrəsi] n. Autocracia, *f.*
autocrat [ˈɔ:təkræt] n. Autócrata, *m.* & *f.*
autocratic [ˌɔ:təˈkrætik] or **autocratical** [—əl] adj. Autocrático, ca.
auto-da-fé or **auto de fé** [ˈɔ:təudɑ:ˈfei] n. REL. Auto de fe, *m.*
autodidact [ˈɔ:tədidækt] n. Autodidacto, ta.

— OBSERV. See SELF-TAUGHT (*Observ.*).

autodidactic [ˌɔ:tədiˈdæktik] adj. Autodidáctico, ca; autodidacto, ta.

— OBSERV. See SELF-TAUGHT (*Observ.*).

autogamy [ɔ:ˈtɔgəmi] n. BOT. Autogamia, *f.*
autogenous [ɔ:ˈtɔdʒənəs] adj. Autógeno, na. || *Autogenous vaccine*, autovacuna, *f.*
autogiro [ˈɔ:təuˈdʒaiərəu] n. AVIAT. Autogiro, *m.*
autograph [ˈɔ:təgrɑ:f] n. Autógrafo, *m.* || Firma, *f.* (signature).
autograph [ˈɔ:təgrɑ:f] v. tr. Poner un autógrafo a. || Firmar (to sign).
autographic [ˌɔ:təˈgræfik] or **autographical** [—əl] adj. Autográfico, ca. || Autógrafo, fa (letter, etc.).
autography [ɔ:ˈtɔgrəfi] n. Autografía, *f.*
autogyro [ˈɔ:təuˈdʒaiərəu] n. AVIAT. Autogiro, *m.*
autoinduction [ˈɔ:təuinˈdʌkʃən] n. Autoinducción, *f.*
autoinfection [ˈɔ:təuinˈfekʃən] n. Autoinfección, *f.*
autointoxication [ˈɔ:təuinˌtɔksiˈkeiʃən] n. Autointoxicación, *f.*
autolysis [ɔ:ˈtɔlisis] n. Autólisis, *f.*
automat [ˈɔ:təmæt] n. U. S. Restaurante (*m.*) en que la comida es distribuida por máquinas automáticas (restaurant). || Aparato (*m.*) mecánico (machine).
automate [ˈɔ:təmeit] v. tr. Automatizar.
automatic [ˌɔ:təˈmætik] adj. Automático, ca.
— N. Arma (*f.*) automática.
automaticity [ˌɔ:təməˈtisiti] n. Automaticidad, *f.*
automation [ˌɔ:təˈmeiʃən] n. Automatización, *f.*
automatism [ɔ:ˈtɔmətizəm] n. Automatismo, *m.*
automatize [ɔ:ˈtɔmətaiz] v. tr. Automatizar.
automaton [ɔ:ˈtɔmətən] n. Autómata, *m.*

— OBSERV. El plural es *automatons* o *automata*.

automobile [ˈɔ:təməubi:l] n. Automóvil, *m.*
automotive [ˌɔ:təˈməutiv] adj. U. S. Automotor, ra.
autonomic [ˌɔ:təˈnɔmik] adj. Autonómico, ca.
autonomist [ɔ:ˈtɔnəmist] n. Autonomista, *m.* & *f.*
autonomous [ɔ:ˈtɔnəməs] adj. Autónomo, ma.
autonomy [ɔ:ˈtɔnəmi] n. Autonomía, *f.*
autoplasty [ˈɔ:təˌplæsti] n. Autoplastia, *f.*
autopsy [ˈɔ:tɔpsi] n. Autopsia, *f.*
autopsy [ˈɔ:tɔpsi] v. tr. MED. Autopsiar.
autosuggestion [ˈɔ:təusəˈdʒestʃən] n. Autosugestión, *f.*
autotomy [ɔ:ˈtɔtəmi] n. Autotomía, *f.*
autovaccine [ˈɔ:təuˈvæksi:n] n. Autovacuna, *f.*
autumn [ˈɔ:təm] n. Otoño, *m.*
autumnal [ɔ:ˈtʌmnəl] adj. Otoñal, de otoño.
autumn crocus [ˈɔ:təmˈkrəukəs] n. BOT. Cólquico, *m.*
auxiliary [ɔ:gˈziljəri] adj. Auxiliar. || *Auxiliary verb*, verbo (*m.*) auxiliar.
— N. Verbo (*m.*) auxiliar. || — Pl. MIL. Tropas (*f.*) auxiliares.
avail [əˈveil] n. Ventaja, *f.*, utilidad, *f.* || — *Of no avail*, sin efecto, inútil. || *Of what avail is it?*, ¿de qué sirve? || *To be of little avail*, no servir para mucho. || *To no avail, without avail*, en vano.
avail [əˈveil] v. tr./intr. Valer, servir. || — *It avails nothing to*, de nada sirve. || *To avail o.s. of*, aprovecharse de, sacar partido de (an opportunity), valerse de (a right, a weapon), utilizar (a service).
availability [əˌveiləˈbiliti] n. Disponibilidad, *f.*
available [əˈveiləbl] adj. Disponible, que sirve (ready for use). || Que se puede conseguir, obtenible (obtainable). || Válido, da (ticket). || Realizable (assets). || Asequible. || — *By all available means*, por todos los medios posibles. || *To make available to*, poner a la disposición de. || *When will he be available?*, ¿cuándo estará libre?
avalanche [ˈævəlɑ:nʃ] n. Avalancha, *f.*, alud, *m.*
avant-garde [ˈævɑ̃:ŋˈgɑ:d] n. Vanguardia, *f.*
avarice [ˈævəris] n. Avaricia, *f.*
avaricious [ˌævəˈriʃəs] adj. Avaro, ra; avaricioso, sa; avariento, ta.
avatar [ˌævəˈtɑ:*] n. Avatar, *m.* (in Hindu religion). || FAM. Manifestación, *f.*, materialización, *f.*
ave [ˈɑ:vi] n. Avemaría, *f.*
Ave Maria [ˈɑ:viməˈriə] n. Avemaría, *f.*
avenge [əˈvendʒ] v. tr. Vengar. || *To avenge o.s.*, vengarse.
— V. intr. Vengarse.
avenger [—ə*] n. Vengador, *m.*
aventurine [əˈventjuri:n] n. MIN. Venturina, *f.*
avenue [ˈævinju:] n. Avenida, *f.* || FIG. Vía, *f.*, senda, *f.*, camino, *m.*
aver [əˈvə:*] v. tr. Afirmar, declarar. || JUR. Establecer la prueba de.
average [ˈævəridʒ] n. Media, *f.*, promedio, *m.* || MAR. Avería, *f.* || *On average*, por término medio, como promedio, como media.
— Adj. Medio, dia (in statistics): *the average price*, el precio medio. || Regular (so-so). || Mediano, na (middling): *a man of average build*, un hombre de estatura mediana. || *The average age of the pupils*, el promedio de edad *or* la edad media de los alumnos.
average [ˈævəridʒ] v. tr. Calcular *or* sacar la media de, calcular el promedio de (to work out the average). || U. S. Repartir proporcionalmente, prorratear. || — *He averaged 50 kilometres per hour*, hizo una media de cincuenta kilómetros por hora. || *He averages ten hours of work a day*, trabaja una media de diez horas diarias. || *The age of the class averages 15*, la edad media de la clase es quince años. || *Sales average 1 000 copies a week*, las ventas arrojan un promedio de 1 000 ejemplares por semana.
— V. intr. *To average out at, to average up to*, ser por término medio, alcanzar un promedio de.
averment [əˈvə:mənt] n. Afirmación, *f.*
Averrhoes or **Averroes** [əˈverəui:z] pr. n. Averroes.
averse [əˈvə:s] adj. Contrario, ria (*to*, a), enemigo, ga (*to*, de): *I am averse to drinking*, soy enemigo de la bebida.
averseness [—nis] n. Repugnancia, *f.*, aversión, *f.*
aversion [əˈvə:ʃən] n. Aversión, *f.*, repugnancia, *f.*: *aversion for work*, aversión al trabajo. || — *Pet aversion*, pesadilla, *f.* || *To take an aversion to s.o.*, tomar antipatía a alguien.
avert [əˈvə:t] v. tr. Apartar, alejar.
avian [ˈeivjən] adj. Aviar.
aviary [ˈeivjəri] n. Pajarera, *f.*
aviation [ˌeiviˈeiʃən] n. Aviación, *f.*
aviator [ˈeivieitə*] n. Aviador, ra.
aviculture [ˈeivikʌltʃə*] n. Avicultura, *f.*
avid [ˈævid] adj. Ávido, da.
avidity [əˈviditi] n. Avidez, *f.*
Avignon [ˈævinjɔ̃] pr. n. GEOGR. Aviñón.
aviso [əˈvaizəu] n. MAR. Aviso, *m.* (boat).
avitaminosis [ˈeivitamiˈnəusis] n. Avitaminosis, *f.*

— OBSERV. El plural de la palabra inglesa es *avitaminoses*.

avocado [ˌævəˈkɑ:dəu] n. BOT. Aguacate, *m.* [*Amer.*, palta, *f.*] || — *Avocado pear*, aguacate, *m.* || *Avocado plantation*, aguacatal, *m.*

avocation [ˌævəˈkeiʃən] n. Distracción, *f.*, ocupación, *f.*, pasatiempo, *m.*
avocet [ˈævəuset] n. ZOOL. Avoceta, *f.*
avoid [əˈvɔid] v. tr. Evitar: *I can't very well avoid asking him to stay to dinner*, no puedo evitar pedirle que se quede a cenar. ‖ Eludir (a duty). ‖ Huir (to shun). ‖ JUR. Anular.
avoidable [—əbl] adj. Evitable. ‖ JUR. Anulable.
avoidance [—əns] n. El evitar, *m.* ‖ JUR. Anulación, *f.*
avoirdupois [ˌævədəˈpɔiz] n. Sistema (*f.*) de pesas en países de habla inglesa.
avoset [ˈævəuset] n. ZOOL. Avoceta, *f.*
avouch [əˈvautʃ] v. tr. Afirmar, sostener (to state). ‖ Garantizar (to guarantee). ‖ Reconocer, confesar (to avow).
avow [əˈvau] v. tr. Reconocer, admitir, confesar.
avowal [—əl] n. Confesión, *f.*
avowed [—d] adj. Declarado, da; reconocido, da.
avulsion [əˈvʌlʃən] n. Avulsión, *f.*
avuncular [əˈvʌŋkjulə*] adj. De tío.
await [əˈweit] v. tr. Esperar.
awake [əˈweik] adj. Despierto, ta (not asleep). ‖ Alerta (alert). ‖ — *To be awake to*, ser consciente de. ‖ *To keep s.o. awake*, impedir dormir a uno, desvelar a uno.
awake* [əˈweik] v. intr. Despertarse (to stop sleeping). ‖ Darse cuenta (*to*, de) [to realize].
— V. tr. Despertar.
— OBSERV. Pret. ***awoke;*** p.p. ***awoken, awaked, awoke.***
awaken [əˈweikən] v. tr. Despertar.
— V. intr. Despertarse.
awakening [—iŋ] n. Despertar, *m.*
award [əˈwɔ:d] n. JUR. Concesión, *f.*, adjudicación, *f.* | Sentencia, *f.*, fallo, *m.* (judgment). ‖ Premio, *m.*, recompensa, *f.* (prize). ‖ MIL. Condecoración, *f.*
award [əˈwɔ:d] v. tr. Conceder, otorgar. ‖ JUR. Adjudicar.
awardee [əˈwɔ:ˈdi:] n. Adjudicatario, ria.
awarder [əˈwɔ:də*] n. Adjudicador, ra.
awarding [—iŋ] n. Atribución, *f.*, concesión, *f.*, otorgamiento, *m.*
aware [əˈwɛə*] adj. Consciente (conscious). ‖ Al corriente (up to date). ‖ — *Are you aware of the risk involved?*, ¿se da cuenta del riesgo que corre? ‖ *Are you aware of the time?*, ¿sabe Vd. la hora que es? ‖ *As far as I am aware*, que yo sepa. ‖ *I am aware of that*, lo sé, me doy cuenta de ello. ‖ *Not that I am aware of*, no que yo sepa. ‖ *To become aware of*, enterarse de (to find out), darse cuenta de, llegar a tener conciencia de (to realize).
awareness [—nis] n. Conciencia, *f.*, conocimiento, *m.*
awash [əˈwɔʃ] adj./adv. Inundado, da (flooded). ‖ A flor de agua. ‖ Flotando (floating).
away [əˈwei] adv. Fuera (in a different place): *I am sorry, my father is away*, lo siento, mi padre está fuera. ‖ A: *we are five miles away from the station*, estamos a cinco millas de la estación; *the house is ten miles away*, la casa está a diez millas. ‖ Lejos: *away from the din*, lejos del bullicio; *from away*, desde lejos. ‖ Incesantemente, sin parar (continuously): *he worked away for two days*, trabajó sin parar durante dos días; *they fired away till they ran out of ammunition*, dispararon incesantemente hasta que se les acabaron las municiones. ‖ En sentido opuesto (in the opposite direction): *the arrow pointed away from the door*, la flecha apuntaba en sentido opuesto a la puerta. ‖ — *Away with you!*, ¡fuera de aquí! ‖ *Far and away*, sin la menor duda, sin ninguna duda. ‖ *Far away*, lejos: *the house is not far away*, la casa no está lejos. ‖ *I must away*, tengo que irme o marcharme. ‖ *Right away*, inmediatamente, en seguida: *I will do it right away*, lo haré inmediatamente. ‖ *Sing, dance, talk away!*, ¡sigan cantando, bailando, hablando! ‖ SP. *To play away*, jugar fuera, jugar en campo contrario.
— Adj. SP. *Away ground*, campo (*m.*) contrario. | *Away match*, partido (*m.*) de ida. | *Away team*, equipo (*m.*) de fuera.
— N. SP. Partido (*m.*) jugado fuera.
— OBSERV. Hay muchos casos en los cuales el advervio *away* no se traduce literalmente, sino que se incluye en el verbo español: *to go away*, irse; *to throw away*, tirar; *to take away*, quitar. Por lo tanto hay que consultar los verbos correspondientes.
awe [ɔ:] n. Temor, *m.* (fear and respect): *awe of God*, temor de Dios. ‖ Asombro, *m.*, admiración, *f.* (wonder): *he looked in awe at the mountain*, contempló la montaña con admiración; *to fill with awe*, llenar de admiración. ‖ — *To go o to stand in awe of*, temer pavorosamente a, tener un miedo pavoroso a: *he stands in awe of his father*, tiene un miedo pavoroso a su padre. ‖ *To hold o to keep in awe*, tener sometido por el temor.
awe [ɔ:] v. tr. Atemorizar: *he was awed by his solemn words*, sus solemnes palabras le atemorizaron.
awe-inspiring [—inˌspaiəriŋ] adj. Impresionante.
awesome [—səm] adj. Impresionante.
awestricken [—ˌstrikən] adj. Atemorizado, da.
awestruck [—strʌk] adj. Atemorizado, da.
awful [ˈɔ:ful] adj. Horrible, espantoso, sa; terrible (appalling). ‖ Atroz, horrible (ugly). ‖ FAM. Enorme, tremendo, da (tremendous). ‖ — *An awful lot*, un montón, muchísimo, ma. ‖ *How awful!*, ¡qué horror!
awfully [ˈɔ:fuli] adv. Terriblemente, atrozmente: *he is awfully stupid*, es terriblemente estúpido. ‖ Muchísimo: *I am awfully sorry*, lo siento muchísimo; *it has been awfully hot today*, ha hecho muchísimo calor hoy. ‖ Muy: *awfully good*, muy bueno; *that's awfully good of you*, es usted muy amable.
— OBSERV. En muchos casos el adverbio *awfully* se traduce en español por un adjetivo en grado superlativo: *she is awfully nice*, es simpatiquísima; *it is awfully easy*, es facilísimo.
awfulness [ˈɔ:fulnis] n. Horror, *m.*, atrocidad, *f.*
awhile [əˈwail] adv. Durante un rato, un rato. ‖ *Not yet awhile*, no tan pronto.
awkward [ˈɔ:kwəd] adj. Difícil (difficult): *an awkward problem*, un problema difícil. ‖ Torpe, torpón, ona (clumsy): *she is very awkward on her feet*, es muy torpe andando. ‖ Desgarbado, da (graceless). ‖ Inoportuno, na; inadecuado, da (inconvenient): *an awkward time to meet*, una hora inadecuada para encontrarse. ‖ Embarazoso, sa; molesto, ta (embarrassing): *an awkward situation*, una situación embarazosa. ‖ Incómodo, da; violento, ta (ill at ease). ‖ Poco manejable (tool). ‖ Pesado, da (style). ‖ FAM. *The awkward age*, see AGE.
awkwardness [—nis] n. Dificultad, *f.* ‖ Molestia, *f.*, carácter (*m.*) molesto, incomodidad, *f.* (of a situation). ‖ Torpeza, *f.* (clumsiness).
awl [ɔ:l] n. Lezna, *f.*
awn [ɔ:n] n. BOT. Arista, *f.*
awning [ˈɔ:niŋ] n. Toldo, *m.* ‖ Marquesina, *f.* (at hotel door). ‖ MAR. Toldilla, *f.*
awoke [əˈwəuk] pret. & p.p. See AWAKE.
awoken [əˈwəuken] p. p. See AWAKE.
AWOL [ˈeiwol] adv./adj. Ausente sin permiso.
awry [əˈrai] adj./adv. Torcido, da. ‖ — *To go awry*, salir mal. ‖ *To look awry*, mirar de soslayo.
ax or **axe** [æks] n. Hacha, *f.* (tool). ‖ FIG. Reducción, *f.* (of prices). ‖ — FAM. *To get the ax*, ser despedido. | *To have an axe to grind*, tener intereses personales.
ax or **axe** [æks] v. tr. Cortar (to cut). ‖ FIG. Reducir (to reduce). | Suprimir (to do away with). | Despedir (personnel).
axial [ˈæksiəl] adj. Axial, del eje.
axil [ˈæksil] n. BOT. Axila, *f.*
axilla [ækˈsilə] n. ANAT. Axila, *f.* (armpit).
— OBSERV. El plural de *axilla* es *axillae* o *axillas.*
axillary [—ri] adj. Axilar.
axiology [ˌæksiˈɔlədʒi] n. Axiología, *f.*
axiom [ˈæksiəm] n. Axioma, *m.*
axiomatic [ˌæksiəˈmætik] adj. Axiomático, ca. ‖ FAM. Evidente, patente.
axis [ˈæksis] n. Eje, *m.* ‖ BOT. Eje, *m.* ‖ ANAT. Axis, *m.*
— OBSERV. El plural de la palabra inglesa es *axes.*
axle [ˈæksl] n. Eje, *m.*: *rear axle*, eje trasero.
axle box [—bɔks] n. TECH. Caja (*f.*) del eje.
axletree [—tri:] n. Eje, *m.*
axolotl [ˌæksəˈlɔtl] n. ZOOL. Ajolote, *m.*
aye [ei] adv. (Ant.). Siempre. ‖ *For aye*, para siempre.
aye or **ay** [ai] adv. Sí.
— N. *Ayes and noes*, votos (*m.*) a favor y en contra. ‖ *The ayes have it*, hay una mayoría de votos a favor.
Aymara [aiməˈrɑ:] n. Aimara, *m.* & *f.*, aimará, *m.* & *f.* (people). ‖ Aimara, *m.*, aimará, *m.* (language).
Aymaran [—n] adj. Aimara, aimará.
— N. Aimara, *m.*, aimará, *m.* (language).
azalea [əˈzeiljə] n. BOT. Azalea, *f.*
azimuth [ˈæziməθ] n. Acimut, *m.*
azoic [əˈzəuik] adj. Azoico, ca.
Azores [əˈzɔ:z] pl. pr. n. GEOGR. Azores, *f.*
azote [əˈzəut] n. CHEM. Ázoe, *m.*, nitrógeno, *m.*
Aztec [ˈæztek] adj./n. Azteca.
azure [ˈæʒə*] adj. Azul (*m.*) celeste. ‖ HERALD. Azur.
— N. Azul (*m.*) celeste. ‖ HERALD. Azur, *m.*
azygous [ˈæzigəs] adj. ANAT. Ácigos.
azygous [ˈæzigəs] adj. BIOL. Ácigos.
— N. Ácigos, *f.*
azyme [ˈæzaim] n. Pan (*m.*) ázimo.

B

b [bi:] n. B, *f.* (letter). || Segundo, da (in a series). || MUS. Si, *m.*

baa [bɑ:] n. Balido, *m.*

baa [bɑ:] v. intr. Balar, dar balidos.

babbitt [ˈbæbit] v. tr. TECH. Revestir de metal antifricción.

Babbitt [ˈbæbit] n. Burgués (*m.*) tradicionalista.

babbitt metal [—metl] n. Metal (*m.*) antifricción.

babble [ˈbæbl] or **babbling** [—iŋ] n. Balbuceo, *m.* (of a baby). || Murmullo (of a brook). || Charloteo, *m.*, parloteo, *m.* (of people). || Farfulla, *f.* (confused speech). || Cháchara, *f.* (idle talk).

babble [ˈbæbl] v. intr. Murmurar (brook). || Charlotear, parlotear (people). || Cotillear (to gossip). || Balbucear (baby). || Ladrar fuera de la pista (hound).

— V. tr. Farfullar (to utter incoherently). || Soltar: *to babble nonsense*, soltar necedades. || Revelar (a secret).

babbler [ə*] n. Charlatán, ana; parlanchín, ina (chatterer). || Cotilla, *m.* & *f.* (gossiper).

babe [beib] n. Nene, *m.*, nena, *f.*, bebé, *m.* (baby). || Niño, *m.*, niña, *f.* (naïve person). || U. S. POP. Monada, *f.* (attractive girl). || *Babe in arms*, niño (*f.*) de pecho.

babel [ˈbeibəl] n. Jaleo, *m.* (confused noise). || *Tower of Babel*, torre (*f.*) de Babel.

babirusa or **babiroussa** [ˌbæbiˈru:sə] n. ZOOL. Babirusa, *f.*

Babism [ˈbɑ:bizm] n. Babismo, *m.* (Persian religion).

baboon [bəˈbu:n] n. ZOOL. Zambo, *m.*, babuino, *m.* (monkey).

babouche [bəˈbu:ʃ] n. Babucha, *f.* (slipper).

baby [ˈbeibi] n. Nene, *m.*, nena, *f.*, bebé, *m.* (infant). || Niño, *m.*, niña, *f.* (young child). || Cría, *f.* (of an animal). || Benjamín, *m.* (youngest member of a family). || Niño, *m.*, niña, *f.* (childish person). || FAM. Hijo, *m.* (product). || U. S. POP. Monada, *f.* (attractive girl). || FAM. *To be left holding the baby*, cargar con el muerto *or* con el mochuelo.

— Adj. De niño (of a baby). || Infantil (like a baby): *baby face*, cara infantil. || Pequeño, ña (small): *a baby car*, un coche pequeño.

baby carriage [—ˌkæridʒ] n. U. S. Coche (*m.*) de niño.

baby farm [—fɑ:m] n. U. S. Guardería (*f.*) infantil.

baby grand [—grænd] n. MUS. Piano (*m.*) de media cola.

babyhood [—hud] n. Infancia, *f.*, niñez, *f.*

babyish [—iʃ] adj. De niño, infantil (infantile). || Pueril (childish).

Babylon [ˈbæbilən] pr. n. Babilonia, *f.* (town).

Babylonia [ˌbæbiˈləunjə] pr. n. Babilonia, *f.* (kingdom).

Babylonian [—n] adj. Babilónico, ca; babilonio, nia.

— N. Babilonio, nia.

baby-sit [ˈbeibiˌsit] v. intr. Cuidar a los niños.

baby-sitter [—ə*] n. Persona (*f.*) que cuida a los niños.

baby sitting [—iŋ] n. Vigilancia (*f.*) de los niños.

baby tooth [ˈbeibiˌtu:θ] n. Diente (*m.*) de leche.

baby walker [ˈbeibiˌwɔ:kə*] n. Tacataca, *m.*, tacatá, *m.*, pollera, *f.*

baby-weighing scales [ˈbeibiˌweiiŋˌskeilz] n. Pesabebés, *m. inv.*

bacca [ˈbækə] n. Baya, *f.*

— OBSERV. El plural de *bacca* es *baccae*.

baccalaureate [ˌbækəˈlɔ:riit] n. Bachillerato, *m.*

baccarat [ˈbækərɑ:] n. Cristal (*m.*) de Baccarat.

baccarat or **baccarra** [ˈbækərɑ:] n. Bacarrá, *m.*, bacará, *m.* (gambling game).

baccate [ˈbækeit] adj. Abayado, da (berry-shaped).

bacchanal [ˈbækənəl] n. Bacante, *f.* (follower of Bacchus). || Bacanal, *f.* (orgy). || Juerguista, *m.* & *f.* (carouser).

— Adj. Báquico, ca.

Bacchanalia [ˌbækəˈneiljə] pl. n. Bacanales, *f.*

bacchanalian [—n] adj. Báquico, ca.

bacchante [bəˈkænti:] n. Bacante, *f.*, ménade, *f.*

bacchic [ˈbækik] adj. Báquico, ca.

Bacchus [ˈbækəs] pr. n. Baco, *m.*

bach [bætʃ] v. intr. U. S. FAM. Llevar una vida de soltero.

bachelor [ˈbætʃələ*] n. Soltero, *m.* (unmarried man): *bachelor flat*, piso de soltero. || Bachiller, ra (student). || — *Bachelor of Arts*, licenciado (*m.*) en letras. || *Bachelor of Laws*, licenciado (*m.*) en derecho. || *Bachelor of Science*, licenciado (*m.*) en ciencias. || BOT. *Bachelor's button*, botón (*m.*) de oro, ranúnculo, *m.* (yellow flower), aciano, *m.* (blue flower in U.S.A.). || *In my bachelor days*, en mi época de soltero. || *Old bachelor*, solterón, *m.*

— OBSERV. No hay equivalencia exacta entre los títulos otorgados por las universidades de lengua española y los de Gran Bretaña y Estados Unidos.

bachelor girl [—gə:l] n. Soltera, *f.*

bachelorhood [—hud] n. Soltería, *f.*, celibato, *m.*

bacillar [bəˈsilə*] or **bacillary** [bəˈsiləri] adj. MED. Bacilar.

bacilliform [bəˈsilifɔ:m] adj. MED. Baciliforme.

bacillus [bəˈsiləs] n. MED. Bacilo, *m.*

back [bæk] n. Espalda, *f.*, espaldas, *f. pl.* (of person). || Lomo, *m.* (of animal, book, sword). || Canto, *m.* (of knife). || Respaldo, *m.*, espaldar, *m.*, respaldar, *m.* (of chair). || Dorso, *m.*, revés, *m.*, envés, *m.* (of hand). || Dorso, *m.*, reverso, *m.*, respaldo, *m.* (of sheet of paper). || Revés, *m.* (of fabric). || Reverso, *m.* (of medal). || Forzal, *m.*, canto, *m.* (of comb). || Parte (*f.*) posterior *or* de atrás (of head, house, car, mountain). || Fondo, *m.* (of room). || SP. Defensa, *f.*, zaga, *f.* (defensive position). | Defensa, *m.*, zaguero, *m.* (player). || Dorso, *m.*, respaldo, *m.* (of cheque). || Foro, *m.* (of stage). || ARCH. Extradós, *m.* (of vault). || — *At one's back*, detrás de uno. || *At the back of*, en la parte de atrás de. || FAM. *At the back of beyond*, en el quinto pino. || *Back to back*, de espaldas. || *Behind one's back*, por detrás de uno, a espaldas de uno. || *Excuse my back*, perdone que le vuelva las espaldas. || U. S. *In back of*, detrás de. || *In the back of one's mind*, en lo más recóndito del pensamiento. || *To be on one's back*, estar acostado boca arriba (to be lying), estar encamado (to be ill). || *To break one's back*, deslomarse (to fall down, to overwork). || FIG. *To break the back of a task*, hacer la parte más difícil de un trabajo. || *To carry on one's back*, llevar a cuestas. || *To carry sth. across one's back*, llevar algo terciado. || *To fall (flat) on one's back*, caerse de espaldas. || FIG. *To get one's back up*, picarse (to become annoyed). || *To have a broad back*, tener anchas las espaldas. || FIG. *To have one's back to the wall*, estar entre la espada y la pared. | *To have s.o. at one's back*, estar respaldado por alguien. | *To have s.o. on one's back*, tener a uno encima, tener que cargar con uno. | *To know like the back of one's hand*, conocer como la palma de la mano. || *To lend a back to*, aupar. || FIG. *To put one's back into it*, echar el resto. | *To put s.o.'s back up*, picar a uno (to annoy). | *To see the back of*, librarse de, deshacerse de. || *To stand with one's back to*, dar la espalda a. || FIG. *To turn one's back on o to*, volver la espalda a.

— Adj. Trasero, ra; posterior: *the back seat of a car*, el asiento trasero de un coche. || De vuelta (on returning). || Atrasado, da (in arrears): *back rent*, alquiler atrasado. || TECH. De retroceso. || GRAMM. Velar (vowel). || U. S. Del interior (remote). || *Back pay o wages*, atrasos, *m. pl.*

— Adv. Detrás, atrás (to the rear). || Atrás: *to step back a pace*, dar un paso atrás. || De vuelta: *he is back*, está de vuelta; *journey back*, viaje de vuelta. || De nuevo, otra vez (again). || — *Back from*, de vuelta *or* de regreso de (on returning), no alineado con (house). || *Back in*, allá por: *back in the forties*, allá por los años cuarenta. || U. S. *Back of*, detrás de. || *To answer s.o. back*, replicar a uno. || *To beat back*, see BEAT. || *To bow back to*, devolver el saludo a. || *To come back*, see COME. || *To get back*, volver (to return), recobrar (to recover). || *To give back*, devolver. || *To go back*, see GO. || *To go back on*, see GO. || *To hold back*, retener. || *To keep back*, see KEEP. || *To make one's way back*, volver. || *To pay back*, devolver, reembolsar. || *To pay s.o. back*, devolverle el dinero a uno (to return money), pagarle a uno con la misma moneda (to avenge o.s.). || *To play back*, see PLAY. || *To put back*, poner en su sitio. || *To walk back*, volver andando. || *Two years back*, hace dos años. || *Years back*, años atrás.

— OBSERV. Además de todos los sentidos que indicamos en el artículo, tenemos que señalar que el adverbio *back* puede dar al verbo que acompaña una idea de devolución (*to send back a letter*, devolver una carta) o de repetición (*to fall back into the water*, volver a caer al agua).

back [bæk] v. tr. Apoyar, respaldar (to support): *to back a colleague*, apoyar a un colega; *to back a venture*, respaldar una empresa. || Reforzar (to line, to strengthen). || Hacer retroceder, dar marcha atrás a (to cause to move backwards). || Dominar (to lie at the back of): *the hills that back the town*, las colinas que dominan la ciudad. || Apostar por (to bet on). || Montar (to mount a horse). || Enlomar (a book). || Endosar (a cheque). || Avalar (a bill). || Hacer marcha atrás con (a car). || — *Foam-backed raincoat*, impermeable con un forro de espuma. || *Leather-backed chair*, silla con un respaldo de cuero. || *To back up*, apoyar. || MAR. *To back water*, ciar.

— V. intr. Retroceder (to move backwards). || Dar marcha atrás (a car). || — *To back down*, echarse atrás, volverse atrás. || *To back out*, salir dando marcha atrás (in a car), retractarse, volverse atrás (of a commitment). || *To back up*, retroceder.

backache [—eik] n. Dolor (*m.*) de espalda.

back and forth [—ənd'fɔ:θ] adv. phr. De acá para allá (to walk). || Para adelante y para atrás (to sway). || — *Back and forth motion*, movimiento de vaivén. || *To go back and forth*, ir y venir, ir de un sitio para otro.
backband [—bænd] n. Sufra, *f.* (of harness). || Lomera, *f.* (of book).
back bench [—'bentʃ] n. Una de las filas traseras de los escaños en el Parlamento donde se sientan los diputados que no pertenecen ni al gabinete en el poder ni al de la oposición.
backbencher [—'benʃə*] n. Miembro (*m.*) del Parlamento que ocupa un escaño en una de las filas traseras.
backbite [—bait] v. tr. Maldecir de, hablar mal de.
— V. intr. Murmurar.
backbiter [—baitə*] n. Maldiciente, murmurador, ra.
backbiting [—baitiŋ] n. Maledicencia, *f.*, murmuración, *f.*
backboard [—bɔ:d] n. Respaldo, *m.*, espaldar, *m.* (of bench). || Tabla (*f.*) trasera (of bookshelves, etc.).
backbone [—bəun] n. ANAT. Columna (*f.*) vertebral, espina (*f.*) dorsal, espinazo, *m.* || FIG. Carácter, *m.* (strength of character). | Elemento (*m.*) principal, pilar, *m.* (mainstay): *farmers are the backbone of the nation*, los campesinos son el elemento principal de la nación. || Lomo, *m.* (of book). || FIG. *English to the backbone*, inglés hasta la médula *or* los tuétanos.
backbreaking [—,breikiŋ] adj. FAM. Matador, ra; deslomador, ra: *backbreaking task*, trabajo matador.
backchat [—tʃæt] n. Impertinencia, *f.* || *I want none of your backchat!*, ¡déjate de impertinencias!, ¡no seas tan respondón!
back-cloth [—klɔθ] n. Telón (*m.*) de foro.
back comb [—kəum] n. Peineta, *f.*
back current [—,kʌrent] n. ELECTR. Contracorriente, *f.*
backdate [—'deit] v. tr. Antedatar (a document). || Dar efecto retroactivo a (to make retroactive).
back door [—'dɔ:*] n. Puerta (*f.*) trasera. || FIG. Puerta (*f.*) falsa *or* trasera.
back-door [—'dɔ:*] adj. De la puerta trasera. || FIG. Clandestino, na; secreto, ta (surreptitious).
backdown [—daun] n. FAM. Retractación, *f.*
backdrop [—drɔp] n. Telón (*m.*) de foro (of theatre). || FIG. Fondo, *m.* (background).
backer ['bækə*] n. Comanditario, ria (financial supporter). || Fiador, ra (guarantor). || Apostante, *m.* & *f.* (who bets). || Partidario, ria (supporter).
backfire [—faiə*] n. AUT. Petardeo, *m.*, explosión, *f.* || Encendido (*m.*) prematuro (of engine). || Retorno (*m.*) de llama (of Bunsen burner). || Contrafuego, *m.* (to stop a fire).
backfire [—'faiə*] v. intr. AUT. Petardear. || Encenderse prematuramente (engine). || Dar retorno de llama (burner). || FIG. Fallar, salir rana (to fail). || FIG. *The scheme backfired on us*, nos salió el tiro por la culata.
back-formation [—fɔ:'meiʃən] n. Derivación (*f.*) regresiva.
backgammon [—'gæmən] n. Chaquete, *m.*, tablas (*f. pl.*) reales.
background [—graund] n. Fondo, *m.*: *red triangles on a green background*, triángulos rojos en un fondo verde. || Último plano, *m.* (of picture, photograph). || FIG. Segundo plano, *m.*, segundo término, *m.* (less prominent position). | Antecedentes, *m. pl.* (events leading up to): *the background to the revolution*, los antecedentes de la revolución. | Ambiente, *m.*, medio, *m.* (atmosphere). | Bases, *f. pl.* (basic knowledge). | Origen, *m.* (origin): *he has an English background*, es de origen inglés. | Conocimientos, *m. pl.*, experiencia, *f.* (experience). | Educación, *f.* | Pasado, *m.* (past life). || *Background music, noise*, música, ruido de fondo.
backhand [—hænd] adj. Dado con el dorso de la mano. || *Backhand stroke*, revés (in tennis, etc.).
— N. Revés, *m.* (blow, stroke). || Letra (*f.*) inclinada hacia la izquierda (handwriting).
backhanded [—'hændid] adj. Dado con el revés de la mano (blow). || Inclinado hacia la izquierda (handwriting). || FIG. Ambiguo, gua; equívoco, ca (compliment). | Que vacila (hesitant): *he is not backhanded in asking for more*, no vacila en pedir más.
backing [—iŋ] n. Apoyo, *m.* (support). || Refuerzo, *m.*: *a cloth belt with a leather backing*, un cinturón de tela con un refuerzo de cuero. || Entretela, *f.* (in sewing). || Soporte, *m.* (of picture). || *Financial backing*, respaldo financiero.
backlash [—læʃ] n. TECH. Retroceso, *m.* (backward movement). | Holgura, *f.*, juego, *m.* (looseness). | Sacudida, *f.* (jarring reaction). || FIG. Reacción, *f.* (antagonistic reaction).
backlighting [—laitiŋ] n. Contraluz, *m.*
backlog [—lɔg] n. Leño (*m.*) en el fondo del hogar (of a fire). || Reserva, *f.* (reserve): *this backlog of orders assures the continued growth of the company*, esta reserva de pedidos garantiza el constante desarrollo de la compañía. || Atrasos, *m. pl.* (outstanding work). || Acumulación, *f.* (accumulation).
back number [—'nʌmbə*] n. Número (*m.*) atrasado (of a publication). || FIG. Cosa (*f.*) *or* persona (*f.*) anticuada (old-fashioned). | Vieja gloria, *f.* (has-been).
back of beyond [—əvbi'jɔnd] n. FAM. Quinto pino, *m.* (remote place): *he lives in the back of beyond*, vive en el quinto pino.
backpedal [—'pedl] v. intr. Pedalear hacia atrás. || FIG. Volverse atrás (to back down).
backplate [—pleit] n. Espaldar, *m.*
backrest [—rest] n. Respaldo, *m.* (of chair).
back room [—ru:m] n. Cuarto (*m.*) trasero. || FIG. *Decisions taken in the back room*, decisiones tomadas entre bastidores.
back scratcher [—,skrætʃə*] n. Rascador, *m.*
back seat [—'si:t] n. Asiento (*m.*) trasero. || — *Backseat driver*, persona (*f.*) que abruma de consejos al conductor (in a car), persona entrometida (meddler). || FIG. *To take a back seat*, pasar al segundo plano; estar en el segundo plano.
backset [—set] n. Revés (setback). || Contracorriente, *f.* (of water).
back shop [—'ʃɔp] n. Trastienda, *f.*
backside [—'said] n. FAM. Trasero, *m.*
backslapper [—,slæpə*] n. Persona (*f.*) campechana.
backslide [—'slaid] v. intr. Desviarse, salir del buen camino (to become corrupted). || Reincidir, volver a caer (to relapse).
backslider [—'slaidə*] n. Reincidente, *m.* & *f.* || REL. Apóstata, *m.* & *f.*
backsliding [—'slaidiŋ] n. Reincidencia, *f.* || REL Apostasía, *f.*
backspacer [—,speisə*] n. Tecla (*f.*) de retroceso (of typewriter).
backspin [—spin] n. Efecto *m.*: *to put a backspin on a ball*, dar efecto a una pelota.
backstage [—steidʒ] n. Bastidores, *m. pl.*
— Adj. De bastidores. || FIG. De la vida privada (of theatre people). | Oculto, ta; secreto, ta: *backstage deals*, acuerdos ocultos. || — *Backstage noises*, ruidos (*m.*) que vienen de los bastidores. || *Backstage workers*, hombres (*m.*) que trabajan entre bastidores.
— Adv. Entre bastidores. || A *or* en los camerinos (to or in the dressing rooms).

— OBSERV. *Entre basidores* may not be used with a verb of motion (*they went backstage*, se fueron a los camerinos; but *it happened backstage*, ocurrió entre bastidores).

back stairs [—'stɛəz] pl. n. Escalera (*f. sing.*) de servicio.
backstairs [—'stɛəz] adj. FIG. Secreto, ta (secret). | Barato, ta: *backstairs novels*, novelas baratas. | Sórdido, da (sordid). || FIG. *To get a job through backstairs influence*, conseguir un puesto por enchufe.
backstay [—stei] n. MAR. Estay, *m.*, brandal, *m.* || Soporte, *m.* (support). || Contrafuerte, *m.* (of shoe).
backstitch [—stitʃ] n. Pespunte, *m.* (in sewing).
backstitch [—stitʃ] v. tr. Pespuntear (in sewing).
back street [—stri:t] n. Calle (*f.*) pequeña, callejuela, *f.*
backstroke [—strəuk] n. Braza (*f.*) de espalda (in swimming). || Revés, *m.* (in tennis).
backsword [—sɔ:d] n. Sable, *m.* (sword). || Bastón, *m.* (singlestick).
back talk [—tɔ:k] n. U. S. See BACKCHAT.
backtrack [—træk] v. intr. Volver hacia atrás. || FIG. Volverse atrás.
backward [—wəd] adj. Hacia atrás: *a backward glance*, una mirada hacia atrás. || Atrasado, da: *a backward country, child*, un país, un niño atrasado. || Tardío, a (fruit). || — *Backward in*, tímido para (shy), remiso en (reluctant), tardo en (slow). || *Backward motion*, retroceso, *m.*
— Adv. See BACKWARDS.
backwardness [—wədnis] n. Atraso, *m.*, retraso, *m.* (mental, economic). || Timidez, *f.* (shyness). || Falta (*f.*) de entusiasmo (reluctance). || Tardanza, *f.* (slowness).
backwards [—wədz] adv. Hacia atrás: *to lean backwards*, inclinarse hacia atrás. || De espaldas: *to fall backwards*, caerse de espaldas. || Al revés: *to do things backwards*, hacer las cosas al revés. || — *Backwards and forwards*, de acá para allá. || *To know sth. backwards* o *backwards and forwards*, saber algo al dedillo *or* como el padre nuestro. || FIG. *To look backwards in time*, mirar hacia atrás. || *To move backwards*, retroceder. || *To read backwards*, leer al revés. || *To stroke the cat backwards*, acariciar el gato a contrapelo.
backwash [—wɔʃ] n. Remolinos (*m. pl.*) de agua. || Resaca, *f.* (of waves). || FIG. Repercusión, *f.*
backwater [—,wɔ:tə*] n. Agua (*f.*) estancada (behind an obstruction). || Remanso, *m.* (still water). || Brazo (*m.*) de mar (of sea). || FIG. Lugar (*m.*) apartado (remote place). | Lugar (*m.*) atrasado (backward place).
backwoods [—wudz] pl. n. Selvas (*f.*) del interior [de América del Norte]. || FIG. Región (*f. sing.*) apartada (remote area). | Lugar (*m.*) apartado *or* perdido (remote place).
— Adj. Tosco, ca; rústico, ca.
backwoodsman [—wudzmən] n. Persona (*f.*) que vive en un lugar perdido. || Patán, *m.* (peasant). || Lord (*m.*) que no presencia casi nunca las sesiones del Parlamento.

— OBSERV. El plural es *backwoodsmen*.

backyard [—'jɑ:d] n. Traspatio, *m.*, patio (*m.*) interior.

bacon [ˈbeikən] n. Tocino (*m.*) entreverado, "bacon", *m.* || — FAM. *To bring home the bacon*, ganarse el cocido *or* el pan (to earn a living), llevarse la palma (to succeed). | *To save one's bacon*, salvar el pellejo.

Baconian [beiˈkəunjən] adj./n. Baconiano, na.

bacterial [bækˈtiəriəl] adj. Bacteriano, na.

bactericidal [bæk,tiəriˈsaidəl] adj. Bactericida.

bactericide [bækˈtiərisaid] n. Bactericida, *m.*

bacteriological [bæk,tiəriəˈlɔdʒikəl] adj. Bacteriológico, ca: *bacteriological warfare*, guerra bacteriológica.

bacteriologist [bæk,tiəri:ˈɔlədʒist] n. Bacteriólogo, ga.

bacteriology [bæk,ti:əriˈɔlədʒi] n. Bacteriología, *f.*

bacterium [bækˈtiəriəm] n. Bacteria, *f.*

— OBSERV. El plural de *bacterium* es *bacteria*.

bad [bæd] adj. Malo, la: *bad habits*, malas costumbres; *bad blood*, mala sangre; *to keep bad company*, tener malas compañías; *a bad light for reading*, una luz mala para leer; *these apples are bad*, estas manzanas están malas; *bad news*, malas noticias; *I have got a bad taste in my mouth*, tengo mal sabor de boca; *smoking is bad for the health*, el fumar es malo para la salud; *to be bad at arithmetic*, ser malo en aritmética; *a bad boy*, un niño malo. || Fuerte (headache). || Severo, ra; intenso, sa (cold). || Grave (mistake, accident, disease). || Falso, sa (coin). || Incobrable (debt). || Viciado, da (blood). || Cruel (defeat). || — *A bad type*, un mal tipo. || FAM. *Bad egg* o *bad lot*, mala persona. || *Bad form*, mala educación. || *Bad language*, palabrotas, *f. pl.* || *From bad to worse*, de mal en peor. || FAM. *He is a bad one*, es un tipo de cuidado, es un mal sujeto. || U. S. *I am in bad with my friend*, mi amigo está enfadado conmigo. || *In a bad sense*, en mal sentido. || *In a bad way*, en mal estado (in a bad state), en un mal paso (in a tight spot). || *It's not bad*, no está mal. || *To be bad*, estar malo (to be ill). || *To be bad for*, ser malo para. || *To feel bad*, encontrarse mal. || FIG. *To feel bad about sth. one has done*, sentir haber hecho algo. || *To go bad*, echarse a perder, estropearse. || *To have a bad leg*, dolerle a uno la pierna. || *To look bad*, tener mala cara. || FAM. *Too bad!*, ¡qué pena! (what a shame!), ¿qué le vamos a hacer? (never mind). || *To use bad language*, ser mal hablado.

— N. Lo malo. || Gente (*f.*) mala (bad people). || — *I am ten pounds to the bad*, tengo un déficit de diez libras. || *To go to the bad*, echarse a perder.

bade [beid] pret. See BID.

badge [bædʒ] n. Insignia, *f.* (of office). || Distintivo, *m.* (distinctive device). || Medalla, *f.* (award). || FIG. Símbolo, *m.* || *Red Cross badge*, brazalete (*m.*) de la Cruz Roja.

badger [—ə*] n. ZOOL. Tejón, *m.*

badger [—ə*] v. tr. Importunar, acosar [con preguntas].

badinage [ˈbædinɑ:ʒ] n. Discreteo, *m.* (playful teasing). || Broma, *f.* (joking).

badlands [ˈbæd,lændz] pl. n. Páramos, *m.*, tierras (*f.*) yermas.

bad-looking [ˈbædˈlukiŋ] adj. Feo, a.

badly [ˈbædli] adv. Mal: *to behave badly*, portarse mal. || Gravemente: *badly hurt*, gravemente herido. || Mucho: *to miss s.o. badly*, echar mucho de menos a alguien. || — *He needs money badly*, tiene mucha necesidad de dinero. || *To be badly off*, andar mal de dinero (hard up). || *To be badly off for*, andar mal de.

badminton [ˈbædmintən] n. Bádminton, *m.*, juego (*m.*) del volante.

badness [ˈbædnis] n. Maldad, *f.* (of a person). || Rigor, *m.* (of climate, weather). || Mal estado, *m.* (of a road). || COMM. Mala calidad, *f.*

bad-tempered [ˈbædˈtempəd] adj. De mal genio (permanently). || De mal humor, malhumorado, da (occasionally).

baffle [ˈbæfl] n. Deflector, *m.* || "Baffle", *m.*, pantalla (*f.*) acústica (of loudspeaker). || *Baffle plate*, deflector, *m.*

baffle [ˈbæfl] v. tr. Desconcertar (to puzzle). || Frustrar (to frustrate). || Impedir (to hamper). || TECH. Desviar (to deflect). | Detener (to stop). || *To baffle all description*, escapar a cualquier descripción.

baffling [—iŋ] adj. Desconcertante.

bag [bæg] n. Bolsa, *f.*: *shopping bag*, bolsa para la compra; *paper bag*, bolsa de papel. || Saco, *m.* (sack). || Bolso, *m.* (handbag). || Cartera, *f.* (satchel). || Chistera, *f.* (for carrying fish). || Morral, *m.* (for carrying game). || Caza, *f.* (animals taken in a hunt). || Pesca, *f.* (fish caught). || Bolsa, *f.* (of animals): *poison, ink bag*, bolsa de veneno, de tinta. || Bolsa, *f.* (under the eye). || Bolsa, *f.*, rodillera, *f.* (in trousers). || ANAT. Bolsa, *f.* || — Pl. Pantalón, *m. sing.*, pantalones, *m.* || — FIG. FAM. *Bag of bones*, costal (*m.*) de huesos. | *Bags of*, montones de: *bags of money*, montones de dinero; mucho, mucha: *there's bags of room*, hay mucho sitio. || *Diplomatic bag*, valija diplomática. || FAM. *It's in the bag*, está en el bote. || *Laundry bag*, bolsa para la ropa sucia. || FIG. *The whole bag of tricks*, todo. || FAM. *To be a bag of bones*, estar en los huesos. || U. S. FAM. *To be left holding the bag*, cargar con el muerto. || FAM. *To pack up bag and baggage*, liar el petate. || *Travelling bag*, bolsa de viaje.

bag [bæg] v. tr. Empaquetar, ensacar (to put in bags). || Cazar (animals). || Pescar (fish). || FIG. Pescar, coger: *the police bagged the whole gang*, la policía pescó toda la banda. | Coger: *he bagged the best seat*, cogió el mejor sitio; *who has bagged my matches?*, ¿quién ha cogido mis fósforos?

— V. intr. Hacer bolsas (clothing). || Hincharse (to swell).

bagasse [bæˈgæs] n. Bagazo, *m.* (of grapes).

bagatelle [bægəˈtel] n. Bagatela, *f.*, fruslería, *f.* (trifle). || Billar (*m.*) inglés (game).

bagful [ˈbægful] n. Bolsa, *f.*, saco, *m.*: *they picked three bagfuls of apples*, recogieron tres sacos de manzanas. || Montón, *m.*: *bagfuls of money*, montones de dinero.

— OBSERV. El plural es *bagfuls* o *bagsful*.

baggage [ˈbægidʒ] n. Equipaje, *m.* (luggage). || MIL. Bagaje, *m.* || (Ant.). Picaruela, *f.* (saucy girl). | Ramera, *f.* (prostitute). || — U. S. *Baggage car*, furgón (*m.*) de equipajes. | *Baggage check*, talón (*m.*) de equipajes. | *Baggage rack*, redecilla, *f.* || *Baggage room*, consigna (*f.*) de equipajes.

baggy [ˈbægi] adj. Que hace bolsas: *a baggy suit*, un traje que hace bolsas. || Holgado, da (loose). || *Trousers baggy at the knees*, pantalón con rodilleras.

Baghdad [bægˈdæd] pr. n. GEOGR. Bagdad.

bagpipes [ˈbægpaips] pl. n. Gaita, *f. sing.*, cornamusa, *f. sing.*

bagpiper [ˈbægpaipə*] n. Gaitero, ra.

baguette [bæˈget] n. ARCH. Junquillo, *m.*

bah! [bɑ:] interj. ¡Bah!

bail [beil] n. JUR. Fianza, *f.*: *a bail of two hundred dollars*, una fianza de doscientos dólares; *on bail*, bajo fianza; *to admit to bail*, libertar bajo fianza. || Asa, *f.* (of pail, kettle). || Arco, *m.* [que sostiene un toldo]. || Achicador, *m.* (for scooping water). || Barra (*f.*) que separa los compartimientos de un establo. || Muro (*m.*) exterior (of castle). || — *To be on bail*, estar en libertad bajo fianza. || *To forfeit bail*, perder la fianza. || *To go bail* o *to put up bail for s.o.*, salir fiador por uno, dar fianza por uno. || *To jump bail*, huir estando bajo fianza.

bail [beil] v. tr. JUR. Poner en libertad bajo fianza (to free). | Dar fianza por, salir fiador por (to put up bail for). || Achicar (water out of a boat). || FIG. *To bail out*, sacar de apuro.

— V. intr. Achicar (in a boat). || *To bail out* (*of an aeroplane*), saltar en paracaídas de un avión.

bailee [beiˈli:] n. JUR. Depositario, *m.*

bailer [ˈbeilə*] n. MAR. Achicador, *m.* || JUR. Fiador, ra.

bailey [ˈbeili] n. Muralla (*f.*) exterior.

bailie [ˈbeili] n. Magistrado (*m.*) municipal escocés.

bailiff [ˈbeilif] n. Administrador, *m.*, mayordomo, *m.* (of estate). || Alguacil, *m.* (debt collector). || (Ant.). Baile, *m.* (magistrate).

bailiwick [ˈbeiliwik] n. (Ant.). Bailía, *f.*

bailment [ˈbeilmənt] n. JUR. Puesta (*f.*) en libertad bajo fianza. | Entrega (*f.*) de bienes al depositario.

bailor [ˈbeilə*] or **bailsman** [ˈbeilzmən] n. JUR. Fiador, *m.*

bain-marie [,bɛ̃mæˈri] n. Baño (*m.*) maría, baño (*m.*) de maría.

bairn [bεən] n. Niño, ña.

bait [beit] n. Cebo, *m.*, carnada, *f.* (in fishing and hunting). || FIG. Cebo, *m.*, señuelo, *m.* (enticement). || — *To lay the bait*, poner el cebo. || *To take the bait*, picar, tragar el anzuelo.

bait [beit] v. tr. Poner el cebo en, cebar: *to bait the hook*, poner el cebo en el anzuelo. || (Ant.). Azuzar (bears, etc.). || FIG. Hostigar (to torment).

baize [beiz] n. Bayeta, *f.* || *Green baize*, tapete (*m.*) verde (in games).

bake [beik] n. Cocción, *f.* (baking).

bake [beik] v. tr. Cocer en el horno (in an oven): *to bake a cake*, cocer un pastel en el horno. || Secar (to dry). || Endurecer (to harden). || *Baked bricks*, ladrillos cocidos.

— V. intr. Cocer, cocerse. || FIG. FAM. *It's baking hot*, hace un calor achicharrante.

Bakelite [—əlait] n. Baquelita, *f.*

baker [—ə*] n. Panadero, ra (who makes and sells bread). || Pastelero, ra (who makes and sells cakes). || — *Baker's*, panadería, *f.* || FIG. *Baker's dozen*, docena (*f.*) del fraile.

bakery [—əri] n. Panadería, *f.*

baking [—iŋ] n. Cocción, *f.* || Hornada, *f.* (batch). || TECH. Cochura, *f.* (of bricks). || — *Baking powder*, levadura (*f.*) en polvo. || *Baking soda*, bicarbonato (*m.*) de sosa.

baksheesh [ˈbækʃi:ʃ] n. Gratificación, *f.*, guante, *m.* (tip).

balaclava [,bæləˈklɑ:və] n. *Balaclava helmet*, pasamontañas, *m. inv.*

balalaika [,bæləˈlaikə] n. MUS. Balalaica, *f.*

balance [ˈbæləns] n. Balanza, *f.* (scales). || Equilibrio, *m.* (physical, mental, artistic): *to lose one's balance*, perder el equilibrio. || Volante, *m.* (of clock). || COMM. Saldo, *m.* (difference between the debit and credit sides): *credit balance*, saldo positivo. | Balance, *m.* (financial statement). | Balanza, *f.*: *balance of payments, of trade*, balanza de pagos, comercial. || Resto, *m.* (remainder). || — COMM. *Balance due*, saldo deudor. || *Balance in hand*, saldo disponible. || *Balance of power*, equilibrio de fuerzas. || *Balance pole*, balancín, *m.* (of acrobat). || MAR. *Balance reef*, faja (*f.*) de rizos.

|| *Balance sheet*, balance, *m.*, estado (*m.*) de cuentas. || *Balance spring*, espiral (*f.*) del volante (of clock). || *Balance wheel*, volante, *m.* (of clock). || *Off one's balance*, desequilibrado, da. || *On balance*, mirándolo bien. || FIG. *To be* o *to hang in the balance*, estar en juego: *his reputation is in the balance*, su reputación está en juego; estar en la balanza: *love and duty were in the balance*, el amor y el deber estaban en la balanza; estar pendiente de un hilo (in a critical position). || *To hold one's balance*, mantener *or* guardar el equilibrio. || FIG. *To hold the balance*, llevar la voz cantante. || *To throw s.o. off his balance*, hacerle a uno perder el equilibrio (to topple), desconcertar a uno (to bewilder).

balance [ˈbæləns] v. tr. Pesar (to weigh). || Comparar: *to balance the advantages against the disadvantages*, comparar las ventajas con los inconvenientes. || Poner en equilibrio: *to balance a plate on the end of a stick*, poner un plato en equilibrio en la punta de un palo. || Equilibrar (to equilibrate). || Compensar (to compensate). || Contrarrestar (s.o.'s power). || Sopesar (to ponder). || COMM. Equilibrar: *to balance the budget*, equilibrar el presupuesto. | Saldar (to settle). || Igualar (an equation). || COMM. *To balance the books*, hacer el balance.

— V. intr. Hacer equilibrios (an acrobat): *to balance on a tightrope*, hacer equilibrios en la cuerda floja. || Guardar el equilibrio, quedarse en equilibrio (to remain in equilibrium). || Equilibrarse (to weigh the same). || COMM. Cuadrar: *the accounts do not balance*, las cuentas no cuadran. || FIG. Compensarse (to compensate each other). || Balancearse (to swing). || Vacilar, dudar (to hesitate).

balanced [—t] adj. Equilibrado, da: *a balanced mind*, una mente equilibrada; *a balanced diet*, una alimentación equilibrada.

balancer [—ə*] n. Equilibrista, *m.* & *f.* (acrobat). || TECH. Balancín, *m.* | Fiel (*m.*) de la balanza (of scales).

balas [ˈbæləs] n. Balaje, *m.* (ruby).

balboa [bælˈbəuə] n. Balboa, *m.* (Panamanian currency).

balcony [ˈbælkəni] n. Balcón, *m.* (of house). || Anfiteatro, *m.* (of theatre). || Entresuelo, *m.* (of cinema).

bald [bɔ:ld] adj. Calvo, va (people): *I am going bald*, me estoy quedando calvo. || Pelado, da (countryside, landscape). || FIG. Franco, ca: *bald statement*, declaración franca. | Desnudo, da; escueto, ta (style). | Sencillo, lla; simple, sin adornos (straightforward). || — *Bald patch*, calva, *f.* || *Bald tyre*, neumático desgastado. || FAM. *To be as bald as a coot*, estar calvo como una bola de billar.

baldachin or **baldaquin** [—əkin] n. Baldaquín, *m.*, baldaquino, *m.*

balderdash [—ədæʃ] n. Tonterías, *f. pl.*, disparates, *m. pl.*

baldhead [—hed] n. Cabeza (*f.*) calva (head). || Calvo, va; persona (*f.*) calva (person).

bald-headed [—ˈhedid] adj. Calvo, va. || FIG. *To go at it bald-headed*, lanzarse ciegamente a ello.

baldness [—nis] n. Calvicie, *f.* || FIG. Lo pelado (of countryside, landscape). | Lo escueto (of style).

baldpate [—peit] n. Calva, *f.*

bald-pated [—ˌpeitid] adj. Calvo, va.

baldric [—rik] n. Tahalí, *m.*

bale [beil] n. Bala, *f.*, fardo, *m.* (of goods). || Bala, *f.*, paca, *f.* (of cotton). || MAR. Achicador, *m.* (bail). || Dolor, *m.*, pena, *f.* (suffering). || Desgracia, *f.* (misfortune).

bale [beil] v. tr. Embalar (to pack). || Empacar, embalar (cotton). || MAR. Achicar (water).

Bâle [bɑ:l] pr. n. GEOGR. Basilea.

Balearic [ˌbæliˈærik] adj. Balear, baleárico, ca. || *The Balearic Islands*, las Islas Baleares, las Baleares.

baleen [bəˈli:n] n. Ballena, *f.* (whalebone).

baleful [ˈbeilful] adj. Funesto, ta; pernicioso, sa; siniestro, tra: *baleful influence*, influencia funesta. || Tétrico, ca (sight).

baler [ˈbeilə*] n. Achicador, *m.* (for scooping water). || Embaladora, *f.* (for packing).

balk [bɔ:k] n. AGR. Caballón, *m.* || Viga, *f.* (beam). || Relinga (*f.*) *or* cuerda (*f.*) superior (of fishing net). || Cabaña, *f.* (billiards). || FIG. Obstáculo, *m.*

balk [bɔ:k] v. tr. Frustrar (to frustrate). || Obstaculizar, poner obstáculos a (to hinder). || Evitar, esquivar (to evade). || Perder (to miss).

— V. intr. Plantarse, repropiarse (a horse). || Negarse (to refuse): *to balk at doing sth.*, negarse a hacer algo. || — *To balk at a difficulty*, echarse atrás ante una dificultad. || *To balk at the work*, resistirse *or* negarse a hacer el trabajo.

Balkan [ˈbɔ:lkən] adj. Balcánico, ca. || *The Balkan Mountains*, los Balcanes.

Balkans [—z] pl. pr. n. GEOGR. Balcanes, *m.*

balkline [ˈbɔ:klain] n. Línea (*f.*) que separa la cabaña del resto de la mesa (billiards).

balky [ˈbɔ:ki] adj. Repropio, pia (a horse). || Reacio, cia; recalcitrante (people).

ball [bɔ:l] n. Bola, *f.* (spherical object). || Pelota, *f.* (used in games): *to play ball*, jugar a la pelota. || SP. Balón, *m.* (football, etc.). | Pelota, *f.* (tennis, baseball). | Bola, *f.* (billiards, golf, hockey). || Bola, *f.* (of snow). || Borla, *f.* (of a fringe). || Esfera, *f.*, globo, *m.* (planetary body). || Bola, *f.* (used in voting). || Ovillo, *m.* (wool, string). || MIL. Bala, *f.* (of cannon, rifle). || MED. Globo (*m.*) ocular (of the eye). || CULIN. Albóndiga, *f.* (of meat). || ANAT. Eminencia (*f.*) tenar (of thumb). | Eminencia (*f.*) metatarsiana (of foot). || Baile, *m.* (dance): *dress ball*, baile de etiqueta; *fancy dress ball*, baile de disfraces. || FIG. Responsabilidad, *f.* || POP. Huevo, *m.* (testicle). || — FIG. *To be on the ball*, estar atento, estar ojo avizor (to be alert), ser espabilado *or* despierto (to be lively). | *To catch the ball on the bounce*, coger la ocasión al vuelo. || FAM. *To have a ball*, pasarlo en grande. || FIG. *To have the ball at one's feet*, tenerlo todo resuelto. | *To keep the ball rolling* o *to keep the ball up*, mantener [conversación, etc.]. | *To play ball*, cooperar. | *To start* o *to get* o *to set the ball rolling*, empezar [conversación, etc.].

ball [bɔ:l] v. tr. Hacer una bola de (to make into a ball). || Hacer un ovillo con *or* de (wool, string). || Apelotonarse alrededor de (bees). || FAM. *To ball up*, hacer un lío, embrollar.

— V. intr. Hacerse una bola. || Hacer bolitas (wool).

ballad [ˈbæləd] n. POET. Balada, *f.*, romance, *m.* || MUS. Balada, *f.*, copla, *f.*

ballade [bæˈlɑ:d] n. POET. Balada, *f.*

ball-and-socket joint [ˈbɔ:ləndˈsɔkitˌdʒɔint] n. TECH. Articulación (*f.*) de rótula.

ballast [ˈbæləst] n. Lastre, *m.* (in boats and balloons). || Balasto, *m.* (on roads, for railway lines). || — *Ballast bed*, firme, *m.* (roads). || MAR. *To be in ballast*, ir en lastre.

ballast [ˈbæləst] v. tr. Lastrar (boats, balloons). || Balastar (roads, railway lines). || FIG. Estabilizar.

ballasting [—iŋ] n. Lastrado, *m.* (boats, balloons). || Tendido (*m.*) del balasto (roads, railway lines).

ball bearing [ˈbɔ:lˈbɛəriŋ] n. TECH. Cojinete (*m.*) de bolas, rodamiento (*m.*) de bolas. | Bola, *f.* (steel ball).

ball boy [ˈbɔ:lbɔi] n. Recogepelotas, *m. inv.*

ball cock [ˈbɔ:lkɔk] n. TECH. Llave (*f.*) de bola, grifo (*m.*) de flotador.

ballerina [ˌbæləˈri:nə] n. Bailarina, *f.*

ballet [ˈbælei] n. Ballet, *m.*, baile (*m.*) clásico. || *Ballet skirt*, tutú, *m.*

ballet dancer [—ˌdɑ:nsə*] n. Bailarín, ina.

ballet girl [—gə:l] n. Bailarina, *f.*

balletomane [ˈbælitəumein] n. Aficionado (*m.*) *or* aficionada (*f.*) al ballet.

ballista [bæˈlistə] n. Balista, *f.* (weapon).

— OBSERV. El plural de *ballista* es *ballistae*.

ballistic [bəˈlistik] adj. Balístico, ca: *ballistic missiles*, proyectiles balísticos.

ballistics [—s] n. Balística, *f.*

balloon [bəˈlu:n] AVIAT. Globo, *m.*: *to go up in a balloon*, montar en globo. || Globo, *m.* (toy). || CHEM. Matraz, *m.*, balón, *m.* || ARCH. Bola, *f.* || Copa, *f.* (drinking glass). || Balón, *m.*, bocadillo, *m.* (in cartoons). || — *Balloon barrage*, barrera (*f.*) de globos. || *Balloon sleeves*, mangas (*f. pl.*) de jamón. || *Barrage balloon*, globo de barrera. || *Captive balloon*, globo cautivo. || *Sounding balloon*, globo sonda.

balloon [bəˈlu:n] v. intr. Ir *or* montar en globo (to fly). || Hincharse (to swell out). || Subir rápidamente (to increase).

balloonist [—ist] n. Aeronauta, *m.* & *f.*

balloon tyre (U. S. **balloon tire**) [bəˈlu:nˌtaiə*] n. Neumático (*m.*) balón *or* de baja presión.

ballot [ˈbælət] n. Papeleta, *f.* (voting paper). || Balota, *f.* (voting ball). || Votación, *f.* (vote): *secret ballot*, votación secreta. || Lista (*f.*) de candidatos. || Sorteo, *m.* (drawing of lots). || — *Ballot box*, urna, *f.* || *To take a ballot on*, someter *or* poner a votación.

ballot [ˈbælət] v. intr. Votar (to vote): *to ballot for s.o.*, votar por alguien. || Sortear (to draw lots): *to ballot for a place*, sortear un puesto.

— V. tr. Invitar a votar.

ballotade [ˌbæləˈteid] n. Balotada, *f.* (of a horse).

ballot paper [ˈbælətˌpeipə*] n. Papeleta, *f.*

ball-point [ˈbɔ:lpɔint] or **ball-point pen** [—ˈpen] n. Bolígrafo, *m.*

ballroom [ˈbɔ:lrum] n. Sala (*f.*) *or* salón (*m.*) de baile.

ball valve [ˈbɔ:lvælv] n. Válvula (*f.*) de bola.

ballyhoo [ˌbæliˈhu:] n. Propaganda (*f.*) *or* publicidad (*f.*) exagerada *or* sensacionalista, bombo (*m.*) publicitario (blatant publicity). || Tontería, *f.* (nonsense). || Jaleo, *m.* (fuss).

ballyhoo [ˌbæliˈhu:] v. tr. Hacer una propaganda exagerada de, dar mucho bombo a.

balm [bɑ:m] n. Bálsamo, *m.* (resin, ointment). || BOT. Melisa, *f.*, citronela, *f.*, toronjil, *m.* || FIG. Bálsamo, *m.* (soothing influence).

balmy [—i] adj. Balsámico, ca (of or like balm). || FIG. Balsámico, ca (soothing). | Fragante (fragrant). || FAM. Chiflado, da (crazy).

balneotherapy [ˈbælniəˈθerəpi] n. Balneoterapia, *f.*

baloney [bəˈləuni] n. U. S. FAM. Camelo, *m.*

balsa [ˈbɔ:lsə] n. Balsa, *f.* (tree, wood, raft).

balsam [ˈbɔ:lsəm] n. Bálsamo, *m.* (plant, tree, medicine). || CHEM. Oleorresina, *f.* || FIG. Bálsamo, *m.* || — *Balsam apple*, balsamina, *f.* || *Balsam fir*, balsamero, *m.* || *Balsam poplar*, álamo balsámico.

balsamic [bɔ:lˈsæmik] adj. Balsámico, ca.

Baltic [ˈbɔ:ltik] adj. Báltico, ca: *Baltic Sea*, Mar Báltico.

— N. GEOGR. Báltico, *m.*

baluster [ˈbæləstə*] n. Balaustre, *m.* || — Pl. Barandilla, *f. sing.* (handrail).

balustrade [ˌbæləsˈtreid] n. Balaustrada, *f.*, barandilla, *f.* (row of balusters).

bamboo [bæmˈbu:] n. Bot. Bambú, *m.*

bamboozle [bæmˈbu:zl] v. tr. Engañar, embaucar, engatusar (to trick).

ban [bæn] n. Prohibición, *f.*, interdicción, *f.* || Jur. Bando, *m.* (proclamation). || Rel. Interdicto, *m.*: *Papal ban*, interdicto papal. || (Ant.). Maldición, *f.* (curse). || — Pl. Amonestaciones, *f.* (banns). || *To put a ban on*, prohibir.

ban [bæn] v. tr. Prohibir: *to ban nuclear weapons*, prohibir las armas nucleares. || Rechazar (to reject): *public opinion bans drug addiction*, la opinión pública rechaza la toxicomanía. || Poner fuera de la ley (to make illegal): *to ban war*, poner la guerra fuera de la ley. || Sp. Suspender (a player). || — *He was banned from driving for three months*, le quitaron el carnet de conducir durante tres meses. || *To be banned by society*, estar excluido de la sociedad.

banal [bəˈnɑ:l] adj. Banal, trivial.

banality [bəˈnæliti] n. Banalidad, *f.*, trivialidad, *f.*

banana [bəˈnɑ:nə] n. Plátano, *m.*, banana, *f.* [*Amer.*, banano, *m.*] (fruit). || Plátano, *m.*, banano, *m.* (tree).

band [bænd] n. Banda, *f.* (group): *a rebel band*, una banda de rebeldes; *band of birds*, banda de pájaros. || Pandilla, *f.*, grupo, *m.*: *a band of friends*, una pandilla de amigos. || Mus. Banda, *f.*: *military band*, banda militar. | Orquesta, *f.*: *jazz band*, orquesta de jazz. || Banda, *f.* (of material, colour): *a dress with a red band around the waist*, un vestido con una banda roja en la cintura. || Cinta, *f.* (ribbon): *the band of a hat*, la cinta de un sombrero. || Tira, *f.* (thin strip): *band of paper*, tira de papel. || Venda, *f.* (bandage). || Faja, *f.* (girdle). || Brazalete, *m.* (armband). || Vitola, *f.*, faja, *f.* (of cigar). || Faja, *f.* (around newspaper). || Lomera, *f.* (in bookbinding). || Min. Capa, *f.*, estrato, *m.* || Faja, *f.* (of territory). || Haz, *m.* (of light). || Tech. Cinta, *f.*, correa, *f.* (driving belt). | Fleje, *m.* (round cart wheel). || Zuncho, *m.*, abrazadera, *f.* (of a gun). || Phys. Rad. Banda, *f.*: *frequency band*, banda de frecuencia. || — Pl. Alzacuello, *m. sing.* || — *Band brake*, freno (*m.*) de cinta. || *Band conveyor*, cinta transportadora. || *Band saw*, sierra (*f.*) de cinta. || *Brake band*, cinta de freno. || *Elastic band*, goma, *f.* || *One-man band*, hombre (*m.*) orquesta.

band [bænd] v. tr. Atar (to tie). || Vendar (to bandage). || Fajar (to put a girdle on). || Poner bandas en, rayar (to stripe). || Fig. *To band together*, unir.
— V. intr. *To band together*, unirse, juntarse.

bandage [ˈbændidʒ] n. Venda, *f.* (for blindfolding). || Med. Venda, *f.*, vendaje, *m.*

bandage [ˈbændidʒ] v. tr. Vendar.

bandanna or **bandana** [bænˈdɑ:nə] n. Pañuelo, *m.*

bandbox [ˈbændbɔks] n. Sombrerera, *f.* || Fig. *To look as if one had just stepped out of a bandbox*, ir de punta en blanco.

banderole or **banderol** [ˈbændərəul] n. Banderola, *f.*

bandit [ˈbændit] n. Bandido, *m.* || Fig. *One-armed bandit*, máquina (*f.*) tragaperras.

banditry [—ri] n. Bandidaje, *m.*, bandolerismo, *m.*

bandmaster [ˈbændˌmɑ:stə*] n. Mus. Director (*m.*) de una banda.

bandolier or **bandoleer** [ˌbændəˈliə*] n. Bandolera, *f.* (for carrying rifle). || Cartuchera, *f.*, canana, *f.* (for cartridges).

bandsman [ˈbændzmæn] n. Mus. Músico, *m.*
— Observ. El plural de esta palabra es *bandsmen*.

bandstand [ˈbændstænd] n. Quiosco (*m.*) de música.

bandwagon [ˈbændˌwægən] n. Carro (*m.*) de la banda de música. || Fig. Partido (*m.*) político que triunfa. || Fig. *To jump on the bandwagon*, arrimarse al sol que más calienta (to side with the strongest), seguir la corriente (to follow the crowd).

bandy [ˈbændi] adj. Patizambo, ba; con las piernas arqueadas (bowlegged).

bandy [ˈbændi] v. tr. Pasarse, tirarse (a ball). || Fig. Juguetear con (to play about with). | Intercambiar (words, insults). | Repetir (to repeat).

bandy-legged [—legd] adj. Patizambo, ba; con las piernas arqueadas.

bane [bein] n. Perdición, *f.*, ruina, *f.* (ruin, woe, curse): *drink will be the bane of him*, la bebida será su perdición. || Plaga, *f.* (pernicious element). || Veneno, *m.* (poison). || *It has been the bane of my life*, me ha amargado la vida.

baneful [ˈbeinful] adj. Nocivo, va (noxious). || Nocivo, va; funesto, ta; pernicioso, sa (harmful).

bang [bæŋ] n. Flequillo, *m.* (fringe). || Golpe, *m.* (blow): *a bang on the head*, un golpe en la cabeza. || Ruido, *m.* (noise). || Estampido, *m.*, detonación, *f.* (of firearm). || Explosión, *f.* (explosion). || Energías, *f. pl.*, vitalidad, *f.* (energy): *he's got no bang left in him*, no le quedan energías. || Bot. Cáñamo, *m.* (bhang). || — Aviat. *Supersonic bang*, estampido supersónico. || *To fall to the floor with a bang*, caer ruidosamente al suelo. || *To give three bangs on the door*, dar tres golpes en la puerta. || *To go off with a bang*, dar un estallido (fireworks), ser un éxito (to be a success): *the party went off with a bang*, la fiesta fue un éxito. || *To shut sth. with a bang*, cerrar algo de golpe. || *To shut the door with a bang*, dar un portazo.
— Adv. Fam. Justo: *to arrive bang on time*, llegar justo a la hora; *to hit the target bang in the middle*, dar justo en el centro de la diana. || — Fam. *Bang in the middle of the war*, justo en plena guerra. | *Bang on*, acertado.
— Interj. ¡Cataplum! (when sth. falls). || ¡Pum! (of a shot): *bang, bang! you're dead*, ¡pum, pum! muerto. || ¡Zas! (of a blow).

bang [bæŋ] v. tr. Golpear, dar un golpe, dar golpes (to hit): *to bang s.o. on the head*, golpear a alguien en la cabeza. || Golpear: *I banged his head on a stone*, le golpeé la cabeza contra una piedra. || Golpearse en, darse un golpe en: *to fall and bang one's head*, caer y golpearse en la cabeza. || Golpear, dar golpes en: *stop banging the desk*, deja de dar golpes en la mesa. || Golpear con, dar golpes con: *the child was banging a ruler on the desk*, el niño estaba golpeando la mesa con una regla, el niño estaba dando golpes en la mesa con una regla. || Tocar (to beat a drum). || Aporrear (to play piano, drum, etc. badly). || Sacudir (a carpet). || — *To bang about*, maltratar: *don't bang the radio about*, no maltrates la radio. || *To bang a nail in*, poner un clavo en, clavar (to nail), remachar un clavo (to drive home). || *To bang down*, tirar: *he banged the book down on the table*, tiró el libro contra la mesa; poner bruscamente (to put roughly), colgar de un golpe (telephone). || *To bang one's fist on the table*, dar un puñetazo en la mesa. || *To bang one's hair*, dejarse flequillo. || *To bang sth. shut*, cerrar algo de golpe. || *To bang the door*, dar un portazo. || *To bang up*, estropear.
— V. intr. Golpear, dar golpes: *to bang at the door*, dar golpes en la puerta, golpear la puerta; *the door was banging all night*, la puerta estuvo dando golpes toda la noche. || Dar un golpe, golpear: *the falling chair banged against the wall*, al caer la silla dio un golpe contra la pared. || Chocar (to bump). || Explotar (to explode). || Estallar (a balloon). || — *To bang about*, armar jaleo (to make noise). || *To bang away*, aporrear: *he is banging away on the piano*, está aporreando el piano; retumbar incesantemente (guns). || *To bang shut*, cerrarse de un golpe.
— Observ. El verbo *to bang* implica una acción hecha con violencia y ruido (*to bang the lid down on the saucepan*, tapar la cacerola bruscamente).

banger [ˈbæŋə*] n. Petardo, *m.* (of fireworks). || Fam. Salchicha, *f.* (sausage).

bangle [ˈbæŋgl] n. Ajorca, *f.*, brazalete, *m.*

banish [ˈbæniʃ] v. tr. Desterrar: *to banish s.o. from a place*, desterrar a alguien de un sitio; *to banish fear, worries*, desterrar el miedo, las preocupaciones.

banishment [—mənt] n. Destierro, *m.*

banister [ˈbænistə*] n. Balaustre, *m.* (upright support). || Barandilla, *f.* (handrail).

banjo [ˈbændʒəu] n. Mus. Banjo, *m.*
— Observ. El plural de la palabra inglesa es *banjos* o *banjoes*.

bank [bæŋk] n. Comm. Banco, *m.* (banking establishment): *bank clerk*, empleado de banco. || Banca, *f.* (in gambling): *to break the bank*, hacer saltar la banca. || Orilla, *f.*, ribera, *f.* (of river): *on the banks of*, a orillas de, en la ribera de. || Dique, *m.* (artificial). || Loma, *f.* (raised ground). || Pendiente, *f.* (slope). || Terraplén, *m.*, talud, *m.* (along road, railway line, etc.). || Peralte, *m.* (in sharp bend). || Fila, *f.*, hilera, *f.* (row). || Banco, *m.*, bajo, *m.*, bajío, *m.* (underwater elevation). || Grupo, *m.* (of clouds). || Montón, *m.* (of snow). || Min. Boca (*f.*) de pozo. || Mus. Teclado, *m.* (of organ). || Teclado, *m.* (of typewriter). || Electr. Batería, *f.* || U. S. Banda, *f.* (in billiards). | Escora, *f.*, inclinación (*f.*) lateral (of an aeroplane). || (Ant.). Banco, *m.* (in galleys). | Hilera, *f.* (of oars). || — Pl. Banca, *f. sing.* (banking industry). || — *Blood bank*, banco de sangre. || Comm. *Farmer's, issuing, joint-stock, lending* [U. S. *loans*], *mortgage bank*, banco agrícola, de emisión, por acciones, de préstamos, hipotecario. | *Savings bank*, caja (*f.*) de ahorros. || *World Bank*, Banco Mundial.
— Observ. See observation in *banca*.

bank [bæŋk] v. tr. Depositar *or* ingresar en el banco (to deposit). || Amontonar (earth). || Peraltar (a sharp bend). || Encauzar (river). || Formar hileras de (to line). || Tech. Cubrir (fire). | Juntar en batería (cells). || Ladear (a plane). || U. S. *To bank a ball*, jugar por banda.
— V. intr. Tener una cuenta (*with*, en). || Tener como banquero a. || Dedicarse a la banca. || Ser banquero (in gambling). || Amontonarse (to pile up). || Inclinarse lateralmente al virar (aeroplanes). || — *To bank on*, contar con. || *To bank up*, amontonarse.

bank account [—əˌkaunt] n. Cuenta (*f.*) bancaria, cuenta (*f.*) corriente.

bank bill [—bil] n. Letra (*f.*) de cambio (bill of exchange). || U. S. Billete (*m.*) de banco (bank note).

bankbook [—buk] n. Libreta (*f.*) de depósitos. || Cartilla, *f.* (of savings banks).

bank credit [—ˌkredit] n. Crédito (*m.*) bancario.

bank draft [—drɑ:ft] n. Letra (*f.*) bancaria.

banker [—ə*] n. Banquero, *m.*

bank holiday [—ˈhɔlədei] n. Día (*m.*) festivo. || U. S. Período (*m.*) en que cierran los bancos por orden del gobierno.

— OBSERV. En Inglaterra hay varios "*bank holidays*": el lunes de Pascua, el lunes de Pentecostés, el primer lunes de septiembre y el día 26 de diciembre.

banking [ˈbæŋkiŋ] n. Banca, *f.* (business). || AVIAT. Inclinación (*f.*) lateral. || — *Banking account*, cuenta bancaria. || *Banking house*, casa (*f.*) de banca.
bank note [ˈbæŋknəut] n. Billete (*m.*) de banco.
bank of issue [ˈbæŋkəvˈiʃu] n. Banco (*m.*) emisor.
bank paper [ˈbæŋk,peipə*] n. Papel (*m.*) moneda.
bank rate [ˈbæŋkreit] n. Tipo (*m.*) de descuento bancario.
bankrupt [ˈbæŋkrəpt] adj. Quebrado, da; en quiebra (company). || Insolvente. || Arruinado, da (ruined). || FIG. Falto de, carente de (lacking). || *To go* o *to become bankrupt*, quebrar, declararse en quiebra.
— N. Quebrado, *m.* || — *Bankrupt's certificate*, concordato, *m.* || *Bankrupt's estate*, masa (*f.*) de la quiebra. || MED. *Mental bankrupt*, demente, *m.* || *To adjudge* o *adjudicate s.o. bankrupt*, declarar en quiebra a alguien.
bankrupt [ˈbæŋkrəpt] v. tr. Hacer quebrar (company). || Arruinar (to ruin).
bankruptcy [ˈbæŋkrəptsi] n. Insolvencia, *f.* (insolvency). || Quiebra, *f.* (of a company). || Bancarrota, *f.* (usually fraudulent). || Ruina, *f.* (ruin). || FIG. Falta, *f.*, carencia, *f.* (lack). | Quiebra, *f.* (failure).
bank statement [ˈbæŋk,steitmənt] n. Extracto (*m.*) de cuenta.
banner [ˈbænə*] n. Bandera, *f.* (flag). || REL. Pendón, *m.*, estandarte, *m.* || Pancarta, *f.* (in demonstrations). || *Banner headlines*, grandes titulares, *m.*
— Adj. U. S. Sobresaliente, excepcional.
banns [bænz] pl. n. Amonestaciones, *f.*, proclamas, *f.*: *to call* o *to publish* o *to ask* o *to put up the banns*, correr las amonestaciones.
banquet [ˈbæŋkwit] n. Banquete, *m.*
banquet [ˈbæŋkwit] v. tr./intr. Banquetear.
banquette [bæŋˈket] n. Banqueta, *f.* (railway, fortification). || U. S. Acera, *f.* (pavement).
banshee [bænˈʃi] n. Hada (*f.*) maligna que anuncia la muerte (in Ireland and Scotland).
bantam [ˈbæntəm] n. Gallo (*m.*) *or* gallina (*f.*) bántam (domestic fowl). || FIG. Gallito, *m.* (small, aggressive person).
bantamweight [—weit] n. Peso (*m.*) gallo (boxer).
banter [ˈbæntə*] n. Broma, *f.*, chanza, *f.*, guasa, *f.*
banter [ˈbæntə*] v. tr. Burlarse de, chancearse de, guasearse de.
— V. intr. Bromear.
bantling [ˈbæntliŋ] n. Niño, *m.*, crío, *m.*
baobab [ˈbeiəubæb] n. BOT. Baobab (tree).
baptism [ˈbæptizəm] n. Bautismo, *m.* (sacrament). || Bautizo, *m.* (christening). || MIL. *Baptism of fire*, bautismo de fuego.
baptismal [bæpˈtizməl] adj. Bautismal. || — *Baptismal certificate*, fe (*f.*) de bautismo. || *Baptismal font*, pila (*f.*) del bautismo. || *Baptismal name*, nombre (*m.*) de pila.
Baptist [ˈbæptist] n. Bautista, *m.* & *f.*, baptista, *m.* & *f.* || *Saint John the Baptist*, San Juan Bautista, El Bautista.
baptistery [ˈbæptistəri] or **baptistry** [ˈbæptistri] n. Bautisterio, *m.*, baptisterio, *m.*
baptize [bæpˈtaiz] v. tr./intr. Bautizar.
bar [bɑ:*] n. Barra, *f.*: *metal bar*, barra de metal. || Barrote, *m.* (of prison): *behind bars*, entre barrotes. || Barra, *f.* (of gold, silver). || Pastilla, *f.* (of soap). || Barra, *f.* (of chocolate). || Bocado, *m.*, barra, *f.* (of horse's bit). || Barra, *f.* (of medal). || Franja, *f.* (of light, colour). || Barra, *f.* (in ballet). || Barra, *f.* (counter). || Bar, *m.* (drinking room). || Barra, *f.* (for the public in an assembly). || TECH. Palanca, *f.*, barra, *f.* (lever). || Tranca, *f.* (of door). || MIL. Galón, *m.* (chevron). || MAR. Barra, *f.* (of sand). || MUS. Barra, *f.* (bar line). | Compás, *m.* (measure). || PHYS. Bar, *m.* | Baria, *f.* (barye). || JUR. Desestimación, *f.* (of a claim). | Tribunal, *m.* (court): *to summon the prisoner to the bar*, hacer comparecer al prisionero ante el tribunal. | Barra, *f.* (dock). | Colegio (*m.*) de abogados (body of lawyers). | Abogacía, *f.* (profession): *to be called to the bar*, ser admitido al ejercicio de la abogacía. || HERALD. Barra, *f.* || FIG. Obstáculo, *m.*, barrera, *f.* (obstacle). | Tribunal, *m.*: *to be judged at the bar of public opinion*, ser juzgado por el tribunal de la opinión pública. || — *Colour bar*, segregación (*f.*) racial. || SP. *Horizontal bar*, barra fija. | *Parallel bars*, barras paralelas. || *The prisoner at the bar*, el acusado.
bar [bɑ:*] prep. Excepto, salvo (except). || *Bar none*, sin excepción.
bar [bɑ:*] v. tr. Atrancar, poner una tranca a: *to bar the door*, atrancar la puerta. || Poner barrotes a (a window). || Excluir: *to bar foreigners from important posts*, excluir a los extranjeros de los puestos importantes; *barring the possibility of rain*, excluyendo la posibilidad de lluvia. || Impedir (to prevent). || Prohibir (to prohibit). || Cortar, interceptar (a road). || JUR. Desestimar. || MUS. Acompasar.
Barabbas [bəˈræbəs] pr. n. Barrabás.
barb [bɑ:b] n. Lengüeta, *f.* (of arrow, fishhook, etc.). || Barbilla, *f.* (of fish). || Barba, *f.* (of feather). || Caballo (*m.*) árabe (horse). || FIG. Dardo, *m.*, flecha, *f.* (malicious remark).
barb [bɑ:b] v. tr. Poner lengüetas en (arrow, etc.).
Barbados [bɑ:ˈbeidəuz] pr. n. GEOGR. Barbados.
Barbara [ˈbɑ:bərə] pr. n. Bárbara, *f.*
barbarian [bɑ:ˈbɛəriən] adj./n. Bárbaro, ra.
barbaric [bɑ:ˈbærik] adj. Barbárico, ca; bárbaro, ra.
barbarism [ˈbɑ:bərizəm] n. GRAMM. Barbarismo, *m.* || Barbarie, *f.* (condition).
barbarity [bɑ:ˈbæriti] n. Barbarie, *f.* (barbarism). || Barbaridad, *f.* (cruelty).
barbarize [ˈbɑ:bəraiz] v. tr. Barbarizar (language). || Volver bárbaro, embrutecer.
— V. intr. Caer en la barbarie. || Emplear barbarismos (speaking).
barbarous [ˈbɑ:bərəs] adj. Bárbaro, ra (uncivilized, cruel, uncouth). || Lleno de barbarismos (language).
Barbary [ˈbɑ:bəri] pr. n. HIST. Berbería, *f.* || ZOOL. *Barbary ape*, macaco, *m.*
barbate [ˈbɑ:beit] adj. BOT. Barbado, da.
barbecue [ˈbɑ:bikju:] n. Barbacoa, *f.*
barbecue [ˈbɑ:bikju:] v. tr. Asar a la parrilla.
barbed [ˈbɑ:bd] adj. Con lengüeta (arrow, etc.). || FIG. Mordaz (word).
barbed wire [—ˈwaiə*] n. Alambre (*m.*) de espino *or* de púas. || *Barbed-wire entanglement*, alambrada, *f.*
barbel [ˈbɑ:bəl] n. Barbilla, *f.* (barb of fish). || ZOOL. Barbo, *m.* (fish).
barbell [ˈbɑ:bel] n. Barra (*f.*) con pesas.
barber [ˈbɑ:bə*] n. Peluquero, *m.*, barbero, *m.* || *Barber's*, peluquería, *f.*, barbería, *f.*
barbershop [—,ʃɔp] n. Peluquería, *f.*, barbería, *f.*
barbette [bɑ:ˈbet] n. MIL. Barbeta, *f.* (of fortress, warship).
barbican [ˈbɑ:bikən] n. MIL. Barbacana, *f.*
barbiturate [bɑ:ˈbitjurit] n. CHEM. Barbitúrico, *m.*
barbituric [,bɑ:biˈtjuərik] adj. Barbitúrico, ca.
barbwire [ˈbɑ:bwaiə*] n. U. S. Alambre (*m.*) de espino *or* de púas.
barcarole or **barcarolle** [ˈbɑ:kərəul] n. MUS. Barcarola, *f.*
Barcelona [,bɑ:siˈləunə] pr. n. GEOGR. Barcelona.
bard [bɑ:d] n. Bardo, *m.*, vate, *m.* (poet). || Barda, *f.* (of a horse). || CULIN. Albardilla, *f.*
bard [bɑ:d] v. tr. Bardar (horse). || CULIN. Emborrizar.
bare [bɛə*] adj. Desnudo, da (naked): *bare from the waist up*, desnudo de cintura para arriba. || Descubierto, ta (head). || Descalzo, za (foot). || Descubierto, ta (uncovered). || Pelado, da; raso, sa (landscape). || Raído, da; gastado, da (worn). || Vacío, a (empty): *bare cupboard*, armario vacío. || Escaso, sa; exiguo, gua (scant): *bare majority*, escasa mayoría. || Puro, ra (truth). || Simple (simple). || Escueto, ta; conciso, sa (style). || Desnudo, da (walls, trees, wire). || Con pocos muebles (room). || Desenvainado, da (sword). || — *A bare chance*, una remota posibilidad. || *Bare of*, desprovisto de. || *To earn a bare living*, ganar lo justo para vivir. || *To lay bare*, revelar, descubrir (secret), poner al descubierto (surface). || *To sleep on the bare ground*, dormir en el mismo suelo. || *With one's bare hands*, con sus propias manos.
bare [bɛə*] v. tr. Desnudar. || Descubrir (to uncover). || Desenvainar (sword). || Revelar (feelings, etc.). || *To bare one's head*, descubrirse.
bareback [—bæk] adj./adv. A pelo: *to learn bareback riding*, aprender a montar a pelo.
barefaced [—feist] adj. Descarado, da (shameless). || Lampiño, ña (without beard). || Sin máscara (unmasked).
barefoot [—fut] adj./adv. Descalzo, za.
barefooted [—ˈfutid] adj. Descalzo, za.
bareheaded [—ˈhedid] adj./adv. Descubierto, ta; con la cabeza descubierta.
barely [—li] adv. Apenas (hardly): *I barely know him*, le conozco apenas. || Escasamente (insufficiently): *a barely furnished room*, una habitación escasamente amueblada.
bareness [—nis] n. Desnudez, *f.* || Lo escueto (of style).
bargain [ˈbɑ:gin] n. Trato, *m.* (agreement). || Negocio, *m.* (deal). || Ganga, *f.* (advantageous purchase). || — *At a bargain price*, a precio de saldo. || *Bargain counter* o *basement*, sección (*f.*) de oportunidades. || *Bargain day*, día (*m.*) de saldos. || *Bargain driver*, regateador, ra. || *Bargain price*, precio irrisorio. || *Bargain sale*, saldos, *m. pl.*, venta (*f.*) de saldos. || *Into the bargain*, además, por añadidura. || *It's a bargain!*, ¡trato hecho! || *To drive a hard bargain*, imponer duras condiciones, pedir mucho. || *To get the best of the bargain*, salir ganando. || *To make* o *to strike* o *to drive a bargain*, cerrar un trato. || *To make the best of a bad bargain*, poner a mal tiempo buena cara.
bargain [ˈbɑ:gin] v. tr. Ofrecer (to offer to exchange): *he bargained his life in return for his son's safety*, ofreció su vida a cambio de la seguridad de su hijo. || Regatear (to haggle over). || Trocar (to barter). || *To bargain away*, malbaratar.
— V. intr. Negociar: *to bargain with s.o. for sth.*, negociar algo con alguien. || Regatear (to haggle). || *To bargain for* o *on*, esperar (to expect), contar con (to count on).
bargaining [—iŋ] n. Negociación, *f.* || Regateo, *m.* (haggling). || *Collective bargaining*, negociaciones colectivas, contrato colectivo.

barge [bɑ:dʒ] n. Barcaza, *f.*, gabarra, *f.* (for river transport). || Falúa, *f.* (of naval officers, royalty). || SP. Carga, *f.* (in football): *fair barge*, carga legal.
barge [bɑ:dʒ] v. intr. *To barge about*, moverse torpemente, dar tumbos (to move clumsily). || *To barge in*, entrometerse (to interfere). || *To barge in on s.o.*, importunar *or* molestar a alguien. || *To barge into s.o.*, tropezar con alguien. || *To barge into the room*, irrumpir en la habitación.
— V. tr. Transportar en barcazas. || Empujar (to push). || SP. Cargar (in football). || *To barge one's way through the crowd*, abrirse paso entre la multitud a empujones.
bargee [bɑ:ˈdʒi:] n. Gabarrero, *m.*, barquero, *m.* || FAM. *To swear like a bargee*, jurar como un carretero.
bargeman [ˈbɑ:dʒmən] n. U. S. See BARGEE.
barge pole [ˈbɑ:dʒpəul] n. Bichero, *m.* || FIG. *I wouldn't touch it with a barge pole*, no lo cogería ni con pinzas (unpleasant object), no quiero saber nada de eso (unpleasant matter).
barhop [ˈbɑ:rˏhɔp] v. intr. U. S. *To go barhopping*, ir de copeo.
barilla [bəˈriljə] n. BOT. Barrilla, *f.*
barite [ˈbærait] n. CHEM. Baritina, *f.*
baritone [ˈbæritəun] n. MUS. Barítono, *m.*
barium [ˈbɛəriəm] n. CHEM. Bario, *m.*
bark [bɑ:k] n. Corteza, *f.* (of tree, bush). || Ladrido, *m.* (of dog). || Estampido, *m.* (of cannon, pistol). || Tos (*f.*) fuerte, tos (*f.*) perruna (cough). || TECH. Casca, *f.* (for tanning). || MAR. Bricbarca, *f.* (barque). || — FIG. *His bark is worse than his bite*, perro ladrador poco mordedor. || MED. *Peruvian bark*, quina, *f.*
bark [bɑ:k] v. tr. Descortezar (a tree). || Despellejar, desollar (to graze). || Curtir (to tan). || FIG. Vociferar, gritar: *to bark an order*, gritar una orden.
— V. intr. Ladrar (*at*, a) [dogs]. || FIG. Rugir (people, cannon). || FAM. Toser (to cough). || FAM. *To bark up the wrong tree*, equivocarse.
barkeeper [ˈbɑ:ˏki:pə*] n. Tabernero, *m.*
barkentine [ˈbɑ:kəntain] n. MAR. Goleta, *f.*
barker [ˈbɑ:kə*] n. Pregonero, *m.* (in fairgrounds, etc.). || FIG. Gritón, ona (shouter). || Máquina (*f.*) para descortezar (for barking trees). || Pistola, *f.* (pistol). || Cañón, *m.* (cannon).
barley [ˈbɑ:li] n. Cebada, *f.* (cereal): *pearl, peeled barley*, cebada perlada, mondada.
barleycorn [—kɔ:n] n. Grano (*m.*) de cebada.
barley field [—fi:ld] n. Cebadal, *m.*
barley sugar [—ˏʃugə*] n. Azúcar (*m.*) cande.
barley water [—ˏwɔ:tə*] n. Hordiate, *m.*
barm [bɑ:m] n. Levadura (*f.*) de cerveza.
barmaid [ˈbɑ:meid] n. Camarera, *f.* [*Amer.*, moza].
barman [ˈbɑ:mən] n. Camarero, *m.* [*Amer.*, mozo].
— OBSERV. El plural de esta palabra es *barmen*.

barmy [ˈbɑ:mi] adj. Espumoso, sa (frothy). || FAM. Chiflado, da; chalado, da (stupid).
barn [bɑ:n] n. Granero, *m.* (for storing grain). || U. S. Establo, *m.* (for cows). | Cuadra, *f.* (for horses). || Cobertizo, *m.* (for vehicles). || PHYS. Barnio, *m.*, barn, *m.* || FIG. Caserón, *m.* (big, bare house). || U. S. *Barn dance*, baile (*m.*) popular que tiene lugar en un granero. | *Streetcar barn*, cochera, *f.*
Barnabas [ˈbɑ:nəbəs] or **Barnaby** [ˈbɑ:nəbi] pr. n. Bernabé, *m.*
Barnabite [ˈbɑ:nəbait] n. Bernabita, *m.* (monk).
barnacle [ˈbɑ:nəkl] n. ZOOL. Percebe, *m.* (crustacean). | Barnacla, *m.* (Arctic goose). || FAM. Lapa, *f.* || — Pl. Acial, *m. sing.* (to restrain horse).
barn owl [ˈbɑ:naul] n. ZOOL. Lechuza, *f.*
barnstorm [ˈbɑ:nstɔ:m] v. intr. U. S. Recorrer el campo representando comedias (actors). | Recorrer el campo pronunciando discursos políticos para una campaña electoral (politicians).
barnyard [ˈbɑ:njɑ:d] n. Corral, *m.* || *Barnyard fowl*, aves (*f. pl.*) de corral.
barograph [ˈbærəgrɑ:f] n. Barógrafo, *m.*
barometer [bəˈrɔmitə*] n. Barómetro, *m.*: *aneroid, cistern, mercury, recording barometer*, barómetro aneroide, de cubeta, de mercurio, registrador.
barometric [ˏbærəˈmetrik] or **barometrical** [—əl] adj. Barométrico, ca.
baron [ˈbærən] n. Barón, *m.* (nobleman). || Doble solomillo, *m.* (joint of meat). || FIG. Magnate, *m.* (magnate): *oil baron*, magnate del petróleo.

— OBSERV. Los barones ingleses tienen derecho al título de *Lord*, los barones extranjeros al de *Baron*.

baronage [ˈbærənidʒ] n. Baronía, *f.* (class, domain, rank). || Lista (*f.*) de lores (book).
baroness [ˈbærənis] n. Baronesa, *f.*
baronet [ˈbærənit] n. Baronet, *m.*
baronial [bəˈraunjəl] adj. De barón, *m.* || FIG. Señorial.
barony [ˈbærəni] n. Baronía, *f.*
baroque [bəˈrɔk] adj. Barroco, ca.
— N. Barroco, *m.*
baroque pearl [—ˏpə:l] n. Barrueco, *m.*, berrueco, *m.* (irregularly shaped pearl).
baroscope [ˈbærəskəup] n. PHYS. Baroscopio, *m.*
barque [bɑ:k] n. MAR. Bricbarca, *f.* || POET. Barca, *f.*
barquentine [ˈbɑ:kəntiːn] n. MAR. Goleta, *f.*
barrack [ˈbærək] v. tr. Acuartelar (soldiers). || Abuchear (to jeer).
barracking [—iŋ] n. MIL. Acuartelamiento, *m.* || Abucheo, *m.* (jeer).
barrack room [ˈbærəkrum] n. Dormitorio (*m.*) de tropa. || *Barrack-room joke*, chiste (*m.*) verde.
barracks [ˈbærəks] pl. n. Cuartel, *m. sing.* || FIG. Caserón, *m. sing.* (large, drab house). || U. S. *Barracks bag*, mochila, *f.*
barrack square [ˈbærəkˈskwɛə*] n. MIL. Plaza (*f.*) de armas.
barracuda [ˏbærəˈku:də] n. Barracuda, *f.* (fish).
barrage [ˈbærɑ:ʒ] n. Presa, *f.* (dam). || Barrera (*f.*) de fuego (of shellfire): *creeping barrage*, barrera de fuego móvil. || Barrera, *f.* (of balloons). || FIG. Bombardeo, *m.*, andanada, *f.* (of questions).
barrage [ˈbærɑ:ʒ] v. tr. Bombardear (to bombard).
barrator or **barrater** [ˈbærətə*] n. JUR. Pleitista, *m.*, picapleitos, *m. inv.* || MAR. Persona (*f.*) culpable de baratería.
barratry [ˈbærətri] n. JUR. Propensión (*f.*) a ocasionar pleitos (incitement of litigations). | Baratería, *f.* || MAR. Baratería *f.* (of the captain).
barred [ˈbɑ:d] adj. Listado, da; rayado, da (striped). || Atrancado, da (door). || See BAR.
barrel [ˈbærəl] n. Tonel, *m.*, cuba, *f.*, barril, *m.* (of wine, etc.). || Barril, *m.* (of herrings). || Cañón, *m.* (of firearm, feather). || Tronco, *m.* (of quadruped). || Depósito, *m.* (of pen). || Cubo, *m.*, tambor, *m.* (of watch). || Caja, *f.* (of drum). || TECH. Tambor, *m.* || — ANAT. *Barrel of the ear*, caja del tímpano. || FAM. *To be over a barrel*, estar con el agua al cuello. | *To scrape the bottom of the barrel*, valerse del último recurso.
barrel [ˈbærəl] v. tr. Embarrilar, entonelar, poner en barriles (to put in barrels).
— V. intr. FAM. Correr mucho.
barrel organ [—ˏɔ:gən] n. MUS. Organillo, *m.*
barrel roll [—ˏrəul] n. AVIAT. Tonel (flying stunt).
barrel vault [—ˏvɔ:lt] n. ARCH. Bóveda (*f.*) de cañón.
barren [ˈbærən] adj. Estéril (sterile). || Árido, da; yermo, ma; estéril (land). || FIG. Infructuoso, sa; inútil (fruitless, vain). | Vacío, a; estéril (mind, ideas). | Seco, ca (style). || *Barren of*, desprovisto de, sin, falto de.
— N. Tierra (*f.*) yerma.
barrenness [—nis] n. Esterilidad, *f.* (sterility). || Aridez, *f.*, esterilidad, *f.* (of land).
barrette [bæˈret] n. Pasador, *m.* (hair slide).
barricade [ˏbæriˈkeid] n. Barricada, *f.*
barricade [ˏbæriˈkeid] v. tr. Levantar barricadas en (a street). || FIG. *To barricade o.s.*, parapetarse.
barrier [ˈbæriə*] n. Barrera, *f.* || FIG. Barrera, *f.*: *customs barriers*, barreras arancelarias. || *Sonic* o *sound barrier*, barrera del sonido.
barrier reef [—ˏri:f] n. Banco (*m.*) *or* barrera (*f.*) de coral. || *The great Barrier Reef*, la gran Barrera.
barring [ˈbɑ:riŋ] prep. Excepto, salvo: *barring death*, salvo la muerte.
barrister [ˈbæristə*] or **barrister-at-law** [—ətˈlɔ:] n. Abogado (*m.*) que puede defender causas en los tribunales superiores británicos.
barroom [ˈbɑ:rum] n. Bar, *m.*
barrow [ˈbærəu] n. Carretilla, *f.* (wheelbarrow). || Carro, *m.*, carreta, *f.* (handcart). || Túmulo, *m.* (grave mound). || GEOGR. Colina, *f.* || *Barrow boy*, vendedor (*m.*) ambulante de fruta.
barstool [ˈbɑ:stul] n. Taburete (*m.*) de bar.
bartender [ˈbɑ:ˏtendə*] n. Camarero (*m.*) de bar, "barman" *m.*
barter [ˈbɑ:tə*] n. Trueque, *m.*, permuta, *f.*
barter [ˈbɑ:tə*] v. intr. Trocar: *to barter for furs with spirits*, trocar licores por pieles.
— V. tr. Trocar (to trade).
Bartholomew [bɑ:ˈθɔləmju:] pr. n. Bartolomé, *m.*
barycentre (U. S. **barycenter**) [ˏbæriˏsentə*] n. Baricentro, *m.*
barye [ˈbæri] n. PHYS. Baria, *f.* (unit of pressure).
barysphere [ˈbæriˏsfi:ə*] n. Barisfera, *f.*
baryta [bæˈri:tə] n. CHEM. Barita, *f.*
barytes [bæˈraiti:z] n. MIN. Baritina, *f.*
barytone [ˈbæritəun] n. Barítono, *m.*
basal [ˈbeisl] adj. Fundamental, básico, ca (essential). || MED. Basal (metabolism).
basalt [ˈbæsɔ:lt] n. Basalto, *m.*
basaltic [bəˈsɔ:ltik] adj. Basáltico, ca.
basan [ˈbæsən] n. Badana, *f.*
bascule [ˈbæskju:l] n. TECH. Báscula, *f.* || *Bascule bridge*, puente basculante *or* levadizo.
base [beis] n. Base, *f.* (lowest part, foundation, stand, etc.). || Raíz, *f.* (of word). || Pie, *m.* (of mountain). || MATH. CHEM. Base, *f.* || MIL. Base, *f.*: *naval, air-force base*, base naval, aérea. || ARCH. Basa, *f.* (of column). || SP. Base, *f.* || FIG. Base, *f.* || — *A drink with a rum base*, una bebida a base de ron. || *Base line*, línea (*f.*) de saque (in tennis). || *Off base*, equivocado, da (mistaken), desprevenido, da (unawares), de improviso (unexpectedly). || FAM. *To get to first base*, vencer la primera dificultad.
— Adj. Despreciable, bajo, ja. | Degradante (degrading). || Bajo, ja; de baja ley (metals). || Bajo, ja: *base Latin*, bajo latín. || De base, básico, ca (basic). || MUS. Bajo, ja (bass).
base [beis] v. tr. Basar, fundar, fundamentar (*on*, en) [arguments, etc.]. || Estacionar (troops).

baseball [—bɔ:l] n. Béisbol, *m.*
baseboard [—bɔ:d] n. U. S. Zócalo, *m.*
baseborn [—bɔ:n] adj. De baja estirpe, de humilde cuna (humble). || Bastardo, da (illegitimate).
Basel [ˊbɑ:zəl] pr. n. GEOGR. Basilea.
baseless [ˊbeislis] adj. Infundado, da; que carece de base *or* de fundamento (groundless).
basement [ˊbeismənt] n. ARCH. Basamento, *m.* (substructure). || Sótano, *m.* (cellar).
baseness [ˊbeisnis] n. Bajeza, *f.*, vileza, *f.* (vileness). || Ilegitimidad, *f.* (illegitimacy).
bash [bæʃ] n. FAM. Golpetazo, *m.*, golpazo, *m.* (blow). || Bollo, *m.* (dent). || FIG. Intento, *m.*, tentativa, *f.* (attempt). || — FIG. FAM. *To have a bash*, intentarlo. | *To have a bash at doing sth.*, intentar hacer algo.
bash [bæʃ] v. tr. FAM. Asestar un golpe a (to hit). || *To bash one's head on a wall*, darse con la cabeza en la pared.
— V. intr. FAM. *To bash into s.o.*, darse un porrazo contra uno, estrellarse contra uno.
bashful [—ful] adj. Tímido, da; vergonzoso, sa (shy).
bashfulness [—fulnis] n. Timidez, *f.*, vergüenza, *f.*
bashing [—iŋ] n. FAM. Paliza, *f.*, tunda, *f.*
basic [ˊbeisik] adj. Básico, ca: *basic industries*, industrias básicas. || Básico, ca; fundamental, esencial (fundamental). || Básico, ca (metals). || Elemental: *basic Spanish*, español elemental. || CHEM. GEOL. Básico, ca.
basically [—əli] adv. Esencialmente, fundamentalmente.
basicity [beiˊsisiti] n. CHEM. Basicidad. *f.*
basidiomycete [bæˌsidiəˊmaisi:t] n. Basidiomiceto, *m.* (fungus).
basidiomycetous [bæˌsidiəmaiˊsi:təs] adj. Basidiomiceto.
basidium [bæˊsidiəm] n. Basidio, *m.* (fungus).
— OBSERV. El plural de *basidium* es *basidia*.
basil [bæzl] n. BOT. Albahaca, *f.* (planta).
Basil [bæzl] pr. n. Basilio, *m.*
basilar [bəˊzilə*] or **basilary** [—ri] adj. ANAT. Basilar.
basilic [bəˊzilik] adj. ANAT. Basílico, ca (vein).
basilica [bəˊzilikə] n. Basílica, *f.* (church).
basilisk [ˊbæzilisk] n. Basilisco, *m.* (legendary animal, lizard).
basin [ˊbeisn] n. Palangana, *f.*, jofaina, *f.* (washbowl). || Lavabo, *m.* (washbasin). || Barreño, *m.* (for washing up). || Cuenco, *m.* (dish). || Taza, *f.* (of fountain). || Dársena, *f.* (in port). || Platillo, *m.* (of scales). || GEOGR. Cuenca, *f.* (containing river, lake). | Depresión, *f.* (depression).
basinet [ˊbæsinet] n. Bacinete, *m.* (helmet).
basinful [ˊbeisnful] n. FAM. *To have had a basinful*, estar harto.
basis [ˊbeisis] n. Base, *f.*
— OBSERV. El plural de *basis* es *bases*.
bask [bɑ:sk] v. intr. Tomar el sol (to sunbathe). || Dejarse acariciar (to be caressed): *to bask in the soft breeze*, dejarse acariciar por la suave brisa. || FIG. Gozar, disfrutar (*in*, de): *to bask in the king's favour*, gozar del favor del rey. || *To bask in the sun*, tomar el sol.
basket [ˊbɑ:skit] n. Cesto, *m.*, cesta, *f.* || Canasta, *f.* (with two handles). || Cesta, *f.* (for shopping). || Barquilla, *f.* (in balloons). || Canasta, *f.*, cesta, *f.* (in basketball). || SP. *To score a basket*, encestar.
basketball [—bɔ:l] n. SP. Baloncesto, *m.* [*Amer.*, basketball, *m.*] (game). | Balón (*m.*) de baloncesto, balón (ball).
basketful [—ful] n. Cesto, *m.*, cesta, *f.*, canasta, *f.*
basket-handle [—ˌhændl] adj. ARCH. *Basket-handle arch*, arco (*m.*) rebajado *or* carpanel *or* apainelado.
basket lunch [—ˌlʌntʃ] n. U. S. Merienda, *f.*
basketry [ˊbɑ:skətri] n. Cestería, *f.*
basketwork [ˊbɑ:skit-wɔ:k] n. Cestería, *f.*
Basle [bɑ:l] pr. n. GEOGR. Basilea.
basque [bæsk] n. Jubón, *m.*
Basque [bæsk] pr. n. GEOGR. Vasco, ca. || Vasco, *m.*, vascuence, *m.* (language).
— Adj. Vasco, ca. || — *Basque country*, País Vasco [parte francesa]. || *Basque provinces*, Provincias Vascongadas (in Spain).
bas-relief [ˊbæsriˌli:f] n. ARCH. Bajorrelieve, *m.*, bajo relieve, *m.*
bass [bæs] n. ZOOL. Perca, *f.* (freshwater fish). | Róbalo, *m.*, lubina, *f.* (marine fish). || BOT. Tilo, *m.*
bass [beis] n. MUS. Bajo, *m.* (part, singer). | Contrabajo *m.*, violón, *m.* (instrument).
— Adj. MUS. Bajo, ja. || — MUS. *Bass clef*, clave (*f.*) de fa. | *Bass drum*, bombo, *m.* | *Bass fiddle*, contrabajo, *m.* | *Bass horn*, tuba, *f.* | *Double bass*, violón, *m.*, contrabajo, *m.*
basset [ˊbæsit] n. GEOL. Afloramiento, *m.* (of stratum). || Perro (*m.*) basset (dog).
basset [ˊbæsit] v. intr. GEOL. Aflorar.
basso [ˊbæsəu] n. MUS. Bajo, *m.*
bassoon [bəˊsu:n] n. MUS. Fagot, *m.* || MUS. *Double bassoon*, contrafagot, *m.*
bassoonist [—ist] n. MUS. Bajonista, *m.*, fagotista, *m.*
bast [bæst] n. BOT. Líber, *m.*
bastard [ˊbæstəd] n. Bastardo, da. || POP. Cabrón, *m.*, hijo (*m.*) de perra.
— Adj. Bastardo, da (illegitimate). || FIG. Falso, sa; espurio, ria (not genuine). | Degenerado, da; corrompido, da (degenerate). || Híbrido, da (hybrid). || TECH. Bastardo, da: *bastard file*, lima bastarda; *bastard sugar*, azúcar bastarda. || *Bastard title*, anteportada, *f.*, portadilla, *f.*
bastardize [ˊbæstədaiz] v. tr. Declarar bastardo *or* ilegítimo. || FIG. Degradar, corromper (to debase).
— V. intr. FIG. Degenerar.
bastardy [ˊbæstədi] n. Bastardía, *f.*
baste [beist] v. tr. CULIN. Rociar (a joint). || U. S. Hilvanar (in sewing). || FAM. Zurrar, apalear (to beat).
bastinado [ˌbæstiˊneidəu] n. Tunda (*f.*) de palos, zurra, *f.* (beating).
basting [ˊbeistiŋ] n. U. S. Hilván, *m.*, hilvanado, *m.* (tacking). | Hilo (*m.*) de hilvanar (thread). || Zurra, *f.*, paliza, *f.* (beating).
bastion [ˊbæstiən] n. MIL. FIG. Baluarte, *m.*, bastión, *m.*
bat [bæt] n. ZOOL. Murciélago, *m.* || SP. Bate, *m.* (in cricket, baseball). | Raqueta, *f.* (in table tennis). | Turno, *m.* (turn to bat). || Golpe, *m.* (blow). || Pala, *f.*, paleta, *f.* (of washerwoman). || FAM. Juerga, *f.* (spree): *to go on a bat*, ir de juerga. | Ritmo, *m.*, paso, *m.*, velocidad, *f.* (pace). || — *At a rare bat*, a toda velocidad. || FIG. *Off one's own bat*, por su cuenta. | *Right off the bat*, inmediatamente (immediately), sin más deliberación (without thinking). | *To be as blind as a bat*, no ver tres en un burro, ser más ciego que un topo. | *To have bats in the belfry*, estar mal de la azotea.
bat [bæt] v. intr. Batear (in cricket, baseball). || FIG. *To go to bat for s.o.*, acudir en ayuda de alguien, respaldar a alguien.
— V. tr. Golpear (to hit). || — FIG. *Nobody batted an eyelid*, nadie pestañeó, nadie se inmutó. | *To bat an idea around o back and forth*, debatir una idea. | *To bat down s.o.'s arguments*, echar por tierra los argumentos de uno. || *To bat one's eyelashes*, parpadear. || *To bat the ball out of the cricket ground*, mandar la pelota fuera del campo. || FIG. *Without batting an eye o an eyelid*, sin pestañear, sin inmutarse.
batata [bəˊtɑ:tə] n. BOT. Batata, *f.*
Batavian [bəˊteiviən] adj./n. Bátavo, va.
batch [bætʃ] n. Hornada, *f.* (of loaves, cakes). || Partida, *f.*, lote, *m.*, serie, *f.*, remesa, *f.* (of goods). || Montón, *m.* (of letters). || MIL. Partida, *f.* (of soldiers). || Tanda, *f.*, grupo, *m.* (of people). || *Batch process*, proceso discontinuo.
bate [beit] n. Solución (*f.*) alcalina.
bate [beit] v. tr. Disminuir, rebajar (to reduce). || *With bated breath*, en voz baja.
bath [bɑ:θ] n. Baño, *m.*: *to have* o *to take a bath*, tomar un baño. || Bañera, *f.* (bathtub). || CHEM. PHOT. Baño, *m.* || U. S. Cuarto (*m.*) de baño (bathroom). || — Pl. Piscina, *f. sing.* (swimming pool). || Casa (*f.*) de baños (for bathing). || Balneario, *m. sing.* (medicinal). || — *Steam bath*, baño de vapor. || *Turkish bath*, baño turco.
— Adj. De baño: *bath towel*, toalla de baño; *bath mat*, alfombra de baño; *bath salts*, sales de baño.
bath [bɑ:θ] v. tr. Bañar, dar un baño a.
— V. intr. Bañarse, tomar un baño.
Bath chair [—tʃɛə*] n. Silla (*f.*) de ruedas.
bathe [beið] n. Baño, *m.* (in river, sea, etc.).
bathe [beið] v. tr. Bañar (to wash). || MED. Lavar (a wound). | Bañarse (one's eyes). || Bañar: *the lake bathed the foot of the mountain*, el lago bañaba el pie de la montaña. || Bañar (with light). || *Face bathed in tears*, cara bañada en lágrimas.
— V. intr. Bañarse (in river, sea, etc.): *to go bathing*, ir a bañarse. || FIG. Bañarse.
bather [ˊbeiðə*] n. Bañista, *m.* & *f.*
bathetic [bəˊθetik] adj. Ridículo, la; que pasa de lo sublime a lo ridículo *or* trivial.
bathhouse [ˊbɑ:θhaus] n. U. S. Caseta, *f.* (on the beach). | Casa (f.) de baños (public baths).
bathing [ˊbeiðiŋ] n. Baños, *m. pl.*: *sea bathing*, baños de mar. || *No bathing*, prohibido bañarse.
bathing beauty [—ˊbju:ti] n. Belleza (*f.*) de la playa.
bathing cap [—kæp] n. Gorro (*m.*) de baño.
bathing costume [—ˌkɔstju:m] n. Traje (*m.*) de baño, bañador, *m.*
bathing resort [—riˌzɔ:t] n. Estación (*f.*) balnearia.
bathing suit [—sju:t] n. Bañador, *m.*, traje (*m.*) de baño.
bathing trunks [—trʌŋks] pl. n. Bañador, *m. sing.*, calzón (*m. sing.*) de baño (for men).
bathos [ˊbeiθɔs] n. Paso (*m.*) de lo sublime a lo ridículo *or* trivial (in literature). || Trivialidad, *f.* (triteness). || Sensiblería, *f.* (excessive sentimentality).
bathrobe [ˊbɑ:θrəub] n. Albornoz, *m.*
bathroom [ˊbɑ:θrum] n. Cuarto (*m.*) de baño.
bathtub [ˊbɑ:θtʌb] n. Bañera, *f.*, baño, *m.*
bathymeter [bæˊθimitər] n. Batímetro, *m.*
bathymetry [bæˊθimitri] n. Batimetría, *f.*
bathyscaphe [ˊbæθiskæf] n. Batíscafo, *m.*
bathysphere [ˊbæθisfiə*] n. Batisfera, *f.*
batiste [bæˊti:st] n. Batista, *f.* (material).
batman [ˊbætmən] n. MIL. Ordenanza, *m.*
— OBSERV. El plural de esta palabra es *batmen*.
baton [ˊbætən] n. Porra, *f.* (of a policeman). || MUS. Batuta, *f.* || Bastón (*m.*) de mando (symbol of office). || SP. Testigo, *m.* (in relay races).

batrachian [bə'treikjən] adj. ZOOL. Batracio, cia.
— N. ZOOL. Batracio, *m.*
bats [bæts] adj. FAM. Chiflado, da.
batsman [bætsmən] n. SP. Bateador, *m.* || Oficial (*m.*) que dirige los aterrizajes [en portaaviones].
— OBSERV. El plural de esta palabra es *batsmen.*
battalion [bə'tæljən] n. MIL. Batallón, *m.* || — Pl. FIG. Batallón, *m. sing.*, ejército, *m. sing.*: *battalions of ants*, un ejército de hormigas.
batten ['bætn] n. Listón, *m.* (strip of wood). || Varal, *m.* (of loom). || Varal, *m.* (in a theatre).
batten ['bætn] v. tr. Listonar, reforzar con listones (to strengthen with battens). || MAR. *To batten down the hatches*, fijar con listones los encerados de escotilla.
— V. intr. Cebarse (*on*, de) [to glut o.s.]. || FIG. Enriquecerse, prosperar (*on*, a costa de) [to another's detriment]: *to batten on the State*, enriquecerse a costa del Estado. | Deleitarse, refocilarse (to delight in). | Agarrarse a (an argument).
batter ['bætə*] n. Bateador, *m.* (in cricket, baseball). || Pasta, *f.*, albardilla, *f.* (in cooking). || PRINT. Defecto, *m.* (defect).
batter ['bætə*] v. tr. Apalear, moler a palos (people). || Azotar: *the giant waves battered the ship*, las gigantescas olas azotaban el barco. || Estropear (to ruin): *a battered old hat*, un viejo sombrero estropeado. || Abollar (to dent): *a battered car*, un coche abollado. || Magullar (to bruise). || MIL. Cañonear, destruir a cañonazos (with cannons). || ARCH. Dar inclinación a (a wall). || Vapulear, criticar violentamente (to criticize). || — *To batter about*, maltratar. || *To batter s.o. to death*, matar a uno a palos. || *To batter sth. down*, derribar algo, echar algo abajo. || *To batter the door in*, derribar la puerta, echar la puerta abajo.
— V. intr. Chocar, golpearse (*on* o *against*, contra). [to beat, to pound]. || ARCH. Inclinarse (a wall). || *To batter at the door*, golpear la puerta.
battering [—riŋ] n. MIL. Cañoneo, *m.*, destrucción (*f.*) a cañonazos.
battering ram [—riŋræm] n. Ariete, *m.*
battery ['bætəri] n. Batería, *f.* (of kitchen utensils). || Batería, *f.* (of hens). || Serie, *f.*, grupo, *m.*, juego, *m.* (series, set). || JUR. Agresión, *f.* || MUS. Batería, *f.* (percussion section). || MIL. MAR. Batería, *f.* (of artillery, guns). || ELECTR. Batería, *f.* (set of cells): *car battery*, batería de coche. | Pila, *f.* (of transistor radio, etc.). || SP. El lanzador y el bateador (in baseball). || — MAR. *Battery deck*, batería. || *Storage battery*, acumulador, *m.*, batería, *f.*
batting ['bætiŋ] n. Guata, *f.* (cotton fibre). || SP. Bateo, *m.*, acción (*f.*) de batear (cricket, baseball).
battle ['bætl] n. Batalla, *f.*, combate, *m.*: *to fight a battle*, librar una batalla. || FIG. Lucha, *f.* || — *Battle array* o *formation*, orden (*m.*) de combate. || FIG. *Battle royal*, batalla campal. || *Line of battle*, frente (*m.*) de batalla. || *Pitched battle*, batalla campal. || FIG. *That's half the battle*, ya hay medio camino andado. || *To do battle*, librar batalla. || FIG. *To do battle for*, luchar por. | *To fight a losing battle*, luchar por una causa perdida. || *To give battle*, dar la batalla. || *To join battle*, trabar batalla. || *To offer battle*, presentar batalla.
battle ['bætl] v. tr. Combatir, luchar contra. || *To battle one's way through the crowd*, abrirse camino entre la multitud.
— V. intr. Combatir, luchar (*against*, contra; *for*, por). || FIG. Luchar: *to battle for one's rights*, luchar por sus derechos.
battle-axe (U. S. **battle-ax**) [—æks] n. Hacha (*f.*) de armas (weapon). || FIG. Arpía, *f.*
battle cruiser [—,kru:zə*] n. MAR. Crucero, *m.*
battle cry [—krai] n. MIL. Grito (*m.*) de guerra. || FIG. Lema, *m.* (slogan).
battledore [—dɔ:*] n. Raqueta, *f.* (racket). || Pala, *f.*, paleta, *f.* (for washing clothes). || Pala, *f.* (for placing loaves).
battle dress [—dres] n. MIL. Uniforme (*m.*) de campaña.
battlefield [—fi:ld] n. MIL. Campo (*m.*) de batalla.
battlemented [—məntid] adj. ARCH. Almenado, da.
battlement [—mənt] n. ARCH. Almena, *f.*
battleship [—ʃip] n. Acorazado, *m.*
battue [bæ'tu:] n. Batida, *f.* (hunting). || FIG. Matanza, *f.* (mass killing).
batty ['bæti] adj. FAM. Chalado, da (crazy).
bauble ['bɔ:bl] n. Chuchería, *f.*, baratija, *f.* (worthless object). || Cetro (*m.*) de bufón (of a jester). || Juguete, *m.* (toy).
baulk [bɔ:k] n./v. tr. See BALK.
bauxite ['bɔ:ksait] n. Bauxita, *f.*
Bavaria [bə'vɛəriə] pr. n. GEOGR. Baviera, *f.*
Bavarian [—n] adj./n. Bávaro, ra.
bawd [bɔ:d] n. Patrona (*f.*) de burdel. || Alcahueta, *f.* (go-between).
bawdy [—i] adj. Obsceno, na; indecente, verde. || *Bawdy house*, lupanar, *m.*
bawl [bɔ:l] v. intr. Gritar, chillar (to shout). || Berrear (to bellow). || *To bawl at s.o.*, gritarle a uno.
— V. tr. Gritar, vociferar. || — *To bawl out*, gritar, vociferar: *to bawl out s.o.'s name*, vociferar el nombre de uno. || FAM. *To bawl s.o. out*, echar una bronca a uno.
bay [bei] n. GEOGR. Bahía, *f.*: *Bay of Pigs*, bahía de Cochinos. | Golfo, *m.* (large): *bay of Biscay*, golfo de Vizcaya. | Abra, *f.* (small). | Abra, *f.*, entrada (*f.*) de un llano en una cordillera (opening between mountains). || Bayo, *m.* (colour). || Caballo (*m.*) bayo (horse). || Crujía, *f.* (division of a building). || Nave, *f.* (of factory). || Pajar, *m.* (in a barn). || Tramo, *m.* (of bridge). || Vano, *m.*, hueco *m.* (window). || Ladrido, *m.*, aullido, *m.* (barking, howling). || BOT. Laurel, *m.* (laurel). || — Pl. Corona (*f. sing.*) de laurel (crown). || FIG. Laureles, *m.* (glory). || — *At bay*, acorralado, da (an animal). || *Bomb bay*, compartimiento (*m.*) de bombas. || *To bring a wild boar to bay*, acorralar a un jabalí. || *To carry off the bays*, ganar laureles. || || *To keep* o *to hold the enemy at bay*, mantener a raya al enemigo.
— Adj. Bayo, ya.
bay [bei] v. intr. Ladrar (to bark). || Aullar (to howl).
— V. tr. Ladrar a: *to bay the moon*, ladrar a la luna. || Acorralar (to corner).
bayadere ['baiə,di:ə*] n. Bayadera, *f.*
baying ['beiiŋ] n. Ladrido, *m.*, aullido, *m.* (of dogs).
bayonet ['beiənit] n. MIL. Bayoneta, *f.*: *to fix bayonets*, armar *or* calar la bayoneta; *bayonet charge*, carga a la bayoneta. || TECH. Bayoneta, *f.*
bayonet ['beiənit] v. tr. MIL. Pasar a la bayoneta.
Bayonne [bæ'jɔ:n] pr. n. GEOGR. Bayona.
bayou ['bæju:] n. U. S. Brazo (*m.*) pantanoso [de un río].
bay window ['bei'windəu] n. Ventana (*f.*) salediza. || FAM. Barriga, *f.* (potbelly).
bazaar [bə'zɑ:*] n. Bazar, *m.* (Oriental market). || Venta (*f.*) benéfica (for charity).
bazan ['beizən] n. Badana, *f.*
bazooka [bə'zu:kə] n. Bazooka, *m.*, bazuca, *m.*
be* [bi:] v. intr.

1. Cases where *to be* is translated by *ser.* — **2.** Translated by *estar.* — **3.** Verbs which may replace *ser* and *estar.* — **4.** *To be* in the passive voice. — **5.** *To be* with a gerund. — **6.** Other translations. — **7.** Impersonal *to be.* — **8.** *To be* as a compound verb. — **9.** *To be* in elliptical constructions. — **10.** Expressions with *to be.*

1. "TO BE" IS TRANSLATED BY *ser.*
a) When followed by a noun, a pronoun, a numeral, a clause or an infinitive: *he is a doctor*, es médico; *the prettiest of the girls is Catherine*, la más guapa de las chicas es Catalina; *that is nothing*, eso no es nada; *it was you who did it*, eres tú quien lo hizo; *we were four*, eramos cuatro; *the treasure is what interests him*, el tesoro es lo que le interesa; *his ambition is to write an opera*, su ambición es escribir una ópera.
b) When followed by an adjective which indicates an essential or inherent characteristic of the subject: *ice is cold*, el hielo es frío; *this child is naughty*, este niño es malo; *the Mediterranean is blue*, el Mediterráneo es azul; *he is rich, obstinate*, es rico, obstinado; *he is happy*, es feliz.
c) In certain cases when used as an auxiliary verb in the passive voice (see no. 4 below).
d) When used with certain adjectives such as *feliz, infeliz, cierto, indudable, notorio, evidente, frecuente, posible, imposible, probable, improbable, necesario.*
e) When the complement indicates possession, authorship, provenance, composition, cause or purpose: *this watch is Raymond's*, este reloj es de Ramón; *it's a Gainsborough*, es de Gainsborough; *Barry is from London*, Barry es de Londres; *this table is mahogany*, esta mesa es de caoba; *it was because of his brother that he was arrested*, fue a causa de su hermano que le detuvieron; *this polish is for black shoes*, este betún es para zapatos negros.
2. "TO BE" IS TRANSLATED BY *estar.*
a) When used with an adjective or a phrase which indicates an accidental or temporary state: *my tea is cold*, mi té está frío; *the child is unhappy when his mother is not there*, el niño está triste cuando no está su madre; *the sky was overcast when the storm broke*, el cielo estaba encapotado cuando estalló la tormenta; *my uncle is ill*, mi tío está enfermo; *how are you?*, ¿cómo estás?; *Mary is very pretty today*, María está muy guapa hoy; *the soup is too salty*, la sopa está demasiado salada; *yesterday you were in a bad mood*, ayer estabas de mal humor.
b) To express position in space or time: *he is in the garden*, está en el jardín; *Paris is in France*, París está en Francia; *we are in summer*, estamos en verano.
c) In certain cases when used as an auxiliary verb in the passive voice (see no. 4 below).
d) When used with certain adjectives such as *contento, descontento, satisfecho, insatisfecho, solo, enfermo.*
3. VERBS WHICH MAY REPLACE *ser* AND *estar.*
Ser and *estar* may occasionally be replaced by several semi-auxiliary verbs:
a) By *resultar* or *quedar* when the predicate indicates the consequence of a previous action or event: *he was injured in an accident*, resultó herido en un accidente; *he was transformed by his journey*, quedó transformado por su viaje.
b) By *ir* (*he is always well dressed*, siempre va bien vestido), *andar* (*he is always in a bad mood*, anda siempre de mal humor), *encontrarse* or *hallarse* (*we*

were in Madrid when it happened, nos encontrábamos en Madrid cuando ocurrió), *llegar* (*he is always on time*, siempre llega a la hora).
c) By *seguir* or *continuar* to indicate a continued state: *he is still ill*, sigue enfermo; *he is still at university*, continúa en la universidad.
4. "To be" as an auxiliary in the passive voice.
a) *Ser* is used as the auxiliary verb in Spanish if the agent, whether expressed or not, is active: *he was arrested by the police*, fue arrestado por la policía; *to be loved is every woman's ideal*, ser amada es el ideal de toda mujer.
b) *Estar* is used as the auxiliary verb to emphasize the result of an action rather than the action itself: *Spain is separated from France by the Pyrenees*, España está separada de Francia por los Pirineos.
c) In Spanish the use of the passive form is often avoided, being replaced by the active form if the agent is expressed or by the reflexive form if the agent is not expressed: *he was knocked down by a car*, le atropelló un coche; *English is spoken the world over*, se habla inglés en el mundo entero.
5. "To be" with a gerund.
To be with a gerund is translated:
a) In most cases by *estar* with the gerund of the accompanying verb: *he is always smoking*, siempre está fumando; *they are eating*, están comiendo.
b) By the present or future indicative of the accompanying verb when the idea expressed is one of action in the near future: *he is leaving for Madrid tomorrow*, se marcha a Madrid mañana.
6. Other translations of "to be".
a) *To be*, when followed by certain adjectives, and when the subject is a person or an animal, is often translated by *tener* with the corresponding noun: *he is hot, cold, hungry, thirsty, ashamed, sleepy, in a hurry*, tiene calor, frío, hambre, sed, vergüenza, sueño, prisa; *my hands are cold*, tengo las manos frías; *to be right*, tener razón; *how old are you?*, ¿cuántos años tienes?; *I am twenty years old*, tengo veinte años.
b) With adjectives expressing emotion caused by a certain event *to be* is translated by *quedarse: I was flabbergasted*, me quedé boquiabierto; *he was utterly astonished*, se quedó extrañadísimo; *he was very disappointed*, se quedó muy desilusionado.
7. Impersonal "to be".
a) In the expression *there is* (there are, there were, etc.) *to be* is translated by *haber: there were not many cars on the road*, no había muchos coches en la carretera; *there is no bread*, no hay pan.
b) When followed by an adverb or adverbial phrase of time or place *to be* is translated by *ser* if the subject is impersonal: *do you know where he lives? — I think it's here*, ¿sabes dónde vive? — Creo que es aquí; *it is late*, es tarde; *it will be in summer*, será en verano; *it is one o'clock*, es la una; *it was five o'clock*, eran las cinco.
c) When used with an adjective in an impersonal expression *to be* is translated by *ser*: *it is important that I see him*, es importante que le vea; *it is useless going now*, es inútil ir ahora (notice, however, that with the adjective *claro* the verb *estar* must be used: *it is obvious that he is drunk*, está claro que está borracho).
d) Other impersonal expressions: *as though it were nothing at all*, como quien no quiere la cosa: *he did it as though it were nothing at all*, lo hizo como quien no quiere la cosa. || *It is time to*, ya es hora de. || *It's about time!*, ¡ya era hora!
8. "To be" as a compound verb.
a) *To be after.* — Estar después de: *you are after me in the queue*, usted está después de mí en la cola. || Perseguir (to chase): *the hunters were after a fox*, los cazadores perseguían un zorro. || Estar buscando: *what are you after there?*, ¿qué estás buscando allí?; *I'm after a job*, estoy buscando trabajo.
b) *To be at.* — Estar haciendo: *what are you at?*, ¿qué estás haciendo? || — *They have been at it a long time*, ya llevan mucho tiempo con ello. || *While we are at it*, de paso, ya que estamos.
c) *To be away.* — Estar fuera, estar ausente: *he has been away the whole week*, ha estado fuera toda la semana. || — *To be away on business*, estar en viaje de negocios. || *To be well away*, estar bebido (to be drunk), estar completamente ensimismado (to be deeply engrossed), estar profundamente dormido (to be asleep).
d) *To be before.* — Estar antes que *or* de: *you are before me*, Vd. está antes que yo *or* antes de mí.
e) *To be for.* — Ser para: *is this tea for me?*, ¿este té es para mí? || Servir *or* ser para (to be used for): *this is for cutting your nails*, esto sirve para cortarse las uñas. || Estar por, ser partidario de: *I'm for leaving it until tomorrow*, yo estoy por dejarlo hasta mañana; *what team are you for?*, ¿por qué equipo estás?
f) *To be from.* — Ser de.
g) *To be in.* — See in.
h) *To be in for.* — See in.
i) *To be off.* — See off.
j) *To be on.* — See on.
k) *To be out.* — See out.
l) *To be over.* — See over.
m) *To be to.* — Tener que, deber (to have to): *you are to go immediately*, tienes que ir inmediatamente. || Deber (to intend to): *she was to stay two weeks*, debía quedarse dos semanas. || Poder ser (to be possible): *it was not to be denied*, no podía ser negado. || Ir a, deber (to be going to): *he was to die a week later*, iba a morir una semana más tarde.
n) *To be up.* — Haberse levantado (out of bed): *is he up yet?*, ¿ya se ha levantado? || Estar procesado, da (for trial): *he is up for armed robbery*, está procesado por robo a mano armada. || Acabarse: *our time is up*, se nos acabó el tiempo. (See up.)
9. "To be" in elliptical constructions.
In such cases *to be* is often not translated into Spanish: *are you happy? — I am*, ¿estás contento? — Sí; *are you ready? — No, I'm not*, ¿estás listo? — No; *he's back. — Is he?*, está de vuelta. — ¿Ah sí?
10. Expressions with "to be".
As it were, digamos, por decirlo así (so to speak). || *As things are*, tal [y] como están las cosas. || *Be that as it may*, sea lo que fuere. || *Father to be*, futuro padre. || *God is love*, Dios es amor. || *Here I am and here I'll stay*, aquí estoy y aquí me quedo. || *How much is it?*, ¿cuánto es?, ¿cuánto vale? || *If I were you*, si yo fuera Vd., yo en su lugar. || *I think, therefore I am*, pienso, luego existo. || *It's four months since I saw her*, hace cuatro meses que no la veo. || *It's not that...*, no es que... || *It's the 15th of August*, estamos a quince de agosto, es el quince de agosto. || *Leave* o *let me be*, déjame estar, déjame en paz. || *Let it be!*, ¡déjalo! || *Not to be missed*, que no se debe perder. || *Not to be o.s.*, encontrarse raro. || *Potatoes are ten pence*, las patatas están a diez peniques *or* cuestan diez peniques. || *So be it*, así sea. || *To be about to do*, estar a punto de hacer. || *To be a long time doing sth.*, tardar mucho en hacer algo. || *To be a mother to s.o.*, ser una verdadera madre para uno || *To be had* o *to be taken in*, dejarse engañar. || *To be or not to be*, ser o no ser. || *To be sure*, ¡claro está! (interjection), estar seguro (to be certain). || *To be with it*, see with. || *To be with s.o. on sth.*, estar [de acuerdo] con alguien acerca de algo. || *We have been in this country (for) two months*, llevamos dos meses en este país, hace dos meses que estamos aquí. || *Were it not for*, de no ser por. || *What is it to be?*, ¿qué va a ser? (in bar). || *What is it to you?*, ¿qué te importa? || *What is the date today?*, ¿a cuántos estamos hoy? || *You are working enough as it is*, ya trabajas bastante.

— Observ. Ver la conjugación de este verbo en el compendio de gramática.

— Pret. ***was, were;*** p. p. ***been.***

beach [bi:tʃ] n. Playa, *f.*: *on the beach*, en la playa. || *Beach umbrella*, quitasol, *m.*, parasol, *m.*
beach [bi:tʃ] v. tr./intr. Varar.
beachcomber [—ˌkəumə*] n. Raquero, *m.* (man). || Ola, *f.* (wave). || Fig. Inútil, *m.* (good-for-nothing).
beachhead [—hed] n. Cabeza (*f.*) de playa.
beacon [ˈbi:kən] n. Almenara, *f.* (fire). || Faro, *m.* (lighthouse). || Mar. Aviat. Baliza, *f.* || Fig. Faro, *m.*, guía, *m.* || *Aerial beacon*, aerofaro, *m.*
beacon [ˈbi:kən] v. tr. Mar. Aviat. Balizar. || Fig. Guiar.
bead [bi:d] n. Cuenta, *f.* (for rosary, necklace): *to thread beads*, ensartar cuentas. || Abalorio, *m.* (of glass). || Gota, *f.* (drop): *a bead of sweat*, una gota de sudor. || Punto (*m.*) de mira (sight of gun). || Burbuja, *f.* (bubble). || Talón, *m.* (of tyre). || Arch. Junquillo, *m.*, astrágalo, *m.* (astragal). || Chem. Perla, *f.* (in analysis). || — Pl. Rosario, *m. sing.* (rosary). || Collar, *m. sing.* (necklace). || — *String of beads*, collar. || *To draw a bead on*, apuntar a. || *To tell one's beads*, rezar el rosario, pasar las cuentas del rosario.
bead [bi:d] v. tr. Adornar con abalorios (to adorn). — V. intr. Gotear.
beading [—iŋ] n. Arch. Astrágalo, *m.*, junquillo, *m.* || Cuentas, *f. pl.*, abalorios, *m. pl.* (beads).
beadle [ˈbi:dl] n. Pertiguero, *m.*, macero, *m.* (in church). || Bedel, *m.* (in university). || Alguacil, *m.* (in law courts).
beadledom [—dəm] n. Papeleo, *m.*
beady [—i] adj. De forma de abalorio. || *Beady eyes*, ojos pequeños, redondos y brillantes.
beagle [ˈbi:gl] n. Beagle, *m.* (dog).
beak [bi:k] n. Pico, *m.* (of bird). || Nariz (*f.*) ganchuda (hooked nose). || Pitorro, *m.* (spout). || Promontorio, *m.* (promontory). || Mar. Espolón, *m.* (in galleys). || Punta, *f.* (of anvil). || Jur. Juez (*m.*) de paz (justice of the peace). | Magistrado, *m.* (magistrate). || Mus. Boquilla, *f.*
beaked [bi:kt] adj. Picudo, da.
beaker [ˈbi:kə*] n. Cubilete, *m.*, copa, *f.* (drinking vessel). || Jarra, *f.* (tumbler in plastic, pottery, etc.). || Chem. Cubeta (*f.*) de precipitación.
beakiron [ˈbi:kaiən] n. Bigornia, *f.* (anvil).
be-all [ˈbiɔ:l] n. *The be-all and end-all*, la única razón de la existencia de uno, lo único que importa: *money must not be our be-all and end-all*, el dinero no debe ser la única razón de nuestra existencia *or* lo único que nos importe.
beam [bi:m] n. Arch. Viga, *f.* (for supporting roof, etc.). || Rayo, *m.* (of light). || Destello, *m.* (gleam).

|| Sonrisa (*f.*) radiante (broad smile). || TECH. Plegador, *m.* (in loom). | Astil, *m.* (of balance). | Balancín, *m.* (of engine). | Lanza, *f.* (of carriage). | Cama, *f.* (of plough). || MAR. Bao, *m.* (timber joining two sides of ship). | Manga, *f.* (breadth). || PHYS. Haz, *m.* (parallel rays): *electron beam*, haz electrónico. | Onda (*f.*) dirigida (radio signal). || — FAM. *Broad in the beam*, ancho de caderas. || MAR. *On the port beam*, a babor. || FAM. *To be off the beam*, estar equivocado (wrong). || *To fly* o *to ride the beam*, seguir el haz radioeléctrico.

beam [bi:m] v. intr. Irradiar. || Sonreír (to smile). || Rebosar (*with*, de) [satisfaction, health].

— V. tr. Difundir, emitir (a broadcast). || Irradiar (rays, warmth). || Emitir (light). || Transmitir (message).

beam compass [—ˈkʌmpəs] n. Compás (*m.*) de vara.

beam-ends [—ˈendz] pl. n. MAR. Cabezas (*f.*) de los baos. || — MAR. *On her beam-ends*, escorado. || FIG. FAM. *To be on one's beam-ends*, no tener ni un céntimo (to have no money).

beaming [ˈbi:miŋ] adj. Radiante.

bean [bi:n] n. BOT. Judía, *f.*, alubia, *f.*, habichuela, *f.* [*Amer.*, frijol, *m.*, fríjol, *m.*, poroto, *m.*] (seed). | Haba, *f.* (broad bean). | Grano, *m.* (of coffee, etc.). || U. S. FAM. Chola, *f.*, cabeza, *f.* || — BOT. *French beans*, judías *or* habichuelas verdes. | *Kidney beans*, fríjoles, *m. pl.* || FAM. *Not to be worth a bean*, no valer un comino. | *Not to know beans about*, no saber ni jota de. | *Old bean*, viejo (friend). || BOT. *Stick bean*, judía verde. || FAM. *To be full of beans*, rebosar de vitalidad. | *To be without a bean*, no tener un cuarto. | *To spill the beans*, descubrir el pastel.

beanfeast [—fi:st] or **beano** [ˈbi:nəu] n. FAM. Comilona, *f.* (big meal). | Juerga, *f.* (binge).

bear [bɛə*] n. ZOOL. Oso, osa: *black, brown, white bear*, oso negro, pardo, blanco. || FIG. Oso, *m.* || Bajista, *m.* (in stock exchange). || — ZOOL. *Bear cub* o *young bear*, osezno, *m.* || ASTR. *Great, Little Bear*, Osa Mayor, Menor. || FAM. *To be like a bear with a sore head*, estar de un humor de perros.

bear* [bɛə*] v. tr. Soportar (to support): *will it bear the weight?*, ¿soportará el peso? || Llevar (to carry): *they bore the chest on their shoulders*, llevaron el cofre a hombros; *the letter bears his signature*, la carta lleva su firma. || Tener (a name, title, reputation, relation, expression, aspect, meaning, price). || Aguantar, soportar (to tolerate): *he can't bear the pain*, no puede soportar el dolor; *I can't bear him*, no puedo aguantarle. || Admitir (to admit): *it bears several interpretations*, admite varias interpretaciones; *it doesn't bear comparison*, no admite comparación. || Merecer: *to bear mentioning*, merecer ser mencionado. || Ser apropiado para (to be suitable for): *his joke doesn't bear repetition*, su chiste nos es apropiado para ser repetido. || Ejercer (power, pressure). || Pagar, correr con: *to bear the cost of*, pagar los gastos de. || Dar a luz, tener (to give birth to): *she has borne a girl*, ha dado a luz a una niña. || Dar (to give): *she bore him a son*, le dio un hijo; *to bear fruit*, dar fruto. || Resistir: *his alibi doesn't bear close examination*, su coartada no resiste un examen a fondo. || Profesar, tener: *the love she bore him*, el amor que le profesaba. || — *Can you bear me to touch it?*, ¿me dejas tocarlo? || *To bear a grudge against s.o.*, guardar rencor a alguien. || *To bear a hand*, echar una mano. || *To bear a part in*, compartir. || *To bear a part* o *a role in sth.*, desempeñar un papel en algo. || *To bear a person company*, acompañar a una persona, hacer compañía a una persona. || *To bear arms*, tener armas (to possess), llevar armas (to carry). || *To bear in mind*, tener presente, recordar, tener en cuenta. || *To bear interest*, producir *or* devengar interés. || *To bear o.s. well*, portarse *or* comportarse bien. || *To bear reference to*, relacionarse con. || *To bear resemblance to*, parecerse a. || *To bear the responsibility for*, ser responsable de.

— V. intr. Torcer (to turn): *the road bears to the right*, la carretera tuerce a la derecha. || Producir (to produce): *the tree bears well*, el árbol produce mucho. || Dirigirse hacia: *the ship bore east*, el barco se dirigía hacia el este. || *To bear hard* o *heavily on s.o.*, pesar mucho sobre alguien.

— ***To bear away,*** llevarse: *she bore the prize away*, se llevó el premio. | Arribar (a ship). || ***To bear down,*** vencer (enemy, opposition). | Abatirse (a bird). | Navegar con el viento (to sail with the wind). | — *To bear down on*, pesar sobre (to weigh on), acercarse a, dirigirse hacia (to draw near). || ***To bear off,*** llevarse (to carry off). | MAR. Alejarse. || ***To bear on,*** referirse a. || ***To bear out,*** confirmar, corroborar (to confirm). || ***To bear up,*** sostener, ayudar (to support). | — *To bear up against*, resistir, aguantar. || ***To bear with,*** tener paciencia con.

— OBSERV. *To bear* va seguido por el infinitivo o por el gerundio.
— El pretérito de *bear* es ***bore***. El participio pasivo es ***borne*** en el sentido de "llevado" y ***born*** cuando significa "nacido".

bearable [ˈbɛərəbl] adj. Soportable, llevadero, ra (life). || Soportable, aguantable (person, work).

beard [biəd] n. Barba, *f.*, barbas, *f. pl.* (of people, animals): *to have a beard*, llevar *or* gastar barba. || BOT. Arista, *f.*, barba, *f.* (awn). || Lengüeta, *f.* (of an arrow). || Barba, *f.* (of a pen).

beard [biəd] v. tr. Desafiar, retar (to defy).

bearded [—id] adj. Con barba, barbado, da; barbudo, da (fam.) [person]. || BOT. Aristado, da (wheat).

beardless [—lis] adj. Barbilampiño, imberbe.

bearer [ˈbɛərə*] n. Soporte, *m.* (support). || Porteador, *m.* (carrier). || Portador, ra (of message). || Portador, *m.* (of cheque). || Poseedor, ra (of passport). || — *Bearer bond*, título (*m.*) al portador. || *Bearer cheque*, cheque (*m.*) al portador. || *Mace bearer*, macero, *m.* || *Stretcher bearer*, camillero, *m.* || *This tree is a poor bearer*, este árbol no da mucho fruto.

bear garden [ˈbɛəˌgɑ:dn] n. FIG. Casa (*f.*) de locos (noisy place).

bearing [ˈbɛəriŋ] n. Transporte, *m.* (transportation). || Porte, *m.*: *a man of noble bearing*, un hombre de noble porte; *majestic bearing*, porte majestuoso. || Conducta, *f.* (behaviour): *his courageous bearing in the battle*, su valiente conducta en la batalla. || Importancia, *f.*, alcance, *m.* (importance): *he didn't realize the bearing of her words*, no se dio cuenta del alcance de sus palabras. || Relación, *f.*, conexión, *f.* (*on*, con) [relevance]. || Producción, *f.* || ARCH. Soporte, *m.* (support). || TECH. Cojinete, *m.*: *ball, needle, roller, thrust bearing*, cojinete de bolas, de agujas, de rodillos, de empuje. || MED. Alumbramiento, *m.*, parto, *m.* || — Pl. Blasón, *m. sing.* (coat of arms). || Aspectos, *m.* (of a question). || — *Beyond all bearing*, insoportable, inaguantable, intolerable. || MAR. *Magnetic bearing*, acimut magnético. || FIG. *To get* o *to find one's bearings*, orientarse. || MAR. *To give one's bearings*, dar su posición. || FIG. *To have no bearing on the matter*, no tener nada que ver con el asunto. || FAM. *To lose one's bearings*, desorientarse. || ARCH. *To take its bearing on sth.*, apoyarse en algo. || *To take one's bearings*, tomar marcaciones, marcarse (in a ship), orientarse (to find one's bearings).

— Adj. Que produce: *interest bearing*, que produce interés.

— OBSERV. Compound adjectives formed by adding *-bearing* to a noun may often be rendered in Spanish by the suffix *ífero, ra* (*fruit-bearing*, fructífero, ra; *coal-bearing*, carbonífero, ra).

bearish [ˈbɛəriʃ] adj. FIG. Huraño, ña (person). || *Bearish tendency*, tendencia a la baja (in stock exchange).

bearskin [ˈbɛəskin] n. Piel (*f.*) de oso (fur, rug). || Gorro, *m.* [de piel de oso] (cap).

beast [bi:st] n. Bestia, *f.* || FIG. Bestia, *f.*, bruto, *m.*, animal, *m.* || — Pl. Reses, *f.*, ganado, *m. sing.* (livestock). || — *Beast of burden*, bestia de carga. || FAM. *It's a beast of a day, of a job*, es un día, un trabajo espantoso. || *The King of the beasts*, el rey de los animales. || *Wild beast*, fiera, *f.*

beastliness [—linis] n. Bestialidad, *f.*

beastly [ˈbi:stli] adj. Bestial. || FAM. Asqueroso, sa; repugnante (awful). | Maldito, ta: *where's that beastly hat?*, ¿dónde está ese maldito sombrero? || FAM. *Beastly weather*, tiempo de perros.

— Adv. FAM. Terriblemente: *beastly difficult*, terriblemente difícil. || *It is beastly hot*, hace un calor bestial.

beat [bi:t] n. Latido, *m.* (of heart, pulse). || Pulsación, *f.* (pulsation). || Martilleo, *m.* (hammering): *the beat of the rain on the roof*, el martilleo de la lluvia en el tejado. || Batir, *m.*: *the beat of the waves against the rocks*, el batir de las olas contra las rocas. || Sonido, *m.*, ruido, *m.* (sound, noise). || Redoble, *m.* (of drums). || Ritmo, *m.* (of verse). || Ritmo, *m.* (of song): *this song has a good beat*, esta canción tiene mucho ritmo. || Ronda, *f.* (round of duty): *a policeman's beat*, la ronda de un policía. || Competencia, *f.* (sphere of action): *that is not my beat*, eso no es de mi competencia. || Noticia (*f.*) sensacional que se tiene en exclusiva (scoop). || Batida, *f.* (in hunting). || MUS. Tiempo, *m.*: *the third beat of the bar*, el tercer tiempo del compás. | Ritmo (*m.*) *or* compás (*m.*) marcado por el director de orquesta. || — *Off beat*, excéntrico, ca (eccentric), fuera de tiempo (out of time), sin ritmo (music), fuera de lo común *or* de lo corriente (unusual). || *The beat of the birds' wings*, el aleteo de los pájaros.

— Adj. See BEATEN. || FAM. Derrengado, da (tired). || — *He has me beat*, aquí me ha cogido. || *The beat generation*, la generación perdida.

beat* [bi:t] v. tr. Pegar (to spank). || Golpear (to hit): *they beat him senseless*, le golpearon hasta dejarle inconsciente. || Dar golpes en, golpear (to pound): *to beat the door, the table*, dar golpes en la puerta en la mesa. || Abrirse: *to beat a path through the jungle, the crowd*, abrirse paso en la jungla, entre la multitud. || Batir, golpear: *the waves beat the cliffs*, las olas batían los acantilados. || Sacudir (carpet, cushions, etc.). || Batir, vencer (to defeat): *the enemy was beaten all along the line*, el enemigo fue batido en toda la línea. || Batir (in cooking). || Llegar antes que: *he beat me to the door*, llegó a la puerta antes que yo. || Batir (the wings). || Batir (in hunting). || Tocar (the drum). || Marcar, llevar (rhythm, time): *to beat time*, marcar el compás. || Meter en la cabeza: *he tried to beat some sense into him*, intentó meterle un poco de sentido común en la cabeza. || Dejar perplejo (to baffle). || TECH. Batir (metals). || SP. Ganar: *he beat me by five seconds*, me ganó por

cinco segundos. | Vencer: *do you think Germany will beat France?*, ¿crees que Alemania vencerá a Francia? | Batir: *to beat the record*, batir el récord. || Pisar (the ground). || Recorrer, batir (the countryside). || — *Beat it!*, ¡lárgate! || *That beats all!*, ¡eso es el colmo! || *To beat a nail into*, poner un clavo en. || *To beat a retreat*, batirse en retirada. || *To beat black and blue*, dar una paliza soberana. || FIG. *To beat one's brains*, devanarse los sesos. || FAM. *To beat s.o. to it*, ganarle a uno por la mano. || U. S. *To beat the band*, a más no poder. || *To beat the breast*, golpearse el pecho, darse golpes de pecho. || *To beat to death*, matar a palos.
— V. intr. Latir (the heart). || Tener pulsaciones (pulse). || Batir, golpear: *the rain beat against the window panes*, la lluvia golpeaba contra los cristales. || Dar golpes (*on*, en) [a door]. || Dar una batida (in hunting). || Resonar, redoblar (drums).
— ***To beat about***, barloventear (ship). | — *To beat about the bush*, andarse con rodeos. || ***To beat against***, estrellarse contra. || ***To beat back***, hacer retroceder, rechazar (to repel). || ***To beat down***, derribar (door, etc.). | Superar (to overcome). | Vencer (opponent). | Regatear (to haggle): *to beat down the price of*, regatear el precio de. | Conseguir que [el vendedor] baje el precio. | Caer de plomo (sun). | AGR. Acamar. || ***To beat in***, derribar (door, etc.). || ***To beat off***, rechazar (to repel). | Dejar atrás (in racing). || ***To beat out***, abrir (path). | Martillear (metals). | Marcar (rythm). || ***To beat up***, batir (in cooking). | Dar una paliza (to thrash).
— OBSERV. Pret. ***beat***; p. p. ***beaten***, ***beat***.

beaten [bi:tn] adj. Trillado, da: *a beaten track*, un camino trillado. || MIL. Vencido, da; batido, da. || Batido, da; martillado, da (metals). || Agotado, da (worn-out, exhausted). || FIG. *Off the beaten track*, aislado, da; retirado, da (isolated), que se sale de lo común: *his ideas are off the beaten track*, sus ideas se salen de lo común.
beater [ˈbi:tə*] n. Batidora, *f.* (in cooking). || Ojeador, *m.*, batidor, *m.* (in hunting). || Sacudidor, *m.* (duster).
beatific [ˌbi:əˈtifik] adj. Beatífico, ca.
beatification [bi:ˌætifiˈkeiʃən] n. Beatificación, *f.*
beatify [bi:ˈætifai] v. tr. Beatificar.
beating [ˈbi:tiŋ] n. Paliza, *f.* (thrashing): *he took a beating*, recibió una paliza. || Derrota, *f.* (defeat): *to take a beating*, sufrir una derrota. || Latido, *m.* (of the heart). || Pulsación, *f.* (pulsation). || Ojeo, *m.*, batida, *f.* (in hunting). || — *Beating of wings*, aleteo, *m.* || *Beating up*, paliza, *f.*
beatitude [biˈætitju:d] n. Beatitud, *f.* || REL. Bienaventuranza, *f.*
beatnik [ˈbi:tnik] n. "Beatnik", *m.* & *f.*
Beatrice [ˈbiətris] or **Beatrix** [ˈbiətriks] pr. n. Beatriz, *f.*
beau [bəu] n. Galán, *m.* (gallant). || Novio, *m.* (sweetheart). || Pretendiente, *m.* (suitor). || Lechuguino, *m.*, pisaverde, *m.* (dandy).
— Adj. *Beau geste*, buen detalle, *m.* || *Beau ideal*, tipo (*m.*) ideal.
— OBSERV. El plural de *beau* es *beaux* o *beaus*.

beauteous [ˈbju:tjəs] adj. Bello, lla; hermoso, sa.
beautician [bju:ˈtiʃən] n. Especialista (*m.* y *f.*) de un instituto de belleza.
beautiful [ˈbju:təful] adj. Bello, lla; hermoso, sa: *a beautiful painting, poem*, un hermoso cuadro, un bello poema. || Hermoso, sa (child, animal). || Guapa, guapísima (woman): *there were some beautiful girls at the party*, había unas chicas guapísimas en la fiesta. || Precioso, sa: *a beautiful dress*, un traje precioso; *a beautiful face*, una cara preciosa. || Magnífico, ca: *it was a beautiful meal*, fue una comida magnífica.
— N. *The beautiful*, lo bello, lo hermoso, la belleza.
— OBSERV. In a literary context a woman may be described as *bella* or *hermosa* in Spanish. *Guapa*, on the other hand, is used in everyday spoken Spanish.

beautify [ˈbju:tifai] v. tr. Embellecer.
— V. intr. Embellecerse.
beauty [ˈbju:ti] n. Belleza, *f.*, hermosura, *f.* (quality). || Belleza, *f.* (beautiful person or thing): *she is a beauty*, es una belleza. || — *Beauty and the Beast*, la Bella y la Bestia. || *Beauty contest*, concurso (*m.*) de belleza. || *Beauty cream*, crema (*f.*) de belleza. || FIG. *Beauty is but skin deep*, las apariencias engañan. || *Beauty is in the eye of the beholder*, la belleza es subjetiva. || *Beauty treatment*, tratamiento (*m.*) de belleza. || FAM. *She o it is a real beauty*, es una preciosidad. || *Sleeping Beauty*, la Bella durmiente del bosque. || FAM. *That was a beauty!*, ¡qué golpe más bueno! || FIG. *The beauty of it is that*, lo bueno es que.
beauty parlour (U. S. **beauty parlor**) [—ˌpɑ:lə*] n. Salón (*m.*) de belleza, instituto (*m.*) de belleza.
beauty sleep [—sli:p] n. Primer sueño, *m.*
beauty spot [—spɔt] n. Lunar, *m.* (on face). || Sitio (*m.*) pintoresco (place).
beaver [ˈbi:və*] n. ZOOL. Castor, *m* (animal, fur). || Babera, *f.* (of helmet).
bebop [ˈbi:bɔp] n. MUS. "Be-bop", *m.*
becalm [biˈkɑ:m] v. tr. Calmar, sosegar. || MAR. Detener por falta de viento (a sailing boat). || *To be becalmed*, estar encalmado.

became [biˈkeim] pret. See BECOME.
because [biˈkɔz] conj. Porque: *he can't come because he is very busy*, no puede venir porque está muy ocupado. || — *Because of*, a causa de: *he can't come because of the transport strike*, no puede venir a causa de la huelga de transportes. || *The more powerful because*, tanto más potente cuanto que.
beccafico [ˌbekəˈfikəu] n. ZOOL. Becafigo, *m.* (bird).
béchamel [ˈbeʃəmel] n. Besamel, *f.*, bechamel, *f.* (white sauce).
beck [bek] n. Arroyo, *m.*, riachuelo, *m.* (brook). || FAM. *To be at s.o.'s beck and call*, estar al servicio de uno, estar a la disposición de uno.
becket [ˈbekit] n. MAR. Vinatera, *f.* (for ropes).
beckiron [ˈbekaiən] n. Bigornia, *f.* (anvil).
beckon [ˈbekən] v. tr. Hacer señas (to motion): *he beckoned him to approach*, le hizo señas para que se acercase. || FIG. Atraer, llamar (to entice): *the prospect of becoming rich beckoned him*, la perspectiva de enriquecerse le atraía.
— V. intr. Hacer señas (*to*, a).
becloud [biˈklaud] v. tr. FIG. Oscurecer (to darken).
become* [biˈkʌm] v. intr. Volverse: *she has become much nicer since she got married*, se ha vuelto mucho más simpática desde que se casó. || Hacerse (on one's own merits): *to become a doctor*, hacerse médico; *to become famous*, hacerse famoso. || Ponerse: *to become sad*, ponerse triste; *to become fat*, ponerse gordo. || Llegar a, llegar a ser (to get to be): *despite his low birth he became president*, pese a su humilde origen llegó a ser presidente. || Quedarse: *to become deaf, blind*, quedarse sordo, ciego. || Llegar a ser: *his daughter became his only consolation*, su hija llegó a ser su único consuelo. || Cumplir: *he'll become 21 next week*, cumplirá 21 años la semana que viene. || Convertirse en, transformarse en: *he became another man*, se convirtió en otro hombre; *tadpoles become frogs*, los renacuajos se transforman en ranas. || — *To become king*, subir al trono. || *To become known*, empezar a ser conocido. || *To become of*, ser de: *what has become of your friend?*, ¿qué ha sido de tu amigo?; *I wonder what has become of them*, no sé qué habrá sido de ellos.
— V. tr. Sentar bien, favorecer: *that dress really becomes her*, ese vestido le sienta muy bien. || Ser propio de, convenir a: *such language does not become a young lady*, ese lenguaje no es propio de una señorita.
— OBSERV. Pret. ***became***; p. p. ***become***.
— *Volverse* generally indicates a permanent state; *ponerse* a temporary state; *llegar a* a transformation which implies an effort; *quedarse*, an involuntary transformation.
— *To become* followed by an adjective may often be rendered in Spanish by a verb alone: *to become rich*, enriquecerse; *to become old*, envejecer; *to become thin*, adelgazar.

becoming [—iŋ] adj. Favorecedor, ra (attractive). || Apropiado, da (proper): *becoming to the occasion*, apropiado para el caso.
— N. PHIL. Devenir, *m.*
bed [bed] n. Cama, *f.*: *I can't sleep in this bed*, no puedo dormir en esta cama; *a hospital with five hundred beds*, un hospital con quinientas camas. || Lecho, *m.* (for animals). || Colchón, *m.* (mattress). || Macizo, *m.*, cuadro, *m.*, arriate, *m.* (of flowers): *a bed of roses*, un macizo de rosas. || Lecho, *m.*, fondo, *m.*, cauce, *m.* (of river). || Fondo, *m.* (of sea). || Banco, *m.*: *oyster bed*, banco de ostras; *coral bed*, banco de coral. || Firme, *m.* (of road, railway). || Capa, *f.* (of plaster). || GEOL. Capa, *f.*, yacimiento, *m.*, estrato, *m.* (stratum). || PRINT. Pletina, *f.* (of press). || TECH. Bancada, *f.* (of machine). | Base, *f.*, apoyo, *m.* (support). | Lecho, *m.*: *pig bed*, lecho de colada. || MIL. Armón, *m.* (of gun carriage). || MAR. Basada, *f.* (cradle). | Cama, *f.* (of ship's bottom in the mud). || — *Bed and board*, pensión completa. || *Bed and breakfast*, cama y desayuno. || *Child of the second bed*, hijo (*m.*) del segundo matrimonio. || *Death bed*, lecho de muerte. || *Double bed*, cama de matrimonio. || *Separation from bed and board*, separación (*f.*) matrimonial. || *Single bed*, cama individual. || *To be brought to bed of a boy*, dar a luz un niño. || FIG. *To be on a bed of roses*, estar en un lecho de rosas. | *To get out of bed on the wrong side*, levantarse con el pie izquierdo. || *To give s.o. a bed for the night*, alojar *or* hospedar a alguien una noche. || *To go to bed*, acostarse. || *To make the beds*, hacer las camas. || *To put s.o. to bed*, acostar a alguien. || *To stay in bed*, guardar cama (because of an illness). || *To take to one's bed*, meterse en la cama, guardar cama. || *Twin beds*, camas separadas *or* gemelas.
bed [bed] v. tr. Alojar, dar cama a: *he was unable to bed all the guests*, no pudo alojar a todos los invitados. || Fijar, asentar, colocar (to fix). || — *To bed down*, acostar, meter en la cama. || *To bed out*, plantar en un macizo (flowers).
— V. intr. *To bed down*, acostarse.
bedaub [biˈdɔ:b] v. tr. Embadurnar (with paint, etc.).
bedazzle [biˈdæzl] v. tr. Deslumbrar.
bedbug [ˈbedbʌg] n. Chinche, *f.* (insect).
bedchamber [ˈbedˌtʃeimbə*] n. Alcoba, *f.*, dormitorio, *m.*
bedclothes [ˈbedkləuðz] pl. n. Ropa (*f. sing.*) de cama.

bedcover [ˈbed,kʌvə*] n. Colcha, *f.*, cubrecama, *m.*
bedding [ˈbediŋ] n. Ropa (*f.*) de cama (bedclothes). || Cama, *f.*, lecho, *m.* (for animals). || ARCH. Asiento, *m.*, fundamento, *m.* || GEOL. Estratificación, *f.*
bedeck [biˈdek] v. tr. Adornar, engalanar.
bedevil [biˈdevl] v. tr. Endemoniar (to beset with devils). || Molestar, importunar (to pester): *to bedevil s.o. with questions*, importunar con preguntas a alguien. || Agravar, empeorar (to aggravate). || Estropear (to spoil). || Complicar (to make more complex).
bedevilment [—mənt] n. Molestia, *f.* (vexation). || Posesión (*f.*) diabólica (possession by a devil).
bedew [biˈdju:] v. tr. Humedecer, bañar.
bedfellow [ˈbed,feləu] n. Compañero (*m.*) *or* compañera (*f.*) de cama.
bedgown [ˈbedgaun] n. Camisón, *m.*, camisa (*f.*) de dormir.
bedhead [ˈbedhed] n. Cabecera, *f.*
bedim [biˈdim] v. tr. Nublar, oscurecer (to cloud). || Amortiguar (the light).
bedizen [biˈdaizn] v. tr. Engalanar (to overadorn).
bed jacket [ˈbed,dʒækit] n. Mañanita, *f.*
bedlam [ˈbedləm] n. Algarabía, *f.*, alboroto, *m.* (uproar, confusion). || Casa (*f.*) de locos (madhouse).
bed linen [ˈbed,linən] n. Ropa (*f.*) blanca.
Bedouin [ˈbeduin] adj./n. Beduino, na.
bedpan [ˈbedpæn] n. Cuña, *f.*, orinal (*m.*) de cama. || Calentador (*m.*) de cama (to warm the bed).
bedplate [ˈbedpleit] n. Bancada, *f.*, placa (*f.*) de asiento.
bedpost [ˈbedpəust] n. Columna (*f.*) *or* pilar (*m.*) de la cama. || FIG. *Between you and me and the bedpost*, dicho sea entre nosotros.
bedraggled [biˈdrægld] adj. Manchado de barro (stained). || FIG. En ruinas: *bedraggled buildings*, edificios en ruinas.
bedrid [ˈbedrid] or **bedridden** [ˈbedridn] adj. Postrado en cama.
bedrock [ˈbedrɔk] n. GEOL. Roca (*f.*) de fondo, roca (*f.*) firme. || FIG. Base, *f.* (basis). | Fondo (*m.*) de la cuestión: *to get down to bedrock*, ir al fondo de la cuestión.
bedroom [ˈbedrum] n. Dormitorio, *m.*, alcoba, *f.*, cuarto, *m.* [de dormir], habitación, *f.* [*Amer.*, recámara, *f.*]: *John is working in his bedroom*, Juan está trabajando en su cuarto. || — *Bedroom farce*, vodevil, *m.*, comedia ligera. || *Bedroom slipper*, zapatilla, *f.*
bedroomed [—d] adj. *A three-bedroomed house*, una casa con tres dormitorios.
bedside [ˈbedsaid] adj. De noche: *bedside table, lamp*, mesilla, lámpara de noche. || De cabecera: *bedside book*, libro de cabecera. || MED. *Bedside manner*, comportamiento (*m.*) con un enfermo.
— N. Cabecera, *f.*: *she was at his bedside when he died*, estaba a su cabecera cuando murió.
bed-sitter [ˈbed,sitə*] or **bed-sitting-room** [ˈbedˈsitiŋrum] n. Estudio, *m.*, apartamento, *m.* (one-room apartment). || Salón (*m.*) con cama (in a flat).
bedsore [ˈbedsɔ:*] n. MED. Escara, *f.*, llaga, *f.*, úlcera, *f.*
bedspread [ˈbedspred] n. Colcha, *f.*, cubrecama, *m.*
bedstead [ˈbedsted] n. Marco (*m.*) *or* armazón (*m.*) de la cama, cuja, *f.*
bedtime [ˈbedtaim] n. Hora (*f.*) de acostarse.
Beduin [ˈbeduin] adj./n. Beduino, na.
bed warmer [ˈbed,wɔ:mə*] n. (Ant.). Calentador (*m.*) de cama.
bee [bi:] n. Abeja, *f.* (insect). || MAR. Violín, *m.* (of bowsprit). || U. S. Reunión, *f.*, tertulia, *f.* (social gathering). | Concurso, *m.* (contest). || — FIG. *Busy as a bee*, muy ocupado. || *Carpenter bee*, abeja carpintera. || *Queen bee*, abeja maesa *or* maestra *or* reina. || FIG. *To have a bee in one's bonnet*, estar obsesionado (to have an obsession), estar mal de la cabeza (to be mad). || *Worker bee*, abeja obrera *or* neutra.
beech [bi:tʃ] n. BOT. Haya, *f.* (tree). || BOT. *Beech grove*, hayal, *m.*
beechen [ˈbi:tʃən] adj. De haya.
beech mast [ˈbi:tʃmɑ:st] n. BOT. Hayucos, *m. pl.*
beechnut [ˈbi:tʃnʌt] n. BOT. Hayuco, *m.*
beech tree [ˈbi:tʃtri:] n. BOT. Haya, *f.*
bee-eater [ˈbi:,i:tə*] n. ZOOL. Abejaruco, *m.* (bird).
beef [bi:f] n. Carne (*f.*) de vaca, vaca, *f.* (meat). || Ganado (*m.*) vacuno (cattle). || FAM. Fuerza (*f.*) muscular, músculos, *m. pl.* (strength). | Corpulencia, *f.*, carnes, *f. pl.* (fat). || U. S. FAM. Queja, *f.* (complaint). || — *Chilled beef*, carne de vaca refrigerada. || *Roast beef*, rosbif, *m.* || *Salt beef*, carne de vaca salada.
— OBSERV. El plural de *beef* puede ser *beeves* o *beefs*, este último sobre todo en Estados Unidos.
beef [bi:f] v. intr. U. S. Quejarse.
beefeater [ˈbi:f,i:tə*] n. Alabardero (*m.*) de la Torre de Londres.
beefsteak [ˈbi:fˈsteik] n. Bistec, *m.* [*Amer.*, bife, *m.*].
beef tea [ˈbi:fˈti:] n. Concentrado (*m.*) de carne.
beefy [ˈbi:fi] adj. Fornido, da; fuerte.
bee glue [ˈbi:,glu:] n. Propóleos, *m.*
beehive [ˈbi:haiv] n. Colmena, *f.*
Beirut [beiˈru:t] pr. n. GEOGR. Beirut.
beekeeper [ˈbi:,ki:pə*] n. Apicultor, ra.
beekeeping [ˈbi:,ki:piŋ] n. Apicultura, *f.*
beeline [ˈbi:lain] n. Línea (*f.*) recta. || *To make a beeline for sth.*, ir derecho hacia algo.
Beelzebub [biˈelzibʌb] pr. n. Belcebú, *m.*
been [bi:n] p. p. See BE.
beer [biə*] n. Cerveza, *f.*: *dark, light beer*, cerveza negra, dorada. || — *Draught beer*, cerveza de barril. || FIG. *It's not all beer and skittles*, no todo es coser y cantar. | *Life is not all beer and skittles*, la vida no es un lecho de rosas. | *To think no small beer of o.s.*, creerse alguien.
beer glass [—glɑ:s] n. Jarra (*f.*) de cerveza, bock, *m.*
beerhouse [—haus] n. Cervecería, *f.*
beery [ˈbiəri] adj. Que huele a cerveza (smelling of beer). || — *Beery voice*, voz aguardentosa. || *It was a beery affair*, allí se bebió mucho.
beestings [ˈbi:stiŋz] pl. n. Calostro (*m.*) de la vaca.
beeswax [ˈbi:zwæks] n. Cera (*f.*) de abejas.
beeswing [ˈbi:zwiŋ] n. Capa (*f.*) de tártaro [en el vino añejo].
beet [bi:t] n. Remolacha, *f.*: *sugar beet*, remolacha azucarera.
— Adj. Remolachero, ra (industry).
beetle [ˈbi:tl] n. Escarabajo, *m.* (insect). || Mano, *f.* (of a mortar). || Mazo, *m.* (mallet). || TECH. Batán, *m.* (cloth-beating machine). | Martinete, *m.* (tool for crushing). | Pisón, *m.* (for paving). || FIG. FAM. *To be blind as a beetle*, no ver tres en un burro.
beetle [ˈbi:tl] v. tr. Golpear (to beat). || Aplastar con pisón.
— V. intr. Sobresalir amenazadoramente (to jut out): *the beetling crags*, los peñascos que sobresalen amenazadoramente.
beetle-browed [—braud] adj. Cejijunto, ta (having bushy eyebrows). || Ceñudo, da (frowning).
beetle-crusher [—,krʌʃə*] n. FAM. Zapato, *m.*, bota, *f.* (boot).
beetroot [ˈbi:tru:t] n. Remolacha, *f.*
beet sugar [ˈbi:t,ʃugə*] n. Azúcar (*m.*) de remolacha.
befall* [biˈfɔ:l] v. tr. Acontecer a: *all the misfortunes which befell the family*, todas las desgracias que acontecieron a la familia.
— V. intr. Acontecer (to happen).
— OBSERV. Pret. **befell**; p. p. **befallen**.
— Este verbo se usa únicamente en tercera persona.
befallen [biˈfɔ:lən] p. p. See BEFALL.
befell [biˈfel] pret. See BEFALL.
befit [biˈfit] v. tr. Convenir a, corresponder a: *he should behave as befits a man of his age*, debería comportarse como corresponde a un hombre de su edad.
befitting [—iŋ] adj. Propio, pia; conveniente.
befog [biˈfɔg] v. tr. Envolver en niebla: *the town was befogged*, la ciudad estaba envuelta en niebla. || FIG. Nublar, oscurecer: *smoke befogged the room*, el humo nublaba la habitación; *the drink befogged his senses*, la bebida nublaba sus sentidos. | Confundir (to confuse).
befool [biˈfu:l] v. tr. Engañar (to deceive).
before [biˈfɔ:*] adv. Antes (earlier): *two weeks before*, dos semanas antes; *I will give it to you tomorrow, not before*, te lo daré mañana, no antes; *why didn't you tell me before?*, ¿por qué no me lo dijiste antes? || Anterior, antes: *the night before*, la noche anterior, la noche antes. || Anterior: *the page before*, la página anterior. || Delante, por delante: *there were trees before and behind*, había árboles delante y detrás *or* por delante y por detrás. || Ya (already): *have you been to England before?*, ¿ha estado usted ya en Inglaterra?; *we have tried that before*, ya lo hemos intentado. || — *A short time before* o *not long before*, poco antes. || *As never before*, como nunca. || *Before long*, dentro de poco. || *Have you seen him before?*, ¿le ha visto usted alguna vez? || *I have never seen him before*, no le he visto nunca. || *I have seen him before somewhere*, le he visto en alguna parte. || *Long before* o *a long time before*, mucho antes. || *The one before*, el anterior, la anterior. || *To go on before*, adelantarse.
— Prep. Delante de: *to stand before the fire*, estar de pie delante del fuego; *to tell s.o. off before the whole class*, regañarle a uno delante de toda la clase. || Antes de (with an idea of order): *the last street before the traffic lights*, la última calle antes de los semáforos; *the day before the wedding*, el día antes de la boda. || Ante: *before God and men*, ante Dios y ante los hombres; *to appear before the judge*, comparecer ante el juez; *he had a brilliant future before him*, un brillante futuro se abría ante él. || Antes que: *he arrived before me*, llegó antes que yo; *I would choose this coat before any other*, escogería este abrigo antes que cualquier otro. || — *Before all else*, ante todo (above all), antes que nada (first of all). || *Before Christ*, antes de Jesucristo. || *Before speaking*, antes de hablar. || *Income before tax*, renta (*f.*) antes de deducir los impuestos. || *Ladies before gentlemen*, las señoras primero. || *The day before yesterday*, antes de ayer. || *The motion before the House*, la moción presentada ante las Cortes *or* sometida a las Cortes (in Parliament). || *The question before us*, el asunto que tenemos que discutir. || *The work I have before me*, el trabajo que tengo por delante. || *To have before one*, tener ante los ojos. || *To put love before honour*, anteponer el amor al honor.
— Conj. Antes de que (followed by the subjunctive): *before anybody notices*, antes de que nadie se dé cuenta. || Antes de (followed by an infinitive): *before I go out I must write to my parents*, antes de salir

tengo que escribir a mis padres. || FAM. *Before you know where you are*, antes de que te des cuenta.

— OBSERV. *Antes de* may only be used to translate the conjunction *before* when the subject of the two clauses is the same: *before we go we must call John*, antes de salir tenemos que llamar a Juan: but *before we go I must tell you something*, antes de que salgamos tengo que decirte algo.

beforehand [bi'fɔ:hænd] adv. Antes: *to come an hour beforehand*, venir una hora antes; *you should have told me beforehand*, me lo deberías haber dicho antes. || De antemano, con anticipación: *to make preparations beforehand*, hacer preparativos de antemano. || Por adelantado: *to ask to be paid beforehand*, pedir ser pagado por adelantado. || Ya (already).

befoul [bi'faul] v. tr. Ensuciar (to make dirty). || FIG. Manchar.

befriend [bi'frend] v. tr. Ofrecer amistad a (to offer friendship to). || Ayudar (to help).

befuddled [bi'fʌdld] adj. Atontado, da [por la bebida]. || Perplejo, ja; atónito, ta (perplexed).

beg [beg] v. intr. Mendigar (to ask for charity): *he begged from door to door*, mendigaba de puerta en puerta. || Pedir limosna (to ask for alms). || Rogar: *make less noise, I beg of you*, les ruego que no hagan tanto ruido. || Pedir (animals). || — *I beg to differ*, siento disentir. || *I beg to inform you that*, tengo el honor de informarles de que. || *I beg to remind you that*, ruego que me permita recordarle que. || FIG. *It's going begging*, nadie lo quiere [aceptar, comprar, etc.]. || *To beg for mercy*, implorar compasión. || *To beg off*, disculparse. || *To beg off the afternoon*, pedir la tarde libre.

— V. tr. Mendigar: *she begged a meal*, mendigó una comida. || Pedir (to ask for): *they begged forgiveness*, pidieron perdón. || Rogar, suplicar (to entreat): *she begged him not to do it*, le rogó que no lo hiciese; *I beg you!*, ¡se lo suplico! || — *Begging the question*, petición (*f.*) de principio. || *I beg your pardon!*, see PARDON. || *To beg s.o. off from a duty*, pedir que dispensen a alguien de una obligación. || *To beg the question*, incurrir en una petición de principio.

began [bi'gæn] pret. See BEGIN.

beget* [bi'get] v. tr. Engendrar, procrear (children). || FIG. Engendrar (consequences). || REL. *The Only Begotten of the Father*, el Unigénito del Padre.

— OBSERV. Pret. **begot, begat** (ant.): p. p. **begotten.**

beggar ['begə*] n. Mendigo, ga; pordiosero, ra (one who begs). || FAM. Tío, tía: *the silly beggar!*, ¡qué tío más tonto! || — *Beggars can't be choosers*, a caballo regalado no le mires el diente. || *Beggar's opera*, ópera (*f.*) de cuatro peniques. || *Poor beggar!*, ¡pobre diablo! || *You little beggar!*, ¡sinvergüenza!

beggar ['begə*] v. tr. Arruinar, empobrecer (to impoverish). || *To beggar description*, superar toda descripción.

beggarly [—li] adj. Miserable, pobre (miserable). || Mezquino, na (mean). || *Beggarly wage*, sueldo (*m.*) de hambre.

beggar-my-neighbour (U. S. **beggar-my-neighbor**) [—mi'neibə*] n. Juego (*m.*) de naipes infantil parecido a la guerrilla.

beggary [—ri] n. Mendicidad, *f.* || Miseria, *f.* (extreme poverty). || Mendigos, *m. pl.* (beggars).

begin* [bi'gin] v. tr./intr. Empezar, comenzar: *begin when you are ready*, empiecen Uds. cuando estén listos; *when the world began*, cuando comenzó el mundo; *to begin a letter*, empezar una carta. || — *Beginning from Monday*, a partir del lunes. || *Not to begin to*, distar mucho de, estar muy lejos de: *he does not begin to meet the requirements*, está muy lejos de satisfacer los requisitos; no encontrar palabras para: *I can't even begin to thank you for your hospitality*, no encuentro palabras para agradecerle su hospitalidad. || *To begin at the beginning*, empezar por el principio. || *To begin by doing sth.*, empezar por hacer algo *or* haciendo algo. || *To begin on sth.*, emprender algo. || *To begin talks*, entablar negociaciones. || *To begin to do sth.* o *doing sth.*, empezar a hacer algo. || *To begin with*, para empezar, en primer lugar (first of all), empezar con (to start with).

— OBSERV. *To begin* va seguido por el infinitivo o por el gerundio.
— Pret. **began;** p. p. **begun.**

beginner [bi'ginə*] n. Principiante, ta. || Iniciador, ra.

beginning [bi'giniŋ] n. Principio, *m.*, comienzo, *m.*: *the beginning of the end*, el principio del fin; *the beginning of the world, of the book*, el principio del mundo, del libro. || Origen, *m.*, causa, *f.* (cause): *nobody knew what the beginning of the feud was*, nadie sabía cuál era el origen de la enemistad. || Orígenes, *m. pl.* (origins): *the political beginning of a country*, los orígenes políticos de un país. || Principios, *m. pl.*: *at the beginning of the month, the year*, a principios de mes, de año. || — *Beginning with*, a partir de. || *From beginning to end*, desde el principio hasta el final. || *In the beginning*, al principio. || *To make a beginning*, empezar.

begone! [bi'gɔn] interj. (Ant.). ¡Retiraos!, ¡fuera de aquí!

begonia [bi'gəunjə] n. BOT. Begonia, *f.*

begoniaceae [bigəun'jəsii] pl. n. BOT. Begoniáceas, *f.*

begot [bi'gɔt] pret. See BEGET.

begotten [bi'gɔtn] p. p. See BEGET.

begrime [bi'graim] v. tr. Tiznar, ennegrecer, ensuciar (to blacken): *the begrimed faces of the miners*, las caras tiznadas de los mineros.

begrudge [bi'grʌdʒ] v. tr. Regatear, escatimar (to quibble over): *the government does not begrudge the money it spends on education*, el gobierno no regatea el dinero que gasta en la educación. || Doler [a uno]: *he begrudges spending money on repairs*, le duele gastar dinero en reparaciones. || Envidiar (to envy): *to begrudge s.o. his good fortune*, envidiarle a alguien su buena suerte.

— OBSERV. The idea of reluctance given by the verb *to begrudge* may often be rendered in Spanish by the adverbial phrases *a disgusto, de mala gana* (reluctantly): *to begrudge giving, doing sth.*, dar, hacer algo a disgusto.

begrudgingly [—iŋli] adv. A disgusto, de mala gana, a regañadientes.

beguile [bi'gail] v. tr. Engañar (to deceive): *he realized he had been beguiled*, se dio cuenta de que le habían engañado. || Seducir (to seduce): *beguiled by vague promises*, seducido por vagas promesas. || Entretener (one's leisure). || Aliviar (to relieve): *to beguile the tedium of a long voyage*, aliviar el tedio de un largo viaje. || — *To beguile s.o. into doing sth.*, inducir a alguien a hacer algo. || *To beguile s.o. out of sth.*, robar algo a alguien engañándole (to steal sth. from s.o.). || *To beguile the time doing sth.*, entretenerse haciendo algo.

Beguine ['begi:n] n. REL. Beguina, *f.*

begum ['beigəm] n. Begum, *f.*

begun [bi'gʌn] p. p. See BEGIN.

behalf [bi'hɑ:f] n. *On behalf of*, en nombre de: *I thank you on behalf of my country*, les doy las gracias en nombre de mi país; en nombre de, de parte de: *they asked me to thank you on their behalf*, me pidieron que les diese las gracias en su nombre *or* de su parte; de parte de: *he went to see the boss on my behalf*, fue de mi parte a ver al jefe; por: *don't worry yourself on my behalf*, no te preocupes por mí; en favor de, por: *to plead on s.o.'s behalf*, abogar por alguien, hablar en favor de alguien; para: *a collection on behalf of old people*, una colecta para los ancianos. || *On behalf of my colleagues and myself*, en nombre de mis colegas y en el mío propio.

behave [bi'heiv] v. intr. Comportarse, portarse, conducirse (to conduct o.s.): *to behave badly*, comportarse mal. || Portarse *or* comportarse bien: *tell the children to behave*, di a los niños que se porten bien. || Funcionar (a machine). || — *Behave yourself!*, ¡pórtate bien! || *That is no way to behave*, no es manera de portarse. || *To behave towards*, tratar.

behaviour (U. S. **behavior**) [bi'heivjə*] n. Conducta, *f.*, comportamiento, *m.* (conduct). || TECH. Funcionamiento, *m.* (of a machine). | Comportamiento, *m.*: *the behaviour of steel under pressure*, el comportamiento del acero bajo presión. || *To be on one's best behaviour*, portarse de la mejor manera posible.

behaviourism (U. S. **behaviorism**) [—rizəm] n. Behaviorismo, *m.*

behead [bi'hed] v. tr. Decapitar, degollar, descabezar.

beheld [bi'held] pret. & p. p. See BEHOLD.

behest [bi'hest] n. Mandato, *m.* (command): *at divine behest*, por mandato divino. || Petición, *f.*, requerimiento, *m.* (request): *he did it at his friends' behest*, lo hizo a petición de sus amigos.

behind [bi'haind] adv. Detrás, atrás: *there are two cars behind*, hay dos coches detrás; *is there anything behind?*, ¿hay algo atrás? || Detrás: *they approached me from behind*, se acercaron a mí por detrás. || Por detrás (around the back). || De atrás: *the one behind*, el de atrás. || — *The holidays already seem a long way behind*, las vacaciones parecen muy lejanas. || *To attack s.o. from behind*, atacar a alguien por la espalda. || *To be behind*, estar atrasado (a clock), ir con *or* llevar retraso (train, etc.): *the train was an hour behind*, el tren iba con *or* llevaba una hora de retraso; estar retrasado *or* atrasado: *to be behind in one's studies, with one's rent*, estar atrasado en los estudios, en el pago del alquiler. || *To be behind with one's work*, tener trabajo atrasado. || *To fall* o *to lag behind*, quedarse atrás. || *To follow close behind*, seguir muy de cerca. || *To leave behind*, dejar: *we can't leave the dog behind*, no podemos dejar el perro; dejar atrás (in a race, etc.): *they left him a long way behind*, le dejaron muy atrás; olvidarse, dejarse (to forget). || *To look behind*, mirar [hacia] atrás. || *To stay* o *to remain behind*, quedarse: *only a small group stayed behind*, sólo un pequeño grupo se quedó; quedar (to be left).

— Prep. Detrás de: *behind the house*, detrás de la casa; *I would like to know what is behind all that*, me gustaría saber qué hay detrás de todo eso. || Por debajo de (below): *our sales are far behind those of last year*, nuestras ventas están muy por debajo de las del año pasado. || Tras, detrás de: *he left a good memory behind him*, dejó un buen recuerdo tras él; *the storm left a trail of destruction behind it*, la tormenta dejó un rastro de destrucción tras ella. || — *Behind one's back*, see BACK. || *Behind the scenes*, entre bastidores. || *To be behind schedule*, llevar retraso (train, boat, etc.), estar atrasado (with one's work). || *To be behind s.o.*, apoyarle a uno (to support s.o.), estar más atrasado que uno: *this country is far behind its neighbours*, este país está mucho más atrasado que sus vecinos; *she is rather behind the rest of the class*, está bastante más atrasada que el resto de la clase. || *To look behind one*, volver la cabeza, mirar hacia atrás. || *To put one's worries behind one*, relegar sus preocupaciones al olvido, dejar de lado sus preocupaciones.

— N. Trasero, *m.* (buttocks). || *To fall on one's behind*, caerse sentado.

behindhand [—hænd] adv./adj. Retrasado, da; atrasado, da: *to be behindhand with the rent*, estar retrasado en el pago del alquiler.

behold* [biˈhəuld] v. tr. (Ant.). Percibir, advertir (to see). || Considerar, ver (to envisage). || *Behold!*, ¡mirad!

— OBSERV. Pret. & p. p. **beheld.**

beholden [biˈhəuldən] adj. Agradecido, da (grateful): *I am very beholden to you*, le estoy muy agradecido.

beholder [biˈhəuldə*] n. Espectador, ra.

behove [biˈhəuv] (U. S. **behoove**) [biˈhu:v] v. impers. Incumbir (to be necessary for): *it behoves the scientist to work objectively*, incumbe al científico trabajar objetivamente. || Corresponder (to befit): *he plays as behoves the son of a great pianist*, toca como corresponde al hijo de un gran pianista; *it ill behoves him to criticize*, no le corresponde criticar.

— V. intr. Ser propio (to be fitting). || Ser menester (to be necessary).

beige [beiʒ] adj. Beige, de color beige.

— N. Beige, *m.*

being [ˈbi:iŋ] n. Ser, *m.*: *human being*, ser humano. || Existencia, *f.*, ser, *m.* (existence): *the mother who gave me my being*, la madre que me dio el ser. || Esencia, *f.* (essence). || REL. PHIL. Ser, *m.*: *the Supreme Being*, el Ser Supremo. || — *In being*, existente. || *To bring into being*, realizar (a plan), engendrar (to beget), crear (to create). || *To come into being*, nacer, aparecer.

— Adj. *For the time being*, por el momento, de momento.

— Conj. *Being as* o *being that*, puesto que, ya que.

Beirut [beiˈru:t] pr. n. GEOGR. Beirut.

bejesus [biˈdʒi:zəs] interj. FAM. ¡Vaya por Dios! || FAM. *To kick the bejesus out of s.o.*, molerle a palos a uno.

bejewel [biˈdʒu:əl] v. tr. Enjoyar, alhajar.

bel [bel] n. PHYS. Bel, *m.*, belio, *m.*

belabour (U. S. **belabor**) [biˈleibə*] v. tr. (Ant.). Azotar, apalear (to beat). || Extenderse sobre (a subject).

belated [biˈleitid] adj. Tardío, a; demorado, da: *belated congratulation*, felicitación tardía. || Atrasado, da (out of date). || Retrasado, da (delayed).

belaud [biˈlɔ:d] v. tr. Alabar, ensalzar.

belay [biˈlei] n. Asidero, *m.* (hold in mountaineering).

belay [biˈlei] v. tr. MAR. Amarrar (to secure). || Asegurar (in mountaineering).

— V. intr. Amarrarse (cables). || FIG. *Belay!*, ¡basta ya!

belaying pin [—iŋpin] n. MAR. Cabilla, *f.*

belch [beltʃ] n. Eructo, *m.*, regüeldo, *m.* (burp).

belch [beltʃ] v. tr. FIG. Arrojar, vomitar: *to belch fire*, arrojar fuego.

— V. intr. Eructar (to burp).

beleaguer [biˈli:gə*] v. tr. Sitiar, asediar, cercar.

belemnite [ˈbeləmnait] n. Belemnita, *f.* (fossil).

belfry [ˈbelfri] n. Campanario, *m.*

Belgian [ˈbeldʒən] adj./n. Belga.

Belgium [ˈbeldʒəm] pr. n. GEOGR. Bélgica, *f.*

Belgrade [belˈgreid] pr. n. GEOGR. Belgrado.

belie [biˈlai] v. tr. Desmentir, contradecir (to contradict): *to belie a proverb*, desmentir un refrán. || Contrastar con (to contrast with): *his hard eyes belied his delicate features*, sus ojos fríos contrastaban con sus delicadas facciones. || Defraudar (to disappoint): *to belie one's expectations*, defraudar sus esperanzas.

— OBSERV. El gerundio de este verbo es **belying.**

belief [biˈli:f] n. Creencia, *f.*: *my political, religious beliefs*, mis creencias políticas, religiosas; *belief in God*, creencia en Dios. || REL. Fe, *f.* (faith): *the war of belief against unbelief*, la guerra de la fe contra la incredulidad. || Confianza, *f.* (confidence): *he has no belief in doctors*, no tiene confianza en los médicos. || Crédito, *m.*: *unworthy of belief*, que no merece crédito. || — *Beyond belief*, increíble. || *In the firm belief that*, en la firme creencia de que. || *It is common belief that*, es creencia popular que. || *It is my belief that*, estoy convencido de que. || *To the best of my belief*, a mi entender, que yo sepa.

believable [biˈli:vəbl] adj. Creíble, verosímil: *a believable explanation*, una explicación verosímil.

believe [biˈli:v] v. intr. Creer: *to believe in God*, creer en Dios. || Ser partidario de (to be in favour of): *I don't believe in smoking*, no soy partidario del tabaco. || — *I believe not*, creo que no. || *I believe so*, creo que sí. || *To make believe*, fingir.

— V. tr. Creer: *I believe you*, te creo; *I believe it is going to rain*, creo que va a llover. || — *Believe me!*, ¡créeme! || *Don't you believe it!*, ¡no te lo creas! || *He is believed to be in London*, se cree *or* se supone que está en Londres. || *To believe one's ears, one's eyes*, dar crédito a sus oídos, a sus ojos.

believer [—ə*] n. Creyente, *m.* & *f.* || Partidario, ria: *a firm believer in corporal punishment*, un firme partidario del castigo corporal.

Belisarius [beliˈsɛəriəs] pr. n. Belisario, *m.*

belittle [biˈlitl] v. tr. Empequeñecer, hacer parecer más pequeño: *the new tower belittles the surrounding houses*, la nueva torre hace parecer más pequeñas las casas de alrededor. || Minimizar: *to belittle one's efforts*, minimizar los esfuerzos de uno. || Despreciar, hacer poco caso de: *don't belittle his advice*, no desprecies su consejo. || *To belittle o.s.*, rebajarse, quitarse importancia, darse poca importancia.

Belize [beˈli:z] pr. n. GEOGR. Belice, *m.*

bell [bel] n. Campana, *f.*: *church bell*, campana de la iglesia. || Campanilla, *f.* (handbell). || Timbre, *m.*: *he rang the bell and entered*, tocó el timbre y entró. || Cencerro, *m.* (of animals). || Cascabel, *m.* (of collar, toys, etc.). || Timbre, *m.* (of bicycle, alarm clock, etc.). || Bramido, *m.* (of stag). || MUS. Pabellón, *m.* (of an instrument). || BOT. Campanilla, *f.* (of flower). || MAR. Campanada, *f.* || — *Diving bell*, campana de buzo. || FIG. *It doesn't ring a bell with me*, no me suena. || *Passing bell*, campana que toca a muerto. || FIG. *Sound as a bell*, más sano que una manzana (healthy), muy seguro (very safe). | *That rings a bell*, eso me suena. || *To set all the bells ringing* o *to ring all the bells full peal*, echar las campanas al vuelo.

bell [bel] v. intr. Acampanarse (to become bell-shaped). || Bramar (a stag). || Tocar el timbre (to ring).

— V. tr. Poner un cencerro a (animals). || Poner un cascabel a (cats). || Acampanar (to make bell-shaped). || FIG. *To bell the cat*, poner el cascabel al gato.

belladonna [ˌbeləˈdɔnə] n. BOT. Belladona, *f.*

bell-bottomed [ˈbelbɔtəmd] adj. Acampanado, da.

bellboy [ˈbelbɔi] n. Botones, *m. inv.* (at the hotel).

bell buoy [ˈbelbɔi] n. Boya (*f.*) de campana.

belle [bel] n. Beldad, *f.*, belleza, *f.* (beautiful woman). || *The belle of the ball*, la reina del baile.

belles lettres [ˈbelˈletr] pl. n. Bellas letras, *f.*

bellflower [ˈbelˌflauə*] n. BOT. Campanilla, *f.*

bell gable [ˈbelgeibl] n. ARCH. Espadaña, *f.*

bell glass [ˈbelglα:s] n. See BELL JAR.

bellhop [ˈbelhɔp] n. U. S. Botones, *m. inv.* (bellboy).

bellicose [ˈbelikəus] adj. Belicoso, sa; agresivo, va (aggressive). || Guerrero, ra (warlike).

bellicosity [ˌbeliˈkɔsiti] n. Belicosidad, *f.*

bellied [ˈbelid] adj. Panzudo, da.

belligerence [biˈlidʒərəns] or **belligerency** [biˈlidʒərənsi] n. Agresividad, *f.* || Beligerancia, *f.*

belligerent [biˈlidʒərənt] adj. Beligerante (at war). || Agresivo, va (aggressive).

— N. Beligerante, *m.* & *f.*

bell jar [ˈbel-dʒα:*] n. Campana, *f.*, fanal, *m.* (to protect objects). || Campana, *f.* (to protect food). || CHEM. Campana (*f.*) de cristal.

bell-mouthed [ˈbelˌmauðd] adj. Acampanado, da.

bellow [ˈbeləu] n. Bramido, *m.*, mugido, *m.* (of animals). || Bramido, *m.*, rugido, *m.* (of guns, men in anger). || Bramido, *m.* (of tempest). || Fragor, *m.* (of thunder).

bellow [ˈbeləu] v. intr. Bramar (a bull, a cow). || FIG. Bramar, rugir, vociferar.

— V. tr. Cantar a voz en cuello (a song).

bellows [—z] pl. n. Fuelle, *m. sing.* (of a camera, etc.). || MUS. Fuelles, *m.* || *A pair of bellows*, un fuelle.

bellpull [ˈbelpul] n. Tirador, *m.*

bell ringer [ˈbelˌriŋə*] n. Campanero, *m.* || FIG. Éxito, *m.*

bell-shaped [ˈbelʃeipt] adj. Acampanado, da.

bell tent [ˈbeltent] n. Pabellón, *m.*, tienda (*f.*) de campaña cónica.

bell tower [ˈbelˌtauə*] n. Campanario, *m.*

bellwether [ˈbelˌweðə*] n. Manso, *m.* (sheep). || FIG. Cabecilla, *m.*, jefe, *m.* (leader).

belly [ˈbeli] n. Vientre, *m.*, barriga, *f.* (fam.), tripa, *f.* (fam.) [of person]. || Panza, *f.* (of animals, things): *the belly of an aeroplane*, la panza de un avión. || MAR. Seno, *m.* (of sail). || MUS. Tabla (*f.*) de armonía (of an instrument).

— OBSERV. Excepto para los animales, la palabra *belly* se emplea poco en inglés con el sentido de vientre. Se le prefiere *stomach* o incluso *tummy*, que pertenece al lenguaje infantil.

belly [ˈbeli] v. tr. Hinchar (to make swell out).

— V. intr. Hincharse (to swell out). || Pandearse (a wall).

bellyache [—eik] n. FAM. Dolor (*m.*) de tripa *or* de barriga *or* de vientre.

bellyache [—eik] v. intr. FAM. Quejarse.

bellyband [—bænd] n. Barriguera, *f.* (of horses). || Faja, *f.* (for babies).

belly button [—ˌbʌtn] n. FAM. Ombligo, *m.* (navel).

bellyflop [—flɔp] n. Panzada, *f.*, panzazo, *m.*: *the diving champion did a bellyflop*, el campeón de salto dio un panzazo. || ***Bellyflop landing*, aterrizaje (*m.*) sobre la panza.**

bellyflop [—flɔp] v. intr. Dar un panzazo. || Aterrizar sobre la panza (aircraft).

bellyful [—ful] n. FIG. FAM. Panzada, *f.*: *I have had a bellyful of studying*, me he dado una panzada de estudiar.
belly landing [—ˌlændiŋ] n. Aterrizaje (*m.*) sobre la panza (aircraft). || *To make a belly landing*, aterrizar sobre la panza.
belly laugh [—lɑ:f] n. FAM. Carcajada, *f.*: *he gave a belly laugh*, soltó una carcajada.
belong [biˈlɔŋ] v. intr. Pertenecer a, ser de: *this money belongs to him*, este dinero le pertenece, este dinero es suyo. || Ser miembro de (to a party, a society, etc.). || Ser socio: *do you belong to that country club?*, ¿eres socio de ese club de campo? || Ser de (to be native, resident): *he belongs here*, es de aquí. || Deber estar: *this dictionary belongs in every office*, este diccionario debe estar en todas las oficinas; *books placed where they don't belong*, libros colocados donde no deben estar. || Incumbir a, competir a (to be incumbent upon). || Ser propio de, corresponder a: *such amusements do not belong to his age*, tales diversiones no son propias de su edad. || Ir bien: *cheese belongs with lettuce*, el queso va bien con la lechuga. || Ir, hacer juego: *this hat doesn't belong with your coat*, este sombrero no va con tu abrigo; *stockings that don't belong*, medias que no hacen juego. || Estar en su ambiente: *you can live in Paris but you'll never belong there*, puedes vivir en París, pero nunca estarás en tu ambiente.
belongings [—iŋz] pl. n. Cosas, *f.*, pertenencias, *f.*, bártulos, *m.*, efectos (*m.*) personales.
beloved [biˈlʌvd] adj. Querido, da; amado, da.
— N. Amado, da.
below [biˈləu] adv. Abajo: *below there are people waiting*, abajo hay gente esperando. || De abajo: *the neighbours below*, los vecinos de abajo. || Por debajo: *the underground runs below*, el metro pasa por debajo. || Más abajo: *five houses below on the right*, cinco casas más abajo a la derecha; *the passage quoted below*, el pasaje citado más abajo. || *Here below*, aquí abajo (on earth).
— Prep. Debajo de: *my mother-in-law lives below us*, mi suegra vive debajo de nosotros. || Por debajo de: *below the knee*, por debajo de la rodilla; *below sea level*, por debajo del nivel del mar; *below the average*, por debajo de la media. || Inferior a: *temperatures below normal*, temperaturas inferiores a lo normal. || — *Below cost*, a un precio inferior al de coste. || *Below zero*, bajo cero. || *It is below me to answer*, no me rebajo a contestar.
belowdecks [—deks] adv. MAR. Bajo cubierta. || MAR. *To go belowdecks*, bajar.
Belshazzar [belˈʃæzə*] pr. n. Baltasar, *m.*
belt [belt] n. Cinturón, *m.*: *a leather belt*, un cinturón de cuero. || Bandolera, *f.* (shoulder belt). || Cinto, *m.* (for carrying weapons). || Zona, *f.* (area): *cotton belt*, zona algodonera. || Cinturón, *m.* (of mountains). || TECH. Correa, *f.*, cinta, *f.* || MED. Faja, *f.* || SP. Cinturón, *m.*: *black belt*, cinturón negro. || FAM. Golpe, *m.* (blow). || — *Blow below the belt*, golpe bajo. || TECH. *Continuous* o *endless belt*, correa sin fin. | *Conveyor belt*, cinta transportadora. | *Drive* o *driving belt*, correa de transmisión. || *Life belt*, cinturón salvavidas. || *Loading belt*, cinta, *f.* (of machine gun). || *Seat* o *safety belt*, cinturón de seguridad. || FIG. *To tighten one's belt*, apretarse el cinturón.
belt [belt] v. tr. Ceñir: *a dress belted with a golden chain*, un traje ceñido con una cadena dorada. || Rodear (to surround): *a house belted by trees*, una casa rodeada de árboles. || Pegar con una correa (to thrash). || Pegar (to hit). || *To belt out*, cantar a voz en grito (to sing out).
— V. intr. FAM. *To belt along*, ir a todo gas. | *To belt past*, pasar zumbando. | *To belt out*, salir pitando. | *To belt up*, cerrar el pico, callarse.
belt highway [—ˈhaiwei] n. U. S. Carretera (*f.*) de circunvalación (ring road).
belting [—iŋ] n. TECH. Correas (*f. pl.*) de transmisión. | Transmisión, *f.* || FAM. Tunda, *f.*, zurra, *f.*, paliza, *f.* (beating).
belt line [—lain] n. Línea (*f.*) de circunvalación.
belvedere [ˈbelvidiə*] n. Belvedere, *m.*, mirador, *m.*
bely [biˈlai] v. tr. See BELIE.
belying [—iŋ] pres. part. See BELIE.
bemire [biˈmaiə*] v. tr. Encenagar.
bemoan [biˈməun] v. tr. Lamentar, llorar (sth.). || Llorar (s.o.).
bemused [biˈmju:zd] adj. Abstraído, da; absorto, ta (plunged in thought). || Perplejo, ja (perplexed).
Ben [ben] pr. n. Benjamín, *m.* [diminutivo de *Benjamin*].
bench [bentʃ] n. Banco, *m.*: *she sat on a bench in the park*, se sentó en un banco en el parque. || Banco, *m.* (work table): *carpenter's bench*, banco de carpintero. || JUR. Estrado, *m.* (judge's seat). | Tribunal, *m.* (court): *the opinion of the bench*, la opinión del tribunal. || Escaño, *m.* (in Parliament). || Desnivel, *m.* (shelf of ground). || Plataforma, *f.* (at a dog show). || — *Testing bench*, banco de pruebas. || JUR. *The Bench*, la magistratura. | *To be appointed* o *raised to the bench*, ser nombrado juez. | *To be on the bench*, ser magistrado, ser juez. | *To bring before the bench*, llevar a los tribunales.
bench [bentʃ] v. tr. Exhibir (a dog). || U.S. SP. Expulsar del campo (punishment). | Retirar del juego (to rest).
bencher [—ə*] n. Decano (*m.*) del Colegio de Abogados.
bench mark [—mɑ:k] n. Cota (*f.*) de referencia (in topography). || Punto (*m.*) de referencia.
bend [bend] n. Curva, *f.* (curve): *a bend in the road*, una curva en la carretera. || Vuelta, *f.*, recodo, *m.* (turn). || Meandro, *m.*, curva, *f.* (of river). || Recodo, *m.*, ángulo, *m.* (of pipe, path). || Inclinación, *f.* (of the body). || ANAT. Sangría, *f.*, sangradura, *f.* (of elbow). || Combadura, *f.* (sag). || MAR. Nudo, *m.* (knot). || HERALD. Banda, *f.* || — Pl. Enfermedad (*f. sing.*) de los buzos. || — *Hairpin bend*, curva muy cerrada. || *Sharp bend*, curva cerrada. || FIG. *To go round the bend*, volverse loco.
bend* [bend] v. tr. Curvar, doblar: *it is not easy to bend a bar of iron*, no es fácil curvar una barra de hierro; *pain prevents him from bending his back*, el dolor le impide doblar la espalda. || Doblar (on posting magazines, photographs, etc.): *do not bend*, no doblar. || Inclinar (one's head). || Encorvar (one's back). || Combar (to cause to sag). || Doblar (one's knee). || Armar (a bow). || FIG. Dirigir (one's steps, one's eyes, military forces). | Desviar (conversation). | Dirigir, concentrar: *to bend all one's efforts to a task*, dirigir todos sus esfuerzos hacia una tarea; *he couldn't bend his mind to his studies*, no podía concentrar la mente en sus estudios. || MAR. Envergar (sail). || — *On bended knee*, arrodillado, da; de rodillas. || *To bend a key out of shape*, doblar *or* torcer una llave. || *To bend back*, doblar hacia atrás (an object), reflejar (light). || *To bend down*, inclinar. || *To bend s.o.'s will* o *to bend s.o. to one's will*, someter a alguien, someter a alguien a la voluntad de uno: *he bent her to his will*, la sometió a su voluntad. || *To bend straight*, enderezar.
— V. intr. Curvarse, doblarse: *the iron bar bent under the weight*, la barra de hierro se curvó bajo el peso. || Encorvarse (a person). || Combarse (to sag). || Desviarse, torcer (to change direction): *the road bends to the right*, la carretera se desvía a la derecha. || Inclinarse, agacharse (to stoop): *I bent to pick up the book*, me incliné para recoger el libro. || Someterse: *to bend to s.o.'s will*, someterse a la voluntad de uno. — *To bend back*, inclinarse hacia atrás. || *To bend down*, inclinarse.
— OBSERV. Pret. ***bent;*** p. p. ***bent, bended*** (ant.)
bender [—ə*] n. FAM. Juerga, *f.*: *to go on a bender* irse de juerga.
bending [—iŋ] n. Flexión, *f.*
beneath [biˈni:θ] adv. Debajo: *an awning with tables and chairs beneath*, un toldo con mesas y sillas debajo. || Abajo: *the sky above and the earth beneath*, el cielo arriba y la tierra abajo; *the mountains and the little towns beneath*, las montañas y los pueblecitos abajo.
— Prep. Bajo: *the trees bent beneath the weight*, los árboles se doblaban bajo el peso. || Debajo de: *beneath his coat*, debajo de su abrigo. || — FIG. *It's beneath you to lie*, mentir es indigno de ti. || *To be far beneath s.o.*, ser muy inferior a alguien. || *To marry beneath o.s.*, casarse con alguien de categoría *or* de clase inferior. || *You are beneath contempt*, ni siquiera eres digno de desprecio.
benedicite [ˌbeniˈdaisiti] n. REL. Benedícite, *m.*
Benedict [ˈbenidikt] pr. n. Benito, *m.* || Benedicto, *m.* (popes).
benedictine [ˌbeniˈdikti:n] n. Benedictino, *m.* (liqueur).
Benedictine [ˌbeniˈdiktin] adj./n. REL. Benedictino, na.
benediction [ˌbeniˈdikʃən] n. Bendición, *f.*: *the Pope's benediction*, la bendición papal *or* del Papa.
benedictory [ˌbeniˈdiktəri] adj. Bendecidor, ra.
benefaction [ˌbeniˈfækʃən] n. Beneficio, *m.*, favor, *m.* (contribution). || Obra (*f.*) de beneficencia (act of charity). || Donación, *f.* (charitable donation).
benefactor [ˈbenifæktə*] n. Benefactor, *m.*, bienhechor, *m.*
benefactress [ˈbenifæktris] n. Benefactora, *f.*, bienhechora, *f.*
benefice [ˈbenifis] n. REL. Beneficio, *m.*
beneficence [biˈnefisəns] n. Beneficencia, *f.*
beneficent [biˈnefisənt] adj. Benéfico, ca (influence). || Benefactor, ra (person).
beneficial [ˌbeniˈfiʃəl] adj. Beneficioso, sa; provechoso, sa (advantageous). || Benéfico, ca: *beneficial rain*, lluvia benéfica. || JUR. Usufructuario, ria.
beneficiary [ˌbeniˈfiʃəri] n. Beneficiario, ria: *contingent beneficiary*, beneficiario condicional *or* eventual. || REL. Beneficiado, *m.*
benefit [ˈbenifit] n. Beneficio, *m.*, provecho, *m.*: *to derive benefit from*, sacar beneficio de. || Ganancia, *f.* (gain). || Ventaja, *f.* (advantage). || Bien, *m.*: *I did it for your benefit*, lo hice por tu bien. || Subsidio, *m.* (allowance): *family, old age, unemployment benefit*, subsidio familiar, de vejez, de paro. || Función (*f.*) benéfica (performance). || — *Benefit match*, partido (*m.*) de homenaje (upon the retirement of a player), partido (*m.*) benéfico (for charity purposes). || JUR. *Benefit of clergy*, fuero eclesiástico. || *Benefit of the doubt*, beneficio de la duda. || U. S. *Benefit society*, mutualidad, *f.* || *For the benefit of*, en beneficio de, en provecho de: *performance for the benefit of the poor*, función en beneficio de los pobres; en honor de: *she*

put on a new hat for his benefit, se puso un nuevo sombrero en su honor. || *Let me add for your benefit that*, añadiré para su gobierno que. || *Marriage without benefit of clergy*, matrimonio que no ha sido sancionado por la Iglesia. || *To be of benefit for*, ser provechoso *or* de provecho para. || *Under the benefit of inventory*, a beneficio de inventario. || *Without benefit of*, sin la ayuda de.
benefit [ˈbenifit] v. tr. Beneficiar: *to benefit humanity*, beneficiar al género humano.
— V. intr. Beneficiar, beneficiarse: *to benefit from* o *by a law*, beneficiarse de una ley; *to benefit from the help of*, beneficiar de la ayuda de. || Sacar provecho, aprovecharse: *she benefited by his advice*, sacó provecho de su consejo.
Benelux [ˈbenilʌks] pr. n. Benelux, *m.*
benevolence [biˈnevələns] n. Benevolencia, *f.* (kindheartedness). || Generosidad, *f.* (generosity).
benevolent [biˈnevələnt] adj. Benévolo, la. || Caritativo, va (charitable). || De beneficencia (society).
Bengal [beŋˈgɔ:l] pr. n. GEOGR. Bengala, *m.* || *Bengal light*, luz (*f.*) de Bengala, bengala, *f.*
Bengalese [ˌbeŋgɔ:ˈli:z] adj./n. Bengalí.
Bengali [beŋˈgɔ:li] adj. Bengalí.
— N. Bengalí, *m.* & *f.* (people). || Bengalí, *m.* (language).
bengaline [ˈbeŋgəli:n] n. Bengalina, *f.* (material).
benighted [biˈnaitid] adj. Anochecido, da; sorprendido por la noche. || FIG. Ignorante (mind).
benign [biˈnain] adj. Benigno, na. || Favorable.
benignant [biˈnignənt] adj. Benigno, na. || Favorable.
benignity [biˈnigniti] n. Benignidad, *f.* || Bondad, *f.*
benjamin [ˈbendʒəmin] n. Benjuí, *m.*
Benjamin [ˈbendʒəmin] pr. n. Benjamín, *m.*
Benjaminite [ˈbendʒəminait] or **Benjamite** [ˈbendʒəmait] adj./n. Benjamita.
bent [bent] pret. & p. p. See BEND.
— Adj. Curvado, da; torcido, da; doblado, da. || FIG. Decidido, da; empeñado, da: *he is bent on succeeding*, está decidido a *or* empeñado en triunfar. | Inclinado, da (disposed). || — *To be bent on mischief*, abrigar malas intenciones. || *With eyes bent on*, con los ojos fijos en.
— N. Inclinación, *f.* (*for*, *towards*, a, hacia): *he followed his bent*, obró de acuerdo con sus inclinaciones. || Facilidad, *f.*: *to have a bent for languages*, tener facilidad para los idiomas. || Curvatura, *f.* (curve). || *To the top of one's bent*, hasta el máximo.
bentonite [ˈbentənait] n. GEOL. Bentonita, *f.*
benumb [biˈnʌm] v. tr. Entumecer: *benumbed by the cold*, entumecido por el frío. || FIG. Embotar, entorpecer (mind). | Dejar paralizado (shock).
benzamide [benzəˈmaid] n. CHEM. Benzamida, *f.*
benzedrine [ˈbenzəˌdrin] n. MED. Bencedrina, *f.*
benzene [ˈbenzi:n] n. CHEM. Benceno, *m.*
benzilic [benˈzilik] adj. Bencílico, ca.
benzine [ˈbenzi:n] n. CHEM. Bencina, *f.*
benzoate [ˈbenzəueit] n. CHEM. Benzoato, *m.*
benzoic [benˈzəuik] adj. CHEM. Benzoico, ca.
benzoin [ˈbenzəuin] n. CHEM. Benzoína, *f.* || BOT. CHEM. Benjuí, *m.*
benzol [ˈbenzɔl] n. CHEM. Benzol, *m.*
bequeath [biˈkwi:ð] v. tr. Legar (to will).
bequest [biˈkwest] n. Legado, *m.*
berate [biˈreit] v. tr. Regañar, reñir (to scold).
Berber [ˈbə:bə*] adj./n. Beréber, berebere, berberisco, ca.
bereave* [biˈri:v] v. tr. Privar: *the war had bereft him of all hope*, la guerra le había privado de toda esperanza; *an accident had bereft him of his father*, un accidente le había privado de su padre. || Despojar: *he was bereft of his possessions*, fue despojado de sus bienes. || — *His bereaved wife*, su desconsolada esposa. || *The bereaved*, su desconsolada familia.

— OBSERV. El verbo *to bereave* tiene dos pretéritos y dos participios pasivos: uno regular, ***bereaved***, y otro irregular, ***bereft***. El primero se emplea generalmente como participio pasivo y adjetivo con el sentido de *desconsolado*, y el segundo se utiliza como pretérito y participio pasivo cuando significa *privar* o *despojar*.

bereavement [—mənt] n. Pérdida, *f.* (of a relative). || Duelo, *m.*, luto, *m.* (mourning): *owing to a recent bereavement*, por reciente luto. || Aflicción, *f.* (sorrow).
bereft [biˈreft] pret. & p. p. See BEREAVE.
beret [ˈberei] n. Boina, *f.*
bergamot [ˈbə:gəmɔt] n. Bergamota, *f.* (fruit, perfume). || *Bergamot tree*, bergamoto, *m.*
beriberi [ˈberiˈberi] n. MED. Beriberi, *m.*
berkelium [ˈbə:kliəm] n. Berkelio, *m.*
Berlin [bə:ˈlin] pr. n. GEOGR. Berlín.
berlin [bə:ˈlin] or **berline** [bə:ˈli:n] n. Berlina, *f.*
Berliner [bə:ˈlinə*] n. Berlinés, esa.
berm [bə:m] n. Berma, *f.* (of a fortification).
Bermuda [bəˈmju:də] pr. n. GEOGR. Islas (*f. pl.*) Bermudas, Bermudas, *f. pl.*
Bermuda grass [—grɑ:s] n. BOT. Grama, *f.*
Bermuda shorts [—ˈʃɔ:ts] pl. n. Pantalones (*m.*) bermudas, bermudas, *m.*
Bern or **Berne** [bə:n] pr. n. GEOGR. Berna.
Bernadette [ˈbə:nəˈdet] pr. n. Bernarda, *f.*
Bernard [ˈbə:nəd] pr. n. Bernardo, *m.*
Bernardine [ˈbə:nədin] adj./n. REL. Bernardo, da.
Bernese [bə:ˈni:z] adj./n. Bernés, esa.
berry [ˈberi] n. BOT. Baya, *f.* || Grano, *m.* (of coffee, wheat). || Hueva, *f.* (of fish and crustacean).
berry [ˈberi] v. intr. Dar fruto.
berserk [ˈbə:sə:k] adj. Enloquecido, da. || *To go berserk*, volverse loco.
berth [bə:θ] n. Litera, *f.* (in trains). || MAR. Litera, *f.* (bunk). | Camarote, *m.* (cabin). | Atracadero, *m.*, amarradero, *m.* (at a dock). || Empleo, *m.*, puesto, *m.* (job). || FIG. *To give s.o. a wide berth*, evitar a alguien.
berth [bə:θ] v. tr. MAR. Atracar, amarrar (to moor). | Dar camarote a (to furnish with a berth). || Dar una litera a (in train).
Bertha [ˈbə:θə] pr. n. Berta, *f.*
beryl [ˈberil] n. MIN. Berilo, *m.*
beryllium [beˈriljəm] n. CHEM. Berilio, *m.*
besant [ˈbesənt] n. Bezante, *m.*, besante, *m.*
beseech* [biˈsi:tʃ] v. tr. Implorar, suplicar: *I beseech you for pardon*, le suplico que me perdone.

— OBSERV. Pret. & p. p. ***besought, beseeched.***

beseecher [—ə*] n. Suplicante, *m.* & *f.*
beseeching [—iŋ] adj. Suplicante, implorante.
beseem [biˈsi:m] v. impers. (Ant.). Convenir, ser conveniente.
beset* [biˈset] v. tr. Rodear (to surround): *the problem is beset with difficulties*, el problema está rodeado de dificultades. || Llenar (*with*, de) [to stud]. || Asaltar (to assail): *to be beset by doubts*, estar asaltado por las dudas. || Acosar, perseguir (to pursue). || Sitiar, cercar (to besiege). || Obstruir (a road). || Engastar (to enchase).

— OBSERV. Pret. & p. p. ***beset.***

besetting [—iŋ] adj. Dominante, principal (principal). || Obsesionante (temptation).
beside [biˈsaid] prep. Al lado de, junto a: *he sat beside me*, se sentó junto a mí. || Cerca de (near). || Al lado de, comparado con: *his efforts look feeble beside yours*, sus esfuerzos parecen débiles comparados con los tuyos. || Además de (in addition to). || Fuera de (aside from). || — *To be beside the point*, no tener nada que ver, no venir al caso. || *To be beside o.s.*, estar fuera de sí.
besides [—z] adv. Además: *the play is excellent, and besides the tickets cost little*, la obra es excelente y además las entradas cuestan poco. || También (also).
— Prep. Además de (in addition to): *besides being dear, it is badly made*, además de ser caro, está mal hecho. || Menos, excepto (except): *no one besides you*, nadie excepto tú.
besiege [biˈsi:dʒ] v. tr. MIL. Sitiar, asediar. || FIG. Asediar, acosar.
besieger [—ə*] n. Sitiador, ra.
besmear [biˈsmiə*] v. tr. Embadurnar, untar (to smear).
besmirch [biˈsmə:tʃ] v. tr. Manchar, ensuciar. || FIG. Manchar, mancillar.
besom [ˈbi:zəm] n. Escoba, *f.*
besot [biˈsɔt] v. tr. Atontar, embrutecer.
besought [biˈsɔ:t] pret. & p. p. See BESEECH.
bespangle [biˈspæŋgl] v. tr. Salpicar (*with*, de).
bespatter [biˈspætə*] v. tr. Salpicar (*with*, de).
bespeak* [biˈspi:k] v. tr. Apalabrar (to hire, to engage). || Dirigir la palabra a (to speak). || Demostrar, indicar (to indicate). || Encargar (a meal). || Reservar (a room).

— OBSERV. Pret. ***bespoke;*** p. p. ***bespoken, bespoke.***

bespectacled [biˈspektəkld] adj. Que lleva gafas, con gafas.
bespoke [biˈspəuk] pret. & p. p. See BESPEAK.
— Adj. Hecho a la medida (clothing). || Que confecciona a la medida (tailor).
bespoken [biˈspəukən] p. p. See BESPEAK.
besprinkle [biˈspriŋkl] v. tr. Salpicar (*with*, de) [a liquid]. || Espolvorear (*with*, de) [a powder].
Bess [bes], **Bessie** or **Bessy** [—i] pr. n. Isabelita, *f.* (diminutive of Elizabeth).
best [best] adj. [El] mejor, [la] mejor: *this colour is best for you*, este color es el mejor para ti; *the best teacher of this subject*, el mejor profesor de esta asignatura. || — *Best man*, amigo (*m.*) del novio que hace las veces de padrino en una boda. || *Best seller*, éxito (*m.*) de librería, "best seller", *m.* (book): *this novel is the best seller of the week*, esta novela es el éxito de librería de la semana. || *Best seller list*, lista (*f.*) de éxitos. || *In the best condition for*, en las mejores condiciones para. || *The best one*, el mejor, la mejor: *this is the best one*, éste es el mejor. || *The best part of*, la mayor parte de. || *To know what is best for s.o.*, saber lo que más conviene a uno.
— Adv. Mejor: *the engine runs best at night*, el motor funciona mejor por la noche. || Más: *the best looking girl*, la chica más guapa. || — *As best he could*, lo mejor que pudo. || *Honey is what bears like best*, la miel es lo que más gusta a los osos *or* lo que prefieren los osos. || *To come off best*, salir ganando. || *You had best go*, es mejor que te vayas, más vale que te vayas.
— N. Lo mejor: *I want the best for you*, quiero lo mejor para ti. || El mejor, la mejor: *she is the best of women*, es la mejor de las mujeres. || — *All the best*, felicidades, *f. pl.* (congratulations), que le vaya

bien (good luck). || *At best*, a lo más, en el mejor de los casos. || *At one's best*, en plena forma, como nunca. || *Even the best of us*, todo el mundo. || *I did it for the best*, lo hice con la mejor intención. || *It's all for the best*, es mejor así, más vale que sea así. || *It's the best there is*, es lo mejor que hay. || *Sunday best*, traje (*m.*) de los domingos, trapitos (*m. pl.*) de cristianar. || *The best of it*, lo mejor del caso. || *To be dressed in one's best*, estar de punta en blanco. || *To be the best of friends*, ser excelentes amigos, ser los mejores amigos del mundo. || *To do one's best*, hacer todo lo posible (to do one's utmost), hacer lo mejor posible (to do as well as one can). || *To do sth. to the best of one's ability*, hacer algo lo mejor posible. || *To get the best of it*, salir ganando. || *To get the best of. s.o.*, vencer *or* derrotar a alguien. || *To get the best out of*, sacar todo lo posible de. || *To look one's best*, estar muy bien, tener muy buen aspecto. || *To make the best of*, sacar el mejor partido de. || *To make the best of it*, conformarse. || *To the best of my knowledge* o *of my recollection*, que yo sepa, que yo recuerde. || *With the best (of them)*, como el que más: *he can sing with the best*, canta como el que más.

best [best] v. tr. Vencer, ganar: *she can best him at swimming*, le gana nadando.

bestial [ˈbestjəl] adj. Bestial.

bestiality [ˌbestiˈæliti] n. Bestialidad, *f.*

bestialize [ˈbestiəlaiz] v. tr. Bestializar.

bestiary [ˈbestiəri] n. Bestiario, *m.*

bestir [biˈstə:*] v. tr. *To bestir o.s.*, moverse.

bestow [biˈstəu] v. tr. Conceder, otorgar: *to bestow a medal on s.o.*, conceder una medalla a alguien. || Conferir (a title). || Dar (to give). || Dedicar (thought, time). || Colocar (to place). || Hacer: *to bestow a compliment on s.o.*, hacer un cumplido a alguien.

bestowal [biˈstəuəl] n. Concesión, *f.*, otorgamiento, *m.*

bestraddle [biˈstrædl] v. tr. See BESTRIDE.

bestrew* [biˈstru:] v. tr. Sembrar, cubrir: *bestrew with leaves*, sembrado de hojas. || Desparramar, esparcir (to scatter).

— OBSERV. Pret. ***bestrewed;*** p. p. ***bestrewed, bestrewn.***

bestrewn [—n] p. p. See BESTREW.

bestridden [biˈstridn] p. p. See BESTRIDE.

bestride* [biˈstraid] v. tr. Montar, cabalgar (a horse). || Estar sentado a horcajadas en (a chair). || Salvar, franquear (a stream).

— OBSERV. Pret. ***bestrode;*** p. p. ***bestridden.***

bestrode [biˈstrəud] pret. See BESTRIDE.

bet [bet] n. Apuesta, *f.*, puesta, *f.*, postura, *f.* || — *To lay* o *to make a bet*, hacer una apuesta. || *To lay* o *to make a bet on*, apostar a. || FIG. *Your best bet is to go at once*, lo mejor que puedes hacer es irte en seguida.

bet* [bet] v. tr. Apostar (*on*, a): *to bet two pounds on a horse*, apostar dos libras a un caballo; *I bet you two shillings that*, te apuesto dos chelines a que. || Poner (to put). || — *I bet you can't!*, ¿a que no puedes? || *You bet we had a good time!*, ¡te aseguro que lo pasamos muy bien! || *You bet!*, *you bet your life!*, ya lo creo!

— V. intr. Apostar.

— OBSERV. Pret. & p. p. ***bet, betted.***

beta [ˈbi:tə] n. Beta, *f.* || — PHYS. *Beta particle*, partícula (*f.*) beta. | *Beta ray*, rayo (*m.*) beta.

betake* [biˈteik] v. tr. (Ant.). *To betake o.s. to*, ir a (to go), entregarse a: *to betake o.s. to drink*, entregarse a la bebida.

— OBSERV. Pret. ***betook;*** p. p. ***betaken.***

betaken [—ən] p. p. See BETAKE.

betatron [ˈbi:təˌtrɔn] n. PHYS. Betatrón, *m.*

betel [ˈbi:təl] n. BOT. Betel, *m.*

betel nut [—nʌt] n. BOT. Areca, *f.* (fruit).

betel palm [—pɑ:m] n. BOT. Areca, *f.* (tree).

bête noire [ˈbeitˈnwɑ:*] n. Pesadilla, *f.* (pet aversion).

bethel [ˈbeθəl] n. Templo (*m.*) no conformista. || U. S. Capilla (*f.*) para marinos.

bethink* [biˈθiŋk] v. tr. *To bethink o.s. of*, acordarse de, recordar (to remember), pensar en (to think).

— OBSERV. Pret. & p. p. ***bethought.***

Bethlehem [ˈbeθlihem] pr. n. GEOGR. Belén.

bethought [biˈθɔ:t] pret. & p. p. See BETHINK.

betide [biˈtaid] v. tr./intr. (Ant.). Acontecer, ocurrir (to happen). || *Woe betide you!*, ¡maldito sea!, ¡maldito seas!

— OBSERV. Este verbo se emplea sólo en tercera persona del singular del presente de subjuntivo.

betimes [biˈtaimz] adv. (Ant.). Al alba, temprano (early). | A tiempo (in good time).

betoken [biˈtəukən] v. tr. Acusar, denotar, revelar (to be sign of). || Presagiar, anunciar (to foreshow).

betook [biˈtuk] pret. See BETAKE.

betray [biˈtrei] v. tr. Traicionar: *to betray one's country*, traicionar a su país. || Entregar: *to betray s.o. to the enemy*, entregar a alguien al enemigo. || Revelar (to reveal): *to betray a secret*, revelar un secreto. || Demostrar, dar muestras de: *he betrayed little intelligence*, demostró poca inteligencia. || Engañar (a woman). || Defraudar (hope, trust).

betrayal [—əl] n. Traición, *f.* (treason). || Revelación, *f.* (of ignorance, etc.). || Engaño, *m.* (of a woman).

betroth [biˈtrəuð] v. tr. Prometer en matrimonio. || *To be betrothed*, desposarse.

betrothal [—əl] n. Esponsales, *m. pl.*, desposorios, *m. pl.*

betrothed [biˈtrəuðd] adj./n. Prometido, da. || *The betrothed*, los prometidos.

— OBSERV. Las palabras *betrothal* y *betrothed* son más corrientes en Estados Unidos que en Gran Bretaña donde se prefiere usar *engagement* y *engaged*.

better [ˈbetə*] adj. Mejor: *he is better today*, está mejor hoy; *this book is better than the other one*, este libro es mejor que el otro. || Mayor: *the better part of the day*, la mayor parte del día. || — FAM. *Better half*, media naranja, cara mitad (one's wife). | *That's better*, eso está mejor, eso va mejor. | *That's better!*, ¡eso es! || *They have seen better days*, han conocido días mejores. || *To be better than one's word*, cumplir su promesa con creces. || *To be no better than*, no ser más que: *he is no better than a beggar*, no es más que un mendigo. || *To get better*, mejorar. || *To go one better*, hacer mejor todavía. || *To make sth. better*, mejorar algo.

— Adv. Mejor. || — *All the better, so much the better*, mejor, tanto mejor. || *Better and better*, cada vez mejor: *he sings better and better*, canta cada vez mejor; cada día más: *to like s.o. better and better*, apreciar a alguien cada día más. || *Better late than never*, más vale tarde que nunca. || *Better off*, más rico. || *Better than a pound*, más de una libra. || *Much better*, mucho mejor. || *The sooner the better*, cuanto antes mejor. || *To be all the better for*, haber mejorado mucho a causa de. || FAM. *To be better off*, estar mejor de dinero (economically), encontrarse mejor (happier). || *To know better*, see KNOW. || *To like better*, preferir. || *To think all the better of s.o. for*, estimar todavía más a alguien por. || *To think better of it*, cambiar de opinión. || *You had better*, es mejor que, más vale que: *you had better go*, es mejor que te vayas, más vale que te vayas.

— N. El mejor, la mejor: *the better of the two*, el mejor de los dos. || Superior, *m.*: *you must respect your betters*, debes respetar a tus superiores. || — *A change for the better*, una mejora. || *For better or worse*, para lo bueno y para lo malo, en la suerte y en la desgracia. || *For the better*, para mejorar. || *To get the better of s.o.*, vencer a alguien (to defeat), engañar a alguien (to cheat).

better [ˈbetə*] v. tr. Mejorar (to improve): *to better housing conditions*, mejorar las condiciones de alojamiento. || Superar (to surpass): *he bettered his record by five seconds*, superó su marca en cinco segundos. || *To better o.s.*, mejorar, mejorar de posición.

— V. intr. Mejorar (to improve).

better [ˈbetə*] n. Apostante, *m.* & *f.*

betterment [ˈbetəmənt] n. Mejora, *f.*, mejoría, *f.*, mejoramiento, *m.* (improvement). || JUR. Plusvalía, *f.*

betting shop [ˈbetiŋʃɔp] n. Agencia (*f.*) de apuestas hípicas.

bettor [ˈbetə*] n. Apostante, *m.* & *f.*

between [biˈtwi:n] prep. Entre: *the house is between two oaks*, la casa está entre dos robles; *between sixty and seventy*, entre sesenta y setenta; *they arrived between two and three*, llegaron entre las dos y las tres; *the difference between a mule and a horse*, la diferencia entre una mula y un caballo; *we did it between the three of us*, lo hicimos entre los tres. || — MAR. *Between decks*, entrecubierta, *f.* || *Between now and then*, de aquí a entonces. || *Between September and November*, de septiembre a noviembre. || *Between you and me, between ourselves*, entre tú y yo, entre nosotros. || *Closed between 1 and 3*, cerrado de 1 a 3. || *In between*, entre. || *To divide* o *to share between*, dividir *or* repartir entre.

— Adv. En medio, por medio, entremedias. || — *Far between*, a grandes intervalos. || *In between*, mientras tanto (meanwhile), en medio. || *To come between*, interponerse.

betweentimes [—taimz] or **betweenwhiles** [—wailz] adv. De vez en cuando (at intervals). || En el intervalo, [en el] entretanto (meanwhile).

betwixt [biˈtwikst] prep. Entre.

— Adv. En medio (between). || — *Betwixt and between*, ni una cosa ni otra: *it's betwixt and between*, no es ni una cosa ni otra. || *The truth lies betwixt and between*, hay parte de verdad en ambos casos.

bevatron [ˈbevətrən] n. PHYS. Bevatrón, *m.*

bevel [ˈbevəl] n. MATH. Ángulo oblicuo (angle). || Bisel, *m.* (surface). || — *Bevel edge*, chaflán, *m.* || *Bevel gear*, engranaje cónico. || *Bevel square*, falsa escuadra.

bevel [ˈbevəl] v. tr. Biselar.

bevelling [—iŋ] n. Biselado, *m.*

beverage [ˈbevəridʒ] n. Bebida, *f.*

bevy [ˈbevi] n. Grupo, *m.* (women). || Bandada, *f.* (birds). || Manada, *f.* (deer, etc.).

bewail [biˈweil] v. tr. Lamentar, llorar.

— V. intr. Lamentarse.

beware [biˈwɛə*] v. intr. Tener cuidado: *beware of the dog*, tenga cuidado con el perro. || *Beware!*, ¡atención!, ¡cuidado!

bewilder [biˈwildə*] v. tr. Desconcertar, desorientar, dejar perplejo (to perplex).

bewildering [—riŋ] adj. Desconcertante.
bewilderingly [—riŋli] adv. De una manera desconcertante. || *Bewilderingly beautiful*, de una belleza desconcertante.
bewilderment [—mənt] n. Desconcierto, *m.*, perplejidad, *f.*
bewitch [bi'witʃ] v. tr. Embrujar, hechizar. || FIG. Encantar, fascinar, hechizar (to fascinate).
bewitching [—iŋ] adj. Fascinante.
bey [bei] n. Bey, *m.*
beyond [bi'jɔnd] adv. Más allá, más lejos: *the river and the mountains beyond*, el río y más allá las montañas; *let us go beyond*, vayámonos más lejos.
— Prep. Más allá de: *we went beyond the river*, fuimos más allá del río; *beyond his hopes*, más allá de sus esperanzas. || Fuera de: *beyond his reach*, fuera de su alcance; *beyond his plans*, fuera de sus planes; *beyond logic*, fuera de la lógica. || Además de (besides): *beyond your regular work, you must type*, además de tu trabajo normal tienes que escribir a máquina. || Pasado, da: *beyond a certain date*, pasada cierta fecha; *beyond twelve o'clock*, pasadas las doce. || Más de: *nothing beyond what I already knew*, nada más de lo que yo ya sabía; *he is beyond sixty*, tiene más de sesenta años. || — *Beyond bearing*, intolerable. || *Beyond belief*, increíble; increíblemente. || *Beyond description*, indescriptible. || *Beyond doubt*, indudable, fuera de duda; indudablemente. || *Beyond help*, irremediable (incurable), perdido, da (lost). || *Beyond measure*, inmenso; inmensamente. || *Beyond praise*, por encima de todo elogio. || *Beyond question*, incuestionable; incuestionablemente. || *Beyond the seas*, allende los mares. || *It is beyond me*, eso está fuera de mi alcance (incomprehensible), es superior a mis fuerzas (difficult to do). || *To be living beyond one's means*, vivir por encima de sus posibilidades. || *To go beyond one's duties*, no caer dentro de las atribuciones de alguien.
beyond [bi'jɔnd] n. *The beyond*, el más allá.
Beyrouth [bei'ru:t] pr. n. GEOGR. Beirut.
bezant ['bezənt] n. Bezante, *m.*, besante, *m.*
bezel ['bezl] n. Faceta, *f.* (of cut gem). || Engaste, *m.* (holding a gem). || Bisel, *m.* (in tools).
bezoar ['bezəə*] n. Bezar, *m.*, bezaar, *m.*
bhang [bæŋ] n. BOT. Cáñamo, *m.* (hemp). | Mariguana, *f.*, marijuana, *f.*, marihuana, *f.*
biacid [bai'æsid] adj. CHEM. Biácido, da (diacid).
biannual [,bai'ænjuəl] adj. Semestral.
bias ['baiəs] n. Tendencia, *f.*: *strong liberal bias*, fuerte tendencia liberal. || Prejuicio, *m.*, prevención, *f.* (prejudice): *you judge her with bias*, le juzgas con prejuicio. || Inclinación, *f.* (*towards*, hacia, por). || SP. Descentramiento, *m.* (of the bowl). || Bies, *m.* (in sewing). || ELECTR. Voltaje (*m.*) de polarización. || — *Cut on the bias*, cortado al sesgo *or* al bies. || *Vocational bias*, deformación (*f.*) profesional.
— Adj. Al bies (in sewing).
bias ['baiəs] v. tr. Influir en, influenciar. || — *To be biased*, ser parcial. || *To be biased against*, tener prejuicio en contra de. || *To be biased in favour of*, ser partidario de.
— OBSERV. En pret. y p. p. se puede emplear tanto *biassed* como *biased*.
biaxial [bai'æksjəl] or **biaxal** [bai'æksəl] adj. Biaxial.
bib [bib] n. Babero, *m.* (for children). || Peto, *m.* (of apron, overalls). || FAM. *In one's best bib and tucker*, vestido de punta en blanco.
bibasic [bai'beisik] adj. CHEM. Bibásico, ca (dibasic).
bibber ['bibə*] n. FAM. Bebedor, *m.*
bibcock ['bibkɔk] n. Grifo, *m.*
bibelot ['bi:bələu] n. Bibelot, *m.*
Bible ['baibl] pr. n. Biblia, *f.*: *the Holy Bible*, la Santa Biblia. || *Bible paper*, papel biblia.
biblical ['biblikəl] adj. Bíblico, ca.
bibliographer [,bibli'ɔgrəfə*] n. Bibliógrafo, fa.
bibliographic [,biblia'græfik] or **bibliographical** [,biblia'græfikəl] adj. Bibliográfico, ca.
bibliography [,bibli'ɔgrəfi] n. Bibliografía, *f.*
bibliomania [,bibliəu'meinjə] n. Bibliomanía, *f.* (excessive love of books).
bibliomaniac [,bibliəu'meiniæk] n. Bibliómano, na.
bibliophile ['bibliəufail] n. Bibliófilo, la.
bibliophilism [bibli'ɔfilizəm] n. Bibliofilia, *f.*
bibulous ['bibjuləs] adj. Bebedor, ra (person). || Absorbente (paper).
bicameral ['bai'kæmərəl] adj. Bicameral.
bicameralism [bai'kæmərəlizəm] n. Bicameralismo, *m.*
bicarbide [bai'kɑ:baid] n. CHEM. Bicarburo, *m.*
bicarbonate [bai'kɑ:bənit] n. CHEM. Bicarbonato, *m.*: *bicarbonate of soda*, bicarbonato de sosa; *sodium bicarbonate*, bicarbonato sódico.
bice [bais] n. Azul (*m.*) de cobalto.
bicentenary [,baisen'ti:nəri] n. Bicentenario, *m.*
bicentennial [,baisen'tenjəl] adj. Que ocurre cada doscientos años.
— N. Bicentenario, *m.*
bicephalous [bai'sefələs] adj. Bicéfalo, la.
biceps ['baiseps] n. ANAT. Bíceps, *m.*
bichloride ['bai'klɔ:raid] n. CHEM. Bicloruro, *m.*
bichromate ['bai'krəumit] n. CHEM. Bicromato, *m.*
bicipital [bai'sipitəl] adj. Bicipital.
bicker ['bikə*] n. Disputa, *f.*, pendencia, *f.*
bicker ['bikə*] v. intr. Discutir, reñir (persons). || Murmurar (stream). || Vacilar (light).
bickiron ['bikaiən] n. Bigornia, *f.* (anvil).
bicolour (U. S. **bicolor**) ['baikʌlə*] adj. Bicolor.
biconcave [bai'kɔnkeiv] adj. Bicóncavo, va.
biconvex [bai'kɔnveks] adj. Biconvexo, xa.
bicycle ['baisikl] n. Bicicleta, *f.*: *to go by bicycle*, ir en bicicleta; *he doesn't know how to ride a bicycle*, no sabe montar en bicicleta.
bicycle ['baisikl] v. intr. Ir en bicicleta; montar en bicicleta.
bicyclist ['baisiklist] n. Ciclista, *m.* & *f.*
bid [bid] n. Oferta, *f.* (offer). || Puja, *f.*, postura, *f.* (at an auction sale). || Declaración, *f.* (in bridge). || Intento, *m.*, tentativa, *f.*: *he failed in his bid for liberty*, fracasó en su intento por conseguir la libertad. || U. S. FAM. Invitación, *f.* (to become a member). || — *Higher bid*, sobrepuja, *f.* || *To make a bid*, pujar (in an auction), declarar (to make a contract in bridge), cumplir el contrato (to score in bridge). || *To make a bid for*, intentar conseguir.
bid* [bid] v. tr. Mandar, ordenar (to command): *she bade him work*, le ordenó que trabajase. || Rogar, pedir: *I bid you be silent*, le ruego que guarde silencio. || Invitar: *to bid s.o. to dinner*, invitar a alguien a cenar. || Dar: *to bid s.o. welcome*, dar la bienvenida a alguien. || Decir (good-bye). || Ofrecer, pujar, licitar (at an auction sale): *to bid fifty pounds for*, ofrecer cincuenta libras por. || Declarar (in bridge). || — *To bid defiance to*, desafiar a. || *To bid farewell to*, despedirse de, decir adiós a. || *To bid s.o. up to twenty pounds*, obligar a alguien a hacer una postura de veinte libras.
— V. intr. Pujar, hacer una oferta (*for*, por) [at an auction sale]. || Declarar (in bridge). || — *The expedition bade fair to be successful*, parecía que la expedición iba a ser un éxito. || *To bid over s.o.*, ofrecer más que alguien. || *To bid up*, pujar.
— OBSERV. Pret. **bade** o **bid;** p. p. **bidden** o **bid**. *Bade* y *bidden* se emplean en todos los sentidos, excepto en los que se refieren a una subasta y a juegos de cartas en cuyos casos sólo se utiliza *bid*.
— En la forma activa *to bid* va seguido por el infinitivo sin *to* (*I bid him sit down*) y en la forma pasiva por el infinitivo con *to* (*he was bidden to sit down*).
biddable [—əbl] adj. Dócil, sumiso, sa.
bidden ['bidn] p. p. See BID.
bidder ['bidə*] n. Licitador, *m.*, postor, *m.* (at an auction sale): *the highest bidder*, el mejor postor. || Declarante, *m.* & *f.* (at bridge).
bidding ['bidiŋ] n. Orden, *f.* (command): *to do s.o.'s bidding*, cumplir la orden de alguien. || Ofertas, *f. pl.*, licitación, *f.*, puja, *f.* (at an auction sale). || Subasta, *f.* (in bridge).
bide* [baid] v. tr. *To bide one's time*, esperar el momento oportuno.
— OBSERV. Pret. ***bode;*** p. p. ***bided***.
bidet ['bi:dei] n. Bidé, *m.*
biennial [bai'eniəl] adj. Bienal.
— N. Bienal, *f.* (exhibition).
biennium [bai'eniəm] n. Bienio, *m.*
— OBSERV. El plural de *biennium* es *biennia*.
bier [biə*] n. Andas, *f. pl.* (for coffin). || Féretro, *m.* (coffin).
bifacial [bai'feiʃəl] adj. Bifacial.
biff [bif] n. FAM. Tortazo, *m.* (cuff).
biff [bif] v. tr. FAM. Pegar un tortazo a.
bifid ['bai,fid] adj. Bífido, da.
bifocal ['bai'fəukəl] adj. Bifocal.
— Pl. n. Lentes (*f.*) bifocales.
bifurcate ['baifə:keit] v. intr. Bifurcarse.
— V. tr. Dividir en dos.
bifurcation [,baifə:'keiʃən] n. Bifurcación, *f.*
big [big] adj. Grande (large): *a big book*, un libro grande. || Mayor: *a big girl*, una chica mayor; *his big sister*, su hermana mayor. || Grande (important): *to do big things*, hacer grandes cosas. || Fuerte (voice). || — FAM. *Big bug* o *boy* o *daddy* o *name* o *gun* o *noise* o *shot* o *wheel*, pez gordo. || TECH. *Big end*, cabeza (*f.*) de biela. || *Big finger*, dedo (*m.*) pulgar. || *Big game*, see GAME. || *Big heart*, gran corazón, *m.* || *Big sounding*, altisonante. || *Big talk*, fanfarronadas, *f. pl.* || *Big toe*, dedo gordo del pie. || BOT. *Big tree*, secoya, *f.* || *Big with child*, embarazada, encinta (woman). || *Big with consequences*, de consecuencias graves. || *Big with young*, preñada (animals). || *The Big Four*, los cuatro Grandes. || FAM. *To live in a big way*, vivir a todo tren. | *Too big for one's boots* [U. S., *breeches* o *pants*], creído, da; engreído, da. | *To think o.s. big*, dárselas de listo. || *You are a big liar!*, ¡menudo embustero eres!, ¡eres un embustero de tomo y lomo!
— Adv. FAM. *To go over big*, tener un éxito enorme. || *To talk big*, fanfarronear.
— OBSERV. The adjective *grande* in Spanish is apocopated before a singular noun: *a large house*, una gran casa *or* una casa grande.
bigamist ['bigəmist] n. Bígamo, ma.
bigamous ['bigəməs] adj. Bígamo, ma.
bigamy ['bigəmi] n. Bigamia, *f.*
bigaroon [,bigə'ru:n] or **bigarreau** ['bigərəu] n. BOT. Cereza (*f.*) gordal *or* garrafal.

big-bellied [ˈbigˈbelid] adj. FAM. Barrigón, ona; tripudo, da. | Embarazada (pregnant).
big-boned [ˈbigˈbəund] adj. FAM. Huesudo, da.
Big Dipper [ˈbigˈdipə*] n. ASTR. Osa (*f.*) Mayor.
big-eared [ˈbigiəd] adj. Orejudo, da.
bigheaded [ˈbigˈhedid] adj. FAM. Engreído, da.
bighearted [ˈbigˈhɑ:tid] adj. Generoso, sa.
bighorn [ˈbighɔ:n] n. ZOOL. Carnero (*m.*) de las Montañas Rocosas.
bight [bait] n. Entrante, *m.* (bend in a coast, river). || Ensenada, *f.*, cala, *f.* (small bay). || MAR. Seno, *m.* (of a rope).
big mouth [ˈbigmauθ] n. FAM. Bocazas, *m & f. inv.*
big-mouthed [ˈbigmauðd] adj. FAM. Hablador, ra.
bigness [ˈbignis] n. Grandeza, *f.*
bignoniaceae [bigˈnəunjəsi:i] pl. n. BOT. Bignoniáceas, *f.*
bigot [ˈbigət] n. Fanático, ca.
bigotry [—ri] n. Fanatismo, *m.*, intolerancia, *f.*
big-time [ˈbigtaim] adj. Influyente.
big top [ˈbigˈtɔp] n. Tienda (*f.*) principal [*Amer.*, carpa (*f.*) principal] (of a circus).
bigwig [ˈbigwig] n. FAM. Pez (*m.*) *or* pájaro (*m.*) gordo.
bike [baik] n. FAM. Bici, *f.* (bicycle).
bike [baik] v. intr. Ir en bicicleta; montar en bicicleta.
bikini [biˈki:ni] n. Bikini, *m.* (bathing suit).
bilabial [baiˈleibjəl] adj. Bilabial.
— N. Bilabial, *f.*
bilabiate [baiˈleibjeit] adj. BOT. Bilabiado, da.
bilateral [baiˈlætərəl] adj. Bilateral.
bilberry [ˈbilbəri] n. BOT. Arándano, *m.*
bile [bail] n. MED. Bilis, *f.* inv. || FIG. Bilis, *f. inv.* || — ANAT. *Bile duct*, conducto (*m.*) biliar. || MED. *Bile stone*, cálculo (*m.*) biliar.
bilge [bildʒ] n. MAR. Sentina, *f.* (inner hull). | Pantoque, *m.* (outer hull). | Agua (*f.*) de sentina (water). || Barriga, *f.* (of barrel). || FAM. Idioteces, *f. pl.* || MAR. *Bilge keel*, quilla (*f.*) de balance.
bilge [bildʒ] v. tr. MAR. Desfondar.
— V. intr. MAR. Hacer agua.
bilharzia [bilˈhɑ:ziə] or **bilharziasis** [ˌbilhɑ:ˈzaiəsis] or **bilharziosis** [ˌbilhɑ:ziˈəusis] n. MED. Bilharciasis, *f.*, bilarciasis, *f.*
biliary [ˈbiljəri] adj. Biliar, biliario, ria; de la bilis.
bilingual [baiˈliŋgwəl] adj. Bilingüe.
bilingualism [—izəm] n. Bilingüismo, *m.*
bilious [ˈbiljəs] adj. MED. Bilioso, sa. || FIG. Malhumorado, da. || MED. *Bilious attack*, trastorno (*m.*) biliar.
biliousness [—nis] n. MED. Crisis (*f.*) hepática, trastorno (*m.*) biliar.
bilk [bilk] v. tr. Engañar, defraudar, estafar (to swindle). || Escapársele [a uno] (to evade): *he bilked us*, se nos escapó.
bill [bil] n. Factura, *f.* (invoice): *electricity bill*, factura de la electricidad. || Cuenta, *f.* (in restaurants, shops, etc.). || Minuta, *f.* (law and other professions). || Programa, *f.* (in theatres). || Hoja, *f.* (advertising leaflet). || Lista, *f.* (list). || Cartel, *m.* (poster). || JUR. Proyecto (*m.*) de ley: *to pass a bill*, adoptar un proyecto de ley. || COMM. Efecto, *m.*, letra, *f.*: *to protest a bill*, protestar una letra. | Bono, *m.* (bond). || Pico, *m.* (of bird). || Promontorio, *m.* (promontory). || MAR. Uña, *f.* (of anchor). || U. S. Billete (*m.*) de banco (bank note). || — *Bill broker*, agente (*m.*) de cambio y bolsa. || JUR. *Bill of appeal*, demanda (*f.*) de apelación. || *Bill of costs*, relación (*f.*) *or* estado (*m.*) de gastos. || *Bill of credit*, carta (*f.*) de crédito. || *Bill of exchange*, letra (*f.*) de cambio. || *Bill of fare*, menú, *m.* || MAR. *Bill of health*, patente (*f.*) de sanidad. | *Bill of lading*, conocimiento (*m.*) de embarque. || *Bill of sale*, contrato (*m.*) *or* escritura (*f.*) de venta. || *Post* o *stick no bills*, prohibido fijar carteles. || FIG. *To fill the bill*, servir, valer (object), satisfacer los requisitos (person), mantenerse en el cartel (play). || FAM. *To foot the bill*, cascar, pagar. || *To head* o *to top the bill*, encabezar el reparto (an artist).
bill [bil] v. tr. Facturar. || Extender *or* pasar la factura: *you may bill me at the end of the month*, puede pasarme la factura a final de mes. || Anunciar (to advertise).
— V. intr. Juntar los picos (birds). || FAM. *To bill and coo*, estar como dos tórtolos.
Bill [bil] pr. n. Guillermo, *m.* [diminutivo de *William*].
billboard [ˈbilbɔ:d] n. U. S. Cartelera, *f.*
billet [ˈbilit] n. Leño, *m.* (for firewood). || ARCH. Moldura, *f.* || TECH. Palanquilla, *f.* || HERALD. Billete, *m.* || MIL. Alojamiento, *m.*, acantonamiento, *m.* (assigned quarters). | Boleta (*f.*) de alojamiento (official order). || FAM. Colocación, *f.*, puesto, *m.* (job).
billet [ˈbilit] v. tr. Alojar, acantonar.
billet-doux [ˈbileiˈdu:] n. Esquela (*f.*) amorosa, carta (*f.*) amorosa.

— OBSERV. El plural de *billet-doux* es *billets-doux*.

billfold [ˈbilfəuld] n. U. S. Cartera, *f.*, billetero, *m.*
billhook [ˈbilhuk] n. Podadera, *f.*
billiard [ˈbiljəd] adj. De billar: *billiard ball, cue, table*, bola, taco, mesa de billar. || *Billiard cloth*, tapete, *m.*, paño, *m.*
billiard player [—ˌpleiə*] n. Jugador (*m.*) de billar, billarista, *m.*
billiards [ˈbiljədz] n. Billar, *m.*
billing [ˈbiliŋ] n. Facturación, *f.* (of invoices). || Orden (*m.*) de importancia (spectacles). || *Top billing*, estrellato, *m.*
billingsgate [ˈbiliŋzgit] n. FAM. Lenguaje (*m.*) grosero.
billion [ˈbiljən] n. Billón, *m.*, millón (*m.*) de millones (in Great Britain). || U. S. Mil millones.
billionth [ˈbiljənθ] adj./n. Billonésimo, ma (in Great Britain). || U. S. Mil millonésimo, ma.
billow [ˈbiləu] n. Ola, *f.* (of water). || FIG. Oleada, *f.*: *billows of people*, oleadas de gente.
billow [ˈbiləu] v. intr. Ondular (to undulate). || Hincharse, inflarse (to swell).
billowy [—i] adj. Ondulante (undulating). || Agitado, da; encrespado, da: *the billowy sea*, el mar agitado. || Hinchado, da; inflado, da (swollen).
billposter [ˈbilˌpəustə*] or **billsticker** [ˈbilˌstikə*] n. Cartelero, *m.*
billy [ˈbili] n. U. S. Porra, *f.* (policeman's truncheon).
Billy [ˈbili] pr. n. Guillermo, *m.* [diminutivo de *William*].
billycan [—kæn] n. Cazo, *m.*
billycock [—kɔk] n. FAM. Hongo, *m.* (hat).
billy goat [—gəut] n. Macho (*m.*) cabrío. || *Billy-goat beard*, perilla, *f.*, pera, *f.*
billy-oh [—əu] adv. *It's raining like billy-oh*, llueve a cántaros. || *They fought like billy-oh*, lucharon encarnizadamente.
bilobate [baiˈləubeit] or **bilobed** [baiˈləubd] adj. BOT. Bilobulado, da.
bilocular [baiˈlɔkjulə*] or **biloculate** [baiˈlɔkjulit] adj. BOT. Bilocular.
biltong [ˈbiltɔŋ] n. Cecina, *f.*
bimanal [ˈbaimənəl] or **bimanous** [ˈbaimənəs] adj. Bímano, na.
bimane [ˈbaimein] n. Bímano, na.
bimester [baiˈmestə*] n. Bimestre, *m.*
bimestrial [baiˈmestriəl] adj. Bimestral, cada dos meses.
bimetallic [ˈbaimeˈtælik] adj. Bimetálico, ca.
bimetallism [baiˈmetəlizəm] n. Bimetalismo, *m.*
bimetalist [baiˈmetəlist] adj./n. Bimetalista.
bimonthly [ˈbaiˈmʌnθli] adj. Bimestral (every two months). || Bimensual (twice a month).
— N. Publicación (*f.*) bimestral *or* bimensual.
— Adv. Bimestralmente (every two months). || Bimensualmente (twice a month).
bin [bin] n. Cajón, *m.*, arca, *f.* || Compartimiento, *m.* (storage compartment). || Recipiente, *m.* (recipient). || Carbonera, *f.* (for coal). || Botellero, *m.* (for wine). || Cubo (*m.*) de la basura (dustbin). || Papelera, *f.* (for waste paper).
binary [ˈbainəri] adj. Binario, ria.
bind [baind] n. Lazo, *m.* (tie). || TECH. Atasco, *m.* || FAM. Lata, *f.*: *this job is a real bind*, este trabajo es una verdadera lata. | Pesado, da (boring person). || U. S. FIG. FAM. *To be in a bind*, estar metido en un lío.
bind* [baind] v. tr. Atar, liar (to tie up): *to bind a package with string*, atar un paquete con una cuerda. || Atar (hands, legs). || Agavillar (corn). || Rematar (to edge). || Ribetear (to trim). || Encuadernar (pages, fascicles). || Obligar (to place under obligation): *to bind s.o. to pay a debt*, obligar a alguien a pagar una deuda. || Ligar (to cause to adhere). || Endurecer (to make hard). || Ceñir (to encircle). || Apretar (the clothes). || Vincular: *a treaty binds your country to ours*, un tratado vincula su país con el nuestro. || Unir (to unite). || Ratificar (a bargain, a treaty). || Recogerse (one's hair). || MED. Estreñir (to constipate). | Vendar (to bandage). || Hacer (an insurance). || — *To bind off*, menguar: *to bind off three stitches*, menguar tres puntos. || *To bind o.s. to*, comprometerse a. || JUR. *To bind over to*, obligar legalmente a. || *To bind s.o. as an apprentice to*, poner a alguien de aprendiz en casa de. || *To bind s.o. down to*, obligar a alguien a. || MED. *To bind up*, vendar.
— V. intr. Endurecerse (to grow stiff, hard). || Fraguar (cement). || TECH. Unirse, trabarse (to stick together). | Atascarse (to jam). || Tener fuerza obligatoria.

— OBSERV. Pret. & p. p. **bound**.

binder [—ə*] n. Encuadernador, *m.* (of books). || AGR. Agavilladora, *f.* || Carpeta, *f.* (for papers). || Cubierta, *f.* (for magazines). || MED. Faja, *f.* (strip of material). || ARCH. Tirante, *m.* (tie beam). || CHEM. Aglutinante, *m.*
binding [—iŋ] n. Atadura, *f.* (fastening). || Encuadernación, *f.* (book cover). || Ribete, *m.* (edging): *blanket binding*, ribete de la manta. || Galón, *m.* (of seam, of hem). || SP. Ataduras, *f. pl.* (of skis).
— Adj. Que hay que cumplir, que compromete: *binding promise*, promesa que hay que cumplir. || Obligatorio, ria (*on, upon*, para): *decision binding on all parties*, decisión obligatoria para todas las partes. || Astringente, que estriñe (astringent). || *Binding energy*, energía (*f.*) de unión *or* de enlace.
bindweed [ˈbaindwi:d] n. BOT. Correhuela, *f.*, enredadera, *f.*
binge [bindʒ] n. FAM. Borrachera, *f.* || *To go on a binge* o *to have a binge*, ir de juerga, ir de parranda.
bingo [ˈbiŋgəu] n. Bingo, *m.* (game).
binnacle [ˈbinəkl] n. MAR. Bitácora, *f.*
binocular [biˈnɔkjulə*] adj. Binocular.
binoculars [—z] pl. n. Prismáticos, *m*, gemelos, *m.*

binomial [baiˈnəumjəl] n. MATH. Binomio, *m.*
— Adj. Binomio, mia.
biochemical [ˈbaiəuˈkemikəl] adj. Bioquímico, ca.
biochemist [ˈbaiəuˈkemist] n. Bioquímico, ca.
biochemistry [—ri] n. Bioquímica, *f.*
biodegradable [ˈbaiəudiˈgreidəbl] adj. Biodegradable.
biogenesis [ˈbaiəuˈdʒenisis] n. Biogénesis, *f.*
biogenetic [ˌbaiəudʒəˈnetik] or **biogenetical** [—əl] adj. Biogenético, ca.
biographer [baiˈɔgrəfə*] n. Biógrafo, fa.
biographic [ˌbaiəuˈgræfik] or **biographical** [—əl] adj. Biográfico, ca.
biography [baiˈɔgrəfi] n. Biografía, *f.*
biologic [ˌbaiəuˈlɔdʒik] or **biological** [—əl] adj. Biológico, ca: *biological warfare*, guerra biológica.
biologist [ˌbaiˈɔlədʒist] n. Biólogo, *m.*
biology [ˌbaiˈɔlədʒi] n. Biología, *f.*
biomechanics [ˈbaiəmiˈkæniks] n. Biomecánica, *f.*
biophysics [ˌbaiəuˈfiziks] n. Biofísica, *f.*
biopsy [ˈbaiəpsi] n. MED. Biopsia, *f.*
biosphere [ˈbaiəsfiə*] n. Biosfera, *f.*
biosynthesis [ˌbaiəuˈsinθəsis] n. Biosíntesis, *f.*
biotherapy [ˌbaiəuˈθerəpi] n. MED. Bioterapia, *f.*
biotite [ˈbaiətait] n. MIN. Biotita, *f.*
bipartisan [baiˈpɑːtizən] adj. U. S. De dos partidos políticos.
bipartite [baiˈpɑːtait] adj. Bipartido, da (having two parts). || Bipartito, ta (of two parties): *bipartite agreement*, acuerdo bipartito.
bipartition [ˌbaipɑːˈtiʃən] n. Bipartición, *f.*
biped [ˈbaiped] adj. Bípedo, da.
— N. Bípedo, *m.*
biplane [ˈbaiplein] n. AVIAT. Biplano, *m.*
bipolar [baiˈpəulə*] adj. Bipolar.
bipolarity [ˌbaipəuˈlæriti] n. Bipolaridad, *f.*
biquadratic [ˌbaikwɔˈdrætik] adj. Bicuadrado, da.
birch [bəːtʃ] n. Abedul, *m.* (tree, wood). || *Birch* o *birch rod*, vara, *f.* [de abedul] (for flogging).
birch [bəːtʃ] v. tr. Azotar (to flog).
birchen [ˈbəːtʃən] adj. De abedul.
bird [bəːd] n. ZOOL. Ave, *f.*, pájaro, *m.* (See OBSERV.) || Caza (*f.*) de pluma (game). || SP. Volante, *m.* (badminton). || FAM. Individuo, *m.*, tipo, *m.* (man). | Niña, *f.*, chica, *f.* (girl). | Novia, *f.*, amiga, *f.* (girlfriend). || — FIG. *A bird in the hand is worth two in the bush*, más vale pájaro en mano que ciento volando. | *A little bird told me*, me lo dijo un pajarito, me lo ha dicho el pajarito verde. || U. S. *Bird dog*, perro (*m.*) de caza. || FIG. *Bird of ill omen*, pájaro de mal agüero. || *Bird of paradise*, ave del Paraíso. || *Bird of passage*, ave de paso (animal, person). || *Bird of peace*, paloma (*f.*) de la paz. || *Bird of prey*, ave de presa *or* de rapiña. || *Bird shot*, perdigones, *m. pl.* || *Bird's nest*, nido (*m.*) de pájaro. || *Bird's nest soup*, sopa (*f.*) de nido de golondrina. || FIG. *Birds of a feather*, lobos (*m. pl.*) de la misma camada. | *Birds of a feather flock together*, Dios los cría y ellos se juntan. | *Early bird*, madrugador, ra. || *Migratory bird*, ave de paso. || *Night bird*, ave nocturna (animal, person). || FIG. *Not to eat enough to feed a bird*, comer como un pajarito. | *The bird has flown*, el pájaro voló. | *The early bird catches the worm*, al que madruga, Dios le ayuda. | *To get the bird*, ser abucheado (artist, speaker). | *To give s.o. the bird*, abuchear a alguien (artist, speaker). | *To kill two birds with one stone*, matar dos pájaros de un tiro.
— OBSERV. *Pájaro* is applied to small birds whereas *ave* is used for larger ones.
birdbath [—bɑːθ] n. Pila (*f.*) para pájaros.
birdbrain [—brein] n. FAM. Majadero, ra; mentecato, ta.
birdcage [—keidʒ] n. Jaula, *f.* || Pajarera, *f.* (large).
birdcall [—kɔːl] n. Canto (*m.*) del pájaro (sound of a bird). || Reclamo, *m.* (for attracting birds).
birdie [—i] n. Pajarito, *m.*
birdlime [—laim] n. Liga, *f.*
birdseed [—siːd] n. BOT. Alpiste, *m.*
bird's-eye [—zˌai] n. Ojo (*m.*) de perdiz. || *Bird's-eye view*, vista panorámica.
bird's-nest [—znest] v. intr. Sacar los pájaros del nido.
birefringence [ˌbairiˈfrindʒəns] n. PHYS. Birrefringencia, *f.*
birefringent [ˌbairiˈfrindʒənt] n. PHYS. Birrefringente.
bireme [ˈbairiːm] n. MAR. Birreme, *f.*
biretta [biˈretə] n. REL. Birrete, *m.*, birreta, *f.*
biro [ˈbaiərəu] n. Bolígrafo, *m.*
birth [bəːθ] n. Nacimiento, *m.*: *the birth of his first child*, el nacimiento de su primer hijo. || MED. Parto, *m.*: *a difficult birth*, un parto difícil. || FIG. Nacimiento, *m.*, comienzo, *m.*: *birth of a nation*, nacimiento de una nación. | Origen, *m.* (origin). | Linaje, *m.*, cuna, *f.*, origen, *m.*: *of noble birth*, de noble linaje. || — *A person of birth*, una persona bien nacida. || *Birth certificate*, partida (*f.*) de nacimiento. || *Birth control*, control (*m.*) de la natalidad, regulación (*f.*) de nacimientos, limitación (*f.*) de la natalidad. || *By* o *from birth*, de nacimiento. || *To give birth to*, dar a luz (to a child), dar origen a (to cause).
birthday [ˈbəːθdei] n. Cumpleaños, *m.*: *birthday party*, fiesta de cumpleaños. || Fecha (*f.*) de nacimiento (day of birth). || — *Birthday honours*, honores que se otorgan con motivo del cumpleaños del rey. || FIG. FAM. *To be in one's birthday suit*, estar como Dios le trajo al mundo.
birthmark [ˈbəːθmɑːk] n. Marca (*f.*) *or* mancha (*f.*) de nacimiento.
birthplace [ˈbəːθpleis] n. Lugar (*m.*) de nacimiento.
birthrate [ˈbəːθreit] n. Natalidad, *f.*, índice (*m.*) de natalidad.
birthright [ˈbəːθrait] n. Derechos (*m. pl.*) de nacimiento. || Derechos (*m. pl.*) de primogenitura. || FIG. Patrimonio, *m.*
birthstone [ˈbəːθstəun] n. Piedra (*f.*) preciosa que corresponde al mes de nacimiento.
bis [bis] adv. MUS. Bis.
Biscay [ˈbiskei] pr. n. GEOGR. Vizcaya, *f.* || *Bay of Biscay*, mar Cantábrico, golfo (*m.*) de Vizcaya.
Biscayan [—ən] adj./n. Vizcaíno, na.
biscuit [ˈbiskit] n. Galleta, *f.* || U. S. Bollo, *m.* (bun). || Bizcocho, *m.*, biscuit, *m.* (pottery). || Beige, *m.* (colour). || FAM. *That takes the biscuit!*, ¡eso es el colmo!
bisect [baiˈsekt] v. tr. MATH. Bisecar (angles). || Dividir en dos partes.
— V. intr. Bifurcarse (to fork).
bisecting [—iŋ] adj. Bisector, bisectriz.
bisection [baiˈsekʃən] n. MATH. Bisección, *f.* || División (*f.*) en dos partes.
bisector [baiˈsektə*] or **bisectrix** [baiˈsektriks] n. MATH. Bisectriz, *f.*
bisexual [baiˈseksjuəl] adj. Bisexual.
bishop [ˈbiʃəp] n. REL. Obispo, *m.* || Alfil, *m.* (in chess). || Bebida (*f.*) caliente a base de vino de Oporto (drink). || BOT. *Bishop's weed*, biznaga, *f.*
bishopric [—rik] n. Obispado, *m.*
bisk [bisk] n. CULIN. Sopa (*f.*) de mariscos.
bismuth [ˈbizməθ] n. Bismuto, *m.*
bison [ˈbaisn] n. ZOOL. Bisonte, *m.*
bisque [bisk] n. Sopa (*f.*) de mariscos (soup). || U. S. Helado (*m.*) de avellana (ice cream). || Bizcocho, *m.*, biscuit, *m.* (pottery). || SP. Ventaja, *f.*
bissextile [biˈsekstail] adj. Bisiesto.
— N. Año (*m.*) bisiesto (leap year).
bister [ˈbistə*] n. U. S. Bistre, *m.* (colour).
bistort [ˈbistɔːt] n. BOT. Bistorta, *f.*
bistoury [ˈbisturi] n. MED. Bisturí, *m.* (scalpel).
bistre [ˈbistə*] n. Bistre, *m.* (colour).
bisulcate [baiˈsʌlkeit] adj. ZOOL. Bisulco, ca.
bisulfate or **bisulphate** [baiˈsʌlfeit] n. CHEM. Bisulfato, *m.*
bisulfide or **bisulphide** [baiˈsʌlfaid] n. CHEM. Bisulfuro, *m.*
bisulfite or **bisulphite** [baiˈsʌlfait] n. CHEM. Bisulfito, *m.*
bit [bit] n. Trozo, *m.*, pedazo, *m.* (small piece): *a bit of bread*, un trozo de pan. || Poco, *m.* (small amount): *a bit of milk*, un poco de leche. || Poco, *m.*, rato, *m.* (short time): *wait a bit*, espera un poco. || Parte, *f.* (part): *one of the best bits of the play*, una de las mejores partes de la obra. || Bocado, *m.* (of the bridle). || TECH. Boca, *f.*, filo, *m.* (in tools). | Broca, *f.*, taladro, *m.* (of the brace). | Paletón, *m.* (of a key). || — *A bit*, un poco: *he is a bit older than I*, es un poco mayor que yo. || *A bit of advice*, un consejo. || *A bit of garden*, un jardincito. || *A bit of luck*, una suerte (stroke of luck), un poco de suerte (a little luck). || *A bit of news*, una noticia. || *A good bit*, bastante. || *Bit actor*, actor secundario. || *Bit brace*, berbiquí, *m.* || *Bit by bit*, poco a poco. || *Bit part*, papel secundario. || *I have got a bit of a headache*, tengo un ligero dolor de cabeza. || *It's not a bit of use*, no sirve absolutamente para nada. || *It was a bit of a surprise*, fue una gran sorpresa. || *Not a bit*, no hay de qué: *thank you! — Not a bit*, ¡gracias! — No hay de qué; en absoluto: *are you tired? — Not a bit*, ¿estás cansado? — En absoluto. || *Threepenny bit*, moneda (*f.*) de tres peniques. || *To be a bit of*, ser un poco: *he's a bit of an artist*, es un poco artista. || *To be a bit of all right*, estar muy bien. || *To be every bit a man*, ser un hombre por los cuatro costados. || *To blow to bits*, hacer añicos, hacer saltar en pedazos. || *To do one's bit*, hacer *or* poner de su parte. || FIG. *To give s.o. a bit of one's mind*, decirle a uno cuatro verdades. | *To go to bits*, venirse abajo. || *To smash to bits*, romper en pedazos, hacer añicos. || FIG. *To take the bit in one's teeth*, desbocarse. || U. S. *Two bits*, veinticinco centavos.
bit [bit] pret. & p. p. See BITE.
bitch [bitʃ] n. Hembra, *f.* (female). || Perra, *f.* (dog). || Loba, *f.* (wolf). || FAM. Bruja, *f.* (bad tempered woman). | Zorra, *f.* (prostitute). || U. S. FAM. Queja, *f.* (complaint). || FAM. *Son of a bitch*, hijo (*m.*) de perra.
bitch [bitʃ] v. intr. U. S. FAM. Quejarse, protestar.
bite [bait] n. Mordisco, *m.*, dentellada, *f.* (act). || Mordedura, *f.* (wound). || Piscolabis, *m.*, bocado, *m.*, refrigerio, *m.* (a snack). || Bocado, *m.* (mouthful): *give me a bite of your cake*, dame un bocado de tu pastel. || Picadura, *f.* (of insect, snake). || Dolor (*m.*) agudo (sharp pain). || FIG. Mordacidad, *f.*: *his criticism lacks bite*, su crítica carece de mordacidad. || Adherencia, *f.* (tyres). || TECH. Agarre, *m.* (grip). || PRINT. Lardón, *m.* || Mordida, *f.*, picada, *f.* (in fishing). || — *I haven't had a bite all day*, no he probado bocado en todo el día (nothing to eat), no han picado en todo el día (in fishing). || FIG. FAM. *To put the bite on s.o.*, pedir dinero prestado a alguien.

bite* [bait] v. tr. Morder: *the dog will bite you*, el perro te morderá. || Picar (insect, snake, fish). || Penetrar (to pierce). || Cortar: *the wind bit her face*, el viento le cortaba la cara. || Quemar: *frost bit the flowers*, la helada quemó las flores. || Picar (pepper). || Engañar (to deceive). || TECH. Agarrarse, agarrar (to grip). | Corroer, atacar (to corrode). | Morder (file). || MAR. Agarrar, morder (the anchor). || — FIG. *Bitten with*, poseído de. | *Once bitten twice shy*, gato escaldado del agua fría huye. || *To bite off*, arrancar con los dientes. || FIG. *To bite off more than one can chew*, abarcar demasiado. | *To bite one's lips* o *tongue*, morderse los labios *or* la lengua. || *To bite one's nails*, morderse las uñas. || FIG. FAM. *To bite s.o.'s head off*, echarle una bronca a alguien. | *To bite the dust*, morder el polvo. | *To get bitten*, dejarse engañar, picar. | *What's biting you?*, ¿qué mosca le ha picado?
— V. intr. Morder: *be careful, the dog bites*, ten cuidado, el perro muerde. || Picar (fish, snake, insect). || Cortar (cold, wind). || FIG. Picar (to yield to a lure). || TECH. Corroer, atacar. | Agarrar (on a road). || *To bite at*, atacar, intentar morder (a dog).
— OBSERV. Pret. ***bit;*** p. p. ***bitten, bit.***

biter [—ə*] n. *The biter bit*, el cazador cazado.
Bithynia [bi'θiniə] pr. n. Bitinia, *f.*
biting ['baitiŋ] adj. Cortante, penetrante (cold). || FIG. Mordaz, cáustico, ca; sarcástico, ca (words, etc.).
bitt [bit] n. MAR. Bita, *f.*, noray, *m.* (bollard).
bitten ['bitn] p. p. See BITE.
bitter ['bitə*] adj. Amargo, ga: *bitter almonds*, almendras amargas. || Ácido, da; agrio, gria: *a very bitter lemon*, un limón muy ácido. || Penetrante, cortante, glacial: *bitter cold*, frío penetrante. || Glacial, riguroso, sa: *bitter weather*, tiempo glacial. || FIG. Amargo, ga (experience, disappointment, words, person). | Acerbo, ba (critic). | Encarnizado, da; enconado, da (fight). | Profundo, da (contempt). | Implacable (enemy, hatred). || — *Bitter apple*, coloquíntida, *f.* || *Bitter orange*, naranja (*f.*) de Sevilla, naranja agria. || *To the bitter end*, hasta el final.
— N. Cerveza (*f.*) amarga (beer). || — Pl. "Bitter", *m. sing.* (drink).
bitterly [—li] adv. Amargamente. || FIG. Con amargura. || *It's bitterly cold*, hace un frío glacial.
bittern ['bitə:n] n. ZOOL. Avetoro, *m.*
bitterness ['bitənis] n. Amargura, *f.* || Acidez, *f.*, amargor, *m.* (of lemon). || Crudeza, *f.*, rigor, *m.* (of winter). || FIG. Encono, *m.*, enconamiento, *m.*, encarnizamiento, *m.* (of fight). | Mordacidad, *f.*, lo punzante (of words).
bittersweet ['bitəswi:t] adj. Agridulce.
bitumen ['bitjumin] n. Betún, *m.*
bituminous [bi'tju:minəs] adj. Bituminoso, sa.
bivalence [bai'veiləns] n. CHEM. Bivalencia, *f.*
bivalent [bai'veilənt] adj. CHEM. Bivalente.
bivalve ['baivælv] adj. Bivalvo, va.
— N. Bivalvo, *m.*
bivouac ['bivuæk] n. Vivaque, *m.*, vivac, *m.*
bivouac ['bivuæk] v. intr. Vivaquear.
— OBSERV. Pret. & p. p. ***bivouacked.***
biweekly ['bai'wi:kli] adj. Bisemanal (twice a week). || Quincenal (every two weeks).
— Adv. Dos veces por semana (twice a week). || Cada quincena (every two weeks).
— N. Publicación (*f.*) bisemanal (twice a week). || Publicación (*f.*) quincenal (every two weeks).
biyearly ['bai'jə:li] adj. Semestral.
bizarre [bi'zɑ:*] adj. Extraño, ña; curioso, sa (strange). || Estrafalario, ria (eccentric).
— OBSERV. The word *bizarro* exists in Spanish but means "brave", "generous", "dashing".

blab [blæb] n. FAM. Chismoso, sa; cotilla, *m.* & *f.* (person). | Chisme, *m.* (gossip).
blab [blæb] v. intr. FAM. Chismorrear, cotillear (to talk indiscreetly). | Ir con el soplo, ir con el cuento (to inform). | Descubrir el pastel (to spill the beans). | No parar de hablar (to chatter).
— V. tr. FAM. Revelar, contar (to reveal).
black [blæk] adj. Negro, gra (colour, race). || Ennegrecido, da: *black with age*, ennegrecido por el tiempo. || FIG. Negro, gra; aciago, ga; funesto, ta: *it was a black year*, fue un año aciago. | Negro, gra: *he has a black future*, le espera un negro porvenir. | | Ruin, perverso, sa (wicked): *a black deed*, una acción ruin. | De estraperlo: *black petrol*, gasolina de estraperlo. | Boicoteado, da: *black goods*, productos boicoteados. || — FIG. *As black as coal*, negro como el carbón *or* el tizón. | *As black as pitch*, negro como el carbón; oscuro como boca de lobo. || *Black amber*, azabache, *m.* || FIG. *Black and blue*, lleno de cardenales. || *Black and white*, por escrito: *put it down in black and white*, ponlo por escrito; en blanco y negro (photography, art, etc.). || *Black art* o *black magic*, magia negra. || *Black bear*, oso negro. || SP. *Black belt*, cinturón negro. || *Black book*, lista negra: *to be in one's black book*, estar en la lista negra de uno. || AVIAT. *Black box*, caja negra, registrador (*m.*) de vuelo. || *Black bread*, pan negro. || HIST. *Black cap*, birrete (*m.*) que usaban los jueces británicos en el momento de pronunciar la sentencia de muerte. || *Black coffee*, café solo. || GEOGR. *Black country*, región (*f.*) de los Midlands [en Inglaterra]. || BOT. *Black currant*, grosella negra. || HIST. *Black Death*, peste negra. || *Black eye*, ojo morado *or* en compota *or* a la funerala. || *Black flag*, pabellón (*m.*) pirata. || GEOGR. *Black Forest*, Selva Negra. || REL. *Black Friar*, fraile dominico. || *Black hole*, calabozo, *m.* || *Black lead*, grafito, *m.* || PRINT. *Black letter*, letra gótica. || *Black man*, negro, *m.* || *Black Maria*, coche (*m.*) celular (prison van). || FIG. *Black mark*, mala nota. || *Black mass*, misa negra. || REL. *Black Monk*, monje benedictino. || *Black pepper*, pimienta negra. || HIST. *Black Prince*, Príncipe Negro. || *Black pudding*, morcilla, *f.* || *Black Rod*, funcionario (*m.*) de la Cámara de los Lores que mantiene el orden. || GEOGR. *Black Sea*, Mar Negro. || FIG. *Black sheep*, oveja negra, garbanzo negro. || ZOOL. *Black snake*, culebra inofensiva americana. || FIG. *Black spot*, see SPOT. || *Black tie*, corbata negra de lazo (tie), traje (*m.*) de etiqueta (dinner jacket). || *Black-tie dinner*, cena de etiqueta. || MED. *Black vomit*, vómito negro. || FIG. *Black with rage*, rojo de ira. || *Black woman*, negra, *f.* || FIG. *To be in a black mood*, estar de mal humor. | *To declare sth. black*, boicotear algo. | *To give a black look*, mirar con mala cara.
— N. Negro, *m.* (colour). || Negro, gra (person). || Luto, *m.* (mourning): *she was in black* o *wearing black*, estaba de luto.
black [blæk] v. tr. Ennegrecer (to make black). || Embetunar, limpiar (to polish). || — *To black out*, apagar las luces de: *to black out a house*, apagar las luces de una casa; tapar (to cover), censurar (to censor). || FAM. *To black s.o.'s eye*, ponerle a uno el ojo a la funerala. || *We were blacked out last night*, nos quedamos sin luz anoche.
— V. intr. Ennegrecer. || *To black out*, perder el conocimiento (to go unconscious).
blackball [—bɔ:l] n. Bola (*f.*) negra (ballot).
blackball [—bɔ:l] v. tr. Echar bola negra.
blackbeetle [—'bi:tl] n. Cucaracha, *f.*
blackberry [—bəri] n. BOT. Zarzamora, *f.*
blackbird [—bə:d] n. Mirlo, *m.* (bird).
blackboard [—bɔ:d] n. Pizarra, *f.*, encerado, *m.*
black-coated [—ˌkəutid] adj. *Black-coated workers*, oficinistas, *m. pl.*
blackdamp [—dæmp] n. MIN. Mofeta, *f.*
blacken [—ən] v. intr. Ennegrecer, ennegrecerse.
— V. tr. Ennegrecer (to make black). || FIG. Denigrar (to defame). | Manchar (one's reputation).
black-eyed [—'aid] adj. De ojos negros.
blackface [—feis] n. PRINT. Negrita, *f.* || Maquillaje (*m.*) del actor que interpreta el personaje de un negro.
blackfellow [—feləu] n. Aborigen (*m.*) australiano.
blackguard ['blægɑ:d] n. Sinvergüenza, *m.* & *f.*, canalla, *m.*
blackguard ['blægɑ:d] v. tr. Vilipendiar.
blackhead ['blækhed] n. MED. Espinilla, *f.*
blacking ['blækiŋ] n. Betún, *m.* (for shoes).
blackish ['blækiʃ] adj. Negruzco, ca.
blackjack ['blækdʒæk] n. Pabellón (*m.*) pirata (pirate flag). || Veintiuna, *f.* (card game). || Porra, *f.*, cachiporra, *f.* (truncheon).
blackjack ['blækdʒæk] v. tr. Aporrear.
blackleg ['blækleg] n. Tahúr, *m.* (swindler). || Esquirol, *m.* (strikebreaker).
blackleg ['blækleg] v. tr./intr. Romper [una huelga].
blacklist ['blæklist] n. Lista (*f.*) negra.
blacklist ['blæklist] v. tr. Poner en la lista negra.
blackmail ['blækmeil] n. Chantaje, *m.*
blackmail ['blækmeil] v. tr. Hacer chantaje, chantajear.
blackmailer ['blækmeilə*] n. Chantajista, *m.* & *f.*
black market ['blæk'mɑ:kit] n. Mercado (*m.*) negro, estraperlo, *m.*
blackmarketeer [—iə*] n. Estraperlista, *m.* & *f.*
blackness ['blæknis] n. Negrura, *f.* || Oscuridad, *f.* (darkness).
blackout ['blækaut] n. Apagón, *m.* (of lights). || Pérdida (*f.*) del conocimiento (of consciousness). || Censura, *f.*
Blackshirt ['blækʃə:t] n. HIST. Camisa negra, *m.*
blacksmith ['blæksmiθ] n. Herrero, *m.* || *Blacksmith's workshop*, herrería, *f.*
blackthorn ['blækθɔ:n] n. BOT. Endrino, *m.* || Porra, *f.*, bastón, *m.* (cudgel).
bladder ['blædə*] n. ANAT. Vejiga, *f.* || Cámara (*f.*) de aire (of a ball, tyre). || BOT. Vesícula, *f.* (in seaweeds). || — MED. *Bladder worm*, cisticerco, *m.* || *Gall bladder*, vesícula biliar.
blade [bleid] n. Hoja, *f.* (of knife, sword, saw, etc.). || Hoja, *f.*, cuchilla, *f.* (of razor). || Cuchilla, *f.* (of ice skate, etc.). || Aspa, *f.* (of a mill). || BOT. Brizna, *f.* (of grass). | Limbo, *m.* (of leaf). || Espada, *f.* (sword). || Pala, *f.* (of an oar). || TECH. Paleta, *f.*, pala, *f.* (fan, propeller). | Álabe, *m.*, paleta, *f.* (of paddle wheel). | Rasqueta, *f.* (of windscreen or windshield wiper). | Cuchilla, *f.* (of guillotine). | Cuchilla, *f.*, hoja, *f.* (of machine). || AGR. Pala, *f.* (of hoe). || ANAT. Paletilla, *f.* || FAM. Galán, *m.* (dashing young man). || — FAM. *Jolly* o *gay old blade*, jaranero, *m.* || *Razor blade*, cuchilla *or* hoja de afeitar.
blamable or **blameable** ['bleiməbl] adj. Censurable. || Culpable (guilty).
blame [bleim] n. Culpa, *f.* (responsibility): *the blame is mine*, la culpa es mía. || Censura, *f.*, reproche, *m.* (censure). || — *To bear the blame*, tener la culpa. ||

To lay o *to put the blame for sth. on* o *upon*, echar la culpa de algo a.

blame [bleim] v. tr. Culpar, echar la culpa: *they blamed him for the crime, they blamed the crime on him*, le culparon del crimen, le echaron la culpa del crimen. || Censurar (to reproach). || — *To be to blame*, ser el culpable *or* el responsable, tener la culpa: *he is to blame for the accident*, él es el culpable del accidente. || *You have only yourself to blame*, la culpa es suya.

blameless [—lis] adj. Inocente (innocent). || Libre de culpa (free from fault). || Irreprochable, intachable (irreproachable).

blameworthy [ˈbleim,wəːði] adj. Censurable, culpable: *his conduct is blameworthy*, su conducta es censurable.

blanch [blɑːntʃ] v. tr. Blanquear (to make white). || Pelar (to peel). || Escaldar (to boil). || Blanquear, blanquecer (metals).
— V. intr. Palidecer (to grow pale).

blancmange [bləˈmɔnʒ] n. Manjar (*m.*) blanco.

bland [blænd] adj. Templado, da; suave (climate). || Afable, suave, amable (manners, person). || Suave, poco fuerte (diet).

blandish [—iʃ] v. tr. Lisonjear, halagar (to coax).
— V. intr. Valerse de halagos.

blandishment [—iʃmənt] n. Halago, *m.*, zalamería, *f.*, lisonja, *f.*

blank [blæŋk] adj. En blanco: *leave a blank space*, deja un espacio en blanco. || Liso, sa; sin adornos (wall). || Falso, sa (door, window). || Mudo, da (map). || FIG. Sin expresión (look). | Vacío, a (empty): *a blank life*, una vida vacía; *blank mind*, mente vacía. | Absoluto, ta (impossibility). | Profundo, da (despair). | Tajante, categórico, ca (definite): *blank denial*, denegación categórica. | Desconcertado, da; perplejo, ja (confused). || — MIL. *Blank cartridge*, cartucho (*m.*) de fogueo. || *Blank cheque*, cheque (*m.*) en blanco (cheque), carta blanca (permission). || PRINT. *Blank page*, guarda, *f.* || *Blank verse*, verso blanco *or* suelto.
— N. Blanco, *m.*, hueco, *m.*, espacio (*m.*) en blanco (in document, etc.): *to leave blanks*, dejar espacios en blanco. || Vacío, *m.*, laguna, *f.*: *that is a blank in American history*, eso es una laguna en la historia americana. || Laguna, *f.* (in one's education). || PRINT. Puntos (*m. pl.*) suspensivos, guión, *m.* [para sustituir una palabra malsonante]. || MIL. Cartucho (*m.*) de fogueo. | Blanco, *m.* (target). || Número (*m.*) no premiado (lottery ticket). || Papeleta (*f.*) en blanco (ballot). || U. S. Impreso, *m.*, formulario, *m.* (form). || TECH. Cospel, *m.* (coin). | Llave (*f.*) ciega (key). || — *Double blank*, blanca doble (in dominoes). || *In blank*, en blanco. || FIG. *My mind was a complete blank*, me falló la memoria. | *To draw a blank*, llevarse un chasco.

blank [blæŋk] v. tr. Tachar, borrar (to erase). || U.S. SP. Impedir que el equipo contrario marque un tanto. || *To blank off*, tapar.

blanket [—it] n. Manta, *f.* [*Amer.*, frazada, *f.*] (bed cover, covering for animals, cloak): *electric blanket*, manta eléctrica. || FIG. Capa, *f.*, manto, *m.*: *a white blanket of snow*, una blanca capa de nieve. | Manto, *m.*: *the blanket of the night*, el manto de la noche. || — FIG. *Security blanket*, medidas (*f. pl.*) de seguridad. || FIG. FAM. *To throw a wet blanket over*, echar un jarro de agua fría a. | *Wet blanket*, aguafiestas, *m.* & *f.*
— Adj. General. || FIG. *Blanket insurance policy*, póliza (*f.*) a todo riesgo.

blanket [—it] v. tr. Tapar con una manta (to cover up). || Envolver (to wrap up). || Cubrir con una capa *or* manto: *the city was blanketed in snow*, la ciudad estaba cubierta con un manto de nieve. || Acallar (rumours, questions). || Tapar (scandal). || Amortiguar (noise). || RAD. Interferir (radio transmissions). || MAR. Robar *or* quitar el viento. || U. S. Cubrir (to apply to).

blankety [—ti] or **blanky** [—i] adj. FAM. Maldito, ta.

blankly [ˈblæŋkli] adv. Con la mirada vacía (without expression). || Completamente (utterly). || Tajantemente, categóricamente.

blare [blɛə*] n. Trompetazo, *m.* (of trumpet). || Estruendo, *m.* (loud sound).

blare [blɛə*] v. intr. Sonar, resonar: *the trumpets blared*, las trompetas sonaron. || Berrear (to blast).
— V. tr. Pregonar, proclamar, anunciar a gritos: *the loudspeakers blared the news*, los altavoces anunciaron a gritos la noticia.

blarney [ˈblɑːni] n. FAM. Coba, *f.*

blarney [ˈblɑːni] v. tr./intr. FAM. Dar coba.

blasé [ˈblɑːzei] adj. Hastiado, da; de vuelta de todo.

blaspheme [blæsˈfiːm] v. tr./intr. Blasfemar.

blasphemer [—ə*] n. Blasfemador, ra; blasfemo, ma.

blasphemous [ˈblæsfiməs] adj. Blasfemador, ra; blasfematorio, ria; blasfemo, ma.

blasphemy [ˈblæsfimi] n. Blasfemia, *f.*

blast [blɑːst] n. Ráfaga, *f.* (gust): *a blast of air*, una ráfaga de aire. || TECH. Inyección (*f.*) de aire. | Explosión, *f.* (explosion). | Chorro, *m.* (of air through a jet). | Onda (*f.*) de choque (of an explosion). || MUS. Toque, *m.* (of a trumpet). || Soplo, *m.* (of bellows). || MIN. Barreno, *m.* (amount of dynamite). || AGR. Añublo, *m.*, tizón, *m.* || FIG. Explosión, *f.*, estallido, *m.* (of anger). || — *At full blast*, a toda marcha. || *Blast furnace*, alto horno, *m.* || *Blast on the whistle*, pitido, *m.*, silbido, *m.* || *Blast wave*, onda de choque. || FIG. FAM. *To have a blast*, pasarlo bomba.

blast [blɑːst] v. tr. Volar (to blow up): *to blast a rock*, volar una roca. || Abrir, perforar [con barrenos]: *to blast a tunnel*, abrir un túnel con barrenos. || Explotar (to explode). || Marchitar (a plant). || Derribar (by lightning). || FIG. Acabar con (hopes). | Criticar (to criticize). | Manchar (one's reputation). || — FAM. *Blast you!*, ¡maldito sea! || MIL. *To blast one's way through*, abrirse camino por medio de bombas.
— V. intr. Seguir disparando (with firearms). || FIG. FAM. Salir pitando. || *To blast off*, despegar.

blasted [—id] adj. Maldito, ta; condenado, da (damnable).

blastema [blæsˈtiːmə] n. BIOL. Blastema, *m.*

blast-hole [ˈblaːst,həul] n. Barreno, *m.*

blasting [ˈblɑːstiŋ] n. Voladura, *f.* (explosion). || — *Blasting cap*, detonador, *m.* || *Blasting charge*, carga explosiva.

blastoderm [ˈblæstəudəːm] n. BIOL. Blastodermo, *m.*

blast-off [ˈblɑːstɔf] n. Despegue, *m.* (of missiles).

blastomere [ˈblæstəmiə*] n. BIOL. Blastómero, *m.*

blastomycetes [ˈblæstə,maiˈsiːtiːz] pl. n. Blastomicetos, *m.* (fungi).

blastomycosis [ˈblæstəmaiˈkəusis] n. MED. Blastomicosis, *f.*

blastula [ˈblæstjulə] n. BIOL. Blástula, *f.*

blatancy [ˈbleitənsi] n. Descaro, *m.*: *the blatancy of his words*, el descaro de sus palabras. || Aspecto (*m.*) chillón *or* llamativo. || Evidencia, *f.* (obviousness).

blatant [ˈbleitənt] adj. Evidente, patente (very obvious): *a blatant lie*, una mentira patente. || Estridente, vocinglero, ra (voices). || Chillón, ona (colour). || Llamativo, va (clothes). || Descarado, da (brazen).

blather [ˈblæðə*] n. Tonterías, *f. pl.*

blather [ˈblæðə*] v. intr. Decir tonterías.

blaze [bleiz] n. Llamarada, *f.* (burst of flame). || Fuego, *m.* (fire). || Resplandor, *m.* (of sun, diamonds, etc.): *the blaze of the spotlights*, el resplandor de los focos. || Arranque, *m.*, rapto, *m.*: *in a blaze of anger*, en un arranque de ira. || Estrella, *f.*, mancha (*f.*) blanca en la frente (in animals). || Señal, *f.*, marca, *f.* (on a tree). || — FAM. *Go to blazes!*, ¡vete a la porra!, ¡vete al diablo! | *Like blazes*, como un rayo (like lightning), como un demonio (like mad). || *To be in a blaze*, estar en llamas. || FAM. *To run like blazes*, correr como un descosido. | *What the blazes...?*, ¿qué demonios...?

blaze [bleiz] v. intr. Arder: *the forest was blazing*, el bosque estaba ardiendo. || Resplandecer, brillar (to shine brightly): *the city was blazing with light*, la ciudad resplandecía de luz. || — *To blaze away*, seguir disparando. || *To blaze down on*, caer de plano en. || *To blaze past*, pasar como un rayo. || *To blaze up*, encenderse (sth.), ponerse furioso (s.o.). || *To blaze with anger*, echar chispas (to be furious).
— V. tr. Proclamar (to proclaim). || Publicar *or* gritar a los cuatro vientos (to spread news). || Señalar, marcar (a tree). || *To blaze a trail*, abrir un camino.

blazer [ˈbleizə*] n. Chaqueta (*f.*) de sport.

blazon [ˈbleizn] n. Blasón, *m.* (coat of arms, shield). || FIG. Ostentación, *f.*

blazon [ˈbleizn] v. tr. Blasonar. || FIG. Publicar *or* gritar a los cuatro vientos (to blaze).

blazonry [ˈbleiznri] n. Blasón, *m.* (art, coat of arms).

bleach [bliːtʃ] n. Decolorante, *m.* (chemical). || Lejía, *f.*: *put some bleach in the wash*, pon un poco de lejía en la colada. || Blanqueo, *m.* (whitening).

bleach [bliːtʃ] v. tr. Blanquear (to whiten). || Descolorar (to decolorize). || Decolorar (the hair).
— V. intr. Blanquear.

bleacher [—ə*] n. Blanqueador (worker). || — Pl. U. S. Graderío, *m. sing.*, gradas, *f.* (seats).

bleaching powder [—iŋ,paudə*] n. Polvo (*m.*) de blanquear.

bleak [bliːk] adj. Desolado, da; pelado, da (countryside). || Desapacible (weather). || Frío, a (wind). || Triste (cheerless): *a bleak smile*, una sonrisa triste. || Frío, a (lacking in kindliness): *a bleak reception*, una fría acogida. || Poco prometedor, ra (outlook).

bleak [bliːk] n. Breca, *f.*, albur, *m.* (fish).

blear [bliə*] adj. Nublado, da (eyes). || Borroso, sa; impreciso, sa (outline).

blear [bliə*] v. tr. Nublar (eyes). || Difuminar (outline).

bleary [—ri] adj. Nublado, da (eyes). || Borroso, sa; impreciso, sa (outline). || Agotado, da (worn-out).

bleat [bliːt] n. Balido, *m.* (of sheep, etc.). || FIG. FAM. Gemido, *m.*

bleat [bliːt] v. intr. Balar (sheep). || FIG. FAM. Gimotear, gemir (to speak plaintively).
— V. tr. Decir con voz quejumbrosa.

bleb [bleb] n. Ampolla, *f.* (blister). || Burbuja, *f.* (bubble).

bled [bled] pret. & p. p. See BLEED.

bleed* [bliːd] v. intr. Sangrar. || Exudar (plants). || PRINT. Refilar demasiado. || Desteñirse (material). || FIG. Sufrir (to suffer): *her heart bleeds for the misfortunes of mankind*, su corazón sufre por las desgracias de la humanidad. || Dar su vida, derramar su sangre (*for*, por). || Salirse (water, gas). || FAM. Escupir (to pay). || — *My nose is bleeding*, estoy sangrando *or* echo sangre por la nariz. || FAM. *To bleed like*

a pig, echar sangre como un cochino *or* un toro. || *To bleed to death*, morir desangrado.
— V. tr. Sangrar, sacar sangre a (to draw blood from). || BOT. Sangrar (plants). || FAM. Sacar dinero (to extort money from). || PRINT. Refilar demasiado. || — FAM. *To bleed o.s. white*, sacrificarse. | *To bleed s.o. white* o *dry*, sacar a uno hasta el último céntimo, esquilmarle a uno, chuparle la sangre a uno.

— OBSERV. Pret. & p. p. **bled.**

bleeder [—ə*] n. MED. Hemofílico, ca.
— Adj. TECH. De purga.

bleeding [—iŋ] adj. Sangrante, sangriento, ta. || POP. Pijotero, ra (damned).
— N. MED. Sangría, *f.* || Salida, *f.* (of water, gas). || Sangría, *f.* (of plants). || TECH. Purga, *f.*

blemish [ˈblemiʃ] n. Defecto, *m.*, imperfección, *f.* || Mancha, *f.*, tacha, *f.* (moral defect): *without blemish*, sin tacha.

blemish [ˈblemiʃ] v. tr. Manchar, mancillar (reputation, etc.). || Estropear, echar a perder (to spoil).

blench [blentʃ] v. intr. Retroceder, echarse atrás (to recoil). || Pestañear: *without blenching*, sin pestañear.

blend [blend] n. Mezcla, *f.*, combinación, *f.* || Mezcla, *f.* (of tea, tobacco, etc.).

blend [blend] v. tr. Mezclar, combinar. || Casar, armonizar (colours). || Armonizar (styles, etc.).
— V. intr. Mezclarse, combinarse. || Casarse, armonizar (colours).

— OBSERV. Aunque este verbo sea regular se emplea a veces la forma *blent* en los tiempos pasados.

blende [blend] n. MIN. Blenda, *f.*

blending [—iŋ] n. Mezcla, *f.*, combinación, *f.*

blennorrhagia [ˌblenəˈreidʒə] n. MED. Blenorragia, *f.*

blennorrhoea [ˌblenəˈriːə] n. MED. Blenorrea, *f.*

bless [bles] v. tr. Bendecir: *God bless you!*, ¡Dios le bendiga! || — *Bless you!*, ¡Jesús, María y José! (to s.o. who sneezes). || *God bless me!* or *God bless my soul!*, ¡Dios mío! || *I'll be blessed if I know*, que me maten si lo sé. || *To bless o.s.*, santiguarse.

— OBSERV. Aunque este verbo sea regular se emplea a veces la forma *blest* en los tiempos pasados.
— See BENDECIR (*Observ.*)

blessed [ˈblesid] or **blest** [blest] adj. Bendito, ta. || Santo, ta: *the blessed martyrs*, los santos mártires. || Beato, ta (beatified in Roman Catholicism). || Bienaventurado, da: *blessed are the poor in spirit*, bienaventurados sean los pobres de espíritu. || Feliz: *of blessed memory*, de feliz memoria. || Dotado, da: *blessed with an easygoing nature*, dotado de un natural apacible. || FAM. Maldito, ta: *that blessed boy!*, ¡ese maldito niño! || — *Blessed be Thy Name*, bendito sea tu Nombre. || *Blessed event*, feliz acontecimiento, *m.* || *Blessed Sacrament*, Santísimo Sacramento. || FAM. *Every blessed day*, todos los días. | *Not a blessed one*, ni uno, ni una. || FIG. *Not to know a blessed thing about*, no saber maldita la cosa de. || *The Blessed Virgin*, la Santa Virgen. || FAM. *The whole blessed day*, todo el santo día.

— OBSERV. See BENDITO (*Observ.*).

blessedness [ˈblesidnis] n. Bienaventuranza, *f.*, beatitud, *f.* || FIG. Felicidad, *f.*

blessing [ˈblesiŋ] n. Bendición, *f.*: *to give the blessing*, echar *or* dar la bendición. || Beneficio, *m.*, ventaja, *f.* (advantage): *the blessings of civilization*, las ventajas de la civilización. || — FIG. *It's a blessing in disguise*, no hay mal que por bien no venga. || FAM. *What a blessing!*, ¡qué suerte!

blest [blest] adj., pret. & p. p. See BLESSED.

blew [bluː] pret. See BLOW.

blight [blait] n. AGR. Roya, *f.* (rust). | Añublo, *m.*, tizón, *m.* (mildew). || FIG. Plaga, *f.*

blight [blait] v. tr. AGR. Producir la roya *or* el añublo *or* el tizón. || Marchitar (to wither). || FIG. Destrozar, destruir, arruinar (to spoil). | Frustrar (to frustrate): *to blight s.o.'s hopes*, frustrar las esperanzas de alguien.

blighter [ˈblaitə*] n. FAM. Sinvergüenza, *m.*, canalla, *m.* (rogue). | Tipo, *m.*, tío, *m.* (fellow).

Blighty [ˈblaiti] n. MIL. FAM. Inglaterra, *f.*

blimey [ˈblaimi] interj. FAM. ¡Caray!, ¡leñe!

blimp [blimp] n. Dirigible (*m.*) no rígido. || FIG. Patriotero, *m.* (jingoist).

blind [blaind] adj. Ciego, ga: *blind from birth*, ciego de nacimiento. || ARCH. Falso, sa (window, door). | Ciego, ga (wall). || Escondido, da (hidden): *a blind crossroad*, un cruce escondido. || FIG. Ciego, ga. || — *A blind man*, un ciego. || *A blind woman*, una ciega. || *Blind alley*, callejón (*m.*) sin salida. || *Blind curve*, curva (*f.*) sin visibilidad. || FAM. *Blind date*, cita (*f.*) concertada con alguien a quien no se conoce. || *Blind flying*, vuelo (*m.*) sin visibilidad. || *Blind gut*, intestino ciego. || *Blind in one eye*, tuerto, ta. || *Blind landing*, aterrizaje (*m.*) sin visibilidad *or* a ciegas. || *Blind letter*, carta (*f.*) cuya dirección es ilegible. || *Blind search*, registro (*m.*) a ciegas. || ANAT. *Blind spot*, punto ciego del ojo. || FAM. *Blind to the world*, borracho como una cuba. || FIG. *Blind with anger*, ciego de ira. | *In blind man's holiday*, al anochecer, entre dos luces. || *The blind*, los ciegos. || FIG. *It is the blind leading the blind*, están tan ciegos uno como otro. | *The blind side of s.o.*, el punto flaco de uno. | *This job is a blind alley*, este trabajo no tiene porvenir. | *To apply the blind eye to sth.*, hacer la vista gorda a una cosa. | *To be blind to*, no ver (not to see), hacer la vista gorda a (to be unwilling to see). || FAM. *To drink o.s. blind*, coger una buena trompa. || *To go blind*, quedarse ciego. || FIG. FAM. *To turn a blind eye*, hacer la vista gorda.
— N. Persiana, *f.*: *Venetian blind*, persiana veneciana. || Toldo, *m.* (awning). || FIG. Pretexto (a cover-up): *it was only a blind*, no era más que un pretexto. || Máscara, *f.* (mask). || MIL. Blinda, *f.* || U. S. Escondrijo, *m.* (a hide). | Anteojera, *f.* (of harness). || FIG. *To act as a blind for*, servir de pantalla a.
— Adv. A ciegas: *to go at a thing blind*, lanzarse a ciegas a algo. || — FAM. *To be blind drunk*, estar como una cuba, estar morado *or* ciego. || *To fly blind*, volar sin visibilidad *or* a ciegas.

blind [blaind] v. tr. Cegar, dejar ciego (to deprive of sight). || FIG. Deslumbrar (to dazzle). | Cegar: *blinded by passion*, cegado por la pasión. || *He was blinded in the war*, se quedó ciego durante la guerra.
— V. intr. AUT. *To blind along*, correr a toda velocidad.

blindage [ˈblaindidʒ] n. MIL. Blindaje, *m.*

blinder [ˈblaində*] n. U. S. Anteojera, *f.*

blindfold [ˈblaindfəuld] n. Venda, *f.*
— Adj./adv. Con los ojos vendados.

blindfold [ˈblaindfəuld] v. tr. Vendar los ojos.

blinding [ˈblaindiŋ] adj. Cegador, ra. || FIG. Deslumbrante, cegador, ra.
— N. Relleno, *m.* (filling in of cracks). || Gravilla, *f.* (material). || FIG. Deslumbramiento, *m.*

blindly [ˈblaindli] adv. A ciegas, ciegamente.

blindman's buff [ˈblaindmænzˈbʌf] n. Gallina (*f.*) ciega (game).

blindness [ˈblaindnis] n. MED. Ceguera, *f.*, ceguedad, *f.* || FIG. Obcecación, *f.*, ceguera, *f.*

blindworm [ˈblaindwəːm] n. ZOOL. Lución, *m.*

blink [bliŋk] n. Parpadeo, *m.* (of the eyes). || Destello, *m.* (gleam). || *On the blink*, averiado, da; estropeado, da.

blink [bliŋk] v. intr. Parpadear, pestañear (eyes). || Destellar (to glimmer). || Parpadear (light). || Mirar con asombro (in surprise). || — *Blinking lights*, luces (*f.*) intermitentes. || FIG. *To blink at a fault*, pasar por alto una falta, hacer caso omiso de una falta.
— V. tr. Guiñar (to wink the eyes). || FIG. Eludir: *to blink the question*, eludir la cuestión. | Negarse a ver (facts). || FIG. *To blink an eye*, hacer la vista gorda.

blinker [—ə*] n. Anteojera, *f.* (for horses). || AUT. Intermitente, *m.*, luz (*f.*) intermitente. || AVIAT. Faro (*m.*) intermitente. || POP. Ojo, *m.* (eye).

blinking [—iŋ] adj. FAM. Maldito, ta; condenado, da.

bliss [blis] n. Beatitud, *f.*, dicha, *f.*, felicidad, *f.* || FIG. *It was bliss!*, ¡fue maravilloso!

blissful [—ful] adj. Feliz, dichoso, sa. || Maravilloso, sa.

blister [ˈblistə*] n. MED. Ampolla, *f.* (in the skin). || Burbuja, *f.* (in a surface). || Vejiga, *f.* (in a film of paint). || ZOOL. *Blister beetle*, cantárida, *f.*

blister [ˈblistə*] v. tr. MED. Producir ampollas en, levantar ampollas en. || FIG. Criticar, censurar.
— V. intr. MED. Cubrirse de ampollas, formarse ampollas.

blistering [—riŋ] adj. Abrasador, ra (sun). || Mordaz (letter). || Candente (issue).

blithe [blaið] adj. Alegre.

blithering [ˈbliðəriŋ] adj. *A blithering idiot*, un tonto perdido *or* de capirote.

blithesome [ˈblaiðsəm] adj. Alegre.

blitz [blits] n. Bombardeo (*m.*) aéreo (air attack). || Ataque (*m.*) por sorpresa (sudden attack).

blitz [blits] v. tr. Bombardear.

blitzkrieg [—kriːg] n. Guerra (*f.*) relámpago.

blizzard [ˈblizəd] n. Ventisca, *f.*

bloat [bləut] v. tr. Hinchar, inflar (to swell). || Ahumar (fish). || FIG. Envanecer (to make vain). || FIG. *Bloated with pride*, hinchado de orgullo.
— V. intr. Hincharse, inflarse, abotagarse, abotargarse.

bloater [—ə*] n. Arenque (*m.*) ahumado.

blob [blɔb] n. Gota, *f.* (drop). || Borrón, *m.* (of ink). || Mancha, *f.* (of colour). || FAM. SP. *To score a blob*, no marcar ningún punto *or* tanto.

blob [blɔb] v. tr. Salpicar.

bloc [blɔk] n. Bloque, *m.* (in politics).

block [blɔk] n. Bloque, *m.* (large piece): *a block of marble*, un bloque de mármol. || Zoquete, *m.*, taco, *m.* (of wood). || Tajo, *m.* (butcher's, executioner's). || Horma, *f.* (wooden mould). || Fraustina, *f.* (of a milliner). || Pella, *f.* (of butter). || Polea, *f.* (pulley). || MAR. Motón, *m.* || Zapata, *f.* (of brake). || Calzo, *m.* (wedge). || Cubo, *m.* (toy). || PRINT. Cliché, *m.*, clisé, *m.* || || ARCH. Bloque, *m.* (for building). || Adoquín, *m.* (for paving). || Bloque (*m.*) *or* edificio (*m.*) comercial (building with shops, offices, etc.). || Manzana, *f.* [*Amer.*, cuadra, *f.*] (city block). || Bloque, *m.* (of cylinder). || Embotellamiento, *m.*, atasco, *m.* (traffic). || Plataforma, *f.* (for auction). || Cepo, *m.* (of anvil). || Taco, *m.* (of calendar). || SP. Bloqueo, *m.* (of a player). || Obstrucción, *f.* (obstruction). || Obstáculo, *m.*, estorbo, *m.* (obstacle). || Grupo, *m.*: *a block of seats*, un grupo de asientos. || Ramal, *m.*, tramo, *m.* (railway line). || Tren, *m.* (train). || COMM. Serie (*f.*) de acciones (group of shares). || FAM. Chola, *f.* (head). | Zoquete, *m.* (idiot). || — *Block and tackle*, aparejo (*m.*) de poleas. || *Block chain*, cadena articulada. || *Block diagram*, bloque diagrama. || *Block letters*, letras (*f. pl.*) de molde. || *Block of flats*, bloque (*m.*) de viviendas, casa (*f.*) de vecindad *or* de alquiler. || *Block printing*, estampado (*m.*) con molde. || *Block system*, bloqueo automático. || *Block tin*, estaño (*m.*) en lingotes *or* en galápagos. || *Note block*, bloc, *m.* || *To go to the block*, ir al cadalso. || *To put on the block*, vender en subasta.

block [blɔk] v. tr. Obstruir (to cause obstruction). || Obstaculizar, estorbar (to put obstacles). || Bloquear (in Parliament, in finances). || Cerrar: *to block the way*, cerrar el paso. || Dar forma a [un sombrero] (to shape a hat). || Bloquear (wheel). || Estampar (in bookbinding). || Calzar (a wheel). || SP. Bloquear (a ball). | Obstaculizar (a player). || — *"Road blocked"*, "calle interceptada". || *To block in* o *out*, bosquejar, esbozar (to sketch). || *To block up*, obstruir (to obstruct), calzar (to wedge), tapar (hole, window, etc.). — V. intr. Obstruirse (to become blocked).

blockade [blɔ'keid] n. Bloqueo, *m.*: *to raise a blockade*, levantar un bloqueo; *to run a blockade*, romper un bloqueo.

blockade [blɔ'keid] v. tr. Bloquear.

blockade-runner [—ˌrʌnə*] n. Persona (*f.*) *or* barco (*m.*) que intenta romper un bloqueo.

blockage ['blɔkidʒ] n. Bloqueo, *m.* || Obstrucción, *f.*

blockhead ['blɔkhed] n. FAM. Alcornoque, *m.*, zoquete, *m.*, tarugo, *m.*, mentecato, ta.

blockhouse ['blɔkhaus] n. MIL. Blocao, *m.*

bloke [bləuk] n. FAM. Tipo, *m.*, individuo, *m.*, tío, *m.*

blond [blɔnd] adj./n. Rubio, *m.*

blonde [blɔnd] adj./n. Rubia, *f.*

blood [blʌd] n. BIOL. Sangre, *f.* || FIG. Sangre, *f.* (character). | Sangre, *f.*, familia, *f.* (family). | Parentesco, *m.* (kinship). | Sangre, *f.*, raza, *f.* (race). | Petimetre, *m.*, currutaco, *m.* (dandy). || — FIG. *Bad blood*, odio, *m.* (hatred), rabia, *f.* (anger). || *Blood bank*, banco (*m.*) de sangre. || *Blood brother*, hermano (*m.*) carnal. || *Blood cell*, glóbulo, *m.* || *Blood clot*, coágulo, *m.* || *Blood count*, recuento (*m.*) de glóbulos sanguíneos. || *Blood donor*, donante (*m.* & *f.*) de sangre. || *Blood feud*, enemistad (*f.*) mortal. || *Blood group*, grupo sanguíneo. || *Blood horse*, pura sangre, *m.* || *Blood money*, precio (*m.*) de la sangre. || *Blood orange*, sanguina, *f.*, naranja (*f.*) de sangre. || *Blood plasma*, plasma sanguíneo. || *Blood platelet*, plaqueta (*f.*) de sangre. || *Blood poisoning*, envenenamiento (*m.*) de la sangre. || *Blood pressure*, tensión (*f.*) arterial. || *Blood pudding*, morcilla, *f.* || *Blood relation*, pariente consanguíneo, parienta consanguínea. || *Blood relationship*, consanguinidad, *f.* || *Blood sausage*, morcilla, *f.* || *Blood serum*, suero sanguíneo. || MED. *Blood sugar*, glicemia, *f.*, glucemia, *f.* || *Blood test*, análisis (*m.*) de sangre. || *Blood transfusion*, transfusión (*f.*) de sangre. || *Blood type*, grupo sanguíneo. || *Blood vessel*, vaso sanguíneo. || FIG. *Blue blood*, sangre azul. || *High blood pressure*, hipertensión, *f.* || FIG. *His blood ran cold*, se le heló la sangre. | *In cold blood*, a sangre fría. | *It is* o *it runs in his blood*, lo lleva en la sangre. | *Of the blood royal*, de sangre real. | *The call of blood*, la voz de la sangre. | *To be bathed in blood*, estar bañado en sangre. || *To be gushing blood*, estar chorreando sangre. || FIG. *To have blood on one's hands*, tener las manos manchadas de sangre. || FIG. FAM. *To have got s.o. in one's blood*, llevar *or* tener a alguien en la sangre, llevar a alguien en la masa de la sangre. | *To have no blood in one's veins*, no tener sangre en las venas, tener sangre de horchata. | *To have one's blood up*, estar de un humor de perros. || FIG. *To infuse new blood in an undertaking*, infundir nueva savia en una empresa. | *To make one's blood boil*, freírle *or* quemarle la sangre a uno. | *To make s.o.'s blood run cold*, helarle la sangre a uno. || *To shed blood*, derramar sangre. || *To sweat blood*, sudar sangre. || *Whole blood*, de pura sangre. || *With blood and iron*, a sangre y fuego. || *Without shedding of blood*, sin efusión de sangre.

blood [blʌd] v. tr. MED. Sangrar (to bleed). || Encarnar, iniciar [a perros de caza haciendo que prueben sangre de una presa]. || FIG. Acostumbrar.

bloodbath [—bɑ:θ] n. Matanza, *f.*, carnicería, *f.*

bloodcurdling ['blʌdˌkə:dliŋ] adj. Espeluznante, que hiela la sangre.

blooded [blʌdid] adj. De pura sangre. || *Cold blooded*, de sangre fría.

bloodguilty ['blʌdˌgilti] adj. Culpable de derramamiento de sangre.

bloodhound ['blʌdhaund] n. Sabueso, *m.* || FIG. Sabueso, *m.*, policía, *m.*

bloodily ['blʌdili] adv. Sangrientamente, sanguinariamente (in a bloody manner). || Cruelmente (cruelly).

bloodiness ['blʌdinis] n. Ensangrentamiento, *m.* (state of being bloody). || Crueldad, *f.* (cruelty).

bloodless ['blʌdlis] adj. Incruento, ta; sin efusión de sangre (without bloodshed). || Exangüe (without blood). || Anémico, ca (anaemic). || Insensible, frío, a (lacking emotion). || Cruel. || FAM. Que tiene sangre de horchata, débil (having little energy).

bloodlessly [—li] adv. Sin efusión de sangre.

bloodletting ['blʌdˌletiŋ] n. Sangría, *f.*

bloodred ['blʌd'red] adj. De color rojo sangre.

bloodroot ['blʌdrut] n. BOT. Sanguinaria, *f.*

bloodshed ['blʌdʃed] n. Matanza, *f.* (slaughter). || Derramamiento (*m.*) *or* efusión (*f.*) de sangre (shedding of blood).

bloodshot ['blʌdʃɔt] adj. Sanguinolento, ta; inyectado de sangre (eyes).

bloodstain ['blʌdstein] n. Mancha (*f.*) de sangre.

bloodstock ['blʌdstɔk] n. Caballos (*m. pl.*) de pura sangre.

bloodstone ['blʌdstəun] n. Sanguinaria, *f.* (semiprecious stone).

bloodstream ['blʌdstri:m] n. Sangre, *f.*: *to inject sth. in the bloodstream*, inyectar algo en la sangre.

bloodsucker ['blʌdˌsʌkə*] n. Sanguijuela, *f.* (animal, person).

bloodthirsty ['blʌdˌθə:sti] adj. Sediento *or* ávido de sangre, sanguinario, ria.

bloody ['blʌdi] adj. Sangriento, ta: *a bloody battle*, una batalla sangrienta. || Manchado de sangre; ensangrentado, da: *your shirt is bloody*, tu camisa está manchada de sangre. || Sanguinolento, ta: *a bloody boil*, un furúnculo sanguinolento. || Sanguinario, ria (murderous): *a bloody tyrant*, un tirano sanguinario. || POP. Condenado, da; puñetero, ra: *that bloody dog!*, ¡ese condenado perro!
— Adv. POP. Sumamente, terriblemente. || POP. *Not bloody likely*, ni hablar.

bloody ['blʌdi] v. tr. Manchar de sangre, ensangrentar.

bloody-minded [—'maindid] adj. POP. Desagradable (unpleasant). | Que tiene mal genio (bad-tempered). | Malintencionado, da (wicked).

bloody-mindedness [—'maindidnis] n. POP. Mal genio, *m.* (bad temper). | Mala intención, *f.*, mala idea, *f.* (wickedness).

bloom [blu:m] n. Florecimiento, *m.* (state of flowering). || Floración, *f.* (period of flowering). || Flor, *f.* (blossom): *in bloom*, en flor. || Color (*m.*) encendido, rubor, *m.* (on the cheek). || Vello, *m.*, pelusa, *f.* (in fruit). || Brillo, *m.* (of new coin). || TECH. Desbaste, *m.*, "bloom", *m.* || Aroma, *m.* (of wine). || — *A flower in its first bloom*, una flor recién abierta. || *Beauty that has lost its bloom*, belleza que ha perdido su lozanía. || *In full bloom*, en flor, florecido, da. || FIG. *In the full bloom of her beauty*, en la plenitud de su belleza. | *In the very bloom of one's youth, of life*, en la misma flor de la juventud, de la vida. || *To burst into bloom*, florecer. || *To take the bloom off*, quitar la frescura a.

bloom [blu:m] v. intr. Florecer (to blossom). || FIG. Florecer. | Resplandecer (to look radiant). | Convertirse (*into*, en) [to become].

bloomer [—ə*] n. FAM. Metedura (*f.*) de pata. || FAM. *To make a bloomer*, meter la pata.

bloomers [—əz] n. Pantalones (*m. pl.*) bombachos, pololos, *m. pl.*

blooming [—iŋ] adj. Floreciente (blossoming). || Radiante de salud, resplandeciente (radiant with health). || POP. Pijotero, ra; pajolero, ra (bloody).

blooper ['blu:pə*] n. U. S. FAM. Metedura (*f.*) de pata.

blossom ['blɔsəm] n. Flor, *f.* (flower). || *In blossom*, en flor.

blossom ['blɔsəm] v. intr. Florecer. || — *To blossom into*, llegar a ser, convertirse en. || *To blossom out*, abrirse (flower), alcanzar su plenitud (person).

blot [blɔt] n. Borrón, *m.*, mancha, *f.* (of ink). || FIG. Mancha, *f.* (on s.o.'s honour). || Monstruosidad, *f.* (eyesore). || FIG. *These big buildings are a blot on the landscape*, estos grandes edificios afean el paisaje.

blot [blɔt] v. tr. Emborronar, manchar de tinta (with ink). || Secar (with blotting paper). || Manchar, ensuciar (to stain). || — *To blot one's record*, manchar su hoja de servicio. || *To blot out*, tachar (to erase), borrar (memories), ocultar (to hide from view), suprimir, liquidar (to kill).
— V. intr. Emborronarse, mancharse de tinta (to become blotted). || Hacer borrones (to make blots). || Correrse (the ink).

blotch [blɔtʃ] n. Mancha, *f.* (of ink, colour). || Pústula, *f.* (pimple). || Rojez, *f.*, mancha, *f.* (in the skin).

blotch [blɔtʃ] v. tr. Manchar (to cover with blotches). || Cubrir de pústulas (to cover with pimples). || Enrojecer (the skin).

blotched [—t] or **blotchy** [—i] adj. Cubierto de manchas (stained). || Enrojecido, da (the skin).

blotter ['blɔtə*] n. Secante, *m.*, papel (*m.*) secante (blotting paper). || U. S. Registro, *m.* (record book).

blotting paper ['blɔtiŋˌpeipə*] n. Papel (*m.*) secante.

blouse [blauz] n. Blusa, *f.* (woman's shirt). || MIL. Guerrera, *f.* || MAR. Marinera, *f.* || *Sailor blouse*, blusón, *m.* (for women).

blow [bləu] n. Soplo, *m.*, soplido, *m.* (blast of air). || Ráfaga (*f.*) de viento (strong gust of wind). || Golpe, *m.* (stroke, shock): *to deal* o *to strike s.o. a blow*, dar *or* asestar un golpe a alguien. || SP. Golpe, *m.* (punch). || FIG. Golpe, *m.*: *he suffered a severe blow when his mother died*, sufrió un golpe duro con la muerte de su madre. || POP. Información (*f.*) secreta. || — *At one blow*, de un golpe. || MUS. *Blow at* o *on one's trumpet*, trompetazo, *m.* || *Blow patch*, parche, *m.* || *Give your nose a good blow*, suénate bien las narices. || FIG. *To aim a blow at s.o.'s authority*, hacer mella en la autoridad de alguien. || *To come to blows*, llegar *or* venir a las manos. || *To exchange blows*, pegarse. || *To feel the blow*, acusar el golpe. || FIG.

To go for a blow, ir a dar una vuelta. || *To miss one's blow*, errar el golpe. || FIG. *Without striking a blow*, sin mover un dedo.

— OBSERV. When "blow with" is followed by the name of an instrument or weapon, it is generally translated by the noun with the suffix *-ada* if the instrument is pointed (*a blow with a knife*, una cuchillada; *a blow with a dagger*, una puñalada, etc.) or with the suffix *-azo* if the instrument is blunt (*a blow with a hammer*, un martillazo; *a blow with a fist*, un puñetazo; *a blow with the hand*, un manotazo; *a blow with a cane*, un bastonazo, etc.). There are of course exceptions, like *a blow with a stone*, una pedrada.

blow* [bləu] v. intr. Soplar (wind, mouth). || Soplarse: *to blow on one's fingers to warm them*, soplarse los dedos para calentárselos. || Jadear, resollar (to be out ot breath). || Volar: *to blow out of the window*, volar por la ventana. || Sonar (to sound): *the whistle blew*, el silbato sonó. || Resoplar, expulsar aire (whales). || Bufar (horses, bulls). || Reventar (tyres). || Fundirse (a fuse). || FAM. Chivarse, soplonear (to denounce). | Alardear, fanfarronear (to boast). | Irse, largarse (to go). || — FAM. *It's blowing great guns*, hace un viento que arranca las chimeneas. || *To be blowing*, hacer viento. || *To be blown*, estar sin aliento. || *To blow on an instrument*, tocar un instrumento. || *To blow open, shut*, abrirse, cerrarse de golpe. || FIG. *To blow upon s.o.'s reputation*, empañar la reputación de alguien. || *To puff and blow*, jadear (person), resoplar (horse).

— V. tr. Llevar (the wind): *to blow a ship ashore*, llevar un barco hacia la costa. || Soplar, aventar: *to blow the fire*, soplar el fuego. || Soplar (a whistle). || Echar (air, smoke). || Sonarse (the nose). || Soplar (the glass). || Reventar (a tyre). || MUS. Tocar: *to blow the trumpet*, tocar la trompeta. | Dar aire a (an organ). || Azotar: *the wind blows the trees*, el viento azota los árboles. || Dejar sin aliento (to put out of breath). || Poner huevos en (flies). || Fundir (fuse). || Vaciar: *to blow a boiler*, vaciar una caldera. || TECH. Inyectar (air). || FAM. Convidar a (to invite). | Regalar con (to offer a gift). | Malgastar (to waste). | Maldecir (to curse). | Perder (an opportunity). || — POP. *Blow the expense!* o *expense be blowed!*, ¡al cuerno el gasto! | *I'll be blowed if...!*, ¡que me aspen si...! || *To blow bubbles*, hacer pompas (with soap), hacer globos (with bubble gum), hacer burbujas (in a liquid). || FIG. *To blow hot and cold*, jugar con dos barajas (to play a double game), cambiar de opinión cada dos por tres (to hesitate). | *To blow one's lid* o *one's top*, salir de sus casillas. || FIG. FAM. *To blow one's own trumpet* o *horn*, echarse flores, darse bombo. || *To blow s.o. a kiss*, enviar un beso a alguien. || AUT. *To blow the horn*, tocar el claxon. || FIG. *To know which way the wind blows*, saber de qué lado sopla el viento. || FAM. *Well, I'm blowed!*, ¡caramba! | *What good wind blows you here?*, ¿qué te trae por aquí?

— ***To blow about***, dispersar (to scatter). | Revolotear (leaves). || ***To blow away***, arrastrar, llevarse (the wind). | Soplar en (dust, etc.). | Disipar (fog). || ***To blow down***, derribar. || ***To blow in***, derribar (door, window-pane). | FAM. Disipar (one's money), entrar de sopetón (to come in), visitar de paso (to call on). | — *To blow in at*, entrar por. || ***To blow off***, quitar (to remove). | Volar (to destroy). | Vaciar (boiler). | Salir volando (a hat). | Salirse, escaparse (the steam). | — *To blow off about*, lamentarse de. | FIG. *To blow off steam*, desfogarse. | U. S. FAM. *To blow the lid off*, descubrir el pastel. || ***To blow on***, denunciar. || ***To blow out***, apagar, soplar (to extinguish). | Apagarse (to become extinguished). | Hinchar (cheeks). | Reventar, estallar (tyre). | Fundirse (fuse). | TECH. Vaciar (boiler). || ***To blow over***, derribar (tree). | Encamar, tumbar (crops). | Calmarse (a storm). | Olvidarse (scandal). || ***To blow up***, inflar, hinchar (to inflate). | Volar (to destroy). | Ampliar (photograph). | Explotar (to explode). | Reventar (to burst). | Soplar, aventar (fire). | FAM. Dar un bocinazo a (to rebuke), salir de sus casillas (to lose one's temper). | — *It's blowing up for rain*, este viento anuncia lluvia. | FIG. *To be blown up with conceit*, estar henchido de orgullo.

— OBSERV. Pret. ***blew;*** p. p. ***blown***.

blower [—ə*] n. Soplador, *m*. [de vidrio] (glass worker). || Fuelle, *m*. (bellows). || Escape (*m*.) de gas (in a coal mine). || Cortina, *f*., pantalla, *f*. (of chimney). || FAM. Teléfono, *m*.

blowfly [—flai] n. ZOOL. Moscarda, *f*., mosca (*f*.) azul de la carne.

blowgun [—gʌn] n. Cerbatana, *f*. || Pistola, *f*. (for painting).

blowhole [—həul] n. Ventilador, *m*. (in tunnel). || Sopladura, *f*., venteadura, *f*. (flaw in a metal casting). || Respiradero, *m*. (in ice). || Orificio (*m*.) nasal (of whales).

blowing [—iŋ] n. Sopladura, *f*. (of glass). || Soplo, *m*., soplido, *m*. (of wind). || Silbido, *m*. (wind noise).

blowlamp [—læmp] n. Lámpara (*f*.) de soldar, soplete, *m*.

blown [bləun] p. p. See BLOW.

— Adj. Jadeante, sin aliento (breathless). || Hinchado, da; lleno de gases (the stomach). || Estropeado, da (food). || *Blown glass*, vidrio soplado.

blowoff [ˈbləuɔf] n. Tubo (*m*.) de extracción (for blowing off steam, water, etc.). || Escape, *m*., salida, *f*. (expelling of air, water, etc.). || Explosión, *f*. (outburst). || *Blowoff valve*, válvula (*f*.) de escape.

blowout [ˈbləuaut] n. Reventón, *m*., pinchazo, *m*. (in a tyre). || Fusión, *f*. (of a fuse). || Escape, *m*., salida, *f*. (of gas, steam). || FAM. *To have a good blowout*, darse un banquetazo.

blowpipe [ˈbləupaip] n. Soplete, *m*. (for producing high intensity heat): *oxyhydrogen blowpipe*, soplete oxhídrico. || Cerbatana, *f*. (blowgun). || Caña (*f*.) de soplador (blowtube). || MED. Sonda, *f*.

blowtorch [ˈbləutɔ:tʃ] n. U.S. See BLOWLAMP.

blowtube [ˈbləutju:b] n. Caña (*f*.) de soplador (in glassworking). || Cerbatana, *f*. (blowgun).

blowup [ˈbləuʌp] n. Ampliación, *f*. (of photograph). || Explosión, *f*. || FIG. Estallido, *m*. (of anger). | Escándalo, *m*. | Riña, *f*., agarrada, *f*. (quarrel).

blowy [bləui] adj. Ventoso, sa.

blowzy [ˈblauzi] adj. Desastrado, da; desaliñado, da (untidy). || Coloradote, ta (ruddy).

blub [blʌb] v. intr. FAM. Lloriquear.

blubber [—ə*] n. Grasa (*f*.) de ballena (whale fat). || Lloriqueo, *m*., gimoteo, *m*. (weeping). || FAM. Medusa, *f*. (jellyfish). || *Blubber lip*, bezo, *m*.

blubber [—ə*] v. intr. Lloriquear, gimotear.

— V. tr. *To blubber out sth*., decir algo entre llantos.

bludgeon [ˈblʌdʒən] n. Maza, *f*., clava, *f*., cachiporra, *f*.

bludgeon [ˈblʌdʒən] v. tr. Aporrear, apalear (to hit). || *To bludgeon s.o. into doing sth*., obligar a alguien a hacer algo.

blue [blu:] adj. Azul (colour). || Amoratado, da (body): *face blue with cold*, cara amoratada de frío. || Deprimente (depressing). || Triste, melancólico, ca (melancholy). || FIG. Azul (blood). || MED. Azul: *blue disease*, enfermedad azul. || Conservador, ra (Tory). || — *Blue blood*, sangre (*f*.) azul. || *Blue book*, libro (*m*.) azul, publicación (*f*.) oficial (government report), guía (*f*.) de personas eminentes (register). || *Blue cheese*, queso (*m*.) de tipo Roquefort *or* de pasta verde. || U. S. FIG. *Blue chip*, valor (*m*.) de primera clase. || *Blue devils*, melancolía, *f*. || FAM. *Blue funk*, miedo (*m*.) cerval. || *Blue jeans*, pantalones vaqueros. || *Blue joke*, chiste (*m*.) verde. || *Blue law*, ley inspirada por los puritanos. || *Blue lead*, galena, *f*. || *Blue mould*, moho, *m*. || FIG. *Blue ribbon*, galardón máximo, primer premio. || FAM. *Blue rum*, matarratas, *m. inv*. || *Blue streak*, rayo, *m*., relámpago, *m*. || ZOOL. *Blue tit*, alionín, *m*. || FIG. *I've told you till I'm blue in the face*, me canso de repetírselo. | *Once in a blue moon*, de Pascuas a Ramos, de higos a brevas. | *To feel blue*, sentirse deprimido. || *To look blue*, estar triste. || FAM. *To talk blue*, decir verdulerías. | *To tell blue stories*, contar chistes verdes. | *To turn the air blue*, jurar como un carretero.

— N. Azul, *m*. (colour): *light, dark blue*, azul claro, oscuro. || Añil, *m*., azulete, *m*. (in laundering). || FIG. Conservador, ra (Tory). | Mar, *m*. (sea). | Cielo, *m*. (sky). || — *Cobalt, deep, pale, navy, Prussian, sky, ultramarine blue*, azul cobalto, oscuro, claro, marino, de Prusia, celeste, de ultramar. || FIG. *Out of the blue*, como llovido del cielo, de repente.

blue [blu:] v. tr. Azular. || Dar azulete a (in laundering). || Pavonar (steel). || FAM. Despilfarrar (money).

— V. intr. Amoratarse (the skin). || Azularse (to become blue).

Bluebeard [—biəd] pr. n. Barba Azul.

bluebell [—bel] n. BOT. Campanilla, *f*., campánula, *f*. (flower).

blueberry [—beri] n. BOT. Arándano, *m*.

bluebird [—bə:d] n. ZOOL. Azulejo, *m*.

bluebottle [—bɔtl] n. ZOOL. Moscarda, *f*., mosca (*f*.) azul. || BOT. Azulejo, *m*.

blue-collar [—ˈkɔlə*] adj. Obreril.

blue-eyed [—aid] adj. De ojos azules. || FIG. *Blue-eyed boy*, ojo derecho, preferido, *m*.

blueing [—iŋ] n. Azulado, *m*., azuleo, *m*. || U. S. Añil, *m*. (bluing).

bluejack [—dʒæk] n. Vitriolo (*m*.) azul.

bluejacket [—ˌdʒækit] n. Marinero, *m*.

bluenose [—nəuz] n. U. S. Puritano, na.

blue-pencil [—ˈpensl] v. tr. Tachar, censurar (to obliterate). || Corregir (to correct).

bluepoint [—pɔint] n. U. S. ZOOL. Ostra, *f*. (oyster).

blueprint [—print] n. Cianotipo, *m*. (photographic reproduction). || Proyecto (*m*.) original (plan).

blues [—z] n. "Blues", estilo (*m*.) de jazz. || FAM. Melancolía, *f*., nostalgia, *f*., morriña, *f*., tristeza, *f*.

bluestocking [—ˌstɔkiŋ] n. Literata, *f*., marisabidilla, *f*., cultalatiniparla, *f*.

bluestone [—stəun] n. CHEM. Sulfato (*m*.) de cobre.

bluff [blʌf] n. Fanfarronada, *f*., farol, *m*. (act of bluffing). || Farol, *m*. (in poker). || Farolero, ra; fanfarrón, ona (bluffer). || Acantilado, *m*. (cliff). || *To call s.o.'s bluff*, hacer que alguien ponga las cartas boca arriba.

— Adj. Brusco, ca (frank). || Cortado a pico, escarpado, da (cliff). || Abultado, da (prow).

bluff [blʌf] v. intr. Tirarse un farol, farolear, fanfarronear.

— V. tr. Engañar (to deceive). || *To bluff s.o. into thinking that*, hacer creer a uno que.

bluffer [—ə*] n. Farolero, ra; fanfarrón, ona.

bluing [ˈblu:iŋ] n. U. S. Añil, *m*., azulete, *m*.

bluish [ˈbluːiʃ] adj. Azulado, da; azulino, na; azulenco ca; azuloso, sa.
blunder [ˈblʌndə*] n. Pifia, *f.*, metedura (*f.*) de pata patinazo, *m.*
blunder [ˈblʌndə*] v. intr. Cometer un error, pifiar, meter la pata (fam.) [to make a mistake]: *I blundered in telling him to go*, cometí un error diciéndole que se fuese. || — *To blunder against* o *into*, tropezar contra. || *To blunder one's way along*, avanzar a ciegas. || *To blunder upon sth.*, tropezar con algo.
— V. tr. *To blunder away*, dejar escapar, perder (an opportunity). || *To blunder out*, dejar escapar (a secret).
blunderbuss [ˈblʌndəbʌs] n. Trabuco (*m.*) naranjero.
blunderer [ˈblʌndərə*] n. Torpe, *m.* & *f.*, persona (*f.*) que mete la pata.
blunt [blʌnt] adj. Embotado, da; desafilado, da (edge, knife). || Despuntado, da (pencil). || MATH. Obtuso, sa (angle). || FIG. Embotado, da (mind). | Franco, ca (straightforward). | Terminante, categórico, ca: *a blunt answer*, una contestación categórica. | Brusco, ca (person). || *Blunt instrument*, instrumento (*m.*) contundente.
blunt [blʌnt] v. tr. Embotar, desafilar (edge, knife). || Despuntar (pencil). || FIG. Embotar: *life had blunted his feelings*, la vida había embotado sus sentimientos.
bluntly [—li] adv. Francamente, sin rodeos.
bluntness [—nis] n. Embotadura, *f.*, embotamiento, *m.* (of edge, knife). || Despuntadura, *f.*, despunte, *m.* (of pencil). || FIG. Franqueza, *f.* | Brusquedad, *f.*
blur [bləː*] n. Mancha, *f.* (stain). || Vaho, *m.* (of breath). || Aspecto (*m.*) borroso. || FIG. *To cast a blur on s.o.'s name*, empañar la reputación de alguien.
blur [bləː*] v. tr. Empañar, enturbiar (to smear): *the rain blurs the window panes*, la lluvia empaña los cristales. || Enturbiar (sight). || Desdibujar, difuminar: *the fog blurs the outline of the hills*, la niebla desdibuja el contorno de las colinas. || Manchar de tinta, emborronar (to stain). || *To blur out*, borrar, ocultar.
— V. intr. Empañarse (to smear). || Desdibujarse, difuminarse (sight).
blurb [bləːb] n. Propaganda, *f.*
blurred [bləːrd] or **blurry** [ˈbləːri] adj Empañado, da (glass). || Borroso, sa (photograph, etc.): *blurred letters*, letras borrosas. || Confuso, sa; borroso, sa; vago, ga: *blurred memories*, recuerdos confusos. || *Eyes blurred with tears*, ojos empañados en lágrimas.
blurt [bləːt] v. tr. *To blurt out*, dejar escapar (a word, a secret), contar de buenas a primeras (a story), decir bruscamente.
blush [blʌʃ] n. Sonrojo, *m.*, rubor, *m.* (of cheeks). || Arrebol, *m.* (red glow). || Color (*m.*) de rosa (rosy glow). || Encarnado, *m.* (of flowers). || Vistazo, *m.*, ojeada, *f.* (look). || *At the first blush*, a primera vista.
blush [blʌʃ] v. intr. Ruborizarse, sonrojarse, ponerse colorado (a person): *to blush for shame*, ruborizarse de vergüenza. || Enrojecer, ponerse rojo *or* colorado (to become red). || Arrebolarse (sky). || — *I blush for you*, me das vergüenza. || *I blush to say that*, me da vergüenza *or* me avergüenza decir que. || *To blush to the roots of one's hair*, ponerse como un pavo, ponerse rojo como una amapola.
blushing [—iŋ] adj. Ruborizado, sa. || Tímido, da (bashful).
— N. Rubor, *m.*, sonrojo, *m.* (blush).
bluster [ˈblʌstə*] n. Estruendo, *m.* (of storm). || FIG. Fanfarronada, *f.*, bravatas, *f. pl.* (swaggering talk). | Ruido, *m.*, estruendo, *m.* (noise).
bluster [ˈblʌstə*] v. intr. Bramar (sea). || Bramar, soplar con fuerza (wind). || FIG. Echar bravatas, fanfarronear (to swagger). | Vociferar (*against*, contra).
— V. tr. *To bluster out*, soltar, proferir (insults, threats).
blusterer [—rə*] n. Fanfarrón, *m.*
blustering [—riŋ] adj. Violento, ta (wind). || Furioso, sa (sea). || FIG. Fanfarrón, ona.
boa [ˈbəuə] n. Boa, *f.* (snake). || Boa, *m.* (fur).
boar [bɔː*] n. Verraco, *m.* (hog). || — *Wild boar*, jabalí, *m.* || *Young wild boar*, jabato, *m.*
board [bɔːd] n. Madero, *m.* (long piece of sawn timber). || Tabla, *f.* (plank). || Tablero, *m.*: *drawing board*, tablero de dibujo. || Tablero, *m.*, cuadro, *m.* (control panel). || Mesa, *f.* (table): *ironing board*, mesa de planchar. || Tablón, *m.* [de anuncios] (for notices). || Cartón, *m.*: *corrugated board*, cartón ondulado. || Cartoné, *m.* (in bookbinding). || Tablero, *m.* (for chess). || MAR. Bordo, *m.*: *on board the ship*, a bordo del barco. | Bordada, *f.*: *to make a board*, dar una bordada. || Junta, *f.*, consejo, *m.* (authoritative body): *board of directors*, junta directiva, consejo de administración. || Comisión, *f.* (committee). || Pensión, *f.*: *full board*, pensión completa. || — Pl. Tablas, *f.* (theatre): *to tread the boards*, pisar las tablas. || — *Above board*, en regla: *his papers were above board*, sus papeles estaban en regla; franco, ca; sincero, ra (sincere). || *Board and lodging*, casa y comida. || *Board of examiners*, tribunal (*m.*) de exámenes. || *Board room*, sala (*f.*) del consejo. || COMM. *Board of Trade*, Ministerio (*m.*) de Comercio [U. S. Cámara (*f.*) de Comercio]. || *Board of trustees*, junta directiva. || COMM. *Free on board*, franco a bordo. || *In boards*, en cartoné (books). || *To be on the boards*, pisar las tablas (theatre). || FIG. *To go by the board*, irse al traste, frustrarse: *his plans went by the board because he had no money*, sus planes se fueron al traste porque no tenía dinero. || MAR. *To go on board*, subir a bordo. || FIG. *To let go by the board*, abandonar: *he let his plan to visit Egypt go by the board*, abandonó el proyecto de visitar Egipto. | *To sweep the board*, limpiar la mesa (in gambling), llevarse todas las medallas: *Spain swept the board in the championship*, España se llevó todas las medallas en el campeonato; llevarse todos los puestos (in an election). | *To throw over board*, tirar *or* echar *or* arrojar por la borda.
board [bɔːd] v. tr. Alojar, hospedar (to lodge). || Embarcarse en, embarcar en (ship, plane): *we boarded the Queen Mary*, embarcamos en el Queen Mary. || Subir a (train, bus): *we boarded the train as it was moving off*, subimos al tren cuando ya estaba en marcha. || MAR. Abordar. || Entarimar, entablar (floor). || Encartonar (book). || *To board up*, tapar (window, door), vallar (field).
— V. intr. Alojarse, hospedarse (*with*, en casa de). || Estar interno: *to board at the school*, ser interno en el colegio.
boarder [—ə*] n. Huésped, *m.* & *f.* (in a boarding-house). || Interno, na (at school).
boarding [—iŋ] n. Entablado, *m.*, entarimado, *m.* (of floor). || Encartonado, *m.* (of books). || Pensión, *f.* || AVIAT. MAR. Embarque, *m.*
boardinghouse [—iŋhaus] n. Pensión, *f.*, casa (*f.*) de huéspedes.
boarding school [—iŋ-skuːl] n. Internado, *m.*
boardwalk [—wɔːk] n. U. S. Paseo (*m.*) construido con tablas a lo largo de una playa.
boast [bəust] n. Jactancia, *f.*, alarde, *m.*, presunción, *f.* || *To be the boast of*, ser el orgullo de.
boast [bəust] v. intr. Jactarse, alardear, presumir (*of*, *about*, de): *he boasts that he can do it*, se jacta de que puede hacerlo. || *That's nothing to boast of*, no hay por qué vanagloriarse.
— V. tr. Presumir de, alardear de: *Germany can boast excellent roads*, Alemania puede presumir de excelentes carreteras. || Tener, vanagloriarse de tener: *he boasts two cars and a helicopter*, tiene dos coches y un helicóptero.
boaster [—ə*] n. Jactancioso, sa; presumido, da.
boastful [—ful] adj. Jactancioso, sa; presumido, da.
boasting [—iŋ] n. Jactancia, *f.*, vanagloria, *f.*
boat [bəut] n. MAR. Barco, *m.* (any ship). | Buque, *m.*, navío, *m.* (large). | Barca, *f.*, bote, *m.* (small vessel). || Salsera, *f.* (for gravy). || — *Boat race*, regata, *f.* || *Boat train*, tren (*m.*) que enlaza con un barco. || *By boat*, en barco. || *Cargo boat*, buque de carga, carguero, *m.* || REL. *Incense boat*, naveta, *f.* || *Merchant boat*, barco mercante. || *Pilot boat*, barco del práctico. || *Pleasure boat*, barco de recreo. || *Sailing boat*, barco de vela, velero, *m.* || FIG. *To be in the same boat*, remar en la misma galera, estar en el mismo caso. | *To burn one's boats*, quemar las naves. | *To miss the boat*, perder el tren, perder una oportunidad. | *To rock the boat*, causar perturbaciones.
boat [bəut] v. tr. Transportar en barco.
— V. intr. Dar un paseo en barco.
boater [—ə*] n. Canotié, *m.*, canotier, *m.*, sombrero (*m.*) de paja.
boathook [—huk] n. Bichero, *m.*
boathouse [—haus] n. Cobertizo, *m.*
boating [—iŋ] n. Paseo (*m.*) en barco. || Transporte (*m.*) en barco.
boatload [—ləud] n. Barcada, *f.*
boatman [—mən] n. Barquero, *m.*

— OBSERV. El plural de esta palabra es *boatmen*.

boatswain [ˈbəusn] n. MAR. Contramaestre, *m.* || — *Boatswain's chair*, guindola, *f.* || *Boatswain's mate*, segundo contramaestre.
boatyard [ˈbəutjɑːd] n. MAR. Astillero, *m.*
bob [bɔb] n. Movimiento (*m.*) brusco, sacudida, *f.* (movement). || Reverencia, *f.* (bow). || Corcho, *m.*, flotador, *m.* (for fishing). || Rizo, *m.* (curl). || Pelo (*m.*) corto (haircut). || Peluca, *f.* (wig). || Cola (*f.*) cortada (of horse). || Borla, *f.* (of ribbons, etc.). || Pendiente, *m.* (of the ear). || FAM. Chelín, *m.* (shilling). || TECH. Volante, *m.* (of machine). | Lenteja, *f.* (of pendulum). | Plomo, *m.* (of plumb line). || SP. Bobsleigh, *m.* || FAM. *A bob a nob*, un chelín por barba.
bob [bɔb] v. intr. Agitarse, menearse. || Balancearse (in the air, water): *the boat is bobbing on the water*, el barco se balancea en el agua. || Hacer una reverencia (to curtsy): *he bobbed to the Queen*, hizo una reverencia ante la Reina. || — *To bob down*, agacharse: *he bobbed down to avoid the blow*, se agachó para evitar el golpe. || *To bob for apples*, intentar coger manzanas con la boca. || *To bob in*, entrar [un momento]. || *To bob up*, salir a la superficie (sth. in the water), surgir, presentarse: *the same problem bobbed up again*, el mismo problema surgió otra vez.
— V. tr. Mover, menear. || Cortar [el pelo de una mujer o el rabo de un animal] (to cut). || — *He bobbed his head up and down*, subía y bajaba la cabeza.
Bob [bɔb] pr. n. Roberto, *m.* (diminutive of *Robert*).
bobber [—ə*] n. U. S. Corcho, *m.*, flotador, *m.* (cork float).
bobbery [ˈbɔbəri] n. FAM. Jaleo, *m.*, alboroto, *m.* (hubbub).

BOATS — BARCOS, m.

I. Different types. — Distintos tipos, *m.*

aircraft carrier	portaaviones *m. inv.*
barge	barcaza *f.*, gabarra *f.*
battleship	acorazado *m.*
boat	barco *m.* (general term), buque *m.*, navío *m.* (large), barca *f.*, bote *m.* (small)
brig, brigantine	bergantín *m.*
canoe	canoa *f.*
caravel	carabela *f.*
cargo boat	carguero *m.*, buque (*m.*) de carga
coaster	barco (*m.*) de cabotaje
coastguard cutter *o* vessel	guardacostas *m. inv.*
cod-fishing boat	bacaladero *m.*
collier	barco (*m.*) carbonero
corvette	corbeta *f.*
cruiser	crucero *m.* (warship)
destroyer	destructor *m.*
ferry, ferryboat	transbordador *m.*
fishing boat	barco (*m.*) de pesca *or* pesquero
freighter	buque (*m.*) de carga, carguero *m.*
frigate	fragata *f.*
galleon; galley	galeón *m.*; galera *f.*
gunboat	cañonero *m.*, lancha (*f.*) cañonera
hovercraft	aerodeslizador *m.*
icebreaker	rompehielos *m. inv.*
launch	lancha *f.*
lifeboat	bote (*m.*) salvavidas, lancha (*f.*) de salvamento
lighter	barcaza *f.*, gabarra *f.*
liner, ocean liner	transatlántico *m.*
merchant ship, merchantman	buque (*m.*) mercante
minelayer	minador *m.*
minesweeper	dragaminas *m. inv.*
motorboat	motora *f.*, lancha (*f.*) motora
outboard	fuera bordo *or* borda *m. inv.*
paddle steamer *o* boat	vapor (*m.*) de ruedas
passenger boat	barco (*m.*) de pasajeros
patrol boat	patrullero *m.*
piragua, pirogue	piragua *f.*
raft	balsa *f.*
revenue cutter	guardacostas *m. inv.*
rowing boat	bote (*m.*) de remos
sailing boat *o* ship	velero *m.*, barco (*m.*) de vela
schooner	goleta *f.*
shallop	chalupa *f.*
ship	barco *m.*, buque *m.*, navío *m.*
skiff	esquife *m.*
sloop	balandro *m.*
steamer, steamship	vapor *m.*, buque (*m.*) de vapor
submarine	submarino *m.*
tanker	buque (*m.*) aljibe, petrolero *m.*
torpedo boat	torpedero *m.*
trawler	trainera *f.*
tug, tugboat	remolcador *m.*
vessel	nave *f.*, navío *m.*, buque *m.*, barco *m.*
whaler	ballenero *m.*
yacht	yate *m.*
yawl	yola *f.*

II. Main parts. — Partes (*f.*) principales.

anchor	ancla *f.*
ballast	lastre *m.*
beam	bao *m.* (crosspiece), manga *f.* (breadth)
berth, bunk	litera *f.*
berth, cabin, stateroom	camarote *m.*
bilge	sentina *f.* (inner hull), pantoque *m.* (outer hull)
bow, prow	proa *f.*
bowline	bolina *f.*
bridge	puente (*m.*) de mando
bull's eye	ojo (*m.*) de buey, portilla *f.*
bulwark	borda *f.*
capstan	cabrestante *m.*
cathead	serviola *f.*, pescante *m.*
compass	brújula *f.*, compás *m.*
conning tower	torre (*f.*) de mando (of ship), torrecilla *f.* (of submarine)
cutwater	tajamar *m.*, espolón *m.*
deck	cubierta *f.*
engine room	sala (*f.*) de máquinas
figurehead	mascarón (*m.*) de proa
forecastle	castillo (*m.*) de proa
frame	cuaderna *f.* (rib), armazón *f.* (entire framework)
funnel	chimenea *f.*
galley	cocina *f.*
gangplank	plancha *f.*
gangway	pasamano *m.* (platform), portalón *m.* (opening), plancha *f.* (gangplank)
grapnel, grappling iron	rezón *m.*
gun turret	torreta *f.*
gunwale, gunnel	regala *f.*, borda *f.*
hammock	coy *m.*
hatchway	escotilla *f.*
hawsehole, hawse	escobén *m.*
helm	timón *m.*
hold	bodega *f.*
hull; keel	casco *m.*; quilla *f.*
lantern	farol *m.*, fanal *m.*
length	eslora *f.*
logbook	cuaderno (*m.*) de bitácora
midship	crujía *f.*
midship frame	cuaderna (*f.*) maestra
oar	remo *m.*
oarlock, rowlock	escálamo *m.*, tolete *m.*
orlop	sollado *m.*
periscope	periscopio *m.*
poop, stern	popa *f.*
poop deck	castillo (*m.*) de popa, toldilla *f.*
port, gun port	porta *f.*
port, port side	babor *m.*
porthole	portilla *f.*, porta *f.*
powder magazine	santabárbara *f.*, pañol (*m.*) de municiones
quarterdeck	alcázar *m.*
rib	cuaderna *f.*, costilla *f.*
rudder	timón *m.*
screw, propeller	hélice *f.*
scuttle	escotilla *f.*
starboard	estribor *m.*
steerage	entrepuente *m.*
stem	roda *f.*
sternpost	codaste *m.*
storeroom	pañol *m.*
tiller	caña (*f.*) del timón
torpedo tube	tubo (*m.*) lanzatorpedos
waterline	línea (*f.*) de flotación
windlass, winch	molinete *m.*, chigre *m.*, maquinilla *f.*

III. Rigging. — Aparejo, *m.*

mast	palo *m.*, mástil *m.*
mainmast	palo (*m.*) mayor
mizzenmast	palo (*m.*) de mesana
foremast	palo (*m.*) de trinquete
topmast	mastelero *m.*
topgallant mast	mastelerillo *m.*
yard	verga *f.*
boom	tangón *m.*, botalón *m.*
bowsprit; top	bauprés *m.*; cofa *f.*
canvas	velamen *m.* (sails), vela *f.* (sail)
lateen sail	vela (*f.*) latina
mainsail	vela (*f.*) mayor
staysail	vela (*f.*) de estay
jib; shroud	foque *m.*; obenque *m.*
halyard; lanyard	driza *f.*; acollador *m.*

See also SAILING

bobbin [ˈbɔbin] n. Bobina, *f.*, carrete, *m.* (in spinning machine). || Canilla, *f.* (in sewing machine). || Bolillo, *m.* (for making lace). || *Bobbin lace*, encaje (*m.*) de bolillos.

bobby [ˈbɔbi] n. FAM. Poli, *m.*

Bobby [ˈbɔbi] pr. n. Roberto, *m.* (diminutive of *Robert*).

bobby pin [—pin] n. U. S. Pasador, *m.*

bobby socks or **bobby sox** [ˈbɔbisɔks] pl. n. U. S. Medias (*f.*) cortas, calcetines, *m.*

bobby-soxer [—ə*] n. Jovencita, *f.*, tobillera, *f.*

bobsled [ˈbɔbsled] or **bobsleigh** [ˈbɔbslei] n. SP. Bobsleigh, *m.*

bobstay [ˈbɔbstei] n. MAR. Barbiquejo (*m.*) de bauprés.

bobtail [ˈbɔbteil] adj. Rabicorto, ta.
— N. Cola (*f.*) cortada (tail). || Rabicorto, ta (horse).

bobtail [ˈbɔbteil] v. tr. Cortar el rabo a.

bode [bəud] v. tr./intr. Presagiar: *it bodes no good*, no presagia nada bueno. || *To bode well, ill*, ser de buen, mal agüero.

bodeful [—ful] adj. Ominoso, sa.

bodice [ˈbɔdis] n. Cuerpo, *m.* (of a dress). || Corpiño, *m.* (sleeveless waist).

bodiless [ˈbɔdilis] adj. Sin cuerpo: *a bodiless head*, una cabeza sin cuerpo. || Incorpóreo, a: *a bodiless form walked through the wall*, una forma incorpórea atravesó la pared.

bodily [bɔdili] adj. Corporal, físico, ca: *he was charged with having caused bodily harm to his wife*, fue acusado de haber causado daños corporales a su mujer; *bodily and mental diseases*, enfermedades físicas y mentales.
— Adv. En conjunto, en masa, en pleno: *the teaching staff resigned bodily*, el cuerpo docente dimitió en pleno. || En persona (in person).

boding [bəudiŋ] n. Presentimiento, *m.*
— Adj. Ominoso, sa.

bodkin [ˈbɔdkin] n. Punzón, *m.* (for making holes). || Pasacintas, *m. inv.* (for ribbon). || PRINT. Punta, *f.*

body [ˈbɔdi] n. Cuerpo, *m.* (of man or animal): *the human body*, el cuerpo humano. || Cadáver, *m.*, cuerpo, *m.* (corpse): *there were five thousand bodies on the battlefield*, había cinco mil cadáveres en el campo de batalla; *the victim's body was found in the kitchen*, el cuerpo de la víctima fue encontrado en la cocina. || Tronco, *m.* (trunk). || Cuerpo, *m.* (of a dress). || CHEM. PHYS. Cuerpo, *m.* || MATH. Sólido, *m.* || Organismo, *m.*: *a body such as the League of Nations*, un organismo como la Sociedad de Naciones. || Cuerpo, *m.*, gremio, *m.* (corporation). || MIL. Cuerpo, *m.* || Cuerpo, *m.* (profession): *the body of lawyers*, el cuerpo de abogados. || Cuerpo, *m.* (of a book). || Recopilación, *f.*: *body of laws*, recopilación de leyes. || Cuerpo, *m.* (of wine, sauce, paint, etc.). || Masa, *f.* (mass): *a body of water*, una masa de agua. || Masa, *f.* (of clay). || Conjunto, *m.*, grupo, *m.* (group). || Número, *m.*: *a large body of people*, un gran número de personas. || Parte (*f.*) principal (main part): *the body of the speech*, la parte principal del discurso. || Tronco, *m.* (of a tree). || ASTR. Cuerpo, *m.*: *heavenly body*, cuerpo celeste. || PRINT. Cuerpo, *m.* [de letra]. || TECH. Bastidor, *m.* (frame). | Vientre, *m.* (of blast furnace). || AUT. Carrocería, *f.*, caja, *f.* || MAR. Casco, *m.* || AVIAT. Fuselaje, *m.* || ARCH. Cuerpo, *m.* (of a building). | Nave, *f.* (of a church). || MUS. Caja, *f.* || FAM. Individuo, *m.*, persona, *f.* (person). || — *Body corporate*, corporación, *f.*; persona jurídica. || *Body snatcher*, ladrón (*m.*) de cadáveres. || *Constituent body*, cuerpo electoral. || *He earns enough money to keep body and soul together*, gana lo justo para vivir. || *In a body*, en masa, en pleno, todos juntos. || *Learned body*, docta asamblea. || *Legislative body*, cuerpo *or* órgano legislativo. || *Public body*, organismo público. || *The main body of*, la mayor parte de: *the main body of the citizens*, la mayor parte de los ciudadanos; el grueso de (the army). || ANAT. *Yellow body*, cuerpo amarillo.

body [ˈbɔdi] v. tr. Dar cuerpo a. || Representar, encarnar, simbolizar.

body-builder [—ˌbildə*] n. AUT. Carrocero, *m.* || Aparato (*m.*) para desarrollar los músculos.

bodyguard [—gɑːd] n. Guardaespaldas, *m. inv.* (of a person). || Guardia (*m.*) de corps (of sovereign).

bodywork [—wəːk] n. AUT. Carrocería, *f.*

Boeotia [biˈəuʃjə] pr. n. Beocia, *f.*

Boeotian [—n] adj./n. Beocio, cia.

Boer [ˈbəuə*] adj./n. Bóer.

bog [bɔg] n. Ciénaga, *f.*, pantano, *m.* || POP. Cagadero, *m.*

bog [ˈbɔg] v. tr. *To bog down*, atascar (a car, etc.): *the rain bogged the car down in the mud*, la lluvia atascó el coche en el barro; obstaculizar: *petty arguments bogged down the progress of the conference*, discusiones nimias obstaculizaron el progreso de la conferencia. || *To get bogged down*, atascarse.

bogey [ˈbəugi] n. Espectro, *m.*, fantasma, *m.*: *the bogey of war hung over Europe*, el espectro de la guerra se cernía sobre Europa. || Trasgo, *m.* (evil goblin). || Carretón, *m.*, bogie, *m.* (of train). || SP. Recorrido (*m.*) normal (golf). || FIG. Pesadilla, *f.* (bugbear).

bogeyman [—mæn] n. FAM. Coco, *m.*

boggle [ˈbɔgl] v. intr. Sobresaltarse. || *To boggle at*, vacilar ante (to hesitate).

boggy [ˈbɔgi] adj. Pantanoso, sa.

bogie [ˈbəugi] n. Carretón, *m.*, bogie, *m.* (of a wagon).

bogus [ˈbəugəs] adj. Falso, sa (false). || Fingido, da; simulado, da (sham). || — *Bogus company*, compañía fantasma. || *Bogus transactions*, transacciones dudosas.

bogy [ˈbəugi] n. See BOGEY.

bohea [bəuˈhiː] n. Té (*m.*) de calidad inferior.

Bohemia [bəuˈhimjə] pr. n. GEOGR. Bohemia, *f.*

Bohemian [—n] adj./n. Bohemio, mia.

bohemianism [—nizəm] n. Bohemia, *f.* (Bohemian life).

boil [bɔil] n. MED. Furúnculo, *m.*, divieso, *m.* || Punto (*m.*) de ebullición (boiling point): *to bring to the boil*, calentar hasta el punto de ebullición. || Remolino, *m.* (in a stream). || — *To be on the boil*, estar hirviendo. || *To come to the boil*, empezar a hervir.

boil [bɔil] v. intr. Hervir (a liquid). || Cocer (to cook). || FIG. Bullir (to seethe). || — *To boil dry* o *away*, consumirse (water), pegarse (vegetables, etc.). || *To boil down*, reducirse: *the problem boils down to this*, el problema se reduce a esto. || *To boil over*, salirse: *the milk has boiled over*, la leche se ha salido. || *To boil with rage*, estar furioso, estar [uno] que rabia. || FIG. *To keep the pot boiling*, ganarse el cocido, calentar el puchero (to earn a living).

— V. tr. Cocer (to cook). || Hervir (to heat to the boiling point). || Pasar por agua (eggs). || *To boil down*, reducir.

boiled [bɔild] adj. Hervido, da. || Pasado por agua (egg). || Almidonado, da (shirt). || U. S. FAM. Borracho, cha (drunk).

boiler [ˈbɔilə*] n. Caldera, *f.* || FAM. Pollo (*m.*) demasiado viejo para asarse. || — TECH. *Boiler house*, sala (*f.*) de calderas. || *Boiler room*, sala (*f.*) de calderas (in a boat). || *Boiler suit*, mono, *m.* (for workers).

boilermaker [—ˌmeikə*] n. Calderero, *m.*

boilermaking [—ˌmeikiŋ] n. Calderería, *f.*

boiling [ˈbɔiliŋ] adj. Hirviendo, hirviente: *boiling water*, agua hirviendo. || *It's boiling hot*, hace un calor espantoso (weather), está ardiendo (object, food).

— N. Ebullición, *f.*: *boiling point*, punto de ebullición.

boisterous [ˈbɔistərəs] adj. Bullicioso, sa; alborotador, ra (persons). || Tumultuoso, sa (crowd). || Exuberante (character). || Revoltoso, sa (children). || Furioso, sa; agitado, da (sea). || Borrascoso, sa; violento, ta (wind). || Tempestuoso, sa (weather). || Estrepitoso, sa (laugh).

bold [bəuld] adj. Intrépido, da; valiente (fearless): *his bold actions won him the Military Cross*, sus valientes hazañas le valieron la Cruz Militar. || Audaz: *a bold piece of architecture*, una audaz obra arquitectónica. || Marcado, da; pronunciado, da (marked): *bold features*, rasgos marcados. || Acentuado, da (relief). || Fuerte, vigoroso, sa (style). || Atrevido, da; audaz: *a bold look*, una mirada atrevida; *bold ideas*, ideas atrevidas. || Descarado, da (shameless). || Resuelto, ta (resolute). || Escarpado, da (steep). || — PRINT. *Bold type*, negrita, *f.* || *To make bold to*, atreverse a, permitirse.

boldface [—feis] n. PRINT. Negrita, *f.*

bold-faced [—feist] adj. Descarado, da; atrevido, da. || PRINT. *Bold-faced type*, negrita, *f.*

boldness [—nis] n. Audacia, *f.*, valor, *m.*, osadía, *f.* (courage). || Descaro, *m.* (shamelessness). || Fuerza, *f.*, vigor, *m.* (of style). || Lo escarpado (steepness).

bole [bəul] n. Tronco, *m.* (of a tree). || Bolo, *m.* (clay): *Armenian bole*, bolo arménico. || Alacena, *f.* (cupboard).

bolero [bəˈlɛərəu] n. Bolero, *m.* (dance and jacket).

boletus [bəuˈliːtəs] n. BOT. Boleto, *m.* (fungus).

bolide [ˈbɔlid] n. Bólido, *m.*

bolivar [bɔˈliːvə*] n. Bolívar, *m.* (monetary unit).

Bolivarian [ˌbɔliˈvɛəriən] adj. Bolivariano, na.

Bolivia [bəˈliviə] pr. n. GEOGR. Bolivia, *f.*

Bolivian [—n] adj./n. Boliviano, na.

boll [bəul] n. BOT. Cápsula, *f.*

bollard [ˈbɔləd] n. Noray, *m.* (on quayside). || Poste, *m.* (for closing roads to traffic).

Bologna [bəˈləunjə] pr. n. GEOGR. Bolonia.

Bolognan [—n] or **Bolognian** [—n] or **Bolognese** [ˈbɔlənjiːz] adj./n. Boloñés, esa.

bolometer [bəuˈlɔmitə*] n. PHYS. Bolómetro, *m.*

Bolshevik [ˈbɔlʃivik] adj./n. Bolchevique.

— OBSERV. El plural es *Bolsheviks* o *Bolsheviki*.

Bolshevism [ˈbɔlʃivizəm] n. Bolchevismo, *m.*, bolcheviquismo, *m.*

Bolshevist [bɔlʃivist] adj./n. Bolchevista.

bolster [ˈbəulstə*] n. Cabezal, *m.*, travesaño, *m.* (pillow). || ARCH. Collarín, *m.* (of a column). || TECH. Apoyo, *m.*, soporte, *m.* (support).

bolster [ˈbəulstə*] v. tr. *To bolster up*, sostener, apoyar (to support), reforzar (to strengthen), rellenar (to pad), animar, entonar: *her presence bolstered him up*, su presencia le animaba.

bolt [bəult] n. Cerrojo, *m.* (heavy bolt). || Pestillo, *m.* (small bolt). || Cerrojo, *m.* (of rifle). || Pestillo, *m.* (of lock). || TECH. Perno, *m.*, tornillo, *m.* || Cuadrillo, *m.*, saeta, *f.* (of crossbow). || Rayo, *m.* (of lightning). || Pieza, *f.* (of cloth). || Rollo, *m.* (of paper). || Desbocamiento, *m.* (of a horse). || Huida, *f.*, fuga, *f.* (flight). || — FIG. *As a bolt from the blue*, como una bomba: *the news came as a bolt from the blue*, la noticia cayó como una bomba. | *Bolt from the blue*, acontecimiento imprevisto. || TECH. *Key bolt*, clavija, *f.* || FIG. *To have shot one's last bolt*, haber quemado su último cartucho. | *To make a bolt for it*, escaparse. | *To make a bolt for sth.*, lanzarse hacia algo.

— Adv. *Bolt upright*, rígido, da; derecho, cha.

bolt [bəult] v. tr. Cerrar con cerrojo *or* pestillo, echar el cerrojo a: *he bolted the door*, cerró la puerta con pestillo. || TECH. Empernar, sujetar con pernos *or* tornillos. || FAM. Engullir (to eat quickly). || Cerner (flour). || U. S. Abandonar (a party). || — *To bolt out*, decir a boca de jarro. || *To bolt s.o. in*, encerrar a alguien echando el cerrojo. || *To bolt s.o. out*, dejar a alguien fuera echando el cerrojo.

— V. intr. Largarse, irse (to escape). || Desbocarse (horse). || U. S. Retirarse (to withdraw).

bolter [—ə*] n. Caballo (*m.*) desbocado (horse). || Cedazo, *m.* (sieve). || U. S. Disidente, *m.* & *f.*

boltrope [ˈbəultrəup] n. MAR. Relinga, *f.*

bolus [ˈbəuləs] n. Bolo, *m.* (pill). || *Alimentary bolus*, bolo alimenticio.

bomb [bɔm] n. Bomba, *f.*: *atomic bomb*, bomba atómica; *hydrogen bomb*, bomba de hidrógeno. || — *Bomb bay*, compartimiento (*m.*) de bombas (in a plane). || *Bomb crater*, hoyo producido por una bomba, embudo (*m.*) de granada. || *Bomb release*, lanzamiento (*m.*) de bombas. || *Bomb release mechanism*, dispositivo (*m.*) lanzabombas. || *Bomb shelter*, refugio antiaéreo. || *Bomb thrower*, lanzabombas, *m. inv.* || MED. *Cobalt bomb*, bomba de cobalto. || *Smoke bomb*, bomba de humo. || *Stink bomb*, bomba fétida. || *Time bomb*, bomba de efecto retardado. || FIG. *To drop* o *to burst like a bomb*, caer como una bomba. || *Volcanic bomb*, bomba volcánica.

bomb [bɔm] v. tr./intr. Bombardear.

bombard [ˈbɔmbɑːd] n. MIL. Bombarda, *f.* (gun).

bombard [bɔmˈbɑːd] v. tr. Bombardear (with guns or shells). || FIG. Bombardear, acosar: *the press reporters bombarded him with questions*, los periodistas le bombardearon a preguntas *or* le acosaron con preguntas. || PHYS. Bombardear.

bombardier [ˌbɔmbəˈdiə*] n. Bombardero, *m.*

bombardment [bɔmˈbɑːdmənt] n. MIL. PHYS. Bombardeo, *m.*

bombardon [bɔmˈbɑːdən] n. MUS. Bombarda, *f.*, bombardón, *m.*

bombasine [ˈbɔmbəziːn] n. Bombasí, *m.* (material).

bombast [ˈbɔmbæst] n. Ampulosidad, *f.*, prosopopeya, *f.*, rimbombancia, *f.*
bombastic [bɔmˈbæstik] adj. Ampuloso, sa; rimbombante.
bombazine [ˈbɔmbəzi:n] n. Bombasí, *m.* (material).
bomber [ˈbɔmə*] n. Bombardero, *m.*
bombing [ˈbɔmiŋ] n. Bombardeo, *m.*
bombproof [ˈbɔm-pru:f] adj. A prueba de bombas.
bombshell [ˈbɔmʃəl] n. MIL. Obús, *m.*, granada, *f.* ‖ FIG. FAM. Bomba, *f.*: *to drop* o *to burst like a bombshell*, caer como una bomba. | Sensación, *f.*: *Sophia, latest Hollywood bombshell*, Sofía, la última sensación de Hollywood.
bombsight [ˈbɔmsait] n. Visor (*m.*) de bombardeo.
bomb-site [ˈbɔmsait] n. MIL. Objetivo, *m.*
bombyx [ˈbɔmbiks] n. Bómbice, *m.*, bómbix, *m.* (silkworm).
bona fide [—ˈfaidi] adj. De buena fe, serio, ria (offer). ‖ Auténtico, ca (traveller).
bonanza [bəuˈnænzə] n. Bonanza, *f.* (rich deposit of ore). ‖ FIG. Mina, *f.* [de oro] (source of wealth).
Bonaventura [bɔnəvenˈtju:rə] pr. n. Buenaventura, *m.*
bonbon [ˈbɔnbɔn] n. Caramelo, *m.*
bond [bɔnd] n. Lazo, *m.*, vínculo, *m.*: *bonds of friendship*, lazos de amistad. ‖ Bono, *m.*: *Treasury bonds*, bonos del Tesoro; *bond issue*, emisión de bonos. ‖ JUR. Obligación, *f.* | Título, *m.* (security). ‖ Fianza, *f.* (bail). ‖ COMM. Depósito, *m.* ‖ CHEM. Enlace, *m.* (of atoms, ions, etc.). ‖ ARCH. Aparejo, *m.* (of bricks): *English bond*, aparejo inglés. ‖ ELECTR. Conexión, *f.* ‖ U. S. Seguro (*m.*) de fianza, garantía, *f.* ‖ — Pl. Cadenas, *f.* (shackles). ‖ FIG. Cautiverio, *m. sing.*: *to be in bonds*, estar en cautiverio. ‖ — *To be in bond*, estar en depósito, estar depositado. ‖ *To take out of bond*, sacar de la aduana.
— Adj. Esclavo, va.
bond [bɔnd] v. tr. ARCH. Aparejar. ‖ Depositar (in customs). ‖ Hipotecar (to mortgage). ‖ Garantizar (a debt, etc.). ‖ Unir (to bind).
bondage [—idʒ] n. Esclavitud, *f.*
bonded [—id] adj. Depositado, da; en depósito (goods). ‖ Garantizado, da (debt). ‖ *Bonded warehouse*, almacén (*m.*) de depósito.
bonderizing [ˈbɔndəraiziŋ] n. TECH. Bonderización, *f.* (protection against corrosion).
bondholder [ˈbɔnd,həuldə*] n. Obligacionista, *m.* & *f.*
bondmaid [ˈbɔndmeid] n. Esclava, *f.*
bondman [ˈbɔndmən] n. Esclavo, *m.*, siervo, *m.*
— OBSERV. El plural de *bondman* es *bondmen.*
bondsman [ˈbɔndzmən] n. Fiador, *m.* ‖ Esclavo, *m.*, siervo, *m.* (bondman).
— OBSERV. El plural de *bondsman* es *bondsmen.*
bondstone [ˈbɔndstəun] n. ARCH. Perpiaño, *m.*
bone [bəun] n. Hueso, *m.* (of body). ‖ Ballena, *f.* (of corset, etc.). ‖ Barba, *f.* (of whale). ‖ Espina, *f.*, raspa, *f.* (of fish). ‖ Hueso, *m.* (of fruits). ‖ Hueso, *m.* (substance): *buttons made of bone*, botones de hueso. ‖ — Pl. Huesos, *m.*, restos, *m.* (remains). ‖ Cuerpo, *m. sing.*: *my old bones*, mi pobre cuerpo. ‖ MUS. Tarreñas, *f.* ‖ FAM. Dados, *m.* (dice). ‖ — FIG. *As dry as a bone* o *bone dry*, más seco que una pasa. | *Bone of contention*, manzana (*f.*) de la discordia. | *Bred in the bone*, en la masa de la sangre. | *Funny bone*, hueso de la alegría *or* de la suegra. | *He won't make old bones*, no llegará a hacer huesos viejos. | *To be a bag of bones*, estar en los huesos. | *To break every bone in s.o.'s body*, no dejarle a uno un hueso sano. | *To feel it in one's bones*, tener el presentimiento de ello. | *To have a bone to pick with s.o.*, tener que ajustarle las cuentas a uno. | *To make no bones about doing sth.*, no vacilar en hacer algo. | *To make no bones about it*, no andarse con rodeos. ‖ *Wet to the bones*, calado hasta los huesos.
bone [bəun] v. tr. Deshuesar (meat). ‖ Quitar el hueso (of fruits). ‖ Quitar las espinas *or* las raspas a (fish). ‖ Emballenar, poner ballenas a (a corset). ‖ FAM. Birlar (to steal). ‖ U. S. FAM. *To bone up*, empollar (to study).
bone black [—blæk] n. Carbón (*m.*) animal.
bone china [—ˈtʃainə] n. Porcelana (*f.*) blanca y translúcida.
boned [—d] adj. Sin huesos, deshuesado, da (meat, fruit). ‖ Sin espinas, sin raspas (fish).
bone-dry [—ˈdrai] adj. Completamente seco. ‖ Sediento, ta (thirsty).
bonehead [—hed] n. FAM. Tonto, ta; majadero, ra.
bone-idle [—ˈaidl] adj. Vago, ga.
boneless [—lis] adj. See BONED.
bone meal [—mi:l] n. Harina (*f.*) de huesos.
boner [—ə*] n. U. S. FAM. Metedura (*f.*) de pata, pifia, *f.*, plancha, *f.* ‖ U. S. FAM. *To pull a boner*, meter la pata, tirarse una plancha.
bonesetter [—,setə*] n. Ensalmador, *m.*
bone shaker [—,ʃeikə*] n. FAM. Cacharro, *m.* (car).
bonfire [ˈbɔn,faiə*] n. Hoguera, *f.*
bongo drum [ˈbɔŋgəu-drʌm] n. MUS. Bongó, *m.*
bonhomie [ˈbɔnəmi:] n. Afabilidad, *f.*, bondad, *f.*
boniness [ˈbəuninis] n. Delgadez, *f.*, demacración, *f.*
bon mot [bɔ̃ˈməu] n. Ocurrencia, *f.*, agudeza, *f.*
Bonn [bɔn] pr. n. GEOGR. Bona.
bonnet [ˈbɔnit] n. Gorro, *m.*, gorra, *f.* (for children). ‖ Gorra (*f.*) escocesa (for men). ‖ Toca, *f.* (for women). ‖ Capó, *m.* (of cars). ‖ Campana, *f.* (of fireplace). ‖ MAR. Boneta, *f.* ‖ TECH. Sombrerete, *m.* (of valve).
bonny [ˈbɔni] adj. Hermoso, sa (babies). ‖ Lindo, da; majo, ja: *a bonny lass*, una chica muy maja.
bonus [ˈbəunəs] n. Prima, *f.*, gratificación, *f.* (gratuity). ‖ Beneficio, *m.* (earned on production). ‖ Dividendo (*m.*) extraordinario (stocks and shares). ‖ Beneficio, *m.* (paid to insurance policy holders). ‖ *Cost of living bonus*, plus (*m.*) de carestía de vida.
bony [ˈbəuni] adj. Huesudo, da (with prominent bones). ‖ Esquelético, ca (thin). ‖ Lleno de huesos (meat). ‖ Lleno de espinas (fish). ‖ De hueso (of bone). ‖ Óseo, a (like bone).
bonze [bɔnz] n. Bonzo, *m.*
boo [bu:] n. Abucheo, *m.*, pateo, *m.* ‖ — FIG. *He wouldn't say boo to a goose*, es de lo más tímido que hay. | *Not to say boo*, no decir ni pío.
boo [bu:] v. tr./intr. Abuchear, patear.
boob [bu:b] n. FAM. Bobo, ba (fool). | Teta, *f.* (breast).
booby [ˈbu:bi] n. Bobo, ba. ‖ Último, ma (in a competition).
booby prize [—praiz] n. Premio (*m.*) al peor *or* al último.
booby trap [—træp] n. Trampa, *f.* ‖ MIL. Trampa (*f.*) explosiva.
booing [ˈbu:iŋ] n. Abucheo, *m.*, pateo, *m.*
book [buk] n. Libro, *m.* (printed work, literary composition, of Bible, etc.): *bound book*, libro encuadernado *or* empastado; *reference book*, libro de consulta; *sacred books*, libros sagrados. ‖ Talonario, *m.* (of cheques, coupons). ‖ Carnet, *m.* (of stamps, tickets). ‖ Registro, *m.* (of bets). ‖ Carterilla, *f.* (of matches). ‖ Cartilla, *f.* (of savings). ‖ — Pl. Libros, *m.*, cuentas, *f.*, contabilidad, *f. sing.* (accounting). ‖ — *Account book*, libro de contabilidad. ‖ *Address book*, libro de señas *or* de direcciones. ‖ *By the book*, según las reglas. ‖ *Book of Common Prayer*, libro de oraciones. ‖ *Book of Hours*, libro de horas. ‖ *Book of knight-errantry*, libro de caballerías. ‖ *Book review*, reseña (*f.*) de libros. ‖ *Complaints book*, libro de reclamaciones. ‖ *Counterfoil book*, [libro] talonario. ‖ *Exercise book*, cuaderno, *m.* ‖ *In one's book*, según el parecer de uno. ‖ COMM. *Letter book*, libro copiador. ‖ *Minute book*, libro de actas. ‖ *Music book*, libro de música. ‖ *One for the books*, hecho (*m.*) memorable. ‖ *On the books*, registrado en los libros. ‖ U. S. *Pocket book*, libro de bolsillo (paperback). ‖ *Record book*, libro borrador. ‖ *Ship's book*, libro *or* registro de a bordo. ‖ *Text book*, libro de texto. ‖ *The Good Book*, la Biblia. ‖ *The Great Book of the Public Debt*, el Gran Libro. ‖ FIG. *To be in s.o.'s bad books*, estar en la lista negra de alguien. | *To be in s.o.'s good books*, estar en buenos términos con alguien. | *To bring s.o. to book*, pedir cuentas a alguien. | *To burn one's books* o *to throw one's books away*, ahorcar los libros. | *To go by the book*, seguir las reglas. ‖ COMM. *To keep the books*, llevar los libros *or* las cuentas. ‖ *To make a book*, registrar las apuestas. ‖ FIG. *To read s.o. like a book*, leer los pensamientos de alguien. | *To suit s.o.'s book*, convenirle a uno. | *To take a leaf out of s.o.'s book*, tomar ejemplo de alguien. ‖ *To talk like a book*, hablar como un libro.
book [buk] v. tr./intr. Reservar, hacer la reserva de (theatre, hotel, travel, etc.). ‖ Contratar (speakers, performers, etc.). ‖ Anotar, registrar, asentar (to record in a book). ‖ Fichar (suspect). ‖ *To be booked up*, estar completo, no haber localidades (theatre, etc.), tener compromisos (a person).
bookbinder [—,baində*] n. Encuadernador, *m.*
bookbinding [—,baindiŋ] n. Encuadernación, *f.*
bookcase [—keis] n. Biblioteca, *f.*, estantería (*f.*) para libros.
bookend [—end] n. Sujetalibros, *m. inv.*
bookie [—i] n. FAM. Corredor (*m.*) de apuestas.
booking [—iŋ] n. Reserva, *f.* [*Amer.*, reservación, *f.*] (of seats, etc.). ‖ Contratación, *f.* (of artists).
booking office [—iŋ,ɔfis] n. Taquilla, *f.*, despacho (*m.*) de billetes.
bookish [—iʃ] adj. Libresco, ca (style). ‖ Pedante: *a bookish writer*, un escritor pedante. ‖ Aficionado a la lectura (fond of reading). ‖ Estudioso, sa (fond of studying). ‖ FIG. Enteradillo, lla (know-all).
book jacket [—,dʒækət] n. Sobrecubierta, *f.*
bookkeeper [—,ki:pə*] n. Tenedor (*m.*) de libros, contable, *m.* & *f.*
bookkeeping [—,ki:piŋ] n. Teneduría (*f.*) de libros, contabilidad, *f.*
book learning [—,lə:niŋ] n. Conocimientos (*m. pl.*) librescos.
booklet [—lit] n. Folleto, *m.*
booklover [—,lʌvə*] n. Bibliófilo, la.
bookmaker [—,meikə*] n. Corredor (*m.*) de apuestas, "bookmaker", *m.* (in races). ‖ Encuadernador, ra (of books).
bookmark [—mɑ:k] n. Señal, *f.*, registro, *m.*
bookmobile [—məu,bil] n. Biblioteca (*f.*) ambulante.
bookplate [—pleit] n. Ex libris, *m.* (label).
bookrest [—rest] n. Atril, *m.* (support).
bookseller [—,selə*] n. Librero, ra.
bookshelf [—ʃelf] n. Estante, *m.* ‖ — Pl. Estantería, *f. sing.*
bookshop [—ʃɔp] n. Librería, *f.*
bookstall [—stɔ:l] or **bookstand** [—stænd] n. Quiosco, *m.*, puesto (*m.*) de libros (open-air stand).

|| Caseta, *f.* (in book exhibitions). || Quiosco, *m.*, puesto (*m.*) de periódicos (newsstand).
bookstore [—stɔ:*] n. U. S. Librería, *f.*
book value [—ˌvælju:] n. Valor (*m.*) contable.
bookworm [—wə:m] n. Polilla (*f.*) que roe los libros (larva). || FIG. Ratón (*m.*) de biblioteca (person).
boom [bu:m] n. Estampido, *m.* (explosion). || Tronido, *m.* (of cannon). || Mugido, *m.* (of a bittern). || Bramido *m.* (of waves). || Retumbo, *m.* (of thunder). || Auge, *m.*, "boom," *m.* (sudden increase). || MAR. Botalón, *m.*, botavara, *f.* (to stretch the sail foot). | Palo (*m.*) de carga (for lifting). | Cadena (*f.*) de troncos, barrera (*f.*) de un puerto (floating barrier). || Aguilón, *m.*, brazo, *m.*, pluma, *f.* (of crane). || CINEM. RAD. Jirafa, *f.* || — CINEM. *Boom operator*, jirafista, *m.* || *Boom years*, años (*m. pl.*) de prosperidad. || *Population boom*, explosión demográfica.
boom [bu:m] v. intr. Retumbar (thunder). || Tronar (cannon). || Resonar (large bell, etc.). || Zumbar (to buzz). || Mugir (a bittern). || Prosperar, estar en auge (to be prosperous or in demand).
— V. tr. Hacer prosperar (to promote). || Hacer tronar (the cannon).
boomerang [ˈbu:məræŋ] n. Bumerang, *m.* || FIG. Acción (*f.*) contraproducente.
boomerang [ˈbu:məræŋ] v. intr. Ser contrapoducente.
booming [ˈbu:miŋ] adj. Que truena (cannon, etc.). || Resonante (voice). || En auge (industry, etc.). || Próspero, ra (years).
boomtown [ˈbu:mtaun] n. U. S. Ciudad (*f.*) de crecimiento rápido.
boon [bu:n] n. Bendición, *f.* (blessing). || Favor, *m.* (favour).
— Adj. Alegre (gay).
boor [buə*] n. Patán, *m.* (peasant, uncouth man).
boorish [—riʃ] adj. Tosco, ca (uncouth).
boorishness [—riʃnis] n. Tosquedad, *f.*
boost [bu:st] n. Empujón (*m.*) hacia arriba. || FIG. Estímulo, *m.* (incentive). || *To give s.o. a boost*, aupar a uno (to lift up), estimular a uno (to encourage), lanzar a uno (to make famous).
boost [bu:st] v. tr. Levantar (to hoist). || Impulsar (to thrust). || Elevar, aumentar (to increase). || Promover, fomentar (to promote). || Ayudar (to help). || Levantar (spirits). || ELECTR. Elevar [el voltaje] (in a battery).
booster [—ə*] n. ELECTR. Elevador (*m.*) de voltaje. || TECH. Motor (*m.*) auxiliar de propulsión (engine). | Aumentador (*m.*) de presión (for increasing pressure). || MED. *Booster injection* o *shot*, revacunación, *f.*
booster pump [—əˌpʌmp] n. Bomba (*f.*) para aumentar la presión.
booster rocket [—əˌrɔkit] n. Cohete (*m.*) acelerador.
boot [bu:t] n. Bota, *f.* (footwear). || Maleta, *f.*, maletero, *m.*, portaequipajes, *m. inv.* (in a car). || MUS. Tubo (*m.*) de enchufe (of an organ). || Caña, *f.* (of stocking). || Calceta, *f.* (torture device). || FAM. Puntapié, *m.*, patada, *f.* (kick). | Despido, *m.* (dismissal). || U. S. FAM. Recluta, *m.* (marine recruit). || — FIG. FAM. *I'd bet my boots that*, me juego la cabeza a que. | *I wouldn't like to be in his boots*, no me gustaría estar en su pellejo. | *Like old boots*, estupendamente. | *The boot is on the other foot*, ha dado la vuelta la tortilla. | *To be too big for one's boots*, ser un engreído. | *To boot*, además, por añadidura. | *To die with one's boots on*, morir con las botas puestas. | *To get the boot*, ser puesto de patitas en la calle. | *To give the boot*, poner de patitas en la calle. | *To have one's heart in one's boots*, estar con *or* tener el alma en un hilo. | *To lick s.o.'s boots*, hacer la pelotilla a alguien. | *To wipe one's boots on s.o.*, tratar con la punta del pie a uno. || *You can bet your boots that*, puedes estar seguro de que.
boot [bu:t] v. tr. Dar una patada a (to kick). || Calzar a (to supply o to put boots on). || — FIG. FAM. *To boot it*, ir a pie. | *To boot s.o. out*, poner a alguien de patitas en la calle.
bootblack [—blæk] n. U. S. Limpiabotas, *m. inv.* [*Amer.*, lustrabotas, *m. inv.*].
bootee [ˈbu:ti] n. Patín, *m.*, calzado (*m.*) de punto para niños (for babies). || Bota, *f.*, botín, *m.*, botina, *f.* (for ladies).
Boötes [bəuˈəuti:z] pl. n. ASTR. Boyero.
booth [bu:ð] n. Puesto, *m.* (in a market). || Cabina, *f.* (to isolate): *telephone booth*, cabina telefónica.
boot hook [ˈbu:thuk] n. Tirabotas, *m. inv.*
bootjack [ˈbu:tdʒæk] n. Sacabotas, *m. inv.*, tirabotas, *m. inv.*
bootlace [ˈbu:tleis] n. Cordón, *m.*
bootleg [ˈbu:tleg] n. Caña, *f.* [de bota].
— Adj. U. S. FAM. De contrabando: *bootleg liquor*, licor de contrabando.
bootleg [ˈbu:tleg] v. tr. U. S. FAM. Pasar de contrabando (to smuggle). | Hacer *or* vender ilegalmente (to make or to sell illegally).
bootlegger [—ə*] n. U. S. Contrabandista (*m.*) de licores.
bootlegging [—iŋ] n. U. S. Contrabando (*m.*) de licores.
bootless [ˈbu:tlis] adj. Inútil, vano, na.
bootlick [ˈbu:tlik] v. tr./intr. FAM. Hacer la pelotilla (to flatter).
bootlicker [—ə*] n. FAM. Pelotillero, ra (adulator).
boots [bu:ts] n. Limpiabotas, *m. inv.* [*Amer.*, lustrabotas, *m. inv.*] (shoeshine boy). || Botones, *m. inv.* (bellboy).
bootstrap [ˈbu:t-stræp] n. Oreja, *f.*
boot tree [ˈbu:t-tri:] n. Horma, *f.*
booty [ˈbu:ti] n. Botín, *m.* (spoils).
booze [bu:z] n. FAM. Bebida (*f.*) alcohólica. | Borrachera, *f.* (drunkenness). || — FAM. *To be on the booze*, estar de copeo. | *To go on the booze*, ir de copeo (to go drinking), empezar a beber (to take to drink).
booze [bu:z] v. intr. FAM. Beber [bebidas alcohólicas]. || FAM. *To be boozed up*, estar borracho.
boozer [—ə*] n. FAM. Borracho, *m.* | Tasca, *f.* (bar).
boozy [ˈbu:zi] adj. FAM. Borracho, cha (person). | En que se bebe mucho (party).
bop [bɔp] n. MUS. Be-bop, *m.*
bop [bɔp] v. tr. Golpear.
bo-peep [bəuˈpi:p] n. FAM. *To play bo-peep*, jugar [con un niño] tapándose la cara y descubriéndola de repente.
boracic [bəˈræsik] adj. CHEM. Bórico, ca.
boracite [ˈbɔrəsait] n. MIN. Boracita, *f.*
borage [ˈbɔridʒ] n. BOT. Borraja, *f.*
borate [ˈbɔ:reit] n. CHEM. Borato, *m.*
borax [ˈbɔ:ræks] n. CHEM. Bórax, *m.*
bordeaux [bɔ:ˈdəu] adj. Burdeos.
— N. Burdeos, *m.* (wine, colour).
Bordeaux [bɔ:ˈdəu] pr. n. GEOGR. Burdeos.
border [ˈbɔ:də*] n. Borde, *m.*, margen, *m.* (edge). || Orilla, *f.* (of river, sea, etc.). || Ribete, *m.* (stripe): *the border of a handkerchief*, el ribete de un pañuelo. || Frontera, *f.*: *to cross the Spanish border*, cruzar la frontera española. || Arriate, *m.* (of plants). || THEATR. Bambalina, *f.* || *Border areas*, zonas fronterizas.
border [ˈbɔ:də*] v. tr. Bordear. || Ribetear (in sewing).
— V. intr. *To border on*, lindar con: *Iowa borders on Missouri*, Iowa linda con el Misuri; rayar en: *his remarks bordered upon rudeness*, sus observaciones rayaron en la grosería.
borderer [—rə*] n. Fronterizo, za.
borderland [—lænd] n. Zona (*f.*) fronteriza. || FIG. Límites, *m. pl.* (limits). | Margen, *m.* (fringe area). | Zona (*f.*) imprecisa (vague zone).
border line [—lain] n. Frontera, *f.*
borderline [—lain] adj. Fronterizo, za; limítrofe. || FIG. Dudoso, sa: *borderline case*, caso dudoso.
bordure [ˈbɔ:djuə*] n. HERALD. Bordura, *f.*
bore [bɔ:*] n. Taladro, *m.* (deep hole). || Alma, *f.*, ánima, *f.* (interior tube of a gun). || Calibre, *m.* (calibre). || FAM. Pelmazo, za; pesado, da (annoying person). | Tostón, *m.*, lata, *f.*, rollo, *m.* (dull person or thing). || MAR. Subida (*f.*) de la marea.
bore [bɔ:*] v. tr. Taladrar, perforar, horadar. || Barrenar (with a drill). || Perforar (a tunnel). || FAM. Aburrir (to weary). | Fastidiar, dar la lata, dar el rollo *or* el tostón [to annoy]. || — FAM. *To be bored stiff* o *to tears*, aburrirse como una ostra. | *To be bored with*, estar harto de. || *To bore one's way through the crowd*, abrirse paso entre la multitud.
— V. intr. Taladrar, perforar, horadar.
bore [bɔ:*] pret. See BEAR.
boreal [ˈbɔ:riəl] adj. Boreal, septentrional.
Boreas [ˈbɔriæs] n. Bóreas, *m.* (north wind).
boredom [ˈbɔ:dəm] n. Aburrimiento, *m.* || Fastidio, *m.* (nuisance).
borer [ˈbɔ:rə*] n. Taladrador, ra; perforador, ra (person). || Taladro, *m.*, barrena, *f.* (tool). || Taladradora, *f.*, perforadora, *f.* (machine). || ZOOL. Barrenillo, *m.*
boresome [ˈbɔ:səm] adj. Aburrido, da.
boric [ˈbɔ:rik] adj. CHEM. Bórico, ca.
boring [ˈbɔ:riŋ] adj. Aburrido, da; pesado, da.
— N. Taladro, *m.* (hole). || Taladrado, *m.*, perforación, *f.* (process). || Perforación, *f.* (of a tunnel).
born [bɔ:n] p. p. & adj. See BEAR. || Nacido, da: *born under a lucky star*, nacido con buena estrella. || Nato, ta: *a born poet*, un poeta nato. || De nacimiento: *a born fool*, tonto de nacimiento; *Spanish-born*, español de nacimiento. || — *Her first, latest born*, su primero, su último hijo. || *He was born in 1928*, nació en 1928. || *In all my born days*, desde que nací, en toda mi vida. || *To be born*, nacer. || *To be born again*, volver a nacer. || FIG. *To be born of*, ser engendrado por, ser el fruto de.
borne [bɔ:n] p. p. See BEAR.
boron [ˈbɔ:rɔn] n. CHEM. Boro, *m.*
borough [ˈbʌrə] n. Villa, *f.*, ciudad, *f.* (town). || Barrio, *m.*, distrito, *m.* (urban constituency). || Municipio, *m.* (municipality).
Borromean [bɔrəˈmiən] adj. *Borromean Islands*, Islas Borromeas.
borrow [ˈbɔrəu] v. tr. Pedir *or* tomar prestado: *to borrow a book from s.o.*, pedir a alguien un libro prestado. || FIG. Apropiarse: *to borrow s.o.'s ideas*, apropiarse las ideas de alguien. | Tomar (to quote): *to borrow a phrase from an author*, tomar una frase de un autor.
— V. intr. Tomar a préstamo.
borrower [—ə*] n. Prestatario, ria. || FIG. Sablista, *m.* & *f.* (cadger).
borrowing [—iŋ] n. El tomar prestado: *the borrowing of valuables is not advisable*, el tomar prestado objetos

valiosos no es recomendable. || Préstamo, *m.* (borrowed thing). || FIG. Adopción, *f.*

bort [bɔ:t] n. Diamante (*m.*) negro, "bort", *m.* (poor quality diamond).

bosh [bɔʃ] n. Necedades, *f. pl.* || TECH. Etalaje, *m.* (of furnace).

bosket [ˈbɔskit] n. Bosquecillo, *m.* (grove). || Matorral, *m.* (thicket).

Bosnia [ˈbɔzniə] pr. n. GEOGR. Bosnia, *f.*

Bosnian [—n] adj./n. Bosnio, nia; bosniaco, ca.

bosom [ˈbuzəm] n. Pecho, *m.* (breast). || Pechos, *m. pl.*, senos, *m. pl.* (woman's breasts). || Pechera, *f.* (of a dress). || Seno, *m.*: *she put the letter in her bosom*, guardó la carta en el seno. || FIG. Seno, *m.*: *in the bosom of the church*, en el seno de de la Iglesia.
— Adj. Íntimo, ma; entrañable: *a bosom friend*, un amigo íntimo.

bosom [ˈbuzəm] v. tr. Guardar.

Bosphorus [ˈbɔsfərəs] or **Bosporus** [ˈbɔspərəs] pr. n. GEOGR. Bósforo, *m.*

boss [bɔs] n. Patrón, ona (employer). || Jefe, fa (person in charge). || Bulto, *m.*, protuberancia, *f.* (protuberance). || Bollo, *m.*, chichón, *m.* (bump). || Joroba, *f.*, giba, *f.*, corcova, *f.* (hunchback). || (Ant.). Ombligo, *m.* (of a shield). || ARCH. Crucería, *f.* (of a vault), almohadilla, *f.* (ornamentation). || Repujado, *m.* (on leather, on silver). || Copa, *f.* (of a bridle). || U. S. Jefe, *m.* (in a party organization). | Cacique, *m.* (with dictatorial authority).

boss [bɔs] v. tr. Dirigir (to manage). || ARCH. Almohadillar. || Repujar (leather, silver). || *To boss about* o *around*, marimandonear, mangonear.

bossage [ˈbɔsidʒ] n. ARCH. Almohadillado, *m.* || Repujado, *m.* (leather, silver).

boss-eyed [bɔsˈaid] adj. FAM. Bizco, ca.

bossiness [ˈbɔsinis] n. Carácter (*m.*) mandón.

bossism [ˈbɔsizəm] n. Caciquismo, *m.*

bossy [ˈbɔsi] adj. FAM. Mandón, ona.

boston [ˈbɔstən] n. Bostón, *m.* (game, walz).

bosun [ˈbəusn] n. MAR. Contramaestre, *m.* (boatswain).

bot or **bott** [bɔt] n. Larva (*f.*) del moscardón, rezno, *m.* (parasitic larva of the botfly).

botanic [bəˈtænik] or **botanical** [—əl] adj. Botánico, ca: *botanical garden*, jardín botánico.

botanist [ˈbɔtənist] n. Botánico, ca; botanista.

botanize [ˈbɔtənaiz] v. intr. Herborizar.

botany [ˈbɔtəni] n. Botánica, *f.*

botany wool [—wul] n. Lana (*f.*) merina.

botch [bɔtʃ] n. Chapucería, *f.*, chapuza, *f.*

botch [bɔtʃ] v. tr. Chapucear. || *To botch it*, meter la pata, cometer una pifia.

botcher [—ə*] n. Chapucero, ra.

botchy [—i] adj. Chapucero, ra.

botfly [ˈbɔtflai] n. Moscardón, *m.*

both [bəuθ] adj./pron. Ambos, ambas, los dos, las dos: *both girls are pretty*, ambas *or* las dos chicas son guapas; *both are pretty*, ambas *or* las dos son guapas. || — *Both expensive and ugly*, caro y feo a la vez. || *Both of them*, ellos dos, los dos, ambos. || *Both of us*, nosotros dos. || *Both of you*, vosotros dos. || *Both she and her mother are pretty*, tanto su madre como ella son guapas.
— Adv. Al mismo tiempo, a la vez.

bother [ˈbɔðə*] n. Preocupación, *f.* (worry). || Molestia, *f.* (disturbance). || Lata, *f.*, fastidio, *m.* (nuisance). || — *Bother!*, ¡caramba!, ¡caray! || *I am giving you a lot of bother*, te estoy dando la lata, te estoy fastidiando *or* molestando.

bother [ˈbɔðə*] v. tr. Preocupar (to worry): *don't bother your head about it*, no te preocupes por eso. || Molestar (to disturb). || Dar la lata, fastidiar (to be a nuisance).
— V. intr. Preocuparse (to worry). || *To bother about* o *with*, tomarse la molestia de, molestarse por (to take the trouble), preocuparse de *or* por (to worry).

bothersome [—səm] adj. Fastidioso, sa; molesto, ta.

bottle [ˈbɔtl] n. Botella, *f.*: *a bottle of wine*, una botella de vino. || Biberón, *m.* (for babies): *brought up on the bottle*, criado con biberón. || Bombona, *f.* (for butane). || — FIG. *To hit* o *to take to* o *to go on the bottle*, darse a la bebida. | *To sit over the bottle with s.o.*, beber una botella entre dos. || *To speak over a bottle*, hablar tomando una copa.

bottle [ˈbɔtl] v. tr. Embotellar: *to bottle wine*, embotellar vino. || Enfrascar, envasar (to preserve). || *To bottle up*, contener, reprimir (feelings, etc.).

bottlebrush [—brʌʃ] n. Escobilla, *f.*, limpiabotellas, *m. inv.*

bottle drainer [—ˌdreinə*] n. Escurrebotellas, *m.*

bottle-fed [—fed] adj. Criado con biberón.

bottleneck [—nek] n. Cuello (*m.*) [de la botella]. || FIG. Estrangulamiento, *m.* (narrowing). | Embotellamiento, *m.*, atasco, *m.* (obstruction). | Obstáculo, *m.* (obstacle). | Callejón (*m.*) sin salida (dead end).

bottle party [—ˌpɑ:ti] n. Asalto, *m.*, reunión (*f.*) de amigos en la que cada uno lleva la bebida.

bottler [—ə*] n. Embotellador, ra.

bottle rack [—ræk] n. Botellero, *m.*, portabotellas, *m. inv.*

bottling [—iŋ] n. Embotellado, *m.*, embotellamiento, *m.* (of wine, etc.).

bottling machine [—iŋməˈʃi:n] n. Embotelladora, *f.*

bottom [ˈbɔtəm] adj. Más bajo: *bottom price*, precio más bajo. || Último, ma: *bottom dollar*, último dólar. || Del fondo (at the end). || Fundamental, esencial (essential). || FIG. *To bet one's bottom dollar*, apostar la cabeza, apostar hasta el último céntimo.
— N. Fondo, *m.*: *the bottom of a box, of a valley*, el fondo de una caja, de un valle. || Asiento, *m.* (seat of a chair, etc.). || Culo, *m.* (of a bottle). || Fondo, *m.* (of a cask). || Trasero, *m.* (buttocks). || Fondo, *m.* (of sea, river, etc.). || Pie, *m.* (of mountain, page, etc.). || Fondo, *m.* (far end): *the bottom of a corridor, of a street*, el fondo de un pasillo, de una calle. || Final, *m.* (inferior level): *to be at the bottom of the class*, estar al final de la clase. || MAR. Obra (*f.*) viva (of ship). || Bajo, *m.* (of a dress). || Bajos, *m. pl.* (of trousers). || Pantalón, *m.* (of pyjamas). || Vega, *f.* (low-lying land). || FIG. Origen, *m.*, causa, *f.* (cause): *he was at the bottom of*, fue la causa de. | Base, *f.*, fundamento, *m.* (basis). | Meollo, *m.*, fondo, *m.*: *the bottom of the matter*, el meollo del asunto. | Fondo, *m.*: *to get to the bottom of a mystery*, llegar al fondo de un misterio. || — *At bottom* o *at the bottom*, en el fondo: *he was at bottom modest*, en el fondo era modesto. || *Bottom up*, boca abajo. || FAM. *Bottoms up!*, ¡apurar las copas! || FIG. *From the bottom of one's heart*, de todo corazón. || *From the bottom up*, desde el principio (from the beginning). || MAR. *To go to the bottom*, irse a pique, irse al fondo. || *To knock the bottom out of an argument*, echar por tierra un argumento. || MAR. *To send to the bottom*, echar a pique, hundir (a ship). || *To touch bottom*, tocar fondo. || *To work one's way up from the bottom*, empezar desde el principio (career, enterprise, etc.). || *Who is at the bottom of the scheme?*, ¿quién está detrás de todo esto?

bottom [ˈbɔtəm] v. intr. Tocar fondo (a submarine).
— V. tr. Poner fondo a (a chair, armchair, etc.). || FIG. Basar, fundamentar (to base). | Llegar al fondo de (a case). || MAR. Hacer tocar fondo a.

bottom drawer [—ˈdrɔ:*] n. Ajuar, *m.*

bottom gear [—ˈgiə*] n. Primera, *f.* (of a car).

bottomless [—lis] adj. Insondable, sin fondo (pit, etc.). || Inescrutable, insondable (mystery). || Infundado, da (accusation). || FIG. *The bottomless pit*, el infierno.

bottommost [—məust] adj. Último, ma: *on the bottommost shelf*, en el último estante. || Insondable, inescrutable (mystery, etc.).

bottomry [—ri] n. MAR. Contrato (*m.*) a la gruesa.

bottomry [—ri] v. tr. MAR. Dar en prenda [un barco].

botulism [ˈbɔtjulizəm] n. MED. Botulismo, *m.*

boudoir [ˈbu:dwɑ:*] n. "Boudoir", *m.*, tocador, *m.*, gabinete, *m.*

bougainvillea [ˌbu:gənˈviljə] n. BOT. Buganvilla, *f.*

bough [bau] n. Rama, *f.* (of a tree).

bought [bɔ:t] pret. & p. p. See BUY.

bougie [ˈbu:ʒi:] n. MED. Sonda, *f.* || Vela, *f.* (candle).

bouillabaisse [ˈbujəbes] n. Bullabesa, *f.*, sopa (*f.*) de pescado.

bouillon [ˈbu:jɔ̃:] n. Caldo, *m.*

boulder [ˈbəuldə*] n. Canto (*m.*) rodado.

boulder clay [—klei] n. Depósito (*m.*) errático.

boulevard [ˈbu:lvɑ:*] n. Bulevar, *m.*

boulter [ˈbəultə*] n. Palangre, *m.* (fishing line).

bounce [bauns] n. Bote, *m.* (of a ball). || Salto, *m.* (jump). || Vitalidad, *f.* || Fanfarronería, *f.* (boastfulness).

bounce [bauns] v. tr. Hacer botar (a ball). || U. S. FAM. Botar, poner de patitas en la calle.
— V. intr. Saltar (to jump). || Botar, rebotar (a ball). || Jactarse, alardear (to boast). || Ser rechazado (a cheque). || — FIG. *To bounce back*, recuperarse. | *To bounce back on*, repercutir en contra de. || *To bounce into*, irrumpir en.

bouncer [—ə*] n. Persona (*f.*) encargada de echar a los alborotadores de un club nocturno.

bouncing [—iŋ] adj. Fuerte, robusto, ta (strong).

bound [baund] pret. & p. p. See BIND.

bound [baund] adj. Destinado, da: *the Greek civilization was bound to disappear*, la civilización griega estaba destinada a desaparecer. || FIG. Obligado, da; ligado, da: *she is bound by her word to fulfil what she promised*, está obligada por su palabra a cumplir lo que prometió. | Vinculado, da; ligado, da: *bound by ties of friendship*, vinculado por lazos de amistad. || Encuadernado, da (a book). || U. S. Determinado, da; decidido, da: *she is bound to get up whatever the doctor says*, está decidida a levantarse diga lo que diga el médico. || — *Bound hand and foot*, atado de pies y manos. || *Bound up in*, absorbido por: *he is bound up in his work*, está absorbido por su trabajo. || *Bound up with*, muy relacionado con, estrechamente ligado a: *the welfare of the citizen is bound up with the welfare of the nation*, el bienestar del ciudadano está muy relacionado con el bienestar de la nación. || *It's bound to happen*, sucederá seguramente. || *She is bound to come*, seguramente vendrá. || *To be bound for*, dirigirse a, ir con destino a.
— N. Salto, *m.* (jump). || Bote, *m.*, rebote, *m.* (of a ball, etc.). || Límite, *m.*, frontera, *f.* (boundary). || — Pl. Límites, *m.*: *beyond the bounds of decency*, más allá de los límites de la decencia. || *To be out of bounds*, estar en zona prohibida.

bound [baund] v. intr. Saltar (to jump). || Botar (a ball, etc.). || Moverse dando saltos *or* botes: *boulders were bounding down the hillside*, los cantos rodados bajaban dando botes por la ladera.
— V. tr. Señalar los límites de. || Confinar con, lindar con (to border on). || *To be bounded by*, lindar con.
boundary [—əri] n. Límite, *m.*, frontera, *f.* (real or imaginary). || SP. Jugada (*f.*) que consiste en lanzar la pelota fuera de los límites marcando cuatro o seis puntos (cricket). || *Boundary stone*, mojón, *m.*, hito, *m.*
bounder [—ə*] n. Grosero, *m.*, hortera, *m.*
boundless [—lis] adj. Ilimitado, da; sin límites.
bounteous [ˈbauntiəs] adj. Generoso, sa: *a bounteous gift*, un regalo generoso. || Abundante: *a bounteous crop*, una cosecha abundante.
bountied [ˈbauntid] adj. Favorecido, da.
bountiful [ˈbauntiful] adj. See BOUNTEOUS.
bounty [ˈbaunti] n. Generosidad, *f.*, liberalidad, *f.* (generosity). || Regalo, *m.* (gift). || Subsidio, *m.* (subsidy). || Prima, *f.*, gratificación, *f.* (premium).
bouquet [buˈkei] n. Ramo, *m.* (of flowers). || Aroma, *m.*, buqué, *m.* (of wine).
bourbon [ˈbə:bən] n. Whisky (*m.*) americano [de maíz y centeno].
Bourbon [ˈbuəbən] n. pr. Borbón.
— Adj. Borbónico, ca: *Bourbon nose*, nariz borbónica.
bourdon [ˈbuədn] n. MUS. Bordón, *m.*
bourgeois [ˈbuəʒwɑ:] adj./n. Burgués, esa.
bourgeoisie [ˌbuəʒwɑ:ˈzi:] n. Burguesía, *f.*
bout [baut] n. Combate, *m.*, encuentro, *m.*: *a wrestling bout*, un combate de lucha libre. || Asalto, *m.* (in boxing). || Ataque, *m.* (of illness). || Rato, *m.* (period of time). || Turno, *m.*, tanda, *f.* (of work).
boutonniere [bu:tənˈjɛə] n. U. S. Flor (*f.*) en el ojal.
bovidae [ˈbəuvidei] pl. n. Bóvidos, *m.*
bovine [ˈbəuvain] adj. Bovino, na; vacuno, na. || FIG. *Bovine face*, cara bovina.
— N. Bovino, *m.*
bow [bau] n. MAR. Proa, *f.* || Saludo, *m.* (with the head). || Reverencia, *f.*: *he answered with a light bow*, contestó con una ligera reverencia. || Inclinación, *f.* (bending).
bow [bau] v. tr. Inclinar, doblar (head or body): *he bowed his head*, inclinó la cabeza. || Doblar (knee). || Someter (a will). || — *To bow down*, doblegar (to bend), agobiar (to overburden). || *To bow one's appreciation*, demostrar su satisfacción con una inclinación de cabeza. || *To bow s.o. in, out*, recibir, despedir a alguien con una reverencia.
— V. intr. Someterse a: *to bow to the inevitable*, someterse a lo inevitable. || Inclinarse. || — *Bowing acquaintance*, conocido, *m.* (person), amistad (*f.*) superficial (friendship). || *To bow and scrape*, hacer zalemas. || *To bow out*, retirarse.
bow [bəu] n. Arco, *m.* (for shooting arrows). || Arco, *m.* (of a violin). || Movimiento (*m.*) del arco del violín. || Arco (*m.*) iris (rainbow). || Lazo, *m.* (in shoelace, ribbon, etc.). || FIG. *To draw the long bow*, exagerar.
bow [bəu] v. tr. Arquear, doblar: *the wind bowed the tree*, el viento dobló el árbol. || MUS. Tocar (violin).
— V. intr. Arquearse, combarse: *the wall bows inward*, la pared se comba hacia dentro.
bow compass [—ˈkʌmpəs] n. Bigotera, *f.*
bowdlerize [ˈbaudləraiz] v. tr. Expurgar.
bowed [baud] adj. Cabizbajo, ja (with grief). || Encorvado, da (with age).

— OBSERV. Este adjetivo con frecuencia va seguido de la preposición *down* sin que ésta altere su significado.

bowel [ˈbauəl] n. Intestino, *m.* (intestine). || — Pl. Entrañas, *f.* (entrails). || FIG. Entrañas, *f.*: *the bowels of the earth*, las entrañas de la tierra. || *Bowel movement*, evacuación (*f.*) intestinal.
bower [ˈbauə*] n. Casita (*f.*) rústica (small house). || Cenador, *m.*, emparrado, *m.* (leafy shelter). || MAR. Ancla (*f.*) de leva.
bowerbird [—bə:d] n. Ave (*f.*) del Paraíso.
bowery [ˈbauəri] n. Plantación (*f.*) holandesa en Estados Unidos. || *The Bowery*, distrito (*m.*) de la parte baja de Manhattan donde viven personas sin hogar.
bowie knife [ˈbəuinaif] n. Cuchillo (*m.*) de monte. || Machete, *m.* (of the U. S. Army).
bowing [ˈbauiŋ] n. Reverencia, *f.*
bowl [bəul] n. Tazón, *m.* (large cup). || Cuenco, *m.* (large hollow dish): *she gave me a bowl of rice*, me dio un cuenco de arroz. || Palangana, *f.*, jofaina, *f.* (for washing). || Cazoleta, *f.* (of a pipe). || Paleta, *f.* (of a spoon). || Escudilla, *f.* (hollow dish for eating). || Pila, *f.* (of a fountain). || Taza, *f.* (of a toilet). || Platillo, *m.* (of a beggar). || Globo, *m.* (of a lamp). || GEOGR. Cuenca, *f.* (of a river). || Bola, *f.* (ball in bowling). || U. S. Anfiteatro, *m.* (amphitheatre). | Estadio, *m.* (stadium). || — Pl. Bolos, *m.*, bochas, *f.*: *to play bowls*, jugar a las bochas. || — *Salad bowl*, ensaladera, *f.* || *Sugar bowl*, azucarero, *m.*
bowl [bəul] v. tr. Hacer rodar (a hoop, a barrel, etc.). || Lanzar, tirar (cricket ball, bowls, etc.).
— V. intr. Jugar a los bolos *or* a las bochas (bowls, bowling). || — *To bowl along*, deslizarse: *the car bowls along the road*, el coche se desliza por la carretera. || *To bowl over*, derribar (to knock over), desconcertar (to surprise). || *To bowl s.o. out*, eliminar, poner fuera de juego (cricket).
bowlegged [ˈbəuˈlegd] adj. Con las piernas arqueadas, patizambo, ba; estevado, da.
bowler [ˈbəulə*] n. Sombrero (*m.*) hongo, bombín, *m.* (hat). || SP. Lanzador, *m.*, jugador (*m.*) que lanza la pelota (in cricket). | Jugador (*m.*) de bolos.
bowline [ˈbəulin] n. MAR. Bolina, *f.* (of a sail): *on a bowline*, de bolina. || Nudo (*m.*) marinero (knot).
bowling [ˈbəuliŋ] n. Bolos, *m. pl.* (game). || Lanzamiento, *m.* (of cricket ball).
bowling alley [—ˌæli] n. Bolera, *f.*
bowling green [—gri:n] n. Campo (*m.*) de bolos.
bowman [ˈbəumən] n. Arquero, *m.*

— OBSERV. El plural de *bowman* es *bowmen*.

bow saw [ˈbəusɔ:] n. Sierra (*f.*) de arco.
bowshot [ˈbəuʃɔt] n. Tiro (*m.*) de flecha. || *At a bowshot*, a tiro de ballesta.
bowsprit [ˈbəusprit] n. MAR. Bauprés, *m.*
bowstring [ˈbəustriŋ] n. Cuerda (*f.*) del arco.
bow tie [ˈbəuˈtai] n. Corbata (*f.*) de lazo.
bow window [ˈbəuˈwindəu] n. Mirador, *m.*
bow-wow [ˈbauwau] n. Guau guau, *m.* (dog in children's language). || Guau, *m.* (bark).
box [bɔks] n. Caja, *f.*: *a box of chocolates*, una caja de bombones. || Arca, *f.*, arcón, *m.*, cofre, *m.* (large wooden case). || Estuche, *m.* (casket). || Palco, *m.* (in a theatre). || Compartimiento, *m.* (of train, etc.). || "Box", *m.*, departamento (*m.*) de una cuadra (of stable). || Pescante, *m.* (coach box). || Caseta, *f.*, garita, *f.* (of sentry). || Apartado (*m.*) de correos [*Amer.*, casilla, *f.*] (post office). || Corte, *m.*, incisión, *f.* (in a tree). || Bofetón, *m.* (blow on the ear). || Cama, *f.* (of cart). || BOT. Boj, *m.* || TECH. Caja (*f.*) de chumacera. || PRINT. Cajetín, *m.* || Recuadro, *m.* (on a newspaper). || SP. Boxeo, *m.* (boxing). | Puesto (*m.*) donde se sitúa el bateador *or* el lanzador (baseball). | Plinto, *m.* (in gymnastics). || — *Christmas box*, aguinaldo, *m.* || FIG. *In the wrong box*, en difícil postura. || *Jury box*, tribuna (*f.*) *or* banco (*m.*) del jurado. || FIG. *To put in the box*, meter en la hucha, ahorrar. || *Witness box*, barra (*f.*) de los testigos.
box [bɔks] v. tr. Embalar, encajonar. || PRINT. Encerrar en un recuadro. || — *To box s.o.'s ears*, abofetear a alguien. || *To box the compass*, cuartear la aguja (to turn the ship round), cambiar completamente (to change), volver al punto de partida (to come back to the starting point). || *To box up*, encerrar.
— V. intr. Boxear.
box calf [—kɑ:f] n. "Boxcalf", *m.*, becerro (*m.*) curtido (tanned calfskin).
boxcar [—kɑ:*] n. U. S. Furgón, *m.*
boxer [—ə*] n. SP. Boxeador, *m.* || Bóxer, *m.* (dog).
boxfish [—fiʃ] n. Cofre, *m.*
boxful [—ful] n. Caja, *f.* (contents).
boxhaul [—hɔ:l] v. tr. Virar en redondo (a ship).
boxing [—iŋ] n. SP. Boxeo, *m.* || Embalaje, *m.*, envase, *m.* (packing).
Boxing Day [—iŋdei] n. Día (*m.*) laborable después de Navidad en que se suelen dar los aguinaldos.
boxing gloves [—iŋglʌvz] pl. n. Guantes (*m.*) de boxeo.
box kite [—kait] n. Cometa, *f.*
box office [—ˌɔfis] n. Taquilla, *f.* [*Amer.*, boletería, *f.*]
box-office [—ˌɔfis] adj. Taquillero, ra: *a good box-office film*, una película taquillera.
box spanner [—ˈspænə*] n. Llave (*f.*) de tubo.
box spring [—spriŋ] n. Colchón (*m.*) de muelles.
box stall [—stɔ:l] n. "Box", *m.*, departamento (*m.*) de una cuadra (for animals in a stable).
boxwood [—wud] n. Boj, *m.*
boy [bɔi] n. Niño, *m.*, chico, *m.*, muchacho, *m.* (young man). || Hijo, *m.*, chico, *m.*, niño, *m.* (son). || MAR. Grumete, *m.* || Sirviente (*m.*) indígena, boy, *m.* (in colonies). || *Oh, boy!*, ¡vaya!
boyar [bɔjə*] n. Boyardo, *m.*
boycott [ˈbɔikət] n. Boicot, *m.*, boicoteo, *m.*
boycott [ˈbɔikət] v. tr. Boicotear.
boycotting [—iŋ] n. Boicoteo, *m.*
boyfriend [ˈbɔifrend] n. Novio, *m.* (fiancé). || Amigo, *m.* (friend).
boyhood [ˈbɔihud] n. Infancia, *f.*, niñez, *f.*
boyish [ˈbɔiiʃ] adj. Infantil (immature). || De muchacho (tastes, manners, etc.).
boy scout [ˈbɔiˈskaut] n. Explorador, *m.*,
bra [brɑ:] n. Sostén, *m.* (for women).
Brabant [brəˈbænt] pr. n. GEOGR. Brabante, *m.*
brace [breis] n. Abrazadera, *f.* (for clasping). || Berbiquí, *m.* (of drill). || Par, *m.* (of pistols, partridge, etc.): *a brace of cats*, un par de gatos. || Puntal, *m.* (prop). || PRINT. Llave, *f.* || Aparato, *m.* (for teeth). || MED. Braguero, *m.* (truss). | Aparato (*m.*) ortopédico (orthopedic device). || MUS. Corchete, *m.* || ARCH. Riostra, *f.*; tirante, *m.* || MAR. Braza, *f.* || — Pl. Tirantes, *m.* (of trousers).
brace [breis] v. tr. Atar, ligar (with a rope). || ARCH. Reforzar (to strengthen). | Apuntalar (to prop). || Tensar (to tighten). || PRINT. Poner una llave a. || MAR. Bracear (a sail, rope, oar, etc.). || — *To brace o.s. for sth.*, prepararse para algo. || *To brace s.o. up*, fortalecer a alguien.
— V. intr. *To brace up*, cobrar ánimo.

bracelet [ˈbreislit] n. Pulsera, *f.*, brazalete, *m.* ‖ — Pl. FAM. Esposas, *f.* (handcuffs).
bracer [ˈbreisə*] n. Estimulante, *m.*, tónico, *m.* (tonic): *the news was a bracer for him*, la noticia fue un estimulante para él. ‖ Muñequera, *f.* (wristband).
brachial [ˈbreikjəl] adj. Braquial.
brachiopod [ˈbrækiəpɔd] n. ZOOL. Braquiópodo, *m.*
brachycephalic [ˌbrækikeˈfælik] adj. Braquicéfalo, la.
brachycephalism [ˌbrækiˈkefəlizəm] n. Braquicefalismo, *m.*
brachycephaly [ˌbrækiˈkefəli] n. Braquicefalia, *f.*
brachyuran [brækˈju:rən] n. Braquiuro, *m.*

— OBSERV. El plural de la palabra inglesa es *brachyura.*

bracken [ˈbrækən] n. BOT. Helecho, *m.*
bracket [ˈbrækit] n. Brazo, *m.* (of a lamp). ‖ Soporte, *m.* (support). ‖ PRINT. Paréntesis, *m.* | Llave, *f.* (brace). ‖ ARCH. Ménsula, *f.* (of a roof, balcony, etc.). ‖ Repisa, *f.* (on a wall). ‖ Grupo, *m.*, categoría, *f.* (category of taxpayers).
bracket [ˈbrækit] v. tr. Poner entre paréntesis. ‖ Agrupar (to group together). ‖ Relacionar (to associate). ‖ Sujetar (a shelf on the wall). ‖ MIL. Precisar [el blanco].
brackish [ˈbrækiʃ] adj. Salobre (water).
bract [brækt] n. BOT. Bráctea, *f.*
brad [bræd] n. Puntilla, *f.* (short nail).
bradawl [ˈbrædɔ:l] n. Lezna, *f.*, punzón, *m.*
bradypepsia [brædiˈpepsiə] n. MED. Bradipepsia, *f.*
brae [brei] n. Ladera, *f.*, pendiente, *f.* (in Scotland).
brag [bræg] n. Jactancia, *f.*, alarde, *m.* (boast).
brag [bræg] v. tr./intr. Jactarse, alardear.
braggart [ˈbrægət] n. Fanfarrón, ona; jactancioso, sa.
Brahma [ˈbrɑ:mə] pr. n. Brahma, *m.*
Brahman [ˈbrɑ:mən] n. Brahmán, *m.*
Brahmanic [brɑ:ˈmænik] or **Brahmanical** [—əl] adj. Brahmánico, ca.
Brahmanism [ˈbrɑ:mənizəm] n. Brahmanismo, *m.*
Brahmin [ˈbrɑ:min] n. Brahmán, *m.*, brahmín, *m.*
Brahminic [brɑ:ˈminik] or **Brahminical** [—əl] adj. Brahmánico, ca.
Brahminism [ˈbrɑ:minizəm] n. Brahmanismo, *m.*
braid [breid] n. Trenza, *f.* (of hair). ‖ Galón, *m.* (of uniform, blazer, etc.).
braid [breid] v. tr. Trenzar (hair). | Galonear (uniform, blazer, etc.).
brail [breil] n. MAR. Candaliza, *f.*
brail [breil] v. tr. MAR. Cargar [las velas].
Braille [breil] n. Braille, *m.* (writing for the blind).
brain [brein] n. ANAT. Cerebro, *m.* ‖ — Pl. FIG. Inteligencia, *f. sing.*, seso, *m. sing.* ‖ CULIN. Sesos, *m.* ‖ — FIG. *Brain drain*, fuga (*f.*) de cerebros. | *To blow one's brains out*, levantarse or saltarse la tapa de los sesos. | *To have sth. on the brain*, tener algo metido en la cabeza. | *To rack* o *to cudgel* o *to beat one's brains*, calentarse *or* estrujarse *or* devanarse los sesos. | *To turn s.o.'s brains*, volverle a uno loco.
brain [brein] v. tr. FAM. Romper la crisma.
braincase [—keis] n. Caja (*f.*) del cráneo.
brainchild [—tʃaild] n. Invento, *m.*, idea, *f.* [genial].
brain fever [—ˌfi:və*] n. MED. Encefalitis, *f.*
brainless [—lis] adj. Tonto, ta; memo, ma; mentecato, ta (silly). ‖ Insensato, ta (thoughtless).
brainpan [—pæn] n. Cráneo, *m.*
brainpower [—ˌpauə*] n. Capacidad (*f.*) intelectual.
brainsick [—sik] adj. Trastornado mentalmente.
brainstorm [—stɔ:m] n. Ataque (*m.*) de locura. ‖ FAM. Inspiración, *f.*, idea (*f.*) genial.
brain trust [—trʌst] n. Grupo (*m.*) de expertos, cerebros, *m. pl.*
brain tumour [—ˌtjumə*] or **brain tumor** [—ˌtjumə] n. Tumor (*m.*) cerebral.
brainwash [—wɔʃ] v. tr. FIG. Lavar el cerebro.
brainwashing [—ˌwɔʃiŋ] n. FIG. Lavado (*m.*) del cerebro.
brain wave [—weiv] n. Inspiración, *f.*, idea (*f.*) genial. ‖ MED. Onda (*f.*) telepática.
brain work [—wə:k] n. Trabajo (*m.*) intelectual.
brainy [ˈbreini] adj. FAM. Inteligente, listo, ta.
braise [breiz] v. tr. Cocer a fuego lento.
brake [breik] n. Freno, *m.*: *foot brake*, freno de pedal; *drum, disc, power-assisted brake*, freno de tambor, de disco, asistido; *front, back brake*, freno delantero, trasero; *to apply the brake*, poner el freno; *to release the brake*, soltar el freno. ‖ FIG. Freno, *m.* ‖ Furgoneta, *f.* (car). ‖ Matorral, *m.*, maleza, *f.* (thicket). ‖ BOT. Helecho, *m.* (bracken). ‖ AGR. Agramadera, *f.* (for beating hemp). | Grada, *f.*, rastra, *f.* (harrow). ‖ ‖ *Brake horsepower*, potencia (*f.*) al freno.
brake [breik] v. tr. Frenar (to slow down). ‖ Agramar (hemp).
— V. intr. Frenar.
brake band [—bænd] n. Cinta (*f.*) del freno.
brake blocks [—blɔks] pl. n. Zapatas (*f.*) del freno.
brake drum [—drʌm] n. Tambor (*m.*) del freno.
brake lining [—ˌlainiŋ] n. Guarnición (*f.*) del freno.
brakeman [—mən] n. Guardafrenos, *m. inv.*

— OBSERV. El plural de *brakeman* es *brakemen.*

brake shoe [—ʃu:] n. TECH. Zapata, *f.*
braking [—in] n. Frenaje, *m.*, frenado, *m.*
bramble [ˈbræmbl] n. BOT. Zarza, *f.*, zarzamora, *f.*
brambleberry [—ˌberi] n. BOT. Zarzamora, *f.*
brambling [ˈbræmbliŋ] n. Pinzón, *m.* (bird).
brambly [ˈbræmbli] adj. Zarzoso, sa.
bran [bræn] n. Salvado, *m.*, afrecho, *m.*
branch [brɑ:ntʃ] n. Rama, *f.* (of a tree). ‖ Brazo, *m.* (of candlestick, horns, etc.). ‖ Brazo, *m.* (of a river). ‖ FIG. Rama, *f.* (of a family). ‖ Ramo, *m.*, rama, *f.* (a part of science, etc.). ‖ Ramificación, *f.* (subdivision). ‖ Ramal, *m.* (railways). ‖ COMM. Sucursal, *f.* ‖ TECH. Derivación, *f.*
branch [brɑ:ntʃ] v. intr. Echar ramas (trees). ‖ Ramificarse (to subdivide). ‖ Bifurcarse (to bifurcate). ‖ — *To branch away*, bifurcarse. ‖ *To branch from*, derivarse de. ‖ *To branch off*, bifurcarse. ‖ FIG. *To branch off into*, extender sus actividades a. ‖ *To branch out*, bifurcarse (to divide), extender sus actividades (to expand one's scope).
branchia [ˈbræŋkiə] n. Branquia, *f.*

— OBSERV. El plural de *branchia* es *branchiae.*

branchial [—l] adj. Branquial.
branching [ˈbrɑ:ntʃiŋ] n. Bifurcación, *f.*, derivación, *f.*
branchiopodes [ˈbræŋkiəˌpɔdz] pl. n. ZOOL. Branquiópodos, *m.*
branch line [ˈbrɑ:ntʃ-lain] n. Ramal, *m.* (of railway).
branch office [ˈbrɑ:ntʃˌɔfis] n. Sucursal, *f.*
brand [brænd] n. Hierro, *m.* (on cattle, prisoners, etc.). ‖ Marca, *f.* (trademark). ‖ Tea, *f.*, tizón, *m.* (charred wood). ‖ BOT. Roya, *f.*, tizón, *m.* (plant disease). ‖ FIG. Estigma, *m.* (stigma). ‖ POET. Acero, *m.*, espada, *f.* (sword).
brand [brænd] v. tr. Marcar con hierro candente, herrar (cattle, prisoners, etc.). ‖ Marcar, poner marca de fábrica en. ‖ FIG. Tildar de: *to brand a man a liar*, tildar a un hombre de mentiroso. | Estigmatizar. | Grabar (in mind). | Motejar (to nickname).
Brandenburg [ˈbrændənbə:g] pr. n. Brandeburgo, *m.*, Brandenburgo, *m.*
branding [ˈbrændiŋ] n. Herradero, *m.*
branding iron [ˈbrændiŋˌaiən] n. Hierro (*m.*) de marcar (to brand cattle, etc.).
brandish [ˈbrændiʃ] v. tr. Blandir, esgrimir.
brandling [ˈbrændliŋ] n. Lombriz (*f.*) para cebo.
brand name [ˈbrændneim] n. Marca (*f.*) de fábrica.
brand-new [ˈbrænd-ˈnju:] adj. Completamente nuevo, flamante.
brandy [ˈbrændi] n. Coñac, *m.*, brandy, *m.* (spirit). ‖ Aguardiente, *m.* (liquor): *cherry brandy*, aguardiente de cerezas.
brant [brænt] n. Barnacla, *m.* (wild goose).
brash [bræʃ] adj. Descarado, da; insolente (impudent). ‖ Temerario, ria (daring).
— N. Escombros, *m. pl.* (of rocks, etc.).
brass [brɑ:s] n. Latón, *m.*, cobre (*m.*) amarillo (alloy of copper and zinc). ‖ FIG. Descaro, *m.*, desfachatez, *f.* (impudence). ‖ FIG. FAM. Dinero, *m.*, parné, *m.*, pasta, *f.* [*Amer.*, plata, *f.*] (money). ‖ MUS. Cobres, *m. pl.* (instruments). ‖ — FAM. *The brass*, el alto mando. | *To be as bold as brass*, tener mucha cara. | *To get down to brass tacks*, ir al grano. | *Top brass*, peces gordos.
brassard [ˈbræsɑ:d] n. Brazalete, *m.*, brazal, *m.*
brass band [ˈbrɑ:sˈbænd] n. MUS. Banda, *f.*
brass hat [ˈbrɑ:sˈhæt] n. MIL. FAM. Oficial (*m.*) de Estado Mayor.
brassie [ˈbrɑ:si] n. Palo (*m.*) de golf.
brassière [ˈbræsiə*] n. Sostén, *m.*
brass knuckles [ˈbrɑ:sˈnʌklz] pl. n. Manopla, *f. sing.*
brasswork [ˈbrɑ:swə:k] n. Objetos (*m. pl.*) de latón *or* de cobre amarillo. ‖ Trabajo (*m.*) del cobre amarillo.
brassworker [—ə*] n. Latonero, *m.*
brassy [ˈbrɑ:si] adj. De latón. ‖ De color de cobre. ‖ Metálico, ca (metallic). ‖ Estridente (harsh). ‖ FIG. Descarado, da (impudent).
brat [bræt] n. FAM. Mocoso, sa (bad-mannered child).
— N. Palo (*m.*) de golf.
brattice [ˈbrætis] n. Tabique (*m.*) de ventilación. ‖ Parapeto (*m.*) de madera en una fortaleza.
brattle [ˈbrætəl] v. intr. Traquetear.
bravado [brəˈvɑ:dəu] n. Baladronada, *f.*, bravata, *f.* (boast). ‖ *Piece of bravado*, baladronada, bravata.

— OBSERV. El plural de *bravado* es *bravadoes* o *bravados.*

brave [breiv] adj. Valeroso, sa; valiente (courageous). ‖ Espléndido, da (splendid).
— N. Valiente, *m.* ‖ U. S. Guerrero (*m.*) indio.
brave [breiv] v. tr. Hacer frente a, arrostrar, afrontar (to face). ‖ Desafiar (to defy): *to brave death*, desafiar la muerte. ‖ *To brave it out*, aguantar hasta el final.
bravery [—ri] n. Valor, *m.*, valentía, *f.* ‖ Esplendor, *m.* (fine appearance).
bravo [ˈbrɑ:ˈvəu] interj. ¡Bravo!
bravura [brəˈvuərə] n. Arrojo, *m.*, bravura, *f.* (show of daring). ‖ MUS. Ejecución (*f.*) brillante.
brawl [brɔ:l] n. Pendencia, *f.*, reyerta, *f.* (fight).
brawl [brɔ:l] v. intr. Pelearse (to fight).
brawler [—ə*] n. Alborotador, ra; pendenciero, ra.
brawn [brɔ:n] n. Fuerza (*f.*) muscular (muscular strength). ‖ Músculo, *m.* (in arm, leg). ‖ Carne (*f.*) de cerdo adobada (pickled pork). ‖ Queso (*m.*) de cerdo (headcheese).
brawny [ˈbrɔ:ni] adj. Musculoso, sa.
bray [brei] n. Rebuzno, *m.* (of an ass). ‖ FIG. Sonido (*m.*) ronco (of trumpets, etc.).

bray [brei] v. intr. Rebuznar (an ass). || *To bray out*, sonar roncamente (trumpets, etc.).
brayer [—ə*] n. PRINT. Rodillo, *m.*
braze [breiz] v. tr. Soldar (copper and zinc, zinc and silver, etc.). || Broncear (to decorate with brass).
brazen [ˈbreizn] adj. De latón. || Bronceado, da (of a harsh yellow colour). || Bronco, ca (harsh and loud). || FIG. Descarado, da (shameless).
brazen [ˈbreizn] v. tr. *To brazen it out*, aguantar una dificultad con descaro.
brazenfaced [breiznfeist] adj. Descarado, da.
brazier [ˈbreizjə*] n. Brasero, *m.* (for heating). || Latonero, *m.* (brassworker). || *Perfume brazier*, pebetero, *m.*
Brazil [brəˈzil] pr. n. GEOGR. Brasil, *m.*
brazil [brəˈzil] n. Palo (*m.*) del Brasil, palo (*m.*) brasil, brasil, *m.* (brazilwood). || Tinte (*m.*) de color rojo extraído del palo del Brasil (red dye).
brazilette [brəziˈlet] n. BOT. Brasilete, *m.*
Brazilian [brəˈziljən] adj./n. Brasileño, ña; brasilero, ra.
Brazil nut [brəˈzilˈnʌt] n. BOT. Nuez (*f.*) del Brasil.
brazilwood [brəˈzilˈwud] n. Palo (*m.*) del Brasil, palo (*m.*) brasil, brasil, *m.*
brazing [ˈbreiziŋ] n. Soldadura, *f.*
breach [bri:tʃ] n. Brecha, *f.* (in a wall, etc.). || Incumplimiento, *m.*: *breach of contract*, incumplimiento de contrato; *breach of promise*, incumplimiento de una promesa. || Violación, *f.*, infracción, *f.*, contravención, *f.*: *breach of the law*, violación de la ley. || Rompimiento, *m.* (of waves). || Ruptura, *f.* (break in friendly relations). || Desgarramiento, *m.* (of material). || — *Breach of faith*, abuso (*m.*) de confianza. || *Breach of the peace*, perturbación (*f.*) del orden público. || *Breach of trust*, abuso (*m.*) de confianza. || FIG. *To stand in the breach*, estar en la brecha. | *To throw o.s. into the breach*, echarse al ruedo.
breach [bri:tʃ] v. tr. Abrir una brecha en (to break through). || Violar, infringir, contravenir, quebrantar (a law). || Violar (a contract).
bread [bred] n. Pan, *m.*: *piece of bread*, pedazo de pan; *bread and butter*, pan con mantequilla. || FIG. Pan, *m.* (living): *to earn one's bread*, ganarse el pan. || FAM. Pasta, *f.*, parné, *m.* [*Amer.*, plata, *f.*] (money). || — *Brown bread*, pan bazo, pan moreno. || *Communion bread*, pan bendito. || *Fine wheaten bread*, pan de flor. || FIG. *For a crust of bread*, por un mendrugo de pan. || *Fresh bread*, pan tierno. || *Homemade bread*, pan casero. || FIG. *Man does not live on bread alone*, no sólo de pan vive el hombre. || *Milk bread*, pan de Viena. || *Our daily bread*, el pan nuestro de cada día. || *Ration bread*, pan de munición. || *Rye bread*, pan de centeno. || *Sliced bread*, pan de molde, pan francés. || *Stale bread*, pan duro. || *To be on bread and water*, estar a pan y agua. || FIG. *To cast one's bread upon the waters*, hacer el bien sin mirar a quien. | *To know which side one's bread is buttered on*, saber lo que más le conviene a uno. | *To take the bread out of s.o.'s mouth*, quitarle a uno el pan de la boca. || *Unleavened bread*, pan ácimo. || *White bread*, pan blanco, pan candeal. || *Wholemeal bread*, pan integral.
bread-and-butter [—əndˌbʌtə*] adj. Corriente (commonplace). || Juvenil (youthful). || De agradecimiento (letter).
breadbasket [—ˌbɑ:skət] n. Panera, *f.*, cesto (*m.*) para el pan. || FIG. Granero, *m.* || FAM. Barriga, *f.* (stomach).
breadcrumb [—krʌm] n. Migaja (*f.*) de pan. || — Pl. Pan (*m. sing.*) rallado. || CULIN. *In breadcrumbs*, empanado, da.
breadfruit [—fru:t] n. Fruto (*m.*) del árbol del pan. || *Breadfruit tree*, árbol (*m.*) del pan.
breadline [—lain] n. U. S. Cola (*f.*) para recibir alimentos gratuitamente.
breadstuff [—stʌf] n. Harina, *f.* (flour). || Cereales, *m. pl.* (grain).
breadth [—θ] n. Anchura, *f.*, ancho, *m.* (width). || Amplitud, *f.* (extent). || FIG. Largueza, *f.*, generosidad, *f.*
breadthways [—weiz] or **breadthwise** [—waiz] adv. A lo ancho.
breadwinner [—ˌwinə*] n. Sostén (*m.*) de la familia.
break [breik] n. Rotura, *f.*, ruptura, *f.* (rupture). || Abertura, *f.*, grieta, *f.* (breach). || Interrupción, *f.*, pausa, *f.*, descanso, *m.* (pause). || Recreo, *m.* (in schools, etc.). || Tacada, *f.* (in billiards). || Break, *m.* (car). || FIG. Claro, *m.* (in the clouds). | Amanecer, *m.* (dawn). | Huida, *f.*, fuga, *f.*, evasión, *f.* (from prison). | Golpe (*m.*) de suerte (piece of good luck). | Ruptura, *f.* (between friends, family, etc.) | Comienzo, *m.*, principio, *m.* (beginning). | Espacio, *m.* (blank space). | Gallo, *m.* (in the voice). | Cambio, *m.*, alteración, *f.*: *a break in the weather*, un cambio de tiempo. || FIG. FAM. Oportunidad, *f.* (opportunity). || Cesura, *f.* (in poetry). || COMM. Baja, *f.* (of the stock market). || ELECTR. Corte, *m.*, interrupción, *f.*: *a break in a wiring circuit*, un corte en el circuito eléctrico. || SP. Cambio (*m.*) de dirección (of ball). | Internada, *f.* (of a player with the ball). | Separación, *f.* (of boxers). || — *Bad* o *unlucky break*, mala suerte. || *Lucky break*, golpe (*m.*) de suerte. || *Without a break*, sin parar.
break* [breik] v. tr. Romper, quebrar: *to break a chair*, romper una silla. || Destrozar (to shatter). || Amortiguar: *the hedge broke the force of the wind*, el seto amortiguó la fuerza del viento. || Romper: *to break silence, an appointment*, romper el silencio, un compromiso; *to break a strike*, romper una huelga. || Quebrantar, violar: *to break the law*, quebrantar la ley. || Degradar (to demote a soldier). || Violar, romper: *to break a contract*, violar un contrato. || Faltar a (one's word). || Descubrir la clave de, descifrar (a code). || Resolver (a case, mystery). || Moderar (strength, speed). || Batir: *to break a record*, batir un récord. || Abrir: *to break a path*, abrir un camino. || Deshacer: *to break a set of books*, deshacer una colección de libros. || Destrozar (morally). || Arruinar (to reduce to poverty): *this venture will either make you or break you*, esta empresa te hará rico o te arruinará. || Sofocar: *to break a rebellion*, sofocar una rebelión. || Dar: *he broke the news*, dio la noticia. || Domar: *to break a horse*, domar un caballo. || Interrumpir, cortar (to interrupt). || Alterar: *to break the peace*, alterar el orden. || Empezar (to begin). || Cambiar (a bank note). || — FIG. *To break a lance with*, batirse con. || *To break asunder*, dividir en dos. || *To break bounds*, entrar en zona prohibida. || *To break camp*, levantar el campo. || *To break cover*, salir al descubierto. || *To break ground*, see GROUND. || *To break jail*, escaparse de la cárcel. || *To break one's back*, deslomarse. || *To break one's fast*, romper el ayuno. || *To break one's health*, quebrantar la salud. || *To break one's neck*, see NECK. || *To break open*, abrir forzando (to force open). || *To break o.s. of a habit*, quitarse de una costumbre. || MIL. *To break ranks*, romper filas. || FIG. *To break s.o.'s heart*, partirle el corazón a uno. || *To break the bank*, hacer saltar la banca (in gambling). || FIG. *To break the ice*, romper el hielo: *he broke the ice by telling a joke*, rompió el hielo contando un chiste. || *To break to pieces*, hacer pedazos.
— V. intr. Romperse: *the glass fell off the table and broke*, el vaso se cayó de la mesa y se rompió. || FIG. Estallar: *the storm broke*, la tormenta estalló. | Terminarse (to come to an end): *the bad weather broke*, el mal tiempo se terminó. | Interrumpirse (to stop). | Quebrantarse, resentirse: *his health broke under the strain*, su salud se resintió por el esfuerzo. | Cambiar, mudar: *John's voice is breaking*, la voz de Juan está cambiando. | Bajar: *the stock market broke*, la bolsa bajó. | Arruinarse (to go bankrupt). || Dispersarse (troops, clouds, crowd). || Romper (waves). || Romper, apuntar, rayar (the day). || Brotar (plants). || Reventarse (an abscess). || Divulgarse, propalarse (news, scandal). || SP. Desviarse (a ball). | Separarse (in boxing, dancing): *the referee told them to break*, el árbitro les ordenó que se separaran. || *To break open*, abrirse de par en par (a door).
— **To break away**, separarse (to withdraw). | Escaparse (to escape). || **To break down**, derribar (to knock down): *the mob broke down the barricades*, la multitud derribó las barricadas. | Acabar con: *to break down the enemy resistance*, acabar con la resistencia enemiga. | Desglosar (expenses). | Hundirse (a bridge). | FIG. Derrumbarse (morally), debilitarse: *his health broke down*, su salud se debilitó; averiarse (car, machine). || **To break in**, intervenir: *to break in on a conversation*, intervenir en una conversación. | Irrumpir (to burst in). | Escalar, forzar (burglars). || **To break into**, escalar, forzar: *the burglars broke into the house*, los ladrones escalaron la casa. | Ponerse a: *to break into song*, ponerse a cantar. || **To break off**, romper: *they broke off the engagement*, rompieron el compromiso. | Cortar: *break a few branches off the tree*, corta unas cuantas ramas del árbol. | Interrumpirse (talks). | Pararse, detenerse: *he broke off in the middle of the speech*, se detuvo en medio del discurso. | Reñir, terminar (to end a relationship). | Desprenderse (to become detached). | — *To break it off*, reñir. || **To break out**, escaparse (to escape). | Salirle a uno: *to break out in spots*, salirle a uno manchas. | Estallar (war, epidemic). || **To break through**, romper, atravesar, abrirse paso por: *the crowd broke through the police cordon*, la muchedumbre rompió el cordón de policía. | Atravesar: *the sun broke through the heavy mist*, el sol atravesó la densa niebla. || **To break up**, romper: *to break up a box*, romper una caja. | Desglosar, separar (words). | Desguazar (car, ship). | Mullir (soil). | Disolver (crowd). | Acabar con (to put an end to). | Levantarse (meeting, etc.). | Separarse (husband and wife, partners, etc.). | Acabar (to finish): *school breaks up tomorrow*, el colegio acaba mañana. | Terminarse (strike). | Disolverse: *the mob broke up*, la multitud se disolvió. | Reñir, terminar (to end a relationship). || **To break with**, romper con: *to break with the family*, romper con la familia. | Violar, quebrantar (a convention).

— OBSERV. Pret. **broke**; p. p. **broken.**

breakable [ˈbreikəbl] adj. Quebradizo, za; frágil.
breakage [ˈbreikidʒ] n. Rotura, *f.* (breaking). || Objetos (*m. pl.*) rotos (broken things). || Indemnización (*f.*) por objetos rotos (allowance).
breakaway [ˈbreikəˌwei] adj. Disidente.
— N. Escapada, *f.* || Ruptura, *f.*
breakaxe (U.S. **breakax**) [ˈbreikˌæks] n. Quebracho, *m.* (hardwood).
breakdown [ˈbreikdaun] n. MED. Depresión (*f.*) nerviosa. || Avería, *f.* (of a car, machine). || CHEM. Descomposición, *f.*, análisis, *m.* || Análisis, *m.* (division

into categories). || Desglose, *m.*: *breakdown of expenses*, desglose de los gastos. || Ruptura, *f.* (of talks, etc.). || Interrupción, *f.* (suspension). || Fracaso, *m.* (failure). — *Breakdown gang*, equipo (*m.*) de arreglo de averías. || *Breakdown lorry*, grúa, *f.*, camión (*m.*) grúa.
breaker [ˈbreikə*] n. MAR. Cachón, *m.*, ola (*f.*) grande. || TECH. Trituradora, *f.* || ELECTR. Interruptor (*m.*) automático.
breakfast [ˈbrekfəst] n. Desayuno, *m.*
breakfast [ˈbrekfəst] v. intr. Desayunar.
breaking [ˈbreikiŋ] n. Rotura, *f.* || Interrupción, *f.* || — *Breaking and entering*, allanamiento (*m.*) de morada. || *Breaking point*, punto (*m.*) de ruptura; extremo, *m.*
breakneck [ˈbreiknek] adj. Suicida: *breakneck speed*, velocidad suicida.
breakthrough [ˈbreikˌθru:] n. Ruptura, *f.* || MIL. Ruptura, *f.* (of a front). | Penetración, *f.* || Progreso, *m.*, adelanto, *m.*, avance, *m.*: *the discovery of penicillin was a significant breakthrough*, el descubrimiento de la penicilina ha sido un gran adelanto.
breakup [ˈbreikʌp] n. Desintegración, *f.*, desmembramiento, *m.*: *the breakup of an empire*, el desmembramiento de un imperio. || División, *f.* (of a state, etc.). || Ruptura, *f.* (of talks). || Deshielo, *m.* (thaw). || Separación, *f.* (of partners, husband and wife, etc.). || Dispersión, *f.* (of a crowd).
breakwater [ˈbreikˌwɔ:tə*] n. Rompeolas, *m. inv.*
bream [bri:m] n. Brema, *f.* (fish).
breast [brest] n. Pecho, *m.* (of a person). || Seno, *m.*, pecho, *m.* (of a woman). || Pechuga, *f.* (of a bird). || Peto, *m.* (of armour). || Reja, *f.* (of a plough). || Corazón, *m.*: *in the depths of my breast*, en lo más profundo de mi corazón. || FIG. Repecho, *m.*: *the breast of a hill*, el repecho de una colina. | Antepecho, *m.*: *the chimney breast*, el antepecho de la chimenea. || — *To beat one's breast*, darse golpes de pecho. || FIG. *To make a clean breast of (it)*, confesar.
breast [brest] v. tr. Hacer frente a, arrostrar, enfrentarse a (to brave).
breastbone [—bəun] n. ANAT. Esternón, *m.*
breast-feed [—fi:d] v. tr. Amamantar, dar el pecho a.
breast-feeding [—ˌfi:diŋ] n. Amamantamiento, *m.*
breastpin [—pin] n. Alfiler (*m.*) de corbata. || U. S. Broche, *m.* (brooch).
breastplate [—pleit] n. Peto, *m.* (of armour). || Petral, *m.* (of harness).
breaststroke [—strəuk] n. SP. Braza (*f.*) de pecho.
breast wall [—wɔ:l] n. Muro (*m.*) de contención (retaining wall). || MIL. Parapeto, *m.*
breastwork [—wə:k] n. MIL. Parapeto, *m.*
breath [breθ] n. Aliento, *m.*: *his breath smelled of whisky*, su aliento olía a whisky. || Respiración, *f.*, (breathing). || FIG. Soplo, *m.*: *there was not a breath of air*, no había un soplo de aire. || Hálito, *m.* (of animals). || FIG. Fragancia, *f.*: *the breath of spring*, la fragancia de la primavera. | Vida, *f.*, aliento, *m.* (life). | Pausa, *f.*, respiro, *m.* (breather). | Rumor, *m.*: *a breath of scandal*, un rumor de escándalo. || Espiración, (*f.*) de aire (in phonetics). || — FIG. *A breath of air*, un aire renovador. | *Below one's breath*, en voz baja. | *In the next breath*, inmediatamente después. | *In the same breath*, en el mismo momento, al mismo tiempo. || *Out of breath*, sin aliento. || *To be short of breath*, perder fácilmente el aliento. || *To catch one's breath*, see CATCH. || *To draw breath*, respirar. || *To draw a deep breath*, respirar a fondo. || *To draw one's last breath*, exhalar el último suspiro. || *To gasp for breath*, jadear, respirar con dificultad. || *To get one's breath back*, recobrar la respiración *or* el aliento. || *To get out of breath*, quedarse sin aliento. || *To go out for a breath of air*, salir a tomar el aire. || FIG. *To save one's breath*, ahorrar palabras. | *To take one's breath away*, dejar sin respiración. | *To waste one's breath*, hablar *or* gastar saliva en balde.
breathable [ˈbri:ðəbl] adj. Respirable.
breathalyser [ˈbreθəlaizə*] n. Alcohómetro, *m.*
breathe [bri:ð] v. intr. Respirar. || FIG. Vivir, respirar (to live). || — FIG. *To breathe again*, respirar. | *To breathe down one's neck*, atosigar (to harass), pisar los talones (to follow). || *To breathe in*, aspirar. || *To breathe out*, espirar.
— V. tr. Aspirar: *to breathe in gulps of fresh air*, aspirar grandes bocanadas de aire fresco. || FIG. Respirar: *her look breathed innocence*, su aspecto respiraba inocencia. | FIG. Susurrar (to whisper). || — FIG. *Not to breathe a word of*, no decir una palabra de, no decir nada de. || *To breathe air into*, inflar soplando. || *To breathe a sigh*, dar un suspiro. || FIG. *To breathe new life into*, dar nueva vida a. || *To breathe one's last breath*, exhalar el último suspiro. || *To breathe out*, exhalar.
breather [—ə*] n. FAM. Descanso, *m.*, pausa, *f.*, respiro, *m.* (short break): *ten-minute breather*, descanso *or* pausa de diez minutos, diez minutos de respiro.
breathing [—iŋ] n. Respiración, *f.* || GRAMM. Espíritu, *m.* (in Greek). || *Breathing space* o *spell*, descanso, *m.*, pausa, *f.*, respiro, *m.* (rest).
breathless [ˈbreθlis] adj. Jadeante, sin aliento (gasping for breath). || Sin vida (lifeless). || FIG. Intenso, sa: *breathless silence*, silencio intenso. | Sin resuello (astonished). | Sin viento, sin aire (stifling).
breathtaking [ˈbreθˌteikiŋ] adj. Punzante, que corta la respiración: *a breathtaking pain*, un dolor punzante. || FIG. Asombroso, sa (astonishing): *a breathtaking experience*, una experiencia asombrosa. | Emocionante (thrilling). | Impresionante, imponente: *a breathtaking view*, una vista impresionante.
breathy [ˈbreθi] adj. Velado, da (voice).
bred [bred] pret. & p. p. See BREED.
breech [bri:tʃ] n. Recámara, *f.* (of a firearm). || Trasero, *m.* (buttocks). || — Pl. Pantalones, *m.* (trousers). || Pantalones (*m.*) de montar (knee-length trousers). || — *Breeches buoy*, salvavidas (*m.*) en forma de pantalón. || FIG. *To wear the breeches*, llevar los pantalones.
breechblock [ˈbri:tʃblɔk] n. Obturador, *m.* (in gun).
breeching [ˈbri:tʃiŋ] n. Retranca, *f.* (of harness).
breech-loading [ˈbri:tʃˌləudiŋ] adj. De retrocarga (arm).
breed [bri:d] n. Raza, *f.* (of animals). || BOT. Variedad, *f.* (of plants).
breed* [bri:d] v. tr. Criar (to produce, to raise). || FIG. Engendrar, producir: *familiarity breeds contempt*, la familiaridad produce el menosprecio. || Criar (to bring up): *country bred*, criado en el campo. || Educar: *well bred*, bien educado.
— V. intr. Reproducirse. || Criarse.
— OBSERV. Pret. & p. p. *bred*.
breeder [—ə*] n. Criador, ra (of animals). || Ganadero, ra (of cattle). || Reproductor, ra (breeding animal).
breeder reactor [ˈbri:də*-riˈæktə*] n. TECH. Reactor generador, *m.*
breeding [bri:diŋ] n. Cría, *f.* (of plants or animals). || FIG. Clase, *f.* (background). | Educación, *f.*: *to lack breeding*, carecer de educación. || — *Breeding animal*, reproductor, ra. || *Breeding place*, criadero, *m.* || *Breeding season*, época (*f.*) de la reproducción.
breeze [bri:z] n. Brisa, *f.* (gentle wind). || MAR. Viento, *m.*: *stiff breeze*, viento fuerte. || FIG. Cosa (*f.*) fácil. || Carbonilla, *f.* (coke).
breeze [bri:z] v. intr. *To breeze in, out*, entrar, salir despreocupadamente. || *To breeze through*, pasar fácilmente (an examination), leer por encima (to read). || *To breeze to*, lograr fácilmente.
breeziness [—inis] n. FIG. Alegría, *f.*, despreocupación, *f.*
breezy [—i] adj. Ventoso, sa: *a breezy afternoon*, una tarde ventosa. || FIG. Despreocupado, da; alegre (brisk, cheerful). || *It is breezy*, hace viento, hace aire.
Bremen [ˈbreimən] pr. n. GEOGR. Brema, Bremen.
Bren gun [ˈbrengʌn] n. MIL. Fusil (*m.*) ametrallador.
brer [brə:*] n. Hermano, *m.* (in fables).
brethren [ˈbreðrin] pl. n. REL. Hermanos, *m.*
Breton [ˈbretən] adj./n. Bretón, ona.
breve [bri:v] n. MUS. Breve, *f.* || GRAMM. Breve, *f.* (short vowel, syllable). || REL. Breve, *m.* (pope's letter).
brevet [ˈbrevit] adj. MIL. Honorario, ria.
— N. MIL. Graduación (*f.*) honoraria.
brevet [ˈbrevit] v. tr. MIL. Conferir un grado honorario a.
breviary [ˈbri:vjəri] n. REL. Breviario, *m.*
brevier [brəˈviə*] n. PRINT. Breviario, *m.* (old size of type).
brevity [ˈbreviti] n. Brevedad, *f.*
brew [bru:] n. Infusión, *f.*
brew [bru:] v. tr. Fabricar, hacer, elaborar (beer). || Preparar, hacer (tea). || FIG. Fomentar (to stir up). | Tramar (to plot).
— V. intr. Fabricar *or* elaborar cerveza. || Fermentar (to ferment). || Reposar: *let the tea brew a few minutes*, deja que el té repose unos minutos. || FIG. Prepararse, amenazar: *a storm is brewing*, se prepara una tormenta.
brewer [—ə*] n. Cervecero, *m.* || *Brewer's yeast*, levadura, *f.*
brewery [ˈbruəri] n. Fábrica (*f.*) de cerveza, cervecería, *f.*
brewing [bruiŋ] n. Elaboración (*f.*) *or* fabricación (*f.*) de la cerveza.
briar [ˈbraiə*] n. BOT. Zarza, *f.* (prickly bush). | Brezo, *m.* (used for pipes). || Pipa (*f.*) de madera de brezo (pipe). || *Briar rose*, gavanza, *f.*
bribe [braib] n. Soborno, *m.* || *To take bribes*, dejarse sobornar.
bribe [braib] v. tr./intr. Sobornar.
bribery [ˈbraibəri] n. Soborno, *m.*
bric-a-brac [ˈbrikəbræk] n. Baratijas, *f. pl.* (small cheap articles). || Curiosidades, *f. pl.* (curiosities).
brick [brik] n. Ladrillo, *m.*: *brick kiln*, horno de ladrillos. || Tarugo, *m.*, taco, *m.* (for children). || Lingote, *m.* (of gold). || Bloque, *m.* (ice cream). || Color (*m.*) ladrillo. || FIG. FAM. Buen chico, *m.* (affable person). || — *Hollow, mock, solid brick*, ladrillo hueco, visto, macizo. || FIG. FAM. *To come down on s.o. like a ton of bricks*, echarle una bronca a alguien. | *To drop a brick*, meter la pata, cometer una pifia.
brick [brik] v. tr. Enladrillar. || *To brick up* o *in*, tapiar con ladrillos.
brickbat [ˈbrikbæt] n. Trozo (*m.*) de ladrillo. || FIG. Palabra (*f.*) hiriente, pulla, *f.*
bricklayer [ˈbrikˌleiə*] n. Enladrillador, *m.*, albañil, *m.*
brickmaker [ˈbrikˌmeikə*] n. Ladrillero, *m.*
brick partition [ˈbrikpɑ:ˈtiʃən] n. Tabique (*m.*) de panderete.

brickwork [ˈbrikwəːk] n. Enladrillado, *m.*, ladrillos, *m. pl.*
brickworks [—s] n. Ladrillar, *m.*, fábrica (*f.*) de ladrillos.
brickyard [ˈbrikjɑːd] n. Almacén (*m.*) *or* fábrica (*f.*) de ladrillos.
bridal [ˈbraidl] adj. Nupcial: *bridal suite*, suite nupcial; *bridal bed*, tálamo nupcial.
— N. Boda, *f.*
bride [braid] n. Novia, *f.* || Desposada, *f.*, novia, *f.* (after wedding). || *The bride and groom*, los novios.
bridegroom [—gruːm] n. Novio, *m.* || Desposado, *m.*, novio, *m.* (after wedding).
bridesmaid [—zmeid] n. Dama (*f.*) de honor.
bridge [bridʒ] n. Puente, *m.*: *stone bridge*, puente de piedra. || MAR. Puente, *m.* || Puente, *m.* (of spectacles). || Caballete, *m.* (of nose). || Puente, *m.* (in dentistry). || Puente, *m.*, caballete, *m.* (of violin). || ELECTR. Puente: *Wheatstone bridge*, puente de Wheatstone. || Bridge, *m.* (card game). || — *Boat* o *pontoon bridge*, puente de barcas *or* de pontones. || *Counterpoise bridge*, puente de báscula. || FIG. *Golden bridge*, puente de plata. | *Much water has flowed under the bridge since then*, ha llovido mucho desde entonces. || *Railway bridge*, puente ferroviario. || *Skew bridge*, puente en esviaje. || *Suspension bridge*, puente colgante. || *To throw a bridge over*, tender un puente sobre.
bridge [bridʒ] v. tr. Tender un puente sobre (a river). || FIG. Recorrer (distance). || FIG. *To bridge the gap*, llenar un vacío, colmar la laguna.
bridgehead [—hed] n. MIL. Cabeza (*f.*) de puente.
Bridget [ˈbridʒit] pr. n. Brígida, *f.*
bridgework [ˈbridʒwəːk] n. Construcción (*f.*) de puentes. || Puente, *m.* (for teeth).
bridle [ˈbraidl] n. Brida, *f.* (of the harness). || Frenillo, *m.* (of tongue). || FIG. Freno, *m.* (restraining influence). || TECH. Tirante, *m.* || MAR. Poa, *f.*
bridle [ˈbraidl] v. tr. Embridar, poner la brida a. || FIG. Reprimir, refrenar (emotions, etc.).
— V. intr. FIG. Picarse (to take offence).
bridle path [—pɑːθ] n. Camino (*m.*) de herradura.
bridoon [briˈduːn] n. MIL. Bridón, *m.*
brief [briːf] adj. Breve: *a brief remark*, una breve observación. || Conciso, sa (concise). || Muy corto, ta: *a brief bathing suit*, un bañador muy corto.
— N. Informe, *m.* (report). || Sumario, *m.*, resumen, *m.* (summary). || REL. Breve, *m.* || JUR. Expediente, *m.* || MIL. Instrucciones, *f. pl.* || — Pl. Calzoncillos, *m.* (underpants), bragas, *f.* (knickers). || — *In brief*, en pocas palabras, en resumen. || JUR. *To hold no brief for*, no abogar por.
brief [briːf] v. tr. Informar (to inform): *he briefed me about the latest developments*, me informó sobre los últimos acontecimientos. || Dar instrucciones a: *to brief a lawyer*, dar instrucciones a un abogado. || Resumir (to sum up).
briefcase [—keis] n. Cartera, *f.* [*Amer.*, portafolio, *m.*].
briefing [—iŋ] n. Sesión (*f.*) de información. || Instrucciones, *f. pl.*
briefness [—nis] n. Brevedad, *f.*, concisión, *f.*
brier [ˈbraiə*] n. See BRIAR.
brig [brig] n. MAR. Bergantín, *m.* || U. S. FAM. Calabozo, *m.* (prison).
brigade [briˈgeid] n. MIL. Brigada, *f.* || FIG. *One of the old brigade*, un veterano.
brigade [briˈgeid] v. tr. MIL. Formar una brigada con.
brigadier [ˌbrigəˈdiə*] n. General (*m.*) de brigada.
brigand [ˈbrigənd] n. Bandido, *m.*, bandolero, *m.*
brigandage [—idʒ] n. Bandolerismo, *m.*, bandidaje, *m.*
brigantine [ˈbrigəntain] n. MAR. Bergantín, *m.*
bright [brait] adj. Vivo, va: *bright colour*, color vivo. || Claro, ra: *a bright day*, un día claro. || De sol (sunny). || Resplandeciente, brillante (sun). || Brillante (light, surface). || FIG. Vivo, va; alegre (cheerful). | Despierto, ta; listo, ta (clever). | Radiante (smile, beauty). | Prometedor, ra: *a bright future*, un futuro prometedor. | Luminoso, sa (idea). || — *Bright interval*, clara, *f.*, claro, *m.* (weather). || FIG. *Bright spark*, listillo, *m.* | *To look on the bright side of things*, mirar el lado bueno de las cosas. | *You're a bright one!*, ¡te has lucido!
— Adv. Brillantemente.
brighten [ˈbraitn] v. tr. Aclarar (to make lighter). || Pulir (to polish). || *To brighten up*, hacer más alegre (house, etc.), alegrar, animar (person).
— V. intr. Aclararse, despejarse: *then the weather brightened up*, luego se aclaró el tiempo. || FIG. Animarse, alegrarse (to cheer up). | Iluminarse (face).
brightly [ˈbraitli] adv. Brillantemente. || FIG. Alegremente (happily). | Ingeniosamente (wittily).
brightness [ˈbraitnis] n. Claridad, *f.*: *the brightness of dawn*, la claridad del amanecer. || Brillo, *m.*, resplandor, *m.* (of sun). || Luminosidad, *f.*, intensidad (*f.*) luminosa (luminosity). || FIG. Inteligencia, *f.*, viveza, *f.* (cleverness).
Bright's disease [ˈbraits-diˈziːz] n. MED. Mal (*m.*) de Bright, nefritis, *f.*
brill [bril] n. ZOOL. Rodaballo, *m.* (fish).
brilliance [ˈbriljəns] or **brilliancy** [—i] n. Brillantez, *f.*, brillo, *m.* || FIG. Brillantez, *f.*
brilliant [ˈbriljənt] adj. Brillante (very bright). || FIG. Brillante: *a brilliant painter, performance*, un pintor, una interpretación brillante. | Genial, luminoso, sa (idea). | Clamoroso, sa (success).
— N. Brillante, *m.* (diamond).
brillantine [ˌbriljənˈtiːn] n. Brillantina, *f.*
brim [brim] n. Borde, *m.* (of cup, bowl, etc.). || Ala, *f.* (of hat). || *Full to the brim*, lleno hasta los topes.
brim [brim] v. intr. Estar lleno hasta los topes. || FIG. Rebosar: *to brim over with happiness*, rebosar de alegría. || — *Broad-brimmed hat*, sombrero (*m.*) de ala ancha. || *To be brimming with*, estar rebosante de.
— V. tr. Llenar hasta el borde *or* hasta los topes.
brimful [—ful] adj. Lleno hasta el borde. || FIG. Rebosante: *brimful of ideas*, rebosante de ideas.
brimmer [—ə*] n. Copa (*f.*) llena hasta el borde.
brimming [—iŋ] adj. See BRIMFUL.
brimstone [—stəun] n. MIN. Azufre, *m.* || FIG. Fuego (*m.*) del infierno.
brindle [ˈbrindl] adj. Abigarrado, da; berrendo, da.
— N. Animal abigarrado *or* berrendo.
brine [brain] n. Salmuera, *f.* || POET. Piélago, *m.*, mar, *f.* (sea).
bring* [briŋ] v. tr. Traer: *to bring news*, traer noticias; *bring her home*, tráela a casa; *to bring bad luck*, traer mala suerte. || Llevar, conducir (to take): *he was brought before the magistrate*, le llevaron ante el magistrado. || FIG. Persuadir, convencer: *try to bring him to accept*, trata de persuadirle para que acepte. | Llevar: *to bring negotiations to a successful conclusion*, llevar las negociaciones a un feliz desenlace; *the series of catastrophes brought him to the brink of despair*, la serie de catástrofes le llevó al borde de la desesperación. || JUR. Intentar: *to bring an action*, intentar una acción judicial. | Hacer, formular: *to bring a complaint*, hacer una reclamación. || Introducir: *to bring somebody into the conversation*, introducir a alguien en la conversación. || Dar: *the picture will bring at least 100 pounds*, el cuadro dará 100 libras como mínimo. || —*To bring near*, acercar. || *To bring suit*, entablar un pleito. || *To bring support*, prestar ayuda.
— **To bring about,** ocasionar, provocar, causar: *to bring about an accident*, causar un accidente. | Efectuar: *to bring about a change*, efectuar un cambio. | MAR. Hacer virar (a ship). || **To bring along,** traer: *may I bring my friend along?*, ¿puedo traer a mi amigo? || **To bring away,** llevarse: *to bring away a prize*, llevarse un premio. || **To bring back,** volver a traer (to bring again). | Devolver (to return): *to bring back a book*, devolver un libro. | Traer: *he brought back news of the defeat*, trajo noticias de la derrota. | Recordar: *it brings back my childhood*, me recuerda mi infancia. || **To bring before,** someter a: *to bring a matter before Parliament*, someter una cuestión al Parlamento. || **To bring down,** bajar: *bring a chair down from the bedroom*, baja una silla del dormitorio. | Derribar (horseman, dictator, house, aeroplane). | Hacer bajar: *to bring down prices, the temperature*, hacer bajar los precios, la temperatura. | MATH. Bajar. || — *To bring down the house*, hacer que el teatro se venga abajo con los aplausos. || **To bring forth,** dar a luz (a child). | Producir (fruit). || **To bring forward,** acercar (to move nearer). | Traer: *bring forward the prisoner*, que traigan al preso. | Presentar: *to bring forward a subject for discussion*, presentar un tema para la discusión. | Plantear (a question). | Adelantar (a date). | — *Brought forward*, suma y sigue. || **To bring in,** traer: *to bring in some wood for the fire*, traer madera para el fuego. | Presentar (an argument, a bill). | Introducir (the fashion, a topic, a quotation). | Hacer entrar, hacer pasar (to show in). | Recoger (harvest). | COMM. Rendir, dar, producir: *an investment that brings in 6%*, una inversión que rinde el seis por ciento. | JUR. Pronunciar: *to bring in a verdict of guilty*, pronunciar un veredicto de culpabilidad. | Atraer (crowds). || **To bring into,** comprometer. | — *To bring into play*, poner en juego. | *To bring into the world*, traer al mundo. || **To bring off,** lograr, conseguir: *to bring off a master coup*, lograr un golpe maestro. | Rescatar (to rescue). | Conducir al éxito (to make a success). || **To bring on,** causar, provocar: *to bring on a fainting attack*, causar un desmayo. | Conducir a (to lead). || **To bring out,** sacar: *to bring sth. out of one's pocket*, sacar algo del bolsillo. | Publicar, sacar a luz: *to bring a new atlas out*, publicar un nuevo atlas. | Poner en escena (theatre). | Hacer resaltar: *to bring out the differences between two points of view*, hacer resaltar las diferencias entre dos puntos de vista. | Poner de manifiesto, sacar a relucir: *his teacher brought out his self-confidence, his gift for languages*, el profesor puso de manifiesto su confianza en sí mismo, su don de lenguas. | Ayudar a tener confianza en sí mismo (to build up s.o.'s self-confidence) | Presentar en sociedad (a debutante). || **To bring round,** o **around,** traer: *can she bring her brother round?*, ¿puede traer a su hermano? | Convencer, persuadir: *I shall bring him round*, yo le convenceré. | Reanimar, hacer volver en sí: *he brought her round after she had fainted*, le reanimó después del desmayo. | Llevar: *to bring the conversation round to a subject*, llevar la conversación hacia un tema. || **To bring through,** mantener vivo (to keep

alive). | Salvar (to save). | — *To bring a patient through*, operar con éxito a un paciente. || **To bring to,** reanimar (after fainting). | Parar, detener (to stop). | — *To bring a smile to one's lips*, hacer sonreír a alguien. | *To bring one's mind to bear on a problem*, examinar un problema. | *To bring o.s. to*, resignarse a. | *To bring sth. to s.o.'s knowledge*, poner algo en conocimiento de alguien. | *To bring to bear*, concentrar (attention), hacer: *to bring pressure to bear on s.o.*, hacer presión sobre alguien. | *To bring to book*, pedir cuentas a. | *To bring to light*, revelar, sacar a luz. | *To bring to mind*, recordar. | *To bring to ruin*, arruinar. | *To bring to task*, llamar a capítulo, reprender. || **To bring together,** reunir (to put together). | Reconciliar (enemies). || **To bring under,** someter. || **To bring up,** subir (sth. from downstairs). | Acercar (to move nearer). | Educar, criar: *a well brought-up child*, un niño bien educado. | Sacar a colación (a topic). | Plantear, poner sobre el tapete (a question). | Devolver (to vomit). | Parar (to stop). | — *To bring up a matter before s.o.*, someter algo a la atención de alguien. | *To bring up the rear*, see REAR. || **To bring upon o.s.,** buscarse (misfortune).

— OBSERV. Pret. & p. p. ***brought***.

brink [briŋk] n. Borde, *m.* (edge). || Orilla, *f.* (of a river). || FIG. *On the brink of*, al borde de: *on the brink of disaster*, al borde del desastre; a punto de: *on the brink of collapse*, a punto de hundirse.

brinkmanship [—manʃip] n. Política (*f.*) arriesgada *or* en la cuerda floja.

briny [ˈbraini] adj. Salado, da; salobre.
— N. Mar, *m.*

brio [ˈbriəu] n. Brío, *m.*

briquette or **briquet** [briˈket] n. Briqueta, *f.* (coal).

brisk [brisk] adj. Lleno de vida (lively). || Enérgico, ca; vigoroso, sa (energetic). || Fresco, ca (breeze). || Activo, va (trade). || — *At a brisk pace*, con paso ligero. || *To take a brisk walk*, dar un paseo rápido.

brisk [brisk] v. tr. Animar, avivar.
— V. intr. Animarse, avivarse.

brisket [ˈbriskit] n. CULIN. Falda, *f.* (of beef, etc.).

briskness [ˈbrisknis] n. Ligereza, *f.* (of step). || Energía, *f.* || Vivacidad, *f.* || Actividad, *f.* (of trade).

brisque [brisk] n. Brisca, *f.*

bristle [ˈbrisl] n. Cerda, *f.*

bristle [ˈbrisl] v. intr. Erizarse, ponerse de punta. || — FIG. *Bristling with rage*, congestionado de rabia. | *To bristle with*, estar erizado *or* lleno de: *bristling with difficulties*, erizado de dificultades.
— V. tr. Erizar, poner de punta.

bristly [ˈbrisli] adj. Erizado, da. || Cerdoso, sa. || *To have a bristly chin*, tener la barba crecida.

Bristol board [ˈbristl-bɔːd] n. Bristol, *m.*, cartulina, *f.*

Britain [ˈbritn] pr. n. GEOGR. Gran Bretaña, *f.* || *Battle of Britain*, batalla de Inglaterra.

Britannia [briˈtænjə] pr. n. Britania, *f.*

Britannic [briˈtænik] adj. Británico, ca: *Her* o *His Britannic Majesty*, Su Majestad Británica.

Briticism [ˈbritisizəm] n. Anglicismo, *m.*, palabra (*f.*) *or* expresión (*f.*) típicamente inglesa.

British [ˈbritiʃ] adj. Británico, ca.
— Pl. pr. n. Británicos, *m.*

British Columbia [—kəˈlʌmbiə] pr. n. GEOGR. Colombia (*f.*) Británica.

Britisher [—ə*] n. Natural (*m.*) de Gran Bretaña.

British Guiana [—gaiˈænə] pr. n. GEOGR. Guayana (*f.*) Británica, Guyana, *f.*

British Isles [—ails] pl. pr. n. GEOGR. Islas (*f.*) Británicas.

Briton [ˈbritn] n. HIST. Britano, na. || Británico, ca.

Brittany [ˈbritəni] pr. n. GEOGR. Bretaña, *f.*

brittle [ˈbritl] adj. Quebradizo, za; frágil. || FIG. Susceptible (person).

broach [brəutʃ] n. Brocheta, *f.*, espetón, *m.* (spit). || TECH. Punzón, *m.* (punch). | Broca, *f.*, mecha, *f.* (of a drill). | Escariador, *m.*, mandril, *m.* (to enlarge a hole). | Lezna, *f.* (in shoemaking). || ARCH. Aguja, *f.* (of spire). || Broche, *m.* (brooch).

broach [brəutʃ] v. tr. Poner en la brocheta, espetar (to put on a spit). || Espitar (a barrel, a cask). || FIG. Empezar, abrir (to begin). | Sacar a colación: *to broach the subject*, sacar el tema a colación.

broad [brɔːd] adj. Ancho, cha (wide): *a broad avenue*, una ancha avenida. || Extenso, sa; amplio, plia: *a broad stretch of water*, una superficie de agua extensa. || FIG. Claro, ra: *a broad hint*, una insinuación clara. | Amplio, plia: *in a broad sense*, en sentido amplio. | General (term). | Atrevido, da; verde (joke, story). | General: *a broad outline*, un esquema general. | Principal, esencial (essential). | Comprensivo, va; liberal, tolerante. | Abierto, ta (smile). || GRAMM. Abierto, ta (vowel). || — FIG. *Broad accent*, acento cerrado. || *In broad daylight*, en pleno día. || *On broad lines*, en grandes líneas, en líneas generales. || FIG. *To be as broad as it is long*, dar igual, dar lo mismo.
— N. Anchura, *f.* (width). || U. S. FAM. Gachí, *f.* (woman).

broad bean [—biːn] n. Haba, *f.*

broadcast [ˈbrɔːdkɑːst] n. RAD. Emisión, *f.* || *Repeat broadcast*, reposición, *f.*

broadcast* [ˈbrɔːdkɑːst] v. tr. Emitir, radiar (by radio). || Transmitir (by television). || AGR. Sembrar al voleo. || FIG. Propalar, difundir: *to broadcast a rumour, a piece of news*, propalar un rumor, difundir una noticia.

— OBSERV. Pret. & p. p. ***broadcast***.

broadcaster [—ə*] n. Locutor, ra (announcer).

broadcasting [—iŋ] n. Radiodifusión, *f.* (by radio). || Transmisión, *f.*, difusión, *f.* (by television). || — *Broadcasting program*, programa (*m.*) de radiodifusión. || *Broadcasting station*, emisora, *f.*

broadcloth [ˈbrɔːdkləθ] n. Paño (*m.*) fino. || Popelín, *m.*, popelina, *f.* (poplin).

broaden [ˈbrɔːdn] v. tr. Ensanchar. || FIG. Ampliar: *to broaden one's outlook*, ampliar las perspectivas.
— V. intr. Ensancharse. || FIG. Ampliarse.

broad jump [ˈbrɔːd-dʒʌmp] n. U.S. SP. Salto (*m.*) de longitud.

broadly [ˈbrɔːdli] adv. En general, en términos generales: *broadly speaking*, hablando en general.

broad-minded [ˈbrɔːdˈmaindid] adj. Tolerante, liberal, de miras amplias, comprensivo, va.

broad-mindedness [—nis] n. Amplitud (*f.*) de miras, tolerancia, *f.*

broadness [ˈbrɔːdnis] n. Anchura, *f.* (width). || FIG. Grosería, *f.* (vulgarity). || *The broadness of his speech*, su acento cerrado.

broad-shouldered [ˈbrɔːdˈʃəuldəd] adj. Ancho de espaldas.

broadside [ˈbrɔːdsaid] n. MAR. Costado, *m.* (side of a ship): *broadside on*, de costado. | Batería (*f.*) del costado (guns). | Andanada, *f.* (shots). || FIG. Retahíla, *f.*, andanada, *f.*, sarta, *f.*: *a broadside of insults*, una retahíla de insultos.
— Adv. MAR. De costado.

broadsword [ˈbrɔːdsɔːd] n. Sable, *m.*

broadways [ˈbrɔːdweiz] or **broadwise** [—waiz] adv. A lo ancho.

brocade [brəˈkeid] n. Brocado, *m.*

brocade [brəˈkeid] v. tr. Decorar con brocados.

brocatelle [brɔkəˈtel] n. Brocatel, *m.* (fabric).

broccoli [ˈbrɔkəli] n. BOT. Brécol, *m.*, bróculi, *m.*

brochette [brɔˈʃet] n. Brocheta, *f.*, pincho, *m.* (skewer). || CULIN. Pincho, *m.*: *to eat brochettes*, comer pinchos.

brochure [ˈbrəuʃjuə] n. Folleto, *m.*

brock [brɔk] n. ZOOL. Tejón, *m.* (badger).

brocket [—it] n. ZOOL. Cervato, *m.*

brocoli [ˈbrɔkəli] n. Brécol, *m.*, bróculi, *m.*

brogue [brəug] n. Zapato (*m.*) grueso (shoe). || Acento (*m.*) regional [sobre todo irlandés].

broil [brɔil] n. Carne (*f.*) asada a la parrilla (meat). || FIG. Pelea, *f.* (quarrel).

broil [brɔil] v. tr. Asar [a la parrilla]. || FIG. Asar.
— V. intr. Asarse. || FIG. Asarse. | Pelearse (to quarrel).

broiler [—ə*] n. Parrilla, *f.* (grill). || Pollo (*m.*) tomatero [para asar] (chicken).

broke [brəuk] pret. See BREAK.
— Adj. FIG. FAM. Bollado, da; pelado, da; sin blanca (penniless).

broken [ˈbrəukən] p.p. See BREAK.
— Adj. Roto, ta. || Fracturado, da (bones). || Interrumpido, da (sleep). || Accidentado, da; desigual (ground). || Accidentado, da; quebrado, da (relief). || Incierto, ta; variable (weather). || Violado, da; quebrantado, da (promise, oath, law). || MATH. Quebrado, da: *broken line*, línea quebrada. || FIG. Deshecho, cha; destrozado, da: *a broken man*, un hombre destrozado. | Abatido, da (tone). | Quebrado, da (voice). | Arruinado, da; quebrantado, da; estragado, da (health). | Chapurreado, da (language): *to speak broken English*, hablar un inglés chapurreado. | Arruinado, da (bankrupt).

broken-down [—ˈdaun] adj. Roto, ta; estropeado, da: *a broken-down old car*, un viejo coche estropeado. || FIG. Destrozado, da; deshecho, cha (person).

brokenhearted [—ˈhɑːtid] adj. Con el corazón destrozado.

brokenly [—li] adv. Con la voz quebrada, con palabras entrecortadas

broken-winded [—ˈwindid] adj. Jadeante. || Corto de resuello (horse).

broker [ˈbrəukə*] n. COMM. Corredor, *m.*, agente (*m.*) de Bolsa (stockbroker). | Agente (*m.*) comercial, corredor, *m.* (of a company). || *Insurance broker*, agente (*m.*) de seguros.

brokerage [ˈbrəukəridʒ] or **broking** [ˈbrəukiŋ] n. COMM. Corretaje, *m.*, correduría, *f.*

brolly [ˈbrɔli] n. FAM. Paraguas, *m. inv.*

bromate [ˈbrəumeit] n. CHEM. Bromato, *m.*

bromic [ˈbrəumik] adj. CHEM. Brómico, ca.

bromide [ˈbrəumaid] n. CHEM. Bromuro, *m.* || FIG. FAM. Pelmazo, za (boring person). | Trivialidad, *f.* (trite saying).

bromine [ˈbrəumiːn] n. CHEM. Bromo, *m.*

bronchia [ˈbrɔŋkiə] pl. n. ANAT. Bronquios, *m.*

bronchial [ˈbrɔŋkjəl] adj. ANAT. Bronquial. || *Bronchial tube*, bronquio, *m.*

bronchioles [ˈbrɔŋkiəulz] pl. n. ANAT. Bronquiolos, *m.*

bronchiopneumonia [ˈbrɔŋkjəunjuˈməunjə] n. MED. Bronconeumonía, *f.*

bronchitic [brɔŋˈkitik] adj. MED. Bronquítico, ca.

bronchitis [brɔŋˈkaitis] n. MED. Bronquitis, *f.*

broncho [ˈbrɔŋkəu] n. U. S. See BRONCO.

bronchopneumonia [—njuˈməunjə] n. MED. Bronconeumonía, *f.*

bronchoscope [—skəup] n. MED. Broncoscopio, *m.*
bronchus [ˈbrɔŋkəs] n. ANAT. Bronquio, *m.*

— OBSERV. El plural de *bronchus* es *bronchi*.

bronco [ˈbrɔŋkəu] n. U. S. Mustango, *m.*, potro (*m.*) cerril.
broncobuster [ˈbrɔŋkəu͵bʌstə*] n. U. S. Domador (*m.*) de potros cerriles.
bronze [brɔnz] n. Bronce, *m.* (alloy). || Objeto (*m.*) de bronce. || Color (*m.*) de bronce.
— Adj. De bronce. || De color de bronce.
bronze [brɔnz] v. tr. Broncear.
— V. intr. Broncearse.
bronzesmith [—smiθ] n. Broncista, *m.*
bronzing [—iŋ] n. Bronceado, *m.*, bronceadura, *f.*
brooch [brəutʃ] n. Broche, *m.*
brood [bru:d] n. Cría, *f.*, nidada, *f.* (of birds). || FIG. Progenie, *f.*, prole, *f.* (children). || — *Brood hen*, gallina clueca. || *Brood mare*, yegua (*f.*) de vientre.
brood [bru:d] v. tr. Empollar.
— V. intr. Empollar. || — FIG. *To brood on* o *over*, rumiar, dar vueltas a: *to brood over a problem*, darle vueltas a un problema. | *To brood over*, cernerse sobre (to hang over).
brooder [—ə*] n. Gallina (*f.*) clueca (hen). || Incubadora, *f.*, pollera, *f.* (for raising young fowl).
broody [—i] adj. Clueca: *broody hen*, gallina clueca. || FIG. Melancólico, ca (moody). | Pensativo, va (pensive).
brook [bruk] n. Arroyo, *m.*
brook [bruk] v. tr. Soportar, aguantar.
brooklet [ˈbruklit] n. Arroyuelo, *m.*
broom [bru:m] n. Escoba, *f.* (for sweeping). || BOT. Retama, *f.*, hiniesta, *f.* || FIG. *A new broom sweeps clean*, las nuevas personas siempre hacen reformas.
broom [bru:m] v. tr. Barrer.
broomstick [—stik] n. Palo (*m.*) de escoba. || Escoba, *f.* (of a witch).
broth [brɔθ] n. Caldo, *m.*
brothel [ˈbrɔθl] n. Burdel, *m.*, lupanar, *m.*
brother [ˈbrʌðə*] n. Hermano, *m.*: *older, younger brother*, hermano mayor, menor; *the oldest brother*, el hermano mayor. || Colega, *m.* & *f.* (colleague). || Camarada, *m.* & *f.* (comrade). || Cofrade, *m.* (in brotherhood). || Compañero, *m.*, amigo, *m.* (friend). || REL. Hermano, *m.*: *lay brother*, hermano lego. || — *Brothers and sisters*, hermanos. || *Full brother*, hermano carnal. || *Half brother*, medio hermano.
brother [ˈbrʌðə*] v. tr. Hermanar.
brotherhood [—hud] n. Fraternidad, *f.*, hermandad, *f.* (condition of being a brother). || Cofradía, *f.*, hermandad, *f.* (religious group). || Gremio, *m*: *the literary brotherhood*, el gremio de los literatos.
brother-in-law [ˈbrʌðərinlɔ:] n. Cuñado, *m.*, hermano (*m.*) político.

— OBSERV. El plural es *brothers-in-law*.

brotherly [ˈbrʌðəli] adj. Fraternal, fraterno, na.
— Adv. Fraternalmente.
brougham [ˈbruəm] n. Berlina, *f.* (car).
brought [brɔ:t] pret. & p. p. See BRING.
brow [brau] n. Frente, *f.* (forehead). || Ceja, *f.* (eyebrow). || Cima, *f.*, cumbre, *f.* (of a hill). || FIG. Cara, *f.*, semblante, *m.* || *To knit one's brows*, fruncir el ceño.
browbeat [ˈbraubi:t] v. tr. Intimidar (to bully). || *To browbeat into*, obligar a.
brown [braun] n. Marrón, *m.*, castaño, *m.*
— Adj. Marrón: *brown shoes*, zapatos marrones. || Castaño, ña (hair). || Moreno, na (by the sun). || Pardo, da (bear). || Moreno, na (bread, sugar). || — *As brown as a berry*, muy moreno [por el sol]. || *Brown paper*, papel (*m.*) de estraza. || *Brown race*, raza cobriza. || *Brown study*, ensimismamiento, *m.* (mental abstraction).
brown [braun] v. tr. CULIN. Dorar. || Broncear, tostar, poner moreno (by the sun). || — FIG. FAM. *To be browned off with*, estar hasta las narices de. | *To brown s.o. off*, fastidiar a alguien.
— V. intr. CULIN. Dorarse. || Broncearse, tostarse, ponerse moreno (in the sun).
brown coal [—ˈkəul] n. MIN. Lignito, *m.*
Brownian [—iən] adj. PHYS. Browniano (movement).
brownie [—i] n. Duende, *m.* (goblin). || Niña (*f.*) exploradora (junior girl guide). || U. S. Bizcocho (*m.*) de chocolate y nueces.
browning [—iŋ] n. Browning, *m.* (gun). || Colorante, *m.*
brownish [—iʃ] adj. Pardusco, ca.
brownout [—aut] n. U. S. Apagón, *m.* (of ligths).
brownstone [—stəun] n. U. S. Piedra (*f.*) arenisca de color pardo.
browse [brauz] n. Ramoneo, *m.* || FIG. Vistazo, *m.*, ojeada, *f.*: *to have a quick browse*, echar un vistazo rápido.
browse [brauz] v. tr./intr. Ramonear (leaves). || Pacer (grass). || — FIG. *I am just browsing*, estoy mirando (en una tienda, etc.). | *To browse through a book*, hojear un libro.
brucellosis [͵bru:səˈləusis] n. MED. Brucelosis, *f.*
Bruges [bru:z] pr. n. GEOGR. Brujas.
Bruin [ˈbruin] pr. n. Oso, *m.* (name used in fairy tales).
bruise [bru:z] n. Magulladura, *f.*, contusión, *f.*, cardenal, *m.* (on the body). || Daño, *m.*, machucadura, *f.* (in fruit). || FIG. Herida, *f.* (wound).
bruise [bru:z] v. tr. Magullar, contusionar (the body): *to have a bruised arm*, tener el brazo magullado. || Dañar, machucar (fruit). || Majar, machacar (to crush). || Abollar (metal). || FIG. Herir (feelings).
— V. intr. Magullarse. || Dañarse, machacarse (fruits). || Abollarse (metal). || FIG. Sentirse herido (feelings). || *He bruises easily*, le salen cardenales con facilidad.
bruiser [—ə*] n. FAM. Matón, *m.* (aggressive man). | Boxeador, *m.* (professional boxer).
bruit [bru:t] n. Rumor, *m.*
bruit [bru:t] v. tr. Difundir, divulgar (a rumour).
brunch [ˈbrʌntʃ] n. U. S. FAM. Desayuno (*m.*) tardío (late morning meal).
brunette [bru:ˈnet] n. Morena, *f.*
brunt [brʌnt] n. Lo más fuerte, lo más recio: *to bear the brunt of an attack*, aguantar lo más recio de un ataque. || La mayor parte (of the work).
brush [brʌʃ] n. Cepillo, *m.*, escobón, *m.* (floor brush). || Cepillo, *m.* (for clothes, shoes, teeth, hair, etc.). || Brocha, *f.* (for painting walls). || Pincel, *m.* (artist's). || Bruza, *f.* (for horses). || Escobilla, *f.*, limpiabotellas, *m. inv.* (for bottles). || Cepillado, *m.* (brushing). || Maleza, *f.*, broza, *f.* (undergrowth). || Leña, *f.* (twigs). || ELECTR. Escobilla, *f.* || PHYS. Haz (*m.*) de rayos. || FIG. Cola (*f.*) muy poblada, hopo, *m.* (of squirrel, fox, etc.). | Escaramuza, *f.* (skirmish). || — *Shaving brush*, brocha de afeitar. || FIG. *To have a brush with the law*, tener un roce con la policía.
brush [brʌʃ] v. tr. Cepillar: *to brush the floor*, cepillar el suelo. || Pintar con brocha (walls). || Pintar con pincel (painting). || Frotar, restregar (to rub hard). || TECH. Cardar (wool). || Rozar: *to brush the wall with one's sleeve*, rozar la pared con la manga. || FIG. *To brush one's way through a crowd*, abrirse paso entre la multitud.
— V. intr. Cepillar. || *To brush against* o *by* o *past*, pasar rozando, rozar al pasar.
— ***To brush aside***, dejar de lado. || ***To brush away***, quitar (dust). || ***To brush down***, cepillar. | Almohazar (a horse). || ***To brush off***, quitar (dust). | Quitarse de encima (to get rid of). | Despedir bruscamente (to dismiss). || ***To brush over***, aplicar [una ligera capa de pintura]. || FIG. ***To brush up***, refrescar: *to brush up one's French*, refrescar sus conocimientos de francés. | Pulir (to polish up). | — *To brush up against*, rozar.
brushing [—iŋ] n. Cepillado, *m.*
brush-off [—ɔf] n. Despedida (*f.*) brusca.
brushstroke [—strəuk] n. Brochazo, *m.* (with a large brush). || Pincelada, *f.* (with an artist's brush).
brushup [—ʌp] n. FIG. *To give one's French a brushup*, refrescar sus conocimientos de francés. | *To have a wash and brushup*, arreglarse.
brushwood [—wud] n. Maleza, *f.*, broza, *f.* (undergrowth). || Leña, *f.* (chopped off tree branches).
brushwork [—wə:k] n. Pintura, *f.* (painting). || Técnica, *f.* (technique). || Pincelada, *f.*: *Renoir's brushwork*, la pincelada de Renoir.
brusque [brusk] adj. Brusco, ca; áspero, ra.
brusqueness [—nis] or **brusquerie** [—əri] n. Brusquedad, *f.*
Brussels [ˈbrʌslz] pr. n. GEOGR. Bruselas. || *Brussels sprouts*, coles (*f. pl.*) de Bruselas.
brutal [ˈbru:tl] adj. Brutal (violent). || Cruel: *a brutal punishment*, un castigo cruel. || FIG. *The brutal truth*, la verdad cruda.
brutality [bru:ˈtæliti] n. Brutalidad, *f.* (violence). || Crueldad, *f.* (cruelty).
brutalization [brutəlaiˈzeiʃən] n. Embrutecimiento, *m.*
brutalize [ˈbru:təlaiz] v. tr. Embrutecer (to make brutal). || Tratar brutalmente (to treat brutally).
— V. intr. Embrutecerse.
brute [bru:t] adj. Bruto, ta: *a brute beast*, una bestia bruta. || Brutal: *brute instincts*, instintos brutales. || *By brute force*, a viva fuerza.
— N. Bruto, *m.*, bestia, *f.* (animal). || FIG. Bestia, *f.* (brutal person). || — FIG. *A brute of a job*, un trabajo horrible. || FAM. *You brute!*, ¡bestia!
brutish [—iʃ] adj. Bestial (savage). || Bruto, ta (stupid). || Brutal.
brutishness [—iʃnis] n. Brutalidad, *f.* (violence). || Bestialidad, *f.* (savagery, stupidity).
bryology [braiˈɔlədʒi] n. BOT. Briología, *f.*
bryony [ˈbraiəni] n. BOT. Brionia, *f.*
bryophyte [ˈbraiəfait] n. BOT. Briofita, *f.*
bryozoan or **bryozoon** [͵braiəˈzəuən] n. ZOOL. Briozoario, *m.*, briozoo, *m.*

— OBSERV. Los plurales de *bryozoan* y *bryozoon* son *bryozoans* y *briozoa*.

bubble [ˈbʌbl] n. Burbuja, *f.* || Pompa (*f.*) de jabón: *to blow bubbles*, hacer pompas de jabón. || Burbujeo, *m.* (bubbling). || TECH. Sopladura, *f.* || FIG. Estafa, *f.* (swindle). | Cosa (*f.*) efímera (sth. short-lived). | Ilusión, *f.* (fantasy). || — *Bubble bath*, producto (*m.*) para baño de espuma. || *Bubble gum*, chicle (*m.*) de globo. || *Bubble point*, punto (*m.*) de ebullición. || *Soap bubble*, pompa de jabón. || FIG. *To prick s.o.'s bubble*, desengañar a uno.
bubble [ˈbʌbl] v. intr. Burbujear. || Borbotear (when heated): *the water in the pan is beginning to bubble*, el agua de la cacerola empieza a borbotear. || Eructar (to belch, a baby). || — FIG. *To bubble over with joy*,

rebosar de alegría. | *To bubble with laughter*, reventar de risa.
— V. tr. Hacer borbotear.
bubble and squeak [—ənd'skwi:k] n. CULIN. Carne (*f.*) picada frita con patatas y coles.
bubble car [—kɑ:*] n. FAM. Huevo, *m.* [coche].
bubble chamber [—'tʃeimbə*] n. PHYS. Cámara (*f.*) de burbujas.
bubbly ['bʌbli] adj. Burbujeante, con burbujas. || Efervescente, espumoso, sa (drinks).
— N. FAM. Champaña, *f.*, champán, *m.*
bubi ['bu:bi] n. Bubi, *m.* (of Fernando Poo).
bubo ['bju:bəu] n. MED. Bubón, *m.*, buba, *f.*

— OBSERV. El plural de la palabra inglesa es *buboes*

bubonic [bju:'bɔnik] adj. MED. Bubónico, ca.
buccal ['bʌkəl] adj. ANAT. Bucal.
buccaneer [,bʌkə'niə*] n. Bucanero, *m.*
buccaneer [,bʌkə'niə*] v. intr. Piratear.
buccinator ['bʌksineitə*] n. ANAT. Buccinador, *m.*
Bucephalus [bju'sefələs] pr. n. Bucéfalo, *m.*
Bucharest [,bju:kə'rest] pr. n. GEOGR. Bucarest.
buck [bʌk] n. ZOOL. Macho, *m.* (of certain animals). | Gamo, *m.*, ciervo, *m.* (male deer). | Macho (*m.*) cabrío (goat). | Conejo (*m.*) macho (rabbit). | Liebre (*f.*) macho (hare). || Ficha, *f.* (in poker). || Brinco, *m.* (of a horse). || SP. Potro, *m.* (in gymnasium). | Carga, *f.* (in American football). || Petimetre, *m.* (dandy). || U. S. FAM. Dólar, *m.* | Joven (*m.*) indio. | Burro, *m.* (sawhorse). || FAM. *To pass the buck to s.o.*, echarle el muerto a uno.
— Adj. Macho (male). || Raso (soldier).
buck [bʌk] v. tr. U. S. FAM. Resistir porfiadamente a. | Cargar (in American football). || — *To buck off*, desmontar, derribar (its rider). || *To buck up*, animar.
— V. intr. Corcovear (a horse). || Dar sacudidas (a car, machine, etc.). || FIG. Empeñarse. || — *To buck up*, animarse (to cheer up), darse prisa (to hurry).
bucket [—it] n. Cubo, *m.*: *a bucket of water*, un cubo de agua. || TECH. Cangilón, *m.* (of waterwheel). | Paleta, *f.* (of turbine). | Cuchara, *f.* (of dredge). || — FAM. *It's raining buckets*, está lloviendo a cántaros. | *To kick the bucket*, estirar la pata, hincar el pico.
bucket [—it] v. tr. Sacar [con cubo].
— V. intr. Apresurarse (to hurry).
bucketful [—itful] n. Cubo, *m.* || FIG. *By the bucketful*, en grandes cantidades.
bucket seat [—it,si:t] n. Asiento (*m.*) de coche deportivo.
buckeye [—ai] n. U. S. BOT. Castaño (*m.*) de Indias.
buckle [—l] n. Hebilla, *f.* (of shoes, etc.). || Pandeo, *m.* (of wall). || Alabeo, *m.* (of wheel).
buckle [—l] v. tr. Abrochar (to fasten): *to buckle up one's shoes*, abrocharse los zapatos. || Torcer, combar, pandear (to bend sharply). || Alabear (a wheel). || Doblar (the knees). || *To buckle on one's sword*, ceñirse la espada.
— V. intr. Pandearse, combarse, torcerse: *to buckle under impact*, torcerse con un choque. || Alabearse (wheel). || Doblarse (knees). || FIG. FAM. *To buckle down to*, dedicarse con empeño a.
buckler [—lə*] n. HIST. Rodela, *f.*, escudo, *m.* (shield). || FIG. Escudo, *m.*, defensa, *f.*
buckler [—lə*] v. tr. Escudar.
buckling [—liŋ] n. Pandeo, *m.*
buck private [—'praivit] n. U. S. FAM. Recluta, *m.*, soldado (*m.*) raso.
buckram [—rəm] n. Bucarán, *m.* (cloth).
buckshee [—'ʃi:] adj. FAM. Gratuito, ta.
— Adv. FAM. De balde.
buckshot [—ʃɔt] n. Posta (*f.*) zorrera.
buckskin [—skin] n. Ante, *m.* (the skin of a buck).
buckthorn [—θɔ:n] n. BOT. Espino (*m.*) cerval.
bucktooth [—'tu:θ] n. Diente (*m.*) saliente.
buckwheat [—wi:t] n. BOT. Alforfón, *m.*, trigo (*m.*) sarraceno.
bucolic [bju'kɔlik] adj. Bucólico, ca.
— N. Bucólica, *f.* (pastoral poem).
bud [bʌd] n. BOT. Brote, *m.*, yema, *f.* (shoot). | Capullo, *m.* (half-opened flower): *in bud*, en capullo. || AGR. Escudete, *m.* || FIG. *To nip in the bud*, cortar de raíz.
bud [bʌd] v. tr. AGR. Injertar de escudete. || Echar (leaves). || *To bud horns*, salirle [a un animal] los cuernos.
— V. intr. BOT. Brotar, echar brotes. || FIG. Florecer.
Budapest ['bju:də'pest] pr. n. GEOGR. Budapest.
Buddha ['budə*] pr. n. REL. Buda, *m.*
Buddhism ['budizəm] pr. n. REL. Budismo, *m.*
Buddhist ['budist] adj./n. REL. Budista.
budding ['bʌdiŋ] adj. FIG. En ciernes: *a budding poet*, un poeta en ciernes.
buddle ['bʌdl] n. MIN. Artesa, *f.*, lavadero, *m.*
buddle ['bʌdl] v. tr. MIN. Lavar.
buddy ['bʌdi] n. U.S. FAM. Compañero, *m.*, camarada, *m.*, amigote, *m.*, amigo, *m.*
budge [bʌdʒ] v. tr. Mover (to move). || FIG. Hacer ceder (to make yield).
— V. intr. Moverse (to move). || FIG. Ceder (to yield).
budgerigar [—ərigɑ:*] n. Periquito, *m.* (bird).
budget ['bʌdʒit] n. Presupuesto, *m.* || — *Budget reform*, reforma presupuestaria. || FAM. *To be on a tight budget*, tener que limitar los gastos.
budget ['bʌdʒit] v. tr./intr. Presupuestar, hacer un presupuesto: *to budget for a new hospital*, hacer un presupuesto para un nuevo hospital.
budgetary [—əri] adj. Presupuestario, ria.
Buenos Aires ['bwenəs'aiəriz] pr. n. Buenos Aires.
buff [bʌf] adj. De color de ante, amarillo, lla.
— N. Piel (*f.*) de búfalo (buffalo skin). || Color (*m.*) de ante, amarillo, *m.* || Pulidor, *m.* (polishing device). || Rueda (*f.*) pulidora (polishing wheel). || U. S. FAM. Entusiasta, *m.* & *f.* || FIG. *In the buff*, en cueros (naked).
buff [bʌf] v. tr. Dar brillo a: *to buff the floor*, dar brillo al suelo. || Pulir, pulimentar (to smooth). || Teñir de color ante *or* amarillo (to dye). || Aterciopelar (to give a velvety surface).
buffalo ['bʌfələu] n. ZOOL. Búfalo, *m.* || Piel (*f.*) de búfalo. || *Buffalo robe*, piel (*f.*) de búfalo [empleada como manta, alfombra, etc.].

— OBSERV. El plural de la palabra *buffalo* es *buffalo*, *buffaloes* y *buffalos*.

buffalo ['bʌfələu] v. tr. U. S. FAM. Engañar, embaucar (to bamboozle). | Confundir (to baffle).
buffer ['bʌfə*] n. Amortiguador, *m.* (deadening device). || Tope, *m.* (of railway wagons). || Parachoques, *m. inv.* (of cars). || CHEM. Regulador, *m.* || — *Buffer state*, estado (*m.*) tapón. || *Buffer stop*, tope, *m.* || FAM. *Old buffer*, carca, *m.*
buffet ['bʌfit] n. Aparador, *m.* (sideboard). || Alacena, *f.* (for display). || Cantina, *f.*, fonda, *f.* (in a railway station). || Bar, *m.* (refreshment bar). || Golpe, *m.* (blow). || Bofetada, *f.* (with the hand). || FIG. Golpe (*m.*) de mala suerte. || — *Buffet car*, coche (*m.*) bar (in train). || *Buffet lunch* o *cold buffet*, buffet, *m.*, comida fría en la cual cada uno se sirve. || *Buffet supper*, cena fría.
buffet ['bʌfit] v. tr. Golpear (to strike). || Abofetear (to slap). || Zarandear (to knock about): *ship buffeted about by the wind and the waves*, barco zarandeado por el viento y las olas.
buffoon [bə'fu:n] n. Bufón, *m.*, payaso, *m.*
buffoonery [—əri] n. Bufonada, *f.*, payasada, *f.*
bug [bʌg] n. Bicho, *m.* (insect). || Chinche, *f.* (bedbug). || FAM. Microbio, *m.* (bacterium). | Fallo, *m.* [*Amer.*, falla, *f.*] (default). | Micrófono (*m.*) oculto. | Afición, *f.*, vicio, *m.*: *to catch the smoking bug*, coger el vicio de fumar. | Molestia, *f.* (nuisance). || FAM. *Big bug*, pez gordo.
bug [bʌg] v. tr. FAM. Ocultar un micrófono en (a room). | Escuchar por medio de un micrófono oculto. | Fastidiar, molestar: *it bugs me not having any money*, me molesta no tener dinero. || — *Bugging device*, micrófono oculto. || FAM. *What's bugging you?*, ¿qué te preocupa?
bugaboo ['bʌgəbu:] or **bugbear** ['bʌgbɛə*] n. Pesadilla, *f.* (worry). || Espantajo, *m.* (object of horror). || Coco, *m.* (bogeyman).
bug-eyed ['bʌgaid] adj. FAM. De ojos saltones.
bugger ['bʌgə*] n. Sodomita, *m.* || POP. Tío, *m.*, sujeto, *m.* (person). | Cabrón, *m.* (contemptible person). || POP. *His son is a little bugger*, su hijo es un sinvergüenza.
buggery ['bʌgəri] n. Sodomía, *f.*
buggy ['bʌgi] n. Calesa, *f.*, "buggy", *m.* (light carriage). || Cochecillo (*m.*) de niño (pram).
bugle ['bju:gl] n. MUS. Bugle, *m.* || Abalorio, *m.* (ornament).
bugle ['bju:gl] v. intr. Tocar el bugle.
bugloss ['bju:glɔs] n. BOT. Buglosa, *f.*, lengua (*f.*) de buey.
bugs [bʌgz] adj. U. S. FAM. Loco, ca; chalado, da (crazy).
buhl [bu:l] n. Taracea, *f.*, marquetería, *f.*
build [bild] n. Tipo, *m.*, figura, *f.* (physique). || Estructura, *f.*, forma, *f.* (shape).
build* [bild] v. tr. Construir: *to build a ship*, construir un barco. || Construir, edificar (a building). || Hacer (a nest). || Preparar (a fire). || FIG. Trazar, formar, hacer (plans). | Basar, fundamentar (to establish). || FAM. *I'm not built that way*, no soy así.
— V. intr. Ser constructor. || Construirse (a house).
— ***To build in***, empotrar: *to build in a cupboard*, empotrar un armario. | Incorporar. || FIG. ***To build on***, basar, fundamentar: *to build one's argument on solid facts*, basar un argumento en hechos concretos. | Contar con (promises, hopes, etc.). || ***To build up***, urbanizar, edificar en: *the area is completely built up*, la zona está completamente urbanizada. | Montar, armar (from parts). | Elaborar: *to build up a theory*, elaborar una teoría. | FIG. Reunir, hacer: *to build up a collection*, hacer una colección. | Crear: *to build up the image of a product*, crear la imagen de un producto. | Aumentar: *to build up sales*, aumentar las ventas. | Fortalecer: *to build up one's health*, fortalecer la salud. | Entonar, animar; *to build s.o. up*, entonar a alguien. | Hacerse: *to build up a clientèle*, hacerse una clientela; *to build up a mental picture of sth.*, hacerse una idea de algo; *to build up a reputation for o.s.*, hacerse una buena reputación. | — SP. *To build up a lead*, tomar la delantera.

— OBSERV. Pret. & p. p. **built**.

builder ['bildə*] n. Constructor, *m.* || ARCH. Contratista, *m.* (contractor). | Maestro (*m.*) de obras (master builder). || FIG. Fundador, *m.* (of an empire, etc.).

building [ˈbildiŋ] n. Edificio, *m.*, construcción, *f.* (house, factory, etc.). ‖ Construcción, *f.* (work of constructing). ‖ *Public building*, edificio público.
building lease [—li:s] n. Arriendo (*m.*) enfitéutico.
building site [—sait] or **building lot** [—lɔt] n. Solar, *m.* (for sale, etc.). ‖ Obra, *f.* (under construction).
building society [—səˌsaiəti] n. Sociedad (*f.*) de préstamo inmobiliario.
building trade [—treid] n. Construcción, *f.*
buildup [ˈbildʌp] n. Fig. Aumento, *m.: a gradual buildup in the traffic*, un aumento gradual de la circulación. | Concentración, *f.* (of forces). | Propaganda, *f.: the film has had big buildup*, se ha hecho mucha propaganda sobre esta película. ‖ Elaboración, *f.* (development). ‖ Enredo, *m.* (in a drama).
built [bilt] pret. & p. p. See BUILD.
built-in [—ˈin] adj. Empotrado, da: *a built-in bookcase*, una biblioteca empotrada. ‖ Incorporado, da: *built-in aerial*, antena incorporada.
built-up [—ˈʌp] adj. Urbanizado, da: *built-up area*, zona urbanizada.
bulb [bʌlb] n. Bot. Bulbo, *m.* ‖ Anat. Bulbo, *m.* (enlargement). | Bulbo (*m.*) raquídeo (medulla oblongata). ‖ Cubeta, *f.* (of thermometer). ‖ Bombilla, *f.* (lamp).
bulbous [ˈbʌlbəs] adj. Bulboso, sa.
Bulgaria [bʌlˈgɛəriə] pr. n. Geogr. Bulgaria, *f.*
Bulgarian [—n] adj./n. Búlgaro, ra.
bulge [bʌldʒ] n. Protuberancia, *f.* ‖ Pandeo, *m.* (in a wall). ‖ Fig. Alza, *f.: bulge in the birthrate*, alza en el índice de natalidad.
bulge [bʌldʒ] v. intr. Pandearse (to warp). ‖ Hincharse (to swell). ‖ Sobresalir (to project). ‖ Estar abultado (to be bulky).
— V. tr. Pandear (a wall). ‖ Abultar (to bulk).
bulginess [—inis] n. Protuberancia, *f.* ‖ Bulto, *m.*
bulging [—iŋ] adj. Abultado, da. ‖ Hinchado, da (swollen). ‖ Pandeado, da (a wall). ‖ *Bulging eyes*, ojos saltones.
— N. Abultamiento, *m.* ‖ Pandeo, *m.* (of a wall).
bulgy [—i] adj. Protuberante. ‖ Abultado, da.
bulimia [ˈbjulimiə] n. Med. Bulimia, *f.*
bulk [bʌlk] n. Masa, *f.* (mass). ‖ Grosor, *m.*, espesor, *m.* (thickness). ‖ Volumen, *m.*, magnitud, *f.* (volume). ‖ Corpulencia, *f.* (corpulence). ‖ La mayor parte, *f.*, la mayoría, *f.: the bulk of them are on holiday*, la mayoría de ellos están de vacaciones. ‖ Mar. Carga, *f.* ‖ — *In bulk*, a granel, suelto, ta (not packaged). ‖ Mar. *To break bulk*, desestibar.
bulk [bʌlk] v. tr. Amontonar (to pile up). ‖ Hinchar (to swell). ‖ Rellenar: *to bulk out a journal with advertisements*, rellenar una revista con anuncios.
— V. intr. Abultar (to occupy space). ‖ Aumentar (to increase). ‖ Fig. *To bulk large*, ser importante.
bulkhead [—hed] n. Mar. Mamparo, *m.* (upright partition).
bulkiness [—inis] n. Volumen, *m.*, magnitud, *f.*
bulky [—i] adj. Voluminoso, sa; abultado, da. ‖ Pesado, da; de difícil manejo (difficult to handle).
Bull [bul] n. Astr. Tauro, *m.*
bull [bul] adj. Macho: *bull elephant, whale*, elefante, ballena macho. ‖ Grande (big). ‖ En alza, que sube (values). ‖ Fig. *Bull neck*, cuello (*m.*) de toro (short neck).
— N. Zool. Toro, *m.: fighting bull*, toro de lidia. | Macho, *m.* (of the elephant, whale, seal, etc.). ‖ Fig. fam. Bola, *f.*, trola, *f.* (lie). | Tonterías, *f. pl.*, sandeces, *f. pl.: that article is a load of bull*, ese artículo es una sarta de tonterías. | Toro, *m.* (strong man). ‖ Comm. Alcista, *m.* ‖ Rel. Bula, *f.: Golden Bull*, Bula de oro. ‖ — Fig. fam. *To shoot the bull*, charlar: *we spent the afternoon shooting the bull*, hemos pasado la tarde charlando; decir tonterías (to talk nonsense). | *To take the bull by the horns*, coger al toro por los cuernos.
bull [bul] v. tr. Comm. Hacer subir el valor de, jugar al alza con (stocks). ‖ Comm. *To bull the market*, jugar al alza.
— V. intr. Comm. Subir (stocks).
bulla [ˈbulə] n. Bula, *f.* (Roman ornament).
bulldog [—dɔg] n. "Buldog", *m.*, dogo, *m.* ‖ Fam. Bedel, *m.* (usher). ‖ — Fig. *Bulldog edition*, edición (*f.*) de provincia (of a newspaper). ‖ Fig. fam. *The bulldog breed*, los ingleses [como hombres valientes].
bulldog [—dɔg] v. tr. U. S. Derribar [un animal] agarrándolo por los cuernos.
bulldoze [—dəuz] v. tr. Mover [la tierra] con una excavadora. ‖ Fig. Intimidar (to bully). ‖ Fig. *To bulldoze one's way into*, forzar la entrada de (a room), abrirse paso a codazos entre (a crowd), meterse en (conversation).
bulldozer [—ˌdəuzə*] n. "Bulldozer", *m.*, excavadora, *f.*
bullet [ˈbulit] n. Bala, *f.*
bulletin [ˈbulitin] n. Boletín, *m.* ‖ Mil. Parte, *m.*, comunicado, *m.* ‖ — U. S. *Bulletin board*, tablón (*m.*) de anuncios. ‖ *News bulletin*, boletín informativo.
bulletproof [ˈbulitpru:f] adj. A prueba de balas.
bullet wound [ˈbulitwu:nd] n. Balazo, *m.*
bullfight [ˈbulfait] n. Corrida, *f.* [de toros].
bullfighter [—ə*] n. Torero, *m.*
bullfighting [—iŋ] n. Tauromaquia, *f.*, (art). ‖ Toros *m. pl.: I like bullfighting*, me gustan los toros.
bullfinch [ˈbulfintʃ] n. Zool. Piñonero, *m.*, pinzón (*m.*) real.
bullfrog [ˈbulfrɔg] n. Zool. Rana (*f.*) mugidora.
bullhead [ˈbulhed] n. Zool. Siluro, *m.* (fish).
bullheaded [—id] adj. Obstinado, da; terco, ca (obstinate). ‖ Impetuoso, sa (impetuous).
bullhorn [ˈbulhɔ:n] n. U. S. Megáfono, *m.*
bullion [ˈbuljən] n. Oro (*m.*) *or* plata (*f.*) en lingotes *or* barras. ‖ Entorchado, *m.* (fringe).
bullock [ˈbulək] n. Buey, *m.*, toro (*m.*) castrado.
bullpen [ˈbulpen] n. Toril, *m.*
bullring [ˈbulriŋ] n. Plaza (*f.*) de toros (the whole stadium). ‖ Ruedo, *m.* (the central part).
bull session [ˈbulˌseʃən] n. U. S. Tertulia, *f.* (informal discussion).
bull's-eye [ˈbulzai] n. Blanco, *m.*, diana, *f.: to hit the bull's-eye, to score a bull's-eye*, dar en el blanco. ‖ Acierto, *m.*, tiro (*m.*) que da en el blanco (shot). ‖ Fig. Acierto, *m.* (remark). ‖ Caramelo (*m.*) redondo y duro (sweet). ‖ Mar. Ojo (*m.*) de buey, portilla, *f.* (porthole). | Guardacabo (thimble). ‖ Cristal (*m.*) abombado (windowpane). ‖ — *Bull's-eye lens*, lente abombada. ‖ Arch. *Bull's-eye window*, ojo de buey.
bullshit [bulʃit] n. Pop. Porquería, *f.* | Jilipolladas, *f. pl.* (nonsense).
bullterrier [bulˈteriə*] n. Bulterrier, *m.* (dog).
bully [ˈbuli] n. Peleón, *m.* (fighter). ‖ Sp. Saque, *m.* (in hockey). ‖ Carne (*f.*) de vaca en conserva (beef).
— Adj. Fam. Formidable.
— Interj. *Bully for you!*, ¡qué bien!, ¡bravo!
bully [ˈbuli] v. tr. Intimidar (to intimidate). ‖ Tiranizar (to tyrannize). ‖ *To bully s.o. into doing sth.*, forzar a alguien a que haga algo.
— V. intr. Fanfarronear.
bully beef [—ˈbi:f] n. Carne (*f.*) de vaca en conserva.
bully-off [—ɔf] n. Sp. Saque, *m.*
bulrush [ˈbulrʌʃ] n. Bot. Espadaña, *f.*, anea, *f.*
bulwark [ˈbulwək] n. Baluarte, *m.*, bastión, *m.* (defensive wall). ‖ Mar. Borda, *f.* ‖ Rompeolas, *m. inv.* (breakwater). ‖ Fig. Baluarte, *m.*, bastión, *m.: bulwark of liberty*, baluarte de la libertad.
bum [bʌm] adj. U. S. Fam. Malo, la; de mala calidad (poor quality). | Inútil, que no vale, sin valor: *bum information*, información inútil.
— N. Fam. Culo, *m.* (backside). ‖ U. S. Fam. Vagabundo, *m.* (tramp). | Holgazán, *m.*, vago, *m.* (loafer). | Pobre tipo, *m.* (worthless person). | Sablista, *m.*, gorrón, *m.* (scrounger). ‖ Fam. *To be on the bum*, vivir de gorra (to sponge), vagabundear (to loaf around), no funcionar (to be out of order).
bum [bʌm] v. tr. U. S. Fam. Sablear, dar un sablazo de: *he bummed $ 5 off me*, me sableó cinco dólares
— V. intr. U. S. Fam. Gorronear (to sponge). | Holgazanear, vagabundear (to idle). ‖ Canturrear (to hum).
bumbailiff [ˌbʌmˈbeilif] n. Alguacil, *m.* (bailiff).
bumble [ˈbʌmbl] v. intr. Fam. Fallar (to miss). | Hablar a tropezones (to speak). | Andar a tropezones (to walk). | Dar traqueteos (a car). ‖ Zumbar (insects).
— V. tr. See BUNGLE.
bumblebee [ˈbʌmblbi:] n. Zool. Abejorro, *m.*
bumbling [ˈbʌmbliŋ] adj. Fam. Torpe.
bumboat [ˈbʌmbəut] n. Barco (*m.*) de aprovisionamiento.
bummer [ˈbʌmə*] n. Fam. Sablista, *m.* & *f.*, gorrón, ona.
bump [bʌmp] n. Choque, *m.*, topetón, *m.* (blow). ‖ Porrazo, *m.*, golpazo, *m.* (forceful blow). ‖ Sacudida, *f.* (jolt). ‖ Porrazo, *m.*, batacazo, *m.* (on falling). ‖ ‖ Chichón, *m.*, hinchazón, *f.* (swelling). ‖ Protuberancia, *f.*, bulto, *m.*, bollo, *m.* (lump). ‖ Choque, *m.* (in bumping race). ‖ Bache, *m.* (in the road).
bump [bʌmp] v. tr. Golpear, dar un golpe: *to bump one's head*, darse un golpe en la cabeza. ‖ Mantear (to toss s.o. up and down). ‖ Chocar contra (in boat racing). ‖ Tech. Enderezar (metal). ‖ — Fig. *To bump off*, cargarse (to kill). | *To bump one's head against the wall*, dar con la cabeza contra la pared.
— V. intr. Darse un golpe, chocar: *to bump into o against the wall*, darse un golpe contra la pared. ‖ — *Fancy bumping into you!*, ¡qué casualidad encontrarle aquí! ‖ *To bump along*, avanzar dando tumbos. ‖ Fig. *To bump into*, tropezar con (to meet).
bumper [—ə*] adj. Abundante: *bumper harvest*, cosecha abundante. ‖ — *Bumper cars*, coches (*m. pl.*) que chocan. ‖ *Bumper Christmas issue*, edición (*f.*) especial de Navidad. ‖ *Bumper guard*, tope, *m.*
— N. Parachoques, *m. inv.* (of a car). ‖ (Ant.). Vaso (*m.*) lleno hasta el borde (of ale, etc.).
bumpily [—ili] adv. Dando tumbos.
bumping post [—iŋˌpəust] n. Tope, *m.*
bumpkin [—kin] n. Paleto, *m.*, cateto, m., patán, *m.*
bumptious [—ʃəs] adj. Presuntuoso, sa; engreído da.
bumpy [—i] adj. Desigual, lleno de baches: *bumpy road*, carretera llena de baches. ‖ Zarandeado, da: *a bumpy journey*, un viaje zarandeado.
bun [bʌn] n. Bollo, *m.* (cake). ‖ Moño, *m.* (chignon).
bunch [bʌntʃ] n. Ramo, *m.*, ramillete, *m.: a bunch of flowers*, un ramo de flores. ‖ Puñado, *m.* (handful). ‖ Manojo, *m.: six pencils tied in a bunch*, seis lápices atados en un manojo. ‖ Mechón, *m.* (of hair). ‖ Racimo, *m.* (of grapes, bananas). ‖ Ristra, *f.* (of onions). ‖ Fam. Grupo, *m.*, montón, *m.* (of people).

bunch [bʌntʃ] v. tr. Atar en un manojo (to put in a bunch). || Agrupar, juntar: *to bunch all the adjectives at the end of the sentence*, agrupar todos los adjetivos al final de la frase. || Fruncir (material).
— V. intr. *To bunch together*, juntarse, agruparse.
bundle [ˈbʌndl] n. Bulto, *m.*, fardo, *m.*, lío, *m.*: *a bundle of old clothes*, un bulto de ropa vieja. || Manojo, *m.*, haz, *m.*: *a bundle of firewood*, un haz de leña. || Ramillete, *m.* (of flowers). || — *Bundle of papers*, fajo (*m.*) de papeles. || FIG. *To be a bundle of nerves*, ser un manojo de nervios. || FAM. *To have a bundle with s.o.*, pelearse con alguien.
bundle [ˈbʌndl] v. tr. Poner desordenadamente. || — FAM. *To bundle off*, despachar. | *To bundle s.o. into the street*, poner a alguien de patitas en la calle. || *To bundle up*, atar en un bulto, liar: *to bundle up some old clothes*, atar ropa vieja en un bulto.
bung [bʌŋ] n. Tapón, *m.*, bitoque, *m.* (of barrel).
bung [bʌŋ] v. tr. Taponar [con bitoque]. || FAM. Largar, arrojar: *bung that knife over here*, lárgame ese cuchillo. | Poner (to put). || *To bung up*, atascar, obturar, atorar (to clog up): *the carburettor is bunged up*, el carburador está atascado; magullar (to bruise).
bungalow [ˈbʌŋgələu] n. "Bungalow", *m.*, chalé, *m.*
bunghole [ˈbʌŋhəul] n. Piquera, *f.*, boca (*f.*) de tonel.
bungle [ˈbʌŋgl] n. Chapucería, *f.*
bungle [ˈbʌŋgl] v. tr. Chapucear: *to bungle a piece of work*, chapucear un trabajo. || FAM. *To bungle it*, desperdiciar una oportunidad (to miss one's chance), fastidiarlo (to mess it up).
— V. intr. Chapucear.
bungler [—ə*] n. Chapucero, ra.
bungling [—iŋ] adj. Chapucero, ra. || Torpe (clumsy).
— N. Torpeza, *f.*
bunion [ˈbʌnjən] n. Juanete, *m.* (on the big toe).
bunk [bʌŋk] n. Litera, *f.* (bed). || FAM. Tonterías, *f. pl.* (nonsense). || FAM. *To do a bunk*, tomar las de Villadiego (to run away).
bunk [bʌŋk] v. intr. U. S. Acostarse. | Poner pies en polvorosa (to flee). || *To bunk down*, dormir.
bunker [—ə*] n. Arcón, *m.* (large bin). || Carbonera, *f.* (for fuel). || MAR. Pañol (*m.*) del carbón. || SP. Obstáculo (*m.*) artificial, bunker, *m.* (golf). || MIL. Refugio (*m.*) subterráneo. | Casamata, *f.*, bunquer, *m.*, bunker, *m.*
bunker [—ə*] v. tr. Meter en la carbonera (fuel). || MAR. Abastecer de combustible (to fuel). || SP. Meter en un bunker (a ball). || FIG. *To be bunkered*, estar en un atolladero.
— V. intr. MAR. Abastecerse de combustible, repostar.
bunkhouse [ˈbʌŋkhaus] n. Barracón, *m.*
bunkum [ˈbʌŋkəm] n. Tonterías, *f. pl.* (bunk).
bunny [ˈbʌni] n. Conejito, *m.*, (rabbit).
bunt [bʌnt] n. Seno, *m.* (of a net). || SP. Golpe (*m.*) ligero [dado a la pelota] (baseball). || BOT. Tizón, *m.*, añublo, *m.*
bunt [bʌnt] v. tr./intr. Golpear ligeramente [la pelota] (in baseball).
bunting [—iŋ] n. ZOOL. Verderón, *m.* || Estameña, *f.* (fabric). || MAR. Empavesado, *m.*, banderas, *f. pl.*
buntline [—lain] n. MAR. Briol, *m.*
buoy [bɔi] n. MAR. Boya, *f.*: *light buoy*, boya luminosa.
buoy [bɔi] v. tr. Mantener a flote (to keep afloat). || Balizar, señalar con boyas (to mark with buoys). || FIG. Apoyar, sostener (to support). | Alentar: *to buoy up s.o.'s hopes*, alentar las esperanzas de uno.
buoyancy [ˈbɔiənsi] n. Flotabilidad, *f.*, facultad (*f.*) de flotar. || PHYS. Empuje, *m.* [de un fluido]. || AVIAT. Fuerza (*f.*) de sustentación. || COMM. Firmeza, *f.* (of stock exchange). | Estabilidad, *f.* (of prices). || FIG. Optimismo, *m.*
buoyant [ˈbɔiənt] adj. Flotante, boyante (able to float). || FIG. Optimista (cheerful). || COMM. Sostenido, da (stock exchange).
bur [bə:*] n. See BURR.
burble [ˈbə:bl] n. Borboteo, *m.* (of water).
burble [ˈbə:bl] v. intr. Borbotar, borbollar (water). || FIG. Hacer gorgoritos (baby). | Murmurar (brook). | Hervir (with anger). || *To burble with laughter*, reír ahogadamente.
burbot [ˈbə:bət] n. ZOOL. Lota, *f.* (fish).
burden [ˈbə:dn] n. Carga, *f.* (load): *beast of burden*, animal de carga. || FIG. Carga, *f.*, gravamen, *m.* (moral). | Peso, *m.*: *the burden of years*, el peso de los años. | Carga, *f.*: *to be a burden to s.o.*, ser una carga para alguien. || MAR. Arqueo, *m.* || MUS. Estribillo, *m.* (refrain). || Tema (*m.*) *or* idea (*f.*) central (of poem, speech, etc.). || Responsabilidad, *f.*: *the white man's burden*, la responsabilidad de los blancos. || JUR. *Burden of proof*, carga de la prueba.
burden [ˈbə:den] v. tr. Cargar (to load). || FIG. Cargar: *I don't want to burden you with my problems*, no te quiero cargar con mis problemas. | Gravar: *to burden the people with taxes*, gravar a la población con impuestos. | Agobiar: *burdened with pain*, agobiado de dolor.
burdensome [—səm] adj. FIG. Pesado, da (heavy): *burdensome responsibility*, responsabilidad pesada. || Oneroso, sa; gravoso, sa (expenses, etc.).
burdock [ˈbə:dɔk] n. BOT. Bardana, *f.*
bureau [ˈbjərəu] n. Escritorio, *m.*, mesa, *f.*, (writing desk). || Agencia, *f.*, oficina, *f.*: *employment bureau*, agencia de colocaciones. || Mesa, *f.* (of a meeting). || U. S. Cómoda, *f.* (chest of drawers). | Departamento, *m.* [del Estado].
bureaucracy [bjuəˈrɔkrəsi] n. Burocracia, *f.*
bureaucrat [ˈbjuərəuˌkræt] n. Burócrata, *m.* & *f.*
bureaucratic [ˌbjuərəuˈkrætik] adj. Burocrático, ca.
burette (U.S. **buret**) [bjuəˈret] n. CHEM. Bureta, *f.* (graduated glass tube).
burg [bə:g] n. HIST. Burgo, *m.*
burgee [ˈbə:dʒi:] n. MAR. Gallardete, *m.*
burgeon [ˈbə:dʒən] n. BOT. Brote, *m.*, retoño, *m.*
burgeon [ˈbə:dʒən] v. intr. BOT. Brotar, retoñar. || FIG. Desarrollarse.
burgess [ˈbə:dʒis] n. Ciudadano, na (citizen). || Diputado, *m.* (member of parliament).
burgh [ˈbʌrə] n. Burgo, *m.*, villa, *f.* (in Scotland).
burgher [ˈbə:gə*] n. Burgués, esa; ciudadano, na.
burglar [ˈbə:glə*] n. Ladrón, ona.
burglar alarm [—əˈlɑ:m] n. Alarma (*f.*) antirrobo.
burglary [ˈbə:gləri] n. Robo (*m.*) con allanamiento de morada, robo (*m.*) con fractura.
burgle [ˈbə:gl] v. tr./intr. Robar [con allanamiento de morada *or* con fractura].
burgomaster [ˈbə:gəˌmɑ:stə*] n. Burgomaestre, *m.*
Burgundian [bə:ˈgʌndjən] adj./n. Borgoñón, ona.
Burgundy [ˈbə:gəndi] pr. n. Borgoña, *f.*
burial [ˈberiəl] n. Entierro, *m.*
burial ground [—graund] n. Cementerio, *m.*, camposanto, *m.*
burin [ˈbjuərin] n. TECH. Buril, *m.*
burl [bə:l] n. Mota, *f.* (in wool, thread or cloth). || U. S. Nudo, *m.* (in wood).
burl [bə:l] v. tr. Desmotar (cloth).
burlap [ˈbə:læp] n. Arpillera, *f.*
burlesque [bə:ˈlesk] adj. Burlesco, ca.
— N. Género (*m.*) burlesco. || Parodia, *f.* || U. S. Espectáculo (*m.*) de variedades.
burlesque [bə:ˈlesk] v. tr. Parodiar.
burly [ˈbə:li] adj. Fuerte, fornido, da.
Burma [ˈbə:mə] pr. n. GEOGR. Birmania, *f.*
Burman [ˈbə:mən] adj./n. Birmano, na.
Burmese [bə:ˈmi:z] adj./n. Birmano, na.
burn [bə:n] n. Quemadura, *f.* (damage, injury). || Arroyo, *m.* (brook).
burn* [bə:n] v. tr. Quemar: *to burn coal*, quemar carbón; *he burnt his hand with acid*, se quemó la mano con ácido. || Tostar (almonds). || Funcionar con (to run on): *engine which burns diesel oil*, motor que funciona con gasoil. || Gastar, consumir: *an appliance which burns a lot of electricity*, un aparato que consume mucha electricidad. || Cocer (bricks). || Calcinar (to calcine). || Fundir (metals). || MED. Cauterizar, quemar (to cauterize). || FAM. Derrochar, tirar (money). | Enfurecer, encolerizar (to anger). | Engañar (to trick). || — *To be burned to death*, morir quemado. || FIG. *To burn a hole in one's pocket*, quemarle a uno en el bolsillo (money). || *To burn a hole in paper*, hacer un agujero en el papel quemándolo. || *To burn a house to the ground*, incendiar completamente una casa. || FIG. *To burn one's bridges* o *one's ships*, quemar las naves. | *To burn the midnight oil*, quemarse las pestañas. || *To burn to ashes*, reducir a cenizas. || *To have a burnt taste*, saber a quemado.
— V. intr. Arder: *the fire is burning brightly*, el fuego está ardiendo vivamente. || Quemarse, arder: *the house is burning*, la casa está ardiendo. || Quemarse: *if you sit in the sun you will burn*, si te sientas al sol te quemarás. || Estar encendido: *the light is burning*, la lámpara está encendida. || BOT. Abrasarse, quemarse (plants). || Escocer (a sore). || FIG. Arder: *to burn with rage*, arder de ira. || CULIN. Quemarse, pegarse. || Quemarse (in games). || — FIG. *To burn to* o *to burn with desire for*, desear ardientemente. | *To burn with impatience*, consumirse de impaciencia.
— **To burn away,** consumirse. || **To burn down,** incendiar (to set fire to). | Incendiarse. || **To burn in,** marcar a fuego. || **To burn into,** quemar (acid). | FIG. Grabar en. || **To burn off,** quemar. || **To burn out,** quemar. | Consumirse. | Extinguirse, apagarse (light, fire). | Fundirse (bulb, fuse). | Hacer salir por medio del fuego. || **To burn up,** consumir completamente. | Consumirse completamente. | Abrasar (to scorch). | Enfurecer (to make angry). | Enfurecerse (to become angry).
— OBSERV. Pret. & p. p. ***burnt, burned.***
burner [—ə*] n. Quemador, *m.*: *gas burner*, quemador de gas. || Mechero, *m.*: *Bunsen burner*, mechero Bunsen.
burnet [—it] n. BOT. Pimpinela, *f.*
burning [—iŋ] adj. Ardiente, abrasador, ra: *beneath a burning sun*, bajo un sol abrasador. || FIG. Ardiente: *to have a burning desire to do sth.*, tener un deseo ardiente de hacer algo. || — FIG. *A burning question*, una cuestión candente. || *It's burning hot*, está que quema (food), hace un calor abrasador (weather).
— N. Quemadura, *f.* (burn, sunburn). || Ardor, *m.* (in the mouth, etc.). || Incendio, *m.* (fire). || Abrasamiento, *m.*, quemadura, *f.* (of plants). || Cocción, *f.* (of bricks). || Combustión, *f.*
burning bush [—iŋˈbuʃ] n. BOT. Bonetero, *m.* (wahoo). || REL. Zarza (*f.*) ardiente.
burning glass [—iŋˈglɑ:s] n. Espejo (*m.*) ustorio (mirror that concentrates the sun's rays).
burnish [—iʃ] n. Bruñido, *m.*, pulido, *m.*, brillo, *m.*
burnish [—iʃ] v. tr. Bruñir, pulir.
burnous [bə:ˈnu:s] n. Albornoz, *m.*
burnt [bə:nt] pret & p. p. See BURN.

burnt offering [— ɔfəriŋ] n. REL. Holocausto, *m.* (sacrifice).
burnt-out [—ˊaut] adj. Apagado, da. || Consumido, da.
burp [bə:p] n. Eructo, *m.*
burp [bə:p] v. tr. U. S. Hacer eructar (a child).
— V. intr. Eructar.
burr [bə:*] n. BOT. Cubierta (*f.*) espinosa. | Erizo, *m.* (of chestnut). || Pronunciación (*f.*) gutural de la *r.* || Acento (*m.*) rústico *or* basto. || Zumbido, *m.* (sound). || Torno, *m.*, fresa, *f.* (dentistry). || TECH. Rebaba, *f.* (roughness). | Arandela, *f.* (washer). | Piedra (*f.*) amoladera (whetstone). || Halo (*m.*) luminoso (round the moon, etc.). || BOT. Nudo, *m.* (on wood). || U. S. FAM. Lapa, *f.*, persona (*f.*) pegajosa.
burr [bə:*] v. intr. Pronunciar guturalmente la *r.* || Zumbar (to make a humming sound).
burrow [ˊbʌrəu] n. Madriguera, *f.* (animal's hole). || Conejera, *f.* (rabbit's hole). || FIG. Escondrijo, *m.*
burrow [ˊbʌrəu] v. tr. Excavar, cavar. || *To burrow one's way into*, cavar la tierra para entrar en.
— V. intr. Hacer una madriguera (animals). || Esconderse (people). || FIG. *To burrow into an affair*, ahondar en un asunto.
bursa [ˊbə:sə] n. ANAT. Bolsa, *f.*, saco, *m.*
bursar [ˊbə:sə*] n. Tesorero, ra (of a college). || Becario, ria (holder of a scholarship).
bursary [—ri] n. Tesorería, *f.* (accounts office). || Beca, *f.* (scholarship).
burst [bə:st] n. Estallido, *m.*, explosión, *f.* || Reventón, *m.* (of a tyre). || MIL. Ráfaga, *f.* (of fire). || — FIG. *Burst of activity*, explosión (*f.*) de actividad. | *Burst of anger*, arranque (*m.*) de cólera. | *Burst of applause*, salva (*f.*) de aplausos. | *Burst of laughter*, carcajada, *f.* | *Burst of speed*, sprint, *m.* (in sport), carrera, *f.* (running faster), aceleración, *f.* (of a car).
burst* [bə:st] v. intr. Estallar, reventar, explotar: *the pipe has burst*, la cañería ha reventado. || Romperse (dam). || Reventar, abrirse (bud). || Estallar: *to burst into flames*, estallar en llamas. || Irrumpir (into a room). || FIG. Desencadenarse (storm). | Brillar repentinamente (sun). | Prorrumpir, deshacerse: *to burst into tears*, deshacerse en lágrimas. | Reventar: *to burst with laughter*, reventar de risa; *to burst with impatience*, reventar de impaciencia. | Rebosar: *he is bursting with health*, rebosa de salud. || — FIG. *To be bursting to do sth.*, reventar por hacer algo. | *To be full to bursting*, estar lleno a reventar, estar reventando. | *To burst forth*, brotar (from the ground), salir a chorro (to spurt out), abrirse (flowers). | *To burst into song*, romper a cantar. | *To burst into view*, aparecer repentinamente. | *To burst open*, abrirse violentamente. | *To burst out*, salir corriendo (of a room), gritar (to shout). | *To burst out laughing*, echarse a reír, prorrumpir en carcajadas. || *To burst with*, reventar de (laughter, eating), rebosar de (emotion, etc.).
— V. tr. Reventar, explotar: *to burst a balloon with a pin*, reventar un globo con un alfiler. || — *The river will burst its banks*, el río se va a salir de madre. || *To burst open the door*, abrir la puerta de golpe.
— OBSERV. Pret. & p. p. *burst*.
burton [ˊbə:tn] n. TECH. Aparejo, *m.*, polipasto, *m.* || FIG. FAM. *To go for a burton*, fastidiarse.
bury [ˊberi] v. tr. Enterrar: *the dog is burying a bone*, el perro está enterrando un hueso. || Sepultar, enterrar (a body). || FIG. Esconder, ocultar: *he buried his face in his hands*, escondió la cara entre las manos. || — FIG. *Buried memories*, recuerdos sepultados. | *To be buried in thought*, estar ensimismado, estar absorto en sus pensamientos. || *To bury at sea*, dar sepultura en el mar. || FIG. *To bury one's head in the sand*, esconder la cabeza debajo del ala. | *To bury o.s. in a book*, enfrascarse en la lectura. | *To bury o.s. in the country*, enterrarse en el campo. | *To bury the hatchet*, enterrar el hacha de la guerra.
burying beetle [ˊberiiŋˏbi:tl] n. ZOOL. Enterrador, *m.*
bus [bʌs] n. Autobús, *m.* || — *Bus line*, línea (*f.*) de autobuses. || FIG. *To miss the bus*, perder la ocasión *or* la oportunidad.
bus [bʌs] v. intr. Ir en autobús.
— V. tr. Llevar en autobús.
busboy [—bɔi] n. U. S. Mozo, *m.*, ayudante (*m.*) de camarero (in a restaurant).
busby [ˊbʌzbi] n. MIL. Gorro (*m.*) alto de piel negra.
bush [buʃ] n. Arbusto, *m.*, matorral, *m.* (shrub). || Breña, *f.* (rough country). || Monte, *m.* (in Australia). || HIST. Ramo (*m.*) de hiedra [que indica la venta de vino]. || TECH. Cojinete, *m.* (bearing). | Forro, *m.* (lining). || FIG. FAM. *To beat about the bush*, andarse con rodeos.
bush [buʃ] v. intr. Crecer espesamente.
— V. tr. Poner arbustos en. || TECH. Forrar.
bush baby [—ˏbeibi] n. ZOOL. Lemúrido, *m.*
bushed [buʃt] adj. Cubierto de malezas. || FAM. Agotado, da; hecho polvo (exhausted).
bushel [ˊbuʃl] n. Medida (*f.*) de áridos.
— OBSERV. En Inglaterra esta medida equivale a 36,367 litros y en Estados Unidos a 35,237 litros.
bushhammer [ˊbuʃˏhæmə*] n. Escoda, *f.*
bushiness [ˊbuʃinis] n. Espesor, *m.* (of foliage).
bushing [buʃiŋ] n. TECH. Cojinete, *m.* (bearing). | Forro, *m.* (lining).
bushman [ˊbuʃmən] n. Campesino (*m.*) australiano.
Bushman [ˊbuʃmən] adj./n. Bosquimano, na.
bushranger [ˊbuʃˏreindʒə*] n. HIST. Bandido, *m.*
bush telegraph [ˊbuʃˏteligrɑ:f] n. FIG. Radio (*f.*) macuto.
bushwhacker [ˊbuʃwækə*] n. Montonero, *m.*, guerrillero, *m.*
bushy [ˊbuʃi] adj. Breñoso, sa (ground). || Parecido a un arbusto (plant). || Tupido, da; espeso, sa: *a bushy moustache*, bigotes espesos.
busily [ˊbizili] adv. Afanosamente.
business [ˊbiznis] n. Negocios, *m. pl.*: *in the business world*, en el mundo de los negocios. || Negocio, *m.*, comercio, *m.*, empresa, *f.*: *to run a television repair business*, llevar un negocio de reparaciones de televisores. || Empleo, *m.*, ocupación, *f.*, oficio, *m.* (occupation). || Profesión, *f.* (profession). || Asunto, *m.*, cuestión, *f.*: *as regards the business of the broken window*, en cuanto al asunto de la ventana rota. || Asunto, *m.* (personal): *that is your business*, eso es asunto tuyo. || — *Big business*, grandes negocios. || *Business as usual*, continúa la venta en el interior. || *Business before pleasure*, primero es la obligación que la devoción. || *Business card*, tarjeta (*f.*) comercial. || *Business college*, escuela (*f.*) de comercio. || *Business connections*, relaciones (*f.*) de negocio. || *Business cycle*, ciclo (*m.*) comercial. || *Business deal*, trato (*m.*) comercial. || *Business district*, zona (*f.*) comercial. || *Business hours*, horas (*f.*) de trabajo. || *Business is business*, los negocios son los negocios. || *Business letterhead*, membrete, *m.* || *Business machines*, máquinas (*f.*) de oficina. || *Business of the day*, orden (*m.*) del día. || *Business premises*, local (*m. sing.*) comercial. || *Business reply envelope*, sobre (*m.*) con franqueo concertado. || *Business school*, escuela (*f.*) de comercio. || *Business suit*, traje (*m.*) de calle. || *Business trip*, viaje (*m.*) de negocios. || *Good business!*, ¡perfecto!, ¡bien hecho! || *It's my business*, eso es cosa mía. || *It's my business to do it*, me corresponde hacerlo. || *It's no business of mine*, no tengo nada que ver con eso, no es asunto mío. || *I will make it my business to*, me encargaré de. || *To be in a place on business*, estar en un sitio por razones profesionales. || *To be sick of the whole business*, estar harto del asunto. || *To do business with*, comerciar con. || FIG. *To get down to business*, ir al grano. || FIG. FAM. *To give one the business*, darle una zurra a uno (to beat), despachar *or* pasaportar a uno (to kill). || *To go about one's business*, ocuparse de sus asuntos. || *To have no business to do sth.*, no tener derecho de hacer algo, no tener por qué hacer algo. || *To make it one's business to do sth.*, proponerse hacer algo. || FAM. *To mean business*, hablar *or* actuar en serio. | *To mind one's own business*, no meterse donde no le llaman, ocuparse de sus propios asuntos. | *To send s.o. about his business*, mandarle a uno a paseo. || *To set up in business as a butcher*, montar un negocio de carnicería. || FAM. *What a business!*, ¡qué lío!
businesslike [—laik] adj. Serio, ria; formal (serious-minded). || Práctico, ca; eficaz (practical-minded). || Metódico, ca; ordenado, da (methodical).
businessman [—mən] n. Hombre (*m.*) de negocios.
— OBSERV. El plural de *businessman* es *businessmen*.
businesswoman [—ˊwumən] n. Mujer (*f.*) de negocios.
— OBSERV. El plural es *businesswomen*.
busker [ˊbʌskə*] n. Músico (*m.*) ambulante.
buskin [ˊbʌskin] n. Borceguí, *m.* (half boot). || Coturno, *m.* (worn by Greek actors).
busman [ˊbʌsmən] n. Conductor (*m.*) de autobús (driver). || Cobrador (*m.*) de autobús (conductor). || FIG. *Busman's holiday*, día (*m.*) de fiesta que uno pasa trabajando.
— OBSERV. El plural de *busman* es *busmen*.
bus stop [ˊbʌs-stɔp] n. Parada (*f.*) de autobús.
bust [bʌst] n. Busto, *m.* (sculpture). || Busto *m.*, pecho, *m* [de mujer]. || FAM. Reventón, *m.* (burst). | Juerga, *f.* (spree): *he went on a bust*, fue de juerga. | Fracaso, *m.* (failure). | Quiebra, *f.* (bankruptcy). || *Bust measurement*, perímetro torácico.
— Adj. FAM. Destrozado, da; hecho polvo (broken). | Reventado, da (burst). | En bancarrota; arruinado, da (bankrupt). || FAM. *To go bust*, quebrar.
bust [bʌst] v. tr. FAM. Destrozar, hacer polvo (to break). || Degradar (to demote a soldier). || Reventar (to burst). || COMM. Llevar a la quiebra. || Domar (a horse). || FAM. Dar un puñetazo a.
— V. intr. FAM. Hacerse polvo. | Reventar (laughing). | Fracasar (to fail). || COMM. Quebrar.
bustard [ˊbʌstəd] n. ZOOL. Avutarda, *f.* (bird).
bustle [ˊbʌsl] n. Bullicio, *m.*, agitación, *f.*, animación, *f.*: *the bustle of the market place*, la animación del mercado. || HIST. Polisón, *m.* (of a skirt).
bustle [ˊbʌsl] v. intr. Ir y venir, apresurarse, ajetrearse.
— V. tr. Apresurar.
bustling [—iŋ] adj. Bullicioso, sa (place). || Activo, va (person).
busy [ˊbizi] adj. Ocupado, da; atareado, da: *she was busy sewing*, estaba ocupada cosiendo; *I had a very busy day*, tuve un día muy ocupado. || Concurrido, da; bullicioso, sa: *a busy street*, una calle muy concurrida. || Ocupado, da (telephone line). || — *As busy as a bee*, see BEE. || — *Busy hours*, horas (*f.*) punta. || U. S. *Busy signal*, señal (*f.*) de comunicando. | *It is busy*, está comunicando (telephone). || *To get busy*,

ponerse a trabajar. || *To keep busy*, estar ocupado (o.s.), ocupar (s.o.).

busy [ˈbizi] v. tr. Ocupar. || *To busy o.s. about the house*, ocuparse en las tareas domésticas.

busybody [—ˌbɔdi] n. Entrometido, da.

but [bʌt] conj. Pero, mas: *the work is hard, but you are well paid*, el trabajo es duro, pero te pagan bien. || Sino (with "not"): *he is not poor, but rich*, no es pobre sino rico. || Sino que (with "not" and a verb): *he told her not to stay, but to go to the cinema*, le dijo que no se quedase sino que fuese al cine. || Sin (without): *I can't speak to him but I get annoyed*, no puedo hablar con él sin enfadarme. || Sin que: *he never speaks but she contradicts him*, nunca habla sin que ella le contradiga. || Que: *I don't doubt but he will answer*, no dudo que conteste. || Al menos: *you can but try it*, al menos puede probarlo.
— Adv. No más que, nada más que, solamente, sólo, no... sino: *she is but a child*, no es [nada] más que una niña, no es sino una niña; *you have but to tell me*, no tienes más que decírmelo, sólo tienes que decírmelo; *it is nothing but meanness*, no es [nada] más que mezquindad, no es sino mezquindad; *I saw her but a moment ago*, sólo hace un momento que la vi, la vi hace nada más que un momento. || *Had I but known*, si lo hubiera sabido.
— Prep. Excepto, salvo, menos: *any day but Thursday suits me*, me conviene cualquier día excepto los jueves; *all but they* o *but them*, todos salvo ellos. || Sino: *what could I do but say yes?*, ¿qué podía hacer sino decir que sí? || — *All but*, casi, medio (almost): *he was all but dead with fatigue*, estaba medio muerto de cansancio. || *But for*, sin, a no ser por (without): *you couldn't have done it but for him*, no hubiera podido hacerlo sin él. || *Last but one*, penúltimo, ma. || *The last but two*, el segundo antes del último, el antepenúltimo.
— N. Pero, *m.* || *There are no buts about it*, no hay pero que valga.

butadiene [ˌbjutəˈdi:n] n. Chem. Butadieno, *m.*

butane [ˈbjutein] n. Chem. Butano, *m.* || *Butane gas*, gas (*m.*) butano.

butcher [ˈbutʃə*] n. Carnicero, ra. || Fig. fam. Carnicero, ra (bad surgeon). | Sanguinario, ria (cruel person). || *Butcher's*, carnicería, *f.*

butcher [ˈbutʃə*] v. tr. Matar (animals). || Fig. Hacer una carnicería con (to kill cruelly). | Destrozar (a piece of work).

butcher-bird [—bə:d] n. Alcaudón, *m.*

butcher's broom [ˈbutʃə:zˈbru:m] n. Bot. Brusco, *m.*

butchery [ˈbutʃəri] n. Carnicería, *f.* || Fig. Carnicería, *f.*, matanza, *f.*

butler [ˈbʌtlə*] n. Mayordomo, *m.*

butt [bʌt] n. Extremo, *m.* (end). || Culata, *f.*: *rifle butt*, culata de fusil. || Tonel, *m.*, pipa, *f.* (barrel). || Aljibe, *m.* (for rainwater). || Pie, *m.*, base, *f.* (of a plant). || Tocón, *m.* (of a tree). || Colilla, *f.* (of cigarette). || Pez (*m.*) plano (flatfish). || Blanco, *m.* (target). || Fig. Blanco, *m.*: *to be the butt of other people's jokes*, ser el blanco de las bromas de otros. || Topetazo, *m.*, cabezazo, *m.* (blow). || Cuero (*m.*) curtido del lomo (leather). || U. S. Fam. Trasero, *m.* (buttocks). || — Pl. Campo (*m. sing.*) de tiro al blanco.

butt [bʌt] v. tr. Topar (a ram). || Dar un golpe con la cabeza a (a person). || Ensamblar, empalmar, unir a tope (to join).
— V. intr. Dar topetazos (a ram). || Dar golpes con la cabeza. || Golpearse (to bump). || Fig. *To butt in*, meterse en (a conversation).

butter [ˈbʌtə*] n. Mantequilla, *f.*: *fresh, salted, melted, browned butter*, mantequilla fresca, salada, derretida, requemada. || — *Butter dish*, mantequera, *f.* || *Butter knife*, cuchillo (*m.*) para la mantequilla. || Fig. *Butter wouldn't melt in his mouth*, es una mosquita muerta.

butter [ˈbʌtə*] v. tr. Untar con mantequilla (to spread with butter). || Guisar con mantequilla (to cook with butter). || Fig. *To butter up*, hacer la pelotilla a (to flatter).

butter bean [—bi:n] n. Bot. Judía, *f.*

buttercup [—kʌp] n. Bot. Ranúnculo, *m.*, botón (*m.*) de oro.

butterfat [—fæt] n. Grasa (*f.*) de la leche.

butter-fingered [—ˌfiŋgəd] adj. Fam. Torpe.

butterfingers [—ˌfiŋgəz] n. Torpe, *m.* & *f.*, manazas, *m.* & *f.* || *To be a butterfingers*, tener manos de trapo.

butterfly [—flai] n. Mariposa, *f.* || Sp. Braza (*f.*) mariposa (in swimming). || Fig. Mariposón, ona. || Fig. *To have butterflies in one's stomach*, tener un cosquilleo en el estómago.

butterfly nut [—flaiˌnʌt] n. Tech. Tuerca (*f.*) de mariposa.

butterfly valve [—flaiˌvælv] n. Tech. Válvula (*f.*) de mariposa.

butteris [—is] n. Pujavante, *m.*

buttermilk [—milk] n. Suero, *m.* [de la leche].

butterscotch [—skɔtʃ] n. Caramelo (*m.*) de azúcar con mantequilla.

buttery [ˈbʌtəri] adj. Mantecoso, sa. || Fig. fam. Pelotillero, ra (adulator).
— N. Despensa, *f.* (storeroom).

butt hinge [ˈbʌtˌhindʒ] n. Bisagra, *f.*

butt joint [ˈbʌtˌdʒɔint] n. Tech. Junta (*f.*) a tope.

buttock [ˈbʌtək] n. Nalga, *f.* || — Pl. Fam. Trasero, *m. sing.* (of a person). || Grupa, *f. sing.* (of a horse).

button [ˈbʌtn] n. Botón, *m.*: *coat button*, botón de abrigo. || Botón, *m.*, pulsador, *m.* (on machine, bell, etc.): *to press the button*, pulsar el botón. || Tirador, *m.* (of a door). || Bot. Botón, *m.*, yema, *f.*, capullo, *m.* (bud). || Sp. Botón, *m.*, zapata, *f.* (in fencing). || U. S. Insignia, *f.*, distintivo, *m.* (badge). || — Pl. Botones, *m. sing.* (hotel errand boy). || — Fam. *On the button*, perfecto, ta (perfect), en punto (right on time). | *To be a button short*, ser duro de entendederas.

button [ˈbʌtn] v. tr. Abrochar, abotonar: *to button up one's overcoat*, abrocharse el abrigo. || Poner botones en. || Fig. fam. *Button your lip!*, ¡cósete la boca!
— V. intr. Abrocharse (to fasten). || Tener botones. || Fig. fam. *To button up*, coserse la boca.

buttonhole [—həul] n. Ojal, *m.* (stitched slit). || Presilla, *f.* (loop). || Flor (*m.*) que se lleva en el ojal (flower). || *Buttonhole stitch*, punto (*m.*) de ojal.

buttonhole [—həul] v. tr. Hacer ojales en (to make buttonholes in). || Fig. Enganchar (to detain).

buttonhook [—huk] n. Abrochador, *m.*

buttress [ˈbʌtris] n. Arch. Contrafuerte, *m.* || Geogr. Estribación, *f.* || Fig. Apoyo, *m.*, sostén, *m.*

buttress [ˈbʌtris] v. tr. Arch. Apuntalar, reforzar. || Fig. Apoyar, reforzar: *to buttress up one's theory with statistics*, apoyar una teoría con estadísticas.

buttstock [ˈbʌtstɔk] n. Culata, *f.* (of firearm).

butt weld [ˈbʌtweld] n. Tech. Soldadura (*f.*) a tope.

butty [ˈbʌti] n. Fam. Bocadillo, *m.*, sandwich, *m.*

butyl [ˈbjutil] n. Chem. Butilo, *m.*

butylene [—i:n] n. Chem. Butileno, *m.*

butyric [bjuˈtirik] adj. Chem. Butírico, ca.

buxom [ˈbʌksəm] adj. Metida en carnes (woman). || Rollizo, za (baby).

buy [bai] n. Compra, *f.* (purchase). || *Good buy*, ganga, *f.*, buena compra (bargain).

buy* [bai] v. tr. Comprar (to purchase): *I bought a house*, compré una casa. || Sobornar, comprar (to bribe): *he cannot be bought*, no se le puede sobornar. || — Fig. fam. *I'll buy it*, me doy por vencido, me rindo (I give in). | *They'll never buy it*, no se lo tragarán, no cuajará. || *To buy back*, volver a comprar. || *To buy off*, librarse de alguien comprándole. || Mil. *To buy o.s. out*, redimirse [del servicio militar] pagando. || *To buy out*, comprar la parte de (a partner, etc.). || *To buy over*, sobornar. || *To buy up*, comprar [grandes cantidades de], acaparar.
— V. intr. Comprar. || *To buy into*, comprar acciones de (a company).
— Observ. Pret. & p. p. **bought**.

buyer [—ə*] n. Comprador, ra. || Comm. *Head buyer*, jefe (*m.*) de compras.

buyer's market [baiə:zˈmɑ:kit] n. Mercado (*m.*) favorable al comprador.

buzz [bʌz] n. Zumbido, *m.* (of bees, etc.). || Cuchicheo, *m.* (whispering). || Murmullo, *m.*: *buzz of conversation*, murmullo de voces. || Fam. Telefonazo, *m.* (call).

buzz [bʌz] v. tr. Murmurar al oído de (to whisper). || Pasar rozando (to fly low and fast over). || Fam. Llamar, dar un telefonazo a.
— V. intr. Zumbar (to make a humming sound). || Murmurar, cuchichear (to murmur). || Fig. Circular: *the rumour buzzed round the village*, el rumor circuló por todo el pueblo. || — *The hall buzzed with anticipation*, se oyó un murmullo de expectación en la sala. || *To buzz about* o *around*, zascandilear. || Fig. fam. *To buzz off*, largarse.

buzzard [ˈbʌzəd] n. Zool. Águila (*f.*) ratonera (hawk). | Buitre, *m.* (vulture).

buzzer [ˈbʌzə*] n. Zumbador, *m.*

buzzing [ˈbʌziŋ] n. Zumbido, *m.*

buzz saw [ˈbʌz-sɔ:] n. Tech. Sierra (*f.*) circular.

by [bai] prep. Por: *painted by a famous artist*, pintado por un artista famoso; *to go by the quickest road*, ir por el camino más rápido; *to win by five minutes*, ganar por cinco minutos; *by rail*, por ferrocarril; *to travel by sea*, viajar por mar *or* por vía marítima; *to take s.o. by the hand*, coger a uno por la mano; *to swear by God*, jurar por Dios; *panel of wood sixty inches by twenty*, panel de madera de sesenta pulgadas por veinte; *to be paid by the hour*, estar pagado por horas. || Math. Por (multiplication): *to multiply four by nine*, multiplicar cuatro por nueve. | Entre: *to divide ten by five*, dividir diez entre cinco. || Al lado de, junto a, cerca de (beside, near): *to sit by the fire*, sentarse junto al fuego; *I walked by the house this morning*, pasé al lado de la casa esta mañana. || Según, de acuerdo con (according to): *to go by the rules*, actuar según las reglas. || De (at): *by night*, de noche. || De (origin): *Spanish by blood*, de sangre española. || De (from): *two children by a previous wife*, dos niños de una esposa anterior. || Para (not later than): *we must be there by three o'clock*, tendremos que estar allí para las tres; *by then*, para entonces. || Antes de: *by the end of the century*, antes de fines de siglo. || Con: *what do you mean by that?*, ¿qué quiere decir con eso? || En (in): *to go by car, by boat*, ir en coche, en barco. || A (on): *to travel by horse*, ir a caballo. | A (indicating progression): *little by little*, poco a poco; *day by day*, día a día; *to go forward by*

small steps, by leaps and bounds, avanzar a pequeños pasos, a pasos agigantados. || A, por (indicating quantity): *they died by the thousand,* murieron a millares; *by hundreds,* por centenares. || — *By appearances,* por las apariencias. || *By chance,* por casualidad. || *By far,* con mucho. || *By heart,* de memoria. || *By lamplight,* a la luz de la lámpara. || *By me, by you, by him,* a mi lado, a tu lado, a su lado. || *By means of,* mediante, por medio de. || *By now,* ya. || *By o.s.,* solo, la. || *By studying you can pass your exam,* estudiando puedes aprobar el examen. || *By the dozen,* por docenas. || *By the light of,* a la luz de. || *By the by,* por cierto, a propósito (incidentally), de paso (in passing). || *Made by hand,* hecho a mano. || *North by east,* norte cuarta al nordeste. || *Side by side,* lado a lado. || *To be known by the name of,* ser conocido por *or* con el nombre de. || *To cut production by a quarter,* reducir la producción en una cuarta parte.
— Adv. Al lado, cerca, delante: *he walked by without greeting us,* pasó delante sin saludarnos. || A un lado, aparte: *to put some money by,* poner dinero a un lado. || — *By and by,* luego, más tarde. || *By and large,* en general. || *Close by,* muy cerca. || *Gone by,* pasado, da: *in years gone by,* en años pasados.
by-by or **bye-bye** [ˈbaibai] interj. FAM. Adiós, hasta luego.
bye [bai] n. SP. Carrera (*f.*) hecha sin haber golpeado la pelota (cricket). | Hoyo (*m.*) que queda sin ser jugado (golf). | Jugador que queda de non.
by-election or **bye-election** [ˈbaiiˌlekʃən] n. Elección (*f.*) parcial.
byelaw [ˈbailɔ:] n. See BYLAW.
bygone [ˈbaigɔn] adj. Pasado, da; del pasado.
— N. Cosa (*f.*) pasada. || *Let bygones be bygones,* olvidemos lo pasado; lo pasado, pasado está.
bylaw [ˈbailɔ:] n. Ordenanza (*f.*) municipal (of a local authority). || Estatuto, *m.* (statute). || Reglamento, *m.* (regulations).
byname [ˈbaiˌneim] n. Apodo, *m.* (nickname).
bypass [ˈbaipɑ:s] n. Carretera (*f.*) de circunvalación || TECH. Tubo (*m.*) de desviación. || ELECTR. Derivación, *f.*
bypass [ˈbaipɑ:s] v. tr. Desviar: *to bypass the traffic,* desviar el tráfico. || Evitar (to avoid).
bypath [ˈbaipɑ:θ] n. Camino, *m.,* vereda, *f.*
byplay [ˈbaiplei] n. THEATR. Juego (*m.*) escénico secundario. | Aparte, *m.* (in conversation).
by-product [ˈbaiˌprɔdʌkt] n. Subproducto, *m.,* derivado, *m.* || FIG. Consecuencia, *f.*
byre [baiə*] n. Establo, *m.,* vaquería, *f.*
byroad [ˈbairəud] n. Carretera (*f.*) secundaria.
Byronic [baiˈrɔnik] adj. Byroniano, na.
Byronism [ˈbairɔnizəm] n. Byronismo, *m.*
bystander [ˈbaiˌstændə*] n. Espectador, ra; mirón, ona; curioso, sa (onlooker). || Persona (*f.*) presente. || *Several innocent bystanders were injured,* varios inocentes fueron heridos.
bystreet [ˈbaistri:t] n. Callejuela, *f.,* calle (*f.*) lateral *or* secundaria.
byway [ˈbaiwei] n. Camino (*m.*) apartado.
byword [ˈbaiwə:d] n. Comidilla, *f.: he is the byword of the village,* es la comidilla del pueblo. || Dicho, *m.* (familiar saying). || Refrán, *m.,* proverbio, *m.* (proverb). || Prototipo, *m.* (type).
Byzantine [biˈzæntain] adj./n. Bizantino, na.
Byzantium [biˈzæntiəm] pr. n. HIST. Bizancio.

C

c [si:] C, *f.* (letter).
C [si:] n. MUS. Do, *m.*
cab [kæb] n. Taxi, *m.* || Cabina, *f.* (cabin of truck, locomotive, etc.). || Cabriolé, *m.* (horse-drawn carriage).
cabal [kəˈbæl] n. Cábala, *f.* (plot). || Camarilla, *f.,* grupo (*m.*) de conspiradores (association of persons). || HIST. Gabinete (*m.*) secreto de ministros que gobernó Inglaterra bajo Carlos II.
cabal [kəˈbæl] v. intr. Conspirar, intrigar.
cabala [kəˈbɑ:lə] n. REL. Cábala, *f.*
cabalist [ˈkəˈbælist] n. Cabalista, *m.* & *f.*
cabalistic [ˌkæbəˈlistik] adj. Cabalístico, ca.
cabaret [ˈkæbərei] n. Cabaret, *m.* (establishment). || Atracciones, *f. pl.,* espectáculo, *m.* (entertainment).
cabbage [ˈkæbidʒ] n. Col, *f.,* berza, *f.* || *Cabbage white,* mariposa (*f.*) de la col.
cabbage palm [—pɑ:m] or **tree** [—tri:] n. BOT. Palma (*f.*) real, palmito, *m.*
cabby [ˈkæbi] n. FAM. Taxista, *m.* & *f.* || Cochero, *m.* (of a carriage).
cabdriver [ˈkæbˌdraivə*] n. U. S. Taxista, *m.* & *f.*
cabin [ˈkæbin] n. Cabaña, *f.,* choza, *f.* (small house). || MAR. Camarote, *m.* || Cabina, *f.* (of plane, etc.).
cabin boy [—bɔi] n. MAR. Camarero (*m.*) de a bordo (servant). | Grumete, *m.* (sailor).
cabin class [—klɑ:s] n. MAR. Segunda (*f.*) clase.
cabin cruiser [—ˌkru:zə*] n. MAR. Yate (*m.*) de recreo.
cabinet [ˈkæbinit] n. Armario, *m.* (cupboard). || Bargueño, *m.* (piece of furniture with drawers). || Vitrina, *f.* (for display). || Caja, *f.* (of a radio). || Gabinete, *m.,* consejo (*m.*) de ministros (ministers). || — *Cabinet council,* consejo (*m.*) de ministros. || *Medicine cabinet,* botiquín, *m.*
cabinetmaker [—ˌmeikə*] n. Ebanista, *m.*
cabinetmaking [—ˌmeikiŋ] n. Ebanistería, *f.*
cabinetwork [—wə:k] n. Ebanistería, *f.*
cable [ˈkeibl] n. Cable, *m.* (rope). || Cablegrama, *m.,* telegrama, *m.* (message). || *Overhead cable,* línea eléctrica aérea.
cable [ˈkeibl] v. tr./intr. Cablegrafiar, telegrafiar.
cable address [—əˈdres] n. Dirección (*f.*) telegráfica.
cable car [—kɑ:*] n. Teleférico, *m.* (telpher). || Funicular, *m.* (cable railway).
cablegram [—græm] n. Cablegrama, *m.,* telegrama, *m.*
cable length [—leŋθ] n. MAR. Cable, *m.*
cable railway [—ˈreilwei] n. Funicular, *m.*
cable ship [—ʃip] n. MAR. Cablero, *m.*
cablet [—it] n. MAR. Cabo (*m.*) pequeño.
cable tape [—teip] n. ELECTR. Cinta (*f.*) aisladora.
cabman [ˈkæbmən] n. Taxista, *m.* & *f.* || Cochero, *m.* (of a carriage).
— OBSERV. El plural de *cabman* es *cabmen.*
cabochon [ˈkæbəʃən] n. Cabujón, *m.* (gem).
caboodle [kəˈbu:dl] n. FAM. *The whole caboodle,* toda la pesca.
caboose [kəˈbu:s] n. MAR. Cocina, *f.* || U. S. Furgón (*m.*) de cola (of a train). | Cabaña, *f.* (cabin).
cabotage [ˈkæbətɑ:ʒ] n. AVIAT. MAR. Cabotaje, *m.*
cab rank [ˈkæb-ræŋk] n. Parada (*f.*) de taxis.
cabriole [ˈkæbriəul] n. Pata (*f.*) encorvada de los muebles estilo reina Ana y Chippendale.
cabriolet [ˌkæbriəˈlei] n. Cabriolé, *m.*
cab stand [ˈkæbstænd] n. Parada (*f.*) de taxis.
cacao [kəˈkɑ:əu] n. BOT. Cacao, *m.* || — BOT. *Cacao bean,* cacao, *m.* || *Cacao butter,* manteca (*f.*) de cacao.
cachalot [ˈkæʃəlɔt] n. ZOOL. Cachalote, *m.*
cache [kæʃ] n. Escondite, *m.,* escondrijo, *m.* (hiding place). || Reserva (*f.*) escondida (of food, etc.).
cache [kæʃ] v. tr. Esconder, poner en un escondrijo.
cachectic [kəˈkektik] adj. MED. Caquéctico, ca.
cachet [ˈkæʃei] n. MED. Sello, *m.,* cápsula, *f.* (capsule). || FIG. Sello, *m.: a work which bears the cachet of genius,* una obra que lleva el sello del genio.
cachexia [kəˈkeksiə] or **cachexy** [kəˈkeksi] n. MED. Caquexia, *f.*
cachinnate [ˈkækineit] v. intr. (Ant.). Reír a carcajadas.
cachou [ˈkæʃu:] n. Cachú, *m.*
cacique [kæˈsi:k] n. Cacique, *m.*
caciquism [—ˌizəm] n. Caciquismo, *m.*
cackle [ˈkækl] n. Cacareo, *m.* (of hen). || FIG. FAM. Risa (*f.*) aguda (raucous laugh). | Cháchara, *f.* (idle talk). || FIG. FAM. *Cut the cackle,* corta y navega, corta el rollo.
cackle [ˈkækl] v. intr. Cacarear (hen). || FIG. FAM. Chacharear (to talk). | Reírse agudamente (to laugh).
cacochymy [ˈkækəuˌkimi] n. Cacoquimia, *f.*
cacodylate [kækəˈdileit] n. CHEM. Cacodilato, *m.*
cacophonous [kæˈkɔfənəs] adj. Cacofónico, ca.
cacophony [kæˈkɔfəni] n. Cacofonía, *f.*
cactaceous [kækˈteiʃəs] adj. BOT. Cactáceo, a; cácteo, a.
cactus [ˈkæktəs] n. BOT. Cactus, *m.,* cacto, *m.*
— OBSERV. El plural de *cactus* es *cacti.*
cad [kæd] n. Sinvergüenza, *m.*
cadastral [kəˈdæstrəl] adj. Catastral.

cadastre [kəˈdæstə*] n. JUR. Catastro, *m.*
cadaver [kəˈdeivə*] n. Cadáver, *m.*
cadaveric [kəˈdævərik] or **cadaverous** [kəˈdævərəs] adj. Cadavérico, ca.
caddie [ˈkædi] n. SP. "Caddy", *m.*, persona (*f.*) que lleva los palos (golf). | Carrito, *m.* (trolley).
caddis fly [ˈkædisflai] n. ZOOL. Frígano, *m.*
caddish [ˈkædiʃ] adj. Desvergonzado, da (behaviour, etc.). || *Caddish trick*, canallada, *f.*, granujada, *f.*
caddishness [—nis] n. Falta (*f.*) de vergüenza.
caddy [ˈkædi] n. See CADDIE. || Caja (*f.*) para el té.
cade [keid] n. BOT. Enebro, *m.* (juniper).
cadence [ˈkeidəns] n. Cadencia, *f.*, ritmo, *m.* (of sound, voice). || MUS. Cadencia, *f.*
cadency [—i] n. Cadencia, *f.* (cadence). || Descendencia (*f.*) de la rama menor (in a family).
cadenza [kəˈdenzə] n. MUS. Cadencia, *f.*
cadet [kəˈdet] n. MIL. Cadete, *m.* || Hijo (*m.*) menor (youngest son).
cadge [kædʒ] v. tr./intr. Gorronear (to sponge). || *To cadge money off s.o.*, darle un sablazo a uno.
cadger [—ə*] n. Gorrón, ona; sablista, *m.* & *f.*
cadi [ˈkɑːdi] n. Cadí, *m.* (judge).
Cádiz [kəˈdiz, U.S. ˈkædiz] pr. n. GEOGR. Cádiz.
cadmic [ˈkædmik] adj. CHEM. Cádmico, ca.
cadmium [ˈkædmiəm] n. CHEM. Cadmio, *m.*
cadre [ˈkɑːdə*, U.S. ˈkædri] n. Cuadro, *m.*
caduceus [kəˈdjuːsjəs] n. MYTH. Caduceo, *m.*
caducity [kəˈdjuːsiti] n. Caducidad, *f.*
caducous [kəˈdjukəs] adj. Caduco, ca.
caecal [ˈsiːkl] n. ANAT. Cecal.
caecum [ˈsiːkəm] n. ANAT. Ciego, *m.*, intestino (*m.*) ciego.
Caesar [ˈsiːzə*] pr. n. HIST. César, *m.* || *Render therefore unto Caesar the things which are Caesar's and unto God the things which are God's*, hay que dar a Dios lo que es de Dios y al César lo que es del César.
Caesarean or **Caesarian** [siˈzɛərjən] adj. Cesariano, na; cesáreo, a. || MED. *Caesarean section* o *operation*, cesárea, *f.*, operación cesárea.
— N. MED. Cesárea, *f.*, operación (*f.*) cesárea.
caesarism [ˈsiːzərizəm] n. Cesarismo, *m.*, dictadura, *f.*
caesium [ˈsiːzjəm] n. Cesio, *m.* (metal).
caesura [siːˈzjuərə] n. Cesura, *f.* (pause).

— OBSERV. El plural es *caesuras* o *caesurae.*

café [ˈkæfei, ˈkæfi] n. Café, *m.*, restaurante, *m.* || Café, *m.* (for drinks). || Cafetería, *f.*
café society [—səˈsaiəti] n. U. S. Gente (*f.*) famosa que frecuenta los cafés de moda.
cafeteria [kæfiˈtiəriə] n. Restaurante (*m.*) de autoservicio.
caffeine [ˈkæfiːn] n. Cafeína, *f.*
caftan [ˈkæftən] n. Caftán, *m.*
cage [keidʒ] n. Jaula, *f.* (for keeping birds, animals, etc.). || SP. Portería, *f.* (goal). | Canasta, *f.* (in basketball). | Campo (*m.*) de entrenamiento (baseball). || *Lift cage*, jaula de ascensor.
cage [keidʒ] v. tr. Enjaular. || SP. Encestar (to basket).
cagey or **cagy** [ˈkeidʒi] adj. FAM. Cauteloso, sa; reservado, da.
cahoots [kəˈhuːts] pl. n. FAM. *In cahoots with*, conchabado con.
Caiaphas [ˈkaiəfæs] pr. n. Caifás, *m.*
caiman [ˈkeimən] n. ZOOL. Caimán, *m.*
Cain [kein] pr. n. Caín, *m.* || FIG. *To raise Cain*, armar jaleo.
caique [kaiˈiːk] n. MAR. Caique, *m.*, esquife, *m.*
cairn [kɛən] n. Montón (*m.*) de piedras [como señal]. || ZOOL. Tipo (*m.*) peludo de terrier (dog).
Cairo [ˈkaiərəu, U.S. ˈkɛərəu] pr. n. GEOGR. El Cairo, *m.*
caisson [kəˈsuːn] n. TECH. Cajón, *m.*, campana, *f.* | Compuerta (*f.*) de dique (used as gate). || MIL. Cajón (*m.*) de municiones. || MED. *Caisson disease*, enfermedad (*f.*) de los buzos.
cajole [kəˈdʒəul] v. tr. Engatusar. || *To cajole s.o. into doing sth.*, conseguir que uno haga algo engatusándole.
cajoler [—ə*] n. Engatusador, ra.
cajolery [—ri] n. Engatusamiento, *m.*
cake [keik] n. Bizcocho, *m.* (without filling). || Tarta, *f.* (with filling). || Pastel, *m.* (individual): *half a dozen cream cakes*, media docena de pasteles de nata. || Pasta, *f.* (small). || Pastilla, *f.*: *cake of soap*, pastilla de jabón. || — *Christmas cake*, tarta de Navidad. || *Fish cake*, croqueta (*f.*) de pescado. || *Fruit cake*, bizcocho con frutas secas, "cake", *m.* || FIG. FAM. *To be a piece of cake*, ser pan comido, estar tirado. | *To sell like hot cakes*, venderse como rosquillas. | *To take the cake*, llevarse la palma, ser el colmo. || *Wedding cake*, tarta nupcial. || FIG. FAM. *You can't have your cake and eat it*, no se puede estar en misa y repicando.
cake [keik] v. intr. Endurecerse, apelmazarse.
calabash [ˈkæləbæʃ] n. BOT. Calabaza, *f.*
calaboose [kæləˈbuːs] n. U. S. FAM. Calabozo, *m.*
Calabrian [kəˈlæbriən] adj./n. Calabrés, esa.
calamar [ˈkæləmɑː] or **calamary** [ˈkæləməri] n. ZOOL. Calamar, *m.*
calamine [ˈkæləmain] n. CHEM. Calamina, *f.*
calamitous [kəˈlæmitəs] adj. Calamitoso, sa.
calamity [kəˈlæmiti] n. Calamidad, *f.*, desgracia, *f.*
calandra lark [kəˈlændrəˈlɑːk] n. ZOOL. Calandria, *f.*
calash [kəˈlæʃ] n. Calesa, *f.*
calcaneum [kælˈkeiniəm] n. Calcáneo, *m.*, calcañar, *m.*
calcareous, calcarious [kælˈkɛəriəs] adj. Calcáreo, a.
calceolaria [ˌkælsiəˈlɛəriə] n. BOT. Calceolaria, *f.*
calceolate [ˈkælsjəleit] adj. BOT. Calceolado, da.
calces [ˈkælsiːz] pl. n. See CALX.
Calchas [ˈkælkæs] pr. n. Calcas, *m.*
calcic [ˈkælsik] adj. CHEM. Cálcico, ca.
calciferol [kælˈsifərol] n. CHEM. Calciferol, *m.*
calciferous [kælˈsifərəs] adj. Calcífero, ra.
calcification [ˌkælsifiˈkeiʃən] n. Calcificación, *f.*
calcify [ˈkælsifai] v. tr. Calcificar.
— V. intr. Calcificarse.
calcimine [ˈkælsimain] n. Encalado, *m.* (whitewash).
calcimine [ˈkælsimain] v. tr. Encalar, blanquear.
calcination [ˌkælsiˈneiʃən] n. Calcinación, *f.*
calcine [ˈkælsain] v. tr. Calcinar.
— V. intr. Calcinarse.
calcite [ˈkælsait] n. MIN. Calcita, *f.*
calcium [ˈkælsiəm] n. CHEM. Calcio, *m.* || *Calcium oxide*, óxido cálcico.
calcspar [ˈkælkspɑː*] n. MIN. Calcita, *f.*, carbonato (*m.*) de calcio.
calculable [ˈkælkjuləbl] adj. Calculable.
calculate [ˈkælkjuleit] v. tr. Calcular: *to calculate the area of a circle*, calcular el área de un círculo. || FIG. Calcular, suponer (to figure out). | Hacer a propósito [para], hacer con el fin [de], calcular: *a promise calculated to win votes*, una promesa hecha con el fin de ganar votos.
— V. intr. Hacer cálculos, calcular. || FIG. Contar, confiar: *we are calculating on having good weather*, contamos con *or* confiamos en tener buen tiempo.
calculated [—id] adj. FIG. Intencional, calculado, da; deliberado, da
calculating [—iŋ] adj. De calcular, calculador, ra. || FIG. Calculador, ra: *to be cool and caclulating*, ser frío y calculador.
calculating machine [—iŋ-məˈʃiːn] n. Máquina (*f.*) de calcular, calculadora, *f.*, calculador, *m.*
calculation [ˌkælkjuˈleiʃən] n. Cálculo, *m.* || FIG. Cálculo, *m.*
calculator [ˈkælkjuleitə*] n. Calculador, *m.* (s.o. who calculates). || Calculista, *m.* & *f.* (of a project). || Tablas, *f. pl.* (set of tables). || Calculadora, *f.*, calculador, *m.* (machine).
calculous [ˈkælkjuləs] adj. MED. Calculoso, sa.
calculus [ˈkælkjuləs] n. MED. Cálculo, *m.* || MATH. Cálculo, *m.*: *differential, integral calculus*, cálculo diferencial, integral.

— OBSERV. El plural es *calculi* o *calculuses.*

caldron [ˈkɔːldrən] n. Caldero, *m.* (cauldron).
calèche [kəlɛʃ] n. Calesa, *f.*
Caledonia [kæliˈdounjə] pr. n. Caledonia, *f.* || *New Caledonia*, Nueva Caledonia.
calefaction [ˌkæliˈfækʃən] n. Calefacción, *f.*
calendar [ˈkælində*] n. Calendario, *m.* || JUR. Lista, *f.*, registro, *m.* (list). || Orden (*m.*) del día (agenda). || Santoral, *m.* (of saints). || — *Calendar month*, mes (*m.*) civil. || *Calendar year*, año (*m.*) civil.
calendar [ˈkælində*] v. tr. Poner en un calendario *or* en una lista. || Clasificar (documents).
calender [ˈkælində*] n. TECH. Calandria, *f.*
calender [ˈkælində*] v. tr. TECH. Calandrar.
calends [ˈkælindz] pl. n. Calendas, *f.*
calendula [kəˈlendjulə] n. BOT. Caléndula, *f.*
calenture [ˈkæləntjuə*] n. MED. Fiebre (*f.*) tropical.
calf [kɑːf] n. ANAT. Pantorrilla, *f.* || Becerro, rra; ternero, ra (young cow). || Cría, *f.* (young elephant, whale, seal, etc.). || Becerro, *m.*, piel (*f.*) de becerro (leather). || Masa (*f.*) de hielo. || — *In calf*, preñada (pregnant). || *The golden calf*, el becerro de oro. || FIG. FAM. *To kill the fatted calf*, echar la casa por la ventana [para celebrar la llegada de una persona].

— OBSERV. El plural de *calf* es *calves.*

calf bone [—bəun] n. ANAT. Peroné, *m.*
calf love [—lʌv] n. Amor (*m.*) de jóvenes.
calfskin [—skin] n. Becerro, *m.*, piel (*f.*) de becerro.
caliber [ˈkælibə*] n. U. S. See CALIBRE.
calibrate [ˈkælibreit] v. tr. Calibrar (guns, cylinders). || Graduar (thermometer).
calibration [ˌkæliˈbreiʃən] n. Calibración, *f.*, calibrado, *m.* || Graduación, *f.*
calibre [ˈkælibə*] n. Calibre, *m.* || FIG. Calibre, *m.*, capacidad, *f.* (of a person).
calices [ˈkæləˌsiz] pl. n. See CALIX.
caliche [kaˈliːtʃi] n. MIN. Caliche, *m.*, nitrato (*m.*) sódico.
calico [ˈkælikəu] n. Calicó, *m.*, percal, *m.*
calif [ˈkælif] n. Califa, *m.* (caliph).
califate [—eit] n. Califato, *m.*
California [ˌkæliˈfɔːnjə] pr. n. GEOGR. California, *f.*
Californian [—n] adj./n. Californiano, na.
californium [—niəm] n. CHEM. Californio, *m.*
caliginous [kəˈlidʒinəs] adj. Caliginoso, sa.
caliper [ˈkælipə*] n. or **calipers** [—z] pl. n. TECH. See CALLIPER.
caliph [ˈkælif] n. Califa, *m.*
caliphate [—eit] n. Califato, *m.*
calix [ˈkæliks] n. Copa, *f.* || REL. Cáliz, *m.*

— OBSERV. El plural de *calix* es *calices*.

calk [kɔ:lk] n. Ramplón, *m.* (in horseshoe).

calk [kɔ:lk] v. tr. Herrar (shoes). || Herrar a ramplón (horseshoe). || U. S. MAR. Calafatear (to caulk).

calkin [ˈkælkin] n. Clavo, *m.* (of shoe). || Ramplón, *m.* (of horseshoe).

calking [ˌkɔ:lkiŋ] n. U. S. MAR. Calafateo, *m.*

call [kɔ:l] n. Llamada, *f.*, llamamiento, *m.* [*Amer.*, llamado, *m.*]: *to come at s.o.'s call*, acudir a la llamada de alguien. || Llamada, *f.*, grito, *m.*: *a call for help*, un grito de socorro. || Llamada, *f.*: *a telephone call*, una llamada telefónica. || Visita (*f.*) corta (visit to a house, etc.): *to pay* o *to make a call on s.o.*, hacer una visita corta a alguien. || Canto, *m.* (of a bird). || Reclamo, *m.* (instrument imitating the cry of an animal). || MIL. Llamamiento, *m.* (of an annual contingent). | Toque, *m.* (music). || FIG. Llamada, *f.*: *call to the priesthood*, llamada al sacerdocio; *the call of the sea*, la llamada del mar. || Demanda, *f.* (claim on time, money). || MAR. AVIAT. Escala, *f.*: *port of call*, puerto de escala. || JUR. Citación, *f.*, convocación, *f.* || COMM. Demanda, *f.*, pedido, *m.* (demand). | Opción (*f.*) de compra (in stock market). | Solicitación (*f.*) de fondos. || Acción (*f.*) de igualar y de hacer enseñar las cartas (in poker). || Anuncio, *m.*, declaración, *f.* (in bridge). || FIG. Motivo, *m.*: *there's no call for you to be upset*, no hay motivo para que te molestes. || — *A call to order*, una llamada al orden. || *Curtain call*, llamada a escena. || *On call*, de guardia (a doctor, etc.), disponible (available), pagadero a la vista (money). || *Reverse-charge call*, conferencia (*f.*) a cobro revertido (telephone call). || *The actor got several calls*, el actor tuvo que salir a saludar varias veces. || *To give s.o. a call*, llamar a alguien. || FIG. *To have a close call*, librarse por los pelos. || *Trunk* o *long-distance call*, conferencia, *f.* [interurbana]. || *Within call*, al alcance de la voz.

call [kɔ:l] v. tr. Llamar: *to call somebody in a loud voice*, llamar a alguien a voces. || Convocar (to summon): *to call a meeting*, convocar una reunión. || Llamar, despertar (to awaken). || Telefonear a, llamar a (to phone). || Llamar: *he was called to the priesthood*, fue llamado al sacerdocio. || Llamar, poner (to give a Christian name to). || Llamar, decir (to give a nickname to). || Llamar: *I call it a swindle*, lo llamo una estafa. || Calcular (to estimate): *I'd call it a good 20 miles*, lo calcularía en unas 20 millas largas. || Reclamar (to attract animals). || JUR. Convocar, citar (a witness). || COMM. Pedir el reembolso de (a loan). || Hacer enseñar las cartas (in poker). || Declarar, anunciar (in bridge). || — *Manchester has called you*, lo han llamado de Manchester. || *To be called*, llamarse: *I am called González*, me llamo González. || *To be called to the bar*, ser recibido de abogado. || SP. *To call a game*, dar por concluido un partido (baseball). || *To call a strike*, declarar una huelga. || *To call it a day*, see DAY. || *To call o.s.*, llamarse. || FAM. *To call s.o. names*, see NAME. || *To call s.o.'s attention to*, llamar la atención de alguien sobre. || *To call the roll*, pasar lista. || *To call to account*, pedir cuentas. || *To call to mind*, traer a la memoria, recordar. || *To call to order*, llamar al orden. || MIL. *To call to the colours*, llamar a filas.

— V. intr. Llamar, gritar, dar voces. || Cantar (bird). || Llamar, hacer una llamada (to telephone). || Hacer una visita (to pay a visit). || Pasar: *I only called to see how you were*, pasé sólo para saber cómo estabas; *to call at the butcher's*, pasar por la carnicería. || Hacer escala: *to call at a port*, hacer escala en un puerto. || Parar: *the train calls at every station*, el tren para en todas las estaciones. || Reclamarse (birds). || Declarar (in bridge). || — *This is Charles calling, is John in?*, soy Carlos, ¿está Juan? || *This is Radio X calling*, aquí Radio X. || *Who is calling?*, ¿de parte de quién?

— **To call after,** llamar a. || **To call again,** venir de nuevo. || **To call aside,** llamar aparte. || **To call at,** pasar por, hacer una visita a (to visit). | MAR. Hacer escala en. || **To call away,** llamar (to another place). | Distraer (s.o.'s attention). || **To call back,** volver a llamar (by telephone). | Recordar (to remember). | Hacer volver: *she called back her son*, hizo volver a su hijo. | Volver (to come back). | — *To call back an ambassador*, retirar a un embajador. || **To call down,** hacer bajar. | Invocar. | U. S. Regañar, reprender (to scold). || **To call for,** llamar a: *to call loudly for s.o.*, llamar a alguien a gritos. | Pedir (to ask for). | Ir a buscar, ir a recoger (to fetch). | Exigir, pedir (attention, measures, volunteers, etc.). | — *To call for help*, pedir auxilio or socorro. || **To call forth,** sacar (to draw out). | Inspirar, provocar (admiration). | Hacer surgir (memories). | Suscitar, provocar (protestation). || **To call in,** retirar [de la circulación]: *to call in old coinage*, retirar moneda antigua de la circulación. | Hacer pasar (to let in). | Llamar a: *to call in the fire brigade*, llamar a los bomberos. | COMM. Exigir el pago de (debts, etc.). | Entrar (to come in). | — *To call in question*, poner en tela de juicio. || **To call off,** cancelar, anular (to cancel). | Dar por terminado (to put an end to). | Llamar (dogs). || **To call on,** visitar (to visit). | Dar or ceder la palabra a: *I call on the next speaker*, doy la palabra al siguiente orador. | Acudir a, recurrir a (for help). | Censurar por (to blame). | Invocar, apelar a (to invoke). || **To call out,** hacer salir: *I don't want to call the doctor out at this time of night*, no quiero hacer salir al médico a estas horas de la noche. | Gritar (to shout). | Llamar a la huelga (workers). | Desafiar, retar (to challenge). | Hacer intervenir (to summon for emergency service). | — *To call out for sth.*, reclamar algo con insistencia. || **To call over,** llamar. || **To call together,** convocar. || **To call up,** llamar (by telephone, radio) | MIL. Llamar a filas. | Hacer subir (to tell to come up). | Hacer surgir (memories). || **To call upon,** invocar (God's name). | Recurrir a, acudir a (s.o.'s generosity). | Dar or ceder la palabra a (speaker). | — *To call upon s.o. to do sth.*, pedir a alguien que haga algo.

calla [ˈkælə] n. BOT. Cala, *f.* || *Calla lily*, lirio (*m.*) de agua.

call-board [—bɔ:d] n. THEATR. Tablón (*m.*) de anuncios [para los ensayos de los artistas].

call box [—bɔks] n. Cabina (*f.*) telefónica.

callboy [—bɔi] n. THEATR. Traspunte, *m.* || Botones, *m. inv.* (bellboy).

caller [—ə*] n. Persona (*f.*) que llama, el que llama (person making a telephone call). || Visita, *f.* (visitor). || Cliente, ta (at a shop).

call girl [—gə:l] n. FAM. Prostituta, *f.*

call house [—həus] n. Casa (*f.*) de citas.

calligraph [kəˈligrəf] v. tr. Caligrafiar.

calligrapher [—ə*] n. Calígrafo, fa.

calligraphic [ˌkæliˈgræfik] adj. Caligráfico, ca.

calligraphy [kəˈligrəfi] n. Caligrafía, *f.*

calling [ˈkɔ:liŋ] n. Llamamiento, *m.*, llamada, *f.* [*Amer.*, llamado, *m.*] (call). || Profesión, *f.* (occupation). || Vocación, *f.* (spiritual summons). || REL. Llamada, *f.* || Visita, *f.*: *calling card, hours*, tarjeta, horas de visita. || Celo, *m.* (of female cat).

Calliope [kəˈlaiəpi] pr. n. MYTH. Calíope, *f.*

calliper [ˈkælipə*] n. or **callipers** [—z] pl. n. TECH.: Compás (*m. sing.*) de calibre, calibrador, *m. sing.*: *vernier calliper*, calibrador micrométrico. || MED. Aparato (*m.*) ortopédico. || *Slide calliper*, pie (*m.*) de rey, compás de corredera.

calliper gauge [—geidʒ] n. Calibrador (*m.*) de mordazas.

callisthenics [ˌkælisˈθeniks] n. Calistenia, *f.*

call loan [ˈkɔ:l-ləun] or **call money** [ˈkɔ:lˈmʌni] n. COMM. Dinero (*m.*) pagadero a la vista.

callosity [kæˈlɔsiti] n. Callosidad, *f.* || FIG. Insensibilidad, *f.*

callous [ˈkæləs] adj. Calloso, sa (skin). || FIG. Insensible, duro, ra.

— N. Callo, *m.* (callus).

— OBSERV. El plural de *callous* es *callouses* y *calli*.

callow [ˈkæləu] adj. Inexperto, ta; inmaduro, ra (lacking experience). || Implume (young birds).

call sign [ˈkɔ:lsain] n. RAD. Sintonía, *f.*, indicativo, *m.*

call-up [ˈkɔ:lʌp] n. MIL. Llamada (*f.*) a filas.

callus [ˈkæləs] n. Callo, *m.*

— OBSERV. El plural de callus es *calluses* o *calli*.

calm [kɑ:m] adj. Sosegado, da; tranquilo, la (person). || Calmoso, sa (weather). || Tranquilo, la (sea).

— N. Calma, *f.*, tranquilidad, *f.*, sosiego, *m.* || MAR. *Dead calm*, calma chicha.

calm [kɑ:m] v. tr. Calmar, sosegar, tranquilizar.

— V. intr. Calmarse, sosegarse, tranquilizarse. || Calmarse (wind, temper).

— OBSERV. El verbo *to calm* va seguido frecuentemente por *down*, sin cambiar por ello su sentido: *the sea was calming down*, el mar se calmaba.

calmative [ˈkælmətiv] adj. Calmante.

— N. Calmante, *m.*

calmly [ˈkɑ:mli] adv. Con calma, tranquilamente.

calmness [ˈkɑ:mnis] n. Calma, *f.*, tranquilidad, *f.*

calomel [ˈkæləməl] n. MED. Calomel, *m.*, calomelanos, *m. pl.*

caloric [kəˈlɔrik] adj. PHYS. Calórico, ca; térmico, ca.

— N. PHYS. Calórico, *m.*

calorie [ˈkæləri] n. BIOL. PHYS. Caloría, *f.*: *large calorie*, caloría grande; *small calorie*, pequeña caloría; *gramme calorie*, caloría gramo.

calorific [ˌkæləˈrifik] adj. Calorífico, ca: *calorific value* o *power*, potencia calorífica.

calorimeter [ˌkæləˈrimitə*] n. PHYS. Calorímetro, *m.*

calorimetric [kæləˈrimitrik] or **calorimetrical** [ˌkæləriˈmetrikəl] adj. PHYS. Calorimétrico, ca.

calorimetry [ˌkæləˈrimitri] n. PHYS. Calorimetría, *f.*

calory [ˈkæləri] n. BIOL. PHYS. Caloría, *f.* (calorie).

calotte [kəˈlɔt] n. Solideo, *m.* (of a priest).

caltrop [ˈkæltrəp] n. MIL. BOT. Abrojo, *m.*

calumet [ˈkæljumet] n. "Calumet", *m.*, pipa (*f.*) de la paz.

calumniate [kəˈlʌmnieit] v. tr. Calumniar.

calumniation [kəˌlʌmniˈeiʃən] n. Calumnia, *f.*

calumniator [kəˈlʌmnieitə*] n. Calumniador, ra.

calumniatory [kəˌlʌmniˈeitəri] or **calumnious** [kəˈlʌmniəs] adj. Calumnioso, sa.

calumny [ˈkæləmni] n. Calumnia, *f.*

calvary [ˈkælvəri] n. FIG. Calvario, *m.*

Calvary [ˈkælvəri] n. Calvario, *m.*

calve [kɑ:v] v. intr. Parir (cow). || Desprenderse (mass of ice).

— V. tr. Parir (a calf).

calves [—z] pl. n. See CALF.

Calvin [ˈkælvin] pr. n. HIST. Calvino.
Calvinism [—izəm] n. REL. Calvinismo, *m.*
Calvinist [—ist] adj./n. REL. Calvinista.
Calvinistic [ˌkælviˈnistik] adj. REL. Calvinista.
calx [kælks] n. TECH. Residuos (*m. pl.*) *or* escorias (*f. pl.*) de la calcinación.
— OBSERV. El plural de *calx* es *calces* o *calxes.*
calyces [ˈkælisi:z] pl. n. See CALYX.
calypso [kəˈlipsəu] n. MUS. Calipso, *m.* (dance).
Calypso [kəˈlipsəu] pr. n. MYTH. Calipso, *f.* (nymph).
calyx [ˈkeiliks] n. BOT. Cáliz, *m.* || ANAT. Cáliz, *m.* (of the kidney). || TECH. Corona (*f.*) dentada.
— OBSERV. El plural de esta palabra es *calyces* o *calyxes.*
cam [kæm] n. TECH. Leva, *f.*
camaraderie [ˌkæməˈrɑ:dəri] n. Compañerismo, *m.*, camaradería, *f.*
camarilla [ˌkæməˈrilə] n. Camarilla, *f.*
camaron [ˌkæməˈrɔn] n. ZOOL. Camarón, *m.* [de agua dulce].
camber [ˈkæmbə*] n. Comba, *f.*, combadura, *f.* || Curvatura, *f.*, peralte, *m.* (of road). || AUT. Inclinación, *f.* (of wheels). || Torsión, *f.*, alabeo, *m.* (of beams).
camber [ˈkæmbə*] v. tr. Combar, arquear.
— V. intr. Combarse, arquearse.
cambist [ˈkæmbist] n. Cambista, *m.*
Cambodia [kæmˈbəudjə] pr. n. GEOGR. Camboya, *f.*
Cambodian [—n] adj./n. Camboyano, na.
cambrel [ˈkæmbrəl] n. Garabato, *m.* (butcher's hook).
Cambrian [ˈkæmbriən] adj. Cambriano, na (Welsh). || GEOL. Cámbrico, ca.
cambric [ˈkeimbrik] n. Cambray, *m.*, batista, *f.*
came [keim] n. TECH. Barra (*f.*) de plomo [en una vidriera o ventana].
came [keim] pret. See COME.
camel [ˈkæməl] n. ZOOL. MAR. Camello, *m.*
cameleer [ˌkæmiˈliə*] n. Camellero, *m.*
camel hair or **camel's hair** [ˈkæməl-hεə*] n. Pelo (*m.*) de camello (fabric).
camellia or **camelia** [kəˈmi:ljə] n. BOT. Camelia, *f.*
cameo [ˈkæmiəu] n. Camafeo, *m.*
camera [ˈkæmərə] n. PHOT. Máquina (*f.*) fotográfica. || Cámara, *f.* (cinema or television). || JUR. Cámara (*f.*) del juez. || — PHOT. *Camera obscura*, cámara oscura. || *Camera stand*, trípode, *m.* || JUR. *In camera*, a puerta cerrada.
cameraman [—mən] n. Cámara, *m.*, cameraman, *m.*, operador (*m.*) de cine *or* de televisión.
Cameroons [ˈkæməru:nz] pl. pr. n. GEOGR. Camerún, *m. sing.* (former protectorate).
Cameroon or **Cameroun** [ˈkæməru:n] pr. n. GEOGR. Camerún, *m.* (republic).
Camilla or **Camille** [kəˈmilə] pr. n. Camila, *f.*
Camillus [kəˈmiləs] pr. n. Camilo, *m.*
camisole [ˈkæmisəul] n. Cubrecorsé, *m.*
camomile [ˈkæməmail] n. BOT. Camomila, *f.*, manzanilla, *f.* || *Camomile tea*, manzanilla, *f.*
camouflage [ˈkæmuflɑ:ʒ] n. MIL. Camuflaje, *m.* || FIG. Enmascaramiento, *m.*, disimulación, *f.*
camouflage [ˈkæmuflɑ:ʒ] v. tr. MIL. Camuflar. || FIG. Enmascarar, disimular (to disguise).
camp [kæmp] n. Campo, *m.*: *concentration camp*, campo de concentración. || Campamento, *m.* (military, for holidays). || FIG. Campo, *m.*, grupo, *m.*: *the existentialist camp*, el campo existencialista. | MIL. Vida (*f.*) militar. || — *Holiday camp*, campamento *or* colonia (*f.*) de vacaciones. || *Internment camp*, campo de internamiento. || *Labour camp*, colonia penitenciaria. || *Summer camp*, campamento de verano (in tents), colonia (*f.*) de verano (in houses). || *Work camp*, campo de trabajo. || *To break* o *to strike camp*, levantar el campo. || *To pitch camp*, instalar el campo, acampar.
camp [kæmp] v. tr. Acampar (soldiers). || Alojar.
— V. intr. Acampar. || — *To camp out*, vivir en tiendas de campaña. || *To camp out at s.o. else's house*, alojarse temporalmente en casa de otro.
camp [kæmp] adj. Afectado, da; amanerado, da (affected). || Afeminado, da (effeminate).
— N. Afectación, *f.* || Afeminación, *f.*
campaign [kæmˈpein] n. Campaña, *f.*: *military, advertising campaign*, campaña militar, publicitaria; *election campaign*, campaña electoral.
campaign [kæmˈpein] v. intr. Hacer [una] campaña. || Luchar (to fight).
campaigner [—ə*] n. FIG. Paladín, *m.* || MIL. *Old campaigner*, veterano, *m.*
campanile [ˌkæmpəˈni:li] n. ARCH. Campanil, *m.*, campanario, *m.*
campanology [ˌkæmpəˈnɔlədʒi] n. Campanología, *f.*
campanula [kəmˈpænjulə] n. BOT. Campánula, *f.*, farolillo, *m.*
campanulaceae [kəmˌpænjuˈleisii] pl. n. BOT. Campanuláceas, *f.*
campanulate [kəmˈpænjuleit] adj. Campaniforme, acampanado, da.
camp bed [ˈkæmp-bed] n. Catre (*m.*) de tijera.
camp chair [ˈkæmptʃεə*] n. Silla (*f.*) de tijera.
campeachy wood [kæmˈpi:tʃi-wud] n. Palo (*m.*) [de] campeche.
camper [ˈkæmpə*] n. SP. Campista, *m. & f.* (person). || Caravana, *f.* (vehicle).
campfire [ˈkæmpˈfaiə*] n. Fuego (*m.*) de campamento.
campfire girl [—gə:l] n. U. S. Muchacha (*f.*) exploradora.
camp follower [ˈkæmpˈfɔləuə*] n. Cantinera, *f.*
campground [ˈkæmpˌgraund] n. U. S. Camping, *m.*
camphor [ˈkæmfə*] n. Alcanfor, *m.*
camphorate [—reit] v. tr. Alcanforar.
camp hospital [ˈkæmpˈhɔspitəl] n. MIL. Hospital (*m.*) de sangre.
camping [ˈkæmpiŋ] n. Camping, *m.*: *to go camping*, ir de camping. || — *Camping chair*, silla (*f.*) de tijera. || *Camping ground* o *site*, camping, *m.*
camp meeting [ˈkæmpˈmi:tiŋ] n. U. S. REL. Concentración (*f.*) religiosa al aire libre.
camporee [ˌkæmpəˈri] n. Reunión (*f.*) de exploradores.
campsite [ˈkæmpsait] n. Camping, *m.*, sitio (*m.*) donde se acampa. || Campamento, *m.* (for boy scouts).
campus [ˈkæmpəs] n. Recinto (*m.*) universitario, ciudad (*f.*) universitaria, campus, *m.*
camshaft [ˈkæmˌʃɑ:ft] n. TECH. Árbol (*m.*) de levas.
can [kæn] n. Lata, *f.*: *a can of beer*, una lata de cerveza. || Bote, *m.*, lata, *f.* (tin): *can of peaches*, bote de melocotones. || Bidón, *m.*: *a gallon can of oil*, un bidón de aceite de un galón. || U. S. Lata, *f.* (flat tin): *can of sardines*, lata de sardinas. || U. S. FAM. Chirona, *f.* (jail). | Retrete, *m.* (toilet). | Carga (*f.*) de profundidad (depth charge). || FIG. FAM. *To carry the can*, pagar el pato.
can* [kæn] v. aux. Poder (to be able to): *can you come to dinner tomorrow?*, ¿puedes venir a cenar mañana? || Poder (to be allowed to): *you can go now*, te puedes marchar. || Saber: *she can speak French*, sabe hablar francés. || Ser capaz de, poder: *I cannot do that type of work*, no soy capaz de hacer esa clase de trabajo. || — *Can you hear me?*, ¿me oyes? || *I can't see him*, no lo veo. || *I could have smacked his face*, no le di una torta de milagro, casi le doy una torta. || *Ugly as could be*, de lo más feo.
— V. tr. Enlatar, envasar, conservar en lata (to preserve in a can). || FAM. Echar del colegio (to expel). | Despedir (from a job). | Grabar (records, tapes). || FAM. *Can it!*, ¡basta!
— OBSERV. El verbo auxiliar *can* es defectivo y sólo se conjuga en presente, pretérito y condicional. El infinitivo y los participios no existen y se sustituyen por *to be able to*. La forma negativa es *cannot* o *can't;* el pretérito y el condicional son *could.*
Canada [ˈkænədə] pr. n. GEOGR. Canadá, *m.*
Canadian [kəˈneidjən] adj./n. Canadiense.
canal [kəˈnæl] n. Canal, *m.* (for navigation). || Canal, *m.*, acequia, *f.* (for irrigation). || ANAT. Canal, *m.*, conducto, *m.* || ARCH. Mediacaña, *f.*, estría, *f.* || — ANAT. *Alimentary canal*, tubo digestivo. || *Canal rays*, rayos (*m.*) canales.
canalizable [ˌkænəlaizəbl] adj. Canalizable.
canalization [ˌkænəlaiˈzeiʃən] n. Canalización, *f.*
canalize [ˈkænəlaiz] v. tr. Canalizar.
canapé [ˈkænəpei] n. CULIN. Canapé, *m.*
canard [kæˈnɑ:d] n. Bulo, *m.* (false piece of news).
Canarian [kæˈnεərjən] adj./n. Canario, ria.
canary [kəˈnεəri] n. Canario, *m.* (bird). || Amarillo (*m.*) canario (colour). || Vino (*m.*) de Canarias.
canary grass [—grɑ:s] n. Alpiste, *m.*
Canary Islands [—ˌailəndz] pl. pr. n. GEOGR. Islas Canarias, *f.*, Canarias, *f.*
canary seed [—si:d] n. Alpiste, *m.*
canasta [kəˈnæstə] n. Canasta, *f.* (card game).
cancan [ˈkænkæn] n. Cancán, *m.* (dance).
cancel [ˈkænsəl] n. Cancelación, *f.*, anulación, *f.*
cancel [ˈkænsəl] v. tr. Cancelar (a decree, contract etc.): *to cancel a contract*, cancelar un contrato. || Anular, invalidar: *to cancel a cheque*, anular un cheque. || Anular: *to cancel an order, a telephone call, an invitation*, anular un pedido, una llamada telefónica, una invitación. || Tachar, suprimir, borrar (to delete, to cross out): *to cancel a name from a list*, borrar un nombre de una lista. || Matar (postage stamp). || MATH. Eliminar. || Contrarrestar (to balance): *the profits cancel the losses*, los beneficios contrarrestan las pérdidas.
— V. intr. MATH. *To cancel out*, anularse.
cancellate [ˈkænsəleit] or **cancellated** [—id] adj. BIOL. Reticular, reticulado, da.
cancellation [ˌkænsəˈleiʃən] n. JUR. Cancelación, *f.*, anulación, *f.* || Matado, *m.* (on a stamp). || Supresión, *f.* (deletion).
canceller [ˈkænsələ] n. Matasellos, *m. inv.*
cancellous [ˈkænsələs] adj. Esponjoso, sa (bone).
cancer [ˈkænsə*] n. MED. Cáncer, *m.*
Cancer [ˈkænsə*] n. ASTR. Cáncer, *m.*
cancerigenic or **cancerogenic** [ˌkænsərəˈdʒenik] adj. MED. Cancerígeno, na.
cancerologist [ˈkænsəˈrɔlədʒist] n. Cancerólogo, *m.*
cancerous [ˈkænsərəs] adj. MED. Canceroso, sa.
cancroid [ˈkæŋˌkrɔid] adj. MED. Cancroideo, a.
— N. MED. Cancroide, *m.*
candela [kænˈdi:lə] n. ELECTR. Candela, *f.* (unit).
candelabra [ˌkændiˈlɑ:brə] n. Candelabro, *m.*
candelabrum [—m] n. Candelabro, *m.*
— OBSERV. El plural es *candelabra* o *candelabrums.*
candescence [kænˈdesns] n. Candencia, *f.*
candescent [kænˈdesnt] adj. Candente.

candid [ˈkændid] adj. Sincero, ra; franco, ca (frank). || Imparcial, justo, ta. || *Candid camera*, cámara indiscreta.

— OBSERV. The Spanish word *cándido* means "naïve".

candidacy [—əsi] n. Candidatura, *f.*
candidate [—eit] n. Candidato, ta: *candidate for a post*, candidato a *or* para un puesto. || Opositor, ra (in a competitive examination).
candidature [—itʃə*] n. Candidatura, *f.*
candidness [ˈkændidnis] n. Franqueza, *f.*, sinceridad, *f.*
candied [ˈkændid] adj. Escarchado, da (cooked in sugar). || Cande, candi (sugar).
candle [ˈkændl] n. Vela, *f.* (of tallow, wax). || Cirio, *m.* (in a church). || Candela, *f.* (unit of intensity). || — FIG. *He is not fit to hold a candle to him*, no le llega a la suela del zapato. | *The game is not worth the candle*, la cosa no vale la pena. | *To burn the candle at both ends*, hacer de la noche día.
candle [ˈkændl] v. tr. Mirar al trasluz.
candleberry [—ˌberi] n. BOT. Árbol (*m.*) de la cera.
candleholder [—ˌhəuldə*] n. Candelero, *m.*
candlelight [—lait] n. Luz (*f.*) de una vela: *by candlelight*, a la luz de una vela. || FIG. Atardecer, *m.*, crepúsculo, *m.*
Candlemas [ˈkændlməs] n. REL. Candelaria, *f.*
candlepower [ˈkændlˌpauə*] n. Candela, *f.*, bujía, *f.* (unit).
candlestick [ˈkændlstik] n. Candelero, *m.*, palmatoria, *f.* || Cirial, *m.* (in a church).
candlewick [ˈkændlwik] n. Pábilo, *m.*, mecha (*f.*) de la vela. || Tela (*f.*) de algodón afelpada (fabric).
candour (U. S. **candor**) [ˈkændə*] n. Sinceridad, *f.*, franqueza, *f.* (frankness). || Imparcialidad, *f.*, justicia, *f.*

— OBSERV. The Spanish words *candor* and *candidez* mean "naïveté".

candy [ˈkændi] n. Azúcar (*m.*) cande. || U. S. Caramelo, *m.* (sweet), bombón, *m.* (made of chocolate).
candy [ˈkændi] v. tr. Escarchar (fruit, etc.). || Cristalizar (sugar).
— V. intr. Escarcharse (fruit). || Cristalizarse (sugar).
candy floss [—flɔs] n. Algodón, *m.* (spun sugar).
candy store [—stɔ:*] n. Confitería, *f.*
candytuft [—tʌft] n. BOT. Carraspique, *m.*
cane [kein] n. Caña, *f.*: *sugar cane*, caña de azúcar. || Bastón, *m.* (thin walking stick). || Mimbre, *m.*: *cane furniture*, muebles de mimbre. || Palmeta, *f.*, vara, *f.* (instrument of punishment). || — *Cane seat*, asiento (*m.*) de mimbre *or* de rejilla. || *Cane sugar*, azúcar (*m.*) de caña.
cane [kein] v. tr. Poner un asiento de mimbre a (a chair). || Castigar con la palmeta *or* las varas (to punish).
canebrake [ˈkeinbreik] n. U. S. Cañaveral, *m.*
canicular [kəˈnikjələ*] adj. Canicular.
canidae [ˈkænidei] pl. n. ZOOL. Cánidos, *m.*
canine [ˈkeinain] adj. Canino, na. || *Canine tooth*, canino, *m.*, colmillo, *m.*, diente canino.
— N. Diente (*m.*) canino, colmillo, *m.*, canino, *m.* (tooth). || U. S. Perro, *m.*, can, *m.* (dog).
caning [ˈkeiniŋ] n. Castigo (*m.*) con la palmeta *or* las varas.
canister [ˈkænistə*] n. Bote, *m.*, lata, *f.* (can). || MIL. Bote (*m.*) de metralla. || REL. Hostiario, *m.*
canker [ˈkæŋkə*] n. MED. Úlcera (*f.*) en la boca. || VET. Cancro, *m.*, llaga (*f.*) gangrenosa. || BOT. Cancro, *m.* (in fruit trees). || FIG. Cáncer, *m.* || MED. *Canker rash*, escarlatina, *f.*
canker [ˈkæŋkə*] v. tr. MED. Ulcerar, gangrenar. || FIG. Corromper.
— V. intr. MED. Ulcerarse, gangrenarse. || FIG. Corromperse.
cankerous [—rəs] adj. Gangrenoso, sa; ulceroso, sa.
cankerworm [ˈkæŋkəˌwə:m] n. ZOOL. Gusano, *m.* [que se come las hojas].
canna [ˈkænə] n. BOT. Cañacoro, *m.*
cannabis [—bis] n. Cáñamo (*m.*) de la India (hemp).
canned [kænd] adj. Enlatado, da; en lata, en bote, en conserva: *canned goods*, productos enlatados. || FAM. Grabado, da: *canned music*, música grabada; *canned speech*, discurso grabado. | Estereotipado, da (stereotyped). | Expulsado, da (expelled). | Despedido, da (from a job). | Borracho, cha; trompa (drunk).
cannel [ˈkænl] or **cannel coal** [—kəul] n. MIN. Carbón (*m.*) bituminoso.
cannelons [ˈkænəlˌɔns] or **canneloni** [ˌkænəlˈouni] pl. n. Canelones, *m.*
canner [ˈkænə*] n. Conservero, ra.
cannery [ˈkænəri] n. Fábrica (*f.*) de conservas.
cannibal [ˈkænibəl] adj./n. Caníbal.
cannibalism [—izəm] n. Canibalismo, *m.*
cannibalistic [ˌkænibəˈlistik] adj. Caníbal.
cannibalize [ˈkænibəlaiz] v. tr. Recuperar las piezas aprovechables de [un coche, etc.].
canniness [ˈkæninis] n. Astucia, *f.*
canning [ˈkæniŋ] n. Enlatado, *m.* || *Canning industry*, industria conservera.
cannon [ˈkænən] n. MIL. Cañón, *m.* (gun). | Artillería, *f.* || Carambola, *f.* (in billiards). || Tija, *f.* (of a key). || Cañón, *m.* (of a horse's bit).

— OBSERV. El plural de *cannon* cuando significa "cañón" (pieza de artillería) es generalmente *cannon*. En los demás sentidos es *cannons*.

cannon [ˈkænən] v. intr. Hacer carambola (in billiards). || — *To cannon into* o *against*, chocar contra. || *To cannon off*, rebotar contra.
— V. tr. Cañonear.
cannonade [ˌkænəˈneid] n. Cañoneo, *m.*
cannonade [ˌkænəˈneid] v. tr./intr. Bombardear, cañonear.
cannonball [ˈkænənbɔ:l] n. HIST. Bala (*f.*) de cañón. || Servicio (*m.*) fuerte (tennis).
cannon bone [ˈkænənbəun] n. ZOOL. Caña, *f.*
cannon fodder [ˈkænənˌfɔdə*] n. FIG. Carne (*f.*) de cañón.
cannonry [ˈkænənri] n. Fuego (*m.*) de artillería.
cannon-shot [ˈkænənʃɔt] n. Cañonazo, *m.* (shot). || Bala (*f.*) de cañón (cannonball). || Alcance (*m.*) de un cañón (range).
cannot [ˈkænɔt] See CAN.
cannula [ˈkænjələ] n. MED. Cánula, *f.*

— OBSERV. El plural de *cannula* es *cannulae*.

canny [ˈkæni] adj. Astuto, ta (shrewd). || Prudente, cauto, ta (cautious).
canoe [kəˈnu:] n. Canoa, *f.* || SP. Piragua, *f.* || FIG. FAM. *To paddle one's own canoe*, arreglárselas solo.
canoe [kəˈnu:] v. intr. Ir en canoa.
canoeing [—iŋ] n. SP. Piragüismo, *m.*
canoeist [—ist] n. SP. Piragüista, *m.* & *f.*
canon [ˈkænən] n. REL. Canon, *m.* (church rule, books regarded as a holy unit, part of the Mass). | Canónigo, *m.* (member of the chapter). || FIG. Canon, *m.*, norma, *f.*, regla, *f.* (principle). || Catálogo, *m.* (catalogue). || MUS. Canon, *m.* || PRINT. Doble canon, *m.* || REL. *Canon law*, Derecho canónico.
cañon [ˈkænjən] n. Cañón, *m.* (canyon).
canoness [ˈkænənis] n. REL. Canonesa, *f.*
canonical [kəˈnɔnikəl] adj. REL. Canónico, ca. || FIG. Ortodoxo, xa (authorized). || REL. *Canonical dress*, hábitos (*m. pl.*) sacerdotales.
canonicals [—z] pl. n. REL. Hábitos (*m.*) sacerdotales.
canonist [ˈkænənist] n. Canonista, *m.*
canonization [ˌkænənaiˈzeiʃən] n. Canonización, *f.*
canonize [ˈkænənaiz] v. tr. REL. Canonizar.
canonry [ˈkænənri] n. REL. Canonjía, *f.*
canoodle [kəˈnu:dl] v. intr. FAM. Besuquearse.
can opener [ˈkænoupnə*] n. Abrelatas, *m. inv.*
canopy [ˈkænəpi] n. Toldo, *m.* (awning). || Dosel, *m.*, baldaquín, *m.*, baldaquino, *m.* (over a bed). | Dosel, *m.* (over a throne). || ARCH. Doselete, *m.* (over niche, etc.). || REL. Dosel, *m.* (fixed). | Palio, *m.* (portable). || FIG. Bóveda, *f.*: *canopy of heaven*, bóveda celeste. || AVIAT. Casquete, *m.* (of parachute). || AVIAT. *Ejectable canopy*, cubierta (*f.*) de cristal eyectable.
canopy [ˈkænəpi] v. tr. Endoselar.
canorous [kəˈnɔrəs] adj. Canoro, ra.
can't [kɑ:nt] contraction of *I cannot*. See CAN.
cant [kænt] adj. Trivial, vulgar (trite). || Insincero, ra; hipócrita (insincere). || De jerga, esotérico, ca (used by a particular group). || Sesgado, da (on the bias). || ARCH. Achaflanado, da.
— N. Hipocresías, *f. pl.* (insincere talk). || Tópicos, *m. pl.*, trivialidades, *f. pl.* (trivial statements). || Gazmoñería, *f.* (insincere piety). || Jerga, *f.*, argot, *m.* (jargon). || Germanía, *f.* (slang of thieves, etc.). || TECH. Esquina, *f.*, chaflán, *m.* (of a building). | Inclinación, *f.* (slope). | Bisel, *m.* (bevelled edge).
cant [kænt] v. tr. Inclinar (to tilt). || Biselar (to bevel). || Poner en ángulo (to set at an angle). || Volcar (to overturn). || ARCH. Chaflanar.
— V. intr. Inclinarse (to slant). || MAR. Escorar. || Decir hipocresías (to speak insincerely).
cantabile [kænˈtɑ:bili] adj. MUS. Cantábile.
— N. MUS. Cantable, *m.*
Cantabrian [kænˈteibriən] adj. GEOGR. Cantábrico, ca. || — *Cantabrian Mountains*, Cordillera Cantábrica. || — Adj./n. Cántabro, bra.
Cantabrigian [ˌkæntəˈbridʒiən] adj. De Cambridge.
— N. Estudiante *or* licenciado de la Universidad de Cambridge (student). || Nativo de Cambridge (native).
cantaloup or **cantaloupe** [ˈkæntəlu:p] n. Melón (*m.*) cantalupo, cantalupo, *m.*
cantankerous [kænˈtæŋkərəs] n. Arisco, ca; intratable (ill-natured). || Malhumorado, da (bad-tempered). || Irritable. || Pendenciero, ra (quarrelsome).
cantata [kænˈtɑ:tə] n. Cantata, *f.*
canteen [kænˈti:n] n. Cantina, *f.* (restaurant). || MIL. Cantina, *f.* (shop, kit). | Cantimplora, *f.* (bottle). || — *Canteen cup*, taza metálica. || *Canteen of cutlery*, juego (*m.*) de cubiertos.
canter [ˈkæntə*] n. Medio galope, *m.* || FIG. FAM. *To win in a canter*, ganar cómodamente.
canter [ˈkæntə*] v. intr. Ir a medio galope.
Canterbury [ˈkæntəbəri] pr. n. GEOGR. Cantorbery. || BOT. *Canterbury bell*, campánula, *f.*, farolillo, *m.*
cantharides [kænˈθæridi:z] pl. n. MED. Cantárida, *f. sing.* (pharmaceutical preparation).
cantharis [ˈkænθəris] n. ZOOL. Cantárida, *f.*

— OBSERV. El plural de *cantharis* es *cantharides*.

cant hook [ˈkænt-huk] n. TECH. Gancho (*m.*) maderero.
canticle [ˈkæntikl] n. REL. Cántico, *m.* || — Pl. REL. Cantar (*m. sing.*) de los Cantares.
cantilena [ˌkæntilˈeinə] n. Cantilena, *f.*
cantilever [ˈkæntili:və*] adj. TECH. Voladizo, za; en voladizo, [de] cantilever: *cantilever bridge*, puente

de cantilever. | Voladizo, za; en voladizo (roof). || *Cantilever spring*, ballesta (*f.*) cantilever.
— N. TECH. Viga (*f.*) voladiza. || ARCH. Ménsula, *f.*
cantle [ˈkæntl] n. Arzón (*m.*) trasero (of a saddle). || Rodaja, *f.*, raja, *f.* (slice). || Trozo, *m.* (piece).
canto [ˈkæntəu] n. Canto, *m.* (division of a poem).
canton [ˈkæntən] n. Cantón, *m.* (of Switzerland, etc.). || HERALD. Cantón, *m.*
canton [ˈkæntən] v. tr. Dividir en cantones.
canton [kənˈtu:n] v. tr. MIL. Acantonar, acuartelar (to quarter).
cantonal [ˈkæntənl] adj. Cantonal.
cantonment [kænˈtu:nmənt] n. MIL. Acantonamiento, *m.*, acuartelamiento, *m.* (of troops). | Cuartel, *m.*, campamento, *m.* (temporary quarters).
cantor [ˈkæntɔ:*] n. REL. Chantre, *m.*
canvas [ˈkænvəs] n. Lona, *f.* (fabric). || Toldo, *m.* (awning). || Tienda (*f.*) de campaña [*Amer.*, carpa, *f.*] (tent). || Cañamazo, *m.* (for embroidery). || FIG. Circo, *m.* || ARTS. Lienzo, *m.* || MAR. Velamen, *m.*, velas, *f. pl.* (sails). || — *Canvas chair*, silla (*f.*) de tijera. || *Canvas shoes*, zapatos (*m.*) de lona. || *On the canvas*, en la lona, derribado, da. || *Under canvas*, bajo lona (in tents), con velamen desplegado (ship).
canvass [ˈkænvəs] n. Campaña (*f.*) en busca de votos *or* de pedidos (soliciting for votes or orders). || Sondeo, *m.* (of public opinion).
canvass [ˈkænvəs] v. tr. Solicitar votos de (from potential supporters). || Solicitar (votes). || COMM. Buscar pedidos de (from potential clients). | Buscar clientes en (a town). || Sondear (public opinion). || Proponer (an idea). || Discutir a fondo (a subject). || U. S. Hacer el escrutinio (election returns).
— V. intr. Hacer una campaña electoral (*for*, a favor de). || Solicitar votos (*for*, a favor de). || COMM. Buscar clientes.
canvasser [—ə*] n. Agente (*m.*) electoral. || COMM. Corredor, *m.* || U. S. Escrutador, *m.*
canvassing [—iŋ] n. Campaña (*f.*) electoral.
canyon [ˈkænjən] n. Cañón, *m.*
canzonet [ˌkænzəˈnet] n. MUS. Cantinela, *f.*, cancioncilla, *f.*
caoutchouc [ˈkautʃuk] n. Caucho, *m.*
cap [kæp] n. Gorra, *f.*: *peaked cap*, gorra de visera. || Gorro, *m.*: *military*, *swimming o bathing cap*, gorro militar, de baño. || Cofia, *f.* (of waitress, maid). || Birrete, *m.* (of judge, professor). || REL. Birrete, *m.*, bonete, *m.* (of priest). | Capelo, *m.* (of cardinal). | Solideo, *m.* (of Pope). | Toca, *f.* (of nun). || Tapa, *f.* (cover). || Cápsula, *f.*, chapa, *f.* (of a bottle). || Capuchón, *m.* (of pen). || Sombrerete, *m.* (of mushroom). || Puntera, *f.* (of shoe). || GEOGR. Casquete, *m.*: *polar cap*, casquete polar. || TECH. Cofia, *f.* (of a fuse). | Caja (*f.*) protectora (of magnetic needle). | Guardapolvo, *m.*, tapa, *f.* (of watch). || MAR. Tamborete, *m.* || SP. Gorra (*f.*) entregada a cada jugador seleccionado. | Jugador (*m.*) seleccionado (player). || Pistón, *m.*, fulminante, *m.* (for children): *cap gun*, pistola de fulminantes. || ARCH. Capitel, *m.* (of column). || — *Cap and bells*, gorro (*m.*) de campanillas. || *Cap and gown*, toga (*f.*) y bonete. || FIG. *Cap in hand*, con el sombrero en la mano, humildemente. || *Cap of liberty* o *Phrygian cap*, gorro frigio. || SP. *He's got three hundred caps*, ha sido seleccionado trescientas veces. || FIG. *If the cap fits, wear it*, aplíquese el cuento; el que se pica, ajos come. | *To put on one's thinking cap*, reflexionar. | *To set one's cap at*, poner sus miras en (girl, woman).
cap [kæp] v. tr. Poner una gorra a (s.o.). || Poner cápsula *or* chapa a (a bottle). || Poner tapa a (a vessel). || TECH. Cebar (a fuse). || FIG. Coronar: *mountain capped with snow*, montaña coronada de nieve. | Poner remate a (job). | Superar (to do better than). || SP. Seleccionar (a player). || Conceder un título universitario a (in Scottish university). || — FIG. *That caps all!*, ¡es el colmo! | *To cap it all*, para colmo.
capability [ˌkeipəˈbiliti] n. Capacidad, *f.*, competencia, *f.*, aptitud, *f.* (of s.o.). || Posibilidad, *f.* (of sth.).
capable [ˈkeipəbl] adj. Capaz: *are you capable of mending the radio?*, ¿es usted capaz de arreglar la radio? || Capaz, competente: *he's a very capable person*, es una persona muy competente. || Susceptible: *apartment capable of being converted into offices*, piso susceptible de ser transformado en oficinas.
capacious [kəˈpeiʃəs] adj. Espacioso, sa; amplio, plia (room). || Grande (vessel). || Holgado, da (clothes).
capacitance [kəˈpæsitəns] n. ELECTR. Capacitancia, *f.*
capacitate [kəˈpæsiteit] v. tr. JUR. Capacitar, habilitar (to empower).
capacitor [kəˈpæsitə] n. ELECTR. Condensador, *m.*
capacity [kəˈpæsiti] n. Capacidad, *f.*, cabida, *f.*: *capacity of a vessel*, capacidad de un recipiente. || FIG. Capacidad, *f.*: *no capacity for concentration*, ninguna capacidad de concentración; *work capacity*, capacidad de trabajo. | Calidad, *f.*: *in his capacity as chairman*, en su calidad de presidente. || JUR. ELECTR. Capacidad, *f.* || AUT. Cilindrada, *f.* || — THEATR. *Capacity house*, lleno (*m.*) total. || *This room has a sitting capacity of thirty*, esta habitación tiene capacidad para treinta personas. || *To fill to capacity*, llenar completamente. || *To work to capacity*, producir a pleno rendimiento (factory).

cap-a-pie [ˌkæpəˈpi] adv. HIST. De pies a cabeza (entirely).
caparison [kəˈpærisn] n. Caparazón, *m.* (for horse). || Galas, *f. pl.* (ceremonial dress).
caparison [kəˈpærisn] v. tr. Engualdrapar (a horse). || Engalanar (s.o.).
cape [keip] n. Esclavina, *f.* (short cloak). || Capa, *f.* (cloak). || Chubasquero, *m.* (for sailors). || Impermeable (*m.*) de hule (for cyclists). || GEOGR. Cabo, *m.*, promontorio, *m.*
Cape Dutch [ˈkeip-dʌtʃ] n. Afrikaans, *m.* (language).
Cape Horn [ˈkeip-hɔ:n] pr. n. GEOGR. Cabo (*m.*) de Hornos.
capeline [ˈkæpəˌlin] n. Capellina, *f.* (hat, bandage).
Cape of Good Hope [ˈkeipəv-gud-həup] pr. n. GEOGR. Cabo (*m.*) de Buena Esperanza.
caper [ˈkeipə*] n. BOT. Alcaparro, *m.* (shrub). | Alcaparra, *f.* (bud). || Cabriola, *f.* (jump). || FIG. Travesura, *f.* (prank, antic). || — FIG. *He's up to his usual capers*, está haciendo una de las suyas. || *To cut capers*, hacer cabriolas (to caper), hacer el loco (to play the fool).
caper [ˈkeipə*] v. intr. Hacer cabriolas (animals). || Corretear, brincar (children).
capercaillie [ˌkæpəːˈkeilji] n. ZOOL. Urogallo, *m.*
Capernaum [kəˈpə:njəm] pr. n. HIST. Cafarnaúm.
Capetian [kəˈpi:ʃən] adj. HIST. De los Capetos.
— Pr. n. HIST. Capeto, *m.*
Cape Town or **Capetown** [ˈkeiptaun] pr. n. GEOGR. Ciudad (*f.*) del Cabo, El Cabo.
Cape Verde Islands [ˈkeipˈvə:dˌailəndz] pl. pr. n. GEOGR. Islas (*f.*) de Cabo Verde.
capillaceous [ˌkæpiˈleiʃəs] adj. Capilar.
capillarity [ˌkæpiˈlæriti] n. Capilaridad, *f.*
capillary [kəˈpiləri] adj. Capilar: *capillary tube*, tubo capilar.
— N. ANAT. Capilar, *m.*, vaso (*m.*) capilar.
capital [ˈkæpitəl] adj. Capital: *capital punishment*, pena capital. || Primordial, capital: *of capital importance*, de capital importancia. || COMM. De capital: *capital reserves*, reservas de capital. || FAM. Excelente, estupendo, da; magnífico, ca: *a capital entertainment*, un espectáculo magnífico. || GRAMM. Mayúscula (letter). || — *Capital assets*, activo fijo. || *Capital city*, capital, *f.* || *Capital expenditure*, inversión (*f.*) de capital. || *Capital gains*, ganancias (*f. pl.*) sobre el capital. || *Capital goods*, bienes (*m.*) de equipo. || *Capital levy*, impuesto (*m.*) sobre el capital. || *Capital ship*, acorazado, *m.* (battleship). || *Capital sin*, pecado (*m.*) capital *or* mortal. || *Capital stock*, capital social.
— N. Capital, *f.* (chief city). || GRAMM. Mayúscula, *f.* (letter). || COMM. Capital, *m.* || ARCH. Capitel, *m.* (of column). || — *Capital and labour*, capital y trabajo. || PRINT. *Small capitals*, versalitas, *f.* || FIG. *To make capital out of*, sacar provecho de, aprovechar. || COMM. *Working capital*, fondo (*m.*) de operaciones.

— OBSERV. En el sentido comercial la palabra inglesa *capital* es invariable (*investment of capital*, inversión de capitales).

capitalism [—izəm] n. Capitalismo, *m.*
capitalist [—ist] adj./n. Capitalista.
capitalistic [ˌkæpitəˈlistik] adj. Capitalista.
capitalizable [ˌkæpitəlaiˈzeibl] adj. Capitalizable.
capitalization [ˌkæpitəlaiˈzeiʃən] n. Capitalización, *f.*
capitalize [kæˈpitəlaiz] v. tr. COMM. Capitalizar. || Escribir *or* imprimir con mayúsculas.
— V. intr. *To capitalize on*, sacar provecho de, aprovechar.
capitation [ˌkæpiˈteiʃən] n. Capitación, *f.*
Capitol [ˈkæpitəl] pr. n. Capitolio, *m.*
capitular [kəˈpitjulə*] adj. Capitular.
— N. REL. Capitular, *m.* (member of a chapter). || — Pl. HIST. Capitulares, *f.*
capitulary [—ri] adj./n. See CAPITULAR.
capitulate [kəˈpitjuleit] v. intr. Capitular: *to capitulate to the enemy*, capitular ante el enemigo.
capitulation [kəˌpitjuˈleiʃən] n. Capitulación, *f.*
capitulum [kəˈpitjuləm] n. BOT. ANAT. Capítulo, *m.*

— OBSERV. El plural de *capitulum* es *capitula*.

capon [ˈkeipən] n. Capón, *m.* (castrated cock).
capotasto [ˌkæpəuˈtæstəu] n. MUS. Cejilla, *f.*, ceja, *f.*
capote [kəˈpəut] n. Capote, *m.* (a cloak with a hood).
capriccio [kəˈpritʃiəu] n. Capricho, *m.*
caprice [kəˈpri:s] n. Capricho, *m.*, antojo, *m.* (whim). || MUS. Capricho, *m.*
capricious [kəˈpriʃəs] adj. Caprichoso, sa.
Capricorn [ˈkæprikɔ:n] pr. n. ASTR. Capricornio, *m.*
caprification [kæprifiˈkeiʃən] n. Cabrahigadura, *f.*
caprifig [ˈkæprifig] n. BOT. Cabrahigo, *m.*
capriole [ˈkæpriəul] n. Cabriola, *f.*
capsicum [ˈkæpsikəm] n. Pimiento, *m.*, chile, *m.*
capsize [kæpˈsaiz] v. tr. MAR. Hacer zozobrar (a boat). || [Hacer] volcar (to turn over).
— V. intr. MAR. Zozobrar. || Volcar (to turn over).
capstan [ˈkæpstən] n. MAR. Cabrestante, *m.*
capstan lathe [—ˈleið] n. TECH. Torno (*m.*) revólver.
capstone [ˈkæpstəun] n. ARCH. Albardilla, *f.* || FIG. Coronamiento, *m.*
capsular [ˈkæpsjulə*] adj. Capsular.
capsule [ˈkæpsju:l] n. ANAT. BIOL. BOT. Cápsula, *f.* || Cápsula, *f.* (of medicine, of spacecraft, metal top).
captain [ˈkæptin] n. Capitán, *m.*: *captain of a ship*, *of a team*, capitán de un barco, de un equipo.

captain [ˈkæptin] v. tr. Capitanear.
captaincy [—si] n. Capitanía, *f.* || *Captaincy General*, capitanía general (of a viceroyship).
captainship [—ʃip] n. Capitanía, *f.*
caption [ˈkæpʃən] n. Encabezamiento, *m.*, título, *m.* (of a chapter, article). || Pie, *m.*, leyenda, *f.* (of illustration, cartoon). || CINEM. Subtítulo, *m.* || JUR. Indicación (*f.*) de origen (part of a document). | Detención, *f.* (legal arrest).
caption [ˈkæpʃən] v. tr. Titular (a chapter, article). || Poner pie a (an illustration, cartoon).
captious [ˈkæpʃəs] adj. Capcioso, sa; insidioso, sa: *a captious question*, una pregunta capciosa. || Criticón, ona; reparón, ona (critical).
captiousness [—nis] n. Capciosidad, *f.* (trickiness). || Espíritu (*m.*) crítico (critical mind).
captivate [ˈkæptiveit] v. tr. Encantar, cautivar, fascinar.
captivating [—iŋ] adj. Cautivador, ra; fascinador, ra; fascinante, encantador, ra.
captivation [kæptiˈveiʃən] n. Fascinación, *f.*, encanto, *m.* (fascination).
captivator [ˈkæptiveitə*] n. Cautivador, ra; fascinador, ra.
captive [ˈkæptiv] adj./n. Cautivo, va (imprisoned). || FIG. Cautivado, da; fascinado, da. || — *Captive balloon*, globo cautivo. || *To hold captive*, mantener cautivo (a prisoner), cautivar, fascinar (to fascinate).
captivity [kæpˈtiviti] n. Cautividad, *f.*, cautiverio, *m.*
captor [ˈkæptə*] n. Apresador, ra; capturador, ra.
capture [ˈkæptʃə*] n. Captura, *f.*, apresamiento, *m.* || MIL. Toma, *f.* (taking): *the capture of a town*, la toma de una ciudad. || Preso, sa (person captured). || Presa, *f.*, botín, *m.* (thing captured).
capture [ˈkæptʃə*] v. tr. Capturar, apresar (to take prisoner). || MIL. Tomar (a place). || FIG. Atraer, captar (s.o.'s attention, etc.). | Acaparar: *to capture a market*, acaparar un mercado. | Captarse, ganarse: *to capture s.o.'s friendship*, captarse la amistad de alguien. | Captar: *the painter captured her expression very well*, el pintor captó muy bien su expresión. | Comer (in chess).
capuchin [ˈkæpuʃin] n. Capuchón, *m.*
Capuchin [ˈkæpjuʃin] n. REL. Capuchino, *m.* (monk).
capuchin monkey [—mʌŋki] n. ZOOL. Mono (*m.*) capuchino, capuchino, *m.*
capybara [kæpiˈbærə] n. ZOOL. Capibara, *m.*, carpincho, *m.* (rodent).
car [kɑ:*] n. Coche, *m.*, automóvil, *m.* [*Amer.*, carro, *m.*]: *to travel by car*, viajar en coche. || Coche, *m.*, vagón, *m.* (of a train). || Tranvía, *m.* (tramcar). || Jaula, *f.*, cabina, *f.* (of lift). || Cabina, *f.* (of cable car, etc.). || Barquilla, *f.* (of balloon). || — *Car park*, aparcamiento, *m.* || *Car wash*, lavado (*m.*) de coches. || *Dining car*, coche restaurante, coche comedor. || *Racing car*, coche de carreras. || *Sleeping car*, coche cama.
carabao [kærəˈbau] n. ZOOL. Carabao, *m.*
caracara [ˌkærəˈkærə] n. ZOOL. Caracará, *m.*
Caracas [kəˈrækəs] pr. n. GEOGR. Caracas.
caracole [ˈkærəkəul] n. Caracoleo, *m.*
caracole [ˈkærəkəul] v. intr. Caracolear, hacer caracolas.
caracul [ˈkærəku:l] n. Caracul, *m.* (astrakhan).
carafe [kəˈræf] n. Garrafa, *f.*
caramel [ˈkærəmel] n. Caramelo, *m.* (sweet). || Pastilla (*f.*) de leche y azúcar. || Azúcar (*m.*) quemado (sugar). || Color (*m.*) de caramelo (colour).
caramelize [—aiz] v. tr. Caramelizar.
carapace [ˈkærəpeis] n. ZOOL. Caparazón, *m.*
carat [ˈkærət] n. Quilate, *m.*: *18 carat gold*, oro de 18 quilates.
caravan [ˈkærəvæn] n. Caravana, *f.* (of travellers). || Carromato, *m.* (gipsy waggon). || Remolque, *m.*, caravana, *f.* (towed by a car).
caravaneer [—ˈiə*] n. Caravanero, *m.*
caravansary [ˌkærəˈvænsəri] or **caravanserai** [ˌkærəˈvænsərai] n. Caravanseray, *m.*, caravasar, *m.*, caravanserrallo, *m.*
caravel [ˈkærəvel] n. MAR. Carabela, *f.*
caraway [ˈkærəwei] n. BOT. Alcaravea, *f.* || *Caraway seed*, carvi, *m.*
carbide [ˈkɑ:baid] n. CHEM. Carburo, *m.*
carbine [ˈkɑ:bain] n. Carabina, *f.*
carbohydrate [ˈkɑ:bəuˈhaidreit] n. CHEM. Carbohidrato, *m.*, hidrato (*m.*) de carbono.
carbolic [kɑ:ˈbɔlik] adj. CHEM. Fénico, ca.
carbon [ˈkɑ:bən] n. CHEM. Carbono, *m.*: *carbon cycle*, ciclo del carbono. || ELECTR. Carbón, *m.* (in batteries, arc lamps, etc.). || Papel (*m.*) carbón (carbon paper). || *Carbon dioxide*, bióxido *or* dióxido de carbono, anhídrido carbónico.
carbonaceous [ˌkɑ:bəˈneiʃəs] adj. Carbonoso, sa.
carbonado [ˌkɑ:bəˈneidəu] n. MIN. Carbonado, *m.*, diamante (*m.*) negro. || Carbonada, *f.* (meat, fish).
— OBSERV. El plural de la palabra inglesa es *carbonadoes* o *carbonados*.
Carbonaro [kɑ:bəˈnɑ:rəu] n. HIST. Carbonario, *m.*
— OBSERV. El plural de *Carbonaro* es *Carbonari*.
carbonatation [ˌkɑ:bəniˈteiʃən] n. CHEM. Carbonatación, *f.* (carbonation).
carbonate [ˈkɑ:bənit] n. CHEM. Carbonato, *m.*
carbonate [ˈkɑ:bəneit] v. tr. CHEM. Carbonatar.
carbonation [kɑ:bəˈneiʃən] n. CHEM. Carbonatación, *f.*
carbon copy [ˈkɑ:bənˈkɔpi] n. Copia (*f.*) hecha con papel carbón. || FIG. *He is a carbon copy of his father*, es calcado a su padre.
carbonic [kɑ:ˈbɔnik] adj. CHEM. Carbónico, ca. || CHEM. *Carbonic-acid gas*, anhídrido carbónico.
carboniferous [ˌkɑ:bəˈnifərəs] adj. Carbonífero, ra. — N. GEOL. Período (*m.*) carbonífero.
carbonization [ˌkɑ:bənaiˈzeiʃən] n. Carbonización, *f.*
carbonize [ˈkɑ:bənaiz] v. tr. Carbonizar. — V. intr. Carbonizarse.
carbon paper [ˈkɑ:bənˌpeipə*] n. Papel (*m.*) carbón.
carborundum [ˌkɑ:bəˈrʌndəm] n. Carborundo, *m.*
carboy [ˈkɑ:bɔi] n. Bombona, *f.*
carbuncle [ˈkɑ:bʌŋkl] n. Carbúnculo, *m.* (semiprecious stone). || MED. Carbunco, *m.*, carbunclo, *m.*
carburant [ˈkɑ:bjurənt] n. Carburante, *m.*
carburate [ˈkɑ:bjureit] v. tr. Carburar.
carburation [ˌkɑ:bjuˈreiʃən] n. Carburación, *f.*
carburet [ˈkɑ:bjuret] v. tr. Carburar, combinar con carbono.
carbureter or **carburetor** [—ə*] n. Carburador, *m.*
carburetion [kɑ:bjuˈreiʃən] n. Carburación, *f.*
carburetter or **carburettor** [ˈkɑ:bjuretə*] n. TECH. Carburador, *m.*
carburetting [ˈkɑ:bjuretiŋ] n. CHEM. Carburación, *f.*
carburization [ˌkɑ:bjuraiˈzeiʃən] n. Carburación (in metallurgy).
carburize [ˈkɑ:bjuˌraiz] v. tr. CHEM. Carburar.
carcass [ˈkɑ:kəs] n. Res (*f.*) muerta (dead animal). || Res (*f.*) abierta en canal (in butchery). || Esqueleto, *m.*, armazón, *m.* (of a ship, building). || Armadura, *f.* (of tyre). || FAM. Cuerpo, *m.* (human body). || FAM. *To save one's carcass*, salvar el pellejo.
carcinogen [ˈkɑ:sinədʒən] n. MED. Agente (*m.*) cancerígeno *or* carcinógeno.
carcinoma [ˌkɑ:siˈnəumə] n. MED. Carcinoma, *m.*
— OBSERV. El plural es *carcinomas* o *carcinomata*.
carcinomatous [—təs] adj. MED. Carcinomatoso, sa.
card [kɑ:d] n. Tarjeta, *f.*: *visiting card*, tarjeta de visita. || Tarjeta (*f.*) postal, postal, *f.* (postcard). || Carta, *f.*, naipe, *m.* (playing card): *to cut, to deal, to shuffle the cards*, cortar, repartir, barajar las cartas. || Ficha, *f.* (in a file). || Carnet, *m.*: *member's card*, carnet de miembro. || Cartulina, *f.* (thin cardboard). || TECH. Carda, *f.* (for carding textiles). || (Ant.). Gracioso, sa (comic person). || — Pl. Cartas, *f.*, naipes, *m.*: *to play cards*, jugar a las cartas; *game of cards*, partida de cartas. || — *Card game*, juego (*m.*) de cartas. || *Card index* o *catalogue*, fichero, *m.* || *Card table*, mesa (*f.*) de juego. || *Card trick*, truco (*m.*) de cartas. || || *Christmas card*, tarjeta de Navidad, crismas, *m.* || *Credit card*, tarjeta de crédito. || *Face* o *court card*, figura, *f.* || FIG. *Like a house of cards*, como un castillo de naipes. || *Pack of cards*, baraja, *f.* || *Punch card*, tarjeta perforada. || FAM. *Queer card*, bicho raro. || FIG. *To be on the cards*, estar previsto. | *To have a card up one's sleeve*, traer algo en la manga. | *To hold all the cards*, tener todos los triunfos en la mano. | *To lay one's cards on the table*, poner las cartas boca arriba. | *To play one's cards right*, actuar adecuadamente. | *To play one's last card*, jugarse la última carta. | *To show one's cards*, mostrar las cartas. | *To speak by the card*, hablar con seguridad. || *Wedding card*, participación (*f.*) de boda.
card [kɑ:d] v. tr. TECH. Cardar (textiles). || Poner en una tarjeta.
cardamom [ˈkɑ:dəməm] n. BOT. Cardamomo, *m.*
cardan [ˈkɑ:dæn] adj. TECH. De cardán: *cardan joint*, junta de cardán. || *Cardan shaft*, eje (*m.*) con junta de cardán.
cardboard [ˈkɑ:dbɔ:d] n. Cartón, *m.* || *Cardboard binding*, encuadernación (*f.*) en pasta.
card case [ˈkɑ:dkeis] n. Tarjetero, *m.*
carder [ˈkɑ:də*] n. TECH. Cardadora, *f.*, carda, *f.* (machine). | Cardador, ra (person).
cardia [ˈkɑ:diə] n. ANAT. Cardias, *m.* (in the stomach).
cardiac [ˈkɑ:diæk] adj./n. Cardiaco, ca; cardíaco, ca: *cardiac muscle*, músculo cardiaco.
cardigan [ˈkɑ:digən] n. Chaqueta (*f.*) de punto, rebeca, *f.*
cardinal [ˈkɑ:dinl] adj. Cardinal. || Esencial, fundamental, principal (of fundamental importance). || Purpúreo, a (deep red). || ZOOL. Purpúreo, a. || — *Cardinal number*, número (*m.*) cardinal. || *Cardinal point*, punto (*m.*) cardinal. || *Cardinal sins*, pecados (*m.*) capitales. || *Cardinal virtues*, virtudes (*f.*) cardinales.
— N. REL. Cardenal, *m.* || ZOOL. Cardenal, *m.* (bird). || Púrpura, *f.* (colour). || MATH. Cardinal, *m.*, número (*m.*) cardinal.
cardinalate [—eit] or **cardinalship** [—ʃip] n. REL. Cardenalato, *m.*
carding [ˈkɑ:diŋ] n. TECH. Cardadura, *f.*, carda, *f.* || *Carding machine*, cardadora, *f.*, carda, *f.*
cardiogram [ˈkɑ:diəgræm] n. MED. Cardiograma, *m.*
cardiograph [ˈkɑ:diəgrɑ:f] n. MED. Cardiógrafo, *m.*
cardiographic [ˌkɑ:diəˈgræfik] adj. MED. Cardiográfico, ca.
cardiography [kɑ:diˈɔgrəfi] n. MED. Cardiografía, *f.*
cardiologist [kɑ:diˈɔlədʒist] n. MED. Cardiólogo, ga.
cardiology [kɑ:diˈɔlədʒi] n. MED. Cardiología, *f.*
carditis [kɑ:ˈdaitis] n. MED. Carditis, *f.*

cardoon [kɑ:ˈdu:n] n. BOT. Cardo, *m.*
cardsharp [ˈkɑ:d,ʃɑ:p] or **cardsharper** [—ə*] n. Fullero, ra.
care [kɛə*] n. Cuidado, *m.*, atención, *f.*: *to do sth. with great care*, hacer algo con mucho cuidado. || Cuidado, *m.*: *to be in s.o.'s care*, estar al cuidado de alguien. || Asistencia, *f.*: *medical care*, asistencia médica. || Inquietud, *f.*, preocupación, *f.*: *not to have a care in the world*, no tener ninguna preocupación en la vida. || Cargo, *m.*: *this matter is in his care*, este asunto está a su cargo. || — *Care of* (*c/o*), para entregar a (on a letter): *Sr. X, c/o Sr. Y*, Sr. Y, para entregar al Sr. X. || *Handle with care*, frágil (on a parcel). || FIG. *I'll take care of him!*, ¡ya me encargaré yo de él! || *It can take care of itself*, eso se resolverá por sí mismo. || *Take care!*, ¡ojo!, ¡cuidado! || *The cares of State*, las responsabilidades del gobierno. || *To be in the care of a good doctor*, atenderle a uno un buen médico. || *To take care*, tener cuidado. || *To take care not to*, guardarse de. || *To take care of*, cuidar de (a person), guardar (an object), ocuparse de (a matter). || *To take care of o.s.*, cuidarse. || *With care!*, ¡cuidado!
care [kɛə*] v. tr. Preocuparse por: *to care what people say*, preocuparse por el qué dirán. || *I don't care what happens*, no me importa lo que pase.
— V. intr. Importarle a uno: *I don't care a damn* o *tuppence*, no me importa un bledo *or* un comino. || — *For all I care you can go ahead*, por mí lo puedes hacer. || *I couldn't care less!*, ¡me trae completamente sin cuidado!, ¡me importa un pepino! || *I don't care either way*, me da completamente igual. || FAM. *I don't care if I do*, no me disgutaría. || *The trouble is he just doesn't care*, el problema es que le trae sin cuidado. || *To care about*, interesarse por, tener interés en. || *To care for*, cuidar de (to look after): *the nursemaid cares for the children*, la niñera cuida de los niños; *a well cared-for lawn*, un césped bien cuidado; gustarle a uno (to like): *I do not care for ice cream*, no me gusta el helado; querer (to love): *he cares for her a lot*, la quiere mucho; apetecerle a uno, querer: *would you care for an ice cream?*, ¿te apetece un helado?, ¿quieres un helado? || *To care to*, querer: *would you care to try it on?*, ¿quiere usted probárselo? || FAM. *What do I care?*, y a mí ¿qué me importa? || *Would you care to give me your address?*, ¿tiene usted inconveniente en darme su dirección?
careen [kəˈri:n] n. MAR. Carena, *f.*, carenadura, *f.*
careen [kəˈri:n] v. tr. MAR. Inclinar, volcar (to turn a ship on its side). | Carenar (to clean, to repair).
— V. intr. MAR Dar de banda.
careenage [—idʒ] n. Carenero, *m.* (place). || Gastos (*m. pl.*) de carena (expenses). || Carena, *f.*, carenadura, *f.* (careen).
career [kəˈriə*] adj. De carrera: *career diplomat*, diplomático de carrera.
— N. Carrera, *f.* (swift movement): *in full career*, en plena carrera. || Carrera, *f.*: *to choose a career*, escoger una carrera. || Profesión, *f.* (profession). || Curso, *m.* (of life). || Carrera, *f.* (of stars).
career [kəˈriə*] v. intr. Correr a toda velocidad.
careerism [kəˈri:rizəm] n. Arribismo, *m.*
careerist [kəˈriərist] n. Arribista, *m.* & *f.*
carefree [ˈkɛəfri:] adj. Despreocupado, da.
careful [ˈkɛəful] adj. Cuidadoso, sa; cauteloso, sa; prudente (cautious). || Cuidadoso, sa; esmerado, da (painstaking). || Acicalado, da; esmerado, da (appearance). || Cuidado, da; esmerado, da (piece of work). || Atento, ta: *careful of the rights of others*, atento a los derechos de los demás. || — *Be careful!*, ¡ten cuidado! || *Be careful what you do*, ten cuidado con lo que haces. || *Careful!*, ¡cuidado!, ¡ojo! || *Careful with one's money*, económico, ca. || *To be careful*, tener cuidado (*of*, con). || *To be careful to*, tener cuidado en.
carefully [—i] adv. Con cuidado, cuidadosamente.
carefulness [—nis] n. Cuidado, *m.*, esmero, *m.* (attention to details). || Prudencia, *f.*, cautela, *f.* (cautiousness).
careless [ˈkɛəlis] adj. Descuidado, da; negligente (negligent). || Despreocupado, da (carefree). || Irreflexivo, va; imprudente (thoughtless). || Desaliñado, da; descuidado, da (clothes, appearance). || Hecho a la ligera *or* sin cuidado: *a careless piece of work*, un trabajo hecho a la ligera.
carelessness [—nis] n. Descuido, *m.*, negligencia, *f.* (negligence). || Desaliño, *m.* (of clothes, appearance). || Despreocupación, *f.*, indiferencia, *f.* (indifference). || *Through sheer carelessness*, por simple descuido.
caress [kəˈres] n. Caricia, *f.*
caress [kəˈres] v. tr. Acariciar.
caressing [—iŋ] adj. Acariciador, ra; acariciante.
caret [ˈkærət] n. PRINT. Signo (*m.*) de intercalación.
caretaker [ˈkɛə,teikə*] n. Vigilante, *m.*, guarda, *m.* || Portero, ra (of a block of flats). || FIG. *Caretaker government*, gobierno (*m.*) provisional.
careworn [ˈkɛəwɔ:n] adj. Agobiado por las inquietudes.
carfare [ˈkɑ:fɛə*] n. U. S. Precio (*m.*) del trayecto (public transport). | Cambio, *m.* (money).
cargo [ˈkɑ:gəu] n. MAR. Carga, *f.*, cargamento, *m.*: *mixed* o *general cargo*, carga mixta. || MAR. *Cargo boat*, buque (*m.*) de carga, carguero, *m.*
— OBSERV. El plural de *cargo* es *cargoes* o *cargos*.
car-hire firm [ˈkɑ:haiə,fə:m] n. Compañía (*f.*) de coches de alquiler.
carhop [ˈkɑ:hɔp] n. U. S. Camarero, ra [en un restaurante donde se sirve a los clientes en su coche].
Carib [ˈkærib] n. Caribe, *m.* & *f.*
Cariban [—ən] n. Caribe, *m.* (language).
Caribbean [,kæriˈbiən] adj. Caribe. || — GEOGR. *Caribbean Islands*, Islas (*f.*) del Caribe, Antillas, *f.* | *Caribbean Sea*, Mar (*m.*) Caribe.
caribou [ˈkæribu:] n. ZOOL. Caribú, *m.*
caricatural [,kærikəˈtjuərəl] adj. Caricaturesco, ca; caricatural.
caricature [,kærikəˈtjuə*] n. Caricatura, *f.*
caricature [,kærikəˈtjuə*] v. tr. Caricaturizar.
caricaturist [,kærikəˈtjuərist] n. Caricaturista, *m.* & *f.*
caries [ˈkɛərii:z] inv. n. MED. Caries, *f.*
carillon [ˈkæriljən] n. Carillón, *m.* (bells and sound).
carillon [ˈkæriljən] v. intr. Repicar, repiquetear.
cariole [ˈkæriəul] n. U. S. See CARRIOLE.
carious [ˈkɛəriəs] adj. MED. Cariado, da.
carking [ˈkɑ:kiŋ] adj. Atormentador, ra (burdensome).
Carlism [ˈkɑ:lizəm] pr. n. Carlismo, *m.*
Carlist [ˈkɑ:list] adj./n. Carlista: *Carlist Wars*, guerras carlistas.
carload [ˈkɑ:ləud] n. U. S. Carga (*f.*) de un carro (load of a freight car). | Carga (*f.*) mínima que se beneficia de una tarifa reducida (minimum weight).
Carlovingian [,kɑ:ləuˈvindʒiən] adj./n. Carlovingio, gia; carolingio, gia.
carmagnole [ˈkɑ:mənjəul] n. Carmañola, *f.*
Carmel [ˈkɑ:məl] pr. n. Carmelo, *m.* (in Palestine).
Carmelite [ˈkɑ:milait] adj./n. REL. Carmelita.
carminative [ˈkɑ:minətiv] adj. MED. Carminativo, va.
— N. MED. Carminativo, *m.*
carmine [ˈkɑ:main] adj. Carmín, *inv.*
— N. Carmín, *m.*
carnage [ˈkɑ:nidʒ] n. Carnicería, *f.*, matanza, *f.* (great bloodshed).
carnal [ˈkɑ:nl] adj. Carnal. || *Carnal knowledge*, ayuntamiento (*m.*) carnal.
carnality [kɑ:ˈnæliti] n. Sensualidad, *f.*
carnation [kɑ:ˈneiʃən] n. BOT. Clavel, *m.* (flower).
carnelian [kəˈni:ljən] n. MIN. Cornalina, *f.*
carnival [ˈkɑ:nivəl] n. Carnaval, *m.* || U. S. Feria, *f.*, verbena, *f.* (travelling amusements).
carnivore [ˈkɑ:nivɔ:*] n. Carnívoro, ra.
carnivorous [kɑ:ˈnivərəs] adj. Carnívoro, ra.
carob [ˈkærəb] n. BOT. Algarrobo, *m.* (tree). || BOT. *Carob bean*, algarroba, *f.* (fruit).
carol [ˈkærəl] n. Villancico, *m.* (Christmas hymn). || Canto, *m.* (of birds).
carol [ˈkærəl] v. intr. Cantar villancicos. || Cantar (birds).
— V. tr. Cantar.
Caroline [ˈkærəlain] adj. HIST. Carolino, na. || GEOGR. *Caroline Islands*, Islas Carolinas.
Carolingian [,kærəˈlindʒjən] adj./n. HIST. Carolingio, gia; Carlovingio, gia.
carom [ˈkærəm] n. U. S. Carambola, *f.* (in billiards).
carotene [ˈkærəti:n] n. CHEM. Caroteno, *m.*
carotid [kəˈrɔtid] adj. ANAT. Carótida (artery).
— N. ANAT. Carótida, *f.*
carotin [ˈkærətin] n. CHEM. Caroteno, *m.*
carousal [kəˈrauzəl] or **carouse** [kəˈrauz] n. Juerga, *f.*, jarana, *f.*
carouse [kəˈrauz] v. intr. Estar de juerga *or* de jarana, correrse una juerga, juerguearse.
carousel [,kæru:ˈzəl] n. See CARROUSEL.
carouser [kəˈrauzə*] n. Juerguista, *m.* & *f.*
carp [kɑ:p] n. ZOOL. Carpa, *f.* (fish).
carp [kɑ:p] v. intr. Quejarse (to complain). || *To carp at*, criticar.
carpal [ˈkɑ:pəl] adj. ANAT. Carpiano, na.
— N. ANAT. Carpo, *m.* (bone).
Carpathian Mountains [kɑ:ˈpeiθjənˈmauntinz] pl. pr. n. GEOGR. Cárpatos, *m.*
carpel [ˈkɑ:pel] n. BOT. Carpelo, *m.*
carpenter [ˈkɑ:pintə*] n. Carpintero, *m.* || — ZOOL. *Carpenter ant, bee, moth*, hormiga, abeja, polilla carpintera. || *Carpenter's horse*, caballete, *m.*
carpentry [ˈkɑ:pintri] n. Carpintería, *f.*
carpet [ˈkɑ:pit] n. Alfombra, *f.* || Moqueta, *f.* (fitted). — *Carpet beetle*, insecto (*m.*) que ataca las alfombras. || *Carpet slippers*, zapatillas, *f.* || *Carpet sweeper*, escoba mecánica. || FIG. *To be on the carpet*, estar sobre el tapete (to be under discussion), estar recibiendo una regañina *or* un rapapolvo (to be reprimanded). | *To roll out the red carpet for s.o.*, recibir a alguien con todos los honores.
carpet [ˈkɑ:pit] v. tr. Alfombrar. || Poner moqueta en (fitted carpet). || FIG. Echar un rapapolvo a (to scold).
carpetbag [ˈkɑ:pitbæg] n. HIST. Bolsa (*f.*) de viaje [hecha de tejido de alfombra].
carpetbagger [ˈkɑ:pit,bægə*] n. U. S. HIST. Politicastro (*m.*) del norte de Estados Unidos que intentaba triunfar en el Sur (politician). || Aventurero, *m.*, estafador, *m.* (adventurer).
carpeting [ˈkɑ:pitiŋ] n. Alfombrado, *m.* (carpets). || Moqueta, *f.* (fitted). || Tejido (*m.*) para alfombras (carpet fabric).
carpi [ˈkɑ:pai] pl. n. See CARPUS.

carping [ˈkɑːpiŋ] adj. Criticón, ona.
carpological [kɑːpəˈlɔdʒikəl] adj. Bot. Carpológico, ca.
carpology [kɑːˈpɔlədʒi] n. Bot. Carpología, *f.*
carport [ˈkɑːpɔːt] n. Cobertizo (*m.*) para guardar el coche.
carpus [ˈkɑːpəs] n. Anat. Carpo, *m.*
— Observ. El plural de *carpus* es *carpi.*
carriage [ˈkæridʒ] n. Carruaje, *m.*, coche, *m.*: *carriage and pair*, coche de dos caballos. || Carroza, *f.*: *the Queen's carriage*, la carroza de la Reina. || Vagón, *m.*, coche, *m.* (railway). || Andares, *m. pl.*, manera (*f.*) de andar, porte, *m.* (manner of holding o.s.). || Comportamiento, *m.*, conducta, *f.* (behaviour). || Manejo, *m.*, dirección, *f.* (of a business). || Transporte, *m.*, porte, *m.* (of goods). || Mil. Cureña, *f.* (of gun). || Tech. Carro, *m.* (of typewriter, etc.). || — *Carriage builder*, carrocero, *m.* || *Carriage entrance*, entrada (*f.*) de carruajes, puerta cochera. || Comm. *Carriage free, carriage paid*, franco de porte, porte pagado.
carriageable [—əbl] adj. Transitable, abierto al tránsito rodado.
carriageway [ˈkæridʒwei] n. Aut. Calzada, *f.* || *Dual carriageway*, carretera (*f.*) de doble calzada.
carrier [ˈkæriə*] n. Transportista, *m.* (person). || Empresa (*f.*) de transportes (company). || Mensajero, ra (messenger). || Portaequipajes, *m. inv.* (on a bicycle). || Aviat. Transportista, *m.* || Med. Portador, ra (of a disease). || Mil. Portaaviones, *m. inv.* (aircraft carrier). || — *Carrier bag*, bolsa *f.* || *Carrier pigeon*, paloma mensajera. || Rad. *Carrier wave*, onda portadora.
carriole [ˈkæriəul] n. Carruaje (*m.*) ligero para una persona.
carrion [ˈkæriən] n. Carroña, *f.* || Zool. *Carrion crow*, corneja, *f.* (bird).
carrot [ˈkærət] n. Bot. Zanahoria, *f.*
carrotene or **carrotin** [—iːn] n. Chem. Caroteno, *m.*
carroty [—i] adj. Color (*m.*) zanahoria: *a carroty dress*, un traje color zanahoria. || Rojo, ja; rojizo, za (hair). || Pelirrojo, ja (red-haired).
carrousel [ˌkæruːˈzel] n. Carrusel, *m.* || Tiovivo, *m.*, caballitos, *m. pl.* (merry-go-round). || Torneo, *m.*, carrusel, *m.* (tournament).
carry [ˈkæri] n. Alcance, *m.* (of a weapon). || Transporte (*m.*) entre dos vías navegables (portage). || Sp. Trayecto, *m.* (of a golf ball).
carry [ˈkæri] v. tr. Llevar (to convey): *to carry a parcel under one's arm*, llevar un paquete bajo el brazo. || Traer (to bring). || Llevar, transportar (a load): *a lorry carrying logs*, un camión que transporta troncos; *a car which carries five persons*, un coche que lleva cinco personas. || Llevar, conducir (a liquid): *these pipes carry oil*, estas tuberías llevan petróleo. || Llevar, tener consigo (on one's person): *I never carry my passport*, nunca llevo el pasaporte. || Sostener (to support): *flyover carried on concrete piles*, paso elevado sostenido por pilotes de hormigón. || Prolongar, extender (to prolong): *the wall is carried to the end of the street*, el muro se extiende hasta el final de la calle. || Tener (on a list). || Fig. Tener, gozar (to enjoy): *he carries no authority*, no tiene ninguna autoridad. | Llevar consigo, entrañar, implicar (to be accompanied by): *a job which carries great responsibility*, un cargo que lleva consigo mucha responsabilidad. | Acarrear (to give rise to): *an act which will carry serious consequences*, una acción que acarreará serias consecuencias. | Tener (meaning). | Retener (in the mind). | Sufrir, aguantar, soportar (grief, etc.). || Hacer aprobar (to get the approval of). || Aprobar (to approve): *carried unanimously*, aprobado por unanimidad. || Llevar: *a number which carries a prize*, un número que lleva premio. || Ganar (to win): *her husband carried the election*, su marido ganó las elecciones. || Salvar (an obstacle). || Ganarse, captarse (to capture): *an outstanding performance which carried the audience*, una interpretación extraordinaria que se captó al público. || Llevar (to hold): *she carries her head well*, lleva la cabeza con garbo. || Comm. Tener en existencia (to have in stock). | Producir (interest, crop). || Mil. Conquistar, tomar (a position). | Ganar (a war). || Mar. Llevar puesto (sail). || Rastrear, seguir (hunting). || Math. Llevarse (in addition): *two down, carry one*, pongo dos y me llevo uno. || U. S. Cantar afinado (a tune). || — *To carry a child*, estar embarazada. || *To carry all before one*, ir arrollándolo todo, tener un éxito arrollador. || *To carry a person with one*, convencer a alguien. || *To carry conviction*, ser convincente. || *To carry insurance*, estar asegurado. || Fig. *To carry one's head high*, llevar la cabeza alta. || *To carry o.s.*, portarse, conducirse. || *To carry o.s. well*, andar con garbo. || Fig. *To carry sth. too far*, llevar algo demasiado lejos. | *To carry the day*, triunfar, salir bien. | *To have had as much as one can carry*, haber bebido todo lo que se puede beber.
— V. intr. Alcanzar, llegar, tener alcance: *this rifle carries half a mile*, este fusil tiene un alcance de media milla. || Llegar, oírse: *a sound which carries a long way*, un sonido que llega muy lejos *or* que se oye desde muy lejos. || Tener efecto (to be effective). || Ser aprobado (a law, a project, etc.).
— ***To carry about***, llevar consigo (to have on one). | Llevar de un lado para otro. || ***To carry along***, arrastrar: *he was carried along with the wreckage of his boat*, fue arrastrado con los restos del barco. | Llevar. || ***To carry away***, llevarse (sth.). | Entusiasmar, exaltar (emotionally): *don't get carried away*, no te exaltes. | Arrebatar (passion). | Arrancar, arrebatar: *the masts were carried away by the storm*, los mástiles fueron arrancados por la tormenta. || ***To carry back***, devolver (to return). | Recordar (to remind). || ***To carry down***, bajar. || ***To carry forward***, pasar a la página *or* a la columna siguiente (bookkeeping). | — *Carried forward*, suma y sigue. || ***To carry into***, llevar. | — *To carry into effect*, llevar a cabo, realizar. || ***To carry off***, llevarse (to take away): *to carry off a prize, a prisoner*, llevarse un premio, a un preso. | Ganar (an election). | Matar (to cause the death of). | Realizar, llevar a cabo (a plan). | Salir airoso de, salir bien de (difficult situation). || ***To carry on***, seguir, continuar (to continue). | Mantener (to hold): *to carry on a conversation*, mantener una conversación. | Ejercer (a profession). | Dirigir, llevar adelante (a business). | Insistir (to insist). | Reñir, discutir (to argue). | Hacer una escena (to make a scene). | Comportarse (to behave). | Fam. Tener una aventura. | — *Carry on!*, ¡siga! | *To carry on somehow*, ir tirando. | Fam. *You do carry on!*, ¡dale que dale! || ***To carry out***, realizar, llevar a cabo (a plan). | Hacer, llevar a cabo (repairs, test). | Cumplir (a promise, threat). || ***To carry over***, llevar a la columna *or* a la página siguiente (bookkeeping). | Conservarse (to survive): *customs which have carried over from the last century*, costumbres que se han conservado desde el siglo pasado. | Llevar al otro lado (to transfer). | Guardar (to hold over). | Convencer (a person). || ***To carry through***, llevar a cabo (a course of action). | Ayudar [a salir de un mal paso] (s.o.). || ***To carry up***, subir.
carryall [ˈkæriɔːl] n. Bolsa, *f.* (bag). || U. S. Carruaje (*m.*) cubierto y tirado por un solo caballo.
carrycot [ˈkærikɔt] n. Cuna (*f.*) portátil.
carry-on [ˈkæriˈɔn] n. Fam. Lío, *m.*, jaleo, *m.* (fuss). | Pelea, *f.* (quarrel).
carry-over [ˈkæriˈəuvə*] n. Comm. Suma (*f.*) *or* saldo (*m.*) anterior (in bookkeeping). || Remanente, *m.* (remainder).
carsick [ˈkɑːsik] adj. Mareado, da. || *I get carsick*, me mareo en coche.
carsickness [—nis] n. Mareo, *m.*
cart [kɑːt] n. Carro, *m.* (drawn by horses). || Carreta, *f.* (drawn by oxen). || Carretilla, *f.*, carro (*m.*) de mano (handcart). || Carromato, *m.* (covered). || Cochecito, *m.*, carrito, *m.* (child's). || Mesa (*f.*) de ruedas, carrito, *m.* (trolley for tea, etc.). || Carrito, *m.* (supermarket trolley). || — *Cart horse*, caballo (*m.*) de tiro. || *Cart rut* o *track*, carril, *m.*, rodada, *f.* || Fig. *To be on the cart*, estar en un aprieto. | Fig. *To put the cart before the horse*, empezar la casa por el tejado.
cart [kɑːt] v. tr. Acarrear, carretear (to convey by cart). || Fig. Fam. Llevar: *the demonstrators were carted off to the police station*, los manifestantes fueron llevados a la comisaría. || Fam. *To cart about*, llevar.
cartage [ˈkɑːtidʒ] n. Acarreo, *m.*, porte, *m.*
carte [kɑːt] n. Cuarta, *f.* (fencing). || — *A la carte*, a la carta (in restaurant). || Fig. *Carte blanche*, carta blanca.
cartel [kɑːˈtel] n. Comm. Cártel, *m.*
carter [ˈkɑːtə*] n. Carretero, *m.* (cart driver). || Transportista, *m.* (carrier).
Cartesian [kɑːˈtiːzjən] adj./n. Cartesiano, na.
Cartesianism [kɑːˈtiːzjənizəm] n. Cartesianismo, *m.*
Carthage [ˈkɑːθidʒ] pr. n. Hist. Cartago.
Carthaginian [ˌkɑːθəˈdʒiniən] adj./n. Hist. Cartaginés, esa; cartaginense. || *Carthaginian wars*, Guerras Púnicas.
Carthusian [kɑːˈθjuːzjən] adj./n. Rel. Cartujo, *m.*
cartilage [ˈkɑːtilidʒ] n. Anat. Cartílago, *m.*
cartilaginoid [ˌkɑːtiˈlædʒinɔid] adj. Cartilaginoso, sa; cartilagíneo, a.
cartilaginous [ˌkɑːtiˈlædʒinəs] adj. Cartilaginoso, sa.
cartload [ˈkɑːtləud] n. Carretada, *f.*: *by cartloads*, a carretadas.
cartogram [ˈkɑːtəgræm] n. Cartograma, *m.*
cartographer [kɑːˈtɔgrəfə*] n. Cartógrafo, fa.
cartographic [kɑːtəˈgræfik] or **cartographical** [—əl] adj. Cartográfico, ca.
cartography [kɑːˈtɔgrəfi] n. Cartografía, *f.*
cartomancy [ˈkɑːtəumænsi] n. Cartomancia, *f.*, cartomancía, *f.*
carton [ˈkɑːtən] n. Caja (*f.*) de cartón (cardboard box). || Cartón, *m.* (of cigarettes). || Diana, *f.* (of a target).
cartoon [kɑːˈtuːn] n. Caricatura, *f.* (caricature). || Chiste, *m.* (illustrated joke). || Arts. Cartón, *m.* (preliminary sketch). || Tira (*f.*) humorística, historieta, *f.* (comic strip). || Dibujos (*m. pl.*) animados (film).
cartoonist [—ist] n. Caricaturista, *m.* & *f.* (caricaturist). || Humorista, *m.* & *f.*, dibujante, *m.* & *f.* (s.o. who draws cartoons). || Realizador (*m.*) de dibujos animados (of films).
cartouche [kɑːˈtuːʃ] n. Arch. Tarjeta, *f.*
cartridge [ˈkɑːtridʒ] n. Cartucho, *m.* (in firearms): *blank cartridge*, cartucho sin bala *or* de fogueo. || Phot. Cartucho, *m.* || Recambio, *m.* (for pen). || — *Cartridge belt*, cartuchera, *f.*, canana, *f.* (round the waist), cinta, *f.* (of a machinegun). || *Cartridge clip*, cargador, *m.*, peine, *m.* (holder for cartridges).

cartulary [ˈkɑ:tjuləri] n. Cartulario, *m.*

cartwheel [ˈkɑ:twi:l] n. Rueda (*f.*) de carro (wheel of a cart). || FIG. Voltereta (*f.*) lateral [sobre pies y manos] (somersault). || FAM. Moneda (*f.*) de un dólar.

cartwright [ˈkɑ:trait] n. Carretero, *m.*

caruncle [ˈkærəŋkl] n. ZOOL. BOT. Carúncula, *f.* (excrescence, outgrowth).

carve [kɑ:v] v. tr./intr. Cortar (to cut). || Tallar, esculpir, cincelar (in stone, wood). || Grabar (on a tree). || CULIN. Trinchar (meat): *to carve the chicken*, trinchar el pollo. || — FIG. *To carve one's way through*, abrirse camino entre. || *To carve out*, tallar, esculpir: *to carve out a sculpture*, tallar una escultura; labrar, hacer (by effort): *to carve out a future*, labrarse un porvenir; separar (to separate from), adueñarse de (to take over). || *To carve up*, dividir (to divide), cortar (to cut up), acuchillar (to stab).

— V. intr. Esculpir. || CULIN. Trinchar carne.

carvel [ˈkɑ:vəl] n. MAR. Carabela, *f.*

carver [ˈkɑ:və*] n. Escultor, ra; tallista, *m.* & *f.* (person who carves). || CULIN. Cuchillo (*m.*) de trinchar, trinchante, *m.* (knife). || — Pl. CULIN. Cubierto (*m. sing.*) de trinchar.

carving [ˈkɑ:viŋ] n. Talla, *f.*, escultura, *f.* (sculpture). || CULIN. Arte (*m.*) cisoria (ability of carving). || *Carving knife*, cuchillo (*m.*) de trinchar, trinchante, *m.*

caryatid [ˌkæriˈætid] n. Cariátide, *f.*

— OBSERV. El plural de *caryatid* es *caryatids* o *caryatides.*

caryopsis [ˌkæriˈɔpsis] n. BOT. Cariópside, *f.*

cascade [kæsˈkeid] adj. Escalonado, da; en cascada. — N. Cascada, *f.*, salto (*m.*) de agua. || FIG. Chorro *m.*, torrente, *m.*

cascade [kæsˈkeid] v. intr. Caer en forma de cascada.

cascarilla [ˌkæskəˈrilə] n. Cascarillo, *m.* (tree).

case [keis] n. Caja, *f.* (box and its contents). || Estuche, *m.* (rigid; for spectacles, instruments, scissors, knives, etc.). || Funda, *f.* (soft; for pistol, guitar, etc.). || Maleta, *f.* (suitcase). || Caja, *f.* (of watch). || MUS. Caja, *f.* (of piano). || TECH. Camisa, *f.* || Vitrina, *f.* (showcase). || Bastidor, *m.*, marco, *m.* (of a door, window). || Pasta, *f.* (bookbinding). || PRINT. Caja, *f.* (where type is kept): *lower*, *upper case*, caja baja, alta. || Caso, *m.*: *in that case*, en ese caso; *in most cases*, en la mayoría de los casos; *that is not my case*, ése no es mi caso. || Asunto, *m.*, caso, *m.*: *the police is working on a drug-smuggling case*, la policía está investigando en un asunto de contrabando de drogas. || MED. Caso, *m.*: *a case of tonsillitis*, un caso de amigdalitis. || Motivo, *m.* (motive). || FAM. Caso, *m.* (strange person). || JUR. Causa, *f.*, pleito, *m.*, proceso, *m.* || GRAMM. Caso, *m.* || — *As the case may be*, según el caso. || MED. *Case history*, historial clínico, historia clínica. || *Case law*, precedentes, *m. pl.*, jurisprudencia, *f.* || *Case of conscience*, caso de conciencia. || *He is a case!*, ¡es un caso! || *If such is the case*, si ése es el caso. || *In any case*, en todo caso, en cualquier caso, de todas formas. || *In case*, en caso de que, por si acaso. || *In case of*, en caso de. || *In no case*, de ningún modo. || *In such a case*, en un caso así, en tal caso. || *In the case of*, en cuanto a, en lo que se refiere a. || *It's not a case of*, no se trata de. || *It's not the case*, ése no es el caso. || *Just in case*, por si acaso, por si las moscas. || *That alters the case*, eso cambia la cosa. || *That being the case*, si ése es el caso. || JUR. *The case for the defence*, la defensa. | *The case for the prosecution*, la acusación. || *The case in point*, el asunto de que se trata. || JUR. *To bring a case against*, poner un pleito a. | *To get up a case*, instruir un caso. || FIG. *To have a good* o *a strong case*, tener argumentos fuertes *or* convincentes. | *To make out one's case*, demostrar su punto de vista. | *To put forward a good case*, presentar argumentos convincentes. | *To put* o *to state one's case*, presentar sus argumentos, exponer su caso. || JUR. *To rest one's case*, terminar su alegato. | *To state the case*, exponer los hechos.

case [keis] v. tr. Embalar, encajonar. || Poner en un estuche. || Enfundar (to sheathe). || TECH. Revestir. || U. S. FAM. *To case the joint*, reconocer el terreno.

casebook [—buk] n. JUR. Repertorio (*m.*) de jurisprudencia. || MED. Registro (*m.*) que contiene las historias clínicas de los enfermos.

case harden [—hɑ:dn] v. tr. TECH. Cementar. || FIG. Insensibilizar, endurecer.

case-hardened [—hɑ:dnd] adj. FIG. Insensible.

casein [ˈkeisi:in] n. CHEM. Caseína, *f.*

casemate [ˈkeismeit] n. MIL. Casamata, *f.*

casement [ˈkeismənt] n. Marco, *m.* (of a window). || Ventana (*f.*) de bisagras (hinged window).

caseous [ˈkeisjəs] adj. Caseoso, sa.

casette [kaˈset] n. See CASSETTE.

casework [ˈkeiswə:k] n. Estudio (*m.*) de los antecedentes personales *or* familiares.

caseworker [—ə*] n. Asistente (*m.*) social, asistenta (*f.*) social.

cash [kæʃ] n. Dinero (*m.*) contante *or* efectivo, metálico, *m.* (ready money): *to convert into cash*, convertir en dinero efectivo. || COMM. Pago (*m.*) al contado. | Caja, *f.* || — COMM. *Cash account*, cuenta (*f.*) de caja. | *Cash book*, libro (*m.*) de caja. | *Cash discount*, descuento (*m.*) por pago al contado. | *Cash down*, al contado. | *Cash flow*, "cash flow", *m.*, corriente (*f.*) en efectivo, movimientos (*m. pl.*) de efectivos. | *Cash in hand* o *on hand*, efectivo (*m.*) en caja, metálico (*m.*) *or* líquido (*m.*) disponible. | *Cash on delivery*, envío (*m.*) *or* entrega (*f.*) contra reembolso. | *Cash payment*, pago (*m.*) al contado. | *Cash price*, precio (*m.*) al contado. | *Cash prize*, premio (*m.*) en metálico. | *Cash register*, caja registradora. | *Cash value*, valor efectivo. | *For cash*, al contado. | *Hard cash*, dinero contante y sonante. | *In cash*, en metálico. | *Petty cash*, dinero para gastos menores. || FAM. *To be out of cash*, estar sin una gorda, estar sin blanca. || *To pay cash for sth.*, pagar algo al contado.

cash [kæʃ] v. tr. Cobrar en efectivo. || Cobrar, hacer efectivo (a cheque). || FIG. *To cash in on*, sacar provecho de.

cash-and-carry [—ænd-ˈkæri] adj. *Cash-and-carry system*, sistema (*m.*) de pago al contado sin entrega a domicilio.

cashbox [—bɔks] n. Caja, *f.*

cashdesk [—desk] n. Caja, *f.*

cashew [kæˈʃu:] n. BOT. Anacardo, *m.* || *Cashew nut*, anacardo, *m.*

cashier [kæˈʃiə*] n. Cajero, ra.

cashier [kæˈʃiə*] v. tr. Destituir (to dismiss). || Despedir (to fire). || MIL. Dar de baja. || FIG. Eliminar.

cashmere [kæʃˈmiə*] n. Cachemira, *f.* (fabric).

Cashmere [kæʃˈmiə*] pr. n. GEOGR. Cachemira, *f.*

cashoo [kæˈʃu] n. Cato, *m.*

casing [ˈkeisiŋ] n. Cubierta, *f.*, envoltura, *f.* (for wrapping). || Funda, *f.* || Estuche, *m.* (case). || Bastidor, *m.*, marco, *m.* (of a door, window). || Revoque, *m.* (of a wall). || Cubierta, *f.* (of a tyre). || MIN. Encofrado, *m.*, entibación, *f.* || Camisa, *f.* (of a cylinder). || Revestimiento, *m.* (of boilers, etc.). || Jareta, *f.* (in sewing).

casino [kəˈsi:nəu] n. Casino, *m.*

cask [kɑ:sk] n. Barril, *m.*, tonel, *m.*

cask [kɑ:sk] v. tr. Entonelar, embarrilar.

casket [—it] n. Cofre, *m.*, joyero, *m.* (for holding jewels, etc.). || Urna, *f.* (for the ashes of a cremated person). || U. S. Ataúd, *m.* (coffin).

Caspian Sea [ˈkæspiənˈsi:] pr. n. GEOGR. Mar (*m.*) Caspio.

casque [kæsk] n. HIST. Yelmo, *m.* (helmet).

Cassandra [kəˈsændrə] pr. n. Casandra, *f.*

cassation [kæˈseiʃən] n. JUR. Casación, *f.*

cassava [kəˈsɑ:və] n. BOT. Mandioca, *f.*, yuca, *f.* (plant). || Mandioca, *f.* (flour). || Cazabe, *m.* (bread).

casserole [ˈkæsərəul] n. Cacerola, *f.* (container). || CULIN. Cazuela, *f.* (cooked food).

cassette [ˈkəˈset] n. PHOT. Cartucho, *m.* || "Cassette", *f.* (tape recording).

cassia [ˈkæsiə] n. BOT. Casia, *f.*

Cassiopeia [ˌkæsiəˈpi:ə] pr. n. MYTH. ASTR. Casiopea, *f.*

cassiterite [kəˈsitərait] n. MIN. Casiterita, *f.*

Cassius [ˈkæsiəs] pr. n. Casio, *m.*

cassock [ˈkæsək] n. Sotana, *f.*

cassowary [ˈkæsəwɛəri] n. Casuario, *m.* (bird).

cast [kɑ:st] n. Lanzamiento, *m.* (throw). || Distancia, *f.*, alcance, *m.* (range). || Apariencia, *f.*, aspecto, *m.* (appearance). || Matiz, *m.*, tinte, *m.*, toque, *m.* (of colour). || Naturaleza, *f.*, carácter, *m.* (kind). || Disposición, *f.* (of mind). || Tirada, *f.*, jugada, *f.* (of dice). || Número (*m.*) que sale al tirar los dados (number thrown). || Caída, *f.* (of drapery). || Cálculo, *m.* (calculation). || THEATR. CINEM. Reparto, *m.* || TECH. Molde, *m.*, forma, *f.* (where metal is poured). | Pieza (*f.*) fundida (moulded product). || MATH. Suma, *f.* (addition). || ZOOL. Regurgitación, *f.* (made by birds of prey). | Piel, *f.* (of reptile). || MED. Ligero estrabismo, *m.* (slight squint). | Escayola, *f.* (for immobilizing a broken limb). || — *Cast of features*, facciones, *f. pl.* || *Cast of mind*, mentalidad, *f.*, temperamento, *m.*

cast* [kɑ:st] v. tr. Tirar, arrojar, lanzar (to throw). || Tirar (dice). || Proyectar (shadow). || Cambiar, mudar: *the snake casts its skin*, la serpiente cambia la piel. || Emitir (a vote): *not many votes were cast in his favour*, no fueron emitidos muchos votos a favor suyo. || Dar: *I cast my vote for you*, le doy mi voto. || Descartarse de (cards). || Echar (a look): *to cast a glance*, echar una ojeada. || Echar (the blame on s.o.). || Sumar (to add up). || Calcular. || Vaciar (molten metal, plaster). || Fundir (metals). || Arrojar, echar (in fishing): *he cast the line into the water*, arrojó el sedal al agua. || Parir antes de tiempo (cow). || THEATR. Hacer el reparto de: *to cast a play*, hacer el reparto de una obra. | Adjudicar el papel de, dar el papel de, asignar el papel de (to assign): *he was casted as Othello*, le fue asignado el papel de Otelo. || Hacer (a horoscope). || PRINT. Estereotipar. || MAR. Hacer virar (a boat). || Combar, alabear (a beam, etc.). || — *The die is cast*, la suerte está echada. || MAR. *To cast anchor*, echar el ancla, anclar, fondear. || *To cast an eye at sth.*, echar una mirada *or* un vistazo *or* una ojeada a algo. || *To cast a shoe*, desherrarse (a horse). || *To cast a spell on*, hechizar. || *To cast doubt upon*, poner en duda. || *To cast feathers*, pelechar. || *To cast into prison*, meter en la cárcel. || FIG. *To cast light on*, aclarar, arrojar luz sobre. || *To cast loose*, soltar. || *To cast lots for*, sortear, echar a suertes. || *To cast one's cares upon*, hacer partícipe de sus preocupaciones. || *To cast one's eyes on s.o.*, mirar a alguien. || *To cast the evil eye on*, hechizar, aojar.

— V. intr. Volver, virar (to tack). || Echar el sedal (fishing). || Echar los dados (to throw dice). || Vomitar,

devolver (to vomit). || Combarse, alabearse (a beam). || MATH. Sumar (to add up). || *To cast loose*, soltar las amarras.
— ***To cast about for***, buscar (to look for). || ***To cast aside* o *away***, desechar, descartar (to discard). | Abandonar (to abandon). | — *To be cast away*, naufragar. || ***To cast down***, bajar: *to cast one's eyes down*, bajar los ojos. | Desanimar, abatir (to depress). | Derribar. || ***To cast forth***, despedir. || ***To cast off***, abandonar (to abandon). | Deshacerse de (a burden). | Desechar (old clothes). | Cerrar (in knitting). | Desamarrar, soltar (a ship). || ***To cast on***, echar los puntos (in knitting). || ***To cast out***, echar, arrojar (to expel). | — *To cast out devils*, exorcizar a los demonios. || ***To cast up***, vomitar (to vomit). | Levantar: *to cast one's eyes up*, levantar los ojos. | Sumar (an account).

— OBSERV. Pret. & p. p. ***cast***.

castanet [ˌkæstəˈnet] n. MUS. Castañuela, *f.*
castaway [ˈkɑːstəwei] adj./n. Náufrago, ga (shipwrecked). || Paria (outcast).
caste [kɑːst] n. Casta, *f.* || FIG. *To lose caste*, perder categoría.
castellated [ˈkæsteleitid] adj. Almenado, da (with battlements). || Encastillado, da (like a castle).
caster [ˈkɑːstə*] n. TECH. Vaciador, *m.* || See CASTOR.
castigate [ˈkæstigeit] v. tr. Reprobar, censurar (to rebuke). || Castigar (to punish).
castigation [ˌkæstiˈgeiʃən] n. Castigo, *m.* (punishment). || Reprobación, *f.*, censura, *f.* (rebuke).
castigator [ˈkæstigeitə*] n. Castigador, ra.
Castile [kæsˈtiːl] pr. n. GEOGR. Castilla, *f.*
Castilian [kæsˈtiliən] adj./n. Castellano, na (people). || Castellano, *m.* (language).
casting [ˈkɑːstiŋ] n. Pieza (*f.*) fundida. || TECH. Vaciado, *m.*, colada, *f.*: *casting bed*, lecho de colada. || THEATR. Reparto, *m.* || Piel, *f.* (of a reptile). || Plumas, *f. pl.* (of a bird).
casting net [—net] n. MAR. Esparavel, *m.*
casting vote [—ˈvəut] n. Voto (*m.*) de calidad.
cast iron [ˈkɑːstˈaiən] n. Hierro (*m.*) colado, arrabio, *m.*, fundición, *f.*
cast-iron [ˈkɑːstˈaiən] adj. FIG. Inquebrantable, férreo, a (will). | Irrefutable (argument). | Irrebatible.
castle [ˈkɑːsl] n. Castillo, *m.* || Torre, *f.* (in chess). || — FIG. *An Englishman's home is his castle*, cada uno es rey en su casa. | *Castles in Spain* o *in the air*, castillos en el aire.
castle [ˈkɑːsl] v. tr./intr. Enrocar (chess).
cast-off [ˈkɑːstˈof] adj. Desechado, da; de desecho.
castoff [ˈkɑːstof] n. Persona (*f.*) *or* cosa (*f.*) desechada, desecho, *m.*
castor [ˈkɑːstə*] n. Salero, *m.* (salt container). || Pimentero, *m.* (pepper container). || Azucarero, *m.* (sugar container). || Ruedecilla, *f.* (wheel). || MED. Castóreo, *m.* (substance). || PRINT. Fundidora, *f.* || ZOOL. Castor, *m.* || Castor, *m.* (hat). || — Pl. Angarillas, *f.*, convoy, *m. sing.* (cruet stand).
Castor [ˈkɑːstə*] pr. n. Cástor, *m.*
castoreum [kɑːsˈtɔːriəm] n. Castóreo, *m.*
castor oil [ˈkɑːstərˈɔil] n. Aceite (*m.*) de ricino.
castor-oil plant [—plɑːnt] n. BOT. Ricino, *m.*
castrate [kæsˈtreit] v. tr. Castrar.
castration [kæsˈtreiʃən] n. Castración, *f.*
castrator [kæsˈtreitə*] n. Castrador, *m.*
casual [ˈkæʒjuəl] adj. Casual, fortuito, ta: *a casual meeting*, un encuentro casual. || Informal (without formality). || Al azar: *to go for a casual stroll*, dar un paseo al azar. || Ocasional, temporero, ra: *casual labour*, trabajo ocasional. || Despreocupado, da (carefree). || Desenfadado, da (answer). || Hecho de paso (in passing): *a casual suggestion*, una sugerencia hecha de paso. || Sin trascendencia: *casual remark*, observación sin trascendencia. || — *Casual conversation*, conversación (*f.*) en que se habla de todo un poco. || *Casual glance*, ojeada, *f.* || *Casual wear*, ropa (*f.*) de sport. || *Casual worker*, temporero, *m.* || *To try to be casual*, intentar hacer como si nada *or* no dar importancia a la cosa.
casually [—i] adv. De paso, sin darle importancia (to say). || De sport (to dress).
casualty [—ti] n. Accidente, *m.* || Víctima, *f.*: *there were three casualties in the accident*, hubo tres víctimas en el accidente. || MIL. Baja, *f.*: *there were no casualties in the battle*, no hubo bajas en la batalla.
casuist [ˈkæzjuist] n. Casuista, *m.* & *f.*
casuistic [ˌkæzjuˈistik] or **casuistical** [—əl] adj. Casuístico, ca.
casuistry [ˈkæzjuistri] n. Casuística, *f.*
cat [kæt] n. ZOOL. Gato, ta. | Felino, na (feline). || Piel (*f.*) de gato (fur). || FIG. Arpía, *f.*, pécora, *f.* (bad woman). || MAR. Gata, *f.* || Azote, *m.* (whip). || — FIG. *A cat in mittens catches no mice*, gato con guantes no caza ratones. || *Angora cat*, gato de Angora. || *Cat burglar*, ladrón, ona. || FIG. *There's no room to swing a cat*, no cabe un alfiler. | *To be like a cat on hot bricks*, estar sobre ascuas. | *To bell the cat*, ponerle el cascabel al gato. | *To lead a cat-and-dog existence* o *to get along like cats and dogs*, llevarse como perros y gatos. | *To let the cat out of the bag*, descubrir el pastel, irse de la lengua. | *To rain cats and dogs*, llover a cántaros, caer chuzos de punta. | *To see which way the cat jumps*, ver de qué lado sopla el viento. | *To set the cat among the pigeons*, meter el lobo en el redil. | *When candles are away all cats are grey*, de noche todos los gatos son pardos. | *When the cat's away the mice will play*, cuando el gato no está, bailan los ratones.
cat [kæt] v. tr. MAR. Izar (the anchor).
catabolic [ˌkætəˈbɔlik] adj. Catabólico, ca.
catabolism [kəˈtæbəlizəm] n. Catabolismo, *m.* (destructive metabolism).
catachresis [ˌkætəˈkriːsis] n. Catacresis, *f.*

— OBSERV. El plural de *catachresis* es *catachreses*.

cataclysm [ˈkætəklizəm] n. Cataclismo, *m.*
catacomb [ˈkætəkuːm] n. Catacumba, *f.*
catafalque [ˈkætəfælk] n. Catafalco, *m.*
Catalan [ˈkætələn] adj./n. Catalán, ana. || Catalán, *m.* (language).
catalepsy [ˈkætəlepsi] n. MED. Catalepsia, *f.*
cataleptic [ˌkætəˈleptik] adj./n. MED. Cataléptico, ca.
catalogue (U. S. **catalog**) [ˈkætəlɔg] n. Catálogo, *m.*
catalogue [ˈkætəlɔg] v. tr. Catalogar.
Catalonia [ˌkætəˈləunjə] pr. n. GEOGR. Cataluña, *f.*
Catalonian [—n] adj./n. Catalán, ana.
catalysis [kəˈtælisis] n. CHEM. Catálisis, *f.*
catalyse [ˈkætəlaiz] v. tr. CHEM. Catalizar.
catalyst [kætəlist] n. CHEM. Catalizador, *m.*
catalytic [ˌkætəˈlitik] adj. CHEM. Catalítico, ca; catalizador, ra.
catalyze [ˈkætəlaiz] v. tr. U. S. Catalizar.
catamaran [ˌkætəməˈræn] n. MAR. Catamarán, *m.*
cat-a-mountain [ˌkætəˈmauntin] n. ZOOL. Gato (*m.*) montés (wildcat). | Leopardo, *m.*
cat-and-mouse [ˈkætənˈmaus] adj. *To play a cat-and-mouse game with s.o.*, jugar al ratón y al gato con uno.
cataplasm [ˈkætəplæzəm] n. MED. Cataplasma, *f.*
catapult [ˈkætəpʌlt] n. Catapulta, *f.* || Tirador, *m.*, tiragomas, *m. inv.* (toy).
catapult [ˈkætəpʌlt] v. tr. Catapultar.
cataract [ˈkætərækt] n. Catarata, *f.*
catarrh [kəˈtɑː*] n. MED. Catarro, *m.*
catarrhal [—rəl] adj. MED. Catarral.
catastrophe [kəˈtæstrəfi] n. Catástrofe, *f.*
catastrophic [ˌkætəˈstrɔfik] adj. Catastrófico, ca.
catbird [ˈkætbəːd] n. Tordo (*m.*) cantor de América y de Australia (bird).
catboat [ˈkætbəut] n. MAR. Laúd, *m.*
catcall [ˈkætkɔːl] n. Pitido, *m.*, silbido, *m.*
catcall [ˈkætkɔːl] v. tr./intr. Pitar, silbar.
catch [kætʃ] n. Cogida, *f.* (the act of catching). || Pesca, *f.*, presa, *f.*, captura, *f.* (in fishing). || Pestillo, *m.* (bolt). || Cerradura, *f.* (of a small box). || Hebijón, *m.* (of a buckle). || MUS. Canon, *m.* (popular round). || Fragmento, *m.* (fragment). || Juego (*m.*) de pelota (ball game). || FIG. Truco, *m.*, trampa, *f.* (trick). | Pega, *f.* (in a question). || SP. Parada, *f.* (of the ball). || — *Safety catch*, fiador, *m.* || FIG. *The catch is that*, la pega es que. | *To be a good catch*, ser un buen partido (man or woman). || *To play catch*, jugar a la pelota. || *With a catch in one's voice*, con la voz entrecortada.
catch* [kætʃ] v. tr. Coger, agarrar (to seize). || Coger, atrapar, prender (to capture). || Coger, tomar (the train, bus). || Alcanzar, dar: *the stone caught him on the head*, la piedra le alcanzó en la cabeza. || Coger, sorprender: *to catch s.o. in the act*, coger a alguien in fraganti. || SP. Coger (the ball). || Coger, contraer (a disease). || FIG. Contagiarse: *she caught his enthusiasm*, se le contagió su entusiasmo. || FAM. Coger, oír: *to catch s.o.'s name*, oír el nombre de alguien. | Coger, entender: *I did not catch the joke*, no he cogido el chiste. || Llamar, captar (attention). || Captar, coger: *the painter has caught her expression*, el pintor ha sabido captar su expresión. || Adquirir, coger (a habit, an accent). || Engancharse: *he caught his jumper on a nail*, se enganchó el jersey en un clavo. || Coger: *he caught his finger in the door*, se cogió el dedo en la puerta. || Darse: *I caught my knee on that table*, di con la rodilla contra esa mesa. || Recibir (a blow, a shot). || — *I only just caught the bus*, por poco perdía el autobús. || *To catch a glimpse of*, vislumbrar. || *To catch a likeness*, coger el parecido. || *To catch fire*, incendiarse (to burst into flames), encenderse, prenderse (to start burning). || *To catch hold of*, agarrarse a. || *To catch it*, ganarse una paliza (a beating), ganarse una bronca (a reprimand). || *To catch one's breath*, quedarse sin respiración (from surprise, etc.), recobrar el aliento (to get one's breath back). || *To catch o.s.*, darse cuenta (to realize), contenerse. || FAM. *To catch s.o. a blow*, pegarle un golpe a uno. | *To catch s.o. red-handed*, coger a alguien con las manos en la masa. || *You'll never catch me doing that*, nunca me verás a mí hacer eso, nunca me cogerás en ésa. || *You will catch it!*, ¡te la vas a ganar!
— V. intr. Engancharse (*on*, en): *her sleeve caught on a nail*, se le enganchó la manga en un clavo. || Quebrarse (the voice). || Prenderse, encenderse (to take fire). || SP. Jugar de "catcher" (in baseball).
— ***To catch at***, tratar de coger. || ***To catch in***, coger con. || ***To catch on***, comprender (to understand). | Caer en la cuenta, darse cuenta (to become aware). | Coger el truco (to get the knack). | Hacerse muy po-

pular (to become popular). || ***To catch out,*** sorprender, coger: *to catch s.o. out in a lie*, coger a alguien mintiendo. | SP. Eliminar. || ***To catch up,*** alcanzar: *you go ahead and I'll catch you up*, id por delante que yo os alcanzaré. | Enredarse (to become entangled). | Poner al día: *I have to catch up with* o *I have to catch up on my work*, tengo que poner al día todo el trabajo. | Ponerse al corriente *or* al día: *to catch up on* o *with the news*, ponerse al corriente de las noticias. | Adquirir, coger (a habit, accent). | Interrumpir (to interrupt).

— OBSERV. In certain Latin American countries the word *coger* is not in decent use and is usually replaced by *tomar* or *agarrar*.

— Pret. & p. p. ***caught***.

catch-as-catch-can [—əz,kætʃ'kæn] adj. U. S. Hecho de cualquier manera.
— N. SP. Lucha (*f.*) libre.

catcher [—ə*] n. SP. "Catcher", *m.*, receptor, *m.*, jugador (*m.*) que para la pelota (baseball).

catching [—iŋ] adj. Contagioso, sa. || FIG. Pegadizo, za (song, music). | Que se pega (habit).

catchment [—mənt] n. Captación, *f.*

catchpenny [—peni] adj. De pacotilla (of low quality). || Facilón, ona: *catchpenny jokes*, chistes facilones.

catchphrase [—freiz] n. Lema, *m.*, "slogan", *m.* || Estribillo, *m.* (pet phrase).

catchword [—wə:d] n. Lema, *m.*, "slogan", *m.* || PRINT. Reclamo, *m.* || THEATR. Pie, *m.* || Estribillo, *m.* (pet word).

catchy [—i] adj. Pegadizo, za: *a catchy melody*, una melodía pegadiza. || Insidioso, sa; capcioso, sa (question).

catechesis [,kæti'kisis] n. Catequesis, *f.*

— OBSERV. El plural de *catechesis* es *catecheses*.

catechetic [,kæti'ketik] or **catechetical** [—əl] adj. Catequístico, ca.

catechism ['kætikizəm] n. Catecismo, *m.*

catechist ['kætikist] n. Catequista, *m.* & *f.*

catechization [,kætikai'zeiʃən] n. Catequización, *f.* || FIG. Interrogatorio, *m.*

catechize ['kætikaiz] v. tr. Catequizar, enseñar el catecismo. || FIG. Preguntar (to question).

catechizer [—ə*] n. Catequizador, ra.

catechu ['kætitʃu:] n. Cato, *m.*

catechumen [,kæti'kju:men] n. Catecúmeno, na.

categoric [,kæti'gɔrik] or **categorical** [—əl] adj. Categórico, ca; rotundo, da; terminante: *a categorical denial*, una negación rotunda. || PHIL. *Categorical imperative*, imperativo categórico.

categorize ['kætigəraiz] v. tr. Clasificar [por categorías].

category ['kætigəri] n. Categoría, *f.*

catena [kə'ti:nə] n. Cadena, *f.* (connected series).

— OBSERV. El plural de *catena* es *catenae* o *catenas*.

catenary [kə'ti:nəri] adj. Catenario, ria. || *Catenary bridge*, puente (*m.*) colgante.
— N. Catenaria, *f.*

catenate ['kætineit] v. tr. Encadenar, enlazar, concadenar.

catenation [,kæti'neiʃən] n. Encadenamiento, *m.*, enlace, *m.*

cater ['keitə*] v. intr. Proveer *or* abastecer de comida (*for*, a). || *To cater for all tastes*, atender a todos los gustos.

catercorner ['kætə,kɔ:nə*] or **cater-cornered** [—d] adj. Diagonal.
— Adv. Diagonalmente, en diagonal.

caterer ['keitərə*] n. Proveedor, ra; abastecedor, ra [de comidas de encargo].

catering ['keitəri:ŋ] n. Abastecimiento, *m.* [de comidas de encargo]. || AVIAT. Mayordomía, *f.*

caterpillar ['kætəpilə*] n. ZOOL. Oruga, *f.* || TECH. Oruga, *f.* || — *Caterpillar tractor*, tractor (*m.*) oruga. || *Caterpillar tread*, oruga, *f.*

caterwaul ['kætəwɔ:l] n. Maullido, *m.*

caterwaul ['kætəwɔ:l] v. intr. Maullar. || Pelearse (to quarrel like cats). || FIG. Berrear, chillar (like cats).

catfish ['kætfiʃ] n. ZOOL. Siluro, *m.*, bagro, *m.* (fish).

— OBSERV. El plural de *catfish* es *catfishes* o *catfish*.

catgut ['kætgʌt] n. Cuerda (*f.*) de tripa (for violin, tennis racket). || MED. Catgut, *m.*

Catharine ['kæθərin] pr. n. Catalina, *f.*

catharsis [kə'θα:sis] n. MED. Purga, *f.*, catarsis, *f.* || PHIL. Catarsis, *f.*

— OBSERV. El plural de la palabra inglesa es *catharses*.

cathartic [kə'θα:tik] adj. Catártico, ca; purgativo, va. || PHIL. Catártico, ca.
— N. MED. Purgante, *m.*

cathead ['kæthed] n. MAR. Serviola, *f.*, pescante, *m.*

cathedra [kə'θi:drə] n. *To speak ex cathedra*, hablar ex cátedra.

cathedral [kə'θi:drəl] adj. Catedral, catedralicio, cia. || *Cathedral city*, ciudad (*f.*) episcopal.
— N. Catedral, *f.*

Catherine ['kæθrin] pr. n. Catalina, *f.*

Catherine wheel [—wi:l] n. Rosetón, *m.* (window). || Girándula, *f.*, rueda, *f.* (firework). || Voltereta (*f.*) lateral (cartwheel). || TECH. Rueda (*f.*) catalina.

catheter ['kæθitə*] n. MED. Catéter, *m.*

catheterism [—rizəm] n. MED. Cateterismo, *m.*

cathetometer [,kæθi'tɔmitə*] n. Catetómetro, *m.*

cathode ['kæθəud] n. ELECTR. Cátodo, *m.* || — PHYS. *Cathode ray*, rayo catódico. | *Cathode-ray tube*, tubo (*m.*) de rayos catódicos.

cathodic [kə'θɔdik] adj. Catódico, ca.

Catholic ['kæθəlik] adj. REL. Católico, ca. || FIG. Universal. | Liberal. || — FIG. *A person of catholic tastes*, una persona a quien le gusta todo. || *Roman Catholic Church*, Iglesia Católica Romana.
— N. Católico, ca.

Catholicism [kə'θɔlisizəm] n. REL. Catolicismo, *m.*

catholicity [,kæθəu'lisiti] n. Universalidad, *f.* || Liberalidad, *f.* || REL. Catolicidad, *f.*, catolicismo, *m.*

catholicize [kə'θɔlisaiz] v. tr. Catolizar.

cation ['kætaiən] n. PHYS. Catión, *m.*

catkin ['kætkin] n. BOT. Candelilla, *f.*, amento, *m.*

cat-lick ['kætlik] n. FAM. Lavado (*m.*) rápido, lavoteo, *m.*

catlike ['kætlaik] adj. Gatuno, na; felino, na.

catmint ['kætmint] n. BOT. Nébeda, *f.*

catnap ['kætnæp] n. Siesta (*f.*) corta.

catnip ['kætnip] n. U. S. BOT. Nébeda, *f.*

Cato ['keitəu] pr. n. Catón, *m.*

cat-o'-nine-tails ['kætə'nain-teilz] n. Gato (*m.*) de nueve colas (whip).

catoptrics [kə'tɔptriks] n. Catóptrica, *f.*

cat's cradle ['kæts,kreidl] n. Juego (*m.*) de la cuna.

cat's eye ['kæts'ai] n. MIN. Ojo (*m.*) de gato. || — Pl. Catafaros, *m.* [por la carretera].

cat's paw ['kæts-pɔ:] n. MAR. Ahorcaperro, *m.* (knot). | Ventolina, *f.* (breeze). || FIG. FAM. Pelele, *m.*, instrumento, *m.* (dupe).

catsup ['kætsəp] n. Salsa (*f.*) de tomate (ketchup).

cattail ['kæt,teil] n. BOT. Anea, *f.*, espadaña, *f.*

cattish ['kætiʃ] adj. Malévolo, la; malicioso, sa.

cattle ['kætl] n. Ganado, *m.* [vacuno]. || — *Cattle bell*, esquilón, *m.* || *Cattle crossing*, paso (*m.*) de ganado (on roads). || *Cattle lifter*, ladrón (*m.*) de ganado, cuatrero, ra. || *Cattle pass*, paso (*m.*) de ganado. || *Cattle plague*, peste bovina. || *Cattle raising*, ganadería, *f.* || *Cattle ranch*, ganadería, *f.* [*Amer.*, hacienda, *f.*, estancia, *f.*]. || U. S. *Cattle rustler*, ladrón (*m.*) de ganado, cuatrero, ra. || *Cattle show*, feria (*f.*) de ganado. || *Cattle truck*, camión (*m.*) de ganado (lorry), vagón (*m.*) de ganado (on a train).

cattleman ['kætlmən] n. Ganadero, *m.*

— OBSERV El plural de esta palabra es *cattlemen*.

catty ['kæti] adj. Gatuno, na; felino, na. || FIG. Malicioso, sa.

Catullus [kə'tʌləs] pr. n. Cátulo, *m.*

catwalk ['kætwɔ:k] n. Pasarela, *f.* (footway). || CINEM. Batería (*f.*) de focos. || THEATR. Puente (*m.*) de trabajo.

Caucasian [kɔ:'keizjən] adj./n. Caucásico, ca; caucasiano, na.

Caucasus ['kɔ:kəsəs] pr. n. GEOGR. Cáucaso, *m.* (mountains). | Caucasia, *f.* (country).

caucus ['kɔ:kəs] n. U. S. Reunión (*f.*) electoral, reunión (*f.*) de dirigentes (of a party). || Comité, *m.*

caucus ['kɔ:kəs] v. intr. U. S. Celebrar una reunión electoral, reunir a los dirigentes.

caudal ['kɔ:dl] adj. Caudal.

caudate ['kɔ:deit] adj. Caudado, da.

Caudine ['kɔ:dain] adj. HIST. *Caudine Forks*, Horcas Caudinas.

caught [kɔ:t] pret. & p. p. See CATCH.

caul [kɔ:l] n. ANAT. Redaño, *m.* (part of the peritoneum). | Amnios, *m.* (enclosing the foetus).

cauldron ['kɔ:ldrən] n. Caldera, *f.*, caldero, *m.*

caulescent [kɔ:'lesnt] adj. BOT. Caulescente.

cauliflower ['kɔliflauə*] n. BOT. Coliflor, *f.*

caulk [kɔ:lk] v. tr. Calafatear.

caulker [—ə*] n. MAR. Calafate, *m.*

caulking [—iŋ] n. Calafateo, *m.*

causal ['kɔ:zəl] adj. Causal.

causality [kɔ:'zæliti] n. Causalidad, *f.*

causation [kɔ:'zeiʃən] n. Causalidad, *f.*

causative ['kɔ:zətiv] adj. Causativo, va.

cause [kɔ:z] n. Causa, *f.*, motivo, *m.*, razón, *f.* (motive). || Causante, *m.* & *f.*, causa, *f.*: *they were the cause of the accident*, ellos fueron los causantes del accidente. || Causa, *f.* (matter of interest and concern): *to fight for a just cause*, luchar por una causa justa. || JUR. Causa, *f.*, pleito, *m.* (lawsuit). || — *Cause célèbre*, proceso (*m.*) célebre. || *Common cause*, causa común. || *In the cause of*, por. || *To plead a cause*, defender una causa.

cause [kɔ:z] v. tr. Causar: *to cause damage*, causar perjuicio. || Causar, provocar: *to cause an accident*, causar un accidente. || *To cause s.o. to do sth.*, hacer que alguien haga algo, obligar a alguien a hacer algo.

causeless [—lis] adj. Sin causa, sin motivo.

causerie ['kəuzəri:] n. Charla, *f.* (chat). || Artículo (*m.*) breve (short article).

causeway ['kɔ:zwei] n. Carretera (*f.*) elevada (raised roadway). || Terraplén, *m.* (embankment).

caustic ['kɔ:stik] adj. CHEM. Cáustico, ca. || FIG. Cáustico, ca; mordaz (sharply biting). || — *Caustic lime*, cal viva. || *Caustic soda*, sosa cáustica.
— N. PHYS. Cáustico, *m.*

causticity [kɔ:s'tisiti] n. FIG. Causticidad, *f.*, mordacidad, *f.*

cauterization [,kɔ:tərai'zeiʃən] n. Cauterización, *f.*

cauterize ['kɔ:təraiz] v. tr. Cauterizar.

cautery [ˈkɔ:təri] n. Cauterio, *m.* (instrument). || Cauterización, *f.*
caution [ˈkɔ:ʃən] n. Cautela, *f.*, prudencia, *f.*, cuidado, *m.* (wariness). || Advertencia, *f.* (warning). || U. S. Fianza, *f.*, garantía, *f.* (money deposit). | Persona (*f.*) que da una fianza, fiador, ra. || — *Caution!*, ¡cuidado!, ¡atención! || *Caution money*, fianza, *f.*, garantía, *f.* || FAM. *He's a caution!*, ¡es un caso!
caution [ˈkɔ:ʃən] v. tr. Amonestar (to reprimand). || Advertir, avisar (to warn).
cautionary [ˈkɔ:ʃnəri] adj. Admonitorio, ria. || Aleccionador, ra: *cautionary tales*, cuentos aleccionadores. || Preventivo, va (preventive).
cautious [ˈkɔ:ʃəs] adj. Cauteloso, sa; precavido, da; cauto, ta; prudente.
cautiousness [—nis] n. Cautela, *f.*, prudencia, *f.*, precaución, *f.*
cavalcade [ˌkævəlˈkeid] n. Cabalgata, *f.* || FIG. Desfile, *m.* (parade).
cavalier [ˌkævəˈliə*] adj. Arrogante (haughty). || Desenvuelto, ta (carefree).
— N. Jinete, *m.* (horseman). || HIST. Caballero, *m.* (knight). | Monárquico (*m.*) partidario de Carlos I de Inglaterra. || Galán, *m.*, acompañante, *m.* (partner).
cavalry [ˈkævəlri] n. MIL. Caballería, *f.*
cavalryman [—mən] n. MIL. Soldado (*m.*) de caballería.
— OBSERV. El plural de *cavalryman* es *cavalrymen*.
cavatina [ˌkævəˈti:nə] n. MUS. Cavatina, *f.*
cave [keiv] n. Cueva, *f.* (natural). || Caverna, *f.* (man-made).
cave [keiv] v. tr. Cavar (earth).
— V. intr. *To cave in*, derrumbarse, hundirse.
caveat [ˈkeiviæt] n. JUR. Aviso (*m.*) de aplazamiento de un proceso. || Advertencia, *f.* (warning): *to enter a caveat*, hacer una advertencia.
cave dweller [ˈkeivˌdwelə*] n. Troglodita, *m.* & *f.*, cavernícola, *m.* & *f.*
cave-in [ˈkeivin] n. Derrumbamiento, *m.* || Socavón, *m.* (in the street).
caveman [ˈkeivmən] n. Hombre (*m.*) de las cavernas (prehistoric human being). || FIG. Bruto, *m.*
— OBSERV. El plural de *caveman* es *cavemen*.
cave painting [ˈkeivˌpeintiŋ] n. ARTS. Pintura (*f.*) rupestre.
cavern [ˈkævən] n. Caverna, *f.*, cueva, *f.* (cave).
cavernous [—əs] adj. Cavernoso, sa.
cavetto [kəˈvetəu] n. ARCH. Caveto, *m.*, mediacaña, *f.*
caviar or **caviare** [ˈkævia:*] n. Caviar, *m.*
cavil [ˈkævil] n. Reparo, *m.*, pero, *m.*
cavil [ˈkævil] v. intr. Poner reparos *or* peros (*at*, *about*, a). || Criticar.
cavitation [kæviˈteiʃən] n. MAR. AVIAT. Cavitación, *f.*
cavity [ˈkæviti] n. Cavidad, *f.*, hueco, *m.* || Caries, *f. inv.* (in a tooth).
cavort [kəˈvɔ:t] v. intr. Corvetear. || FIG. Retozar, juguetear (to romp). | Divertirse.
cavy [ˈkeivi] n. ZOOL. Cobayo, *m.*, conejillo (*m.*) de Indias.
caw [kɔ:] n. Graznido, *m.* (of crow, etc.).
caw [kɔ:] v. intr. Graznar.
cay [kei] n. Cayo, *m.* (of rock). || Banco, *m.* (of sand).
cayenne pepper [ˈkeienˈpepə*] n. Pimienta (*f.*) sacada del chile.
cayman [ˈkeimən] n. ZOOL. Caimán, *m.*
cease [si:s] n. *Without cease*, sin cesar, incesantemente.
cease [si:s] v. tr. Cesar, suspender (to interrupt). || Cesar (to stop). || Poner fin a (to bring to an end). || *To cease firing*, cesar el fuego.
— V. intr. Cesar, dejar (*from*, *to*, de).
cease-fire [—ˈfaiə*] n. MIL. Alto (*m.*) el fuego.
ceaseless [—lis] adj. Incesante, continuo, nua.
ceasing [—iŋ] n. Cese, *m.*, cesación, *f.*, cesamiento, *m.*
cecal [ˈsi:kl] adj. ANAT. Cecal.
Cecil [ˈsesl] pr. n. Cecilio, *m.*
Cecily [ˈsisili] pr. n. Cecilia, *f.*
cecum [ˈsi:kəm] n. ANAT. Intestino (*m.*) ciego, ciego, *m.*
— OBSERV. El plural de *cecum* es *ceca*.
cedar [ˈsi:də*] n. BOT. Cedro, *m.* (tree).
cede [si:d] v. tr. Ceder.
cedilla [siˈdilə] n. Cedilla, *f.*
ceiba [ˈseibə] n. BOT. Ceiba, *f.*
ceibo [ˈseibəu] n. BOT. Ceibo, *m.*
ceil [si:l] v. tr. Revestir el techo de.
ceiling [ˈsi:liŋ] n. Techo, *m.* || AVIAT. Altura (*f.*) máxima, techo, *m.* || FIG. Tope, *m.*, límite, *m.*, máximo, *m.* (upper limit): *ceiling price*, precio tope. || FAM. *To hit the ceiling*, subirse por las paredes (with anger).
celadon [ˈselədən] n. Verdeceledón, *m.* (colour).
celandine [ˈseləndain] n. BOT. Celidonia, *f.*
celebrant [ˈselibrənt] n. Celebrante, *m.*
celebrate [ˈselibreit] v. tr. Celebrar (a religious ceremony): *to celebrate a wedding*, celebrar una boda. || Celebrar, festejar: *to celebrate a birthday*, celebrar un cumpleaños. || Celebrar, alabar (to praise).
— V. intr. Celebrar (to say mass). || Divertirse, pasarlo bien (to amuse o.s.).
celebrated [—id] adj. Famoso, sa; célebre (*for*, por).
celebration [ˌseliˈbreiʃən] n. Celebración, *f.* || Conmemoración, *f.* (of an event). || Fiesta, *f.* (party). || Festividades, *pl.* (festivities).
celebrity [siˈlebriti] n. Celebridad, *f.*, fama, *f.* (fame). || Celebridad, *f.* (famous person).
celeriac [siˈleriæk] n. BOT. Apio (*m.*) nabo.
celerity [siˈleriti] n. Celeridad, *f.*
celery [ˈseləri] n. BOT. Apio, *m.*
celeste [siˈlest] adj. Celeste.
— N. Celeste, *m.*
celestial [siˈlestjəl] adj. Celestial (divine). || Celeste, astronómico, ca (pertaining to the sky). || — *Celestial Empire*, Celeste Imperio. || *Celestial equator*, ecuador (*m.*) celeste. || *Celestial navigation*, navegación astronómica. || *Celestial sphere*, esfera (*f.*) celeste.
celiac [ˈsi:ljæk] adj. See COELIAC.
celibacy [ˈselibəsi] n. Celibato, *m.*, soltería, *f.*
celibate [ˈselibit] adj./n. Célibe, soltero, ra.
cell [sel] n. Celda, *f.* (in prisons, monasteries, etc.). || Célula, *f.* (political group). || BIOL. Célula, *f.* || ZOOL. Celdilla, *f.* (of bees). | Ventosa, *f.* (of octopus). || ELECTR. Pila, *f.*: *dry cell*, pila seca. || — BIOL. *Cell division*, mitosis, *f.*, división (*f.*) celular. || *Photoelectric cell*, célula fotoeléctrica.
cellar [ˈselə*] n. Sótano, *m.* || Bodega, *f.* (for wines).
cellarage [—ridʒ] n. Almacenaje, *m.* (storage, price). || Bodega, *f.* (cellar).
cellarer [—rə*] n. Cillerero, *m.* (in a monastery).
cellaret [ˌseləˈret] n. Fresquera, *f.* (for bottles).
cellist [ˈtʃelist] n. MUS. Violoncelista, *m.* & *f.*
cello or **'cello** [ˈtʃeləu] n. MUS. Violoncelo, *m.*
cellophane [ˈseləfein] n. Celofán, *m.*
cellular [ˈseljulə*] adj. Celular.
cellule [ˈselju:l] n. BIOL. Célula, *f.*
cellulitis [ˌseljuˈlaitis] n. MED. Celulitis, *f.*
celluloid [ˈseljulɔid] n. Celuloide, *m.*
cellulose [ˈseljuləus] n. CHEM. Celulosa, *f.*
— Adj. Celulósico, ca.
celt [selt] n. Hacha (*f.*) prehistórica.
Celt [kelt] n. HIST. Celta, *m.* & *f.*
Celtiberia [ˌkeltiˈbiərjə] pr. n. Celtiberia, *f.*
Celtiberian [—n] adj./n. Celtíbero, ra; celtibérico, ca; celtiberio, ria.
Celtic [ˈkeltik] adj. Céltico, ca; celta.
— N. Celta, *m.* (language).
Celticism [ˈkeltisizəm] n. Celtismo, *m.*
Celtologist [kelˈtɔlədʒist] n. Celtista, *m.* & *f.*
cement [siˈment] n. Cemento, *m.* || Cola, *f.*, pegamento, *m.* (glue). || MED. Cemento, *m.* (for filling teeth).
cement [siˈment] v. tr. Cementar, unir con cemento (to join with cement). || Revestir de cemento (to cover with cement). || FIG. Cimentar, fortalecer: *to cement a friendship*, cimentar una amistad.
cementation [ˌsi:menˈteiʃən] n. TECH. Cementación, *f.* || FIG. Consolidación, *f.*, cimentación, *f.*, fortalecimiento, *m.*
cemetery [ˈsemitri] n. Cementerio, *m.*
cenobite [ˈsi:nəbait] n. Cenobita, *m.* & *f.*
cenobitic [sinəˈbitik] or **cenobitical** [—əl] adj. Cenobítico, ca; cenobial.
cenobitism [sinəˈbitizəm] n. Cenobitismo, *m.*
cenotaph [ˈsenəta:f] n. Cenotafio, *m.*
Cenozoic [ˈsi:nəˌzəuik] adj. GEOL. Cenozoico, ca.
cense [sens] v. tr. Incensar.
censer [—ə*] n. Incensario, *m.*
censor [—ə*] n. Censor, *m.*
censor [—ə*] v. tr. Censurar. || Tachar (to delete).
censorious [senˈsɔ:riəs] adj. Censurador, ra; reprobador, ra.
censorship [ˈsensəʃip] n. Censura, *f.*
censurable [ˈsenʃərəbl] adj. Censurable.
censure [ˈsenʃə*] n. Censura, *f.*
censure [ˈsenʃə*] v. tr. Censurar.
census [ˈsensəs] n. Censo, *m.*, empadronamiento, *m.* || — *Census taker*, empadronador, *m.* || *To take a census of*, empadronar, levantar el censo de.
cent [sent] n. Centavo, *m.* (coin). || COMM. Ciento, *m.* (percentage): *ten per cent*, diez por ciento. || FAM. *I haven't got a cent*, no tengo un céntimo *or* un centavo.
cental [ˈsentl] n. Quintal, *m.*
centaur [ˈsentɔ:*] n. MYTH. Centauro, *m.*
centaury [—ri] n. BOT. Centaura, *f.*, centaurea, *f.*
centenarian [ˌsentiˈneəriən] adj./n. Centenario, ria.
centenary [senˈti:nəri] adj. Centenario, ria.
— N. Centenario, *m.*
centennial [senˈteniəl] adj. Centenario, ria.
— N. Centenario, *m.*
center [ˈsentə*] n. U. S. See CENTRE.
centerboard [—bɔ:d] n. U. S. MAR. Orza (*f.*) de deriva.
centering [—iŋ] n. U. S. Centrado, *m.*
centerpiece [—pi:s] n. U. S. Centro (*m.*) de mesa.
centesimal [senˈtesiməl] adj. Centesimal.
— N. Centésimo, *m.*
centiare [ˈsentia:r] n. Centiárea, *f.*
centigrade [ˈsentigreid] adj. Centígrado, da: *centigrade scale*, escala centígrada: *20 degrees centigrade*, 20 grados centígrados.
centigramme (U. S. **centigram**) [ˈsentigræm] n. Centigramo, *m.*
centilitre (U. S. **centiliter**) [ˈsentiˌlitə*] n. Centilitro, *m.*
centime [ˈsa:nti:m] n. Céntimo, *m.*
centimetre (U. S. **centimeter**) [ˈsentiˌmi:tə*] n. Centímetro, *m.* || *Centimetre-gram-second system*, sistema (*m.*) cegesimal.
centipede [ˈsentipi:d] n. ZOOL. Ciempiés, *m. inv.*

centner [ˈsentnə*] n. Quintal (*m.*) métrico.

central [ˈsentrəl] adj. Central. || Céntrico, ca: *I live in a central district*, vivo en un barrio céntrico. || — *Central bank*, banco (*m.*) central. || *Central heating*, calefacción (*f.*) central. || *Central nervous system*, sistema nervioso central. || *Central standard time*, hora (*f.*) legal correspondiente al meridiano 90° W. || *To take a central position on a problem*, tomar una postura intermedia en un problema.

— N. Central (*f.*) telefónica. || Telefonista, *m.* & *f.* (operator).

Central America [—əˈmerikə] pr. n. GEOGR. América (*f.*) Central, Centroamérica, *f.*

Central American [—əˈmerikən] adj./n. Centroamericano, na.

Central European [—ˌjuərəˈpi:ən] adj./n. Centroeuropeo, a.

centralism [ˈsentrəlizəm] n. Centralismo, *m.*

centralist [ˈsentrəlist] adj./n. Centralista.

centrality [senˈtræliti] n. Posición (*f.*) central.

centralization [ˌsentrəlaiˈzeiʃən] n. Centralización, *f.*

centralize [ˈsentrəlaiz] v. tr. Centralizar.

centralizer [—ə*] n. Centralizador, *m.*

centralizing [—iŋ] adj. Centralizador, ra.

— N. Centralización, *f.*

centre (U. S. center) [ˈsentə*] n. Centro, *m.*: *the centre of the circle*, el centro del círculo; *city centre*, centro de la ciudad. || Eje, *m.* (axis). || Alma, *f.* (of cable). || ARCH. Cimbra, *f.* || SP. Centro, *m.* || ANAT. Centro, *m.* || — TECH. *Centre bit* o *drill*, broca (*f.*) de centrar. | *Centre distance*, distancia (*f.*) entre ejes. || SP. *Centre forward*, delantero (*m.*) centro. | *Centre half*, medio (*m.*) centro. || *Centre of gravity*, centro de gravedad. || *Community centre*, centro social. || U. S. *Railroad center*, centro ferroviario. || *The motor centre*, el centro motor.

centre [ˈsentə*] v. tr. Centrar (to place in the middle, to find the centre). || Concentrar, centrar: *to centre one's efforts on doing sth.*, concentrar sus esfuerzos en hacer algo. || SP. Centrar (the ball).

— V. intr. Concentrarse, centrarse (*at, in, on, upon*, en) [to concentrate]. || Centrarse (*on*, sobre): *the conversation centred on tennis*, la conversación se centró sobre el tenis.

centreboard [—bɔ:d] n. MAR. Orza (*f.*) de deriva.

centrepiece [—pi:s] n. Centro (*m.*) de mesa.

centric [ˈsentrik] or **centrical** [—əl] adj. Céntrico, ca; central.

centrifugal [senˈtrifjugəl] adj. Centrífugo, ga: *centrifugal pump*, bomba centrífuga. || Centrifugador, ra: *centrifugal machine*, máquina centrifugadora.

centrifuge [ˈsentrifju:ʒ] n. TECH. Centrifugadora, *f.*

centrifuge [ˈsentrifju:ʒ] v. tr. Centrifugar.

centripetal [senˈtripitl] adj. Centrípeto, ta: *centripetal acceleration, force*, aceleración, fuerza centrípeta.

centring [ˈsentəriŋ] n. Centrado, *m.*

centrist [ˈsentrist] n. Centrista, *m.* & *f.*

centrosome [ˈsentrəˌsəum] n. BIOL. Centrosoma, *m.*

centrosphere [ˈsentrəsfiə*] n. Centro (*m.*) de la Tierra. || BIOL. Centrosfera, *f.*

centuple [ˈsentjupl] adj. Céntuplo, pla.

— N. Céntuplo, *m.*

centuple [ˈsentjupl] or **centuplicate** [senˈtju:plikeit] v. tr. Centuplicar.

centuplicate [senˈtju:pliket] n. Céntuplo, *m.*

— Adj. Céntuplo, pla.

centuries-old [ˈsentʃurizˌəuld] adj. Secular.

centurion [senˈtjuəriən] n. HIST. Centurión, *m.*

century [ˈsentʃuri] n. Siglo, *m.*: *the 17th century*, el siglo XVII. || Siglo, *m.*, centuria, *f.*: *it happened two centuries ago*, sucedió hace dos siglos. || HIST. Centuria, *f.* (in the Roman army). || BOT. *Century plant*, pita, *f.*, agave, *m.*

cephalalgia [sefəˈlældʒə] n. MED. Cefalalgia, *f.*

cephalic [keˈfælik] adj. Cefálico, ca.

cephalopod [ˈsefələpɔd] n. ZOOL. Cefalópodo, *m.*

— Adj. Cefalópodo, da.

cephalothorax [ˈsefələˈθɔ:ræks] n. Cefalotórax, *m.*

ceraceous [siˈreiʃəs] adj. Ceroso, sa (waxy).

ceramic [siˈræmik] adj. Cerámico, ca.

ceramics [—s] n. Cerámica, *f.*

ceramist [ˈseramist] n. Ceramista, *m.* & *f.* (potter).

cerastes [siˈræsti:z] n. ZOOL. Cerasta, *f.*, cerastes, *m.* (horned viper).

cerate [ˈsiərit] n. Cerato, *m.*

ceratin [ˈkerətin] n. Queratina, *f.*

Cerberus [ˈsə:bərəs] pr. n. MYTH. Cerbero, *m.*, Cancerbero, *m.*

cercopithecus [ˌsə:kəu piθikəs] n. Cercopiteco, *m.*

cereal [ˈsiəriəl] adj. Cereal: *cereal plant*, planta cereal. || *Cereal production*, producción cerealista *or* de cereales.

— N. Cereal, *m.*

cerebellum [ˌseriˈbeləm] n. ANAT. Cerebelo, *m.*

— OBSERV. El plural es *cerebellums* o *cerebella*.

cerebral [ˈseribrəl] adj. Cerebral. || MED. *Cerebral palsy*, parálisis (*f.*) cerebral.

cerebrate [ˈseribreit] v. intr. Pensar.

cerebration [ˌseriˈbreiʃən] n. Actividad (*f.*) mental, función (*f.*) cerebral.

cerebrospinal [ˌseribrəuˈspainl] adj. Cerebroespinal. || MED. *Cerebrospinal fluid*, líquido cefalorraquídeo. | *Cerebrospinal meningitis*, meningitis (*f.*) cerebroespinal.

cerebrum [ˈseribrəm] n. ANAT. Cerebro, *m.*

— OBSERV. El plural es *cerebrums* o *cerebra*.

cerecloth [ˈsiəkləθ] or **cerement** [ˈsiəmənt] n. Mortaja (*f.*) encerada.

ceremonial [ˌseriˈməunjəl] adj. Ceremonial. || De gala: *ceremonial uniform*, uniforme de gala.

— N. Ceremonial, *m.*

ceremonious [seriˈməunjəs] adj. Ceremonioso, sa.

ceremony [ˈseriməni] n. Ceremonia, *f.*: *a religious ceremony*, una ceremonia religiosa. || — *Master of ceremonies*, see MASTER. || *To stand on ceremony*, andarse con ceremonias *or* cumplidos. || *Without ceremony*, sin ceremonias, sin cumplidos.

cereus [ˈsiəriəs] n. BOT. Cirio, *m.*

cerin [ˈsiərin] n. Cerina, *f.*

cerise [səˈri:z] adj. De color cereza.

— N. Color (*m.*) cereza.

cerite [ˈsiərait] n. MIN. Cerita, *f.*

cerium [ˈsiəriəm] n. CHEM. Cerio, *m.*

ceroplastics [ˈsiərəuplɑ:stiks] n. Ceroplástica, *f.*

cert [sə:t] n. FAM. *It's a cert!*, ¡eso está hecho!, ¡es cosa segura!

certain [ˈsə:tn] adj. Seguro, ra; cierto, ta: *I am certain that it is not true*, estoy seguro de que no es verdad; *it is certain that*, es cierto que. || Cierto, ta; un tal, una tal: *a certain Mrs. Brown*, una tal señora Brown. || Cierto, ta: *a certain resistance*, cierta resistencia; *a certain day*, cierto día. || — *Be certain to do that*, no dejes de hacerlo. || *For certain*, seguro, con toda seguridad. || *He is certain to be there*, es seguro que estará. || *I'll make certain*, lo averiguaré, lo comprobaré. || *To make certain of*, asegurarse de.

certainly [—li] adv. Desde luego, naturalmente, por supuesto (of course). || Naturalmente, con mucho gusto: *certainly, sir!*, ¡con mucho gusto, señor! || Seguro, sin falta: *I shall certainly do that*, lo haré seguro *or* sin falta. || — *Certainly not!*, ¡de ninguna manera!, ¡por supuesto que no!, ¡ni hablar! || *He certainly can run fast*, ése sí que corre rápido.

certainty [—ti] n. Certeza, *f.*, certidumbre, *f.* || Seguridad, *f.*: *there is no certainty about him coming tomorrow*, no hay seguridad de que venga mañana. || — *For a certainty*, con toda seguridad, a ciencia cierta. || *It's a certainty*, es cosa segura. || *With certainty*, a ciencia cierta.

certifiable [ˈsə:tiˈfaiəbl] adj. Certificable (capable of being certified). || Loco, ca; demente (mad).

certificate [səˈtifikit] n. Certificado, *m.* (attesting some fact). || Diploma, *m.*, título, *m.* (academic, etc.). || — *Birth certificate*, partida (*f.*) de nacimiento. || *Certificate of baptism*, partida (*f.*) *or* fe (*f.*) de bautismo. || *Death certificate*, partida (*f.*) de defunción. || *Marriage certificate*, certificado (*m.*) de matrimonio, partida (*f.*) de matrimonio.

certificate [səˈtifikeit] v. tr. Dar un certificado a (to grant a certificate to). || Dar un título *or* un diploma a (an academic title).

certificated [—id] adj. Diplomado, da.

certification [ˌsə:tifiˈkeiʃən] n. Certificación, *f.* || Certificado, *m.*

certifier [ˈsə:tifaiə*] n. Certificador, *m.*

certify [ˈsə:tifai] v. tr. Certificar, atestiguar (to attest). || Declarar loco. || *Certified copy*, copia legalizada.

certifying [—iŋ] adj. Certificativo, va; certificatorio, ria.

certitude [ˈsə:titju:d] n. Certeza, *f.*, certidumbre, *f.*

cerulean [siˈru:ljən] adj. Cerúleo, a.

— N. Azul (*m.*) celeste (colour).

cerumen [siˈru:mən] n. Cerumen, *m.* (of ears).

ceruse [ˈsiəru:s] n. Cerusa, *f.*, albayalde, *m.*

cerussite [ˈsiərəsait] n. MIN. Cerusita, *f.*

Cervantine [səˈvænˌtain] adj. Cervantesco, ca; cervantino, na.

Cervantist [səˈvænˌtist] n. Cervantista, *m.* & *f.*

cervical [ˈsə:vikəl] adj. Cervical.

cervid [ˈsə:vid] n. Cérvido, *m.*

— OBSERV. El plural de *cervid* es *cervidae*.

cervine [ˈsə:vain] adj. ZOOL. Cervino, na; cerval.

cervix [ˈsə:viks] n. ANAT. Cerviz, *f.* (back part of the neck). | Cuello (*m.*) del útero (neck of the uterus).

— OBSERV. El plural de *cervix* es *cervices* o *cervixes*.

Cesarean or **Cesarian** [siˈzeərjən] adj./n. See CAESAREAN.

cesium [ˈsiziəm] n. CHEM. Cesio, *m.*

cessation [seˈseiʃən] n. Cese, *m.*, cesación, *f.*, cesamiento, *m.*

cession [ˈseʃən] n. Cesión, *f.*

cessionary [ˈseʃənəri] n. Cesionario, ria.

cesspit [ˈsespit] n. Pozo (*m.*) negro.

cesspool [ˈsespu:l] n. Pozo (*m.*) negro. || FIG. Sentina, *f.*

cestode [ˈsestəud] n. ZOOL. Cestodo, *m.*

cesura [sizˈjurə] n. Cesura, *f.* (pause).

cetacean [siˈteiʃjən] n. ZOOL. Cetáceo, *m.*

cetonia [seˈtəunjə] n. ZOOL. Cetonia, *f.*

Ceylon [siˈlɔn] pr. n. GEOGR. Ceilán.

Ceylonese [siləˈni:z] adj./n. Ceilanés, esa.

chaconne [ʃəˈkɔn] n. MUS. Chacona, *f.*

chafe [tʃeif] n. Rozadura, *f.* || Irritación, *f.* (irritation). || Desgaste, *m.* (wear caused by rubbing).

chafe [tʃeif] v. tr. Irritar (to irritate). || Desgastar (to wear). || Rozar (to rub). || Excoriar. || Frotar (for warmth). || FIG. Irritar, enfadar (to annoy).

— V. intr. Rozarse: *the cars chafed against each other*

los coches se rozaron. || Desgastarse (to become worn by rubbing). || FIG. Irritarse, enfadarse (*at*, por, a causa de, debido a).

chafer [—ə*] n. ZOOL. Abejorro, *m.*

chaff [tʃɑ:f] n. Ahechaduras, *f. pl.*, barcia, *f.* (of wheat). || Granzas, *f. pl.* (of other grain). || Paja (*f.*) cortada (for animal fodder). || FIG. Paja, *f.*, broza, *f.* (useless writing, talk, etc.). | Broma, *f.*, chanza, *f.* (banter). || FIG. *To separate the chaff from the grain*, separar la cizaña del buen grano.

chaff [tʃɑ:f] v. tr. Cortar (hay or straw). || FIG. Tomar el pelo a (to tease).

chaffer [ˈtʃɑ:fə*] n. Bromista, *m.* & *f.* (teaser). || Regateo, *m.* (of price).

chaffer [ˈtʃɑ:fə*] v. intr. Regatear (to bargain). — V. tr. Intercambiar (words).

chaffinch [ˈtʃæfintʃ] n. ZOOL. Pinzón, *m.*

chafing dish [ˈtʃeifiŋ,diʃ] n. Calientaplatos, *m. inv.*

chagrin [ˈʃægrin] n. Disgusto, *m.*, contrariedad, *f.* (grief). || Desilusión, *f.*, desengaño, *m.* (disappointment). || Mortificación, *f.* (mortification).

chagrin [ˈʃægrin] v. tr. Contrariar, disgustar (to grieve). || Desilusionar, decepcionar (to disappoint). || Mortificar (to mortify).

chain [tʃein] n. Cadena, *f.*: *the links of the chain were very strong*, los eslabones de la cadena eran muy sólidos; *a chain of hotels*, una cadena de hoteles. || Sucesión, *f.*, cadena, *f.* (of facts). || — Pl. Cadenas, *f.* (prisoner's fetters). || — *Chain armour*, cota (*f.*) de malla. || *Chain bridge*, puente (*m.*) colgante. || *Chain coupling*, cadena de enganche (for linking rail cars). || *Chain gang*, cadena [de presidiarios], cuerda (*f.*) de presos. || *Chain letter*, carta (*f.*) que forma parte de una cadena. || U. S. *Chain lightning*, relámpagos (*m. pl.*) en zigzag. || *Chain lock*, cadena antirrobo. || *Chain mail*, cota (*f.*) de mallas (armour). || *Chain of mountains*, cordillera, *f.*, cadena (*f.*) de montañas. || *Chain pump*, noria (*f.*) de cangilones. || CHEM. *Chain reaction*, reacción (*f.*) en cadena. || MIL. *Chain shot*, bala (*f.*) de cadena. || FAM. *Chain smoker*, fumador (*m.*) que enciende un cigarrillo con otro. || *Chain stitch*, punto (*m.*) de cadeneta, cadeneta, *f.* || *Chain store*, sucursal, *f.* [de una cadena de establecimientos]. || *Chain wheel*, plato, *m.* (de bicicleta), rueda dentada de cadena. || *Driving chain*, cadena de transmisión. || *Land chain, measuring chain*, cadena de agrimensor. || *Safety chain*, cadena de seguridad.

chain [tʃein] v. tr. Encadenar.

chain-react [—riˈækt] v. intr. Tener reacción en cadena.

chain-smoke [—sməuk] v. intr. Encender un cigarrillo con otro, fumar pitillo tras pitillo.

chair [tʃɛə*] n. Silla, *f.* (seat): *cane chair*, silla de rejilla; *folding chair*, silla de tijera *or* plegable; *swivel chair*, silla giratoria. || Cátedra, *f.* (in a university). || Presidencia, *f.*: *to appeal to the chair*, apelar a la presidencia. || Sillón, *m.* (of chairman). || Presidente, *m.* (chairman): *to address the chair*, dirigirse al presidente. || Silla (*f.*) eléctrica (electric chair). || TECH. Cojinete (*m.*) de riel. || Coche (*m.*) salón (railway carriage). || Silla (*f.*) de la reina (child's game). || — *Gestatorial chair*, silla gestatoria (of the Pope). || *Please, take a chair*, siéntese por favor. || *Sedan chair*, silla de manos. || *To be in the chair* o *to occupy the chair*, ocupar la presidencia, presidir. || *To leave the chair*, levantar la sesión. || *To take the chair*, tomar la presidencia, presidir. || *Wing chair*, sillón (*m.*) de orejas.

chair [tʃɛə*] v. tr. Llevar a hombros (to shoulder). || Llevar en triunfo (to carry in triumph). || Presidir (a meeting).

chair car [—kɑ:*] n. U. S. Coche (*m.*) salón (rail car).

chair lift [—lift] n. Telesilla, *m.* (for skiers).

chairman [—mən] n. Presidente, *m.*

— OBSERV. El plural de esta palabra es *chairmen.*

chairman [—mən] v. tr. Presidir.

chairmanship [—mənʃip] n. Presidencia, *f.*

chair rail [—reil] n. Guardasilla, *f.*

chairwoman [—,wumən] n. Presidenta, *f.*

— OBSERV. El plural de *chairwoman* es *chairwomen.*

chaise [ʃeiz] n. Tílburi, *m.* (carriage). || *Chaise longue*, tumbona, *f.* (long chair).

chalaza [kəˈleizə] n. BIOL. BOT. Chalaza, *f.*

chalcedony [kælˈsedəni] n. MIN. Calcedonia, *f.*

chalcographer [kælˈkɔgrəfə*] n. Calcógrafo, *m.*

chalcography [kælˈkɔgrəfi] n. Calcografía, *f.*

chalcopyrite [,kælkəˈpairait] n. MIN. Calcopirita, *f.*

Chaldaic [kælˈdeik] adj. Caldaico, ca.

Chaldea or **Chaldaea** [kælˈdi:ə] pr. n. Caldea, *f.*

Chaldean [—n] adj./n. Caldeo, a.

chalet [ˈʃælei] n. Chalet, *m.*, chalé, *m.*

chalice [ˈtʃælis] n. REL. Cáliz, *m.*

chalk [tʃɔ:k] adj. Cretáceo, a: *chalk hills*, colinas cretáceas. || Hecho con tiza, a tiza: *a chalk drawing*, un dibujo a tiza.
— N. GEOL. Creta, *f.* || Tiza, *f.* (for writing on blackboards, etc.). || — FAM. *Not by a long chalk*, ni mucho menos. | *To be as different as chalk from cheese*, parecerse como el día a la noche, parecerse como un huevo a una manzana.

chalk [tʃɔ:k] v. tr. Escribir *or* marcar con tiza. || Poner tiza a (billiard cue). || — *To chalk out*, trazar (to sketch out a plan, etc.). || *To chalk up*, apuntar (on a board), apuntarse: *to chalk up a victory*, apuntarse una victoria.

chalkiness [—inis] n. Naturaleza (*f.*) cretácea.

chalk pit [—pit] n. Cantera (*m.*) de creta.

chalkstone [—stəun] n. MED. Concreción (*f.*) cálcica.

chalky [ˈtʃɔ:ki] adj. Cretáceo, a; gredoso, sa. || Calcáreo, a (water).

challenge [ˈtʃælindʒ] n. Desafío, *m.*, reto, *m.* || MIL. Quién vive, *m.*, alto, *m.* (of sentry). || FIG. Estímulo, *m.*, incentivo, *m.* (stimulus). | Tentativa, *f.* [para conquistar algo] (attempt). || JUR. Recusación, *f.* || SP. "Challenge", *m.* || — *To issue a challenge to s.o.*, desafiar a alguien. || *To take up the challenge*, aceptar el desafío *or* el reto.

challenge [ˈtʃælindʒ] v. tr. Desafiar, retar (to a duel, game, etc.). || Poner en duda, poner en tela de juicio: *to challenge a statement*, poner en duda una declaración. || Requerir: *this matter challenges attention*, este asunto requiere atención. || Poner a prueba (to test). || FIG. Estimular (to stimulate). || JUR. Recusar. || MIL. Dar el quién vive a. || U. S. Impugnar (a vote). || — *To challenge s.o. to do sth.*, desafiar a alguien a que haga algo. || *To challenge the speaker*, hacer objeciones *or* pedir aclaraciones al orador.

challenger [—ə*] n. Retador, *m.*, desafiador, *m.* (to a duel, etc.). || SP. "Challenger", *m.*, aspirante, *m.* [a un título].

challenging [—iŋ] adj. Desafiante. || Estimulante (work). || Provocativo, va (smile).

chalybeate [kəˈlibiit] adj. Ferruginoso, sa: *chalybeate water*, agua ferruginosa.

chalybite [ˈkælibait] n. MIN. Siderita, *f.*

chamber [ˈtʃeimbə*] n. Cámara, *f.*, aposento, *m.* (private room). || Cámara, *f.* (legislative or judicial body). || TECH. Recámara, *f.* (of a gun). | Cámara, *f.* (of a motor, sluice, furnace). || — Pl. JUR. Despacho, *m. sing.*, bufete, *m. sing.* (of a lawyer). || — *Chamber music*, música (*f.*) de cámara. || *Chamber of commerce*, cámara de comercio. || *Chamber orchestra*, orquesta (*f.*) de cámara. || *Chamber of Deputies*, cámara de diputados. || *Chamber pot*, orinal, *m.* || *Compression chamber*, cámara de compresión. || *Funeral chamber*, cámara mortuoria. || *Gas chamber*, cámara de gas. || *Upper, lower chamber*, cámara alta, baja.

chamberlain [ˈtʃeimbəlin] n. Chambelán, *m.*

chambermaid [ˈtʃeimbəmeid] n. Doncella, *f.*, camarera, *f.*

chameleon [kəˈmi:ljən] n. ZOOL. Camaleón, *m.* || FIG. Camaleón, *m.* (person).

chameleonic [,kəmi:ljˈɔnik] adj. FIG. Inconstante, que cambia mucho de opinión.

chamfer [ˈtʃæmfə*] n. Bisel, *m.*, chaflán, *m.*

chamfer [ˈtʃæmfə*] v. tr. Biselar, chaflanar, achaflanar.

chamois [ˈʃæmwɑ:] n. ZOOL. Gamuza, *f.* || *Chamois leather*, gamuza, *f.*

— OBSERV. La pronunciación de *chamois* en la expresión *chamois leather* es [ˈʃæmi]. El plural de esta palabra es *chamois* o *chamoix.*

chamomile [ˈkæməmail] n. BOT. Manzanilla, *f.*, camomila, *f.*

champ [tʃæmp] n. FAM. Campeón, *m.*

champ [tʃæmp] v. tr./intr. Mascar haciendo ruido: *he champed his food*, mascaba la comida haciendo ruido. || Mordiscar, mordisquear (to bite on). || FIG. *To champ at the bit*, tascar el freno (to show impatience).

champagne [ʃæmˈpein] n. Champán, *m.*, champaña, *m.*

champion [ˈtʃæmpjən] adj. Campeón, ona: *a champion team*, un equipo campeón. || FAM. De primera, estupendo, da: *that's champion!*, ¡eso es de primera!
— N. Campeón, ona: *a tennis champion*, un campeón de tenis. || FIG. Paladín, *m.*, defensor, *m.*, adalid, *m.*: *champion of liberty*, paladín de la libertad.

champion [ˈtʃæmpjən] v. tr. Defender, hacerse el paladín de, hacerse el campeón de, ser el adalid de.

championship [—ʃip] n. Campeonato, *m.*: *league championship*, campeonato de liga. || FIG. Defensa, *f.*: *the championship of a cause*, la defensa de una causa.

chance [tʃɑ:ns] adj. Casual, fortuito, ta: *a chance meeting*, un encuentro casual.
— N. Casualidad, *f.*, azar, *m.*: *I found it by chance*, lo encontré por casualidad. || Casualidad, *f.*: *have you a car by any chance?*, ¿tiene un coche por casualidad? || Azar, *m.*: *game of chance*, juego de azar. || Destino, *m.*, fortuna, *f.*: *chance willed that*, el destino quiso que. || Suerte, *f.*: *chance was against me*, la suerte me fue contraria. || Oportunidad, *f.*, ocasión, *f.*: *it was a chance to see the queen*, fue una oportunidad de ver a la reina. || Posibilidad, *f.*, probabilidad, *f.* [*Amer.*, chance, *f.*]: *he has no chance of escaping*, no tiene ninguna posibilidad de escapar; *the chances are that we are going*, la probabilidad es que vayamos. || Riesgo, *m.*: *it's a chance I have to take*, es un riesgo que tengo que correr. || — *By sheer chance*, por mera casualidad. || *It's a long chance*, es poco probable. || *On the chance that*, con la esperanza de que. || *To give s.o. a chance*, darle a alguien una oportunidad. || *To leave it to chance*, dejarlo al azar. || *To stand a chance*, tener probabilidades *or* posibilidades. || *To take a chance*, correr un riesgo, arriesgarse. || *To take no chances*, no arriesgarse. || *To take one's chance*, arriesgarse, tentar la suerte.

chance [ˈtʃɑːns] v. tr. Arriesgar. || Probar: *to chance one's luck*, probar fortuna. || *To chance it*, arriesgarse.
— V. intr. Acaecer, suceder: *it chanced that*, sucedió que. || Tener la suerte *or* la oportunidad de. || — *He chanced to see me*, me vio por casualidad. || *To chance upon*, tropezar con, encontrar por casualidad: *I chanced upon a friend*, tropecé con un amigo.
chancel [ˈtʃɑːnsəl] n. Presbiterio, *m.*, antealtar, *m.*
chancellery [ˈtʃɑːnsələri] n. Cancillería, *f.*
chancellor [ˈtʃɑːnsələ*] n. Canciller, *m.* (of a state, of an embassy). || Rector, *m.* (of a university). || U. S. JUR. Magistrado, *m.* || — *Chancellor of the Exchequer*, ministro (*m.*) de Hacienda. || *Lord Chancellor*, presidente (*m.*) de la Cámara de los Lores.
chancellory [—ri] n. Cancillería, *f.*
chancery [ˈtʃɑːnsəri] n. Cancillería, *f.* (office of a chancellor or of public records). || U. S. Juzgado, *m.*
Chancery [ˈtʃɑːnsəri] n. JUR. Tribunal (*m.*) de justicia, chancillería, *f.*
chancre [ˈʃæŋkə*] n. MED. Chancro, *m.*
chancy [ˈtʃɑːnsi] adj. Arriesgado, da (risky). || Incierto, ta (uncertain).
chandelier [ˌʃændiˈliə*] n. Araña, *f.* (of lights).
chandler [ˈtʃɑːndlə*] n. (Ant.) Cerero, ra; velero, ra (person who sells candles). || Proveedor, *m.* (supplier). || Droguista, *m.* (who sells paint, etc.).
chandlery [—ri] n. Cerería, *f.* || Droguería, *f.*
change [tʃeindʒ] n. Cambio, *m.* (of opinion, position, state, government, etc.): *change of address*, cambio de domicilio; *change in the weather*, cambio de tiempo. || Cambio, *m.*, trueque, *m.* (exchange for). || Cambio, *m.*, vuelta, *f.* (money returned): *he kept the change*, se quedó con la vuelta. || Cambio, *m.* (money changed). || Calderilla, *f.*, suelto, *m.* (small coins). || Cambio, *m.*, transbordo, *m.* (of trains). || Relevo, *m.*, cambio, *m.* (of horses). || Muda, *f.*, cambio, *m.* (of skin, clothes). || — *Change of heart*, cambio de opinión *or* de parecer. || *Change of life*, menopausia, *f.* || *Change of scene*, cambio escénico, mutación, *f.* || *For a change*, para variar. || *It's a change for the better*, es un cambio beneficioso. || *No change given*, se ruega moneda fraccionaria. || *On Change*, que trabaja en la Bolsa. || FIG. *To get no change out of s.o.*, no sacarle nada a uno. || *To ring the changes*, tocar las variaciones de un carillón (campanology), decir *or* hacer una cosa de varias maneras, agotar todas las formas posibles.
change [tʃeindʒ] v. tr. Cambiar: *to change a wheel*, cambiar una rueda; *they have changed the timetable*, han cambiado el horario. || Cambiar, mudar (clothes, nappies, sheets, skin, etc.). || Cambiar de: *to change the subject*, cambiar de tema; *to change one's shoes*, cambiar de zapatos. || Cambiar, trocar (one thing for another). || — *All change!*, ¡bájense por favor! || *To change books, habits*, cambiar de libros, de costumbres. || *To change gear*, cambiar de velocidad. || *To change hands*, cambiar de manos *or* de mano: *this car has changed hands many times*, este coche ha cambiado de mano muchas veces. || MUS. *To change key*, cambiar de tono. || *To change money*, cambiar dinero. || *To change one's clothes*, cambiarse de ropa. || *To change one's mind*, cambiar de idea. || *To change step*, cambiar el paso. || *To change the guard*, relevar la guardia. || *To get changed*, cambiarse.
— V. intr. Cambiar: *he has changed a lot*, ha cambiado mucho. || Cambiarse, mudarse (clothes). || Transbordar, hacer transbordo: *when I came by train I had to change twice*, cuando vine en tren tuve que hacer transbordo dos veces. || Transformarse, convertirse (to become): *the snow is changing into water*, la nieve se está transformando en agua. || FIG. *To change with the wind*, cambiar más que una veleta.
— ***To change about***, cambiar de dirección. || ***To change around***, cambiar de arriba abajo. || ***To change down*** o ***up***, cambiar a una velocidad inferior *or* superior (gears). || ***To change over***, cambiar: *we changed over to the decimal system*, cambiamos al sistema métrico decimal.
changeability [ˌtʃeindʒəˈbiliti] n. Variabilidad, *f.*
changeable [ˈtʃeindʒəbl] adj. Variable (weather, character, etc.). || Cambiable (which can be changed). || Cambiadizo, za (inconsistent).
changeful [ˈtʃeindʒful] adj. Variable, cambiante.
changeless [ˈtʃeindʒlis] adj. Invariable, inmutable.
changeling [ˈtʃeindʒliŋ] n. Niño (*m.*) cambiado por otro.
changeover [ˈtʃeindzˌəuvə*] n. Cambio, *m.*
changer [ˈtʃeindʒə*] n. Cambiador.
changing [ˈtʃeindʒiŋ] adj. Que cambia, cambiante.
— N. Cambio, *m.*: *the changing of a wheel*, el cambio de una rueda.
changing room [—ruːm] n. Vestuario, *m.*
channel [ˈtʃænl] n. Canal, *m.* (course for running water). || Cauce, *m.* (the deepest part of a river). || FIG. Vía, *f.*, conducto, *m.*: *legislation must go through the usual channels*, las leyes deben seguir las vías usuales. | Canal (commercial). || Canal, *m.*, cadena, *f.*: *television channel*, canal de televisión. || Ranura, *f.* (groove). || — GEOGR. *Channel Islands*, Islas Anglonormandas. | *English Channel* o *The Channel*, el Canal de la Mancha. || *Irrigation channel*, acequia, *f.*, canal (*m.*) de riego.

channel [ˈtʃænl] v. tr. Construir canales en, canalizar (to make channels). || Canalizar, encauzar: *to channel water*, canalizar agua. || Formar barrancos en (to make ravines). || FIG. Encauzar, canalizar (ideas, etc.).
chanson [ʃanˈsɔn] n. MUS. Canción, *f.* || *Chanson de Geste*, cantar (*m.*) de gesta.
chant [tʃɑːnt] n. MUS. REL. Cántico, *m.* (psalm). || MUS. Canción, *f.*, canto, *m.* (song). || Melopea, *f.* (rythmic repetitive singing). || FIG. Sonsonete, *m.*, cantinela, *f.* (singsong). || *Gregorian chant*, canto gregoriano.
chant [tʃɑːnt] v. tr. Cantar (to sing). || FIG. Salmodiar, cantar con monotonía (to sing monotonously).
— V. intr. Salmodiar (psalms).
chanter [—ə*] n. Cantor, ra (singer). || REL. Chantre, *m.* (of a choir). || MUS. Caramillo, *m.* (of bagpipes).
chanterelle [ˌtʃæntəˈrel] n. BOT. Mízcalo, *m.* (fungus).
chantry [ˈtʃɑːntri] n. REL. Capellanía, *f.* (endowment). | Capilla (*f.*) *or* altar (*m.*) para decir misas por el fundador (chapel or altar).
chanty [ˈtʃɑːnti] n. MAR. Saloma, *f.*
chaos [ˈkeiɔs] n. Caos, *m.*
chaotic [keiˈɔtik] adj. Caótico, ca.
chap [tʃæp] n. FAM. Tipo, *m.*, tío, *m.* || Grieta, *f.* (crack in the skin). || ANAT. Mandíbula, *f.* (jaw). | Mejilla, *f.* (cheek). || Quijada, *f.* (of animals). || TECH. Mordaza, *f.* (of a vice). || — *Be a good chap and do it*, sé buen chico y hazlo. || *Listen, old chap*, escucha, hombre. || *Poor chap*, pobre hombre, *m.*, pobrecillo, *m.*
chap [tʃæp] v. tr. Agrietar.
— V. intr. Agrietarse.
chaparral [ˌtʃæpəˈræl] n. Chaparral, *m.*
chapbook [ˈtʃæpbuk] n. (Ant.). Libro (*m.*) de coplas vendido por las calles.
chape [tʃeip] n. Contera, *f.*, regatón, *m.* (of scabbard).
chapel [ˈtʃæpəl] n. REL. Capilla, *f.* (small church, part of church containing an altar). || Servicio (*m.*) religioso: *tomorrow chapel will be at nine o'clock*, mañana el servicio religioso será a las nueve. | Templo, *m.* (nonconformists' place of worship). || Gremio, *m.* [de impresores] (association of printers). || — *Chapel master*, maestro (*m.*) de capilla. || *Chapel of ease*, capilla sufragánea. || *Funeral chapel*, capilla ardiente.
chaperon or **chaperone** [ˈʃæpərəun] n. Carabina, *f.*, señora (*f.*) de compañía.
chaperon or **chaperone** [ˈʃæpərəun] v. tr. Hacer de carabina con, acompañar [a una señorita].
chapfallen [ˈtʃæpˌfɔlən] adj. Abatido, da; deprimido, da; alicaído, da.
chaplain [ˈtʃæplin] n. REL. Capellán, *m.*
chaplaincy [—si] n. REL. Capellanía, *f.*
chaplet [ˈtʃæplit] n. Guirnalda, *f.* (of flowers or jewels). || Sarta (*f.*) de cuentas (string of beads). || REL. Rosario, *m.* (part of rosary). || ARCH. Moldura (*f.*) de cuentas. || FIG. Sarta, *f.*, rosario, *m.*, retahíla, *f.* (series).
chapman [ˈtʃæpmən] n. Vendedor (*m.*) ambulante.
— OBSERV. El plural de *chapman* es *chapmen*.
chaps [tʃæps] pl. n. Zajones, *m.*, zahones, *m.* (leggings).
chapter [ˈtʃæptə*] n. Capítulo, *m.*: *a chapter of a book*, un capítulo de un libro; *with his death ended a chapter of history*, con su muerte se termina un capítulo de la historia. || REL. Cabildo, *m.* (of canons). || — *Chapter house*, sala (*f.*) capitular. || *Chapter of accidents*, serie (*f.*) de accidentes *or* desgracias. || *To give chapter and verse for sth.*, indicar algo con pelos y señales. || *To quote chapter and verse*, citar literalmente.
chapter [ˈtʃæptə*] v. tr. Dividir en capítulos.
char [tʃɑː*] n. Asistenta, *f.* (charwoman). || Carbón (*m.*) de leña (charcoal). || FAM. Té, *m.* (tea). || Umbra, *f.* (fish).
char [tʃɑː*] v. tr. Carbonizar (to reduce to carbon). || Chamuscar (to scorch).
— V. intr. Carbonizarse. || Chamuscarse (to be scorched). || Trabajar de asistenta (a charwoman).
charabanc [ˈʃærəbæŋ] n. Autocar, *m.*
character [ˈkæriktə*] adj. De carácter: *character actor*, actor de carácter.
— N. Carácter, *m.*: *they have very strong characters*, tienen caracteres muy fuertes. || Personaje, *m.*: *the leading character of this play*, el personaje principal de esta obra; *a well-known public character*, un personaje muy conocido. || Papel (role): *in the character of*, en el papel de. || FIG. FAM. Tipo, *m.*, individuo, *m.*: *he's an odd character!*, ¡es un tipo raro! || Reputación, *f.*: *he is a bad character*, tiene mala reputación. || PRINT. Carácter, *m.*, tipo, *m.* (symbol, letter). || — *Character disorder*, inadaptación (*f.*) social. || *Character reference*, informe, *m.* || *In character of*, en calidad de. || *Main o chief character*, protagonista, *m. & f.* || *To be in character with*, ser característico de. || *To be out of character with*, no ser nada característico de.
characteristic [—ˈristik] adj. Característico, ca.
— N. Característica, *f.*
characterization [—raiˈzeiʃən] n. Caracterización, *f.*
characterize [—raiz] v. tr. Caracterizar: *his big nose characterizes him*, su gran nariz le caracteriza. || Describir (to portray): *he characterized his brother very well*, describió muy bien a su hermano.
characterless [—lis] adj. Sin carácter, sin personalidad.
characterology [—ˈrɔlədʒi] n. Caracterología, *f.*
charade [ʃəˈrɑːd] n. Charada, *f.* || FIG. Charada, *f.*

charcoal [ˈtʃɑ:kəul] n. Carbón (*m.*) vegetal, carbón (*m.*) de leña (carbon). || Arts. Carboncillo, *m.* || *Charcoal drawing*, dibujo (*m.*) al carbón, carboncillo, *m.*

charge [ˈtʃɑ:dʒ] n. Cargo, *m.* (responsibility, safekeeping): *take charge of the administration*, hazte cargo de la administración. || Cargo, *m.* (post). || Tarea, *f.*, trabajo, *m.* (task). || Carga, *f.*, peso, *m.* (load): *my brother is a charge on me*, mi hermano es una carga para mí. || Carga, *f.* (of battery, furnace, firearm). || Min. Barreno, *m.* (explosive). || Mil. Carga, *f.* (attack): *to return to the charge*, volver a la carga. || Jur. Cargo, *m.*, acusación, *f.* (legal accusation). | Extracto (*m.*) de los debates (of judge to jury). || Embestida, *f.* (of bull). || Carga, *f.* (sports). || Electr. Carga, *f.* || Precio, *m.* (price). || Blasón, *m.* (heraldry). || — *At my own charge*, a expensas mías, a mi costa. || Comm. *Charge account*, cuenta (*f.*) a cargo. || *In charge*, encargado, da (in command), detenido, da (under arrest). || *In charge of*, encargado, da: *he is in charge of the class*, está encargado de la clase; al cargo de, al cuidado de (under the supervision of). || *The person in charge*, el encargado. || *To bring charges against*, formular acusaciones contra. || *To lay sth. to a person's charge*, culpar a alguien de algo. || *To make a charge for*, facturar a. || *To reverse the charges*, poner una conferencia a cobro revertido. || *To take charge of*, encargarse de, hacerse cargo de (responsibility), tomar el mando de (direction).

charge [ˈtʃɑ:dʒ] v. tr. Acusar: *they charged him with murder*, le acusaron de asesinato. || Ordenar: *he charged her to be careful*, le ordenó que tuviera cuidado. || Exhortar: *the bishop charged the priests to give it careful consideration*, el obispo exhortó a los sacerdotes a que examinaran detenidamente la cuestión. || Encargar (to entrust). || Cargar: *they charged him with presents for the family*, le cargaron de regalos para la familia. || Cobrar: *they charged me 10 pounds*, me cobraron 10 libras. || Cargar: *charge it to my account*, cárguemelo en mi cuenta. || Cargar: *the lorry was charged with wooden planks*, el camión estaba cargado con tablas de madera; *to charge a battery, a furnace*, cargar una batería, un horno; *to charge a gun*, cargar un arma; *the clouds were charged with electricity*, las nubes estaban cargadas de electricidad. || Atacar, cargar (to attack). || Cargar (sports). || Embestir (a bull). || Blasonar (heraldry).

— V. intr. Cargar (soldiers, etc.). || Cobrar: *he charges for his services*, cobra por sus servicios. || Cargar (sports). || Embestir (a bull). || — Fam. *To charge in*, irrumpir [en]. | *To charge off*, salir corriendo.

chargeable [—dʒəbl] adj. Acusable (liable to be accused). || *Chargeable to the customer*, a cargo del cliente.

chargé d'affaires [ˈʃɑ:ʒeidæˈfɛə*] n. Encargado (*m.*) de negocios.

charger [ˈtʃɑ:dʒə*] n. Electr. Mil. Cargador, *m.* || Poet. Corcel, *m.* (horse).

charily [ˈtʃɛərili] adv. Cautelosamente (warily). || Parcamente (sparingly).

chariness [ˈtʃɛərinis] n. Cautela, *f.* (caution). || Parsimonia, *f.* (parsimony).

chariot [ˈtʃæriət] n. Carro, *m.*

charioteer [ˌtʃæriəˈtiə*] n. Auriga, *m.*

charism [kærizəm] **charisma** [kəˈrizmə] n. Carisma, *m.*

— Observ. El plural de *charisma* es *charismata*.

charismatic [ˌkærizˈmætik] adj. Carismático, ca.

charitable [ˈtʃæritəbl] adj. Caritativo, va: *he is very charitable towards the poor*, es muy caritativo con los pobres. || Tolerante (tolerant). || Comprensivo, va (understanding). || *Charitable society*, institución benéfica.

charity [ˈtʃæriti] n. Caridad, *f.*: *to live on charity*, vivir de la caridad. || Institución (*f.*) benéfica (charitable society). || Caridad, *f.*, limosna, *f.* (alms). || Comprensión, *f.* (tolerance). || Benevolencia, *f.*, indulgencia, *f.* || — *Charity bazaar*, venta benéfica. || Fig. *Charity begins at home*, la caridad bien entendida empieza por uno mismo. || *Charity child*, inclusero, *m.*, hospiciano, *m.* || Rel. *Sister of charity*, hermana (*f.*) de la Caridad. || *To be out of charity with*, no ser muy caritativo con.

charivari [ˈʃɑ:riˈvɑ:ri] n. Alboroto, *m.*, guirigay, *m.* (noise). || Cencerrada, *f.* (mock serenade).

charlady [ˈtʃɑ:ˈleidi] n. Asistenta, *f.*

charlatan [ˈʃɑ:lətən] n. Charlatán, ana.

charlatanic [ˈʃɑ:ləˈtænik] adj. Charlatanesco, ca.

charlatanism [ˈʃɑ:lətənizəm] n. Charlatanismo, *m.*

charlatanry [ˈʃɑ:lətənri] n. Charlatanería, *f.*

Charlemagne [ˈʃɑ:ləˈmein] pr. n. Carlomagno, *m.*

Charles [tʃɑ:lz] n. pr. Carlos, *m.* || Astr. *Charles's Wain*, Carro (*m.*) Mayor, Osa (*f.*) Mayor.

charleston [ˈtʃɑ:lstən] n. Charlestón, *m.* (dance).

charley horse [ˈtʃɑ:lihɔ:s] n. U. S. Fam. Calambre, *m.*

charlock [ˈtʃɑ:lɔk] n. Bot. Mostaza (*f.*) silvestre.

Charlotte [ˈʃɑ:lət] pr. n. Carlota, *f.*

charm [tʃɑ:m] n. Encanto, *m.* (attraction). || Atractivo, *m.* (appeal). || Hechizo, *m.* (magic spell). || Amuleto, *m.* (amulet). || Dije, *m.* (trinket). || — Fig. fam. *Like a charm*, a las mil maravillas, perfectamente: *my ruse worked like a charm*, mi truco resultó perfectamente. || *To be under s.o.'s charm*, estar bajo el encanto de alguien. || *To fall a victim to s.o.'s charms*, sucumbir ante los encantos de alguien. || *To turn on the charm*, deshacerse en cumplidos.

charm [tʃɑ:m] v. tr. Encantar (to delight): *I was charmed by her kindness*, estaba encantado con su amabilidad. || Hechizar, encantar (snakes). || — *To charm away*, hacer desaparecer como por ensalmo: *my troubles were charmed away*, mis dificultades desaparecieron como por ensalmo. || *To lead a charmed life*, ser muy afortunado *or* tener mucha suerte en la vida.

charmer [—ə*] n. Persona (*f.*) encantadora (delightful person). || Encantador, *m.* (of snakes).

charming [—iŋ] adj. Encantador, ra.

charnel house [ˈtʃɑ:nəlhaus] n. Osario, *m.*

chart [tʃɑ:t] n. Mar. Carta (*f.*) de marear *or* marina. || Mapa, *m.* (map). || Tabla, *f.* (table). || Gráfico, *m.* (graph).

chart [tʃɑ:t] v. tr. Poner en una carta marina. || Trazar: *to chart a course*, trazar un derrotero.

charter [—ə*] n. Carta, *f.* (official document granting rights). || Estatutos, *m. pl.* (of a society). || Fletamento, *m.*, fletamiento, *m.* (boat, aeroplane). || Alquiler, *m.* (bus, train). || — *Charter flight*, vuelo (*m.*) "charter" *or* fletado. || *Charter member*, socio fundador.

charter [—ə*] v. tr. Conceder carta a (to grant a charter). || Fletar (ship, plane). || Alquilar (bus, train).

chartered accountant [ˈtʃɑ:tədəˈkauntənt] n. Perito (*m.*) contable, perito (*m.*) mercantil.

charterer [ˈtʃɑ:tərə*] n. Fletador, *m.*

charterhouse [ˈtʃɑ:təhaus] n. Cartuja, *f.*

charter party [tʃɑ:təˌpɑ:ti] n. Contrato (*m.*) de flete.

chartreuse [ʃɑ:ˈtrə:z] n. Cartuja, *f.* (monastery). || "Chartreuse", *m.* (liqueur). || Color (*m.*) amarillo verdoso.

charwoman [ˈtʃɑ:ˌwumən] n. Asistenta, *f.*

— Observ. El plural de *charwoman* es *charwomen*.

chary [ˈtʃɛəri] adj. Cauto, ta; cauteloso, sa (wary). || Parco, ca (sparing): *he is chary in his praise*, es parco en alabanzas. || Avaro, ra (stingy). || Tímido, da (shy).

Charybdis [kəˈribdis] pr. n. See scylla.

chase [tʃeis] n. Persecución, *f.*, caza, *f.* (pursuit). || Caza, *f.* (hunting). || Caña, *f.* (of gun). || Ranura, *f.* (groove). || Tech. Canal, *m.* (in wall). || Mar. Caza, *f.* || Print. Rama, *f.* || *To give chase to*, dar caza a.

chase [tʃeis] v. tr. Perseguir (to run after). || Cazar (to hunt). || Fig. Dar caza a, cazar (a girl). || Tech. Cincelar (to ornament silver, etc.). | Acanalar (to groove). | Engastar (jewel). | Repujar (to emboss). | Aterrajar, filetear, roscar (a screw). || Fam. *Go chase yourself!*, ¡vete al diablo!

— V. intr. Ir corriendo (to hurry).

— Fig. **To chase after**, ir detrás de, perseguir a: *Andrew was chasing after Christine*, Andrés iba detrás de Cristina. || **To chase away**, ahuyentar. || **To chase from**, echar *or* expulsar de. || **To chase off**, ahuyentar. || **To chase out**, echar fuera, expulsar.

chaser [—ə*] n. Tech. Cincel, *m.* (chisel). || Cazador, ra (hunter). || Perseguidor, ra (pursuer). || U. S. Caza, *m.* (plane). || Grabador, ra (engraver). || Tech. Roscador, *m.*, terraja, *f.* || Bebida (*f.*) ligera tomada después de otra más fuerte.

chasm [ˈkæzəm] n. Sima, *f.*, abismo, *m.* (cleft). || Fig. Abismo, *m.*

chassis [ˈʃæsi] n. Aut. Chasis, *m.*, bastidor, *m.* || U. S. Fam. Cuerpo, *m.* (body).

chaste [tʃeist] adj. Casto, ta (virtuous). || Sobrio, bria; escueto, ta (style).

chasten [ˈtʃeisn] v. tr. Limar, pulir, depurar (style). || Castigar (to punish). || Corregir (to correct). || Escarmentar (to teach a lesson).

chasteness [ˈtʃeistnis] n. Castidad, *f.*

chastise [tʃæsˈtaiz] v. tr. Castigar.

chastisement [ˈtʃæstizmənt] n. Castigo, *m.*

chastiser [tʃæsˈtaizə*] n. Castigador, *m.*

chastity [ˈtʃæstiti] n. Castidad, *f.*: *chastity belt*, cinturón de castidad. || Pureza, *f.* (of style).

chasuble [ˈtʃæzjubl] n. Rel. Casulla, *f.*

chat [tʃæt] n. Charla, *f.*, palique, *m.* (talk). || *To have a chat about sth.*, hablar de algo.

chat [tʃæt] v. intr. Charlar, estar de palique.

château [ˈʃætəu] n. Castillo, *m.*

— Observ. El plural es *châteaus* o *châteaux*.

chattel [ˈtʃætl] n. Jur. Bien (*m.*) mueble. || *Chattel mortgage*, hipoteca (*f.*) sobre bienes muebles.

chatter [ˈtʃætə*] n. Charla, *f.*, palique, *m.*, cháchara, *f.* (talk). || Chillido, *m.* (of apes). || Gorjeo, *m.*, piada, *f.* (of birds). || Murmullo, *m.* (murmur). || Castañeteo, *m.* (of teeth). || Picado, *m.* (of engine). || Ruido, *m.* (noise).

chatter [ˈtʃætə*] v. intr. Parlotear, estar de cháchara, charlar (to chat). || Hablar por los codos (to be talkative). || Chillar (apes). || Piar (birds). || Castañetear (teeth). || Picar (an engine). || Hacer ruido (tool).

chatterbox [—bɔks] or **chatterer** [—rə*] n. Parlanchín, ina; charlatán, ana.

chattiness [ˈtʃætinis] n. Charloteo, *m.*: *his chattiness annoyed me*, su charloteo me molestaba.

chatty [ˈtʃæti] adj. Hablador, ra; parlanchín, ina (person). || Familiar (informal). || *Chatty letter*, carta llena de noticias.

chauffeur [ˈʃəufə*] n. Chófer, *m.* [*Amer.*, chofer], conductor, ra.

chauffeur [ˈʃəufə*] v. tr. Conducir.
chauvinism [ˈʃəuvinizəm] n. Chauvinismo, *m.*, patriotería, *f.*
chauvinist [ˈʃəuvinist] adj./n. Chauvinista, patriotero, ra.
chauvinistic [ʃəuviˈnistik] adj. Chauvinista, patriotero, ra.
chaw [tʃɔ:] v. tr. U. S. Masticar. || U. S. FAM. *To chaw s.o. up*, poner a uno verde, poner a uno como chupa de dómine.
chayote [tʃaˈjəuti] n. BOT. Chayote, *m.*
cheap [tʃi:p] adj. Barato, ta (price). || De precio reducido, económico, ca (reduced ticket). || Fácil: *a cheap victory*, una victoria fácil. || Bajo, ja; vil (mean). || FIG. Malo, la; de poca calidad, barato, ta; charro, rra (tawdry). || — *Cheap and nasty*, malo y barato. || *Cheap money*, préstamo obtenido a bajo interés. || *Cheap sterling*, libra (*f.*) esterlina vendida a bajo precio. || *Dirt cheap*, baratísimo, ma. || *On the cheap*, a bajo precio, barato. || FIG. *That's pretty cheap*, eso es vergonzoso. | *To feel cheap*, tener vergüenza. || *To hold life cheap*, tener en poco la vida. || *To make cheaper*, abaratar. || *To make o.s. cheap*, subestimarse, rebajarse. || *To turn out cheap*, salir barato.
— Adv. Barato: *he got it very cheap*, lo obtuvo muy barato.
cheapen [ˈtʃi:pən] v. tr. Rebajar el precio, abaratar (to lower the price). || Degradar (to degrade). || FIG. *To cheapen o.s.*, rebajarse.
— V. intr. Bajar de precio, abaratarse.
cheap-jack [ˈtʃi:pdʒæk] n. Buhonero, *m.* (hawker)
cheaply [ˈtʃi:pli] adv. Barato, a bajo precio.
cheapness [ˈtʃi:pnis] n. Baratura, *f.*, lo barato. || FIG. Poca calidad, *f.* (low quality). || Bajeza, *f.* (lowness).
cheat [tʃi:t] n. Tramposo, sa; fullero, ra (in games). || Estafador, ra; timador, ra (swindler). || Timo, *m.*, estafa, *f.* (swindle). || Trampa, *f.* (trick).
cheat [tʃi:t] v. tr. Estafar, timar (to swindle). || Engañar, burlarse de (to deceive). || Escapar de, burlar a: *he cheated death on a number of occasions*, escapó de la muerte en numerosas ocasiones. || *To cheat s.o. out of sth.*, estafar algo a alguien.
— V. intr. Hacer trampas (in games). || Copiar (in exams).
cheater [—ə*] n. Estafador, ra; timador, ra (swindler). || Tramposo, sa; fullero, ra (in games).
cheating [—iŋ] adj. Tramposo, sa (deceiving). || Fraudulento, ta (swindling).
— N. Trampa, *f.* (trickery). || Timo, *m.*, estafa, *f.* (swindle).
check [tʃek] n. Detención, *f.*, parada, *f.* (stop). || Restricción, *f.*, freno, *m.* (restraint). || Comprobación, *f.*, inspección, *f.* (control). || Repaso, *m.*, examen, *m.*, inspección, *f.* (test). || Ficha, *f.* (counter). || MIL. Revés, *m.*, contratiempo, *m.* (reverse). || Pérdida (*f.*) de la pista (in hunting). || Jaque, *m.* (chess). || Cuadros, *m. pl.* (pattern). || Cuadro, *m.* (each square of the pattern). || Tela (*f.*) de cuadros (cloth). || TECH. Tope, *m.* || U. S. Grieta, *f.* (crack). | Marca, *f.*, señal, *f.* (mark of approval). | Inspector, ra (inspector). | Cuenta, *f.* (bill in a restaurant). | Talón, *m.* (deposit receipt). | Cheque, *m.* (cheque) [See CHEQUE]. || — *To keep a check on*, controlar. || *To keep* o *to hold in check*, contener (to restrain), mantener a raya (a person).
— Adj. De control: *check list*, lista de control. || *Check suit*, traje de cuadros.
— Interj. ¡Jaque! (in chess). || U. S. ¡Bien! (right!).
check [tʃek] v. tr. Parar, detener: *he checked his horse and dismounted*, paró el caballo y bajó; *the window ledge checked his fall*, el antepecho de la ventana detuvo su caída. || Obstaculizar (to hinder). || Reprimir, refrenar, contener (to restrain). || Inspeccionar, examinar (to examine). || Comprobar, averiguar (facts). || Poner contraseña a (to mark). || Cuadricular (to square). || Dar jaque a (chess). || MIL. Censurar, reprender (to rebuke). || U. S. Depositar (to deposit). | Facturar (to forward luggage). || *To check sth. against sth. else*, cotejar *or* comprobar una cosa con otra.
— V. intr. Detenerse, pararse (to stop). || Dar jaque (in chess). || Perder la pista (in hunting). || Concordar (to agree). || Comprobar, averiguar (to make sure). || U. S. Rajarse, agrietarse (to crack).
— ***To check in,*** registrarse (at a hotel). || ***To check off,*** marcar (to mark). | Contar uno por uno (to count individually). || Eliminar (to eliminate). || ***To check on,*** comprobar, averiguar (to verify). | Inspeccionar. || ***To check out,*** averiguar, comprobar. | Sacar prestado (books). | Retirar sacar: *he went to the bank to check out some money*, fue al banco a sacar dinero. | Pagar la cuenta y marcharse (from a hotel). || ***To check up,*** averiguar, comprobar. || ***To check with,*** cotejar con, comparar con (to compare), consultar (a person).
checkbook [—buk] n. U. S. Talonario (*m.*) de cheques, chequera, *f.*
checked [—t] adj. A cuadros.
checker [—ə*] n. U. S. Ficha, *f.* (in draughts). || Cuadro, *m.* (square). || Cuadros, *m. pl.* (pattern).
checker [—ə*] v. tr. Marcar con cuadros.
checkerboard [—əˌbɔ:d] n. U. S. Tablero (*m.*) de damas *or* de ajedrez.
checkered [ˈtʃekəd] adj. A cuadros (cloth). || FIG. Con altibajos (uneven). | Variado, da (varied).
checkers [ˈtʃekəz] n. U. S. Damas, *f. pl.* (game).
checking account [ˈtʃekiŋəˌkaunt] n. U. S. Cuenta (*f.*) corriente.
checkmate [ˈtʃekˈmeit] n. Jaque (*m.*) y mate (in chess). || FIG. Fracaso, *m.* (failure).
checkmate [ˈtʃekˈmeit] v. tr. Dar jaque y mate (in chess). || FIG. Ganarle a uno por la mano (to beat). | Frustrar (s.o.'s plans). || FIG. *To be checkmated*, estar en un callejón sin salida.
checkoff [ˈtʃekɔ:f] n. U. S. Deducción (*f.*) de cierta cantidad del sueldo para pagar la cuota sindical.
checkpoint [ˈtʃekpɔint] n. Control, *m.*
checkrein [ˈtʃekrein] n. Falsa (*f.*) rienda.
checkroom [ˈtʃekru:m] n. U. S. Guardarropa, *m.* (cloakroom). || Consigna, *f.* (left-luggage office).
checkup [ˈtʃekʌp] n. Chequeo, *m.*, reconocimiento (*m.*) médico general (physical examination). || Comprobación, *f.* (verification). || Revisión, *f.*, examen, *m.*
Cheddar [ˈtʃedə*] n. Queso (*m.*) de Cheddar.
cheek [tʃi:k] n. Carrillo, *m.* (side wall of mouth). || Mejilla, *f.* (the flesh on the cheekbone). || ARCH. Jamba, *f.* || FAM. Caradura, *f.* (impudence): *to have the cheek of the devil*, tener una caradura de mil diablos. || — Pl. TECH. Mordaza, *f. sing.* (of a vice). || — ZOOL. *Cheek pouch*, abazón, *m.* || *Cheek to cheek*, con las caras juntas (together), como los dos dedos de una mano (very friendly). || FIG. *To go cheek by jowl*, ir codo con codo. | *To turn the other cheek*, poner la otra mejilla. || FAM. *What a cheek!*, ¡qué caradura!
cheek [tʃi:k] v. tr. FAM. Tener caradura con, insolentarse con.
cheekbone [ˈtʃi:kbəun] n. ANAT. Pómulo, *m.*
cheekily [ˈtʃi:kili] adv. Descaradamente, con caradura.
cheekiness [ˈtʃi:kinis] n. FAM. Caradura, *f.*, frescura, *f.*
cheeky [ˈtʃi:ki] adj. FAM. Descarado, da; fresco, ca; caradura.
cheep [tʃi:p] n. Gorjeo, *m.*, piada, *f.*
cheep [tʃi:p] v. intr. Piar, gorjear (birds).
cheer [tʃiə*] n. Viva, *m.*, vítor, *m.* (shout of joy). || Consuelo, *m.* (comfort). || Comida, *f.* (food). || Humor, *m.*, estado (*m.*) de ánimo (mood). || Ánimo, *m.*, regocijo, *m.* (joy). | — *Cheers!*, ¡salud! (drinking). || *Loud cheers*, nutridos aplausos, ovación cerrada. || *To be of good cheer*, sentirse animoso. || *To give three cheers*, dar tres hurras. || *To make good cheer*, comer como un rey.
cheer [tʃiə*] v. tr. Vitorear, aclamar, ovacionar (to shout with joy). || Alegrar, animar (to gladden). || Reconfortar (to comfort). || — *To cheer on*, animar (fans). || *To cheer up*, animar, alentar (morally).
— V. intr. Alegrarse, animarse (to brighten up). || *Cheer up!*, ¡ánimo!, ¡anímese!
cheerful [ˈtʃiəful] adj. Alegre, animado, da (joyful). || Alentador, ra; prometedor, ra (encouraging).
cheerfulness [—nis] n. Alegría, *f.*
cheerily [ˈtʃiərili] adv. Alegremente.
cheeriness [ˈtʃiərinis] n. Alegría, *f.*
cheering [ˈtʃiəriŋ] adj. Esperanzador, ra; alentador, ra; prometedor, ra (encouraging).
— N. Ovaciones, *f. pl.*, aplausos, *m. pl.*, vítores, *m. pl.*
cheerio [ˈtʃiəriˈəu] interj. FAM. ¡Adiós!, ¡chao!, (at parting). | ¡Salud! (drinking).
cheerleader [ˈtʃiəli:də*] n. U. S. Persona (*f.*) que inicia los vivas en un partido (in football, etc.).
cheerless [ˈtʃiəlis] adj. Melancólico, ca; triste.
cheery [ˈtʃiəri] adj. Alegre, animado, da.
cheese [tʃi:z] n. Queso, *m.*: *grated cheese*, queso rallado. || — U. S. FAM. *Big cheese*, pez gordo (important person). || *Cheese cutter*, cuchillo (*m.*) para cortar queso. || *Cheese rennet*, cuajaleche, *m.* || *Cheese straws*, palitos (*m.*) de queso (cocktail biscuits). || *Dutch cheese*, queso de bola. || FIG. FAM. *Hard cheese*, mala potra, mala suerte.
cheesecake [—keik] n. Pastel (*m.*) de queso. || FAM. Fotos (*f. pl.*) sugestivas.
cheesecloth [—klɔθ] n. Estopilla, *f.*
cheeseparing [ˈtʃi:zˌpɛəriŋ] adj. Tacaño, ña; avaro, ra (mean).
— N. Tacañería, *f.*, avaricia, *f.* (miserliness). || *Cheeseparing economy*, economías (*f. pl.*) de chicha y nabo.
cheesy [ˈtʃi:zi] adj. Que sabe a queso (tasting of cheese). || Caseoso, sa (resembling cheese).
cheetah [ˈtʃi:tə] n. ZOOL. Onza, *f.*, leopardo (*m.*) cazador.
chef [ʃef] n. Jefe (*m.*) de cocina.
chef-d'oeuvre [ʃeiˈdə:vr] n. Obra (*f.*) maestra.
— OBSERV. El plural de *chef-d'œuvre* es *chefs-d'œuvre*.
chela [ˈki:lə] n. ZOOL. Pinza, *f.* || REL. Novicio (*m.*) budista.
— OBSERV. El plural de *chela*, cuando significa pinza, es *chelae*.
chelonian [keˈləuniən] n. ZOOL. Quelonio, *m.*
chemical [ˈkemikəl] adj. Químico, ca: *chemical symbol*, símbolo químico; *chemical engineer*, ingeniero químico; *chemical warfare*, guerra química.
— N. Sustancia (*f.*) química, producto (*m.*) químico.
chemin de fer [ʃəˌmɛ̃dəˈfɛə*] n. Ferrocarril, *m.* (card game).
chemise [ʃəˈmi:z] n. Camisa, *f.* (for women).
chemist [ˈkemist] n. Químico, ca (in chemistry). || Farmacéutico, ca (in pharmacy). || *Chemist's*, farmacia, *f.*: *all-night chemist s*, farmacia de guardia.

chemistry [—ri] n. Química, *f.*
chemotherapy [ˌkeməuˈθerəpi] n. Quimioterapia, *f.*
chenille [ʃəˈni:l] n. Felpilla, *f.* (textile). || U. S. Tela (*f.*) de algodón afelpada (candlewick).
chenopodiaceae [ˌki:nəpəudiˈeisii] pl. n. BOT. Quenopodiáceas, *f.*
cheque (U. S. **check**) [tʃek] n. Cheque, *m.*: *to write a cheque* o *to make out a cheque for a thousand pounds*, extender un cheque de mil libras; *to cash a cheque*, cobrar un cheque. || — *Bearer cheque*, cheque al portador. || *Blank cheque*, see BLANK. || *Cheque to order* o *order cheque*, cheque nominativo *or* nominal. || *Cheque without cover* o *dud cheque* (fam.) o *cheque that bounces* (fam.), cheque sin fondos. || *Crossed cheque*, cheque cruzado. || *Open cheque*, cheque al portador. || *Traveller's cheque*, cheque de viaje.
chequebook [ˈtʃekbuk] n. Talonario (*m.*) de cheques, chequera, *f.*
chequer [ˈtʃekə*] n. Cuadro, *m.* (square). || Cuadros, *m. pl.* (pattern).
chequer [ˈtʃekə*] v. tr. Marcar con cuadros.
chequerboard [—bɔ:d] n. Tablero (*m.*) de damas *or* de ajedrez.
chequered [—d] adj. A cuadros (cloth). || FIG. Con altibajos (uneven). | Variado, da (varied).
cherimoya [tʃeriˈmɔiə] n. BOT. Chirimoyo, *m.* (árbol). || *Cherimoya fruit*, chirimoya, *f.*
cherish [ˈtʃeriʃ] v. tr. Querer, amar (to love). || FIG. Abrigar (hopes, fears, etc.). | Cuidar (to take care of).
cheroot [ʃəˈru:t] n. Puro (*m.*) cortado en ambos extremos.
cherry [ˈtʃeri] adj. De color cereza (colour).
— N. BOT. Cerezo, *m.* (tree). | Cereza, *f.* (fruit): *cherry brandy*, aguardiente de cereza. || Rojo (*m.*) cereza (colour). || — BOT. *Cherry laurel*, lauroceraso, *m.* | *Cherry wood*, madera (*f.*) de cerezo.
cherrystone [—stəun] n. ZOOL. Almeja (*f.*) redonda. || Hueso (*m.*) de cereza (bone). || FIG. *It's not worth a cherrystone*, no vale un pepino.
chert [ˈtʃə:t] n. MIN. Sílex, *m.*, pedernal, *m.*
cherub [ˈtʃerəb] n. Querubín, *m.*
— OBSERV. El plural es *cherubs* o *cherubim*.
chervil [ˈtʃə:vil] n. BOT. Perifollo, *m.*
chess [tʃes] n. Ajedrez, *m.*
chessboard [ˈtʃesbɔ:d] n. Tablero (*m.*) de ajedrez.
chessel [ˈtʃesəl] n. Encella, *f.* (for cheese).
chessman [ˈtʃesmæn] n. Pieza (*f.*) de ajedrez.
— OBSERV. El plural de *chessman* es *chessmen*.
chess player [ˈtʃespleiə*] n. Ajedrecista, *m.* & *f.*
chest [tʃest] n. ANAT. Pecho, *m.* || Caja, *f.* (for tea, opium). || Cofre, *m.* (coffer). || FIG. Dinero, *m.*, fondos, *m. pl.* (funds). || — *Chest cavity*, cavidad torácica. || *Chest of drawers*, cómoda, *f.* || *Chest protector*, pechera, *f.* || *Chest voice*, voz (*f.*) de bajo. || FIG. FAM. *To get it off one's chest*, desahogarse, echarlo fuera. | *To throw out one's chest*, sacar el pecho.
chesterfield [ˈtʃestəfi:ld] n. Sofá, *m.* (settee). || Abrigo (*m.*) elegante (overcoat).
chestnut [ˈtʃesnʌt] n. BOT. Castaño, *m.* (tree). | Castaña, *f.* (fruit). | Castaño (*m.*) de Indias (horse chestnut). || Castaño, *m.*, marrón, *m.* (colour). || FAM. Chiste (*m.*) viejo. || Alazán, *m.* (horse). || VET. Espejuelo, *m.* (callus). || FIG. *To pull s.o.'s chesnusts out of the fire*, sacar a uno las castañas del fuego.
— Adj. Castaño, ña; marrón (colour). || Alazán, ana (horse).
chesty [ˈtʃesti] adj. FAM. Ancho de pecho. || FIG. FAM. Delicado de los bronquios. | Presumido, da; postinero, ra (boasting). || *Chesty cough*, tos (*f.*) de pecho.
cheval-de-frise [ʃəˈvældəˈfri:z] n. Caballo (*m.*) de frisa.
— OBSERV. El plural es *chevaux-de-frise*.
cheval glass [ʃəˈvælglɑ:s] n. Espejo (m.) de cuerpo entero.
chevalier [ˌʃevaˈliə*] n. Caballero, *m.*
cheviot [ˈtʃeviət] n. Cordero (*m.*) de Cheviot (animal). || Cheviot, *m.* (fabric).
chevron [ˈʃevrən] n. HERALD. Cheurón, *m.* || MIL. Galón, *m.*
chew [tʃu:] n. Masticación, *f.* (mastication). || Mascada (*f.*) de tabaco (tobacco).
chew [tʃu:] v. tr. Masticar, mascar. || Mascar (tobacco). || Morder (one's nails). || — FIG. FAM. *To chew one's ear off*, dar la lata. | *To chew one's nails*, morderse los puños. | *To chew out*, echar una bronca. | *To chew the fat* o *the rag*, estar de palique. | *To chew sth. over*, rumiar algo. | *To chew the cud*, rumiar. | *To chew up*, estropear (sth.), echar una bronca (to a person).
— V. intr. Mascar tabaco. || Mascar, masticar.
chewing [—iŋ] n. Masticación, *f.*, mascadura, *f.* || *Chewing gum*, chicle, *m.*
chi [kai] n. Ji, *f.* (Greek letter).
chiaroscuro [kiˌɑ:rəsˈkuərəu] n. Claroscuro, *m.*
chiasma [kaiˈæzmə] n. ANAT. Quiasma, *m.*
— OBSERV. El plural es *chiasmata* o *chiasmas*.
Chibcha [ˈtʃibtʃə] n. Chibcha, *m.* & *f.*
Chibchan [ˈtʃibtʃən] adj. Chibcha.
chibouque or **chibouk** [tʃiˈbu:k] n. Chibuquí, *m.* (pipe).
chic [ʃi:k] adj. Elegante, distinguido, da; de buen gusto.
— N. Elegancia, *f.*, distinción, *f.*, "chic", *m.*
chicane [ʃiˈkein] n. Triquiñuela, *f.* (trickery). || Fallo, *m.* (cards). || Argucia, *f.*, trapacería, *f.* (legal trick). || Través, *m.* (car racing).
chicane [ʃiˈkein] v. tr. Engañar con triquiñuelas (to trick). || Embrollar, enredar (to quibble).
— V. intr. Hacer triquiñuelas [*Amer.*, chicanear].
chicaner [ʃiˈkeinə*] n. Chicanero, ra.
chicanery [—ri] n. Argucia, *f.*, trapacería, *f.*
Chicano [ʃiˈkɑ:nəu] adj./n. Chicano, na.
chichi [ˈʃi:ʃi:] adj. Cursi.
chichimec [ˈtʃitʃimek] or **chichimeca** [ˌtʃitʃiˈmekɔ] or **chichimeco** [—ˈmekəu] n. Chichimeco, ca.
chichimecan [ˌtʃitʃiˈmekən] adj. Chichimeco, ca.
chick [tʃik] n. Polluelo, *m.* (chicken). || U. S. FAM Chavala, *f.* (girl).
chickadee [ˈtʃikədi:] n. Paro, *m.* (bird).
chicken [ˈtʃikin] n. Pollo, *m.* (bird). || FAM. Gallina, *m.* (coward). | Chavala, *f.* (young girl). || — FIG. FAM. *Don't count your chickens before they're hatched*, no hay que vender la piel del oso antes de haberlo matado, eso es el cuento de la lechera. | *To be chicken*, ser un gallina. | *To be no spring chicken*, no haber nacido ayer. | *To go to bed with the chickens*, acostarse con las gallinas.
chicken [ˈtʃikin] v. intr. FAM. *To chicken out*, rajarse.
chicken farmer [—ˌfɑ:mə*] n. Avicultor, ra.
chicken farming [—ˌfɑ:miŋ] n. Avicultura, *f.*
chicken feed [—fi:d] n. Alimento (*m.*) para las gallinas (food for hens). || FIG. FAM. Muy poco dinero, una miseria (money).
chickenhearted [—ˌhɑ:tid] adj. FIG. Gallina, cobarde (cowardly).
chicken pox [—pɔks] n. MED. Varicela, *f.*
chicken run [—rʌn] n. Gallinero, *m.*
chick-pea [ˈtʃikpi:] n. Garbanzo, *m.*
chickweed [ˈtʃikwi:d] n. BOT. Pamplina, *f.*
chicle [ˈtʃikəl] n. Chicle, *m.*, gomorresina, *f.*
chicory [ˈtʃikəri] n. Achicoria, *f.* (in coffee). || Escarola, *f.* (in salads).
chid [tʃid] pret. & p. p. See CHIDE.
chide* [tʃaid] v. tr./intr. Reprender, regañar.
— OBSERV. Pret. ***chid, chided***: p. p. ***chid, chidden, chided***.
chidden [ˈtʃidən] p. p. See CHIDE.
chief [tʃi:f] n. Jefe, *m.* & *f.* (leader, head). || Jefe, *m.*, cacique, *m.* (of tribe). || HERALD. Jefe, *m.* (upper part of a shield). || — *Chief executive*, jefe del ejecutivo. || MIL. *Chief of staff*, jefe del estado mayor. || *In chief*, en jefe.
— Adj. Principal: *the chief export is oil*, la exportación principal es el petróleo.
chiefly [—li] adv. Principalmente, sobre todo.
chieftain [ˈtʃi:ftən] n. Cacique, *m.*, jefe, *m.* (of a clan).
chieftaincy [—si] or **chieftainship** [—ʃip] n. Jefatura, *f.*
chiffon [ˈʃifɔn] n. Gasa, *f.* (material).
chiffonier [ˌʃifəˈniə*] n. Cómoda (*f.*) estrecha y alta, "chiffonier", *m.* (chest of drawers).
chigger [ˈtʃigə*] n. ZOOL. Nigua, *f.*
chignon [ˈʃi:njɔ̃] n. Moño, *m.* (hair).
chigoe [ˈtʃigəu] n. ZOOL. Nigua, *f.*
chilblain [ˈtʃilblein] n. MED. Sabañón, *m.*
child [tʃaild] n. Niño, ña (young boy or girl): *child prodigy*, niño prodigio. || Hijo, ja (son or daughter): *adopted, legitimate, natural child*, hijo adoptivo, legítimo, natural; *foster child*, hijo de leche. || Discípulo, la; hijo, ja: *child of the devil*, hijo del diablo. || FIG. Producto, *m.*, hijo, *m.*, hija, *f.*: *child of his imagination*, producto de su imaginación. || — *Child care*, puericultura, *f.* || *Child care centre*, guardería (*f.*) infantil. || *Child labour*, trabajo (*m.*) de menores, explotación (*f.*) de menores. || FIG. *Child's play*, juego (*m.*) de niños. || *Child welfare*, protección (*f*) de la infancia. || *With child*, embarazada, encinta, en estado.
— OBSERV. El plural de *child* es *children*.
childbearing [—ˌbeəriŋ] n. Maternidad, *f.* || *Childbearing woman*, mujer fecunda.
childbed [—bed] n. Sobreparto, *m.* || *Woman in childbed*, mujer de parto.
childbirth [—bə:θ] n. Parto, *m.*, alumbramiento, *m.* || *To die in childbirth*, morir de sobreparto.
Childermas [ˈtʃildəmæs] n. Día (*m.*) de los Inocentes.
childhood [ˈtʃaildhud] n. Niñez, *f.*, infancia, *f.* || — *Early childhood*, primera infancia. || FIG. *Second childhood*, segunda infancia.
childish [ˈtʃaildiʃ] adj. Infantil, pueril. || *Don't be childish!*, ¡no seas niño!
childishness [ˈtʃaildiʃnis] n. Puerilidad, *f.*, infantilismo, *m.*, niñería, *f.*
childless [ˈtʃaildlis] adj. Sin hijos.
childlike [ˈtʃaildlaik] adj. Infantil, de niño || FIG. Inocente, ingenuo, nua.
children [ˈtʃildrən] pl. n. See CHILD.
Chile [ˈtʃili] pr. n. GEOGR. Chile, *m.*
Chilean [—ən] adj./n. Chileno, na.
chili [ˈtʃili] n. BOT. Chile, *m.*
chill [tʃil] adj. Helador, ra; helado, da: *a chill wind*, un viento helador. || FIG. Frío, a (reception, etc.).
— N. Frío, *m.* (of temperature). || MED. Tiritona, *f.*, escalofrío, *m.* (shiver). || FIG. Frialdad, *f.* || TECH. Lingotera, *f.* || — *Chills and fever*, fiebre (*f.*) intermitente. || *There was a chill in the air*, hacía fresquito (weather), había un ambiente frío (atmosphere). || FIG. *To cast a chill over one's spirits*, caerle a uno como un jarro de agua fría. || *To catch a chill*, enfriarse, coger frío. || *To take the chill off*, entibiar, templar.

chill [tʃil] v. tr. Enfriar (to make cold). || Refrigerar (meat). || TECH. Templar (metal).
— V. intr. Enfriarse (to become cold). || Tiritar, tener escalofríos (to shiver). || TECH. Endurecerse al temple.
chiller [—ə*] n. Historia (*f.*) espeluznante.
chilli [ˈtʃili] n. BOT. Chile, *m.*
chilliness [—nis] n. Frío, *m.* || FIG. Frialdad, *f.*
chilling [ˈtʃiliŋ] n. Refrigeración, *f.* (of meat).
— Adj. Espeluznante.
chilly [ˈtʃili] adj. Fresco, ca: *a chilly morning*, una mañana fresca. || Frío, a: *his attitude was rather chilly*, su actitud fue bastante fría. || Friolero, ra (sensitive to cold).
chimaera [kaiˈmi:rə] n. See CHIMERA.
chime [tʃaim] n. Carillón, *m.* (bells, sound). || MUS. Vibráfono, *m.* || — Pl. Carillón, *m. sing.*
chime [tʃaim] v. tr. Tocar (to ring). || Dar: *the clock chimed six o'clock*, el reloj dio las seis.
— V. intr. Sonar, repicar. || — *To chime in*, intervenir en la conversación: *he chimed in with a stupid remark*, intervino en la conversación soltando una tontería. || FIG. FAM. *To chime in with*, estar de acuerdo con (to agree with), concordar con (to fit in with).
chimera [kaiˈmiərə] n. MYTH. Quimera, *f.* || FIG. Quimera, *f.* (foolish idea).
chimere [tʃiˈmiə*] n. REL. Especie de sobrepelliz, *f.* (bishop's robe).
chimeric [kaiˈmerik] or **chimerical** [kaiˈmerikəl] adj. Quimérico, ca.
chimney [ˈtʃimni] n. Chimenea, *f.* (of a house, train, mountain, etc.). || Chimenea (*f.*) volcánica (in a volcano). || Tubo (*m.*) de cristal del quinqué (of a lamp). || — *Chimney corner*, espacio (*m.*) junto a la chimenea. || *Chimney flue*, cañón (*m.*) de chimenea. || *Chimney pot*, cañón (*m.*) de chimenea. || *Chimney stack*, fuste (*m.*) de la chimenea. || *Chimney sweep*, deshollinador, *m.*, limpiachimeneas, *m. inv.* || *Chimney sweep's brush*, deshollinador, *m.* || *Sitting in the chimney corner*, sentado al amor de la lumbre. || FIG. *To smoke like a chimney*, fumar como una chimenea.
chimneypiece [—pi:s] n. Manto (*m.*) de chimenea.
chimpanzee [ˌtʃimpənˈzi] n. ZOOL. Chimpancé, *m.*
chin [tʃin] n. Barbilla, *f.*, mentón, *m.* || — *Chin strap*, barboquejo, *m.* || *Double chin*, papada, *f.* || FIG. *Keep your chin up!*, ¡ánimo!, ¡anímese! | *To keep one's chin up*, no desanimarse. || U. S. FAM. *To take it on the chin*, mantenerse firme. || FAM. *Up to the chin o chin deep*, hasta el cuello.
china [ˈtʃainə] adj. De loza, de porcelana. || *China closet*, chinero, *m.* (a piece of furniture).
— N. China, *f.* (ceramic). || Porcelana, *f.* (porcelain). || Loza, *f.* (crockery). || *China clay*, caolín, *m.*
China [ˈtʃainə] pr. n. GEOGR. China, *f.*
chinaberry [ˈtʃainəˌberi] n. BOT. Jaboncillo, *m.*
Chinaman [ˈtʃainəmən] n. Chino, *m.*

— OBSERV. El plural de *Chinaman* es *Chinamen.*

Chinatown [ˈtʃainətaun] n. U. S. Barrio (*m.*) chino.
chinaware [ˈtʃainəwεə*] n. China, *f.* (ceramic).
chinch bug [ˈtʃintʃbʌg] n. ZOOL. Chinche, *f.*
chinchilla [tʃinˈtʃilə] n. Chinchilla, *f.* (animal and fur).
chin-chin [ˈtʃinˈtʃin] interj. ¡Salud!
chincough [ˈtʃinkɔf] n. MED. Tos ferina, *f.*
chine [tʃain] n. Lomo, *m.* (meat). || GEOL. Cresta, *f.*, cumbre, *f.* (ridge). | Barranco, *m.* (gully).
chine [tʃain] v. tr. Deslomar.
Chinese [ˈtʃaiˈni:z] adj. Chino, na.
— N. Chino, na (native of China). || Chino, *m.* (language). || — *Chinese lantern*, farolillo (*m.*) de papel. || *Chinese puzzle*, rompecabezas (*m. inv.*) chino.
chink [tʃiŋk] n. Raja, *f.*, grieta, *f.* (fissure). || Resquicio, *m.* (crack). || Sonido (*m.*) metálico, tintineo, *m.* (light sound). || FAM. Chino, na (Chinese). | Pasta, *f.*, moni, *m.* [*Amer.*, plata, *f.*] (money). || FIG. *A chink in s.o.'s armour*, el punto flaco de alguien.
chink [tʃiŋk] v. tr. Hacer sonar, hacer tintinear. || FAM. *To chink glasses*, chocar las copas, brindar.
— V. intr. Sonar, tintinear.
chinook [tʃiˈnuk] n. Viento (*m.*) cálido de las montañas Rocosas, Oregón y Washington.
chintz [tʃints] n. Zaraza, *f.* (cloth).
chintzy [—i] adj. U. S. De oropel.
chin-wag [ˈtʃinwæg] n. FAM. Palique, *m.*
chin-wag [ˈtʃinwæg] v. intr. FAM. Parlotear, estar de cháchara *or* de palique.
chip [tʃip] n. Pedacito, *m.*, trocito, *m.* (piece of glass, etc.). || Viruta, *f.* (of metal, of wood). || Astilla, *f.* (splinter). || Lasca, *f.* (of a stone). || Muesca, *f.* (mark made by chipping). || Mella, *f.*, melladura, *f.* (in a knife). || Desportilladura, *f.* (on china): *there is a chip on the rim of this cup*, hay una desportilladura en el borde de esta taza. || Ficha, *f.* (gambling). || CULIN. Patata (*f.*) frita. || — *Chip ax*, hachuela, *f.* || *Chip basket*, cestito, *m.* || *Chip shot*, chip, *m.* (golf). || FAM. *He has had his chips*, está perdido. || FIG. (*He is*) *a chip off the old block*, de tal palo, tal astilla. || U. S. FAM. *In the chips*, forrado de dinero. || FAM. *The chips are down*, la suerte está echada. || FIG. *To have a chip on one's shoulder*, guardar un resentimiento.
chip [tʃip] v. tr. Astillar (to splinter). || Mellar (a knife). || Desportillar (a plate). || Cepillar (with a plane). || Cascar (an egg). || Trabajar con el escoplo (with a chisel). || Cortar (potatoes). || FAM. Tomar el pelo a (to pull one's leg). || SP. Picar (a ball).
— V. intr. Astillarse. || Desportillarse (plate): *this china chips easily*, esta porcelana se desportilla fácilmente. || Mellarse (a knife). || Cascarse (an egg). || Hacer un "chip" (in golf). || FAM. *To chip in*, decir (to say), apostar (to bet), compartir los gastos (to share expenses), poner (to contribute).
chipboard [ˈtʃipbɔ:d] n. Cartón, *m.* (cardboard). || Madera (*f.*) aglomerada (wood).
chipped beef [ˈtʃiptˈbi:t] n. U. S. Carne (*f.*) ahumada de vaca cortada en lonchas finas.
chipper [ˈtʃipə*] adj. U. S. FAM. Alegre, jovial, animado, da.
chi-rho [ˈkaiˈrəu] n. REL. Monograma (*m.*) de Cristo.
chiromancer [ˈkaiərəmænsə*] n. Quiromántico, ca.
chiromancy [ˈkaiərəmænsi] n. Quiromancia, *f.*
chiropodist [kiˈrɔpədist] n. MED. Pedicuro, ra; callista *m.* & *f.*
chiropody [kiˈrɔpədi] n. MED. Quiropodia, *f.*
chiropractic [ˈkairəˌpræktik] n. Quiropráctica, *f.*
chiropractor [ˈkairəˌpræktə*] n. Quiropráctico, ca.
chiropter [ˈkaiərɔptə*] n. ZOOL. Quiróptero, *m.*
chiropteran [kaírɔptəren] adj. Quiróptero, ra.
— N. Quiróptero, *m.*

— OBSERV. El plural de *chiropteran* es *chiroptera.*

chirp [tʃə:p] n. Gorjeo, *m.* (of birds). || Canto, *m.*, chirrido, *m.* (of crickets).
chirp [tʃə:p] v. tr./intr. Gorjear (birds). || Cantar, chirriar (crickets).
chirpiness [—inis] n. FAM. Alegría, *f.*, animación, *f.*
chirpy [—i] adj. FAM. Alegre, animado, da.
chirr [tʃə:*] n. Chirrido, *m.* (of crickets, etc.).
chirr [tʃə:*] v. intr. Chirriar.
chirrup [ˈtʃirəp] n./v.tr./intr. See CHIRP.
chisel [ˈtʃizl] n. TECH. Cincel, *m.*, escoplo, *m.* (tool). | Cortafrío, *m.* (cold chisel). || FIG. Estafa, *f.*, timo, *m.*
chisel [ˈtʃizl] v. tr. TECH. Cincelar (to tool). | Escoplear (to mortice). || FIG. FAM. Estafar, timar.
chiselled or **chiseled** [—d] adj. Cincelado, da. || FIG. Cincelado, da: *chiselled features*, rostro cincelado.
chiseller [—ə*] n. TECH. Cincelador, *m.* || FIG. FAM. Estafador, *m.*, timador, *m.*
chit [tʃit] n. Chica, *f.*, muchacha, *f.* (girl). || Niño, *m* (boy). || Nota, *f.*, tarjeta, *f.* (note). || Vale, *m.*, cuenta, *f.*, nota, *f.* (of a sum owed).
chitchat [ˈtʃittʃæt] n. Cháchara, *f.*, palique, *m.* (gossip).
chitin [ˈkaitin] n. Quitina, *f.*
chitinous [—əs] adj. Quitinoso, sa.
chitterlings [ˈtʃitəliŋʒ] pl. n. Mondongo (*m. sing.*) frito *or* cocido.
chitty [ˈtʃiti] n. FAM. Nota, *f.*
chivalric [ˈʃivəlrik] adj. Caballeresco, ca.
chivalrous [ˈʃivəlrəs] adj. Caballeroso, sa.
chivalry [ˈʃivəlri] n. Caballerosidad, *f.* (conventions). || Caballería, *f.* (order).
chive [tʃaiv] n. BOT. Cebolleta, *f.*
chivy or **chivvy** [ˈtʃivi] v. tr. Perseguir (to chase). || *To chivy s.o. about*, no dejar a alguien en paz.
chlamys [ˈklæmis] n. Clámide, *f.*
Chloe [ˈkləui] pr.n. Cloe, *f.*
chloral [ˈklɔ:rəl] n. CHEM. Cloral, *m.* || CHEM. *Chloral hydrate*, hidrato (*m.*) de cloral.
chlorate [ˈklɔ:rit] n. CHEM. Clorato, *m.*
chloric [ˈklɔ:rik] adj. CHEM. Clórico, ca.
chloride [ˈklɔ:raid] n. CHEM. Cloruro, *m.*: *chloride of lime*, cloruro de cal.
chlorinate [ˈklɔ:rineit] v. tr. CHEM. Tratar con cloro.
chlorination [ˌklɔ:riˈneiʃən] n. Desinfección (*f.*) con cloro.
chlorine [ˈklɔ:ri:n] n. CHEM. Cloro, *m.*
chloroform [ˈklɔrəfɔ:m] n. CHEM. Cloroformo, *m.*
chloroform [ˈklɔrəfɔ:m] v. tr. Cloroformizar.
chloromycetin [ˌklɔ:rəumaiˈsi:tin] n. MED. Cloromicetina, *f.*
chlorophyll, chlorophyl [ˈklɔrəfil] n. Clorofila, *f.*
chlorophyllian [ˌklɔrəˈfiliən] adj. Clorofílico, ca: *chlorophyllian function*, función clorofílica.
chlorophyllose [ˌklɔrəˈfiləuz] or **chlorophyllous** [ˌklɔrəˈfiləs] adj. Clorofílico, ca.
chloroplast [ˈklɔrəplæst] n. BOT. Cloroplasto, *m.*
chlorosis [kləˈrəusis] n. MED. BOT. Clorosis, *f.*
chlorotic [kləˈrɔtik] adj. Clorótico, ca.
chock [tʃɔk] n. Calzo, *m.*, cuña, *f.* (wedge).
chock [tʃɔk] v. tr. Calzar (to wedge). || *To chock up*, llenar hasta el máximo *or* hasta los topes.
chockablock [ˈtʃɔkəˈblɔk] adj. Hasta los topes, atestado, da; de bote en bote.
chock-full [ˈtʃɔkˈful] adj. Hasta los topes, atestado, da; de bote en bote.
chocolate [ˈtʃɔkəlit] adj. De chocolate (made of chocolate). || De color chocolate. || U. S. *Chocolate candy*, bombón, *m.*
— N. Chocolate, *m.*: *drinking chocolate*, chocolate a la taza; *plain chocolate*, chocolate para crudo. || Bombón, *m.*, chocolatina, *f.* (sweet). || — *Bar of chocolate*, tableta (*f.*) *or* barra (*f.*) de chocolate. || *Chocolate factory*, chocolatería, *f.* || *Chocolate pot*, chocolatera, *f.* || *Chocolate shop*, chocolatería, *f.*
choice [tʃɔis] adj. Escogido, da; selecto, ta. || De primera calidad (wine, etc.).
— N. Elección, *f.*, selección, *f.* (act of choosing). ||

Opción, *f.* (right to choose). || Preferencia, *f.*, elección, *f.* (sth. chosen). || Surtido, *m.* (variety). || FAM. Flor (*f.*) y nata, crema *f.* (best). || — *By choice*, por gusto. || *Of one's choice*, elegido, da; de su elección. || *To have no choice*, no tener alternativa. || *To have no choice but to*, no tener más remedio que. || *To have plenty of choice*, tener donde escoger. || *To make* o *to take one's choice*, escoger, elegir.

choiceness [—nis] n. Lo escogido, calidad, *f.*

choir [ˈkwaiə*] n. MUS. Coro, *m.*, coral, *f.* || ARCH. Coro, *m.*

choir [ˈkwaiə*] v. tr./intr. MUS. Cantar a coro: *to choir a hymn*, cantar un himno a coro.

choirboy [—bɔi] n. MUS. REL. Niño (*m.*) de coro.

choirmaster [—ˌmɑːstə*] n. Director (*m.*) de coro (of a choral society). || REL. Maestro (*m.*) de capilla.

choke [tʃəuk] n. TECH. Obturador, *m.* (valve). || ELECTR. Bobina, (*f.*) de reactancia. || AUT. Estrangulador, *m.* || MED. Ahogo, *m.*, sofocamiento, *m.* || Obstrucción, *f.* || Pelusa, *f.* (of artichokes).

choke [tʃəuk] v. tr. Estrangular (to strangle). || Asfixiar, ahogar (to asphyxiate). || Apagar, sofocar, extinguir (fire). || Obstruir, atascar: *weeds were choking the river*, las hierbas obstruían el río. || Ahogar (voice). || TECH. Obturar. || — *To choke back* o *down*, contener, reprimir, sofocar (feelings). || *To choke down sobs*, ahogar el llanto. || *To choke s.o. off*, callar *or* silenciar a uno (to silence), fastidiar (to annoy). || *To choke up*, obstruir, atascar.

— V. intr. Asfixiarse, ahogarse (to suffocate). || Obstruirse, atascarse (to get blocked up). || FIG. Quedarse sin respiración (with emotion). || Atragantarse (*on*, con): *to choke on a fishbone*, atragantarse con una espina. || — *To choke up*, atascarse, obstruirse. || *To choke with laughter*, reír ahogadamente.

chokebore [—bɔː*] n. Estrangulamiento, *m.* (of a sporting gun).

chokecherry [—ˌtʃeri] n. BOT. Cereza (*f.*) silvestre (fruit). | Cerezo (*m.*) silvestre (tree).

choke coil [—kɔil] n. ELECTR. Bobina (*f.*) de reactancia.

chokedamp [—dæmp] n. Mofeta, *f.* (gas).

choker [ˈtʃəukə*] n. TECH. Obturador, *m.* || AUT. Estrangulador, *m.* || Estola, *f.* (narrow fur piece). || Gargantilla, *f.* (necklace). || Cuello (*m.*) alto (collar).

choky [ˈtʃəuki] adj. Ahogado, da: *a choky voice*, una voz ahogada. || Sofocante, asfixiante: *choky atmosphere*, atmósfera sofocante.

choledoc [ˈkəlidək] adj. ANAT. Colédoco.

— N. ANAT. Colédoco, *m.*

choler [ˈkələ*] n. (Ant.) Cólera, *f.* || (Ant.) MED. Bilis, *f.*

cholera [ˈkələrə] n. MED. Cólera, *m.*: *cholera morbus*, cólera morbo.

choleric [ˈkələrik] adj. Colérico, ca. || MED. Colérico, ca.

cholesterine [kəˈlestəriːn] n. Colesterina, *f.*

cholesterol [kəˈlestərəl] n. Colesterol, *m.*

choose* [tʃuːz] v. tr. Escoger, elegir (to select). || — REL. *The chosen ones*, los elegidos. || *The Chosen People*, El Pueblo Elegido.

— V. intr. Escoger, elegir (to make a choice). || Querer (to like): *as you choose*, como quiera. || Preferir (to prefer). || Decidir (to decide). || — *He cannot choose but*, no tiene más remedio que, no tiene otra alternativa que. || *There is nothing to choose between them*, son iguales, vale tanto el uno como el otro. || *To choose to do sth.*, optar por hacer algo, decidirse por hacer algo. || *To pick and choose*, ser muy exigente.

— OBSERV. Pret. **chose;** p. p. **chosen.**

chooser [—ə*] n. Persona (*f.*) que escoge, el que escoge.

choosing [—iŋ] n. Elección, *f.*, selección, *f.*

choosy or **choosey** [—i] adj. FAM. Quisquilloso, sa; exigente; difícil (fussy).

chop [tʃɔp] n. Golpe, *m.*, tajo, *m.* (a cut). || Hachazo, *m.*, tajo, *m.* (with an axe). || Chuleta, *f.* (meat). || Chapoteo, *m.* (of the sea). || COMM. Sello, *m.* (seal). | Marca, *f.* (brand). | Licencia, *f.* || — Pl. FAM. Morros, *m.* (mouth). | Quijada, *f. sing.* (jaws of an animal). || — *Chops and changes*, cambios, *m. pl.* || FIG. FAM. *To get the chop*, ser despedido. | *To lick one's chops*, relamerse.

chop [tʃɔp] v. tr. Cortar: *to chop wood*, cortar leña. || CULIN. Picar (to mince). || Cortar, tajar (to cut up). || Tronchar: *to chop a branch off a tree*, tronchar una rama de un árbol. || SP. Dar efecto a, cortar: *to chop the ball*, dar efecto a la pelota. || MED. Cortar. || FIG. Cortar (one's words). || — *To chop down*, disminuir. || FIG. *To chop logic*, discutir. || *To chop off s.o.'s head*, cortar la cabeza a alguien, degollar a alguien. || *To chop trees down*, talar *or* cortar árboles. || *To chop up*, cortar en trozos (to cut in pieces), picar (meat).

— V. intr. MAR. Saltar (the wind). | Chapotear (the sea). || — *To chop at*, hacer cortes en. || *To chop and change*, cambiar [de opinión]. || *To chop back*, dar media vuelta. || FAM. *To chop in*, intervenir, meter baza.

chop-chop [ˈtʃɔpˈtʃɔp] interj. FAM. ¡De prisa!, ¡rápido! (quickly). || ¡En seguida! (at once).

chopine [ˈtʃɔpin] n. Chapín, *m.* (shoe).

chopper [ˈtʃɔpə*] n. Hacha, *f.* (axe). || Cuchilla, *f.*, tajadera, *f.* (of butcher). || FAM. Helicóptero, *m.* || AGR. Cortarraíces, *m. inv.*, cortadora (*f.*) de raíces.

chopping [ˈtʃɔpiŋ] n. Corte, *m.* (of wood). || Picadura, *f.* (of tobacco, etc.). || — FAM. *Chopping and changing*, fluctuaciones, *f. pl.*, cambios (*m. pl.*) frecuentes. || *Chopping block* o *chopping board*, tajo, *m.* || *Chopping knife*, tajadera, *f.*, cuchilla, *f.*

choppy [ˈtʃɔpi] adj. Picado, da (sea). || Variable (wind). || FIG. Inconexo, xa (ideas). | Cortado, da (style).

chopstick [ˈtʃɔpstik] n. Palillo, *m.* (eating utensil).

choral [ˈkɔːrəl] adj. MUS. Coral. || *Choral society*, orfeón, *m.*

choral or **chorale** [kəˈrɑːl] n. MUS. Coral, *f.*

chord [kɔːd] n. MUS. Acorde, *m.* (combination of notes). | Cuerda, *f.* (string). || FIG. Fibra, *f.*: *to touch the right chord*, tocar la fibra sensible. || MATH. Cuerda, *f.* (of an arc). || AVIAT. Profundidad (*f.*) del ala. || ANAT. Cuerda, *f.*: *vocal chords*, cuerdas vocales. || Solera, *f.* (of a beam). || MUS. *Broken* o *spread chord*, arpegio, *m.*

chordate [ˈkɔːdit] adj. ZOOL. Cordado, da.

— N. Cordado, *m.*

chore [tʃɔː*] n. Faena, *f.*, quehacer, *m.*: *household chores*, faenas de la casa. || Tarea (*f.*) penosa (hard task). || Trabajo (*m.*) rutinario (routine task).

chorea [kɔˈriə] n. MED. Corea, *f.*, baile (*m.*) de San Vito.

choreographer [ˌkɔriˈɔgrəfə*] n. Coreógrafo, *m.*

choreographic [ˌkɔriəˈgræfik] adj. Coreográfico, ca.

choreography [ˌkɔriˈɔgrəfi] n. Coreografía, *f.*

choriamb [ˈkɔriæmb] n. Coriambo, *m.*

chorioid [ˈkɔːriɔid] adj./n. See CHOROID.

chorion [ˈkɔːriən] n. ANAT. Corión, *m.*

chorister [ˈkɔristə*] n. Corista, *m.* (choir singer). || U. S. Director (*m.*) de un coro.

chorography [kəˈrɔgræfi] n. Corografía, *f.*

choroid [ˈkɔːrɔid] adj. Coroideo, a.

— N. Coroides, *f. inv.*

chortle [ˈtʃɔːtl] n. Risa (*f.*) ahogada.

chortle [ˈtʃɔːtl] v. intr. Reír entre dientes, reír ahogadamente. || *"Not I", he chortled*, Yo no, dijo riéndose.

chorus [ˈkɔːrəs] n. MUS. Coro, *m.* || Conjunto, *m.* (of chorus girls). || Estribillo, *m.* (of a song). || — *Chorus girl*, corista, *f.* || FIG. *Chorus of protests*, coro de protestas. || *In chorus*, en coro.

chorus [ˈkɔːrəs] v. tr. Cantar *or* decir en coro.

— V. intr. Cantar *or* hablar en coro.

chose [tʃəuz] pret. See CHOOSE.

chosen [—n] p. p. See CHOOSE.

chough [tʃʌf] n. ZOOL. Chova, *f.* (bird).

chouse [tʃaus] v. tr. Estafar, timar (to swindle): *to chouse sth. out of s.o.*, estafar algo a alguien.

chow [tʃau] n. Perro (*m.*) chino. || U. S. FAM. Jamancia, *f.*, manduca, *f.*, comida, *f.* (food).

chowder [ˈtʃaudə*] n. U. S. CULIN. Sopa (*f.*) de pescado.

chrematistic [ˌkreməˈtistik] adj. Crematístico, ca.

chrematistics [—s] n. Crematística, *f.*

chrestomathy [kresˈtɔməθi] n. Crestomatía, *f.*

chrism [ˈkrizəm] n. REL. Crisma, *m.*

chrismal [ˈkrizməl] n. REL. Capillo (*m.*) de cristianar.

Christ [kraist] pr. n. REL. Cristo, *m.* || — *Jesus Christ*, Jesucristo. || *The Christ child*, el Niño Jesús.

— Interj. FAM. ¡Por Dios!

christen [ˈkrisn] v. tr. REL. Bautizar. || Bautizar, llamar: *they christened him David*, lo llamaron David. || FIG. Bautizar (a ship, building, etc.).

Christendom [ˈkrisndəm] n. Cristiandad, *f.*

christening [ˈkrisniŋ] n. Bautismo, *m.*, bautizo, *m.*

— Adj. Bautismal.

Christian [ˈkristjən] adj./n. REL. Cristiano, na. || — REL. *Christian Brothers*, Hermanos de la Doctrina Cristiana. | *Christian era*, era cristiana. || *Christian name*, nombre (*m.*) de pila.

christiania [ˌkristiˈɑːnjə] n. Cristiania, *m.* (in skiing).

Christianity [ˌkristiˈæniti] n. REL. Cristianismo, *m.* (religion). | Cristiandad, *f.* (Christendom).

Christianization [ˌkristjənaiˈzeiʃən] n. Cristianización, *f.*

Christianize [ˈkristjənaiz] v. tr. Cristianizar.

Christine [ˈkristiːn] pr. n. Cristina, *f.*

Christlike [ˈkraistlaik] adj. Como Cristo.

Christliness [ˈkraistlinis] n. Espíritu (*m.*) cristiano.

Christmas [ˈkrisməs] n. Navidad, *f.* || — *At Christmas*, por Navidades. || *Christmas box*, aguinaldo, *m.* || *Christmas cake*, tarta (*f.*) de Navidad. || *Christmas card*, tarjeta (*f.*) de Navidad, christmas, *m. inv.*, crismas, *m. inv.* || *Christmas carol*, villancico, *m.* || *Christmas Day*, día (*m.*) de Navidad. || *Christmas Eve*, Nochebuena, *f.*, Noche Buena. || *Christmas pudding*, pastel (*m.*) de Navidad. || *Christmas rose*, eléboro negro. || *Christmas stocking*, zapatos (*m. pl.*) de Reyes. || *Christmas time*, Navidades, *f. pl.* || *Christmas tree*, árbol (*m.*) de Navidad (tree; part of oil well). || *Father Christmas*, Papá Noel, *m.* || *Merry Christmas*, ¡Felices Pascuas!

Christmastide [ˈkrisməstaid] n. Pascuas, *f. pl.*, Navidades, *f. pl.*

Christopher [ˈkristəfə*] pr. n. Cristóbal, *m.*

christ's-thorn [ˈkraistsθɔːn] n. BOT. Espina (*f.*) santa.

christy [ˈkristi] n. Cristiania, *m.* (in skiing).

chromate [ˈkrəumit] n. CHEM. Cromato, *m.*

chromatic [krəˈmætik] adj. Cromático, ca. || — MED. *Chromatic aberration*, aberración cromática. || *Chroma-*

tic printing, impresión (*f.*) en color. || *Chromatic scale*, escala cromática.

chromaticism [krəˈmætisizəm] n. Mus. Cromatismo, *m.*

chromatin [ˈkrəumətin] n. Biol. Cromatina, *f.*

chromatism [ˈkrəumətizəm] n. Cromatismo, *m.*

chrome [krəum] n. Cromo, *m.* || — *Chrome green*, verde (*m.*) de cromo. || *Chrome red*, rojo (*m.*) de cromo. || *Chrome steel*, acero (*m.*) al cromo.

chrome [krəum] v. tr. Cromar.

chromic [—ik] adj. Crómico, ca.

chromium [ˈkrəumjəm] n. Chem. Cromo, *m.*

chromium-plate [—pleit] v. tr. Tech. Cromar.

chromium-plating [—ˌpleitiŋ] n. Tech. Cromado, *m.*

chromolithograph [ˈkrəuməuˈliθəgrɑ:f] n. Cromolitografía, *f.*

chromolithographer [ˈkrəuməuliˈθɔgrəfə*] n. Cromolitógrafo, *m.*

chromolithography [ˈkrəuməuliˈθɔgrəfi] n. Cromolitografía, *f.*

chromosome [ˈkrəuməsəum] n. Biol. Cromosoma, *m.*

chromosphere [ˈkrəuməsfiə*] n. Astr. Cromosfera, *f.*

chronic [ˈkrɔ:nik] adj. Crónico, ca (deep-seated). || Fig. Empedernido, da: *a chronic gambler*, un jugador empedernido. || Fam. Terrible, fatal (very bad): *the actor gave a chronic performance*, el actor tuvo una actuación terrible.

chronicity [krəˈnisiti] n. Cronicidad, *f.*

chronicle [ˈkrɔnikl] n. Crónica, *f.*

chronicle [ˈkrɔnikl] v. tr. Hacer la crónica de.

chronicler [—ə*] n. Cronista, *m.* & *f.*

chronograph [ˈkrɔnəgrɑ:f] n. Cronógrafo, *m.*

chronographer [—ə*] n. Cronógrafo, *m.*

chronologer [krəˈnɔlədzə*] n. Cronólogo, *m.*

chronologic [ˌkrɔnəˈlɔdʒik] adj. Cronológico, ca.

chronological [ˌkrɔnəˈlɔdʒikəl] adj. Cronológico, ca.

chronologist [krəˈnɔlədʒist] n. Cronologista, *m.*, cronólogo, *m.*

chronology [krəˈnɔlədʒi] n. Cronología, *f.*

chronometer [krəˈnɔmitə*] n. Cronómetro, *m.*

chronometric [ˌkrɔnəˈmetrik] or **chronometrical** [—əl] adj. Cronométrico, ca.

chronometry [krəˈnɔmitri] n. Cronometría, *f.*

chrysalid [ˈkrisəlid] n. Zool. Crisálida, *f.*

chrysalis [ˈkrisəlis] n. Zool. Crisálida, *f.*

— Observ. El plural es *chrysalises* o *chrysalides*.

chrysanthemum [kriˈsænθəməm] n. Crisantemo, *m.*

chub [tʃʌb] n. Zool. Cacho, *m.* (fish).

chubby [ˈtʃʌbi] adj. Gordinflón, ona; rechoncho, cha (body). || Mofletudo, da (face).

chubby-cheeked [—tʃi:kt] adj. Mofletudo, da.

chuck [tʃʌk] n. Culin. Paletilla, *f.* (of meat). || Calzo, *m.* (chock). || Tech. Mandril, *m.* || Mamola, *f.* (tap under the chin). || Fam. Tiro, *m.* (throw). || Cloqueo, *m.* (of hens, etc.). || Chasquido, *m.* (of the tongue). || Sp. Disco, *m.* (in ice hockey). || U. S. Fam. Jamancia, *f.*, comida, *f.* (food). || Fam. *To give s.o. the chuck*, echar a alguien, poner a alguien de patitas en la calle.

chuck [tʃʌk] v. tr. Golpear en la barbilla, hacer la mamola a (tap under the chin). || Fam. Tirar, arrojar, echar (to throw). | Abandonar, dejar (to give up). || Tech. Sujetar con el mandril. || — Fam. *Chuck it!*, ¡basta! | *To chuck away*, tirar (to throw away), despilfarrar (money), desperdiciar, perder (a chance). | *To chuck out*, tirar (things), poner de patitas en la calle, echar (people). | *To chuck up*, mandar a paseo (to give up).

chucker-out [ˈtʃʌkərˈaut] n. Fam. Matón, *m.* [encargado de echar a los alborotadores de un club].

— Observ. El plural de *chucker-out* es *chuckers-out*.

chuckhole [ˈtʃʌkˌhəul] n. Bache, *m.*

chuckle [ˈtʃʌkl] n. Risa (*f.*) ahogada, risita, *f.* || *To have a good chuckle over sth.*, reírse mucho de algo.

chuckle [ˈtʃʌkl] v. intr. Reír entre dientes (to laugh). || Cloquear (a hen). || *To chuckle at* o *over*, reírse de.

chucklehead [—hed] n. Fam. Alcornoque, *m.*, zoquete, *m.* (blockhead).

chuck wagon [ˈtʃʌkˌwægən] n. U. S. Fam. Carromato (*m.*) con provisiones.

chufa [ˈtʃufə] n. Bot. Chufa, *f.* (earth almond).

chuffed [tʃʌft] adj. Fam. Contento, ta.

chug [tʃʌg] n. Resoplido, *m.* (of steam engine). || Traqueteo, *m.* (of an internal combustion engine).

chug [tʃʌg] v. intr. Resoplar (a steam engine). || Traquetear (an internal combustion engine).

chukkar or **chukker** [ˈtʃʌkə*] n. Sp. Período (*m.*) de juego (in polo).

chum [tʃʌm] n. Fam. Compinche, *m.*, compañero, *m.* || *To be great chums*, ser buenos compañeros *or* muy amigos.

chum [tʃʌm] v. intr. Fam. Ser muy amigos. || — Fam. *To chum up*, hacerse amigos. | *To chum up with s.o.*, hacerse amigo de alguien.

chummy [—i] adj. Fam. Amistoso, sa (friendly). || — Fam. *To be chummy*, ser muy amigos. | *To be chummy with s.o.*, ser muy amigo de alguien.

chump [tʃʌmp] n. Cadera, *f.* (meat). || Tarugo, *m.* (of wood). || Fam. Majadero, ra (silly person). | Azotea, *f.*, chaveta, *f.* (head): *to be off one's chump*, estar mal de la azotea.

chump chop [—tʃɔp] n. Chuleta, *f.*

chunk [tʃʌŋk] n. Pedazo, *m.* (of bread, etc.). || Tarugo, *m.* (of wood). || Cantidad (*f.*) grande (large amount). || Parte, *f.* (part).

chunky [—i] adj. Fornido, da (person). || Grueso y pesado (things).

church [tʃə:tʃ] n. Rel. Iglesia, *f.* (catholic). | Templo, *m.*, iglesia, *f.* (protestant). | Oficio (*m.*) religioso (service). | Misa, *f.* (mass): *after church*, después de la misa. || — Rel. *Church of England*, iglesia anglicana. | *Church of Jesus Christ of Latter-day Saints*, iglesia de los mormones. | *Mother Church*, la Santa Madre Iglesia.

— Adj. De la iglesia: *the church roof*, el tejado de la iglesia. || Eclesiástico, ca: *the Church authorities*, las autoridades eclesiásticas. || — *Church militant*, iglesia militante. || *Church music*, música sacra. || *Church service*, oficio religioso. || Fig. *Poor as a church mouse*, más pobre que las ratas.

church [tʃə:tʃ] v. tr. Rel. Purificar.

churchgoer [—gəuə*] n. Rel. Practicante, *m.* & *f.*, persona (*f.*) que va a misa.

churchgoing [—ˌgəuiŋ] n. Rel. Práctica, *f.*

— Adj. Practicante.

churching [—iŋ] n. Rel. Ceremonia (*f.*) de purificación.

churchman [ˈtʃə:tʃmən] n. Rel. Clérigo, *m.*, eclesiástico, *m.*, sacerdote, *m.* (of Roman Catholic Church). | Pastor, *m.* (of Protestant Church). | Anglicano, *m.*

— Observ. El plural de *churchman* es *churchmen*.

churchwarden [ˈtʃə:tʃˈwɔ:dn] n. Rel. Mayordomo, *m.* || Pipa (*f.*) larga.

churchwoman [ˈtʃə:tʃˌwumən] n. Anglicana, *f.*

— Observ. El plural es *churchwomen*.

churchy [ˈtʃə:tʃi] adj. Fam. Beato, ta.

churchyard [ˈtʃə:tʃˈjɑ:d] n. Cementerio, *m.*, campo (*m.*) santo (cemetery). || Patio (*m.*) de la iglesia (yard).

churl [tʃə:l] n. Patán, *m.*, palurdo, *m.* (boor). || Fam. Refunfuñón, *m.* (grouser). | Tacaño, *m.* (niggard).

churlish [ˈtʃə:liʃ] adj. Grosero, ra (boorish). || Fam. Refunfuñón, ona (grumpy). | Tacaño, ña (miserly).

churlishness [ˈtʃə:liʃnis] n. Patanería, *f.* || Fam. Malhumor, *m.* (peevishness). | Tacañería, *f.* (stinginess).

churn [tʃə:n] n. Mantequera, *f.* (for making butter). || Lechera, *f.* (milk container).

churn [tʃə:n] v. tr. Batir (milk). || Hacer (butter). || Remover, agitar: *the propeller churned the water*, la hélice agitaba el agua. || — *To churn out*, producir en profusión. || *To churn up*, remover, revolver: *the plough churned up the earth*, el arado removía la tierra.

— V. intr. Agitarse, revolverse: *the sea churned all round us*, el mar se agitaba a nuestro alrededor. || Culin. Hacer mantequilla (to make butter).

churrigueresque [tʃurigeəˈresk] adj. Arts. Churrigueresco, ca.

chute [ʃu:t] n. Salto (*m.*) de agua (waterfall). || Conducto, *m.* (pipe). || Tolva, *f.* (hopper). || Rampa, *f.* (ramp). || Tobogán, *m.* (in swimming pool). || Fam. Paracaídas, *m. inv.* (parachute).

chutney [ˈtʃʌtni] n. Salsa (*f.*) picante.

chyle [kail] n. Quilo, *m.*

chyme [kaim] n. Biol. Quimo, *m.*

ciao! [tʃau] interj. ¡Chao!

ciborium [siˈbɔ:riəm] n. Rel. Copón, *m.* (for Host). || Ciborio, *m.* (altar canopy).

— Observ. El plural de *ciborium* es *ciboria*.

cicada [siˈkɑ:də] n. Zool. Cigarra, *f.*

cicatrice [ˈsikətris] n. Cicatriz, *f.*

cicatricial [sikəˈtriʃəl] adj. Cicatrizal.

cicatricle [siˈkætrikəl] n. Cicatriz, *f.* (cicatrice). || Cicatrícula, *f.* (in bird and reptile eggs).

cicatrix [ˈsikətriks] n. Cicatriz, *f.*

— Observ. El plural de *cicatrix* es *cicatrices* o *cicatrixes*.

cicatrization [ˌsikətriˈzeiʃən] n. Cicatrización, *f.*

cicatrizant [ˈsikətraizənt] n. Med. Cicatrizante, *m.*

cicatrize [ˈsikətraiz] v. tr. Med. Cicatrizar.

— V. intr. Med. Cicatrizarse, cicatrizar.

cicatrizing [—iŋ] adj. Med. Cicatrizante.

cicely [ˈsisili] n. Bot. Perifollo, *m.*

Cicero [ˈsisərəu] pr. n. Cicerón, *m.*

cicerone [ˌtʃitʃəˈrəuni] n. Cicerone, *m.*

— Observ. El plural de *cicerone* es *ciceroni* o *cicerones*.

Ciceronian [ˌsisəˈrəunjən] adj. Ciceroniano, na.

cicindela [sisinˈdelə] n. Zool. Cicindela, *f.*

cider [ˈsaidə*] n. Sidra, *f.* || U. S. Zumo (*m.*) de manzana (apple juice). || — *Cider house*, fábrica (*f.*) de sidra, sidrería, *f.* || *Cider press*, lagar, *m.* || U. S. *Hard cider*, sidra.

C.I.F. [si:-ai-ef] abbrev. of *cost, insurance and freight*, coste, seguro y flete.

cigar [siˈgɑ:*] n. Cigarro (*m.*) puro, puro, *m.* || — *Cigar band*, vitola, *f.* || *Cigar case*, cigarrera, *f.*, petaca, *f.* || *Cigar cutter*, cortapuros, *m. inv.* || *Cigar holder*, boquilla, *f.* || *Cigar maker*, cigarrera, *f.* || *Cigar shop* o *store*, estanco, *m.*, expendeduría (*f.*) de tabaco [*Amer.*, cigarrería, *f.*]

cigarette [ˌsigəˈret] n. Cigarrillo, *m.*, pitillo, *m.* (fam.). || — *Cigarette case*, pitillera, *f.* || *Cigarette end*, colilla, *f.* || *Cigarette holder*, boquilla, *f.* || *Cigarette lighter*, encendedor, *m.*, mechero, *m.* || *Cigarette paper*, papel (*m.*) de fumar.

cigarillo [ˌsigəˈriləu] n. Purito, *m.* [de señoritas].

cilia [ˈsiliə] pl. n. Cilios, *m.*

ciliary [ˈsiliəri] adj. Anat. Ciliar.

ciliate [ˈsilieit] adj. Ciliado, da.
— N. Ciliado, *m.*
ciliated [ˈsilieitid] adj. Ciliado, da.
cilice [ˈsilis] n. Cilicio, *m.*
cilium [ˈsiliəm] n. Cilio, *m.*
— OBSERV. El plural de *cilium* es *cilia.*
cinch [sintʃ] n. Cincha, *f.* (of saddle). || FIG. FAM. Apretón, *m.* (grip). | Control, *m.*, dominio, *m.* || FAM. *It's a cinch*, está tirado (easy), es cosa segura (sure).
cinch [sintʃ] v. tr. Cinchar (a saddle). || FIG. FAM. Asegurar (to assure).
cinchona [siŋˈkəunə] n. BOT. Quino, *m.* || *Cinchona bark*, quina, *f.*
cincture [ˈsiŋktʃə*] n. (Ant.). Cinto, *m.* || ARCH. Filete, *m.*
cinder [ˈsində*] n. Carbonilla, *f.* (of burnt coal). || Escoria, *f.* (slag from a furnace). || — Pl. Cenizas (*f.*) volcánicas (from a volcano). || Ceniza, *f. sing.*, cenizas, *f.* (residue of burnt coal). || *Cinder track*, pista (*f.*) de ceniza.
Cinderella [ˌsindəˈrelə] pr. n. Cenicienta, *f.*
cindery [ˈsindəri] adj. Ceniciento, ta.
cinecamera [ˈsiniˌkæmərə] n. Tomavistas, *m. inv.*, cámara (*f.*) cinematográfica.
cinema [ˈsinəmə] n. Cine, *m.*: *continuous performance cinema*, cine de sesión continua; *silent cinema*, cine mudo; *talking cinema*, cine sonoro.
cinemagoer [—ˌgəuə*] n. Aficionado (*m.*) al cine.
Cinemascope [ˈsinəməˌskəup] n. Cinemascope, *m.*
cinematic [ˌsinəˈmætik] adj. Cinemático, ca.
cinematics [—s] n. Cinemática, *f.* (kinematics).
cinematograph [ˌsinəˈmætəgrɑːf] n. Cinematógrafo, *m.*
cinematographer [sinəməˈtɔgrəfə*] n. Cámara, *m.*, operador, *m.*, cameraman, *m.*
— OBSERV. *Cameraman* is an Anglicism which, though frequently used, is better replaced by *operador* or *cámara.*
cinematographic [ˌsinəmætəˈgræfik] adj. Cinematográfico, ca.
cinematography [ˌsinəməˈtɔgrəfi] n. Cinematografía, *f.*
cinerama [ˌsinəˈrɑːmə] n. Cinerama, *m.*
cineraria [ˌsinəˈrɛəriə] n. BOT. Cineraria, *f.*
cinerarium [ˌsinəˈrɛəriəm] n. Nicho (*m.*) para urnas cinerarias.

CINEMATOGRAPHY. — CINEMATOGRAFÍA, *f.*

I. General terms. — Generalidades, *f.*

film industry	industria (*f.*) cinematográfica
cinematograph	cinematógrafo *m.*
cinema, pictures *pl.* [U.S., movies *pl.*]	cine *m. sing.*
cinema, picture house [U.S., movie theater]	cine *m.*, sala (*f.*) de cine
first-run cinema	cine (*m.*) de estreno
second-run cinema	cine (*m.*) de reestreno
art theatre	cine (*m.*) de arte y ensayo
film society [U.S., film club]	cineclub *m.*
film library	cinemateca *f.*, filmoteca *f.*
continuous performance cinema	cine (*m.*) de sesión continua
première	estreno *m.*
release	salida *f.*, estreno *m.*
film festival	festival (*m.*) de cine
distributor	distribuidor *m.*
shooting schedule	plan (*m.*) de rodaje
Board of Censors	censura *f.*
censor's certificate	visado (*m.*) de la censura
banned film	película (*f.*) prohibida
A-certificate	prohibida a menores de 16 años
U-certificate	apta para todos
X-certificate	reservada para mayores
direction	dirección *f.*, realización *f.*
production	producción *f.*
adaptation	adaptación *f.*
scenario, screenplay, script	guión *m.*
scene	escena *f.*
exterior	exteriores *m. pl.*
lighting	luminotecnia *f.*
shooting	rodaje *m.*
to shoot	rodar
dissolve	encadenado *m.*
fade-out; fade-in	fundido *m.*
recording	grabado *m.*, grabación *f.*
sound recording	toma (*f.*) del sonido
slow motion	cámara (*f.*) lenta
sound effects	efectos (*m.*) sonoros
special effects	efectos (*m.*) especiales, trucajes *m.*
mix, mixing	mezcla *f.*
editing, cutting	montaje *m.*
dubbing	doblaje *m.*
postsynchronization	postsincronización *f.*
studio	estudio *m.*
(motion) film studio	estudio (*m.*) cinematográfico
set, stage, floor	plató *m.*, escenario *m.*
properties, props	accesorios *m.*, atrezzo *m. sing.*
dolly	plataforma (*f.*) rodante, travelling *m.*, travelín *m.*
spotlight	proyector *m.*, foco *m.*
clapper boards	claqueta *f. sing.*
microphone	micrófono *m.*
boom	jirafa *f.*
scenery	decorados *m. pl.*

II. Filming, shooting. — Toma (*f.*) de vistas.

camera	cámara *f.*
shooting angle	ángulo (*m.*) de toma de vistas
high angle shot	picado *m.*
long shot	plano (*m.*) largo *or* de conjunto
full shot	plano (*m.*) general
close-up, close shot	primer plano *m.*
medium shot	plano (*m.*) medio
background	segundo plano *m.*
three-quarter shot	plano (*m.*) americano
pan	panorámica *f.*
frame, picture	imagen *f.*
still	fotograma *m.*
double exposure	doble exposición *f.*
superimposition	sobreimpresión *f.*
exposure meter	fotómetro *m.*, exposímetro *m.*
printing	positivado *m.*, tiraje *m.*

III. Films. — Películas, *f.*

film, motion picture, picture [U.S., movie]	película *f.*, filme *m.*
newsreel	actualidades *f. pl.*, noticiario *m.*
documentary (film)	documental *m.*
serial	película (*f.*) en jornadas *or* de episodios
trailer	avance *m.*, trailer *m.*
cartoon (film)	dibujos (*m. pl.*) animados
footage	metraje *m.*
full-length film, feature film	largometraje *m.*
short (film)	cortometraje *m.*
colour film [U.S., color film]	película (*f.*) en color
silent film	película (*f.*) muda
silent cinema *o* films	cine (*m. sing.*) mudo
sound motion picture, talkie	película (*f.*) sonora
cinemascope	cinemascope *m.*
cinerama	cinerama *m.*
title	título *m.*
original version	versión (*f.*) original
dialogue	diálogo *m.*
dubbed film	película (*f.*) doblada
subtitles, subtitling	subtítulos *m. pl.*
credits, credit titles	ficha (*f. sing.*) técnica
telefilm	telefilm *m.*

IV. Actors. — Actores, *m.*

cast	reparto *m.*
film star, movie star	estrella (*f.*) de cine
star, lead	intérprete (*m.* y *f.*) principal
double, stand-in	doble *m.* y *f.*
stunt man	doble (*m.*) especial
extra, walker-on	extra *m.* y *f.*

V. Technicians. — Técnicos, *m.*

adapter	adaptador *m.*
scenarist, scriptwriter	guionista *m.* y *f.*
dialogue writer	dialoguista *m.* y *f.*
production manager	director (*m.*) de producción
producer	productor *m.*
film director	director (*m.*) de cine, realizador *m.*
assistant director	ayudante (*m.*) de dirección
cameraman	operador *m.*
assistant cameraman	ayudante (*m.*) del operador
set photographer	fotógrafo *m.*
property manager, props man	attrezzista *m.*, accesorista *m.*
art director [U.S., set decorator]	decorador *m.*
stagehand	maquinista *m.*
lighting engineer	luminotécnico *m.*
sound engineer, recording director	ingeniero (*m.*) del sonido
film cutter	montador *m.*
script girl, continuity girl	script girl, secretaria (*f.*) de rodaje

VI. Projection. — Proyección, *f.*

reel, spool	bobina *f.*
sound track	banda (*f.*) sonora
showing, screening, projection	proyección *f.*
projector	proyector *m.*
projection booth *o* room	cabina (*f.*) de proyección
panoramic screen	pantalla (*f.*) panorámica

See also PHOTOGRAPHY

— OBSERV. El plural de *cinerarium* es *cineraria*.

cinerary [ˈsinərəri] adj. Cinerario, ria: *cinerary urn*, urna cineraria.
cineration [sinəˈreiʃən] n. Incineración, *f.*
cinerator [ˈsinəreitə*] n. U. S. Horno (*m.*) crematorio.
cinereous [siˈniəriəs] adj. Cinéreo, a; ceniciento, ta.
Cingalese or **Cinghalese** [ˌsiŋgəˈli:z] adj./n. Cingalés, esa.
cinnabar [ˈsinəbɑ:*] n. MIN. Cinabrio, *m.*
cinnamic [siˈnæmik] adj. CHEM. Cinámico, ca.
cinnamon [ˈsinəmən] n. BOT. Cinamomo, *m.*, canelo, *m.* || Canela, *f.* (spice).
cinqfoil [ˈsiŋkfɔil] n. BOT. Cincoenrama, *f.*
cinque [siŋk] n. Cinco, *m.*
cinquefoil [ˈsiŋkfɔil] n. BOT. Cincoenrama, *f.*
cipher [ˈsaifə*] n. MATH. Cero, *m.* (zero). || Cifra, *f.*, número, *m.* (numeral). || Clave, *f.*, código, *m.*, cifra, *f.* (code): *cipher message*, mensaje en clave. || Cifra, *f.*, monograma, *m.* (monogram). || Zumbido, *m.* (of an organ). || FIG. *He is a mere cipher*, es un cero a la izquierda.
cipher [ˈsaifə*] v. tr. Cifrar (to put in ciphers). || MATH. Calcular. || Poner en clave (using a code).
— V. intr. MATH. Cifrar, calcular. || Zumbar (an organ note).
cipolin [ˈsipəlin] n. Cipolino, *m.*
cippus [ˈsipəs] n. Cipo, *m.* (memorial stone).

— OBSERV. El plural de esta palabra es *cippi*.

circa [ˈsə:kə] prep. Hacia: *circa 1920*, hacia 1920.
circle [ˈsə:kl] n. Círculo, *m.*, corro, *m.*, rueda, *f.*: *to stand in circle*, hacer un corro. || MATH. Círculo, *m.* || FAM. Circunferencia, *f.* (circumference). || FIG. Círculo, *m.*: *circle of friends*, círculo de amigos. || Ojera, *f.* (round the eyes). || THEATR. Piso (*m.*) principal. || ASTR. Órbita, *f.* (orbit). | Halo, *m.* (of the moon). | Revolución, *f.*, vuelta, *f.* || GEOGR. Círculo, *m.*: *polar circle*, círculo polar. || AVIAT. Diámetro, *m.* (of the propeller). || Línea (*f.*) de circunvalación (in the underground). || — Pl. Círculos, *m.*, medios, *m.*, esferas, *f.*: *in high circles*, en las altas esferas; *from well-informed circles*, de círculos bien informados. || — *Antarctic, Arctic Circle*, Círculo Polar Antártico, Ártico. || MAR. *Azimuth circle*, círculo acimutal. || *Family circle*, círculo familiar. || MATH. *Great, small circle*, círculo máximo, menor. || *In a circle*, en círculo. || *To be in a vicious circle*, estar en un círculo vicioso. || *To come full circle*, volver al punto de partida (in arguments). || *To go round in circles*, tomar el camino más largo (to take the longest road), dar vueltas (to walk round and round), estar en un círculo vicioso (in arguments). || FIG. *To square the circle*, encontrar la cuadratura del círculo. || AUT. *Turning circle*, radio (*m.*) de giro. || THEATR. *Upper circle*, segundo piso.
circle [ˈsə:kl] v. tr. Rodear, cercar (to put a circle round). || Dar la vuelta a (to go round). || Ceñir, rodear, circundar (to surround). || Dar vueltas *or* gi.ar alrededor de (to move around).
— V. intr. Girar, dar vueltas: *the planes circle overhead*, los aviones dan vueltas en el aire. || *To circle round*, circular (news, object).
circlet [ˈsə:klit] n. Círculo (*m.*) pequeño. || Venda, *f.* (band). || Anillo, *m.* (ring).
circuit [ˈsə:kit] n. Circuito, *m.* (route). || Gira, *f.* (journey). || Perímetro, *m.* (perimeter). || Recorrido, *m.* (course). || Rodeo, *m.* (long way round): *to make a wide circuit*, dar un gran rodeo. || ELECTR. Circuito, *m.* || JUR. Distrito, *m.*, jurisdicción, *f.* || Cadena, *f.* (of cinemas, theatres). || SP. Circuito, *m.*, recorrido, *m.* || ASTR. Revolución, *f.*, vuelta, *f.* || FIG. Serie, *f.* (of acts). || — ELECTR. *Circuit breaker*, cortacircuitos, *m. inv.* || JUR. *Circuit court*, tribunal (*m.*) de distrito. || U. S. *Circuit rider*, predicador (*m.*) ambulante. || ELECTR. *Short circuit*, cortocircuito, *m.*
circuit [ˈsə:kit] v. tr. Dar la vuelta a.
circuitous [sə:ˈkjuitəs] adj. Indirecto, ta.
circular [ˈsə:kjulə*] adj. Circular: *circular motion*, movimiento circular. || De circunvalación (railway). || FIG. Indirecto, ta. || — *Circular letter*, circular, *f.* || MATH. *Circular measure*, medición (*f.*) del círculo. || *Circular saw*, sierra (*f.*) circular. || *Circular tour*, circuito, *m.*
— N. Circular, *f.* (letter).
circularize [ˈsə:kjuləraiz] v. tr. Mandar circulares a. || Anunciar por circulares.
circulate [ˈsə:kjuleit] v. tr. Circular: *to circulate an order*, circular una orden. || Hacer circular, divulgar (news). || Hacer circular (a letter, a paper, etc.).
— V. intr. Circular.
circulating [—iŋ] adj. Circulante: *circulating library*, biblioteca circulante. || COMM. *Circulating capital*, capital (*m.*) disponible *or* circulante.
circulation [ˌsə:kjuˈleiʃən] n. Circulación, *f.* || Difusión, *f.* (of news). || Tirada, *f.* (of a newspaper). || — *Blood circulation*, circulación de la sangre. || COMM. *Notes in circulation*, billetes (*m.*) en circulación. || *To put into circulation*, poner en circulación. || *To withdraw from circulation*, retirar de la circulación.
circulatory [ˌsə:kjuˈleitəri] adj. Circulatorio, ria: *circulatory system*, aparato circulatorio.
circumambiency [ˌsə:kəmˈæmbiənsi] n. Ambiente, *m.*, medio ambiente, *m.*
circumambient [ˌsə:kəmˈæmbiənt] adj. Ambiente, circundante.
circumambulate [ˌsə:kəmˈæmbjuleit] v. tr. Dar la vuelta a.
— V. intr. Andar de un lado para otro. || FIG. Andar con rodeos.
circumbendibus [ˌsə:kəmˈbendibəs] n. FAM. Circunloquios, *m. pl.*, rodeos, *m. pl.*
circumcise [ˈsə:kəmsaiz] v. tr. Circuncidar.
circumcised [—d] adj. Circunciso, sa.
circumcision [ˌsə:kəmˈsiʒən] n. Circuncisión, *f.*
circumference [ˌsə:ˈkʌmfərəns] n. Circunferencia, *f.*
circumflex [ˈsə:kəmfleks] adj. Circunflejo.
— N. Circunflejo, *m.*, acento (*m.*) circunflejo.
circumflex [ˈsə:kəmfleks] v. tr. Poner acento circunflejo en.
circumfuse [ˌsə:kəmˈfju:z] v. tr. Echar, difundir (to spread). || Derramar (a liquid). || Rodear (to surround). || *Circumfused with light*, bañado de luz.
circumjacent [ˌsə:kəmˈdʒeisənt] adj. Circunyacente.
circumlocution [ˌsə:kəmləˈkju:ʃən] n. Circunlocución, *f.*, circunloquio, *m.*
circumnavigate [ˌsə:kəmˈnævigeit] v. tr. Circunnavegar.
circumnavigation [ˈsə:kəmnæviˈgeiʃən] n. Circunnavegación, *f.*
circumpolar [ˈsə:kəmˈpəulə*] adj. ASTR. Circumpolar.
circumscribe [ˈsə:kəmskraib] v. tr. Circunscribir. || Limitar (powers).
circumscribed [—d] adj. Circunscrito, ta; circunscripto, ta.
circumscription [ˌsə:kəmˈskripʃən] n. Circunscripción, *f.* || Límite, *m.* || Contorno, *m.* (outline). || Inscripción (*f.*) circular (of a coin).
circumspect [ˈsə:kəmspekt] adj. Circunspecto, ta.
circumspection [ˌsə:kəmˈspekʃən] n. Circunspección, *f.* (caution).
circumstance [ˈsə:kəmstəns] n. Circunstancia, *f.* (essential fact): *in* o *under the circumstances*, en estas circunstancias. || Detalle, *m.* (detail). || Ceremonia, *f.* (stiff ceremonial). || — Pl. Posición, *f. sing.*, situación, *f. sing.* (material welfare). || — JUR. *Extenuating circumstances*, circunstancias atenuantes. || *In bad circumstances*, apurado, da; en un apuro. || *In easy circumstances*, acomodado, da. || *Narrow circumstances*, mal paso, *m.* || *Under no circumstances*, en ningún concepto.
circumstantial [ˌsə:kəmˈstænʃəl] adj. Circunstancial (incidental). || Circunstanciado, da (detailed). || JUR. Indirecto, ta (evidence).
circumstantiality [ˈsə:kəmˌstænʃiˈæliti] n. Acumulación (*f.*) de detalles. || Detalle, *m.* (detail).
circumstantially [ˌsə:kəmˈstænʃəli] adv. Con todo detalle, detalladamente. || Circunstancialmente.
circumstantiate [ˌsə:kəmˈstænʃjeit] v. tr. Corroborar, confirmar.
circumvallate [ˌsə:kəmˈvælit] v. tr. Circunvalar.
circumvallation [—væˈleiʃən] n. Circunvalación, *f.*
circumvent [ˌsə:kəmˈvent] v. tr. Embaucar, engañar (to baffle). || Burlar, circunvenir (the law). || Rodear, evitar (to avoid). || MIL. Rodear.
circumvolution [ˌsə:kəmvəˈlju:ʃən] n. Circunvolución, *f.* (turn).
circus [ˈsə:kəs] n. Circo, *m.* (entertainment). || Plaza (*f.*) circular, glorieta, *f.* (road junction). || HIST. Circo, *m.* (Roman arena). || AVIAT. Escuadrilla, *f.*
— Adj. Circense.
cirque [sə:k] n. GEOL. Circo, *m.*
cirrhosis [siˈrəusis] n. MED. Cirrosis, *f.*
cirrhotic [siˈrɔtik] adj. MED. Cirroso, sa.
cirriped [ˈsiriped] n. ZOOL. Cirrípedo, *m.*
cirrocumulus [ˈsirəuˈkju:mjuləs] n. Cirrocúmulo, *m.*

— OBSERV. El plural de *cirrocumulus* es *cirrocumuli*.

cirrostratus [sirəuˈstrɑ:təs] n. Cirroestrato, *m.*

— OBSERV. El plural de *cirrostratus* es *cirrostrati*.

cirrous [ˈsirəs] adj. BOT. ZOOL. Cirroso, sa.
cirrus [ˈsirəs] n. Cirro, *m.* (cloud). || BOT. ZOOL. Cirro, *m.* (tendril, feeler).

— OBSERV. El plural de *cirrus* es *cirri*.

cisalpine [sisˈælpain] adj. Cisalpino, na.
cissie or **cissy** [ˈsisi] n. See SISSY.
cissoid [ˈsisɔid] n. MATH. Cisoide, *f.*
cist [sist] n. Cista, *f.*
Cistercian [sisˈtə:ʃjən] adj. Cisterciense. || *Cistercian Order*, Orden (*f.*) del Cister, Cister, *m.*, Cistel, *m.*
— N. Cisterciense, *m.* & *f.*
cistern [ˈsistən] n. Cisterna, *f.*, aljibe, *m.* (for rainwater). || Tanque, *m.*, depósito, *m.* (at the top of a house). || Cisterna, *f.*, cisternilla, *f.* (in a water closet). || Cubeta, *f.* (of a barometer).
cistus [ˈsistəs] n. BOT. Cisto, *m.*
citadel [ˈsitədl] n. Ciudadela, *f.* || FIG. Baluarte, *m.*, ciudadela, *f.* (stronghold).
citation [saiˈteiʃən] n. Cita, *f.*, citación, *f.* (quotation). || JUR. Citación, *f.* || MIL. Mención, *f.*, citación, *f.*
cite [sait] v. tr. Citar. || MIL. Mencionar, citar. || JUR. Citar.
cithara [ˈsiθərə] n. MUS. Cítara, *f.*
citify [ˈsitifai] v. tr. Urbanizar.
citizen [ˈsitizn] n. Ciudadano, na; habitante (inhabitant). || Súbdito, ta; ciudadano, na (of a country). || Ciudadano, na (of a town). || Paisano, *m.* (civilian).

citizenry [—ri] n. Ciudadanos, *m. pl.*
citizenship [—ʃip] n. Ciudadanía, *f.*
citrate [ˈsitrit] n. CHEM. Citrato, *m.*
citric [ˈsitrik] adj. Cítrico, ca.
citron [ˈsitrən] n. Cidra, *f.* (fruit). || Cidro, *m.* (tree).
citronella [sitrəˈnelə] n. BOT. Citronela, *f.*
citrus [ˈsitrəs] n. BOT. Fruta (*f.*) agria *or* cítrica. || — Pl. Agrios, *m.*, cítricos, *m.*

— OBSERV. El plural de *citrus* es *citrus* o *citruses.*

city [ˈsiti] n. Ciudad, *f.* || — *City block*, manzana, *f.* [*Amer.*, cuadra, *f.*] || *City Council*, ayuntamiento, *m.*, concejo (*m.*) municipal. || *City edition*, edición (*f.*) local (of a newspaper). || *City editor*, redactor (*m.*) financiero (of financial section of a newspaper), redactor (*m.*) local (in United States). || *City father*, concejal, *m.* || *City hall*, ayuntamiento, *m.* (building), municipalidad, *f.*, municipio, *m.* || U. S. *City manager*, administrador (*m.*) municipal. || *City planning*, urbanización, *f.* || FAM. *City slicker*, capitalino, na. || *Garden city*, ciudad jardín. || *The City*, centro financiero de Londres. || *The Eternal City*, la Ciudad Eterna.
— Adj. De la ciudad, municipal. || COMM. Financiero, ra.

— OBSERV. Generalmente la palabra *city* se aplica a una ciudad de mayor amplitud que la que designa *town.*

cityscape [—skeip] n. Paisaje (*m.*) urbano.
city-state [—steit] n. Ciudad (*f.*) estado.
civet [ˈsivit] n. ZOOL. Civeta, *f.* || Algalia, *f.* (used in perfume). || *Civet cat*, gato (*m.*) de Algalia, civeta, *f.*
civic [ˈsivik] adj. Cívico, ca: *civic rights*, derechos cívicos. || Municipal: *civic authorities*, autoridades municipales. || *Civic centre*, parte (*f.*) de la ciudad donde están los edificios públicos.
civics [—s] n. Educación (*f.*) cívica.
civil [ˈsivl] adj. Civil: *civil war, marriage*, guerra, matrimonio civil. || JUR. Civil: *civil law*, derecho civil. || Educado, da; urbano, na (well-bred). || Cortés (polite). || Pasivo, va (defence). || Civil, paisano, na (not military). || Laico, ca (lay). || — *Civil death*, muerte (*f.*) civil. || *Civil disobedience*, resistencia pasiva. || *Civil engineer*, ingeniero (*m.*) civil. || *Civil engineering*, ingeniería (*f.*) civil. || *Civil list*, presupuesto (*m.*) de la casa real aprobado por el Parlamento. || JUR. *Civil procedure*, procedimiento (*m.*) civil. || *Civil rights*, derechos (*m.*) civiles. || *Civil servant*, funcionario, ria. || *Civil service*, administración (*f.*) pública. || *Civil year*, año (*m.*) civil.
civilian [siˈviljən] adj. Civil, de paisano: *civilian clothes*, traje de paisano.
— N. Civil, *m.*, paisano, *m.*
civility [siˈviliti] n. Urbanidad, *f.*, civilidad, *f.*, cortesía, *f.* (politeness).
civilizable [ˈsivilaizəbl] adj. Civilizable.
civilization [ˌsivilaiˈzeiʃən] n. Civilización, *f.*
civilize [ˈsivilaiz] v. tr. Civilizar.
— V. intr. Civilizarse.
civilizer [—ə*] n. Civilizador, ra.
civilly [ˈsivili] adv. Cortésmente.
civism [ˈsivizəm] n. Civismo, *m.*
civvies [ˈsiviz] pl. n. FAM. Traje (*m. sing.*) de paisano. || *In civvies*, de paisano, vestido de paisano.
clack [klæk] n. Ruido (*m.*) seco (sound). || Castañeteo, *m.* (of teeth). || FAM. Charla, *f.* (chat). || TECH. *Clack valve*, chapaleta, *f.*
clack [klæk] v. intr. Hacer un ruido seco (to make a sound). || FAM. Charlar (to chatter). || Castañetear (teeth). || Cloquear (hen).
clad [klæd] adj. Vestido, da (*in*, de): *clad in velvet*, vestido de terciopelo.

— OBSERV. La palabra inglesa *clad* es el pretérito y el participio pasivo arcaicos de *to clothe.*

clad [klæd] v. tr. Revestir.
cladding [ˈklædiŋ] n. TECH. Revestimiento, *m.*
claim [kleim] n. Demanda, *f.*, petición, *f.* (the demanding of sth.). || Derecho, *m.* (right): *to have a claim on s.o., on sth.*, tener derecho sobre alguien, a algo. || JUR. Demanda, *f.*: *to put in a claim*, presentar una demanda. || Reclamación, *f.*, reivindicación, *f.* (of a right to a possession). || Pretensión, *f.* (to a title). || Demanda, *f.* (insurance.) || Declaración, *f.*, afirmación, *f.* (statement). || Propiedad, *f.* (land). || U. S. MIN. Concesión, *f.* || — *Claim agent*, agente (*m.*) de reclamaciones. || *Claim check*, comprobante, *m.* || *To assert one's claim to*, hacer valer su derecho a. || *To have a claim against*, tener motivo para reclamar contra. || *To have a claim on s.o.'s attention*, merecer la atención de alguien.
claim [kleim] v. tr. Exigir, pedir: *to claim a thousand pounds damage*, exigir mil libras por daños y perjuicios. || Reclamar, reivindicar: *to claim a right*, reclamar un derecho. || Declarar, afirmar, pretender (to assert). || Necesitar, requerir (to need). || *To claim s.o.'s attention*, requerir la atención de alguien.
claimable [ˈkleiməbəl] adj. Reclamable.
claimant [ˈkleimənt] n. JUR. Demandante, *m.* & *f.* || Pretendiente, *m.*: *the claimant to the throne*, el pretendiente al trono. || JUR. *Rightful claimant*, derechohabiente, *m.*
claimless [ˈkleimlis] adj. JUR. Sin derecho.
clairvoyance [kleəˈvɔiəns] n. Clarividencia, *f.*
clairvoyant [kleəˈvɔiənt] adj./n. Clarividente.
clam [klæm] n. ZOOL. Almeja, *f.* || Grapa, *f.* (clamp). || FAM. *To shut up like a clam*, callarse como un muerto.
clam [klæm] v. intr. Pescar almejas. || FAM. *To clam up*, callarse como un muerto.
clamant [ˈkleimənt] adj. Estrepitoso, sa (noisy). || Urgente, acuciante, apremiante (demanding attention).
clambake [ˈklæmbeik] n. U. S. Reunión (*f.*) donde se guisan almejas y otros alimentos al aire libre (social gathering). || U. S. FAM. Mitin, *m.* (political rally).
clamber [ˈklæmbə*] n. Subida (*f.*) a gatas.
clamber [ˈklæmbə*] v. intr. Gatear, subir gateando.
clammy [ˈklæmi] adj. Frío y húmedo (damp). || Pegajoso, sa (sticky).
clamor [ˈklæmə*] n./v. intr. U. S. See CLAMOUR.
clamorous [ˈklæmərəs] adj. Clamoroso, sa; vociferante (vociferous). || Ruidoso, sa (noisy). || FIG. Acuciante, apremiante, urgente (clamant).
clamorously [—li] adv. A voces.
clamour (U. S. **clamor**). [ˈklæmə*] n. Clamor, *m.* (noise). || Vociferaciones, *f. pl.*, clamor, *m.* (outcry). || Reclamación, *f.*, reivindicación, *f.* (claim).
clamour (U. S. **clamor**) [ˈklæmə*] v. intr. Clamar, vociferar (to make an outcry). || Hacer ruido (to make noise). || *To clamour for sth.*, pedir algo a voces.
clamp [klæmp] n. TECH. Abrazadera, *f.* (brace). | Grapa, *f.* (for fastening). | Cárcel, *f.* (in carpentry). | Tornillo, *m.* (of a bench). | Borne, *m.* (in electricity). || Montón, *m.* (pile).
clamp [klæmp] v. tr. TECH. Sujetar con abrazadera *or* grapa. || Amontonar (to pile up). || Sujetar (to grasp).
— V. intr. Andar con paso lento. || — FIG. *To clamp down on*, suprimir (to wipe out), reprimir. || FAM. *To clamp down on s.o.*, apretarle los tornillos a uno.
clan [klæn] n. Clan, *m.* (a social group, a large family). || Tribu, *f.* (tribe). || Facción, *f.* (clique).
clandestine [klænˈdestin] adj. Clandestino, na.
clang [klæŋ] n. Sonido (*m.*) *or* ruido (*m.*) metálico.
clang [klæŋ] v. tr. Hacer sonar.
— V. intr. Sonar. || Tener un sonido metálico.
clanger [—ə*] n. FAM. Plancha, *f.*, metedura (*f.*) de pata. || FAM. *To drop a clanger*, meter la pata, tirarse una plancha.
clangorous [ˈklæŋgərəs] adj. Resonante, sonoro, ra; estrepitoso, sa.
clangour (U. S. **clangor**) [ˈklæŋgə*] n. Sonido (*m.*) metálico. || Estrépito, *m.*, estruendo, *m.* (noise).
clank [klæŋk] n. Ruido (*m.*) metálico.
clank [klæŋk] v. tr. Hacer sonar.
— V. intr. Sonar. || Hacer un ruido metálico.
clannish [ˈklæniʃ] adj. Que tiene espíritu de clan. || Exclusivista (cliquish).
clannishness [—nis] n. Espíritu (*m.*) de clan. || Exclusivismo, *m.*
clansman [ˈklænzmən] n. Miembro (*m.*) de un clan.
— OBSERV. El plural de esta palabra es *clansmen.*
clap [klæp] n. Ruido (*m.*) seco, estampido, *m.* (sharp noise). || Palmada, *f.* (with hands). || FAM. Purgaciones, *f. pl.* (blennorrhagia). || *A clap of thunder*, un trueno.
clap [klæp] v. tr. Aplaudir (to applaud). || FAM. Poner (to put). || — *To clap in jail*, meter en la cárcel. || *To clap one's eyes on*, ver. || *To clap one's hands*, dar palmadas, batir palmas. || *To clap on the back*, dar palmadas en la espalda. || *To clap on the brakes*, frenar en seco. || *To clap shut*, cerrar de golpe.
— V. intr. Aplaudir (to applaud). || Dar palmadas (for rhythm).
clapboard [—bɔ:d] n. U. S. ARCH. Chilla, *f.*, tablilla, *f.*
clapboard [—bɔ:d] v. tr. U. S. ARCH. Revestir con chillas *or* tablillas.
clapper [—ə*] n. Badajo, *m.* (of a bell). || Tarabilla, *f.* (of a mill). || Chapaleta, *f.* (of a pump). || Carraca, *f.* (rattle). || — *Clapper boards*, claqueta, *f. sing.* || *Clapper boy*, claquetista, *m.* || FAM. *To run like the clappers*, correr como un loco.
clapping [—iŋ] n. Aplausos, *m. pl.* || Palmadas, *f. pl.*
claptrap [ˈklæptræp] n. FAM. Charlatanería, *f.* (insincere talk). | Perorata, *f.* (pretentious talk). | Música (*f.*) celestial (nonsense).
— Adj. Vacío, a; huero, ra.
claque [klæk] n. THEATR. Claque, *f.*
Clare [klɛə] n. REL. Clarisa, *f.*
claret [ˈklærət] adj. Clarete (wine). || Burdeos (colour).
— N. Clarete, *m.* (wine).
clarification [ˌklærifiˈkeiʃən] n. Clarificación, *f.* (of liquid, etc.). || Aclaración, *f.*, clarificación, *f.* (of situation).
clarifier [ˈklærifaiə*] n. Clarificador, *m.* (for wine). || Clarificadora, *f.* (for sugar).
clarify [ˈklærifai] v. tr. Clarificar (a liquid). || Aclarar, clarificar: *the teacher clarified the matter*, el profesor aclaró la cuestión.
— V. intr. Aclararse, clarificarse.
clarinet [ˌklæriˈnet] n. MUS. Clarinete, *m.*
clarinettist (U. S. **clarinetist**) [—ist] n. Clarinetista, *m.* & *f.*, clarinete, *m.*
clarion [ˈklæriən] adj. Claro y potente, sonoro, ra.
— N. MUS. Clarín, *m.* (musical instrument, organ stop). || HIST. Corneta, *f.* (war trumpet).
clarity [ˈklæriti] n. Claridad, *f.*
clash [klæʃ] n. Ruido (*m.*) metálico (as of cymbals) || Estruendo, *m.*, estrépito, *m.* (noise). || Ruido, *m.*,

choque, *m.* (of weapons). || Choque, *m.*, encuentro, *m.* (between forces, persons). || Desacuerdo, *m.*, conflicto, *m.* (between opinions, interests, etc.). || Disparidad, *f.*, contraste, *m.* (of colours). || Coincidencia, *f.* (of dates). || — *Timetable clash*, incompatibilidad (*f.*) de horario. || *Verbal clash*, choque verbal.

clash [ˈklæʃ] v. tr. Golpear: *to clash cymbals*, golpear los platillos. || Hacer sonar (bells). || Hacer chocar.
— V. intr. Sonar: *the cymbals clashed*, los platillos sonaron. || Chocar, encontrarse (forces). || Chocar (to collide). || Estar en desacuerdo, chocar (opinions, interests, etc.). || Coincidir (dates): *his party clashed with my theatre engagement*, su fiesta coincidió con mi cita para ir al teatro. || Matarse, desentonar: *these colours clash*, estos colores se matan.

clasp [klɑ:sp] n. Cierre, *m.* (fastening device). || Broche, *m.* (of belt, book, etc.). || Apretón, *m.* (of hands). || || MIL. Pasador, *m.* || — *Clasp knife*, navaja (*f.*) de muelle. || *Hair clasp*, pasador (*m.*) para el pelo.

clasp [klɑ:sp] v. tr. Abrazar (to embrace). || Agarrar (to grasp). || Abrochar (to fasten). || Estrechar, apretar (hand).
— V. intr. *The two hands clasped in token of agreement*, las dos manos se estrecharon en señal de acuerdo.

class [klɑ:s] n. Clase, *f.*: *working class*, clase obrera *or* trabajadora. || Clase, *f.* (on a train, ship, plane): *first class*, primera clase. || Clase, *f.* (group of students): *a class of twenty-five students*, una clase de veinticinco estudiantes. || Clase, *f.* (lesson): *evening class*, clase nocturna. || Clase, *f.* (excellence): *she has real class*, tiene mucha clase. || Clase, *f.*, calidad, *f.* (quality): *grapes of the first class*, uvas de primera calidad. || BIOL. Clase, *f.* || Categoría, *f.*, clase, *f.* (kind). || U. S. Promoción, *f.*: *1972 class*, promoción de 1972. || — *Class struggle* o *warfare*, lucha (*f.*) de clases. || *First class degree*, sobresaliente, *m.* || *Governing, lower, middle, upper class*, clase dirigente, baja, media, alta. || *In a class apart* o *in a class by itself*, sin par, sin igual. || U. S. *Senior class*, curso (*m.*) superior.

class [klɑ:s] v. tr. Clasificar.

class-conscious [—ˈkɔnʃəs] adj. Que tiene conciencia de clase.

class-consciousness [—ˈkɔnʃəsnis] n. Conciencia (*f.*) de clase.

classic [ˈklæsik] adj. Clásico, ca.
— N. Clásico, *m.* (writer, literary work). || Estudiante (*m.* & *f.*) de lengua y literatura clásicas (student).

classical [—əl] adj. Clásico, ca: *classical music*, música clásica. || — *Classical architecture*, arquitectura neoclásica (of the eighteen century), arquitectura renacentista (of the Renaissance). || *Classical Latin*, latín clásico. || *Classical scholar*, erudito (*m.*) en lenguas clásicas.

classicism [ˈklæsisizəm] n. Clasicismo, *m.* || Humanismo, *m.*

classicist [ˈklæsisist] n. Clasicista, *m.* & *f.* || Humanista, *m.* & *f.*

classics [ˈklæsiks] pl. n. Lenguas (*f.*) clásicas (Greek and Latin). || Clásicos, *m.*, autores (*m.*) clásicos: *the classics of English literature*, los clásicos de la literatura inglesa. || Obras (*f.*) clásicas, clásicos, *m.* (literary works).

classifiable [ˈklæsifaiəbl] adj. Clasificable.

classification [ˌklæsifiˈkeiʃən] n. Clasificación, *f.*

classified [ˈklæsifaid] adj. Clasificado, da. || — *Classified advertisements*, anuncios (*m. pl.*) por palabras [clasificados por secciones]. || *Classified information*, información (*f.*) de difusión secreta *or* reservada.

classifier [ˈklæsifaiə*] n. Clasificador, ra (person). || MIN. Clasificador, *m.* (machine).

classify [ˈklæsifai] v. tr. Clasificar (*in, into, under*, en).

classmate [ˈklɑ:smeit] n. Compañero (*m.*) de clase, compañera (*f.*) de clase.

classroom [ˈklɑ:srum] n. Clase, *f.*, aula, *f.* (in school). || Aula, *f.* (in university).

classy [ˈklɑ:si] adj. FAM. Elegante, con clase.

clastic [ˈklæstik] adj. GEOL. Clástico, ca.

clatter [ˈklætə*] n. Estrépito, *m.*: *the dishes fell down with a great clatter*, los platos se cayeron con gran estrépito. || Choque, *m.* (of several things striking). || Trápala, *f.*, chacoloteo, *m.* (of hooves). || Triquitraque, *m.* (of train). || Guirigay, *m.*, algarabía, *f.* (confused chatter).

clatter [ˈklætə*] v. tr. Hacer sonar con estrépito. || Chocar.
— V. intr. Sonar con estrépito. || FAM. Charlar (to talk). || Chacolotear (hooves). || *To clatter down the stairs*, bajar las escaleras estrepitosamente.

Claud or **Claude** [klɔ:d] pr. n. Claudio, *m.*

clause [klɔ:z] n. Cláusula, *f.*: *a clause in the will*, una cláusula en el testamento. || GRAMM. Oración, *f.*, cláusula, *f.* || — *Additional clause*, cláusula adicional. || *Escape clause*, cláusula de excepción. || *Most-favoured-nation clause*, cláusula del país más favorecido.

claustral [klɔ:strəl] adj. Claustral.

claustrophobia [ˌklɔ:strəˈfəubjə] n. Claustrofobia, *f.*

clavecin [ˈklævisin] n. MUS. Clavecín, *m.*

clavichord [ˈklævikɔ:d] n. MUS. Clavicordio, *m.*

clavicle [ˈklævikl] n. ANAT. Clavícula, *f.*

clavicymbal [ˌklæviˈsimbəl] n. MUS. Clavicímbalo, *m.*

clavier [kləˈviə*] n. Teclado, *m.*

claw [klɔ:] n. ZOOL. Garra, *f.* (hooked nail of bird, animal). | Uña, *f.* (of cat). | Garra, *f.*, zarpa, *f.* (clawed foot). | Pinza, *f.* (of crab, etc.). || TECH. Garfio, *m.* (claw-shaped implement). || FAM. Garra, *f.*, mano, *f.* (hand). || — *Claw bar*, pata (*f.*) de cabra, sacaclavos, *m. inv.* || *Claw coupling*, acoplamiento dentado. || *Claw hammer*, martillo (*m.*) de orejas. || FAM. *To show one's claws*, enseñar las uñas.

claw [klɔ:] v. tr. Arañar (to scratch). || Desgarrar (to tear). || Agarrar (to clutch). || FAM. Rascar.
— V. intr. Arañar (to scratch at). || Dar zarpazos (to make grasping motions). || Agarrarse (to grasp at). || MAR. *To claw off*, barloventear.

clawed [—d] adj. Con zarpas (having claws). || Arañado, da (scratched). || TECH. Dentado, da.

clay [klei] n. Arcilla, *f.* || FIG. Barro, *m.* || — SP. *Clay pigeon*, plato, *m.* || *Clay pit*, gredal, *m.*

clayey [—i] or **clayish** [—iʃ] adj. Arcilloso, sa.

claymore [ˈkleimɔ:*] n. Claymore, *f.* (Scottish sword).

clean [kli:n] adj. Limpio, pia: *a very clean little boy*, un niño muy limpio; *clean shirt*, camisa limpia; *clean cut*, corte limpio. || Puro, ra; limpio, pia (pure). || Puro, ra; limpio, pia (food, person). || Bien proporcionado, da: *a car with clean lines*, un coche con líneas bien proporcionadas. || Fino, na (ankle). || Hábil, diestro, tra (deft). || Despejado, da (unobstructed). || En blanco (paper). || SP. Limpio, pia: *clean player, jump*, jugador, salto limpio. || FIG. Vacío, a; limpio, pia: *his pockets were clean*, tenía los bolsillos vacíos. | Limpio, pia (broke). | Sin mancha, sin tacha (irreproachable): *to lead a clean life*, llevar una vida sin tacha. | Decente. || — FIG. *Clean as a new pin*, limpio como una patena *or* como los chorros del oro *or* como un espejo. || *Clean bill of health*, patente de sanidad limpia. || *Clean police record* o *clean sheet*, registro de antecedentes penales limpio. || *To make a clean copy of*, poner en limpio.
— Adv. Completamente, por completo: *I clean forgot*, se me ha olvidado completamente. || Limpiamente. || — FAM. *Clean broke*, pelado, da; limpio, pia. || FIG. *To get clean away*, desaparecer sin dejar rastro.
— N. Limpiado, *m.*, limpiada, *f.*: *I'm going to give it a clean*, le voy a dar un limpiado.

clean [kli:n] v. tr. Limpiar: *to clean the windows*, limpiar las ventanas. || Pelar (vegetables). || MIN. Limpiar: *to clean gold*, limpiar oro. || Limpiar en seco (to dry-clean). || — *To clean down*, limpiar. || *To clean off*, quitar. || *To clean one's nails*, limpiarse las uñas. || *To clean one's teeth*, lavarse los dientes. || *To clean o.s. up*, lavarse, asearse. || *To clean out*, vaciar (to empty), limpiar (to make clean). || FIG. FAM. *To clean s.o. out*, limpiar *or* desplumar a alguien. || *To clean up*, ordenar (to tidy up), ganarse (a fortune), limpiar a fondo (to make neat), acabar con (to finish with), lavarse, asearse (to wash). | *To clean up a town*, limpiar una ciudad de sitios indeseables.
— V. intr. Hacer la limpieza. || *To clean up*, hacer la limpieza (to tidy), ganarse una fortuna.

clean-cut [—ˈkʌt] adj. Bien cortado, da. || Claro, ra. || FAM. Bien hecho, cha (figure). | Perfilado, da (features). | Sano, na (wholesome).

cleaner [—ə*] n. Limpiador, ra (person). || Asistenta, *f.* (charwoman). || Producto (*m.*) para la limpieza (product). || Aparato (*m.*) de limpieza (device). || — Pl. Tinte, *m. sing.*, tintorería, *f. sing.* || *Vacuum cleaner*, aspiradora, *f. sing.*

cleanhanded [—ˈhændid] adj. FIG. Con las manos limpias.

cleaning [ˈkli:niŋ] n. Limpieza, *f.*: *dry cleaning*, limpieza en seco. || — *Cleaning fluid*, quitamanchas, *m. inv.* || *Cleaning rag*, trapo (*m.*) de la limpieza.

clean-limbed [kli:nˈlimbd] adj. De miembros bien formados.

cleanliness [ˈklenlinis] n. Limpieza, *f.*

cleanly [kli:nli] adv. Limpiamente.

cleanly [ˈklenli] adj. Limpio, pia.

cleanness [ˈkli:nnis] n. Limpieza, *f.*

clean-out [ˈkli:naut] n. Limpiado, *m.*

cleanse [klenz] v. tr. Purificar, limpiar (from sin). || Limpiar: *to cleanse the wound*, limpiar la herida. || Curar, limpiar (of leprosy).

cleanser [—ə*] n. Producto (*m.*) para la limpieza.

clean-shaven [ˈkli:nˈʃeivn] adj. Bien afeitado, da. || Lampiño, ña (smooth-faced).

cleansing [ˈklensiŋ] n. Purificación, *f.* (purification). || Limpieza, *f.* (of a wound). || Curación, *f.* (of a leper).
— Adj. Limpiador, ra. || *Cleansing cream* o *milk*, desmaquillador, *m.*

cleanup [ˈkli:nˈʌp] n. Limpieza, *f.* (cleaning). || Eliminación, *f.*

clear [kliə*] adj. Claro, ra: *clear view, voice*, vista, voz clara; *clear statement*, declaración clara; *clear handwriting*, letra clara. || Claro, ra; transparente (a liquid). || Claro, ra; evidente: *a clear proof*, una prueba clara. || Claro, ra; neto, ta: *a clear majority*, una clara mayoría. || Tranquilo, la: *clear conscience*, conciencia tranquila. || Libre (of sorrow, care, debts, obstacles, etc.). || Libre: *the way is clear*, el camino está libre. || Despejado, da: *clear sky*, cielo despejado. || Terso, sa: *clear complexion*, cutis terso. || Completo, ta; entero, ra: *six clear months*, seis meses enteros. || COMM. Neto, ta; líquido, da. || SP. Sin faltas (round). || — *All clear!*, ¡no hay peligro! || FIG. *As clear as crystal* o *as day*, más claro que el agua. | *As clear as mud*, nada claro. || *Clear of*, libre de. || *Clear profit*, beneficio neto. || *He was perfectly clear about it*, lo dijo muy claramente. || *I'm not very clear on the matter*, no tengo una idea muy clara del asunto. || *Is that clear?*, ¿está claro? || *I want to make it clear that*, quiero dejar claro *or* bien sentado que. || *The all clear (signal)*, la señal de fin de alarma. || FIG. *The coast is clear*, see COAST. || *To be clear of debts*, no tener deudas, estar libre de deudas. || *To get sth. clear*, dejar algo bien sentado. || *To make o.s. clear*, explicarse claramente *or* con claridad.

— Adv. Claramente. || MAR. A la altura (*of*, de). || — *I can hear you loud and clear*, le oigo claramente *or* muy bien. || *To get clear away*, desaparecer sin dejar rastro. || *To jump clear* o *to crawl clear*, quitarse de en medio de un salto *or* a gatas. || *To keep clear of*, evitar. || *To shine clear*, brillar con claridad. || *To speak loud and clear*, hablar alto y claro. || *To stand clear of*, mantenerse a distancia de, apartarse de. || *To steer clear of*, evitar.

— N. Claro, *m.*, espacio (*m.*) libre. || *To be in the clear*, estar fuera de peligro (out of danger), estar libre de deudas (of debts), estar *or* quedar fuera de toda sospecha (from suspicion).

clear [kliə*] v. tr. Limpiar: *to clear a street of snow*, limpiar la calle de nieve. || Despejar (of obstruction). || Dispersar (a crowd). || Aclarar (to make clear). || Quitar (to remove). || AGR. Rozar (a field). || Clarificar (wine). || JUR. Probar *or* demostrar la inocencia de: *the evidence cleared him*, las pruebas demostraron su inocencia. | Acreditar, habilitar, capacitar (by Security). || Saltar (to jump). || Salvar (an obstacle). || Ganar, sacar [beneficio] (net profit). || Pagar, liquidar, saldar (a debt). || Satisfacer (a mortgage). || Quitar: *to clear the table*, quitar la mesa. || Aclararse (the throat). || Evacuar, aliviar (the bowels). || MED. Depurar, limpiar (blood). || Pasar sin rozar: *the lorry cleared the bridge*, el camión pasó sin rozar el puente. || Abrir: *to clear the way*, abrir el camino. || Descargar (to unload). || Evacuar, desalojar: *to clear the court*, evacuar la sala. || Liquidar (to sell off unwanted stocks). || Aprobar: *the boss cleared their proposals*, el jefe aprobó sus propuestas. || FIG. Aclarar (a question). | Limpiar (of suspicion, blame, etc.). | Descargar, aliviar (one's conscience). || MAR. Sacar de la aduana (goods), salir de (the harbour). || Autorizar (an aircraft to take off, etc.). || COMM. Compensar (a cheque). || SP. Despejar (the ball in football). || Desatorar (a pipe). || — MIL. *To clear the decks for action*, tocar zafarrancho de combate. || *To clear sth. with s.o.*, proponer algo a alguien. || *To clear the air*, aclarar las cosas. || FAM. *To clear the ground*, despejar el terreno.

— V. intr. Aclararse (to become clear). || Volverse más claro (to become clearer). || Derretirse (snow). || Despejarse (weather, sky). || MAR. Zarpar. || SP. Despejar (in football). || Dispersarse (the crowd). || Desaparecer (a symptom). || Venderse (goods).

— **To clear away**, quitar (to take away). | Disiparse (fog, clouds). | Largarse, irse (to go). || **To clear off**, irse, largarse (to go away). | Liquidar (debts, goods). || **To clear out**, limpiar (to clean). | Vaciar (to empty). | COMM. Liquidar. | Echar (s.o.). | Irse, largarse (to go away). | — *To clear out of the way*, quitar de en medio. || **To clear through**, pasar por. | Ser aprobado por. || **To clear up**, limpiar (to clean). | Ordenar (to tidy up). | Aclarar: *to clear up a problem*, aclarar un problema. | Resolver, disipar (doubt). | Aclararse, despejarse (weather). | Despejarse (the sky). | Terminar, comerse (food).

clearance [ˈkliərəns] n. Espacio (*m.*) libre (between two objects). || Altura (*f.*) libre, margen (*m.*) de altura (of a bridge). || Gálibo, *m.* (of a wagon). || Despeje, *m.* (removal of obstructions). || MAR. Despacho (*m.*) de aduanas (by the customs). | Certificado (*m.*) de aduana (clearance papers). || Acreditación, *f.*, habilitación, *f.* (by Security). || COMM. Compensación, *f.* (of a cheque). | Liquidación, *f.* (of goods). || Holgura, *f.* (between two parts in machinery). || SP. Despeje, *m.* (in football). || Distancia (*f.*) al suelo (of vehicles). || Permiso, *m.* (permission). || AGR. Desmonte, *m.*, roza, *f.* || — *Clearance sale*, liquidación, *f.* || *Slum clearance*, supresión (*f.*) del chabolismo.

clear-cut [ˈkliəˈkʌt] adj. Bien definido, da. || Claro, ra.

clear-eyed [ˈkliəˈraid] adj. De ojos claros. || FIG. Clarividente, perspicaz.

clearheaded [ˈkliəˈhedid] adj. Lúcido, da. || Perspicaz.

clearing [ˈkliəriŋ] n. Aclaramiento, *m.* (the making clear). || Claro, *m.*: *a clearing in a wood*, un claro en un bosque. || Clara, *f.*, escampada, *f.* (of the weather). || COMM. Compensación, *f.* (of a cheque). | Liquidación, *f.* (of account). || Recogida, *f.* (of the letter box). || Despeje, *m.* (removal of obstructions). || CULIN. Clarificación, *f.* (of a liquid). || AGR. Roza, *f.*, desmonte, *m.* || MED. Evacuación, *f.*, alivio, *m.* (of the bowels). || MAR. Despacho (*m.*) de aduanas.

clearinghouse [—haus] n. COMM. Cámara (*f.*) de compensación. || Agencia (*f.*) distribuidora (of news).

clearly [ˈkliəli] adv. Claramente. || Evidentemente, con toda evidencia.

clearness [ˈkliənis] n. Claridad, *f.*

clear-sighted [ˈkliəˈsaitid] adj. Clarividente, perspicaz.

clearway [ˈkliəwei] n. Carretera (*f.*) en la que no se puede aparcar.

cleat [kli:t] n. TECH. Abrazadera, *f.* (to secure a rope, etc.). || MAR. Cornamusa, *f.* || Clavo, *m.* (of shoes).

cleavage [ˈkli:vidʒ] n. Hendidura, *f.* (splitting). || BIOL. División, *f.* (of a cell). || CHEM. Desdoblamiento, *m.* (of molecules). || MIN. Crucero, *m.* || División, *f.* (of opinion, etc.). || Escote, *m.* (in dress). || Canal, *f.* (in body).

cleave* [kli:v] v. tr. Hender, partir (to split). || FIG. Cortar, surcar: *the ship cleft the waves*, el barco cortaba las olas. | Separar (to separate). | Abrirse [camino]: *he cleft his way through the jungle*, se abrió camino a través de la jungla.

— V. intr. Partirse, henderse (to split). || (Ant). Pegarse, adherirse (to adhere). | Ser fiel (*to*, a) [to be faithful].

— OBSERV. El verbo *to cleave* tiene tres pretéritos (*clove, cleaved* y *cleft*) y tres participios pasivos (*cloven, cleaved* y *cleft*), excepto cuando significa *pegarse, adherirse* y *ser fiel*, en cuyo caso el pasado y el participio pasivo son regulares (*cleaved*).

cleaver [kli:və*] n. Cuchilla, *f.* (of a butcher).

clef [klef] n. MUS. Clave, *f.*

cleft [kleft] adj. Hendido, da; partido, da (split). || Dividido, da (divided). || MED. *Cleft palate*, fisura palatina.

— Pret. & p. p. See CLEAVE.

— N. Grieta, *f.*, hendidura, *f.* (a split).

clematis [ˈklemətis] n. BOT. Clemátide, *f.*

clemency [ˈklemənsi] n. Clemencia, *f.*

clement [ˈklemənt] adj. Clemente.

Clement [ˈklemənt] pr. n. Clemente, *m.*

Clementine [—ain] pr. n. Clementina, *f.*

clench [klentʃ] n. Apretón, *m.* (a pressing). || Agarrón, *m.* (grip).

clench [klentʃ] v. tr. Apretar, presionar (to press). || Apretar (one's fists, teeth). || Remachar (rivet, nail). || Sujetar, agarrar (to grip).

clencher [—ə*] n. See CLINCHER.

Cleopatra [kliəˈpætrə] pr. n. Cleopatra, *f.*

clepsydra [ˈklepsidrə] n. Clepsidra, *f.* (water clock).

— OBSERV. El plural de *clepsydra* es *clepsydrae* o *clepsydras*.

clerestory [ˈkliəstəri] n. ARCH. Triforio, *m.* (church window).

clergy [ˈklə:dʒi] n. REL. Clero, *m.*

clergyman [—mən] n. REL. Clérigo, *m.*, sacerdote, *m.* (priest). | "Clergyman", *m.*, pastor (*m.*) protestante (protestant).

— OBSERV. El plural de esta palabra es *clergymen*.

cleric [ˈklerik] n. REL. (Ant.) Clérigo, *m.*

clerical [—əl] adj. Clerical (of the clergy). || De oficina, oficinesco, ca (of the work of a clerk). || — *Clerical error*, error (*m.*) de copia. || *Clerical work*, trabajo (*m.*) de oficina. || *Clerical worker*, oficinista, *m.* & *f.*

— N. Clerical, *m.* (clericalist). || Clérigo, *m.* (priest).

clericalism [—əlizəm] n. Clericalismo, *m.*

clericalist [—əlist] n. Clerical, *m.*

clerisy [ˈklerisi] n. Intelectualidad, *f.*

clerk [klɑ:k] n. Oficinista *m.* & *f.*, empleado (*m.*) de oficina (office worker). || Empleado, da (of a bank). || Recepcionista, *m.* & *f.* (at a hotel). || Funcionario, ria (in a Ministry, council, etc.). || (Ant.) Clérigo, *m.* (clergyman). || Sacristán, *m.* (in a parish). || JUR. Pasante, *m.* (of an attorney). || SP. Juez, *m.* (in horse racing). || U. S. Dependiente, ta (shop assistant). || — *Clerk of the works*, maestro (*m.*) de obras. || JUR. *Clerk of the court*, escribano (*m.*) forense. || *Town clerk*, secretario (*m.*) del Ayuntamiento.

clerkship [—ʃip] n. Oficio (*m.*) *or* ocupación (*f.*) *or* empleo (*m.*) de oficinista. || JUR. Pasantía, *f.* (of an attorney's clerk). | Escribanía, *f.* (of a clerk of the court).

clever [ˈklevə*] adj. Listo, ta; inteligente (intelligent). || Hábil (skilful): *he's very clever with his hands*, es muy hábil con sus manos. || Ingenioso, sa (ingenious): *that's clever!*, ¡qué ingenioso! || Astuto, ta (cunning).

cleverness [—nis] n. Inteligencia, *f.*, listeza, *f.* (intelligence). || Habilidad, *f.* (skill). || Ingenio, *m.*

clew [klu:] n. Ovillo, *m.* (of thread). || MAR. Puño (*m.*) de escota (lower corner of a sail). | Anillo (*m.*) del puño de escota (loop). || Indicio, *m.*, pista, *f.* (clue). || — Pl. Cabuyeras, *f.* (of hammock). || *Clew line*, chafaldete, *m.*

clew [klu:] v. tr. Hacer un ovillo, enrollar (thread). || FIG. Dar una pista, dar un indicio. || MAR. *To clew up*, cargar (a sail).

cliché [ˈkli:ʃei] n. PRINT. Cliché, *m.*, clisé, *m.* || FIG. Tópico, *m.*, lugar (*m.*) común, frase (*f.*) estereotipada.

click [klik] n. Chasquido, *m.* || Taconeo, *m.* (of heels). || Tecleo, *m.* (of typewriter). || TECH. Trinquete, *m.* || *Click!*, ¡clic!

click [klik] v. tr. Chascar, chasquear (the tongue, etc.). || *To click one's heels*, taconear (repeatedly), dar un taconazo (a soldier).

— V. intr. Chascar, chasquear (to make a clicking sound). || FIG. FAM. Gustarse, llevarse bien: *the two clicked immediately*, los dos se gustaron en seguida. | Tener éxito (to be a success). || FIG. FAM. *I didn't understand and suddenly it clicked*, no lo entendía y de pronto caí en lo que significaba.

client [ˈklaiənt] n. Cliente, *m.* & *f.*

clientele [ˌkli:ɑ:nˈtel] n. Clientela, *f.*, clientes, *m. pl.*
cliff [klif] n. Acantilado, *m* (on coast). || SP. Escalamiento (*m.*) de peñascos (in mountaineering).
cliff dweller [—dwelə*] n. U. S. Troglodita, *m.* & *f.*
cliff-hanging [—hæŋiŋ] adj. Tenso, sa; de tensión (moment). || Emocionante, de suspense (film, etc.).
cliffy [ˈklifi] adj. Escarpado, da.
climacteric [klaiˈmæktərik] adj. Climatérico, ca. || FIG. Crítico, ca.
— N. MED. Climaterio, *m.* || FIG. Momento (*m.*) crítico.
climacterium [klaimækˈtiriəm] n. MED. Climaterio, *m.*
climactic [klaiˈmæktik] adj. Culminante.
climate [ˈklaimit] n. Clima, *m.* (weather condition). || Región, *f.*, país, *m.* (region). || FIG. Atmósfera, *f.*, ambiente, *m.* (atmosphere).
climatic [klaiˈmætik] adj. Climático, ca.
climatological [ˌklaimətəˈlɔdʒikəl] adj. Climatológico, ca.
climatology [ˌklaiməˈtɔlədʒi] n. Climatología, *f.*
climax [ˈklaimæks] n. Punto (*m.*) culminante (culmination). || Clímax, *m.* (ascending scale). || Clímax, *m.* (of a play).
climax [ˈklaimæks] v. tr. Llevar al punto culminante.
— V. intr. Llegar al punto culminante.
climb [klaim] n. Subida, *f.*, escalada, *f.*, ascensión, *f.* (of a mountain). || AVIAT. Subida, *f.* (of an aircraft). || FIG. Ascenso, *m.*
climb [klaim] v. tr. Subir, escalar (mountain). || Subir (hill, stairs). || Subir a, trepar a: *the boys are climbing the trees*, los niños están subiendo a los árboles.
— V. intr. Subir (road, aeroplane). || Subir, elevarse: *the mercury in the thermometer is climbing*, el mercurio del termómetro está subiendo. || Trepar (plants). || Escalar, hacer alpinismo (mountaineering). || ASTR. Ascender, subir (sun). || FIG. Subir, ascender (in social rank, in power, etc.). || — *To climb down*, bajar (to go down), volverse atrás (to abandon an attitude, opinion, etc.). || *To climb out*, salir trepando (of a hole), bajar (of a vehicle). || *To climb over*, salvar trepando. || *To climb up*, subir trepando, trepar por.
climber [—ə*] n. Trepador, ra; escalador, ra (person who climbs). || Alpinista, *m.* & *f.*, montañero, ra (mountaineer). || Escalador, ra (in cycling). || FIG. Arribista, *m.* || BOT. Enredadera, *f.*, planta (*f.*) trepadora. || ZOOL. Trepadora, *f.*
climbing [—iŋ] adj. Trepador, ra. || — *Climbing irons*, trepadoras, *f. pl.*, garfios (*m.*) para trepar. || ZOOL. *Climbing perch*, perca trepadora. || *Climbing rope*, cuerda (*f.*) de nudos para trepar.
— N. Escalada, *f.*, alpinismo, *m.*, montañismo, *m.* || FIG. Arribismo, *m.*
clime [klaim] n. Región, *f.* || Clima, *m.* (climate).
clinch [klintʃ] n. SP. Cuerpo a cuerpo, *m.* || MAR. Entalingadura, *f.* || Remache, *m.* (of nail, rivet). || Fin, *m.*, término, *m.*, conclusión, *f.*, cierre, *m.* (of a deal, etc.). || FAM. Abrazo (*m.*) apasionado (embrace).
clinch [klintʃ] v. tr. Cerrar: *to clinch a deal*, cerrar un trato. || Remachar (rivet, nail). || Apretar (teeth, fists). || Afianzar (to secure). || FIG. Resolver definitivamente (to solve). | Remachar (argument). | Confirmar (suspicions). | Ganarse (a post, title, etc.). || MAR. Entalingar. || FIG. *That clinches it!*, ¡no hay más que hablar!
— V. intr. SP. Luchar cuerpo a cuerpo. || FAM. Abrazarse estrechamente (to embrace).
clincher [—ə*] n. Argumento (*m.*) decisivo (argument that settles a dispute). || Remachador, *m.* (riveter). || Clavo (*m.*) remachado (nail). || MAR. Entalingadura, *f.*
cling* [kliŋ] v. intr. *To cling to*, agarrarse: *the child clung to its mother*, el niño se agarró a su madre; ceñirse a, ir ceñido a: *the boat clung to the coastline*, el barco iba ceñido a la costa; pegarse a (clothes), aferrarse a: *to cling to the past, to a hope*, aferrarse al pasado, a una esperanza; colgar: *the village clung to the mountain side*, el pueblo colgaba en la ladera de la montaña; apegarse a (a friend, habit, etc.), persistir en (to persist in). || *To cling to one another*, abrazarse fuertemente *or* estrechamente.

— OBSERV. Pret. & p. p. **clung**.

clinger [—ə*] n. FAM. Lapa, *f.*
clinging [-iŋ] adj. Ceñido, da; ajustado, da (dress). || Pegajoso, sa; tenaz (odour). || Pegajoso, sa (person).
clingstone [—stəun] n. BOT. Pavía, *f.*, albérchigo, *m.* (peach).
clinic [ˈklinik] n. MED. Dispensario, *m.*, ambulatorio, *m.* (part of hospital, place for free medical assistance). || Clínica, *f.* (medical instruction, private place of consultation).
clinical [—əl] adj. Clínico, ca. || *Clinical thermometer*, termómetro clínico.
clinician [kliˈniʃən] n. Clínico, *m.*
clink [kliŋk] n. FAM. Chirona, *f.*, cárcel, *f.* (prison): *in the clink*, en chirona. || Tintín, *m.*, sonido (*m.*) metálico, tintineo, *m.* (sound). || Choque, *m.* (of glasses).
clink [kliŋk] v. tr. Hacer tintinear. || Chocar: *to clink glasses with*, chocar copas con.
— V. intr. Tintinear.
clinker [—ə*] n. TECH. Escoria (*f.*) de hierro, cagafierro, *m.* (of iron). | Escoria (*f.*) de hulla (of coal). | Ladrillo (*m.*) vitrificado *or* holandés (brick). || FAM. Persona (*f.*) *or* cosa (*f.*) estupenda.
clinker-built [—ə*ˌbilt] adj. MAR. De tingladillo.
clinkstone [—stəun] n. Fonolita, *f.*
clinometer [klaiˈnɔmitə*] n. Clinómetro, *m.*
clip [klip] n. Clip, *m.*, sujetapapeles, *m. inv.* (for fastening things together). || Broche, *m.* (brooch). || Pinza, *f.* (for hair rollers). || Horquilla, *f.*, clip, *m.* (for hair). || Prendedor, *m.*, sujetador, *m.* (of a pen, biro). || Cargador, *m.* (of cartridges). || Esquileo, *m.* (action of clipping). || Vellón, *m.* (quantity of wool clipped from a sheep). || Tijeretada, *f.* (with scissors). || Lana (*f.*) esquilada en una temporada (season's yield of wool). || Recorte, *m.* (a cutting). || TECH. Collar, *m.*, abrazadera, *f.* || Fragmento, *m.* (of film). || FAM. Bofetada, *f.*, torta, *f.* (a cuff with the hand). || SP. Zancadilla, *f.* (in American football). || — U. S. *Clip joint*, bar *o* cabaret sumamente caro. | *To go at a fair clip*, ir a buen paso.
clip [klip] v. tr. Sujetar (to fasten together). || Esquilar (animals). || Recortar (to trim). || Desbarbar (coins). || FAM. Abofetear (to cuff). || Cortar (hair, wings). || Picar (tickets). || SP. Poner la zancadilla a, zancadillear (in American football). || — *Clipped form*, forma abreviada. || *To clip one's words*, comerse las palabras. || FIG. *To clip s.o.'s wings*, cortarle las alas a alguien. || *To clip sth. on to*, prender algo en.
— V. intr. U. S. FAM. *To clip along*, ir a buen paso.
clipper [ˈklipə*] n. Esquilador, *m.* (of sheep). || MAR. AVIAT. Clíper, *m.* (ship and plane). || — Pl. Esquiladora, *f. sing.* (for animals). || Maquinilla (*f. sing.*) para cortar el pelo (for people). | Tijeras (*f.*) de podar (for hedges). || *Nail clippers*, cortaúñas, *m. inv.*
clippie [ˈklipi] n. FAM. Cobradora, *f.* (in the bus).
clipping [ˈklipiŋ] n. Esquileo, *m.* (of sheep). || Recorte, *m.* (of metal, material). || Corte, *m.* (of hair). || Recorte, *m.* (of newspaper). || *Hedge clippings*, ramas cortadas.
— Adj. Cortante (cutting). || Rápido, da (swift). || FAM. Estupendo, da.
clique [kli:k] n. Pandilla, *f.*, camarilla, *f.*
cliquey [—i] or **cliquish** [—iʃ] or **cliquy** [—i] adj. Exclusivista.
clitoris [ˈklitəris] n. ANAT. Clítoris, *m.*
cloaca [kləuˈeikə] n. Cloaca, *f.*
cloak [kləuk] n. Capa, *f.* (sleeveless outer garment). || MIL. Capote, *m.* || FIG. Manto, *m.*: *cloak of snow*, manto de nieve. || — FIG. *A cloak of mystery*, un velo de misterio. | *Under the cloak of*, al amparo de: *under the cloak of religion they committed many atrocities*, al amparo de la religión cometieron muchas atrocidades; so capa de, con el pretexto de (under a pretext).
cloak [kləuk] v. tr. Encubrir, disimular (to hide): *to cloak one's disapproval with a smile*, disimular su desaprobación con una sonrisa. || Cubrir, encapotar: *the hills were cloaked with mist*, la niebla cubría las colinas.
cloak-and-dagger [—ənˈdægə*] adj. De capa y espada: *cloak-and-dagger story*, novela de capa y espada. || De espionaje (of spies). || *The cloak-and-dagger boys*, el Servicio Secreto.
cloakroom [ˈkləukrum] n. Guardarropa, *m.* (in a theatre, etc.). || Servicios, *m. pl.* (lavatory). || Consigna, *f.*, depósito (*m.*) de equipajes (for deposit of luggage).
clobber [ˈklɔbə*] n. FAM. Pingos, *m. pl.*, trapos, *m. pl.* (clothes). | Trastos, *m. pl.* (personal effects).
clobber [ˈklɔbə*] v. tr. FAM. Dar una paliza (to beat).
cloche [klɔʃ] n. Campana (*f.*) de cristal (to protect plants). || Sombrero (*m.*) de mujer de forma acampanada (bell-shaped hat).
clock [klɔk] n. Reloj, *m.* (timepiece). || Cronómetro, *m.* (chronometer). || TECH. Contador, *m.* (instrument connected to a machine). | Reloj (*m.*) de fichar, reloj (*m.*) registrador (time clock). | Velocímetro, *m.* (speedometer). | Cuentakilómetros, *m. inv.* (milometer). | Taxímetro, *m.* (taximeter). || FAM. Molinillo, *m.* (of dandelion). | Jeta, *f.* (face). || Dibujo, (*m.*) lateral (of socks or stockings). || — *Against the clock*, contra reloj. || *Alarm clock*, despertador *m.*, reloj despertador. || *Around the clock*, durante 24 horas. || *Cuckoo clock*, reloj de cuco. || *Electric clock*, reloj eléctrico. || *To put a clock on*, cronometrar. || *To put the clocks back*, atrasar los relojes. || FIG. *To set* o *to turn the clock back*, volver el reloj atrás. || *To sleep the clock round*, dormir doce horas seguidas.
clock [klɔk] v. tr. Cronometrar, tomar el tiempo de (with a stopwatch). || Registrar (with a speedometer).
— V. intr. *To clock in* o *on*, fichar, picar (in factory), llegar al trabajo (to arrive at work). || *To clock out* o *off*, fichar la salida.
clockdial [—daiəl] or **clockface** [-feis] n. Esfera (*f.*) del reloj.
clocklike [—laik] adj. Puntual como un reloj.
clockmaker [—ˌmeikə*] n. Relojero, *m.*
clockwise [—waiz] adv. En el sentido de las agujas del reloj.
clockwork [—wə:k] adj. De cuerda: *a clockwork car*, un cochecito de cuerda. || Puntual.
— N. Maquinaria (*f.*) de reloj (mechanism of a clock). || Mecanismo (*m.*) de relojería: *machinery driven by clockwork*, maquinaria movida por un mecanismo de relojería. || Mecanismo, *m.* (of a toy). || FIG. *Like clockwork*, como un reloj, con precisión.

clod [klɔd] m. AGR. Terrón, *m.* (of earth). | Tierra, *f.* (soil). || CULIN. Aguja, *f.* (of beef). || FAM. Patán, *m.*, paleto, *m.*

clod crusher [—ˌkrʌʃə*] n. AGR. Desterronadora, *f.*

cloddish [—iʃ] adj. FAM. Memo, ma; tonto, ta; paleto, ta.

clodhopper [ˈklɔdˌhɔpə*] n. Patán, *m.*, paleto, *m.*, destripaterrones, *m. inv.* (country lout). || — Pl. FAM. Zapatos, *m.*, zapatones, *m.* (big heavy shoes).

Clodowig [ˈklɔdəvig] pr. n. Clodoveo, *m.*

clog [klɔg] n. Zueco, *m.* (wooden shoe). || Traba, *f.* (fetter for animals). || FIG. Traba, *f.*

clog [klɔg] v. tr. Atascar, obstruir, atorar: *leaves clogged the drain*, las hojas atascaban el desagüe. || Embarrar (with mud). || Llenar, cubrir: *wet clay clogged our shoes*, la arcilla húmeda nos cubría los zapatos. || Entorpecer (to hinder movement). || Estorbar, obstaculizar (to be an encumbrance to). || Trabar (animals).

— V. intr. Atascarse, obstruirse, atorarse (to become blocked up). || Espesarse (to become thick).

clogging [—iŋ] n. Atasco, *m.*, atoramiento, *m.*

cloisonné [klwæzɔˈnei] adj. Tabicado, da.

— N. Esmalte (*m.*) tabicado.

cloister [ˈklɔistə*] n. ARCH. Claustro, *m.* (covered walk). || REL. Monasterio, *m.*, convento, *m.*, claustro, *m.* (monastery, convent). || *The cloister*, la clausura, la vida conventual *or* monástica, el claustro (monastic life).

cloister [ˈklɔistə*] v. tr. Enclaustrar (to confine in a convent, etc.). || FIG. Encerrar, aislar (to isolate).

cloistered [—d] adj. Enclaustrado, da (isolated from the outside world). || Monástico, ca; conventual (monastic). || — FIG. *Cloistered life*, vida (*f.*) de ermitaño. || *Cloistered walk*, arcadas, *f. pl.*

cloistral [ˈklɔistrəl] adj. Claustral.

close [kləus] adj. Cercano, na: *close relative*, pariente cercano. || Íntimo, ma: *close friend*, amigo íntimo. || Unido, da: *I am close to my brother*, estoy muy unido a mi hermano. || Cercano, na (near). || Cerrado, da (shut). || Minucioso, sa; detallado, da; detenido da; profundo, da: *close examination*, examen minucioso. || Fiel, exacto, ta: *close translation*, traducción fiel. || Preciso, sa (argument). || Mal ventilado, da (room). || Cargado, da (air). || A cerrado (smell). || Sofocante, bochornoso, sa (weather). || GRAMM. Cerrado, da: *close vowels*, vocales cerradas. || COMM. Restringido, da (credit). | Justo, ta (price). || Estrecho, cha: *a close watch*, una estrecha vigilancia. || Secreto, ta (secretive). || Cerrado, da; poco accesible (society). || Estrecho, cha (contact). || Cerrado, da; reservado, da (character). || Profundo, da (silence). || Oculto, ta (hidden). || Prohibido, da (forbidden). || Ajustado, da; ceñido, da (clothes). || Compacto, ta (compact). || Apretado, da (writing). || Tupido, da: *close texture*, tejido tupido. || Recio, cia (rain). || Parecido, da: *a texture close to that of wool*, una contextura parecida a la de la lana. || Reñido, da: *close game*, partido reñido. || Igualado, da; reñido, da: *the voting was very close*, la votación estaba muy igualada. || Cerrado, da (chess). || FAM. Tacaño, ña; agarrado, da (stingy). || — *A close resemblance*, un gran parecido. || *At close quarters* o *at close range*, de cerca. || MIL. *Close column*, columna cerrada. || *Close combat*, combate (*m.*) cuerpo a cuerpo. || *Close quarters*, lugar estrecho. || *Close season*, veda, *f.* (for hunting and fishing), temporada (*f.*) de descanso (in sports). || *Close shave*, afeitado muy apurado. || *Close time*, veda, *f.* || FAM. *It was a close shave*, ha faltado el canto de un duro. || *To pay close attention*, prestar mucha atención.

— N. Recinto, *m.* (enclosed place). || Calle, *f.* (street).

— Adv. Cerca (near). || Completamente: *the door was shut close*, la puerta estaba completamente cerrada. || — *According to people close to the Prime Minister*, según personas allegadas al Primer Ministro. || *Close at hand*, a mano. || *Close by*, muy cerca. || *Close on nine o'clock*, casi las nueve. || *Close to*, cerca de, junto a: *my house is close to the river*, mi casa está cerca del río; casi (almost). || *Close together*, muy juntos. || *They finished the race very close*, terminaron la carrera casi a la vez. || *To be close on sixty*, rondar *or* pisar los sesenta. || *To come close*, acercarse. || *To cut one's hair close*, cortar el pelo al rape. || *To fit close*, estar apretado *or* ajustado. || *To get close to*, acercarse a. || *To keep close*, mantenerse oculto. || *To keep close to the text*, ajustarse al texto. || *To run s.o. close* o *to run s.o. close second*, seguir a alguien muy de cerca.

close [kləuz] n. Final, *m.*, fin, *m.* (an end). || MIL. SP. Cuerpo (*m.*) a cuerpo. || MUS. Cadencia, *f.* (cadence). || — *At the close of the day*, al caer el día. || *To bring sth. to a close*, terminar algo. || *To come to a close*, terminar.

close [kləuz] v. tr. Cerrar: *to close the door*, cerrar la puerta. || Tapar (a hole, view). || Acabar, terminar (to finish). || COMM. Saldar (an account). | Cerrar (a deal). | Cerrar, liquidar (a bank account). || Clausurar (a meeting, ceremony, etc.). || Cerrar (a list, a vote). || Cerrar, clausurar (a debate). || Acortar (a distance). || MIL. Cerrar (ranks). || ELECTR. Cerrar (circuit).

— V. intr. Cerrarse (to shut). || Acabarse, terminarse (to come to an end). || Acercarse (to draw near). || Estar de acuerdo (to agree). || Llegar a las manos (to grapple). || MIL. Cerrar filas (ranks).

— ***To close about***, rodear. || ***To close down***, cerrar [definitivamente]: *to close down through lack of money*, cerrar por falta de dinero. | Cerrar, cerrar la emisión (a radio station, etc). || ***To close in***, rodear (to surround). | Acercarse (to draw near). | Encerrar (to shut in). | Acortarse: *the days are closing in*, los días se están acortando. | Caer, cerrarse: *the night was closing in*, la noche caía *or* se cerraba. | — *To close in on* o *upon s.o.*, envolver a alguien, rodear *or* cercar a alguien. || U. S. ***To close out***, liquidar. || ***To close round***, rodear. || ***To close up***, cerrar (to shut). | Cerrar (a shop). || Cerrarse (flowers, ranks). | Taparse (aperture). | Arrimarse más, juntarse más (to crowd together). | Cicatrizarse (a wound). | Callarse (to fall silent).

close-cropped [—ˌkrɔpt] adj. Rapado, da; al rape.

closed [kləuzd] adj. Cerrado, da (shut, inaccessible). || Cerrado, da (road). || Concluido, da; acabado, da (finished). || Exclusivo, va; reservado, da (reserved). || Vedado, da (hunting). || Cerrado, da (vowel). || De miras estrechas, cerrado, da (mind). || Cerrado, da (society, etc.). || — *Closed chapter*, asunto concluido. || *Closed circuit*, circuito cerrado. || U. S. *Closed primary*, votación (*f.*) preliminar. || *Closed season*, veda, *f.* || JUR. *Closed session*, sesión (*f.*) a puerta cerrada. || *Closed shop*, establecimiento (*m.*) que contrata solamente a miembros sindicados.

closed-door [—ˈdɔ:*] adj. A puerta cerrada.

closed-end [—ˈend] adj. COMM. De capital limitado.

closedown [ˈkləuzdaun] n. Cierre, *m.* (radio, television). || Cierre, *m.* (of a factory). || Caída, *f.* (of night).

closefisted [ˈkləusˈfistid] adj. FAM. Tacaño, ña; agarrado, da (stingy).

close-fitting [ˈkləusˈfitiŋ] adj. Ajustado, da; ceñido, da.

close-grained [ˈkləusˈgreind] adj. Tupido, da (fibre). || MIN. De grano fino.

close-hauled [ˈkləusˈhɔ:ld] adj. MAR. De bolina.

close-knit [ˈkləusˈnit] adj. Unido, da (family, etc.).

close-lipped [ˈkləuslipt] adj. Callado, da;reservado, da (not talking much).

closely [kləusli] adv. Cerca, de cerca (near). || Atentamente (carefully). || Estrechamente: *closely connected with*, estrechamente relacionado con. || Densamente (built, populated, etc.). || Apretadamente (writing). || Exactamente, fielmente (a translation). || — *Closely contested*, muy reñido. || *Closely packed*, muy apretados unos contra otros (objects). || *You resemble David very closely*, te pareces mucho a David.

closemouthed [ˈkləusˈmauðd] adj. Discreto, ta; callado, da.

closeness [ˈkləusnis] n. Cercanía, *f.*, proximidad, *f.* (nearness). || Intimidad, *f.* (intimacy). || Minuciosidad, *f.*, detalle, *m.* (thoroughness). || Fidelidad, *f.* (of a translation). || Tacañería, *f.* (meanness). || Exactitud, *f.* (of a resemblance). || Mala ventilación, *f.* (stuffiness). || Bochorno, *m.*, pesadez, *f.* (of weather). || GRAMM. Cerrazón, *f.* (of vowels). || Inaccesibilidad, *f.* (of a society, club, etc.). || Lo reñido (of competition, voting). || Lo compacto, compacidad, *f.* (compactness). || Densidad, *f.* (density). || Lo tupido (of a texture). || Carácter (*m.*) poco comunicativo (of a person).

closeout [ˈkləuzaut] n. Liquidación, *f.* (of stock).

close-set [ˈkləuˈset] adj. Junto, ta (eyes, etc.).

close-shaven [ˈkləus-ˈʃeivən] adj. Bien afeitado.

closet [ˈklɔzit] n. U. S. Armario, *m.*, ropero, *m.* (for clothes). || Retrete, *m.*, water, *m.* (water closet). || Gabinete, *m.* (private room). || — *Closet drama*, teatro [para ser] leído. || FAM. *Closet strategist*, estratega (*m.*) de café.

closet [ˈklɔzit] v. tr. Encerrar. || *To closet o.s. with*, encerrarse con.

close-tongued [ˈkləuz-tʌŋd] adj. Callado, da.

close-up [ˈkləusʌp] n. Primer plano, *m.* (in photography, cinema).

closing [ˈkləuziŋ] adj. Final, último, ma. || COMM. De cierre (prices).

— N. Cierre, *m.* || Conclusión, *f.* (concluding portion). || COMM. Cierre, *m.* (inventory). | Liquidación, *f.* (account).

closure [ˈkləuʒə*] n. Fin, *m.* (end). || Cierre, *m.* (closing). || Conclusión, *f.* (conclusion). || Clausura, *f.* (in Parliament). || Cierre, *m.* (of T.V., etc.).

clot [klɔt] n. Grumo, *m.* (of a liquid). || Coágulo, *m.* (of blood). || FAM. Bobo, ba; tonto, ta.

clot [klɔt] v. tr. Coagular, cuajar.

cloth [klɔθ] n. Tela, *f.*, paño, *m.* (fabric). || Trapo, *m.* (rag). || Mantel, *m.* (tablecloth). || THEATR. Telón, *m.* || MAR. Vela, *f.* || FIG. Clero, *m.* (the clerical profession). || — *American cloth*, hule, *m.* || *Bound in cloth*, encuadernado en tela. || *Cloth of gold*, tisú (*m.*) de oro. || *To lay the cloth*, poner la mesa.

— Adj. De tela.

— OBSERV. El plural de esta palabra es *cloths*.

clothe* [kləuð] v. tr. Vestir (*in, with, as,* de). || FIG. Revestir, cubrir (to cover).

— OBSERV. Pret. & p. p. ***clothed, clad*** (ant.).

clothes [—z] pl. n. Ropa, *f. sing.* (bedclothes, laundry). || Vestidos, *m.*, ropa, *f. sing.* (garments). || — *Clothes bag*, bolsa (*f.*) de la ropa sucia. || *Clothes basket*, cesta (*f.*) de la ropa sucia (of clothes to be washed), canasta (*f.*) de la plancha (of clothes waiting to be ironed). || *Clothes brush*, cepillo (*m.*) de la ropa. || *Clothes hanger*, percha, *f.* || ZOOL. *Clothes moth*, polilla, *f.* || *Clothes peg*, pinza, *f.* || *Clothes tree*, perchero, *m.*, percha, *f.* || *In plain clothes*, de paisano. || *Suit of clothes*, traje, *m.*

clotheshorse [—zhɔ:s] n. Tendedero, *m.* (for airing).

clothesline [—zlain] n. Cuerda (*f.*) para tender la ropa, tendedero, *m.*

clothespin [—zpin] n. U. S. Pinza, *f.*

clothespole [—zpəul] n. Palo (*m.*) del tendedero.

clothier [ˈkləuðiə*] n. Fabricante (*m.* & *f.*) de paños (person who makes cloth). || Pañero, ra (person who sells cloth). || Sastre, *m.* (tailor). || *Clothier's shop*, pañería, *f.* (for cloth), sastrería, *f.* (for clothes).

Clothilda [kləuˈðildə*] pr. n. Clotilde, *f.*

clothing [ˈkləuðiŋ] n. Vestir, *m.* (act). || Ropa, *f.* (clothes). || — *Article of clothing*, prenda (*f.*) de vestir. || *Clothing trade*, industria (*f.*) de la confección.

Clotilda [kləuˈtildə] pr. n. Clotilde, *f.*

cloture [ˈkləuˈtʃə*] n. U. S. Clausura, *f.*

cloud [klaud] n. Nube, *f.* (in the sky, a liquid, a precious stone). || Vaho, *m.* (in a mirror). || Nube, *f.* (of dust, smoke, locusts). || Capa, *f.* (of gas). || FIG. Sombra (*f.*) de tristeza, nube, *f.* | Nube, *f.* (crowd). || — *Cloud chamber*, cámara (*f.*) de niebla. || FIG. *Every cloud has a silver lining*, no hay mal que por bien no venga. | *On cloud seven*, en el séptimo cielo. | *Passing cloud*, nube de verano. | *To have one's head in the clouds*, estar en las nubes. | *Under a cloud*, bajo sospecha (under suspicion), deprimido, da (depressed). | *Under the cloud of night*, amparado por la noche. | *Up in the clouds*, en las nubes.

cloud [klaud] v. tr. Nublar: *smoke clouded the room*, el humo nublaba la habitación. || Ensombrecer, nublar (to darken). || Empañar (glass). || Vetear (wood). || FIG. Oscurecer, obcecar, obnubilar (s.o.'s mind). | Empañar, manchar (s.o.'s reputacion). | Entristecer (s.o.'s face).

— V. intr. Nublarse (to become cloudy). || Ensombrecerse (to darken). || Enturbiarse (liquid). || Empañarse (glass). || FIG. Obnubilarse, obcecarse (mind). | Empañarse, mancharse (reputation). | Entristecerse (face).

cloudburst [—bə:st] n. Chaparrón, *m.* (heavy shower).

cloud-capped [ˈ—kæpt] adj. Coronado de nubes.

cloudiness [ˈklaudinis] n. Nubosidad, *f.*, nebulosidad, *f.* || Lo turbio (of liquid). || FIG. Tristeza, *f.* (of s.o.'s face). | Lo oscuro, nebulosidad, *f.* (of style).

cloudland [ˈklaudlænd] n. FIG. Mundo (*m.*) imaginario.

cloudless [ˈklaudlis] adj. Despejado, da; sin nubes.

cloudlet [ˈklaudlit] n. Nube (*f.*) pequeña.

cloudy [ˈklaudi] adj. Nuboso, sa (resembling clouds). || Nublado, da; encapotado, da: *cloudier sky*, cielo más nublado; *it is cloudy today*, hoy está nublado. || Empañado, da: *cloudy glass*, cristal empañado. || Turbio, bia (liquid). || FIG. Vago, ga; nebuloso, sa: *cloudy ideas*, ideas vagas. | Triste (person).

clough [klʌf] n. Barranco, *m.* (ravine).

clout [klaut] n. FAM. Tortazo, *m.* (blow). || Pieza, *f.* (for patching). || Blanco, *m.* (target). || Tiro (*m.*) que da en el blanco (hit). || Chapa, *f.* (shoes). || FIG. Influencia, *f.* || FIG. *Ne'er cast a clout till May is out*, hasta el cuarenta de mayo no te quites el sayo.

clout [klaut] v. tr. FAM. Abofetear, pegar un tortazo (to slap). || Remendar (to patch).

clove [kləuv] n. BOT. Clavo, *m.* (spice). | Clavero, *m.* (tree). || Diente, *m.* (of garlic). || *Clove hitch*, ballestrinque, *m.* (knot).

clove [kləuv] pret. See CLEAVE.

cloven [—ən] p. p. See CLEAVE.

— Adj. Hendido, da: *cloven hoof*, pezuña hendida. || FAM. *To show the cloven hoof*, enseñar la oreja.

cloven-hoofed [—hu:ft] adj. De pezuña hendida.

clover [ˈkləuvə*] n. BOT. Trébol, *m.* || FAM. *To be in clover*, vivir a cuerpo de rey.

cloverleaf [—li:f] n. TECH. Cruce (*m.*) en trébol. || BOT. Hoja (*f.*) de trébol.

— OBSERV. El plural de esta palabra es *cloverleaves*.

Clovis [ˈkləuvis] pr. n. Clodoveo, *m.*

clown [klaun] n. Payaso, *m.*, clown, *m.* (in circus). || FIG. Patán, *m.* (boor). || Villano, *m.* (peasant).

clown [klaun] v. intr. Ser un payaso (to be a clown). || Hacer el payaso (to make people laugh).

clownery [—əri] n. Payasadas, *f. pl.*

clownish [—iʃ] adj. Bufón, ona (comical). || Patán, grosero, ra (boorish). || Torpe (clumsy).

clownishness [—iʃnis] n. Payasadas, *f. pl.* (clownery). || Bufonería, *f.* (buffoonery).

cloy [klɔi] v. tr./intr. Empalagar. || FIG. Hartar, saciar.

cloying [—iŋ] adj. Empalagoso, sa.

club [klʌb] n. Garrote, *m.*, cachiporra, *f.* (stout stick). || SP. Palo, *m.* (golf, hockey). || Asociación, *f.* (association). || Club, *m.* (circle). || Casino, *m.* (for gaming). || Cotización, *f.* (subscription). || — Pl. Bastos, *m.* (in Spanish cards). || Trébol, *m. sing.* (in standard pack). || — *Club sandwich*, sandwich (*m.*) vegetal con pollo y bacon. || *Club soda*, agua (*f.*) de seltz. || *Club steak*, filete (*m.*) de solomillo. || FIG. FAM. *To be in the club*, estar preñada (pregnant).

club [klʌb] v. tr. Dar garrotazos a, aporrear, dar cachiporrazos a (to beat). || Reunir (persons, resources).

— V. intr. Reunirse. || — *To club together*, reunirse: *they clubbed together to buy a present*, se reunieron para comprar un regalo. || *To club with*, asociarse con, aliarse a.

clubfoot [ˈfut] n. Pie (*m.*) zopo.

— OBSERV. El plural de esta palabra es *clubfeet*.

clubfooted [—ˈfutid] adj. De pie zopo.

clubhaul [—ˈhɔ:l] v. tr. MAR. Virar sobre el ancla.

clubhouse [—ˌhaus] n. Sede (*f.*) de un club, club, *m.*

clubman [—mən] n. Miembro (*m.*) *or* socio (*m.*) de un club (member). || U. S. Aficionado (*m.*) a la vida de club (who spends much time in clubs).

— OBSERV. El plural de *clubman* es *clubmen*.

clubroom [—rum] n. Sala (*f.*) de reunión de un club.

cluck [klʌk] n. Cloqueo, *m.* (of hens). || FIG. FAM. Mentecato, ta (simpleton).

cluck [klʌk] v. intr. Cloquear (hens). || Chascar (with the tongue). || FAM. Parlotear (a person).

clue [klu:] n. Pista, *f.* (lead for police, etc.). || Indicio, *m.* (isolated piece of evidence). || Clave, *f.* (key to problem, mystery, etc.). || Indicación, *f.* (in crossword). || *I haven't a clue*, no tengo ni idea, no tengo la menor idea.

clueless [ˈklulis] adj. Desorientado, da; despistado, da.

clump [klʌmp] n. Grupo, *m.* (of trees). || Macizo, *m.*, mata, *f.* (of flowers). || Terrón, *m.* (of earth). || FAM. Pisada (*f.*) fuerte (sound). | Tortazo, *m.* (blow).

clump [klʌmp] v. tr. Agrupar.

— V. intr. Agruparse (to form clumps). || FAM. Andar con pisadas fuertes (to tramp).

clumpish [—iʃ] adj. Torpe.

clumsiness [ˈklʌmzinis] n. Torpeza, *f.* (awkwardness). || Desmaña, *f.* (unskilfulness). || FIG. Falta (*f.*) de delicadeza *or* de tacto (lack of tact). | Chabacanería, *f.* (lack of refinement). || Pesadez, *f.* (of objects).

clumsy [ˈklʌmzi] adj. Torpe (awkward). || Desmañado, da (unskilful). || FIG. Chabacano, na (without refinement). | Indelicado, da; sin tacto (tactless). || Pesado, da (object).

clung [klʌŋ] pret. & p. p. See CLING.

Cluniac [ˈklu:niæk] adj. REL. Cluniacense.

— N. REL. Cluniacense, *m.*

cluster [ˈklʌstə*] n. Grupo, *m.* (of people, trees, houses). || Racimo, *m.* (of fruits): *a cluster of grapes*, un racimo de uvas. || ASTR. Enjambre, *m.* (of stars). || Macizo, *m.*, mata, *f.* (of shrubs). || Enjambre, *m.* (of bees). || Hato, *m.*, manada, *f.* (of cattle).

cluster [ˈklʌstə*] v. intr. Arracimarse, apiñarse, agruparse (people). || BOT. Arracimarse (plants).

clutch [klʌtʃ] n. Agarrón, *m.* (grip). || AUT. Embrague, *m.* | Pedal (*m.*) del embrague, embrague, *m.* (clutch pedal). || TECH. Cuchara, *f.* (of a crane). || Nidada, *f.* (of eggs). || Garra, *f.* (of animals). || SP. Llave, *f.*, presa, *f.* (in wrestling). || POP. Garra, *f.* (hand). || — AUT. *Clutch disc*, disco (*m.*) de embrague. | *Clutch pedal*, pedal del embrague, embrague. | *Plate clutch*, embrague de discos. | *To disengage the clutch*, desembragar. | *To engage* o *to let in* o *to throw in the clutch*, embragar. | FIG. *To fall into s.o.'s clutches*, caer en las garras de alguien.

clutch [klʌtʃ] v. tr. Agarrar, asir. || AUT. Embragar. || — FIG. *To clutch s.o. into one's arms*, estrechar a alguien entre sus brazos. | *To clutch to one's breast*, estrechar contra su corazón *or* su pecho.

— V. intr. Agarrarse. || — *To clutch at*, agarrarse a, agarrar. || FIG. *To clutch at a hope*, aferrarse a una esperanza.

clutter [ˈklʌtə*] n. FAM. Desorden, *m.*, confusión, *f.* (untidy mess). || Montón, *m.* (of things).

clutter [ˈklʌtə*] v. tr. Desordenar (to make untidy). || *To clutter up*, llenar, atestar: *the table was cluttered up with books*, la mesa estaba llena de libros.

— V. intr. Desordenar las cosas. || Ajetrearse (to bustle).

clyster [ˈklistə*] n. MED. Clister, *m.*, clistel, *m.*

coach [kəutʃ] n. Coche, *m.* (carriage). || Carroza, *f.* (ceremonial carriage). || Diligencia, *f.* (stagecoach). || AUT. Autocar, *m.* || Vagón, *m.*, coche, *m.* (of a train). || Profesor (*m.*) particular (tutor). || SP. Entrenador, ra. || — *Coach box*, pescante, *m.* || *Coach house*, cochera *f.*, cobertizo, *m.*

coach [kəutʃ] v. tr. Dar clases particulares, preparar intensamente [para un examen]: *he coaches me in Spanish*, me da clases particulares de español. || SP. Entrenar, preparar (to train).

— V. intr. Dar clases particulares. || Viajar en diligencia *or* en coche.

coachbuilder [—ˌbildə*] n. Carrocero, *m.*

coacher [—ə*] n. Entrenador, *m.*

coaching [—iŋ] n. Clases (*f. pl.*) particulares. || Preparación, *f.* (for an examination). || SP. Entrenamiento, *m.*, preparación, *f.* (training).

coachman [ˈkəutʃmən] n. Cochero, *m.*

— OBSERV. El plural de *coachman* es *coachmen*.

coachwork [ˈkəutʃwə:k] n. AUT. Carrocería, *f.*

coaction [kəuˈækʃən] n. Coacción, *f.* (coercion). || Acción (*f.*) conjunta (joint action).

coadjutant [kəuˈædʒutənt] adj. Coadyuvante.

— N. Ayudante, *m.* & *f.*, auxiliar *m.* & *f.*

coadjutor [kəuˈædʒutə*] n. REL. Coadjutor, *m.*, coadyutor, *m.*

coagulable [kəuˈægjuləbl] adj. Coagulable.

coagulant [kəu'ægjulənt] n. Coagulante, *m.*
coagulate [kəu'ægjuleit] v. tr. Coagular (to cause to congeal). || CHEM. Precipitar.
— V. intr. Coagularse (to congeal).
coagulation [kəu,ægju'leiʃən] n. Coagulación, *f.*
coagulative [kəu'ægjulətiv] adj. Coagulador, ra; coagulante.
coagulator [kəu'ægjuleitə*] n. Coagulador, *m.*, coagulante, *m.*
coagulum [kəu'ægjuləm] n. Coágulo, *m.*
— OBSERV. El plural de *coagulum* es *coagula.*
coal [kəul] n. GEOL. Carbón, *m.*, hulla, *f.*: *coal mine,* mina de carbón. || — *Anthracite coal,* antracita, *f.* || MAR. *Coal bunker,* carbonera, *f.* || *Coal cellar,* carbonera, *f.* || *Coal cutter,* rozadora, *f.*, máquina rozadora. || *Coal dust,* carbón en polvo, polvo (*m.*) de carbón, cisco, *m.* || *Coal face,* frente (*m.*) de arranque del carbón. || *Coal gas,* gas (*m.*) del alumbrado, gas (*m.*) de hulla. || *Coal measures,* rocas carboníferas. || *Coal merchant,* carbonero, *m.* || *Coal miner,* minero (*m.*) de carbón. || *Coal mining,* explotación hullera. || U. S. *Coal oil,* petróleo, *m.* (petroleum), queroseno, *m.* (kerosene). || *Coal scuttle,* cubo (*m.*) para el carbón. || *Coal tar,* alquitrán (*m.*) de hulla. || *Live coal,* ascua, *f.*, brasa, *f.* || FIG. *To blow the coals,* echar leña al fuego, avivar la llama. | *To carry coals to Newscastle,* ir a vendimiar y llevarse de postre uvas, echar agua en el mar. || FIG. FAM. *To rake* o *to haul over the coals,* echar un rapapolvo *or* una bronca.
coal [kəul] v. tr. Proveer de carbón (a ship, etc.).
— V. intr. Proveerse de carbón.
coal-black [—'blæk] adj. Negro como el carbón *or* como un tizón.
coaler ['kəulə*] n. MAR. Barco (*m.*) carbonero. || Tren (*m.*) de carbón.
coalesce [,kəuə'les] v. intr. Fundirse (to merge). || Unirse (to unite in coalition). || MED. Soldarse.
coalescence [—ns] n. Unión, *f.* (coalition). || Fusión, *f.* (merger). || MED. Soldadura, *f.*
coalfield ['kəulfi:ld] n. Yacimiento (*m.*) de carbón (deposit). || Mina (*f.*) de carbón (mine). || Cuenca (*f.*) carbonífera (region).
coalheaver ['kəul,hi:və*] n. Carbonero, *m.*
coalition [,kəuə'liʃən] n. Coalición, *f.*
coalitionist [—ist] n. Coalicionista, *m.* & *f.*
coalman ['kəulmæn] n. Carbonero, *m.*
— OBSERV. El plural de *coalman* es *coalmen.*
coalmouse ['kəulmaus] n. Paro (*m.*) carbonero (bird).
— OBSERV. El plural de esta palabra es *coalmice.*
coalpit ['kəulpit] n. Mina (*f.*) de carbón.
coaming ['kəumiŋ] n. MAR. Brazola, *f.*
coarse [kɔ:s] adj. Tosco, ca; basto, ta; burdo, da: *coarse stockings,* medias bastas. || Basto, ta (badly-made). || Grosero, ra; basto, ta: *coarse person,* persona basta; *coarse joke,* chiste grosero. || Áspero, ra (hands, skin). || Agudo, da; estridente (noise, voice). || De grano grueso (sugar). || Grueso, sa (flour, sand, etc.). || — *Coarse file,* lima (*f.*) de desbastar. || *Coarse grinding,* esmerilado basto.
coarse-grained [—greind] adj. De grano grueso. || FIG. Basto, ta; grosero, ra.
coarse-minded [—maindid] adj. Grosero, ra; basto, ta.
coarsen ['kɔ:sn] v. tr. Volver grosero, embrutecer (a person). || Volver basto (thing). || Curtir (skin).
— V. intr. Volverse grosero, embrutecerse (person). || Volverse basto (things). || Curtirse (skin).
coarseness [—is] n. Tosquedad, *f.*, basteza, *f.* (poor quality). || Ordinariez, *f.*, grosería, *f.* (rudeness). || Indecencia, *f.*, basteza, *f.*, grosería, *f.* (of a joke). || Aspereza, *f.* (of hands, skin).
coast [kəust] n. Costa, *f.* (seashore). || Costa, *f.*, litoral, *m.* (coastline). || Deslizamiento, *m.* (free-wheeling). || U. S. Cuesta, *f.*, pendiente, *f.* (slope). || FIG. *The coast is clear,* no hay moros en la costa (there is no one about), pasó el peligro (the danger has passed).
coast [kəust] v. tr. MAR. Hacer cabotaje en (from port to port). | Bordear la costa de, costear: *we coasted Spain,* bordeamos la costa de España.
— V. intr. MAR. Hacer cabotaje. | Bordear la costa, costear (to follow the coast). || Deslizarse cuesta abajo [sin pedalear o sin motor] (to freewheel).
coastal [—əl] adj. Costero, ra; costanero, ra. || *Coastal trading* o *traffic,* cabotaje, *m.*
coaster [—ə*] n. MAR. Barco (*m.*) de cabotaje. || Tabla (*f.*) para el queso (cheeseboard). || Carrito, *m.* (for drinks). || Montaña (*f.*) rusa (big dipper). || U. S. Salvamantel, *m.* (mat).
coastguard [—gɑ:d] n. MAR. Guardacostas, *m. inv.* || *Coastguard cutter* o *vessel,* guardacostas.
coasting [—iŋ] adj. MAR. De cabotaje. || *Coasting trade,* cabotaje, *m.*
coastland [—lænd] n. Litoral, *m.*, costa, *f.*
coastline [—lain] n. Litoral, *m.*, costa, *f.*
coastwards [—wədz] adv. Hacia la costa.
coastwise [—waiz] adv. A lo largo de la costa, bordeando la costa.
coat [kəut] n. Abrigo, *m.* (overcoat). || Chaqueta, *f.*, americana, *f.* [*Amer.*, saco, *m.*] (man's jacket). || Lana, *f.* (of sheep). || Pelo, *m.* (of horse, dog, etc.). || MIL. Capote, *m.* || Mano, *f.*, capa, *f.*: *a coat of paint,* una mano de pintura. || BOT. Binza, *f.*, tela, *f.* (of an onion). | Piel, *f.* (of fruits). || ANAT. Membrana, *f.* || FIG. Capa, *f.*, manto, *m.* || — *Coat armour* (U. S. *coat armor*), escudos (*m. pl.*) de armas. || *Coat hanger,* percha, *f.* || *Coat of arms,* escudo (*m.*) de armas. || *Coat of mail,* cota (*f.*) de malla. || FIG. *To cut one's coat according to one's cloth,* vivir según las posibilidades de uno, gobernar su casa según su bolsa, saber adaptarse a las circunstancias. | *To dust one's coat,* sacudir el polvo a uno. | *To turn one's coat,* cambiar de camisa, chaquetear, volver [la] casaca. || *To wear the king's coat,* servir al rey (as a soldier). || *White coat,* bata, *f.* (of a doctor, chemist, etc.).
coat [kəut] v. tr. Cubrir, revestir (*with,* de) [to cover]. || Dar una mano *or* capa de pintura (with paint). || CULIN. Rebozar (meat, fish, etc.). | Bañar (*with,* en) [with a liquid]. || ELECTR. Forrar.
coated [—id] adj. Cuché (paper). || MED. Sucio, cia; saburroso, sa (tongue).
— P. p. See COAT.
coatee [kəu'ti:] n. Chaquetilla (*f.*) corta. || MIL. Guerrera, *f.*
coati [kəu'ɑ:ti] n. ZOOL. Coatí, *m.*
coating ['kəutiŋ] n. Capa, *f.*, mano, *f.* (of paint, etc.). || Rebozado, *m.*, rebozo, *m.* (of meat, fish, etc.). || Baño, *m.* (with a liquid). || Paño (*m.*) de abrigo (cloth).
coattail ['kəutteil] n. Faldón, *m.* (of a coat).
coauthor ['kəu'ɔ:θə*] n. Coautor, ra.
coax [kəuks] v. tr. Engatusar, persuadir con halagos (to persuade): *to coax s.o. into doing sth.,* engatusar a alguien para que haga algo. || Lograr con paciencia (to obtain). || — *To coax s.o. along,* engatusar a uno. || *To coax sth. out of s.o.,* sonsacarle algo a alguien halagándolo *or* engatusándolo.
coaxer [—ə*] n. Adulador, ra; engatusador, ra.
coaxial ['kəu'æksjəl] or **coaxal** ['kəu'æksəl] adj. Coaxial: *coaxial cable,* cable coaxial.
coaxing ['kəuksiŋ] adj. Zalamero, ra; adulador, ra (flattering). || Engatusador, ra (wheedling).
— N. Halagos, *m. pl.*, zalamerías, *f. pl.* (flattery). || Engatusamiento, *m.* (wheedling).
cob [kɔb] n. ZOOL. Cisne, *m.* (swan). | Jaca, *f.* (horse). || Avellana, *f.* (nut). || Mazorca, *f.* (maize). || Pan (*m.*) redondo (loaf). || Trozo (*m.*) redondo de carbón (coal). || ARCH. Adobe, *m.*
cobalt [kəubɔ:lt] n. CHEM. Cobalto, *m.* || — *Cobalt blue,* azul (*m.*) cobalto. || *Cobalt bomb,* bomba (*f.*) de cobalto.
cobaltic [kəu'bɔ:ltik] adj. Cobáltico, ca.
cobble ['kɔbl] n. Adoquín, *m.* (square stone). || Guijarro, *m.* (round stone).
cobble ['kɔbl] v. tr. Adoquinar (to pave with square stones). || Empedrar con guijarros (with round stones). || Remendar (to mend).
cobbler [—ə*] n. Zapatero, *m.*, zapatero (*m.*) remendón (shoemender). || U. S. Tarta (*f.*) de fruta. | Bebida (*f.*) helada de vino, azúcar y limón.
cobblestone ['kɔblstəun] n. Adoquín, *m.* (square stone). || Guijarro, *m.* (round stone).
cobnut ['kɔbnʌt] n. BOT. Avellana, *f.*
cobra ['kəubrə] n. ZOOL. Cobra, *f.* (snake).
cobweb ['kɔbweb] n. Telaraña, *f.* || FIG. Red, *f.*, tejido, *m.*
cobwebbed [—d] or **cobwebby** [—i] adj. Cubierto de telarañas, telarañoso, sa.
coca ['kəukə] n. BOT. Coca, *f.* || Coca, *f.* (drink).
Coca-cola ['kəukə'kəulə] n. Coca-cola, *f.*, coca, *f.*
cocaine [kə'kein] n. CHEM. Cocaína, *f.* || — *Cocaine addict,* cocainómano, na. || *Cocaine addiction,* cocainomanía, *f.*
cocainize [—aiz] v. tr. MED. Anestesiar con cocaína.
coccus ['kɔkəs] n. MED. Coco, *m.*
— OBSERV. El plural de *coccus* es *cocci.*
coccygeal [kɔk'sidʒiəl] adj. Coccígeo, a.
coccyx ['kɔksiks] n. ANAT. Cóccix, *m.*, coxis, *m.*
— OBSERV. El plural de *coccyx* es *coccyges* o *coccyxes.*
Cochin-China ['kɔtʃin'tʃainə] pr. n. GEOGR. Cochinchina, *f.*
cochineal ['kɔtʃini:l] n. Cochinilla, *f.* (dye, insect).
cochlea ['kɔkliə] n. ANAT. Caracol (*m.*) óseo, cóclea, *f.*
— OBSERV. El plural de *cochlea* es *cochleae.*
cochlear [—*] adj. Coclear.
cochleate ['kɔkliit] or **cochleated** ['kɔklieitid] adj. Coclear.
cock [kɔk] n. Gallo, *m.* (the male of the fowl). || Macho, *m.* (male bird): *cock sparrow,* gorrión macho. || Veleta, *f.* (weathercock). || Aguja, *f.*, fiel, *m.* (of balance). || Estilo, *m.* (of sundial). || Grifo, *m.* (tap). || Percutor, *m.* (of a gun). || Inclinación, *f.* (tilting). || Pico, *m.* (of a cocked hat). || Montón (*m.*) de heno (of hay). || POP. Polla, *f.* (male organ). || FAM. Amigo, *m.* (mate). || — *At full cock,* amartillado, da (firearms). || *Cock of the eye,* guiñada, *f.*, mirada, *f.* || *Cock of the rock,* gallo de roca. || FIG. FAM. *Cock of the walk,* gallito (*m.*) del lugar. || *Cock of the wood,* gallo de monte *or* silvestre, urogallo, *m.* || FIG. *Cock sparrow,* gallito, *m.* || *Fighting cock,* gallo de pelea. || FAM. *Old cock!,* ¡viejales! || *The cock of his nose,* su nariz respingona.

cock [kɔk] v. tr. Erguir, levantar: *the dog cocked its ears*, el perro levantó las orejas. || Ladear (to tilt a hat). || Montar, amartillar (a gun). || Amontonar (hay). || — *To cock a snook*, hacer burla con la mano. || *To cock one's eye at*, dirigir una mirada a (s.o.), echar un vistazo a (sth.). || FIG. *To cock the ears*, aguzar el oído.
— V. intr. Erguirse, levantarse (to lift). || FIG. Gallear (to show off).
cockade [kɔ'keid] n. Escarapela, *f.*
cock-a-doodle-doo ['kɔkədu:dl'du:] n. Quiquiriquí, *m.*
cock-a-hoop ['kɔkə'hu:p] adj. Jubiloso, sa; rebosante de alegría. || *To be cock-a-hoop*, brillarle a uno los ojos de alegría.
— Adv. Alegremente, jubilosamente.
Cockaigne [kɔ'kein] n. Tierra (*f.*) de Jauja.
cock-a-leekie ['kɔkə'li:ki] n. CULIN. Caldo (*m.*) de pollo y puerros.
cock-and-bull story ['kɔkən'bul'stɔ:ri] n. FAM. Cuento (*m.*) chino, patraña, *f.*, camelo, *m.*
cockatoo [ˌkɔkə'tu:] n. ZOOL. Cacatúa, *f.* (parrot).
cockatrice ['kɔkətrais] n. MYTH. Basilisco, *m.*
cockboat ['kɔkbəut] n. MAR. Bote, *m.*
cockchafer ['kɔkˌtʃeifə*] n. ZOOL. Abejorro, *m.*
cockcrow ['kɔkkrəu] n. Canto (*m.*) del gallo. || FIG. Amanecer, *m.*, alba, *f.* (dawn). || *At cockcrow*, al amanecer, al cantar el gallo, al despuntar el alba.
cocked ['kɔkt] adj. *Cocked hat*, sombrero de tres picos. || FIG. FAM. *To knock into a cocked hat*, dar or pegar una paliza (to beat completely), dar ciento y raya a (to be superior), destruir totalmente (to ruin).
cocker ['kɔkə*] n. Cocker, *m.* (dog). || Gallero, *m.* (breeder of gamecocks). || *Cocker spaniel*, cocker, *m.*
cockerel [—rəl] n. ZOOL. Pollo, *m.*, gallo (*m.*) joven.
cockeyed ['kɔkaid] adj. FAM. Bizco, ca (cross-eyed). | Torcido, da (awry). | Disparatado, da (absurd). | Trompa, *inv.* (drunk).
cockfight ['kɔkfait] or **cockfighting** [—iŋ] n. Pelea (*f.*) de gallos.
cockhorse ['kɔk'hɔ:s] n. Caballo (*m.*) de juguete.
— Adv. A horcajadas (riding).
cockiness ['kɔkinis] n. Descaro, *m.*, caradura, *f.*, frescura, *f.* (cheek). || Presunción, *f.*, engreimiento, *m.* (cocksureness).
cockish ['kɔkiʃ] adj. FAM. Engreído, da.
cockle ['kɔkl] n. ZOOL. Berberecho, *m.* | Concha (*f.*) de berberecho (shell). || BOT. Neguilla, *f.* || Arruga, *f.* (wrinkle). || MAR. Cascarón (*m.*) de nuez. || Estufa, *f.* (stove). || FIG. *The cockles of the heart*, las entretelas del corazón.
cockle ['kɔkl] v. tr. Arrugar.
— V. intr. Arrugarse.
cockleboat [—bəut] n. MAR. Cascarón (*m.*) de nuez.
cockleshell ['kɔklʃəl] n. Concha (*f.*) de berberecho (shell). || Cascarón (*m.*) de nuez (small boat).
cockloft ['kɔklɔft] n. Desván, *m.* (garret).
cockney ['kɔkni] n. Lenguaje (*m.*) *or* acento (*m.*) característico de los barrios bajos de Londres. || Habitante (*m. & f.*) de los barrios bajos de Londres. || Londinense (*m.*) que habla con un acento chabacano.
cockpit ['kɔkpit] n. AVIAT. Cabina (*f.*) del piloto, carlinga, *f.* || MAR. Caseta (*f.*) del timón. || Reñidero, *m.* [*Amer.*, cancha, *f.*] (for cockfights). || Campo (*m.*) de batalla (battleground). || FIG. Palestra, *f.*, arena, *f.*
cockroach ['kɔkrəutʃ] n. ZOOL. Cucaracha, *f.*
cockscomb ['kɔkskəum] n. Cresta (*f.*) de gallo.
cockshut ['kɔkʃʌt] n. Crepúsculo, *m.*
cockspur ['kɔkspə:*] n. ZOOL. Espolón, *m.*
cocksure ['kɔk'ʃuə*] adj. FAM. Engreído, da; presumido, da (self-confident). | Completamente seguro, ra (absolutely sure).
cocksureness [—nis] n. FAM. Presunción, *f.*, engreimiento, *m.* (self-confidence). | Seguridad, *f.*
cocktail ['kɔkteil] n. Cóctel, *m.*, cocktail, *m.* (drink, appetizer, etc.). || Caballo (*m.*) de raza cruzada y de cola recortada (horse). || — *Cocktail cabinet*, mueble bar, *m.* || *Cocktail party*, cóctel, *m.*, cocktail, *m.* || *Cocktail shaker*, coctelera, *f.* || *Cockail snacks*, tapas, *f. pl.*
cockup ['kɔkʌp] n. PRINT. Inicial, *f.*
cocky ['kɔki] adj. FAM. Engreído, da; presumido, da (cocksure). | Fresco, ca; descarado, da (pert).
coco ['kəukəu] n. BOT. Coco, *m.* (fruit). | Cocotero, *m.*, coco, *m.* (tree). || FAM. Chola, *f.* (head).
cocoa ['kəukəu] n. Cacao, *m.* (drink, powder). || — *Cocoa bean*, grano (*m.*) de cacao. || *Cocoa butter*, manteca (*f.*) de cacao.
coconut or **cocoanut** ['kəukənʌt] n. BOT. Coco, *m.* (fruit). || — BOT. *Coconut o cocoanut grove*, cocotal, *m.* | *Coconut o cocoanut palm*, cocotero, *m.*, coco, *m.*
cocoon [kə'ku:n] n. Capullo, *m.* (of silkworm, etc).
cod [kɔd] n. ZOOL. Bacalao, *m.* (fish).
coda ['kəudə] n. MUS. Coda, *f.*
coddle ['kɔdl] v. tr. Mimar (to pamper). || U. S. Cocer a fuego lento (to cook slowly).
code [kəud] n. JUR. Código, *m.* || Clave, *f.*, cifra, *f* (system of signals). || FIG. Código, *m.* (of concepts). || — *Area code o code number*, prefijo, *m.* (telephone). || *Code of honour*, código del honor. || *Code word*, palabra (*f.*) en clave. || *Highway code*, código de la circulación. || *Morse code*, alfabeto (*m.*) Morse.
code [kəud] v. tr. Cifrar, poner en clave.
codefendant [ˌkəudi'fendənt] n. JUR. Coacusado, da.
codeine ['kəudi:n] n. MED. Codeína, *f.*
codex ['kəudeks] n. Códice, *m.*
— OBSERV. El plural de *codex* es *codices*.
codfish ['kɔdˌfiʃ] n. ZOOL. Bacalao, *m.* (fish).
codger ['kɔdʒə*] n. FAM. Vejete, *m.* (old man).
codicil ['kɔdisil] n. Codicilo, *m.*
codicillary [ˌkɔdi'siləri] adj. Codicilar.
codification [ˌkɔdifi'keiʃən] n. Codificación, *f.*
codifier [kɔdi'faiə*] n. Codificador, ra.
codify ['kɔdifai] v. tr. JUR. Codificar. || Poner en clave (to code).
codling ['kɔdliŋ] n. Bacalao (*m.*) pequeño (fish).
cod-liver oil ['kɔdlivər'ɔil] n. Aceite (*m.*) de hígado de bacalao.
co-driver ['kəuˌdraivə*] n. Copiloto, *m.*
co-ed or **coed** ['kəu'ed] n. U. S. FAM. Alumna (*f.*) de un colegio mixto.
coeducation ['kəuˌedju'keiʃən] n. Coeducación, *f.*, enseñanza (*f.*) mixta.
coeducational [—l] adj. Coeducacional, mixto, ta.
coefficient [ˌkəui'fiʃənt] n. Coeficiente, *m.*
coelacanth ['si:ləkænθ] n. ZOOL. Celacanto, *m.*
coelenterate [si:'lentəreit] n. ZOOL. Celentéreo, *m.*
coeliac ['si:liæk] adj. ANAT. Celíaco, ca; celiaco, ca. || MED. *Coeliac disease*, celiaca, *f.*
coendou [kəu'endu:] n. ZOOL. Coendú, *m.*
coenobite ['si:nəbait] n. REL. Cenobita, *m. & f.*
coenobitic [ˌsi:nə'bitik] or **coenobitical** [—əl] adj. Cenobítico, ca; cenobial.
coenobitism ['si:nəˌbaitizəm] n. Cenobitismo, *m.*
coequal [kəu'i:kwəl] adj./n. Igual [a otro]
coequality [ˌkəui'kwɔliti] n. Igualdad, *f.* [con otro].
coerce [kəu'ə:s] v. tr. JUR. PHYS. Coercer. || Forzar, obligar, coaccionar (*into*, a) [to force].
coercible [kəu'ə:sibl] adj. JUR. PHYS. Coercible.
coercion [kəu'ə:ʃən] n. JUR. PHYS. Coerción, *f.* || Coacción, *f.* (by force).
coercive [kəu'ə:siv] adj. Coactivo, va (compelling). || JUR. PHYS. Coercitivo, va.
coercivity [ˌkəuə:'siviti] n. Coercitividad, *f.*
coetaneous [ˌkəui:'teiniəs] adj. Coetáneo, a.
coeternal [ˌkəui:'tə:nl] adj. Coeterno, na.
coeval [kəu'i:vəl] adj./n. Coetáneo, a.
coexist ['kəuig'zist] v. intr. Coexistir, convivir.
coexistence [—əns] n. Coexistencia, *f.*, convivencia, *f.*
coexistent ['kəuig'zistənt] adj. Coexistente.
coffee ['kɔfi] n. Café, *m.* (bean and drink): *black, white coffee*, café solo, con leche. || BOT. Café, *m.*, cafeto, *m.* (plant). || — *Coffee bar*, café, *m.* || *Coffee bean*, grano (*m.*) de café. || *Coffee break*, descanso (*m.*) para tomar café. || *Coffee cup*, taza (*f.*) de café. || *Coffee grounds*, poso, *m. sing.*, zurrapa, *f. sing.* || *Coffee grower o planter*, cafetalero, *m.*, cafetero, *m.* || *Coffee mill*, molinillo (*m.*) de café. || *Coffee plantation*, plantación (*f.*) de café, cafetal, *m.* || *Coffee roaster*, tostador (*m.*) de café. || *Coffee shop*, café, *m.* || *Coffee spoon*, cucharilla (*f.*) de café. || *Coffee tree*, cafeto, *m.* || *Roasted coffee*, café torrefacto.
— Adj. Cafetalero, ra; cafetero, ra; de café: *coffee production*, producción cafetalera. || Color café, de color café (coffee-coloured): *a coffee dress*, un traje color café.
coffeehouse [—haus] n. Café, *m.*
coffeepot [—pɔt] n. Cafetera, *f.*
coffeeroom [—rum] n. Café, *m.*
coffer ['kɔfə*] n. Caja, *f.*, arca, *f.* (for storing money). || ARCH. Artesón, *m.* || — Pl. Fondos, *m.* (funds).
coffer ['kɔfə*] v. tr. ARCH. Artesonar. || Atesorar (money).
cofferdam [—dæm] n. Ataguía, *f.* (dam). || MAR. Compartimiento (*m.*) estanco.
coffin ['kɔfin] n. Ataúd, *m.*, féretro, *m.* (for funerals). || Cavidad (*f.*) del casco (of hoof). || PRINT. Carro, *m.* (of a machine). || — *Coffin bone*, bolillo, *m.* (of horse). || FAM. *Coffin nail*, pitillo, *m.* (cigarette).
coffin ['kɔfin] v. tr. Poner en el ataúd. || FAM. Enterrar.
cog [kɔg] n. TECH. Diente, *m.* (of wheel, gear). | Rueda (*f.*) dentada (wheel). | Espiga, *f.* (in carpentry). || FIG. Eslabón, *m.*, pieza, *f.* (person).
cog [kɔg] v. tr. Hacer trampas con (to cheat). || Cargar (a die). || TECH. Endentar, poner dientes a. | Ensamblar con espigas (in carpentry).
— V. intr. TECH. Engranarse. || Hacer trampa.
cogency ['kəudʒənsi] n. Fuerza, *f.*, poder, *m.* (of an argument). || JUR. Lo bien fundado, legitimidad, *f.*
cogent ['kəudʒənt] adj. Fuerte, convincente, poderoso, sa.
cogged ['kɔgd] adj. TECH. Dentado, da (wheel). || Cargado, da; falso, sa (dice).
cogitable ['kɔdʒitəbl] adj. Concebible.
cogitate ['kɔdʒiteit] v. tr./intr. Reflexionar, meditar, cavilar, cogitar.
cogitation [ˌkɔdʒi'teiʃən] n. Reflexión, *f.*, meditación, *f.*, cogitación, *f.*
cogitative ['kɔdʒitətiv] adj. Pensativo, va; reflexivo, va.
cognac ['kɔnjæk] n. Coñac, *m.* (brandy).
cognate ['kɔgneit] adj. JUR. Cognado, da. || GRAMM. Afín. || Similar (alike).
— N. JUR. Cognado, *m.* || GRAMM. Palabra (*f.*) afín.
cognation [kɔg'neiʃən] n. JUR. Cognación, *f.*
cognition [kɔg'niʃən] n. Percepción, *f.* || PHIL. Cognición, *f.*

cognitive [ˈkɔgnitiv] adj. PHIL. Cognoscitivo, va.
cognizable [ˈkɔgnizəbl] adj. Cognoscible. || JUR. Enjuiciable.
cognizance [ˈkɔgnizəns] n. Conocimiento, *m.* (knowledge). || JUR. Competencia, *f.*, incumbencia, *f.* || HERALD. Emblema, *m.* || — *Beyond one's cognizance*, fuera de la competencia de uno. || *To have cognizance of*, tener conocimiento de. || *To take cognizance of*, tener en cuenta. || *Within my cognizance*, de mi incumbencia, de mi competencia.
cognizant [ˈkɔgnizənt] adj. Conocedor, ra; sabedor, ra. || JUR. Competente (*of*, para). || *To be cognizant of*, saber.
cognize [kɔgˈnaiz] v. tr. Conocer.
cognomen [kɔgˈnəumen] n. Cognomen, *m.* (in ancient Rome). || Apodo, *m.* (nickname). || Apellido, *m.* (surname).

— OBSERV. El plural de *cognomen* es *cognomens* o *cognomina*.

cognoscible [kɔgˈnɔsibl] adj. Cognoscible.
cogwheel [ˈkɔgwi:l] n. Rueda (*f.*) dentada.
cohabit [kəuˈhæbit] v. intr. Cohabitar, vivir juntos.
cohabitation [ˌkəuhæbiˈteiʃən] n. Cohabitación, *f.*
coheir [ˈkəuˈɛə*] n. Coheredero, *m.*
coheiress [ˈkəuˈɛəris] n. Coheredera, *f.*
cohere [kəuˈhiə*] v. intr. Adherirse, pegarse (to stick together). || FIG. Ser coherente (style, planning, etc.).
coherence [kəuˈhiərəns] or **coherency** [—i] n. Coherencia, *f.*, adherencia, *f.*, cohesión, *f.* || FIG. Coherencia, *f.*
coherent [kəuˈhiərənt] adj. Coherente.
coherer [kəuˈhiərə*] n. RAD. Cohesor, *m.*
cohesion [kəuˈhi:ʒən] n. Cohesión, *f.*
cohesive [kəuˈhi:siv] adj. Cohesivo, va.
cohesiveness [—nis] n. Cohesión, *f.*
cohibit [kəuˈhibit] v. tr. Cohibir.
cohort [ˈkəuhɔ:t] n. Cohorte, *f.*
coif [kɔif] n. Cofia, *f.* (cap). || JUR. Birrete, *m.* || MIL. Cofia, *f.* || BOT. Cofia, *f.*
coiffure [kwɑ:ˈfjuə] n. Peinado, *m.*
coign [kɔin] n. Pico, *m.*, parte (*f.*) saliente. || *Coign of vantage*, posición ventajosa.
coil [kɔil] n. Rizo, *m.* (of hair). || Rollo, *m.* (of rope). || MAR. Aduja, *f.* || ELECTR. Carrete, *m.*, bobina, *f.* (in electromagnetics). || Anillo, *m.* (of snake). || Espiral, *f.* (of smoke). || Vuelta, *f.* (a single turn). || Serpentín, *m.* (of pipe). || *Coil spring*, muelle (*m.*) en espiral.
coil [kɔil] v. tr. Enrollar, arrollar. || MAR. Adujar. || ELECTR. Embobinar, enrollar.
— V. intr. Enrollarse, arrollarse (to wind itself up). || Enroscarse (a snake). || Serpentear (a river, etc.). || *To coil up*, hacerse un ovillo.
coin [kɔin] n. Moneda, *f.* || — FIG. *To pay s.o. in his own coin*, pagar a alguien con la misma moneda. || *To toss a coin*, echar una moneda al aire, echar a cara o cruz.
coin [kɔin] v. tr. Acuñar (coins). || FIG. Inventar (tales). | Acuñar, inventar, crear (words, expressions). || FIG. FAM. Amasar, amontonar (money). || FIG. *To coin money*, amasar una fortuna.
coinage [ˈkɔinidʒ] n. Acuñación, *f.* (making of coins). || Moneda, *f.* (money). || Sistema (*m.*) monetario (monetary system). || FIG. Invención, *f.* (of tales, words, sentences, etc.).
coincide [ˌkəuinˈsaid] v. intr. Coincidir.
coincidence [kəuˈinsidəns] n. Coincidencia, *f.* || Casualidad, *f.* (chance).
coincident [kəuˈinsidənt] adj. Coincidente.
coincidental [kəuˌinsiˈdentl] adj. Coincidente (coinciding). || Casual (chance).
coiner [kɔinə*] n. Acuñador, *m.* (who makes coins). || Falsificador (*m.*) de moneda (counterfeiter). || FIG. Inventor, ra; creador, ra (of words, etc.).
coir [ˈkɔiə*] n. Bonote, *m.*, fibra (*f.*) de coco.
coition [kəuˈiʃən] or **coitus** [ˈkəuitəs] n. Coito, *m.*
coke [kəuk] n. Cok, *m.*, coque, *m.* (coal). || FAM. Coca, *f.* (Coca-cola). | Cocaína, *f.* (cocaine).
coke [kəuk] v. tr. Convertir en cok, coquizar, coquificar.
— V. intr. Convertirse en cok.
cokernut [ˈkəukənʌt] n. Coco, *m.* (coconut).
coking [kaukiŋ] n. Coquefacción, *f.*, coquificación, *f.*, coquización, *f.*
cola [ˈkəulə] n. BOT. Cola, *f.*
colander [ˈkʌləndə*] n. Colador, *m.*
colander [ˈkʌləndə*] v. tr. Colar.
colchicum [ˈkɔltʃikəm] n. BOT. Cólquico, *m.*
Colchis [ˈkɔlkis] pr. n. GEOGR. Cólquida, *f.*
colcothar [ˈkɔlkəθɑ:*] n. Colcótar, *m.*
cold [kəuld] adj. Frío, a: *a cold day*, un día frío; *a cold meal*, una comida fría. || Frigorífico, ca (room, store). || FAM. Frío, a; muerto, ta (dead). || FIG. Frío, a; indiferente (without enthusiasm). | Frío, a (frigid). | Frío, a; poco amistoso, sa: *a cold reception*, un recibimiento frío. | Frío, a; desapasionado, da; objetivo, va (calm, objective). | Deprimente (dispiriting). | Frío, a (far from the thing sought). | Viejo, ja (news). | Sin conocimiento, inconsciente, fuera de combate: *to knock s.o. cold*, dejar a alguien fuera de combate. || ARTS. Frío, a (colours). || SP. Débil, vago, ga (scent). || — *As cold as ice*, más frío que el hielo, helado, da. || *Cold chisel*, cortafrío, *m.* || *Cold comfort*, poco consuelo. || *Cold cream*, "cold cream", *m.*, crema (*f.*) para el cutis. || *Cold cuts*, fiambres variados. || FAM. *Cold feet*, mieditis, *f.* | *Cold fish*, persona pesada. || *Cold forging*, forjado en frío. || *Cold frame*, cajonera, *f.* (for plants). || *Cold front*, frente frío (in meteorology). || *Cold meat*, fiambres, *m. pl.* (food), fiambre, *m.* (corpse). || *Cold pack*, compresa fría. || *Cold riveting*, remachado en frío. || FAM. *Cold shoulder*, frialdad, *f.* || *Cold snap*, ola (*f.*) de frío. || *Cold sore*, herpes (*m.*) labial. || *Cold spell*, ola (*f.*) de frío. || *Cold steel*, arma blanca. || *Cold storage*, conservación (*f.*) en cámara frigorífica. || *Cold sweat*, sudor frío. || FIG. *Cold war*, guerra fría. || *Cold wave*, ola (*f.*) de frío. || FIG. *In cold blood*, a sangre fría. || *It's bitterly cold*, hace un frío que pela *or* un frío de perros. || *To be cold*, hacer frío (weather): *it's very cold today*, hoy hace mucho frío; tener frío (persons), estar frío (things). || *To be very cold*, hacer mucho frío (weather), tener mucho frío (persons), estar muy frío (things). || *To get cold*, enfriarse (things), refrescar, empezar a hacer frío (weather). || FIG. *To have s.o. cold*, tener a alguien en el bolsillo. | *To leave s.o. cold*, dejar a uno frío. | *To make s.o.'s blood run cold*, hacer que a alguien se le hiele la sangre. | *To put into cold storage*, echar en el olvido, dejar en suspenso.
— Adv. De repente, en seco (suddenly). || De plano, llanamente (plainly). || Perfectamente (perfectly).
— N. Frío, *m.* (low temperature). || MED. Constipado, *m.*, resfriado, *m.*, catarro, *m.* || — *To catch cold*, coger frío. || MED. *To catch a cold*, resfriarse, acatarrarse, coger un resfriado. | *To have a cold*, estar constipado *or* resfriado *or* acatarrado. || FIG. *To leave s.o. out in the cold*, dejar a alguien al margen *or* en la estacada.
cold-blooded [ˈkəuldˈblʌdid] adj. FIG. Insensible (insensitive). | Cruel, despiadado, da (callous). || ZOOL. De sangre fría.
cold-bloodedness [—nis] n. Sangre (*f.*) fría.
cold-draw* [ˈkəuldˌdrɔ:] v. tr. Estirar en frío.

— OBSERV. Pret. ***cold-drew;*** p. p. ***cold-drawn.***

cold-drawn [—n] p. p. See COLD-DRAW.
cold-drew [ˈkəuldˌdru:] pret. See COLD-DRAW.
coldhearted [ˈkəuldˈhɑ:tid] adj. Insensible, frío de corazón.
coldheartedness [—nis] n. Frialdad, *f.*
coldish [ˈkəuldiʃ] adj. Fresquito, ta.
coldness [ˈkəuldnis] n. Frialdad, *f.* || Frío, *m.*, temperatura (*f.*) fría (cold). || FIG. Frialdad, *f.*
cold-press [ˈkəuldˈpres] v. tr. Prensar en frío.
cold-setting [ˈkəuldˈsetiŋ] n. Fraguado (*m.*) en frío.
cold-short [ˈkəuldˈʃɔ:t] adj. Quebradizo, za (metal).
cold-shoulder [ˈkəuldˈʃəuldə*] v. tr. Tratar con frialdad (to treat with coldness). || Volver la espalda a (to rebuff).
cole [kəul] n. BOT. Colza, *f.* (rape).
colegatee [kəulegəˈti:] n. Colegatario, ria.
coleopteron [ˌkɔliˈɔptərən] n. ZOOL. Coleóptero, *m.*

— OBSERV. El plural de *coleopteron* es *coleoptera*.

coleslaw [ˈkəulslɔ:] n. Ensalada (*f.*) de col.
colewort [ˈkəulwə:t] n. BOT. Col, *f.*
colic [ˈkɔlik] n. MED. Cólico, *m.*: *hepatic, nephritic colic*, cólico hepático, nefrítico. || MED. *Lead* o *painter's colic*, cólico saturnino.
— Adj. Cólico, ca.
colicky [—i] adj. Que tiene *or* causa cólico.
Coliseum [ˌkɔliˈsiəm] pr. n. Coliseo, *m.*
colitis [kɔˈlaitis] n. MED. Colitis, *f.*
collaborate [kəˈlæbəreit] v. intr. Colaborar.
collaboration [kəˌlæbəˈreiʃən] n. Colaboración, *f.* || Colaboracionismo, *m.* (in politics).
collaborationist [—ist] n. Colaboracionista, *m.* & *f.*
collaborator [kəˈlæbəreitə*] n. Colaborador, ra (in a work, etc.). || Colaboracionista, *m.* & *f.* (in politics).
collage [kɔˈlɑ:ʒ] n. ARTS. Collage, *m.*
collapse [kəˈlæps] n. Derrumbamiento, *m.*, desplome, *m.* (a falling down). || MED. Colapso, *m.* || FIG. Fracaso, *m.* (failure). | Ruina, *f.* (financial ruin). | Hundimiento, *m.*, derrumbamiento, *m.* (of business, government). | Caída (*f.*) vertical (of prices). || TECH. Pandeo, *m.* (of a beam).
collapse [kəˈlæps] v. tr. Derrumbar, echar abajo (to cause to collapse). || Plegar: *to collapse a tent*, plegar una tienda de campaña.
— V. intr. Derrumbarse, desplomarse, caerse (to fall down). || Desinflarse (balloon). || MED. Tener *or* sufrir un colapso. || Plegarse (to fold). || FIG. Fracasar (to fail). | Arruinarse (to go bankrupt). | Derrumbarse, hundirse, venirse abajo (a business, government). | Bajar verticalmente (prices). || TECH. Pandearse (beam). | Alabearse (wheel).
collapsible [—əbl] adj. Plegable.
collar [ˈkɔlə*] n. Cuello (of a shirt, dress, etc.). || Collar, *m.* (of animals). || Collera, *f.* (of a harness). || TECH. Collarín, *m.*, abrazadera, *f.* || Collar, *m.* (of an order). || CULIN. Carne (*f.*) atada para guisar. || BOT. Cuello, *m.* || — ARCH. *Collar beam*, falso tirante. || *Stiff collar*, cuello duro. || FAM. *To get hot under the collar*, acalorarse (to get angry).
collar [ˈkɔlə*] v. tr. Agarrar *or* coger por el cuello (to seize). || Acollarar, poner collar a (to put a collar

on). || FIG. Coger, capturar (to capture). || FAM. Acorralar (to stop and talk to). | Mangar (to appropriate). || CULIN. Atar (fish, meat). || TECH. Poner abrazadera a.
collarbone [ˈkɔləbəun] n. ANAT. Clavícula, *f.*
collaret or **collarette** [ˌkɔləˈret] n. Cuello (*m.*) de encaje.
collate [kɔˈleit] n. Confrontar, cotejar (to compare). || Ordenar (pages, illustrations). || Verificar, comprobar (to verify). || REL. Colacionar, conferir (an ecclesiastical benefice). || JUR. Colacionar.
collateral [kɔˈlætərəl] adj. Paralelo, la: *collateral arguments*, argumentos paralelos. || Colateral (accompanying, secondary). || JUR. Auxiliar, adicional. || COMM. Subsidiario, ria: *collateral security*, garantía subsidiaria. || Colateral (a relative).
— N. Colateral, *m.* & *f.* (relative). || COMM. Garantía (*f.*) subsidiaria.
collation [kɔˈleiʃən] n. Cotejo, *m.*, comparación, *f.*, confrontación, *f.* (of texts). || REL. Colación, *f.* (of a benefice). || (Ant.) Colación, *f.* (snack). || JUR. *Collation of property*, colación de bienes.
collator [kɔˈleitə*] n. REL. Colador, *m.*
colleague [ˈkɔli:g] n. Colega, *m.* & *f.*
collect [kəˈlekt] adj./adv. U. S. A cobro revertido (telephone call, telegram, etc.).
collect [ˈkɔlekt] n. REL. Colecta, *f.*
collect [kəˈlekt] v. tr. Coleccionar (to gather as a hobby). || Reunir, juntar (to gather together). || Reunir (to gather people together). || Recaudar (taxes, money for charity). || Allegar (funds). || Cobrar (rents, bills, etc.). || Recoger (to gather in, to pick up): *the teacher collected the examination papers*, el profesor recogió los exámenes; *I'm going to collect my skirt from the cleaners*, voy a recoger la falda a la tintorería. || Amontonar (wealth). || Poner en orden (one's thoughts). || Inferir, deducir (to deduce). || *To collect o.s.*, recobrar el dominio de sí mismo.
— V. intr. Congregarse, reunirse (people). || Acumularse, amontonarse (things). || Cobrar (rent, bill, etc.). || REL. Hacer una colecta (to take up a collection). || Ser coleccionista (to be a collector). || *To collect on delivery*, contra reembolso (cash on delivery).
collectable [—əbl] adj. Cobrable.
collected [kəˈlektid] adj. FIG. Sosegado, da (calm). | Recogido, da (pensive). || See COLLECT. || — *Collected short stories*, colección (*f.*) de novelas cortas. || *Collected works*, obras completas.
collection [kəˈlekʃən] n. Colección, *f.* (pictures, fashion, stamps, models, etc.). || Colecta, *f.*, cuestación, *f.* (money for charity). || Grupo, *m.*, reunión, *f.* (of people). || Reunión, *f.* (of things). || Montón, *m.* (mass). || Cobro, *m.* (of rent, bill, etc.). || Recaudación, *f.* (of taxes). || Recogida, *f.* (of post, eggs). || REL. Colecta, *f.* (in church). || — Pl. Examen (*m. sing.*) final.
collective [kəˈlektiv] adj. Colectivo, va. || — *Collective agreement*, convenio colectivo. || *Collective bargaining*, negociaciones colectivas, contrato colectivo. || *Collective farm*, granja colectiva. || GRAMM. *Collective noun*, nombre *or* sustantivo colectivo, colectivo, *m.* || *Collective security*, garantía colectiva.
— N. Colectividad, *f.*
— OBSERV. Los nombres colectivos van seguidos de un verbo en singular cuando predomina el concepto de unidad y de un verbo en plural cuando prevalece el concepto de pluralidad (*is the family at home?*, ¿está la familia en casa?: *the family were stricken with grief*, todos los miembros de la familia se afligieron).
collectivism [—izəm] n. Colectivismo, *m.*
collectivist [—ist] adj./n. Colectivista.
collectivity [ˌkəlekˈtiviti] n. Colectividad, *f.*
collectivization [kəˌlektiviˈzeiʃən] n. Colectivización, *f.*
collectivize [kəˈlektivaiz] v. tr. Colectivizar.
collector [kəˈlektə*] n. Recaudador, ra (of taxes). || Empleado (*m.*) que recoge los billetes (of tickets). || Cobrador, *m.* (of rents, bills, etc.). || Coleccionista, *m.* & *f.* (of stamps, coins, etc.). || TECH. Colector, *m.*
college [ˈkɔlidʒ] n. Colegio, *m.*: *the college of barristers, doctors*, el colegio de abogados, de médicos; *Eton college*, colegio de Eton. || Colegio (*m.*) mayor (as in Oxford, Cambridge, etc.). || Facultad, *f.* (part of the university). || Escuela, *f.* (technical). || MUS. Conservatorio, *m.* || U. S. Universidad (*f.*) autónoma. || — *College of Cardinals or Sacred College*, colegio de cardenales *or* cardenalicio. || *Electoral college*, colegio electoral.
collegial [kəˈli:dʒjəl] adj. Colegial. || U. S. Universitario, ria.
collegian [kəˈli:dʒjən] n. Estudiante, *m.* & *f.* (at University). || Colegiado, da (of a college of doctors, etc.).
collegiate [kəˈli:dʒiit] adj. Colegiado, da: *collegiate member*, miembro colegiado. || Colegial (relating to a college). || Superior (school). || U. S. Universitario, ria. || *Collegiate church*, colegiata, *f.*, iglesia (*f.*) colegial, colegial, *f.*
collet [ˈkɔlit] n. TECH. Collar, *m.* || Engaste, *m.* (for gems).
collet [ˈkɔlit] v. tr. Engastar.
collide [kəˈlaid] v. intr. Chocar (*with*, con, contra). || FIG. Chocar, estar en conflicto.
collie [ˈkɔli] n. Perro (*m.*) pastor escocés.
collier [ˈkɔliə*] n. Minero, *m.* (coal miner). || MAR. Barco (*m.*) carbonero.
colliery [ˈkɔljəri] n. Mina (*f.*) de carbón.
colligate [ˈkɔligeit] v. tr. Relacionar (to relate). || Unir (to bind).
collimation [ˌkɔliˈmeiʃən] n. PHYS. Colimación, *f.*
collimator [ˈkɔlimeitə*] n. PHYS. Colimador, *m.*
collision [kəˈliʒən] n. Colisión, *f.*, choque, *m.*: *there was a collision between a bus and a lorry*, hubo un choque entre un autobús y un camión. || FIG. Choque, *m.*, conflicto, *m.* (of ideas).
collocate [ˈkɔləkeit] v. tr. Colocar, ordenar, disponer.
collocation [ˌkɔləˈkeiʃən] n. Colocación, *f.*, ordenación, *f.*, disposición, *f.*
collodion [kəˈləudjən] n. CHEM. Colodión, *m.*
collogue [kəˈləug] v. intr. Tener una entrevista privada.
colloid [ˈkɔlɔid] adj. CHEM. Coloide.
— N. CHEM. Coloide, *m.*
colloidal [kɔˈlɔidəl] adj. CHEM. Coloidal.
collop [ˈkɔləp] n. Filete, *m.* (slice of meat).
colloquial [kəˈləukwiəl] adj. Familiar.
colloquialism [—izəm] n. Expresión (*f.*) familiar. || Lengua (*f.*) familiar.
colloquist [ˈkɔləkwist] n. Participante (*m.* & *f.*) en un coloquio, interlocutor, ra.
colloquy [ˈkɔləkwi] n. Coloquio, *m.*
collude [kəˈlu:d] v. intr. Estar de connivencia.
collusion [kəˈlu:ʒən] n. JUR. Colusión, *f.* || *To enter into collusion with*, estar de connivencia con.
collusive [kəˈlu:siv] adj. JUR. Colusorio, ria.
collyrium [kɔˈliriəm] n. MED. Colirio, *m.*
— OBSERV. El plural es *collyria* o *collyriums*.
collywobbles [ˈkɔliˌwɔblz] pl. n. FAM. Ruidos (*m.*) de tripas, borborigmos, *m.* || FAM. *It gives me the collywobbles*, me pone los pelos de punta.
Cologne [kəˈləun] pr. n. GEOGR. Colonia.
Colombia [kəˈlɔmbiə] pr. n. GEOGR. Colombia, *f.*
Colombian [—n] adj./n. Colombiano, na.
colon [ˈkəulən] n. ANAT. Colon, *m.* || PRINT. Dos puntos (:).
colon [kəˈləun] n. Colono, *m.* (colonial).
colón [kɔˈlɔn] n. Colón, *m.* (Costa Rican money).
colonel [ˈkə:nl] n. MIL. Coronel, *m.*
colonial [kəˈləunjəl] adj. Colonial: *colonial period*, época colonial. || Colonizador, ra (power).
— N. Colono, *m.* (inhabitant of a colony).
colonialism [—izəm] n. Colonialismo, *m.*
colonialist [—ist] adj./n. Colonialista.
colonist [ˈkɔlənist] n. Colonizador, ra (person who colonizes). || Colono, *m.* (inhabitant of a colony).
colonization [ˌkɔlənaiˈzeiʃən] n. Colonización, *f.*
colonize [ˈkɔlənaiz] v. tr. Colonizar.
— V. intr. Establecer una colonia (to found a colony). || Establecerse en una colonia (to settle in a colony).
colonizer [—ə*] n. Colonizador, ra.
colonnade [ˌkɔləˈneid] n. ARCH. Columnata, *f.*
colony [ˈkɔləni] n. Colonia, *f.*
colophon [ˈkɔləfən] n. Colofón, *m.*
colophony [ˈkɔləˌfəuni] n. CHEM. Colofonia, *f.*
color [ˈkʌlə*] n. U. S. See COLOUR.
color [ˈkʌlə*] v. tr./intr. U. S. See COLOUR.
colorable [ˈkʌlərəbl] n. U. S. See COLOURABLE.
Colorado [ˌkɔləˈrɑ:dəu] pr. n. GEOGR. Colorado, *m.* || ZOOL. *Colorado beetle*, escarabajo (*m.*) de la patata.
colorant [ˈkʌlərənt] n. U. S. Colorante, *m.*
coloration [ˌkʌləˈreiʃən] n. U. S. Coloración, *f.* | Colorido, *m.*
color-bearer [ˈkʌləˌbɛərə*] n. U. S. MIL. Abanderado, *m.*
color-blind [ˈkʌləblaind] adj. U. S. Daltoniano, na.
color-blindness [—nis] n. U. S. Daltonismo, *m.*
colorcast [ˈkʌləkɑ:st] n. U. S. Televisión (*f.*) en color.
colorcast [ˈkʌləkɑ:st] v. tr./intr. U. S. Televisar en color.
colored [ˈkʌləd] adj. U. S. See COLOURED.
colorful [ˈkʌləful] adj. U. S. See COLOURFUL.
colorimeter [ˌkʌləˈrimitə*] n. Colorímetro, *m.*
coloring [ˈkʌləriŋ] n. U. S. See COLOURING.
colorist [ˈkʌlərist] n. U. S. Colorista, *m.* & *f.*
colorless [ˈkʌləlis] adj. U. S. See COLOURLESS.
colossal [kəˈlɔsl] adj. Colosal (huge).
Colossians [kəˈlɔʃənz] pl. n. REL. Colosenses, *m.*: *Epistle to the Colossians*, Epístola a los colosenses.
colossus [kəˈlɔsəs] n. Coloso, *m.* || *The Colossus of Rhodes*, El Coloso de Rodas.
— OBSERV. El plural de *colossus* es *colossi* o *collosuses*.
colostrum [kəˈlɔstrəm] n. Calostro, *m.*, colostro, *m.*
colour (U. S. **color**) [ˈkʌlə*] n. Color, *m*: *this dress is a nice colour*, este vestido tiene un color bonito; *complementary colours*, colores complementarios; *what colour is it?*, ¿de qué color es? || Color, *m.*, tez, *f.* (complexion). || Color, *m.*, tinte, *m.* (dye). || Color, *m.* (racial complexion): *a man of colour*, un hombre de color. || ARTS. Colorido, *m.*, tonos, *m. pl.* (effect of colours). || MUS. Calidad (*f.*) de tono. || Ambiente, *m.*, color, *m.* (in literature): *local colour*, color local. || Color, *m.*, opinión, *f.*, tendencia, *f.* (of a newspaper). || PRINT. Color, *m.* || — Pl. MIL. Ceremonia (*f. sing.*) de izar o de arriar la bandera. || MAR. Pabellón, *m. sing.*, colores, *m.* (flag). || MIL. Colores, *m.*, bandera, *f. sing.* || Distintivo, *m. sing.*, colores, *m.* (of athletic team). || — *Colour bar*, barrera (*f.*) racial. || *Colour*

box, caja (*f.*) de pinturas. || U. S. *Colour line*, barrera (*f.*) racial. || *Colour photography*, fotocromía, *f.*, fotografía (*f.*) en colores. || PRINT. *Colour printing*, cromolitografía, *f.* || *Colour scheme*, combinación (*f.*) de colores. || *Colour television*, televisión (*f.*) en color. || *Fast colour*, color sólido. || *High colour*, color subido. || *In colour*, en colores. || *In full colour*, a todo color. || FAM. *Let's see the colour of your money!*, ¡a ver la pasta! || *Off colour*, descolorido, da (colourless), indispuesto, ta (sick), verde (joke). || *That skirt is green in colour*, esa falda es de color verde. || MIL. *To call to the colours*, llamar a filas. || FIG. *To change colour*, mudar de color. | *To come through with flying colours*, salir airoso. || MIL. *To hoist the colours*, izar la bandera. | *To join the colours*, alistarse en el ejército. || FIG. *To lend* o *to give colour to sth.*, dar una apariencia de verdad a algo, hacer que algo parezca verosímil. || *To lose colour*, palidecer. || FIG. *To nail one's colours to the mast*, mantenerse firme. | *To paint in dark colours*, pintar con negros colores. | *To put false colours upon*, presentar bajo un falso color. || MIL. *To serve with the colours*, servir en el ejército. || FIG. *To show one's true colours*, quitarse la máscara. | *To stick to one's colours*, mantenerse fiel a sus principios. | *To take all the colour out of sth.*, quitarle toda la gracia a algo. | *Under colour of*, con el pretexto de, so pretexto de, so color de. || MIL. *With flying colours*, con banderas desplegadas. || MIL. *With the colours*, en filas.

colour (U. S. **color**) [ˈkʌlə*] v. tr. Colorear, colorar (to impart colour to). || Teñir (to dye). || Pintar (to paint). || FIG. Adornar, embellecer, colorear, amenizar (a description, report, one's style). | Alterar, desvirtuar (feelings, opinions, views). || FAM. Curar, quemar, ennegrecer (a pipe).
— V. intr. Colorearse. || Cambiar de color. || Sonrojarse, ruborizarse, ponerse colorado (to blush).

colourable (U. S. **colorable**) [—rəbl] adj. Verosímil (plausible). || Engañoso, sa (deceptive). || JUR. *Colourable imitation*, imitación fraudulenta.

colourant [—rənt] n. Colorante, *m.*

colouration [ˌkʌləˈreiʃən] n. Coloración, *f.* || Colorido, *m.* (colour).

colour-bearer [ˈkʌləˌbɛərə*] n. MIL. Abanderado, *m.*

colour-blind [ˈkʌləblaind] adj. Daltoniano, na.

colour-blindness [—nis] n. Daltonismo, *m.*

coloured (U. S. **colored**) [ˈkʌləd] adj. De color, coloreado, da (having colour). || De color (of race). || FIG. Tendencioso, sa (biased). || FIG. *Highly coloured narrative*, relato lleno de colorido.

colourful (U. S. **colorful**) [ˈkʌləful] adj. Lleno de color (full of colour). || Animado, da (lively, interesting). || Pintoresco, ca (person, character).

colouring (U. S. **coloring**) [ˈkʌləriŋ] n. Coloración, *f.* || Color, *m.*, colorido, *m.* (colour). || ARTS. Colorido, *m.* || Colorido, *m.* (of skin). || Colorante, *m.* (colouring matter). || FIG. Alteración, *f.* (of facts). | Apariencia, *f.* (aspect). || *Colouring book*, libro (*m.*) para colorear.
— Adj. Colorante.

colourist [ˈkʌlərist] n. Colorista, *m.* & *f.*

colourless (U. S. **colorless**) [ˈkʌləlis] adj. Incoloro, ra; sin color (without colour). || Descolorido, da; sin color (having lost its colour). || FIG. Soso, sa (dull).

colt [kəult] n. ZOOL. Potro, *m.* (young horse). || FIG. Joven (*m.*) inexperto, pipiolo, *m.*, novato, *m.* (young and inexperienced person). | Juvenil, *m.* (young cricketer). || MIL. Colt, *m.* (revolver). || MAR. Azote, *m.*

colter [—ə*] n. U. S. Cuchilla, *f.* [del arado].

coltish [—iʃ] adj. FIG. Novato, ta; inexperto, ta (young). | Juguetón, ona (frisky).

coltsfoot [—sfut] n. BOT. Tusilago, *m*

— OBSERV. El plural de *coltsfoot* es *coltsfoots*.

columbarium [ˌkɔləmˈbɛəriəm] n. Columbario, *m.* || Palomar, *m.* (dovecot).

— OBSERV. El plural de *columbarium* es *columbaria*.

Columbia [kəˈlʌmbiə] pr. n. GEOGR. Columbia, *f.*, Colombia, *f.*: *British Columbia*, Colombia Británica.

Columbian [—n] adj. Colombino, na.

columbine [ˈkɔləmbain] n. BOT. Aguileña, *f.*
— Adj. Columbino, na.

Columbus [kəˈlʌmbəs] pr. n. Colón. || — *Christopher Columbus*, Cristóbal Colón. || *Columbus Day*, Día (*f.*) de la Raza *or* de la Hispanidad.

column [ˈkɔləm] n. ARCH. Columna, *f.*: *Corinthian column*, columna corintia. || Columna, *f.* (of a newspaper, book). || MIL. Columna, *f.*: *in columns of three*, en columnas de a tres. || — FIG. *Fifth column*, quinta columna. || TECH. *Fractionating column*, columna de fraccionamiento. || ARCH. *Rostral column*, columna rostrada *or* rostral. || ANAT. *Spinal column*, columna vertebral. || AUT. *Steering column*, columna de dirección.

columnar [kəˈlʌmnə*] adj. De forma de columna.

columnist [ˈkɔləmnist] n. U. S. Columnista, *m.* & *f.*, periodista, *m.* & *f.* (journalist).

colza [ˈkɔlzə] n. BOT. Colza, *f.*

coma [ˈkəumə] n. MED. Coma, *m.* || ASTR. Cabellera, *f.* (of a comet): *Coma Berenices*, cabellera de Berenice. || BOT. Coma, *f.* (of leaves or hairs). || Coma, *f.* (imperfection in lens). || MED. *In a coma*, en estado comatoso.

— OBSERV. El plural de la palabra inglesa *coma* es *comae*.

Comanche [kəˈmæntʃi] adj./n. Comanche (Indian).

comate [ˈkəumeit] adj. Cabelludo, da.
— N. Compañero, ra.

comatose [ˈkəumətəus] adj. MED. Comatoso, sa.

comb [kəum] n. Peine, *m.* || Peineta, *f.* (ornamental). || TECH. Carda, *f.* (for wool). || Almohaza, *f.* (currycomb). || Cresta, *f.* (crest of bird, wave or mountain). || Panal, *m.* (honeycomb). || MIL. Cimera, *f.* (of helmet). || ELECTR. Escobilla, *f.* || — FAM. *To cut s.o.'s comb*, bajarle los humos a alguien. || *To give one's hair a comb*, peinarse.

comb [kəum] v. tr. Peinar (to arrange hair). || Cardar (wool). || Almohazar (a horse). || Registrar a fondo (to search). || — *To comb one's hair*, peinarse. || *To comb out*, limpiar (to clean out), desenmarañar (hair).
— V. intr. Romperse, romper (the waves).

combat [ˈkɔmbət] n. Combate, *m.* || — *Combat mission, post, zone*, misión, puesto, zona de combate. || U. S. MIL. *Combat team*, equipo (*m.*) de combate.

combat [ˈkɔmbət] v. tr. Combatir, luchar contra.
— V. intr. Combatir, luchar.

combatant [ˈkɔmbətənt] adj./n. Combatiente.

combative [ˈkɔmbətiv] adj. Combativo, va.

combativeness [—nis] n. Combatividad, *f.*

combe [ku:m] n. Valle (*m.*) estrecho.

comber [ˈkəumə*] n. Cardador, ra (person who combs wool). || TECH. Máquina (*f.*) cardadora. || Ola (*f.*) grande y encrespada (wave).

combination [ˌkɔmbiˈneiʃən] n. Combinación, *f.* (act of combining). || Asociación, *f.* (of persons). || Combinación, *f.* (underwear). || MATH. CHEM. Combinación, *f.* || FIG. Cúmulo, *m.*, conjunto, *m.* (of circumstances). || *Combination lock*, cerradura (*f.*) de combinación.

combinatorial [ˌkɔmbinəˈtɔ:rjəl] adj. MATH. Combinatorio, ria: *combinatorial analysis*, análisis combinatorio.

combine [ˈkɔmbain] n. Asociación, *f.* (of people). || COMM. Cártel, *m.* || AGR. Segadora trilladora, *f.*, cosechadora, *f.* || — *Combine harvester*, cosechadora, *f.*, segadora trilladora, *f.* || COMM. *Horizontal combine*, consorcio, *m.*

combine [ˈkɔmˈbain] v. tr. Unir, fusionar: *he has combined his business with his brother's*, ha unido su negocio con el de su hermano. || Combinar: *he combined business with pleasure*, combinó el negocio con la diversión. || CHEM. Combinar.
— V. intr. Unirse, asociarse, fusionarse: *the two businesses have combined*, los dos negocios se han unido. || CHEM. Combinarse. || JUR. Sindicarse. || FIG. Ligarse, unirse (*against*, contra).

combined [—d] adj. MIL. Combinado, da (operation). || Unido, da (*with*, a). || *Combined set*, microteléfono, *m.*, pesa, *f.* (telephone).

combing [ˈkəumiŋ] n. Peinada, *f.* (of hair). || TECH. Peinado, *m.*, cardadura, *f.* || — Pl. Peinaduras, *f.*

combo [ˈkɔmbəu] n. FAM. Conjunto (*m.*) de jazz.

comb-out [ˈkəumaut] n. FAM. *To give a place a comb-out*, registrar un lugar a fondo.

combustible [kəmˈbʌstəbl] adj. Combustible. || FIG. Ardiente.
— N. Combustible, *m.*

combustion [kəmˈbʌstʃən] n. Combustión, *f.* || — *Combustion chamber*, cámara (*f.*) de combustión. || *Combustion engine*, motor (*m.*) de combustión.

combustor [kəmˈbʌstə*] n. Cámara (*f.*) de combustión (of gas turbine, jet engine).

come* [kʌm] v. intr. Venir: *he came to the party*, vino a la fiesta; *take life as its comes*, toma la vida como viene; *spring comes after winter*, la primavera viene después del invierno. || Llegar: *the water comes up to my chin*, el agua me llega a la barbilla. || Hacer, recorrer (a distance): *he has come ten miles*, ha recorrido diez millas. || Pasar: *he came through the wood*, pasó por el bosque. || Recaer: *the title came to the younger son*, el título recayó en el hijo más pequeño. || Venir, proceder: *he comes from a wealthy family*, procede de una familia rica. || Producirse, surgir: *a misunderstanding came between us*, se produjo un malentendido entre nosotros. || Salir, resultar: *good wines come expensive*, los vinos buenos salen caros; *nothing came of it*, no resultó nada de ello. || Ocurrir, suceder, pasar (to happen): *you know what comes of drinking too much*, ya sabes lo que sucede por beber mucho; *a change has come over his life*, ha ocurrido un cambio en su vida. || Existir, hacerse: *it comes in two sizes*, se hace en dos tamaños. || POP. Correrse (to have an orgasm). || — FAM. *Come again?*, ¿cómo? || *Come, come!*, ¡vamos! || *Come here!*, ¡ven!, ¡ven aquí! || *Come now!*, ¡vamos! || *Come summer and I will see him again*, el próximo verano lo volveré a ver. || *Come what may*, pase lo que pase. || *Coming!*, ¡voy! || *Don't come the young innocent*, no te hagas el inocente. || FIG. *Easy come, easy go*, del mismo modo que viene se va. | *First come, first served*, el que se adelanta nunca pierde. || *He had it coming*, tuvo *or* recibió su merecido. || *How come?*, ¿cómo es eso? || *I could see it coming*, lo veía venir. || *It came as a great surprise to us*, fue una gran sorpresa para nosotros. || *It comes to this*, en resumen. || *It will be a year come Monday*, hará un año el próximo lunes. || *Time to come*, tiempos futuros. || *To come a cropper*, darse un batacazo. || *To come* *again*, venir de nuevo, volver. || *To come and go*, ir y venir. || *To come apart*, see APART. || *To come asunder*, deshacerse. || *To come between*, interponerse entre. || *To come clean*, confesarlo todo. || *To come easy to*, costar poco esfuerzo, ser fácil para. || *To come from*, venir de. || *To come loose*, soltarse, desatarse. || *To come near*, acercarse a (s.o.), estar a punto de *or* a dos dedos de, faltar poco para: *I came near fainting*, estuve a punto de desmayarme. || *To come next*, seguir. || *To come of age*, alcanzar la mayoría de edad. || *To come short of*, no llegar a, no alcanzar. || *To come to power, to the throne*, subir al poder, al trono. || *To come to the wrong person*, acudir a la persona menos indicada. || *To come true*, hacerse realidad, realizarse. || *To come undone* o *unstuck*, deshacerse. || *What do you come here for?*, ¿a qué vienes?, ¿qué vienes a hacer aquí?

— **To come about,** suceder, ocurrir: *how did this accident come about?*, ¿cómo sucedió este accidente? | MAR. Virar (ship). | Cambiar (wind). || **To come across,** encontrarse con, tropezar con (person). | Encontrar (thing). | U. S. FAM. Apoquinar (to fork out). | Hacer lo que se pide (to do as one is told). | Ser comprendido (to be understood). | Ser apreciado (to be appreciated). || **To come after,** venir detrás de. | Venir en busca de. || **To come along,** ir, andar. | Venir también. | — *Come along!*, ¡venga! || **To come around,** see TO COME ROUND. || **To come at,** encontrar, llegar a (to reach): *I came at the solution*, encontré la solución. | Atacar (to attack). || **To come away,** desprenderse (to become detached). || Salir, irse (to leave). || **To come back,** volver (to return). | Volver en sí (to regain consciousness). | Venir *or* volver a la memoria: *the name has just come back to me*, el nombre me acaba de venir a la memoria. | Replicar (to answer). | Desquitarse (to get even). | — *To come back with*, contestar diciendo. || **To come before,** llegar antes. | Ser sometido a. | Anteceder. | JUR. Comparecer ante (the court). || **To come by,** conseguir, lograr, obtener (to obtain). | Pasar por [un sitio]: *he came by this morning*, pasó por aquí esta mañana. || **To come down,** bajar: *he came down the stairs*, bajó las escaleras. | Desplomarse, derrumbarse (building, etc.). | Caerse (to fall). | Llegar (to reach). | Venir a menos (to lose status). | — *All these houses are coming down*, se van a derribar estas casas. | *To come down on*, echarse encima: *the authorities came down on him*, las autoridades se le echaron encima. | *To come down to*, llegar a *or* hasta (to reach), reducirse a (to amount to). | *To come down with*, caer enfermo con. || **To come for,** venir a buscar: *he came for a paper*, vino a buscar un periódico. || **To come forth,** aparecer. || **To come forward,** presentarse. | Avanzar. | Responder a la llamada. || **To come in,** entrar (to enter): *that is where you come in*, ahí es donde tú entras. | Llegar: *he came in first in the hundred metres*, llegó el primero en los cien metros. | Ponerse de moda (to become fashionable). | Empezar (season). | Estar (to be). | Sacar, ganar (to get). | Subir (tide). | Ser presentado (an invoice). | Ser cobrado (a sum). | Llegar al poder (a party). | Llegar a ser (to become). | — *Come in*. ¡pase!, ¡adelante! | FAM. *To come in for*, recibir (scolding, praise). | *To come in handy* o *useful*, resultar útil. || **To come into,** entrar en (a room, etc.): *to come into play*, entrar en juego. | Llegar a (power). | Participar en (to take part). | Recibir (inheritance). | Heredar (to inherit). | Entrar en posesión de (to acquire). | — *To come into one's own*, hacer valer sus méritos. | *To come into sight*, aparecer. | *To come into the world*, venir al mundo. | *To come into trouble*, meterse en un lío. || **To come off,** caerse (to fall off). | Desprenderse (page, wheel). | Salir (stain). | Quitarse (to be removed). | Salir: *it came off all right*, salió bien. | Ser un éxito, salir bien (to be a success). | Tener lugar: *the wedding comes off next week*, la boda tendrá lugar la semana que viene. | — *Come off it!*, ¡vamos, anda! || **To come on,** avanzar (to advance). | Encontrar (to find). | Progresar, mejorar (to make progress). | Llegar (season, storm). | Caer (night). | Ser discutido (question). | THEATR. Salir a escena (actor). | Ser representado, representarse (play). | — *Come on!*, ¡vamos!, ¡venga! | FAM. *I have two parties coming on*, tengo dos fiestas en perspectiva. | *It came on to rain*, empezó a llover. || **To come out,** salir: *he came out of the house*, salió de la casa. | Declararse: *they came out on strike*, se declararon en huelga. | Salir: *ten photographs came out*, salieron diez fotografías; *you have come out well*, has salido bien. | Salir, publicarse: *the magazine comes out monthly*, la revista se publica mensualmente. | Ser presentada [en sociedad]: *she came out at eighteen*, fue presentada en sociedad a los dieciocho años. | BOT. Crecer, salir. | MED. Salir: *I came out in spots*, me salieron granos. | THEATR. Empezar, salir. | Salir, descubrirse (truth). | Salir, quitarse (stain). || — *To come badly out of*, salir mal parado de. | *To come out with*, publicar (news), revelar (to reveal), saltar con, salir con (a remark, idea, etc.), soltar (a curse). || **To come over,** venir: *he is coming over next summer*, vendrá el verano que viene. | Pasar (to happen): *I don't know what came over me*, no sé lo que me pasó. | Sobrevenir, invadir: *a great sadness came over them*, les invadió una gran tristeza. | Ponerse: *he came over all funny*, se puso muy raro. | Llegar: *his voice came over clearly*, su voz llegó con claridad. | Ser comprendido (to be understood). | Ser apreciado (to be appreciated). | — *To come over to*, pasarse a (s.o.'s side), dejarse convencer por (an opinion). || **To come round,** (U. S. **to come around**), venir: *he came round to see us*, vino a vernos. | Volver en sí: *he came round one hour after the accident*, volvió en sí una hora después del accidente. | Restablecerse (from an illness). | Cambiar de dirección. | MAR. Virar (a ship). | Ceder (to yield). | Hacer una visita (to visit). || — *He came round to my point of view*, me dio la razón, se dejó convencer, aceptó mi punto de vista. || **To come through,** calar: *the rain comes through my coat*, el agua me cala el abrigo. | Pasar por (sufferings). | Sobrellevar, vencer (difficulties). | Salir: *he came through the accident unhurt*, salió ileso del accidente. | Pasar [sin detenerse] (train). | Concretarse (to materialize). || **To come to,** llegar a: *how did you come to do that?*, ¿cómo llegaste a hacer eso?; *to come to an end*, llegar a su término. | Pasar (to happen). | Ir a ver (s.o.) | Ceder, dejarse convencer (to yield). | Ascender: *what does the bill come to?*, ¿a cuánto asciende la cuenta? | Volver en sí: *he came to*, volvió en sí. | Venir a la mente, ocurrírsele [a uno] (an idea). | — *To come to a point*, acabar en punta. | *To come to blows*, llegar a las manos. | *To come to light*, salir a luz. || **To come together,** reunirse, juntarse (to join). | Venir juntos. || **To come under,** venir bajo. | Caer bajo (s.o.'s influence). | Entrar en (a heading). | — *To come under s.o.'s notice*, llegar al conocimiento de uno. || **To come up,** subir: *he came up the stairs*, subió las escaleras. | Brotar, salir (plants). | Salir (fashion). | JUR. Comparecer. | Surgir: *the matter came up at the last meeting*, el asunto surgió en la última reunión. | — *To come up against*, tropezarse con. | *To come up to*, ascender a (a degree), satisfacer (expectations), estar a la altura de (s.o., a task), acercarse a (to approach), llegar a *or* hasta (to reach). | *To come up with*, alcanzar (to overtake), proponer, sugerir (to suggest). || **To come upon,** tropezar con, encontrar a (s.o.). | Encontrar (sth.). | Descubrir (a secret). | Caer encima de, precipitarse contra (the enemy). | Reclamar (to ask). | — *It came upon me that*, se me ocurrió que. || **To come within,** entrar en. | — *To come within s.o.'s jurisdiction*, competer a, ser de la incumbencia *or* de la competencia de.

— OBSERV. Pret. **came;** p. p. **come.**

come-at-able [kʌmˈætəbl] adj. Accesible.
comeback [ˈkʌmbæk] n. Reaparición, *f.* (return). || Vuelta, *f.* || Réplica, *f.* (retort). || *To make a comeback*, volver a escena, reaparecer (actors, etc.).
comedian [kəˈmi:diən] n. Comediante, *m.*, actor, *m.*, cómico, *m.* (infr.) [in theatre]. || Cómico, *m.* (in variety) || Autor (*m.*) cómico (writer). || FIG. Cómico, *m.*
comedienne [kə,mediˈen] n. Comedianta, *f.*, actriz, *f.*, cómica, *f.* (infr.) [in theatre]. || Cómica, *f.* (in variety).
comedo [ˈkəmi:dəu] n. MED. Comedón, *m.*

— OBSERV. El plural de *comedo* es *comedones* o *comedos.*

comedown [ˈkʌmdaun] n. Humillación, *f.* || Decadencia, *f.*, bajón, *m.* (loss of status). || Desilusión (disappointment). || Revés, *m.* (setback).
comedy [ˈkəmidi] n. Comedia, *f.* || — *Comedy of character*, comedia de carácter *or* de figurón. || *Comedy of intrigue*, comedia de enredo. || *Comedy of manners*, comedia de costumbres. || *Comedy of situation*, comedia de enredo. || *Light comedy*, comedia ligera. || *Musical comedy*, comedia musical.
come-hither [ˈkʌmhiðə*] adj. Seductor, ra; sugestivo, va.
comeliness [ˈkʌmlinis] n. Atractivo, *m.*, encanto, *m.*
comely [ˈkʌmli] adj. Atractivo, va.
come-on [ˈkʌmən] n. Llamada, *f.* (inviting gesture). || U. S. Incentivo, *m.*, atractivo, *m.*, aliciente, *m.*
comer [ˈkʌmə*] n. El que llega, la que llega. || U. S. FAM. Promesa, *f.*, persona (*f.*) que promete. || — *All comers*, todos los que vengan. || *The first comer*, el primer llegado *or* venido, el que llega primero. || *To challenge all comers*, desafiar a todos.
comestible [kəˈmestibl] adj. Comestible.
comestibles [—z] pl. n. Comestibles, *m.*
comet [ˈkəmit] n. Cometa, *m.*
comeuppance [kʌˈmʌpəns] n. U. S. Castigo, *m.* [merecido], merecido, *m.*
comfit [ˈkʌmfit] n. Dulce, *m.*, confite, *m.*
comfort [ˈkʌmfət] n. FIG. Consuelo, *m.* (consolation). | Alivio, *m.* (relief). || Bienestar, *m.*, "confort", *m.* (well being). || Comodidad, *f.*: *this house has many comforts*, esta casa tiene muchas comodidades. || — U. S. *Comfort station*, servicios, *m. pl.* (lavatory). || *To live in comfort*, vivir cómodamente.
comfort [ˈkʌmfət] v. tr. Consolar (to solace). || Aliviar (to be a relief). || Animar, confortar (to hearten).
comfortable [—əbl] adj. Cómodo, da; confortable: *is your bed comfortable?*, ¿es cómoda su cama? || Cómodo, da: *to make o.s. comfortable*, ponerse cómodo. || Agradable: *a comfortable atmosphere*, un ambiente agradable. || Decente, bueno, na: *a comfortable income*, ingresos decentes. || Suficiente (sufficient). || Holgado, da (living). || Tranquilo, la (unworried).
comfortableness [—nis] n. Comodidad, *f.*

comfortably [—i] adv. Confortablemente, cómodamente. || Fácilmente (easily). || *To be comfortably off,* vivir con holgura *or* con desahogo.
comforter [ˈkʌmfətə*] n. Consolador, ra (one who comforts). || Chupete, *m.* (for babies). || Bufanda, *f.* (scarf). || U. S. Edredón, *m.* (eiderdown). || REL. *The Comforter,* el Espíritu Santo.
comforting [ˈkʌmfətiŋ] adj. Consolador, ra; reconfortante, alentador, ra.
comfortless [ˈkʌmfətlis] adj. Incómodo, da (lacking comfort). || Abandonado, da; desamparado da.
comfort-loving [ˈkʌmfət,lʌviŋ] adj. Comodón, ona.
comfy [ˈkʌmfi] adj. FAM. Cómodo, da.
comic [ˈkɔmik] adj. Cómico, ca. || — *Comic book,* tebeo, *m.* || *Comic opera,* ópera bufa. || *Comic strip,* tira cómica, historieta, *f.*
— N. Cómico, ca (comedian). || Tebeo, *m.* (magazine). || — FIG. *He is a comic!,* ¡es un cómico! || *The comic of life,* el lado cómico de la vida.
comical [ˈkɔmikəl] adj. Cómico, ca; divertido, da; gracioso, sa.
comicality [kɔmiˈkæliti] or **comicalness** [ˈkɔmikəlnis] n. Comicidad, *f.*, lo cómico.
coming [ˈkʌmiŋ] adj. Próximo, ma; venidero, ra; que viene: *the coming year,* el año próximo. || FIG. Prometedor, ra: *a coming actor,* un actor prometedor.
— N. Venida, *f.*, llegada, *f.* || REL. Advenimiento, *m.* || — *Coming away,* salida, *f.* || *Coming back,* vuelta, *f.* || *Coming on,* principio, *m.* || *Coming out,* salida, *f.*; presentación (*f.*) en sociedad (of a débutante). || *Comings and goings,* idas (*f.*) y venidas. || *Coming up,* ascensión, *f.*; llegada, *f.*; acercamiento, *m.*
comitia [kɔˈmiʃiə] pl. n. HIST. Comicios, *m.*
comity [ˈkɔmiti] n. Cortesía, *f.* || *Comity of nations,* acuerdo (*m.*) entre naciones.
comma [ˈkɔmə] n. GRAMM. Coma, *f.* || MUS. Coma, *f.* || MED. Vírgula, *f.*, vibrión (*m.*) del cólera. || — *In inverted commas,* entre comillas. || *Inverted commas,* comillas, *f. pl.*: *to open, to close the inverted commas,* abrir, cerrar las comillas.
command [kəˈmɑːnd] n. Orden, *f.*, mandato, *m.* (order). || Mando, *m.* (authority). || Dominio, *m.*: *command of a language,* dominio de una lengua; *command over o.s.,* dominio de sí mismo. || MIL. Mando, *m.*: *command word,* voz de mando; *command post,* puesto de mando. | Unidad (*f.*) militar: *defence command,* unidad militar de defensa. | Comandancia, *f.* (zone). | Dominio, *m.*: *the guns had command over the valley,* las armas tenían dominio sobre el valle. || — *At* o *by s.o.'s command,* por orden de alguien. || *High command,* alto mando. || *His command was the fifth artillery division,* estaba al mando de la quinta división de artillería, mandaba la quinta división de artillería. || *In command of,* al mando de. || *Money at one's command,* dinero (*m.*) disponible. || *To be at s.o.'s command,* estar a las órdenes de alguien, estar a la disposición de alguien. || *To be in command of,* estar al mando de, mandar (person), dominar (pass, fort). || *To have at one's command* o *to have a command of,* dominar (languages). || *To take command,* tomar el mando. || *Under the command of,* bajo el mando de.
command [kəˈmɑːnd] v. tr. Mandar (to control). || Dominar: *to command one's temper,* dominar el mal genio; *the house commands the whole bay,* la casa domina toda la bahía; *to command the market,* dominar el mercado. || Mandar, ordenar: *he commanded them to leave,* les ordenó que se marcharan; *to command sth. to be done,* ordenar que se haga algo. || Merecer (to deserve). || Disponer de, poseer (to have at one's disposal). || Exigir (a good salary). || Tener (view). || Llamar, atraer, captar (attention). || Infundir (respect). || Suscitar (admiration). || Venderse a (to be sold). || *Yours to command!,* ¡a sus órdenes!
— V. intr. Mandar.
commandant [,kɔmənˈdænt] n. MIL. Comandante, *m.*
commandeer [,kɔmənˈdiə*] v. tr. Expropiar, requisar [para uso militar]. || Reclutar por fuerza (men). || FAM. Apoderarse de.
commander [kəˈmɑːndə*] n. MIL. Comandante, *m.* || MAR. Capitán (*m.*) de fragata. || Jefe, *m.* (leader). || Comendador, *m.* (in knighthood). || *Commander in chief,* comandante en jefe.
— OBSERV. El plural de la expresión *commander in chief* es *commanders in chief.*
commandership [—ʃip] n. Mando, *m.* (command). || Comandancia, *f.* (position). || MAR. Cargo (*m.*) de capitán de fragata.
commandery [—ri] n. Encomienda, *f.*
commanding [kəˈmɑːndiŋ] adj. Dominante (dominating). || Imponente (demanding respect). || Dominante: *a commanding position,* una posición dominante. || || MIL. Que está al mando. || MIL. *Commanding officer,* jefe, *m.*, comandante, *m.*
commandment [kəˈmɑːndmənt] n. REL. Mandamiento, *m.*: *the Ten Commandments,* los diez mandamientos.
commando [kəˈmɑːndəu] n. MIL. Comando, *m.*
— OBSERV. El plural de *commando* es *commandos* o *commandoes.*
commeasurable [kəˈmeʒərəbl] adj. Proporcionado, da.
commemorate [kəˈmeməreit] v. tr. Conmemorar.
commemoration [kə,meməˈreiʃən] n. Conmemoración, *f.*
commemorative [kəˈmemərətiv] adj. Conmemorativo, va.
commence [kəˈmens] v. tr./intr. Comenzar, empezar.
commencement [—mənt] n. Comienzo, *m.*, principio, *m.* (beginning). || U. S. Ceremonia (*f.*) de entrega de diplomas (university).
commend [kəˈmend] v. tr. Encomendar confiar (to entrust): *to commend one's soul to God,* encomendar su alma a Dios. || Recomendar (to recommend). || Alabar (to praise): *to commend s.o. for his bravery,* alabar a alguien por su valentía. || Aprobar (to approve). || — (Ant.) *Commend me to him,* salúdele de mi parte. || *To commend itself to,* gustar a.
commendable [kəˈmendəbl] adj. Recomendable. || Digno de elogio (praiseworthy).
commendably [—i] adv. De un modo digno de elogio.
commendam [kəˈmendəm] n. REL. Encomienda, *f.*
commendation [,kɔmenˈdeiʃən] n. Alabanza, *f.*, encomio, *m.*, elogio, *m.* (praise). || Recomendación, *f.* (recommendation).
commendatory [kəˈmendətəri] adj. REL. Comendatario. || Elogioso, sa (laudatory).
commensal [kəˈmensəl] n. Comensal, *m.*
commensurability [kə,menʃərəˈbiliti] n. Conmensurabilidad, *f.*
commensurable [kəˈmenʃərəbl] adj. Conmensurable. || Proporcionado, da.
commensurate [kəˈmenʃərit] adj. Proporcionado, da.
comment [ˈkɔment] n. Comentario, *m.* (explanatory note). || Observación, *f.* (remark). || *No comment,* sin comentarios.
comment [ˈkɔment] v. intr. Comentar, hacer comentarios *or* observaciones (*on, upon,* sobre). || Criticar (to criticize).
commentary [ˈkɔməntəri] n. Comentario, *m.* || Observación, *f.* (remark). || RAD. *Running commentary,* reportaje (*m.*) en directo.
commentate [ˈkɔmen,teit] v. tr. Comentar. || Narrar [las incidencias de] (a match, show, etc.).
commentator [ˈkɔmenteitə*] n. Comentarista, *m.* & *f.* (who analyzes). || Locutor, ra (who reports).
commerce [ˈkɔməːs] n. Comercio, *m.* (trade). || Comercio, *m.*, ayuntamiento, *m.* (sexual intercourse).
commercial [kəˈməːʃəl] adj. Comercial: *commercial treaty,* tratado comercial; *commercial street,* calle comercial. || Mercantil: *commercial law,* derecho mercantil. || — *Commercial agency,* agencia (*f.*) comercial. || *Commercial bank,* banco (*m.*) comercial. || *Commercial college,* escuela (*f.*) de comercio. || *Commercial traveller,* viajante (*m.*) de comercio. || *Commercial value,* valor (*m.*) comercial.
— N. RAD. Anuncio, *m.* (advertisement). | Programa (*m.*) publicitario (publicity programme). || Viajante (*m.*) de comercio (commercial traveller).
commercialism [—izəm] n. Mercantilismo, *m.*
commercialization [kə,məːʃəlaiˈzeiʃən] n. Comercialización, *f.*
commercialize [kəˈməːʃəlaiz] v. tr. Comercializar.
comminate [ˈkɔmineit] v. tr. Conminar.
commination [,kɔmiˈneiʃən] n. Conminación, *f.*
comminatory [ˈkɔminətəri] adj. Conminatorio, ria.
commingle [kɔˈmiŋgl] v. tr. Mezclar.
— V. intr. Mezclarse.
comminute [ˈkɔminjuːt] v. tr. Triturar, pulverizar (to crush). || JUR. Parcelar (property). || *Comminuted fracture,* fractura conminuta.
comminution [kɔmiˈnjuːʃən] n. Trituración, *f.*, pulverización, *f.* (crushing). || JUR. Parcelación, *f.* (of property).
commiserable [kəˈmizərəbl] adj. Lastimoso, sa; que da lástima.
commiserate [kəˈmizereit] v. intr. Compadecerse (*with,* de).
— V. tr. Compadecer.
commiseration [kə,mizəˈreiʃən] n. Conmiseración, *f.*, compasión, *f.*, lástima, *f.*
commiserative [kəˈmizərətiv] adj. Compasivo, va; conmiserativo, va.
commissar [,kɔmiˈsɑː*] n. Comisario, *m.* (in U.S.S.R.).
commissarial [,kɔmiˈsɛəriəl] adj. Del comisario.
commissariat [,kɔmiˈsɛəriət] n. Comisaría, *f.* (government department). || MIL. Intendencia, *f.*
commissary [ˈkɔmisəri] n. Comisario, *m.* (representative commissar). || REL. Comisario, *m.* || Comisario, *m.* (senior police officer). || U. S. Economato, *m.* (government store).
commission [kəˈmiʃən] n. Nombramiento, *m.* (to a post, a task, etc.). || Comisión, *f.*: *a commission of nine per cent,* una comisión del nueve por ciento; *the commission to investigate the disaster,* la comisión para investigar el desastre. || Cometido, *m.* (assignment). || Encargo, *m.* (charge). || Misión, *f.* (mission). || Perpetración, *f.*, ejecución, *f.* (of a crime). || Delegación, *f.* (of authority). || MIL. Despacho (*m.*) de oficial (certificate). | Grado (*m.*) de oficial (rank). || — *Commission agent,* comisionista, *m.* || *Commission merchant,* comisionista, *m.* || U. S. *Commission plan,* gobierno (*m.*) municipal que ejerce funciones legislativas y ejecutivas. || *Done on commission,* hecho por encargo. || *In commission,* en servicio activo. || *On commission,* como comisionista. || *Out of commission,*

inservible (thing), fuera de servicio (person). || MAR. *To put a ship in, out of commission*, armar, desarmar un barco. || *To work on a commission basis*, trabajar a comisión.
commission [kəˈmiʃən] v. tr. Comisionar (to give a commission). || Encargar (to order): *to commission a portrait*, encargar un retrato. || Poner en servicio (a ship). || MIL. Nombrar (an officer). || MIL. *Commissioned officer*, oficial, *m*.
commissionaire [kə,miʃəˈnεə*] n. Portero, *m*. (doorkeeper). || Recadero, *m*. (messenger).
commissioner [kəˈmiʃənə*] n. Comisionado, *m*., miembro (*m*.) de una comisión (member of commission). || Comisario, *m*.: *High Commissioner*, Alto Comisario.
commissure [ˈkɔmisjuə*] n. Comisura, *f*.
commit [kəˈmit] v. tr. Confiar (to entrust). || Cometer (a crime). || Cometer, hacer (error). || Comprometer: *committed literature*, literatura comprometida. || Entregar (to the flames, to the waves). || Encarcelar (to prison). || Encerrar, internar (a madman). || JUR. Someter a una comisión. || Encomendar (one's soul to God). || — *To commit for trial*, citar ante los tribunales. || *To commit o.s.*, comprometerse. || *To commit sth. to paper* o *to writing*, consignar algo por escrito. || *To commit to memory*, aprender de memoria.
commitment [—mənt] n. Compromiso, *m*. (pledge). || Cometido, *m*. (assignment). || JUR. Encarcelamiento, *m*. (to prison). | Auto (*m*.) de prisión (order). || Internamiento, *m*., reclusión, *f*. (of a madman). || Devolución (*f*.) a una comisión (of a bill). || Presentación, *f*. (of a project). || Ejecución, *f*. (of a crime). || COMM. Compromiso, *m*. || Entierro, *m*. (burial). || Inmersión, *f*. (in water).
committal [kəˈmitl] n. See COMMITMENT.
committee [kəˈmiti] n. Comité, *m*., comisión, *f*. (body of people): *committee of experts*, comisión de expertos. || JUR. Curador, *m*. || — *Committee of honour*, comité de honor. || *Committee of the whole (house)*, pleno, *m*. || *Committee of ways and means*, comisión del presupuesto. || *Joint committee*, comisión conjunta *or* paritaria. || *Management committee*, consejo (*m*.) de administración. || *Standing committee*, comisión permanente. || *To sit on a committee*, ser miembro de una comisión.
committeeman [—mən] n. Miembro (*m*.) de un comité *or* de una comisión.
— OBSERV. El plural de esta palabra es *committeemen*.
commix [kəˈmiks] v. tr. Mezclar.
— V. intr. Mezclarse.
commixture [kəˈmikstjə*] n. Mezcla, *f*.
commode [kəˈməud] n. Cómoda, *f*. (chest of drawers). || Silla (*f*.) con orinal, silla (*f*.) retrete.
commodious [kəˈməudjəs] adj. Espacioso, sa.
commodity [kəˈmɔditi] n. Mercancía, *f*. [*Amer*., mercadería, *f*.], artículo, *m*., producto, *m*. || *Commodity agreement*, acuerdo (*m*.) comercial.
commodore [ˈkɔmədɔ:*] n. MAR. Comodoro, *m*.
common [ˈkɔmən] adj. Común: *common staircase*, escalera común. || Público, ca; común: *common opinion*, opinión pública. || Ordinario, ria; vulgar: *common manners*, modales ordinarios. || MATH. Común: *common factor*, factor común; *common multiple*, común múltiplo. || Normal, usual: *it is common to dine at eight o'clock*, es usual cenar a las ocho. || Común, corriente (frequent). || GRAMM. Común: *common gender, noun*, género, nombre común. || MIL. Raso (soldier). || Municipal (council). || Consuetudinario, ria (law). || — *Common as dirt*, de lo más ordinario. || MUS. *Common chord*, acorde (*m*.) simple. || *Common carrier*, empresa pública de transporte. || *Common cold*, constipado, *m*., catarro, *m*. || *Common council*, ayuntamiento, *m*., concejo (*m*.) municipal. || *Common councilman*, concejal, *m*. || *Common crier*, pregonero, *m*. || MATH. *Common denominator*, común denominador, *m*. | *Common divisor*, divisor (*m*.) común. || U. S. *Common fraction*, fracción ordinaria. || *Common ground*, tema (*m*.) de interés mutuo. || *Common informer*, confidente (*m*.) de la policía. || *Common herd*, vulgo, *m*., masa, *f*. || *Common man*, hombre medio, hombre (*m*.) de la calle. || *Common Market*, Mercado (*m*.) Común. || FIG. *Common or garden*, ordinario, ria. || REL. *Common Prayer*, liturgia anglicana. || JUR. *Common property*, bienes (*m. pl*.) que pertenecen a la colectividad. || *Common room*, sala (*f*.) común. || *Common sense*, buen sentido, *m*., sentido (*m*.) común. || COMM. *Common stock*, acciones ordinarias. || MUS. *Common time*, compás (*m*.) de cuatro por cuatro. || *Common touch*, contacto (*m*.) con el pueblo. || *Common year*, año (*m*.) común. || *In common*, en común. || *In common use*, de uso corriente. || *In common with*, de acuerdo con. || *It is common knowledge that*, see KNOWLEDGE. || *Of a common accord*, de común acuerdo. || *The common people*, el pueblo. || *The common run of humanity*, el común de los mortales.
— N. Ejido, *m*., terreno (*m*.) comunal (area of land). || — Pl. Pueblo, *m. sing*. (common people). || Cámara (*f. sing*.) de los Comunes (of Parliament). || Refectorio, *m. sing*. (in a college). || Víveres, *m*. (food). || — REL. *Common of martyrs*, común de mártires. || *Common of pasturage*, derecho (*m*.) de pasto. || *On short commons*, a media ración. || *Out of the common*, fuera de lo corriente. || *The House of Commons*, la Cámara de los Comunes.
commonage [—idʒ] n. JUR. Pasto (*m*.) libre (land). | Derecho (*m*.) de pasto (right). || Comunidad, *f*. || Pueblo, *m*. (commonalty).
commonalty [—əlti] n. Vulgo, *m*. (people not of the upper classes). || Pueblo, *m*. (people in general). || Comunidad, *f*. || JUR. Corporación, *f*.
commoner [—ə*] n. Plebeyo, ya (not a peer). || Estudiante sin beca (in Oxford University). || Miembro (*m*.) de la Cámara de los Comunes (in Parliament).
commonly [—li] adj. Comúnmente, generalmente (usually). || De un modo común *or* vulgar.
commonness [—nis] n. Frecuencia, *f*. (of an event). || Vulgaridad, *f*. (of a person).
commonplace [—pleis] adj. Común, vulgar. || *Commonplace book*, libro (*m*.) de citas.
— N. Tópico, *m*., lugar (*m*.) común.
commons [—z] pl. n. See COMMON.
— OBSERV. Aunque esta palabra sea plural se construye con el singular.
commonsense [—sens] adj. Lógico, ca.
commonweal [—wi:l] n. (Ant.) Bien (*m*.) público. | Estado, *m*.
commonwealth [—welθ] n. República, *f*., democracia, *f*. || Estado, *m*. (state). || Bien (*m*.) público (commonweal).
Commonwealth [—welθ] pr. n. "Commonwealth", *f*., Comunidad (*f*.) de Naciones.
commotion [kəˈməuʃən] n. Disturbio, *m*., agitación, *f*. (disturbance). || Alboroto, *m*. (noisy disturbance). || Conmoción, *f*. (mental turmoil).
communal [ˈkɔmjunəl] adj. Comunal.
communalism [—izəm] n. JUR. Descentralización (*f*.) del poder, regionalización, *f*.
communalist [—ist] n. Comunalista, *m*. & *f*.
commune [ˈkɔmju:n] n. Municipio, *m*. (administrative unit). || *The Commune*, la Comuna (in Paris).
commune [kəˈmju:n] v. intr. Comunicarse (to communicate). || REL. Comulgar (to receive communion).
communicability [kə,mju:nikəˈbiliti] n. Comunicabilidad, *f*.
communicable [kəˈmju:nikəbl] adj. Comunicable. || Contagioso, sa (disease).
communicant [kəˈmju:nikənt] n. Comunicante, *m*. & *f*. (person who communicates information). || REL. Comulgante, *m*. & *f*. (who receives Communion).
communicate [kəˈmju:nikeit] v. tr. Comunicar (information, feelings, etc.). || Contagiar (a disease).
— V. intr. REL. Comulgar. || Comunicarse: *the rooms communicate*, las habitaciones se comunican.
communication [kə,mju:niˈkeiʃən] n. Comunicación, *f*.: *radio communication*, comunicación por radio; *road communication*, comunicación por carretera. || Comunicado, *m*., comunicación, *f*.: *an official communication*, un comunicado oficial. || — Pl. Comunicaciones.
communicative [kəˈmju:nikətiv] adj. Comunicativo, va; expansivo, va.
communion [kəˈmju:njən] n. Comunión, *f*.
communiqué [kəˈmju:nikei] n. Comunicado (*m*.) oficial.
communism [ˈkɔmjunizəm] n. Comunismo, *m*.
communist [ˈkɔmjunist] adj./n. Comunista.
communistic [,kɔmjuˈnistik] adj. Comunista.
community [kəˈmju:niti] n. Comunidad, *f*.: *community of goods*, comunidad de bienes; *community of interest*, comunidad de intereses. || Vecindario, *m*. (local inhabitants). || Colectividad, *f*., sociedad, *f*. (people in general). || FIG. Comunidad, *f*. (of ideas). || — *Community centre*, centro (*m*.) social. || U. S. *Community chest*, fondo (*m*.) para beneficencia pública. || *Community property*, comunidad de bienes; bienes (*m*.) municipales.
communization [kɔmjunaiˈzeiʃən] n. Comunización, *f*.
communize [ˈkɔmju:naiz] v. tr. Convertir en propiedad comunal: *the king communized the church lands*, el rey convirtió las tierras de la iglesia en propiedad comunal. || Hacer comunista (people, countries).
commutability [kə,mju:təˈbiliti] n. JUR. Conmutabilidad, *f*.
commutable [kəˈmju:təbl] adj. JUR. Conmutable.
commutate [ˈkɔmjuteit] v. tr. ELECTR. Conmutar.
commutation [,kɔmjuˈteiʃən] n. JUR. Conmutación, *f*. || ELECTR. Conmutación, *f*., cambio (*m*.) de dirección de la corriente. || Conmutación, *f*. (of payment). || U. S. *Commutation ticket*, abono, *m*.
commutative [kəˈmju:tətiv] adj. Conmutativo, va.
commutator [ˈkɔmjuteitə*] n. Conmutador, *m*.
commute [kəˈmju:t] v. tr. JUR. ELECTR. Conmutar.
— V. intr. Viajar: *he commutes daily between Windsor and London*, viaja diariamente de Windsor a Londres.
commuter [—ə*] n. Viajero, ra [que hace diariamente el mismo trayecto y tiene un abono].
comose [ˈkəuməus] adj. BOT. Cabelludo, da.
compact [kəmˈpækt] adj. Compacto, ta: *a compact mass*, una masa compacta. || Recogido, da: *a compact house*, una casa recogida. || Conciso, sa: *a compact book*, un libro conciso. || Denso, sa (dense). || *Compact of*, compuesto de.
compact [ˈkɔmpækt] n. Pacto, *m*., convenio, *m*. (agreement). || Coche (*m*.) no muy grande. || —

General compact, común acuerdo, *m.* || *Powder compact*, polvera, *f.*
compact [kəmˈpækt] v. tr. Condensar. || Apretar, comprimir. || Componer.
companion [kəmˈpænjən] n. Compañero, ra: *a travelling companion*, un compañero de viaje. || Acompañante, *m.* & *f.*: *companion wanted for elderly lady*, se requiere acompañante para señora mayor. || Caballero (*m.*) de grado inferior (in knighthood). || — MAR. *Companion hatch*, cubierta (*f.*) de escotilla. | *Companion hatchway*, escotilla, *f.* | *Companion ladder*, escala (*f.*) de toldilla.
companionable [—əbl] adj. Sociable.
companionably [—i] adv. Sociablemente.
companionship [—ʃip] n. Compañerismo, *m.* (fellowship). || Compañeros, *m. pl.* (companions).
companionway [—wei] n. MAR. Escalera (*f.*) de toldilla.
company [ˈkʌmpəni] n. COMM. Compañía: *he owns an insurance company*, es propietario de una compañía de seguros. | Empresa, *f.*: *building company*, empresa constructora. || Compañía, *f.*: *her mother was good company for me*, su madre me hizo mucha compañía. || Compañías, *f. pl.*: *he keeps bad company*, tiene malas compañías. || Compañero, ra (companion). || Compañerismo, *m.* (companionship). || Invitado, da: *I have company for lunch*, tengo invitados para almorzar. || Visita, *f.* (visitors). || MAR. Tripulación, *f.* (crew). || MIL. THEATR. Compañía, *f.* || — *Better alone than in bad company*, más vale estar solo que mal acompañado. || *Company manners*, buenos modales. || *Company union*, sindicato (*m.*) libre [de una empresa]. || *In company*, en compañía. || *Joint-stock company*, sociedad anónima. || *Limited-liability company*, sociedad [de responsabilidad] limitada. || *Present company excepted*, mejorando lo presente. || *To bear company*, acompañar. || *To be expecting company*, estar esperando visita. || *To keep company with*, asociarse con (to associate), salir con (lovers). || *To keep s.o. company*, hacer compañía a alguien. || *To part company*, separarse: *the two travellers parted company*, los dos viajeros se separaron; terminar (to end a friendship). || *Touring company*, compañía teatral que se dedica a hacer giras. || *Two's company, three's a crowd*, ni amor ni señoría quieren compañía.
comparable [ˈkɔmpərəbl] adj. Comparable.
comparative [kəmˈpærətiv] adj. Comparativo, va. || Relativo, va: *her party was a comparative success*, su fiesta fue un éxito relativo. || Comparado, da: *comparative studies*, estudios comparados. || GRAMM. *Comparative degree*, grado comparativo.
— N. GRAMM. Comparativo, *m.*
comparatively [—li] adv. En comparación, comparativamente. || Relativamente.
comparator [kɔmˈpærətə*] n. PHYS. Comparador, *m.*
compare [kəmˈpɛə*] n. Comparación, *f.* || *Beyond compare* o *past compare*, sin comparación, sin par.
compare [kəmˈpɛə*] v. tr. Comparar: *to compare a film with a play*, comparar una película con una obra de teatro; *to compare notes*, comparar apuntes. || GRAMM. Formar el comparativo de. || — *As compared with*, comparado con. || *They are not to be compared*, no se pueden comparar.
— V. intr. Poderse comparar. || *To compare favourably with*, no ser inferior a.
comparison [kəmˈpærisn] n. Comparación, *f.*: *beyond comparison*, sin comparación; *it bears no comparison with the other*, no admite comparación con el otro.
compartment [kəmˈpɑ:tmənt] n. Compartimiento, *m.*, departamento, *m.* (in a railway carriage). || MAR. Compartimiento, *m.*: *watertight compartment*, compartimiento estanco. || Sección, *f.* (in parliamentary business). || Departamento, *m.*, sección, *f.* (department).
compass [ˈkʌmpəs] n. Brújula, *f.* (for determining direction). || MAR. AVIAT. Compás, *m.*, brújula, *f.*, aguja, *f.* || Compás, *m.* (for making circles). || Círculo, *m.* (circle). || Límites, *m. pl.* (limits). || Espacio, *m.* (space). || Alcance, *m.* (range). || Extensión, *f.* (extent). || MUS. Extensión, *f.* (of the voice). || — *Compass bearing*, rumbo, *m.* || *Compass card*, rosa náutica, rosa (*f.*) de los vientos. || TECH. *Compass plane*, cepillo redondo. || *Compass rose*, rosa (*f.*) de los vientos. || *Compass saw*, sierra (*f.*) de contornar. || *Pair of compasses*, compás, *m.* || *Points of the compass*, puntos (*m.*) de la brújula.
compass [ˈkʌmpəs] v. tr. Dar la vuelta a (to go round). || Rodear (to surround). || Comprender, captar (to grasp mentally). || Urdir, tramar (to plot). || Lograr, conseguir (to obtain).
compassion [kəmˈpæʃən] n. Compasión, *f.* || *To move s.o. to compassion*, mover a uno a compasión.
compassionate [—it] adj. Compasivo, va (sympathetic, understanding).
compassionate [—eit] v. tr. Compadecer, compadecerse de.
compatibility [kəmˌpætəˈbiliti] n. Compatibilidad, *f.*
compatible [kəmˈpætəbl] adj. Compatible.
compatriot [kəmˈpætriət] n. Compatriota, *m.* & *f.*
compeer [kɔmˈpiə*] n. Igual, *m.* (equal). || Compañero, ra (companion).
compel [kəmˈpel] v. tr. Compeler, obligar (to oblige). || Imponer: *his honesty compels respect*, su honradez impone respeto.
compellation [kɔmpəˈleiʃən] n. Tratamiento, *m.* || Nombre, *m.* (name).
compelling [kəmˈpeliŋ] adj. Apremiante (urgent). || Obligatorio, ria (compulsory). || Irresistible (driving). || Fuerte (personality). || *Compelling urge*, necesidad (*f.*) urgente.
compendious [kəmˈpendiəs] adj. Compendioso, sa; conciso, sa.
compendiousness [—nis] n. Concisión, *f.*
compendium [kəmˈpəndiəm] n. Compendio, *m.*

— OBSERV. El plural de *compendium* es *compendiums* o *compendia*.

compensate [ˈkɔmpenseit] v. tr. Indemnizar (to repay). || PHYS. Compensar. || Compensar (to make up for).
— V. intr. *To compensate for*, compensar.
compensating [—iŋ] adj. TECH. *Compensating gear*, engranaje (*m.*) diferencial. || *Compensating pendulum*, péndulo compensador.
compensation [ˌkɔmpenˈseiʃən] n. Compensación, *f.* (the act of compensating). || Indemnización, *f.* (indemnity). || Remuneración, *f.* || Recompensa, *f.* (reward). || TECH. PHYS. Compensación, *f.* || *Compensation balance*, balanza (*f.*) de compensación.
compensative [kəmˈpensətiv] adj. Compensativo, va; compensador, ra.
compensator [ˈkɔmpenseitə*] n. Compensador, *m.*
compensatory [kəmˈpensətəri] adj. Compensatorio, ria. || — *Compensatory damages*, indemnización (*f. sing.*) por daños y perjuicios. || *Compensatory lengthening*, alargamiento compensatorio (of vowels).
compère [ˈkɔmpɛə*] n. Presentador *m.*
compère [ˈkɔmpɛə*] v. tr./intr. Presentar.
compete [kəmˈpi:t] v. intr. Competir.
competence [ˈkɔmpitəns] n. Competencia, *f.*, aptitud, *f.* (sufficient ability). || Sueldo (*m.*) suficiente para vivir (modest income). || JUR. Competencia, *f.*
competency [—i] n. See COMPETENCE.
competent [ˈkɔmpitənt] adj. Competente, apto, ta; capaz (having necessary qualities). || Adecuado, da (suitable). || JUR. Competente.
competition [ˌkɔmpiˈtiʃən] n. Competición, *f.*: *an athletic competition*, una competición atlética. || COMM. Competencia, *f.* || Oposición, *f.* (examination for certain posts). || Concurso, *m.* (contest).
competitive [kəmˈpetitiv] adj. De competencia (spirit). || De libre competencia (market). || — *Competitive examination*, oposición, *f.* || *Competitive price*, precio competitivo.
competitor [kəmˈpetitə*] n. Competidor, ra; rival, *m.* & *f.* || COMM. Competidor, *m.* || Opositor, ra (for certain posts). || Concursante, *m.* & *f.* (in a contest).
compilation [ˌkɔmpiˈleiʃən] n. Compilación, *f.*
compile [kəmˈpail] v. tr. Compilar.
compiler [—ə*] n. Compilador, ra.
complacence [kəmˈpleisəns] or **complacency** [kəmˈpleisnsi] n. Satisfacción (*f.*) de sí mismo.
complacent [kəmˈpleisnt] adj. Satisfecho de sí mismo.
complain [kəmˈplein] v. intr. Quejarse, lamentarse (*of*, *about*, de; *that*, de que). || JUR. Presentar una demanda.
complainant [kəmˈpleinənt] n. JUR. Demandante, *m.* & *f.*, querellante, *m.* & *f.*
complaint [kəmˈpleint] n. Queja, *f.* (expression of dissatisfaction): *he made a complaint to the police*, presentó una queja a la policía. || Reclamación, *f.* (about quality of service, etc.). || Enfermedad, *f.*: *he suffers from a stomach complaint*, tiene una enfermedad del estómago. || JUR. Demanda, *f.*: *he lodged a complaint*, entabló una demanda. || U. S. JUR. Acusación, *f.*
complaisance [kəmˈpleizəns] n. Complacencia, *f.*, amabilidad, *f.*
complaisant [kəmˈpleizənt] adj. Complaciente, amable.
complection [kəmˈplekʃən] n. See COMPLEXION.
complement [ˈkɔmplimənt] n. Complemento, *m.*: *wine is the complement to a good dinner*, el vino es el complemento de una buena comida. || MIL. Efectivo, *m.* || GRAMM. Complemento, *m.* || MAR. Dotación, *f.* || MATH. Complemento, *m.* || MED. *Complement fixation*, fijación (*f.*) del complemento.
complement [ˈkɔmpliment] v. tr. Complementar.
complemental [ˌkɔmpliˈmentl] adj. Complementario, ria.
complementary [ˌkɔmpliˈmentəri] adj. Complementario, ria: *complementary angles, colours*, ángulos, colores complementarios.
complete [kəmˈpli:t] adj. Completo, ta: *the complete works of Shakespeare*, las obras completas de Shakespeare; *a complete stranger*, un completo desconocido. || Acabado, da; concluido, da; terminado, da: *his work is complete*, su trabajo está concluido. || Total: *a complete surprise*, una sorpresa total. || Consumado, da (consummate). || Perfecto, ta.
complete [kəmˈpli:t] v. tr. Completar: *he wants two more volumes to complete the set*, le faltan dos volúmenes para completar su colección. || Terminar, acabar, concluir (to finish). || Completar, complemen-

tar: *travel completes an education*, el viajar complementa la educación. || Llenar: *to complete a form*, llenar un formulario.

completion [kəm'pli:ʃən] n. Terminación, *f.*, conclusión, *f.* || Realización, *f.* (execution).

complex ['kɔmpleks] adj. Complejo, ja (not simple): *a complex idea*, una idea compleja. || Complejo, ja; complicado, da (having many parts): *complex machinery*, maquinaria complicada. || CHEM. Complejo, ja. || — MATH. *Complex fraction*, fracción compuesta. | *Complex number*, número complejo. || GRAMM. *Complex sentence*, oración compuesta.
— N. Complejo, *m.*: *an industrial complex*, un complejo industrial. || Complejo, *m.* (in psychology).

complexion [kəm'plekʃən] n. Cutis, *m.*, tez, *f.* || FIG. Aspecto, *m.*, cariz, *m.*: *matters took on a new complexion*, los asuntos tomaron un nuevo cariz.

complexioned [—d] adj. De tez, de cutis: *fair complexioned*, de tez clara.

complexity [kəm'pleksiti] n. Complejidad, *f.*

compliance [kəm'plaiəns] n. Obediencia, *f.* (submission). || Conformidad, *f.* (aquiescement). || *In compliance with*, de acuerdo con.

compliant [kəm'plaiənt] adj. Acomodaticio, cia (accommodating). || Dócil, sumiso, sa (obedient).

complicacy ['kɔmplikəsi] n. Complicación, *f.* || Complejidad, *f.* (complexity).

complicate ['kɔmplikeit] adj. Complicado, da; complejo, ja.

complicate ['kɔmplikeit] v. tr. Complicar.
— V. intr. Complicarse.

complicated [—id] adj. Complicado, da; complejo, ja.

complication [,kɔmpli'keiʃən] n. Complicación, *f.*

complicity [kəm'plisiti] n. Complicidad, *f.*

compliment ['kɔmplimənt] n. Cumplido, *m.* (expression of praise): *he paid compliments*, hizo cumplidos. || Atención, *f.* (kind attention). || Detalle, *m.* (kind gesture). || Piropo, *m.* (amorous flattery). || — Pl. Saludos, *m.*: *pay my compliments to your wife*, mis saludos a su mujer. | Enhorabuena, *f. sing.*: *my compliments to the chef*, mi enhorabuena al cocinero. || — *Compliments of the season*, felices Pascuas. || *With the publisher's compliments*, obsequio (*m. sing.*) de la editorial.

compliment ['kɔmplimənt] v. tr. Cumplimentar, felicitar. || Alabar (to praise). || Requebrar, piropear (a woman).

complimentary [,kɔmpli'mentəri] adj. Elogioso, sa; halagador, ra (eulogistic). || — *Complimentary copy*, obsequio (*m.*) del autor. || *Complimentary ticket*, billete (*m.*) *or* entrada (*f.*) de favor.

compline or **complin** ['kɔmplin] n. REL. Completas, *f. pl.* (last service of the day).

complot ['kɔmplɔt] n. Complot, *m.*, conspiración, *f.*

complot ['kəmplɔt] v. intr. Complotar, conspirar.

comply [kəm'plai] v. intr. Acceder, conformarse (with wishes). || Obedecer (to obey). || *To comply with*, cumplir con (the rules), acatar (the law).

component [kəm'pəunənt] adj. Componente, constituyente.
— N. Componente, *m.*

comport [kəm'pɔ:t] v. tr./intr. Concordar. || *To comport o.s.*, portarse, conducirse, comportarse.

comportment [—mənt] n. Comportamiento, *m.*, conducta, *f.*

compose [kəm'pəuz] v. tr. Componer. || Calmar, sosegar (to make calm). || *To compose o.s.*, calmarse, sosegarse.
— V. intr. Componer.

composed [—d] adj. Tranquilo, la; sereno, na.

composedness [—dnis] n. Tranquilidad, *f.*, serenidad, *f.*, calma, *f.*

composer [—ə*] n. MUS. Compositor, ra.

composing [—iŋ] adj. De composición. || — *Composing machine*, máquina (*f.*) de componer. || PRINT. *Composing stick*, componedor, *m.*
— N. Composición, *f.*

compositae [kəm'pɔsiti:] pl. n. BOT. Compuestas, *f.*

composite ['kɔmpəzit] adj. Compuesto, ta: *composite number*, número compuesto. || BOT. Compuesto, ta. || ARCH. Compuesto, ta.
— N. BOT. Compuesta, *f.* || CHEM. Compuesto, *m.* || ARCH. Orden (*m.*) compuesto.

composition [,kɔmpə'ziʃən] n. Composición, *f.* || Redacción, *f.*, composición, *f.* (an essay). || Ejercicio, *m.* (exercise). || MATH. Composición (*f.*) de fuerzas. || COMM. Transacción, *f.*, acuerdo, *m.*

compositor [kəm'pɔzitə*] n. PRINT. Cajista, *m.*

compos mentis ['kɔmpɔs'mentis] adj. En su sano juicio.

compost ['kɔmpɔst] n. Abono, *m.*, estiércol (*m.*) vegetal.

compost ['kɔmpɔst] v. tr. Abonar (to fertilize). || Convertir en abono.

composure [kəm'pəuʒə*] n. Calma, *f.*, serenidad, *f.*, compostura, *f.*

compote ['kɔmpɔt] n. CULIN. Compota, *f.*

compound ['kɔmpaund] adj. Compuesto, ta. || — *Compound circuit*, circuito combinado. || ZOOL. *Compound eye*, ojo compuesto. || MATH. *Compound fraction*, fracción compuesta. || MED. *Compound fracture*, fractura complicada. || COMM. *Compound interest*, interés compuesto. || BOT. *Compound leaf*, hoja digitada. || *Compound lens*, lente compuesta. || MATH. *Compound number*, número compuesto. || GRAMM. *Compound sentence*, oración compuesta.
— N. Compuesto, *m.* || Recinto (*m.*) cercado (enclosed land). || Palabra (*f.*) compuesta (word).

compound [kəm'paund] v. tr. Componer (to make by combining). || Combinar, mezclar (to combine). || Arreglar (to arrange). || Agravar (an error). || COMM. Liquidar [una deuda] pagando sólo una parte. | Calcular [interés compuesto].
— V. intr. Arreglarse, llegar a un acuerdo (to compromise). || Combinarse, mezclarse (to combine).

comprehend [,kɔmpri'hend] v. tr. Comprender.

comprehensibility ['kɔmpri,hensə'biliti] n. Comprensibilidad, *f.*

comprehensible [,kɔmpri'hensəbl] adj. Comprensible.

comprehension [,kɔmpri'henʃən] n. Comprensión, *f.*

comprehensive [,kɔmpri'hensiv] adj. Amplio, plia; de gran amplitud, extenso, sa: *politics is a comprehensive term*, el término política es muy amplio. || De conjunto, general, global (survey, view). || Comprensivo, va: *a comprehensive mind*, una mente comprensiva. || A todo riesgo (insurance). || — *Comprehensive charge*, precio (*m.*) todo incluido. || U. S. *Comprehensive examination*, reválida, *f.* || *Comprehensive school*, instituto (*m.*) de segunda enseñanza.

comprehensiveness [—nis] n. Comprensión, *f.* || Amplitud, *f.*, gran extensión, *f.*

compress ['kɔmpres] n. MED. Compresa, *f.* || TECH. Prensa (*f.*) para comprimir el algodón en balas.

compress [kəm'pres] v. tr. Comprimir (to reduce by pressure). || FIG. Condensar (to condense).

compressed [—t] adj. Comprimido, da (pressed together). || FIG. Condensado, da (condensed). || — *Compressed air*, aire comprimido. || *Compressed air brake*, freno neumático.

compressibility [kəm,presi'biliti] n. Compresibilidad, *f.* (capacity to be compressed).

compressible [kəm'presəbl] adj. Compresible, comprimible.

compression [kəm'preʃən] n. Compresión, *f.*: *compression chamber*, cámara de compresión.

compressive [kəm'presiv] adj. Compresivo, va.

compressor [kəm'presə*] n. Compresor, *m.*

comprise (U. S. **comprize**) [kəm'praiz] v. tr. Comprender (to include). || Constar de (to consist of).

compromise ['kɔmprəmaiz] n. Compromiso, *m.*, acomodo, *m.*, arreglo, *m.*: *we shall have to come to a compromise over this point*, tendremos que llegar a un arreglo sobre este punto. || Término (*m.*) medio: *a compromise between two different opinions*, un término medio entre dos opiniones distintas. || *To be a compromise to*, comprometer.

compromise ['kɔmprəmaiz] v. intr. Llegar a un arreglo (to agree): *if you disagree with me, we shall have to compromise*, si no estás de acuerdo conmigo, tendremos que llegar a un arreglo. || Transigir (to yield): *I am willing to compromise over the price*, estoy dispuesto a transigir sobre el precio.
— V. tr. Comprometer (to endanger). || Arreglar (a quarrel, etc.).

compromising [—iŋ] adj. Comprometedor, ra.

comptometer [kɔmp'tɔmitə*] n. TECH. Máquina (*f.*) de calcular.

comptroller [kən'trəulə*] n. (Ant.). Administrador, *m.* || COMM. Interventor, *m.*

compulsion [kəm'pʌlʃən] n. Obligación, *f.*, fuerza, *f.*: *he did it under compulsion*, lo hizo por obligación *or* a la fuerza. || Coacción, *f.* (coercion). || Impulso, *m.* (impulse). || *To be under compulsion to do sth.*, estar obligado a hacer algo.

compulsive [kəm'pʌlsiv] adj. Obligatorio, ria (obligatory). || Coercitivo, va (coercive). || Incorregible, empedernido, da: *a compulsive gambler*, un jugador empedernido.

compulsorily [kəm'pʌlsərili] adv. Obligatoriamente.

compulsory [kəm'pʌlsəri] adj. Obligatorio, ria (obligatory). || Coercitivo, va (coercive).

compunction [kəm'pʌŋkʃən] n. REL. Compunción, *f.* || Remordimiento, *m.* (pricking of conscience). || *Without compunction*, sin escrúpulo.

compunctious [kəm'pʌŋkʃəs] adj. Compungido, da.

computable [kəm'pju:təbl] adj. Computable, calculable.

computation [,kɔmpju:'teiʃən] n. Cómputo, *m.*, cálculo, *m.*

compute [kəm'pju:t] n. Cómputo, *m.*, cálculo, *m.*

compute [kəm'pju:t] v. tr. Computar, calcular.

computer [—ə*] n. Computador, *m.*, computadora, *f.*, ordenador, *m.*, calculador, *m.*, calculadora, *f.* || *Computer language*, lenguaje (*m.*) de máquina.

computerize [—əraiz] v. tr. Tratar (data). || Poner computadoras en. || *To be computerized*, tener computadoras.

comrade ['kɔmrid] n. Camarada, *m.* & *f.*

comrade-in-arms [—in'ɑ:mz] n. Compañero (*m.*) de armas.

comradeship [—ʃip] n. Camaradería, *f.*

con [kɔn] n. Contra, *m.*: *pros and cons*, los pros y los contras. || — FAM. *Con game*, estafa, *f.* | *Con man*, estafador, *m.*

con (U. S. **conn**) [kɔn] v. tr. MAR. Gobernar.

COMPUTER — COMPUTADORA, *f.*, ORDENADOR, *m.*

access arm	brazo (*m.*) de acceso
access time	tiempo (*m.*) de acceso
adder	sumadora *f.*
address	dirección *f.*
alphanumeric	alfanumérico, ca
analog computer	calculador (*m.*) analógico
analyst	analista *m.* & *f.*
area	área *f.*
array	serie *f.*, matriz *f.*
assembler	ensamblador *m.*
automation	automatización *f.*
band	banda *f.*
batch processing	tratamiento (*m.*) por lotes
binary code	código (*m.*) binario
binary digit, bit	dígito (*m.*) binario, "bit" *m.*
branch	bifurcación *f.*
brush	escobilla *f.*
buffer storage	memoria (*f.*) intermedia
calculator	calculadora *f.*
call instruction	instrucción (*f.*) de llamada
card punch	perforadora (*f.*) de tarjetas
card reader	lector (*m.*) de tarjetas
cell	célula *f.*
channel	canal *m.*
character	carácter *m.*
check digit	dígito (*m.*) de comprobación
circuit	circuito *m.*
clear (to)	borrar
clock	reloj *m.*
code; code (to)	código *m.*; codificar
coder	codificador *m.*
command	orden *f.*, instrucción *f.*
compiler	compilador *m.*
computer language	lenguaje (*m.*) de máquina
console	pupitre *m.*, consola *f.*
control unit	unidad (*f.*) de control
core storage *o* store	memoria (*f.*) de núcleos
counter	contador *m.*
cybernetics	cibernética *f.*
cycle	ciclo *m.*
data	datos *m.*, información *f. sing.*
data processing	informática *f.* (science), tratamiento (*m.*) de la información, procesamiento (*m.*) *or* proceso (*m.*) de datos
debugging	depuración *f.*
decision	decisión *f.*
digit	dígito, *m.*
digital computer	calculador (*m.*) digital
disc, disk	disco *m.*
display unit	unidad (*f.*) de representación visual
drum	tambor *m.*
edit (to)	editar, revisar
electronics	electrónica *f.*
emitter	emisor *m.*
encode (to)	codificar
erase (to)	borrar
feed	alimentación *f.*
feed (to)	alimentar
feedback	realimentación *f.*
field	campo *m.*
file	archivo *m.*, fichero *m.*
flow chart	organigrama *m.*
frame	encuadre *m.*
hardware	hardware *m.*, maquinaria *f.*, equipos (*m. pl.*) y dispositivos
identifier	identificador *m.*
index	índice *m.*
information	información *f.*
inline processing	proceso (*m.*) lineal
input	entrada *f.*
inquiry	consulta *f.*, interrogación *f.*
instruction	instrucción *f.*
integrated circuit	circuito (*m.*) integrado
interpret (to)	interpretar
item	unidad (*f.*) de información (characters), registro *m.* (of a file)
jump	salto *m.*
key	tecla *f.*
keyboard	teclado *m.*
latency time	tiempo (*m.*) de espera
library	biblioteca *f.*
linkage	enlace *m.*
load (to)	cargar
location	posición *f.*
logger	registrador (*m.*) automático
loop	circuito *m.*; bucle *m.*
machine language	lenguaje (*m.*) de máquina
magnetic storage	memoria (*f.*) magnética
magnetic tape	cinta (*f.*) magnética
matrix	matriz *f.*
memory	memoria *f.*
message	mensaje *m.*
module	módulo *m.*
monitor	monitor *m.*
nanosecond	nanosegundo *m.*
network	red *f.*
numeric, numerical	numérico, ca
octet	octeto *m.*
operator	operador *m.*
optical character reader	lector (*m.*) óptico de caracteres
optical scanner	explorador (*m.*) óptico
output	salida *f.*
overflow	exceso (*m.*) de capacidad
panel	tablero *m.*
parameter	parámetro *m.*
perforator	perforadora *f.*
peripheral equipment	equipo (*m.*) periférico
printed circuit	circuito (*m.*) impreso
printer	impresora *f.*
process (to)	tratar
processing unit	unidad (*f.*) de tratamiento
program; program (to)	programa *m.*; programar
programmer	programador *m.*
programming	programación *f.*
pulse	impulso *m.*
punch; punch (to)	perforadora *f.*; perforar
punched *o* punch card	tarjeta (*f.*) *or* ficha (*f.*) perforada
punched *o* punch tape	cinta (*f.*) perforada
punch hole	perforación *f.*
random access	acceso (*m.*) al azar
read (to); reader	leer; lector *m.*
reading	lectura *f.*
real time	tiempo (*m.*) real
record, register	registro *m.*
redundancy	redundancia *f.*
routine	rutina *f.*
selector	selector *m.*
sentinel	centinela *m.*
sequence; sequential	secuencia *f.*; secuencial
serial	en serie
shift	desplazamiento *m.*
signal	señal *f.*
simulation	simulación *f.*
simulator	simulador *m.*
software	"software" *m.*, programas (*m. pl.*) y procedimientos
sort (to); sort	clasificar; clasificación *f.*
sorter	clasificadora *f.*
storage	almacenamiento *m.* (operation), memoria *f.* (device).
store (to)	almacenar
subprogram	subprograma *m.*
subroutine	subrutina *f.*
switch	conmutador *m.*
symbol	símbolo *m.*
symbolic language	lenguaje (*m.*) simbólico
system	sistema *m.*
tabulator	tabuladora *f.*
teleprinter	teleimpresor *m.*
terminal	terminal *m.*
terminal unit	unidad (*f.*) terminal
timer	cronómetro
time sharing	tiempo (*m.*) compartido
timing	sincronización *f.*
track	pista *f.*
transducer	transductor *m.*
translater	traductor *m.*
update (to)	actualizar
working storage	memoria (*f.*) de trabajo

con [kɔn] v. tr. Aprender de memoria, memorizar (to learn by heart). || Estudiar: *to con a lesson*, estudiar una lección. || FAM. Estafar, timar: *he conned me out of five pounds*, me estafó cinco libras. || FAM. *To con s.o. into doing sth.*, persuadir a alguien para que haga algo.

conation [kəuˈneiʃən] n. PHIL. Volición, *f.*

conative [ˈkəunətiv] adj. PHIL. Volitivo, va.

concatenate [kɔnˈkætineit] adj. Concatenado, da; concadenado, da.

concatenate [kɔnˈkætineit] v. tr. Concatenar, concadenar, enlazar.

concatenation [kɔnˌkætiˈneiʃən] n. Concatenación, *f.*, encadenamiento, *m.*, serie, *f.*

concave [ˈkɔnkeiv] adj. Cóncavo, va.
— N. Concavidad, *f.*

concavity [kɔnˈkæviti] n. Concavidad, *f.*

concavo-concave [kɔnˈkeivəuˈkɔnkeiv] adj. PHYS. Bicóncavo, va.

concavo-convex [kɔnˈkeivəuˈkɔnveks] adj. PHYS. Cóncavoconvexo, xa.

conceal [kənˈsi:l] v. tr. Ocultar. || JUR. Encubrir.

concealment [—mənt] n. Ocultación, *f.* || JUR. Encubrimiento, *m.* || Escondite, *m.* (hiding place).

concede [kənˈsi:d] v. tr. Reconocer, admitir (to admit). || Conceder, otorgar (to grant). || *To concede the game, to concede victory*, darse por vencido.
— V. intr. Ceder, hacer una concesión.

conceit [kənˈsi:t] n. Presunción, *f.*, vanidad, *f.*, engreimiento, *m.* (pride). || Agudeza, *f.*, dicho (*m.*) ingenioso, concepto, *m.* (literary). || Noción, *f.*, concepto, *m.* (notion).

conceited [kənˈsi:tid] adj. Engreído, da; presumido, da; vanidoso, sa.

conceitedness [—nis] n. Presunción, *f.*, vanidad, *f.*, engreimiento, *m.*

conceivable [kənˈsi:vəbl] adj. Concebible, imaginable.

conceive [kənˈsi:v] v. tr. Concebir: *to conceive an idea*, concebir una idea. || BIOL. Concebir.
— V. intr. Concebir. || *To conceive of*, concebir, imaginarse.

concenter [kɔnˈsentə*] v. tr./intr. U. S. See CONCENTRE.

concentrate [ˈkɔnsəntreit] v. tr. Concentrar (troops). || Concentrar (attention). || Enfocar, concentrar (rays).

— V. intr. Concentrarse: *we must concentrate on our work*, debemos concentrarnos en nuestro trabajo. || Concentrarse (troops).
concentrate [ˈkɔnsəntreit] n. Concentrado, *m*.
concentration [ˌkɔnsənˈtreiʃən] n. Concentración, *f*. || *Concentration camp*, campo (*m*.) de concentración.
concentrative [ˈkɔnsəntreitiv] adj. Concentrable.
concentre (U. S. **concenter**) [kɔnˈsentə*] v. tr. Concentrar, hacer converger *or* convergir.
— V. intr. Concentrarse, converger, convergir.
concentric [kɔnˈsentrik] or **concentrical** [—l] adj. Concéntrico, ca.
concentricity [kɔnsenˈtrisiti] n. Concentricidad, *f*.
concept [ˈkɔnsept] n. Concepto, *m*.
conception [kənˈsepʃən] n. Concepción, *f*. (of child, idea). || Idea, *f*.: *he has no conception of the work involved*, no tiene ni idea del trabajo que eso supone.
conceptional [—əl] adj. Concepcional.
conceptism [ˈkənseptizəm] n. Conceptismo, *m*.
conceptive [kənˈseptiv] adj. Conceptivo, va.
conceptual [kənˈseptjuəl] adj. Conceptual.
conceptualism [—izəm] n. PHIL. Conceptualismo, *m*.
conceptualist [—ist] n. PHIL. Conceptualista, *m*. & *f*.
conceptualistic [—ˈistik] adj. Conceptualista.
concern [kənˈsəːn] n. Asunto, *m*., cosa, *f*.: *it's no concern of yours*, no es asunto tuyo. || Intereses, *m. pl*.: *he has a concern in the industry*, tiene intereses en la industria. || Empresa, *f*. (business). || Preocupación, *f*., inquietud, *f*. (worry): *he regarded his sick mother with concern*, miró a su madre enferma con inquietud. || Conexión, *f*., relación, *f*.: *it has no concern with them*, no tiene relación con ellos. || — Pl. Asuntos, *m*. (private affairs). || — *A matter of some concern to us*, un asunto que nos interesa *or* que nos preocupa mucho. || *Of concern*, de interés. || *Of what concern is it to you?*, ¿a Ud qué le importa?
concern [kənˈsəːn] v. tr. Tratar de (to have as a subject): *this book concerns fencing*, este libro trata de esgrima. || Meterse: *don't concern yourself with politics*, no te metas en la política. || Complicar, implicar: *he was concerned in a scuffle*, fue complicado en una pelea. || Afectar, atañer, concernir (to affect): *it concerns him only indirectly*, le afecta sólo indirectamente. || Estar relacionado con, relacionarse con, referirse a (to be related to). || Preocupar (to worry): *your behaviour concerns me deeply*, tu comportamiento me preocupa mucho. || — *As concerns*, respecto de, respecto a, refiriéndose a. || *As far as I am concerned*, por lo que a mí se refiere. || *To whom it may concern*, a quien corresponda.
concerned [—d] adj. Preocupado, da; inquieto, ta (worried): *he has a concerned face*, tenía cara preocupada; *she was concerned to know*, estaba preocupada por saber. || *Those concerned*, los interesados.
concerning [—iŋ] prep. Con respecto a, acerca de, concerniente a, refiriéndose a, referente a.
concert [ˈkɔnsət] n. Concierto, *m*., acuerdo, *m*. (agreement): *to work in concert with*, obrar de concierto *or* de común acuerdo con. || Concierto, *m*. (musical performance). || — MUS. *Concert grand*, piano (*m*.) de cola. | *Concert pitch*, diapasón (*m*.) normal.
concert [kənˈsəːt] v. tr. Concertar.
— V. intr. Obrar de concierto.
concerted [—id] adj. Concertado, da.
concertgoer [ˈkɔnsətˌgəuə*] n. Aficionado (*m*.) a los conciertos, melómano, na.
concertina [ˌkɔnsəˈtiːnə] n. MUS. Concertina, *f*.
concertina [ˌkɔnsəˈtiːnə] v. intr. Arrugarse (on impact).
concertmaster [ˈkɔnsətˌmɑːstə*] n. U. S. MUS. Concertino, *m*.
concerto [kənˈtʃəːtəu] n. MUS. Concierto, *m*.

— OBSERV. El plural de *concerto* es *concerti* o *concertos*.

concession [kənˈseʃən] n. Concesión, *f*.
concessionaire or **concessionnaire** [kənˌseʃəˈnɛə*] n. Concesionario, ria.
concessionary [kənˈseʃənəri] adj. Del concesionario (rights). || Concesionario, ria.
concessive [kənˈsesiv] adj. Concesivo, va.
conch [kɔŋk] n. ZOOL. Caracol (*m*.) marino (sea snail). || Concha, *f*. (shell). || ARCH. Bóveda (*f*.) de concha. || ANAT. Concha, *f*.
concha [ˈkɔŋkə] n. ANAT. Concha, *f*.

— OBSERV. El plural de *concha* es *conchae*.

conchiferous [kɔnˈkifərəs] adj. Conchífero, ra.
conchoid [ˈkɔŋkɔid] n. MATH. Concoide, *f*.
conchoidal [kɔŋˌkɔidəl] adj. Concoideo, a.
concierge [ˌkɔ̃ːnsiˈɛəʒ] n. Portero, ra.
conciliar [kənˈsiliə*] adj. Conciliar.
conciliate [kənˈsilieit] v. tr. Conciliar.
conciliation [kənˌsiliˈeiʃən] n. Conciliación, *f*.: *conciliation board*, tribunal de conciliación laboral; *conciliation court*, tribunal de conciliación. || Reconciliación, *f*. (reconcilement).
conciliative [kənˈsiliətiv] adj. Conciliativo, va.
conciliator [kənˈsilieitə*] n. Conciliador, ra.
conciliatory [kənˈsiliətəri] adj. Conciliatorio, ria; conciliador, ra.
concise [kənˈsais] adj. Conciso, sa.
conciseness [kənˈsaisnis] or **concision** [kənˈsiʒən] n. Concisión, *f*.

conclave [ˈkɔnkleiv] n. Cónclave, *m*.
conclavist [—ist] n. Conclavista, *m*.
conclude [kənˈkluːd] v. tr. Concluir, acabar (to end). || Firmar, concertar (a treaty, etc.). || Concluir (to deduce).
— V. intr. Concluirse, terminarse (to come to an end). || Concluir, terminar: *he concluded by saying*, terminó diciendo. || Decidir (to decide).
conclusion [kənˈkluːʒən] n. Conclusión, *f*. (finish, deduction). || Firma, *f*. (of a treaty). || — *In conclusion*, en conclusión. || *To jump to conclusions*, see JUMP.
conclusive [kənˈkluːsiv] adj. Conclusivo, va; concluyente. || *Conclusive evidence*, pruebas definitivas.
concoct [kənˈkɔkt] v. tr. CULIN. Confeccionar (to mix). || FIG. Urdir, fraguar, maquinar (to plot). | Inventar.
concoction [kənˈkɔkʃən] n. Mezcla, *f*. (mixture). || Brebaje, *m*. (brew). || FIG. Maquinación, *f*. (of a plot). | Fabricación, *f*. (of lies). | Invento, *m*. (lie).
concomitance [kənˈkɔmitəns] or **concomitancy** [—i] n. Concomitancia, *f*.
concomitant [kənˈkɔmitənt] adj. Concomitante.
— N. Cosa (*f*.) que acompaña otra.
concord [ˈkɔŋkɔːd] n. Concordia, *f*. (state of agreement). || MUS. Acorde, *m*. || GRAMM. Concordancia, *f*.
concordance [kənˈkɔːdəns] n. Concordancia, *f*. (agreement). || Concordancias, *f. pl*. (index).
concordant [kənˈkɔːdənt] adj. Concordante, concorde. || MUS. Armonioso, sa.
concordat [kɔnˈkɔːdæt] n. REL. Concordato, *m*.
concourse [ˈkɔŋkɔːs] n. Concurrencia, *f*. (coming together). || Confluencia, *f*. (of rivers). || U. S. Encrucijada, *f*. (in a park). | Vestíbulo, *m*. (in railway station).
concrete [ˈkɔnkriːt] n. Hormigón, *m*. [*Amer*., concreto, *m*.] (for building): *concrete steel* o *reinforced concrete*, hormigón armado.
— Adj. Concreto, ta (not abstract). || TECH. De hormigón (made of concrete). || *Concrete mixer*, hormigonera, *f*.
concrete [ˈkɔnkriːt] v. tr. Cubrir con hormigón (to cover). || Solidificar (to harden).
concreting [—iŋ] n. Hormigonado, *m*.
concretion [kənˈkriːʃən] n. Concreción, *f*. || MED. Cálculo, *m*.
concretize [ˈkɔnkritaiz] v. tr. Concretar.
concubinage [kɔnˈkjuːbinidʒ] n. Concubinato, *m*.
concubine [ˈkɔŋkjubain] n. Concubina, *f*.
concupiscence [kənˈkjuːpisəns] n. Concupiscencia, *f*.
concupiscent [kənˈkjuːpisənt] adj. Concupiscente.
concur [kənˈkəː*] v. intr. Estar de acuerdo (to agree). || Concurrir, coincidir (to coincide). || — *To concur in*, convenir en. || *To concur with*, estar de acuerdo con.
concurrence [kənˈkʌrəns] or **concurrency** [—i] n. Concurrencia, *f*. || Coincidencia, *f*. (coincidence). || Acuerdo, *m*. (agreement).
concurrent [kənˈkʌrənt] adj. Concurrente (coinciding). || JUR. Común: *concurrent powers*, poderes comunes. | Opuesto, ta (rights).
concuss [kənˈkʌs] v. tr. MED. Conmocionar. || MED. *To be concussed*, sufrir una conmoción cerebral.
concussion [kənˈkʌʃən] n. MED. Conmoción (*f*.) cerebral.
condemn [kənˈdem] v. tr. Condenar (to censure, to punish): *the papers condemned the strike*, los periódicos condenaron la huelga; *he was condemned to death*, le condenaron a muerte. || Declarar en ruina: *the house was condemned*, la casa fue declarada en ruina. || Confiscar (smuggling).
condemnable [—nəbl] adj. Condenable, censurable.
condemnation [ˌkɔndemˈneiʃən] n. Condenación, *f*. (judgment). || Condena, *f*. (punishment). || FIG. Condena, *f*.
condemnatory [kənˈdemnətəri] adj. Condenatorio, ria.
condemned [kənˈdemd] adj. Condenado, da. || *Condemned cell*, celda (*f*.) de los condenados a muerte.
condensability [kənˌdensəˈbiliti] n. Condensabilidad, *f*.
condensable [kənˈdensəbl] adj. Condensable.
condensation [ˌkɔndenˈseiʃən] n. Condensación, *f*. (action). || Vaho, *m*. (vapour). || Resumen, *m*. (of a document or speech). || *Condensation trail*, estela (*f*.) de condensación.
condense [kənˈdens] v. tr. PHYS. Condensar. || Condensar, resumir (document, speech, etc.). || *Condensed milk*, leche condensada.
— V. intr. Condensarse.
condenser [kənˈdensə*] n. Condensador, *m*.
condescend [ˌkɔndiˈsend] v. intr. Condescender, dignarse: *the king condescended to receive his subjects*, el rey condescendió a recibir a sus súbditos; *he condescended to say hello*, se dignó saludar.
condescendence [kɔndiˈsendəns] n. Condescendencia, *f*. (condescension).
condescending [ˌkɔndiˈsendiŋ] adj. Condescendiente.
condescension [ˌkɔndiˈsenʃən] n. Condescendencia, *f*.
condign [kənˈdain] adj. Merecido, da: *condign punishment*, castigo merecido.
condiment [ˈkɔndimənt] n. Condimento, *m*.
condisciple [ˈkɔndiˈsaipl] n. Condiscípulo, la.
condition [kənˈdiʃən] n. Condición, *f*. (stipulation): *the conditions of the contract*, las condiciones del contrato; *I shall do it on one condition*, lo haré con una condición. || Condición, *f*. (social status): *people of every condition*, gente de toda condición. || Estado,

m. (state): *in a liquid condition,* en estado líquido; *a bicycle in good condition,* una bicicleta en buen estado. || Condiciones, *f. pl.*: *to be in no condition to do sth.*, no estar en condiciones de hacer algo; *this merchandise arrived in bad condition,* estas mercancías llegaron en males condiciones. || Estado (*m.*) de salud: *his condition is very grave,* su estado de salud es muy grave. || Oración (*f.*) condicional. || — Pl. Condiciones, *f.* (terms). || Circunstancias, *f.* (circumstances). || — *On condition that,* a condición de que. || *Under any condition,* de ningún modo. || *Weather conditions permitting,* si el tiempo no lo impide. || *We try to keep in condition,* intentamos mantenernos en forma. || *Working conditions,* condiciones de trabajo.

condition [kən'diʃən] v. tr. Condicionar: *supply is conditioned by demand,* la oferta está condicionada por la demanda. || Poner en condiciones, preparar: *to condition a horse for a race,* poner en condiciones a un caballo para una carrera. || Acondicionar (a place, a substance, the air): *to condition a room for a dance,* acondicionar un salón para un baile.

conditional [kən'diʃənl] adj. Condicional. || GRAMM. Potencial, condicional (mood). | Condicional: *conditional clause,* oración condicional. || *To be conditional on,* depender de.

— N. GRAMM. Potencial, *m.* condicional, *m.* | Oración (*f.*) condicional.

conditioned [kən'diʃənd] adj. Condicionado, da: *conditioned reflexes,* reflejos condicionados. || Acondicionado, da (place, substance, air).

conditioner [kən'diʃənə*] n. Acondicionador, *m.* || *Air conditioner,* acondicionador (*m.*) de aire.

conditioning [kən'diʃəniŋ] n. Condicionamiento, *m.* || Acondicionamiento, *m.* (of place, substance, air). || *Air conditioning,* aire acondicionado.

condole [kən'dəul] v. intr. Condolerse, compadecer (to commiserate): *to condole with s.o.*, condolerse de *or* compadecer a alguien. || Dar el pésame.

condolence [kən'dəuləns] n. Condolencia, *f.* || — *Please accept my condolences,* le acompaño en el sentimiento. || *To express* o *to send one's condolences for,* dar el pésame por.

condom ['kɔndəm] n. Condón, *m.* (contraceptive).

condominium ['kɔndə'miniəm] n. Condominio, *m.*

condonation [,kɔndəu'neiʃən] n. Condonación, *f.*, perdón, *m.*

condone [kən'dəun] v. tr. Condonar, perdonar (to forgive). || Permitir que continúe (what ought to be stopped).

condor ['kɔndɔ:*] n. Cóndor, *m.* (bird, coin).

conduce [kən'dju:s] v. intr. Conducir: *to conduce to a result,* conducir a un resultado.

conducive [kən'dju:siv] adj. Conducente: *measures conducive to a solution,* medidas conducentes a una solución. || Conveniente: *exercise is conducive to good health,* el ejercicio es conveniente para la buena salud. || Propicio, cia (helpful).

conduct ['kɔndʌkt] n. Conducta, *f.*, comportamiento, *m.* (behaviour). || Dirección, *f.*, conducción, *f.* (direction).

conduct [kən'dʌkt] v. tr. Conducir, llevar: *he conducted me to my room,* me condujo a mi habitación. || Dirigir: *he conducted his business from his home,* dirigía su negocio en su casa; *he conducted the orchestra at that concert,* dirigió la orquesta en ese concierto. || Conducir: *steel conducts electricity,* el acero conduce la electricidad. || — *Conducted tour,* visita acompañada. || *To conduct o.s.*, comportarse, conducirse.

— V. intr. Dirigir una orquesta. || Conducir (a way). || ELECTR. Ser conductor.

conductance [—əns] n. ELECTR. Conductancia, *f.*

conductibility [kən,dʌktə'biliti] n. Conductibilidad, *f.*

conduction [kən'dʌkʃən] n. Conducción, *f.*

conductive [kən'dʌktiv] adj. Conductivo, va; conductor, ra.

conductivity [,kəndʌk'tiviti] n. Conductividad, *f.*

conductor [kən'dʌktə*] n. Guía, *m.* (guide). || Director, *m.* (of orchestra, choir). || Cobrador, *m.* (of a bus). || PHYS. Conductor, *m.* || U. S. Revisor, *m.* (of trains). || *Lightning conductor,* pararrayos, *m. inv.*

conductress [kən'dʌktris] n. Cobradora, *f.* (of a bus). || Directora, *f.*

conduit ['kɔndit] n. Conducto, *m.* || ELECTR. Tubo, *m.*

condyle ['kɔndil] n. ANAT. Cóndilo, *m.*

condyloid ['kɔndilɔid] adj. BOT. Condiloideo, a.

condyloma [kɔndi'ləumə] n. MED. Condiloma, *m.*

— OBSERV. El plural de *condyloma* es *condylomata.*

cone [kəun] n. MATH. Cono, *m.* || BOT. Piña, *f.* || Cucurucho, *m.*: *ice-cream cone,* cucurucho de helado. || TECH. *Cone gear,* engranaje cónico.

cone [kəun] v. tr. Dar forma cónica a.

cone-shaped [—ʃeipt] adj. Cónico, ca; coniforme.

coney or **cony** ['kəuni] n. ZOOL. Conejo, *m.* (rabbit). || Piel (*f.*) de conejo (rabbit fur).

confab ['kɔnfæb] n. FAM. Cháchara, *f.*, palique, *m.*

confab ['kɔnfæb] v. intr. FAM. Charlotear, estar de cháchara *or* de palique.

confabulate [kən'fæbjuleit] v. intr. Charlar.

confabulation [kən'fæbju'leiʃən] n. Charla, *f.*

confect ['kɔnfekt] v. tr. Confeccionar, preparar (to prepare). || Forjar (to invent lies).

confection [kən'fekʃən] n. CULIN. Dulce, *m.*, confite, *m.* || COMM. Confección, *f.* (of clothes). || Mixtura, *f.*, confección, *f.* (compound of drugs).

confectioner [—ə*] n. Confitero, ra. || Repostero, ra (pastrycook). || U. S. *Confectioner's sugar,* azúcar glaseado.

confectionery [kən'fekʃnəri] n. Confitería, *f.* (shop, trade). || Dulces, *m. pl.* (sweets). || Repostería, *f.* (cake shop).

confederacy [kən'fedərəsi] n. Confederación, *f.*

confederal [kən'fedərəl] adj. Confederal.

confederate [kən'fedərit] adj. Confederado, da

— N. Cómplice, *m.* (an accomplice). || Confederado, da (ally).

confederate [kən'fedəreit] v. intr. Confederarse.

— V. tr. Confederar.

confederation [kən,fedə'reiʃən] n. Confederación, *f.*

confederative [kən'fedərətiv] adj. Confederativo, va.

confer [kən'fə*] v. intr. Consultar: *to confer with s.o.*, consultar con alguien. || Conferenciar (to hold a conference).

— V. tr. Conferir, otorgar (*on,* a).

conference ['kɔnfərəns] n. Consulta, *f.* (consultation). || Conferencia, *f.*, congreso, *m.* (meeting). || Entrevista, *f.*, reunión, *f.* (talks). || U. S. Federación (*f.*) deportiva (sporting league).

conferment [kən'fə:mənt] n. Concesión, *f.*

confess [kən'fes] v. tr. Confesar: *we must confess our sins,* debemos confesar nuestros pecados; *Father Smith confessed me,* el padre Smith me confesó.

— V. intr. Confesarse (a sinner). || Confesar (a confessor). || *To confess to a crime,* confesar un crimen.

confessed [—t] adj. Declarado, da. || Confesado, da.

confession [kən'feʃən] n. Confesión, *f.* || Tumba, *f.* (tomb). || — *Confession of faith,* profesión (*f.*) de fe. || *On their own confession,* según propia confesión. || *The seal of confession,* el secreto de confesión. || *To go to confession,* confesarse. || *To hear confession,* confesar. || *To make a full confession,* confesar de plano.

confessional [kən'feʃənl] adj. Confesional.

— N. Confesionario, *m.*, confesonario, *m.* (where confession is heard). || Confesión, *f.* (practice).

confessor [kən'fesə*] n. Confesor, *m.* || Director (*m.*) espiritual (spiritual adviser).

confetti [kən'feti] n. Confeti, *m. pl.*, papelillos, *m., pl.*

confidant [,kɔnfi'dænt] n. Confidente, *m.*

confidante [,kɔnfi'dænt] n. Confidente, *f.* || THEATR. Confidenta, *f.*

confide [kən'faid] v. tr. Confiar.

— V. intr. *To confide in,* fiarse de (to trust), confiarse a (to share secrets).

confidence ['kɔnfidəns] n. Confianza, *f.* (trust). || Confidencia, *f.* (secret). || Confianza, *f.*, seguridad (*f.*) en sí mismo. || — *Confidence man,* estafador, *m.* || *Confidence trick,* estafa, *f.*, fraude, *m.* || *In confidence,* en confianza. || *To betray s.o.'s confidence,* defraudar la confianza de alguien. || *To take s.o. into one's confidence,* depositar su confianza en alguien.

confident ['kɔnfidənt] adj. Seguro, ra; convencido, da (certain). || Seguro de sí mismo (self-assured). || Presuntuoso, sa (presumptuous). || — *He is confident of the future,* tiene fe en el futuro. || *He said it in a confident tone,* lo dijo en un tono seguro.

— N. Confidente, *m.* & *f.*

confidential [,kɔnfi'denʃəl] adj. Confidencial. || De confianza: *a confidential secretary,* una secretaria de confianza. || Íntimo, ma (friend).

confiding [kən'faidiŋ] adj. Confiado, da.

configurate [kən,figju'reit] v. tr. Configurar, dar forma.

configuration [kən,figju'reiʃən] n. Configuración, *f.*

configure [kən'figjuə*] v. tr. Configurar, dar forma.

confine ['kɔnfain] n. Confín, *m.*, límite, *m.*

confine [kən'fain] v. tr. Confinar (to isolate, to imprison). || Limitar (to restrict): *confine your remarks to the main issue,* limite usted sus observaciones al tema en cuestión. || — *He was confined to his bed,* tenía que guardar cama. || *To be confined,* estar de parto (a woman). || *To confine o.s. to,* limitarse a.

— V. intr. Ser fronterizos, estar contiguos.

confinement [—mənt] n. Confinamiento, *m.* (state of being confined). || Limitación, *f.*, límite, *m.* (restriction). || Obligación (*f.*) de guardar cama (to bed). || Parto, *m.* (childbirth). || Prisión, *f.* (prison).

confirm [kən'fə:m] v. tr. Confirmar. || Ratificar: *to confirm a treaty,* ratificar un tratado. || REL. Confirmar.

confirmand [kɔnfə'mænd] n. REL. Confirmando, da.

confirmation [,kɔnfə'meiʃən] n. Confirmación, *f.* || Ratificación, *f.* (of treaty). || REL. Confirmación, *f.*

confirmative [kən'fə:mətiv] adj. Confirmativo, va; confirmatorio, ria.

confirmatory [kən'fə:mətəri] adj. Confirmativo, va; confirmatorio, ria.

confirmed [kən'fə:md] adj. Confirmado, da. || Empedernido, da: *a confirmed bachelor,* un solterón empedernido. || Crónico, ca (illness).

confiscable [kən'fiskəbl] adj. Confiscable.

confiscate ['kɔnfiskeit] v. tr. Confiscar, incautarse de.

confiscation [,kɔnfis'keiʃən] n. Confiscación, *f.*, incautación, *f.*

confiscator ['kɔnfiskeitə*] n. Confiscador, ra.

confiscatory [kən'fiskətəri] adj. De confiscación.

CONFERENCES. — CONFERENCIAS, *f.*

I. Meetings. — Reuniones, *f.*

assembly	asamblea *f.*
convention	reunión *f.*, congreso *m.*
general meeting *o* assembly	asamblea (*f.*) general
congress	congreso *m.*
seat, headquarters	sede *f. sing.*
governing body	órgano (*m.*) director
board of directors	consejo (*m.*) de administración
executive council *o* board	consejo (*m.*) ejecutivo
standing body	organismo (*m.*) permanente
committee, commission	comisión *f.*
subcommittee	subcomisión *f.*
general committee, officers, bureau	mesa *f. sing.*
secretariat	secretaría *f.*
budget committee	comisión (*f.*) de presupuestos
drafting committee	comisión (*f.*) de redacción
committee of experts	comisión (*f.*) de expertos
advisory *o* consultative committee	comisión (*f.*) asesora *or* consultiva
round table	mesa (*f.*) redonda
symposium	simposio *m.*
study group	grupo (*m.*) de estudios
seminar	seminario *m.*
working party	grupo (*m.*) de trabajo
sit (to), meet (to), to hold a meeting	celebrar sesión, reunirse
sitting, meeting [U.S., session]	sesión *f.*
session [U.S., meeting]	período (*m.*) de sesiones, reunión *f.*
meeting in camera [U.S., executive session]	sesión (*f.*) a puerta cerrada
opening, final sitting	sesión (*f.*) de apertura, de clausura
formal sitting	sesión (*f.*) solemne
plenary meeting	sesión (*f.*) plenaria, plenaria *f.*, pleno *m.*

II. Participants. — Participantes, *m.*

head of delegation	jefe (*m.*) de delegación
permanent delegate	delegado (*m.*) permanente
membership	calidad (*f.*) de miembro
member	miembro *m.*
member as of right	miembro (*m.*) de derecho
life member	miembro (*m.*) vitalicio
full-fledged member	miembro (*m.*) con plenos poderes
full powers	plenos poderes *m.*
terms of reference	mandato *m. sing.*
representative	representante *m.*
alternate, substitute	suplente *m.* y *f.*, sustituto, ta
with a right to vote	con voz y voto
observer	observador *m.*
technical adviser	asesor (*m.*) técnico
auditor	interventor (*m.*) de cuentas
office	cargo *m.*, puesto *m.*
holder of an office	titular (*m.*) de un cargo
honorary president	presidente (*m.*) honorario
chairman	presidente *m.*
presidency, chairmanship, chair	presidencia *f.*
interim chairman	presidente (*m.*) interino
chair (to)	presidir
vice-president, vice-chairman	vicepresidente *m.*
rapporteur	ponente *m.* [*Amer.*, relator *m.*]
former chairman [U.S., past chairman]	ex presidente *m.*
director general	director (*m.*) general
deputy director general	director (*m.*) general adjunto.
secretary general	secretario (*m.*) general
executive secretary	secretario (*m.*) ejecutivo
treasurer	tesorero *m.*
officials	funcionarios *m.*
consultant	consultor *m.*
precis writer	secretario (*m.*) *or* redactor (*m.*) de actas
ushers	ordenanzas *m.*

III. Debate. — Debate, *m.*

hall	sala *f.*
rostrum	tribuna (*f.*) de oradores
public gallery	tribuna (*f.*) pública
notice board	tablón (*m.*) de anuncios
convene (to), convoke (to)	convocar
convocation	convocatoria *f.*
standing orders, by-laws	reglamento (*m. sing.*) general
rules of procedure	reglamento (*m. sing.*) interno
constitution, statutes	estatutos *m.*
procedure	procedimiento *m.*
agenda	orden (*m.*) del día
item on the agenda	punto (*m.*) del orden del día
(any) other business	asuntos (*m. pl.*) varios, cuestiones (*f. pl.*) varias
to place on the agenda	incluir *or* inscribir en el orden del día
working paper	documento (*m.*) de trabajo
timetable, schedule	horario *m.*
opening	apertura *f.*
the sitting is open	se abre la sesión
appointment	nombramiento *m.*
appoint (to)	nombrar
general debate	debate (*m.*) general
speaker	orador *m.*
to ask for the floor	pedir la palabra
to give the floor to [U.S., to recognize]	dar *or* conceder la palabra a
to take the floor, to address the meeting	hacer uso de la palabra, tomar la palabra
to make *o* to deliver a speech	pronunciar un discurso
declaration, statement	declaración *f.*
am I in order?	¿me lo permite el reglamento?
call to order	llamada (*f.*) al orden
to raise a point of order	plantear una cuestión de orden
receivability	admisibilidad *f.*
stand	posición *f.*
consensus	opinión *f.*
advisory opinion	dictamen *m.*
proposal	propuesta *f.*
to table a proposal	presentar una propuesta
clarification	aclaración *f.*
comment	comentario *m.*, observación *f.*
second (to), support (to)	apoyar
adopt (to)	aprobar; adoptar
oppose (to)	oponerse a
to raise an objection	formular una objeción
to move an amendment	proponer una enmienda
to amend	enmendar
second reading	segunda lectura *f.*
substantive motion	moción (*f.*) sobre el fondo de la cuestión
decision	decisión *f.*
ruling	decisión (*f.*) del presidente
reject (to)	rechazar
resolution	resolución *f.*
draft resolution	proyecto (*m.*) de resolución
first *o* preliminary draft	anteproyecto *m.*
whereases	considerandos *m.*
motivations	exposición (*f. sing.*) de motivos
operative part	parte (*f.*) dispositiva *or* resolutiva
report	informe *m.*, ponencia *f.*
factual report	exposición (*f.*) de hechos
minutes, record	actas *f. pl.*, acta *f. sing.*
summary record	actas (*f. pl.*) analíticas
verbatim record	actas (*f. pl.*) taquigráficas *or* literales
memorandum	memorándum *m.*
postpone (to), adjourn (to), put off (to)	aplazar, diferir
closure	clausura *f.*
closing speech	discurso (*m.*) de clausura
to adjourn *o* to close the meeting	levantar la sesión

See also POLITICS

confiteor [kən'fitiɔ:*] n. REL. Confíteor, *m.*
conflagration [ˌkɔnflə'greiʃən] n. Conflagración, *f.* (war). ‖ Incendio, *m.* (fire).
conflation [kən'fleiʃən] n. Combinación (*f.*) de dos textos.
conflict ['kɔnflikt] n. Conflicto, *m.*: *conflict of interest*, conflicto de intereses.
conflict [kən'flikt] v. intr. Luchar (to struggle, to contend). ‖ Chocar (to clash).
conflicting [—iŋ] adj. Contrario, ria; contrapuesto, ta.
confluence ['kɔnfluəns] n. Confluencia, *f.*
confluent ['kɔnfluənt] adj. Confluente.
— N. Confluente, *m.*, tributario, *m.* (river).
conflux ['kɔnflʌks] n. Confluencia, *f.*
conform [kən'fɔ:m] v. intr. Conformarse. ‖ Someterse: *you must conform to discipline*, tienes que someterte a la disciplina. ‖ Ajustarse: *to conform to the regulations*, ajustarse a las reglas.
— V. tr. Conformar. ‖ Ajustar (to adapt).
conformability [kənˌfɔ:mə'biliti] n. Conformidad, *f.*
conformable [kən'fɔ:məbl] adj. Conforme: *conformable to*, conforme con.
conformance [kən'fɔ:məns] n. Conformidad, *f.*
conformation [ˌkɔnfɔ:'meiʃən] n. Conformación, *f.* ‖ Ajuste, *m.*, amoldamiento, *m.*, adaptación, *f.*
conformism [kən'fɔ:mizəm] n. Conformismo, *m.*
conformist [kən'fɔ:mist] n. Conformista, *m.* & *f.*
conformity [kən'fɔ:miti] n. Conformidad, *f.* ‖ *In conformity with*, conforme a *or* con.
confound [kən'faund] v. tr. Confundir (to confuse). ‖ Frustrar (to foil). ‖ Desconcertar (to disconcert). ‖ Maldecir (to damn). ‖ — FAM. *Confound him!*, ¡maldito sea! | *Confound it*, ¡caray!
confounded [—id] adj. FAM. Maldito, ta; condenado, da. | Desconcertado, da.
confraternity [ˌkɔnfrə'tə:niti] n. Hermandad, *f.*, confraternidad, *f.*
confront [kən'frʌnt] v. tr. Hacer frente a: *a robber confronted me*, un ladrón me hizo frente. ‖ Enfrentar, confrontar (to bring face to face). ‖ Presentarse: *many difficulties confronted us*, se nos presentaban muchas dificultades. ‖ Confrontar (to compare).
confrontation [kənfrʌn'teiʃən] n. Confrontación, *f.*
Confucius [kən'fju:ʃjəs] pr. n. Confucio, *m.*
confuse [kən'fju:z] v. tr. Confundir (to mix up, to perplex). ‖ Desconcertar (to disconcert). ‖ — *To*

confuse the issue, complicar las cosas. || *To get confused*, hacerse un lío.
confusedness [—dnis] n. Confusión, *f.*
confusing [—iŋ] adj. Confuso, sa (confused). || Desconcertante.
confusion [kən'fju:ʒən] n. Confusión, *f.*, desorden, *m.* || Confusión, *f.*, desconcierto, *m.* (bewilderment). || Confusión, *f.* (embarrassment). || — *A sea of confusion*, un mar de confusiones. || *To be in confusion*, estar en desorden (untidy), estar confuso, sa (embarrassed).
confutation [ˌkɔnfju:'teiʃən] n. Refutación, *f.*
confute [kən'fju:t] v. tr. Refutar, confutar.
congeal [kən'dʒi:l] v. intr. Congelarse (to freeze). || Coagularse (to coagulate) || Fig. Petrificarse, anquilosarse.
— V. tr. Congelar (to freeze). || Coagular (to coagulate).
congealable [—əbl] adj. Congelable (freezable). || Coagulable (coagulable).
congealment [—mənt] or **congelation** [ˌkɔndʒi'leiʃən] n. Congelación, *f.* (a freezing). || Coagulación, *f.* (coagulation).
congener ['kɔndʒinə*] n. Congénere, *m.* & *f.*
congeneric [ˌkɔndʒi'nerik] adj. Congénere.
congenerous [kən'dʒenərəs] adj. Congénere.
congenial [kən'dʒi:njəl] adj. Agradable (agreeable). || Apropiado, da; conveniente (suitable). || Similar (kindred). || Compatible.
congenital [kən'dʒenitl] adj. Congénito, ta.
conger ['kɔŋgə*] or **conger eel** [—i:l] n. Zool. Congrio, *m.*
congeries [kɔn'dʒiəri:z] inv. n. Montón, *m.*
congest [kən'dʒest] v. tr. Congestionar.
— V. intr. Congestionarse.
congested [—id] adj. Congestionado, da. || Bot. Apiñado, da. || Superpoblado, da (overpopulated).
congestion [kən'dʒestʃən] n. Congestión, *f.* || Superpoblación, *f.* (overpopulation).
congestive [kən'dʒestiv] adj. Congestivo, va.
conglobate ['kɔngləubeit] v. tr. Conglobar.
conglomerate [kən'glɔmərit] adj. Conglomerado, da.
— N. Geol. Conglomerado, *m.* || Conglomeración, *f.*
conglomerate [kən'glɔməreit] v. tr. Conglomerar.
— V. intr. Conglomerarse.
conglomeration [kənˌglɔmə'reiʃən] n. Conglomeración, *f.* || Fam. Montón, *m.* (of things).
conglutinate [kən'glu:tineit] v. tr. Conglutinar.
— V. intr. Conglutinarse.
conglutination [kənglu:ti'neiʃən] n. Conglutinación, *f.*
Congo ['kɔŋgəu] pr. n. Geogr. Congo, *m.*
Congolese [ˌkɔngəu'liz] adj./n. Congolés, esa; congoleño, ña.
congratulate [kən'grætjuleit] v. tr. Felicitar, dar la enhorabuena, congratular: *I congratulated him on the birth of his daughter*, le felicité por el nacimiento de su hija. || *To congratulate o.s.*, congratularse.
congratulation [kənˌgrætju'leiʃən] n. Congratulación, *f.*, felicitación, *f.*: *I send you my sincerest congratulations*, reciba Ud. mis más sinceras congratulaciones. || *Congratulations!*, ¡enhorabuena!, ¡felicidades!, ¡muchas felicidades!
congratulatory [kən'grætjulətəri] adj. Congratulatorio, ria; de felicitación.
congregate ['kɔŋgrigit] adj. Congregado, da.
congregate ['kɔngrigeit] v. intr. Congregarse.
— V. tr. Congregar.
congregation [ˌkɔngri'geiʃən] n. Congregación, *f.* || Rel. Feligreses, *m. pl.*, fieles, *m. pl.* (of a parish). | Congregación, *f.* (of monks, nuns, etc.).
congregational [—əl] adj. De la congregación. || *The Congregational Church*, la Iglesia Congregacionalista.
Congregationalism [ˌkɔŋgri'geiʃnəlizəm] n. Rel. Congregacionalismo, *m.*
Congregationalist [ˌkɔŋgri'geiʃnəlist] adj./n. Congregacionalista.
congress ['kɔŋgres] n. Congreso, *m.* (formal meeting). || Congreso, *m.*: *the U. S. Congress*, el Congreso de los Estados Unidos.
congressional [kɔŋ'greʃənl] adj. Del congreso.
congressman ['kɔŋgresmən] n. Miembro (*m.*) del Congreso de los Estados Unidos. || Congresista, *m.* (of a meeting).

— Observ. El plural de *congressman* es *congressmen.*

congruence ['kɔŋgruəns] or **congruency** [—i] n. Congruencia, *f.*
congruent ['kɔŋgruənt] adj. Congruente.
congruity [kɔŋ'gru:iti] n. Congruencia, *f.*
congruous ['kɔŋgruəs] adj. Congruo, grua; congruente.
conic ['kɔnik] adj. Cónico, ca.
— N. Geometría (*f.*) cónica.
conical [—əl] adj. Cónico, ca.
conidium [kəu'nidjəm] n. Bot. Conidio, *m.*

— Observ. El plural de *conidium* es *conidia.*

conifer ['kəunifə*] n. Bot. Conífera, *f.*
coniferous [kəu'nifərəs] adj. Bot. Conífero, ra.
coniform ['kəunifɔ:m] adj. Coniforme, cónico, ca.
conium [kəu'naiəm] n. Bot. Cicuta, *f.* (hemlock).
conjectural [kən'dʒektʃərəl] adj. Conjetural.
conjecture [kən'dʒektʃə] n. Conjetura, *f.*
conjecture [kən'dʒektʃə] v. tr. Conjeturar.
— V. intr. Hacer conjeturas.
conjoin [kən'dʒɔin] v. tr. Unir.
— V. intr. Unirse.
conjoint ['kɔndʒɔint] adj. Conjunto, ta: *conjoint efforts*, esfuerzos conjuntos.
conjugable ['kɔndʒugəbl] adj. Conjugable.
conjugal ['kɔndʒugəl] adj. Conyugal.
conjugate ['kɔndʒugit] adj. Enlazado, da (joined together). || Conjugado, da: *conjugate points*, puntos conjugados. || Gramm. Congénere (word).
conjugate ['kɔndʒugeit] v. tr. Conjugar.
— V. intr. Conjugarse (a verb, etc.).
conjugation [ˌkɔndʒu'geiʃən] n. Conjugación, *f.*
conjunct [kən'dʒʌŋkt] adj. Conjunto, ta; unido, da.
conjunction [kən'dʒʌŋkʃən] n. Conjunción, *f.* || *In conjunction with*, conjuntamente con.
conjunctiva [ˌkɔndʒʌŋk'taivə] n. Anat. Conjuntiva, *f.*

— Observ. El plural de la palabra inglesa es *conjunctivae* o *conjunctivas.*

conjunctive [kən'dʒʌŋktiv] adj. Anat. Conjuntivo, va: *conjunctive tissue*, tejido conjuntivo. || Gramm. Conjuntivo, va.
— N. Conjunción, *f.*
conjunctivitis [kənˌdʒʌŋkti'vaitis] n. Med. Conjuntivitis, *f.*
conjuncture [kən'dʒʌŋktʃə*] n. Coyuntura, *f.*
conjuration [ˌkɔndʒuə'reiʃən] n. Rel. Conjuro, *m.*
conjure [kən'dʒuə*] v. tr. Suplicar.
conjure ['kʌndʒə*] v. tr. Conjurar (to invoke a spirit). || Hacer aparecer (by sleight of hand): *to conjure a rabbit from a hat*, hacer aparecer un conejo de un sombrero. || *To conjure up*, evocar.
— V. intr. Hacer juegos de manos.
conjurer or **conjuror** [—rə*] n. Prestidigitador, *m.*
conk [kɔŋk] n. Fam. Napia, *f.* (nose). | Coco, *m.* (head).
conk [kɔŋk] v. tr. Fam. Golpear [en la cabeza].
— V. intr. Fam. *To conk out*, fastidiarse, estropearse.
conker [—ə*] n. Bot. Castaño (*m.*) de Indias.
conn [kɔn] v. tr. Mar. Gobernar.
connate ['kɔneit] adj. Innato, ta; congénito, ta (inborn). || Similar (alike).
connatural [kə'nætʃərəl] adj. Connatural, innato, ta; congénito, ta (innate). || Similar (alike).
connect [kə'nekt] v. tr. Conectar (to join together). || Relacionar (to relate). || Poner [en comunicación] (*with*, con) [on the phone]. || Electr. Conectar, enchufar (to plug in).
— V. intr. Juntarse, unirse (to join). || Empalmar, enlazar (trains). || Cambiar a (to change train). || Electr. Conectarse. || *To connect with*, ponerse en relación con (people), comunicarse con (a room), relacionarse con (to be related to).
connected [—id] adj. Conectado, da (joined together). || Relacionado, da (associated). || Empalmado, da (two wagons). || Coherente (coherent). || Emparentado, da (related). || Enchufado, da (plugged in).
connecter [—ə*] n. Conectador, *m.* || Empalme, *m.* (joint).
connecting [—iŋ] adj. *Connecting gear*, embrague, *m.* || *Connecting link*, eslabón, *m.*, lazo, *m.*, vínculo, *m.*, nexo, *m.* || *Connecting rod*, biela, *f.*
connection [kə'nekʃən] n. Electr. Tech. Conexión, *f.* | Empalme, *m.*, unión, *f.* || Empalme, *m.*, enlace, *m.* (of trains, buses, etc.). || Unión, *f.* (joint). || Fig. Pariente, *m.* (relative). | Relación, *f.* (between persons): *to have good connections*, tener buenas relaciones. || Respecto, *m.*: *in this connection*, a este respecto; *in connection with*, con respecto a.
connective [kə'nektiv] adj. Conectivo, va. || *Connective tissue*, tejido conjuntivo.
— N. Gramm. Conjunción, *f.*
connector [kə'nektə*] n. Conectador, *m.* || Empalme, *m.* (joint).
connexion [kə'nekʃən] n. See connection.
conning ['kɔniŋ] adj. Mar. *Conning tower*, torre (*f.*) de mando (of a ship), torrecilla, *f.* (of a submarine).
conniption [kə'nipʃən] n. U. S. Fam. Rabieta, *f.*
connivance or **connivence** [kə'naivəns] n. Connivencia, *f.*
connive [kə'naiv] v. intr. Confabularse: *he connived with Andrew to rob the bank*, se confabuló con Andrés para robar el banco. || *To connive at*, hacer la vista gorda a.
conniver [kə'naivə*] n. Cómplice, *m.* & *f.*
connoisseur [ˌkɔnə'sə:*] n. Conocedor, ra; experto, ta; perito, ta.
connotation [ˌkɔnəu'teiʃən] n. Connotación, *f.*
connote [kə'nəut] v. tr. Connotar. || Implicar, traer consigo (to imply).
connubial [kə'nju:bjəl] adj. Connubial, conyugal.
conoid ['kəunɔid] n. Math. Conoide, *m.*
— Adj. Math. Conoidal, conoideo, a.
conquer ['kɔŋkə*] v. tr. Conquistar. || Vencer: *to conquer a habit*, vencer un hábito.
— V. intr. Triunfar, vencer.
conquering [—riŋ] adj. Victorioso, sa.
conqueror [—rə*] n. Conquistador, *m.*: *William the Conqueror*, Guillermo el Conquistador. || Vencedor, ra; triunfador, ra.
conquest ['kɔŋkwest] n. Conquista, *f.*
conquistador [kɔŋ'kistadɔ:*] n. Conquistador, *m.*

— Observ. El plural en inglés es *conquistadores* o *conquistadors.*

Conrad ['kɔnræd] pr. n. Conrado, *m.*
consanguineous [,kɔnsæŋ'gwiniəs] adj. Consanguíneo, a (related by blood).
consanguinity [,kɔnsæŋ'gwiniti] n. Consanguinidad, *f.*
conscience ['kɔnʃəns] n. Conciencia, *f.*: *to have a clear conscience*, tener la conciencia tranquila *or* limpia. || — *Case of conscience*, caso (*m.*) de conciencia. || *Conscience money*, dinero (*m.*) que se da para descargar la conciencia. || *For conscience's sake*, en descargo de conciencia. || *Guilty conscience*, conciencia sucia. || *In all conscience* en conciencia. || *Matter of conscience*, caso (*m.*) de conciencia. || *To have a guilty conscience*, remorderle a uno la conciencia. || *To have sth. on one's concience*, tener un peso en la conciencia.
conscienceless [—lis] adj. Sin escrúpulo, sin conciencia.
conscience-stricken [—,strikən] adj. Contrito, ta; arrepentido, da.
conscientious [,kɔnʃi'enʃəs] adj. Concienzudo, da. || *Conscientious objector*, objetor (*m.*) de conciencia.
conscientiousness [—nis] n. Escrupulosidad, *f.*
conscious ['kɔnʃəs] adj. Consciente. || — *To become conscious*, volver en sí. || *To become conscious of*, darse cuenta de. || *To be conscious*, tener conocimiento. || *To be conscious of*, tener conciencia de, saber.
consciousness [—nis] n. Conciencia, *f.* || MED. Conocimiento, *m.*: *he lost consciousness*, perdió el conocimiento.
conscript ['kɔnskript] n. MIL. Recluta, *m.*
— Adj. Alistado, da. || *Conscript father*, padre conscripto.
conscript [kən'skript] v. tr. MIL. Reclutar, alistar.
conscription [kən'skripʃən] n. MIL. Reclutamiento, *m.*
consecrate ['kɔnsikrit] adj. Consagrado, da.
consecrate ['kɔnsikreit] v. tr. Consagrar.
consecration [,kɔnsi'kreiʃən] n. Consagración, *f.*
consecrator ['kɔnsikreitə*] n. Consagrante, *m.*
consecratory ['kɔnsikreitəri] adj. Consagrante.
consecution [,kɔnsi'kju:ʃən] n. Ilación, *f.* (logical sequence). || Sucesión, *f.*
consecutive [kən'sekjutiv] adj. Consecutivo, va. || Sucesivo, va; consecutivo, va (following in regular order).
consensual [kən'sensjuəl] adj. Consensual.
consensus [kən'sensəs] n. Consenso, *m.*: *consensus of opinion*, consenso general.
consent [kən'sent] n. Consentimiento, *m.* || — *By common consent*, de mutuo acuerdo, de común acuerdo. || *Silence gives consent*, quien calla otorga.
consent [kən'sent] v. intr. Consentir: *to consent to*, consentir en.
consentient [kən'senʃənt] adj. Acorde, unánime. || Que consiente.
consequence ['kɔnsikwəns] n. Consecuencia, *f.* || — *In consequence*, por consiguiente. || *In consequence of*, a consecuencia de, como resultado de. || *Of no consequence*, sin importancia. || *Persons of consequence*, personas (*f.*) importantes. || *To take the consequences*, aceptar las consecuencias.
consequent ['kɔnsikwənt] n. Consecuencia, *f.* || GRAMM. MATH. Consecuente, *m.*
— Adj. Consiguiente. || *Consequent on* o *upon*, consecutivo a.
consequential [,kɔnsi'kwenʃəl] adj. Consecuente. || Suficiente (self-important). || *Consequential damages*, daños indirectos.
consequently ['kɔnsikwəntli] adv. Consecuentemente, en consecuencia, por lo tanto, por consiguiente.
conservancy [kən'sə:vənsi] n. Conservación, *f.*, preservación, *f.* (of natural resources). || Comisión (*f.*) portuaria.
conservation [,kɔnsə:'veiʃən] n. Conservación, *f.* || Conservación, *f.*, preservación, *f.* (of natural resources).
conservatism [kən'sə:vətizəm] n. Conservadurismo, *m.* [*Amer.*, conservatismo, *m.*]
conservative [kən'sə:vətiv] adj. Conservador, ra. || Por lo bajo, moderado, da: *conservative estimate*, cálculo moderado. || Prudente: *a conservative investment*, una inversión prudente. || *Conservative party*, partido conservador.
— N. Conservador, ra (person). || Producto (*m.*) para la conservación (preservative).
conservatoire [kən'sə:vətwɑ:*] n. MUS. Conservatorio, *m.*
conservator [kən'sə:vətə*] n. Conservador, *m.*
conservatory [kən'sə:vətri] n. Invernadero, *m.* (for plants). || MUS. Conservatorio, *m.* (conservatoire).
conserve [kən'sə:v] n. Conserva, *f.*
conserve [kən'sə:v] v. tr. Conservar.
consider [kən'sidə*] v. tr. Considerar. || Darse cuenta de (to realize). || Examinar (to study). || Pensar [en] (to think). || Tener en cuenta (to take into account). || — *All things considered*, considerándolo bien. || *Consider yourself lucky*, date por satisfecho.
considerable [kən'sidərəbl] adj. Considerable. || Importante, considerable (amount).
considerably [—i] adv. Considerablemente.
considerate [kən'sidərit] adj. Considerado, da; atento, ta.
considerately [—li] adv. Con consideración.
consideration [kən,sidə'reiʃən] n. Consideración, *f.* || Retribución, *f.* (payment). || — *After due consideration*, después de un detenido examen de la cuestión. || *A little consideration costs you nothing*, un poco de consideración no te cuesta nada. || *For a consideration*, por una gratificación. || *He shows consideration for others*, trata a los demás con consideración. || *In consideration of his age*, en consideración a su edad. || *On no consideration will I do it*, no lo haré bajo ningún concepto. || *Out of consideration for s.o.*, por consideración a alguien. || *To take into consideration*, tomar en consideración. || *The question under consideration*, la cuestión que se está estudiando *or* examinando. || *To act without due consideration*, actuar sin reflexionar. || *To give consideration to*, considerar.
considered [kən'sidəd] adj. Considerado, da.
considering [kən'sidəriŋ] prep. Teniendo en cuenta, considerando (in view of).
— Adv. Después de todo: *it's not too bad, considering*, después de todo, no está mal.
consign [kən'sain] v. tr. Consignar. || COMM. Consignar. || Enviar (to send). || Confiar (to entrust).
consignatary [kən'signətəri] n. Consignatario, ria.
consignation [,kɔnsig'neiʃən] n. Consignación, *f.*
consignee [,kɔnsai'ni:] n. COMM. Consignatario, *m.*
consignment [kən'sainmənt] n. COMM. Consignación, *f.* (deposit). | Envío, *m.*, expedición, *f.* (of goods). || *On consignment*, en consignación, en depósito.
consigner or **consignor** [kən'sainə*] n. Consignador, *m.*
consist [kən'sist] v. intr. Consistir, radicar (to lie essentially): *its advantage consists in its simplicity*, su ventaja consiste en su simplicidad. || Componerse, constar (to be composed of): *the human body consists of many parts*, el cuerpo humano se compone de muchas partes.
consistence [kən'sistəns] n. Consistencia, *f.*
consistency [—i] n. Consistencia, *f.* (of density). || Firmeza, *f.* (of behaviour): *his behaviour lacks consistency*, su conducta carece de firmeza. || Conformidad, *f.*, acuerdo, *m.* (agreement): *consistency between versions*, conformidad entre las versiones. || Coherencia, *f.* (coherence).
consistent [kən'sistənt] adj. De acuerdo, consecuente: *his conduct is not consistent with his promises*, su conducta no está de acuerdo con sus promesas; *his behaviour is not consistent with his teaching*, su comportamiento no es consecuente con sus enseñanzas. || Firme (going on without change): *a consistent advocate of peace*, un firme defensor de la paz. || Coherente (coherent).
consistorial [,kɔnsis'tɔ:riəl] adj. REL. Consistorial.
consistory [kən'sistəri] n. REL. Consistorio, *m.*
consolable [kən'səuləbl] adj. Consolable.
consolation [,kɔnsə'leiʃən] n. Consuelo, *m.* || *Consolation prize*, premio (*m.*) de consolación.
consolatory [kən'sɔlətəri] adj. Consolador, ra.
console [kən'səul] v. tr. Consolar.
console ['kɔnsəul] n. Ménsula, *f.*, soporte, *m.* (shelf support). || Consola, *f.* (table). || MUS. Consola, *f.* (of organ). || Mesa (*f.*) de control (in theatre, in television studio). || Mueble (*m.*) para aparato de radio *or* televisión (cabinet for radio or television). || TECH. Pupitre, *m.*, consola, *f.* || *Console table*, consola, *f.*
consoler [kən'səulə*] n. Consolador, ra.
consolidate [kən'sɔlideit] v. tr. Consolidar, reforzar (to strengthen). || Comprimir (to compress). || Consolidar (debts).
— V. intr. Comprimirse (to become compressed). || COMM. Fusionarse (to merge). || Consolidarse (to become strengthened).
consolidation [kən,sɔli'deiʃən] n. Consolidación, *f.* || COMM. Fusión, *f.* (merger). | Consolidación, *f.* (of debts).
consoling [kən'səuliŋ] adj. Consolador, ra.
consols [kən'sɔlz] pl. n. Fondos (*m.*) consolidados.
consommé [kən'sɔmei] n. Consomé, *m.*, caldo, *m.*
consonance ['kɔnsənəns] n. Consonancia, *f.* (in music, in poetry). || PHYS. Resonancia, *f.*
consonant ['kɔnsənənt] adj. De acuerdo, conforme (consistent): *behaviour consonant with principles*, conducta de acuerdo con *or* conforme a unos principios. || Consonante (in music, poetry, grammar). || PHYS. Resonante.
— N. GRAMM. Consonante, *f.*
consonantal [,kɔnsə'næntl] adj. GRAMM. Consonántico, ca.
consonantism ['kɔnsənæntizəm] n. Consonantismo, *m.*
consort ['kɔnsɔ:t] n. Consorte, *m.* & *f.* (of reigning monarch). || MAR. Escolta, *f.* || Asociación, *f.* || *In consort with*, de acuerdo con.
consort [kən'sɔ:t] v. intr. Asociarse (to associate). || Estar de acuerdo, concordar (to be in accord).
consortium [kən'sɔ:tjəm] n. Consorcio, *m.*

— OBSERV. El plural es *consortia* o *consortiums.*

conspectus [kən'spektəs] n. Estudio (*m.*) general (comprehensive survey). || Sinopsis, *f*, cuadro (*m.*) sinóptico (synopsis).
conspicuous [kən'spikjuəs] adj. Visible: *a conspicuous landmark*, un punto de referencia visible. || Llamativo, va (attracting attention): *a conspicuous tie*, una corbata llamativa. || Notable, insigne (remarkable): *conspicuous gallantry*, notable galantería. || Manifiesto, ta; patente (obvious): *a conspicuous violation*, una violación manifiesta. || — *To be conspicuous by one's absence*, brillar

por su ausencia. || *To make o.s. conspicuous*, llamar la atención. || *To play a conspicuous part*, desempeñar un papel importante.
conspicuousness [—nis] n. Evidencia, *f*. || Lo llamativo.
conspiracy [kən'spirəsi] n. Conspiración, *f*.
conspirator [kən'spirətə*] n. Conspirador, ra.
conspire [kən'spaiə*] v. intr. Conspirar.
— V. tr. Urdir, maquinar (a plot).
constable ['kʌnstəbl] n. Policía, *m*., guardia, *m*. (policeman). || (Ant.) Condestable, *m*. || Administrador (*m*.) de un castillo real.
constabulary [kən'stæbjuləri] n. Policía, *f*.: *the mounted constabulary*, la policía montada.
— Adj. De policía, policial.
Constance ['kɔnstəns] pr. n. Constanza.
constancy ['kɔnstənsi] n. Constancia, *f*. (steadfastness). || Fidelidad, *f*., lealtad, *f*. (loyalty). || Fortaleza, *f*. (endurance). || Invariabilidad, *f*. (stability).
constant ['kɔnstənt] adj. Constante (unceasing, stable). || Leal, fiel (loyal).
— N. MATH. PHYS. Constante, *f*.
Constantine ['kɔnstəntain] pr. n. Constantino, *m*.
Constantinople [ˌkɔnstænti'nəupl] pr. n. GEOGR. Constantinopla.
constellate ['kɔnstəleit] v. tr. Tachonar, sembrar (to stud). || Agrupar (to group). || Constelar (to spangle).
— V. intr. Agruparse. || ASTR. Formar una constelación.
constellation [ˌkɔnstə'leiʃən] n. Constelación, *f*.
consternate ['kɔnstəneit] v. tr. Consternar. || *To be consternated*, consternarse.
consternation [ˌkɔnstə'neiʃən] n. Consternación, *f*.
constipate ['kɔnstipeit] v. tr. Estreñir.
constipation [ˌkɔnsti'peiʃən] n. Estreñimiento, *m*.
constituency [kən'stitjuənsi] n. Distrito (*m*.) electoral, circunscripción, *f*. (area). || Colegio (*m*.) electoral, electorado, *m*. (body of voters).
constituent [kən'stitjuənt] n. Componente, *m*. (component). || Votante, elector, ra (votes). || JUR. Poderdante, *m*.
— Adj. Constitutivo, va; constituyente (component). || Electoral (having power to elect). || Constituyente (modifying a constitution): *constituent assembly*, asamblea constituyente.
constitute ['kɔnstitju:t] v. tr. Constituir (to set up, to make up). || Nombrar (to appoint).
constitution [ˌkɔnsti'tju:ʃən] n. Constitución, *f*. (setting up, physical condition, principles). || Estatutos, *m. pl*. (statutes).
constitutional [ˌkɔnsti'tju:ʃənl] adj. Constitucional. || *Constitutional law*, derecho político.
— N. Paseo (*m*.) higiénico.
constitutionalism [ˌkɔnsti'tju:ʃnəlizəm] n. Constitucionalismo, *m*.
constitutionalist [kɔnst'itju:ʃnəlist] n. Especialista (*m*.) en derecho político (student of constitutionalism). || Partidario (*m*.) del constitucionalismo, constitucionalista, *m. & f*. (supporter of constitutionalism).
constitutionality [ˌkɔnstitju:ʃə'næliti] n. Constitucionalidad, *f*.
constitutionalize [ˌkɔnsti'tju:ʃnəlaiz] v. tr. Constitucionalizar.
constitutionally [ˌkɔnsti'tju:ʃnəli] adv. JUR. Constitucionalmente. || Físicamente.
constitutive ['kɔnstitju:tiv] adj. Constitutivo, va.
constrain [kən'strein] v. tr. Constreñir, obligar, forzar (to compel). || Encerrar (to confine). || Incomodar, violentar (to embarrass).
constrained [—d] adj. Incómodo, da; violento, ta (embarrassed). || Forzado, da; obligado, da (compelled). || Encerrado, da (confined). || *Constrained smile*, risa forzada.
constraint [kən'streint] n. Coacción, *f*., imperativo, *m*., fuerza, *f*. (compulsion). || Turbación, *f*., confusión, *f*., molestia, *f*. (sense of embarrassment). || Encierro, *m*. (restriction of liberty). || Represión, *f*. (of feelings).
constrict [kən'strikt] v. tr. Estrechar (to make narrower). || Oprimir (to compress). || Estrangular (a vein).
constricted [—id] adj. Estrecho, cha; limitado, da: *constricted outlook*, visión estrecha.
constriction [kən'strikʃən] n. Constricción, *f*. || Estrangulamiento, *m*. (of a vein).
constrictive [kən'striktiv] adj. Constrictivo, va.
constrictor [kən'striktə*] n. ANAT. Músculo (*m*.) constrictor, constrictor, *m*. || ZOOL. Constrictor, *m*., boa (*f*.) constrictor.
constringent [kən'strindʒənt] adj. Constringente.
construable [kən'stru:əbl] adj. Analizable (able to be analysed). || Interpretable (interpretable). || Explicable (explicable).
construct [kən'strʌkt] v. tr. Construir.
constructer [kən'strʌktə*] n. Constructor, *m*.
construction [kən'strʌkʃən] n. Construcción, *f*. || Composición (*f*.) escultórica (sculpture). || Estructura, *f*. (structure). || — *To put a good, a bad construction on s.o.'s words*, interpretar bien, mal las palabras de alguien. || *Under construction*, en construcción.
constructional [—l] adj. De la construcción. || Estructural.
constructionist [—ist] n. U. S. Persona (*f*.) que interpreta la ley a su manera.
constructive [kən'strʌktiv] adj. Constructivo, va. || JUR. Por deducción, implícito, ta.
constructiveness [—nis] n. Carácter (*m*.) constructivo.
constructor [kən'strʌktə*] n. Constructor, *m*.
construe [kən'stru:] v. tr. GRAMM. Construir (to combine in syntax). || Analizar (a sentence). || Traducir literalmente (to translate). || Interpretar (to interpret).
— V. intr. GRAMM. Tener construcción gramatical. || *Not to construe*, estar mal construido, da.
consubstantial [ˌkɔnsəb'stænʃəl] adj. REL. Consubstancial.
consubstantiality [ˌkɔnsəbˌstænʃi'æliti] n. REL. Consubstancialidad, *f*.
consubstantiate [ˌkɔnsəb'stænʃieit] v. tr. REL. Unir en una sola y misma substancia.
consubstantiation ['kɔnsəbˌstænʃi'eiʃən] n. REL. Consubstanciación, *f*.
consuetude ['kɔnswitju:d] n. Costumbre, *f*.
consuetudinary [ˌkɔnswi'tju:dinəri] adj. Consuetudinario, ria.
— Pl. n. Devocionario, *m. sing*. (book).
consul ['kɔnsəl] n. Cónsul, *m*.
consular ['kɔnsjulə*] adj. Consular.
consulate ['kɔnsjulit] n. Consulado, *m*.
consulship ['kɔnsəlʃip] n. Consulado, *m*.
consult [kən'sʌlt] v. tr./intr. Consultar.
consultant [kən'sʌltənt] n. JUR. Asesor (*n*.) jurídico. || MED. Especialista, *m*. (doctor). || TECH. Consejero (*m*.) técnico. || *Engineering consultant*, ingeniero consultor.
consultation [ˌkɔnsəl'teiʃən] n. Consulta, *f*.
consultative [kən'sʌltətiv] adj. Consultivo, va.
consultatory [kən'sʌltətəri] adj. Consultivo, va.
consulting [kən'sʌltiŋ] adj. Consultor, ra. || — *Consulting hours*, horas (*f*.) de consulta. || *Consulting office* o *room*, consultorio, *m*., consulta, *f*.
consultor [kən'sʌltə*] n. Consultor, *m*.
consumable [kən'sju:məbl] adj. COMM. Consumible, de consumo.
— N. Artículo (*m*.) de consumo.
consume [kən'sju:m] v. tr. COMM. Consumir. || Comerse (to eat). || Beberse (to drink). || Consumir (fire). || Tomar (time). || *To be consumed with envy*, estar muerto de envidia *or* carcomido por la envidia.
consumer [—ə*] n. Consumidor, ra. || — *Consumer goods*, bienes (*m*.) de consumo. || *Consumer society*, sociedad (*f*.) de consumo. || *Consumer tax*, impuesto (*m*.) de consumo.
consummate [kʌn'sʌmit] adj. Consumado, da: *consummate liar*, mentiroso consumado.
consummate ['kɔnsəmeit] v. tr. Consumar. || Satisfacer (a wish).
consummation [ˌkɔnsə'meiʃən] n. Consumación, *f*. (act of completing). || Culminación, *f*. (fulfilment): *the consummation of a life's work*, la culminación del trabajo de una vida.
consumption [kən'sʌmpʃən] n. Consumo, *m*. (in economy). || Destrucción, *f*. (destruction): *the consumption of the forest by the flames*, la destrucción del bosque por el fuego. || Consumo, *m*., consumición, *f*. (act of consuming). || FAM. Tisis, *f*., consunción, *f*. (tuberculosis). || *Consumption tax*, impuesto (*m*.) de consumo.
consumptive [kən'sʌmptiv] adj. Destructivo, va (destructive). || FAM. Tísico, ca (tuberculous).
— N. FAM. Tísico, ca.
contact ['kɔntækt] n. Contacto, *m*. || — *To be in contact with*, estar en contacto con. || ELECTR. *To break contact*, interrumpir el contacto. || *To come into contact with*, tocar (to touch), chocar con (to clash), entrar en contacto con (to deal with), encontrar (to meet). || *To get into contact with*, ponerse en contacto con. || *To have contacts*, tener relaciones.
— Adj. De contacto: *contact lens*, lente de contacto. || — ELECTR. *Contact breaker*, interruptor, *m*. || *Contact flying*, vuelo (*m*.) con visibilidad. || *We were the contact men of the firm*, éramos los representantes de la empresa.
contact ['kɔntækt] v. tr. Ponerse en contacto con.
contactor [—ə*] n. ELECTR. Interruptor (*m*.) automático.
contagion [kən'teidʒən] n. Contagio, *m*., contaminación, *f*.
contagious [kən'teidʒəs] adj. Contagioso, sa.
contagiousness [—nis] n. Contagiosidad, *f*.
contagium [kən'teidʒiəm] n. Virus, *m*.

— OBSERV. El plural de *contagium* es *contagia*.

contain [kən'tein] v. tr. Contener (to enclose, to include). || Contener (to restrain): *she couldn't contain her laughter*, no pudo contener la risa. || MATH. Ser divisible por. || *To contain o.s.*, contenerse.
container [—ə*] n. Recipiente, *m*. (receptacle). || Contenedor, *m*. (for transporting goods). || Envase, *m*. (package).
containerize [—əraiz] v. tr. Poner en contenedores.
containment [kən'teinmənt] n. Contención, *f*.
contaminant [kən'tæminənt] n. Contaminador, *m*., contaminante, *m*.
contaminate [kən'tæmineit] v. tr. Contaminar (disease, environment). || Contaminar, corromper (morally).

contamination [kən,tæmi'neiʃən] n. Contaminación, *f.*, contagio, *m.* (of a disease). || Contaminación, *f.* (of environment). || Corrupción, *f.*, contaminación, *f.* (corruption).
contemn [kən'tem] v. tr. Desdeñar, despreciar.
contemplate ['kɔntempleit] v. tr. Contemplar (to look attentively). || Considerar, examinar (to consider). || Contar con, prever (to expect). || Estar pensando en (to be considering).
— V. intr. Reflexionar.
contemplation [,kɔntem'pleiʃən] n. Contemplación, *f.* (act of looking). || Contemplación, *f.*, meditación, *f.* || Consideración, *f.*, examen, *m.* (study). || Proyecto, *m.*, perspectiva, *f.* (plan): *no changes are in contemplation*, no hay cambios en perspectiva.
contemplative ['kɔntempleitiv] adj./n. Contemplativo, va.
contemplator ['kɔntempleitə*] n. Contemplador, ra.
contemporaneity [kən,tempərə'ni:iti] n. Contemporaneidad, *f.*
contemporaneous [kən,tempə'reinjəs] adj. Contemporáneo, a.
contemporary [kən'tempərəri] adj./n. Contemporáneo, a.
contemporize [kən'tempəraiz] v. tr. Volver contemporáneo.
contempt [kən'tempt] n. Desprecio, *m.*, desdén, *m.* || — *Contempt of court*, desacato (*m.*) a los tribunales. || *To hold in contempt*, despreciar.
contemptibility [kən,temptə'biliti] n. Bajeza, *f.*
contemptible [kən'temptəbl] adj. Despreciable, desdeñable.
contemptuous [kən'temptjuəs] adj. Despreciativo, va; desdeñoso, sa; despectivo, va (gesture). || Desdeñoso, sa (person).
contemptuousness [—nis] n. Desprecio, *m.*, desdén, *m.* (contempt).
contend [kən'tend] v. intr. Contender, luchar (to struggle). || Disputar (to argue). || Competir (to compete).
— V. tr. Afirmar, sostener: *he contended that he was right*, afirmó que tenía razón. || Disputar (to argue).
contender [—ə*] n. Competidor, ra; contendiente, *m.* & *f.* (rival).
contending [—iŋ] adj. En conflicto; opuesto, ta: *contending passions*, pasiones en conflicto. || Litigante: *contending parties*, partes litigantes.
content [kən'tent] v. tr. Contentar. || *To content o.s. with*, contentarse con.
content [kən'tent] adj. Contento, ta. || *To rest content*, conformarse, darse por contento.
content [kən'tent] n. Contento, *m.* || Voto (*m.*) a favor (vote). || — *Not content*, voto en contra. || *To one's heart's content*, hasta quedarse satisfecho.
content ['kɔntent] n. Contenido, *m.* (substance contained). || Capacidad, *f.* (capacity). || Índice (*m.*) de materias (index). || Contenido, *m.* (of speech, argument, book). || Significado, *m.* (significance). || Contenido, *m.*, proporción, *f.*: *gold content*, contenido en oro, proporción de oro.
contented [kən'tentid] adj. Contento, ta.
contention [kən'tenʃən] n. Contienda, *f.* (struggle). || Controversia, *f.*, discusión, *f.* (controversy). || Opinión, *f.* (opinion).
contentious [kən'tenʃəs] adj. Peleón, ona; pendenciero, ra; belicoso, sa (people). || Discutible (issue). || JUR. Contencioso, sa.
contentiousness [—nis] n. Carácter (*m.*) pendenciero.
contentment [kən'tentmənt] n. Contento, *m.*
conterminal [kɔn'tə:minl] adj. Limítrofe.
conterminous [kɔn'tə:minəs] adj. Limítrofe.
contest ['kɔntest] n. Competición, *f.*, prueba, *f.* (competition). || Concurso, *m.*: *beauty contest*, concurso de belleza. || Lucha, *f.*, contienda, *f.* (struggle). || Controversia, *f.*, discusión, *f.* (controversy). || *Beyond contest*, impugnable, incontestable.
contest [kən'test] v. tr. Impugnar, rebatir (to question). || Disputar (to dispute). || Presentarse como candidato a (election, seat in Parliament).
— V. intr. Luchar, contender.
contestable [kən'testəbl] adj. Discutible.
contestant [kən'testənt] n. Contrincante, *m.* (in a match, fight). || Candidato, ta (in election, etc.). || Concursante, *m.* & *f.*
contestation [kɔntes'teiʃən] n. Controversia, *f.*, disputa, *f.* (controversy). || Impugnación, *f.* (a questioning).
context ['kɔntekst] n. Contexto, *m.*
contextual [kɔn'tekstjuəl] adj. Según el contexto (depending on the context). || Del contexto.
contexture [kɔn'tekstjə*] n. Contextura, *f.*
contiguity [,kɔnti'gju:iti] n. Contiguidad, *f.*
contiguous [kən'tigjuəs] adj. Contiguo, gua.
continence ['kɔntinəns] n. Continencia, *f.*
continent ['kɔntinənt] adj. Continente.
— N. Continente, *m.* || *The Continent*, el continente europeo.
continental [,kɔnti'nentl] adj. Continental. || De Europa continental. || — *Continental drift*, deriva (*f.*) de los continentes. || *Continental shelf*, plataforma (*f.*) continental.
— N. Habitante (*m.*) del continente europeo.
contingency [kən'tindʒənsi] n. Contingencia, *f.*, eventualidad, *f.* (possibility). || Acontecimiento (*m.*) fortuito (event). || PHIL. Contingencia, *f.* || — Pl. Gastos (*m.*) accesorios (expenses).
contingent [kən'tindʒənt] adj. Contingente, eventual (liable to happen). || Aleatorio, ria (aleatory). || Derivado, da (incidental): *risks contingent to mining*, riesgos derivados de la minería. || Supeditado, da; subordinado, da (dependent). || Accidental, fortuito, ta (accidental). || Contingente (in logic). || *Contingent on* o *upon*, dependiente de.
— N. MIL. Contingente, *m.* (of troops). || Representación, *f.*: *the Spanish contingent at the Olympics*, la representación española en los Juegos Olímpicos. || Contingencia, *f.* (which may or may not happen).
continual [kən'tinjuəl] adj. Continuo, nua.
continuance [kən'tinjuəns] n. Permanencia, *f.* (in office, place). || Duración, *f.* (duration). || Continuación, *f.* || Perpetuación, *f.* (of species). || JUR. Aplazamiento, *m.*
continuant [kən'tinjuənt] n. GRAMM. Consonante (*f.*) continua.
— Adj. GRAMM. Continuo, nua (consonant).
continuation [kən,tinju'eiʃən] n. Continuación, *f.*
continuative [kən'tinjuətiv] adj. Continuativo, va.
continuator [kən'tinjueitə*] n. Continuador, ra.
continue [kən'tinju:] v. tr. Continuar (to go on with, to resume, to prolong). || Seguir, continuar: *to continue working*, seguir trabajando. || Mantener (to prolong the employment of s.o.). || Prolongar (to lengthen). || JUR. Aplazar.
— V. intr. Continuar. || Seguir, continuar: *he continues to be chairman*, sigue en la presidencia. || Prolongarse (to extend). || *To be continued*, continuará.
continuity [,kɔnti'nju:iti] n. Continuidad, *f.* || Guión, *m.* (cinema, radio). || Intervalo (*m.*) hablado *or* musical (between two programs). || MATH. Continuidad, *f.* || *Continuity girl*, secretaria (*f.*) de rodaje.
continuous [kən'tinjuəs] adj. Continuo, nua.
continuum [kən'tinjuəm] n. MATH. Cantidad (*f.*) *or* serie (*f.*) continua.

— OBSERV. El plural es *continua* o *continuums*.

contort [kən'tɔ:t] v. tr. Retorcer, torcer.
contortion [kən'tɔ:ʃən] n. Contorsión, *f.* (a twisting). || FIG. Deformación, *f.*: *contortion of the truth*, deformación de la verdad.
contortionist [kən'tɔ:ʃənist] n. Contorsionista, *m.* & *f.*
contour ['kɔntuə*] n. Contorno, *m.* (outline). || Curva (*f.*) de nivel (of map). || — *Contour line*, curva de nivel. || *Contour map*, mapa topográfico.
contour ['kɔntuə*] v. tr. Levantar curvas de nivel en (to mark with contours). || Trazar [una carretera] siguiendo las curvas de nivel. || Contornear, perfilar.
contraband ['kɔntrəbænd] n. Contrabando, *m.* || *Contraband of war*, contrabando de guerra.
— Adj. De contrabando.
contrabandist ['kɔntrəbændist] n. Contrabandista, *m.* & *f.*
contrabass ['kɔntrə'beis] n. MUS. Contrabajo, *m.* (instrument).
contrabassist [—ist] n. Contrabajo, *m.* (musician).
contrabassoon ['kɔntrəbə'su:n] n. MUS. Contrafagot, *m.* (instrument).
contraception [,kɔntrə'sepʃən] n. Contracepción, *f.*
contraceptive [,kɔntrə'septiv] adj. Anticonceptivo, va; contraceptivo, va.
— N. Contraceptivo, *m.*
contract ['kɔntrækt] n. Contrato, *m.*: *contract of purchase and sale*, contrato de compraventa. || Contrato, *m.* (in bridge). || Contrata, *f.* (of public works).
contract [kən'trækt] v. tr. Contraer (debts). || Contratar (to make a contract). || Coger (a chill, a cold). || Fruncir (eyebrow). || Contraer (to shrink, to shorten). || Contraer (muscles).
— V. intr. Contraerse (to shrink). || Hacer un contrato (to enter into a contract).
contractile [kən'træktail] adj. Contráctil.
contractility [,kɔntræk'tiliti] n. Contractilidad, *f.*
contracting [kən'træktiŋ] adj. Contratante: *contracting party*, parte contratante.
— N. Contratación, *f.* (engagement).
contraction [kən'trækʃən] n. MED. Contracción, *f.* || GRAMM. Contracción, *f.*
contractive [kən'træktiv] adj. Contractivo, va.
contractor [kən'træktə*] n. Contratista, *m.* (person or firm undertaking work). || ANAT. Músculo (*m.*) que se contrae.
contractual [kən'træktjuəl] adj. Contractual.
contradict [,kɔntrə'dikt] v. tr. Contradecir. || *To contradict o.s.*, contradecirse.
contradiction [,kɔntrə'dikʃən] n. Contradicción, *f.* || *To be a contradiction in terms*, ser contradictorio.
contradictious [,kɔntrə'dikʃəs] adj. Contradictorio, ria (contrary). || Contradictor, ra (person).
contradictorily [,kɔntrə'diktərili] adv. Contradictoriamente.
contradictoriness [,kɔntrə'diktərinis] n. Contradicción, *f.*, carácter (*m.*) contradictorio.
contradictory [,kɔntrə'diktəri] adj. Contradictorio, ria.
— N. Contradictoria, *f.* (in logic).
contradistinction [,kɔntrədis'tiŋkʃən] n. Oposición, *f.*, contraste, *m.*
contradistinguish [,kɔntrədis'tiŋgwiʃ] v. tr. Diferenciar, contrastar.

contrail [ˈkɔntreil] n. Estela, *f.*
contraindicant [ˌkɔntrəˈindikənt] n. Contraindicación, *f.*
contraindicate [ˌkɔntrəˈindikeit] v. tr. Contraindicar.
contraindication [ˌkɔntrəindiˈkeiʃən] n. Contraindicación, *f.*
contraindicative [ˌkɔntrəinˈdikətiv] adj. Contraindicante.
contralto [kənˈtræltəu] n. Contralto, *m.*
— Adj. De contralto.
contraposition [ˌkɔntrəpəˈziʃən] n. Contraposición, *f.*
contraption [kənˈtræpʃən] n. Artefacto, *m.*, aparato, *m.*, artilugio, *m.* (contrivance). || FAM. Chisme, *m.* (thing).
contrapuntal [ˌkɔntrəˈpʌntl] adj. MUS. De contrapunto.
contrapuntist [ˈkɔntrəpʌntist] n. Contrapuntista, *m.*
contrariety [ˌkɔntrəˈraiəti] n. Oposición, *f.* || Inconsistencia, *f.* (inconsistency).
contrarily [ˈkɔntrərili] adv. Contrariamente.
contrariness [ˈkɔntrərinis] n. Espíritu (*m.*) de contradicción. || Oposición, *f.*
contrariwise [ˈkɔntrəriwaiz] adv. Al contrario (on the contrary). || En sentido opuesto (the opposite way). || Viceversa.
contrary [ˈkɔntrəri] adj. Contrario, ria (opposed). || Que siempre está llevando la contraria: *he was a very contrary child*, era un niño que siempre estaba llevando la contraria. || *Don't be so contrary!*, ¡no me lleves la contraria!
— N. Lo contrario. || — Pl. TECH. Impurezas, *f.*, cuerpos (*m.*) extraños. || — *On the contrary*, al contrario, por el contrario. || *Quite the contrary!*, ¡todo lo contrario! || *To the contrary*, en contra: *I have nothing to say to the contrary*, no tengo nada que decir en contra.
— Adv. Contrariamente: *contrary to public opinion*, contrariamente a lo que la opinión pública cree.
contrast [ˈkɔntrɑːst] n. Contraste, *m.*: *in contrast*, por contraste. || *To be a contrast to*, contrastar con.
contrast [kənˈtrɑːst] v. tr. Contrastar, hacer contrastar.
— V. intr. Contrastar.
contrasting [kənˈtrɑːstiŋ] adj. Contrastante.
contrasty [kənˈtrɑːsti] adj. Que tiene mucho contraste (in optics).
contravene [ˌkɔntrəˈviːn] v. tr. JUR. Contravenir (to infringe). || Ir en contra de (to go against). || Negar (to deny). || Oponerse a (to oppose).
contravener [—ə*] n. JUR. Contraventor, ra.
contravening [—iŋ] adj. JUR. Contraventor, ra.
contravention [ˌkɔntrəˈvenʃən] n. JUR. Contravención, *f.*
contredanse [ˈkɔ̃ntrədɑ̃ns] n. Contradanza, *f.*
contretemps [ˈkɔ̃ntrətɑ̃ːŋ] n. Contratiempo, *m.*
contribute [kənˈtribjuːt] v. tr. Contribuir [con] (to donate). || Escribir (newspaper articles). || Aportar (to provide information, etc.).
— V. intr. Contribuir. || Colaborar (to a newspaper).
contribution [ˌkɔntriˈbjuːʃən] n. Contribución, *f.* || Artículo, *m.*, colaboración, *f.* (to a newspaper). || Intervención, *f.* (in discussion). || Aportación, *f.* (of funds, information, etc.). || *To lay under contribution*, hacer contribuir.
contributive [kənˈtribjutiv] adj. Contributivo, va; contribuyente.
contributor [kənˈtribjutə*] n. Contribuyente, *m.* & *f.* || Colaborador, ra (of a newspaper, etc.).
contributory [—ri] adj. Contribuyente, cooperante. || — *Contributory negligence*, responsabilidad (*f.*) de la víctima en un accidente. || *Contributory pension*, pensión (*f.*) de retiro.
— N. Accionista (*m.*) que en caso de liquidación de una sociedad debe contribuir al pago de las deudas.
contrite [ˈkɔntrait] adj. Contrito, ta.
contrition [kənˈtriʃən] n. Contrición, *f.*
contrivable [kənˈtraivəbl] adj. Realizable, factible (feasible). || Imaginable (imaginable).
contrivance [kənˈtraivəns] n. Invención, *f.* (invention). || Artefacto, *m.*, aparato, *m.* (mechanical appliance). || Ingenio, *m.* (resourcefulness): *it required considerable contrivance to get us there in time*, necesitamos mucho ingenio para llegar allí a tiempo. || Invento, *m.*, invención, *f.*: *his excuse was a mere contrivance*, su excusa era una pura invención.
contrive [kənˈtraiv] v. tr. Inventar, idear: *he contrived a means of getting out of classes*, ideó una estratagema para no ir a clase; *he contrived a new kind of tool*, inventó un nuevo tipo de herramienta. || Conseguir (to manage): *he contrived to raise his family on very little money*, consiguió sacar adelante a su familia con muy poco dinero.
contrived [—d] adj. Artificial.
contriver [—ə*] n. Autor, ra.
control [kənˈtrəul] n. Control, *m.* (direction, restraint, regulation). || Autoridad, *f.* (authority). || Control, *m.*, dominación, *f.* (power). || Control, *m.*, comprobación, *f.*, verificación, *f.* || Control, *m.* (checkpoint in rally, etc.). || Testigo, *m.* (standard of comparison). || Espíritu (*m.*) que controla al médium. || — Pl. Mandos, *m.* (of aircraft, vehicle). || — *Birth control*, regulación (*f.*) de nacimientos, limitación (*f.*) de la natalidad, control de natalidad. || *Control board*, tablero (*m.*) de mando. || *Control column*, palanca (*f.*) de mando. || *Control desk*, pupitre, *m.*, consola, *f.* || *Control knob*, botón, *m.* [de mando]. || *Control panel*, tablero (*m.*) de instrumentos. || *Control point*, punto (*m.*) de control. || *Control room*, sala (*f.*) de control. || *Control tower*, torre (*f.*) de control. || *Dual control*, doble mando, *m.* || *Remote control*, mando (*m.*) a distancia. || *The epidemic is beyond our control*, la epidemia está fuera de nuestro control. || *To be in control*, tener el mando. || *To be out of control*, estar fuera de control. || *To be under control*, estar bajo control. || *To get under control*, conseguir dominar. || *To lose control of*, perder el control de. || *To lose control of o.s.*, perder el control de sí mismo.
control [kənˈtrəul] v. tr. Controlar (to restrain, to regulate): *control your temper*, controla el mal humor. || Tener autoridad sobre *or* bajo su mando: *he controls two thousand men*, tiene autoridad sobre dos mil hombres. || Controlar (to direct): *he controls the steel industry*, controla la industria del acero. || Verificar, comprobar, controlar (to verify). || Manejar (vehicle). || TECH. Regular, controlar (to regulate). | Poner en marcha, accionar (to work).
controllable [—əbl] adj. Controlable.
controlled [—d] adj. Controlado, da. || Dirigido, da (economy).
controller [—ə*] n. Director, *m.* (director). || COMM. Interventor, *m.* || Inspector, *m.* (inspector). || Control, *m.* (controlling device). || ELECTR. Combinador, *m.* || AVIAT. Controlador, *m.*: *air traffic controller*, controlador del tráfico aéreo.
controlling [—iŋ] adj. Predominante: *controlling interest*, interés predominante. || Dirigente (governing). || Determinante (decisive).
controversial [ˌkɔntrəˈvəːʃəl] adj. Polémico, ca; controvertible, discutible (disputable). || Discutidor, ra; polémico, ca (person).
controversialist [ˌkɔntrəˈvəːʃəlist] n. Controversista, *m.* & *f.*, polemista, *m.* & *f.*
controversy [ˈkɔntrəvəːsi] n. Controversia, *f.*, polémica, *f.*, discusión, *f.* || *Beyond* o *without controversy*, incuestionable, incontrovertible.
controvert [ˈkɔntrəvəːt] v. tr. Controvertir, discutir, debatir (to discuss). || Contradecir (to deny).
controvertible [—əbl] adj. Controvertible.
controvertist [ˈkɔntrəvəːtist] n. Controversista, *m.* & *f.*, polemista, *m.* & *f.*
contumacious [ˌkɔntjuˌmeiʃəs] adj. Contumaz.
contumacy [ˈkɔntjuməsi] n. Contumacia, *f.*
contumelious [ˌkɔntjuˈmiːljəs] adj. Afrentoso, sa; ofensivo, va.
contumely [ˈkɔntjuːmli] n. Contumelia, *f.*, ofensa, *f.*, afrenta, *f.*
contuse [kənˈtjuːz] v. tr. Contusionar.
contusion [kənˈtjuːʒən] n. Contusión, *f.*
conundrum [kəˈnʌndrəm] n. Adivinanza, *f.* (riddle). || Enigma, *m.* (problem).
conurbation [ˌkɔnəːˈbeiʃən] n. Conurbación, *f.*
convalesce [ˌkɔnvəˈles] v. intr. Convalecer.
convalescence [ˌkɔnvəˈlesns] n. Convalecencia, *f.*
convalescent [ˌkɔnvəˈlesnt] adj. Convaleciente. || *Convalescent home*, casa (*f.*) de convalecencia, clínica (*f.*) de reposo.
— N. Convaleciente, *m.* & *f.*
convection [kənˈvekʃən] n. PHYS. Convección, *f.*
convector [kənˈvektə*] n. Estufa (*f.*) de convección.
convene [kənˈviːn] v. tr. Convocar (to call together). || Citar (to summon).
— V. intr. Reunirse.
convenience [kənˈviːnjəns] n. Conveniencia, *f.*: *marriage of convenience*, matrimonio de conveniencia. || Ventaja, *f.* (advantage): *living near one's work is a great convenience*, vivir cerca de donde uno trabaja es una gran ventaja. || Comodidad, *f.*, confort, *m.* (comfort). || Dispositivo (*m.*) útil (useful device). || — Pl. Servicios, *m.* (toilets). || — *At your convenience*, cuando guste, cuando le sea posible. || *At your earliest convenience*, tan pronto como lo sea posible. || *It is a great convenience*, es muy cómodo. || *To make a convenience of s.o.*, abusar de alguien. || *To suit one's convenience*, convenirle a uno.
convenient [kənˈviːnjənt] adj. Cómodo, da (handy). || Conveniente (suitable). || Práctico, ca (tool). || Oportuno, na (time). || Bien situado, da (place). || *If it is convenient for you*, si le conviene.
convent [ˈkɔnvənt] n. Convento, *m.*
convention [kənˈvenʃən] n. Convenio, *m.* (agreement between nations). || Convención, *f.* (usage). || Congreso, *m.*, asamblea, *f.* (conference). || — Pl. Conveniencias, *f.* (polite practices). || Convencionalismo, *m. sing.* (conventionalism).
conventional [—əl] adj. Convencional (deriving from convention, not original). || Clásico, ca (traditional): *conventional weapons*, armas clásicas.
conventionalism [—əlizəm] n. Convencionalismo, *m.*
conventionalist [—əlist] n. Convencionalista, *m.* & *f.*
conventionality [kənˌvenʃəˈnæliti] n. Convencionalismo, *m.*
conventionalize [kənˈvenʃənəlaiz] v. tr. Hacer convencional (to make conventional). || ARTS. Estilizar (to stylize).
conventual [kənˈventjuəl] adj. Conventual.
— N. REL. Miembro (*m.*) de un convento.

converge [kən'və:dʒ] v. intr. Converger, convergir.
— V. tr. Hacer converger *or* convergir.
convergence [kən'və:dʒəns] n. Convergencia, *f.*
convergency [—i] n. Convergencia, *f.*
convergent [kən'və:dʒənt] or **converging** [kən'və:dʒiŋ] adj. Convergente.
conversable [kən'və:səbl] adj. Sociable, tratable (sociable). || Conversador, ra (fond of conversation). || A propósito para la conversación.
conversance [kən'və:səns] or **conversancy** [—i] n. Familiaridad, *f.* || Conocimiento, *m.* (acquaintance through study).
conversant [kən'və:sənt] adj. Versado, da; entendido, da (informed about): *conversant with the matter*, versado en la materia. || Familiarizado, da; conocedor, ra (well acquainted). || *To become conversant with*, familiarizarse con.
conversation [,kɔnvə'seiʃən] n. Conversación, *f.* [*Amer.*, plática, *f.*]: *to make conversation*, dar conversación. || JUR. Trato (*m.*) carnal. || — Pl. Conversaciones, *f.* || — *Conversation piece*, tema (*m.*) de conversación (something that arouses conversation), interior, *m.*, escena (*f.*) de interior (genre painting). || *Criminal conversation*, adulterio, *m.*
conversational [—l] adj. Locuaz, hablador, ra (person). || Familiar, de la conversación (tone).
conversationalist [—list] n. Conversador, ra; hablador, ra.
converse ['kɔnvə:s] n. Proposición (*f.*) recíproca (in logic). || Lo opuesto, lo contrario (opposite). || MATH. Recíproca, *f.*
— Adj. Opuesto, ta; contrario, ria.
converse [kən'və:s] v. intr. Conversar, hablar [*Amer.*, platicar].
conversely [kɔn'və:sli] adv. A la inversa.
conversion [kən'və:ʃən] n. Conversión, *f.*, transformación, *f.* (from one state to another). || JUR. Apropiación (*f.*) ilícita (of property). || SP. Transformación, *f.* || REL. COMM. MATH. Conversión, *f.*
convert [kən'və:t] v. tr. Convertir, transformar (to change, to transform). || REL. COMM. MATH. Convertir. || SP. Transformar (a try in rugby). || JUR. Apropiarse ilícitamente.
— V. intr. Convertirse. || SP. Transformar un ensayo.
convert ['kɔnvə:t] n. Converso, sa.
converter [kən'və:tə*] n. TECH. Convertidor, *m.* || ELECTR. Transformador, *m.*
convertibility [kən,və:tə'biliti] n. Convertibilidad, *f.*
convertible [kən'və:təbl] adj. Convertible (able to be converted). || Transformable. || COMM. Convertible. || GRAMM. Intercambiable (interchangeable). || Descapotable (car).
— N. Descapotable, *m.* (car).
convex ['kɔn'veks] adj. Convexo, xa.
convexity [kɔn'veksiti] n. Convexidad, *f.*
convexo-convex [kɔn'veksəu'kɔnveks] adj. Biconvexo, xa.
convey [kən'vei] v. tr. Transportar, llevar (to carry). || Transmitir (to transmit, to pass on). || Sugerir, dar a entender: *what does his speech convey to you?*, ¿qué te sugiere su discurso? || Expresar, dar (meaning). || JUR. Hacer cesión de, transferir.
conveyable [kən'veiəbl] adj. Transportable (transportable). || Comunicable (communicable). || Transmisible (transmissible). || Conductible (current). || JUR. Transferible, transmisible.
conveyance [kən'veiəns] n. Transporte, *m.* (means and act of conveyance). || Transmisión, *f.* (transmission). || JUR. Traspaso, *m.* | Escritura (*f.*) de traspaso (deed).
conveyancer [—ə*] n. JUR. Notario (*m.*) que hace escrituras de traspaso.
conveyancing [—iŋ] n. Redacción (*f.*) de una escritura de traspaso.
conveyer or **conveyor** [kən'veiə*] n. Transportador, *m.* || Cinta (*f.*) transportadora. || Conductor, *m.* || JUR. Cedente, *m.* || *Conveyor belt*, cinta transportadora.
convict ['kɔnvikt] n. Presidiario, ria (criminal serving a sentence). || Convicto, ta (one convicted of crime).
convict [kən'vikt] v. tr. Declarar culpable, condenar (to prove guilty). || Hacer admitir (of an error, etc.). || Traicionar (to betray). || Condenar (to condemn).
conviction [kən'vikʃən] n. JUR. Condena, *f.*, sentencia, *f.* | Declaración (*f.*) de culpabilidad. || Convicción, *f.* (strong belief). || *To carry conviction*, ser convincente.
convince [kən'vins] v. tr. Convencer.
convincible [kən'vinsəbl] adj. Que se deja convencer.
convincing [kən'vinsiŋ] adj. Convincente.
convivial [kən viviəl] adj. Amigo de la buena mesa. || Alegre, sociable, jovial, festivo, va (person). || Alegre (occasion, atmosphere).
convocation [,kɔnvəu'keiʃən] n. Convocación, *f.* (calling together). || Asamblea, *f.*, junta, *f.* (academic, legislative, etc.). || REL. Sínodo, *m.*
convoke [kən'vəuk] v. tr. Convocar.
convolute ['kɔnvəlu:t] adj. Retorcido, da; enroscado, da (coiled, rolled on itself). || ZOOL. Enrollado, da.
— N. Enroscadura, *f.* (a coil).
convolute ['kɔnvəlu:t] v. intr. Enrollarse.
— V. tr. Enrollar.
convolution [,kɔnvə'lu:ʃən] n. Circunvolución, *f.*
convolve [kən'vɔlv] v. tr. Arrollar, enrollar.
— V. intr. Arrollarse, enrollarse.
convolvulaceae [kənvɔlvju'leiʃii] pl. n. BOT. Convolvuláceas, *f.*
convolvulaceous [kən,vɔlvju'leiʃəs] adj. BOT. Convolvuláceo, a.
convolvulus [kən'vɔlvjuləs] n. BOT. Enredadera, *f.*

— OBSERV. El plural de *convolvulus* es *convolvuluses* o *convolvuli*.

convoy ['kɔnvɔi] n. Convoy, *m.* || Escolta, *f.* (escort). || *Under* o *in convoy*, en convoy.
convoy ['kɔnvɔi] v. tr. Escoltar.
convoyer [—ə*] n. Escolta, *f.* (boat).
convulse [kən'vʌls] v. tr. Convulsionar (to throw into convulsions). || Hacer dislocarse de risa (to make laugh). || — *To be convulsed with anger, fear*, descomponerse de ira, de miedo. || *To be convulsed with laughter*, dislocarse de risa. || *To be convulsed with pain*, contorsionarse de dolor.
convulsion [kən'vʌlʃən] n. Convulsión, *f.* (involuntary spasm). || Conmoción, *f.* (earthquake, etc.). || — Pl. Conmociones, *f.* (political, social upheaval). | Carcajadas, *f.* (uncontrollable laughter).
convulsionary [kən'vʌlʃənəri] adj. Convulsionario, ria.
convulsive [kən'vʌlsiv] adj. Convulsivo, va.
cony ['kəuni] n. Piel (*f.*) de conejo. || Conejo, *m.* (rabbit).
coo [ku:] n. Arrullo, *m.*
— Interj. ¡Toma!, ¡anda!, ¡vaya!
coo [ku:] v. intr. Arrullar (pigeons, lovers). || Hacer gorgoritos (babies).
cooing [—iŋ] n. Arrullos, *m. pl.*
cook [kuk] n. Cocinero, ra. || FIG. *Too many cooks spoil the broth*, muchas manos en un plato hacen mucho garabato.
cook [kuk] v. tr. Guisar, cocinar. || Asar (to roast). || FAM. Falsificar (the accounts). | Urdir, maquinar (a plot). || — FAM. *He is cooked*, está aviado, está perdido. || *To cook a meal*, hacer *or* preparar una comida. || *To cook lunch*, hacer la comida. || FAM. *To cook up*, inventar: *to cook up an excuse*, inventar una excusa; preparar, tramar: *he is cooking something up*, está tramando algo.
— V. intr. Cocinar, guisar: *I like cooking*, me gusta cocinar. || Guisarse (food). || Ser cocinero, ra. || FAM. *What's cooking?*, ¿qué sucede?, ¿qué ocurre?
cookbook [—buk] n. U. S. Libro (*m.*) de cocina.
cooker ['kukə*] n. Cocina, *f.* (stove). || Olla, *f.*: *a pressure cooker*, una olla de presión, una olla exprés. || Fruta (*f.*) para cocer (fruit to be eaten cooked). || Verdura (*f.*) que cuece fácilmente.
cookery ['kukəri] n. Arte (*m.*) culinario, cocina, *f.*
cookery book [—buk] n. Libro (*m.*) de cocina.
cookhouse ['kukhaus] n. Cocina *f.* [de un barco].
cookie ['kuki] n. U. S. Galleta, *f.* || U. S. FAM. Tipo, *m.* (fellow). | Guapa, *f.* (girl).
cooking ['kukiŋ] n. Cocción, *f.* (act). || Cocina, *f.*: *French cooking*, cocina francesa. || *To do the cooking*, guisar.
— Adj. De cocina. || Para cocer (fruit).
cooky ['kuki] n. See COOKIE. || FAM. Cocinero, ra (cook).
cool [ku:l] adj. Fresco, ca (refreshingly cold, chilly): *it is cool*, hace fresco. || Tranquilo, la (calm). || Frío, a (unenthusiastic): *to be cool towards s.o.*, ser frío con alguien. || Insolente; fresco, ca (impudent). || Sereno, na; frío, a (in a crisis). || Frío, a (colours). || Fresco, ca (garments). || FAM. Fenómeno, na (excellent). || — FAM. *As cool as a cucumber*, más fresco que una lechuga. | *It costs a cool ten thousand*, cuesta la friolera de diez mil. || FIG. *Keep cool* o *play it cool*, no te pongas nervioso, tómatelo con calma. || *Keep in a cool place*, conservar en un lugar fresco. || FAM. *To be a cool hand* o *a cool one*, ser un fresco. || *To go* o *to get cool*, enfriarse (a liquid), refrescarse (a person). || *To leave to get cool*, dejar enfriarse.
— N. Frescor, *m.*, fresco, *m.* (fresh air). || *In the cool*, al fresco.
cool [ku:l] v. tr. Enfriar. || Refrigerar (to refrigerate). || FIG. Calmar. || FAM. *Cool it!*, ¡calma!
— V. intr. Enfriarse. || Refrescarse (weather). || FIG. Calmarse. || — *To cool down*, enfriarse (machines), calmarse (persons), enfriarse (feelings). || *To cool off*, enfriarse (enthusiasm), calmarse (persons).
coolant ['ku:lənt] n. Líquido (*m.*) refrigerante.
cooler ['ku:lə*] n. Enfriador, *m.* || Refrigerador, *m.* (refrigerator). || FAM. Bebida (*f.*) refrescante, refresco, *m.* (drink). | Sombra, *f.*, chirona, *f.* (prison).
cool-headed ['ku:l'hedid] adj. Sereno, na.
coolie or **cooly** ['ku:li] n. Coolí, *m.*, culi, *m.*
cooling ['ku:liŋ] adj. Refrescante. || TECH. Refrigerante, refrigerador, ra; de refrigeración: *cooling system*, sistema de refrigeración.
— N. Refrigeración, *f.*
coolish ['ku:liʃ] adj. Fresquito, ta.
coolly ['ku:li] adv. Fríamente. || Tranquilamente (calmly). || FAM. Con frescura, con descaro.
coolness ['ku:lnis] n. Frescor, *m.*, fresco, *m.* (quality of being cool). || Frialdad, *f.* (lack of enthusiasm). || Serenidad, *f.*, calma, *f.*, frialdad, *f.* (self-assurance). || Sangre (*f.*) fría (composure). || Frescura, *f.* (boldness).
cooly ['ku:li] n. Coolí, *m.*, culi, *m.*
coombe [ku:m] n. Valle (*m.*) estrecho.
coon [ku:n] n. U. S. ZOOL. Mapache, *m.* || FAM. Negro, *m.*

coop [ku:p] n. Gallinero, *m.* (for poultry). || Caseta, *f.* (cabin). || FIG. FAM. Cárcel, *f.*, chirona, *f.* || FIG. *To fly the coop*, fugarse, escaparse.

coop [ku:p] v. tr. Encerrar. || FIG. FAM. *To coop up*, encerrar, enjaular (to confine).

co-op (U. S. **coop**) [ˈkəuɔp] n. FAM. Cooperativa, *f.* || *Co-op apartment*, copropiedad, *f.*

cooper [ˈku:pə*] n. Tonelero, *m.* || Fabricante (*m.*) de vinos (wine merchant).

cooper [ˈku:pə*] v. tr. Fabricar *or* reparar [toneles *or* barriles]. || Embarrilar (to put into casks).

cooperage [ˈku:pəridʒ] n. Tonelería, *f.*

cooperate [kəuˈɔpəreit] v. intr. Cooperar.

cooperation [kəuˌɔpəˈreiʃən] n. Cooperación, *f.*

cooperative [kəuˈɔpərətiv] adj. Cooperativo, va. || Servicial, dispuesto a ayudar (helpful).
— N. Cooperativa, *f.*

cooperator [kəuˈɔpəreitə*] n. Cooperador, ra.

coopery [ˈku:pəri] n. Tonelería, *f.*

co-opt [kəuˈɔpt] v. tr. Cooptar, elegir por votación colectiva.

co-optation [ˌkəuɔpˈteiʃən] n. Cooptación, *f.*, elección (*f.*) por votación colectiva.

co-option [kəuˈɔpʃən] n. Cooptación, *f.*, elección (*f.*) por votación colectiva.

coordinate [kəuˈɔ:dinit] adj. Igual, semejante (equal). || Coordinado, da (coordinated). || — *Coordinate geometry*, geometría analítica. || *Coordinate paper*, papel cuadriculado.
— N. MATH. Coordenada, *f.* || Igual, *m.* & *f.*, semejante, *m.* & *f.*

coordinate [kəuˈɔ:dineit] v. tr. Coordinar.
— V. intr. Coordinarse.

coordinating [kəuˈɔ:dineitiŋ] adj. Coordinador, ra.

coordination [kəuˌɔ:diˈneiʃən] n. Coordinación, *f.*

coordinative [kəuˈɔ:dinətiv] adj. Coordinativo, va.

coordinator [kəuˈɔ:dineitə*] n. Coordinador, ra.

coot [ku:t] n. Fúlica, *f.* (bird). || FAM. Memo, ma (idiot).

cootie [ˈku:ti] n. U. S. FAM. Piojo, *m.*

cop [kɔp] n. FAM. Poli, *m.* (copper). || Canilla, *f.* (of yarn). || *Cops and robbers*, justicias y ladrones (game).

cop [kɔp] v. tr. FAM. Cargarse: *he copped 20 years*, se cargó 20 años. | Pillar, pescar, coger (to seize). || — FAM. *He was* o *he got copped by the police*, le pilló la policía. | *To cop it*, ganársela, pagarla: *now you'll cop it*, ahora te la vas a ganar.

copaiba [kɔˈpaibə] n. BOT. Copaiba, *f.*

copal [ˈkəupəl] n. Copal, *m.*

coparcenary [ˈkəuˈpɑ:sinəri] n. Participación (*f.*) en una herencia. || Copropiedad, *f.*

coparcener [ˈkəuˈpɑ:sinə*] n. Coheredero, ra.

co-participant [ˈkəu-pɑ:ˈtisipənt] n. Copartícipe, *m.* & *f.*

copartner [ˈkəuˈpɑ:tnə*] n. Copartícipe, *m.*, consocio, *m.*

copartnership [—ʃip] n. Asociación, *f.* || Coparticipación, *f.*

cope [kəup] n. REL. Capa (*f.*) pluvial (cape). || ARCH. Albardilla, *f.* (coping). || FIG. Bóveda, *f.* (of heaven).

cope [kəup] v. tr. REL. Poner la capa pluvial. || Poner albardilla (a wall). || Poner una bóveda (to vault).
— V. intr. FAM. Arreglárselas: *don't worry, I can cope*, no te preocupes, ya me las arreglaré. | Dar abasto: *I have so many things to do that I can't cope*, tengo tantas cosas que hacer que no puedo dar abasto. || *To cope with a situation*, hacer frente a *or* enfrentarse con una situación. || *We can't cope with the children*, no podemos con los niños.

copeck [ˈkəupek] n. Copec, *m.*, kopeck, *m.*

Copernicus [kəuˈpə:nikəs] pr. n. Copérnico, *m.*

copestone [ˈkəupstəun] n. Piedra (*f.*) de albardilla *or* de remate. || FIG. Remate, *m.*

copier [ˈkɔpiə*] n. Imitador, ra (imitator). || Copista, *m.* (copyist). || Multicopista, *f.* (machine).

copilot [ˈkəuˈpailət] n. AVIAT. Copiloto, *m.*

coping [ˈkəupiŋ] n. Albardilla, *f.* || *Coping stone*, piedra (*f.*) de albardilla *or* de remate. || FIG. Remate, *m.*

copious [ˈkəupjəs] adj. Copioso, sa; abundante (plentiful). || Prolífico, ca (an author). || Rico, ca (language). || Prolijo, ja (style).

copiousness [—nis] Abundancia, *f.*, profusión, *f.*, copiosidad, *f.*

coplanar [ˌkəuˈpleinə*] adj. MATH. *Coplanar forces*, fuerzas coplanarias.

copper [ˈkɔpə*] n. Cobre, *m.* (metallic element). || FAM. Perra, *f.* (small coin). | Penique, *m.* (penny). | Calderilla, *f.*, dinero (*m.*) suelto (small change). || Caldera, *f.* (boiler). || FAM. Poli, *m.* (policeman).
— Adj. De cobre (made of copper). || Cobrizo, za (copper-coloured). || — *Copper pyrites*, calcopirita, *f.* || *Copper sulphate*, sulfato (*m.*) de cobre.

copper [ˈkɔpə*] v. tr. Cubrir *or* revestir con cobre.

copperas [ˈkɔpərəs] n. Caparrosa (*f.*) verde.

copperbottomed [ˈkɔpəˌbɔtəmd] adj. Con fondo de cobre.

copper-coloured (U. S. **copper-colored**) [ˈkɔpəˌkʌləd] adj. Cobrizo, za.

copperplate [ˈkɔpəpleit] n. Lámina (*f.*) de cobre (plate of copper for engraving). || Grabado (*m.*) en cobre (impression). || Letra (*f.*) caligrafiada (handwriting).

coppersmith [ˈkɔpəsmiθ] n. Calderero (*m.*) en cobre.

coppery [ˈkɔpəri] adj. Cobrizo, za.

coppice [ˈkɔpis] n. Soto, *m.*, bosquecillo, *m.*

copra [ˈkɔprə] n. BOT. Copra, *f.*

coprolite [ˈkɔprəlait] n. GEOL. Coprolito, *m.*

coprology [kəˈprɔlədʒi] n. Escatología, *f.*

copse [kɔps] n. Soto, *m.*, bosquecillo, *m.*

Copt [kɔpt] n. Copto, ta.

Coptic [ˈkɔptik] adj. Copto, ta.
— N. Copto, *m.* (language).

copula [ˈkɔpjulə] n. Cópula, *f.*

copulate [ˈkɔpjuleit] v. intr. Copular.

copulation [ˌkɔpjuˈleiʃən] n. Cópula, *f.*

copulative [ˈkɔpjulətiv] adj. Copulativo, va. || *Copulative verb*, verbo copulativo.
— N. Cópula, *f.*, palabra (*f.*) copulativa.

copy [ˈkɔpi] n. Copia, *f.* (reproduction, duplicate). || Original, *m.*, manuscrito, *m.*, texto, *m.* (of an article). || Ejemplar, *m.* (of book). || Número, *m.*, ejemplar, *m.* (of paper). || Modelo, *m.* (pattern). || Asunto, *m.*: *the case made good copy for the reporters*, el proceso fue un buen asunto para los reporteros. || — *Carbon copy*, papel (*m.*) carbón. || JUR. *Certified copy*, copia legalizada. || *Fair copy*, copia en limpio. || *Rough copy*, borrador, *m.* || *To make a fair copy of*, pasar en limpio.

copy [ˈkɔpi] v. tr./intr. Copiar. || Copiar, imitar.

copybook [ˈkɔpibuk] n. Cuaderno (*m.*) de caligrafía *or* de ejercicios. || COMM. Libro (*m.*) copiador. || — FIG. *Copybook maxims*, tópicos, *m.*, lugares (*m.*) comunes. | *To blot one's copybook*, manchar su reputación.

copycat [ˈkɔpikæt] n. FAM. Copión, ona; mono (*m.*) de imitación.

copydesk [ˈkɔpidesk] n. Mesa (*f.*) del redactor.

copy-edit [ˈkɔpiˌedit] v. tr. Corregir [el manuscrito].

copy editor [ˈkɔpiˌeditə*] n. Corrector (*m.*) de manuscritos. || Redactor (*m.*) jefe (of a newspaper).

copyholder [ˈkɔpiˌhəuldə*] n. PRINT. Atendedor, ra.

copying ink [ˈkɔpiiŋˌiŋk] n. PRINT. Tinta (*f.*) de copiar.

copyist [ˈkɔpiist] n. Copista, *m.*

copyreader [ˈkɔpiˌri:də*] n. Corrector (*m.*) de manuscritos.

copyright [ˈkɔpirait] n. "Copyright", *m.*, propiedad (*f.*) literaria. || Derechos (*m. pl.*) de autor (royalties). || *Copyright reserved*, reservado el derecho de reproducción.
— Adj. Protegido por la propiedad literaria.

copyright [ˈkɔpirait] v. tr. Registrar [una publicación] en el registro de la propiedad literaria.

copywriter [ˈkɔpiˈraitə*] n. Redactor (*m.*) de textos publicitarios.

coquet or **coquette** [kɔˈket] v. intr. Coquetear (to flirt). || FIG. Acariciar (to toy with): *to coquet with a suggestion*, acariciar una sugerencia.

coquetry [ˈkɔkitri] n. Coquetería, *f.*

coquette [kɔˈket] n. Coqueta, *f.*

coquettish [kɔˈketiʃ] adj. Coqueto, ta; coquetón, ona.

cor! [kɔ:*] interj. POP. ¡Diablos!

coracle [ˈkɔrəkl] n. Barquilla (*f.*) de cuero *or* de hule.

coral [ˈkɔrəl] n. Coral, *m.*
— Adj. De coral, coralino, na. || — *Coral reef*, arrecife (*m.*) de coral. || ZOOL. *Coral snake*, coral, *f.*, coralillo, *m.*

coralliferous [kɔrəˈlifərəs] adj. Coralífero, ra.

coralline [ˈkɔrəlain] n. Coralina, *f.*
— Adj. Coralino, na.

corallite [ˈkɔrəlait] n. Coral (*m.*) fósil (fossil coral). || Mármol (*m.*) coralino.

coralloid [ˈkɔrəlɔid] adj. Coralino, na.

cor anglais [ˈkɔ:rɑ̃ŋˈglei] n. MUS. Corno (*m.*) inglés.

corbel [ˈkɔ:bəl] n. ARCH. Ménsula, *f.*

corbel [ˈkɔ:bəl] v. tr. ARCH. Poner ménsulas.
— V. intr. Formar un voladizo.

corbelling [—iŋ] n. Saledizo, *m.*

corbie [ˈkɔ:bi] n. Cuervo, *m.* (bird). || *Corbie gable*, hastial escalonado.

cord [kɔ:d] n. Cuerda, *f.* (string, rope). || Cordón, *m.* (of habit). || Canutillo, *m.* (on textiles). || Pana, *f.* (corduroy). || Cordón, *m.* (insulated wire). || FIG. Lazo, *m.*, vínculo, *m.* || — Pl. Pantalón (*m. sing.*) de pana (trousers). || — ANAT. *Spinal cord*, médula (*f.*) espinal. | *Umbilical cord*, cordón (*m.*) umbilical. | *Vocal cords*, cuerdas (*f.*) vocales.

cord [kɔ:d] v. tr. Atar con cuerda.

cordage [ˈkɔ:didʒ] n. Cordaje, *m.* (ropes). || MAR. Jarcias, *f. pl.*

cordate [ˈkɔ:deit] adj. En forma de corazón.

corded [ˈkɔ:did] adj. Atado con cuerdas (fastened). || Perlado, da; "perlé" (cotton). || De canutillo (fabric).

cordial [ˈkɔ:djəl] adj. Cordial.
— N. Cordial, *m.*

cordiality [ˌkɔ:diˈæliti] n. Cordialidad, *f.*

cordillera [ˌkɔ:diˈljeərə] n. Cordillera, *f.*

córdoba [ˈkɔ:dəbə] n. Córdoba, *m.* (monetary unit of Nicaragua).

Córdoba [ˈkɔ:dəbə] pr. n. Córdoba (in Argentina).

cordon [ˈkɔ:dn] n. Cordón, *m.* || *Cordon bleu*, cocinero (*m.*) de primera clase (cook).

cordon [ˈkɔ:dn] v. tr. *To cordon off*, acordonar.

Cordova [ˈkɔ:dəvə] pr. n. GEOGR. Córdoba (Spanish town).

Cordovan [—n] adj. Cordobés, esa. || De cuero cordobés (made of leather).
— N. Cuero (*m.*) cordobés, cordobán, *m.* (leather). || Cordobés, esa (from Cordova).

corduroy [ˈkɔːdərɔi] n. Pana, *f.* || — Pl. Pantalones (*m.*) de pana (trousers).
— Adj. De pana. || U. S. *Corduroy road,* camino (*m.*) de troncos.

cordwood [ˈkɔːdwud] n. Haz (*m.*) de leña. || Leña, *f.*

core [kɔː*] n. Bot. Corazón, *m.* (of fruit). || Corazón, *m.* (of timber). || Fig. Corazón, *m.*, núcleo, *m.*, centro, *m.* (innermost part). | Núcleo, *m.*, foco, *m.* (of resistance, etc.). | Esencia, *f.* (essence or gist). || Med. Clavo, *m.* (of a boil). | Foco, *m.* (of infection). || Geol. Núcleo, *m.* | Testigo, *m.* (drilling). || Electr. Núcleo, *m.* || Alma, *f.* (of ropes, cables). || — Fig. *Rotten to the core,* podrido hasta la médula. | *Spaniard to the core,* español hasta los huesos, español hasta la médula.

core [kɔː*] v. tr. Quitar el corazón de.

coreligionary [ˈkəuriˈlidʒənəri] or **coreligionist** [ˈkəuriˈlidʒənist] n. Correligionario, ria.

corer [ˈkɔːrə*] n. Despepitadora, *f.*, deshuesadora, *f.*

corespondent [ˈkəurisˌpɔndənt] n. Cómplice (*m.*) del demandado (in divorce).

corf [kɔːf] n. Min. Vagoneta, *f.* || Cesta, *f.* (in fishing).

corgi [ˈkɔːgi] n. Zool. Perro (*m.*) galés.

coriaceous [ˌkɔriˈeiʃəs] adj. Coriáceo, a.

coriander [ˌkɔriˈændə*] n. Bot. Coriandro, *m.*, cilantro, *m.*, culantro, *m.*

corindon [kəˈrindən] n. Corindón, *m.*

Corinth [ˈkɔrinθ] pr. n. Geogr. Corinto.

Corinthian [kəˈrinθiən] adj./n. Corintio, tia.

corium [ˈkɔːriəm] n. Anat. Dermis, *f.*, piel, *f.*

— Observ. El plural de *corium* es *coria.*

cork [kɔːk] n. Bot. Corcho, *m.* || Corcho, *m.*, tapón, *m.* (stopper). || Corcho, *m.*, flotador, *m.* (for fishing). || — *Cork jacket,* chaleco (*m.*) salvavidas. || Bot. *Cork oak,* alcornoque, *m.* || Bot. *Cork tree,* alcornoque, *m.* || *To draw the cork of a bottle,* descorchar una botella.

cork [kɔːk] v. tr. Poner el tapón, taponar (to stop a bottle). || Tiznar con corcho quemado (to blacken).

corkage [ˈkɔːkidʒ] n. Derecho (*m.*) que se paga en un restaurante por el descorche de una botella que no es de la casa.

corked [kɔːkt] adj. Que sabe a corcho (wine). || Con tapón, taponado, da (bottle). || Tiznado con corcho quemado (face).

corker [ˈkɔːkə*] n. Fam. Bola, *f.*, mentira, *f.* (lie). | Tipo (*m.*) formidable. | Cosa (*f.*) formidable. | Argumento (*m.*) irrefutable. || Máquina (*f.*) de taponar.

corking [ˈkɔːkiŋ] adj. Fam. Estupendo, da; formidable.

corklike [ˈkɔːklaik] adj. Corchoso, sa.

corkscrew [ˈkɔːkskruː] n. Sacacorchos, *m. inv.*
— Adj. De caracol: *a corkscrew staircase,* una escalera de caracol. || En espiral (curl).

corkscrew [ˈkɔːkskruː] v. intr./tr. Girar en espiral (to curl). || Serpentear (a path, river, etc.).

cork-tipped [ˈkɔːktipt] adj. Con boquilla *or* filtro de corcho.

corkwood [ˈkɔːkwud] n. Bot. Balsa, *f.*

corky [ˈkɔːki] adj. De corcho, acorchado, da (like cork). || Bot. Suberoso, sa. || Fig. Caprichoso, sa.

corm [kɔːm] n. Bot. Bulbo, *m.*

cormorant [ˈkɔːmərənt] n. Zool. Cormorán, *m.*, mergo, *m.*, cuervo (*m.*) marino.

corn [kɔːn] n. U. S. Maíz, *m.* (maize). || Grano, *m.* (grain of pepper, etc.) || Trigo, *m.* (wheat). || Avena, *f.* (oats). || Granos, *m. pl.*, cereales, *m. pl.* (cereals). || Med. Callo, *m.* || Fam. Chiste (*m.*) malo (bad joke). || U. S. Fam. Whisky (*m.*) de maíz (drink). || *Corn on the cob,* maíz en la mazorca.

corn [kɔːn] v. tr. Salar.

cornaceae [kɔːˈneisii] pl. n. Bot. Córneas, *f.*

corn bread [ˈkɔːnbred] n. U. S. Borona, *f.*, pan (*m.*) de maíz.

corn cake [ˈkɔːnkeik] n. Borona, *f.*

corn chandler [ˈkɔːnˌtʃɑːndlə*] n. Triguero, *m.*

corncob [ˈkɔːnkɔb] n. Mazorca, *f.* (central part of an ear of maize). || Pipa (*f.*) hecha de mazorca (pipe).

corn cockle [ˈkɔːnˌkɔkl] n. Neguilla, *f.*, neguillón, *m.*

corncrake [ˈkɔːnkreik] n. Zool. Rey (*m.*) de codornices (bird).

corncrib [ˈkɔːnkrib] n. Granero, *m.*

corn cutter [ˈkɔːnˌkʌtə*] n. Cortacallos, *m. inv.*

cornea [ˈkɔːniə] n. Córnea, *f.*

corned beef [ˈkɔːndˈbiːf] n. Carne (*f.*) en conserva *or* en lata.

cornel [ˈkɔːnl] n. Bot. Cornejo, *m.*

cornelian [kɔːˈniːljən] n. Cornalina, *f.*

corneous [ˈkɔːniəs] adj. Córneo, a; calloso, sa.

corner [ˈkɔːnə*] n. Esquina, *f.* (outside angle): *the corner house,* la casa de la esquina. || Rincón, *m.* (inside angle). || Pico, *m.* (of a table, etc.). || Curva, *f.* (bend, curve). || Fig. Rincón, *m.*, parte, *f.* (region). || Cantonera, *f.* (for protecting photographs, edges, etc.). || Sp. Córner, *m.*, saque (*m.*) de esquina (in football). || Rabillo, *m.* (of the eye). || Comisura, *f.* (of mouth). || Monopolio, *m.* (in commerce). || — *Corner piece,* rinconera, *f.* || *Done in a corner,* hecho a escondidas. || *In the chimney corner,* al amor de la lumbre. || *It's round the corner,* está a la vuelta de la esquina. || *Out of the corner of one's eye,* con el rabillo del ojo. || Fig. *To be in a tight corner,* estar en un apuro *or* en un aprieto. || Fig. *To cut corners,* tomar atajos (to shorten the distance), economizar esfuerzos *or* dinero. || *To drive s.o. into a corner,* arrinconar, acorralar. || Fig. *To go to the four corners of the earth,* ir a las cinco partes del mundo. | *To rub the corners off. s.o.,* pulir a alguien. || *To turn the corner,* doblar la esquina (of a street), salir del apuro *or* del mal paso.

corner [ˈkɔːnə*] v. tr. Poner cantoneras (to provide a book with corners). || Poner en una esquina (to set in a corner). || Acorralar, arrinconar (to drive someone into a corner). || Monopolizar, acaparar: *to corner the market,* acaparar el mercado. || Abordar (to accost). || Fig. Poner en un apuro *or* en un aprieto.
— V. intr. Hacer esquina (a house). || Doblar una esquina. || Tomar una curva (a car).

cornered [—d] adj. Esquinado, da; angulado, da; que tiene ángulos. || Fig. En un apuro, en un aprieto (in trouble). || Arrinconado, da; acorralado, da. || — *A three-cornered hat,* un sombrero de tres picos. || *Four-cornered competition,* competición entre cuatro participantes.

corner kick [ˈkɔːnə*kik] n. Sp. Córner, *m.*, saque (*m.*) de esquina.

cornerstone [ˈkɔːnəstəun] n. Arch. Piedra (*f.*) angular.

cornerways [ˈkɔːnəweiz] adv. Diagonalmente.

cornerwise [ˈkɔːnəwaiz] adv. Diagonalmente.

cornet [ˈkɔːnit] n. Mus. Corneta, *f.* || Cucurucho, *m.* (paper, ice cream, etc.). || Mar. Insignia, *f.*, corneta, *f.* (flag). || Toca, *f.* (of nun).

cornetist or **cornettist** [ˈkɔːnitist] n. Corneta, *m.*

cornfield [ˈkɔːnfiːld] n. Trigal, *m.*, campo (*m.*) de trigo (of wheat). || U. S. Maizal, *m.*, campo (*m.*) de maíz.

cornflakes [ˈkɔːnfleiks] pl. n. Copos (*m.*) de maíz.

cornflour [ˈkɔːnflauə*] n. Harina (*f.*) de maíz.

cornflower [ˈkɔːnflauə*] n. Bot. Aciano, *m.*

corn husk [ˈkɔːnhʌsk] n. U. S. Vaina (*f.*) de maíz.

cornice [ˈkɔːnis] n. Arch. Cornisa, *f.*

Cornish [ˈkɔːniʃ] adj. De Cornualles.
— N. Idioma (*m.*) de Cornualles.

corn liquor [ˈkɔːnˌlikə*] n. U.S. Whisky (*m.*) de maíz.

cornmeal [ˈkɔːnmiːl] n. Harina (*f.*) de maíz.

corn pone [ˈkɔːn pəun] n. U. S. Borona, *f.*, pan (*m.*) de maíz.

corn silk [ˈkɔːnsilk] n. Barbas (*f. pl.*) de maíz.

cornstalk [ˈkɔːnstɔːk] n. Bot. Tallo (*m.*) del maíz.

cornstarch [ˈkɔːnstɑːtʃ] n. U. S. Maicena, *f.*

corn sugar [ˈkɔːnˌʃugə*] n. U. S. Azúcar (*m.*) de almidón de maíz.

corn syrup [ˈkɔːnˌsirəp] n. U. S. Glucosa, *f.*

cornucopia [ˌkɔːnjuˈkəupjə] n. Cornucopia, *f.* cuerno (*m.*) de la abundancia.

Cornwall [ˈkɔːnwəl] n. Cornualles, *m.*

corn whiskey [ˈkɔːnˈwiski] n. U. S. Whisky (*m.*) de maíz.

corny [ˈkɔːni] adj. Productor de trigo (of wheat). || U. S. Productor de maíz. || Fam. Viejo, ja (old). | Rancio, cia; trillado, da; sobado, da (stale). | Malo, la (bad): *a corny joke,* un chiste malo. || Med. Calloso, sa.

corolla [kəˈrɔlə] n. Bot. Corola, *f.*

corollary [kəˈrɔləri] n. Math. Corolario, *m.* || Fig. Consecuencia, *f.*, corolario, *m.*
— Adj. Consecuente.

corona [kəˈrəunə] n. Corona, *f.*

— Observ. El plural de *corona* en inglés es *coronae.*

coronal [ˈkɔrənəl] n. Guirnalda, *f.* (wreath). || Cerco, *m.* (of gold, stones, etc.).

coronary [ˈkɔrənəri] adj. Coronario, ria (like a crown). || Anat. Coronario, ria: *coronary artery,* arteria coronaria; *coronary thrombosis,* trombosis coronaria.

coronate [ˈkɔrənit] adj. Coronado, da.

coronation [ˌkɔrəˈneiʃən] n. Coronación, *f.*

coroner [ˈkɔrənə*] n. Oficial (*m.*) de justicia de la Corona que investiga los casos de muerte violenta o accidentes [especie de juez de primera instancia].

coronet [ˈkɔrənit] n. Corona, *f.* (of nobility). || Tortillo, *m.* (of a baron). || Diadema, *f.* (decorative headdress for ladies). || Zool. Corona (*f.*) del casco.

corozo [kəˈrəuzə] n. Bot. Corozo, *m.*, corojo, *m.*

corpora [ˈkɔpərə] pl. n. See corpus.

corporal [ˈkɔːpərəl] adj. Corporal: *corporal punishment,* castigo corporal.
— N. Rel. Corporal, *m.* || Mil. Cabo, *m.*: *corporal of the guard,* cabo de guardia.

corporality [ˌkɔːpəˈræliti] n. Corporalidad, *f.*

corporate [ˈkɔːpərit] adj. Corporativo, va (of a corporation). || Colectivo, va. || Combinado, da: *corporate efforts,* esfuerzos combinados. || Jur. Constituido, da (body). | Constituido en sociedad (business). | Municipal (land, office). || — *Corporate name,* nombre (*m.*) social. || *Corporate town,* municipalidad, *f.* || *Status of body corporate,* personalidad jurídica.

corporation [ˌkɔːpəˈreiʃən] n. Corporación, *f.* || Sociedad (*f.*) anónima. || Fam. Panza, *f.*, barriga, *f.* (abdomen). || *Municipal corporation,* ayuntamiento, *m.*

corporative [ˈkɔːpərətiv] adj. Corporativo, va.

corporativism [—izəm] n. Corporativismo, *m.*

corporativist [ˈkɔːpərətivist] adj./n. Corporativista.

corporeal [kɔːˈpɔːriəl] adj. Corpóreo, a. || Jur. Material.

corporeality [kɔːpɔːriˈæliti] or **corporeity** [ˈkɔːpəˈriiti] n. Corporeidad, *f.*, materialidad, *f.*

corposant [ˈkɔːpəznt] n. Fuego (*m.*) de San Telmo.

corps [kɔː] inv. n. Mil. Cuerpo, *m.* || — *Corps de ballet,* cuerpo de ballet. || *Corps diplomatique,* cuerpo

diplomático. || *Medical corps*, cuerpo de sanidad. || *Service Corps*, cuerpo de intendencia.
corpse [kɔ:ps] n. Cadáver, *m.*
corpsman [kɔ:mən] n. U. S. MIL. Miembro (*m.*) del cuerpo de sanidad. | Ambulanciero, *m.*
— OBSERV. El plural de *corpsman* es *corpsmen*.
corpulence [ˈkɔ:pjuləns] or **corpulency** [—i] n. Corpulencia, *f.*
corpulent [ˈkɔ:pjulənt] adj. Corpulento, ta.
corpus [ˈkɔ:pəs] n. Cuerpo, *m.*, recopilación, *f.* || Capital, *m.* || — ANAT. *Corpus callosum*, cuerpo calloso. || *Corpus Christi*, Corpus Cristi, *m.* || *Corpus delicti*, cuerpo del delito.
— OBSERV. El plural de *corpus* es *corpora*.
corpuscle [ˈkɔ:pʌsl] n. ANAT. Corpúsculo, *m.*, glóbulo, *m.*: *red corpuscles*, glóbulos rojos. || PHYS. Corpúsculo, *m.* (atom, etc.)
corpuscular [kɔ:ˈpʌsjulə*] adj. Corpuscular: *corpuscular theory*, teoría corpuscular.
corpuscule [ˈkɔ:pʌsl] n. See CORPUSCLE.
corral [kɔ:ˈrɑ:l] n. Corral, *m.*
corral [kɔ:ˈrɑ:l] v. tr. Encorralar, acorralar (animals). || Cercar con (wagons). || FAM. Hacerse con (to lay hold of).
correct [kəˈrekt] adj. Correcto, ta (behaviour, person). || Exacto, ta (accurate). || Bueno, na (taste). || Justo, ta (right). || — *Am I correct in telling that...?*, ¿no es cierto que...? || *They are perfectly correct*, tienen toda la razón.
correct [kəˈrekt] v. tr. Corregir.
correction [kəˈrekʃən] n. Corrección, *f.* || — *House of correction*, reformatorio, *m.*, correccional, *m.* || *Under correction*, salvo error u omisión.
correctional [kəˈrekʃənl] adj. Correccional.
correctitude [kəˈrektitju:d] n. Corrección, *f.*
corrective [kəˈrektiv] adj. Correctivo, va. || *Corrective glasses*, gafas correctoras.
— N. Correctivo, *m.*
correctness [kəˈrektnis] n. Corrección, *f.* (of behaviour, of style). || Rectitud, *f.* (of judgment). || Exactitud, *f.* (accuracy).
corrector [kəˈrektə*] n. Corrector, *m.*
correlate [ˈkɔrileit] n. Correlativo, *m.*
correlate [ˈkɔrileit] v. tr. Poner en correlación, correlacionar.
— V. intr. Tener correlación, estar en correlación.
correlation [ˌkɔriˈleiʃən] n. Correlación, *f.*
correlative [kɔˈrelətiv] adj. Correlativo, va.
— N. Correlativo, *m.*
correspond [ˌkɔrisˈpɔnd] v. intr. Corresponder.
correspondence [ˌkɔrisˈpɔndəns] adj. Correspondencia, *f.* || — *Correspondence course*, curso (*m.*) por correspondencia. || *Correspondence school*, escuela (*f.*) por correspondencia.
correspondency [—i] n. Correspondencia, *f.*
correspondent [ˌkɔrisˈpɔndənt] n. Corresponsal, *m.* & *f.* (of a newspaper, a firm).
— Adj. Correspondiente.
corresponding [ˌkɔrisˈpɔndiŋ] adj. Correspondiente. || *Corresponding member*, miembro (*m.*) correspondiente.
corrida [kɔˈri:də] n. Corrida, *f.* (bullfight).
corridor [ˈkɔridɔ:*] n. Pasillo, *m.*, corredor, *m.* || GEOGR. Corredor, *m.*
corrie [ˈkɔri] n. GEOG. Circo, *m.*
corrigenda [ˌkɔriˈdʒendə] pl. n. Erratas, *f.*, fe (*f. sing.*) de erratas.
corrigendum [ˈkɔriˈdʒendəm] n. Errata, *f.*
— OBSERV. El plural es *corrigenda*.
corrigible [ˈkɔridʒəbl] adj. Corregible, enmendable.
corroborant [kəˈrɔbərənt] adj. Corroborante.
— N. MED. Tónico, *m.*, corroborante, *m.*
corroborate [kəˈrɔbəreit] v. tr. Corroborar.
corroboration [kəˌrɔbəˈreiʃən] n. Corroboración, *f.*
corroborative [kəˈrɔbərətiv] adj. Corroborativo, va.
corroborator [kəˈrɔbəreitə*] n. Testigo, *m.*
corroboratory [kəˈrɔbərətəri] adj. U. S. Corroborativo, va.
corrode [kəˈrəud] v. tr. Corroer.
— V. intr. Corroerse.
corrodible [kəˈrəudibl] adj. Corrosible.
corrosion [kəˈrəuʒən] n. Corrosión, *f.*
corrosive [kəˈrəusiv] adj. Corrosivo, va.
— N. Corrosivo, *m.*
corrosiveness [—nis] n. Corrosividad, *f.*
corrugate [ˈkɔrugeit] v. tr. Ondular (cardboard, iron). || Estriar (glass). || Gofrar, estampar (paper).
corrugation [ˌkɔruˈgeiʃən] n. Estrías, *f. pl.* || Ondulado, *m.* (of cardboard, iron). || Gofrado, *m.* (of paper).
corrupt [kəˈrʌpt] adj. Corrompido, da; corrupto, ta. || Estragado, da (taste). || Corrompido, da; pervertido, da (perverted). || Venal (open to bribery). || *Corrupt practices*, corrupción, *f. sing.*
corrupt [kəˈrʌpt] v. tr. Corromper. || Sobornar (to bribe). || Alterar (a text).
— V. intr. Corromperse.
corrupter [—ə*] n. Corruptor, ra.
corruptibility [kəˌrʌptəˈbiliti] n. Corruptibilidad, *f.*
corruptible [kəˈrʌptəbl] adj. Corruptible.
corrupting [kəˈrʌptiŋ] adj. Corruptor, ra.
corruption [kəˈrʌpʃən] n. Corrupción, *f.*
corruptive [kəˈrʌptiv] adj. Corruptivo, va.
corruptness [kəˈrʌptnis] n. Venalidad, *f.*, corruptela, *f.*, corrupción, *f.*
corsage [kɔ:ˈsɑ:ʒ] n. Cuerpo, *m.* (of a dress). || Ramillete, *m.* (flowers).
corsair [ˈkɔ:sɛə*] n. Corsario, *m.*
corselet [ˈkɔ:slit] n. Coselete, *m.* (armour). || Faja, *f.* (undergarment). || ZOOL. Coselete, *m.*
corset [ˈkɔ:sit] n. Corsé, *m.* (for women). || MED. Corsé (*m.*) ortopédico.
corsetière [ˌkɔ:səˈtjɛə*] n. Corsetera, *f.*
Corsica [ˈkɔ:sikə] pr. n. GEOGR. Córcega, *f.*
Corsican [—n] adj./n. Corso, sa.
corslet [ˈkɔ:slit] n. See CORSELET.
cortège [kɔ:ˈteiʒ] n. Cortejo, *m.*, séquito, *m.*, comitiva, *f.*
Cortes [ˈkɔ:tes] pl. n. Cortes, *f.* (Spanish parliament).
cortex [ˈkɔ:teks] ANAT. BOT. Corteza, *f.*
— OBSERV. El plural es *cortices* o *cortexes*.
cortical [ˈkɔ:tikəl] adj. ANAT. Cortical.
cortisone [ˈkɔ:tizəun] n. MED. Cortisona, *f.*
corundum [kəˈrʌndəm] n. MIN. Corindón, *m.*
Corunna [kɔˈrʌnə] pr. n. GEOGR. La Coruña.
coruscate [ˈkɔrəskeit] v. intr. Centellear, brillar. || FIG. Brillar.
coruscation [ˌkɔrəsˈkeiʃən] n. Brillo, *m.*, centelleo, *m.* (brilliance). || FIG. Destello, *m.* (of wit).
corvette (U. S. **corvet**) [kɔ:ˈvet] n. MAR. Corbeta, *f.*
corvina [kɔ:ˈvinə] n. ZOOL. Corvina, *f.* (fish).
corymb [ˈkɔrimb] n. BOT. Corimbo, *m.*
coryphaeus [ˌkɔriˈfi:əs] n. Corifeo, *m.*
— OBSERV. El plural de *coryphaeus* es *coryphaei*.
coryphée [ˌkɔriˈfei] n. Primer bailarín, *m.*, primera bailarina, *f.*
coryza [kəˈraizə] n. MED. Coriza, *f.*, catarro (*m.*) nasal.
cos [kɔs] n. Lechuga (*f.*) romana.
cosecant [ˈkəuˈsi:kənt] n. MATH. Cosecante, *f.*
cosh [kɔʃ] n. Porra, *f.*, cachiporra, *f.*
cosh [kɔʃ] v. tr. Dar un porrazo a.
cosher [ˈkɔʃə*] v. tr. Mimar.
cosignatory [ˈkəuˈsignətəri] n. Cosignatario, ria.
cosily [ˈkəuzili] adv. Confortablemente, cómodamente (comfortably). || Cariñosamente (affectionately).
cosine [ˈkəusain] n. MATH. Coseno, *m.*
cosiness [ˈkəuzinis] n. Comodidad, *f.*
cosmetic [kɔzˈmetik] adj. Cosmético, ca.
— N. Cosmético, *m.*
cosmetician [ˈkɔzməˈtiʃən] n. Vendedor (*m.*) de productos de belleza.
cosmic [ˈkɔzmik] adj. Cósmico, ca: *cosmic rays*, rayos cósmicos; *cosmic dust*, polvo cósmico; *cosmic radiation*, radiación cósmica.
cosmogonic [ˌkɔzməˈgɔnik] adj. Cosmogónico, ca.
cosmogony [kɔzˈmɔgəni] n. Cosmogonía, *f.*
cosmographer [kɔzˈmɔgrəfə*] n. Cosmógrafo, *m.*
cosmographic [ˌkɔzməˈgræfik] adj. Cosmográfico, ca.
cosmography [kɔzˈmɔgrəfi] n. Cosmografía, *f.*
cosmological [ˌkɔzməˈlɔdʒikəl] adj. Cosmológico, ca.
cosmology [kɔzˈmɔlədʒi] n. Cosmología, *f.*
cosmonaut [ˈkɔzmənɔ:t] n. Cosmonauta, *m.*
cosmonautics [ˌkɔzməˈnɔ:tiks] n. Cosmonáutica, *f.*
cosmopolitan [ˌkɔzməˈpɔlitən] adj./n. Cosmopolita.
cosmopolitanism [—izəm] n. Cosmopolitismo, *m.*
cosmopolite [kɔzˈmɔpəlait] n. Cosmopolita, *m.* & *f.*
cosmorama [ˌkɔzməˈrɑ:mə] n. Cosmorama, *m.*
cosmos [ˈkɔzmɔs] n. Cosmos, *m.*
Cossack [ˈkɔsæk] adj./n. Cosaco, ca.
cosset [ˈkɔsit] n. U. S. Animal (*m.*) favorito.
cost [kɔst] n. Costo, *m.*, coste, *m.*: *cost price*, precio de coste. || Precio, *m.* (price). || Gastos, *m. pl.* (expenses): *cost free*, sin gastos. || — Pl. JUR. Costas, *f.* || — *At all costs* o *at any cost*, cueste lo que cueste, a toda costa. || FIG. *At great cost*, tras grandes esfuerzos. || *At small cost*, a buen precio. || *At the cost of*, a costa de. || *Cost of living*, coste de vida. || *Cost-of-living allowance* o *cost-of-living bonus*, plus (*m.*) de carestía de vida. || *He'll do it whatever the cost*, lo hará cueste lo que cueste. || *To count the cost*, considerar los riesgos. || *To one's cost*, a expensas de uno: *I learnt it to my cost*, lo supe a mis expensas.
cost* [kɔst] v. tr. Calcular el coste de.
— V. intr. Costar: *it cost 1 000 pesetas*, costó 1 000 pesetas. || Valer, costar: *how much does this cost?*, ¿cuánto vale esto? || FIG. Costar: *his foolishness cost him his life*, su insensatez le costó la vida. || *Cost what it may*, cueste lo que cueste.
— OBSERV. Pret. & p. p. **cost.**
cost accounting [—əˈkauntiŋ] n. Contabilidad (*f.*) de costos.
costal [ˈkɔstl] adj. Costal (relating to ribs).
co-star [ˈkəustɑ:] n. Cada uno de los actores principales en una película.
Costa Rica [ˈkɔstəˈrikə] pr. n. GEOGR. Costa Rica, *f.*
Costa Rican [—n] adj./n. Costarriqueño, ña; costarricense.
coster [ˈkɔstə*] or **costermonger** [—ˌmʌŋgə*] n. Vendedor (*m.*) ambulante.
costing [ˈkɔstiŋ] n. Cálculo (*m.*) del coste. || Fijación (*f.*) del precio.
costive [ˈkɔstiv] adj. Estreñido, da (constipated). || FIG. FAM. Tacaño, na (stingy).

costiveness [—nis] n. Estreñimiento, *m.* || Fig. fam. Tacañería, *f.* (stinginess).
costless [ˈkɔstlis] adj. Gratis.
costliness [ˈkɔstlinis] n. Alto precio, *m.*, precio (*m.*) elevado, lo caro. || Fig. Suntuosidad, *f.*
costly [ˈkɔstli] adj. Caro, ra; costoso, sa. || U. S. Fig. Suntuoso, sa.
cost-plus [ˈkɔstˈplʌs] n. Precio (*m.*) de coste más el beneficio.
costume [ˈkɔstju:m] n. Traje, *m.* (style of clothing, etc.): *local costume*, traje típico de la región, traje regional. || Disfraz, *m.* (disguise): *costume ball*, baile de disfraces. || Traje (*m.*) sastre (lady's suit). || Traje (*m.*) de baño (bathing suit). || — Pl. Theatr. Vestuario, *m. sing.* || — *Costume jewellery*, bisutería, *f.*, joyas (*f. pl*). de fantasía. || *Costume piece*, obra (*f.*) de teatro de época.
costume [ˈkɔstju:m] v. tr. Vestir (to dress). || Disfrazar (to disguise).
costumier (U. S. **costumer**) [kɔsˈtju:miə*] n. Theatr. Encargado (*m.*) del vestuario.
cosy [ˈkəuzi] adj. Confortable, cómodo, da (comfortable): *it is very cosy here*, aquí se está muy confortable. || Cariñoso, sa; agradable (people). || Íntimo, ma; acogedor, ra (place). || *To play it cosy*, obrar con cautela.
— N. Cubreterera, *m.* (tea cosy).
cot [kɔt] n. Cuna, *f.* (children's bed). || U. S. Cama (*f.*) de campaña, catre, *m.* (camp bed). || Hamaca, *f.* (hammock). || Cabaña, *f.* (shelter). || Dedil, *m.* (fingerstall).
cotangent [ˈkəuˈtændʒənt] n. Math. Cotangente, *f.*
cote [kəut] n. Palomar, *m.* (dovecote). || Redil, *m.* (sheepcot).
co-tenant [ˈkəuˈtenənt] n. Coinquilino, na.
coterie [ˈkəutəri] n. Tertulia, *f.*, peña, *f.* (people meeting regularly). || Círculo, *m.* (literary). || Camarilla, *f.* (clique).
cothurnus [kəˈθə:nəs] n. Coturno, *m.* (buskin).

— Observ. El plural de *cothurnus* es *cothurni*.

cotillion [kəˈtiljən] n. Cotillón, *m.* (ball).
cotta [ˈkɔtə] n. Sobrepelliz, *f.*
cottage [ˈkɔtidʒ] n. Casa (*f.*) de campo (country house). || Chalet, *m.*, chalé, *m.* (villa). || Choza, *f.* (farm labourer's dwelling).
cottage cheese [—ˈtʃi:z] n. Requesón, *m.*
cottage industry [—ˈindʌstri] n. Industria (*f.*) casera.
cottage loaf [—ˈləuf] n. Pan (*m.*) casero.
cottager [ˈkɔtidʒə*] n. Labrador, *m.* || Inquilino (*m.*) de una casa de campo.
cotter [ˈkɔtə*] n. Tech. Chaveta, *f.* || *Cotter pin*, pasador (*m.*) de chaveta.
cotton [ˈkɔtn] n. Algodón, *m.*: *printed cotton*, algodón estampado; *absorbent cotton*, algodón hidrófilo. || Algodonero, *m.* (plant).
— Adj. De algodón, algodonero, ra: *cotton industry*, industria algodonera.
cotton [ˈkɔtn] v. intr. *To cotton on* o *up to*, atraer (to attract), coger cariño a (s.o.), comprender, captar (a meaning), aficionarse a (to take a liking).
cotton batting [—ˈbætiŋ] n. Algodón (*m.*) en rama.
cotton belt [—belt] n. U. S. Zona (*f.*) algodonera.
cotton candy [—ˈkændi] n. Algodón, *m.* (sweet).
cotton gin [—dʒin] n. Desmotadora, *f.*
cotton plant [—plɑ:nt] n. Algodonero, *m.*
cotton plantation [—plɑ:nˌteiʃən] n. Algodonal, *m.*, plantación (*f.*) de algodón.
cotton print [—print] n. Estampado (*m.*) de algodón.
cottonseed [—si:d] n. Semilla (*f.*) de algodón.
cottontail [—teil] n. Zool. Conejo (*m.*) de rabo blanco.
cotton thistle [—ˌθisl] n. Bot. Cardo (*m.*) borriquero.
cotton waste [—weist] n. Borra (*f.*) de algodón.
cottonwood [—wud] n. Bot. Álamo (*m.*) de Virginia.
cotton wool [—wul] n. Algodón (*m.*) en rama, guata, *f.* || Med. Algodón (*m.*) hidrófilo. || Fig. *He was brought up in cotton wool*, fue criado entre algodones.
cottony [ˈkɔtni] adj. Algodonoso, sa.
cotyledon [ˌkɔtiˈli:dən] n. Bot. Cotiledón, *m.*
couch [kautʃ] n. Sofá, *m.* (a sofa). || Lecho, *m.*, cama, *f.* (bed). || Capa (*f.*) de cebada (in brewing). || Guarida, *f.* (animal's lair). || *Couch grass*, grama, *f.*
couch [kautʃ] v. tr. Expresar (to express). || Poner en ristre (a lance). || Acostar (in bed). || Redactar (in writing). || Fig. Disimular, encubrir. || *To couch o.s.*, acostarse.
— V. intr. Tumbarse (to lay o.s. down). || Emboscarse (to hide). || Acostarse (to have sexual intercourse). || Recogerse (an animal). || *To couch down*, agacharse.
couchant [ˈkautʃənt] adj. Herald. Acostado, da.
cougar [ˈku:gə*] n. Zool. Puma, *m.*
cough [kɔf] n. Tos, *f.*: *to have a cough*, tener tos; *cough drop*, pastilla para la tos.
cough [kɔf] v. intr. Toser.
— V. tr. *To cough out*, escupir al toser, expectorar. || *To cough up*, escupir (to spit), expectorar (to expectorate), escupir, cascar (to pay).
could [kud] pret. See can.
couldn't [ˈkudənt] contraction of *could not.*
coulee [ˈku:li:] n. Geol. Corriente (*f.*) *or* torrente (*m.*) de lava. || Barranco, *m.* (ravine).
coulisse [ku:ˈli:s] n. Theatr. Bastidor. || Bolsín, *m.* (stock exchange). || Corredera, *f.* (groove, slot).
coulomb [ˈku:lɔm] n. Electr. Culombio, *m.* (unit of electric charge).
coulter [ˈkəultə*] n. Cuchilla, *f.* [del arado].
council [ˈkaunsl] n. Consejo, *m.* (advisory assembly): *council of ministers*, consejo de ministros. || Ayuntamiento, *m.* (of towns and cities). || Rel. Concilio, *m.* || — *City* o *town council*, concejo (*m.*) municipal, ayuntamiento, *m.* || *Council house*, vivienda protegida. || *Council of war*, consejo de guerra.
councillor [U. S. **councilor**] [ˈkaunsilə*] n. Concejal, *m.* || Rel. Conciliar, *m.*
councillorship [U. S. **councilorship**] [—ʃip] n. Cargo (*m.*) de concejal.
councilman [ˈkaunsəlmən] n. Concejal, *m.*

— Observ. El plural de *councilman* es *councilmen.*

counsel [ˈkaunsəl] n. Consejo, *m.* (advice). || Abogado, *m.* (lawyer). || Abogados, *m. pl.* (lawyers). || Asesor (*m.*) jurídico (legal adviser). || — *Counsel for the defence*, abogado defensor. || *Counsel for the prosecution*, fiscal, *m.* || *Counsel of perfection*, consejo (*m.*) imposible de seguir. || *To be counsel for*, defender a, abogar por. || *To keep one's own counsel*, guardar un secreto, callarse. || *To take counsel with*, pedir consejo a, consultar a.
counsel [ˈkaunsəl] v. tr. Aconsejar.
— V. intr. Pedir consejo, consultar.
counselling (U. S. **counseling**) [—iŋ] n. Asesoramiento, *m.*
counsellor (U. S. **counselor**) [ˈkaunsələ*] n. Consejero, *m.* (of an embassy). || Asesor, *m.*, consejero, *m.* (adviser). || U. S. Abogado, *m.* (lawyer).
counsellor-at-law [—ætlɔ:] n. Asesor (*m.*) jurídico.

— Observ. El plural es *counsellors-at-law.*

count [kaunt] n. Cuenta, *f.*, cálculo, *m.* (a calculation). || Total, *m.*, suma, *f.* (sum). || Recuento, *m.* (recount). || Escrutinio, *m.* (of votes). || Conde, *m.* (a noble). || Jur. Cargo, *m.* || Sp. Cuenta, *f.* (in boxing). || — *Out for the count*, fuera de combate. || *To keep count of*, llevar la cuenta de. || *To lose count of*, perder la cuenta de.
count [kaunt] v. tr. Contar: *count the mistakes*, cuenta los errores. || Contar hasta: *I counted ten*, conté hasta diez. || Contar, tener *or* tomar en cuenta (to include): *not counting*, sin contar. || Considerar (to consider). || Calcular (to calculate).
— V. intr. Contar: *to count on one's fingers*, contar con los dedos de la mano; *that doesn't count*, eso no cuenta. || Ser, haber (to number). || *Counting from tomorrow*, a partir de mañana.
—***To count against***, ir en contra de.||***To count down***, contar hacia atrás. || ***To count for***, valer por. || ***To count in***, incluir. || ***To count off***, separar. || ***To count on***, contar con: *to count on winning*, contar con la victoria. || ***To count out***, ir contando (to reckon up), declarar fuera de combate (in boxing), no contar con (not to count on), eliminar (to eliminate). | — *To count out the House*, aplazar la sesión [porque no hay quórum]. || ***To count up***, contar. | — *To count up to*, ascender a, sumar.
countable [—əbl] adj. Contable, que se puede contar.
countdown [ˈkauntdaun] n. Cuenta (*f.*) atrás, cuenta (*f.*) hacia atrás.
countenance [ˈkauntinəns] n. Semblante, *m.*, cara, *f.*, expresión, *f.*: *sad countenance*, cara triste; *to change countenance*, cambiar de cara. || — *To be out of countenance*, estar turbado *or* desconcertado. || *To give countenance to*, apoyar. || *To keep one's countenance*, no perder la serenidad *or* la seriedad. || *To lend countenance to*, apoyar. || *To lose countenance*, turbarse. || *To put s.o. out of countenance*, desconcertar a uno.
countenance [ˈkauntinəns] v. tr. Apoyar (to support). || Aprobar (to approve).
counter [ˈkauntə*] adj. Contrario, ria; opuesto, ta.
— Adv. En dirección contraria. || *To go counter to*, oponerse a, ir en contra de.
— N. Pecho, *m.* (of a horse). || Mar. Bovedilla, *f.* || Mostrador, *m.* (shops). || Ficha, *f.* (in games, for telephones). || Contra, *f.* (in boxing, fencing). || Ventanilla, *f.* (in banks). || Contrafuerte, *m.* (in shoes). || Computadora, *f.* (a computer). || Contador, *m.*: *Geiger counter*, contador Geiger. || Mus. Contrapunto, *m.* (counterpoint). || — *Over the counter*, al contado. || *Under the counter*, bajo mano.
counter [ˈkauntə*] v. intr. Contraatacar (to answer an attack). || Pelear a la contra (in boxing).
— V. tr. Contestar a: *to counter a threat*, contestar a una amenaza. || Oponerse a (to oppose). || Contrariar, ir en contra de (schemes, plans). || Parar (to parry in fencing).
counteraccusation [ˈkauntərˌækjuˈzeiʃən] n. Contraacusación, *f.*
counteract [ˌkauntəˈrækt] v. tr. Contrarrestar (to neutralize). || Frustrar, contrariar (to frustrate): *I counteracted his plans*, frustré sus planes. || Oponerse a (to act in opposition to): *I counteracted his instructions*, me opuse a sus instrucciones.
counteraction [ˌkauntəˈrækʃən] n. Oposición, *f.* || Neutralización, *f.*
counteractive [ˌkauntəˈræktiv] adj. Contrario, ria.
counterattack [ˈkauntərəˌtæk] n. Contraataque, *m.*
counterattack [ˈkauntərəˈtæk] v. tr./intr. Contraatacar.

counter attraction [ˈkauntərəˈtrækʃən] n. Atracción (*f.*) contraria.
counterbalance [ˈkauntəˏbæləns] n. Contrapeso, *m.* || Compensación, *f.*
counterbalance [ˈkauntəˈbæləns] v. tr./intr. Contrapesar, contrabalancear. || Compensar.
counterblast [ˈkauntəblɑ:st] n. Réplica, *f.* (retort). || Contraataque, *m.*
counterblow [ˈkauntəˏbləu] n. Contragolpe, *m.*
counterbrace [ˈkauntəbreis] v. tr. ARCH. Afirmar con riostras.
counterchange [kauntəˈtʃeindʒ] v. tr. Intercambiar, cambiar.
countercharge [ˈkauntətʃɑ:dʒ] n. JUR. Reconvención, *f.* || MIL. Contraataque, *m.*
countercharge [ˈkauntətʃɑ:dʒ] v. tr. JUR. Reconvenir. || MIL. Contraatacar.
countercheck [ˈkauntətʃek] n. Fuerza (*f.*) antagonista *or* contraria. || Obstáculo, *m.*, impedimento, *m.*, traba, *f.* (obstacle). || Segundo control, *m.*, comprobación (*f.*) de una verificación (a checking of a check).
countercheck [ˈkauntətʃek] v. tr. Contrarrestar (to counter). || Comprobar por segunda vez (to verify).
counterclaim [ˈkauntəkleim] n. JUR. Contradenuncia, *f.*, reconvención, *f.*
counterclaim [ˈkauntəkleim] v. tr. reconvenir.
counterclockwise [ˈkauntəˈklɔkwaiz] adj./adv. En sentido opuesto a las agujas del reloj.
countercurrent [ˈkauntəˏkʌrənt] n. Contracorriente, *f.*
counter-demonstrate [ˈkauntəˈdemənstreit] v. intr. Contramanifestar.
counter-demonstration [ˈkauntəˏdemənsˈtreiʃən] n. Contramanifestación, *f.*
counterespionage [ˈkauntəˈrespiənɑ:ʒ] n. Contraespionaje, *m.*
counterfeit [ˈkauntəfit] adj. Falsificado, da (falsified). || Simulado, da; fingido, da (feigned).
— N. Falsificación, *f.*, imitación, *f.* || Moneda (*f.*) falsa.
counterfeit [ˈkauntəfit] v. tr. Falsificar (to falsify). || Simular, fingir (to feign).
counterfeiter [ˈkauntəˏfitə*] n. Falsificador, *m.* (of money). || Simulador, *m.*
counterfoil [ˈkauntəfɔil] n. Talón, *m.*, matriz, *f.* (of a cheque, etc.). || *Counterfoil book*, talonario, *m.*
counterfort [ˈkauntəfɔ:t] n. Contrafuerte, *m.*
counterfugue [ˈkauntəfju:g] n. MUS. Contrafuga, *f.*
counterinquiry [ˈkauntərinˈkwaiəri] n. Nueva información, *f.*, nueva investigación, *f.*
counterinsurance [ˈkauntərinˈʃuərəns] n. Contraseguro, *m.*
counterintelligence [ˈkauntərinˈtelidʒəns] n. Contraespionaje, *m.*
counterirritant [kauntərˈiritənt] n. Revulsivo, *m.*
counterman [ˈkauntəmən] n. Dependiente, *m.*

— OBSERV. El plural de *counterman* es *countermen.*

countermand [ˏkauntəˈmɑ:nd] n. Contraorden, *m.*
countermand [ˏkauntəˈmɑ:nd] v. tr. Anular, revocar (a command). || COMM. Anular (an order).
countermarch [ˈkauntəmɑ:tʃ] n. Contramarcha, *f.*
countermarch [ˈkauntəmɑ:tʃ] v. intr. Contramarchar.
countermark [ˈkauntəmɑ:k] n. Contramarca, *f.*, contraseña, *f.*
countermeasure [ˈkauntəˏmeʒə*] n. Contramedida, *f.*
countermine [ˈkauntəmain] n. MIL. Contramina, *f.* || FIG. Contramaniobra, *f.* (counterplot).
countermine [ˈkauntəmain] v. tr. MIL. Contraminar. || FIG. Frustrar (to thwart).
countermove [ˈkauntəmu:v] n. Contraataque, *m.*
countermure [ˈkauntəmjuə*] n. Contramuralla, *f.*, contramuro, *m.*
counteroffensive [ˈkauntərəˈfensiv] n. MIL. Contraofensiva, *f.*
counterorder [ˈkauntərˏɔ:də*] n. Contraorden, *f.*
counterpane [ˈkauntəpein] n. Cubrecama, *m.*, colcha, *f.* (bedspread).
counterpart [ˈkauntəpɑ:t] n. Colega, *m.* & *f.* (colleague): *the American ambassador met his Russian counterpart*, el embajador americano se entrevistó con su colega ruso. || Sosia, *m.*, doble, *m.* (double). || Réplica, *f.* (replica). || FIG. Complemento, *m.* (complement). || MUS. Contrapaso, *m.* || Duplicado, *m.*, doble, *m.* (copy). || Pareja, *f.* (of ornament, picture). || JUR. Contrapartida, *f.*
counterplan [ˈkauntəplæn] n. Contraproyecto, *m.*
counterplea [ˈkauntəpli:] n. JUR. Contrarréplica, *f.*
counterplot [ˈkauntəplɔt] n. Contramaniobra, *f.*
counterplot [ˈkauntəplɔt] v. intr. Preparar una contramaniobra.
counterpoint [ˈkauntəpɔint] n. MUS. Contrapunto, *m.*
counterpoise [ˈkauntəpɔiz] n. Contrapeso, *m.*
counterpoise [ˈkauntəpɔiz] v. tr. Contrapesar, hacer contrapeso a. || FIG. Contrapesar, compensar.
counterpoison [ˈkauntəpɔizn] n. Contraveneno, *m.*, antídoto, *m.*
counterproductive [ˈkauntəprəˈdʌktiv] adj. Contraproducente.
counterproject [ˈkauntəˏprɔdʒekt] n. Contraproyecto, *m.*
counterproof [ˈkauntəpru:f] n. Contraprueba, *f.*
counterproposal [ˈkauntəprəˈpəuzəl] n. Contrapropuesta, *f.*
counterpunch [ˈkauntəpʌntʃ] n. Contragolpe, *m.*
Counter-Reformation [ˈkauntərefəˈmeiʃən] n. Contrarreforma, *f.*
counterrevolution [ˈkauntərevəˈlu:ʃən] n. Contrarrevolución, *f.*
counterrevolutionary [—əri] adj./n. Contrarrevolucionario, ria.
countersank [ˈkauntəsæŋk] pret. See COUNTERSINK.
counterscarp [ˈkauntəskɑ:p] n. Contraescarpa, *f.*
counterseal [ˈkauntəsi:l] n. Contrasello, *m.*
counterseal [ˈkauntəsi:l] v. tr. Contrasellar.
countershaft [ˈkauntəʃɑ:ft] n. Eje (*m.*) secundario, transmisión (*f.*) intermedia.
countersign [ˈkauntəsain] n. MIL. Contraseña, *f.*, consigna, *f.* (password). || Contrafirma, *f.*, refrendata, *f.*
countersign [ˈkauntəsain] v. tr. Contrafirmar, refrendar. || Ratificar.
countersignature [ˈkauntəˈsignitʃə*] n. Contrafirma, *f.*, refrendata, *f.*
countersink [ˈkauntəsiŋk] n. TECH. Avellanador, *m.*, broca, *f.* (tool). || Agujero (*m.*) avellanado (hole).
countersink* [ˈkauntəsiŋk] v. tr. TECH. Avellanar.

— OBSERV. Pret. ***countersank;*** p. p. ***countersunk.***

counterstatement [ˈkauntəˏsteitmənt] n. Contradeclaración, *f.*
counterstroke [ˈkauntəstrəuk] n. Contragolpe, *m.*
countersunk [ˈkauntəsʌŋk] p. p. See COUNTERSINK.
countertenor [ˈkauntəˈtenə*] n. MUS. Contralto, *m.*
counterterm [ˈkauntətə:m] n. GRAMM. Antónimo, *m.*
countervail [ˈkauntəveil] v. tr. Compensar. || Contrarrestar.
— V. intr. *To countervail against*, prevalecer contra.
counterweigh [ˈkauntəwei] v. tr. Contrapesar, hacer contrapeso a. || Sopesar, pesar (to think over).
— V. intr. Servir de contrapeso.
counterweight [ˈkauntəweit] n. Contrapeso, *m.*
counterweight [ˈkauntəweit] v. tr. Poner contrapeso a.
counterword [ˈkauntəwə:d] n. Palabra (*f.*) de significado poco preciso.
countess [ˈkauntis] n. Condesa, *f.*
counting [ˈkauntiŋ] n. Cuenta, *f.* (count).
countinghouse [—haus] n. Oficina (*f.*) de contabilidad.
countless [ˈkauntlis] adj. Incontable, innumerable, sin número.
countrified [ˈkʌntrifaid] adj. Rústico, ca. || Provinciano, na.
country [ˈkʌntri] n. País, *m.* (region, land, political state, people of a country). || Campo, *m.* (as opposed to town): *to live in the country*, vivir en el campo. || — *Cattle country*, país ganadero. || *Mother country*, madre (*f.*) patria. || *To appeal* o *to go to the country*, convocar elecciones generales.
— Adj. Del campo.
country cousin [—ˈkʌzn] n. Provinciano, na.
country-dance [—ˈdɑ:ns] n. Baile (*m.*) regional.
country estate [—isˈteit] n. Finca, *f.* [*Amer.*, hacienda, *f.*, estancia, *f.*]
countryfolk [—fəuk] n. Gente (*f.*) del campo, campesinos, *m. pl.*
country house [—ˈhaus] n. Casa (*f.*) de campo (house in the country). || Casa (*f.*) solariega (of a nobleman).
countryman [—mən] n. Campesino, *m.* (who lives in the country). || Compatriota, *m.* (a compatriot). || Habitante, *m.* (of a specified district).

— OBSERV. El plural de *countryman* es *countrymen.*

country people [—ˏpi:pl] pl. n. Campesinos, *m.*, gente (*f. sing.*) del campo.
country road [—ˈrəud] n. Camino (*m.*) vecinal.
countryseat [—ˈsi:t] n. Finca, *f.*
countryside [—said] n. Campo, *m.* (rural area, inhabitants). || Paisaje, *m.* (landscape).
countrywoman [—ˏwumən] n. Campesina, *f.* (who lives in the country). || Compatriota, *f.* (a compatriot). || Habitante, *f.* (of a specified district).

— OBSERV. El plural de *countrywoman es countrywomen.*

countship [ˈkauntʃip] n. Condado, *m.*
county [ˈkaunti] n. Condado, *m.* || — *County borough*, ciudad (*f.*) de más de 50 000 habitantes. || *County council*, ayuntamiento, *m.* (organization), municipio, *m.* (territory). || *County court*, juzgado (*m.*) municipal. || U. S. *County seat*, capital (*f.*) de un condado. || *County town*, capital (*f.*) de un condado.
coup [ku:] n. Golpe, *m.* || — *Coup de grâce*, golpe de gracia. || *Coup d'état*, golpe de estado. || *Coup de théâtre*, sorpresa, *f.*, lance imprevisto.
coupé [ˈku:pei] n. Cupé, *m.*
couple [ˈkʌpl] n. Par, *m.* (pair). || Pareja, *f.* (married or engaged pair, partner in a dance). || PHYS. Par, *m.* | Enganche, *m.* (a coupler). || Yunta, *f.* (of oxen). || Pareja (*f.*) de perros de caza (two hounds). || Traílla (*f.*) doble (leash). || *I have a couple of things to do*, tengo un par de cosas que hacer.
couple [ˈkʌpl] v. tr. Emparejar (to pair). || Enganchar (wagons). || Asociar (to associate). || ELECTR. Conectar, acoplar. || TECH. Acoplar. | Empalmar (two cables).
— V. intr. Aparearse (animals). || Emparejarse (to join in pairs). || Conectarse (radio). || Copular (to copulate).

coupler [ˈkʌplə*] n. Aparato (*m.*) de conexión (in radio). || Enganche, *m.* (of wagons). || ELECTR. Acoplamiento, *m.* | Empalme, *m.*

couplet [ˈkʌplit] n. Pareado, *m.* (verse).

coupling [ˈkʌpliŋ] n. Conexión, *f.* (action of connecting). || Enganche, *m.* (wagons, cars). || Empalme, *m.* || Acoplamiento, *m.* || Asociación, *f.* (ideas). || Cópula, *f.* (sexual intercourse).

coupon [ˈku:pɔn] n. Cupón, *m.* || Boleto, *m.* (in football pools). || *Coupon bond*, vale, *m.*

courage [ˈkʌridʒ] n. Valor, *m.*, valentía, *f.* || — *Courage!*, ¡ánimo! || *Take courage!*, ¡anímate! || *To have the courage of one's convictions*, ser consecuente con sus principios. || *To lose courage*, desanimarse. || *To pluck up courage* o *to screw up one's courage*, armarse de valor. || *To take courage*, cobrar ánimo. || *To take one's courage in both hands*, hacer de tripas corazón.

courageous [kəˈreidʒəs] adj. Valiente, valeroso, sa.

courier [ˈkʌriə*] n. Guía, *m.* & *f.* (a guide). || Mensajero, *m.*, correo, *m.* (letter carrier). || Correo, *m.* (diplomatic).

course [kɔ:s] n. Curso, *m.* (progress in space or time): *the course of life*, el curso de la vida; *the course of the river*, el curso del río. || ASTR. Curso, *m.*, trayectoria, *f.* (of the sun, moon). || Recorrido, *m.*, trayectoria, *f.* (of a bullet). || Recorrido, *m.* (of a piston). || Dirección, *f.*, rumbo, *m.*, ruta, *f.* (direction): *change course and head for London*, cambia de dirección y dirígete a Londres. || Dirección, *f.* (of a lode). || Curso, *m.* (development): *the course of events*, el curso de los acontecimientos. || Camino, *m.*, vía, *f.* (way, means): *several courses are open to us*, varios caminos se abren ante nosotros. || Línea, *f.*: *course of action, of conduct*, línea de acción, de conducta. || Curso, *m.* (series of lessons). || Carrera, *f.* (university career). || Programa, *m.* (of education). || Ciclo, *m.*: *a course of lectures*, un ciclo de conferencias. || Plato, *m.* (any of the parts of a meal). || Servicio, *m.* (sitting). || Pista, *f.* (track). || Hipódromo, *m.* (racecourse). || Campo, *m.* (for golf). || MED. Curso, *m.* (of a disease). | Serie, *f.* (of injections). | Reglas, *f. pl.* (periods). | Tratamiento, *m.*: *to put s.o. on a course of medicine*, recetar a uno un tratamiento médico. || ARCH. Hilada, *f.* || AGR. Rotación (*f.*) de cultivos. || COMM. Corriente, *f.* | Cotización, *f.* (of exchange). || MAR. Vela (*f.*) baja (sail). | Rumbo, *m.* (way): *to change one's course*, cambiar de rumbo. || Galería, *f.* (in a mine). || — *As a matter of course*, naturalmente. || *By course of law*, según las leyes. || *Close course*, circuito cerrado. || *First course*, entrada, *f.*, principio, *m.* (of a meal). || *In course of*, en curso de. || *In due course*, a su debido tiempo. || *In the course of*, en el transcurso de, durante. || *In the ordinary course of events*, normalmente, lógicamente. || *Last course*, postre, *m.* || *Main course*, plato fuerte. || *Of course*, claro, por supuesto, desde luego. || *That's a matter of course*, esto cae de su peso. || *To hold one's course*, seguir el camino trazado. || *To set course for*, poner *or* hacer rumbo a. || *To take a middle course*, tirar por la calle de en medio, evitar los extremos. || *To take one's own course*, seguir su camino. || *To take* o *to run its course*, seguir su curso.

course [kɔ:s] v. tr. Cazar (to hunt). || Hacer correr (to race).
— V. intr. Correr (blood, liquid).

courser [—ə*] n. Corcel, *m.* (horse). || ZOOL. Corredora, *f.* (bird).

coursing [—iŋ] n. Cacería, *f.*

court [kɔ:t] n. Patio, *m.* (courtyard). || Callejón (*m.*) sin salida (alley). || Plaza, *f.* (of a church). || Sala, *f.* (big room). || Corte, *f.* (of royalty). || Palacio, *m.* (palace). || JUR. Audiencia, *f.* (audience): *open court*, audiencia pública. | Tribunal, *m.*: *High Court*, Tribunal Supremo. || Comisión, *f.* (of inquiry). || Corte, *m.* (wooing): *to pay court to s.o.*, hacer la corte a alguien. || SP. Cancha, *f.* || — *Court of last resort*, tribunal de última instancia. || *Court order*, orden (*f.*) judicial. || *Juvenile court*, tribunal de menores. || *To bring* o *to take to court*, llevar a los tribunales. || *To fall out of court with*, perder el favor de. || *To go to court*, acudir a los tribunales. || *To rule out of court*, desestimar [una demanda]. || *To settle a case out of court*, llegar a un arreglo amistoso.

court [kɔ:t] v. tr. Cortejar, hacer la corte a (to woo). || Buscar, solicitar (to look for). || Incitar a: *to court s.o. into doing sth.*, incitar a uno a que haga algo. || Exponerse a, ir al encuentro de (disappointment, failure). || Pedir, solicitar: *to court inquiry*, solicitar una investigación.
— V. intr. Ser novios, estar en relaciones (two people). || Tener novio, tener novia: *is she courting?*, ¿tiene novio?

court card [—kɑ:d] n. Figura, *f.*

court day [—dei] n. Día (*m.*) hábil.

courteous [ˈkə:tjəs] adj. Cortés, atento, ta.

courteousness [—nis] n. Cortesía, *f.*

courtesan [ˌkɔ:tiˈzæn] n. Cortesana, *f.* (prostitute).

courtesy [ˈkə:tisi] n. Cortesía, *f.* || *To exchange courtesies*, intercambiar cumplidos.

courtezan [ˌkɔ:tiˈzæn] n. Cortesana, *f.* (prostitute).

court hand [ˈkɔ:tˈhænd] n. Letra (*f.*) gótica.

courthouse [ˈkɔ:thaus] n. Palacio (*m.*) de Justicia.

courtier [ˈkɔ:tjə*] n. Cortesano, *m.*

courtliness [ˈkɔ:tlinis] n. Cortesía, *f.* || Distinción, *f.*, elegancia, *f.*

courtly [ˈkɔ:tli] adj. Cortés. || Distinguido, da; elegante.

court-martial [ˈkɔ:tˈmɑ:ʃəl] n. Consejo (*m.*) de guerra, tribunal (*m.*) militar.

— OBSERV. El plural es *courts-martial* o *court-martials*.

court-martial [ˈkɔ:tˈmɑ:ʃəl] v. tr. Juzgar en consejo de guerra.

Court of Appeals [ˈkɔ:təvəˈpi:lz] n. Tribunal (*m.*) de apelación.

courtroom [ˈkɔ:tru:m] n. Sala (*f.*) de un tribunal.

courtship [ˈkɔ:tʃip] n. Cortejo, *m.* (action of courting). || Noviazgo, *m.* (engagement).

courtshoe [ˈkɔ:tʃu:] n. Escarpín, *m.*

courtyard [ˈkɔ:tjɑ:d] n. Patio, *m.*

couscous [ˈkuskus] n. Cuscús, *m.*

cousin [ˈkʌzn] n. Primo, ma: *first cousin*, primo hermano *or* carnal. || *First cousin once removed*, sobrino segundo (one's first cousin's child), tío segundo (one's parent's first cousin).

cousin-german [—ˈdʒə:mən] n. Primo (*m.*) hermano, prima (*f.*) hermana; primo (*m.*) carnal, prima (*f.*) carnal.

— OBSERV. El plural es *cousins-german*.

cousinhood [—hud] n. Primazgo, *m.*, parentesco (*m.*) de primo.

cousinship [—ʃip] n. See COUSINHOOD.

couturier [ku:ˈtu:riei] n. Modisto, *m.*, modista, *m.*

cove [kəuv] n. Cala, *f.*, ensenada, *f.* (bay). || ARCH. Bovedilla, *f.* || Cueva, *f.* (cave). || FAM. Tío, *m.*, sujeto, *m.* (guy).

cove [kəuv] v. intr. ARCH. Abovedarse.

covenant [ˈkʌvənənt] n. Convenio, *m.* (agreement). || Pacto, *m.*: *covenant of the League of Nations*, Pacto de la Sociedad de Naciones. || Contrato, *m.* (contract). || REL. Alianza, *f.*

covenant [ˈkʌvənənt] v. tr. Concertar.
— V. intr. Convenir. || Pactar.

covenanter [—ə*] n. Parte (*f.*) contratante.

Coventry [ˈkɔvəntri] pr. n. GEOGR. Coventry. || FIG. FAM. *To send s.o. to Coventry*, hacer el vacío a alguien.

cover [ˈkʌvə*] n. Cubierta, *f.* (in general). || Tapa, *f.* (a lid). || Tapa, *f.* (binding of a book). || Forro, *m.* (protection of books). || Portada, *f.* (of magazine). || Funda, *f.* (a fitted covering). || Cubierta, *f.* (of a tyre). || Envoltura, *f.* (of a parcel). || Refugio, *m.* (a concealing shelter). || Cobertura, *f.*, fondos, *m. pl.* (money to meet liabilities). || Tapete, *m.* (of a table). || Cobertor, *m.*, colcha, *f.* (on bed). || Cubierto, *m.* (table service). || Sobre, *m.* (envelope). || Faja, *f.*, banda, *f.* (of newspaper). || Pretexto, *m.*, excusa, *f.* (pretence). || Protección, *f.*, amparo, *m.* (protection). || — Pl. Ropa (*f. sing.*) de cama (bedclothes). || — *From cover to cover*, de cabo a rabo. || *To break cover*, salir al descubierto. || *To take cover*, ponerse a cubierto. || *Under cover*, al abrigo; bajo techo, a cubierto. || *Under registered cover*, certificado, da. || *Under separate cover*, por separado. || *Under (the) cover of*, al amparo de. || *Under the same cover*, adjunto, ta.

cover [ˈkʌvə*] v. tr. Tapar (to put a cover on). || Cubrir: *the field was covered with snow*, el campo estaba cubierto de nieve. || Cubrirse (the head). || Cubrir, proteger (to protect). || Cubrir, defender (to defend). || Apuntar (to aim a gun). || MIL. Cubrir. || Ocupar una extensión de (to occupy). || Cubrir (a bet). || Encuadernar (to bind a book). || Forrar (to protect a book). || Cubrir (to include in an insurance policy). || Asegurar (to insure). || Cubrir (to defray costs). || Estar encargado de, ocuparse de (to be responsible for): *he covers the north of the country*, está encargado del norte del país. || SP. Cubrir. || Abarcar, cubrir (to embrace). || Cubrir, recorrer (a distance). || Dominar, cubrir (a landscape). || Informar sobre (to report). || Cubrir (animals). || Empollar (to hatch). || — *To cover o.s. with glory*, cubrirse de gloria. || *To cover up*, cubrir completamente (to cover thoroughly), encubrir (offence), copar (gambling), disimular, ocultar (to conceal). || *To cover with honours*, cubrir de honores.
— V. intr. Cubrir. || *To cover up for*, encubrir.

coverage [ˈkʌvəridʒ] n. Alcance, *m.* (reach). || Circulación, *f.* (of a newspaper). || Reportaje, *m.* (report). || Respaldo, *m.* (of money). || Fondos, *m. pl.* (of a cheque). || Extensión, *f.*, riesgos (*m. pl.*) cubiertos (of an insurance). || FIG. Protección, *f.*, amparo, *m.*

coveralls [ˈkʌvərɔ:lz] n. Bata, *f.* (coat). || Mono, *m.* (overalls).

cover charge [ˈkʌvətʃɑ:dʒ] n. Precio (*m.*) del cubierto.

covered waggon (U. S. **covered wagon**) [ˈkʌvədˈwægən] n. Carromato, *m.*

covered way [ˈkʌvədˈwei] n. MIL. Camino (*m.*) cubierto, corredor, *m.*

cover girl [ˈkʌvəgə:l] n. Modelo (*f.*) fotográfica.

covering [ˈkʌvəriŋ] n. Cubierta, *f.*, envoltura, *f.* (wrapping). || Abrigo, *m.* (dress, etc.). || — *A covering of snow*, una capa de nieve. || *Covering action*, acción (*f.*) de cobertura. || *Covering fire*, fuego (*m.*) de protección. || *Covering letter*, carta explicatoria.

coverlet [ˈkʌvəlit] n. Colcha, *f.*, cubrecama, *m.* (bedspread). || Cubrepiés, *m. inv.* (counterpane).

covert [ˈkʌvət] n. Matorral, *m.* (thicket). || Refugio, *m.*, abrigo, *m.* (shelter). || — Pl. Plumas, *f.*
— Adj. Furtivo, va: *covert glance*, mirada furtiva. || Secreto, ta (secret). || Cubierto, ta; abrigado, da (sheltered).
coverture [ˈkʌvətjuə*] n. Envoltura, *f.* (of a package). || Refugio, *m.*, abrigo, *m.* (refuge). || Escondrijo, *m.* (concealment). || Jur. Estado (*m.*) legal de una mujer casada.
cover-up [ˈkʌvərʌp] n. Fam. Coartada, *f.* (alibi). || Encubrimiento, *m.* (concealment).
covet [ˈkʌvit] v. tr. Codiciar.
covetous [ˈkʌvitəs] adj. Codicioso, sa; ávido, da.
covetousness [—nis] n. Codicia, *f.*, avidez, *f.*
covey [ˈkʌvi] n. Nidada, *f.* (brood). || Bandada, *f.* (flock). || Fig. Grupo, *m.*
covings [ˈkəuviŋz] pl. n. Arch. Dovelas, *f.*
cow [kau] n. Zool. Vaca, *f.* (of ox family): *milch cow*, vaca lechera. || Hembra, *f.* (of other animals): *cow seal*, foca hembra. || *Cow elephant*, elefanta, *f.* || — Fig. *The time of the lean cows*, la época de las vacas flacas. | *To wait till the cows come home*, esperar sentado, esperar hasta que las ranas críen pelos.
cow [kau] v. tr. Acobardar, intimidar.
coward [—əd] n. Cobarde, *m.* & *f.*
cowardice [—ədis] n. Cobardía, *f.*
cowardliness [—ədlinis] n. Cobardía, *f.*
cowardly [—ədli] adj. Cobarde.
— Adv. Cobardemente.
cowbell [—bel] n. Cencerro, *m.*
cowboy [—bɔi] n. Vaquero, *m.*
cowcatcher [—ˌkætʃə*] n. U. S. Rastrillo (*m.*) delantero, quitapiedras, *m. inv.*
cower [—ə*] v. intr. Acobadarse, encogerse (from fear). || Agacharse (to crouch).
cowfish [—fiʃ] n. Zool. Manatí, *m.* (sea cow).
cowgirl [—gə:l] n. Vaquera, *f.*
cowhand [—hænd] n. U. S. Vaquero, *m.*
cowherd [—hə:d] n. Vaquero, *m.*
cowhide [—haid] n. Cuero, *m.* || Látigo (*m.*) de cuero (whip).
cowl [kaul] n. Rel. Capucha, *f.* || Capirote, *m.* (of penitent). || Sombrerete (*m.*) de chimenea. || Capó, *m.* (of a car). || Capota, *f.* (of plane).
cowlick [ˈkaulik] n. Remolino, *m.*, mechón, *m.* (of hair).
cowling [ˈkauliŋ] n. Capota, *f.* (of plane).
cowman [ˈkaumən] n. Vaquero, *m.* (cowherd). || U. S. Ganadero, *m.* (cattle owner).
— Observ. El plural de *cowman* es *cowmen.*

co-worker [ˈkəuˈwə:kə*] n. Colaborador, ra.
cowpox [ˈkaupɔks] n. Vet. Vacuna, *f.*
cowpuncher [ˈkauˌpʌntʃə*] n. U. S. Vaquero, *m.*
cowrie or **cowry** [ˈkauri] n. Zool. Cauri, *m.*
— Observ. El plural de estas palabras es *cowries.*

cowshed [ˈkauʃed] n. Establo, *m.*
cowslip [ˈkauslip] n. Bot. Prímula, *f.*
cox [kɔks] n. Sp. Timonel, *m.*
cox [kɔks] v. tr. Sp. Gobernar.
— V. intr. Sp. Hacer de timonel.
coxa [ˈkɔksə] n. Anat. Zool. Cadera, *f.* (hip).
— Observ. El plural de *coxa* es *coxae.*

coxalgia [kɔksˈældʒjə] n. Med. Coxalgia, *f.*
coxcomb [ˈkɔkskəum] n. Fatuo, tua.
coxcombical [kɔksˈkəumikəl] adj. Fatuo, tua.
coxswain [ˈkɔksn, ˈkɔkswein] n. Timonel, *m.* (helmsman). || Patrón, *m.* (person in charge of a boat).
coy [kɔi] adj. Tímido, da (shy). || Remilgado, da (demure). || *Coy of speech*, parco en palabras.
coyly [—li] adv. Tímidamente.
coyness [—nis] n. Timidez, *f.* || Afectación, *f.*
coyote [kɔiˈəut] n. Zool. Coyote, *m.*
coypu [ˈkɔipu:] n. Zool. Coipo, *m.*, coipu, *m.*
cozily [ˈkəuzili] adv. See cosily.
coziness [ˈkəuzinis] n. See cosiness.
cozy [ˈkəuzi] adj. See cosy.
crab [kræb] n. Zool. Cangrejo, *m.* (crustacean). || Astr. Cáncer, *m.* || Tech. Torno, *m.* || Aviat. Deriva, *f.* || Ladilla, *f.* (insect). || Fig. Gruñón, *m.* (grumbly). || Sp. Fam. *To catch a crab*, dar un falso golpe de remo.
crab [kræb] v. tr. Aviat. Hacer ir a la deriva. || Fig. Criticar (to find fault with). | Estropear (to frustrate).
— V. intr. Aviat. Ir a la deriva. || Pescar cangrejos (to catch crabs). || Fig. Refunfuñar, quejarse.
crab apple [—ˌæpl] n. Bot. Manzana (*f.*) silvestre.
crabbed [ˈkræbid] adj. Malhumorado, da (morose). || Enrevesado, da (intricate).
crabber [ˈkræbə*] n. Cangrejero, ra (person). || Barca (*f.*) para pescar cangrejos (boat). || Fig. Gruñón, *m.*
crabbiness [ˈkræbinis] n. Malhumor, *m.*, mal genio, *m.*
crabby [ˈkræbi] adj. Malhumorado, da; gruñón, ona (grumbly). || Hosco, ca (peevish).
crab louse [ˈkræblaus] n. Zool. Ladilla, *f.*
crack [kræk] n. Restallido, *m.*, chasquido, *m.*, traquido, *m.*: *the crack of a whip*, el chasquido de un látigo. || Crujido, *m.* (of branches, etc.). || Detonación, *f.* (of a firearm). || Golpe, *m.* (blow). || Raja, *f.*, resquebrajadura, *f.* (split): *a cup with a crack*, una taza con una raja. || Grieta, *f.*, hendidura, *f.* (in the ground, in walls). || Abertura, *f.* (opening). || Rendija, *f.* (slit): *the light came in through a crack in the door*, la luz entraba por una rendija en la puerta. || Fam. Murmuración, *f.*, chismorreo, *m.*, habladuría, *f.* (gossip). | Chiste, *m.* (joke). | Favorito, *m.* (favourite). | Campeón, *m.*, as, *m.* (star). | Tipo (*m.*) curioso (strange person). || Gallo, *m.* (in the voice). || Momento, *m.*, instante, *m.* (trice): *in a crack*, en un momento. || Fam. Robo (*m.*) con fractura. || U. S. Fam. Pulla, *f.*, chacota, *f.* (gibe). | Intento, *m.* (attempt). || — *At the crack of dawn*, al amanecer, al romper el alba. || *Crack of doom*, día (*m.*) del Juicio Final. || *Nasty crack*, observación malintencionada, broma pesada. || *To have a crack at*, intentar. || *To take a crack at*, dar un golpe a, pegar a (to strike), intentar (to try).
— Adj. De primera (excellent).
crack [kræk] v. tr. Restallar, chasquear: *to crack a whip*, restallar un látigo. || Golpear, pegar (to hit). || Chasquear (the fingers). || Crujir (the knuckles). || Cascar (to break a nut). || Romper, partir (to break). || Agrietar, hender (the earth). || Rajar, resquebrajar (glass, stone). || Agrietar, cuartear (a wall). || Astillar (a bone). || Agrietar (the skin). || Cascar (the voice). || Fam. Forzar (a safe). || Chem. Craquear, fraccionar (oil). || Fig. Arruinar, echar abajo (s.o.'s credit). | Perturbar, trastonar (the calm). | Hacer (pun). | Contar (to tell a joke). | Gastar (to play a joke). | Derribar, vencer (an obstacle). | Encontrar la solución a, resolver (a difficulty). | Explicar (a mystery). | Descifrar (a code). | Abrir, destapar (a bottle). || — *He isn't as good as he is cracked up to be*, no es tan bueno como lo pintan *or* como dicen. || *To crack up*, destrozar (to break), alabar, ensalzar (to praise).
— V. intr. Agrietarse, resquebrajarse (to split). || Restallar, chasquear (a whip). || Reventar (to burst). || Crujir (the knuckles). || Romperse, partirse, abrirse (to break). || Rajarse, resquebrajarse (glass, stone). || Agrietarse, cuartearse (a wall). || Astillarse (a bone). || Agrietarse (the skin). || Detonar (a rifle). || Fraccionarse (petrol, oil). || Cascarse, quebrarse (voice). || Mudar (boy's voice). || Fig. Ceder, rendirse, darse por vencido (to give in). | Fallar (to fail). | Perder el control de sí mismo (to lose control). | Volverse loco (to go crazy). | Arruinarse, venirse abajo, hundirse (to break down). | Charlar (to chatter). | Bromear, decir bromas (to joke). || — Fig. *At a cracking pace*, a todo correr. || *To crack down on*, tomar medidas enérgicas contra. || *To crack on sail*, avanzar a toda vela, desplegar todas las velas. || *To crack up*, destrozarse, hacerse pedazos (to fall into pieces), volverse loco, ca (to break down mentally), venirse abajo, agotarse (to break down physically), estrellarse (a plane), quebrar (economy), darse autobombo, darse pisto (to boast), reírse a carcajadas (to laugh). || *To get cracking*, darse prisa, apresurarse (to hurry), empezar (to start).
crackbrain [—brein] n. Fam. Chiflado, da; loco, ca.
crackbrained [—breind] adj. Fam. Chiflado, da; loco, ca.
crackdown [—daun] n. Medidas (*f. pl.*) enérgicas.
cracked [krækt] adj. Agrietado, da (split). || Resquebrajado, da; rajado, da (glass, stone). || Cuarteado, da; agrietado, da (wall). || Fam. Chiflado, da (crazy). | Desafinado, da (tuneless). | Cascado, da (old man's voice).
cracker [ˈkrækə*] n. Galleta, *f.* (biscuit). || Buscapiés, *m. inv.* (firework). || Sorpresa, *f.*: *to pull a Christmas cracker*, abrir una sorpresa. || — Pl. Papillotes, *m.* (hair curlers).
crackerjack [—dʒæk] adj. Fam. Magnífico, ca; maravilloso, sa; de primera.
— N. Fam. Maravilla, *f.* (first-rate thing). | Campeón, *m.*, as, *m.* (skilful person).
crackers [ˈkrækəz] adj. Fam. Loco, ca; chiflado, da.
cracking [ˈkrækiŋ] n. Cracking, *m.*, craqueo, *m.* (of oil).
— Adj. Fig. fam. Extraordinario, ria.
crackle [ˈkrækl] n. Crepitación, *f.*, chisporroteo, *m.* (of fire, wood). || Crujido, *m.* (of leaves). || Grieteado, *m.* (in glassware). || Ruido (*m.*) parásito, fritura, *f.* (on the telephone).
crackle [ˈkrækl] v. intr. Crepitar, chisporrotear (fire). || Crujir (leaves, etc,) || Agrietarse (glaze).
— V. tr. Estrujar, hacer crujir (papers, etc.).
crackling [—iŋ] n. See crackle. || — Pl. Chicharrones, *m.* (roasted pork skin).
crackly [—i] adj. Crepitante, chisporroteante (fire). || Quebradizo, za (fragile).
cracknel [ˈkræknəl] n. Galleta, *f.* (biscuit). || — Pl. U. S. Torreznos, *m.* (small pieces of fat). | Chicharrones (cracklings).
crackpot [ˈkrækpɔt] adj./n. Fam. Chiflado, da; chalado, da.
cracksman [ˈkræksmən] n. Fam. Atracador, *m.*
— Observ. El plural de *cracksman* es *cracksmen.*

crack-up [ˈkrækʌp] n. Fam. Caída, *f.* (of a plane). | Choque, *m.* (collision). | Depresión (*f.*) nerviosa (mental breakdown). | Colapso, *m.* (physical breakdown). | Quiebra, *f.* (of a firm).
cracky [ˈkræki] adj. Agrietado, da (full of cracks). || Resquebrajadizo, za (liable to crack). || Fam. Chiflado, da (crazy). || *By cracky!*, ¡córcholis!
Cracow [ˈkrækəu] pr. n. Geogr. Cracovia, *f.*
cradle [ˈkreidl] n. Cuna, *f.*: *a baby in its cradle*, un niño en su cuna; *the cradle of civilization*, la cuna de la civilización. || Soporte, *m.*, horquilla, *f.* (for phone). || Mar. Basada, *f.*, cuna (*f.*) de botadura (support for ships under construction). | Boya (*f.*) pantalón

(lifesaving device). || MIN. Criba, *f.* || MED. Arco, *m.* | Entablillado, *m.* (for fractures). || Soporte, *m.* (of a plane). || AGR. Armazón (*f.*) de la guadaña (for scythe). || Andamio (*m.*) volante (used by house painters, etc.). || Rascador (*m.*) dentado (engraving tool). || *Cradle car*, vagoneta (*f.*) basculante.

cradle [ˈkreidl] v. tr. Acostar, poner en la cuna (to put a baby in a cradle). || Acunar, mecer (to hold a baby). || AGR. Segar. || MIN. Lavar, pasar por la criba. || FIG. *Cradled in luxury*, criado en buenos pañales.

cradlesong [—sɔŋ] n. Canción (*f.*) de cuna, nana, *f.*

craft [krɑːft] n. Arte, *m.* (a trade requiring skill, or that skill). || Gremio, *m.* (a guild). || Trabajo (*m.*) manual, oficio, *m.* (trade). || Astucia, *f.*, habilidad, *f.*, maña, *f.* (cunning). || Embarcación, *f.*, navío, *m.* (boat). || Aparato, *m.*, avión, *m.* (aircraft). || — *Craft union*, gremio, *m.*, corporación, *f.* || *The Craft*, la masonería.

— OBSERV. El plural de *craft* cuando significa embarcación o avión es *craft*.

craftily [—ili] adv. Astutamente.

craftiness [—inis] n. Astucia, *f.*, maña, *f.*, habilidad, *f.*

craftsman [ˈkrɑːftsmən] n. Artesano, *m.* (artisan). || Artista, *m.* (an artist in his trade). || FIG. Artífice, *m.*, realizador, *m.*

— OBSERV. El plural de *craftsman* es *craftsmen*.

craftsmanship [—ʃip] n. Artesanía, *f.* || Oficio, *m.* (of writer). || Habilidad, *f.*, destreza, *f.* (skill). || Ejecución, *f.*, realización, *f.* (execution).

crafty [ˈkrɑːfti] adj. Astuto, ta; hábil, mañoso, sa.

crag [kræg] n. Despeñadero, *m.* (steep, rugged cliff). || Risco, *m.* (projecting rock).

cragged [ˈkrægid] adj. Peñascoso, sa; rocoso, sa; escarpado, da.

craggedness [—nis] or **cragginess** [ˈkræginis] n. Rocosidad, *f.*, carácter (*m.*) escarpado.

craggy [ˈkrægi] adj. Peñascoso, sa; escarpado, da; rocoso, sa.

crake [kreik] n. ZOOL. Rascón, *m.*, rey (*m.*) de codornices.

cram [kræm] n. Apretura, *f.* (of people). || FAM. Estudio (*m.*) de última hora. | Bola, *f.*, mentira, *f.* (lie).

cram [kræm] v. tr. Abarrotar, atiborrar, atestar (to fill very full). || Meter a la fuerza (to force sth. in). || Meter (in the pocket). || Cebar (fowl). || Hartar (to stuff). || U. S. Atiborrarse de (to eat sth. greedily). || FAM. Llenar (one's memory). | Dar clases intensivas a (to teach intensively).

— V. intr. Atiborrarse, atracarse (with food). || FAM. Empollar (before an exam). | Bromear (to joke).

crambo [ˈkræmbəu] n. Juego (*m.*) consistente en rimar palabras.

— OBSERV. El plural de *crambo* es *cramboes*.

crammer [ˈkræmə*] n. Empollón, ona (student).

cramp [kræmp] n. Pinza (*f.*) de unión (metal wall support). || Grapa, *f.* (staple). || Cárcel, *f.* (clamp). || FIG. Obstáculo, *m.*, traba, *f.* || MED. Calambre, *m.* (contraction of muscles). || — Pl. MED. Retortijones, *m.* (intestinal pain). || FIG. *Under the cramp of*, atenazado por.

cramp [kræmp] v. tr. Poner trabas a, obstaculizar (to hinder). || Dar calambre a (a muscle). || Apretar (to secure with a cramp). || Poner grapas a (papers). || Girar, dar vueltas a (a wheel). || FIG. FAM. *To cramp s.o.'s style*, cohibir a alguien, cortar las alas a alguien.

— V. intr. Tener un calambre.

cramped [—t] adj. Apiñado, da: *we are cramped in this room*, estamos apiñados en esta habitación. || Exiguo, gua (place). || Apretado, da (writing). || Molesto, ta; violento, ta (awkward). || *In cramped circumstances*, en la estrechez.

cramp iron [ˈkræmpˌaiən] n. Grapa, *f.*

crampon [ˈkræmpən] n. Garfio, *m.* (grappling hook). || SP. Crampón, *m.* (in climbing).

cranberry [ˈkrænbəri] n. BOT. Arándano, *m.*

crane [krein] n. ZOOL. Grulla, *f.* (bird). || Grúa, *f.* (machine for raising and lowering weights): *bridge, gantry crane*, grúa de puente, de pórtico. || Jirafa, *f.* (for camera). || MAR. Pescante, *m.* (davit). || Sifón, *m.* (siphon). || — *Crane boom*, aguilón (*m.*) de grúa. || *Crane driver*, see CRANEMAN. || ZOOL. *Crane fly*, típula, *f.*

crane [krein] v. tr. Estirar (the neck). || TECH. Levantar con grúa.

— V. intr. Estirar el cuello.

craneman [ˈkreinmən] n. Conductor (*m.*) de grúa, gruísta, *m.*

— OBSERV. El plural de esta palabra es *cranemen*.

cranesbill [ˈkreinzbil] n. BOT. Geranio, *m.*

cranial [ˈkreinjəl] adj. Craneal, craneano, na.

craniologist [ˌkreiniˈɔlədʒist] n. Craneólogo, ga.

craniology [ˌkreiniˈɔlədʒi] n. Craneología, *f.*

cranium [ˈkreinjəm] n. Cráneo, *m.*

— OBSERV. El plural de *cranium* es *crania* o *craniums*.

crank [kræŋk] n. TECH. Manivela, *f.* (handle). | Cigüeñal, *m.* (crankshaft). || Chiflado, da (fool). || Excéntrico, ca (an excentric person). || Chifladura, *f.* (craziness). || Manía, *f.*, capricho, *m.* (whim). || Extravagancia, *f.*

— Adj. Estropeado, da.

crank [kræŋk] v. tr. Arrancar [un coche] con la manivela. || Poner una manivela a (to provide with a crank). || Acodar (to square).

— V. intr. Arrancar con la manivela.

crankcase [—keis] n. TECH. Cárter, *m.*

crankily [ˈkræŋkili] adv. De mala manera. || Caprichosamente.

crankiness [ˈkræŋkinis] n. Irritabilidad, *f.*, mal humor, *m.* (irritability). || Excentricidad, *f.* (excentricity). || Capricho, *m.*, manía, *f.* (whim). || Chifladura, *f.* (craziness). || Mal funcionamiento, *m.* (of machines).

crankpin [ˈkræŋkpin] n. Muñón (*m.*) del cigüeñal.

crankshaft [ˈkræŋʃɑːft] n. Cigüeñal, *m.*: *crankshaft gear*, piñón del cigüeñal.

cranky [ˈkræŋki] adj. Irritable (irritable). || Chiflado, da (crazy). || Excéntrico, ca (eccentric). || Caprichoso, sa (capricious). || Estropeado, da; descompuesto, ta (machines).

crannied [ˈkrænid] adj. Agrietado, da.

cranny [ˈkræni] n. Grieta, *f.*

crap [kræp] n. U. S. Juego (*m.*) de dados. || POP. Porquería, *f.* (rubbish). | Disparate, *m.* (nonsense). | Trola, *f.* (lie). | Mierda, *f.* (excrement).

crap [kræp] v. intr. Tirar los dados. || POP. Cagar (to defecate).

crape [kreip] n. Crespón, *m.*

craps [kræps] pl. n. U. S. Dados, *m.*: *to shoot craps*, jugar a los dados, tirar los dados.

crapulence [ˈkræpjuləns] n. Crápula, *f.* (debauchery). || Embriaguez, *f.* (drunkenness).

crapulent [ˈkræpjulənt] or **crapulous** [ˈkræpjuləs] adj. Crapuloso, sa (debauched). || Borracho, cha (drunk).

crash [kræʃ] n. Estrépito, *m.* (loud noise). || Estallido, *m.*, estampido, *m.* (of a gun). || Choque, *m.* (collision). || Accidente, *m.* (of railway, car). || Caída, *f.*, accidente, *m.* (of aircraft). || Quiebra, *f.* (of a business). || Tela (*f.*) para toallas.

— Adj. Intensivo, va (course). || Rápido, da (dive). || De emergencia, forzoso, sa (landing). || Protector, ra (helmet).

crash [kræʃ] v. intr. Retumbar (to make a violent noise): *the thunder crashed*, el trueno retumbó. || Estallar (to explode). || Dar un estallido (to detonate). || Chocar (to collide). || Estrellarse, caer (aeroplane): *to crash into a hill*, estrellarse contra una colina. || Quebrar (business). || Fracasar (to fail). || Romperse, hacerse pedazos (to break). || Tener un accidente (to have an accident). || Derrumbarse (to fall in). || — *To crash about o around*, andar de un lado a otro armando mucho ruido. || *To crash down*, caer con gran estrépito. || *To crash into*, irrumpir: *he crashed into the room*, irrumpió en la habitación; estrellarse contra, chocar contra: *the car crashed into the tree*, el coche chocó contra el árbol.

— V. tr. Estrellar. || — *To crash a party*, colarse en una fiesta. || *To crash one's way through*, abrirse camino arrollándolo todo.

crash-dive [—daiv] v. intr. MAR. Sumergirse rápidamente.

crashing [—iŋ] adj. FAM. Arrollador, ra (success). | Completo, ta (utter). | Impresionante (stunning).

crash-land [—lænd] v. intr. AVIAT. Hacer un aterrizaje forzoso *or* de emergencia.

crasis [ˈkreisis] n. GRAMM. Crasis, *f. inv.*

— OBSERV. El plural de *crasis* es *crases*.

crass [kræs] adj. Craso, sa (ignorance). || Obtuso, sa; estúpido, da (person). || Burdo, da; tosco, ca (coarse). || Grueso, sa (thick).

crassness [ˈkræsnis] n. Enormidad, *f.* (of an error). || Tosquedad, *f.*, grosería, *f.* (coarseness). || Estupidez, *f.* (stupidity).

crate [kreit] n. Cajón, *m.*, embalaje, *m.* || FAM. Cacharro, *m.* (car).

crate [kreit] v. tr. Embalar.

crater [ˈkreitə*] n. Cráter, *m.*

cravat [krəˈvæt] n. Corbata, *f.* (tie). || Pañuelo, *m.* (scarf).

crave [kreiv] v. tr. Desear ardientemente, ansiar, anhelar (to desire strongly). || Implorar, suplicar (to beg). || Reclamar, solicitar (attention).

— V. intr. *To crave after o for*, desear ardientemente, ansiar, anhelar, consumirse por.

craven [ˈkreivən] adj. Cobarde, timorato, ta.

— N. Cobarde, *m.* & *f.*

cravenness [—is] n. Cobardía, *f.*

craving [ˈkreiviŋ] n. Deseo (*m.*) ardiente, ansia, *f.*, anhelo, *m.* (*for*, de) || Antojo, *m.* (in pregnancy).

— Adj. Voraz, insaciable (appetite). || Intenso, sa; ardiente (desire). || Tiránico, ca (need).

craw [krɔː] n. Buche, *m.* (of a bird). || FIG. FAM. *It sticks in my craw*, no me lo trago.

crawfish [ˈkrɔːfiʃ] n. ZOOL. Cangrejo (*m.*) de río (freshwater crustacean). | Langosta, *f.* (spiny lobster).

crawl [krɔːl] n. Arrastramiento, *m.*, deslizamiento, *m.* (of a snake). || Criadero, *m.* (enclosure for fish). || Marcha (*f.*) lenta (slow movement). || SP. "Crawl", *m.* (swimming). || *At a crawl*, a paso lento.

crawl [krɔːl] v. intr. Andar a cuatro patas, andar a gatas, gatear (to move on hands and knees). || Andar a paso de tortuga, avanzar lentamente (to move slowly). || Deslizarse, reptar (a snake). || Arrastrarse: *he crawled to the hole*, se arrastró hasta el agujero. || Trepar (plants). || Sentir un hormigueo (the flesh):

I crawl all over, siento un hormigueo por todo el cuerpo. || SP. Nadar el "crawl". || Circular lentamente en busca de clientes (a taxi). || FIG. Arrastrarse a los pies de, humillarse ante: *I crawled to him*, me arrastré a sus pies. || — *To crawl along*, avanzar paso a paso. || *To crawl by*, pasar lentamente. || *To crawl under*, meterse debajo de. || *To crawl with*, estar lleno de, hervir de (to be full), sentir un hormigueo a causa de (to creep).

crawler [—ə*] n. Oruga, *f.* (of a tractor). || Tractor (*m.*) oruga (tractor). || Reptil, *m.* || FIG. Persona (*f.*) rastrera.

crawly [—i] adj. FAM. Espeluznante, horripilante.

crayfish [ˈkreifiʃ] n. ZOOL. Crangrejo (*m.*) de río (fresh-water crustacean). | Langosta, *f.* (spiny lobster).

crayon [ˈkreiən] n. Carboncillo, *m.* (charcoal). || Pastel, *m.*, lápiz (*m.*) de pastel. || Dibujo (*m.*) al pastel (drawing). || ELECTR. Carbón, *m.* || FIG. Esbozo, *m.*, bosquejo, *m.*

crayon [ˈkreiən] v. tr. Dibujar al pastel *or* con carboncillo. || FIG. Esbozar, bosquejar.

craze [kreiz] n. Manía, *f.* (fad). || Capricho, *m.* (whim). || Moda, *f.* (fashion). || Chifladura, *f.*, locura, *f.* (exaggerated enthusiasm).

craze [kreiz] v. tr. Enloquecer.
— V. intr. Cuartearse, agrietarse.

crazed [—d] adj. Loco, ca: *half crazed*, medio loco. || Agrietado, da (pottery).

crazily [—ili] adv. Locamente.

craziness [—inis] n. Locura, *f.* (madness).

crazy [ˈkreizi] adj. Loco, ca (foolish, insane). || Disparatado, da; loco, ca (idea). || En ruina (unsound). || Desvencijado, da (furniture). || De baldosas irregulares (paving). || — FAM. *To be crazy about s.o.*, estar loco por alguien. || *To be crazy with joy*, estar loco de algería. || *To drive* o *to send s.o. crazy*, volver loco a alguien. || *To go crazy*, volverse loco. || *To run like crazy*, correr como un loco.

crazy bone [—bəun] n. U. S. Hueso (*m.*) de la alegría (funny bone).

crazy quilt [—kwilt] n. Centón, *m.*, colcha (*f.*) hecha con retales de distintos colores y tamaños. || FIG. Lío, *m.* (jumble).

creak [kri:k] n. Crujido, *m.* (of floorboards). || Chirrido, *m.* (of door hinges).

creak [kri:k] v. intr. Crujir (floor). || Chirriar (hinges).

creaky [ˈkri:ki] adj. Chirriante (door hinges). || Que cruje (floorboards). || FIG. Poco seguro, ra.

cream [kri:m] n. Nata, *f.*, crema, *f.* (of milk). || Nata, *f.* (in confectionery): *whipped cream*, nata batida. || Crema, *f.* (soup). || CHEM. Crema, *f.* || Crema, *f.* (cosmetics). || FIG. Crema, *f.* (best part of anything). || Crema, *f.* (liqueur). || — FIG. *The cream of the crop*, la flor y nata, la crema. | *The cream of the joke*, lo más gracioso del caso.
— Adj. Crema, color crema.

cream [kri:m] v. tr. Batir (to beat). || Descremar, desnatar (to skim cream from milk). || Poner crema (in tea, coffee, on one's face).
— V. intr. Formar nata (milk). || Hacer espuma (to foam).

cream cheese [—ˈtʃi:z] n. Queso (*m.*) de nata.

creamer [—ə*] n. Desnatadora, *f.*

creamery [—əri] n. Lechería, *f.* (where milk is sold). || Mantequería, *f.* (for cheese, butter and cream).

cream of tartar [—əvˈtɑ:tə*] n. Crémor (*m.*) tartárico.

creamy [ˈkri:mi] adj. Cremoso, sa.

crease [kri:s] n. Doblez, *m.*, pliegue, *m.* (fold). || Arruga, *f.* (wrinkle). || Raya, *f.* (of trousers). || SP. Línea (*f.*) de la puerta. | Línea (*f.*) del bateador (in cricket).

crease [kri:s] v. tr. Doblar, plegar (to fold). || Arrugar (to wrinkle). || Hacer la raya de (one's trousers).
— V. intr. Arrugarse (to wrinkle). || Doblarse, plegarse (to fold).

creaseless [—lis] adj. Inarrugable.

creasy [—i] adj. Arrugado, da.

create [kriˈeit] v. tr. Crear.
— V. intr. FAM. Protestar, armar jaleo (to protest).

creation [kriˈeiʃən] n. Creación, *f.* || FAM. Alboroto, *m.*, jaleo, *m.* (fuss).

creative [kriˈeitiv] adj. Creador, ra.

creativeness [—nis] n. Creatividad, *f.*, facultad (*f.*) creadora, inventiva, *f.*

creativity [ˌkrieiˈtiviti] n. Facultad (*f.*) creadora, inventiva, *f.*, creatividad, *f.*

creator [kriˈeitə*] n. Creador, ra.

creature [ˈkri:tʃə*] n. Criatura, *f.* (a living human or animal). || Animal, *m.*, bicho, *m.* (animal). || FIG. Fruto, *m.*, obra, *f.*, producto, *m.*, creación, *f.*: *a creature of the imagination*, una obra de la imaginación. | Instrumento, *m.*, juguete, *m.* (a servile tool of s.o. else). || — *Creature comforts*, comodidades (*f.*) materiales. || *Poor creature!*, ¡pobrecito!, ¡pobrecita!

crèche [kreiʃ] n. Guardería, *f.* (nursery). || Nacimiento, *m.* (a model of the Nativity).

credence [ˈkri:dəns] n. Creencia, *f.* (belief). || Crédito, *m.* (credit): *I gave credence to him*, le di crédito. || *Letters of credence*, cartas (*f.*) credenciales.

credential [kriˈdenʃəl] adj. Credencial.

credentials [kriˈdənʃəlz] pl. n. Credenciales, *f.*

credibility [ˌkrediˈbiliti] n. Credibilidad, *f.*, verosimilitud, *f.*

credible [ˈkredəbl] adj. Creíble, verosímil.

credit [ˈkredit] n. Crédito, *m.*: *I have credit at the butcher's*, tengo crédito en la carnicería. || COMM. Haber, *m.*: *on the credit side*, en el haber; *credit and debit*, debe y haber. | Crédito, *m.* || Honor, *m.*, prestigio, *m.* (good name): *he is a credit to the school*, hace honor a la escuela. || Influencia, *f.* (influence). || Fe, *f.*, creencia, *f.*, crédito, *m.* (belief). || U. S. Asignatura, *f.* (to get a degree). || — Pl. Ficha (*f. sing.*) técnica (of a film). || — *Credit balance*, saldo acreedor. || *Credit card*, tarjeta (*f.*) de crédito. || *Credit line*, nota (*f.*) que indica la procedencia de lo mencionado. || *Credit rating*, solvabilidad, *f.* || *Credit union*, banco (*m.*) de crédito. || *Credit where it's due*, el honor a quien le corresponda. || *It does him credit*, le honra, dice mucho a su favor. || *On credit*, a crédito, a plazos [*Amer.*, a cuotas] (terms). || *Tax credits*, deducciones tributarias. || *To buy on credit*, comprar a crédito, comprar a plazos. || *To come out of sth. with credit*, salir bien de algo. || *To gain credit*, confirmarse. || *To give credit*, dar crédito. || *To give credit to*, dar crédito a. || *To give s.o. credit for sth.*, atribuir *or* reconocer a alguien el mérito de algo. || *To his credit*, en su haber, a su favor. || *To lend credit to*, acreditar. || *To pass with credit*, sacar un notable. || *To take credit for*, atribuirse el mérito de. || *We do not give credit*, no se fía (shop). || *With credit*, muy decentemente, muy bien.

credit [ˈkredit] v. tr. Creer, dar crédito a (to believe). || FIG. Atribuir, reconocer: *he is credited with great intelligence*, se le atribuye una gran inteligencia. || Ingresar, abonar en cuenta (to enter money in an account). || Poner en el haber (to enter on the credit side of a balance sheet).

creditable [—əbl] adj. Digno de elogio, encomiable, loable (praiseworthy). || Digno de crédito (believable). || De buena reputación (of good repute).

creditably [—əbli] adv. De forma encomiable. || Honrosamente.

creditor [—ə*] n. Acreedor, ra.

credo [ˈkri:dəu] n. Credo, *m.*

credulity [kriˈdju:liti] n. Credulidad, *f.*

credulous [ˈkredjuləs] adj. Crédulo, la.

creed [kri:d] n. Credo, *m.*

creek [kri:k] n. Cala, *f.* (small bay). || U. S. Riachuelo, *m.* (small arm of a river). || FAM. *Up the creek*, en un aprieto.

creel [kri:l] n. Nasa, *f.* (angler's basket).

creep [kri:p] n. Arrastramiento, *m.*, deslizamiento, *m.* (act or pace of creeping). || GEOL. Deslizamiento, *m.* || Hormigueo, *m.* (in the skin). || FAM. Pelotillero, ra (toady). | Desgraciado, da (unpleasant person). || — Pl. FAM. Carne (*f. sing.*) de gallina (gooseflesh): *to give s.o. the creeps*, poner a alguien la carne de gallina. | Pavor, *m.*, miedo, *m.* (fear).

creep* [kri:p] v. intr. Arrastrarse, deslizarse, reptar (to move with body prone to the floor). || Gatear, andar a gatas (babies on their hands and knees). || Deslizarse (to move stealthily). || Ir muy despacio (to go slowly). || Deslizarse (an error). || Trepar (plants). || FAM. Ponérsele a uno la carne de gallina: *my flesh crept*, se me puso la carne de gallina. || FIG. Arrastrarse a los pies de, humillarse ante (to humble o.s.) || Sentir hormigueo (to tingle). || — *To creep about on tiptoe*, ir de puntillas. || *To creep by*, pasar lentamente. || *To creep in, out*, entrar, salir silenciosamente. || *To creep to s.o.*, hacer la pelotilla *or* dar la coba a uno. || *To creep up on s.o.*, acercarse sigilosamente a uno.
— OBSERV. Pret. & p. p. **crept**.

creeper [—ə*] n. BOT. Enredadera, *f.* || Trepador, *m.* (for climbing). || ZOOL. Ave (*f.*) trepadora (bird). || MAR. Rezón, *m.* || U. S. Pelele, *m.* (for baby). || — Pl. U. S. Tacos, *m.* (for boots).

creeping [—iŋ] adj. MED. Progresivo, va. || MIL. Móvil (barrage).
— N. See CREEP.

creepy [—i] adj. Espeluznante, horripilante.

creepy-crawly [ˈkri:piˈkrɔ:li] n. Bicho, *m.*

creese [kri:s] n. Puñal (*m.*) malayo, cris, *m.*

cremate [kriˈmeit] v. tr. Incinerar.

cremation [kriˈmeiʃən] n. Cremación, *f.*, incineración, *f.* (of the dead).

cremator [kriˈmeitə*] n. Horno (*m.*) crematorio (place of cremation). || Incinerador, *m.* (person).

crematorium [ˌkreməˈtɔ:riəm] n. Crematorio, *m.*, horno (*m.*) crematorio.
— OBSERV. El plural de *crematorium* es *crematoria* o *crematoriums*.

crematory [ˈkremətəri] n. Crematorio, *m.*, horno (*m.*) crematorio.
— Adj. Crematorio, ria.

crenate [ˈkri:neit] adj. BOT. Dentado, da.

crenel or **crenelle** [ˈkrenəl] n. Almena, *f.*

crenellate or **crenelate** [ˈkrenileit] v. tr. Almenar.

crenellation or **crenelation** [ˌkreniˈleiʃən] n. Almenaje, *m.*, almenas, *f. pl.*

Creole [ˈkri:əul] adj./n. Criollo, lla.

creosol [ˈkriəsəl] n. CHEM. Creosol, *m.*, aceite (*m.*) de creosota.

creosote [ˈkriəsəut] n. CHEM. Creosota, *f.*

creosote [ˈkriəsəut] v. tr. Creosotar.

creosoting [—iŋ] n. TECH. Creosotado, *m.*

crêpe or **crepe** [kreip] n. Crespón, *m.* (fabric). || Crepé, *m.* (rubber).
crepitant [ˈkrepitənt] adj. Crepitante.
crepitate [ˈkrepiteit] v. tr. Crepitar (to crackle). || Crujir (joints).
crepitation [krepiˈteiʃən] n. Crepitación, *f.*
crept [krept] pret. & p. p. See CREEP.
crepuscular [kriˈpəskjulə*] adj. Crepuscular.
crescendo [kriˈʃendəu] adj./adv. MUS. Crescendo.
— N. MUS. Crescendo, *m.*
crescent [ˈkresnt] n. Luna (*f.*) creciente (the waxing moon). || Medialuna, *f.* (any half-moon shape). || Media Luna, *f.* (emblem).
— Adj. Creciente.
cresol [ˈkrisɔl] n. CHEM. Cresol, *m.*
cress [kres] n. BOT. Berro, *m.*
crest [krest] n. Cresta, *f.* (on the head of animals). || Cimera, *f.* (on helmet). || Penacho, *m.* (plume of helmet). || Cresta, *f.* (top of wave). || Cima, *f.*, cumbre, *f.*, cresta, *f.* (of hill). || Copa, *f.* (of tree). || Crines, *f. pl.* (a mane). || ARCH. Caballete, *m.*, cumbrera, *f.* || HERALD. Timbre, *m.*
crest [krest] v. tr. Coronar (a wall). || Poner un penacho a. || ARCH. Poner un caballete a. || FIG. Subir hasta la cima *or* cumbre de (a hill, etc.).
— V. intr. Encresparse (wave).
crested lark [—idˈlɑ:k] n. ZOOL. Cogujada, *f.*
crestfallen [—ˌfɔ:lən] adj. Alicaído, da; cabizbajo, ja.
cretaceous [kriˈteiʃəs] adj. Gredoso, sa; cretáceo, a.
Cretaceous [kriˈteiʃəs] adj. Cretáceo, a.
— N. Cretáceo, *m.*
Cretan [ˈkri:tən] adj./n. Cretense.
Crete [kri:t] pr. n. GEOGR. Creta, *f.*
cretin [ˈkretin] n. Cretino, na.
cretinism [ˈkretinizəm] n. Cretinismo, *m.*
cretinous [ˈkretinəs] adj. Cretino, na.
cretonne [kreˈtɔn] n. Cretona, *f.* (material).
crevasse [kriˈvæs] n. GEOL. Grieta, *f.*
crevice [ˈkrevis] n. Grieta, *f.*
crew [kru:] n. Tripulación, *f.* (of ship, aircraft). || MIL. Dotación, *f.* (of tank, gun). || Equipo, *m.* (body of men working together). || Banda, *f.*, cuadrilla, *f.* (a mob). || *Ground crew*, personal (*m.*) de tierra.
crew [kru:] pret. See CROW.
crew cut [—kʌt] n. Pelo (*m.*) cortado al cepillo (very short hairstyle).
crewel [ˈkru:il] n. Estambre, *m.*
crib [krib] n. Pesebre, *m.* (rack). || Cuadra, *f.* (stable). || U. S. Cuna, *f.* (cot). || Belén, *m.*, nacimiento, *m.* (crèche). || Traducción (*f.*) literal de una obra clásica para uso en los colegios. || FAM. Plagio, *m.* (a plagiarism). | Chuleta, *f.* (in exam). | Caja (*f.*) de caudales (in banks). || Nasa, *f.* (trap for fish). || FAM. Cuadra, *f.* (room). | Casucha, *f.* (house). || ARCH. Encofrado, *m.* || MIN. Entibación, *f.* (framework of a mine shaft). || Puntales, *m. pl.* (heavy timber supports). || U. S. Arca, *f.* (bin for grain).
crib [krib] v. tr. FAM. Copiar (to copy unfairly). | Plagiar (to plagiarize). || MIN. Entibar (to line with timber). || ARCH. Poner encofrado a. || Almacenar (grains). || Encerrar, confinar (to lock in). || FAM. Birlar, robar (to steal).
— V. intr. FAM. Usar chuletas (a student). || Plagiar (to plagiarize).
cribwork [—wə:k] n. Entibación, *f.*, encofrado, *m.*
crick [krik] n. Calambre, *m.* (cramp). || Tortícolis, *m.* & *f.* (in the neck). || Lumbago, *m.* (in the back).
crick [krik] v. tr. Dar tortícolis (in the neck). || Dar lumbago (in the back). || Dar un calambre.
cricket [ˈkrikit] n. ZOOL. Grillo, *m.* || SP. Criquet, *m.*, cricket, *m.* || FIG. *It's not cricket!*, ¡esto no es jugar limpio!
cricketer [—ə*] n. Jugador (*m.*) de cricket.
cricoid [ˈkraikɔid] adj. ANAT. Cricoides.
— N. ANAT. Cricoides, *m. inv.*
crier [ˈkraiə*] n. Pregonero, *m.*: *town crier*, pregonero público.
crime [kraim] n. Crimen, *m.* (a violation of the law): *crime wave*, ola de crímenes. || Criminalidad, *f.*: *an increase in crime*, un aumento de la criminalidad.
Crimea [kraiˈmiə] pr. n. GEOGR. Crimea, *f.*
criminal [ˈkriminl] adj./n. Criminal: *a criminal action*, una acción criminal; *to arrest a criminal*, detener a un criminal. || — *Criminal law*, derecho (*m.*) penal. || *Criminal lawyer*, penalista, *m.* & *f.*, criminalista, *m.* & *f.* || *Criminal record*, antecedentes (*m. pl.*) penales.
criminalist [—əlist] n. Criminalista, *m.* & *f.*
criminality [ˌkrimiˈnæliti] n. Criminalidad, *f.*
criminate [ˈkrimineit] v. tr. Incriminar. || Condenar.
crimination [ˌkrimiˈneiʃən] n. Incriminación, *f.*
criminative [ˈkriminətiv] or **criminatory** [ˈkriminətəri] adj. Acusatorio, ria.
criminological [ˌkriminəˈlɔdʒikəl] adj. Criminológico, ca.
criminilogist [ˌkrimiˈnɔlədʒist] n. Criminologista, *m.* & *f.*, criminalista, *m.* & *f.*
criminology [ˌkrimiˈnɔlədʒi] n. Criminología, *f.*
crimmer [ˈkrimə*] n. Variedad (*f.*) de caracul.
crimp [krimp] n. Rizos, *m. pl.* (in hair). || Ondulación, *f.* (corrugation). || Reclutador, ra (of soldiers, etc.). || U. S. FAM. Obstáculo, *m.*, traba, *f.*
crimp [krimp] v. tr. Ondular (to wave). || Rizar (to curl). || Fruncir, plisar (cloth). || Encañonar (linen). || Estrechar (a tube). || Acanalar (to make flutings in). || Acuchillar (to gash newly killed fish). || Dar forma (to mould). || MIL. Reclutar. || U. S. Estorbar, obstaculizar, poner trabas a.
crimson [ˈkrimzn] adj. Carmesí. || *To turn crimson*, enrojecer, ponerse rojo (sky), ponerse colorado, sonrojarse (s.o.).
— N. Carmesí, *m.*
crimson [ˈkrimzn] v. tr. Teñir de carmesí.
— V. intr. Sonrojarse, ponerse colorado (to blush).
cringe [krindʒ] v. intr. Encogerse, acobardarse (to shrink). || Agacharse (to cower). || Humillarse, rebajarse (to lower o.s.)
cringing [—iŋ] adj. Servil. || Rastrero, ra (abject).
cringle [ˈkriŋgl] n. MAR. Garrucho *m.*
crinkle [ˈkriŋkl] n. Arruga, *f.* (wrinkle). || Ondulado, *m.* || Rizado, *m.* (of hair). || Frunce, *m.*, pliegue, *m.* (pleat). || Crujido, *m.* (crisp sound).
crinkle [ˈkriŋkl] v. intr. Arrugarse (to wrinkle). || Rizarse (to ridge). || Ondularse (to ripple). || Crujir (to rustle). || Crepitar (the fire, etc.).
— V. tr. Arrugar (to wrinkle). || Ondular (to wave). || Rizar (hair).
crinkly [—i] adj. Arrugado, da (wrinkled). || Ondulado, da (wavy). || Rizado, da (hair). || Crujiente (leaves, silk, etc.).
crinoid [ˈkrainɔid] n. ZOOL. Crinoideo, *m.*
crinoline [ˈkrinəli:n] n. Miriñaque, *m.* (a hopped petticoat). || Crinolina, *f.* (fabric of horsehair).
cripes [kraips] interj. FAM. ¡Caramba!
cripple [ˈkripl] adj./n. Tullido, da; lisiado, da.
cripple [ˈkripl] v. tr. Lisiar, tullir (a person). || Estropear (a ship, etc.). || FIG. Paralizar.
crisis [ˈkraisis] n. Crisis, *f. inv.*: *cabinet crisis*, crisis ministerial. || *To draw to a crisis*, llegar al punto crucial *or* crítico.
— OBSERV. El plural de la palabra inglesa es *crises*.
crisp [krisp] adj. Fresco, ca: *crisp lettuce*, lechuga fresca. || Vivificante (air). || Directo, ta; vigoroso, sa: *a crisp style*, un estilo directo. || Crespo, pa; rizado, da: *crisp hair*, pelo crespo. || Curruscante (bread, biscuit). || Decidido, da; resuelto, ta (resolute). || Crujiente (snow). || Claro, ra; preciso, sa (analysis). || Animado, da (dialogue). || Tajante (tone).
— N. Patata (*f.*) frita a la inglesa.
crisp [krisp] v. tr. Encrespar, rizar (cloth, hair). || Volver curruscante (bread, etc.).
— V. intr. Encresparse, rizarse (hair). || Ponerse curruscante (bread, etc.).
crispation [krisˈpeiʃən] n. Crispamiento, *m.* (of the skin). || Rizado, *m.* (curling).
crisper [ˈkrispə*] n. Tenacillas (*f. pl.*) de rizar, rizador (*m.*) para el pelo.
crispness [ˈkrispnis] n. Encrespado, *m.*, rizado, *m.* (of hair). || Frío (*m.*) vivificante (air). || Crujido, *m.* (of snow). || Consistencia (*f.*) curruscante (of bread, etc.). || Claridad, *f.* (of style, music, etc.). || FIG. Vivacidad, *f.*
crispy [ˈkrispi] adj. See CRISP.
crisscross [ˈkriskrɔs] n. Entrecruzamiento, *m.* || Cruz, *f.* (signature). || FIG. Enredo, *m.*, enmarañamiento, *m.*
— Adj. Entrecruzado, da.
crisscross [ˈkriskrɔs] v. tr. Entrecruzar.
— V. intr. Entrecruzarse.
criterion [kraiˈtiəriən] n. Criterio, *m.*
— OBSERV. El plural de *criterion* es *criteria*.
critic [ˈkritik] n. Crítico, *m.* (reviewer). || Criticón, ona (faultfinder).
critical [ˈkritikəl] adj. Exigente, criticón, ona (demanding). || Crítico, ca: *critical faculty*, sentido crítico; *critical point*, punto crítico. || PHYS. MATH. Crítico, ca. || *To be critical of*, criticar.
criticaster [ˈkritiˌkæstə*] n. Criticastro, *m.*
criticism [ˈkritisizəm] n. Crítica, *f.*
criticizable [ˈkritisaizəbl] adj. Criticable.
criticize [ˈkritisaiz] v. tr./intr. Criticar.
criticizer [—ə*] n. Criticón, ona.
critique [kriˈti:k] n. Crítica, *f.*
croak [krəuk] n. Croar, *m.*, canto, *m.* (of frog). || Graznido, *m.* (of raven). || Gruñido, *m.* (of people).
croak [krəuk] v. intr. Croar, cantar (frog). || Graznar (raven). || FIG. Gruñir, refunfuñar (to complain). | Augurar desgracias (to predict evil). || FAM. Reventar, palmar (to die).
— V. tr. Decir refunfuñando (to grumble). || FIG. Pronosticar, presagiar (to forebode). || FAM. Apiolar, liquidar (to kill).
Croat [krəuət] adj./n. Croata.
Croatian [krəuˈeiʃjən] adj./n. Croata.
crochet [ˈkrəuʃei] n. Ganchillo, *m.*, "croché", *m.*
crochet [ˈkrəuʃei] v. tr. Hacer a ganchillo.
— V. intr. Hacer ganchillo.
crock [krɔk] n. Cántaro, *m.* (earthenware pot). || FAM. Carcamal, *m.* (worn-out person). | Cacharro, *m.* (worn-out thing). | Jamelgo, *m.* (nag).
crock [krɔk] v. tr. Lisiar.
— V. intr. Lisiarse.
crockery [ˈkrɔkəri] n. Loza, *f.*
crocket [ˈkrɔkit] n. ARCH. Follaje, *m.*
crocodile [ˈkrɔkədail] n. ZOOL. Cocodrilo, *m.* || FIG. Fila (*f.*) de a dos (double file). || FIG. *To shed crocodile tears*, llorar lágrimas de cocodrilo.

crocodilians [krɔkəˈdiliəns] pl. n. Cocodriloideos, *m.*
crocus [ˈkrəukəs] n. BOT. Azafrán, *m.*

— OBSERV. El plural de *crocus* es *crocuses* o *croci.*

Croesus [ˈkri:səs] pr. n. Creso, *m.*
croft [krɔft] n. Huerta (*f.*) arrendada (small rented holding). || Huerto, *m.* (adjoining a cottage).
crofter [ˈkrɔftə*] n. Colono, *m.*
cromlech [ˈkrɔmlek] n. Crómlech, *m.*
crone [krəun] n. FAM. Arpía, *f.*, bruja, *f.*
crony [ˈkrəuni] n. FAM. Amigote, *m.* (chum).
crook [kruk] n. Cayado, *m.* (for shepherds). || Báculo, *m.* (of a bishop). || Gancho, *m.* (a hook). || Recodo, *m.* (of a path, river, etc.). || Ángulo, *m.*, curva, *f.*, codo, *m.* (of anything hooked). || Corva, *f.* (of leg). || Pliegue, *m.* (of elbow). || FAM. Ladrón, *m.*, timador, *m.* (swindler).
crook [kruk] v. tr. Encorvar, doblar (to bend). || Enganchar (to grasp with a hook). || FAM. Estafar, timar (to swindler). || FAM. *To crook the elbow*, empinar el codo.
— V. intr. Encorvarse, doblarse.
crooked [—id] adj. Torcido, da; doblado, da (twisted). || Retorcido, da (wood). || Curvo, va; curvado, da (bent). || Encorvado, da (bent with age). || Tortuoso, sa; sinuoso, sa (path). || Zambo, ba (leg). || Corvo, va; ganchudo, da (nose). || FIG. Tortuoso, sa (means). | Poco limpio, pia (person, practice).
crookedness [—nis] n. Sinuosidad, *f.* (of a path). || FIG. Falta (*f.*) de honradez.
croon [kru:n] n. Tarareo, *m.*, canturreo, *m.*
croon [kru:n] v. tr. Tararear, cantar a media voz, canturrear.
crooner [—ə*] n. Cantante (*m.*) melódico.
crop [krɔp] n. Cosecha, *f.* (harvest). || Cultivo, *m.* (cultivated produce): *crop rotation*, rotación de cultivos. || Buche, *m.* (gullet of bird). || Fusta, *f.* (hunting whip). || Mango, *m.*, empuñadura, *f.* (handle of whip). || Corte (*m.*) de pelo (haircut). || Pelo (*m.*) muy corto (style): *she wears her hair in a crop*, lleva el pelo muy corto. || Cuero, *m.* (a hide). || Espaldilla, *f.* (meat). || FIG. Montón, *m.*: *a crop of difficulties*, un montón de dificultades. | Cosecha, *f.* (collection). || — *Crop year*, campaña (*f.*) agrícola. || *In crop*, cultivado, da. || *Out of crop*, sin cultivo. || *To have a fine crop of hair*, tener una buena mata de pelo.
crop [krɔp] v. tr. Cortar muy corto (hair). || Cortar (the grass). || Recortar (to cut off ends). || Podar (shrubs, etc.). || Desmochar (branches). || Desorejar, cortar las puntas de las orejas a (to clip ears). || Cortar la cola de (to cut the tail). || Cosechar (to harvest). || Cultivar (to cultivate). || Plantar, sembrar (to plant with): *to crop a field with clover*, plantar un campo de trébol. || Tundir (textiles).
— V. intr. Rendir (land). || Pacer (sheep). || — *To crop out* o *up*, aflorar. || FIG. *To crop up*, surgir, aparecer.
crop-eared [—iəd] adj. Con las orejas cortadas.
cropper [ˈkrɔpə*] n. Tundidora, *f.* (textiles). || Cortacéspedes, *m.* inv. (for grass). || Cultivador, *m.*, agricultor, *m.* (one who cultivates). || Segador, *m.* (harvestman). || FAM. *To come a cropper*, darse un batacazo (to fall), ser cateado: *I came a cropper in history*, me catearon en historia.
croquet [ˈkrəukei] n. SP. Croquet, *m.*
croquette [krɔˈket] n. Croqueta, *f.*
crosier [ˈkrəuʒə*] n. Báculo, *m.*
cross [krɔs] n. Cruz, *f.* || Cruce, *m.* (of streets). || Cruce, *m.* (of phone lines, etc.). || Golpe (*m.*) cruzado (in boxing). || Cruce, *m.* (between breeds). || Trazo (*m.*) horizontal (as on the letter "t"). || FIG. Mezcla, *f.* (mixing). | Cruz, *f.*, prueba, *f.* (burden). || FAM. Estafa, *f.*, timo, *m.* (swindle). || — *On the cross*, sesgado, da; al bies (woodwork, textiles), fraudulentamente. || *Red Cross*, Cruz Roja. || FIG. *To be a cross between*, ser una mezcla de. | *To bear one's cross*, llevar su cruz. || *To make the sign of the cross*, hacer la señal de la cruz, santiguarse. || *To take the Cross*, ir a una cruzada.
— Adj. Cruzado, da; transversal (transverse). || Cruzado, da (breed). || Contrario, ria; opuesto, ta (contrary). || Enfadado, da (angry): *he is cross with me*, está enfadado conmigo. || — FAM. *As cross as two sticks*, de un humor de perros. || *To get cross*, enfadarse.
cross [krɔs] v. tr. Cruzar (to place crosswise, to mark a cheque, to interbreed). || Cruzar (the arms, legs). || Atravesar, cruzar (to go across): *to cross the road*, cruzar la calle; *bridge crossing the river*, puente que atraviesa el río. || Cruzarse con (a person). || Contrariar (to oppose). || Frustrar (to thwart, to frustrate). || Marcar con una cruz (to mark with a cross). || REL. Hacer la señal de la cruz a. || Poner un trazo horizontal a (a letter). || Montar a horcajadas sobre (a horse, a saddle). || — *To cross off* o *out*, tachar. || *To cross one's arms*, cruzarse de brazos. || *To cross one's mind*, ocurrírsele a alguien, pasar por la mente: *suddenly an idea crossed my mind*, de pronto se me ocurrió una idea. || *To cross o.s.*, santiguarse. || *To cross over*, atravesar. || *To cross s.o.'s palm with silver*, llenar las manos de alguien de monedas de plata. || *To cross swords with*, see SWORD. || *To cross the border*, pasar *or* cruzar *or* atravesar la frontera.
— V. intr. Cruzarse (roads, letters, breeds, etc.). || Pasar, cruzar, atravesar (to go over).
crossbar [—bɑ:*] n. Travesaño, *m.* || Tranca, *f.* (of the door). || Barra, *f.* (on bicycle). || Larguero, *m.* (of the goal). || PRINT. Crucero, *m.*
crossbeam [—bi:m] n. Viga (*f.*) transversal.
crossbearer [—ˌbɛərə*] n. REL. Crucero, *m.*
crossbench [—bentʃ] n. Escaño (*m.*) de los diputados independientes en el parlamento británico.
crossbow [—bəu] n. Ballesta, *f.*
crossbred [—bred] pret. & p. p. See CROSSBREED.
— Adj. Cruzado, da; híbrido, da.
crossbreed [—bri:d] n. Híbrido, *m.*
crossbreed* [—bri:d] v. tr. Cruzar.

— OBSERV. Pret. & p. p. ***crossbred.***

crossbreeding [—ˌbri:diŋ] n. Cruce, *m.*
cross-check [—tʃek] v. intr./tr. Comprobar otra vez.
cross-country [—ˈkʌntri] adj. A campo traviesa. || *Cross-country race*, "cross-country", *m.*, "cross", *m.*, carrera (*f.*) a campo traviesa *or* a campo través.
crosscurrent [—ˈkʌrənt] n. Contracorriente, *f.*
crosscut [—kʌt] n. Corte (*m.*) transversal (a diagonal cut). || Atajo, *m.* (path running crosswise). || MIN. Crucero, *m.*
crosscut [—kʌt] v. tr. Cortar transversalmente.
cross-examination [—igˌzæmiˈneiʃən] n. Interrogatorio (*m.*) hecho para comprobar lo declarado anteriormente.
cross-examine [—igˈzæmin] v. tr. Interrogar [para comprobar lo declarado anteriormente].
cross-eye [—ai] n. Bizquera, *f.*
cross-eyed [—aid] adj. Bizco, ca.
cross-fertilization [—ˌfə:tilaiˈzeiʃən] n. Fecundación (*f.*) cruzada.
cross-fertilize [—ˈfə:tilaiz] v. tr. Fecundar por fecundación cruzada.
cross fire [—faiə*] n. Fuego (*m.*) cruzado. || FIG. *Exposed to cross fire*, cogido entre dos fuegos.
cross-grained [—greind] adj. De fibras irregulares *or* cruzadas (wood). || FIG. Intratable (people). | Intrincado, da; enmarañado, da (problem, etc.).
cross hairs [—hɛəz] pl. n. Retículo, *m. sing.*, retícula, *f.* sing.
crosshatch [—hætʃ] v. tr. Sombrear.
crosshead [—hed] n. TECH. Cruceta, *f.* || Subtítulo, *m.* (in a newspaper).
crossing [—iŋ] n. Travesía, *f.* (sea voyage). || Cruce, *m.* (intersection). || Paso (*m.*) de peatones, cruce, *m.* (for crossing roads). || Paso (*m.*) a nivel (rail). || Paso, *m.* (for crossing rivers). || Cruce, *m.*, cruzamiento, *m.* (of races). || *Crossing gate*, barrera (*f.*) de paso a nivel.
crossing out [—iŋˌaut] n. Tachadura, *f.*
crossing-over [—iŋˌəuvə*] n. Entrecruzamiento, *m.*
cross-legged [—legd] adj. Con las piernas cruzadas.
cross-linkage [—ˈliŋkidʒ] n. CHEM. Eslabón, *m.*
crossly [—li] adv. Con enfado, malhumoradamente.
crossover [—ˌəuvə*] n. Paso, *m.*
crosspatch [—pætʃ] n. FAM. Gruñón, ona.
crosspiece [—pi:s] n. Travesaño, *m.*
cross-purposes [—ˈpə:pəsiz] pl. n. Fines (*m.*) opuestos, objetivos (*m.*) opuestos. || *We are* (*talking*) *at cross-purposes*, hay un malentendido.
cross-question [—ˈkwestʃən] n. Pregunta (*f.*) hecha para comprobar declaraciones anteriores.
cross-question [—ˈkwestʃən] v. tr. Interrogar [para comprobar declaraciones anteriores].
cross-refer [—riˈfə*] v. tr. Remitir a.
— V. intr. Hacer una remisión.
cross-reference [—ˈrefrəns] n. Referencia, *f.*, remisión, *f.*
crossroad [—rəud] n. Cruce, *m.* (road crossing another). || — Pl. Cruce, *m. sing.* || FIG. Encrucijada, *f. sing.*: *at the crossroads*, en la encrucijada.
cross ruling [—ˈru:liŋ] n. Cuadrícula, *f.*
cross section [ˈsekʃən] n. Sección (*f.*) *or* corte (*m.*) transversal (a transverse section). || MATH. Sección (*f.*) recta. || FIG. Muestra (*f.*) representativa (a representative sample).
cross stitch [—stitʃ] n. Punto (*m.*) de cruz.
cross talk [—tɔ:k] n. Réplicas (*f. pl.*) ocurrentes. || Cruce (*m.*) de líneas (of phone). || RAD. Interferencia, *f.*
crosstie [—tai] n. U. S. Traviesa, *f.*
crosstrees [—tri:z] pl. n. MAR. Crucetas, *f.*
crosswalk [—ˌwɔ:k] n. Cruce, *m.*, paso (*m.*) de peatones.
crossway [—ˌwei] n. Encrucijada, *f.*
crosswind [—wind] n. Viento (*m.*) de costado.
crosswise [—waiz] adv. En forma de cruz (in the form of a cross). || Transversalmente.
crossword [—wə:d] n. Crucigrama, *m.*
crotch [krɔtʃ] n. Horquilla, *f.* (of a tree). || Cruz, *f.*, entrepierna, *f.*, entrepiernas, *f. pl.* (of a person).
crotchet [ˈkrɔtʃit] n. MUS. Negra, *f.* || FIG. Idea (*f.*) fija, manía, *f.*, capricho, *m.*
crotchety [ˈkrɔtʃiti] adj. De mal genio, arisco, ca (surly). || Fantasioso, sa; caprichoso, sa; excéntrico, ca (eccentric).
Croton bug [—bʌg] n. ZOOL. Cucaracha *f.*
crouch [krautʃ] v. intr. Estar en cuclillas *or* agachado (to be squatting). || Agacharse, ponerse en cuclillas (to squat). || Encogerse (before springing). || FIG. Rebajarse. || *To crouch down*, agacharse, ponerse en cuclillas.
croup [kru:p] n. MED. Garrotillo, *m.*, crup, *m.*

croup or **croupe** [kru:p] n. Grupa, *f.* (of a horse).
croupier [ˈkru:piə*] n. "Croupier", *m.*
crouton [kruˈtɔ̃n] n. Cuscurro, *m.*, cuscurrón, *m.*
crow [krəu] n. ZOOL. Cuervo, *m.* (bird). || Quiquiriquí, *m.*, cacareo, *m.* (call of a cock). || Balbuceo, *m.* (of a baby). || TECH. Palanca, *f.* || — FIG. *As the crow flies*, a vuelo de pájaro, en línea recta. || U. S. FAM. *To eat crow*, reconocer su error.
crow* [krəu] v. intr. Cantar, cacarear (a cock). || Balbucear (baby). || Gritar con entusiasmo. || — *To crow over*, pavonearse *or* jactarse de. || *To crow over s.o.*, salir triunfante de alguien.
— OBSERV. Pret. **crew, crowed;** p. p. **crowed.**
crowbar [ˈkrəubɑ:*] n. Palanca, *f.*
crowd [kraud] n. Multitud, *f.*, muchedumbre, *f.* (many people). || Pandilla, *f.*, grupo, *m.* (a clique). || Público, *m.*, espectadores, *m. pl.* (spectators). || Vulgo, *m.* (common people). || FIG. FAM. Montón, *m.*, gran cantidad, *f.* (heap): *a crowd of things*, un montón de cosas. || THEATR. Comparsas, *m. pl.* || CINEM. Extras, *m. pl.* || — *In a crowd*, en tropel, todos juntos. || *There was quite a crowd*, había un gran gentío *or* mucha gente. || *To follow the crowd*, dejarse llevar por los demás.
crowd [kraud] v. tr. Atestar, llenar (to fill space). || Amontonar, apiñar, reunir (to collect). || Empujar (to push). || Apresurar (to hurry). || Apremiar (to put under pressure). || *To crowd (on) sail*, hacer fuerza de vela.
— V. intr. Amontonarse, apiñarse (to throng). || Reunirse, congregarse (to assemble).
— ***To crowd around*** o ***together***, agolparse, amontonarse, apiñarse. || ***To crowd down***, bajar en tropel. || ***To crowd in***, entrar en tropel. || ***To crowd out***, salir en tropel: *they crowded out of the house*, salieron de la casa en tropel; dejar fuera, excluir: *your report was crowded out*, su informe fue dejado fuera [del periódico]. | — *He was crowded out of the race*, en la carrera le estorbaron el paso. || ***To crowd round***, apiñarse en torno [de].
crowded [—id] adj. Lleno, na; atestado, da. || Muy concurrido, con mucho público (spectacle). || — *Crowded together*, apretados unos contra otros. || *The theater was crowded*, el teatro estaba atestado de gente, había mucha gente en el teatro.
crowfoot [ˈkrəufut] n. BOT. Ranúnculo, *m.* || MAR. Cabuyera, *f.* || MIL. Abrojo, *m.*
— OBSERV El plural de *crowfoot* es *crowfeet*, excepto en el sentido botánico para el cual se usa *crowfoots*.
crown [kraun] n. Corona, *f.* || ARCH. Coronamiento, *m.*, remate, *m.* || Parte (*f.*) central (of a road). || Copa, *f.* (of a hat). || Cumbre, *f.*, cima, *f.* (of a hill). || Copete, *m.*, cresta, *f.* (of a bird). || Caballete, *m.* (of a roof). || Coronilla, *f.* (of the head). || Corona, *f.* (coin): *half a crown*, media corona. || ANAT. Corona, *f.* (of a tooth). || Copa, *f.* (of a tree). || Mesa, *f.* (of an anvil). || FIG. Coronación, *f.*, coronamiento, *m.*, remate, *m.* (of life's work). || Cápsula, *f.* (of a bottle). || Parte (*f.*) superior (of a bell). || Clave, *f.* (of a vault). || MAR. Diamante, *m.* (of the anchor). || — MIN. *Crown block*, caballete (*m.*) portapoleas. || *Crown cap* o *crown cork*, cápsula, *f.* || *Crown colony*, colonia (*f.*) de la Corona. || *Crown glass*, crownglass, *m.* || *Crown jewels*, joyas (*f.*) reales *or* de la Corona. || *Crown land*, patrimonio (*m.*) de la Corona. || *Crown law*, derecho (*m.*) penal. || *Crown lens*, lente convexa. || *Crown prince*, príncipe heredero. || TECH. *Crown wheel*, corona dentada. || *The Crown*, la Corona.
crown [kraun] v. tr. Coronar (a monarch, a building): *crowned head*, testa coronada. || FIG. Coronar, completar, rematar (to complete). || Poner una corona a (a tooth). || Coronar (in draughts). || FIG. Coronar, recompensar, galardonar (to reward). || Dar forma convexa, bombear (a road). || FAM. Dar un golpe en la cabeza a (to hit on the head). || *To crown it all*, para rematarlo todo.
crowning [—iŋ] adj. Supremo, ma.
— N. Coronación, *f.*
crow's-foot [ˈkrəuzfut] n. Pata (*f.*) de gallo (of the eyes). || MIL. Abrojo, *m.* (caltrop).
— OBSERV. El plural de esta palabra es *crow's-feet*.
crow's nest [ˈkrəuznest] n. Torre (*f.*) de vigía, atalaya, *f.*
crozier [ˈkrəuʒə*] n. REL. Báculo, *m.*
crucial [ˈkru:ʃəl] adj. Crucial, decisivo, va; crítico, ca: *crucial problems*, problemas cruciales. || ANAT. En forma de cruz, crucial.
cruciate [ˈkru:ʃieit] adj. BOT. Cruciforme. || ZOOL. Cruzado, da.
crucible [ˈkru:sibl] n. Crisol, *m.* || FIG. Crisol, *m.* || *Crucible steel*, acero (*m.*) de crisol.
crucifer [ˈkru:sifə*] n. REL. Cruciferario, *m.* || BOT. Crucífera, *f.*
cruciferae [kruˈsifəri] pl. n. BOT. Crucíferas, *f.*
cruciferous [kru:ˈsifərəs] adj. Crucífero, ra.
crucified [ˈkru:sifaid] adj. Crucificado, da.
crucifix [ˈkru:sifiks] n. REL. Crucifijo, *m.*
crucifixion [ˌkru:siˈfikʃən] n. Crucifixión, *f.*
cruciform [ˈkru:sifɔ:m] adj. Cruciforme.
crucify [ˈkru:sifai] v. tr. Crucificar (to put to death on a cross). || FIG. Mortificar (to mortify). | Martirizar (to torment).
crude [kru:d] adj. Crudo, da (raw). || Bruto, ta (steel, etc.). || Sin refinar, crudo, da; bruto, ta (oil, petrol). || Crudo, da; vivo, va (light). || Crudo, da; brutal (reality, statement). || Basto, ta; ordinario, ria (vulgar). || Tosco, ca; mal acabado, da: *crude furniture*, muebles toscos. || Verde (fruit). || MED. Latente (disease). | Sin asimilar (undigested).
— M. Crudo, *m.*, petróleo (*m.*) crudo *or* sin refinar.
crudeness [—nis] or **crudity** [—iti] n. Crudeza, *f.* (rawness). || Ordinariez, *f.* (vulgarity). || Tosquedad, *f.* (coarseness).
cruel [kruəl] adj. Cruel.
cruelty [ˈkruəlti] n. Crueldad, *f.* || *Society for the prevention of cruelty to animals*, sociedad protectora de animales.
cruet [ˈkru:it] n. Vinagreras, *f. pl.*, angarillas, *f. pl.* (for oil and vinegar). || REL. Vinajera, *f.*
cruet stand [—stænd] n. Vinagreras, *f. pl.*, angarillas, *f. pl.*
cruise [kru:z] n. MAR. Crucero, *m.*
cruise [kru:z] v. intr. MAR. Hacer un crucero (to make a sea voyage). | Patrullar (to be in search of enemy ships). || Ir a una velocidad de crucero (at cruising speed). || Circular lentamente (to drive slowly). || FIG. Andar, ir.
cruiser [kru:zə*] n. MAR. Crucero, *m.* (warship). | Barco (*m.*) para cruceros (passenger boat).
cruiserweight [—weit] n. Semipesado, *m.* (in boxing).
cruising [kru:ziŋ] adj. De crucero. || *Cruising speed*, velocidad (*f.*) de crucero (of aircraft), velocidad económica (of cars).
— N. Crucero, *f.*
crumb [krʌm] n. Migaja, *f.*, trozo, *m.*, pedazo, *m.* (a fragment). || Miga, *f.* (the inside of a loaf of bread).
crumb [krʌm] v. tr. Empanar (to coat with bread). || Desmigar, desmigajar (to break into crumbs).
crumble [ˈkrumbl] v. tr. Desmenuzar (to break into small pieces). || Desmigar, desmigajar (bread).
— V. intr. Derrumbarse (to fall). || Deshacerse (to fall to pieces). || Desmigajarse, desmigarse (bread). || Desmoronarse (walls). || FIG. Pulverizarse.
crumbly [ˈkrʌmbli] adj. Desmenuzable. || Desmoronadizo, za (a wall, house, etc.).
crumby [ˈkrʌmi] adj. Empanado, da (covered with crumbs). || Blando, da (soft).
crummy [ˈkrʌmi] adj. FAM. Que no vale nada, malísimo, ma (bad). | De mala muerte (place).
crump [krʌmp] n. Golpe (*m.*) fuerte (hard hit). || Explosión, *f.* (of bombs).
crumpet [ˈkrʌmpit] n. Bollo (*m.*) blando. || FIG. FAM. Cholla, *f.*, cabeza, *f.* (head). || FIG. FAM. *To be off one's crumpets*, estar chiflado.
crumple [ˈkrʌmpl] n. Arruga, *f.*
crumple [ˈkrʌmpl] v. tr. Arrugar.
— V. intr. Arrugarse. || *To crumple up*, desplomarse (to fall), aplastarse (to be squashed).
crunch [krʌntʃ] n. Crujido, *m.* (noise). || Mascadura, *f.* (action). || FIG. Momento (*m.*) decisivo.
crunch [krʌntʃ] v. tr. Masticar [haciendo ruido] (to crush with the teeth). || Triturar (to grind). || Hacer crujir: *to crunch one's way through snow*, hacer crujir la nieve a su paso.
— V. intr. Crujir.
crunchy [krʌntʃi] adj. Que cruje, crujiente.
cruor [ˈkru:ɔ:*] n. MED. Crúor, *m.*
crupper [ˈkrʌpə*] n. Baticola, *f.* (of harness). || Grupa, *f.* (of a horse): *on the crupper*, a la grupa.
crural [ˈkruərəl] adj. ANAT. Crural, femoral.
crusade [kru:ˈseid] n. Cruzada, *f.* (war). || FIG. Campaña, *f.*, cruzada, *f.*: *crusade against drink*, campaña contra el alcohol.
crusade [kru:ˈseid] v. intr. Hacer una cruzada: *El Cid crusaded against the Moors*, el Cid hizo una cruzada contra los moros. || FIG. Hacer una campaña *or* una cruzada: *they crusade against drink*, hacen una campaña contra la bebida.
crusader [—ə*] n. Cruzado, *m.*
crush [krʌʃ] n. Aglomeración, *f.*, multitud, *f.* (crowd): *there was a great crush in the train*, había una gran aglomeración en el tren. || Aplastamiento, *m.* (squashing). || Apretón, *m.* (squeeze). || Choque, *m.*, colisión, *f.* (collision). || Pasaje (*m.*) estrecho (fenced passage for sheep). || — *I hate the crush of public transport*, odio los apretones de los transportes públicos. || FAM. *I have a crush on her*, estoy loco perdido por ella. || *Orange crush*, naranjada, *f.*
crush [krʌʃ] v. tr. Aplastar (to squash, to spoil by pressure). || Arrugar, aplastar (to crease). || Estrujar (paper). || Machacar, triturar (to reduce to powder, to small pieces). || Exprimir, prensar (grapes). || Apiñar (people). || FIG. Aplastar (to subdue, to silence). | Apretar (to hug violently). | Aplastar, reprimir (a revolt). | Abrumar (to overwhelm).. || — *Crushed rock* o *stone*, grava, *f.* || *To crush one's way through the crowd*, abrirse paso con dificultad entre la muchedumbre.
— V. intr. Amontonarse, apretujarse: *hundreds crushed into the small room*, cientos de personas se amontonaban en la pequeña habitación. || Aplastarse (to squash).
crusher [—ə*] n. FIG. Argumento (*m.*) aplastante, respuesta (*f.*) contundente. || TECH. Trituradora, *f.*
crush hat [—ˈhæt] n. Clac, *m.*

crushing [—iŋ] adj. Aplastante (argument, defeat, etc.). || Abrumador, ra (overwhelming).
— N. Trituración, *f.*
crust [krʌst] n. Corteza, *f.* (of a loaf). || Mendrugo, *m.* (dry piece of bread). || CULIN. Pasta, *f.*, pastel, *m.* (of a pie). || GEOL. Corteza, *f.*: *crust of the Earth*, corteza terrestre. || BOT. Corteza, *f.* || MED. Postilla, *f.*, costra, *f.* || Poso, *m.*, depósito, *m.* (in a wine bottle or barrel). || Capa (*f.*) dura (of snow, ice, etc.). || ZOOL. Caparazón, *m.* || FIG. Máscara, *f.* (outer appearance). || U. S. FAM. Caradura, *f.*, frescura, *f.* (cheek). || FIG. *The upper crust*, la flor y nata.
crust [krʌst] v. tr. Encostrar, formar una costra en. || MED. Formar una postilla en.
— V. intr. Encostrarse, formarse una costra. || MED. Formarse una postilla.
crustacean [krʌsˈteiʃjən] adj. Crustáceo, a.
— N. Crustáceo, *m.*
crustaceous [krʌsˈteiʃjəs] adj. Crustáceo, a.
crustily [ˈkrʌstili] adv. Bruscamente.
crustiness [ˈkrʌstinis] n. Brusquedad, *f.*, malhumor, *m.* || Dureza, *f.* (of bread).
crusty [ˈkrʌsti] adj. Crujiente. || De corteza dura (bread). || FAM. Brusco, ca; desabrido, da; malhumorado, da.
crutch [krʌtʃ] n. MED. Muleta, *f.* (support). || Cruz, *f.*, entrepierna, *f.*, entrepiernas, *f. pl.* (crotch). || ARCH. Puntal, *m.* || MAR. Candelero, *m.* || Soporte, *m.* (for motorcycles). || FIG. Apoyo, *m.*, soporte, *m.*
crux [krʌks] n. Quid, *m.* (of a matter). || Punto (*m.*) crucial. || Lo esencial. || Enigma, *m.* (literary problem).
— OBSERV. El plural de *crux* es *cruxes* o *cruces*.
cruzeiro [kruˈzeirəu] n. Cruceiro, *m.*, cruzeiro, *m.* (Brazilian coin).
cry [krai] n. Grito, *m.* (shout): *to utter* o *to give a cry*, dar un grito. || Pregón, *m.* (of a street vendor, etc.). || Lloro, *m.*, llanto, *m.* (weeping). || — *To be a far cry from*, mediar un gran abismo entre: *virtue is a far cry from vice*, media un gran abismo entre la virtud y el vicio. || *To be in full cry after*, estar persiguiendo. || *To have a good cry*, llorar a lágrima viva.
cry [krai] v. tr. Gritar (to shout). || Pregonar (to call out wares, news, etc.). || Llorar (to weep).
— V. intr. Gritar (to call out in pain, anger, etc.). || Llorar (to weep): *he cried for joy*, lloraba de alegría. || Aullar (animals).
— **To cry down**, despreciar (to belittle). | Desacreditar (to disparage). | Hacer callar por medio de gritos. || **To cry for**, pedir: *to cry for mercy*, pedir merced. | Requerir, necesitar (to need). || **To cry off**, romper, deshacer: *to cry off a deal*, romper un trato. | Rajarse: *at the last moment he cried off*, en el último momento se rajó. || **To cry out**, clamar, exclamar. | — *To cry out against*, clamar contra. | *To cry out for sth.*, pedir algo a gritos. || **To cry over**, lamentarse de. || **To cry to**, clamar: *to cry to heaven*, clamar al cielo. || **To cry up**, exaltar, enaltecer, glorificar.
crybaby [ˈkraiˌbeibi] n. Llorón, ona.
crying [ˈkraiiŋ] adj. Llorón, ona. || FIG. Escandaloso, sa; que clama al cielo: *a crying injustice*, una injusticia que clama al cielo.
— N. Grito, *m.* (shout). || Lloro, *m.*, llanto, *m.* (weeping). || Pregón, *m.* (of a street vendor, etc.).
cryogen [ˈkraiədʒən] n. Criógeno, *m.*
cryolite [ˈkraiəlait] n. Criolita, *f.*
cryometry [kraiˈəmitri] or **cryoscopy** [kraiˈəskəpi] n. Crioscopia, *f.*
crypt [kript] n. Cripta, *f.* (cell or cavity). || ANAT. Cripta, *f.*, folículo, *m.*
cryptic [ˈkriptik] adj. Secreto, ta; oculto, ta (secret, hidden). || Enigmático, ca (enigmatic).
cryptically [ˈkriptikəli] adv. A medias palabras (to speak).
cryptogam [ˈkriptəugæm] n. BOT. Criptógama, *f.*
cryptogamous [kripˈtɔgəməs] adj. Criptógamo, ma.
cryptogram [ˈkriptəugræm] n. Criptograma, *m.*
cryptographer [kripˈtɔgrəfə*] n. Criptógrafo, fa.
cryptographic [kriptəˈgræfik] adj. Criptográfico, ca.
cryptography [kripˈtɔgrəfi] n. Criptografía, *f.*
crystal [ˈkristl] adj. De cristal (of crystal). || Cristalino, na (very clear). || — *Crystal ball*, bola (*f.*) de cristal. || *Crystal detector*, detector (*m.*) de galena. || *Crystal gazer*, pitonisa, *f.*
— N. Cristal, *m.*
crystalline [ˈkristəlain] adj. De cristal (of or like crystal). || Cristalino, na (extremely clear). || *Crystalline lens*, cristalino, *m.* (of the eye).
crystallizable [ˈkristəlaizəbl] adj. Cristalizable.
crystallization [ˌkristəlaiˈzeiʃən] n. Cristalización, *f.*
crystallize [ˈkristəlaiz] v. tr. Cristalizar.
— V. intr. Cristalizarse.
crystallized [—d] adj. Cristalizado, da. || Escarchado, da (fruta).
crystallizer [—ə*] n. Cristalizador, *m.*
crystallizing [—iŋ] adj. Cristalizador, ra; cristalizante.
crystallographic [kristələˈgræfik] adj. Cristalográfico, ca.
crystallography [kristəˈlɔgrəfi] n. Cristalografía, *f.*
crystalloid [ˈkristəlɔid] adj. Cristaloide.
— N. Cristaloide, *m.*
crystalloidal [ˌkristəˈlɔidəl] adj. Cristaloideo, a.
cub [kʌb] n. Cachorro, *m.* (of lion, bear, tiger, wolf). || Cría, *f.* (of other animals). || Novato, ta: *cub reporter*, periodista novato. || Niño (*m.*) explorador (boy scout).
cub [kʌb] v. tr./intr. Parir.
Cuba [ˈkju:bə] pr. n. GEOGR. Cuba.
cubage [ˈkju:bidʒ] n. Cubicación, *f.*
Cuban [ˈkju:bən] adj./n. Cubano, na.
cubanism [—izəm] n. Cubanismo, *m.*
cubature [ˈkju:bətjuə*] n. Cubicación, *f.*
cubbyhole [ˈkʌbihəul] n. Armario (*m.*) pequeño (small cupboard). || Habitación (*f.*) pequeña, chiribitil, *m.* (workroom).
cube [kju:b] n. MATH. Cubo, *m.* || — MATH. *Cube root*, raíz cúbica. || *Sugar cube*, terrón (*m.*) de azúcar.
cube [kju:b] v. tr. MATH. Elevar al cubo, cubicar. || Cortar en forma de cubo (to cut into cubes).
cubic [ˈkju:bik] adj. Cúbico, ca: *cubic equation*, ecuación cúbica.
cubicle [—l] n. Cubículo, *m.* || Caseta, *f.* (changing room). || Camarilla, *f.* (in a dormitory).
cubiform [ˈkju:bifɔ:m] adj. De forma cúbica.
cubism [ˈkju:bizəm] n. Cubismo, *m.*
cubist [ˈkju:bist] adj./n. Cubista.
cubit [ˈkju:bit] n. Codo, *m.* (measure).
cubital [—l] adj. Cubital.
cubitus [—əs] n. MED. Cúbito, *m.*
cuboid [ˈkju:bɔid] adj. De forma cúbica.
— N. ANAT. Cuboides, *m. inv.* (bone).
cuckold [ˈkʌkəuld] n. Cornudo, *m.* (husband).
cuckold [ˈkʌkəuld] v. tr. Poner los cuernos a.
cuckoo [ˈkuku:] n. Cuco, *m.*, cuclillo, *m.* (bird). || Cucú, *m.* (song). || *Cuckoo clock*, reloj (*m.*) de cuco.
— Adj. FAM. Mentecato, ta; majadero, ra (silly).
cuckoopint [ˈkuku:pint] n. BOT. Aro, *m.*
cucumber [ˈkju:kʌmbə*] n. BOT. Pepino, *m.* || U. S. *Cucumber tree*, magnolio, *m.*, magnolia, *f.*
cucurbit [kju:ˈkə:bit] n. BOT. Cucúrbita, *f.*
cucurbitaceous [kjuˌkə:biˈteiʃəs] adj. BOT. Cucurbitáceo, a.
cud [kʌd] n. Bolo (*m.*) alimenticio (of ruminants). || *To chew the cud*, rumiar (animals, people).
cuddle [ˈkʌdl] n. Abrazo, *m.*
cuddle [ˈkʌdl] v. tr. Abrazar.
— V. intr. Abrazarse.
cuddlesome [—səm] or **cuddly** [ˈkʌdli] adj. Mimoso, sa; cariñoso, sa.
cuddy [ˈkʌdi] n. Camarote (*m.*) pequeño (in a ship). || Alacena, *f.* (closet). || Armario, *m.* (cupboard). || FAM. Borrico, *m.*
cudgel [ˈkʌdʒəl] n. Garrote, *m.* (big stick). || Porra, *f.* (weapon). || FIG. *To take up the cudgels for*, sacar la cara por, salir en defensa de.
cudgel [ˈkʌdʒəl] v. tr. Dar garrotazos a (with a big stick). || Golpear con la porra a, apporrear (with a weapon). || FIG. *To cudgel one's brains*, devanarse los sesos.
cudgelling [—iŋ] n. Tunda (*f.*) de palos, paliza, *f.*
cue [kju:] n. THEATR. MUS. Entrada, *f.*, pie, *m.* || Señal, *f.*, seña, *f.* (signal). || Indicación (*f.*) convenida: *don't do anything until he has given you the cue*, no hagas nada antes de que te haya dado la indicación convenida. || Norma *f.*, ejemplo, *m.*: *New York takes its cue from Paris fashions*, Nueva York sigue las normas de la moda de París. || Humor, *m.* (temper). || Taco, *m.* (in billiards). || U. S. See QUEUE. || *Cue ball*, bola blanca (in billiards).
cue [kju:] v. tr. Trenzar (to braid). || Indicar (to indicate).
— V. intr. U. S. Hacer cola.
cuff [kʌf] n. Puño, *m.* (of sleeves). || Vuelta, *f.* (of trousers). || Bofetada, *f.* (blow). || — Pl. Esposas, *f.* (handcuffs). || — FAM. *Off the cuff*, espontáneo, a (adj.), de improviso (adv.) | *On the cuff*, a plazos.
cuff [kʌf] v. tr. Abofetear (to slap). || Poner puños a (sleeves). || Esposar (to handcuff).
cuff links [—liŋks] pl. n. Gemelos, *m.*
Cufic [ˈkjufik] adj. Cúfico, ca.
cuirass [kwiˈræs] n. Coraza, *f.* (armour). || ZOOL. Coraza, *f.*, caparazón, *m.*
cuirass [kwiˈræs] v. tr. Poner coraza.
cuirassier [ˌkwirəˈsiə*] n. Coracero, *m.*
cuisine [kwiˈzi:n] n. Cocina, *f.* (cooking).
cul-de-sac [ˈkuldəˈsæk] n. Callejón (*m.*) sin salida. || ANAT. Conducto (*m.*) con un solo orificio.
culinary [ˈkʌlinəri] adj. Culinario, ria.
cull [kʌl] n. Desecho, *m.*
cull [kʌl] v. tr. Entresacar, escoger (to select). || Coger (flowers).
cullender [ˈkʌlində*] n. Colador, *m.*, escurridor, *m.* (colander).
cullender [ˈkʌlində*] v. tr. Colar, escurrir.
cullet [ˈkʌlit] n. Desperdicios (*m. pl.*) de vidrio.
culm [kʌlm] n. BOT. Caña, *f.*, tallo, *m.* || Cisco, *m.* (coal dust). || Antracita, *f.* (anthracite).
culminant [ˈkʌlminənt] adj. Culminante.
culminate [ˈkʌlmineit] v. intr. Culminar.
— V. tr. Hacer culminar, llevar a su culminación.
culmination [ˌkʌlmiˈneiʃən] n. Culminación, *f.*
culottes [kju:ˈlɔts] pl. n. Falda (*f. sing.*) pantalón.
culpability [ˌkʌlpəˈbiliti] n. Culpabilidad, *m.*
culpable [ˈkʌlpəbl] adj. Culpable.
culprit [ˈkʌlprit] n. Culpable, *m.* & *f.* (guilty person). || JUR. Acusado, da (accused).

cult [kʌlt] n. Culto, *m.* (*of*, a) [religious worship]. || Culto, *m.* (*of*, a) [admiration]. || *Personality cult*, culto de la personalidad.
cultivable [ˈkʌltivəbl] or **cultivatable** [ˈkʌltiveitəbl] adj. Cultivable.
cultivate [ˈkʌltiveit] v. tr. Cultivar: *to cultivate land, friendship, an art*, cultivar la tierra, la amistad, un arte. || Criar (oysters, silkworms, etc.).
cultivated [—id] adj. AGR. Cultivado, da. || Culto, ta (person).
cultivation [ˌkʌltiˈveiʃən] n. AGR. Cultivo, *m.* || Cultura, *f.* (of a person). || Cría, *f.* (of oysters, etc.).
cultivator [ˈkʌltiveitə*] n. Cultivador, *m.* || Criador, ra (of oysters, silkworms, etc.).
cultural [ˈkʌltʃərəl] adj. Cultural. || *Cultural Revolution*, Revolución (*f.*) cultural.
culture [ˈkʌltʃə*] n. Cultura, *f.*: *popular, physical culture*, cultura popular, física. || Cultivo, *m.* (development by study). || Cultivo, *m.* (of soil, plants). || Cría, *f.* (of oysters, silkworms, etc.). || BIOL. Cultivo, *m.*: *culture medium*, caldo de cultivo.
culture [ˈkʌltʃə*] v. tr. Cultivar.
cultured [—d] adj. AGR. Cultivado, da. || Culto, ta (person). || *Cultured pearl*, perla cultivada, perla (*f.*) de cultivo.
culver [ˈkʌlvə*] n. Paloma (*f.*) torcaz *or* zurita (dove).
culverin [ˈkʌlvərin] n. MIL. Culebrina, *f.*
culvert [ˈkʌlvət] n. Alcantarilla, *f.* (sewer). || ELECTR. Conducto (*m.*) subterráneo.
cumber [ˈkʌmbə*] v. tr. Estorbar, molestar.
cumber [ˈkʌmbə*] n. Estorbo, *m.*, molestia, *f.*
cumbersome [ˈkʌmbəsəm] or **cumbrous** [ˈkʌmbrəs] adj. Molesto, ta; incómodo, da (annoying). || Pesado, da (heavy). || De mucho bulto, voluminoso, sa (big).
cumin or **cummin** [ˈkʌmin] n. BOT. Comino, *m.*
cummerbund [ˈkʌməbʌnd] n. Faja, *f.*
cumulate [ˈkju:mjuleit] v. tr. Acumular, amontonar.
— V. intr. Acumularse, amontonarse.
cumulation [ˌkju:mjuˈleiʃən] n. Acumulación, *f.*, amontonamiento, *m.*
cumulative [ˈkju:mjulətiv] adj. Acumulativo, va. || Plural (voting). || Acumulado, da (condemnation, interest). || — JUR. *Cumulative evidence*, pruebas acumuladas. || *Cumulative preference shares*, acciones (*f.*) preferentes acumulativas.
cumulocirrus [ˈkju:mjuləuˈsirəs] n. Cirrocúmulo, *m.* (cloud).
cumulonimbus [ˈkju:mjuləuˈnimbəs] n. Cumulonimbo, *m.* (cloud).
cumulostratus [ˈkju:mjuləuˈstreitəs] n. Estratocúmulo, *m.* (cloud).
cumulous [ˈkju:mjuləs] adj. En forma de cúmulo. || Compuesto de cúmulos.
cumulus [ˈkju:mjuləs] n. Cúmulo, *m.* (cloud). || Cúmulo, *m.*, acumulación, *f.* (a great quantity).

— OBSERV. El plural de *cumulus* es *cumuli*.

cuneate [ˈkju:niit] adj. Cuneiforme (wedge-shaped).
cuneiform [ˈkju:niifɔ:m] adj. Cuneiforme (writing). || *Cuneiform bone*, hueso (*m.*) cuneiforme, cuña, *f.*
— N. Escritura (*f.*) cuneiforme.
cunning [ˈkʌniŋ] adj. Astuto, ta (clever). || Ingenioso, sa; hábil, mañoso, sa (skilful). || Astuto, ta; taimado, da (sly). || U. S. Mono, na; lindo, da (sweet, charming).
— N. Astucia, *f.* (slyness). || Ingenio, *m.*, ingeniosidad, *f.*, habilidad, *f.*, maña, *f.* (skill). || Agudeza, *f.*, sutileza, *f.* (keenness).
cunt [kʌnt] n. POP. Coño, *m.*
cup [kʌp] n. Taza, *f.* (bowl-shaped vessel): *cup of tea*, taza de té. || Copa, *f.* (trophy). || REL. Cáliz, *m.* || Cubilete, *m.*, vaso (*m.*) metálico (metal cup). || Cap, *m.* (drink). || BOT. Cáliz, *m.* (of a flower). || ANAT. Cavidad, *f.* (of bones). || MED. Ventosa, *f.* (glass bowl). || Cangilón, *m.* (of water wheel). || FIG. Cáliz, *m.* (of sorrow, bitterness, etc.). | Copa, *f.* (of pleasures). || Cazuela, *f.*, copa, *f.* (of bikini, bra). || Hoyo, *m.* (hollow). || — FAM. *In one's cups*, trompa, curda (drunk). | *It is not my cup of tea*, no me gusta mayormente.
cup [kʌp] v. tr. Ahuecar (the hands). || MED. Aplicar ventosas a. || *To cup one's hands to one's mouth*, hacer bocina con las manos (to shout).
cupbearer [ˈkʌpˌbɛərə*] n. Copero, *m.*
cupboard [ˈkʌbəd] n. Aparador, *m.* (sideboard). || Alacena, *f.* (built in). || Armario, *m.* (wardrobe). || FIG. FAM. *Cupboard love*, amor interesado.
cupel [ˈkju:pəl] n. Copela, *f.*
cupel [ˈkju:pəl] v. tr. Copelar.
cupellation [—eiʃən] n. Copelación, *f.*
cupful [ˈkʌpful] n. Taza, *f.* (contents of a cup).
Cupid [ˈkju:pid] n. Cupido, *m.*: *Cupid's bow*, arco de Cupido.
cupidity [kju:ˈpiditi] n. Codicia, *f.*
cupola [ˈkju:pələ] n. ARCH. Cúpula, *f.* (rounded roof). | Linterna, *f.* (dome-shaped superstructure). || MAR. MIL. Cúpula, *f.* || TECH. Cubilote, *m.*
cupped [kʌpt] adj. En forma de bocina (the hands).
cupping [ˈkʌpiŋ] n. MED. Aplicación (*f.*) de ventosas.
cupreous [ˈkju:priəs] adj. Cuproso, sa.
cupressaceae [kju:prəˈsæsii] pl. n. BOT. Cupresáceas, *f.*
cupric [ˈkju:prik] adj. Cúprico, ca.
cupriferous [kju:ˈprifərəs] adj. Cuprífero, ra.
cuprite [ˈkju:prait] n. MIN. Cuprita, *f.*
cupronickel [ˌkju:prəˈnikəl] n. Cuproníquel, *m.*
cuprous [ˈkju:prəs] adj. Cuproso, sa.
cupule [ˈkju:pjul] n. BOT. Cúpula, *f.*
cur [kə:*] n. Perro (*m.*) que no es de raza (dog). || FAM. Perro, *m.*, canalla, *m.* (person). || FAM. *Mangy cur*, perro sarnoso.
curability [ˌkjuərəˈbiliti] n. Curabilidad, *f.*
curable [ˈkjuərəbl] adj. Curable.
curaçao [ˌkjuərəˈsəu] n. Curasao, *m.* (liqueur).
Curaçao [ˌkjuərəˈsəu] pr. n. Curazao.
curacy [ˈkjuərəsi] n. REL. Coadjutoría, *f.*
curare or **curari** [kjuˈrɑ:ri] n. Curare, *m.* (poison).
curassow [ˈkjuərəsəu] n. ZOOL. Guaco, *m.* (bird).
curate [ˈkjuərit] n. REL. Coadjutor, *m.*
curative [ˈkjuərətiv] adj. Curativo, va.
— N. Remedio, *m.*
curator [kjuəˈreitə*] n. Conservador, ra (of a museum, art gallery, etc.). || JUR. Curador, *m.*, tutor, *m.* || Miembro (*m.*) del cuerpo administrativo de la universidad.
curb [kə:b] n. Barbada, *f.* (of harness). || Bordillo, *m.* (kerb). || Brocal, *m.* (of well). || Barandilla, *f.* (protective barrier). || FIG. Restricción, *f.*, freno, *m.* (a restraint): *I put a curb on his abuses*, puse freno a sus abusos. | Estorbo, *m.* (obstacle). || U. S. COMM. Bolsín, *m.* || — *Curb bit*, freno, *m.*, bocado, *m.* || ARCH. *Curb roof*, tejado abuhardillado.
curb [kə:b] v. tr. Poner la barbada a (a horse). || Poner bordillo a (a pavement). || FIG. Contener, reprimir, refrenar (to restrain).
curbstone [ˈkə:bstəun] n. Piedra (*f.*) del bordillo.
curculio [kəkˈju:ljəu] n. ZOOL. Gorgojo, *m.*
curd [kə:d] n. Cuajada, *f.*, requesón, *m.*
curdle [ˈkə:dl] v. tr. Cuajar.
— V. intr. Cuajarse, coagularse (to form into curds). || FAM. *It made my blood curdle*, se me heló la sangre en las venas.
curdy [ˈkə:di] adj. Cuajado, da; coagulado, da.
cure [kjuə*] n. Cura, *f.* (course of treatment). || Remedio, *m.* (remedy). || Curación, *f.*, cura, *f.* (successful treatment). || REL. Cura, *f.*: *cure of souls*, cura de almas. || Cura, *f.* (of food, by smoking). || Salazón, *f.* (by salting). || Curtido, *m.* (of leather).
cure [kjuə*] v. tr. Curar (to restore to health). || Remediar (to remedy). || Curar (by smoking). || Salar (by salting). || Vulcanizar (rubber). || Curtir (leather). || FIG. Remediar, poner remedio a.
— V. intr. Curarse.
cure-all [—ɔ:l] n. Panacea, *f.*, curalotodo, *m.*
cureless [—lis] adj. Incurable.
curettage [kjuˈretidʒ] n. MED. Raspado, *m.*, legrado, *m.*
curette [kjuəˈret] n. MED. Raspador, *m.*, cureta, *f.*, legra, *f.*
curette [kjuəˈret] v. tr. MED. Hacer un raspado a, raspar.
curfew [ˈkə:fju:] n. Toque (*m.*) de queda (signal). || Queda, *f.* (time).
curia [ˈkjuəriə] n. REL. Curia, *f.* || *Curia* (*Romana*), Curia Romana.

— OBSERV. El plural de *curia* es *curiae*.

curial [—l] adj. Curial.
curie [ˈkjuəri] n. PHYS. Curie, *m.* (unit of measurement).
curietherapy [—ˈθerəpi] n. MED. Curieterapia, *f.*
curio [ˈkjuəriəu] n. Curiosidad, *f.*, fruslería, *f.*
curiosity [ˌkjuəriˈɔsiti] n. Curiosidad, *f.* (inquisitiveness, strangeness). || Curiosidad, *f.*, objeto (*m.*) curioso (curious object). || — FIG. *Curiosity killed the cat*, por la boca muere el pez. || *Curiosity shop*, tienda (*f.*) de antigüedades.
curious [ˈkjuəriəs] adj. Curioso, sa (inquisitive). || Curioso, sa; extraño, ña (odd). || *I am curious of*, tengo curiosidad por.
curiously [—li] adv. Curiosamente. || *Curiously enough*, aunque parezca extraño, por muy curioso que parezca.
curium [ˈkjuəriəm] n. PHYS. Curio, *m.* (radioactive element).
curl [kə:l] n. Rizo, *m.*, bucle, *m.* (of hair). || Espiral, *m.*, voluta, *f.* (of smoke). || Encrespamiento, *m.* (of waves). || Veta (*f.*) redondeada (in wood grain). || Sinuosidad, *f.*, zigzag, *m.*, serpenteo, *m.* (sinuousness). || Torcedura, *f.* (twisting). || BOT. Zarcillo, *m.* || FIG. *With a curl of the lip*, con una mueca de desprecio.
curl [kə:l] v. tr. Rizar (the hair). || Arrollar (paper). || — *To curl o.s. up*, acurrucarse, hacerse un ovillo. || *To curl the lip*, hacer una mueca de desprecio.
— V. intr. Rizarse (hair). || Arrollarse (to roll up). || Abarquillarse (to wrinkle). || Encresparse (waves). || Hacer espirales *or* volutas (smoke). || Zigzaguear, serpentear (a path, etc.).
curler [—ə*] n. Rulo, *m.*, bigudí, *m.* (hair roller). || Ola (*f.*) al romper (wave). || SP. Jugador, ra [de curling]. || — Pl. Tenacillas (*f.*) de rizar (curling iron).
curlew [ˈkə:lju:] n. Zarapito, *m.* (bird).
curlicue [ˈkə:likju:] n. Floritura, *f.*, floreo, *m.*, adorno, *m.* (in handwriting).
curliness [ˈkə:linis] n. Rizado, *m.*, ensortijamiento, *m.*
curling [ˈkə:liŋ] n. Rizado, *m.* (of hair). || SP. "Curling", *m.* || — *Curling iron*, tenacillas (*f. pl.*) de rizar. || *Curling paper*, papillote, *m.* || *Curling pin*, bigudí, *m.*
curlpaper [ˈkə:lˌpeipə*] n. Papillote, *m.*

curly [ˈkə:li] adj. Rizado, da (hair). || En espiral (in spiral). || Sinuoso, sa (winding).
curmudgeon [kə:ˈmʌdʒən] n. Cascarrabias, *m. & f. inv.*, persona (*f.*) de mal genio *or* de malas pulgas.
currant [ˈkʌrənt] n. BOT. Grosella, *f.* (berry). || Pasa, *f.* (dried grape). || *Black currant*, grosella negra (fruit), grosellero negro (bush).
currency [ˈkʌrənsi] n. Moneda, *f.* [en circulación] (money): *currency convertibility*, convertibilidad de la moneda. || Dinero (*m.*) en circulación. || Uso (*m.*) corriente (general use): *it had a certain currency*, tuvo un uso bastante corriente. || Extensión, *f.* (general acceptance). || Temporada, *f.* (time during which a thing is current). || — *Currency allocation*, cupo (*m.*) de divisas que se permite sacar de un país. || *Floating currency*, moneda flotante. || *Foreign currency*, divisa, *f.*, moneda extranjera. || *To gain currency*, llegar a ser creído.
current [ˈkʌrənt] adj. Corriente (in general use). || General (prevalent): *current opinion*, la opinión general. || Actual (of the present time): *the current crisis*, la crisis actual. || Admitido, da; aceptado, da (accepted). || En curso: *current year*, año en curso. || Último, ma (magazine): *current issue*, último número. || Corriente (expenses). || Abierto, ta (credit, etc.). || De curso legal (money). || — COMM. *Current account*, cuenta corriente. || *Current assets*, activo (*m.*) disponible. || ELECTR. *Current breaker*, interruptor eléctrico. | *Current density*, densidad (*f.*) de corriente. || *Current liabilities*, pasivo (*m.*) exigible. || *Current meter*, hidrómetro, *m.* || *Current rate of exchange*, cambio (*m.*) del día.
— N. Corriente, *f.* (of air, water). || Curso (*m.*) de agua (stream). || ELECTR. Corriente, *f.*: *alternating, direct current*, corriente alterna, continua. || Marcha, *f.*, curso, *m.* (of events).
currently [ˈkʌrəntli] adv. Corrientemente (generally). || Actualmente (at present).
curricle [ˈkʌrikl] n. Coche (*m.*) de dos caballos.
curricular [kəˈrikjulə*] adj. Del plan de estudios.
curriculum [kəˈrikjuləm] n. Plan (*m.*) de estudios, programa (*m.*) de estudios. || *Curriculum vitae*, curriculum vitae, *m.*, historial (*m.*) profesional.

— OBSERV. El plural de la palabra *curriculum* es *curricula* o *curriculums*.

currier [ˈkʌriə*] n. Zurrador, *m.*, adobador, *m.*
currish [ˈkəriʃ] adj. Arisco, ca; huraño, ña (surly).
curry [ˈkʌri] n. "Curry", *m.*, cari, *m.* (spice).
curry [ˈkʌri] v. tr. Guisar con "curry" (to cook with curry). || Almohazar (a horse). || Zurrar, adobar (leather). || — *To curry favour*, buscar favores. || *To curry favour with s.o.*, buscar el favor de alguien.
— V. intr. Guisar con "curry".
currycomb [—kəum] n. Almohaza, *f.*
curse [kə:s] n. Maldición, *f.*: *under a curse*, bajo una maldición. || Blasfemia, *f.* (oath). || Palabrota, *f.* (rude word). || Reniego, *m.*, voto, *m.* (imprecation). || REL. Excomunión, *f.*, anatema, *m.* || FIG. Calamidad, *f.*, maldición, *f.* (bane). || *A curse on him!*, ¡maldito sea!
curse [kə:s] v. tr. Maldecir (to utter a curse on s.o.). || Afligir (to afflict). || REL. Excomulgar, anatematizar. || *Curse him!*, ¡maldito sea!
— V. intr. Blasfemar (to blaspheme). || Decir palabrotas (to say rude words).
cursed [ˈkə:sid] adj. Maldito, ta (under a curse). || FAM. Maldito, ta (blasted).
cursing [ˈkə:siŋ] adj. Maldiciente. || Blasfemador, ra. || Palabrotero, ra.
— N. Maldición, *f.* || Blasfemias, *f. pl.* (oaths). || Palabrotas, *f. pl.* (rude words).
cursive [ˈkə:siv] adj. Cursivo, va; bastardilla.
— N. Letra (*f.*) cursiva, cursiva, *f.*, letra (*f.*) bastardilla, bastardilla, *f.*
cursor [ˈkə:sə*] n. Cursor, *m.*
cursoriness [—rinis] n. Rapidez, *f.*, superficialidad, *f.*
cursory [—ri] adj. Precipitado, da; rápido, da; superficial: *cursory reading*, lectura rápida.
curst [kə:st] adj. See CURSED.
curt [kə:t] adj. Breve, conciso, sa (short in speech). || Lacónico, ca (laconic). || Brusco, ca; seco, ca (blunt).
curtail [kə:ˈteil] v. tr. Abreviar, acortar (to cut short). || Reducir (to reduce, to cut down).
curtailment [—mənt] n. Acortamiento, *m.*, abreviación, *f.* || Reducción, *f.* (of expenses, credits).
curtain [ˈkə:tn] n. Cortina, *f.* (for windows, of rain, fire, etc.): *to draw the curtain*, correr la cortina; *to draw back the curtain*, descorrer la cortina. || THEATR. Telón, *m.*: *to lower the curtain*, bajar el telón. || Subida (*f.*) *or* bajada (*f.*) del telón (raising or lowering of the curtain). || MIL. Cortina, *f.* (of ramparts). || FIG. Cortina, *f.*, velo, *m.* (veil). || — Pl. FAM. Final, *m. sing.*, fin, *m. sing.* (the end, death). || — *Blind curtain*, persiana, *f.* || THEATR. *Curtain call*, llamada (*f.*) a escena [para saludar]. | *Curtain raiser*, sainete, *m.* (short play), introducción, *f.* (introduction). | *Curtain wall*, paneles, *m. pl.* | *Front curtain*, telón (*m.*) de boca. || FIG. *Iron curtain*, telón (*m.*) de acero. || *Net o lace curtain*, visillo, *m.* || THEATR. *Safety curtain*, telón metálico. | *The curtain falls*, baja el telón. | *The curtain rises*, sube el telón.
curtain [ˈkə:tn] v. tr. Poner cortinas en. || FIG. Encubrir, tapar. || *To curtain off*, separar con cortina.
curtly [ˈkə:tli] adv. Secamente, bruscamente. || Brevemente, de manera concisa. || Lacónicamente.
curtness [ˈkə:tnis] n. Sequedad, *f.*, brusquedad, *f.* || Concisión, *f.*, brevedad, *f.* (conciseness). || Laconismo, *m.*
curtsy or **curtsey** [ˈkə:tsi] n. Reverencia, *f.*: *to drop a curtsy*, hacer una reverencia.
curtsy or **curtsey** [ˈkə:tsi] v. intr. Hacer una reverencia.
curule [ˈkjuəru:l] adj. Curul.
curvaceous [kə:ˈveiʃəs] adj. Curvilíneo, a.
curvature [ˈkə:vətʃə*] n. Curvatura, *f.* (curve). || Esfericidad, *f.* (of the Earth). || Encorvamiento, *m.*: *curvature of the spine*, encorvamiento de la columna vertebral. || MAR. Cimbra, *f.*
curve [kə:v] n. Curva, *f.* || Curva, *f.*, vuelta, *f.* (of a road). || Pistola, *f.* (of draftsman).
curve [kə:v] v. tr. Doblar, encorvar.
— V. intr. Doblarse, encorvarse (to take the shape of a curve). || Torcerse, hacer una curva (a road).
curved [kə:vd] adj. Curvo, va: *curved line*, línea curva. || Doblado, da; encorvado, da.
curvet [kə:ˈvet] n. Corveta, *f.* (of a horse).
curvet [kə:ˈvet] v. intr. Hacer corvetas, corvetear (a horse). || FIG. Retozar, juguetear.
curvilinear [ˌkə:viˈliniə*] or **curvilineal** [ˌkə:viˈliniəl] adj. Curvilíneo, a.
curving [ˈkə:viŋ] adj. Que hace una curva. || Que se dobla.
— N. Curva, *f.*
curvometer [kə:ˈvɔmitə*] n. Curvímetro, *m.*
curvy [ˈkə:vi] adj. Curvilíneo, a.
cusec [ˈkjusek] n. Pie (*m.*) cúbico por segundo (of the flow of a fluid).
cushat [ˈkʌʃət] n. Paloma (*f.*) torcaz *or* zurita (dove).
cushion [ˈkuʃən] n. Cojín, *m.*, almohadón, *m.* (for sitting on, etc.). || Banda, *f.* (of billiard table). || Acerico, *m.*, almohadilla, *f.* (for pins). || VET. Ranilla, *f.* (of horse's hoof). | Cuarto trasero, *m.* (buttocks of animal). || TECH. Colchón, *m.*: *air cushion*, colchón de aire. || Almohadilla, *f.* (for office stamp). || FIG. Amortiguador, *m.*, colchón, *m.*: *the grass acted as a cushion to his fall*, la hierba hizo de amortiguador en su caída. || FAM. Rosca, *f.* (of fat).
cushion [ˈkuʃən] v. tr. Poner almohadones *or* cojines en. || Poner en un cojín (to seat). || Rellenar (a seat, etc.). || Almohadillar, acolchar (to pad). || FIG. Amortiguar (to absorb shock). | Proteger (to shield from). | Sofocar (to suppress). | Mimar (to cosset). || Recostar (to lean as on a cushion). || Dejar [la bola] pegada a la banda (billiards).
cushy [ˈkuʃi] adj. FIG. FAM. Fácil, cómodo, da. || — *Cushy life*, vida tranquila *or* facilona. || *Cushy number* o *job*, chollo, *m.*, momio, *m.*, ganga, *f.*
cusp [kʌsp] n. Cúspide, *f.* (apex). || MATH. Vértice, *m.* || ARCH. Vértice, *m.* || Cuerno, *m.* (of the moon).
cuspid [ˈkʌspid] n. Diente (*m.*) canino, colmillo, *m.*
cuspidal [ˈkʌspidəl] adj. Puntiagudo, da.
cuspidor [ˈkʌspido:*] n. U. S. Escupidera, *f.*
cuss [kʌs] n. FAM. Maldición, *f.* (curse). | Individuo, *m.*, tipo, *m.*, tío, *m.* (fellow). | Palabrota, *f.* (rude word).
cuss [kʌs] v. tr./intr. FAM. Maldecir. || Decir palabrotas (to say rude words).
cussed [ˈkʌsid] adj. FAM. Terco, ca; cabezón, ona (stubborn). | Maldito, ta (cursed).
cussedness [—nis] n. Espíritu (*m.*) de contradicción. || Terquedad, *f.*, obstinación, *f.* (stubbornness).
custard [ˈkʌstəd] n. CULIN. Natillas, *f. pl.* || — *Caramel custard*, flan, *m.* || *Custard apple*, chirimoya, *f.*, anona, *f.* (fruit), chirimoyo, *m.*, anona, *f.* (tree).
custodial [kʌsˈtəudjəl] adj. De la custodia (of custody). || Del guardián (of custodian).
— N. REL. Custodia, *f.*
custodian [kʌsˈtəudjən] n. Guardián, ana; custodio, *m.* || Portero, ra (of a building). || Conservador, ra (of a museum).
custody [ˈkʌstədi] n. Custodia, *f.*, guardia, *f.* || Prisión, *f.*, detención, *f.* (prison). || — *In custody*, bajo custodia, custodiado, da; detenido, da. || *Remanded in custody*, mantenido bajo custodia. || *To give into custody*, entregar a la policía. || *To take s.o. into custody*, detener a uno.
custom [ˈkʌstəm] n. Costumbre, *f.* (habit): *as is the custom*, según costumbre; *ill custom*, mala costumbre. || Clientela, *f.* (customers). || JUR. Derecho (*m.*) consuetudinario. || — Pl. Derechos (*m.*) de aduana, aranceles *m.*, derechos (*m.*) arancelarios (duty). | Aduana, *f. sing.*: *to go through* (*the*) *customs*, pasar la aduana.
— Adj. Aduanero, ra; de aduana. || U. S. Hecho de encargo, a la medida (made-to-order). || Que trabaja por encargo (dealer in made-to-order goods).
customarily [ˈkʌstəmərili] adv. Acostumbradamente, comúnmente.
customariness [ˈkʌstəmərinis] n. Costumbre, *f.*
customary [ˈkʌstəməri] adj. Acostumbrado, da; de costumbre, habitual. || JUR. Consuetudinario, ria. || *It is customary to*, es costumbre.
custom-built [ˈkʌstəmˈbilt] adj. Hecho de encargo, a la medida.
customer [ˈkʌstəmə*] n. Cliente, *m. & f.* (purchaser): *to attract customers*, atraer a clientes. || FAM. Individuo,

m., tipo, *m.*, tío, *m.*: *an awkward customer*, un tipo difícil.

custom-free [ˈkʌstəmfriː] adj. Exento de aranceles, libre de derechos arancelarios.

customhouse [ˈkʌstəmhaus] n. Aduana, *f.* || — *Customhouse broker*, agente (*m.*) de aduana. || *Customhouse officer*, aduanero, ra; vista (*m.*) de aduana.

custom-made [ˈkʌstəmˈmeid] adj. Hecho de encargo, a la medida.

customs [ˈkʌstəmz] pl. n. See CUSTOM.

customshouse [—haus] n. See CUSTOMHOUSE.

customs union [—ˈjuːnjən] n. Unión (*f.*) aduanera.

custom-tailor [ˈkʌstəmˌteilə*] n. U. S. Sastre (*m.*) a la medida.

cut [kʌt] adj. Cortado, da: *cut flowers*, flores cortadas; *a well cut suit*, un traje bien cortado. || Castrado (castrated). || Reducido, da: *cut prices*, precios reducidos. || Tallado, da (glass, diamond). || Picado, da (tobacco).

— N. Corte, *m.* (incision). || Muesca, *f.* (notch). || Herida, *f.* (gash). || Corte, *m.*, cortadura, *f.* (small wound). || Tajo, *m.*, chirlo, *m.* (on the face). || Filo, *m.*, corte, *m.* (cutting edge). || Reducción, *f.* (in prices, wages, etc.). || Corte, *m.* (in an article, a play). || Corte, *m.*, interrupción, *f.* (on TV, films, radio). || Recorte, *m.* (clipping). || Golpe, *m.* (thrashing stroke). || Latigazo, *m.* (with a whip). || Cuchillada, *f.* (with a knife). || FAM. Parte, *f.*: *his cut was 10 %*, su parte era el 10 %. || Trozo, *m.*, corte, *m.* (piece of meat). || Tajada, *f.* (slice). || Rebanada, *f.* (of bread). || Corte, *m.* (of hair, clothes). || MED. Incisión, *f.*, corte, *m.* || SP. Corte, *m.* || Zanja, *f.* (railway cutting). || Corte, *m.* (of a pack of cards). || GEOGR. Entrada, *f.* || FIG. FAM. Corte, *m.* (verbal attack). | Golpe, *m.* (misfortune). || PRINT. Grabado, *m.* || Grabado (*m.*) en madera (woodcut). || Talla, *f.* (of jewels). || FAM. Ausencia, *f.* (from school). || TECH. Pasada, *f.* (of a machine tool). || — *Cold cuts*, fiambres, *m.* || FIG. FAM. *Cut of one's jib*, semblante, *m.*, aspecto, *m.* || *Short cut*, atajo, *m.* || *Sword cut*, estocada, *f.* || FIG. *The cut and thrust*, la lucha (the struggle). | *There is no short cut to fame*, no se consigue fácilmente la gloria. | *To be a cut above the rest*, ser superior a los demás, estar por encima de los demás. || *Whose cut is it?*, ¿quién corta? (in cards).

cut* [kʌt] v. tr. Cortar (to make an incision, to wound, to sever, to separate into pieces, slices, to halve a pack of cards). || Segar (to reap). || Talar (trees). || Cortar: *to cut the lawn*, cortar el césped. || Cortar (clothes, in tailoring). || Acortar (to make smaller or shorter). || Cruzar (to insersect). || Bajar, reducir: *to cut the price of meat by 2 %*, reducir el precio de la carne en un 2 por ciento. || Cortar, romper (connections). || Cortar, parar (an engine). || Cortar (communications). || Reducir, acortar, abreviar (a speech, visit, etc.). || Repartir, dividir (benefits, booty). || Cortar, hacer cortes en: *to cut a film*, hacer cortes en una película. || Excavar, abrir (trench, canal). || Abrir (an opening). || FIG. Herir, lastimar (to hurt one's feelings). | Dejarse de, acabar con: *cut the clowning!*, ¡déjese de payasadas! || Penetrar (the cold). || FAM. Faltar a, fumarse (classes, lectures). || Cortar (alcohol, wine). || Disolver (grease). || Diluir (a liquid). || Picar (tobacco). || Castrar (to castrate). || Echar, salir (teeth): *he cut his teeth*, echó los dientes, le salieron los dientes. || ARTS. Grabar, tallar, esculpir. || Hacer: *to cut a notch*, hacer una muesca. || Tallar (stones). || Tallar, labrar (diamond). || Aterrajar, roscar (screw). || MAR. Soltar, largar (one's moorings). || SP. Cortar, dar efecto a (a ball). || Grabar (a record). || MED. Abrir (an abscess). || Desglosar (a film). || — *To cut a corner*, coger una curva en diagonal. || *To cut a dash*, see DASH. || *To cut adrift*, desatar. || FIG. *To cut a fine figure*, causar buena impresión (to give a good impression), tener buen tipo (appearance), ser elegante (smartness). || *To cut a long story short*, en pocas palabras, para abreviar. || *To cut asunder*, separar. || *To cut capers*, see CAPER. || *To cut corners*, see CORNER. || *To cut it fine*, calcular muy justo. || *To cut loose*, see LOOSE. || FIG. *To cut no ice*, no convencer; no tener importancia. | *To cut one's coat according to one's cloth*, gobernar su boca según su bolsa. | *To cut one's losses*, abandonar algo muy costoso. || *To cut one's nails*, cortarse las uñas. || FIG. *To cut one's throat*, arruinarse. || *To cut one's way through*, abrirse paso entre. || *To cut open*, abrir con un corte. || FIG. *To cut short*, cortar en seco (discussion). | *To cut s.o. dead*, negar el saludo a uno, pasar cerca de uno sin saludarle. | *To cut s.o. short*, interrumpir bruscamente *or* cortar en seco a uno (to interrupt), dejarle cortado a uno (to silence). || *To cut the prices*, vender a precio reducido. || *To cut the thread of the argument*, cortar el hilo del discurso. || *To cut to pieces*, hacer pedazos *or* trizas. | FIG. *To cut to the bone*, reducir a lo mínimo. | *To cut to the heart* o *to the quick*, herir en lo vivo (to hurt s.o.'s feelings). || *To have one's hair cut*, cortarse el pelo.

— V. intr. Cortar: *this knife cuts badly*, este cuchillo corta mal. || Cortar: *we cut through the forest*, cortamos por el bosque. || Cortarse: *this stone cuts easily*, esta piedra se corta con facilidad. || Cruzarse (two roads). || Cortar, penetrar (the cold). || Cortar (at cards). || — CINEM. *Cut!*, ¡corten! || FIG. *To cut and run*, salir pitando (to go), levar anclas (a ship). | *To cut both ways*, ser un arma de dos filos. || *To cut loose*, escaparse. || *To cut to the left*, doblar a la izquierda. || *To cut through s.o.'s coat*, atravesar el abrigo de alguien. || *To cut through the air*, hendir el aire.

— **To cut across**, cortar completamente. | Cortar por: *to cut across the town*, cortar por la ciudad. | FIG. Ir en contra de: *this cuts across all my principles*, esto va en contra de todos mis principios. | — *To cut across a field*, pasar a campo traviesa. || **To cut along**, irse deprisa. || **To cut away**, cortar. | FAM. Salir pitando (to run away). || **To cut back**, acortar (to make shorter). | Podar (to trim). | CINEM. Retroceder. | Reducir, disminuir (expenses). | Volver (to come back). || **To cut down**, cortar (trees). | Acortar (to shorten). | AGR. Segar (corn). | Reducir (expenses). | Cortar, hacer cortes en (a speech). | — *To cut down on smoking*, fumar menos (to smoke less), gastar menos en cigarrillos. || **To cut in**, interrumpir (to interrupt). | Colarse (to push in). | Insertar (to insert). | Meterse en la conversación. | AUT. Cerrar el paso, cerrarse. | Conectar (an engine). | Sacar a bailar a la pareja de otra persona (in dancing). | — *To cut in and out*, colarse. | *To cut in on*, hacer partícipe en (benefits), incluir en (to include), interrumpir (a conversation), entrar en (card game). | FIG. *To cut s.o. in on a deal*, meterle a uno en un asunto. || **To cut into**, acortar, reducir (to shorten). | Cortar (cake). | Mermar (savings). || **To cut off**, cortar. | Llevarse: *death cut him off in his prime*, la muerte se lo llevó en la flor de la edad. | Separar (to separate). | Aislar: *we were cut off by the flood*, estuvimos aislados por la inundación. | Amputar (to amputate). | Tapar (the view). | Cortar, parar (an engine). | Pararse, dejar de funcionar (a car, etc.). | Cortar (telephone, current). | Desheredar (to disinherit). | MIL. Cortar la retirada a. | Romper (negotiations). | Cortar el camino a (to bar s.o.'s way). | Marcharse, irse (to go). || **To cut out**, recortar: *to cut a photo out of a paper*, recortar una foto en un periódico. | Cortar (a garment). | Hacer, cavar (a hole). | Suplantar (to supplant). | Omitir, excluir (to omit). | Eliminar (to eliminate). | Suprimir (to suppress). | Dejar de: *to cut out smoking*, dejar de fumar. | Dejarse de: *cut out the nonsense*, déjate de tonterías. | Pararse (engine). | U. S. Separar (of the herd). | — FAM. *Cut it out!*, ¡basta ya! | *To be cut out for* o *to*, estar hecho para: *he is not cut out to be a farmer*, no está hecho para ser agricultor. || **To cut up**, cortar en pedazos (to cut into pieces). | Cortar, trinchar (meat in slices), picar (in small pieces). | Cortar (paper, wood). | Destrozar (to destroy). | FIG. Poner por los suelos (to criticize harshly). | Apenar (to distress). | Alardear (to boast). | Dejar carriles en (a road). | U. S. Hacer tonterías (to play the fool).

— OBSERV. Pret. & p. p. **cut**.

cut-and-dried [—ənˈdraid] adj. Previsto [hasta el más mínimo detalle].

cutaneous [kjuːˈteinjəs] adj. Cutáneo, a.

cutaway [ˈkʌtəwei] n. Corte, *m.*, sección, *f.* (of a machine).

cutback [ˈkʌtbæk] n. Reducción, *f.* || Restricción, *f.* || Resumen (*m.*) de lo anterior (of a serialized story).

cute [kjuːt] adj. U. S. Listo, ta; astuto, ta (sharp-witted). || Mono, na; lindo, da (attractive).

cuteness [—nis] n. Astucia, *f.* (cleverness). || U. S. Monería, *f.* [*Amer.*, lindura, *f.*]

cut glass [ˈkʌtˈglɑːs] n. Cristal (*m.*) tallado.

cuticle [ˈkjuːtikl] n. Cutícula, *f.*

cutis [ˈkjuːtis] n. ANAT. Cutis, *m.*

— OBSERV. El plural de la palabra inglesa *cutis* es *cutes* o *cutises*.

cutlass [ˈkʌtləs] n. MIL. Alfanje, *m.* || U. S. Machete, *m.*

cutler [ˈkʌtlə*] n. Cuchillero, *m.*

cutlery [—ri] n. Cubiertos, *m. pl.*, cubertería, *f.* (used at table). || Objetos (*m. pl.*) cortantes (razors, shears, etc.). || Cuchillería, *f.* (the trade of a cutler).

cutlet [ˈkʌtlit] n. Chuleta, *f.* (chop). || Croqueta, *f.* (of chopped meat or fish).

cutoff [ˈkʌtɔf] n. Corte, *m.*, cese, *m.* || U. S. Brazo (*m.*) muerto (of a river). | Atajo, *m.* (short cut). || TECH. Obturador, *m.* (of a cylinder). | Cierre (*m.*) de admisión.

cutout [ˈkʌtaut] n. Recorte, *m.*, figura (*f.*) recortada (design made by cutting). || Recortable, *m.*, dibujo (*m.*) para recortar (design prepared for cutting). || TECH. Válvula (*f.*) de escape. | Escape (*m.*) libre. || ELECTR. Cortacircuitos, *m. inv.*, interruptor, *m.* | Fusible, *m.*, plomo, *m.* (fuse).

cut-price [ˈkʌtprais] adj. A precio reducido.

cutpurse [ˈkʌtpəːs] n. Carterista, *m.* & *f.*, ratero, ra.

cut-rate [ˈkʌtreit] adj. Rebajado, da.

cutter [ˈkʌtə*] n. Cortador, ra (person who cuts). || Cantero, *m.*, tallista, *m.* & *f.* (of stone). || Tallista, *m.* & *f.* (of precious stones). || Desglosador, ra (of film). || TECH. Cizalla, *f.* (wire cutter). || MAR. Cúter, *m.* (single-masted boat). | Patrullero, *m.*, guardacostas, *m. inv.* (coastguard boat). || Incisivo, *m.* (tooth). || U. S. Trineo, *m.* (sledge). || *Coastguard* o *revenue cutter*, guardacostas, *m. inv.*

cutthroat [ˈkʌtθrəut] adj. Sanguinario, ria (murderous). || Implacable: *cutthroat competition*, una rivalidad implacable. || A tres (card games).

— N. Asesino, na (murderer). || Navaja (*f.*) barbera (razor).
cutting [ˈkʌtiŋ] adj. Cortante (sharp): *cutting edge*, filo cortante. || Cortante (wind). || Penetrante (rain). || Mordaz, incisivo, va; hiriente (remarks, etc.).
— M. Corte, *m.* || Bot. Tala, *f.* (of trees). | Poda, *f.* (of rose trees). | Esqueje, *m.* (slip). || Talla, *f.* (of a diamond). || Corte, *m.* (of a garment). || Recorte, *m.* (piece cut off). || Retal, *m.* (of cloth). || Recorte, *m.* (from a newspaper). || Zanja, *f.* (for road, railway). || Abertura, *f.* (of a channel). || Paso, *m.* (in a wood). || Reducción, *f.* (of prices, wages). || Desglose, *m.* (of a film). || *Cutting iron*, cortafrío, *m.*
cuttle [ˈkʌtl] n. Zool. Jibia, *f.*
cuttlebone [—bəun] n. Zool. Jibión, *m.*
cuttlefish [—fiʃ] n. Zool. Jibia, *f.*
cutty [ˈkʌti] adj. Corto, ta.
cutwater [ˈkʌtˌwɔ:tə*] n. Mar. Tajamar, *m.*, roda, *f.*, espolón, *m.* || Tajamar, *m.* (of a bridge).
cutwork [ˈkʌtwə:k] n. Calado, *m.* (in lace).
cutworm [ˈkʌtwə:m] n. U. S. Zool. Oruga, *f.*
cyanidation [saiənaiˈdeiʃən] or **cyaniding** [ˈsaiənaidiŋ] n. Cianuración, *f.*
cyanide [ˈsaiənaid] n. Chem. Cianuro, *m.* || *Cyanide process*, cianuración, *f.*
cyanite [ˈsaiənait] n. Min. Cianita, *f.*
cyanogen [saiˈænədʒin] n. Chem. Cianógeno, *m.*
cyanosis [saiəˈnəusis] n. Med. Cianosis, *f.*
cyanotype [saiˈænətaip] n. Cianotipo, *m.* (blueprint).
Cybele [ˈsibəli:] pr. n. Myth. Cibeles, *f.*
cybernetics [ˌsaibə:ˈnetiks] n. Cibernética, *f.*
cyclamen [ˈsikləmən] n. Ciclamen, *m.*, ciclamino, *m.*
cycle [ˈsaikl] n. Ciclo, *m.*: *life cycle*, ciclo de la vida. || Astr. Órbita, *f.* || Bicicleta, *f.* (bicycle). || *Cycle race*, carrera (*f.*) ciclista.
cycle [ˈsaikl] v. intr. Pasar por un ciclo (to move in cycles). || Ir en bicicleta: *I cycled home last night*, anoche fui a casa en bicicleta. || Montar en bicicleta (to ride a bicycle).
cyclic [ˈsaiklik] or **cyclical** [—əl] adj. Cíclico, ca.
cycling [ˈsaikliŋ] n. Ciclismo *m.*
— Adj. Ciclista: *cycling race*, carrera ciclista. || En bicicleta (tour).
cyclist [ˈsaiklist] n. Ciclista, *m.* & *f.*
cyclo-cross [ˈsaikləkrɔs] n. Sp. Ciclocrós, *m.*
cycloid [ˈsaiklɔid] n. Math. Cicloide. *f.*
cycloidal [saiˈklɔidl] adj. Cicloidal, cicloideo, a.
cyclometer [saiˈklɔmitə*] n. Contador (*m.*) kilométrico de bicicleta.
cyclonal [ˈsaiklənəl] adj. Ciclonal, ciclónico, ca.
cyclone [ˈsaikləun] n. Ciclón, *m.* || U. S. *Cyclone cellar*, refugio (*m.*) anticiclones.
cyclonic [saiˈklɔnik] adj. Ciclónico, ca.
cyclopaedia [ˌsaikləˈpi:djə] n. Enciclopedia, *f.*
cyclopean [saiˈkləupjən] adj. Ciclópeo, a.
cyclopedia [ˌsaikləˈpi:djə] n. Enciclopedia, *f.*
Cyclops [ˈsaiklɔps] n. Myth. Cíclope, *m.*

— Observ. El plural de *Cyclops* es *Cyclopes.*

cyclorama [ˌsaikləˈrɑ:mə] n. Ciclorama, *m.*
cyclostomes [ˈsaikləstəumz] or **cyclostomi** [ˈsaikləstəumi] pl. n. Zool. Ciclóstomos, *m.*
cyclostyle [ˈsaikləstail] n. Ciclostilo, *m.*
cyclothymia [ˌsaikləˈθaimiə] n. Med. Ciclotimia, *f.*
cyclotron [ˈsaiklətrɔn] n. Ciclotrón, *m.*
cygnet [ˈsignit] n. Zool. Pollo (*m.*) de cisne.
cygnus [ˈsignəs] n. Astr. Cisne, *m.*
cylinder [ˈsilində*] n. Cilindro, *m.* || — *Cylinder block*, bloque (*m.*) de cilindros. || *Cylinder capacity* o *charge*, cilindrada, *f.* || *Cylinder press*, rotativa, *f.*
cylindric [siˈlindrik] or **cylindrical** [—əl] adj. Cilíndrico, ca.
cyma [ˈsaimə] n. Arch. Gola, *f.*, cimacio, *m.*
cymbal [ˈsimbəl] n. Mus. Címbalo, *m.*, platillo, *m.*
cymbalist [—ist] n. Mus. Cimbalero, *m.*, cimbalista, *m.*
cyme [saim] n. Bot. Cima, *f.*
cynegetic [ˌsainiˈdʒetik] adj. Cinegético, ca.
cynegetics [—s] n. Cinegética, *f.*
cynic [ˈsinik] adj./n. Cínico, ca. || See cynical.
cynical [ˈsinikəl] adj. Cínico, ca. || Escéptico, ca; desengañado, da (disillusioned). || Sarcástico, ca (sarcastic). || Burlón, ona; despreciativo, va (sneering).
cynically [—i] adj. Cínicamente. || Escépticamente. || Burlonamente, despreciativamente.
cynicism [ˈsinisizəm] n. Cinismo, *m.* || Escepticismo, *m.*, desengaño, *m.* (disillusion). || Burla, *f.*, desprecio, *m.* || Carácter (*m.*) sarcástico.
cynocephalus [ˌsainəuˈsefələs] n. Cinocéfalo, *m.* (monkey).
cynosure [ˈsinəzjuə*] n. Centro (*m.*) de atracción. || Astr. Osa Menor, *f.* || *Cynosure of every eye*, blanco (*m.*) de las miradas.
cypher [ˈsaifə*] n. See cipher.
cyphosis [saiˈfəusis] n. Cifosis, *f.*
cypress [ˈsaipris] n. Bot. Ciprés, *m.* (tree).
cyprinid [ˈsiprənid] n. Zool. Ciprino, *m.*
Cyprian [ˈsipriən] adj./n. Chipriota.
Cypriot or **Cypriote** [ˈsipriət] adj./n. Chipriota.
Cyprus [ˈsaiprəs] pr. n. Geogr. Chipre.
Cyrenaica [ˌsaiərəˈneiikə] pr. n. Geogr. Cirenaica, *f.*
cyrenian [saiˈri:njən] adj./n. Cirineo, a.
Cyril [ˈsiril] pr. n. Cirilo, *m.*
Cyrillic [siˈrilik] adj. Cirílico, ca.
cyst [sist] n. Quiste, *m.* (growth). || Vesícula, *f.* (bladder).
cystic [ˈsistik] adj. Enquistado, da (like a cyst). || Anat. Cístico, ca.
cysticercus [sistiˈsə:kəs] n. Zool. Cisticerco, *m.* (tapeworm larva).

— Observ. El plural de *cysticercus* es *cysticerci.*

cystitis [sisˈtaitis] n. Med. Cistitis, *f.*
cystotomy [sisˈtɔtəmi] n. Cistotomía, *f.*
cytisus [ˈsitisəs] n. Bot. Citiso, *m.*, codeso, *m.*
cytology [saiˈtɔlədʒi] n. Citología, *f.*
cytoplasm [ˈsaitəuplæzəm] n. Biol. Citoplasma, *m.*
czar [zɑ:*] n. Zar, *m.*
czardas [ˈtʃɑrˌdæʃ] n. Czarda, *f.* (dance).
czarevitch [ˈzɑ:rivitʃ] n. Zarevitz, *m.*
czarina [zɑ:ˈri:nə] n. Zarina, *f.*
czarism [ˈzɑ:rizəm] n. Zarismo, *m.*
Czech [tʃek] adj./n. Checo, ca.
Czechoslovak [ˈtʃekəˈsləuvæk] adj./n. Checoslovaco, ca.
Czechoslovakia [ˈtʃekəsləˈvækiə] pr. n. Geogr. Checoslovaquia, *f.*
Czechoslovakian [—n] adj./n. Checoslovaco, ca.

D

d [di:] n. D, *f.* (letter). || Mus. Re, *m.* || Signo (*m.*) que representa un penique antiguo (English old penny). || *D day*, día (*m.*) D.

— Observ. La *d* que representa el penique antiguo es una abreviatura de la palabra latina *denarius.*

dab [dæb] adj. Fam. *To be a dab hand at*, ser un hacha en.
— Adv. U. S. Fam. *Right dab in the middle*, justo en el centro, en pleno centro.
— N. Fam. Hacha, *m.* (expert). || Golpe (*m.*) ligero (a light blow or stroke). || Toque, *m.*: *a dab of paint*, un toque de pintura. || Pizca, *f.*, poquito, *m.* (bit). || Mancha, *f.* (of mud). || Platija, *f.*, gallo, *m.* (fish). || — Pl. Huellas (*f.*) digitales *or* dactilares.
dab [dæb] v. tr. Golpear ligeramente (to strike). || Dar unos toques de: *to dab paint on the wall*, dar unos toques de pintura en la pared. || *To dab a stain with a sponge*, quitar una mancha con una esponja.
dabber [—ə*] n. Tampón, *m.* (for inking).
dabble [ˈdæbl] v. tr. Salpicar (to splash). || Rociar (to sprinkle). || Mojar (to wet).
— V. intr. Chapotear (in water). || Fig. Interesarse superficialmente (*in*, *at*, en, por) [to do sth. superficially]. | Meterse: *to dabble in politics*, meterse en política.
dabbler [—ə*] n. Diletante, *m.*
dabchick [ˈdæbtʃik] n. Somorgujo, *m.* (bird).
dabster [ˈdæbstə*] n. Fam. Diletante, *m.* (dabbler). | Hacha, *m.* (dab).
dace [deis] n. Albur, *m.* (fish).
Dacian [ˈdeisjən] adj./n. Dacio, cia.
dactyl [ˈdæktil] n. Dáctilo, *m.* (in poetry).
dad [dæd] n. Papá, *m.*
Dada [ˈdɑ:dɑ:] or **Dadaism** [—izəm] n. Dadaísmo, *m.*
Dadaist [ˈdɑ:dɑ:ist] adj./n. Dadaísta.
daddy [ˈdædi] n. Fam. Papá, *m.*, papaíto, *m.*

daddy longlegs [—'lɔŋlegz] n. Zool. Tipula, *f.* (crane fly). || U. S. Zool. Segador, *m.* (arachnid).
dado ['deidəu] n. Arch. Dado, *m.* (of a pedestal). | Rodapié, *m.*, friso, *m.* (of a wall).
daedal ['di:dəl] or **daedalian** [—iən] adj. Ingenioso, sa; habilidoso, sa (skilful). || Complejo, ja (intricate).
Daedalus ['di:dələs] pr. n. Myth. Dédalo, *m.*
daemon ['di:mən] n. See demon.
daffodil ['dæfədil] n. Bot. Narciso, *m.*
daffy ['dæfi] adj. U. S. Fam. Chalado, da; chiflado, da.
daft [dɑ:ft] adj. Fam. Tonto, ta. || *To go daft over*, chiflarse por.
daftness [—nis] n. Fam. Chifladura, *f.*
dagger ['dægə*] n. Daga, *f.*, puñal, *m.* (weapon). || Print. Obelisco, *m.* || — Fig. *To be at daggers drawn*, estar a matar. | *To look daggers at s.o.*, fulminar a alguien con la mirada.
dago ['deigəu] n. Término despectivo aplicado a españoles, portugueses e italianos.
daguerreotype [də'gerəutaip] n. Daguerrotipo, *m.*
daguerreotypy [də'gerəutaipi] n. Daguerrotipia, *f.*
dahlia ['deiljə] n. Bot. Dalia, *f.* (plant, flower).
Dahoman [də'həumən] adj./n. Dahomeyano, na.
Dahomey [də'həumi] pr. n. Geogr. Dahomey, *m.*
daily ['deili] adj. Diario, ria; cotidiano, na. || — Fam. *Daily dozen*, ejercicios (*m. pl.*) matinales. || Rel. *Our daily bread*, el pan nuestro de cada día.
— Adv. Diariamente, a diario, cada día.
— N. Diario, *m.* (newspaper). || Asistenta, *f.* (charwoman).
daimon ['daimən] n. See demon.
daintily ['deintili] adv. Delicadamente. || Elegantemente. || De una manera refinada, finamente.
daintiness ['deintinis] n. Delicadeza, *f.* (delicacy). || Elegancia, *f.* || Remilgos, *m. pl.* (squeamishness).
dainty ['deinti] n. Bocado (*m.*) exquisito.
— Adj. Delicado, da; fino, na (taste). || Exquisito, ta; delicado, da (food). || Delicado, da; difícil (fussy). || Elegante, primoroso, sa (delicately pretty). || Precioso, sa (lovely). || Remilgado, da (affected).
dairy ['dɛəri] n. Vaquería, *f.* (part of a farm). || Lechería, *f.* (where milk, cheese and butter are sold). || — *Dairy cattle*, vacas lecheras. || *Dairy farm*, granja (*f.*) de vacas. || *Dairy products*, productos lácteos.
dairymaid [—meid] n. Lechera, *f.*
dairyman [—mən] n. Lechero, *m.*

— Observ. El plural de *dairyman* es *dairymen*.

dais ['deiis] n. Tarima, *f.*, estrado, *m.*
daisy ['deizi] n. Margarita, *f.* (flower). || Fig. Perla, *f.*, joya, *f.* (pearl). || — Dep. *Daisy cutter*, pelota (*f.*) rasante. || Fig. fam. *To push up daisies*, criar malvas (to be dead).
Dalai Lama ['dælai'lɑ:mə] pr. n. Rel. Dalai Lama, *m.*
dale [deil] n. Valle, *m.*
dalesman ['deilzmən] n. Habitante de una región con valles, situada en el norte de Inglaterra y llamada "The Dales"

— Observ. El plural de esta palabra es *dalesmen*.

dalliance ['dæliəns] n. Flirteo, *m.*, coqueteo, *m.* (flirting). || Frivolidad, *f.* (trifling).
dally ['dæli] v. intr. Flirtear, coquetear (amorously). || Remolonear (to loiter). || Perder el tiempo (to waste time). || Juguetear (to play). || Entretenerse (with an idea). || Fig. Burlarse, reírse (*with*, de). | Tomar a la ligera (to take lightly).
— V. tr. *To dally the time away*, perder el tiempo.
Dalmatia [dæl'meiʃjə] pr. n. Geogr. Dalmacia, *f.*
Dalmatian [—n] adj. Dálmata (from Dalmatia).
— N. Dálmata, *m.* & *f.* (person). || Dálmata, *m.* (dog).
dalmatic [dæl'mætik] n. Dalmática, *f.*
daltonian [dɔl'təuniən] adj./n. Daltoniano, na.
daltonism ['dɔltənizəm] n. Med. Daltonismo, *m.*
dam [dæm] n. Dique, *m.* (barrier across a water flow). || Presa, *f.*, embalse, *m.* (a reservoir of water). || Madre, *f.* (female parent of animals).
dam [dæm] v. tr. Embalsar, represar (water). || Construir un dique en (a river). || Construir una presa sobre (a lake, etc.). || Fig. *To dam up*, poner un dique a, contener.
damage ['dæmidʒ] n. Daño, *m.*: *the damage caused by hail*, el daño causado por el granizo. || Fig. Perjuicio, *m.* || — Pl. Jur. Daños (*m.*) y perjuicios. || Fig. fam. *What's the damage?*, ¿cuánto le debo?
damage ['dæmidʒ] v. tr. Dañar (to harm). || Estropear (to spoil). || Fig. Perjudicar.
— V. intr. Dañarse.
damageable [—əbl] adj. Que se puede dañar.
damaging [—iŋ] adj. Perjudicial.
Damascene ['dæməsi:n] adj. Damasceno, na; damasquino, na. || *Damascene work*, damasquinado, *m.*
— N. Damasceno, na.
damascene ['dæməsi:n] v. tr. Damasquinar.
Damascus [də'mɑ:skəs] pr. n. Geogr. Damasco. || Rel. *Road to Damascus*, camino (*m.*) de Damasco.
damask ['dæməsk] adj. Adamascado, da; damascado, da; damasquino, na (linen). || De color (*m.*) rosa de Damasco. || Damasquino, na (metal).
— N. Damasco, *m.* (linen). || Acero (*m.*) damasquino *or* de Damasco. || Damasquinado, *m.* (Damascene work).
damask ['dæməsk] or **damaskeen** [—i:n] v. tr. Damasquinar (to damascene). || Adamascar (to weave patterns into a fabric).
dame [deim] n. Dama, *f.* || U. S. Fam. Mujer, *f.* (woman). || Fam. *An old dame*, una señora de edad.

— Observ. El título de *dame* se concede a las mujeres que tienen ciertas condecoraciones.

dammit! ['dæmit] interj. Fam. ¡Córcholis!, ¡mecachis!
damn [dæm] n. Fam. *I don't give* o *I don't care a damn*, no me importa un comino, me trae sin cuidado. | *It's not worth a damn*, no vale un comino.
— Adj. Fam. Maldito, ta: *that damn car*, ese maldito coche.
— Adv. Fam. Muy: *it's damn good*, está muy bueno.
damn [dæm] v. tr. Condenar (to condemn). || Maldecir (to curse). || Fig. Echar a perder. || — Fam. *Damn!* o *damn it!*, ¡córcholis!, ¡mecachis! | *I'll be damned if I know*, no tengo la menor idea de eso. | *It is as near to lying as damn is to swearing*, si no es una mentira se le parece mucho. | *Well, I'm damned!*, ¡mecachis!
— V. intr. Soltar tacos (to swear).
damnable ['dæmnəbl] adj. Condenable (deserving condemnation). || Detestable (detestable). || Molesto, ta; fastidioso, sa (annoying).
damnation [dæm'neiʃən] n. Rel. Condenación, *f.* || Fig. Crítica (*f.*) mordaz, vapuleo, *m.* (of a play, an author, etc.).
— Interj. ¡Maldición!
damnatory ['dæmnətɔri] adj. Condenatorio, ria. || Fig. Abrumador, ra; irrecusable (evidence).
damned [dæmd] adj. Condenado, da (doomed). || Condenado, da; réprobo, ba (condemned to eternal punishment). || Fam. Maldito, ta: *that damned boy*, ¡ese maldito niño! | Tremendo, da: *a damned lie*, una mentira tremenda. || *To do one's damnedest*, hacer lo humanamente posible.
— N. Rel. *The damned*, los réprobos, los condenados.
— Adv. Sumamente. || *It's damned cold!*, ¡hace un frío horrible *or* terrible!
damnify ['dæmnifai] v. tr. Damnificar, perjudicar.
damning ['dæmiŋ] adj. Irrecusable (proof). || Mortal (sin).
Damocles ['dæməkli:z] pr. n. Damocles: *Damocles' sword*, espada de Damocles.
damp [dæmp] adj. Húmedo, da.
— N. Humedad, *f.* (moisture). || Min. Mofeta, *f.* (in general). | Grisú, *m.* (firedamp). || Fig. Desánimo, *m.*, desaliento, *m.* (depression). || *Damp course*, aislante hidrófugo (in a wall).
damp [dæmp] or **dampen** [dæmpən] v. tr. Humedecer (to moisten). || Mojar (to wet). || Sofocar, apagar (a fire). || Phys. Amortiguar. || Mus. Amortiguar, apagar. || Fig. Desanimar, desalentar, descorazonar (to discourage). | Cortar (the appetite). | Disminuir (ardour, zeal). || Fig. *To damp s.o.'s spirits*, desanimar *or* desalentar a alguien.
— V. intr. Humedecerse (to moisten). || Mojarse (to get wet). || Amortiguarse (waves, sounds, etc.). || Agr. *To damp off*, pudrir por exceso de humedad.
dampener [—ənə*] n. Amortiguador, *m.*
damper ['dæmpə*] n. Mus. Sordina, *f.*, apagador, *m.* || Humedecedor, *m.*, humectador, *m.* (for moistening stamps, envelopes, etc.). || Regulador (*m.*) de tiro (for chimney). || Tech. Registro, *m.* || Phys. Amortiguador, *m.* || Fam. Aguafiestas, *m. inv.* (person). | Chasco, *m.* (disappointment). || Fig. *To put a damper on*, apagar (the enthusiasm), caer como un jarro de agua fría en (a gathering), frenar (the economy).
damping ['dæmpiŋ] n. Humedecimiento, *m.* || Phys. Amortiguación, *f.*, amortiguamiento, *m.*
dampish ['dæmpiʃ] adj. Algo húmedo, ligeramente húmedo.
dampness ['dæmpnis] n. Humedad, *f.*
damsel ['dæmzəl] n. Damisela, *f.*
damson ['dæmzən] n. Bot. Ciruela (*f.*) damascena (fruit). | Ciruelo (*m.*) damasceno (tree).
Danaids [dæ'neiidz] pr. n. Myth. Danaides, *f.*
dance [dɑ:ns] n. Baile, *m.* || Danza, *f.* (ritual or tribal): *sword dance*, danza de las espadas. || — *Dance band*, orquesta (*f.*) de baile. || *Dance floor*, pista (*f.*) de baile. || *Dance hall*, sala (*f.*) de baile. || *Dance music*, música (*f.*) de baile. || *Dance of death*, danza de la muerte. || Med. *St Vitus's dance*, baile de San Vito. || Fig. *To lead s.o. a dance*, traerle a uno al retortero.
dance [dɑ:ns] v. intr./tr. Bailar. || Fig. Saltar, bailar, danzar. || — *Shall we dance?*, ¿bailas?, ¿quieres bailar? || *To dance on points*, bailar de puntas. || Fig. *To dance to another tune*, mudar de tono.
dancer [—ə*] n. Bailarín, ina (professional dancer). || Bailaor, ra (of flamenco). || Persona (*f.*) que baila.
dancing [—iŋ] adj. De baile: *dancing partner*, pareja de baile. || *Dancing girl*, corista, *f.*
— N. Baile, *m.*
dandelion ['dændilaiən] n. Bot. Diente (*m.*) de león.
dander ['dændə*] n. Caspa, *f.* (dandruff). || U. S. Fam. Malhumor, *m.* (temper). | Rabia, *f.* (anger). || — U. S. Fam. *To get one's dander up*, salir de sus casillas. | *To get s.o.'s dander up*, sacar a alguien de sus casillas.
dandify ['dændifai] v. tr. Acicalar, poner de tiros largos.
dandle ['dændl] v. tr. Hacer saltar sobre las rodillas (a child). || Mimar (to caress).

dandruff [ˈdændrʌf] n. Caspa, *f.* (in hair).
dandy [ˈdændi] n. Dandi, *m.*, dandy, *m.*, petimetre, *m.* (man). || MAR. Balandra, *f.* || Carro (*m.*) del lechero (cart).
— Adj. U. S. Excellente (very good). | Muy elegante (smart).
dandyish [ˈdændiiʃ] adj. Elegantón, ona.
dandyism [ˈdændiizəm] n. Dandismo, *m.*
Dane [dein] n. Danés, esa. || ZOOL. *Great Dane*, perro danés.
danger [ˈdeindʒə*] n. Peligro, *m.* || — *Danger*, peligro de muerte (sign). || *Danger signal*, señal (*f.*) de peligro. || *Danger zone*, área de peligro *or* peligrosa. || *In danger of*, en peligro de. || *No danger of*, no hay peligro de. || *To be out of danger*, estar fuera de peligro.
dangerous [ˈdeindʒerəs] adj. Peligroso, sa.
dangle [ˈdæŋgl] v. tr. Balancear en el aire (to swing). || Colgar, dejar colgado (to hang). || FIG. Hacer brillar, dejar entrever (to let see).
— V. intr. Balancearse (to swing). || Colgar (to hang). || — FIG. *To dangle after*, ir tras de. | *To keep s.o. dangling*, tener a alguien pendiente.
Danish [ˈdeiniʃ] n. Danés, *m.* (language).
— Adj. Danés, esa.
dank [dæŋk] adj. Malsano y húmedo (damp). || Que huele a humedad (which smells damp).
dankness [—nis] n. Humedad, *f.* || Olor (*m.*) a humedad.
danse macabre [ˈdɑ̃:nsmækɑ:br] n. Danza (*f.*) macabra.
Dantean [dænˈti:ən] or **Dantesque** [dænˈtesk] adj. Dantesco, ca.
Danube [ˈdænju:b] pr. n. GEOGR. Danubio, *m.*
dap [dæp] n. Rebote, *m.* (of a ball). || Muesca, *f.* (in wood).
dap [dæp] v. tr. Hacer rebotar (a ball). || Hacer muescas en (wood).
— V. intr. Rebotar (ball, stone). || Zambullirse (bird).
Daphne [dæfni] pr. n. Dafne, *f.*
Daphnis [ˈdæfnis] pr. n. Dafnis, *m.*
dapper [ˈdæpə*] adj. Atildado, da; apuesto, ta (spruce). || Vivo, va (active).
dapple [ˈdæpl] n. Moteado, *m.*
dapple [ˈdæpl] v. tr. Motear.
— V. intr. Motearse (skin). || Aborregarse (sky).
dappled [—d] adj. Moteado, da (horse).
dapple-grey [ˈdæplˈgrei] adj. Tordo, da (horse).
Dardanelles [ˌdɑ:dəˈnelz] pl. pr. n. GEOGR. Dardanelos, *m.*
dare [dɛə*] n. Desafío, *m.*, reto, *m.* (challenge): *to take a dare*, aceptar un reto.
dare [dɛə*] v. tr. Desafiar: *to dare s.o. to do sth.*, desafiar a alguien a hacer algo. || Desafiar, arrostrar (to face). || Atreverse a: *how dare you say that?*, ¿cómo se atreve a decir eso? || *I dare say*, a mi parecer (in my opinion), quizás, tal vez (perhaps).
— V. intr. Atreverse, osar.
— OBSERV. Ademas del pretérito regular *dared*, el verbo *to dare* tiene una forma antigua, *durst*.

daredevil [—ˌdevl] adj./n. Temerario, ria; atrevido, da.
daredevilry [—ri] (U. S. **daredeviltry**) [—tri] n. Temeridad, *f.*, audacia, *f.*, atrevimiento, *m.*
daresay [ˈdɛəˈsei] v. tr./intr. U. S. *I daresay*, a mi parecer; quizás.
daring [ˈdɛəriŋ] adj. Atrevido, da; osado, da.
— N. Atrevimiento, *m.*, osadía, *f.*
Darius [dəˈraiəs] pr. n. Darío, *m.*
dark [dɑ:k] adj. Oscuro, ra; obscuro, ra: *dark room*, habitación oscura; *dark green*, verde oscuro. || Moreno, na (hair, complexion). || Negro, gra (race). || FIG. Amenazador, ra (threatening). | Triste, sombrío, a: *the dark days of winter*, los tristes días del invierno. | Sombrío, a; negro, gra (the future). | Oculto, ta: *dark practices*, actividades ocultas. | Enigmático, ca; misterioso, sa (mysterious). | Tenebroso, sa (designs). | Oscuro, ra; obscuro, ra (a prophecy). | Ignorante. || FAM. Siniestro, tra: *he is a dark one*, es un tipo siniestro. || — *Dark Ages*, Edad (*f.*) de las tinieblas, primeros años de la Edad Media. || FIG. *Keep it dark!*, ¡no digas nada! || *The Dark Continent*, el Continente Negro. || FIG. *To be a dark horse*, no ser favorito, ser un "outsider" (horse), tenérselo bien callado (person). || *To become* o *to get* o *to grow dark*, anochecer, hacerse de noche (at nightfall), oscurecerse (room, etc.).
— N. Oscuridad, *f.*, obscuridad, *f.* (absence of light). || Noche, *f.* (night). || Sombra, *f.* (in painting). || — *After dark*, después del anochecer. || *At dark*, al anochecer, al caer la noche. || FIG. *Leap in the dark*, salto (*m.*) en el vacío. || *To be in the dark*, estar a oscuras. || *To be left in the dark*, quedarse a oscuras. || FIG. *To keep s.o. in the dark*, ocultarle algo a uno.
darken [ˈdɑ:kən] v. tr. Oscurecer. || Poner moreno (the complexion). || FIG. Entristecer (to sadden). | Ensombrecer (the future). | Nublar, oscurecer (s.o.'s mind). || FAM. *Not to darken s.o.'s door*, no poner los pies en casa de alguien.
— V. intr. Oscurecerse. || Ponerse moreno (complexion). || FIG. Ponerse negro *or* sombrío (future). | Oscurecerse, nublarse (mind).
darkie [ˈdɑ:ki] n. FAM. Negro, gra.
darkish [ˈdɑ:kiʃ] adj. Que tira a oscuro. || Que tira a moreno (hair). || U. S. FAM. Negro, gra (person).
darkle [ˈdɑ:kəl] v. intr. Oscurecerse (to darken). || Ocultarse (to hide).
darkling [dɑ:kliŋ] adj. Oscuro, ra.
— Adv. A oscuras.
darkly [ˈdɑ:kli] adv. Tristemente (gloomily). || Misteriosamente (mysteriously).
darkness [ˈdɑ:knis] n. Oscuridad, *f.* || — *Prince of Darkness*, Ángel (*m.*) de las tinieblas. || *To be in darkness*, estar a oscuras. || *To cast s.o. into outer darkness*, condenar a uno a las penas del infierno.
darkroom [ˈdɑ:krum] n. PHOT. Cámara (*f.*) oscura.
darling [ˈdɑ:liŋ] adj./n. Querido, da: *my darling David*, mi querido David. || — *A darling little house*, una monada *or* una preciosidad de casa. || *He is a darling*, es un encanto. || *Mother's darling* o *spoilt darling*, niño mimado. || *Yes, darling*, sí, querido *or* sí, querida.
darn [dɑ:n] adj. FAM. Maldito, ta: *that darn car*, ¡ese maldito coche!
— Adv. Muy, sumamente.
— N. Zurcido, *m.* (mended hole). || FAM. Comino, *m.*: *I don't give a darn*, me importa un comino.
— Interj. FAM. *Darn it!*, ¡córcholis!, ¡mecachis!
darn [dɑ:n] v. tr. Zurcir (to mend). || See DAMN.
darned [—d] adj. Zurcido, da (mended). || FAM. Maldito, ta (damned).
darnel [ˈdɑ:nl] n. BOT. Cizaña, *f.*
darner [ˈdɑ:nə*] n. Huevo (*m.*) de madera para zurcir (ball). || Aguja (*f.*) de zurcir (needle). || Zurcidor, ra (person).
darning [dɑ:niŋ] n. Zurcido, *m.* || *Darning needle*, aguja (*f.*) de zurcir.
dart [dɑ:t] n. Dardo, *m.* (pointed missile). || Movimiento (*m.*) rápido (swift movement). || Punzada, *f.* (of pain). || Pinza, *f.* (in dressmaking). || SP. Lanzamiento, *m.* || Lengua, *f.*, résped, *m.*, réspede, *m.* (of snake). || Aguijón, *m.* (of insects). || — Pl. Dardos, *m.* (game). || *To make a dart for the door*, precipitarse hacia la puerta.
dart [dɑ:t] v. tr. Lanzar.
— V. intr. Precipitarse (*for*, hacia). || FIG. *To dart away*, salir como una flecha, salir disparado.
dartboard [—bɔ:d] n. Blanco, *m.* (target).
dartre [ˈdɑ:tə*] n. MED. Herpes, *m. pl.* or *f. pl.*
dartrous [ˈdɑ:trəs] adj. MED. Herpético, ca.
Darwinian [dɑ:ˈwiniən] adj. Darviniano, na.
Darwinism [ˈdɑ:winizəm] n. Darvinismo, *m.*
Darwinist [ˈdɑ:winist] adj./n. Darvinista.
dash [dæʃ] n. Choque, *m.*: *the dash of oars striking the water*, el choque de los remos con el agua. || Romper, *m.* (breaking): *the dash of the waves on the rocks*, el romper de las olas contra las rocas. || Carrera, *f.* (rush). || Raya, *f.* (in telegraphy). || PRINT. Guión, *m.* (small). | Raya, *f.* (large). || CULIN. Poco, *m.*, gotas, *f. pl.* (of brandy, etc.): *tea with a dash of milk*, té con un poco de leche. | Pizca, *f.*, poco, *m.* (of garlic, vanilla). | Chorrito, *m.* (of vinegar). || SP. Carrera (*f.*) corta de velocidad (sprint). || Plumada, *f.*, trazo, *m.* (with a pen). || Pincelada, *f.*, toque, *m.* (of an artist). || Brochazo, *m.* (of a decorator). || AUT. Salpicadero, *m.* (instrument panel). | Guardabarros, *m. inv.* (mudguard). || FIG. Garbo, *m.* (grace). | Brío, *m.* (verve). | Empuje, *m.*, dinamismo, *m.*, energía, *f.* (drive). || — *A dash of colour*, una nota de color. || *At a dash*, de un golpe. || FIG. *To cut a dash*, ser elegante (to be smart), darse pisto (to make a display of o.s.), causar sensación (to cause a sensation), hacer buen papel (to do well). || *To make a dash at*, lanzarse sobre (the enemy). || *To make a dash for*, precipitarse hacia: *to make a dash for the exit*, precipitarse hacia la salida. || *To make a dash for it*, huir precipitadamente: *the thieves made a dash for it*, los ladrones huyeron precipitadamente. || *You'll have to make a dash for it*, tendréis que correr.
— Interj. ¡Demonios!
dash [dæʃ] v. tr. Estrellar, romper (to shatter). || Chocar (to knock). || Tirar, lanzar, arrojar (to throw violently). || Salpicar (*with*, de) [to splash]. || CULIN. Sazonar (with spices). | Mezclar, cortar (with water). || Realzar (with colour). || FIG. Defraudar (hopes). | Desanimar (to dishearten). || — *To dash sth. to pieces*, hacer algo pedazos. || *To dash to the ground*, tirar al suelo (objects), echar por tierra (argument).
— V. intr. Ir de prisa (people and vehicles). || Precipitarse (to rush). || Chocar (*into*, contra).
— ***To dash against***, estrellarse contra, romperse contra: *the waves dashed against the cliff*, las olas se rompían contra el acantilado. | Lanzar contra. || ***To dash along***, ir corriendo. || ***To dash at***, lanzarse sobre. || ***To dash away***, irse corriendo. | Quitar rápidamente (to remove). || ***To dash by*** o ***past***, pasar corriendo: *the thief dashed past*, el ladrón pasó corriendo. || ***To dash down***, tirar al suelo (to throw on the floor). | Anotar (to write down). || ***To dash in***, entrar precipitadamente. || ***To dash off***, escribir deprisa: *he dashed off a letter*, escribió una carta deprisa. | Hacer muy deprisa: *he dashed off his homework*, hizo sus deberes muy deprisa. | Irse corriendo: *he dashed off*, se fue corriendo. || ***To dash out***, salir precipitadamente. || ***To dash up***, llegar corriendo: *the boy dashed up to the door*, el niño llegó corriendo a la puerta. | Subir corriendo: *to dash up the stairs*, subir las escaleras corriendo.

dashboard [—bɔ:d] n. Salpicadero, *m.* (instrument panel). ‖ U. S. Guardabarros, *m. inv.* (mudguard).
dasher [dæʃə*] n. Batidor, *m.*, paleta, *f.* (in a churn). ‖ FAM. Presuntuoso, sa; farolero, ra. ‖ U. S. AUT. Guardabarros, *m. inv.*
dashing [ˈdæʃiŋ] adj. Fogoso, sa (horse). ‖ Garboso, sa; gallardo, da (debonair). ‖ Elegante, apuesto, ta (elegant). ‖ Dinámico, ca; enérgico, ca (spirited). ‖ Presuntuoso, sa (showy).
dastard [ˈdæstəd] n. Cobarde, *m.* (coward).
dastardliness [—linis] n. Cobardía, *f.*
dastardly [—li] adj. Cobarde (cowardly). ‖ Ruin, vil (crime).
data [ˈdeitə] pl. n. See DATUM.
date [deit] n. Fecha, *f.*: *what is today's date?*, ¿cuál es la fecha de hoy?; *to put the date on a letter*, poner la fecha en una carta. ‖ Época, *f.*: *of medieval date*, de época medieval. ‖ COMM. Plazo, *m.* ‖ BOT. Dátil, *m.* (fruit). | Datilero, *m.* (tree). ‖ Cita, *f.*: *to have a date*, tener una cita. ‖ U. S. Novio, *m.*, novia, *f.*, amigo, ga. ‖ — *At an early date*, en fecha próxima. ‖ *Final* o *closing date*, fecha tope. ‖ *On a fixed date*, a fecha fija. ‖ *Out of date*, anticuado, da; pasado de moda (old-fashioned). ‖ *To be up to date*, ser moderno (modern), estar al día (facts, etc.). ‖ *To be up to date in one's work*, estar al día en el trabajo, tener el trabajo al día. ‖ *To be up to date on the news*, estar al corriente de las noticias. ‖ *To bring s.o. up to date*, poner a alguien al corriente. ‖ *To bring sth. up to date*, poner algo al día. ‖ *To date* o *up to date*, hasta la fecha. ‖ *To make a date*, citarse, darse cita. ‖ *To make a date with*, citar, dar cita. ‖ *Who is your date?*, ¿con quién sales?
date [deit] v. tr. Datar, fechar (to write a date on, to assign a date to). ‖ Dar cita, citar (to make an appointment with). ‖ Salir con: *she has been dating him for a long time*, sale con él desde hace mucho tiempo. ‖ *To date back*, antedatar.
— V. intr. Datar: *a friendship dating from before the war*, una amistad que data de antes de la guerra. ‖ Poner la fecha. ‖ Quedar anticuado (to become old-fashioned). ‖ *To date back to*, remontarse a.
dated [ˈdeitid] adj. Fechado, da (bearing a date). ‖ Anticuado, da (old-fashioned).
dateless [ˈdeitlis] adj. Sin fecha (undated). ‖ Inmemorial (very ancient). ‖ Eterno, na (everlasting).
dateline [ˈdeitlain] n. Fecha, *f.* (in a letter, etc.).
date line [ˈdeitlain] n. Meridiano (*m.*) de cambio de fecha.
date palm [ˈdeitpɑ:m] n. BOT. Palmera (*f.*) datilera.
dater [ˈdeitə*] n. Fechador, *m.*
date stamp [ˈdeitstæmp] n. Fechador, *m.*
dation [ˈdeiʃən] n. JUR. Dación, *f.*
dative [ˈdeitiv] adj. GRAMM. Dativo, va. ‖ JUR. Dativo, va: *tutor dative*, tutor dativo.
— N. GRAMM. Dativo, *m.*: *in the dative*, en dativo.
datum [ˈdeitəm] n. Dato, *m.* (known fact). ‖ — Pl. Datos, *m.*: *we need more data*, necesitamos más datos. ‖ — *Data processing*, informática, *f.* (science), tratamiento (*m.*) de la información, procesamiento (*m.*) *or* proceso (*m.*) de datos. ‖ *Datum line*, línea (*f.*) de referencia. ‖ *Datum point*, punto (*m.*) de referencia.
— OBSERV. El plural de la palabra *datum* es *data*.
daub [dɔ:b] n. Revestimiento, *m.* (coating). ‖ Mancha, *f.* (smear). ‖ Pintarrajo, *m.*, mamarracho, *m.* (unskilfully painted picture).
daub [dɔ:b] v. tr. Revestir [con] (to coat). ‖ Embadurnar (to smear). ‖ Pintarrajear (to paint unskifully).
— V. intr. Pintarrajear.
dauber [—ə*] or **daubster** [ˈdɔ:bstə*] n. Embadurnador, ra (who smears). ‖ Pintamonas, *m.* & *f. inv.* (poor painter).
dauby [—i] adj. Pegajoso, sa (sticky). ‖ Embadurnado, da (smeared). ‖ Pintarrajeado, da (poorly painted).
daughter [ˈdɔ:tə*] n. Hija, *f.*
daughter-in-law [ˈdɔ:tərinlɔ:] n. Nuera, *f.*, hija (*f.*) política.
— OBSERV. El plural es *daughters-in-law*.
daughterly [ˈdɔ:təli] adj. Filial.
daunt [dɔ:nt] v. tr. Intimidar (to intimidate). ‖ Desanimar, desalentar (to dishearten).
dauntless [—lis] adj. Intrépido, da.
dauntlessness [—linis] n. Intrepidez, *f.*
dauphin [ˈdɔ:fin] n. Delfín, *m.*
dauphine [ˈdɔ:fi:n] or **dauphiness** [—is] n. Delfina, *f.*
davenport [ˈdævnpɔ:t] n. Escritorio (*m.*) pequeño (small writing desk). ‖ U. S. Sofá cama, *m.*
davit [ˈdævit] n. MAR. Pescante, *m.*
Davy Jones's locker [ˈdeiviˈdʒəunzˈlɔkə*] n. FIG. Fondo (*m.*) del mar [en cuanto hace de tumba].
Davy lamp [ˈdeivilæmp] n. MIN. Lámpara (*f.*) de seguridad.
daw [dɔ:] n. ZOOL. Chova, *f.* (bird).
dawdle [ˈdɔ:dl] v. tr. *To dawdle away*, malgastar (time).
— V. intr. Holgazanear (to loiter). ‖ Andar despacio (to walk slowly). ‖ Perder el tiempo (to waste time).
dawdler [—ə*] n. Holgazán, ana (lazy person). ‖ Persona (*f.*) que anda despacio, rezagado, da (slow walker).
dawn [dɔ:n] n. Alba, *m.*, aurora, *f.*, amanecer, *m.* (daybreak). ‖ FIG. Alborear, *m.*, albores, *m. pl.*: *the dawn of civilization*, los albores de la civilización. ‖ — *At dawn*, al alba. ‖ *Dawn breaks*, raya el alba. ‖ *To work from dawn to dusk*, trabajar de sol a sol.
dawn [dɔ:n] v. intr. Amanecer, alborear (to begin to grow light). ‖ FIG. Esbozarse (a smile). ‖ — FIG. *A new era has dawned*, ha nacido una nueva era. | *Then it dawned on me*, entonces caí en la cuenta.
day [dei] n. Día, *m.*: *all day*, todo el día; *every day*, todos los días; *the day we were married*, el día en que nos casamos; *a few days after I met him*, a los pocos días de conocerle, pocos días después de conocerle; *it's not his day today*, hoy no es su día. ‖ Jornada, *f.* (of work): *a six hour day*, una jornada de seis horas. ‖ Fiesta, *f.*: *Labour Day*, Fiesta del Trabajo. ‖ Época, *f.*: *the best singer of his day*, el mejor cantante de su época. ‖ Tiempo, *m.* (time). ‖ — Pl. Días, *m.*: *her dancing days are over*, sus días de bailarina se han acabado; *to the end of his days*, hasta el fin de sus días; *in the days of*, en los días de.
— *All day long*, durante todo el día, todo el santo día. ‖ *Another day* o *some other day*, otro día. ‖ *Any day*, cualquier día. ‖ *At the close of the day*, al caer el día. ‖ *By day*, de día. ‖ *By the day*, al día; a jornal (to work). ‖ *Day after day* o *day in day out*, día tras día. ‖ *Day and night*, día y noche. ‖ *Day by day*, día a día. ‖ *Day off*, día libre, día de descanso. ‖ *Days of grace*, plazo (*m.*) de respiro. ‖ *Day of obligation*, día de precepto. ‖ *Day of reckoning*, día de ajustar cuentas (for settling accounts), día del Juicio Final (Last Judgment). ‖ *Every other day*, cada dos días, un día sí y otro no. ‖ *From day to day*, de día en día (gradually), al día: *to live from day to day*, vivir al día. ‖ *From one day to the next*, de un día al otro. ‖ *From this day onward*, de hoy en adelante. ‖ *Good day!*, ¡buenos días! ‖ REL. *Holy day*, fiesta, *f.* ‖ *In his day*, en sus tiempos. ‖ FIG. *It's all in a day's work*, son gajes del oficio. ‖ *It's early days yet*, todavía es pronto. ‖ *It was a black day for the country*, fue un día aciago para el país. ‖ *It was broad day*, era muy de día. ‖ *Mother's Day*, día de la madre. ‖ *One day* o *one fine day*, un día *or* un buen día. ‖ *One of these days*, un día de éstos, uno de estos días. ‖ *Some day*, algún día. ‖ *The day after*, al día siguiente. ‖ *The day after tomorrow*, pasado mañana. ‖ *The day before*, el día anterior. ‖ *The day before his death*, la víspera de su muerte. ‖ *The day before yesterday*, anteayer, antes de ayer. ‖ *The next day*, al día siguiente, el día siguiente. ‖ *The next day but one*, dos días después, a los dos días. ‖ *The other day*, el otro día. ‖ *These days*, hoy en día. ‖ *This day*, hoy. ‖ *This day week*, dentro de ocho días. ‖ *This very day*, hoy mismo. ‖ *To a day*, exactamente. ‖ FIG. *To call it a day*, dar por acabado el día, dejarlo. ‖ *To have had one's day*, estar fuera de uso; haber pasado de moda. ‖ *To have seen better days*, haber conocido días mejores. ‖ FIG. *To know the time of day*, saber cuántas son cinco. | *Tomorrow is another day*, mañana será otro día. | *To save for a rainy day*, ahorrar para los momentos difíciles. ‖ *To take a day off*, coger un día libre *or* un día de descanso. ‖ *To win the day*, llevarse la palma, triunfar. ‖ *Twice a day*, dos veces al *or* por día. ‖ *Working day*, día laborable (weekday), jornada, *f.* (number of hours).
daybed [—bed] n. Meridiana, *f.*
daybook [—buk] n. Diario, *m.*
day boy [—bɔi] n. Externo, *m.* (pupil).
daybreak [—breik] n. Amanecer, *m.*, alba, *f.*
daydream [—dri:m] n. Ensueño, *m.* (reverie). ‖ Ilusión, *f.* (a wish or plan not likely to be realized).
daydream [—dri:m] v. intr. Soñar despierto.
daydreamer [—ˌdri:mə*] n. Soñador, ra.
day girl [—gə:l] n. Externa, *f.* (pupil).
day labourer (U. S. **day laborer**) [—ˈleibərə*] n. Jornalero, *m.*, peón, *m.*
daylight [—lait] n. Luz (*f.*) del día. ‖ Luz, *f.* (open space). ‖ Amanecer, *m.*, alba, *f.* (dawn). ‖ — *By daylight*, de día (by day), a la luz del día (by the light of day). ‖ *In broad daylight*, en pleno día. ‖ *In daylight*, a la luz del día. ‖ U. S. *To burn daylight*, perder el tiempo. ‖ FIG. *To let daylight into s.o.*, pegar un tiro a alguien. | *To let in some daylight on a subject*, aclarar un asunto. | *To see daylight*, ver claro, llegar a comprender (to understand), ver la luz del día (to be published), ver el final de un trabajo (to conclude). | *To throw daylight on*, aclarar (to clarify), sacar a luz (to disclose).
daylight-saving time [—laitˌseiviŋˈtaim] n. Hora (*f.*) de verano.
daylong [—lɔŋ] adj. Que dura todo el día.
— Adv. Todo el día.
day nursery [—ˈnə:səri] n. Guardería (*f.*) infantil.
day-old [—əuld] adj. De un día: *a day-old baby*, un niño de un día.
days [deiz] adv. De día.
day school [ˈdeisku:l] n. Externado, *m.*, colegio (*m.*) sin internado.
day shift [ˈdeiʃift] n. Turno (*m.*) de día.
dayspring [ˈdeispriŋ] n. Aurora, *f.*, alba, *f.*
daystar [ˈdeistɑ:*] n. Lucero (*m.*) del alba (Venus). ‖ Sol, *m.* (the sun).
daytime [ˈdeitaim] n. Día, *m.*: *in the daytime*, de día.
day-to-day [ˈdeitəˈdei] adj. Cotidiano, na: *day-to-day life*, vida cotidiana.

daywork [ˈdeiwəːk] n. Trabajo (*m.*) a jornal. || Trabajo (*m.*) hecho en un día.
daze [deiz] n. Aturdimiento, *m.*: *to come out of one's daze*, salir del aturdimiento. || Atolondramiento, *m.* (bewilderment). || Deslumbramiento, *m.* (dazzle). || *In a daze*, aturdido, da.
daze [deiz] v. tr. Aturdir (to stun). || Atolondrar, atontar (to bewilder). || Deslumbrar (to dazzle).
dazedly [—dli] adv. Con un aire atolondrado *or* atontado.
dazzle [ˈdæzl] n. Deslumbramiento, *m.* || Resplandor, *m.* (brightness). || FIG. Deslumbramiento, *m.*
dazzle [ˈdæzl] v. tr./intr. Deslumbrar: *dazzled by the headlights*, deslumbrado por los faros. || FIG. Deslumbrar: *the conjuror dazzled his audience*, el prestidigitador deslumbró al público.
dazzling [—iŋ] adj. Deslumbrante, deslumbrador, ra: *a dazzling success*, un éxito deslumbrante.
— N. Deslumbramiento, *m.*
DDT [ˈdiːdiːˈtiː] n. D.D.T., *m.* (abbreviation of dichlorodiphenyltrichloroethane).
deacon [ˈdiːkən] n. Diácono, *m.*
deacon [ˈdiːkən] v. tr. Adulterar (to adulterate). || *To deacon a basket of fruit*, llenar un cesto de fruta poniendo lo mejor en la parte de arriba.
deaconate [ˈdiːkənit] n. Diaconado, *m.*
deaconess [ˈdiːkənis] n. Diaconisa, *f.*
deaconry [ˈdiːkənri] n. Diaconato, *m.*, diaconado, *m.*
deaconship [ˈdiːkənʃip] n. Diaconato, *m.*, diaconado, *m.*
dead [ded] adj. Muerto, ta: *to be dead*, estar muerto; *dead city*, ciudad muerta; *dead language*, lengua muerta; *dead weight*, peso muerto. || Difunto, ta: *the dead king*, el difunto rey. || Absoluto, ta: *dead cert*, certeza absoluta; *dead secret*, secreto absoluto. || | Absoluto, ta; completo, ta (silence, quietness). || Insensible: *dead to remorse*, insensible a los remordimientos. || Apagado, da (fire, colour, volcano, oven). || Marchito, ta; seco, ca (leaf). || Mate (gold). || Sin vida (picture). || Sordo, da (voice, ache, etc.): *dead sound*, sonido sordo. || Estancado, da (water). || Agotado, da (well, mine). || Descargado, da (battery). || Gastado, da (used): *dead matches*, cerillas gastadas. || Anticuado, da (obsolete). || Inerte: *dead matter*, materia inerte. || Adormecido, da; entumecido, da (limb). || AGR. Improductivo, va; estéril (soil). || ARCH. Ciego, ga (arch, window). || FAM. Muerto, ta (very tired). || SP. Fuera de juego (ball). || ELECTR. Sin corriente, desconectado, da. || Inmóvil (part of machine). || COMM. Estancado, da (business). | Ficticio, cia (account). | Irrecuperable, incobrable (loan). | Completo, ta; total (loss). | Muerto, ta; improductivo, va (money). || JUR. En desuso (law). | Muerto, ta (letter). || — *Dead and gone* o *dead and buried* o *dead as a doornail* o *dead as a mutton*, muerto y bien muerto. || *Dead hours*, horas muertas. || *Dead letters*, cartas desechadas. || *Dead loss*, pérdida (*f.*) total (of money), nulidad, *f.*, birria, *f.* (things): *the film is a dead loss*, la película es una birria; inútil, *m.* & *f.*, nulidad, *f.* (person). || *Dead man*, muerto, *m.* || *Dead march*, marcha (*f.*) fúnebre. || FIG. *Dead men*, cascos (*m. pl.*) de botella. | *Dead men tell no tales*, los muertos no hablan. || *Dead shot*, tiro certero (which hits the target), tirador certero (person). || *Dead silence*, silencio sepulcral *or* completo. || FIG. *Dead spit*, vivo retrato. || *Dead stop*, parada (*f.*) en seco. || FAM. *Dead to the world*, borracho perdido (drunk), como un leño (asleep). || *Dead water*, aguas muertas *or* mansas *or* estancadas. || *Dead woman*, muerta, *f.* || FAM. *Drop dead!*, ¡vete al cuerno! || *He has been dead 2 years*, hace dos años que se murió. || *I wouldn't be seen dead there*, allí no se me ha perdido nada. || *More dead than alive*, más muerto que vivo. || *On a dead level*, a nivel, de nivel. || *The dead calm* o *still*, la calma chicha. || *The dead hours of night*, la quietud de la noche. || *The wire has gone dead*, la línea está cortada. || *To drop down dead*, caerse muerto. || *To fall dead*, caer muerto; amainar (the wind). || *To give s.o. up for dead*, dar por muerto a uno. || *To go dead*, dormirse, entumecerse (a limb), dejar de funcionar, cortarse (radio, phone, etc.). || *To strike* o *to kill s.o.* (*stone*) *dead*, matar a uno. || *Wanted dead or alive*, se busca vivo o muerto.
— Adv. FAM. Completamente (completely): *dead sure*, completamente seguro. || Muy: *dead slow*, muy lento. || Justo: *dead in the centre*, justo en medio; *dead on time*, justo a tiempo. || — *Dead tired*, muerto de cansancio. || *To be dead set against*, estar resueltamente opuesto a. || *To be dead set on sth.*, estar empeñado en algo. || *To stop dead*, pararse en seco.
— N. *In the dead of night*, en plena noche. || *In the dead of winter*, en pleno invierno, en lo más recio del invierno. || *The dead*, los muertos. || *The dead of night*, el silencio de la noche. || *To rise from the dead*, resucitar de entre los muertos.
dead beat [ˈdedˈbiːt] adj. FAM. Muerto, ta; rendido, da (exhausted).
deadbeat [ˈdedˈbiːt] adj. TECH. Aperiódico, ca.
— N. FIG. y FAM. Gorrón, ona; aprovechado, da.
dead centre (U. S. **dead center**) [ˈdedˈsentə*] n. TECH. Punto (*m.*) muerto.
dead-drunk [ˈdedˈdrʌŋk] adj. Borracho perdido.
deaden [ˈdedn] v. tr. Amortiguar: *to deaden a sound, a blow*, amortiguar un sonido, un golpe. || Calmar, aliviar: *to deaden pain*, calmar el dolor. || Embotar (feeling). || Insonorizar (a wall, etc.). || Volver mate (gold). || Disminuir (vitality).
— V. intr. Amortiguarse (sound, blow). || Desbravarse (wine). || Embotarse (sensibility). || Disminuir (vitality).
dead end [ˈdedˈend] n. Callejón (*m.*) sin salida (street with no exit, situation without solution).
dead-end [ˈdedˈend] adj. Sin salida (street). || Barriobajero, ra (of the slums). || *Dead-end job*, trabajo (*m.*) sin porvenir.
deadening [ˈdedniŋ] adj. Aislante (for walls, etc.)
deadeye [ˈdedai] n. MAR. Vigota, *f.*
deadfall [ˈdedfɔːl] n. Trampa, *f.*
deadhead [ˈdedhed] n. Persona (*f.*) que tiene pase (for the cinema, theatre, etc.).
dead heat [ˈdedˈhiːt] n. Empate, *m.*
deadline [ˈdedlain] n. Fecha (*f.*) tope, plazo, *m.*, límite, *m.*: *the deadline for the construction*, la fecha tope para la construcción. || U. S. Línea (*f.*) vedada (of a prison). || *To meet one's deadline*, respetar el plazo fijado.
dead load [ˈdedˈləud] n. Peso (*m.*) muerto.
deadlock [ˈdedlɔk] n. Punto (*m.*) muerto. || TECH. Cerradura (*f.*) con pestillo de golpe.
deadlock [ˈdedlɔk] v. tr. Llevar a un punto muerto.
— V. intr. Llegar a un punto muerto.
deadly [ˈdedli] adj. Mortal: *a deadly wound*, una herida mortal; *deadly sin*, pecado mortal; *deadly enemy*, enemigo mortal. || A muerte (fight). || Absoluto, ta: *with deadly skill*, con destreza absoluta. || JUR. Abrumador, ra (evidence). || Devastador, ra (critics). || Nocivo, va; pernicioso, sa (habit, effect, etc.). || Certero, ra (shot). || Cadavérico, ca (pallor). || FAM. Fatal, terrible (very bad).
— Adv. Extremadamente, terriblemente: *deadly boring*, extremadamente aburrido.
deadness [ˈdednis] n. Falta (*f.*) de vida. || Color (*m.*) mate (of gold). || COMM. Estancamiento, *m.* || Entumecimiento, *m.* (of limb). || CULIN. Desbravación, *f.* (of wine).
deadpan [ˈdedpæn] adj. FAM. Inexpresivo, va.
dead reckoning [ˈdedˈrekniŋ] n. AVIAT. MAR. Estima, *f.*
Dead Sea [ˈdedˈsiː] pr. n. GEOGR. Mar (*m.*) Muerto.
deadweight [ˈdedweit] n. Peso (*m.*) muerto (weight of an inert mass). || MAR. Carga (*f.*) máxima, peso (*m.*) muerto. || FIG. Lastre, *m.*, carga, *f.* (burden).
deadwood [ˈdedwud] n. Rama (*f.*) muerta (dead branch). || Persona (*f.*) *or* cosa (*f.*) inútil (useless person *or* thing). || Mercancía (*f.*) inservible. || MAR. Durmientes, *m. pl.*
deaf [def] adj. Sordo, da: *he went deaf*, se quedó sordo. || FIG. Sordo, da. || — *Deaf and dumb*, sordomudo, da. || FAM. *To be as deaf as a post*, estar más sordo que una tapia. || FIG. *To turn a deaf ear*, hacerse el sordo, no prestar oídos.
— N. *The deaf*, los sordos.
deaf-aid [—eid] n. Aparato (*m.*) para sordos.
deaf-and-dumb [—ənˈdʌm] adj. Sordomudo, da. || *Deaf-and-dumb alphabet*, alfabeto (*m.*) de los sordomudos.
deafen [ˈdefn] v. tr. Ensordecer (to make deaf). || Amortiguar (a sound). || ARCH. Insonorizar.
deafening [—iŋ] adj. Ensordecedor, ra.
deaf-mute [ˈdefˈmjuːt] adj./n. Sordomudo, da.
deafness [ˈdefnis] n. Sordera, *f.*
deal [diːl] n. Reparto, *m.* (of cards). || Vez, *f.*, turno, *m.* (a turn to distribute cards). || Transacción, *f.*, negocio, *m.*, trato, *m.* (business transaction). || Trato, *m.*, tratamiento, *m.* (treatment): *raw deal*, trato injusto. || Convenio, *m.*, arreglo, *m.* (agreement). || Cantidad, *f.* (large amount). || Tablón, *m.*, madero, *m.* (board of wood). || Pino, *m.*, abeto, *m.* (wood). || — *A good deal, a great deal*, mucho, una gran cantidad. || *It's a deal!*, ¡trato hecho! || *Square deal*, trato equitativo *or* justo, justicia, *f.* || *To make a great deal of*, dar importancia a (sth.), tener en mucho a (s.o.). || *Your deal*, tu vez, te toca.
deal [diːl]* v. tr. Repartir, distribuir (to distribute). || Dar, repartir, distribuir (cards). || Asestar, dar: *to deal s.o. a blow*, asestarle un golpe a alguien.
— V. intr. Dar *or* repartir *or* distribuir las cartas.
— ***To deal by,*** comportarse *or* portarse con. || ***To deal in,*** comerciar en. || ***To deal out,*** repartir, distribuir. || ***To deal with,*** tratar con: *I deal with large business organizations*, trato con grandes empresas. | Tratar a: *to deal justly with s.o.*, tratar con justicia a alguien. | Comportarse *or* portarse con (to behave). | Enfrentarse con (to meet a situation). | Resolver (a difficulty). | Tratar de *or* sobre (a subject). | Ocuparse de, encargarse de: *I'll deal with him*, yo me encargaré de él. | Castigar: *the murderer will be dealt with*, el asesino será castigado. | Hacer sus compras en (one's regular tradesman).
— OBSERV. Pret. & p. p. ***dealt.***
dealer [—ə*] n. Negociante, *m.* & *f.*, comerciante, *m.* & *f.* (merchant). || Mano, *f.* (in cards).
dealing [—iŋ] n. Trato, *m.* (treatment). || Comportamiento, *m.*, conducta, *f.* (behaviour). || COMM. Comercio, *m.* || — Pl. Relaciones, *f.*, trato, *m. sing.* | Transacciones, *f.*
dealt [delt] pret. & p. p. See DEAL.
dean [diːn] n. REL. Deán, *m.* || Decano, *m.* (in university). || U. S. Decano, *m.* (senior member).

deanery [ˈdi:nəri] n. REL. Deanato, *m.*, deanazgo, *m.* (the office of dean). | Residencia (*f.*) del deán (residence). || Decanato, *m.* (of university).
deanship [ˈdi:nʃip] n. REL. Deanato, *m.*, deanazgo, *m.* || Decanato, *m.* (of university).
dear [diə*] adj. Querido, da : *dear Patrick*, querido Patricio. || Costoso, sa; caro, ra (costly). || Caro, ra; carero, ra (charging high prices). || Sincero, ra; profundo, de (sincere). || FIG. Costoso, sa : *a dear victory*, una victoria costosa. || — *Dear Madam*, estimada Señora. || *Dear me!* o *oh dear!*, ¡ Dios mío! || *Dear Sir*, muy señor mio. || *He is dear to me*, le quiero mucho, le tengo mucho cariño. || *It is dear to me*, le tengo mucho cariño (jewel), lo aprecio mucho (place, idea). || *My dear George*, querido Jorge. || FAM. *To run for dear life*, correr desesperadamente.
— Adv. Caro (dearly): *it will cost you dear*, te va a costar caro. || *To hold dear*, querer (s.o.), apreciar.
— N. Querido, da: *my dear*, querido mío. || — *An old dear*, una viejecita encantadora. || *Be a dear!*, ¡sé bueno! || *He is such a dear*, es un encanto.
dearly [—li] adv. Cariñosamente (very affectionately). || Caro: *it will cost you dearly*, te va a costar caro. || — *The peace we so dearly seek*, la paz que tanto deseamos. || *To love s.o. dearly*, querer muchísimo a uno. || *We would dearly love to know*, nos encantaría saber.
dearness [—nis] n. COMM. Carestía, *f.*, lo caro (of life, etc.). || Afecto, *m.*, cariño, *m.* (love).
dearth [də:θ] n. Escasez, *f.*, carestía, *f.*
deary [ˈdiəri] n. FAM. Querido, da
death [deθ] n. Muerte, *f.*: *to die a violent death*, morir de muerte violenta. || Defunción, *f.*, fallecimiento, *m.*: *to notify a death*, notificar una defunción. || FIG. Fin, *m.*, muerte, *f.*: *the death of all hopes*, el fin de todas las esperanzas. || — Pl. Necrología, *f. sing.* (in newspaper). || — *A living death*, una vida horrible. || *Black Death*, peste negra. || *Death to traitors!*, ¡mueran los traidores! || *Pale as death*, pálido como un muerto. || *Proof of death*, acta (*f.*) de defunción. || *To be at death's doors*, estar a las puertas de la muerte. || *To be death to*, ser muy peligroso. || FIG. *To be the death of one*, matarle a uno. || *To be working o.s. to death*, matarse trabajando. || FAM. *To catch one's death of cold*, agarrar un constipado de campeonato. | *To death*, muerto de: *bored to death*, muerto de aburrimiento. || *To do to death*, matar, dar muerte. || *To hold on like grim death*, agarrarse fuertemente (to hold on tightly), resistir firmemente (to resist). || *To put to death*, matar, dar muerte (to kill), ejecutar, ajusticiar (to execute). || *To the death*, hasta la muerte. || *To work one's employees to death*, matar a sus empleados trabajando. || *Wounded to the death*, herido de muerte.
deathbed [—bed] n. Lecho (*m.*) de muerte. || FAM. *Deathbed repentance*, arrepentimiento (*m.*) de última hora.
death bell [—bel] n. Tañido (*m.*) fúnebre, toque (*m.*) a muerto.
deathblow [—bləu] n. Golpe (*m.*) mortal.
death certificate [—səˈtifikit] n. Certificado (*m.*) de defunción, partida (*f.*) de defunción.
death-dealing [—di:liŋ] adj. Mortífero, ra.
death duty [—ˌdju:ti] n. Derechos (*m. pl.*) de sucesión, impuesto (*m.*) sobre sucesiones.
death house [—haus] n. Pabellón (*m.*) de los condenados a muerte. || *To be in the death house*, estar en capilla.
death knell [—nel] n. Toque (*m.*) a muerto. || FIG. Golpe (*m.*) de gracia.
deathless [—lis] adv. Inmortal.
deathlessness [lisnis] n. Inmortalidad, *f.*
deathlike [—laik] adj. Cadavérico, ca (face). || Sepulcral (silence). || Como muerto, inmóvil (person). || *To look deathlike*, tener cara de muerto.
deathly [—li] adj. Mortal, de muerte, mortífero, ra (illness, wound, etc.). || Sepulcral (silence). || Cadavérico, ca (face).
— Adv. Mortalmente. || *Deathly pale*, más pálido que un muerto, pálido como un muerto.
death mask [—mɑ:sk] n. Mascarilla, *f.*
death penalty [—ˌpenəlti] n. Pena (*f.*) de muerte.
death rate [—reit] n. Mortalidad, *f.*, índice (*m.*) de mortalidad.
death rattle [—rætl] n. Estertor (*m.*) de la muerte.
death roll [—rəul] n. Lista (*f.*) de víctimas (list of dead persons). || Número (*m.*) de muertos: *the death roll stands at 87*, el número de muertos asciende a 87. || MIL. Lista (*f.*) de bajas.
death's-head [—shed] n. Calavera, *f.* (skull). || ZOOL. Mariposa (*f.*) de la muerte.
death tax [—tæks] n. Derechos (*m. pl.*) de sucesión, impuesto (*m.*) sobre sucesiones.
deathtrap [—træp] n. Lugar (*m.*) peligroso (unsafe place).
death warrant [—ˌwɔrənt] n. Sentencia (*f.*) de muerte.
deathwatch [—wɔtʃ] n. Velatorio, *m.* (watch over dead person). || Guardia (*f.*) de un condenado a muerte. || ZOOL. *Deathwatch beetle*, reloj (*m.*) de la muerte.
deb [deb] n. FAM. Debutante, *f.*
debacle or **débacle** [deiˈbɑ:kl] n. Desastre, *m.* (collapse, disaster). || MIL. Derrota, *f.* || Deshielo, *m.* (breaking-up of ice).
debar [diˈbɑ:*] v. tr. Excluir (*from*, de). || Prohibir : *to debar s.o. from doing sth.*, prohibir a alguien que haga algo. || Privar de (a right). || Impedir (to prevent).
debark [diˈbɑ:k] v. tr./intr. Desembarcar.
debarkation [ˌdi:bɑ:ˈkeiʃən] n. Desembarque, *m.* (of goods). || Desembarco, *m.* (of people, soldiers).
debase [diˈbeis] v. tr. Alterar (coinage). || Desvalorizar (to devalue). || FIG. Degradar, rebajar.
debasement [—mənt] n. Alteración, *f.* (coinage). || FIG. Degradación, *f.*
debatable [diˈbeitəbl] adj. Discutible (questionable). || En litigio: *debatable territory*, territorio en litigio.
debate [diˈbeit] n. Discusión, *f.*, debate, *m.* (discussion). || Controversia, *f.* (controversy). || *The problem under debate*, el problemo que se está discutiendo.
debate [diˈbeit] v. tr. Discutir, debatir (a question). || Controvertir, discutir (a statement). || Considerar (to consider).
— V. intr. Discutir (*with*, con).
debater [—ə*] n. Persona (*f.*) que toma parte en una discusión *or* debate. || Polemista, *m.* & *f.*
debating [—iŋ] adj. Controvertido, da: *debating point*, punto controvertido. || *Debating society*, asociación (*f.*) que organiza debates.
debauch [diˈbɔ:tʃ] n. Libertinaje, *m.*, disolución, *f.* (dissipation). || Orgía, *f.* (orgy). || Corrupción, *f.*
debauch [diˈbɔ:tʃ] v. tr. Corromper, pervertir. || Seducir (a woman).
— V. intr. Pervertirse.
debauchee [ˌdebɔ:ˈtʃi:] n. Libertino, na.
debauchery [diˈbɔ:tʃəri] n. Libertinaje, *m.*, disolución, *f.* (dissipation). || Corrupción, *f.*, perversión, *f.*: *debauchery of youth*, corrupción de menores.
debenture [diˈbentʃə*] n. COMM. Obligación, *f.*
debilitate [diˈbiliteit] v. tr. Debilitar.
debilitation [dibiliˈteiʃən] n. Debilitación, *f.*
debility [diˈbiliti] n. Debilidad, *f.*
debit [ˈdebit] n. Débito, *m.* (entry of money owed). || Debe, *m.*, pasivo, *m.* (left-hand side of an account). || — *Debit balance*, saldo (*m.*) deudor. || *Debit entry*, débito.
debit [ˈdebit] v. tr. Cargar en cuenta.
debonair (U. S. **debonaire**) [ˌdebəˈnɛə*] adj. Jovial, alegre (cheerful). || Cortés, afable (polite). || Agraciado, da (graceful). || Gallardo, da; garboso, sa (charming, elegant).
debouch [diˈbautʃ] v. intr. Salir (to emerge). || Desembocar (river, street).
debouchment [—mənt] n. Salida, *f.* (emergence). || Desembocadura, *f.* (of a river, of a street).
debride [diˈbraid] v. tr. MED. Desbridar.
debris [ˈdebri:] n. Escombros, *m. pl.* (broken remains). || GEOL. Detritos, *m. pl.*
debt [det] n. Deuda, *f.*: *in debt to*, en deuda con; *out of debt*, libre de deudas; *public* o *national debt*, deuda pública; *I was deeply in debt*, tenía muchas deudas; *floating debt*, deuda flotante; *consolidated* o *funded debts*, deudas consolidadas. || — *Bad debt*, deuda incobrable *or* morosa. || *Debt of honour*, deuda de honor. || *To be in s.o.'s debt*, estar en deuda con uno. || *To run into debt*, contraer deudas.
debtor [ˈdetə*] n. Deudor, ra (person owing money). || COMM. Debe, *m.* (in bookkeeping).
debunk [ˈdi:ˈbuŋk] v. tr. FAM. Desenmascarar (to unmask). | Desacreditar, desprestigiar (to discredit).
début (U. S. **debut**) [ˈdeibju:] n. Debut, *m.*, presentación, *f.* (first appearance). || Presentación (*f.*) en sociedad, puesta (*f.*) de largo (of girls). || *To make one's début*, ponerse de largo, ser presentada en sociedad (girl), hacer sus primeras armas (in a job), debutar (in the theatre).
débutante (U. S. **debutante**) [ˈdebjutɑ̃:nt] n. Joven (*f.*) que hace su presentación en sociedad, "debutante", *f.*
decade [ˈdekeid] n. Decenio, *m.* (ten years). || Década, *f.* (ten days). || Decena, *f.* (of a rosary).
decadence [ˈdekədəns] n. Decadencia, *f.*
decadent [ˈdekədənt] adj./n. Decadente. || ARTS. *The Decadents*, los decadentes.
decaffeinate [di:ˈkæfi:neit] or **decaffeinize** [di:ˈkæfi:naiz] v. tr. Descafeinar.
decagon [ˈdekəgən] n. MATH. Decágono, *m.*
decagonal [deˈkægənal] adj. Decagonal.
decagram or **decagramme** [ˈdekəgræm] n. Decagramo, *m.*
decahedron [dekəˈhi:drən] n. MATH. Decaedro, *m.*
decalcification [di:ˌkælsifiˈkeiʃən] n. Descalcificación, *f.*
decalcify [di:ˈkælsifai] v. tr. Descalcificar. || *To become decalcified*, descalcificarse.
decalcomania [diˌkælkəˈmeiniə] n. Calcomanía, *f.*
decalitre (U. S. **decaliter**) [ˈdekəˌli:tə*] n. Decalitro, *m.* (measure of capacity).
Decalogue (U. S. **Decalog**) [ˈdekələg] n. REL. Decálogo, *m.*
decametre (U. S. **decameter**) [ˈdekəˌmi:tə*] n. Decámetro, *m.*
decamp [diˈkæmp] v. intr. FAM. Largarse, pirarse (to go away). || MIL. Decampar, levantar el campo.
decant [diˈkænt] v. tr. Decantar.
decantation [ˌdi:kænˈteiʃən] n. Decantación, *f.*
decanter [diˈkæntə*] n. Garrafa, *f.* || TECH. Decantador, *m.*
decanting [diˈkæntiŋ] n. Decantación, *f.*
decapitate [diˈkæpiteit] v. tr. Decapitar (to behead).

decapitation [di,kæpi'teiʃən] n. Decapitación, *f.*
decapod ['dekəpɔd] n. ZOOL. Decápodo, *m.*
decarbonate [di:'kɑ:bəneit] v. tr. CHEM. Descarbonatar.
decarbonization [di:'kɑ:bənai'zeiʃən] n. TECH. Descarburación, *f.*
decarbonize [di:'kɑ:bənaiz] v. tr. Descarburar.
decarbonizer [—ə*] n. TECH. Descarburante, *m.*
decarbonizing [—iŋ] adj. TECH. Descarburante.
— N. TECH. Descarburación, *f.*
decarburization [di:,kɑ:bjuərai'zeiʃən] n. TECH. Descarburación, *f.*
decarburize [di:'kɑ:bjuəraiz] v. tr. TECH. Descarburar.
decarburizer [—ə*] n. TECH. Descarburante, *m.*
decarburizing [—iŋ] adj. TECH. Descarburante.
— N. TECH. Descarburación, *f.*
decastere ['dekəsti:ə*] n. Diez estéreos, *m. pl.*
decasyllabic ['dekəsi'læbik] or **decasyllable** ['dekəsiləbl] adj. Decasílabo, ba.
— N. Decasílabo, *m.*
decathlon [de'kæθlɔn] n. SP. Decatlón, *m.*
decay [di'kei] n. Caries, *f.* (of a tooth). || Descomposición, *f.* (decomposition). || PHYS. Desintegración (*f.*) progresiva (of radioactive materials). || Decadencia, *f.* (of morals, culture, country, etc.). || Ruina, *f.*, deterioro, *m.* (of buildings). || Debilitamiento, *m.* (of health, sight). || Disminución, *f.* (of sounds, etc.). || Marchitamiento, *m.* (of plants). || Putrefacción, *f.* (rotting). || *To fall into decay*, caer en ruinas.
decay [di'kei] v. intr. Cariarse (tooth). || Descomponerse (to decompose). || PHYS. Desintegrarse (radioactive materials). || Decaer (morals, culture, country, etc.). || Deteriorarse (to deteriorate). || Caerse, caer en ruinas (buildings). || Debilitarse (health, sight). || Disminuir (sounds, etc.). || Marchitarse (plants). || Pudrirse (to rot). || Marchitarse (beauty). || FIG. Desvanecerse (hope). | Desaparecer (friendships).
— V. tr. Pudrir : *water decays wood*, el agua pudre la madera. || Cariar (tooth).
decease [di'si:s] n. Fallecimiento, *m.*, defunción, *f.*
decease [di'si:s] v. intr. Morir, fallecer.
deceased [—t] adj./n. Difunto, ta.
deceit [di'si:t] n. Engaño, *m.* (cheating). || Decepción, *f.* (disappointment). || Fraude, *m.* (fraud). || Mentira, *f.* (lying). || Superchería, *f.* (trick).
deceitful [—ful] adj. Engañoso, sa (deceiving). || Fraudulento, ta (fraudulent). || Mentiroso, sa (lying). || Falso, sa (two-faced).
deceitfulness [—fulnis] n. Lo engañoso, *m.* || Falsedad, *f.*
deceive [di'si:v] v. tr. Engañar. || Defraudar (hopes). || — *If my memory does not deceive me*, si la memoria no me falla, si mal no recuerdo. || *To deceive o.s.*, engañarse.
deceiver [—ə*] n. Embustero, ra.
deceiving [—iŋ] adj. Decepcionante, desilusionante (disappointing). || Engañoso, sa (deceptive).
— N. Decepción, *f.*
decelerate [di:'seləreit] v. tr. Aminorar *or* disminuir la velocidad de.
— V. intr. Ir más despacio, decelerar.
deceleration ['di:,selə'reiʃən] n. Deceleración, *f.*, disminución (*f.*) de la velocidad.
December [di'sembə*] n. Diciembre, *m.*: *December 25 o 25th*, el 25 de diciembre.
decemvir [di'semvə*] n. Decenviro, *m.*
decency ['di:snsi] n. Decencia, *f.*, decoro, *m.* || Decoro, *m.* (in language, behaviour, etc.).
decennary [di'senəri] adj. Decenal.
— N. Decenio, *m.*, decenario, *m.*
decennial [di'senjəl] adj. Decenal.
— N. Décimo aniversario, *m.*
decent ['di:snt] adj. Decente, decoroso, sa (observing propriety). || Razonable, decente (satisfactory): *decent wages*, un sueldo decente. || FAM. Bueno, na; formal: *a decent chap*, un buen chico. | Amable, simpático, ca: *to be decent to s.o.*, ser amable con alguien. | Visible, presentable (not naked).
decentralization [di:,sentrəlai'zeiʃən] n. Descentralización, *f.*
decentralize [di:'sentrəlaiz] v. tr. Descentralizar.
decentralizer [—ə*] n. Descentralizador, ra.
decentralizing [—iŋ] adj. Descentralizador, ra.
decentre [di:'sentə*] v. tr. PHYS. Descentrar.
deception [di'sepʃən] n. Engaño, *m.*
deceptive [di'septiv] adj. Engañoso, sa.
deceptiveness [—nis] n. Apariencia (*f.*) engañosa.
dechristianization [di:,kristjənai'zeiʃən] n. Descristianización, *f.*
dechristianize [di:'kristjənaiz] v. tr. Descristianizar.
decibel ['desibel] n. PHYS. Decibel, *m.*, decibelio, *m.*
decide [di'said] v. tr. Decidir. || Resolver (a conflict).
— V. intr. Decidir. || *To decide on o upon*, decidir (sth. being done), determinar, fijar (a line of action), optar por (to choose).
decided [—id] adj. Decidido, da; resuelto, ta; determinado, da (determined). || Marcado, da (difference). || Determinado, da; claro, ra (opinion). || Indudable (undeniable). || Categórico, ca; tajante (refusal).
decidedness [di'saididnis] n. Determinación, *f.*
deciding [di'saidiŋ] adj. Decisivo, va.
decidua [di'sidjuə] n. ANAT. Membrana (*f.*) caduca.

— OBSERV. El plural de *decidua* es *deciduae.*

deciduous [di'sidjuəs] adj. Caduco, ca (leaf). || De hoja caduca (trees). || FIG. Efímero, ra.
decigram, decigramme ['desigræm] n. Decigramo, *m.*
decilitre (U.S. **deciliter**) ['desi,li:tə*] n. Decilitro, *m.*
decimal ['desiməl] adj. Decimal. || — *Decimal fraction*, fracción (*f.*) decimal. || *Decimal point*, coma, *f.* (of decimal fraction). || *Decimal system*, sistema decimal.
— N. MATH. Decimal, *m.*
decimalize ['desiməlaiz] v. tr. Aplicar el sistema decimal a.
decimate ['desimeit] v. tr. Diezmar.
decimation [,desi'meiʃən] n. Acción (*f.*) de diezmar.
decimetre (U. S. **decimeter**) ['desi,mi:tə*] n. Decímetro, *m.*
decipher [di'saifə*] n. Descifrado, *m.*
decipher [di'saifə*] v. tr. Descifrar.
decipherable [di'saifərəbl] adj. Descifrable.
decipherer [di'saifərə*] n. Descifrador, ra.
deciphering [—iŋ] adj. Descifrador, ra.
— N. Desciframiento, *m.*, descifrado, *m.*
decipherment [di'saifəmənt] n. Desciframiento, *m.*, descifrado, *m.*
decision [di'siʒən] n. Decisión, *f.*: *the decision is final*, la decisión es definitiva; *to make o to take a decision*, tomar una decisión. || Resolución, *f.*, determinación, *f.* (resoluteness). || JUR. Fallo, *m.*
decisive [di'saisiv] adj. Decisivo, va: *decisive proof*, prueba decisiva. || Concluyente: *a decisive experiment*, una experiencia concluyente. || Tajante (tone). || Decidido, da (manner).
deck [dek] n. MAR. Cubierta, *f.* (of ship). || Piso, *m.* (of bus). || Baraja, *f.* (pack of cards). || FAM. Suelo, *m.* || TECH. Tablero, *m.*, piso, *m.* (of bridge). | Techo, *m.* (of wagon). || — MAR. *Below decks*, en la bodega (of a ship). | *Between decks*, entrepuente, *m.*, entrecubierta, *f.* || FAM. *Hit the deck!*, ¡cuerpo a tierra! || *On deck*, en cubierta. || *To clear the decks*, tocar zafarrancho de combate.
deck [dek] v. tr. Adornar, engalanar (to trim). || MAR. Poner cubierta a. || FAM. *To deck o.s. out*, ponerse de tiros largos *or* de punta en blanco.
deck chair [—tʃɛə*] n. Tumbona, *f.*
decker [—ə*] n. *Single-decker*, autobús (*m.*) de un piso (bus), barco (*m.*) de una cubierta (boat).
deckhand [—hænd] n. Marinero (*m.*) de cubierta.
deckhouse [—haus] n. MAR. Camareta (*f.*) alta.
deckle edge ['dekledʒ] n. Barbas, *f. pl.* (of paper).
declaim [di'kleim] v. tr./intr. Declamar.
declamation [,deklə'meiʃən] n. Declamación, *f.*
declamatory [di'klæmətəri] adj. Declamatorio, ria.
declaimer [di'kleimə*] n. Declamador, ra.
declarant [di'klærənt] n. JUR. Declarante, *m.* & *f.*
declaration [,deklə'reiʃən] n. Declaración, *f.*: *declaration of war*, declaración de guerra; *customs declaration*, declaración de aduana; *to make a declaration to the police*, hacer una declaración a la policía. || Proclamación, *f.*: *declaration of the poll*, proclamación de los resultados. || — *Declaration of bankruptcy*, declaración de quiebra. || *Declaration of Human Rights*, Declaración de los Derechos Humanos; *Declaration of the Rights of Man*, Declaration de los Derechos del Hombre. || *Declaration of love*, declaración de amor.
declaratory [di'klærətəri] adj. Declaratorio, ria.
declare [di'klɛə*] v. tr. Declarar: *to declare war on a country*, declarar la guerra a un país; *have you anything to declare?*, ¿tiene usted algo que declarar? || Proclamar: *to declare s.o. the winner*, proclamar a alguien ganador; *to declare one's innocence*, proclamar la inocencia de uno. || Cantar, acusar (in card games). || Declarar (in bridge). || — *To declare off*, abandonar. || *To declare o.s.*, declararse; confesar: *I declare myself completely at a loss*, confieso que estoy completamente perdido.
— V. intr. Declarar (in cricket). || *To declare against, for*, pronunciarse *or* declararse en contra, a favor. || *Well I declare!*, ¡vaya por Dios!
declared [—d] adj. Declarado, da: *declared profits*, beneficios declarados. || Declarado, da; manifiesto, ta (opinion).
declaredly [di'klɛəridli] adv. Abiertamente, declaradamente.
declarer [di'klɛərə*] n. Declarante, *m.* & *f.*
declension [di'klənʃən] n. GRAMM. Declinación, *f.* || Desviación, *f.* (from a definite direction). || Inclinación, *f.*, declive, *m.* (slope). || Decadencia, *f.* (decline).
declinable [di'klainəbl] adj. Declinable.
declination [,dekli'neiʃən] n. Negativa, *f.* (refusal). || PHYS. ASTR. Declinación, *f.* || Declive, *m.* (slope). || Decadencia, *f.* (decline).
decline [di'klain] n. Disminución, *f.* (decrease). || Decaimiento, *m.* (decay). || Decadencia, *f.*, ocaso, *m.*: *the decline of the Roman Empire*, la decadencia del Imperio Romano. || Ocaso, *m.* (of life). || Baja, *f.* (in price or number). || Declive, *m.* (downward slope). || Caída, *f.*, ocaso, *m.* (of the day). || Ocaso, *m.* (of the sun). || MED. Enfermedad (*f.*) de postración. || Negativa, *f.* (refusal). || *To be on the decline*, debilitarse: *his health is on the decline*, su salud se está debilitando; disminuir: *the crime rate is on the decline*, la criminalidad está disminuyendo; estar en decadencia.
decline [di'klain] v. tr. Rehusar, rechazar (an offer, etc.). || Negarse (*to*, a) [to do sth.]. || Inclinar (to incline). || GRAMM. Declinar.

— V. intr. Rehusar, negarse (to refuse). || Decaer (to decay). || Decaer, debilitarse (strength). || Disminuir (to diminish). || Bajar (prices). || Inclinarse (to slope down). || Declinar (the sun, the day). || MED. Debilitarse.
declining [—iŋ] adj. Declinante. || *In his declining years*, en sus últimos años, en el ocaso de su vida.
declivity [diˈkliviti] n. Declive, *m.*
declutch [ˈdi:klʌtʃ] v. intr. AUT. Desembragar.
declutching [—iŋ] n. AUT. Desembrague, *m.*
decoct [diˈkɔkt] v. tr. Extraer por medio de la decocción.
decoction [diˈkɔkʃən] n. Decocción, *f.* (decocting). || Extracto, *m.* (extract).
decode [ˈdi:ˈkəud] v. tr. Descifrar.
decoder [—ə*] n. Descifrador, ra (person). || Decodificador, *m.* (machine).
decoding [—iŋ] n. Desciframiento, *m.*, descifrado, *m.*
decoke [ˈdi:ˈkəuk] v. tr. Descarburar (un motor).
décolletage [ˈdeikɔlˈtɑ:ʒ] n. Escote, *m.*
décolleté [ˈdeikɔlˈtei] adj. Escotado, da.
— N. Escote, *m.*
decolonization [di:ˌkɔlənaiˈzeiʃən] n. Descolonización, *f.*
decolonize [di:ˈkɔlənaiz] v. tr. Descolonizar.
decolourize (U. S. **decolorize**) [di:ˈkɔləraiz] v. tr. Descolorir, descolorar.
decompensation [di:ˌkɔmpənˈseiʃən] n. Descompensación, *f.*
decomposable [ˌdi:kəmˈpəuzəbl] adj. Descomponible.
decompose [ˌdi:kəmˈpəuz] v. tr. Descomponer (to break up into parts). || Pudrir, descomponer, corromper (to cause to rot). || CHEM. Descomponer. || FIG. Analizar, descomponer.
— V. intr. Descomponerse (to break up into parts). || Pudrirse, descomponerse, corromperse (to rot).
decomposition [ˌdi:kɔmpəˈziʃən] n. Descomposición, *f.* (into parts). || Descomposición, *f.*, putrefacción, *f.* (rotting).
decompound [ˌdi:kəmˈpaund] v. tr. Descomponer.
decompress [ˌdi:kəmˈpres] v. tr. Descomprimir.
decompression [ˌdi:kəmˈpreʃən] n. Descompresión, *f.*: *decompression chamber*, cámara de descompresión.
decompressor [ˌdi:kəmˈpresə*] n. Descompresor, *m.*
decongestion [ˌdi:kənˈdʒestʃən] n. Descongestión, *f.*
deconsecrate [di:ˈkɔnsikreit] v. tr. Secularizar (a church).
decontaminate [ˈdikənˈtæmineit] v. tr. Descontaminar, desinfectar.
decontamination [ˌdikəntæmiˈneiʃən] n. Descontaminación, *f.*, desinfección, *f.*
decontrol [ˈdi:kənˈtrəul] n. Liberalización, *f.* (abolition of controls).
decontrol [ˈdi:kənˈtrəul] v. tr. Liberalizar.
décor (U. S. **decor**) [ˈdeikɔ:*] n. THEATR. Decorado, *m.* || Decoración, *f.* (decoration).
decorate [ˈdekəreit] v. tr. Decorar, adornar (to adorn). || Pintar (to paint). || Empapelar (to paper). || Condecorar (with a medal).
decoration [ˌdekəˈreiʃən] n. Decoración, *f.* (décor). || Adorno, *m.* (sth. decorative). || Condecoración, *f.* (medal, ribbon, etc.).
decorative [ˈdekərətiv] adj. Decorativo, va (ornamental). || *Decorative arts*, artes decorativas.
decorator [ˈdekəreitə*] n. Decorador, ra (who plans interior design). || Pintor, *m.* (painter). || Empapelador, *m.* (paperhanger).
decorous [ˈdekərəs] adj. Decoroso, sa.
decorticate [di:ˈkɔ:tikeit] v. tr. Descortezar (trees). || Pelar, descascarar, quitar la cáscara a (to peel). || Descascarillar (rice).
decortication [ˈdi:kɔ:tiˈkeiʃən] n. Descortezamiento, *m.* (of trees). || Descascaramiento, *m.*, peladura, *f.* (peeling). || Descascarillamiento, *m.* (of rice).
decorum [diˈkɔ:rəm] n. Decoro, *m.*
decoy [diˈkɔi] n. Señuelo, *m.* (artificial bird to lure game). || Cimbel, *m.* (real bird to lure game). || Cebo, *m.* (bait). || FIG. Gancho, *m.*, señuelo, *m.* (person used as bait).
decoy [diˈkɔi] v. tr. Atraer con señuelo (an animal). || FIG. Atraer. | Seducir (a woman).
decrease [ˈdi:kri:s] n. Disminución, *f.*: *decrease in value*, disminución de valor. || *To be on the decrease*, ir disminuyendo.
decrease [di:ˈkri:s] v. tr. Disminuir (to diminish). || Menguar (in knitting).
— V. intr. Disminuir.
decreasing [—iŋ] adj. Decreciente, menguante.
decree [diˈkri:] n. Decreto, *m.* (of a ruling body or authority): *to issue a decree*, promulgar un decreto. || JUR. Sentencia, *f.* || JUR. *Decree nisi*, sentencia provisional de divorcio.
decree [diˈkri:] v. tr. Decretar (to appoint or order by decree). || Pronunciar (a penalty).
— V. intr. Promulgar un decreto.
decree-law [—lɔ:] n. JUR. Decreto ley, *m.*
decrement [ˈdekrimənt] n. MATH. ELECTR. Decremento, *m.* || Disminución, *f.* (decrease).
decrepit [diˈkrepit] adj. Decrépito, ta.
decrepitate [diˈkrepiteit] v. intr. Decrepitar, crepitar.
decrepitude [diˈkrepitju:d] n. Decrepitud, *f.*
decrescendo [ˌdi:kriˈʃendəu] adj./adv. MUS. Decrescendo.
— N. MUS. Decrescendo, *m.*
decrescent [diˈkresənt] adj. Decreciente, menguante.
decretal [diˈkri:təl] n. REL. Decretal, *f.*
decretist [diˈkri:tist] n. Canonista, *m.*
decry [diˈkrai] v. tr. Censurar, criticar (to censure). || COMM. Depreciar, desvalorizar (money).
decubitus [diˈkju:bitəs] n. MED. Decúbito, *m.*: *supine, prone decubitus*, decúbito supino, prono.
decuple [ˈdekjupl] adj. Décuplo, pla.
— N. Décuplo, *m.*
decuple [ˈdekjupl] v. tr. Decuplar, decuplicar.
— V. intr. Decuplarse, decuplicarse.
decurrent [diˈkʌrənt] adj. BOT. Decurrente.
dedicate [ˈdedikeit] v. tr. Dedicar (a book, one's life). || Dedicar, consagrar (a church). || U. S. Inaugurar. || *To dedicate o.s. to*, dedicarse a.
dedication [ˌdediˈkeiʃən] n. Dedicación, *f.* (devotion, act of dedicating). || Dedicatoria, *f.* (inscription).
dedicatory [ˈdedikətəri] adj. Dedicatorio, ria.
deduce [diˈdju:s] v. tr. Deducir (to infer).
deducible [—əbl] adj. Deducible.
deduct [diˈdʌkt] v. tr. Deducir, restar, descontar.
deductible [—əbl] adj. Deducible.
deduction [diˈdʌkʃən] n. Deducción, *f.*, descuento, *m.*, rebaja, *f.* (a subtracting, the amount deducted). || || Conclusión, *f.*, deducción, *f.* (conclusion).
deductive [diˈdʌktiv] adj. Deductivo, va.
deed [di:d] n. Acto, *m.*, acción, *f.* (any act). || Hecho, *m.* (sth. done). || Hazaña, *f.*, proeza, *f.* (outstanding feat). || Ejecución, *f.*, realización, *f.* (fulfilment). || JUR. Escritura, *f.* || — *In deed*, de hecho. || *In word and deed*, de palabra y obra. || *To change one's name by deed poll*, cambiar su apellido por escritura legal.
deem [di:m] v. tr. Considerar, juzgar, creer. || *To deem highly of s.o.*, tener muy buena opinión de alguien.
deep [di:p] adj. Profundo, da; hondo, da: *deep well*, pozo profundo; *deep sight*, suspiro hondo. || De profundidad: *a well twenty feet deep*, un pozo de veinte pies de profundidad. || De fondo: *a cupboard a metre deep*, un armario de un metro de fondo. || De ancho: *a wall twenty feet deep*, una pared de veinte pies de ancho. || Ancho, cha (wide). || Hundido, da (eyes). || Profundo, da (sleep, wound, wrinkle). || Metido, da; hundido, da: *with his hands deep in his pockets*, con las manos hundidas en los bolsillos. || FIG. Cargado, da; lleno, na: *deep in debt*, cargado de deudas. | Absorto, ta (in thought, meditation). | A fondo, profundo, da: *deep study*, estudio a fondo. | Riguroso, sa (mourning). | Profundo, da (despair, feelings, learning, character): *deep sorrow*, tristeza profunda. | Profundo, da; grave (voice, sound). | Grande (disgrace, shame, interest, secrets). | Profundo, da; completo, ta (mystery, silence). | Oscuro, ra (night). | Poco claro, oscuro, ra (scheme). | Espeso, sa (shadow). | Grave (sin). | Difícil de entender (conduct). | Astuto, ta (shrewd). || Subido, da; oscuro, ra (colours). || MUS. Grave (sound). || — *Deep drinker*, gran bebedor. || FIG. FAM. *To go off the deep end*, perder los estribos (to lose one's control), obrar con precipitación (to act rashly).
— Adv. Profundamente: *to dig deep*, cavar profundamente; *to sleep deep*, dormir profundamente. || — *Deep in his heart*, en lo más profundo de su corazón. || *Deep into the night*, hasta muy entrada la noche. || *Deep-lying cause*, causa profunda, causa principal. || *The difference runs deep*, hay una gran diferencia. || *To be deep in love*, estar profundamente enamorado. || *To drink deep*, beber mucho [de una vez]. || *To form up four deep*, formarse de cuatro en fondo. || *To play deep*, jugar fuerte.
— N. Piélago, *m.* (sea). || Abismo, *m.* (abyss). || Profundidad, *f.* || *In the deep of winter*, muy entrado el invierno, en pleno invierno.
deep-chested [—ˈtʃestid] adj. Ancho de pecho.
deep-dyed [—ˈdaid] adj. U.S. Completamente teñido. || U. S. FAM. Redomado, da; completo, ta (total).
deepen [—ən] v. tr. Hacer más profundo, ahondar (a hole, etc.). || Intensificar (colour, emotion). || MUS. Hacer más grave (sound). || FIG. Profundizar.
— V. intr. Hacerse más hondo *or* profundo. || Intensificarse (colour, emotion). || Aumentar (to increase).
deepfreeze [—ˈfri:z] n. Congelador, *m.* (freezer). || Congelación, *f.* (freezing). || FIG. *In deepfreeze*, archivado, da (project).
deepfreeze [—ˈfri:z] v. tr. Congelar.
deep-laid [—leid] adj. Muy bien preparado (plan).
deeply [—li] adv. Profundamente, hondamente. || Intensamente: *deeply coloured*, intensamente coloreado. || Profundamente, muy: *deeply offended*, profundamente ofendido. || *To breathe deeply*, respirar hondo, respirar a pleno pulmón.
deepness [—nis] n. Profundidad, *f.*, hondura, *f.*
deep-rooted [—ˈru:tid] adj. Profundamente arraigado.
deep-sea [—ˈsi:] adj. De alta mar. || *Deep-sea fishing*, pesca (*f.*) de altura.
deep-seated [—ˈsi:tid] adj. Profundamente arraigado, da. || De origen profundo (earthquake, etc.). || De origen interno (illness, etc.).
deep-set [—set] adj. Hundido, da (eyes). || Profundamente arraigado, da (deep-rooted).
deep water [—ˈwɔ:tə*] n. Dificultad, *f.*, apuro, *m.*, aprieto, *m.* || FIG. *To get into deep water*, meterse en dificultades.

deepwater [—ˈwɔ:tə*] adj. Profundo, da (deep). ‖ De alta mar, de altura (fishing, navigation).
deer [diə*] inv. n. ZOOL. Ciervo, *m.*, venado, *m.*
deerhound [—haund] n. Galgo (*m.*) para cazar ciervos.
deerskin [—skin] n. Gamuza, *f.*
deerstalker [—ˌstɔ:kə*] n. Cazador (*m.*) [de venado] al acecho (hunter). ‖ Gorro (*m.*) de cazador de ciervos (cap).
deerstalking [—ˈstɔ:kiŋ] n. Caza (*f.*) de venado al acecho.
de-escalate [di:ˈeskəleit] v. tr. Desescalar.
de-escalation [ˌdi:eskəˈleiʃən] n. Desescalada, *f.*
deface [diˈfeis] v. tr. Desfigurar (to spoil appearance). ‖ Mutilar (a statue). ‖ Estropear, deteriorar (a wall, a door). ‖ Desgarrar (a poster). ‖ Matar (a stamp). ‖ Borrar (an inscription).
defacement [—mənt] n. Desfiguración, *f.* (spoiling of appearance). ‖ Mutilación, *f.* (of statue). ‖ Deterioro, *m.* (of wall, door). ‖ Desgarramiento, *m.* (of poster). ‖ Matado, *m.* (of stamp). ‖ Borradura, *f.* (erasure).
de facto [di:ˈfæktəu] adj./adv. De hecho, de facto.
defaecate [ˈdefikeit] v. tr./intr. Defecar.
defaecation [ˌdefiˈkeiʃən] n. Defecación, *f.*
defalcate [ˈdi:fælkeit] v. intr. Desfalcar, malversar fondos.
defalcation [ˌdi:fælˈkeiʃən] n. Desfalco, *m.*, malversación (*f.*) de fondos.
defalcator [ˌdi:fælkeitə*] n. Malversador, ra; desfalcador, ra.
defamation [ˌdefəˈmeiʃən] n. Difamación, *f.*
defamatory [diˈfæmətəri] adj. Difamatorio, ria; difamante.
defame [diˈfeim] v. tr. Difamar.
defamer [—ə*] n. Difamador, ra.
default [diˈfɔ:lt] n. JUR. Contumacia, *f.*, rebeldía, *f.*: *judgment by default*, sentencia en rebeldía. ‖ Descuido, *m.*, negligencia, *f.* (of duty). ‖ SP. Incomparecencia, *f.* ‖ Falta, *f.*, ausencia, *f.* (absence). ‖ Incumplimiento, *m.*, falta (*f.*) de pago (of debt). ‖ — *In default of*, a falta de, en ausencia de. ‖ JUR. *In default whereof*, en cuyo defecto. ‖ SP. *To win by default*, ganar por incomparecencia del adversario.
default [diˈfɔ:lt] v. tr. JUR. Condenar en rebeldía. ‖ Dejar de pagar (a debt, etc.). ‖ SP. Dejar de presentarse a, perder por incomparecencia (a contest).
— V. intr. JUR. Estar en rebeldía. ‖ Dejar de cumplir el pago, faltar a sus compromisos (to fail to pay a debt). ‖ SP. Dejar de presentarse, perder por incomparecencia.
defaulter [—ə*] n. JUR. Contumaz, *m.* & *f.*, rebelde, *m.* & *f.* (absentee). | Delincuente, *m.* (offender). ‖ COMM. Moroso, sa (s.o. who fails to pay his debts). | Desfalcador, ra; malversador, ra (embezzler). ‖ MIL. Rebelde, *m.*
defeasance [diˈfi:zəns] n. JUR. Anulación, *f.* ‖ JUR. *Defeasance clause*, cláusula resolutoria.
defeasible [diˈfi:zəbl] adj. JUR. Anulable.
defeat [diˈfi:t] n. MIL. Derrota, *f.* ‖ Fracaso, *m.* (failure). ‖ JUR. Anulación, *f.*
defeat [diˈfi:t] v. tr. Vencer, derrotar. ‖ Derrotar (the government). ‖ Hacer fracasar, desbaratar (projects). ‖ JUR. Anular. ‖ — *To defeat s.o. in his hopes*, defraudar las esperanzas de alguien. ‖ *To defeat s.o. in his plans*, desbaratar los planes de alguien.
defeatism [diˈfi:tizəm] n. Derrotismo, *m.*
defeatist [diˈfi:tist] adj./n. Derrotista.
defeature [diˈfi:tʃə*] v. tr. Desfigurar.
defecate [di:fikeit] v. tr./intr. Defecar.
defecation [ˌdi:fiˈkeiʃən] n. Defecación, *f.*
defect [diˈfekt] n. Defecto, *m.*
defect [diˈfekt] v. intr. Desertar: *to defect from a political party*, desertar de un partido político. ‖ *To defect to a country*, huir a un país.
defection [diˈfekʃən] n. Deserción, *f.*, defección, *f.*
defective [diˈfektiv] adj. Defectuoso, sa (having faults). ‖ Incompleto, ta (incomplete). ‖ GRAMM. Defectivo, va: *defective verb*, verbo defectivo. ‖ Anormal (abnormal).
— N. Persona (*f.*) anormal (abnormal person). ‖ GRAMM. Verbo (*m.*) defectivo.
defectiveness [—nis] n. Defectuosidad, *f.*, imperfección, *f.*
defence [diˈfens] n. Defensa, *f.*: *defence of a town, of an idea*, defensa de una ciudad, de una idea. ‖ JUR. Defensa, *f.*: *to call upon the defence to speak*, conceder la palabra a la defensa. ‖ SP. Defensa, *f.* (defenders). ‖ — Pl. MIL. Defensas, *f.* ‖ — JUR. *Counsel for the defence*, abogado defensor. ‖ *In the defence of*, en defensa de. ‖ *Passive defence*, defensa pasiva. ‖ *To come out in s.o.'s defence*, salir en defensa de alguien.
defenceless [—lis] adj. Indefenso, sa.
defend [diˈfend] v. tr. Defender (*against*, contra; *from*, de): *to defend a country, an idea*, defender un país, una idea. ‖ *To defend o.s.*, defenderse.
defendant [diˈfendənt] adj./n. JUR. Demandado, da (in civil case). | Acusado, da (in criminal case).
defender [diˈfendə*] n. Defensor, ra. ‖ SP. Defensa, *m.* ‖ — Pl. SP. Defensa, *f. sing.* ‖ *Defender of the Faith*, defensor de la fe.
defending [diˈfendiŋ] adj. Defensor, ra. ‖ *Defending champion*, campeón (*m.*) titular.
defenestration [diˌfenə:ˈstreiʃən] n. Defenestración, *f.*
defense [diˈfens] n. U. S. See DEFENCE.
defenseless [—lis] adj. U. S. Indefenso, sa.
defensible [diˈfensəbl] adj. Defendible (easily defended). ‖ Justificable (justifiable).
defensive [diˈfensiv] adj. Defensivo, va.
— N. Defensiva, *f.* ‖ *On the defensive*, a la defensiva.
defer [diˈfə:*] v. tr. Diferir, aplazar (to postpone). ‖ MIL. Dar una prórroga a. ‖ Delegar (an affair, function, etc.). ‖ Someter (to submit).
— V. intr. Deferir, remitirse (*to*, a). ‖ Tardar: *without deferring any longer*, sin tardar más.
deferable [diˈfə:rəbl] adj. Diferible, aplazable.
deference [ˈdefərəns] n. Deferencia, *f.* ‖ — *In deference to* o *out of deference to*, por respeto a, por deferencia a. ‖ *With all due deference to you*, con perdón de usted.
deferent [ˈdefərənt] adj. ANAT. Deferente.
deferential [ˌdefəˈrenʃəl] adj. Deferente, respetuoso, sa.
deferment [diˈfə:mənt] n. Aplazamiento, *m.* ‖ MIL. Prórroga, *f.*
deferrable [diˈfə:rəbl] adj. Diferible, aplazable.
— N. U. S. MIL. Persona (*f.*) con derecho a prórroga.
deferred [diˈfə:d] adj. Diferido, da; aplazado, da. ‖ COMM. Diferido, da. ‖ MIL. Que beneficia de una prórroga. ‖ *Deferred annuity*, renta vitalicia de pago diferido.
defiance [diˈfaiəns] n. Desafío, *m.*, reto, *m.* ‖ — *In defiance of*, con desprecio de. ‖ *To bid defiance to*, desafiar a. ‖ *To set s.o. at defiance*, desafiar a alguien.
defiant [diˈfaiənt] adj. Provocativo, va; provocador, ra; desafiante (challenging). ‖ De desafío, desafiante, retador, ra (tone).
defiantly [—li] adv. Con tono *or* aire retador.
deficiency [diˈfiʃənsi] n. Deficiencia, *f.* ‖ COMM. Déficit, *m.* (of budget). | Descubierto, *m.* (of account). ‖ — MED. *Deficiency disease*, enfermedad (*f.*) por carencia. | *Mental deficiency*, debilidad (*f.*) mental.
deficient [diˈfiʃənt] adj. Deficiente. ‖ MED. Atrasado, da. ‖ *To be deficient in*, carecer de.
— N. MED. Atrasado (*m.*) mental.
deficit [ˈdefisit] n. COMM. Déficit, *m.* (of balance). | Descubierto, *m.* (of account).
defier [diˈfaiə*] n. Desafiador, ra; retador, ra.
defilade [ˌdefiˈleid] n. MIL. Desenfilada, *f.*
defilade [ˌdefiˈleid] v. tr. MIL. Desenfilar.
defile [ˈdi:fail] n. Desfiladero, *m.* (gully).
defile [ˈdifail] v. intr. MIL. Desfilar.
defile [diˈfail] v. tr. Ensuciar, manchar (to soil). ‖ Profanar (to desecrate). ‖ Desflorar, deshonrar, violar (a woman). ‖ Deshonrar, mancillar (reputation).
defilement [diˈfailmənt] n. Mancha, *f.*, ensuciamiento, *m.* (soiling). ‖ Profanación, *f.* (desecration). ‖ Mancha, *f.*, mancilla, *f.* (of the reputation, etc.). ‖ Deshonra, *f.*, desfloración, *f.* (of a woman).
definable [diˈfainəbl] adj. Definible.
define [diˈfain] v. tr. Definir (to give a definition of). ‖ Caracterizar, definir (to characterize). ‖ Formular, definir (to formulate). ‖ Precisar, definir (to outline the function of). ‖ Determinar, definir: *to define the limits of a field*, determinar los límites de un campo.
definite [ˈdefinit] adj. Definido, da; determinado, da (limiting). ‖ Claro, ra (clear). ‖ Claro, ra; preciso, sa; categórico, ca (answer). ‖ Preciso, sa (needs). ‖ Determinado, da (date). ‖ Definitivo, va (final). ‖ GRAMM. Definido, da; determinado, da: *definite article*, artículo definido. ‖ Limitado, da (powers). ‖ Seguro, ra (certain). ‖ — *It's definite that*, no hay duda que. ‖ *To arrange a definite date*, fijar una fecha determinada.
definitely [—li] adv. Claramente. ‖ Categóricamente, rotundamente (categorically). ‖ Sin duda alguna, seguramente (without doubt). ‖ De modo definitivo, definitivamente. ‖ — *He is definitely mad*, está completamente loco. ‖ *They are definitely not coming*, es completamente seguro que no vienen.
— Interj. ¡Desde luego!, ¡por supuesto!
definiteness [—nis] n. Lo definido. ‖ Precisión, *f.*
definition [ˌdefiˈniʃən] n. Definición, *f.* ‖ TECH. Definición, *f.* (telescope, television). ‖ PHOT. Claridad, *f.*, nitidez, *f.* ‖ Limitación, *f.* (of powers). ‖ *By definition*, por definición.
definitive [diˈfinitiv] adj. Definitivo, va.
definitiveness [—nis] n. Carácter (*m.*) definitivo.
deflagrate [ˈdefləgreit] v. tr. Hacer deflagar.
— V. intr. Deflagar.
deflagration [ˌdefləˈgreiʃən] n. Deflagración, *f.*
deflagrator [ˈdeflagreitə*] n. Deflagrador, *m.*
deflate [diˈfleit] v. tr. Deshinchar, desinflar (ball, tyre). ‖ COMM. Provocar la deflación de. ‖ FIG. Rebajar (vanity, pride). | Reducir (hopes).
— V. intr. Desinflarse, deshincharse.
deflation [diˈfleiʃən] n. Desinflado, *m.*, desinflamiento, *m.* ‖ COMM. Deflación, *f.*
deflationary [diˈfleiʃənəri] adj. Deflacionista.
deflator [diˈfleitə*] n. Índice (*m.*) de deflación.
deflect [diˈflekt] v. tr. Desviar. ‖ AUT. Hacer girar (wheels).
— V. intr. Desviarse.
deflection [diˈflekʃən] n. Desviación, *f.* (of stream, light, compass). ‖ AUT. Giro, *m.*
deflector [diˈflektə*] n. Deflector, *m.*
deflexion [diˈflekʃən] n. Desviación, *f.* ‖ AUT. Giro, *m.*
defloration [ˌdi:flɔ:ˈreiʃən] n. Desfloración, *f.*, desfloramiento, *m.*

deflower [di:ˈflauə*] v. tr. Desflorar.
deflowering [—riŋ] n. Desfloración, *f.*, desfloramiento, *m.* (defloration).
defoliate [di:ˈfəulieit] v. tr. Deshojar.
— V. intr. Deshojarse.
defoliation [di:fəuliˈeiʃən] n. Defoliación, *f.*
deforcement [diˈfɔ:smənt] n. JUR. Detentación, *f.*, usurpación, *f.*
deforciant [diˈfɔ:ʃənt] n. JUR. Detentador, ra.
deforest [diˈfɔrist] v. tr. Despoblar de árboles, desmontar, talar.
deforestation [difɔrisˈteiʃən] n. Despoblación (*f.*) forestal, desmonte, *m.*, tala, *f.*
deform [diˈfɔ:m] v. tr. Deformar (body, thing). || Desfigurar, afear (person).
— V. intr. Deformarse. || Desfigurarse.
deformation [ˌdifɔˈmeiʃən] n. Deformación, *f.* (of body, thing). || Desfiguración, *f.* (of people).
deformed [diˈfɔ:md] adj. Deformado, da (changed in form). || Deforme (misshappen). || Disforme (ugly).
deformity [diˈfɔ:miti] n. Deformidad, *f.*
defraud [diˈfrɔ:d] v. tr. Defraudar, estafar. || FIG. Perjudicar.
defraudation [ˌdifrɔˈdeiʃən] n. Defraudación, *f.*
defrauder [diˈfrɔ:də*] n. Defraudador, ra; estafador, ra.
defray [diˈfrei] v. tr. Costear, pagar, sufragar.
defrayal [—əl] or **defrayment** [—mənt] n. Pago, *m.*
defrock [ˈdiˈfrɔk] v. tr. Obligar a colgar los hábitos.
defrost [diˈfrɔst] v. tr. Deshelar. || Descongelar (fridge).
defrosting [—iŋ] n. Descongelación, *f.*
deft [deft] adj. Hábil, diestro, tra (skilful).
deftly [—li] adv. Con destreza, con habilidad.
deftness [—nis] n. Destreza, *f.*, habilidad, *f.*
defunct [diˈfʌŋkt] adj./n. Difunto, ta (dead). || FIG. Que ya no existe (extinct).
defy [diˈfai] v. tr. Desafiar, retar (to challenge). || Resistir a (to resist). || *It defies description*, es imposible describirlo.
degauss [ˈdiˈgaus] v. tr. MAR. Desimantar, desimanar.
degeneracy [diˈdʒenərəsi] n. Degeneración, *f.*
degenerate [diˈdʒenərit] adj./n. Degenerado, da.
degenerate [diˈdʒenəreit] v. intr. Degenerar (*into*, en).
degeneration [diˌdʒenəˈreiʃən] n. Degeneración, *f.*
degenerative [diˈdʒenərətiv] adj. Degenerativo, va; degenerante.
deglutition [ˌdiglu:ˈtiʃən] n. Deglución, *f.*
degradation [ˌdegrəˈdeiʃən] n. Degradación, *f.*
degrade [diˈgreid] v. tr. Degradar (to lower in rank, to humiliate). || Degradar, envilecer (to debase morally). || Rebajar (the quality). || GEOL. Desgastar. || PHYS. Degradar.
— V. intr. Degenerar (race, etc.). || GEOL. Desgastarse.
degrading [—iŋ] adj. Degradante: *degrading conduct*, conducta degradante.
degrease [ˈdiˈgri:s] v. tr. Desengrasar.
degree [diˈgri:] n. Grado, *m.* (step). || Grado, *m.*, punto, *m.* (pitch). || Categoría, *f.*, rango, *m.*: *of low degree*, de baja categoría. || Grado, *m.* (of relationship). || Título, *m.* (of university). || GRAMM. MATH. GEOGR. PHYS. Grado, *m.*: *to stand at fifteen degrees*, marcar quince grados. || Grada, *f.* (of the altar). || — *Bachelor's degree*, licenciatura, *f.* || *By degrees*, gradualmente, progresivamente, poco a poco. || *Doctor's degree*, doctorado, *m.* || JUR. *First-degree murder*, asesinato, *m.* || *Honorary degree*, doctorado (*m.*) "honoris causa". || JUR. *Second-degree murder*, homicidio (*m.*) por imprudencia. || MED. *Third-degree burns*, quemaduras (*f. pl.*) de tercer grado. || *To a certain degree* o *to some degree* o *in some degree*, hasta cierto punto. || *To a degree*, sumamente. || JUR. *To give s.o. the third degree*, sacudir a uno. || *To take a degree in*, licenciarse en. || *To the highest degree*, en sumo grado.
degression [diˈgreʃən] n. Disminución, *f.*
degressive [diˈgresiv] adj. Decreciente.
degust [diˈgʌst] v. tr. Probar (to taste).
degustation [digʌsˈteiʃən] n. Degustación, *f.*
dehisce [diˈhis] v. intr. BOT. Abrirse.
dehiscent [diˈhisnt] adj. BOT. Dehiscente.
dehorn [di:ˈhɔ:n] v. tr. Descornar (an animal).
dehumanization [di:ˈhju:mənaiˈzeiʃən] n. Deshumanización, *f.*
dehumanize [di:ˈhju:mənaiz] v. tr. Deshumanizar.
dehumidify [di:hjuˈmidifai] v. tr. Deshumedecer.
dehydrate [di:ˈhaidreit] v. tr. Deshidratar.
dehydration [di:haiˈdreiʃən] n. Deshidratación, *f.*
dehydrogenate [di:haiˈdrɔdʒeneit] v. tr. Deshidrogenar.
dehydrogenation [di:haidrədʒəˈneiʃən] n. Deshidrogenación, *f.*
dehydrogenize [di:haiˈdrɔdʒenaiz] v. tr. Deshidrogenar.
dehypnotize [ˈdi:ˈhipnətaiz] v. tr. Deshipnotizar.
deice [ˈdi:ˈais] v. tr. Descongelar, deshelar.
deicer [—ə*] n. Descongelador, *m.* || AVIAT. Dispositivo (*m.*) antihielo.
deicidal [ˈdi:iˈsaidl] adj. Deicida.
deicide [ˈdi:isaid] n. Deicidio, *m.* (killing of a god). || Deicida, *m.* & *f.* (killer of a god).
deicing [ˈdi:ˈaisiŋ] n. Descongelación, *f.*
deification [ˌdi:ifiˈkeiʃən] n. Deificación, *f.*
deify [ˈdi:ifai] v. tr. Divinizar, deificar.
deign [dein] v. tr. Dignarse a: *to deign a reply*, dignarse a dar una respuesta.
— V. intr. Dignarse (*to*, a).
deism [ˈdi:izəm] n. REL. Deísmo, *m.*
deist [ˈdi:ist] n. REL. Deísta, *m.* & *f.*
deistic [di:ˈistik] adj. Deísta.
deity [ˈdi:iti] n. Deidad, *f.*, divinidad, *f.* (divine nature). || Deidad, *f.*, dios, *m.*, diosa, *f.* (god). || *The Deity*, Dios, *m.*
deject [diˈdʒekt] v. tr. Descorazonar, desanimar, desalentar.
dejecta [diˈdʒektə] pl. n. Excrementos, *m.*, deyecciones, *f.* || GEOGR. Deyecciones, *f.*
dejected [diˈdʒektid] adj. Descorazonado, da; desanimado, da; desalentado, da.
dejection [diˈdʒekʃən] n. Desaliento, *m.*, abatimiento, *m.* (low spirits). || MED. Deyección, *f.*
delate [diˈleit] v. tr. Denunciar, delatar.
delation [diˈleiʃən] n. Denuncia, *f.*, delación, *f.*
delator [diˈleitə*] n. Delator, ra.
delay [diˈlei] n. Retraso, *m.*, dilación, *f.* || Demora, *f.* (wait). || — *To take no delay in*, no demorarse en. || *Without delay*, sin dilación, sin demora, en seguida.
delay [diˈlei] v. tr. Retrasar (to make late). || Aplazar, demorar (to postpone). || Estorbar (to hinder). || Entretener (to hold up).
— V. intr. Tardar. || *Don't delay!*, ¡no te entretengas!
delayed action [diˈleidˈækʃən] n. Efecto (*m.*) retardado: *delayed-action bomb*, bomba de efecto retardado.
delaying [diˈleiiŋ] adj. Dilatorio, ria: *delaying tactics*, tácticas dilatorias.
dele [ˈdi:li] n. PRINT. Dele, *m.*, deleátur, *m.*
dele [ˈdi:li] v. tr. Suprimir, tachar (to delete).
delectable [diˈlektəbl] adj. Deleitable, delicioso, sa.
delectation [di:lekˈteiʃən] n. Delectación, *f.*, deleite, *m.*
delegacy [ˈdeligəsi] n. Delegación, *f.*
delegate [ˈdeligit] n. Delegado, da. || U. S. Diputado, da (in the Chamber of Representatives).
delegate [ˈdeligeit] v. tr. Delegar: *to delegate one's powers to s.o.*, delegar sus poderes a *or* en alguien.
delegation [deliˈgeiʃən] n. Delegación, *f.* (act, body).
delegatory [deliˈgeitəri] adj. Delegatorio, ria.
delete [diˈli:t] v. tr. Tachar, suprimir.
deleterious [ˌdeliˈti:riəs] adj. Deletéreo, a (physically harmful). || Perjudicial (morally harmful).
deletion [diˈli:ʃən] n. Tachadura, *f.*, supresión, *f.*
delft [delft] or **delftware** [—wɛə*] n. Cerámica (*f.*) de Delft.
deliberate [diˈlibərit] adj. Deliberado, da (intentional). || Prudente (cautious). || Premeditado, da (premeditated). || Lento, ta; pausado, da (unhurried).
deliberate [diˈlibəreit] v. tr. Reflexionar, meditar.
— V. intr. Reflexionar (to ponder). || Deliberar (*on*, sobre): *the judges deliberated behind closed doors*, los jueces deliberaron a puerta cerrada.
deliberately [diˈlibəritli] adv. A propósito, deliberadamente (voluntarily). || Prudentemente (circumspectly). || Lentamente, pausadamente (slowly).
deliberation [diˌlibəˈreiʃən] n. Deliberación, *f.*, discusión, *f.* (debate). || Reflexión, *f.* || Lentitud, *f.* (slowness). || *After due deliberation*, después de pensarlo bien.
deliberative [diˈlibərətiv] adj. Deliberativo, va; deliberante: *deliberative assembly*, asamblea deliberante.
delible [ˈdelibl] adj. Deleble.
delicacy [ˈdelikəsi] n. Delicadeza, *f.*, fragilidad, *f.* (fragility). || Delicadeza, *f.* (elegance, consideration, sensitivity, tenuousness, skill). || Manjar (*m.*) exquisito (choice food). || MED. Debilidad, *f.* || TECH. Sensibilidad, *f.* (of compass).
delicate [ˈdelikit] adj. Delicado, da (needing great skill or tact). || Delicado, da; frágil (fragile). || Delicado, da; primoroso, sa (work). || Suave (colours). || Sutil (subtle): *a delicate hint*, una indirecta sutil; *a delicate distinction*, una distinción sutil. || Fino, na: *a delicate sense of smell*, un olfato muy fino. || Delicado, da; escrupuloso, sa (scrupulous). || Delicado, da; fino, na (taste). || Ligero, ra (touch). || Delicado, da; suave (odour). || Refinado, da: *a delicate upbringing*, una educación refinada. || Exquisito, ta (food). || Delicado, da (tactful, considerate). || MED. Delicado, da; frágil (health). || TECH. Sensible (compass).
delicateness [—nis] n. Delicadeza, *f.*
delicatessen [ˌdelikəˈtesn] n. Tienda (*f.*) de platos preparados (shop). || Platos (*m. pl.*) preparados.
delicious [diˈliʃəs] adj. Delicioso, sa; exquisito, ta.
delict [diˈlikt] n. JUR. Delito, *m.*: *in flagrant delict*, en flagrante delito.
delight [diˈlait] n. Deleite, *m.*, delicia, *f.* || Encanto, *m.*: *one of the delights of England*, uno de los encantos de Inglaterra. || — *Much to my delight*, con gran regocijo mío. || *The poem is sheer delight*, el poema es una verdadera maravilla. || *To take delight in sth.*, *in doing sth.*, deleitarse con algo, en hacer algo.
delight [di lait] v. tr. Deleitar: *music delights the ear*, la música deleita el oído. || Encantar: *to be delighted with sth.*, estar encantado con algo; *I am delighted to meet you*, estoy encantado de conocerle.
— V. intr. Deleitarse. || — *To delight in doing sth.* deleitarse en hacer algo. || *To delight in sth.*, deleitarse con algo.
delightful [—ful] adj. Delicioso, sa; encantador, ra.
delightfulness [—fulnis] n. Encanto, *m.*
Delilah [diˈlailə] pr. n. Dalila, *f.*

delimit [di'limit] or **delimitate** [—eit] v. tr. Delimitar.
delimitation [di,limi'teiʃən] n. Delimitación, *f.*
delineate [di'linieit] v. tr. Delinear, trazar (to outline). || Bosquejar, esbozar (to sketch). || Delimitar (to delimit). || FIG. Describir, pintar (to describe).
delineation [di,lini'eiʃən] n. Delineación, *f.* (outlining). || Dibujo, *m.* (drawing). || Boceto, *m.*, bosquejo, *m.* (sketch). || FIG. Descripción, *f.*
delineator [di'linieitə*] n. Dibujante, *m.* & *f.*
delinquency [di'liŋkwənsi] n. JUR. Delincuencia, *f.*: *juvenile delinquency*, delincuencia juvenil. | Delito, *m.* (fault). | Culpa, *f.* (guilt).
delinquent [di'liŋkwənt] adj./n. Delincuente. || *Juvenile delinquent*, delincuente juvenil, joven delincuente.
deliquesce [,deli'kwes] v. intr. Licuarse.
deliquescence [,deli'kwesns] n. Delicuescencia, *f.*
deliration [dili'reiʃən] n. MED. Delirio, *m.*
delirious [di'liriəs] adj. Delirante. || *To be delirious*, delirar.
delirium [di'liriəm] n. MED. FIG. Delirio, *m.* || MED. *Delirium tremens*, delírium tremens, *m.*

— OBSERV. El plural de la palabra inglesa es *deliriums* o *deliria.*

deliver [di'livə*] v. tr. Repartir, entregar (goods). || Entregar (to hand over). || Repartir (mail). || Dar (a message). || Expresar, formular (an opinion). || Pronunciar (a speech). || Dar (a lecture). || Rendir (accounts). || Lanzar (the ball). || Pegar, dar, asestar (a blow). || MED. Asistir para dar a luz (a woman). || Liberar (to free). || JUR. Pronunciar. || MIL. Iniciar (an attack). | Librar (a battle). | Lanzar (a missile). || — REL. *Deliver us from evil*, líbranos del mal. || *Stand and deliver!*, ¡la bolsa o la vida! || *The doctor delivered her of her child*, el médico le asistió en el nacimiento de su hijo. || *To be delivered of a child*, dar a luz a un niño. || *To deliver o.s. of*, expresar (an opinion). || *To deliver o.s. over o up to justice*, entregarse a la justicia. || *To deliver over o up*, entregar. || COMM. "*We deliver*", entrega (*f.*) a domicilio.
deliverance [di'livərəns] n. Liberación, *f.* (a rescuing or being rescued). || Declaración, *f.* (opinion). || JUR. Fallo, *m.*, veredicto, *m.*
deliverer [di'livərə*] n. Libertador, ra; liberador, ra. || COMM. Repartidor, ra.
delivery [di'livəri] n. Entrega, *f.* (of a parcel, shop orders). || Reparto, *m.* (of mail). || Distribución, *f.* (distribution). || Expedición, *f.* (of goods). || Pronunciación, *f.* (of a speech, lecture, etc.). || Manera (*f.*) de expresarse (manner of speaking). || Liberación, *f.* (saving). || MED. Parto, *m.*, alumbramiento, *m.* || SP. Lanzamiento, *m.* (in cricket, baseball, etc.). || JUR. Cesión, *f.* || TECH. Caudal, *m.* (of water). || — *Delivery boy*, recadero, *m.*, chico (*m.*) de los recados. || *Delivery note*, nota (*f.*) de entrega. || MED. *Delivery room*, sala (*f.*) de partos. || *Delivery service*, servicio (*m.*) a domicilio. || *Delivery van*, furgoneta (*f.*) de reparto. || U. S. *General Delivery*, lista (*f.*) de Correos [*Amer.*, poste restante]. || *To take delivery of*, recibir.
deliveryman [—mən] n. Repartidor, *m.*

— OBSERV. El plural de *deliveryman* es *deliverymen.*

dell [del] n. Pequeño valle, *m.* (small valley).
delouse ['di:'laus] v. tr. Despiojar, espulgar.
Delphi ['delfai] pr. n. GEOGR. Delfos.
delphinium [del'finiəm] n. BOT. Espuela (*f.*) de caballero.
delta ['deltə] n. Delta, *f.* (Greek letter). || Delta, *m.* (of a river). || AVIAT. *Delta-winged*, con alas en forma de delta.
deltaic [del'teiik] adj. Deltaico, ca.
deltoid ['deltɔid] adj. Deltoideo, a; deltoides.
— N. ANAT. Deltoides, *m. inv.*
deltoidal [del'tɔidl] adj. Deltoideo, a; deltoides.
delude [di'lu:d] v. tr. Engañar. || *To delude o.s. with false hopes*, forjarse ilusiones.
deluge ['delju:dʒ] n. Inundación, *f.* (flood). || Diluvio, *m.* (heavy fall of rain). || FIG. Avalancha, *f.*, alud, *m.* (of people, letters, etc.).
deluge ['delju:dʒ] v. tr. Inundar. || FIG. Abrumar (with requests). | Inundar de. || — FIG. *Deluged with tears*, bañado en lágrimas. | *To be deluged with presents*, lloverle a uno los regalos.
delusion [di'lu:ʒən] n. Engaño, *m.*, error, *m.* || Ilusión, *f.* || MED. Alucinación, *f.* || — *Delusions of grandeur*, megalomanía, *f.*, delirio (*m.*) de grandezas. || *To labour under a delusion*, estar equivocado *or* engañado.
delusive [di'lu:siv] adj. Engañoso, sa (deceiving). || Ilusorio, ria (illusory).
delusiveness [—nis] n. Lo engañoso, lo ilusorio.
de luxe [də'lʌks] adj. De lujo.
delve [delv] v. intr. AGR. Cavar. || Bajar, inclinarse (a road, etc.). || FIG. *To delve into*, ahondar (a problem), hurgar en (one's pocket, a drawer).
— V. tr. AGR. Cavar. || FIG. Explorar.
demagnetization ['di:mægnitai'zeiʃən] n. Desmagnetización, *f.*, desimantación, *f.*, desimanación, *f.*
demagnetize ['di:'mægnitaiz] v. tr. Desmagnetizar, desimantar, desimanar.
demagog ['deməgɔg] n. U. S. Demagogo, *m.*
demagogic [,demə'gɔgik] or **demagogical** [—əl] adj. Demagógico, ca.
demagogism ['deməgɔgizəm] n. Demagogia, *f.*
demagogue ['deməgɔg] n. Demagogo, *m.*
demagogy ['deməgɔgi] n. Demagogia, *f.*
demand [di'mɑ:nd] n. Petición, *f.*, solicitud, *f.* (request). || Reclamación, *f.* (for payment). || Exigencia, *f.* (urgent claim). || COMM. Demanda, *f.*: *a big demand for cotton dresses*, una gran demanda de vestidos de algodón. || — *By popular demand*, a petición del público. || *He has many demands on his time*, sus asuntos le tienen muy ocupado. || *In demand*, muy solicitado. || *It makes great demands on my strength*, requiere muchos esfuerzos. || *On demand*, a petición. || *The pressing demands for housing*, la urgente necesidad de viviendas.
demand [di'mɑ:nd] v. tr. Exigir (to ask for emphatically). || Requerir (to require): *the matter demands careful consideration*, la cuestión requiere un examen detenido. || Reclamar: *he demanded his rights*, reclamó sus derechos. || *He demanded to see it*, insistió en verlo.
demandable [—əbl] adj. Exigible.
demandant [—ənt] n. JUR. Demandante, *m.* & *f.*
demand bill [—bil] n. COMM. Letra (f.) a la vista.
demand deposit [—di'pɔzit] n. COMM. Depósito (*m.*) a la vista.
demand draft [—drɑ:ft] n. COMM. Letra (*f.*) a la vista.
demanding [—iŋ] adj. Exigente (person). || Absorbente (absorbing). || Agotador, ra (exhausting).
demand loan [—ləun] n. COMM. Préstamo (*m.*) reembolsable a petición.
demarcate ['di:mɑ:keit] v. tr. Demarcar.
demarcation [,di:mɑ:'keiʃən] n. Demarcación, *f.* || *Demarcation line*, línea (*f.*) de demarcación.
démarche ['deimɑ:ʃ] n. Gestión, *f.*, diligencia, *f.*
dematerialization ['di:mə,tiəriəlai'zeiʃən] n. Desmaterialización, *f.*
dematerialize ['di:mə'tiəriəlaiz] v. tr. Hacer *or* volver inmaterial.
— V. intr. Hacerse *or* volverse inmaterial.
demean [di'mi:n] v. tr. Rebajar. || *To demean o.s.*, rebajarse (to lower o.s.).
demeanour (U. S. **demeanor**) [—ə*] n. Conducta, *f.*, comportamiento, *m.* (behaviour). || Porte, *m.* (bearing).
dement [di'ment] n. U. S. MED. Demente, *m.* & *f.*, loco, ca.
dement [di'ment] v. tr. MED. Volver loco a.
demented [—id] adj. MED. Demente, loco, ca.
dementedly [—idli] adj. Como un loco.
dementia [di'menʃiə] n. MED. Demencia, *f.* || MED. *Dementia praecox* (U. S. *dementia precox*), demencia precoz.
demerara [,demə'rɛərə] n. Azúcar (*m.*) terciado.
demerit [di:'merit] n. Demérito, *m.*, desmerecimiento, *m.* (fault).
demesne [di'mein] n. Propiedad, *f.* (estate). || Casa (*f.*) y tierras solariegas (of a lord). || JUR. Plena propiedad, *f.* || FIG. Esfera, *f.* (of activity).
demigod ['demigɔd] n. Semidiós, *m.*
demijohn ['demidʒɔn] n. Damajuana, *f.*
demilitarization ['di:,militərai'zeiʃən] n. Desmilitarización, *f.*
demilitarize ['di:'militəraiz] v. tr. Desmilitarizar.
demimonde ['demi'mɔ̃:nd] n. Mujeres (*f. pl.*) de vida alegre.
demineralization [di:minərəlai'zeiʃən] n. Desmineralización, *f.*
demineralize [di:'minərəlaiz] v. tr. Desmineralizar.
demise [di'maiz] n. Defunción, *f.*, fallecimiento, *m.* (death). || JUR. Cesión, *f.* | Transmisión, *f.* (transfer of sovereignty).
demise [di'maiz] v. tr. JUR. Legar (by will or lease). | Transmitir (to transfer).
— V. intr. JUR. Transmitirse por herencia. || Morir (to die).
demisemiquaver ['demisemi,kweivə*] n. Fusa, *f.*
demission [di'miʃən] n. Dimisión, *f.*
demist [di:'mist] v. tr. Eliminar el vaho de.
demit [di'mit] v. intr. Dimitir.
— V. tr. Dimitir de.
demitasse ['demi,tæs] n. U. S. Taza (*f.*) de café.
Demiurge ['di:miə:dʒ] n. Demiurgo, *m.*
demob ['di:mɔb] n. FAM. Soldado (*m.*) desmovilizado.
demob ['di:'mɔb] v. tr. FAM. Desmovilizar.
demobilization [,dimaubilai'zeiʃən] n. Desmovilización, *f.*
demobilize [di:'məubilaiz] v. tr. Desmovilizar.
democracy [di:'mɔkrəsi] n. Democracia, *f.*
democrat ['deməkræt] n. Demócrata, *m.* & *f.* || *Christian Democrat*, demócratacristiano, na.
democratic [,demə'krætik] adj. Democrático, ca. || — *Christian Democratic*, demócratacristiano, na. || *Democratic party*, partido demócrata.
democratization [di'mɔkrətai'zeiʃən] n. Democratización, *f.*
democratize [di'mɔkrətaiz] v. tr. Democratizar.
— V. intr. Democratizarse.
Democritus [di'mɔkritəs] pr. n. Demócrito, *m.*
démodé [,deiməu'dei] adj. Pasado de moda.
demographer [di:'mɔgrəfə*] n. Demógrafo, *m.*
demographic [,di:mə'græfik] adj. Demográfico, ca.
demography [di'mɔgrəfi] n. Demografía, *f.*
demoiselle [,dəmwa'zel] n. ZOOL. Libélula, *f.* (dragonfly). || Damisela, *f.* (damsel).
demolish [di'mɔliʃ] v. tr. Echar abajo, derribar, demoler (a building). || Destruir (to raze). || FIG.

Destruir, echar abajo *or* por tierra (an argument). || FAM. Zamparse (to eat).

demolisher [—ə*] n. Demoledor, ra.

demolition [ˌdemə'liʃən] n. Demolición, *f.*, derribo, *m.* (of a building). || Destrucción, *f.*

demon ['di:mən] n. Demonio, *m.* || Espíritu, *m.* (spirit). || Demonio, *m.*, diablo, *m.*: *this child is a demon*, este niño es un demonio. || Demonio, *m.*: *driven by a demon of avarice*, impulsado por el demonio de la avaricia. || FIG. Hacha, *m.* (ace). || FIG. *To be a demon for work*, ser una fiera para el trabajo.

demonetization [di:ˌmʌnitai'zeiʃən] n. Desmonetización, *f.*

demonetize [di:'mʌnitaiz] v. tr. Desmonetizar.

demoniac [di'məuniæk] adj. Endemoniado, da; demoniaco, ca (possessed by a demon). || Demoniaco, ca; diabólico, ca (fiendish).
— N. Demoniaco, ca; endemoniado, da.

demoniacal [ˌdi:məu'naiəkəl] or **demonic** [di:'mɔnik] adj. Demoniaco, ca; diabólico, ca.

demonism ['di:mənizəm] n. Creencia (*f.*) en los demonios.

demonstrability [ˌdemənstrə'biliti] n. Posibilidad (*f.*) de ser demostrado.

demonstrable ['demənstrəbl] adj. Demostrable.

demonstrate ['demənstreit] v. tr. Demostrar, probar (to prove). || Demostrar (to make clear). || Mostrar, hacer la demostración de (the working of a machine, etc.). || MATH. Demostrar. || FIG. Manifestar.
— V. intr. Manifestarse, hacer una manifestación (to show public simpathy, to protest). || MIL. Hacer una demostración.

demonstration [ˌdemənstreiʃən] n. Manifestación, *f.* (expression of public feeling for or against sth.). || Demostración, *f.*, prueba, *f.*: *demonstration of affection*, demostración de cariño; *fruit falling offers a demonstration of gravity*, la caída de la fruta es una demostración de la fuerza de gravedad; *to give a demonstration of how a piece of equipment works*, hacer una demostración de cómo funciona un aparato. || MIL. Demostración, *f.*

demonstrative [di'mɔnstrətiv] adj. GRAM. Demostrativo, va: *demonstrative adjectives*, adjetivos demostrativos. || Convincente (convincing). || Demostrativo, va; expansivo, va (person).
— N. GRAMM. Demostrativo, *m.*

demonstrator ['demənstreitə*] n. Demostrador, ra. || Manifestante, *m.* & *f.* (participant in a public protest meeting). || Auxiliar, *m.* & *f.* (in a laboratory).

demoralization [diˌmɔrəlaizeiʃən] n. Desmoralización, *f.*

demoralize [di'mɔrəlaiz] v. tr. Desmoralizar.

demoralizer [—ə*] n. Desmoralizador, ra.

demoralizing [—iŋ] adj. Desmoralizador, ra; desmoralizante.

Demosthenes [di'mɔsθəni:z] pr. n. Demóstenes, *m.*

demote [di'məut] v. tr. Degradar.

demotic [di'mɔtik] adj. Popular (popular). || Demótico, ca (of ancient Egyptian writing).

demotion [di'məuʃən] n. Degradación, *f.*

demount [di'maunt] v. tr. Desmontar, desarmar.

demountable [—əbl] adj. Desmontable, desarmable.

demulcent [di'mʌlsənt] adj. MED. Emoliente.
— N. MED. Emoliente, *m.*

demur [di'mə:*] n. Objeción, *f.* || Vacilación, *f.* (hesitation).

demur [di'mə:*] v. intr. Hacer objeciones (to object). || Vacilar (to hesitate).

demure [di'mjuə*] adj. Comedido, da (sober). || Recatado, da (modest). || Remilgado, da (affectedly modest). || Gazmoño, ña (prudish).

demurely [—li] adv. Recatadamente (modestly). || Con gazmoñería.

demureness [—nis] n. Recato, *m.* (of a girl, dress, etc.). || Gazmoñería, *f.* (prudery).

demurrage [di'mʌridʒ] n. MAR. Sobrestadía, *f.* || Almacenaje, *m.* (storage fee). || Cantidad (*f.*) cobrada por el Banco de Inglaterra por lingote depositado.

demurrer [di'mə:rə*] n. JUR. Excepción (*f.*) perentoria.

den [den] n. Guarida, *f.* (animal's lair). || Guarida, *f.* (gang hideout): *den of thieves*, guarida de ladrones. || Cuchitril, *m.* (dirty little room). || Antro, *m.*: *den of vice*, antro de perversión. || U. S. Estudio, *m.* (small room).

denarius [di'nɛəriəs] n. Denario, *m.*

— OBSERV. El plural de *denarius* es *denarii*.

denary ['di:nəri] adj. Denario, ria; decimal.

denationalization ['di:ˌnæʃnəlai'zeiʃən] n. Desnacionalización, *f.*

denationalize [di:'næʃnəlaiz] v. tr. Desnacionalizar.

denaturalization ['di:ˌnætʃrəlai'zeiʃən] n. Desnaturalización, *f.*

denaturalize [di:'nætʃrəlaiz] v. tr. Desnaturalizar.

denaturation [di:ˌneitʃəreiʃən] n. CHEM. Desnaturalización, *f.*

denature [di:ˌneitʃə*] v. tr. Desnaturalizar. || *Denatured alcohol*, alcohol desnaturalizado.

dendrite ['dendrait] n. Dendrita, *f.*

dene [di:n] n. Duna, *f.* (dune). || Pequeño valle, *m.*, vallejo, *m.* (valley).

denegation [ˌdi:ni'geiʃən] n. Denegación, *f.*

dengue ['deŋgi] n. MED. Dengue, *m.*

deniable [di'naiəbl] adj. Negable.

denial [di'naiəl] n. Negación, *f.* (an assertion that sth. is not true, disavowal). || Negativa, *f.* (refusal). || Rechazamiento, *m.* (rejection). || Mentís, *m.* (to a statement). || Abnegación, *f.* (self-denial). || JUR. *Denial of justice*, denegación (*f.*) de justicia.

denicotinize [di'nikətinaiz] v. tr. Desnicotinizar.

denier [di'naiə*] n. Negador, ra.

denier ['deniei] n. Denier, *m.* (of stockings).

denigrate ['denigreit] v. tr. Denigrar.

denigration [ˌdeni'greiʃən] n. Denigración, *f.*

denigrator ['denigreitə*] n. Denigrante, *m.* & *f.*, denigrador, ra.

denigratory [ˌdeni'greitəri] adj. Denigrante, denigrador, ra.

denim ['denim] n. Mahón, *m.* (cotton fabric). || — Pl. Pantalones (*m.*) vaqueros (jeans). || Mono, *m. sing.* (overall).

denitrate ['di:'naitreit] v. tr. Desnitrificar.

denitration [ˌdi:nai'treiʃən] or **denitrification** ['di:ˌnaitrifi'keiʃən] n. Desnitrificación, *f.*

denitrify [di:'naitrifai] v. tr. Desnitrificar.

denizen ['denizn] n. Ciudadano, na; habitante, *m.* & *f.* (people). || Habitante, *m.* & *f.*: *the lion is a denizen of the jungle*, el león es un habitante de la selva. || JUR. Residente (*m.*) extranjero. || GRAM. Palabra (*f.*) extranjera naturalizada. || BOT. Planta (*f.*) aclimatada. || ZOOL. Animal (*m.*) aclimatado.

Denmark ['denmɑ:k] pr. n. GEOGR. Dinamarca, *f.*

denominate [di'nɔmineit] v. tr. Denominar.

denomination [diˌnɔmi'neiʃən] n. Denominación, *f.* || Unidad, *f.* (of weight, measure). || Secta, *f.*, confesión, *f.*: *Baptist denomination*, secta baptista. || Valor, *m.* (of coins). || Clase, *f.*, tipo, *m.* (kind).

denominational [diˌnɔmi'neiʃənl] adj. REL. Sectario, ria (sectarian). || Religioso, sa; confesional (education).

denominative [di'nɔminətiv] adj. Denominativo, va.

denominator [di'nɔmineitə*] n. MATH. Denominador, *m.*: *the least* o *the lowest common denominator*, el mínimo común denominador.

denotation [ˌdi:nəu'teiʃən] n. Indicación, *f.* || Designación, *f.* (name). || Señal, *f.*, indicio, *m.* (sign). || Significado, *m.* (meaning). || Extensión, *f.* (of a word).

denotative [di'nəutətiv] adj. Revelador, ra (*of*, de).

denote [di'nəut] v. tr. Denotar (to mark). || Indicar (to indicate). || Significar (to stand for).

dénoument (U. S. **denouement**) [dei'nu:mɑ̃:ŋ] n. Desenlace, *m.* (of a play or story). || FIG. Desenlace, *m.*

denounce [di'nauns] v. tr. Denunciar (a thief, a treaty). || FIG. Alzarse contra (an abuse). | Censurar (to criticize).

denouncement [—mənt] n. See DENUNCIATION.

denouncer [—ə*] n. Denunciante, *m.* & *f.*, denunciador, ra.

dense [dens] adj. Denso, sa (thick, packed together). || FAM. Torpe (person). | Craso, sa (ignorance). || PHYS. Denso, sa (body, metal). | Opaco, ca (negative).

densely [—li] adv. Densamente. || *Densely ignorant*, de una ignorancia supina *or* crasa.

denseness ['densnis] n. See DENSITY.

densify ['densifai] v. tr. Densificar.

densimeter [den'simetə*] n. PHYS. Densímetro, *m.*

density ['densiti] n. Densidad, *f.* (thickness). || FAM. Torpeza, *f.* (slowness). || PHYS. Densidad, *f.*

dent [dent] n. Bollo, *m.*, abolladura, *f.* (hollow). || Mella, *f.* (in blade).

dent [dent] v. tr. Abollar (surface). || Mellar (blade).
— V. intr. Abollarse (surface). || Mellarse (blade).

dental ['dentl] adj. Dental: *dental prothesis*, prótesis dental. || GRAMM. Dental. || MED. *Dental surgeon*, odontólogo, *m.*
— N. GRAMM. Dental, *f.*

dentate ['denteit] adj. BOT. Dentado, da: *dentate leaf*, hoja dentada. || Dentado, da (notched).

dentation [den'teiʃən] n. Borde (*m.*) dentado.

denticle ['dentikl] n. ARCH. Dentículo, *m.* || Dientecillo, *m.* (small tooth).

denticulate [den'tikjələt] or **denticulated** [dentikjəleitid] adj. Denticulado, da.

denticulation [ˌdentikjə'leiʃən] n. Borde (*m.*) dentado.

dentrifrice ['dentifris] n. Dentífrico, *m.*

dentil ['dentil] n. ARCH. Dentículo, *m.*

dentine (U. S. **dentin**) ['denti:n] n. ANAT. Dentina, *f.*, esmalte (*m.*) de los dientes.

dentist ['dentist] n. MED. Dentista, *m.* & *f.* || *To go to the dentist's*, ir al dentista.

dentistry [—ri] n. Odontología, *f.*

dentition [den'tiʃən] n. Dentición, *f.*

denture ['dentʃə*] n. Dentadura (*f.*) postiza.

denudate ['denjudeit] v. tr. See DENUDE.

denudation [ˌdi:nju:'deiʃən] n. GEOL. Denudación, *f.*

denude [di'nju:d] v. tr. Desnudar (to make naked). || Descarnar (bone). || Descortezar (a tree). || GEOL. Denudar. || FIG. Despojar (to strip).

denunciation [diˌnʌnsi'eiʃən] n. Denuncia, *f.* (of a thief). || Denuncia, *f.*, anulación, *f.*, ruptura, *f.* (of a treaty). || FIG. Condena, *f.* (of an abuse). | Censura, *f.* (criticism).

denunciative [di'nʌnsiətiv] adj. Denunciador, ra.

denunciator [di'nʌnsieitə*] n. Denunciador, ra; denunciante, *m.* & *f.*

deny [di'nai] v. tr. Negar (to dispute): *I don't deny it*, no lo niego. || Desmentir (to give the lie to). || Repudiar (s.o., faith). || Rechazar (charge). || Denegar, rechazar (request). || Negar (to refuse). || — *To be denied to*, ser negado a. || *To deny o.s. sth.*, privarse de algo. || *To deny the door to s.o.*, cerrar la puerta a alguien.

deodorant [di:'əudərənt] adj. Desodorante.
— N. Desodorante, *m.*

deodorize [di:'əudəraiz] v. tr. Desodorizar.

deodorizer [—ə*] n. Desodorante, *m.*

deontological [di,ɔntə'lɔdʒikəl] adj. Deontológico, ca.

deontology [,di:ɔn'tɔlədʒi] n. Deontología, *f.*

deoxidation [di:,ɔksi'deiʃən] or **deoxidization** [di:,ɔksidai'zeiʃən] n. CHEM. Desoxidación, *f.*

deoxidize [di:'ɔksidaiz] v. tr. CHEM. Desoxidar.

deoxidizer [—ə*] n. CHEM. Desoxidante, *m.*

deoxidizing [—iŋ] adj. Desoxidante.

deoxygenate [di:'ɔksidʒəneit] v. tr. CHEM. Desoxigenar.

deoxyribonucleic [di:'ɔksi'raibəu'nju:kliik] adj. CHEM. Desoxirribonucleico, ca (acid).

depart [di'pɑ:t] v. intr. Marcharse, irse (to go away). || Salir (to set off or out). || Apartarse, salirse (*from*, de) [to deviate]. || Morir (to die).
— V. tr. *To depart this life*, pasar a mejor vida.

departed [—id] adj. Pasado, da (bygone). || Difunto, ta: *my departed husband*, mi difunto marido.
— N. *The departed*, el difunto, la difunta, los difuntos.

department [di'pɑ:tmənt] n. Departamento, *m.*, sección, *f.* (in a store). || Sección, *f.* (in a college, university). || Servicio, *m.*: *the accounting department*, el servicio de contabilidad. || Ramo, *m.* (branch). || Negociado, *m.* (in a ministry). || Departamento, *m.* (administrative district in France). || FIG. Esfera, *f.* (sphere of activity). || U. S. Departamento, *m.*, ministerio, *m.*: *Department of State*, Departamento de Estado, Ministerio de Asuntos Exteriores; *Department of Labor, of the Interior, of the Navy*, Ministerio de Trabajo, de Gobernación [*Amer.*, del Interior], de Marina.

departmental [,di:pɑ:t'mentl] adj. Departamental. || *Departmental head*, jefe (*m.*) de servicio.

department store [di:'pɑ:tmənt,stɔ:*] n. Gran almacén, *m.*

departure [di'pɑ:tʃə*] n. Marcha, *f.*, partida, *f.* (a going away). || Salida, *f.*: *the departure of the train is at nine o'clock*, la salida del tren es a las nueve. || Desviación, *f.* (deviation). || FIG. Orientación, *f.*: *to make a new departure in physics*, dar una nueva orientación a la física. || MAR. Diferencia (*f.*) de longitud contada desde el punto de partida. || *To take one's departure*, marcharse, irse.

depauperate [di:'pɔ:pəreit] v. tr. Empobrecer, depauperar.

depauperation [di:,pɔ:pə'reiʃən] n. Empobrecimiento, *m.*, depauperación, *f.* (impoverishment). || MED. Depauperación, *f.*

depend [di'pend] v. intr. Depender: *it depends on whether you are in a hurry or not*, depende de si tienes prisa o no; *I depend upon my father*, dependo de mi padre. || Contar con: *we are depending on you!*, ¡contamos contigo! || Fiarse de: *you can never depend on what he says*, no se puede uno fiar nunca de lo que dice. || JUR. Estar pendiente (suit). || — *That depends*, eso depende, según. || *To depend on one's work for one's living*, vivir de su trabajo. || *To depend on o.s.*, bastarse a sí mismo. || *You may depend on it*, puede estar seguro.

dependability [di,pendə'biliti] n. Formalidad, *f.*, seriedad, *f.* (of s.o.). || Seguridad, *f.* (of a machine).

dependable [di'pendəbl] adj. Fiable, seguro, ra; formal (trustworthy). || Seguro, ra (things).

dependance [di'pendəns] n. U. S. See DEPENDENCE.

dependant [di'pendənt] n. Persona (*f.*) a cargo. || — Pl. Servidumbre, *f. sing.* (servants).

dependence [di'pendəns] n. Dependencia, *f.*: *the dependence of one person on another*, la dependencia de una persona de otra. || Dependencia, *f.* (*upon*, de), subordinación, *f.* (*upon*, a) [subordination]. || Confianza, *f.* (*on, upon*, en) [trust].

dependency [—i] n. Dependencia, *f.*

dependent [di'pendənt] adj. Dependiente (*on*, de) [persons, lands]. || Subordinado, da (*on*, a) [subordinate]. || GRAMM. Subordinado, da: *dependent clause*, oración subordinada. || *To be dependent on*, depender de.
— N. Persona (*f.*) a cargo.

depeople [di'pi:pl] v. tr. Despoblar.

depersonalization [di,pə:snəlai'zeiʃən] n. Despersonalización, *f.*

depersonalize [di'pə:snəlaiz] v. tr. Despersonalizar.

dephase [di:'feiz] v. tr. ELECTR. Defasar.

dephasing [—iŋ] n. Defasaje, *m.*

dephosphorize [di:'fɔsfəraiz] v. tr. Desfosforar.

depict [di'pikt] v. tr. ARTS. Pintar, representar. || FIG. Describir, pintar (to describe).

depiction [di'pikʃən] n. ARTS. Pintura, *f.* || Descripción, *f.*, pintura, *f.* (description).

depilate ['depileit] v. tr. Depilar.

depilation [,depi'leiʃən] n. Depilación, *f.*

depilatory [di'pilətəri] adj. Depilatorio, ria.
— N. Depilatorio, *m.*

deplenish [di'pleniʃ] v. tr. Vaciar. || COMM. Desproveer.

deplete [di'pli:t] v. tr. Agotar (to exhaust provisions, ammunition). || Reducir (to reduce). || MIL. Desguarnecer (a garrison). || MED. Descongestionar.

depletion [di'pli:ʃən] n. Agotamiento, *m.* (exhaustion of provisions, ammunition, etc.). || Disminución, *f.*, reducción, *f.* (lessening). || MED. Descongestión, *f.*

deplorable [di'plɔ:rəbl] adj. Deplorable, lamentable.

deplore [di'plɔ:*] v. tr. Deplorar, lamentar. || *It is to be deplored*, es de lamentar, es deplorable.

deploy [di'plɔi] v. tr. MIL. FIG. Desplegar.
— V. intr. MIL. Desplegarse.

deployment [—mənt] n. MIL. Despliegue, *m.*

deplume [di:'plu:m] v. tr. Desplumar (to pluck). || FIG. Despojar.

depolarization ['di:,pəulərai'zeiʃən] n. PHYS. Despolarización, *f.*

depolarize [di:'pəuləraiz] v. tr. PHYS. Despolarizar.

depolarizer [—ə*] n. PHYS. Despolarizador, *m.*

depone [di'pəun] v. intr. JUR. Deponer.

deponent [di'pəunənt] adj. GRAMM. Deponente.
— N. GRAMM. Verbo (*m.*) deponente. || Deponente, *m.* & *f.*, declarante, *m.* & *f.* (witness).

depopulate [di:'pɔpjuleit] v. tr. Despoblar.
— V. intr. Despoblarse.

depopulation [di:,pɔpju'leiʃən] n. Despoblación, *f.*

deport [di'pɔ:t] v. tr. JUR. Expulsar (an alien). | Deportar (a convict). || *To deport o.s.*, comportarse, portarse.

deportation [,di:pɔ:'teiʃən] n. JUR. Expulsión, *f.* (of an alien). | Deportación, *f.* (of a convict).

deportee [,di:pɔ:'ti] n. JUR. Deportado, da.

deportment [di'pɔ:tmənt] n. Porte, *m.* (bearing). || Conducta, *f.*, comportamiento, *m.* (behaviour).

deposal [di'pəuzəl] n. Deposición, *f.*, destronamiento, *m.* (of a king). || Destitución, *f.* (from office).

depose [di'pəuz] v. tr. Deponer, destronar (to dethrone). || Destituir (to remove from office). || JUR. Deponer, declarar.
— V. intr. JUR. Deponer, declarar.

deposit [di'pɔzit] n. Depósito, *m.* (in a bank). || Poso, *m.*, sedimento, *m.*, depósito, *m.* (sediment). || Depósito, *m.* (in electrolysis). || MIN. Yacimiento, *m.* || Señal, *f.* (pledge): *to leave ten pounds deposit on a refrigerator*, dejar una señal de diez libras para un refrigerador. || Entrada, *f.*: *to put a deposit on a flat*, dar una entrada para un piso.

deposit [di'pɔzit] v. tr. Depositar (to put sth. down). || Depositar, sedimentar (to leave a layer or coating of). || Depositar (money in bank). || Ingresar (money in one's account). || Dar de señal (to pledge). || Dar una entrada de, hacer un desembolso inicial de (when buying houses, cars, etc.). || Poner (eggs).

deposit account [—ə,kaunt] n. Cuenta (*f.*) de depósitos a plazo.

depositary [di'pɔzitəri] n. Depositario, ria (person). || Depositaría, *f.* (storehouse).

deposition [,depə'ziʃən] n. Deposición, *f.*, destronamiento, *m.* (of a king). || Destitución, *f.* (from office). || JUR. Deposición, *f.*, declaración, *f.* || Depósito, *m.* (deposit). || REL. Descendimiento, *m.* (of Christ).

depositor [di'pɔzitə*] n. Depositador, ra; depositante, *m.* & *f.* || Cuentacorrentista, *m.* & *f.* (person who holds an account).

depository [—ri] n. Depositario, ria (person). || Depositaría, *f.* (storehouse).

depot ['depəu] n. Almacén, *m.* (storehouse). || MIL. Depósito, *m.* || Cochera, *f.*, depósito, *m.* (for buses). || U. S. Estación, *f.* (station).

depravation [,deprə'veiʃən] n. Depravación, *f.*, perversión, *f.*

deprave [di'preiv] v. tr. Depravar, pervertir.

depraver [—ə*] n. Depravador, ra.

depravity [di'præviti] n. Depravación, *f.* (perversion).

deprecate ['deprikeit] v. tr. Desaprobar.

deprecation [,depri'keiʃən] n. Desaprobación, *f.* (disapproval). || Deprecación, *f.* (prayer).

deprecative [,depri'keitiv] or **deprecatory** ['deprikətəri] adj. De desaprobación (disapproving): *a deprecative murmur*, un murmullo de desaprobación. || Tímido, da (smile).

depreciate [di'pri:ʃieit] v. tr. Depreciar (money). || Abaratar (goods). || Despreciar, menospreciar (to belittle).
— V. intr. Depreciarse (money). || Bajar (in price).

depreciation [di,pri:ʃi'eiʃən] n. Depreciación, *f.* (of money). || Abaratamiento, *m.* (of goods). || FIG. Desprecio, *m.*

depreciator [di'pri:ʃieitə*] n. Depreciador, ra.

depreciative [di'pri:ʃieitiv] or **depreciatory** [di'pri:ʃjətəri] adj. Depreciador, ra (lessening in value). || Peyorativo, va; despectivo, va (pejorative).

depredate ['deprideit] v. tr. Depredar.

depredation [,depri'deiʃən] n. Depredación, *f.* || — Pl. Estragos, *m.* (ravages).

depredator ['deprideitə*] n. Depredador, *m.*

depredatory [di'predətəri] adj. Depredador, ra.

depress [di'pres] v. tr. Deprimir (to dispirit). || Debilitar (to weaken). || Bajar (to lower). || Disminuir (to lessen). || Presionar, apretar (to push down). || AUT. Pisar (the pedal). || MATH. Reducir (an equation). || COMM. Reducir (trade). | Deprimir (economy). | Hacer bajar (prices).

depressant [—ənt] adj. MED. Calmante, sedante.
— N. MED. Calmante, *m.*, sedante, *m.*
depressed [—t] adj. Deprimido, da; desanimado, da (miserable). || Necesitado, da (needy): *depressed areas*, áreas necesitadas. || COMM. De depresión (period). | Deprimido, da (economy).
depressing [—iŋ] adj. Deprimente.
depression [di'preʃən] n. GEOGR. MED. Depresión, *f.* || Depresión, *f.*, crisis (*f.*) económica (slump). || FIG. Abatimiento, *m.*, depresión, *f.* (dejection).
depressive [di'presiv] adj. Deprimente, depresivo, va (depressing). || Propenso a la depresión (easily depressed).
depressor [di'presə*] n. ANAT. MED. Depresor, *m.* || ELECTR. Elevador (*m.*) de voltaje.
depressurization ['di:,preʃərai'zeiʃən] n. Descompresión, *f.*
depressurize ['di:'preʃəraiz] v. tr. Descomprimir.
deprival [di'praivəl] n. Privación, *f.*
deprivation [,depri'veiʃən] n. Privación, *f.* || Pérdida, *f.* (loss). || JUR. *Deprivation of office*, suspensión (*f.*) de empleo.
deprive [di'praiv] v. tr. Privar: *to deprive s.o. of food*, privar a alguien de alimento. || JUR. Destituir (to remove from office). || *To deprive o.s.*, privarse.
deprived [—d] adj. Desheredado, da: *the deprived ones of the world*, los desheredados de la fortuna. || *Deprived child*, niño desgraciado.
de profundis [deiprəu'fʌndis] n. REL. De profundis, *m.*
depth [depθ] n. Profundidad, *f.*: *the depth of the ocean*, la profundidad del océano; *depth of field*, profundidad de campo; *depth of feeling*, profundidad de sentimiento. || Lo más profundo, lo más hondo: *in the depth of his heart*, en lo más profundo de su corazón. || Intensidad, *f.* (of colour). || Corazón, *m.*: *the depth of the forest*, el corazón del bosque. || MUS. Gravedad, *f.* || — Pl. Abismo, *m. sing.* || — *In depth*, a fondo: *to study a matter in depth*, estudiar una cuestión a fondo; en profundidad (defence). || *In the depth of winter*, en pleno invierno, en lo más crudo del invierno. || *In the depths of despair*, completamente desesperado. || *The lake is ten feet in depth*, el lago tiene una profundidad de diez pies. || *To be out of one's depth*, perder pie (in water), estar perdido, no entender nada (not to understand). || *To get out of one's depth*, perder pie (in water), meterse en honduras.
depth charge [—tʃɑ:dʒ] n. Carga (*f.*) de profundidad.
depth gauge [—geidʒ] n. Sonda, *f.*
depthless [—lis] adj. Sin fondo.
depurate ['depjuəreit] v. tr. Depurar.
— V. intr. Depurarse.
depuration [,depjuə'reiʃən] n. Depuración, *f.*
depurative ['depjuərətiv] adj. MED. Depurativo, va. || Depuratorio, ria (cleansing).
— N. MED. Depurativo, *m.*
depurator ['depjuəreitə*] n. Depurador, *m.*
deputation [,depju'teiʃən] n. Delegación, *f.*
depute [di'pju:t] v. tr. Delegar.
deputize ['depjutaiz] v. tr. Delegar.
— V. intr. Sustituir (*for*, a).
deputy ['depjuti] n. Delegado, *m.* (member of a deputation). || Suplente, *m.*, sustituto, *m.* (substitute). || Diputado, *m.* (member of a legislative body): *Chamber of Deputies*, Cámara de Diputados. || — *Deputy Chairman*, vicepresidente, *m.* || *Deputy Director General*, Director General Adjunto. || *Deputy head*, subdirector, ra. || *Deputy judge*, juez suplente *or* adjunto. || *Deputy mayor*, teniente (*m.*) de alcalde.
deracinate [di'ræsineit] v. tr. Desarraigar.
derail [di'reil] v. tr. Hacer descarrilar.
— V. intr. Descarrilar.
derailment [—mənt] n. Descarrilamiento, *m.*
derange [di'reindʒ] v. tr. Trastornar el juicio a, enloquecer (to make insane). || Desarreglar (to throw into confusion). || Estropear (to cause to go out of order). || Perturbar, molestar (to annoy).
derangement [—mənt] n. MED. Trastorno (*m.*) mental. || Desorden, *m.*, desarreglo, *m.* (disorder).
derat [di:'ræt] v. tr. Desratizar.
derate [di:'reit] v. tr. Desgravar, reducir los impuestos sobre.
deratization [di:,rætai'zeiʃən] n. Desratización, *f.*
derby ['dɑ:bi] n. U. S. Hongo, *m.* (hat).
Derby ['dɑ:bi] pr. n. GEOGR. Derby. || Derby, *m.* (horse race).
derelict ['derilikt] adj. Abandonado, da.
— N. MAR. Derrelicto, *m.*, pecio, *m.* || FIG. Deshecho, *m.* (worthless thing or person).
dereliction [,deri'likʃən] n. Abandono, *m.* (abandonment). || Descuido, *m.*, negligencia, *f.* (of duty). || MAR. Retirada, *f.* (of the sea).
deride [di'raid] v. tr. Mofarse de, burlarse de.
derision [di'riʒən] n. Mofa, *f.* || Irrisión, *f.* (laughing-stock). || *To hold s.o. in derision*, mofarse de uno, hacer mofa de uno.
derisive [di'raisiv] or **derisory** [di'raisəri] adj. Burlón, ona; mofador, ra (mocking). || Irrisorio, ria (petty, ridiculous).
derivable [di'raivəbl] adj. Derivable.
derivation [,deri'veiʃən] n. Derivación, *f.*
derivative [di'rivətiv] adj. Derivado, da.
— N. CHEM. GRAMM. Derivado, *m.* || MATH. Derivada, *f.* (differential coefficient).
derive [di'raiv] v. tr. Derivar. || Sacar (profit, ideas, etc.).
— V. intr. Derivar, derivarse (to be derived). || Provenir, proceder: *his money derives from the savings he made in Germany*, su dinero procede de lo que ahorró en Alemania.
derm [də:m] or **derma** [—ə] n. ANAT. Dermis, *f.*
dermal [—əl] adj. ANAT. Dérmico, ca.
dermatitis [,də:mə'taitis] n. MED. Dermatitis, *f.*, dermitis, *f.*
dermatologist [,də:mə'tɔlədʒist] n. MED. Dermatólogo, *m.*
dermatology [,də:mə'tɔlədʒi] n. MED. Dermatología, *f.*
dermatosis [,də:mə'təusis] n. MED. Dermatosis, *f.*

— OBSERV. El plural de *dermatosis* es *dermatoses.*

dermic ['də:mik] adj. ANAT. Dérmico, ca.
dermis ['də:mis] n. ANAT. Dermis, *f.*
dermoskeleton [,də:mə'skelitn] n. ANAT. Dermatoesqueleto, *m.*
derogate ['derəgeit] v. intr. *To derogate from*, atentar contra, ir en contra de (rights, liberty), ir contra (one's dignity), rebajarse de (one's rank).
derogation [,derə'geiʃən] n. Menosprecio, *m.* (contempt). || Derogación, *f.* [de una ley] (of a law). || *To the derogation of*, en detrimento de.
derogatory [di'rɔgətəri] adj. Despectivo, va (disparaging). || JUR. Derogatorio, ria. || FIG. *Derogatory to*, que va en contra de (s.o.'s dignity), indigno de (s.o.'s rank).
derrick ['derik] n. Grúa, *f.* (crane). || Torre (*f.*) de perforación, "derrick", *m.* (of an oil well).
derring-do ['deriŋ'du:] n. Valor, *m.* || *Deeds of derring-do*, hazañas, *f. pl.*
dervish ['də:viʃ] n. REL. Derviche, *m.*
desalinate [di:'sælineit] v. tr. Desalar, desalinizar.
desalination [,di:sæli'neiʃən] n. Desalación, *f.*, desalinización, *f.*
desalt [di:'sɔlt] v. tr. Desalar.
desalting [—iŋ] n. Desalazón, *f.*
descale ['di:'skeil] v. tr. Desincrustar.
descaling [—iŋ] n. Desincrustación, *f.*
descant ['deskænt] n. MUS. Contrapunto, *m.* || FIG. *A descant on religion*, una larga conferencia sobre religión.
descant [dis'kænt] v. intr. MUS. Cantar en contrapunto. || FIG. Disertar largamente (to discourse at large).
descend [di'send] v. intr. Descender, bajar (to come or to go down). || ASTR. Ponerse (the sun). || — *To descend from*, descender de. || *To descend on* o *upon*, caer sobre. || *To descend to*, rebajarse a (to lower o.s. to), pasar a (a property).
— V. tr. Descender, bajar: *to descend the stairs*, bajar la escalera.
descendant or **descendent** [di'sendənt] n. Descendiente, *m.* & *f.*
descended [di'sendid] adj. *To be descended from*, descender de. || *Well descended*, de buena familia.
descendible [di'sendibl] adj. JUR. Transmisible (property).
descending [di'sendiŋ] adj. Descendiente, descendente.
descent [di'sent] n. Descenso, *m.*, bajada, *f.* (a going down). || Declive, *m.*, pendiente, *f.* (slope). || Descenso, *m.* (a way down). || Descendencia, *f.* (lineage). || SP. Descenso, *m.* || Incursión, *f.* (raid). || JUR. Transmisión, *f.* || REL. Descendimiento, *m.*: *Descent from the Cross*, Descendimiento de la Cruz. || FIG. Decadencia, *f.* (decline).
describable [dis'kraibəbl] adj. Describible, descriptible.
describe [dis'kraib] v. tr. Describir. || Calificar: *to describe s.o. as intelligent*, calificar a uno de inteligente. || Trazar (a geometrical figure). || *To describe o.s. as an actor*, presentarse como actor.
describing [—iŋ] n. Descripción, *f.*
description [dis'kripʃən] n. Descripción, *f.* (account, explanation): *it answers your description*, corresponde a su descripción. || Clase, *f.*, tipo, *m.* (kind, sort): *toys of every description*, juguetes de todas clases.
descriptive [dis'kriptiv] adj. Descriptivo, va: *descriptive geometry*, *anatomy*, geometría, anatomía descriptiva. || GRAMM. Calificativo, va (adjective).
descry [dis'krai] v. tr. Divisar, columbrar (to see). || Descubrir (to discover).
desecrate ['desikreit] v. tr. REL. Profanar.
desecration [,desi'kreiʃən] n. REL. Profanación, *f.*
desecrator ['desikreitə*] n. REL. Profanador, ra.
desegregate ['di:'segrigeit] v. tr. Suprimir la segregación racial en.
desegregation [,di:sægri'geiʃən] n. Supresión (*f.*) de la segregación racial.
desensitization [,di:sensiti'zeiʃən] n. Insensibilización, *f.*
desensitize ['di:'sensitaiz] v. tr. Insensibilizar.
desert ['dezət] adj. Desierto, ta; desértico, ca.
— N. Desierto, *m.*
desert [di'zə:t] v. tr. Abandonar: *his courage deserted him*, su valor le abandonó. || MIL. Desertar de.
— V. intr. MIL. Desertar: *to desert from the army*, desertar del ejército.
deserter [—ə*] n. Desertor, *m.*
desertion [di'zə:ʃən] n. MIL. Deserción, *f.* || Abandono, *m.* (abandon).

deserts [di zə:tz] pl. n. *To get one's deserts*, tener *or* llevarse su merecido.
deserve [di'zə:v] v. tr. Merecer: *he deserves punishing*, merece castigo; *he deserves to win*, merece ganar. || Ser digno de: *to deserve praise*, ser digno de elogios. || *You'll get what you deserve*, tendrás *or* te llevarás tu merecido.
— V. intr. *To deserve well of*, merecer el reconocimiento de. || *To deserve well of one's country*, hacerse digno de la patria.
deserved [—d] adj. Merecido, da.
deserving [—iŋ] adj. Digno, na: *he is deserving of our esteem*, es digno de nuestro aprecio. || Meritorio, ria (action). || De mérito (person).
déshabillé (U. S. **deshabille**) [ˌdeizæ'bi:ei] n. See DISHABILLE.
desiccant ['desikənt] adj. Desecativo, va.
— N. Desecativo, *m.*
desiccate [desikeit] v. tr. Desecar.
— V. intr. Desecarse.
desiccation [ˌdesi'keiʃən] n. Desecación, *f.*
desiccative [de'sikətiv] adj. Desecativo, va.
— N. Desecativo, *m.*
desiccator ['desikeitə*] n. Desecador, *m.*
desiderative [di'zidərətiv] adj. GRAMM. Desiderativo, va.
desideratum [diˌzidə'reitəm] n. Desiderátum, *m.*

— OBSERV. El plural de *desideratum* es *desiderata*.

design [di'zain] n. Dibujo, *m.* (pattern, drawing). || Bosquejo, *m.* (in painting). || Boceto, *m.* (in sculpture). || Estilo, *m.*, diseño, *m.* (style). || ARCH. Plano, *m.* || Propósito, *m.*, intención, *f.* (intention). || Mala intención, *f.* (bad intention). || Proyecto, *m.* (scheme). || — *By design*, intencionalmente, a propósito. || *To have designs on sth.*, haber puesto sus miras en.
design [di'zain] v. tr. Diseñar (to prepare plans or sketches for). || Dibujar (to draw). || ARTS. Esbozar. || Inventar (to invent). || Crear (to create). || Concebir: *a well designed building*, un edificio bien concebido. || Planear, proyectar (to intend). || Imaginar (to contrive). || Destinar (to destine).
— V. intr. Hacer diseños *or* dibujos.
designate ['dezignit] adj. Designado, da. || Nombrado, da (appointed).
designate ['dezigneit] v. tr. Designar (to name for a duty). || Nombrar (to appoint): *to designate s.o. for a post*, nombrar a alguien para un puesto. || Señalar (to point out). || Denominar (to name).
designation [ˌdezig'neiʃən] n. Designación, *f.* || Nombramiento, *m.* (appointment). || Denominación, *f.* (naming).
designedly [di'zainidli] adv. A propósito.
designer [di'zainə*] n. Diseñador, ra. || Delineante, *m.* (draughtsman). || FIG. Autor, ra. || — *Dress designer*, modista, *m.* || THEATR. *Stage designer*, escenógrafo, *m.*
designing [di'zainiŋ] n. Diseño, *m.* (of a machine). || Creación, *f.* (of a dress).
— Adj. Intrigante. || *A designing old man*, un viejo intrigante.
desilver [di:'silvə*] or **desilverize** [di:'silvəraiz] v. tr. Desplatar.
desinence ['desinəns] n. GRAMM. Desinencia, *f.*
desinential ['desinənʃəl] adj. GRAMM. Desinencial.
desirability [diˌzaiərə'biliti] n. Lo atractivo, lo apetecible. || Conveniencia, *f.* (advisability): *the desirability of a reform*, la conveniencia de una reforma. || Atractivo, *m.* (of a woman).
desirable [di:'zaiərəbl] adj. Deseable. || Conveniente, deseable (proper): *I don't think it desirable to go*, no creo que sea conveniente ir. || Atractivo, va (attractive).
desire [di'zaiə*] n. Deseo, *m.*: *all his desires have been met*, todos sus deseos han sido satisfechos. || Petición, *f.* (request). || Deseo, *m.*, instinto (*m.*) sexual (sexual).
desire [di'zaiə*] v. tr. Desear. || Rogar, pedir: *I desire you to come at three o'clock*, le ruego que venga a las tres. || Querer (to want). || — *It is to be desired that*, es deseable que. || *It leaves much to be desired*, deja mucho que desear.
desirous [di'zaiərəs] adj. Deseoso, sa. || *To be desirous of* o *to*, desear.
desist [di'zist] v. intr. Desistir (*from*, de). || *To desist from smoking*, dejar de fumar.
desistance [di'zistəns] n. Desistimiento, *m.*
desk [desk] n. Pupitre, *m.* (at school). || Mesa (*f.*) de despacho, despacho, *m.*, escritorio, *m.* (in an office). || COMM. Caja, *f.* || REL. Atril, *m.* (lectern). || U. S. Redacción, *f.* (editorial department of a newspaper).
desman ['desmən] n. ZOOL. Desmán, *m.*, ratón (*m.*) almizclero.
desolate ['desəlit] adj. Solitario, ria (lonely). || Deshabitado, da (uninhabited). || Asolado, da; desolado, da (waste). || Desierto, ta (deserted). || Afligido, da; desconsolado, da (disconsolate).
desolate ['desəleit] v. tr. Asolar, arrasar (to lay waste): *the town was desolated by an earthquake*, la ciudad fue asolada por un terremoto. || Despoblar (to depopulate). || Abandonar (to forsake). || Afligir, desconsolar (to distress).
desolating [—iŋ] adj. Desolador, ra.
desolation [ˌdesə'leiʃən] n. Asolamiento, *m.* (destruction). || Desolación, *f.* (barren state). || Aflicción, *f.*, desconsuelo, *m.* (grief). || Desierto, *m.* (desert). || Soledad, *f.* (loneliness).
desoxyribonucleic [de'sɔksi'raibəun'ju:kliik] adj. CHEM. Desoxirribonucleico, ca (acid).
despair [dis'pɛə*] n. Desesperación, *f.*: *to be the despair of*, ser la desesperación de. || *To be in despair*, estar desesperado.
despair [dis'pɛə*] v. intr. Desesperar, desesperarse: *I despair at not hearing from him*, me desespero por no recibir noticias suyas. || *Her life is despaired of*, se ha perdido toda esperanza de salvarle la vida.
despairing [—riŋ] adj. Desesperado, da.
despatch [dis'pætʃ] n./v. tr. See DISPATCH.
despatcher [—ə*] n. Expedidor, ra.
desperado [ˌdespə'rɑ:dəu] n. Forajido, *m.*, bandido, *m.*

— OBSERV. El plural es *desperadoes* o *desperados*.

desperate ['despərit] adj. Desesperado, da. || Apremiante (urgency, need). || Capaz de cualquier cosa (ruthless). || Encarnizado, da (conflict). || Enérgico, ca (resistance). || Muy grave, mortal (wound, illness). || Muy grave, desesperado, da (situation). || Heroico, ca (remedy). || — *Desperate ills call for desperate measures*, a grandes males grandes remedios. || *I am desperate for*, necesito con gran urgencia. || *They are getting desperate*, empiezan a desesperarse.
desperately [—li] adv. Desesperadamente. || Encarnizadamente (to fight). || Locamente: *desperately in love*, locamente enamorado. || — *Desperately ill*, gravemente enfermo, enfermo de gravedad. || *He was desperately afraid*, tenía muchísimo miedo, tenía un miedo espantoso.
desperation [ˌdespə'reiʃən] n. Desesperación, *f.* || *In desperation*, a la desesperada: *they operated on him in desperation*, le operaron a la desesperada; desesperado, da (in despair).
despicable [dis'pikəbl] adj. Despreciable, desdeñable.
despicableness [—nis] n. Bajeza, *f.*, vileza, *f.*
despise [dis'paiz] v. tr. Despreciar, menospreciar, desdeñar.
despite [dis'pait] prep. A pesar de: *despite what he says*, a pesar de lo que dice.
— N. Despecho, *m.* (offended pride). || Odio, *m.* (hatred). || *In despite of*, a pesar de.
despoil [dis'pɔil] v. tr. Despojar: *to despoil s.o. of sth.*, despojar a alguien de algo. || Saquear (to plunder).
despoiler [—ə*] n. Expoliador, ra.
despoilment [—mənt] or **despoliation** [ˌdispɔi'leiʃən] n. Expoliación, *f.* (spoliation). || Saqueo, *m.* (plundering).
despond [dis'pɔnd] v. intr. Desanimarse, descorazonarse, desalentarse.
despondence [dis'pɔndəns] or **despondency** [—i] n. Desánimo, *m.*, desaliento, *m.*, descorazonamiento, *m.*
despondent [dis'pɔndənt] adj. Desanimado, da; desalentado, da; descorazonado, da (disheartened). || Pesimista (pessimistic).
despot ['despɔt] n. Déspota, *m.*: *Nero was a cruel despot*, Nerón fue un déspota cruel; *the child is a real despot*, el niño es un verdadero déspota.
despotic [des'pɔtik] adj. Despótico, ca: *a despotic government, husband*, un gobierno, un marido despótico.
despotically [—əli] adv. Despóticamente.
despotism ['despətizəm] n. Despotismo, *m.*: *enlightened despotism*, el despotismo ilustrado.
despumate ['despjumeit] v. tr. Espumar.
desquamate ['deskwəmeit] v. intr. MED. Descamarse.
desquamation [ˌdeskwə'meiʃən] n. MED. Descamación, *f.*
dessert [di'zə:t] n. Postre, *m.*: *what is there for dessert?*, ¿qué hay de postre?
dessertspoon [—spu:n] n. Cuchara (*f.*) de postre.
destination [ˌdesti'neiʃən] n. Destino, *m.*: *the destination of a ship*, el destino de un barco; *to arrive at* o *to reach one's destination*, llegar a destino.
destine ['destin] v. tr. Destinar (*for, to*, a). || — MAR. *To be destined for*, salir con destino a. || *To be destined to be Prime Minister*, estar llamado a ser Primer Ministro. || *To be destined to fail*, estar condenado al fracaso.
destiny ['destini] n. Destino, *m.*
destitute ['destitju:t] adj. Indigente, desvalido, da; necesitado, da. || — *Destitute of*, desprovisto de. || *The destitute*, los indigentes, los desvalidos, los necesitados. || *To be destitute*, estar en la miseria.
destitution [ˌdesti'tju:ʃən] n. Indigencia, *f.*, miseria, *f.*, desvalimiento, *m.* (poverty). || Falta, *f.*, carencia, *f.* (lack). || Destitución, *f.* (deprivation of office).
destroy [dis'trɔi] v. tr. Destruir (to demolish). || Matar (to kill). || Matar, sacrificar (horse, etc.). || Aniquilar (to annihilate). || FIG. Destruir (reputation, etc.). | Anular (influence, etc.).
destroyable [—əbl] adj. Destructible, destruible.
destroyer [—ə*] n. MAR. Destructor, *m.*
destructible [dis'trʌktəbl] adj. Destructible.
destruction [dis'trʌkʃən] n. Destrucción, *f.* (demolition). || FIG. Ruina, *f.*, perdición, *f.*: *to rush to one's destruction*, correr a la ruina.
destructive [dis'trʌktiv] adj. Destructivo, va; destructor, ra. || Destrozón, ona (child). || Dañino, na (animal). || *Destructive of* o *to*, perjudicial para.
destructiveness [—nis] n. Destructividad, *f.* (tendency). || Poder (*m.*) destructivo *or* de destrucción (power).

destructor [dis'trʌktə*] n. Incinerador (*m.*) *or* quemadero (*m.*) de basuras.
desuetude [di'sjuitju:d] n. Desuso, *m.*: *to fall into desuetude*, caer en desuso.
desultorily ['desəltərili] adv. Sin orden ni concierto.
desultoriness ['desəltərinis] n. Falta (*f.*) de ilación.
desultory ['desəltəri] adj. Inconexo, xa (disconnected). || Poco metódico, ca (work, person, etc.). || Sin orden ni concierto (conversation).
detach [di'tætʃ] v. tr. Separar (*from*, de) [to separate]. || MIL. Destacar.
detachable [—əbl] adj. Separable. || Postizo, za (collar). || Amovible, desmontable (parts of machine).
detached [—t] adj. Independiente (independent): *detached house*, casa independiente. || Suelto, ta: *detached extracts*, trozos sueltos. || Separado, da (separate). || Objetivo, va (objective). || Indiferente, despreocupado, da (unworried). || Desenvuelto, ta (manners). || MIL. Destacado, da. || — *To become detached*, separarse. || *To live detached from the world*, vivir aislado del mundo.
detachment [—mənt] n. Separación, *f.* (separation). || MIL. Destacamento, *m.* || Objetividad, *f.* (objectivity). || Despreocupación, *f.*, despego, *m.*, indiferencia, *f.* (indifference). || MED. Desprendimiento, *m.* (of retina). || Desenganche, *m.* (of trains).
detail ['di:teil] n. Detalle, *m.*, pormenor, *m.*: *in full detail*, con todo detalle, con todos los pormenores. || ARTS. Detalle, *m.* || MIL. Destacamento, *m.* || — *To go into detail*, entrar en detalles. || *To tell sth. in detail*, contrar algo detalladamente *or* con todo detalle.
detail ['di:teil] v. tr. Detallar, pormenorizar (to relate in detail). || Enumerar (to itemize). || MIL. Destacar (*for*, *to*, para).
detain [di'tein] v. tr. Retener (to keep). || JUR. Detener. || — *He was detained at the meeting*, se entretuvo en la reunión. || *To be detained by snow*, retrasarse a causa de la nieve.
detainee [,di:tei'ni:] n. Detenido, da; preso, sa.
detainer [di'teinə*] n. JUR. Toma (*f.*) de posesión (of property). | Orden (*f.*) de detención (of incarceration). | Detención, *f.* (of an object).
detainment [di'teinmənt] n. Detención, *f.*
detect [di'tekt] v. tr. Advertir (to note). || Percibir (to perceive). || Descubrir (to discover). || TECH. Detectar: *to detect enemy aircraft*, detectar aviones enemigos.
detectable [—əbl] adj. Perceptible.
detecting [—iŋ] adj. Detector, ra.
detection [di'tekʃən] n. Descubrimiento, *m.* || Detección, *f.*: *mine detection*, detección de minas.
detective [di'tektiv] n. Detective, *m.*
detective story [—,stɔ:ri] n. Novela (*f.*) policiaca.
detector [di'tektə*] n. Detector, *m.*: *lie detector*, detector de mentiras; *mine detector*, detector de minas. || Descubridor, *m.*
detent [di'tent] n. TECH. Escape, *m.* (of a watch). | Trinquete, *m.* (of a machine).
détente [deitɑ̃nt] n. Relajación (*f.*) de la tensión [entre países].
detention [di'tenʃən] n. Detención, *f.*, arresto, *m.* || MIL. Arresto, *m.* || *Detention barracks*, calabozo, *m. sing.*
deter [di'tə*] v. tr. Disuadir (to dissuade): *he deterred me from doing it*, me disuadió de hacerlo. || Desanimar (to dishearten): *don't let the rain deter you*, que no te desanime la lluvia. || *Your threats will not deter me*, no me asustarás *or* no me harás desistir con amenazas.
deterge [di'tə:dʒ] v. tr. Deterger.
detergent [—ənt] adj. Detergente.
— N. Detergente, *m.*
deteriorate [di'tiəriəreit] v. tr. Empeorar (to make worse). || Deteriorar (to wear out). || Depreciar, desvalorizar (to lower the value of).
— V. intr. Empeorar (to become worse): *the situation is deteriorating*, la situación está empeorando. || Deteriorarse (to wear out). || Degenerar (race).
deterioration [di,tiəriə'reiʃən] n. Empeoramiento, *m.* (worsening). || Deterioro, *m.* (wearing out). || Degeneración, *f.* (of race). || Decadencia, *f.* (decline).
determent [di'tə:mənt] n. Disuasión, *f.* || *For the determent of*, para disuadir a, para asustar a.
determinable [di'tə:minəbl] adj. Determinable.
determinant [di'tə:minənt] adj. Determinante.
— N. MATH. Determinante, *m.* || Factor (*m.*) *or* elemento determinante (determining factor).
determinate [di'tə:minit] adj. Determinado, da.
determination [di,tə:mi'neiʃən] n. Determinación, *f.*, resolución, *f.*, decisión, *f.* (firmness of purpose). || Determinación, *f.*, decisión, *f.* (decision). || Fijación, *f.* (of a date, etc.). || JUR. Resolución, *f.*, fallo, *m.* (decision). | Fijación, *f.* (of penalty). | Rescisión, *f.*, anulación, *f.* (of a contract). || Determinación, *f.* (determining). || *In his determination to win*, estando resuelto a ganar.
determinative [di'tə:minətiv] adj. Determinante. || GRAMM. Determinativo, va: *determinative adjective*, adjetivo determinativo.
— N. GRAMM. Determinativo, *m.*
determine [di'tə:min] v. tr. Determinar (to fix): *to determine the causes of an accident*, determinar las causas de un accidente: *that determined me to try*, eso me determinó a intentar. || Causar, provocar (to cause). || Resolver (to settle). || Fijar, determinar (date). || Definir, determinar (limits). || Decidir (to decide): *to determine to do sth.*, decidir hacer algo. || JUR. Rescindir, anular (a contract). || *To be determined by*, depender de: *his answer will be determined by what happens today*, su respuesta depende de lo que pase hoy.
— V. intr. JUR. Expirar. || *To determine on*, decidirse por.
determined [—d] adj. Decidido, da; resuelto, ta: *a determined person*, una persona decidida. || Determinado, da (date, price). || *To be determined to do sth.*, estar decidido *or* resuelto a hacer algo.
determining [—iŋ] adj. Decisivo, va; determinante.
determinism [di'tə:minizəm] n. PHIL. Determinismo, *m.*
determinist [di'tə:minist] adj./n. PHIL. Determinista, *m.* & *f.*
deterministic [di,tə:mi'nistik] adj. Determinista.
deterrence [di'terəns] n. Disuasión, *f.*
deterrent [di'terənt] adj. Disuasivo, va.
— N. Freno, *m.* (obstacle). || Fuerza (*f.*) de disuasión, fuerza (*f.*) disuasoria (armaments). || *To act as a deterrent to*, disuadir.
detersion [di'tə:ʃən] n. Detersión, *f.*
detersive [di'tə:siv] adj. Detergente, detersivo, va.
— N. Detergente, *m.*
detest [di'test] v. tr. Detestar, odiar: *to detest a person, travelling*, detestar a una persona, los viajes.
detestable [di'testəbl] adj. Detestable, odioso, sa.
detestation [,di:tes'teiʃən] n. Odio, *m.*, aborrecimiento, *m.* || *To hold in detestation*, odiar, aborrecer.
dethrone [di'θrəun] v. tr. Destronar.
dethronement [—mənt] n. Destronamiento, *m.*
detonate ['detəneit] v. intr. Detonar.
— V. tr. Hacer detonar.
detonating [—iŋ] adj. Detonante. || *Detonating fuse*, detonador, *m.*, fulminante, *m.*
detonation [,detə'neiʃən] n. Detonación, *f.*
detonator [,detəneitə*] n. Detonador, *m.*, fulminante, *m.*
detour ['di:tuə*] n. Desvío, *m.*, desviación, *f.* (deviation). || Vuelta, *f.*, rodeo, *m.* (to avoid some obstacle): *he made a detour*, dio un rodeo.
detoxicate [di:'tɔksikeit] or **detoxify** [di:'tɔksifai] v. tr. Desintoxicar.
detract [di'trækt] v. intr. *To detract from*, quitar: *to detract from s.o.'s merit*, quitarle mérito a alguien; empañar, deslucir (s.o.'s reputation).
— V. tr. Disminuir, reducir (to reduce). || Quitar (to take away). || Denigrar (to disparage).
detraction [di'trækʃən] n. Denigración, *f.*
detractor [di'træktə*] n. Detractor, ra.
detrain [di:,trein] v. intr. Bajarse del tren.
— V. tr. Desembarcar de un tren (troops, etc.).
detriment ['detrimənt] n. Detrimento, *m.*, perjuicio, *m.*: *to the detriment of*, en detrimento de; *without detriment to*, sin causar detrimento *or* perjuicio a.
detrimental [,detri'mentl] adj. Perjudicial (*to*, a, para).
detritus [di'traitəs] n. GEOL. Detrito, *m.*
detruncate [di:'trʌŋkeit] v. tr. Truncar.
deuce [dju:s] n. Dos, *m.* (cards, dice). || Cuarenta iguales, *m. pl.* (in tennis). || FIG. Demonio, *m.*, diablo, *m.*: *what the deuce is that?*, ¿qué diablos es esto?, ¿qué demonios es esto? || — FAM. *A deuce of a noise*, un ruido tremendo, un ruido de mil demonios. | *To play the deuce with*, estropear (sth.), arruinar (s.o.'s health).
— Interj. ¡Diablos!
deuced [—t] adj. FAM. De mil demonios, tremendo, da (tremendous). | Maldito, ta (damned).
— Adv. FAM. Terriblemente, sumamente (very).
deuterium [dju:'tiəriəm] n. CHEM. Deuterio, *m.*
deuteron ['dju:tərɔn] n. PHYS. Deuterón, *m.*
Deuteronomy [,dju:tə'rɔnəmi] pr. n. REL. Deuteronomio, *m.*
devaluate [di:'væljueit] v. tr. Devaluar, desvalorizar.
devaluation [,di:vælju'eiʃən] n. Devaluación, *f.*, desvalorización, *f.*
devalue ['di:'vælju:] v. tr. Devaluar, desvalorizar.
devastate ['devəsteit] v. tr. Devastar, asolar (to ravage). || FIG. *I was devastated*, me quedé anonadado.
devastating [—iŋ] adj. Devastador, ra. || Arrollador, ra: *the devastating force of the wind*, la fuerza arrolladora del viento. || Entristecedor, ra; desconsolador, ra: *devastating news*, noticias entristecedoras. || Aplastante, abrumador, ra (argument).
devastation [,devəs'teiʃən] n. Devastación, *f.*
devastator ['devəsteitə*] n. Devastador, ra.
develop [di'veləp] v. tr. Desarrollar (to expand): *to develop one's body, industry*, desarrollar el cuerpo, la industria. || Hacer desarrollar: *the rain and sun develop the seed*, la lluvia y el sol hacen desarrollar la semilla. || Echar (to begin to have). || Aprovechar (resources). || Urbanizar (land). || Explotar (a business, mine, etc.). || Fomentar (to promote). || Perfeccionar (process). || Realizar (a new technique). || Empezar a tener (difficulties). || Adquirir, tomar, coger (taste, hatred). || Contraer, coger (to catch an illness). || Incubar: *I think my child is developing measles*, creo que mi hijo está incubando el sarampión. || Contraer

(a habit). || Mostrar (a talent). || Manifestar (a tendency). || MIL. Desplegar (troops). || PHOT. Revelar. || MATH. Desarrollar. || MUS. Desarrollar. || — *He developed a pain in his leg this morning*, le empezó a doler la pierna esta mañana. || *To develop a speed of...*, desarrollar una velocidad de...
— V. intr. Desarrollarse (mind, body, species, to expand, etc.): *this country's industry has developed a lot*, la industria de este país se ha desarrollado mucho. || Producirse (to arise). || Aparecer (to appear): *a cloud has developed*, ha aparecido una nube. || Aumentar, crecer (interest, hatred, taste, etc.). || Ir: *how is the work developing?*, ¿cómo va el trabajo?

developer [—ə*] n. PHOT. Revelador, *m.*

developing [—iŋ] adj. En [vías de] desarrollo: *developing countries*, países en vías de desarrollo.
— N. Desarrollo, *m.*

development [—mənt] n. Desarrollo, *m.* (expansion, evolution): *the development of a plant, of an industry*, el desarrollo de una planta, de una industria; *child at the most rapid stage of development*, niño en pleno desarrollo. || Evolución, *f.*: *the development of the situation*, la evolución de la situación. || Tendencia, *f.* (tendency). || Acontecimiento, *m.*, hecho, *m.* (event). || Cambio, *m.* (change). || Explotación, *f.*, aprovechamiento, *m.* (of resources). || Urbanización, *f.* (of towns, cities). || Fomento, *m.* (promotion). || Progreso, *m.* (progress). || PHOT. Revelado, *m.* || MIL. Despliegue, *m.* (of troops). || MUS. MATH. Desarrollo, *m.* || — *Any developments?*, ¿hay algo nuevo? || *Development area*, polo (*m.*) de desarrollo. || *Development plan*, plan (*m.*) de desarrollo. || *His works represent a new development in literature*, sus obras señalan una nueva tendencia en literatura. || *New developments in medecine enable us to cure tuberculosis*, los últimos descubrimientos de la medicina nos permiten curar la tuberculosis.

developmental [di,veləp'mentl] adj. De desarrollo (project, etc.). || Para el desarrollo (aid, etc.). || Experimental. || Del desarrollo (disease).

deviate ['di:vieit] n. U. S. Invertido (*m.*) sexual. || Extravagante, *m.* & *f.*

deviate ['di:vieit] v. intr. Desviarse.
— V. tr. Desviar.

deviation [,di:vi'eiʃən] n. Desviación, *f.*: *deviation of light, of a magnetic needle*, desviación de la luz, de la aguja imantada. || Alejamiento, *m.* (from the truth). || MATH. Desviación, *f.* || Inversión, *f.* (sexual).

deviationism [,di:vi'eiʃənizəm] n. Desviacionismo, *m.*

deviationist [,di:vi'eiʃənist] n. Desviacionista, *m.* & *f.*

device [di'vais] n. FIG. Ardid, *m.*, estratagema, *f.* (scheme). || Dispositivo, *m.*, aparato, *m.* (mechanical contrivance). || Mecanismo, *m.* || Ingenio, *m.*, artefacto, *m.*: *nuclear device*, ingenio nuclear. || HERALD. Emblema, *m.* | Lema, *m.* (motto). || FAM. *To leave s.o. to his own devices*, dejar a uno que se las arregle solo.

devil ['devl] n. Diablo, *m.*, demonio, *m.* (evil spirit). || FIG. Diablo, *m.* || Aprendiz, *m.*: *printer's devil*, aprendiz de imprenta. || Secretario, *m.* (lawyer's). || Negro, *m.* (writer's). || — FIG. *A devil of a problem*, un problema dificilísmo *or* diabólico *or* de todos los diablos. | *A devil of a mess*, un lío tremendo. | *A devil of a noise*, un ruido de mil demonios, un ruido infernal. | *A poor devil*, un pobre diablo. | *A she-devil*, una arpía. | *Better the devil we know* (*than the devil we don't know*), más vale malo conocido que bueno por conocer. | *Between the devil and the deep blue sea*, entre la espada y la pared. | *Devil a one!*, ¡ni uno! || FAM. *Devil's bones*, dados, *m. pl.* | *Devil's books*, cartas, *f.*, naipes, *m.* || FIG. *Go to the devil!*, ¡vete al diablo! | *It's the devil*, es dificilísmo. | *He is a bit of a devil*, es un conquistador (a man), es un diablillo (child). | *How the devil?*, ¿cómo demonios?, ¿cómo diablos? | *Like the devil*, como llevado por el diablo (to go), muchísimo (to work, to study). | *Little devil*, demonio, diablillo. | *Talk of the devil!*, hablando del rey de Roma por la puerta asoma. || *The Devil*, El Diablo, El Demonio. || FIG. *The devil!*, ¡qué diablos! | *The devil finds work for idle hands*, cuando el diablo no tiene nada que hacer con el rabo mata moscas. | *The devil is not so black as he is painted*, el diablo no es tan feo como lo pintan. || *The devil on two sticks*, el diablo cojuelo. || FIG. *The devil's advocate*, el abogado del diablo. || FAM. *The devil take it!*, ¡al diablo! | *There'll be the devil to pay!*, ¡la vamos a pagar! || FIG. *To be a real devil*, ser el mismísimo demonio. | *To be possessed of the devil*, tener el diablo en el cuerpo, ser de la piel del diablo, estar poseído por el demonio. | *To do it for the devil of it*, hacerlo porque le da a uno la gana. | *To give the devil his due*, ser justo. | *To play the devil with*, arruinar, estropear. | *To raise the devil*, armarla, armar un escándalo. | *To run like the devil*, correr como un descosido. | *To send to the devil*, enviar al diablo, mandar a paseo. | *To work like the devil*, trabajar como un negro. | *We had the devil of a job* (*to*), nos costó muchísimo trabajo. | *What the devil...?*, ¿qué diablos...?, ¿qué demonios...?

devil ['devil] v. tr. CULIN. Sazonar con mucho picante. || U. S. Molestar, fastidiar (to annoy).
— V. intr. Trabajar de aprendiz *or* de secretario *or* de negro.

devilfish [—fiʃ] n. ZOOL. Pulpo, *m.* (octopus). | Mantarraya, *f.* (ray).

devilish [—iʃ] adj. Diabólico, ca.
— Adv. Sumamente, terriblemente.

devilishly [—iʃli] adv. REL. Diabólicamente. || FAM. Terriblemente, sumamente.

devilishness [—iʃnis] n. Carácter (*m.*) diabólico.

devilism [—izəm] n. Satanismo, *m.*

devil-may-care [—mei'keə*] adj. Despreocupado, da (carefree). || Temerario, ria (rash).

devilment [—mənt] n. Diablura, *f.* (mischief). || Maldad, *f.* (wickedness). || FIG. *To be full of devilment*, tener el diablo en el cuerpo, ser de la piel del diablo.

devilry [—ri] n. Diablura, *f.* (mischief). || Maldad, *f.* (wickedness). || Magia (*f.*) negra (black magic). || Osadía, *f.*, atrevimiento, *m.* (daring).

deviltry [—tri] n. See DEVILRY.

devious ['di:vjəs] adj. Sinuoso, sa; tortuoso, sa (road). || Tortuoso, sa (person). || Poco limpio, pia (means).

deviousness [—nis] n. Tortuosidad, *f.*

devirginate [di:'və:dʒineit] v. tr. Desvirgar.

devisable [di'vaizəbl] adj. Concebible, imaginable.

devise [di'vais] n. JUR. Disposiciones (*f. pl.*) testamentarias (clause). | Legado, *m.* (gift).

devise [di'vaiz] v. tr. Concebir, idear, imaginar (a plan, etc.). || Inventar (to invent). || Tramar, maquinar (to plot). || JUR. Legar.

devisee [,devi'zi:] n. JUR. Legatario, ria.

deviser [di'vaizə*] n. Inventor, ra; autor, ra.

devisor [,devi'zɔ:*] n. JUR. Testador, ra.

devitalize [di:'vaitəlaiz] v. tr. Debilitar. || Desvitalizar (a tooth).

devitrification [di:,vitrifi'keiʃən] n. Desvitrificación, *f.*

devitrify [di:'vitrifai] v. tr. Desvitrificar.

devoid [di'vɔid] adj. *Devoid of*, desprovisto de, sin. || *Devoid of cares*, libre de cuidados.

devolution [,di:və'lu:ʃən] n. JUR. Transmisión, *f.* (inheritance). || BIOL. Degeneración, *f.* || Delegación, *f.* (of powers).

devolve [di'vɔlv] v. tr. Transmitir. || Delegar (powers).
— V. intr. Recaer (*on, to, upon*, sobre): *the responsibility devolved upon his successor*, la responsabilidad recayó sobre su sucesor. || Incumbir, corresponder (*upon*, a) [to be incumbent upon].

Devonian [de'vəunjən] adj. Devoniano, na; devónico, ca. || *The Devonian*, el devónico, el devoniano.

devote [di'vəut] v. tr. Dedicar: *to devote one's life to helping the poor*, dedicar su vida a ayudar a los pobres. || — *To be devoted to s.o.*, querer mucho a uno. || *To devote o.s. to*, dedicarse a.

devoted [—id] adj. Leal, fiel (loyal). || Devoto, ta (devout). ||Dedicado, da (dedicated).

devotedly [—idli] adv. Con devoción.

devotedness [—idnis] n. Devoción, *f.* (devotion). || Dedicación, *f.* (dedication).

devotee [,devəu'ti:] Partidario, ria; devoto, ta (supporter). || Devoto, ta (devout person).

devotion [di'vəuʃən] n. Devoción, *f.*, afecto, *m.* (affection). || Lealtad, *f.* (loyalty). || Dedicación, *f.* (to studies, etc.). || Afición, *f.* (addiction). || Devoción, *f.*, piedad, *f.*, fervor, *m.* (devoutness). || — Pl. REL. Oraciones, *f.* || *Book of devotions*, devocionario, *m.*

devotional [—l] adj. Piadoso, sa; devoto, ta (attitude, soul). || Piadoso, sa (articles).

devotionalist [—list] n. Beato, ta; santurrón, ona.

devour [di'vauə*] v. tr. Devorar. || FIG. Devorar: *he devoured the book in one evening*, devoró el libro en una noche; *the flames devoured the building*, las llamas devoraron el edificio. || *To be devoured with envy*, morirse de envidia, carcomerse de envidia.

devouring [—riŋ] adj. Devorador, ra.

devouringly [—riŋli] adv. Ávidamente.

devout [di'vaut] adj. Devoto, ta (very religious). || Sincero, ra (earnest).

devoutly [—li] adv. Con devoción.

devoutness [—nis] n. Devoción, *f.*

dew [dju:] n. Rocío, *m.* (morning damp). || FIG. Flor, *f.* (of youth). | Gotas, *f. pl.* (drops).

dew [dju:] v. intr. Rociar.
— V. tr. Bañar de rocío.

dewberry [—beri] n. BOT. Zarzamora, *f.*

dewclaw [—klɔ:] n. Garra, *f.* (of dogs, etc.).

dewdrop [—drɔp] n. Gota (*f.*) de rocío.

dewfall [—fɔ:l] n. Relente, *m.* (evening dew). || Caída (*f.*) del rocío.

dewlap [—læp] n. Papada, *f.* (of animals).

dew point [—pɔint] n. Punto (*m.*) de condensación.

dewy ['dju:i] adj. Rociado, da; cubierto de rocío. || Húmedo, da (wet). || FIG. Puro, ra; virginal.

dewy-eyed [—áid] adj. Ingenuo, nua.

dexter ['dekstə*] adj. A mano derecha. || HERALD. Diestro, tra.

dexterity [deks'teriti] n. Destreza, *f.*, habilidad, *f.*

dexterous ['dekstərəs] adj. Diestro, tra; hábil.

dextrin ['dekstrin] n. CHEM. Dextrina, *f.*

dextrorotary [,dekstrəu'rəutəri] adj. U. S. PHYS. Dextrógiro, ra.

dextrorotatory [,dekstrəu'rəutətəri] adj. PHYS. Dextrógiro, ra.

dextrorse [deks'trɔ:s] adj. Dextrorso, sa.

dextrose ['dekstrəus] n. Dextrosa, *f.*

dextrous ['dekstrəs] adj. Diestro, tra; hábil.

dey [dei] n. Dey, *m.* (prince of Algiers).

diabetes [ˌdaiəˈbi:ti:z] n. MED. Diabetes, *f.*
diabetic [ˌdaiəˈbetik] adj./n. MED. Diabético, ca.
diabolic [ˌdaiəˈbɔlik] or **diabolical** [—əl] adj. Diabólico, ca.
diabolism [daiˈæbəlizəm] n. Brujería, *f.* (sorcery). || Magia (*f.*) negra (black magic). || Satanismo, *m.*
diabolo [diˈɑ:bələu] n. Diábolo, *m.* (toy).
diacid [daiˈasid] adj. CHEM. Biácido, da.
diaconal [daiˈækənl] adj. REL. Diaconal.
diaconate [daiˈækənit] n. REL. Diaconato, *m.*, diaconado, *m.*
diacritic [ˌdaiəˈkritik] adj. Diacrítico, ca.
— N. Signo (*m.*) diacrítico.
diacritical [—əl] adj. Diacrítico, ca.
diad [ˈdaiæd] n. Pareja, *f.* (couple).
diadem [ˈdaiədem] n. Diadema, *f.*
diaeresis [daiˈiərisis] n. GRAMM. Diéresis, *f.*
— OBSERV. El plural de *diaeresis* es *diaereses.*
diagnose [ˈdaiəgnəuz] v. tr. MED. Diagnosticar.
— V. intr. MED. Hacer un diagnóstico.
diagnosis [ˌdaiəgˈnəusis] n. MED. Diagnóstico, *m.* (of a disease). | Diagnosis, *f. inv.* (science).
— OBSERV. El plural de la palabra inglesa es *diagnoses.*
diagnostic [ˌdaiəgˈnɔstik] adj. MED. Diagnóstico, ca.
— N. MED. Síntoma, *m.* (symptom). | Diagnosis, *f. inv.* (science). | Diagnóstico, *m.* (statement).
diagonal [daiˈægənəl] adj. Diagonal.
— N. Diagonal, *f.*
diagonally [—i] adv. En diagonal, diagonalmente.
diagram [ˈdaiəgræm] n. Diagrama, *m.* (to explain a phenomenon). || Gráfico, *m.* (chart). || Esquema, *m.* (sketch). || MATH. Figura, *f.*
diagram [ˈdaiəgræm] v. tr. Representar por un diagrama *or* por un gráfico. || Esquematizar.
diagrammatic [ˌdaiəgrəˈmætik] adj. Esquemático, ca.
dial [ˈdaiəl] n. Esfera, *f.* (of a clock). || Esfera, *f.*, dial, *m.* (of radio). || Botón (*m.*) selector. || Cuadrante, *m.* (of a sundial). || Reloj (*m.*) de sol (sundial). || Disco, *m.* (of a telephone). || Limbo, *m.* (of measuring instruments). || FAM. Cara, *f.*, jeta, *f.* (face).
dial [ˈdaiəl] v. tr. Marcar [un número]. || Sintonizar (the radio).
— V. intr. Marcar [un número].
dialect [ˈdaiəlekt] n. Dialecto, *m.*
dialectal [ˌdaiəˈlektl] adj. Dialectal.
dialectalism [ˌdaiəˈlektəlizəm] n. Dialectalismo, *m.*
dialectic [ˌdaiəˈlektik] adj. PHIL. Dialéctico, ca.
— N. PHIL. Dialéctica, *f.*
dialectical [—əl] adj. PHIL. Dialéctico, ca.
dialectician [ˌdaiəlekˈtiʃən] n. PHIL. Dialéctico, ca.
dialectics [ˌdaiəˈlektiks] n. Dialéctica, *f.*
dialectology [ˌdaiəlekˈtɔlədʒi] n. Dialectología, *f.*
dialling tone [ˈdaiəliŋ-təun] n. Señal (*f.*) para marcar (of telephone).
dialog [ˈdaiəlɔg] n. U. S. Diálogo, *m.*
dialogist [daiˈælədʒist] n. Dialoguista, *m.* & *f.* (dialogue writer). || Interlocutor, ra (speaker).
dialogue [ˈdaiəlɔg] n. Diálogo, *m.* || *Dialogue writer*, dialoguista, *m.* & *f.*
dialogue [ˈdaiəlɔg] or **dialogize** [ˈdaiəlɔgaiz] v. intr. Dialogar.
dial tone [ˈdaiəl-təun] n. U. S. Señal (*f.*) para marcar (of telephone).
dialysis [daiˈælisis] n. CHEM. Diálisis, *f.*
dialyze [ˈdaiəlaiz] v. tr. CHEM. Dializar.
diamagnetism [ˌdaiəˈmægnitizəm] n. ELECTR. Diamagnetismo, *m.*
diamantiferous [daiəmənˈtifərəs] adj. Diamantífero, ra.
diameter [daiˈæmitə*] n. MATH. Diámetro, *m.*
diametral [daiˈæmitrəl] or **diametric** [ˌdaiəˈmetrik] or **diametrical** [—əl] adj. MATH. Diametral.
diametrically [—əli] adv. Diametralmente.
diamond [ˈdaiəmənd] n. Diamante, *m.* (stone): *rough diamond*, diamante en bruto. || Oro, *m.* (in Spanish cards), diamante, *m.* (in standard cards). || MATH. Rombo, *m.* || Cortavidrios, *m. inv.* (glass cutter). || Aguja, *f.*, diamante, *m.* (of record players). || U. S. SP. Campo (*m.*) de béisbol. || PRINT. Tipo (*m.*) muy pequeño.
— Adj. Diamantado, da (like a diamond). || Diamantífero, ra (containing diamond): *diamond field*, región diamantífera. || De diamante (made of diamond). || MATH. Rombal. || Diamantino, na (sparkling). || *Diamond wedding*, bodas (*f. pl.*) de diamante.
diamond [ˈdaiəmənd] v. tr. Adornar con diamantes.
diamond-bearing [—ˌbɛəriŋ] adj. Diamantífero, ra.
diamond cutter [—ˌkʌtə*] n. Diamantista, *m.*
diamond-shaped [—ʃeipt] adj. Romboidal.
diamond-yielding [—ˌji:ldiŋ] adv. Diamantífero, ra.
diapason [ˌdaiəˈpeisn] n. MUS. Diapasón, *m.* (of an organ, of pitch, tuning fork). | Crescendo (*m.*) armonioso (of a choir). | Armonía, *f.* (harmony).
diaper [ˈdaiəpə*] n. ARCH. Motivo (*m.*) romboidal *or* geométrico. || Tela (*f.*) bordada *or* adamascada (linen). || MED. Paño (*m.*) higiénico (sanitary towel). || U. S. Pañal, *m.* (for babies). || U. S. *Diaper rash*, sarpullido, *m.* (inflammation).
diaper [ˈdaiəpə*] v. tr. U. S. Poner el pañal a (a baby).
diaphaneity [ˌdaiəfəˈniiti] or **diaphanousness** [daiˈæfənəsnis] n. Diafanidad, *f.*
diaphanous [daiˈæfənəs] adj. Diáfano, na (filmy).

diaphragm [ˈdaiəfræm] n. Diafragma, *m.*
diaphragm [ˈdaiəfræm] v. tr. Diafragmar.
diaphragmatic [ˌdaiəfrægˈmætik] adj. Diafragmático, ca.
diarchy [ˈdaiɑ:ki] n. Diarquía, *f.*
diarist [ˈdaiərist] n. Diarista, *m.* & *f.*
diarrhea or **diarrhoea** [ˌdaiəˈriə] n. MED. Diarrea, *f.*
diary [ˈdaiəri] n. Diario, *m.* (of personal experiences). || Agenda, *f.* (for appointments, etc.).
Diaspora [daiˈæspərə] n. Diáspora, *f.*
diastase [ˈdaiəsteis] n. BIOL. Diastasa, *f.*
diastole [daiˈæstəli] n. ANAT. GRAMM. Diástole, *f.*
diastolic [daiəˈstɔlik] adj. ANAT. Diastólico, ca.
diathermy [ˈdaiəˌθə:mi] n. MED. Diatermia, *f.*
diathesis [daiˈæθəsis] n. Diátesis, *f.*
— OBSERV. El plural de *diathesis* es *diatheses.*
diatomic [ˌdaiəˈtɔmik] adj. CHEM. Diatómico, ca (with two atoms). | Bivalente (bivalent).
diatonic [ˌdaiəˈtɔnik] adj. MUS. Diatónico, ca: *diatonic scale*, escala diatónica.
diatribe [ˈdaiətraib] n. Diatriba, *f.*: *to pronounce a diatribe*, lanzar una diatriba.
diazo [daiˈæzəu] adj. CHEM. Diazoico, ca; *diazo compounds*, compuestos diazoicos.
dibasic [daiˈbeisik] adj. CHEM. Dibásico, ca.
dibber [ˈdibə*] or **dibble** [ˈdibl] n. Plantador, *m.*, almocafre, *m.*
dibble [ˈdibl] v. intr. Plantar con plantador *or* almocafre.
dibs [dibz] pl. n. Tabas, *f.* (game). || FAM. Parné, *m. sing.* (money).
dice [dais] pl. n. Dados, *m.* || — *Dice box*, cubilete (*m.*) de dados. || FAM. *No dice*, no hay nada que hacer, ni hablar. || *To load the dice*, cargar los dados.
dice [dais] v. intr. Jugar a los dados. || FIG. *To dice with death*, jugar con la muerte.
— V. tr. Cortar en cuadritos. || *To dice away a fortune*, perder una fortuna jugando a los dados.
dicey [ˈdaisi] adj. Peligroso, sa (dangerous). || Incierto, ta; dudoso, sa (uncertain).
dichloride [daiˈklɔ:raid] n. CHEM. Bicloruro, *m.*
dichotomize [daiˈkɔtəmaiz] v. tr. Dividir en dos.
— V. intr. Dividirse en dos. || Formar una dicotomía, *f.*
dichotomy [daiˈkɔtəmi] n. Dicotomía, *f.*
dichroism [ˈdaikrəuizəm] n. Dicroísmo, *m.*
dichromate [ˈdaiˈkrəumeit] n. CHEM. Bicromato, *m.*
dichromatic [ˈdaikrəˈmætik] adj. Dicromático, ca.
dichromatism [daiˈkrəumætizəm] n. Dicromatismo, *m.*
dick [dik] n. POP. Polla, *f.* (penis). || U. S. POP. Sabueso, *m.*, detective, *m.*
Dick [dik] pr. n. FAM. Ricardo, *m.* [diminutivo de Richard].
dickens [ˈdikinz] n. FAM. Diablo, *m.* || *What the dickens...?*, ¿qué diablos...?, ¿qué demonios...?
dicker [ˈdikə*] n. COMM. Decena, *f.* || U. S. Regateo, *m.* (bargaining).
dicker [ˈdikə*] v. intr. U. S. Regatear (to bargain).
dicky or **dickey** [ˈdiki] n. Pechera (*f.*) postiza (on shirt). || Babero, *m.* (bib, pinafore). || AUT. Spider, *m.* || ZOOL. Burrito, *m.* (ass). | Pajarito, *m.* (bird).
— Adj. FAM. Debilucho, cha (person). | Defectuoso, sa (thing).
dicotyledon [ˈdaiˌkɔtiˈli:dən] n. BOT. Dicotiledónea, *f.*
dicotyledoneae [daiˌkɔtiliˈdəuni:i] pl. n. BOT. Dicotiledóneas, *f.*
dicotyledonous [daikɔtiˈli:dənəs] adj. BOT. Dicotiledóneo, a.
dictaphone [ˈdiktəfəun] n. Dictáfono, *m.*
dictate [ˈdikteit] n. Mandato, *m.*, orden, *f.* (authoritative command). || Dictado, *m.*: *the dictates of conscience*, los dictados de la conciencia.
dictate [ˈdikteit] v. tr. Dictar (to say aloud). || Mandar, ordenar (to order). || FIG. Inspirar, dictar. || *To dictate terms*, imponer condiciones.
— V. intr. Mandar. || Dictar (to a secretary). || *I won't be dictated to*, a mí no me manda nadie.
dictation [dikˈteiʃən] n. Dictado, *m.*: *to take dictation*, escribir al dictado; *musical dictation*, dictado musical. || Mandato, *m.*, orden, *f.* (dictate).
dictator [dikˈteitə*] n. Dictador, *m.*
dictatorial [ˌdiktəˈtɔ:riəl] adj. Dictatorial: *dictatorial powers*, poderes dictatoriales.
dictatorship [dikˈteitəːʃip] n. Dictadura, *f.*: *dictatorship of the proletariat*, dictadura del proletariado.
diction [ˈdikʃən] n. Dicción, *f.* (enunciation). || Estilo, *m.*, lenguaje, *m.* (choice of words).
dictionary [ˈdikʃənəri] n. Diccionario, *m.* || FIG. *Walking o living dictionary*, enciclopedia (*f.*) ambulante.
dictum [ˈdiktəm] n. Máxima, *f.*, sentencia, *f.* (maxim). || Dicho, *m.* (saying). || Afirmación, *f.*, declaración, *f.* (statement). || JUR. Dictamen, *m.*
— OBSERV. El plural de *dictum* es *dicta* o *dictums.*
did [did] pret. See DO.
didactic [diˈdæktik] adj. Didáctico, ca.
didacticism [diˈdæktisizəm] n. Didáctica, *f.*
didactics [diˈdæktiks] n. Didáctica, *f.*
didapper [ˈdaidæpə*] n. Somorgujo, *m.* (bird).
diddle [ˈdidl] v. tr. FAM. Timar, estafar (to swindle): *she diddled me out of one hundred pounds*, me timó cien libras. || U. S. FAM. Menear (to move). || U. S. *To diddle away*, perder (time).
diddler [—ə*] n. FAM. Timador, ra; estafador, ra.

didn't [ˈdidnt] n. Contraction of *did not.*
dido [ˈdaidəu] n. U. S. FAM. Travesura, *f.* (prank).
— OBSERV. El plural es *didoes* o *didos.*
die [dai] n. Dado, *m.* (cube used in playing dice). || ARCH. Dado, *m.* (pedestal). || CULIN. Cuadrito, *m.* || TECH. Matriz, *f.* (for shaping). | Troquel, *m.* (for minting). | Hilera, *f.* (for drawing wire). | Terraja, *f.* (for screwing). | Punzón, *m.* (for hand punching). || — FIG. *As straight as a die,* más derecho que una vela (not bent), de una perfecta honradez (honest). | *The die is cast,* la suerte está echada.
— OBSERV. El plural de *die,* cuando significa "dado para jugar" o "cuadrito" es *dice.* En los demás casos es regular (*dies*).
die [dai] v. intr. Morir, morirse: *he died of cancer,* murió de cáncer; *he died a hero,* murió como un héroe; *the word died on his lips,* la palabra murió en sus labios. || Extinguirse (light). || Desaparecer (to disappear). || Calarse, pararse (motor). || — *His secret died with him,* se llevó su secreto a la tumba. || *I am dying!,* ¡me muero! || *I nearly died of shame!,* ¡me morí de vergüenza! || *Never say die!,* no hay que darse por vencido, mientras hay vida hay esperanza. || *Old habits die hard,* genio y figura hasta la sepultura. || *To be dying for,* morirse por. || *To be dying to do sth.,* morirse por hacer algo. || *To die a violent death,* morir de muerte violenta. || *To die away,* desvanecerse (sound), difuminarse (colour), amainar (wind), desmayarse (to faint). || *To die down,* apagarse (a fire), desvanecerse (sound), amainar (wind), decaer (conversation), disminuir (agitation). || *To die hard,* tardar en desaparecer. || *To die in one's bed,* morir en la cama. || *To die like flies,* caer como chinches *or* como moscas. || *To die of laughter* o *laughing,* morirse de risa. || *To die off,* desaparecer, ir desapareciendo, extinguirse, ir extinguiéndose (race, family), marchitarse (leaves). || *To die out,* desaparecer; apagarse (fire). || *To die suddenly,* morir de repente. || *To die with one's boots on,* morir con las botas puestas. || *To do or die,* vencer o morir.
die-cast [—kɑ:st] v. tr. TECH. Fundir a presión, troquelar.
die-casting [—ˌkɑ:stiŋ] n. TECH. Pieza (*f.*) fundida a presión *or* troquelada.
diehard [ˈdaihɑ:d] adj./n. Intransigente.
dielectric [ˌdaiiˈlektrik] adj. ELECTR. Dieléctrico, ca.
— N. ELECTR. Dieléctrico, *m.*
dieresis [daiˈiərisis] n. U. S. GRAMM. Diéresis, *f.*
— OBSERV. El plural de *dieresis* es *diereses.*
diesel [ˈdi:zəl] adj. TECH. Diesel: *diesel engine,* motor diesel. || *Diesel oil* o *fuel,* gasoil, *m.,* gas-oil, *m.,* aceite pesado.
— M. Diesel.
diesinker [ˈdaisiŋkə*] n. TECH. Grabador (*m.*) de troqueles.
diesis [ˈdaiisis] n. PRINT. Signo (*m.*) de referencia. || MUS. Sostenido, *m.,* diesi, *f.*
— OBSERV. El plural de *diesis* es *dieses.*
diestock [ˈdaistɔk] n. TECH. Terraja, *f.*
diet [ˈdaiət] n. Alimentación, *f.* (daily fare). || Régimen, *m.,* dieta, *f.* (prescribed course of food): *to be on a diet,* estar a régimen; *to put on a diet,* poner a régimen. || Dieta, *f.* (for convalescents, sick people).
diet [ˈdaiət] v. tr. Poner a régimen *or* a dieta.
— V. intr. Estar a régimen *or* a dieta.
Diet [ˈdaiət] n. Dieta, *f.* (assembly).
dietary [ˈdaiətəri] adj. Dietético, ca.
— N. Alimentación, *f.,* régimen (*m.*) alimenticio (in hospital, prison).
dietetic [ˌdaiiˈtetik] adj. Dietético, ca.
dietetics [—s] n. MED. Dietética, *f.*
dietician or **dietitian** [ˌdaiiˈtiʃən] n. MED. Bromatólogo, *m.,* médico (*m.*) dietético.
differ [ˈdifə*] v. intr. Ser distinto, ser diferente (to be unlike): *their jobs differ,* sus trabajos son distintos. || No estar de acuerdo (to disagree): *they differ on this point,* no están de acuerdo en este punto. || — *I beg to differ,* siento disentir *or* no estar de acuerdo. || *They differ widely in their tastes,* tienen gustos completamente distintos, sus gustos difieren completamente.
difference [ˈdifrəns] n. Diferencia, *f.*: *a difference between two figures,* una diferencia entre dos cifras; *the difference in age,* la diferencia de edad. || Discrepancia, *f.,* desacuerdo, *m.* (disagreement). || HERALD. Lambel, *m.* || — *Difference of opinions,* contraste (*m.*) de pareceres (in Parliament). || *It makes a great difference,* no es lo mismo, es muy diferente. || *It makes no difference,* da lo mismo, da igual. || *It makes no difference to me,* me da igual, me da lo mismo. || *To make a difference between two things,* diferenciar dos cosas, hacer una distinción entre dos cosas. || *To pay the difference,* pagar la diferencia. || *To split the difference,* partir la diferencia. || *What difference does it make?,* ¿qué más da?
different [ˈdifrənt] adj. Diferente, distinto, ta (*from,* de).
differential [ˌdifəˈrenʃəl] adj. Diferencial: *differential calculus, equation,* cálculo, ecuación diferencial.
— N. TECH. Diferencial, *f.* (of a car). || MATH. Diferencial, *f.* || U. S. Tarifa (*f.*) diferencial (in transport, cost).
differentiate [ˌdifəˈrenʃieit] v. tr. Diferenciar, distinguir.
— V. intr. Diferenciarse (to become differentiated). || Distinguir: *to differentiate between two things,* distinguir entre dos cosas.
differentiation [ˌdifərenʃiˈeiʃən] n. Diferenciación, *f.*
differing [ˈdifəriŋ] adj. Discordante (discrepant). || Diferente (unlike).
difficult [ˈdifikəlt] adj. Difícil. || *You are making life difficult for me,* me haces la vida imposible.
difficulty [—i] n. Dificultad, *f.*: *I overcame a difficulty,* vencí una dificultad; *he makes difficulties,* crea dificultades.
— *Financial difficulties,* apuros (*m.*), económicos problemas financieros. || *He is having difficulties with his son,* tiene problemas con su hijo. || *I find difficulty in talking,* tengo dificultad en hablar. || *Ship in difficulties,* barco (*m.*) en peligro. || *The difficulty is to,* lo difícil es. || *To be in difficulties,* estar en un apuro *or* en un aprieto. || *To get into difficulties,* meterse en un lío (to get into trouble), verse en un apuro (to be in trouble). || *To get out of one's difficulties,* salir de apuro. || *We have no difficulty in getting spare parts,* no nos es difícil encontrar piezas de recambio. || *With difficulty,* difícilmente, con dificultad.
diffidence [ˈdifidəns] n. Timidez, *f.,* falta (*f.*) de confianza en sí mismo.
diffident [ˈdifidənt] adj. Tímido, da; que no tiene confianza en sí mismo.
diffidently [—li] adv. Con timidez, tímidamente.
diffract [diˈfrækt] v. tr. PHYS. Difractar.
diffraction [diˈfrækʃən] n. PHYS. Difracción, *f.*
diffractive [diˈfræktiv] adj. PHYS. Difrangente.
diffuse [diˈfju:s] adj. Difuso, sa.
diffuse [diˈfju:z] v. tr. Difundir: *to diffuse light,* difundir luz. || Desprender (heat).
— V. intr. Difundirse: *perspiration diffuses through pores,* la transpiración se difunde por los poros.
diffused [—d] adj. Difuso, sa.
diffuser [—ə*] n. TECH. Difusor, *m.*
diffusible [diˈfju:zəbl] adj. Difusible.
diffusion [diˈfju:ʒən] n. Difusión, *f.*
diffusive [diˈfju:siv] adj. Difuso, sa.
diffusor [diˈfjuzə*] n. TECH. Difusor, *m.*
dig [dig] n. Golpe, *m.*: *a dig in the ribs,* un golpe en las costillas. || Empujón, *m.* (push). || Codazo, *m.* (with the elbow). || FIG. Pinchazo, *m.,* pulla, *f.* (sarcastic remark). || Excavación, *f.*: *an archeological dig,* una excavación arqueológica. || U. S. FAM. Empollón, *m.* (at school). || — Pl. FAM. Pensión, *f. sing.* (boardinghouse). | Alojamiento, *m. sing.* (lodgings). || FIG. *To have a dig at s.o.,* meterse con alguien.
dig* [dig] v. tr. Cavar (to break the ground). || Excavar (to excavate). || Hacer (a hole). || Escarbar (animals). || Extraer, sacar (coal). || Hincar, clavar: *to dig spurs into a horse,* hincar las espuelas en un caballo. || FAM. Gustar: *do you dig electronic music?,* ¿te gusta la música electrónica? | Comprender, captar (to understand). || — *To dig in,* enterrar (manure), clavar (nails, claws, etc.). || *To dig into,* hundir, clavar. || Fig. *To dig one's heels in,* mantenerse en sus trece. || *To dig o.s. in,* atrincherarse (soldier). || *To dig out,* excavar (hole), sacar, extraer (buried object), sacar (to bring out), encontrar (to find). || *To dig s.o. with one's elbow,* dar codazos a uno. || *To dig up,* desenterrar (buried object), arrancar, desarraigar (plant), roturar (land), levantar (street), descubrir (to discover).
— V. intr. Cavar. || FAM. Alojarse (to lodge). || — U. S. FAM. *To dig at* o *into,* empollar (to study hard). || *To dig deeper into a subject,* ahondar en un tema, profundizar un tema. || *To dig for gold,* buscar oro. || FAM. *To dig in,* atacar (to start eating). || *To dig into,* investigar. || FAM. *To dig into a cake,* hincarle el diente a un pastel. || *To dig into one's pocket,* hurgar en el bolsillo.
— OBSERV. Pret. & p. p. **dug**.
digest [ˈdaidʒest] n. Resumen, *m.* || JUR. Digesto, *m.*
digest [ˈdaidʒest] v. tr. Digerir: *to digest food,* digerir la comida. || Resumir (to summarize). || Ordenar (to arrange). || FIG. Asimilar: *have you digested everything that is important in the book?,* ¿ha asimilado todo lo importante del libro? | Tragarse, digerir (to stomach).
— V. intr. Digerirse: *this food digests very well,* esta comida se digiere muy bien. || Digerir la comida.
digestibility [diˈdʒestəbiliti] n. Digestibilidad, *f.*
digestible [diˈdʒestəbl] adj. Digerible, digestible.
digestion [diˈdʒestʃən] n. Digestión, *f.* || FIG. Asimilación, *f.*
digestive [diˈdʒestiv] adj. Digestivo, va: *digestive system,* aparato digestivo.
— N. Digestivo, *m.*
digger [ˈdigə*] n. Cavador, *m.* (s.o. who digs). || Excavador, ra (on an archaeological site). || Excavadora, *f.* (machine). || Minero, *m.* (gold miner). || AGR. Plantador, *m.* (dibble). | Roturador, *m.* (grubber). || FAM. Australiano, *m.*
digging [ˈdigiŋ] n. AGR. Cava, *f.* || — Pl. Mina, *f. sing.* (mine). || Excavaciones, *f.* (archaeological). || FAM. Pensión, *f. sing.* (boardinghouse). | Alojamiento, *m. sing.* (lodgings).
digit [ˈdidʒit] n. Dedo, *m.* (finger, toe). || MATH. Dígito, *m.*

digital [ˈdidʒitl] adj. Digital.
— N. Mus. Tecla, *f.*

digitalin [ˌdidʒiˈteilin] n. Med. Digitalina, *f.*

digitalis [ˌdidʒiˈteilis] n. Bot. Digital, *f.* || Med. Digitalina, *f.*

digitate [ˈdidʒitit] or **digitated** [ˈdidʒiteitid] adj. Zool. Bot. Digitado, da.

digitation [didʒiˈteiʃən] n. Digitación, *f.*

digitiform [ˈdidʒitifɔ:m] adj. Digitiforme.

digitigrade [ˈdidʒitigreid] adj. Zool. Digitígrado, da.
— N. Zool. Digitígrado, *m.*

diglot [ˈdaiglɔt] adj. U. S. Bilingüe.
— N. U. S. Edición (*f.*) bilingüe.

dignified [ˈdignifaid] adj. Solemne (solemn): *to speak in a dignified tone*, hablar con tono solemne. || Digno, na; decoroso, sa (act).

dignify [ˈdignifai] v. tr. Dignificar. || Realzar (to give distinction). || Fam. Dar un nombre rimbombante a.

dignifying [—iŋ] adj. Dignificante, honroso, sa.

dignitary [ˈdignitəri] n. Rel. Dignatario, *m.*

dignity [ˈdigniti] n. Dignidad, *f.* || — *It is beneath your dignity to accept*, no puede dignarse a aceptar. || *To stand on one's dignity*, hacerse respetar.

digress [daiˈgres] v. intr. Desviarse, apartarse (to deviate): *he digressed from the main subject*, se apartó del tema principal. || Hacer una digresión (to divagate).

digression [daiˈgreʃən] n. Digresión, *f.*

dihedral [daiˈhi:drəl] adj. Math. Diedro.
— N. Math. Diedro, *m.*

dihedron [daiˈhi:drən] n. Math. Diedro, *m.*

dike [daik] n. Dique, *m.* (protective bank). || Arroyo, *m.* (waterway). || Tapia, *f.* (wall). || Zanja, *f.* (ditch). || Terraplén, *m.* (causeway). || Min. Dique, *m.* || Fig. Dique, *m.*, barrera, *f.* (obstacle).

dike [daik] v. tr. Proteger con un dique. || Retener con diques.

dilacerate [diˈlæsəreit] v. tr. Dilacerar, desgarrar.

dilaceration [diˌlæsəˈreiʃən] n. Dilaceración, *f.*, desgarramiento, *m.*

dilapidate [diˈlæpideit] v. intr. Desmoronarse (house).
— V. tr. Deteriorar (a building). || Estropear (one's clothes, etc.).

dilapidated [—id] adj. Derruido, da (building). || Desvencijado, da (car). || Muy estropeado (clothes).

dilapidation [diˌlæpiˈdeiʃən] n. Estado (*m.*) ruinoso (disrepair). || Jur. Deterioro, *m.* || Geol. Desprendimiento, *m.*

dilatability [daiˌleitəˈbiliti] n. Dilatabilidad, *f.*

dilatable [daiˈleitəbl] adj. Dilatable.

dilatation [ˌdaileiˈteiʃən] n. Dilatación, *f.*

dilate [daiˈleit] v. tr. Dilatar.
— V. intr. Dilatarse (to swell). || Fig. Dilatarse: *to dilate upon a subject*, dilatarse sobre un tema.

dilation [daiˈleiʃən] n. Dilatación, *f.*

dilative [daiˈleitiv] adj. Dilatador, ra.

dilator [daiˈleitə*] n. Dilatador, *m.*

dilatoriness [ˈdilətərinis] n. Tardanza, *f.*, demora, *f.*, dilación, *f.*

dilatory [ˈdilətəri] adj. Jur. Dilatorio, ria. || Lento, ta (people).

dilemma]diˈlemə] n. Dilema, *m.*

dilettante [ˌdiliˈtænti] n. Diletante, *m.* & *f.*

— Observ. El plural de la palabra inglesa es *dilettanti* o *dilettantes.*

dilettantism [ˌdiliˈtæntizəm] n. Diletantismo, *m.*

diligence [ˈdiliʒɑ̃:ns] n. Diligencia, *f.* (coach).

diligence [ˈdilidʒəns] n. Diligencia, *f.* (care).

diligent [ˈdilidʒənt] adj. Diligente.

dill [dil] n. Bot. Eneldo, *m.*

dilly-dally [ˈdilidæli] v. intr. Vacilar, titubear (to hesitate). || Perder el tiempo (to waste time).

diluent [ˈdiljuənt] adj. Diluyente, diluente, disolvente.
— N. Disolvente, *m.*

dilute [daiˈlju:t] adj. Diluido, da (liquid). || Suavizado, da; diluido, da (colour). || Fig. Suavizado, da; atenuado, da.

dilute [daiˈlju:t] v. tr. Diluir (liquid). || Suavizar, diluir (colours). || Fig. Atenuar, suavizar.
— V. intr. Diluirse. || Fig. Atenuarse, suavizarse.

dilution [daiˈlu:ʃən] n. Dilución, *f.*

diluvial [daiˈlu:vjəl] or **diluvian** [daiˈlu:vjən] adj. Diluvial: *diluvial sediments*, sedimentos diluviales. || Diluviano, na: *diluvian rain*, lluvia diluviana.

diluvium [daiˈlu:vjəm] n. Geol. Diluvial, *m.*

— Observ. El plural de *diluvium* es *diluviums* o *diluvia.*

dim [dim] adj. Oscuro, ra (not bright, dark). || Débil, pálido, da: *the dim light of a candle*, la luz pálida de una vela. || Lejano, na: *dim memory*, recuerdo lejano. || Borroso, sa (vague, blurred): *the dim outline of a mountain*, la silueta borrosa de una montaña. || Apagado, da; sin brillo (colour). || Sordo, da; apagado, da (sound). || Turbio, bia: *his sight is dim*, tiene la vista turbia. || Fig. Sombrío, a (view). || Fam. Tonto, ta; torpe. || — *To grow dim*, oscurecerse (light), nublarse (sight), borrarse, difuminarse (outline, memory). || *To take a dim view of sth.*, ver algo con malos ojos.
— N. Aut. Luz (*f.*) de cruce (dipped headlights).

dim [dim] v. tr. Bajar (light). || Oscurecer (room). || Borrar, difuminar (outline). || Nublar (sight). || Empañar, nublar: *tears dimmed her eyes*, las lágrimas le empañaban los ojos. || Apagar (colour). || Amortiguar, apagar (sound). || Fig. Borrar, difuminar (memory). | Empañar (s.o.'s glory). || Aut. *To dim one's lights*, poner luz de cruce, bajar los faros.
— V. intr. Oscurecerse (light). || Apagarse (colour). || Borrarse, difuminarse (outline). || Amortiguarse, apagarse (sound). || Nublarse (sight). || Fig. Borrarse, difuminarse (memory). | Desvanecerse (beauty). | Empañarse (s.o.'s glory).

dime [daim] n. U. S. Moneda (*f.*) de 10 centavos. || — U. S. *Dime novel*, novelucha, *f.*, novela barata. | *Dime store*, almacén (*m.*) donde se venden artículos baratos. | *They were a dime a dozen*, los había a porrillo.

dimension [diˈmenʃən] n. Dimensión, *f.*: *overall* o *external dimensions*, dimensiones exteriores.

dimensional [diˈmenʃənl] adj. Dimensional.

diminish [diˈminiʃ] v. tr./intr. Disminuir.

diminuendo [diˌminjuˈendəu] adv. Mus. Diminuendo.
— N. Mus. Diminuendo, *m.*

diminution [ˌdimiˈnju:ʃən] n. Disminución, *f.*

diminutive [diˈminjutiv] adj. Diminuto, ta (very small). || Gramm. Diminutivo, va.
— N. Gramm. Diminutivo, *m.*

diminutively [—li] adv. Gramm. Como diminutivo.

dimissory [diˈmisəri] adj. De dimisión. || *Dimissory letters*, dimisorias, *f. pl.*

dimity [ˈdimiti] n. Bombasí, *m.* (fabric).

dimly [ˈdimli] adv. Poco: *dimly lit*, poco iluminado. || Vagamente, de una manera confusa (to remember). || Vagamente, indistintamente (to see).

dimmer [ˈdimə*] n. Electr. Regulador (*m.*) de voltaje. || — Pl. Aut. Luces (*f.*) de estacionamiento *or* de cruce.

dimness [ˈdimnis] n. Lo apagado (of colours). || Palidez, *f.* (of light). || Lo oscuro, oscuridad, *f.* (of a room). || Debilidad, *f.* (of sight). || Lo borroso (of outline, memory).

dimorphic [daiˈmɔ:fik] adj. Dimorfo, fa.

dimorphous [daiˈmɔ:fəs] adj. Dimorfo, fa.

dimple [ˈdimpl] n. Hoyuelo, *m.* (on cheek).

dimple [ˈdimpl] v. tr. Formar hoyuelos en (the cheeks). || Rizar (water).
— V. intr. Tener hoyuelos (to show dimples). || Rizarse (water).

dimwit [ˈdimwit] n. Fam. Tonto, ta.

dim-witted [ˈdimˈwitid] adj. Fam. Tonto, ta.

din [din] n. Jaleo, *m.*, estrépito, *m.*: *to kick up a din*, armar jaleo, formar un estrépito. || Clamoreo, *m.*, alboroto, *m.* (of a crowd).

din [din] v. tr. Meter en la cabeza: *to din Spanish verbs into a pupil*, meterle los verbos españoles en la cabeza a un alumno. || Machacar con (to repeat insistently): *to din sth. into s.o.'s ears*, machacar los oídos de uno con algo. || *The noise dinned my ears*, el ruido me ensordecía.
— V. intr. Armar jaleo. || Hacer mucho ruido.

dinar [ˈdi:nɑ:*] n. Dinar, *m.* (coin).

dine [dain] v. intr. Cenar. || — *To dine in*, cenar en casa. || *To dine on* o *off sth.*, cenar algo. || *To dine out*, cenar fuera.
— V. tr. Dar de cenar: *we dined them well*, les dimos bien de cenar. || Ser capaz para, tener cabida para (to have room for): *the table dines ten*, la mesa tiene cabida para diez personas.

diner [ˈdainə*] n. Comensal, *m.* & *f.* || U. S. Coche (*m.*) restaurante (in a train). | Restaurante (*m.*) barato (cheap restaurant).

dinette [daiˈnet] n. U. S. Comedor (*m.*) pequeño.

ding [diŋ] v. intr. Sonar.
— V. tr. Repetir insistentemente, machacar con.

ding dong [ˈdiŋˈdɔŋ] n. Tintineo, *m.* (of a hand bell). || Talán talán, *m.* (of a big bell).
— Adj. Reñido, da (battle).

dinghy [ˈdiŋgi] n. Mar. Bote, *m.* (small boat). || Bote (*m.*) neumático (inflatable boat).

dinginess [ˈdindʒinis] n. Sordidez, *f.* (of city, house). || Color (*m.*) apagado, lo deslustrado (of curtains). || Lo sucio (of furniture, clothes, etc.).

dingle [ˈdiŋgl] n. Geogr. Valle (*m.*) arbolado.

dingo [ˈdiŋgəu] n. Dingo, *m.* (dog).

dingy [ˈdindʒi] adj. Sórdido, da (dirty looking). || Deslustrado, da (dull). || Sucio, cia (dirty).

dining [ˈdainiŋ] n. Cena, *f.*

dining car [—kɑ:*] n. Coche (*m.*) restaurante, coche (*m.*) comedor.

dining hall [—hɔ:l] n. Refectorio, *m.*

dining room [—rum] n. Comedor, *m.*

dinky [ˈdiŋki] adj. Fam. Mono, na; bonito, ta; lindo, da (pretty). || U. S. Fam. Diminuto, ta (small).

dinner [ˈdinə*] n. Cena, *f.* (in the evening). || Comida, *f.* (at midday). || Banquete, *m.* (formal). || Servicio, *m.*, turno, *m.* (in trains). || — *Dinner hour* o *dinner time*, la hora de cenar *or* de comer. || *Dinner jacket* o *dinner coat*, esmoquin, *m.*, smoking, *m.* || *Dinner pail*, fiambrera, *f.* || *Dinner party*, cena, *f.* || *Dinner service* o *dinner set*, vajilla, *f.* || *Dinner table*, mesa (*f.*) de comedor. || *Dinner waggon*, carrito, m. || *To go out to dinner*, cenar fuera. || *To have dinner*, cenar (in the evening), comer (at midday).

dinosaur [ˈdainəsɔ:*] n. Dinosaurio, *m.*

dint [dint] n. Bollo, *m.*, abolladura, *f.* || *By dint of*, a fuerza de.

dint [dint] v. tr. Bollar, abollar.
diocesan [daiˈɔsisən] adj./n. Diocesano, na.
diocese [ˈdaiəsis] n. Diócesis, *f.*, diócesi, *f.*
diode [ˈdaiəud] n. Diodo, *m.*
Dionysia [ˌdaiəˈniziə] pl. n. Dionisiacas, *f.*
Dionisyac [ˌdaiəˈnisiæk] or **Dionysian** [ˌdaiəˈnisiən] adj. Dionisiaco, ca; dionisíaco, ca.
Dionysus or **Dionysos** [ˌdaiəˈnaisəs] pr. n. MYTH. Dioniso, *m.*, Dionisos, *m.*
diopter or **dioptre** [daiˈɔptə*] n. PHYS. Dioptría, *f.*
dioptric [daiˈɔptrik] or **dioptrical** [—əl] adj. PHYS. Dióptrico, ca.
dioptrics [—s] n. PHYS. Dióptrica, *f.*
diorite [ˈdaiərait] n. MIN. Diorita, *f.*
dioxide [daiˈɔksaid] n. CHEM. Bióxido, *m.*
dip [dip] n. Inmersión, *f.* (of sth. in water). || Baño, *m.*, chapuzón, *m.* (a quick swim): *to have a dip*, darse un chapuzón. || Depresión, *f.* (of ground, road, horizon). || Baño, *m.* (liquid). || Picado, *m.* (of a plane). || Vela (*f.*) de sebo (candle). || GEOL. Buzamiento, *m.* || Declive, *m.*, pendiente, *f.* (downward slope). || Inclinación, *f.* (inclination). || Inclinación (*f.*) de la aguja magnética (of compass). || Baja, *f.*, bajada, *f.* (of prices, etc.). || MAR. Calado, *m.* (of a ship). || CULIN. Salsa, *f.*
dip [dip] v. tr. Mojar, bañar (into a liquid). || Sumergir (to immerse). || Dar un baño, dar un chapuzón, zambullir (s.o.). || Mojar (pen). || Meter (one's hand, face, etc.). || Sacar (to scoop). || Inclinar (the scale). || MAR. Inclinar [la bandera] en señal de saludo (flag). || TECH. Tratar por inmersión *or* con un baño. | Teñir (to dye). || — FIG. FAM. *To dip one's fingers into*, entremeterse en. || AUT. *To dip one's lights*, poner luz de cruce, bajar los faros.
— V. intr. Sumergirse (to plunge). || Darse un baño, darse un chapuzón, zambullirse (to have a swim). || Meter la mano (to put a hand into): *he dipped into the drawer*, metió la mano en el cajón. || Descender: *the sun dipped behind the hill*, el sol descendió por detrás de la colina. || Bajar en picado (aeroplane). || Bajar (ground, road). || Bajar (prices). || Inclinarse (scale). || GEOL. Buzar. || FIG. Hojear (to browse through): *I dipped into the dictionary*, hojeé el diccionario. | Meterse (to meddle): *to dip into politics*, meterse en política. || — FIG. *To dip into one's capital*, echar mano a su dinero. | *To dip into the future*, prever el futuro.
dip circle [—ˈsəːkl] n. Aguja (*f.*) de inclinación.
diphase [ˈdaifeiz] adj. Difásico, ca.
diphteria [difˈθiəriə] n. MED. Difteria, *f.*
diphtheric [difˈθerik] or **diphtheritic** [ˌdifθəˈritik] adj. MED. Diftérico, ca.
diphthong [ˈdifθɔŋ] n. GRAMM. Diptongo, *m.*
diphthongization [ˌdifθɔŋgaiˈzeiʃən] n. GRAMM. Diptongación, *f.*
diphthongize [ˈdifθɔŋgaiz] v. tr. GRAMM. Diptongar.
— V. intr. GRAMM. Diptongarse.
diplodocus [diˈplɔdəkəs] n. ZOOL. Diplodoco, *m.*
diploma [diˈpləumə] n. Diploma, *m.*
diplomacy [diˈpləuməsi] n. Diplomacia, *f.* || FIG. Diplomacia, *f.*
diplomat [ˈdipləmæt] n. Diplomático, *m.*
diplomate [ˈdipləmeit] n. Diplomado, da.
diplomatic [ˌdipləˈmætik] adj. Diplomático, ca. || — *Diplomatic bag* (U. S., *diplomatic pouch*), valija diplomática. || *Diplomatic corps*, cuerpo diplomático. || *Diplomatic immunity*, inmunidad diplomática.
diplomatics [—s] n. Diplomática, *f.*
diplomatist [diˈpləumətist] n. Diplomático, *m.*
dip needle [ˈdipˈniːdl] n. Aguja (*f.*) de inclinación.
dipolar [daiˈpəulə*] adj. PHYS. Bipolar.
dipper [ˈdipə*] n. Somorgujo, *m.* (bird). || CULIN. Cucharón, *m.* (for table). | Cazo, *m.*, cacillo, *m.* (for kitchen). || TECH. Cuchara, *f.* (of excavator). | Conmutador (*m.*) de luces de cruce (in cars). | Pinzas, *f. pl.* (in photography). || — U. S. *Big dipper*, montaña rusa. | *The Great* o *Big Dipper*, la Osa Mayor (in astronomy). | *The Little Dipper*, la Osa Menor.
dipsomania [ˌdipsəuˈmeinjə] n. Dipsomanía, *f.*
dipsomaniac [ˌdipsəuˈmeinjæk] adj./n. Dipsómano, na.
dipsomaniacal [—əl] adj. Dipsómano, na.
dipstick [ˈdipstik] n. Varilla (*f.*) graduada, indicador (*m.*) de nivel.
dipteral [ˈdiptərəl] adj. ARCH. Díptero, ra: *a dipteral temple*, un templo díptero.
dipteran [ˈdiptərən] adj. ZOOL. Díptero, ra.
— N. Díptero, *m.*
dipteron [ˈdiptəˌrɔn] n. ZOOL. Díptero, *m.*

— OBSERV. El plural de la palabra inglesa es *diptera*.

dipterous [ˈdiptərəs] adj. ZOOL. Díptero, ra.
diptych [ˈdiptik] n. Díptico, *m.*
dire [ˈdaiə*] adj. Horrible, terrible, espantoso, sa (dreadful). || Extremo, ma (extreme): *dire measures*, medidas extremas. || *To be in dire need of*, necesitar urgentemente.
direct [diˈrekt,daiˈrekt] adj. Directo, ta (straight). || Franco, ca (frank). || Tajante (blunt). || Directo, ta (immediate): *the direct causes of his illness*, las causas directas de su enfermedad; *the direct results of the catastrophe*, las consecuencias directas de la catástrofe. || Directo, ta (descent, taxation). || Textual, literal (quotation). || GRAMM. Directo, ta: *direct object*, complemento directo. || ELECTR. Continuo, nua: *direct current*, corriente continua. || — U. S. *Direct discourse*, estilo directo. || *The direct opposite of sth.*, exactamente lo contrario de algo.
— Adv. Directamente: *the train goes direct to London*, el tren va directamente a Londres.
direct [diˈrekt, daiˈrekt] v. tr. Dirigir (letter, instrument, steps, film, orchestra, company, etc.). || Mandar, ordenar: *he directed me to draw up detailed plans*, me mandó elaborar planes detallados. || Indicar: *can you direct me to the station?*, ¿me puede indicar dónde está la estación? || — *To direct one's attention to*, fijar la atención en. || *To direct one's gaze towards*, dirigir la mirada hacia. || *To direct s.o.'s attention to sth.*, señalar algo a la atención de uno, llamar la atención de alguien sobre algo.
— V. intr. Dirigir.
direction [diˈrekʃən, daiˈrekʃən] n. Dirección, *f.*: *they entrusted him with the direction of the work*, le confiaron la dirección de la obra; *we are going in the same direction*, vamos en la misma dirección. || Dirección, *f.* (of film, company, etc.). || — Pl. Instrucciones, *f.* || — *Directions for use*, instrucciones para el uso, modo (*m.*) de empleo. || CINEM. *Executive direction*, dirección general de producción. || *In the direction of*, en dirección a.
directional [—l] adj. Direccional, orientable.
direction finder [—ˌfaində*] n. Radiogoniómetro, *m.*
direction indicator [—ˌindikeitə*] n. AUT. Intermitente, *m.*
directive [diˈrektiv, daiˈrektiv] adj. Directivo, va.
— N. Orden, *f.*, instrucción, *f.* (order). || — Pl. Directrices, *f.*, directivas, *f.*: *I have given them perfectly clear directives*, les he dado directrices perfectamente claras.
directly [diˈrektli, daiˈrektli] adv. Directamente (in a direct manner). || Inmediatamente, en seguida (immediately): *he came in directly*, entró en seguida. || Exactamente, justo: *he lives directly opposite the church*, vive exactamente en frente de la iglesia.
— Conj. En cuanto (as soon as).
directness [diˈrektnis, daiˈrektnis] n. Franqueza, *f.*
director [diˈrektə*, daiˈrektə*] n. Director, *m.* || — *Board of directors*, consejo (*m.*) de administración, junta directiva. || *Director general*, director general. || *Director of production*, director de producción. || *Film director*, director de cine. || *Managing director*, director gerente. || *Spiritual director*, director espiritual.
directorate [diˈrektərit, daiˈrektərit] n. Cargo (*m.*) de director, dirección, *f.* (post). || Consejo (*m.*) de administración, junta (*f.*) directiva (board of directors).
directorial [ˌdirekˈtɔːriəl, ˌdairekˈtɔːriəl] adj. Directoral: *directorial powers*, poderes directorales. || Directivo, va.
directorship [diˈrektəʃip, daiˈrektəʃip] n. Cargo (*m.*) de director, dirección, *f.*
directory [diˈrektəri, daiˈrektəri] n. Guía (*f.*) telefónica (telephone). || Directorio, *m.* (book of directions). || Libro (*m.*) de instrucciones (set of rules). || Consejo (*m.*) de administración, junta (*f.*) directiva (directorate).
— Adj. Directorio, ria.
Directory [diˈrektəri,daiˈrektəri] n. HIST. Directorio, *m.*
direct primary [diˈrektˈpraiməri] n. U. S. Elección (*f.*) preliminar en la que el candidato es designado directamente por el pueblo.
directress [diˈrektris, daiˈrektris] n. Directora, *f.*
directrix [diˈrektriks, daiˈrektriks] n. Directriz, *f.*

— OBSERV. El plural de *directrix* es *directrices* o *directrixes*.

direful [ˈdaiəful] adj. Horrible, espantoso, sa; terrible.
dirge [dəːdʒ] n. Canto (*m.*) fúnebre (funeral hymn). || Endecha, *f.* (lament).
dirigible [ˈdiridʒəbl] adj. AVIAT. Dirigible.
— N. AVIAT. Dirigible, *m.*
diriment [ˈdirimənt] adj. JUR. Dirimente: *diriment impediment*, impedimento dirimente.
dirk [dəːk] n. Puñal, *m.*
dirk [dəːk] v. tr. Apuñalar.
dirt [dəːt] n. Suciedad, *f.* (dirtiness). || Mugre, *f.* (filth). || Porquería, *f.* (soiling matter). || Basura, *f.* (litter). || Barro, *m.* (mud). || Excremento, *m.* (of animals). || Porquerías, *f. pl.* (obscenities): *to talk dirt*, decir porquerías. || Cochinada, *f.* (dirty trick). || TECH. Tierra (*f.*) aurífera. || U. S. Tierra, *f.* (earth). || — FIG. *To do dirt to s.o.*, hacer una cochinada a alguien. | *To eat dirt*, tragar quina. | *To throw dirt at s.o.*, poner a alguien como un trapo. | *To treat s.o. like dirt*, tratar a alguien como a una zapatilla.
dirt-cheap [ˈdəːtˈtʃiːp] adj. FAM. Baratísimo, ma; tirado, da.
dirt farmer [ˈdəːtˈfɑːmə*] n. U. S. FAM. Cultivador, *m.*
dirtiness [ˈdəːtinis] n. Suciedad, *f.* || Porquería, *f.* (obscenity). || FIG. Bajeza, *f.* (meanness).
dirt track [ˈdəːt-træk] n. Pista (*f.*) de ceniza (for motorcycle racing).
dirty [ˈdəːti] adj. Sucio, cia (unclean): *a dirty handkerchief*, un pañuelo sucio. || Lleno de barro (muddy). || FAM. Malísimo, ma; de perros (weather): *a dirty night*, una noche de perros. || FIG. Sucio, cia: *dirty business*, negocios sucios; *a dirty mind*, una mente sucia. | Sucio, cia: *dirty grey*, gris sucio. | Lascivo, va (look). || FAM. Verde (obscene): *a dirty joke*, un chiste

verde; *a dirty old man*, un viejo verde. | Grosero, ra; obsceno, na (language). || — *Dirty trick*, mala pasada, mala jugada. || FIG. *Don't wash your dirty linen in public*, los trapos sucios se lavan en casa. || FIG. FAM. *To do the dirty on s.o.* o *to play a dirty trick on s.o.*, jugar una mala pasada a uno, hacer una mala jugada *or* una cochinada a uno.

dirty [ˈdəːti] v. tr. Ensuciar. || Embarrar, enlodar (to muddy). || FIG. Manchar (to stain).
— V. intr. Ensuciarse. || FIG. Mancharse.

disability [ˌdisəˈbiliti] n. MED. Incapacidad (*f.*) física *or* mental. || JUR. Incapacidad, *f.* || Desventaja, *f.* (disadvantage).

disable [disˈeibl] v. tr. Incapacitar (*from*, para) [to incapacitate legally]. || Dejar imposibilitado (to incapacitate physically). || Lisiar (to cripple). || Dejar mentalmente incapacitado (to incapacitate mentally). || Poner fuera de uso, volver inservible (to render useless). || Impedir (to prevent).

disabled [—d] adj. Inválido, da; imposibilitado, da. || JUR. Incapacitado, da. || *The disabled*, los inválidos.

disablement [—mənt] n. Incapacidad, *f.*

disabuse [ˌdisəˈbjuːz] v. tr. Desengañar.

disaccord [ˌdisəˈkɔːd] n. Desacuerdo, *m.*

disaccord [ˌdisəˈkɔːd] v. intr. Estar en desacuerdo, no estar de acuerdo.

disaccustom [ˈdisəˈkʌstəm] v. tr. Desacostumbrar.

disadvantage [ˌdsədˈvɑːntidʒ] n. Desventaja, *f.*, inconveniente, *m.* || — *To be at a disadvantage*, estar en situación desventajosa. || *To the disadvantage of*, en perjuicio de, en detrimento de.

disadvantage [ˌdisədˈvɑːntidʒ] v. tr. Perjudicar.

disadvantageous [ˌdisædvɑːnˈteidʒəs] adj. Desventajoso, sa.

disaffect [ˌdisəˈfekt] v. tr. Indisponer.

disaffected [—id] adj. Desafecto, ta.

disaffection [ˌdisəˈfekʃən] n. Desafección, *f.*, desafecto, *m.* || Descontento, *m.* (discontent).

disaffirm [ˌdisəˈfəːm] v. tr. Desmentir (to contradict). || JUR. Casar, anular (a sentence). | Denunciar (a contract).

disagree [ˌdisəˈgriː] v. intr. No estar de acuerdo, estar en desacuerdo (to differ). || Discrepar: *their testimonies disagree*, sus testimonios discrepan. || No aprobar, no estar de acuerdo: *I disagree with your policy*, no apruebo su política. || No convenir, sentar mal (to be unsuitable): *the climate disagrees with him*, el clima no le conviene. || Sentar mal (to upset the digestion). || Reñir (to quarrel).

disagreeable [ˌdisəˈgriəbl] adj. Desagradable (unpleasant). || Desagradable, antipático, ca (ill-natured).

disagreement [ˌdisəˈgriːmənt] n. Desacuerdo, *m.* (lack of agreement). || Disconformidad, *f.*: *there is a disagreement between their versions*, hay disconformidad entre sus versiones. || Riña, *f.*, altercado, *m.* (squabble).

disallow [ˈdisəˈlau] v. tr. Rechazar (to refuse to admit). || Anular (in sport). || Prohibir (to forbid).

disallowance [—əns] n. Rechazo, *m.*

disannul [ˌdisəˈnʌl] v. tr. Anular (to annul).

disappear [ˌdisəˈpiə*] v. intr. Desaparecer.

disappearance [ˌdisəˈpiərəns] n. Desaparición, *f.*

disappoint [ˌdisəˈpɔint] v. tr. Decepcionar, desilusionar: *the film disappointed me*, la película me ha decepcionado. || Defraudar, decepcionar: *her son disappointed her*, su hijo le ha defraudado. || Faltar a su palabra (to break a promise): *you promised to come but you disappointed me*, prometiste venir pero faltaste a tu palabra.

disappointed [—id] adj. Decepcionado, da; desilusionado, da; defraudado, da. || Desengañado, da (love). || — *I was disappointed by his performance*, me decepcionó su actuación. || *To be disappointed in love*, sufrir un desengaño amoroso *or* desengaños amorosos.

disappointing [—iŋ] adj. Decepcionante.

disappointment [—mənt] n. Decepción, *f.*, desilusión, *f.* || Disgusto, *m.* (displeasure). || — *Disappointment in love*, desengaño amoroso. || *To be a disappointment to s.o.*, decepcionar a alguien.

disapprobation [ˌdisæprəuˈbeiʃən] n. Desaprobación, *f.* (disapproval).

disapprobatory [ˌdisæprəuˈbeitəri] adj. Desaprobador, ra; desaprobatorio, ria.

disapproval [ˌdisəˈpruːvəl] n. Desaprobación, *f.*

disapprove [ˈdisəˈpruːv] v. tr. Desaprobar.
— V. intr. No gustarle a uno (people): *I disapprove of him*, no me gusta. || Desaprobar: *he disapproved of my conduct*, desaprobó mi comportamiento. || Estar en contra: *to disapprove of sth. being done*, estar en contra de que se haga algo.

disapproving [—iŋ] adj. Desaprobador, ra.

disapprovingly [—iŋli] adv. Con desaprobación.

disarm [disˈɑːm] v. tr. Desarmar.
— V. intr. Desarmar, deponer las armas.

disarmament [disˈɑːməmənt] n. Desarme, *m.*

disarming [disˈɑːmiŋ] adj. Que desarma.
— N. Desarme, *m.*

disarrange [ˈdisəˈreindʒ] v. tr. Desordenar, desarreglar (to untidy). || Desbaratar (plans).

disarrangement [—mənt] n. Desorden, *m.*, desarreglo, *m.* (disorder). || Desbaratamiento, *m.* (of plans).

disarray [ˈdisəˈrei] n. Desorden, *m.* (lack of order): *a room in disarray*, una habitación en desorden. || Desaliño, *m.* (of dress). || *To flee in disarray*, huir a la desbandada.

disarray [ˈdisəˈrei] v. tr. Hacer huir (the enemy). || Desarreglar, desordenar (to untidy). || Desarreglar (s.o.'s dress).

disarticulate [ˈdisɑːˈtikjuleit] v. tr. Desarticular.
— V. intr. Desarticularse.

disarticulation [ˌdisɑːˌtikjuˈleiʃən] n. Desarticulación, *f.*

disassemble [ˌdisəˈsembl] v. tr. Desmontar, desarmar.

disassembly [—i] n. Desmontaje, *m.*, desarme, *m.*

disassociate [ˌdisəˈsəuʃieit] v. tr. See DISSOCIATE.

disassociation [ˌdisəˌsəuʃiˈeiʃən] n. Disociación, *f.*

disaster [diˈzɑːstə*] n. Desastre, *m.* (catastrophe). || FIG. Desastre, *m.* (complete failure): *the dance was a disaster*, el baile fue un desastre. || *To court disaster*, correr al desastre.

disastrous [diˈzɑːstrəs] adj. Desastroso, sa.

disavow [ˈdisəˈvau] v. tr. Renegar de (one's faith, one's family, friends). || Negarse a aceptar la responsabilidad de (an action). || Desaprobar (to disapprove).

disavowal [—əl] n. Negación, *f.* || Desaprobación, *f.*

disband [disˈbænd] v. tr. Disolver (an organization). || Dispersar (people). || Licenciar (troops).
— V. intr. Disolverse. || Dispersarse.

disbandment [—mənt] n. Disolución, *f.* (of an organization). || Dispersión, *f.* (of people). || Licenciamiento, *m.* (of troops).

disbar [disˈbɑː*] v. tr. JUR. Expulsar del colegio de abogados.

disbarment [—mənt] n. JUR. Expulsión (*f.*) del colegio de abogados.

disbelief [ˈdisbiˈliːf] n. Incredulidad, *f.*

disbelieve [ˈdisbiˈliːv] v. tr. No creer.
— V. intr. No creer. || Ser incrédulo.

disbeliever [—ə*] n. Descreído, da; incrédulo, la.

disbranch [disˈbrɑːntʃ] v. tr. Podar.

disbud [disˈbʌd] v. tr. Desyemar (plants). || Descornar (cattle).

disburden [disˈbəːdn] v. tr. Descargar. || FIG. *To disburden o.s.*, desahogarse, aliviarse.

disburse [disˈbəːs] v. tr. Desembolsar.

disbursement [disˈbəːsmənt] n. Desembolso, *m.*

disc [disk] n. See DISK.

discalceate [disˈkælsiit] or **discalced** [disˈkælst] adj. REL. Descalzo, za.

discard [ˈdiskɑːd] n. Descarte, *m.* (in card games). || Desecho, *m.* (sth. rejected).

discard [disˈkɑːd] v. tr. Descartarse de, descartar (cards). || Desechar, descartar (to cast aside). || Desechar: *to discard an old suit*, desechar un traje viejo. || Tirar (to throw away). || FIG. Renunciar a (to abandon).
— V. intr. Descartarse.

discarding [—iŋ] n. Descarte, *m.*

discern [diˈsəːn] v. tr. Discernir, distinguir: *to discern good from evil*, discernir el bien del mal. || Percibir (to perceive).

discernible [diˈsəːnibl] adj. Distinguible, discernible. || Perceptible.

discerning [diˈsəːniŋ] adj. Perspicaz.

discernment [diˈsəːnmənt] n. Discernimiento, *m.*, perspicacia, *f.* (discrimination). || Criterio, *m.*, discernimiento, *m.*: *to act with discernment*, actuar con discernimiento.

discharge [ˈdisˈtʃɑːdʒ] n. Descarga, *f.*: *the discharge of the ship*, la descarga del barco. || Descarga, *f.*, disparo, *m.*: *he heard the discharge of a gun*, oyó la descarga de una escopeta. || Disparo, *m.* (of arrows). || Escape, *m.* (of gases). || JUR. Liberación, *f.* (of a prisoner). | Rehabilitación, *f.* (of a bankrupt). | Absolución, *f.* (of the accused in court). || MIL. Licencia (*f.*) absoluta. || Descargo, *m.*, exoneración, *f.* (of taxes, etc.). || Descargo, *m.*, pago, *m.* (of a debt). || Recibo, *m.* (certificate of payment). || Cumplimiento, *m.*, ejercicio, *m.*, desempeño, *m.*: *in the discharge of his duties*, en el ejercicio de sus funciones. || Cumplimiento, *m.* (of a vow). || MED. Supuración, *f.* | Pus, *m.* (pus). | Alta, *f.* (from hospital). || ELECTR. PHYS. Descarga, *f.* || Decoloración, *f.* (process of removing dye). || Decolorante, *m.* (chemical for removing dye). || Destitución, *f.* (from a post). || Despido, *m.* (of a worker). || — *Discharge tube*, tubo luminoso. || *Discharge valve*, válvula (*f.*) de escape. || *To the discharge of*, en descargo de.

discharge [disˈtʃɑːdʒ] v. tr. Descargar: *to discharge a cargo*, descargar un cargamento. || Verter: *the factory discharges waste into the river*, la fábrica vierte los residuos en el río. || Saldar (a debt). || Disparar, descargar (a gun). || Disparar (arrows). || Lanzar (a bomb). || Despedir (a worker). || JUR. Absolver (the accused). | Liberar, poner en libertad (a prisoner). | Rehabilitar (a bankrupt). || Dar de alta, dar el alta (a patient). || MIL. Dar de baja (disabled soldier). | Licenciar (soldiers). || Desempeñar: *to discharge one's duties*, desempeñar sus funciones. || Cumplir con, cumplir: *to discharge one's duty*, cumplir con su deber. || Eximir, descargar (to free from an obligation). || Arrojar, echar (pus). || Perder (its colour). || Desprender (gas). || ELECTR. PHYS.

Descargar. || *To discharge s.o. from doing sth.*, dispensar a alguien de hacer algo.
— V. intr. Descargar (a ship). || Supurar (to suppurate). || Descargarse, dispararse (a gun). || ELECTR. PHYS. Descargarse. || Verter: *the sewers discharge in the river*, las cloacas vierten en el río. || Descargar (river). || Desteñirse, correrse (colour).
discharger [—ə*] n. Descargador, *m.*
disciple [di'saipl] n. Discípulo, la.
disciplinant ['disiplinənt] n. Disciplinante, *m.* & *f.* (in Holy Week).
disciplinarian [ˌdisipli'neəriən] adj. Disciplinario, ria.
— N. Ordenancista, *m.* & *f.*, partidario (*m.*) de una disciplina rigurosa.
disciplinary ['disiplinəri] adj. Disciplinario, ria: *disciplinary batallion*, batallón disciplinario.
discipline ['disiplin] n. Disciplina, *f.*
discipline ['disiplin] v. tr. Disciplinar (to submit to discipline). || Castigar (to punish).
disc jockey ['diskˌdʒɔki] n. Locutor (*m.*) que presenta discos en la radio, "disc jockey", *m.* || Pinchadiscos, *m. inv.*, "disc jockey", *m.* (in a discotheque).
disclaim [dis'kleim] v. tr. Rechazar (authority, responsibility). || JUR. Renunciar a (a legal claim). || *I disclaim any part in the murder*, niego rotundamente haber tomado parte en el asesinato.
— V. intr. Renunciar.
disclaimer [—ə*] n. JUR. Renuncia, *f.* (of a right). || Denegación, *f.* (denial). || Rectificación, *f.*: *he sent a disclaimer to the newspaper*, envió una rectificación al periódico.
disclose [dis'kləuz] v. tr. Revelar (to reveal): *to disclose a secret*, revelar un secreto.
disclosure [dis'kləuzə*] n. Revelación, *f.* (of a secret). || Descubrimiento, *m.* (of hidden objects).
discobolus [dis'kɔbələs] n. Discóbolo, *m.*
discography [dis'kɔgrəfi] n. Catálogo (*m.*) de discos.
discoid ['diskɔid] or **discoidal** [dis'kɔidəl] adj. Discoidal, discoideo, a.
discolour [U. S. **discolor**] [dis'kʌlə*] v. tr. Descolorar, desteñir: *the sun discolours the curtains*, el sol descolora las cortinas. || Manchar, desteñir en (to stain): *the red shirt has discoloured the sheets*, la camisa roja ha desteñido en las sábanas.
discolouration [U. S. **discoloration**] [disˌkʌlə'reiʃən] n. Descoloración, *f.*, descoloramiento, *m.*
discomfit [dis'kʌmfit] v. tr. Desconcertar.
discomfiture [dis'kʌmfitʃə*] n. Desconcierto, *m.*
discomfort [dis'kʌmfət] n. Molestia, *f.* (physical pain). || Malestar, *m.* (feeling of uneasiness). || Incomodidad, *f.* (lack of comfort). || Preocupación, *f.* (worry). || Aflicción, *f.*, pesar, *m.* (sorrow).
discomfort [dis'kʌmfət] v. tr. Molestar (to cause uneasiness). || Preocupar (to worry). || Afligir (to sadden).
discommode [ˌdiskə'məud] v. tr. Incomodar, molestar.
discompose [ˌdiskəm'pəuz] v. tr. Perturbar, turbar (s.o.). || Descomponer (s.o.'s countenance).
discomposure [ˌdiskəm'pəuʒə*] n. Desconcierto, *m.* (of a person). || Alteración, *f.* (of the face).
disconcert [ˌdiskən'sə:t] v. tr. Desconcertar (to confuse). || Perturbar, trastornar: *this disconcerts my plans*, esto trastorna mis planes.
disconcerting [—iŋ] adj. Desconcertante.
disconcertment [—mənt] n. Desconcierto, *m.* (confusion). || Trastorno, *m.*, perturbación, *f.* (upsetting).
disconnect ['diskə'nekt] v. tr. ELECTR. Desconectar. || Desarticular (two parts). || Separar (one part from another). || Desenganchar (wagons).
disconnected [—id] adj. Desconectado, da: *a disconnected television*, una televisión desconectada. || Sin conexión, sin relación: *disconnected events*, sucesos sin conexión. || Deshilvanado, da; inconexo, xa (speech, style).
disconnection or **disconnexion** [diskə'nekʃən] n. Desconexión, *f.* || Desarticulación, *f.* (of two parts). || Separación, *f.* || FIG. Falta (*f.*) de conexión, incoherencia, *f.*
disconsolate [dis'kɔnsəlit] adj. Desconsolado, da.
disconsolateness [—nis] or **disconsolation** [disˌkɔnsə'leiʃən] n. Desconsuelo, *m.*
discontent ['diskən'tənt] n. Descontento, *m.*
— Adj. Descontento, ta.
discontent ['diskən'tənt] v. tr. Descontentar.
discontented [—id] adj. Descontento, ta.
discontentedness [—idnis] or **discontentment** [—mənt] n. Descontento, *m.*
discontinuance [ˌdiskən'tinjuəns] n. Cesación, *f.*, interrupción, *f.* || JUR. Suspensión, *f.* (of a suit). | Sobreseimiento, *m.* (of a case).
discontinuation [ˌdiskənˌtinju'eiʃən] n. Cesación, *f.*, interrupción, *f.*, discontinuación, *f.*
discontinue ['diskən'tinju:] v. tr. Discontinuar, interrumpir (to stop). || Suspender (one's subscription). || JUR. Sobreseer (a case). || *To discontinue doing sth.*, dejar de hacer algo.
— V. intr. Cesar, interrumpirse, suspenderse.
discontinuity ['disˌkɔnti'njuiti] n. Discontinuidad, *f.* (lack of continuity). || Interrupción, *f.* || Falta (*f.*) de ilación: *discontinuity of ideas*, falta de ilación en las ideas.
discontinuous ['diskən'tinjuəs] adj. Discontinuo, nua. || Interrumpido, da.
discophile ['diskəfail] n. Discófilo, la.
discord ['diskɔ:d] n. Discordia, *f.*, disensión, *f.* (disagreement): *to sow discord*, sembrar la discordia. || MUS. Disonancia, *f.*
discord ['diskɔ:d] v. intr. Discrepar, discordar.
discordance [dis'kɔ:dəns] or **discordancy** [—i] n. Discordancia, *f.*: *discordance between the statements and the facts*, discordancia entre los dichos y los hechos. || Discordia, *f.*, disensión, *f.* (disagreement). || MUS. Discordancia, *f.*, disonancia, *f.*
discordant [dis'kɔ:dənt] adj. Discordante (opinions, notes). || Discorde, en desacuerdo (people). || MUS. Discorde. || *Discordant with*, opuesto a, en desacuerdo con.
discotheque ['diskəutek] n. Discoteca, *f.*
discount ['diskaunt] n. Descuento, *m.*: *to give a discount to*, conceder un descuento a; *bank discount*, descuento bancario. || — *At a discount*, a precio reducido, con descuento (goods), por debajo de la par (shares). || FIG. *Politeness is at a discount*, ya no se cotiza la cortesía.
discount ['dis'kaunt] v. tr. Descontar (in finance). || Rebajar, disminuir (to reduce). || No hacer caso de (to disregard): *you must discount half of what he says*, no debes hacer caso de la mitad de lo que dice. || Dejar de lado (to leave out). || Contar con (to anticipate): *we had already discounted this loss*, ya habíamos contado con esa pérdida.
— V. intr. Descontar letras de cambio.
discountable [—əbl] adj. COMM. Descontable.
discountenance [dis'kauntinəns] v. tr. Estar en contra de (to be against). || Desaprobar (to disapprove of). || Desconcertar, turbar (to abash).
discount house ['diskaunt-haus] n. Tienda (*f.*) que vende artículos a precio reducido.
discount rate ['diskaunt-reit] n. Tipo (*m.*) de descuento.
discourage [dis'kʌridʒ] v. tr. Desanimar, desalentar, descorazonar: *this hard work discourages them*, este duro trabajo les desanima. || No fomentar: *inflation discourages saving*, la inflación no fomenta el ahorro. || *To discourage from*, recomendar que no (to advise against): *the police discourage people from driving too fast*, la policía recomienda a la gente que no conduzca muy de prisa; hacer desistir de, disuadir (to dissuade from): *the sight of the enemy discouraged them from attacking*, la vista del enemigo les hizo desistir de atacar.
discouragement [—mənt] n. Desánimo, *m.*, desaliento, *m.*, desmoralización, *f.* || Desaprobación, *f.*
discouraging [—iŋ] adj. Desalentador, ra; descorazonador, ra; desmoralizador, ra.
discourse [dis'kɔ:s] n. Discurso, *m.* (speech). || Conversación, *f.* [*Amer.*, plática, *f.*]. || Disertación, *f.* (dissertation). || Tratado, *m.*, discurso, *m.* (treatise).
discourse [dis'kɔ:s] v. intr. Disertar (*upon*, sobre). || Conversar [*Amer.*, platicar] (to talk).
discourser [—ə*] n. Disertante, *m.* & *f.*
discourteous [dis'kə:tjəs] adj. Descortés.
discourtesy [dis'kə:tisi] n. Descortesía, *f.*
discover [dis'kʌvə*] v. tr. Descubrir: *to discover a new antibiotic*, descubrir un nuevo antibiótico. || Darse cuenta de (to realize).
discoverer [—rə*] n. Descubridor, ra.
discovery [dis'kʌvəri] n. Descubrimiento, *m.* || — *Discovery Day*, Día (*m.*) de la Raza. || *The age of discovery*, la época de los descubrimientos.
discredit [dis'kredit] n. Descrédito, *m.* (loss of reputation). || Duda, *f.* (disbelief): *to throw discredit upon a statement*, poner una declaración en duda. || — *To be a discredit to*, deshonrar a. || *To be to the discredit of*, ir en descrédito de. || *To bring discredit on o.s.* o *to fall into discredit*, desacreditarse. || *To cast* o *to throw discredit on s.o.*, desacreditar a uno.
discredit [dis'kredit] v. tr. Desacreditar (to destroy s.o.'s trustworthiness). || Poner en duda, dudar de, no dar crédito a (to refuse to believe): *to discredit s.o.'s evidence*, poner en duda el testimonio de alguien. || Deshonrar (to dishonour).
discreditable [dis'kreditəbl] adj. Indigno, na: *conduct discreditable to a doctor*, conducta indigna de un médico. || Vergonzoso, sa (shameful). || *Her performance was far from discreditable*, su actuación, fue bastante buena.
discreet [dis'kri:t] adj. Discreto, ta. || Circunspecto, ta.
discreetness [—nis] n. Discreción, *f.* || Circunspección, *f.*
discrepancy [dis'krepənsi] n. Discrepancia, *f.*: *there is a discrepancy between the two versions*, hay discrepancia entre las dos versiones. || Diferencia, *f.* (between numbers).
discrepant [dis'krepənt] adj. Discrepante (*with*, *from*, de). || Diferente.
discrete [dis'kri:t] adj. MATH. MED. Discreto, ta. || PHIL. Abstracto, ta. || Distinto, ta (separate).
— OBSERV. No se confunda esta palabra con *discreet*.
discreteness [—nis] n. Distinción, *f.*
discretion [dis'kreʃən] n. Discreción, *f.* (prudence). || Circunspección, *f.* || Juicio, *m.*, razón, *f.* (judgment). || — *Age of discretion*, edad (*f.*) del juicio, uso (*m.*) de razón. || *At discretion*, a discreción. || *At the discre-*

tion of, a juicio de. || *At your discretion*, como usted guste, a su gusto. || *To use one's own discretion*, hacer lo que a uno le parezca.

discretionary [dis'kreʃnəri] adj. Discrecional: *discretionary power*, poder discrecional.

discriminant [dis'kriminənt] n. MATH. Discriminante, *m.* (mathematical expression).

discriminate [dis'krimineit] v. tr. Discriminar, distinguir: *to discriminate good from bad*, discriminar lo bueno de lo malo. || Distinguir: *his height discriminates him from his friends*, su estatura le distingue de sus amigos.

— V. intr. Discriminar, distinguir: *to discriminate between good and bad*, discriminar entre lo bueno y lo malo. || — *To discriminate against*, discriminar, hacer discriminaciones en contra de. || *To discriminate in favour of*, hacer discriminaciones en favor de.

discriminating [—iŋ] adj. Juicioso, sa (people). || Discriminatorio, ria (laws, tariff, etc.). || Muy bueno (taste). || Distintivo, va (sign). || Fino, na; muy bueno (ear).

discrimination [dis,krimi'neiʃən] n. Discriminación, *f.*, distinción, *f.* || Discriminación, *f.*: *racial discrimination*, discriminación racial. || Discernimiento, *m.* (discernment). || Buen gusto, *m.* (good taste).

discriminative [dis'kriminətiv] adj. See DISCRIMINATING.

discriminatory [dis'kriminətəri] adj. Discriminatorio, ria.

discrown [dis'kraun] v. tr. Descoronar (a king).

discursive [dis'kə:siv] adj. Divagador, ra (rambling). || Deshilvanado, da (speech). || Discursivo, va (proceeding by reasoning): *discursive method*, método discursivo.

discus ['diskəs] n. SP. Disco, *m.*: *throwing the discus*, lanzamiento del disco. || SP. *Discus thrower*, lanzador (*m.*) de disco.

— OBSERV. El plural de *discus* es *discuses* o *disci*.

discuss [dis'kʌs] v. tr. Discutir (to exchange ideas about, to debate). || Hablar de (to talk about).

discussion [dis'kʌʃən] n. Discusión, *f.*: *subject for discussion*, tema de discusión. || — *To be under discussion*, estar en discusión, estar siendo discutido. || *To come up for discussion*, ser sometido a discusión.

disdain [dis'dein] n. Desdén, *m.*, desprecio, *m.*

disdain [dis'dein] v. tr. Desdeñar, despreciar (to have contempt for). || No dignarse: *to disdain to answer*, no dignarse a contestar.

disdainful [—ful] adj. Desdeñoso, sa; despectivo, va (expressing disdain). || Desdeñoso, sa (aloof).

disease [di'zi:z] n. Enfermedad, *f.*: *occupational disease*, enfermedad profesional; *contagious disease*, enfermedad contagiosa. || FIG. Mal, *m.*, enfermedad, *f.*

diseased [—d] adj. Enfermo, ma.

disembark ['disim'ba:k] v. tr./intr. Desembarcar.

disembarkation [,disemba:'keiʃən] or **disembarkment** [,disim'ba:kmənt] n. Desembarco, *m.* (of people). || Desembarque, *m.* (of goods).

disembarrass ['disim'bærəs] v. tr. Desembarazar.

disembodied ['disim'bɔdid] adj. Incorpóreo, a.

disembody ['disim'bɔdi] v. tr. Separar del cuerpo.

disembogue [,disim'beug] v. tr. Verter.

— V. intr. Desembocar, desaguar.

disembowel [,disim'bauəl] v. tr. Desentrañar, destripar.

disembowelment [—mənt] n. Desentrañamiento, *m.*, destripamiento, *m.*

disembroil [,disim'brɔil] v. tr. Desenmarañar, desembrollar.

disenchant ['disin'tʃa:nt] v. tr. Desencantar, desilusionar.

disenchantment [—mənt] n. Desencanto, *m.*, desilusión, *f.*

disencumber ['disinkʌmbə*] v. tr. Desembarazar, librar.

disendow ['disin'dau] v. tr. Privar de una dotación (a church).

disengage [,disin'geidʒ] v. tr. Desenganchar (to uncouple, to unhook). || Soltar (to detach). || Liberar (to free). || Desengranar (gears). || MIL. Retirar (troops). || AUT. *To disengage the clutch*, desembragar.

— V. intr. Desengancharse. || Soltarse. || Liberarse. || MIL. Retirarse.

disengaged [—d] adj. Libre (free). || Suelto, ta (loose). || Desenganchado, da. || AUT. Desembragado, da (clutch).

disengagement [—mənt] n. Retirada, *f.* (in fencing). || MIL. Retirada (*f.*) de las tropas. || Liberación, *f.* || AUT. Desembrague, *m.* || Ruptura (*f.*) de compromiso matrimonial.

disentail ['disin'teil] v. tr. Liberar, desamortizar (property).

disentailment [—mənt] n. Desamortización, *f.* (of property).

disentangle ['disin'tæŋgl] v. tr. Desenredar, desenmarañar (to unravel): *to disentangle one's hair*, desenredar el pelo. || Desenmarañar, desenredar, poner en claro (an intrigue). || Descubrir (a puzzle).

— V. intr. Desenredarse, desenmarañarse.

disentanglement [,disin'tæŋglmənt] n. Desenmarañamiento, *m.*, desenredo, *m.* || FIG. Solución, *f.*

disentomb [,disin'tu:mb] v. tr. Desenterrar.

disequilibrium ['disekwi'libriəm] n. Desequilibrio, *m.*

disestablish ['disis'tæbliʃ] v. tr. Separar [la Iglesia] del Estado.

disestablishment [,disis'tæbliʃmənt] n. Separación (*f.*) [de la Iglesia] del Estado.

disesteem ['disis'ti:m] n. Poco aprecio, *m.* || Descrédito, *m.* (discredit).

disesteem ['disis'ti:m] v. tr. Desestimar, despreciar.

disfavour (U. S. **disfavor**) ['dis'feivə*] n. Desgracia, *f.* || Desaprobación, *f.* (disapproval). || Desventaja, *f.* (disadvantage). || *To fall into disfavour*, caer en desgracia (people), caer en desuso (word, custom).

disfavour (U. S. **disfavor**) [dis'feivə*] v. tr. Desfavorecer. || Desaprobar (to disapprove).

disfeature [dis'fi:tʃə*] v. tr. Desfigurar.

disfiguration [dis,figjuəreiʃən] n. Desfiguración, *f.*

disfigure [dis'figə*] v. tr. Desfigurar. || Afear (to spoil): *pylons which disfigure the landscape*, postes que afean el paisaje.

disfigurement [dis'figəmənt] n. Desfiguración, *f.* || Afeamiento, *m.* (spoiling).

disfranchise ['dis'fræntʃaiz] v. tr. Privar de los derechos civiles *or* del derecho de votación.

disgorge [dis'gɔ:dʒ] v. tr. Devolver, vomitar (to vomit). || Verter, descargar (a river). || Devolver (to give back). || Desembuchar (birds).

disgrace [dis'greis] n. Deshonra, *f.* (loss of honour). || Ignominia, *f.* (ignominy). || Vergüenza, *f.* (cause of shame). || Desgracia, *f.* (disfavour). || — *This room is a disgrace*, esta habitación es una vergüenza. || *To be in disgrace*, haber caído en desgracia (person), estar castigado (child). || *To bring disgrace on*, deshonrar. || *To fall into disgrace*, caer en desgracia.

disgrace [dis'greis] v. tr. Deshonrar (to bring shame upon): *to disgrace one's family*, deshonrar a la familia. || *He was disgraced for his behaviour*, su comportamiento le hizo caer en desgracia.

disgraceful [—ful] adj. Vergonzoso, sa (shameful). || Deshonroso, sa (dishonourable): *disgraceful act*, acto deshonroso. || *Disgraceful!*, ¡qué vergüenza!

disgracefulness [—fulnis] n. Lo vergonzoso.

disgruntle [dis'grʌntl] v. tr. Disgustar, contrariar.

disgruntled [—d] adj. Contrariado, da; descontento, ta (*at*, de). || Disgustado, da (*with*, con).

disguisable [dis'gaizəbl] adj. FIG. Disimulable.

disguise [dis'gaiz] n. Disfraz, *m.* || FIG. Disfraz, *m.*

disguise [dis'gaiz] v. tr. Disfrazar. || FIG. Disimular (to hide). | Disfrazar: *to disguise the voice*, disfrazar la voz. || *To disguise o.s. as*, disfrazarse de.

disgust [dis'gʌst] n. Repugnancia, *f.*, asco, *m.* || *To fill with disgust*, repugnar, dar asco.

disgust [dis'gʌst] v. tr. Repugnar, dar asco a (to fill with loathing). || Indignar (to make indignant).

disgusted [—id] adj. Asqueado, da.

disgusting [—iŋ] adj. Repugnante, asqueroso, sa.

disgustingly [—iŋli] adv. De una manera asquerosa, asquerosamente. || *He is disgustingly mean*, es de una tacañería que da asco.

dish [diʃ] n. Plato, *m.* (eating vessel). || Fuente, *f.* (serving vessel). || Plato, *m.* (food). || PHOT. Cubeta, *f.*

— Pl. Platos, *m.*: *to wash the dishes*, fregar los platos. || — FAM. *Reading is not my dish*, no me gusta mayormente leer. | *She is quite a dish*, es un bombón.

dish [diʃ] v. tr. Dar forma cóncava *or* convexa a (to shape). || Ahuecar (to hollow). || Servir (food). || Arruinar (chances). || FAM. Vencer (to outmanoeuvre). || — FAM. *To dish out*, dar (news), dar, asestar (blows), infligir (a punishment), pagar (to pay), gastar (to spend). || *To dish up*, servir (food), sacar, presentar: *to dish up the same arguments time and again*, sacar siempre los mismos argumentos.

dishabille [,disæ'bi:l] n. Traje (*m.*) de casa, bata, *f.*: *to be in dishabille*, estar en traje de casa.

disharmonious [,disha:'məuniəs] adj. Disonante (sounds). || Discorde, discordante (opinions).

disharmonize [dis'ha:mənaiz] v. tr. Desarmonizar.

disharmony ['dis'ha:məni] n. Falta (*f.*) de armonía. || MUS. Disonancia, *f.*

dishcloth ['diʃklɔθ] n. Bayeta, *f.*, trapo (*m.*) de fregar.

dishearten [dis'ha:tn] v. tr. Descorazonar, desanimar, desalentar.

disheartening [—iŋ] adj. Desalentador, ra; descorazonador, ra.

disheartenment [—mənt] n. Descorazonamiento, *m.*, desaliento, *m.*, desánimo, *m.*

dishevel [di'ʃevəl] v. tr. Despeinar (one's hair). | Desaliñar, desarreglar (clothes).

dishevelled (U. S. **disheveled**) [—d] adj. Despeinado, da (hair). || Desaliñado, da; desarreglado, da (clothes).

dishevelment [—mənt] n. Desorden, *m.* (of hair). || Desaliño, *m.* (of clothes).

dishful ['diʃful] n. Plato, *m.*

dishonest [dis'ɔnist] adj. Poco íntegro, gra; poco honrado, da (people). || Fraudulento, ta (dealings).

dishonesty [dis'ɔnisti] n. Falta (*f.*) de honradez (lack of honesty). || Fraude, *m.* (fraud).

dishonour (U. S. **dishonor**) [dis'ɔnə*] n. Deshonra, *f.*, deshonor, *m.* || Falta (*f.*) de pago, rechazo, *m.* (of a bill, etc.).

dishonour (U. S. **dishonor**) [dis'ɔnə*] v. tr. Deshonrar (to bring shame on): *to dishonour a woman*, deshonrar a una mujer. || Faltar a: *to dishonour one's word*, faltar a su palabra. || Rechazar, negarse a pagar (a cheque).

dishonourable (U. S. **dishonorable**) [dis ɔnərəbl] adj. Deshonroso, sa.
dishouse [dis'hauz] v. tr. Expulsar.
dishpan ['diʃpæn] n. U. S. Barreño, *m.*
dishrack ['diʃræk] n. Escurreplatos, *m. inv.*
dish towel ['diʃ,tauəl] U. S. Trapo (*m.*) *or* paño (*m.*) de cocina.
dishwarmer ['diʃ,wɔ:mə*] n. Calientaplatos, *m. inv.*
dishwasher ['diʃ,wɔʃə*] n. Lavaplatos, *m.* & *f. inv.* (person). || Máquina (*f.*) lavaplatos, lavaplatos, *m. inv.*, lavavajillas, *m. inv.* (machine).
dishwater ['diʃ,wɔ:tə*] n. Agua (*f.*) de fregar platos. || FAM. Agua (*f.*) sucia (weak tea or coffee).
dishy ['diʃi] adj. FAM. Guapo, pa; atractivo, va.
disillusion [,disi'lu:ʒən] n. Desilusión, *f.*
disillusion [,disi'lu:ʒən] v. tr. Desilusionar: *to be disillusioned with*, quedar desilusionado con *or* de.
disillusionment [—mənt] n. Desilusión, *f.*
disincentive [,disin'sentiv] n. Freno, *m.*
disinclination [,disinkli'neiʃən] n. Aversión, *f.*, poca inclinación, *f.*
disincline ['disin'klain] v. tr. Quitar las ganas de. || *To be disinclined to*, estar poco dispuesto a, tener pocas ganas de.
disinfect [,disin'fekt] v. tr. Desinfectar.
disinfectant [,disin'fektənt] n. Desinfectante, *m.*
— Adj. Desinfectante.
disinfection [,disin'fekʃən] n. Desinfección, *f.*
disinfest [,disin'fest] v. tr. Desinfestar.
disinfestation [,disinfes'teiʃən] n. *Rat disinfestation*, desratización, *f.*
disinflationary [,disin'fleiʃənəri] adj. Desinflacionista, deflacionista.
disingenuous [,disin'dʒenjuəs] adj. Insincero, ra; falso, sa; disimulado, da.
disinherit ['disin'herit] v. tr. Desheredar.
disinheritance [,disin'heritəns] or **disinheriting** ['disin'heritiŋ] n. Desheredamiento, *m.*, desheredación, *f.*
disintegrable [dis'intigrəbl] adj. Desintegrable.
disintegrate [dis'intigreit] v. tr. Desintegrar, disgregar.
— V. intr. Desintegrarse, disgregarse.
disintegration [dis,inti'greiʃən] n. Desintegración, *f.*: *atomic disintegration*, desintegración atómica.
disinter ['disin'tə:*] v. tr. Desenterrar.
disinterest [dis'intrist] n. Desinterés, *m.*
disinterest [dis'intrist] v. tr. Desinteresar.
disinterested [dis'intristid] adj. Desinteresado, da (without vested interest). || Imparcial (unbiased). || Indiferente.
disinterestedness [—nis] n. Desinterés, *m.*
disinterment [,disin'tə:mənt] n. Desenterramiento, *m.*, exhumación, *f.*
disjoin [dis'dʒɔin] v. tr. Separar, desunir.
— V. intr. Separarse, desunirse.
disjoint [dis'dʒɔint] v. tr. Desarticular. || Trinchar (a fowl).
disjointed [—id] adj. Sin conexión, inconexo, xa (incoherent). || Desarticulado, da. || Desunido, da (disunited).
disjunction [dis'dʒʌŋkʃən] n. Separación, *f.* || GRAMM. PHIL. Disyunción, *f.*
disjunctive [dis'dʒʌŋktiv] adj. GRAMM. PHIL. Disyuntivo, va.
— N. GRAMM. Conjunción (*f.*) disyuntiva. || PHIL. Proposición (*f.*) disyuntiva.
disk [disk] n. Disco, *m.*: *Newton's disk*, disco de Newton. || ANAT. Disco, *m.* (of bone). || SP. Disco, *m.*: *disk thrower*, lanzador de disco. || TECH. Disco, *m.* (of brake). | Disco, *m.* (of plough). || Disco, *m.* (record). || *Parking disk*, disco de control.
dislikable [dis'laikəbl] adj. Antipático, ca; odioso, sa.
dislike [dis'laik] n. Aversión, *f.*, antipatía, *f.* (*for*, *of*, a). || *To take a dislike to s.o.*, cogerle antipatía a uno.
dislike [dis'laik] v. tr. Tener antipatía a, no gustarle a uno, tener aversión a: *he dislikes me*, me tiene antipatía, no le gusto, me tiene aversión. || No gustarle a uno: *I dislike music*, no me gusta la música. || *I don't dislike him*, no me disgusta, no le encuentro antipático.
— OBSERV. El verbo *dislike* se construye siempre con el gerundio (*I dislike working*, no me gusta trabajar).
dislocate ['disləukeit] v. tr. Dislocar (to put out of joint). || Desarreglar, trastornar (plans). || *To dislocate one's jaw, one's shoulder*, desencajarse la mandíbula, dislocarse el hombro.
dislocation [,disləu'keiʃən] n. Dislocación, *f.*, desarticulación, *f.* (putting out of joint). || Trastorno, *m.*, desarreglo, *m.* (of plans). || Dislocación, *f.* (of a bone). || Desencajamiento, *m.* (of jaw).
dislodge [dis'lɔdʒ] v. tr. Desalojar (to oust): *to dislodge the enemy from the fort*, desalojar al enemigo del fuerte. || Sacar (to remove). || Desalojar, hacer salir (an animal).
dislodgement [—mənt] or **dislodging** [—iŋ] n. Desalojamiento, *m.*
disloyal ['dis'lɔiəl] adj. Desleal: *disloyal to his brother*, desleal con su hermano.
disloyalty [—ti] n. Deslealtad, *f.*
dismal ['dizməl] adj. Deprimente, triste: *dismal landscape*, paisaje triste. || Triste, sombrío, a (face). || Tenebroso, sa (dark). || Deprimido, da (depressed). || Lúgubre, triste (voice). || Catastrófico, ca (failure). || Lamentable (very bad). || FAM. *The dismals*, nostalgia, *f.*, morriña, *f.*
dismantle [dis'mæntl] v. tr. Desmantelar. || Desarmar, desmontar: *to dismantle a watch*, desarmar un reloj.
dismantlement [—mənt] or **dismantling** [—iŋ] n. Desarme, *m.*, desmontaje, *m.* (of machine). || Desmantelamiento, *m.* (of a place).
dismast ['dis'mɑ:st] v. tr. MAR. Desarbolar.
dismasting [—iŋ] n. MAR. Desarboladura, *f.*
dismay [dis'mei] n. Consternación, *f.*: *to look in dismay*, mirar con consternación. || Desaliento, *m.* (discouragement). || Espanto, *m.* (fright). || *To fill s.o. with dismay*, consternarle a uno.
dismay [dis'mei] v. tr. Consternar. || Espantar (to frighten). || Desalentar (to discourage).
dismember [dis'membə*] v. tr. Desmembrar: *to dismember an empire*, desmembrar un imperio.
dismemberment [—mənt] n. Desmembramiento, *m.*
dismiss [dis'mis] v. tr. Despedir: *after supper, he dismissed the servant and went to bed*, después de cenar, despidió al criado y fue a acostarse; *he was dismissed from his job*, le despidieron de su trabajo. || Destituir (high officials). || MIL. Licenciar (to discharge). || Dar permiso para retirarse (to send away). || Disolver (an assembly). || Alejar (to discard mentally): *dismiss those sad thoughts*, aleja esos tristes pensamientos. || Descartar (an idea). || Despachar, acabar con (to treat briefly): *he dismissed the subject in a few words*, despachó el asunto en pocas palabras. || JUR. Desestimar (a claim). | Absolver (the accused). || MIL. *Dismiss!*, ¡rompan filas!
— V. intr. MIL. Romper filas.
dismissal [dis'misəl] n. Despido, *m.* (of servants, employees). || Destitución, *f.* (of high officials). || Disolución, *f.* (of an assembly). || Abandono, *m.* (of an idea, thought, etc.). || JUR. Rechazamiento, *m.*, desestimación, *f.* || MIL. Licenciamiento, *m.*
dismount ['dis'maunt] v. intr. Apearse, bajarse, desmontarse (from a horse, etc.).
— V. tr. Desmontar. || TECH. Desarmar, desmontar. || Desengastar (a jewel).
disobedience [,disə'bi:djəns] n. Desobediencia, *f.*
disobedient [,disə'bi:djənt] adj. Desobediente.
disobey ['disə'bei] v. tr./intr. Desobedecer.
disoblige ['disə'blaidʒ] v. tr. Contrariar, disgustar (to displease). || No hacer un favor a, no complacer (not to oblige).
disobliging [—iŋ] adj. Poco servicial, poco complaciente (not obliging). || Desagradable, molesto, ta (unpleasant).
disorder [dis'ɔ:də*] n. Desorden, *m.* (untidiness, state of confusion). || Desorden, *m.*, disturbio, *m.* (riot). || Trastorno, *m.* (ailment): *nervous disorders*, trastornos nerviosos.
disorder [dis'ɔ:də*] v. tr. Desordenar (to disarrange). || Trastornar (to upset the health of).
disorderliness [—linis] n. Desorden, *m.*
disorderly [—li] adj. Desordenado, da; desarreglado, da (room, etc.). || Desordenado, da (person). || Alborotado, da (debate, meeting). || Escandaloso, sa (scandalous). || Desarreglado, da (life). || — *Disordely conduct*, conducta escandalosa (behaviour), alteración (*f.*) del orden público. || FIG. *Disorderly house*, casa (*f.*) de lenocinio (brothel), casa (*f.*) de juego (gambling house).
disorganization [dis,ɔ:gənai'zeiʃən] n. Desorganización, *f.*
disorganize [dis'ɔ:gənaiz] v. tr. Desorganizar.
disorganizer, [—ə*] n. Desorganizador, ra.
disorient [dis'ɔ:rient] or **disorientate** [—eit] v. tr. Desorientar. || ARCH. Orientar mal (a church).
disorientation [disɔ:rien'teiʃən] n. Desorientación, *f.*
disown [dis'əun] v. tr. No reconocer como suyo (one's offspring). || Repudiar (to repudiate). || Negar (to deny). || No reconocer (one's signature). || Desautorizar (an agent).
disparage [dis'pæridʒ] v. tr. Menospreciar, despreciar (to belittle). || Denigrar (to speak badly of). || Desacreditar (to discredit).
disparagement [—mənt] n. Descrédito, *m.* (discredit). || Denigración, *f.* (detraction). || Menosprecio, *m.* (underestimation). || *I haven't written it in disparagement of him*, no lo he escrito para desprestigiarle.
disparager [—ə*] n. Detractor, ra.
disparaging [—iŋ] adj. Despectivo, va; menospreciativo, va (word, look). || Denigrante (speech).
disparagingly [—iŋli] adv. Con desprecio, despectivamente.
disparate ['dispərit] adj. Dispar.
disparity [dis'pæriti] n. Disparidad, *f.*
dispassionate [dis'pæʃnit] adj. Desapasionado, da (without emotion). || Imparcial (unbiased).
dispatch [dis'pætʃ] n. Expedición, *f.*, despacho, *m.* (of letter, message). || Envío, *m.* (of messenger). || Expedición, *f.*, envio, *m.* (of parcels). || Despacho, *m.* (official report). || MIL. Parte, *m.* || COMM. Servicio (*m.*) de expedición. || Ejecución, *f.* (a putting to death). || Despacho, *m.* (of business, duty). || Diligencia, *f.* (promptitude).
dispatch [dis'pætʃ] v. tr. Expedir, remitir (a letter, parcels). || Enviar (messenger). || Matar, despachar (to kill). || Despachar (meal, work, business, etc.).
dispatch boat [—bəut] n. MAR. Aviso, *m.*

dispatcher [dis'pætʃə*] n. Expedidor, ra.
dispel [dis'pel] v. tr. Disipar.
dispensable [dis'pensəbl] adj. Prescindible, innecesario, ria (not necessary). || REL. Dispensable.
dispensary [dis'pensəri] n. Dispensario, *m.* (hospital). || Farmacia, *f.* (laboratory).
dispensation [,dispen'seiʃən] n. Dispensa, *f.*, exención, *f.* (exemption from a rule, law, etc.). || Decreto (*m.*) divino, designio (*m.*) divino (fate ordained by providence). || Distribución, *f.*, reparto, *m.* (of rewards, alms). || JUR. Administración, *f.* || Ley, *f.*: *the Mosaic dispensation*, la Ley mosaica.
dispense [dis'pens] v. tr. Distribuir, repartir (to distribute). || Preparar (drugs). || Administrar (justice). || Aplicar (laws, rules). || Administrar (sacrament). || Eximir, dispensar (to exempt).
— V. intr. Dar dispensa. || *To dispense with*, prescindir de.
dispenser [—ə*] n. Distribuidor, ra (s.o. who distributes). || Dispensador, ra (of favours). || Farmacéutico, ca (chemist). || Administrador, ra (of justice). || Distribuidor (*m.*) automático (machine).
dispeople ['dis'pi:pl] v. tr. Despoblar.
dispersal [dis'pə:səl] n. Dispersión, *f.*
disperse [dis'pə:s] v. tr. Dispersar: *the wind dispersed the clouds*, el viento dispersó las nubes; *the police dispersed the demonstrators*, la policía dispersó a los manifestantes. || Situar, apostar (to put in position): *to disperse troops along the road*, apostar tropas a lo largo de la carretera. || Dispersar, diseminar (news). || PHYS. Dispersar (light).
— V. intr. Dispersarse. || *We dispersed to our homes*, nos fuimos cada uno a nuestra casa.
dispersed [—t] adj. Disperso, sa.
dispersion [dis'pə:ʃən] n. Dispersión, *f.*
dispersive [dis'pə:siv] adj. Dispersivo, va.
dispirit [di'spirit] v. tr. Desalentar, desanimar.
dispiteous [dis'pitiəs] adj. Despiadado, da.
displace [dis'pleis] v. tr. Desplazar, cambiar de lugar, trasladar (to remove from its usual place). || Destituir (to remove from office). || Quitar el puesto a (to oust). || Sustituir, reemplazar (to substitute). || Desplazar (to take the place of): *a ship displaces water*, un barco desplaza agua. || CHEM. PHYS. Desplazar. || *Displaced person*, persona desplazada, expatriado, da.
displacement [—mənt] n. Desplazamiento, *m.*, traslado, *m.*, cambio (*m.*) de sitio (move). || Destitución, *f.* (from office). || Sustitución, *f.*, reemplazo, *m.* (substitution). || MAR. CHEM. PHYS. Desplazamiento, *m.*
display [dis'plei] n. Exhibición, *f.* (a showing): *on display*, en exhibición. || Exposición, *f.* (a show). || Alarde, *m.* (of emotion). || Despliegue, *m.* (of energy). || Demostración, *f.* (demonstration). || MIL. Desfile, *m.*, parada, *f.* || Pompa, *f.*: *a parade with great display*, un desfile con mucha pompa. || TECH. Representación (*f.*) visual (data processing). || — *Display artist*, escaparatista, *m.* & *f.* || *Display window*, escaparate, *m.* [*Amer.*, vidriera, *f.*].
display [dis'plei] v. tr. Exhibir, exponer (to show): *shops display their goods in the windows*, las tiendas exhiben sus artículos en los escaparates. || Demostrar, mostrar: *he displays great intelligence*, muestra una gran inteligencia. || Desplegar (energy). || Lucir: *he displayed a new tie*, lucía una nueva corbata.
displease [dis'pli:z] v. tr./intr. Disgustar, desagradar, molestar.
displeased [—d] adj. Disgustado, da; molesto, ta: *displeased at*, disgustado con.
displeasing [—iŋ] adj. Desagradable.
displeasure [dis'pleʒə*] n. Disgusto, *m.*, desagrado, *m.*: *to show displeasure*, mostrar desagrado; *to my great displeasure*, con gran disgusto mío. || *To incur s.o.'s displeasure*, enojar *or* disgustar a alguien.
disport [dis'pɔ:t] v. tr. *To disport o.s.*, entretenerse (to amuse o.s.).
disposable [dis'pəuzəbl] adj. Disponible (available). || Para tirar: *disposable wrapping*, envase para tirar.
disposal [dis'pəuzəl] n. Arreglo, *m.*, colocación, *f.*, disposición, *f.* (arrangement). || Destrucción, *f.*, eliminación, *f.*: *disposal of refuse*, destrucción de las basuras. || Neutralización, *f.* (of bombs). || Evacuación, *f.*: *sewage disposal*, evacuación de las aguas residuales. || Resolución, *f.* (of question, difficulty). || COMM. Venta, *f.* (sale). || Traspaso, *m.* (of property). || — *At the disposal of*, a la disposición de. || *At your disposal*, a la disposición de usted, a su disposición. || *To have at one's disposal*, tener a su disposición, disponer de.
dispose [dis'pəuz] v. tr. Disponer, colocar (to place). || Inclinar, disponer (to incline). || Mover (to move). || Determinar, disponer (to determine).
— V. intr. Disponer: *man proposes, God disposes*, el hombre propone y Dios dispone. || *To dispose of*, tirar (to throw away), disponer de (to have at one's disposal), echar por tierra (arguments), deshacerse de (to get rid of), traspasar (to transfer), vender (to sell), despachar (a matter), poner fin a (to stop), resolver (to settle), despachar, liquidar (to kill), consumir, comer (to eat), apabullar (an interlocutor), emplear, ocupar (one's time).
disposed [—d] adj. Dispuesto, ta.
disposition [,dispə'ziʃən] n. Disposición, *f.*: *at the disposition of*, a la disposición de. || Disposición, *f.*, colocación, *f.* (arrangement). || Traspaso, *m.* (transfer of property). || Disposición, *f.*, carácter, *m.* (nature). || Predisposición, *f.* (tendency). || Propensión, *f.* (inclination). || Designio, *m.* (dispensation). || Preparativo, *m.*, disposición, *f.* (plan). || — JUR. *Disposition inter vivos*, donación (*f.*) entre vivos. | *Dispositions of a will*, disposiciones testamentarias.
dispossess ['dispə'zes] v. tr. Desposeer. || JUR. Desahuciar (to expropriate). || *To dispossess o.s. of*, desposeerse de, desprenderse de.
dispossession [,dispə'zeʃən] n. Desposeimiento, *m.* || JUR. Desahucio, *m.* (expropriation).
dispraise [dis'preiz] n. Crítica, *f.* (blame). || Desprecio, *m.* (contempt).
dispraise [dis'preiz] v. tr. Criticar (to blame). || Despreciar (to contempt).
disproof ['dis'pru:f] n. Refutación, *f.*
disproportion ['disprə'pɔ:ʃən] n. Desproporción, *f.*
disproportion ['disprə'pɔ:ʃən] v. tr. Desproporcionar.
disproportional [—l] or **disproportionate** [—it] or **disproportioned** [—d] adj. Desproporcionado, da.
disprovable [dis'pru:vəbl] adj. Refutable.
disproval ['dis'pru:vəl] n. Refutación, *f.*
disprove ['dis'pru:v] v. tr. Refutar.
disputable [dis'pju:təbl] adj. Discutible, controvertible, disputable.
disputant [dis'pju:tənt] n. Discutidor, ra; controversista, *m.* & *f.*
disputation [,dispju'teiʃən] n. Controversia, *f.* || Discusión, *f.*, debate, *m.* (discussion).
disputatious [,dispju'teiʃəs] adj. Disputador, ra. || Disputable, discutible, controvertible.
dispute [dis'pju:t] n. Disputa, *f.* (quarrel). || Controversia, *f.* (controversy). || Discusión, *f.*, debate, *m.* || JUR. Litigio, *m.*: *under dispute*, en litigio. || — *Beyond dispute*, indiscutible, incontrovertible. || *In dispute*, en debate. || *Labour dispute*, conflicto (*m.*) laboral. || *Territory in dispute*, territorio (*m.*) en litigio.
dispute [dis'pju:t] v. intr. Discutir (*about, over*, de, sobre). || Disputarse (to quarrel).
— V. tr. Poner en duda (to question the truth of). || Discutir (an order, a question). || Disputar (to fight for): *to dispute a prize*, disputar un premio. || *A much disputed question*, un asunto muy controvertido.
disputer [—ə*] n. Disputador, ra.
disqualification [dis,kwɔlifi'keiʃən] n. Incapacidad, *f.*, inhabilitación, *f.*, (incapacity). || SP. Descalificación, *f.* (of a competitor). | Desclasificación, *f.* (of a team).
disqualify [dis'kwɔlifai] v. tr. Incapacitar, inhabilitar (to render unfit, to take legal right from). || SP. Descalificar (a competitor). | Desclasificar (a team). || *I was disqualified from driving for a year*, me retiraron el carnet de conducir por un año.
disquiet [dis'kwaiət] n. Preocupación, *f.*, inquietud, *f.*, intranquilidad, *f.*
— Adj. Preocupado, da; inquieto, ta; intranquilo, la.
disquiet [dis'kwaiət] v. tr. Preocupar, inquietar, intranquilizar.
disquieting [—iŋ] adj. Preocupante, inquietante.
disquietude [dis'kwaiitju:d] n. Preocupación, *f.*, inquietud, *f.* (worry). || Agitación, *f.* || Malestar, *m.* (uneasiness).
disquisition [,diskwi'ziʃən] n. Disquisición, *f.*
disrate [dis'reit] v. tr. MAR. Degradar.
disregard ['disri'gɑ:d] n. Indiferencia, *f.* || Despreocupación, *f.*, descuido, *m.* (neglect). || JUR. Violación, *f.*, desacato, *m.* (of the law). || *With disregard for his own life*, con desprecio de su vida.
disregard ['disri'gɑ:d] v. tr. No hacer caso de, desatender, hacer caso omiso de: *to disregard s.o.'s advice*, no hacer caso de los consejos de uno. || Despreocuparse de, descuidar (to neglect). || JUR. Violar, desacatar (the law).
disregardful [—ful] adj. Que no hace caso de (of s.o.'s advice). || Negligente (neglectful). || Despreocupado, da (careless). || Poco respetuoso, sa (of the law).
disrelish [dis'reliʃ] n. Repugnancia, *f.*, aversión, *f.*
disrelish [dis'reliʃ] v. tr. No gustarle a uno, tener repugnancia por
disrepair ['disri'pɛə*] n. Mal estado, *m.*, desarreglo, *m.* || *To fall into disrepair*, descomponerse, deteriorarse (machinery), caer en ruina (house).
disreputable [dis'repjutəbl] adj. De mala reputación *or* fama (not respectable). || Vergonzoso, sa (shameful). || Lamentable (shabby).
disrepute ['disri'pju:t] n. Mala reputación, *f.*, desprestigio, *m.*, descrédito, *m.* || — *To bring into disrepute*, desprestigiar, desacreditar. || *To fall into disrepute*, desprestigiarse, desacreditarse.
disrespect ['disris'pekt] n. Falta (*f.*) de respeto. || *He meant no disrespect*, no quería ofenderle.
disrespect [,disris'pekt] v. tr. Faltar al respeto a.
disrespectful [—ful] adj. Irrespetuoso, sa.
disrobe ['dis'rəub] v. intr. Desvestirse, desnudarse.
— V. tr. Desvestir, desnudar.
disroot [dis'ru:t] v. tr. Arrancar de raíz, desarraigar.
disrupt [dis'rʌpt] v. tr. Trastornar, alterar (to upset). || Romper (to break up). || Interrumpir: *to disrupt the traffic*, interrumpir el tráfico. || Desbaratar, trastornar (plans). || Desorganizar (to disorganize).
disruption [dis'rʌpʃən] n. Ruptura, *f.* || Interrupción, *f.* || Desbaratamiento, *m.*, trastorno, *m.* (of plans). || Desorganización, *f.*

disruptive [dis'rʌptiv] adj. ELECTR. Disruptivo, va. || Que trastorna *or* desorganiza. || Perjudicial (harmful).
disruptor [dis'rʌptə*] n. Disruptor, *m.*
dissatisfaction ['dis,sætis'fækʃən] n. Descontento, *m.*, insatisfacción, *f.* (*at, with*, de, con).
dissatisfactory ['dis,sætis'fæktəri] adj. Poco satisfactorio, ria.
dissatisfied ['dis'sætisfaid] adj. Descontento, ta; insatisfecho, cha.
dissastify ['dis'sætisfai] v. tr. No satisfacer (to fail to satisfy). || Disgustar, descontentar, desagradar (to make discontented).
dissect [di'sekt] v. tr. Disecar (to cut open for examination). || Abrir (to open up). || FIG. Examinar detenidamente (to examine in detail). || *Dissecting room*, sala (*f.*) de disección.
dissection [di'sekʃən] n. Disección, *f.*, disecación, *f.* (act of dissecting). || Examen (*m.*) detenido (close examination).
dissector [di'sektə*] n. Disecador, ra; disector, ra (person). || Escalpelo, *m.* (instrument).
disseise or **disseize** [dis'si:z] v. tr. JUR. Desposeer.
disseisin or **disseizin** [dis'si:zin] n. JUR. Desposesión (*f.*) *or* desposeimiento (*m.*) ilegal.
dissemble [di'sembl] v. tr. Ocultar, disimular. || Simular, fingir (a virtue, etc.).
— V. intr. Disimular.
dissembler [di'semblə*] n. Disimulador, ra.
disseminate [di'semineit] v. tr. Diseminar (to scatter). || Difundir, propagar (beliefs, propaganda, etc.).
— V. intr. Diseminarse. || Difundirse, propagarse.
dissemination [di,semi'neiʃən] n. Diseminación, *f.* (a spreading). || Difusión, *f.*, propagación, *f.* (of beliefs, propaganda).
disseminator [di'semineitə*] n. Difusor, ra; propagador, ra.
dissension [di'senʃən] n. Disensión, *f.* || *To sow dissension*, sembrar la discordia.
dissent [di'sent] n. Disensión, *f.* || Disidencia, *f.* || Disentimiento, *m.* (disagreement).
dissent [di'sent] v. intr. Disentir (*from*, de) [not to agree with]. || Disidir (to refuse to accept a doctrine).
dissenter [di'sentə*] n. Disidente, *m.* & *f.*
dissentient [di'senʃiənt] adj./n. Disidente.
dissenting [di'sentiŋ] adj. Disidente.
dissert [di'sə:t] or **dissertate** ['disəteit] v. intr. Disertar (*on*, de).
dissertation [,disə'teiʃən] n. Disertación, *f.* || Informe, *m.* (treatise). || Tesis, *f.* (for a doctorate).
dissertator ['disəteitə*] n. Disertador, ra; disertante, *m.* & *f.*
disserve [dis'sə:v] v. tr. Perjudicar.
disservice [—is] n. Perjuicio, *m.* || *To do s.o. a disservice*, perjudicar a alguien.
dissever [dis'sevə*] v. tr. Separar, desunir.
— V. intr. Separarse, desunirse.
dissidence ['disidəns] n. Disidencia, *f.* || Disentimiento, *m.*, desacuerdo, *m.* (disagreement).
dissident ['disidənt] adj./n. Disidente.
dissimilar ['di'similə*] adj. Distinto, ta; desigual, diferente, desemejante (*to*, de).
dissimilarity [,disimi'læriti] n. Disimilitud, *f.*, desemejanza, *f.*, desigualdad, *f.*, diferencia, *f.*
dissimilate [di'simileit] v. tr. Desasimilar. || Disimilar (in phonetics).
dissimilation ['disimi'leiʃən] n. Disimilación, *f.* (in phonetics). || Desasimilación, *f.* (catabolism).
dissimilitude [,disi'militju:d] n. Disimilitud, *f.*
dissimulate [di'simjuleit] v. tr./intr. Disimular.
dissimulation [di,simju'leiʃən] n. Disimulo, *m.*, disimulación, *f.*
dissimulator [di'simjuleitə*] n. Disimulador, ra.
dissipate ['disipeit] v. tr. Disipar (clouds, doubts). || Dispersar (efforts). || Disipar, derrochar (one's resources). || Dispersar (a crowd).
— V. intr. Disiparse. || Dispersarse.
dissipated [—id] adj. Disipado, da. || Disoluto, ta: *dissipated life*, vida disoluta.
dissipation [,disi'peiʃən] adj. Disipación, *f.* || Dispersión, *f.* (of efforts). || Disipación, *f.*, derroche, *m.* (of resources). || Disolución, *f.* (debauchery).
dissociable [di'səuʃjəbl] adj. Disociable.
dissocial [di'səuʃəl] adj. Insociable.
dissociate [di'səuʃieit] v. tr. Disociar. || *To dissociate o.s. from*, desolidarizarse de, disociarse de.
— V. intr. Disociarse.
dissociation [di,səusi'eiʃən] n. Disociación, *f.*
dissolubility [di,sɔlju'biliti] n. Disolubilidad, *f.*
dissoluble [di'sɔljubl] adj. Disoluble.
dissolute ['disəlu:t] adj. Disoluto, ta.
dissoluteness [—nis] n. Disolución, *f.*
dissolution [,disə'lu:ʃən] n. Disolución, *f.* (of meeting, society, marriage). || Disolución, *f.* (melting). || Rescisión, *f.* (of a contract).
dissolvable [di'zɔlvəbl] adj. Soluble. || JUR. Disoluble.
dissolve [di'zɔlv] v. tr. Disolver. || Disipar (illusions). || Descomponer, desintegrar (to disintegrate). || JUR. Rescindir (a contract). | Disolver (a society). || FIG. Dispersar, desvanecer (clouds). | Dispersar (crowd).
— V. intr. Disolverse. || Descomponerse, desintegrarse. || FIG. Deshacerse : *she dissolved into tears*, se deshizo en lágrimas. || CINEM. Fundirse (to fade into another picture).
dissolve [di'zɔlv] n. CINEM. Fundido, *m.*
dissolved [—d] adj. Disuelto, ta.
dissolvent [di'zɔlvənt] adj. Disolvente.
— N. Disolvente, *m.*
dissonance ['disənəns] n. MUS. Disonancia, *f.* || FIG. Desacuerdo, *m.*, disentimiento, *m.*
dissonant ['disənənt] adj. Disonante, discordante (discordant). || FIG. En desacuerdo (*from, to*, con).
dissuade [di'sweid] v. tr. Disuadir (*from*, de). || Desaconsejar (to advise against).
dissuasion [di'sweiʒən] n. Disuasión, *f.*
dissuasive [di'sweisiv] adj. Disuasivo, va.
dissyllabic ['disi'læbik] adj. Bisilábico, ca; bisílabo, ba; disílabo, ba; disilábico, ca.
dissyllabe [di'siləbl] n. Bisílabo, *m.*, bisilábico, *m.*, disílabo, *m.*, disilábico, *m.*
dissymmetric ['disi'metrik] or **dissymmetrical** [—əl] adj. Disimétrico, ca.
dissymmetry ['di'simitri] n. Disimetría, *f.*
distaff ['distɑ:f] n. Rueca, *f.*
— Adj. *The distaff side of a family*, la rama femenina de una familia.
distance ['distəns] n. Distancia, *f.* (an interval in space): *at a distance of two kilometers*, a dos kilómetros de distancia. || Lejanía, *f.* (remoter part of a view). || FIG. Distancia, *f.* (reserve, aloofness). || MUS. Intervalo, *m.* || — *At* o *from a distance*, de lejos. || *At a distance of ten years*, después de diez años. || *At a respectable distance*, a respetable *or* respetuosa distancia. || *In the distance*, en la lejanía, a lo lejos. || *Long-distance aeroplane*, avión (*m.*) de larga distancia. || SP. *Long-distance race*, carrera (*f.*) de fondo. | *Middle-distance runner*, corredor (*m.*) de medio fondo. || *To cut down* o *to reduce the distance*, acortar las distancias. || *To keep at a distance*, mantener *or* tener a distancia. || *To keep one's distance*, guardar la distancia (of vehicles in a convoy), guardar las distancias (to remain aloof). || *Town within walking distance*, ciudad adonde se puede ir andando. || *Within speaking distance*, al alcance de la voz.
distance ['distəns] v. tr. Alejar (to maintain at a distance). || Distanciar (to outdistance).
distant ['distənt] adj. Distante, lejano, na (far away). || Lejano, na (remote in time, far removed in relationship, likeness, etc.): *a distant cousin*, un primo lejano; *a distant resemblance*, un lejano parecido. || FIG. Distante. || *Ten miles distant*, a diez millas.
distantly [—li] adv. De lejos. || FIG. Con frialdad. || *To be distantly related*, ser parientes lejanos.
distaste ['dis'teist] n. Aversión, *f.* (*for*, por, a).
distasteful [dis'teistful] adj. Desagradable.
distemper [dis'tempə*] n. Moquillo, *m.* (dog's disease). || Malestar, *m.* (uneasiness). || Malhumor, *m.*, mal genio, *m.* (bad temper). || Temple, *m.* (paint). || Pintura (*f.*) al temple (method of painting). || JUR. Desorden, *m.* (turnmoil).
distemper [dis'tempə*] v. tr. Pintar al temple (to paint). || Poner de malhumor (to anger).
distend [dis'tend] v. tr. Distender. || Hinchar (to swell). || Dilatar (to dilate).
— V. intr. Distenderse. || Hincharse.
distensible [dis'tensəbl] adj. Extensible. || Dilatable, hinchable.
distension (U. S. **distention**) [dis'tenʃən] n. Distensión, *f.* || Hinchazón, *f.* (swelling). || Dilatación, *f.* (dilatation).
distich ['distik] n. POET. Dístico, *m.*
distil or **distill** [dis'til] v. tr./intr. Destilar.
distillate ['distilit] n. Destilado, *m.*
distillation [,disti'leiʃən] n. Destilación, *f.*
distiller [dis'tilə*] n. Destilador, *m.* (person, still).
distiller [dis'tiləri] n. Destilería, *f.*
distinct [dis'tiŋkt] adj. Distinto, ta (*from*, de) [different]. || Claro, ra (clear). || Marcado, da; señalado, da; bien determinado, da (marked, definite): *distinct tendency*, tendencia bien determinada. || *As distinct from*, a diferencia de.
distinction [dis'tiŋkʃən] n. Distinción, *f.* || — *In distinction from* o *to*, a distinción de. || *Of distinction*, distinguido, da: *a man of distinction*, un hombre distinguido; notable, eminente, distinguido, da: *a writer of distinction*, un escritor notable. || *To gain distinction*, distinguirse. || *With distinction*, con sobresaliente (qualification).
distinctive [dis'tiŋktiv] adj. Distintivo, va. || *Distinctive to*, característico de.
distinctness [dis'tiŋktnis] n. Claridad, *f.* || Diferencia, *f.*
distinguish [dis'tiŋgwiʃ] v. tr./intr. Distinguir: *to distinguish one thing from another*, distinguir una cosa de otra. || *To distinguish o.s.*, distinguirse.
distinguishable [—əbl] adj. Distinguible.
distinguished [—t] adj. Distinguido, da (elegant). || Eminente, distinguido, da; notable: *a distinguished writer*, un escritor eminente.
distort [dis'tɔ:t] v. tr. Retorcer, torcer, deformar (to twist out of shape). || FIG. Desvirtuar: *to distort the meaning of a text*, desvirtuar el sentido de un texto.
distortion [dis'tɔ:ʃən] n. Deformación, *f.*, torcimiento, *m.* (twisting). || PHOT. PHYS. Distorsión, *f.* || FIG. Desnaturalización, *f.*, deformación, *f.*, desvirtuación, *f.*

distract [dis'trækt] v. tr. Distraer (to divert the attention of). || Distraer, apartar (attention). || Aturdir, confundir (to confuse). || Enloquecer (to drive mad). || *To distract the enemy*, distraer al enemigo.
distraction [dis'trækʃən] n. Distracción, *f.* (being distracted). || Aturdimiento, *m.*, confusión, *f.* (bewilderment). || Locura, *f.* (frenzy). || Distracción, *f.*, entretenimiento, *m.*, diversión, *f.* (amusement). || *To drive to distraction*, volver loco.
distrain [dis'trein] v. intr. JUR. Embargar.
distrainee [ˌdistrei'ni:] n. JUR. Embargado, da.
distrainer or **distrainor** [ˌdistrei'nə*] n. JUR. Embargador, ra.
distraint [dis'treint] n. JUR. Embargo, *m.*
distrait [dis'trei] adj. Distraído, da.
distraught [dis'trɔ:t] adj. Loco, ca; enloquecido, da. || Muy turbado, da (upset).
distress [dis'tres] n. Aflicción, *f.*, desolación, *f.* || Congoja, *f.*, angustia, *f.* (anguish). || Miseria, *f.* (poverty). || Peligro, *m.*, apuro, *m.* (danger or difficulty): *ship in distress*, barco en peligro. || MED. Agotamiento, *m.* || JUR. Embargo, *m.* || — MAR. *Distress signal*, señal (*f.*) de socorro. || FIG. *To be in distress*, estar en un apuro.
distress [dis'tres] v. tr. Afligir, desolar (to afflict). || Angustiar (to anguish). || MED. Agotar. || JUR. Embargar.
distressed [—t] adj. Afligido, da (afflicted). || Angustiado, da (anguished). || En la miseria (poor). || En peligro (in danger). || MED. Agotado, da.
distressing [—iŋ] adj. Angustioso, sa (grievous).
distribute [dis'tribjut] v. tr. Distribuir, repartir; *to distribute money among the poor*, distribuir dinero entre los pobres. || Clasificar (statistical information). || COMM. PRINT. Distribuir.
distributing [—iŋ] adj. Distribuidor, ra.
distribution [ˌdistri'bju:ʃən] n. Distribución, *f.*, reparto, *m.* || Clasificación, *f.* (in statistics). || COMM. PRINT. Distribución, *f.*
distributive [dis'tribjutiv] adj. Distributivo, va.
— N. GRAMM. Adjetivo (*m.*) distributivo.
distributor [dis'tribjutə*] n. Distribuidor, ra. || AUT. Distribuidor, *m.*, delco, *m.*
district ['distrikt] n. Región, *f.* (region). || Barrio, *m.* (of a town). || Distrito, *m.* (political or geographical division). || — U. S. *District attorney*, fiscal (*m.*) de un distrito judicial. | *District court*, tribunal (*m.*) federal. | *District manager*, representante (*m.*) regional. || *Federal, postal district*, distrito federal, postal. || *University district*, distrito universitario.
distrust [dis'trʌst] n. Desconfianza, *f.*, recelo, *m.* (mistrust). || Sospechas, *f. pl.* (suspicion).
distrust [dis'trʌst] v. tr. Desconfiar de. || Sospechar.
distrustful [—ful] adj. Desconfiado, da; receloso, sa (distrusting). || Sospechoso, sa (suspicious).
distrustfully [—fuli] adv. Con recelo, desconfiadamente.
disturb [dis'tə:b] v. tr. Molestar (to bother): *don't disturb yourself*, no se moleste. || Mover, agitar (to agitate). || Preocupar (to worry). || Desordenar (to move out of order). || Perturbar, alterar (the peace). || Trastornar (s.o.'s mind). || Perturbar, alterar (plans). || PHYS. Perturbar. || *Do not disturb*, se ruega no molestar.
disturbance [dis'tə:bəns] n. Alboroto, *m.* (row). || Disturbio, *m.* (public disorder). || Preocupación, *f.* (worry). || Molestia, *f.* (trouble). || Perturbación, *f.* (atmospheric, magnetic, etc.). || Trastorno, *m.* (of the mind). || — *Disturbance in the night*, escándalo nocturno. || *Disturbance of the peace*, alteración (*f.*) del orden público.
disturbing [dis'tə:biŋ] adj. Perturbador, ra. || Molesto, ta (annoying). || Preocupante (worrying).
disunion ['dis'ju:njən] n. Desunión, *f.*
disunite ['disju:'nait] v. tr. Desunir.
— V. intr. Desunirse.
disunity [dis'ju:niti] n. Desunión, *f.*
disuse ['dis'ju:s] n. Desuso, *m.*: *to fall into disuse*, caer en desuso. || Abandono, *m.*
disuse ['dis'ju:z] v. tr. Dejar de usar.
disyllabic ['disi'læbik] adj. Bisilábico, ca; disilábico, ca; bisílabo, ba; disílabo, ba.
disyllable [di'siləbl] n. Bisílabo, *m.*, bisilábico, *m.*, disílabo, *m.*, disilábico, *m.*
ditch [ditʃ] n. Zanja, *f.* (trench). || Canal, *m.* (for drainage). || Acequia, *f.* (for irrigation). || Cuneta, *f.* (at the side of a road). || Foso, *m.* (surrounding a castle). || SP. Foso, *m.* || — FIG. FAM. *The Ditch*, el Canal de la Mancha. | *To the last ditch*, hasta el final.
ditch [ditʃ] v. intr. Abrir zanjas (to make ditches). || Hacer acequias (for irrigation). || AUT. Volcar en la cuneta (a car). || Hacer un amaraje forzoso (a plane).
— V. tr. Hacer zanjas *or* acequias en. || AUT. Hacer volcar en la cuneta (to overturn). || FAM. Abandonar (to abandon). | Tirar, deshacerse de (to get rid of).
ditcher [—ə*] n. Peón (*m.*) caminero.
dither ['diðə*] n. *To be in a dither o to be all of a dither*, estar muy excitado, estar muy nervioso (in an excited condition), estar temblando (trembling).
dither ['diðə*] v. intr. Estar nervioso (to be excited). || Temblar (to tremble).
dithery [—ri] adj. Nervioso, sa.
dithyramb ['diθiræmb] n. Ditirambo, *m.*
dithyrambic [diθi'ræmbik] adj. Ditirámbico, ca.
— N. Ditirambo, *m.*
dittany ['ditəni] n. BOT. Díctamo, *m.*
ditto ['ditəu] n. Comillas, *f. pl.* (mark used to indicate repetition). || Ídem, *m.* || Duplicado, *m.* (duplicate).
— Adv. Ídem, del mismo modo.
ditto ['ditəu] v. tr. Repetir (to repeat). || Hacer un duplicado de, reproducir (to duplicate).
ditto machine [—mə'ʃi:n] n. Multicopista, *f.*
ditty ['diti] n. Cancioncilla, *f.* || FIG. Cantinela, *f.*
ditty bag [—bæg] n. MAR. Bolsa, *f.*
diuresis [ˌdaijuə'ri:sis] n. MED. Diuresis, *f.*
— OBSERV. El plural de la palabra inglesa es *diureses*.
diuretic [ˌdaijuə'retik] adj. MED. Diurético, ca.
— N. MED. Diurético, *m.*
diurnal [dai'ə:nl] adj. Diurno, na.
— N. REL. Diurno, *m.* (book).
diuturnity [daiə'tə:niti] n. Diuturnidad, *f.*
diva ['di:və] n. Diva, *f.* (singer).
divagate ['daivəgeit] v. intr. Divagar.
divagation [ˌdaivə'geiʃən] n. Divagación, *f.*
divalent ['daiˌveilənt] adj. Bivalente.
divan [di'væn] n. Diván, *m.* (council, sofa, poetry). || Fumadero, *m.* (smoking room).
divaricate [dai'værikeit] v. intr. Bifurcarse (to fork).
divarication [daiˌværi'keiʃən] n. Bifurcación, *f.* || FIG. Divergencia, *f.*
dive [daiv] n. Zambullida, *f.* (a diving into water). || Salto, *m.* [*Amer.*, clavado, *m.*] (in competitions). || Inmersión, *f.*, sumersión, *f.* (of a submarine). || Picado, *m.*, descenso (*m.*) en picado (of aircraft, birds). || Estirada, *f.* (of a goalkeeper). || FAM. Tasca, *f.* (bar). || FIG. FAM. *To make a dive into*, meterse en.
dive* [daiv] v. intr. Saltar (into water with controlled grace). || Tirarse de cabeza, zambullirse de cabeza (into water head first). || Bucear (underwater). || Sumergirse (a submarine). || Bajar en picado (planes). || Zambullirse (birds). || Hacer una estirada, tirarse (a goalkeeper). || Meterse: *he dived under the table*, se metió debajo de la mesa. || FIG. Lanzarse, meterse (into an affair, etc.). || — *To dive into*, meterse en. || *To dive into one's pocket*, meterse la mano en el bolsillo.
— OBSERV. Pret. ***dived, dove;*** p. p. ***dived.***
dive-bomb [—bɔm] v. tr. Bombardear en picado.
dive bomber [—ˌbɔmə*] n. Avión (*m.*) de bombardeo en picado.
dive-bombing [—ˌbɔmiŋ] n. Bombardeo (*m.*) en picado.
diver [—ə*] n. Buzo, *m.* || SP. Saltador, ra. || ZOOL. Somorgujo, *m.* || *Pearl diver*, pescador (*m.*) de perla.
diverge [dai'və:dʒ] v. intr. Bifurcarse, separarse, divergir (to go in branching directions). || FIG. Apartarse (to turn aside): *to diverge from the truth*, apartarse de la verdad. | Salirse (from the normal).
— V. tr. Desviar.
divergence [dai'və:dʒəns] n. Divergencia, *f.*
divergency [—i] n. Divergencia, *f.*
divergent [daivə:dʒənt] adj. Divergente.
divers ['daivəz] adj. Varios, rias; diversos, sas (several).
diverse [dai'və:s] adj. Diverso, sa; distinto, ta; diferente (different). || Diverso, sa; variado, da (varied).
diversification [daiˌvə:sifi'keiʃən] n. Diversificación, *f.*, variación, *f.*
diversiform [dai'və:sifɔ:m] adj. Diversiforme.
diversify [dai'və:sifai] v. tr. Diversificar.
diversion [dai'və:ʃən] n. Desviación, *f.* (of river, road, etc.). || Diversión, *f.* (mental distraction). || MIL. Diversión, *f.*
diversionary [dai'və:ʃənəri] adj. MIL. De diversión.
diversity [dai'və:siti] n. Diversidad, *f.*
divert [dai'və:t] v. tr. Desviar: *to divert an aeroplane*, desviar un avión. || Distraer: *to divert s.o.'s attention*, distraer la atención de alguien. || Divertir (to amuse). || *To divert o.s.*, divertirse.
diverting [dai'və:tiŋ] adj. Divertido, da.
divertissement [di'və:tismənt] n. Diversión, *f.* (entertainment). || MUS. Divertimento, *m.* (piece of light instrumental music). | Intermedio, *m.* (short interlude between the acts of a play).
divest [dai'vest] v. tr. Desposeer (of possessions). || Despojar (of honours). || Quitar (clothing). || *To divest o.s. of one's rights*, renunciar a sus derechos.
divestiture [—itʃə*] or **divestment** [—mənt] n. Desposeimiento, *m.* (of possessions). || Despojo, *m.* (of honours).
dividable [di'vaidəbl] adj. Divisible.
divide [di'vaid] v. tr. Dividir: *to divide into five groups*, dividir en cinco grupos. || MATH. Dividir. || *To divide the House*, hacer que la Cámara vote.
— V. intr. Dividirse. || Votar: *the House divided*, el Parlamento votó. || — *Divide and conquer*, divide y vencerás. || MATH. *To divide into*, estar contenido en: *5 divides into 20 four times*, cinco está contenido cuatro veces en veinte.
divide [di'vaid] n. U. S. Línea (*f.*) divisoria de las aguas (watershed).
dividend ['dividend] n. MATH. COMM. Dividendo, *m.* || COMM. *Accrued, interim dividend*, dividendo acumulado, provisional.

divider [diˈvaidə*] n. Divisor, ra. || — Pl. Compás (*m. sing.*) de punta fija *or* seca.
dividing [diˈvaidiŋ] adj. Divisor, ra; divisorio, ria.
divi-divi [ˈdiviˈdivi] n. Bot. Dividivi, *m.*
divination [ˌdiviˈneiʃən] n. Adivinación, *f.*
divinatory [ˈdiviˌneitəri] adj. Divinatorio, ria.
divine [diˈvain] n. Teólogo, *m.* (theologian). || Eclesiástico, *m.* (clergyman).
— Adj. Divino, na: *divine punishment*, castigo divino. || Fig. Divino, na.
divine [diˈvain] v. tr./intr. Adivinar.
diviner [—ə*] n. Adivinador, ra; adivino, na.
diving [ˈdaiviŋ] n. Sp. Salto, *m.* [*Amer.*, clavado, *m.*] (in competitions). || Buceo, *m.* (underwater). || Aviat. Picado, *m.*
diving bell [—bel] n. Campana (*f.*) de buzo.
diving board [—bɔ:d] n. Trampolín, *m.*
diving suit [—sju:t] n. Escafandra, *f.*
divining [diˈvainiŋ] adj. Adivinatorio, ria. || *Divining rod*, varilla (*f.*) de zahorí.
divinity [diˈviniti] n. Divinidad, *f.* (quality of being divine). || Teología, *f.*
divinize [ˈdivinaiz] v. tr. Divinizar.
divisibility [diˌviziˈbiliti] n. Divisibilidad, *f.*
divisible [diˈvizəbl] adj. Divisible.
division [diˈviʒən] n. División, *f.* || Distribución, *f.*, reparto, *m.* (distribution). || Separación, *f.*, división, *f.* (partition). || Sección, *f.*, ramo, *m.* (section). || Math. Mil. División, *f.* || Votación, *f.* (in Parliament): *to insist on a division*, exigir una votación. || Graduación, *f.* (of a thermometer, etc.). || Fig. División, *f.*, desunión, *f.*, discordia, *f.* (discord). | División, *f.*, discrepancia, *f.* (of opinions). || *To come to a division*, votar (to vote), someterse a votación (a bill).
divisional [diˈviʒənl] adj. Divisionario, ria; divisional. || *Divisional coin*, moneda fraccionaria.
divisor [diˈvaizə*] n. Math. Divisor, *m.*
divorce [diˈvɔ:s] n. Divorcio, *m.*: *to sue for a divorce*, pedir el divorcio. || Fig. Divorcio, *m.* || *To get a divorce from*, divorciarse de.
divorce [diˈvɔ:s] v. tr. Divociarse de: *he divorced her*, se divorció de ella. || Divorciar: *the judge divorced them*, el juez les divorció.
divorcee [diˌvɔ:ˈsi:] n. Divorciado, da.
divorcement [diˈvɔ:smənt] n. Divorcio, *m.*
divulgation [ˌdaivʌlˈgeiʃən] n. Divulgación, *f.*
divulge [daiˈvʌldʒ] v. tr. Divulgar.
divulgement [—mənt] or **divulgence** [daiˈvʌldʒəns] n. Divulgación, *f.*
divulger [—ə*] n. Divulgador, ra.
divulsion [daiˈvʌlʃən] n. Med. Divulsión, *f.*
dixie or **dixy** [ˈdiksi] n. Marmita, *f.*, olla, *f.*
dizziness [ˈdizinis] n. Mareo, *m.*, vértigo, *m.*
dizzy [ˈdizi] adj. Mareado, da; atacado de vértigo (feeling dizziness). || Vertiginoso, sa (heights, speed). || U. S. Fam. Bobo, ba; alelado, da (stupid). || *To feel dizzy*, estar mareado, tener vértigo.
dizzy [ˈdizi] v. tr. Marear, dar vértigo.
DNA [ˈdi:ˈenˈei] abbrev. of *deoxyribonucleic acid*. A.D.N.
do [dəu] n. Mus. Do, *m.*
do [du:] n. Fam. Fiesta, *f.* (party). | Ceremonia, *f.* | Estafa, *f.*, timo, *m.* (swindle). | Lío, *m.* (trouble). || — *The do's and do nots of society*, las reglas que hay que respetar en la sociedad. || Fam. *That's not fair do's!*, ¡es injusto!
do* [du:] v. tr. Hacer (to carry out an action): *what is he doing now?*, ¿qué está haciendo ahora? || Dedicarse a (to have as occupation): *he does painting*, se dedica a la pintura. || Ocuparse de (to deal with): *to do the suburbs*, ocuparse de los suburbios. || Cumplir con, hacer (to fulfil): *to do one's duty*, cumplir con su deber. || Hacer (to cover a distance): *he did Madrid to Paris in twenty hours*, hizo Madrid París en veinte horas; *my car does a hundred miles an hour*, mi coche hace cien millas por hora. || Recorrer (to tour): *we are doing Italy this year*, vamos a recorrer Italia este año. || Visitar (to visit). || Hacer (to render): *to do s.o. a favour*, hacer un favor a alguien. || Venir bien, convenir (to serve): *this hotel will do us*, este hotel nos vendrá bien. || Hacer (a part). || Hacer de (to play the part of): *who's doing Orpheus in the film?*, ¿quién hace de Orfeo en la película? || Representar (to present a play). || Traducir (to translate): *to do Milton into Spanish*, traducir Milton al castellano. || Vender, hacer (to sell): *we do you this article at ten pounds*, le vendemos este artículo por diez libras. || Trabajar (to work). || Estudiar: *I am doing medicine*, estoy estudiando medicina. || Fam. Timar, estafar (to swindle): *you've been done*, te han timado. | Coger (to catch): *the police did him for speeding*, la policía le cogió por exceso de velocidad. | Entrar a robar en: *the burglars did my house last night*, los ladrones entraron a robar en mi casa anoche. || Cumplir (a sentence). || Tratar: *he did me well*, me trató bien. || Peinar (hair). || Lavar (teeth). || Hacer, afeitar (beard). || Arreglar (nails). || Fregar (the dishes). || Limpiar (a room). || Resolver (a problem). || Hacer (to cook): *a steak well done*, un filete muy hecho. || Dárselas de (to feign).
— *Do what she would, she couldn't*, por más que hizo no lo consiguió. || *I've done it!*, ¡lo conseguí! || Fam. *Nothing doing!*, ¡ni hablar! || *Now you've done it!*, ¡buena la has hecho! || *To be done*, estar agotado (tired), estar hecho, estar terminado (finished). || *To do battle*, luchar, librar batalla. || *To do duty as*, servir de. || *To do harm*, hacer daño (to hurt), perjudicar (to prejudice). || *To do justice*, hacer justicia. || *To do one credit*, decir mucho en su favor. || *To do one good*, hacer bien a uno, sentarle bien a uno. || *To do one's best*, see BEST. || *To do one's bit*, see BIT. || *To do one's hair*, peinarse. || *To do one's nails*, arreglarse las uñas. || *To do one's shoes*, limpiarse los zapatos. || *To do one's teeth*, lavarse los dientes. || *To do o.s. well*, darse buena vida (to live well), no privarse de nada (to lack nothing). || *To do right by s.o.*, tratar bien a alguien. || Fam. *To do s.o. out of sth.*, birlar algo a alguien. || *To do the honours of*, hacer los honores de. || Fam. *To do the trick*, servir [para el caso], resolver el problema. || Fam. *To do time*, estar en prisión. || *To do to death*, matar. || *To do wonders*, hacer maravillas. || *To have one's hair done*, arreglarse el pelo. || *What can I do about it?*, ¿qué quiere que le haga? || *What can I do for you?*, ¿en qué puedo servirle? || *What else can be done?*, ¿qué más se puede hacer? || *What's done is done*, a lo hecho, pecho.
— V. intr. Hacer: *do as I did*, haz como hice yo. || Irle a alguien (to make progress): *how is she doing*, ¿qué tal le va? || Estar, sentirse, irle a uno (to feel). || Valer (to be suitable): *this book will not do*, este libro no vale. || Ocurrir, pasar: *what's doing here?*, ¿qué pasa aquí? || — *Do well and dread no shame*, haz bien y no mires a quien. || *He did right*, hizo bien. || *How do you do?*, encantado, da; mucho gusto (when introduced), ¿cómo está ústed? (how are you?). || *It doesn't do to*, no conviene. || *That will do*, ya está bien. || *That will never do*, eso no puede ser. || *To do or die*, vencer o morir. || *To do well*, ir bien (business), ir por buen camino, medrar (person), estar recuperándose (invalid), darse bien (plant), salir bien: *he did well in his exam*, salió bien del examen; hacer bien: *he would do well to see the dentist*, haría bien en ir al dentista. || *To do well by*, portarse bien con. || *To make do with*, arreglárselas con.
— V. aux. En interrogaciones: *do you speak Spanish?*, ¿habla usted español? || En negaciones: *I do not speak English*, no hablo inglés; *do not lie*, no mientas. || Con una inversión: *never did I say anything of the sort*, nunca dije tal cosa. || Para dar mayor énfasis al imperativo: *do tell me*, dímelo, por favor. || Para acentuar el significado del verbo: *I do love Mary*, quiero a María de verdad; *do come and see me*, no deje de venir a verme; *he did transmit your request to her*, seguramente le transmitió tu petición.
— V. substitute. Hacer: *I'll tell him.* — *Don't*, se lo voy a decir. — No lo haga; *he painted these flowers much better than she could have done*, él pintó estas flores mucho mejor que ella hubiera podido hacerlo. || Para evitar la repetición del verbo: *sing as I do*, canta como yo; *do you sing?* — *Yes, I do*, ¿cantas? — Sí; *do you play piano?* — *No, I don't*, ¿sabes tocar el piano? — No; *he dances well.* — *Does he?*, baila bien. — ¿De verdad?; *he dances well, so does she*, él baila bien, ella también. || — *He doesn't live here, does he?*, no vive aquí, ¿verdad? || *He writes well, doesn't he?*, escribe bien, ¿verdad? || *Please do*, por supuesto, naturalmente, por favor.
— **To do again**, volver a hacer, hacer otra vez, hacer de nuevo. || **To do away with**, suprimir (s.o., sth.). | Abolir (a custom). || **To do by**, tratar. || **To do down**, timar. || **To do for**, llevar la casa a (to work in s.o.'s house). | Servir de (to serve as). | Fam. Matar, cargarse (to kill). | Hundir (to ruin). | — Fam. *We're done for!*, ¡estamos perdidos! || Fam. **To do in**, cargarse a (to kill). | Agotar, derrengar (to exhaust). || **To do out**, arreglar (to tidy). | Decorar (to decorate). | Vestir (to dress). | Fam. Robar (to steal). || **To do over**, volver a hacer (to do again). | Revisar (to revise). | Retocar (a painting). | Cubrir (*with*, con). || **To do up**, atarse (shoelaces). | Abrocharse (belt, buttons). | Envolver (to wrap up). | Poner pañales a (a baby). | Cerrar (a letter). | Arreglar (an old garment). | Renovar (to renovate). | Arreglar, ordenar (to arrange). | Preparar, guisar (food). | Fam. Reventar, derrengar (to exhaust). | — *To do up one's face*, maquillarse, pintarse. || **To do with**, hacer con: *what did you do with my hat?*, ¿qué has hecho con mi sombrero? | Aguantar (to tolerate): *I can't do with him*, no le puedo aguantar. | Conformarse con: *I do with very little food*, me conformo con muy poca comida. | Tener que ver con: *I have nothing to do with this matter*, no tengo nada que ver con este asunto. | Estar relacionado con (to be related to). | — *I could do with a cup of tea*, no me vendría mal *or* me gustaría tomarme una taza de té. || *To have done with*, haber acabado con. || **To do without**, prescindir de, arreglárselas sin. | — *I can do without your remarks*, puede ahorrarse sus comentarios.

— Observ. Pret. ***did;*** p. p. ***done.***

doable [ˈdu:əbl] adj. Factible, realizable.
dobbin [ˈdobin] n. Caballo (*m.*) de tiro. || U. S. Fam. Jamelgo, *m.*
doc [dɔk] n. Fam. Galeno, *m.*, doctor, *m.*
docent [dəuˈsent] n. U. S. Profesor (*m.*) auxiliar.
docile [ˈdəusail] adj. Dócil.
docility [dəuˈsiliti] n. Docilidad, *f.*

dock [dɔk] n. Maslo, *m.* (of an animal's tail). || Muñón (*m.*) de la cola (stump). || Baticola, *f.* (crupper of saddle). || Banquillo (*m.*) de los acusados (in courtroom). || Dársena, *f.* (for boats). || Muelle, *m.* (platform). || Andén, *m.* (of railway). || U. S. Malecón, *m.* (pier). || — Pl. Puerto, *m. sing.* || — *Dry dock*, dique seco. || *Floating dock*, dique (*m.*) flotante. || AUT. *In dock*, averiado (car). || *Loading dock*, embarcadero, *m.*
dock [dɔk] v. tr. Cortar (to cut). || Descolar, cortar la cola a (to shorten the tail of). || Acortar, reducir (to shorten). || Deducir, descontar (*off*, de) [to deduct a sum of money]. || Multar (to fine). || Hacer entrar en dársena (to bring a ship into the dock).
— V. intr. Atracar al muelle (ship). || Llegar (to arrive). || Acoplarse (spacecraft).
dockage [—idʒ] n. MAR. Muellaje, *m.*, derechos (*m. pl.*) por atracar. || Reducción, *f.*
docker [ˈdɔkə*] n. Cargador (*m.*) *or* descargador (*m.*) de muelle, cargador (*m.*) *or* descargador (*m.*) de puerto, "docker", *m.*, estibador, *m.*
docket [ˈdɔkit] n. Rótulo, *m.*, etiqueta, *f.* (label). || Lista, *f.* (list). || Certificado (*m.*) de aduana (custom warrant). || U. S. Orden (*m.*) del día, agenda, *f.* || JUR. Registro (*m.*) de sumarios de causas.
docket [ˈdɔkit] v. tr. Rotular, poner un rótulo en (to label). || Registrar (to register).
dockhand [ˈdɔkˌhænd] n. See DOCKER.
docking [ˈdɔkiŋ] n. MAR. Atracamiento, *m.* || Acoplamiento, *m.* (spacecraft).
dockyard [ˈdɔkjɑ:d] n. Astillero, *m.* (shipbuilder's yard). || Arsenal, *m.* (naval yard).
doctor [ˈdɔktə*] n. Médico, ca (person qualified in medicine): *family doctor*, médico de cabecera. || Doctor, ra (university title): *Doctor of Laws, of Science*, doctor en derecho, en ciencias. || REL. Doctor, *m.*: *doctor of the Church*, doctor de la Iglesia. || — *Honorary doctor*, doctor honoris causa. || *To be under the doctor's care*, seguir un tratamiento médico. || *Woman doctor*, médica, *f.*
doctor [ˈdɔktə*] v. tr. Atender, asistir (to administer medical attention to). || Adulterar (food, text). || Falsificar, amañar (accounts). || Apañar, arreglar (to patch up). || Conceder el título de doctor (in university). || POP. Capar (to castrate).
— V. intr. Ser médico (to be a doctor). || Tomar medicinas (a patient).
doctoral [—rəl] adj. Doctoral.
doctorate [—rit] n. Doctorado, *m.* || *To take one's doctorate*, presentar la tesis de doctorado.
doctrinaire [ˌdɔktriˈnɛə*] adj./n. Doctrinario, ria.
doctrinairism [—rizəm] n. Doctrinarismo, *m.*
doctrinal [dɔkˈtrainəl] adj. Doctrinal.
doctrine [ˈdɔktrin] n. Doctrina, *f.*: *Aristotelian, Buddhist doctrine*, doctrina aristotélica, budista. || *It is a matter of doctrine that*, es teoría corriente que.
document [ˈdɔkjumənt] n. Documento, *m.* || JUR. Escritura, *f.*: *legal document*, escritura pública.
document [ˈdɔkjumənt] v. tr. Documentar. || Probar con documentos.
document case [—keis] n. Portadocumentos, *m. inv.*, cartera, *f.* [*Amer.*, portafolio, *m.*].
documentary [ˌdɔkjuˈmentəri] adj. Documental: *documentary proof*, prueba documental. || *Documentary film*, documental, *m.*
— N. Documental, *m.* (film).
documentation [ˌdɔkjumenˈteiʃən] n. Documentación, *f.*
dodder [ˈdɔdə*] n. BOT. Cuscuta, *f.*
dodder [ˈdɔdə*] v. intr. Temblequear (to tremble). || Tambalearse, andar con paso inseguro (to totter). || AUT. *To dodder along*, ir tranquilamente.
dodderer [—ə*] n. FAM. *An old dodderer*, un viejo chocho.
doddering [—riŋ] adj. Chocho, cha.
dodecagon [dəuˈdekəgən] n. MATH. Dodecágono, *m.*
dodecagonal [dəudeˈkægənəl] adj. MATH. Dodecágono, na.
dodecahedron [ˈdəudikəˈhedrən] n. MATH. Dodecaedro, *m.*
dodecaphonic [ˌdəudekəˈfɔnik] adj. MUS. Dodecafónico, ca.
dodecaphony [ˌdəuˈdekəfəni] n. MUS. Dodecafonismo, *m.*
dodecasyllabic [ˌdəudekasiˈlæbik] adj. Dodecasílabo, ba.
dodecasyllable [ˌdəudekəˈsiləbl] n. Dodecasílabo, *m.*
dodge [dɔdʒ] n. Regate, *m.* (quick evasive movement). || Truco, *m.* (trick): *he is up to all the dodges*, conoce todos los trucos. || Esquiva, *f.*, finta, *f.* (of a boxer). || Sistema, *m.*, truco, *m.* (trick).
dodge [dɔdʒ] v. intr. Echarse a un lado, hurtar el cuerpo, esquivarse (to move to one side): *he dodged when I tried to hit him*, se echó a un lado cuando intenté pegarle. || Esconderse, echarse (*behind*, detrás) [to hide]. || Andar con rodeos (in speech). || SP. Hacer un regate, regatear (in football, etc.). | Hacer una finta (in boxing). || *To dodge about*, andarse con rodeos.
— V. tr. Eludir: *to dodge a question*, eludir una pregunta. || Zafarse: *he dodged military service*, se zafó del servicio militar. || Esquivar (a blow, etc.). || Regatear (in football, etc.). || Evitar (to avoid): *to dodge the traffic*, evitar el tráfico. || Despistar, dar esquinazo a (a pursuer). || Mover, desplazar (to move). || FAM. Fumarse (to skive): *to dodge a class*, fumarse una clase. || *To dodge it*, escurrir el bulto.
dodgems [ˈdɔdʒəms] pl. n. Coches (*m.*) que chocan.
dodger [ˈdɔdʒə*] n. Tramposo, sa (tricky person). || Tunante, ta; marrullero, ra (shifty rascal). || MIL. Emboscado, *m.* || U. S. Octavilla, *f.* (handbill).
dodgy [ˈdɔdʒi] adj. Astuto, ta; marrullero, ra.
dodo [ˈdəudəu] n. FIG. *As old as a dodo*, más viejo que la nana, un vejestorio.

— OBSERV. El plural es *dodoes* o *dodos*.

doe [dəu] n. Coneja, *f.* (female rabbit). || Liebre, *f.* (female hare). || Gama, *f.* (female deer).
doer [ˈdu:ə*] n. Persona (*f.*) activa. || Autor, ra (*of*, de).
does [dʌz] 3rd pers. sing. pres. See DO.
doeskin [ˈdəuskin] n. Ante, *m.* (deer skin).
doesn't [ˈdʌzənt] contraction of *does not*.
doff [dɔf] v. tr. Quitarse (to take off). || Librarse de (to get rid of).
dog [dɔg] n. Perro, *m.* (animal). || Macho, *m.* (of fox, jackal, wolf). || TECH. Cabezal, *m.* (mechanical gripping device). | Grapa, *f.* (iron bar for joining timbers together). || ASTR. Can, *m.*: *Great Dog, Little* o *Lesser Dog*, Can Mayor, Can Menor. || FAM. Perro, *m.* (person). | Desastre, *m.*, fracaso, *m.* (of a play). || — Pl. Morillos, *m.* (pair of supports for logs in an open hearth).
— FIG. *Barking dogs don't bite*, perro ladrador poco mordedor. | *Beware of the dog*, cuidado con el perro. || FIG. *Dead dog*, persona (*f.*) que ha venido a menos. | *Dead dogs don't bite*, muerto el perro se acabó la rabia. || FAM. *Dirty dog*, canalla, *m.*, tío cochino. || *Dog collar*, collar (*m.*) de perro. || *Dog fox*, zorro, *m.* || *Dog show*, exposición canina. || FIG. *Dog tired*, rendido, da. || *Dog wolf*, lobo, *m.* || FIG. *Every dog has his day*, a cada cerdo le llega su San Martín. || *Hot dog*, perro caliente. || FIG. *Let sleeping dogs lie*, más vale no meneallo. || FAM. *Lucky dog*, tío (*m.*) con suerte. || *Newfoundland dog*, perro de Terranova. || FIG. *Not to have a dog's chance*, no tener la menor probabilidad. || *Pedigree dog*, perro de casta. || *Stray dog*, perro sin dueño. || FIG. FAM. *The dog in the manger*, el perro del hortelano [que ni come ni deja comer]. || FAM. *The dogs*, carrera (*f. sing.*) de galgos. || FIG. FAM. *To be as sick as a dog*, estar más malo que los perros. | *To be top dog*, ser el gallito del lugar (to rule the roost), ser el mejor (to be first). | *To die a dog's death*, morir como un perro. | *To go to the dogs*, ir a la ruina (business), malearse (person). | *To lead a dog's life*, llevar una vida de perros. || U. S. FAM. *To put on the dog*, darse pisto. || FIG. *To treat s.o. like a dog*, tratar a alguien como a un perro. || U. S. FIG. *To work like a dog*, trabajar como un condenado.
dog [dɔg] v. tr. Seguir: *to dog s.o.'s footsteps*, seguir los pasos de alguien. || Perseguir (to pursue).
dogaressa [ˌdɔgəˈresə] n. Dogaresa, *f.*
dogberry [ˈdɔgberi] n. BOT. Fruto (*m.*) del cornejo. || *Dogberry tree*, cornejo, *m.*
dog biscuit [ˈdɔgˌbiskit] n. Galleta (*f.*) de perro.
dogcart [ˈdɔgkɑ:t] n. Coche (*m.*) de dos ruedas.
dogcatcher [ˈdɔgˌkætʃə*] n. Perrero, *m.*
dog days [ˈdɔgdeiz] pl. n. Canícula, *f. sing.* (summer).
doge [dəudʒ] n. Dux, *m.* (in Venice).
dog-ear [ˈdɔgiə*] n. Esquina (*f.*) doblada de una página.
dog-ear [ˈdɔgiə*] v. tr. Doblar la esquina de (a page).
dog-eared [—d] adj. Sobado, da (book).
dogfight [ˈdɔgfait] n. Pelea (*f.*) entre perros. || Combate (*m.*) aéreo. || FAM. Trifulca, *f.* (brawl).
dogfish [ˈdɔgfiʃ] n. Cazón, *m.*, lija, *f.* (fish).
dogged [ˈdɔgid] adj. Obstinado, da; tenaz.
doggedness [—nis] n. Obstinación, *f.*, tenacidad, *f.*
doggerel [ˈdɔgərəl] n. Aleluyas, *f. pl.* (bad verse).
doggie [ˈdɔgi] n. Perrito, *m.*
doggish [ˈdɔgiʃ] adj. Que se parece a un perro, perruno, na; de perros. || FIG. Arisco, ca (surly). || U. S. FAM. Aparatoso, sa (showy).
doggo [ˈdɔgəu] adj. FAM. *To lie doggo*, estar escondido.
doggone [ˈdɔgˌgɔn] adj. U. S. FAM. Maldito, ta
— Interj. U. S. FAM. ¡Caray!
doggy [ˈdɔgi] n. Perrito, *m.*
— Adj. Perruno, na; de perros (dog-like). || FIG. Arisco, ca (surly). || Aficionado a los perros (fond of dogs). || U. S. Aparatoso, sa (showy). || *There is a doggy smell*, huele a perros.
doghouse [ˈdɔghaus] n. U. S. Perrera, *f.* (kennel). || FIG. *To be in the doghouse*, haber caído en desgracia.
dog Latin [ˈdɔgˈlætin] n. Latín (*m.*) macarrónico.
dogma [ˈdɔgmə] n. Dogma, *m.*

— OBSERV. El plural de la palabra inglesa es *dogmas* o *dogmata*.

dogmatic [dɔgˈmætik] adj. Dogmático, ca.
dogmatical [—əl] adj. Dogmático, ca.
dogmatics [dɔgˈmætiks] n. Dogmática, *f.*
dogmatism [ˈdɔgmətizəm] n. Dogmatismo, *m.*
dogmatist [ˈdɔgmətist] n. Dogmatista, *m.* (believer in dogmatism). || Dogmatizador, ra; dogmatizante, *m.* & *f.* (who states categorically).
dogmatize [ˈdɔgmətaiz] v. tr./intr. Dogmatizar.
dogmatizer [—ə*] n. Dogmatizador, ra; dogmatizante, *m.* & *f.*
do-gooder [du:ˈgudə*] n. Persona (*f.*) bien intencionada, bienhechor, ra.

dog rose [ˈdɔgrəuz] n. Bot. Escaramujo, *m.*, rosal (*m.*) silvestre.
dog's age [ˈdɔgzeidʒ] n. U. S. Fig. fam. Siglos, *m. pl.*, miles (*m. pl.*) de años (a long time).
dogsbody [ˈdɔgsbɔdi] n. Fam. Burro (*m.*) de carga (drudge).
dogsled [ˈdɔgsled] n. Trineo (*m.*) tirado por perros.
Dog Star [ˈdɔgstɑ:*] n. Astr. Sirio, *m.*
dog tag [ˈdɔgtæg] n. U. S. Placa (*f.*) de identificación.
dog-tired [ˈdɔgˈtaiəd] adj. Fam. Rendido, da.
dogvane [ˈdɔgvein] n. Mar. Cataviento, *m.*
dogwatch [ˈdɔgwɔtʃ] n. Mar. Guardia (*f.*) de 4 a 6 y de 6 a 8 de la tarde.
dogwood [ˈdɔgwud] n. Bot. Cornejo, *m.*
doily [ˈdɔili] n. Tapete, *m.*
doing [ˈdu:iŋ] n. Obra, *f.*: *it is not of my doing*, no es obra mía. || — Pl. Actuación, *f. sing.* (behaviour). || Actividades, *f.* (activities). || Acontecimientos, *m.* (happenings, events). || Fiestas, *f.* (social events). || Chisme, *m. sing.*, cachivache, *m. sing.* (thing).
doit [dɔit] n. Ochavo, *m.* (old coin). || Fam. *I don't care a doit for it*, me importa un bledo.
do-it-yourself [ˈdu:itjɔ:ˈself] adj. Que uno hace o construye uno mismo. || Hágalo usted mismo (book titles). || *A do-it-yourself man*, un hombre mañoso.
doldrums [ˈdɔldrəmz] pl. n. Mar. Zona (*f. sing.*) de las calmas, calmas (*f.*) ecuatoriales. || Fig. *To be in the doldrums*, estar deprimido (person), estar parado (business), estar estancado (economy), estar en calma (stock exchange).
dole [dəul] n. Subsidio (*m.*) de paro (unemployment pay). || Distribución, *f.*, reparto, *m.* (distribution). || Parte, *f.* (share). || Limosna, *f.* (alms). || *To be on the dole*, estar acogido al paro, estar parado.
dole [dəul] v. tr. *To dole out*, repartir [parcamente].
doleful [—ful] adj. Triste (appearance, news). || Triste, afligido, da (person). || Lastimero, ra; quejumbroso, sa (cry). || Lúgubre (dreary).
dolefulness [—nis] n. Tristeza, *f.*, melancolía, *f.*
dolichocephal [ˌdɔlikəuˈkefəl] n. Dolicocéfalo, la.
dolichocephalic [ˈdɔlikəukeˈfælik] adj. Anat. Dolicocéfalo, la.
dolichocephalism [ˌdɔlikəuˈkefəlizəm] or **dolichocephaly** [ˈdɔlikəuˈkefəli] n. Dolicocefalia, *f.*
doll [dɔl] n. Muñeca, *f.* (toy, girl).
doll [dɔl] v. tr. Fam. *To doll o.s. up*, emperejilarse, empingorotarse. | *To doll up*, emperejilar, empingorotar.
dollar [ˈdɔlə*] n. Dólar, *m.* || U. S. *Dollar diplomacy*, diplomacia (*f.*) del dólar.
dollhouse [ˈdɔlhaus] n. U. S. Casa (*f.*) de muñecas.
dollop [ˈdɔləp] n. Fam. Masa, *f.*
doll's house [ˈdɔlzhaus] n. Casa (*f.*) de muñecas.
dolly [ˈdɔli] n. Muñeca, *f.* (doll). || Batidor, *m.* (for thumping clothes). || Carretilla (*f.*) de ruedas (wheeled trolley). || Cinem. Travelín, *m.*, plataforma (*f.*) rodante.
dolman [ˈdɔlmən] n. Dormán, *m.* (jacket). || *Dolman sleeve*, manga japonesa.
dolmen [ˈdɔlmən] n. Dolmen, *m.*
Dolomites [ˈdɔləmaits] pl. pr. n. Geogr. Dolomitas, *f.*
dolomitic [ˌdɔləˈmitik] adj. Geol. Dolomítico, ca.
dolor [ˈdəulər] n. U. S. Dolor, *m.*
dolorous [ˈdɔlərəs] adj. Doloroso, sa.
dolose [dəˈləus] adj. Jur. Doloso, sa (fraudulent).
dolour [ˈdəulə*] n. Dolor, *m.*
dolphin [ˈdɔlfin] n. Zool. Delfín, *m.* (mammal). | Dorado, *m.* (fish).
dolt [dəult] n. Idiota, *m.* & *f.*, bobo, ba.
doltish [ˈdəultiʃ] adj. Idiota, bobo, ba.
domain [dəˈmein] n. Dominio, *m.* (territory under one ruler). || Finca, *f.* (estate). || Fig. Campo, *m.*, ámbito, *m.*, esfera, *f.* (field of activity).
dome [dəum] n. Arch. Cúpula, *f.*, domo, *m.* || Fig. Bóveda, *f.* | Cumbre (*f.*) redondeada (of a hill). || U. S. Fam. Chola, *f.* (head).
dome [dəum] v. tr. Cubrir con una cúpula (to cover). || Dar forma de cúpula a (to shape).
domestic [dəˈmestik] adj. Doméstico, ca: *domestic service*, servicio doméstico. || Hogareño, ña; casero, ra (home-loving). || Doméstico, ca; de uso doméstico (appliance). || Nacional, interior (trade, market, flight, etc.). || Zool. Doméstico, ca: *domestic animal*, animal doméstico. || — *Domestic arts*, artes domésticas. || *Domestic help*, doméstico, ca. || *Domestic life*, vida (*f.*) de familia. || *Domestic quarrels*, riñas (*f.*) conyugales (between married people), luchas intestinas (in politics). || *Domestic science*, economía doméstica.
— N. Doméstico, ca (servant).
domesticable [dəˈmestikəbl] adj. Domesticable.
domesticate [dəˈmestikeit] v. tr. Domesticar (animals). || Civilizar (savages). || Aclimatar (plants). || Volver casero (person). || *Domesticated woman*, mujer de su casa.
— V. intr. Volverse casero.
domestication [dəˌmestiˈkeiʃən] n. Domesticación, *f.* (of animals). || Civilización, *f.* (of savages). || Aclimatación, *f.* (of plants). || Carácter (*m.*) casero (of people).
domesticity [ˌdəumesˈtisiti] n. Domesticidad, *f.* (of animals). || Vida (*f.*) casera. || — Pl. Asuntos (*m.*) domésticos.
domicile [ˈdɔmisail] n. Domicilio, *m.*
domicile [ˈdɔmisail] v. tr. Domiciliar.
— V. intr. Domiciliarse, tener domicilio.
domiciliary [ˌdɔmisˈiljəri] adj. Domiciliario, ria.
domiciliate [—ieit] v. tr. Domiciliar.
— V. intr. Domiciliarse, tener domicilio.
domiciliation [dɔmisiliˈeiʃən] n. Domiciliación, *f.*
dominance [ˈdɔminəns] or **dominancy** [—si] n. Dominación, *f.* || Predominio, *m.* (predominance).
dominant [ˈdɔminənt] adj. Dominante. || *To be dominant over*, dominar.
— N. Mus. Biol. Dominante, *f.*
dominate [ˈdɔmineit] v. tr./intr. Dominar.
dominating [—iŋ] adj. Dominador, ra; dominante.
domination [ˌdɔmiˈneiʃən] n. Dominación, *f.* || — Pl. Rel. Dominaciones, *f.* (dominions).
domineer [ˌdɔmiˈniə*] v. tr. *To domineer over*, dominar tiránicamente a, tiranizar a.
domineering [—iŋ] adj. Dominante, autoritario, ria.
Dominic [ˈdɔminik] pr. n. Domingo, *m.*
Dominica [ˌdɔmiˈni:kə] pr. n. Geogr. Dominica, *f.*
dominical [dəˈminikəl] adj. Dominical.
Dominican [dəˈminikən] adj./n. Dominicano, na (of Dominican Republic). || Rel. Dominico, ca; dominicano, na.
Dominican Republic [—riˈpʌblik] pr. n. Geogr. República (*f.*) Dominicana.
dominion [dəˈminjən] n. Dominio, *m.* || — Pl. Rel. Dominaciones, *f.*
domino [ˈdɔminəu] n. Dominó, *m.* (game, dress): *to play dominoes*, jugar a los dominós.

— Observ. El plural de la palabra inglesa es *dominoes* o *dominos*.

don [dɔn] n. Catedrático, *m.* (university teacher). || Don, *m.* (Spanish and Italian title). || Hidalgo, *m.* (nobleman). || Fam. As, *m.*, hacha, *m.* (*at*, en) [ace].
don [dɔn] v. tr. Ponerse (a garment). || Vestirse de (a certain colour or material).
donate [dəuˈneit] v. tr. Donar, hacer donación de: *he donated 15 000 pesetas*, donó 15 000 pesetas; *he donated his house*, hizo donación de su casa. || Dar, donar (blood).
donating [—iŋ] adj. Donante.
donation [dəuˈneiʃən] n. Jur. Donación, *f.*: *donation inter vivos*, donación entre vivos. || Donativo, *m.* (gift, contribution).
donative [ˈdəunətiv] n. Donativo, *m.*
donator [dəuˈnəitə*] n. Donatario, ria.
done [dʌn] p. p. See do. || Terminado, da (finished). || Hecho, cha (cooked). || Gastado, da (worn-out). || Rendido, da; agotado, da (tired). || — *Done!*, ¡trato hecho! || *Done to a turn*, en su punto (meat). || *Done with*, acabado, da. || *It is not done*, esto no se hace. || *It is not done to*, no es elegante, es de mal gusto. || *Leave it like that and have done with it*, déjalo así y ya está. || *To have done with*, haber acabado con. || *Well done*, muy hecho, cha (meat). || *Well done!*, ¡muy bien!
donee [dəuˈni:] n. Donatario, ria.
donjon [ˈdɔndʒən] n. Calabozo, *m.*, mazmorra, *f.* (prison). || Torre (*f.*) del homenaje (keep of a castle).
donkey [ˈdɔŋki] n. Burro, *m.*, asno, *m.* || Fam. Burro, rra; bruto, ta. || Fam. *Donkey's years*, siglos, *m. pl.*, miles de años, *m. pl.*
donkey engine [—ˌendʒin] n. Motor (*m.*) auxiliar. || Locomotora (*f.*) pequeña.
donnish [ˈdɔniʃ] adj. Pedante. || Profesoral.
donor [ˈdəunə*] n. Donante, *m.* & *f.*: *blood donor*, donante de sangre. || Jur. Donatario, ria.
don't [dəunt] contraction of *do not*.
donzel [ˈdɔnzl] n. (Ant.). Doncel, *m.* (pageboy).
doodad [ˈdu:dæd] n. U. S. Fam. Chisme, *m.*, cosa, *f.*
doodle [ˈdu:dl] n. Garabatos, *m. pl.* (writing). || Dibujitos, *m. pl.* (drawing).
doodle [ˈdu:dl] v. intr. Garabatear, hacer garabatos (in writing). || Pintarrajear (in drawing).
doodlebug [ˈdu:dlbʌg] n. Bomba (*f.*) teledirigida (flying bomb). || U. S. Varilla (*f.*) de zahorí.
doom [du:m] n. Destino, *m.* [funesto] (calamitous fate). || Perdición, *f.* (ruin). || Muerte, *f.* (death). || Rel. Juicio (*m.*) final. || Jur. Juicio, *m.*
doom [du:m] v. tr. Rel. Jur. Condenar (*to*, a). || Predestinar (to predestine). || *Doomed to failure*, condenado al fracaso.
doomsday [ˈdu:mzdei] n. Rel. Día (*m.*) del juicio final. || Fam. *Till doomsday*, hasta el juicio final.
door [dɔ:*] n. Puerta, *f.*: *revolving door*, puerta giratoria. || — Fig. *At death's door*, a las puertas de la muerte. || *Automatic door*, puerta automática. || *Back door*, puerta trasera. || *Behind closed doors*, a puerta cerrada. || *Door-to-door salesman*, vendedor (*m.*) a domicilio. || *From door to door*, de puerta en puerta. || *Front door*, puerta de entrada. || *Glass door*, puerta de cristal, puerta vidriera. || *Hidden door*, puerta excusada o falsa. || *Next door*, en la casa de al lado. || *Out of dors*, al aire libre (in the open air), fuera (outside). || *Secret door*, puerta secreta. || *Sliding door*, puerta de corredera. || Fig. *There's the door!*, ¡ahí tienes la puerta! | *This is next door to*, esto raya en. || *To break the door open*, echar la puerta abajo. || Fig. *To close the door upon*, cerrar la puerta a. | *To find all doors closed*, encontrar todas las puertas cerradas. | *To have an open door*, tener puerta abierta. | *To knock the door down*, echar la puerta abajo. | *To lay a charge at the door of*, echar la culpa a. | *To leave a door open*, dejar una puerta abierta. | *To lie at s.o.'s door*, recaer sobre alguien. | *To open the door to*, abrir la puerta a. | *To*

show s.o. the door, enseñar la puerta a uno. || *To show s.o. to the door*, acompañar a alguien hasta la puerta. || *To slam the door*, dar un portazo. || FIG. *To slam the door in s.o.'s face*, dar a uno con la puerta en las narices, cerrarle a uno la puerta en las narices. | *When one door closes another always opens*, cuando una puerta se cierra, cien se abren. || *Within doors*, en casa.
doorbell [ˈdɔ:bel] n. Timbre, *m.* [de la puerta].
doorcase [ˈdɔ:keis] n. Marco (*m.*) de la puerta.
doorframe [ˈdɔ:freim] n. Marco (*m.*) de la puerta.
doorhead [ˈdɔ:hed] n. Dintel, *m.*
doorjamb [ˈdɔ:dʒæm] n. Jamba (*f.*) de la puerta.
doorkeeper [ˈdɔ:ˌki:pə*] n. Portero, *m.* (of a hotel). || Conserje, *m.* (of public building). || REL. Ostiario, *m.*
doorknob [ˈdɔ:nɔb] n. Pomo (*m.*) de la puerta.
doorman [ˈdɔ:mən] n. Portero, *m.*

— OBSERV. El plural de esta palabra es *doormen*.

doormat [ˈdɔ:mæt] n. Felpudo, *m.*, estera, *f.*
doornail [ˈdɔ:neil] n. Clavo (*m.*) de puerta. || — FIG. *Dead as a doornail*, see DEAD. | *Deaf as a doornail*, más sordo que una tapia.
doorplate [ˈdɔ:pleit] n. Placa, *f.* [que se pone en la puerta].
doorpost [ˈdɔ:pəust] n. Jamba (*f.*) de puerta.
doorstep [ˈdɔ:step] n. Umbral, *m.* (threshold). || Peldaño, *m.* (step).
doorstop [ˈdɔ:stɔp] n. Tope (*m.*) de puerta (wooden strip). || Retenedor, *m.* (to hold a door open).
doorway [ˈdɔ:wei] n. Portal, *m.* || FIG. Puerta, *f.*
dooryard [ˈdɔ:jɑ:d] n. U. S. Patio, *m.*
dope [dəup] n. FAM. Droga, *f.* (narcotic). | Información, *f.*, informes, *m. pl.* (information). | Idiota, *m.* & *f.* (idiot). || Barniz, *m.* (varnish). || Lubricante, *m.* (lubricant).
dope [dəup] v. tr. Drogar. || SP. Dopar. || U. S. FAM. *To dope out*, sacar (to deduce).
dope fiend [—fi:nd] n. U. S. FAM. Toxicómano, na.
dopey [ˈdəupi] adj. Tonto, ta (stupid). || Atontado, da (fuddled).
doping [ˈdəupiŋ] n. SP. Doping, *m.*, drogado, *m.*
dor [dɔ:*] n. ZOOL. Escarabajo (*m.*) pelotero (dung beetle). | Abejorro, *m.* (flying beetle).
dorado [dəˈrɑ:dəu] n. ZOOL. Dorado, *m.* (fish).
Dorian [ˈdɔ:riən] adj./n. Dorio, ria.
Doric [ˈdɔrik] adj. Dórico, ca: *Doric order*, orden dórico.
— N. Dórico, *m.* (Greek dialect).
dormancy [ˈdɔ:mənsi] n. Letargo, *m.* (of animals). || Sueño, *m.* (sleep). || Inactividad, *f.*
dormant [ˈdɔ:mənt] adj. Inactivo, va: *to lie dormant*, estar inactivo. || Letárgico, ca (animals). || Inactivo, va (volcano). || Latente (latent). || JUR. Caído en desuso (a title). | Inaplicado, da (a law).
dormer [ˈdɔ:mə*] n. Buhardilla, *f.*
dormitory [ˈdɔ:mitri] n. Dormitorio, *m.*
dormouse [ˈdɔ:maus] n. Lirón, *m.* (animal).

— OBSERV. El plural de esta palabra es *dormice*.

dorsal [ˈdɔ:səl] adj. ANAT. Dorsal.
dory [ˈdɔ:ri] n. Pez (*m.*) de san Pedro (fish). || U. S. Bote, *m.* (fishing boat).
dosage [ˈdəusidʒ] n. Dosificación, *f.* (determination). || Dosis, *f. inv.* (amount). || Administración (*f.*) de un medicamento (giving). || FIG. Dosis, *f. inv.*
dose [dəus] n. Dosis, *f. inv.* (amount of medicine). || FIG. Dosis, *f. inv.*
dose [dəus] v. tr. Dosificar (to determine the dose of). || Administrar un medicamento a, medicinar. || Alcoholizar (wine). || *To dose o.s. with*, seguir un tratamiento a base de.
dosimeter [dəuˈsimitə*] n. Dosímetro, *m.*
dosing [ˈdəusiŋ] n. Dosificación, *f.*
doss [dɔs] n. FAM. Piltra, *f.*, catre, *m.* (bed).
doss [dɔs] v. intr. FAM. Dormir. || FAM. *To doss down*, dormir.
dossal [ˈdɔsəl] n. Dosel, *m.*
doss house [ˈdɔshaus] n. FAM. Fonducha, *f.*, posada (*f.*) del peine, pensión (*f.*) de mala muerte.
dossier [ˈdɔsiei] n. Expediente, *m.*
dot [dɔt] n. Punto, *m.* (point). || FAM. Chaval, *m.* (boy). || — FAM. *Off one's dot*, loco, ca. || *On the dot*, puntualmente: *to arrive on the dot*, llegar puntualmente; en punto: *it's two o'clock on the dot*, son las dos en punto; a toca teja: *to pay on the dot*, pagar a toca teja. || *Three dots*, puntos suspensivos.
dot [dɔt] v. tr. Poner el punto a (to put a dot on). || Puntear (a line). || Salpicar (to scatter). || MUS. Puntear. || — *Dotted line*, línea (*f.*) de puntos, punteado, *m.* || FAM. *I dotted him one*, le di un porrazo. || FIG. *To dot one's i's and cross one's t's*, poner los puntos sobre las íes.
dotage [ˈdəutidʒ] n. Chochez, *f.* || *To be in one's dotage*, estar chocho, cha.
dotal [ˈdəutəl] adj. Dotal.
dotard [ˈdəutəd] n. Viejo (*m.*) chocho, vieja (*f.*) chocha.
dotation [dəuˈteiʃən] n. Dotación, *f.*
dote [dəut] v. intr. Chochear (an old person). || *To dote on*, adorar, estar chocho por.
doting [—iŋ] adj. Chocho, cha.
dotty [ˈdɔti] adj. FAM. Chiflado, da; chalado, da (daft). || Punteado, da (with dots).
double [ˈdʌbl] adj. Doble. || En dos ejemplares (in duplicate). || Doblado, da (folded). || Repetido, da (repeated). || Para dos personas (room). || FIG. Doble: *to lead a double life*, llevar una doble vida; *double meaning*, doble sentido. || — *I am double your age*, soy dos veces mayor que tú. || *Your income is double what it was last year*, sus ingresos son dos veces lo que eran el año pasado *or* el doble de lo que eran el año pasado.
— Adv. Doble: *to see double*, ver doble. || — *Double as long as*, dos veces más largo que. || *Double or nothing, double or quits*, doble o nada. || *To pay double*, pagar el doble. || *To ride double*, montar dos en un caballo. || *To sleep double*, dormir dos en una cama.
— N. Doble, *m.* (quantity, actor). || MIL. Paso (*m.*) ligero. || — Pl. Doble, *m. sing.*: *men's, ladies, mixed doubles*, doble caballeros, damas, mixto. || FAM. *At the double*, corriendo. | *On the double*, con toda rapidez.
double [ˈdʌbl] v. tr. Doblar, duplicar (in quantity, size, weight). || Redoblar (efforts). || Doblar (to fold). || Cerrar (the fist). || THEATR. Doblar. || Doblar (in bridge). || — *To double back* o *up*, doblar (to fold).
— V. intr. Duplicarse, doblarse (to become double). || Doblarse (to fold up). || Servir al mismo tiempo de (to serve as). || Correr a paso ligero (to run). || — *To double back*, volver sobre sus pasos (person), dar un rodeo (river). || CINEM. *To double for*, doblar a. || *To double round*, dar la vuelta por. || *To double up*, doblarse (from pain), compartir una habitación (to share a room), compartir una cama (to share a bed). || FIG. FAM. *To double up with laughter*, mondarse *or* partirse de risa.
double-acting [—ˈæktiŋ] adj. De doble efecto.
double bar [—ˈbɑ:*] n. MUS. Barras, *f. pl.*
double-barrelled [—ˈbærəld] adj. De dos cañones (gun). || FAM. Compuesto, ta (surname). || FIG. De doble efecto.
double bass [—ˈbeis] n. MUS. Contrabajo, *m.*, violón, *m.*
double bassoon [—bəˈsu:n] n. MUS. Contrafagot, *m.*
double bed [—ˈbed] n. Cama (*f.*) de matrimonio, cama (*f.*) camera, cama (*f.*) doble.
double-bedded [—ˈbedid] adj. Con dos camas.
double bill [—ˈbil] n. CINEM. Programa (*m.*) doble.
double boiler [—ˈbɔilə*] n. Baño (*m.*) maría.
double-bottomed [—ˌbɔtəmd] adj. De doble fondo.
double-breasted [—ˈbrestid] adj. Cruzado, da (coat).
double chin [—ˈtʃin] n. Papada, *f.*
double-cross [—ˈkrɔs] n. Traición, *f.*
double-cross [—ˈkrɔs] v. tr. Traicionar.
double-crosser [—ˈkrɔsə*] n. FAM. Hipócrita, *m.* & *f.* | Traidor, ra.
double dagger [—ˈdægə*] n. PRINT. Obelisco (*m.*) doble, signo (*m.*) de referencia.
double-dealer [—ˈdi:lə*] n. Embustero, *m.* (cheat). || Traidor, *m.* (traitor).
double-dealing [—ˈdi:liŋ] n. Doblez, *f.*, duplicidad, *f.*
double-decker [—ˈdekə*] n. Autobús (*m.*) de dos pisos. || MAR. Barco (*m.*) de dos cubiertas. || U. S. Sandwich (*m.*) *or* emparedado (*m.*) doble.
double Dutch [—dʌtʃ] n. FAM. Chino, *m.* (gibberish): *to talk double Dutch*, hablar chino.
double-edged [—ˈedʒd] adj. De dos filos.
double-entendre [ˈdu:blɑ̃:nˈtɑ̃:ndr] n. Expresión (*f.*) con doble sentido.
double entry [ˈdʌblˈentri] n. COMM. Partida (*f.*) doble. || *Double-entry bookkeeping*, contabilidad (*f.*) por partida doble.
double-faced [ˈdʌblˈfeist] adj. De dos caras. || FIG. Doble.
double feature [ˈdʌblˈfi:tʃə*] n. Programa (*m.*) doble, dos películas, *f. pl.*
double-headed [ˈdʌblˈhedid] adj. Bicéfalo, la.
double-jointed [ˈdʌblˈdʒɔintid] adj. Con articulaciones dobles.
double-lock [ˈdʌblˈlɔk] v. tr. Cerrar con dos vueltas.
double-quick [ˈdʌblˈkwik] adj. Ligero (step).
— Adv. A paso ligero.
double-spaced [ˈdʌblˈspeist] adj. Con doble espacio (in typewriting).
doublet [ˈdʌblit] n. Jubón, *m.* (garment). || Doblete, *m.* (jewel, linguistics). || PHYS. Objetivo (*m.*) doble.
double-talk [ˈdʌbltɔ:k] n. Palabras (*f. pl.*) con doble sentido.
double-talk [ˈdʌbltɔ:k] v. intr. Hablar con segundas.
double time [ˈdʌblˈtaim] n. Paso (*m.*) ligero.
doubleton [ˈdʌbltən] n. Dos cartas del mismo palo, doblete, *m.*
doubloon [dʌbˈlu:n] n. Doblón, *m.* (coin).
doubly [ˈdʌbli] adv. Doblemente: *doubly magnanimous*, doblemente magnánimo. || Por duplicado (in duplicate).
doubt [daut] n. Duda, *f.* (*about, as, to*, de): *to call in doubt*, poner en duda. || — *Beyond doubt*, fuera de duda. || *In doubt*, dudoso, sa. || *Make no doubt about it*, puede estar seguro de ello. || *No doubt*, sin duda. || *There is no doubt about it*, no cabe la menor duda. || *There is no doubt that*, no cabe duda de que. || *To be in doubt about* o *to have one's doubts about*, tener sus dudas acerca de. || *To clear up s.o.'s doubts*, sacar de dudas a uno. || *To put in a doubt*, hacer dudar (to give doubt to), poner en duda (to question). || *To shed one's doubts*, salir de dudas. || *When in doubt, don't* o *when in doubt, abstain*, en la duda abstente. || *Without a* o *any doubt*, sin duda alguna. || *Without the shadow of*

a doubt, sin sombra de duda. || *Without the slightest doubt*, sin la menor duda.

doubt [daut] v. tr. Dudar: *I doubt it*, lo dudo. || Dudar de, poner en tela de juicio (to question). || Desconfiar de (to distrust).

— V. intr. Dudar (*about, of*, de). || *I doubt whether he'll come*, no sé si vendrá, no estoy seguro de que venga, dudo que venga.

doubter [—ə*] n. Escéptico, ca.

doubtful [—ful] adj. Dudoso, sa; poco seguro, ra: *the results are doubtful*, los resultados son dudosos. || Indeciso, sa (irresolute). || Dudoso, sa; sospechoso, sa (character, place, society). || Dudoso, sa (taste). || Vago, ga (vague). || — *To be doubtful of* o *about*, dudar de. || *We were still doubtful about speaking to her*, no nos decidíamos todavía a hablarle.

doubting Thomas [ˈdautiŋˈtɔməs] n. Fig. Incrédulo, la.

doubtless [ˈdautlis] adv. Sin duda, indudablemente.

douceur [du:ˈsə:*] n. Propina, *f.* (gratuity). || Guante, *m.*, mamelas, *f. pl.* (bribe).

douche [du:ʃ] n. Ducha, *f.* (jet of water). || Irrigador, *m.* (instrument used). || Med. Irrigación, *f.*

douche [du:ʃ] v. tr. Irrigar.

— V. intr. Irrigarse.

doucine [du:ˈsi:n] n. Arch. Cimacio, *m.*

dough [dəu] n. Masa, *f.*, pasta, *f.* || U. S. Fam. Pasta, *f.* [*Amer.*, plata, *f.*] (money).

doughboy [—bɔi] n. U. S. Mil. Soldado (*m.*) de infantería.

doughnut [—nʌt] n. Rosquilla, *f.*, buñuelo, *m.*

doughty [ˈdauti] adj. Valiente.

doughy [ˈdəui] adj. Pastoso, sa.

dour [duə*] adj. Austero, ra (sullen). || Severo, ra (severe). || Terco, ca; obstinado, da (obstinate).

Douro [ˈduərəu] pr. n. Geogr. Duero, *m.*

douse [daus] v. tr. Mojar (to soak or to put in water). || Mar. Arriar (sails). || Fam. Apagar (to extinguish).

dove [dʌv] n. Zool. Paloma, *f.* || Fig. fam. *My dove*, mi cielo, mi amor.

dove [dəuv] pret. See DIVE.

dovecot or **dovecote** [ˈdʌvkɔt] n. Palomar, *m.*

dovetail [ˈdʌvteil] n. Tech. Cola (*f.*) de milano.

dovetail [ˈdʌvteil] v. tr. Ensamblar a cola de milano (in carpentry). || Fig. Enlazar, unir (to link). | Encajar (to fit).

— V. intr. Fig. Enlazar (to be linked). | Encajar (to fit).

dowager [ˈdauədʒə*] n. Viuda (*f.*) que goza de una pensión *or* viudedad *or* del título de su marido. || Fam. Señora (*f.*) mayor. || *Queen dowager*, reina viuda.

dowdiness [ˈdaudinis] n. Desaliño, *m.* (slovenliness). || Falta (*f.*) de elegancia.

dowdy [ˈdaudi] adj. Desaliñado, da (slovenly). || Poco elegante (not smart).

dowel [ˈdauəl] n. Clavija, *f.*

dowel [ˈdauəl] v. tr. Sujetar con una clavija, enclavijar.

dower [ˈdauə*] n. Viudedad, *f.* (property retained by a widow). || Dote, *f.* (dowry). || Don, *m.* (natural gift).

dower [ˈdauə*] v. tr. Dotar (a girl). || Dar una viudedad a (a widow). || Fig. Dotar.

down [dauŋ] n. Plumón, *m.* (on birds). || Vello, *m.* (any fine hair growth). || Pelusa, *f.* (fuzz, on fruit). || Loma, *f.* (treeless upland). || U. S. Duna, *f.* (dune). || U. S. Sp. "Down", *m.* || — *His ups and downs*, sus más y sus menos, sus altibajos. || Fig. fam. *To have a down on s.o.*, tenerle manía a uno, tenerle tirria a uno.

— Adj. Descendente: *a down current*, una corriente descendente. || Bajo, ja: *the river is down*, el río está bajo; *prices are down now*, los precios están bajos ahora. || Deprimido, da (depressed). || Agotado, da (tired). || Comm. Al contado, inicial (payment). || Sp. Fuera de juego. | Fuera de combate (in boxing). || Desinflado, da (tyre). || *Down train*, tren que sale de la capital, tren descendente.

— Adv. Hacia abajo: *they rolled the ball down*, hicieron rodar la pelota hacia abajo. || En el suelo: *to hit a man when he is down*, pegar a un hombre cuando está en el suelo. || Por escrito: *to take s.o.'s name down*, poner el nombre de alguien por escrito. || Comm. Al contado (to pay). || — Fam. *Down and out*, sin una perra, sin un cuarto (broke), fuera de combate (in boxing). || *Down below*, abajo. || *Down, boy!*, ¡quieto! (to a dog). || *Down here*, por aquí. || *Down to*, hasta: *down to date*, hasta la fecha. || *Down to where?*, ¿hasta dónde? || *Down under*, en Australia, en Nueva Zelanda, en las antípodas. || *¡Down with the king!*, ¡abajo el rey! || *Face down*, boca abajo. || *Further down*, más abajo. || *He is twenty francs down*, le faltan veinte francos. || *The curtains are down*, se han bajado las cortinas. || *The team was three down*, el equipo iba perdiendo por tres puntos. || *The wind is down*, ha amainado el viento. || Fig. *To be down*, haber acabado el curso (a student). || Fam. *To be down on s.o.*, tenerle manía *or* tirria a alguien. || *To be down with*, estar con: *he is down with flu*, está con gripe. || *To come down in the world*, venir a menos. || *To copy down*, copiar. || *To fall down*, caerse. || *To go down*, see GO. || *To lie down*, see LIE. || *To take* o *to write down*, apuntar. || *Two down, one to go*, dos fuera, uno me queda. || *Up and down*, de arriba abajo.

— Prep. Abajo: *it is down the street a little*, está un poco más abajo de la calle. || — *Down the centuries*, a través de los siglos. || *Down the road*, más abajo. || *To go down the river*, ir río abajo. || *To go down the street*, bajar la calle. || *To run down the street*, bajar la calle corriendo.

— Observ. Existen muchos casos en los cuales el adverbio *down* modifica el sentido del verbo que le antecede (*to go down, to let down, to pull down*, etc.) y no puede traducirse separadamente. Es imprescindible por consiguiente consultar el verbo correspondiente donde las distintas acepciones están tratadas con todo detalle (ver "to pull down" en el artículo dedicado a "pull").

down [daun] v. tr. Tirar al suelo: *to down s.o.*, tirar a alguien al suelo. || Derribar (a plane). || Vaciar de un trago (a drink). || Tragar (food). || *To down tools*, declararse en huelga.

down-and-out [ˈdaunəndˈaut] adj. Pobre, pobrísimo, ma; sin un céntimo.

— N. Pobre, *m.* & *f.*

down-at-heel [ˈdaunəthi:l] adj. Desaliñado, da (slovenly). || Gastado, da; destaconado, da (shoes). || Fam. Pelado, da; sin un cuarto (penniless).

downcast [ˈdaunkɑ:st] adj. Abatido, da (depressed). || Bajo, ja (directed downwards): *downcast eyes*, ojos bajos.

— N. Min. Pozo (*m.*) de ventilación.

downfall [ˈdaunfɔ:l] n. Chaparrón, *m.* (a fall of rain). || Caída, *f.* (of snow). || Caída, *f.* (a fall from greatness): *the downfall of an empire, of a ministry*, la caída de un imperio, de un ministerio. || Perdición, *f.* (cause of ruin): *drink will be his downfall*, la bebida será su perdición. || Ruina, *f.* || U. S. Trampa, *f.* (trap).

downgrade [ˈdaungreid] n. Bajada, *f.*, descenso, *m.* || Fig. *To be on the downgrade*, ir cuesta abajo, estar en decadencia.

downgrade [ˈdaungreid] v. tr. Degradar.

downhaul [ˈdaunhɔ:l] n. Mar. Candaliza, *f.*

downhearted [daunˈhɑ:tid] adj. Descorazonado, da; abatido, da. || *To make downhearted*, descorazonar, desanimar.

downheartedness [—nis] n. Descorazonamiento, *m.*, desánimo, *m.*

downhill [ˈdaunhil] adj. En pendiente. || Sp. *Downhill race*, carrera (*f.*) de descenso (ski).

— Adv. Cuesta abajo. || *To go downhill*, bajar, ir cuesta abajo (road, car), ir cuesta abajo, estar en decadencia (person).

— N. Bajada, *f.*, pendiente, *f.*, declive, *m.*

downiness [ˈdauninis] n. Vellosidad, *f.*

downpour [ˈdaunpɔ:] n. Aguacero, *m.*, chaparrón, *m.*

downright [ˈdaunrait] adj. Categórico, ca (straightforward). || Sincero, ra; franco, ca (sincere). || Patente, evidente, manifiesto, ta: *a downright lie*, una mentira patente. || Verdadero, ra: *a downright swindle*, un verdadero timo. || *Downright fool*, tonto rematado.

— Adv. Categóricamente, rotundamente: *he refused downright*, se negó rotundamente. || Realmente, verdaderamente (positively). || Completamente.

downrightness [—nis] n. Franqueza, *f.*, sinceridad, *f.*

downstage [ˈdaunsteidʒ] adj./adv. Theatr. En *or* hacia la parte delantera del escenario.

— N. Theatr. Proscenio, *m.*

downstair [ˈdaunˈstɛə*] or **downstairs** [—z] adj. De abajo.

— Adv. Abajo. || *To go* o *to come downstairs*, bajar la escalera.

— N. U. S. Planta (*f.*) baja (ground floor).

downstream [ˈdaunstri:m] adj./adv. Río abajo.

downstroke [ˈdaunstrəuk] n. Palo, *m.* (of a letter). || Tech. Carrera (*f.*) descendente (of a piston).

downthrow [ˈdaunθrəu] n. Geol. Corrimiento, *m.*

down-to-earth [ˈdauntuˈə:θ] adj. Prosaico, ca.

downtown [ˈdauntaun] adv. U. S. Al *or* en el centro de la ciudad.

— Adj. Céntrico, ca; del centro de la ciudad.

— N. U. S. Centro, *m.*

downtrodden [ˈdaun,trɔdn] adj. Pisoteado, da: *downtrodden grass*, hierba pisoteada. || Fig. Oprimido, da (oppressed).

downturn [ˈdauntə:n] n. Vuelta (*f.*) hacia abajo. || Comm. Baja, *f.*

downward [ˈdaunwəd] adj. Descendente (road, movement). || Ulterior (time). || Comm. A la baja (tendency).

— Adv. Hacia abajo.

downwards [—z] adv. Hacia abajo. || *From the fourteenth century downwards*, desde el siglo XIV.

downwind [ˈdaunwind] adj./adv. A favor del viento, con el viento (in the same direction as the wind).

downy [ˈdauni] adj. Velloso, sa. || Suave (soft).

dowry [ˈdauəri] n. Dote, *f.* (of a girl). || Fig. Don, *m.*, dote, *m.* (talent).

dowse [dauz] v. intr. Buscar agua con una varilla de zahorí.

— V. tr. See DOUSE.

dowser [—ə*] n. Zahorí, *m.*

doxy [ˈdɔksi] n. Pop. Ramera, *f.*, zorra, *f.* (whore). | Querida, *f.* (mistress).

doyen [ˈdɔiən] n. Decano, *m.*

doze [dəuz] n. Cabezada, *f.*: *to have a doze after lunch*, echar una cabezada después del almuerzo.

doze [dəuz] v. intr. Dormitar. || *To doze off*, dormirse, echar una cabezada.

dozen [ˈdʌzn] n. Docena, *f.* (twelve): *a dozen eggs*, una docena de huevos. || — Pl. Docenas, *f.*, miles, *m.*: *dozens of times*, miles de veces. || — FIG. *A dozen words*, unas cuantas palabras. | *Baker's dozen*, docena (*f.*) del fraile. || *By the dozen*, por docenas, a docenas (goods), a docenas (in great quantity). || FIG. *In dozens*, a docenas.

— OBSERV. La palabra *dozen* es invariable cuando va seguida por un sustantivo y precedida por una cifra o su equivalente (*three dozen eggs*, tres docenas de huevos; *how many dozen?*, ¿cuantas docenas?).

dozy [ˈdəuzi] adj. Soñoliento, ta; medio dormido, da.

drab [dræb] adj. Pardo, da (colour). || FIG. Monótono, na; gris: *a drab existence*, una vida gris.
— N. Pardo, *m.* (colour). || Sayal, *m.* (cloth). || FIG. Lo gris, monotonía, *f.* || Marrana, *f.*, mujer (*f.*) sucia (slut). || Mujer (*f.*) perdida (prostitute).

drabble [ˈdræbl] v. tr. Manchar de barro.
— V. intr. Chapotear (through the mud). || Mancharse de barro (to get stained).

drachm [dræm] or **drachma** [ˈdrækmə] n. Dracma, *f.*

— OBSERV. El plural de las palabras inglesas *drachm* y *drachma* es *drachmas*, *drachmae* o *drachmai*.

Draconian [dreiˈkəunjən] or **Draconic** [dreiˈkəunik] adj. Draconiano, na.

draff [dræf] n. Heces, *f. pl.*, poso, *m.* (dregs). || Aguas (*f. pl.*) sucias (slops). || Residuo (*m.*) de la cebada utilizado en la fabricación de la cerveza (in brewery). || FIG. Heces, *f. pl.*

draft [drɑ:ft] n. Borrador, *m.* (in writing). || Boceto, *m.*, esbozo, *m.* (in drawing). || Bosquejo, *m.* (a rough plan of work). || Redacción, *f.*, versión, *f.*: *first draft of a novel*, primera redacción de una novela. || JUR. Minuta, *f.* (of an act). | Proyecto, *m.* (of an agreement). || COMM. Libramiento, *m.* (payment from an account). | Letra (*f.*) de cambio, giro, *m.* (bill). || MIL. Quinta, *f.* (conscription). | Destacamento, *m.* (of troops). || Forma (*f.*) acampanada (of a mould). || Trazo, *m.* (in masonry). || U. S. Corriente, *f.* (of air). | Tiro, *m.* (of a chimney). | Trago, *m.* (of liquid). | Calado, *m.* (of a boat). || — Pl. Juego (*m. sing.*) de damas. || — *Draft bill*, anteproyecto (*m.*) de ley. || *Draft horse*, caballo (*m.*) de tiro. || *On draft*, de barril, a presión (beer).

draft [drɑ:ft] v. tr. Hacer un proyecto de (to sketch). || Hacer un borrador de (in writing). || Redactar (to draw up): *to draft a text*, redactar un texto. || Esbozar (in drawing). || ARCH. Trazar una línea en (in masonry). || MIL. Destacar (troops). | Llamar a filas, reclutar (conscript).

draftee [drɑ:fˈti:] n. U.S. MIL. Quinto, *m.*, recluta, *m.*

draftsman [ˈdrɑ:ftsmən] n. Delineante, *m.*, dibujante, *m.* (designer). || Pieza, *f.*, dama, *f.* (in draughts). || JUR. Redactor (*m.*) de proyectos de ley.

— OBSERV. El plural de esta palabra es *draftsmen*.

draftsmanship [—ʃip] n. Dibujo (*m.*) lineal.

drafty [ˈdrɑ:fti] adj. Que tiene corrientes de aire.

drag [dræg] n. Arrastre, *m.* (towing). || AGR. Grada, *f.*, rastro, *m.*, rastra, *f.* || Rastra, *f.* (device for searching the river bed). || Estorbo, *m.* (sth. or s.o. which hinders): *to be a drag on*, ser un estorbo para. || FAM. Calada, *f.*, chupada, *f.* (a draw on a cigarette). || AVIAT. Resistencia (*f.*) aerodinámica. || TECH. Galga, *f.* (brake). || THEATR. Disfraz (*m.*) de mujer. || FAM. Cuña, *f.*, enchufe, *m.* (influence). | Calle, *f.* (street). | Carrera (*f.*) de velocidad (race). | Guateque, *m.*, fiesta, *f.* (party). | Rollo, *m.*, pesado, *m.* (boring person). | Lata., *f.* (bother). || — MAR. *Drag anchor*, ancla (*f.*) flotante. || *In drag*, disfrazado de mujer. || FAM. *What a drag!*, ¡qué lata!

drag [dræg] v. tr. Arrastrar (to haul or pull): *to drag a table*, arrastrar una mesa; *to drag one's feet*, arrastrar los pies. || Dragar, rastrear (river, lake, etc.). || AGR. Rastrillar. || TECH. Engalgar, calzar (a wheel). || FAM. Dar la lata, dar el rollo (to bore). || FIG. Distraer, entretener (from one's work). || — *To drag along*, arrastrar. || FIG. *To drag down*, hundir: *to drag s.o. down*, hundir a alguien. || *To drag in*, hacer entrar a la fuerza (sth., s.o.), traer por los cabellos (a subject). || *To drag on*, arrastrar, llevar (one's life), alargar (a speech). || *To drag out*, sacar: *to drag s.o. out of bed*, sacar a alguien de la cama; dar largas a (an affair), arrastrar, llevar (one's life). || MAR. *To drag the anchor*, garrar. || *To drag up*, sacar (sth., s.o.), sacar a colación (an old story), dejar que se críe solo (a child).
— V. intr. Arrastrarse. || Rezagarse (to lag behind). || AGR. Rastrillar. || Hacerse largo: *this film is beginning to drag*, esta película empieza a hacerse larga. || MAR. Garrar (an anchor). || *To drag on*, no acabar nunca, ser interminable, ir para largo.

dragging [ˈdrægiŋ] n. Dragado, *m.*

draggle [ˈdrægl] v. tr. Manchar de barro.
— V. intr. Mancharse de barro. || Rezagarse (to lag behind).

draggletail [ˈdrægl̩teil] n. Mujer (*f.*) desarreglada (slut).

drag link [ˈdrægliŋk] n. Barra (*f.*) de acoplamiento.

dragnet [ˈdrægnet] n. Red (*f.*) barredera.

dragoman [ˈdrægəumən] n. Dragomán, *m.*

dragon [ˈdrægən] n. Dragón, *m.* (mythical animal). || FIG. Arpía, *f.*, fiera, *f.* (fierce woman). || ZOOL. *Flying dragon*, dragón, *m.* (reptile).

dragonfly [—flai] n. ZOOL. Libélula, *f.*

dragon tree [—tri:] n. BOT. Drago, *m.*

dragoon [drəˈgu:n] n. MIL. Dragón, *m.*

dragoon [drəˈgu:n] v. tr. Tiranizar. || Forzar, obligar (*into*, a) [to bully s.o. into a course of action].

dragrope [ˈdrægrəup] n. Cable (*m.*) de arrastre (a towing rope). || Freno, *m.* (for an aerostat).

drain [drein] n. Tubo (*m.*) de desagüe, desaguadero, *m.* (pipe for carrying away water). || Canal (*m.*) de drenaje (for draining off water). || Boca (*f.*) de alcantarilla, sumidero, *m.* (inlet to a sewer). || MED. Tubo (*m.*) de drenaje. || TECH. Purga, *f.* || FIG. Sangría, *f.* (of money). | Pérdida, *f.*, disminución, *f.* (of strength). || — Pl. Alcantarillado, *m. sing.* (sewage system). || — FIG. *Brain drain*, fuga (*f.*) de cerebros. || FAM. *To throw money down the drain*, tirar el dinero por la ventana.

drain [drein] v. tr. Desaguar (to conduct water away from). || AGR. Avenar. || Secar (linen). || Escurrir (bottles, etc.). || Apurar, vaciar (to empty by drinking). || MED. Drenar (an abscess). || Desecar (a marsh). || Desaguar (mine). || TECH. Purgar (a cylinder, a machine). | Vaciar (boilers). | Descebar (a pump). || FIG. Agotar (resources, strength). || FAM. *To drain s.o. dry*, esquilmarle a uno.
— V. intr. Escurrirse (bottles, etc.). || Desaguar (river).

drainage [—idʒ] n. Desagüe, *m.* || AGR. Avenamiento, *m.* || Desecación, *f.* (of a marsh). || Alcantarillado, *m.* (sewage system). || — GEOGR. *Drainage basin*, cuenca hidrográfica. || MED. *Drainage tube*, tubo (*m.*) de drenaje.

drainer [—ə*] n. Escurridero, *m.* || Escurreplatos, *m. inv.* (for dishes). || AGR. Avenador, *m.*

draining [—iŋ] n. Desagüe, *m.* || AGR. Avenamiento, *m.* || Desecación, *f.* (of a marsh).

draining board [—iŋbɔ:d] n. Escurridero, *m.*

drainpipe [ˈdreinpaip] n. Tubo (*m.*) de desagüe. || FAM. *Drainpipe trousers*, pantalones muy estrechos.

drake [dreik] n. ZOOL. Pato, *m.* || Mosca, *f.* (in fishing).

dram [dræm] n. Dracma, *f.* (weight). || FAM. Copita, *f.* (of alcoholic drink): *a dram of whisky*, una copita de whisky. | Pizca, *f.* (bit).

drama [ˈdrɑ:mə] n. Drama, *m.*: *lyric drama*, drama lírico. || FIG. Drama, *m.*

dramatic [drəˈmætik] or **dramatical** [—əl] adj. Dramático, ca.

dramatics [—s] n. THEATR. Teatro, *m.* || FIG. Teatro, *m.* (dramatic behaviour).

dramatism [ˈdræmətizəm] n. Dramatismo, *m.*

dramatist [ˈdræmətist] n. THEATR. Dramaturgo, ga.

dramatize [ˈdræmətaiz] v. tr. Adaptar al teatro (to adapt a novel for a play). || FIG. Dramatizar.
— V. intr. Adaptarse al teatro.

dramaturge [ˈdræmətə:dʒ] or **dramaturgist** [—ist] n. Dramaturgo, ga.

dramaturgy [ˈdræməˌtə:dʒi] n. Dramaturgia, *f.*

drank [dræŋk] pret. See DRINK.

drape [dreip] n. Caída, *f.* (the manner of hanging): *the drape of a dress*, la caída de un traje. || Colgadura, *f.* (hanging). || U. S. Cortina, *f.* (curtain).

drape [dreip] v. tr. Adornar con colgaduras, tapizar (to decorate). || Cubrir: *walls draped with flags*, muros cubiertos de banderas. || Drapear (a cloth). || ARTS. Disponer los ropajes. || FAM. *To drape o.s. in one's dignity*, encastillarse en su dignidad.

draper [ˈdreipə*] n. Pañero, ra.

drapery [ˈdreipəri] n. Pañería, *f.* (draper's shop). || Telas, *f. pl.* (fabrics). || Colgaduras, *f. pl.*, tapices, *m. pl.* (hangings). || ARTS. Ropaje, *m.* (of a statue). || Drapeado, *m.* (artistic arrangement of clothing).

drastic [ˈdræstik] adj. Drástico, ca (measures, action, etc.). || Importante (reduction). || MED. Drástico, ca.

drastically [—əli] adv. De una manera drástica.

drat [dræt] interj. FAM. ¡Caramba!

draught [drɑ:ft] n. Rastreo, *m.* (the act of dragging with a net). || Redada, *f.* (amount of fish in a net). || Tracción, *f.* (pulling of a vehicle). || Sorbo, *m.*, trago, *m.* (act of drinking): *at a draught*, de un trago. || Corriente, *f.* (current of air). || Aire, *m.*: *to make draught with a fan*, hacer aire con un abanico. || Tiro, *m.* (of a chimney). || MAR. Calado, *m.* || Bosquejo, *m.* (a rough plan of work). || Trazo, *m.* (in masonry). || Dama, *f.*, pieza, *f.* (a piece in the game of draughts). || MED. Poción, *f.* || — Pl. Juego (*m. sing.*) de damas. || FIG. FAM. *To feel a draught*, sufrir las consecuencias.
— Adj. De tiro (animals): *draught horse*, caballo de tiro. || De barril, a presión (drawn from a barrel): *draught beer*, cerveza de barril.

draught [drɑ:ft] v. tr. See DRAFT.

draughtboard [—bɔ:d] n. Tablero (*m.*) de damas.

draughtsman [—smən] n. See DRAFTSMAN.

— OBSERV. El plural de esta palabra es *draughtsmen*.

draughtsmanship [—smənʃip] n. Dibujo (*m.*) lineal.

draughty [ˈdrɑ:fti] adj. Que tiene corrientes de aire.

Dravidian [drəˈvidiən] n. Drávida, *m.* & *f.*

draw [drɔ:] n. SP. Empate, *m.* (game or match that ends without a winner). || Tablas, *f. pl.* (in chess). || Chupada, *f.*, calada, *f.* (smoking). || Sorteo, *m.* (of lots). || Lotería, *f.* (lottery). || Tracción, *f.*, tiro, *m.* (of a horse, a vehicle). || Tiro, *m.* (of a chimney). || CULIN. Infusión, *f.* || COMM. Artículo (*m.*) de reclamo. || Obra (*f.*) taquillera (play). || FAM. Atracción, *f.* (thing that attracts). | Artilugios (*m. pl.*) para conseguir confidencias.

|| TECH. Estirado, *m.* || U. S. Parte (*f.*) movible de un puente levadizo (of a drawbridge). || — *Draw works*, torno, *m.* (in oil wells). || *Quick on the draw*, rápido en sacar la pistola.

draw* [drɔ:] v. tr. Tirar de: *to draw a cart*, tirar de un carro. || Atraer (to attract): *to draw s.o.'s eye*, atraer la mirada de alguien. || FIG. Atraer (public). || Extraer (to pull out, to extract). || Limpiar, destripar: *to draw fish*, limpiar el pescado. || Destripar, vaciar (fowl). || Dibujar (to make a picture): *to draw in ink, in pencil, freehand, from nature, by gouache*, dibujar con *or* a pluma, con *or* a lápiz, a mano alzada, del natural, a la aguada. || Trazar (a line). || Levantar, hacer, trazar (a map). || Trazar(to delineate in words): *the book's characters are well drawn*, los personajes del libro están bien trazados. || Sacar: *to draw water from a well*, sacar agua de un pozo; *to draw a nail*, sacar un clavo; *to draw a tooth*, sacar una muela; *to draw conclusions*, sacar conclusiones; *to draw a confession from s.o.*, sacar una confesión a alguien; *to draw profit from*, sacar provecho de; *to draw money from a bank account*, sacar dinero de una cuenta bancaria. || Formular, decir (an opinion, etc.). || Hacer (comparisons). || JUR. Redactar (a document). || Aspirar (to inhale). || Tomar (breath). || Estirar (to stretch). || Alargar (a speech). || Hacer madurar: *to draw an abscess*, hacer madurar un absceso. || Acarrear, traer consigo (to entail). || Llevar, incitar: *to draw s.o. into doing sth.*, llevar a alguien a que haga algo. || Recibir, cobrar (to earn): *he draws a very high salary*, recibe un salario muy elevado. || Librar, extender (a cheque). || Girar, librar (a bill). || Ganar, llevarse (a prize). || Sortear (lots). || MAR. Calar, tener un calado de (a ship). || Rastrear, batir (woods, etc.). || Hinchar (to swell). || Correr (to close curtains, a bolt). || Descorrer (to open curtains, a bolt). || Bajar (the blinds). || Quitar (to take away). || Desenfundar, sacar (pistol, knife). || Desenvainar, sacar (sword). || Tensar (a bow). || Robar (a card from the pack). || Arrastrar, hacer echar (trumps). || Levantar (a drawbridge). || TECH. Estirar (a wire). | Vaciar (a casting). | Extraer, sacar (coal). || AUT. Remolcar, tirar de (a car). || Hacer hablar: *to try to draw s.o.*, intentar hacer hablar a alguien. || Fruncir, arrugar (the face). || MIL. Provocar (enemy fire). || — FIG. *His face was drawn*, tenía la cara cansada. || *To draw a blank*, llevarse un chasco. || *To draw a distinction* o *a line between*, distinguir entre, hacer una distinción entre. || *To draw a game with*, empatar con. || *To draw attention*, llamar *or* atraer la atención. || *To draw blood*, hacer sangrar. || *To draw lots*, sortear: *to draw lots for a bottle of wine*, sortear una botella de vino; echar a suertes: *they drew lots to see who would go*, echaron a suertes a ver quién iría. || *To draw one's hand across one's forehead*, pasarse la mano por la frente. || *To draw s.o. from*, apartar a alguien de. || *To draw s.o. into conversation*, entablar conversación con alguien. || *To draw straws*, echar pajas. || *To draw tight*, apretarse (the belt). || *To feel drawn to*, sentirse atraído por.

— V. intr. Tirar (horse). || Dibujar (pictures). || Sortear (lots). || Tirar (a chimney). || Reposar (tea). || Sacar el arma (the pistol). || SP. Empatar. || Hacer tablas (in chess). || Dirigirse (*towards*, hacia). || THEATR. Ser taquillero (a play). || — *To draw ahead*, destacarse (a runner). || *To draw alongside*, ponerse de costado. || *To draw near to*, acercarse a.

— ***To draw apart,*** separar. | Separarse. || ***To draw aside,*** apartar (sth.). | Llamar aparte (s.o.). | Descorrer (curtain). | Apartarse. || ***To draw asunder,*** separar. || ***To draw away,*** llevarse. | Apartar (s.o. from sth.). | Alejarse: *the car drew away*, el coche se alejó. | Destacarse: *the favourite drew away from the rest of the runners*, el favorito se destacó del resto de los corredores. || ***To draw back,*** retirar. | Descorrer (curtains). | Retroceder (to move back). | FIG. Retirar (one's word), volverse atrás, echarse para atrás (to back down). || ***To draw down,*** bajar (the blinds). || ***To draw forth,*** hacer salir (s.o.). | Sacar (sth.). | Provocar (to provoke). | Hacer saltar (tears). || ***To draw in,*** tirar hacia adentro (s.o., sth.). | Retraer (claws). | Tirar de (reins). | Aspirar (air). | Entrar (to enter). | Entrar en la estación (trains). | Aparcar (a car). | Acortarse, hacerse más cortos (days). | FIG. Comprometer. || ***To draw off,*** quitarse (one's shoes). | Retirar (troops). | Sacar (wine). | MED. Sacar (blood). | Desviar, apartar (the attention). || ***To draw on,*** ponerse (clothing). | Incitar (to induce). | Recurrir a: *to draw on one's imagination*, recurrir a la imaginación. | Inspirarse en (to get one's ideas from). | Ocasionar, causar (to cause). | Pasar: *time draws on*, el tiempo pasa. | Acercarse: *evening was drawing on*, la noche se acercaba. || ***To draw out,*** sacar (sth.). | Sacar, arrancar (a nail). | Alargar, estirar (to stretch). | TECH. Estirar (a wire). | ARTS. Trazar (patterns, plan). | COMM. Sacar (money). | Redactar (a document). | Salir de la estación (trains). | FIG. Hacer durar, dar largas a (an affair), alargar, hacer durar (speech). | FAM. Hacer hablar, desatar la lengua (s.o.). || ***To draw to,*** correr (curtains). | — *To draw to an end*, llegar a su fin. || ***To draw together,*** juntar (two things). | Unir (people). | Unirse. | Reunirse. || ***To draw up,*** subir (a blind). | Subirse, remangarse (sleeves, etc.). | Acercar: *draw up a chair and sit down*, acerca una silla y siéntate. | Redactar (a document). | Preparar (the budget). | Hacer (an account). | Elaborar (a plan). | Trazar (an itinerary). | MIL. Ordenar para el combate. | TECH. Apretar (a nut). | Sacar del agua (a boat). | Acercarse (to get close). | Pararse (to stop): *to draw up short*, pararse en seco. | — *To draw o.s. up*, enderezarse (to straighten o.s.), incorporarse (in bed), erguirse (with pride). | *To draw up with s.o.*, alcanzar a alguien.

— OBSERV. Pret. ***drew;*** p. p. ***drawn.***

drawback [ˈdrɔ:bæk] n. Inconveniente, *m.* (*to*, de) [shortcoming]. || Desventaja, *f.* (disadvantage). || COMM. "Drawback", *m.*, reintegro (*m.*) de los derechos de aduana pagados por las materias primas que sirvieron para productos de exportación, prima (*f.*) a la exportación.

drawbar [ˈdrɔ:ˌbɑ:*] n. Barra (*f.*) de tracción.

drawbench [ˈdrɔ:bentʃ] n. TECH. Hilera, *f.*

drawbridge [ˈdrɔ:bridʒ] n. Puente (*m.*) levadizo.

drawee [drɔ:ˈi:] n. COMM. Girado, *m.*, librado, *m.*

drawer [ˈdrɔ:ə*] n. Dibujante, *m.* & *f.* (artist). || Cajón, *m.* (of table, sideboard, etc.). || COMM. Girador, *m.*, librador, *m.* || — Pl. FAM. Calzoncillos, *m.* (underpants). || Bragas, *f.* (knickers).

drawing [ˈdrɔ:iŋ] n. Dibujo, *m.* (picture, action): *charcoal, pencil, ink, freehand drawing*, dibujo al carbón, a lápiz, a pluma, a mano alzada. || Extracción, *f.* (extraction). || TECH. Vaciado, *m.* (of casting). | Estirado, *m.* (of wire). | Extracción, *f.* (of coal). || COMM. Giro, *m.*: *drawing rights*, derechos de giro. || U. S. Sorteo, *m.* || — *Drawing from nature* o *life*, dibujo del natural. || *Mechanical drawing*, dibujo industrial

drawing account [—əˌkaunt] n. U. S. Cuenta (*f.*) de depósito a la vista.

drawing board [—bɔ:d] n. Tablero (*m.*) de dibujo.

drawing card [—kɑ:d] n. FAM. Atracción, *f.*

drawing knife [—naif] n. TECH. Plana, *f.*

drawing mill [—mil] n. Trefilería, *f.*, fábrica (*f.*) de alambre.

drawing paper [—ˌpeipə*] n. Papel (*m.*) de dibujo.

drawing pen [—pen] n. Tiralíneas, *m. inv.*

drawing pin [—pin] n. Chincheta, *f.*, chinche, *f.*

drawing room [—rum] n. Salón, *m.* (sitting room). || Recepción, *f.* (formal reception).

drawing up [—ʌp] n. Redacción, *f.* || Elaboración, *f.* (of a plan). || Preparación, *f.* (of the budget).

drawknife [ˈdrɔ:naif] n. TECH. Plana, *f.*

drawl [drɔ:l] n. Voz (*f.*) cansina.

drawl [drɔ:l] v. intr. Hablar lenta y cansinamente, hablar con una voz cansina.

— V. tr. Arrastrar: *to drawl the words*, arrastrar las palabras. || Decir con una voz cansina.

drawn [drɔ:n] p. p. See DRAW. || *Drawn butter*, mantequilla derretida.

drawnwork [—wə:k] n. Calado, *m.*

drawplate [ˈdrɔ:pleit] TECH. Hilera, *f.*

draw poker [ˈdrɔ:ˈpəukə*] n. Póker (*m.*) cerrado.

drawshave [ˈdrɔ:ʃeiv] n. TECH. Plana, *f.*

dray [drei] n. Narria, *f.* (cart).

drayage [ˈdreiidʒ] n. Acarreo, *m.*, porte, *m.*

dray horse [ˈdreihɔ:s] n. Caballo (*m.*) de tiro.

drayman [ˈdreimən] n. Transportista, *m.*

— OBSERV. El plural de *drayman* es *draymen*.

dread [dred] n. Pavor, *m.*, terror, *m.* (great fear). || Aprensión, *f.* (apprehension). || — *In dread of*, con el temor de. || *To be in dread of*, temer a, tener temor *or* pavor a.

— Adj. Espantoso, sa (dreadful).

dread [dred] v. tr. Temer, tener temor *or* pavor a. || *He dreads flying*, le horroriza ir en avión.

dreadful [—ful] adj. Espantoso, sa (fearful). || FIG. Horrible: *I've heard dreadful things about him*, he oído cosas horribles acerca de él. | Malísmo, ma; fatal (very bad). || — FIG. *How dreadful!*, ¡qué horror! | *I feel dreadul about it*, me da vergüenza.

dreadfully [—fuli] adv. Terriblemente: *dreadfully ugly*, terriblemente feo. || Fatal (very badly). || — *I'm dreadfully sorry*, lo siento en el alma. || *I was dreadfully frightened*, tuve *or* pasé un miedo espantoso.

dreadnought [ˈdrednɔ:t] n. MAR. Acorazado, *m.*

dream [dri:m] n. Sueño, *m.* (when sleeping): *the dream came true*, el sueño se volvió realidad. || Ensueño, *m.* (when awake). || FIG. Sueño, *m.*, ilusión, *f.* || — *Bad dream*, pesadilla, *f.* || *Life's dream*, sueño dorado. || FIG. *My greatest dream is to be a millionaire*, el sueño de mi vida es ser millonario. | *She was wearing a dream of a hat*, llevaba un sombrero de sombrero *or* un sombrero precioso. || *Sweet dreams!*, ¡que sueñes con los angelitos! || *To be in a dream*, estar soñando. || *To see sth. in a dream*, ver algo en sueños.

dream* [dri:m] v. tr./intr. Soñar (*about*; *of*, con). || FIG. Soñar: *to dream of wealth*, soñar con riquezas. | Pensar: *to dream of one's youth*, pensar en su juventud. | Imaginarse (to fancy). || — *I would not dream of doing it*, no se me ocurriría hacerlo, no lo haría ni soñando. || *To dream away*, pasar soñando (one's time). || *To dream up*, idear, inventar.

— OBSERV. Pret. & p. p. ***dreamed, dreamt.***

dreamer [—ə*] n. Soñador, ra.

dreamily [ˈdri:mili] adv. Como si estuviera soñando.

dreamland [ˈdri:mlænd] n. País (*m.*) de los sueños. || Mundo (*m.*) de ensueño (lovely place).

dreamless [ˈdri:mlis] adj. Sin sueños. || Sin ilusiones.
dreamlike [ˈdri:mlaik] adj. De ensueño.
dreamt [dremt] pret. & p. p. See DREAM.
dreamworld [ˈdri:mwəld] n. Mundo (*m.*) de ensueño.
dreamy [ˈdri:mi] adj. Soñador, ra (people). || Vago, ga (vague). || De ensueño (delightful). || Lleno de sueños (sleep). || *Isn't it dreamy!*, ¡qué preciosidad!
dreariness [ˈdriərinis] n. Monotonía, *f.*, tristeza, *f.* (of life, etc.). || Insipidez, *f.*, falta (*f.*) de interés (of a book).
dreary [ˈdriəri] adj. Monótono, na; triste (life, countryside). || Insípido, da; sin interés (book). || Aburrido, da (boring).
dredge [dredʒ] n. Draga, *f.*
dredge [dredʒ] v. tr. Dragar (to clear a harbour, river). || Espolvorear (to sprinkle).
— V. intr. Dragar (to use a dredge).
dredger [—ə*] n. Draga, *f.* (dredge). || Espolvoreador, *m.* (for sprinkling flour, sugar, etc.).
dredging [—iŋ] n. Dragado, *m.* || *Dredging machine*, draga, *f.*
dreg [dreg] n. Rastro, *m.*, resto, *m.* (small amount). || — Pl. Poso, *m. sing.*, heces, *f.* (of liquids). || FIG. Hez, *f. sing.*: *the dregs of society*, la hez de la sociedad; *he drained the cup to the dregs*, apuró la copa hasta las heces.
drench [drentʃ] n. VET. Pócima, *f.*, poción, *f.* || Chaparrón, *m.*, aguacero, *m.* (of rain).
drench [drentʃ] v. tr. Empapar, calar (to soak). || VET. Administrar una pócima a. || — *Drenched in blood*, bañado en sangre. || *To be drenched to the skin*, estar calado hasta los huesos.
drencher [—ə*] n. Chaparrón, *m.* (a heavy shower).
dress [dres] n. Vestimenta, *f.* (attire). || Ropa, *f.* (clothing). || Vestido, *m.*, traje, *m.* (woman's frock). || Traje, *m.*: *court dress*, traje de corte. || — *Evening dress*, traje de etiqueta (for men), traje de noche (for women). || *Full dress*, traje de etiqueta (for men), traje de noche (for women), uniforme de gala (for military men). || *Morning dress*, traje de calle (man), traje de casa (woman). || *Wedding dress*, traje de novia.
dress [dres] v. tr. Vestir (to put clothes on, to wear clothes): *to be dresssed in silk*, estar vestido *or* ir vestido de seda. || Decorar, arreglar (shop windows). || Adornar (to decorate). || Peinar, arreglar (hair). || MIL. Alinear (troops). || MED. Vendar (a wound). || Almohazar, (a horse). || AGR. Abonar (soil). | Cultivar (garden). | Podar (fruit tree). || TECH. Adobar, curtir (skins). | Labrar (stone). | Aderezar, aprestar (cloth). | Preparar (cotton, wool). | Desbastar (timber). | Cepillar (wood). || CULIN. Aderezar (food). | Aliñar (salad). || MAR. Empavesar (a ship). || — FAM. *Dressed to kill*, de tiros largos, de punta en blanco. | *To be dressed up to the nines*, estar de punta en blanco. | *To dress down*, echar un rapapolvo (to scold), pegar una paliza (to thrash). || *To dress one's hair*, peinarse. || *To dress out*, ataviar. || *To dress up*, vestir, poner de tiros largos. || *To dress up as*, disfrazar de. || *To get dressed*, vestirse, arreglarse.
— V. intr. Vestirse, vestir: *to dress with taste*, vestirse con gusto. || Vestirse (on a ceremonial occasion). || MIL. Alinearse. || — *To dress up*, vestirse, ponerse de tiros largos. || *To dress up as*, disfrazarse de.
dress ball [—bɔ:l] n. Baile (*m.*) de etiqueta.
dress circle [—ˈsə:kl] n. THEATR. Piso (*m.*) principal.
dress coat [—ˈkəut] n. Frac, *m.*
dress designer [—diˌzainə*] n. Modelista, *m.* & *f.*
dresser [ˈdresə*] n. Aparador, *m.* (cupboard). || THEATR. Camarero, ra (person who helps an actor). || MED. Ayudante, *m.* (surgeon's assistant). || MIN. Punterola, *f.* || TECH. Adobador, *m.* (of skins). || U. S. Tocador, *m.*, coqueta, *f.* (dressing table).
dressing [ˈdresiŋ] n. Vestir, *m.*, vestirse, *m.* (act). || Ropa, *f.* (clothes). || MED. Vendaje, *m.* (for an injury). || CULIN. Aliño, *m.* (for food, salad, etc.). || AGR. Abono, *m.* (fertilizer). || MAR. Empavesado, *m.* || MIL. Formación, *f.* (of troops). || TECH. Adobo, *m.*, curtido, *m.* (of skins). | Labrado, *m.* (of stone). | Aderezo, *m.*, apresto, *m.* (of cloth). | Preparación, *f.* (of cotton, wool). | Desbaste, *m.* (of timber). | Cepilladura, *f.* (of wood).
dressing case [—keis] n. Neceser, *m.*
dressing down [—ˈdaun] n. FAM. Rapapolvo, *m.* (talking-to): *to give s.o. a dressing down*, echar un rapapolvo a alguien. | Paliza, *f.* (thrashing).
dressing gown [—gaun] n. Bata, *f.*
dressing room [—rum] n. Tocador, *m.*, cuarto (*m.*) de vestir (in a house). || THEATR. Camerino, *m.*, camarín, *m.*
dressing station [—ˌsteiʃən] n. MIL. Puesto (*m.*) de socorro.
dressing table [—ˌteibl] n. Tocador, *m.*, coqueta, *f.*
dressmaker [ˈdresˌmeikə*] n. Modista, *m.* & *f.*
dressmaking [ˈdresˌmeikiŋ] n. Costura, *f.*
dress rehearsal [ˈdresriˈhə:səl] n. Ensayo (*m.*) general.
dress shield [ˈdresʃi:ld] n. Sobaquera, *f.*
dress shirt [ˈdresʃə:t] n. Camisa (*f.*) de frac.
dress suit [ˈdressju:t] n. Traje (*m.*) de etiqueta.
dress uniform [ˈdresˈju:nifɔ:m] n. MIL. Uniforme (*m.*) de gala.
dressy [ˈdresi] adj. Elegante. || *A dressy gown*, un traje de vestir.
drew [dru:] pret. See DRAW.
dribble [ˈdribl] n. Goteo, *m.* (of a liquid). || SP. Regate, *m.*, drible, *m.*, finta, *f.* || Llovizna, *f.* (rain).
dribble [ˈdribl] v. intr. Babear (babies). || Gotear (to trickle). || SP. Driblar, regatear.
— V. tr. Derramar *or* dejar caer gota a gota (to cause to flow in a trickle). || SP. Driblar con, regatear con.
driblet or **dribblet** [ˈdriblit] n. Pequeña cantidad, *f.* || *By* o *in driblets*, poco a poco.
dribs [dribz] pl. n. *In dribs and drabs*, poco a poco, en pequeñas cantidades.
dried [draid] adj. Seco, ca. || Seco, ca; paso, sa (fruit).
drier [ˈdraiə*] n. Secador, *m.* (device). || Secadora, *f.* (machine for drying clothes). || Tendedero, *m.* (rack for drying clothes). || TECH. Secadero, *m.* || Secante, *m.* (for painting).
drift [drift] n. Arrastramiento, *m.*, arrastre, *m.* (process of being driven by the wind). || MAR. AVIAT. Deriva, *f.* || Ventisquero, *m.* (of snow). || Nube, *f.* (of dust). || Ráfaga, *f.* (of rain). || Montón, *m.* (of sand, etc.). || Desplazamiento, *m.*, movimiento, *m.* (of people). || Significado, *m.* (meaning). || Propósito, *m.*, objetivo, *m.* (purpose). || Curso, *m.* (of affairs). || Tendencia, *f.* (trend). || MIL. Desviación, *f.* (of a shell or projectile). || ARCH. Empuje (*m.*) horizontal (of an arch). || GEOL. Terrenos (*m. pl.*) de acarreo (debris accumulated by water). | Derrubios (*m. pl.*) depositados por los glaciares (debris accumulated by ice). | Deriva, *f.* (of continents). || MAR. Corriente (*f.*) oceánica (current). | Velocidad, *f.* (speed of a current). | Dirección, *f.* (course of a current). || TECH. Punzón, *m.* | Botador (*m.*) de roblones (for rivets). || — MAR. *Drift anchor*, ancla (*f.*) flotante. || *Drift angle*, ángulo (*m.*) de deriva. || *Drift sand*, arena movediza. || *I get the drift of it*, lo entiendo. || *The drift from the land*, el éxodo rural, el abandono del campo.
drift [drift] v. intr. Ser arrastrado por la corriente (to be carried by a current of water or wind). || Derivar, ir a la deriva (to be carried off course). || Amontonarse (sand, snow). || FIG. Ir a la deriva, vivir sin rumbo (to live without aim). | Encaminarse, tender (questions, events). || — *To drift along*, vagar. || *To drift around*, pasearse. || *To drift in*, llegar. || *To drift with the current*, dejarse llevar por la corriente. || *To let things drift*, dejarse llevar por los acontecimientos.
— V. tr. Empujar, llevar (to carry along). || Empujar (clouds). || Amontonar (sand, snow). || Acarrear (downstream). || Conducir en armadía (wood). || TECH. Escariar.
drifter [—ə*] n. Trainera, *f.* (fishing boat). || FIG. Vagabundo, *m.* (aimless person).
drifting [—iŋ] adj. A la deriva.
drift net [—net] n. MAR. Traína, *f.*, red (*f.*) barredera.
driftpin [ˈdriftpin] n. Mandril, *m.*
driftwood [ˈdriftwud] n. Madera (*f.*) flotante.
drill [dril] n. Instrucción, *f.* (training, instruction). || Ejercicios, *m. pl.* (series of exercises). || TECH. Taladro, *m.*, broca, *f.*, barrena, *f.* (tool for boring holes). | Berbiquí, *m.* (brace). | Taladradora, *f.* (machine). | Fresa, *f.* (of a dentist). || MIN. Barrena, *f.* | Perforadora, *f.*, trépano, *m.* (in oil prospecting). || AGR. Surco, *m.* (furrow). | Hilera, *f.* (row of seeds or plants). | Sembradora, *f.* (machine for sowing). || Dril, *m.* (cotton fabric). || Dril, *m.* (monkey). || FAM. Manera, *f.*: *what is the drill for doing this?*, ¿cuál es la manera de hacer esto? || — *Drill chuck*, portabroca, *f.* || *Drill press*, perforadora, *f.*
drill [dril] v. tr. MIL. Enseñar la instrucción a, ejercitar. || Enseñar por medio de ejercicios o repeticiones (to teach). || FIG. Entrenar (to train). || TECH. Taladrar (to bore holes in). | Perforar (a well). | Sondear, perforar (looking for oil, etc.). | Hacer (a hole). || AGR. Sembrar en hileras (to sow).
— V. intr Hacer un agujero. || TECH. Perforar. || MIL. Hacer la instrucción. || Hacer ejercicios (to do exercises). || FIG. Entrenarse (to train).
drilling [ˈdriliŋ] n. Perforación, *f.* (boring). || MIL. Instrucción, *f.*
drily [ˈdraili] adv. Secamente. || Con guasa, con un tono guasón: *to answer drily*, contestar con un tono guasón.
drink [driŋk] n. Bebida, *f.* (liquid to be consumed). || Copa, *f.* (alcoholic liquid): *to stand s.o. a drink*, convidar a alguien a una copa; *I took a drink*, tomé una copa. || Algo de beber: *would you like a drink?*, ¿quieres algo de beber? || Vaso, *m.* (of water, milk). || Bebida, *f.* (excessive drinking): *drink will be the death of you*, la bebida será tu perdición. || FIG. Mar, *m.* (sea). || — *After-dinner drink*, licor, *m.*, copa, *f.* || *Long drink*, bebida larga. || *Soft drink*, bebida no alcohólica *or* sin alcohol. || *Strong drink*, bebida alcohólica. || *To have a drink*, tomar algo. || *To take to drink*, darse a la bebida.
drink* [driŋk] v. tr./intr. Beber (beer, water, etc.): *to drink from the bottle*, beber de la botella. || Absorber (plants). || Beber (to be an habitual drinker). || Tomar: *would you like something to drink?*, ¿quieres tomar algo?; *I never drink tea*, nunca tomo té; *to drink the waters*, tomar las aguas. || FIG. Beberse: *to drink one's wages*, beberse todo lo que se gana. || Brindar por (to toast). || — FIG. *To drink away*, beberse (one's fortune), ahogar (one's sorrows). || *To drink down*, beber de un trago. || *To drink hard*, beber mucho. || FIG. *To drink in*, beber, beberse. || FIG. FAM. *To drink*

like a fish, beber como una esponja *or* como un cosaco. || *To drink off*, beber de un trago. || *To drink o.s. into debt*, beberse la fortuna. || *To drink s.o. under the table*, aguantar más bebiendo que otro. || *To drink to*, brindar por, beber a la salud de. || *To drink up*, bebérselo todo; terminar de beber.

— OBSERV. Pret. ***drank;*** p. p. ***drunk.***

drinkable [ˈdriŋkəbl] adj. Potable, bebible.
— Pl. n. FAM. Bebida, *f. sing.*
drinker [ˈdriŋkə*] n. Bebedor, ra.
drinking [ˈdriŋkiŋ] n. Beber, *m.* (act): *excessive drinking can have bad consequences*, el beber en exceso puede tener malas consecuencias. || FIG. Bebida, *f.*: *to take to drinking*, darse a la bebida.
drinking bout [—baut] n. Juerga, *f.*, orgía, *f.*, borrachera, *f.*
drinking fountain [— fauntin] n. Fuente (*f.*) de agua potable.
drinking song [—sɔŋ] n. Canción (*f.*) báquica.
drinking trough [—trɔf] n. Bebedero, *m.*, abrevadero *m.* (water trough).
drinking water [—, wɔ:tə*] n. Agua (*f.*) potable.
drip [drip] n. Goteo, *m.* (a falling in drops). || Gota, *f.* (drop). || ARCH. Goterón, *m.* || FAM. Tonto, *m.*, mentecato, *m.* (simpleton). | Pelma, *m.*, pesado, *m.* (bore).
drip [drip] v. intr. Gotear (to fall in drops). || Chorrear (to be soaked).
— V. tr. Dejar caer gota a gota.
drip-dry [ˈdripˈdrai] adj. Que seca rápidamente y no necesita planchado.
dripping [ˈdripiŋ] n. Goteo, *m.* (act). || Gotas, *f. pl.* (drops). || CULIN. Grasa, *f.*, pringue, *f.* (from meat).
— Adj. Que gotea. || — *Dripping with perspiration*, bañado en sudor. || *To be dripping wet*, estar calado hasta los huesos.
dripping pan [—pæn] n. CULIN. Grasera, *f.*
dripping tube [—tju:b] n. Cuentagotas, *m. inv.*
dripstone [ˈdripstəun] n. ARCH. Goterón, *m.*
drive [draiv] n. Vuelta (*f.*) en coche, paseo (*m.*) en coche (short ride). || Excursión, *f.* (round trip). || Viaje, *m.* (journey). || Trayecto, *m.*: *it's an hour's drive*, es un trayecto de una hora. || Ojeo, *m.*, batida, *f.* (in hunting). || Conducción (*f.*) del ganado (of cattle). || MIL. Ofensiva, *f.* (major offensive). || FIG. Vigor, *m.*, energía, *f.*, empuje, *m.* (energy). | Expansión, *f.* (of a nation). | Campaña, *f.* (campaign). | Apremio, *m.* (pressure). | Instinto, *m.*, impulso, *m.*: *the sex drive*, el instinto sexual. || SP. "Drive", *m.*, pelota (*f.*) rasante (in tennis). | "Drive", *m.* (in golf). || AUT. Tracción, *f.*: *front-wheel drive*, tracción delantera. | Conducción, *f.* [*Amer.*, manejo, *m.*]: *right-hand drive*, conducción a la derecha. || TECH. Transmisión, *f.* | Propulsión, *f.* || Camino (*m.*) de entrada (private road, parking space in front of a garage). || Calle, *f.* (road). || Camino, *m.* (through a forest). || Flotación, *f.* (floating of logs). || Armadía, *f.* (floating logs). || Torneo, *m.* (of bridge, etc.). || — AUT. *Direct drive*, directa, *f.* | *Drive belt, gear, shaft*, correa (*f.*), engranaje (*m.*), eje (*m.*) de transmisión. | *To go for a drive*, ir a dar una vuelta en coche.
drive* [draiv] v. tr. Conducir [*Amer.*, manejar] (to control a vehicle). || Llevar (to convey in a vehicle). || Recorrer (a distance). || Llevar (wind, water). || Guiar, llevar, conducir (cattle). || Empujar (to push forward). || Arrojar: *the sea drove the ship on to the rocks*, el mar arrojó el barco contra las rocas. || Echar (to force a person to leave): *to drive s.o. from* o *out of the house*, echar a alguien de la casa. || Asestar (a blow). || Lanzar (a projectile). || COMM. Tratar (business). | Cerrar: *to drive a bargain*, cerrar un trato. | Ejercer (a trade). || SP. Mandar (a ball). || Ojear, batir (in hunting). || FIG. Hacer trabajar mucho (to make work hard). | Conducir, llevar: *to drive s.o. to despair*, llevar a alguien a la desesperación. | Empujar: *his bad luck drove him to drink*, su mala suerte le empujó a la bebida. | Forzar, obligar (to compel). | Aplazar (to postpone). || TECH. Abrir, perforar: *to drive a tunnel*, abrir un túnel. | Construir (to build a railway, road, etc.). | Hacer funcionar, poner en movimiento, accionar (a machine). | Clavar (a nail). | Apretar (a nut). | Hacer (a hole). | Hincar: *to drive a stake into the ground*, hincar una estaca en el suelo. | Meter, hacer entrar, introducir (to put in). || — *To drive an idea out of s.o.'s mind*, sacarle a uno una idea de la cabeza. || FIG. *To drive a point home*, remachar el clavo. || *To drive a way through*, abrirse paso por. || *To drive into a corner*, acorralar. || *To drive s.o. mad*, volverle a uno loco. || *To drive s.o. wild*, sacarle a uno de sus casillas. || *To drive sth. into s.o.'s head*, meterle a uno algo en la cabeza. || SP. *To drive the ball*, jugar una pelota rasante (in tennis).
— V. intr. Ir en coche (to travel by car): *to drive to a place*, ir en coche a un sitio. || Conducir [*Amer.*, manejar]: *can you drive?*, ¿sabes conducir? || Golpear, azotar: *the snow was driving against the windows*, la nieve azotaba los cristales. || TECH. Entrar (a nail). || MAR. Derivar. || SP. Dar el "drive" (golf). | Jugar una pelota rasante (tennis).
— ***To drive at,*** insinuar, querer decir (to mean). | Pretender (to aim at). | Consagrarse intensamente a (a work). | Dirigirse hacia (in a car). | — *To let drive at*, asestar un golpe a. || ***To drive away,*** alejar, apartar (s.o., sth.). | Irse [en coche]. || ***To drive back,*** hacer retroceder. | Acompañar en coche: *I'll drive you back to your house*, te acompañaré en coche a tu casa. | Volver *or* regresar en coche (to return by car). || ***To drive by,*** pasar [por]. || ***To drive in,*** entrar (by car). | Clavar (nail, dagger). || ***To drive into,*** atropellar (s.o.). | Chocar contra (a tree, etc.). | Entrar en (a garage). || ***To drive off,*** alejar, apartar. | Irse en coche. || ***To drive on,*** seguir su camino. || ***To drive out,*** echar. | Hacer salir (to oblige to come out). | Sacar (a nail). | Salir en coche. || ***To drive over,*** atropellar: *to drive over a dog*, atropellar un perro. | Ir en coche (to go by car). || ***To drive through,*** pasar [por]. || ***To drive up,*** acercarse (to approach). | Llegar (to arrive).

— OBSERV. Pret. ***drove;*** p. p. ***driven.***

drive-in cinema [ˈdraivinˈsinəmə] n. Cine (*m.*) donde se ven las películas desde el coche.
drive-in bank [ˈdraivinˈbæŋk] n. Banco (*m.*) donde se atiende a los clientes sin que bajen de su coche.
drive-in restaurant [ˈdraivinˈrestərɔ̃ŋ] n. Restaurante (*m.*) donde sirven a los clientes sin que bajen del coche.
drivel [ˈdrivəl] n. Tonterías, *f. pl.*: *to talk drivel*, decir tonterías.
drivel [ˈdrivl] v. intr. Babear (to slaver). || FAM. Decir tonterías. || *To drivel away*, malgastar (time).
driven [ˈdrivn] p. p. See DRIVE.
driver [ˈdraivə*] n. Conductor, ra; chófer, *m.* (person who drives a car, bus). || Camionero, *m.* (of lorries). || Maquinista, *m.* (of trains). || Taxista, *m.* & *f.* (of taxi). || Corredor, *m.*, piloto, *m.* (of racing car). || Cochero, *m.* (of coach). || TECH. Rueda (*f.*) motriz. || *Driver's licence*, permiso (*m.*) de conducir *or* de conducción, carnet (*m.*) de conducir.
driveway [ˈdraivwei] n. Camino (*m.*) de entrada (leading to the street). || Camino, *m.* (way). || Calle, *f.* (street).
driving [draiviŋ] n. Conducción, *f.* [*Amer.*, manejo, *m.*]: *driving lesson*, lección de conducción. || TECH. Transmisión, *f.*: *driving belt*, correa de transmisión. || — *Driving licence*, permiso (*m.*) de conducción *or* de conducir, carnet (*m.*) de conducir. || *Driving mirror*, retrovisor, *m.* || *Driving school*, autoescuela, *f.* || *Driving test*, examen (*m.*) para sacar el carnet de conducir. || *Driving wheel*, rueda motriz.
— Adj. Torrencial (rain).
drizzle [ˈdrizl] n. Llovizna, *f.*
drizzle [ˈdrizl] v. intr. Lloviznar.
droit [drɔit] n. JUR. Derecho, *m.* (right).
droll [drəul] adj. Divertido, da (amusing). || Extraño, ña; raro, ra (odd).
drollery [ˈdrəuləri] n. Gracia, *f.* (act, quality, remark).
dromedary [ˈdrʌmədəri] n. ZOOL. Dromedario, *m.*
drone [drəun] n. ZOOL. Zángano, *m.* (male bee). || AVIAT. Avión (*m.*) teledirigido. || MUS. Roncón, *m.* (pipe of a bagpipe). | Gaita, *f.* (bagpipe). || Zumbido, *m.* (noise made by bees, aircraft, machinery, etc.). || Murmullo, *m.* (of people, voices, etc.). || FAM. Zángano, *m.*, holgazán, *m.*, vago, *m.* (loafer). || MUS. *Drone bass*, bajo continuo.
drone [drəun] v. tr. Murmurar, ronronear. || *To drone away*, malgastar (time).
— V. intr. Murmurar (people). || Zumbar (bees, machinery, etc.). || FAM. Holgazanear.
drool [dru:l] n. Tonterías, *f. pl.*
— V. intr. Babear. || FIG. *To drool over*, caérsele a uno la baba por.
droop [dru:p] n. Inclinación, *f.* (of head). || Caída, *f.* (of eyelids). || Encorvamiento, *m.* (of shoulders). || Caída, *f.* (of branches, trees). || FIG. Languidez, *f.*
droop [dru:p] v. intr. Inclinarse (to hang down). || Caerse (eyelids). || Estar encorvado (people). || Marchitarse (flowers). || FIG. Debilitarse (to lose strength). | Desanimarse (to become dispirited). | Decaer (to decline).
— V. tr. Inclinar (head). || Bajar (eyelids). || Encorvar (shoulders).
drooping [—iŋ] adj. Inclinado, da (head). || Bajado, da (eyes). || Caído, da (shoulders). || Gacho, cha; caído, da (ears). || Marchito, ta (flower). || FIG. Lánguido, da. | Abatido, da.
drop [drɔp] n. Gota, *f.* (of blood, rain, sweat, water). || Colgante, *m.* (of chandelier). || Pendiente, *m.* [*Amer.*, arete, *m.*] (earring). || Colgante, *m.*, dije, *m.* (of necklace). || Pastilla, *f.* (sweet). || Gota, *f.*, pizca, *f.* (a bit). || FAM. Gota, *f.*, poquito, *m.* (small amount of drink). | Gota, *f.* (small amount of rain). || Caída, *f.* (fall). || Bajada, *f.* (in pressure, voltage, etc.). || Baja, *f.* (in prices). || Descenso, *m.*, baja, *f.* (in temperature). || Disminución, *f.* (in values, sales, etc.). || Pendiente, *f.*, bajada, *f.* (slope): *there is a drop from the hill to the valley*, hay una pendiente de la colina al valle. || Desnivel, *m.* (sudden descent, difference in level). || Precipicio, *m.* (abyss). || Altura, *f.* (the height of fall). || MED. Gota, *f*: *drop by drop*, gota a gota. || THEATR. Telón, *m.* (curtain). || Trampa, *f.* (of gallows). || Caída, *f.* (of a person being hung). || Descenso, *m.* (of a parachute). || Lanzamiento, *m.* (of sth. by parachute). || MIL. Aprovisionamiento (*m.*) aéreo. || TECH. Escudo, *m.* (of a lock). || SP. Botepronto, *m.* (kick). || — FIG. *A drop in the ocean* o *in a bucket*, una gota de agua en el mar. | *At the drop of a hat*,

en seguida (at once), con cualquier pretexto (on the least pretext). | *To get* o *to have the drop on*, llevar la delantera a. | *To have had a drop too much*, haber bebido más de la cuenta. | *To take a drop*, tomar una gota *or* un trago.

drop [drɔp] v. tr. Dejar caer (to let fall): *I dropped the handkerchief*, dejé caer el pañuelo. || Soltar (to let go off): *he dropped the hot plate*, soltó el plato hirviendo. || Echar gota a gota (a liquid). || Derramar (tears). || Dejar escapar [un punto] (to miss a stitch in knitting). || Echar (a letter). || Derribar (to knock down). || FIG. Dejar de (to give up a habit): *I have to drop smoking*, tengo que dejar de fumar. | Dejar (conversation, friend, work). | Interrumpir (to break off a conversation). | Renunciar a (an idea). | Echar, expulsar (to throw out). || Soltar (to say): *to drop a coarse word*, soltar un taco. || Dejar: *I'll drop you at the station*, te dejaré en la estación. || Lanzar [en paracaídas] (to land by parachute). || Bajar (eyes, voice, prices, hem): *they dropped their eyes*, bajaron la mirada. || THEATR. Bajar (the curtain). || ZOOL. Parir (to give birth to). || MATH. Trazar, tirar (to draw a line). || MIL. Lanzar (bombs). || Perder (points, games). || SP. Marcar, meter (to score a goal). | Dar al bote-pronto a (a ball). || FIG. Comerse (not to pronounce in speech). | No usar, omitir: *cases in which the article is dropped*, casos en que el artículo no se usa. || Despegarse de (to leave behind, to advance ahead of). || FAM. Perder (money). | Cargarse (to kill). || MAR. Echar (anchor). || AUT. Rebajar (the chassis). || — U. S. FAM. *To drop a brick*, see BRICK. || *To drop a curtsey*, hacer una reverencia. || *To drop a hint*, tirar *or* soltar una indirecta. || *To drop a line* o *a card*, poner unas líneas *or* una postal a alguien.
— V. intr. Caerse, caer (to fall): *he dropped dead*, se cayó muerto. || Dejarse caer (to flop down). || Caerse de cansancio, desplomarse (from exhaustion). || Gotear (to drip). || Bajar (temperature, prices, voice, etc.). || Disminuir, bajar (value, sales, etc.). || Amainar (wind). || Bajar, descender (ground). || Acabarse, terminarse (conversation). || Escaparse (remark). || — *To drop around* o *by* o *over*, pasar. || *To drop asleep*, quedarse dormido. || *To drop away*, irse uno tras otro (persons), disminuir (to diminish), quedarse atrás (a runner). || *To drop behind*, quedarse atrás. || *To drop in on s.o.*, pasar por casa de alguien. || *To drop into the habit of*, coger la costumbre de. || *To drop off*, caer (leaves), disminuir (to diminish), caerse, desprenderse (part), dormirse (to fall asleep), morir (to die). || FIG. *To drop on*, reñir (to scold). || *To drop on one's knees*, caer de rodillas. || *To drop out*, dejar caer (sth.), omitir (a syllable, a name, etc.), abandonar, retirarse (of a contest), desaparecer (letter), irse: *it has dropped out of my mind*, se me ha ido de la cabeza. || *To drop to the rear*, quedarse atrás, dejarse adelantar.

drop curtain [ˈdrɔp,kəːtn] n. THEATR. Telón, *m.*

drop-forge [ˈdrɔpˈfɔːdʒ] v. tr. Forjar a martillo.

drop hammer [ˈdrɔp,hæmə*] n. Martillo (*m.*) pilón.

dropkick [ˈdrɔpkik] n. Botepronto, *m.*

drop leaf [ˈdrɔpliːf] n. Ala (*f.*) abatible (of a table).

droplet [ˈdrɔplit] n. Gotita, *f.*

droplight [ˈdrɔplait] n. ELECTR. Lámpara (*f.*) transportable.

dropout [ˈdrɔpaut] n. Abandono, *m.* || U. S. Estudiante que abandona la universidad antes de graduarse. | Marginado, da (hippies, etc.).

dropper [ˈdrɔpə*] n. MED. Cuentagotas, *m. inv.*

dropping [ˈdrɔpiŋ] n. Caída, *f.* (fall). || MED. Descendimiento, *m.* (of womb). || Parto, *m.* (of an animal). || — Pl. Gotas, *f.* (drops). || Migas, *f.* (of food, etc.) || Excrementos, *m.* (of animals), cagadas, *f.* (of birds, mice, etc.), cagarrutas, *f.* (of sheep, goats, etc.), cagajones, *m.* (of horses, donkeys, etc.).
— Adj. Goteante, chorreante (dripping).

drop press [ˈdrɔppres] n. Martillo (*m.*) pilón (drop hammer).

drop shot [ˈdrɔpʃɔt] n. SP. Dejada, *f.* (in tennis).

dropsical [ˈdrɔpsikəl] adj. MED. Hidrópico, ca. || FIG. Hinchado, da.

dropsy [ˈdrɔpsi] n. MED. Hidropesía, *f.*

dross [drɔs] n. TECH. Escoria, *f.*

drought [draut] or **drouth** [drauθ] n. Sequía, *f.*

droughty [—i] adj. Árido, da; seco, ca.

drove [drəuv] n. Manada, *f.* (herd of cattle). || Cincel, *m.* (chisel). || — Pl. FIG. Manadas, *f.*: *in droves*, a manadas.

drove [drəuv] pret. See DRIVE.

drove [drəuv] v. tr. Conducir (cattle).

drover [—ə*] n. Boyero, *m.*, vaquero, *m.*

drown [draun] v. intr. Ahogarse.
— V. tr. Ahogar (to kill by suffocation). || Anegar (to flood). || FIG. Anegar, bañar: *eyes drowned in tears*, ojos anegados en lágrimas. | Ahogar: *words drowned by applause*, palabras ahogadas por los aplausos. || — FIG. *To drown one's sorrows*, ahogar sus penas. || *To drown o.s.*, ahogarse. || FIG. *We were drowned in letters*, fuimos inundados de cartas.

drowse [drauz] n. Somnolencia, *f.*, modorra, *f.*

drowse [drauz] v. intr. Estar medio dormido, da; estar adormecido, da. || *To drowse off*, adormecerse.
— V. tr. Adormecer. || *To drowse away one's time*, pasar el tiempo dormitando.

drowsiness [—inis] n. Somnolencia, *f.*, modorra, *f.* || FIG. Apatía, *f.*

drowsy [—i] adj. Soñoliento, ta (sleepy). || Soporífero, ra (lulling). || FIG. Apático, ca (apathetic).

drub [drʌb] v. tr. Apalear (to cudgel). || Pegar una paliza (to thrash). || FIG. Derrotar, pegar una paliza (fam.) [to defeat overwhelmingly]. || *To drub sth. into s.o.*, meter algo en la cabeza de alguien.

drubbing [—iŋ] n. Paliza, *f.* (beating). || FIG. Derrota, *f.*, paliza, *f.* (fam.) [defeat].

drudge [drʌdʒ] n. FAM. Esclavo, *m.* [del hogar o del trabajo].

drudge [drʌdʒ] v. intr. Apencar, currelar (to work).

drudgery [ˈdrʌdʒəri] n. Trabajo (*m.*) pesado.

— OBSERV. Esta palabra nunca va precedida por el artículo indefinido *a*.

drug [drʌg] n. Medicamento, *m.*, medicina, *f.* (medicament). || Droga, *f.* (narcotic). || FIG. *Drug on the market*, artículo (*m.*) imposible de vender.

drug [drʌg] v. tr. Drogar (s. o.). || Echar una droga en (a drink). || — FIG. *To be drugged with*, estar harto de. || *To drug o.s.*, drogarse.

drug addict [—,ædikt] n. Toxicómano, na; drogadicto, ta.

drug addiction [—ə,dikʃən] n. Toxicomanía, *f.*

druggist [ˈdrʌgist] n. Farmacéutico, ca.

drugstore [ˈdrʌgstɔː*] n. U. S. Farmacia, *f.* (a chemist's). | "Drugstore", *m.*, almacén (*m.*) donde se venden productos farmacéuticos, comestibles, tabacos, periódicos, etc.

druid [ˈdruːid] n. Druida, *m.*

drum [drʌm] n. MUS. Tambor, *m.* || Bidón, *m.* (metal container). || ANAT. Tímpano, *m.* || TECH. Tambor, *m.* (cylinder). | Tambor, *m.*, cilindro, *m.* (of a revolver). | Bobina, *f.*, carrete, *m.* (in electricity). || ARCH. Tambor, *m.* || Tamborileo, *m.*, repiqueteo, *m.* (sound). || — Pl. Batería, *f. sing.* (in an orchestra). || — MUS. *Bass drum*, bombo, *m.* || MIL. *Drum major* tambor mayor. || FIG. *To beat the drum for*, dar bombo a.

drum [drʌm] v. tr./intr. MUS. Tocar el tambor. || FIG. Tamborilear con: *to drum one's fingers*, tamborilear con los dedos. || — FIG. *To drum out*, expulsar. | *To drum sth. into s.o.'s ears*, machacar los oídos de alguien con algo. | *To drum sth. into s.o.'s head*, meterle a alguien algo en la cabeza. | *To drum up*, conseguir (support, trade).

drumbeat [ˈdrʌmbiːt] n. MUS. Toque (*m.*) del tambor.

drumfire [ˈdrʌm,faiə*] n. MIL. Fuego (*m.*) graneado.

drumhead [ˈdrʌmhed] n. MUS. Piel, *f.*, parche, *m.* [del tambor]. || *Drumhead court-martial*, consejo (*m.*) de guerra sumarísimo.

drummer [ˈdrʌmə*] n. MUS. Tambor, *m.* (in a band). | Batería, *m.* (in a group). || U. S. Viajante (*m.*) de comercio.

drumming [ˈdrʌmiŋ] n. Tamborileo, *m.*

drumstick [ˈdrʌmstik] n. Palillo (*m.*) de tambor (for drum). || Muslo (*m.*) de ave (of birds). || FAM. Zanca, *f.* (leg).

drunk [drʌŋk] p. p. & adj. See DRINK. || Borracho, cha (through drinking). || FIG. Ebrio, a: *drunk with happiness*, ebrio de alegría. || — FAM. *To be as drunk as a lord*, estar borracho como una cuba. || *To be drunk on brandy*, haberse emborrachado con coñac, estar borracho de coñac. || *To get drunk*, emborracharse.
— N. Borracho, cha (drunk person). || U. S. Juerga, *f.*: *to go on a drunk*, irse de juerga.

drunkard [—əd] n. Borracho, cha.

drunken [—ən] adj. Borracho, cha: *a drunken man*, un hombre borracho. || De borrachos (of drunkards). || De embriaguez: *drunken state*, estado de embriaguez.

drunkenness [—ənnis] n. Embriaguez, *f.*, borrachera, *f.*

drupe [druːp] n. BOT. Drupa, *f.*

druse [druːz] n. MIN. Drusa, *f.*

dry [drai] adj. Seco, ca (not wet; arid, etc.). || Firme: *dry land*, tierra firme. || Para áridos (measure). || Seco, ca; desecado, da (leaf, wood). || Seca (a cow). || Seco, ca (wine, bread). || FIG. Sin inspiración, acabado, da: *a dry poet*, un poeta sin inspiración. | Aburrido, da (boring): *this book is very dry*, este libro es muy aburrido. | Agudo, da (wit, etc.). | Sediento, ta; seco, ca (thirsty). | Árido, da (a subject). | Simple (simple): *dry facts*, hechos simples. | Seco, ca (answer, character, style). || ELECTR. Seco, ca: *dry battery* o *cell*, pila seca. || COMM. Líquido, da (money). || De práctica (shooting). || U. S. Prohibicionista (country). || — *Dry fly*, mosca (*f.*) flotante [para pescar]. || U. S. *Dry goods*, mercería, *f.* || CHEM. *Dry ice*, nieve carbónica. || U. S. *Dry law*, ley seca. || *Dry nurse*, ama seca. || *I am dry*, tengo sed. || FAM. *Not to be dry behind the ears yet*, tener la leche en los labios. || *To go dry*, secarse. || *To run dry*, secarse, agotarse.
— N. U. S. FAM. Prohibicionista, *m.* & *f.*

dry [drai] v. tr. Secar. || Secar, agotar (a well). || CULIN. Desuerar (butter). | Poner a secar (fruit). || *To dry up*, secar completamente.
— V. intr. Secarse. || Secarse, agotarse (to run dry). || *To dry up*, secarse completamente (to become dry), callarse (to be quiet): *dry up!*, ¡cállate!

dryad [ˈdraiəd] n. MYTH. Dríada, *f.*, dríade, *f.*

dryasdust [ˈdraiəz,dʌst] adj. Aburridísimo, ma.

dry-clean [ˈdraiˈkliːn] v. tr. Limpiar en seco.

dry cleaner [—ə*] n. Tintorero, ra. || *Dry cleaner's*, tintorería, *f.*, tinte, *m.*
dry cleaning [—iŋ] n. Limpieza (*f.*) en seco.
dryer [draiə*] n. See DRIER.
dry-eyed [ˈdraiˈaid] adj. Sin lágrimas.
dry farm [ˈdraiˈfɑ:m] n. Finca (*f.*) de secano.
dry farming [—iŋ] n. Cultivo (*m.*) de secano.
drying [ˈdraiiŋ] adj. Secante.
dryly [ˈdraili] adv. See DRILY.
dryness [drainis] n. Sequedad, *f.*
dry point [ˈdraipɔint] n. Punta (*f.*) seca (needle for engraving). || Grabado (*m.*) con punta seca (engraving).
dry rot [ˈdraiˈrɔt] n. Putrefacción (*f.*) de la madera. || FIG. Putrefacción, *f.*, desintegración, *f.*
dry-salt [ˈdraiˈsɔ:lt] v. tr. Salar (meat).
dry-shod [ˈdraiˈʃɔd] adj./adv. A pie enjuto.
dry wash [ˈdraiˈwɔʃ] n. Ropa (*f.*) lavada pero no planchada.
dual [ˈdjuəl] adj. Doble: *dual citizenship*, doble nacionalidad; *dual ignition*, encendido doble; *dual personality*, doble personalidad. || GRAMM. Dual.
— N. GRAMM. Dual, *m.*
dualism [ˈdjuəlizəm] n. Dualismo, *m.*
dualist [ˈdjuəlist] n. Dualista, *m.* & *f.*
dualistic [ˌdjuəˈlistik] adj. Dualista.
duality [djuˈæliti] n. Dualidad, *f.*
dual-purpose [ˈdjuəlˈpə:pəs] adj. De dos usos.
dub [dʌb] v. tr. Armar [caballero] (to knight). || Apodar (to nickname). || Doblar (film). || Volver a grabar (to rerecord). || Adobar (skins).
dubbin [ˈdʌbin] n. Adobo, *m.* || Cera, *f.* (for boots).
dubbing [ˈdʌbiŋ] n. Adobo, *m.* (dubbin). || Doblaje, *m.* (of a film).
dubiety [djuˈbaiəti] n. Incertidumbre, *f.*
dubious [ˈdju:bjəs] adj. Dudoso, sa; poco seguro, ra: *dubious result*, resultado dudoso. || Ambiguo, gua; equívoco, ca (not clear). || Indeciso, sa (irresolute). || Discutible, controvertible (questionable). || Sospechoso, sa (shady). || — *To be dubious about*, tener dudas sobre. || *To be dubious of*, dudar de.
dubiously [—li] adv. Dudosamente, con duda. || De una manera sospechosa.
dubiousness [—nis] n. Incertidumbre, *f.*, duda, *f.* (uncertainty). || Lo ambiguo, lo equívoco (of a compliment).
dubitable [ˈdju:bitəbl] adj. Dudoso, sa.
dubitation [ˌdju:biˈteiʃən] n. Duda, *f.*
dubitative [ˈdju:bitətiv] adj. Dubitativo, va.
Dublin [ˈdʌblin] pr. n. GEOGR. Dublín.
ducal [ˈdju:kəl] adj. Ducal.
ducat [ˈdʌkət] n. Ducado, *m.* (coin).
duchess [ˈdʌtʃis] n. Duquesa, *f.*: *Her Grace The Duchess*, la señora duquesa.
duchy [ˈdʌtʃi] n. Ducado, *m.* (territory).
duck [dʌk] n. Pato, *m.* (drake): *wild duck*, pato salvaje. || Pata, *f.* (female duck). || CULIN. Pato, *m.* || SP. Cero, *m.* (in cricket). | Esquiva, *f.* (in boxing). || AUT. Camión (*m.*) anfibio. || Dril, *m.* (cloth). || Zambullida, *f.*, chapuzón, *m.* (in water). || Agachada, *f.* (preventive move). || FIG. FAM. Pichoncito, *m.*, cariño, *m.* || — Pl. Pantalones (*m.*) de dril. || — FAM. *Fine weather for the ducks*, tiempo lluvioso. || FIG. *In two shakes of a duck's tail*, en un periquete, en un santiamén. | *Lame duck*, see LAME DUCK. | *The words glanced off him like water off a duck's back*, oía las palabras como quien oye llover. || *To play ducks and drakes*, hacer pijotas *or* cabrillas en el agua. || FIG. *To play ducks and drakes with one's money*, despilfarrar el dinero. || *To take to sth. like a duck to water*, adaptarse fácilmente a algo, hallarse en su elemento con algo.
duck [dʌk] v. tr. Agachar (to lower suddenly). || FAM. Fumarse: *to duck a class*, fumarse una clase. || Zambullir (in water). || Esquivar (a blow). || FIG. Eludir (a problem).
— V. intr. Agacharse (to bob down suddenly). || Zambullirse (in water). || — *To duck out*, desaparecer. || *To duck out on*, eludir.
duckbill [ˈdʌkbil] n. Monotrema, *m.*, ornitorrinco, *m.* (animal).
duckboard [ˈdʌkbɔ:d] n. Enrejado (*m.*) de madera.
ducker [dʌkə*] n. Somorgujo, *m.* (bird).
duck-footed [ˈdʌkfutid] adj. Palmípedo, da.
ducking [ˈdʌkiŋ] n. Zambullida, *f.*, chapuzón, *m.* || *Ducking stool*, silla (*f.*) en que se zambullía a los condenados a modo de castigo.
duckling [ˈdʌkliŋ] n. ZOOL. Patito, *m.* || *The ugly duckling*, el patito feo.
duckweed [ˈdʌkwi:d] n. Lenteja (*f.*) de agua.
ducky [ˈdʌki] adj. Mono, na; precioso, sa.
— N. Querido, da; cariño, *m.*
duct [dʌkt] n. Conducto, *m.* (of gas). || ELECTR. Tubo, *m.* || ANAT. Canal, *m.*, conducto, *m.*: *tear duct*, canal *or* conducto lagrimal. || ANAT. *Auditory duct*, conducto auditivo.
ductile [ˈdʌktail] adj. Dúctil.
ductility [dʌkˈtiliti] n. Ductilidad, *f.*
ductless [ˈdʌktlis] adj. ANAT. Endocrino, na; de secreción interna: *ductless glands*, glándulas endocrinas.
dud [dʌd] adj. Falso, sa (false): *a dud note*, un billete falso. || Sin fondos (a cheque). || Incapaz (a person). || Inútil (useless). || Defectuoso, sa (faulty). || COMM. *Dud stock*, mercancía (*f.*) invendible.
— N. MIL. Proyectil (*m.*) que no estalla (shell). || COMM. Mercancía (*f.*) invendible. || FAM. Desastre, *m.*, calamidad, *f.*: *a dud at mathematics*, un desastre en matemáticas. || — Pl. FAM. Trapos, *m.*, ropa, *f. sing.* (clothes). || *To be a dud*, ser falso (coin).
dude [dju:d] n. U. S. Petimetre, *m.* || U. S. *Dude ranch*, rancho (*m.*) para turistas.
dudgeon [ˈdʌdʒən] n. Cólera, *f.*, ira, *f.* (anger). || *In high dudgeon*, muy enojado, da; iracundo, da.
due [dju:] adj. COMM. Pagadero, ra (payable). || Debido, da: *with due care*, con el debido cuidado; *in due time*, a su debido tiempo. || — COMM. *Debts due by us*, deudas nuestras. | *Debts due to us*, créditos (*m. pl.*) a nuestro favor. | *Due bill*, reconocimiento (*m.*) de deuda. | *Due date*, vencimiento, *m.* || *Due to*, debido a. || COMM. *Falling due*, vencimiento, *m.* || *He is due to arrive next month*, debe llegar el mes que viene. || *To be due to*, deberse a: *it's due to your negligence*, se debe a su negligencia. || *To be due to s.o.*, corresponder a (to fall to). || COMM. *To fall* o *to become due*, vencer. || *Train due at four o'clock*, tren que debe llegar a las cuatro.
— N. Merecido, *m.* (that which s.o. deserves): *he got his due*, se llevó su merecido; *to give s.o. his due*, dar a alguien su merecido. || COMM. Deuda, *f.*: *to pay one's dues*, pagar sus deudas. || — Pl. Derechos, *m.*: *harbour dues*, derechos de fondeo *or* anclaje. || Cuota, *f. sing.* (for the rights of membership). || FIG. *We must give him his due*, hay que ser justo con él.
— Adv. MAR. Derecho hacia: *due north*, derecho hacia el norte.
duel [ˈdjuəl] n. Duelo, *m.*: *to fight a duel*, batirse en duelo; *it was a duel to the death*, fue un duelo a muerte.
duel [ˈdjuəl] v. intr. Batirse en duelo.
duellist (U. S. **duelist**) [—ist] n. Duelista, *m.*
duenna [djuˈenə] n. (Ant.). Dueña, *f.*
Duero [ˈdweirə] pr. n. GEOGR. Duero, *m.*
duet [djuˈet] n. MUS. Dúo, *m.*
duettist [djuˈetist] n. MUS. Duetista, *m.* & *f.*
duff [dʌf] n. CULIN. Budín, *m.*, pudín, *m.* || Cisco, *m.* (coal). || U. S. Humus, *m.*, mantillo, *m.*
— Adj. FAM. Sin valor.
duff [dʌf] v. tr. Falsificar (to fake).
duffel [ˈdʌfəl] n. Muletón, *m.* (cloth). || U. S. Ropa (*f.*) para cambiarse.
duffel bag [—bæg] n. Bolsa (*f.*) de lona.
duffel coat [—kəut] n. Trenca, *f.* (overcoat).
duffer [ˈdʌfə*] n. FAM. Zoquete, *m.* (stupid person). | Desastre, *m.*, calamidad, *f.* (incompetent person). || Vendedor (*m.*) ambulante, buhonero, *m.* (peddler).
duffle [ˈdʌfəl] n. Muletón, *m.*
duffle coat [—kəut] n. Trenca, *f.* (overcoat).
dug [dʌg] n. Teta, *f.* (of animal). || Ubre, *f.* (of cow).
dug [dʌg] pret. & p. p. See DIG.
dugout [ˈdʌgaut] n. MAR. Piragua, *f.* || MIL. Refugio (*m.*) subterráneo, trinchera, *f.* (shelter). || FAM. Militarote, *m.*
duke [dju:k] n. Duque, *m.*: *His Grace The Duke*, el señor duque. || — Pl. FAM. Puños, *m.* (fists).
dukedom [ˈdju:kdəm] n. Ducado, *m.* (title).
dulcet [ˈdʌlsit] adj. Dulce, suave.
dulcify [ˈdʌlsifai] v. tr. Dulcificar.
dulcimer [ˈdʌlsimə*] n. MUS. Dulcimer, *m.*
Dulcinea [ˌdʌlsiˈniə] n. Dulcinea, *f.*
dulia [dju:ˈlaiə] n. REL. Dulía, *f.*
dull [dʌl] adj. Lerdo, da; torpe (obtuse). || Lento, ta; tardo, da (slow). || Monótono, na; insulso, sa (drab). || Sin sabor, insulso, sa (flat). || Sin relieve (lacklustre). || Sin vida (lifeless). || Pesado, da (tedious). || Soso, sa (uninteresting). || Apagado, da (colours). || Mate (surface). || Pálido, da (light). || Sordo, da (pain, sounds). || Embotado, da (sense). || Flojo, ja: *trade is dull*, los negocios están flojos. || Muerto, ta (season, etc.). || Gris, desapacible (weather). || Triste (cheerless). || Deprimido, da (depressed). || Taciturno, na; sombrío, a (sullen). || Oscuro, ra (dark). || Embotado, da (blunt). || *To have a dull sense of hearing*, ser duro de oído.
dull [dʌl] v. tr. Aliviar (to lessen pain). || Oscurecer (to darken). || Enfriar (emotions). || Embotar (senses). || Entorpecer (mind). || Apagar (colours). || Deslustrar, volver mate (surface). || Amortiguar, apagar (sounds). || Embotar (a knife). || Debilitar (attention). || Entristecer (to sadden).
— V. intr. Aliviarse (pain). || Oscurecerse (to become dark). || Enfriarse (emotions). || Embotarse (senses). || Entorpecerse (mind). || Embotarse (a knife). || Debilitarse (attention). || Entristecerse (to become sad). || Volverse mate (surface). || Apagarse (colours). || Amortiguarse, apagarse (sounds).
dullard [ˈdʌləd] n. FAM. Lelo, la; burro, rra.
dullish [ˈdʌliʃ] adj. Torpe, de cortos alcances (person). || Pesado, da (tedious). || Con poco brillo (colour). || Apagado, da; sordo, da (sound).
dullness [ˈdʌlnis] n. Torpeza, *f.* (stupidity). || Monotonía, *f.*, insulsez, *f.* (drabness). || Insipidez, *f.*, lo soso (flatness). || Tristeza, *f.* (sadness). || Pesadez, *f.* (tediousness). || Falta (*f.*) de vida (lifelessness). || Lo apagado (of colours). || Falta (*f.*) de brillo (of surface). || Flojedad, *f.* (of trade). || Embotamiento, *m.* (of senses). || TECH. Embotamiento, *m.* (bluntness). || *Dullness of hearing*, sordera, dureza (*f.*) de oído.
dully [dʌli] adv. Lentamente (slowly). || Torpemente (stupidly). || Sordamente. || De una manera aburrida.

duly [ˈdju:li] adv. Debidamente (properly). || A su debido tiempo (on time). || COMM. *I duly received your favour of*, acuso recibo de su atenta del.
Duma [ˈdu:mə] n. HIST. Duma, *f.*
dumb [dʌm] adj. Mudo, da (not speaking): *born dumb*, mudo de nacimiento. || FIG. Mudo, da (*with*, de). || FAM. Estúpido, da; tonto, ta (stupid). || — *Dumb animal*, animal, *m.* || *Dumb motions*, señas, *f.* || *Dumb show*, pantomima, *f.* || *The dumb*, los mudos. || *To strike s.o. dumb*, dejar a alguien sin habla *or* mudo.
dumbbell [—bel] n. SP. Pesa, *f.* || U.S. FAM. Bobo, ba.
dumbfound [dʌmˈfaund] v. tr. Dejar sin habla, enmudecer. || *To be dumbfounded*, quedarse sin habla *or* pasmado.
dumbly [dʌmli] adv. Sin decir nada. || En silencio. || FAM. Estúpidamente.
dumbness [dʌmnis] n. MED. Mudez, *f.* || FIG. Mutismo, *m.* || FAM. Estupidez, *f.*
dumbwaiter [ˈdʌmˈweitə*] n. Carrito, *m.* (trolley). || U. S. Montaplatos, *m. inv.* (lift).
dumdum [ˈdʌmdʌm] n. Dum-dum, *f.* (bullet).
dumfound [dʌmˈfaund] v. tr. See DUMBFOUND.
dummy [ˈdʌmi] n. Objeto (*m.*) ficticio (display article). || Maniquí, *m.* (of tailor). || Títere, *m.*, muñeco, *m.* (puppet). || Chupete, *m.* (for babies). || Muerto, *m.* (in cards). || PRINT. Maqueta, *f.* || FIG. Testaferro, *m.* (cover). || FAM. Tonto, ta; bobo, ba. || SP. *To sell the dummy*, hacer una finta de pase, fintar (in rugby).
— Adj. Falso, sa; ficticio, cia.
dummy [ˈdʌmi] v. intr. SP. Fintar (in rugby).
dump [dʌmp] n. Vertedero, *m.* (scrap heap). || FIG. FAM. Tugurio, *m.* (hovel). | Poblacho, *m.* (village). || MIL. Depósito, *m.* || — *Dump lorry* o *truck* volquete, *m.* || FIG. *To be down in the dumps*, tener murria *or* ideas negras.
dump [dʌmp] v. tr. Descargar, verter [algo de un camión, tren, etc.] (to unload). || Tirar (to throw down, to throw away). || Deshacerse de (to get rid of). || COMM. Inundar el mercado con. || Expulsar a un país extranjero (immigrants).
dumping [—iŋ] n. Descarga, *f.* || "Dumping", *m.*, venta (*f.*) de un producto en el extranjero a un precio inferior al aplicado en el interior.
dumpish [—iʃ] adj. FAM. Desalentado, da; que tiene ideas negras *or* murria.
dumpling [—liŋ] n. CULIN. Budín (*m.*) relleno de carne *or* fruta. | Masa (*f.*) hervida.
dumpy [dʌmpi] adj. FAM. Regordete, ta.
dun [dʌn] adj. Pardo, da.
— N. Color (*m.*) pardo. || Caballo (*m.*) pardo (horse). || COMM. Petición (*f.*) de reembolso (demand). | Acreedor (*m.*) insistente (insistent creditor).
dun [dʌn] v. tr. COMM. Apremiar (a debtor).
dunce [dʌns] n. FAM. Burro, *m.* || FAM. *Dunce's cap* (U. S., *dunce cap*), orejas (*f. pl.*) de burro.
dunderhead [ˈdʌndəhed] n. Idiota, *m.* & *f.*, burro, rra.
dune [dju:n] n. Duna, *f.*
dung [dʌŋ] n. Excrementos, *m. pl.* (of animals). || Boñiga, *f.* (of cow). || Cagajón, *m.* (of horse). || AGR. Estiércol, *m.* (manure).
dung [dʌŋ] v. tr. AGR. Estercolar (a field).
dungarees [ˌdʌŋgəˈri:z] pl. n. Mono, *m. sing.* (overall).
dung beetle [ˈdʌŋˌbi:tl] n. ZOOL. Escarabajo (*m.*) pelotero.
dungeon [ˈdʌndʒən] n. Calabozo, *m.*, mazmorra, *f.* (prison). || Torre (*f.*) del homenaje (keep).
dunghill [ˈdʌŋhil] n. Estercolero, *m.*
dunk [dʌŋk] v. tr. Mojar, remojar.
— V. intr. Tirarse al agua.
dunnage [ˈdʌnidʒ] n. Maderos (*m. pl.*) de estibar.
duo [ˈdju:əu] n. Dúo, *m.*
duodecimal [ˌdjuəuˈdesiməl] adj. MATH. Duodecimal.
duodecimo [ˌdjuəuˈdesiməu] adj. En dozavo (book).
duodenal [ˌdjuəˈdi:nl] adj. ANAT. Duodenal. || MED. *Duodenal ulcer*, úlcera (*f.*) del duodeno.
duodenitis [ˌdjuəudiˈnaitis] n. MED. Duodenitis, *f.*
duodenum [ˌdjuəuˈdi:nəm] n. ANAT. Duodeno, *m.*

— OBSERV. El plural es *duodenums* o *duodena*.

duologue [ˈdjuələg] n. Diálogo, *m.*
dupe [dju:p] n. FAM. Primo, ma.
dupe [dju:p] v. tr. Embaucar, engañar (to cheat). || Timar (to swindle).
duper [—ə*] n. Embaucador, ra; engañador, ra (cheater). || Timador, ra (swindler).
dupery [ˈdju:pəri] n. Engaño, *m.* (cheating). || Timo, *m.* (swindle).
duplex [dju:pleks] adj. TECH. Dúplex: *duplex line* o *link*, enlace dúplex. || Doble (double).
— N. Dúplex, *m.*
duplex [ˈdju:pleks] v. tr. ELECTR. Establecer un enlace dúplex en.
duplexer [—ə*] n. Dispositivo (*m.*) para enlace dúplex.
duplicate [ˈdju:plikit] adj. Duplicado, da. || De recambio, de repuesto (parts).
— N. Doble, *m.*, copia, *f.*, duplicado, *m.* (copy). || *In duplicate*, por duplicado.
duplicate [ˈdju:plikeit] v. tr. Duplicar: *to duplicate a document, the locks on a door*, duplicar un documento, las cerraduras de una puerta. || Multicopiar, hacer *or* tirar con multicopista, reproducir.
duplicating [—iŋ] n. Duplicación, *f.* || Tirada (*f.*) con multicopista, reproducción (*f.*) con multicopista. || *Duplicating machine*, multicopista, *f.*
— Adj. Duplicador, ra.
duplication [ˌdju:pliˈkeiʃən] n. Duplicación, *f.* || Reproducción, *f.* || Duplicado, *m.*, copia, *f.* (copy).
duplicative [ˈdju:plikətiv] adj. Duplicativo, va.
duplicator [ˈdju:plikeitə*] n. Multicopista, *f.* [*Amer.*, mimeógrafo, *m.*].
duplicity [djuˈplisiti] n. Doblez, *f.*, duplicidad, *f.*
durability [ˌdjuərəˈbiliti] n. Durabilidad, *f.*, duración, *f.*, lo duradero.
durable [ˈdjuərəbl] adj. Duradero, ra. || *Durable goods*, productos no perecederos.
durably [ˈdjuərəbli] adv. Duraderamente.
duralumin [djuəˈræljumin] or **duraluminium** [djuərˌæljuˈminjəm] n. CHEM. Duraluminio, *m.*
dura mater [ˈdjuərəˈmeitə*] n. ANAT. Duramáter, *f.*, duramadre, *f.*
duramen [djuəˈreimen] n. BOT. Duramen, *m.*
durance [ˈdjuərəns] n. JUR. Detención, *f.*, prisión, *f.*
duration [djuəˈreiʃən] n. Duración, *f.* || FAM. *For the duration*, mientras dure la guerra.
Dürer [ˈdjuərə*] pr. n. Durero.
duress [djuəˈres] n. JUR. Coacción, *f.*, coerción, *f.* (compulsion). | Prisión, *f.* (imprisonment).
during [ˈdjuəriŋ] prep. Durante.
durst [də:st] pret. See DARE.
dusk [dʌsk] n. Crepúsculo, *m.* (twilight). || Oscuridad, *f.* (gloom). || *At dusk*, al atardecer, al anochecer.
— Adj. Oscuro, ra.
dusk [dʌsk] v. tr. Oscurecer.
— V. intr. Oscurecerse.
duskiness [ˈdʌskinis] n. Oscuridad, *f.* || Color (*m.*) moreno (of complexion).
dusky [ˈdʌski] adj. Oscuro, ra (gloomy). || Moreno, na (complexion).
dust [dʌst] n. Polvo, *m.*: *covered with dust*, cubierto de polvo. || Cenizas, *f. pl.* (remains of dead person). || BOT. Polen, *m.* || — FIG. *To bite the dust*, morder el polvo. | *To let the dust settle*, esperar que se calme la borrasca. | *To lick the dust*, morder el polvo. || *To make* o *to raise a dust*, levantar una polvareda. || FIG. *To raise* o *to kick up a dust*, armar un escándalo. | *To throw dust in s.o.'s eyes*, engañar a alguien con falsas apariencias.
dust [dʌst] v. tr. Limpiar el polvo de, quitar el polvo a (to clean dust off). || Espolvorear (to powder). || FIG. FAM. *To dust s.o.'s jacket* o *s.o.'s coat*, sacudirle el polvo a uno.
— V. intr. Limpiar el polvo. || U. S. FAM. *To dust out*, poner pies en polvorosa.
dustbin [ˈdʌstbin] n. Cubo (*m.*) de la basura.
dust bowl [ˈdʌstbəul] n. Terreno (*m.*) pelado por la erosión.
dust cart [—kɑ:t] n. Camión (*m.*) de la basura.
dustcloth [—klɔθ] n. U. S. Trapo, *m.* (duster). || Funda, *f.* (cover).
dust cloud [—klaud] n. Polvareda, *f.*, nube (*m.*) de polvo.
dustcoat [—ˌkəut] n. Guardapolvo, *m.*
dust cover [—ˈkʌvə*] n. Sobrecubierta, *f.* (of books). || Funda, *f.*, guardapolvo, *m.* (of furniture).
dust devil [—ˌdevl] n. Tormenta (*f.*) de polvo.
duster [ˈdʌstə*] n. Trapo, *m.* (cloth). || Plumero, *m.* (with feathers). || Borrador, *m.* (for blackboard). || U. S. Guardapolvo, *m.* (overalls). | Pulverizador, *m.* (spray).
dustiness [ˈdʌstinis] n. Lo polvoriento.
dusting [ˈdʌstiŋ] n. Limpieza, *f.* (cleaning). || FAM. Paliza, *f.* (thrashing). || Espolvoreo, *m.* (light sprinkling). || Capa (*f.*) de polvo.
dust jacket [ˈdʌstˌdʒækit] n. Sobrecubierta, *f.* (of a book).
dustman [ˈdʌstmən] n. Basurero, *m.*

— OBSERV. El plural es *dustmen*.

dustpan [ˈdʌstpæn] n. Recogedor, *m.*
dust sheet [ˈdʌstʃi:t] n. Funda, *f.*, guardapolvo, *m.*
dust shot [ˈdʌstʃɔt] n. MIL. Mostacilla, *f.*
dust storm [ˈdʌststɔ:m] n. Tormenta (*f.*) de polvo.
dustup [ˈdʌstʌp] n. FAM. Riña, *f.*, pelea, *f.*
dusty [ˈdʌsti] adj. Polvoriento, ta (powdery). || Cubierto de polvo (covered with dust). || Ceniciento, ta (dust-coloured). || Vago, ga (answer). || FAM. *It's not so dusty*, no está nada mal.
Dutch [dʌtʃ] adj. Holandés, esa.
— N. Holandés, *m.* (language). || — Pl. Holandeses, *m.* || — FIG. *To beat the Dutch*, ser extraordinario. | *To go Dutch*, pagar cada uno lo suyo, pagar a escote.
Dutchman [—mən] n. Holandés, *m.* || — MUS. *Flying Dutchman*, buque (*m.*) fantasma. || FIG. FAM. *If that picture is genuine I'm a Dutchman*, que me corten la mano si este cuadro es auténtico.

OBSERV. El plural de esta palabra es *Dutchmen*.

Dutchwoman [—ˌwumən] n. Holandesa, *f.*

— OBSERV. El plural de esta palabra es *Dutchwomen*.

duteous [ˈdju:tjəs] adj. Deferente (respectful). || Obediente.
dutiable [ˈdju:tjəbl] adj. JUR. Sujeto a derechos arancelarios *or* de aduana.
dutiful [ˈdju:tiful] adj. Obediente, sumiso, sa (obedient). || Deferente (respectful). || Servicial (obliging).
dutifully [—i] adv. Con deferencia *or* sumisión.
duty [ˈdju:ti] n. Deber, *m.*, obligación, *f.*: *to do one's duty*, cumplir con su obligación; *to fail in one's duty*,

faltar a su deber. || TECH. Rendimiento, *m.* || Impuesto, *m.* (tax). || Derechos (*m. pl.*) arancelarios, derechos (*m. pl.*) de aduana, aranceles, *m. pl.* (at customs). || Función, *f.*: *to fulfil one's duties*, desempeñar sus funciones. || — *As in duty bound*, como es debido. || *For duty's sake* o *from a sense of duty*, por cumplido, para cumplir. || *In duty to*, en consideración a. || *In the line of duty*, en cumplimiento de los deberes de uno. || *I shall make it my duty to*, me encargaré de. || *On duty*, de servicio. || *To be off duty*, estar libre, no estar de servicio. || MIL. *To be on sentry duty*, estar de guardia. || *To be s.o.'s duty to*, incumbirle a uno, corresponderle a uno. || *To do duty for s.o.*, sustituir a alguien. || *To do duty for sth.*, servir de algo, hacer las veces de algo. || *To do one's duty by* o *to s.o.*, cumplir con alguien. || *To pay a duty call*, hacer una visita de cumplido. || *To pay one's duty to*, saludar respetuosamente a. || *To take up one's duties*, tomar posesión de un empleo *or* cargo, entrar en funciones.

duty-free [ˈdju:tiˈfri:] adj. Libre *or* exento de derechos de aduana, en franquicia aduanera.

duty-paid [ˈdju:tiˈpeid] adj./adv. Con los derechos arancelarios pagados.

duumvir [djuˈʌmvə*] n. Duumviro, *m.*

dwarf [dwɔ:f] adj./n. Enano, na.

dwarf [dwɔ:f] v. tr. Achicar, empequeñecer (to make seem small). || Impedir que crezca (to prevent from growing).

dwarfish [ˈdwɔ:fiʃ] adj. Enano, na.

dwarfishness [ˌdwɔ:fiʃnis] n. MED. Enanismo, *m.* || Tamaño (*m.*) diminuto, pequeñez, *f.*

dwarfism [ˈdwɔ:fizəm] n. MED. Enanismo, *m.*

dwell [dwel] n. TECH. Parada (*f.*) momentánea.

dwell* [dwel] v. intr. Morar, vivir (to live). || *To dwell on*, extenderse en, hablar extensamente de (a subject), insistir en, hacer hincapié en (to emphasize), acentuar (a syllable), fijarse en (gaze), detenerse en (a thought).

— OBSERV. Pret. & p. p. **dwelt**.

dweller [ˈdwelə*] n. Habitante, *m.* & *f.* (*in*, *on*, de).

dwelling [ˈdweliŋ] n. Morada, *f.*, vivienda, *f.* || FIG. Insistencia, *f.*

dwelling house [—haus] n. Casa (*f.*) particular.

dwelt [dwelt] pret. & p. p. See DWELL.

dwindle [ˈdwindl] v. intr. Menguar, disminuir. || *To dwindle to nothing*, quedar reducido a nada.

dyad [ˈdaiæd] n. Pareja, *f.* (couple).

dyarchy [ˈdaiɑ:ki] n. Diarquía, *f.*

dye [dai] n. Tinte, *m.* (colouring matter). || Color, *m.*, tono, *m.* (colour). || — *Fast dye*, color sólido. || FIG. *Of the deepest dye*, de la peor catadura.

dye [dai] v. tr. Teñir. || *To have a coat dyed black*, mandar teñir un abrigo de negro.

— OBSERV. El gerundio de este verbo es *dyeing*. No se confunda con *dying*, gerundio del verbo *to die* (morir).

dyeing [—iŋ] n. Tinte, *m.*

dyer [—ə*] n. Tintorero, ra.

dyer's-weed [ˈdaiəzwi:d] n. BOT. Gualda, *f.*

dyestuff [ˈdaistʌf] n. Tinte, *m.*, materia (*f.*) colorante.

dyewood [ˈdaiwud] n. Madera (*f.*) tintórea.

dying [ˈdaiiŋ] adj. Moribundo, da (about to die). || FIG. Mortecino, na (waning, failing). | En vías de desaparición (about to disappear). || — *Dying words*, últimas palabras. || FAM. *I'm dying to see you*, me muero de ganas de verte.

dyke [daik] n. See DIKE.

dynamic [daiˈnæmik] adj. Dinámico, ca.

dynamics [daiˈnæmiks] n. PHYS. Dinámica, *f.*

dynamism [ˈdainəmizəm] n. Dinamismo, *m.*

dynamist [ˈdainəmist] n. Dinamista, *m.* & *f.*

dynamistic [ˌdainəˈmistik] adj. Dinamista.

dynamite [ˈdainəmait] n. Dinamita, *f.* || FIG. *This story is dynamite*, esta historia es explosiva.

dynamite [ˈdainəmait] v. tr. Dinamitar, volar con dinamita.

dynamiter [—ə*] n. Dinamitero, ra.

dynamiting [—iŋ] n. Voladura (*f.*) con dinamita.

dynamo [ˈdainəməu] n. Dinamo, *f.*, dínamo, *f.*

dynamoelectric [ˌdainəmauiˈlektrik] or **dynamoelectrical** [—əl] adj. Dinamoeléctrico, ca.

dynamometer [ˌdainəˈmɔmitə*] n. Dinamómetro, *m.*

dynamometry [ˌdainəˈmɔmitri] n. Dinamometría, *f.*

dynastic [diˈnæstik] or **dynastical** [—əl] adj. Dinástico, ca.

dynasty [ˈdinəsti] n. Dinastía, *f.*

dyne [dain] n. PHYS. Dina, *f.*

dysenteric [ˌdisnˈterik] adj. MED. Disentérico, ca.

dysentery [ˈdisəntri] n. MED. Disentería, *f.*

dyslogistic [ˌdisləˈdʒistik] adj. Peyorativo, va; despectivo, va.

dyspepsia [disˈpepsiə] or **dyspepsy** [disˈpepsi] n. MED. Dispepsia, *f.*

dyspeptic [disˈpeptik] adj./n. MED. Dispéptico, ca.

dysphasia [disˈfeiʒjə] n. MED. Disfasia, *f.*

dyspnoea (U. S. **dyspnea**) [disˈpniə] n. Disnea, *f.*

distrophia [disˈtrəufiə] or **dystrophy** [ˈdistrəfi] n. MED. Distrofia, *f.*

dysuric [disˈjuərik] adj. MED. Disúrico, ca.

E

e [i:] n. E, *f.* (letter). || MUS. Mi, *m.*: *E major, minor, flat, sharp*, mi mayor, menor, bemol, sostenido.

each [i:tʃ] adj. Cada: *each child had a book*, cada niño tenía un libro. || *Each and every man*, todos los hombres sin excepción.

— Pron. Cada uno, cada una: *one of each*, uno de cada uno; *he gave us a pound each*, nos dio una libra a cada uno; *they are two pesetas each*, valen dos pesetas cada uno. || — *Each for himself*, cada cual por su cuenta. || *To each his own*, a cada cual lo suyo. || *Two bottles each*, dos botellas por persona.

each other [—ˈʌðə*] pron. Uno a otro, una a otra, unos a otros, unas a otras, el uno al otro, etc.: *the two of them help each other a lot*, los dos se ayudan mucho uno a otro; *John and David complain of each other*, Juan y David se quejan el uno del otro *or* uno de otro.

— OBSERV. *Each other* sólo debe emplearse cuando se trata de dos personas. Si hay una más, ha de decirse *one another*.

— The reciprocal sense of *each other* is often conveyed in Spanish by a simple reflexive verb (*they greeted each other*, se saludaron). This may, however, result in ambiguity in Spanish between the reciprocal and the reflexive meanings (*se hirieron* can mean "they hurt each other" or "they hurt themselves"). In this case "they hurt each other" would be better translated by *se hirieron uno a otro*.

— The appropriate preposition must be inserted as follows: *they laughed at each other*, se han reído uno de otro.

— Two alternative translations expressing the idea of reciprocal action are "mutuamente" and "recíprocamente" (*they envy each other*, se envidian mutuamente).

eager [ˈi:gə*] adj. Grande: *eager hopes*, grandes esperanzas; *eager appetite*, gran apetito. || Ávido, da; ansioso, sa (hungry): *eager for riches, for fame, for knowledge*, ávido de riquezas, de fama, de saber. || Apasionado, da: *an eager student*, un estudiante apasionado. || Deseoso, sa: *eager to start*, deseoso de empezar; *eager to please*, deseoso de contentar a la gente *or* de gustar. || Apremiante, vehemente, vivo, va; ardiente: *eager desire*, deseo ardiente. || — *An eager glance*, una mirada de deseo (desirous), una mirada entusiasta (excited). || *An eager public*, un público anhelante. || *Don't be so eager!*, ¡ten paciencia! || *Eager cold*, frío agudo *or* penetrante. || *To be eager for*, ansiar, anhelar, tener gran deseo de. || *To be eager to do sth.*, anhelar *or* ansiar hacer algo, desear vivamente hacer algo. || *To be in eager pursuit of*, perseguir ansiosamente.

— N. U. S. MAR. Macareo, *m.*, barra, *f.*

eagerly [—li] adv. Ávidamente (to eat, to read, etc.). || Ansiosamente (to desire). || Atentamente (to listen). || Impacientemente (impatiently).

eagerness [—nis] n. Impaciencia, *f.* (impatience). || Ansia, *f.*, anhelo, *m.*: *his eagerness to succeed, to learn*, su ansia de tener éxito, de aprender.

eagle [ˈi:gl] n. ZOOL. Águila, *f.* (bird): *golden eagle*, águila real *or* caudal. || Águila, *f.* (emblem). || ASTR. Águila, *f.* (constellation). || SP. Hoyo (*m.*) conseguido en dos golpes menos que la media (in golf). || — *The Black Eagle of Prussia*, el águila negra de Prusia. || *The Imperial Eagle*, el águila imperial.

eagle eye [—ˈai] n. FIG. Ojo (*m.*) de lince.

eagle-eyed [—áid] adj. *To be eagle-eyed*, tener ojos de lince.
eagle owl [—aul] n. Búho (*m.*) real (bird).
eagle ray [—rei] n. Águila (*f.*) de mar (fish).
eaglet [ˈi:glit] n. Aguilucho, *m.* (young eagle).
eagre [ˈeigə*] n. MAR. Macareo, *m.*, barra, *f.*
ear [iə*] n. ANAT. Oreja, *f.* (outer part): *to have big ears*, tener grandes orejas; *pricked, drooping ears*, orejas tiesas, gachas. | Oído, *m.*: *inner, middle ear*, oído interno, medio. || Oído, *m.* (sense): *to have a good ear*, tener buen oído. || Espiga, *f.* (of corn). || Oreja, *f.*, asa, *f.* (of vase, etc.). || — MUS. *By ear*, de oído. || || FIG. *It goes in at one ear and out at the other*, por un oído le entra y por otro le sale. | *My ears are burning*, me están pitando *or* silbando los oídos. | *To be all ears*, ser todo oídos. | *To believe one's ears*, dar crédito a sus oídos. || TAUR. *To cut an ear, two ears*, cortar una oreja, dos orejas. || FIG. *To fall down about one's ears*, venirse abajo (plans). | *To fall on deaf ears*, caer en saco roto. | *To give* o *to lend an ear to*, prestar oído *or* oídos a. || FAM. *To give s.o. a thick ear* o *to clip s.o.'s ear*, darle una torta a uno. || *To have no ear for music*, tener mal oído. || *To have sharp ears*, tener el oído fino. || FIG. *To have the ear of*, gozar de la confianza de, tener influencia con, hacerse escuchar por. | *To keep* o *to have one's ear to the ground*, mantenerse alerta, mantenerse al corriente. | *To listen with half an ear*, escuchar a medias. | *To open one's ears*, abrir los oídos. | *To play by ear*, tocar de oído. | *To play it by ear*, improvisar sobre la marcha. | *To prick up one's ears*, aguzar el oído. | *To set people by the ears*, sembrar la discordia entre la gente. | *To turn a deaf ear*, no prestar oídos, hacerse el sordo, hacer oídos de mercader. | *Up to the ears in debt*, abrumado de deudas, empeñado hasta la camisa. | *Walls have ears*, las paredes oyen.
ear [iə*] v. intr. Espigar.
earache [ˈiəreik] n. Dolor (*m.*) de oídos.
eardrop [ˈiədrɔp] n. Pendiente, *m.*, arete, *m.* (earring).
eardrum [ˈiədrʌm] n. ANAT. Tímpano, *m.*
earflap [ˈiəflæp] n. Orejera, *f.* (of hat). || ANAT. Pabellón (*m.*) de la oreja.
earing [ˈiəriŋ] n. MAR. Empuñidura, *f.*
earl [ə:l] n. Conde, *m.*
earlap [ˈiəlæp] n. ANAT. Pabellón (*m.*) de la oreja.
earldom [ə:ldəm] n. Condado, *m.*
earlier [ˈə:liə*] adv. Más temprano. || Anterior.
early [ˈə:li] adj. Temprano, na: *at an early age*, a temprana edad; *early vegetables*, verduras tempranas. || Primero, ra (first): *the early stages*, las primeras etapas; *an early model of a car*, uno de los primeros modelos de un coche; *the early poets*, los primeros poetas; *early youth*, primera juventud. || Rápido, da; pronto, ta (quick): *an early reply*, una contestación rápida. || Temprano, na; prematuro, ra; precoz (premature): *his early death*, su muerte prematura; *an early summer*, un verano precoz. || Próximo, ma (imminent): *at an early date*, en fecha próxima. || Matutino, na (of the early morning): *the early silence*, el silencio matutino. || Primitivo, va: *early art*, arte primitivo. || — *At an early date*, en fecha próxima, muy pronto (soon), muy pronto (in the past). || *At the earliest*, como muy pronto. || *At the earliest possible moment*, lo más pronto posible. || *At your earliest convenience*, con la mayor brevedad. || *Earliest youth*, tierna *or* primera infancia (infancy). || *Early closing day*, día en que las tiendas cierran por la tarde. || *Early education*, primera enseñanza. || *Early life*, juventud, *f.*, años (*m. pl.*) juveniles (youth): *in my early life*, en mi juventud. || *Early riser*, madrugador, ra. || CINEM. *Early show*, primera función. || *In the early afternoon*, al principio de la tarde. || *In the early morning*, de madrugada, muy de mañana. || *The earliest times*, los tiempos más remotos. || *The early ages*, los primeros días *or* tiempos. || *The early morning*, la madrugada. || *To be early days yet*, ser todavía demasiado pronto. || *To have an early dinner*, cenar temprano. || *To keep early hours*, levantarse y acostarse temprano. || *We are in our early thirties*, tenemos poco más de treinta años.
— Adv. Temprano: *to get up, to arrive early*, levantarse, llegar temprano; *it was early in the morning*, fue por la mañana temprano. || Al principio de, a principios de (at the beginning of): *early* (*on*) *in the winter*, a principios del invierno; *early in one's life, one's career*, al principio de su vida, de su carrera; *early on the list*, al principio de la lista. || Antes (before): *he let me off five minutes early*, dejó que me fuese cinco minutos antes. || Pronto: *man learnt to use tools early on*, el hombre aprendió pronto a emplear las herramientas. || Con tiempo, con mucha anticipación, con mucha antelación (in advance): *to book one's tickets early*, comprar las entradas con tiempo. || — *As early as possible*, lo más pronto posible, cuanto antes. || *As early as the tenth century*, ya en el siglo x (diez). || *Bright and early*, muy temprano. || *Earlier on*, antes. || *Early enough*, a tiempo (in time), bastante temprano. || *To die early*, morir joven *or* prematuramente.
early bird [—bə:d] n. FIG. Madrugador, ra (early riser). | Persona (*f.*) que llega temprano. || FIG. *The early bird catches the worm*, al que madruga, Dios le ayuda.
Early Bird [—bə:d] n. Pájaro (*m.*) del Alba (satellite).
earmark [ˈiəmɑ:k] n. Señal (*f.*) en la oreja (of livestock). || FIG. Marca (*f.*) distintiva, característica, *f.*, señal, *f.*
earmark [ˈiəmɑ:k] v. tr. Poner una señal en la oreja (livestock). || Dejar una señal en. || Reservar, poner aparte (*for*, para) [to put aside]. || Destinar (*for*, a) [to destine]. || Consignar, asignar (credits).
earn [ə:n] v. tr. Ganar: *I earn twenty pounds a week*, gano veinte libras por semana. || Merecer, merecerse, hacerse acreedor a, ganarse (to deserve): *he had earned a rest*, había merecido un descanso. || Valer: *the theft earned him three months in gaol*, el robo le valió tres meses de cárcel. || Obtener, conseguir (to obtain). || COMM. Devengar: *shares which earn interest*, acciones que devengan interés. || *To earn one's living*, ganarse la vida.
— V. intr. Trabajar, ganarse la vida: *her sons are all earning now*, sus hijos ya trabajan todos. || COMM. Devengar interés (shares).
earnest [ˈə:nist] n. Prenda, *f.*, señal, *f.* (token): *an earnest of his good intentions*, una prenda de sus buenas intenciones. || Arras, *f. pl.*, fianza, *f.* (deposit to confirm a contract). || *In earnest*, en serio: *to be in earnest*, hablar en serio; sinceramente (sincerely).
— Adj. Sincero, ra (sincere): *an earnest appeal*, una llamada sincera. || Aplicado, da (hard-working). || Serio, ria (serious): *life is earnest*, la vida es seria. || Ardiente (eager).
earnestness [—nis] n. Seriedad *f.* (seriousness). || Sinceridad, *f.* (sincerity). || Ardor, *m.* (of pleadings).
earning power [ˈə:niŋ,pauə*] n. Rentabilidad, *f.*
earnings [ˈə:niŋz] pl. n. Ingresos, *m.* (income). || Sueldo, *m. sing.* (salary). || Ganancias, *f.*, beneficios, *m.*, utilidades, *f.* (profits).
earphone [ˈiəfəun] n. Auricular, *m.* [*Amer.*, audífono, *m.*]
earpick [ˈiəpik] n. Escarbaorejas, *m. inv.*, mondaoídos, *m. inv.*
earpiece [ˈiəpi:s] n. Auricular, *m.* (of a telephone).
earring [ˈiəriŋ] n. Pendiente, *m.* [*Amer.*, arete, *m.*]
earshell [iəʃel] n. ZOOL. Oreja (*f.*) de mar.
earshot [ˈiəʃɔt] n. Alcance (*m.*) del oído: *within earshot*, al alcance del oído; *out of earshot*, fuera del alcance del oído.
ear-splitting [ˈiəsplitiŋ] adj. Ensordecedor, ra (deafening). || Estridente (strident).
earth [ə:θ] n. Tierra, *f.* (planet): *the Earth is divided into continents*, la Tierra está dividida en continentes. || Tierra, *f.* (soil, solid surface of planet). || Guarida, *f.*, madriguera. *f.* (of fox, badger). || ELECTR. Cable (*m.*) de toma de tierra. || AGR. Tierra, *f.* || — FIG. *Down to earth*, prosaico, ca. || *On earth*, en el mundo (in the world), diablo, demonios: *who on earth is it?*, ¿quién diablo es?; *where on earth have you been?*, ¿dónde demonios has estado? || REL. *On Earth as it is in Heaven*, así en la Tierra como en el Cielo. || FIG. *To come back* o *down to earth*, bajar de las nubes, volver a la realidad. || FAM. *To cost the earth*, costar un potosí *or* un ojo de la cara. || FIG. *To move heaven and earth*, mover cielo y tierra. | *To promise the earth*, prometer el oro y el moro. || *To run to earth*, cazar [un animal] hasta que se meta en su guarida (an animal), encontrar *or* descubrir por fin (a person, information, etc.).
earth [ə:θ] v. tr. Acollar (to heap soil on or round). || ELECTR. Conectar a tierra.
earth almond [—,ɑ:mənd] n. BOT. Chufa, *f.*
earthborn [—bɔ:n] adj. Mortal (mortal). || Humano, na (human).
earthbound [—baund] adj. Terrestre. || FIG. Prosaico, ca.
earthen [ˈə:θən] adj. De barro (pottery, etc). || De tierra (walls, dams, etc.).
earthenware [—wɛə*] n. Alfarería, *f.*, objetos (*m. pl.*) de barro. || *Glazed earthenware*, loza, *f.*
— Adj. De barro.
earthlight [ˈə:θlait] n. Luz (*f.*) cenicienta (of the moon).
earthliness [ˈə:θlinis] n. Lo terrenal. || Mundanalidad, *f.* (worldliness).
earthling [ˈə:θliŋ] n. Terrícola, *m.* & *f.* (an inhabitant of the earth). || Criatura (*f.*) humana (a mortal human). || Persona (*f.*) mundana (worldly-minded person).
earthly [ˈə:θli] adj. Terrenal, terreno na: *earthly passions*, pasiones terrenas. || Mundanal (not spiritual). || — *Earthly paradise*, paraíso (*m.*) terrenal. || FAM. *To be of no earthly use*, no servir absolutamente para nada. | *To see no earthly reason*, no ver ninguna razón. | *You haven't an earthly*, no tienes ninguna posibilidad de salir bien.
earthmover [ˈə:θ,mu:və*] n. Excavadora, *f.*
earthnut [ˈə:θnʌt] n. Cacahuete, *m.*, maní, *m.* (peanut). || Chufa, *f.* (earth almond). || Trufa, *f.* (truffle).
earthquake [ˈə:θkweik] n. Terremoto, *m.*, temblor (*m.*) de tierra (tremor). || FIG. Convulsión, *f.*, conmoción, *f.* (upheaval).
earthshine [ˈə:θʃain] n. Luz (*f.*) cenicienta.
earthward [ˈə:θwəd] or **earthwards** [—z] adv. Hacia la tierra.
earthwork [ˈə:θwə:k] n. Terraplén, *m.* (bank of earth). || Movimiento (*m.*) de tierras (in construction work).
earthworm [ə:θwə:m] n. Gusano, *m.*, lombriz, *f.*

earthy [ˈəːθi] adj. Terroso, sa (like earth). || FIG. Grosero, ra; tosco, ca (bawdy, gross). | Terrenal, mundano, na (worldly).
ear trumpet [ˈiəˌtrʌmpit] n. Trompetilla (*f.*) acústica.
earwax [ˈiəwæks] n. Cerumen, *m.*
earwig [ˈiəwig] n. Tijereta, *f.* (insect).
ease [i:z] n. Facilidad, *f.*: *he lifted the load with great ease*, levantó la carga con mucha facilidad. || Facilidad, *f.*, soltura, *f.*: *she speaks with ease*, habla con soltura. || Tranquilidad, *f.*, seguridad, *f.* (tranquillity): *a kind of ease came over him*, le entró una especie de tranquilidad. || Naturalidad, *f.* (naturalness): *his ease of manner*, la naturalidad de su comportamiento. || Alivio, *m.* (from pain). || Comodidad, *f.* (comfort). || — *At ease*, a gusto, cómodo, da; a sus anchas (relaxed), en posición de descanso (soldiers). || *Ease of mind*, tranquilidad, *f.* || *Ill at ease*, see ILL. || *Put yourself at ease*, póngase cómodo. || MIL. *Stand at ease!*, en su lugar, ¡descanso! || *To live a life of ease*, llevar una vida cómoda (comfortably), vivir con desahogo (to be well-off). || *To take one's ease*, descansar. || *With ease*, fácilmente.
ease [i:z] v. tr. Aliviar, mitigar (pain). || Facilitar (to make easy). || Aflojar (a screw, bolt, pressure). || Tranquilizar (one's mind). || Aligerar (weight). || Suavizar, mitigar (to soften). || Relajar (tension). || Mover [poner, etc.] con cuidado: *to ease a cupboard away from the wall*, apartar un armario de la pared con cuidado. || MAR. Arriar, largar. || *To ease o.s. of a burden*, quitarse un peso de encima.
— V. intr. Relajarse (tensions). || Aliviarse (pain). || Amainar (wind). || Disminuir (rain). || *To ease off* o *up*, bajar (to go down): *the fever has eased up*, la fiebre ha bajado; *sales have eased off*, las ventas han bajado; trabajar menos (to work less), descansar (person), volverse menos tenso (a situation).
— OBSERV. En inglés las preposiciones *off* y *up* se añaden a menudo al verbo *to ease* sin que cambie por eso su sentido inicial.
easeful [—ful] adj. Tranquilo, la.
easel [ˈi:zl] n. Caballete, *m.* (of a painter).
easement [ˈi:zmənt] n. JUR. Servidumbre, *f.*
easily [ˈi:zili] adv. Fácilmente, con facilidad (without difficulty). || Fácilmente: *it could easily happen*, podría ocurrir fácilmente. || Con tranquilidad, con calma: *to take things easily*, tomarse las cosas con calma. || Fácilmente, con mucho (by far): *this one is easily the best*, éste es fácilmente el mejor. || Bien: *the motor runs easily*, el motor funciona bien. || Muy: *easily breakable*, muy frágil. || — *Easily operated*, de fácil manejo. || *It could easily be*, podría ser así. || *More easily said than done*, más fácil decirlo que hacerlo.
easiness [ˈi:zinis] n. Facilidad, *f.* || Comodidad, *f.* (comfort). || Tranquilidad, *f.* (tranquillity). || Soltura, *f.* (of action). || COMM. Flojedad, *f.* (of market).
east [i:st] adj. Del este: *east wind*, viento del este. || Oriental, del Este: *East Africa*, África Oriental; *East Germany*, Alemania Oriental; *East coast*, costa oriental. || Que da al este (a window, door, etc.). || Este: *the east wing of the house*, el ala este de la casa.
— Adv. Hacia el este: *to travel east*, viajar hacia el este. || Al este: *my house lies east of London*, mi casa está al este de Londres. || — *My window looks east*, mi ventana da al este. || *The wind blows east*, hay viento del este.
— N. Este, *m.* (cardinal point). || Este, *m.*, parte (*f.*) oriental (of a country or region): *I live in the East of England*, vivo en el este de Inglaterra. || Oriente, *m.* (Orient): *Near East*, Próximo *or* Cercano Oriente; *Middle East*, Oriente Medio; *Far East*, Lejano *or* Extremo Oriente. || Levante, *m.* (direction of the rising sun, Eastern Mediterranean countries). || — *East by north*, este cuarta al nordeste. || *East by south*, este cuarta al sudeste. || U. S. *The East*, estados situados en el Nordeste de los EE.UU.
East End [—ˈend] pr. n. La parte más oriental de Londres [donde están los muelles].
Easter [ˈi:stə*] n. Pascua (*f.*) de Resurrección, Pascua (*f.*) Florida. || Semana (*f.*) Santa (period): *are you going away at Easter?*, ¿vas de vacaciones en Semana Santa?
— Adj. De Pascua de Resurrección (service, etc.). || De Semana Santa (festivities). || — *Easter Day* o *Sunday*, Domingo (*m.*) de Resurrección. || *Easter egg*, huevo (*m.*) de Pascua. || *Easter Island*, Isla (*f.*) de Pascua. || *Easter Saturday*, Sábado (*m.*) de Gloria, Sábado Santo. || *Easter week*, Semana Santa.
easterly [ˈi:stəli] adj. Del este (wind). || Este (direction).
— Adv. Hacia el este (toward the east). || Del este (from the east).
— N. Viento (*m.*) del este.
eastern [i:stən] adj. Oriental, este: *the eastern part of the house*, la parte este de la casa. || Del este: *the eastern provinces*, las provincias del este. || Hacia el este (motion). || Oriental (Oriental). || *The eastern hemisphere*, el hemisferio oriental.
Eastern Church [—tʃəːtʃ] n. REL. Iglesia (*f.*) Oriental.
Easterner [ˈi:stənə*] n. U. S. Habitante (*m.*) de la parte nordeste de los EE. UU.
easternmost [ˈi:stənməust] adj. Más oriental.
Eastern time [ˈi:stəntaim] or **Eastern standard time** [ˈi:stənˈstændədˌtaim] n. Hora (*f.*) del meridiano 75 al oeste de Greenwich [tiene cinco horas de retraso con relación a la hora de Greenwich].
Eastertide [ˈi:stətaid] n. REL. Tiempo (*m.*) pascual.
East Indian [i:stˈindjən] adj. De las Indias Orientales.
East Indies [i:stˈindiz] pl. pr. n. GEOGR. Indias (*f.*) Orientales.
easting [ˈi:stiŋ] n. MAR. Marcha (*f.*) hacia el este.
east-northeast [ˈi:stnɔ:θˈi:st] n. Estenordeste, *m.*
East Pakistan [ˈi:st-ˌpɑ:kisˈtɑ:n] pr. n. GEOGR. Pakistán (*m.*) Oriental.
east-southeast [ˈi:stsauθˈi:st] n. Estesudeste, *m.*
eastward [ˈi:stwəd] adj./adv. Hacia el este.
eastwards [—z] adv. Hacia el este.
easy [ˈi:zi] adj. Fácil: *an easy problem to solve*, un problema fácil de resolver; *easy style*, estilo fácil; *an easy opponent*, un adversario fácil; *an easy woman*, una mujer fácil. || Tranquilo, la (conscience, mind). || Natural, afable (manner). || Suelto, ta (not awkward). || Flexible, tolerante (tractable). || Pausado, da (pace). || Suave (gentle). || Leve (punishment). || Flojo, ja (loose). || Cómodo, da; desahogado, da (life). || Cómodo, da (person). || Fácil de engañar (gullible). || Laxo, xa (morals, virtue). || COMM. Abundante (plentiful). | Con poca demanda (trade). | Flojo, ja (market). | Bajo, ja (interest rate). || FAM. Agradable. || — *An easy*, un buen, unos buenos: *it cost him an easy million*, le costó un buen millón. || *By easy payments* o *on easy terms*, con facilidades de pago. || *Easy come, easy go*, lo que el agua trae, el agua lleva. || *Easy to get on with*, muy amable. || *Easy to run*, de fácil manejo. || *He is an easy person to live with*, es fácil vivir con él. || *He is easy*, le da igual *or* lo mismo. *It is only too easy to yield to temptation*, es muy fácil caer en la tentación. || *To be an easy fit*, estarle cómodo a uno. || FAM. *To be as easy as pie* o *as falling off a log* o *as shelling peas* o *as ABC* o *as winking* o *as can be* o *as anything*, estar tirado, ser muy fácil. || FIG. *To be on easy street*, llevar una vida acomodada. || *To feel easy in one's mind*, estar tranquilo. || COMM. *To get easier*, bajar (prices).
— Adv. FAM. Fácilmente (easily). || — *Easier said than done*, más fácil es decirlo que hacerlo. || *Easy does it!*, ¡cuidado!, ¡despacito! || *To go easy with* o *on*, tener cuidado con, no gastar demasiado (not to waste), ser benévolo con (to be kind to), tener cuidado con (to be careful with). || MIL. *To stand easy*, quedarse en posición de descanso. || *To take it easy*, descansar (to rest), ir despacio (to go slowly), tomárselo con calma, no preocuparse (not to worry): *take it easy!*, ¡tómatelo con calma!; no ponerse nervioso (to remain calm); ir con cuidado (carefully), perder el tiempo (to idle).
— N. Descanso, *m.*
easy chair [—tʃɛə*] n. Butacón, *m.*, sillón, *m.*
easy game [—ˈgeim] n. FIG. Presa (*f.*) fácil.
easygoing [—gəuiŋ] adj. Tolerante (tolerant). || Despacioso, sa; lento, ta (slow). || Indolente, descuidado, da (careless). || De trato fácil (good-natured).
easy mark [—ˈmɑ:k] n. U. S. FIG. Presa (*f.*) fácil.
easy money [—ˈmʌni] n. Dinero (*m.*) fácilmente ganado.
eat* [i:t] v. tr. Comer: *he ate an apple*, comió una manzana; *horses eat oats*, los caballos comen cebada. || FIG. Tragar, consumir: *this old car eats oil*, este viejo coche traga aceite. | Corroer (to corrode): *acid eats metals*, el ácido corroe los metales. || — FIG. *To be eaten up with envy*, consumirse de envidia. | *To be hungry enough to eat a horse*, tener un hambre canina. || *To eat away*, corroer (to corrode), desgastar (to wear away), devorar. || *To eat breakfast*, tomar el desayuno, desayunar. || FIG. *To eat crow* o *humble pie*, reconocer su error. || *To eat dinner*, tomar la cena, cenar. || FIG. *To eat like a horse*, comer como un sabañón *or* como un regimiento. || *To eat lunch*, tomar el almuerzo, almorzar. || *To eat off*, devorar. || *To eat one's fill*, comer bien. || FIG. *To eat one's heart out*, consumirse [de dolor]. | *To eat one's words*, tragarse las palabras. || *To eat out*, roer. || FIG. *To eat s.o. out of house and home*, dejar a alguien sin un céntimo [por haber comido mucho]. | *To eat s.o.'s head off*, comerse vivo a alguien. || *To eat up*, comerse: *he ate it all up*, se lo comió todo; devorar: *the car ate up the kilometres*, el coche devoraba los kilómetros. || FIG. *What's eating you?*, ¿qué mosca te ha picado? (why are you angry?), ¿qué te está carcomiendo? (what is troubling you?).
— V. intr. Comer: *they are eating*, están comiendo. || Comerse (to be eaten). || Ser sabroso: *this meat eats well*, esta carne es muy sabrosa. || — *To eat into*, corroer (metal, etc.), mermar (one's savings), desgastar (to wear away). || *To eat through*, corroer (to corrode). || FIG. *To have s.o. eating out of one's hand*, tener dominado a alguien.
— OBSERV. pret. ***ate***; p. p. ***eaten***.
eatable [—əbl] adj. Comible, comestible.
— Pl. Comestibles, *m.*
eaten p. p. See EAT.
eater [—ə*] n. Comedor, ra (person who eats). Fruta (*f.*) de mesa (fruit). || — *He is a big eater*, es un comilón. || *He is a slow eater*, come lentamente.
eating [—iŋ] n. El comer, acción (*f.*) de comer. || Comida, *f.* (food). || — *Eating house*, restaurante, *m.* || *To be good eating*, ser sabroso, sa.

eats [—s] pl. n. Comestibles, *m.*, comida, *f. sing.* (things to eat).

eau de Cologne [ˈəudəkəˈləun] n. Agua (*f.*) de colonia, colonia, *f.*

eaves [i:vz] pl. n. ARCH. Alero, *m. sing.* || ARCH. *Eaves trough*, canalón, *m.*

eavesdrop [—drɔp] v. intr. Escuchar indiscretamente.

eavesdropper [—drɔpə*] n. Indiscreto, ta; persona (*f.*) que escucha indiscretamente.

ebb [eb] n. MAR. Menguante, *m.*, reflujo, *m.* || FIG. Caída, *f.*, decadencia, *f.* || — FIG. *At a low ebb in*, en el punto más bajo de. || *Ebb tide*, marea (*f.*) menguante (of the sea), decadencia, *f.* (decline). || *The ebb and flow*, el flujo y reflujo (of tide), los altibajos, *m. pl.* (ups and downs). || FIG. *To be at a low ebb*, estar decaído. | *To be on the ebb*, ir disminuyendo.

ebb [eb] v. intr. MAR. Bajar, menguar (tide). || FIG. Decaer, disminuir.

ebenaceae [ˌebəˈneisi:i] pl. n. BOT. Ebenáceas, *f.*

ebon [ˈebən] adj. De ébano.

ebonite [—ait] n. Ebonita, *f.* (rubber).

ebony [ˈebəni] n. BOT. Ébano, *m.* (tree, wood).
— Adj. De ébano (made of ebony). || Color de ébano (colour).

Ebro [ˈi:brəu] pr. n. GEOGR. Ebro, *m.* (river).

ebullience [iˈbʌljəns] or **ebulliency** [—i] n. Ebullición, *f.* || FIG. Exaltación, *f.*, entusiasmo, *m.*, exuberancia, *f.*

ebullient [iˈbʌljənt] adj. FIG. Exaltado, da; entusiasta, exuberante.

ebullition [ˌebəˈliʃən] n. Ebullición, *f.* (boiling). || FIG. Arranque, *m.*, arrebato, *m.* (outburst).

eburnean [iˈbə:niən] adj. Ebúrneo, a.

ecce homo [ˈeksiˈhəuməu] n. Eccehomo, *m.*, ecce homo, *m.*

eccentric [ikˈsentrik] adj. Excéntrico, ca: *eccentric circles*, círculos excéntricos; *eccentric behaviour*, comportamiento excéntrico.
— N. Excéntrico, ca (person). || TECH. Excéntrica, *f.*

eccentricity [ˌeksenˈtrisiti] n. Excentricidad, *f.*

ecchymosis [ekiˈməusis] n. MED. Equimosis, *f.*

Ecclesiastes [iˌkli:ziˈæsti:z] n. REL. Eclesiastés, *m.*

ecclesiastic [iˌkli:ziˈæstik] n. REL. Eclesiástico, *m.*
— Adj. Eclesiástico, ca.

ECONOMIC AND COMMERCIAL TERMS — VOCABULARIO (*m.*) DE ECONOMÍA Y COMERCIO

ECONOMIC TERMS — VOCABULARIO (*m.*) DE ECONOMÍA

I. General terms. — Términos (*m.*) generales.

economist	economista *m.* y *f.*
rural economics	economía (*f.*) rural
capitalist, socialist, collective, planned, controlled, liberal, mixed, political economy	economía (*f.*) capitalista, socialista, colectivista, planificada, dirigida, liberal, mixta, política
protectionism	proteccionismo *m.*
autarchy	autarquía *f.*
primary sector	sector (*m.*) primario
public, private sector	sector (*m.*) público, privado
economic channels, balance	circuito (*m.*), equilibrio (*m.*) económico
economic fluctuation, depression, stability, policy, recovery	fluctuación (*f.*), depresión (*f.*), estabilidad (*f.*), política (*f.*), reactivación (*f.*) económica
understanding	acuerdo *m.*
concentration	concentración *f.*
holding company	holding *m.*
trust	trust *m.*
cartel	cártel *m.*
rate of growth	índice (*m.*) de crecimiento
economic trend, economic situation	coyuntura *f.*, situación (*f.*) económica
infrastructure	infraestructura *f.*
standard of living	nivel (*m.*) de vida
purchasing power, buying power	poder (*m.*) adquisitivo
scarcity	escasez *f.*, carestía *f.*
stagnation	estancamiento *m.*
underdevelopment	subdesarrollo *m.*
underdeveloped	subdesarrollado, da
developing	en vías de desarrollo

II. Capital. — Capital, *m.*

share	acción *f.*
shareholder, stockholder	accionista *m.* y *f.*
bond, debenture	obligación *f.*
security, stock	título *m.*, valor *m.*
dividend	dividendo *m.*
initial capital	capital (*m.*) inicial
frozen capital *o* assets	capital (*m. sing.*) congelado
fixed assets	capital (*m. sing.*) fijo
real estate	capital (*m.*) inmobiliario
circulating *o* working capital	capital (*m.*) circulante
available capital	capital (*m.*) disponible
capital goods	bienes (*m.*) de equipo
reserve	reserva *f.*
calling up of capital	solicitación (*f.*) de fondos
allocation of funds	asignación (*f.*) de fondos
contribution of funds	aportación (*f.*) de fondos
working capital fund	fondo (*m.*) de operaciones
revolving fund	fondo (*m.*) de rotación
contingency *o* reserve fund	fondo (*m.*) de reserva
buffer fund	fondo (*m.*) regulador
sinking fund	fondo (*m.*) de amortización
investment	inversión *f.*
investor	inversionista *m.* y *f.*
self-financing	autofinanciación *f.*
bank	banco *m.*, banca *f.*
current account [U.S., checking account]	cuentacorriente *f.*
current-account holder [U.S., checking-account holder]	cuentacorrentista *m.* y *f.*
cheque [U.S., check]	cheque *m.*
bearer cheque, cheque payable to bearer	cheque (*m.*) al portador
crossed cheque	cheque (*m.*) cruzado
traveller's cheque	cheque (*m.*) de viaje
chequebook [U.S., checkbook]	talonario (*m.*) de cheques
endorsement	endoso *m.*
transfer	transferencia *f.*
money	dinero *m.*
issue	emisión *f.*
ready money	dinero (*m.*) líquido
cash	dinero (*m.*) efectivo *or* en metálico
change	dinero (*m.*) suelto, cambio *m.*
banknote, note [U.S., bill]	billete *m.*
to pay (in) cash	pagar en efectivo
domestic *o* local currency	moneda (*f.*) nacional
convertibility	convertibilidad *f.*
convertible currencies	monedas (*f.*) convertibles
foreign exchange	divisas *f. pl.*
exchange rate	tipo (*m.*) de cambio
hard currency	moneda (*f.*) fuerte
stock exchange	bolsa *f.*
quotation	cotización *f.*
speculation	especulación *f.*
saving	ahorro *m.*
depreciation	depreciación *f.*
devaluation	devaluación *f.*
revaluation	revaluación *f.*
runaway inflation	inflación (*f.*) galopante
deflation	deflación *f.*
capital flight	fuga (*f.*) de capitales

III. Loan and credit. — Préstamo (*m.*) y crédito, *m.*

lender	prestamista *m.* y *f.*
short, long, medium term loan	préstamo (*m.*) a corto, largo, medio plazo
borrower	prestatario *m.*
borrowing	empréstito *m.*, préstamo *m.*
interest	interés *m.*, rédito *m.*
rate of interest	tipo (*m.*) de interés
discount	descuento *m.*
rediscount	redescuento *m.*
annuity	anualidad *f.*
maturity	vencimiento *m.*
amortization, redemption	amortización *f.*
insurance	seguro *m.*
mortgage	hipoteca *f.*
allotment	habilitación (*f.*) de créditos
short term credit	crédito (*m.*) a corto plazo
creditor	acreedor *m.*
debtor	deudor *m.*
consolidated *o* funded, floating debt	deuda (*f.*) consolidada, flotante
drawing	giro *m.*
aid	ayuda *f.*
allowance, grant, subsidy	subsidio *m.*, subvención *f.*

IV. Production. — Producción, *f.*

output	producción *f.*
overproduction	superproducción *f.*
productive, producing	productivo, va
producer	productor *m.*
products, goods	productos *m.*, mercancías *f.* [*Amer.*, mercaderías *f.*]
article	artículo *m.*
raw material	materia (*f.*) prima
raw product	producto (*m.*) en bruto
manufactured, finished goods	productos (*m.*) manufacturados, acabados
semifinished goods	productos (*m.*) semimanufacturados
consumer goods	bienes (*m.*) de consumo
foodstuffs	productos (*m.*) alimenticios
by-product	subproducto *m.*
supply	abastecimiento *m.*, aprovisionamiento *m.*, suministro *m.*
input	insumo *m.*
productivity, productiveness	productividad *f.*

V. Expenses. — Gastos, *m.*

cost	costo *m.*
expenditure, outgoings	gastos *m. pl.*
running expenses	gastos (*m.*) corrientes

miscellaneous costs	gastos (*m.*) diversos
overhead expenses *o* costs, overheads	gastos (*m.*) generales
operating costs *o* expenses	gastos (*m.*) de funcionamiento *or* de explotación
upkeep *o* maintenance costs	gastos (*m.*) de mantenimiento
fixed costs	gastos (*m.*) fijos
transport costs	gastos (*m.*) de transporte
social charges	cargas (*f.*) sociales
contingent expenses, contingencies	gastos (*m.*) imprevistos
apportionment of expenses	prorrateo (*m.*) de gastos

VI. Profit. — Beneficio, *m.*

income	ingresos *m. pl.*, renta *f.*
earnings	ganancias *f.*
net, average income	renta (*f.*) neta, media
gross income, gross earnings	renta (*f. sing.*) bruta
gross profit *o* benefit	beneficio (*m.*) bruto
national income	renta (*f.*) nacional
profitability, profit earning capacity	rentabilidad *f.*
yield	rendimiento *m.*

increase in value, appreciation	plusvalía *f.*

VII. Taxes. — Impuestos, *m.*

duty	impuesto *m.*
taxation	imposición *f.*
fiscal charges	gravámenes (*m.*) fiscales
value added tax	impuesto (*m.*) al valor añadido *or* agregado
progressive taxation, graduated tax	impuesto (*m.*) progresivo
income tax	impuesto (*m.*) sobr la renta
land tax	contribución (*f.*) territorial
excise tax	impuesto (*m.*) indirecto
basis of assessment	base (*f.*) del impuesto
taxable income	líquido (*m.*) imponible
fiscal authorities	fisco *m. sing.*, hacienda *f. sing.*
taxation system	régimen (*m.*) fiscal
fiscality	fiscalidad *f.*
tax-free	libre de impuestos
tax exemption	exención (*f.*) *or* exoneración (*f.*) fiscal
taxpayer	contribuyente *m.* y *f.*
tax collector	recaudador (*m.*) de impuestos

COMMERCIAL TERMS — VOCABULARIO (*m.*) COMERCIAL

I. General terms. — Términos (*m.*) generales.

commerce, trade, trading	comercio *m.*
commercial channels	circuito (*m. sing.*) comercial
international trade	comercio (*m.*) internacional
terms of trade	términos (*m.*) del intercambio
free-trade area	zona (*f.*) de libre cambio [*Amer.*, de libre comercio]
import, importation	importación *f.*
importer	importador *m.*
export, exportation	exportación *f.*
exporter	exportador *m.*
customs	aduana *f. sing.*
customs duty	derechos (*m. pl.*) de aduana *or* arancelarios
quota	cupo *m.*, cuota *f.*, contingente *m.*
item	partida *f.*
inland *o* home *o* domestic *o* internal *o* interior trade	comercio (*m.*) nacional *or* interior
foreign *o* external trade	comercio (*m.*) exterior
commercial transaction	operación (*f.*) comercial
manufacturer	fabricante *m.*
middleman	intermediario *m.*
wholesaler	mayorista *m.* y *f.*
retailer	minorista *m.* y *f.*, detallista *m.* y *f.*
dealer	vendedor *m.*
merchant, tradesman	comerciante *m.*
concessionaire, licensed dealer	concesionario *m.*
consumer	consumidor *m.*
client, customer	cliente *m.* y *f.*
stocks	existencias *f.*
purchase	compra *f.*
buyer	comprador *m.*
sale	venta *f.*
bulk sale	venta (*f.*) a granel
wholesale	comercio (*m.*) al por mayor
retail trade	comercio (*m.*) al por menor
cash sale	venta (*f.*) al contado
hire-purchase [U.S., installment plan]	venta (*f.*) a plazos
competition	competencia *f.*
competitor	competidor *m.*
competitive	competitivo, va
unfair competition	competencia (*f.*) desleal
dumping	dumping *m.*
profit margin	margen (*m.*) de beneficio
trademark	marca (*f.*) registrada
registered *o* head office	domicilio (*m.*) social

II. Market. — Mercado, *m.*

Latin-American Free Trade Association	Asociación (*f.*) Latino-americana de Libre Comercio
home market	mercado (*m.*) nacional *or* interior
open market	mercado (*m.*) libre
black market	mercado (*m.*) negro, estraperlo *m.*
monopoly	monopolio *m.*
marketing	comercialización *f.* (of goods), estudio (*m.*) *or* investigación (*f.*) de mercados (market research)
consumption	consumo *m.*
offer	oferta *f.*
demand	demanda *f.*
outlet	salida *f.*

III. Management and organization. — Gestión (*f.*) y organización, *f.*

foresight, forecast	previsión *f.*
plan	plan *m.*
planning	planificación *f.*
programme [U.S., program]	programa *m.*
estimation, estimate, valuation	estimación *f.*
budget	presupuesto *m.*

IV. Accounting, bookkeeping. — Contabilidad, *f.*

accountant, bookkeeper	contable *m.* y *f.*
double-entry, single-entry bookkeeping	contabilidad (*f.*) por partida doble, simple
account book	libro (*m.*) de contabilidad
cashbook	libro (*m.*) de caja
journal	diario *m.*
inventory, stocktaking	inventario *m.*
balance (sheet)	balance *m.*
financial *o* trading year	año (*m.*) *or* ejercicio (*m.*) económico
income and expenditure, receipts and expenditure, output and input	gastos (*m. pl.*) e ingresos
assets	haber *m. sing.*, activo *m. sing.*
liabilities	debe *m. sing* , pasivo *m. sing.*
debit	débito *m.*
cash on hand	efectivo (*m.*) en caja
cash balance	saldo (*m.*) de caja
credit balance	saldo (*m.*) acreedor *or* positivo
debit balance	saldo (*m.*) deudor *or* negativo
turnover, volume of business	volumen (*m.*) de negocios *or* de ventas, facturación *f.*
statement of accounts	estado (*m.*) de cuentas
deficit	déficit *m.*
balance of trade, of payments	balanza (*f.*) comercial, de pagos

V. Price. — Precio, *m.*

cost price	precio (*m.*) de coste
prime cost, first cost *o* price, initial cost *o* price	precio (*m.*) inicial
factory *o* manufacturer's price	precio (*m.*) de fábrica
net price	precio (*m.*) neto
price free on board	precio (*m.*) franco a bordo
purchase, sale price	precio (*m.*) de compra, de venta
wholesale price	precio (*m.*) al por mayor
retail price	precio (*m.*) al por menor
fixed price	precio (*m.*) fijo
guaranteed price	precio (*m.*) garantizado
cash price	precio (*m.*) al contado
piece *o* unit price	precio (*m.*) por unidad
market price	precio (*m.*) de mercado, precio (*m.*) corriente
preferential price	precio (*m.*) de favor
price control	control (*m.*) de precios, intervención *f.*
maximum *o* ceiling price	precio (*m.*) máximo *or* tope
minimum price	precio (*m.*) mínimo
price freeze	bloqueo (*m.*) *or* congelación (*f.*) de precios

price fixing	fijación (*f.*) de los precios
price index	índice (*m.*) de precios
price fall	baja (*f.*) de precios
rise in price	subida (*f.*) *or* aumento (*m.*) *or* alza (*f.*) de precios
all-inclusive	todo comprendido
on a lump-sum basis	a tanto alzado

VI. Payment. — Pago, *m.*

sum	suma *f.*
amount	importe *m.* [*Amer.*, monto, *m.*]
bill [U.S., check]	cuenta *f.*
pro forma invoice	factura (*f.*) pro forma
voucher	comprobante *m.*
receipt	recibo *m.*
advance (payment)	anticipo *m.*, adelanto *m.*
cash payment	pago (*m.*) al contado
deferred payment, payment by instalments	pago (*m.*) a plazos
cash on delivery	entrega (*f.*) contra reembolso
down payment	pago (*m.*) inicial
monthly payment	mensualidad *f.*
payment in kind	pago (*m.*) en especie
payment in specie	pago (*m.*) en metálico
bill of exchange	letra (*f.*) de cambio
promissory note	pagaré *m.*
refund, repayment	reembolso *m.*
payment in arrears, outstanding payment	pago (*m.*) atrasado
remuneration	remuneración *f.*
compensation	indemnización *f.*

ecclesiastical [—əl] adj. REL. Eclesiástico, ca.
ecclesiasticism [i,kli:zi'æstisizəm] n. Clericalismo, *m.*
Ecclesiasticus [i,kli:'æstikəs] n. REL. Eclesiástico, *m.*
echelon ['eʃələn] n. MIL. Escalón, *m.* || Grado, *m.* (grade). || Nivel, *m.* (level).
echelon ['eʃələn] v. tr. Escalonar.
echinite ['ekinait] n. Erizo (*m.*) de mar fósil.
echinoderm [e'kainəu,də:m] n. Equinodermo, *m.*
echinoid [e'kainɔid] n. Equinoideo, *m.*, erizo (*m.*) de mar.
echinus [e'kainəs] n. ZOOL. Equino, *m.*, erizo (*m.*) de mar. || ARCH. Equino, *m.*
— OBSERV. El plural de *echinus* es *echini*.

echo ['ekəu] n. Eco, *m.* || FIG. Eco, *m.*, resonancia, *f.* (sympathetic reaction). | Repetición, *f.*: *his latest book is an echo of his previous one*, su último libro es una repetición del anterior. || — *Echo chamber*, cámara (*f.*) de resonancia. || *Echo sounder*, sonda acústica. || *To cheer to the echo*, ovacionar.
— OBSERV. El plural de *echo* es *echoes*.

echo ['ekəu] v. intr. Resonar, hacer eco. || — *Echoed wave*, onda reflejada. || *The footsteps echoed in the room*, se oía el eco de los pasos en la habitación.
— V. tr. Repetir: *the mountains echoed back his shout*, las montañas repitieron su grito. || Imitar (to imitate). || Adherirse a, hacerse eco de (to second).
éclair ['eikleə*] n. Relámpago, *m.* (cake).
eclampsia [i'klæmpsiə] n. MED. Eclampsia, *f.*
éclat ['eiklɑ:] n. Brillo, *m.* || Éxito (*m.*) clamoroso (great success).
eclectic [ek'lektik] adj./n. Ecléctico, ca.
eclecticism [ek'lektisizəm] n. Eclecticismo, *m.*
eclipse [i'klips] n. ASTR. Eclipse, *m.* || FIG. Eclipse, *m.*
eclipse [i'klips] v. tr. ASTR. Eclipsar. || FIG. Eclipsar, deslucir (to outshine).
ecliptic [i'kliptik] n. ASTR. Eclíptica, *f.*
— Adj. Eclíptico, ca.
eclogue ['eklɔg] n. Égloga, *f.* (poem).
ecological [,ekə'lɔdʒikəl] adj. Ecológico, ca.
ecologist [i:'kɔlədʒist] n. Ecólogo, *m.*
ecology [i:'kɔledʒi] n. Ecología, *f.*
econometrician [i,kɔnəmitriʃən] n. Especialista (*m.* & *f.*) en econometría.
econometrics [i:,kɔnə'metriks] n. Econometría, *f.*
economic [i:,kə'nɔmik] adj. Económico, ca: *economic crisis*, crisis económica; *European Economic Community*, Comunidad Económica Europea.
economical [—əl] adj. Económico, ca: *an economical car*, un coche económico; *an economical person*, una persona económica.
economics [—s] n. Economía, *f.*, economía (*f.*) política (science): *to study economics*, estudiar economía. || Rentabilidad, *f.*: *the economics of advertising*, la rentabilidad de la publicidad. || *School of Economics*, Escuela (*f.*) de Ciencias Económicas.
economist [i'kɔnəmist] n. Economista, *m.* & *f.* || FAM. Persona (*f.*) ahorrativa.
economize [i'kɔnəmaiz] v. tr./intr. Economizar (*on*, en).
economy [i'kɔnəmi] n. Economía, *f.*: *capitalist, planned economy*, economía capitalista, planificada. || Economía, *f.*, ahorro, *m.* (saving): *for economy's sake*, por ahorro. || — *Economy class*, clase económica *or* turista. || *To practise economy*, economizar.
écru (U. S. **ecru**) ['eikru:] adj. Crudo, da (colour).
ecstasize ['ekstəsaiz] v. tr. Extasiar.
— V. intr. Extasiarse.
ecstasy ['ekstəsi] n. Éxtasis, *f.*: *to go into ecstasy*, caer en éxtasis. || Arrebato, *m.*: *in an ecstasy of love*, en un arrebato de amor. || *To go into ecstasies over*, extasiarse ante.
ecstatic [eks'tætik] adj. Extático, ca.
ecstatically [—əli] adv. Con éxtasis.
ectoderm ['ektəudə:m] n. BIOL. Ectodermo, *m.*
ectoparasite ['ektəu'pærəsait] n. Ectoparásito, *m.*
ectoparasitic ['ektəu,pærə'sitik] adj. Ectoparásito, ta.
ectoplasm ['ektəuplæzəm] n. Ectoplasma, *m.*
Ecuador [,ekwə'dɔ:] pr. n. GEOGR. Ecuador, *m.*
— OBSERV. The official name of this country is *El Ecuador*.

Ecuadoran [—rən] or **Ecuadorean** or **Ecuadorian** [—riən] adj./n. Ecuatoriano, na.
ecumene ['i:kjumi:n] n. Ecumene, *m.*
ecumenical [,i:kju'menikəl] adj. Ecuménico, ca.
ecumenicalism [—izəm] n. Ecumenismo, *m.*
ecumenism [i:'kju:menizəm] n. Ecumenismo, *m.*
eczema ['eksimə] n. MED. Eczema, *m.*
eczematous [ek'semətəs] adj. MED. Eczematoso, sa.
edacious [i'deiʃəs] adj. Voraz, devorador, ra.
edacity [i'dæsiti] n. Voracidad, *f.*
eddy ['edi] n. Remolino, *m.* (whirling movement). || Contracorriente, *f.* (countercurrent). || *Eddy current*, corriente parásita, corriente (*f.*) de Foucault.
eddy ['edi] v. intr. Arremolinarse, formar remolinos.
edelweiss ['eidlvais] n. BOT. Edelweiss, *m.*
edema [i'di:mə] n. MED. Edema, *m.*
edematous [i'demətəs] adj. MED. Edematoso, sa.
Eden ['i:dn] n. Edén, *m.* (garden).
Edenic [i'denik] adj. Edénico, ca.
edentate [i'denteit] adj. Desdentado, da.
— N. ZOOL. Desdentado, *m.*
edge [edʒ] n. Borde, *m.*: *the edge of a cliff, of a table*, el borde de un acantilado, de una mesa; *he was on the edge of disaster*, estaba al borde del desastre. || Orilla, *f.*, borde, *m.* (of water): *at the edge of the pond*, a orillas *or* en la orilla del estanque. || Canto, *m.* (vertical part): *the top of the table is red and the edge yellow*, la parte superior de la mesa es roja y el canto amarillo. || Filo, *m.*, corte, *m.* (of cutting tools). || Margen, *m.* (of page). || Límite, *m.*, linde, *m.* (limit). || Extremidad, *f.* (outside part, farthest part). || Borde, *m.* (border). || Cresta, *f.* (of a mountain). || Línea (*f.*) saliente (of nose). || Labio, *m.* (of a wound). || Limbo, *m.* (of sun, moon). || Arista, *f.*: *a cube has twelve edges*, un cubo tiene doce aristas. || Ángulo, *m.* (angle). || Canto, *m.* (of a coin, book). || FIG. Ventaja, *f.*: *to have the edge on s.o.*, llevar ventaja a alguien. || Afueras, *f. sing.* (of town). || — *A knife with a sharp* o *keen edge*, un cuchillo bien afilado. || *Blunt edge*, canto, *m.* (of a knife). || *Cutting edge*, corte, *m.*, filo, *m.* || FIG. *His nerves are on edge*, tiene los nervios de punta. || AVIAC. *Leading edge*, borde (*m.*) de ataque. || *Milled edge*, cordoncillo, *m.* || FIG. *Not to put too fine an edge on it...*, hablando en plata... || *To be on edge*, estar de canto (to be edgeways), tener los nervios de punta (to be nervous). || FIG. *To give s.o. the sharp edge of one's tongue*, echarle una bronca a alguien. || *To put an edge on a blade*, afilar una hoja. || FIG. *To set one's nerves on edge*, ponerle a uno los nervios de punta. | *To set one's teeth on edge*, darle dentera a uno. || *To stand a board on edge*, poner una tabla de canto. || *To take the edge off*, embotar (to blunt), acallar (one's appetite), embotar (one's feelings), quitarle fuerza a (an argument). || *Words with an edge to them*, palabras (*f.*) mordaces.
edge [edʒ] v. tr. Bordear: *trees edged the lake*, unos árboles bordeaban el lago. || Afilar (to sharpen). || Ribetear (in sewing). || Mover *or* meter *or* acercar (etc.) poco a poco *or* con cuidado: *they edged the piano back to the wall*, acercaron el piano a la pared con cuidado. || — FIG. *To edge on*, incitar. | *To edge one's way through*, abrirse paso poco a poco. | *To edge o.s. in*, introducirse poco a poco. | *To edge out*, eliminar poco a poco, conseguir eliminar.
— V. intr. Andar de lado (to move sideways). || Avanzar con cautela (to move carefully): *he edged along the top of the wall*, avanzaba con cautela por el muro. || — *To edge away*, alejarse poco a poco. || *To edge in*, abrirse paso poco a poco, conseguir meterse. || *To edge up*, trepar lentamente *or* con cuidado (to climb). || *To edge up to s.o.*, acercarse cautelosamente a alguien.
edgebone ['edʒbəun] n. Cadera, *f.* (aitchbone).
edged [edʒd] adj. Cortante (blade). || Ribeteado, da (in sewing).
edge tool ['edʒtu:l] n. Herramienta (*f.*) cortante.
edgeless [edʒlis] adj. Embotado, da (blunt).
edgeways ['edʒweiz] or **edgewise** ['edʒwaiz] adv. De lado, de costado (sideways). || De canto (on end). || FIG. *Not to be able to get a word in edgeways*, no poder meter baza.

edging [edʒiŋ] n. Orla, *f.*, ribete, *m.* (in sewing). || Borde, *m.* (of path).
edgy [edʒi] adj. Afilado, da. || FIG. Nervioso, sa.
edible [ˊedibl] adj. Comestible (eatable).
— Pl. n. Comestibles, *m.*
edict [ˊi:dikt] n. Edicto, *m.*
edification [ˏedifiˊkeiʃən] n. Edificación, *f.*
edificatory [ˊedifiˏkeitəri] adj. Edificante.
edifice [ˊedifis] n. Edificio, *m.* [imponente]. || FIG. Estructura, *f.*, edificio, *m.* (of ideas, science, etc.).
edify [ˊedifai] v. tr. Edificar: *to edify by one's example*, edificar con el ejemplo.
edifying [—iŋ] adj. Edificante.
edile [ˊi:dail] n. Edil, *m.* (Roman magistrate).
Edinburgh [ˊedinbərə] pr. n. GEOGR. Edimburgo, *m.*
edit [ˊedit] v. tr. Preparar para la imprenta (to prepare for printing). || Redactar (to prepare articles). || Dirigir (to direct a newspaper). || Corregir (to correct). || Montar (film). || Adaptar (to adapt). || Quitar, suprimir (to cut out).
editing [—iŋ] n. Redacción, *f.* (writing). || Dirección, *f.* (of newspaper). || Corrección, *f.*, revisión, *f.* (correction). || Montaje, *m.* (of film).
edition [iˊdiʃən] n. Edición, *f.*: *first edition*, primera edición; *paperback edition*, edición en rústica. || Tirada, *f.*: *an edition of 50 000*, una tirada de 50 000. || FIG. Versión, *f.*: *he is a smaller edition of his brother*, es una versión de su hermano en más pequeño.
editio princeps [iˊdiʃiəuˊprinseps] n. Edición (*f.*) príncipe.
— OBSERV. El plural de *editio princeps* es *editiones principes*.
editor [ˊeditə*] n. Redactor (*m.*) jefe (head of editorial staff). || Director, *m.*: *editor of a dictionary*, director de un diccionario. || *Editor's note*, nota (*f.*) de la redacción.
editorial [ˏediˊtɔ:riəl] adj. Editorial. || De la dirección || — *Editorial staff*, redacción, *f.* || U.S. *Editorial writer*, editorialista, *m.* & *f.*
— N. Editorial, *m.*, artículo (*m.*) de fondo (article).
editorialist [ˏediˊtɔ:riəlist] n. Editorialista, *m.* & *f.*
editor in chief [ˊeditərinˊtʃi:f] n. Redactor (*m.*) jefe, jefe (*m.*) de redacción.
editorship [ˊeditəʃip] n. Dirección, *f.*: *under the editorship of*, bajo la dirección de. || Redacción, *f.* (in a publishing house). || Cargo (*m.*) de redactor jefe (of a newspaper).
educable [ˊedjukəbl] adj. Educable.
educate [ˊedjukeit] v. tr. Educar: *he was educated in France*, fue educado en Francia. || Dar carrera de: *they educated their son for the law*, dieron a su hijo la carrera de derecho. || Instruir: *to educate s.o. in elementary psychology*, instruir a alguien en psicología elemental. || Educar (one's palate, etc.). || Amaestrar (an animal).
educated [—id] adj. Cultivado, da; culto, ta: *he seems very educated*, parece muy culto. || Instruido, da: *educated in the art of...*, instruido en el arte de... || Culto, ta: *educated speech*, lenguaje culto. || Bien educado, da (well-bred). || Amaestrado, da animal).
education [ˏedjuˊkeiʃən] n. Enseñanza, *f.* (schooling, teaching): *primary, secondary education*, primera, segunda enseñanza. || Educación, *f.* (upbringing): *hunting was part of his education*, la caza formaba parte de su educación. || Formación, *f.*: *they gave me a good education at that school*, recibí una buena formación en esa escuela. || Instrucción, *f.* (in specific field): *education in the art of ...*, instrucción en el arte de... || Cultura, *f.* (culture). || Amaestramiento, *m.* (of animals). || — *Further education*, estudios universitarios, enseñanza superior. || *Ministry of Education*, Ministerio (*m.*) de Educación. || *Physical education*, educación física. || *To have a classical education*, haber hecho estudios clásicos.
educational [ˏedjuˊkeiʃənl] adj. Educativo, va: *new educational methods*, nuevos métodos educativos; *an educational film*, una película educativa. || Docente (teaching): *educational centre*, centro docente.
educationalist [ˏedjuˊkeiʃnəlist] or **educationist** [ˏedjuˊkeiʃənist] n. Especialista (*m.*) en pedagogía.
educative [ˊedjukətiv] adj. Educativo, va.
educator [ˊedjukeitə*] n. Educador, ra. || Especialista (*m.* & *f.*) en pedagogía (educationist).
educe [iˊdju:s] v. tr. Deducir, sacar.
educt [ˊi:dʌkt] n. CHEM. Producto (*m.*) de descomposición. || FIG. Deducción, *f.*
eduction [iˊdʌkʃən] n. TECH. Evacuación, *f.*, descarga, *f.* | Escape, *m.* (of steam). || FIG. Deducción, *f.*
edulcorate [iˊdʌlkəreit] v. tr. Edulcorar, endulzar.
Edward [ˊedwəd] pr. n. Eduardo, *m.*
Edwardian [edˊwɔ:djən] adj. Eduardiano, na.
eel [i:l] n. ZOOL. Anguila, *f.* (fish).
eelworm [ˊi:lwə:m] n. ZOOL. Anguílula, *f.*
e'en [i:n] adv. See EVEN.
e'er [ɛə*] adv. See EVER.
eerie or **eery** [ˊiəri] adj. Misterioso, sa (mysterious). || Horripilante (frightening). || Extraño, ña (strange).
efface [iˊfeis] v. tr. Borrar (to rub out). || FIG. Borrar: *to efface a memory*, borrar un recuerdo. | Eclipsar (to outshine). || *To efface o.s.*, conseguir pasar desapercibido.
effaceable [—əbl] adj. Borrable.
effacement [—mənt] n. Borradura, *f.* || FIG. Desaparición, *f.*
effect [iˊfekt] n. Efecto, *m.*: *cause and effect*, causa y efecto; *his words had no effect on her*, sus palabras no le hicieron ningún efecto; *of no effect*, sin efecto; *the Compton effect*, el efecto Compton. || Efecto, *m.*, resultado, *m.*, consecuencia, *f.* (result). || Impresión, *f.*, efecto, *m.*: *clothes which create an effect of youthfulness*, ropa que da impresión de juventud. || Fin, *m.*, propósito, *m.*, intención, *f.* (purpose): *to speak to that effect*, hablar con esa intención. || Sentido, *m.*, tenor, *m.* (sense). || — Pl. Efectos, *m.*: *special effects*, efectos especiales; *sound effects*, efectos sonoros; *personal effects*, efectos personales. || — *For effect*, para causar efecto, para impresionar. || *In effect*, en efecto, en realidad (in fact), vigente (a law). || *No effects*, sin fondos (on a cheque). || *Or words to that effect*, o algo por el estilo. || *Side effect*, efecto secundario. || *Striving after effect*, efectismo, *m.* || *To be in effect*, estar vigente (a law). || *To bring* o *to put into effect*, poner en vigor (a law), aplicar, empezar a aplicar (a rule). || *To carry into effect*, llevar a cabo, realizar, ejecutar. || *To create a good, a bad effect*, ser de buen, de mal efecto. || *To give effect to*, hacer efectivo. || *To go into effect*, entrar en vigor. || *To have no effect*, no dar resultado. || *To have the desired effect*, producir el efecto deseado. || *To no effect*, en vano, inútilmente, sin resultado. || *To take effect*, surtir efecto (medicine, etc.), entrar en vigor, tener efecto (law, timetable, etc.). || *To the effect that...*, con el propósito de... (with the intention of), en el sentido de que... (in order that), especificando que... (specifying that). || *To the same effect* o *to that effect*, por el estilo, en el mismo sentido. || *To this effect*, con este fin. || *With effect from*, con efecto a partir de, que surte efecto a partir de.
effect [iˊfekt] v. tr. Efectuar, realizar, llevar a cabo: *the crossing was effected without difficulty*, la travesía se realizó sin dificultad. || Hacer (saving).
effective [iˊfektiv] adj. Eficaz: *those pills are very effective*, esas píldoras son muy eficaces. || Efectivo, va; real: *effective power*, potencia efectiva. || Impresionante (striking). || Vigente, en vigor, en vigencia (in force): *the rules effective at the present time*, las normas vigentes en la actualidad. || MIL. Disponible: *effective troops*, tropas disponibles. || — TECH. *Effective capacity, force*, capacidad (*f.*), fuerza (*f.*) útil. || *To become effective*, entrar en vigor (law), [empezar a] aplicarse (measures).
— Pl. n. Efectivos, *m.*
effectiveness [—nis] n. Eficacia, *f.* (efficiency). || Efecto, *m.* (effect). || Vigencia, *f.* (of a law).
effectual [iˊfektʃuəl] adj. Eficaz. || Válido, da (valid).
effectuate [iˊfektjueit] v. tr. Efectuar, realizar, ejecutar.
effectuation [ifektjuˊeiʃən] n. Realización, *f.*, ejecución, *f.* (execution).
effeminacy [iˊfeminəsi] n. Afeminación, *f.*, afeminamiento, *m.*
effeminate [iˊfeminit] adj. Afeminado, da.
— N. Afeminado, *m.*
effeminate [iˊfemineit] v. tr. Afeminar.
— V. intr. Afeminarse.
efferent [ˊefərənt] adj. Eferente: *efferent blood vessels*, vasos eferentes.
effervesce [ˏefəˊves] v. intr. Estar *or* entrar en efervescencia (to fizz). | Ser efervescente (to be effervescent). || FIG. Hervir, bullir (in anger). || FIG. *To effervesce with joy*, rebosar de alegría.
effervescence [—ns] or **effervescency** [—nsi] n. Efervescencia, *f.*
effervescent [ˏefəˊvesnt] adj. Efervescente.
effete [eˊfi:t] adj. Agotado, da (land). || Ineficaz, estéril, vano, na (ineffective). || Gastado, da (worn-out). || Agotado, da (exhausted). || Degenerado, da (degenerate). || Decadente (decadent).
efficacious [ˏefiˊkeiʃəs] adj. Eficaz.
efficaciousness [—nis] or **efficacy** [ˊefikəsi] n. Eficacia, *f.*
efficiency [iˊfiʃənsi] n. Eficacia, *f.*, eficiencia, *f.*: *he works with great efficiency*, trabaja con mucha eficacia. || Rendimiento, *m.*: *the efficiency of a machine*, el rendimiento de una máquina.
efficient [iˊfiʃənt] adj. Eficaz, eficiente: *an efficient secretary*, una secretaria eficaz. || Eficaz (effective). || De buen rendimiento (machine). || *Efficient cause*, causa (*f.*) eficiente.
effigy [ˊefidʒi] n. Efigie, *f.*: *to burn s.o. in effigy*, quemar a alguien en efigie.
effloresce [ˏeflɔ:ˊres] v. intr. BOT. Florecer (to blossom).
efflorescence [—ns] n. CHEM. Eflorescencia, *f.* || BOT. Florecimiento, *m*
efflorescent [—nt] adj. CHEM. Eflorescente. || BOT. Floreciente.
effluence [ˊefluəns] n. Emanación, *f.*
effluent [ˊefluənt] n. Chorro, *m.*
effluvium [eˊflu:vjəm] n. Efluvio, *m.*
— OBSERV. El plural de *effluvium* es *effluvia* o *effluviums*.
efflux [ˊeflʌks] n. Flujo, *m.* (of liquid). || Escape, *m.* (of gas). || Transcurso, *m.* (of time).
effort [ˊefət] n. Esfuerzo, *m.*: *to make an effort to*, hacer un esfuerzo para; *I spared no effort*, no escatimé esfuerzos; *without effort*, sin esfuerzo; *wasted efforts*, esfuerzos vanos. || FAM. Obra, *f.*: *have you seen his last effort?*, ¿has visto su última obra? | Tentativa, *f.* (attempt). || PHYS. Fuerza (*f.*) efectiva.

effortless [—lis] adj. Fácil, sin ningún esfuerzo.
effraction [iˈfrækʃən] n. Efracción, *f.*
effrontery [iˈfrʌntəri] n. Descaro, *m.*, desfachatez, *f.*, desvergüenza, *f.*, caradura, *f.*, frescura, *f.*
effulgence [eˈfʌldʒəns] n. Refulgencia, *f.*, resplandor, *m.*
effulgent [eˈfʌldʒənt] adj. Refulgente, resplandeciente.
effuse [eˈfju:z] v. tr. Verter, derramar (to pour out). || Difundir (to spread).
— V. intr. Derramarse.
effusion [iˈfju:ʒən] n. Efusión, *f.* (shedding). || Fig. Efusión, *f.*, desahogo, *m.*, expansión, *f.* (of emotion). || Med. Derrame, *m.* || Chem. Efusión, *f.*
effusive [iˈfju:siv] adj. Efusivo, va.
effusiveness [—nis] n. Carácter (*m.*) efusivo.
e.g. [ˈi:ˈdʒi:] abbrev. v.g., verbi gratia, verbigracia.
— Observ. E.g. es la abreviatura de *exempli gratia.*
egalitarian [iˌgæliˈtɛəriən] adj./n. Igualitario, ria.
Egeria [iˈdʒiəriə] pr. n. Egeria, *f.*
egg [eg] n. Huevo, *m.*: *fried egg*, huevo frito. || Fam. Bomba, *f.* (bomb). || — Fig. fam. *A bad egg*, una mala persona. | *A good egg*, una buena persona. | *As sure as eggs*, tan cierto como que dos y dos son cuatro. || *Bad egg*, huevo podrido. || *Boiled egg*, huevo pasado por agua. || *Darning egg*, huevo de zurcir. || *Easter egg*, huevo de Pascuas. || *Hard-boiled egg*, huevo duro. || *In the egg*, en embrión. || *New-laid egg*, huevo fresco. || *Poached egg*, huevo escalfado. || *Scrambled eggs*, huevos revueltos. || *Soft-boiled egg*, huevo pasado por agua. || *To boil an egg*, pasar un huevo por agua. || Fig. *To kill the goose that lays the golden egg*, matar la gallina de los huevos de oro. || *To lay an egg*, poner un huevo. || Fig. *To put all one's eggs in one basket*, jugárselo todo a una carta. | *To tread on eggs*, andar *or* ir pisando huevos.
egg [eg] v. tr. *To egg on*, incitar.
eggbeater [ˈegˌbi:tə] n. U. S. Batidor (*m.*) de huevos.
egg cell [ˈegsel] n. Med. Óvulo, *m.*
eggcup [ˈegkʌp] n. Huevera, *f.*
egg flip [ˈegflip] n. "Flip", *m.*, ponche (*m.*) de huevo.
egghead [ˈeghed] n. Fam. Intelectual, *m.* | Científico, *m.*
eggnog [ˈegnɔg] n. "Flip", *m.*, ponche (*m.*) de huevo.
eggplant [ˈegplɑ:nt] n. Bot. Berenjena, *f.*
egg-shaped [ˈegʃeipt] adj. Oviforme, ovoide.
eggshell [ˈegʃel] n. Cascarón (*m.*) de huevo.
— Adj. Frágil.
egg-whisk [ˈegwisk] n. Batidor (*m.*) de huevos.
egg white [ˈegwait] n. Clara (*f.*) de huevo.
egis [ˈi:dʒis] n. See aegis.
eglantine [ˈegləntain] n. Bot. Escaramujo, *m.*
ego [ˈegəu] n. Phil. Ego, *m.*, yo, *m.* || Fam. Amor (*m.*) propio (self-esteem). | Egoísmo, *m.* (selfishness).
egocentric [ˌegəuˈsentrik] or **egocentrical** [—əl] adj./n. Egocéntrico, ca.
egocentricity [ˌegəusenˈtrisiti] or **egocentrism** [ˌegəuˈsentrizəm] n. Egocentrismo, *m.*
egoism [ˈegəuizəm] n. Egoísmo, *m.*
egoist [ˈegəuist] n. Egoísta, *m.* & *f.*
egoistic [ˌegəuˈistik] or **egoistical** [—əl] adj. Egoísta.
egotism [ˈegəutizəm] n. Egoísmo, *m.* (selfishness). || Egotismo, *m.* (self-importance).
egotist [ˈegəutist] n. Egoísta, *m.* & *f.* (selfish person). || Egotista, *m.* & *f.* (self-important person).
egotistic [ˌegəuˈtistik] or **egotistical** [—əl] adj. Egoísta (selfish). || Egotista (self-important).
egregious [iˈgri:dʒəs] adj. Notorio, ria (flagrant). || Atroz (atrocious). || Extraordinario, ria (extraordinary). || Enorme (error).
egregiousness [—nis] n. Notoriedad, *f.* (notoriety). || Atrocidad, *f.* (atrocity). || Enormidad, *f.* (of an error).
egress [ˈi:gres] or **egression** [iˈgreʃən] n. Salida, *f.* (exit). || Astr. Emersión, *f.*
egret [ˈi:gret] n. Zool. Garceta, *f.* (bird).
Egypt [ˈi:dʒipt] pr. n. Geogr. Egipto, *m.*
Egyptian [iˈdʒipʃən] adj./n. Egipcio, cia.
Egyptologist [ˌi:dʒipˈtɔlədʒist] n. Egiptólogo, ga.
Egyptology [ˌi:dʒipˈtɔlədʒi] n. Egiptología, *f.*
eh! [ei] interj. ¡Eh!
eider [ˈaidə*] n. Eider, *m.*, pato (*m.*) de flojel (bird).
eiderdown [ˈaidədaun] n. Edredón, *m.*
eight [eit] adj. Ocho.
— N. Ocho, *m.*: *the eight of clubs*, el ocho de trébol. || Ocho, *f. pl.* (time): *I'll come at eight*, vendré a las ocho; *five past eight*, las ocho y cinco. || Sp. Equipo (*m.*) de ocho (team). || Ocho, *m.* (boat). || Carrera (*f.*) para ocho (race). || — *A boy of eight*, un niño de ocho años. || Fig. *To have had one over the eight*, llevar una copa de más.
eight ball [—bɔ:l] n. U. S. Sp. Bola (*f.*) negra (in pool). || Fig. fam. *To be behind the eight ball*, estar en un apuro.
eighteen [ˈeiˈti:n] adj. Dieciocho, diez y ocho.
— N. Dieciocho, *m.*, diez y ocho, *m.*
eighteenth [ˈeiˈti:nθ] adj. Decimoctavo, va (ordinal). || Dieciochavo, va (partitive): *eighteenth part*, dieciochava parte. || *The eighteenth century*, el siglo XVIII [dieciocho].
— N. Decimoctavo, va; diez y ocho, *m.* & *f.*, dieciocho, *m.* & *f.* (in a series). || Dieciochavo, *m*, dieciochava (*f.*) parte (fraction). || Diez y ocho, dieciocho: *John XVIII* (*the eighteenth*), Juan XVIII [diez y ocho]. || Dieciocho, *m.*, día (*m.*) dieciocho (date): *the eighteenth of January*, el dieciocho de enero.

eightfold [ˈeitfəuld] adj. Multiplicado por ocho.
— Adv. Ocho veces.
eighth [eitθ] adj. Octavo, va.
— Adv. En octavo lugar. || *To come eighth*, salir el octavo (in a competition).
— N. Octavo, va (in a series). || Octavo, *m.*, octava parte, *f.* (fraction). || Ocho, *m.*, día (*m.*) ocho (date): *he is coming on the eighth*, viene el día ocho. || Octavo: *Henry VIII* (*the eighth*), Enrique VIII [octavo]. || Mus. Octava, *f.*
eighth note [—nəut] n. U.S. Mus. Corchea, *f.*
eight hundred [ˈeitˈhʌndrəd] adj. Ochocientos, tas.
— N. Ochocientos, *m.*
eight hundredth [—θ] adj./n. Octingentésimo, ma.
eightieth [ˈeitiiθ] adj. Octogésimo, ma.
— N. Octogésimo, ma; ochenta, *m.* & *f.* (in eightieh position). || Octogésimo, *m.*, octogésima parte, *f.* (fraction).
— Observ. When the word *eightieth* means "in eightieth position" it is more often translated by *ochenta* than by *octogésimo.*
eighty [ˈeiti] adj. Ochenta.
— N. Ochenta, *m.* || — Pl. Años (*m.*) ochenta: *in the eighties*, en los años ochenta. || *She is in her eighties*, tiene unos ochenta años.
eikon [ˈaikən] n. Icono, *m.* (ikon).
einsteinium [ˈainstainjəm] n. Chem. Einstenio, *m.*
Eire [ˈɛərə] pr. n. Geogr. Eire, *m.*
either [ˈaiðə* U.S., ˈi:ðə*] adj. Cada, ambos (both): *there were cars parked on either side of the street*, había coches aparcados en cada lado *or* en ambos lados de la calle. || Cualquiera de los dos: *either of the tables will do*, cualquiera de las dos mesas valdrá. || Ninguno de los dos (with negation): *I can't find either book*, no encuentro ninguno de los dos libros.
— Pron. Cualquiera de los dos, uno u otro: *you can use either of them*, te puedes servir de cualquiera de los dos. || Ninguno de los dos, ni uno ni otro (with negation): *I didn't see either of them*, no vi ni a uno ni a otro. || *Either of us*, cualquiera de nosotros.
— Adv. Tampoco: *I don't like him or his family or his friends either*, no me gusta él, ni su familia, ni sus amigos tampoco; *I can't find my pencil either*, no encuentro mi lápiz tampoco.
— Conj. *Either... or*, o ... o: *either he goes or I go*, o se va él o me voy yo.
ejaculate [iˈdʒækjuleit] v. tr. Exclamar, proferir de repente (to exclaim). || Lanzar (a cry). || Eyacular (semen).
ejaculation [iˌdʒækjuˈleiʃən] n. Exclamación, *f.* (exclamation). || Jaculatoria, *f.* (prayer). || Eyaculación, *f.* (of semen).
ejaculatory [iˈdʒæljulətəri] adj. Exclamatorio, ria. || Jaculatorio, ria (prayer).
eject [idˈʒeikt] v. tr. Expulsar (flames, cartridge, etc.). || Expulsar, echar: *they ejected the demonstrators*, expulsaron a los manifestantes. || Desahuciar (a tenant). || Expulsar (from a party, a job, etc.). || Eyectar, expeler (from a plane, etc.).
ejecta [iˈ:dʒektə] pl. n. Deyecciones, *f.* (of volcano). || Materias (*f.*) expulsadas.
ejection [iˈdʒekʃən] n. Expulsión, *f.* || Desahucio, *m.* (of a tenant). || *Ejection seat*, asiento (*m.*) eyectable *or* lanzable.
ejectment [iˈdʒektmənt] n. Expulsión, *f.* || Desahucio, *m.* (of tenants).
ejector [iˈdʒektə*] n. Eyector, *m.* (of firearm). || *Ejector seat*, asiento (*m.*) eyectable *or* lanzable.
eke [i:k] v. tr. Escatimar, hacer durar (to make last): *to eke out the provisions*, escatimar los víveres. || Suplir las deficiencias de, complementar (one's salary, etc.). || *To eke out a livelihood*, ganarse la vida a duras penas.
el [el] n. U.S. Ferrocarril (*m.*) elevado.
elaborate [iˈlæbərit] adj. Complicado, da (complicated). || Detallado, da (detailed). || Trabajado, da (style, artistic works). || Primoroso, sa (decoration). || Rebuscado, da (affected). || De muchos platos (meal).
elaborate [iˈlæbəreit] v. tr. Elaborar (to produce). || Elaborar: *to elaborate a plan*, elaborar un proyecto. || Ampliar, desarrollar (to enlarge upon, to develop).
— V. intr. Explicarse (to explain o.s.). || Explicarse con muchos detalles (in great detail). || — *To elaborate on*, explicar con más detalles. || *To refuse to elaborate*, negarse a dar más detalles.
elaborately [iˈlæbəritli] adv. Con cuidado, cuidadosamente (carefully). || De modo complicado, complicadamente. || Con detalles, detalladamente.
elaborateness [iˈlæbəritnis] n. Esmero, *m.* cuidado, *m.* (care). || Complejidad, *f.* (of a mechanism).
elaboration [iˈlæbəˈreiʃən] n. Explicación, *f.* (of texts, etc.). || Elaboración, *f.* (of a plan). || Complicación, *f.*
eland [ˈi:lənd] n. Zool. Alce (*m.*) africano.
élan vital [eiˈlɑ̃:ŋvi:ˈtæl] n. Impulso, *m.*, elan (*m.*) vital (vital force).
elapse [iˈlæps] v. intr. Pasar, transcurrir (time).
elastic [iˈlæstik] adj. Elástico, ca: *gases are very elastic*, los gases son muy elásticos. || Fig. Elástico, ca; flexible: *an elastic plan*, un proyecto elástico. || — *Elastic band*, goma [elástica]. || *Elastic limit*, límite (*m.*) de elasticidad, límite elástico.
— N. Elástico, *m.*
elasticity [ˌelæsˈtisiti] n. Elasticidad, *f.* || Fig. Elasticidad, *f.*, flexibilidad, *f.*

elate [i'leit] v. tr. Regocijar: *she was elated at her triumph*, su triunfo le regocijó.
elated [—id] adj. De regocijo, de alegría (cry, etc.).
elaterid [i'lætərid] adj. ZOOL. Elatérido, da.
elation [i'leiʃən] n. Regocijo, *m.*, júbilo, *m.*
Elba ['elbə] pr. n. GEOGR. Elba, *f.* (island).
Elbe ['elbə] pr. n. GEOGR. Elba, *m.* (river).
elbow ['elbəu] n. Codo, *m.* (of arm). ‖ Codillo, *m.* (of animals). ‖ Recodo, *m.* (bend in road). ‖ Codo, *m.* (in pipe). ‖ — FAM. *At one's elbow*, al alcance de la mano. ‖ *Out at elbows*, raído, da (clothes), desharrapado, da (person). ‖ FIG. *To bend* o *to crook* o *to lift the elbow*, empinar el codo (to drink). | *To be up to the elbows in work*, estar agobiado de trabajo. ‖ *To lean one's elbows on*, apoyar los codos en, acodarse en. ‖ FIG. *To rub elbows with*, codearse con.
elbow ['elbəu] v. tr. Dar un codazo a: *he elbowed him in the stomach*, le dio un codazo en el estómago. ‖ Empujar con el codo (to push). ‖ Apartar con el codo (to push aside). ‖ *To elbow one's way through the crowd*, abrirse paso a codazos entre la muchedumbre.
— V. intr. Abrirse paso a codazos. ‖ Formar un codo or recodo.
elbow grease [—gri:s] n. FIG. Fuerza (*f.*) de puños, energía, *f.*
elbowroom [—rum] n. FIG. Sitio, *m.*, espacio, *m.* (space). | Libertad (*f.*) de acción, campo (*m.*) libre (freedom to act).
elder ['eldə*] adj. Mayor: *his elder daughter*, su hija mayor. ‖ *Pliny the Elder*, Plinio el Viejo.
— N. Mayor, *m.*: *respect for one's elders*, respeto a los mayores. ‖ Anciano, *m.* (of a village, tribe, etc.). ‖ REL. Anciano, *m.* ‖ BOT. Saúco, *m.* (tree). ‖ *He is two years my elder*, es dos años mayor que yo.
elderberry ['eldə,beri] n. BOT. Baya (*f.*) del saúco (fruit). | Saúco, *m.* (tree).
elderly ['eldəli] adj. Mayor, de edad. ‖ — *Elderly people*, la gente mayor. ‖ *To be getting elderly*, ir para viejo.
eldest ['eldist] adj. Mayor: *John is the eldest of the children*, Juan es el mayor de los niños.
El Dorado [,eldə'rɑ:dəu] pr. n. Eldorado, *m.*
Eleanor ['elinə*] pr. n. Leonor, *f.*
elecampane [,elikæm'pein] n. BOT. Helenio, *m.*
elect [i'lekt] adj. Elegido, da (chosen). ‖ Electo, ta: *the President-elect*, el Presidente electo.
— Pl. n. *The elect*, los elegidos, *m.*
elect [i'lekt] v. tr. Elegir: *to elect a chairman*, elegir a un presidente; *he elected to leave*, eligió marcharse.
— V. intr. Elegir.
election [i'lekʃən] n. Elección, *f.* ‖ — *Election returns*, resultados (*m. pl.*) electorales. ‖ *Election time*, periodo (*m.*) electoral. ‖ *General election*, elecciones generales. ‖ *To call* o *to hold an election*, convocar elecciones. ‖ *To stand for an election*, presentar su candidatura, presentarse a una elección.
electioneer [i'lekʃə'niə*] v. intr. Hacer campaña electoral.
electioneering [—riŋ] n. Campaña (*f.*) electoral (campaign). ‖ Maniobras (*f. pl.*) electorales (election rigging).
elective [i'lektiv] adj. Electivo, va: *an elective post*, un puesto electivo. ‖ Electoral: *an elective system, body*, un sistema, un cuerpo electoral. ‖ U.S. Facultativo, va (study). ‖ *Elective affinity*, afinidad electiva.
— N. U.S. Asignatura (*f.*) facultativa.
elector [i'lektə*] n. Elector, ra. ‖ HIST. Elector, *m.*
electoral [i'lektərəl] adj. Electoral. ‖ — U.S. *Electoral college*, colegio (*m.*) electoral. ‖ *Electoral roll*, censo (*m.*) electoral.
electorate [i'lektərit] n. Electorado, *m.* ‖ Distrito (*m.*) electoral (district).
Electra [i'lektrə] pr. n. Electra, *f.*
electress [i'lektris] n. Electriz, *f.*
electric [i'lektrik] adj. Eléctrico, ca: *electric guitar*, guitarra eléctrica. ‖ FIG. Cargado de electricidad, muy tenso, sa (atmosphere). ‖ — *Electric appliances*, aparatos eléctricos. ‖ *Electric blanket*, manta eléctrica. ‖ *Electric blue*, azul eléctrico. ‖ *Electric chair*, silla eléctrica. ‖ *Electric cooker*, cocina eléctrica. ‖ *Electric eye*, célula fotoeléctrica. ‖ *Electric fixtures*, instalación eléctrica. ‖ *Electric generator*, electrógeno, *m.* ‖ *Electric heating*, calefacción eléctrica. ‖ *Electric light*, luz eléctrica. ‖ *Electric lighting*, alumbrado eléctrico. ‖ *Electric motor*, motor eléctrico, electromotor, *m.* ‖ *Electric pump*, electrobomba, *f.* ‖ *Electric ray*, torpedo, *m.* (fish). ‖ *Electric razor* o *shaver*, maquinilla de afeitar eléctrica. ‖ *Electric shock*, electrochoque, *m.* ‖ *Electric tape*, cinta aisladora. ‖ *Electric welding*, soldadura eléctrica. ‖ *Electric wiring*, instalación eléctrica.
electrical [—əl] adj. Eléctrico, ca. ‖ FIG. Cargado de electricidad, muy tenso, sa (atmosphere). ‖ — *Electrical engineer*, ingeniero electrotécnico. ‖ *Electrical engineering*, electrotecnia, *f.*, ingeniería eléctrica. ‖ *Electrical household appliances*, aparatos electrodomésticos. ‖ *Electrical supplies*, material eléctrico.
electrically [—əli] adv. Por electricidad.
electrician [ilek'triʃən] n. Electricista, *m.* & *f.*
electricity [ilek'trisiti] n. Electricidad, *f.*: *static electricity*, electricidad estática.
electrification [i,lektrifi'keiʃən] n. Electrificación, *f.*
electrify [i'lektrifai] v. tr. Electrificar (railway, industry, etc.). ‖ Electrizar (to produce electricity in). ‖ FIG. Electrizar.
electrize [i'lektraiz] v. tr. Electrizar.
electroacoustics [i'lektrəuə'ku:stiks] n. PHYS. Electroacústica, *f.*
electroanalysis [i'lektrəuə'næləsis] n. CHEM. Electroanálisis, *m.*
electrocardiogram [i'lektrəu'kɑ:djəugræm] n. MED. Electrocardiograma, *m.*
electrocardiograph [i'lektrəu'kɑ:djəugrɑ:f] n. MED. Electrocardiógrafo, *m.*
electrocardiography [i'lektrəu,kɑ:di'ɔgrəfi] n. MED. Electrocardiografía, *f.*
electrocautery [i'lektrəu'kɔ:təri] n. MED. Electrocauterio, *m.*
electrochemical [i'lektrəu'kemikəl] adj. Electroquímico, ca.
electrochemistry [i'lektrəu'kemistri] n. Electroquímica, *f.*
electrocoagulation [i'lektrəukəu,ægju'leiʃən] n. MED. Electrocoagulación, *f.*
electrocute [i'lektrəkju:t] v. tr. Electrocutar.
electrocution [i,lektrə'kju:ʃən] n. Electrocución, *f.*
electrode [i'lektrəud] n. PHYS. Electrodo, *m.*
electrodynamic [i'lektrəudai'næmik] adj. Electrodinámico, ca.
electrodynamics [—s] n. Electrodinámica, *f.*
electrodynamometer [i'lektrəu,dainə'mɔmitə] n. Electrodinamómetro, *m.*
electroencephalogram [i'lektrəuen'sefələugræm] n. MED. Electroencefalograma, *m.*
electroencephalograph [i'lektrəuen'sefələugrɑ:f] n. MED. Electroencefalógrafo, *m.*
electroencephalography [i'lektrəu,en,sefə'lɔgrəfi] n. MED. Electroencefalografía, *f.*
electrokinetics [i'lektrəukai'netiks] n. Electrocinética, *f.*
electrolier [i,lektrə'li:ə*] n. Araña, *f.* (chandelier).
electrolysis [ilek'trɔlisis] n. CHEM. Electrólisis, *f.*
electrolyte [i'lektrəulait] n. CHEM. Electrólito, *m.*
electrolytic [i'lektrə'litik] adj. CHEM. Electrolítico, ca.
electrolyze [i'lektrəulaiz] v. tr. Electrolizar.
electromagnet [i'lektrəu'mægnit] n. PHYS. Electroimán, *m.*
electromagnetic [i'lektrəumæg'netik] adj. Electromagnético, ca: *electromagnetic wave*, onda electromagnética.
electromagnetism [i'lektrəu'mægnitizəm] n. PHYS. Electromagnetismo, *m.*
electromechanical [i'lektrəumi'kænikəl] adj. Electromecánico, ca.
electromechanics [i'lektrəumi'kæniks] n. Electromecánica, *f.*
electrometallurgy [i'lektrəume'tælədʒi] n. Electrometalurgia, *f.*
electrometer [ilek'trɔmitə] n. Electrómetro, *m.*
electrometry [ilek'trɔmitri] n. PHYS. Electrometría, *f.*
electromotive [i'lektrəuməutiv] adj. Electromotor, ra. ‖ *Electromotive force*, fuerza electromotriz.
electromotor [i'lektrəu'məutə*] n. Electromotor, *m.*
electron [i'lektrɔn] n. PHYS. Electrón, *m.* ‖ *Electron beam, microscope, tube, bombardment*, haz, microscopio, tubo, bombardeo electrónico.
electronegative [i'lektrəu'negətiv] adj. PHYS. Electronegativo, va.
electronic [ilek'trɔnik] adj. Electrónico, ca.
electronics [—s] n. Electrónica, *f.*
electron volt [i'lektrɔnvəlt] n. PHYS. Electronvoltio, *m.*
electropathy [ilek'trɔpəθi] n. Electroterapia, *f.*
electrophone [i'lektrəfəun] n. Electrófono, *m.*
electrophorus [ilek'trɔfərəs] n. PHYS. Electróforo, *m.*

— OBSERV. El plural es *electrophori*.

electroplate [i'lektrəupleit] v. tr. Galvanizar.
electroplating [—iŋ] n. Galvanoplastia, *f.*
electropositive [i'lektrəu'pɔzətiv] adj. Electropositivo, va.
electroscope [i'lektrəskəup] n. PHYS. Electroscopio, *m.*
electroshock [i'lektrəu,ʃɔk] n. MED. Electrochoque, *m.*
electrostatic [i'lektrəu'stætik] adj. Electrostático, ca.
electrostatics [—s] n. Electrostática, *f.*
electrotechnical [i'lektrəu'teknikəl] adj. Electrotécnico, ca.
electrotechnics [i'lektrəu'tekniks] n. Electrotecnia, *f.*
electrotherapy [i'lektrəu'θerəpi] n. MED. Electroterapia, *f.*
electrothermic [i'lektrəu'θə:mik] adj. PHYS. Electrotérmico, ca.
electrothermy [i'lektrəu,θə:mi] n. PHYS. Electrotermia, *f.*
electrotype [i'lektrəutaip] n. Galvano, *m.*
electrotype [i'lektrəutaip] v. tr. Galvanotipar.
electrotyping [—iŋ] n. Galvanotipia, *f.*
electrotypy [i'lektrəu'taipi] n. Galvanotipia, *f.*
electuary [i'lektjuəri] n. MED. Electuario, *m.*
eleemosynary [,elii:'mɔsinəri] adj. Limosnero, ra; caritativo, va (charitable). ‖ De caridad. ‖ Que vive de limosnas.
elegance ['eligəns] n. Elegancia, *f.*
elegant ['eligənt] adj. Elegante. ‖ Elegante, refinado, da (refined).
elegiac [,eli'dʒaiək] or **elegiacal** [—əl] adj. Elegiaco, ca; elegíaco, ca. ‖ *Elegiac couplet*, dístico elegiaco.

elegize [ˈelidʒaiz] v. tr. Escribir una elegía a.
elegy [ˈelidʒi] n. Elegía, *f.* (poem).
element [ˈelimənt] n. Elemento, *m.* (part of a whole). || Parte, *f.*: *there is an element of truth in what he said,* hay una parte de verdad en lo que dijo. || Factor, *m.*, parte, *f.*: *the personal element,* el factor personal. || BIOL. CHEM. PHYS. REL. ELECTR. Elemento, *m.* || — Pl. Elementos, *m.* (rudiments): *elements of mathematics,* elementos de matemáticas. || Elementos, *m.* (of Nature): *the four elements,* los cuatro elementos. || FIG. *To be in one's element,* estar en su elemento.
elemental [ˌeliˈmentl] adj. Elemental (elementary). || De los elementos (of the elements). || CHEM. Elemental.
elementary [ˌeliˈmentəri] adj. Elemental, fundamental (basic). || CHEM. Elemental. || U.S. *Elementary school,* escuela primaria.
elephant [ˈelifənt] n. ZOOL. Elefante, *m.* || — *Cow elephant,* elefanta, *f.* || *Elephant seal,* elefante marino. || *Young elephant,* elefantillo, *m.*
elephantiasic [ˌelifənˈtaiəsik] adj. MED. Elefantiásico, ca; elefanciaco, ca; elefancíaco, ca.
elephantiasis [ˌelifənˈtaiəsis] n. MED. Elefantiasis, *f.*, elefancía, *f.*
elephantine [ˌeliˈfæntain] adj. FIG. Colosal, enorme (big). | Torpe (awkward). | Pesado, da: *elephantine wit,* humor pesado.
elevate [ˈeliveit] v. tr. Elevar (to raise). || Elevar (style, dignity, temperature). || Aumentar (price). || Alzar, levantar (eyes, voice). || Ascender (rank of a person). || Levantar (one's mind). || Regocijar (to elate). || REL. Elevar, alzar (the Host). || MIL. Elevar (a gun). || *To elevate s.o.'s hopes,* alimentar las esperanzas de uno.
elevated [—id] adj. Elevado, da. || Aéreo, a (railway). || Elevado, da (road). || FAM. Alegre (gay).
— N. U. S. Metro (*m.*) aéreo.
elevation [ˌeliˈveiʃən] n. Elevación, *f.* (action, angle, hill). || Ascenso, *m.* (of a person). || Altitud, *f.*, altura, *f.* (of a plane). || GEOGR. Elevación, *f.* || ARCH. Alzado, *m.* (plan). || REL. *The Elevation,* la Elevación.
elevator [ˈeliveitə*] n. Elevador, *m.* (a machine for raising things). || Timón, (*m.*) de profundidad (of aeroplane). || ANAT. Elevador, *m.* (muscle). || U. S. Ascensor, *m.* [*Amer.*, elevador, *m.*] (lift for people). | Montacargas (goods lift). | Silo (*m.*) con elevador (a grain storage building).
eleven [iˈlevn] adj. Once.
— N. Once, *m.* (number). || Once, *f. pl.* (time): *he arrived at eleven,* llegó a las once. || SP. Once, *m.*, equipo, *m.* (team): *the Madrid eleven,* el once madrileño.
eleven-plus [—plʌs] n. Ingreso, *m.*, examen (*m.*) de ingreso.
— OBSERV. El *eleven-plus* es un examen que hacen los niños al final de la primera enseñanza para saber en qué escuela secundaria pueden ingresar.
elevens [iˈlevnz] or **elevenses** [iˈlevnziz] pl. n. Comida (*f. sing.*) ligera, once, *f. pl.*
eleventh [iˈlevənθ] adj. Onceavo, va; undécimo, ma; onceno, na. || FIG. *At the eleventh hour,* en el último momento.
— N. Undécimo, ma; onceno, na: *the eleventh on the list,* el undécimo en la lista. || Onzavo, *m.*, undécima parte, *f.* (fraction). || Once, *m.*, día (*m.*) once (date): *on the eleventh of August,* el once de agosto. || Once, *m.*: *Pius XI (the eleventh),* Pío XI [once].
elf [elf] n. Duende, *m.*
— OBSERV. El plural de *elf* es *elves.*
elfin [ˈelfin] adj. De los duendes (of elves). || Mágico, ca.
— N. Duendecillo, *m.*
elfish [ˈelfiʃ] adj. De los duendes (of elves). || Mágico, ca. || FIG. Travieso, sa (mischievous). | Pequeño, ña (small).
elicit [iˈlisit] v. tr. Sacar (the truth). || Provocar (to cause). || Obtener (to obtain).
elide [iˈlaid] v. tr. Elidir (in speech). || Suprimir (to strike out).
eligibility [ˌelidʒəˈbiliti] n. Elegibilidad, *f.*
eligible [ˈelidʒəbl] adj. Elegible (by votation). || Adecuado, da (suitable). || Deseable (desirable). || Atractivo, va (attractive). || — *An eligible young man,* un buen partido. || *To be eligible for a pension,* tener derecho a una pensión.
eliminate [iˈlimineit] v. tr. Eliminar.
elimination [iˌlimiˈneiʃən] n. Eliminación, *f.*
eliminative [iˈliminətiv] adj. Eliminador, ra.
eliminator [iˈlimineitə*] n. Eliminador, ra.
eliminatory [iˈliminətəri] adj. Eliminatorio, ria. || SP. *Eliminatory heat* o *round,* eliminatoria, *f.*
elinvar [ˈelinvɑ:] n. Elinvar, *m.* (of nickel and chrome).
Elisha [iˈlaiʃə] pr. n. Eliseo, *m.*
elision [iˈliʒən] n. Elisión, *f.*
élite (U. S. **elite**) [eiˈli:t] n. Élite, *f.*, lo más selecto, minoría (*f.*) selecta.
elixir [iˈliksə*] n. Elixir, *m.*
Elizabeth [iˈlizəbəθ] pr. n. Isabel, *f.*
Elizabethan [iˌlizəˈbi:θən] adj. Elisabetiano, na; isabelino, na (of Elizabeth I of England).
elk [elk] n. ZOOL. Alce, *m.* || U. S. Wapití, *m.*
ell [el] n. Ana, *f.* (former measure).
ellipse [iˈlips] n. MATH. Elipse, *f.*
ellipsis [—is] n. GRAMM. Elipsis, *f.*
— OBSERV. El plural de la palabra inglesa es *ellipses.*
ellipsoid [iˈlipsɔid] n. MATH. Elipsoide, *m.*
ellipsoidal [ˌelipˈsɔidl] adj. Elipsoidal.
elliptic [iˈliptik] or **elliptical** [—əl] adj. Elíptico, ca.
elm [elm] n. Olmo, *m.* (tree).
elocution [ˌeləˈkju:ʃən] n. Elocución, *f.* (manner). || Declamación, *f.* (art).
elocutionary [ˌeləˈkju:ʃnəri] adj. Declamatorio, ria.
elocutionist [ˌeləˈkju:ʃnist] n. Profesor (*m.*) de elocución. || Declamador, ra.
elongate [ˈi:lɔŋgit] adj. Extendido, da; alargado, da.
elongate [ˈi:lɔŋgeit] v. tr. Extender, alargar.
elongation [ˌi:lɔŋˈgeiʃən] n. Elongación, *f.* || Alargamiento, *m.* (extension).
elope [iˈləup] v. intr. Fugarse [con un amante]. || Fugarse para contraer matrimonio.
elopement [—mənt] n. Fuga, *f.*
eloquence [ˈeləkwəns] n. Elocuencia, *f.*
eloquent [ˈeləkwənt] adj. Elocuente.
El Salvador [ˌelˌsælvəˈdɔ:*] pr. n. GEOGR. El Salvador, *m.*
else [els] adj./adv. Otro, otra: *have you anything else to do?,* ¿tienes otra cosa que hacer?; *anyone else would have failed,* cualquier otro hubiera fracasado; *anything else is unworkable,* cualquier otra cosa es irrealizable. || Más: *nothing else,* nada más; *no one* o *nobody else,* nadie más; *who else?,* ¿quién más?; *what else?,* ¿qué más?; *anything else, sir?,* ¿algo más, señor?; *I could not do else than laugh,* no pude hacer más que reírme. || — *All else, everything else,* todo lo demás. || *Anyone* o *anybody else,* cualquier otra persona, cualquier otro, cualquier otra. || *Anywhere else,* en cualquier otro sitio, en cualquier otra parte (position): *if it had been anywhere else,* si hubiera sido en cualquier otro sitio; a cualquier otro sitio, a cualquier otra parte (motion): *take me anywhere else but there,* llévame a cualquier otro sitio menos allí; ningún otro sitio (after negative): *he can't be anywhere else,* no puede estar en ningún otro sitio. || *Everyone else,* todos los demás. || *Everywhere else,* en todas partes (position), a todas partes (motion). || *How else?,* ¿de qué otra manera? || *Little else remains to be done,* fuera de esto queda muy poco por hacer. || *Much else,* todavía mucho: *much else remains to be done,* queda todavía mucho por hacer. || *No one else could have done it but him,* nadie más que él hubiera podido hacerlo. || *Nowhere else,* en ningún otro sitio, en ninguna otra parte (position), a ningún otro sitio, a ninguna otra parte (motion). || *Or else,* si no: *telephone him tomorrow or else it will be too late,* llámale mañana si no será demasiado tarde; *do as I say or else...,* haz lo que yo digo si no... || *Say anything else except that,* di lo que quieras menos eso, di cualquier cosa menos eso. || *Someone else, somebody else,* otro, otra: *you are taking me for s.o. else,* me está tomando por otro. || *Something else,* otra cosa: *let us speak of something else,* vamos a hablar de otra cosa; algo más, otra cosa: *I have something else to tell you,* tengo algo más que decirle. || *They didn't see anyone else,* no vieron a nadie más, no vieron a ninguna otra persona. || *When else?,* ¿en qué otro momento? || *Where else?,* ¿en qué otro sitio? (position), ¿a qué otro sitio? (motion).
elsewhere [ˈelsˈwɛə*] adj. En otro sitio, en otra parte (at another place). || A otro sitio, a otra parte (to another place).
elucidate [iˈlu:sideit] v. tr. Dilucidar, aclarar, poner en claro.
elucidation [iˌlu:siˈdeiʃən] n. Aclaración, *f.*, elucidación, *f.*, dilucidación, *f.*
elucidator [iˈlu:sideitə*] n. Dilucidador, ra.
elucidatory [iˌlu:siˈdeitəri] adj. Aclaratorio, ria.
elude [iˈlu:d] v. tr. Eludir (a question). || Esquivar, evitar (a blow). || Despistarse de (one's pursuer). || Escapar de (to escape). || Zafarse de (an obligation). || Burlar (the law). || — *The answer eluded me,* no pude encontrar la solución. || *Their names elude me,* se me han ido de la memoria sus nombres.
eludible [—ibl] adj. Evitable, eludible.
elusion [iˈlu:ʒən] n. Escapatoria, *f.*, evasión, *f.*
elusive [iˈlu:siv] adj. Evasivo, va (evasive). || Escurridizo, za (slippery). || Difícil de conseguir.
elusiveness [—nis] n. Carácter (*m.*) evasivo.
elusory [iˈlu:səri] adj. Evasivo, va.
elver [ˈelvə*] n. ZOOL. Angula, *f.*
elves [elvz] pl. n. See ELF.
elvish [ˈelviʃ] adj. See ELFISH.
Elysian [iˈliziən] adj. MYTH. Elíseo, a: *Elysian Fields,* Campos Elíseos.
Elysium [iˈliziəm] pr. n. Elíseo, *m.*
elytron [ˈelitrɔn] n. ZOOL. Élitro, *m.*
— OBSERV. El plural de *elytron* es *elytra.*
elytrum [ˈelitrəm] n. ZOOL. Élitro, *m.*
— OBSERV. El plural de *elytrum* es *elytra.*
elzevir [ˈelziviə] n. PRINT. Elzevir, *m.*, elzevirio, *m.*
em [em] n. Eme, *f.* (letter). || PRINT. Cuadratín, *m.*
emaciate [iˈmeiʃieit] v. tr. Adelgazar (person). || Demacrar (face). || AGR. Empobrecer (soil).
emaciated [—id] adj. Demacrado, da (face).
emaciation [iˌmeisiˈeiʃən] n. Demacración, *f.* (of face). || Adelgazamiento, *m.* (of a person).

emanate [ˈeməneit] v. intr. Proceder, emanar.
emanation [ˌeməˈneiʃən] n. Emanación, *f.*
emancipate [iˌmænsipeit] v. tr. Emancipar.
emancipation [iˌmænsiˈpeiʃən] n. Emancipación, *f.*
emancipator [iˈmænsipeitə*] n. Emancipador, ra.
emancipatory [iˈmænsiˌpeitəri] adj. Emancipador, ra.
emarginate [iˈmɑːdʒinit] adj. Emarginado, da.
emasculate [iˈmæskjuleit] v. tr. Castrar, emascular. || FIG. Mutilar.
emasculation [iˌmæskjuˈleiʃən] n. Castración, *f.*, emasculación, *f.* || FIG. Mutilación, *f.*
embalm [imˈbɑːm] v. tr. Embalsamar (a corpse, to perfume). || FIG. Conservar.
embalmer [—ə*] n. Embalsamador, ra.
embalmment [—mənt] n. Embalsamamiento, *m.*
embank [imˈbæŋk] v. tr. Construir un muro de contención, terraplenar (a roadway). || Encauzar con diques, poner diques a (a river).
embankment [—mənt] n. Terraplenado, *m.* (action). || Terraplén, *m.* (bearing road, railway). || Muro (*m.*) de contención, terraplén, *m.* (wall). || Dique, *m.* (of a river).
embarcation [ˌembɑːˈkeiʃən] n. See EMBARKATION.
embargo [emˈbɑːgəu] n. Prohibición, *f.* || MAR. JUR. Embargo, *m.* || — *To be under an embargo*, estar prohibido. || *To put an embargo on*, prohibir.

— OBSERV. El plural de la palabra inglesa es *embargoes.*

embargo [emˈbɑːgəu] v. tr. MAR. JUR. Embargar. || Prohibir (to forbid).
embark [imˈbɑːk] v. tr. Embarcar.
— V. intr. Embarcarse (*for*, con rumbo a; *on*, en). || FIG. *To embark on*, emprender (to start).
embarkation [ˌembɑːˈkeiʃən] n. Embarco, *m.* (of people). || Embarque, *m.* (of goods).
embarrass [imˈbærəs] v. tr. Desconcertar, turbar, embarazar (to disconcert). || Poner en un aprieto (to put in a tight spot). || Molestar, estorbar, embarazar (to hinder). || Complicar, dificultar (to complicate). || — *To be embarrassed*, pasar vergüenza, sentirse molesto, estar violento. || *To be financially embarrassed*, estar mal de dinero, tener apuros económicos.
embarrassing [—iŋ] adj. Violento, ta; molesto, ta; embarazoso, sa.
embarrassment [—mənt] n. Desconcierto, *m.*, confusión, *f.*, turbación, *f.* (confusion). || Vergüenza, *f.* (shame). || Molestia, *f.* (trouble). || Estorbo, *m.* (nuisance). || *Financial embarrassment*, apuros (*m. pl.*) de dinero, dificultades económicas, apuros económicos.
embassy [ˈembəsi] n. Embajada, *f.*
embattle [imˈbætl] v. tr. MIL. Formar en orden de batalla. || ARCH. Almenar (walls). | Fortificar (a castle).
embay [imˈbei] v. tr. MAR. Abrigar en una ensenada. || FIG. Rodear.
embed [imˈbed] v. tr. Empotrar. || Clavar, hincar (weapon, etc.). || FIG. Meter, fijar (in mind).
embellish [imˈbeliʃ] v. tr. Embellecer (to beautify). || Adornar (to adorn).
embellishment [—mənt] n. Embellecimiento, *m.* || Adorno, *m.* (adornment).
ember [ˈembə*] n. Ascua, *f.*, rescoldo, *m.*
Ember days [—deiz] pl. n. REL. Témporas, *f.*
embezzle [imˈbezl] v. tr. Malversar, desfalcar.
embezzlement [—mənt] n. Malversación, *f.*, desfalco, *m.*
embezzler [—ə*] n. Malversador, ra; desfalcador, ra.
embitter [imˈbitə*] v. tr. FIG. Envenenar (a quarrel). | Agriar, amargar (a person).
embittered [—d] adj. Amargado, da (bitter). || Resentido, da; rencoroso, sa (resentful).
emblaze [imˈbleiz] v. tr. Iluminar (to light up). || Encender (to kindle). || Engalanar (to adorn).
emblazon [imˈbleizən] v. tr. HERALD. Blasonar. || FIG. Ensalzar, alabar (to extol).
emblazonry [—ri] n. HERALD. Blasón, *m.* || FIG. Adorno (*m.*) brillante.
emblem [ˈembləm] n. Símbolo, *m.*, emblema, *m.* (symbol). || HERALD. Divisa, *f.*, emblema, *m.*
emblematic [ˌembliˈmætik] or **emblematical** [—əl] adj. Simbólico, ca; emblemático, ca.
emblematize [emˈblemətaiz] v. tr. Simbolizar, ser el emblema de.
emblements [ˈemblmənts] pl. n. JUR. Frutos (*m.*) de la tierra.
embodiment [imˈbɔdimənt] n. Personificación, *f.*, encarnación, *f.*: *he is the very embodiment of vice*, es la misma personificación del vicio. || Incorporación, *f.*
embody [imˈbɔdi] v. tr. Personificar, encarnar (to be the concrete expression of). || Materializar, dar cuerpo a (to give clear form to). || Incluir (to include). || Expresar (an idea).
embog [imˈbɔg] v. tr. Atascar.
embolden [imˈbəuldən] v. tr. Dar ánimo a, alentar, envalentonar.
embole [ˈembəli] n. Embolia, *f.*
embolism [ˈembəlizəm] n. MED. Embolia, *f.*
emboly [ˈembəli] n. Embolia, *f.*
embosom [imˈbuzəm] v. tr. Abrazar, apretar contra sí (to embrace). || Rodear, cercar, encerrar (to enclose).
emboss [imˈbɔs] v. tr. Grabar en relieve. || Gofrar (paper). || Repujar (leather, silver).
embossment [—mənt] n. Gofrado, *m.* (of paper). || Grabado (*m.*) en relieve (engraving). || Repujado, *m.* (of leather, silver).
embouchure [ˌɔmbuˈʃuə*] n. Desembocadura, *f.* (of a river). || MUS. Embocadura, *f.*
embowel [imˈbauəl] v. tr. Sacar las tripas, destripar.
embower [imˈbauə*] v. tr. Enramar, esconder entre las ramas.
embrace [imˈbreis] n. Abrazo, *m.*
embrace [imˈbreis] v. tr. Abrazar (to hug). || Aprovecharse de, aprovechar (to seize): *to embrace an opportunity*, aprovechar una oportunidad. || Abarcar, contener, incluir (to encompass): *"democracy" embraces many concepts*, la palabra "democracia" abarca muchos conceptos. || Aceptar (an offer). || Adoptar, abrazar (a doctrine, a conduct). || Dedicarse a (a profession).
— V. intr. Abrazarse: *they embraced*, se abrazaron.
embracement [—mənt] n. Abrazo, *m.*
embranchment [imˈbrɑːntʃmənt] n. Ramificación, *f.*, bifurcación, *f.* || Brazo, *m.* (of a river).
embrasure [imˈbreiʒə*] n. ARCH. Alféizar, *m.* (of a window). || MIL. Tronera, *f.*, cañonera, *f.* (loophole).
embrocate [ˈembrəukeit] v. tr. MED. Dar fricciones.
embrocation [ˌembrəuˈkeiʃən] n. MED. Embrocación, *f.* (liniment).
embroglio [emˈbrəuljəu] n. Embrollo, *m.*
embroider [imˈbrɔidə*] v. tr. Bordar: *embroidered by hand*, bordado a mano. || FIG. Adornar, embellecer (a story, etc.).
— V. intr. Bordar.
embroiderer [—rə*] n. Bordador, ra.
embroideress [—ris] n. Bordadora, *f.*
embroidery [—ri] n. Bordado, *m.* || FIG. Adorno, *m.* (of a story, etc.).
embroil [imˈbrɔil] v. tr. Embrollar, enredar (to entangle). || Enredar, envolver (to involve). || Sembrar la discordia entre (to set at odds).
embroilment [—mənt] n. Embrollo, *m.*, enredo, *m.*
embrown [imˈbraun] v. tr. Oscurecer.
embryo [ˈembriəu] n. Embrión, *m.* || FIG. Embrión, *m.*, germen, *m.*: *in embryo*, en embrión.
— Adj. Embrionario, ria.
embryologic [ˌembrieuˈlɔdʒik] or **embryological** [—əl] adj. Embriológico, ca.
embryologist [ˌembriˈɔlədʒist] n. Embriólogo, *m.*
embryology [ˌembriˈɔlədʒi] n. Embriología, *f.*
embryonic [ˌembriˈɔnik] adj. Embrionario, ria.
emcee [ˈemsiː] n. U. S. Maestro (*m.*) de ceremonias (at a formal event), presentador, *m.* (of a show).
emend [iˈmend] or **emendate** [—eit] v. tr. Enmendar.
emendation [ˌiːmenˈdeiʃən] n. Enmienda, *f.*
emendatory [iˈmendətəri] adj. De enmienda.
emerald [ˈemərəld] n. Esmeralda, *f.* (stone). || Color (*m.*) esmeralda (colour).
— Adj. Esmeralda, *inv.* (colour). || *The Emerald Isle*, la verde Erín (Ireland).
emerge [iˈməːdʒ] v. intr. Salir, emerger (to rise from a fluid). || Surgir, salir (to come out). || Sacarse (to be brought out by investigation). || JUR. Deducirse. || Aparecer, surgir (to be dicovered). || *It emerges that*, resulta que.
emergence [iˈməːdʒəns] n. Salida, *f.*, emergencia, *f.* (the act of emerging). || BOT. Excrecencia, *f.*
emergency [iˈməːdʒənsi] n. Emergencia, *f.* (unexpected event). || Situación (*f.*) crítica, crisis, *f.* (crisis). || MED. Urgencia, *f.* || Necesidad (*f.*) urgente (need). || — *Case of emergency*, caso (*m.*) de emergencia *or* de urgencia. || *In an emergency*, en caso de emergencia. || *National emergency*, crisis (*f.*) nacional. || *State of emergency*, estado (*m.*) de emergencia; estado de excepción (for political reasons). || *To provide for emergencies*, prevenirse contra toda eventualidad. || *To rise to the emergency*, mostrarse a la altura de las circunstancias.
— Adj. De emergencia: *emergency exit*, salida de emergencia. || De urgencia (measure). || Forzoso, sa (forced): *emergency landing*, aterrizaje forzoso. || De seguridad: *emergency brake*, freno de seguridad. || De alarma (bell). || Provisional (bridge, dwelling). || Extraordinario, ria.
emergent [iˈməːdʒənt] adj. Emergente (emerging). || Inesperado, da (unexpected). || Joven (nation).
emeritus [iˈmeritəs] adj. Honorario, ria; emérito, ta.
emersion [iˈməːʃən] n. ASTR. Emersión, *f.*, reaparición, *f.*
emery [ˈeməri] n. MIN. Esmeril, *m.* || — *Emery board*, lima (*f.*) de uñas. || *Emery cloth*, tela (*f.*) de esmeril. || *Emery paper*, papel (*m.*) esmerilado *or* de lija, lija *f.*
emetic [iˈmetik] adj. Emético, ca; vomitivo, va.
— N. Emético, *m.*, vomitivo, *m.*
emigrant [ˈemigrənt] adj./n. Emigrante.
emigrate [ˈemigreit] v. intr. Emigrar.
emigration [ˌemiˈgreiʃən] n. Emigración, *f.*
emigratory [ˈemigrətəri] adj. Emigratorio, ria.
émigré [ˈemigrei] n. Emigrado, da.
eminence [ˈeminəns] n. Eminencia, *f.* || — FIG. *Grey eminence*, eminencia gris. || REL. *His Eminence*, Su Eminencia.
éminence grise [ˈeimiːnɑ̃nsˈgriːz] n. Eminencia (*f.*) gris.
eminent [ˈeminənt] adj. Eminente.
emir [eˈmiə*] n. Emir, *m.*
emirate [eˈmiərit] n. Emirato, *m.*
emissary [ˈemisəri] n. Emisario, ria.

emission [iˈmiʃən] n. Emisión, *f.*
emissive [iˈmisiv] adj. Emisivo, va; de emisión.
emit [iˈmit] v. tr. Emitir (a sound, light, money). ‖ Emitir, expresar (opinion, etc.). ‖ Desprender (heat). ‖ Despedir, desprender (an odour). ‖ Echar, arrojar (smoke). ‖ Dar (a cry).
emitter [—ə*] n. RAD. Emisora, *f.*
Emmanuel [iˈmænjuəl] pr. n. Manuel, *m.*
emmetrope [ˈemətrəup] n. Emétrope, *m. & f.*
emmetropia [ˌemˈətrəupjə] n. MED. Emetropía, *f.*
emmetropic [ˌeməˈtrɔpik] adj. MED. Emétrope.
emollient [iˈmɔliənt] adj. Emoliente.
— N. Emoliente, *m.*
emolument [iˈmɔljumənt] n. Emolumento, *m.*
emote [iˈməut] v. intr. Manifestar emoción. ‖ U. S. FAM. Comportarse de forma demasiado teatral.
emotion [iˈməuʃən] n. Emoción, *f.*
emotional [iˈməuʃənl] adj. Emocional (relating to the emotions, appealing to the emotions). ‖ Emotivo, va; conmovedor, ra: *an emotional farewell*, una despedida conmovedora. ‖ Emotivo, va: *an emotional person*, una persona emotiva.
emotionalism [iˈməuʃnəlizəm] n. Emotividad, *f.*, sentimentalismo, *m.*
emotionalist [iˈməuʃnəlist] n. Persona (*f.*) sensible *or* emotiva *or* emocionable.
emotionality [iˌməuʃəˈnæliti] n. Emotividad, *f.*, emocionabilidad, *f.*, sensibilidad, *f.*
emotive [iˈməutiv] adj. Emotivo, va.
emotiveness [—nis] or **emotivity** [iməuˈtiviti] n. Emotividad, *f.*
empale [imˈpeil] v. tr. See IMPALE.
empanel [imˈpænl] v. tr. JUR. Seleccionar (to select). | Inscribir (to list).
empennage [imˈpenidʒ] n. AVIAT. Planos (*m. pl.*) de estabilización, estabilizador, *m.*, empenaje, *m.* ‖ Aleta, *f.* (of a bomb). ‖ Plumas, *f. pl.* (of an arrow).
emperor [ˈempərə*] n. Emperador, *m.* ‖ ZOOL. Pavón, *m.* (butterfly).
emperorship [—ʃip] n. Imperio, *m.*
emphasis [ˈemfəsis] n. GRAMM. Acento, *m.*, acentuación, *f.* (stress). ‖ FIG. Acento, *m.*, énfasis, *m.* (to call special attention). | Importancia, *f.* | Insistencia, *f.* (insistence). ‖ *To lay emphasis on a fact, on a word*, subrayar un hecho, una palabra, hacer hincapié en un hecho, en una palabra.

— OBSERV. El plural de *emphasis* es *emphases*.

emphasize [ˈemfəsaiz] v. tr. GRAMM. Acentuar, poner el acento en. ‖ FIG. Subrayar, recalcar, hacer hincapié en, poner de relieve, acentuar [*Amer.*, enfatizar].
emphatic [imˈfætik] adj. Enfático, ca (adding emphasis). ‖ Enérgico, ca (strongly marked). ‖ GRAMM. Acentuado, da (stressed). ‖ Decidido, da (resolute). ‖ Categórico, ca (categorical): *I was most emphatic*, fui muy categórico.
emphatically [—əli] adv. Enérgicamente, categóricamente. ‖ Enfáticamente.
emphysema [ˌemfiˈsiːmə] n. MED. Enfisema, *m.*
emphysematous [ˌemfiˈsemətəs] adj. MED. Enfisematoso, sa.
emphyteusis [ˌemfiˈtjuːsis] n. JUR. Enfiteusis, *f.* (lease).
emphyteuta [ˌemfiˈtjuːtə] n. JUR. Enfiteuta, *m. & f.*
emphyteutic [ˌemfiˈtjuːtik] adj. JUR. Enfitéutico, ca.
empire [ˈempaiə*] n. Imperio, *m.* ‖ — *The Empire*, el Sacro Imperio Romano Germánico (Holy Roman Empire), el Imperio [de Napoleón] (of Napoleon), el Imperio Británico (British Empire). ‖ *The Empire State*, el estado de Nueva York.
— Adj. Imperio (style).
empiric [emˈpirik] adj./n. Empírico, ca.
empirical [—əl] adj. Empírico, ca.
empiricism [emˈpirisizəm] n. Empirismo, *m.*
empiricist [emˈpirisist] n. Empírico, ca.
emplacement [imˈpleismənt] n. Emplazamiento, *m.*
employ [imˈplɔi] n. Empleo, *m.* ‖ — *In s.o.'s employ*, empleado por alguien, al servicio de alguien. ‖ *They are in my employ*, son empleados míos.
employ [imˈplɔi] v. tr. Emplear.
employable [—əbl] adj. Utilizable, empleable.
employé [ɔmˈplɔiei] n. Empleado, da.
employee [ˌemplɔiˈiː] n. Empleado, da.
employer [imˈplɔiə*] n. Empresario, ria; empleador, ra (who employs people): *employer's union*, sindicato de empresarios. ‖ Usuario, ria (user).
— Adj. Empresarial, de empresarios.
employment [imˈplɔimənt] n. Empleo, *m.*: *full employment*, pleno empleo. ‖ Trabajo, *m.* (work). ‖ Ocupación, *f.* (occupation). ‖ Uso, *m.* (use). ‖ — *Employment agency*, agencia (*f.*) de colocaciones. ‖ *Employment contract*, contrato (*m.*) de trabajo. ‖ *Employment exchange* o *bureau*, bolsa (*f.*) de trabajo. ‖ *Employment legislation*, legislación (*f.*) laboral. ‖ *Employment offered*, puesto (*m.*) vacante. ‖ *Employment wanted*, solicitan trabajo. ‖ *To be in employment*, tener trabajo. ‖ *To give employment to*, emplear a. ‖ *To look for employment*, buscar empleo *or* trabajo.
empoison [imˈpɔizn] v. tr. Envenenar.
emporium [emˈpɔːriəm] n. Emporio, *m.* (a big market). ‖ (Ant.). Emporio, *m.*, almacén, *m* (a store).

— OBSERV. El plural es *emporiums* o *emporia*.

empower [imˈpauə*] v. tr. Facultar, autorizar, habilitar.
empress [ˈempris] n. Emperatriz, *f.*
emptiness [ˈemptinis] n. Vacío, *m.* ‖ FIG. Vaciedad, *f.*, vacuidad, *f.* (of a person, words, etc.).
empty [ˈempti] adj. Vacío, a (with nothing in it). ‖ Vacío, a; desocupado, da (a house). ‖ Desierto, ta (place). ‖ Vacante (an employment). ‖ Vacío, a (words, etc.). ‖ Sin sentido (meaningless). ‖ FAM. Vacío, a; hambriento, ta (hungry). ‖ AGR. Vacía, *f.* (not pregnant). ‖ *Empty of*, sin, desprovisto de.
— N. Envase (*m.*) vacío, recipiente (*m.*) vacío. ‖ *Returnable empties*, cascos (*m.*) *or* envases (*m.*) en depósito.
empty [ˈempti] v. tr. Vaciar, dejar vacío (to make empty). ‖ Vaciar (the contents). ‖ Despojar, quitar (of meaning).
— V. intr. Vaciarse (to become empty). ‖ Quedarse vacío (a car). ‖ Quedar desocupado (a flat). ‖ Quedarse vacante (an employment). ‖ Desaguar, desembocar (a river).
empty-handed [—ˈhændid] adj. Con las manos vacías.
empty-headed [—ˈhedid] adj. Casquivano, na; sin nada en la cabeza.
empurple [imˈpəːpl] v. tr. Enrojecer.
empyreal [ˌempaiˈriːəl] adj. Empíreo, a.
Empyrean [ˌempaiˈriːən] n. Empíreo, *m.*
emu [ˈiːmjuː] n. Emú, *m.* (bird).
emulate [ˈemjuleit] v. tr. Emular.
emulation [ˌemjuˈleiʃən] n. Emulación, *f.* ‖ *In emulation of each other*, a cual mejor, a cual más.
emulative [ˈemjulətiv] adj. Emulador, ra.
emulator [ˈemjuleitə*] n. Emulador, ra; émulo, la.
emulous [ˈemjuləs] adj. Émulo, la. ‖ *To be emulous of honours*, ambicionar honores.
emulsifier [iˈmʌlsifaiə*] n. Emulsor, *m.*
emulsify [iˈmʌlsifai] v. tr. Emulsionar.
emulsion [iˈmʌlʃən] n. Emulsión, *f.*
emulsive [iˈmʌlsiv] adj. Emulsivo, va.
en [en] n. PRINT. Cuadratín, *m.* ‖ Ene, *f.* (letter).
enable [iˈneibl] v. tr. Permitir (to permit). ‖ JUR. Permitir, autorizar, capacitar, habilitar.
enact [iˈnækt] v. tr. JUR. Promulgar (a law). | Dar fuerza de ley a (a bill). | Decretar (to decree). ‖ Representar (to act, to represent). ‖ Hacer, efectuar (to do).
— V. intr. Actuar.
enactment [—mənt] n. Promulgación, *f.* (of a law). ‖ Estatuto, *m.* (statute). ‖ Decreto, *m.* (decree).
enamel [iˈnæməl] n. Esmalte, *m.* ‖ *Enamel paint*, esmalte, *m.*
enamel [iˈnæməl] v. tr. Esmaltar.
enamelled [—d] adj. Esmaltado, da.
enameller [—ə*] n. Esmaltador, *m.*
enamelling [—iŋ] n. Esmaltado, *m.*
enamelware [—ˌwɛə] n. Utensilios (*m. pl.*) de hierro esmaltado.
enamour (U. S. **enamor**) [iˈnæmə*] v. tr. Enamorar (to inspire love). ‖ FIG. Cautivar, seducir.
enamoured (U. S. **enamored**) [—d] adj. Enamorado, da: *she was enamoured of me*, estaba enamorada de mí. ‖ Aficionado, da (of a thing): *she was enamoured of*, era muy aficionada a. ‖ Aferrado, da (of an idea).
en bloc [ɑ̃ːˈblɔk] adj. En bloque.
encaenia [enˈsiːnjə] n. Conmemoración, *f.*
encaged [inˈkeidʒd] adj. Enjaulado, da.
encamp [inˈkæmp] v. intr. MIL. Acamparse.
— V. tr. MIL. Acampar.
encampment [—mənt] n. MIL. Campamento, *m.*
encase [inˈkeis] v. tr. Encajonar (in a box). ‖ Encerrar (to enclose). ‖ Cubrir (to cover).
encash [inˈkæʃ] v. tr. Hacer efectivo, cobrar.
encashment [—mənt] n. Cobro, *m.*
encaustic [enˈkɔːstik] n. Encausto, *m.*
— Adj. Encáustico, ca.
enceinte [ɑ̃ːˈsɛ̃ːnt] n. Recinto, *m.* (fortress).
encephalic [ˌenkəˈfælik] adj. ANAT. Encefálico, ca.
encephalitis [ˌenkefəˈlaitis] n. MED. Encefalitis, *f.*
encephalogram [enˈsefələugræm] n. MED. Encefalograma, *m.*
encephalograph [enˈsefələugrɑːf] n. MED. Electroencefalógrafo, *m.* (apparatus). | Encefalograma, *m.* (result).
encephalography [ˌensefəˈlɔgrəfi] n. MED. Encefalografía, *f.*
encephalomyelitis [enˈsefələuˌmaiəˈlaitis] n. Encefalomielitis, *f.*
encephalon [enˈsefəlɔn] n. ANAT. Encéfalo, *m.*

— OBSERV. El plural de *encephalon* es *encephala*.

enchain [inˈtʃein] v. tr. Encadenar.
enchainment [—mənt] n. Encadenamiento, *m.*
enchant [inˈtʃɑːnt] v. tr. Encantar.
enchanter [—ə*] n. Hechicero, *m.* (sorcerer). ‖ Encanto, *m.*, hechizo, *m.* (s.o. who fascinates).
enchanting [—iŋ] adj. Encantador, ra.
enchantment [—mənt] n. Encanto, *m.* (charm). ‖ Encantamiento, *m.*, hechizo, *m.* (of a sorcerer).
enchantress [—ris] n. Hechicera, *f.* (sorceress). ‖ Encanto, *m.*, hechicera, *f.* (s.o. who fascinates).
enchase [inˈtʃeis] v. tr. Engastar, engarzar (to set a gem). ‖ Incrustar (to inlay). ‖ Grabar (to engrave). ‖ Embutir (to emboss). ‖ Repujar (leather).
encina [inˈsiːnə] n. BOT. Encina, *f.*

encircle [inˈsə:kl] v. tr. Rodear, cercar. || Ceñir (to fasten round). || MIL. Envolver.
encirclement [—mənt] n. Circunvalación, *f.* (a surrounding). || MIL. Envolvimiento, *m.* (of troops). | Cerco, *m.* (of a town).
encircling [inˈsə:kliŋ] adj. Que circunvala. || MIL. Envolvente.
enclasp [inˈklɑ:sp] v. tr. Abrazar.
enclave [ˈenkleiv] n. Enclave, *m.*
enclave [ˈenkleiv] v. tr. Enclavar.
enclisis [ˈenkləsis] n. GRAMM. Énclisis, *f.*
enclitic [inˈklitik] adj. GRAMM. Enclítico, ca.
— N. GRAMM. Enclítica, *f.*
enclose [inˈkləuz] v. tr. Encerrar (to shut in). || Rodear, cercar (to surround). || Adjuntar, remitir adjunto (to include in a letter): *the enclosed letter*, la carta adjunta; *enclosed herewith*, encontrará adjunto. || Encerrar, incluir, abarcar (to contain). || REL. Enclaustrar. || *I enclose herewith*, remito adjunto.
enclosure [inˈkləuʒə*] n. Encierro, *m.* (act of shutting in). || Cerco, *m.*, cercado, *m.* (fence). || Recinto, *m.* (space included within certain limits). || REL. Enclaustramiento, *m.* || Carta (*f.*) adjunta, documento (*m.*) adjunto *or* anexo (in a letter).
encomiast [enˈkəumiæst] n. Encomiasta, *m.* & *f.*, panegirista, *m.* & *f.*
encomiastic [en,kəumiˈæstik] or **encomiastical** [—əl] adj. Encomiástico, ca; laudatorio, ria; panegírico, ca.
encomium [enˈkəumjəm] n. Encomio, *m.*, elogio, *m.*
— OBSERV. El plural es *encomiums* o *encomia.*
encompass [inˈkʌmpəs] v. tr. Abarcar (to include). || Cercar, rodear (to surround). || Envolver (to envelop). || Llevar a cabo (to accomplish).
encore [ɔŋˈkɔ:*] interj. ¡Otra vez!, ¡otra!, ¡bis!, ¡que se repita!
— N. Repetición, *f.* || *To give an encore*, repetir *or* bisar a petición del público.
encore [ɔŋˈkɔ:*] v. tr. Pedir la repetición a *or* de (to call for an encore). || Repetir, bisar (to repeat).
encounter [inˈkauntə*] n. Encuentro, *m.*
encounter [inˈkauntə*] v. tr. Encontrarse con, encontrar, tropezar con (to meet by chance). || Encontrar, tropezar con, enfrentarse a (to face a difficulty). || MIL. Enfrentarse con.
encourage [inˈkʌridʒ] v. tr. Animar, alentar (to help by sympathetic interest): *the spectators encouraged the players*, los espectadores alentaron a los jugadores; *I encouraged him to do it*, le animé para que lo hiciese. || Incitar: *he was encouraged to steal*, le incitaron a robar. || Estimular, fomentar (to promote, to stimulate): *to encourage industry*, estimular la industria. || Fortalecer (to strengthen a belief).
encouragement [—mənt] n. Ánimo, *m.*, aliento, *m.* (courage). || Incitación, *f.* (incitement). || Estímulo, *m.*, fomento, *m.* (promotion, stimulation of industry, etc.). || Incentivo, *m.* (incentive). || *To give encouragement to*, dar ánimo *or* ánimos a.
encouraging [—iŋ] adj. Alentador, ra: *encouraging results*, resultados alentadores. || Prometedor, ra; halagüeño, ña (promising): *encouraging prospects*, perspectivas halagüeñas. || Que da ánimos: *to be an encouraging person*, ser una persona que da ánimos.
encouragingly [—iŋli] adv. En tono alentador.
encroach [inˈkrəutʃ] v. intr. *To encroach on*, usurpar (s.o.'s rights), meterse en, inmiscuirse en (to intrude on): *he encroached on my affairs*, se metía en mis asuntos; abusar de (to abuse): *to encroach on s.o.'s good nature*, abusar de la amabilidad de alguien; quitar: *to encroach on s.o.'s time*, quitar tiempo a alguien; invadir (to invade).
encroachment [—mənt] n. Usurpación, *f.* (appropriation). || Abuso, *m.* (abuse). || Intrusión, *f.* || Invasión, *f.*
encrust [inˈkrʌst] v. tr. Incrustar: *encrusted with*, incrustado de.
— V. intr. Incrustarse, cubrirse de costra.
encumber [inˈkʌmbə*] v. tr. Estorbar (to hamper). || Cargar: *encumbered with parcels*, cargado de paquetes. || Sobrecargar (the market). || Llenar: *encumbered with footnotes*, lleno de notas. || Obstruir (to block). || Gravar (with taxes, etc.).
encumbrance [inˈkʌmbrəns] n. Estorbo, *m.*, obstáculo, *m.* (hindrance). || JUR. Carga, *f.*, gravamen, *m.*: *free from encumbrances*, libre de gravámenes. || *Without encumbrance*, sin familia.
encyclic [enˈsiklik] or **encyclical** [—kəl] adj. REL. *Encyclical letter*, encíclica, *f.*
— N. REL. Encíclica, *f.*
encyclopedia or **encyclopaedia** [en,saikləuˈpi:djə] n. Enciclopedia, *f.*
encyclopedic or **encyclopaedic** [en,saikləuˈpi:dik] or **encyclopedical** or **encyclopaedical** [—əl] adj. Enciclopédico, ca.
encyclopedism or **encyclopaedism** [en,saikləuˈpi:dizəm] n. Enciclopedismo, *m.* || Conocimientos (*m. pl.*) enciclopédicos (knowledge).
encyclopedist or **encyclopaedist** [en,saikləuˈpi:dist] n. Enciclopedista, *m.* & *f.*
encyst [inˈsist] v. tr. MED. Enquistar.
— V. intr. MED. Enquistarse.
encystment [—mənt] or **encystation** [insisˈteiʃən] n. MED. Enquistamiento, *m.*
end [end] adj. Final: *the end result*, el resultado final; *end product*, producto final.
— N. Fin, *m.*, final, *m.* (finish): *until the end*, hasta el final. || Fin, *m.*: *the end of a reel*, el fin de un carrete. || Extremo, *m.*: *the other end of the street*, el otro extremo de la calle. || Parte, *f.*: *the fashionable end of town*, la parte elegante de la ciudad. || Extremo, *m.*, límite, *m.* (limit). || Pedazo, *m.*, trozo, *m.*, resto, *m.* (remnant). || Cabo, *m.* (tail end): *a candle end*, un cabo de vela. || Punta, *f.* (point). || PHIL. Fin, *m.*, causa (*f.*) final. || Pie, *m.* (of a perpendicular). || Colilla, *f.* (of a cigarette). || Término, *m.* (termination). || Muerte, *f.*, fin, *m.* (death): *a tragic end*, un trágico fin. || Destrucción, *f.* (destruction). || Propósito, *m.*, fin, *m.*, objetivo, *m.* (aim): *she achieved her ends*, consiguió sus fines; *to what end?*, ¿con qué propósito? || Método, *m.* (means). || SP. Lado, *m.* || — FAM. *And that's the end of it*, y sanseacabó. || *At the end of the year*, al final del año, a fines de año. || *At the end of two years*, después de dos años, al cabo de dos años. || *End on*, de frente. || *End to end*, unidos por los extremos (next to), uno tras otro (one behind the other). || *For days on end*, día tras día. || *From end to end*, de un extremo a otro, desde el principio hasta el final. || FAM. *He is no end of a fellow*, es un chico estupendo. || *I did it in the end*, acabé haciéndolo *or* por hacerlo. || *In the end*, al final, al fin. || *It did me no end of good*, me hizo un bien inmenso. || *Latter end of s.o.'s life*, los últimos años de uno. || *No end of*, muchísimos, muchísimas. || *On end*, erizado, de punta (hair), derecho, de pie (upright), incesantemente, sin parar (nonstop), seguido, da (consecutive). || *That's the end of the money*, se acabó el dinero. || *That will be the end of him*, esto acabará con él. || *The end justifies the means*, el fin justifica los medios. || *The end of the world*, el fin del mundo. || *There is an end to everything*, principio y fin quieren las cosas. || *To be at an end*, estar acabado (finished), tocar a su fin (finishing). || *To be at one's wit's end*, no saber qué hacer. || *To bring to an end*, llevar a su fin, terminar. || *To come to an end*, llegar a su fin, terminarse. || *To gain one's ends*, lograr sus propósitos. || FIG. *To get hold of the wrong end of the stick*, tomar el rábano por las hojas. | *To go off the deep end*, see DEEP. | *To keep one's end up*, hacer bien lo que a uno le corresponde. || *To make an end of*, acabar con. || FIG. *To make an end of s.o.*, enviar a alguien a paseo. | *To make ends meet* o *to make both ends meet*, hacer equilibrios para vivir. | *To meet one's end*, encontrar la muerte. || *To no end*, en vano, inútilmente. || *To put an end to*, poner fin a. || *To reach its end*, tocar a su fin. || *To stand on end*, ponerse de punta (hair). || *To start at the wrong end*, empezar por el final. || *To the end that*, para que, a fin de que, con el objeto de que. || FIG. *To think no end of s.o.*, tener muy buen concepto de uno. || *To this end*, con este fin, para este fin. || *We are at the end of our patience*, se nos ha agotado la paciencia. || *You'll never hear the end of it*, no te dejarán olvidarlo nunca.
end [end] v. tr. Acabar, terminar, finalizar, poner fin a (to finish). || Acabar con (abuses, etc.). || Terminar (one's days). || FAM. *To end it all*, acabar con la vida.
— V. intr. Terminarse, acabarse (to terminate). || Terminar sus días (to die). || Acabar, terminar: *he ended by eating*, acabó comiendo. || — *To end in*, terminar en. || *To end off*, acabar: *to end off a story*, acabar una historia; terminarse: *the path ends off abruptly*, el sendero se termina de repente. || *To end up*, acabar, terminar (to finish), ir a parar: *the car ended up in my garden*, el coche fue a parar a mi jardín.
end-all [—ɔ:l] n. Objetivo (*m.*) final. || See BE-ALL.
endamage [inˈdæmidʒ] v. tr. Dañar, perjudicar.
endanger [inˈdeindʒə*] v. tr. Poner en peligro.
endear [inˈdiə*] v. tr. Hacer querer (*to*, por). || *To endear o.s. to*, hacerse querer por, granjearse las simpatías de: *he endeared himself to his friends*, se hizo querer por sus amigos.
endearing [—riŋ] adj. Simpático, ca; atractivo, va (attractive). || Encantador, ra (charming).
endearment [—mənt] n. Palabra (*f.*) *or* frase (*f.*) cariñosa (word or phrase which expresses affection). || Caricia, *f.* (caress). || Cariño, *m.*, afecto, *m.*, encariñamiento, *m.* (affection).
endeavour (U. S. **endeavor**) [inˈdevə*] n. Esfuerzo, *m.*, empeño, *m.* (effort). || Tentativa, *f.*, intento, *m.* (attempt). || *To use every endeavour to*, no regatear esfuerzos para.
endeavour (U. S. **endeavor**) [inˈdevə*] v. intr. Esforzarse (*to*, por), intentar, procurar.
endemic [enˈdemik] adj. Endémico, ca.
— N. Endemia, *f.*
endemical [—əl] adj. Endémico, ca.
end-grain [ˈendˈgrein] adj./adv. A contrahílo.
ending [ˈendiŋ] n. Fin, *m.*, final, *m.* || Final, *m.*, desenlace, *m*: *the book has a happy ending*, el libro tiene un desenlace feliz. || GRAMM. Desinencia, *f.*, terminación, *f.*
endive [ˈendiv] n. BOT. Endibia, *f.*
endleaf [ˈendli:f] n. Guarda, *f.* (of a book).
endless [ˈendlis] adj. Interminable, inacabable. || Infinito, ta. || TECH. Sin fin.
endmost [ˈendməust] adj. Más remoto, último, ma.
endocardial [endəuˈkɑ:djəl] adj. Endocardiaco, ca.
endocarditis [endəukɑ:ˈdaitis] n. MED. Endocarditis, *f.*

endocardium [ˌendəuˈkɑːdjəm] n. ANAT. Endocardio, *m.*

— OBSERV. El plural de *endocardium* es *endocardia.*

endocarp [ˈendəukɑːp] n. ANAT. Endocarpio, *m.*
endocranium [ˌendəuˈkreinjəm] n. ANAT. Endocráneo, *m.*

— OBSERV. El plural de *endocranium* es *endocrania.*

endocrine [ˈendəukrain] adj. ANAT. Endocrino, na.
— N. ANAT. Glándula (*f.*) endocrina.
endocrinal [ˌendəuˈkrainəl] or **endocrinic** [ˌendɔˈkrinik] or **endocrinous** [enˈdɔkrinəs] adj. Endocrino, na.
endocrinologist [ˌendəukriˈnɔlədʒist] n. Endocrinólogo, ga.
endocrinology [ˌendəukriˈnɔlədʒi] n. MED. Endocrinología, *f.*
endoderm [ˈendəudəːm] n. Endodermo, *m.*
endodermis [ˌendəuˈdəːmis] n. Endodermis, *f.*
endogamy [enˈdɔgəmi] n. Endogamia, *f.*
endogenous [enˈdɔdʒənəs] adj. Endógeno, na.
endogeny [enˈdɔdʒəni] n. Endogénesis, *f.*
endoparasite [ˈendəuˈpærəsait] n. ZOOL. Endoparásito, *m.*
endoparasitic [ˈendəuˌpærəˈsitik] adj. Endoparásito, ta.
endoplasm [ˈendəuplæzəm] n. Endoplasma, *m.*
endorse [inˈdɔːs] v. tr. COMM. Endosar (a cheque). | Avalar (a bill). || Aprobar (to approve). || Aceptar (to accept). || Apoyar, respaldar (to support). || Confirmar (to confirm). || Escribir los detalles de una sanción en (a driving licence, etc.). || Visar (a passport). || *To endorse over*, transferir.
endorsee [ˌendɔːˈsiː] n. Endosatario, ria.
endorsement [inˈdɔːsmənt] n. COMM. Endoso, *m.* (of a cheque). | Aval, *m.*, respaldo, *m.* (guarantee). || Aprobación, *f.* (approval). || Apoyo, *m.*, respaldo, *m.* (support).
endorser [inˈdɔːsə*] n. Endosador, ra; endosante, *m.* & *f.*
endoscope [ˈendəuskəup] n. MED. Endoscopio, *m.*
endoscopy [enˈdɔskəpi] n. MED. Endoscopia, *f.*
endoskeleton [ˈendəuˈskelitən] n. ANAT. Endoesqueleto, *m.*
endosmometer [ˌendɔzˈmɔmitə*] n. Endosmómetro, *m.*
endosmosis [ˌendɔzˈməusis] n. CHEM. Endósmosis, *f.*
endosmotic [ˈendɔzˈmɔtik] adj. CHEM. Endosmótico, ca.
endosperm [ˈendəuspəːm] n. BOT. Endosperma, *m.*
endothelium [ˌendəuˈθiːljəm] n. ANAT. Endotelio, *m.*

— OBSERV. El plural de *endothelium* es *endothelia.*

endothermal [ˌendəuˈθəːməl] or **endothermic** [ˌendəuˈθəːmik] adj. Endotérmico, ca.
endotoxin [ˌendəuˈtɔksin] n. BIOL. Endotoxina, *f.*
endow [inˈdau] v. tr. Dotar. || Hacer una donación a (to a hospital). || FIG. Dotar: *endowed with intelligence*, dotado de inteligencia.
endowment [—mənt] n. Donación, *f.* (act of endowing, money given). || Fundación, *f.*, creación, *f.* (foundation). || FIG. Don, *m.*, dote, *f.* (natural gift).
endpaper [ˈendˌpeipə*] n. Guarda, *f.* (of a book).
endue [inˈdjuː] v. tr. Dotar (with virtues). || Ponerse (a garment). || Poner (with a garment). || Investir (with an office).
endurable [inˈdjuərəbl] adj. Soportable, tolerable, aguantable (bearable).
endurance [inˈdjuərəns] n. Aguante, *m.*, resistencia, *f.* (capacity to put up with pain). || AVIAT. Autonomía (*f.*) de vuelo. || Duración, *f.* (duration). || — *Beyond* o *past endurance*, inaguantable, insoportable. || *Endurance race*, carrera (*f.*) de resistencia.
endure [inˈdjuə*] v. tr. Aguantar, soportar, sobrellevar (to suffer patiently). || Tolerar (to tolerate).
— V. intr. Aguantarse (to remain set in purpose). || Durar, perdurar (to last for a long time).
enduring [—riŋ] adj. Perdurable, duradero, ra (lasting). || Resistente (resistant). || Paciente, sufrido, da (patient).
endways [ˈendweiz] or **endwise** [—waiz] adv. De pie (upright). || De canto (edgewise). || Unidos por los extremos (next to). || Uno tras otro (one behind the other). || Longitudinalmente (lengthwise).
enema [ˈenimə] n. MED. Enema, *m.*, lavativa, *f.*

— OBSERV. El plural de *enema* es *enemas* o *enemata.*

enemy [ˈenimi] adj. Enemigo, ga.
— N. Enemigo, ga. || — *To go over to the enemy*, pasarse al enemigo. || *To make enemies*, hacerse enemigos.
energetic [ˌenəˈdʒetik] adj. Enérgico, ca (forceful). || PHYS. Energético, ca.
energetics [—s] n. Energética, *f.*
energize [ˈenədʒaiz] v. tr. Vigorizar, dar energía a, dar vigor a (to give energy to). || ELECTR. Excitar (an electromagnet). | Imanar (a coil). || FIG. Activar, estimular.
— V. intr. Obrar con energía *or* con vigor. || FIG. Activarse.
energumen [ˌenəːˈgjuːmən] n. Energúmeno, na. || FIG. Fanático, ca.
energy [ˈenədʒi] n. Energía, *f.*: *atomic energy*, energía atómica; *a person with lots of energy*, una persona que tiene mucha energía.

enervate [ˈenəːvit] adj. Deprimido, da; decaído, da (depressed). || Debilitado, da (weakened). || Falto de vigor (lacking vitality).
enervate [ˈenəːveit] v. tr. Debilitar (to weaken). || Deprimir (to depress).
enervating [—iŋ] adj. Enervador, ra; enervante. || Deprimente (depressing).
enervation [ˌenəːˈveiʃən] n. Debilitación, *f.* (weakening). || Depresión, *f.* (depression).
enfeeble [inˈfiːbl] v. tr. Debilitar (to weaken).
enfeeblement [—mənt] n. Debilitación, *f.*, debilitamiento, *m.*
enfeoff [inˈfef] v. tr. Enfeudar.
enfeoffment [—mənt] n. Enfeudación, *f.*, enfeudamiento, *m.* (investing with a fief). || Acta (*f.*) de enfeudación (document).
enfetter [inˈfetə*] v. tr. Poner los grilletes a. || FIG. Encadenar.
enfilade [ˌenfiˈleid] n. MIL. Enfilada, *f.*
enfilade [ˌenfiˈleid] v. tr. MIL. Batir por el flanco *or* en enfilada, enfilar. || *Enfilading fire*, tiro (*m.*) de enfilada.
enfold [inˈfəuld] v. tr. Envolver (to wrap up). || Estrechar: *to enfold in an embrace*, estrechar en un abrazo. || Rodear (to surround).
enforce [inˈfɔːs] v. tr. Imponer: *to enforce obedience*, imponer la obediencia. || Insistir en (to insist). || Dar fuerza a, reforzar (to give strength). || Hacer valer (claims). || Forzar (one's way). || Hacer respetar (rights). || Poner en vigor (to put into effect). || Hacer cumplir: *the purpose of the police is to enforce the law*, la policía tiene que hacer cumplir la ley.
enforceable [inˈfɔːsibl] adj. Ejecutorio, ria (contract). || Aplicable (law).
enforced [inˈfɔːst] adj. Forzado, da. || Inevitable.
enforcement [inˈfɔːsmənt] n. JUR. Entrada (*f.*) en vigor (putting into effect). | Aplicación, *f.* (of the law). || Coacción, *f.* (coercion).
enframe [inˈfreim] v. tr. Encuadrar.
enfranchise [inˈfræntʃaiz] v. tr. Conceder derechos políticos (to a person, etc.). || Conceder derechos municipales (to a town). || Conceder el derecho de votar (to give the right to vote). || Libertar, liberar (to free). || FIG. Liberar, emancipar.
enfranchisement [inˈfræntʃizmənt] n. Liberación, *f.* (from slavery). || Concesión (*f.*) de derechos políticos (to a person, etc.). || Concesión (*f.*) de derechos municipales (to a town). || Concesión (*f.*) del derecho de votar. || FIG. Liberación, *f.*, emancipación, *f.*
engage [inˈgeidʒ] v. tr./intr. Comprometer, empeñar (one's honour). || Empeñar, dar (one's word). || Comprometerse: *he engaged to do it*, se comprometió a hacerlo. || Prometer en matrimonio (one's daughter). || Contratar (a worker). || Ajustar, apalabrar, tomar a su servicio (a servant). || Reservar (theatre seats, room, etc.). || Alquilar (a taxi). || Ocupar (telephone): *to engage the line for twenty minutes*, ocupar la línea durante veinte minutos. || Ocupar (to keep busy). || Llamar (s.o.'s attention). || Requerir (efforts). || Atraer, granjearse (s.o.'s affection). || Entablar con: *to engage s.o. in conversation*, entablar conversación con alguien. || MIL. Librar, entablar, trabar (a battle). | Entablar un combate con: *to engage the enemy*, entablar un combate con el enemigo. | Emplear, utilizar (troops). | Reclutar (soldiers). || TECH. Meter, poner: *he engaged the first gear*, metió la primera velocidad. | Embragar (the clutch). | Engranar (gear wheel). | Hacer funcionar (a machine). || — *To be engaged in conversation*, estar hablando. || *To be engaged in the textile business*, trabajar en la industria textil. || *To be engaged in war*, participar en la guerra (to take part), estar en guerra (to be fighting). || *To engage for*, prometer. || *To engage in battle*, entablar un combate. || *To engage in conversation with s.o.*, entablar conversación con alguien. || *To engage in politics*, meterse en política. || *To engage o.s. to do sth.*, comprometerse a hacer algo.
engaged [—d] adj. Prometido, da (pledged to marry). || Ocupado, da (busy, not free). || Comprometido, da: *I am engaged tomorrow*, estoy comprometido para mañana. || MIL. Combatiente (fighting). || Contratado, da (a worker). || Ajustado, da; apalabrado, da (a servant). || TECH. Metido, da (gear). | Embragado, da (clutch). | Engranado, da (gear wheel). || ARCH. Empotrado, da (column). || — *Engaged tone*, señal (*f.*) de comunicando (telephone). || *The engaged couple*, los novios. || *To be engaged*, estar comunicando (telephone). || *We've been engaged for five years*, somos novios desde hace cinco años.
engagement [—mənt] n. Compromiso, *m.*: *to carry out one's engagements*, cumplir con sus compromisos. || Compromiso, *m.*: *social engagements*, compromisos sociales; *I have a prior engagement*, ya tengo un compromiso. || Cita, *f.* (appointment). || Contratación, *f.*, contrata, *f.* (of workers). || Ajuste, *m.*, apalabramiento, *m.* (of servants). || Colocación, *f.*, empleo, *m.*, puesto, *m.* (job). || Petición (*f.*) de mano (betrothal). || Noviazgo, *m.*: *we had a very long engagement*, tuvimos un noviazgo muy largo. || MIL. Combate, *m.* (battle). || SP. Encuentro, *m.* (match). || TECH. Engranaje, *m.* (of gear wheels). | Embrague, *m.* (of a car). || *Engagement ring*, sortija (*f.*) de pedida.
engaging [—iŋ] adj. Simpático, ca; atractivo, va.
engarland [inˈgɑːlənd] v. tr. Adornar con guirnaldas.

engender [in'dʒendə*] v. tr. Engendrar (a child). || FIG. Engendrar, causar.
engine ['endʒin] n. Motor, *m.*: *internal-combustion engine*, motor de combustión interna; *jet engine*, motor de reacción. || Máquina, *f.* (machine). || Artefacto, *m.*, ingenio, *m.*, máquina, *f.* (of warfare). || Locomotora, *f.* (locomotive): *steam engine*, locomotora de vapor. || FIG. Medio, *m.* (means). || — *Engine block*, bloque (*m.*) del motor. || *Engine driver*, maquinista, *m.* || *Engine nacelle*, bloque (*m.*) del motor (of aircraft). || *Engine room*, sala (*f.*) de máquinas. || *Engine shed*, depósito (*m.*) de locomotoras.
engineer [,endʒi'niə*] n. Ingeniero, *m.*: *consulting, mining, sound, army, chemical engineer*, ingeniero consultor, de minas, del sonido, militar, químico. || Mecánico, *m.* (workman). || MIL. Ingeniero (*m.*) militar (officer). | Soldado (*m.*) del Cuerpo de Ingenieros (soldier). || FIG. Autor, *m.* || U.S. Maquinista, *m.* (of railways). || *Civil engineer*, ingeniero civil, ingeniero de Caminos, Canales y Puertos.
engineer [,endʒi'niə*] v. tr. Construir (roads, bridges, etc.). || FIG. FAM. Lograr (to achieve). | Idear (to conceive). | Maquinar (a plot).
engineering [—riŋ] n. Ingeniería, *f.*: *civil engineering*, ingeniería civil. || Técnica, *f.*: *hydraulic engineering*, técnica hidráulica. || FIG. Maniobras, *f. pl.*, maquinaciones *f. pl.*
enginery ['endʒinəri] n. Maquinaria, *f.*, máquinas, *f. pl.* || FIG. Maniobras, *f. pl.*, maquinaciones, *f. pl.*
engird [in'gə:d] v. tr. Ceñir.
England ['iŋglənd] pr. n. GEOGR. Inglaterra, *f.*
English ['iŋgliʃ] adj. Inglés, esa. || — *English Channel*, Canal (*m.*) de la Mancha. || BOT. *English daisy*, margarita, *f.* || MUS. *English horn*, corno (*m.*) inglés.
— N. Inglés, *m.* (language): *I study English*, estudio inglés. || — *The English*, los ingleses. || *To speak the King's English* o *the Queen's English*, hablar un inglés correcto. || *What is the English for "mesa"?*, ¿cómo se dice mesa en inglés?
English ['iŋgliʃ] v. tr. Traducir al inglés.
Englishism ['iŋgliʃizəm] n. Anglicismo, *m.* (word, etc.). || Costumbre (*f.*) inglesa (habit).
Englishman ['iŋgliʃmən] n. Inglés, *m.*

— OBSERV. El plural es *Englishmen*.

Englishwoman ['iŋgliʃ,wumən] n. Inglesa, *f.*

— OBSERV. El plural es *Englishwomen*.

englut [in'glʌt] v. tr. Engullir, tragar.
engorge [in'gɔ:dʒ] v. tr. Devorar (to devour). || MED. Congestionar. | Obstruir.
— V. intr. Tragar.
engorgement [—mənt] n. MED. Congestión, *f.* | Obstrucción, *f.*
engraft [in'grα:ft] v. tr. Injertar (to graft in). || FIG. Inculcar (principles, habits, etc.).
engrailed [in'greild] adj. HERALD. Angrelado, da.
engrain [in'grein] v. tr. Inculcar (habits, tastes, etc.). || Teñir (to dye).
engrave [in'greiv] v. tr. Grabar: *to engrave with a burin*, grabar al buril. || FIG. Grabar, imprimir.
engraver [—ə*] n. Grabador, ra.
engraving [—iŋ] n. Grabado, *m.*: *stipple engraving*, grabado punteado; *intaglio engraving*, grabado en hueco.
engross [in'grəus] v. tr. Absorber (s.o.'s attention). || Acaparar, monopolizar (conversation, products, etc.). || Copiar, pasar a limpio (to make a fair copy of).
engrossing [—iŋ] adj. Absorbente.
engrossment [—mənt] n. Absorción, *f.* (of attention). || Redacción (*f.*) de una copia (of documents). || Monopolio, *m.*, acaparamiento, *m.* (of products, etc.).
engulf [in'gʌlf] v. tr. Sepultar, tragarse: *the river engulfed the island*, el río se tragó la isla. || Sumergir, hundir (to sink). || Rodear (to surround completely).
enhance [in'hα:ns] v. tr. Acrecentar, aumentar, intensificar. || Incrementar, aumentar (prices, etc.). || Realzar, dar realce a (beauty, etc.).
enhancement [—mənt] n. Acrecentamiento, *m.*, aumento, *m.* || Incremento, *m.*, aumento, *m.* (of prices). || Realce, *m.* (of beauty).
enigma [i'nigmə] n. Enigma, *m.*

— OBSERV. El plural es *enigmas* o *enigmata*.

enigmatic [,enig'mætik] or **enigmatical** [—əl] adj. Enigmático, ca.
enjambment or **enjambement** [in'dʒæmmənt] n. Encabalgamiento, *m.* (in poetry).
enjoin [in'dʒɔin] v. tr. Imponer: *to enjoin obedience*, imponer obediencia. || Ordenar (to command). || JUR. Prohibir (to forbid).
enjoy [in'dʒɔi] v. tr. Disfrutar de, gozar de (to delight in): *to enjoy life*, disfrutar de la vida. || Disfrutar de, gozar de (to have the use of). || Divertirse en, pasarlo bien en: *did you enjoy the party?*, ¿lo pasaste bien en la fiesta? || Gustar: *did you enjoy the book?*, ¿te gustó el libro?; *he enjoys writing*, le gusta escribir. || — *Enjoy your meal!*, ¡que aproveche! || *Enjoy yourself!*, ¡que lo pase bien!, ¡que se divierta! || *To enjoy o.s.*, divertirse, pasarlo bien.
enjoyable [in'dʒɔiəbl] adj. Agradable (pleasant). || Divertido, da (amusing).
enjoyment [in'dʒɔimənt] n. Placer, *m.*, fruición, *f.*: *with real enjoyment*, con verdadero placer. || Diversión, *f.* (sth. enjoyed). || Uso, *m.* (the use of sth.). || Disfrute, *m.* (possession).
enkindle [in'kindl] v. tr. Encender (to light up). || FIG. Atizar, avivar (passions). | Acalorar, encender, inflamar (to inflame).
enlace [in'leis] v. tr. Entrelazar (to entwine). || Rodear (to encircle).
enlacement [—mənt] n. Entrelazamiento, *m.*
enlarge [in'lα:dʒ] v. tr. Ampliar, agrandar (to make bigger). || Ensanchar (a town). || Extender, ampliar (to expand): *to enlarge the field of one's activities*, extender el campo de su actividad. || Ampliar (an organization). || PHOT. Ampliar. || Desarrollar (intelligence). || PHYS. MED. Dilatar. || U. S. Poner en libertad (to free).
— V. intr. Agrandarse, ampliarse (to become bigger). || Ensancharse (a town). || PHOT. Ampliarse. || *To enlarge on* o *upon*, extenderse sobre, tratar detalladamente, hablar extensamente sobre.
enlargement [—mənt] n. Aumento, *m.* (development). || Apéndice, *m.* (to a book). || PHOT. Ampliación, *f.* || Extensión, *f.* (extension). || Ensanche, *m.*, ensanchamiento, *m.* (of a town, etc.). || Ampliación, *f.* (of an organization): *the enlargement of the Common Market*, la ampliación del Mercado Común. || Ampliación, *f.* (of a shop). || Aumento, *m.* (of s.o.'s fortune). || Explicación (*f.*) detallada (of a subject). || PHYS. MED. Dilatación, *f.* || Liberación, *f.* (from prison).
enlarger [—ə*] n. PHOT. Ampliadora, *f.*
enlighten [in'laitn] v. tr. Aclarar, dar aclaraciones sobre (a problem). || Informar, instruir (to give information to s.o.). || Iluminar, ilustrar (mind).
enlightened [in'laitnd] adj. Culto, ta. || Bien informado, da (well informed). || Ilustrado, da (despot).
enlightening [in'laitniŋ] adj. Informativo, va. || Instructivo, va.
enlightenment [in'laitnmənt] n. Aclaración, *f.* (an enlightening). || Ilustración, *f.* (illustration). || *The Age of Enlightenment*, el Siglo Ilustrado *or* de la Ilustración, el Siglo de las Luces.
enlist [in'list] v. tr. MIL. Reclutar, alistar (to recruit). || FIG. Conseguir, lograr, obtener (help, support). | Reclutar (helpers).
— V. intr. MIL. Alistarse. || *To enlist before the usual age*, alistarse voluntario.
enlisted man [—id,mən] n. U. S. Soldado (*m.*) de tropa.

— OBSERV. El plural es *enlisted men*.

enlistment [—mənt] n. MIL. Alistamiento, *m.*, reclutamiento, *m.* || FIG. Reclutamiento, *m.*
enliven [in'laivn] v. tr. Animar, avivar (to give animation). || Alegrar, animar (to make gayer). || Estimular, animar (business).
en masse [α̃:ŋ'mæs] adv. En masa.
enmesh [in'meʃ] v. tr. Enredar, coger en una red.
enmity ['enmiti] n. Enemistad, *f.*
ennoble [i'nəubl] v. tr. Ennoblecer.
ennoblement [—mənt] n. Ennoblecimiento, *m.*
ennobling [i'nəubliŋ] n. Ennoblecimiento, *m.*
ennui [α̃:'nwi:] n. Aburrimiento, *m.* (boredom).
enology [i:'nɔlədʒi] n. Enología, *f.*
enormity [i'nɔ:miti] n. Atrocidad, *f.*, monstruosidad, *f.* (a shocking crime or error). || Enormidad, *f.* (huge size).
enormous [i'nɔ:məs] adj. Enorme (in amount, degree, size). || Monstruoso, sa; atroz (crime, error).
enormousness [—nis] n. See ENORMITY.
enough [i'nʌf] adj. Bastante, suficiente: *it's enough to*, hay bastante para; *he has enough money to buy it*, tiene bastante dinero para comprarlo.
— Adv. Suficientemente, bastante: *he is tall enough to*, es bastante alto para. || Bastante (quite, fairly): *she looks well enough*, tiene bastante buena cara. || U. S. FAM. Muy: *he was happy enough to meet you*, estaba muy contento de verte. || — *It's good enough*, está bien. || *Oddly enough*, por extraño que parezca. || *Sure enough*, más que seguro, sin duda alguna. || *Well enough*, bastante bien.
— Interj. ¡Basta! || *Enough of your nonsense!*, ¡basta de tonterías.
— N. Lo bastante, lo suficiente: *he has enough to live on*, tiene lo suficiente para vivir. || — *Enough and to spare*, de sobra. || *Enough is enough*, basta y sobra. || *It is enough for me to know that*, me basta saber que. || *That's enough*, ya está bien, con eso basta. || *There's more than enough for all of us*, hay más que bastante para todos nosotros. || *We have had enough of her*, estamos hartos de ella.
enounce [i'nauns] v. tr. Proclamar (to proclaim). || Enunciar (to state). || Pronunciar (to pronounce).
enouncement [—mənt] n. Declaración, *f.* || Enunciación, *f.*
enplane [in'plein] v. intr. Subirse a un avión, tomar el avión.
enquire [in'kwaiə*] v. tr./intr. See INQUIRE.
enquiry [in'kwaiəri] n. See INQUIRY.
enrage [in'reidʒ] v. tr. Enfurecer, poner furioso (to make furiously angry). || Enloquecer: *enraged by thirst*, enloquecido por la sed.
enrapture [in'ræptʃə*] v. tr. Arrebatar, extasiar, embelesar.
enrich [in'ritʃ] v. tr. Enriquecer. || Fertilizar, abonar (soil). || FIG. Enriquecer. || *To enrich o.s.*, enriquecerse.

enrichment [in'ritʃmənt] n. Enriquecimiento, *m.* || Fertilización, *f.*, abono, *m.* (of soil).
enrobe [in'rəub] v. tr. Vestir.
enrol or **enroll** [in'rəul] v. tr. Inscribir, apuntar en la lista (to include in a list). || Registrar (to enter in a register). || Matricular (a student). || MIL. Alistar.
— V. intr. Inscribirse (in a list). || Matricularse (to join an establishment). || MIL. Alistarse.
enrolment or **enrollment** [—mənt] n. Alistamiento, *m.* (in the forces). || Matriculación, *f.* (in university). || Inscripción, *f.* (in a list). || Registro, *m.* (in a register).
enroot [in'ru:t] v. tr. Arraigar.
en route [ã:'ru:t] adv. En el camino. || *To be en route for*, ir camino de, ir en dirección de.
ens [enz] n. PHIL. Ente, *m.*
— OBSERV. El plural de *ens* es *entia*.
ensanguine [in'sæŋgwin] v. tr. Ensangrentar.
ensconce [in'skɔns] v. tr. Esconder, ocultar (to conceal). || *To be ensconced in*, estar cómodamente instalado en, estar arrellanado en.
ensemble [ã:n'sã:mbl] n. Conjunto, *m.* || MUS. Conjunto, *m.* | Orquesta (*f.*) de cámara. || THEATR. Compañía, *f.* || Conjunto, *m.* (dress).
enshrine [in'ʃrain] v. tr. REL. Poner en un relicario. || Encerrar (to enclose). || FIG. Conservar religiosamente (to put in an honoured place).
enshroud [in'ʃraud] v. tr. Envolver. || Disimular.
ensign ['ensain] n. Enseña, *f.*, pabellón, *m.* (flag). || Abanderado, *m.* (standard bearer). || Insignia, *f.*, distintivo, *m.* (badge). || U.S. MAR. Alférez, *m.*
ensilage ['ensilidʒ] n. Ensilaje, *m.*, ensilado, *m.*
ensilage ['ensilidʒ] or **ensile** ['ensail] v. tr. Ensilar.
enslave [in'sleiv] v. tr. Esclavizar.
enslavement [—mənt] n. Esclavitud, *f.*
enslaver [—ə*] n. Esclavista, *m.* & *f.*
ensnare [in'snɛə*] v. tr. Coger en una trampa.
ensphere [in'sfiə*] v. tr. Abarcar.
ensue [in'sju:] v. intr. Resultar (to result). || Seguirse, seguir (to follow). || Originarse (to be caused).
ensuing [—iŋ] adj. Consiguiente, resultante. || Siguiente (year).
ensure [in'ʃuə*] v. tr. Asegurar.
enswathe [in'sweið] v. tr. Envolver. || Fajar, poner pañales (a baby).
entablature [en'tæblətʃə*] n. ARCH. Entablamento, *m.*
entail [in'teil] n. JUR. Vínculo, *m.* (link).
entail [in'teil] v. tr. Traer consigo, acarrear, ocasionar (to bring as a consequence). || Suponer, implicar (to involve). || JUR. Vincular.
entailment [—mənt] n. JUR. Vinculación, *f.*
entangle [in'tæŋgl] v. tr. Enredar, enmarañar: *to entangle a ball of wool*, enredar un ovillo de lana; *he got entangled in the rope*, se enredó en la cuerda. || Complicar, enredar, liar (to involve in difficulties). || FIG. *To get entangled*, meterse en un lío.
entanglement [—mənt] n. Enredo, *m.*, embrollo, *m.* (an entangling or being entangled). || MIL. Alambrada, *f.* || FIG. Lío, *m.*: *to keep out of the entanglement*, no meterse en el lío. | Lío, *m.* (love affair).
entasis ['entəsis] n. ARCH. Éntasis, *f.*
entelechy [en'teləki] n. Entelequia, *f.*
entente [ã:n'tã:nt] n. Convenio, *m.*, alianza, *f.*, acuerdo, *m.* || HIST. *Entente Cordiale*, Entente (*f.*) Cordial.
enter ['entə*] v. tr. Entrar en: *to enter a room*, entrar en una habitación; *to enter the age of space travel*, entrar en la era de los vuelos espaciales. || Penetrar en, entrar en (to penetrate into). || Pasarse por: *it never entered my head*, nunca se me pasó por la cabeza. || Meterse en: *to enter politics*, meterse en política. || Entrar en, tomar parte en, participar en (a conversation, competition, plot, etc.). || Entrar en, ingresar en: *to enter a firm*, entrar en una empresa. || Hacerse miembro de (to join). || Abrazar (a profession). || Inscribir: *to enter a car for a race*, inscribir un coche para una carrera. || Inscribir, apuntar (in a list). || Registrar (to record). || Matricular (a child in a school). || Matricularse en: *to enter one's name for the summer school*, matricularse en los cursos de verano. || Presentar (a request, claim, etc.). || Formular, elevar: *she entered a protest*, elevó una protesta. || JUR. Entablar, intentar (an action), interponer (an appeal), depositar, registrar en el depósito legal (a book), declarar (a cargo). || MIL. Alistarse en. || Declarar (for customs). || — FAM. *To enter an appearance*, hacer acto de presencia. || *To enter religion*, abrazar el estado religioso.
— V. intr. Entrar (to go or to come in). || THEATR. Entrar en *or* salir a escena.
— ***To enter for***, tomar parte en, participar en (race). | Presentarse como candidato a (post). || ***To enter into***, empezar (to start upon). | Entablar, iniciar (negotiations). | Tomar parte en, participar en (a conversation). | Establecer (relations). | Concertar (agreement). | Celebrar (contract). | Cerrar (bargain). | Contraer (obligation). | Comprender (a joke). | Entrar en, meterse en: *to enter into details*, entrar en detalles. | Compartir (feelings). | Entrar en: *this never entered into the plans*, esto nunca entró en los planes. | || ***To enter up***, registrar (in accounts). || ***To enter upon*** o ***on***, comenzar, emprender, empezar (to begin). | Tomar posesión de (a property).
enteralgia [,entər'ældʒiə] n. MED. Enteralgia, *f.*
enteric [en'terik] adj. MED. Entérico, ca; intestinal. || *Enteric fever*, fiebre entérica *or* tifoidea.
enteritis [,entə'raitis] n. MED. Enteritis, *f.*
enterprise ['entəpraiz] n. Empresa, *f.*: *a business enterprise*, una empresa comercial; *a dangerous enterprise*, una empresa peligrosa. || Iniciativa, *f.* (personal characteristic): *spirit of enterprise*, espíritu de iniciativa. || Carácter (*m.*) emprendedor. || *Private enterprise*, sector privado, empresa privada.
enterprising [—iŋ] adj. Emprendedor, ra. || Lleno de iniciativa. || Decidido, da (resolute).
entertain [,entə'tein] v. tr. Recibir (to receive as a guest). || Entretener, divertir (to amuse). || Mantener (conversation, relations). || Albergar, abrigar (to have in one's mind): *to entertain the hope that*, abrigar la esperanza de que. || Considerar (to consider). || *To entertain friends to dinner*, invitar a unos amigos a cenar.
— V. intr. Recibir invitados.
entertainer [—ə*] n. Artista, *m.* & *f.* (in show business). || Animador, ra (amusing person). || Anfitrión, ona (host, hostess).
entertaining [—iŋ] adj. Entretenido, da; divertido, da.
entertainment [—mənt] n. Entretenimiento, *m.*, diversión, *f.*, distracción, *f.* (amusement). || Espectáculo, *m.* (public performance). || Hospitalidad, *f.*, recibimiento, *m.* (hospitality). || Recepción, *f.* (reception). || — *Entertainment allowance*, gastos (*m. pl.*) de representación. || *Entertainment tax*, impuesto aplicado a los espectáculos.
enthral or **enthrall** [in'θrɔ:l] v. tr. Cautivar.
enthraling or **enthralling** [—iŋ] adj. Cautivador, ra.
enthralment or **enthrallment** [—mənt] n. Encanto, *m.*, embeleso, *m.*
enthrone [in'θrəun] v. tr. Entronizar.
enthronement [—mənt] n. Entronización, *f.*
enthuse [in'θju:z] v. intr. Entusiasmarse: *to enthuse over sth.*, entusiasmarse por algo.
enthusiasm [in'θju:ziæzəm] n. Entusiasmo, *m.*
enthusiast [in'θju:ziæst] n. Entusiasta, *m.* & *f.*
enthusiastic [in,θju:zi'æstik] adj. Entusiástico, ca (praise, etc.). || Entusiasta (person). || *To be enthusiastic about* o *to become enthusiastic over*, entusiasmarse por.
entia ['enʃiə] pl. n. See ENS.
entice [in'tais] v. tr. Seducir (to seduce). || Atraer (to attract). || Convencer: *to entice s.o. away from his duty*, convencer a uno para que abandone su obligación.
enticement [—mənt] n. Atractivo, *m.* (attraction). || Seducción, *f.* (seduction). || Tentación, *f.*
enticing [—iŋ] adj. Atractivo, va; seductor, ra. || Tentador, ra.
entire [in'taiə*] adj. Entero, ra; completo, ta: *the entire fleet*, la flota entera. || Total, todo, da; entero, ra: *the entire population*, toda la población. || Intacto, ta: *the stocks are still entire*, las existencias están aún intactas. || BOT. Entero, ra. || Entero (a horse).
— N. Semental, *m.* (horse). || FIG. Totalidad, *f.*
entirely [in'taiəli] adv. Completamente, totalmente, enteramente (wholly). || Únicamente (solely).
entirety [in'taiərəti] n. Totalidad, *f.*: *the country in its entirety*, el país en su totalidad.
entitle [in'taitl] v. tr. Dar derecho a (to empower): *this ticket entitles you to a seat*, este billete le da derecho a sentarse. || Titular, dar el título de (to give a title to). || *To be entitled*, tener derecho: *you are entitled to think what you want*, tienes derecho a pensar lo que quieras; titularse (a book, a film, etc.).
entity ['entiti] n. PHIL. Entidad, *f.* || *Legal entity*, persona jurídica.
entomb [in'tu:m] v. tr. Enterrar, sepultar.
entomologic [,entəmə'lɔdʒik] or **entomological** [—əl] adj. Entomológico, ca.
entomologist [,entə'mɔlədʒist] n. Entomólogo, *m.*
entomology [,entə'mɔlədʒi] n. Entomología, *f.*
entomophagous [,entə'mɔfəgəs] adj. ZOOL. Entomófago, fa.
entomophily [,entə'mɔfili] n. Entomofilia, *f.*
entourage [,ɔntu'rɑ:ʒ] n. Séquito, *m.* (retinue). || Allegados, *m. pl.* (people who are close to). || Ambiente, *m.*, entorno, *m.* (surroundings).
entozoan [,entə'zəuən] n. ZOOL. Entozoario, *m.*
entr'acte ['ɔntrækt] n. Entreacto, *m.*
entrails ['entreilz] pl. n. Entrañas, *f.*
entrain [in'trein] v. tr. Poner en un tren (troops).
— V. intr. Tomar el tren (troops).
entrance ['entrəns] n. Entrada, *f.* || Admisión, *f.*, ingreso, *m.*: *entrance examination*, examen de ingreso. || Bocacalle, *f.* (to a street). || THEATR. Salida (*f.*) a escena. || — *Entrance hall*, vestíbulo, *m.*, entrada, *f.* || *No entrance*, prohibida la entrada. || *Tradesmen's entrance*, entrada de servicio. || *To pay one's entrance fee*, pagar los derechos de entrada *or* de admisión.
entrance [in'trɑ:ns] v. tr. Arrebatar, extasiar (to overcome with joy). || Poner en trance (to put into a trance).
entrancement [—mənt] n. Arrebato, *m.*, éxtasis, *m.* || Trance, *m.*
entrancing [—iŋ] adj. Encantador, ra; fascinante.
entrant ['entrənt] n. Participante, *m.* & *f.* (candidate). || Principiante, *m.* & *f.* (beginner). || Persona (*f.*) que entra: *late entrants are a nuisance in a theatre*,

ENTERTAINMENTS. — DIVERSIONES *f.*

I. Circus. — Circo, *m.*

travelling circus	circo (*m.*) ambulante
circus wagon	carromato *m.*
big top	toldo (*m.*) de circo, carpa *f.*
tent	tienda *f.*, carpa *f.*
ring, arena	pista *f.*
tier	grada *f.*
master of ceremonies, M.C.	presentador *m.*
parade, cavalcade	desfile *m.*
show	espectáculo *m.*
circus act	número (*m.*) de circo
equitation, riding	equitación *f.*
equestrian, rider	artista (*m.* y *f.*) ecuestre
horse trainer	domador (*m.*) de caballos
trick rider, equestrian acrobat	acróbata (*m.* y *f.*) ecuestre
lion tamer	domador (*m.*) de leones
wild animal	fiera *f.*
wild animal trainer	domador (*m.*) de fieras
cage	jaula *f.*
whip	látigo *m.*
performing animal	animal (*m.*) amaestrado
contortionist	contorsionista *m.* y *f.*
acrobat	acróbata *m.* y *f.*
mountebank, tumbler	saltimbanqui *m.* y *f.*
tights, *pl.*, leotard	leotardo *m. sing.*
tumble	pirueta *f.*, trecha *f.*
double somersault	doble salto (*m.*) mortal
human pyramid	pirámide (*f.*) *or* torre (*f.*) humana
balance	equilibrio *m.*
balancer	equilibrista *m.* y *f.*
rings	aros *m.*
springboard	trampolín *m.*
trampoline	cama (*f.*) elástica
trapeze	trapecio *m.*
trapeze artist	trapecista *m.* y *f.*
flier [U.S., aerialist]	volatinero *m.*
safety net	red *f.*
tightrope, walker, rope-walker funambulist	funámbulo, la
tightrope	cuerda (*f.*) floja
balancing pole	contrapeso *m.*
juggler	malabarista *m.* *f.*
clown	payaso *m.*
giant	gigante *m.*
midget, dwarf	enano *m.*
sword swallower	tragasables *m. inv.*
fire eater	tragafuego *m.*
snake charmer	encantador (*m.*) de serpientes
fakir; magician	faquir *m.*; mago *m.*
illusionist	ilusionista *m.* y *f.*
conjurer, conjuror	prestidigitador *m.*, escamoteador *m.*
ventriloquist	ventrílocuo *m.*

II. Fun fair. — Parque (*m.*) de atracciones.

fair	feria *f.*; verbena *f.*
amusement park	parque (*m.*) de atracciones
merry-go-round, roundabout [U.S., carrousel]	tiovivo *m.*, caballitos *m. pl.*
switchback, scenic railway, big dipper [U.S., roller coaster]	montaña (*f.*) rusa
ghost train	tren (*m.*) fantasma
big wheel, Ferris wheel	noria *f.*
dodgems, bumper cars	coches (*m.*) que chocan
slide, helter-skelter	tobogán *m.*
sideshow, stall, booth	barraca (*f.*) de feria
fortune teller	pitonisa *f.*
rifle range, shooting gallery	barraca (*f.*) de tiro
wheel of fortune	rueda (*f.*) de la fortuna
tombola	tómbola *f.*, rifa *f.*
Punch and Judy show, puppet show	teatro (*m.*) de marionetas *or* de títeres
greasy pole	cucaña *f.*

III. Dancing. — Baile, *m.*

dance	baile *m.*, danza *f.*
classical dancing	baile (*m.*) clásico
ballet	ballet *m.*
corps de ballet	cuerpo (*m.*) de ballet
ballet dancer	bailarina (*f.*) de ballet
tutu, ballet skirt	tutú *m.*, tonelete *m.*
ballet shoe	zapatilla (*f.*) de ballet
choreography	coreografía *f.*
steps	pasos *m.*
ballroom dance	baile (*m.*) de sociedad
ballroom, dance hall	sala (*f.*) de baile
dance orchestra	orquesta (*f.*) de baile
dancing partner	pareja (*f.*) de baile
folk dance	baile (*m.*) tradicional *or* folklórico

IV. Other entertainments. — Otras diversiones, *f.*

ice skating	patinaje (*m.*) sobre hielo
figure skating	patinaje (*m.*) artístico
ice skates	patines (*m.*) de cuchilla
roller skating	patinaje (*m.*) sobre ruedas
roller skates	patines (*m.*) de ruedas
festival	festival *m.*
discotheque	discoteca *f.*
records	discos *m.*
jukebox	máquina (*f.*) de discos
party	guateque *m.*
masked ball, fancy dress ball	baile (*m.*) de disfraces
face mask	máscara *f.*, careta *f.*
half mask, small mask	antifaz *m.*
costume	disfraz *m.*
carnival	carnaval *m.*
carnival parade	cabalgata (*f.*) de carnaval
float	carroza *f.*
paper lantern	farolillo *m.*
paper streamer	serpentina *f.*
confetti	papelillos *m. pl.*, confeti *m. pl.*
firework display, fireworks, *pl.*	fuegos (*m. pl.*) artificiales
jumping jack *o* cracker	buscapiés *m. inv.*
banger	petardo *m.*
rocket	cohete *m.*
variety show	espectáculo (*m.*) de variedades
cabaret	cabaret *m.*
vaudeville	vodevil *m.* (comedy), variedades *f. pl.* (variety show)
music hall	teatro (*m.*) de variedades
nightclub	sala (*f.*) de fiestas
floor show	atracciones *f. pl.*
comedian	comediante, ta
singer	cantante *m.* y *f.*
chorus girls	coristas *f.*
stripper, stripteaser	mujer (*f.*) que hace strip-tease
pub	taberna *f.*, bar *m.*
jazz club	club (*m.*) de jazz
one-armed bandit, fruit machine	máquina (*f.*) tragaperras
casino	casino *m.*
club	círculo *m.*, casino *m.*, peña *f.*
excursion, outing	excursión *f.*
a day in the country	partida (*f.*) de campo, gira (*f.*) campestre
picnic	comida (*f.*) campestre
pleasure trip	viaje (*m.*) de recreo
to go for a walk	dar un paseo
park	parque *m.*
flower gardens	jardines *m.*
playground	campo (*m.*) de juego
swing	columpio *m.*
balloon	globo *m.*
sandpit [U.S., sandbox]	cajón (*m.*) de arena
bucket and spade	cubo (*m.*) y pala *f.*
sandcastle	castillo (*m.*) de arena
miniature golf	minigolf *m.*
rowing boat	barco (*m.*) de remos
paddle boat	hidropedal *m.*
sailing boat	velero *m.*
zoo	parque (*m.*) zoológico

See also DEPORTE, VIAJES, CINEMATOGRAPHY, GAMES, RADIO AND TELEVISION

las personas que entran tarde en un teatro molestan mucho.

entrap [inˈtræp] v. tr. Coger en una trampa.

entreat [inˈtri:t] v. tr. Suplicar, implorar, rogar.

entreatingly [—iŋli] adv. Encarecidamente.

entreaty [inˈtri:ti] n. Súplica, *f.*, ruego, *m.*

entrechat [ɑ̃ntrəˈʃɑ:] n. Trenzado, *m.* (dance).

entrée (U. S. **entree**) [ˈɔntrei] n. Entrada, *f.* || CULIN. Entrada, *f.*, principio, *m.* || U. S. Plato (*m.*) fuerte (main course).

entrench [inˈtrentʃ] v. tr. Atrincherar. || *The enemy entrenched themselves on the hill*, el enemigo se atrincheró en la colina.
— V. intr. Atrincherarse. || See ENCROACH.

entrenchment [—mənt] n. Atrincheramiento, *m.* || See ENCROACHMENT.

entrepôt [ˈɔntrəpəu] n. Centro (*m.*) comercial de importación y distribución. || Almacén, *m.* (storehouse).

entrepreneur [ˌɔntrəprəˈnə:*] n. Empresario, *m.* (man who runs a business). || Intermediario, *m.* (middleman). || Contratista, *m.* (of works).

entresol [ˈɔntrəsɔl] n. Entresuelo, *m.*

entrust [inˈtrʌst] v. tr. Confiar (to commit). || Encargar (*with*, de) [s.o.]

entry [ˈentri] n. Entrada, *f.* (entrance). || Acceso, *m.* (access). || Vestíbulo, *m.*, recibidor, *m.*, entrada, *f.* (hall). || Pasadizo, *m.* (a narrow lane leading to a building). || Bocacalle, *f.* (to a street). || Entrada, *f.*, artículo, *m.* (in a dictionary). || JUR. Toma (*f.*) de posesión. || Asiento, *m.* (in bookkeeping). || Anotación, *f.*, registro, *m.* (in a book, etc.). || Ingreso, *m.* (into profession, etc.). || SP. Participante, *m.* & *f.* (entrant). | Lista (*f.*) de participantes (list). || COMM. Partida, *f.* (item): *double-entry, single-entry bookkeeping*, contabilidad por partida doble, simple. || — *No entry*, dirección prohibida (streets), prohibida la entrada (on a door). || *Forcible entry*, violación (*f.*) de domicilio, allanamiento (*m.*) de morada. || *To force an entry*, allanar la morada.

entryway [—wei] n. U. S. Entrada, *f.*

entwine [inˈtwain] v. tr. Entrelazar (to plait). || Enroscar (to twist around).
— V. intr. Entrelazarse. || Enroscarse.

entwist [inˈtwist] v. tr. Enroscar.

enucleate [iˈnju:kliit] adj. Sin núcleo.

enucleate [i'nju:klieit] v. tr. Deshuesar, desosar (to extract the stone from a fruit, etc.). || BIOL. Extraer el núcleo de. || MED. Extirpar, enuclear (a tumour). || FIG. Explicar, aclarar, esclarecer.
enucleation [i,nju:kli'eiʃən] n. BIOL. Extracción (*f.*) del núcleo. || MED. Extirpación (*f.*) de un tumor, enucleación, *f.* || FIG. Aclaración, *f.*, esclarecimiento, *m.* (of a problem).
enumerate [i'nju:məreit] v. tr. Enumerar.
enumeration [i,nju:mə'reiʃən] n. Enumeración, *f.*
enumerative [i'nju:mərətiv] adj. Enumerativo, va.
enunciate [i'nʌnsieit] v. tr. Enunciar (a principle). || Formular, enunciar (to state). || Pronunciar, articular (sounds, syllables, etc.). || Proclamar (to proclaim).
— V. intr. Articular (to articulate).
enunciation [i,nʌnsi'eiʃən] n. Enunciado, *m.*, enunciación, *f.* (of a principle). || Pronunciación, *f.*, articulación, *f.* (of sounds, syllables). || Proclamación, *f.*, declaración, *f.*
enunciative [i'nʌnʃjətiv] adj. Enunciativo, va.
enunciator [i'nʌnsieitə*] n. Persona (*f.*) que enuncia *or* declara algo.
envelop [in'veləp] v. tr. Envolver.
envelop or **envelope** ['envələup] n. Sobre, *m.* (for letters). || Funda, *f.* (cover). || Envoltura, *f.*, cubierta, *f.* (of an airship). || ANAT. BOT. Túnica, *f.* || MATH. Envolvente, *f.*
enveloping [in'veləpiŋ] adj. Envolvente.
envelopment [in'veləpmənt] n. Envoltura, *f.* (wrapper). || Envolvimiento, *m.* (wrapping up).
envenom [in'venəm] v. tr. Envenenar, emponzoñar.
enviable ['enviəbl] adj. Envidiable.
envious ['enviəs] adj. Envidioso, sa. || — *It made him envious of their riches*, le dio envidia de su riqueza. || *To be envious of*, tener envidia de, envidiar a. (s.o.).
enviousness [—nis] n. Envidia, *f.*
environ [in'vaiərən] v. tr. Rodear.
environment [in'vaiərənmənt] n. Medio ambiente, *m.*, entorno, *m.*: *pollution of the environment*, contaminación del medio ambiente. || Ambiente, *m.* (surroundings).
environmental [in,vaiərən'mentəl] adj. Ambiental.
environs [in'vaiərənz] pl. n. Alrededores, *m.*, cercanías, *f.*
envisage [in'vizidʒ] v. tr. Imaginarse, concebir, pensar en (to have a mental picture of). || Pensar, creer: *I do not envisage arriving before ten o'clock*, no pienso llegar antes de las diez. || Proyectar, tener la intención de: *I envisage going to France*, proyecto irme a Francia. || Enfocar, ver (to look at): *I had not envisaged the matter in that light*, no había enfocado la cuestión de esta manera. || Pretender llegar a: *I don't envisage an agreement*, no pretendo llegar a un acuerdo. || Prever (to foresee).
envision [in'viʒən] v. tr. U. S. Imaginar.
envoy ['envɔi] n. Enviado, *m.*, mensajero, *m.* (s.o. sent on a mission). || *Envoy extraordinary*, enviado extraordinario.
envy ['envi] n. Envidia, *f.*: *he could not hide his envy*, no podía ocultar su envidia. || Cosa (*f.*) envidiada (sth. desired). || *She was the envy of the other girls*, las otras chicas la envidiaban.
envy ['envi] v. tr. Envidiar, tener envidia de: *I don't envy you*, no te envidio.
— V. intr. Tener envidia.
enwrap [in'ræp] v. tr. Envolver (to envelop). || FIG. Absorber (to engross).
enwreathe [in'ri:ð] v. tr. See ENGARLAND.
enzootic [,enzəu'ɔtik] n. Enzootia, *f.*
enzyme ['enzaim] n. Enzima, *f.*
eocene ['i:əusi:n] adj. GEOL. Eoceno.
— N. Eoceno, *m.*
eolith ['i:əuliθ] n. Eolito, *m.*
eparch ['epɑ:k] n. Eparca, *m.*
epaulet or **epaulette** ['epəulet] n. MIL. Charretera, *f.*
épée ['eipei] n. Espada, *f.*
epeira [e'pairə] n. ZOOL. Epeira, *f.*
epenthesis [e'penθisis] n. GRAMM. Epéntesis, *f.*
epergne [i'pə:n] n. Centro (*m.*) de mesa.
ephebe [i'fib] or **ephebus** [—əs] n. Efebo, *m.*

— OBSERV. El plural de *ephebus* es *ephebi*.

ephedrine ['efidrin] n. Efedrina, *f.*
ephemera [i'femərə] n. ZOOL. Efímera, *f.*, cachipolla, *f.* || Cosa (*f.*) efímera.

— OBSERV. El plural de la palabra *ephemera* es *ephemerae* o *ephemeras*, pero es preferible emplear este último.

ephemeral [i'femərəl] adj. Efímero, ra.
ephemeris [i'feməris] n. Efemérides, *f. pl.*

— OBSERV. El plural de *ephemeris* es *ephemerides*.

ephemeron [i'femərɔn] n. ZOOL. Efímera, *f.*, cachipolla, *f.*

— OBSERV. El plural es *ephemera* o *ephemerons*.

Ephesus ['efisəs] pr. n. GEOGR. Éfeso.
epiblast ['epiblæst] n. BIOL. Epiblasto, *m.*
epic ['epik] n. Poema (*f.*) épico, épica, *f.* epopeya. *f.*
— Adj. Épico, ca. || FIG. Épico, ca.
epicarp ['epikɑ:p] n. BOT. Epicarpio, *m.*
epicene ['episi:n] adj. GRAMM. Epiceno. || Hermafrodita.
— N. Hermafrodita.

epicentre (U. S. **epicenter**) ['epi,sentə*] n. Epicentro, *m.*
epicentral [,epi'sentrəl] adj. Epicéntrico, ca.
epicure ['epikjuə*] n. Epicúreo, a (pleasure seeker). || Gastrónomo, ma; sibarita, *m.* & *f.* (gastronome).
Epicurean [,epikjuə'ri:ən] adj./n. Epicúreo, a.
epicureanism [—izəm] or **epicurism** ['epikjuərizəm] n. Epicureísmo, *m.*
Epicurus [,epi'kjuərəs] pr. n. Epicuro, *m.*
epicycle ['episaikl] n. Epiciclo, *m.*
epicyclic [,epi'saiklik] adj. Epicíclico, ca.
epicycloid [,epi'saiklɔid] n. MATH. Epicicloide, *f.*
epicycloidal [,episai'klɔidəl] adj. Epicicloidal.
epidemic [,epi'demik] n. MED. Epidemia, *f.* || FIG. Ola, *f.*
— Adj. Epidémico, ca.
epidemical [—əl] adj. Epidémico, ca.
epidermal [,epi'də:məl] or **epidermic** [,epi'də:mik] adj. Epidérmico, ca.
epidermis [,epi'də:mis] n. Epidermis, *f.*

— OBSERV. El plural de la palabra inglesa es *epidermes*.

epididymis [,epi'didəmis] n. ANAT. Epidídimo, *m.*
epigastric [,epi'gæstrik] adj. ANAT. Epigástrico, ca.
epigastrium [,epi'gæstriəm] n. ANAT. Epigastrio, *m.*

— OBSERV. El plural de *epigastrium* es *epigastria*.

epigeal [,epi'dʒiəl] or **epigean** [,epi'dʒiən] adj. BOT. ZOOL. Epigeo, a.
epigenesis [,epi'dʒenisis] n. Epigénesis, *f.*
epigenetic [,epidʒə'netik] adj. Epigenético, ca.
epigeous [,epi'dʒiəs] adj. Epigeo, a.
epiglottis [,epi'glɔtis] n. Epiglotis, *f.*
epigone ['epigəun] n. Epígono, *m.*
epigram ['epigræm] n. Epigrama, *m.*
epigrammatic [,epigrə'mætik] or **epigrammatical** [—əl] adj. Epigramático, ca.
epigrammatist [,epi'græmətist] n. Epigramista, *m.*, epigramatista, *m.*
epigraph ['epigrɑ:f] n. Epígrafe, *m.*
epigraphic [,epi'græfik] or **epigraphical** [—əl] adj. Epigráfico, ca.
epigraphist [e'pigrəfist] n. Epigrafista, *m.* & *f.*
epigraphy [e'pigrəfi] n. Epigrafía, *f.*
epilepsy ['epilepsi] n. Epilepsia, *f.*
epileptic [,epi'leptik] adj./n. MED. Epiléptico, ca.
epilogue (U. S. **epilog**) ['epilɔg] n. Epílogo, *m.*
Epiphany [i'pifəni] n. REL. Epifanía, *f.*
epiphenomenalism [,epifi'nɔminəlizəm] n. Epifenomenismo, *m.*
epiphenomenon [,epifi'nɔminən] n. Epifenómeno, *m.*

— OBSERV. El plural de *epiphenomenon* es *epiphenomena*.

epiphysis [i'pifəsis] n. ANAT. Epífisis, *f.*

— OBSERV. El plural de *epiphysis* es *epiphyses*.

epiphyte ['epifait] n. BOT. Epifita, *f.*
epiphytic [,epi'fitik] or **epiphytical** [—əl] adj. BOT. Epifito, ta.
episcopacy [i'piskəpəsi] n. REL. Episcopado, *m.*
episcopal [i'piskəpəl] adj. REL. Episcopal.
episcopalian [i,piskə'peiljən] adj./n. REL. Episcopalista.
episcopalism [i'piskəpəlizəm] n. REL. Episcopalismo, *m.*
episcopate [i'piskəupit] n. REL. Episcopado, *m.*
episode ['episəud] n. Episodio, *m.*
episodic [,epi'sɔdik] or **episodical** [—əl] adj. Episódico, ca.
episternum [,epis'tə:nəm] n. ANAT. Episternón, *m.*

— OBSERV. El plural de *episternum* es *episterna*.

epistle [i'pisl] n. Epístola, *f.*
Epistle [i'pisl] n. REL. Epístola, *f.*
epistolary [i'pistələri] adj. Epistolar.
— N. Epistolario, *m.*
epistyle ['epistail] n. ARCH. Arquitrabe, *m.*
epitaph ['epitɑ:f] n. Epitafio, *m.*
epithalamial [,epiθə'leimjəl] or **epithalamic** [,epiθə'læmik] adj. Epitalámico, ca.
epithalamion [,epiθə'leimjən] n. Epitalamio, *m.*

— OBSERV. El plural de *epithalamion* es *epithalamia*.

epithalamium [,epiθə'leimjəm] n. Epitalamio, *m.*

— OBSERV. El plural es *epithalamiums* o *epithalamia*.

epithelial [,epi'θi:ljəl] adj. Epitelial.
epithelioma [,epi,θi:li'əumə] n. MED. Epitelioma, *m.*
epithelium [,epi'θi:ljəm] n. ANAT. Epitelio, *m.*

— OBSERV. El plural es *epitheliums* o *epithelia*.

epithet ['epiθet] n. Epíteto, *m.*
epitome [i'pitəmi] n. Epítome, *m.*, resumen, *m.*, compendio, *m.* (summary). || FIG. Personificación, *f.*
epitomize [i'pitəmaiz] v. tr. Resumir, compendiar. || FIG. Ser la personificación de.
epizootic [,epizəu'ɔtik] n. Epizootia, *f.*
epizooty [,epizəu'ɔti] n. Epizootia, *f.*
epoch ['i:pɔk] n. Época, *f.*: *to mark an epoch*, hacer época.
epoch-making [—,meikiŋ] adj. Que hace época.
epode ['epəud] n. POET. Epodo, *m.*
eponym ['epəunim] n. Epónimo, *m.*
eponymic [,epə'nimik] or **eponymous** [i'pɔniməs] adj. Epónimo, ma.
epopee ['epəpi:] or **epopoeia** [,epə'piə] n. Epopeya, *f.*
epos ['epɔs] n. Epopeya, *f.*

epsilon [ep'sailən] n. Épsilon, *f.*
Epsom ['epsəm] pr. n. GEOGR. Epsom. || CHEM. *Epsom salts*, sulfato (*m.*) de magnesio, sal (*f.*) de la Higuera.
equability [,ekwə'biliti] n. Ecuanimidad, *f.* (composure). || Uniformidad, *f.*, igualdad, *f.*
equable ['ekwəbl] adj. Regular, uniforme: *an equable climate*, un clima regular. || Ecuánime (calm): *equable disposition*, temperamento ecuánime.
equal ['i:kwəl] adj. Igual: *she is equal to you*, ella es igual que tú; *equal in value*, de igual valor. || Igualado, da: *an equal match*, un partido igualado. || Igual, mismo, ma: *you have equal rights*, tienes los mismos derechos. || Equitativo, va (treatment). || Regular, uniforme (uniform). || — *All things being equal*, si todo sigue igual. || *Equal distance*, equidistancia, *f.* || SP. *Equal on points*, empatados. || *Equal pay*, igualdad (*f.*) de salario. || *Equal rights*, igualdad (*f.*) de derechos. || *Equal sign*, signo (*m.*) de igualdad. || *Equal to*, igual que: *her share is equal to his*, su parte es igual que la de él; equivalente a (equivalent to). || *On equal terms*, en un plano de igualdad. || *Other things being equal*, si todo sigue igual, en igualdad de condiciones. || *To be equal to*, tener fuerzas *or* ánimo para (a task), estar a la altura de (a situation). || *To feel equal to a task*, sentirse con fuerzas para hacer un trabajo. || *With equal ease*, con la misma facilidad, con igual facilidad.
— N. Igual, *m.* & *f.* || *To treat s.o. as an equal*, tratar a uno de igual a igual.
equal ['i:kwəl] v. tr. Igualar, ser igual a (to be or become equal to). || Igualar (to come up to the standard of). || Ser igual a, ser: *three and five equals eight*, tres más cinco son ocho.
equalitarian [ik,wɔli'tɛərjən] adj. Igualitario, ria.
equality [i:'kwɔliti] n. Igualdad, *f.* || *To be on an equality with*, estar en un pie de igualdad con.
equalization [,i:kwəlai'zeiʃən] n. Igualación, *f.*, igualamiento, *m.* || SP. Empate, *m.* || Compensación, *f.*: *equalization fund*, fondo de compensación.
equalize ['i:kwəlaiz] v. tr./intr. Igualar. || SP. Empatar, igualar.
equalizer [—ə*] n. SP. Tanto (*m.*) del empate. || ELECTR. Compensador, *m.*
equally ['i:kwəli] adv. Igualmente (to the same degree). || Equitativamente (equitably). || *Equally matched*, de igual fuerza.
equanimity [,ekwə'nimiti] n. Ecuanimidad, *f.*
equate [i'kweit] v. tr. MATH. Poner en ecuación. || FIG. Igualar, equiparar (to regard as equal). | Comparar (to compare).
equation [i'kweiʒən] n. MATH. Ecuación, *f.*: *quadratic equation*, ecuación de segundo grado. || CHEM. Ecuación (*f.*) química. || MATH. *Simple equation*, ecuación de primer grado.
equator [ik'weitə*] n. Ecuador, *m.*
equatorial [,ekwə'tɔ:riəl] adj. Ecuatorial.
— N. Ecuatorial, *m.*
equerry ['ekwəri] n. Caballerizo (*m.*) de la casa real.
equestrian [i'kwestriən] adj. Ecuestre.
— N. Caballista, *m.*, jinete, *m.*
equestrienne [i,kwestri'en] n. Amazona, *f.*, caballista, *f.* (woman who rides on horseback).
equiangular [,i:kwi'æŋgjulə*] adj. MATH. Equiángulo, la.
equidistance ['i:kwi'distəns] n. Equidistancia, *f.*
equidistant ['i:kwi'distənt] adj. Equidistante.
equilateral ['i:kwi'lætərəl] adj. Equilátero, ra.
— N. MATH. Lado (*m.*) equilátero (side). | Figura (*f.*) equilátera (figure).
equilibrant [i'kwilibrənt] n. TECH. Fuerza (*f.*) equilibrante.
equilibrate [i'kwilibreit] v. tr. Equilibrar.
— V. intr. Mantenerse en equilibrio, estar en equilibrio.
equilibration [i'kwili'breiʃən] n. Equilibrio, *m.*
equilibrist [i:'kwilibrist] n. Equilibrista, *m.* & *f.*
equilibrium [,i:kwi'libriəm] n. Equilibrio, *m.*

— OBSERV. El plural es *equilibriums* o *equilibria*.

equimolecular [,ikwiməu'lekjulə*] adj. CHEM. Equimolecular.
equine ['ekwain] adj. Equino, na.
— N. Caballo, *m.*
equinoctial [,i:kwi'nɔkʃəl] adj. Equinoccial. || *Equinoctial circle* o *line*, línea (*f.*) equinoccial.
equinox ['i:kwinɔks] n. Equinoccio, *m.*
equip [i'kwip] v. tr. Equipar, proveer.
equipage ['ekwipidʒ] n. Equipo, *m.* (materials for an expedition). || Carruaje, *m.*, carroza, *f.* (carriage).
equipment [i'kwipmənt] n. Equipo, *m.* || Herramientas, *f. pl.* (tools). || FIG. Aptitud, *f.*, dotes, *f. pl.* || Material (*m.*) móvil (railways).
equipoise ['ekwipɔiz] n. Contrapeso, *m.* (counterweight). || Equilibrio, *m.* (the state of equilibrium).
equipollence [,i:kwi'pɔləns] n. Equivalencia, *f.*
equipollent [,i:kwi'pɔlənt] adj. Equivalente.
— N. Equivalente, *m.*
equiponderant [,i:kwi'pɔndərənt] adj. Del mismo peso.
equiponderate [,i:kwi'pɔndəreit] v. tr. Hacer del mismo peso (to make equal in weight). || Contrapesar (to counterbalance).
— V. intr. Equiponderar.
equitable ['ekwitəbl] adj. Justo, ta; equitativo, va.
equitableness [—nis] n. Equidad, *f.*
equitation [,ekwi'teiʃən] n. Equitación, *f.*
equity ['ekwiti] n. Equidad, *f.*, justicia, *f.* (justice). || U. S. Valor (*m.*) de una propiedad después de haber deducido la cantidad en que está hipotecada. || — *Equity capital*, capital (*m.*) en acciones ordinarias. || *Equity of a statute*, espíritu (*m.*) de una ley. || *Equity of redemption*, derecho (*m.*) de redimir una hipoteca. || *Equity securities*, acciones (*f.*) ordinarias.
equivalence [i'kwivələns] or **equivalency** [—i] n. Equivalencia, *f.*
equivalent [i'kwivələnt] adj. Equivalente. || *To be equivalent to*, equivaler a, ser equivalente a.
— N. Equivalente, *m.*
equivocal [i'kwivəkəl] adj. Equívoco, ca (ambiguous). || Dudoso, sa (suspect, doubtful).
equivocally [—i] adv. Equívocamente.
equivocate [i'kwivəkeit] v. intr. Usar equívocos, dar una respuesta ambigua.
equivocation [i,kwivə'keiʃən] n. Ambigüedad, *f.*
equivocator [i'kwivəkeitə*] n. Persona (*f.*) que se vale siempre de equívocos.
equivoque ['ekwivəuk] n. Equívoco, *m.* (quibble).
era ['iərə] n. Era, *f.*: *the Christian era*, la era cristiana: *the atomic era*, la era atómica. || *To mark an era*, hacer época.
eradiate [i'reidieit] v. tr. Irradiar.
eradiation [i,reidi'eiʃən] n. Irradiación, *f.*
eradicable [i'rædikəbl] adj. Desarraigable. || FIG. Extirpable, erradicable.
eradicate [i'rædikeit] v. tr. AGR. Desarraigar (plants). || FIG. Erradicar, extirpar (habits, etc.).
eradication [i,rædi'keiʃən] n. AGR. Desarraigo, *m.* || FIG. Erradicación, *f.*, extirpación, *f.*
eradicator [i'rædikeitə*] n. Extirpador, *m.* || Borratintas, *m. inv.* (ink remover).
erasable [i'reizəbl] adj. Borrable.
erase [i'reiz] v. tr. Borrar.
eraser [i'reizə*] n. Borrador, *m.*, goma (*f.*) de borrar (a rubber for pencil). || Borrador, *m.* (a cloth pad for rubbing chalk). || Raspador, *m.* (knife).
erasing head [i'reiziŋ,hed] n. Cabeza (*f.*) supresora (of tape recorder).
Erasmian [i'ræzmiən] adj./n. Erasmista.
Erasmianism [izəm] n. Erasmismo, *m.*
Erasmus [i'ræzməs] pr. n. Erasmo, *m.*
erasure [i'reiʒə*] n. Borradura, *f.* || Raspadura, *f.*
erbium ['ə:bjəm] n. CHEM. Erbio, *m.*
ere [ɛə*] prep. (Ant.). Antes de.
— Conj. (Ant.). Antes de que.
erect [i'rekt] adj. Erguido, da: *to stand erect*, estar erguido. || Erizado, da; de punta (hair, etc.). || Derecho, cha; de pie (upright). || Vertical.
erect [i'rekt] v. tr. Levantar, erigir: *to erect a monument*, levantar un monumento; *to erect a barrier between two people*, levantar una barrera entre dos personas. || Levantar (to set upright). || Montar, armar (to assemble). || MATH. Trazar, levantar: *to erect a perpendicular*, trazar una perpendicular. || Establecer (to establish). || Erigir (a principle).
— V. intr. Erguirse.
erectile [—ail] adj. Eréctil.
erection [i'rekʃən] n. Erección, *f.* || Erección, *f.*, construcción, *f.* (of a building). || Constitución, *f.*, establecimiento, *m.* (of a court). || TECH. Montaje, *m.* (of a machine). || Construcción, *f.*, edificio, *m.* (building).
erector [i'rektə*] n. Erector, *m.* || TECH. Montador, *m.*
eremite ['erimait] n. Eremita, *m.*, ermitaño, *m.*
eremitic [,eri'mitik] or **eremitical** [—əl] adj. Eremítico, ca.
erethism ['erəθizəm] n. MED. Eretismo, *m.*
erewhile [ɛə'wail] adv. Hace poco.
erg [ə:g] n. PHYS. Ergio, *m.*, erg, *m.*
ergosterol [ə:'gɔstərəl] n. Ergosterol, *m.*
ergot ['ə:gət] n. Cornezuelo, *m.* (of rye).
ergotism [—izəm] n. Ergotismo, *m.*
ergotize [—aiz] v. tr. AGR. Atacar del cornezuelo. || *Ergotized corn*, trigo atacado del cornezuelo.
— V. intr. Ergotizar.
Erin ['iərin] pr. n. (Ant.) GEOGR. Erín, *f.*, Irlanda, *f.*
eristic [e'ristik] adj. Polémico, ca.
Eritrea [,eri'treiə] pr. n. GEOGR. Eritrea, *f.*
ermine ['ə:min] n. Armiño, *m.* (animal and fur). || HERALD. Armiño, *m.*
ermined [—d] adj. Forrado de armiño (garment). || Vestido de armiño (person).
Ernest ['ə:nist] pr. n. Ernesto, *m.*
erode [i'rəud] v. tr. Corroer, desgastar: *acid erodes metal*, el ácido corroe los metales. || Erosionar (to wear away).
— V. intr. Corroerse, desgastarse. || Erosionarse.
erogenous [i'rɔdʒənəs] adj. Erógeno, na.
Eros ['erɔs] pr. n. MYTH. Eros, *m.*
erosion [i'rəuʒən] n. Erosión, *f.* (of rocks, etc.). || Corrosión, *f.*, desgaste, *m.* (of metals).
erosive [i'rəusiv] adj. Erosivo, va.
erotic [i'rɔtik] adj. Erótico, ca.
— N. Poema (*m.*) erótico.
erotica [i'rɔtikə] n. Literatura (*f.*) erótica.
erotical [—l] adj. Erótico, ca.
erotically [i'rɔtikəli] adv. Eróticamente.

eroticism [eˈrɔtisizəm] or **erotism** [ˈerətizəm] n. Erotismo, *m.*
erotomania [iˌrɔtəˈmeinjə] n. MED. Erotomanía, *f.*
erotomaniac [iˌrɔtəˈmeinjæk] n. Erotómano, na.
err [əː*] v. intr. Errar, equivocarse (to make a mistake). || *She does not err on the side of modesty*, no peca de modesta.
errancy [ˈerənsi] n. Error, *m.*
errand [ˈerənd] n. Recado, *m.*: *to run an errand*, hacer un recado. || — *Errand boy*, recadero, *m.* || *To be on an errand*, estar haciendo un recado. || *To go on an errand*, hacer un recado. || *What errand brings you here?*, ¿qué le trae por aquí?
errant [ˈerənt] adj. Errante, que yerra (erring or straying). || Errante (wandering). || *Errant knight*, caballero (*m.*) andante.
errantry [—ri] n. Caballería (*f.*) andante. || Vida (*f.*) errante.
errata [eˈrɑːtə] pl. n. Fe (*f. sing.*) de erratas.
erratic [iˈrætik] adj. Irregular: *erratic attendance*, asistencia irregular. || Irregular, desigual: *his writings are brilliant but erratic*, sus escritos son muy buenos pero desiguales. || Excéntrico, ca; extravagante, original (eccentric). || Voluble (changing). || GEOL. MED. Errático, ca.
— N. GEOL. Canto (*m.*) rodado.
erratically [—əli] adv. De manera irregular.
erratum [eˈrɑːtəm] n. Errata, *f.*

— OBSERV. El plural de la palabra inglesa es *errata.*

erroneous [iˈrəunjəs] adj. Erróneo, a; equivocado, da.
error [ˈerə*] n. Error, *m.*, equivocación, *f.* (a mistake): *to fall into error*, caer en un error, cometer una equivocación. || Extravío, *m.*, yerro, *m.* (wrongdoing). || SP. Error, *m.* (in baseball). || MATH. Error, *m.* || *Errors and omissions excepted*, salvo error u omisión.
ersatz [ˈɛəzæts] adj. Sucedáneo, a.
— N. Sucedáneo, *m.*
Erse [əːs] adj. Gaélico, ca.
— N. Gaélico, *m.* (language).
erstwhile [ˈəːstwail] adv. Antiguamente.
— Adj. Antiguo, gua.
erubescent [ˌeruˈbesns] adj. Ruboroso, sa.
eruct [iˈrʌkt] or **eructate** [—eit] v. tr. Arrojar (to spew out): *a volcano eructs molten lava*, el volcán arroja lava fundida.
— V. intr. Eructar (to belch).
eructation [ˌiːrʌkˈteiʃən] n. Eructo, *m.* (belch).
erudite [ˈerudait] adj./n. Erudito, ta.
erudition [ˌeruˈdiʃən] n. Erudición, *f.*
erupt [iˈrʌpt] v. tr. Arrojar (volcano, geyser, etc.).
— V. intr. Estar *or* entrar en erupción (volcano). || Brotar, surgir (geyser). || Estallar (to burst out). || MED. Hacer erupción (on the skin). | Salir (teeth, etc.). || FIG. *To erupt into a house*, irrumpir en una casa.
eruption [iˈrʌpʃən] n. Erupción, *f.* (of a volcano). || Brote, *m.*, surgimiento, *m.* (of a geyser). || Estallido, *m.*, explosión, *f.* (of violence). || Arrebato, *m.* (of passion, etc.). || MED. Erupción, *f.*
eruptive [iˈrʌptiv] adj. Eruptivo, va.
erysipelas [ˌeriˈsipiləs] n. MED. Erisipela, *f.*
erythema [ˌiriˈθiːmə] n. MED. Ericema, *m.*
erythroblast [iˈriθəblæst] n. BIOL. Eritroblasto, *m.*
erythrocyte [iˈriθrəsait] n. BIOL. Eritrocito, *m.*
escalade [ˌeskəˈleid] n. MIL. Escalada, *f.* || FIG. Escalada, *f.*
escalade [ˌeskəˈleid] v. tr. Escalar.
escalate [ˈeskəleit] v. tr. Agravar, intensificar (war). || Subir (prices).
— V. intr. Agravarse, intensificarse (war). || *To escalate into*, desembocar en (a problem, etc.).
escalation [ˌeskəˈleiʃən] n. Agravación, *f.*, agravamiento, *m.*, intensificación, *f.*, escalada, *f.* (of war). || FIG. Subida, *f.* (of prices). | Escalada, *f.*
escalator [ˈeskəleitə*] n. Escalera (*f.*) mecánica, escalera (*f.*) automática. || *Escalator clause*, cláusula (*f.*) en un contrato que permite variar las condiciones de éste de acuerdo con un índice económico.
escalop or **escallop** [isˈkɔləp] n. ZOOL. Venera, *f.*
escapade [ˌeskəˈpeid] n. Aventura, *f.*
escape [isˈkeip] n. Escapatoria, *f.*, fuga, *f.* (flight). || Escape, *m.* (of gas, steam). || Salida, *f.* (of liquid). || Escapatoria, *f.* (loophole, way out). || Evasión, *f.* (from worries, responsibilities, etc.). || — JUR. *Escape clause*, cláusula de excepción. || AVIAT. *Escape hatch*, escotilla (*f.*) de salvamento. || *Escape pipe*, tubo (*m.*) de escape. || *Fire escape*, escalera (*f.*) de incendios. || *To have a narrow escape*, escaparse por los pelos *or* por un pelo. || *To make one's escape*, escapar.
escape [isˈkeip] v. tr. Escaparse: *a cry of pain escaped him*, se le escapó un grito de dolor. || Escapar de, librarse de (punishment, death, etc.). || Evadir, rehuir (to avoid). || Eludir, evitar (to elude). || — *His name escapes me*, no me sale su nombre, su nombre se me ha ido de la memoria. || *It would not have escaped the notice of anyone*, no se le habría escapado a nadie. || *We just escaped being caught*, por poco nos cogieron.
— V. intr. Escaparse, escapar, fugarse (to get free). || Librarse, salvarse (to avoid an accident, etc.). || Salirse, escaparse (to leak). || Evadirse (to escape from one's troubles).
escapee [ˌeskeiˈpiː] n. Fugitivo, va; evadido, da.
escapement [isˈkeipmənt] n. TECH. Escape, *m.*
escapeway [isˈkeipwei] n. Salida (*f.*) de socorro.

escapism [isˈkeipizəm] n. FIG. Evasión, *f.*
escapist [isˈkeipist] adj. De evasión.
escapologist [ˌeskeiˈpɔlədʒist] n. Rey (*m.*) de la evasión.
escarp [isˈkɑːp] n. Escarpadura, *f.*, escarpa, *f.* (steep slope). || Escarpa, *f.* (of a fortress).
escarp [isˈkɑːp] v. tr. Escarpar.
escarpment [—mənt] n. See ESCARP.
eschalot [ˈeʃəlɔt] n. BOT. Ascalonia, *f.*, chalote, *m.*
eschar [ˈeskɑː*] n. MED. Escara, *f.*
eschatological [ˌeskətəˈlɔdʒikəl] adj. Escatológico, ca.
eschatology [ˌeskəˈtɔlədʒi] n. Escatología, *f.*
escheat [isˈtʃiːt] n. JUR. Reversión (*f.*) de bienes al señor feudal *or* a la corona *or* al Estado. || Tierras (*f. pl.*) entregadas al señor feudal *or* a la corona *or* al Estado.
escheat [isˈtʃiːt] v. tr./intr. Revertir tierras al señor feudal *or* a la corona *or* al Estado.
eschew [isˈtʃuː] v. tr. Evitar, abstenerse de.
eschewal [—əl] n. Abstención, *f.*
escort [ˈeskɔːt] n. Escolta, *f.* (to give protection or guard or out of courtesy). || Séquito, *m.*, acompañamiento, *m.* (suite). || MAR. Escolta, *f.* | Buque escolta, *m.* (ship). || Acompañante, *m.* (a male companion). || *Under escort*, bajo escolta.
escort [isˈkɔːt] v. tr. Escoltar (to accompany as an escort). || Acompañar (to accompany as a courtesy).
escritoire [ˌeskriˈtwɑː*] n. Escritorio, *m.*
escrow [ˈeskrəu] n. Plica, *f.* || *In escrow*, en depósito.
escudo [esˈkuːdəu] n. Escudo, *m.* (Portuguese and Chilean monetary unit).
esculent [ˈeskjulənt] adj. Comestible (eatable).
escutcheon [isˈkʌtʃən] n. Escudo (*m.*) de armas (shield). || MAR. Espejo (*m.*) de popa, escudo, *m.* || Escudo, *m.*, escudete, *m.* (plate round a lock). || FIG. *A blot on one's escutcheon*, una mancha en su hoja de servicio.
Eskimo [ˈeskiməu] adj./n. Esquimal. || *Eskimo dog*, perro (*m.*) esquimal.

— OBSERV. El plural es *Eskimos* o *Eskimo.*

esophagus [iːˈsɔfəgəs] n. ANAT. Esófago, *m.*

— OBSERV. El plural de *esophagus* es *esophagi.*

esoteric [ˌesəuˈterik] adj. Esotérico, ca (doctrine, literature). || Confidencial (plan).
esoterism [ˌesəuˈterizəm] n. Esoterismo, *m.*
espadrille [ˌespəˈdril] n. Alpargata, *f.*
espagnolette [esˌpænjəˈlet] n. Falleba, *f.*
espalier [isˈpæljə*] n. Árbol (*m.*) en espaldera. || Espaldera, *f.* (for fruit tree). || Emparrado, *m.* (trellis).
esparto [esˈpɑːtəu] n. BOT. Esparto, *m.*
especial [isˈpeʃəl] adj. Especial, particular: *of especial importance*, de importancia especial. || Excepcional (exceptional). || *In especial*, en especial, en particular (in particular), especialmente (especially).
especially [—i] adv. Especialmente, particularmente. || Sobre todo (mainly).
Esperantist [ˌespəˈræntist] adj./n. Esperantista.
Esperanto [ˌespəˈræntəu] n. Esperanto, *m.*
espial [isˈpaiəl] n. Espionaje, *m.* (espionage). || Observación, *f.* (observation). || Descubrimiento, *m.*, revelación, *f.*
espionage [ˌespiəˈnɑːʒ] n. Espionaje, *m.*
esplanade [ˌespləˈneid] n. Explanada, *f.* || Paseo (*m.*) marítimo (on the seafront).
espousal [isˈpauzəl] n. Adopción, *f.* (of a doctrine). || Adhesión, *f.* (*of*, a) [of a cause].
espouse [isˈpauz] v. tr. Casarse con, desposar (to marry). || Casar (to give in marriage). || FIG. Adherirse a, abrazar (a cause). | Adoptar (an idea).
espresso [esˈpresəu] n. Café (*m.*) exprés.
esprit de corps [ˈespriːdəˈkɔː*] n. Sentido (*m.*) de solidaridad.
espy [isˈpai] v. tr. Percibir, divisar, columbrar.
Esquimau [ˈeskiməu] adj./n. Esquimal.
Esquire [isˈkwaiə*] n. Señor Don: *John Bull Esq.* (*Esquire*), Sr. D. (señor don) John Bull.

— OBSERV. El título "esquire" se emplea en lugar de *Mister (Mr)* y siempre se pone detrás del nombre y apellido.

essay [ˈesei] n. Redacción, *f.*, composición, *f.* (in schools). || Ensayo, *m.* (erudite work). || Tentativa, *f.*, intento, *m.* (attempt). || Prueba, *f.* (of a rejected design for a stamp or for paper money).
essay [ˈesei] v. tr. Probar, someter a prueba (to test). || Intentar, probar, ensayar (to attempt).
— V. intr. Intentar, hacer un intento.
essayist [—ist] n. Ensayista, *m.* & *f.*
esse [ˈesi] n. PHIL. Existencia, *f.* (actual existence). | Esencia, *f.* (essential being).
essence [ˈesns] n. Esencia, *f.* || Esencia, *f.*, perfume, *m.* (concentrated extract). || Extracto, *m.* (extract). || Fondo, *m.*: *the essence of the matter*, el fondo de la cuestión. || *In essence*, esencialmente.
essential [iˈsenʃəl] adj. Esencial, imprescindible, necesario, ria (necessary). || Fundamental: *an essential difference*, una diferencia fundamental. || Innato, ta: *his essential selfishness*, su egoísmo innato. || *Essential oil*, aceite (*m.*) esencial.
— N. Lo esencial (sth. basic or fundamental). || — Pl. Elementos (*m.*) esenciales. || *To stick to essentials*, ir al grano.
establish [isˈtæbliʃ] v. tr. Establecer, fundar: *to establish a university*, fundar una universidad. || Establecer, constituir (a government). || Establecer:

to establish law and order, establecer la ley y el orden; *to establish communication,* establecer comunicación. || Sentar, establecer: *to establish a precedent,* sentar un precedente. || Comprobar (to verify). || Hacer constar (one's rights). || Establecer, probar, demostrar (a fact, one's innocence). || Entablar (relations). || Hacer oficial, reconocer (to make into the official national Church). || Demostrar, probar (to prove). || Instalar: *her father established them in a house,* su padre los instaló en una casa. || *To establish o.s.,* establecerse (to set o.s. up), crearse una reputación (to make a reputation), arraigar (sth.).

established [—t] adj. Establecido, da. || Arraigado, da: *an established custom,* una costumbre arraigada. || De plantilla (staff). || Oficial, de Estado (Church). || De buena reputación, de buena fama (highly reputed). || Sabido, da; conocido, da (fact). || Constituido, da (authorities).

establishment [—mənt] n. Establecimiento, *m.* (a being established). || Servidumbre, *f.* (the servants of a household). || Personal, *m.* (staff). || Establecimiento, *m.*, fundación, *f.*, institución, *f.* (foundation). || Establecimiento, *m.* (place of business). || Fijación, *f.* (of a residence). || Demostración, *f.* || Comprobación, *f.* (of facts). || MIL. Fuerzas, *f. pl.*, efectivos, *m. pl.* (troops). || *To be on the establishment,* formar parte del personal, estar en plantilla.

Establishment [—mənt] n. Clase (*f.*) dirigente (ruling class). || Iglesia (*f.*) *or* religión (*f.*) oficial *or* del Estado (official national Church).

estate [isˈteit] n. Propiedad, *f.* (property). || Finca, *f.* [*Amer.*, hacienda, *f.*, estancia, *f.*] (land). || Urbanización, *f.* (a tract of land developed for residential purposes). || Fortuna, *f.* (fortune). || Herencia, *f.* (inheritance). || Estado, *m.* (a class in society): *third estate,* estado llano. || JUR. Balance, *m.* (of a bankrupt). | Testamentaría, *f.* (of a dead person). || — *Real estate,* bienes (*m. pl.*) raíces. || *The fourth estate,* la prensa. || *To come to man's estate,* llegar a la edad viril. || *To leave a large estate,* dejar una gran fortuna.

estate agency [—ˌeidʒənsi] n. Agencia (*f.*) inmobiliaria.

estate agent [—ˌeidʒənt] n. COMM. Agente (*m.*) inmobiliario. || Administrador, *m.* (manager of an estate).

estate car [—kɑ:*] n. Furgoneta, *f.*, break, *m.*

estate duty [—ˌdju:ti] n. Impuesto (*m.*) de sucesión.

esteem [isˈti:m] n. Estima, *f.*, estimación, *f.*, aprecio, *m.* || *I hold him in high esteem,* le tengo en gran estima, le estimo en mucho, le aprecio mucho.

esteem [isˈti:m] v. tr. Estimar, apreciar (to have a high opinion of). || Considerar, estimar (to regard): *to esteem it a privilege,* considerarlo un privilegio. || *To esteem o.s. lucky,* considerarse afortunado.

ester [ˈestə*] n. CHEM. Éster, *m.*

esterification [esˌterifiˈkeiʃən] n. CHEM. Esterificación, *f.* (of an acid).

esterify [esˈterifai] v. tr. Esterificar.
— V. intr. Esterificarse.

esthete [ˈi:sθi:t] n. Esteta, *m.* & *f.*

esthetic [i:sˈθetik] adj. Estético, ca.

estimable [ˈestiməbl] adj. Estimable.

estimableness [—nis] n. Estimabilidad, *f.*

estimate [ˈestimit] n. Estimación, *f.*, apreciación, *f.*, cálculo (*m.*) aproximado (a judgment of size, number, quantity, value, etc.). || Presupuesto, *m.* (a statement of the cost of a piece of work). || — Pl. Presupuesto, *m. sing.* || — *At a rough estimate,* haciendo un cálculo aproximado. || *Estimate of quantities and costs,* presupuesto aproximado.

estimate [ˈestimeit] v. tr. Estimar, apreciar, calcular aproximadamente. || FIG. Estimar, juzgar (to gauge).
— V. intr. *To estimate for,* hacer un presupuesto de.

estimation [ˌestiˈmeiʃən] n. Juicio, *m.*, parecer, *m.*, opinión, *f.*: *in my estimation,* a mi juicio, a mi parecer, en mi opinión. || Estima, *f.*, aprecio, *m.* (esteem). || Estimación, *f.* (estimate).

estimative [ˈestimətiv] adj. Estimatorio, ria.

estimator [ˈestimeitə*] n. Tasador, *m.*, estimador, *m.*

estival [i:sˈtaivəl] adj. Estival.

estivate [ˈi:stiveit] v. intr. Pasar el verano en estado de letargo.

estop [isˈtɔp] v. tr. JUR. Desestimar una demanda [por imposibilidad legal de admitir una afirmación o alegación contraria a lo que se ha afirmado anteriormente].

estoppel [—əl] n. JUR. Desestimación (*f.*) de una demanda [por afirmar algo que contradice lo dicho anteriormente].

estovers [isˈtəuvəz] pl. n. JUR. Derecho (*m. sing.*) de hacer leña. | Pensión (*f. sing.*) alimenticia (to a wife divorced from her husband).

estrange [isˈtreindʒ] v. tr. Alejar, separar. || Hacer perder el afecto *or* el cariño (from a person). || Hacer perder la afición a (from a thing). || *To become estranged from,* enajenarse la amistad de, alejarse de.

estrangement [—mənt] n. Alejamiento, *m.*, separación, *f.* || Pérdida (*f.*) del afecto (loss of affection). || Desavenencia, *f.* (discord).

estreat [iˈstri:t] n. JUR. Extracto (*m.*) de las minutas de un tribunal.

estrogen [ˈi:strədʒin] n. Estrógeno, *m.*

estrogenic [ˌi:strəˈdʒenik] adj. Estrógeno, na.

estrum [ˈi:strəm] or **estrus** [ˈi:strəs] n. U. S. Celo, *m.*, estro, *m.* || FIG. Estro, *m.*

estuarial [ˌestjuˈɛərjəl] or **estuarine** [ˈestjuərain] adj. Del estuario.

estuary [ˈestjuəri] n. Estuario, *m.*

esurience [iˈsjuəriəns] or **esuriency** [—i] n. Voracidad, *f.*

esurient [iˈsjuəriənt] adj. Voraz, ávido de comida, hambriento, ta.

eta [ˈi:tə] n. Eta, *f.* (Greek letter).

et cetera [itˈsetrə] adv. Etcétera, etc.

etceteras [—z] pl. n. Cosas, *f.*

etch [etʃ] v. tr. Grabar al agua fuerte.

etcher [etʃə*] n. Acuafortista, *m.* & *f.*, aguafuertista, *m.* & *f.*

etching [ˈetʃiŋ] n. Grabado (*m.*) al agua fuerte, aguafuerte, *m.*

eternal [iˈtə:nl] adj. Eterno, na (lasting for ever). || Incesante, eterno, na: *stop this eternal arguing!,* ¡para esta incesante discusión! || — *The Eternal City,* la Ciudad Eterna. || *The Eternal Father,* el Padre Eterno.

eternity [iˈtə:niti] n. Eternidad, *f.*

eternize [i:ˈtə:naiz] v. tr. Perpetuar, eternizar.

ethane [ˈeθein] n. CHEM. Etano, *m.*

ethanol [ˈeθənɔl] n. Alcohol (*m.*) etílico.

ether [ˈi:θə*] n. Éter, *m.* || *Ether addict,* eterómano, na.

ethereal [iˈθiəriəl] adj. Etéreo, a: *the ethereal vault,* la bóveda etérea.

etherify [ˈi:θerifai] v. tr. Convertir en éter, eterificar.

etherism [ˈi:θərizəm] n. Eterismo, *m.*

etherize [ˈi:θəraiz] v. tr. Eterizar, anestesiar con éter.

ethic [ˈeθik] adj. Ético, ca.
— N. PHIL. Ética, *f.* || Ética, *f.*, moralidad, *f.*

ethical [—əl] adj. Ético, ca. || Honrado, da (honourable). || Moral.

ethics [—s] n. PHIL. Ética, *f.* || Ética, *f.*, moralidad, *f.*

Ethiopia [ˌi:θiˈəupjə] pr. n. GEOGR. Etiopía, *f.*

Ethiopian [—n] adj./n. Etíope.

ethmoid [ˈeθmɔid] adj. ANAT. Etmoides.
— N. ANAT. Etmoides, *m.*

ethmoidal [eθˈmɔidəl] adj. Etmoides, etmoidal.

ethnarch [ˈeθnɑ:k] n. Etnarca, *m.*

ethnarchy [—i] n. Etnarquía, *f.*

ethnic [ˈeθnik] or **ethnical** [—əl] adj. Étnico, ca.

ethnographer [eθˈnɔgrəfə] n. Etnógrafo, *m.*

ethnographic [ˌeθnəuˈgræfik] or **ethnographical** [—əl] adj. Etnográfico, ca.

ethnography [eθˈnɔgrəfi] n. Etnografía, *f.*

ethnologic [ˌeθnəuˈlɔdʒik] or **ethnological** [—əl] adj. Etnológico, ca.

ethnologist [eθˈnɔlədʒist] n. Etnólogo, *m.*

ethnology [eθˈnɔlədʒi] n. Etnología, *f.*

ethnos [ˈeθnɔs] n. Etnia, *f.*

ethos [ˈi:θɔs] n. Genio, *m.*, carácter (*m.*) distintivo (of a group of people).

ethyl [ˈeθil] n. CHEM. Etilo, *m.* || *Ethyl alcohol,* alcohol etílico.

ethylene [ˈeθili:n] n. CHEM. Etileno, *m.*

etiolate [ˈi:tiəuleit] v. tr. Descolorar (the skin). || BOT. Ajar, marchitar (plants).

etiolation [ˌi:tiəuˈleiʃən] n. Marchitamiento, *m.*, ajamiento, *m.* (of plants). || Descoloración, *f.*, palidez, *f.* (of skin). || Debilitamiento, *m.*, debilitación, *f.* (weakening).

etiological [ˌi:tiəˈlɔdʒikəl] adj. Etiológico, ca.

etiology [ˌi:tiˈɔlədʒi] n. Etiología, *f.*

etiquette [ˈetiket] n. Etiqueta, *f.*, ceremonial, *m.*, protocolo, *m.* (in polite society). || Buenos modales, *m. pl.* (decorum). || Normas (*f. pl.*) profesionales, ética (*f.*) profesional (of professional conduct). || Protocolo, *m.*: *court etiquette,* el protocolo de la corte. || *It is not etiquette to...,* no está bien...

Etruscan [iˈtrʌskən] adj./n Etrusco, ca.

étude [ˈeitju:d] n. MUS. Estudio, *m.*

etymological [ˌetiməˈlɔdʒikəl] adj. Etimológico, ca.

etymologist [ˌetiˈmɔlədʒist] n. Etimólogo, ga; etimologista, *m.* & *f.*

etymologize [ˌetiˈmɔlədʒaiz] v. tr. Buscar la etimología de.
— V. intr. Estudiar etimología.

etymology [ˌetiˈmɔlədʒi] n. Etimología, *f.*

etymon [ˈetimɔn] n. Raíz, *f.* (of a word).

— OBSERV. El plural es *etymons* o *etyma.*

eucalyptol [ˌju:kəˈliptəl] n. Eucaliptol, *m.*

eucalyptus [ˌju:kəˈliptəs] n. BOT. Eucalipto, *m.*

— OBSERV. El plural es *eucalypti* o *eucalyptuses.*

Eucharist [ˈju:kərist] n. REL. Eucaristía, *f.*

Eucharistic [ˌju:kəˈristik] or **Eucharistical** [—əl] adj. Eucarístico, ca.

euchre (U. S. **eucher**) [ˈju:kə*] n. Juego (*m.*) de cartas.

euchre (U. S. **eucher**) [ˈju:kə*] v. tr. Derrotar.

Euclid [ˈju:klid] pr. n. Euclides: *Euclid's postulate,* el postulado de Euclides.

Euclidean [ju:ˈklidiən] adj. Euclidiano, na.

eudaemonism or **eudemonism** [ju:ˈdi:mənizəm] n. Eudemonismo, *m.*

eugenic [ju:ˈdʒenik] adj. Eugenésico, ca.

eugenics [—s] n. Eugenesia, *f.*

eulogia [ju:ˈləudʒjə] n. REL. Eulogia, *f.*

eulogist [ˈju:lədʒist] n. Elogiador, ra; panegirista, *m.* & *f.*; encomiador, ra.

eulogistic [ˌju:ləˈdʒistik] adj. Laudatorio, ria; elogiador, ra; encomiástico, ca.
eulogize [ˈju:lədʒaiz] v. tr. Elogiar, encomiar, loar.
eulogy [ˈju:lədʒi] n. Elogio, *m.*, encomio, *m.* (high praise). || Panegírico, *m.* (speech, statement).
eunuch [ˈju:nək] n. Eunuco, *m.*
euonymus [juˈɔniməs] n. BOT. Bonetero, *m.*
eupatorium [ju:pəˈtɔ:rjəm] n. BOT. Eupatorio, *m.*
eupeptic [ju:ˈpeptik] adj. Eupéptico, ca.
euphemism [ˈju:fimizəm] n. Eufemismo, *m.*
euphemistic [ˌju:fiˈmistik] adj. Eufemístico, ca.
euphemize [ˈju:fimaiz] v. tr. Expresar por medio de eufemismos.
— V. intr. Usar eufemismos.
euphonic [ju:ˈfɔnik] or **euphonious** [ju:ˈfəunjəs] adj. Eufónico, ca.
euphony [ˈju:fəni] n. Eufonía, *f.*
euphorbia [ju:ˈfɔ:bjə] n. BOT. Euforbio, *m.*
euphorbium [ju:ˈfɔ:bjəm] n. Euforbio, *m.*
euphoria [ju:ˈfɔ:riə] n. Euforia, *f.*
euphoric [ju:ˈfɔ:rik] adj. Eufórico, ca.
euphuism [ˈju:fju:izəm] n. Eufuismo, *m.*
euphuist [ˌju:fju:ist] adj./n. Eufuista.
euphuistic [ˌju:fju:ˈistik] adj. Eufuístico, ca. || FIG. Ampuloso, sa; rimbombante.
Eurasia [juəˈreiʒjə] pr. n. GEOGR. Eurasia, *f.*
Eurasian [—n] adj./n. Eurasiático, ca.
eureka! [juəˈri:kə] interj. ¡Eureka!
eurhythmic [ju:ˈriðmik] or **eurhythmical** [—ikəl] adj. Eurítmico, ca.
eurhythmics [—s] n. Euritmia, *f.*
Euripides [juəˈripidi:z] pr. n. Eurípides, *m.*
Europe [ˈjuərəp] pr. n. GEOGR. Europa, *f.*
European [ˌjuərəˈpi:ən] adj./n. Europeo, a.
Europeanism [ˌjuərəˈpiənizəm] n. Europeísmo, *m.*
Europeanization [ˌjuərəˌpiənaiˈzeiʃən] n. Europeización.
Europeanize [ˌjuərəˈpiənaiz] v. tr. Europeizar.
europium [juˈrəupjəm] n. CHEM. Europio, *m.*
Eurovision [ˈjuərəˌviʒən] n. Eurovisión, *f.*
eurythmic [ju:ˈriðmik] or **eurythmical** [—əl] adj. Eurítmico, ca.
eurythmics [—s] n. Euritmia, *f.*
eurythmy [ju:ˈriðmi] n. Euritmia, *f.*
Euskarian [ju:sˈkeəriən] adj./n. Éuscaro, ra.
Eustachian tube [ju:sˈteiʃjənˈtju:b] n. ANAT. Trompa (*f.*) de Eustaquio.
Eustachius [ju:sˈteikjəs] pr. n. Eustaquio, *m.*
euthanasia [ˌju:θəˈneizjə] n. Eutanasia, *f.*
evacuant [iˈvækjuənt] n. MED. Evacuativo, va; evacuatorio, ria; evacuante.
— N. MED. Evacuativo, *m.*, evacuante, *m.*
evacuate [iˈvækjueit] v. tr. Evacuar (a dangerous place). || Hacer salir: *to evacuate air from a cylinder*, hacer salir el aire de un cilindro. || Evacuar (from the body). || Desocupar, vaciar (a house). || PHYS. Hacer el vacío en.
evacuation [iˌvækjuˈeiʃən] n. Evacuación, *f.* || Escape, *m.* (of a gas). || Deposición, *f.* (from the body).
evacuee [iˌvækju:ˈi:] n. Evacuado, da.
evadable [iˈveidəbl] adj. Evitable, eludible.
evade [iˈveid] v. tr. Evadir, eludir, evitar, esquivar (to avoid). || Escaparse de (to escape). || Sustraerse a (taxes).
— V. intr. Usar evasivas.
evaginate [iˈvædʒineit] v. tr. Volver de dentro afuera, volver al revés (a tubular organ).
evaluate [iˈvæljueit] v. tr. Valuar, valorar, valorizar, evaluar (to determine the monetary value of). || Calcular, estimar (to estimate). || Evaluar (to weigh up). || Juzgar (to judge). || Interpretar (to interpret). || MATH. Hallar el valor numérico de.
evaluation [iˌvæljuˈeiʃən] n. Evaluación, *f.*, valoración, *f.*, valuación, *f.* || Evaluación, *f.* || Cálculo, *m.* (estimation). || Interpretación, *f.*
evanesce [ˌi:vəˈnes] v. intr. Desvanecerse, esfumarse, desaparecer (to vanish).
evanescence [—ns] n. Desvanecimiento, *m.*, evanescencia, *f.*, desaparición, *f.*
evanescent [—nt] adj. Evanescente, efímero, ra.
evangelic [ˌi:vænˈdʒelik] or **evangelical** [—l] adj. Evangélico, ca. || *Evangelical Church*, Iglesia Evangélica.
evangelism [iˈvændʒilizəm] n. Propagación (*f.*) del Evangelio, evangelización, *f.* (effort to spread the Gospel). || Evangelismo, *m.* (Evangelical Church doctrines).
evangelist [iˈvændʒilist] adj./n. Evangelista, evangelizador, ra. || *Saint John the Evangelist*, San Juan Evangelista.
evangelistic [iˌvændʒiˈlistik] adj. Evangélico, ca.
evangelization [iˌvændʒelaiˈzeiʃən] n. Evangelización, *f.*
evangelize [iˈvændʒilaiz] v. tr. Evangelizar.
evangelizing [—iŋ] n. Evangelización, *f.*
evaporable [iˈvæpərəbl] adj. Evaporable.
evaporate [iˈvæpəreit] v. tr. Evaporar. || Deshidratar (milk, vegetables, etc.). || *To evaporate down*, reducir por evaporación.
— V. intr. Evaporarse. || FIG. Desvanecerse, evaporarse.
evaporation [iˌvæpəˈreiʃən] n. Evaporación, *f.* || Deshidratación (*f.*) por evaporación (of milk, vegetables, etc.).
evaporator [iˈvæpəreitə*] n. Evaporador, *m.*
evasion [iˈveiʒən] n. Evasión, *f.*, escapatoria, *f.* (the act of evading the law, a danger, etc.). || Evasión, *f.*, fuga, *f.* (flight). || Evasión, *f.*, evasiva, *f.* (avoidance of a question, of the truth). || Evasión, *f.* (of taxes).
evasive [iˈveisiv] adj. Evasivo, va.
Eve [i:v] pr. n. Eva, *f.*
eve [i:v] n. Víspera, *f.*: *on the eve of his departure*, en la víspera de su partida. || REL. Vigilia, *f.* || Crepúsculo, *m.* (dusk). || — *Christmas Eve*, Nochebuena, *f.* || *New Year's Eve*, Noche (*f.*) Vieja. || FIG. *On the eve of*, en vísperas de.
evection [iˈvekʃən] n. ASTR. Evección, *f.*
even [ˈi:vən] adj. Regular, uniforme, constante (uniform). || Suave (smooth). || Llano, na (level). || Liso, sa (flat). || Ecuánime (calm). || Imperturbable (not easily ruffled). || Tranquilo, la; sereno, na; apacible (placid). || Equitativo, va; justo, ta (fair). || A nivel (at the same level). || Igual, semejante, idéntico, ca (equal). || Par (number). || Exacto, ta: *an even ten seconds*, diez segundos exactos. || Redondo, da (sum of money). || — *Even with*, al mismo nivel que, al nivel de. || FIG. *I'll get even with you yet!*, ¡me las pagarás! || *Of even date*, del actual. || SP. *To become even*, empatar, igualar. || *To be even with s.o.*, estar en paz con alguien. || *To break even*, quedar igual (gambling), cubrir los gastos. || *To get even*, desquitarse. || *To make even*, allanar, alisar. || *To stand an even chance*, tener tantas posibilidades de éxito como de fracaso. || *To stay even*, cubrir los gastos.
— Adv. Siquiera: *he didn't even answer three of the questions*, ni siquiera contestó a tres preguntas. || Incluso, hasta, aun: *even if, even now*, incluso si, incluso ahora; *even John would have done it*, incluso Juan lo hubiera hecho; *she wears a coat even when it is hot*, lleva abrigo incluso cuando hace calor. || Aún, todavía: *it is even colder than yesterday*, hace aún más frío que ayer. || Incluso (indeed). || — *Even as*, en cuanto: *even as he opened the door*, en cuanto abrió la puerta; del mismo modo que (as). || *Even if* o *even though*, aunque, aun cuando. || *Even so*, aun así.
even [ˈi:vən] v. tr. Nivelar, igualar, allanar (ground). || Igualar (to make equal).
— V. intr. Nivelarse. || *To even up on s.o.*, desquitarse con uno.
evenfall [—fɔl] n. Atardecer, *m.*
evenhanded [—ˈhændid] adj. Imparcial.
evening [ˈi:vniŋ] n. Tarde, *f.*: *yesterday evening*, ayer por la tarde; *in the evening*, por la tarde. || Anochecer, *m.*, noche, *f.* (between sunset and bedtime). || FIG. Ocaso, *m.* (of a man's life, a civilization, etc.). || Velada, *f.*: *musical evening*, velada musical. || — *Evening class*, clase nocturna. || *Evening dress*, traje (*m.*) de etiqueta (for men), traje (*m.*) de noche (for women). || *Evening gown*, traje (*m.*) de noche. || *Evening paper*, periódico (*m.*) de la tarde. || THEATR. *Evening performance*, función (*f.*) de noche. || *Evening star*, estrella (*f.*) vespertina, lucero (*m.*) de la tarde. || *Evening was coming on*, estaba anocheciendo. || *Good evening!*, ¡buenas tardes! (early), ¡buenas noches! (at sunset).
evenly [ˈi:vənli] adv. Uniformemente. || Imparcialmente, equitativamente (fairly).
even-minded [ˈi:vən-maindid] adj. Ecuánime.
evenness [ˈi:vənnis] n. Igualdad, *f.* || Lo liso (smoothness). || Calma, *f.*, serenidad, *f.*, ecuanimidad, *f.* (of mind). || Uniformidad, *f.*, regularidad, *f.* (of temperature, speed, etc.). || Imparcialidad, *f.* (of treatment). || Ecuanimidad, *f.*, justicia, *f.* (fairness).
evensong [ˈi:vənsɔŋ] n. REL. Vísperas, *f. pl.*
event [iˈvent] n. Suceso, *m.*, acontecimiento, *m.* (an occurrence). || Acontecimiento, *m.*: *going to the opera is quite an event for us*, ir a la ópera es un gran acontecimiento para nosotros. || Consecuencia, *f.*, resultado, *m.* (outcome). || Caso, *m.*: *in the event of raining*, en caso de que llueva. || Número, *m.* (in a programme). || Encuentro, *m.* (in boxing, etc.). || SP. Prueba, *f.* (separate item in a programme of games). || — *At all events* o *in any event*, en todo caso, pase lo que pase. || *Current events*, actualidades, *f.* || *In the normal course of events*, si todo sigue bien. || *The event will show*, ya veremos lo que pasa. || *To be expecting a happy event*, estar esperando un feliz acontecimiento.
even-tempered [ˈi:vən-tempəd] adj. Ecuánime, sereno, na.
eventful [iˈventful] adj. Lleno de acontecimientos, agitado, da (full of interesting events). || Memorable: *on that evenful morning*, en aquella memorable mañana.
eventide [ˈi:vəntaid] n. Anochecer, *m.*, noche, *f.*
eventless [iˈventlis] adv. Sin incidentes.
eventual [iˈventʃuəl] adj. Final (ultimate). || Posible, eventual (contingent).
eventuality [iˌventjuˈæliti] n. Eventualidad, *f.*, caso, *m.*: *in all eventualities*, en cualquier caso.
eventually [iˈventʃuəli] adv. Finalmente, en definitiva, al fin y al cabo: *he will do it eventually*, finalmente lo hará. || Con el tiempo (in the long run).
eventuate [iˈventjueit] v. intr. Resultar (to come as a result). || Acabarse, terminarse (*in*, por) [to finish]. || U.S. Acontecer, suceder (to happen).

ever ['evə*] adv. Siempre (always): *he came late, as ever,* vino tarde, como siempre. || Nunca, jamás: *no man has ever doubt my word,* nunca ha dudado nadie de mi palabra. || Nunca: *they hardly ever go to the cinema,* casi nunca van al cine; *better than ever,* mejor que nunca; *it is hotter than ever,* hace más calor que nunca. || Alguna vez: *have they ever met?,* ¿se han visto alguna vez? || — *As soon as ever I can,* en cuanto pueda. || FAM. *Did you ever?,* ¿habrase visto? || *Did you ever buy it?,* ¿lo compraste por fin? || *Ever after* o *ever since,* desde entonces (since then), desde [que] (after). || *Ever and anon,* de vez en cuando. || *Ever so,* muy: *I am ever so happy,* estoy muy contento. || *Ever so little,* muy poco. || *Ever so much,* mucho, muchísimo: *I thank you ever so much,* se lo agradezco mucho. || *For ever,* para siempre. || *For ever and a day* o *for ever and ever,* para *or* por siempre jamás. || *If he ever comes back,* si se le ocurre volver, si vuelve alguna vez. || *It is ever so hot,* hace un calor terrible. || *Not ever,* nunca jamás. || *The coldest day ever,* el día más frío que he conocido. || *What ever did she say?,* ¿qué demonios dijo? || *What ever's the matter with you?,* ¿qué demonios te pasa? || *Worst ever,* sin precedente, único. || *Yours ever,* cordialmente suyo (letter).

everchanging [—'tʃeindʒiŋ] adj. Cambiadizo, za.

everglade ['evəgleid] n. U. S. Terreno (*m.*) pantanoso cubierto de hierbas altas.

evergreen ['evəgri:n] adj. De hoja perenne. || FIG. Imperecedero, ra; vivo, va: *evergreen memories,* recuerdos imperecederos.
— N. Árbol (*m.*) *or* planta (*f.*) de hoja perenne.

everlasting [ˌevə'lɑ:stiŋ] adj. Eterno, na; perpetuo, tua; sin fin (eternal). || Interminable, eterno, na (never ceasing). || BOT. *Everlasting flower,* siempreviva, *f.*
— N. Eternidad, *f.* || Ser (*m.*) eterno (God). || BOT. Siempreviva, *f.*

evermore ['evə'mɔ:*] adv. Eternamente, siempre. || *For evermore,* por *or* para siempre jamás.

evert [i'və:t] v. tr. Volver de dentro afuera.

every ['evri] adj. Todo, da: *have every confidence in him,* ten toda confianza en él; *you have every reason to fear him,* tiene toda la razón en temerle. || Todo, da; todos los, todas las, cada: *every man knows it,* todos los hombres lo saben. || Todos los, todas las: *every day,* todos los días; *she was given every chance to,* se le dieron todas las posibilidades para. || Cada: *every other day, every two days,* cada dos días. || — *Every bit a man,* todo un hombre, un hombre por los cuatro costados. || *Every man for himself,* ¡sálvese quien pueda! || *Every man jack of them,* todos sin excepción. || *Every now and again* o *every now and then,* de vez en cuando. || *Every once in a while,* alguna que otra vez. || *Every one,* cada uno, cada cual (each), todos, todas: *every one of them,* todos ellos. || *Every other Saturday,* un sábado sí y otro no, cada dos sábados. || *Every so often,* alguna que otra vez. || *Every time,* siempre, cada vez: *you win every time,* ganas siempre. || *Every way,* en todos los aspectos. || *Every which way,* por todas partes. || *He is every bit as pleased as you are,* está igual de contento que tú, está tan contento como tú. || *He is every inch a patriot,* es patriota hasta la médula *or* de pies a cabeza. || *To give every assistance,* ayudar en todo lo posible.

everybody ['evribɔdi] pron. Todo el mundo, todos, das.

everyday ['evridei] adj. Diario, ria; de todos los días. || Rutinario, ria (routine). || Corriente (usual). || — *An everyday event,* un suceso cotidiano *or* corriente. || *For everyday use,* de uso diario.

Everyman ['evrimæn] n. Hombre (*m.*) de la calle, ciudadano (*m.*) medio.

everyone ['evriwʌn] pron. Todo el mundo, todos, das.

everything ['evriθiŋ] pron. Todo: *I like everything,* me gusta todo.

everywhere ['evriwεə*] adv. Por *or* en todas partes (in every place, position): *everywhere in England,* en todas partes de Inglaterra. || A todas partes, por todas partes (to every place, motion): *he wants to go everywhere,* quiere ir a todas partes. || Dondequiera que (wherever): *everywhere he goes,* dondequiera que vaya. || Totalmente: *his evidence is everywhere coherent,* su declaración es totalmente coherente.

evict [i'vikt] v. tr. Desahuciar, desalojar, expulsar (from a house). || Excluir.

eviction [i'vikʃən] n. Desahucio, *m.*

evidence ['evidəns] n. Evidencia, *f.* || Indicio, *m.,* prueba, *f.* (sign). || Hechos, *m. pl.,* datos, *m. pl.* (facts). || JUR. Prueba, *f.* (proof). | Testimonio, *m.,* declaración (*f.*) de un testigo (information given by a witness). | Testigo, *m.* & *f.* (witness): *evidence for the defence, for the prosecution,* testigo de descargo, de cargo. || Justificante, *m.,* comprobante, *m.* (of indebtedness). || — *In evidence,* manifiesto, ta; evidente. || *To call s.o. in evidence,* llamar a alguien como testigo. || *To give evidence,* declarar como testigo, prestar declaración. || *To show evidence of,* presentar señales de. || FIG. *To turn Queen's evidence,* delatar a un cómplice.

evidence ['evidəns] v. tr. Evidenciar, probar, manifestar, demostrar (to show up). || JUR. Declarar (a witness). | Justificar (to show proofs).

evident ['evidənt] adj. Evidente, patente, manifiesto, ta.

evidential [ˌevi'denʃəl] adj. JUR. Probatorio, ria.

evidently ['evidəntli] adv. Por supuesto, desde luego, naturalmente, manifiestamente, evidentemente.

evil ['i:vl] adj. Malo, la; perverso, sa; depravado, da (immoral). || Malo, la; malvado, da; perverso, sa (wicked). || Malo, la; funesto, ta; nefasto, ta (baleful). || Malo, la; nocivo, va (harmful). || Aciago, ga (unlucky). || Horrible (smell). || Maligno, na: *evil spirit,* espíritu maligno.
— N. Mal, *m.* (what is morally wrong). || Desgracia, *f.* (what is materially harmful). || *Evil eye,* mal de ojo, aojamiento, *m.*
— OBSERV. Los comparativos y superlativos de *evil* son *worse* y *worst,* aunque también se emplean *more evil* y *most evil.*

evildoer [—'du:ə*] n. Malhechor, ra; malvado, da.

evildoing [—'duiŋ] n. Fechoría, *f.*

evil-eyed [—'aid] adj. Que echa mal de ojo.

evil-looking [—'lukiŋ] adj. De aspecto siniestro.

evil-minded [—'maindid] adj. Malpensado, da (salacious). || Malintencionado, da (malevolent). || Malvado, da; malo, la (malicious).

evil-smelling [—'smeliŋ] adj. Maloliente, fétido, da.

evil-tongued [—tʌŋd] adj. Que habla mal de la gente, de mala lengua.

evince [i'vins] v. tr. Mostrar, manifestar (a desire). || Dar pruebas *or* muestras de, revelar (a quality).

eviscerate [i'visəreit] v. tr. Destripar (to disembowel). || FIG. Debilitar, quitar la sustancia a.

evocable [i'vəukəbl] adj. Evocable.

evocation [ˌevəu'keiʃən] n. Evocación, *f.*

evocative [i'vɔkətiv] adj. Evocador, ra.

evocatory [i'vɔkətəri] adj. Evocador, ra; evocatorio, ria.

evoke [i'vəuk] v. tr. Provocar, producir: *his words evoked laughter,* sus palabras provocaron la risa. || Evocar (to bring to mind). || Llamar (spirits).

evolute ['i:vəlu:t] n. Evoluta, *f.* (curve).

evolution [ˌi:və'lu:ʃən] n. Evolución, *f.* || PHYS. Desprendimiento, *m.* (of gas, etc.). || MATH. Extracción (*f.*) de raíces. | Evolución, *f.* (of a curve). || FIG. Desarrollo, *m.*

evolutionary [ˌi:və'lu:ʃnəri] adj. Evolutivo, va.

evolutionism [ˌi:və'lu:ʃənizəm] n. Evolucionismo, *m.*

evolutionist [ˌi:və'lu:ʃənist] n. Evolucionista, *m.* & *f.*

evolve [i'vɔlv] v. intr. Evolucionar. || Desarrollarse (to develop). || MATH. Extraer raíces.
— V. tr. Desarrollar (to develop). || PHYS. Desprender, despedir (gas, heat). || FIG. Desarrollar (an argument). | Sacar (a conclusion).

evolvement [—mənt] n. Desarrollo, *m.* (development). || MATH. Extracción (*f.*) de raíces. || Desprendimiento, *m.* (of gas, heat). || Deducción, *f.* (of a conclusion).

evulsion [i'vʌlʃən] n. MED. Extracción, *f.*

ewe [ju:] n. ZOOL. Oveja, *f.*

ewer ['ju:ə*] n. Jarra, *f.,* aguamanil, *m.*

ex [eks] prep. Sin (without). || Fuera de (out). || — *Ex dividend,* sin cupón. || *Ex dock,* en el muelle. || *Ex factory,* en fábrica, franco en fábrica. || *Ex store price,* precio (*m.*) en almacén. || *Ex tax value,* precio (*m.*) sin impuestos. || *Ex works price,* precio (*m.*) en fábrica.

ex- [eks] pref. Ex: *ex-minister,* ex ministro; *ex-servicemen,* ex combatientes. || Antiguo, gua: *an ex-pupil,* un antiguo alumno.

exacerbate [eks'æsə:beit] v. tr. Exacerbar.

exacerbation [eksˌæsə'beiʃən] n. Exacerbación, *f.*

exact [ig'zækt] adj. Exacto, ta.

exact [ig'zækt] v. tr. Exigir (*of, from,* a) [to demand]. || Lograr por la fuerza (money).

exactable [—əbl] adj. Exigible.

exacting [—iŋ] adj. Exigente (person). || Severo, ra; riguroso, sa (conditions). || Duro, ra (work). || Agotador, ra (exhausting).

exaction [ig'zækʃən] n. Exacción, *f.*: *exaction of taxes,* exacción de impuestos.

exactitude [ig'zæktitju d] n. Exactitud, *f.*

exactly [ig'zæktli] adv. Exactamente (precisely): *to reveal exactly what one is thinking,* revelar exactamente lo que uno está pensando. || Precisamente: *he was not exactly pleased,* no estaba precisamente contento. || Exactamente, en punto (in time).

exactness [ig'zæktnis] n. Exactitud, *f.*

exaggerate [ig'zædʒəreit] v. tr. Exagerar.

exaggerated [—id] adj. Exagerado, da.

exaggeration [igˌzædʒə'reiʃən] n. Exageración, *f.*

exalt [ig'zɔ:lt] v. tr. Exaltar, elevar (to raise up). || Exaltar, arrebatar (to elate). || Ensalzar, exaltar (to praise). || Intensificar, avivar (colours).

exaltation [ˌegzɔ:l'teiʃən] n. Exaltación, *f.* || *Exaltation of the Holy Cross,* Exaltación de la Santa Cruz.

exalted [ig'zɔ:ltid] adj. Exaltado, da. || Elevado, da (style). || Eminente (person). || Muy favorable (an opinion, etc.).

exalting [ig'zɔ:ltiŋ] adj. Exaltador, ra; exaltante.

exam [ig'zæm] n. FAM. Examen, *m.*: *to pass an exam,* aprobar un examen.

examinant [—inənt] n. Examinador, ra.

examination [igˌzæmi'neiʃən] n. Examen, *m.*: *to sit* o *to take* o *to do* o *to go in for an examination,* hacer *or* sufrir un examen, presentarse a un examen; *qualifying examination,* examen eliminatorio. || Examen, *m.* (of a matter). || MED. Reconocimiento, *m.* || JUR. Instrucción, *f.,* sumario, *m.* (of a case).

| Interrogatorio, *m.* (of a defendant). | Inspección, *f.*, registro, *m.* (of customs). | Investigación, *f.* (inquiry). | Revisión, *f.* (of accounts). || — *Entrance examination*, examen de ingreso. || *Examination paper*, preguntas (*f. pl.*) del examen (questions), respuestas (*f. pl.*) del examen (answers). || *To take an examination in history*, examinarse de historia. || *Under examination*, sometido a examen, que se está examinando.

examine [ig'zæmin] v. tr. Examinar (sth.). || Examinar a, someter a un examen (a student). || JUR. Instruir (a case). | Interrogar a (a defendant). | Hacer declarar a (a witness). | Revisar (accounts). | Investigar (to inquiry). | Registrar (customs). || MED. Reconocer, hacer un reconocimiento médico a.

— V. intr. Interrogar (to question).

examinee [ig,zæmi'ni:] n. Examinando, da; candidato, ta.

examiner [ig'zæminə*] n. Examinador, ra.

examining magistrate [ig'zæminiŋ'mædʒistreit] n. JUR. Juez (*m.*) de instrucción.

example [ig'zɑ:mpl] n. Ejemplo, *m.*: *after* o *following the example of*, siguiendo el ejemplo de, a ejemplo de; *beyond example*, sin ejemplo. || Ejemplar, *m.* (copy). || MATH. Problema, *m.* || — *For example*, por ejemplo. || *For example's sake*, para ejemplo, como ejemplo. || *To follow s.o.'s example*, tomar ejemplo de uno. || *To hold s.o. up as an example*, citar a uno como ejemplo. || *To make an example of s.o.*, dar a alguien un castigo ejemplar. || *To set an example*, dar ejemplo. || *To take as an example*, tomar por *or* como ejemplo. || FIG. *Without example*, sin ejemplo, sin precedente.

exanimate [ig'zænimit] adj. MED. Exánime, inanimado, da. || FIG. Sin vida, poco animado.

exanthem [ig'zænθəm] or **exanthema** [,egzæn'θi:mə] n. MED. Exantema, *m.*

— OBSERV. El plural es *exanthemas* o *exanthemata*.

exarch ['eksɑ:k] n. Exarca, *m.*

exarchate [—eit] n. Exarcado, *m.*

exasperate [ig'zɑ:spəreit] v. tr. Exasperar (to irritate). || Exacerbar (to exacerbate). || *To get exasperated*, exasperarse.

exasperating [—iŋ] adj. Exasperante. || Irritante.

exasperation [ig,zɑ:spə'reiʃən] n. Exasperación, *f.*

ex cathedra ['ekskə'θi:drə] adj./adv. Ex cátedra.

excavate ['ekskəveit] v. tr. Excavar.

excavation [,ekskə'veiʃən] n. Excavación, *f.* (digging).

excavator ['ekskəveitə*] n. TECH. Excavadora, *f.* (machine). | Excavador, *m.* (person).

exceed [ik'si:d] v. tr. Exceder (quantity): *income exceeds expenditure by a hundred pounds*, los ingresos exceden los gastos en cien libras. || Superar (hopes). || Rebasar, sobrepasar (a limit). || Excederse en: *he exceeded his duty*, se excedió en sus funciones.

exceeding [—iŋ] adj. Excesivo, va.

exceedingly [—iŋli] adv. Sumamente, extremadamente.

excel [ik'sel] v. tr. Superar.

— V. intr. Sobresalir.

excellence ['eksələns] n. Excelencia, *f.*

Excellency [—i] n. Excelencia, *f.*: *His Excellency*, Su Excelencia.

excellent ['eksələnt] adj. Excelente.

excelsior [ek'selsiɔ:*] n. U. S. Virutas (*f. pl.*) que se emplean para rellenar.

except [ik'sept] prep. Excepto, salvo, exceptuando a, con excepción de. || — *Except for*, excepto. || *Except that*, excepto que, sólo que, salvo que.

except [ik'sept] v. tr. Excluir, exceptuar. || JUR. Recusar (a witness).

— V. intr. *To except against*, hacer objeciones a.

excepting [—iŋ] prep. Excepto, exceptuando a, salvo, con excepción de.

exception [ik'sepʃən] n. Exclusión, *f.* (exclusion). || Excepción *f.* (something excepted): *to be an exception to the rule*, ser una excepción a la regla; *the exception proves the rule*, la excepción confirma la regla. || JUR. Recusación, *f.* (of a witness). || Objeción, *f.* (objection). || — *By way of an exception*, por excepción, a título excepcional. || *To make an exception*, hacer una excepción. || *To take exception to*, ofenderse por, molestarse por (to resent), objetar (to object). || *With the exception of*, con *or* a excepción de.

exceptionable [ik'sepʃnəbl] adj. Recusable (witness). || Reprochable, censurable (open to objection).

exceptionably [—i] adv. Con ciertas reservas.

exceptional [ik'sepʃənl] adj. Excepcional.

excerpt ['eksə:pt] n. Extracto, *m.*

excerpt [ek'sə:pt] v. tr. Sacar extractos de, extractar.

excerption [ek'sə:pʃən] n. Extracto, *m.*

excess [ik'ses] n. Exceso, *m.* || COMM. Excedente, *m.* (surplus). || FIG. Exceso, *m.* || — *In excess*, en exceso. || *In excess of*, superior a. || *To excess*, en *or* con exceso: *to eat to excess*, comer con exceso.

— Adj. Excedente. || — *Excess luggage*, exceso de equipaje. || *Excess weight*, exceso de peso.

excessive [ik'sesiv] adj. Excesivo, va.

excess-profits tax [—'prɔfittæks] n. Impuestos (*m. pl.*) sobre beneficios excesivos.

exchange [iks'tʃeindʒ] n. Cambio, *m.* (change). || Intercambio, *m.* (interchange): *exchange of students*, intercambio de estudiantes. || Cambio, *m.* (of foreign currency). || Canje, *m.* (of prisoners). || Bolsa, *f.* (stocks, shares, etc.): *exchange quotation*, cotización de la Bolsa. || Central (*f.*) telefónica (for telephones). || Lonja, *f.* (for commodities). || — *Bill of exchange*, letra (*f.*) de cambio. || *Exchange broker*, cambista, *m.* || *Exchange control*, control (*m.*) de divisas. || *Exchange of views*, cambio de impresiones. || *Exchange premium*, agio, *m.* || *Foreign exchange*, divisas, *f. pl.* || *In exchange for*, a cambio de. || *Rate of exchange*, tipo (*m.*) de cambio. || *Stock Exchange*, bolsa (*f.*) de valores. || *The Labour exchange*, la bolsa (*f.*) del trabajo.

exchange [iks'tʃeindʒ] v. tr. Cambiar (to change): *to exchange an old car for a new one*, cambiar un coche viejo por uno nuevo. || Canjear (prisoners). || Intercambiar (to interchange). || Cambiar (foreign currency). || Cambiar: *to exchange views with*, cambiar impresiones con. || Hacerse (courtesies). || Cruzar: *to exchange words*, cruzar palabras. || Darse, propinarse (blows). || — *They exchanged glances*, cruzaron una mirada, sus miradas se cruzaron. || *To exchange for*, cambiarse por. || *To exchange greetings*, saludarse, cambiar saludos. || *To exchange greetings with*, saludar a. || *To exchange signs*, hacerse señas.

exchangeable [—əbl] adj. Cambiable. || Canjeable. || Intercambiable.

exchequer [iks'tʃekə*] n. Hacienda, *f.* (finances). || Tesoro (*m.*) público, fisco, *m.*, erario, *m.* (treasury). || JUR. Tribunal, *m.* (court). || — *Chancellor of the Exchequer*, Ministro (*m.*) de Hacienda. || *Exchequer bonds*, bonos (*m. pl.*) del Tesoro.

excipient [ik'sipiənt] n. MED. Excipiente, *m.*

excise [ek'saiz] n. Impuestos (*m. pl.*) sobre el consumo, impuestos (*m. pl.*) indirectos (tax). || Patente, *f.* (licence).

excise [ek'saiz] v. tr. Gravar con unos impuestos (to tax). || Extirpar (to cut out). || Suprimir (to omit). || MED. Sajar.

exciseman [—mən] n. Recaudador (*m.*) de impuestos

— OBSERV. El plural de *exciseman* es *excisemen*.

excision [ek'siʒən] n. MED. Extirpación, *f.*, excisión, *f.* (removal). | Incisión, *f.* (incision). || FIG. Corte, *m.* (cut out). | Supresión, *f.*

excitability [ik,saitə'biliti] n. Excitabilidad, *f.*

excitable [ik'saitəbl] adj. Excitable. || FIG. Nervioso, sa (nervous). | Emocionable (emotional).

excitant ['eksitənt] n. Excitante, *m.*

excitation [,eksi'teiʃən] n. Excitación, *f.* || FIG. Nerviosismo, *m.* | Emoción, *f.*

excitative [ek'saitətiv] adj. Excitante.

excitatory [ek'saitətəri] adj. Excitante.

excite [ik'sait] v. tr. Emocionar: *the news has excited me*, la noticia me ha emocionado. || Entusiasmar: *I'm excited with my new car*, estoy entusiasmado con mi coche nuevo. || Excitar (to stimulate). || Incitar (to urge). || Poner nervioso (to irritate). || Provocar (admiration, jealousy, etc.). || Despertar (one's imagination). || Excitar (a crowd). || ELECTR. Excitar: *to excite a dynamo*, excitar una dinamo.

excited [—id] adj. Entusiasmado, da (enthused). || Emocionado, da (deeply moved). || Excitado, da (agitated). || Nervioso, sa (nervous). || ELECTR. Excitado, da. || — *Don't get excited*, no te excites. || *To get excited*, emocionarse (to be deeply moved), entusiasmarse (to enthuse), alborotarse, agitarse (the crowd), acalorarse (a discussion).

excitedly [—idli] adv. Con entusiasmo.

excitement [—mənt] n. Excitación, *f.* || Entusiasmo, *m.* (enthusiasm). || Emoción, *f.*: *the news caused great excitement*, la noticia causó gran emoción. || Alboroto, *m.* (disturbance). || Agitación, *f.* (agitation).

exciter [ik'saitə*] n. PHYS. Excitador, *m.*

exciting [ik'saitiŋ] adj. Apasionante: *an exciting life*, una vida apasionante. || Excitante. || Emocionante: *how exciting!*, ¡qué emocionante!

exclaim [iks'kleim] v. intr. Exclamar. || *To exclaim against* o *at* o *upon*, clamar en contra.

— V. tr. Gritar.

exclamation [,ekskla'meiʃən] n. Exclamación, *f.* || GRAMM. *Exclamation mark*, signo (*m.*) de admiración.

exclamative [,ekskla'meitiv] adj. Exclamativo, va.

exclamatory [eks'klæmətəri] adj. Exclamatorio, ria.

exclave ['ekskleiv] n. Parte (*f.*) de un Estado situada fuera de sus fronteras.

exclude [iks'klu:d] v. tr. Excluir (to leave out): *to exclude all possibility of doubt*, excluir cualquier posibilidad de duda. || No admitir (not to admit).

excluding [—iŋ] prep. Excepto, con exclusión de, exceptuando a.

exclusion [iks'klu:ʒən] n. Exclusión, *f.*: *to the exclusion of*, con exclusión de.

exclusive [iks'klu:siv] adj. Exclusivo, va (sole): *exclusive model*, modelo exclusivo; *exclusive selling rights*, derechos exclusivos de venta. || Selecto, ta (select): *exclusive neighbourhood*, vecindad selecta. || Cerrado, da: *exclusive society*, sociedad cerrada. || Exclusivista (policy). || — *Exclusive interview*, entrevista en exclusiva. || *Exclusive rights*, exclusividad, *f.* || *Mutually exclusive possibilities*, posibilidades que se excluyen. || *To have exclusive rights to*, tener la exclusiva de.

— N. Exclusiva, *f.*, exclusividad, *f.*

— Adv. Exclusive (not counting the first and last mentioned). || *Exclusive of*, excluyendo, sin tener en cuenta.

exclusiveness [iks'klu:sivnis] n. Exclusividad, *f.*

exclusivism [eks'klu:sivizəm] n. Exclusivismo, *m.*
exclusivist [eks'klu:sivist] adj./n. Exclusivista.
exclusivity [eksklu:'siviti] n. Exclusividad, *f.*, exclusiva, *f.*
excogitate [eks'kɔdʒiteit] v. tr. Inventar, imaginar (to contrive). || Maquinar, tramar (to plot).
excogitation [eks,kɔdʒi'teiʃən] n. Invención, *f.*
excommunicant [,ekskə'mju:nikənt] n. Excomulgado, da.
excommunicate [,ekskə'mju:nikeit] adj./n. REL. Excomulgado, da.
excommunicate [,ekskə'mju:nikeit] v. tr. REL. Excomulgar.
excommunication ['ekskə,mju:ni'keiʃən] n. Excomunión, *f.*
ex-convict ['eks'kɔnvikt] n. Ex presidiario, *m.*
excoriate [eks'kɔ:rieit] v. tr. Excoriar.
excoriation [eks,kɔ:ri'eiʃən] n. Excoriación, *f.*
excrement ['ekskrimənt] n. Excremento, *m.*
excremental [,ekskri'mentl] adj. Excrementicio, cia.
excrescence [iks'kresns] or **excrescency** [—i] n. Excrecencia, *f.*, excrescencia, *f.*
excrescent [iks'kresnt] adj. Saliente (forming excrescence). || Superfluo, flua (superfluous).
excreta [eks'kri:tə] pl. n. Excrementos, *m.*
excrete [eks'kri:t] v. intr. Excretar.
excretion [eks'kri:ʃən] n. Excreción, *f.*
excretory [eks'kri:təri] adj. Excretorio, ria; excretor, ra.
— N. Órgano (*m.*) excretorio.
excruciate [iks'kru:ʃieit] v. tr. Torturar, atormentar.
excruciating [—iŋ] adj. Intolerable, insoportable (hard to bear). || Atroz, insoportable (pain).
excruciatingly [—iŋli] adv. Atrozmente. || FAM. *It is excruciatingly funny*, es para morirse de risa.
excruciation [iks,kru:ʃi'eiʃən] n. Suplicio, *m.*, tortura, *f.*, tormento, *m.*
exculpate ['ekskʌlpeit] v. tr. Disculpar. || *To exculpate o.s. from*, disculparse de.
exculpation [,ekskʌl'peiʃən] n. Disculpa, *f.*
exculpatory [eks'kʌlpətəri] adj. Justificante, justificativo, va. || De disculpa (letter).
excurrent [eks'kʌrənt] adj. Que brota, que mana (blood). || De salida.
excursion [iks'kə:ʃən] n. Excursión, *f.* (trip). || MIL. Incursión, *f.*, correría, *f.* || ASTR. Desviación, *f.* || FIG. Digresión, *f.* (in speech). || — *Excursion train*, tren (*m.*) de recreo. || *Excursion trip*, viaje (*m.*) de recreo.
excursionist [—ist] n. Excursionista, *m.* & *f.*
excursive [eks'kə:siv] adj. Digresivo, va (speech, etc.). || Inclinado a la digresión (people). || Errabundo, da (imagination). || Superficial (reading). || De recreo (trip).
excursus [eks'kə:səs] n. Apéndice, *m.* (in a book). || Digresión, *f.* (in a literary work).

— OBSERV. El plural es *excursuses* o *excursus.*

excusable [iks'kju:zəbl] adj. Excusable, disculpable, perdonable.
excuse [iks'kju:s] n. Excusa, *f.*, disculpa, *f.*: *to make excuses*, dar excusas; *to admit of no excuse*, no tener disculpa; *to make sth. one's excuse*, dar algo como excusa. || Razón, *f.*, justificación, *f.* (reason). || Pretexto, *m.* (pretext).
excuse [iks'kju:z] v. tr. Excusar, disculpar, perdonar: *nothing can excuse such carelessness*, nada puede excusar tal descuido. || Dispensar de, eximir de (a duty): *you are excused work today*, está dispensado de trabajar hoy; *the teacher excused him from coming to school*, el profesor le dispensó de venir al colegio. || Perdonar: *to excuse s.o. sth.*, perdonar algo a alguien. || — *Excuse me!*, ¡perdón!, ¡discúlpeme!, ¡perdone Ud.! || *Excuse my saying so*, perdone mi atrevimiento. || *May I be excused for a moment*, ¿puedo salir un momento? || *To excuse o.s.*, pedir permiso (before leaving). || *To excuse o.s. for*, disculparse de, excusarse de.
exeat ['eksiæt] n. Permiso (*m.*) de salida (in colleges). || REL. Exeat, *m.*, permiso, *m.*, licencia, *f.*
execrable ['eksikrəbl] adj. Execrable, abominable, odioso, sa; detestable.
execrate ['eksikreit] v. tr. Execrar, abominar, odiar (to abhor). || Maldecir (to curse).
— V. intr. Proferir maldiciones (to curse).
execration [,eksi'kreiʃən] n. Odio, *m.*, execración, *f.*, abominación, *f.* || Maldición, *f.* (curse).
executable ['eksikju:təbl] adj. Ejecutable.
executant [ig'zekjutənt] n. Ejecutante, *m.* & *f.*
execute ['eksikju:t] v. tr. Ejecutar, cumplir: *to execute an order*, ejecutar una orden. || Ejecutar: *to execute a dance*, ejecutar un baile; *to execute a prisoner*, ejecutar a un prisionero; *to execute a will*, ejecutar un testamento. || Realizar, llevar a cabo, ejecutar, hacer (to carry out). || Desempeñar, llevar a cabo: *to execute the duties of director*, desempeñar las funciones de director. || Servir, despachar (a trade order). || Hacer (a banker's order). || Firmar (a treaty, a contract). || JUR. Legalizar (a document).
execution [,eksi'kju:ʃən] n. Ejecución, *f.* (of a criminal). || Cumplimiento, *m.*, ejecución, *f.* (of orders). || Realización, *f.*, ejecución, *f.* (carrying out). || Desempeño, *m.* (of one's duty). || MUS. Ejecución, *f.* || JUR. Legalización, *f.* (of a document). || Firma, *f.* (of a treaty, contract). || Ejecución, *f.* (of a judgment). || Ejecución (*f.*) de embargo (distress). || *Writ of execution*, ejecutoria, *f.*
executioner [,eksi'kju:ʃnə*] n. Verdugo, *m.*
executive [ig'zekjutiv] adj. Ejecutivo, va (government, power). || De ejecución (ability). || Ejecutivo, va; dirigente (function). || — *Executive board*, consejo (*m.*) de dirección. || U. S. *Executive Mansion*, la Casa Blanca (in Washington), el Palacio del Gobernador (in a State capital). | *Executive officer*, segundo comandante, *m.* || *Executive secretary*, secretario ejecutivo.
— N. Poder (*m.*) ejecutivo (branch of government). || Ejecutivo, *m.* (businessman).
executor [ig'zekjutə*] n. Ejecutor, ra. || JUR. Albacea, *m.*, ejecutor (*m.*) testamentario.
executorship [—ʃip] n. Ejecutoría, *f.*
executory [ig'zekjutəri] adj. JUR. Ejecutorio, ria. || Ejecutivo, va. || U. S. Administrativo, va.
executrix [ig'zekjutriks] n. Albacea, *f.*, ejecutora (*f.*) testamentaria.

— OBSERV. El plural es *executrices* o *executrixes.*

exegesis [eksi'dʒi:sis] n. Exégesis, *f.*

— OBSERV. El plural de la palabra inglesa es *exegeses.*

exegete ['eksidʒi:t] n. Exegeta, *m.*
exegetic [,eksi'dʒetik] or **exegetical** [—əl] adj. Exegético, ca.
exegetics [—s] pl. n. Teología (*f. sing.*) exegética, exégesis, *f.*
exemplar [ig'zemplə*] n. Ejemplo, *m.*, modelo, *m.* (a model). || Ejemplar, *m.* (a copy).
exemplariness [ig'zemplərinis] or **exemplarity** [,egzem'plæriti] n. Ejemplaridad, *f.*
exemplary [ig'zempləri] adj. Ejemplar: *an exemplary husband*, un marido ejemplar; *an exemplary punishment*, un castigo ejemplar. || Típico, ca (typical).
exemplification [ig,zemplifi'keiʃən] n. Ejemplificación, *f.*, desmostración (*f.*) por el ejemplo (an exemplifying). || Ejemplo, *m.* (an example). || JUR. Copia (*f.*) legalizada.
exemplify [ig'zemplifai] v. tr. Demostrar con ejemplos, ilustrar con ejemplos. || Servir de ejemplo para, ilustrar. || JUR. Hacer una copia legalizada de.
exempt [ig'zempt] adj. Exento, ta; libre; eximido, da; dispensado, da (*from*, de).
exempt [ig'zempt] v. tr. Eximir, dispensar (*from*, de).
exemption [ig'zempʃən] n. Exención, *f.* || Franquicia, *f.* (from custom duties).
exequatur [,eksi'kweitə*] n. Exequátur, *m. inv.*
exequies ['eksikwiz] pl. n. Exequias, *f.*
exercise ['eksəsaiz] n. Ejercicio, *m.*: *in the exercise of my duties*, en el ejercicio de mis funciones; *breathing exercises*, ejercicios respiratorios. || — *Exercise book*, cuaderno, *m.* || *Exercise yard*, patio, *m.* || *Practical exercises*, clases prácticas. || *To take exercise*, hacer ejercicio.
exercise ['eksəsaiz] v. tr. Ejercer (rights, duties, authority, influence, profession). || Usar de, proceder con (patience). || Entrenar (to train an animal, a team). || Hacer ejercicios con (one's body). || Sacar de paseo (a dog). || Ejercitar: *to exercise charity*, ejercitar la caridad; *to exercise children in mathematics*, ejercitar a los niños en las matemáticas. || Preocupar: *this problem has exercised the best brains in the country*, este problema ha preocupado a los cerebros más insignes del país. || MIL. Instruir a. || — *To exercise care*, tener cuidado. || *To exercise o.s.*, ejercitarse.
— V. intr. Entrenarse (to take physical exercise). || Ejercitarse. || MIL. Hacer la instrucción.
exercitation [eg,zə:si'teiʃən] n. Ejercicio, *m.*
exergue [ek'sə:g] n. Exergo, *m.*
exert [ig'zə:t] v. tr. Ejercer. || *To exert o.s.*, esforzarse, hacer esfuerzos.
exertion [ig'zə:ʃən] n. Esfuerzo, *m.* [excesivo] (effort). || Ejercicio, *m.* (of authority). || Empleo, *m.* (of strength).
exeunt ['eksiʌnt] v. intr. THEATR. Salen, se van (the actors).
exfoliate [eks'fəulieit] v. tr. Exfoliar.
exfoliation [eks,fəuli'eiʃən] n. Exfoliación, *f.*
exfoliative [eksfəu'lieitiv] adj. Exfoliativo, va.
exhalation [,ekshə'leiʃən] n. Exhalación, *f.*
exhale [eks'heil] v. tr./intr. Exhalar. || Despedir (gas, smell).
exhaust [ig'zɔ:st] n. Escape, *m.* (the expulsion of steam or gases). || Gas (*m.*) de escape (gases or steam expelled). || Tubo (*m.*) de escape (pipe).
exhaust [ig'zɔ:st] v. tr. Agotar: *he exhausted my patience*, me agotó la paciencia; *they exhausted the ammunition*, agotaron las municiones; *to exhaust a topic of conversation*, agotar un tema de conversación; *I am exhausted*, estoy agotado. || Vaciar (to empty a container). || Extraer (to remove a liquid, gas). || Empobrecer (soil).
exhausted [—id] adj. Exhausto, ta; agotado, da (worn-out).
exhaustible [—ibl] adj. Agotable.
exhausting [—iŋ] adj. Agotador, ra.
exhaustion [ig'zɔ:stʃən] n. Agotamiento, *m.*
exhaustive [ig'zɔ:stiv] adj. Exhaustivo, va; completo, ta.
exhaustless [ig'zɔ:stlis] adj. Inagotable.

exhibit [igˈzibit] n. Objeto (*m.*) expuesto. || JUR. Documento, *m.* || U. S. Exposición, *f.* || *On exhibit*, expuesto, ta.
exhibit [igˈzibit] v. tr. Mostrar, dar muestras de (to display): *to exhibit symptoms of hysteria*, mostrar síntomas de histeria. || Presentar (documents, passport, ticket). || Mostrar al público (theater, sports). || Exponer (paintings, sculpture, object for sale).
— V. intr. Exponer, hacer una exposición.
exhibition [ˌeksiˈbiʃən] n. Exposición, *f.* (a display of art). || Beca, *f.* (scholarship). || Presentación, *f.* (of documents, tickets, etc.). || FIG. Ostentación, *f.*, alarde, *m.* | Demostración, *f.*, manifestación, *f.* || — *Ideal Home Exhibition*, Salón (*m.*) de Artes Domésticas. || *To make an exhibition of o.s.*, ponerse en ridículo, hacer el ridículo.
exhibitioner [ˌeksiˈbiʃnə*] n. Becario, ria.
exhibitionism [ˌeksiˈbiʃnizəm] n. Exhibicionismo, *m.*
exhibitionist [ˌeksiˈbiʃnist] n. Exhibicionista, *m.* & *f.*
exhibitor [igˈzibitə*] n. Expositor, ra. || U. S. CINEM. Exhibidor, *m.*
exhilarant [igˈzilərənt] adj. Estimulante, tónico, ca; regocijante.
exhilarate [igˈzilərei̯t] v. tr. Alegrar, animar, levantar el ánimo, regocijar.
exhilarating [—iŋ] adj. Estimulante, tónico, ca.
exhilaration [igˌziləˈreiʃən] n. Alegría, *f.*, regocijo, *m.* (high spirits). || Efecto (*m.*) estimulante.
exhilarative [igˈzilərətiv] adj. Estimulante, tónico, ca; vivificante.
exhort [igˈzɔːt] v. tr. Exhortar. || Recomendar (action, measures).
exhortation [ˌegzɔːˈteiʃən] n. Exhortación, *f.*
exhortative [igˈzɔːtətiv] adj. Exhortativo, va.
exhortatory [igˈzɔːtətəri] adj. Exhortatorio, ria.
exhumation [ˌekshjuːˈmeiʃən] n. Exhumación, *f.*
exhume [eksˈhjuːm] v. tr. Exhumar. || FIG. Desenterrar.
exigence [ˈeksidʒəns] or **exigency** [—i] n. Exigencia, *f.* (need). || Caso (*m.*) de emergencia (emergency).
exigent [ˈeksidʒənt] adj. Exigente (exacting). || Urgente (urgent).
exigible [ˈeksidʒibl] adj. Exigible (*against*, *from*, a).
exiguity [ˌeksiˈgjuːiti] n. Exigüidad, *f.*
exiguous [egˈzigjuəs] adj. Exiguo, gua.
exile [ˈeksail] n. Exilio, *m.* (banishment from one's country, voluntary living outside one's country): *government in exile*, gobierno en el exilio. || Exiliado, da; exilado, da (person). || Cautiverio, *m.* (of Jews). || *To go into exile*, exiliarse, exilarse.
exile [ˈeksail] v. tr. Exiliar, exilar.
exist [igˈzist] v. intr. Existir: *do angels exist?*, ¿existen los ángeles?; *after we have ceased to exist*, después de que hayamos dejado de existir. || Subsistir, vivir: *how do you manage to exist on such little money?*, ¿cómo te las arreglas para subsistir con tan poco dinero?
existence [igˈzistəns] n. Existencia, *f.* || PHIL. Ser, *m.*, entidad, *f.* || — *To have been in existence for ten years*, existir desde hace diez años. || *To come into existence*, nacer, empezar a existir.
existent [igˈzistənt] adj. Existente (that exists). || Actual, presente (present).
existential [ˌegzisˈtenʃəl] adj. Existencial.
existentialism [—izəm] n. Existencialismo, *m.*
existentialist [—ist] adj./n. Existencialista.
existing [igˈzistiŋ] adj. Existente.
exit [ˈeksit] n. Salida, *f.* (a way out): *emergency exit*, salida de emergencia. || Mutis, *m.* (an actor's leaving of the stage). || FAM. Fin, *m.* (death).
exit [ˈeksit] v. intr. THEATR. Hacer mutis. || Morir (to die).
ex libris [eksˈlaibris] n. Ex libris (bookplate).
exocarp [ˈeksəukɑːp] n. BOT. Epicarpio, *m.*
exocrine [ˈeksəukrin] adj. Exocrino, na.
exodus [ˈeksədəs] n. Éxodo, *m.*: *rural exodus*, éxodo rural.
ex officio [ˌeksəˈfiʃiəu] adv./adj. *To act ex officio*, actuar de oficio. || *Member ex officio*, miembro de oficio, miembro de derecho.
exogamic [ˌeksəuˈgæmik] or **exogamous** [ˌeksəuˈgæməs] adj. Exógamo, ma.
exogamy [ekˈsɔgəmi] n. Exogamia.
exogenous [ekˈsɔdʒinəs] adj. Exógeno, na.
exonerate [igˈzɔnəreit] v. tr. Exonerar de, dispensar de, eximir de (a burden, an obligation). || Disculpar (to exculpate).
exoneration [igˌzɔnəˈreiʃən] n. Exoneración, *f.*, dispensa, *f.* (freeing). || Disculpa, *f.* (exculpation).
exophthalmus or **exophthalmos** [ˌeksɔfˈθælməs] n. MED. Exoftalmía, *f.*
exorbitance [igˈzɔːbitəns] or **exorbitancy** [—i] n. Carácter (*m.*) desorbitado, exorbitancia, *f.*
exorbitant [igˈzɔːbitənt] adj. Exorbitante, desorbitado, da; excesivo, va; desmesurado, da.
exorcise [ˈeksɔːsaiz] v. tr. Exorcizar, conjurar.
exorciser [—ə*] n. Exorcista, *m.*
exorcism [ˈeksɔːsizəm] n. Exorcismo, *m.*
exorcist [ˈeksɔːsist] n. Exorcista, *m.*
exorcize [ˈeksɔːsaiz] v. tr. Exorcizar, conjurar.
exordial [ekˈsɔːdjəl] adj. Introductorio, ria.
exordium [ekˈsɔːdjəm] n. Exordio, *m.*
— OBSERV. El plural de *exordium* es *exordiums* o *exordia*.
exoskeleton [eksɔsˈskelitn] n. Dermatoesqueleto, *m.*
exosmosis [eksɔsˈməusis] n. Exósmosis, *f.*
exoteric [ˌeksəuˈterik] adj. Exotérico, ca.
exothermic [ˌeksəuˈθəːmik] adj. Exotérmico, ca.
exotic [igˈzɔtik] adj. Exótico, ca.
— N. Planta (*f.*) exótica. || Palabra (*f.*) exótica.
exoticism [igˈzɔtisizəm] o **exotism** [igˈzɔtizəm] n. Exotismo, *m.*
expand [iksˈpænd] v. tr. Dilatar (to make larger): *heat expands metals*, el calor dilata los metales. || Desarrollar (to cause to increase): *to expand trade*, desarrollar el comercio. || Ensanchar, extender, ampliar (to enlarge). || Ampliar: *the pocket dictionary was expanded*, el diccionario de bolsillo fue ampliado. || Desarrollar (a topic, a formula, an algebraic expression). || Extender, abrir, desplegar (wings).
— V. intr. Dilatarse (to become larger): *metals expand when they are heated*, los metales se dilatan cuando se les calienta. || Extenderse (to extend). || Ensancharse (to broaden): *the river expands and forms a lake*, el río se ensancha y forma un lago. || Desarrollarse: *Japanese trade expanded after the war*, el comercio japonés se desarrolló después de la guerra. || Volverse expansivo (to become affable): *he is expanding lately*, se está volviendo expansivo últimamente. || Abrirse (flowers).
expandability [ikspændəˈbiliti] n. Expansibilidad, *f.*
expandable [iksˈpændəbl] adj. Expansible, dilatable. || Extensible.
expanse [iksˈpæns] n. Extensión, *f.* (extent). || Expansión, *f.* || Envergadura, *f.* (of wings).
expansibility [iksˌpænsəˈbiliti] n. Expansibilidad, *f.*
expansible [iksˈpænsəbl] adj. Extensible. || PHYS. Expansible, dilatable.
expansile [iksˈpænsail] adj. Expansible.
expansion [iksˈpænʃən] n. Expansión, *f.*, dilatación, *f.* (of gas). || Dilatación, *f.* (of metals). || Ampliación, *f.* (of a subject). || Extensión, *f.* (extent). || Ensanche, *m.* (of a town). || MATH. Desarrollo, *m.* || Expansión, *f.*, desarrollo, *m.* (of trade).
expansionism [—izəm] n. Expansionismo, *m.*
expansionist [—ist] adj./n. Expansionista.
expansive [iksˈpænsiv] adj. Expansivo, va; comunicativo, va (people). || Extenso, sa; amplio, plia (broad, wide). || Expansivo, va (tending to expand): *the expansive energy of steam*, la energía expansiva del vapor. || Dilatable (metals).
expansiveness [—nis] n. FIG. Expansibilidad, *f.*, carácter (*m.*) expansivo. || PHYS. Expansibilidad, *f.*, dilatabilidad, *f.*
ex parte [ˈeksˈpɑːti] adj. Unilateral, de una de las partes.
expatiate [eksˈpeiʃieit] v. intr. Extenderse.
expatiation [eksˌpeiʃiˈciʃən] n. Disertación, *f.*
expatriate [eksˈpætriit] adj./n. Expatriado, da.
expatriate [eksˈpætrieit] v. tr. Desterrar, expatriar. || *To expatriate o.s.*, expatriarse.
— V. intr. Expatriarse.
expatriation [eksˌpætriˈeiʃən] n. Expatriación, *f.*
expect [iksˈpekt] v. tr. Suponer (to think likely): *I expect the train will be late*, supongo que el tren llegará con retraso; *I expect so*, así supongo. || Esperar (to anticipate the coming of): *we're all expecting you*, todos te esperamos; *he's expecting the bill any day*, espera la cuenta un día de estos. || Esperar (to hope for): *you can't expect any money*, no esperes ningún dinero. || Esperar, contar con (to require sth. of s.o.): *a speech will be expected of you*, se espera que haga usted un discurso; *you are expected to work late if need be*, esperamos que se quede trabajando si es necesario. || *I expected as much*, ya me lo esperaba.
— V. intr. FAM. *To be expecting*, estar esperando (to be pregnant).
expectancy [iksˈpektensi] n. Expectación, *f.*, expectativa, *f.* (state of expectation). || Esperanza, *f.*: *life expectancy*, esperanza de vida.
expectant [iksˈpektənt] adj. Expectante. || Candidato, ta (to a job). || Ilusionado, da (hopeful). || *Expectant mother*, mujer embarazada, futura madre.
expectantly [—li] adv. Con expectación.
expectation [ˌekspekˈteiʃən] n. Esperanza, *f.* (hope): *we work in the expectation of being paid*, trabajamos con la esperanza de que nos paguen; *it is beyond our expectations*, supera nuestras esperanzas. || Previsión, *f.* (anticipation): *contrary to all expectations*, en contra de todas las previsiones. || Expectativa, *f.*: *to live in expectation*, vivir a la expectativa. || Perspectiva, *f.*: *happiness in expectation*, felicidad en perspectiva. || — *A man of great expectations*, un futuro heredero. || *Contrary to expectations*, contrariamente a lo esperado. || *Expectation of life*, esperanza (*f.*) de vida, vida media. || *In expectation of*, en expectación de, en espera de. || *To come up to s.o.'s expectations*, estar a la altura de las esperanzas de uno, colmar las esperanzas de uno. || *To fall short of s.o.'s expectations*, defraudar las esperanzas de uno. || *To live up to one's expectations*, estar a la altura de lo que uno esperaba. || *To succeed beyond one's expectations*, tener más éxito de lo previsto.
expectorant [eksˈpektərənt] adj. Expectorante.
— N. Expectorante, *m.*
expectorate [eksˈpektəreit] v.tr./intr. Escupir, expectorar (to spit).
expectoration [eksˌpektəˈreiʃən] n. Expectoración, *f.*

expedience [iks'pi:djəns] or **expediency** [—i] n. Conveniencia, *f.*, oportunidad, *f.* || *On grounds of expediency*, por conveniencia propia.
expedient [iks'pi:djənt] adj. Conveniente, oportuno, na.
— N. Expediente, *m.*, recurso, *m.*
expedite ['ekspidait] v. tr. Acelerar (to hasten). || Dar curso a (a petition, legal matter). || Despachar, expedir (business, task). || Facilitar (progress).
expedition [,ekspi'diʃən] n. Expedición, *f.*: *rescue expedition*, expedición de salvamento.
expeditionary [—əri] adj. Expedicionario, ria: *expeditionary force*, cuerpo expedicionario.
expeditious [,ekspi'diʃəs] adj. Expeditivo, va; expedito, ta.
expel [iks'pel] v. tr. Expulsar (person). || Expulsar, arrojar, expeler: *to expel smoke through the mouth*, expulsar humo por la boca.
expellant or **expellent** [iks'pelənt] adj. Expelente.
expend [iks'pend] v. tr. Gastar (to spend). || Emplear (time). || Agotar (to use up completely). || Dedicar, consagrar (efforts). || Poner (care).
expendable [iks'pendəbl] adj. Prescindible (people). || Gastable (things).
expenditure [iks'penditʃə*] n. Gasto, *m.*, desembolso, *m.* (of money). || Gasto, *m.*, empleo, *m.* (of time). || Gasto, *m.* (of energy).
expense [iks'pens] n. Gasto, *m.*: *overhead expenses*, gastos generales. || JUR. Costa, *f.*: *legal expenses*, costas judiciales. || — *All expenses paid*, con todos los gastos pagados. || *At great expense*, con mucho gasto. || *At my expense*, a costa mía, a mi costa. || *At the expense of*, a costa *or* a expensas de. || *Expense account*, cuenta (*f.*) de gastos de representación. || *Incidental expenses*, gastos imprevistos. || *Regardless of expense*, sin escatimar gastos. || *To go to any expense*, hacer todo lo posible. || *To go to expense*, meterse en gastos. || *To go to the expense of*, meterse en gastos para. || *To meet expenses*, hacer frente a los gastos. || *To put to expense*, obligar a gastar mucho dinero. || *To spare no expense*, no escatimar gastos.
expensive [—iv] adj. Caro, ra; costoso, sa.
expensiveness [—ivnis] n. Carestía, *f.*, lo caro, precio (*m.*) elevado.
experience [iks'piəriəns] n. Experiencia, *f.*: *to know from one's own experience*, saber por experiencia propia. || *It hasn't happened in my experience*, nunca me ocurrió tal cosa.
experience [iks'piəriəns] v. tr. Experimentar: *I experienced great joy*, experimenté gran placer. || Sufrir (a loss). || Tener (difficulties). || Saber por experiencia (to know from experience).
experienced [—t] adj. Experimentado, da (with experience). || Experto, ta (expert).
experiential [ekspiə'rienʃəl] adj. Experimental, empírico, ca.
experiment [iks'perimənt] n. Experimento, *m.*: *a chemistry experiment*, un experimento químico. || — *As an experiment*, como experimento. || *Experiment station*, estación experimental.
experiment [iks'perimənt] v. intr. Hacer experimentos, experimentar.
experimental [eks,peri'mentl] adj. Experimental.
experimentalist [eks,peri'mentəlist] n. Experimentador, ra.
experimentation [iks,perimentiŋ] n. Experimentación, *f.*
experimenter [iks'perimənta*] n. Experimentador, ra.
expert ['ekspə:t] adj. Experto, ta (skilful). || JUR. Pericial (provided by an expert).
— N. Experto, ta; perito, ta. || — *According to expert opinion*, a juicio de peritos. || *To be an expert in the matter* o *on the subject*, ser experto en la materia. || *With the eye of an expert*, con ojos de perito.
expertise [,ekspə:'ti:z] n. Pericia, *f.*, habilidad, *f.* (skilfulness). || Competencia, *f.* (competence).
expertness ['ekspə:tnis] n. Pericia *f.*, habilidad, *f.*
expiable ['ekspiəbl] adj. Expiable.
expiate ['ekspieit] v. tr. Expiar.
expiation [,ekspi'eiʃən] n. Expiación, *f.*
expiatory ['ekspiətəri] adj. Expiatorio, ria.
expiration [,ekspaiə'reiʃən] n. Expiración, *f.*, terminación, *f.* (a coming to an end). || Espiración, *f.* (a breathing out). || Expiración, *f.* (death). || COMM. Vencimiento, *m.* (of a bill, etc.).
expire [iks paiə*] v. tr. Espirar, expeler (air, etc.).
— V. intr. Expirar, terminar (to come to an end). || Expirar (to die). || COMM. Expirar, vencer. || Caducar (to become void).
expiry [iks'paiəri] n. Expiración, *f.*, terminación, *f.* (ending). || COMM. Vencimiento, *m.*
explain [iks'plein] v. tr. Explicar: *explain to me how it happened*, explícame cómo ha ocurrido. || Exponer: *to explain one's thought*, exponer su pensamiento. || — *To be explained*, explicarse. || *To explain away*, justificar. || *To explain o.s.*, explicarse: *explain yourself!*, ¡explíquese usted!
— V. intr. Dar explicaciones.
explainable [—əbl] adj. Explicable.
explanation [,eksplə'neiʃən] n. Explicación, *f.* || Aclaración, *f.* (of an obscure point). || FIG. *To come to an explanation with s.o.*, tener una explicación con alguien.
explanative [iks'plænətiv] adj. Explicativo, va.
explanatory [iks'plænətəri] adj. Explicativo, va. || Aclaratorio, ria (clarifying).
expletive [eks'pli:tiv] adj. GRAMM. Expletivo, va.
— N. GRAMM. Voz (*f.*) expletiva (used to pad out a sentence). || Taco, *m.* (an oath).
explicable ['eksplikəbl] adj. Explicable.
explicate ['eksplikeit] v. tr. Explicar (a text). || Aclarar (an obscure point). || Exponer (to expound).
explication [,ekspli'keiʃən] n. Explicación, *f.* || Exposición, *f.* (detailed account).
explicative [eks'plikətiv] or **explicatory** [eks'plikətəri] adj. Explicativo, va.
explicit [iks'plisit] adj. Explícito, ta.
explicitness [—nis] n. Claridad, *f.*, precisión, *f.*
explode [iks'pləud] v. tr. Hacer explotar, estallar (to cause to burst). || Refutar (a myth, theory). || Desmentir (rumours). || *Exploded view*, vista esquemática.
— V. intr. Explotar, estallar. || FIG. Explotar, reventar (with anger, etc.). || FIG. *To explode with laughter*, prorrumpir en risa.
exploit ['eksplɔit] n. Hazaña, *f.*, proeza, *f.*
exploit [eks'plɔit] v. tr. Explotar.
exploitable [iks'plɔitəbl] adj. Explotable.
exploitation [,eksplɔi'teiʃən] n. Explotación, *f.*
exploiter [iks'plɔitə*] n. Explotador, *m.*
exploration [,ekplɔ:'reiʃən] n. Exploración, *f.*: *underwater exploration*, exploración submarina.
explorative [eks'plɔ:rətiv] or **exploratory** [eks'plɔ:rətəri] adj. Exploratorio, ria.
explore [iks'plɔ:*] v. tr. Explorar. || FIG. Explorar, sondear.
— V. intr. *To explore for oil*, explorar el terreno en busca de petróleo.
explorer [—rə*] n. Explorador, ra (person). || MED. Sonda, *f.*
explosion [iks'pləuʒən] n. Explosión, *f.*; *the explosion of a bomb*, la explosión de una bomba. || — *Explosion engine*, motor (*m.*) de explosión. || *Population explosion*, explosión demográfica.
explosive [iks'pləusiv] adj. Explosivo, va.
— N. Explosivo, *m.* || Explosiva, *f.* (consonant).
explosiveness [—nis] n. Carácter (*m.*) explosivo.
exponent [eks'pəunənt] n. Intérprete, *m.* & *f.*: *an exponent of the Bible*, un intérprete de la Biblia; *an exponent of Bach's music*, un intérprete de la música de Bach. || Defensor, ra: *an exponent of aid to underdeveloped countries*, un defensor de la ayuda a los países subdesarrollados. || Experto, ta; perito, ta: *an exponent of the art of engraving*, un experto en el arte de grabar. || FIG. Exponente, *m.* & *f.*: *the leading exponent of this art*, el máximo exponente de este arte. || MATH. Exponente, *m.* (index).
exponential [ekspəu'nenʃəl] adj. MATH. Exponencial.
export ['ekspɔ:t] adj. Exportador, ra. || De exportación: *export duty*, derechos de exportación.
— N. Exportación, *f.* (trade, act). || Artículo (*m.*) de exportación (commodity).
export [eks'pɔ:t] v. tr. Exportar: *to export oranges from Spain*, exportar naranjas de España.
exportable [—əbl] adj. Exportable.
exportation [,ekspɔ:'teiʃən] n. Exportación, *f.*
exporter [eks'pɔ:tə*] n. Exportador, ra.
exporting [—iŋ] n. Exportación, *f.*
— Adj. De exportación, exportador, ra.
expose [iks'pəuz] v. tr. Exponer (to leave uncovered, unprotected): *to expose one's head to the sun*, exponer la cabeza al sol; *to expose the soldiers to unnecessary risks*, exponer a los soldados a peligros innecesarios. || Descubrir, exponer (to leave open to attack): *to expose one's flank to the enemy*, descubrir el flanco al enemigo. || Descubrir (a plot, an impostor, a crime). || COMM. Exponer (goods). || Revelar (to reveal). || REL. Exponer. || Abandonar (to abandon). || PHOT. Exponer. || Exponer (to display). || Demostrar, revelar, poner al descubierto (to uncover). || *To be exposed*, estar orientado: *the house is exposed to the south*, la casa está orientada al sur; estar poco protegido: *the house on the hill is very exposed*, la casa de la colina está muy poco protegida.
exposé [eks'pəuzei] n. Exposición, *f.* (of a theme). || Desenmascaramiento, *m.* (an exposure of sth. shameful). || Revelación, *f.*
exposed [iks'pəuzd] adj. Expuesto, ta. || Descubierto, ta.
exposition [,ekspəu'ziʃən] n. Exposición, *f.* (to a danger, of goods, of facts, etc.). || Introducción, *f.* || Comentario, *m.* (of a literary work). || MUS. PHOT. REL. Exposición, *f.* || Abandono, *m.* (of a child). || Exposición, *f.* (exhibition).
expositive [eks'pɔzitiv] or **expository** [eks'pɔzitəri] adj. Expositivo, va; descriptivo, va.
expositor [eks'pɔzitə*] n. Expositor, ra. || Comentador, ra (commentator).
ex post facto [ekspəust'fæktəu] adj. JUR. Con efecto retroactivo.
expostulate [iks'pɔstjuleit] v. intr. Reconvenir, amonestar (*with*, a) || Protestar.
expostulation [iks,pɔstju'leiʃən] n. Amonestación, *f.*, reconvención, *f.* (reproach). || Protesta, *f.*
expostulatory [iks'pɔstjulətəri] adj. De amonestación, recriminatorio, ria.

exposure [iks'pəuʒə*] n. Exposición, *f.* (to light, cold, heat, etc.). || PHOT. Fotografía, *f.* (a piece of a film): *to make an exposure*, sacar una fotografía. | Exposición, *f.* (an exposing of a piece of film): *time of exposure*, tiempo de exposición. || Denuncia, *f.* (a denouncing). || Orientación, *f.*, situación, *f.* (aspect of a house). || Abandono, *m.* (of a child). || FIG. Revelación, *f.*, (of a secret). | Descubrimiento, *m.* (of a criminal). || PHOT. *Exposure meter*, exposímetro, *m.*, fotómetro, *m.*
expound [iks'paund] v. tr. Comentar, explicar (to interpret). || Exponer (to state with great detail).
express [iks'pres] adj. Expreso, sa (explicit, special): *express order*, orden expresa; *he left with the express intention of calling*, salió con la expresa intención de llamar. || Rápido, da (service). || Urgente (fast): *an express letter*, una carta urgente; *express post*, correo urgente. || Exacto, ta (image). || Expreso (train). || De tiro rápido (rifle).
— N. Expreso, *m.* (train). || Correo (*m.*) urgente. || U. S. Servicio (*m.*) de urgencia (a fast delivery service).
— Adv. Por correo urgente (by post). || Por tren expreso (by express train).
express [iks'pres] v. tr. Expresar: *to express an opinion*, expresar una opinión; *his work expresses his attitude to life*, su obra expresa su actitud ante la vida. || MATH. Expresar. || Exprimir (to press). || U. S. Enviar por expreso. || *To express o.s.*, expresarse.
expressage [iks'presidʒ] n. Envío (*m.*) por servicio de urgencia.
expressible [iks'presəbl] adj. Posible de expresar (which can be stated). || Exprimible (which can be pressed).
expression [iks'preʃən] n. Expresión, *f.* || *As an expression of thanks*, en señal de agradecimiento. || *Beyond expression*, más de lo que uno se puede figurar.
expressionism [—izəm] n. Expresionismo, *m.*
expressionist [—ist] adj./n. Expresionista.
expressionless [—lis] adj. Inexpresivo, va. || Sin significado.
expressive [iks'presiv] adj. Expresivo, va. || *Expressive of*, que expresa, que denota.
expressiveness [—nis] n. Expresividad, *f.*
expressman [—mən] n. Empleado del servicio de urgencia.

— OBSERV. El plural de *expressman* es *expressmen*.

expressway [iks'preswei] n. U. S. Autopista, *f.* (road).
expropriate [eks'prəuprieit] v. tr. Expropiar. || FIG. Desposeer (*from*, de).
expropriation [eks,prəupri'eiʃən] n. Expropiación, *f.* || FIG. Desposeimiento, *m.*
expropriator [eks'prəuprieitə*] n. Expropiador, ra.
expulsion [iks'pʌlʃən] n. Expulsión, *f.*
expulsive [iks'pʌlsiv] adj. Expulsivo, va.
expunction [iks'pʌŋkʃən] n. Borradura, *f.*, tachadura, *f.* (erasure). || Supresión, *f.*
expunge [eks'pʌndʒ] v. tr. Borrar, tachar (to erase). || Suprimir (to suppress).
expurgate ['ekspə:geit] v. tr. Expurgar.
expurgation [,ekspə:'geiʃən] n. Expurgación, *f.*
expurgatorial [eks,pə:gə'tɔ:riəl] adj. Expurgatorio, ria.
expurgatory [eks'pə:gətəri] adj. Expurgatorio, ria.
exquisite ['ekskwizit] adj. Exquisito, ta. || Perfecto, ta (perfect). || Delicado, da; fino, na (delicate). || MED. Intenso, sa (pain).
— N. Petimetre, *m.*, figurín, *m.*
exquisiteness [—nis] n. Exquisitez. *f.* || Perfección, *f.* || Delicadeza, *f.* (refinement). || MED. Intensidad, *f.*
exsanguine [eks'sæŋgwin] adj. Exangüe (bloodless). || Anémico, ca (anaemic).
exscind [ek'sind] v. tr. Cortar, escindir.
exsert [ek'sə:t] v. tr. Proyectar, sacar.
exsertion [—ʃən] n. Proyección, *f.*
ex-serviceman [eks'sə:vismən] n. Excombatiente, *m.*

— OBSERV. El plural es *ex-servicemen*.

exsiccate ['eksikeit] v. tr. Desecar, secar.
exsiccation [,eksi'keiʃən] n. Desecación, *f.*
exsiccator ['eksikeitə*] n. Secante, *m.*
extant [eks'tænt] adj. Existente.
extemporaneous [eks,tempə'reinjəs] adj. Improvisado, da.
extemporarily [iks'tempərərili] adv. U. S. Improvisadamente.
extemporary [iks'tempərəri] adj. Improvisado, da.
extempore [eks'tempəri] adj. Improvisado, da.
— Adv. Improvisadamente, de improviso. || *To speak extempore*, improvisar un discurso.
extemporization [eks,tempərai'zeiʃən] n. Improvisación, *f.*
extemporize [iks'tempəraiz] v. tr./intr. Improvisar.
extend [iks'tend] v. tr. Prolongar (to lengthen): *to extend a holiday, a road*, prolongar unas vacaciones, una calle. || Ampliar (to widen): *to extend the meaning of a word*, ampliar el significado de una palabra. || Extender, ensanchar (to enlarge). || Estirar (one's body). || MIL. Desplegar (troops). || Aumentar (to increase). || Extender, alargar (to hold out): *to extend the arm horizontally*, extender el brazo horizontalmente. || Tender (the hand). || Ofrecer (aid). || Dar (welcome). || Enviar (an invitation). || JUR. Evaluar (to assess). | Embargar (to seize). || Prorrogar (time-limit): *to extend a note*, prorrogar un pagaré. || Conceder: *to extend credits to s.o.*, conceder créditos a alguien. || Llevar a la página siguiente (in book-keeping). || Desarrollar (to write out in full). || Exigir el máximo esfuerzo a (to tax the strength of). || Extender (one's influence, knowledge). || Manifestar (sympathy). || — *To extend an invitation to*, invitar a. || *To extend o.s.*, esforzarse, hacer esfuerzos. || *To extend shorthand*, transcribir taquigrafía.
— V. intr. Extenderse. || Prolongarse. || Llegar, alcanzar (to reach). || *To extend over*, abarcar.
extended [—id] adj. Prolongado, da (lengthened). || Extendido, da (stretched out, widespread). || Alargado, da (the arm). || Tendido, da (the hand). || Aumentado, da (increased). || Prorrogado, da (a period). || Ampliado, da (enlarged in scope, etc.). || Intenso, sa (an effort). || MIL. Desplegado, da (formation). | Abierto, ta (order).
extendible [—ibl] adj. Extensible.
extensibility [iks,tensə'biliti] n. Extensibilidad, *f.*
extensible [iks'tensəbl] adj. Extensible, extensivo, va.
extensile [eks'tensail] adj. Extensible.
extension [iks'tenʃən] n. Extensión, *f.* (an extending or being extended). || Prolongación, *f.* (addition): *a canal extension*, la prolongación de un canal. || Anexo, *m.*: *the hotel extension*, el anexo del hotel. || Aumento, *m.* (increase). || Prórroga, *f.* (of time). || Extensión, *f.* (phone): *put me through to extension 333*, póngame con la extensión 333. || TECH. Larguero, *m.* (of table). || PHYS. MED. PHIL. GRAMM. Extensión, *f.* || Vulgarización, *f.*, divulgación, *f.*, extensión, *f.*: *extension programme*, programa de divulgación. || — *By extension*, por extensión. || *Extension ladder*, escalera (*f.*) extensible. || *Extension spring*, muelle (*m.*) de tracción. || *Extension table*, mesa (*f.*) con largueros *or* extensible.
extensive [iks'tensiv] adj. Extenso, sa (vast). || Extensivo, va (farming).
extensor [iks'tensə*] n. Músculo (*m.*) extensor.
extent [iks'tent] n. Extensión, *f.* (length, area). || Punto, *m.* (degree): *to what extent is our country industrialized?*, ¿hasta qué punto está industrializado nuestro país? || Alcance, *m.* (scope). || JUR. Embargo, *m.* || — *Credit to the extent of forty pounds*, crédito hasta la cantidad de cuarenta libras. || *I would not go to that extent*, no iría tan lejos. || *The extent of the damage*, la importancia de los daños. || *To a certain extent*, hasta cierto punto. || *To a great* o *large extent*, en gran parte. || *To a lesser extent*, en menor grado. || *To such an extent*, hasta tal punto. || *To that extent*, hasta este punto. || *To the extent of*, hasta el punto de. || *To the full extent*, en toda su extensión. || *To the full extent of his power*, hasta el máximo de su capacidad. || *Within the extent of his jurisdiction*, dentro de los límites de su jurisdicción.
extenuate [eks'tenjueit] v. tr. Atenuar, disminuir.
extenuating [—iŋ] adj. JUR. Atenuante: *extenuating circumstances*, circunstancias atenuantes.
extenuation [eks,tenju'eiʃən] n. Atenuación, *f.*
extenuative [eks'tenjuətiv] or **extenuatory** [eks'tenjuətəri] adj. U. S. Atenuante.
exterior [eks'tiəriə*] adj. Exterior (outer). || MATH. Externo, na (angle).
— N. Exterior, *m.* (outside). || Aspecto, *m.* (appearance). || — Pl. CINEM. Exteriores, *m.*
exteriority [eks,tiəri'ɔriti] n. Exterioridad, *f.*
exteriorization [eksti:əriərai'zeiʃən] n. Exteriorización, *f.*
exteriorize [eks'tiəriəraiz] v. tr. Exteriorizar.
exterminate [iks'tə:mineit] v. tr. Exterminar.
exterminating [—iŋ] adj. Exterminador, ra.
extermination [iks,tə:mi'neiʃən] n. Exterminio, *m.*, exterminación, *f.*
exterminator [iks'tə:mineitə*] n. Exterminador, ra.
extern [eks'tə:n] n. U. S. Médico (*m.*) externo (doctor). | Externo, na (pupil).
external [eks'tə:nl] adj. Externo, na (medicine, angle): *for external use only*, sólo para uso externo; *external angle*, ángulo externo. || Exterior (situated on the outside): *external walls*, murallas exteriores. || Exterior (foreign): *external events*, asuntos exteriores. || Exterior (of what lies outside the mind): *external reality*, realidad exterior.
— N. Aspecto (*m.*) exterior, apariencia, *f.*
externalization [eks,tə:nəlai'zeiʃən] n. Exteriorización, *f.*
externalize [eks'tə:nəlaiz] v. tr. Exteriorizar.
externally [eks'tə:nəli] adv. Exteriormente.
exterritorial ['eks,teri'tɔ:riəl] adj. Extraterritorial.
exterritoriality ['eks,teri,tɔ'riæliti] n. Extraterritorialidad, *f.*
extinct [iks'tiŋkt] adj. Extinto, ta; extinguido, da (race). || Extinguido, da; apagado, da (fire, volcano). || *To become extinct*, extinguirse.
extinction [iks'tiŋkʃən] n. Extinción, *f.*
extinguish [iks'tiŋgwiʃ] v. tr. Extinguir (to put out). || Apagar (a light, fire, etc.). || Eclipsar (to outshine completely). || Extinguir, amortizar (a debt). || Extinguir (to put an end to). || Reducir al silencio a (to silence). || JUR. Abolir. || FIG. Destruir (hope). | Extinguir (family, race). | Suprimir, destruir (to eliminate).
extinguishable [—əbl] adj. Extinguible.

extinguisher [—ə*] n. Extintor, *m.* (for putting out a fire). || Apagador, *m.* (for putting out candles). || Apagador, *m.* (s.o. who extinguishes).
extinguishment [—mənt] n. Extinción, *f.*
extirpate [ˈekstə:peit] v. tr. Extirpar.
extirpation [ˌekstə:ˈpeiʃən] n. Extirpación, *f.*
extirpator [ˈekstə:peitə*] n. Extirpador, *m.*
extol (U. S. **extoll**) [iksˈtəul] v. tr. Ensalzar, alabar, (s.o.). || Encomiar, alabar (sth.).
extolling [—iŋ] or **extolment** [—mənt] n. Ensalzamiento, *m.*, alabanza, *f.*, encomio, *m.*, elogio, *m.*
extort [iksˈtɔ:t] v. tr. Arrancar, sacar de mala manera *or* por la fuerza (signature, promise, confession, etc.): *to extort sth. out of s.o.*, sacar algo a alguien por la fuerza.
extortion [iksˈtɔ:ʃən] n. Extorsión, *f.*, exacción, *f.*, concusión, *f.*
extortionate [iksˈtɔ:ʃnit] adj. Exorbitante, excesivo, va; desorbitado, da (price).
extortioner [iksˈtɔ:ʃnə*] or **extortionist** [—ist] n. Concusionario, ria.
extra [ˈekstrə] adj. Extra (of superior quality). || De más, de sobra: *we have two extra beds*, tenemos dos camas de más. || Adicional, suplementario, ria (additional). || Extraordinario, ria (dish). || Suplementario, ria (servant). || No incluido, aparte: *singing lessons are extra*, las clases de canto no están incluidas *or* son aparte. || De recambio, de repuesto (part). || — *Extra charge*, recargo, *m.* || *Extra fare*, suplemento, *m.* || *Extra luggage*, exceso (*m.*) de equipaje. || *Extra pay*, paga extraordinaria. || *Extra postage*, sobretasa, *f.* || *Extra weight*, sobrecarga, *f.* || *Extra work*, horas extraordinarias.
— N. Recargo, *m.* (extra charge). || Suplemento, *m.*: extra, *m.*: *to pay for the extras*, pagar los suplementos. || CINEM. Extra, *m.* & *f.* || Criado (*m.*) suplementario (servant). || Edición (*f.*) especial (newspaper). || U. S. Repuesto, *m.*, recambio, *m.* (spare part).
— Adv. Extraordinariamente: *extra difficult*, extraordinariamente difícil. || *Extra good quality*, de calidad extraordinaria *or* superior.
extract [ˈekstrækt] n. Extracto, *m.*, trozo, *m.* (of a book). || Extracto, *m.*, concentrado, *m.* (of meat, etc.). || CHEM. Extracto, *m.* || *Extract from police records*, certificado (*m.*) de penales.
extract [iksˈtrækt] v. tr. Extraer, sacar: *to extract a tooth*, extraer una muela; *oil is extracted from olives*, el aceite se extrae de las aceitunas. || Sacar (passages from books, sounds). || Sacar (to obtain): *did you manage to extract any information from him?*, ¿conseguiste sacarle alguna información? || MATH. CHEM. Extraer.
extractable [iksˈtræktəbl] or **extractible** [iksˈtræktəbl] adj. Extraíble.
extraction [iksˈtrækʃən] n. Extracción, *f.* (extracting). || Origen, *m.* (descent): *Welsh by extraction*, galés de origen. || *Of low extraction*, de baja extracción.
extractive [iksˈtræktiv] adj. Extractivo, va.
extractor [iksˈtræktə*] n. Extractor, *m.* (of a gun). || Tenazas, *f. pl.*, alicates, *m. pl.* (of dentist).
extracurricular [ˈekstrəkəˈrikjulə] adj. Fuera del programa de estudios. || Extraescolar (out-of-school).
extraditable [ˈekstrədaitəbl] adj. Sujeto a extradición.
extradite [ˈekstrədait] v. tr. Conceder la extradición de, entregar (to hand over). || Obtener la extradición de (to obtain).
extradition [ˌekstrəˈdiʃən] n. Extradición, *f.*
extrados [eksˈtreidɔs] n. Extradós, *m.*, trasdós, *m.*
extrajudicial [ˈekstrədʒu:ˈdiʃəl] adj. Extrajudicial.
extralegal [ekstrəˈli:gəl] adj. Extralegal.
extramundane [ˈekstrəˈmʌndein] adj. Extraterrestre.
extramural [ˈekstrəˈmjuərəl] adj. Situado extramuros (outside the walls). || Para estudiantes libres: *extramural course*, curso para estudiantes libres. || De carácter privado (activities). || *Extramural lecturer*, profesor encargado de cursos dados fuera de la universidad.
extraneous [eksˈtreinjəs] adj. Extraño, ña; externo, na (coming from outside): *extraneous influences*, influencias externas. || Ajeno a la cuestión (not belonging to the matter): *extraneous details*, detalles ajenos a la cuestión.
extraordinary [iksˈtrɔ:dnri] adj. Extraordinario, ria: *ambassador extraordinary*, embajador extraordinario; *extraordinary powers*, poderes extraordinarios. || Extraordinario, ria (remarkable). || Raro, ra (odd). || Sorprendente (astonishing).
extrapolate [eksˈtræpəuleit] v. tr. Extrapolar.
extrapolation [eksˌtræpəuˈleiʃən] n. MATH. Extrapolación, *f.*
extrasensory [ˈekstrəˈsensəri] adj. Extrasensible.
extraterrestrial [ˈekstrətiˈrestrjəl] adj. Extraterrestre.
extraterritorial [ˈekstrəˌteriˈtɔ:riəl] adj. Extraterritorial.
extraterritoriality [ˈekstrəˌteriˌtɔ:riˈæliti] n. Extraterritorialidad, *f.*
extrauterine [ekstrəˈju:tərain] adj. Extrauterino, na.
extravagance [iksˈtrævigəns] n. Despilfarro, *m.*, derroche, *m.* (of spending). || Prodigalidad, *f.* (prodigality). || Extravagancia, *f.* (eccentricity).
extravagancy [—i] n. See EXTRAVAGANCE.
extravagant [iksˈtrævigənt] adj. Despilfarrador, ra; derrochador, ra (wasteful). || Pródigo, ga (lavish). || Dispendioso, sa; de lujo: *extravagant tastes*, gustos dispendiosos. || Extravagante: *extravagant language*, lenguaje extravagante; *extravagant ideas*, ideas extravagantes. || Exorbitante, desorbitado, da (price). || Excesivo, va (praise).
extravaganza [eksˌtrævəˈgænzə] n. THEATR. Farsa, *f.* || MUS. Fantasía, *f.* || Extravagancia, *f.* (in behaviour, speech). || Historia (*f.*) extravagante.
extravasate [eksˈtrævəseit] v. tr. Extravasar.
— V. intr. Extravasarse.
extraversion [ˌekstrəˈvə:ʃən] n. Extraversión, *f.*
extravert [ˈekstrəvə:t] n. Extravertido, da.
extraverted [—id] adj. Extravertido, da.
extreme [iksˈtri:m] adj. Extremo, ma: *extreme cold*, frío extremo; *extreme right wing in politics*, extrema derecha en política. || Excepcional, extremo, ma: *an extreme case*, un caso excepcional. || *Extreme in one's views*, de opiniones extremas.
— N. Extremo, *m.*: *he is worried to the extreme that he doesn't eat*, está preocupado hasta el extremo de no comer. || MATH. Extremo, *m.* || — FIG. *Extremes meet*, los extremos se tocan. || *In the extreme*, extremadamente, en extremo, en sumo grado. || *To carry to extremes*, llevar al extremo. || *To go from one extreme to the other*, pasar de un extremo a otro. || *To go to extremes*, llegar a extremos.
extremely [—li] adv. Extremadamente, sumamente.
Extreme Unction [ˈekstri:mˈʌŋkʃən] n. REL. Extremaunción, *f.*
extremism [iksˈtri:mizəm] n. Extremismo, *m.*
extremist [iksˈtrimist] adj./n. Extremista.
extremity [iksˈtremiti] n. Extremidad, *f.* (the very end). || Situación (*f.*) extrema (dangerous situation). || Necesidad (*f.*) extrema, apuro, *m.* (necessity): *in this extremity*, en semejante apuro. || Extremo, *m.*: *in the extremity of his endurance*, al extremo de su resistencia. || — Pl. Extremidades, *f.* (furthest ends, feet and hands). | Medidas (*f.*) extremas (extreme measures). || — *To be at the last extremity*, estar en las últimas. || *To be driven to extremity*, estar en un gran apuro.
extricable [ˈekstrikəbl] adj. Solucionable.
extricate [ˈekstrikeit] v. tr. Librar, sacar (from a difficulty). || Desenredar (to disentangle). || Liberar, desprender (a gas, heat). || *To extricate o.s. from*, conseguir salir de.
extrication [ˌekstriˈkeiʃən] n. Liberación, *f.*
extrinsic [eksˈtrinsik] adj. Extrínseco, ca.
extrorse [ˈekstrɔ:s] adj. BOT. Extrorso, sa.
extroversion [ˌekstrəuˈvə:ʃən] n. Extroversión, *f.*
extrovert [ˈekstrəuvə:t] n. Extrovertido, da.
extroverted [—id] adj. Extrovertido, da.
extrude [eksˈtru:d] v. tr. TECH. Estirar (metal). || Expulsar (to force out).
— V. intr. Sobresalir.
extrusion [eksˈtru:ʒən] n. Extrusión, *f.*, estirado, *m.* (of metal). || Expulsión, *f.*
exuberance [igˈzju:bərəns] n. Exuberancia, *f.*
exuberant [igˈzju:bərənt] adj. Exuberante.
exudate [ˈeksju:deit] n. Exudado, *m.*
exudation [eksju:ˈdeiʃən] n. Exudación, *f.*
exude [igˈzju:d] v. tr./intr. Exudar, rezumar.
exult [igˈzʌlt] v. intr. Exultar, alegrarse mucho, regocijarse. || *To exult over*, triunfar sobre.
exultancy [igˈzʌltənsi] n. Exultación, *f.*, júbilo, *m.*, regocijo, *m.*
exultant [igˈzʌltənt] adj. Exultante, regocijado, da; jubiloso, sa.
exultation [ˌegzʌlˈteiʃən] n. Exultación, *f.*, júbilo, *m.*, regocijo, *m.*
exutory [egˈzju:təri] n. MED. Exutorio, *m.*
exuviae [igˈzju:vii:] pl. n. Camisa, *f. sing.*, piel, *f. sing.* (of animals).
exuviate [igˈzju:vieit] v. tr. Echar.
exuviation [igˌzju:viˈeiʃən] n. Muda (*f.*) de la piel.
ex-voto [ˈeksˈvəutəu] n. Exvoto, *m.*
eyas [ˈaiəs] n. ZOOL. Halcón (*m.*) niego.
eye [ai] n. Ojo, *m.*: *big eyes*, ojos grandes. || Ojo, *m.* (of a needle). || Hembra (*f.*) de corchete (of a hook). || Ojo, *m.* (in the handle of a tool). || Ojete, *m.* (of a boot). || Lazada, *f.* (of thread). || BOT. Yema, *f.*, botón, *m.* || Ojo, *m.* (of bread, cheese, hurricane). || MIL. Diana, *f.* (on a target). || FIG. Vista, *f.*, visión, *f.*, ojo, *m.* (view): *he has good eyes*, tiene buena vista. | Mirada, *f.* (look): *to follow with one's eyes*, seguir con la mirada. || Ocelo, *m.*, ojo, *m.* (on a peacock's tail). || — *Almond eyes*, ojos achinados *or* rasgados. || FIG. *An eye for an eye*, ojo por ojo. || *As far as the eye can see*, hasta donde alcanza la vista. || *Before my very eyes*, delante de mis propios ojos (before s.o.), a ojos vistas (rapidly). || FIG. FAM. *Black eye*, ojo a la funerala, ojo en compota. | *Bulging* o *protruding eye*, ojo de besugo, ojo saltón. || *By eye*, a ojo. || || *Electric eye*, ojo eléctrico. || *Evil eye*, mal (*m.*) de ojo, aojamiento, *m.* || *Eye bank*, banco (*f.*) de ojos. || *Eye patch*, parche, *m.* || MIL. *Eyes right!*, ¡vista a la derecha! || *Glass eye*, ojo de cristal. || FIG. FAM. *His eyes are bigger than his belly*, llena antes los ojos que la barriga *or* que la tripa. || *His eyes filled with tears*, se le arrasaron los ojos en lágrimas. || MAR. *In the eye of the wind*, contra el viento. || FIG. *In the eyes of*, a los ojos de. | *In the mind's eye*, en la imaginación. | *In the twinkling of an eye*, en un abrir y cerrar de ojos. | *It hits you in the eye*, salta a la vista. || FAM.

It's all my eye!, ¡es puro camelo! | *Keep your eyes peeled!*, ¡ojo alerta! || RAD. *Magic eye*, ojo mágico. || FAM. *My eye!*, ¡por Dios! (astonishment), ¡ni hablar! (contradiction). || FIG. *No eye like the eye of the master*, el ojo del amo engorda al caballo. | *Not to believe one's eyes*, no dar crédito a sus ojos. || *Not to take one's eyes off*, no quitar los ojos de encima, no quitar ojo a. || *Pleasing to the eye* agradable a la vista. || FAM. *Private eye*, detective, *m.* || *Saucy eyes*, ojos pícaros. || *Slant eyes*, ojos oblicuos. || *Sunken eyes*, ojos hundidos. || *Tears came to his eyes*, se le humedecieron los ojos. || FIG. *To be all eyes*, ser todo ojos. | *To be in the public eye*, estar a la vista. | *To be the apple of one's eye*, ser la niña de los ojos de alguien. || FAM. *To be up to one's eyes in work*, estar hasta aquí de trabajo. | *To black s.o.'s eye*, poner a uno un ojo a la funerala. | *To bring s.o. into the public eye*, dar a conocer a alguien al público. | *To catch one's eye*, llamar la atención a uno. | *To close* o *to shut one's eyes*, cerrar los ojos. | *To cock one's eye at*, see COCK. | *To cry one's eyes out*, llorar a lágrima viva. | *To fix one's eyes upon*, clavar los ojos *or* la mirada en. || FAM. *To give s.o. a black eye*, poner a uno un ojo a la funerala. || FIG. *To give s.o. the glad eye* o *to make sheep's eyes at s.o.*, echar miradas cariñosas *or* miraditas a alguien, mirar con ternura a alguien. | *To have a good* o *a sure* o *an accurate eye*, tener buen ojo *or* ojo clínico *or* ojo de buen cubero. | *To have an eye for*, tener buen ojo para (to have a due sense of). | *To have an eye to*, tener en cuenta. | *To have eyes like a hawk*, tener ojos de lince. | *To have one's eyes about one*, andar con cien ojos. || SP. *To have one's eye in*, tener el ojo acostumbrado. || FIG. *To have one's eyes on*, echar el ojo a, tener los ojos puestos en (to watch with interest), vigilar, no perder de vista (to keep under observation). | *To have one's eye on everything*, estar en todo. | *To keep an eye on*, estar pendiente de, echar una mirada a: *keep an eye on the time or we will be late*, estate pendiente de la hora o llegaremos tarde; no perder de vista, vigilar (to keep under observation), no quitar los ojos de encima (to watch with interest). | *To keep one's eyes open*, abrir el ojo, andar ojo alerta. | *To leap to the eye*, saltar a los ojos. | *To look a fool in s.o.'s eyes*, pasar a los ojos de uno como un tonto. | *To look at out of the corner of one's eye*, mirar con el rabillo del ojo. || *To look into s.o.'s eyes* o *face*, mirar a *or* en los ojos. || FIG. *To make eyes at*, echar miraditas a (a girl). | *To make s.o.'s eyes open*, asombrar a alguien. | *To open s.o.'s eyes*, abrir los ojos a alguien. | *To put the evil eye on*, echar mal de ojo a. || *To roll one's eyes*, poner los ojos en blanco. || *To rub one's eyes*, restregarse los ojos. || FIG. *To run one's eye over*, echar un vistazo a, recorrer con la vista. | *To see eye to eye with*, ver con los mismos ojos que, estar de acuerdo con. | *To see with half an eye*, ver a primera vista. || *To set eyes on*, [alcanzar a] ver. || FIG. *To set one's eye on*, poner el ojo *or* los ojos en. | *To sleep with one eye open*, dormir con los ojos abiertos. | *To the eye*, por encima, a primera vista. | *To turn a blind eye*, cerrar los ojos, hacer la vista gorda. | *To view with a jaundiced eye*, mirar con ojos envidiosos. | *Under one's very eyes*, delante de los propios ojos de uno. | *With an eye to*, con miras a. | *With one's eyes open, closed*, con los ojos abiertos, cerrados. | *With the naked eye*, a simple vista. | *You can see it with half an eye*, salta a los ojos.

eye [ai] v. tr. Mirar: *to eye from head to foot*, mirar de pies a cabeza.

eyeball [ˈaibɔ:l] n. ANAT. Globo (*m.*) del ojo.

eyebath [ˈaibɑ:θ] n. Lavaojos, *m. inv.*, ojera, *f.*

eyebolt [ˈaibəult] n. TECH. Armella, *f.*, cáncamo, *m.*

eyebrow [ˈaibrau] n. ANAT. Ceja, *f.*

eye-catcher [ˈaikætʃə*] n. Cosa (*f.*) que llama la atención.

eye-catching [ˈaikætʃiŋ] adj. Llamativo, va.

eyecup [ˈaikʌp] n. U. S. Lavaojos, *m. inv.*, ojera, *f.*

eyed [aid] adj. De ojos: *black-eyed*, de ojos negros.

eyedropper [ˈaidrɔpə*] n. Cuentagotas, *m. inv.*

eyeflap [ˈaiflæp] n. Anteojera, *f.*

eyeful [ˈaiful] n. FAM. Vistazo, *m.*: *to get an eyeful of*, echar un vistazo a.

eyeglass [ˈaiglɑ:s] n. Monóculo, *m.* (monocle). || Lente, *m.* & *f.* (of an optical instrument). || Lavaojos, *m. inv.*, ojera, *f.* (eyebath).

eyehole [ˈaihəul] n. Mirilla, *f.* (in a door). || Agujero, *m.* (a hole). || ANAT. Órbita (*f.*) *or* cuenca (*f.*) del ojo.

eyelash [ˈailæʃ] n. Pestaña, *f.*

eyeless [ˈailis] adj. Ciego, ga.

eyelet [ˈailit] n. Ojete, *m.*

eyelid [ˈailid] n. ANAT. Párpado, *m.* || FIG. FAM. *To hang on by one's eyelids*, estar pendiente de un hilo.

eye-opener [ˈaiˈəupnə*] n. Sorpresa, *f.*

eyepiece [ˈaipi:s] n. Ocular, *m.*

eyeshade [ˈaiʃeid] n. Visera, *f.*

eyeshadow [ˈaiˈʃædəu] n. Sombreador, *m.* (cosmetic).

eyeshot [ˈaiʃɔt] n. Vista, *f.*, alcance (*m.*) de la vista.

eyesight [ˈaisait] n. Vista, *f.*

eyesore [ˈaisɔ:*] n. Algo que ofende la vista, monstruosidad, *f.*

eyespot [ˈaispɔt] n. ZOOL. Mancha (*f.*) ocular.

eyestalk [ˈaistɔ:k] n. ZOOL. Pedúnculo, *m.*

eyestrain [ˈaistrein] n. Vista (*f.*) cansada. || *To get eyestrain*, tener la vista cansada.

eyetooth [ˈaitu:θ] n. Colmillo, *m.* || FIG. *He would give his eyetooth to go with her*, daría un ojo de la cara por acompañarla.

eyewash [ˈaiwɔʃ] n. Colirio, *m.* (lotion for the eyes). || FIG. Tonterías, *f. pl.*, disparates, *m. pl.* (nonsense): *that's all eyewash*, eso son disparates. | Música (*f.*) celestial (drivel).

eyewater [ˈaiˌwɔ:tə*] n. MED. Humor (*m.*) ácueo.

eyewitness [ˈaiˈwitnis] n. Testigo (*m.*) ocular.

eyot [eit] n. GEOGR. Islote, *m.*, isla (*f.*) pequeña.

eyrie [ˈaiəri] n. Aguilera, *f.*

F

f [ef] n. F, *f.* (letter). || MUS. Fa, *m.*: *F clef*, clave de fa.

fa [fɑ:] n. MUS. Fa, *m.* (fixed fa). | Subdominante, *f.* (movable).

fab [fæb] adj. FAM. See FABULOUS.

Fabian [ˈfeibjən] adj. Contemporizador, ra. || *Fabian Society*, Sociedad Fabiana.

fable [ˈfeibl] n. Fábula, *f.*: *the fables of La Fontaine*, las fábulas de La Fontaine. || FIG. Fábula, *f.*, mentira, *f.*, cuento, *m.* (falsehood). | Mito, *m.*, fábula, *f.*, leyenda, *f.* (myth).

fable [ˈfeibl] v. intr. Escribir fábulas. || FIG. Contar fábulas *or* cuentos. || *It is fabled that*, se cuenta que, según la leyenda.

fabled [—d] adj. Legendario, ria (legendary). || FIG. Fabuloso, sa (fictitious, fabulous).

fabler [—ə*] n. Fabulista, *m.* & *f.* (fable writer). || FIG. Cuentista, *m.* & *f.*

fabric [ˈfæbrik] n. Tejido, *m.*, tela, *f.* (material). || Estructura, *f.* (structure). || Textura, *f.* (texture). || Fábrica, *f.*, edificio, *m.* (building). || REL. Fábrica, *f.* || FIG. Índole, *f.* (kind): *people of all fabric*, gente de toda índole.

fabricate [ˈfæbrikeit] v. tr. Fabricar (to construct, to manufacture). || Labrar: *to fabricate steel into plates*, labrar acero en chapas. || FIG. Forjar, inventar: *to fabricate a story*, forjar una historia. | Falsificar (evidence, documents, etc.).

fabrication [ˌfæbriˈkeiʃən] n. Fabricación, *f.* (construction, manufacture). || FIG. Mentira, *f.*, cuento, *m.*, invención, *f.* (lie): *the hole thing is a fabrication*, todo es un cuento. | Falsificación, *f.* (of evidence).

fabricator [ˈfæbrikeitə*] n. Fabricante, *m.* || FIG. Mentiroso, sa; embustero, ra (liar).

fabulist [ˈfæbjulist] n. Fabulista, *m.* & *f.* || FIG. Cuentista, *m.* & *f.* (liar).

fabulous [ˈfæbjuləs] adj. Fabuloso, sa. || FAM. Estupendo, da; fabuloso, sa; macanudo, da (marvellous).

façade [fəˈsɑ:d] n. Fachada, *f.* || FIG. Fachada, *f.* (appearance): *the country's prosperity was nothing but a facade*, la prosperidad del país era pura fachada.

face [feis] n. Cara, *f.*, rostro, *m.*: *a pretty face*, una cara bonita. || Cara, *f.*, semblante, *m.* (countenance): *a sad face*, una cara triste. || FIG. Aspecto, *m.* (aspect). | Cariz, *m.*: *the situation has taken on another face*, la situación ha tomado otro cariz. || Mueca, *f.*, gesto, *m.* (grimace). || Careta, *f.* (mask). || Cara, *f.*, cara (*f.*) dura, caradura, *f.*, descaro, *m.*, desfachatez, *f.* (cheek, nerve). || Superficie, *f.* (surface). || Superficie, *f.*, faz, *f.*

(of the earth). || Lado, *m.*, cara, *f.* (side). || Parte (*f.*) delantera (front). || ARCH. Fachada, *f.*, frente, *m.* (façade). || Cara, *f.* (of cards, coins, cliff). || Esfera, *f.* (of clock). || Recto, *m.* (of a sheet of paper). || Derecho, *m.* (of cloth). || Haz, *f.* (of leaf). || Paramento, *m.* (of wall). || TECH. Cotillo, *m.* (of hammer). | Mesa, *f.*, plana, *f.* (of an anvil). || MIN. Frente (*m.*) de ataque. || PRINT. Ojo, *m.* || — FAM. *A face like a wet weekend*, cara de viernes *or* de Cuaresma. || *Face down*, boca abajo. || *Face massage*, masaje (*m.*) facial. || MIL. *Face to*, frente a, enfrente de. || *Face to face*, cara a cara. || *Face up*, boca arriba. || FAM. *I didn't do it for your pretty face*, no lo hice por tu bella *or* por tu linda cara. || *In the face of*, frente a, ante (in the presence of), a pesar de (despite). || *I said it in his face*, se lo dije en la cara. || FIG. *It's staring you in the face*, lo tiene ante las narices (a thing), salta a la vista (a solution). | *On the face of it* o *of things*, a primera vista. || *The Holy Face*, la Santa Faz. || FIG. *To do sth. until one is blue in the face*, hartarse de hacer algo. || *To fall flat on one's face*, caerse de bruces. || FIG. *To fly in the face of*, burlarse de (convention), hacer caso omiso de (s.o.'s rights). | *To have a face as long as a poker*, tener cara de alma en pena. || *To keep a straight* o *a firm face*, mantenerse impávido. || *To laugh in s.o.'s face*, reírse en la cara de uno. || *To look square in the face*, mirar en los ojos, mirar fijamente. || FIG. *To lose face*, perder prestigio, quedar mal. || *To make* o *to pull a wry face*, torcer el gesto. || *To make* o *to pull faces*, hacer muecas. || *To pull a face like*, poner cara de. || FIG. *To pull* o *to wear a long face*, poner cara larga. | *To put a good face on it*, ponerle buena cara. | *To put on a face of importance*, dárselas de persona importante. | *To put on a face to suit the occasion*, poner cara de circunstancias. | *To save face*, salvar las apariencias. || *To see from the look on one's face that*, poder ver en la cara de alguien que. || *To set face for home*, dirigirse a casa. || FIG. *To set one's face against sth.*, negarse a, oponerse firmemente a. || *To show one's face*, dejarse ver, aparecer. || FAM. *To slam the door in s.o.'s face*, darle a uno con la puerta en las narices. | *To slap s.o.'s face*, abofetear a alguien, darle un tortazo a alguien. | *To smash s.o.'s face in*, romper la cara a uno. || FIG. *To stare death in the face*, ver la muerte de cerca. || *To tell s.o. to his face that*, decirle a uno en la cara que. || FIG. *To throw sth. in s.o.'s face*, echarle algo en cara a alguien. || *To turn red in the face*, ponerse colorado (with shame), ponerse rojo (with anger). || *Unfriendly face*, cara de pocos amigos. || *Wry face*, mueca.

face [feis] v. tr. Mirar hacia, dar a, estar orientado hacia: *our house faces the park*, nuestra casa da al parque. || Estar enfrente de (to be opposite). || Mirar hacia (to look towards). || Volver la cara hacia, mirar hacia (to turn towards): *he faced the orchestra*, volvió la cara hacia la orquesta. || Enfrentarse con, arrostrar: *to face great danger*, enfrentarse con grandes peligros; *to face the facts*, enfrentarse con los hechos. || Hacer frente a, afrontar (a problem). || Arrostrar, hacer frente a (the consequences). || Enfrentarse a *or* con, hacer frente a (the enemy, a person). || Hacer frente a (to stand up to). || Soportar, aguantar (to stand): *I don't think I can face another week here*, creo que no podré soportar otra semana aquí. || Presentarse ante: *he won't dare face her now*, ahora no se atreverá a presentarse ante ella. || Volver, poner boca arriba, enseñar (cards). || Forrar (in sewing). || TECH. Revestir (to put a new surface on). | Alisar (to smoothe). || CULIN. Poner una capa de (caramel). || — *Facing each other*, uno enfrente del otro, uno frente al otro. || *Facing east*, con orientación al este. || *Let's face it*, hay que reconocerlo, reconozcámoslo. || *The problem that faces me*, el problema que se me plantea. || *To be faced with a difficulty*, enfrentarse con una dificultad. || MIL. *To face about*, mandar dar media vuelta. || *To face it out*, mantenerse firme. || *To face s.o. with*, confrontar *or* carear a alguien con. || *To face the music*, afrontar las consecuencias. || *To face the wall*, ponerse de cara a la pared.

— V. intr. Dar a, mirar hacia: *my bedroom faces north*, mi cuarto da al norte. || Volverse (to turn). || — MIL. *About face!*, ¡media vuelta! | *Left face!*, ¡media vuelta a la izquierda! || *To face about*, dar media vuelta (person, soldier). || *To face on to*, mirar hacia, dar a. || *To face up to*, enfrentarse con (danger, etc.), hacer frente a (to stand up to s.o.), soportar (to put up with).

face ache [—eik] n. MED. Neuralgia (*f.*) facial.

face card [—kɑ:d] n. Figura, *f.* (in card games).

facecloth [—klɔθ] n. Guante, *m.*, manopla, *f.*, pañito, *m.* [para lavarse la cara]. || Sudario, *m.* (for a corpse).

face cream [—kri:m] n. Crema (*f.*) de belleza.

face flannel [—flænl] n. Guante, *m.*, manopla, *f.*, pañito, *m.* [para lavarse la cara].

face-harden [—hɑ:dn] v. tr. TECH. Cementar (metals).

faceless [—lis] adj. Sin cara. || Anónimo, ma.

face-lifting [—ˌliftiŋ] n. MED. Operación (*f.*) facial de estética, estiramiento (*m.*) de la piel. || FIG. Lavado, *m.*: *this building needs a face-lifting*, este edificio necesita un lavado.

face powder [—ˈpaudə*] n. Polvos (*m. pl.*) para la cara.

facer [—ə*] n. FAM. Bofetada, *f.* (blow). | Lío, *m.*, engorro, *m.* (difficulty). | Revés, *m.* (setback).

face-saving [—ˈseiviŋ] adj. Para salvar las apariencias.

facet [ˈfæsit] n. Faceta, *f.* (of gem, bone, eye; aspect).

facet [ˈfæsit] v. tr. Labrar en facetas (gems).

faceted [—id] adj. Labrado en facetas, con facetas.

facetiae [fəˈsi:ʃii:] pl. n. Gracias, *f.*, agudezas, *f.* (witticisms). || Libros (*m.*) humorísticos (books).

facetious [fəˈsi:ʃəs] adj. Chistoso, sa; gracioso, sa; jocoso, sa.

facetiousness [—nis] n. Gracia, *f.*, jocosidad, *f.*

face-to-face [ˈfeistəˈfeis] adv. Cara a cara: *to come face-to-face with s.o.*, encontrarse cara a cara con alguien.

face value [feisˈvælju:] n. Valor (*m.*) nominal (of bill, etc.). || Valor (*m.*) facial (of stamps, etc.). || *To take sth. at face value*, creer algo a pie juntillas.

facia [ˈfeiʃə] n. Letrero, *m.* (of a shop). || Tablero (*m.*) de mandos, salpicadero, *m.* (of a car).

facial [ˈfeiʃəl] adj. Facial.

— N. Masaje (*m.*) facial (massage).

facies [ˈfeiʃii:z] inv. n. MED. Facies, *m. inv.*

facile [ˈfæsail] adj. Fácil (easy): *a facile victory*, una victoria fácil. || Fácil: *a man with a facile tongue, pen*, un hombre de palabra, de pluma fácil. || Vivo, va (mind). || Acomodaticio, cia (easygoing). || Superficial.

facilitate [fəˈsiliteit] v. tr. Facilitar: *to facilitate s.o. in sth.*, facilitar algo a alguien.

facilitation [fəˌsiliˈteiʃən] n. Facilitación, *f.*

facility [fəˈsiliti] n. Facilidad, *f.*: *to have a facility for maths*, tener facilidad para las matemáticas; *a task of incredible facility*, una tarea de una facilidad increíble. || — Pl. Facilidades, *f.*: *credit facilities*, facilidades de crédito. || Instalaciones, *f.*: *sports facilities*, instalaciones deportivas. || *Transportation facilities*, medios (*m.*) de comunicación.

facing [ˈfeisiŋ] n. Revestimiento, *m.* (of a wall). || Guarnición, *f.* (decorative trimming). || — Pl. Vueltas, *f.* (of a uniform).

— Adj De enfrente: *on the facing wall*, en la pared de enfrente.

facsimile [fækˈsimili] n. Facsímil, *m.*, facsímile, *m.*

fact [fækt] n. Hecho, *m.*: *the fact is that...*, el hecho es que...: *it is a fact that*, es un hecho que. || Realidad, *f.*: *to distinguish fact from fiction*, distinguir la realidad de la ficción. || — Pl. Datos, *m.* (information). || — *Accomplished fact*, hecho consumado. || *As a matter of fact*, en realidad. || *Hard facts*, las duras realidades de la vida. || *In fact* o *in point of fact*, en realidad. || *It's a matter of fact*, es una realidad, es un hecho, es cosa probada. || *The fact of the matter is that*, la verdad es que. || *The fact remains that*, a pesar de todo. || FAM. *The facts of life*, las cosas de la vida. || *To know for a fact that*, saber a ciencia cierta que. || *To stick to the facts*, atenerse a los hechos.

fact-finding [—ˌfaindiŋ] adj. De investigación, de indagación.

faction [ˈfækʃən] n. Facción, *f.*

factious [ˈfækʃəs] adj. Faccioso, sa.

factiousness [—nis] n. Espíritu (*m.*) faccioso.

factitious [fækˈtiʃəs] adj. Facticio, cia; artificial.

factitiously [—li] adv. De manera facticia, artificialmente.

factor [ˈfæktə*] n. Factor, *m.*, elemento, *m.*: *the factors contributing to his success*, los factores que contribuyen a su éxito. || MATH. Factor, *m.* || BIOL. Factor, *m.*: *rhesus factor*, factor Rhesus. || COMM. Agente (*m.*) de venta. || AGR. Administrador (*m.*) de fincas (in Scotland). || — *Factor of safety*, coeficiente (*m.*) de seguridad. || MATH. *Highest common factor*, máximo común divisor.

factorage [—ridʒ] n. COMM. Corretaje, *m.*, factoría, *f.* (business). | Comisión, *f.* (charges).

factorial [fæk tɔ:riəl] n. MATH. Factorial, *f.*

factorize [ˈfæktəraiz] v. tr. MATH. Descomponer en factores.

factory [ˈfæktəri] n. Fábrica, *f.*

factotum [fækˈtəutəm] n. Factótum, *m.*

factual [ˈfæktʃuəl] adj. Objetivo, va (objective). || Basado en hechos (based on facts). || Real.

factuality [ˌfæktʃuˈæləti] or **factualness** [ˈfæktʃuəlnəs] n. Objetividad, *f.*

facula [ˈfækjulə] n. ASTR. Fácula, *f.*

— OBSERV. El plural de la palabra inglesa es *faculae*.

facultative [ˈfækəltətiv] adj. Facultativo, va (optional). || Eventual.

faculty [ˈfækəlti] n. Facultad, *f.*: *the faculty of speech*, la facultad de hablar. || Facilidad, *f.* [*for*, para], don, *m.* [*for*, de] (gift): *he has a faculty for languages*, tiene facilidad para los idiomas. || Facultad, *f.* (in a university): *faculty of Law*, facultad de Derecho. || Profesorado, *m.*, cuerpo (*m.*) docente, facultad, *f.* (teaching body). || Cuerpo (*m.*) facultativo (physicians). || Facultad, *f.* (authorization). || — Pl. Facultades, *f.*: *in possession of all his faculties*, en posesión de todas sus facultades.

fad [fæd] n. Manía, *f.*, capricho, *m.* (whim). || Novedad, *f.*, moda, *f.*: *the latest fad*, la última novedad.

faddish [—iʃ] or **faddist** [—ist] or **faddy** [—i] adj. Maniático, ca; caprichoso, sa (whimsical). || Aficionado a seguir la moda.

fade [feid] v. intr. Desteñirse (colours when washed). || Descolorarse, decolorarse (to lose colour). || Mar-

chitarse (flowers). || Apagarse (light). || Desvanecerse (sound). || Fig. Desvanecerse (pictures, memories, etc.): *my memory of those days has almost completely faded*, el recuerdo de aquellos días se ha desvanecido casi totalmente. | Desaparecer gradualmente (to disappear gradually). | Decaer (interest). | Desaparecer (to vanish). | Fundirse: *to fade into the distance*, fundirse en la distancia. || — *To fade away*, desvanecerse (to disappear), consumirse (to waste away). || *To fade in*, aparecer progresivamente (picture), subir progresivamente (sound). || *To fade out*, desaparecer progresivamente (picture), desvanecerse (sound).
— V. tr. Descolorar, decolorar (to discolour). || Desteñir (colours when washed). || Marchitar (flowers). — *To fade in*, hacer aparecer progresivamente (picture). || *To fade out*, hacer desaparecer progresivamente (picture).
faded [—id] adj. Descolorido, da (dress). ||Marchito, ta (plants).
fade-in [—in] n. Cinem. Fundido, *m.*
fadeless [—lis] adj. Inmarchitable, inmarcesible (plant). || Que no se destiñe (dress).
fade-out [—aut] n. Cinem. Fundido, *m.*
fading [—iŋ] n. Rad. Desvanecimiento (*m.*) de la señal, "fading", *m.* || Cinem. *Fading in, fading out*, fundido, *m.*
faecal [ˈfi:kəl] adj. Fecal.
faeces [ˈfi:si:z] pl. n. Excrementos, *m.*, heces, *f.*
faery [ˈfeiəri] adj. See fairy.
— N. Mundo (*m.*) *or* país (*m.*) de las hadas.
fag [fæg] n. Faena, *f.*, trabajo (*m.*) penoso (tiresome job). || Cansancio, *m.* (weariness). || Alumno (*m.*) que sirve a otro mayor (in school). || Fam. Pitillo, *m.* (cigarette). || U. S. Pop. Marica, *m.* (homosexual). || *What a fag*, ¡vaya faena!
fag [fæg] v. intr. Trabajar como un negro (to work hard). || *To fag for s.o.*, servir a uno (in school).
— V. tr. Cansar, fatigar (to tire). || *To be fagged out*, estar rendido, estar molido.
fag end [—ˈend] n. Sobras, *f. pl.*, desperdicios, *m. pl.* (leftovers). || Pestañas, *f. pl.* (of cloth). || Fam. Colilla, *f.* (of cigarette).
faggot or **fagot** [ˈfægət] n. Haz (*m.*) de leña (sticks). || Haz (*m.*) de barras de hierro (metal bars). || Haz, *m.*, manojo, *m.* (bundle). || U. S. Pop. Marica, *m.* (homosexual).
faggot or **fagot** [ˈfægət] v. tr. Hacer manojos *or* haces de. || Adornar con vainicas (in sewing).
faggoting or **fagoting** [—iŋ] n. Vainicas, *f. pl.* (in sewing).
Fahrenheit thermometer [ˈfærənhait-θəˈmɔmitə*] n. Termómetro (*m.*) de Fahrenheit.
faience [faiˈɑ̃ns] n. Loza (*f.*) fina.
fail [feil] n. Falta, *f.*: *without fail*, sin falta. || Suspenso, *m.* (in exams).
fail [feil] v. intr. Fallar: *the electricity often fails in winter*, la electricidad falla muchas veces en invierno; *the engine failed*, el motor falló; *when all else failed he had to ask for help*, cuando le falló todo tuvo que pedir ayuda. || Dejar: *I shall not fail to tell him*, no dejaré de decírselo; *don't fail to...*, no deje de... (See Observ.) || Fracasar, fallar (to be unsuccessful): *the experiment failed*, el experimento fracasó; *the attack failed*, el ataque fracasó; *his business failed*, su negocio fracasó. || Frustrarse (hopes). || No conseguir, no lograr (not to succeed). || Fallar (to get worse): *his sight is failing*, le está fallando la vista. || Faltar: *to fail in one's duty*, faltar a su deber. || Acabarse: *when the food supplies failed*, cuando se acabaron los víveres. || Ser suspendido (in exams). || Decaer, debilitarse (to weaken). || Comm. Quebrar. || — *A failed musician*, un músico fracasado. || *I failed in maths*, me suspendieron en matemáticas. || *I fail to see why*, no veo por qué. || *I have an idea that cannot fail*, tengo una idea que no puede fallar. || *To fail by few votes*, perder por pocos votos.
— V. tr. Suspender (a pupil): *they failed me*, me suspendieron. || No aprobar (an exam). || Fallar: *he failed me at the last minute*, me falló en el último momento; *my strength is failing me*, me están fallando las fuerzas; *his memory often fails him*, su memoria le falla a menudo. || Faltar: *words fail me to describe it*, me faltan palabras para describirlo.
— Observ. *To fail to do sth.* may often be translated into Spanish by a simple negative: *he failed to come*, no vino; *he failed to answer the invitation*, no contestó a la invitación.
failing [—iŋ] n. Defecto, *m.* (defect). || Falta, *f.* (fault). || Punto (*f.*) flaco, flaqueza, *f.*, debilidad, *f.* (weakness). || Fracaso, *m.* (failure). || Comm. Quiebra, *f.*
— Prep. A falta de: *failing wine we all drank water*, a falta de vino todos bebimos agua.
faille [feil] n. Falla, *f.* (material).
failure [ˈfeiljə*] n. Fracaso, *m.*: *the failure of the plan, of the experiment*, el fracaso del proyecto, del experimento; *the play was a failure*, la obra fue un fracaso; *as a doctor he is a failure*, como médico es un fracaso; *his failure to make himself understood*, su fracaso en hacerse comprender. || Fallo, *m.* (omission, fault): *his failure to keep his promise*, su fallo en cumplir su promesa. || Fallo, *m.*: *engine failure*, fallo en el motor. || Avería, *f.* (breakdown). || Corte, *m.*, interrupción, *f.* (of electricity). || Incumplimiento, *m.*: *failure to pay the rent*, incumplimiento en el pago del alquiler; *failure to comply with the rules*, incumplimiento de las reglas. || Suspenso, *m.* (in an examination). || Fracasado, da (person who has failed). || Comm. Quiebra, *f.* (bankruptcy). || Med. Ataque, *m.* || — *Failure to pay*, falta (*f.*) de pago. || *His failure to appear caused a scandal*, el hecho de que no se presentase causó un escándalo. || *Power failure*, corte de corriente *or* de luz.
fain [fein] adj. Dispuesto, ta (willing). || Contento, ta (happy). || Forzado, da (compelled).
— Adv. De buena gana (willingly).
faint [—t] adj. Mareado, da; a punto de desmayarse (about to collapse): *to feel faint*, estar mareado. || Débil (weak). || Ligero, ra (slight): *a faint resemblance*, un ligero parecido. || Timorato, ta; temeroso, sa (timid). || Pálido, da; apagado, da (colour). || Casi imperceptible (trace). || Vago, ga; ligero, ra (idea). || Borroso, sa; indistinto, ta: *the faint outline*, la silueta borrosa. || Tenue (thin). || — *Not to have the faintest idea*, no tener la más mínima idea. || *To be faint with hunger*, estar muerto de hambre.
— N. Desmayo, *m.*, desfallecimiento, *m.* (swoon). || — *To be in a faint*, estar desmayado. || *To fall into a faint*, desmayarse.
faint [feint] v. intr. Desmayarse, perder el conocimiento (to swoon). || (Ant.) Debilitarse (to weaken). || *To be fainting with hunger*, morirse de hambre.
fainthearted [—ˈhɑ:tid] adj. Pusilánime, medroso, sa; cobarde.
faintheartedness [—ˈhɑ:tidnis] n. Pusilanimidad, *f.*, miedo, *m.*, cobardía, *f.*
faintness [ˈfeintnis] n. Debilidad, *f.* (weakness). || Desmayo, *m.* (swoon). || Tenuidad, *f.* (thinness). || Palidez, *f.* (of a colour). || Falta (*f.*) de claridad (of an inscription).
faints [feints] pl. n. Alcohol (*m. sing.*) de cabeza [que se recoge en la primera y la última fase de la destilación del whisky].
fair [fɛə*] adj. Bello, lla; hermoso, sa: *a fair maiden*, una hermosa doncella. || Rubio, bia (hair). || Blanco, ca; claro, ra (complexion). || Justo, ta; equitativo, va (just). || Imparcial (impartial). || Honrado, da; íntegro, gra (honest). || Amable: *fair words*, palabras amables. || Bueno, na (reputation). || Favorable, prometedor, ra; esperanzador, ra (prospects). || Favorable, bueno, na (wind). || Bueno, na (weather). || Razonable (price). || Mediano, na; regular (middling). || Acertado, da; atinado, da (comment). || Limpio, pia; *fair play*, juego limpio. || Leal, franco, ca (competition). || En limpio (copy). || Bueno, na: *a fair amount of money*, una buena cantidad de dinero. || — *As is only fair*, como es debido *or* justo. || *But to be fair*, pero en honor a la verdad. || *Fair defeat*, derrota justa. || Fam. *Fair enough!*, ¡vale!, ¡muy bien! || *Fair example*, buen ejemplo. || *Fair to middling*, mediano, bastante bueno. || *In a fair fight*, en buena lid. || *It's not fair!*, ¡no hay derecho! || *It's not fair on the students*, es injusto para los estudiantes. || *The fair sex*, el bello sexo. || *To be fair*, hacer buen tiempo (weather). || *To be fair and square*, ser honrado a carta cabal. || *To be in a fair way to*, estar en buen camino de. || *To give s.o. a fair hearing*, escuchar a uno imparcialmente. || *To give s.o. fair warning*, avisar a uno. || *To have a fair chance of winning*, tener bastantes probabilidades de ganar. || *To have more than one's fair share*, tener más de lo que le corresponde a uno.
— Adv. Exactamente, justo: *it hit him fair between the eyes*, le dio justo entre los ojos. || Amablemente (kindly). || Cortésmente (politely): *to speak s.o. fair*, hablar a alguien cortésmente. || Honradamente (honestly). || Bastante, mucho (enough). || Bien, correctamente (well). || En limpio (copy). || Francamente (squarely). || — *To bid fair to*, tener posibilidades *or* probabilidades de. || *To play fair*, jugar limpio.
fair [fɛə*] n. Verbena, *f.* (sideshows and amusements). || Feria, *f.* (exhibition, market): *agricultural, livestock fair*, feria del campo, de ganado; *trade fair*, feria de muestras. || *Fun fair*, parque (*m.*) de atracciones.
fair copy [—ˈkɔpi] n. Copia (*f.*) en limpio (of a draft, etc.). || *To make a fair copy of*, poner en limpio.
fair game [—geim] n. Caza (*f.*) legal (in hunting). || Fig. Presa (*f.*) fácil: *to be fair game for pickpockets*, ser presa fácil para los rateros. | Hazmerreír, *m.* (target for ridicule). || Fig. *This girl is fair game*, esta chica no es terreno vedado.
fairgoer [—ˈgəuə*] n. Feriante, *m.* & *f.*
fairground [—ˈgraund] n. Parque (*m.*) de atracciones (fun fair). || Real, *m.* (for exhibitions and amusements). || Feria, *f.* (for trade exhibitions).
fair-haired [—hɛəd] adj. Rubio, bia. || Fam. Preferido, da; mimado, da; *fair-haired boy*, niño mimado.
fairing [ˈfɛəriŋ] n. Carena, *f.* (aerodynamic structure).
fairish [ˈfɛəriʃ] adj. Fam. Regular.
fairleader [ˈfɛəˈli:də*] n. Mar. Guía, *f.*
fairly [ˈfɛə:li] adj. Con justicia, equitativamente, imparcialmente (in an equitable manner). || Honradamente (honestly). || Bastante: *he plays fairly well*, juega bastante bien. || Realmente (positively). || Completamente (completely). || Claramente (clearly).
fair-minded [ˈfɛəˈmaindid] adj. Imparcial, justo, ta; equitativo, va.
fairness [ˈfɛənis] n. Hermosura, *f.*, belleza, *f.* (beauty). || Blancura, *f.* (of complexion). || Color (*m.*) rubio

(of hair). || Franqueza, *f.*, lealtad, *f.* (sincerity). || Justicia, *f.*, imparcialidad, *f.*, equidad, *f.* (justice). || Claridad, *f.* (of weather). || Lo limpio (of a copy). || *In all fairness to*, para ser justo con.

fair-spoken [ˈfɛəˈspəukən] adj. Bien hablado, da.

fair-trade [ˈfɛəˈtreid] adj. U. S. *Fair-trade agreement*, acuerdo por el cual un vendedor se compromete a no vender un producto por debajo del precio fijado por el fabricante.

fairway [ˈfɛəwei] n. MAR. Canalizo, *m.* || Calle, *f.* (in golf).

fair-weather [ˈfɛəˌweðə*] adj. FIG. *Fair-weather friend*, amigo (*m.*) no dispuesto a prestar ayuda en la desgracia.

fairy [ˈfɛəri] n. Hada, *f.* (supernatural being). || U. S. POP. Marica, *m.* (effeminate man).
— Adj. De hada, de hadas. || FIG. Encantador, ra (charming). || — *Fairy footsteps*, pasos ligeros. || *Fairy godmother*, hada madrina.

fairy lamps [—ˌlæmps] pl. n. Bombillas (*f.*) de colores (for decoration).

fairyland [—lænd] n. País (*m.*) de las hadas. || FIG. Lugar (*m.*) de ensueño.

fairy ring [—riŋ] n. Anillo (*m.*) mágico (of a fairy). || Círculo (*m.*) oscuro de hierba (of grass).

fairy tale [—teil] n. Cuento (*m.*) de hadas (story). || FIG. Cuento, *m.* (lie).

fait accompli [ˈfeitækomˈpli:] n. Hecho (*m.*) consumado.

faith [feiθ] n. Confianza, *f.* (trust). || Fe, *f.*: *religious faith*, fe religiosa; *profession of faith*, profesión de fe. || — *In bad, in good faith*, de mala, de buena fe. || *In faith*, en verdad. || *Political faith*, doctrina política, credo político. || *To accept* o *to take sth. on faith*, creer algo. || *To break faith with s.o.*, faltar a la palabra dada a alguien. || *To have blind faith in*, tener una fe ciega en. || *To have faith* o *to place one's faith in s.o.* o *to pin one's faith on s.o.*, fiarse de alguien, tener confianza *or* fe en alguien. || *To have faith* o *to place one's faith in sth.* o *to pin one's faith on* o *to sth.*, contar con algo, confiar en algo. || *To keep faith with s.o.*, cumplir con la palabra dada a alguien. || *To plight one's faith*, empeñar su palabra. || (Ant.). *Upon my faith*, a fe mía. || *What faith do you belong to?*, ¿qué religión tiene?

faith cure [—kjuə*] n. Curación (*f.*) por la fe.

faithful [—ful] adj. Fiel: *faithful to one's oath*, fiel a su juramento; *faithful to one's friends*, fiel a *or* con *or* para con sus amigos; *a faithful report of the events*, un relato fiel de los acontecimientos. || Exacto, ta (accurate). || Fidedigno, na (credible). || Digno de confianza (trustworthy). || *The faithful*, los fieles.

faithfully [—fuli] adv. Fielmente. || Fielmente, lealmente. || Con exactitud, fielmente (accurately). || *Yours faithfully, G. Brown*, le saluda atentamente, G. Brown.

faithfulness [—fulnis] n. Fidelidad, *f.*: *faithfulness between husband and wife*, fidelidad conyugal. || Lealtad, *f.*, fidelidad, *f.* (loyalty). || Exactitud, *f.* (accuracy).

faithless [ˈfeiθlis] adj. Desleal (disloyal). || Infiel: *a faithless wife*, una mujer infiel. || Pérfido, da; traidor, ra (treacherous). || Poco seguro, ra (unreliable). || Inexacto, ta (inaccurate). || REL. Infiel, descreído, da.

faithlessness [—nis] n. Infidelidad, *f.* || Deslealtad, *f.* || Perfidia, *f.* || Inexactitud, *f.* (inaccuracy). || REL. Descreimiento, *m.*

fake [feik] n. Falsificación, *f.* || Impostor, ra: *don't trust him, he is a fake*, no te fíes de él, es un impostor. || Tongo, *m.* (in sports, etc.): *the fight was a fake*, el combate era tongo. || MAR. Aduja, *f.* (of a rope). || *This is not the genuine painting, it is a fake*, este cuadro no es auténtico, es falso.
— Adj. Falso, sa: *fake diamonds*, diamantes falsos. || Falsificado, da (counterfeit). || Fingido, da: *a fake friendship*, una amistad fingida.

fake [feik] v. tr./intr. Falsificar (to counterfeit). || Fingir, simular: *a faked reaction*, una reacción fingida. || Adulterar (a text). || Amañar (to rig a fight). || || MAR. Adujar (a rope). || SP. Fintar. || *To fake up*, fabricar (to contrive), inventar (an excuse), falsificar (to counterfeit).

faker [—ə*] n. Impostor, ra. || Estafador, ra (swindler). || Falsificador, ra (counterfeiter).

faking [ˈfeikiŋ] n. Falsificación, *f.*: *the faking of a signature*, la falsificación de una firma.

fakir [ˈfeikiə*] n. Fakir, *m.*, faquir, *m.*

Falange [ˈfælændʒ] pr. n. Falange, *f.*

Falangism [fəˈlændʒizəm] n. Falangismo, *m.*

Falangist [fəˈlændʒist] adj./n. Falangista.

falchion [ˈfɔ:ltʃən] n. Alfanje, *m.*, cimitarra, *f.* (sword).

falcon [ˈfɔ:lkən] n. Halcón, *m.*

falconer [—ə*] n. Halconero, *m.*, cetrero, *m.*

falconet [ˈfɔ:lkənet] n. ZOOL. Halcón (*m.*) de pequeño tamaño.

falconry [ˈfɔ:lkənri] n. Cetrería, *f.*, halconería, *f.*

faldstool [ˈfɔ:ldstu:l] n. Facistol, *m.*, atril, *m.*

Falkland Isles [ˈfɔ:klənd-ailz] pl. pr. n. GEOGR. Islas (*f.*) Malvinas.

fall [fɔ:l] n. Caída, *f.*: *he died from a fall*, se murió de una caída. || Caída, *f.* (of leaves). || Caída, *f.*, derrumbamiento, *m.*: *the fall of the Roman Empire*, la caída del Imperio Romano. || Caída, *f.* (of a stronghold). || Derrumbamiento, *m.* (of earth, rocks, etc.). || Caída, *f.* (of a skirt, etc.). || Baja, *f.*, disminución, *f.* (of price, demand, temperature). || Declive, *m.*, pendiente, *f.* (slope). || Bajada, *f.* (of a theatre curtain). || FIG. Caída, *f.* (from virtue): *the fall of Adam*, la caída de Adán. | Caída, *f.* (of day). | Final, *m.* (of year, etc.). || Aparejo, *m.* (hoisting tackle). || Tira, *f.* (of hoisting tackle). || SP. Caída, *f.* (in wrestling). || MAR. Reflujo, *m.* (of the tide). || Camada, *f.* (of animals). || U. S. Otoño, *m.* (autumn). || — Pl. Cascada, *f. sing.*, salto, *m. sing.* (of water). || — *Fall of snow*, capa (*f.*) de nieve (layer): *a six-inch fall of snow*, una capa de nieve de seis pulgadas; nevada, *f.*, caída de nieve: *a heavy fall of snow*, una fuerte nevada. || *Free fall*, caída libre (of parachutist). || *In the fall of the year*, a fines de año. || *Niagara Falls*, las Cataratas del Niágara. || FIG. *To head* o *to ride for a fall*, ir a la ruina, correr hacia un peligro.
— Adj. U. S. Otoñal, del otoño.

fall* [fɔ:l] v. intr. Caer (by force of gravity). || Caer, caerse: *he fell from the horse*, se cayó del caballo. || Bajar, descender (prices, demand). || Bajar (temperature, fever, floodwater, tide, voice). || Caer (skirt, curtains). || Caerse, derrumbarse, desplomarse (a building). || Bajar (to slope). || Desembocar, ir a dar: *the Ebro falls into the Mediterranean*, el Ebro desemboca en el Mediterráneo. || Caer (a soldier, a stronghold, a government). || Amainar (the wind). || Caer (night, silence, event, date). || Decaer (conversation). || Corresponder, tocar (privilege, task): *it fell to him to do it*, le tocó a él hacerlo. || Tocar, caer: *the prize fell to my uncle*, el premio le tocó a mi tío. || Caer (under s.o.'s influence, etc.): *to fall under s.o.'s power*, caer bajo el dominio de alguien. || Recaer (accent). || Dividirse: *to fall into three categories*, dividirse en tres categorías. || Entrar: *these considerations fall under another category*, estas consideraciones entran en otra categoría. || Decaer (to decay). || Pecar, caer (to sin). || Quedarse, volverse: *to fall dumb*, quedarse mudo. || Quebrar (to go bankrupt). || Dar (a shot, arrow). || Nacer (animals). || — *His face fell*, puso cara larga. || *His glance fell*, bajó los ojos. || *Night was falling*, anochecía. || *To fall across*, dar con. || *To fall apart*, caerse a pedazos. || *To fall a prey to*, caer en manos de (to fall into the hands of), ser víctima de (to be the victim of). || *To fall asleep*, dormirse, quedarse dormido. || FIG. *To fall by the cannon*, morir de un cañonazo. || *To fall due*, vencer (payment). || *To fall flat*, see FLAT. || *To fall foul of*, see FOUL. || REL. *To fall from grace*, perder la gracia. || *To fall from one's lips*, salir de la boca de uno. || *To fall ill*, caer enfermo. || *To fall in love with*, enamorarse de. || *To fall in price*, bajar de precio. || *To fall into disrepair*, deteriorarse. || *To fall into disuse*, caer en desuso. || *To fall into line with*, see LINE. || *To fall into temptation*, caer en la tentación. || *To fall into the habit of*, coger el hábito de, acostumbrarse a. || *To fall short of*, ser insuficiente para (to be insufficient), no alcanzar (not to reach). || *To fall short of the target*, no alcanzar el blanco, no dar en el blanco (a shot). || *To fall to pieces*, hacerse pedazos (to break up), caerse a pedazos (house, person), hundirse (business). || *To fall under s.o.'s competence*, caer dentro de la competencia de alguien, ser de la competencia de alguien. || *To fall under suspicion*, hacerse sospechoso. || *To fall within one's province*, ser de la incumbencia de uno, incumbirle a uno. || *To let fall*, dejar escapar (words, secret). || FIG. *You fell wide of the target*, no acertaste.
— ***To fall away***, desaparecer (to disappear). | Desprenderse (stage of rocket, loose rocks, etc.). | Descender, inclinarse (to slope downwards). | Hundirse (ground). | REL. Apostatar. | MED. Adelgazar. | — *To fall away from*, abandonar. || ***To fall back***, caerse de espaldas. | Retroceder, retirarse (to recede). | MIL. Replegarse. | — *To fall back on*, echar mano a *or* de, recurrir a: *he fell back on his savings*, echó mano a sus ahorros, recurrió a sus ahorros. | *To fall back on one's word*, desdecirse. || ***To fall behind***, retrasarse (to be behind schedule). | Quedarse atrás (to be left behind). || ***To fall down***, caer | Caer *or* caerse al suelo (on the ground). | Postrarse, prosternarse (to prostrate o.s.). | Derrumbarse (house). | Ser suspendido, suspenderle a uno: *he fell down in maths*, le suspendieron en matemáticas, fue suspendido en matemáticas. | Fallar: *to fall down on the job*, fallar en el trabajo. | Fracasar (plan). | — *To fall down a precipice*, caer en un precipicio. || FAM. ***To fall for***, chiflarse por, volverse loco por (to fall in love). | — *To fall for a trick*, caer en la trampa. | FAM. *To fall for it*, tragárselo (to believe), picar (to take the bait). || ***To fall in***, caerse, desplomarse (roof, walls). | Hundirse (cheeks). | COMM. Vencer (term). | JUR. Expirar (lease). || MIL. Formar filas. | — MIL. *Fall in!*, ¡a formar! | *To fall in with*, encontrarse con (to meet), estar de acuerdo con (to agree with), aceptar (a proposal), acceder a (a request), adherirse a (an opinion). || ***To fall off***, caer. | Caer de, caerse de (to drop from): *a tile fell off the roof*, una teja se cayó del tejado. | Desprenderse (to come off): *the door handle fell off*, se desprendió el picaporte. | Caerse: *his bicycle hit a stone and he fell off*, su bicicleta dio con una piedra y se cayó. | Bajar, disminuir (to decrease): *the demand has fallen off*, la demanda ha bajado. | Decaer: *the tourist trade has fallen off*, la industria turística ha

decaído. | Enfriarse (zeal, interest). | Empeorar (to get worse). || MAR. Abatir. || **To fall on** o **upon,** caer en (date, etc.): *his birthday falls on Saturday*, su cumpleaños cae en sábado. | Caer sobre (enemy, food). | Caer en (accent). | Tocar a, corresponder a: *it fell upon me to invite him to lunch*, me tocó a mí invitarle a comer. | — *To fall on one's back*, caerse *or* caer de espaldas. || **To fall out,** caerse (of the window, etc.). | Reñir (to quarrel): *I have fallen out with him*, he reñido con él. | Salir, resultar: *things fell out well*, salieron bien las cosas. | MIL. Romper filas: *fall out!*, ¡rompan filas! | — *To fall out of the habit of*, perder la costumbre de. || **To fall over,** caerse. Tropezar con (an obstacle). | — *To fall over each other for sth.*, disputarse algo. | *To fall over o.s.*, desvivirse. || **To fall through,** venirse abajo, fracasar (project, etc.). || **To fall to,** ponerse a, empezar a (to begin). | Ponerse a trabajar (to start working). | Empezar a comer (to start eating). | Cerrarse (to close by itself). | Tocar a, corresponder a (to be the duty of). | — *To fall to one's lot*, caerle en suerte a uno.

— OBSERV. Pret. **fell**; p. p. **fallen**.

fallacious [fəˈleiʃəs] adj. Falaz (misleading). || Erróneo, a (erroneous).
fallacy [ˈfæləsi] n. Falacia, *f.*, sofisma, *m.* || Idea (*f.*) falsa *or* errónea (mistaken idea). || Engaño, *m.* (deception).
fal-lal [ˈfælˈlæl] n. Faralá, *m.*
fallback [ˈfɔːlbæk] n. Retirada, *f.*
fallen [ˈfɔːlən] p. p. See FALL.
— Adj. Caído, da. || FIG. Perdido, da. || *The fallen*, los caídos.
fall guy [ˈfɔːlgai] n. U. S. FAM. Cabeza (*f.*) de turco (scapegoat).
fallibility [ˌfæliˈbiliti] n. Falibilidad, *f.*
fallible [ˈfæləbl] adj. Falible.
falling [fɔːliŋ] n. Caída, *f.*
falling away [—ˈəwei] n. MED. Adelgazamiento, *m.* || REL. Apostasía, *f.* || FIG. Abandono, *m.* (of supporters).
falling back [—bæk] n. MIL. Repliegue, *m.*, retirada, *f.*
falling in [—in] n. Derrumbamiento, *m.*, hundimiento, *m.* (of a building). || MIL. Formación, *f.* || JUR. Expiración, *f.* || COMM. Vencimiento, *m.* (of a debt).
falling off [—ɔf] n. COMM. Baja, *f.* (of prices). || Disminución, *f.* (lessening). || Empeoramiento, *m.* (worsening). || FIG. Defección, *f.*
falling out [—aut] n. Caída, *f.* (of hair). || FIG. Enfado, *m.*, desacuerdo, *m.*
falling sickness [—ˈsiknis] n. MED. Epilepsia, *f.*
falling star [—stɑː*] n. Estrella (*f.*) fugaz.
Fallopian [fəˈləupiən] adj. ANAT. *Fallopian tube*, trompa (*f.*) de Falopio.
fallout [ˈfɔːlaut] n. Lluvia (*f.*) radiactiva. || *Fallout shelter*, refugio atómico.
fallow [ˈfæləu] adj. AGR. En barbecho: *to lie fallow* estar en barbecho. || FIG. Inculto, ta. || Leonado, da (colour).
— N. Barbecho, *m.*
fallow [ˈfæləu] v. tr. AGR. Barbechar.
fallow deer [—diə*] n. ZOOL. Gamo, *m.*
fallowing [—iŋ] n. Barbecho, *m.*, barbechera, *f.*
false [fɔːls] adj. Falso, sa: *false accusation*, acusación falsa. || Erróneo, a; falso, sa: *a false conclusion*, una conclusión errónea. || Mal entendido, da: *false pride*, orgullo mal entendido. || Postizo, za: *false teeth*, dientes postizos. || Falso, sa (disloyal, fake): *a false friend*, un falso amigo; *a false door*, una puerta falsa. || MUS. Falso, sa; desafinado, da (note). || Falso, sa; forzado, da (not natural). || ANAT. Falso, sa: *false ribs*, costillas falsas. || BOT. Falso, sa: *false acacia*, acacia falsa. || — *False alarm*, falsa alarma. || *False bottom*, doble fondo, *m.* || *False ceiling*, cielo raso. || U. S. *False face*, máscara, *f.* || *False imprisonment*, detención ilegal. || JUR. *False pretences*, estafa, *f.* || SP. *False start*, salida nula. || *False step*, paso (*m.*) en falso. || *False to the core*, más falso que Judas. || *To bear false witness*, jurar en falso. || *To sail under false colours*, navegar bajo pabellón falso (a ship), atribuirse una personalidad falsa (people). || *To take a false step*, dar un paso en falso.
— Adv. Hipócritamente: *to act false*, actuar hipócritamente. || *To play s.o. false*, traicionar a uno.
falsehearted [fɔːlsˈhɑːtid] adj. Pérfido, da; traicionero, ra.
falsehood [ˈfɔːlshud] n. Falsedad, *f.* (falseness). || Mentira, *f.* (lie). || *To distinguish truth from falsehood*, distinguir lo falso de lo verdadero.
falsely [fɔːlsli] adv. Falsamente, con falsedad. || Mal: *to interpret sth. falsely*, interpretar algo mal.
falseness [ˈfɔːlsnis] n. Inexactitud, *f.*, falsedad, *f.* (lack of accuracy). || Infidelidad, *f.* (of a lover, etc.). || Perfidia, *f.* (wickedness). || Falsedad, *f.* (duplicity).
falsetto [fɔːlˈsetəu] n. MUS. Falsete, *m.*
— Adj. De falsete (voice).
— Adv. *In falsetto*, con voz de falsete.
falsies [ˈfɔlsiz] pl. n. Rellenos, *m.* (brassière).
falsification [ˈfɔːlsifiˈkeiʃən] n. Falsificación, *f.* (of documents). || Adulteración, *f.* (of wine, etc.).
falsifier [ˈfɔːlsifaiə*] n. Falsificador, ra.
falsify [ˈfɔːlsifai] v. tr. Falsificar (documents). || Desvirtuar (to distort). || Adulterar (liquor, wine). || Desmentir, refutar (to prove to be false). || Frustrar (hopes, etc.).
falsity [ˈfɔːlsiti] n. Falsedad, *f.*
faltboat [ˈfɔːltbəut] n. Bote (*m.*) plegable.
falter [ˈfɔːltə*] v. intr. Titubear, vacilar (in walking). || Titubear (in speech). || Quebrarse, desfallecer (voice). || Vacilar (in actions). || FIG. Fallar: *his resolution faltered*, le falló la determinación. || *With faltering voice*, con voz titubeante (hesitant), con voz quebrada (through emotion).
— V. tr. Decir balbuceando. || *To falter out*, balbucir (an excuse, etc.).
faltering [riŋ] adj. Vacilante, titubeante.
falteringly [—riŋli] adv. Con voz titubeante (hesitantly). || Con voz quebrada (from emotion). || Con paso vacilante (walking).
fame [feim] n. Fama, *f.*, reputación, *f.*: *ill fame*, mala fama. || — *Sheffield, of stainless steel fame*, Sheffield, ciudad famosa por su acero inoxidable. || *To find fame*, conseguir la fama, triunfar. || *To rise to fame*, hacerse famoso.
famed [—d] adj. Afamado, da; famoso, sa. || *She is not as beautiful as she is famed to be*, no es tan hermosa como dicen.
familial [fəˈmiljəl] adj. Familiar, de familia.
familiar [fəˈmiljə*] adj. Familiar, conocido, da: *a familiar voice*, una voz familiar. || De todos los días (often repeated): *a familiar story*, un cuento de todos los días. || Familiar (colloquial): *a familiar expression*, una expresión familiar. || Íntimo, ma (friend). || — *At times his answers are too familiar*, a veces contesta con demasiada confianza. || *I am familiar with that*, eso me es familiar, estoy familiarizado con eso, conozco bien eso. || *It's the familiar story*, es lo de siempre. || *That sounds familiar*, eso me suena. || *To be on familiar terms with s.o.*, tener confianza con alguien. || *To get too familiar with s.o.*, tomarse demasiadas confianzas con uno. || *To make o.s. familiar with*, familiarizarse con.
— N. Amigo (*m.*) íntimo, familiar, *m.* (close friend). || Demonio (*m.*) familiar (spirit). || REL. Familiar, *m.*
familiarity [fəmiliˈæriti] n. Familiaridad, *f.* (*with*, con), conocimiento, *m.* (*with*, de). || Familiaridad, *f.*, confianza, *f.* (absence of formality). || — Pl. Familiaridades, *f.*, confianzas, *f.*
familiarize [fəˈmiljəraiz] v. tr. Acostumbrar, familiarizar, habituar: *to familiarize s.o. with the procedure*, acostumbrar a uno al sistema. || *To familiarize o.s. with*, familiarizarse con.
family [ˈfæmili] n. Familia, *f.* || BOT. ZOOL. GRAMM. Familia, *f.* || — *His integrity runs in the family*, su integridad le viene de familia. || REL. *The Holy Family*, La Sagrada Familia. || FAM. *To be in the family way*, estar en estado interesante. || *To be one of the family*, ser como de la familia. || *To have a big family*, tener muchos hijos *or* mucha familia. || *With one's family* en familia.
— Adj. Familiar, de familia: *family resemblance* o *likeness*, parecido de familia; *family allowance*, subsidio familiar. || — *Family doctor*, médico (*m.*) de cabecera *or* de familia. || *Family man*, padre (*m.*) de familia (with a family), hombre casero (devoted to his home). || U. S. *Family name*, apellido, *m.* (surname). || *Family planning*, planificación (*f.*) familiar. || *Family room*, cuarto (*m.*) de estar. || *Family skeleton*, vergüenza (*f.*) de la familia, secreto (*m.*) de familia. || *Family tree*, árbol genealógico.
famine [ˈfæmin] n. Escasez, *f.* (shortage of food). || Hambre, *f.*, inanición, *f.* (starvation): *to die of famine*, morir de inanición. || Escasez, *f.*, carestía, *f.* (scarcity): *coal famine*, escasez de carbón.
famish [ˈfæmiʃ] v. tr. (Ant.). Hacer morir de hambre, hacer padecer hambre.
— V. intr. (Ant.). Morirse de hambre, padecer hambre.
famished [—t] adj. Famélico, ca; muerto de hambre. || FIG. *To be famished*, estar muerto de hambre.
famous [ˈfeiməs] adj. Famoso, sa; célebre (renowned). || FIG. FAM. Fabuloso, sa; excelente, magnífico, ca: *a famous idea*, una idea excelente.
famously [—li] adv. FIG. FAM. Estupendamente, a las mil maravillas: *she sings famously*, canta a las mil maravillas.
famulus [ˈfæmjuləs] n. Ayudante (*m.*) de un mago *or* alquimista (of a sorcerer). || Fámulo, *m.* (of a scholar).

— OBSERV. El plural de *famulus* es *famuli*.

fan [fæn] n. Abanico, *m.*: *she hid her face behind her fan*, ocultó su rostro tras el abanico. || TECH. Ventilador, *m.* (mechanically operated). | Paleta, *f.* (blade of a propeller). || AGR. Bieldo, *m.*, aventadora, *f.* (for winnowing). || Aficionado, da; entusiasta, *m.* & *f.*; admirador, ra (devotee). || Admirador, ra (of a pop star). || SP. Hincha, *m.* & *f.* || — *Fan club*, club (*m.*) de admiradores. || *Fan mail*, correspondencia (*f.*) de los admiradores.
fan [fæn] v. tr. Abanicar (a person). || Agitar (the air). || Acariciar: *the breeze fanned her face*, la brisa le acariciaba el rostro. || Avivar (with a bellows): *he took the bellows and fanned the fire*, cogió el fuelle y avivó el fuego. || Soplar sobre (to blow on). || AGR. Aventar (to winnow). || Abrir en abanico (cards, etc.). || TECH. Ventilar. || FIG. Avivar (passion, etc.). | Excitar (curiosity, etc.). || *To fan o.s.*, abanicarse.

— V. intr. Abrirse en abanico: *the soldiers fanned out*, los soldados se abrieron en abanico.
fanatic [fəˈnætik] adj./n. Fanático, ca.
fanatical [—əl] adj. Fanático, ca.
fanatically [—əli] adv. Fanáticamente, con fanatismo.
fanaticism [fəˈnætisizəm] n. Fanatismo, *m.*
fanaticize [fəˈnætisaiz] v. tr. Fanatizar.
— V. intr. Volverse fanático.
fan belt [ˈfænbelt] n. AUT. Correa (*f.*) del ventilador.
fancied [ˈfænsid] adj. Favorito, ta; preferido, da: *his fancied pupil did badly in the test*, su alumno preferido hizo mal el examen. || Imaginario, ria: *fancied illness*, enfermedad imaginaria.
fancier [ˈfænsiə*] n. Aficionado, da. || Soñador, ra (imaginer).
fanciful [ˈfænsiful] adj. Imaginario, ria; fantástico, ca (unreal). || Extravagante (odd): *a fanciful hairstyle*, un peinado extravagante. || Imaginativo, va; fantasioso, sa (imaginative). || Caprichoso, sa (whimsical).
fancy [ˈfænsi] n. Fantasía, *f.*, imaginación, *f.* (imaginative faculty). || Capricho, *m.*, antojo, *m.* (whim). || Idea, *f.* || Ilusión, *f.*, quimera, *f.* (delusion). || Afición, *f.*, gusto, *m.*: *to take a fancy to music, to tennis*, tomar afición a la música, al tenis. || Gusto, *m.* (taste): *a person of delicate fancy*, una persona de gusto delicado. || — *It is my fancy* o *I have a fancy that they are lovers*, tengo la impresión de que son amantes. || *The fancy took me to learn Chinese*, se me antojó aprender chino. || *To take a fancy to s.o.*, tomar cariño a alguien. || *To take a fancy to sth.*, encapricharse por algo. || *To take* o *to catch s.o.'s fancy*, gustarle a uno. || *What takes your fancy most?*, ¿qué es lo que más te apetece?
— Adj. De adorno (ornamental). || De fantasía, de imitación (goods): *fancy jewels*, joyas de fantasía. || De lujo: *fancy shop*, tienda de lujo. || Exorbitante, excesivo, va: *a fancy price*, un precio exorbitante. || Elegante (elegant). || Estrafalario, ria (extravagant). U. S. Selecto, ta; fino, na (foodstuffs).
fancy [ˈfensi] v. tr. Imaginarse, imaginar (to imagine): *I can't fancy him doing that*, no me lo puedo imaginar haciendo eso. || Suponer, creer (to suppose, to believe): *I fancy he is annoyed*, supongo que se ha enfadado. || Tener la impresión de que, parecerle a uno (to suspect): *I fancy you are hiding sth.*, tengo la impresión de que me ocultas algo, me parece que me ocultas algo. || Gustar: *I don't fancy the idea*, no me gusta la idea; *Peter fancies Mary*, a Pedro le gusta María. || Apetecer: *she fancies that dress*, le apetece ese vestido. || — *Fancy!* o *fancy that!* o *just fancy!*, ¡imagínate!, ¡imagínese!, ¡fíjate!, ¡fíjese!, ¡vaya! || *Fancy her becoming a nun!*, ¡parece mentira que se haya metido a monja! || *To fancy o.s.*, ser un creído. || *To fancy o.s. as*, presumir de, dárselas de. || *To fancy o.s. sth.*, creerse *or* imaginarse algo: *she fancies herself a film star*, se cree una estrella de cine.
fancy diving [—ˈdaiviŋ] n. Saltos (*m. pl.*) acrobáticos.
fancy dress [—dres] n. Disfraz, *m.* || — *Fancy-dress ball*, baile (*m.*) de disfraces. || *In fancy dress*, disfrazado, da.
fancy-free [—fri:] adj. Sin compromiso (not committed in love). || Despreocupado, da (carefree).
fancy goods [—gudz] pl. n. Objetos (*m.*) *or* artículos (*m.*) de fantasía.
fancy man [—mən] n. FAM. Chulo, *m.* (pimp). | Amante, *m.*, querido, *m.* (lover).
fancy woman [—ˈwumən] n. FAM. Amante, *f.*, querida, *f.* (mistress). | Mujer (*f.*) de vida alegre (prostitute).
fancywork [—wə:k] n. Labor, *f.* (in sewing).
fandango [fænˈdæŋgəu] n. MUS. Fandango, *m.*
fanfare [ˈfænfεə*] n. Fanfarria, *f.* (of trumpets, etc.).
fanfaronade [ˌfænfærəˈnα:d] n. Fanfarronada, *f.*, baladronada, *f.*
fang [fæŋ] n. Colmillo, *m.* (of tiger, wolf, etc.). || Diente, *m.* (of snake). || Espiga, *f.* (of a tool). || Raíz, *m.* (of a tooth).
fanged [—d] adj. Con colmillos.
fanlight [ˈfænlait] n. ARCH. Montante (*m.*) de abanico.
fanner [ˈfænə*] n. AGR. Aventadora, *f.*
fanon [ˈfænən] n. REL. Manípulo, *m.*
fan palm [ˈfæn-pα:m] n. BOT. Miraguano, *m.*
fantail [ˈfænteil] n. Cola (*f.*) en forma de abanico (tail). || Paloma (*f.*) colipava (pigeon). || Papamoscas, *m. inv.* (flycatcher). || TECH. Cola (*f.*) de milano.
fantasia [fænˈteizjə] n. MUS. Fantasía, *f.*
fantast [ˈfæntæst] n. Soñador, ra.
fantastic [fænˈtæstik] adj. Fantástico, ca; imaginario, ria (unreal). || Fantástico, ca; extraño, ña (quaint).
fantasy [ˈfæntəsi] n. Imaginación, *f.*, fantasía, *f.* (imagination). || Fantasía, *f.* (sth. imagined). || Capricho, *m.* (whim). || Ensueño, *m.* (daydream). || MUS. Fantasía, *f.*
fan tracery [ˈfæntreisəri] n. ARCH. Nervios (*m. pl.*) en abanico.
fan vaulting [ˈfænvɔ:ltiŋ] n. ARCH. Bóveda (*f.*) de abanico.
far [fα:*] adv. Lejos: *is it far?*, ¿está lejos? || Mucho: *far better*, mucho mejor; *far beyond*, mucho más allá de; *far more*, mucho más. || Muy: *far distant*, muy distante. || — *As far as*, hasta: *we went as far as Guadalajara*, fuimos hasta Guadalajara; que: *as far as I know* o *as far as I can tell*, que yo sepa; por lo que: *as far as I can judge*, por lo que puedo juzgar; *as far as I am concerned*, por lo que a mí se refiere. || FIG. *As far as possible*, en lo posible, en la medida de lo posible. || *As far back as we can recall*, hasta donde alcanza la memoria. || *By far*, con mucho: *he's by far the best*, es con mucho el mejor. || FIG. *Far and away*, con mucho: *she's far and away the prettiest*, es con mucho la más guapa. || *Far and near* o *far and wide*, por todas partes. || *Far away*, lejos. || *Far away from*, lejos de. || FIG. *Far be it from me to criticize*, no tengo la menor intención de criticar. || *Far from*, lejos de. || *Far from it*, ni mucho menos. || *Far gone*, see GONE. || *Far into the night*, hasta muy avanzada la noche, hasta muy tarde (very late). || *Far off*, lejos (distant), a lo lejos (in the distance). || *Far too much*, demasiado. || *From far off*, desde lejos, de lejos. || *Having reached this far*, a estas alturas. || *How far can he be trusted?*, ¿hasta qué punto se puede uno fiar de él? || *How far have you got?*, ¿hasta dónde *or* hasta qué punto han llegado? || *How far is it to Madrid?*, ¿cuánto hay de aquí a Madrid? || *In so far as*, en la medida en que. || FIG. *She's not far off sixty*, tiene casi sesenta años. | *She wasn't far from tears*, estaba al borde de las lágrimas, estaba a punto de llorar. || *So far*, tan lejos: *I didn't know he travelled so far*, no sabía que había viajado tan lejos; hasta ahora: *so far so good*, hasta ahora todo va bien; hasta aquí *or* allí (up to here *o* there). || *So far this month*, en lo que va de mes. || FIG. *That's as far as I'll go*, de allí no paso. | *That's going too far!*, ¡esto es demasiado!, ¡es el colmo! || *Thus far*, hasta ahora (until now), hasta aquí *or* allí (up to here o there). || *To carry far*, oírse de lejos (voice, etc.). || FIG. *To carry sth. too far*, llevar algo demasiado lejos *or* al extremo. || *To go far*, llegar lejos: *this boy will go far*, este muchacho llegará lejos; tener valor, servir para mucho: *money doesn't go far these days*, actualmente el dinero tiene poco valor; cundir [mucho]: *this box of soap goes far*, este paquete de jabón cunde mucho; ir lejos, exagerar (to exaggerate): *that's going a bit far*, eso es ir un poco lejos. || *To go far into the desert*, adentrarse mucho en el desierto. || FIG. *To go far towards*, contribuir mucho a. | *To go so far as to say, as to call, etc.*, llegar a decir, a llamar, etc.| *To go too far*, ir demasiado lejos, pasarse de la raya. | *To push s.o. too far*, sacarle a uno de sus casillas. | *You weren't far out*, casi aciertas.
— Adj. Lejano, na; distante, remoto, ta (distant). || Largo, ga (long): *a far journey*, un viaje largo. || Otro, otra; opuesto, ta (other, opposite): *at the far end*, en el otro extremo; *on the far bank*, en la orilla opuesta.
farad [ˈfærəd] n. ELECTR. Faradio, *m.*, farad, *m.*
faraday [ˈfærədi] n. ELECTR. CHEM. Faraday, *m.*
faradic [ˌfærəˈdik] adj. ELECTR. Farádico, ca.
faradism [ˈfærədizəm] or **faradization** [færædaiˈzeiʃən] n. Faradización, *f.*
faraway [ˈfα:rəwei] adj. Remoto, ta; lejano, na: *faraway parts of the world*, las zonas lejanas de la Tierra. || FIG. Ausente, perdido, da: *he has a faraway look in his eyes*, tiene la mirada perdida.
farce [fα:s] n. THEATR. Farsa, *f.* || FIG. Farsa, *f.*: *the trial was a farce*, el proceso fue una farsa. || CULIN. Relleno, *m.*
farce [fα:s] v. tr. CULIN. Rellenar. || FIG. Rellenar.
farceur [fα:ˈsə:*] n. Bromista, *m.* (joker). || Farsante, *m.* (actor).
farcical [ˈfα:sikəl] adj. Absurdo, da; ridículo, la; grotesco, ca: *farcical situation*, situación ridícula. || Divertido, da (funny).
farcicality [—iti] n. Ridiculez, *f.*
farcy [ˈfα:si] n. VET. Muermo, *m.*
fare [fεə*] n. Precio (*m.*) del billete *or* del recorrido *or* del viaje, tarifa, *f.* (in public transport). || Billete, *m.* (ticket). || Pasaje, *m.* (in a boat). || Pasajero, ra; viajero, ra (passenger). || Viajero, ra (in a bus). || Cliente, *m.* & *f.* (in a taxi). || Comida, *f.* (food). || — *Excess fare*, suplemento, *m.* || *Fares please!*, ¡billetes por favor! || *How much is the fare to Madrid?*, ¿cuánto es el billete para Madrid?, ¿cuánto cuesta el viaje a Madrid? || *Minimum fare*, bajada (*f.*) de bandera (in a taxi).
fare [fεə*] v. intr. Viajar (to travel). || Irle a uno: *how did you fare in London?*, ¿cómo te ha ido en Londres?, ¿qué tal te fue en Londres? || Comer (to eat). || — *To fare alike*, correr la misma suerte. || *To fare forth*, irse, ponerse en camino. || *To fare well*, irle bien a uno (to do well), comer bien (to eat well).
Far East [ˈfα:ˈi:st] pr. n. GEOGR. Extremo Oriente, *m.*, Lejano Oriente, *m.*
farewell [ˈfεəˈwel] interj. ¡Adiós!, ¡vaya con Dios!
— N. Adiós, *m.*: *to say farewell*, decir adiós. || *To bid farewell to* o *to take one's farewell of*, despedirse de.
— Adj. De despedida: *a farewell party*, una fiesta de despedida.
farfetched [ˈfα:ˈfetʃt] adj. Inverosímil (not plausible). || Exagerado, da (exaggerated). || Rebuscado, da (complicated). || Traído por los cabellos (forced).
far-flung [ˈfα:ˈflʌŋ] adj. Extenso, sa (of huge extent). || Remoto, ta (remote).
farina [fəˈrainə] n. Harina, *f.* (flour). || Fécula, *f.* (of potatoes). || Almidón, *m.* (starch).
farinaceous [ˌfæriˈneiʃəs] adj. Farináceo, a.
farinose [ˈfærinəus] adj. Harinoso, sa. || BOT. Farináceo, a.

farm [fɑːm] n. Granja, *f.*, finca, *f.* [*Amer.*, hacienda, *f.*] (for cultivation or animal breeding). || Criadero, *m.* (of oysters, fish, mink, etc.).
— Adj. Agrícola, del campo: *farm labour*, trabajo agrícola; *farm products*, productos agrícolas.
farm [fɑːm] v. tr. Cultivar, labrar (to till). || *To farm out*, arrendar (to let), mandar hacer fuera [de una fábrica u oficina] (work).
— V. intr. Cultivar la tierra (to till). || Ser agricultor (to be a farmer).
farmer [—ə*] n. Agricultor, *m.*, cultivador, *m.* || Granjero, ra [*Amer.*, hacendado, *m.*] (farm owner). || Campesino, na (peasant).
farmhand [ˈfɑːmhænd] n. Mozo (*m.*) de labranza, peón, *m.*, trabajador (*m.*) agrícola *or* del campo.
farmhouse [ˈfɑːmhaus] n. Granja, *f.*, finca, *f.*, alquería, *f.* [*Amer.*, hacienda, *f.*].
farming [ˈfɑːmiŋ] n. Labranza, *f.*, cultivo, *m.* (till). || Agricultura, *f.* (agriculture). || Cría, *f.* (of animals).
— Adj. Agrícola: *farming country*, país agrícola; *farming year*, campaña agrícola.
farm labourer (U. S. **farm laborer**) [ˈfɑːmleibərə*] n. Trabajador (*m.*) agrícola *or* del campo, peón, *m.*
farmland [ˈfɑːmlænd] n. Tierras (*f. pl.*) de labrantío.
farmstead [ˈfɑːmsted] n. Granja, *f.*, finca, *f.*
farmyard [ˈfɑːmjɑːd] n. Corral, *m.*
far-off [ˈfɑːˈrɔf] adj. Remoto, ta (in time and space).
farrago [fəˈrɑːgəu] n. Fárrago, *m.*
— Observ. El plural de la palabra inglesa es *farragoes.*
far-reaching [ˈfɑːˈriːtʃiŋ] adj. De mucho alcance, trascendental: *far-reaching consequences*, consecuencias trascendentales.
farrier [ˈfæriə*] n. Herrador, *m.* (smith). || Veterinario, *m.* (veterinary)
farriery [—ri] n. Herrería, *f.* (blacksmithing). || Veterinaria, *f.*
farrow [ˈfærəu] n. Lechigada (*f.*) de cerdos (litter of pigs). || Parto, *m.* (giving birth to pigs).
farrow [ˈfærəu] v. tr./intr. Parir (a sow).
farseeing [ˈfɑːˈsiːiŋ] adj. Prudente, precavido, da; previsor, ra: *farseeing measures*, medidas prudentes. || Perspicaz (perspicacious).
farsighted [ˈfɑːˈsaitid] adj. Med. Hipermétrope. || Perspicaz, clarividente (having foresight). || Prudente, precavido, da (cautious).
farsightedly [—li] adv. Con perspicacia, con clarividencia.
farsightedness [—nis] n. Perspicacia, *f.*, clarividencia, *f.* (foresight). || Prudencia, *f.* (cautiousness). || Med. Hipermetropía, *f.*
fart [fɑːt] n. Pop. Pedo, *m.*
fart [fɑːt] v. intr. Pop. Peerse, echarse un pedo.
farther [ˈfɑːðə*] adj. Más lejano, na (in space or time).
— Adv. Más lejos (in space). || Más adelante (in time). || Más (to a greater degree): *farther on*, más adelante. || Además (moreover). || *To get farther and farther away from*, alejarse cada vez más de.
— Observ. *Farther* es el comparativo de *far.*
farthermost [—məust] adj. Más lejano, na.
farthest [ˈfɑːðist] adj. Más lejano, na (most distant). || Más largo, ga (longest).
— Adv. Más lejos.
— Observ. *Farthest* es el superlativo de *far.*
farthing [ˈfɑːðiŋ] n. Cuarto (*m.*) de penique (old coin). || Fam. Bledo, *m.*, comino, *m.*: *I don't care a farthing*, me importa un bledo. || Fam. *That's not worth a brass farthing*, no vale un real *or* un comino.
farthingale [—geil] n. Verdugado, *m.*, guardainfante, *m.*, miriñaque, *m.* (type of petticoat).
fascia [ˈfeiʃə] n. Faja, *f.* (band). || Med. Venda, *f.*, vendaje, *m.* || Astr. Banda (*f.*) *or* anillo (*m.*) que rodea un planeta. || Arch. Faja, *f.* || Aut. Salpicadero, *m.*, tablero (*m.*) de mandos (dashboard).
fasciate [ˈfæʃiit] adj. Med. Vendado, da. || Zool. Rayado, da; listado, da (striped).
fascicle [ˈfæsikl] n. Fascículo, *m.* (of fibres, nerves). || Bot. Fascículo, *m.* || Ramo, *m.* (of flowers). || Fascículo, *m.* (of a publication).
fascicule [ˈfæsikjuːl] or **fasciculus** [—əs] n. Fascículo, *m.* (of a book). || Anat. Fascículo, *m.*
— Observ. El plural de *fasciculus* es *fasciculi.*
fascinate [ˈfæsineit] v. tr. Fascinar.
fascinating [—iŋ] adj. Fascinante, fascinador, ra.
fascination [ˌfæsiˈneiʃən] n. Fascinación, *f.*, hechizo, *m.* (fascinating). || Encanto, *m.*, atractivo, *m.* (charm).
fascine [fæˈsiːn] n. Mil. Fajina, *f.*
Fascism [ˈfæʃizəm] n. Fascismo, *m.*
Fascist [ˈfæʃist] adj./n. Fascista.
Fascistic [fæˈʃistik] adj. Fascista.
fashion [ˈfæʃən] n. Manera, *f.*, modo, *m.*: *that is his fashion of doing things*, es su modo de hacer las cosas. || Moda, *f.* (of dresses, suits): *what will the fashion be this year?*, ¿cuál será la moda este año? || Elegancia, *f.*, distinción, *f.* (elegance). || Costumbre, *f.* (custom). || — *After a fashion*, en cierto modo (in a manner), más o menos (somehow), hasta cierto punto (to some extent). || *After the fashion of*, a imitación de, a la manera de. || Fam. *All the fashion*, muy de moda. || *Fashion magazine*, revista (*f.*) de modas. || *In fashion*, de moda. || *In one's own fashion*, a su estilo. || *In the Paris fashion*, a la moda de París. || *In the Spanish fashion*, a la española. || *It is not her fashion to act like that*, no acostumbra obrar así. || *Out of fashion*, pasado de moda. || *To be in fashion*, estar de moda, estilarse. || *To come into fashion*, ponerse de moda. || *To dress in the latest fashion*, vestirse a la última moda. || *To go out of fashion*, pasar de moda. || *To set the fashion*, dictar la moda. || *To speak a language after a fashion*, chapurrear un idioma. || *Woman of fashion*, mujer elegante *or* distinguida.
fashion [ˈfæʃən] v. tr. Moldear (to mould). || Hacer: *to fashion a whistle from a piece of wood*, hacer un silbato con un trozo de madera. || Labrar (to work). || Forjar (to forge). || Formar (to shape). || Adaptar, ajustar (to fit).
fashionable [—əbl] adj. De moda: *a fashionable dress, painter*, un traje, un pintor de moda; *it's fashionable to go to Saint Tropez*, está de moda ir a San Tropez. || Elegante: *fashionable summer resort*, lugar elegante de verano.
— N. Persona (*f.*) elegante.
fashionably [—əbli] adv. A la moda, elegantemente.
fashion model [—ˈmɔdl] n. Modelo, *m.* & *f.*
fashion parade [—pəˈreid] n. Desfile (*m.*) de modas *or* de modelos, presentación (*f.*) de modelos.
fashion plate [—pleit] n. Figurín, *m.* (picture). || Fig. Figurín, *m.* | Mujer (*f.*) esclava de la moda (woman).
fashion show [—ʃəu] n. See fashion parade.
fast [fɑːst] adj. Rápido, da; veloz: *fast runner*, corredor veloz. || Rápido, da: *a fast road*, una carretera rápida; *fast train*, tren rápido. || Ligero, ra; ágil: *fast steed*, corcel ligero. || Adelantado, da (a watch): *your watch is ten minutes fast*, su reloj está diez minutos adelantado. || Sólido, da; inalterable: *fast colours*, colores sólidos. || Indeleble (indelible). || Resistente a: *acid-fast*, resistente a los ácidos. || Atascado, da (in mud). || Fiel, constante, seguro, ra: *a fast friend*, un amigo fiel. || Cerrado, da (closed). || Encajado, da; atrancado, da (door, drawer). || Seguro, ra; firme, estable (fixed securely). || Ajetreado, da (active): *to live a fast life*, llevar una vida ajetreada. || Disoluto, ta (dissolute). || Phot. Rápido, da. || Sp. Seco y firme (pitch). || — *Fast money*, dinero que se gana rápidamente. || Fig. *Fast woman*, mujer fresca. || *To make fast*, sujetar (to fix), atar (to tie), amarrar (a boat). || Fig. Fam. *To pull a fast one on s.o.*, jugar una mala jugada *or* pasada a alguien.
— Adv. Rápidamente, de prisa: *don't speak so fast*, no hables tan rápidamente. || Firmemente (firmly, securely). || Profundamente, completamente (thoroughly). || (Ant.) Cerca (near). || — *Hold fast!*, ¡agarraos! (hold tight), ¡para! (stop), ¡alto! (halt). || *Not so fast!*, ¡un momento!, ¡más despacio! || *To be fast asleep*, estar profundamente dormido. || *To be stuck fast*, estar completamente atascado (in mud), estar completamente encajado (a door, etc.). || *To hold fast*, no deshacerse (a knot, etc.), agarrarse bien (a person). || Fig. *To hold fast to*, mantenerse firme en (an argument). | *To play fast and loose with*, jugar con (s.o.'s affections, s.o.). || *To rain fast*, llover a cántaros. || *To run fast*, correr rápidamente (s.o.), adelantar (a watch). || *To stand fast*, mantenerse firme (to be firm).
— N. Ayuno, *m.*: *fast day*, día de ayuno; *to break one's fast*, romper el ayuno. || Mar. Amarra, *f.* (rope).
fast [fɑːst] v. intr. Ayunar.
fastback [—bæk] n. Aut. Coche (*m.*) de forma aerodinámica.
fasten [ˈfɑːsen] v. tr. Sujetar (to attach): *he fastened two sheets of paper with a clip*, sujetó dos hojas de papel con un clip. || Fijar (to fix). || Pegar (with paste). || Abrochar: *she fastens her dress at the back*, se abrocha el vestido por detrás. || Atar (parcels, bundles, shoelaces). || Amarrar (a boat). || Cerrar (to shut). || Encerrar (to enclose). || Fig. Fijar, clavar (one's eyes). | Atribuir (responsibility). | Echar, achacar: *to fasten the blame on s.o.*, echar la culpa a alguien.
— V. intr. Agarrarse, sujetarse: *I fastened on to the handrail*, me agarré al pasamano. || Fijarse (one's attention, eyes, etc.). || Cerrarse (door, window, box etc.). || Abrocharse (garment). || — *To fasten on to an idea*, aferrarse a una idea. || *To fasten on to a pretext*, valerse de un pretexto. || *To fasten on to s.o.*, pegarse a uno (to stick to), fijarse en uno (to stare at).
fastener [—ə*] n. Cierre, *m.* (of a box, window). || Corchete, *m.* (of a dress). || Cremallera, *f.* (zip). || Cerrojo, *m.* (of a door). || Clip, *m.*, sujetador, *m.*, sujetapapeles, *m. inv.* (for papers).
fastening [—iŋ] n. Fijación, *f.* || Abrochamiento, *m.* (of a garment). || See fastener. || — Pl. Tech. Piezas (*f.*) de unión.
fastidious [fəsˈtidiəs] adj. Melindroso, sa; delicado, da (about food, lodgings, etc.). || Quisquilloso, sa: *the boss is very fastidious when he checks the reports*, el jefe es muy quisquilloso cuando revisa los informes. || Exigente (demanding).
— Observ. La palabra "fastidioso" corresponde a *tedious, annoying* o *irksome.*
fastidiousness [—nis] n. Melindre, *m.*, delicadeza (*f.*) excesiva.
fastness [ˈfɑːstnis] n. Firmeza, *f.* (firmness). || Solidez, *f.* (of dyes). || Rapidez, *f.* (speed). || Fortaleza, *f.* (stronghold). || Adelanto, *m.* (of a watch). || Constancia, *f.* (of friendship).

fat [fæt] adj. Grueso, sa; gordo, da; obeso, sa (persons). || Que tiene mucha grasa (meat). || Grasiento, ta (greasy). || Fertil, feraz (land). || Cebado, da (animal for slaughter). || FAM. Lucrativo, va (job, position, etc.). || FIG. Muy hermoso, sa (bank account). | Repleto, ta (purse). | Grande, pingüe: *a fat profit*, un gran beneficio. | Torpe (dull). || — FIG. FAM. *A fat chance he has!*, ¡ni soñarlo! | *A fat lot I care!*, ¡me importa un pepino! | *A fat lot of work you have done this morning!*, ¡pues sí que has hecho mucho trabajo esta mañana! || *To grow fat*, engordar.
— N. Grasa, *f.*, carnes, *f. pl.* (of a fat person). || Gordo, *m.*, grasa, *f.*: *this meat has a lot of fat*, esta carne tiene mucho gordo. || CULIN. Manteca (*f.*) de cerdo (lard). || Sebo, *m.*, grasa, *f.* (grease). || CHEM. Grasa, *f.* || — FIG. FAM. *The fat is in the fire*, se va a armar la gorda. | *To chew the fat*, estar de palique. | *To live on the fat of the land*, vivir a cuerpo de rey.
fat [fæt] v. tr./intr. See FATTEN.
fatal [ˈfeitl] adj. Mortal (accident). || Fatal, funesto, ta (very serious): *his death had fatal consequences*, su muerte tuvo consecuencias funestas. || Fatídico, ca: *the fatal day arrived for David to take a decision*, llegó para David el día fatídico de tomar una decisión. || *The fatal sisters*, las Parcas.
fatalism [ˈfeitəlizəm] n. Fatalismo, *m.*
fatalist [ˈfeitəlist] n. Fatalista, *m.* & *f.*
fatalistic [ˌfeitəˈlistik] adj. Fatalista.
fatality [fəˈtæliti] n. Calamidad, *f.*, desgracia, *f.*: *floods, earthquakes and other fatalities*, inundaciones, terremotos y otras calamidades. || Muerte, *f.* (death). || Muerto, ta; víctima, *f.* (in accidents, wars, etc.). || Fatalidad, *f.*: *the fatality that marked his family*, la fatalidad que pesó sobre su familia.
fatally [ˈfeitəli] adv. Fatalmente (by destiny). || Mortalmente (mortally).
fate [feit] n. Destino, *m.*, suerte, *f.*: *fate stepped in and prevented our meeting*, el destino se interpuso e impidió nuestro encuentro. || Muerte, *f.* (death): *on the 12th of May he met his fate*, el 12 de mayo encontró la muerte. || *We cannot tell what fate has in store for us*, no podemos saber lo que la suerte nos va a deparar.
fate [feit] v. tr. Predestinar. || Condenar: *fated to fail*, condenado al fracaso. || *It is fated that*, está escrito que, es inevitable que.
fateful [ˈfeitful] adj. Profético, ca. || Decisivo, va (decisive). || Fatal (inevitable). || Fatídico, ca.
Fates [feits] pl. pr. n. MYTH. Parcas, *f.*
fathead [ˈfæthed] n. FAM. Imbécil, *m.* & *f.*, tonto, ta.
father [ˈfɑːðə*] n. Padre, *m.* || REL. Padre, *m.*: *Father Bartolomé de las Casas*, el Padre Bartolomé de las Casas. || Padre (*m.*) de familia (civil status). || — FIG. *A miserly father makes a lavish son*, a padre ganador, hijo gastador. || *Conscript father*, padre conscripto. || *Father Christmas*, Papá Noel. || *Father confessor*, padre espiritual. || *Foster father*, padre nutricio. || *From father to son*, de padres a hijos. || *God the Father*, Dios Padre. || *Heavenly Father*, Padre Eterno. || FIG. *Like father like son*, de tal palo, tal astilla. || *Our Father*, Padre Nuestro, *m.*, Padrenuestro, *m.* (prayer). || *The Holy Father*, el Santo Padre, el Padre Santo (the Pope). || *The Fathers of the Christian Church*, los [Santos] Padres de la Iglesia. || FIG. *To be a father to*, ser un padre para. | *To be the father of*, ser el autor de (bill, resolution, etc.).
father [ˈfɑːðə*] v. tr. Engendrar (to create). || FIG. Ser el autor de (to be the author of). | Patrocinar (to support). | Ser el padre de: *he is the father of modern astronomy*, es el padre de la astronomía moderna. | Atribuir (to attribute).
fatherhood [—hud] n. Paternidad, *f.*
father-in-law [—rinlɔː] n. Suegro, *m.*, padre (*m.*) político.
fatherland [—lænd] n. Patria, *f.*, madre (*f.*) patria.
fatherless [—lis] adj. Huérfano de padre (orphan). || Sin padre (bastard).
fatherliness [—linis] n. Paternalismo, *m.*
fatherly [—li] adj. Paternal, paterno, na; de padre (of the father): *fatherly duties*, deberes paternos. || Paternal: *in a fatherly tone*, con un tono paternal.
— Adv. Paternalmente.
fathom [ˈfæðəm] n. MAR. Braza, *f.* (measure, depth). || MAR. *Fathom line*, sonda, *f.*
fathom [ˈfæðəm] v. tr. Sondar, sondear (water depth). || FIG. Comprender, entender: *I can't fathom this theory*, no puedo comprender esta teoría. | Desentrañar (to unravel a mystery). | Penetrar en (to penetrate).
fathomless [—lis] adj. Insondable: *fathomless pit*, pozo insondable. || FIG. Insondable: *fathomless mysteries*, misterios insondables. | Impenetrable.
fatidical [fəˈtidikəl] adj. Fatídico, ca.
fatigue [fəˈtiːg] n. Cansancio, *m.*, fatiga, *f.* (weariness). || Fatiga, *f.* (of metals). || MIL. Fajina, *f.*, faena, *f.* || — MIL. *Fatigue dress*, traje (*m.*) de faena. | *Fatigue duty*, servicio (*m.*) de fajina. | *Fatigue party* o *fatigue detail*, destacamento (*m.*) de fajina.
fatigue [fəˈtiːg] v. tr. Fatigar, cansar (to tire out).
fatiguing [—iŋ] adj. Fatigoso, sa; agotador, ra.
fatling [ˈfætliŋ] n. Cebón, *m.*
fatness [ˈfætnis] n. Gordura, *f.* (of a person). || FIG. Fertilidad, *f.*, feracidad, *f.* (of land).
fatten [ˈfætn] v. tr. Cebar, engordar (an animal). || Enriquecer, abonar, fertilizar (soil). || FAM. Engordar (a person).
— V. intr. Engordar (to grow fat).
fattening [—iŋ] adj. Que engorda.
— N. Engorde, *m.*, ceba, *f.* || *Fattening animals*, animales (*m. pl.*) de engorde.
fattish [ˈfætiʃ] adj. FAM. Regordete, ta; gordinflón, ona.
fatty [ˈfæti] adj. ANAT. Adiposo, sa (tissue, degeneration). || Graso, sa: *fatty acid*, ácido graso.
— N. FAM. Gordinflón, ona (person).
fatuitous [fəˈtjuitəs] adj. Fatuo, tua; necio, cia.
fatuity [fəˈtjuːiti] n. Fatuidad, *f.*, necedad, *f.*
fatuous [ˈfætjuəs] adj. Fatuo, tua; necio, cia.
fatuousness [—nis] n. Fatuidad, *f.*
faucal [ˈfɔːkəl] adj. Gutural.
fauces [ˈfɔːsiːz] pl. n. ANAT. Fauces, *f.*
faucet [ˈfɔːsit] n. U. S. Grifo, *m.* (tap). | Espita, *f.* (of a barrel).
faugh [fɔː] interj. ¡Fu!
fault [fɔːlt] n. Culpa, *f.*: *it is your fault*, es tu culpa, es culpa tuya; *whose fault is it?*, ¿quién tiene la culpa? || Defecto, *m.*, imperfección, *f.*: *she loves me in spite of all my faults*, me quiere a pesar de todos mis defectos. || Defecto, *m.* (of material, metals, etc.). || GEOL. Falla, *f.* || SP. Falta, *f.* (in tennis). || Error, *m.*, falta, *f.*: *an essay with numerous faults of syntax*, una redacción con muchos errores de sintaxis. || Pérdida (*f.*) del rastro (in hunting). || TECH. Avería, *f.* (breakdown). || (Ant.) Falta, *f.*, carencia, *f.* (lack). || — *John was at fault in the accident*, Juan tuvo la culpa del accidente. || *To a fault*, excesivamente. || *To catch s.o. in fault*, coger a uno en falta. || *To find fault with s.o.* o *sth.*, criticar a alguien *or* algo. || *Your memory is at fault*, usted recuerda mal. || *You were at fault in not warning me*, hizo mal en no avisarme.
fault [fɔːlt] v. tr. Criticar: *you can't fault him in matters of grammar*, no le puedes criticar en cuestiones de gramática. || GEOL. Provocar una falla en.
— V. intr. GEOL. Tener una falla.
faultfinder [—ˌfaində*] n. Criticón, ona.
faultfinding [—ˌfaindiŋ] n. Crítica, *f.* || *Faultfinding is his favourate pastime*, su afición favorita es criticar.
— Adj. Criticón, ona.
faultily [ˈfɔːltili] adv. Imperfectamente, defectuosamente.
faultiness [ˈfɔːltinis] n. Imperfección, *f.*
faultless [ˈfɔːltlis] adj. Intachable, perfecto, ta (irreproachable). || Perfecto, ta; sin defecto: *a faultless diamond*, un diamante sin defecto.
faulty [ˈfɔːlti] adj. Malo, la: *faulty excuse*, excusa mala. || Erróneo, a (mistaken). || Defectuoso, sa (machine). || Imperfecto, ta.
faun [fɔːn] n. MYTH. Fauno, *m.*
fauna [ˈfɔːnə] n. ZOOL. Fauna, *f.*

— OBSERV. El plural de la palabra inglesa es *faunas* o *faunae*.

Faust [faust] pr. n. Fausto, *m.*
fauvism [ˈfəuvizəm] n. Fauvismo, *m.* (a movement in painting).
faux-bourdon [ˈfəubuːˈdoŋ] n. MUS. Fabordón, *m.*
faux pas [ˈfəuˈpɑː] n. Metedura (*f.*) de pata (social blunder).
favor [ˈfeivə*] n./v. tr. U. S. See FAVOUR.
favorable [ˈfeivərəbl] adj. U. S. See FAVOURABLE.
favored [ˈfeivərəd] adj. U. S. See FAVOURED.
favorite [ˈfeivərit] adj./n. U. S. See FAVOURITE.
favorite son [—sʌn] n. U. S. Hijo (*m.*) predilecto (famous man). | Candidato (*m.*) predilecto.
favoritism [—izəm] n. U. S. See FAVOURITISM.
favour [ˈfeivə*] n. Favor, *m.*: *to do s.o. a favour*, hacerle a alguien un favor; *to ask a favour of*, pedir un favor a. || Favoritismo, *m.* (partiality). || Favor, *m.* (advantage): *two points in our favour*, dos puntos a nuestro favor. || COMM. Carta, *f.*, atenta, *f.*: *your favour of the third inst.*, su atenta del tres del corriente. || Favor, *m.*: *to seek the favour of the king*, buscar el favor del rey. || Obsequio, *m.* (gift): *party favours*, obsequios dados en una fiesta. || Permiso, *m.* (permission): *by your favour*, con su permiso. || Favor, *m.* (ribbon). || Favor, *m.* (of a woman). || — *To be in favour*, estar de moda (to be fashionable), ser apreciado (to be popular). || *To be in favour of s.o.* o *of sth.*, estar a favor de alguien *or* de algo. || *To be in favour with s.o.* o *in s.o.'s favour*, gozar del favor *or* de la protección de alguien. || *To be out of favour*, no estar de moda (unfashionable), dejar de ser apreciado (to be no longer popular). || *To be out of favour with s.o.*, haber perdido el favor de alguien, haber caído en desgracia con alguien. || *To fall out of favour with s.o.*, perder el favor de alguien, caer en desgracia con alguien. || *To find favour in s.o.'s eyes* o *to find favour with s.o.*, ganarse el favor de alguien, gustarle a uno. || *To look on s.o.* o *on sth. with favour*, mirar a alguien *or* algo con buenos ojos. || *Under favour of the night*, al amparo de la noche. || *With favour*, favorablemente (favourably).
favour [ˈfeivə*] v. tr. Favorecer: *fortune favours the brave*, la fortuna favorece a los valientes; *this reform favours injustice*, esta reforma favorece las injusticias. || Favorecer: *blue favours you*, el azul te favorece. || Estar a favor de (to approve): *the senator favours his appointment*, el senador está a favor de su nombramiento. || Apoyar (to support). || Preferir (to prefer).

|| Ser favorable a (to be favourable). || Obsequiar (to give a present). || Dotar (with intelligence, etc.). || Parecerse a (to resemble): *she favours her mother*, se parece a su madre. || — *Most favoured nation clause*, cláusula (*f.*) de la nación más favorecida. || *To favour s.o. with a visit*, honrar a alguien con una visita.

favourable [ˈfeivərəbl] adj. Favorable. || Favorable, propicio, cia (conditions).

favoured [ˈfeivəd] adj. Favorecido, da. || Predilecto, ta; preferido, da; favorito, ta (favourite).

favourite [ˈfeivərit] adj. Favorito, ta; preferido, da; predilecto, ta.
— N. Favorito, ta. || Favorito, *m.*, valido, *m.*, privado, *m.* (of a king, etc.). || Querida, *f.* (mistress). || SP. Favorito, ta.

favouritism [—izəm] n. Favoritismo, *m.*

favus [ˈfeivəs] n. MED. Favo, *m.*

fawn [fɔ:n] n. ZOOL. Cervato, *m.*
— Adj. Color de gamuza.

fawn [fɔ:n] v. intr. Hacer fiestas (a dog). || Parir (to give birth to a fawn). || *To fawn on* o *upon*, adular.

fawning [—iŋ] adj. Adulador, ra; servil.
— N. Adulación, *f.*, servilismo, *m.*

fay [fei] n. Hada, *f.*

faze [feiz] v. tr. U. S. Desconcertar.

fealty [ˌfi:əlti] n. Lealtad, *f.*, fidelidad, *f.*

fear [fiə*] n. Miedo, *m.*, temor, *m.*: *fear of God*, temor de *or* a Dios. || — *For fear of*, por miedo de (with verb), por miedo a (with noun). || *For fear that*, por miedo de que *or* a que. || FAM. *No fear!*, ¡ni hablar! || *There is no fear of failure*, no hay ningún riesgo de fracaso. || *To be in fear of*, tener miedo a. || *To go in fear of one's life*, temer por su vida. || FIG. FAM. *To put the fear of God into s.o.*, dar un susto mortal a uno.

fear [fiə*] v. tr. Temer, tener miedo de *or* a (See OBSERV.): *I fear there may be a war*, temo que haya una guerra. || *To be feared*, de temer: *he is to be feared*, es de temer.
— V. intr. Temer, tener miedo. || — *Never fear!*, ¡no temas!, ¡no hay cuidado! || *To fear for*, temer por: *I fear for his sanity*, temo por su salud mental.
— OBSERV. The construction *tener miedo de* usually precedes a verbal complement and *tener miedo a* a noun (*tener miedo de morir*, to be afraid to die; *tener miedo a la muerte*, to fear death). This rule, however, is not strict and is sometimes disregarded in practice.

fearful [ˈfiəful] adj. Espantoso, sa; horrible: *the railway accident was fearful*, el accidente de ferrocarril fue espantoso. || Temeroso, sa (frightened). || FAM. Tremendo, da; espantoso, sa: *what a fearful mess!*, ¡qué lío más espantoso! || — *Fearful of*, temeroso de. || *To be fearful of*, temer. || *To be fearful of doing sth.*, temer hacer algo.

fearfully [—i] adv. FAM. Terriblemente, tremendamente, horriblemente: *it was a fearfully hot day*, era un día terriblemente caluroso. || Con miedo, con temor.

fearfulness [—nis] n. Horror, *m.*, lo horrible (horror). || Pusilanimidad, *f.* (of character).

fearless [fiəlis] adj. Audaz, bravo, va; valiente, intrépido, da.

fearlessly [—li] adv. Audazmente, intrépidamente.

fearlessness [—nis] n. Intrepidez, *f.*, audacia, *f.*

fearsome [ˈfiəsəm] adj. Temible, espantoso, sa (frightful). || Temeroso, sa (frightened). || Timorato, ta (timid).

feasibility [ˌfi:zəˈbiliti] n. Viabilidad, *f.*

feasible [ˈfi:zəbl] adj. Factible, hacedero, ra; viable, posible. || Verosímil, posible, plausible: *his story sounds feasible*, su historia parece verosímil.

feast [fi:st] n. Fiesta (*f.*) religiosa. || Banquete, *m.* (meal). || FAM. Comilona, *f.* (huge meal). || — *Immovable, movable feast*, fiesta fija, movible *or* móvil. || FIG. *To be a feast for the eyes*, regalar la vista, ser un regalo para los ojos.

feast [fi:st] v. tr. Agasajar, festejar. || FIG. *Feast your eyes on that*, regálate la vista con eso.
— V. intr. Deleitarse, regalarse: *he feasted himself on chocolates*, se regaló con bombones. || Banquetear (to eat a rich meal).

feast day [—dei] n. Día (*m.*) festivo *or* de fiesta, fiesta, *f.*

feat [fi:t] n. Proeza, *f.*, hazaña, *f.* (deed): *a remarkable feat*, una gran hazaña. || Prueba, *f.*: *a feat of endurance*, una prueba de resistencia. || *Feat of arms*, hecho (*m.*) de armas.

feather [ˈfeðə*] n. Pluma, *f.* || Plumas, *f. pl.* (of an arrow). || TECH. Barbilla, *f.*, lengüeta, *f.* (for a grove). | Pestaña, *f.*, reborde, *m.* (flange). | Defecto, *m.*, jardín, *m.* (flaw of a gem). || — Pl. Plumas, *f.*, plumaje, *m. sing.* (plumage). || — FIG. *Birds of a feather*, see BIRD. || FIG. *Feather bed*, colchón (*m.*) de plumas. || *Feather duster*, plumero, *m.* || *Feather pillow*, almohada (*f.*) de plumas. || FIG. *That's a feather in your cap*, es un tanto que te apuntas. | *To be in fine feather*, estar en forma. | *To be in high feather*, estar de muy buen humor. | *To show the white feather*, ser un gallina, mostrarse cobarde (to exhibit cowardice). | *You could have knocked me down with a feather*, casi me caigo de espaldas.

feather [ˈfeðə*] v. tr. Emplumar (an arrow). || Adornar *or* ribetear con plumas (to decorate with feathers). || TECH. Machihembrar (to join two pieces). || Alzar (oars in rowing). || AVIAT. Poner en bandera (a propeller in aircraft). || FIG. *To feather one's nest*, hacer su agosto.
— V. intr. Cubrirse de plumas (a bird). || Ondular (to move like feathers).

featherbed [—bed] v. tr. FIG. Obligar [a los empresarios] a emplear más trabajadores de los que necesitan. | Favorecer, subvencionar: *the government featherbeds the miners*, el gobierno favorece a los mineros.

featherbedding [—bediŋ] n. U. S. Disminución (*f.*) de las horas de trabajo por obrero para evitar el paro. | Obligación (*f.*) de emplear un cupo de trabajadores superior al necesario.

featherbed rule [—bedru:l] n. U. S. Medida (*f.*) que adoptan los sindicatos para obligar a los empresarios a emplear más trabajadores de los necesarios.

featherbrain [—brein] n. FAM. Cabeza (*f.*) de chorlito.

featherbrained [—breind] adj. FAM. Estúpido, da; necio, cia: *featherbrained idea*, idea necia. | Casquivano, na (person). || FAM. *Featherbrained idiot*, tonto perdido.

feathered [ˈfeðəd] adj. Emplumado, da (adornment, arrow). || Con plumas (hat). || AVIAT. En bandera (propeller). || Alzado, da (oars). || FIG. Alado, da (winged). | Veloz, ligero, ra (swift). || *Feathered game*, caza (*f.*) de pluma.

featheredge [ˈfeðəredʒ] n. Borde (*m.*) delgado (very thin edge). || Bisel, *m.* (bevelled edge).

featherhead [ˈfeðəhed] n. FAM. Cabeza (*f.*) de chorlito.

feathering [ˈfeðəriŋ] n. Plumaje, *m.* (of birds). || Plumas, *f. pl.* (of an arrow).

featherstitch [ˈfeðəstitʃ] n. Punto (*m.*) de espina.

featherweight [ˈfəðəweit] n. Peso (*m.*) pluma (boxing). || Cosa (*f.*) muy ligera. || SP. *A featherweight fight*, un combate de pesos pluma.
— Adj. De peso pluma (boxing). || Muy ligero, ra (very light). || FIG. De poco peso, de poca entidad.

feathery [ˈfeðəri] adj. Plumoso, sa. || Ligero como una pluma (light): *feathery snow*, nieve ligera como una pluma. || Cubierto de plumas (covered with feathers). || De plumas, con plumas (hat).

feature [ˈfi:tʃə*] n. Característica, *f.* (characteristic). || Rasgo, *m.* (of a face). || Figura, *f.* (shape). || Artículo (*m.*) principal, crónica (*f.*) especial (in a newspaper). || CINEM. Película (*f.*) principal, película (*f.*) de largo metraje: *what feature is showing?*, ¿cuál es la película principal? || — Pl. Rostro, *m. sing.*, semblante, *m. sing.* (face). || Facciones, *f.*, rasgos, *m.*: *he has hard features*, tiene facciones duras. || *Main feature*, película principal (film), atracción (*f.*) principal.

feature [ˈfi:tʃə*] v. tr. Presentar (film, actor). || Representar (to represent). || Describir: *the book features the life of a monk on an island*, el libro describe la vida de un fraile en una isla. || Caracterizar (to be a striking feature of). || Presentar (news, article). || Imaginarse (to imagine): *I can't feature that*, no puedo imaginarme eso. || Destacar, poner de relieve (to emphasize). || *This film features Charlie Chaplin*, en esta película trabaja *or* actúa como protagonista Charlie Chaplin.
— V. intr. Figurar, constar (to appear, to figure).

featured [—d] adj. Destacado, da; puesto de relieve (emphasized). || Principal (actor, etc.). || *He is fine-featured*, tiene rasgos finos.

feature film [—film] n. Película (*f.*) principal.

feature-length [—leŋθ] adj. De largo metraje (film). || Largo, ga; extenso, sa (article).

featureless [—lis] adj. Sin rasgos distintivos. || Monótono, na (monotonous).

febrifugal [fiˈbrifjugəl] adj. MED. Febrífugo, ga.

febrifuge [ˈfebrifju:dʒ] adj. MED. Febrífugo, ga.
— N. MED. Febrífugo, *m.*

febrile [ˈfi:brail] adj. Febril.

February [ˈfebruəri] n. Febrero, *m.*: *it happened on the 27th of February*, ocurrió el 27 de febrero.

fecal [ˈfi:kəl] adj. U. S. Fecal (faecal).

feces [ˈfi:si:z] pl. n. U. S. Excrementos, *m.*, heces, *f.*

feckless [ˈfeklis] adj. Débil (weak). || Incapaz (helpless). || Ineficaz (inefficient). || Inútil (useless). || Irreflexivo, va (irresponsible).

feculence [ˈfekjuləns] n. Feculencia, *f.*

feculent [ˈfekjulənt] adj. Feculento, ta (foul with impurities). || Sucio, cia (filthy).

fecund [ˈfi:kənd] adj. Fecundo, da.

fecundate [ˈfi:kəndeit] v. tr. Fecundar (to make fruitful or prolific). || Fertilizar (the land). || Fecundar (a flower).

fecundation [ˌfi:kənˈdeiʃən] n. Fecundación, *f.*

fecundity [fiˈkʌnditi] n. Fecundidad, *f.*

fed [fed] pret. & p. p. See FEED.

federacy [ˈfedərəsi] n. Federación, *f.*

federal [ˈfedərəl] adj./n. Federal.

federalism [ˈfedərəlizəm] n. Federalismo, *m.*

federalist [ˈfedərəlist] adj./n. Federalista.

federalize [ˈfedərəlaiz] v. tr. Federalizar, federar.

federate [ˈfedərit] adj. Federado, da.
— N. Federado, *m.*

federate [ˈfedəreit] v. tr. Federar.
— V. intr. Federarse.

federation [ˌfedəˈreiʃən] n. Federación, *f.*

federative [ˈfedərətiv] adj. Federativo, va.

fed up [ˈfedʌp] adj. FAM. Harto, ta; hasta la coronilla.

fee [fi:] n. Honorarios, *m. pl.*, emolumentos, *m. pl.* (of a professional, doctor, lawyer, etc.). || Derechos (*m. pl.*) de matrícula, matrícula, *f.* (at a university). || Cuota, *f.* (to a club). || Gratificación, *f.* (gratuity). || HIST. Feudo, *m.* (in Medieval times). || JUR. Hacienda, *f.*, patrimonio, *m.* (in a will). || — *Entrance fee*, entrada, *f.* || *Retaining fee*, anticipo, *m.* || *School fees*, precio (*m.*) de la escolaridad [y de la pensión en el caso de un internado]. || *To hold in fee*, poseer (to own). || *To pay one's school fees*, pagar el colegio.

fee [fi:] v. tr. Contratar (to hire). || Pagar los honorarios a (to pay).

feeble [ˈfi:bl] adj. Débil (weak). || De poco peso, poco convincente: *a feeble argument*, un argumento poco convincente. || Tenue: *a feeble light*, una luz tenue.

feebleminded [—ˈmaindid] adj. Débil mental (mentally deficient). || Tonto, ta (silly). || Irresoluto, ta (irresolute).

feeblemindedness [—ˈmaindidnis] n. Debilidad (*f.*) mental (mental deficiency). || Irresolución, *f.* (irresolution).

feebleness [ˈfi:blnis] n. Debilidad, *f.*

feed [fi:d] n. Pienso, *m.* (food for cattle). || Forraje, *m.* (fodder). || Comida, *f.* (food for babies). || FAM. Comilona, *f.*: *we had a nice feed last night*, tuvimos una buena comilona anoche. || TECH. Alimentación, *f.* (act of feeding a machine): *injection feed*, alimentación por inyección; *feed pump*, bomba de alimentación. | Mineral (*m.*) bruto (of blast furnace). | Avance, *m.* (of machine tool). | Alimentador, *m.* (feeder). || *To be off one's feed*, haber perdido el apetito.

feed* [fi:d] v. tr. Dar de comer a (to give food to): *she fed us well*, nos dio bien de comer; *to feed the chickens*, dar de comer a las gallinas; *she feeds her children a lot of fruit*, les da de comer mucha fruta a los niños. || Alimentar: *he has twelve children to feed*, tiene doce hijos que alimentar; *rice does not feed one properly*, el arroz no alimenta mucho. || Nutrir, alimentar (to nourish). || Dar de mamar, amamantar (to suckle). || Dar el biberón a (a baby with a bottle). || FIG. Alimentar: *to feed coal into a fire*, alimentar un fuego con carbón; *to feed one's mind*, alimentar el espíritu; *this river feeds the reservoir*, este río alimenta el depósito. | Avivar (one's anger). | Dar (hopes). | Acrecentar (to heighten). | Alimentar (one's vanity). | Mantener (to maintain). | Suministrar (to supply): *this pipeline feeds gas to the northern cities*, este gasoducto suministra gas a las ciudades del norte. | Suministrar, abastecer (water). | Suministrar electricidad a: *this generator feeds the whole city*, este generador suministra electricidad a la ciudad entera. || TECH. Alimentar (a blast furnace). | Introducir (pieces into a machine). | Desplazar, hacer avanzar (machine tools). | Alimentar: *to feed information into a computer*, alimentar una computadora con datos. || THEATR. Dar la réplica a (an actor). || SP. Pasar (the ball). || — FAM. *To be fed up with*, estar harto de, estar hasta la coronilla de. || *To feed back*, realimentar. || *To feed up*, sobrealimentar (person), cebar, engordar (animals).

— V. intr. Comer (to eat). || AGR. Pacer, pastar (to graze). || — *To feed back*, proceder (news, etc.), pitar (a microphone). || *To feed off*, vivir de (at the expense of): *to feed off the State*, vivir del Estado. || *To feed on*, alimentarse con (to live on).

— OBSERV. Pret. & p. p. **fed.**

feedback [ˈfi:dbæk] n. ELECTR. Realimentación, *f.* || Reacción, *f.* || Reaprovechamiento, *m.* (of information).

feed bag [ˈfi:dbæg] n. U. S. Morral, *m.* (nose bag). || U. S. FIG. FAM. *To put on the feed bag*, jalar, llenar la tripa.

feeder [ˈfi:də*] n. Alimentador, *m.* (of a machine). || Canal (*m.*) alimentador (of lake, reservoir). || Río (*m.*) tributario, afluente, *m.* (tributary). || Ramal, *m.* (of railway). || Carretera (*f.*) secundaria (road). || ELECTR. Cable (*m.*) alimentador. || SP. Lanzador, *m.* || Biberón, *m.* (feeding bottle). || Babero, *m.* (child's bib). || Animal (*m.*) de engorde (fattening animal). || Alimentador, *m.* (of cattle). || — FAM. *He's a prodigious feeder*, come como una lima. || *This plant is a large feeder*, esta planta requiere mucho abono.

feeding [ˈfi:diŋ] n. Comida, *f.*: *the feeding of the lions takes place at 8 o'clock*, la comida de los leones tiene lugar a las ocho. || Alimentación, *f.* (of domestic animals). || TECH. Alimentación, *f.* (of machine). | Avance, *m.* (of machine tool). || *Feeding time*, la hora de la comida.

feeding bottle [—ˌbɔtl] n. Biberón, *m.*

feeding trough [—trɔf] n. Comedero, *m.*

feed pipe [ˈfi:dpaip] n. Tubo (*m.*) de alimentación.

feed rack [ˈfi:dræk] n. Comedero, *m.*, pesebre, *m.* (for animals). || TECH. Cremallera (*f.*) de avance.

feedstuff [ˈfi:dstʌf] n. Alimentos (*m. pl.*) para el ganado.

feel [fi:l] n. Tacto, *m.*: *soft to the feel*, suave al tacto. || Sensación, *f.* (sensation). || Atmósfera, *f.*: *the empty room had a strange feel about it*, había una atmósfera extraña en la habitación vacía. || Sentido, *m.*: *to have a feel for colours*, tener sentido de los colores. || Disposición, *f.*, aptitudes, *f. pl.*: *to have a feel for the piano*, tener disposición para tocar el piano. || — *To get the feel of sth.*, cogerle el truco a algo (to acquire the knack), acostumbrarse a algo (to get used to). || *To have a feel*, tocar. || *To have a sticky feel*, ser pegajoso al tacto. || *To recognize sth. by its feel*, reconocer algo al tacto.

feel* [fi:l] v. tr. Tocar: *go and feel the water*, ve a tocar el agua. || Mirar: *feel how soft it is*, mira lo blando que es. || Sentir: *I can't feel the heat*, no siento el calor. || Sentir, tener, experimentar: *I don't feel much pity for him*, no tengo mucha compasión por él. || Sentir, [los efectos de]: *the whole country felt the earthquake*, el país entero sintió el terremoto. || Sentir: *to feel the presence of s.o.*, sentir la presencia de alguien. || Tener el presentimiento de que, sentir: *she felt things were about to go wrong*, tuvo el presentimiento de que las cosas iban a tomar mal cariz. || Parecerle [a uno], tener la impresión de que, creer que: *I feel you are right*, me parece que tienes razón. || Darse cuenta de (to realize): *you must feel your position*, debe darse cuenta de su situación. || Tomar (pulse). || MIL. Tantear, sondear (the enemy, the ground). || POP. Sobar, magrear (to caress). || — *I feel a song coming on*, me apetece mucho cantar. || *I have felt the cold this winter*, he pasado frío este invierno. || *To feel interest in*, tener interés por. || *To feel one's way*, ir a tientas (to grope), andar con pies de plomo (to act cautiously), tantear el terreno (to explore). || FIG. *To feel (quite) o.s.*, encontrarse bien. || *To feel out*, sondear. || *To feel s.o.'s vengeance*, sufrir la venganza de alguien. || *To feel strongly that*, estar convencido de que. || *To feel the heat*, ser sensible al calor, no aguantar el calor.

— V. intr. Sentir. || Ser [al tacto]: *it feels smooth*, es liso. || Estar: *it feels cold*, está frío. || Parecer: *the room feels damp*, el cuarto parece húmedo. || Encontrarse, sentirse, estar: *I feel tired*, me encuentro cansado; *how do you feel?*, ¿cómo se encuentra?; *to feel all the better for it*, sentirse mejor. || Tener: *I feel cold, hot, hungry, sleepy*, tengo frío, calor, hambre, sueño. || Hacer: *it feels cold today*, hace frío hoy. || Pensar (to think): *how do you feel about it?*, ¿qué piensas de esto? || — *How does it feel to...?*, ¿qué impresión hace...? || *If you feel like it*, si te parece, si te apetece. || *It feels like rain*, parece que va a llover. || *To feel about in*, ir a tientas por. || *To feel as if*, tener la impresión de que, parecerle [a uno] que: *I feel as if you don't like me*, me parece que no me quieres. || *To feel bad about*, sentir (to regret). || *To feel certain* o *sure that*, estar seguro de que. || *To feel for s.o.*, sentirlo por alguien, compadecer a alguien. || *To feel for sth.*, buscar algo a tientas. || *To feel for the enemy*, buscar al enemigo. || *To feel in (one's pockets)*, registrar [los bolsillos]. || *To feel like*, apetecer: *do you feel like a beer?*, ¿te apetece una cerveza?; tener ganas de: *I feel like going to the pictures*, tengo ganas de ir al cine; parecer: *it feels like wool*, parece lana. || FIG. *To feel like death*, encontrarse fatal. || *To feel sorry for s.o.*, compadecer a alguien. || *To feel sorry for sth.*, sentir algo (to regret). || *To feel strongly about*, tener ideas muy fijas sobre. || *To feel strongly for*, tener sentimientos muy profundos por. || *To feel up to*, sentirse capaz de [hacer algo]. || *We feel with you* o *for you in your loss*, le acompañamos en el sentimiento.

— OBSERV. Pret. & p. p. **felt.**

feeler [—ə*] n. Bigotes, *m. pl.* (cat's whiskers). || Cuerno, *m.* (of a snail). || Antena, *f.* (of insects). || Tentáculo, *m.* (of octopus, etc.). || TECH. Calibrador, *m.* (gauge). || FIG. *To put out a feeler*, lanzar una sonda, efectuar un sondeo.

feeling [—iŋ] n. Sentimiento, *m.*: *feelings of gratitude*, sentimientos de gratitud. || Sensación, *f.*: *feeling of weightlessness*, sensación de ingravidez. || Impresión, *f.*, presentimiento, *m.*: *I have the feeling that this will fail*, tengo la impresión de que eso va a fracasar. || Opinión, *f.*, parecer, *m.*, sentir, *m.* (opinion): *my feeling is that*, mi parecer es que. || Sensibilidad, *f.*: *I have no feeling in my leg*, no tengo sensibilidad en la pierna; *to play the piano with feeling*, tocar el piano con sensibilidad. || Sentido, *m.*: *she has a feeling for music*, tiene el sentido de la música. || Amor, *m.*: *a feeling for his homeland*, amor a su patria. || Ternura, *f.* (tenderness). || Emoción, *f.* (emotion): *to speak with feeling*, hablar con emoción. || Compasión, *f.*: *feeling for the suffering of others*, compasión por el sufrimiento de los demás. || Sentimientos, *m. pl.*: *during the crisis feeling ran high*, durante la crisis los sentimientos estaban exacerbados. || Tacto, *m.* (sense of touch). || — *A man of feeling*, un hombre sensible. || *Good feeling*, buenos sentimientos. || *Hard feelings*, resentimiento, *m. sing.* || *Ill feeling*, malos sentimientos. || *To have a feeling for nature*, ser sensible a la naturaleza. || *To have kind feelings for*, tener sentimientos amistosos por. || *To have no feelings*, no tener sensibilidad, ser insensible. || *To relieve one's feelings*, desahogarse.

— Adj. Sensible: *a feeling heart*, un corazón sensible. || Muy sentido, da (grief).

feelingly [—iŋli] adv. Con emoción: *to speak feelingly*, hablar con emoción. || Con sensibilidad: *to sing feelingly*, cantar con sensibilidad.

feet [fi:t] pl. n. See FOOT.

feign [fein] v. tr. Fingir, aparentar, simular: *to feign indifference*, fingir indiferencia. || Fingir, fingirse: *to feign illness*, fingir estar enfermo, fingirse enfermo; *to feign sleep*, fingirse dormido. || Inventar (an excuse).

— V. intr. Fingir.

feigned [—d] adj. Fingido, da; simulado, da: *feigned joy*, alegría fingida. || Ficticio, cia. || Falso, sa (false).
feint [feint] n. SP. Finta, *f.* | Amago, *m.*, finta, *f.* (in fencing). || MIL. Maniobra (*f.*) fingida. || Amago, *m.* (mock attack). || *To make a feint of working*, fingir estar trabajando.
feint [feint] v. intr. SP. Fintar, hacer una finta.
feints [feints] pl. n. See FAINTS.
feldspar [ˊfeldspɑ:*] or **feldspath** [ˊfeldspɑθ] n. MIN. Feldespato, *m.*
feldspathic [ˊfelds,pæθik] adj. MIN. Feldespático, ca.
felicitate [fiˊlisiteit] v. tr. Congratular, felicitar. || (Ant.) Alegrar.
felicitation [fi,lisiˊteiʃən] n. Congratulación, *f.*, felicitación, *f.*, enhorabuena, *f.*
felicitous [fiˊlisitəs] adj. Oportuno, na; afortunado, da; feliz (well chosen).
felicity [fiˊlisiti] n. Felicidad, *f.* (happiness). || Idea (*f.*) feliz (idea). || Expresión (*f.*) feliz (expression). || *To express o.s. with felicity*, expresarse bien.
felid [ˊfi:lid] n. ZOOL. Félido, *m.*
felidae [ˊfi:lidei] pl. n. ZOOL. Félidos, *m.*
feline [ˊfi:lain] adj. ZOOL. FIG. Felino, na.
— N. ZOOL. Felino, *m.*
fell [fel] n. Páramo, *m.* (moor). || Colina (*f.*) rocosa (hill). || Piel, *f.*, pellejo, *m.* (skin of animal). || Corte, *m.*, tala, *f.*, árboles (*m. pl.*) cortados en una temporada.
— Adj. POET. Cruel, feroz (cruel). || Funesto, ta (deadly). || *In one fell swoop*, de un golpe.
fell [fel] v. tr. Talar, cortar (trees). || Derribar (to knock down). || Sobrecargar (in sewing).
fell [fel] pret. & p. p. See FALL.
feller [felə*] n. Leñador, *m.*, talador, *m.* || U. S. FAM. Individuo, *m.*, tipo, *m.*, tío, *m.* (fellow). | Muchacho, *m.* (boy).
felling [ˊfeliŋ] n. Tala, *f.*, corte, *m.* (of trees).
fellow [ˊfeləu] n. Chico, *m.* (boy): *a nice fellow*, un chico simpático. || Hombre, *m.* (man). || Persona, *f.* (person). || Compañero, *m.*, camarada, *m.*, amigo, *m.* (companion). || Pareja, *f.* (mate, counterpart). || Colega, *m.* (colleague). || FAM. Individuo, *m.*, tipo, *m.*, tío, *m.*: *he is an odd fellow*, es un tío extraño. | Uno, *m.*: *a fellow has to rest from time to time*, uno tiene que descansar de vez en cuando. || Igual, *m.*, par, *m.* (peer): *it has no fellow*, no tiene igual *or* no tiene par. || Becario, *m.* (university researcher). || Miembro (*m.*) del consejo de gobierno de una facultad. || Socio, *m.*, miembro, *m.* (of society). || — Pl. Compañeros, *m.*, amigos, *m.* (friends). || — *He is a poor fellow*, es un pobre diablo. || *My dear fellow!*, ¡hombre! || *Old fellow*, viejo amigo. || *Poor little fellow!*, ¡pobrecito!, ¡pobrecillo! || *Young fellow*, joven, *m.*
— Adj. *Fellow being*, semejante, *m.*, prójimo, *m.* || *Fellow boarder*, comensal, *m.* || *Fellow candidate*, candidato (*m.*) del mismo partido que otro. || *Fellow citizens*, conciudadanos, *m.* || *Fellow countrymen*, compatriotas, *m.* || *Fellow creature*, prójimo, *m.* || *Fellow feeling*, simpatía, *f.*, compañerismo, *m.* || *Fellow member*, consocio, *m.* || *Fellow men*, prójimos, *m.* || *Fellow musician, doctor, etc.*, colega, *m.* [de un músico, doctor, etc.]. || *Fellow partner*, asociado, *m.* || *Fellow passenger*, compañero (*m.*) de viaje. || *Fellow student*, compañero, *m.*, condiscípulo, *m.* || *Fellow sufferer*, compañero (*m.*) de fatigas. || *Fellow traveller*, compañero (*m.*) de viaje (on a trip), simpatizante, *m.* (in politics). || *Fellow worker*, compañero (*m.*) de trabajo, colega, *m.*
fellow [ˊfeləu] v. tr. (Ant.). Aparear (to pair).
fellowman [—mən] n. Semejante, *m.*, prójimo, *m.*
— OBSERV. El plural de *fellowman* es *fellowmen*.
fellowship [—ʃip] n. Comunidad, *f.*: *Christian fellowship*, comunidad cristiana. || Compañerismo, *m.*, camaradería, *f.* (companionship). || Fraternidad, *f.*, solidaridad, *f.* (solidarity). || Comunión, *f.*: *intellectual fellowship*, comunión de ideas. || Comunidad, *f.* (of interests). || Asociación, *f.* (association). || Compañía, *f.*, grupo, *m.* (group). || Asociación, *f.*, sociedad, *f.* (organized association). || Beca, *f.* (scholarship). || Título (*m.*) de miembro *or* socio (position). || Dignidad (*f.*) de miembro del consejo de gobierno de una facultad.
felo-de-se [ˊfi:ləudi:ˊsi:] n. JUR. Suicida, *m.* & *f.* (who has committed suicide). | Suicidio, *m.* (suicide).
— OBSERV. El plural es *felones-de-se* o *felos-de-se*.
felon [ˊfelən] n. JUR. Criminal, *m.* || MED. Panadizo, *m.*, uñero, *m.* (infection).
— Adj. Malvado, da (wicked). || Criminal.
felonious [fiˊləunjəs] adj. JUR. Criminal, delictivo, va; delictuoso, sa. || Malvado, da (wicked).
felonry [ˊfelənri] n. JUR. Criminales, *m. pl.*
felony [ˊfeləni] n. JUR. Crimen, *m.*, delito (*m.*) grave.
felspar [ˊfelspɑ:*] n. MIN. Feldespato, *m.*
felspathic [ˊfels,pæθik] adj. MIN. Feldespático, ca.
felt [felt] n. Fieltro, *m.* || *Roofing felt*, cartón (*m.*) embreado de techumbres.
— Adj. De fieltro: *a felt hat*, un sombrero de fieltro.
felt [felt] v. tr. Enfurtir, convertir en fieltro (to make into felt). || Cubrir con fieltro (to cover). || Poner fieltro debajo de (a carpet).
— V. intr. Ponerse como el fieltro (garments).

felt [felt] pret. & p. p. See FEEL.
felting [—iŋ] n. Enfurtido, *m.* (process). || Fieltro, *m.* (felt).
felucca [feˊlʌkə] n. MAR. Falucho, *m.*
female [ˊfi:meil] adj. Hembra: *a female rhinoceros*, un rinoceronte hembra. || Femenino, na: *the female sex*, el sexo femenino. || De mujer, femenino, na: *a female voice*, una voz de mujer. || De las mujeres: *female education*, educación de las mujeres. || TECH. Hembra: *female screw*, tornillo hembra. || BOT. Femenino, na. || *Female friend, cousin*, amiga, *f.*, prima, *f.*
— N. Hembra, *f.*: *the female of the species*, la hembra de la especie. || Mujer, *f.* (woman). || Chica, *f.* (girl). || TECH. Hembra, *f.* || POP. Hembra, *f.*
feme [fi:m] n. JUR. Mujer, *f.*: *feme sole*, mujer soltera *or* viuda; *feme covert*, mujer casada.
feminality [femiˊnæliti] n. Feminidad, *f.*
femineity [ˊfeminiti] n. Feminidad, *f.*
feminine [ˊfeminin] adj. Femenino, na: *feminine fashion*, moda femenina. || Afeminado, da (effeminate). || GRAMM. Femenino, na.
— N. GRAMM. Femenino, *m.*
femininity [,femiˊniniti] n. Feminidad, *f.* (womanliness). || Mujeres, *f.* (womankind).
femininism [ˊfeminizəm] n. Feminismo, *m.*
feminist [ˊfeminist] adj./n. Feminista.
feminization [,feminaiˊzeiʃən] n. Afeminación, *f.*
feminize [ˊfeminaiz] v. tr. Afeminar.
— V. intr. Afeminarse.
femme fatale [ˊfæmfæˊtɑ:l] n. Vampiresa, *f.*
femoral [ˊfemərəl] adj. Femoral.
femur [ˊfi:mə*] n. ANAT. Fémur, *m.*
— OBSERV. El plural de la palabra inglesa es *femurs* o *femora*.
fen [fen] n. Pantano, *m.*
fence [fens] n. Cerca, *f.*, cercado, *m.*, valla, *f.*, vallado, *m.*: *a fence around a garden*, una valla alrededor de un jardín. || Empalizada, *f.* (wooden fence). || SP. Valla, *f.* (in show jumping). | Esgrima, *f.* (fencing). || Encubridor, ra [de ojetos robados] (receiver). || Sitio (*m.*) donde se ocultan objetos robados (receiving place). || Guarda, *f.* (of a lock). || TECH. Guía, *f.* (of saw, plane). || FIG. Barrera, *f.* (barrier). || — FIG. *To come down on the right side of the fence*, ponerse del lado del que gana. | *To sit on the fence*, nadar entre dos aguas (not to commit o.s.), ver los toros desde la barrera (to wait).
fence [fens] v. intr. SP. Practicar la esgrima: *he fences for a hobby*, practica la esgrima como pasatiempo. | Saltar (to jump). | Luchar: *in the final France will fence against Sweden*, en la final Francia luchará contra Suecia. || FIG. Contestar con evasivas (to answer evasively). || Traficar con objetos robados.
— V. tr. Cercar, vallar: *his land is fenced with barbed wire*, su terreno está cercado con alambre de púas. || Encerrar (animals). || FIG. Proteger. || — *To fence in*, cercar (land), encerrar (animals), arrinconar, acorralar (to corner), limitar (to limit). || *To fence off*, separar con una cerca (to separate two parts), aislar (to isolate), interceptar (road, street, etc.). | *To fence out*, excluir.
fenceless [—lis] adj. Sin cercar, sin valla. || FIG. Indefenso, sa.
fencer [ˊfensə*] n. SP. Esgrimidor, ra (in fencing). | Caballo (*m.*) de saltos (in steeplechasing).
fence season [ˊfenssi:zn] n. Tiempo (*m.*) de veda (in hunting).
fencing [ˊfensiŋ] n. SP. Esgrima, *f.* || Vallado, *m.*, cercado, *m.* (fences). || Material (*m.*) para construir cercas o vallas (material). || Tráfico (*m.*) con objetos robados. || — *Fencing bout*, encuentro (*m.*) de esgrima. || *Fencing foil*, florete, *m.* || *Fencing master*, maestro (*m.*) de armas *or* de esgrima.
fend [fend] v. tr. Defender. || *To fend off*, desviar (a blow), repeler, rechazar (an attack).
— V. intr. *To fend for*, mantener: *three children to fend for*, tres hijos que mantener. || *To fend for o.s.*, arreglárselas, valerse por sí mismo.
fender [ˊfendə*] n. Pantalla, *f.* (of fire). || MAR. Defensa, *f.* (on a boat). || Quitapiedras, *m. inv.*, salvavidas, *m. inv.* (of locomotive). || U. S. Parachoques, *m. inv.* (bumper). | Guardabarros, *m. inv.* (mudguard).
fenestrate [fiˊnestreit] adj. Fenestrado, da.
fenestration [,fenisˊtreiʃən] n. ARCH. Ventanaje, *m.* || MED. Fenestración, *f.*
fen fire [ˊfenˊfaiə*] n. Fuego (*m.*) fatuo.
Fenian [ˊfi:njən] n. HIST. Feniano, *m.*
fenianism [—izəm] n. HIST. Fenianismo, *m.*
fennec [ˊfenik] n. Zorro (*m.*) del Sáhara.
fennel [ˊfenl] n. BOT. Hinojo, *m.*
feoff [fef] n. Feudo, *m.*
feoff [fef] v. tr. Enfeudar.
feoffee [feˊfi:] n. Feudatario, ria.
feoffer [fefə*] n. Persona (*f.*) que enfeuda.
feoffment [ˊfefmənt] n. Feudo, *m.*, enfeudación, *f.*
feoffor [feˊfɔ:*] n. Persona (*f.*) que enfeuda.
feracious [fəˊreiʃəs] adj. Feraz, fértil.
feral [ˊfiərəl] adj. Salvaje (wild). || Feroz, feral (fierce). || Fúnebre (gloomy).
Ferdinand [ˊfə:dinənd] pr. n. Fernando, *m.*
feretory [ˊferitəri] n. REL. Relicario, *m.*

feria [ˈfiəriə] n. REL. Feria, *f.*

— OBSERV. El plural de la palabra inglesa es *feriae.*

ferial [ˈfiəriəl] adj. REL. Ferial.
ferine [ˈfiərain] adj. Salvaje, ferino, na.
fermata [ˈfəːmɑːtə] n. MUS. Calderón, *m.*
ferment [ˈfəːment] n. Fermento, *m.* (fermenting agent). || Fermentación, *f.* (fermentation). || FIG. Agitación, *f.* (commotion).
ferment [ˈfəːment] v. tr. Fermentar, hacer fermentar (to cause fermentation). || FIG. Agitar (to stir up).
— V. intr. Fermentar (to undergo fermentation). || FIG. Fermentar: *social discontent was fermenting,* el descontento social estaba fermentando.
fermentable [—əbl] adj. Fermentable.
fermentation [ˌfəːmen teiʃən] n. Fermentación, *f.* || FIG. Agitación, *f.*
fermium [ˈfɛəmjəm] n. CHEM. Fermio, *m.*
fern [fəːn] n. BOT. Helecho, *m.*
fernery [—əri] n. BOT. Helechal, *m.*
ferny [*—i] adj. Cubierto de helechos.
ferocious [fəˈrəuʃəs] adj. Feroz, fiero, ra (animal): *a ferocious lion,* un león fiero. || Feroz (person, look). || FIG. Violento, ta: *a ferocious attack,* un ataque violento.
ferociousness [—nis] n. Ferocidad, *f.*, crueldad, *f.*
ferocity [fəˈrɔsiti] n. Ferocidad, *f.*
ferrate [ˈfereit] n. CHEM. Ferrato, *m.*
ferreous [ˈferiəs] adj. CHEM. Ferroso, sa.
ferret [ˈferit] n. Hurón. *m.* (animal).
ferret [ˈferit] v. tr. Cazar con hurones. || *To ferret out,* conseguir descubrir (a secret), conseguir encontrar (a person).
— V. intr. Huronear, cazar con hurones. || FIG. Registrar, hurgar: *he ferreted (about) in the drawer for the letter,* registró el cajón para encontrar la carta. | Huronear (to pry).
ferreter [—ə*] n. Huronero, *m.*
ferric [ˈferik] adj. Férrico, ca.
ferricyanide [feriˈsaiənaid] n. CHEM. Ferricianuro, *m.*
ferriferous [feˈrifərəs] adj. Ferrífero, ra.
Ferris wheel [ˈferiswiːl] n. Noria, *f.* (in amusement parks).
ferrite [ˈferait] n. CHEM. Ferrito, *m.* (salt). || MIN. Ferrita, *f.* (ore).
ferroconcrete [ˈferəuˈkɔŋkriːt] n. Hormigón (*m.*) armado.
ferrocyanide [ferəuˈsaiənaid] n. CHEM. Ferrocianuro, *m.*
ferromagnetic [ˈferəumægˈnetik] adj. Ferromagnético, ca.
ferromagnetism [ˈferəuˈmægnitizəm] n. Ferromagnetismo, *m.*
ferromanganese [ˈferəuˈmæŋgəˈniːz] n. Ferromanganeso, *m.*
ferronickel [ˈferəuˈnikl] n. Ferroníquel, *m.*
ferroprusiate [ˈferəuˈprʌʃiit] n. Ferroprusiato, *m.*
ferrous [ˈferəs] adj. Ferroso, sa.
ferruginous [feˈruːdʒinəs] adj. Ferruginoso, sa (containing iron). || Aherrumbrado, da (rust-coloured).
ferrule [ˈferuːl] n. Contera, *f.*, regatón, *m.* (tip of umbrella, stick, etc.). || Abrazadera, *f.*, virola, *f.* (metal ring on tool, pole, etc.).
ferry [ˈferi] n. Transbordador, *m.* (boat). || Embarcadero, *m.* (place).
ferry [ˈferi] v. tr. Transportar (to transport). || Cruzar (a river, etc.). || Entregar [avión, coche, barco] conduciéndolo de la fábrica al comprador (to deliver). || Transportar por avión (to transport by air). || *To ferry across,* transportar *or* llevar por barco.
ferryboat [—bəut] n. Transbordador, *m.*
ferry bridge [—bridʒ] n. Puente (*m.*) transbordador.
ferrying [—iŋ] n. Transbordo, *m.* || Transporte (*m.*) en barco.
ferryman [—mən] n. Barquero, *m.*

— OBSERV. El plural de *ferryman* es *ferrymen.*

fertile [ˈfəːtail] adj. Fértil, feraz, (soil). || BIOL. Fecundo, da. || FIG. Abonado, da: *fertile ground for communism,* campo abonado para el comunismo. | Fecundo, da; fértil: *fertile imagination,* imaginación fecunda.
fertility [fəːˈtiliti] n. Fertilidad, *f.*, feracidad, *f.* (of soil). || BIOL. Fecundidad, *f.*
fertilizable [ˈfəːtilaizəbl] adj. Fertilizable.
fertilization [ˌfəːtilaiˈzeiʃən] n. Fertilización, *f.* (of soil). || BIOL. Fecundación, *f.*
fertilize [ˈfəːtilaiz] v. tr. Abonar, fertilizar (soil). || BIOL. Fecundar.
fertilizer [—ə*] n. Abono, *m.*, fertilizante, *m.*: *nitrate fertilizers,* abonos nitrogenados.
fertilizing [—iŋ] n. Fertilización, *f.*
— Adj. Fertilizante.
ferula [ˈferjulə] n. BOT. Férula, *f.* || Férula, *f.*, palmeta, *f.* (ferule). || (Ant.) Cetro, *m.*
ferule [ˈferuːl] n. Férula, *f.*, palmeta, *f.* (kind of cane).
ferule [ˈferuːl] v. tr. Castigar con la palmeta *or* con la férula.
fervency [ˈfəːvənsi] n. Fervor, *m.*
fervent [ˈfəːvənt] adj. Ferviente, fervoroso, sa; ardiente.
fervid [ˈfəːvid] adj. Ferviente, fervoroso, sa.
fervour (U. S. **fervor**) [ˈfəːvə*] n. Fervor, *m.*, ardor, *m.*: *he spoke with fervour of his leader,* habló con fervor de su jefe. || Fervor, *m.*: *the fervour of his faith,* el fervor de su fe. || Calor (*m.*) intenso (heat).
fescue [ˈfeskjuː] n. Puntero, *m.* (teacher's pointer).
fess or **fesse** [fes] n. HERALD. Faja, *f.*
festal [ˈfestl] adj. Festivo, va (day). || De fiesta (garments, etc.).
fester [ˈfestə*] n. Pústula, *f.*
fester [ˈfestə*] v. intr. MED. Supurar, enconarse (to produce pus). || Pudrirse (to putrefy). || FIG. Enconarse (to become bitter).
— V. tr. FIG. Alimentar, nutrir (hatred). | Envenenar, emponzoñar (to embitter). || MED. Enconar.
festival [ˈfestəvəl] n. Fiesta, *f.* (celebration): *Church festivals,* fiestas religiosas. || Festival, *m.*: *song festival,* festival de la canción.
— Adj. De fiesta. || De festival.
festive [ˈfestiv] adj. Festivo, va; alegre (gay): *to be in a festive mood,* estar de un humor festivo. || De fiestas: *festive season,* temporada de fiestas.
festivity [fesˈtiviti] n. Festividad, *f.*, fiesta, *f.* (celebration). || Regocijo, *m.* (gaiety).
festoon [fesˈtuːn] n. Festón, *m.* (in sewing). || Guirnalda, *f.* (garland). || ARCH. Festón, *m.*
festoon [festuːn] v. tr. Festonear.
festooned [Feˈstuːnd] adj. Festoneado, da.
festoonry [—ri] n. Decoración (*f.*) con guirnaldas *or* festones. || Festoneado, *m.* (in sewing).
fetal [ˈfiːtl] adj. BIOL. Fetal.
fetation [fiːˈteiʃən] n. BIOL. Gestación, *f.*, desarrollo (*m.*) del feto.
fetch [fetʃ] n. Estratagema, *f.* (trick). || Aparición, *f.* (of a living person).
fetch [fetʃ] v. tr. Buscar: *go and fetch the doctor,* ve a buscar al médico. || Traer (to bring). || Ir a buscar, ir por: *fetch water from the river,* ve a buscar agua al río. || Alcanzar (to reach): *to fetch a very high price,* alcanzar un precio muy elevado. || Asestar, pegar (a blow). || Hacer brotar: *a blow which fetched blood,* un golpe que hizo brotar la sangre. || Atraer: *he was fetched by the idea of the voyage,* le atraía la idea del viaje. || Dar: *to fetch a sigh,* dar un suspiro. || — *Fetch it here!,* ¡tráelo! || *How much did it fetch?,* ¿por cuánto se vendió? || *To fetch one's breath,* tomar aliento. || *To fetch tears to one's eyes,* hacerle subir a uno las lágrimas a los ojos. || *You fetched me all this way for nothing,* me has hecho venir desde tan lejos *or* me fuiste a buscar tan lejos para nada.
— V. intr. MAR. Navegar. || — *Fetch and carry!,* ¡busca! (to a dog). || *To fetch and carry for,* hacer los recados de (to do minor tasks).
— ***To fetch about,*** dar bordadas (a sailing boat). || ***To fetch away,*** llevarse. | MAR. Desamarrarse. || ***To fetch back,*** traer: *fetch some wine back with you,* trae vino cuando vuelvas. | Decir *or* hacer que vuelva (a person). || ***To fetch down,*** bajar: *fetch me down the dictionary,* bájame el diccionario. | Derribar (to shoot down game). || ***To fetch in,*** traer para dentro. | Hacer entrar (a person). | Recoger (washing). || ***To fetch out,*** sacar (sth.). | Quitar (a stain). | Hacer salir (s.o.). || ***To fetch through,*** alcanzar el puerto (a boat). | Superar las dificultades (to overcome difficulties). || ***To fetch up,*** subir: *fetch me up a towel,* súbeme una toalla. | Vomitar (to vomit). | Ir a parar (*in,* a) [to end up]. | MAR. Llegar (to arrive). | Pararse (to stop). | U. S. Criar, educar (children).
fetching [—iŋ] adj. Atractivo, va.
fête (U. S. **fete**) [feit] n. Fiesta, *f.* (festival). || Santo, *m.* (saint's day).
fête [feit] v. tr. Festejar.
feticide [ˈfiːtəsaid] n. Feticidio, *m.*
fetid [ˈfetid] adj. Fétido, da; hediondo, da.
fetidity [—iti] or **fetidness** [—nis] n. Fetidez, *f.*, hediondez, *f.*
fetish [ˈfiːtiʃ] n. Fetiche, *m.* (idol). || FIG. Culto, *m.*: *to make a fetish of the past,* tener un culto por el pasado. | Obsesión, *f.*
fetishism [—izəm] n. Fetichismo, *m.*
fetishist [—ist] n. Fetichista, *m. & f.*
fetishistic [—istik] adj. Fetichista.
fetlock [ˈfetlɔk] n. Espolón, *m.* (projection). || Cerneja, *f.* (tuft of hair). || *Fetlock joint,* menudillo, *m.* (of horse).
fetor [ˈfiːtə*] n. Hedor, *m.*, hediondez, *f.*
fetter [ˈfetə*] n. Traba, *f.* (of animal). || — Pl. Grilletes, *m.*, grillos, *m.* (of prisoners, slaves, etc.). || FIG. Trabas, *f.*: *the fetters placed on world trade,* las trabas puestas al comercio internacional. || *To be in fetters,* estar encadenado.
fetter [ˈfetə*] v. tr. Encadenar, poner grillos a, engrillar (people). || Trabar (animals). || FIG. Poner trabas a (to hinder).
fetterlock [—lɔk] n. See FETLOCK.
fettle [ˈfetl] n. Condición, *f.*, estado, *m.*, forma, *f.* (persons, horses, etc.). || Revestimiento (*m.*) del horno de pudelación. || *In fine fettle,* en buenas condiciones (fit), de buen humor (in a good mood).
fettle [ˈfetl] v. tr. Arreglar (to put in order). || Limpiar (to clean). || Desbarbar (moulded ware). || Revestir (a furnace).
fetus [ˈfiːtəs] n. Feto, *m.*

— OBSERV El plural de *fetus* es *fetuses.*

feud [fju:d] n. HIST. Feudo, *m.* (estate): *land in feud*, tierra en feudo. || Enemistad (*f.*) hereditaria, odio (*m.*) heredirario (enmity). || — *At feud with*, peleado a muerte con. || *Family feuds*, disensiones (*f.*) familiares (inveterate strife between families).
feud [fju:d] v. intr. Pelear, luchar.
feudal [ˈfju:dl] adj. Feudal: *feudal lord*, señor feudal.
feudalism [ˈfju:dəlizəm] n. Feudalismo, *m.*
feudality [fju:ˈdæliti] n. Feudalidad, *f.* (state). || Feudo, *m.* (feud).
feudalization [ˌfju:dəlaiˈzeiʃən] n. Enfeudación, *f.*
feudalize [ˈfju:dəlaiz] v. tr. Enfeudar.
feudatory [ˈfju:dətəri] adj./n. Feudatario, ria.
feudist [ˈfju:dist] n. Camorrista, *m.* & *f.* (participant in a quarrel).
fever [ˈfi:və*] n. MED. Fiebre, *f.*, calentura, *f.*: *he has a high fever* o *he is running a high fever*, tiene mucha fiebre. | Fiebre, *f.*: *typhoid, algid, yellow, intermittent fever*, fiebre tifoidea, álgida, amarilla, intermitente. || FIG. Fiebre, *f.*: *election fever*, fiebre electoral. | Agitación, *f.* || — *Milk fever*, fiebre láctea. || *Scarlet fever*, escarlatina, *f.* || *To be in a fever*, tener fiebre.
fever [ˈfi:və*] v. tr. MED. Dar fiebre a. || FIG. Apasionar, inflamar, enardecer.
fevered [—d] adj. Febril.
feverfew [ˈfi:vəˌfju:] n. BOT. Matricaria, *f.*
feverish [ˈfi:vəriʃ] adj. Febril, calenturiento, ta. || FIG. Febril.
feverishness [—nis] n. Febrilidad, *f.*
feverous [ˈfi:vərəs] adj. Febril.
few [fju:] adj. Poco, ca (not many): *few people came*, vino poca gente; *there are few books on the subject*, hay pocos libros sobre este tema. || Raro, ra; poco numeroso, sa (rare): *such occasions are few*, tales ocasiones son raras. || — *A few*, algunos, algunas, unos [cuantos], unas [cuantas], unos pocos, unas pocas: *give me a few cigarettes*, dame algunos cigarrillos. || *A few hundred pounds*, unos centenares de libras. || *A good few* o *some few* o *quite a few*, muchos, muchas, bastantes: *he has quite a few friends*, tiene bastantes amigos. || *During the last few days*, estos últimos días. || *Every few days*, cada dos o tres días. || *Few and far between*, raro, ra; escaso, sa; contadísimo, ma. || *In the next few days*, dentro de unos días. || *Not a few*, no pocos, no pocas, muchos, muchas, bastantes. || *One of the few people who*, uno de los pocos que. || *The buses run every few minutes*, los autobuses pasan cada dos o tres minutos. || *With few exceptions*, con pocas excepciones.
— N. Minoría, *f.*: *laws made for the few*, leyes hechas para una minoría. || Pocos, cas: *few of them can read and write*, pocos saben leer y escribir; *there are very few of us who can remember him*, somos muy pocos en acordarnos de él. || — *A few*, algunos, algunas, unos cuantos, unas cuantas, unos pocos, unas pocas: *only a few understood him*, sólo le entendieron algunos. || *A few of*, algunos de: *a few of us remained*, algunos de nosotros nos quedamos. || *A good few* o *some few* o *quite a few*, un buen número, muchos, muchas, bastantes: *a good few of his friends*, muchos de sus amigos. || *A privileged few*, una minoría privilegiada. || *Many are called but few are chosen*, muchos son los llamados, pocos los escogidos. || *Not a few*, muchos, muchas. || *The happy few*, los privilegiados.
fewer [—ə*] comp. adj. Menos: *there were fewer people than I expected*, había menos gente de lo que esperaba; *he has fewer friends than I*, tiene menos amigos que yo; *no fewer than*, no menos de. || — *The fewer the better*, cuantos menos mejor. || *To become fewer*, ser cada vez menos numeroso.
fewest [—ist] superl. adj. Menos: *I have fewer books than you but she has the fewest*, yo tengo menos libros que tú, pero ella es la que menos tiene.
fewness [—nis] n. Escasez, *f.*, corto número, *m.*
fey [fei] adj. Medio loco, ca (slightly mad). || Destinado a morir (destined to die). || Vidente (clairvoyant).
fez [fez] n. Fez, *m.*, gorro (felt cap).
— OBSERV. El plural de la palabra inglesa es *fezzes*.
fiancé [fiˈɑ̃nsei] n. Novio, *m.*, prometido, *m.*
fiancée [fiˈɑ̃nsei] n. Novia, *f.*, prometida, *f.*
fiasco [fiˈæskəu] n. Fiasco, *m.*, fracaso, *m.*
— OBSERV. El plural de la palabra inglesa es *fiascoes* o *fiascos*.
fiat [ˈfaiæt] n. Fiat, *m.*, autorización, *f.*
— Adj. Fiduciario, ria (money).
fiat [ˈfaiæt] v. tr. Autorizar.
fib [fib] n. FAM. Mentirijilla, *f.*, bola, *f.* (lie): *to tell a fib*, decir una mentirijilla.
fib [fib] v. intr. Decir una mentirijilla *or* mentirijillas, mentir.
fibber [—ə*] n. FAM. Mentirosillo, lla; mentiroso, sa.
fibre (U. S. **fiber**) [ˈfaibə*] n. Fibra, *f.*: *vegetable fibre*, fibra vegetal; *man-made* o *artificial fibres*, fibras artificiales. || FIG. Carácter, *m.* || — *Staple fibre*, fibrana, *f.* || *Textile fibre*, fibra textil.
fibreboard (U. S. **fiberboard**) [—bɔ:d] n. Panel (*m.*) de fibras de madera.
fibreglass (U. S. **fiberglass**) [—glɑ:s] n. Fibra (*f.*) de vidrio.
fibril [ˈfaibril] or **fibrilla** [—ə] n. Fibrilla, *f.*
— OBSERV. El plural de *fibrilla* es *fibrillae*.
fibrillation [faibriˈleiʃən] n. MED. Fibrilación, *f.*
fibrin [ˈfaibrin] n. Fibrina, *f.*
fibrinogen [faiˈbrinədʒin] n. Fibrinógeno, *m.*
fibrocement [ˈfaibrəˌsiˈment] n. Fibrocemento, *m.*
fibroid [ˈfaibrɔid] adj. Fibroso, sa.
— N. MED. Fibroma, *m.*
fibroma [faiˈbrəumə] n. MED. Fibroma, *m.*
— OBSERV. El plural de la palabra inglesa es *fibromata* o *fibromas*.
fibrous [ˈfaibrəs] adj. Fibroso, sa.
fibster [ˈfibstə*] n. FAM. Mentirosillo, lla; mentiroso, sa.
fibula [ˈfibjulə] n. ANAT. Peroné, *m.* (bone). || Fíbula, *f.* (brooch).
— OBSERV. El plural de la palabra inglesa es *fibulae* o *fibulas*.
fibular [—ə*] adj. ANAT. Del peroné, peroneo, a; fibular.
fichu [ˈfi:ʃu:] n. Pañuelo, *m.* (scarf).
fickle [ˈfikl] adj. Inconstante, veleidoso, sa; voluble.
fickleness [—nis] n. Inconstancia, *f.*, veleidad, *f.*, volubilidad, *f.*
fictile [ˈfiktil] adj. Figulino, na.
fiction [ˈfikʃən] n. Ficción, *f.* || Novela, *f.*, novelística, *f.*, género (*m.*) novelístico (literature). || — *Fact and fiction*, la realidad y la ficción. || JUR. *Legal fiction*, ficción de derecho *or* legal. || *That's all fiction*, aquello es pura imaginación.
fictional [ˈfikʃənl] adj. Novelesco, ca (literature). || Ficticio, cia (not restricted to fact).
fictionalize [ˈfikʃnəlaiz] v. tr. Novelar, novelizar.
fictionist [ˈfikʃənist] n. Novelista, *m.* & *f.*
fictionize [ˈfikʃənaiz] v. tr. Novelar, novelizar.
fictitious [fikˈtiʃəs] adj. Ficticio, cia: *fictitious name*, nombre ficticio. || Imaginario, ria (imaginary). || Fingido, da (feigned): *fictitious emotion*, emoción fingida.
fictitiousness [fikˈtiʃəsnis] n. Lo ficticio, carácter (*m.*) ficticio.
fictive [ˈfiktiv] adj. Ficticio, cia. || Imaginario, ria (imaginary). || Fingido, da (feigned).
fid [fid] n. MAR. Pasador, *m.* (to separate rope strands). | Cuña (*f.*) del mastelero (mast support). || Cuña, *f.* (wedge).
fiddle [ˈfidl] n. MUS. Violín, *m.* (instrument). | Violinista, *m.* (musician). || MAR. Tabla (*f.*) de mal tiempo. || FAM. Trampa, *f.*, superchería, *f.* (trick). || — FIG. FAM. *Face as long as a fiddle*, cara larga. | *Fit as a fiddle*, más sano que una manzana, en plena forma. || *Tax fiddle*, evasión (*f.*) fiscal. || FIG. *To play second fiddle*, desempeñar un papel secundario.
fiddle [ˈfidl] v. intr. FAM. Tocar el violín. || Juguetear, enredar: *stop fiddling with that pencil*, deja de juguetear con ese lápiz. || *To fiddle about*, perder el tiempo.
— V. tr. Tocar (a tune). || FAM. Camelar, embaucar: *they fiddled him into buying it*, le camelaron para que lo comprase. | Amañar (to falsify): *to fiddle the accounts*, amañar las cuentas. | Agenciarse (a job). || *To fiddle one's time away*, perder el tiempo.
fiddlededee! [ˈfidldiˈdi:] interj. ¡Pamplinas!, ¡tonterías!, ¡bobadas!
fiddle-faddle [ˈfidlˌfædl] n. Tonterías, *f. pl.*, necedades, *f. pl.*, bobadas, *f. pl.*
fiddle-faddle [ˈfidl ˌfædl] v. intr. Perder el tiempo.
fiddler [ˈfidlə*] n. Violinista, *m.* (musician). || FAM. Tramposo, *m.* (trickster).
fiddler crab [—kræb] n. Barrilete, *m.*
fiddlestick [ˈfidlstik] n. MUS. Arco (*m.*) de violín. || — Pl. FAM. Tonterías, *f.* || *Fiddlesticks!*, ¡tonterías!, ¡bobadas!, ¡pamplinas!
fiddling [ˌfidliŋ] adj. Trivial, insignificante, fútil.
fidelity [fiˈdeliti] n. Fidelidad, *f.* || RAD. *High fidelity*, alta fidelidad.
fidget [ˈfidʒit] n. Agitación (*f.*) nerviosa. || Fuguillas, *m. inv.*, persona (*f.*) que no para de moverse. || FAM. *To have the fidgets*, no poder estarse quieto.
fidget [ˈfidʒit] v. intr. Moverse: *stop fidgeting*, deja de moverte. || Impacientarse, ponerse nervioso. || — *To fidget about*, no poder estarse quieto. || *To fidget with*, juguetear *or* enredar con.
— V. tr. Poner nervioso.
fidgety [ˈfidʒiti] adj. Nervioso, sa; impaciente, febril (nervous). || Agitado, da; que no deja de moverse, que no puede estarse quieto (restless).
fiducial [fiˈdju:ʃjəl] adj. *Fiducial line*, fiducial, *f.*
fiduciary [fiˈdju:ʃjəri] adj. COMM. Fiduciario, ria.
— N. Fiduciario, *m.*
fie! [fai] interj. (Ant.) ¡Qué vergüenza!
fief [fi:f] n. HIST. Feudo, *m.* (property).
field [fi:ld] n. Campo, *m.*: *a field of maize*, un campo de maíz; *a playing field*, un campo de deportes. || Extensión, *f.* (of ice, water). || Campo, *m.* (of snow). || MIL. HERALD. PHYS. Campo, *m.*: *field of battle*, campo de batalla; *magnetic, electric, acoustic field*, campo magnético, eléctrico, acústico. || MIN. Yacimiento, *m.*: *oil field*, yacimiento petrolífero. || FIG. Campo, *m.*, sector, *m.*, esfera, *f.*: *the field of medicine*, el campo de la medicina; *field of activity*, campo de actividad. | Terreno, *m.*: *it's not my field*, ése no es mi terreno. | Campo, *m.* (background). || SP. Participantes, *m. pl.* (in a contest). | Competidores, *m. pl.* (in a race). | Jugadores, *m. pl.* (players). | Equipo, *m.* (team). | Todos los competidores salvo el favorito. || — *Field of vision*, campo visual. || MIL. *In the field*, en campaña. || *Landing field*, campo de aterrizaje. ||

MED. *Operative field*, campo operatorio. || FIG. *To have a clear field*, tener campo libre. || MIL. *To hold the field*, no ceder terreno. || FIG. *To leave the field open* o *clear*, dejar el campo libre. | *To take the field*, entrar en campaña (mil.), salir a la palestra (fig.). || *To work in the field*, trabajar en el terreno (researchers, etc.).
field [fi:ld] v. intr. SP. Parar y devolver la pelota (in cricket and baseball).
— V. tr. SP. Parar y devolver (the ball). || Presentar (a team).
field army [—'α:mi] n. MIL. Ejército (*m.*) de operaciones.
field artillery [—α:'tiləri] n. MIL. Artillería (*f.*) de campaña.
field book [—buk] n. MIL. Libreta (*f.*) de campo.
field day [—dei] n. MIL. Día (*m.*) de maniobras. || Día (*m.*) en el campo (for scientific study). || U. S. Reunión (*f.*) de atletismo. | Fiesta (*f.*) al aire libre. | Gran día, *m.* (great day): *they had a field day*, fue un gran día para ellos.
fielder [—ə*] n. SP. Jugador (*m.*) del equipo que no batea (in cricket and baseball).
field event [—i'vent] n. SP. Competición (*f.*) atlética [salto y lanzamiento].
fieldfare [—fɛə*] n. Zorzal, *m.* (bird).
field glasses [—,glα:siz] pl. n. Gemelos, *m.* [de campaña].
field gun [—gʌn] n. MIL. Cañón (*m.*) de campaña.
field hockey [—'hɔki] n. U. S. SP. Hockey (*m.*) sobre hierba.
field hospital [—'hɔspitl] n. MIL. Hospital (*m.*) de campaña, hospital (*m.*) de sangre.
field kitchen [—'kitʃin] n. MIL. Cocina (*f.*) de campaña.
field magnet [—'mægnit] n. PHYS. Electroimán (*m.*) del campo. || *Field-magnet coil*, bobina (*f.*) de inducción.
field marshal [—'mα:ʃəl] n. MIL. Mariscal (*m.*) de campo.
field mouse [—maus] n. Ratón (*m.*) campesino.

— OBSERV. El plural de *field mouse* es *field mice*.

field officer [—'ɔfisə*] n. MIL. Jefe, *m.*, oficial (*m.*) superior.
field of honour [—əv'ɔnə*] n. Campo (*m.*) del honor (for duel). || Campo (*m.*) de batalla (battlefield).
field of view [—əvvju:] n. Campo (*m.*) visual.
fieldsman [—zmən] n. SP. See FIELDER.

— OBSERV. El plural de *fieldsman* es *fieldsmen*.

field sports [—spɔ:ts] pl. n. Deportes (*m.*) al aire libre.
field winding [—,waindiŋ] n. Arrollamiento (*m.*) *or* devanado (*m.*) inductor.
fieldwork [—wə:k] n. Trabajo (*m.*) en el terreno (on the spot). || — Pl. MIL. Obras (*f.*) de campaña.
fiend [fi:nd] n. Demonio, *m.*, diablo, *m.* (devil, demon). || Desalmado, da; malvado, da (cruel person). || U. S. FAM. Fanático, ca (fanatic). || — *Dope fiend*, toxicómano, na. || *Fresh-air fiend*, enamorado del aire libre. || *To be a fiend for*, ser una fiera para.
fiendish [—iʃ] adj. Diabólico, ca; demoniaco, ca: *to take a fiendish delight in*, experimentar un placer diabólico en.
fiendishness [—iʃnis] n. Maldad, *f.*, crueldad, *f.*
fierce [fiəs] adj. Feroz, fiero, ra (animal). || Cruel, violento, ta (person). || Horroroso, sa (weather). || Intenso, sa (heat). || Fortísimo, ma: *the wind was fierce*, hacía un viento fortísimo. || Ardiente, furioso, sa (desire). || Violento, ta (envy, hatred). || Furioso, sa (attack). || Encarnizado, da (battle, struggle). || Feroz (look). || Acérrimo, ma; fanático, ca (supporter).
fierceness [—nis] n. Ferocidad, *f.*, fiereza, *f.* (of animal). || Crueldad, *f.* (of a person). || Violencia, *f.* (violence). || Ardor, *m.* (ardour). || Lo horroroso (of weather). || Intensidad, *f.* (intensity). || Encarnizamiento, *m.* (of battle).
fieriness ['faiərinis] n. Ardor, *m.* (of sun, passion). || Pasión, *f.*, acaloramiento, *m.*, apasionamiento, *m.* (of speech). || Lo picante (of food). || Fogosidad, *f.* (of a horse).
fiery ['faiəri] adj. Llameante (flaming). || Ardiente (burning). || Apasionado, da (passionate). || Fogoso, sa (temper). || Brioso, sa; fogoso, sa (horse). || Acalorado, da (speech). || Encendido, da (eyes, colour). || Rojo, ja (hair). || Fuerte, picante (taste). || Abrasador, ra (sun). || Inflamable (gas). || Con grisú (mine). || *A fiery sunset*, un ocaso arrebolado.
fiesta ['fiestə] n. Fiesta, *f.*
fife [faif] n. MUS. Pífano, *m.* (instrument).
fife [faif] v. intr. Tocar el pífano.
— V. tr. Tocar con el pífano (a tune).
fifteen ['fif'ti:n] adj. Quince: *she is fifteen years old*, tiene quince años de edad.
— N. Quince, *m.*
fifteenth [—θ] adj. Decimoquinto, ta.
— N. Decimoquinto, ta. || Quinzavo, *m.*, quinzava parte, *f.* (fraction). || Quince, *m.*, día (*m.*) quince: *we shall go on the fifteenth of March*, iremos el día quince de marzo. || Quince: *Louis XV* (*the fifteenth*), Luis XV [quince].
fifth [fifθ] adj. Quinto, ta: *the fifth door*, la quinta puerta.
— N. Quinto, ta. || Quinto, *m.*, quinta parte, *f.* (fraction). || Cinco, *m.*, día (*m.*) cinco: *today is the fifth of June*, hoy es el día cinco *or* el cinco de junio. || Quinto, ta: *Henry V* (*the fifth*), Enrique V [quinto]. || MUS. Quinta, *f.*
fifth column [—'kɔləm] n. Quinta columna, *f.*
fifth columnist [—'kɔləmnist] n. Quintacolumnista, *m.*
fifthly ['fifθli] adv. En quinto lugar.
fiftieth ['fiftiəθ] adj. Quincuagésimo, ma.
— N. Quincuagésimo, ma. || Quincuagésimo, *m.*, quincuagésima parte, *f.* (fraction).
fifty ['fifti] adj./n. Cincuenta. || — Pl. Años (*m.*) cincuenta (sixth decade of a century). || *She is in her fifties*, tiene unos cincuenta años.

— OBSERV. *Fifty-first, fifty-second*, etc. is translated by *quincuagésimo primero, quincuagésimo segundo*, etc.

fifty-fifty [—'fifti] adv. FAM. A medias: *let's go fifty-fifty*, vayamos a medias.
fiftyish [—tiʃ] adj. Cincuentón, ona.
fig [fig] n. BOT. Higo, *m.* (fruit). | Higuera, *f.* (tree). || FAM. Bledo, *m.*, comino, *m.*, higo, *m.*, pepino, *m.*: *I don't care a fig*, me importa un bledo *or* un comino, no se me da un higo. | Atavío, *m.* (dress). | Forma, *f.* (condition). || — FAM. *A fig for it!*, ¡me importa un pepino! || *Fig leaf*, hoja (*f.*) de higuera (of tree), hoja (*f.*) de parra (of statue).
fight [fait] n. Lucha, *f.*, pelea, *f.*: *street fights*, luchas callejeras; *a fight to the death*, una lucha a muerte. || Disputa, *f.* (argument). || MIL. Batalla, *f.*, combate, *m.* (battle). || SP. Combate, *m.* (in boxing). || Combatividad, *f.* (fighting spirit): *to show fight*, mostrar combatividad. || Ánimo, *m.* (courage). || FIG. Lucha, *f.*: *the fight for life*, la lucha por la vida. || — *In fair fight*, en buena lid. || *There was no fight left in him*, ya no tenía ánimo para luchar. || *To have a fight*, pelearse. || *To pick a fight with s.o.*, provocar a alguien, meterse con uno. || *To put up a good fight*, defenderse bien.
fight* [fait] v. tr. Pelearse con, pelear con, luchar con (a person). || Luchar contra, combatir: *to fight disease, vandalism*, luchar contra la enfermedad, contra el vandalismo. || Combatir (fire). || Luchar contra (in a war). || Discutir, impugnar (a point). || — *To fight a battle*, librar una batalla, librar combate. || *To fight a bull*, torear *or* lidiar un toro. || *To fight a duel*, batirse en duelo. || *To fight a war*, hacer una guerra. || *To fight a war against a country*, hacer la guerra a un país. || *To fight cocks*, echar los gallos a pelear. || *To fight one's way*, luchar por abrirse camino. || *To fight one's way out*, abrirse camino luchando. || *To fight the good fight*, combatir por una causa justa.
— V. intr. Luchar, combatir: *to fight against* o *with the enemy*, luchar *or* combatir contra el enemigo. || Pelear: *I saw two men fighting*, vi a dos hombres que estaban peleando. || SP. Boxear, combatir (in boxing), luchar, combatir (in wrestling). || FIG. Luchar. || FAM. Reñir (to quarrel). || — *To fight fair*, luchar limpiamente. || *To fight for*, luchar *or* combatir por. || *To fight like a tiger* o *a wildcat*, luchar como un gato panza arriba. || *To fight shy of*, evitar. || *To fight through difficulties*, superar *or* vencer dificultades. || *To fight to a finish*, luchar hasta el final.
— **To fight back**, rechazar (the enemy, an attack). | Contener, retener (tears, laughter). | Reprimir (emotions). | Defenderse, resistir. || **To fight down**, reprimir. || **To fight off**, luchar contra (disease, sleep). | Rechazar (an attack). || **To fight out**, aguantar (to endure). | — *To fight it out*, luchar hasta resolverlo, luchar hasta llegar a una decisión.

— OBSERV. Pret. & p. p. **fought**.

fighter [—ə*] n. MIL. Combatiente, *m.*, guerrero, *m.* (soldier). || AVIAT. Avión (*m.*) de caza, caza, *m.* || FIG. Luchador, ra; persona combativa. || SP. Púgil, *m.*
fighter bomber [—'bɔmə*] n. Cazabombardero, *m.*
fighter plane [—plein] n. AVIAT. Avión (*m.*) de caza, caza, *m.*
fighting ['faitiŋ] adj. Combatiente. || *Fighting spirit*, combatividad, *f.*
— N. Lucha, *f.*, pelea, *f.* || MIL. SP. Combate, *m.*
fighting chance [—tʃα:ns] n. Mucha posibilidad (*f.*) de tener éxito (if great efforts are made).
fighting cock [—kɔk] n. Gallo (*m.*) de pelea.
figment ['figmənt] n. Ficción, *f.*, invención, *f.* || *A figment of one's imagination*, un producto de su imaginación.
figpecker ['figpekə*] n. Papafigo, *m.*, papahigo, *m.* (bird).
figurant ['figjurənt] n. Figurante, *m.*
figurante [,figju'rɑ̃:nt] n. Figurante, *f.*
figuration [,figju'reiʃən] n. Figuración, *f.* (action). || Forma, *f.*, configuración, *f.* (shape). || Perfil, *m.*, contorno, *m.*, silueta, *f.* (outline).
figurative ['figjurətiv] adj. Figurado, da: *figurative language*, lenguaje figurado. || Figurativo, va (art). || Metafórico, ca (style).
figure ['figə*] n. Cifra, *f.*, número, *m.*, guarismo, *m.* (number). || Cifra, *f.*: *the production figures are low*, las cifras de producción son bajas. || COMM. Precio, *m.* (price). || Suma, *f.*, cantidad, *f.* (sum). || Figura, *f.*, estatua, *f.* (statue). || Figura, *f.*: *geometric figures*, figuras geométricas. || Dibujo, *m.* (sketch). || Ilustración, *f.* (illustration in book). || Figura, *f.*, personaje, *m.* (person): *important historic figure*, importante figura histórica. || Tipo, *m.*, figura, *f.*: *she has a*

lovely figure, tiene un tipo estupendo. || Línea, *f.*: *to keep one's figure*, guardar la línea. || Forma, *f.*, silueta, *f.*: *a figure loomed up out of the mist*, una silueta apareció en la niebla. || Figura, *f.* (in dancing, skating). || GRAMM. MUS. Figura, *f.* || — *A fine figure of a woman*, una mujer bien hecha *or* que tiene buen tipo. || *Central figure*, figura central (in a drama). || *Figure of speech*, tropo, *m.*, figura (*f.*) retórica (rethoric), manera (*f.*) de hablar. || SP. *Figure skating*, patinaje artístico. || *In round figures*, en números redondos. || *To be good at figures*, dársele bien los números a uno: *I'm very good at figures*, se me dan muy bien los números. || *To cut a (brilliant) figure*, hacer un buen papel. || *To have a good figure*, tener buena presencia.

figure [ˈfigə*] v. tr. Representar (to portray). || Imaginar, representarse (to picture mentally). || Estampar (materials). || MATH. Poner en cifras. || FAM. Imaginarse, suponer, figurarse (to consider): *I figure it will take twenty years*, me imagino que tardará veinte años. || — *Figured language*, lenguaje figurado. || *To figure out*, comprender (to understand), explicarse: *I can't figure out why it doesn't work*, no me explico por qué no marcha; calcular (to calculate), resolver (a problem), descifrar (writing).

— V. intr. Hacer cálculos (to calculate). || Figurar: *to figure briefly in history*, figurar brevemente en la historia; *his name figured on the guest list*, su nombre figuraba en la lista de invitados. || U. S. FAM. Ser probable. || — THEATR. *To figure as*, hacer el papel de. || *To figure on*, contar con (to count on), tener la intención de (to plan). || *To figure out at*, sumar, ascender a (to amount to).

figured bass [—d bæs] n. MUS. Bajo (*m.*) cifrado.

figurehead [—hed] n. MAR. Mascarón (*m.*) de proa. || FIG. Testaferro, *m.*

figurine [ˈfigjuri:n] n. Figurilla, *f.*, estatuilla, *f.*

filagree [ˈfiləgri:] n./v.tr. See FILIGREE.

filament [ˈfiləmənt] n. Filamento, *m.*

filament lamp [—læmp] n. Lámpara (*f.*) incandescente.

filamentous [ˌfiləˈmentəs] adj. Filamentoso, sa.

filar [ˈfailə] adj. *Filar microscope*, microscopio (*m.*) de ocular reticulado.

filaria [fiˈlɛərjə] n. MED. Filaria, *f.*

— OBSERV. El plural de la palabra inglesa *filaria* es *filariae*.

filariasis [filəˈraiəsis] or **filariosis** [filəˈraiəsis] n. MED. Filariosis, *f.*, filariasis, *f.*

filature [ˈfilətʃə*] n. Hilandería, *f.*, fábrica (*f.*) de hilados (place). || Devanadera, *f.* (reel). || Devanado, *m.* (reeling).

filbert [ˈfilbə:t] n. Avellana, *f.* (nut). || Avellano, *m.* (bush).

filch [filtʃ] v. tr. Hurtar, robar.

filcher [—ə*] n. Ratero, ra.

filchering [—riŋ] n. Robo, *m.*, hurto, *m.*

file [fail] n. Lima, *f.* (tool): *dead-smooth file*, lima sorda. || Ficha, *f.*: *personal file*, ficha personal. || Carpeta, *f.* (folder). || Fichero, *m.* (container for cards). || Archivador, *m.*, archivo, *m.* (container for documents). || Archivo, *m.* (archive): *police files*, archivos de la policía. || Expediente, *m.* (dossier). || Fila, *f.* (line). || MIL. Fila, *f.*: *in file*, en fila. || — *Card-index file*, fichero, *m.* || *Indian file*, fila india. || *In single file*, en fila de a uno. || *To be on file*, estar archivado. || *To close the file on a case*, dar carpetazo a un asunto, dar por terminado un asunto. || *To take one's place in the file*, ponerse en cola.

file [fail] v. tr. Limar: *to file one's nails*, limarse las uñas. || Archivar, clasificar (a card, a document). || JUR. Presentar (a petition): *to file a petition for divorce*, presentar una demanda de divorcio.

— V. intr. Marchar en fila. || — U. S. *To file for a pension*, hacer una petición de *or* solicitar una pensión. || *To file in, out*, entrar, salir en fila *or* uno tras otro. || *To file past*, desfilar ante.

file card [—kɑ:d] n. Ficha, *f.*

filer [ˈfailə*] n. TECH. Limador, *m.* || Archivero, ra (filing clerk).

filet [fiˈlei] n. Encaje, *m.* (lace). || CULIN. Filete, *m.*

filial [ˈfiljəl] adj. Filial.

filiation [ˌfiliˈeiʃən] n. JUR. Filiación, *f.* (father-son relationship). || Filiación, *f.*: *to determine the filiation of a language*, determinar la filiación de una lengua.

filibuster [ˈfilibʌstə*] n. Filibustero, *m.* (pirate). || U. S. Obstruccionista, *m.* (person who delays proceedings). | Obstruccionismo, *m.* (use of delaying tactics).

filibuster [ˈfilibʌstə*] v. intr. Ser un filibustero. || U. S. Practicar el obstruccionismo.

— V. tr. U. S. Obstruir (the passage of a bill, etc.).

filibusterer [—rə*] n. U. S. Obstruccionista, *m.*

filibustering [—riŋ] n. Filibusterismo, *m.* || U. S. Obstruccionismo, *m.*

filiform [ˈfilifɔ:m] adj. Filiforme.

filigree [ˈfiligri:] n. Filigrana, *f.*

filigree [ˈfiligri:] v. tr. Afiligranar.

filing [ˈfailiŋ] n. Limadura, *f.* (action of filing metals, etc.). || Colocación (*f.*) en un archivo *or* en un fichero. || Clasificación, *f.*: *the filing of papers*, la clasificación de papeles. || — Pl. Limaduras, *f.*: *iron filings*, limaduras de hierro.

filing cabinet [—ˈkæbinit] n. Archivo, *m.*, fichero, *m.*

filing card [—kɑ:d] n. Ficha, *f.*

filing clerk [klɑ:k] n. Archivero, ra; archivista, *m.* & *f.*

Filipino [filiˈpi:nəu] adj./n. Filipino, na.

fill [fil] n. Hartura, *f.*, hartazgo, *m.* || Pipa, *f.* (of tobacco). || Terraplén, *m.* (embankment). || — *To eat one's fill*, hartarse de comer (very much), comer lo suficiente *or* bien (just enough). || *To have had one's fill of sth.*, estar harto de algo. || *To take a fill of tobacco*, cargar la pipa.

fill [fil] v. tr. Llenar: *he filled my glass*, me llenó el vaso; *smoke filled the room*, el humo llenaba el cuarto. || Ocupar (space, post). || Cubrir (a vacancy). || Ocupar, llenar (time). || Llenar (food). || Empastar (a tooth). || Cargar (to load). || Tapar, rellenar, llenar (a crack, a hole). || CULIN. Rellenar. || Chapar (with gold). || Hinchar: *the wind filled the sails*, el viento hinchaba las velas. || Inflar (a tyre). || Cumplir con, satisfacer (requirements). || FIG. Llenar: *to fill s.o. with rage, with confusion*, llenar a uno de ira, de confusión. || U. S. Despachar (an order). | Extender, hacer (prescription). || — *Fill her up!*, ¡llénelo! (petrol tank). || *The thoughts which filled his mind*, las ideas que le llenaban la cabeza. || *To be filled to capacity*, estar completamente lleno. || *To fill one's part well*, desempeñar bien su papel.

— V. intr. Llenarse.

— ***To fill in***, terraplenar, rellenar (a hole in the ground). | Rellenar, llenar (a form). | Poner (the date in a form). | Extender (a cheque). | Completar (an outline). | — *To fill in for somebody*, reemplazar a alguien. | *To fill s.o. in*, poner a alguien al corriente. || ***To fill out***, rellenar (a form, essay, speech). | Hinchar (a balloon). | Hincharse (sails in the wind). | Llenarse (cheeks). | Engordar (to grow fatter). || ***To fill up***, llenar: *fill my glass up, please*, lléname el vaso por favor. | Llenarse: *the tank filled up with water*, el depósito se llenó de agua. | Rellenar, llenar (a form). | Hartar, llenar: *the meal filled me up*, la comida me llenó. | — *To fill up with fuel*, repostar a tope (a plane, a boat).

filler [—ə*] n. Relleno, *m.* (to increase weight or bulk). || Tripa, *f.* (of a cigar). || Masilla, *f.* (to fill in cracks). || Artículo, *m.* [de relleno] (in a newspaper, etc.).

fillet [ˈfilit] n. CULIN. Filete, *m.* (of meat, fish). || Cinta, *f.* (band). || || ARCH. PRINT. Filete, *m.*

fillet [ˈfilit] v. tr. Recoger con una cinta (hair). || CULIN. Cortar en filetes. || Filetear (to adorn with a fillet).

filling [ˌfiliŋ] n. Relleno, *m.* || Terraplenado, *m.* (of a ditch). || Empaste, *m.* (of a tooth). || Trama, *f.* (of a material).

— Adj. Que llena mucho (food).

filling station [—ˈsteiʃən] n. Estación (*f.*) de servicio.

fillip [ˈfilip] n. Capirotazo, *m.* (flick of the finger). || Papirotazo, *m.* (quick blow). || FIG. Estímulo, *m.* (stimulus).

fillip [ˈfilip] v. tr. Dar un capirotazo a (to flick). || Dar un papirotazo a (to strike). || FIG. Estimular (to stimulate).

fillister [ˈfilistə*] n. Guillame, *m.* (plane).

fill-up [ˈfilʌp] n. Relleno, *m.*

filly [ˈfili] n. Potra, *f.* (young mare). || FIG. Muchacha, *f.* (girl).

film [film] n. Película, *f.*, capa, *f.* (thin layer). || PHOT. Película, *f.* || CINEM. Película, *f.*, filme, *m.*: *to shoot a film*, rodar una película; *to make a film*, hacer una película. || Cine, *m.*, cinema, *m.*: *film fan*, aficionado al cine; *film producer*, productor de cine. || Nube, *f.* (in the eye). || FIG. Velo, *m.* (of smoke, mist, etc.). || — *Film industry*, industria cinematográfica. || *Film library*, cinemateca, *f.*, filmoteca, *f.* || PHOT. *Roll of film*, carrete, *m.*, rollo, *m.* || CINEM. *Silent film*, película muda.

film [film] v. tr. CINEM. Rodar, filmar (a scene, a story). | Filmar (people, events): *to film a sunset*, filmar una puesta de sol. | Hacer una versión cinematográfica de (a book). || Cubrir con una película *or* capa (to coat with a layer).

— V. intr. Rodar. || *To film over*, cubrirse con una película *or* capa.

filmgoer [—gəuə*] n. Aficionado (*m.*) al cine.

filminess [—inis] n. Diafanidad, *f.*, transparencia, *f.* (transparency).

filming [—iŋ] n. Filmación, *f.*, rodaje, *m.*

film star [—stɑ:*] n. Astro (*m.*) de cine (man). || Estrella (*f.*) de cine (woman).

filmstrip [—strip] n. Película, *f.* [para ilustrar una conferencia *or* una lección].

film studio [—ˈstju:diəu] n. Estudio, *m.* [de cine].

filmy [ˈfilmi] adj. Diáfano, na; transparente (transparent). || Nublado, da (misty).

filose [ˈfailəus] adj. Filiforme.

filter [ˈfiltə*] n. Filtro, *m.*: *air filter*, filtro de aire; *oil, petrol filter*, filtro de aceite, de gasolina. || PHYS. PHOT. Filtro, *m.* || *Filter paper*, papel (*m.*) de filtro.

filter [ˈfiltə*] v. tr. Filtrar.

— V. intr. Filtrarse: *to filter through a paper*, filtrarse a través de *or* por un papel. || — FIG. *To filter into*, infiltrarse en. || *To filter through* o *out*, llegar a saberse, filtrarse.

filtering [—riŋ] n. Filtración, *f.*

— Adj. Filtrante.

filter tip [ˈfiltətip] n. Boquilla (*f.*) con filtro (tip). || Cigarrillo (*m.*) con filtro (cigarette).

filter-tipped [ˈfiltətipt] adj. Con filtro, emboquillado, da.

filth [filθ] n. Suciedad, *f.*, porquería, *f.*, inmundicia, *f.* (dirt). || FIG. Obscenidades, *f. pl.*, porquerías, *f. pl.* (bad language, thoughts).

filthiness [—inis] n. Suciedad, *f.* (dirtiness). || FIG. Obscenidad, *f.*

filthy [—i] adj. Asqueroso, sa; mugriento, ta; inmundo, da (very dirty). || Obsceno, na; asqueroso, sa (obscene). || FIG. De perros (weather, temper). || — FIG. *Filthy lucre*, vil metal, *m.* (money). | *Filthy rich*, asquerosamente rico.

filtrate [ˈfiltrit] n. Líquido (*m.*) filtrado.

filtrate [ˈfiltreit] v. tr. Filtrar.

— V. intr. Filtrarse (to filter). || FIG. Filtrarse: *revolutionary elements have filtrated into the country*, elementos revolucionarios se han filtrado en el país.

filtration [filˈtreiʃən] n. Filtración, *f.*

fin [fin] n. Aleta, *f.* (of fish). || Rebaba, *f.* (of metal casting). || AVIAT. Plano (*m.*) de deriva. || AUT. Aleta, *f.* || U. S. FAM. Mano, *m.* (hand). | Billete (*m.*) de cinco dólares (bill).

fin [fin] v. tr. TECH. Proveer de aletas.

— V. intr. Aletear.

finable [ˈfainəbl] adj. Castigado con multa.

finagle [fiˈneigl] v. tr. U. S. Conseguir con artimañas.

— V. intr. U. S. Trampear.

final [ˈfainl] adj. Último, ma; final: *final performance*, última representación: *final chapter*, último capítulo. || Decisivo, va; terminante, definitivo, va (decisive). || Último, ma (ultimate): *that is my final word*, es mi última palabra. || GRAMM. Final: *final conjunction*, conjunción final. || — *And that's final*, y sanseacabó. || PHIL. *Final cause*, causa (*f.*) final.

— N. Final, *f.* (deciding race, game): *the cup final*, la final de copa. || Última tirada, *f.* (of a newspaper). || MUS. Nota (*f.*) final. || — Pl. Exámenes (*m.*) finales (examinations).

finale [fiˈnɑːli] n. MUS. Final, *m.* || THEATR. Escena (*f.*) final. || FIG. Final, *m.* (end).

finalism [ˈfainəlizəm] n. PHIL. Finalismo, *m.*

finalist [ˈfainəlist] n. SP. Finalista, *m. & f.*

finality [faiˈnæliti] n. Determinación, *f.* (determination). || Carácter (*m.*) definitivo (decisiveness). || Irrevocabilidad, *f.* || PHIL. Finalidad, *f.* || *He said it with finality*, lo dijo de modo terminante.

finalize [ˈfainəlaiz] v. tr. Finalizar (to complete). || Aprobar de modo definitivo (to give final approval).

finally [ˈfainəli] adv. Finalmente, por último: *finally, I should like to add*, finalmente, quisiera añadir. || Por fin: *so you finally came!*, ¡por fin has llegado! || Definitivamente (once and for all).

finance [faiˈnæns] n. Finanzas, *f. pl.* || — Pl. Fondos, *m.* (resources). || — *Finance bill*, ley presupuestaria. || *Finance company*, compañía financiera. || *Minister of Finance*, Ministro (*m.*) de Hacienda [*Amer.*, Ministro (*m.*) de Finanzas].

finance [faiˈnæns] v. tr. Financiar.

financial [faiˈnænʃəl] adj. Financiero, ra. || Económico, ca: *financial year*, año *or* ejercicio económico. || *Financial statement*, estado financiero.

financier [faiˈnænsiə*] n. Financiero, *m.*

financing [faiˈnænsiŋ] n. Financiación, *f.*, financiamiento, *m.*

finback [ˈfinˌbæk] n. Rorcual, *m.* (whale).

finch [fintʃ] n. Pinzón, *m.* (bird).

find [faind] n. Hallazgo, *m.*, descubrimiento, *m.*:

find* [faind] v. tr. Encontrar, hallar: *I found that money I lost*, he encontrado el dinero que perdí. || Encontrar: *to find one's way*, encontrar el camino; *how do you find the wine?*, ¿cómo encuentras el vino?; *to find sth. easy*, encontrar algo fácil; *to find s.o. boring*, encontrar aburrido a alguien. || Proporcionar, facilitar (to provide): *the employer finds them accommodation*, el empresario les proporciona alojamiento. || JUR. Declarar: *the jury found him guilty*, el jurado lo declaró culpable. | Pronunciar (sentence). || FIG. Sorprender: *I found him looking through the keyhole*, lo sorprendí mirando por la cerradura. || Comprobar: *it has been found that it was not true*, se ha comprobado que no era verdad. || — *All found*, con comida y alojamiento, todo incluido (salary). || *I find the job dull*, el trabajo me resulta pesado. || *If you can find time*, si tienes tiempo. || *Leave everything as you find it*, deja todo como lo has encontrado. || *The arrow found its mark*, la flecha dio en el blanco. || *The statement found its way to the newspapers*, la declaración llegó hasta los periódicos. || *To be found*, encontrarse. || *To find fault with*, criticar. || *To find favour with s.o.*, caerle en gracia a uno. || *To find it in one's heart to*, ser capaz de. || *To find o.s.*, encontrarse a sí mismo (to discover one's possibilities), encontrarse (to feel): *how do you find yourself?*, ¿cómo te encuentras?; verse: *to find o.s. obliged to*, verse obligado a; encontrar: *did you find yourself a flat?*, ¿encontraste piso? || *To find s.o. out*, sorprender a alguien (to catch s.o.), descubrir a alguien (to discover). || *To find sth. out*, averiguar algo, enterarse de algo (to check up on), descubrir algo, enterarse de algo (to discover). || *To find the courage to*, tener el valor de. || *To try to find*, buscar. || *We found it impossible*, nos fue imposible, lo encontramos imposible.

— V. intr. JUR. Fallar: *how did the jury find?*, ¿cómo falló el jurado?; *to find for*, fallar a favor de. || — *Seek and ye shall find*, busca y hallarás. || *To find out about*, averiguar, enterarse de.

— OBSERV. Pret & p. p. ***found***.

finder [—ə*] n. Descubridor, ra; hallador, ra. || Inventor, ra; descubridor, ra (inventor). || PHOT. Visor, *m.* (of a camera). || Anteojo (*m.*) buscador (of telescope).

finding [—iŋ] n. Descubrimiento, *m.* (discovery). || JUR. Fallo, *m.*, decisión, *f.* || — Pl. Hallazgos, *m.*: *to exhibit the findings of an archeological expedition*, exponer los hallazgos de una expedición arqueológica. || Resultados: *to publish the findings of one's research*, publicar los resultados de su investigación. || Conclusiones, *f.* (conclusions). || Herramientas, *f.* (tools).

fine [fain] adj. Excelente: *a fine performance*, una excelente representación. || Hermoso, sa (beautiful). || Elegante (smart): *fine clothes*, ropa elegante. || Admirable, excelente (person). || Agradable (pleasant): *a fine feeling*, una sensación agradable. || Magnífico, ca; bueno, na: *a fine future*, un magnífico porvenir. || Refinado, da; fino, na (refined): *fine taste*, gusto refinado. || Primoroso, sa: *fine hand*, letra primorosa. || Bueno, na (good): *fine weather*, buen tiempo. || Fino, na; delicado, da: *a fine lace*, un encaje fino. || Fino, na: *fine sand*, arena fina. || Agudo, da; fino, na (sharp): *a fine point*, una punta fina; *a fine sense of justice*, un agudo sentido de la justicia. || Ligero, ra; sutil (slight): *a fine distinction*, una ligera diferencia. || Puro, ra; fino, na (metals): *fine gold*, oro puro. || FAM. Menudo, da: *that's a fine mess we're in!*, ¡en menudo lío estamos metidos!; *a fine friend you are!*, ¡menudo amigo eres tú! || — *Fine fellow*, buen mozo. || *Fine sentiments*, buenos sentimientos. || *Gold eighteen carats fine*, oro de dieciocho quilates. || *Is it fine out?*, ¿hace buen tiempo? || *One of these fine days*, un día de éstos. || *That's fine!*, ¡muy bien!, ¡estupendo! || *To make a fine job of sth.*, hacer un buen trabajo con algo.

— Adv. En trozos pequeños: *she chopped garlic fine*, cortó el ajo en trozos pequeños. || Fino: *to grind coffee fine*, moler fino el café. || Mucho: *that would suit me fine*, esto me convendría mucho. || Muy bien (well). || — FIG. *To cut it fine*, llegar justo a tiempo (to arrive just in time), calcular muy justo. || *To cut one's profits too fine*, reducir demasiado sus beneficios. || *To feel fine*, sentirse bien.

— N. Multa, *f.* (as a punishment): *a heavy fine*, una multa de mucha cuantía. || *In fine*, en resumidas cuentas.

fine [fain] v. tr. Multar, poner una multa a (to punish). || Purificar (to purify). || Refinar (to refine). || *To fine down*, afinar: *to fine down the lines of a car*, afinar la línea de un coche; afilar (a pencil), purificar (to purify), refinar (to refine).

— V. intr. Purificarse. || Afinarse (to become slimmer).

fine arts [—ɑːts] pl. n. Bellas artes, *f.*

fine-draw [—drɔː] v. tr. Zurcir (torn materials). || Estirar (wire). || FIG. Sutilizar.

fine-drawn [—drɔːn] adj. Fino, na (features). || Invisible (mend). || Estirado, da (wire). || Sutil (subtle).

fine-grained [—greind] adj. De grano fino.

fineness [—nis] n. Finura, *f.*, fineza, *f.*, delicadeza, *f.* (delicacy). || Finura, *f.*, tenuidad, *f.* (thinness). || Elegancia, *f.* (elegance). || Belleza, *f.* (beauty). || Excelencia, *f.* (excellence). || Agudeza, *f.* (sharpness). || Pureza, *f.* (purity). || Ley, *f.* (of metals).

finery [—əri] n. Refinería, *f.* (refinery). || Galas, *f. pl.*: *to dress up in all one's finery*, vestirse con sus mejores galas.

finespun [—sˈpʌn] adj. Fino, na; hilado muy fino (silk, etc.). || Sutil (subtle).

finesse [fiˈnes] n. Fineza, *f.*, delicadeza, *f.* (delicacy). || Estratagema, *f.*, treta, *f.* (strategy). || Diplomacia, *f.*, tacto, *m.* (diplomacy). || Astucia, *f.* (cunning). || Discernimiento, *m.* (subtlety of judgment). || Impase, *m.*, impás, *m.* (in bridge).

finesse [fiˈnes] v. intr. Hacer el impase (in bridge).

— V. tr. Conseguir por artimañas: *to finesse one's way into a position*, conseguir un puesto por artimañas.

fine-tooth comb [ˈfaintuːθˈkəum] or **fine-toothed comb** [ˈfaintuːθtˈkəum] n. Peine (*m.*) espeso. || *To go through a room with a fine-tooth comb*, registrar un cuarto a fondo.

finger [ˈfiŋgə*] n. Dedo, *m.* (of hand, glove): *little, middle, ring, index finger*, dedo meñique, del corazón, anular, índice. || Dedo, *m.* (measure): *two fingers of whisky*, dos dedos de whisky. || TECH. Trinquete, *m.* || — FIG. *His fingers are all thumbs*, es muy desmañado. | *I can't quite put my finger on it*, no veo lo que puede ser. | *Let's keep our fingers crossed!*, ¡ojalá salga todo bien! | *To burn one's fingers*, cogerse los dedos. || FIG. FAM. *To have a finger in every pie*, see PIE. | *To have green fingers*, tener habilidad para la jardinería. | *To lay a finger on s.o.*, alzar la mano a alguien. | *To lift a finger*, mover un dedo. | *To put one's finger on*, señalar (to indicate), dar informaciones sobre (to inform on), denunciar, delatar (to denounce). | *To put one's finger on it*, dar en el clavo (to guess right). | *To put one's finger on the sore spot*, poner el dedo en la llaga. | *To slip through one's fingers*, escapársele a uno de las manos. | *To snap one's*

fingers at s.o., burlarse de alguien. | *To twist s.o. round one's little finger*, manejar a uno a su antojo.
finger [ˈfiŋgə*] v. tr. Tocar (to touch). || Mus. Tocar, tañer, pulsar (a stringed instrument). | Teclear (a tune on the piano). | Marcar la digitación en (written music). || Fam. Robar (to steal).
finger biscuit [—ˈbiskit] n. Culin. Lengua (*f.*) de gato.
fingerboard [—bɔ:d] n. Mus. Diapasón, *m.* (of a stringed instrument). | Teclado, *m.* (of a piano).
finger bowl [—bəul] n. Enjuague, *m.*
fingerbreadth [—bredθ] n. Dedo, *m.* (dimension).
fingered [—d] adj. Con dedos. || Bot. Mus. Digitado, da.
fingering [—riŋ] n. Manoseo, *m.* (action of touching). || Mus. Digitación, *f.*
fingerling [—liŋ] n. Zool. Salmoncillo, *m.* (young salmon). || U. S. Pececillo, *m.* (small fish).
fingernail [—neil] n. Uña, *f.*
finger plate [—pleit] n. Chapa (*f.*) de protección (of doors).
finger post [—pəust] n. Poste (*m.*) indicador.
fingerprint [—print] n. Hueila (*f.*) dactilar *or* digital.
fingerprint [—print] v. tr. Tomar las huellas dactilares *or* digitales a.
fingerstall [—stɔ:l] n. Dedil, *m.* (protective covering of rubber, etc.).
fingertip [—tip] n. Punta (*f.*) *or* yema (*f.*) de los dedos. || Dedil, *m.* (protection). || — Fig. *To have sth. at one's fingertips*, saber algo al dedillo. | *To one's fingertips*, de pies a cabeza (completely).
finial [ˈfainiəl] n. Florón, *m.*
finical [ˈfinikəl] adj. Melindroso, sa; remilgado, da; afectado, da.
finickiness [ˈfiniknis] n. Melindre, *m.*, remilgo, *m.*
finicking [ˈfinikiŋ] adj. See finicky.
finicky [ˈfiniki] adj. Melindroso, sa; remilgado, da; afectado, da.
finish [ˈfiniʃ] n. Fin, *m.*, final, *m.*, conclusión, *f.* (end). || Acabado, *m.* (of a surface): *a gloss finish*, un acabado brillante. || Perfección, *f.* || Sp. Llegada, *f.* (in a race). || Arts. Última mano, *f.* || Buenos modales, *m. pl.* (social polish). || — *That was the finish of him*, aquello fue su ruina. || *To be in at the finish*, presenciar el final. || *To fight to the finish*, luchar hasta el final.
finish [ˈfiniʃ] v. tr. Terminar, acabar: *to finish a book, a story*, terminar un libro, un relato. || Llegar al final de (a journey). || Acabar con: *the fever almost finished him*, la fiebre casi acabó con él. || Dar el último toque *or* los ultimos toques *or* la última mano a, rematar (to add the finishing touch). || Tech. Acabar. || — *To finish off*, rematar (to complete, to kill). || *To finish up*, acabar, terminar.
— V. intr. Acabar, terminar: *how does the play finish?*, ¿cómo acaba la obra?; *he finished by saying...*, terminó diciendo..., terminó por decir... || Sp. Llegar: *he finished second*, llegó el segundo. || — *To finish with*, acabar con. || *To finish with one's boyfriend*, reñir con *or* acabar con el novio. || Fig. fam. *Wait till I've finished with him!*, ¡ya verás cómo le dejo!
finished [—t] adj. Acabado, da; terminado, da: *is the job finished?*, ¿está terminado el trabajo? || Fig. Consumado, da; excelente (perfect): *a finished speaker*, un orador excelente. || Tech. Acabado, da. || Agotado, da; rendido, da (tired). || *He is finished as a politician*, está acabado como político.
finisher [—ə*] n. Sp. Participante (*m.*) que llega a la meta. || Tech. Máquina (*f.*) acabadora (machine). | Acabador, ra (person). || Fam. Golpe (*m.*) de gracia (final blow).
finishing [—iŋ] adj. Último, ma: *finishing touch*, último toque, última mano. || — Sp. *Finishing line*, línea (*f.*) de llegada; meta, *f.* || *Finishing school*, escuela (*f.*) privada de educación social para señoritas.
— N. Acabado, *m.*
finite [ˈfainait] adj. Math. Phil. Finito, ta. || Gramm. Conjugado, da (form of verb).
fink [fiŋk] n. U. S. Fam. Esquirol, *m.*, rompehuelgas, *m. inv.* (strikebreaker).
Finland [ˈfinlənd] pr. n. Geogr. Finlandia, *f.*
Finn [fin] n. Finlandés, esa.
finnan haddie [ˌfinənˈhædi] or **finnan haddock** [—ˈhædək] n. Bacalao (*m.*) ahumado.
finned [find] adj. Con aletas.
Finnic [ˈfinik] adj. Finés, esa; finlandés, esa.
— N. Finés, *m.* (language).
finnicking [—iŋ] adj. Melindroso, sa; remilgado, da; afectado, da.
finnicky [—i] adj. Melindroso, sa; remilgado, da; afectado, da.
Finnish [ˈfiniʃ] adj. Finlandés, esa.
— N. Finlandés, *m.* (language).
fiord [fjɔ:d] n. Fiordo, *m.*
fir [fə:*] n. Abeto, *m.*
fire [ˈfaiə*] n. Fuego, *m.*: *to light a wood fire*, encender un fuego de leña; *to put out the fire*, apagar el fuego. || Incendio, *m.*: *the factory was destroyed by fire*, la fábrica fue destruida por un incendio; *forest fire*, incendio forestal. || Estufa, *f.*: *electric, gas fire*, estufa eléctrica, de gas. || Mil. Fuego, *m.*: *artillery fire*, fuego de artillería; *to come under the enemy's fire*, caer bajo el fuego del enemigo. || Fig. Fuego, *m.*, ardor, *m.* (passion). || — Fig. *A rapid fire of questions*, una serie de preguntas. | *Between two fires*, entre dos fuegos. | *Fire and brimstone*, fuegos (*m. pl.*) del infierno. || Mil. *Fire at will*, fuego a discreción. || *Greek fire*, fuego griego. || Mil. *Heavy, running fire*, fuego nutrido, graneado. || Culin. *On a slow fire*, a fuego lento. || Fig. *There is no smoke without fire*, cuando el río suena, agua lleva. | *To add fuel to the fire*, echar leña al fuego. || *To be on fire*, estar ardiendo. || *To be under fire*, estar bajo el fuego del enemigo (troops), estar sometido a críticas, ser atacado (under criticism). || *To catch* o *to take fire*, prenderse, encenderse (to start burning), incendiarse (to burst into flames). || Fig. *To go through fire and water*, afrontar toda clase de peligros. || *To miss fire*, fallar. || *To open fire*, romper el fuego. || Fig. *To play with fire*, jugar con fuego. || *To set sth. on fire* o *to set fire to sth.*, prenderle fuego a algo. || Fig. *To set the world on fire*, cubrirse de gloria. || *To sit by the fire*, estar sentado al amor de la lumbre, estar sentado al lado de la chimenea. || *Trial by fire*, prueba del fuego.
— Interj. Mil. ¡Fuego! (order). || ¡Fuego! (call for help).
fire [faiə*] v. tr. Disparar (a gun, bullet). || Tirar: *to fire a salute*, tirar una salva. || Lanzar (rocket, torpedo, etc.). || Explotar (a mine). || Prender (a fuse). || Aut. Encender. || Incendiar, prender fuego a (to set fire to). || Lanzar, arrojar (to throw). || Fig. Soltar (remark, insults, etc.): *to fire a question at s.o.*, soltar una pregunta a alguien. | Inflamar (passion). | Infundir: *to fire s.o. with enthusiasm*, infundir entusiasmo a alguien. | Enardecer: *his speech fired the crowd*, su discurso enardeció a la multitud. | Echar (to dismiss). || Cocer (bricks, pottery). || Cargar, alimentar (to supply with fuel). || Calentar (oven). || Secar al fuego (to dry). || — *To fire off*, disparar (a shot), soltar (a question, etc.). || *To fire questions at s.o.*, bombardear a alguien con preguntas. || *To fire up*, calentar (oven), cargar, alimentar (to supply with fuel).
— V. intr. Encenderse. || Hacer fuego, disparar: *to fire at s.o.*, hacer fuego contra alguien. || Dispararse (a gun). || Explotar (explosives). || Encenderse: *one of the cylinders is not firing*, uno de los cilindros no se enciende. || Funcionar (to run, to work). || — Mil. *Fire at will!*, ¡fuego a discreción! || Fig. *Fire away!*, ¡adelante! || *To fire on*, hacer fuego sobre *or* contra. || U. S. *To fire up*, enfurecerse.
fire alarm [—ˌlɑ:m] n. Alarma (*f.*) de incendios.
firearm [—ɑ:m] n. Arma (*f.*) de fuego.
fireball [—bɔ:l] n. Bola (*f.*) de fuego. || Bólido, *m.* (meteor).
fireboat [—bəut] n. Barco (*m.*) bomba.
fire bomb [—bɔm] n. Bomba (*f.*) incendiaria.
firebox [—bɔks] n. Fogón, *m.*
firebrand [—brænd] n. Tea, *f.* (burning wood). || Botafuego, *m.* (lighted torch). || Fig. Agitador, *m.* (agitator).
firebreak [—breik] n. Cortafuego, *m.*
firebrick [—brik] n. Ladrillo (*m.*) refractario.
fire brigade [—briˌgeid] n. Bomberos, *m. pl.*, cuerpo (*m.*) de bomberos.
firebug [—bʌg] n. U. S. Fam. Incendiario, ria; pirómano, na.
fireclay [—klei] n. Arcilla (*f.*) refractaria.
fire control [—kənˌtrəul] n. Mil. Dirección (*f.*) *or* conducción (*f.*) de tiro. || Extinción (*f.*) de incendios.
firecracker [—ˈkrækə*] n. U. S. Petardo, *m.*
fire curtain [—ˈkə:tn] n. Cortina (*f.*) de fuego.
firedamp [—dæmp] n. Grisú, *m.* (in mines).
fire department [—diˈpɑ:tmənt] n. U. S. Bomberos, *m. pl.*, cuerpo (*m.*) de bomberos.
firedog [—dɔg] n. Morillo, *m.*
fire drill [—dril] n. Simulacro (*m.*) de incendio [para enseñar a la gente cómo puede escapar en caso de incendio].
fire-eater [—ˌi:tə*] n. Tragafuegos, *m. inv.* (in a circus). || Fig. Matamoros, *m.* (aggressive person).
fire engine [—ˌendʒin] n. Coche (*m.*) de bomberos.
fire escape [—isˌkeip] n. Escalera (*f.*) de incendios *or* de emergencia (in buildings).
fire extinguisher [—iksˌtiŋgwiʃə*] n. Extintor (*m.*) de incendios.
firefly [—flai] n. Luciérnaga, *f.* (beetle).
fireguard [—gɑ:d] n. Pantalla, *f.* (of a fireplace) || Cortafuego, *m.* (firebreak).
firehouse [—haus] n. U. S. Parque (*m.*) de bomberos.
fire hydrant [—ˈhaidrənt] n. Boca (*f.*) de incendio.
fire insurance [—inˌʃuərəns] n. Seguro (*m.*) contra incendios.
fire irons [—ˌaiənz] pl. n. Útiles (*m.*) de chimenea.
firelight [—lait] n. Luz (*f.*) del hogar, lumbre, *f.*
fire-lighter [—ˌlaitə*] n. Astillas (*f. pl.*) para encender el fuego.
firelock [—lɔk] n. Trabuco (*m.*) de pedernal.
fireman [—mən] n. Bombero, *m.* (member of a fire brigade). || Fogonero, *m.* (of locomotive, etc.).

— Observ. El plural de esta palabra es *firemen*.

fire opal [— əupəl] n. Min. Girasol, *m.*
fire pan [—pæn] n. Brasero, *m.*
fireplace [—pleis] n. Chimenea, *f.*
fireplug [—plʌg] n. Boca (*f.*) de incendio.
firepower [—ˌpauə*] n. Mil. Potencia (*f.*) de fuego.
fireproof [—pru:f] adj. Ininflamable, incombustible, ignífugo, ga. || Refractario, ria (brick, clay, etc.).

fireproof [—pru:f] v. tr. Hacer ininfamable *or* ignífugo, ignifugar.
fire-raiser [—reizə*] n. Incendiario, ria.
fire-raising [—ˏreiziŋ] n. Incendio (*m.*) premeditado.
fire screen [—skri:n] n. Pantalla, *f.*
fire ship [—ʃip] n. Brulote, *m.*
fireside [—said] n. Hogar, *m.* || *To sit down by the fireside*, sentarse al amor de la lumbre, sentarse al lado de la chimenea.
— Adj. Al amor de la lumbre. || U. S. Sin protocolo, familiar (informal).
fire station [—ˈsteiʃən] n. Parque (*m.*) de bomberos.
firestone [—stəun] n. Pedernal, *m.* (flint). || Piedra (*f.*) refractaria.
firetrap [—træp] n. Edificio (*m.*) con salidas de emergencia insuficientes en caso de incendio.
fire wall [—wɔ:l] n. Cortafuego, *m.*
fire warden [—ˈwɔ:dn] n. U. S. Funcionario (*m.*) encargado de la protección contra los incendios.
firewater [—ˏwɔ:tə*] n. FAM. Aguardiente, *m.*, matarratas, *m. inv.*
firewood [—wud] n. Leña, *f.*
firework [—wə:k] n. Fuego (*m.*) de artificio. || — Pl. Fuegos (*m.*) artificiales (display). || FIG. *Then the fireworks started*, entonces se armó la gorda.
firing [ˈfaiəriŋ] n. Disparos, *m. pl.*: *firing could be heard*, podían oírse disparos. || Combustible, *m.* (fuel). || Carga, *f.*, alimentación, *f.* (of furnace). || Cocción, *f.* (of pottery). || AUT. Encendido, *m.* || VET. Cauterización, *f.* || FIG. Despido, *m.*, expulsión, *f.* (dismissal). || *The firing of the ships' cannons*, el cañoneo de los barcos.
firing line [—lain] n. Línea (*f.*) de fuego.
firing party [—ˏpɑ:ti] n. U. S. Pelotón (*m.*) de ejecución.
firing pin [—pin] n. Percutor, *m.*, percusor, *m.*
firing squad [—skwɔd] n. Pelotón (*m.*) de ejecución. || U. S. Piquete (*m.*) de salvas (who fires a salute).
firm [fə:m] adj. Firme, sólido, da: *firm foundation*, base sólida. || Firme: *firm decision*, decisión firme. || Estable (stable). || Estable, firme (prices). || COMM. En firme: *firm offer*, *order*, oferta, pedido en firme. | Firme (shares). || *To rule a country with a firm hand*, gobernar un país con mano dura.
— Adv. Firme: *to stand firm*, mantenerse firme. || *To hold firm to*, agarrarse bien a (an object), mantenerse firme en (one's opinions).
— N. Empresa, *f.*, firma, *f.* (company). || Razón (*f.*) social (name).
firm [fə:m] v. tr. Afirmar, afianzar.
— V. intr. Ponerse firme. || COMM. Afirmarse, consolidarse.
firmament [ˈfə:məmənt] n. Firmamento, *m.*
firmer chisel [ˈfə:mə*ˈtʃizl] n. Formón, *m.*
firmly [ˈfə:mli] adv. Firmemente, sólidamente. || Firmemente: *I firmly believe that*, creo firmemente que.
firmness [ˈfə:mnis] n. Firmeza, *f.* (stability). || FIG. Firmeza, *f.* (resolution, strength): *firmness in one's convictions*, *of character*, firmeza de convicciones, de carácter.
firn [ˈfə:n] n. Nevero, *m.*
first [fə:st] adj. Primero, ra (see OBSERV.): *the first three months*, los tres primeros meses; *first row*, primera fila; *the first man*, el primer hombre; *first secretary*, primer secretario. || Básico, ca; fundamental (basic): *first principles*, principios básicos. || Elemental, rudimentario, ria (elementary). || Más mínimo, ma: *he hasn't the first idea about drawing*, no tiene la más mínima idea del dibujo. || — *At first hand*, de primera mano. || *At first sight*, a primera vista. || PHIL. REL. *First cause*, causa primera. || *First edition*, primera edición, edición príncipe (of a book), primera edición (of a newspaper). || AUT. *First gear*, primera, *f.*, primera velocidad: *to put a car in first gear*, poner un coche en primera. || GRAMM. *First person*, primera persona. || *First things first*, lo primero es lo primero. || *In the first place*, en primer lugar. || *I shall do it first thing tomorrow*, es lo primero que haré mañana. || *Not to know the first thing about*, no tener la más mínima idea de. || *The first house but one*, la segunda casa.
— Adv. Por primera vez: *we first went there last year*, fuimos allí por primera vez el año pasado. || En primer lugar, primero (firstly). || Antes, primero: *you must finish your work first*, tienes que acabar el trabajo antes. || — *First and foremost*, antes que nada, ante todo. || *First and last*, en todos los aspectos. || *First come, first served*, el que se adelanta nunca pierde. || *First of all*, en primer lugar, ante todo. || *First or last*, tarde o temprano. || *Head first*, de cabeza. || *I would die first!*, ¡antes morir! || *Ladies first*, las señoras primero. || *To come first*, llegar primero (in a race), ser lo primero: *my family comes first*, mi familia es lo primero. || FIG. *To get in first*, adelantarse a los demás. || *To go first*, ir *or* entrar el primero (to be the first), viajar en primera (to travel first-class). || *To say first one thing, then another*, decir primero una cosa, luego otra. || *To travel first*, viajar en primera clase. || *Women and children first*, las mujeres y los niños primero. || *You go first*, Ud. primero.
— N. Primero, ra: *the first of the speakers*, el primero de los oradores; *Isabel I (the first)*, Isabel I [primera]. || Sobresaliente, *m.* (degree): *to get a first*, sacar sobresaliente. || Día (*m.*) uno, uno, *m.*, primero, *m.* (date): *the first of January*, el día uno de enero. || AUT. Primera, *f.* (gear). || — Pl. Artículos (*m.*) de primera calidad. || — *At first*, al principio. || *From first to last*, desde el principio hasta el final. || *From the first*, desde el principio. || *That's the first I've heard about it*, es la primera noticia que tengo. || *The first to arrive*, el primero [*or* los primeros] en llegar. || *To be the first to*, ser el primero en.
— OBSERV. The adjective *primero* is apocopated to *primer* when preceeding a masculine noun: *the first day*, el primer día.
first aid [—eid] n. MED. Primeros auxilios, *m. pl.* (emergency treatment).
first-aid kit [—eidkit] n. Botiquín (*m.*) de urgencia.
first-aid post [—eidpəust] n. Casa (*f.*) de socorro.
first base [beis] n. U. S. SP. Primera base, *f.* (in baseball). || U. S. *To get to first base*, hacer algún progreso, haber dado el primer paso.
firstborn [—bɔ:n] adj./n. Mayor, primogénito, ta.
first-class [—klɑ:s] adj. De primera clase: *first-class ticket*, billete de primera clase. || De primera calidad, de primera categoría (of the best quality): *a first-class film*, una película de primera calidad. || Sobresaliente (examination marks).
— Adv. En primera: *to travel first-class*, viajar en primera.
first cousin [—ˈkʌzn] n. See COUSIN.
first day [—dei] n. U. S. Día (*m.*) de emisión (of a stamp). | Domingo, *m.* (used by Quakers).
first-day cover [—deiˈkʌvə*] n. Sobre (*m.*) del día de emisión de un sello.
first floor [flɔ:*] n. Primer piso, *m.* || U. S. Planta (*f.*) baja.
firstfruits [—fru:ts] pl. n. Frutas (*f.*) tempranas. || FIG. Primeros frutos, *m.*
firsthand [—hænd] adv./adj. De primera mano. || *At firsthand*, directamente.
First Lady [—ˈleidi] n. Primera Dama, *f.*
first lieutenant [—lefˈtenənt] n. U. S. Teniente, *m.*
firstling [—liŋ] n. Primogénito, *m.* (of animals). || FIG. Primeros frutos, *m. pl.*
firstly [—li] adv. En primer lugar, primero.
first mate [—meit] n. MAR. Segundo oficial, *m.*
first mortgage [—ˈmɔ:gidʒ] n. Primera hipoteca, *f.*
first name [—neim] n. Nombre (*m.*) de pila, nombre, *m.*
first night [—nait] n. Noche (*f.*) de estreno, estreno, *m.*
first nighter [—ˈnaitə*] n. Persona (*f.*) que asiste a todos los estrenos.
first offender [—əˈfendə*] n. JUR. Persona (*f.*) que comete un delito por primera vez.
first officer [—ˈɔfisə*] n. MAR. Primer piloto, *m.*
first papers [—ˈpeipəz] pl. n. U. S. Solicitud (*f. sing.*) de naturalización.
first quarter [—ˈkwɔ:tə*] n. Cuarto (*m.*) creciente (of the moon).
first-rate [—reit] adj. De primera clase *or* calidad *or* categoría (finest quality).
— Adv. Muy bien.
first sergeant [—ˈsɑ:dʒənt] n. U. S. Sargento, *m.*
first water [—ˈwɔ:tə*] n. Primera calidad, *f.* (of diamond). || FIG. Primera categoría, *f.*
firth [—fə:θ] n. Estuario, *m.*, brazo (*m.*) de mar.
fisc [fisk] n. Fisco, *m.*, tesoro (*m.*) público, erario, *m.*
fiscal [ˈfiskəl] adj. Fiscal. || *Fiscal year*, año *or* ejercicio económico.
— N. Fiscal, *m.*
fish [fiʃ] n. Pez, *m.* (in water). || Pescado, *m.* (food). || Refuerzo, *m.* (for building). || MAR. Jimelga, *f.* || Eclisa, *f.*, mordaza, *f.* (fishplate). || FIG. FAM. Tipo, *m.*, tío, *m.* (fellow). || ASTR. Piscis, *m. pl.* || — FIG. *A different kettle of fish*, harina de otro costal. || *Fish and chips*, pescado frito con patatas fritas. || *Flying fish*, pez volador. || *Freshwater fish*, pez de agua dulce. || FIG. *He's a queer fish*, es un tipo extraño. | *Neither fish nor fowl*, ni chicha ni limonada, ni carne ni pescado. | *Poor fish*, pobre hombre. | *There are lots more fish in the sea*, no es la única persona en el mundo. | *To be like a fish in water*, estar como pez en el agua. | *To drink like a fish*, beber como una esponja. | *To feed the fishes*, ahogarse (to drown). | *To feel like a fish out of water*, sentirse como gallo en corral ajeno *or* como pez fuera del agua. | *To have other fish to fry*, tener algo mejor que hacer. || *Salt-water fish*, pez de agua salada.
fish [fiʃ] v. intr. Pescar (to go fishing). || FIG. Buscar: *to fish for compliments*, buscar elogios; *to fish in one's pocket*, buscar en el bolsillo. || — FIG. *To fish in troubled waters*, pescar en río revuelto. || *To go fishing*, ir de pesca.
— V. tr. Pescar en: *to fish a river*, pescar en un río. || Pescar (fish, pearls). || FIG. Sacar: *to fish a coin out of one's pocket*, sacar una moneda del bolsillo. || TECH. Unir con eclisas (rails, etc.). || — *To fish out a river*, vaciar de peces un río. || FAM. *To fish secrets out of s.o.*, sonsacar a alguien.
fish ball [—bɔ:l] n. Croqueta (*f.*) de pescado.
fish bone [—bəun] n. Espina, *f.*
fishbowl [—bəul] n. Pecera, *f.*
fish breeding [—ˈbri:diŋ] n. Piscicultura, *f.*
fish cake [—keik] n. Croqueta (*f.*) de pescado.
fish carver [—ˈkɑ:və*] n. Cuchillo (*m.*) para el pescado.
fisher [—ə*] n. Pescador, *m.* (man). || Barco (*m.*) pesquero (boat). || ZOOL. Marta (*f.*) de América (marten).

fisherman [ˈfiʃə:mən] n. Pescador, *m.* (person). || Barco (*m.*) pesquero (boat).

— OBSERV. El plural es *fishermen.*

fisherwoman [ˈfiʃə:wumən] n. Pescadora, *f.*

— OBSERV. El plural es *fisherwomen.*

fishery [ˈfiʃəri] n. Pesquería, *f.*, industria (*f.*) pesquera, pesca, *f.* (industry). || Pesquería, *f.* (fishing area). || Criadero (*m.*) de peces (place where fish are bred). || Derecho (*m.*) de pesca (right).
fish finger [fiʃˈfiŋgə*] n. CULIN. Filete (*m.*) de pescado empanado.
fish flour [fiʃˈflauə*] n. Harina (*f.*) de pescado.
fish glue [ˈfiʃ-glu:] n. Cola (*f.*) de pescado.
fish hatchery [ˈfiʃˈhætʃəri] n. Vivero (*m.*) *or* criadero (*m.*) de peces.
fish hawk [ˈfiʃhɔ:k] n. ZOOL. Pigargo, *m.*
fishhook [ˈfiʃhuk] n. Anzuelo, *m.*
fishing [ˈfiʃiŋ] n. Pesca, *f.*
fishing boat [—bəut] n. Barco (*m.*) de pesca *or* pesquero.
fishing ground [—graund] n. Pesquería, *f.*, zona (*f.*) de pesca.
fishing line [—lain] n. Sedal, *m.*
fishing net [—net] n. Red (*f.*) de pesca.
fishing rod [—rɔd] n. Caña (*f.*) de pescar.
fishing tackle [—ˈtækl] n. Aparejo (*m.*) de pescar.
fish joint [fiʃdʒɔint] n. Junta (*f.*) de eclisa (railway).
fish kettle [fiʃˈketl] n. Besuguera, *f.*
fishline [ˈfiʃlain] n. U. S. Sedal, *m.*
fish market [fiʃˈmɑ:kit] n. Mercado (*m.*) de pescado.
fish meal [ˈfiʃmi:l] n. Harina (*f.*) de pescado.
fishmonger [ˈfiʃ,mʌŋgə*] n. Pescadero, *m.* || *Fishmonger's shop* o *fishmonger's*, pescadería, *f.*
fishplate [ˈfiʃpleit] n. Eclisa, *f.*, mordaza, *f.* (of a railway line).
fish pole [ˈfiʃpəul] n. U. S. Caña (*f.*) de pescar.
fishpond [ˈfiʃpɔnd] n. Vivero, *m.*, criadero, *m.* (for breeding). || Estanque (*m.*) con peces (in a garden). || FAM. Mar, *m.* (sea).
fish story [ˈfiʃˈstɔ:ri] n. FAM. Cuento (*m.*) inverosímil, historia (*f.*) increíble.
fishtail [ˈfiʃteil] v. intr. AVIAT. Colear.
fishtailing [—iŋ] n. AVIAT. Coleo, *m.*
fish trap [ˈfiʃtræp] n. Nasa, *f.*
fishwife [ˈfiʃwaif] n. Pescadera, *f.* || FIG. FAM. Verdulera, *f.*, mujer (*f.*) malhablada.

— OBSERV. El plural de esta palabra es *fishwives.*

fishworm [ˈfiʃwə:m] n. Gusano, *m.*
fishy [ˈfiʃi] adj. A pescado: *a fishy smell*, un olor a pescado. || Rico en peces, abundante en peces (rich in fish). || Sin brillo (eyes). || FAM. Sospechoso, sa (suspicious). | Poco claro, ra; turbio, bia (not clear). || — FIG. *There's sth. fishy going on*, hay gato encerrado. | *To smell fishy*, oler mal, oler a chamusquina. || *To taste fishy*, saber a pescado.
fissile [ˈfisail] adj. Fisible, físil, escindible, fisionable.
fission [ˈfiʃən] n. PHYS. Fisión, *f.*, escisión, *f.* (of nucleus). || Fisión, *f.*, escisión, *f.* (splitting of cell).
fissionable [ˈfiʃnəbl] adj. Fisionable, fisible.
fissirostral [,fisiˈrɔstrəl] adj. Fisirrostro, tra.
fissure [ˈfiʃə*] n. Grieta, *f.*, hendidura, *f.*, fisura, *f.* (a cleft or split): *the earthquake opened up fissures in the rocks*, el terremoto abrió grietas en las rocas. || ANAT. Fisura, *f.*
fissure [ˈfiʃə*] v. tr. Rajar, agrietar, hender, cuartear.
— V. intr. Cuartearse, agrietarse, rajarse, henderse.
fist [fist] n. Puño, *m.* || FIG. Letra, *f.* (writing). || FAM. Mano, *f.* (hand). || — *To clench one's fists*, apretar los puños. || *To shake one's fist at*, amenazar con el puño. || *To strike s.o. with one's fist*, dar un puñetazo *or* puñetazos a alguien.
fist [fist] v. tr. Dar puñetazos a (to hit). || Asir (to grasp).
fistic [ˈfistik] adj. Pugilístico, ca.
fisticuffs [ˈfistikʌf] pl. n. Pelea (*f. sing.*) a puñetazos (fight). || Puñetazos, *m.* (blows).
fistula [ˈfistjulə] n. MED. Fístula, *f.*

— OBSERV. El plural de la palabra inglesa es *fistulas* o *fistulae.*

fistular [—ə*] or **fistulous** [—əs] adj. Fistular, fistuloso, sa.
fit [fit] adj. Conveniente, apropiado, da: *do what you think fit*, haz lo que te parezca conveniente. || Apto, ta; capaz (competent): *he isn't fit to do the job*, no es apto para hacer el trabajo, no es capaz de hacer el trabajo. || Capacitado, da (qualified). || Apropiado, da; adecuado, da (suitable): *I need a dress fit for a wedding*, necesito un traje apropiado para una boda. || Justo, ta (just). || Digno, na (worthy): *he is not fit to live*, no es digno de vivir. || Sano, na; bien de salud, en buen estado físico (healthy): *to be very fit*, estar muy bien de salud. || SP. En forma (in good form): *the captain is not fit today*, el capitán no está en forma hoy. || — *Fit for a king*, digno de un rey. || U. S. *He is fit to be tied*, está que echa chispas. || *I'm not fit to be seen right now*, no estoy visible de momento. || *It is not fit to be seen*, no es digno de verse (film, etc.). || *That's all he is fit for*, no sirve para otra cosa, no sirve para más. || *The meat is not fit to eat*, la carne no se puede comer. || *This car is not fit for the road*, este coche no está en buenas condiciones. || *This dress is not fit to wear*, no me puedo poner este vestido. || *To be as fit as a fiddle*, estar más sano que una manzana, estar en plena forma. || *To be fit to drop*, estar a punto de caerse de agotamiento. || *To get fit*, entrenarse (to train), reponerse, recuperarse (from an illness). || *To keep fit*, mantenerse en forma. || *To see fit*, juzgar conveniente. || *To think fit to*, estimar conveniente.
— Adv. *To cry fit to break one's heart*, llorar a lágrima viva. || *To laugh fit to burst*, partirse *or* desternillarse de risa. || *To run fit to collapse*, correr como un descosido.
— N. Arrebato, *m.* (short spell): *he had a fit of anger*, le dio un arrebato de cólera. || Ataque, *m.* (outburst): *he went into a fit of laughter*, le dio un ataque de risa. || MED. Ataque, *m.*, acceso, *m.*: *a fit of madness*, un ataque de locura. || — *A fit of energy*, un arranque de energía. || *By fits and starts*, a trompicones, a rachas. || *Fainting fit*, síncope, *m.* || *To be a good fit*, estar bien ajustado, tener buen corte (clothes), encajar bien (machine part). || FIG. *To be in fits (of laughter)*, morirse de risa. || *To have* o *to throw a fit*, darle a uno un ataque: *he had a fit*, le dio un ataque.
fit [fit] v. tr. Capacitar (to qualify): *his experience fits him for the job*, su experiencia lo capacita para el trabajo. || Cuadrar con, corresponder a, responder a, estar de acuerdo con (to tally with): *he fits the description*, responde a la descripción. || Adaptar, adecuar, ajustar (to adapt): *to fit a policy to a new situation*, adaptar una política a una nueva situación. || Preparar (to prepare). || Sentar bien a, ir bien a: *his coat fits him well*, el abrigo le sienta bien. || Hacer juego con (a colour scheme). || Tomar medidas a (to measure): *to fit s.o. for a suit*, tomar medidas a alguien para un traje. || Probar (to try on): *to fit a suit on s.o.*, probarle un traje a alguien. || Entallar (to tailor a dress). || Encontrar sitio para, meter (to find room for): *I can't fit this cupboard anywhere*, no puedo meter este armario en ninguna parte. || Encajar: *to fit one part into another*, encajar una pieza en otra. || Unir (to join together). || Entrar en: *the key doesn't fit the lock*, la llave no entra en la cerradura. || Colocar (to put): *I'm going to fit it on the wall*, lo voy a colocar en la pared; *to fit a new window*, colocar una nueva ventana. || Poner (a carpet): *they fitted my carpet yesterday*, me pusieron la moqueta ayer. || Equipar con, proveer de (to supply with): *to fit new headlamps to a car*, equipar un coche con nuevos faros. || Introducir (to introduce). || Incluir (to include). || — *A meal to fit the occasion*, una comida apropiada para la ocasión. || *To fit in*, intercalar, meter: *to fit in an extra commercial between programmes*, intercalar otro anuncio entre los programas; tener tiempo para: *can we fit in one more game before dinner?*, ¿tenemos tiempo para jugar otro partido antes de cenar?; meter, encajar: *to fit a television in between two cupboards*, encajar un televisor entre dos armarios; atender (a customer): *we could fit you in at five o'clock*, le podríamos atender a las cinco. || *To fit out*, equipar (to equip), armar (a ship). || *To fit up*, equipar. || *To make the punishment fit the crime*, adaptar el castigo al crimen.
— V. intr. Encajar: *pieces that fit together*, piezas que encajan una con otra. || Caber: *the cupboard doesn't fit in the car*, el armario no cabe en el coche. || Sentar (clothes): *how does the suit fit?*, ¿cómo te sienta el traje?; *it fits you very well*, le sienta muy bien. || Adaptarse, ajustarse (to adjust o.s.). || Corresponder, estar de acuerdo, cuadrar (facts, figures, etc.). || — FIG. *If the cap fits, wear it*, see CAP. | *It all fits now!*, ¡ahora está todo claro!, ¡ya lo veo todo claro! || *To fit in with*, cuadrar con (things), congeniar con, llevarse bien con: *he doesn't fit in with my friends*, no congenia con mis amigos. || *To fit to a T*, sentar como anillo al dedo (clothes), encajar perfectamente (into a space).
fitch [fitʃ] or **fitchet** [—et] or **fitchew** [—tʃu:] n. ZOOL. Turón, *m.* (polecat). | Mofeta, *f.* (skunk).
fitful [ˈfitful] adj. MED. Espasmódico, ca. || Cambiadizo, za (changeable). || Caprichoso, sa (capricious). || Irregular.
fitfully [—i] adv. A rachas.
fitment [ˈfitmənt] n. Mueble, *m.* (piece of furniture). || — Pl. Mobiliario, *m. sing.* (fittings).
fitness [ˈfitnis] n. Conveniencia, *f.*, oportunidad, *f.* (suitability). || Salud, *f.* (health). || Aptitud, *f.* (aptitude).
fitted [ˈfitid] adj. Apto, ta; capacitado, da (qualified, suited): *to be fitted for sth.*, estar capacitado para algo, ser apto para algo. || Entallado, da; ceñido, da (tailored). || Hecho a la medida (made-to-measure). || Empotrado, da (cupboard).
fitter [ˈfitə*] n. Ajustador, *m.* (mechanic). || Probador, ra (in tailoring).
fitting [ˈfitiŋ] adj. Oportuno, na; apropiado, da (just): *a fitting remark*, una observación apropiada. || Propio, pia; justo ta: *it is fitting that he be elected president*, es justo que sea elegido presidente. || Digno, na (worthy). || — *A badly fitting suit*, un traje que sienta mal. || *It is not fitting that*, no está bien que.
— N. Ajuste, *m.* (of two pieces). || Colocación, *f.*, instalación, *f.* (of a machine, etc.). || Mueble, *m.* (piece of furniture). || Prueba, *f.* (of clothes). || Medida, *f.* (size). || Horma, *f.* (width of shoe). || — Pl. Mobiliario, *m. sing.*, muebles, *m.* (furniture). || Accesorios, *m.* (accessories). || — *Bathroom fittings*, aparatos sanitarios. || *Electrical fittings*, accesorios eléctricos.
five [faiv] adj. Cinco. || — *Five hundred*, quinientos, *m.* (number), quinientos, tas (adjective): *five hundred*

apples, quinientas manzanas. || *Five hundredth*, quingentésimo, ma.
— N. Cinco, *m.* (number, card, figure). || SP. Equipo (*m.*) de cinco jugadores. || U. S. FAM. Billete (*m.*) de cinco dólares. || — *Five o'clock*, las cinco. || *Ten past five*, las cinco y diez.
five-and-ten [ˈfaivəntən] n. U. S. Tienda (*f.*) donde todo vale cinco *or* diez centavos.
five-day week [ˈfaivdeiˈwi:k] n. Semana (*f.*) de cinco días laborables.
fivefold [ˈfaivfəuld] adj. Multiplicado por cinco, quíntuplo, pla. || *To increase fivefold*, multiplicar por cinco, quintuplicar.
fiver [ˈfaivə*] n. FAM. Billete (*m.*) de cinco libras (note). || SP. Jugada (*f.*) que vale cinco puntos. || U. S. FAM. Billete (*m.*) de cinco dólares (bill).
fives [ˈfaivz] n. SP. Juego (*m.*) inglés de pelota parecido al frontón.
five-year [ˈfaivjə:] adj. Quinquenal: *five-year plan*, plan quinquenal.
fix [fiks] n. Aprieto, *m.*, apuro, *m.* (difficult situation). || MAR. AVIAT. Situación, *f.*, posición, *f.*, localización, *f.* || — *To be in a bad* o *in a tight fix*, estar en un apuro *or* en un aprieto, estar con el agua al cuello. || MAR. AVIAT. *To get a fix on*, localizar. || FIG. FAM. *To have a fix*, tomar una dosis de droga.
fix [fiks] v. tr. Fijar, asegurar, sujetar (to secure). || Ajustar (to fasten firmly). || Fijar, decidir: *nothing has been fixed yet*, no se ha decidido nada todavía. || Fijar, determinar, establecer (prices). || Fijar, señalar (date). || Precisar, determinar (a position). || Fijar (attention). || Clavar, fijar (eyes). || Poner (hopes). || Grabar (in one's memory). || Echar: *to fix the blame on s.o.*, echar la culpa a alguien. || Arreglar, componer (to mend). || FAM. Arreglar, amañar: *they fixed the race*, arreglaron la carrera. | Untar la mano, sobornar (to bribe): *they fixed him so he would not talk*, le untaron la mano para que no hablase. || CHEM. Fijar (to make solid). || PHOT. Fijar (a negative). || MIL. Calar (bayonet). | Acampar (to set up camp). || U. S. Arreglar (hair, nails). | Preparar, servir, dar (food, drink): *she fixed me a drink*, me sirvió una copa; *I'm fixing your breakfast*, te estoy preparando el desayuno. | Resolver. || — *How are we fixed for time?*, ¿cómo andamos de tiempo? || FAM. *I'll fix him*, ya le arreglaré las cuentas, yo me encargo de él. || *It's all fixed*, ya está todo arreglado. || SP. FAM. *It was fixed*, hubo tongo. || FAM. *That ought to fix him*, con esto tendría que callarse. || *To fix o.s. up*, arreglarse. || *To fix up*, proveer, proporcionar: *they fixed him up with everything he needed*, le proveyeron *or* le proporcionaron todo lo que necesitaba; organizar (to arrange): *they fixed up a return match*, organizaron un partido de vuelta; conseguir una cita (to arrange an interview), instalar (to set up): *he fixed up a darkroom*, instaló un cuarto oscuro; colocar (to place): *the cupboard was fixed up in the corner*, se colocó el armario en la esquina; acondicionar: *he fixed up the room as a workshop*, acondicionó la habitación para taller; arreglar, componer (to mend), curar (to cure), arreglarse, ponerse de acuerdo: *fix it up with him*, ponte de acuerdo *or* arréglate con él.
— V. intr. Fijarse. || *To fix on* o *upon*, decidirse por, escoger (to choose).
fixate [ˈfikseit] v. tr. U. S. Fijar.
— V. intr. U. S. Concentrarse, fijar la mirada, fijarse (*on*, *upon*, en).
fixation [fikˈseiʃən] n. Fijación, *f.*
fixative [ˈfiksətiv] n. Fijador, *m.* (for hair, photos, etc.).
— Adj. Fijador, ra.
fixed [fikst] adj. Fijo, ja: *a fixed seat*, una silla fija; *a fixed income*, una renta fija; *fixed salary*, sueldo fijo. || CHEM. Fijo, ja (nonvolatile): *a fixed acid*, un ácido fijo. || FAM. Amañado, da; arreglado, da: *a fixed election*, una elección arreglada. || — *Fixed bayonet*, bayoneta calada. || *Fixed idea*, idea fija. || U. S. *To be well fixed*, estar acomodado.
fixedness [—nis] n. Fijeza, *f.*
fixer [ˈfiksə*] n. PHOT. Fijador, *m.* || U. S. Sobornador, *m.* (briber).
fixing [ˈfiksiŋ] n. Fijación, *f.* || PHOT. Fijado, *m.*, fijación, *f.* || — Pl. Guarnición, *f. sing.* (of a dish). || Accesorios, *m. pl.* (accessories).
fixity [ˈfiksiti] n. Fijeza, *f.* || Estabilidad, *f.*, fijeza, *f.* (stability).
fixture [ˈfikstʃə*] n. Instalación (*f.*) fija (sth. permanent). || Aparato, *m.*, dispositivo, *m.* (device). || Accesorio, *m.* (accessory). || Artefacto, *m.* (contrivance). || SP. Fecha (*f.*) fijada (date). | Encuentro, *m.*, partido, *m.* (match). || FIG. FAM. *He is a fixture here*, parece que siempre ha estado aquí.
fizz [fiz] n. Burbujeo, *m.* (sparkle). || Efervescencia, *f.* (effervescence). || FAM. Gaseosa, *f.*, bebida (*f.*) gaseosa (effervescent drink). | Champaña, *f.*, champán, *m.* (champagne). || Ruido (*m.*) sibilante (hissing).
fizz [fiz] v. intr. Burbujear (effervescent liquid). || Hacer un ruido sibilante.
fizzle [ˈfizl] n. FAM. Fracaso, *m.*, fallo, *m.* (failure).
fizzle [ˈfizl] v. intr. See FIZZ. || FIG. FAM. *To fizzle out*, fallar, fracasar.
fizzy [ˈfizi] adj. Efervescente, gaseoso, sa (mineral water, etc.). || Espumoso, sa (wine).
fjord [fjɔ:d] n. Fiordo, *m.*
flabbergast [ˈflæbəgɑ:st] v. tr. Pasmar, asombrar: *I was flabbergasted by his success*, su éxito me dejó pasmado, me quedé pasmado ante su éxito.
flabbiness [ˈflæbinis] n. Blandura, *f.*, flaccidez, *f.*, flacidez, *f.* (of muscles). || Flaccidez, *f.*, flacidez, *f.* (of flesh).
flabby [ˈflæbi] adj. Fláccido, da; flácido, da; fofo, fa; flojo, ja (skin, muscles, etc.). || FIG. Soso, sa (style). | Blandengue (lacking character). | Debilucho, cha (weak).
flabellum [fləˌbeləm] n. Flabelo, *m.*
— OBSERV. El plural de *flabellum* es *flabella*.
flaccid [ˈflæksid] adj. Fláccido, da; flácido, da.
flaccidity [flækˈsiditi] n. Flaccidez, *f.*, flacidez, *f.*
flag [flæg] n. Bandera, *f.*, pabellón, *m.* (banner): *the French flag*, la bandera francesa; *the regiment's flag*, la bandera del regimiento. || Banderín, *m.* (pennant). || Banderín, *m.* (in sports). || Banderita, *f.* (charity). || Bandera, *f.* (in a taxi). || Pluma (*f.*) secundaria (of birds). || BOT. Lirio, *m.* || Baldosa, *f.*, losa, *f.* (paving stone). || Rabo, *m.* (of a hunting dog). || — *Answering flag*, bandera de inteligencia. || *Flag at half-mast*, bandera a media asta. || *Flag of truce*, bandera de parlamento *or* de paz. || *Quarantine flag*, bandera amarilla. || *To deck a building with flags*, engalanar un edificio con banderas. || *To dip the flag*, arriar [la] bandera. || *To hoist the flag*, izar la bandera. || FIG. *To keep the flag flying*, mantener alto el pabellón. | *To show the flag*, hacer acto de presencia (to make an appearance). || *To strike the flag*, arriar [la] bandera. || *To take the pledge of allegiance to the flag*, jurar la bandera. || *White flag*, bandera blanca.
flag [flæg] v. tr. Embaldosar, enlosar (to pave). || Hacer señales con banderas a (to signal). || Transmitir por señales (a message). || *To flag down*, detener haciendo señales.
— V. intr. Colgar (to hang). || Flaquear (to weaken). || Decaer (interest, enthusiasm). || Languidecer (conversation). || Marchitarse (plants).
Flag Day [—dei] n. Día (*m.*) de la banderita. || U. S. Catorce (*m.*) de junio.
flagellant [ˈflædʒilənt] adj./n. Flagelante.
flagellatae [flædʒeˈleitiː] pl. n. BIOL. Flagelados, *m.*
flagellate [ˈflædʒelit] adj. Flagelado, da.
flagellate [ˈflædʒeleit] v. tr. Flagelar, azotar.
flagellation [ˌflædʒeˈleiʃən] n. Flagelación, *f.*
flagellator [ˈflædʒeleitə*] n. Flagelador, ra.
flagellum [fləˈdʒeləm] n. BIOL. Flagelo, *m.*
— OBSERV. El plural de *flagellum* es *flagella* o *flagellums*.
flageolet [ˌflædʒəuˈlet] n. MUS. Chirimía, *f.*
flagging [flægiŋ] adj. Flojo, ja; desmadejado, da.
— N. Embaldosado, *m.*, enlosado, *m.* (paving stones).
flagitious [fləˈdʒiʃəs] adj. Malvado, da (wicked). || Infame (vile).
flagitiousness [—nis] n. Maldad, *f.*, infamia, *f.*
flagman [ˈflægmən] n. Guardavía, *m.*
— OBSERV. El plural de esta palabra es *flagmen*.
flag officer [ˈflægˌɔfisə*] n. Oficial (*m.*) general de Marina [almirante, vicealmirante o contralmirante].
flagon [ˈflægən] n. Jarra, *f.* (with a handle). || REL. Vinajera, *f.* || Botella, *f.* [de dos litros] (large bottle).
flagpole [ˈflægpəul] n. Asta (*f.*) de bandera.
flagrancy [ˈfleigrənsi] n. Flagrancia, *f.*, lo escandaloso.
flagrant [ˈfleigrənt] adj. Flagrante (conspicuous). || Escandaloso, sa; descarado, da (scandalous).
flagrante delicto [flæˈgræntidiˈliktə] n. JUR. Flagrante delito, *m.*
flagship [ˈflægʃip] n. MAR. Buque (*m.*) insignia *or* almirante.
flagstaff [ˈflægstɑ:f] n. Asta (*f.*) de bandera.
flag station [ˈflægˈsteiʃən] n. Apeadero, *m.* (railway).
flagstone [ˈflægstəun] n. Baldosa, *f.*, losa, *f.*
flail [fleil] n. AGR. Mayal, *m.*, desgranador, *m.*
flail [fleil] v. tr. Desgranar (to thresh). || Azotar (to thrash). || Sacudir (to beat). || Agitar (to wave).
— V. intr. Agitarse (to wave about).
flair [flɛə*] n. Instinto, *m.* (instinct). || Don, *m.*: *he has a flair for saying the wrong thing*, tiene el don de decir lo que no debe; *he has a flair for languages*, tiene don de lenguas. || Talento, *m.*: *he has a flair for acting*, tiene talento de actor. || *To have a flair for bargains*, tener buena vista *or* buen olfato para las gangas.
flak [flæk] n. MIL. Fuego (*m.*) antiaéreo. | Artillería (*f.*) antiaérea (guns).
flake [fleik] n. Copo, *m.* (thin fragment): *flake of snow*, copo de nieve. || Escama, *f.* (of mica). || Desconchón, *m.* (thin scale): *flake of paint*, desconchón de pintura. || Trozo, *m.*, pedazo, *m.*: *flakes of fish*, pedazos de pescado. || Chispa, *f.* (of fire). || Copo, *m.* (of cereal). || Cañizo, *m.* (for drying fish). || — *Flake pastry*, hojaldre, *m.* || *Soap flakes*, jabón (*m. sing.*) en escamas, escamas de jabón.
flake [fleik] v. tr. Desconchar: *to flake paint off a wall*, desconchar la pintura de una pared. || Cubrir de copos (to cover with flakes). || FAM. *To be flaked out*, estar agotado *or* rendido.
— V. intr. Desconcharse, desprenderse (to come away in pieces). || Caer en copos (to fall like snow). || FAM. *To flake out*, caer rendido.
flake white [—ˈwait] n. Albayalde, *m.*
flaky [ˈfleiki] adj. Escamoso, sa. || CULIN. Hojaldrado, da. || *Flaky pastry*, hojaldre, *m.*

flambé [ˈflɑmbei] adj. CULIN. Flameado, da: *flambé bananas*, plátanos flameados.

flambeau [ˈflæmbəu] n. Hachón, *m.*, antorcha, *f.*

— OBSERV. El plural es *flambeaux* o *flambeaus*.

flamboyance [flæmˈbɔiəns] n. Extravagancia, *f.*

flamboyant [flæmˈbɔiənt] adj. Llamativo, va; vistoso, sa (clothes, etc.). || Extravagante (ostentatious). || Flameante (flame-like). || Rimbombante, florido, da (style). || ARCH. Flamígero, ra; florido, da (Gothic style).

— N. BOT. Framboyán, *m.*

flame [fleim] n. Llama, *f.* (burning gas). || Llamarada, *f.* (a sudden blaze). || Destello, *m.*, reflejo, *m.* (of a diamond). || Brillo, *m.* (of a colour). || FIG. Llama, *f.* (of passion). || FAM. Amor, *m.* (boy or girlfriend): *and old flame of mine*, un antiguo amor mío. || — Pl. Fuego, *m. sing.*: *the flames of sunset*, el fuego del ocaso. || — *In flames*, en llamas. || FIG. *The flame of youth*, el ardor juvenil. || *To burst into flames*, incendiarse (house), empezar a arder (papers, etc.). || *To commit a manuscript to the flames*, entregar un manuscrito a las llamas. || *To commit s.o. to the flames*, condenar a alguien a la hoguera. || *To go up in flames*, arder.

flame [fleim] v. tr. MED. Flamear (to sterilize). || CULIN. Flamear.

— V. intr. Arder, llamear (to burn). || Brillar (to shine). || Encenderse (face). || — *To flame up*, inflamarse (people): *he flamed up with passion*, se inflamó de pasión; arder, inflamarse (objects).

flamenco [fləˈmeŋkəu] n. Flamenco, *m.*

— Adj. Flamenco, ca: *flamenco guitar*, guitarra flamenca. || *Flamenco song*, cante flamenco.

flameout [ˈfleimaut] n. AVIAT. Avería (*f.*) en el sistema de combustión (jet engines).

flameproof [ˈfleimpru:f] adj. Ininflamable, a prueba de fuego.

flamethrower [ˈfleimθrəuə*] n. MIL. Lanzallamas, *m. inv.* (weapon).

flaming [ˈfleimiŋ] adj. Llameante (in flames). || Abrasador, ra (very hot). || FIG. Ardiente, apasionado, da (passionate). || FAM. Maldito, ta.

— N. Flameado, *m.*

flamingo [fləˈmiŋgəu] n. Flamenco, *m.* (bird).

— OBSERV. El plural es *flamingos* o *flamingoes*.

flammability [ˌflæməˈbiliti] n. Inflamabilidad, *f.*

flammable [ˈflæməbl] adj. Inflamable.

flan [flæn] n. Tarta (*f.*) de frutas (fruit tart). || Flan, *m.* (baked custard).

Flanders [ˈflɑ:ndəz] pr. n. GEOGR. Flandes, *m.*

flange [flændʒ] n. Pestaña, *f.*, reborde, *m.* (projecting rim). || Pestaña, *f.*, ceja, *f.* (of a wheel). || Collarín, *m.* (of a pipe). || Base, *f.* (of a rail).

flange [flændʒ] v. tr. Rebordear.

flanger [—ə*] n. TECH. Rebordeador, *m.*

flank [flæŋk] n. Ijada, *f.*, ijar, *m.* (of an animal). || Costado, *m.* (of a person). || MIL. Flanco, *m.*: *they attacked on the right flank*, atacaron por el flanco derecho. || Ladera, *f.*, falda, *f.* (of a hill). || Lado, *m.* (side).

flank [flæŋk] v. tr. Bordear: *the trees flanked the road*, los árboles bordeaban el camino. || Lindar con (to adjoin). || MIL. Flanquear. || *Flanked by mountains*, flanqueado por montañas.

flanking [—iŋ] n. Flanqueo, *m.*

flannel [ˈflænl] n. Franela, *f.* (material). || Pañito (*m.*) para lavarse la cara, guante, *m.*, manopla, *f.* (for washing). || Trapo, *m.* (duster). || FAM. Coba, *f.* (flattery). || — Pl. Pantalones (*m.*) de franela (trousers). || Ropa (*f. sing.*) interior de franela (underwear).

— Adj. De franela.

flannel [ˈflænl] v. tr. Frotar con un pañito. || FAM. Dar coba a (to flatter).

flannelette [ˌflænlˈet] n. Franela (*f.*) de algodón.

flap [flæp] n. Solapa, *f.* (of envelopes, book cover, etc.). || Carterita, *f.* (of pocket). || Faldón, *m.* (of coat). || Ala, *f.* (of hat). || Oreja, *f.* (of shoe). || Ala (*f.*) abatible (of table). || Trampa, *f.* (of counter). || Chasquido, *m.* (noise). || Gualdrapazo, *m.* (movement of sail). || Aleteo, *m.* (of wings, etc.). || Aletazo, *m.* (stroke of the wing). || Bofetada, *f.* (slap). || FAM. Confusión, *f.* (loss of self-confidence). | Jaleo, *m.* (fuss). | Crisis, *f.* || AVIAT. Alerón, *m.*, "flap", *m.* (of aircraft). || MED. Colgajo, *m.* (piece of skin). || ANAT. Lóbulo, *m.* (of the ear). || — FAM. *There was a big flap about it*, se armó un lío *or* un jaleo. | *To get into a flap*, ponerse nervioso.

flap [flæp] v. tr. Batir (wings). || Agitar (arms). || Sacudir (to shake). || Dar una bofetada a (to slap).

— V. intr. Aletear (wings). || Restallar, chasquear (flag). || Gualdrapear (sail). || FAM. Ponerse nervioso.

flapdoodle [—ˌdu:dl] n. FAM. Tonterías, *f. pl.*, bobadas, *f. pl.* (nonsense).

flapjack [—dʒæk] n. Torta, *f.* (cake). || Polvera, *f.* [plana y redonda] (powder compact).

flapper [—ə*] n. Batidor, *m.* (thing that flaps). || Matamoscas, *m. inv.* (fly swatter). || Polluelo, *m.* (young duck or partridge). || ZOOL. Aleta, *f.* [ancha] (large flipper). | Cola, *f.* (tail of crustacean). || Joven (*f.*) emancipada de los años veinte.

flapping [—iŋ] n. Aleteo, *m.* (of wings). || Ondeo, *m.* (of flag). || Gualdrapazo, *m.* (of sail).

flare [fleə*] n. Fulgor, *m.* (shine). || Llamarada, *f.* (blaze). || MIL. MAR. AVIAT. Cohete (*m.*) de señales, bengala, *f.* (signal). || Ensanchamiento, *m.* (widening). || Vuelo, *m.*: *the skirt needs more flare*, la falda necesita más vuelo. || PHOT. Mancha (*f.*) luminosa. || FIG. Arrebato, *m.* (of anger). || — *A skirt with a flare*, una falda acampanada. || *Solar flare*, erupción (*f.*) solar.

flare [fleə*] v. tr. Hacer llamear (to cause to emit flames). || Ensanchar (to make wider). || Acampanar (trousers, skirt).

— V. intr. Llamear (fire, flames). || Acampanarse (clothes). || Ensancharse (to get wider). || Resplandecer (light). || *To flare up*, llamear (flames, light), encolerizarse, ponerse furioso (in anger), estallar (to break out), declararse (epidemic).

flareback [—bæk] n. Llamarada, *f.* (in a furnace).

flare path [—pɑ:θ] n. AVIAT. Pista (*f.*) iluminada con balizas.

flare-up [—ʌp] n. Llamarada, *f.* (flames). || FIG. Arrebato (*m.*) de cólera (anger). | Pelea, *f.*, riña, *f.* (quarrel). | Estallido, *m.* (of a revolution). | Declaración, *f.* (of an epidemic).

flaring [—iŋ] adj. Resplandeciente (light). || Llamativo, va (colour). || Acampanado, da (skirt).

flash [flæʃ] adj. FAM. Chillón, ona; llamativo, va (gaudy). | Elegante (elegant). | Chulo, la (vulgarly pretentious). || *Flash language*, germanía, *f.*

— N. Destello, *m.* (sudden burst of light). || Centelleo, *m.* (sparkle, glitter). || PHOT. Flash, *m.*, luz (*f.*) relámpago. || Fogonazo, *m.* (flame of gun). || Instante, *m.*, momento, *m.* (short space of time): *in a flash*, en un momento. || FIG. Resquicio, *m.*: *a flash of hope*, un resquicio de esperanza. | Rasgo, *m.* (sudden manifestation): *a flash of genious* o *of wit*, un rasgo de ingenio. | Ráfaga, *f.*: *a flash of inspiration*, una ráfaga de inspiración. | Ostentación, *f.* || Noticia (*f.*) de última hora, flash, *m.* (on radio, television, etc.). || — FIG. *A flash in the pan*, una llamarada, una cosa que no dura. || *A flash of lightning*, un relámpago. || FIG. *Like a flash*, como un relámpago.

flash [flæʃ] v. tr. Despedir, lanzar (to emit light). || Transmitir (to transmit a message). || Esgrimir (a sword, knife). || Dirigir: *flash the torch this way*, dirige la linterna por aquí. || Encender (to light): *flash the torch on*, enciende la linterna. || Reflejar (to reflect). || FIG. Echar (a smile). | Lanzar (a glance). | Enseñar con ostentación: *he flashed a wad of banknotes at me*, me enseñó con ostentación un fajo de billetes. || TECH. Chapar (to coat). | Laminar (glass). || — *He flashed the light in my eyes*, me deslumbró con la linterna. || *To flash about* o *around*, hacer ostentación de: *he always flashes his money around*, siempre hace ostentación de su dinero.

— V. intr. Echar destellos, destellar (to emit momentary light). || Centellear (a light, stars, jewel, etc.). || Brillar (to shine): *his knife flashed in the sun*, su cuchillo brilló al sol. || — FIG. *An idea flashed across* o *through my mind*, se me ocurrió una idea, una idea me pasó por la cabeza. | *His eyes flashed with anger*, echaba chispas. || CINEM. *To flash back*, retroceder. || FIG. *To flash past, across, etc.*, pasar, cruzar, etc. como un rayo.

flashback [—bæk] n. Escena (*f.*) retrospectiva (cinema, novel, etc.). || Retroceso (*m.*) de la llama (in a furnace).

flashboard [—bɔ:d] n. Alza (*f.*) móvil (of a dam).

flashbulb [—bʌlb] n. PHOT. Flash, *m.*, bombilla (*f.*) de magnesio.

flasher [—ə*] n. Luz (*f.*) intermitente.

flash flood [—flʌd] n. U. S. Riada, *f.*

flashgun [—gʌn] n. PHOT. Disparador (*m.*) de flash.

flashily [—ili] adv. Ostentosamente.

flashiness [—inis] n. Ostentación, *f.* || Color (*m.*) *or* aspecto (*m.*) llamativo (of clothes).

flashing [—iŋ] adj. Intermitente (light). || Brillante (eyes).

flash lamp [—læmp] n. Linterna, *f.* (torch). || PHOT. Flash, *m.*, luz (*f.*) relámpago, lámpara (*f.*) relámpago.

flashlight [—ˈlait] n. Linterna, *f.* (torch). || PHOT. Flash, *m.*, luz (*f.*) relámpago. || MAR. Luz (*f.*) intermitente (of a lighthouse).

flashover [—ˈəuvə*] n. ELECTR. Descarga, *f.*

flash point [—pɔint] n. Punto (*m.*) de inflamación.

flashy [—i] adj. Chillón, ona; llamativo, va (showy). || Ostentoso, sa (ostentatious). || De relumbrón (jewel).

flask [flɑ:sk] n. CHEM. Matraz, *m.* || Frasco, *m.* (pocket container). || Termo, *m.* (thermos). || Polvorín, *m.* (for powder). || Caja (*f.*) de moldear (in foundries).

flat [flæt] adj. Llano, na (level): *flat countryside*, paisaje llano. || Plano, na (object, surface). || Uniforme, liso, sa (uniform). || Suave (curve). || Chato, ta (nose). || Plano, na (foot). || Arrasado, da (after a bombing). || Horizontal (horizontal). || Tendido, da (taut). || Mate (without gloss). || Sin relieve (picture). || FIG. Categórico, ca; rotundo, da; terminante (outright): *a flat refusal*, una negativa rotunda. | Soso, sa; insípido, da (style, taste, etc.). | Monótono, na (monotonous): *flat existence*, vida monótona. | Aburrido, da; pesado, da (boring). | Deprimido, da (depressed). || COMM. Inactivo, va (market). | Uniforme (price). | Fijo, ja (rate). | Sin intereses (shares). || MUS. Bemol: *C flat*, do bemol. | Desafinado, da (below correct pitch). | Sordo, da; apagado, da (sound). || AUT. Desinflado, da (tyre). | Descargado, da (battery). || SP. Sin obstáculos (horse racing). | Liso, sa: *100 metres flat*, 100 metros lisos. || MAR. En calma (sea). || — *Bombed flat*, arrasado por las bombas. || FAM. *Flat as a pancake*, completamente llano, na; liso como la palma de la mano (ground), totalmente liso (uniform), aplastado, da (crushed). || *Flat beer*, cerveza muerta *or* que ha perdido el gas. || *Flat joke*, chiste malo *or* grosero. || *In ten seconds flat*, en diez segundos justos. || FIG. *That's flat!*, ¡es mi última palabra! | *To feel flat*, no estar en forma, estar abatido *or* deprimido. | *To fall flat*, fracasar (to fail), no hacer ninguna gracia (joke). || *To fall flat on one's back*, caer *or* caerse de espaldas. || *To fall flat on one's face*, caer *or* caerse de bruces. || *To lay flat*, see LAY.

— Adv. Completamente (absolutely). || Terminantemente, categóricamente, rotundamente: *he told me flat I could not go*, me dijo categóricamente que yo no podía ir. || — FAM. *To be flat broke*, estar sin blanca, no tener un céntimo. | *To go flat out*, ir a todo gas, ir a toda mecha. | *To go flat out for*, hacer todo lo posible para conseguir. || MUS. *To play* o *to sing flat*, desafinar. || *To turn sth. down flat*, rechazar algo de plano.

— N. Superficie (*f.*) plana (surface). || Plano, *m.* (of a sword). || Palma, *f.* (of hand). || Llano, *m.* (flat land). || THEATR. Trasto, *m.*, decorado (*m.*) móvil (portable scenery). || Piso, *m.* (set of rooms). || Apartamento, *m.* (small dwelling). || MUS. Bemol, *m.* || Pinchazo, *m.* (flat tyre). || Batea, *f.* (flatcar). || MAR. Chata, *f.*, chalana, *f.* (boat). | Bajo, *m.*, bajío, *m.* (shallow). || MUS. *Sharps and flats*, teclas negras (of a piano), sostenidos y bemoles (in written music).

flat [flæt] v. tr. MUS. Bemolar.

flatboat [—bəut] n. Chalana, *f.*, chata, *f.* (boat).

flatcar [—kɑ:*] n. Batea, *f.* (railway carriage).

flat-chested [—ˌtʃestid] adj. Lisa, sin pecho (a woman).

flatfish [—fiʃ] n. Platija, *f.* (fish).

flatfoot [—fut] n. Pie (*m.*) plano. || FAM. Poli, *m.* (policeman).

flat-footed [—ˈfutid] adj. De pies planos (having flatfeet). || FAM. Patoso, sa (clumsy). || U. S. FAM. Resuelto, ta (determined).

flatiron [—ˌaiən] n. Plancha, *f.* (for pressing).

flatlet [—let] n. Piso (*m.*) pequeño.

flatly [—li] adv. Categóricamente, terminantemente, rotundamente (categorically). || Completamente (absolutely).

flatness [—nis] n. Llanura, *f.*, lo llano (of land). || Lisura, *f.* (smoothness). || Insipidez, *f.* (of taste). || FIG. Monotonía, *f.* (monotonoy).

flat-nosed [—nəuzd] adj. Chato, ta.

flat spin [—spin] n. AVIAT. Barrena (*f.*) plana.

flatten [ˈflætn] v. tr. Aplastar (to crush). || Aplanar, allanar (to make flat). || Alisar (to smooth). || CULIN. FIG. Volver soso *or* insípido. || MUS. Bemolar. || Volver mate (colours, painting). || FIG. Derribar (to knock down). | Aplastar (to defeat). || *To flatten o.s. against the ground*, pegarse al suelo.

— V. intr. Aplanarse, allanarse. || CULIN. FIG. Volverse soso *or* insípido. || Perder el gas (beer, etc.). || AVIAT. *To flatten out*, enderezarse.

flatter [ˈflætə*] v. tr. Adular, halagar, lisonjear (to praise): *to flatter the ladies*, adular a las mujeres. || Halagar (to gratify the vanity): *he was flattered by the invitation*, se sintió halagado con la invitación. || Favorecer (to make look more handsome): *the dress, the hairstyle flatters you*, el vestido, el peinado te favorece; *the portrait flatters you*, estás favorecido en el retrato. || — *To flatter o.s.*, congratularse, jactarse (*on*, de; *that*, de que) [to be pleased], presumir (to show off). || *To flatter o.s. with hopes*, abrigar esperanzas.

flatterer [—rə*] n. Adulador, ra; lisonjero, ra.

flattering [—riŋ] adj. Favorecedor, ra; que favorece: *a flattering dress*, un vestido favorecedor. || Adulador, ra; lisonjero, ra; halagador, ra (person). || Halagüeño, ña; lisonjero, ra (words).

flatteringly [—riŋli] adv. Con palabras lisonjeras.

flattery [—ri] n. Halago, *m.*, adulación, *f.*, lisonja, *f.*: *flattery will get you nowhere*, la adulación no te llevará a ninguna parte. || Halagos, *m. pl.*, adulaciones, *f. pl.*, lisonjas, *f. pl.* (words). || *A piece of flattery*, un halago, una lisonja.

flattop [ˈflætɔp] n. U. S. MAR. Portaaviones, *m. inv.*

flatulence [ˈflætjuləns] n. Flatulencia, *f.* || FIG. Pomposidad, *f.*, ampulosidad, *f.* (of style). | Engreimiento, *m.* (conceit).

flatulent [ˈflætjulənt] adj. MED. Flatulento, ta. || FIG. Ampuloso, sa; pomposo, sa (pretentious). | Engreído, da; hinchado, da (person).

flatus [ˈfleitəs] n. Flato, *m.*

flatware [ˈflætwεə] n. Platos (*m. pl.*) y cubiertos.

flatways [ˈflætweiz] or **flatwise** [ˈflætwaiz] adv. Horizontalmente, de plano.

flatworm [ˈflætwə:m] n. Platelminto, *m.*

flaunt [flɔ:nt] n. Ostentación, *f.*, alarde, *m.*

flaunt [flɔ:nt] v. tr. Ostentar, hacer alarde de (to display proudly): *he flaunts his riches*, hace alarde de su riqueza. || U. S. Burlarse de (to flout).

— V. intr. Ondear (a flag, etc.). || Pavonearse (to show off).

flautist [ˈflɔ:tist] n. Flautista, *m.* & *f.*

flavescent [fləˈvesənt] adj. Amarillento, ta.

flavour (U. S. **flavor**) [ˈfleivə*] n. Sabor, *m.*, gusto, *m.* (taste): *an orange flavour*, un sabor a naranja; *a pleasant flavour*, un sabor agradable. || Aroma, *m.* || Condimento, *m.* (flavouring). || FIG. Sabor, *m.*: *a poem with a classical flavour*, un poema de sabor clásico.

flavour (U. S. **flavor**) [ˈfleivə] v. tr. Condimentar, sazonar. || FIG. *To flavour a novel with mystery*, darle un tinte de misterio a una novela.

flavouring (U. S. **flavoring**) [—riŋ] n. Condimento, *m.*

flavourless (U. S. **flavorless**) [—lis] adj. Insípido, da, soso, sa.

flaw [flɔ:] n. Grieta, *f.* (crack or gap). || Defecto, *m.*, desperfecto, *m.*, imperfección, *f.* (a blemish, defect). || Jardín, *m.* (in a gem). || Defecto, *m.*, pelo, *m.*, quebraza, *f.* (in metal). || Fallo, *m.* (error, weakness): *this was the only flaw in his argument*, era el único fallo en su argumento. || Borrasca, *f.* (squall).

flaw [flɔ:] v. tr. Estropear (to spoil). || Agrietar (to crack). || *I flawed his argument on two points*, encontré dos fallos en su argumento.

— V. intr. Agrietarse. || Estropearse.

flawless [—lis] adj. Sin defecto, perfecto, ta.

flax [flæks] n. BOT. Lino, *m.*

flaxen [—ən] adj. De lino. || Rubio, bia (blond).

flax oil [—ɔil] n. Aceite (*m.*) de linaza.

flaxseed [ˈflæksi:d] n. Linaza, *f.*

flay [flei] v. tr. Desollar (an animal). || FIG. Despellejar, desollar (to criticize harshly). | Desollar (to charge extortionately).

flayer [—ə*] n. Desollador, ra.

flaying [—iŋ] n. Desolladura, *f.*

flea [fli:] n. ZOOL. Pulga, *f.* || *To send s.o. away* o *off with a flea in his ear*, echar a alguien con cajas destempladas, mandar a alguien con viento fresco.

fleabite [ˈfli:bait] n. Picadura (*f.*) de pulga (the bite of a flea). || FIG. Cosa (*f.*) sin importancia.

flea-bitten [ˌfli:ˌbitn] adj. Picado de pulgas. || Infestado de pulgas (flea-infested). || Moteado, da (horse). || FAM. Miserable.

fleam [fli:m] n. VET. Fleme, *m.*

flea market [fli:ˈmɑ:kit] n. Rastro, *m.*, mercado (*m.*) de objetos de segunda mano.

flea pit [ˈfli:pit] n. FAM. Cine (*m.*) de baja categoría.

flèche [fleiʃ] n. ARCH. Aguja, *f.*

fleck [flek] n. Mota, *f.*, pinta, *f.* (small mark, speck). || Mancha, *f.* (patch of light, colour). || Peca, *f.* (freckle). || Partícula, *f.* (of dust).

fleck [flek] v. tr. Motear. || Salpicar (with paint).

flection [ˈflekʃən] n. Flexión, *f.* (a bending). || Curvatura, *f.* (a bent part). || GRAMM. Flexión, *f.*, inflexión, *f.*

fled [fled] pret. & p. p. See FLEE.

fledge [fledʒ] v. intr. Emplumecer.

— V. tr. Emplumar (to provide with feathers). || Criar (to bring up a bird).

fledged [—d] adj. Plumado, da. || *Fully-fledged*, see FULL-FLEDGED.

fledgling or **fledgeling** [—liŋ] n. Pájaro (*m.*) volantón, pajarito, *m.* (bird). || FIG. Novato, *m.* (novice). || Crío, *m.* (youngster). || *Fledgling poet*, poeta (*m.*) en ciernes.

flee* [fli:] v. tr. Huir de (to run away from). || Evitar (to shun): *to flee temptation*, evitar la tentación.

— V. intr. Huir (to run away). || Refugiarse (*to*, en) [to take refuge]. || FIG. Desvanecerse: *night had fled*, la noche se había desvanecido.

OBSERV. Pret. & p. p. *fled*.

fleece [fli:s] n. Lana, *f.* (wool). || Piel, *f.* (animal skin with wool). || Vellón, *m.* (sheared wool). || Muletón, *m.* (for lining). || FIG. Capa, *f.* (of snow, clouds, etc.). || — *The Golden Fleece*, el Vellocino de Oro. || *The Order of the Golden Fleece*, la Orden del Toisón de Oro.

fleece [fli:s] v. tr. Esquilar (sheep). || FIG. Desplumar, pelar (to rob).

fleecy [—i] adj. Lanoso, sa; lanudo, da (covered with wool). || Aborregado, da (sky). || Encrespado, da (sea). || En copos (snow).

fleet [fli:t] n. Flota, *f.*: *fishing, air fleet*, flota pesquera, aérea. || Armada, *f.* (national navy). || Escuadra (of cars).

— Adj. Veloz (swift). || Fugaz (transient). || *Fleet of foot*, veloz, rápido, da.

fleet-footed [—ˌfutid] adj. Veloz, rápido, da.

fleeting [—iŋ] adj. Fugaz, efímero, ra (ephemeral). || Breve (very short).

Fleming [ˈflemiŋ] n. Flamenco, ca.

Flemish [ˈflemiʃ] adj. Flamenco, ca. || *Flemish bond*, aparejo flamenco.

— N. Flamenco, *m.* (language).

flench [flentʃ] or **flense** [flenz] v. tr. Despellejar (whale, seal).

flesh [fleʃ] n. Carne, *f.* (of man, animals). || Pulpa, *f.* (of fruit). || FIG. Carne, *f.* (sensual nature of man): *sins of the flesh*, pecados de la carne. | Género (*m.*) humano (mankind). || Color (*m.*) carne (colour). || — FIG. *Flesh and blood*, la naturaleza humana, el hombre. || *In the flesh* o *in flesh and blood*, en carne y hueso, en persona (in person). | *One's own flesh and blood*, los de su propia sangre. | *To make s.o.'s flesh creep* o *crawl*, ponerle a uno la carne de gallina. | *To put on flesh*, echar carnes.

flesh [fleʃ] v. tr. Encarnar (hunting dogs). || Cebar, engordar (to fatten animals). || Descarnar (to remove flesh). || Clavar (a sword).
flesh-coloured (U. S. **flesh-colored**) [—ˌkʌləd] adj. De color carne.
flesh-eating [—ˌi:tiŋ] adj. Carnívoro, ra.
flesh fly [—flai] n. ZOOL. Moscón, *m.*
fleshiness [ˈfleʃinis] adj. Carnosidad, *f.* (of fruit, animals). || Gordura, *f.* (of person).
fleshings [ˈfleʃiŋz] pl. n. THEATR. Mallas (*f.*) de color carne. || Piltrafas, *f.* (scraps of flesh).
fleshless [ˈfleʃlis] adj. Descarnado, da.
fleshliness [ˈfleʃlinis] n. Apetitos (*m. pl.*) carnales.
fleshly [ˈfleʃli] adj. Carnal. || Sensual.
fleshpots [ˈfleʃpɔts] pl. n. Lujo, *m. sing.* (luxury). || FIG. Lugares (*m.*) de perdición.
flesh wound [ˈfleʃwu:nd] n. MED. Herida (*f.*) superficial.
fleshy [ˈfleʃi] adj. Gordo, da (people). || Carnoso, sa (limb, fruit).
fletch [ˈfletʃ] v. tr. Emplumar.
fleur-de-lis or **fleur-de-lys** [ˈflə:dəˈli:s] n. HERALD. Flor (*f.*) de lis.
— OBSERV. El plural de estas palabras es *fleurs-de-lis* y *fleurs-de-lys.*
fleuron [ˈflə:rən] n. Florón, *m.*
flew [flu:] pret. See FLY.
flews [flu:z] pl. n. Belfos, *m.*, morros, *m.* (of dogs).
flex [fleks] n. ELECTR. Flexible, *m.*
flex [fleks] v. tr. Doblar.
— V. intr. Doblarse.
flexibility [ˌfleksəˈbiliti] n. Flexibilidad, *f.*
flexible [ˈfleksəbl] adj. Flexible (easily bent, pliable). || FIG. Elástico, ca; flexible (able to be modified): *a very flexible plan*, un plan muy elástico. || Flexible, adaptable (responsive to changing conditions). || Flexible (character).
flexion [ˈflekʃən] n. See FLECTION.
flexor [ˈfleksə*] n. Músculo (*m.*) flexor, flexor, *m.*
flexure [ˈflekʃə*] n. Flexión, *f.* (action of being flexed). || Curva, *f.* (bend, curve). || GEOL. Pliegue, *m.*
flibbertigibbet [ˈflibətiˈdʒibit] n. Casquivano, na (irresponsible person). || Chismoso, sa (gossip).
flick [flik] n. Golpecito, *m.* (light stroke). || Latigazo (*m.*) suave (with a whip). || Capirotazo, *m.* (of the fingers). || Pasada, *f.* (of a duster). || Toque, *m.* (with a paintbrush). || Movimiento (*m.*) rápido (of the wrist). || Chasquido, *m.* (sound). || FAM. Película, *f.*, filme, *m.* || — *A flick of the whip*, un latigazo. || FAM. *The flicks*, el cine.
flick [flik] v. tr. Chasquear (a whip, one's fingers). || Tirar (a coin, pellet, etc.). || Dar un golpecito a (to strike). || Dar un capirotazo a (s.o.'s ear). || — *To flick one's tail*, dar un coletazo. || *To flick sth. away* o *off*, quitar algo con un capirotazo *or* un golpecito.
— V. intr. Moverse (to move).
flicker [—ə*] n. Parpadeo, *m.* (of light, eyelids). || Llama (*f.*) vacilante (flame). || FIG. Resquicio, *m.*: *a flicker of hope*, un resquicio de esperanza. || — *A flicker of fear*, un estremecimiento. || FIG. *Not a flicker of life*, ni la menor señal de vida.
flicker [—ə*] v.intr. Vacilar (flames). || Parpadear (light). || Temblar (leaves). || Aletear (birds). || Ondear (flag). || Danzar (shadows). || Oscilar (a needle). || FIG. *His life is flickering out*, su vida se está apagando.
flier [ˈflaiə*] n. Aviador, ra (aviator). || Volatinero, ra (acrobat). || FIG. Bólido, *m.* (a fast vehicle, horse, etc.). | Expreso, *m.* (train). || Aleta, *f.* (of spinning machine). || U. S. Prospecto, *m.* (handbill). | Operación (*f.*) *or* inversión (*f.*) arriesgada (reckless gamble). || — Pl. Escalones, *m.*, peldaños, *m.* (steps).
flight [flait] n. Vuelo, *m.* (act or mode of flying, a journey by air). || Recorrido, *m.*, trayectoria, *f.* (distance flown by aeroplane, bird, etc.). || Trayectoria, *f.* (of bullet). || Bandada, *f.* (group of birds). || Escuadrilla, *f.* (group of aircraft). || Descarga, *f.* (of arrows). || SP. Línea (*f.*) de obstáculos (set of hurdles). | Cucharilla, *f.* (fishing). | Flecha (*f.*) ligera (light arrow). || Vuelo, *m.* (of imagination). || Rasgo, *m.* (of wit). || Huida, *f.*, fuga, *f.* (act of fleeing). || — Pl. ZOOL. Remeras, *f.* (of a bird). || — AVIAT. *Blind flight*, vuelo sin visibilidad. | *Flight crew*, tripulación, *f.* | *Flight deck*, cubierta (*f.*) de aterrizaje (aircraft carriers), cabina (*f.*) del piloto (of an aircraft). | *Flight engineer*, mecánico (*m.*) de a bordo. | *Flight formation*, formación (*f.*) de vuelo. | *Flight leader* o *commander*, jefe (*m.*) de patrulla. || *Flight of capital*, evasión (*f.*) *or* fuga (*f.*) de capitales. || *Flight of fancy*, ilusión, *f.* *f.* || *Flight of steps*, tramo (*m.*) de escalera (staircase), escalinata, *f.* (outside steps). || AVIAT. *Flight path*, trayectoria de vuelo. | *In flight*, en vuelo: *to refuel in flight*, repostar en vuelo; durante el vuelo: *drinks served in flight*, bebidas servidas durante el vuelo; huyendo (fleeing). | *Orbital flight*, vuelo orbital. | *Reconnaissance flight*, vuelo de reconocimiento. || *She lives two flights up*, vive dos pisos más arriba. || *To put to flight*, poner en fuga (the enemy), ahuyentar (to scare away). || *To take flight*, alzar el vuelo. || *To take to flight*, darse a la fuga.
flight [flait] v. intr. Volar en bandadas (birds).
— V. tr. Cazar al vuelo.
flightiness [—inis] n. Ligereza, *f.*
flightless [—lis] adj. Incapacitado para volar.
flighty [—i] adj. Frívolo, la; ligero, ra (frivolous). || Caprichoso, sa (capricious). || Inconstante (changeable). || Casquivano, na (irresponsible).
flimflam [ˈflim-flæm] n. FAM. Fruslería, *f.*, tontería, *f.* || U. S. Engaño, *m.* (deception).
flimsiness [ˈflimzinis] n. Debilidad, *f.*, endeblez, *f.* (weakness). || Fragilidad, *f.* || Ligereza, *f.* (of cloth). || Finura, *f.* (of paper).
flimsy [ˈflimzi] adj. Débil, endeble (weak). || Frágil (fragile). || Ligero, ra (cloth). || Fino, na (paper). || Insustancial (lacking substance). || FIG. Flojo, ja: *a flimsy excuse*, una excusa floja.
— N. Papel (*m.*) cebolla (transfer paper). || FAM. Billete (*m.*) de banco, pápiro, *m.* (banknote). || — Pl. Copias (*f.*) hechas en papel cebolla.
flinch [flintʃ] n. Mueca (*f.*) de dolor *or* de desagrado. || *To bear pain without a flinch*, soportar el dolor sin pestañear.
flinch [flintʃ] v. intr. Retroceder (to draw back). || Echarse atrás, acobardarse: *to flinch from an unpleasant duty*, echarse atrás ante un trabajo desagradable. || Vacilar (to hesitate). || Inmutarse, pestañear: *to bear pain without flinching*, soportar el dolor sin inmutarse. || Encogerse: *he flinched under the lash of the whip*, se encogió bajo el latigazo; *his face flinched*, se le encogió la cara.
flinders [ˈflindəz] pl. n. Astillas, *f. pl.*: *to break into flinders*, hacerse astillas.
fling [fliŋ] n. Lanzamiento, *m.* (a throw). || Baile (*m.*) escocés (dance). || FIG. Pulla, *f.* (sarcastic attack). || FAM. Juerga, *f.* (a wild time). || — FAM. *To go on* o *to have a fling*, echar una cana al aire. | *To have a fling at*, probar, intentar: *have a fling at opening this door*, prueba tú a ver si abres esta puerta. | *To have one's fling*, correrla. | *Youth will have its fling*, hay que aceptar los excesos de la juventud.
fling* [fliŋ] v. tr. Arrojar, lanzar, tirar (to hurl, to throw): *he flung a stone at me*, me tiró una piedra. || Echar (to move violently): *he flung his arms around her neck*, le echó los brazos al cuello. || Precipitar, lanzar (to send into attack). || Soltar (abuse, etc.). || Sumir: *the news flung the crowd into confusion*, la noticia sumió a la multitud en la confusión. || — *He flung the door in my face*, me dio con la puerta en las narices. || *He flung the door open*, abrió la puerta de golpe. || *He flung the door shut*, cerró la puerta de golpe. || *To fling o.s.*, lanzarse, tirarse, arrojarse. || *To fling o.s. into a chair*, dejarse caer en una silla. || *To fling s.o. into jail*, meter a uno en la cárcel, encarcelar a uno.
— V. intr. Precipitarse, lanzarse (to dash).
— ***To fling about***, esparcir (objects). | Agitar (arms etc.). | Despilfarrar (money). || ***To fling aside***, tirar (to throw away). | Dejar de lado: *he flung aside the advice of his friends*, dejó de lado los consejos de sus amigos. || ***To fling away***, tirar (to throw). | Desperdiciar (an opportunity). || ***To fling back***, devolver (ball). | Echar hacia atrás (the head). | Rechazar (the enemy). || ***To fling down***, tirar al suelo. | Derribar (a building). || ***To fling off***, quitarse rápidamente (clothes). | Salir disparado (to go out). || ***To fling out***, cocear (horses). | Soltar (a remark). | Abrir (one's arms). | FAM. Poner de patitas en la calle (to kick s.o. out). | Salir disparado: *he flung out of the room*, salió disparado de la habitación. || FAM. ***To fling up***, abandonar (one's job, etc.).
— OBSERV. Pret. & p. p. **flung**.
flint [flint] n. Pedernal, *m.* (rock). || Hacha (*f.*) de sílex (prehistoric tool). || Piedra, *f.*, pedernal, *m.* (anything hard): *a heart of flint*, un corazón de piedra. || Piedra (*f.*) de chispa, pedernal, *m.* (for striking fire, for guns). || Piedra (*f.*) de mechero (of cigarette lighter). || FIG. FAM. *To skin a flint*, ser tacaño.
flint glass [—glɑ:s] n. Flint-glass, *m.*, flintglas, *m.* (heavy brilliant glass).
flintlock [—lɔk] n. Fusil (*m.*) de chispa (gun). || Llave (*f.*) de chispa (gunlock).
flinty [—i] adj. De pedernal. || FIG. De piedra (heart).
flip [flip] n. Capirotazo, *m.* (flick of the fingers). || Golpe, *m.* (quick blow). || Vuelo, *m.* (short plane flight). || Flip, *m.* (drink). || *With a flip of its tail*, de *or* con un coletazo.
flip [flip] v. tr. Dar un capirotazo a (to flick). || Echar [algo] al aire [con los dedos] (to toss with the fingers). || Quitarse de un manotazo: *he flipped an insect from his face*, se quitó de un manotazo el insecto que tenía en la cara. || — *He flipped the book shut*, cerró el libro de golpe. || *To flip a coin*, echar a cara o cruz (to toss up). || FAM. *To flip one's lid*, see LID.
flippancy [ˈflipənsi] n. Ligereza, *f.* (lack of seriousness). || Impertinencia, *f.* (flippant remark).
flippant [ˈflipənt] adj. Ligero, ra; frívolo, la (frivolous). || Irrespetuoso, sa; impertinente (lacking respect).
flipper [ˈflipə*] n. Aleta, *f.* (of whale, seal). || FAM. Garra, *f.*, mano, *f.* (hand). || — Pl. Aletas, *f.* (of a swimmer).
flirt [flə:t] n. Mariposón, *m.* (man). || Coqueta, *f.* (girl). || Meneo, *m.* (quick movement).
flirt [flə:t] v. tr. Agitar (fan, bird's tail, etc.).
— V. intr. Flirtear, coquetear (to play at courtship). || — FIG. *To flirt with a dangerous situation*, jugar con una situación peligrosa. | *To flirt with an idea*, acariciar una idea.

flirtation [flə:'teiʃən] n. Coqueteo, *m.*, flirteo, *m.*
flirtatious [flə:'teiʃəs] adj. Coqueto, ta (glance, woman). || Mariposón (man).
flirting ['flə:tiŋ] n. Coqueteo, *m.*, flirteo, *m.*
flit [flit] n. Revoloteo, *m.* (of birds). || Mudanza (*f.*) secreta (act of moving out secretly). || *To do a moonlight flit*, mudarse a escondidas, irse a la chita callando (to move out secretly), desaparecer de la noche a la mañana (to disappear overnight).
flit [flit] v. intr. Revolotear (to make short flights). || Mudarse a escondidas (to move out secretly). || — FIG. *An idea flitted through his mind*, le pasó una idea por la cabeza. || *To flit about*, ir y venir sin ruido.
flitch [flitʃ] n. Costero, *m.* (of tree trunk). || — *Flitch beam*, viga (*f.*) de tablones adosados. || *Flitch of bacon*, lonja (*f.*) de tocino.
flitter ['flitə*] v. intr. Revolotear.
flittermouse [—maus] n. Murciélago, *m.* (bat).
flivver ['flivə*] n. U. S. FAM. Cacharro, *m.* (cheap old car or plane).
float [fləut] n. Flotador, *m.* (for aircraft, fishing nets, carburettor, cistern, life raft). || Corcho, *m.* (on a fishing line). || Balsa, *f.* (raft). || ZOOL. Vejiga (*f.*) natatoria (of fish). || Masa (*f.*) flotante (of weeds, ice, etc.). || Carroza, *f.* (for carnivals, displays). || Llana, *f.* (trowel for smoothing). || — Pl. THEATR. Candilejas, *f.*
float [fləut] v. intr. Flotar: *to float on the water, through the air*, flotar en el agua, en el aire. || Ondear, flotar (flag in the wind). || FIG. Flotar: *ideas floated through his mind*, las ideas flotaban en su mente. | Vagar (to wander aimlessly). | Correr (rumours). || COMM. Flotar (a currency). || — *It floated to the surface*, salió a la superficie. || FIG. *To float along with the stream*, dejarse llevar por la corriente. | *To float on air*, estar eufórico. || *To float on one's back*, flotar boca arriba, hacer el muerto. || *To float to the surface*, salir a la superficie.
— V. tr. Hacer flotar (to support). || Poner a flote (to set afloat). || Inundar (to flood). || Lanzar (a company, business). || Hacer correr (rumours, ideas). || COMM. Hacer flotar (a currency). | Emitir (shares, loan). || Allanar (to smooth).
floatability [fləutə'biliti] n. Flotabilidad, *f.*
floatable ['fləutəbl] adj. Flotable.
floatage ['fləutidʒ] n. Flotación, *f.* (act of floating). || Flotabilidad, *f.* (ability to float). || Obra (*f.*) muerta (part of a boat over waterline). || Tonelaje (*m.*) a flote, arqueo, *m.* (tonnage). || Pecios, *m. pl.* (flotsam).
floatation [fləu'teiʃən] n. Flotación, *f.* || COMM. Emisión, *f.* (of loan). | Lanzamiento, *m.* (of a firm).
floater ['fləutə*] n. Flotador, *m.* (thing that floats). || COMM. Título, *m.* (security). || FAM. Persona (*f.*) que cambia a menudo de domicilio o de empleo. || U. S. Persona (*f.*) que vota en más de un colegio electoral.
float-feed ['fləutfi:d] n. AUT. Alimentación (*f.*) por flotador.
floating ['fləutiŋ] adj. Flotante (that floats, not fixed in place, variable). || MED. ANAT. TECH. Flotante: *floating kidney*, riñón flotante; *floating ribs*, costillas flotantes; *floating axle*, eje flotante. || COMM. Circulante: *floating capital*, capital circulante. | Flotante: *floating debt, currency*, deuda, moneda flotante. || — *Floating bridge*, pontón (*m.*) flotante, puente (*m.*) de pontones (pontoon bridge), puente (*m.*) de balsas (of rafts), pontón, *m.* (moveable part of bridge), transbordador, *m.* (ferry). || *Floating dock*, dique (*m.*) flotante. || *Floating island*, isla (*f.*) flotante (floating mass of earth), natillas (*f. pl.*) con merengue *or* crema batida (dessert). || *Floating light*, buque (*m.*) faro (lightship), boya luminosa (light buoy). || *Floating vote* o *votes*, votos indecisos.
— N. Flotación, *f.* (of currency).
floatplane ['fləutplein] n. Hidroavión, *m.*
floatstone ['fləutstəun] n. MIN. Ópalo (*m.*) capaz de flotar.
float valve ['fləutvælv] n. TECH. Válvula (*f.*) de flotador.
floc [flɔk] n. CHEM. Flóculo, *m.*
floccose ['flɔkəus] adj. BOT. Velludo, da.
flocculate ['flɔkjulit] adj. CHEM. Floculado, da.
flocculate ['flɔkjuleit] v. intr. CHEM. Flocular.
flocculation ['flɔkju'leiʃən] n. Floculación, *f.*
floccule ['flɔkju:l] n. CHEM. Flóculo, *m.*
flocculent ['flɔkjulənt] adj. Lanudo, da (woolly). || CHEM. Floculento, ta. || BOT. Velludo, da.
flocculus ['flɔkjuləs] n. Mechón, *m.*, copo, *m.* (tuft). || CHEM. ASTR. Flóculo, *m.*

— OBSERV. El plural de *flocculus* es *flocculi*.

floccus ['flɔkəs] n. Mechón, *m.*, copo, *m.* (tuft).

— OBSERV. El plural de *floccus* es *flocci*.

flock [flɔk] n. Bandada, *f.* (of birds). || Rebaño, *m.* (of goats, sheep). || Muchedumbre, *f.*, tropel, *m.*, multitud, *f.* (of people). || REL. Grey, *f.*, rebaño, *m.* (of Christ). | Feligresía, *f.*, feligreses, *m. pl.* (parishioners). || Mechón, *m.* (tuft). || Borra, *f.* (filling for cushions, etc.). || — *Flocks and herds*, ganado (*m.*) lanar y vacuno. || *To come in flocks*, venir en tropel.
flock [flɔk] v. intr. Congregarse, reunirse (to gather). || Venir en tropel (to come in great numbers). || — *To flock in*, entrar en tropel. || *To flock together*, congregarse, reunirse.
— V. tr. U. S. Rellenar con borra.
flock paper [—peipə*] n. Papel (*m.*) aterciopelado.
floe [fləu] n. Témpano (*m.*) de hielo.
flog [flɔg] v. tr. Azotar (to beat). || FAM. Hacer trabajar demasiado (to drive too hard): *don't flog the engine so hard*, no hagas trabajar tanto el motor. | Vender (to sell). || — FIG. *To flog a dead horse*, azotar el aire. || *To flog to death*, malar a latigazos (a person), machacar los oídos con (a theory, etc.).
flogging [—iŋ] n. Paliza, *f.*, azotaina, *f.* (beating). || Flagelación, *f.* (punishment).
flood [flʌd] n. Inundación, *f.* (of water). || FIG. Flujo, *m.*, torrente, *m.* (of words). | Raudales, *m. pl.* (of light). | Torrente, *m.* (of tears). || Pleamar, *f.* (high tide). || REL. Diluvio, *m.* || — *In flood*, crecido, da: *the river is in flood*, el río está crecido. || FIG. *To weep floods of tears*, llorar a lágrima viva.
flood [flʌd] v. tr. Inundar (to cover with water). || AGR. Anegar (a meadow). | Irrigar (to irrigate). || Hacer crecer *or* desbordar (a river). || FIG. Inundar: *the country was flooded with foreigners*, el país estaba inundado de extranjeros.
— V. intr. Crecer (to rise). || Desbordar (to overflow). || — *To flood in*, entrar a raudales, entrar en tropel (people), llegar a montones (letters, etc.). || *To flood out*, salir a raudales, salir en tropel.
flood control [—kən'trəul] n. Medidas (*f. pl.*) defensivas contra las inundaciones.
floodgate [—geit] n. Esclusa, *f.*, compuerta, *f.*
flooding [—iŋ] n. Inundación, *f.*
floodlight [—lait] n. Foco, *m.*
floodlight [—lait] v. tr. Iluminar con focos.
floodlighting [—'laitiŋ] n. Iluminación (*f.*) con focos.
floodmark [—mɑ:k] n. Nivel (*m.*) de la marea alta.
flood tide [—taid] n. Pleamar, *f.*, marea (*f.*) creciente.
floor [flɔ:*] n. Suelo, *m.*, piso, *m.* (of buildings): *he was sitting on the floor*, estaba sentado en el suelo. || Tablero, *m.*, piso, *m.* (of a bridge). || Piso, *m.* (storey). || Fondo, *m.* (of sea). || Pista, *f.* (of a dance hall). || Nivel (*m.*) mínimo (of prices). || Hemiciclo, *m.* (for debates). || Delegados, *m. pl.*, congresistas, *m. pl.* (in a meeting): *to invite questions from the floor*, invitar a los delegados a que hagan preguntas. || MAR. Varenga, *f.* || — *First floor*, primer piso (in England), planta baja (in U. S.). || *Ground floor*, planta baja. || *Second floor*, segundo piso (in England), primer piso (in U. S.). || *To give the floor*, dar *or* conceder la palabra. || *To have the floor*, tener la palabra. || *Top floor*, ático, *m.*, piso (*m.*) alto. || *To take the floor*, hacer uso de la palabra, tomar la palabra (to speak), salir a bailar (to dance). || FIG. FAM. *To wipe the floor with s.o.*, pegar una paliza a alguien (to defeat).
floor [flɔ:*] v. tr. Solar (a room). || Echar al suelo (to knock down). || FIG. Apabullar (to silence).
floorage ['flɔ:ridʒ] n. Suelo, *m.*, espacio, *m.*
floorboard ['flɔ:bɔ:d] n. Tabla (*f.*) del suelo (plank covering floor). || AUT. Piso, *m*, suelo, *m.*
floorcloth [—klɔθ] n. Trapo, *m.*, bayeta, *f.* [para fregar el suelo]. || Linóleo, *m.* (linoleum).
floorer [—rə*] n. Solador, *m.* (workman). || FAM. Pregunta (*f.*) desconcertante (puzzling question). | Golpe, *m.* (blow).
flooring [—riŋ] n. Solado, *m.* || Entarimado, *m.* (floorboards). || Suelo, *m.* (floor). || Revestimiento (*m.*) para el suelo (material).
floor lamp [—læmp] n. Lámpara (*f.*) de pie.
floor leader [—'li:də*] n. U. S. Jefe (*m.*) de partido.
floor polish [—'pɔliʃ] n. Cera (*f.*) para el suelo.
floor show [—ʃəu] n. Atracciones, *f. pl.* [en la pista de baile].
floor waiter [—weitə*] n. Camarero (*m.*) de piso (in a hotel).
floorwalker [—wɔ:kə*] n. U. S. Jefe (*m.*) de sección *or* de departamento (in a shop).
floozy ['flu:zi] n. U. S. FAM. Mujer (*f.*) de vida airada.
flop [flɔp] n. FAM. Fracaso, *m.* (failure). || Sonido (*m.*) sordo (sound).
flop [flɔp] v. intr. Dejarse caer pesadamente, desplomarse: *he flopped down in his bed*, se dejó caer pesadamente en la cama. || Agitarse (a fish). || Dar aletazos, aletear (birds). || FAM. Fracasar (to be a failure).
— V. tr. Dejar caer pesadamente.
flophouse [—haus] n. U. S. FAM. Posada (*f.*) *or* pensión (*f.*) de mala muerte (doss house).
floppy [—i] adj. Flojo, ja; blando, da (not rigid). || Colgante (hanging).
flora ['flɔ:rə] n. BOT. Flora, *f.*

— OBSERV. El plural de la palabra inglesa es *florae* o *floras*.

floral [—l] adj. Floral.
Florentine ['flɔrəntain] adj./n. Florentino, na.
florescence [flɔ:'resns] n. BOT. Florescencia, *f.*
florescent [flɔ:'resnt] adj. En flor.
floret ['flɔ:rit] n. BOT. Flósculo, *m.*
floriated ['flɔ:rieitid] adj. Floreado, da.
floriculture ['flɔ:rikʌltʃə*] n. Floricultura, *f.*
floriculturist [,flɔ:ri'kʌltʃərist] n. Floricultor, ra.
florid ['flɔrid] adj. Florido, da: *florid style*, estilo florido. || Rojo, ja; colorado, da (face).
floridity [flɔ'riditi] n. Floridez, *f.* || Rubicundez, *f.* (of face).

florilegium [ˌflɔriˈliːdʒjəm] n. Florilegio, *m.*

— OBSERV. El plural de *florilegium* es *florilegia.*

florin [ˈflɔrin] n. Moneda (*f.*) de dos chelines, florín, *m.* (in Great Britain). || Florín, *m.* (in the Netherlands).

florist [ˈflɔrist] n. Florista, *m.* & *f.* (who sells flowers). || *Florist's* or *florist's shop*, florería, *f.*

floss [flɔs] n. Seda (*f.*) floja (silk). || BOT. Seda (*f.*) vegetal. || Borra, *f.* (of cocoon).

floss silk [—ˈsilk] n. Seda (*f.*) floja.

flossy [ˈflɔsi] adj. Sedoso, sa. || FAM. Elegante (smart).

flotage [ˈfləutidʒ] n. See FLOATAGE.

flotation [fləuˈteiʃən] n. See FLOATATION.

flotilla [fləuˈtilə] n. MAR. Flotilla, *f.*

flotsam [ˈflɔtsəm] n. Pecios, *m. pl.* (wreckage of a ship). || Fruslerías, *f. pl.* (objects of little value). || FIG. Vagabundos, *m. pl.* (drifters).

flounce [flauns] n. Volante, *m.* (in sewing). || Movimiento (*m.*) brusco (movement).

flounce [flauns] v. tr. Adornar con volantes.

— V. intr. Moverse bruscamente, forcejear. || *To flounce out*, salir enfadado.

flounder [ˈflaundə*] n. Platija, *f.* (fish).

flounder [ˈflaundə*] v. intr. Andar con dificultad (in mud, water, etc.). || Forcejear (to struggle). || Enredarse, no saber qué decir (in speaking).

flour [ˈflauə*] n. Harina, *f.* || *Pure wheaten flour*, flor (*f.*) de harina, harina de flor.

flour [ˈflauə*] v. tr. Enharinar (to put flour in or on). || Moler (grain).

flourish [ˈflʌriʃ] n. Ostentación, *f.* (ostentation). || Movimiento, *m.*, ademán, *m.* (gesture). || Molinete, *m.*, floreo, *m.* (in fencing). || MUS. Floreo, *m.* || Rúbrica, *f.* (on signature). || Rasgo, *m.*, floreo, *m.* (in writing). || Toque (*m.*) de trompeta (fanfare). || Prosperidad, *f.* (prosperity).

flourish [ˈflʌriʃ] v. intr. Florecer, prosperar (to thrive). || Crecer (plants). || Usar de floreos (in writing, speaking, etc.). || Jactarse (to boast).

— V. tr. Agitar (to wave). || Esgrimir, blandir (to brandish). || Adornar (to ornament). || Hacer alarde de (to display ostentatiously).

flourishing [—iŋ] adj. Floreciente, próspero, ra.

flour mill [ˈflauəmil] n. Molino (*m.*) harinero.

floury [ˈflauəri] adj. Harinoso, sa (like or of flour). || Enharinado, da (covered with flour).

flout [flaut] n. Burla, *f.*

flout [flaut] v. tr. Burlarse de, reírse de.

— V. intr. *To flout at*, burlarse de, reírse de.

flow [fləu] n. Flujo, *m.* (action of flowing). || Caudal, *m.* (volume of liquid). || Chorro, *m.* (jet): *flow of water from a tap*, chorro de agua del grifo. || Corriente, *f.* (current). || Circulación, *f.* (circulation of blood). || Caída, *f.* (of drapery, etc.). || FIG. Flujo, *m.* (of words). | Torrente, *m.* (of tears). | Afluencia, *f.*, flujo, *m.* (of goods, etc.). | Flujo, *m.*, derrame, *m.* (of blood). | Paso, *m.* (passing). | Curso, *m.* (course). || Subida, *f.*, flujo, *m.* (of tide). || Fluidez, *f.* (flowing quality). || Movimiento, *m.* (movement). || COMM. Movimiento, *m.* (of capital).

flow [fləu] v. intr. Fluir (liquid). || Circular (blood in the body). || Derramarse, correr (blood from the body). || Manar, correr (blood of a wound). || Fluir, correr (river). || Subir, crecer (tide). || Correr (tears). || FIG. Correr (to be plentiful): *champagne flowed*, el champán corrió. || Ondear (in the wind). || *To flow past*, pasar [delante de].

— ***To flow away***, irse. || ***To flow back***, refluir. || ***To flow from***, salir de. | Provenir de, proceder de: *wisdom flows from experience*, la sabiduría proviene de la experiencia. || ***To flow in***, entrar a raudales. || ***To flow into***, desembocar en (river). || ***To flow out***, salir a raudales. || ***To flow over*** desbordarse (river). | Rebosar (vessel). || ***To flow together***, confluir (rivers). || ***To flow with*** abundar en.

flow chart [ˈfləutʃɑːt] or **flow diagram** [ˈfləuˈdiagræm] n. Organigrama, *m.*, diagrama, *m.*, gráfico, *m.*

flower [ˈflauə*] n. BOT. Flor, *f.*: *to grow flowers*, cultivar flores. || FIG. Flor, *f.*: *in the flower of youth*, en la flor de la juventud. | Flor (*f.*) y nata, crema, *f.* (the best part): *the flower of the nation's youth*, la flor y nata de los jóvenes del país. || — Pl. Flor, *f. sing.* (del vino, del azufre). || — *Artificial flower*, flor artificial. || *Flower bed*, arriate, *m.*, cuadro, *m.* || *Flower girl*, florista, *f.* || *Flower grower*, floricultor, ra. || *Flower growing*, floricultura, *f.* || *Flower piece*, ramillete, *m.* (a flower arrangement), cuadro (*m.*) de flores (painting of flowers). || *Flower shop*, tienda (*f.*) de flores, florería, *f.* || *Flower show*, exposición (*f.*) de flores. || *Flower vase*, florero, *m.* || *No flowers by request*, no se admiten flores ni coronas. || *Plant in flower*, planta en flor.

flower [ˈflauə*] v. intr. Florecer.

— V. tr. Adornar con flores. || AGR. Hacer florecer.

flower-de-luce [—dəˈluːs] n. HERALD. Flor (*f.*) de lis.

floweret [ˈflauərit] n. BOT. Flósculo, *m.* (floret). || Florecita, *f.* (small flower).

floweriness [ˈflauərinis] n. Floridez, *f.*

flowering [ˈflauəriŋ] n. Floración, *f.*, florecimiento, *m.*

— Adj. Floreciente.

flowerpot [ˈflauəpɔt] n. Maceta, *f.*, tiesto, *m.*

flowery [ˈflauəri] adj. Florido, da: *a flowery garden*, un jardín florido. || FIG. Florido, da (style, language).

flowing [ˈfləuiŋ] adj. Fluido, da (style). || Fluente, fluyente (stream). || Largo, ga (beard). || Suelto, ta (hair). || Ascendente (tide). || De mucho vuelo (dress).

— N. Flujo, *m.*

flown [fləun] p. p. See FLY. || Exaltado, da (exalted). || (Ant.) Hinchado, da.

flow sheet [ˈfləuʃiːt] n. Gráfico, *m.*, diagrama, *m.* (in factory, workshop, etc.).

flu [fluː] n. MED. Gripe, *f.*

fluctuant [ˈflʌktjuənt] adj. Fluctuante.

fluctuate [ˈflʌktjueit] v. intr. Fluctuar, variar, oscilar: *the price fluctuates between nine and ten pounds*, el precio fluctúa entre nueve y diez libras. || Subir y bajar (waves).

— V. tr. Hacer fluctuar.

fluctuating [—iŋ] adj. Fluctuante.

fluctuation [ˌflʌktjuˈeiʃən] n. Fluctuación, *f.*, variación, *f.*, oscilación, *f.*: *market fluctuations*, fluctuaciones del mercado.

flue [fluː] n. MAR. Trasmallo, *m.* (fishing net). || Pelusa, *f.*, borra, *f.* (fluff). || Chimenea, *f.* (chimney). || TECH. Conducto (*m.*) de humos, humero, *m.* (chimney pipe). | Conducto, *m.* (for air conditioning). | Tubo, *m.* (pipe). || MUS. Boca, *f.* (of an organ).

fluency [ˈfluənsi] n. Facilidad, *f.*, soltura, *f.*, fluidez, *f.* (of speech). || Dominio, *m.*: *her fluency in English*, su dominio del inglés.

fluent [ˈfluənt] adj. Bueno, na: *he speaks fluent Spanish*, habla un español bueno. || Fluido, da (in writing). || — *He is fluent in English*, domina el inglés, habla el inglés con soltura. || *To be a fluent speaker*, hablar con soltura.

fluently [—li] adv. De corrido, con soltura (in speaking): *he speaks Spanish fluently*, habla español con soltura. || Con fluidez (in writing).

flue pipe [ˈfluːpaip] n. MUS. Cañón, *m.* (of an organ).

flue stop [ˈfluːstɔp] n. MUS. Flautado, *m.* (of an organ).

fluff [flʌf] n. Pelusa, *f.* (soft mass). || Pelotillas (*f. pl.*) de polvo (dust). || THEATR. Pifia, *f.* || FAM. *A bit of fluff*, un bombón, una chica mona.

fluff [flʌf] v. tr. Mullir (pillow, soil, etc.). || Esponjar (wool, cotton). || FAM. Decir mal, equivocarse en [su papel] (in theatre). | Errar (a shot). || TECH. Afelpar, apomazar (leather). || — FAM. *To fluff one's entrance*, salir al escenario a destiempo (an actor). | *To fluff one's exam*, ser cateado *or* suspendido en un examen.

— V. intr. Esponjarse (wool, cotton).

fluffiness [—inis] n. Esponjosidad, *f.*

fluffy [—i] adj. Que tiene pelusa (cloth). || Cubierto de plumón (chicken, etc.). || Velloso, sa (downy). || Esponjado, da (hair). || Vaporoso, sa (dress). || Mullido, da (pillow, soil, etc.). || Aborregado, da (clouds).

fluid [ˈfluid] n. Fluido, *m.* || — *Fluid drive*, transmisión hidráulica. || *Fluid mechanics*, mecánica (*f.*) de los fluidos.

— Adj. Fluido, da. || Inestable (not settled). || FIG. Cambiadizo, za; variable: *his opinions are fluid*, sus opiniones son cambiadizas. | Flexible (plan).

fluidify [ˌfluidːfai] v. tr. Fluidificar.

fluidity [fluˈiditi] n. Fluidez, *f.* || FIG. Inestabilidad, *f.* | Variabilidad, *f.* (of opinions).

fluke [fluːk] n. MAR. Uña, *f.* (of anchor, harpoon, etc.). || Lengüeta, *f.* (of arrow). || Aleta, *f.* (of whale). || ZOOL. Trematodo, *m.* (worm). | Platija, *f.* (flatfish). || FAM. Chiripa, *f.* (stroke of luck in billiards). | *To win by a fluke*, ganar por *or* de chiripa.

fluke [fluːk] v. tr. Ganar por chiripa.

— V. intr. Tener chiripa (to be lucky). || Ganar por chiripa (in billiards).

fluky [—i] adj. De suerte (lucky). || Variable (breeze).

flume [ˈfluːm] n. Saetín, *m.* (of mill). || Resbaladero, *m.* (for timber). || U. S. Cañada, *f.* (gorge).

flummery [ˈflʌməri] n. Pamplinas, *f. pl.* (nonsense). || Camelo, *m.* (flattery). || Flan, *m.* [dulce hecho esencialmente con harina, leche, huevos].

flummox [ˈflʌməks] v. tr. FAM. Despistar, desconcertar (to confuse).

flump [flʌmp] v. tr. *To flump sth. down*, dejar caer algo [ruidosamente].

— V. intr. *To flump about*, andar con paso pesado. || *To flump down*, desplomarse.

flung [flʌŋ] pret. & p. p. See FLING.

flunk [flʌŋk] v. tr. U. S. FAM. Ser suspendido *or* cateado en: *to flunk an exam*, ser suspendido en un examen. | Suspender, catear: *they flunked me in Chinese*, me suspendieron en chino. || U. S. FAM.. *To flunk s.o. out of college*, echar a alguien del instituto.

— V. intr. U. S. FAM. Ser suspendido *or* cateado (to fail). | Abandonar (to give up).

flunk [flʌŋk] n. U. S. FAM. Suspenso, *m.* (failure).

flunkey (U. S. **flunky**) [ˈflʌŋki] n. Lacayo, *m.* (liveried servant). || FAM. Pelotillero, *m.*, lacayo, *m.* (toady).

flunkeyism (U. S. **flunkyism**) [—izəm] n. Adulación, *f.*, servilismo, *m.*

fluor [ˈfluːɔː*] n. CHEM. Fluorita, *f.*,

fluoresce [fluəˈres] v. intr. Ser fluorescente.

fluorescence [fluəˈresns] n. Fluorescencia, *f.*

fluorescent [fluəˈresnt] adj. Fluorescente: *fluorescent lamp*, lámpara fluorescente.

fluoridation [ˌfluəraiˈdeiʃən] n. Fluoración, *f.*

fluoride [ˈfluəraid] n. CHEM. Fluoruro, *m.*

fluorine [ˈfluəriːn] n. MIN. Flúor, *m.*

fluorite [ˈfluərait] n. MIN. Fluorita, *f.*, espato (*m.*) flúor.

fluorspar [ˈfluəspɑ:*] n. CHEM. Espato (*m.*) flúor.

flurry [ˈflʌri] n. Ráfaga, *f.* (of wind). || Borrasca, *f.*, nevisca, *f.*, nevada, *f.* (of snow). || Chubasco, *m.*, chaparrón, *m.* (of rain). || Convulsión, *f.* (spasm). || Agitación, *f.*, nerviosismo, *m.* (excitement). || Frenesí, *m.*: *a flurry of activity*, un frenesí de actividad. || — *A flurry of alarm*, un gran pánico. || *The death flurry*, los últimos estertores. || *To be in a flurry*, estar nervioso *or* aturrullado.

flurry [ˈflʌri] v. tr. Poner nervioso (to fluster).

flush [flʌʃ] n. Sofoco, *m.* (fever, illness). || Rubor, *m.*, sonrojo, *m.* (embarrassment). || Arrebol, *m.* (of sky). || Transporte, *m.*, arrebato, *m.* (of joy). || Brote, *m.* (of vegetation). || Resplandor, *m.* (of youth, colour, light). || Vuelo (*m.*) repentino (of birds). || Alud, *m.*, lluvia, *f.*, gran cantidad, *f.* (of money, etc.). || Gran limpieza (*f.*) con agua (cleansing). || Cisterna, *f.*, descarga (*f.*) de agua (in a lavatory). || Flux, *m.* (in poker). || — *Hot flush*, sofoco de calor. || *In the flush of victory*, en medio de la euforia de la victoria. || FIG. *Not to be in the first flush of youth*, no estar en su primera juventud. || *Royal, straight flush*, escalera (*f.*) real, de color. || *These words brought a flush to his face*, estas palabras le hicieron ruborizarse. || FIG. *To be in the full flush of health*, estar rebosante de salud.

— Adj. A nivel: *flush with*, a nivel con. || Empotrado, da; encajado, da: *the wardrobe is flush with the wall*, el armario está empotrado en la pared. || Embutido, da (screw). || Próximo a desbordarse, crecido, da (a stream). || Abundante, copioso, sa (abundant). || Lozano, na (full of vigour). || Ruboroso, sa (face). || FAM. Adinerado, da (rich). | Liberal (lavish).

— Adv. A nivel, al mismo nivel. || En pleno, na: *flush in the face*, en plena cara.

flush [flʌʃ] v. intr. Ruborizarse, sonrojarse, ponerse colorado (to blush). || Subir: *the blood flushed into his face*, le subió la sangre a la cara. || Arrebolarse (the sky). || Resplandecer (colour, light). || Brotar (to flow suddenly). || Emprender el vuelo (birds). || BOT. Echar renuevos *or* brotes. || MED. Tener sofocos. || — *To flush with anger*, ponerse rojo de ira. || *To flush over*, desbordarse, salirse de madre (river). || *To flush up*, ruborizarse, ponerse colorado. || FAM. *To flush up to the ears*, subírsele a uno el pavo.

— V. tr. Limpiar [con agua], baldear: *to flush the floor with a bucket of water*, limpiar el suelo con un cubo de agua. || Inundar (a meadow). || Rebosar: *flushed with pride*, rebosante de orgullo. || Levantar (game). || Nivelar (to make level). || Ruborizar, sonrojar (to blush). || BOT. Hacer crecer (plants). || *To flush the toilet*, tirar de la cadena.

fluster [ˈflʌstə*] n. Agitación, *f.*, nerviosismo, *m.*

fluster [ˈflʌstə*] v. tr. Poner nervioso. || *To get flustered*, ponerse nervioso.

— V. intr. Ponerse nervioso.

flute [flu:t] n. MUS. Flauta, *f.*: *transverse* o *German flute*, flauta traversera. | Flautado, *m.* (of organ). || Acanaladura, *f.* (groove). || Estría, *f.* (of glass). || Cañón, *m.*, encañonado, *m.* (of ruffle). || Canón, *m.*, pliegue, *m.* (of cloth). || ARCH. Acanaladura, *f.*, estría, *f.* (of column).

flute [flu:t] v. intr. MUS. Tocar la flauta. || FIG. Hablar *or* cantar con voz aflautada.

— V. tr. Decir con voz aflautada (to say). || MUS. Tocar con la flauta. || Acanalar (to make grooves). || Estriar (glass). || Encañonar (cloth). || ARCH. Acanalar, estriar.

flute player [ˈflu:tpleiə*] n. Flautista, *m.* & *f.*

fluting [ˈflu:tiŋ] n. Acanaladuras, *f. pl.* (grooves). || Encañonado, *m.* (of ruffle). || Acanaladura, *f.*, estriado, *m.* (of column). || *Fluting iron*, plancha (*f.*) de encañonar (for pressing ruffles).

flutist [ˈflu:tist] n. Flautista, *m.* & *f.*

flutter [ˈflʌtə*] n. Ondulación, *f.* (of curtains, flag). || Aleteo, *m.* (of wing). || Parpadeo, *m.* (of eyelids). || FIG. Agitación, *f.* (excitement). | Alboroto, *m.* (confusion). | Emoción (emotion). || MED. Palpitación, *f.* (of heart). | Pulsación (*f.*) irregular (of pulse). || FAM. Impresión, *f.*: *his speech made quite a flutter*, su discurso causó gran impresión. | Apuesta (*f.*) baja (bet). | Especulación (*f.*) de poca importancia (speculation). || AVIAT. Trepidación, *f.*, vibración, *f.* || TECH. Oscilación (*f.*) del sonido (on a recording). || — FIG. *Her heart was in a flutter*, le latía el corazón. | *To be all in a flutter*, estar muy nervioso. | *To cause a flutter in the dovecotes*, sembrar el alboroto, armar un escándalo. || FIG. *To be in a flutter of excitement*, estar excitado *or* emocionado. | *To put s.o. in a flutter*, poner nervioso a alguien.

flutter [ˈflʌtə*] v. intr. Revolotear (birds, leaves, etc.). || Batir (wings of a bird). || Ondear, ondular (curtain, flag). || Palpitar (heart). || Latir irregularmente (pulse). || — FIG. FAM. *His mother is always fluttering round him*, su madre está siempre detrás de él. | *To flutter about* o *around*, dar vueltas. || *To flutter down*, caer revoloteando. || *To make s.o.'s heart flutter*, hacerle latir el corazón a uno.

— V. tr. Agitar (to flap). || Batir (wings). || FIG. Poner nervioso.

fluvial [ˈflu:vjəl] adj. Fluvial.

flux [flʌks] n. Flujo, *m.* (flow). || MAR. Flujo, *m.* || FIG. Torrente, *m.* (of words). | Afluencia, *f.* (of people, ideas, etc.). | Cambios (*m. pl.*) frecuentes (changes). || PHYS. CHEM. Flujo, *m.*: *magnetic flux*, flujo magnético. || TECH. Fundente, *m.* (for metals). | Castina, *f.* (for minerals). | Desoxidante, *m.* (for deoxidizing). || *To be in a state of flux*, estar siempre cambiando.

flux [flʌks] v. tr. Añadir un fundente a (for fusion). || Fundir (to melt).

— V. intr. Fundirse.

fluxion [ˈflʌkʃən] n. MED. Fluxión, *f.* || Flujo, *m.* || MATH. Diferencial, *f.*

fly [flai] n. Vuelo, *m.* (flight). || Mosca, *f.* (insect, bait): *fly rod*, caña de mosca. || Pata, *f.* (on dresses). || Tejadillo, *m.* (entrance of a tent). || Alero, *m.* (outer canvas of a tent). || Extremo (*m.*) de la bandera (edge of a flag). || Envergadura, *f.* (span). || Guarda, *f.* (of book). || Simón, *m.*, coche (*m.*) de punto (carriage). || TECH. Volante, *m.* (flywheel). || U. S. Bragueta, *f.* (of trousers). || — Pl. Bragueta, *f. sing.* (of trousers). || Telares, *m.* (theatrical). || — FIG. FAM. *He's the only fly in the ointment*, es la única pega. | *There are no flies on him*, no se chupa el dedo, no tiene ni pizca de tonto. || U. S. FIG. FAM. *To be on the fly*, ajetrearse. || FIG. FAM. *To catch flies*, cazar *or* papar moscas (to daydream). || *To catch on the fly*, coger al vuelo (a ball). || FIG. FAM. *To die* o *to fall* o *to go down like flies*, caer como moscas. | *To put a fly in the ointment*, poner trabas *or* pegas. || *To rise to* o *to take the fly*, picar (fish), picar al anzuelo (to fall into the trap), tragárselo (to believe): *I don't rise to that fly*, eso no me lo trago. || FIG. *You catch more flies with honey than with vinegar*, más moscas se cogen con miel que con hiel.

— Adj. FAM. Ladino, na; astuto, ta (sly).

fly* [flai] v. intr. Volar (bird, aeroplane). || Ir en avión (to go by plane): *to fly to Paris*, ir a París en avión. || Saltar (sparks, cork, etc.). || Flotar (flag, hair). || FAM. Irse volando *or* corriendo, irse de prisa (to hurry): *I must fly now*, tengo que irme corriendo ahora. || FIG. Huir, escapar (to escape). | Pasar *or* irse volando (time). | Correr (gossip). | Alzarse (to rise). || — FIG. FAM. *His watch has flown*, su reloj ha desaparecido. | *Insults were flying thick and fast*, llovían los insultos. | *The bird has flown*, el pájaro voló. || *To fly asunder*, hacerse pedazos. || *To fly at*, cazar con halcón (hawking), lanzarse sobre (to attack), arremeter contra uno (shouting). || *To fly for one's life*, huir para salvar la vida. || FIG. *To fly from s.o.'s mouth*, salir de la boca de uno (words). || FIG. FAM. *To fly high*, picar alto. || FIG. *To fly in the face of*, see FACE. | *To fly into a temper*, ponerse furioso. || FIG. FAM. *To fly off the handle*, salir *or* salirse de sus casillas. || FIG. *To fly open*, abrirse de un golpe. | *To fly to pieces*, hacerse pedazos. | *To fly to s.o.*, ir a ponerse bajo la protección de alguien. | *To fly to s.o.'s assistance*, correr en ayuda *or* auxilio de uno. | *To fly to the head*, subirse a la cabeza (success). | *To let fly*, disparar (weapon), soltar (insults), salir de sus casillas (with anger), empezar a repartir golpes (to start hitting out). | *To let fly at s.o.*, arremeter contra uno (shouting), asestarle un golpe a uno (to hit out at), disparar contra alguien (with a firearm). | *To make the money fly*, gastar mucho dinero, despilfarrar el dinero. || FIG. FAM. *To send s.o. flying*, tirarle a uno al suelo. | *To send sth. flying*, echar algo a rodar. | *To send sth. flying at s.o.*, tirarle algo a alguien. | *To send the enemy flying*, hacer huir al enemigo.

— V. tr. Echar a volar: *to fly a kite*, echar a volar una cometa. || Pilotar (an aeroplane). || Izar (to hoist): *to fly a flag*, izar una bandera. || Enarbolar: *the ship flies the British flag*, este barco enarbola la bandera británica. || Atravesar *or* cruzar en avión: *to fly the Atlantic*, cruzar el Atlántico en avión. || Transportar *or* llevar en avión: *they flew their troops into France*, llevaron sus tropas a Francia en avión. || Mandar, enviar (a man or rocket into space). || Recorrer en avión: *to fly five thousand miles in a month*, recorrer cinco mil millas en avión en un mes. || Soltar (a hawk). || Cazar (game). || Evitar (to avoid). || Huir de (a country).

— ***To fly about***, revolotear (birds). || ***To fly along***, ir volando. || ***To fly away***, emprender el vuelo. || ***To fly back***, volver rápidamente (to hurry back). | Volver en avión (by plane). | Volver (bird). || ***To fly by***, pasar volando (to hurry by). | Pasar cerca de *or* al lado de: *the aeroplane flew by the Statue of Liberty*, el avión pasó cerca de la estatua de la Libertad. | FIG. Pasar volando (time). || ***To fly off***, emprender el vuelo (birds). | Irse rápidamente (people). | Saltar (buttons). | Desprenderse (to break off). || ***To fly out***, salir (birds). | Irse en avión (by plane). | Salir rápidamente (to hurry out). | — FIG. FAM. *To fly out at s.o.*, arremeter contra alguien. || ***To fly over***, volar sobre, sobrevolar. | ***To fly past***, desfilar (planes in formation). || ***To fly up***, subir volando. | — *To fly up the stairs*, subir corriendo la escalera.

— OBSERV. Pret. **flew**; p. p. **flown**.

fly agaric [—ˈægərik] n. BOT. Amanita, *f.* (mushroom).

flyaway [—əˌwei] adj. Suelto, ta (clothing). || FIG. Casquivano, na; frívolo, la (people). | Descabellado, da (ideas). || Listo para el vuelo (aircraft).

fly ball [—bɔ:l] n. U. S. Pelota (*f.*) bateada al aire (in baseball).
flybelt [—belt] n. Área (*f.*) plagada de moscas tse-tsé.
flyblow [—bləu] n. Cresa, *f.*
flyblown [—bləun] adj. Lleno de cresas (meat). || FIG. Cochambroso, sa (dirty): *a flyblown hotel*, un hotel cochambroso. | Mancillado, da (reputation).
fly-by-night [—bəˌnait] adj. Poco de fiar, poco seguro, ra (unreliable). || Efímero, ra (transitory).
— N. Persona (*f.*) poco de fiar. || FAM. Noctámbulo, *m.*, ave (*f.*) nocturna (night rambler).
flycatcher [—ˌkætʃə*] n. ZOOL. Papamoscas, *m. inv.*
flyer [—ə*] n. See FLIER.
fly-fishing [—ˌfiʃiŋ] n. Pesca (*f.*) con moscas.
flying [—iŋ] adj. Volador, ra: *a flying machine*, un aparato volador. || Volante (able to fly). || Ondeante, flameante (flag). || Rápido, da; muy breve: *a flying visit*, una visita rápida. || Volante: *a flying bridge*, un puente volante; *a flying squad*, un equipo volante. || De vuelo: *a flying suit*, un traje de vuelo. || *De* aviación: *flying club*, club de aviación. || — *Flying fortress*, fortaleza (*f.*) volante. || *Flying scaffold*, andamio suspendido. || MIL. *Flying squadron*, escuadra ligera. || *Flying time*, horas (*f. pl.*) de vuelo (flying hours), duración (*f.*) del vuelo (duration of flight).
— N. Vuelo, *m.* (flight). || Aviación, *f.* || Pilotaje, *m.* (pilotage). || Suelta, *f.* (of hawk, etc.). || — AVIAT. *Blind flying*, vuelo sin visibilidad. || *Trick flying*, acrobacia aérea.
flying boat [—bəut] n. Hidroavión, *m.*
flying bomb [—bɔm] n. MIL. Bomba (*f.*) volante.
flying buttress [—ˌbʌtris] n. ARCH. Arbotante, *m.*
flying colours (U. S. **flying colors**) [—ˈkʌləz] pl. n. FIG. Éxito (*m.*) rotundo. || FIG. *To come off with flying colours*, salir airoso.
Flying Dutchman [—ˈdʌtʃmən] n. Buque (*m.*) fantasma (ghost ship).
flying field [—fi:ld] n. Campo (*m.*) de aviación.
flying fish [—fiʃ] n. ZOOL. Pez (*m.*) volador.
flying jib [—dʒib] n. MAR. Petifoque, *m.*
flying saucer [—ˌsɔ:sə*] n. Platillo (*m.*) volante.
flying squirrel [—ˈskwirəl] n. ZOOL. Ardilla (*f.*) volante.
flying start [—stɑ:t] n. SP. Salida (*f.*) lanzada. || FIG. Principio (*m.*) feliz (good beginning). || FIG. *To get off to a flying start*, empezar muy bien.
flyleaf [ˈflaiˌli:f] n. Guarda, *f.* (of book).
flyover [ˈflaiˌəuvə*] n. Paso (*m.*) elevado (motorway). || U. S. Desfile (*m.*) de aviones (flypast).
flypaper [ˈflaiˌpeipə*] n. Papel (*m.*) matamoscas.
flypast [ˈflaiˌpɑ:st] n. Desfile (*m.*) de aviones.
fly sheet [ˈflaiˌʃi:t] n. Hoja (*f.*) suelta (loose sheet). || Prospecto, *m.* (handbill).
flyspeck [ˈflaiˌspek] n. Cagadita (*f.*) de mosca (fly excrement). || Mancha, *f.* (dirty mark).
flyswatter [ˈflaiˌswɔtə*] n. Matamoscas, *m. inv.*
flytrap [ˈflaiˌtræp] n. BOT. Atrapamoscas, *m. inv.*
flyweight [ˈflaiˌweit] n. SP. Peso (*m.*) mosca.
flywheel [—wi:l] n. TECH. Volante, *m.*
foal [fəul] n. ZOOL. Potro, *m.*, potra, *f.*
foal [fəul] v. tr./intr. Parir.
foam [fəum] n. Espuma, *f.*
foam [fəum] v. intr. Espumar, hacer espuma (liquid). || Hacer espuma (sea). || Echar espumarajos, espumajear (animal). || FIG. *To foam with rage* o *at the mouth*, echar espumarajos de cólera, espumajear de ira.
foaminess [—inis] n. Espumosidad, *f.*
foaming [—iŋ] adj. Espumoso, sa; encrespado, da (sea). || FIG. Furioso, sa (angry).
foam rubber [—ˈrʌbə*] n. Goma (*f.*) espuma, gomespuma, *f.*
foamy [—i] adj. Espumoso, sa.
fob [fɔb] n. Faltriquera (*f.*) *or* bolsillo (*m.*) del reloj (for watch). || U. S. Leontina, *f.* (watch chain).
fob [fɔb] v. tr. *To fob s.o. off*, engañar a alguien (to fool s.o.). || *To fob sth. off as*, hacer pasar algo por. || *To fob sth. off on s.o.*, colar algo a alguien.
f.o.b. [ˈefˈəuˈbi:] abbrev. of *free on board*, franco a bordo.
fob chain [ˈfɔbtʃein] n. Leontina, *f.* (watch chain).
focal [ˈfəukəl] adj. Focal: *focal length*, distancia focal.
focalization [fəukəlaiˈzeiʃən] n. PHYS. Enfoque, *m.* | Focalización, *f.* (in electronics). || MED. Localización, *f.*
focalize [ˈfəukəlaiz] v. tr. PHYS. Enfocar. | Focalizar (in electronics). || MED. Localizar (an infection).
— V. intr. MED. Localizarse.
fo'c'sle [ˈfəuksl] n. MAR. Castillo (*m.*) de proa (forecastle).
focus [ˈfəukəs] n. PHYS. MATH. Foco, *m.* || Distancia (*f.*) focal (focal distance). || Epicentro, *m.* (in seismology). || FIG. Foco, *m.*, centro, *m.*: *the focus of Greek civilization*, el foco de la civilización griega. || MED. Foco, *m.* (of a disorder). || — *Depth of focus*, profundidad (*f.*) de foco. || *Fixed focus*, foco fijo. || *In focus*, enfocado, da. || *Out of focus*, fuera de foco, desenfocado, da. || FIG. *The world in focus* o *focus on the world*, panorama (*m.*) del mundo, ojeada (*f.*) al mundo. || *To bring into focus*, enfocar.

— OBSERV. El plural de *focus* es *foci* o *focuses*.

focus [ˈfəukəs] v. tr. Hacer converger (light). || Enfocar: *to focus the binoculars on a point*, enfocar los prismáticos en un punto. || Ajustar: *to focus a microscope*, ajustar un microscopio. || FIG. Fijar, concentrar: *to focus one's attention on a problem*, fijar su atención en un problema. || *All eyes were focused on her*, todos los ojos estaban clavados en ella.
— V. intr. Converger (light). || FIG. Fijarse, centrarse: *to focus on a problem*, centrarse en un problema. | Enfocar: *we must focus on the racial problem from a humanitarian point of view*, tenemos que enfocar el problema racial desde un punto de vista humanitario.
focusing [—iŋ] n. Convergencia, *f.* (of light). || Enfoque, *m.* (of microscope, camera, etc.).
fodder [ˈfɔdə*] n. Forraje, *m.*, pienso, *m.*: *green, mixed fodder*, forraje verde, mixto.
fodder [ˈfɔdə*] v. tr. Dar forraje a.
foe [fəu] n. Enemigo, *m.*
foehn [fə:n] n. Viento (*m.*) caliente y muy seco (föhn).
foetal [fi:tl] adj. Fetal: *foetal life*, vida fetal.
foetation [fi:ˈteiʃən] n. BIOL. Gestación, *f.*, desarrollo (*m.*) del feto.
foeticide [ˈfi:təsaid] n. Feticidio, *m.*
foetid [ˈfi:tid] adj. Fétido, da; hediondo, da.
foetidity [—iti] or **foetidness** [—nis] n. Fetidez, *f.*, hediondez, *f.*
foetus [ˈfi:təs] n. Feto, *m.*
fog [fɔg] n. Niebla, *f.*, bruma, *f.* || PHOT. Velo, *m.* || AGR. Hierba (*f.*) de segundo corte. || FIG. FAM. *To be in a fog*, estar en un mar de confusiones, no saber a qué atenerse.
fog [fɔg] v. tr. Envolver en niebla. || Empañar (to mist up). || Velar (in photography). || Confundir, ofuscar (to confuse). || Oscurecer (to obscure).
— V. intr. *To fog up*, empañarse (to mist up), velarse (in photography), ofuscarse (a person), nublarse, oscurecerse (landscape).
fog bank [—bæŋk] n. Niebla (*f.*) espesa.
fogbound [—baund] adj. Inmovilizado por la niebla.
fogey [ˈfəugi] n. See FOGY.
fogginess [ˈfɔginis] n. Nebulosidad, *f.* (of the atmosphere). || Niebla, *f.*: *the fogginess of the morning prevented me from going out*, la niebla que había por la mañana me impidió salir.
foggy [ˈfɔgi] adj. Brumoso, sa; nebuloso, sa; de niebla: *a foggy day*, un día brumoso. || Velado, da (in photography). || FIG. Vago, ga: *I have a foggy impression of Barcelona*, tengo una vaga idea de lo que es Barcelona. || FIG. FAM. *I haven't the foggiest idea!*, ¡no tengo la más mínima idea!
foghorn [ˈfɔghɔ:n] n. MAR. Sirena (*f.*) de niebla. || FIG. FAM. *A foghorn voice*, una voz ronca.
fog lamp [ˈfɔglæmp] **fog light** [ˈfɔglait] n. Faro (*m.*) antiniebla.
fogy [ˈfəugi] n. FAM. *Old fogy*, vejestorio, *m.*, carcamal, *m.* (very old person). | *To be (a bit of) an old fogy*, estar chapado a la antigua.
föhn [fə:n] n. Viento (*m.*) caliente y muy seco.
foible [ˈfɔibl] n. Punto (*m.*) flaco, debilidad, *f.* (mild failing). || Extravagancia, *f.* (odd feature). || Manía, *f.* (fad): *this is a foible of his*, es una manía suya. || Parte (*f.*) de la hoja de la espada situada entre la mitad y la punta (in fencing).
foil [fɔil] n. Hoja (*f.*) fina de metal (thin sheet of metal). || Azogue, *m.* (in mirrors). || Laminilla (*f.*) de metal pulido (in jewelry). || Oropel, *m.* (of copper). || Pan, *m.* (of gold). || ARCH. Lóbulo, *m.* || FIG. Contraste, *m.* || Rastro, *m.*, huella, *f.* (trail). || Florete, *m.* (in fencing). || Fracaso, *m.* (failure). || FIG. *To serve as a foil to*, hacer resaltar, realzar.
foil [fɔil] v. tr. Chapar (to plate). || Azogar (a mirror). || Aniquilar, frustrar (efforts). || Hacer fracasar (scheme). || Desbaratar *or* hacer fracasar los planes de: *the police foiled the robber*, la policía desbarató los planes del ladrón. || ARCH. Adornar con lóbulos. || FIG. Realzar, hacer resaltar (to enhance).
foil paper [—ˈpeipə*] n. Papel (*m.*) de aluminio *or* de estaño.
foilsman [—zmən] n. Floretista, *m.*

— OBSERV. El plural de esta palabra es *foilsmen*.

foist [fɔist] v. tr. FAM. Colar: *to foist a bad coin on s.o.*, colar una moneda falsa a alguien. | Meter: *to foist s.o. into a deal*, meter a alguien en un asunto. | Endosar: *to foist a job on s.o.*, endosar un trabajo a alguien. || Imputar, atribuir: *to foist a book on an author*, imputar un libro a un autor. || *To foist o.s. on s.o.*, imponerse a alguien.
fold [fəuld] n. Redil, *m.*, aprisco, *m.* (for sheep). || Rebaño, *m.* (flock): *a fold of sheep*, un rebaño de corderos. || REL. Grey, *f.*, rebaño, *m.* (religious community). | Redil, *m.*: *to bring back a lost sheep to the fold*, hacer volver al redil a una oveja descarriada. || Pliegue, *m.*, doblez, *f.* (crease in clothes or in paper). || Arruga, *f.* (wrinkle). || GEOL. ANAT. Pliegue, *m.*
fold [fəuld] v. tr. Acorralar, encerrar, meter en un aprisco (sheep). || Doblar, plegar: *to fold a blanket*, doblar una manta. || Cruzar: *to fold one's hands*, cruzar las manos. || Plegar, recoger (wings). || Envolver (to wrap, to surround). || — *To fold back*, volver (collar). || *To fold one's arms*, cruzarse de brazos. || *To fold s.o. in one's arms*, abrazar a alguien, estrechar a alguien entre los brazos. || *To fold up*, plegar (umbrella), envolver (to wrap up), doblar, plegar (clothes, blankets, chairs, etc.), cerrar (case, deal), liquidar (business).

— V. intr. Doblarse, plegarse. || FIG. Fracasar (to fail). || *To fold up*, doblarse, plegarse (to bend), fracasar (to fail), quebrar (to go bankrupt), liquidarse (to close down).
foldboat [—bəut] n. Bote (*m.*) plegable.
folder [—ə*] n. Carpeta, *f.*, subcarpeta, *f.* (for documents). || Folleto, *m.*, prospecto, *m.*, desplegable, *m.* (leaflet). || TECH. Máquina (*f.*) plegadora, plegadora, *f.*
folderol [ˈfɔldəˈrɔl] n. U. S. Trasto, *m.*, cachivache, *m.* (unnecessary object). | Tonterías, *f. pl.* (nonsense).
folding [ˈfəuldiŋ] adj. Plegable: *folding table*, mesa plegable. || De tijera, plegable (bed, chair). || De fuelle (camera, door). || — *Folding hood* o *top*, capota (*f.*) plegable. || TECH. *Folding machine*, máquina plegadora, plegadora, *f.* || *Folding screen*, biombo, *m.* || *Folding seat*, traspuntín, *m.*, trasportín, *m.*, traspontín, *m.*, asiento (*m.*) plegable.
— N. GEOL. Plegamiento, *m.*
foliaceous [ˌfəuliˈeiʃəs] adj. BOT. Foliáceo, a.
foliage [ˈfəuliidʒ] n. Follaje, *m.* (leaves).
foliar [ˈfəuliə*] adj. BOT. Foliar.
foliate [ˈfəuliit] adj. BOT. Foliado, da.
foliate [ˈfəulieit] v. tr. Foliar (to number pages). || ARCH. Adornar con lóbulos. || Azogar (a mirror). || Batir (metal).
— V. intr. BOT. Echar hojas. || Hojear (metal).
foliation [ˌfəuliˈeiʃən] n. BOT. Foliación, *f.* || Foliación, *f.* (of pages). || TECH. Chapado, *m.* (plating). | Azogado, *m.* (of mirror). | Laminado, *m.* (lamination). || ARCH. Adorno (*m.*) con lóbulos (ornamentation with foils). | Follaje, *m.* (leaflike decoration). || GEOL. Estructura (*f.*) laminar.
folio [ˈfəuliəu] n. PRINT. Folio, *m.* (leaf): *in folio*, en folio. | Infolio, *m.*, libro (*m.*) en folio (book). || Hoja (*f.*) de un libro de contabilidad que contiene el debe y el haber. || JUR. Unidad (*f.*) de medida para evaluar la extensión de un documento [72 ó 90 palabras en Inglaterra, 100 en Estados Unidos].
— Adj. PRINT. En folio.
folio [ˈfəuliəu] v. tr. Foliar, paginar.
foliole [ˈfəuliəul] n. BOT. Foliolo, *m.*
folk [fəuk] n. Gente, *f.*: *I don't mix with that kind of folk*, no me mezclo con esta clase de gente. || Pueblo, *m.*: *the British folk*, el pueblo británico. || — Pl. FAM. Familia, *f. sing.* (family). | Amigos, *m.* (friends). || — *Common folk*, pueblo, *m.* || *Country folk*, campesinos, *m. pl.* || FAM. *The old folks at home*, los viejos, los padres.
— Adj. Popular: *folk art*, arte popular.
folk dance [—dɑːns] n. Baile (*m.*) tradicional *or* foklórico.
folklore [—lɔː*] n. Folklore, *m.*
folkloric [—ˌlɔːrik] adj. Folklórico, ca.
folklorist [—ˌlɔːrist] n. Folklorista, *m.* & *f.*
folk music [—ˈmjusik] n. Música (*f.*) popular.
folk singer [—ˌsiŋgə*] n. Cantante (*m.* & *f.*) de canciones populares.
folk song [—sɔŋ] n. Canción (*f.*) popular.
folksy [—si] adj. U. S. Popular. | Campechano, na (very sociable).
folk tale [—teil] n. Cuento (*m.*) popular.
folkways [—weiz] pl. n. Costumbres, *f.*
follicle [ˈfɔlikl] n. Folículo, *m.*
follicular [fɔˈlikjulə*] adj. Folicular.
folliculin [fɔˈlikjulin] n. Foliculina, *f.*
folliculitis [fɔlikjuˈlaitis] n. MED. Foliculitis, *f.*
follies [ˈfɔliz] pl. n. THEATR. Revista, *f. sing.*
follow [ˈfɔləu] n. Carambola (*f.*) corrida (in billiards). || Continuación, *f.*
follow [ˈfɔləu] v. tr. Seguir: *Wednesday follows Tuesday*, el miércoles sigue al martes; *he was followed by his mother*, iba seguido por su madre; *to follow a car*, seguir un coche; *to follow fashion*, seguir la moda; *he spoke so fast that I couldn't follow him*, hablaba tan rápidamente que no podía seguirle; *the boat follows the coast*, el barco sigue la costa; *he followed my advice*, siguió mi consejo; *he followed his father's example*, siguió el ejemplo de su padre; *he follows his son's studies*, sigue los estudios de su hijo. || Perseguir (to pursue): *to follow the enemy*, perseguir al enemigo. || Dedicarse a (to dedicate o.s. to). || Ejercer (to practise a profession): *he follows the medical profession*, ejerce la medicina. || — *Do you follow rugby?*, ¿te interesa el rugby? || *Following*, a consecuencia de, como consecuencia de: *following the decision taken by the Board*, a consecuencia de la decisión tomada por el Consejo. || *It follows that*, de ello resulta *or* se deriva que. || *To follow a person in*, entrar detrás de una persona. || *To follow a person out*, salir detrás de una persona. || *To follow suit*, see SUIT.
— V. intr. Seguir: *a long silence followed*, un largo silencio siguió. || Resultar, derivarse (to result). || — *I answered as follows*, contesté lo siguiente. || *That doesn't follow*, no es lógico. || *The requirements are as follows*, los requisitos son los siguientes.
— ***To follow on***, seguir (in the same direction). | Reemplazar, sustituir: *he followed on from his father as director*, sustituyó a su padre como director. | Jugar un segundo turno justo después del primero [el mismo equipo] (in cricket). | — *To follow on behind*, venir *or* ir detrás. | *To follow on from*, ser la consecuencia lógica de. || ***To follow out***, seguir hasta el final. | Llevar a cabo (a plan). || ***To follow through***, llevar a cabo. | SP. Seguir el golpe. || ***To follow up***, seguir de cerca (s.o.). | Perseguir (to pursue). | Seguir (a clue, a case). | Sacar provecho de (a success). | Investigar sobre, profundizar, obtener más detalles sobre (to seek further details). | Dar más detalles sobre (to give further details). | Reforzar (to consolidate). | Hacer seguir: *we followed up the bombardment with an attack*, hicimos seguir el bombardeo por un ataque.
follower [—ə*] n. Seguidor, ra; partidario, ria (supporter). || Secuaz, *m.* (of a gangster). || Partidario, ria (of a party). || Admirador, ra (admirer). || Discípulo, *m.* (disciple). || Aficionado, da (of a sport). || TECH. Pieza (*f.*) movida por otra. || — Pl. Séquito, *m. sing.* (of a king). || *Followers of fashion*, los que siguen la moda.
following [—iŋ] adj. Siguiente: *the following day*, el día siguiente. || MAR. *Following wind*, viento (*m.*) en popa.
— N. Partidarios, *m. pl.*, seguidores, *m. pl.*: *the statesman has quite a following*, el hombre de Estado tiene muchos partidarios. || Discípulos, *m. pl.* (disciples). || Secuaces, *m. pl.* (of a gangster). || Séquito, *m.* (of king). || *The following*, lo siguiente.
— Prep. Después de.
follow-my-leader [—miˈliːdə*] or **follow-the-leader** [—ðəˈliːdə*] n. Juego (*m.*) que consiste en hacer lo que otro manda.
follow-through [—ˈθruː] n. SP. Continuación (*f.*) del movimiento.
follow-up [—ˈʌp] n. Continuación, *f.*: *this record is the follow-up to his last success*, este disco es la continuación de su último éxito. || Consecuencia, *f.* (consequence): *as a follow-up to his latest hit, he is now playing in Hamlet*, a consecuencia de su último éxito, ahora está trabajando en Hamlet. || COMM. Carta (*f.*) de insistencia, recordatorio, *m.* || MED. Tratamiento (*m.*) complementario.
— Adj. Complementario, ria: *follow-up research*, investigaciones complementarias. || COMM. De insistencia (letter).
folly [ˈfɔli] n. Locura, *f.*, desatino, *m.*, disparate, *m.* (foolish act or idea).
foment [fəuˈment] v. tr. Fomentar: *to foment a rebellion*, fomentar una rebelión. || MED. Fomentar, aplicar fomentos *or* paños calientes a.
fomentation [ˌfəumenˈteiʃən] n. Instigación, *f.*, fomento, *m.*: *the fomentation of discord*, la instigación a la discordia, el fomento de la discordia. || MED. Fomento, *m.*, paño (*m.*) caliente (compress).
fomenter [fəuˈmentə*] n. Promotor, ra; fomentador, ra: *fomenter of troubles*, promotor de disturbios.
fond [fɔnd] adj. Cariñoso, sa; afectuoso, sa (affectionate). || Indulgente: *spoiled by a fond father*, mimado por un padre indulgente. || Inocente (naïve). || — *He had fond hopes of*, abrigaba *or* acariciaba esperanzas de. || *I have fond memories of*, recuerdo con cariño. || *To become fond of s.o.*, tomar cariño a alguien. || *To become fond of sth.*, aficionarse a algo. || *To be fond of s.o.*, tenerle cariño a alguien; querer a alguien: *he is fond of his children*, quiere a sus hijos; gustarle alguien a uno: *I am fond of brunettes*, me gustan las morenas; apreciar (to appreciate). || *To be fond of sth.*, gustarle a uno algo: *he is very fond of sweets*, le gustan mucho los caramelos; ser aficionado a algo: *he is very fond of hunting*, es muy aficionado a la caza.
fondant [ˈfɔndənt] n. Pasta (*f.*) de azúcar.
fondle [ˈfɔndl] v. tr. Acariciar (to caress). || Mimar: *the mother was fondling her child*, la madre estaba mimando a su hijo.
fondly [ˈfɔndli] adv. Con cariño, cariñosamente: *he looked fondly at her*, le miró con cariño. || Inocentemente: *he fondly imagined that*, se imaginaba inocentemente que.
fondness [ˈfɔndnis] n. Cariño, *m.*, afecto, *m.* (affection). || Indulgencia, *f.* (indulgence). || Afición, *f.*: *his fondness of hunting*, su afición a la caza.
fondue [ˌfɔ̃duː] n. CULIN. Plato (*m.*) a base de queso derretido o carne frita.
font [fɔnt] n. REL. Pila, *f.* || PRINT. Fundición, *f.*, casta, *f.* || FIG. Fuente, *f.* (source). | Manantial, *m.*, fuente, *f.* (spring).
fontanel, fontanelle [fɔntəˈnel] n. ANAT. Fontanela, *f.*
food [fuːd] n. Alimento, *m.*: *food for animals*, alimento para el ganado. || Comida, *f.*: *food and drink*, comida y bebida. || Comestibles, *m. pl.*: *food shop*, tienda de comestibles. || Suministro, *m.* (supply). || FIG. Alimento, *m.*: *mental food*, alimento para el espíritu. || — *Food allowance*, dietas, *f. pl.* || MED. *Food poisoning*, intoxicación alimenticia. || *Food safe*, fresquera, *f.* || *Food value*, valor nutritivo. || *The food is good and cheap here*, aquí se come bien y barato. || FAM. *To be off one's food*, no tener apetito, no tener ganas de comer. || FIG. *To give food for thought*, dar materia en que pensar. || *To give s.o. food*, dar de comer a alguien.
foodstuff [—stʌf] n. Producto (*m.*) alimenticio.
fool [fuːl] n. Tonto, ta; imbécil, *m.* & *f.* (stupid). || Bufón, *m.* (jester). || — *Any fool could do it*, cualquier tonto lo haría, es pan comido. || *Don't be a fool!*, ¡no seas tonto! || FAM. *I am nobody's fool*, a mí no me la dan, a mí no me toman el pelo. || *More fool you*, allá tú, peor para ti: *more fool you if anything happens*, peor

FOOD AND MEALS. — ALIMENTOS (*m.*) Y COMIDAS, *f.*

I. General terms. — Generalidades, *f.*

feeding	alimentación *f.*
to feed, to nourish	alimentar, nutrir
nutrition	nutrición *f.*
to maintain	mantener, sustentar
subsistence	subsistencia *f.*
to eat	comer
to drink	beber
to chew	mascar, masticar
to swallow	tragar
to nibble, to peck	picar
appetite	apetito *m.*, gana *f.*
hunger; thirst	hambre *f.*; sed *f.*
to be hungry, thirsty	tener hambre, sed
gluttony; greed	glotonería *f.*; gula *f.*
overfeeding	sobrealimentación *f.*
fasting	abstinencia *f.*, ayuno *m.*
diet	dieta *f.*, régimen *m.*
banquet	banquete *m.*

II. Meals. — Comidas, *f.*

breakfast	desayuno *m.*
to have breakfast	desayunar
lunch	almuerzo *m.*
to have lunch	almorzar
afternoon tea	merienda *f.*
high tea	merienda cena *f.*
dinner, supper	cena *f.*
to dine, to have dinner *o* supper	cenar
soup	sopa *f.*
hors d'œuvre	entremés *m.*
entrée	entrada *f.*
main course	plato (*m.*) fuerte
sweet, dessert	postre *m.*
snack	bocado *m.*, piscolabis *m.*, tentempié *m.*
helping, portion	ración *f.*, porción *f.*
sandwich	bocadillo *m.*, emparedado *m.*

III. Foodstuffs and dishes. — Productos (*m.*) alimenticios y platos, *m.*

meat	carne *f.*
beef	carne (*f.*) de vaca
veal	ternera *f.*
lamb	cordero *m.*
sirloin	solomillo *m.*
steak	bistec *m.*
chop, cutlet	chuleta *f.*
stew	estofado *m.*, guisado *m.*
roast	asado *m.*
pork	cerdo *m.*
ham	jamón *m.*
bacon	tocino (*m.*) entreverado
sausage	salchicha *f.*
black pudding, blood sausage	morcilla *f.*
cold meats [U.S., cold cuts]	fiambres *m.*
chicken	pollo *m.*
turkey	pavo *m.*
duck	pato *m.*
fish	pescado *m.*
vegetables	verduras *f.*
dried legumes	legumbres (*f.*) secas
chips [U.S., French fries]	patatas (*f.*) fritas [*Amer.*, papas (*f.*) fritas]
mashed potatoes	puré (*m.*) de patatas [*Amer.*, puré (*m.*) de papas]
pasta	pastas *f.*
macaroni	macarrones *m. pl.*
noodles	fideos *m.* (cylindrical), tallarines *m.* (flat)
consommé; broth	consomé *m*; caldo *m.*
cheese	queso *m.*
butter	mantequilla *f.*
bread	pan *m.*
slice of bread	rebanada (*f.*) de pan
crust	corteza *f.*
crumb	miga *f.*
milk	leche *f.*
egg	huevo *m.*
boiled *o* soft-boiled eggs	huevos (*m.*) pasados por agua
hard-boiled eggs	huevos (*m.*) duros
fried eggs	huevos (*m.*) fritos
poached, scrambled eggs	huevos (*m.*) escalfados, revueltos
omelet	tortilla *f.*
pastry	pastel *m.*
sponge cake	bizcocho *m.*
tart	tarta *f.*
biscuits	galletas *f.*
fruit	fruta *f.*
ice cream	helado *m.*
compote	compota *f.*
jam, preserves *pl.*	mermelada *f. sing.*
marmalade	mermelada (*f.*) de naranjas amargas
salt	sal *f.*
pepper	pimienta *f.*
mustard	mostaza *f.*
vinegar	vinagre *m.*
oil	aceite *m.*
sauce	salsa *f.*
spices	especias *f.*
clove	clavo *m.*

IV. Beverages. — Bebidas, *f.*

drink	bebida *f.*
mineral water	agua (*f.*) mineral
lemonade	gaseosa *f.*; limonada *f.*, limón (*m.*) natural
beer	cerveza *f.*
white, red wine	vino (*m.*) blanco, tinto
claret	clarete *m.*
cider	sidra *f.*
orange juice	zumo (*m.*) de naranja
orangeade; orange squash	naranjada *f.*
lemon juice	zumo (*m.*) de limón
champagne	champán *m.*
liqueur	licor *m.*

V. Restaurant. — Restaurante, *m.*, restorán, *m.*

eating house	casa (*f.*) de comidas
canteen	cantina *f.*
dining hall	comedor *m.*
refectory	refectorio *m.*
waiter	camarero *m.*, mozo *m.*
headwaiter, maître d'hôtel	jefe (*m.*) de comedor
service	servicio *m.*
bill of fare, menu	lista (*f.*) de platos, minuta *f.*, menú *m.*, carta *f.*
winelist	carta (*f.*) de vinos
table	mesa *f.*
to lay *o* to set the table	poner la mesa
to wait at table	servir la mesa
to clear the table	quitar la mesa
tablecloth	mantel *m.*
napkin, serviette	servilleta *f.*
cutlery	cubiertos *m. pl.*
fork	tenedor *m.*
spoon	cuchara *f.*
teaspoon	cucharilla *f.*
ladle	cucharón *m.*
knife	cuchillo *m.*
dishes *pl.*; crockery	vajilla *f. sing.*; loza *f. sing.*
dish, plate	plato *m.*
soup plate *o* dish	plato (*m.*) hondo *or* sopero
(serving) dish [U.S., platter]	fuente *f.*
soup tureen	sopera *f.*
salad bowl	ensaladera *f.*
fruit dish *o* bowl	frutero *m.*
sauce *o* gravy boat	salsera *f.*
glass service, glassware	cristalería *f.*
glass	vaso *m.*; copa *f.*
bottle	botella *f.*
carafe, decanter	garrafa *f.*
cup	taza *f.*
saucer	platillo *m.*
sugar bowl	azucarero *m.*
tea service *o* set	servicio (*m.*) de té
teapot	tetera *f.*
coffee service *o* set	servicio (*m.*) de café
coffeepot	cafetera *f.*
salt shaker	salero *m.*
cruet	vinagreras *f. pl.*
tray	bandeja *f.*

para ti si pasa algo. || FAM. *Silly fool*, pedazo de tonto. || FIG. *There's no fool like an old fool*, a la vejez, viruelas. || *To act* o *to play the fool*, hacer el tonto. || *To be a born fool*, ser tonto de nacimiento, ser más tonto que una mata de habas. || *To make a fool of o.s.*, ridiculizarse, hacer el ridículo. || *To make a fool of s.o.*, ridiculizar a alguien, poner a alguien en ridículo.
— Adj. U. S. Tonto, ta: *to be fool enough to*, ser bastante tonto como para.

fool [fu:l] v. tr. Engañar (to deceive). || Tomar el pelo a (to pull s.o.'s leg). || Estafar: *to fool s.o. out of his money*, estafarle a alguien el dinero. || Dejar perplejo, ja; confundir (to leave puzzled). || — *They fooled me into doing it*, me convencieron de que lo tenía que hacer, me embaucaron de tal manera que lo hice. || *To fool away*, malgastar (time), despilfarrar, malgastar (money).
— V. intr. Bromear (to joke, to kid): *he's only fooling*, sólo está bromeando. || Hacer el tonto (to play the fool). || — *Stop fooling!*, ¡déjate de tonterías! || *To fool about* o *around*, juguetear: *stop fooling around with that gun*, deja de juguetear con esta escopeta; perder el tiempo en tonterías (to waste time), hacer el tonto (to play the fool).

foolery ['fu:ləri] n. Tontería, *f.* || *Stop that foolery!*, ¡déjate de tonterías!

foolhardiness ['fu:l,hα:dinis] n. Temeridad, *f.*

foolhardy ['fu:l,hα:di] adj. Temerario, ria.

fooling ['fu:liŋ] n. Broma, *f.* (joking). || Engaño, *m.* (deception). || *No fooling*, sin broma, en serio.

foolish ['fu:li∫] adj. Insensato, ta (unwise). || Tonto, ta; necio, cia; estúpido, da (silly). || Descabellado, da: *a foolish suggestion*, una sugerencia descabellada. || Ridículo, la (ridiculous). || — *I felt very foolish*, me sentí muy ridículo. || *That was foolish of you*, eso fue una tontería por su parte. || *To make s.o. look foolish*, ridiculizar a uno. || *You foolish thing!*, ¡qué tonto eres!

foolishness [—nis] n. Insensatez, *f.* || Tontería, *f.*, necedad, *f.*, insensatez, *f.* (silly thing). || Locura, *f.*, disparate, *m.* (folly). || Ridiculez, *f.* (ridiculousness).

foolproof ['fu:l,pru:f] adj. Infalible (plan, scheme). || A toda prueba, que no se puede estropear (device).

foolscap [ˈfu:lzkæp] n. Pliego (*m.*) de varios tamaños [12 × 15 pulgadas, 13,5 × 17 pulgadas y 13 × 8 pulgadas].

fool's cap or **foolscap** [ˈfu:lzkæp] n. Gorro (*m.*) de bufón (jester's cap). || Orejas (*f. pl.*) de burro (dunce's cap).

fool's errand [ˈfu:lzˈerənd] n. Empresa (*f.*) descabellada: *to go on a fool's errand*, lanzarse en una empresa descabellada. || *To send on a fool's errand*, mandar hacer algo inútil.

fool's gold [ˈfu:lzˈgəuld] n. Pirita, *f.* [de hierro o de cobre).

fool's paradise [ˈfu:lzˈpærədaiz] n. *To live in a fool's paradise*, vivir entre nubes, no tener la cabeza sobre los hombros.

fool's parsley [ˈfu:lzˈpɑ:sli] n. Bot. Cicuta (*f.*) menor.

foot [fut] n. Anat. Pie, *m.* || Pata, *f.* (of dog, etc.). || Pie, *m.* (of stocking, mountain, wall, verse). || Pie, *m.*, pies, *m. pl.* (of bed): *at the foot of the bed*, al pie de la cama. || Paso, *m.* (step): *to walk with a light foot*, andar con paso ligero. || Pata, *f.* (of piece of furniture). || Pie, *m.*, parte (*f.*) inferior (of a page). || Final, *m.* (of list, etc.). || Pie, *m.* (base). || Arranque, *m.*, pie, *m.* (of stairs). || Pie, *m.* (measure): *running foot*, pie lineal. || Pie, *m.*, parte (*f.*) opuesta a la cabecera (of a table). || Mil. Infantería, *f.* || Print. Pie, *m.* || Mar. Pujamen, *m.* (of a sail). || Tech. Pie (*m.*) prensatelas (of a sewing machine). | Zapata, *f.* (of a rail). || — Pl. Residuos, *m.* (dregs). || — *At one's feet*, a los pies de uno. || *Bound hand and foot*, atado de pies y manos. || *By foot*, a pie, andando. || Fig. *Feet of clay*, pies de arcilla. || Mil. *Foot soldier*, soldado (*m.*) de a pie, infante, *m.* || *From head to foot*, de pies a cabeza, de arriba abajo. || *Hind foot*, pata trasera. || *My hind foot!*, *my foot!*, ¡narices! || *On foot*, a pie, andando (walking), en marcha (under way), en vivo (cattle). || *On one's feet*, de pie (standing). || *Swift* o *fleet of foot*, rápido (animal), veloz, rápido, da (people). || Fig. *To be back on one's feet*, haberse recuperado (person), haber salido a flote (enterprise, etc.), haberse restablecido (economy). || *To be on one's feet all day long*, estar trajinando todo el día. || Fig. *To be swept off one's feet*, volverse loco. | *To carry off one's feet*, arrebatar. | *To catch on the wrong foot*, coger desprevenido. || *To change foot*, cambiar el paso. || *To drag one's feet*, arrastrar los pies (in walking), hacerse el remolón (to stall, to delay). || Fig. *To find one's feet*, acostumbrarse (to accustom o.s.), saber desenvolverse (to manage well). | *To get back on one's feet*, restablecerse (person, economy), salir a flote (enterprise, etc.). | *To get cold feet*, tener miedo. | *To get one's foot in the door*, introducirse. | *To get* o *to be under one's feet*, estar por medio. | *To have a foot in both camps*, jugar con dos barajas. | *To have one foot in the grave*, estar con un pie en el sepulcro. | *To have one's feet on the ground*, tener los pies en la tierra. || *To jump to one's feet*, levantarse de un salto. || Fig. *To keep one's feet*, mantenerse firme. || *To knock s.o. off his feet*, tirar a alguien al suelo (by hitting), tirar de espaldas (by surprise). || *To land* o *to fall on one's feet*, caer de pie. || Fig. *To put one's best foot foreward* o *foremost*, esmerarse. | *To put one's foot down*, pisar el acelerador (in a car), dar prueba de autoridad (to be firm). | *To put one's foot in it*, meter la pata. || *To rise to one's feet*, levantarse, ponerse de pie. || *To set foot on*, pisar: *to set foot on an island*, pisar una isla. || Fig. *To set* o *to put s.o. on his feet*, lanzar a alguien (to put in a good position), hacer levantar cabeza (to help out of difficulty). | *To set sth. back on its feet*, restablecer algo. | *To stand on one's own two feet*, valerse por sí mismo, volar con sus propias alas. | *To start off on the right foot*, entrar con buen pie. | *To stay off one's feet*, no andar mucho. | *To take the load* o *weight off one's feet*, descansar. | *To think on one's feet*, pensar rápidamente. || *Under foot*, see UNDERFOOT.

— Observ. El plural de *foot* es *feet*, excepto cuando significa "residuos" en cuyo caso es *foots*.

foot [fut] v. tr. Hacer el pie de (stocking). || Pisar (to tread). || Sufragar, costear, pagar (expenses). || Sumar (to add up). || Fam. *To foot it*, ir andando *or* a pie (to walk), bailar (to dance).

— V. intr. Avanzar (to proceed). || *To foot up to*, alcanzar.

footage [—idʒ] n. Longitud (*f.*) en pies (length). || Metraje, *m.* (of film).

foot-and-mouth-disease [—ændˈmauθdiˈzi:z] n. Vet. Fiebre (*f.*) aftosa.

football [—bɔ:l] n. Sp. Fútbol, *m.*, balompié, *m.* || Balón, *m.*, pelota, *f.* (ball). || — *Football field*, campo (*m.*) de fútbol [*Amer.*, cancha (*f.*) de fútbol]. || *Football player*, futbolista, *m.*, jugador (*m.*) de fútbol. || *Football pools*, quinielas, *f.* || *Football tournament*, torneo futbolístico. || *Table football*, futbolín, *m.*

footballer [—bɔ:lə*] n. Sp. Futbolista, *m.*

footbath [—bɑ:θ] n. Baño (*m.*) de pies. || Med. Pediluvio, *m.*, baño (*m.*) de pies.

footboard [—bɔ:d] n. Tabla (*f.*) donde están los pedales (in a car). || Tabla (*f.*) del pescante (in a carriage). || Pie, *m.*, pies, *m. pl.* (of bed). || Estribo, *m.* (running board of car).

footboy [—bɔi] n. Lacayo, *m.*, criado, *m.*

foot brake [—breik] n. Freno (*m.*) de pedal.

footbridge [—bridʒ] n. Pasarela, *f.*, puente (*f.*) para peatones.

foot-candle [—ˌkændl] n. Phys. Candela (*f.*) por pie cuadrado.

footcloth [—klɔθ] n. Gualdrapa, *f.* (of horse). || Alfombra, *f.* (carpet).

footed [—id] adj. Con pie: *a footed fruit bowl*, un frutero con pie. || Con patas: *a footed bed*, una cama con patas. || *Four-footed*, con cuatro patas.

footer [—ə*] n. Cosa (*f.*) *or* persona (*f.*) que mide cierto número de pies. || Sp. Fútbol, *m.*, balompié, *m.* || *My yacht is a sixty footer*, mi yate mide sesenta pies de longitud *or* tiene sesenta pies de largo.

footfall [—fɔ:l] n. Paso, *m.*, pisada, *f.*

foot fault [—fɔ:lt] n. Sp. Falta (*f.*) de pie (tennis).

footgear [—giə*] n. Calzado, *m.*

foothill [—hil] n. Colina (*f.*) al pie de una montaña. || — Pl. Estribaciones, *f.* (of a mountain).

foothold [—ˌhəuld] n. Punto (*m.*) de apoyo para el pie. || Fig. Posición, *f.*: *to gain a foothold in the international market*, tomar posición en el mercado internacional. || — Fig. *The rumour had gained a foothold*, el rumor había llegado a ser creído. || *To lose one's foothold*, perder pie.

footing [—iŋ] n. Pie, *m.*, equilibrio, *m.*: *to loose one's footing*, perder pie *or* el equilibrio. || Fig. Base, *m.* (basis). | Pie, *m.*: *on an equal footing*, en un pie de igualdad. | Condición, *f.* (standing). | Posición, *f.* || Colocación (*f.*) del pie (of stocking). || Colocación (*f.*) de los pies (in dancing, fencing). || Math. Suma, *f.* || Arch. Zapata, *f.* (of building). | Zócalo, *m.* (of column). || — *On a war footing*, en pie de guerra. || Fig. *To be on a friendly footing with*, tener relaciones amistosas con. | *To be on a good footing with*, estar en buenos términos con. | *To gain a footing*, conseguir establecerse. || *To miss one's footing*, poner el pie en falso.

footle [—l] v. tr./intr. Fam. Hacer el tonto. || — Fam. *To footle around* o *about*, perder el tiempo en tonterías. | *To footle one's time away*, perder el tiempo.

footless [—lis] adj. Sin pies. || Fig. Sin fundamento.

footlights [—laits] pl. n. Candilejas, *f.* (of stage). || Fig. Teatro, *m.* (the acting profession).

footling [—liŋ] adj. Fam. Fútil (trivial).

footloose [—lu:s] adj. Libre. || *Footloose and fancy free*, libre como el aire.

footman [—mən] n. Lacayo, *m.*, criado, *m.*

— Observ. El plural de esta palabra es *footmen*.

footmark [—mɑ:k] n. Huella, *f.*, pisada, *f.*

footnote [—nəut] n. Nota, *f.* [al pie de la página].

footpace [—peis] n. Paso, *m.* (speed).

footpad [—pæd] n. Bandolero, *m.*, salteador (*m.*) de caminos.

footpath [—pɑ:θ] n. Senda, *f.*, sendero, *m.*, camino, *m.* (in woods, fields). || Acera, *f.* (pavement).

footplate [—pleit] n. Plataforma, *f.* (of railway engine).

foot-pound [—paund] n. Phys. Pie (*m.*) libra (unit of energy).

footprint [—print] n. Huella, *f.*, pisada, *f.*

footrace [—reis] n. Sp. Carrera (*f.*) pedestre.

footrail [—ˌreil] n. Rodapié, *m.*

footrest [—rest] n. Reposapiés, *m. inv.* || Estribo, *m.* (of motorcycle).

footrope [—rəup] n. Mar. Marchapié, *m.*

foot rule [—ru:l] n. Regla (*f.*) de un pie (ruler).

footscraper [—ˌskreipə*] n. Limpiabarros, *m. inv.*

footsie [—si] n. Fam. *To play footsie with*, dar con el pie a.

footslog [—slɔg] v. intr. Andar.

foot soldier [—ˈsəuldʒə*] n. Mil. Soldado (*m.*) de infantería *or* de a pie, infante, *m.*

footsore [—sɔ:*] adj. Con los pies cansados *or* doloridos.

footstalk [—stɔ:k] n. Bot. Pedúnculo, *m.*, pecíolo, *m.* || Pedúnculo, *m.* (of barnacle).

footstep [—step] n. Paso, *m.*, pisada, *f.* || Fig. *To follow in s.o.'s footsteps*, seguir los pasos de alguien.

footstock [—stɔk] n. Contrapunta, *f.* (of a lathe).

footstone [—stəun] n. Arch. Primera piedra, *f.* || Lápida, *f.* [al pie de un sepulcro].

footstool [—stu:l] n. Escabel, *m.*, taburete, *m.*

foot warmer [—ˌwɔ:mə*] n. Calientapiés, *m. inv.*

footway [—wei] n. Acera, *f.* (pavement). || Sendero, *m.*, senda, *f.*, camino, *m.* (pathway).

footwear [—wɛə*] n. Calzado, *m.*

footwork [—wə:k] n. Sp. Juego (*m.*) de piernas.

footworn [—wɔ:n] adj. Trillado, da: *a footworn path*, un camino trillado. || Desgastado, da (stairs). || Con los pies cansados (person).

foozle [ˈfu:zl] v. tr. Fam. Errar (blow).

fop [fɔp] n. Petimetre, *m.*, pisaverde, *m.*, currutaco, *m.*

foppery [ˈfɔpəri] n. Afectación, *f.* || Fatuidad, *f.*, presunción, *f.* (vanity).

foppish [ˈfɔpiʃ] adj. Afectado, da. || Presumido, da; fatuo, tua (conceited).

foppishness [—nis] n. See FOPPERY.

for [fɔ:*]

A. Preposition: **1.** Translated by *para*. — **2.** Translated by *por*. — **3.** Translated by *de*. — **4.** Translated by other prepositions. — **5.** Locutions.
B. Conjunction.

A. Preposition

1. Translated by PARA to express **with the purpose of:** *a book for studying,* un libro para estudiar; **destined to:** *a gift for his mother,* un regalo para su madre; **in the direction of:** *I am leaving for London,* me marcho para Londres; **in effect on:** *bread is good for you,* el pan es bueno para ti; **considering the usual nature of:** *that was a clever remark for John,* aquélla era una observación inteligente para Juan; *he's nice for a teacher,* para ser profesor, es simpático; *you are small for your age,* eres bajo para la edad que tienes; **at** [of time]: *I have got an engagement for 10 o'clock,* tengo una cita para las diez; **during:** *we have work for two years,* tenemos trabajo para dos años.

2. Translated by POR to express **on behalf of:** *I'll sign for you,* firmaré por ti; **in exchange of:** *sold for 10 pounds,* vendido por diez libras; *blow for blow,* golpe por golpe; **because of:** *for this reason,* por esta razón; *he was punished for his crime,* fue castigado por su crimen; *famous for his heroic deeds,* famoso por sus hazañas; **for the benefit of:** *I did it for you,* lo hice por ti; **in spite of:** *for all his studying he will never know anything,* por mucho que estudie no sabrá nunca nada; **compared with:** *for every adult there were ten children,* por cada adulto había diez niños.

3. Translated by DE to express **as the effect of:** *she shouted for joy,* gritó de alegría; **representing:** *A* for *Andrew,* A de Andrés; **to the amount of:** *a bill for 5 pounds,* una cuenta de cinco libras; **to have:** *eager for news,* ávido de noticias; **to:** *the train for Paris,* el tren de París.

4. Translated by OTHER PREPOSITIONS. — Desde hace (in indefinite time): *I have been in Manchester for three months,* estoy en Manchester desde hace tres meses. || Durante (in definite time): *he worked for eight hours,* trabajó durante ocho horas. || Antes de (before): *he won't be back for a week,* no volverá antes de una semana. || En honor de (in honour of): *a banquet for the mayor,* un banquete en honor del alcalde. || A favor de, en favor de (in favour of): *he was for a negotiated peace,* estaba a favor de una paz negociada; *campaign for women's lib,* campaña a favor de la liberación de la mujer. || A, para con (towards): *affection for children,* cariño a los niños; *respect for his parents,* respeto para con sus padres. || En lugar de, en vez de, como (in place of): *he used a cup for a soup bowl,* utilizó una taza en vez de un plato sopero. || Como (as): *I want you for my wife,* te quiero como mujer. || Para que (in order that): *I have brought this for you to see,* he traido esto para que lo veas. || Contra (against): *campaign for pollution control,* campaña contra la contaminación. || En cuanto a (as regards).

5. LOCUTIONS. — *As for,* en cuanto a. || *For all that,* a pesar de todo eso, con todo y con eso. || *For ever,* para siempre (eternally), siempre (always). || *For ever and ever,* para siempre jamás. || *For him to fall now would be fatal,* caerse ahora sería fatal para él, sería fatal que se cayera ahora. || *For o.s.,* solo, la: *I can do it for myself,* lo puedo hacer solo. || *For sale,* en venta. || *For that to be possible,* para que eso sea posible. || *For the time being,* de momento, por ahora. || *I for one,* yo personalmente. || FAM. *I'm all for it,* me parece muy bien. || *I'm for Madrid,* voy a Madrid. || *It is best for you to go,* más vale que te vayas. || *It is for you to,* a ti te toca. || *It is time for lunch,* es la hora de comer. || *I travelled for miles and miles,* recorrí muchas millas. || *I want to see it for myself,* quiero verlo yo mismo. || FAM. *Now we are (in) for it!,* ¡ahora se va a armar! || *Oh, for...!,* ¡ojalá!: *oh, for a fine day!,* ¡ojalá hiciese un buen día!; ¡quién tuviera...!: *oh, for an ice cream!,* ¡quién tuviera un helado! || *Speaking for myself,* hablando en mi nombre *or* en nombre propio. || *There is nothing for it but to,* no hay más remedio que. || *To come for,* venir a por *or* a buscar. || *To go for,* ir a por *or* a buscar. || *To go for a walk,* [ir a] dar un paseo. || FAM. *To go for s.o.,* gustarle a uno alguien: *I really go for him,* me gusta mucho. || *To leave s.o. for dead,* dejar a uno por muerto. || *To make a name for o.s.,* hacerse un nombre. || *To write for the papers,* escribir para *or* en los periódicos. || *Were it not for that,* si no hubiera sido por eso, de no haber sido por eso (in the past tense), de no ser por eso, si no fuera por eso (in the present). || *What for?,* ¿para qué? (with what aim), ¿por qué? (why). || *What is the French for "spoon"?,* ¿cómo se dice "cuchara" en francés? || *What is this for?,* ¿para qué sirve esto? || *Where are you going for your holiday?,* ¿adónde vas de vacaciones?

B. Conjunction. Ya que, pues, puesto que (because, seeing that).

— OBSERV. *For* when used in an expression of duration of time in the future is either not translated in Spanish or translated by *por* or *para* (*I am going to Pamplona for two weeks,* voy a Pamplona dos semanas, voy a Pamplona por *or* para dos semanas).

forage [ˈfɔridʒ] n. Forraje, *m.*

forage [ˈfɔridʒ] v. intr. Forrajear, buscar el forraje (to collect forage). || FIG. Hurgar (to search). || FIG. *To forage for,* buscar hurgando.
— V. tr. Forrajear (hay, etc.). || Dar forraje a (animals). || FIG. Saquear (to plunder).

forage plant [—plænt] n. AGR. Planta (*f.*) forrajera.

forager [ˈfɔridʒə*] n. MIL. Forrajeador, *m.*

foraging [—iŋ] n. Forraje, *m.*

forasmuch as [fərəzˈmʌtʃæz] conj. Puesto que, ya que.

foray [ˈfɔrei] n. Correría, *f.*, incursión, *f.* (raid). || Saqueo, *m.* (pillage).

foray [ˈfɔrei] v. intr. Hacer una incursión *or* una correría.
— V. tr. Saquear (to plunder).

forbad [fəˈbæd] pret. See FORBID.

forbade [fəˈbæd] pret. See FORBID.

forbear [ˈfɔːbɛə*] n. Antepasado, *m.*

forbear* [fɔːˈbɛə*] v. intr. Contenerse (to refrain). || Abstenerse: *to forbear from drinking,* abstenerse de beber. || *To forbear with,* soportar con paciencia.
— V. tr. Abstenerse de.

— OBSERV. Pret. ***forbore;*** p. p. ***forborne.***

forbearance [fɔːbɛərəns] n. Indulgencia, *f.* (tolerance). || Paciencia, *f.* (patience). || Dominio (*m.*) sobre sí mismo (self-control). || Abstención, *f.*

forbearing [fɔːˈbɛəriŋ] adj. Indulgente. || Paciente.

forbid* [fəˈbid] v. tr. Prohibir: *I forbid you to leave the house,* te prohibo que salgas de casa, te prohibo salir de casa; *to forbid sth. to s.o.,* prohibir algo a alguien. || FIG. Impedir (to prevent). || — *Smoking strictly forbidden,* prohibido fumar. || *To forbid s.o. the house,* negarse a recibir a alguien.

— OBSERV. Pret. ***forbad, forbade;*** p. p. ***forbidden.***

forbiddance [fəˈbidəns] n. Prohibición, *f.*

forbidden [fəˈbidn] p. p. See FORBID.

forbidding [fəˈbidiŋ] adj. Impresionante, imponente: *a forbidding task,* una tarea impresionante. || Severo, ra (stern). || Inhóspito, ta: *a forbidding country,* un país inhóspito. || Odioso, sa (repellent). || Amenazador, ra (threatening): *a forbidding sky,* un cielo amenazador. || Terrible (terrifying).

forbore [fɔːˈbɔː*] pret. See FORBEAR.

forborne [fɔːˈbɔːn] p. p. See FORBEAR.

force [fɔːs] n. Fuerza, *f.*: *we had to use force to restrain him,* tuvimos que emplear la fuerza para contenerle; *to resort to force,* recurrir a la fuerza; *the force of an argument,* la fuerza de un argumento; *force of character,* fuerza de carácter. || Contingente, *m.* (contingent). || PHYS. Fuerza, *f.*: *centrifugal, inertial force,* fuerza centrífuga, de inercia. || Policía, *f.*, fuerza (*f.*) pública (police). || MIL. Cuerpo, *m.*: *expeditionary force,* cuerpo expedicionario. || — Pl. MIL. Fuerzas, *f.*: *armed forces,* fuerzas armadas; *land forces,* fuerzas terrestres. || — *Brute force,* fuerza bruta. || *By force,* a la fuerza, por fuerza. || *By force of,* a fuerza de. || *By force of circumstances,* debido a las circunstancias. || *By force of habit,* por costumbre, por la fuerza de la costumbre. || *By sheer force,* a viva fuerza. || *In force,* en vigor, vigente. || *In (full) force,* en masa. || *Labour force,* mano (*f.*) de obra. || *Sales force,* vendedores, *m. pl.* || *To be in force,* estar en vigor, estar vigente, regir. || *To come into force,* entrar en vigor. || *To join forces,* unirse. || *To put into force,* poner en vigor, hacer entrar en vigor, aplicar. || *To yield to force,* rendirse a la fuerza.

force [fɔːs] v. tr. Forzar, obligar: *to force s.o. to do sth.* o *into doing sth.,* obligar a alguien a que haga algo. || Forzar (a door, a lock, a key). || Meter a la fuerza: *to force a coin into a slot,* meter a la fuerza una moneda en una ranura. || AGR. Forzar, activar la maduración de. || MIL. Tomar por asalto, forzar (to take). || GRAMM. Forzar (meaning). || Forzar, violar (a woman). || TECH. Inyectar (air). || — *To be forced to,* verse obligado a, estar forzado a. || *To force a smile,* sonreír de dientes afuera, sonreír forzadamente. || *To force one's way,* abrirse paso: *to force one's way through the crowd,* abrirse paso entre la muchedumbre; entrar por [la] fuerza: *to force one's way into a house,* entrar por la fuerza en una casa. || *To force o.s. into doing sth.,* hacer un esfuerzo por hacer algo, esforzarse por hacer algo. || *To force s.o. into,* hacer entrar por la fuerza a alguien en. || *To force s.o. into a corner* o *against a wall,* arrinconar a uno. || FIG. *To force s.o.'s hand,* forzarle la mano a alguien. || *To force the pace,* forzar *or* apresurar *or* apretar el paso. — ***To force away,*** obligar a alejarse. || ***To force back,*** hacer retroceder (the enemy). | Contener, reprimir (tears). || ***To force down,*** obligar a bajar (to push down). | Tragar por la fuerza (to swallow unwillingly). | Hacer tragar (to force to swallow). | Cerrar por la fuerza (a lid, etc.). | Obligar a aterrizar (a plane). | Hacer bajar (prices). | Inyectar (air). || ***To force from,*** arrancar. || ***To force in,*** conseguir hacer entrar, hacer entrar *or* introducir por la fuerza. || ***To force off,*** quitar por la fuerza, conseguir despegar (sth. which is stuck). | Hacer salir de: *to force a lorry off the road,* hacer salir un camión de la carretera. || ***To force out,*** obligar a salir, hacer salir por la fuerza. | Arrancar (to pull out). | Eliminar [a un jugador] (in baseball). | Pronunciar con dificultad (words). | Sacar (the truth). || — *To force out a few words of congratulation,* pronunciar unas palabras de felicitación de boca para fuera. | *To force the truth out of s.o.,* obligar *or* forzar a uno a decir la verdad. || ***To force through,*** conseguir hacer entrar. || ***To force up,*** obligar a subir, hacer subir por la fuerza. | Hacer subir (prices). || ***To force upon,*** imponer:

he tries to force his ideas upon me, intenta imponerme sus ideas. | Obligar a aceptar *or* tomar: *he forced a drink upon me*, me obligó a tomar una copa.
forced [—t] adj. Forzado, da: *forced smile*, sonrisa forzada. || TECH. A presión (feed). || — *Forced labour*, trabajo obligatorio. || AVIAT. *Forced landing*, aterrizaje forzoso. || *Forced march*, marcha forzada.
forceful [—ful] adj. Fuerte: *a forceful personality*, una personalidad fuerte. || Contundente (convincing): *a forceful speech*, un discurso contundente. || Enérgico, ca; vigoroso, sa (energetic).
forcefulness [—fulnis] n. Fuerza, *f.*, energía, *f.*
force majeure [fɔ:smæ'ʒə*] n. Fuerza (*f.*) mayor.
forcemeat ['fɔ:smi:t] n. Picadillo (*m.*) de relleno, relleno, *m.*
forceps ['fɔ:seps] inv. n. MED. Fórceps, *m.* (in obstetrics). | Gatillo, *m.*, tenazas, *f. pl.* (in dentistry).
force pump ['fɔ:spʌmp] n. TECH. Bomba (*f.*) impelente.
forcible ['fɔ:səbl] adj. Contundente: *a forcible argument*, un argumento contundente. || Fuerte, enérgico, ca (style). || A la fuerza, por fuerza (by force). || — JUR. *Forcible detainer*, posesión ilegal obtenida por la violencia. | *Forcible entry*, violación (*f.*) de domicilio, allanamiento (*m.*) de morada.
forcibly [—i] adv. Por la fuerza (by force). || Enérgicamente (energetically).
forcing ['fɔ:siŋ] n. Forzamiento, *m.*
ford [fɔ:d] n. Vado, *m.*
ford [fɔ:d] v. tr. Vadear.
fordable ['fɔ:dəbl] adj. Vadeable.
fore [fɔ:*] adj. Delantero, ra: *the fore legs*, las patas delanteras. || Anterior, delantero, ra: *the fore part*, la parte anterior. || MAR. De proa.
— Adv. Delante, en la parte delantera.
— Prep. Ante.
— N. MAR. Proa, *f.*, parte (*f.*) delantera. || — *At the fore*, en el palo de trinquete (in ships), en la cabeza (in a leading position). || FIG. *To be to the fore*, ocupar un lugar preeminente. | *To come to the fore*, empezar a destacar *or* a ser conocido. || MIL. *To the fore!*, ¡adelante!
— Interj. ¡Cuidado! (in golf).
fore and aft [—ændɑ:ft] adv. MAR. De proa a popa.
fore-and-aft [—ændɑ:ft] adj. Longitudinal. || De proa a popa.
fore and after [—ænd'ɑ:ftə*] n. MAR. Goleta, *f.*, barco (*m.*) de velas áuricas. || Bicornio, *m.* (hat).
fore-and-aft rig [—ændɑ:ftrig] n. MAR. Aparejo (*m.*) de velas áuricas.
fore-and-aft sail [—ændɑ:ftseil] n. MAR. Vela (*f.*) áurica.
forearm [—r'ɑ:m] n. ANAT. Antebrazo, *m.*
forearm [—r'ɑ:m] v. tr. Prevenir.
forebear [—'bɛə*] n. Antepasado, *m.*
forebode [—'bəud] v. tr. Anunciar, presagiar: *a policy that forebodes disaster*, una política que anuncia un desastre. || Presentir, tener el presentimiento de (to have a presentiment).
foreboding [—'bəudiŋ] n. Presentimiento, *m.* || Presagio, *m.* (sign of things to come).
forebrain [—brein] n. ANAT. Cerebro (*m.*) anterior.
forecast [—kɑ:st] n. Previsión, *f.*, pronóstico, *m.* || Pronóstico, *m.* (in racing). || *Weather forecast*, parte meteorológico (weather report), previsión meteorológica (predicting weather).
forecast [—kɑ:st] v. tr. Pronosticar.
forecaster [—,kɑ:stə*] n. Pronosticador, ra.
forecastle ['fəuksl] n. MAR. Castillo (*m.*) de proa.
foreclose [fɔ:'kləuz] v. tr. Excluir (to preclude). || JUR. Privar del derecho de redimir una hipoteca.
— V. intr. JUR. Ejecutar una hipoteca.
foreclosure [fɔ:k'ləuʒə*] n. Exclusión, *f.* || JUR. Ejecución (*f.*) de una hipoteca.
forecourt ['fɔ:kɔ:t] n. Antepatio, *m.* (of a building). || SP. Parte (*f.*) del campo cercana a la red (tennis, badminton).
foredoom [fɔ:'du:m] n. Destino, *m.*
foredoom [fɔ:'du:m] v. tr. Condenar de antemano: *an attempt that was foredoomed to failure*, un intento que estaba condenado de antemano al fracaso. || (Ant.). Predeterminar, predestinar.
fore edge ['fɔ:redʒ] n. Canal, *f.* (of book).
forefather ['fɔ:,fɑ:ðə*] n. Antepasado, *m.*
forefinger ['fɔ:,fiŋgə*] n. Índice, *m.*, dedo (*m.*) índice.
forefoot ['fɔ:fut] Pata (*f.*) delantera (of an animal). || MAR. Pie (*m.*) de la roda.
forefront ['fɔ:frʌnt] n. Primer plano, *m.*, vanguardia, *f.* || MIL. Primera fila, *f.*, vanguardia, *f.*, frente, *m.* || — *This question is still in the forefront*, esta cuestión sigue en primer plano. || *To come to the forefront*, empezar a destacar.
foregather [fɔ:'gæðə*] v. intr. Reunirse.
forego* [fɔ:'gəu] v. tr. Renunciar a, privarse de (to forgo). || Preceder, anteceder (to precede).
— OBSERV. Pret. ***forewent;*** p. p. ***foregone.***
foregoing [fɔ:'gəuiŋ] adj. Anteriormente mencionado, da (above). || Precedente, anterior (preceeding).
— N. Lo anteriormente dicho.
foregone [fɔ:'gɔn] adj. Conocido de antemano (conclusion, etc.). || Inevitable (determined). || Previsto, ta (anticipated). || Pasado, da (previous).
— P. p. See FOREGO.
foreground ['fɔ:graund] n. Primer plano, *m.*, primer término, *m.* || FIG. Primer plano, *m.*
forehand ['fɔ:hænd] adj. Previo, via (prior). || *Forehand stroke*, golpe derecho *or* directo (in tennis).
— N. Golpe (*m.*) derecho *or* directo (in tennis). || Cuarto (*m.*) delantero (of a horse).
forehanded [—id] adj. U. S. Precavido, da; prudente (prudent). | Acomodado, da (well-off). | Derecho, cha; directo, ta (stroke in tennis).
forehead ['fɔ:hed] n. ANAT. Frente, *f.* || Parte (*f.*) delantera (front part).
foreign ['fɔrin] adj. Extranjero, ra: *foreign languages*, lenguas extranjeras. || Exterior: *foreign trade*, comercio exterior. || Ajeno, na: *this behaviour is foreign to his nature*, este comportamiento es ajeno a su naturaleza. || — *Foreign affairs*, asuntos exteriores [*Amer.*, relaciones exteriores]. || *Foreign body*, cuerpo extraño. || *Foreign correspondent*, corresponsal en el extranjero. || *Foreign currency o exchange*, divisas, *f. pl.* || *Foreign debt*, deuda externa *or* exterior. || *Foreign legion*, legión extranjera. || *Foreign money order*, giro (*m.*) internacional. || *Foreign Office*, Ministerio de Asuntos Exteriores [*Amer.*, Ministerio de Relaciones Exteriores]. || *Foreign parts*, el extranjero. || *Foreign Secretary*, ministro (*m.*) de Asuntos Exteriores [*Amer.*, ministro (*m.*) de Relaciones Exteriores]. || *Foreign travel*, viajes (*m. pl.*) al *or* en el extranjero.
foreign-born [—bɔ:n] adj. Nacido en el extranjero.
foreigner ['fɔrinə*] n. Extranjero, ra (from another country). || Forastero, ra (from another region).
foreignism [—izəm] n. Extranjerismo, *m.*
forejudge [fɔ:'dʒʌdʒ] v. tr. Prejuzgar.
foreknow* [fɔ:'nəu] v. tr. Saber de antemano.
— OBSERV. Pret. ***foreknew;*** p.p. ***foreknown.***
foreknowledge ['fɔ:'nɔlidʒ] n. Presciencia, *f.*
foreland ['fɔ:lənd] n. Promontorio, *m.*, cabo, *m.*
foreleg ['fɔ:leg] n. Pata (*f.*) delantera (of a dog). || Brazo, *m.* (of a horse).
forelock ['fɔ:lɔk] n. Copete, *m.*, mechón (*m.*) de pelo (hair). || TECH. Clavija, *f.* (fastening device). || *To take time by the forelock*, coger la ocasión por los pelos.
foreman ['fɔ:mən] n. Capataz, *m.* (in a factory). || Mayoral, *m.* (in a farm). || ARCH. Capataz, *m.*, maestro (*m.*) de obras, aparejador, *m.* || PRINT. Regente, *m.* || JUR. Presidente (*m.*) del jurado.
— OBSERV. El plural es *foremen.*
foremast ['fɔ:mɑ:st] n. MAR. Palo (*m.*) de trinquete.
forementioned [fɔ:'menʃənd] adj. Anteriormente mencionado, da.
foremost ['fɔ:məust] adj. Primero, ra: *one of the foremost producers of cotton*, uno de los primeros productores de algodón. || *To be first and foremost*, ser el primero de todos.
— Adv. *First and foremost*, ante todo, antes que nada.
forename ['fɔ:neim] n. Nombre, *m.* [de pila].
forenamed [—d] adj. Anteriormente mencionado, da.
forenoon [,fɔ:nu:n] n. Mañana, *f.*
— Adj. Matutino, na; matinal.
forensic [fə'rensik] adj. JUR. Forense: *forensic surgeon*, médico forense; *forensic medicine*, medicina forense. | Del foro: *forensic eloquence*, elocuencia del foro.
foreordain [,fɔ:rɔ:'dein] v. tr. Predestinar, predeterminar.
foreordination [,fɔ:rɔ:də'neiʃən] n. Predestinación, *f.*, predeterminación, *f.*
forepart ['fɔ:pɑ:t] n. Parte (*f.*) delantera. || Principio, *m.* (beginning).
forepeak ['fɔ:pi:k] n. MAR. Bodega (*f.*) de proa.
forequarter ['fɔ:,kwɔ:tə*] n. Cuarto (*m.*) delantero [de la res].
forereach [fɔ:'ri:tʃ] v. tr. MAR. Adelantar, pasar (to overtake).
— V. intr. MAR. Ganar terreno.
forerun [fɔ:'rʌn] v. tr. Preceder.
forerunner [—ə*] n. Precursor, ra. || Predecesor, ra (predecessor). || Anunciador, ra (herald). || Presagio, *m.* (omen). || Antepasado, *m.* (forebear). || *The Forerunner*, el Precursor de Cristo.
foresaid ['fɔ:sed] adj. Anteriormente mencionado, da; susodicho, cha.
foresail ['fɔ:seil] n. MAR. Trinquete, *m.*
foresaw [fɔ:'sɔ:] pret. See FORESEE.
foresee* [fɔ:'si:] v. tr. Prever: *he had foreseen the problem*, había previsto el problema.
— OBSERV. Pret. ***foresaw;*** p. p. ***foreseen.***
foreseeable [—əbl] adj. Previsible.
foreseen [fɔ:'si:n] p. p. See FORESEE.
foreshadow [fɔ:'ʃædəu] v. tr. Presagiar (to presage). || Prefigurar (to prefigure).
foresheet ['fɔ:ʃi:t] n. MAR. Escota (*f.*) del trinquete. || — Pl. MAR. Parte (*f. sing.*) delantera de un barco.
foreshore ['fɔ:ʃɔ:] n. Playa, *f.* [entre los límites de pleamar y bajamar].
foreshorten [fɔ:'ʃɔ:tən] v. tr. ARTS. Escorzar.
foreshortening [—iŋ] n. Escorzo, *m.*
foreshow [fɔ:'ʃəu] v. tr. Presagiar.
foreside ['fɔ:said] n. Parte (*f.*) anterior.
foresight ['fɔ:sait] n. Previsión, *f.* || Punto (*m.*) de mira (of a rifle). || *To have foresight*, ser previsor *or* precavido.
foresighted [—id] adj. Previsor, ra (farsighted). || Precavido, da (cautious).

foreskin [ˈfɔːskin] n. Anat. Prepucio, *m.*

forest [ˈfɔrist] n. Selva, *f.*: *the virgin forest*, la selva virgen. || Bosque, *m.* (wood). || Fig. Intrincamiento, *m.*: *a forest of masts in a harbour*, un intrincamiento de palos en un puerto. || — U. S. Fig. *He can't see the forest for the trees*, los árboles impiden ver el bosque. || *State forests*, patrimonio (*m. sing.*) forestal del Estado.
— Adj. Selvático, ca; de la selva: *forest animals*, animales de la selva. || Forestal: *forest botany, fire*, botánica, incendio forestal.

forest [ˈfɔrist] v. tr. Poblar de árboles.

forestage [ˈfɔːsteidʒ] n. Proscenio, *m.* (in a theatre).

forestal [ˈfɔːristəl] adj. Forestal: *forestal resources*, recursos forestales.

forestall [fɔːˈstɔːl] v. tr. Adelantarse a, anticiparse a (people). || Anticiparse a (circumstances). || Comm. Acaparar, monopolizar (a market).

forestation [ˌfɔrisˈteiʃən] n. Plantación (*f.*) de bosques. || Repoblación (*f.*) forestal (reafforestation).

forestay [ˈfɔːstei] n. Mar. Estay (*m.*) del trinquete.

forester [ˈfɔristə*] n. Guardabosque, *m.* (officer in charge of a forest). || Silvicultor, *m.* (forestry expert). || Habitante (*m.*) de un bosque (who lives in a forest). || Zool. Canguro (*m.*) gigante.

forest ranger [ˈfɔːristˈreindʒə*] n. U. S. Guardabosque, *m.*, guarda (*m.*) forestal.

forestry [ˈfɔristri] n. Bosques, *m. pl.* (woods). || Silvicultura, *f.* || — *Forestry Commission*, Administración (*f.*) de montes. || *Forestry expert*, silvicultor, *m.*

foretaste [ˈfɔːteist] n. Anticipación, *f.*

foretaste [fɔːˈteist] v. tr. Conocer *or* probar de antemano.

foretell* [fɔːˈtel] v. tr. Predecir, pronosticar (to predict). || Presagiar (to forebode).
— Observ. Pret. & p. p. ***foretold***.

foreteller [—ə*] n. Pronosticador, *m.* (forecaster). || Profeta, *m.* (prophet). || Adivino, na (fortune-teller).

forethought [ˈfɔːθɔːt] n. Prudencia, *f.*, previsión, *f.* (prudence). || Premeditación, *f.*: *crime of forethought*, crimen con premeditación.
— Adj. Premeditado, da.

foretoken [fɔːˈtəukən] n. Presagio, *m.*, signo (*m.*) precursor.

foretoken [fɔːˈtəukən] v. tr. Presagiar.

foretold [fɔːˈtəuld] pret. & p. p. See foretell.

foretooth [ˈfɔːtuːθ] n. Anat. Incisivo, *m.*, diente (*m.*) incisivo.
— Observ. El plural de *foretooth* es *foreteeth*.

foretop [ˈfɔːtɔp] n. Mar. Cofa (*f.*) del trinquete.

fore-topgallant mast [ˈfɔːtəpˌgæləntmɑːst] n. Mar. Mastelerillo (*m.*) de juanete de proa.

fore-topgallant sail [ˈfɔːtəpˌgæləntseil] n. Mar. Juanete (*m.*) de proa.

fore-topmast [ˈfɔːtɔpˈmɑːst] n. Mar. Mastelero (*m.*) de velacho.

fore-topsail [ˈfɔːtɔpseil] n. Mar. Velacho, *m.*

for ever (U. S. **forever**) [fəˈrevə*] adv. Para siempre: *he is gone for ever*, se ha ido para siempre. || Fig. Siempre: *he is for ever complaining*, siempre se está quejando. || *For ever and ever*, para siempre jamás.

forevermore [fəˈrevəˈmɔː*] adv. (Ant.). Para siempre jamás.

forewarn [fɔːˈwɔːn] v. tr. Prevenir, avisar, advertir (to warn). || *Forewarned is forearmed*, hombre prevenido vale por dos.

forewent [ˈfɔːwent] pret. See forego.

forewoman [ˈfɔːˌwumən] n. Jur. Presidente (*f.*) del jurado. || Encargada, *f.* (of a workshop, etc.).
— Observ. El plural de esta palabra es *forewomen*.

foreword [ˈfɔːwəːd] n. Prólogo, *m.*, prefacio, *m.*

foreyard [ˈfɔːjɑːd] n. Mar. Verga (*f.*) del trinquete.

forfeit [ˈfɔːfit] n. Multa, *f.* (fine). || Prenda, *f.* (in a game). || Jur. Pérdida (*f.*) de un derecho (loss of a right). || Fig. Pérdida, *f.* (loss). | Castigo, *m.* (punishment). || — Pl. Juego (*m. sing.*) de prendas.
— Adj. Confiscado, da (confiscated). || Perdido, da.

forfeit [ˈfɔːfit] v. tr. Jur. Perder (a right). | Comisar, decomisar, confiscar (a property). || Perder (to lose).

forfeiture [ˈfɔːfitʃə*] n. Pérdida, *f.* (of licence, right). || Confiscación, *f.* (of property).

forgather [ˈfɔːgæðə*] v. intr. Reunirse.

forgave [fəˈgeiv] pret. See forgive.

forge [fɔːdʒ] n. Tech. Fragua, *f.* (furnace). | Herrería, *f.*, forja, *f.*, fundición, *f.* (ironworks).

forge [fɔːdʒ] v. tr. Fraguar, forjar (metal). || Falsificar (to counterfeit): *to forge a signature*, falsificar una firma. || Fig. Fraguar, forjar (project, friendship, etc.).
— V. intr. Avanzar (to move forward). || — *To forge ahead*, hacer grandes progresos (to make progress), avanzar [rápidamente] (to move forward). || *To forge ahead of s.o.*, adelantar a alguien.

forger [—ə*] n. Herrero, *m.*, forjador, *m.* (metal worker). || Falsificador, *m.* (counterfeiter).

forgery [—əri] n. Falsificación, *f.* (counterfeiting). || Documento (*m.*) *or* billete (*m.*) falsificado, moneda (*f.*) falsificada (sth. forged).

forget* [fəˈget] v. tr. Olvidar, olvidarse de: *I forgot my watch*, me olvidé del reloj, olvidé el reloj. || Dejar (to leave): *I forgot it in the train*, lo dejé en el tren. || No fijarse en: *I forgot the time*, no me fijé en la hora. || Olvidar: *try to forget it*, intenta olvidarlo. || — *And don't you forget it!*, ¡que no se te olvide! || *Forget it!*, ¡deja! (don't bother), ¡de nada! (reply to "thank you"), ¡no importa! (it doesn't matter), ¡no se preocupe! (don't worry). || *Never to be forgotten*, inolvidable. || *To forget o.s.*, olvidarse de uno mismo (to act unselfishly), propasarse (to behave thoughtlessly): *he forgot himself and hit her*, se propasó y le pegó. || *To forget to do sth.*, olvidarse de hacer algo, olvidársele a uno hacer algo: *I forgot to ring you up*, se me olvidó llamarte por teléfono.
— V. intr. Tener poca memoria (to have a bad memory). || Olvidar: *I went away to forget*, me marché para olvidar. || — *I forget right now*, no me acuerdo ahora mismo. || *Let's forget about it*, olvidémoslo. || *She had to bring me a book but she forgot*, tenía que traerme un libro pero se le olvidó.
— Observ. Pret. ***forgot;*** p. p. ***forgotten***.

forgetful [—ful] adj. Olvidadizo, za; desmemoriado, da; que tiene muy mala memoria (apt to forget). || Descuidado, da (negligent). || — *Forgetful of his pain*, olvidando su dolor, haciendo caso omiso de su dolor. || *She is very forgetful*, tiene muy mala memoria.

forgetfulness [—fulnis] n. Falta (*f.*) de memoria (lack of memory). || Olvido, *m.*: *a moment of forgetfulness*, un momento de olvido. || Descuido, *m.* (negligence). || Despiste, *m.* (absentmindedness).

forget-me-not [fəˈgetminɔt] n. Bot. Nomeolvides, *f. inv.*, raspilla, *f.*, miosota, *f.*

forgettable [fəˈgetəbl] adj. Olvidable.

forging [ˈfɔdʒiŋ] n. Forja, *f.*

forgivable [fəˈgivəbl] adj. Perdonable.

forgive* [fəˈgiv] v. tr. Perdonar: *to forgive s.o. for sth.*, perdonar algo a alguien; *to forgive s.o. a debt*, perdonar una deuda a uno.
— Observ. Pret. ***forgave;*** p. p. ***forgiven***.

forgiven [—n] p. p. See forgive.

forgiveness [—nis] n. Perdón, *m.*: *to ask for forgiveness*, pedir perdón. || Remisión, *f.*, perdón, *m.* (of sins). || Perdón, *m.* (of a debt). || Indulgencia, *f.* (willingness to forgive).

forgiving [—iŋ] adj. Propenso a perdonar, indulgente, clemente.

forgivingness [—nis] n. Indulgencia, *f.*, clemencia, *f.*

forgo* [fɔːˈgəu] v. tr. Renunciar a, privarse de (to do without). || Desperdiciar (an opportunity). || *I cannot forgo mentioning it*, no puedo dejar de mencionarlo.
— Observ. Pret. ***forwent;*** p. p. ***forgone***.

forgone [fɔːˈgɔn] p. p. See forgo.

forgot [fɔːˈgɔt] pret. See forget.

forgotten [fəˈgɔtn] p. p. See forget.

fork [fɔːk] n. Tenedor, *m.* (cutlery). || Horca, *f.*, horquilla, *f.* (for gardening). || Horquilla, *f.* (to support a branch, etc.). || Bifurcación, *f.* (of road). || Horcadura, *f.* (of a tree). || Zigzag, *m.* (of lightning). || Horcajo, *m.*, confluencia, *f.* (in a river). || Tech. Horquilla, *f.* (of bicycle). || Anat. Horcajadura, *f.* (crotch). || Mus. Diapasón, *m.* (tuning fork).

fork [fɔːk] v. tr. Cargar con la horca, coger con la horca (hay, etc.). || Atacar al mismo tiempo [dos peones] (in chess). || Fam. *To fork out* o *over* o *up*, soltar, aflojar (money).
— V. intr. Bifurcarse. || Fam. *To fork out* o *over* o *up*, aflojar *or* soltar la mosca (to pay).

forked [—t] adj. Ahorquillado, da (fork-shaped). || Bifurcado, da (roads). || Bot. Bífido, da. || *Forked lightning*, relámpago en zigzag.

forklift [ˈfɔːklift] n. Tech. Carretilla (*f.*) elevadora.

forlorn [fəˈlɔːn] n. Triste, melancólico, ca (sad). | Desesperado, da (desperate): *a forlorn cry*, un grito desesperado. || Desolado, da: *a forlorn landscape*, un paisaje desolado. || Abandonado, da (abandoned). || *Forlorn hope*, empresa desesperada (hopeless undertaking), destacamento (*m.*) de soldados encargados de una misión peligrosa (soldiers).

form [fɔːm] n. Forma, *f.* (shape, nature): *it was published in book form*, se publicó en forma de libro; *form and substance*, forma y fondo. || Figura, *f.*, cuerpo, *m.* (figure). || Manera, *f.*, forma, *f.*: *there are several forms of saying it*, hay varias maneras de decirlo. || Clase, *f.*, tipo, *m.*: *two forms of government*, dos tipos de gobierno. || Formulario, *m.* (document): *application form*, formulario de inscripción; *to fill in a form*, llenar un formulario. || Banco, *m.* (bench). || Clase, *f.* (class). || Curso, *m.* (year, at school): *first form*, primer curso. || Forma, *f.*: *to be in good form*, estar en forma; *to be on the top of one's form*, estar en plena forma. || Gramm. Phil. Forma, *f.* || Print. Forma, *f.*, molde, *m.* || Jur. Forma, *f.* || Tech. Molde, *m.*, forma, *f.* (mould). | Encofrado, *m.*, entibación, *f.* (for concrete). || Cama, *f.*, madriguera, *f.* (of hare). || — Pl. Gradas, *f.* (rows of seats). || — *Bad form*, malos modales (bad manners). || *For form o for form's sake*, para cumplir, para que no se diga. || *Form of worship*, ritos, *m. pl.* || *Good form*, buenos modales. || *In due form*, en debida forma, como es debido. || *It is only a form of speech*, es un decir. || *It's just for form's sake* o *it's a mere matter of form*, es para guardar las formas. || *To be off form*, no estar en forma, estar en baja forma. || *To go through the form of refusing*, hacer el paripé de rechazar [algo]. || *To take the form of*, consistir en (to consist of).

form [fɔ:m] v. tr. Hacer (to make): *he formed a statue out of a piece of wood*, hizo una estatua con un trozo de madera. || Modelar, moldear: *to form the clay*, modelar el barro. || Formar: *to form a circle*, formar un círculo. || Formar, construir (to put together): *to form a sentence*, construir una frase. || Formar (s.o.'s character). || Pronunciar, decir (to pronounce): *difficulty in forming certains words*, dificultad en decir ciertas palabras. || Crear (to create a habit). || Adquirir (to acquire a habit). || Hacerse, formarse (ideas, opinion). || Hacer, concebir, elaborar (a plan). || Sacar (conclusion). || Constituir, integrar, componer (to constitute). || Crear (to set up): *to form a society*, crear una sociedad. || Formar (government, team). || Concertar (to conclude): *they decided to form an alliancé*, decidieron concertar una alianza. || GRAMM. Formar: *how do you form the gerund?*, ¿cómo forma Ud. el gerundio? || TECH. Moldear (to mould). || MIL. Formar. || *To form a queue*, ponerse en cola (to make a queue), hacer cola (to queue).
— V. intr. Tomar forma: *an idea is forming in his mind*, una idea está tomando forma en su mente. || Formarse: *clouds began to form*, empezaban a formarse nubes. || — MIL. *Form up!*, ¡a formar!, ¡formen filas! | *To form up*, formar, formarse, formar filas.
formal [ˈfɔ:məl] adj. Formal: *he gave his formal consent*, dio su acuerdo formal. || Solemne: *a formal speech*, un discurso solemne. || Formalista (person): *don't be so formal!*, ¡no seas tan formalista! || Ceremonioso, sa: *he spoke to me in a formal manner*, me habló de una manera ceremoniosa. || Protocolario, ria: *formal terms*, términos protocolarios. || De cumplido, de cortesía: *we had to make a formal visit*, tuvimos que hacer una visita de cumplido. || Oficial: *a formal invitation*, una invitación oficial. || De etiqueta (dinner, ball, etc.): *a formal dress*, un traje de etiqueta. || En debida forma: *a formal receipt*, un recibo en debida forma. || Tradicional (traditional). || Muy correcto, ta: *a formal style*, un estilo muy correcto. || COMM. En firme (order). || PHIL. Esencial. | Formal.
— N. U. S. Traje (*m.*) de etiqueta (dress). | Baile (*m.*) de etiqueta.
formaldehyde [fɔ:ˈmældihaid] n. Formaldehído, *m.*
formalin or **formaline** [ˈfɔ:məlin] n. CHEM. Formalina, *f.*
formalism [ˈfɔ:məlizəm] n. Formalismo, *m.*
formalist [ˈfɔ:məlist] n. Formalista, *m.* & *f.*
formalistic [—ik] adj. Formalista.
formality [fɔ:ˈmæliti] n. Formalidad, *f.*, trámite, *m.* (requirement): *one must go through a lot of formalities to get in*, hay que pasar por muchas formalidades para entrar. || Ceremonia, *f.* (ceremony). || Rigidez, *f.* (of manner). || — Pl. Ceremonial, *m. sing.* (proper procedure). || — *As a mere formality*, para *or* por cumplir. || *To comply with all the necessary formalities*, cumplir con todos los requisitos.
formalize [ˈfɔ:məlaiz] v. tr. Formalizar (to make formal). || Dar forma a (to shape).
— V. intr. Ser formalista (to be formal).
formally [ˈfɔ:məli] adv. Formalmente. || En debida forma, como es debido (in due form). || En cuanto a la forma (with regard to form). || Ceremoniosamente (ceremoniously). || Oficialmente (officially).
format [ˈfɔ:mæt] n. Tamaño, *m.* (dimension). || PRINT. Formato, *m.*, tamaño, *m.* || U. S. Concepción, *f.* (of a radio programme).
formation [fɔ:ˈmeiʃən] n. Formación, *f.*: *geological formation*, formación geológica. || MIL. Formación, *f.*: *close-order formation*, formación en orden cerrado; *formation in threes*, formación de a tres. || FIG. Formación, *f.* || MIL. *In battle formation*, en orden de combate.
formative [ˈfɔ:mətiv] adj. De formación: *formative years*, años de formación. || Formativo, va (which forms): *formative influence*, influencia formativa. || GRAMM. Formativo, va.
former [ˈfɔ:mə*] adj. Anterior (previous): *in a former existence*, en una vida anterior. || Primero, ra (first mentioned). || Antiguo, gua; ex: *the former Prime Minister*, el antiguo Primer Ministro. || Pasado, da; antiguo, gua: *in former days*, en tiempos pasados. || *He is but a shadow of his former self*, no es más que la sombra de sí mismo.
— Pron. Ése, ésa, aquél, aquélla, el primero, la primera.
formerly [—li] adv. Anteriormente (previously). || Antiguamente, antes, en tiempos pasados (before, in olden days).
formic [ˈfɔ:mik] adj. Fórmico.
Formica [fɔ:ˈmaikə] n. (trademark). Formica, *m.*
formicary [ˈfɔ:mikəri] n. Hormiguero, *m.*
formication [ˌfɔ:mikeiʃən] n. MED. Formicación, *f.*
formidable [ˈfɔ:midəbl] adj. Enorme, formidable (task). || Formidable, terrible (adversary). || Terrible (look). || FIG. Impresionante, tremendo, da (impressive).
formless [ˈfɔ:mlis] adj. Sin forma, informe.
form letter [fɔ:mˈletə*] n. U. S. Circular, *f.*
formol [ˈfɔ:məl] n. CHEM. Formol, *m.*
Formosa [fɔ:ˈməusə] pr. n. GEOGR. Formosa, *f.*
formula [ˈfɔ:mjulə] n. Fórmula, *f.*: *courtesy formula*, fórmula de cortesía. || MATH. CHEM. Fórmula, *f.* || AUT. Fórmula, *f.*: *formula one car*, coche de fórmula uno.
— OBSERV. El plural de la palabra inglesa es *formulas* o *formulae*.
formularize [ˈfɔ:mjuləraiz] v. tr. Formular.
formulary [ˈfɔ:mjuləri] n. Formulario, *m.*
formulate [ˈfɔrmjuleit] v. tr. Formular.
formulation [ˌfɔ:mjuˈleiʃən] n. Formulación, *f.*
formulism [ˈfɔ:mjulizəm] n. Formulismo, *m.*
formulization [ˌfɔ:mjuliˈzeiʃən] n. Formulación, *f.*
formulize [ˈfɔ:mjulaiz] v. tr. Formular.
fornicate [ˈfɔ:nikeit] v. intr. Fornicar.
fornicate [ˈfɔ:nikit] adj. ARCH. Abovedado, da.
fornication [ˌfɔ:niˈkeiʃən] n. Fornicación, *f.*
fornicator [ˈfɔ:nikeitə*] n. Fornicador, ra.
fornicatress [ˈfɔ:nikətris] or **fornicatrix** [fɔ:niˈkeitriks] n. Fornicadora, *f.*
fornix [ˈfɔ:niks] n. ARCH. Bóveda, *f.*
forsake* [fəˈseik] v. tr. Abandonar, dejar (to abandon): *she forsook her children*, abandonó a sus hijos. || Renunciar a (to give up).
— OBSERV. Pret. ***forsook***; p. p. ***forsaken***.
forsaken [fəˈseikən] p. p. See FORSAKE.
forsook [fəˈsuk] pret. See FORSAKE.
forsooth [fəˈsu:θ] adv. (Ant.). En verdad.
forspent [fəˈspent] adj. (Ant.) Exhausto, ta.
forswear* [fɔ:ˈswɛə*] v. tr. Abjurar [de], renunciar solemnemente a. || *To forswear o.s.*, perjurar, jurar en falso.
— OBSERV. Pret. ***forswore***; p. p. ***forsworn***.
forswore [fɔ:ˈswɔ:*] pret. See FORSWEAR.
forsworn [—n] p. p. See FORSWEAR.
— Adj. Perjuro, ra.
forsythia [fɔ:ˈsaiθjə] n. BOT. Forsythia, *f.*
fort [fɔ:t] n. Fortaleza, *f.*, fuerte, *m.* || FIG. *To hold the fort*, quedarse vigilando.
forte [ˈfɔ:ti] n. Fuerte *m.* (talent). || MUS. Forte, *m.*
— Adj./adv. MUS. Forte.
forth [fɔ:θ] adv. En adelante. || — *And so forth*, y así sucesivamente. || *Back and forth*, see BACK AND FORTH. || *From that day forth*, desde aquel día en adelante. || *To come forth*, see COME. || *To go forth*, irse, ir: *go forth and tell the world*, id e instruid a todas las naciones. || *To put forth*, echar (leaves).
forthcoming [fɔ:θˈkʌmiŋ] adj. Próximo, ma; venidero, ra (approaching): *in the forthcoming weeks*, en las próximas semanas. || Próximo, ma: *the forthcoming session*, la próxima reunión. || Abierto, ta; amable: *Andalusians are a very forthcoming people*, los andaluces son una gente muy abierta. || De próxima publicación (soon to appear). || *The expected aid was not forthcoming*, no recibimos la ayuda esperada.
forthright [ˈfɔ:θˈrait] adj. Franco, ca; directo, ta (person). || Rotundo, da (refusal).
forthwith [ˈfɔ:θˈwiθ] adv. En seguida, enseguida, inmediatamente, en el acto (at once).
fortieth [ˈfɔ:tiiθ] adj. Cuadragésimo, ma; cuarentavo, va. || Cuarenta: *the fortieth chapter*, el capítulo cuarenta.
— N. Cuarentavo, *m.*, cuadragésima parte, *f.* (one of forty parts). || Cuadragésimo, ma. || *She was the fortieth in the queue*, era la cuarenta de la cola.
fortification [ˌfɔ:tifiˈkeiʃən] n. MIL. Fortificación, *f.* || Reforzamiento, *m.* (of an argument). || Fortalecimiento, *m.* (of a person).
fortifier [ˈfɔ:tifaiə*] n. Fortificante, *m.* (tonic).
fortify [ˈfɔ:tifai] v. tr. MIL. Fortificar (a town). || Fortalecer, fortificar (health). || Reforzar: *to fortify a dam, an argument*, reforzar una presa, un argumento. || Fortalecer (to give moral strength). || U. S. Enriquecer (foodstuff). | Encabezar (wine).
— V. intr. MIL. Construir fortificaciones.
fortifying [—iŋ] adj. Fortalecedor, ra.
fortissimo [fɔ:ˈtisiməu] adj. MUS. Fortísimo, ma.
— Adv. MUS. Fortísimo.
fortitude [ˈfɔ:titju:d] n. Fortaleza, *f.*, fuerza, *f.*, entereza, *f.*
fortitudinous [fɔ:tiˈtju:dinis] adj. Fuerte, valiente.
fortnight [ˈfɔ:tnait] n. Quince días, *m. pl.*, dos semanas, *f. pl.*: *I am going to spend a fortnight in Spain*, voy a pasar quince días en España.
fortnightly [ˈfɔ:tˌnaitli] adj. Quincenal, bisemanal.
— Adv. Quincenalmente, cada quince días, bisemanalmente.
— N. Revista (*f.*) *or* publicación (*f.*) bisemanal.
fortress [ˈfɔ:tris] n. Fortaleza, *f.*
fortuitous [fɔ:ˈtjuitəs] adj. Fortuito, ta; casual.
fortuitously [—li] adv. Fortuitamente, por casualidad.
fortuity [fɔ:ˈtjuiti] n. Casualidad, *f.*
fortunate [ˈfɔ:tʃnit] adj. Afortunado, da (lucky): *a fortunate woman*, una mujer afortunada. || Afortunado, da; feliz (favourable). || Oportuno, na (opportune): *a fortunate arrival*, una llegada oportuna. || — *How fortunate!*, ¡qué suerte! || *It was fortunate that he was there*, fue una suerte que estuviera allí.
fortune [ˈfɔ:tʃən] n. Fortuna, *f.* (destiny): *the wheel of fortune*, la rueda de la fortuna. || Suerte, *f.*, fortuna, *f.* (luck): *stroke of fortune*, golpe de suerte. || Fortuna, *f.* (wealth): *he went to South America to make his fortune*, fue a América del Sur para hacer fortuna. || FAM. Fortuna, *f.*, dineral, *m.*: *it cost a fortune*, costó un dineral. || — FIG. *To marry a fortune*, casarse con una

mujer rica. || *To tell one's fortune*, decirle a alguien la buenaventura. || *To try one's fortune*, probar fortuna.
fortune hunter [—ˌhʌntə*] n. Cazador (*m.*) de dotes (one who marries money). || Aventurero, *m.* (adventurer).
fortune-teller [—ˌtelə*] n. Adivino, na. || Echadora(*f.*) de buenaventura, pitonisa, *f.* (palmist).
forty [ˈfɔːti] n. Cuarenta, *m.* || — *In the forties*, en los años cuarenta. || *To be in ones forties*, tener unos cuarenta años.
— Adj. Cuarenta.
— OBSERV. *Forty-first, forty-second*, etc. is translated by *cuadragésimo primero, cuadragésimo segundo*, etc.
forty-niner [—ˌnainə*] n. U. S. Aventurero (*m.*) que se dirigió hacia California en búsqueda de oro en el año 1849.
forty winks [—wiŋks] pl. n. FAM. Cabezada, *f. sing.*, siestecita, *f. sing.*, sueñecito, *m. sing.*
forum [ˈfɔːrəm] n. Foro, *m.* || FIG. Tribuna, *f.*: *the U. N. is a forum for world discussions*, la O.N.U. es una tribuna para las discusiones internacionales.
— OBSERV. El plural de la palabra *forum* es *forums* o *fora*.
forward [ˈfɔːwəd] adj. Delantero, ra (front): *the forward wheels of a car*, las ruedas delanteras de un coche. || Hacia adelante: *a forward movement*, un movimiento hacia adelante. || Adelantado, da; avanzado, da: *he is forward for his age*, está muy adelantado para su edad; *the book is well forward*, el libro está muy adelantado. || Avanzado, da (progressive). || MIL. Avanzado, da. || MAR. De la proa. || Impertinente, descarado, da (overbold): *I found him a little forward*, le encontré un poco impertinente. || Atrevido, da (bold): *he is very forward with the girls*, es muy atrevido con las chicas. || De avance (gears). || Adelantado, da (crop). || SP. Delantero, ra (line). || COMM. Para entrega futura (buying, etc.). | En fecha futura (delivery). || SP. *Forward pass*, pase adelantado (in rugby).
— Adv. Adelante, hacia adelante: *he gave a step forward*, dio un paso adelante. || Hacia adelante: *he ran forward*, corrió hacia adelante. || En adelante: *from this time forward*, desde ahora en adelante. || MAR. Hacia la proa. || — *Forward!*, ¡adelante! || MIL. *Forward march!*, ¡de frente, ar! || *To look forward to*, esperar [con ansia]. || *We have got forward with our work*, hemos adelantado el trabajo.
— N. Delantero, *m.* (in football).
— OBSERV. Como este adverbio modifica el sentido de varios verbos (to bring, to carry, to put, etc.), se ha tratado en el artículo correspondiente a cada uno de ellos.
forward [ˈfɔːwəd] v. tr. Expedir, enviar (to send). || FIG. Patrocinar: *to forward a project*, patrocinar un proyecto. | Promover (to promote). || *Please forward*, remítase al destinatario *or* a las nuevas señas (in a letter).
forwarder [—ə*] n. COMM. Agente (*m.*) de transporte. || FIG. Promotor, ra.
forwarding [—iŋ] n. Expedición, *f.* (sending). || Transporte, *m.* || *Forwarding agent*, agente (*m.*) de tránsito *or* de transporte.
forwardness [—nis] n. Precocidad, *f.* (precociousness, earliness). || Adelantamiento, *m.* (progress). || Modernismo, *m.*, progresismo, *m.* (progressiveness). || Atrevimiento, *m.*, audacia, *f.* (boldness). || Descaro, *m.*, desfachatez, *f.* (pertness).
forwards [—z] adv. Hacia adelante, adelante.
forwent [fɔːˈwent] pret. See FORGO.
fossa [ˈfɔːsə] n. ANAT. Fosa, *f.*: *nasal fossae*, fosas nasales.
— OBSERV. El plural de *fossa* es *fossae*.
fosse [fɔs] n. Foso, *m.* (ditch).
fossette [fɔˈset] n. Hoyuelo, *m.*
fossil [ˈfɔsl] n. Fósil, *m.* || FIG. FAM. Fósil, *m.*
— Adj. Fósil.
fossilization [ˌfɔsilaiˈzeiʃən] n. Fosilización, *f.*
fossilize [ˈfɔsilaiz] v. intr. Fosilizarse. || FIG. Volverse anticuado (a person).
— V. tr. Fosilizar.
foster [ˈfɔstə*] v. tr. Criar (to bring up). || FIG. Abrigar (ideas, hopes, etc.). | Patrocinar (a project). | Fomentar, promover (to promote). | Favorecer (to favour).
fosterage [—ridʒ] n. Crianza, *f.* (rearing). || Entrega (*f.*) a padres adoptivos. || FIG. Promoción, *f.*, fomento, *m.* (promotion).
foster brother [—brʌðə*] n. Hermano (*m.*) de leche.
foster child [—tʃaild] n. Hijo (*m.*) adoptivo, hija (*f.*) adoptiva.
foster daughter [—ˈdɔːtə*] n. Hija (*m.*) adoptiva.
foster father [—ˌfɑːðə*] n. Padre (*m.*) adoptivo.
fostering [—riŋ] n. Promoción, *f.*, fomento, *m.*
fosterling [—liŋ] n. Hijo (*m.*) adoptivo, hija (*f.*) adoptiva.
foster mother [—ˌmʌðə*] n. Madre (*f.*) adoptiva.
foster nurse [—nəːs] n. Nodriza, *f.*
foster parent [—ˈpeərənt] n. Padre (*m.*) adoptivo, madre (*f.*) adoptiva. || — Pl. Padres (*m.*) adoptivos.
foster sister [—ˌsistə*] n. Hermana (*f.*) de leche.
foster son [—sʌn] n. Hijo (*m.*) adoptivo.
fought [fɔːt] pret. & p. p. See FIGHT.
foul [faul] adj. Asqueroso, sa; sucio, cia (dirty). || Fétido, da (smell). || Viciado, da (air). || Sucio, cia (water). || Horrible (horrible). || Grosero, ra (language). || Asqueroso, sa; espantoso, sa (weather). || Contrario, ria (wind, tide). || Obstruido, da (obstructed). || Peligroso, sa (dangerous). || Ilícito, ta (fraudulent). || MAR. Encepado, da (anchor). | Enmarañado, da (propeller). | Sucio, cia (ship bottom). | Malo, la (sea bottom). || Atascado, da (gun). || SP. Sucio, cia: *foul play*, jugada sucia. | Ilícito, ta: *foul blow*, golpe ilícito. | Bateado fuera de los límites (in baseball). || — *By fair means or foul*, por las buenas o por las malas. || *Foul bill of health*, patente sucia. || *Foul trick*, mala jugada, jugarreta, *f.* || *To be in a foul mood*, estar de un humor de perros. || *To fall o to run foul of*, chocar con.
— Adv. *To play foul*, jugar sucio. || *To play s.o. foul*, hacerle a uno una jugarreta *or* una mala jugada.
— N. Choque, *m.* (collision). || SP. Falta, *f.* (unfair play). | Pelota (*f.*) bateada fuera de los límites (in baseball).
foul [faul] v. tr. Ensuciar (to dirty). || FIG. Mancillar, manchar (one's reputation). || Obstruir, atorar (to obstruct). || Atascar (gun, pipe). || Enmarañar (to entangle). || Chocar con *or* contra (to collide with). || MAR. Encepar (anchor). | Enmarañar (propeller). || SP. Cometer una falta contra (an opponent). | Batear fuera de los límites (in baseball). || FIG. *To foul up*, hacer fallar.
— V. intr. Ensuciarse (to become dirty). || Obstruirse, atorarse (to get obstructed). || Atascarse (gun). || MAR. Enceparse (anchor). | Enmarañarse (propeller). || SP. Cometer una falta.
foulard [fuːˈlɑːd] n. Fular, *m.* (material). || Pañuelo, *m.* (scarf).
foul ball [ˈfaulbɔːl] n. SP. Bola (*f.*) mala (in bowling). | Pelota (*f.*) bateada fuera de los límites (in baseball).
foul line [ˈfaullain] n. SP. Una de las líneas que delimitan el campo y que no se puede pasar.
foulmouthed [ˈfaulmauðd] adj. Malhablado, da.
foulness [ˈfaulnis] n. Suciedad, *f.*, asquerosidad, *f.* (dirtiness). || Fetidez, *f.* (stink). || Atoramiento, *m.* (clogging). || Vileza, *f.*, infamia, *f.* (of a deed). || Grosería, *f.*, obscenidad, *f.* (of language).
foul-smelling [ˈfaulˈsmeliŋ] adj. Hediondo, da.
found [faund] v. tr. TECH. Fundir, vaciar (metal). | Fundir (glass). || Fundar (to establish): *to found a school, a family*, fundar una escuela, una familia. || ARCH. Echar los cimientos de (to lay the foundations). | Construir: *a building founded on solid rock*, un edificio construido sobre roca firme. || FIG. Fundamentar, fundar: *to found one's opinion on*, fundamentar su opinión en. | Basar: *a film founded on facts*, una película basada en los hechos.
— V. intr. Fundarse, fundamentarse, basarse.
found [faund] pret. & p. p. See FIND.
foundation [faunˈdeiʃən] n. Fundación, *f.* (establishment, endowment, institution): *the foundation of a school, of a city*, la fundación de una escuela, de una ciudad. || Cimientos, *m. pl*: *to lay the foundations of a building*, echar los cimientos de un edificio. || Firme, *m.* (roadbed). || FIG. Fundamento, *m.*, base, *f.* (basis, basic principles). || Forro, *m.* (backing of material). || Fondo, *m.* (in embroidery). || Maquillaje (*m.*) de fondo (cosmetic). || — *Foundation member*, miembro fundador. || *Scholar on the foundation*, becario, ria. || FIG. *To lay the foundations of*, sentar las bases de, echar los cimientos de. || *To put s.o. on the foundation*, concederle a uno una beca. || FIG. *To shake the very foundations of a theory*, quebrantar las bases de una teoría.
foundationer [—ə*] n. Becario, ria.
foundation garment [—ˈgɑːmənt] n. Corsé, *m.*
foundation stone [—stəun] n. Primera piedra, *f.* (of a building). || FIG. Piedra (*f.*) angular (cornerstone).
founder [ˈfaundə*] n. Fundador, ra. || TECH. Fundidor, *m.* || VET. Infosura, *f.*, aguadura, *f.* (of horses).
founder [ˈfaundə*] v. intr. Derrumbarse, hundirse (building). || Hundirse, irse a pique (ship). || Derrumbarse, desplomarse (to fall). || VET. Padecer infosura (horse). || Atascarse (to get stuck). || FIG. Hundirse, irse a pique (company). | Fracasar (to fail.)
— V. tr. Hundir (ship). || VET. Producir infosura.
foundering [—riŋ] n. Derrumbamiento, *m.* || MAR. Hundimiento, *m.*
founder's shares [—zˈʃɛə*z] pl. n. Partes (*f.*) de fundador.
founding father [ˈfaundiŋˈfɑːðə*] n. Fundador, *m.* (founder). || Autor(*m.*) de la constitución norteamericana.
foundling [ˈfaundliŋ] n. Expósito, ta (abandoned child). || Inclusero, ra (living in a hospital).
foundling hospital [—ˈhɔspitl] n. Inclusa, *f.*
foundress [ˈfaundris] n. Fundadora, *f.*
foundry [ˈfaundri] n. Fundición, *f.*
fount [faunt] n. Fuente, *f.* (fountain). || Manantial, *m.* (of a river). || Fuente, *f.*: *a fount of wisdom*, una fuente de sabiduría. || PRINT. Fundición, *f.*, casta, *f.* (font).
fountain [ˈfauntin] n. Fuente, *f.* (natural or artificial). || Manantial, *m.* (of a river). || Surtidor, *m.* (water jet). || Depósito, *m.* (for ink, oil). || FIG. Fuente, *f.* (source). || U. S. *Soda fountain*, bar (*m.*) donde sólo se venden bebidas sin alcohol.
fountainhead [—ˈhed] n. Manantial, *m.* (of a river). || FIG. Fuente, *f.*
fountain pen [—pen] n. Pluma (*f.*) estilográfica.
four [fɔː*] adj. Cuatro.
— N. Cuatro, *m.* (number, card, figure). || SP. Equipo

(*m.*) de cuatro personas (team). | Golpe (*m.*) que da cuatro puntos (in cricket). || — *Four o'clock*, las cuatro. || *Four of a kind*, un póker, *m.* (at cards). || *It's five past four*, son las cuatro y cinco. || *On all fours*, a gatas (on hands and knees), análogo, ga (*with*, a) [similar].

four-cornered [—ˈkɔːnəd] adj. Cuadrangular.
four-cycle [—ˌsaikl] adj. De cuatro tiempos.
four-dimensional [—dimenʃənl] adj. Cuadridimensional.
four-door [—dɔː*] adj. De cuatro puertas.
four-engined [—ˈendʒind] adj. Cuadrimotor, cuatrimotor (aeroplane). || *Four-engined plane*, cuadrimotor, *m.*, cuatrimotor *m.*
four-eyes [—aiz] n. FAM. Cuatro ojos, *m.*
four-flush [—flʌʃ] v. intr. U. S. FAM. Tirarse un farol (to bluff).
four-flusher [—ˈflʌʃə*] n. U. S. FAM. Farolero, ra (bluffer). | Embustero, ra (trickster).
fourfold [—fəuld] adj. Cuádruple.
— Adv. Cuatro veces.
four-footed [—futid] adj. Cuadrúpedo, da.
four-handed [—ˈhændid] adj. Para cuatro (game). || MUS. A cuatro manos. || ZOOL. Cuadrúmano, na.
four hundred [—ˈhʌndred] adj. Cuatrocientos, tas.
— N. Cuatrocientos, *m.*
four-in-hand [ˈfɔːrinˈhænd] n. Coche (*m.*) tirado por cuatro caballos (vehicle). || Corbata (*f.*) de nudo corredizo (tie).
four-leaf clover [ˈfɔːliːfˈkləuvə*] n. Trébol (*m.*) de cuatro hojas.
four-letter word [ˈfɔːˈletə*wəːd] n. Palabrota, *f.*, taco, *m.*
four-month [ˈfɔːmʌnθ] adj. Cuatrimestral.
four-monthly [—li] adj. Cuatrimestral.
four-o'clock [ˈfɔːrəˈklɔk] n. BOT. Dondiego (*m.*) de noche.
four-part [ˈfɔːpɑːt] adj. MUS. Para cuatro voces.
fourpence [ˈfɔːpəns] n. Cuatro peniques, *m. pl.*
fourpenny [ˈfɔːpəni] adj. De cuatro peniques.
four-poster [ˈfɔːˈpəustə] n. Cama (*f.*) con cuatro columnas.
fourscore [ˈfɔːskɔː*] adj. Ochenta.
— N. Ochenta, *m.*
foursome [ˈfɔːsəm] Partido (*m.*) de dos contra dos (in golf). || Grupo (*m.*) de cuatro personas.
foursquare [ˈfɔːskweə*] adj. Cuadrado, da (square). || Sincero, ra; franco, ca (forthright).
— Adv. Firmemente (firmly). || Sinceramente, francamente (sincerely).
four-stroke [fɔːsˈtrəuk] adj. De cuatro tiempos (engine).
four-syllable [fɔːˈsiləbl] adj. Cuatrisílabo, ba.
fourteen [ˈfɔːˈtiːn] adj. Catorce.
— N. Catorce, *m.*
fourteenth [—θ] adj. Decimocuarto, ta.
— N. Decimocuarto, ta. || Catorzavo, *m.*, decimocuarta parte, *f.* (fraction). || Catorce, *m.*, día (*m.*) catorce: *he came on the fourteenth*, vino el catorce. || Catorce: *Louis XIV* (*the fourteenth*), Luis XIV [catorce].
fourth [fɔːθ] adj. Cuarto, ta. || MATH. *Fourth dimension*, cuarta dimensión.
— N. Cuarto, ta. || Cuarto, *m.*, cuarta parte, *f.* (fraction). || Cuatro, *m.*, día (*m.*) cuatro: *the fourth of February*, el cuatro de febrero. || Cuarto: *Henry IV* (*the fourth*), Enrique IV [cuarto]. || Cuarta velocidad, *f.* (gear). || MUS. Cuarta, *f.*
— Adv. En cuarto lugar. || *To come fourth*, salir *or* ser el cuarto (in competition).
fourth estate [—isˈteit] n. U. S. FAM. Prensa, *f.*
fourthly [—li] adv. En cuarto lugar.
four-wheel [fɔːˈwiːl] adj. De cuatro ruedas. || *Car with four-wheel drive*, coche (*m.*) de cuatro ruedas motrices.
fowl [faul] n. Aves (*f. pl.*) de corral, ave (*f.*) de corral (poultry). || Gallo, *m.* (cock). || Gallina, *f.* (hen). || Pollo, *m.* (chicken). || Pollo, *m.* (meat). || Aves, *f. pl.* (birds).
fowl [faul] v. intr. Cazar aves.
fowler [—ə*] n. Cazador (*m.*) de aves.
fowling [—iŋ] n. Caza (*f.*) de aves.
fowling piece [ˈfauliŋpiːs] n. Escopeta, *f.*
fowl pest [ˈfaulpest] n. VET. Peste (*f.*) aviar.
fowl plague [ˈfaulpleig] n. VET. Peste (*f.*) aviar.
fox [fɔks] n. ZOOL. Zorra, *f.*, zorro, *m.* || Zorro, *m.* (fur). || FIG. Zorro, *m.* (sly person).

— OBSERV. The word *zorro* is used when referring to the male fox, whereas *zorra* is used to indicate both the female fox and the species in general.

fox [fɔks] v. tr. Engañar (to trick, to fool). || Dejar perplejo, desconcertar (to baffle). || Manchar (to stain). || Remendar (shoes).
— V. intr. Mancharse (paper). || Fingir (to simulate).
fox brush [—brʌʃ] n. Rabo (*m.*) *or* cola (*f.*) de zorra.
foxglove [—glʌv] n. BOT. Digital, *f.*, dedalera, *f.*
fox hole [—həul] n. Zorrera, *f.*
foxhole [—həul] n. MIL. Pozo (*m.*) de tirador.
foxhound [—haund] n. Perro (*m.*) raposero.
fox hunt [—hʌnt] n. Caza (*f.*) de zorros.
foxiness [—inis] n. Astucia, *f.*, zorrería, *f.* (cunning).
foxtail [—teil] n. BOT. Cola (*f.*) de zorra. || Rabo (*m.*) de zorra, cola (*f.*) de zorra (tail).
fox terrier [—ˈteriə*] n. Fox terrier, *m.*, perro (*m.*) raposero (dog).
fox-trot [—trɔt] n. Fox trot, *m.* (dance). || Trote (*m.*) corto (of a horse).
foxy [ˈfɔksi] adj. Astuto, ta (cunning). || Marrón, rojizo, za (colour). || Manchado, da; descolorido, da (stained). || Agrio, agria (sour).
foyer [ˈfɔiei] n. THEATR. Foyer, *m.*
fracas [ˈfrækɑː] n. Gresca, *f.*, riña, *f.*, reyerta, *f.*

— OBSERV. Mientras en Inglaterra el plural de *fracas* es *fracas*, en Estados Unidos es *fracases*.

fraction [ˈfrækʃən] n. MATH. Fracción, *f.*, quebrado, *m.*: *continued, decimal, improper, proper fraction*, fracción continua, decimal, impropia, propia. || Fracción, *f.* (of time). || Parte, *f.*: *a large fraction of the electorate*, una gran parte del electorado. || Pequeña parte, *f.* (small portion). || REL. Fracción, *f.*: *the fraction of the bread*, la fracción del pan. || CHEM. Fracción, *f.* || FIG. *A fraction*, un poco: *a fraction closer*, un poco más cerca.
fraction [ˈfrækʃən] v. tr. Fraccionar.
fractional [—l] adj. MATH. Fraccionario, ria. || Fraccionario, ria (coin). || Ínfimo, ma (very small): *a fractional risk*, un riesgo ínfimo. || CHEM. Fraccionado, da: *fractional distillation*, destilación fraccionada.
fractionalize [ˈfrækʃnəlaiz] v. tr. Fraccionar.
fractionate [ˈfrækʃneit] v. tr. CHEM. Fraccionar.
fractionation [frækʃnˈeiʃən] n. CHEM. Fraccionamiento, *m.*
fractionize [ˈfrækʃnaiz] v. tr. Fraccionar.
fractious [ˈfrækʃəs] adj. Díscolo, la (ungovernable). || Resabiado, da (horse). || Caprichoso, sa (temperamental). || Quejumbroso, sa (complaining). || Malhumorado, da; displicente (peevish).
fracture [ˈfræktʃə*] n. GEOL. Fractura, *f.* || MED. Fractura, *f.*: *comminuted, compound, greenstick fracture*, fractura conminuta, complicada, en tallo verde. || Fractura, *f.*, rotura, *f.*, rompimiento, *m.* (breaking).
fracture [ˈfræktʃə*] v. tr. Fracturar: *fractured skull*, cráneo fracturado. || Agrietar (to crack). || FIG. Quebrantar.
— V. intr. Fracturarse.
fraenulum [ˈfriːnələm] n. ANAT. Frenillo, *m.*

— OBSERV. El plural de esta palabra es *fraenula*.

fraenum [ˈfriːnəm] n. ANAT. Frenillo, *m.*

— OBSERV. El plural es *fraena* o *fraenums*.

fragile [ˈfrædʒail] adj. Frágil: *a fragile glass, mechanism*, un vaso, un mecanismo frágil. || FIG. Frágil, delicado, da (health).
fragility [frəˈdʒiliti] n. Fragilidad, *f.*
fragment [ˈfrægmənt] n. Fragmento, *m.* || *To smash sth. to fragments*, hacer algo añicos *or* pedazos.
fragment [ˈfrægmənt] v. tr. Fragmentar.
fragmental [frægˈmentl] or **fragmentary** [ˈfrægməntəri] adj. Fragmentario, ria.
fragmentation [ˌfrægmenˈteiʃən] n. Fragmentación, *f.*
fragrance [ˈfreigrəns] n. Fragancia, *f.*, perfume, *m.*
fragrant [ˈfreigrənt] adj. Fragante (sweet-smelling).
frail [freil] adj. Frágil (fragile). || Débil (weak). || Delicado, da (delicate).
— N. Capazo, *m.*, capacho, *m.* (for figs or raisins). || U. S. FAM. Gachí, *f.* (woman, girl).
frailty [ˈfreilti] n. Fragilidad, *f.* (fragility). || Delicadeza, *f.* (delicacy). || Debilidad, *f.* (weakness). || FIG. Flaqueza, *f.* (moral weakness).
fraise [freiz] n. TECH. Avellanador, *m.*, fresa, *f.* (drill). || Frisa, *f.* (fortification). || Gorguera, *f.* (ruff).
frame [freim] n. Marco, *m.* (of picture, door, window). || Armazón, *f.* (of building, machine, etc.). || Cuadro, *m.* (of bicycle). || Entramado, *m.* (of wall). || Armadura, *f.* (of armchair). || Armadura, *f.* (of bed). || Marco, *m.* (of tennis racket). || Armazón, *f.* (of umbrella). || Bastidor, *m.* (for embroidery). || Montura, *f.* (of spectacles). || Estatura, *f.*, esqueleto, *m.* (stature). || Cuerpo, *m.* (body). || FIG. Estructura, *f.*: *the frame of society*, la estructura de la sociedad. || AUT. Chasis, *m.*, bastidor, *m.* || AGR. Cajonera, *f.*, cama, *f.* || Panal, *m.* (of beehive). || MAR. Cuaderna, *f.* (rib). | Cuadernas, *f. pl.*, armazón, *f.* (entire framework). || MIN. Entibación, *f.*, entibado, *m.* || Imagen, *f.* (in filmstrips, television). || SP. Jugada, *f.* (turn). | Triángulo, *m.* (snooker triangle). || FIG. *Frame of mind*, estado (*m.*) de ánimo.
frame [freim] v. tr. Enmarcar (to enclose): *to frame a photograph*, enmarcar una fotografía. || Encuadrar (image on a screen). || Elaborar, concebir (to devise): *to frame a plan*, elaborar un plan. || Hacerse (an opinion). || Inventar (a story). || Tramar (a plot). || Formular, expresar: *to frame a question*, formular una cuestión. || Pronunciar (to pronounce). || Hacer la armazón de (to make a frame for). || Ensamblar (to put together). || Formar (to shape). || Adaptar (to adjust). || Construir (a structure, a novel). || FAM. Amañar (an accusation). | Incriminar, culpar, amañar las pruebas de tal manera que sea acusada [una persona inocente].
— V. intr. Ir (to develop).
frame house [—haus] n. Casa (*f.*) de madera.
frame of reference [—əvˈrefrəns] n. MATH. Sistema (*m.*) de coordenadas. || Punto (*m.*) de referencia.
framer [—ə*] n. Autor, ra. || ARTS. Montador (*m.*) *or* fabricante (*m.*) de marcos.

frame-up [—ʌp] n. FAM. Maquinación, *f.*

framework [—wə:k] n. Armazón, *f.* (of buildings, ships, machines). || Estructura, *f.*: *the framework of a novel*, la estructura de una novela. || — *Open framework*, entramado, *m.*, celosía, *f.* || *Within the framework of*, en el marco de.

framing [ˈfreimiŋ] n. Marco, *m.* (of picture). || Colocación (*f.*) del marco (action). || Armazón, *f.* (framework). || Encofrado, *m.* (of concrete). || Expresión, *f.*, formulación, *f.* (of ideas). || Elaboración, *f.* (of plan, constitution). || Maquinación, *f.* (of a plot). || Construcción, *f.* (building). || Formación, *f.* (shaping). || CINEM. Encuadre, *m.*

franc [fræŋk] n. Franco, *m.* (monetary unit).

France [frɑ:ns] pr. n. GEOGR. Francia, *f.*

Frances [ˈfrɑ:nsis] pr. n. Francisca, *f.*

franchise [ˈfræntʃaiz] n. Derecho (*m.*) de voto (suffrage). || U. S. Concesión, *f.*, licencia, *f.*

franchise [ˈfræntʃaiz] v. tr. U. S. Otorgar la concesión de, dar una licencia para.

Francis [ˈfrɑ:nsis] pr. n. Francisco, *m.*

Franciscan [frænˈsiskən] adj./n. Franciscano, na.

francium [ˈfrænsiəm] n. CHEM. Francio, *m.*

Franco-Belgian [ˈfræŋkəuˈbeldʒən] adj. Franco-belga.

Francoist [ˈfræŋkəuist] adj./n. Franquista.

francophile [ˈfræŋkəfil] adj./n. Francófilo, la.

francophobe [ˈfræŋkəfəub] adj./n. Francófobo, ba.

Franco-Spanish [ˈfræŋkəuˈspæniʃ] adj. Francoespañol, la.

frangible [ˈfrændʒibl] adj. Frágil.

frangipane [ˈfrændʒəpein] or **frangipani** [ˌfrændʒəˈpɑ:ni] n. Pastel (*m.*) de almendras (dessert).

frank [fræŋk] adj. Franco, ca; sincero, ra (sincere): *frank look*, mirada franca. || Abierto, ta: *a frank face*, una cara abierta; *a frank rebellion*, una rebelión abierta.
— N. Sello (*m.*) que indica la franquicia (mark). || Franquicia, *f.* (right). || Carta (*f.*) exenta de franqueo (letter).

frank [fræŋk] v. tr. Mandar [una carta] exenta de franqueo (to mail). || Franquear (to stamp).

Frank [fræŋk] n. HIST. Franco, ca. || Francisco, *m.* (Christian name).

frankfurter [ˈfræŋkfə:tə*] n. Salchicha (*f.*) de Francfort.

frankincense [ˈfræŋkinˌsens] n. Incienso, *m.*, olíbano, *m.* (fragrant gum resin).

franking [ˈfræŋkiŋ] n. Franqueo, *m.* (stamping). || *Franking machine*, máquina franqueadora *or* de franquear.

Frankish [ˈfræŋkiʃ] adj. Franco ca.
— N. Franco, *m.* (language).

franklin [ˈfræŋklin] n. HIST. Poseedor (*m.*) de un feudo franco.

frankness [ˈfræŋknis] n. Franqueza, *f.*, sinceridad, *f.*

frantic [ˈfræntik] adj. Frenético, ca (frenzied). || Loco, ca: *frantic with anger*, *with joy*, loco de ira, de alegría. || Desesperado, da: *frantic efforts*, esfuerzos desesperados. || *To drive s.o. frantic*, sacarle de quicio a uno, volverle a uno loco.

frantically [—əli] adv. Frenéticamente (in a frenzy). || Locamente (madly). || Desesperadamente (desperately).

frap [fræp] v. tr. MAR. Apretar (a rope).

frappé [fræˈpei] adj. Granizado, da (drink).
— N. Granizado, *m.*

frater [ˈfreitə*] n. HIST. REL. Refectorio (*m.*) de un monasterio. | Hermano, *m.* (brother).

fraternal [frəˈtə:nl] adj. Fraternal, fraterno, na: *fraternal love*, amor fraterno. || U. S. Fraterno, na (of a fraternity). || *Fraternal twins*, gemelos falsos.

fraternally [—i] adv. Fraternalmente.

fraternity [frəˈtə:niti] n. Fraternidad, *f.* (brotherhood). || REL. Hermandad, *f.*, cofradía, *f.* || Asociación, *f.* (association). || U. S. Club (*m.*) de estudiantes.

fraternization [ˌfrætənaiˈzeiʃən] n. Fraternización, *f.*

fraternize [ˈfrætənaiz] v. intr. Fraternizar, confraternizar.

fratricidal [ˌfreitriˈsaidl] adj. Fratricida.

fratricide [ˈfreitrisaid] n. Fratricida, *m.* & *f.* (murderer). || Fratricidio, *m.* (crime).

fraud [frɔ:d] n. Fraude, *m.* (criminal deception) || Engaño, *m.*, timo, *m.*, supercheria, *f.* (sth. done to deceive). || Impostor, *m.* (person).

fraudulence [ˈfrɔ:djuləns] n. Fraudulencia, *f.*

fraudulent [ˈfrɔ:djulənt] adj. Fraudulento, ta: *fraudulent bankruptcy*, quiebra fraudulenta.

fraught [frɔ:t] adj. *Fraught with*, lleno de, cargado de.

fray [frei] n. Combate, *m.* (fight). || Refriega, *f.*, riña, *f.* (brawl). || Parte (*f.*) deshilachada *or* raída (of cloth). || FIG. *To enter the fray*, salir a la palestra.

fray [frei] v. tr. Desgastar, raer: *a frayed collar*, un cuello raído. || Escodar (a deer). || FIG. *To fray s.o.'s nerves*, atacarle los nervios a uno.
— V. intr. Deshilacharse, desgastarse, raerse (clothing, carpet, rope).

frayed [—d] adj. Deshilachado, da; raído, da (cloth).

fraying [—iŋ] n. Fleco, *m.*, hilacha, *f.* (frayed edge).

frazzle [ˈfræzl] n. Agotamiento, *m.* (exhaustion). || Hilacha, *f.* (frayed edge). || *Worn to a frazzle*, hecho un trapo, completamente agotado.

frazzle [ˈfræzl] v. tr. Desgastar, deshilachar, raer (to fray). || Agotar: *frazzled with the heat*, agotado por el calor.

freak [fri:k] n. Monstruo, *m.* (monster). || Ejemplar (*m.*) anormal (abnormal specimen). || Fenómeno, *m.* (prodigy). || Cosa (*f.*) extraña *or* imprevista *or* inesperada: *it was a freak that he passed the exam*, fue una cosa extraña que aprobara el examen. || Capricho, *m.*: *freaks of fortune*, caprichos de la fortuna. || FAM. Tío (*m.*) extraño *or* estrafalario (strange fellow).
— Adj. Imprevisto, ta; inesperado, da (unexpected). || Extraño, ña; estafalario, ria (strange).

freak [fri:k] v. intr. FAM. *To freak out*, hacer el viaje (to take a drug). | Dejarse llevar por estímulos visuales o auditivos. | Bailar como un loco (to dance wildly).
— V. tr. Abigarrar.

freakish [—iʃ] adj. Extraño, ña; estrafalario, ria (eccentric). || Monstruoso, sa (monstruous). || Anormal (abnormal). || Inesperado, da (unexpected). || Caprichoso, sa (whimsical).

freakishness [—iʃnis] n. Carácter (*m.*) caprichoso. || Monstruosidad, *f.*

freckle [ˈfrekl] n. Peca, *f.*

freckle [ˈfrekl] v. tr. Cubrir de pecas.
— V. intr. Cubrirse de pecas.

freckled [—d] or **freckle-faced** [—feist] or **freckly** [—i] adj. Pecoso, sa; lleno de pecas.

Frederick [ˈfredrik] pr. n. Federico, *m.*

free [fri:] adj. Libre: *a free people*, *man*, un pueblo, un hombre libre; *the free world*, el mundo libre; *when will you be free?*, ¿cuándo estarás libre?; *free society*, sociedad libre: *free translation*, traducción libre. || Libre, desocupado, da (place): *is the flat still free?*, ¿está todavía libre el piso? || Libre, independiente (state). || Libre (unmarried). || Vacante, libre (post). || Gratis, gratuito, ta (which costs nothing): *a free ticket*, una entrada gratis. || Libre: *free of debt*, libre de deudas. || Suelto, ta (loose). || Desatado, da (untied). || Desenvuelto, ta (bearing, manner). || Abierto, ta; sincero, ra (sincere). || Subido de tono (language). || Generoso, sa (generous). || FIG. Libre: *free road*, vía libre. || COMM. Libre (market, competition). | Franco, ca (exempt from taxes): *free port*, puerto franco. | Exento de derechos de aduana (goods). | Espontáneo, a (offer). || Libre (verse). || Autorizado, da; permitido, da (authorized). || CHEM. PHYS. Libre: *free oxygen*, oxígeno libre; *free energy*, energía libre. || — *Admission free*, entrada libre. || FIG. *As free as a bird*, más libre que un pájaro. || *For free*, gratis, gratuitamente. || *Free and easy*, despreocupado, da (carefree), poco ceremonioso, sa (unceremonious). || *Free city*, ciudad (*f.*) libre. || *Free enterprise*, libre empresa, *f.* || *Free gift*, prima, *f.* || TECH. *Free motion*, holgura, *f.* || *Free of charge*, sin gastos, gratis. || *Free of duty*, libre *or* exento de derechos de aduana. || *Free of tax*, exento *or* libre de impuestos. || *Free sample*, muestra gratuita. || *Free speech*, libertad (*f.*) de expresión. || COMM. *Post and package free*, franco de porte y embalaje. || *This place is free from dust*, en este sitio no hay polvo. || *To be free from*, estar libre de (cares, debt, etc.), no tener: *this product is free from defects*, este producto no tiene defectos. || *To be free of s.o.*, haberse librado de alguien. || *To be free of speech*, hablar muy libremente. || *To be free to*, ser libre de. || FIG. *To be free with one's fists*, tener las manos largas. || *To be free with one's money*, no reparar en gastos. || *To be very free with criticism*, criticar muy libremente, criticar mucho. || *To break* o *to get free*, liberarse, soltarse. || *To feel free to*, no tener reparos en. || FIG. *To have a free hand* o *rein*, tener campo libre, tener carta blanca. || *To make free with sth.*, utilizar algo a su antojo *or* como si fuera cosa propia. || *To set free*, liberar (a person), libertar (a slave), libertar, poner en libertad, liberar (a prisoner), soltar (a bird, etc.). || *To work free*, soltarse (to come loose), deshacerse (knot).
— Adv. Sin pagar, gratuitamente, gratis: *we got in free*, entramos sin pagar. || Libremente: *bulls running free in the streets*, toros que corren libremente por las calles.

— OBSERV. Nótese que la palabra *free* se utiliza también como sufijo y significa entonces "sin" (*after ten years of accident-free driving*, después de haber conducido diez años sin accidente).

free [fri:] v. tr. Poner en libertad, soltar, libertar, liberar (a prisoner). || Libertar (a slave). || Liberar (from domination). || Libertar, liberar, librar (from tyranny, etc.). || Liberar (from a debt, obligation). || Salvar (to save). || Soltar (to let loose). || Soltar (something stuck): *he managed to free his hands*, logró soltarse las manos. || Desenredar (to untangle). || Desatar, soltar (to untie). || Desatascar (to unblock a pipe). || Desembarazar, despejar (to clean up). || Exentar, eximir (to exempt). || *To free a property from mortgage*, levantar una hipoteca.

free alongside ship [—əˈlɔŋˈsaidʃip] adj. MAR. Franco en el muelle (goods).

freeboard [—bɔ:d] n. MAR. Obra (*f.*) muerta.

freebooter [—ˌbu:tə*] n. Filibustero, *m.*, pirata, *m.*

freeborn [—ˈbɔ:n] adj. Nacido libre.

freedman [fri:dmæn] n. Liberto, *m.*

— OBSERV. El plural de esta palabra es *freedmen*.

freedom [—dəm] n. Libertad, *f.*: *freedom of movement*, libertad de movimiento. || Exención, *f.*: *freedom from taxation*, exención de impuestos. || Libertad (*f.*) completa: *to give s.o. the freedom of one's flat*, dar a alguien libertad completa para utilizar el apartamento que uno tiene. || Soltura, *f.* (of manner, style). || Desenvoltura, *f.* (ease). || COMM. Entrada (*f.*) libre. || — *Freedom of a city*, ciudadanía (*f.*) de honor. || *Freedom of conscience, of speech*, libertad de conciencia, de expresión. || *Freedom of the individual*, libertad individual. || *Freedom of the press*, libertad de prensa. || *Freedom of the seas*, libertad de los mares. || *Freedom of worship*, libertad de cultos.

freedwoman [—,dwumən] n. Liberta, *f.*

— OBSERV. El plural de esta palabra es *freedwomen.*

free fight [—fait] n. Trifulca, *f.*, refriega, *f.*

free-for-all [—fər,ɔ:l] n. Pelea, *f.*, refriega, *f.* (brawl).

freehand [—hænd] adj. A pulso: *freehand drawing*, dibujo a pulso.

freehanded [—'hændid] adj. Generoso, sa (generous).

freehold [—həuld] n. HIST. Alodio, *m.*, feudo (*m.*) franco. || Propiedad (*f.*) absoluta.

— Adj. HIST. Alodial.

freeholder [— həuldə*] n. HIST. Propietario (*m.*) de un alodio. || Propietario (*m.*) absoluto.

free kick [—kik] n. SP. Golpe (*m.*) franco.

free labour (U. S. **free labor**) [—'leibə*] n. Trabajadores (*m. pl.*) no sindicados.

free lance [—'lɑ:ns] n. Persona(*f.*) que trabaja independientemente (who works independently). || Persona (*f.*) que no pertenece a ningún partido (in politics). || HIST. Mercenario, *m.*

free-lance [—lɑns] adj. Independiente.

free-lance [—lɑns] v. intr. Trabajar independientemente.

free list [—list] n. Lista (*f.*) de personas a las que se envían muestras *or* entradas gratuitas (list of persons). || Lista (*f.*) de productos libres de derechos de aduana (list of goods).

free liver [—'livə*] n. Vividor, ra.

free-living [—'liviŋ] adj. Vividor, ra (person).

free love [—lʌv] n. Amor (*m.*) libre.

freely [—li] adv. Libremente. || Liberalmente (generously). || Abundantemente (profusely). || Francamente, abiertamente (to speak). | Sin cumplidos (without ceremony). || Voluntariamente (willingly). || Gratuitamente, gratis (without paying).

freeman [—mən] n. Ciudadano (*m.*) libre, hombre (*m.*) libre.

— OBSERV. El plural de esta palabra es *freemen.*

freemartin [—'mɑ:tən] n. ZOOL. Ternera (*f.*) estéril.

freemason [—,meisən] n. Francmasón, *m.*, masón, *m.*

freemasonry [—,meisənri] n. Francmasonería, *f.*, masonería, *f.* || FIG. Compañerismo, *m.*

free on board [—ɔn'bɔ:d] adj./adv. Franco a bordo.

free soil [—sɔil] n. Territorio (*m.*) donde la esclavitud era ilegal.

free-spoken [—'spəukən] adj. Franco, ca; sincero, ra.

freestone [—stəun] n. Sillar, *m.*, piedra (*f.*) de sillería (used in building). || Hueso (*m.*) de una fruta que no se adhiere a la carne (stone of a fruit). || Fruta (*f.*) cuyo hueso no se adhiere a la carne (fruit).

freestyle [—stail] n. Estilo (*m.*) libre. || — *Freestyle wrestling*, lucha (*f.*) libre. || *The 100 metres freestyle*, los 100 metros libres.

freethinker [—'θiŋkə*] n. Librepensador, ra.

freethinking [—'θiŋkiŋ] n. Librepensamiento, *m.*

— Adj. Librepensador, ra.

free thought [—θɔ:t] n. Librepensamiento, *m.*

free time [—taim] n. Tiempo (*m.*) libre, momentos (*m. pl.*) de ocio.

free trade [—treid] n. Librecambio, *m.*, libre cambio, *m.* [*Amer.*, libre comercio, *m.*]: *free trade area*, zona de libre cambio.

free-trade [—treid] adj. Librecambista.

free trader [—,treidə*] n. Librecambista, *m.* & *f.*

freeway [—wei] n. U. S. Autopista (*f.*) sin peaje.

freewheel [—'wi:l] n. Rueda (*f.*) libre.

freewheel [—'wi:l] v. intr. Andar con rueda libre (a bicycle). || Ir en punto muerto (car). || U. S. FIG. FAM. Obrar a su antojo [haciendo caso omiso de toda clase de principios].

free will [—wil] n. Libre albedrío, *m.*

freeze [fri:z] n. Helada, *f.*: *crops destroyed by the freeze*, cosechas destruidas por la helada. || Congelación, *f.*, bloqueo, *m.* (of prices, wages, credits).

freeze* [fri:z] v. intr. Helarse, congelarse (from cold). || FIG. Quedarse inmóvil (to avoid being seen). | Quedarse helado *or* paralizado (*with*, de) [fear, etc.]. || — FIG. *To freeze on to*, pegarse a. || FIG. FAM. *To freeze to death*, morirse de frío. || FIG. *To freeze up*, quedarse rígido, da. || *When the lake freezes over*, cuando se hiela el lago.

— V. tr. Helar (to turn to ice). || Congelar (to preserve by refrigeration). || Refrigerar (to chill). || FIG. Congelar, bloquear (credits, prices, wages). | Bloquear (an account). || FIG. *To freeze out*, deshacerse de (to get rid of), excluir (to exclude).

— V. impers. Helar.

— OBSERV. Pret. **froze;** p. p. **frozen.**

freeze-dry [—drai] v. tr. Deshidratar por congelación (food, vaccines).

freezer [—ə*] n. Congelador, *m.* (for frozen foods). || Heladera, *f.* (for making ice cream).

freezing ['fri:ziŋ] adj. Glacial: *freezing weather*, tiempo glacial. || — *Freezing mixture*, mezcla (*f.*) refrigerante. || FIG. *It's freezing (cold)*, hace un frío espantoso *or* un frío que hiela las piedras.

— N. Congelación, *f.* (of foodstuffs). || COMM. Congelación, *f.*, bloqueo, *m.* (of prices, etc.). || Helada, *f.* (of a river). || *Twenty degrees below freezing*, veinte grados bajo cero.

freezing point [—pɔint] n. Punto (*m.*) de congelación.

free zone ['fri:zəun] n. U. S. Zona (*f.*) franca.

Freiburg ['fraibə:g] pr. n. GEOGR. Friburgo.

freight [freit] n. Flete, *m.* (by plane and ship). || Mercancías, *f. pl.* (by other means of transport): *freight train*, tren de mercancías. || Carga, *f.* (load). || Transporte, *m.* (transportation).

freight [freit] v. tr. Fletar (plane, ship). || Cargar (other means of transport). || Transportar (to transport).

freightage [—idʒ] n. Flete, *m.* (by plane and ship). || Carga, *f.* (by other means of transport). || Transporte, *m.*

freight car ['freitkɑ:*] n. U. S. Vagón (*m.*) de mercancías.

freight elevator ['freit'eliveitə*] n. U. S. Montacargas, *m. inv.*

freighter ['freitə*] n. Buque (*m.*) de carga, carguero, *m.* (ship). || Avión (*m.*) de carga (plane). || Transportista, *m.* (carrier). || Fletador, *m.* (maritime or air shipping agent). || U. S. Vagón (*m.*) de mercancías.

French [frentʃ] adj. Francés, esa.

— N. Francés, *m.* (language). || *The French*, los franceses.

French bean [—bi:n] n. Judía (*f.*) *or* habichuela (*f.*) verde.

French chalk [—tʃɔ:k] n. Esteatita, *f.*, jaboncillo (*m.*) de sastre.

French cuff [—kʌf] n. Puño (*m.*) doble.

French doors [—dɔ:z] pl. n. Puertaventana, *f. sing.*

French dressing [—'dresiŋ] n. Vinagreta, *f.*

French fries [—fraiz] pl. n. U. S. Patatas (*f.*) fritas [*Amer.*, papas (*f.*) fritas].

French horn [—hɔ:n] n. MUS. Trompa (*f.*) de llaves.

Frenchification [,frentʃifi'keiʃən] n. Afrancesamiento, *m.*

Frenchify ['frentʃifai] v. tr. Afrancesar.

French kiss [—kis] n. *To give a French kiss*, darse la lengua.

French leave [—li:v] n. *To take French leave*, despedirse a la francesa.

French letter [—'letə*] n. POP. Condón, *m.*

Frenchman [—mən] n. Francés, *m.* || HIST. Buque (*m.*) francés (ship).

— OBSERV. El plural de esta palabra es *Frenchmen.*

French pastry [—'peistri] n. Pequeños pasteles (*m. pl.*) rellenos con crema.

French roll [—rəul] n. Panecillo, *m.*

French-speaking [—,spi:kiŋ] adj. De habla francesa, francófono, na: *French-speaking countries*, países de habla francesa.

French telephone [—'telifəun] n. Microteléfono, *m.*

French toast [—təust] n. Torrija, *f.* (slice of bread dipped in milk and egg).

French window [—'windəu] n. Puertaventana, *f.*

Frenchwoman [—'wumən] n. Francesa, *f.*

— OBSERV. El plural de esta palabra es *Frenchwomen.*

Frenchy ['frentʃi] n. FAM. Franchute, ta.

frenetic [fri'netik] adj. Frenético, ca.

frenulum ['fri:nələm] n. ANAT. Frenillo, *m.*

— OBSERV. El plural de esta palabra es *frenula.*

frenum ['fri:nəm] n. ANAT. Frenillo, *m.*

— OBSERV. El plural de esta palabra es *frena* o *frenums.*

frenzied ['frənzid] adj. Frenético, ca: *frenzied applause*, aplausos frenéticos. || Enloquecido, da: *a frenzied look in his eyes*, una mirada enloquecida en sus ojos. || De frenesí: *the last frenzied moments before curtain call*, los últimos momentos de frenesí antes de que se levante el telón.

frenzy ['frenzi] n. Frenesí, *m.* (near madness). || Arrebato, *m.*: *a frenzy of rage*, un arrebato de cólera. || — *A frenzy of joy*, una alegría loca. || *A frenzy of preparation*, preparaciones frenéticas. || *A frenzy of work*, un trabajo febril. || *To drive to frenzy*, volver loco, poner frenético.

frenzy ['frenzi] v. tr. Volver loco, poner frenético.

frequency ['fri:kwənsi] n. Frecuencia, *f.*: *the frequency of his visits*, la frecuencia de sus visitas. || RAD. PHYS. Frecuencia, *f.*: *high, low frequency*, frecuencia alta, baja. || *Frequency modulation*, frecuencia modulada, modulación (*f.*) de frecuencia.

frequency meter [—'mitə*] n. Frecuencímetro, *m.*

frequent ['fri:kwent] adj. Frecuente: *frecuent visits*, visitas frecuentes. || Corriente: *it is quite a frequent practice*, es una costumbre muy corriente. || Habitual (customer). || Asiduo, dua (visitor). || Rápido, da (pulse).

frequent [fri'kwent] v. tr. Frecuentar (to go often to). || REL. Frecuentar: *to frequent the sacrements*, frecuentar los sacramentos.

frequentation [,frikwen'teiʃən] n. Frecuentación, *f.*

frequentative [fri'kwentetiv] adj. GRAMM. Frecuentativo, va.

— N. Verbo (*m.*) frecuentativo, frecuentativo, *m.*

frequenter [fri'kwentə*] n. Frecuentador, *m.*

frequently [ˈfriːkwəntli] adv. A menudo, frecuentemente.
fresco [ˈfreskəu] n. ARTS. Fresco, *m.* || FIG. Fresco, *m.*: *a vast historical fresco*, un vasto fresco histórico.
— OBSERV. El plural de la palabra inglesa es *frescoes* o *frescos*.
fresco [ˈfreskəu] v. tr. Pintar al fresco.
fresh [freʃ] adj. Fresco, ca: *fresh eggs*, huevos frescos; *fresh fruit*, fruta fresca. || Tierno, na; fresco, ca: *fresh bread*, pan tierno. || Puro, ra (air). || Dulce (river water). || Natural (water from the tap). || Fresco, ca (cold, brisk). || FIG. Fresco, ca; de buen color (complexion). | Fresco, ca (not tired): *to feel as fresh as a daisy*, sentirse fresco como una rosa. | Fresco, ca (recent): *fresh news*, noticias frescas. | Nuevo, va; otro, otra (new, another): *a fresh sheet of paper*, otra hoja de papel; *to start a fresh life*, empezar una vida nueva. | Fresco, ca; descarado, da (cheeky, impertinent). || — FIG. *Fresh from*, recién salido de (factory, etc.), recién llegado de (country, place). || *In the fresh air*, al aire libre. || FIG. *It is still fresh in my memory*, está todavía fresco en mi memoria. | *To get fresh with s.o.*, ponerse fresco con uno. | *To give s.o. fresh courage*, dar nuevos ánimos a alguien. | *To make a fresh start*, empezar de nuevo.
— Adv. Recientemente (recently). || *We're fresh out of tomatoes*, se nos han acabado los tomates.
— N. Frescor, *m.*, fresco, *m.*: *in the fresh of the morning*, en el frescor de la mañana. || Avenida, *f.* (caused by rain, melted snow). || Corriente (*f.*) de agua dulce que penetra en el mar.
freshen [ˈfreʃn] v. tr. Refrescar (to refresh). || Desalar (to remove the salt from). || — *That shower has freshened me up*, la ducha me ha refrescado. || *To freshen o.s. up*, refrescarse.
— V. intr. Refrescar (weather, wind). || *To freshen up*, refrescarse.
freshening [—iŋ] n. Enfriamiento, *m.*
freshet [ˈfreʃit] n. Avenida, *f.* (caused by rain, melted snow). || Corriente (*f.*) de agua dulce que penetra en el mar.
freshly [ˈfreʃli] adv. Recién, recientemente: *freshly picked fruit*, fruta recién cogida. || Frescamente.
freshman [ˈfreʃmən] n. Estudiante (*m.*) de primer año.
— OBSERV. El plural de esta palabra es *freshmen*.
freshness [ˈfreʃnis] n. Frescura, *f.* (coolness). || Frescura, *f.* (of bread, eggs, etc.). || Frescura, *f.*, lozanía, *f.* (of complexion, person). || Novedad, *f.* (novelty). || Frescura, *f.*, descaro, *m.* (cheek).
freshwater [ˈfreʃˌwɔːtə*] adj. De agua dulce (fish, etc.). || U. S. De provincia (college, town).
fret [fret] n. MUS. Traste, *m.* (of stringed instrument). || ARCH. Greca, *f.* (repeated pattern). || Calado, *m.* (network pattern). || Desgaste, *m.* (wearing away). || Parte (*f.*) desgastada (worn spot). || Preocupación, *f.* (worry). || Enfado, *m.* (irritation). || *To be in a fret*, estar preocupado.
fret [fret] v. tr. ARCH. Adornar con grecas. || Desgastar (to wear away). || Cavar: *the river fretted a channel through the rock*, el río cavó un canal en la roca. || Agitar, rizar (water). || Rozar (to rub). || Irritar, molestar (to vex). || Preocupar (to worry). || MUS. Poner trastes a (an instrument).
— V. intr. Preocuparse (to worry): *to fret about one's health*, preocuparse por su salud. || Atormentarse (to torture o.s.). || Lamentarse, quejarse (to complain). || Irritarse, enojarse (to become vexed). || Desgastarse (to wear away). || Rizarse (water). || *To fret at s.o.'s nerves*, ponerle a uno los nervios de punta.
fretful [—ful] adj. Preocupado, da (worried). || Irritable. || Apenado, da (upset). || Descontento, ta (discontented). || Molesto, ta (ill at ease). || Quejumbroso, sa (complaining).
fretfulness [—fulnis] n. Irritabilidad, *f.* || Preocupación, *f.* (worry).
fretsaw [—sɔː] n. Sierra (*f.*) de calar, segueta, *f.*
fretwork [—wəːk] n. Calado, *m.* (openwork). || Grecas, *f. pl.*
Freudian [ˌfrɔidjən] adj./n. Freudiano, na.
Freudianism [frɔiˈdjənizəm] n. Freudismo, *m.*
friability [ˌfraiəˈbiliti] n. Friabilidad, *f.*
friable [ˈfraiəbl] adj. Friable.
friar [ˈfraiə*] n. REL. Fraile, *m.*, monje, *m.*, religioso, *m.* (brother): *to become a friar*, meterse a fraile. || Fray, *m.* (in titles). || PRINT. Fraile, *m.* || — REL. *Black friar*, dominico, *m.* | *White friar*, carmelita, *m.*
friar's balsam [—zˈbɔːlsəm] n. Benjuí, *m.*, tintura (*f.*) de benjuí.
friary [ˈfraiəri] n. REL. Monasterio, *m.*, convento (*m.*) de monjes. | Orden (*f.*) de religiosos.
fribble [ˈfribl] n. Frívolo, la (person). || Fruslería, *f.* (trifle).
— Adj. Frívolo, la.
fribble [ˈfribl] v. intr. Perder el tiempo en fruslerías.
— V. tr. Malgastar, desperdiciar (time, money).
fricandeau [ˈfrikəndəu] n. CULIN. Fricandó, *m.*
fricassee [ˌfrikəˈsiː] n. CULIN. Estofado, *m.*
fricative [ˈfrikətiv] adj. GRAMM. Fricativo, va.
— N. Fricativa, *f.*
friction [ˈfrikʃən] n. Fricción, *f.* || TECH. Fricción, *f.*, rozamiento, *m.* || FIG. Fricción, *f.*, roce, *m.*, desavenencia, *f.*
frictional [—l] adj. De fricción.
friction tape [—teip] n. ELECTR. Cinta (*f.*) aislante.
Friday [ˈfraidi] n. Viernes, *m.*: *he will be here on Friday*, estará aquí el viernes. || *Good Friday*, Viernes Santo.
fridge [fridʒ] n. FAM. Refrigerador, *m.*, nevera, *f.*
fried [fraid] adj. Frito, ta: *fried eggs*, huevos fritos.
friend [frend] n. Amigo, ga: *he's a friend of mine*, es un amigo mío; *lifelong friend*, amigo de toda la vida *or* de siempre. || FIG. Amigo, ga: *friends of the poor*, amigos de los pobres; *friends of the arts*, amigos de las artes. || Cuáquero, ra (Quaker). || Partidario, ria (supporter). || Aliado, *m.* (ally). || — *A doctor friend of mine*, un médico amigo mío. || FIG. *A friend in need is a friend indeed*, en la necesidad *or* en el peligro se conoce al amigo. || *Bosom* o *close friend*, amigo íntimo. || *Friend!*, ¡gente de paz! || *My honourable* o *learned friend*, mi eminente colega. || *To be friends with*, ser amigo de. || *School friend*, compañero *or* compañera de clase. || FIG. *To have a friend at court* o *friends in high places*, tener buenas aldabas *or* enchufe. || *To keep friends with*, seguir siendo amigo de. || *To make friends again*, reconciliarse, hacer las paces. || *To make friends with*, hacerse amigo de, trabar amistad con. || *We are the best of friends*, somos muy amigos. || FIG. *You look like you lost your last friend*, parece que se te ha muerto la madre.
friendless [—lis] adj. Sin amigos, solo, la.
friendliness [—linis] n. Simpatía, *f.*, amabilidad, *f.* (amiability). || Bondad, *f.* (kindness). || Amistad, *f.* (friendship).
friendly [—li] adj. Amable, simpático, ca: *to be friendly with*, ser amable con. || Amistoso, sa: *a friendly smile*, una sonrisa amistosa. || Amigo, ga: *friendly country*, país amigo. || Aliado, da: *friendly forces*, fuerzas aliadas. || Bondadoso, sa: *friendly act*, acción bondadosa. || Favorable: *friendly wind*, viento favorable; *official attitude which is friendly to investors*, actitud oficial que es favorable a los inversionistas. || De amigo: *friendly advice*, consejo de amigo. || De amigos: *friendly gathering*, reunión de amigos. || Acogedor, ra: *a friendly fire burned in the hearth*, un fuego acogedor ardía en el hogar. || JUR. SP. Amistoso, sa. || — *To become friendly with*, hacerse amigo de. || *To be on friendly terms with*, estar en buenos términos con.
friendly society [—səˈsaiəti] n. Mutualidad, *f.*
friendship [ˈfrendʃip] n. Amistad, *f.*
frier [fraiə*] n. See FRYER.
Friesian [ˈfriːzjən] adj./n. Frisio, sia.
Friesland [ˈfriːzlənd] pr. n. GEOGR. Frisia, *f.*
frieze [friːz] n. ARCH. Friso, *m.* || Frisa, *f.* (cloth). || Cenefa, *f.* (of wallpaper).
frigate [ˈfrigit] n. MAR. Fragata, *f.*
frigate bird [—bəːd] n. Fragata, *f.*
fright [frait] n. Susto, *m.* (sudden shock): *he was seized with fright*, le dio un susto. || Miedo, *m.* (fear). || FIG. Espantajo, *m.* (person): *to look a fright*, estar hecho un espantajo. | Horror, *m.* (horrible sight). || *To take fright*, asustarse (*at*, de).
frighten [—n] v. tr. Asustar: *sudden movements frighten the horse*, los movimientos bruscos asustan al caballo. || Dar un susto (to give a fright). || — *He was frightened at the thought of*, le asustaba la idea de. || *He was frightened to do it* o *of doing it*, le asustaba hacerlo. || *To be easily frightened*, ser asustadizo. || *To be frightened*, tener miedo, asustarse. || *To be frightened to death*, morirse de miedo, estar muerto de miedo. || *To frighten away* o *off*, espantar, ahuyentar. || *To frighten s.o. into doing sth.*, conseguir que alguien haga algo amenazándole.
frightening [—niŋ] adj. Espantoso, sa.
frightful [—ful] adj. Espantoso, sa; horrible, horroroso, sa (causing horror, disgust, shock). || FIG. Tremendo, da: *a frightful thirst*, una sed tremenda. | Espantoso, sa; malísimo, ma; pésimo, ma (very bad).
frightfully [—fuli] adv. Terriblemente. || — *She is frightfully pleased*, está la mar de contenta, está contentísima *or* muy contenta. || *We are frightfully sorry*, lo sentimos enormemente *or* en el alma.
frightfulness [—fulnis] n. Horror, *m.* (horror). || Terrorismo, *m.* (in warfare).
frigid [ˈfridʒid] adj. Glacial, muy frío: *frigid climate*, clima muy frío. || FIG. Frío, a: *to be frigid toward s.o.*, ser frío con alguien. || MED. Frígido, da.
frigidity [friˈdʒiditi] or **frigidness** [ˈfridʒidnis] n. Frialdad, *f.* || MED. Frigidez, *f.*
frigidly [ˈfridʒidli] adv. Con frialdad.
frigid zone [ˈfridʒidzəun] n. Zona (*f.*) glacial.
frigorific [frigəˈrifik] adj. Frigorífico, ca.
frill [fril] n. Encañonado, *m.* (fluting). || Volante, *m.*, faralá, *m.* (flared edge). || Pechera, *f.*, chorrera, *f.* (on shirt front). || Gorguera, *f.* (ruff). || CULIN. Adorno (*m.*) de papel. || — Pl. FIG. Adornos, *m.*: *a straightforward story with no frills*, una historia sencilla sin adornos. | Afectación, *f. sing.* (affectation). || Collarín, *m. sing.* (of bird).
frill [fril] v. tr. Encañonar, alechugar (clothes).
— V. intr. PHOT. Arrugarse.
frilled [—d] adj. Encañonado, da; alechugado, da (fluted). || Con volantes (skirt, dress). || Con pechera,

con chorrera (shirt). || Con collarín (bird). || PHOT. Arrugado, da.
frillies [ˈfriliz] pl. n. Ropa (*f. sing.*) interior con perifollos (underwear).
frilling [ˈfriliŋ] n. Volantes, *m. pl.*
frilly [ˈfrili] adj. Con volantes (dress). || Encañonado, da; alechugado, da (fluted). || FIG. Con muchos adornos.
fringe [frindʒ] n. Franja, *f.*, fleco, *m.* (of material): *the fringe of a shawl*, el fleco de un chal. || Flequillo, *m.* (of hair). || Linde, *m.*, lindero, *m.* (of a forest). || Franja, *f.*: *a fringe of trees*, una franja de árboles. || FIG. Margen, *m.*: *to live on the fringe of society*, vivir al margen de la sociedad. | Periferia, *f.*: *to live just on the fringe of London*, vivir justo en la periferia de Londres. | Borde, *m.* (of a lake, etc.). | Pequeña parte, *f.*: *to touch upon the fringe of a problem*, tocar una pequeña parte de un problema. || PHYS. Franja, *f.*: *interference fringe*, franja de interferencia. || — FIG. *Fringe benefits*, beneficios complementarios. || *Fringe groups*, grupos marginales.
fringe [frindʒ] v. tr. Poner una franja a, orlar, franjar, franjear (to put a fringe on). || Bordear (to border). || FIG. Orlar: *fluffy clouds fringed the horizon*, nubes aborregadas orlaban el horizonte.
frippery [ˈfripəri] n. Cursilería, *f.*, afectación, *f.* (affected elegance). || — Pl. Perifollos, *m.* (gaudy ornaments). || Baratijas, *f.* (trashy ornaments).
Frisian [ˈfriziən] adj./n. Frisio, sia. || HIST. Frisón, ona.
frisk [frisk] n. Brinco, *m.*, salto, *m.* (leap). || Diversión, *f.* (gay time). || FAM. Registro, *m.*, cacheo, *m.* (search).
frisk [frisk] v. intr. Retozar, brincar (to leap about). || Juguetear (to play about).
— V. tr. Mover, menear (to shake). || FAM. Registrar, cachear (to search). | Birlar (to steal).
friskily [ˈfriskili] adv. Alegremente (joyfully). || Retozando, jugueteando (playfully).
frisky [ˈfriski] adj. Retozón, ona: juguetón, ona (child, dog). || Fogoso, sa (horse). || Vivo, va (lively).
frit [frit] n. Frita, *f.* (for making glass and glazes).
frit [frit] v. tr. TECH. Fritar, sinterizar, calcinar.
frith [friθ] n. Estuario, *m.*, brazo (*m.*) de mar.
fritter [ˈfritə*] n. CULIN. Buñuelo, *m.*, fruta (*f.*) de sartén.
fritter [ˈfritə*] v. tr. Fragmentar, desmenuzar (to split up). || *To fritter away*, malgastar, desperdiciar.
fritting [ˈfritiŋ] n. TECH. Fritaje, *m.*, fritado, *m.*, calcinación, *f.*, sinterización, *f.*
frivol [ˈfrivəl] v. tr. *To frivol away*, desperdiciar, malgastar.
— V. intr. Perder el tiempo en frivolidades.
frivolity [friˌvɔliti] n. Frivolidad, *f.*
frivolous [ˈfrivələs] adj. Frívolo, la (person). || Fútil, de poca entidad, de poco peso: *a frivolous argument*, un argumento fútil.
frizz [friz] n. Rizo, *m.* (curl). || Pelo (*m.*) crespo (hair).
frizz [friz] v. tr. Rizar (hair). || TECH. Rizar (nap of cloth). || CULIN. Freír.
— V. intr. Rizarse. || CULIN. Chisporrotear (to sizzle). | Quemarse, chamuscarse (to burn).
frizzle [ˈfrizl] n. Rizo, *m.* (curl). || Pelo (*m.*) crespo (hair).
frizzle [ˈfrizl] v. tr. Rizar (hair). || CULIN. Freír.
— V. intr. Rizarse (hair). || CULIN. Chisporrotear (to sizzle). | Quemarse (to burn).
frizzly [ˈfrizli] or **frizzy** [ˈfrizi] adj. Muy rizado, da; crespo, pa (hair).
fro [frəu] adv. *To go to and fro*, ir de un lado para otro, ir y venir.
frock [frɔk] n. Hábito, *m.* (monk's habit). || Bata, *f.* (for women and workmen). || Babero, *m.* (for children). || Jersey (*m.*) de marinero (worn by sailors). || Vestido (*m.*) ligero (dress). || FIG. REL. *To give up the frock*, colgar los hábitos.
frock coat [—ˈkəut] n. Levita, *f.*
frog [frɔg] n. Rana, *f.* (animal). || Anillo, *m.*, anilla, *f.* (on belt). || Alamares, *m. pl.* (fastener). || Ranilla, *f.* (of horse's hoof). || TECH. Cruce, *m.* (of rails). | Aguja (*f.*) aérea (of trolley wires). || FAM. Franchute, ta (Frenchman, Frenchwoman). || — *Frogs' legs*, ancas (*f.*) de rana. || FIG. *To have a frog in one's throat*, tener carraspera.
frogfish [—fiʃ] n. ZOOL. Pejesapo, *m.*
froggy [ˈfrɔgi] n. FAM. Franchute, ta.
frogman [ˌfrɔgmən] n. Hombre (*m.*) rana.
— OBSERV. El plural de *frogman* es *frogmen*.
— The plural of *hombre rana* is *hombres rana*.
frog-march [ˌfrɔgmɑːtʃ] v. tr. Llevar por fuerza [a alguien sujetándole por las piernas y por los brazos].
frolic [ˈfrɔlik] n. Jugueteo, *m.*, juego (*m.*) alegre (playing about). || Travesura, *f.* (mischief). || Fiesta, *f.* (party). || *To have a frolic*, divertirse.
— Adj. Alegre, animado (lively). || Juguetón, ona (playful). || Travieso, sa (mischievous).
frolic [ˈfrɔlik] v. intr. Divertirse (to have fun). || Retozar (to leap about). || Juguetear (to play about). || Hacer travesuras (to get up to mischief).
frolicsome [—səm] adj. Retozón, ona; juguetón, ona (children, animals). || Travieso, sa (mischievous). || Alegre (gay).
from [frɔm] prep. De: *ten miles from London*, a diez millas de Londres; *where are you from?*, ¿de dónde eres?; *he jumped from the wall*, saltó del muro; *to shelter from*, protegerse de; *he suffers from the cold*, sufre del frío; *to tremble from fear*, temblar de miedo; *to escape from*, escapar de; *I received a letter from a friend*, recibí una carta de un amigo. || Desde: *from above*, desde arriba; *the view from the window*, la vista desde la ventana; *to be sick from childhood*, estar enfermo desde su niñez; *from your point of view*, desde su punto de vista. || A partir de, desde: *from that day*, a partir de ese día; *watches from three pounds*, relojes a partir de tres libras. || Con: *fuels made from coal*, combustibles hechos con carbón. || A: *to steal, to take, to buy sth. from s.o.*, robar, quitar, comprar algo a alguien; *I learnt that from reading the papers*, me enteré al leer los periódicos; *to write from s.o.'s dictation*, escribir al dictado. || En: *to drink from a glass*, beber en un vaso; *to learn sth. from a book*, aprender algo en un libro. || De, sacado de (the work of an author, etc.): *a quotation from Shakespeare*, una cita de Shakespeare. || Por: *to speak from one's own experience*, hablar por experiencia propia; *to act from conviction*, actuar por convicción; *from good motives*, por motivos válidos. || Según, por (according to): *from what he has just said*, según lo que acaba de decir; *from what I saw*, por lo que he visto. || Entre (between, among): *chosen from twenty candidates*, escogido entre veinte candidatos. || De parte de (on behalf of): *tell him that from me*, díselo de mi parte; *I have brought it to you from a friend*, te lo traigo de parte de un amigo. || Procedente de, de: *goods from foreign countries*, mercancías procedentes de países extranjeros; *the train from Birmingham*, el tren procedente de Birmingham. || Ante (before): *to shrink from a danger*, retroceder ante un peligro. || — *As from*, a partir de. || *Far from*, lejos de: *far from Madrid*, lejos de Madrid; *he was far from the best*, estaba lejos de ser el mejor. || *From afar*, desde lejos. || *From among*, de entre. || *From birth*, de nacimiento (deaf, blind, etc.). || *From memory*, de memoria. || *From now on*, de ahora en adelante, a partir de ahora. || *From... onwards*, a partir de ... || *From the bottom of my heart*, de todo corazón. || *From ... till*, desde ... hasta. || *From ... to ...*, de .... en ....: *from bad to worse*, de mal en peor; *from house to house*, de casa en casa; de ... a ..., desde ... hasta ...: *from six to eight o'clock*, de seis a ocho, desde la seis hasta las ocho; entre ... y ... (between). || *He prevented me from doing it*, me impidió hacerlo. || *Judging from* o *to judge from*, a juzgar por. || *To be away from home*, estar fuera, no estar en casa. || *To date from*, datar de. || *To die from*, morir de. || *To have known s.o. from childhood*, conocer a alguien de niño. || *To judge from appearances*, juzgar por las apariencias. || *To know good from bad*, distinguir lo bueno de lo malo. || *To paint from nature*, pintar del natural. || MATH. *To substract* o *to take two from four*, restar dos de cuatro. || *To take away books from a child*, quitarle los libros a un niño. || *To translate from English*, traducir del inglés. || *We heard* o *learnt* o *got it from Peter*, nos lo dijo Pedro, nos enteramos por Pedro.
frond [frɔnd] n. BOT. Fronda, *f.*
Fronde [frɔ̃d] pr. n. HIST. Fronda, *f.*
fronded [ˈfrɔndid] adj. BOT. Frondoso, sa.
frondescense [frɔnˈdesəns] n. Fronda, *f.*
frondose [ˈfrɔndəs] adj. Frondoso, sa (leafy).
front [frʌnt] n. Parte (*f.*) delantera: *the front of the train, of the car, of the chair*, la parte delantera del tren, del coche, de la silla. || Fachada, *f.* (of building). || Escaparate, *m.* (of a shop). || Principio, *m.*: *front of the queue, of the book*, principio de la cola, del libro. || Cara, *f.* (face). || Frente, *f.* (forehead). || Playa, *f.* (beach). || Paseo (*m.*) a orillas de la playa (sea front). || Pechera, *f.* (of shirt). || Frente, *m.* (meteorology): *cold, warm front*, frente frío, cálido. || Tupé, *m.* (wig). || FIG. Frente, *m.*: *popular front*, frente popular. | Nivel, *m.*, terreno, *m.*: *the news on the home front is encouraging*, las noticias al nivel nacional son alentadoras. | Apariencia, *f.* (outward demeanour). | Fachada, *f.*: *the florist's served as a front for the dope smugglers*, el florista sirvió de fachada a los traficantes de droga. | Cara, *f.*, caradura, *f.*, rostro, *m.* (effrontery). || MIL. Frente, *m.*: *battle front*, frente de batalla. || Auditorio, *m.* (in theatre). || — *At* o *in the front*, en el frente (of battle), delante (forward). || *From the front*, por delante, de frente: *an attack from the front*, un ataque de frente *or* por delante. || *Front to front*, frente a frente. || *In front*, delante. || *In front of*, delante de: *a terrace in front of the house*, una terraza delante de la casa; en frente de (facing, opposite). || *Seen from the front*, visto de frente. || FIG. *To change front*, mudar de táctica. | *To como to the front*, empezar a destacar. | *To come to the front again*, volver sobre el tapete (a question, problem). || *To go on in front*, ir delante *or* en cabeza. || FIG. *To put on a bold front*, hacer de tripas corazón.
— Adj. Delantero, ra: *front legs*, patas delanteras. || Principal (door, etc.). || Primero, ra (first): *front row*, primera fila. || GRAMM. Palatal (letter). || — *Front steps*, escalinata, *f. sing.* (of important buildings), escaleras (*f.*) de la puerta principal (of a house). || *The front view of the house*, la casa vista de frente.
front [frʌnt] v. tr. Dar a: *the house fronts the lake*, la casa da al lago. || Estar delante de: *a rose garden fronts the house*, un jardín de rosas está delante de la casa. || Poner una fachada a: *to front a house with*

marble, poner una fachada de mármol a una casa. || Revocar (to clean a façade). || Hacer frente a, afrontar (the enemy, problems, etc.). || Carear: *to front two people*, carear a dos personas. || GRAMM. Palatalizar.
— V. intr. Dar a: *my bedroom fronts onto the street*, mi dormitorio da a la calle. || FIG. *To front for*, servir de fachada a (illegal activities).

frontage [—idʒ] n. Extensión (*f.*) de tierras: *the army won a frontage on the ocean*, el ejército conquistó una extensión de tierras a orillas del océano. || Terreno, *m.* [entre una casa y la carretera]. || Fachada, *f.* (face of building). || Orientación, *f.* (direction faced). || Alineación, *f.* (line).

frontal [—l] adj. ANAT. Frontal: *frontal bone*, hueso frontal. || De frente: *frontal attack, view*, ataque, vista de frente. || Del frente (in meteorology).
— N. Frontal, *m.* (of altar). || Fachada, *f.* (façade). || ANAT. Frontal, *m.* (bone).

front bench [—bentʃ] n. Una de las dos filas de escaños ocupados por los ministros del Gobierno y sus equivalentes en la oposición [en la Cámara de Diputados británica].

front bencher [—ˈbentʃə*] n. Ministro (*m.*) del Gobierno o su equivalente en la oposición.

front door [—dɔ:*] n. Entrada (*f.*) *or* puerta (*f.*) principal.

frontier [ˈfrʌntiə*] n. Frontera, *f.* || FIG. Frontera, *f.* || U. S. Zona (*f.*) situada entre regiones colonizadas y las que no han sido todavía exploradas.
— Adj. Fronterizo, za: *frontier dispute*, conflicto fronterizo.

frontiersman [—smən] n. Fronterizo, *m.* (who lives on a frontier). || U. S. Colonizador, *m.*, pionero, *m.*

— OBSERV. El plural de esta palabra es *frontiersmen*.

frontispiece [ˈfrʌntispi:s] n. Frontispicio, *m.*

frontlet [ˈfrʌntlit] n. Venda, *f.* (headband). || Frente, *m.* (animal's forehad). || Frontal, *m.* (of an altar).

front line [ˈfrʌntlain] n. MIL. Primera línea, *f.*

frontline [ˈfrʌntlain] adj. MIL. De la primera línea.

front matter [ˈfrʌntˌmætə*] n. Páginas (*f. pl.*) pre liminares [de un libro].

fronton [ˈfrɔntɔn] n. ARCH. Frontón, *m.*

front page [ˈfrʌntˈpeidʒ] n. Primera plana, *f.* (of newspaper). || *Front page news*, noticia (*f.*) de la primera plana, noticia (*f.*) sensacional.

front room [ˈfrʌntrum] n. Sala (*f.*) de estar.

frontstall [ˈfrʌntstɔ:l] n. Testera, *f.* (of horse's armour).

front-wheel drive [ˈfrʌntwi:lˈdraiv] n. Tracción (*f.*) delantera.

frost [frɔst] n. Escarcha, *f.* (frozen dew). || Helada, *f.* (freezing). || FIG. Frialdad, *f.* (coldness). | Fracaso, *m.* (failure). || — *Ten degrees of frost*, diez grados bajo cero. || *White frost*, escarcha.

frost [frɔst] v. tr. Cubrir de escarcha (to cover with frost). || Helar (to freeze). || Quemar (plants). || CULIN. Escarchar (cakes). || Esmerilar (glass). || Glasear (metals). || U. S. Congelar (vegetables).
— V. intr. Cubrirse de escarcha (windows, etc.). || Helarse (to freeze).

frostbite [—bait] n. MED. Congelación, *f.* || Quemadura, *f.* (of plants).

frostbite [—bait] v. tr. MED. Congelar. || Quemar (plants).

frostbitten [—ˌbitn] adj. MED. Congelado, da. || Quemado, da (plants).

frostiness [—inis] n. FIG. Frialdad, *f.*

frosting [—iŋ] n. CULIN. Azúcar (*m.*) glaseado (mixture). | Glaseado, *m.* (action of icing a cake). || TECH. Glaseado, *m.* (of metal). | Esmerilado, *m.* (of glass). || Escarcha, *f.* (for decoration).

frostwork [—wə:k] n. Escarcha, *f.*

frosty [i] adj. Muy frío, a (very cold). || De helada: *a frosty day*, un día de helada. || Escarchado, da; cubierto de escarcha (frost-covered). || Helado, da (frozen). || Canoso, sa (hair). || FIG. Glacial (reception, etc.). || *It was frosty yesterday*, ayer heló.

froth [frɔθ] n. Espuma, *f.* (foam, bubbles, lather, etc.). || Espumarajos, *m. pl.* (from animal's mouth). || FIG. Palabras (*f. pl.*) al aire (trivial words). || FIG. FAM. *To be on the froth*, echar espumarajos por la boca, espumajear (to be angry).

froth [frɔθ] v. tr. Batir (to whip up).
— V. intr. Espumar, hacer espuma (to foam). || *To froth at the mouth*, echar espumarajos por la boca, espumajear.

frothy [ˈfrɔθi] adj. Espumoso, sa (covered with froth). || Vaporoso, sa (fluffy). || FIG. Vacío, a (words, etc.).

frou-frou [ˈfru:fru:] n. Frufrú, *m.* (rustling noise). || Faralá, *m.* (frilly trimming).

froward [ˈfrəuəd] adj. Obstinado, da (stubborn). || Rebelde (not easily controlled).

frown [fraun] n. Ceño, *m.* || *To say sth. with a frown*, decir algo frunciendo el entrecejo *or* el ceño.

frown [fraun] v. intr. Fruncir el ceño *or* el entrecejo. || — *To frown at*, mirar frunciendo el entrecejo *or* el ceño. || FIG. *To frown on* o *upon*, desaprobar (to disapprove of).
— V. tr. *To frown s.o. into silence*, hacer callar a uno mirándole con severidad.

frowning [—iŋ] adj. Severo, ra; de reprobación (glance). || FIG. Amenazador, ra (menacing).

frowsty [ˈfrausti] adj. Que huele a cerrado.

frowzily [ˈfrauzili] adv. Con descuido (carelessly).

frowziness [ˈfrauzinis] n. Descuido, *m.*, desaliño, *m.*

frowzy [ˈfrauzi] adj. Descuidado, da (slovenly). || Desaliñado, da (dishevelled). || Desordenado, da (disorderly). || Despeinado, da (unkempt). || Que huele a cerrado (musty). || Sucio, cia (dirty).

froze [frəuz] pret. See FREEZE.

frozen [—n] p. p. See FREEZE.
— Adj. Congelado, da (food, etc.). || Helado, da: *children skating on the frozen lake*, niños que patinan en el lago helado. || FIG. Congelado, da; bloqueado, da (prices, credits, wages). | Bloqueado, da (an account). | Paralizado, da (with terror). | Frío, a (not moved).

fructiferous [frʌkˈtifərəs] adj. Fructífero, ra.

fructification [ˌfrʌktifiˈkeiʃən] n. Fructificación, *f.*

fructify [ˈfrʌktifai] v. intr. Fructificar, dar fruto (plants). || FIG. Fructificar, dar fruto.
— V. tr. Fecundar.

fructivorous [frʌkˈtivərəs] adj. Frugívoro, ra.

fructose [ˈfrʌktəs] n. CHEM. Fructosa, *f.*

fructuous [ˈfrʌktjuəs] adj. Fructífero, ra; fructuoso, sa.

frugal [ˈfru:gəl] adj. Frugal: *a frugal meal, life*, una comida, una vida frugal. || Ahorrador, ra; económico, ca (thrifty).

frugality [fru:ˈgæliti] n. Frugalidad, *f.*

frugivorous [fru:dˈʒivərəs] adj. Frugívoro, ra.

fruit [fru:t] n. BOT. Fruto, *m.*: *to bear fruit*, dar fruto; *dehiscent fruit*, fruto dehiscente; *fleshy fruits*, frutos carnosos. || Fruta, *f.* (for eating): *a diet of salads and fruit*, un régimen de ensaladas y fruta; *you don't eat enough fruit*, no comes bastante fruta; *the apple is a fruit*, la manzana es una fruta. || FIG. Fruto, *m.*: *his efforts finally bore fruit*, sus esfuerzos acabaron por dar fruto. || U. S. FAM. Marica, *m.* (homosexual). || — *Candied fruit*, fruta escarchada. || *Dried fruit*, fruta seca. || *Early fruit*, fruta temprana. || FIG. *Forbidden fruit*, fruta prohibida, fruto prohibido. || *Fruit bowl* o *dish*, frutero, *m.* || *Fruit industry*, industria frutera. || *Fruit tree*, árbol (*m.*) frutal. || FIG. *The fruits of the earth*, los frutos de la tierra. | *The tree is known by its fruit*, por el fruto se conoce el árbol.

— OBSERV. *Fruto* is a botanical term, whereas *fruta* is used to denote edible fruits.

fruit [fru:t] v. intr. Dar fruto.

fruitage [—idʒ] n. Fruto, *m.*

fruitcake [—keik] n. Pastel (*m.*) de fruta.

fruiter [—ə*] n. Buque (*m.*) frutero (boat). || Árbol (*m.*) frutal (tree). || *This tree is a poor fruiter*, este árbol da poco fruto.

fruiterer [—ərə*] n. Frutero, ra (merchant). || *Fruiterer's*, frutería, *f.*

fruitful [—ful] adj. Fructífero, ra; fértil (land, etc.). || Productivo, va (productive). || FIG. Fructuoso, sa; provechoso, sa.

fruitfulness [—fulnis] n. Productividad, *f.* (productivity). || Fertilidad, *f.* (fertility). || FIG. Lo fructuoso, lo provechoso.

fruitiness [—tinis] n. Olor (*m.*) *or* sabor (*m.*) a fruta (smell, taste). || Pastosidad, *f.* (of voice). || FIG. FAM. Sabor, *m.* (of a story). | Sal, *f.* (of jokes).

fruition [fruˈiʃən] n. Fruición, *f.*, goce, *m.* (enjoyment). || Fructificación, *f.* (of plants). || FIG. Cumplimiento, *m.*, realización, *f.* (accomplishment). || — *To bring to fruition*, realizar. || *To come to fruition*, realizarse.

fruit juice [ˈfru:tdʒu:s] n. Zumo (*m.*) de fruta, jugo (*m.*) de fruta.

fruitless [ˈfru:tlis] adj. FIG. Infructuoso, sa; inútil. || BOT. Estéril.

fruit machine [ˈfru:tməˈʃi:n] n. Máquina (*f.*) tragaperras.

fruit salad [ˈfru:tˌsæləd] n. Ensalada (*f.*) de frutas.

fruit salts [ˈfru:tsɔ:lts] pl. n. Sales (*f.*) de frutas.

fruit stand [ˈfru:tstænd] n. U. S. Frutería, *f.*

fruit sugar [ˈfru:tˈʃugə*] n. CHEM. Fructosa, *f.*

fruity [ˈfru:ti] adj. Que huele *or* sabe a fruta, con sabor *or* olor a fruta. || FIG. Pastoso, sa (voice). || FIG. FAM. Sabroso, sa (story). | Picante (jokes).

frumentaceous [ˌfru:mənˈteiʃəs] adj. Frumentario, ria; frumenticio, cia.

frumenty [ˈfru:mənti] n. Papilla (*f.*) de trigo.

frump [frʌmp] n. Birria, *f.* (fam.), espantajo, *m.* (unattractive woman). || Persona (*f.*) chapada a la antigua (old-fashioned person). || FAM. *Old frump*, bruja, *f.*

frumpish [—iʃ] or **frumpy** [—i] adj. Desaliñado, da (dowdy). || Anticuado, da; chapado a la antigua (old-fashioned). || Malhumorado, da (ill-tempered).

frustrate [frʌsˈtreit] v. tr. Frustrar: *to frustrate a plot*, frustrar un complot. || Echar a perder, impedir: *the high wind frustrated all attempts at rescue*, el viento fuerte echó a perder toda tentativa de salvamento. || *I feel frustrated*, me siento frustrado.

frustration [frʌsˈtreiʃən] n. Frustración, *f.* || Decepción, *f.* (disappointment).

frustum [ˈfrʌstəm] n. MATH. Tronco, *m.*

— OBSERV. El plural de esta palabra es *frusta* o *frustums*.

fry [frai] n. Fritada, *f.*, fritura, *f.* (fried meal). || Asadura (*f.*) frita, despojos (*m. pl.*) fritos: *pig's fry*, asadura frita de cerdo. || U. S. Fiesta (*f.*) al aire libre en que se comen manjares fritos.

— OBSERV. El plural de *fry* es *fries*.

fry [frai] pl. n. Alevines, *m.* (young fish). || Salmoncillos, *m.* (small salmon). || Morralla, *f. sing.*, pescado (*m.*) menudo (small fish). || *Small fry*, fritura, *f. sing.* (fish), gente (*f. sing.*) menuda (children), gente (*f. sing.*) de poca monta (people).
fry [frai] v. tr. Freír. || U. S. FAM. Electrocutar. || *Fried fish*, pescado frito.
— V. intr. Freírse. || FIG. *To fry in the heat*, asarse de calor.
fryer [—ə*] n. Pollo (*m.*) tomatero (chicken). || Sartén, *f.* (pan).
frying [—iŋ] n. Freidura, *f.*, freimiento, *m.*
frying pan [—iŋpæn] n. Sartén, *f.* || FIG. *To jump out of the frying pan into the fire*, salir de Guatemala y meterse en Guatepeor, salir de Málaga para entrar en Malagón.
fuchsia [ˈfju:ʃə] n. BOT. Fucsia, *f.*
fuchsine or **fuchsin** [ˈfu:ksi:n] n. CHEM. Fucsina, *f.*
fuck [fʌk] v. tr./intr. POP. Joder. || — POP. *Fuck it!*, ¡joder! | *Fuck off!*, ¡vete a la mierda!
fucus [ˈfju:kəs] n. BOT. Fuco, *m.*
— OBSERV. El plural de la palabra *fucus* es *fucuses* o *fuci*.
fuddle [ˈfʌdl] n. Embriaguez, *f.*, borrachera, *f.* (drunken state). || Confusión, *f.* || — *To be in a fuddle*, estar bebido. || *To go on the fuddle*, irse de juerga *or* de jarana.
fuddle [ˈfʌdl] v. tr. Emborrachar (to intoxicate). || Confundir.
— V. intr. Empinar el codo, ser un borracho.
fuddy-duddy [ˈfʌdiˈdʌdi] n. FAM. Carcamal, *m.*, persona (*f.*) chapada a la antigua (old-fashioned). | Quisquilloso, sa (fussy).
fudge [fʌdʒ] n. Dulce (*m.*) de azúcar (sweet). || PRINT. Última noticia, *f.* || Cuento, *m.*, mentira, *f.* (lie). || Tonterías, *f. pl.* (nonsense).
— Interj. ¡Tonterías!
fudge [fʌdʒ] v. intr. Fallar, faltar (*on*, a) [to fail to live up to]. || PRINT. Insertar una noticia de última hora.
— V. tr. Inventar (to invent). || Amañar, arreglar (to fiddle). || Chapucear (to botch). || PRINT. Insertar como noticia de última hora. || Eludir (to dodge).
Fuegian [fjuˈi:dʒiən] adj./n. Fueguino, na.
fuel [fjuəl] n. Combustible, *m.* || Gasolina, *f.* (petrol). || Carburante, *m.*: *they have found a new fuel for the motor car*, han encontrado un nuevo carburante para el automóvil. || FIG. Pábulo, *m.*: *to be fuel for*, dar pábulo a. || FIG. *To add fuel to the fire*, echar leña al fuego.
fuel [fjuəl] v. intr. Repostar, repostarse.
— V. tr. Alimentar (a furnace). || Abastecer de combustible (ships, rockets, etc.). || Echar gasolina a (cars).
fuel oil [—ɔil] n. Fuel, *m.*, fuel-oil, *m.*
fuel pump [—pʌmp] n. Gasolinera, *f.*, surtidor (*m.*) de gasolina.
fug [fʌg] n. Aire (*m.*) espeso *or* cargado *or* viciado.
fugacious [fjuˈgeiʃəs] adj. Fugaz (fleeting). || BOT. Caduco, ca (caducous).
fugacity [fjuˈgæsiti] n. Fugacidad, *f.*
fuggy [ˈfʌgi] adj. Cargado, da; espeso, sa (atmosphere). || *It smells fuggy*, huele a cerrado.
fugitive [ˈfju:dʒitiv] adj. Fugitivo, va (running away). || FIG. Fugitivo, va; efímero, ra: *fugitive happiness*, felicidad efímera. | Pasajero, ra; efímero, ra (changeable). | Fugaz: *fugitive memory, moment*, recuerdo, momento fugaz. | Esparcido, da (scattered). || FIG. *A colour fugitive to light*, un color poco resistente a la luz.
— N. Fugitivo, va. || Refugiado, da.
fugleman [ˈfju:glmæn] n. MIL. Gastador, *m.* || FIG. Jefe, *m.* (leader). | Portavoz, *m.* (spokesman).
— OBSERV. El plural de esta palabra es *fuglemen*.
fugue [fju:g] n. MUS. Fuga, *f.* || MED. Amnesia (*f.*) temporal.
fulcrum [ˈfʌlkrəm] n. Fulcro, *m.* || FIG. Punto (*m.*) de apoyo.
— OBSERV. El plural de *fulcrum* es *fulcra* o *fulcrums*.
fulfil (U. S. **fulfill**) [fulˈfil] v. tr. Cumplir (a promise, an order, a command). || Cumplir con (obligation). || Satisfacer (wishes, requirements, hopes). || Llevar a cabo (a task, a plan). || Desempeñar (a function). || Servir (a purpose). || Seguir (instructions). || Escuchar (prayers). || Realizar (ambitions).
fulfilment (U. S. **fulfillment**) [—mənt] n. Cumplimiento, *m.* (of promise, order, obligation, duties). || Satisfacción, *f.* (of wishes, hopes, requirements). || Ejecución, *f.* (of instructions, task). || Realización, *f.*: *the fulfilment of a plan*, la realización de un proyecto.
fulgent [ˈfʌldʒənt] adj. Fulgente, fúlgido, da.
fulgurant [ˈfʌlgjuərənt] adj. Fulgurante.
fulgurate [ˈfʌlgjuəreit] v. intr. Fulgurar.
fulgurating [—iŋ] adj. MED. Fulgurante.
fulguration [ˌfʌlgjuəˈreiʃən] n. Fulguración, *f.*
fulica [ˈfjuləkə] n. ZOOL. Fúlica, *f.* (coot).
fuliginous [fju:ˈldʒinəs] adj. Fuliginoso, sa.
full [ful] adj. Lleno, na: *a room full of people, of smoke*, una sala llena de gente, de humo; *a dictionary full of examples*, un diccionario lleno de ejemplos; *the bottle is full*, la botella está llena; *to lead a very full life*, llevar una vida muy llena. || Completo, ta; lleno, na (theatre, bus, etc.). || Completo, ta: *a full study of the subject*, un estudio completo del tema; *a full report*, un informe completo; *full payment*, pago completo; *in full retreat*, en completa derrota. || Completo, ta; entero, ra (freedom, liberty). || Lleno, na (voice, moon, animals with young). || Extenso, sa (extensive). || Lleno, na; relleno, na (face). || Relleno, na (figure). || Grueso, sa (lips). || Íntegro, gra (text). || Sin descuento, íntegro, gra; completo, ta (price, fare). || Pleno, na: *in full daylight*, en pleno día; *in full development*, en pleno desarrollo; *in full possession of one's faculties*, con pleno dominio de sus facultades. || Largo, ga (at least): *it will take us two full hours to do it*, tardaremos dos horas largas en hacerlo. || Entero, ra (whole): *I waited a full hour*, esperé una hora entera; *full term of office*, mandato entero. || Holgado, da; amplio, plia (clothes). || De etiqueta (dress). || De gala (uniform). || Todo, da: *at full speed*, a toda velocidad; *to bear the full brunt of the criticism*, soportar todo el peso de la crítica. || Máximo, ma: *full capacity, potency*, capacidad, potencia máxima. || Mucho, cha: *to have a full flavour*, tener mucho sabor. || Completo, ta (meal). || Cargado, da: *I have had a very full day*, he tenido un día muy cargado; *a man full of years*, un hombre cargado de años. || Lleno, na: *full of hope*, lleno de esperanza. || Colmado, da (of honours). || Carnal: *a full brother*, un hermano carnal. || Exacto, ta: *full measure*, medida exacta; *full weight*, peso exacto. || Crecido, da (river, stream). || Titular (teacher). || MAR. Desplegado, da (sails). || GRAMM. Velar (back). || — JUR. *Full age*, mayoría (*f.*) de edad. || MIL. *Full discharge*, licencia absoluta. || *Full employment*, pleno empleo. || *Full heart*, corazón acongojado *or* oprimido (sad). || *Full house*, no hay localidades (notice outside theatre). || *Full member*, miembro (*m.*) de pleno derecho. || FIG. *Full of*, absorto en (thoughts, etc.). || *Full orchestra*, orquesta, *f.* [con todos los instrumentos]. || *Full powers*, plenos poderes. || *Full session*, sesión plenaria, plenò, *m.* || *Full to the brim* o *to overflowing*, lleno hasta los topes. || *Full up*, completamente lleno (very full), lleno, na; completo, ta (bus, etc.), lleno, na; harto, ta; ahito, ta (after a meal). || FAM. *I'm full*, no puedo más (after eating). || *In full agreement*, completamente de acuerdo. || *In full colour*, a todo color. || *In full detail*, con todo detalle. || *In the full sense of the word*, en toda la extensión de la palabra. || *To be full of a subject*, conocer un tema a fondo. || *To be full of o.s.*, ser muy creído. || *To be full of praise for s.o.*, deshacerse en elogios sobre uno. || *To fill sth. full*, llenar algo hasta los topes. || *To make full use of*, emplear al máximo. || *To take full advantage of*, aprovecharse al máximo de. || *With full particulars*, con todos los detalles.
— Adv. Justo (right): *full in the centre*, justo en medio. || Por lo menos (at least): *it was full five miles away*, estaba por lo menos a cinco millas. || Completamente (completely). || — *Full in the face*, en plena cara. || *Full well*, perfectamente, muy bien.
— N. Máximo, *m.* (greatest amount, number, etc.). || Totalidad, *f.* (totality). || — *In full*, con todas sus letras (name, address), íntegro, gra (payment, text), íntegramente (to pay). || *The moon is at the full*, es luna llena. || *To enjoy sth. to the full*, disfrutar lo más posible de algo. || *To have one's full of sth.*, estar harto de algo. || *To the full*, completamente.
full [ful] v. tr. Dar amplitud a (a dress). || Abatanar (textiles).
— V. intr. U. S. Estar llena (the moon).
fullback [—bæk] n. SP. Defensa, *m.* (in football). | Zaguero, *m.* (in rugby, American football).
full-blooded [—ˈblʌdid] adj. De raza, de pura sangre (thoroughbred). || FIG. Verdadero, ra; cabal: *a full-blooded socialist*, un socialista cabal. | Robusto, ta; vigoroso, sa (vigorous). | Apasionado, da (passionate). || MED. Sanguíneo, a.
full-blown [—ˈbləun] adj. Abierto, ta (flower). || Desarrollado, da (fully grown). || FIG. Verdadero, ra: *a full-blown scandal*, un verdadero escándalo. | Con todas las de la ley, hecho y derecho (full-fledged).
full-bodied [—ˈbɔdid] adj. Fuerte (person). || CULIN. De mucho cuerpo (wine).
full-bred [—bred] adj. De raza, de pura sangre. || *Full-bred horse*, caballo (*m.*) de pura sangre, pura sangre, *m.*
full-dress [—dres] adj. De etiqueta (clothes). || De gala (uniform). || De etiqueta, de gala (dinner). || FIG. Completo, ta. || *Full-dress rehearsal*, ensayo (*m.*) general.
fuller [—ə*] n. Abatanador, *m.* (of textiles). || Tajadera, *f.* (of blacksmith). || Estría, *f.* (groove). || — *Fuller's earth*, tierra (*f.*) de batán. || *Fuller's teasel* o *fuller's thistle*, cardencha, *f.*
fullface [—feis] n. PRINT. Negrita, *f.*
full-fashioned [—ˈfæʃənd] adj. U. S. Menguado, da (stockings, etc.).
full-fledged [—ˈfledʒd] adj. Con todas sus plumas (birds). || Desarrollado, da (fully grown). || FIG. Con todas las de la ley, hecho y derecho (doctor, lawyer, man, etc.). || *Full-fledged member*, miembro (*m.*) de pleno derecho.
full-grown [—ˈgrəun] adj. Crecido, da (tree). || Adulto, ta (person).
fullhearted [—ˈhɑ:tid] adj. Completo, ta.
full house [—ˈhaus] n. Full, *m.* (in card games). || Lleno, *m.* (in theatres, etc.). || No hay localidades (notice outside theatre).

full-length [—'leŋθ] adj. De cuerpo entero (portrait, mirror). || De tamaño normal (of the standard length). || *Full-length film*, largo metraje.
full-mouthed [—mauðd] adj. ZOOL. Que tiene todos sus dientes (cattle). || FAM. Sonoro, ra (loud).
fullness [—nis] n. Plenitud, *f*. || Amplitud, *f*. (of skirt). || Abundancia, *f*. (of details). || Riqueza, *f*. (of style). || *In the fullness of time*, a su debido tiempo (at the appointed time), con el tiempo (eventually).
full-scale [—'skeil] adj. De tamaño natural (drawing). || Completo, ta; total.
full-size [—'saiz] or **full-sized** [—'saizd] adj. De tamaño natural.
full stop [—'stɔp] n. Punto, *m*. (punctuation mark). || Punto (*m*.) final (at the end of text). || FIG. *To come to a full stop*, pararse.
full-swing [—swiŋ] adv. En plena actividad.
full tilt [—tilt] adv. A toda velocidad.
full-time [—'taim] adj. De jornada completa, de plena dedicación (job, employee, etc.).
— Adv. *To work full-time*, hacer la jornada completa.
fully ['fuli] adv. Completamente, enteramente (completely): *I fully agree with you*, estoy completamente de acuerdo con Ud. || Por lo menos (at least): *fully fifty people*, por lo menos cincuenta personas.
fully-fashioned [—'fæʃənd] adj. Menguado, da (stockings, etc.).
fulminant ['fʌlminənt] adj. MED. Fulminante.
fulminate ['fʌlmineit] v. intr. Fulminar, explotar, detonar. || FIG. *To fulminate against immorality*, tronar contra la inmoralidad.
— V. tr. Fulminar (decree, invectives, etc.). || Hacer explotar (to make explode).
fulminating [—iŋ] adj. Fulminante: *fulminating powder*, pólvora fulminante.
fulmination [ˌfʌlmi'neiʃən] n. Fulminación, *f*. || Detonación, *f*. (loud explosion).
fulness ['fulnis] n. See FULLNESS.
fulsome ['fulsəm] adj. Obsequioso, sa; servil (person). || Excesivo, va; exagerado, da (compliments). || Hipócrita (insincere).
fulsomeness [—nis] n. Hipocresía, *f*. (lack of sincerity). || Servilismo, *m*., obsequiosidad, *f*. (excessive deference).
fulvous ['fʌlvəs] adj. Leonado, da.
fumarole ['fju:məˌrəul] n. Fumarola, *f*.
fumble ['fʌmbl] n. Torpeza, *f*.
fumble ['fʌmbl] v. tr. Toquetear, manosear (to fiddle with). || Dejar caer (to drop). || — *To fumble one's way*, buscar su camino a tientas. || *To fumble the door open*, abrir la puerta torpemente.
— V. intr. Hurgar: *to fumble in a drawer, in one's pocket*, hurgar en un cajón, en el bolsillo. || Ir *or* andar a tientas (to feel one's way). || — *To fumble for*, buscar (words), buscar a tientas (an object). || *To fumble with*, manejar torpemente.
fumbler [—ə*] n. Torpe, *m*. & *f*.
fume [fju:m] n. Vapor, *m*.: *to give off fumes*, desprender vapores; *fumes of wine*, vapores de vino. || Gas, *m*. || — Pl. Humo, *m. sing.* (smoke): *factory fumes*, humo de las fábricas. || FIG. FAM. *To be in a fume*, estar bufando de cólera.
fume [fju:m] v. intr. Humear, echar humo (to give off smoke). || Echar *or* emitir vapores (to give off vapour). || Desprenderse (smoke, vapour). || FIG. Bufar de cólera (to be angry).
— V. tr. Ahumar (to expose to fumes).
fumigate ['fju:migeit] v. tr. Fumigar.
fumigation [ˌfjumi'geiʃən] n. Fumigación, *f*.
fumigator ['fjumigeitə*] n. Fumigador, *m*.
fumigatory [ˌfjumi'geitəri] adj. Fumigatorio, ria.
fun [fʌn] n. Alegría, *f*. (merriment): *full of fun*, lleno de alegría. || Gracia, *f*.: *to be poor fun*, no tener gracia; *I don't see the fun in that*, no le veo la gracia. || Diversión, *f*. (amusement). || — *All the fun of the fair*, todas las atracciones de la feria. || *For fun*, en broma (jokingly), para reírse (for a laugh). || *For the fun of it*, para reírse. || *In fun*, en broma. || FIG. FAM. *Like fun!*, ¡ni hablar! | *This is where the fun starts*, ahora nos vamos a divertir. || *To be great fun*, ser muy divertido. || *To have fun*, divertirse, pasarlo bien. || *To have great fun*, divertirse mucho, pasarlo en grande. || FAM. *To like one's bit of fun*, gustarle a uno bromear. || *To make fun of* o *to poke fun at*, reírse de. || *To spoil the fun*, aguar la fiesta. || *What fun!*, ¡qué divertido!

— OBSERV. La palabra *fun* nunca va precedida por el artículo *a*.

fun [fʌn] v. intr. U. S. FAM. Bromear.
funambulist [fju'næmbjulist] n. Funámbulo, la.
function ['fʌŋkʃən] n. Función, *f*. (purpose, duty, role): *to fulfil a function*, desempeñar una función. || Acto, *m*., solemnidad, *f*. (official ceremony). || Recepción, *f*. || REL. Ceremonia, *f*. || MATH. GRAMM. CHEM. Función, *f*. || ANAT. Función, *f*.: *functions of the heart*, funciones del corazón. || *In my function as a magistrate*, como magistrado, en mi calidad de magistrado.
function ['fʌŋkʃən] v. intr. Funcionar.
functional ['fʌŋkʃənl] adj. Funcional: *functional architecture*, arquitectura funcional.
functionary ['fʌŋkʃnəri] n. Funcionario, ria.
functioning ['fʌŋkʃəniŋ] n. Funcionamiento, *m*.

fund [fʌnd] n. COMM. Fondo, *m*.: *building fund*, fondo para la construcción; *International Monetary Fund*, Fondo Monetario Internacional. || Reserva, *f*. (reserve). || FIG. Fuente, *f*. (source): *to have a fund of anecdotes*, ser una fuente de anécdotas. | Fondo, *m*. (stock): *a fund of wisdom*, un fondo de sabiduría. || — Pl. Fondos, *m*. (resources): *available funds*, fondos disponibles. || Deuda (*f. sing.*) pública (government debt). || Fondos (*m. pl.*) públicos (public securities).
fund [fʌnd] v. tr. Consolidar (debt). || Colocar (to put in a fund). || Invertir (to invest).
fundament ['fʌndəmənt] n. Ano, *m*. (anus). || Trasero, *m*., nalgas, *f. pl.* (buttocks). || U. S. Fundamento, *m*., base, *f*.
fundamental [ˌfʌndə'mentl] adj. Fundamental.
— Pl. n. Fundamentos, *m*.
fundamentally [—i] adv. Fundamentalmente, esencialmente.
fundus ['fʌndʌs] n. ANAT. Fondo, *m*.

— OBSERV. El plural de *fundus* es *fundi*.

funeral ['fju:nərəl] n. Funeral, *m*., funerales, *m. pl.*, exequias, *f. pl.* (service). || Entierro, *m*. (burial). || Cortejo (*m*.) fúnebre (procession). || — *State funeral*, exequias nacionales. || FIG. FAM. *It's not my funeral*, me trae sin cuidado. | *That's his funeral*, allá él, con su pan se lo coma.
— Adj. Fúnebre: *funeral chant*, canto fúnebre; *funeral procession*, cortejo fúnebre; *funeral march*, marcha fúnebre. || Funerario, ria (urn). || — U. S. *Funeral home* o *parlor*, funeraria, *f*. || *Funeral pyre*, hoguera, *f*. || *Funeral service*, misa (*f*.) de "corpore insepulto" *or* de cuerpo presente.
funerary ['fju:nəreri] adj. Funerario, ria; funeral.
funereal [fju:'niəriəl] adj. Fúnebre (mournful).
fun fair [fʌn'fɛə*] n. Parque (*m*.) de atracciones.
fungi ['fʌŋgai] pl. n. See FUNGUS.
fungible ['fʌndʒibl] adj. JUR. Fungible.
fungicidal ['fʌndʒisaidl] adj. Fungicida.
fungicide ['fʌndʒisaid] n. Fungicida, *m*.
fungosity [fʌŋ'gɔsiti] n. Fungosidad, *f*.
fungous ['fʌŋgəs] adj. Fungoso, sa.
fungus ['fʌŋgəs] n. BOT. Hongo, *m*. || MED. Fungo, *m*.
— OBSERV. El plural de la palabra *fungus* es *fungi* o *funguses*.

funicular [fju:'nikjulə*] adj. Funicular. || *Funicular railway*, funicular, *m*.
— N. Funicular, *m*.
funiculus [fju:'nikjuləs] n. Cordón (*m*.) umbilical.

— OBSERV. El plural de la palabra inglesa es *funiculi*.

funk [fʌŋk] n. FAM. Canguelo, *m*., jindama, *f*. (state of fright): *to be in a funk*, tener canguelo. | Gallina, *m*. (coward).
funk [fʌŋk] v. tr. FAM. Tener miedo a *or* de (to fear). | Rajarse ante (to shirk).
— V. intr. FAM. Tener canguelo. | Rajarse.
funk hole [—həul] n. Trinchera, *f*., refugio (*m*.) subterráneo. || FAM. Refugio, *m*.
funky [—i] adj. FAM. Cobarde, cagueta (coward).
funnel ['fʌnl] n. Embudo, *m*. (for pouring liquids). || Chimenea, *f*. (of boat, steam engine). || Conducto, *m*. (of ventilation, etc.). || TECH. Tolva, *f*. (hopper).
funnel ['fʌnl] v. tr. Verter por un embudo. || Encauzar (to direct).
funneled [—d] adj. En forma de embudo.
funnies ['fʌniz] pl. n. U. S. FAM. Tiras (*f*.) cómicas (cartoon strips).
funnily ['fʌnili] adv. Graciosamente. || FAM. De una manera muy rara.
funny ['fʌni] adj. Divertido, da; gracioso, sa (amusing). || FAM. Raro, ra; extraño, ña (strange): *how funny!*, ¡qué raro!; *this tea tastes funny*, este té tiene un sabor extraño. | Raro, ra (ill): *I feel a bit funny*, me siento algo raro. || — *Don't get funny with me!*, ¡no te hagas el gracioso! || *He's just trying to be funny*, se está haciendo el gracioso. || FAM. *I came over all funny*, me sentí muy raro. | *I find it funny that*, me parece extraño que. | *It strikes me as funny that*, me resulta raro que. || *It was too funny for words*, era de lo más gracioso. || FAM. *Let's have no funny business*, no quiero cosas raras. | *That's funny!*, ¡qué raro! || *The funny part of it*, lo gracioso del caso. || *The funny thing about it is that*, lo raro *or* lo curioso del caso es que.
— N. MAR. Esquife, *m*.
funny bone [—bəun] n. Hueso (*m*.) de la alegría *or* de la suegra (in the elbow).
funnyman [—mæn] n. U. S. Cómico, *m*.
— OBSERV. El plural de esta palabra es *funnymen*.

funny papers [—'peipəz] pl. n. U. S. Tiras (*f*.) cómicas.
fur [fə:*] n. Pelo, *m*., pelaje, *m*. (of living animal). || Piel, *f*. (pelt). || Abrigo (*m*.) *or* chaqueta (*f*.) de piel *or* de pieles (coat). || Sarro, *m*. (in kettle). || Saburra, *f*., sarro, *m*. (on tongue). || Caza (*f*.) de pelo (in hunting). || FIG. *To make the fur fly*, armar la de Dios es Cristo.
— Adj. De pieles, de piel: *fur coat*, abrigo de pieles.
fur [fə:*] v. tr. Forrar con pieles (a coat). || Depositar sarro en, incrustar (to coat with a deposit). || Cubrir de sarro (tongue).
— V. intr. *To fur up*, cubrirse de sarro.
furbelow ['fə:biləu] n. Faralá, *m*. (flounce). || — Pl. FIG. Ringorrangos, *m*. (funny trimmings).

furbish [ˈfəːbiʃ] v. tr. Bruñir, acicalar, pulir (to polish). || *To furbish up*, renovar, restaurar (to renovate), pulir (to brush up).
furcate [ˈfəːkeit] adj. Ahorquillado, da (forked). || Hendido, da (hoof). || Bifurcado, da (road).
furcate [ˈfəːkeit] v. intr. Bifurcarse (a road).
furcation [fəːˈkeiʃən] n. Bifurcación, *f.*
furcula [ˈfəːkjulə] n. Espoleta, *f.* (wishbone).
— OBSERV. El plural de *furcula* es *furculae.*

Furies [ˈfjuəriz] pl. pr. n. MYTH. Furias, *f.*
furious [ˈfjuəriəs] adj. Furioso, sa: *he got furious*, se puso furioso. || Frenético, ca (frantic). || Violento, ta; furioso, sa (violent). || *At a furious pace*, a toda velocidad.
furl [fəːl] n. Rollo, *m.* (of paper, etc.).
furl [fəːl] v. tr. MAR. Aferrar (the sails). || Cerrar (a fan, an umbrella). || Poner a media asta (flag). || Recoger (wings). || Arrollar, enrollar (to roll up).
— V. intr. Enrollarse.
furlong [ˈfəːlɔŋ] n. Estadio, *m.*, medida (*f.*) de 201 metros.
furlough [ˈfəːləu] n. Permiso, *m.*: *to be on furlough*, estar de permiso.
furlough [ˈfəːləu] v. tr. Dar permiso a.
furnace [ˈfəːnis] n. Horno, *m.*: *blast furnace*, alto horno; *open-hearth furnace*, horno de hogar abierto; *reverberatory furnace*, horno de reverbero; *arc furnace*, horno de arco. || Hogar, *m.* (of boiler). || Estufa, *f.* (for domestic heating). || FIG. Horno, *m.* (hot place).
furnace [ˈfəːnis] v. tr. Calentar en un horno.
furnish [ˈfəːniʃ] v. tr. Amueblar (a house, room). || Suministrar, proporcionar, proveer (to supply): *to furnish the soldiers with food*, suministrar comida a los soldados, proveer a los soldados de comida. || Proporcionar, facilitar (to give). || Dar (an opportunity). || Equipar (to equip): *to furnish a fortress with guns*, equipar una fortaleza con cañones. || Aducir (proof). || *Furnished room*, cuarto amueblado.
furnisher [—ə*] n. Proveedor, *m.* (who supplies). || Vendedor (*m.*) de muebles (who sells furniture).
furnishings [—iŋz] pl. n. Muebles, *m.*, mobiliario, *m. sing.* (furniture). || Accesorios, *m.* (accessories). || U.S. Artículos, *m.*, ropa, *f. sing.* (things to wear): *men's furnishings*, artículos para caballeros.
furniture [ˈfəːnitʃə*] n. Muebles, *m. pl.*, mobiliario, *m.* (of a house). || Herraje, *m.* (of door). || Accesorios, *m. pl.* (accessories). || MAR. Aparejo, *m.* (of boat). || — *A piece of furniture*, un mueble. || *Furniture van*, camión (*m.*) de mudanzas. || *Furniture warehouse* o *furniture repository*, guardamuebles, *m. inv.* || *Set of furniture*, muebles, *m. pl.*, mobiliario, *m.*
furor [ˈfjuərɔː*] n. Furor, *m.*
furore [fjuəˈrɔːri] n. Furor, *m.* (enthusiasm): *to make* o *to create a furore*, hacer furor.
furrier [ˈfʌriə*] n. Peletero, *m.* || *Furrier's*, peletería, *f.*
furriery [ˈfʌriəri] n. Peletería, *f.*
furring [ˈfəːriŋ] n. Guarnición (*f.*) *or* forro (*m.*) de piel (trimming, lining). || TECH. Incrustación, *f.* (coating). | Desincrustación, *f.* (cleaning). || ARCH. Revestimiento, *m.* || Sarro, *m.* (on the tongue).
furrow [ˈfʌrəu] n. AGR. Surco, *m.* || Arruga, *f.* (on the face). || ARCH. Estría, *f.* || Ranura, *f.* (groove). || Surco, *m.* (of a ship).
furrow [ˈfʌrəu] v. tr. Surcar. || Arrugar (the face).
— V. intr. Arrugarse (one's face).
furry [ˈfəːri] adj. Peludo, da (hairy). || Sarroso, sa (tongue, deposit).
further [ˈfəːðə*] adj. Otro, otra (more distant): *on the further side of the river*, al otro lado del río. || Nuevo, va; otro, otra (new, another): *a further topic of conversation*, otro tema de conversación; *until further orders*, hasta nueva orden; *until further notice*, hasta nuevo aviso. || Otro, otra; adicional (additional): *further amendment*, enmienda adicional. || Otro, otra; más: *one further question*, una pregunta más, otra pregunta. || Ulterior, posterior (later): *further examination*, examen posterior. || Superior (education). || — *After further consideration*, después de examinarlo con más detenimiento. || COMM. *Further to my letter of the 1th*, con relación a mi carta del 1.
— Adv. Más lejos, más allá: *it is dangerous to go any further*, es peligroso ir más lejos. || Más: *to drive further south*, ir más al sur; *further back*, más atrás; *further off*, más lejos; *further down*, más abajo; *further on* o *along*, más adelante; *not to know any further*, no saber nada más. || Además (moreover): *let us further suppose that*, supongamos además que. || — *How much further?*, ¿qué distancia queda? || *To go further into*, estudiar más a fondo.
further [ˈfəːðə*] v. tr. Favorecer, fomentar: *to further understanding between nations*, favorecer la comprensión entre los pueblos.
furtherance [ˈfəːðərəns] n. Adelantamiento, *m.*, adelanto, *m.* (advancement). || Fomento, *m.* (promotion). || *In furtherance of*, para fomentar, para favorecer.
furthermore [ˈfəːðəˈmɔː*] adv. Además.
furthermost [ˈfəːðəməust] adj. Más lejano, na (most distant).
furthest [ˈfəːðist] adj. Más lejano, na (most distant). || Extremo, ma (extreme). || *To push sth. to its furthest limits*, llevar algo hasta el último extremo.
— Adv. Más lejos.

furtive [ˈfəːtiv] adj. Furtivo, va.
furuncle [ˈfjuərʌŋkl] n. MED. Furúnculo, *m.*
furunculosis [ˌfjurʌŋkjuˈləusis] n. MED. Furunculosis, *f.*
fury [ˈfjuəri] n. Furia, *f.*, furor, *m.* (anger). || Furia, *f.*: *the fury of the wind*, la furia del viento. || Violencia, *f.* (violence). || FIG. Furia, *f.* (angry woman). || — *Like fury*, furiosamente, con furia. || *To be in a fury*, estar hecho una furia.
furze [fəːz] n. BOT. Aulaga, *f.*, aliaga, *f.*
fusain [ˈfjuːzæn] n. Carboncillo, *m.* (charcoal). || Dibujo (*m.*) al carbón (drawing).
fuscous [ˈfʌskəs] adj. Pardo, da.
fuse [fjuːz] n. ELECTR. Fusible, *m.*, plomo, *m.* || Mecha, *f.* (piece of cord, etc.): *to light the fuse*, encender la mecha. || Espoleta, *f.* (detonating device): *the fuse of a grenade*, la espoleta de una granada. || *Fuse box*, caja (*f.*) de fusibles.
fuse [fjuːz] v. tr. Fundir (to melt). || Poner espoleta a (a missile). || FIG. Fusionar (to join together). || *To fuse the lights*, fundir los plomos.
— V. intr. Fundirse (to melt). || Fundirse: *the lights have fused*, se han fundido los plomos. || FIG. Fusionarse (to merge). || MED. Soldarse (broken bones).
fusee [fjuːˈzi] n. Caracol, *m.* (of clock). || Fósforo (*m.*) grande [que no apaga el viento] (match). || Señal (*f.*) luminosa (railway signal). || Sobrecaña, *f.* (of horse).
fuselage [ˈfjuːzilɑːʒ] n. Fuselaje, *m.* (of aircraft).
fusibility [ˌfjuːzəˈbiliti] n. Fusibilidad, *f.*
fusible [ˈfjuːzəbl] adj. Fusible, fundible.
fusilier or **fusileer** [ˌfjuːziˈliə*] n. MIL. Fusilero, *m.*
fusillade [ˌfjuːziˈleid] n. Descarga (*f.*) de fusilería (rapid fire). || Tiroteo, *m.* (repeated fire). || Fusilamiento, *m.* (execution). || FIG. Lluvia, *f.* (of questions).
fusillade [ˌfjuːziˈleid] v. tr. Fusilar (to shoot down). || Atacar con una descarga de fusilería (to attack).
fusion [ˈfjuːʒən] n. Fusión, *f.*: *fusion point*, punto de fusión. || Fusión, *f.*, fundición, *f.* (melting of metals). || FIG. Fusión, *f.* (union).
fusion bomb [—bɔm] n. Bomba (*f.*) termonuclear.
fuss [fʌs] n. Jaleo, *m.*, alboroto, *m.* (commotion): *what is all the fuss about?*, ¿por qué tanto jaleo? || Quejas, *f. pl.* (complaints): *let's have no more fuss from you*, déjate de quejas. || Lío, *m.* (trouble). || Remilgos, *m. pl.* (affectation): *after a great deal of fuss he accepted*, aceptó después de muchos remilgos. || Cumplidos, *m. pl.* (ceremony). || — *A lot of fuss about nothing*, mucho ruido y pocas nueces. || *It's not worth the fuss*, no vale *or* no merece la pena. || *There's no need to make such a fuss*, no es para tanto. || FAM. *To kick up a fuss* or *to make a great fuss*, armar un escándalo. || *To make a fuss of s.o.*, deshacerse en atenciones con alguien, mimar (to pay too much attention), encomiar (to praise). || *To make too much fuss of s.o.*, hacer cumplidos con alguien.
fuss [fʌs] v. intr. Preocuparse [por pequeñeces] (to worry). || Quejarse (to complain). || Agitarse (to bustle). || — *To fuss over s.o.*, deshacerse en atenciones con uno. || *To fuss with*, toquetear.
— V. tr. Molestar, fastidiar (to bother).
fussbudget [—ˌbʌdʒit] n. U. S. FAM. See FUSSPOT.
fussiness [ˈfʌsinis] n. Agitación, *f.* || Cumplidos, *m. pl.* (ceremony). || Afectación, *f.*, falta (*f.*) de sencillez (lack of simplicity).
fusspot [ˈfʌspɔt] n. FAM. Quisquilloso, sa (punctilious). | Remilgado, da; melindroso, sa (finicky). | Quejica, *m.* & *f.* (who complains). | Persona (*f.*) que anda con cumplidos (lacking simplicity).
fussy [ˈfʌsi] adj. Exigente (exacting). || Delicado, da; escrupuloso, sa (about food). || Quisquilloso, sa (punctilious). || Remilgado, da; melindroso, sa (finicky). || Que anda con cumplidos (lacking simplicity). || Rebuscado, da; recargado, da (overornate). || Nervioso, sa (nervous).
fustian [ˈfʌstiən] n. Fustán, *m.* (cloth). || Grandilocuencia, *f.*, prosopopeya, *f.* (pomposity).
— Adj. De fustán (made of fustian). || Ampuloso, sa; grandilocuente (pompous).
fustigate [ˈfʌstigeit] v. tr. Fustigar.
fusty [ˈfʌsti] adj. Mohoso, sa (musty). || Que huele a cerrado (stale-smelling). || Anticuado, da; chapado a la antigua (olf-fashioned).
futile [ˈfjuːtail] adj. Inútil, vano, na (vain): *a futile attempt*, un intento vano. || Frívolo, la; fútil (frivolous). || Pueril (childish).
futility [fjuːˈtiliti] n. Inutilidad, *f.* (uselessness). || Frivolidad, *f.*, futileza, *f.*, futilidad, *f.* (frivolity).
futtock [ˈfʌtək] n. MAR. Genol, *m.*
future [ˈfjuːtʃə*] adj. Futuro, ra: *future events*, sucesos futuros; *future wife*, futura esposa. || Venidero ra; futuro, ra (days, years, etc.). || GRAMM. Futuro (tense).
— N. Futuro, *m.*, porvenir, *m.* || GRAMM. Futuro, *m.* (tense). || FIG. Porvenir, *m.* (situation). || FAM. Futuro, ra (fiancé). || — Pl. COMM. Futuros, *m.*, entregas (*f.*) a plazo. || — GRAMM. *Future perfect*, futuro perfecto *or* anterior. || *In (the) future*, en lo futuro, en el futuro, en lo sucesivo. || *In the near future*, en un futuro próximo.
futurism [ˈfjuːtʃərizəm] n. Futurismo, *m.*
futurist [ˈfjuːtʃərist] adj./n. Futurista.
futuristic [fjuːtʃəˈristik] adj. Futurista.
futurity [fjuːˈtjuəriti] n. Futuro, *m.* (future). || Suceso (*m.*) futuro (future event). || REL. Vida (*f.*) futura.

fuze [fju:z] n. Mecha, *f.* (made of cord, etc.): *to light the fuze*, encender la mecha. || Espoleta, *f.* (detonating device): *the fuze of a grenade*, la espoleta de una granada.
fuze [fju:z] v. tr. Poner espoleta a (a missile).
fuzee [fju:ˊzi:] n. See FUSEE.
fuzz [fʌz] n. Pelusa, *f.* (fluff). || Borra, *f.* (of cotton plant). || Vello, *m.* (on face). || Aspecto (*m.*) borroso (blurred effect). || FAM. Poli, *f.*, policía, *f.*
fuzz [fʌz] v. intr. Soltar pelusa: *this wool tends to fuzz*, esta lana tiene tendencia a soltar pelusa. || Volverse borroso (to get blurred).
— V. tr. Empañar (to blur).
fuzzy [ˊfʌzi] adj. Rizado, da (very curly). || Deshilachado, da (frayed). || Velloso, sa (fluffy). || Borroso, sa (blurred).
fylfot [ˊfilfɔt] n. Esvástica, *f.*, cruz (*f.*) gamada.

G

g [dʒi:] n. G, *f.* (letter of the alphabet).
G n. MUS. Sol, *m.*
gab [gæb] n. FAM. Palique, *m.* (chatter). || — FAM. *Stop your gab*, cierra el pico. | *To have the gift of the gab*, tener mucha labia.
gab [gæb] v. intr. FAM. Estar de palique, charlotear.
gabardine [ˊgæbədi:n] n. Gabardina, *f.*
gabble [ˊgæbl] n. FAM. Farfulla, *f.*, habla (*f.*) atropellada. | Charloteo, *m.* (chatter).
gabble [ˊgæbl] v. intr. FAM. Farfullar, hablar atropelladamente (to jabber). | Charlotear (to chatter).
— V. tr. FAM. Decir atropelladamente (to say).
gabby [ˊgæbi] n. U. S. FAM. Charlatán, ana; parlanchín, ina.
gaberdine [ˊgæbədi:n] n. Gabardina, *f.*
gabion [ˊgeibjən] n. MIL. Gavión, *m.*
gable [geibl] n. ARCH. Aguilón, *m.*, gablete, *m.* || — *Gable end*, hastial, *m.* || *Gable roof*, tejado (*m.*) de dos aguas.
Gabon [ˊgæbən] pr. n. GEOGR. Gabón, *m.*
Gabriel [ˊgeibriəl] pr. n. Gabriel, *m.*
Gabriella [ˊgeibriələ] pr. n. Gabriela, *f.*
gaby [ˊgeibi] n. FAM. Mentecato, ta.
gad [gæd] n. AGR. Aguijón, *m.* || Barra (*f.*) puntiaguda (bar). || Cuña, *f.* (wedge). || FIG. FAM. Callejeo, *m.* (stroll). || *Gad!*, ¡caramba!, ¡cáspita!
gad [gæd] v. intr. *To gad about*, callejear, ir de acá para allá (to stroll).
gadabout [ˊgædəbaut] n. Callejero, ra; trotacalles, *m.* & *f. inv.*, azotacalles, *m.* & *f. inv.*
gadfly [ˊgædflai] n. ZOOL. Tábano, *m.* || FAM. Persona (*f.*) molesta.
gadget [ˊgædʒit] n. Artilugio, *m.*, chisme, *m.* (article of little importance). || Aparato, *m.*, dispositivo, *m.* (device).
gadid [ˊgeidid] or **gadoid** [ˊgeidɔid] adj. Gádido, da.
— N. Gádido, *m.*
Gaditan [gæditən] adj./n. Gaditano, na.
gadolinium [ˌgædəˊlinjəm] n. Gadolinio, *m.*
gadroon [gəˊdru:n] n. ARCH. Moldura (*f.*) ovalada, gallón, *m.*
Gael [geil] n. Gaélico, ca.
Gaelic [ˊgeilik] adj. Gaélico, ca.
— N. Gaélico, *m.* (language).
gaff [gæf] n. Arpón, *m.*, garfio, *m.* (harpoon). || MAR. Cangrejo, *m.* || FAM. Teatrucho, *m.* (theatre). || Espolón (of fighting cock). || — *Gaff sail*, vela (*f.*) cangreja. || FAM. *To blow the gaff*, descubrir el pastel. | *To stand the gaff*, tener aguante.
gaff [gæf] v. tr. Arponear (fish). || Poner un espolón de acero (a fighting cock). || U. S. FAM. Engañar.
gaffe [gæf] n. *To make a gaffe*, meter la pata, tirarse una plancha.
gaffer [ˊgæfə*] n. FAM. Tío, *m.* (fellow). | Jefe, *m.* (boss). | Capataz, *m.* (foreman).
gag [gæg] n. Mordaza, *f.* (to stop s.o. from speaking). || Supresión (*f.*) de la libertad de expresión (prevention of freedom of speech). || Broma, *f.* (hoax). || "Gag", *m.*, chiste, *m.* (joke). || Truco, *m.* (trick). || Clausura (*f.*) de un debate (closure of a debate). || THEATR. Morcilla, *m.* (ad lib).
gag [gæg] v. tr. Amordazar (to prevent from speaking). || Dar náuseas a (to nauseate). || Clausurar (to close). || Obstruir (to obstruct). || FIG. Hacer callar, amordazar.
— V. intr. THEATR. Meter morcilla. || Tener náuseas (to retch). || Bromear (to joke).
gaga [ˊgɑ:gɑ:] adj. FAM. Chocho, cha. || — FAM. *To be going gaga*, chochear. | *To go gaga over*, encapricharse por, volverse chocho por.
gage [geidʒ] n. Desafío, *m.* (challenge). || Prenda, *f.*, garantía, *f.* (pledge). || See GAUGE.
gage [geidʒ] v. tr. Dar como garantía, dar en prenda (to pledge). || FIG. Comprometer. || See GAUGE.
gaggle [ˊgægəl] n. Manada, *f.* (of geese). || FIG. FAM. *A gaggle of housewives*, un corro de comadres.
gaggle [ˊgægəl] v. intr. Graznar (geese).
gaiety [ˊgeiəti] n. Alegría, *f.* || *Gaieties*, regocijos, *m.*, diversiones, *f.*
gain [gein] n. Ganancia, *f.*, beneficio, *m.* (winnings). || Aumento, *m.* (increase): *gain in weight*, aumento de peso. || Ventaja, *f.* (advantage). || Muesca, *f.* (notch).
gain [gein] v. tr. Ganar (to win, to earn). || Llegar a, alcanzar, ganar (to reach). || Conseguir (to obtain). || Recobrar, recuperar (the balance). || Adquirir (to acquire). || Conquistar (to conquer). || Granjearse, captarse (s.o.'s affection, etc.). || Adelantar (a clock). || — *To gain ground*, ganar terreno. || *To gain the upper hand*, tomar la ventaja. || *To gain time*, ganar tiempo. || *You have gained weight*, has engordado.
— V. intr. Adelantar (a clock). || Mejorar (to improve). || Ganar: *to gain by the change*, ganar con el cambio. || Aumentar, acrecentar (to increase). || Subir (shares). || — *To gain in prestige*, ganar prestigio. || *To gain in weight*, engordar. || *To gain on*, ganar terreno a.
gainer [—ə*] n. Ganador, ra. || *To be the gainer*, salir ganando.
gainful [ˊgeinful] adj. Ganancioso, sa; remunerador, ra; lucrativo, va (profitable).
gainings [ˊgeiniŋz] pl. n. Ganancias, *f.*, beneficios, *m.*
gainsay [geinˊsei] v. tr. Negar: *I don't gainsay it*, no lo niego.
gait [geit] n. Andares, *m. pl.*, paso, *m.*, modo (*m.*) de andar: *with unsteady gait*, con paso poco seguro.
gaiter [ˊgeitə*] n. Polaina, *f.*
gal [gæl] n. PHYS. Gal, *m.* || FAM. Chica, *f.* (girl).
gala [ˊgɑ:lə] n. Gala, *f.*, fiesta, *f.* || SP. Competición, *f.* || — *Gala dress*, traje (*m.*) de etiqueta. || *Gala performance*, función (*f.*) de gala.
galactic [gəˊlæktik] adj. ASTR. Galáctico, ca. || MED. Lácteo, a.
galactose [gəˊlæktəus] n. CHEM. Galactosa, *f.*
galalith [ˊgæləliθ] n. Galalita, *f.*
galantine [ˊgælənti:n] n. CULIN. Galantina, *f.*
galanty show [gəˊlæntiʃəu] n. Sombras (*f. pl.*) chinescas.
Galápagos Islands [gəˊlæpəgəsˊailəndz] pl. n. GEOGR. Islas (*f.*) Galápagos.
galaxy [ˊgæləksi] n. ASTR. Galaxia, *f.* || FIG. Constelación, *f.*, pléyade, *f.*
gale [geil] n. Vendaval *m.* (strong wind). || Tempestad, *f.* (storm). || FIG. *Gales of laughter*, carcajadas, *f.*
galena [gəˊli:nə] n. MIN. Galena, *f.*
Galicia [gəˊliʃiə] pr. n. GEOGR. Galicia, *f.* (in Spain). | Galitzia, *f.* (in Central Europe).
Galician [—n] adj. Gallego, ga; galaico, ca.
— N. Gallego, ga (inhabitant of Galicia, Spain). || Gallego, *m.* (language of Galicia, Spain).
Galician [—n] adj. De Galitzia.
— N. Habitante (*m.* & *f.*) de Galitzia.
Galilean [ˌgæliˊliən] adj./n. Galileo, a.
Galilee [ˊgælili:] pr. n. GEOGR. Galilea, *f.*
galipot [ˊgælipɔt] n. Galipote, *m.*
gall [gɔ:l] n. VET. Matadura, *f.*, rozadura, *f.* (injury to a horse's skin). || ANAT. Vesícula (*f.*) biliar (gallbladder). || Bilis, *f.* (bile). || Hiel, *f.* (of an animal). || BOT. Agalla, *f.* (unnatural growth). || FAM. Descaro, *m.*, frescura, *f.*, caradura, *f.* (cheek). || FIG. Amargura, *f.*, hiel, *f.* (bitterness). | Herida (*f.*) en el amor propio (in s.o.'s pride).
gall [gɔ:l] v. tr. VET. Hacer una matadura *or* una rozadura, excoriar (to chafe). || FIG. Molestar (to annoy). | Herir en el amor propio (to mortify).
gallant [ˊgælənt] adj. Valiente, valeroso, sa (courageous). || Elegante, garboso, sa (stately in appearance). || Atento, ta (attentive). || Galante (attentive towards women). || Lucido, da (showy). || Espléndido, da; noble (steed). || De amor (poem).

— N. Elegante, *m.* (man of fashion). || Galán, *m.* (ladies' man).
gallant [ˈgælənt] v. tr. Galantear.
— V. intr. Ser galante.
gallantry [ˈgæləntri] n. Cortesía, *f.* (courtesy). || Galantería, *f.* (chivalrous attention, compliment). || Valor, *m.*, valentía, *f.* (courage). || Heroísmo, *m.* (heroism).
gallbladder [ˈgɔ:l,blædə*] n. ANAT. Vesícula (*f.*) biliar.
galleass [ˈgæliəs] n. MAR. Galeaza, *f.*
galleon [ˈgæliən] n. MAR. Galeón, *m.*
gallery [ˈgæləri] n. Galería, *f.* || Tribuna, *f.* (for spectators). || THEATR. Gallinero, *m.*, paraíso, *m.* || Museo, *m.* (museum). || Galería, *f.* (for works of art). || Galería, *f.* (in mining). || MAR. Galería, *f.* || FIG. *To play to the gallery*, actuar para la galería.
galley [ˈgæli] n. MAR. Galera, *f.* | Cocina, *f.* (kitchen). || PRINT. Galera, *f.* (tray for holding composed type). | Galerada, *f.* (galley proof). || — Pl. Galeras, *f.*: *to condemn to the galleys*, condenar a galeras.
galley proof [—pru:f] n. PRINT. Galerada, *f.*
galley slave [—sleiv] n. Galeote, *m.*
galliard [ˈgæljəd] n. Gallarda, *f.* (dance).
galliass [ˈgæliəs] n. MAR. Galeaza, *f.*
gallic [ˈgælik] adj. CHEM. Gálico, ca.
Gallic [ˈgælik] adj. Gálico, ca; galo, la.
Gallican [ˈgælikən] adj. Galicano, na.
Gallicanism [—izəm] n. Galicanismo, *m.*
Gallicism [ˈgælisizəm] n. GRAMM. Galicismo, *m.*
gallicize [ˈgælisaiz] v. tr. Afrancesar.
— V. intr. Afrancesarse.
gallimaufry [,gæliˈmɔ:fri] n. Mescolanza, *f.*
gallinacean [,gæliˈneiʃən] n. Gallinácea, *f.*
gallinaceous [,gæliˈneiʃəs] adj. ZOOL. Gallináceo, a.
galling [gɔ:liŋ] adj. Mortificante, irritante.
gallinule [ˈgælinju:l] n. ZOOL. Polla (*f.*) de agua.
galliot [ˈgæliət] n. MAR. Galeota, *f.*
gallipot [ˈgælipɔt] n. Galipote, *m.*
gallium [ˈgæljəm] n. CHEM. Galio, *m.*
gallivant [,gæliˈvænt] v. intr. Corretear, callejea (to gad about).
gallon [ˈgælən] n. Gaión, *m.* [medida de líquido equivalente a 4,55 litros en Inglaterra y a 3,79 litros en E.E. U.U.].
galloon [gəˈlu:n] n. Galón, *m.* (braid).
gallop [ˈgæləp] n. Galope, *m.*: *hand gallop*, galope medio *o* sostenido. || — *At a gallop*, a galope. || *At full gallop*, a galope tendido. || *To go at a galop*, galopar, ir a galope.
gallop [ˈgæləp] v. intr. Galopar. || FIG. FAM. *To gallop through a book*, leer un libro por encima.
— V. tr. Hacer galopar.
galloping [ˈgæləpiŋ] adj. Galopante. || MED. *Galloping consumption*, tisis (*f.*) galopante.
Gallo-Roman [ˈgæləuˈrəumən] adj. Galorromano, na.
gallows [ˈgæləuz] pl. n. Cadalso, *m. sing.*, patíbulo, *m. sing.*, horca, *f. sing.* (for those condemned to death). || MIN. Castillete (*m. sing.*) de extracción.
gallows bird [ˈgæləuzbə:d] n. FAM. Carne (*f.*) de horca.
gallstone [ˈgɔ:lstəun] n. MED. Cálculo (*m.*) biliar.
Gallup poll [ˈgæləppəul] n. Sondeo (*m.*) de la opinión pública.
galluses [ˈgæləsiz] pl. n. FAM. Tirantes, *m.*
galop [ˈgæləp] n. Galop, *m.* (dance).
galore [gəˈlɔ:*] adj./adv. En cantidad, en abundancia.
galosh [gəˈlɔʃ] n. Chanclo, *m.*
galumph [gəˈlʌmf] v. intr. FAM. Dar saltos de alegría.
galvanic [gælˈvænik] adj. PHYS. Galvánico, ca. || FIG. Forzado, da (smile).
galvanism [ˈgælvənizəm] n. PHYS. Galvanismo, *m.*
galvanization [,gælvənaiˈzeiʃən] n. PHYS. Galvanización, *f.*
galvanize [ˈgælvənaiz] v. tr. PHYS. Galvanizar. || FIG. Galvanizar.
galvanocautery [ˈgælvənɔˈkɔ:təri] n. MED. Galvanocauterio, *m.*
galvanometer [,gælvəˈnɔmitə*] n. Galvanómetro, *m.*
galvanoplastic [,gælvənɔˈplæstik] adj. Galvanoplástico, ca.
galvanoplastics [—s] or **galvanoplasty** [—ti] n. Galvanoplastia, *f.*
gam [gæm] n. Manada (*f.*) de ballenas. || FAM. Pierna, *f.* (leg).
gam [gæm] v. intr. Formar una banda (ballenas).
gamba [ˈgæmbə] n. MUS. Viola (*f.*) de gamba.
gambado [gæmˈbeidəu] n. Brinco, *m.* (of horse). || FIG. Travesura, *f.* (a prank).
gambit [ˈgæmbit] n. Gambito, *m.* (in chess). || FIG. Táctica, *f.*, estratagema, *f.*
gamble [ˈgæmbl] n. Jugada, *f.* (game). || Empresa, (*f.*) arriesgada (risky undertaking).
gamble [ˈgæmbl] v. tr. Arriesgar (to risk). || Jugar, apostar (to bet). || *To gamble away*, perder en el juego.
— V. intr. Jugar (to play for money). || Arriesgarse (to take a risk). || FIG. *To gamble on*, confiar en [que], contar con.
gambler [—ə*] n. Jugador, ra.
gambling [—iŋ] n. Juego, *m.* || — *Gambling den*, garito, *m.* || *Gambling game*, juego de envite. || *Gambling house*, casa (*f.*) de juego.
gamboge [gæmˈbu:ʒ] n. Gutagamba, *f.*
gambol [ˈgæmbəl] n. Brinco, *m.*
gambol [ˈgæmbəl] v. intr. Brincar, saltar.
gambrel [gæmbrəl] n. Garabato, *m.* (butcher's hook). || ZOOL. Corvejón, *m.* || ARCH. Cubierta (*f.*) a la holandesa (roof).
game [geim] n. Juego, *m.* (for amusement): *game of chance*, juego de azar. || Juego, *m.*: *Olympic games*, juegos olímpicos. || Deporte, *m.* (sport). || Partido, *m.* (in football, baseball, basket, tennis etc.). || Juego, *m.* (in tennis, part of a match). || Juego, *m.* (player's style). || Partida, *f.* (cards, chess, etc.): *to have o to play a game of billiards*, jugar una partida de billar. || Manga, *f.* (bridge). || Caza, *f.* (in hunting). || FAM. Lío, *m.* (fuss). || FIG. Juego, *m.*: *he saw through your game*, vio su juego; *to spoil s.o.'s game*, estropear el juego de uno. || — *Big game*, caza mayor. || FAM. *Fair game for*, buena presa para. || *Game of forfeits*, juego de prendas. || U. S. *Game warden*, guardabosque, *m.*, guarda (*m.*) de caza. || FIG. *Off one's game*, en baja forma. | *Paying game*, empresa lucrativa. | *The game is up!*, ¡se acabó! || *To be game*, haber ganado. || *To be game all*, estar empatados. || FAM. *To be on the game*, ser una mujer de vida alegre. || FIG. *To be on to s.o.'s game*, conocer el juego de alguien. | *To give the game away*, descubrir las cartas. | *To have the game in one's hands*, tener todas las bazas en la mano. | *To make game of*, tomar a broma, burlarse de. | *To play a double game*, hacer doble juego. || *To play a good game*, jugar bien. || FIG. *To play s.o.'s game*, hacer el juego de alguien, servir los propósitos de uno. | *To play the game*, jugar limpio, actuar honradamente. || FAM. *What's your game?*, ¿qué haces?
— Adj. De caza (of hunting). || Valiente (brave). || Tullido, da; lisiado, da (a limb). || — *Are you game?*, ¿te animas? || *To be game for anything*, no tener miedo a nada.
game [geim] v. intr./tr. Jugar.
gamebag [—bæg] n. Morral, *m.* (of hunter).
game bird [—bə:d] n. Ave (*f.*) de caza.
gamecock [—kɔk] n. Gallo (*m.*) de pelea *or* de riña.
gamekeeper [—,ki:pə*] n. Guardabosque, *m.*, guarda (*m.*) de caza, guardamonte, *m.*
game licence [—,laisəns] n. Licencia (*f.*) de caza.
gameness [—nis] n. Valentía, *f.*, valor, *m.*
game preserve [—priˈzə:v] n. Coto (*m.*) de caza, vedado (*m.*) de caza.
gamesome [—səm] adj. Alegre, retozón, ona.
gamester [—stə*] n. Jugador, ra.
gamete [ˈgæmi:t] n. BIOL. Gameto, *m.*
game warden [ˈgeimˈwɔ:dn] n. Guardabosque, *m.*, guarda (*m.*) de caza, guardamonte, *m.*
gamey [ˈgeimi] adj. See GAMY.
gamin [ˈgæmən] n. Golfillo, *m.*
gamine [gæˈmi:n] n. Golfilla, *f.*
gaming [ˈgeimiŋ] n. Juego, *m.*: *gaming house*, casa de juego.
gamma [ˈgæmə] n. Gamma, *f.* || PHYS. *Gamma rays*, rayos (*m. pl.*) gamma.
gammadion [gəˈmeidi:ən] or **gammation** [gəˈmeiʃi:ən] n. Cruz (*f.*) gamada.
— OBSERV. El plural es *gammadia* y *gammatia*.
gammer [ˈgæmə*] n. FAM. Abuela, *f.*, tía, *f.*: *gammer Smith*, la tía Smith.
gammon [ˈgæmən] n. Jamón (*m.*) ahumado (ham). || Tocino (*m.*) ahumado (bacon). || FAM. Mentira, *f.* (lie).
gammon [ˈgæmən] v. tr. Curar [jamón] (ham). || MAR. Trincar. || FAM. Engañar.
— V. intr. FAM. Bromear (to joke). | Fingir (to feign).
gammy [ˈgæmi] adj. FAM. Tullido, da; lisiado, da.
gamopetalous [gæməˈpetələs] adj. Gamopétalo, la.
gamosepalous [,gæməˈsepələs] adj. Gamosépalo, la.
gamp [gæmp] n. FAM. Paraguas, *m. inv.*
gamut [ˈgæmət] n. MUS. Gama, *f.* || FIG. Gama, *f.*, serie, *f.*
gamy [ˈgeimi] adj. Manido, da (meat). || Abundante en caza (wood). || Valiente (courageous). || U. S. Picante, salaz (spicy).
gander [ˈgændə*] n. Ganso, *m.* (goose). || FAM. Mentecato, ta; papanatas, *m. & f. inv.* (idiot). || U. S. FAM. Ojeada, *f.*: *he took a gander at*, echó una ojeada a.
gang [gæŋ] n. Cuadrilla, *f.*, brigada, *f.*, equipo, *m.* (of workers). || Pandilla, *f.*, cuadrilla, *f.* (a band of people who go round together). || Banda, *f.*, gang, *m.* (of gangsters). || Juego, *m.* (of tools). || MIN. Ganga, *f.*
gang [gæŋ] v. intr. Ir (in Scottish). || — *To gang up*, agruparse. || *To gang up on*, conspirar contra, confabularse contra, unirse contra (to conspire against), atacar en grupo (to attack in a gang). || *To gang up with*, unirse a.
ganged [—d] adj. Acoplado, da.
ganger [—ə*] n. Capataz, *m.*, jefe (*m.*) de equipo.
Ganges [ˈgændʒi:z] pr. n. GEOGR. Ganges, *m.*
gang hook [ˈgæŋhuk] n. Anzuelo (*m.*) múltiple.
gangling [ˈgæŋgliŋ] adj. FAM. Larguirucho, cha.
ganglion [ˈgæŋgliən] n. MED. ANAT. Ganglio, *m.* || FIG. Centro, *m.*, foco, *m.* (of activity).
— OBSERV. El plural de *ganglion* es *ganglions* o *ganglia*.
gangly [ˈgæŋgli] adj. U. S. FAM. Larguirucho, cha.
gangplank [ˈgæŋplænk] n. MAR. Plancha, *f.*
gangrene [ˈgæŋgri:n] n. MED. Gangrena, *f.*

GAMES — JUEGOS, m.

I. Parlour games [U.S., parlor games]. — Juegos (m.) de sociedad.

player	jugador, ra
forfeits	juego (*m.*) de prendas
charade	charada *f.*
blindman's buff	gallina (*f.*) ciega
hunt-the-thimble	zurriago (*m.*) escondido
puss-in-the-corner	las cuatro esquinas *f.*
guessing game	acertijo *m.*, adivinanza *f.*
noughts-and-crosses	tres en raya *m.*
battleships	batalla (*f. sing.*) naval
crossword puzzle	crucigrama *m.*, palabras (*f. pl.*) cruzadas
riddle	rompecabezas *m. inv.*
ludo	parchís *m. inv.*, parchesi *m.*
snakes and ladders	juego (*m.*) de la oca
monopoly	monópolis *m.*
lotto	lotería *f.*
dominoes	dominó *m.*
domino	ficha *f.*
double blank	blanca (*f.*) doble
solitaire	solitario *m.*
bingo, lotto	lotería *f.*

II. Chess and draughts. — Ajedrez (m.) y damas, f. pl.

draughts [U.S., checkers]	damas *f. pl.*
board	tablero *m.*
draughtboard [U.S., checkerboard]	damero *m.*
square	casilla *f.*, escaque *m.*
man, piece	pieza *f.*
king	dama *f.*
to crown	coronar
to take	comer
to huff	soplar
chess	ajedrez *m.*
chess player	ajedrecista *m.* & *f.*
start	salida *f.*
gambit	gambito *m.*
castling	enroque *m.*
check	jaque *m.*
mate	mate *m.*
checkmate	jaque mate *m.*
king	rey *m.*
queen	reina *f.*
castle, rook	torre *f.*
knight	caballo *m.*
bishop	alfil *m.*
pawn	peón *m.*
to block	encerrar
to mate, to checkmate	dar mate, dar jaque y mate
to draw	hacer tablas
to win; to lose	ganar; perder

III. Games of chance. — Juegos (m.) de azar.

card games	juegos (*m.*) de cartas
cards	cartas *f.*, naipes *m.*
pack (of cards), deck	baraja *f.*
suit	palo *m.*
joker	comodín *m.*
ace	as *m.*
king	rey *m.*
queen	reina *f.*
Jack	jota *f.*
face cards, court cards	figuras *f.*
clubs	trébol *m. sing.*
diamonds	diamante *m. sing.*
hearts	corazón *m. sing.*
spades	pico *m. sing.*
trumps	triunfos *m.*
to shuffle	barajar
to cut	cortar
to deal	dar, distribuir, repartir
banker	banquero *m.*
hand	mano *m.*
to lead	salir
to lay	poner
to follow suit	servir del palo
to trump	fallar
to overtrump	contrafallar
to win a trick	ganar una baza
to pick up, to draw	robar
stake	apuesta *f.*, puesta *f.*
to stake	apostar
to raise	envidar
to see	aceptar (bet)
bid	declaración *f.*
to bid	declarar
bluff	farol *m.*
to bluff	tirarse un farol
royal flush	escalera (*f.*) real
straight flush	escalera (*f.*) de color
straight	escalera *f.*
four of a kind	póker *m.*
full house	full *m.*
three of a kind	trío *m.*
two pairs	doble pareja *f. sing.*
one pair	pareja *f.*
to go banco	copar la banca
bank	banca *f.*
martingale	martingala *f.*
poker	póquer *m.*, póker *m.*
chemin-de-fer	chemin-de-fer *m.*
baccarat	bacarrá *m.*, bacará *m.*
shoe	carrito *m.*
whist	whist *m.*
bridge	bridge *m.*
rummy	rami *m.*
canasta	canasta *f.*
old maid	mona *f.*
beggar-my-neighbour	guerrilla *f.*
patience	solitario *m.*
roulette	ruleta *f.*
dice	dados *m.*

IV. Children's games. — Juegos (m.) infantiles.

tin soldiers, toy soldiers	soldaditos (*m.*) de plomo
trainset	tren *m.*
cowboys and Indians	vaqueros (*m.*) e indios *m.*
catapult [U.S., slingshot]	tiragomas *m. inv.*, tirador *m.*, tirachinos *m. inv.*
cops and robbers	justicias y ladrones *m.*
peashooter	tirabala *m.*
popgun	fusil (*m.*) de juguete
doll	muñeca *f.*
doll's house	casa (*f.*) de muñecas
to skip	saltar a la comba
skipping rope	comba *f.*
ball	pelota *f.*
tag	pillapilla *m.*
hide and seek	escondite *m.*
hopscotch	tejo *m*, infernáculo *m.*
marbles	canicas *f.*, bolas *f.*
dibs [U.S., jacks]	tabas *f.*
hoop	aro *m.*
stilts	zancos *m.*
spinning top	peonza *f.*, trompo *m.*
kite	cometa *f.*
plasticene, plasticine	arcilla (*f.*) de modelar
meccano	mecano *m.*
aeromodelling	aeromodelismo *m.*
scooter	patineta *f.*
swing	columpio *m.*
slide	tobogán *m.*
sledge [U.S., sled]	trineo *m.*
snowball	bola (*f.*) de nieve
snowman	muñeco (*m.*) de nieve
yo-yo	yoyo *m.*
diabolo	diábolo *m.*, diávolo *m.*

V. Other games. — Otros juegos, m.

darts	dardos *m.*
dartboard	blanco *m.*
quoits	tejo *m.*, chito *m.*
bowls	bochas *f.*
jack	boliche *m.*
tenpins, bowling, skittles	bolos *m. pl.*
billiards	billar *m.*
snooker	billar (*m.*) ruso
cue	taco (*m.*) de billar
pocket	tronera *f.*
table tennis	ping-pong, tenis (*m.*) de mesa
racket	raqueta *f.*
net	red, *f.*
croquet	croquet *m.*

See also DEPORTE and ENTERTAINMENTS

gangrene [ˈgæŋgri:n] v. intr. Gangrenarse.
— V. tr. Gangrenar.
gangrenous [ˈgæŋgrenəs] adj. MED. Gangrenoso, sa.
gangster [ˈgæŋstə*] n. Gángster, *m.*, pistolero, *m.*
gangsterism [—rizəm] n. Gangsterismo, *m.*, bandidaje, *m.* (organized use of violence).
gangue [gæŋ] n. MIN. Ganga, *f.*
gangway [—wei] n. Pasillo, *m.* (passage between rows of seats, etc.). || MAR. Plancha, *f.* (gangplank). | Portalón, *m.* (opening). | Pasamano, *m.* (platform between forecastle and quarterdeck). | Pasarela, *f.* (for disembarking). || THEATR. Pasarela, *f.* || *Gangway!*, ¡paso!
gannet [ˈgænit] n. ZOOL. Alcatraz, *m.* (bird).
gantry [ˈgæntri] n. Caballete, *m.* (for barrels). || Pórtico, *m.* (for crane). || Torre (*f.*) de lanzamiento (of rockets). || *Gantry crane*, grúa (*f.*) de pórtico.
gaol [dʒeil] n. Cárcel, *f.*
gaol [dʒeil] v. tr. Encarcelar.
gaolbird [—bə:d] n. Presidiario (*m.*) reincidente, preso (*m.*) reincidente.
gaolbreak [—breik] n. Evasión, *f.*, fuga, *f.*
gaoler [—ə*] n. Carcelero, *m.*
gap [gæp] n. Portillo, *m.* (in a wall). || Brecha, *f.*, boquete, *m.* (breach). || Desfiladero, *m.*, quebrada, *f.* (between mountains). || Hueco, *m.* (cavity). || Resquicio, *m.* (crack). || Espacio, *m.* (in writing). || Vacío, *m.* (unfilled space). || Laguna, *f.* (in text, s.o.'s education). || Intervalo, *m.* (of time). || Claro, *m.* (in a wood, in traffic). || Pausa, *f.* (pause). || Diferencia, *f.* (difference): *to fill the gap*, suprimir la diferencia. || Desequilibrio, *m.* (imbalance).
gape [geip] n. Bostezo, *m.* (yawn). || Mirada (*f.*) atónita (look).
gape [geip] v. intr. Quedarse boquiabierto (to stare in surprise). || Abrirse [mucho], estar [muy] abierto (to be wide open). || Bostezar (to yawn). || Pensar en las musarañas, papar moscas (to let one's mind wander).
gaper [—ə*] n. Mirón, ona; curioso, sa.
gaping [—iŋ] adj. Abierto, ta (open). || Boquiabierto, ta (surprised).
garage [ˈgærɑ:dʒ, U.S. gəˈrɑ:ʒ] n. Garaje, *m.* || — *Garage attendant*, garajista, *m.* (person in charge). || *Garage owner*, garajista, *m.*
garage [ˈgærɑ:dʒ, U.S. gəˈrɑ:ʒ] v. tr. Dejar en el garaje.

garb [gɑ:b] n. Vestido, *m.*, vestidura, *f.*
garb [gɑ:b] v. tr. Vestir.
garbage [ˈgɑ:bidʒ] n. Basura, *f.* || FIG. Basura, *f.* || — *Garbage can*, cubo (*m.*) de la basura. || *Garbage collector* o *man*, basurero, *m.* || *Garbage disposal*, vertedero (*m.*) *or* colector (*m.*) de basuras. || *Garbage incinerator*, incinerador (*m.*) de basura.
garble [ˈgɑ:bl] v. tr. Amañar, falsificar (to falsify). || Desvirtuar (facts). || Truncar (a quotation). || Mutilar (a text).
garden [ˈgɑ:dn] n. Jardín, *m.* (of flowers). || Huerto, *m.* (where foodstuffs are grown). || Huerta, *f.*, región (*f.*) fértil, jardín, *m.* (large fertile region). || Jardín, *m.* (botany). || — Pl. Parque, *m. sing.*, jardines, *m.* | Calle, *f. sing.* (street). || — *Back* o *kitchen garden*, huerto. || FAM. *To lead s.o. up the garden path*, engañar *or* embaucar a alguien. || *Zoological gardens*, parque zoológico.
— Adj. De jardín (flowers). || De la huerta, del huerto (vegetables). || De jardinería (tools).
garden [ˈgɑ:dn] v. intr. Trabajar en un jardín *or* en un huerto.
garden city [—ˈsiti] n. Ciudad jardín *f.*
gardenal [—əl] n. Gardenal, *m.*
gardener [ˈgɑ:dnə*] n. Jardinero, ra (of flowers). || Hortelano, na (of vegetables). || *Landscape gardener*, jardinero paisajista.
gardenia [gɑ:ˈdi:njə] n. BOT. Gardenia, *f.*
gardening [ˈgɑ:dniŋ] n. Jardinería, *f.* (of flowers). || Horticultura, *f.* (of vegetables).
garden party [ˈgɑ:dnˌpɑ:ti] n. "Garden-party", *m.*, fiesta (*f.*) al aire libre.
garfish [ˈgɑ:fiʃ] n. ZOOL. Aguja, *f.*
garganey [ˈgɑ:gəni] n. Zarceta, *f.* (bird).
Gargantua [gɑ:ˈgæntjuə] pr. n. Gargantúa, *m.*
gargantuan [—n] adj. Enorme, tremendo, da.
garget [ˈgɑ:gət] n. VET. Mastitis, *f.*
gargle [ˈgɑ:gl] n. MED. Gargarismo, *m.* (liquid). | Gárgara, *f.*, gárgaras, *f. pl.*, gargarismo, *m.* (treatment).
gargle [ˈgɑ:gl] v. intr. Hacer gárgaras, gargarizar.
gargling [—iŋ] n. Gárgara, *f.*, gargarismo, *m.*
gargoyle [ˈgɑ:gɔil] n. ARCH. Gárgola, *f.*
garish [ˈgɛəriʃ] adj. Chillón, ona; llamativo, va.
garland [ˈgɑ:lənd] n. Guirnalda, *f.* (wreath). || Antología, *f.* || MAR. Eslinga, *f.*
garland [ˈgɑ:lənd] v. tr. Adornar con guirnaldas, enguirnaldar.
garlic [ˈgɑ:lik] n. BOT. Ajo, *m.*
garment [ˈgɑ:mənt] n. Prenda, *f.* [de vestir]. || — Pl. Ropa, *f. sing.*
garner [ˈgɑ:nə*] n. AGR. Granero, *m.* || FIG. Abundancia, *f.*
garner [ˈgɑ:nə*] v. tr. AGR. Guardar en un granero. || FIG. Acumular.
garnet [ˈgɑ:nit] n. MIN. Granate, *m.*
— Adj. Granate.
garnish [ˈgɑ:niʃ] n. Aderezo, *m.*, adorno, *m.* || CULIN. Guarnición, *f.*, aderezo, *m.*
garnish [ˈgɑ:niʃ] v. tr. Aderezar, adornar (to decorate). || CULIN. Guarnecer, aderezar. || JUR. Embargar (to garnishee). | Citar (to summon). | Retener (payment).
garnishee [ˌgɑ:niˈʃi:] n. JUR. Embargado, da.
garnishee [ˌgɑ:niˈʃi:] v. tr. JUR. Embargar.
garnishment [ˈgɑ:niʃmənt] n. JUR. Embargo, *m.* | Orden (*f.*) de retención de pagos. | Citación, *f.* || Embellecimiento, *m.*, adorno, *m.* (embellishment). || CULIN. Guarnición, *f.*, aderezo, *m.*
garniture [ˈgɑ:nitʃə*] n. Aderezo, *m.* (condiments). || Guarnición, *f.* (additional to main plate).
Garonne [gæˈrɔn] pr. n. GEOGR. Garona, *m.*
garotte [gəˈrɔt] n. Garrote, *m.*
garotte [gəˈrɔt] v. tr. Agarrotar (to garrotte).
garotting [—iŋ] n. Garrote, *m.* (garrotting).
garpike [ˈgɑ:paik] n. ZOOL. Aguja, *f.* (fish).
garret [ˈgærət] n. Buhardilla, *f.* (room), desván, *m.* (attic, loft).
garrison [ˈgærisn] n. MIL. Guarnición, *f.*: *to be in garrison in a city*, estar de guarnición en una ciudad.
garrison [ˈgærisn] v. tr. Guarnecer (a place). || Poner en guarnición (troops).
garrotte (U. S. **garrote**) [gəˈrɔt] n. Garrote, *m.*
garrotte (U. S. **garrote**) [gəˈrɔt] v. tr. Agarrotar.
garrotting (U. S. **garroting**) [—iŋ] n. Garrote, *m.*
garrulity [gæˈru:liti] n. Locuacidad, *f.*, garrulidad, *f.*
garrulous [ˈgæruləs] adj. Locuaz, parlanchín, ina; gárrulo, la (person). || Verboso, sa (style).
garter [ˈgɑ:tə*] n. Liga, *f.* || *Order of the Garter*, orden (*f.*) de la Jarretera.
garter [ˈgɑ:tə*] v. tr. Poner una liga.
garter belt [—belt] n. U. S. Liguero, *m.*, portaligas, *m. inv.*
garth [gɑ:θ] n. Patio, *m.*
gas [gæs] n. Gas, *m.* (substance): *illuminating gas*, gas de alumbrado; *laughing*, *tear gas*, gas hilarante, lacrimógeno. || FAM. Parloteo, *m.*, palique, *m.* (chatter). || Grisú, *m.* (in mining). || U. S. Gasolina, *f.* (petrol). || — *Asphyxiating* o *lethal* o *poison gas*, gas asfixiante *or* de combate. || *By gas*, de gas. || *Coal gas*, gas de hulla. || *Gas burner*, mechero (*m.*) de gas. || *Gas chamber*, cámara (*f.*) de gas. || *Gas cooker*, cocina (*f.*) de gas. || *Gas engine*, motor (*m.*) de gas. || *Gas fire*, estufa (*f.*) de gas. || *Gas fitter*, gasista, *m.*, empleado (*m.*) del gas. || *Gas furnace*, horno (*m.*) de gas. || MED. *Gas gangrene*, gangrena gaseosa. || *Gas lighter*, encendedor (*m.*) de gas. || *Gas lighting*, alumbrado (*m.*) de gas. || *Gas mask*, careta (*f.*) antigás. || *Gas meter*, contador (*m.*) de gas. || *Gas oven*, horno (*m.*) de gas. || *Gas pipe*, tubería (*f.*) de gas. || *Gas pipeline*, gasoducto, *m.* || *Gas plant*, fábrica (*f.*) de gas. || *Gas ring*, hornillo (*m.*) de gas. || U. S. *Gas station*, surtidor (*m.*) de gasolina, gasolinera, *f.* || *Gas welding*, soldadura autógena. || *Marsh gas*, gas de los pantanos. || *Producer gas*, gas pobre. || *Water gas*, gas de agua. || U. S. *To step on the gas*, pisar el acelerador.
gas [gæs] v. tr. Asfixiar con gas (to kill by gas). || *To gas up*, proveer de gas.
— V. intr. Despedir gas (to give off gas). || FAM. Camelar (to cheat). | Charlotear, estar de palique (to chatter).
gasbag [—bæg] n. Cámara (*f.*) de gas. || FAM. Camelista, *m. & f.* (cheater). | Parlanchín, ina (chatterbox).
Gascon [ˈgæskən] adj./n. Gascón, ona.
Gascony [ˈgæskəni] pr. n. GEOGR. Gascuña, *f.*
gaseous [ˈgæsjəs] adj. Gaseoso, sa.
gash [gæʃ] n. Cuchillada, *f.* (wound).
gash [gæʃ] v. tr. Acuchillar.
gasholder [ˈgæsˌhəuldə*] n. U. S. Gasómetro, *m.*
gashouse [ˈgæshaus] n. U. S. Fábrica (*f.*) de gas.
gasification [ˌgæsifiˈkeiʃən] n. Gasificación, *f.*
gasify [ˈgæsifai] v. tr. Gasificar.
— V. intr. Gasificarse.
gas jet [ˈgæsdʒet] n. Mechero (*m.*) de gas (gas burner). || Llama, *f.* (flame).
gasket [ˈgæskit] n. AUT. Junta (*f.*) de culata.
gaslight [ˈgæslait] n. Alumbrado (*m.*) de gas, luz (*f.*) de gas. || TECH. Mechero (*m.*) de gas.
gasman [ˈgæsmæn] n. Gasista, *m.*, empleado (*m.*) del gas.

— OBSERV. El plural de esta palabra es *gasmen*.

gasogene [ˈgæsədʒi:n] n. Gasógeno, *m.*
gasoline or **gasolene** [ˈgæsəli:n] n. U. S. Gasolina, *f.*
gasometer [gæˈsɔmitə*] n. Gasómetro, *m.*
gasp [gɑ:sp] n. Boqueada, *f.* (before dying). || Grito (*m.*) de asombro (of surprise). || Jadeo, *m.* (difficulty in breathing). || *To be at one's last gasp*, estar dando las últimas boqueadas, estar en las últimas.
gasp [gɑ:sp] v. intr. Quedar boquiabierto, ta (with surprise). || Jadear (to pant). || — *To gasp for air*, hacer esfuerzos para respirar. || *To make s.o. gasp*, dejar boquiabierto a uno.
— V. tr. *To gasp out*, decir con voz entrecortada.
gasper [—ə*] n. FAM. Pito, *m.*, pitillo, *m.* (cigarette).
gasping [—iŋ] n. Jadeo, *m.*
gaspy [gɑ:spi] adj. Jadeante.
gassed [gæst] adj. Gaseado, da. || FAM. Borracho, cha.
gassing [ˈgæsiŋ] n. Asfixia (*f.*) con gas (killing by gas). || Gasificación, *f.* (gasification). || MIL. Ataque (*m.*) con gas. || FAM. Charloteo, *m.* (chatter).
gassy [ˈgæsi] adj. Gaseoso, sa.
gasteropod [ˈgæstərəpɔd] n. ZOOL. Gasterópodo, *m.*
gastight [ˈgæstait] adj. A prueba de gas, hermético, ca.
gastralgia [gæsˈtrældʒiə] n. MED. Gastralgia, *f.*
gastric [ˈgæstrik] adj. ANAT. Gástrico, ca: *gastric juice*, jugo gástrico.
gastritis [gæsˈtraitis] n. MED. Gastritis, *f.*
gastroenteritis [ˈgæstrɔinteˌraitis] n. MED. Gastroenteritis, *f.*
gastroenterology [ˈgæstrɔinteˈrɔlədʒi] n. Gastroenterología, *f.*
gastronome [ˈgæstrənəum] n. Gastrónomo, ma.
gastronomic [ˌgæstrəˈnɔmik] or **gastronomical** [—əl] adj. Gastronómico, ca.
gastronomist [gæsˈtrɔnəmist] n. Gastrónomo, ma.
gastronomy [gæsˈtrɔnəmi] n. Gastronomía, *f.*
gastropod [ˈgæstrəuˌpɔd] n. ZOOL. Gasterópodo, *m.*, gastrópodo, *m.*
gasworks [ˈgæswə:ks] n. Fábrica (*f.*) de gas.
gat [gæt] n. U. S. FAM. Revólver, *m.*
gate [geit] n. Verja, *f.* (metal barrier in wall or fence). || Puerta, *f.* (of city, entrance, etc.). || Pórtico, *m.* (of church). || Entrada, *f.* (of a public place, football stadium, etc.). || Puerta, *f.* (at airport). || Barrera, *f.* (of railway crossing). || Puerto, *m.* (of mountains). || Compuerta, *f.* (of sluice). || Recaudación, *f.*, taquilla, *f.* (number of tickets sold). || FAM. U. S. *To give s.o. the gate*, poner a uno en la calle.
gate [geit] v. tr. Castigar sin salir (in school). || Poner puerta a.
gatecrash [—kræʃ] v. tr. FAM. Colarse en.
— V. intr. FAM. Colarse.
gatecrasher [—ˈkræʃə*] n. FAM. Persona (*f.*) que se cuela.
gatehouse [—haus] n. Casa (*f.*) del guarda de un parque (of a park). || Caseta (*f.*) del guardabarrera (of railway crossing).
gatekeeper [—ˌki:pə*] n. Guardabarrera, *m. & f.* (of a railway crossing). || Portero, ra (doorkeeper).
gateleg table [ˈgeitlegˈteibl] n. Mesa (*f.*) plegable, mesa (*f.*) de alas abatibles.
gate money [ˈgeitˌmʌni] n. Recaudación, *f.*, taquilla, *f.* (admission receipts).
gatepost [ˈgeitˌpəust] n. Pilar, *m.*, poste, *m.*
gateway [ˈgeitwei] n. See GATE. || FIG. Puerta, *f.* (means of approach).

gather [ˈgæðə*] n. AGR. Cosecha, *f.* || Pliegue, *m.*, frunce, *m.* (in sewing).
gather [ˈgæðə*] v. tr. Recoger (to pick up). || Juntar, reunir (to put together). || Juntar, unir (to join). || Acumular (to collect, to amass). || Cosechar (to harvest). || Coger (to pick flowers, etc.). || Fruncir (to sew, to pucker). || Recobrar: *to gather breath*, recobrar el aliento. || Cobrar (strength, etc.). || Deducir (to deduce). || Recaudar (money). || SP. Recoger (the ball). || — FIG. *Rolling stone gathers no moss*, agua pasada no mueve molino. || *To gather dirt*, ensuciarse. || *To gather honey*, libar (the bees). || *To gather in*, recaudar (taxes). || *To gather one's energies*, reunir sus fuerzas. || *To gather o.s. together*, reponerse. || *To gather o.s. up*, acurrucarse. || *To gather speed*, ganar velocidad. || *To gather that*, tener entendido que (to understand), sacar la conclusión de que (to deduce). || *To gather together*, reunir, juntar. || *To gather up*, recoger.
— V. intr. Acumularse, amontonarse (things). || Reunirse, juntarse (persons). || Aumentar, incrementar (to increase). || Madurar (abscess). || Formarse (pus).
gathering [—iŋ] n. Reunión, *f.*, asamblea, *f.* || Concurrencia, *f.*, asistentes, *m. pl.* (people present). || Recolección, *f.* (collection). || Cosecha, *f.* (of fruit). || MED. Absceso, *m.* || Pliegue, *m.*, frunce, *m.* (in sewing).
gauche [gəuʃ] adj. Torpe, desmañado, da.
gaucherie [ˈgəuʃəri:] n. Torpeza, *f.*
gaucho [ˈgautʃəu] n. Gaucho, *m.*
— Adj. Gauchesco, ca: *gaucho life*, vida gauchesca.
gaud [gɔ:d] n. Dije, *m.* (trinket).
gaudiness [ˈgɔ:dinis] n. Lo chillón, lo llamativo.
gaudy [ˈgɔ:di] adj. Chillón, ona; llamativo, va.
gauffer [ˈgɔfə*] v. tr. See GOFFER.
gauge [geidʒ] n. Calibre, *m.* (calibre). || Medida, *f.* (measure). || Muestra, *f.*, indicación, *f.* (demonstration): *this work gives us a gauge of his abilities*, este trabajo nos da una muestra de sus capacidades. || Entrevía, *f.*, ancho, *m.* (of railway line). || AUT. Batalla, *f.* (of wheels). || Gramil, *m.* (in carpentry). || TECH. Calibrador, *m.*, galga, *f.* (for measuring diameter). | Indicador, *m.* (meter). | Manómetro, *m.* (for pressure). || MAR. Calado, *m.* (draught). | Barlovento, *m.*: *to have the weather gauge of*, estar a barlovento de. || — TECH. *Marking gauge*, gramil. || FIG. *To take the gauge of*, determinar, estimar.
gauge [geidʒ] v. tr. Calibrar (to measure the diameter of). || Medir (to measure). || Aforar, medir la capacidad de (a cask). || Arquear (ships). || Calcular (to calculate). || Determinar (to assess). || Apreciar, estimar (s.o.'s capacities).
gauger [—ə*] n. Aforador, *m.*
gauging [—iŋ] n. Aforo, *m.* (of cask). || Medida, *f.* (measure). || MAR. Arqueo, *m.*
Gaul [gɔ:l] n. HIST. Galo, la (people). | Galia, *f.* (country).
gaunt [gɔ:nt] adj. Demacrado, da (lean). || FIG. Lúgubre (desolate). | Feroz (grim).
gauntlet [ˈgɔ:ntlit] n. Guantelete, *m.* (in armour). || Guante, *m.* (glove). || — *To run the gauntlet*, correr baquetas (as punishment). || FIG. *To run the gauntlet of*, estar sometido a. | *To take up the gauntlet* recoger el guante. | *To throw down the gauntlet*, arrojar el guante.
gauntness [ˈgɔ:ntnis] n. Delgadez (*f.*) extrema.
gauss [gaus] n. ELECTR. Gauss, *m.*
gauze [gɔ:z] n. Gasa, *f.* (of cloth). || Tela (*f.*) metálica (of wire). || FIG. Bruma, *f.* (thin haze).
gauziness [ˈgɔ:zinis] n. Diafanidad, *f.*
gauzy [ˈgɔ:zi] adj. Diáfano, na.
gave [geiv] pret. See GIVE.
gavel [ˈgævl] n. Martillo, *m.*
gavial [ˈgeiviəl] n. ZOOL. Gavial, *m.*
gavotte [gəˈvɔt] n. MUS. Gavota, *f.*
gawk [gɔ:k] n. Bobo, ba.
gawk [gɔ:k] v. intr. Papar moscas. || *To gawk at*, mirar tontamente [a].
gawky [ˈgɔ:ki] adj. Torpe (awkward). || Desgarbado, da (ungainly).
gay [gei] adj. Alegre. || FAM. Homosexual (homosexual).
gayety [ˈgeiəti] n. Alegría, *f.*
gazabo [gəˈzeibəu] n. FAM. Tipo, *m.*, tío, *m.* (fellow).
gaze [geiz] n. Mirada (*f.*) fija (stare). || Contemplación, *f.* (act).
gaze [geiz] v. intr. Mirar. || — *To gaze at*, mirar fijamente; contemplar. || *To gaze into space*, estar con la mirada perdida.
gazebo [gəˈzi:bəu] n. Belvedere, *m.*

— OBSERV. El plural es *gazebos* o *gazeboes*.

gazelle [gəˈzel] n. ZOOL. Gacela, *f.*
gazette [gəˈzet] n. Gaceta, *f.* || Boletín (*m.*) Oficial (official publication). || *Gazette writer*, gacetero, *m.*
gazette [gəˈzet] v. tr. Publicar en el Boletín Oficial.
gazetteer [ˌgæziˈtiə*] n. Diccionario (*m.*) geográfico.
gazogene [ˈgæzədʒi:n] n. Gasógeno, *m.*
gear [giə*] n. Equipo, *m.* (equipment). || Ropa, *f.* (clothing). || Efectos (*m. pl.*) personales (personal belongings). || Arreos, *m. pl.*, aparejo, *m.* (of a horse). || Herramientas, *f. pl.* (tools). || Mecanismo, *m.* (mechanism). || Dispositivo, *m.* (device). || Engranaje, *m.* (of machinery): *differential gear*, engranaje del diferencial; *timing gear*, engranaje de distribución. || Velocidad, *f.*, cambio, *m.*, marcha, *f.* (for a car). || Embrague, *m.* (clutch). || Desarrollo, *m.* (for a bicycle). || MAR. Aparejo, *m.* || — *Bottom gear*, primera velocidad, || *Gear teeth*, engranaje, *m. sing.* (cogs). || *In gear*, engranado, da. || *In low gear*, en primera velocidad. || *Neutral gear*, punto muerto. || FIG. *Out of gear*, descompuesto, ta. || *Reversing gear*, marcha (*f.*) atrás. || *To change gear*, cambiar de velocidad. || *Top gear*, cuarta velocidad. || *To put into gear*, meter una velocidad, cambiar de velocidad (car), engranar. || *To throw into, out of gear*, embragar, desembragar.
gear [giə*] v. tr. Aparejar, poner los arreos a (a horse). || Engranar (to put into gear). || Adaptar, ajustar (to adapt). || — *To gear down*, desmultiplicar. || *To gear up*, multiplicar.
— V. intr. Engranar.
gearbox [—bɔks] n. Caja (*f.*) de cambios, caja (*f.*) de velocidades.
gear-change lever [—tʃeindʒˈli:və*] n. Palanca (*f.*) de cambio de velocidades.
gear differential [giə*ˌdifəˈrenʃəl] n. Piñón (*m.*) diferencial.
gearing [—iŋ] n. Engranaje, *m.* (gears, meshing).
gearshift [—ʃift] n. U. S. Cambio (*m.*) de velocidades. || *Gearshift lever*, palanca (*f.*) de cambio.
gear wheel [—wi:l] n. Piñón, *m.* (of bicycle). || Rueda (*f.*) dentada.
gecko [ˈgekəu] n. ZOOL. Salamanquesa, *f.*
gee [dʒi:] interj. ¡Caramba! || *Gee up!*, ¡arre! (to a horse).
geese [gi:s] pl. See GOOSE.
geezer [ˈgi:zə*] n. FAM. Tío, *m.*, viejo, *m.*
Gehenna [giˈhenə] n. Gehena, *f.* (hell).
geisha [ˈgeiʃə] n. Geisha, *f.* (Japanese woman).
gel [dʒel] n. CHEM. Gel, *m.*
gel [dʒel] v. intr. Gelificarse.
gelatin or **gelatine** [ˌdʒeləˈti:n] n. Gelatina, *f.*
gelatinous [dʒiˈlætinəs] adj. Gelatinoso, sa.
geld [geld] v. tr. Castrar, capar.
gelder [—ə*] n. Capador, *m.*, castrador, *m.*
Gelderland [ˈgeldəˌlænd] pr. n. GEOGR. Güeldres, *f.*
gelding [ˈgeldiŋ] n. Castración, *f.* (castration). || Caballo (*m.*) castrado (horse).
gelid [ˈdʒelid] adj. Helado, da; gélido, da.
gelignite [ˈdʒelignait] n. Gelignita, *f.* (explosive).
gem [dʒem] n. Gema, *f.*, piedra (*f.*) preciosa (jewel). || FIG. Alhaja, *f.*, joya, *f.* (thing, person). || *A gem of a child*, una preciosidad de niño.
gem [dʒem] v. tr. Adornar con piedras preciosas.
gemelli [dʒeˈmeli] pl. n. ANAT. Músculos (*m.*) gemelos.
geminate [ˈdʒemineit] adj. Geminado, da; gémino, na.
Gemini [ˈdʒeminai] pl. n. ASTR. Géminis, *m.*
gemma [ˈdʒemə] n. BOT. Yema, *f.*

— OBSERV. El plural de *gemm* es *gemmae*.

gemmate [ˈdʒemeit] v. intr. Reproducirse por gemación.
gemmation [dʒeˈmeiʃən] n. Gemación, *f.*
Gemonies [ˈdʒeməniz] pl. pr. n. HIST. Gemonías, *f.*
gen [dʒen] n. FAM. Información, *f.* || FAM. *To get the gen on*, informarse sobre.
gendarme [ˈʒɑ̃:ndɑ:m] n. Gendarme, *m.*
gendarmerie or **gendarmery** [ˌʒɑ̃:ndɑ:məˈri:] n. Gendarmería, *f.*
gender [ˈdʒendə*] n. GRAMM. Género, *m.*: *masculine, feminine, neutral gender*, género masculino, femenino, neutro. || FAM. Sexo, *m.*
gender [ˈdʒendə*] v. tr. Engendrar.
gene [dʒi:n] n. BIOL. Gene, *m.*, gen, *m.*
genealogical [ˌdʒi:njəˈlɔdʒikəl] adj. Genealógico, ca: *genealogical tree*, árbol genealógico.
genealogist [ˌdʒi:niˈælədʒist] n. Genealogista, *m.* y *f.*
genealogy [ˌdʒi:niˈælədʒi] n. Genealogía, *f.*
genera [ˈdʒenərə] pl. n. See GENUS.
general [ˈdʒenərəl] adj. General: *as a general rule*, por regla general; *in a general way*, de modo general; *the general opinion*, la opinión general; *general paralysis*, parálisis general. || *In general*, en general, por lo general, generalmente.
— N. MIL. REL. General, *m.* || Chica (*f.*) para todo (servant).
General Certificate of Education [—səˈtifikeitov ˌedju:ˈkeiʃən] n. Reválida, *f.*
General Court [—kɔ:t] n. U. S. Asamblea (*f.*) Legislativa.
general delivery [—diˈlivəri] n. U. S. Lista (*f.*) de correos.
generalissimo [ˌdʒenərəˈlisiməu] n. MIL. Generalísimo, *m.*
generality [ˌdʒenəˈræliti] n. Generalidad, *f.*
generalization [ˌdʒenərəlaiˈzeiʃən] n. Generalización, *f.*
generalize [ˈdʒenərəlaiz] v. tr./intr. Generalizar.
generalizing [—iŋ] adj. Generalizador, ra.
generally [ˈdʒenərəli] adj. Generalmente, por lo general, en general. || *Generally speaking*, hablando en términos generales.
general meeting [—ˌmi:tiŋ] n. Asamblea (*f.*) general.
general practitioner [ˈdʒenərəlprækˈtiʃnə*] n. Médico (*m.*) de medicina general, internista, *m.*
general-purpose [—ˈpɔ:pəs] adj. De uso general.
generalship [ˈdʒenərəlʃip] n. MIL. Estrategia, *f.*, táctica (*f.*) militar (military skill). | Generalato, *m.* (grade of general). || Don (*m.*) de mando (leadership).

general staff [ˈdʒenərəlstɑ:f] n. MIL. Estado (*m.*) mayor.
general store [ˈdʒenərəlˌstɔ:*] n. Almacén, *m.*
generate [ˈdʒenəreit] v. tr. Engendrar, generar, producir (to produce). || BIOL. Procrear, engendrar. || MATH. ELECTR. Generar: *to generate an electric current*, generar una corriente eléctrica.
generating [—iŋ] adj. Generador, ra: *generating station*, central generadora.
generation [ˌdʒenəˈreiʃən] n. Generación, *f.*: *spontaneous generation*, generación espontánea; *the rising generation*, la nueva generación.
generative [ˈdʒenərətiv] adj. Generativo, va.
generator [ˈdʒenəreitə*] n. TECH Generador, *m.*
generatrix [ˈdʒenəreitriks] n. MATH. Generatriz, *f.*

— OBSERV. El plural de *generatrix* es *generatrices*.

generic [dʒiˈnerik] or **generical** [—kəl] adj. Genérico, ca.
generosity [ˌdʒenəˈrɔsiti] n. Generosidad, *f.*
generous [ˈdʒenərəs] adj. Generoso, sa (*to*, con, para). || AGR. Fértil, rico, ca (soil). || Abundante (copious).
genesis [ˈdʒenisis] n. Génesis, *f.*

— OBSERV. El plural de la palabra inglesa es *geneses*.

Genesis [ˈdʒenisis] n. REL. Génesis, *m.*
genet [ˈdʒenit] n. ZOOL. Jineta, *f.*
genetic [dʒiˈnetik] adj. Genético, ca.
geneticist [dʒiˈnetisist] n. Genetista, *m. & f.*, geneticista, *m. & f.*
genetics [dʒinetiks] n. Genética, *f.*
Geneva [dʒiˈni:və] pr. n. GEOGR. Ginebra.
Genevan [dʒiˈni:vən] or **Genevese** [dʒiˈni:vi:z] adj./n. Ginebrino, na; ginebrés, esa.
genial [ˈdʒi:njəl] adj. Afable, cordial, simpático, ca (people). || Suave, clemente (weather). || Reconfortante, vivificante (warmth). || Genial (talent).
geniality [ˌdʒi:niˈæliti] n. Afabilidad, *f.*, simpatía, *f.*, cordialidad, *f.* (of person). || Clemencia, *f.*, suavidad, *f.* (of climate).
genic [ˈdʒi:nik] adj. Genético, ca.
genie [ˈdʒi:ni] n. Genio, *m.* [en los cuentos árabes].

— OBSERV. El plural de *genie* es *genies* o *genii*.

genipap [ˈdʒenipæp] n. BOT. Mamón, *m.*
genista [dʒiˈnistə] n. BOT. Retama, *f.*
genital [ˈdʒenitl] adj. Genital.
genitalia [ˌdʒeniˈteiljə] or **genitals** [ˈdʒenitlz] pl. n. ANAT. Órganos (*m.*) genitales.
genitival [ˌdʒeniˈtaivəl] adj. GRAMM. Del genitivo.
genitive [ˈdʒenitiv] n. GRAMM. Genitivo, *m.*
genitourinary [ˈdʒenitəuˈjuərinəri] adj. ANAT. Genitourinario, ria.
genius [ˈdʒi:njəs] n. Genio, *m.*: *she is a genius*, ella es un genio; *the genius of the language*, el genio de la lengua. || — *He has a genius for making friends*, tiene don de gente, tiene un don especial para hacerse amigos. || *He has a genius for mathematics*, es un genio para las matemáticas.

— OBSERV. El plural de *genius* es *geniuses* o *genii*.

Genoa [ˈdʒenəuə] pr. n. GEOGR. Génova.
genocide [ˈdʒenəusaid] n. Genocidio, *m.*
Genoese [ˌdʒenəuˈi:z] adj./n. Genovés, esa.
genotype [ˈdʒi:nətaip] n. BIOL. Genotipo, *m.*
genre [ʒɑ̃:ŋr] n. Género, *m.*, tipo, *m.*, clase, *f.* || ARTS. *Genre painting*, pintura (*f.*) de género.
gent [dʒent] n. FAM. Señor, *m.*, sujeto, *m.*, individuo, *m.* (man). || — Pl. Caballeros, *m.* (lavatory).
genteel [dʒenˈti:l] adj. Fino, na; distinguido, da; de buen tono (refined). || Cursi (excessively refined). || Cortés (polite).
gentian [ˈdʒenʃiən] n. BOT. Genciana, *f.*
gentile [ˈdʒentail] adj. Gentil, no judío (not Jewish). || Gentil (pagan). || GRAMM. Gentilicio, cia (gentilic).
— N. Gentil, *m.*
gentilic [dʒenˈtilik] adj. Gentilicio, cia: *gentilic noun, adjective*, nombre, adjetivo gentilicio.
— N. Gentilicio, *m.*
gentilism [dʒenˈtilizəm] n. Gentilismo, *m.*
gentility [dʒenˈtiliti] n. Finura, *f.*, distinción, *f.* (refinement). || Cursilería, *f.* (pretentiousness). || Cortesía, *f.* (politeness).
gentle [ˈdʒentl] adj. Suave (mild). || Bondadoso, sa (kind). || Amable (friendly). || Cortés, fino, na (polite). || Moderado, da (moderate). || Ligero, ra (light, not violent). || Lento, ta (slow). || Manso, sa (tame). || De buena familia, bien nacido, da (of good birth). || — *Gentle reader*, apreciado lector. || *Of gentle birth*, de buena familia, bien nacido, da. || *The gentle sex*, el sexo débil.
gentlefolk [—fəuk] n. Gente (*f.*) bien nacida.
gentleman [ˈdʒentlmən] n. Caballero, *m.*, señor, *m.*, (well-bred man). || Señor, *m.*, caballero, *m.* (man). || Gentilhombre, *m.* (at court). || — Pl. Muy señores míos, muy señores nuestros (in letters). || Caballeros, *m.* (lavatory). || — *Gentleman in waiting*, gentilhombre de cámara. || *Gentleman of the road*, salteador (*m.*) de caminos. || *Ladies and Gentlemen!*, ¡señoras y señores!, ¡señoras y caballeros!

— OBSERV. El plural de esta palabra es *gentlemen*.

gentleman-at-arms [—ətˈɑ:mz] n. Guardia (*m.*) de corps.

— OBSERV. El plural es *gentlemen-at-arms*.

gentleman farmer [—fɑ:mə*] n. Terrateniente, *m.*

— OBSERV. El plural es *gentlemen farmers*.

gentlemanlike [—laik] adj. Caballeroso, sa.
gentlemanliness [—linis] n. Caballerosidad, *f.*
gentlemanly [—li] adj. Caballeroso, sa.
gentleman's agreement [ˈdʒentlmænzəˈgri:mənt] or **gentlemen's agreement** [zəˈgri:mənt] n. Acuerdo (*m.*) entre caballeros.
gentleman's gentleman [ˈdʒentlmənzˈdʒentlmən] n. Ayuda (*m.*) de cámara.
gentleness [ˈdʒentlinis] n. Amabilidad, *f.* (kindness). || Bondad, *f.* (goodness). || Suavidad, *f.* (mildness). || Mansedumbre, *f.* (of animals).
gentlewoman [ˈdʒentlwumən] n. Señora, *f.*, dama, *f.*

— OBSERV. El plural de esta palabra es *gentlewomen*.

gently [ˈdʒentli] adv. Amablemente (kindly). || Suavemente (smoothly). || Despacio, poco a poco (slowly).
gentry [ˈdʒentri] n. Pequeña nobleza, *f.*, alta burguesía, *f.*, pequeña aristocracia, *f.* (people of good family). || Gente, *f.* (people).
genuflect [ˈdʒenjuflekt] v. intr. Doblar la rodilla, hacer una genuflexión.
genuflection or **genuflexion** [ˌdʒenjuˈflekʃən] n. Genuflexión, *f.*
genuine [ˈdʒenjuin] adj. Verdadero, ra (real). || Sincero, ra; franco, ca (frank). || Auténtico, ca; genuino, na; legítimo, ma (authentic).
genuineness [—nis] n. Autenticidad, *f.*
genus [ˈdʒi:nəs] n. Género, *m.*

— OBSERV. El plural de *genus* es *genera*.

geocentric [ˌdʒiəuˈsentrik] or **geocentrical** [—kəl] adj. Geocéntrico, ca.
geode [ˈdʒiəud] n. GEOL. Geoda, *f.*
geodesic [ˌdʒiəuˈdesik] adj. Geodésico, ca.
— N. MATH. Geodésica, *f.*
geodesy [dʒiˈɔdisi] n. Geodesia, *f.*
geodetic [dʒiˈɔdetik] adj. Geodésico, ca.
geodetics [—s] n. Geodésica, *f.*
geographer [dʒiˈɔgrəfə*] n. Geógrafo, *m.*
geographic [dʒiəˈgræfik] adj. Geográfico, ca.
geographical [—əl] adj. Geográfico, ca.
geography [dʒiˈɔgrəfi] n. Geografía, *f.*
geoid [ˈdʒi:ɔid] n. Geoide, *m.*
geologic [dʒiəˈlɔdʒik] or **geological** [—əl] adj. Geológico, ca.
geologist [dʒiˈɔlədʒist] n. Geólogo, *m.*
geologize [dʒiˈɔlədʒaiz] v. intr. Estudiar geología.
geology [dʒiˈɔlədʒi] n. Geología, *f.*
geomagnetic [ˌdʒi:əumægˈnetik] adj. Geomagnético, ca.
geometer [dʒiˈɔmitə*] n. Geómetra, *m.*
geometric [dʒiəˈmetrik] adj. MATH. Geométrico, ca: *geometric progression*, progresión geométrica; *geometric ratio*, razón geométrica; *geometric mean*, media geométrica.
geometrical [—əl] adj. MATH. Geométrico, ca: *geometrical construction*, construcción geométrica.
geometrician [ˌdʒiəuməˈtriʃən] n. Geómetra, *m.*
geometrize [dʒiˈɔmətraiz] v. tr. Representar geométricamente.
geometry [dʒiˈɔmitri] n. MATH. Geometría, *f.*: *plane, descriptive, solid geometry*, geometría plana, descriptiva, del espacio.
geomorphology [ˌdʒi:əumɔ:ˈfɔlədʒi] n. Geomorfología, *f.*
geophysical [ˈdʒi:əuˈfizikəl] adj. Geofísico, ca.
geophysicist [ˈdʒi:əuˈfizist] n. Geofísico, *m.*
geophysics [ˈdʒi:əuˈfiziks] n. Geofísica, *f.*
geopolitics [dʒi:əuˈpɔlitiks] n. Geopolítica, *f.*
George [dʒɔ:dʒ] pr. n. Jorge, *m.*
Georgia [ˈdʒɔ:dʒjə] pr. n. GEOGR. Georgia, *f.*
Georgian [ˈdʒɔ:dʒjən] adj./n. Georgiano, na.
georgic [ˈdʒɔ:dʒik] adj. Geórgico, ca.
— Pl. n. Geórgicas, *f.* (poem by Virgil).
geosynclinal [dʒi:əusinkˈlainəl] adj. GEOL. Geosinclinal.
— N. GEOL. Geosinclinal, *m.*
geosyncline [ˌdʒi:əuˈsinklain] n. GEOL. Geosinclinal, *m.*
Gerald [ˈdʒerəld] or **Gerard** [ˈdʒerɑ:d] pr. n. Gerardo, *m.* (Christian name).
geranium [dʒiˈreinjəm] n. BOT. Geranio, *m.*
gerbil or **gerbille** [ˈdʒə:bil] n. ZOOL. Gerbo, *m.*, jerbo, *m.*
gerfalcon [ˈdʒə:ˌfɔ:lkən] n. ZOOL. Gerifalte, *m.* (bird).
geriatrician [ˌdʒeriəˈtriʃən] n. MED. Geriatra, *m. & f.*
geriatrics [ˌdʒeriˈætriks] n. MED. Geriatría, *f.*
germ [dʒə:m] n. BIOL. Germen, *m.* || MED. Bacilo, *m.* (bacillus). | Microbio, *m.* (of a disease). | Bacteria, *f.* (bacterium). || FIG. Germen, *m.* || — *Germ carrier*, portador (*m.*) de gérmenes. || *Germ cell*, gameto, *m.* || *Germ killer*, germicida, *m.*, microbicida, *m.*, bactericida, *m.* || *Germ warfare*, guerra bacteriológica.
German [ˈdʒə:mən] adj. Alemán, ana.
— N. Alemán, ana (inhabitant of Germany). || Alemán, *m.* (language).
german [ˈdʒə:mən] adj. Hermano, na (cousin). || Carnal (brother). || FIG. Relacionado, da.
germane [dʒə:ˈmein] adj. Relacionado, da.
germane [dʒə:ˈmein] adj. FIG. See GERMAN.
Germania [dʒə:ˈmeinjə] pr. n. Germania, *f.*
Germanic [dʒə:ˈmænik] adj. Germánico, ca.
— N. Germánico, *m.*

Germanism [ˈdʒə:mənizəm] n. Germanismo, *m.*
Germanist [ˈdʒə:mənist] n. Germanista, *m.* & *f.*
germanium [dʒə:ˈmeiniəm] n. CHEM. Germanio, *m.*
German measles [ˈdʒə:mənˈmi:zlz] n. MED. Rubéola, *f.* (infectious disease).
germanophile [dʒə:ˈmænəfail] adj./n. Germanófilo, la.
germanophobe [dʒə:ˈmænəfəub] adj./n. Germanófobo, ba.
German shepherd [ˈdʒə:mənˈʃepəd] n. U. S. Perro (*m.*) pastor alemán (dog).
German silver [ˈdʒə:mənˈsilvə*] n. MIN. Alpaca, *f.*, metal (*m.*) blanco, plata (*f.*) alemana.
Germany [ˈdʒə:məni] pr. n. GEOGR. Alemania, *f.*
germicidal [ˌdʒə:miˈsaidl] adj. Germicida, microbicida, bactericida.
germicide [ˈdʒə:misaid] n. MED. Germicida, *m.*, microbicida, *m.*, bactericida, *m.*
germinal [ˈdʒə:minl] adj. Germinal. || FIG. Embrionario, ria.
germinate [ˈdʒə:mineit] v. intr. Germinar.
— V. tr. Hacer germinar.
germination [ˌdʒə:miˈneiʃən] n. Germinación, *f.*
germinative [ˌdʒə:miˈneitiv] adj. Germinativo, va.
germ-killing [ˈdʒə:mˈkiliŋ] adj. Bactericida.
gerontocracy [ˌdʒerənˈtɔkrəsi] n. Gerontocracia, *f.*
gerontologist [ˌdʒerənˈtɔlədʒist] n. MED. Gerontólogo, ga.
gerontology [ˌdʒerənˈtɔlədʒi] n. MED. Gerontología, *f.*
gerrymander [ˈdʒerimændə*] n. División (*f.*) arbitraria de los distritos electorales para ser favorecido en las elecciones.
gerrymander [ˈdʒerimændə*] v. tr. Dividir [los distritos electorales] para sacar ventaja en las elecciones.
gerund [ˈdʒerənd] n. GRAMM. Gerundio, *m.*
gerundive [dʒiˈrʌndiv] n. GRAMM. Gerundio, *m.*
gesso [ˈdʒesəu] n. Yeso, *m.*
gest [dʒest] n. Gesta, *f.*
Gestapo [gesˈtɑ:pəu] n. Gestapo, *f.*
gestate [ˈdʒesteit] v. tr. Gestar (to carry). || FIG. Concebir, gestar (an idea).
gestation [dʒesˈteiʃən] n. Gestación, *f.*
gestational [dʒesˈteiʃənl] adj. De la gestación.
gestatorial [ˌdʒestəˈtɔ:riəl] adj. Gestatorio, ria: *gestatorial chair*, silla gestatoria.
geste [dʒest] n. *Chanson de geste*, cantar (*m.*) de gesta.
gesticulate [dʒesˈtikjuleit] v. intr. Gesticular, hacer ademanes.
gesticulation [dʒesˌtikjuˈleiʃən] n. Gesticulación, *f.*, ademanes, *m. pl.*, movimientos, *m. pl.*
gesticulative [dʒesˌtikjuˈleitiv] adj. Gesticulador, ra; gestero, ra.
gesture [ˈdʒestʃə*] n. Gesto, *m.*, ademán, *m.*, movimiento, *m.*: *he always makes a lot of gestures with his hands*, siempre hace muchos gestos con las manos. || FIG. Detalle: *what a nice gesture on your part!*, ¡qué buen detalle de tu parte! | Muestra, *f.* (token).
gesture [ˈdʒestʃə*] v. intr. Gesticular, hacer gestos *or* ademanes.
— V. tr. Expresar con gestos *or* con ademanes.
gesundheit [gəˈzuntˌhait] interj. ¡Jesús! (after sneezing).
get* [get] v. tr. Obtener, tener: *did you get an answer?*, ¿tuviste contestación? || Recibir: *I got your letter this morning*, recibí tu carta esta mañana. || Recibir, tener: *he got a lovely present*, tuvo un regalo precioso. || Ir a buscar, traer: *would you get me a cup of tea?*, ¿quieres traerme una taza de té? || Buscar: *go and get a cup of coffee*, vete a buscar una taza de café. || Llamar (to call): *to get the doctor*, llamar al médico. || Comprar (to buy). || Encontrar (to find). || Llevarse, ganar: *who has got the prize?*, ¿quién se llevó el premio? || Llevarse: *he got the worst of it*, se llevó la peor parte. || Lograr, conseguir (to obtain). || Conseguir, proporcionar (to provide): *I'll get you a pen*, te conseguiré una pluma. || Ganar (to earn): *he gets two thousand pesetas a week*, gana dos mil pesetas por semana. || Dar (to hit): *the bullet got him in the arm*, la bala le dio en el brazo. || Recibir (to suffer): *he got a bump on the head*, recibió un porrazo en la cabeza. || Coger [*Amer.*, agarrar] (to catch): *the police got the thief*, la policía cogió al ladrón; *she got the measles*, cogió el sarampión. || Coger (to reproduce): *the artist got the expression well*, el artista cogió bien la expresión. || Sacar (to extract): *to get aluminium from bauxite*, sacar aluminio de la bauxita. || Obtener, caerle a uno, echarle a uno: *he got twenty years for murder*, le echaron veinte años por asesinato. || Marcar (points). || Sacar (profit). || Llevar (to bring): *he got it to my house*, lo llevó a mi casa. || Mandar (to send). || Hacer, preparar (to prepare): *I'm going to get breakfast*, voy a preparar el desayuno. || Convencer (to persuade): *can you get him to come?*, ¿puedes convencerle de que venga? || Conseguir: *we got him to talk on this subject*, conseguimos que hablara de este tema. || Poner: *he gets me angry*, me pone furioso. || FAM. Llegar a comprender (to understand): *I don't get it*, no llego a comprenderlo. | Oír (to hear). | Matar (to kill). | Poner nervioso (to irritate). | Conmover (to move). | Chiflar: *his paintings get me*, sus cuadros me chiflan. || Hablar con: *he couldn't get you by phone*, no pudo hablar con usted por teléfono. || RAD. Captar, sintonizar con. || U. S. FAM. Ver (to see). | Poner en un aprieto (to put in a fix).
— *Adding two and three you get five*, dos y tres son cinco. || *Can I get you a drink?*, ¿quiere tomar algo? || *Could you get me Madrid on the phone?*, ¿me puede poner con Madrid? || FAM. *I'll get you one day!*, ¡ya me las pagarás! || *I've got Madrid on the phone*, tengo Madrid al teléfono. || *She got her man*, encontró al hombre de su vida. || FAM. *That's got me*, no tengo ni idea. || *To get a bad name*, adquirir mala fama. || *To get a wife*, casarse. || *To get going*, poner en marcha. || FAM. *To get it bad*, darle a uno fuerte (disease, love). | *To get it hot*, tener una bronca. || U. S. REL. *To get religion*, convertirse. || *To get some sleep*, dormir un poco. || *To get s.o. on to a subject*, conseguir que alguien hable de un tema. || FIG. *To get one's back up*, see BACK. || *To get sth. by heart*, aprender algo de memoria. || *To get sth. done*, mandar hacer algo (by s.o. else), conseguir hacer *or* terminar algo (o.s.). || *To get things done*, conseguir que se hagan las cosas. || *To get with child*, dejar embarazada. || *To have got*, tener: *I haven't got any money*, no tengo dinero. || *To have got to*, tener que: *she has got to go there*, tiene que ir allí. || FAM. *What's got you?*, ¿qué te pasa?, qué mosca te ha picado? || *What's that got to do with it?*, ¿qué tiene eso que ver? || FAM. *You'll get it from your father!*, ¡tu padre te va a echar una bronca! || *You must get your hair cut*, tienes que hacerte cortar el pelo, tienes que cortarte el pelo. || FAM. *You've got me there*, ya me has cogido.
— V. intr. Ponerse (to become): *he got better*, se puso mejor. || Llegar: *I got there at two o'clock*, llegué allí a las dos. || Ir (to go). || FAM. Irse (to leave). || — FAM. *Get going!*, ¡muévete! || *How far have you got?*, ¿hasta dónde has llegado? || FIG. *To get above o.s.*, subírsele a uno los humos. || *To get doing sth.*, ponerse a or empezar a hacer algo (See OBSERV. II.). || *To get dressed*, vestirse. || *To get married*, casarse. || *To get shaved*, afeitarse. || FIG. *To get somewhere*, abrirse camino (to make one's way), progresar (to progress), sacar algo en claro (to clarify sth.). || *To get used to*, acostumbrarse a. || *To get used to it*, acostumbrarse.
— **To get about**, desplazarse: *he couldn't get about because of his broken leg*, no podía desplazarse con la pierna rota. | Difundirse, propalarse: *rumours quickly get about*, los rumores se difunden rápidamente. | Viajar mucho, ir a muchos sitios (to travel). | Levantarse y salir (after sickness). || **To get across**, atravesar, cruzar: *to get across the road*, cruzar la carretera. | Hacer comprender: *I can't get across to you what I mean*, no puedo hacerte comprender lo que quiero decir. | Ser comprendido (to be understood). | Ser apreciado: *the singer got across to the audience*, el cantante fue apreciado por el público. || **To get along**, hacer progresos, progresar (to progress). | Encontrarse mejor, mejorar: *the patient is getting along*, el enfermo está mejorando. | Ir: *how are you getting along with your work?*, ¿cómo le va el trabajo? | Llevarse bien: *we get along together*, nos llevamos bien. | Ir tirando: *we are not rich but we get along*, no somos ricos pero vamos tirando. | Arreglárselas: *I'll get along somehow*, me las arreglaré de una manera o de otra. | Marcharse, irse (to leave): *I must be getting along*, tengo que marcharme. | Seguir andando (to go on walking). | Hacer venir (to bring s.o.). | Llevar: *we got him along to hospital*, lo llevamos al hospital. | — FAM. *Get along with you!*, ¡déjate de bobadas! | *To get along without*, pasar sin, prescindir de. | U. S. *To get along with sth.*, seguir, continuar: *get along with your work!*, ¡sigue trabajando! || **To get around**, viajar (to travel). | Salir (to go out). | Difundirse, propalarse (rumours). Evitar, soslayar (to avoid). | Saber manejar (s.o.). | — *To get around to*, llegar a. || **To get at**, alcanzar, llegar a (to reach). | Entrar en contacto con (to come into contact). | Conseguir: *I can't get at my money until the bank opens*, no puedo conseguir dinero hasta que abra el banco. | Estar detrás de (to pester): *my mother is always getting at me*, mi madre siempre está detrás mía. | Reñir (to scold). | Meterse con (to tease). | Insinuar: *what are you getting at?*, ¿qué insinúas? | Pretender (to try to obtain). | Averiguar, descubrir (the truth). | Atacar (to criticize). | Estropear (to spoil). | Comprar, sobornar (to bribe). | — *To get at the drink*, ponerse a beber. || **To get away**, escaparse (to escape). | Alejarse: *to get away from the coast*, alejarse de la costa. | Conseguir marcharse (to leave). | Irse (to go away). | Separar (to separate). | Llevar, llevarse (to take away). | Quitar: *I got the gun away from him*, le quité la pistola. | Librarse: *he managed to get away from that boring person*, consiguió librarse de esa persona pesada. | Liberar: *to get s.o. away from the hands of the enemy*, liberar a alguien de las manos del enemigo. | AUT. Arrancar. | — *Get away (from here)!*, ¡fuera [de aquí]! | *Get away with you!*, ¡déjate de tonterías! | *To get away with*, llevarse (to steal). | *To get away with it*, no ser castigado (not to be punished), conseguir hacerlo (to succeed). | *You won't get away with it*, ya lo pagarás. || **To get back**, volver a poner (*into*, en). | Volver, regresar (to return): *he got back home*, volvió a su casa. | — *He didn't get his money back*, no le devol-

vieron el dinero, no recuperó *or* no recobró su dinero. | *To get back at*, vengarse de, desquitarse con. || **To get behind**, atrasarse: *he got behind in his work*, se atrasó en el trabajo. | Quedarse atrás (to lag behind). | Penetrar (to penetrate). | Respaldar (to back). | Conseguir el apoyo *or* el respaldo de (to get support). || **To get by**, arreglárselas (to manage): *we are not rich but we get by*, no somos ricos pero nos las arreglamos. | Defenderse: *he can get by in German*, se defiende en alemán. | Burlar la vigilancia de, conseguir pasar inadvertido delante de. | Conseguir pasar (sth.). || **To get down**, bajar (to descend). | Deprimir (to depress). | Desanimar (to discourage). | Escribir, poner por escrito (to write). | Apuntar: *I'll get your name down on my list*, apuntaré su nombre en mi lista. | Tragarse: *I couldn't get my steak down*, no pude tragarme el filete. | — *To get down on one's knees*, arrodillarse. | *To get down to*, ponerse a: *to get down to work*, ponerse a trabajar; abordar (a problem). | *To get down to the facts*, ir al grano. || **To get in**, entrar. | Llegar: *the train got in at ten o'clock*, el tren llegó a las diez. | Montar en (a car). | Volver, regresar (to come back). | Ser elegido (to be elected). | Recibir (to receive). | Recoger (crops, etc.). | Recaudar (taxes). | Cobrar (debts). | Decir (word). | Asestar (blow). | — Fam. *I could hardly get a word in edgeways*, no pude meter baza. | *To get in the habit of*, coger la costumbre de, acostumbrarse a. | *To get in with*, trabar amistad con. || **To get into**, entrar en (a place). | Subir a, montarse en (to board): *I got into the train*, subí al tren. | Ponerse (to put on): *he got into his pyjamas*, se puso el pijama. | Meterse en: *he got into bed*, se metió en la cama. | Poner en: *to get the key into the lock*, poner la llave en la cerradura. | — *I can't get it into your head*, no puedo metértelo en la cabeza. | *To get into a rage*, ponerse furioso. | *To get into bad habits*, adquirir malas costumbres. | *To get into trouble*, meterse en un lío. | Fam. *What's got into you?*, ¿qué mosca te ha picado? || **To get off**, apearse de, bajarse de, bajar de: *I got off the bus*, me apeé del autobús; *I got off my horse*, me bajé del caballo. | Escapar: *he got off with a light sentence*, escapó con una sentencia poco severa. | Marcharse (to go away). | Arrancar (a car). | Salir (train). | Despegar (aircraft). | Librarse de (a duty). | Librarse: *to get off with a fine*, librarse con una multa. | Quitar (a stain). | Quitarse (clothes): *she can't get her dress off*, no puede quitarse el vestido. | Despachar (work). | Mandar (a letter). | Soltar (a remark). | Jur. Hacer absolver. | Fam. Sacar de apuro (to get s.o. out of a jam). | — Fam. *Get off!*, ¡suelta! | *To get off lightly*, salir bien parado. | *To get off one's chair*, levantarse. | *To get off to sleep*, dormir, conciliar el sueño. | Fam. *To get off with*, ligar con. | Fig. *To tell s.o. where to get off*, cantarle a uno las verdades del barquero. || **To get on**, subir a, subirse a, montarse en: *I got on the train*, subí al tren. | Ponerse en: *the cat got on my lap*, el gato se puso en mi regazo. | Desenvolverse: *he is getting on well at school*, se desenvuelve bien en el colegio. | Hacer progresos, progresar (to make progress). | Medrar (to succeed): *Mary has got on in life*, María ha medrado en la vida. | Llevarse bien: *we get on together*, nos llevamos bien. | Envejecer (to grow old). | Hacerse tarde: *what time is it? — It's getting on*, ¿qué hora es? — Se está haciendo tarde. | Ponerse (clothes). | Irse (to go): *I must be getting on now*, me tengo que ir ahora. | — *Get on with it*, ponte a hacerlo. | *He is getting on for sixty*, está rondando los sesenta. | *How are you getting on?*, ¿qué tal está?, ¿cómo le va? | *I can't get on with Latin*, no me entra el latín. | *It's getting on for six o'clock*, son cerca de las seis. | *To be always getting on at s.o. to do sth.*, estar siempre detrás de uno para que haga algo. | *To get on at s.o. about sth.*, meterse con alguien acerca de algo. | Fam. *To get on s.o.'s nerves*, crisparle los nervios a uno. | *To get on to*, localizar: *how did the police get on to that thief?*, ¿cómo localizó la policía a ese ladrón?; llegar hasta: *how did we get on to that subject?*, ¿cómo hemos llegado a este tema?; descubrir: *to get on to the trick*, descubrir el truco; conseguir hablar con (to speak to), encargarse de: *I'll get on to that for you*, me encargaré de ello para Ud. | *To get on with one's work*, seguir trabajando. || **To get out**, salir (to exit). | Escaparse (to escape). | Bajarse, bajar (of a train). | Sacar (to take out). | Quitar (a stain). | Publicar, sacar (a book). | Resolver (a problem). | Pronunciar (words). | Sacar (a car, a boat). | Hacer (a list). | Trazar (plans). | Difundirse (news). | Hacerse público (secret). | Fig. Sacar: *what do you get out of this?*, ¿qué sacas de esto? | — Fam. *Get out!*, ¡fuera! | *To get out of*, librarse de: *he got out of military service*, se libró del servicio militar; perder: *you must get out of this bad habit*, tienes que perder esta mala costumbre; quitar: *I must get you out of this bad habit*, tengo que quitarte esta mala costumbre; sacar: *to get a secret, money out of s.o.*, sacarle a uno un secreto, dinero; salir: *to get out of trouble*, salir de un apuro; sacar: *I got him out of trouble*, le saqué de apuro | Sp. *To get s.o. out*, sacar a un bateador del campo (in cricket). || **To get over**, cruzar: *I got over the river*, crucé el río. | Recorrer (a distance). | Pasar por encima: *to get over a fence*, pasar por encima de una valla. | Superar, salvar: *to get over an obstacle*, salvar un obstáculo. | Pasar por alto (to overlook). | Vencer (a difficulty). | Sobreponerse (to recover from a loss, a grief). | Reponerse (an illness, a fright). | Perder (a bad habit). | Olvidar (to forget). | Hacer comprender (to make understood). | Ser comprendido (to be understood). | Ser apreciado (a play, etc.). | Acabar con: *we must get it over before Friday*, tenemos que acabar con esto antes del viernes. | — *Let's get it over*, acabemos de una vez. || **To get round**, dar la vuelta a. | Soslayar (difficulty, law). | Persuadir (to convince). | — *To get round the world*, dar la vuelta al mundo. | *To get round to*, llegar a. || **To get through**, [conseguir] pasar por. | Acabar con, terminar (to finish). | Hacer (to do). | Aprobar: *to get through an exam*, aprobar un examen. | Conseguir que apruebe: *he got all his pupils through*, consiguió que aprobaran todos sus alumnos. | Conseguir comunicar: *I got through to Madrid yesterday*, conseguí comunicar con Madrid ayer. | Abrirse paso: *the troops got through to the besieged town*, las tropas se abrieron paso hasta la ciudad sitiada. | Llegar: *at the end the news got through to him*, al final le llegó la noticia. | Meter en la cabeza, hacer comprender (to make understood): *I can't get through to you that smoking is dangerous*, no puedo meterte en la cabeza que el tabaco es peligroso. | Jur. Hacer aprobar; ser aprobado (a bill). | Fam. Gastarse: *I got through a hundred pounds in two days*, me gasté cien libras en dos días. | — *To get through the day*, pasar el día. || **To get to**, llegar a (to succeed in). | Aprender a: *to get to do sth.*, aprender a hacer algo. | — *To get to work*, ponerse a trabajar. || **To get together**, reunir. | Reunirse (to assemble). | Ponerse de acuerdo (to agree). || **To get under**, ponerse debajo de. | — *To get under way*, see way. || **To get up**, levantarse: *I got up late this morning*, me levanté tarde esta mañana. | Levantarse, ponerse de pie (to stand up). | Levantar: *I have to get my husband up for work*, tengo que levantar a mi marido para que vaya a trabajar. | Subirse, trepar (to climb). | Subir: *to get up a slope*, subir una cuesta. | Levantar (to lift). | Subir (to take up). | Desencadenarse (a storm). | Levantarse (wind). | Embravecerse (sea). | Organizar (a party). | Montar (a play). | Tramar (a plot). | Forjar, fraguar (a story). | Preparar (lecture). | Estudiar (to make a special study of). | Repasar (to learn again). | Comm. Presentar (goods). | Disfrazar (to disguise). | Acicalarse (to dress up.) | — *To get o.s. up*, vestirse de, disfrazarse de: *he got himself up as a sailor*, se vistió de marinero; maquillarse (to make up). | *To get up speed*, acelerar. | *To get up to*, llegar a *or* hasta (to reach), hacer (to do). | *To get up to mischief*, hacer de las suyas.

— Observ. I. El verbo *to get* tiene el pretérito y el participio pasivo irregulares, **got**. Además de éste, en Estados Unidos se usa también la forma **gotten** para el participio pasivo.
— II. Cuando el verbo *to get* va seguido por un gerundio se traduce por « ponerse a » o « empezar a » (*once he gets speaking you can't stop him*, cuando se pone a hablar, no hay quien lo pare).
— III. En muchos casos, cuando el verbo *to get* antecede un adjetivo o un participio pasivo, se traduce al castellano por un simple verbo (*to get old*, envejecer; *to get drunk*, emborracharse; *to get fat*, engordar; *to get killed*, matarse; *to get one's hands dirty*, ensuciarse las manos).
— IV. In some Latin-American countries the word "coger" is not in decent use. It is substituted therefore by "agarrar".

get-at-able [— ætəbl] adj. Accesible.

getaway [—əwei] n. Huida, *f.*, fuga, *f.* (escape). || Sp. Salida, *f.* (start). | Escapada, *f.* (breakaway). || Aut. Arranque, *m.*

Gethsemane [geθ′seməni] pr. n. Getsemaní.

getter [′getə*] n. Persona (*f.*) emprendedora.

get-together [′get′tə′geðə*] n. Reunión, *f.* (meeting). || Fiesta, *f.* [sin cumplidos] (informal party).

getup [—ʌp] n. Fam. Vestimenta, *f.*, atavío, *m.* (a style of dressing). | Disfraz, *m.* (fancy dress). | Maquillaje, *m.* (makeup). || Presentación, *f.* (of a publication). || U. S. Energía, *f.*

gewgaw [′gju:gɔ:] n. Chuchería, *f.*, fruslería, *f.*

geyser [′gaizə*] n. Géiser, *m.* (a hot spring). || Calentador (*m.*) de agua (water heater).

Ghanaian [gɑ:′neiən] adj./n. Ghanés, esa.

ghastliness [′gɑ:stlinis] n. Aspecto (*m.*) siniestro. || Palidez (*f.*) cadavérica (pallor).

ghastly [′gɑ:stli] adj. Horroroso, sa (gruesome). || Cadavérico, ca: *a ghastly pallor*, una palidez cadavérica. || Pálido, da; mortecino, na (light). || Fam. Espantoso, sa.
— Adv. Terriblemente, horriblemente.

Ghent [gent] pr. n. Geogr. Gante.

gherkin [′gə:kin] n. Pepinillo, *m.*

ghetto [′getəu] n. Judería, *f.*, ghetto, *m.* (Jewish quarter). || Ghetto, *m.* (where members of a minority live).

ghost [gəust] n. Fantasma, *m.*, aparecido, *m.*, espectro, *m.*: *this castle has ghosts*, este castillo tiene fantasmas. || Imagen (*f.*) fantasma (in optics). || — *Not the ghost of a chance*, ni la más remota posibilidad. || *The Holy Ghost*, el Espíritu Santo. || *To give up the ghost*, entregar el alma, exhalar el último suspiro.

ghost [gəust] v. tr. Escribir [un libro] para otro. || Rondar por (to haunt).
— V. intr. Hacer de negro (to write for another).
ghostly [—li] adj. Fantasmal, espectral (like a ghost). || (Ant.). Espiritual (spiritual).
ghost-writer [—,raitə*] n. Negro, *m.*
ghoul [gu:l] n. Espíritu (*m.*) necrófago (a corpse-devouring spirit). || FAM. Persona (*f.*) macabra. || Profanador (*m.*) de cementerios.
ghoulish [—iʃ] adj. Macabro, bra.
giant [ˈdʒaiənt] n. Gigante, *m.*
— Adj. Gigantesco, ca; gigante.
giantess [ˈdʒaiəntis] n. Giganta, *f.*
giantism [ˈdʒaiəntizəm] n. Gigantismo, *m.*
gib [dʒib] n. TECH. Chaveta, *f.*
gibb [dʒib] v. tr. MAR. See JIB.
gibber [ˈdʒibə*] n. Galimatías, *m.*, jerigonza, *f.*
gibber [ˈdʒibə*] v. intr. Farfullar.
gibberish [ˈdʒibəriʃ] n. Galimatías, *m.*, jerigonza, *f.*
gibbet [ˈdʒibit] n. Horca, *f.*
gibbet [ˈdʒibit] v. tr. Ahorcar. || FIG. Poner en la picota.
gibbon [ˈgibən] n. Gibón, *m.* (monkey).
gibbosity [giˈbɔsiti] n. Gibosidad, *f.*
gibbous [ˈgibəs] adj. Giboso, sa; gibado, da (hump-backed).
gibe [dʒaib] n. Mofa, *f.*, sarcasmo, *m.*
gibe [dʒaib] v. tr. Mofarse de, burlarse de.
— V. intr. Burlarse, mofarse (to scoff).
giblets [ˈdʒiblets] pl. n. Menudillos, *m.*
Gibraltar [ˈdʒiˈbrɔ:ltə*] pr. n. GEOGR. Gibraltar: *the Rock, the Straits of Gibraltar,* el peñón, el estrecho de Gibraltar.
Gibraltarian [,dʒibrɔ:lˈtɛəriən] n. Gibraltareño, ña.
gid [gid] n. VET. Modorra, *f.*
giddiness [ˈgidinis] n. Mareo, *m.*, vértigo, *m.* (dizziness).
giddy [ˈgidi] adj. Mareado, da (dizzy): *I feel giddy,* estoy mareado. || Que da vértigo, vertiginoso, sa (which produces dizziness). || FIG. Frívolo, la; ligero, ra; atolondrado, da (frivolous).
gift [gift] n. Regalo, *m.*, obsequio, *m.* (a present). || JUR. Donación, *f.*: *deed of gift,* donación entre vivos. || Don, *m.* (natural talent): *gift of tongues,* don de lenguas. || Dote, *f.* (of an artist). || REL. Ofrenda, *f.* || COMM. Prima, *f.* || — FIG. *It's a gift!,* ¡está tirado!, ¡es muy fácil! | *To be in the gift of,* estar en manos de. || *To have the gift of the gab,* tener mucha labia. || *You would not have it as a gift,* no lo querrías ni regalado.
gift [gift] v. tr. Dotar (to endow with natural talent). || Regalar, obsequiar (to bestow as a gift).
gifted [ˈgiftid] adj. Dotado, da (endowed by nature). || Talentudo, da; talentoso, sa (talented).
gig [gig] n. Canoa, *f.* (a light boat). || Arpón, *m.* (a fish spear). || Calesa, *f.* (a two-wheeled carriage). || U. S. Sedal (*m.*) con varios anzuelos (for fishing). | Actuación, *f.* (a performance). | Castigo, *m.* (in school).
gigantic [dʒaiˈgæntik] adj. Gigantesco, ca.
gigantism [ˈdʒaigæntizəm] n. Gigantismo, *m.*
giggle [ˈgigl] n. Risita, *f.* || *The giggles,* la risa tonta.
giggle [ˈgigl] v. intr. Reírse tontamente.
giggly [ˈgigli] adj. Propenso a reírse.
gigolo [ˈʒigələu] n. "Gigolo", *m.*, chulo, *m.*
gild [gild] n. See GUILD.
gild [gild] v. tr. Dorar (to make golden). || Dar brillo a (to make attractive). || FIG. *To gild the pill,* dorar la píldora.
gildhall [ˈgildhɔ:l] n. See GUILDHALL.
gilder [—ə*] n. Dorador, ra.
gilding [ˈgildiŋ] n. Dorado, *m.*, doradura, *f.* || FIG. Oropel, *m.*
gill [gil] n. Branquia, *f.*, agalla, *f.* (of fish). || Papada, *f.* (of birds, animals). || Laminilla, *f.* (of plants). || Barranco, *m.* (a ravine). || TECH. Aleta, *f.* || FIG. *To look green about the gills,* tener mala cara.
gill [dʒil] n. Medida (*f.*) de líquidos (one quarter of a pint).
gill [gil] v. tr. Limpiar (to gut a fish). || Atrapar por las agallas (to catch by the gills).
gillie [ˈgili] n. Ayudante, *m.*
gillyflower [ˈdʒili,flauə*] n. (Ant.) BOT. Alhelí, *m.*
gilt [gilt] n. Dorado, *m.* (gilding). || FIG. Oropel, *m.*, brillo (*m.*) superficial (superficial glitter). || FAM. Parné, *m.*, pasta, *f.*, plata, *f.* (money). || Cerda (*f.*) joven (young sow).
— Adj. Dorado, da.
gilt-edged [ˈgiltedʒd] adj. Con cantos dorados. || *Gild-edged securities,* valores (*m. pl.*) *or* títulos (*m. pl.*) de máxima garantía.
gilthead [ˈgilthed] n. Dorada, *f.* (fish).
gimbals [ˈdʒimbəlz] pl. n. MAR. Suspensión (*f. sing.*) de cardán.
gimcrack [ˈdʒimkræk] n. Baratija, *f.*, fruslería, *f.*
— Adj. De lance (furniture). || De bisutería (jewel).
gimlet [ˈgimlit] n. TECH. Barrena (*f.*) de mano.
gimlet [ˈgimlit] v. tr. Barrenar.
gimlet eye [—ai] n. Mirada (*f.*) penetrante.
gimlet-eyed [—aid] adj. De mirada penetrante.
gimmick [ˈgimik] n. FAM. Artefacto, *m.*, artilugio, *m.* (a gadget). | Truco, *m.* (trick).
gimp [gimp] n. Galón, *m.*
gin [dʒin] n. Ginebra, *f.* (drink). || "Gin rummy", *m.* (card game). || Cabria, *f.* (a tripod hoist). || Trampa, *f.* (a snare). || TECH. Desmotadora, *f.* (for removing seeds from fibres). || *Gin fizz,* "gin fizz", *m.* (drink).
gin [dʒin] v. tr. Atrapar (to catch animals). || Desmotar (to clean fibres).
ginger [ˈdʒindʒə*] n. BOT. Jengibre, *m.* || FIG. FAM. Garra, *f.*: *a book that lacks ginger,* un libro al que le falta garra. || Color (*m.*) rojizo (reddish-yellow colour).
— Adj. Rojizo, za.
ginger [ˈdʒindʒə*] v. tr. Echar jengibre a (to add ginger to). || FAM. Animar (to liven up).
ginger ale [—ˈeil] or **ginger beer** [—ˈbiə*] n. "Ginger ale", *m.*, gaseosa (*f.*) de jengibre.
gingerbread [—bred] n. Pan (*m.*) de jengibre. || FIG. *Gingerbread work,* decoración recargada y de mal gusto, decoración cursi.
gingerly [—li] adj. Cauteloso, sa.
— Adv. Cautelosamente.
ginger nut [—nʌt] or **gingersnap** [ˈdʒindʒəs,næp] n. Galleta (*f.*) de jengibre.
gingery [ˈdʒindʒəri] adj. Rojizo, za (reddish-yellow coloured). || Que sabe a jengibre (having the taste of ginger). || FIG. Vivo, va (high-spirited). | Agudo, da; punzante (remark, etc.). | Picante (spicy).
gingham [ˈgiŋəm] n. Guinga, *f.*, guingán, *m.* (fabric).
gingival [dʒinˈdʒaivəl] adj. Gingival.
gingivitis [dʒindʒiˈvaitis] n. MED. Gingivitis, *f.*
ginner [ˈdʒinə*] n. Desmotador, ra.
gin rummy [ˈdʒinˈrʌmi] n. "Gin rummy", *m.*
Gioconda [dʒəˈkɔndə] pr. n. ARTS. Gioconda, *f.*
gipsy [ˈdʒipsi] adj./n. Gitano, na (in Western Europe). || Zíngaro, ra (in central Europe).
gipsy moth [—mɔθ] n. ZOOL. Lagarta, *f.*
giraffe [dʒiˈrɑ:f] n. ZOOL. Jirafa, *f.*
girandole [ˈdʒirəndəul] n. Candelabro, *m.* (a candle holder). || Pendiente, *m.* (an earring). || Girándula, *f.* (a rotating water jet or firework).
girasol or **girasole** [ˈdʒirə,sɔl] n. BOT. Girasol, *m.*
gird* [gə:d] v. tr. Ceñir (to fasten with a belt): *he girded his sword,* ciñó la espada. || Rodear (to surround). || FIG. Investir. || *To gird o.s. for the battle,* prepararse para la lucha.
— OBSERV. Pret. & p. p. **girded, girt.**
girder [ˈgə:də*] n. Viga, *f.*
girdle [ˈgə:dl] n. Faja, *f.* (sash, woman's undergarment). || Arista, *f.* (of a gem). || Cinturón, *m.* (a belt). || FIG. Cinturón, *m.*
girdle [ˈgə:dl] v. tr. Ceñir (to bind). || Rodear (to encircle).
girl [gə:l] n. Chica, *f.*, muchacha, *f.* || Niña, *f.* (small child). || Chica, *f.*, joven, *f.* (a young unmarried woman). || FAM. Chica, *f.* || Muchacha, *f.* (a servant). || Novia, *f.* (a sweetheart). || Alumna, *f.* (of a school).
girl friend [—frend] n. Novia, *f.*, amiga, *f.*, amiguita, *f.* (of a boy). || Amiga, *f.* (of a girl).
girlhood [—hud] n. Juventud, *f.*, niñez, *f.*
girlish [—liʃ] adj. De niña (of a girl). || Afeminado, da (effeminate).
girl scout [—skaut] n. Exploradora, *f.*
Gironde [ʒi:rɔ̃d] pr. n. GEOGR. Gironda, *f.*
Girondist [dʒiˈrɔndist] adj./n. HIST. Girondino, na.
girt [gə:t] pret. & p. p. See GIRD.
girth [gə:θ] n. Cincha, *f.* (strap for securing a pack). || Circunferencia, *f.* (circumference). || Gordura, *f.* (stoutness). || Dimensiones, *f. pl.* (dimensions).
girth [gə:θ] v. tr. Cinchar, ceñir.
gist [dʒist] n. Esencia, *f.*, quid, *m.*, fondo, *m.*, lo esencial (heart of the matter). || JUR. Motivo (*m.*) principal.
give [giv] n. Elasticidad, *f.*
give* [giv] v. tr. Dar: *give me the book,* dame el libro; *I give you twenty francs for that,* te doy veinte francos por eso; *he gave a start,* dio un salto; *they gave a cry of delight,* dieron un grito de alegría; *he gave a sigh,* dio un suspiro; *she gave signs of life,* dio señales de vida; *I'd give my life for you,* daría mi vida por ti; *I would give my eyetooth to go,* daría un ojo de la cara por ir; *I give you my word,* te doy mi palabra; *I'm going to give a lecture,* voy a dar una conferencia; *they will give a show tomorrow,* darán una función mañana. || Regalar, dar (to offer as a present): *I had this book given to me,* me dieron este libro. || Proveer de (to provide with). || Pasar, dar (to hand over). || Entregar (to deliver). || Indicar (pressure, etc.). Hacer (a gesture). || Conceder, dar (to grant): *God has given me what I prayed for,* Dios me ha concedido lo que le pedí. || Administrar, dar (the sacraments). || Conceder: *I'll give you that,* te concedo eso. || Ceder: *to give ground to the enemy,* ceder terreno al enemigo. || Imponer (to inflict). || Dar, poner: *she was given a pretty name,* le han puesto un nombre bonito. || Contagiar: *I gave you a cold,* te contagié el resfriado. || Pronunciar (a speech). || Decir, venir con: *don't give me that,* no me vengas con eso. || Comunicar: *please, give us your decision,* comuníquenos su decisión, por favor. || MED. Poner (to administer). || JUR. Pronunciar: *to give a sentence,* pronunciar un fallo. | Condenar a, dar (punishment). || Dejar (to leave): *he gave money for the poor when he died,* dejó dinero para los pobres cuando murió. || Dejar

(to lend): *give me your watch*, déjame el reloj. || Dedicar (to devote). || Poner con (on the phone): *give me the police*, póngame con la policía. || COMM. BOT. Dar. || Brindar por: *I give you the mayor*, brindo por el alcalde. || — FIG. *Give him an inch and he'll take a yard*, dale la mano y te cogerá el brazo. || *Give him my compliments*, salúdele respetuosamente de mi parte. || *Give him my love*, dale recuerdos. || *He was given to believe that*, le hicieron creer que. || *How long do you give your diet?*, ¿cuánto tiempo crees que va a durar tu régimen? || FAM. *I don't give a damn!*, ¡no me importa un bledo!, ¡no me importa un comino! || *I gave fifty pounds for my car*, el coche me costó cincuenta libras. || FIG. *I gave him what for*, le di su merecido. || FAM. *I'll give it to you!*, ¡te vas a enterar! | *I'll give you bull if I catch you!*, ¡ya te voy a dar yo pelota si te cojo! || *To be much given to*, ser muy aficionado a, gustarle mucho a uno, ser muy dado a. || *To give a laugh*, soltar la risa. || *To give (an account) of*, dar cuenta de. || *To give a recitation*, recitar un poema. || *To give a smile to*, sonreír a. || *To give a thought to*, acordarse de, recordar. || *To give attention to*, prestar atención a. || *To give birth*, see BIRTH. || *To give ear, help to*, prestar oídos, ayuda a. || FAM. *To give it to s.o.*, echarle una bronca a alguien (to scold), pegarle una buena paliza a alguien (to beat). || *To give mouth to*, expresar. || *To give notice*, see NOTICE. || *To give o.s. airs*, darse aires. || *To give o.s. one hour for*, necesitar una hora para. || *To give o.s. to*, dedicarse a, entregarse a. || *To give rise to*, causar, ocasionar. || *To give s.o. a glance*, echarle una mirada a alguien. || *To give s.o. a hand*, echarle una mano a uno. || *To give s.o. a lift*, llevar a alguien en coche. || *To give s.o. a song*, cantar para alguien. || *To give s.o. to understand that*, dar a entender a alguien que. || *To give sth. into s.o.'s hands*, entregar algo a alguien. || *To give sth. to eat*, dar algo de comer. || *Two and two gives four*, dos y dos son cuatro.

— V. intr. Hacer regalos: *he enjoys giving at Christmas*, le gusta hacer regalos por Navidades. || Ceder (to yield to pressure). || Dar de sí (to stretch). || — *To feel one's legs give beneath one*, flaquearle las piernas a uno. || FIG. *To give as good as one gets*, pagar con la misma moneda. || *To give and take*, hacer concesiones mutuas. || *To give on to*, dar a. || FAM. *What gives?*, ¿qué pasa?

— **To give away**, distribuir, repartir (to distribute). | Regalar (a present). | Revelar, descubrir (to discover). | Entregar (prizes). | Deshacerse de (to get rid of). | — *To give away the bride*, llevar la novia al altar. | *To give o.s. away*, traicionarse. | *To give s.o. away*, traicionar *or* denunciar a alguien. | FIG. *To give the show away*, descubrir el pastel, revelar un secreto. || **To give back**, devolver. || **To give forth**, divulgar (news). | Emitir (a sound). | Despedir (smell, gas, etc.). || **To give in**, darse por vencido, rendirse (to admit defeat). | Ceder (to yield). | Dar (one's name). | Entregar (to hand in): *to give in a document*, entregar un documento. | — *To give in to*, ceder ante. || **To give off**, despedir, emitir. || **To give out**, distribuir, repartir (to distribute). | Emitir (to emit). | Anunciar (to proclaim). | Divulgar (to spread). | Agotarse (supplies). | Acabarse (strength, patience). | Sufrir una avería (engine). | — *To give (s.o.) out to be*, hacer pasar por. || **To give over**, entregar (to hand over). | Dejar de (to stop): *to give over crying*, dejar de llorar. | *Give over!*, ¡basta ya! (stop it). | — *To give o.s. over to*, abandonarse a. || **To give up**, dejar, abandonar (to abandon). | Renunciar a, dimitir de (one's appointment). | Dejar (one's business). | Vender (one's property). | Darse por vencido, rendirse (to admit defeat). | Entregar (to hand over). | Dejar por imposible (to renounce an impossible task). | Ceder (to yield). | Desahuciar (a sick person). | Dejar de: *I gave up smoking*, dejé de fumar. | — *To give it up*, darse por vencido. | *To give o.s. up*, entregarse. | *To give o.s. up to*, entregarse a (vice), dedicarse a (study). | *To give s.o. up*, dejar a alguien, acabar con alguien. | *To give s.o. up for lost, for dead*, dar a alguien por perdido, por muerto. | *To give up one's seat to s.o.*, ceder el asiento a alguien. *To give up the crown*, renunciar a la corona.

— OBSERV. Pret. **gave**; p. p. **given**.

give-and-take [ˈgivənˈteik] n. Toma y daca, *m.*, concesiones (*f. pl.*) mutuas.
giveaway [ˈgivəwei] n. Revelación (*f.*) involuntaria (indiscrete disclosure). || FAM. Examen (*m.*) tirado (easy examination). || Ganapierde, *m.* (in draughts). || U. S. Regalo, *m.*, obsequio, *m.* (free gift). | FAM. Concurso (*m.*) radiofónico. || *Giveaway price*, precio de saldo.
given [ˈgivn] p. p. See GIVE.
— Adj. Fijado, da; dado da (fixed). || Dado, da: *he is much given to*, es muy dado a; *given my strength*, dada mi fuerza. || Determinado, da (determined): *in a given moment*, en un momento determinado. || MATH. Dado, da. || — U. S. *Given name*, nombre (*m.*) de pila. || *She is given that way!*, ¡ella es así!
giver [ˈgivə*] n. Donador, ra; donante, *m.* & *f.*
giving [ˈgiviŋ] n. Don, *m.* (gift). || — *Giving away*, reparto, *m.*, distribución, *f.* (of prizes), denuncia, *f.* (of s.o.) || *Giving back*, devolución, *f.*, restitución, *f.* || *Giving forth*, publicación, *f.* (of news), emisión, *f.* (of sound). || *Giving in*, entrega, *f.* || *Giving up*, abandono, *m.*
gizzard [gizəd] n. Molleja, *f.* (of a bird). || FIG. FAM. *That sticks in my gizzard*, no puedo tragar eso.
glabrous [ˈgleibrəs] adj. Lampiño, ña; glabro, bra (face). || BOT. Liso, sa.
glacé [glæˈsei] adj. Escarchado, da (covered with sugar). || Helado, da (frozen). || Glaseado, da (glossy).
glacial [ˈgleiʃəl] adj. Glacial: *glacial period*, período glacial; *glacial zones*, zonas glaciales; *glacial wind*, viento glacial. || Glaciar: *glacial deposits*, depósitos glaciares.
glaciation [ˌglæsiˈeiʃən] n. Glaciación, *f.*
glacier [ˈglæsjə*] n. GEOL. Glaciar, *m.*, ventisquero, *m.* [*Amer.*, helero, *m.*]
glaciology [ˌglæˈsjɔlədʒi] n. GEOL. Glaciología, *f.*
glacis [ˈgleisis] n. Glacis, *m.*, explanada, *f.*

— OBSERV. El plural de la palabra inglesa es *glacis* o *glacises*.

glad [glæd] adj. Contento, ta; alegre (pleased). || Feliz (happy). || Agradable, bueno, na (giving pleasure). || — U. S. *Glad hand*, saludo afectuoso. || *To be glad*, alegrarse: *I am glad to see you*, me alegro de verte. || *To be very glad to help s.o.*, tener mucho gusto en ayudar a alguien. || FAM. *To give s.o. the glad eye*, echar miradas cariñosas a alguien.
gladden [ˈglædn] v. tr. Alegrar.
glade [gleid] n. Claro, *m.* (in a wood).
gladiator [ˈglædieitə*] n. Gladiador, *m.*
gladiolus [ˌglædiˈəuləs] n. BOT. Gladiolo, *m.*, gladíolo, *m.* (flower).

— OBSERV. El plural de *gladiolus* es *gladioli*, *gladiolus* o *gladioluses*.

gladly [ˈglædli] adv. Alegremente. || Con mucho gusto (willingly).
gladness [ˈglædnis] n. Alegría, *f.*
gladsome [ˈglædsəm] adj. Alegre, contento, ta.
Gladstone bag [ˈglædstənbæg] n. Maletín, *m.*
glair [glεə*] n. Clara (*f.*) de huevo.
glairy [—ri] adj. Viscoso, sa.
glamor [ˈglæmə*] n. U. S. Encanto, *m.*, atractivo, *m.*
glamorize [ˈglæməraiz] v. tr. Adornar. || Embellecer.
glamorous [ˈglæmərəs] adj. Encantador, ra; atractivo, va.
glamour [ˈglæmə*] n. Encanto, *m.* || *Glamour girl*, muchacha atractiva, guapa, *f.*
glance [glɑːns] n. Mirada, *f.*, ojeada, *f.*, vistazo, *m.* (look). || Destello, *m.* (of light). || MIN. Mineral (*m.*) lustroso. || Desviación, *f.* (deflection). || SP. Golpe (*m.*) con efecto (in cricket). || — *At a glance*, de un vistazo. || *At first glance*, a primera vista.
glance [glɑːns] v. tr. Golpear con efecto (in cricket). || *To glance one's eye over*, echar una mirada a.
— V. intr. Echar una mirada *or* ojeada *or* vistazo (*at*, a) [to have a look at]. || Brillar (to shine). || Botar con efecto (to bounce at an angle). || — *To glance aside*, apartar la vista. || *To glance off*, tocar, tratar por encima (a subject), rebotar (a bullet). || *To glance over*, mirar por encima, echar un vistazo a. || *To glance over a problem*, tratar un problema por encima.
glancing [—iŋ] adj. Oblicuo, cua. || Indirecto, ta.
gland [glænd] n. ANAT. BOT. Glándula, *f.*: *lachrymal gland*, glándula lagrimal. || TECH. Casquillo, *m.* (of a stuffing box).
glanders [ˈglændəz] pl. n. VET. Muermo, *m. sing.*
glandular [ˈglændjulə*] adj. Glandular.
glandulous [ˈglændjuləs] adj. Glanduloso, sa.
glans [glænz] n. ANAT. Bálano, *m.*, glande, *m.* (of the penis). | Glande (*m.*) clitoridiano (of the clitoris).

— OBSERV. El plural de *glans* es *glandes*.

glare [glεə*] n. Luz (*f.*) deslumbrante (strong light). || Deslumbramiento, *m.* (dazzle). || Mirada (*f.*) feroz *or* airada (fierce look). || Colorido (*m.*) chillón (flashiness). || Ostentación, *f.* (boasting).
glare [glεə*] v. intr. Relumbrar, brillar (to shine). || Deslumbrar (to dazzle). || Mirar airadamente (to stare fiercely). || Saltar a la vista (to be too evident).
glariness [—rinis] n. Resplandor, *m.*
glaring [—riŋ] adj. Deslumbrante; deslumbrador, ra (dazzling). || Resplandeciente, brillante (bright). || Chillón, ona (flashy). || Evidente, manifiesto, ta (conspicuous). || Airado, da; feroz (fierce).
glary [ˈglεəri] adj. See GLARING.
glass [glɑːs] n. Vidrio, *m.* (substance). || Vaso, *m.* (drinking vessel). || Copa, *f.* (drinking vessel with stem). || Espejo, *m.* (mirror). || Cristal, *m.* (protective covering). || Lente, *f.* (lens). || Reloj (*m.*) de arena (hourglass). || Cristalería, *f.* (glassware). || Cristal, *m.* (pane). || Cristal, *m.* (of a picture, watch). || Barómetro, *m.* (barometer). || Catalejo, *m.* (telescope). || Invernadero, *m.* (greenhouse). || Escaparate, *m.* (of a shop). || — Pl. Gafas, *f.*, lentes, *m.* [*Amer.*, anteojos, *m.*, espejuelos, *m.*] (spectacles). || Gemelos, *m.* (binoculars).
glass bead [—biːd] n. Abalorio, *m.*
glassblower [—ˌbləuə*] n. Soplador (*m.*) de vidrio.
glassblowing [—ˌbləuiŋ] n. Soplado (*m.*) del vidrio.
glass case [—keis] n. COMM. Escaparate, *m.* || Campana (*f.*) de cristal (for protecting).
glass cutter [—ˌkʌtə*] n. Cortavidrio, *m.*, diamante, *m.*, grujidor, *m.* (tool).
glass door [—dɔː*] n. Puerta (*f.*) de cristales.
glass eye [—ai] n. Ojo (*m.*) de cristal.
glass factory [—ˈfæktəri] n. Cristalería, *f.*

glassful [—ful] n. Vaso, *m.*
glasshouse [—haus] n. Invernadero, *m.* (greenhouse). || Fábrica (*f.*) de cristal (glassworks). || FAM. MIL. Prisión (*f.*) militar.
glassmaker [—meikə*] n. Vidriero, *m.*
glass paper [—,peipə*] n. Papel (*m.*) de lija.
glassware [—wεə*] n. Cristalería, *f.*, artículos (*m. pl.*) de cristal.
glasswool [—wul] n. Lana (*f.*) de vidrio.
glasswork [—wə:k] n. Cristalería, *f.* (glassware). || — Pl. Fábrica (*f. sing.*) de vidrio.
glassworker [—wə:kə*] n. Vidriero, *m.*
glasswort [—wə:t] n. BOT. Sosa, *f.*
glassy [ˈglɑ:si] adj. Vidrioso, sa (dull, lifeless). || Vítreo, a (like glass). || Liso, sa (smooth). || Cristalino, na (water).
Glaswegian [glæsˈwi:dʒən] adj. De Glasgow.
— N. Persona (*f.*) de Glasgow.
glaucoma [glɔ:ˈkəumə] n. MED. Glaucoma, *m.* (disease of the eye).
glaucous [ˈglɔ:kəs] adj. Glauco, ca.
glaze [gleiz] n. Vidriado, *m.* (for pottery). || Brillo, *m.* (sheen). || Barniz, *m.* (varnish). || U. S. Aguanieve, *f.* (sleet). | Terreno (*m.*) helado (icy ground).
glaze [gleiz] v. tr. Poner cristales a (a window). || Vidriar (pottery). || Barnizar (to varnish). || Sacar brillo a (to polish). || Glasear (cakes, paper). || Poner vidrioso (eye). || *To glaze in*, poner cristales a.
— V. intr. Ponerse vidrioso.
glazier [ˈgleizjə*] n. Vidriero, *m.*
glazing [ˈgleiziŋ] n. Barniz, *m.* (varnish). || Barnizado, *m.* (action of varnishing). || Cristales, *m. pl.* (windowpanes). || Glaseado, *m.* (of cakes, paper).
gleam [gli:m] n. Destello, *m.*, rayo, *m.* || FIG. Resquicio, *m.*: *a gleam of hope*, un resquicio de esperanza. | Punta, *f.* (of irony). | Chispa, *f.* (of intelligence).
gleam [gli:m] v. intr. Destellar, brillar.
gleamy [—i] adj. Reluciente, brillante.
glean [gli:n] v. tr./intr. Espigar. || FIG. Recoger, cosechar.
— V. intr. Espigar.
gleaner [—ə*] n. Espigador, ra.
gleaning [—iŋ] n. Espigueo, *m.* || FIG. Rebusca, *f.*
glebe [gli:b] n. REL. Terreno (*m.*) beneficial.
glee [gli:] n. Regocijo, *m.*, júbilo, *m.* || MUS. Canción (*f.*) para tres o más voces sin acompañamiento. || MUS. *Glee club*, coral, *f.*
gleeful [ˈgli:ful] or **gleesome** [—səum] adj. Regocijado, da; jubiloso, sa; alegre.
gleet [gli:t] n. MED. Gota (*f.*) militar.
glen [glen] n. Cañada, *f.*
glengarry [glenˈgæri] n. Gorro (*m.*) escocés.
glenoid [ˈgli:nɔid] adj. ANAT. Glenoideo, a. || ANAT. *Glenoid cavity*, cavidad glenoidea, glena, *f.*
glib [glib] adj. Fácil (too pat). || De mucha labia (person). || Liso, sa; resbaladizo, za (surface). || *To have a glib tongue*, tener la lengua suelta.
glibness [—nis] n. Labia, *f.*, facundia, *f.* || Soltura, *f.* (of speech).
glide [glaid] n. Deslizamiento, *m.* (gentle movement). || AVIAT. Planeo, *m.*, vuelo (*m.*) sin motor. || MUS. Ligadura, *f.* || GRAMM. Semivocal, *f.*
glide [glaid] v. tr. Hacer deslizar (to make to move gently). || AVIAT. Hacer planear.
— V. intr. Deslizarse (to move smoothly). || AVIAT. Planear. || *The years glide by*, pasan los años.
glider [—ə*] n. AVIAT. Planeador, *m.* || U. S. Columpio, *m.* (swing).
gliding [—iŋ] n. Deslizamiento, *m.* (gentle movement). || AVIAT. Planeo, *m.*, vuelo (*m.*) sin motor (sport of flying in gliders).
glimmer [ˈglimə*] n. Luz (*f.*) tenue, luz (*f.*) trémula (faint light). || Espejeo, *m.* (of water). || FIG. Resquicio, *m.* (of hope). | Chispa, *f.* (of intelligence).
glimmer [ˈglimə*] v. intr. Brillar tenuemente. || Espejear (water).
glimpse [glimps] n. Vislumbre, *f.*, visión (*f.*) momentánea. || *To catch a glimpse of*, vislumbrar.
glimpse [glimps] v. tr./intr. Vislumbrar, entrever. || *To glimpse at*, echar una ojeada a.
glint [glint] n. Destello, *m.*, centelleo, *m.*
glint [glint] v. intr. Destellar, centellear.
— V. tr. Reflejar.
glissade [gliˈsɑ:d] n. Deslizamiento, *m.*
glissade [gli:sɑ:d] v. intr. Deslizarse.
glisten [ˈglisn] n. Brillo, *m.*, resplandor, *m.*
glisten [ˈglisn] v. intr. Relucir, brillar. || FIG. *All that glistens is not gold*, no es oro todo lo que reluce.
glitter [ˈglitə*] n. Brillo, *m.*
glitter [ˈglitə*] v. intr. Relucir, brillar. || FIG. *All that glitters is not gold*, no es oro todo lo que reluce.
glittering [ˈglitəriŋ] adj. Reluciente, brillante.
gloaming [ˈgləumiŋ] n. Crepúsculo, *m.*
gloat [gləut] v. intr. Recrearse con, refocilarse con.
glob [glɔb] n. U. S. Gota, *f.* (drop).
global [ˈgləubəl] adj. Global: *global view*, vista global; *global method*, método global. || Esférico, ca (spherical). || Mundial (of the world).
globate [ˈgləubeit] adj. Esférico, ca.
globe [gləub] n. Globo, *m.*, esfera, *f.* || Esfera (*f.*) terrestre, globo (*m.*) terráqueo (the Earth). || Globo, *m.* (of a lamp).
globefish [ˈgləubfiʃ] n. ZOOL. Orbe, *m.*
globe-trotter [—,trɔtə*] n. Trotamundos, *m. inv.*
globose [ˈgləubəus] adj. Globoso, sa; globular.
globular [ˈglɔbjulə*] adj. Globular.
globule [ˈglɔbjul] n. Glóbulo, *m.*
globulin [ˈglɔbju:lin] n. CHEM. Globulina, *f.*
globulous [ˈglɔbjuləs] adj. Globuloso, sa.
glomerate [ˈglɔmərət] adj. Aglomerado, da.
glomeration [,glɔməˈreiʃən] n. Aglomeración, *f.*
gloom [glu:m] n. Penumbra, *f.* (semidarkness). || Melancolía, *f.*, tristeza, *f.* (melancholy). || Pesimismo, *m.* || *To cast a gloom over*, entristecer.
gloom [glu:m] v. intr. Encapotarse (sky). || Entristecerse.
gloominess [glu:minis] n. See GLOOM.
gloomy [ˈglu:mi] adj. Oscuro, ra; tenebroso, sa (dark). || Melancólico, ca (melancholic). || Deprimente (depressing). || Pesimista: *to feel gloomy*, sentirse pesimista. || Encapotado, da (sky).
gloria [ˈglɔ:riə] n. REL. Gloria, *m.* || ARTS. Gloria, *f.*
glorification [,glɔ:rifiˈkeiʃən] n. Glorificación, *f.*
glorify [ˈglɔrifai] v. tr. Glorificar. || Alabar (to praise).
gloriole [ˈglɔ:riəul] n. ARTS. Halo, *m.*
glorious [ˈglɔ:riəs] adj. Glorioso, sa. || Radiante (day). || Espléndido, da; magnífico, ca (wonderful). || Colosal, enorme, mayúsculo, la: *glorious mess*, lío colosal.
glory [ˈglɔ:ri] n. Gloria, *f.*: *glory be to the Father*, gloria al Padre; *these paintings are the glory of the museum*, estos cuadros son las glorias del museo; *Cervantes is one of the glories of Spain*, Cervantes es una de las glorias de España; *the king in all his glory*, el rey en toda su gloria; *the saints who are in glory*, los santos que están en la Gloria. || Gloria, *f.*, fama, *f.* (renown). || ARTS. Gloria, *f.* (aureole). || Belleza, *f.* (beauty). || — FAM. *Glory hole*, leonera, *f.* (room in disorder). || FIG. *In one's glory*, en la gloria: *he is in his glory*, está en la gloria. | *To cover o.s. in* o *with glory*, cubrirse de gloria. | *To go to glory*, irse al otro mundo.
glory [ˈglɔ:ri] v. intr. Gloriarse, enorgullecerse (*in*, de) [to be proud]. || Exultar (to exult).
gloss [glɔs] n. Glosa, *f.* (comment, interpretation, explanation). || Glosario, *m.* (glossary). || Glosa, *f.* (poetical composition). || Brillo, *m.*, lustre, *m.* (sheen). || FIG. Oropel, *m.*
gloss [glɔs] v. tr. Glosar (a text). || Desvirtuar, glosar (to misinterpret). || Dar brillo a, lustrar (to put a sheen on). || *To gloss over*, encubrir (to cover up), disfrazar (to disguise).
— V. intr. Hacer glosas.
glossarist [ˈglɔsərist] or **glossator** [ˈglɔsətə*] n. Glosador, ra.
glossary [ˈglɔsəri] n. Glosario, *m.*
glossiness [ˈglɔsinis] n. Brillo, *m.*, lustre, *m.*
glossy [ˈglɔsi] adj. Brillante, lustroso, sa. || Brillante (photograph). || Liso, sa (hair). || Glaseado, da (paper).
— N. Revista (*f.*) impresa en papel glaseado.
glottal [ˈglɔtl] or **glottic** [ˈglɔtik] adj. Glótico, ca (pertaining to the glottis).
glottis [ˈglɔtis] n. ANAT. Glotis, *f. inv.*
glove [glʌv] n. Guante, *m.*: *boxing gloves*, guantes de boxeo. || — *Glove box* o *compartment*, guantera, *f.* (in a car). || *Glove factory* o *shop*, guantería, *f.* || *Glove stretcher*, ensanchador (*m.*) de guantes. || FIG. *To fit like a glove*, sentar como anillo al dedo. | *To go hand in glove*, ser uña y carne. | *To take up the glove*, recoger el guante. | *To throw down the glove*, arrojar el guante. | *With the gloves off*, sin miramientos.
glove [glʌv] v. tr. Enguantar.
glover [ˈglʌvə*] n. Guantero, ra.
glow [gləu] n. Incandescencia, *f.* (emission of light without smoke or flame). || Brillo, *m.* (of jewel). || Resplandor, *m.* (glaze). || Color (*m.*) vivo, luminosidad, *f.* (bright colour). || Arrebol, *m.* (of sun). || Calor, *m.* (heat). || Rubor, *m.* (in cheeks). || Calor, *m.*, ardor, *m.* (of feelings).
glow [gləu] v. intr. Estar al rojo vivo (metal). || Brillar (to shine). || Rebosar de: *to glow with health*, rebosar de salud. || Estar encendido (to be lit up). || Enrojecerse (complexion). || Enardecerse, encenderse (with passion).
glower [ˈglauə*] n. Mirada (*f.*) furiosa.
glower [ˈglauə*] v. intr. Lanzar una mirada furiosa.
glowing [gləuiŋ] adj. Incandescente. || Al rojo vivo (metal, etc.). || Rojo, ja (complexion). || Encendido, da (cheeks). || Vivo, va (fire, colour). || Brillante (light). || Entusiasta (enthusiastic). || Cálido, da (style, terms). || *Glowing with health*, rebosante de salud.
glowworm [ˈgləuwə:m] n. ZOOL. Luciérnaga, *f.*, gusano (*m.*) de luz.
gloze [gləuz] v. tr. *To gloze over*, encubrir.
glucemia [gluˈsi:mjə] n. MED. Glucemia, *f.*, glicemia, *f.*
glucide [ˈglu:said] n. CHEM. Glúcido, *m.*
glucinium [glu:ˈsinjəm] or **glucinum** [ˈglu:sinəm] n. CHEM. Glucinio, *m.*
glucometer [glukɔˈmitə*] n. Glucómetro, *m.*
glucose [ˈglu:kəus] n. CHEM. Glucosa, *f.*
glucoside [ˈglu:kəsaid] n. CHEM. Glucósido, *m.*
glue [glu:] n. Pegamento, *m.*, cola, *f.*
glue [glu:] v. tr. Pegar.
— V. intr. Pegarse.
gluey [ˈglu:i] adj. Pegajoso, sa.
glum [glʌm] adj. Sombrío, a; taciturno, na; triste.
glut [glʌt] n. Superabundancia, *f.*, exceso, *m.* (of the market). || Saciedad, *f.*, hartazgo, *m.* (of food).
glut [glʌt] v. tr. Inundar (the market). || Hartar, saciar (to overfeed).

gluteal [ˈglu:ti:əl] adj. ANAT. Glúteo, a.
gluten [ˈglu:tən] n. Gluten, *m.*
gluteus [gluˈtiəs] n. ANAT. Glúteo, *m.* (muscle).
— OBSERV. El plural de *gluteus* es *glutei*.
glutinous [ˈglu:tinəs] adj. Glutinoso, sa; pegajoso, sa.
glutton [ˈglʌtn] n. Glotón, ona (excessive eater). || ZOOL. Glotón, *m.* || — *Glutton for work*, trabajador (*m.*) incansable. || *To be a glutton for sth.*, ser insaciable de algo.
gluttonous [ˈglʌtnəs] adj. Glotón, ona.
gluttony [ˈglʌtni] n. Glotonería, *f.*, gula, *f.* || *Sin of gluttony*, pecado (*m.*) de gula.
glyceride [ˈglisəraid] n. CHEM. Glicérido, *m.*
glycerin [ˈglisərin] or **glycerine** [ˌglisəˈri:n] n. CHEM. Glicerina, *f.*
glycerol [ˈglisərəl] n. CHEM. Glicerol, *m.*
glycerophosphate [ˈglisərəuˈfɔsfeit] n. CHEM. Glicerofosfato, *m.*
glycogen [ˈglikəudʒen] n. CHEM. Glicógeno, *m.*
glycol [ˈglaikɔl] n. CHEM. Glicol, *m.*
glycoside [ˈglaikəsaid] n. CHEM. Glucósido, *m.*
glyph [glif] n. Glifo, *m.*
glyptic [ˈgliptik] n. Glíptica, *f.*
glyptodon [ˈgliptədɔn] or **glyptodont** [ˈgliptədɔnt] n. Gliptodonte, *m.*
glyptography [glipˈtɔgrəfi] n. Gliptografía, *f.*
G-man [ˈdʒi:mæn] n. U. S. FAM. Agente (*m.*) del F.B.I. (Federal Bureau of Investigation).
gnarl [nɑ:l] n. Nudo, *m.* (in wood).
gnarled [—d] or **gnarly** [—i] adj. Nudoso, sa.
gnash [næʃ] v. tr. Rechinar.
gnashing [—iŋ] n. Rechinamiento, *m.*
gnat [næt] n. ZOOL. Mosquito, *m.*
gnaw* [nɔ:] v. tr./intr. Roer.
— OBSERV. Pret. ***gnawed;*** p. p. ***gnawed, gnawn.***
gnawing [—iŋ] n. Roedura, *f.* || Retortijón, *m.* (of stomach).
gneiss [nais] n. GEOL. Gneis, *m.*
gnome [nəum] n. Gnomo, *m.* (small imaginary person). || Duende, *m.* (goblin). || Enano, *m.* (dwarf).
gnomic [ˈnəumik] adj. Gnómico, ca.
gnomon [ˈnəumən] n. Gnomon, *m.*
gnosis [ˈnəusis] n. PHIL. Gnosis, *f.*
gnostic [ˈnɔstik] adj./n. PHIL. Gnóstico, ca.
gnosticism [ˈnɔstisizəm] n. PHIL. Gnosticismo, *m.*
gnu [nu:] n. ZOOL. Ñu, *m.*
go [gəu] n. Energía, *f.* (energy): *to have lots of go*, tener mucha energía. || — *At one go*, en una sola vez. || *Is it a go?*, ¿está resuelto?, ¿estamos de acuerdo? || *It's a go*, trato hecho. || *It's all the go*, está muy en boga. || *It's your go*, te toca a ti. || *No go*, inútil. || *On the go*, ocupado, da (busy). || FAM. *The go*, la moda. || *To have a go at sth.*, intentar algo. || *To make a go of sth.*, tener éxito en algo. || *What a pretty go!*, ¡vaya desastre!
— Adj. Listo, ta.
go* [gəu] v. intr. Ir: *I am going to the cinema*, voy al cine; *I must go to Paris*, tengo que ir a París; *to go and fetch*, ir a buscar; *to go barefoot*, ir descalzo; *salary goes by age*, el sueldo va según la edad; *the meeting was going very well*, la reunión iba muy bien; *to go to school*, ir al colegio; *to go to war*, ir a la guerra; *how are things going?*, ¿cómo van las cosas?; *these colours go very well*, estos colores van muy bien. || Salir (to depart): *the coach goes at seven o'clock*, el autocar sale a las siete. || Irse (to leave): *he went at midnight*, se fue a medianoche. || Irse (to be spent): *all his money goes on wine*, se le va el dinero en vino. || Hacer: *this car goes at 50 miles an hour*, este coche hace 50 millas por hora. || Desaparecer (to disappear): *the pain soon goes*, pronto desaparece el dolor. || Ser suprimido (to be abolished): *Latin is going to go next term*, el latín será suprimido el próximo trimestre. || Llegar (to reach): *the property goes as far as the river*, la finca llega hasta el río. || Funcionar: *this clock does not go*, este reloj no funciona; *a going concern*, una empresa que funciona; *it goes by electricity*, funciona con electricidad. || Quedarse, volverse (to become): *to go blind*, quedarse ciego; *to go mad*, volverse loco. || Ponerse: *he went red*, se puso colorado; *it has gone very cold*, se ha puesto muy frío. || Salir, resultar: *all has gone well*, todo ha salido bien. || Sonar (to sound): *the bell goes at three*, el timbre suena a las tres. || Decir (to say): *the story goes that*, la historia dice que. || Hacer (to carry out an action): *go like this*, haz así. || Pasar: *it went unobserved*, pasó desapercibido. || Escapar (to escape): *he went unpunished*, escapó sin castigo. || Acudir: *you must go to him to get what you want*, tienes que acudir a él para obtener lo que quieres. || Romperse (to break). || Ceder (to give way): *the beam went*, cedió la viga. || Caerse, caer (to fall). || Fundirse (a fuse). || Gastarse (to wear out): *my shoes have gone*, se me han gastado los zapatos. || Caber (to fit): *it won't go into the box*, no cabe en la caja. || Ponerse, ir (to be placed): *coats go on the peg*, los abrigos se ponen en la percha. || Venderse (to be sold): *it went for fifty pounds*, se vendió por cincuenta libras. || Tener curso legal, valer (currency). || Transcurrir, pasar (time). || Contribuir (to be a contributing factor): *it all goes to show that*, todo contribuye a demostrar que. || Pasar (to be given to). || Ser ganado (to be won). || Ser: *how does that story go?*, ¿cómo es esa historia? ||Estar disponible (to be available). || Valer: *anything goes*, todo vale. || Morir (to die).
— *Anything that's going*, lo que haya. || *As far as that goes*, por lo que se refiere a esto. || *As things go*, según y como van las cosas ahora. || *Four into twenty goes five*, veinte entre cuatro son cinco (in mathematics). || *From the word go*, desde el principio, desde que el mundo es mundo. || SP. *Go!*, ¡ya! || JUR. *Going, going, gone!*, ¡a la una... a las dos... a las tres! || *He's a good teacher as teachers go*, es un buen profesor dentro de lo que cabe. || *His sight went*, perdió la vista. || *How goes it?*, ¿cómo va eso?, ¿qué tal? || *It's all right as far as it goes*, está bien dentro de lo que cabe. || *Let's go!*, ¡vamos!, ¡vámonos! || *That goes for me to*, yo también. || *There he goes!*, ¡ahí va! || *There is an hour to go before*, queda una hora antes. || FIG. *There you go again!*, ¡otra vez con la misma canción! || *The song goes like this*, la canción es así. || FAM. *They have gone and done it!*, ¡buena la han hecho! || *To be going sixty*, andar por los sesenta. || *To be going to*, ir a, estar a punto de (to be about to): *I am going to sing*, voy a cantar; ir a (to intend to). || *To come and go*, ir y venir. || *To go bail for*, salir fiador por. || *To go bang*, explotar. || *To go far*, see FAR. || *To go fifty-fifty*, ir a medias. || *To go for a walk*, [ir a] dar un paseo. || *To go hunting*, ir de caza. || *To go near*, acercarse a. || *To go on a journey*, ir de viaje. || *To go on an errand*, ir a hacer un recado. || *To go on strike*, declararse en huelga. || *To go shopping*, ir de compras. || *To go to prove*, demostrar. || *To go to the trouble of*, tomarse la molestia de. || *To keep going*, see KEEP. || *To let go*, see LET. || *To let o.s. go*, see LET. || *To set going*, poner en marcha. || *What I say goes*, aquí se hace lo que yo digo. || MIL. *Who goes there?*, ¿quién va?
— V. tr. Andar, recorrer (to cover): *we have gone five miles*, hemos andado cinco millas. || Apostar, hacer una puesta de (to bet): *to go 5 000 pesetas*, apostar 5 000 mil pesetas. || Declarar (in cards). || Hacer: *to go a journey*, hacer un viaje. || Ir por (to travel by): *to go the short way*, ir por el camino más corto. || Dar (to strike): *it has gone six*, ya han dado las seis. || Ofrecer: *I'll go six pounds for the car*, ofrezco seis libras por el coche. || — *To go it*, ir a toda velocidad (to go fast), echar el resto (to work hard), correrla (to live it up). || *To go it alone*, obrar por su cuenta. || *To go one better on s.o.*, superar a alguien.
— ***To go about***, circular, correr (rumour, story). | Ir de un sitio para otro (to circulate). | MAR. Virar de bordo. | Hacer: *you're not going about it right*, no lo estás haciendo bien. | Ocuparse de (to be occupied with). | Salir: *he goes about a great deal*, sale mucho. | Recorrer: *to go about the country*, recorrer el país. | Emprender (a task). || ***To go after***, perseguir (to chase). | Seguir (to follow). | Andar tras (to try to obtain). || ***To go against***, ir en contra de. || ***To go along***, pasar por (a street). | Seguir, continuar (to continue). | Estar de acuerdo (to agree). | — *As we go along*, sobre la marcha. | FAM. *Go along with you!*, ¡qué va! | *To go along with*, acompañar a. || ***To go around***, see TO GO ROUND. || ***To go at***, atacar, acometer. | FAM. *Go at it!*, ¡venga! || ***To go away***, irse, marcharse (to leave). | Desaparecer (to disappear). | — *To go away with*, llevarse. || ***To go back***, volver, regresar. | Retroceder: *to go back two paces*, retroceder dos pasos. | Volver: *to go back to the beginning*, volver al principio. | Remontarse: *to go back to the Flood*, remontarse al diluvio. | — *To go back on one's steps*, desandar lo andado. | *To go back on one's word*, faltar a su palabra. || ***To go before***, preceder, anteceder (to precede). | Ir delante de (to proceed in front of). | Tener prelación sobre (to be more important). | Ser sometido a (to be submitted to). || ***To go below***, bajar (in a boat). || ***To go between***, interponerse *or* mediar entre. || ***To go by***, pasar, transcurrir (time). | Pasar (to move past). | Pasar cerca de: *I went by him*, pasé cerca de él. | Seguir, atenerse a: *to go by the directions*, seguir las intrucciones. | — *To go by appearances*, juzgar por las apariencias. | *To go by the name of*, llamarse. || ***To go down***, bajar (to descend). | Ponerse (sun). | Hundirse (a ship). | Amainar (wind). | Bajar (temperature, tide). | Ser acogido: *his songs went down well*, sus canciones fueron bien acogidas. | Pasar a la historia: *Columbus went down as a heroe*, Colón pasó a la historia como un héroe. | Ser vencido (to be defeated). | Pasar: *this pill needs water to help it go down*, esta píldora necesita agua para pasar. | Digerirse, pasar (food). | Dejar la universidad (to leave a university). | Desinflarse (tyre). | Disminuir (to disminish). | Decaer (to decline). | Extenderse (to extend). | Estar escrito *or* apuntado (to be written down). | — *To go down before*, sucumbir ante. | *To go down with*, coger, caer enfermo de (an illness). | *To go down with s.o.*, gustarle a uno. || ***To go for***, ir por, ir a buscar (to fetch). | Atacar (to attack). | Valer para (to be applicable to). | Votar por (to be in favour of). | — FAM. *I go for dancing*, me gusta mucho bailar. | *To go for each other*, pelearse. || ***To go in***, entrar (to enter). | Caber (to fit). | Ocultarse (the sun). | Ponerse (clothes). | SP. Entrar (in cricket). | — *To go in for*, presentar su candidatura a (an appointment), seguir (a course of lectures), adoptar (a doctrine), comprarse (to buy), dedicarse a (to engage o.s. in),

entregarse a (a vice), participar en (to participate in). | *To go in for an examination*, examinarse. | *To go in with*, asociarse con. || **To go into**, entrar en (to enter). | Dedicarse a (to engage o.s. in). | Examinar a fondo, profundizar (a question). | — *To go into a discussion about*, entablar una discusión sobre, empezar a discutir sobre. | *To go into hysterics*, ponerse histérico. | *To go into mourning*, ponerse de luto. || **To go off**, marcharse, irse (to leave). | Dispararse (to fire, of a gun). | Explotar (to explode). | Sonar (to ring, to sound). | Estropearse (to go bad). | FAM. Dejar de gustarle a uno: *I've gone off cheese*, ha dejado de gustarme el queso. | THEATR. Hacer mutis. | Salir (to turn out): *everything went off well*, todo salió bien. | Dormirse (to go to sleep). | Desmayarse (to lose consciousness). | Desaparecer (to disappear). | COMM. Venderse. | — *To go off the rails*, descarrilar. | *To go off with sth.*, llevarse algo. || **To go on**, seguir, continuar (to continue): *he went on talking for hours*, siguió hablando horas y horas. | Seguir su camino. | Avanzar, progresar (to progress). | Pasar a (to proceed to): *to go on to the next item*, pasar al punto siguiente. | Partir de, basarse en (to base arguments upon). | THEATR. Salir a escena. | Pasar, transcurrir (time). | Durar (to last). | Estar bien (to fit): *my gloves won't go on*, los guantes no me están bien. | Comportarse (to behave). | Ocurrir (to happen). | Encenderse (lights). | — *Don't go on so!*, ¡no insistas! | FAM. *Go on!*, ¡qué va! (with incredulity), ¡vaya! (with surprise), ¡sigue! (carry on!) | *How are you going on?*, ¿qué tal estás? | *It's going on for two o'clock*, son casi las dos. | *To be going on for sixty*, andar por los sesenta. | *To go on about*, hablar constantemente de. | *To go on at*, regañar, reprender. | *What is going on here?*, ¿qué pasa aquí? || **To go out**, salir (to move out of somewhere). | Salir (to be published). | Apagarse (matches, fire, light). | Desaparecer (to disappear). | Pasar de moda (to cease to be fashionable). | Declararse en huelga, estar en huelga (to strike). | Dejar el poder (a politician). | Tener un desafío (duel). | — *My heart went out to him*, en seguida me resultó simpático, le cogí simpatía en seguida. | FAM. *Out you go!*, ¡fuera de aquí! | *To go out to dinner*, cenar fuera. || **To go over**, cruzar (to cross). | Pasar por encima de: *to go over the wall*, pasar por encima del muro. | Recorrer (a house, the ground). | Ir: *to go over to England*, ir a Inglaterra. | Pasarse a (to change one's allegiance to): *to go over to the enemy*, pasarse al enemigo. | Examinar (to investigate in detail). | Revisar (to revise). | Retocar (a drawing). | Repasar (a lesson). | Ensayar (to rehearse). | Ser acogido (to be received): *the film went over well*, la película fue bien acogida. | Volcar (to overturn). || **To go round**, dar la vuelta (to make one's way around). | Dar un rodeo: *to go ten miles round*, dar un rodeo de unas diez millas. | Girar (to revolve). | Circular, correr (rumour, story, etc.). | Ir a casa de, ir a ver a: *I'm going round to Barry's*, voy a casa de Barry, voy a ver a Barry. | Ir: *I'm going round to the café*, voy al café. | *Is there enough to go round?*, ¿hay para todos? || **To go through**, atravesar (to pass from one side to the other). | Pasar por (window, hole). | Examinar a fondo (to examine). | Pasar por, sufrir (to undergo). | Ser aprobado: *the bill has gone through*, el proyecto de ley ha sido aprobado. | Ejecutar (to perform). | Gastar (to spend). | Vender (to sell out). | — *To go through with*, llevar a cabo. || **To go together**, ir juntos: *they went to the cinema together*, fueron al cine juntos. | Armonizar, ir juntos (colours). | Salir juntos, ir juntos (a boy and girl). || **To go under**, hundirse (to sink). | Ponerse (sun). | Sucumbir (to succumb). | — FAM. *He is going under*, está de capa caída. | *He is gone under*, es un hombre acabado. || **To go up**, subir: *to go up the stairs*, subir las escaleras; *the prices are going up*, los precios van subiendo. | Levantarse (to be erected). | Ingresar: *to go up to the university*, ingresar en la universidad. | Subir, montarse (in an aeroplane). | Explotar (to explode). | Ir: *to go up to town*, ir a la ciudad. | Acercarse, dirigirse: *to go up to s.o.*, acercarse a alguien. | — *To go up a river*, ir aguas arriba. | *To go up for an exam*, examinarse. | *To go up in flames*, quemarse, arder. || **To go with**, acompañar (to accompany). | Hacer juego con, armonizarse con (colours, etc.). | Ir con: *red wine goes with cheese*, el vino tinto va con el queso. | Corresponder: *a salary which goes with the job*, un sueldo que corresponde al trabajo. | FAM. Tener relaciones con (lovers). | — *To go with the times*, ser de su tiempo. || **To go without**, pasar sin, prescindir de. | Arreglárselas (to manage). | — *It goes without saying*, ni que decir tiene (needless to say), eso cae de su peso (it is obvious).

— OBSERV. Pret. ***went;*** p. p. ***gone.***

goad [gəud] n. Aguijada, *f.* (stick for driving cattle). || Pincho, *m.* (wooden spike). || FIG. Aguijón, *m.*, acicate, *m.* (incentive).

goad [gəud] v. tr. Aguijar, aguijonear. || Pinchar (to prick). || FIG. Aguijonear, incitar.

go-ahead [ˈgəuəhed] adj. Emprendedor, ra. || Activo, va.

— N. Vía (*f.*) libre (signal). || FIG. Autorización, *f.*

goal [gəul] n. SP. Gol, *m.*, tanto, *m.*: *to score a goal*, marcar un gol. | Portería, *f.* (structure). || FIG. Objetivo, *m.*, meta, *f.*, fin, *m.*: *his goal was to be a doctor*, su objetivo era ser médico. || — SP. *Goal area*, área (*f.*) de gol. | *Goal average*, goal average, *m.*, cociente (*m.*) de goles.

goalee or **goalie** [—i] n. SP. FAM. Portero, *m.*, guardameta, *m.*

goalkeeper [—ˌki:pə*] n. SP. Portero, *m.*, guardameta, *m.*

goal kick [—kik] n. SP. Saque (*m.*) de puerta.

goal line [—lain] n. SP. Línea (*f.*) de gol (in football). | Línea (*f.*) de meta (in rugby).

goalpost [—pəust] n. SP. Poste, *m.*

goal scorer [—skɔ:rə*] n. SP. Goleador, *m.*

goat [gəut] n. ZOOL. Cabra, *f.* (female). | Macho (*m.*) cabrío (male). || ASTR. Capricornio, *m.* || U. S. FIG. FAM. Cabeza (*f.*) de turco (scapegoat). || FIG. *To get s.o.'s goat*, molestar *or* fastidiar a uno.

goatee [gəuˈti:] n. Barbas (*f. pl.*) de chivo, perilla, *f.*

goatherd [ˈgəuthə:d] n. Cabrero, *m.*, guardacabras, *m.* & *f. inv.*

goatish [ˈgəutiʃ] adj. Cabruno, na. || FIG. Libidinoso, sa.

goatskin [ˈgəutskin] n. Piel (*f.*) de cabra.

goatsucker [ˈgəutˌsʌkə*] n. Chotacabras, *m. inv.*, zumaya, *f.* (bird).

gob [gɔb] n. Trozo, *m.* (piece). || FAM. Boca, *f.* (mouth). | Lapo, *m.* (spit). | U. S. Marinero, *m.* (sailor). | FAM. *Gobs of*, gran cantidad de.

gobbet [ˈgɔbit] n. Fragmento (*m.*) de un texto (extract of a text). || FAM. Bocado, *m.* (mouthful).

gobble [ˈgɔbl] v. tr. Engullir.

— V. intr. Comer mucho (to eat). || Gluglutear (a turkey).

gobble [ˈgɔbl] n. Gluglú, *m.* (of turkey).

gobbledygook or **gobbledegook** [ˌgɔbldiˈguk] n. U. S. FAM. Jerga (*f.*) burocrática.

gobbler [ˈgɔblə*] n. FAM. Pavo (*m.*) macho (turkey). | Tragón, *m.*, comilón, *m.* (eater).

go-between [ˈgəubiˈtwi:n] n. Intermediario, ria; mediador, ra (negotiator). || Mensajero, ra (messenger). || Alcahuete, ta (pimp).

goblet [ˈgɔblit] n. Copa, *f.*

goblin [ˈgɔblin] n. Duende, *m.*

go-by [ˈgəubai] n. *To give s.o. the go-by*, no hacer caso a alguien. || *To give sth. the go-by*, hacer caso omiso de algo.

go-cart [ˈgəukɑ:t] n. Coche (*m.*) silla (pushchair). || Carrillo (*m.*) de juguete (homemade toy). || Carretilla (*f.*) de mano (handcart).

god [gɔd] n. REL. Dios, *m.*: *it was an act of God*, fue obra de Dios. || — Pl. THEATR. FAM. Gallinero, *m. sing.*, paraíso, *m. sing.* || Dioses, *m.*: *the gods of Olympus*, los dioses del Olimpo. || — *Almighty God*, Dios Todopoderoso. || *By God!*, ¡voto a Dios! || *For God's sake!*, ¡por Dios!, ¡por amor de Dios! || *God!*, ¡Dios mío!, ¡Dios Santo! || *God be praised!* o *praise be to God!*, ¡alabado *or* bendito sea Dios! || *God be o go with you!*, ¡anda *or* vete *or* vaya con Dios! || *God bless you!*, ¡Dios le bendiga! || *God forbid!*, ¡no lo permita Dios!, ¡Dios me libre!, ¡no lo quiera Dios! || *God forgive me!*, ¡que Dios me perdone! || *God has forsaken him*, Dios le ha dejado de su mano. || *God helps those who help themselves*, a Dios rogando y con el mazo dando. || *God help us!*, ¡que Dios nos asista *or* nos coja confesados! || *God help you!*, ¡Dios le asista *or* le ayude! || *God knows...*, Dios es testigo..., sabe Dios... || *God protect you!*, ¡Dios le ampare!, ¡que Dios le guarde! || *God repays a hundredfold*, Dios da ciento por uno. || *God's will be done!*, ¡sea lo que Dios quiera! || *God tempers the wind to the shorn lamb*, Dios aprieta pero no ahoga. || *God the Son, God made Man*, Dios Hijo, Dios hecho Hombre. || *God willing*, Dios mediante, si Dios quiere. || *God will provide!*, ¡Dios proveerá! || *May God repay you!*, ¡Dios se lo pagará!, ¡Dios se lo pague! || *My God!*, ¡Dios mío! || *Render therefore unto Caesar the things which are Caesar's and unto God things that are God's*, hay que dar a Dios lo que es de Dios y al César lo que es del César. || *Thank God!*, ¡gracias a Dios!, ¡a Dios gracias! || *To swear by almighty God*, poner a Dios por testigo. || *To thank God, to give thanks to God*, dar gracias a Dios. || *Would to God that*, quiera Dios que.

godchild [ˈgɔdtʃaild] n. Ahijado, da.

— OBSERV. El plural es *godchildren.*

goddaughter [ˈgɔdˌdɔ:tə*] n. Ahijada, *f.*

goddess [ˈgɔdes] n. Diosa, *f.*

godfather [ˈgɔdˌfɑ:ðə*] n. Padrino, *m.* (*to*, de).

God-fearing [ˈgɔdˌfiəriŋ] adj. Temeroso de Dios, piadoso, sa.

godforsaken [ˈgɔdfəˌseikn] adj. Dejado de la mano de Dios.

godhead [ˈgɔdhed] n. Divinidad, *f.*

godhood [ˈgɔdhud] n. Divinidad, *f.*

godless [ˈgɔdlis] adj. Descreído, da; ateo, a.

godlike [ˈgɔdlaik] adj. Divino, na.

godliness [ˈgɔdlinis] n. Santidad, *f.* || Devoción, *f.*, piedad, *f.* (piousness).

godly [ˈgɔdli] adj. Santo, ta. || Devoto, ta; piadoso, sa.

godmother [ˈgɔdˌmʌðə*] n. Madrina, *f.* (*to*, de).

godown [ˈgəudaun] n. Almacén (*m.*) en ciertos países asiáticos.

godparent [ˈgɔdˌpɛərənt] n. Padrino, *m.* (godfather). || Madrina, *f.* (godmother).
God's acre [ˈgɔdzˌeikə*] n. FAM. Cementerio, *m.*, camposanto, *m.*
godsend [ˈgɔdsend] n. Don (*m.*) del cielo.
godship [ˈgɔdʃip] n. Divinidad, *f.*
godson [ˈgɔdsʌn] n. Ahijado, *m.*
godspeed [ˈgɔdˈspi:d] n. Buena suerte, *f.*
goffer [ˈgəufə*] n. TECH. Gofradora, *f.* (for paper).
goffer [ˈgəufə*] v. tr. Encañonar (material). || Gofrar (paper).
goffering [—riŋ] n. Encañonado, *m.* (of material). || Gofrado, *m.* (of paper).
go-getter [ˈgəuˈgetə*] n. FAM. Ambicioso, sa; buscavidas, *m. & f. inv.*
goggle [ˈgɔgl] v. intr. Tener los ojos desorbitados. || *To goggle at*, mirar con los ojos desorbitados.
goggle-eyed [—aid] adj. De ojos saltones.
goggles [—z] pl. n. Gafas, *f.* (of divers, driver, etc.).
Goidelic [gɔiˈdelik] adj. Gaélico, ca.
going [gəuiŋ] n. Salida, *f.*, ida, *f.* || Camino, *m. the going was rough*, el camino era accidentado. || Manera (*f.*) de proceder, conducta, *f.* (behaviour). || Paso, *m.* (speed). || FIG. Progreso, *m.*
— Adj. Que funciona bien: *a going concern*, una empresa que funciona bien. || Existente: *one of the best firms going*, una de las mejores empresas existentes. || Corriente (price).
going-over [—ˈəuvə*] n. Inspección, *f.* || FAM. Paliza, *f.* (beating).
goings-on [ˈgəuiŋzˈɔn] pl. n. FAM. Tejemanejes, *m.*
goitre (U. S. **goiter**) [ˈgɔitə*] n. MED. Bocio, *m.*
goitrous [ˈgɔitrəs] adj. MED. Que tiene bocio.
go-kart [ˈgəukɑ:t] n. SP. Kart, *m.*
gold [gəuld] n. MIN. Oro, *m.* (metal). || Dorado, *m.*, oro, *m.* (colour). || — FIG. *All that glitters is not gold*, no es oro todo lo que reluce. || *Beaten gold*, oro batido. || *Dead gold*, oro mate. || *Fine gold*, oro de ley. || *Gold bars*, oro en barras. || *Gold bath*, baño (*m.*) de oro. || *Gold billet*, lingote (*m.*) de oro. || *Gold dust*, oro en polvo, polvo (*m.*) de oro. || *Gold ingot*, lingote (*m.*) de oro. || *Gold leaf, gold foil*, oro en hojas, pan (*m.*) de oro. || *Gold mine*, mina (*f.*) de oro (where gold is mined), mina, *f.* (profitable concern). || *Gold plate*, vajilla (*f.*) de oro. || *Gold printing*, impresión (*f.*) en oro. || *Gold reserve*, reserva (*f.*) de oro. || *Gold rush*, fiebre (*f.*) del oro. || FIG. *Heart of gold*, corazón (*m.*) de oro. || FIG. *To be worth its weight in gold*, valer su peso en oro. || *White gold*, oro blanco.
— Adj. De oro (necklace, etc.): *gold coin*, moneda de oro. || Oro (colour). || Oro: *gold standard*, patrón oro; *gold value*, valor oro.
gold-bearing [—ˈbɛəriŋ] adj. Aurífero, ra: *gold-bearing land*, terreno aurífero.
goldbeater [—ˌbi:tə*] n. Batidor (*m.*) de oro, batihoja, *m.*
goldbeating [—ˈbi:tiŋ] n. TECH. Batido, *m.*
goldbrick [—brik] n. FIG. FAM. Estafa, *f.*, timo, *m.* (sham). | Oropel, *m.* (glitter). || U. S. FAM. Holgazán, ana (shirker). || FIG. FAM. *To sell s.o. a goldbrick*, vender a alguien gato por liebre, timar a alguien.
goldbrick [—brik] v. intr. U. S. FAM. Holgazanear.
— V. tr. FIG. FAM. Timar, dar gato por liebre.
Gold Coast [—kəust] pr. n. GEOGR. Costa (*f.*) de Oro.
gold digger [—ˈdigə*] n. Buscador (*m.*) de oro (miner). || FAM. Aventurera, *f.* (woman).
gold diggings [—ˈdigiŋz] pl. n. Placer (*m. sing.*) aurífero.
golden [—dən] adj. Dorado, da (colour). || De oro (made of gold). || Áureo, a (number). || De oro (rule, wedding). || ZOOL. Dorado, da: *golden eagle*, águila dorada; *golden pheasant*, faisán dorado. || FIG. Excelente: *a golden opportunity*, una excelente oportunidad. | Dorado, da (flourishing): *the golden day of boxing*, la época dorada del boxeo. || Rubio, bia (hair). || — FIG. *Golden age*, Edad (*f.*) de Oro. || *Golden anniversary*, bodas (*f. pl.*) de oro. || *Golden calf*, becerro (*m.*) de oro. || FIG. *Golden goose*, gallina (*f.*) de los huevos de oro. | *Golden mean*, término medio (moderation).
Golden Fleece [ˈgəuldənˈfli:s] n. MYTH. Vellocino (*m.*) de oro. || *Order of the Golden Fleece*, Orden (*f.*) del Toisón de Oro.
goldenrod [ˈgəuldənˌrɔd] n. BOT. Vara (*f.*) de oro *or* de San José.
goldfield [ˈgəuldfi:ld] n. MIN. Yacimiento (*m.*) de oro.
gold-filled [ˈgəuldfild] adj. Chapado de oro (watch, etc.). || Empastado con oro (tooth).
goldfinch [ˈgəuldfintʃ] n. Jilguero, *m.* (bird).
goldfish [ˈgəuldfiʃ] n. Pez (*m.*) de colores (fish).
gold-plated [ˈgəuldpleitəd] adj. Dorado, da. || Chapado de oro (watch, etc.).
goldsmith [ˈgəuldsmiθ] n. Orfebre, *m.*
goldsmithery [—əri] n. Orfebrería, *f.*
golf [gɔlf] n. SP. Golf, *m.*
golf club [—klʌb] n. Palo (*m.*) de golf (implement). || Club (*m.*) de golf (association).
golf course [—kɔ:s] or **golf links** [—liŋks] n. Campo (*m.*) de golf.
golfer [ˈgɔlfə*] n. SP. Golfista, *m. & f.*, jugador (*m.*) de golf.
Golgotha [ˈgɔlgəθə] pr. n. Gólgota, *m.*
goliard [ˈgəuliɑ:d] n. Goliardo, *m.*
Goliath [gəuˈlaiəθ] pr. n. Goliat, *m.*
golly! [ˈgɔli] interj. ¡Cáspita!, ¡Dios mío!
gollywog or **golliwog** [ˈgɔliwɔg] n. Muñeco (*f.*) negro de trapo.
golosh [gəˈlɔʃ] n. Chanclo, *m.* (galosh).
Gomorrah [gəˈmɔrə] pr. n. HIST. Gomorra.
gonad [ˈgɔnæd] n. BIOL. Gónada, *f.*
gondola [ˈgɔndələ] n. Góndola, *f.* (Venetian boat). || Góndola, *f.*, barquilla, *f.* (of an airship, balloon). || U. S. Barcaza, *f.* (barge). | Batea, *f.* (open railway wagon).
gondolier [ˌgɔndəˈliə*] n. Gondolero, *m.*
gone [gɔn] p. p. See GO.
— Adj. Pasado, da (past). || Dado, da (hour). || JUR. Adjudicado, da. || FAM. Loco, ca (in love with). | Agotado, da (exhausted). | Magnífico, ca; espléndido, da (excellent). | Acabado, da (worn-out). | Muerto, ta: *when I'm gone*, cuando me haya muerto. || — *Gone with child*, embarazada. || *Gone with the wind*, lo que el viento se llevó. || *The coal is all gone*, se acabó el carbón, ya no queda carbón. || *To be far gone*, estar pasado (food), estar bebido (to be drunk), estar muy mal (to be ill). || *To be far gone in*, estar muy metido en (to be deeply involved in). || *To be gone*, estar fuera: *I won't be gone five minutes*, no estaré fuera más de cinco minutos. || FAM. *To be gone on*, estar loco por. || *To be six months gone*, estar de seis meses (pregnant). || *To be too far gone*, estar demasiado avanzado (disease, illness, etc.).
goner [ˈgɔnə*] n. FAM. Enfermo (*m.*) desahuciado (very sick person). | Hombre (*m.*) perdido (ruined man).
gonfalon [ˈgɔnfələn] n. Gonfalón, *m.*, estandarte, *m.*
gonfalonier [ˌgɔnfələˈniə*] n. Gonfalonero, *m.*, abanderado, *m.* (standard bearer).
gong [gɔŋ] n. Gong, *m.*
gongoresque [gɔŋgəresk] or **gongoristic** [gɔŋgəristik] adj. Gongorista, gongorino, na.
gongorism [ˈgɔŋgərizəm] n. Gongorismo, *m.*
goniometer [ˌgəuniˈɔmitə*] n. Goniómetro, *m.*
goniometry [ˌgəuniˈɔmetri] n. Goniometría, *f.*
gonococcus [ˌgɔnəˈkɔkəs] n. Gonococo, *m.*

— OBSERV. El plural de *gonococcus* es *gonococci*.

gonorrhoea (U. S. **gonorrhea**) [ˈgɔnəˈri:ə] n. MED. Gonorrea, *f.*
goo [gu:] n. FAM. Sustancia (*f.*) pegajosa (sticky matter). | Sentimentalismo, *m.* (sentimentalism).
goober [ˈgu:bə*] n. U. S. Cacahuete, *m.* [*Amer.*, maní, *m.*, cacahuate, *m.*] (peanut).
good [gud] adj. Bueno, na: *a good person*, una buena persona; *good soldier*, buen soldado; *milk is good for your health*, la leche es buena para la salud; *a good thrashing*, una buena paliza; *I had a good night*, pasé una buena noche; *he comes from a good family*, es de buena familia. || Amable (kind): *she was very good to me*, fue muy amable conmigo; *that is very good of you*, es Ud. muy amable. || Agradable, bueno, na (pleasant). || Más de, largo, ga: *he has been here for a good hour*, ha estado aquí más de una hora. || Ventajoso, sa (advantageous). || Competente (competent). | Útil (useful). || Válido, da: *this ticket is not good*, este billete no es válido. || — *A good deal*, mucho, cha. || *A good few*, see FEW. || *A good many*, un buen número, muchos, chas. || *A good sort*, una buena persona. || *A good turn*, un favor. || *A good while*, un buen rato. || *All in good time*, todo a su debido tiempo. || *As good as*, como si, prácticamente: *it's as good as done*, es como si estuviera hecho, está prácticamente hecho. || *As good as gold*, bueno como un ángel. || *As good as new*, como nuevo. || *As good as saying that*, tanto como decir que. || *Be good!*, ¡sé bueno! || *Good!*, ¡muy bien! || *Good afternoon* o *good evening*, buenas tardes. || *Good and late*, bien tarde. || *Good and ready*, bien preparado. || *Good Book*, Biblia, *f.* || *Good cheer*, see CHEER. || *Good deal*, buen negocio. || *Good fellow*, buen chico. || *Good for*, bueno para. || *Good for a laugh*, divertido, da. || *Good for you!*, ¡estupendo! || *Good Friday*, Viernes Santo. || *Good Lord, heavens, gracious, grief!*, ¡madre mía! || *Good looks*, belleza, *f.* || *Good luck*, buena suerte. || *Good manners*, buenos modales. || *Good money*, buena cantidad de dinero. || *Good morning*, buenos días. || *Good name*, buena reputación. || *Good night*, buenas noches. || *Good offices*, buenos oficios. || *Good sense*, sentido (*m.*) común, buen sentido, sensatez, *f.*, juicio, *m.* || *Good word*, recomendación, *f.* || *In good spirits*, de buen humor. || *In good time*, see TIME. || *It's a good job*, menos mal que: *it's a good job he came*, menos mal que vino. || *Please be so good as to*, tenga la bondad de. || *That's a good one!*, ¡menuda bola! (that's hard to believe), ¡ésa sí que es buena! (that is good). || *To be as good as one's word*, ser hombre de palabra. || *To be good at*, ser fuerte en, tener capacidad para. || *To be good enough for*, valer para, convenir a: *do you think this paper is good enough for writing letters on?*, ¿cree Ud. que este papel vale para la correspondencia? || FIG. *To be good for*, valer (to be worth), disponer de (money), durar (to be able to last), estar en condiciones de hacer (to have the necessary energy). || *To be good with children*, tener arte para los niños. || *To be too good to be true*, ser demasiado bueno para ser cierto. || *To drink more than is good for one*, beber

más de la cuenta. || *To feel good*, sentirse bien (in health), estar satisfecho (satisfied). || *To give as good as one gets*, pagar con la misma moneda. || *To have a good time*, pasarlo bien. || *To hold good for*, valer para. || *To make good*, prosperar (to prosper), triunfar (to succeed), cubrir (a deficit), compensar, recuperar (expenses, a loss), pagar (to pay), hacer valer (one's rights), reparar (an injustice), cumplir (one's promise), llevar a cabo, realizar (one's purpose), demostrar (a statement), comprobar (accusation). || *To make good a loss to s.o.*, indemnizar a alguien por una pérdida. || *To put in* o *to say a good word for s.o.*, decir unas palabras en favor de alguien. || *Very good*, muy bien. || *Would you be so good as to?*, ¿sería tan amable de?

— N. Bien, *m.*: *the powers of good and evil*, los poderes del bien y del mal; *he did it for his own good*, lo hizo por su propio bien. || Utilidad, *f.* (usefulness). || Buenos, *m. pl.* (persons). || — Pl. See GOODS. || — *For good*, definitivamente, para siempre (for always). || *For good and all*, de una vez para siempre. || *For the good of*, en bien de. || *It's no good...*, de nada sirve... || *No good*, inútil (useless), sin valor (worthless). || *No good will come of it*, nada bueno puede salir de ahí. || *The good*, lo bueno. || *To be no good at*, no servir para. || *To be up to no good*, tener mala idea, estar tramando algo malo. || *To come to no good*, acabar mal. || *To do good*, hacer el bien. || *To do one good*, hacer bien a uno, sentarle bien a uno. || *To the good*, provechoso, sa (beneficial), de beneficio, a favor de uno (in profit). || *What's the good of running?*, ¿de qué sirve correr?

— Adv. Bien. || *It has been a good long time*, hace mucho tiempo.

— OBSERV. El comparativo de *good* es *better* y el superlativo *best*.

good-bye (U.S. **good-by**) [gud'bai] interj. ¡Adiós!

— N. Adiós, *m.*, despedida, *f.* || *To say good-bye to*, despedirse de.

good-fellowship [gud,feləuʃip] n. Compañerismo, *m.*, camaradería, *f.*

good-for-nothing ['gudfə,nʌθiŋ] adj. Inútil, que no sirve para nada.

— N. Inútil, *m. & f.*

good-hearted [gud'hα:tid] adj. De buen corazón.

good humour (U. S. **good humor**) [gud'hju:mə*] n. Buen humor, *m.*

good-humoured (U. S. **good-humored**) [—d] adj. De buen humor, jovial. || Alegre (gay).

goodies ['gudiz] pl. n. U. S. Dulces, *m.*

good-looking [gud'lukiŋ] adj. Guapo, pa; bien parecido, da.

goodly ['gudli] adj. Grande, considerable (big). || Agradable (pleasant). || Bien parecido, da (good-looking).

good-natured [gud'neitʃəd] adj. Amable, bondadoso, sa.

good-neigbour (U. S. **good-neigbor**) [gud'neibə*] adj. De buena vecindad: *good-neigbour policy*, política de buena vecindad.

goodness ['gudnis] n. Bondad, *f.* (quality or state of being good). || Sustancia, *f.* (of food). || Calidad, *f.* (quality). || — *For goodness sake!*, ¡por Dios! || *Goodness gracious!*, ¡Dios mío! || *Goodness knows!*, ¡Dios sabe! || *I wish to goodness!*, ¡ojalá! || *My goodness*, ¡madre mía!, ¡Dios mío! || *Thank goodness!*, ¡gracias a Dios!

goods [gudz] pl. n. See GOOD. || Bienes, *m.* (possessions). || COMM. Géneros, *m.*, artículos, *m.* || Mercancías, *f.* (merchandise): *goods train*, tren de mercancías. || — *By goods*, por tren de mercancías. || *Canned goods*, conservas (*f.*) en lata. || *Consumer goods*, bienes (*m.*) de consumo. || *Goods and chattels*, muebles (*m.*) y enseres, efectos (*m.*) personales. || *Goods wagon*, furgón, *m.* || *To catch with the goods*, coger in fraganti *or* con las manos en la masa. || *To deliver the goods*, repartir las mercancías (merchandise), cumplir sus compromisos (to keep one's promise). || U. S. *To have the goods on s.o.*, tener pruebas de culpabilidad contra alguien.

good-tempered ['gud'tempəd] adj. De buen carácter (not easily angered). || De buen humor (not angry). || Amistoso, sa (friendly).

good-time Charlie [gud'taim'tʃα:li] n. Vividor, *m.*

goodwill ['gud'wil] n. Buena voluntad, *f.*: *a goodwill mission*, una misión de buena voluntad. || Clientela, *f.* (of a business). || Buen nombre, *m.* (reputation).

goody ['gudi] n. Dulce, *m.*

— Interj. ¡Qué bien!

goody-goody ['gudi'gudi] adj./n. Gazmoño, ña; santurrón, ona.

— Interj. ¡Qué bien!, ¡estupendo!, ¡magnífico!

gooey ['gu:i] adj. FAM. Pegajoso, sa (sticky). | Sentimental, empalagoso, sa (sentimental).

goof ['gu:f] n. FAM. Mentecato, ta (person). || U. S. FAM. Pifia, *f.* (a blunder).

goof [gu:f] v. tr. U. S. FAM. Chafallar.

— V. intr. U. S. FAM. Cometer una pifia. || U. S. FAM. *To goof off*, hacerse el remolón.

goofy ['gu:fi] adj. Mentecato, ta.

goon ['gu:n] n. U. S. FAM. Tonto, ta; mentecato, ta. | Terrorista (*m.*) pagado.

goose [gu:s] n. ZOOL. Ganso, *m.*, oca, *f.*, ánsar, *m.* || FIG. Ganso, sa; bobo, ba (silly person). || — Pl. Plancha (*f.*) de sastre (tailor's iron). || — FIG. FAM. *His goose is cooked*, está aviado. || *The geese of the Capitol*, los gansos del Capitolio. || FIG. FAM. *To cook s.o.'s goose*, hacerle la pascua a uno. | *To kill the goose that lays the golden eggs*, matar la gallina de los huevos de oro.

— OBSERV. El plural de *goose* es *geese*.

goose barnacle [—,bα:nəkl] n. ZOOL. Percebe, *m.*

gooseberry ['guzbəri] n. BOT. Grosellero (*m.*) espinoso (plant). | Grosella (*f.*) espinosa (fruit). || — *Gooseberry bush*, grosellero espinoso. || FAM. *He was born under a gooseberry bush*, le trajo la cigüeña. | *To play gooseberry*, hacer de carabina, llevar la cesta.

gooseflesh ['gu:sfleʃ] n. FIG. Carne (*f.*) de gallina.

goosefoot ['gu:sfut] n. BOT. Pata (*f.*) de gallo.

goose pimples ['gu:s'pimplz] pl. n. FIG. Carne (*f. sing.*) de gallina.

goose step ['gu:sstep] n. MIL. Paso (*m.*) de ganso.

goose-step ['gu:sstep] v. intr. Ir a paso de ganso.

gopher ['gəufə*] n. ZOOL. Ardilla (*f.*) terrestre (burrowing rodent).

Gordian ['gɔ:djən] adj. Gordiano (knot).

gore [gɔ:*] n. Sangre (*f.*) coagulada (shed blood). || Nesga, *f.*, cuchillo, *m.* (in a skirt, dress, etc.). || MAR. Cuchillo, *m.*

gore [gɔ:*] v. tr. Cornear, dar cornadas (to wound with horns). || Acuchillar, poner nesgas en (a dress, etc.). || Cortar en triángulo (to cut into a triangular shape).

gorge [gɔ:dʒ] n. Desfiladero, *m.*, garganta, *f.* (between hills). || Gola, *f.* (of a fortification). || Masa (*f.*) que obstruye (choking mass). || FAM. Comilona, *f.* (gluttonous feed). || FIG. *To make one's gorge rise*, revolverle el estómago a uno.

gorge [gɔ:dʒ] v. tr. Atiborrar, hartar (to fill with food). || Engullir, tragar (to gulp down). || Obstruir (to choke). || Llenar (to fill up).

— V. intr. Atracarse, hartarse (*on*, de).

gorgeous ['gɔ:dʒəs] adj. Magnífico, ca; espléndido, da (magnificent). || FAM. Bonito, ta (nice).

gorgeousness [—nis] n. Esplendidez, *f.*, esplendor, *m.*

gorgerin ['gɔ:dʒərin] n. ARCH. Collarino, *m.* (of column).

gorget ['gɔ:dʒit] n. Gola, *f.*, gorguera, *f.*, gorjal, *m.*, colla, *f.* (piece of armour). || Collar, *m.* (on the throat of a bird, etc.). || Toca, *f.*, griñón, *m.* (medieval wimple).

Gorgon ['gɔ:gən] n. MYTH. Gorgona, *f.*

gorgonize ['gɔ:gənaiz] v. tr. Petrificar.

gorilla [gə'rilə] n. ZOOL. Gorila, *m.* (ape).

gormandize ['gɔ:məndaiz] v. intr. Comer con glotonería.

gorse [gɔ:s] n. BOT. Tojo, *m.*, aulaga, *f.*

gory ['gɔ:ri] adj. Ensangrentado, da (person). || Sangriento, ta (fight).

gosh! [gɔʃ] interj. ¡Cielos! || — *By Gosh!*, ¡por Dios! || *Good Gosh!*, ¡Santo Dios! || *My Gosh!*, ¡Dios mío!

goshawk ['gɔshɔ:k] n. Azor, *m.*, halcón (*m.*) palumbario (bird).

gosling ['gɔzliŋ] n. Ansarón, *m.* (bird). || FIG. Ganso, sa; mentecato, ta.

go-slow ['gəu'sləu] n. Tipo (*m.*) de huelga que consiste en trabajar con excesiva meticulosidad y lentitud.

Gospel ['gɔspəl] n. REL. Evangelio, *m.*: *the Gospel according to Saint John*, el Evangelio según San Juan. || — *Gospel book*, evangeliario, *m.* || FIG. *This is the gospel truth*, esto es el evangelio.

gospeller (U. S. **gospeler**) ['gɔspələ*] n. REL. Evangelista, *m.*

gossamer ['gɔsəmə*] n. Telaraña, *f.* (spider's thread). || Gasa, *f.* (gauzy material).

— Adj. Muy fino, na.

gossip ['gɔsip] n. Cotilleo, *m.*, comadreo, *m.*, chismorreo, *m.* (tittle-tattle). || Charla, *f.* (chatter). || Cotilla, *m. & f.*, chismoso, sa (scandalmonger). || — *Gossip column*, ecos (*m. pl.*) de sociedad. || *Gossip shop*, lugar (*m.*) donde se chismorrea, mentidero, *m.* || *Piece of gossip*, chisme, *m.*

gossip ['gɔsip] v. intr. Cotillear, chismorrear, chismear (to talk scandal). || Charlar (to chatter).

gossiper [—ə*] n. Cotilla, *m. & f.*, chismoso, sa (scandalmonger). || Charlatán, ana; hablador, ra (chatterer).

gossiping [—iŋ] adj. Chismoso, sa.

— N. Cotilleo, *m.*, chismorreo, *m.*, comadreo, *m.*

gossipmonger ['gɔsip'mʌŋgə*] n. Cotilla, *m. & f.*, chismoso, sa.

gossipy [—i] adj. Cotilla, chismoso, sa (person). || Anecdótico, ca; familiar (style).

got [gɔt] pret. & p. p. See GET.

Goth [gɔθ] n. Godo, *m.* || FIG. Vándalo, la.

Gotham ['gɔθəm] adj. U. S. FAM. Neoyorquino, na.

— N. Nueva York.

Gothic ['gɔθik] adj. Godo, da (applied to people). || Gótico, ca (art, literature, etc.): *gothic language, type*, lengua, letra gótica.

— N. Lengua (*f.*) gótica (language). || Gótico, *m.*: *flamboyant gothic*, gótico flamígero.

gotten ['gɔtn] p. p. U. S. See GET.

— OBSERV. En inglés el participio pasivo *gotten* no se usa más que en ciertas expresiones como *ill-gotten gains* (bienes adquiridos por medios ilícitos), mientras que se emplea mucho en los Estados Unidos.

gouache [gu'ɑ:ʃ] n. ARTS. Pintura (*f.*) a la aguada, aguada, *f.*
gouge [gaudʒ] n. TECH. Gubia, *f.*, escoplo (*m.*) *or* formón (*m.*) de mediacaña.
gouge [gaudʒ] v. tr. Escoplear con gubia *or* con formón de mediacaña (to chisel out). || FAM. Arrancar, sacar: *to gouge out s.o.'s eyes*, arrancar los ojos a alguien.
gourd [guəd] n. Calabaza, *f.*
gourmand ['guəmənd] n. Goloso, sa; glotón, ona.
gourmet ['guəmei] n. Gastrónomo, ma.
gout [gaut] n. MED. Gota, *f.* || Gota, *f.* (drop).
gouty [—i] adj. MED. Gotoso, sa.
govern ['gʌvən] v. tr. Gobernar, dirigir (to rule): *to govern a country*, gobernar un país. || Dirigir, administrar (affairs). || Dominar (to restrain): *to govern one's passions*, dominar las pasiones. || Guiar (to determine): *self-interest governs her actions*, el egoísmo guía sus actos. || Regir (to serve as a rule for). || Determinar (to determine). || GRAMM. Regir. || Regular (to control the speed or power of).
— V. intr. Gobernar. || Prevalecer, predominar (to prevail).
governable [—əbl] adj. Gobernable. || Manejable.
governance [—əns] n. Gobierno, *m.* || Autoridad, *f.* (authority).
governess [—nis] n. Aya, *f.*, institutriz, *f.* (of children). || Gobernadora, *f.*
governing [—iŋ] adj. Gobernante, dirigente: *governing class*, clase gobernante. || Dominante, rector, ra: *governing idea*, idea rectora. || — *Governing body*, consejo (*m.*) de administración. || *Governing hand*, mano dura.
government [—mənt] n. Gobierno, *m.* (of a state): *federal, totalitarian government*, gobierno federal, totalitario. || Dirección, *f.*, administración, *f.*, gestión, *f.* (of a society). || FIG. Dominio, *m.* (of passions). || GRAMM. Régimen, *m.*
— Adj. Del gobierno, del Estado. || Gubernamental (newspaper, party). || Del gobernador (house). || Administrativo, va.
governmental [,gʌvən'mentl] adj. Gubernamental, gubernativo, va.
governor ['gʌvənə*] n. Gobernador, *m.*: *governor of the Bank of Spain*, gobernador del Banco de España. || Gobernador, *m.* (of a town, province, colony). || Director, *m.* (of a prison). || Administrador, *m.*, director, *m.* (of an institution). || FAM. Jefe, *m.* (boss). | Padre, *m.*, viejo, *m.* (father). || TECH. Regulador, *m.* || *Provincial governor*, gobernador civil.
governor-general [—'dʒenərəl] n. Gobernador (*m.*) general.
— OBSERV. El plural de la palabra inglesa es *governors-general* o *governor-generals*.
governorship [—ʃip] n. Gobierno, *m.*: *civil governorship*, gobierno civil.
gowk [gauk] n. Cuclillo, *m.* (bird). || FAM. Bobo, ba; necio, cia (silly person).
gown [gaun] n. Traje (*m.*) largo (of woman). || Toga, *f.* (of lawyers, academics, etc.). || *Dressing gown*, bata, *f.*
gown [gaun] v. tr. Vestir.
gownsman [—zmən] n. Universitario, *m.*
— OBSERV. El plural de *gownsman* es *gownsmen*.
grab [græb] n. Cuchara, *f.* (mechanical device). || Asimiento, *m.* (the act of snatching). || — FAM. *To be up for grabs*, estar libre. || *To make a grab at sth.*, intentar agarrar algo.
— Adj. Tomado al azar (at random). || De sostenimiento (rail in buses, etc.).
grab [græb] v. tr. Agarrar (to snatch). || Asir, coger, agarrar (to take). || Pillar: *the police grabbed him before he could escape*, la policía le pilló antes de que pudiese escapar. || Apropiarse (to seize illegally, forcibly). || Echar mano a (to lay hands on). || FAM. *To grab a bite*, tomar un bocado.
— V. intr. *To grab at*, tratar de coger *or* de agarrarse a.
grabble ['græbl] v. intr. *To grabble for*, buscar a tientas.
grace [greis] n. Gracia, *f.*, elegancia, *f.*, distinción, *f.* (charm, elegance). || Gracia, *f.*, garbo, *m.* (fine bearing). || Cortesía, *f.*, delicadeza, *f.* (courtesy): *he had the grace to say thank you*, tuvo la cortesía de decir gracias. || Gracia, *f.*, perdón, *m.* (forgiveness). || Bondad, *f.*, benevolencia, *f.*, gracia, *f.* (kindness). || Favor, *m.* (favour). || REL. Gracia, *f.* (God's divine grace): *in a state of grace*, en estado de gracia. | Bendición (*f.*) de la mesa (prayer at meals). || Plazo, *m.*, demora, *f.* (delay). || — Pl. MYTH. Gracias: *the Three Graces*, las Tres Gracias. || — *By the grace of*, gracias a. || *By the grace of God*, por la gracia de Dios. || *Grace cup*, última copa. || FIG. *Her saving grace is her smile*, la sonrisa es lo que la salva. || *In this year of grace*, en este año de gracia. || *To be in s.o. bad graces*, haber caído en desgracia con uno. || *To be in s.o. good graces*, gozar del favor de alguien. || *To fall from grace*, caer en desgracia. || *To get into s.o.'s good graces*, congraciarse con uno. || *To put on airs and graces*, darse aires. || *To say grace*, bendecir la mesa. || *With bad grace*, de mala gana. || *With good grace*, de buena gana. || *Your Grace*, Su Excelencia (a duke), Su Ilustrísima (a bishop), Su Alteza (a prince).
grace [greis] v. tr. Adornar, embellecer (to adorn). || Honrar (to honour).
graceful [—ful] adj. Elegante (elegant). || Agraciado, da (nice). || Gracioso, sa; lleno de gracia, precioso, sa (attractive, pleasing). || Airoso, sa; garboso, sa (a movement). || Cortés, delicado, da (polite).
gracefulness [—fulnis] n. Gracia, *f.*
graceless [—lis] adj. Falto de gracia, sin gracia (lacking grace): *graceless features*, facciones sin gracia. || Desgarbado, da (gawky). || Feo, a (ugly). || Descortés (impolite). || REL. Que no está en estado de gracia.
gracile ['græsil] adj. Grácil.
gracious ['greiʃəs] adj. Gracioso, sa (showing grace). || Cortés, afable (courteous). || Grato, ta; placentero, ra (pleasant). || Amable (kind): *she was very gracious to me*, estuvo muy amable conmigo. || Indulgente (lenient). || REL. Misericordioso, sa. || — *Gracious me!*, ¡válgame Dios! || *His* o *Her Gracious Majesty*, Su Graciosa Majestad.
graciousness [—nis] n. Gracia, *f.* || Benevolencia, *f.*, bondad, *f.* (kindness). || Amabilidad, *f.* (affability). || REL. Misericordia, *f.*
grackle ['grækl] n. Estornino, *m.*, quiscal, *m.* (bird).
gradate [grə'deit] v. tr. Graduar. || Degradar (colours).
— V. intr. Graduarse. || Degradarse (colours).
gradation [grə'deiʃən] n. Gradación, *f.* || Degradación, *f.* (of colours).
grade [greid] n. Grado, *m.* (degree in rank, quality, etc.). || Clase, *f.*, categoría, *f.* (of person or things). || Cruce (*m.*) de un pura sangre y otro que no lo es para mejorar la raza (of animals). || U. S. Curso, *m.* (in school). | Nota, *f.* (mark given to a pupil). | Pendiente, *f.* (gradient). | Nivel, *m.* (level). || — U. S. *Grade crossing*, paso (*m.*) a nivel. || *Grade school*, escuela primaria. || FIG. *To make the grade*, llegar al nivel necesario.
grade [greid] v. tr. Graduar (to arrange in grades, to gradate). || Degradar (colours). || Nivelar (road, railway, etc.). || Cruzar [animales] para mejorar la raza. || Clasificar (goods). || U. S. Calificar (in school). || *To grade up*, cruzar [animales] para mejorar la raza.
gradient ['greidjənt] n. Pendiente, *f.*, declive, *m.* (declivity). || Cuesta, *f.* (slope). || Índice (*m.*) de aumento or de disminución (of temperature, pressure, etc.). || PHYS. Gradiente, *m.*
gradin ['greidin] or **gradine** [grə'di:n] n. Grada, *f.*
gradual ['grædʒuəl] n. adj. Gradual, progresivo, va.
— N. REL. Gradual, *m.*
graduate ['grædʒuət] n. Graduado, da; diplomado, da; titulado, da (from university). || CHEM. Probeta (*f.*) graduada (tube). | Frasco (*m.*) graduado (flask).
graduate ['grædjueit] v. tr. Graduar. || Degradar (colours). || Dar un diploma *or* un título a (a student).
— V. intr. Graduarse, sacar el título, diplomarse (to become a graduate): *to graduate as a doctor of philosophy*, graduarse de doctor en filosofía. || *To graduate into*, convertirse progresivamente en.
graduate school ['grædʒuətsku:l] n. U. S. Escuela (*f.*) para graduados.
graduate student ['grædʒuət'stju:dənt] n. Estudiante (*m.* & *f.*) de una escuela para graduados.
graduation [,grædju'eiʃən] n. Graduación, *f.* || Entrega (*f.*) de un título (by the University).
graduator ['grædjueitə*] n. TECH. Graduador, *m.*
graffito [græ'fi:təu] n. Pintada, *f.*, dibujo (*m.*) *or* inscripción (*f.*) en una pared.

— OBSERV. El plural de *graffito* es *graffiti*.

graft [grɑ:ft] n. AGR. MED. Injerto, *m.* || Guante, *m.*, mamelas, *f. pl.*, soborno, *m.* (corruption of public officer). || FAM. Trabajo, *m.*: *building roads is hard graft*, hacer carreteras es un trabajo duro.
graft [grɑ:ft] v. tr. AGR. MED. Injertar.
— V. intr. Injertarse, unirse [por medio de un injerto]. || Hacer un injerto (to make a graft). || Dar guante, sobornar (to bribe). || FAM. Trabajar: *he has been grafting all day*, ha estado trabajando todo el día.
graftage [—idʒ] or **grafting** [—iŋ] n. Injerto, *m.*: *shield grafting*, injerto de escudete.
grafter [—ə*] n. Injertador, *m.* (person). || Navaja (*f.*) *or* cuchilla (*f.*) de injertar (tool). || Sobornador, ra (briber).
Grail [greil] n. REL. Grial, *m.*: *the Holy Grail*, el Santo Grial.
grain [grein] n. Grano, *m.* (a cereal seed). || Cereales, *m.* (cereals). || Grano, *m.* (of sand, of salt). || Poco, *m.*, pizca, *f.*: *not a grain of common sense*, ni pizca de buen sentido. || Grano, *m.* (the smallest unit of weight). || Veta, *f.* (of stone). || Fibra, *f.*, grano, *m.* (of wood). || Flor, *f.* (of leather). || PHOT. Grano, *m.* || — *Against the grain*, a contrapelo. || FIG. *Take what he says with a grain of salt*, créete la mitad de lo que dice. || *That's a grain of comfort*, ya es un consuelo. || *To saw with the grain*, serrar en la dirección de la veta.
grain [grein] v. tr. Vetear (wood, stone). || Granear (stone for lithographic work). || Granular (to give a granular surface to).
— V. intr. Volverse granulado, granularse.
grain elevator [—'eliveitə*] n. Silo (*m.*) de cereales con elevador.
grainy [—i] adj. Granular. || Granado, da (full of grain). || Granoso, sa: *grainy leather*, cuero granoso. || Veteado, da (stone, marble).

gram [græm] n. Gramo, *m.* (unit of mass). || Garbanzo, *m.* (chick-pea). || — *Gram atom* átomo-gramo, *m.* || *Gram atomic mass* o *weight*, átomo-gramo, *m.* || *Gram molecular mass* o *weight*, molécula (*f.*) gramo. || *Gran molecule*, molécula (*f.*) gramo.

grama [ˈgræmə] n. Bot. Grama, *f.*

graminaceae [ˌgreimiˈneisii] or **gramineae** [ˌgreimiˈnei] pl. n. Bot. Gramíneas, *f.*

graminaceous [ˌgreimiˈneiʃəs] or **gramineous** [greiˈminiəs] adj. Bot. Gramíneo, a.

gramma [ˈgræmə] n. Bot. Grama, *f.*

grammar [ˈgræmə*] n. Gramática, *f.*: *comparative, historical grammar*, gramática comparativa, histórica. || *Grammar school*, instituto (*m.*) de segunda enseñanza (in Great Britain), escuela primaria (in U. S.).

grammarian [grəˈmɛəriən] n. Gramático, ca.

grammatical [grəˈmætikəl] adj. Gramatical.

gramme [græm] n. Gramo, *m.*

gramophone [ˈgræməfəun] n. Gramófono, *m.* (old style). || Tocadiscos, *m. inv.* (record player).

grampus [ˈgræmpəs] n. Zool. Orca, *f.*

granadilla [ˌgrænəˈdilə] n. Bot. Granadilla, *f.*

granary [ˈgrænəri] n. Granero, *m.*

grand [grænd] adj. Grandioso, sa; magnífico, ca; espléndido, da (splendid): *a grand view*, una vista magnífica. || Importante (distinguished). || Grande (great). || Principal (staircase). || Completo, ta; general (total). || Mus. De cola (piano). || Fam. Fenomenal, grandioso, sa; estupendo, da: *it's been a grand day*, ha sido un día fenomenal. || — *That would be grand!*, ¡sería estupendo!, ¡sería grandioso! || *To have a grand time*, pasarlo estupendamente *or* en grande.

— N. Piano (*m.*) de cola. || Fam. Mil dólares, *m. pl.*

grandam [ˈgrændæm] n. Abuelita, *f.*, abuela, *f.*

grandaunt [ˈgrændɑ:nt] n. Tía (*f.*) abuela.

grandchild [ˈgræntʃaild] n. Nieto ta.

granddad [ˈgrændæd] n. Abuelito, *m.*, abuelo, *m.*

granddaughter [ˈgrænˌdɔ:tə*] n. Nieta, *f.*

grand duchess [ˈgrændˈdʌtʃis] n. Gran duquesa, *f.*

grand duke [ˈgrændˈdju:k] n. Gran duque, *m.*

grandee [grænˈdi:] n. Grande, *m.* (nobleman): *Spanish grandee*, grande de España.

grandeur [ˈgrændʒə*] n. Grandiosidad, *f.* (magnificence): *the grandeur of the spectacle*, la grandiosidad del espectáculo. || Nobleza, *f.*, grandeza, *f.* (nobility).

grandfather [ˈgrændˌfɑ:ðə*] n. Abuelo, *m.* || *Grandfather clock*, reloj (*m.*) de caja.

grandfatherly [—li] adj. De abuelo.

grandiloquence [grænˈdiləkwəns] n. Grandilocuencia, *f.*

grandiloquent [grænˈdiləkwənt] adj. Grandilocuente, grandílocuo, cua.

grandiose [ˈgrændiəus] adj. Grandioso, sa.

grandiosity [ˌgrændiˈɔsiti] n. Grandiosidad, *f.*

grand jury [grændˈdʒuəri] n. U. S. Jur. Jurado (*m.*) de acusación.

grand lodge [grændˈlɔdʒ] n. Gran oriente, *m.* (of Freemasons).

grandma [ˈgrænmɑ:] n. Abuelita, *f.*, abuela, *f.*

grand mal [ˈgrændˈmæl] n. Med. Epilepsia, *f.*

grand master [grændˈmɑ:stə*] n. Gran maestre, *m.* (of an order). || Gran maestro, *m.* (in chess).

grandmother [ˈgrændˌmʌðə*] n. Abuela, *f.*

grandmotherly [—li] adj. De abuela.

grandnephew [ˈgrændˌnevju:] n. Sobrino (*m.*) nieto.

grandniece [ˈgrænni:s] n. Sobrina (*f.*) nieta.

grand opera [ˈgrænˈɔpərə] n. Mus. Ópera, *f.*

grandpa [ˈgrænpɑ:] n. Abuelito, *m.*, abuelo, *m.*

grandparent [ˈgrænˌpɛərənt] n. Abuelo, la. || — Pl. Abuelos, *m.*

grand piano [grænpiˈænəu] n. Piano (*m.*) de cola.

grand prize [ˈgrænˌpraiz] n. Premio (*m.*) gordo.

grandsire [ˈgrænˌsaiə*] n. Antepasado, *m.*

grand slam [ˈgrænslæm] n. Bola, *f.* (in bridge). || Fig. Éxito (*m.*) rotundo.

grandson [ˈgrænsʌn] n. Nieto, *m.*

grandstand [ˈgrændstænd] n. Tribuna, *f.*

granduncle [ˈgrændˌʌŋkl] n. Tío (*m.*) abuelo.

grand vizier [ˈgrænˌviˈziə*] n. Gran vizir, *m.*

grange [greindʒ] n. Finca, *f.*, cortijo, *m.* [*Amer.*, hacienda, *f.*, estancia, *f.*] (farm). || Casa (*f.*) solariega (manor house).

granite [ˈgrænit] n. Granito, *m.*

— Adj. Granítico, ca.

granitic [græˈnitik] adj. Granítico, ca.

granivorous [græˈnivərəs] adj. Granívoro, ra.

granny [ˈgræni] n. Abuelita, *f.* (grandmother). || Fam. Comadre, *f.*

grant [grɑ:nt] n. Concesión, *f.*, otorgamiento, *m.* (the act of granting). || Concesión, *f.* (thing granted). || Subvención, *f.* (money donated). || Jur. Cesión, *f.* | Donación, *f.* (gift). || Beca, *f.* (scholarship).

grant [grɑ:nt] v. tr. Conceder, otorgar: *to grant a favour*, conceder un favor. || Admitir: *granted that you are right*, admitiendo que tienes razón; *he doesn't grant that he is wrong*, no admite estar equivocado. || Asentir a (a proposition). || Donar (to give) || Jur. Ceder, transferir. || — *Granted* o *granting that*, dado que. || *To take it for granted that*, dar por supuesto *or* por sentado que.

grant-aided [—ˈeidid] adj. Subvencionado, da.

grantee [grɑ:nti:] n. Jur. Cesionista, *m.* & *f.* | Donante, *m.* & *f.*, donador, ra.

grant-in-aid [grɑ:ntiˈneid] n. Subvención, *f.*

grantor [grɑ:nˈtɔ:*] n. Otorgante, *m.* || Jur. Cesionista, *m.* & *f.* | Donante, *m.* & *f.*, donador, ra.

granular [ˈgrænjulə*] adj. Granular. || Med. Granulado, da.

granulate [ˈgrænjuleit] v. tr. Granular.

— V. intr. Granularse.

granulation [ˌgrænjuleiʃən] n. Granulación, *f.*, granulado, *m.*

granule [ˈgrænju:l] n. Gránulo, *m.*

granulous [ˈgrænjuləs] adj. Granuloso, sa.

grape [greip] n. Bot. Uva, *f.* || — Pl. Vet. Grapas, *f.* || — *Grape harvest*, vendimia, *f.* || *Grape juice*, mosto, *m.* (for wine), zumo (*m.*) de uva (drink). || *Grape sugar*, glucosa, *f.* || Fig. *Sour grapes!*, ¡están verdes!

grapefruit [ˈgreipfru:t] n. Pomelo, *m.*, toronja, *f.* (fruit).

grapeshot [ˈgreipʃɔt] n. Metralla, *f.*

grapevine [ˈgreipvain] n. Vid, *f.* (plant). || Parra, *f.* (in the wall). || Fam. Rumores, *m. pl.* (gossip). | Medio (*m.*) de comunicación *or* de recepción de informaciones. || Fam. *I heard on the grapevine that*, me he enterado de que.

graph [græf] n. Gráfico, *m.*, gráfica, *f.* || *Graph paper*, papel cuadriculado.

graphic [ˈgræfik] adj. Gráfico, ca: *graphics arts*, artes gráficas. || Fig. Gráfico, ca.

graphical [—əl] adj. Gráfico, ca.

graphite [ˈgræfait] n. Grafito, *m.*

graphologic [græfəˈlədʒik] adj. Grafológico, ca.

graphologist [græˈfələdʒist] n. Grafólogo, ga.

graphology [græˈfələdʒi] n. Grafología, *f.*

grapnel [ˈgræpnəl] n. Rezón, *m.* (of anchor).

grapple [ˈgræpl] n. Rezón, *m.* (grapnel). || Lucha (*f.*) cuerpo a cuerpo (fight).

grapple [ˈgræpl] v. tr. Agarrar (to grip). || Mar. Aferrar con el rezón.

— V. intr. Luchar cuerpo a cuerpo (to fight). || Intentar resolver: *to grapple with a problem*, intentar resolver un problema. || Mar. Echar el rezón.

grappling iron [ˈgræpliŋˌaiən] n. Mar. Rezón, *m.*

grasp [grɑ:sp] n. Asimiento, *m.* (grip). || Apretón, *m.* (of hands). || Dominio, *m.*: *a good grasp of grammar*, un gran dominio de la gramática. || Control, *m.* || Alcance, *m.* (range): *beyond my grasp*, fuera de mi alcance. || Comprensión, *f.* (understanding). || — *To fall into s.o.'s grasp*, caer en manos de alguien. || *To have a good grasp of*, dominar. || *To loose one's grasp*, soltar presa. || *Within one's grasp*, al alcance de uno.

grasp [grɑ:sp] v. tr. Agarrar, asir (to seize hold of). || Estrechar, apretar (the hand). || Sujetar (to hold firmly). || Empuñar (weapon). || Entender, comprender, captar (to understand). || Apoderarse de (power).

— V. intr. Aprovechar: *to grasp at an opportunity*, aprovechar una oportunidad. || *To grasp at*, intentar agarrar (an object).

grasper [—ə*] n. Avaro, ra.

grasping [—iŋ] adj. Avaro, ra; codicioso, sa.

grass [grɑ:s] n. Hierba, *f.*, yerba, *f.* (green herbage). || Pasto, *m.* (pasture). || Césped, *m.* (lawn): *grass court*, terreno de césped. || Fam. Mariguana, *f.* || — *Keep off the grass*, prohibido pisar el césped. || Fig. *There's a snake in the grass*, see SNAKE. || *To be at grass*, estar pastando. || Fig. *To hear the grass grow*, sentir crecer la hierba. | *To let the grass grow under one's feet*, perder el tiempo.

grass [grɑ:s] v. tr. Sembrar de hierba (to plant with grass). || U. S. Apacentar, pacer (animals).

— V. intr. Cubrirse de hierba.

grasshopper [ˈgrɑ:sˌhɔpə*] n. Zool. Saltamontes, *m. inv.* (insect).

grassland [ˈgrɑ:slænd] n. Prado, *m.*, pasto, *m.*, pastizal, *m.*

grass roots [ˈgrɑ:sru:ts] n. Población (*f.*) rural (rural population). || Raíz, *f.*, fundamento, *m.*, base, *f.* (the fundamental part).

grass-roots [ˈgrɑ:sru:ts] adj. Básico, ca; fundamental. || Popular. || Rural.

grass widow [ˈgrɑ:sˈwidəu] n. Mujer (*f.*) cuyo marido está ausente. || U. S. Divorciada, *f.* | Mujer (*f.*) separada de su marido.

grassy [ˈgrɑ:si] adj. Cubierto de hierba, herboso, sa (covered with grass). || Herbáceo, a (like grass). || De color verde hierba.

grate [greit] n. Parrilla, *f.* (of a fireplace). || Chimenea, *f.* (fireplace). || Verja, *f.*, reja, *f.*, enrejado, *m.* (of a window). || Criba, *f.*, tamiz, *m.*, cedazo, *m.* (sieve).

grate [greit] v. tr. Poner un enrejado *or* una verja *or* una reja a (to put a grating on). || Rallar: *to grate cheese*, rallar queso. || Hacer rechinar: *to grate one's teeth*, hacer rechinar los dientes.

— V. intr. Chirriar (to make a harsh sound). || Rechinar (the teeth). || *To grate on*, crispar, irritar (the nerves), lastimar, herir (the ear).

grateful [—ful] adj. Agradecido, da (feeling thankfulness). || Agradable, grato, ta (agreeable). || *To be grateful for*, agradecer [por], estar agradecido por.

gratefully [—fuli] adv. Con agradecimiento, con gratitud.

gratefulness [—fulnis] n. Agradecimiento, *m.*, gratitud, *f.*

grater [—ə*] n. Rallador, *m.*

graticule [ˈgrætikju:l] n. Phys. Retícula, *f.*

gratification [—grætifi'keiʃən] n. Gratificación, *f.* (reward). || FIG. Placer, *m.*, satisfacción, *f.*, contento, *m.*: *to her great gratification*, con gran satisfacción suya.
gratifier ['grætifaiə*] n. Gratificador, ra.
gratify ['grætifai] v. tr. Satisfacer, agradar (to satisfy). || Agradar a, dar gusto a (to please). || Satisfacer (a whim). || Gratificar, dar una gratificación a (to reward). || *To be gratified to*, alegrarse de.
gratifying [—iŋ] adj. Satisfactorio, ria; agradable, grato, ta.
gratin ['grætɛ̃:ŋ] n. CULIN. Gratén, *m.*, gratín, *m.*
grating ['greitiŋ] n. Verja, *f.*, enrejado, *m.*, reja, *f.* || PHYS. Retícula, *f.*
— Adj. Áspero, ra (harsh). || Chirriante (sound). || Rechinante (teeth). || Irritante, molesto, ta (irritating).
gratis ['greitis] adv. Gratis.
gratitude ['grætitju:d] n. Gratitud, *f.*, agradecimiento, *m.* (thankfulness).
gratuitous [grə'tju:itəs] adj. Gratuito, ta. || JUR. *Gratuitous contract*, contrato (*m.*) a título gratuito.
gratuitousness [—nis] n. Gratuidad, *f.*
gratuity [grə'tju:iti] n. Propina, *f.* (tip). || Gratificación, *f.* (gift of money). || Aguinaldo, *m.* (at Christmas).
gratulatory ['grætjulətəri, U.S.'grætʃələ,tɔ:ri:] adj. De felicitación.
gravamen [grə'veimən] n. Agravio, *m.* (grievance). || JUR. Fundamento, *m.* (of a charge).
— OBSERV. El plural de la palabra inglesa *gravamen* es *gravamina* o *gravamens*.
grave [greiv] adj. Serio, ria (warranting anxiety). || Solemne (solemn). || Importante (important). || Severo, ra; oscuro, ra (colour). || Grave (critical). || GRAMM. Grave (accent). || MUS. Grave, bajo, ja.
— N. Sepultura, *f.*, tumba, *f.* (tomb). || GRAMM. Acento (*m.*) grave. || — *Pauper's grave*, fosa (*f.*) común. || *With one foot in the grave*, con un pie en el sepulcro.
grave [greiv] v. tr. Grabar, esculpir, tallar (to carve). || FIG. Grabar (in one's mind).
graveclothes ['greivkləuðz] pl. n. Mortaja, *f. sing.*
gravedigger ['greiv,digə*] n. Sepulturero, *m.*, enterrador, *m.*
gravel ['grævəl] n. Grava, *f.*, guijo, *m.* (small stones): *gravel path*, camino de grava. || MED. Arenilla, *f.*
gravel ['grævəl] v. tr. Echar una capa de grava a, cubrir con grava. || FIG. Desconcertar.
gravelly ['grævəli] adj. Lleno de grava.
gravely ['greivli] adv. Gravemente.
graven ['greivən] adj. Esculpido, da; grabado, da; tallado, da.
graven image [—'imidʒ] n. Ídolo, *m.*
graver ['greivə*] n. Buril, *m.*, cincel, *m.* (burin). || Grabador, ra; escultor, ra (person).
gravestone ['greivstəun] n. Lápida (*f.*) sepulcral, lápida (*f.*) mortuoria.
graveyard ['greivjɑ:d] n. Cementerio, *m.*
gravid ['grævid] adj. Embarazada (a woman). || Preñada (an animal). || Siniestro, tra (portentous).
gravimetry [grə'vimətri] n. Gravimetría, *f.*
graving dock ['greiviŋdɔk] n. MAR. Dique (*m.*) de carena.
gravitate ['græviteit] v. intr. PHYS. Gravitar. || FIG. Tender hacia, ser atraído por, dirigirse hacia.
gravitation [,grævi'teiʃən] n. PHYS. Gravitación, *f.*: *universal gravitation*, gravitación universal. || FIG. Tendencia, *f.*
gravitational [—əl] adj. De gravitación, de gravedad.
gravity ['græviti] n. Gravedad, *f.* (of an illness, a situation, an accident). || PHYS. Gravedad, *f.*: *laws of gravity*, leyes de la gravedad; *centre of gravity*, centro de gravedad. || *Specific gravity*, peso específico.
— Adj. De gravedad.
gravure [grə'vjuə*] n. Fotograbado, *m.*
gravy ['greivi] n. CULIN. Salsa, *f.* || U. S. FAM. Ganga, *f.* || *Gravy boat*, salsera, *f.*
gray, graybeard, etc. See GREY, GREYBEARD, etc.
grayling [—liŋ] n. Tímalo, *m.* (fish).
graze [greiz] n. Rozadura, *f.*, roce, *m.* (rubbing). || Pasto, *m.* (grass). || Apacentamiento, *m.* (pasturing).
graze [greiz] v. tr. Rozar (to rub gently). || Raspar (to scrape). || Apacentar (cattle).
— V. intr. Rozar (to rub). || Pastar, pacer (to feed).
grazier ['greizjə*] n. Ganadero, ra.
grazing ['greiziŋ] n. Apacentamiento, *m.*, pastoreo, *m.* (feeding). || Pasto, *m.* (land).
grease [gri:s] n. Grasa, *f.*
grease [gri:z] v. tr. Engrasar. || TECH. Engrasar, lubricar, lubrificar. || FIG. FAM. *To grease the hand* o *palm of*, untar la mano a a.
grease gun [gri:sgʌn] n. TECH. Pistola (*f.*) engrasadora, engrasador, *m.*
greasepaint ['gri:speint] n. Maquillaje, *m.*
grease trap ['gri:stræp] n. TECH. Sifón (*m.*) colector de grasas.
greasiness ['gri:zinis] n. Untuosidad, *f.*, lo grasiento.
greasy ['gri:zi] adj. Grasiento, ta: *greasy food*, comida grasienta. || Resbaladizo, za (slippery). || Ensebado (pole). || Sucio, cia (wool). || Mugriento, ta (filthy). || FIG. Cobista (flattering).
greasy pole [gri:sipəul] n. Cucaña, *f.*
great [greit] adj. Grande (big): *we heard a great noise*, oímos un gran ruido. || Grande (high): *the airplane flies at great altitude*, el avión vuela a gran altura; *great speed*, gran velocidad. || Grande (large): *a great number of people*, un gran número de gente. || FIG. Grande (eminent, splendid): *a great man*, un gran hombre; *I gave a great party*, di una gran fiesta. || Mucho, largo (time): *for a great while*, durante mucho tiempo. || Importante (important). || Favorito, ta (favourite). || Noble (noble). || Principal (stairs). || Avanzado, da (age). || FAM. Estupendo, da; espléndido, da; magnífico, ca (excellent). || — *Alexander the Great*, Alejandro Magno. || *Great at* o *on*, muy bueno en. || *Great at* o *for* o *on*, aficionado a. || *Great big*, enorme, muy grande. || *Great with*, lleno de. || *She is a great friend of mine*, es muy amiga mía. || *To have a great time*, pasarlo en grande *or* estupendamente. || *To my great surprise*, con gran sorpresa mía.
— Adv. FAM. Muy bien, estupendamente.
— N. FIG. Grande, *m.*
great-aunt [—'ɑ:nt] n. Tía (*f.*) abuela.
Great Bear [—bɛə*] n. ASTR. Osa (*f.*) Mayor.
Great Britain [—'britn] pr. n. Gran Bretaña, *f.*
great circle [—'sə:kl] n. Círculo (*m.*) máximo.
greatcoat [—kəut] n. Abrigo, *m.*, gabán, *m.*
Great Dane [—dein] n. Mastín (*m.*) danés (dog).
greater [greitə*] adj. comp. Mayor. || *Greater London*, gran Londres.
Greater Dog ['greitə*,dɔg] n. ASTR. Can (*m.*) Mayor.
greatest [greitist] adj. superl. Mayor: *his greatest enemy*, su mayor enemigo.
great-grandchild [—'grænt∫aild] n. Biznieto, ta; bisnieto, ta.
— OBSERV. El plural es *great-grandchildren*.
great-granddaughter [—'græn,dɔ:tə*] n. Biznieta, *f.*, bisnieta, *f.*
great-grandfather [—'græn,fɑ:ðə*] n. Bisabuelo, *m.*
great-grandmother [—'græn,mʌðə*] n. Bisabuela, *f.*
great-grandparent [—'grænd,pɛərənt] n. Bisabuelo, la. || — Pl. Bisabuelos, *m.*
great-grandson [—'grænsʌn] n. Biznieto, *m.*, bisnieto, *m.*
great-great-grandchild [—greit'græn,t∫aild] n. Tataranieto, ta.
— OBSERV. El plural es *great-great-grandchildren*.
great-great-granddaughter [—greit'græn,dɔ:tə*] n. Tataranieta, *f.*
great-great-grandfather [—greit'græn,fɑ:ðə*] n. Tatarabuelo, *m.*
great-great-grandmother [—greit'græn,mʌðə*] n. Tatarabuela, *f.*
great-great-grandparent [—greit'grænd,pɛərənt] n. Tatarabuelo, la. || — Pl. Tatarabuelos, *m.*
great-great-grandson [—greit'grænsʌn] n. Tataranieto, *m.*
greathearted [—'hɑ:tid] adj. Valiente (brave). || Generoso, sa; magnánimo, ma (magnanimous).
greatheartedness [—'hɑ:tidnis] n. Valentía, *f.* (courage). || Generosidad, *f.*, magnanimidad, *f.* (generosity).
great horned owl [—hɔ:ndaul] n. ZOOL. Búho (*m.*) real.
greatly ['greitli] adv. Enormemente, grandemente, mucho, muy.
great-nephew [greit'nevju:] n. Sobrino (*m.*) nieto.
greatness ['greitnis] n. Grandeza, *f.*
great-niece [greitni:s] n. Sobrina (*f.*) nieta.
great-uncle ['greit'ʌŋkl] n. Tío (*m.*) abuelo.
Great War [—wɔ:*] n. Gran Guerra, *f.*, Primera Guerra (*f.*) Mundial.
greave [gri:v] n. Greba, *f.* (of an armour).
— OBSERV. Esta palabra se usa generalmente en plural.
greaves [gri:vz] pl. n. Chicharrones, *m.*
grebe [gri:b] n. Colimbo, *m.* (bird).
Grecian [gri:ʃən] adj. Griego, ga. || *Grecian nose*, nariz (*f.*) griega.
— N. Helenista, *m.* & *f.*
Grecism ['gri:sizm] n. Grecismo, *m.*, helenismo, *m.*
grecize ['gri:saiz] v. tr. Helenizar.
Greco-Latin ['grekəu'lætin] adj. Grecolatino, na.
Greco-Roman ['grekəu'rəumən] adj. Grecorromano, na.
Greece [gri:s] pr. n. GEOGR. Grecia, *f.*
greed [gri:d] or **greediness** [—inis] n. Avaricia, *f.*, codicia, *f.*, avidez, *f.* (for wealth). || Glotonería, *f.*, gula, *f.* (for food).
greedy [—i] adj. Glotón, ona; goloso, sa (gluttonous). || Avaro, ra; codicioso, sa; ávido, da (*for*, de) (avaricious, ambitious).
Greek [gri:k] adj. Griego, ga. || *Greek fire*, fuego griego.
— N. Griego, ga (native of Greece). || Griego, *m.* (language). || — *Greek language*, griego, *m.* || FIG. FAM. *It's all Greek to me*, es griego *or* chino para mí.
Greek Orthodox Church [—'ɔ:θədɔkst∫ə:t∫] n. REL. Iglesia (*f.*) ortodoxa griega.
green [gri:n] adj. Verde (colour). || Verde (unripe). || Tierno, na (a shoot). || Verde: *green wood*, leña verde. || Crudo, da (meat). || Sin curar (bacon). || En verde: *green hide*, cuero en verde. || Fresco, ca (fresh). || Pálido, da; lívido, da; verde (having a pale complexion). || Lozano, na: *green old age*, vejez lozana. || FIG. Verde (immature). | Novato, ta; inexperimentado, da (inexperienced). | Crédulo, la; simplón, ona (gullible). || — *Green fodder*, forraje (*m.*) verde. || FIG. *He is green with envy*, se lo come la envidia, está verde de envidia.
— N. Verde, *m.* (colour). || Verdor, *m.* (verdure). ||

Césped, *m.* (lawn). || Prado, *m.* (pasture). || Pista, *f.* (for playing). || Campo, *m.*, "green", *m.* (in golf). || Terreno (*m.*) comunal, ejido, *m.* (a stretch of grass for public use). || — Pl. Verduras, *f.* (vegetables). | Ramas (*f.*) y hojas verdes (for decoration).
green [gri:n] v. tr. Poner verde.
— V. intr. Volverse verde, verdear.
greenback [—bæk] n. U. S. FAM. Pápiro, *m.* (banknote).
green bean [—bi:n] n. U. S. Judía (*f.*) verde.
greenbelt [—belt] n. Zona (*f.*) verde.
greenery [—əri] n. Verdor, *m.* (verdure). || Invernadero, *m.* (greenhouse).
green-eyed [—aid] adj. Celoso, sa; envidioso, sa (jealous). || De ojos verdes.
greenfinch [—fintʃ] n. Verderón, *m.* (bird).
greenfly [—flai] n. ZOOL. Pulgón, *m.*
greengage [—geidʒ] n. BOT. Ciruela (*f.*) claudia.
greengrocer [—ˌgrəusə*] n. Verdulero, ra. || *Greengrocer's*, verdulería, *f.*
greengrocery [—ˌgrəusəri] n. Verdulería, *f.* || — Pl. Verduras (*f.*) y frutas.
greenhorn [—hɔ:n] n. Simplón, ona (simpleton). || Novato, ta; bisoño, ña (new).
greenhouse [—haus] n. Invernadero, *m.*
greenish [—iʃ] adj. Verdoso, sa.
Greenland [—lænd] pr. n. GEOGR. Groenlandia, *f.*
Greenlander [—lændə*] n. Groenlandés, esa.
green light [—lait] n. FAM. Luz (*f.*) verde (permission).
green manure [—məˈnjuə*] n. Abono (*m.*) vegetal.
green meat [—mi:t] n. Herbaje, *m.*
greenness [—nis] n. Verdor, *m.*, lo verde. || FIG. Bisoñería, *f.*, inexperiencia, *f.*
green pepper [—pepə*] n. Pimiento (*m.*) verde.
greenroom [—rum] n. THEATR. Camerino, *m.* (dressing room).
greensand [—sænd] n. GEOL. Arenisca (*f.*) verde.
greensickness [—siknis] n. MED. Clorosis, *f.*
greenstone [—stəun] n. Diorita, *f.*
greenstuff [—stʌf] n. Verduras, *f. pl.* (vegetables).
greensward [—swɔ:d] n. Césped, *m.*
green vitriol [—ˈvitriəl] n. CHEM. Caparrosa (*f.*) verde.
Greenwich [ˈgrinidʒ] n. GEOGR. Greenwich. || *Greenwich mean time*, la hora según el meridiano de Greenwich.
greet [gri:t] v. tr. Saludar: *he greeted me with a smile*, me saludó con una sonrisa. || Dar la bienvenida, recibir (to salute the arrival of). || FIG. Acoger. || *To greet the eyes*, presentarse a la vista.
greeting [—iŋ] n. Saludo, *m.* (expression of salutation). || Recibimiento, *m.* (welcome). || Felicitación, *f.*: *greetings telegram*, telegrama de felicitaciones. || — Pl. Recuerdos, *m.* (in a letter).
gregarious [griˈgεəriəs] adj. Gregario, ria: *gregarious instinct*, instinto gregario. || FIG. Sociable.
grège [greiʒ] n. Seda (*f.*) cruda.
Gregorian [griˈgɔ:riən] adj. Gregoriano, na: *Gregorian chant, calendar*, canto, calendario gregoriano.
Gregory [ˈgregəri] pr. n. Gregorio, *m.*
greige [greiʒ] n. Seda (*f.*) cruda.
— Adj. Crudo, da (colour).
gremial [ˈgri:miəl] n. REL. Gremial, *m.*
gremlin [ˈgremlin] n. Duende, *m.*
grenade [griˈneid] n. MIL. Granada, *f.*: *hand grenade*, granada de mano.
grenadier [ˌgrenəˈdiə*] n. MIL. Granadero, *m.*
grenadilla [ˌgrenəˈdilə] n. BOT. Granadilla, *f.*
grenadine [ˌgrenəˈdi:n] n. Granadina, *f.*
gressorial [greˈsɔ:rjəl] adj. ZOOL. Ambulatorio, ria.
grew [gru:] pret. See GROW.
grey [grei] adj. Gris (colour). || Rucio, cia (horse). || Crudo, da (textiles). || Cano, na (hair). || FIG. Triste, gris (sad). | Nublado, da (overcast). | Gris: *grey eminence*, eminencia gris.
— N. Gris, *m.* (colour). || Primeras luces, *f. pl.*: *the first grey of dawn*, las primeras luces del amanecer. || Caballo (*m.*) tordo (horse). || *To turn grey*, volverse gris (to become grey), encanecer (hair).
grey [grei] v. tr. Poner gris.
— V. intr. Volverse gris (to become grey). || Encanecer (hair).
greybeard [—biəd] n. Anciano, *m.* (old man).
Grey Friar [—ˈfraiə*] n. Franciscano, *m.*
grey-haired [—ˈhεəd] or **grey-headed** [—ˈhedid] adj. Canoso, sa.
greyhound [—haund] n. Galgo, *m.* (dog).
greyish [—iʃ] adj. Grisáceo, a (grey). || Entrecano, na; canoso, sa (hair).
grey matter [—ˈmætə*] n. Materia (*f.*) gris, sustancia (*f.*) gris.
greyness [—nis] n. Color (*m.*) gris, gris, *m.*
grey squirrel [—ˈskwirəl] n. ZOOL. Ardilla (*f.*) gris.
grid [grid] n. Verja, *f.*, reja, *f.* (grating). || ELECTR. Red, *f.* (network). | Rejilla, *f.* (lattice). || Cuadrícula (on a map). || CULIN. Parrilla, *f.* (gridiron). || THEATR. Peine, *m.*
griddle [ˈgridl] n. Plancha, *f.* (for cooking). || TECH. Criba, *f.*
griddle [ˈgridl] v. tr. Asar a la plancha (to cook). || TECH. Cribar.
griddlecake [—keik] n. Hojuela, *f.*, "crepe", *f.*
gride [graid] v. intr. Rechinar, chirriar.
gridiron [ˈgridˌaiən] n. Parrilla, *f.* (used for broiling). || Red, *f.* (of pipes, etc.). || MAR. Carenero, *m.*, varadero, *m.* || THEATR. Peine, *m.* || U. S. Campo (*m.*) de fútbol.
grief [gri:f] n. Pena, *f.*, dolor, *m.*, pesar, *m.*, aflicción, *f.*, congoja, *f.* || — *Good grief!*, ¡voto al chápiro verde! || *To bring to grief*, apenar a, causar pesar a. || *To come to grief*, sufrir un accidente: *the car came to grief on the motorway*, el coche sufrió un accidente en la autopista; estropearse: *the lamp came to grief*, la lámpara se estropeó; fracasar, irse al traste: *my plan came to grief*, mi plan fracasó.
grief-stricken [—strikən] adj. Desconsolado, da; apesadumbrado, da.
grievance [ˈgri:vəns] n. Queja, *f.* (complaint). || Motivo (*m.*) de queja (cause for complaint). || Injusticia, *f.*, agravio, *m.* (injury).
grieve [gri:v] v. tr. Afligir, apenar, dar pena: *it grieves me to tell him it*, me da pena decírselo. || Lamentar (to complain). || *To be grieved at* o *by*, afligirse con *or* por *or* de.
— V. tr. Afligirse, apenarse. || *To grieve about* o *at* o *over*, lamentar.
grievous [ˈgri:vəs] adj. Doloroso, sa; penoso, sa (causing pain, trouble, suffering). || Dolorido, da; apenado, da (hurt). || Lastimoso, sa (pitiful). || Grave (serious). || Cruel (loss). || Lamentable (error, fault). || Intenso, sa (pain).
griffin [ˈgrifin] n. MYTH. Grifo, *m.* || U. S. Recién llegado, *m.*
griffon [ˈgrifən] n. Grifón, *m.* (dog). || MYTH. Grifo, *m.* (griffin).
grifter [ˈgriftə*] n. U. S. FAM. Tramposo, sa.
grig [grig] n. Grillo, *m.* (cricket). || Angula, *f.*, cría (*f.*) de la anguila (small eel). || FIG. Persona (*f.*) que tiene azogue en las venas.
grill [gril] n. Parrilla, *f.* (gridiron). || Asado (*m.*) a la parrilla. || Parrillada, *f.* (a dish of grilled food). || Restaurante (*m.*) donde se sirven asados, parrilla, *f.* || See GRILLE. || *Mixed grill*, plato combinado.
grill [gril] v. tr. Asar a la parrilla (to broil on a gridiron). || Torturar con fuego (to torture). || FIG. Someter a un interrogatorio severo (to interrogate).
— V. intr. Asarse a la parrilla. || FIG. Someterse a un interrogatorio severo.
grillage [ˈgrilidʒ] n. Entramado (*m.*) de madera.
grille [gril] n. Rejilla, *f.* (of convent parlour). || Mirilla (*f.*) con enrejado (of a door). || Ventana (*f.*) con reja *or* barrotes (barred window). || Reja, *f.*, verja, *f.* (protective barrier). || Enrejado, *m.* (for ventilation).
grilled [ˈgrild] adj. Asado a la parrilla.
grillroom [ˈgrilrum] n. Parrilla, *f.*, restaurante (*m.*) donde se sirven asados.
grilse [grils] n. ZOOL. Salmón (*m.*) joven que vuelve del mar por primera vez.
grim [grim] adj. Feroz, severo, ra. || Torvo, va; ceñudo, da (expression). || Inflexible, inexorable (unrelenting): *a grim determination*, una determinación inflexible. || Terrible, horrible (threatening, forbidding). || Porfiado, da; muy reñido, da (struggle). || Solemne (solemn). || Frío, a (cheerless). || Macabro, bra; lúgubre, siniestro, tra (sinister). || Desagradable (disagreeable). || *The grim truth*, la pura verdad.
grimace [griˈmeis] n. Mueca, *f.*
grimace [griˈmeis] v. intr. Hacer muecas.
grimalkin [griˈmælkin] n. Gato (*m.*) viejo (cat). || FIG. FAM. Bruja, *f.* (unpleasant woman).
grime [graim] n. Mugre, *f.*, suciedad, *f.*
grime [graim] v. tr. Ensuciar.
griminess [ˈgraiminis] n. Suciedad, *f.*, mugre, *f.*
grimness [ˈgrimnis] n. Aspecto (*m.*) siniestro *or* lúgubre. || Inflexibilidad, *f.* || Porfía, *f.* (of struggle).
grimy [ˈgraimi] adj. Mugriento, ta; sucio, cia.
grin [grin] n. Sonrisa (*f.*) abierta (smile). || Risa (*f.*) burlona *or* socarrona (sneer). || Mueca, *f.* (grimace).
grin [grin] v. tr. Expresar con una sonrisa *or* con una mueca.
— V. intr. Sonreír abiertamente (to smile broadly). || Hacer una mueca de dolor (in pain). || Reír burlonamente (in scorn). || Enseñar los dientes (to bare the teeth). || — FIG. *To grin and bear it*, poner al mal tiempo buena cara. | *To grin like a Cheshire cat*, sonreír abiertamente.
grind [graind] n. Trabajo (*m.*) *or* estudio (*m.*) pesado *or* penoso (hard work). || Pendiente (*f.*) muy empinada (steep slope). || See GRINDING. || SP. Carrera (*f.*) de obstáculos. || U. S. FAM. Empollón, ona (student).
grind* [graind] v. tr. Moler (to mill). || Pulverizar (to pulverize). || Triturar (to crash). || Picar (meat). || Afilar (to sharpen). || Esmerilar (valves, diamonds, glass). || Hacer rechinar (one's teeth). || Tocar (a barrel organ). || Agobiar, oprimir (to oppress). || — *To grind down*, oprimir (to oppress), desgastar (to wear away), reducir: *to grind down to dust*, reducir a polvo; acabar con: *to grind down the opposition*, acabar con la oposición. || *To grind out a tune*, desgranar una canción (a barrel organ). || FAM. *To grind sth. into s.o.'s head*, meterle algo en la cabeza a alguien.
— V. intr. Molerse (to mill). || Triturarse (to crash). || Pulverizarse (to pulverize). || Afilarse (to sharpen). || Picarse (the meat). || Andar con dificultad (to move

laboriously). || FAM. Empollar (to study hard). || Trabajar duramente (to work hard). || Chirriar (to grate).

— OBSERV. Pret. & p. p. **ground**.

grinder [ˈgraində*] n. Afilador, *m.* (of knives). || Afiladora, *f.* (sharpener). || Muela, *f.* (grindstone). || Moledor, *m.* (for sugar cane). || Molinillo, *m.* (for coffee, pepper). || Molino, *m.* (mill). || Trituradora, *f.* (crusher). || — Pl. Muelas, *f. pl.* (teeth).

grindery [ˈgraindəri] n. Materiales (*m. pl.*) de zapatero *or* de talabartero. || Taller (*m.*) de afilador (where tools are ground).

grinding [ˈgraindiŋ] n. Afilado, *m.* (of knives). || Molienda, *f.* (milling). || Trituración, *f.* (crushing). || Esmerilado, *m.* (of valves, glass, etc.). || Chirrido, *m.* (shrill sound). || FIG. Opresión, *f.*

grindstone [ˈgraindstəun] n. Muela, *f.* (for sharpening). || Piedra (*f.*) de amolar (from which stones for grinding are made). || FIG. *To keep one's nose to the grindstone*, trabajar con ahínco, trabajar sin levantar cabeza.

gringo [ˈgriŋgəu] n. Gringo, *m.*

grip [grip] n. Asimiento, *m.* (tight hold). || Mango, *m.* (of racket, etc.). || Asidero, *m.* (handle). || Empuñadura, *f.* (of weapon). || Apretón, *m.* (of hands). || Dominio, *m.*, poder, *m.*, control, *m.* (power). || Comprensión, *f.* (mental grasp). || Interés, *m.*: *the play lost its grip in the third act*, la obra perdió su interés en el tercer acto. || TECH. Sujeción, *f.* || Horquilla, *f.* (for the hair). || Dolor (*m.*) agudo (pain). || U. S. Maletín, *m.*, bolsa (*f.*) de viaje. || — *To come to grips*, luchar a brazo partido, pelear (to fight), enfrentarse: *to come to grips with the situation*, enfrentarse con la situación. || *To get to grips with a problem*, atacar un problema.

grip [grip] v. tr. Agarrar (to grasp). || Empuñar (a weapon). || Apretar, estrechar (hands). || Captar la atención: *the play gripped the audience*, la obra de teatro captó la atención del público. || Sujetar (to hold).

— V. intr. Agarrarse.

gripe [graip] n. See GRASP & GRIP. || Retortijón, *m.* (pain in the bowels). || FAM. *He likes a good gripe*, le gusta quejarse.

gripe [graip] v. tr. See GRASP & GRIP. || Dar retortijones en (in the bowels).

— V. intr. FAM. Quejarse (to complain). || Sentir retortijones (in the bowels).

griper [—ə*] n. U. S. FAM. Gruñón, ona; refunfuñador, ra.

grippe [grip] n. MED. Gripe, *f.*

grippy [ˈgripi] adj. Griposo, sa.

gripsack [ˈgripsæk] n. U. S. Bolsa (*f.*) de viaje, maletín, *m.* (small bag).

grisaille [griˈzeil] n. Grisalla, *f.*

grisly [ˈgrizli] adj. Horroroso, sa; espantoso, sa.

grist [grist] n. Grano (*m.*) para moler (grain for grinding). || Malta (*f.*) molida (malt). || Molienda, *f.* (quantity of grain ground at one time). || FIG. Beneficio, *m.*, ganancia, *f.* || U. S. FAM. Cantidad, *f.*, montón, *m.* || — FIG. *It's all grist to his mill*, saca provecho de todo. | *To bring grist to the mill*, aportar su granito de arena.

gristle [ˈgrisl] n. Cartílago, *m.*

gristly [ˈgrisli] adj. Cartilaginoso, sa.

grit [grit] n. Asperón, *m.*, gres, *m.*, arenisca, *f.* (sandstone). || Granos (*m. pl.*) de arena (tiny particles of sand). || Grano, *m.* (structure of stone). || FIG. Valor, *m.*, valentía, *f.*, ánimo, *m.* (courage). | Resistencia, *f.* (tenacity). | Entereza, *f.*, carácter, *m.* (character). | Firmeza, *f.* (of character).

grit [grit] v. tr./intr. Rechinar. || FIG. *To grit one's teeth*, rechinar los dientes (to grate), apretar los dientes (in determination).

grits [grits] pl. n. Sémola, *f. sing.* || Grava, *f. sing.* (for road surfacing). || U. S. Maíz (*m. sing.*) a medio moler (coarse hominy).

grittiness [ˈgritinis] n. FIG. Valor, *m.*, valentía, *f.*, ánimo, *m.*

gritty [ˈgriti] adj. FIG. Valiente, animoso, sa (plucky). || Arenoso, sa (sandy).

grizzle [ˈgrizl] v. tr. Hacer encanecer.

— V. intr. Encanecer (hair). || Quejarse (to complain). || Lloriquear, gimotear (to cry).

grizzled [—d] adj. Entrecano, na (hair).

grizzly [ˈgrizli] adj. Entrecano, na (hair). || Pardo (bear).

— N. Oso (*m.*) pardo (grizzly bear).

groan [grəun] n. Gemido, *m.*, quejido, *m.* (moan). || Gruñido, *m.* (of disapproval).

groan [grəun] v. tr. Decir con voz quejumbrosa.

— V. intr. Gemir, quejarse (to moan). || Sufrir (to suffer). || Crujir (to creak). || Gruñir, refunfuñar (to grumble).

groat [grəut] n. Moneda (*f.*) de cuatro peniques.

groats [grəuts] pl. n. Avena (*f. sing.*) mondada.

grocer [ˈgrəusə*] n. Tendero, ra [*Amer.*, abarrotero, ra; pulpero, ra]. || *Grocer's*, tienda (*f.*) de ultramarinos *or* de comestibles, ultramarinos, *m.* [*Amer.*, tienda (*f.*) de abarrotes, pulpería, *f.*].

grocery [ˈgrəusəri] n. Tienda (*f.*) de comestibles, *or* de ultramarinos, ultramarinos, *m.* [*Amer.*, tienda (*f.*) de abarrotes, pulpería, *f.*] (grocer's shop). || — Pl. Comestibles, *m.* [*Amer.*, abarrotes, *m.*]

grog [grɔg] n. Grog, *m.*, ponche, *m.* (drink).

grogginess [ˈgrɔginis] n. Inseguridad, *f.*, inestabilidad, *f.* || Atontamiento, *m.* (of a boxer).

groggy [ˈgrɔgi] adj. "Groggy" (a boxer). || Tambaleante (after drinking). || Débil (after illness). || Inestable, poco seguro (unstable). || Con debilidad en las patas delanteras (a horse).

groin [grɔin] n. ANAT. Ingle, *f.* || ARCH. Arista (*f.*) de bóveda (projecting edge). || — Pl. ARCH. Crucería, *f. sing.*

groin [grɔin] v. tr. ARCH. Construir con bóveda de crucería.

grommet [ˈgrʌmet] n. Ojal, *m.*

groom [grum] n. Novio, *m.* (bridegroom). || Mozo (*m.*) de cuadra (of horses). || Ayuda (*m.*) de cámara (in royal palace).

groom [grum] v. tr. Almohazar (a horse). || Preparar (to prepare). || Arreglar, acicalar (to make smart).

groomsman [—zmən] n. Padrino (*m.*) de boda.

— OBSERV. El plural de *groomsman* es *groomsmen*.

groove [gru:v] n. Ranura, *f.* (small rut or channel). || Garganta, *f.* (of a rail, pulley or runner). || Acanaladura, *f.* (of a column). || Estría, *f.* (stria). || Surco, *m.* (of record). || Rodada, *f.* (of car). || PRINT. Cran, *m.* (of letters). || FIG. Rutina, *f.* (routine). || FIG. *In the groove*, en plena forma (on the top of one's form), de moda (in fashion).

groove [gru:v] v. tr. Acanalar, hacer ranuras en. || Rayar, estriar.

grooved [—d] adj. Acanalado, da; estriado, da. || Rayado, da (a gun).

grooving [—iŋ] n. See GROOVE. || *Grooving plane*, acanalador, *m.*

groovy [—i] adj. FAM. Fenómeno, na; estupendo, da (wonderful).

grope [grəup] v. intr./tr. Andar a tientas. || — *To grope for*, buscar a tientas. || *To grope one's way in*, entrar a tientas.

groping [ˈgrəupiŋ] adj. Inseguro, ra.

gropingly [grəupiŋli] adv. A tientas.

grosbeak [ˈgrəusbi:k] n. ZOOL. Piñonero, *m.* (bird of the finch family).

gross [grəus] adj. Gordo, da; grueso, sa (fat). || Grueso, sa (thick). || Denso, sa (dense). || Grande: *gross negligence*, gran negligencia. || Craso, sa; flagrante (glaring): *gross ignorance*, ignorancia crasa. || Grosero, ra; ordinario, ria (vulgar). || Verde, indecente (obscene). || Zafio, fia; lerdo, da (rough). || Basto, ta; grosero, ra (unrefined): *gross humour*, humor grosero. || Bruto, ta: *gross profit*, beneficio bruto; *gross weight*, peso bruto. || Total (overall). || General. || Insensible. || — *Gross amount*, importe (*m.*) total. || *Gross national product*, producto nacional bruto. || *Gross ton*, tonelada larga.

— N. Total, *m.*, totalidad, *f.* (totality). || Gruesa, *f.*, doce docenas, *f. pl.* (twelve dozen): *a gross of pencils*, una gruesa de lápices. || — *By the gross*, al por mayor. || *In gross* o *in the gross*, en total, en conjunto.

gross [grəus] v. tr. U. S. Recaudar en bruto.

grossness [—nis] n. Enormidad, *f.* (of a crime). || Grosería, *f.* (of language). || Magnitud, *f.* (of a body). || Espesor, *m.*, grueso, *m.* (thickness). || Densidad, *f.*

grotesque [grəuˈtesk] adj. ARCH. Grotesco, ca. || Grotesco, ca (absurd).

— N. Obra (*f.*) grotesca (painting, sculpture). || Grotesco, *m.*, grutesco, *m.* (grotesque style).

grotesqueness [—nis] n. Carácter (*m.*) grotesco.

grotesquerie (U. S. **grotesquery**) [grəuˈteskəri] n. Carácter (*m.*) grotesco, lo grotesco.

grotto [ˈgrɔtəu] n. Gruta, *f.*, cueva, *f.*

— OBSERV. El plural de esta palabra es *grottoes* o *grottos*.

grouch [grautʃ] n. Cascarrabias, *m. & f. inv.*, refunfuñón, ona (grumbling person). || Mal humor, *m.*, malhumor, *m.* (bad humour). || Motivo (*m.*) de queja (cause for grumbling). || *To have a grouch against*, estar resentido con alguien.

grouch [grautʃ] v. intr. Refunfuñar (to complain). || Estar de mal humor (to be bad-tempered).

grouchy [—i] adj. Malhumorado, da (bad-tempered). || Refunfuñón, ona (grumbling).

ground [graund] n. Suelo, *m.*, tierra, *f.* (the surface of the earth). || Tierra, *f.* (the upper soil). || Terreno, *m.* (piece of land). || SP. Campo, *m.*, terreno, *m.*: *football ground*, campo de fútbol. || Campo, *m.* (of a battle). || GEOGR. Territorio, *m.*, tierra, *f.* || FIG. Terreno, *m.*, campo, *m.* (field). | Fundamento, *m.*, base, *f.* (basis). | Motivo, *m.*, razón, *f.* (motive). | Tema, *m.* (subject). || ARTS. Fondo, *m.* (background): *on a green ground*, sobre un fondo verde. || Fondo, *m.* (of water, of the sea). || U. S. ELECTR. Tierra, *f.*, toma (*f.*) de tierra. || — Pl. Jardines, *m.*, jardín, *m. sing.* (enclosed land attached to a house). || Poso, *m. sing.* (dregs). || Zurrapa, *f. sing.* (coffee sediment).

— FIG. *Above ground*, en vida, con vida, vivo, va. || *Breeding ground of vice*, terreno abonado para el vicio. || *Camping ground*, camping, *m.* || FIG. *Down to the ground*, completamente. | *From the ground up*, completamente. || *Holy ground*, Tierra Santa. || FIG. *Into the ground*, hasta más no poder. | *On delicate ground*, en situación delicada. || *On the ground*, sobre el terreno. || FIG. *On the grounds of*, por motivos de, por razones de, a causa de (because of). | *On the grounds that*, porque. || *Piece of ground*, terreno, *m.* || FIG. *To be on one's own ground*, estar en su propio terreno, estar en su elemento. | *To break fresh* o *new ground*, abrir un nuevo camino. || *To break ground*, abrir la tierra (the earth), empezar a construir (to begin to build), abrir un nuevo camino (to break fresh ground). || FIG. *To cover the ground*, discutir todos los puntos. | *To cut the ground from under s.o.'s feet*, tomarle la delantera a alguien. | *To drop* o *to throw on the ground*, dar en tierra con. || *To fall to the ground*, caer al suelo (to fall), venirse abajo, fracasar (to fail). || *To gain ground*, ganar terreno. || *To get off the ground*, despegar, quitar tierra (a plane), llevarse a cabo, realizarse (to be carried out). || FIG. *To give ground*, ceder terreno. | *To go over the same ground*, repetir la misma canción. | *To hold one's ground*, mantenerse firme. | *To keep one's* o *both feet on the ground*, tener los pies en la tierra. | *To lose ground*, perder terreno. | *To shift one's ground*, cambiar de táctica. | *To stand one's ground*, mantenerse en sus trece, no ceder. | *To suit s.o. down to the ground*, venirle al pelo *or* de perilla a uno, convenir mucho a alguien (sth.), sentar a alguien como anillo al dedo (a dress). || MAR. *To take the ground*, encallar, varar. || FIG. *To touch ground*, tocar tierra. | *To worship the ground s.o. walks on*, besar la tierra que alguien pisa.

ground [graund] v. tr. MAR. Hacer encallar, varar (a ship). || AVIAT. Obligar a permanecer en tierra (to confine to the ground). || Enseñar los conocimientos básicos a (to teach basic facts). || Preparar el fondo de (in painting). || ELECTR. Conectar con tierra. || Poner en tierra (to place on the ground). || MIL. Descansar (arms). || FIG. Fundar, basar. || — FIG. *Well grounded*, bien fundado. | *Well grounded in*, muy versado en, muy entendido en.

ground [graund] pret. & p. p. See GRIND.
— Adj. A ras de tierra. || Terrestre. || FIG. Fundamental. | Básico, ca. || — De tierra: *ground crew* o *staff*, personal de tierra. || ELECTR. *Ground cable*, cable de toma de tierra. | *Ground connection*, toma de tierra.

ground-cherry [—'tʃeri] n. BOT. Alquequenje, *m.*

ground control [—kən'trəul]. n. Control (*m.*) desde tierra.

grounder [—ə*] n. SP. Pelota (*f.*) rasa.

ground fire [—,faiə*] n. Fuego (*m.*) antiaéreo.

ground floor [—'flɔ:*] n. Planta (*f.*) baja.

groundhog [—'hɔg] n. Marmota, *f.* (animal).

ground ice [—ais] n. Hielo (*m.*) de fondo.

grounding [—iŋ] n. *To have a good grounding in*, tener una buena base en.

ground lead [—li:d] n. ELECTR. Conductor (*m.*) a tierra.

groundless [—lis] adj. Sin fundamento, infundado, da. || Sin base.

ground level [—'levl] n. Nivel (*m.*) del suelo.

groundling [—liŋ] n. Pez (*m.*) que vive en el fondo del agua. || Planta (*f.*) rastrera (creeping plant). || THEATR. Mosquetero, *m.*

groundnut [—nʌt] n. BOT. Cacahuete, *m.* [*Amer.*, cacahuate, *m.*, maní, *m.*] (peanut). | Chufa, *f.* (earth almond).

ground plan [—plæn] n. ARCH. Plano, *m.*, planta, *f.* || FIG. Proyecto (*m.*) fundamental.

ground plate [—pleit] n. U. S. ELECTR. Placa (*f.*) de conexión a tierra. || ARCH. Durmiente, *m.*

ground rent [—rent] n. Alquiler (*m.*) del terreno.

groundsel [—səl] n. BOT. Zuzón, *m.*

groundsheet [—ʃi:t] n. Tela (*f.*) impermeable.

ground speed [—spi:d] n. AVIAT. Velocidad (*f.*) respecto a la tierra.

ground squirrel [—'skwirəl] n. ZOOL. Ardilla (*f.*) terrestre.

ground swell [—'swel] n. Mar (*m.*) de fondo. || Ola (*f.*) de fondo.

groundwater [—wɔ:tə*] n. Agua (*f.*) subterránea.

ground wave [—weiv] n. Onda (*f.*) terrestre.

ground wire [—'waiə*] n. U. S. ELECTR. Cable (*m.*) de toma de tierra.

groundwork [—wə:k] n. Base, *f.* (basis): *to do the groundwork for*, echar las bases de. || Plan (of a novel). || Fundamento, *m.* (foundation). || Fondo, *m.* (background).

group [gru:p] n. Grupo, *m.*, agrupación, *f.* || ARTS. MUS. Conjunto, *m.* || Grupo, *m.* (of figures). || TECH. Haz, *m.* (of rails). || — *Blood group*, grupo sanguíneo. || *Group insurance*, seguro colectivo. || *Pressure group*, grupo de presión.

group [gru:p] v. tr. Agrupar.
— V. intr. Agruparse.

group captain [—'kæptin] n. AVIAT. Jefe (*m.*) de escuadrilla.

grouper ['gru:pə*] n. Mero, *m.* (fish).

grouping ['gru:piŋ] n. Agrupación, *f.*, agrupamiento, *m.*

grouse [graus] n. Urogallo, *m.* (bird). || FAM. Queja, *f.* (complain).

grouse [graus] v. intr. Quejarse (to complain).

grout [graut] n. ARCH. Lechada, *f.*

grout [graut] v. tr. ARCH. Rellenar con lechada.

grove [grəuv] n. Arboleda, *f.*, bosquecillo, *m.* (small group of trees). || *Orange grove*, naranjal, *m.*

grovel ['grɔvl] v. intr. Arrastrarse (to slide). || FIG. Humillarse, rebajarse, arrastrarse (to humiliate o.s.). || FIG. *To grovel in the dust*, morder el polvo.

groveller or **groveler** [—ə*] n. Persona (*f.*) servil.

grovelling or **groveling** [—iŋ] adj. Servil, rastrero, ra (servile).

grow* [grəu] v. tr. Cultivar: *to grow vegetables*, cultivar verduras. || Dejar crecer (to allow to grow): *to grow a beard*, dejarse crecer la barba. || Adquirir: *to grow a habit*, adquirir una costumbre. || FIG. Cultivar.
— V. intr. Crecer (to increase in size). || Desarrollarse (to develop). || Cultivarse, ser cultivado (to be cultivated). || Aumentar, crecer, incrementar (to increase). || Hacerse, volverse (to become): *to grow bolder*, hacerse más atrevido. || Llegar a (to come to). || Ponerse (pale, red, etc.). || — FIG. *They don't grow on every tree*, no se encuentran a la vuelta de la esquina. || *To grow accustomed*, acostumbrarse. || *To grow better*, mejorar. || *To grow dark*, oscurecer. || *To grow old*, envejecer. || *To grow to do sth.*, llegar a hacer algo. || *To grow used to*, acostumbrarse a. || *To grow weary*, cansarse.
— ***To grow from***, derivarse de (to derive from). || ***To grow into***, hacerse, convertirse en, llegar a ser. || ***To grow on*** o ***upon***, llegar a gustar: *a picture that grows on you*, una película que llega a gustar. | Arraigar (custom). || ***To grow out of***, quedársele pequeño: *the child has grown out of his jacket*, al niño la chaqueta se le ha quedado pequeña. | Perder (a habit). | Derivarse de (to stem from). || — *To grow out of fashion*, pasar de moda. || ***To grow up***, crecer mucho (a child). | Hacerse mayor (to reach adulthood). | Establecerse (to become prevalent). | Desarrollarse (to extend). | Madurar (in mind). | — *To grow up together*, criarse juntos.

— OBSERV. Pret. ***grew***; p. p. ***grown***.

grower [—ə*] n. Cultivador, ra (one who grows vegetables). || *This plant is a fast grower*, esta planta crece rápidamente.

growing [—iŋ] n. Crecimiento, *m.* (of a child). || Cultivo, *m.* (of plants). || Desarrollo, *m.* (development).
— Adj. Creciente (increasing). || Que crece, en crecimiento (child). || *Growing pains*, dolores producidos por el crecimiento (of children).

growl [graul] n. Gruñido, *m.* (of person, dog). || Retumbo, *m.* (of a gun).

growl [graul] v. tr. Decir refunfuñando.
— V. intr. Gruñir, refunfuñar (a person). || Gruñir (a dog). || Retumbar (a gun).

growler [—ə*] n. Simón, *m.* (four-wheeled cab). || Témpano (*m.*) de hielo (small iceberg). || FAM. Refunfuñador, ra; refunfuñón, ona (grumbler).

growling [—iŋ] adj. Refunfuñador, ra (person). || Que retumba (gun).

grown [grəun] adj. Adulto, ta. || *Grown over with*, cubierto de.
— P. p. See GROW.

grown-up [—ʌp] adj. Adulto, ta (adult). || Crecido, da (child, plant).
— N. Adulto, ta; mayor, *m.* (person).

growth [grəuθ] n. Crecimiento, *m.* (increase in size): *growth factor*, factor de crecimiento. || Incremento, *m.*, aumento, *m.* (increase). || Desarrollo, *m.* (development): *economic growth*, desarrollo económico. || Cultivo, *m.* (of plants). || Vegetación, *f.* || MED. Bulto, *m.*, excrecencia, *f.* (tumour). || Origen, *m.* (origin): *of foreign growth*, de origen extranjero. || *To reach full growth*, alcanzar su plenitud, alcanzar su pleno desarrollo.

groyne [grɔin] n. Espolón, *m.*, espigón, *m.*

groyne [grɔin] v. tr. Colocar espigones en.

grub [grʌb] n. ZOOL. Larva, *f.*, gusano, *m.* || FAM. Comida, *f.*, manducatoria, *f.*, jamancia, *f.* (food). | Esclavo (*m.*) del trabajo (drudge). | Plumífero, *m.*, escritorzuelo, *m.* (hack). || U. S. Empollón, *m.* (at school).

grub [grʌb] v. tr. Cavar (to dig). || Limpiar de hierbas (a land). || FAM. Dar de comer (to feed). || *To grub up* o *out*, desenterrar, descubrir (to discover), arrancar, extirpar (to extirpate).
— V. intr. Cavar (to dig). || Hozar (a pig). || FIG. Hurgar (to search laboriously). || FAM. Pringar, apencar, acurrelar (to work). | Empollar (to study). | Manducar, jalar, jamar (to eat).

grubber [—ə*] n. AGR. Roturadora, *f.* || FAM. Gran trabajador, *m.* (hard-working person). | Empollón, *m.* (at school). | Comilón, *m.* (eater).

grubbiness [—inis] n. Suciedad, *f.*

grubby [—i] adj. Sucio, cia (dirty). || Agusanado, da (grub-infested).

grubstake [—steik] n. U. S. Subvención (*f.*) *or* ayuda (*f.*) concedida a un prospector con la condición de que éste reparta lo que encuentre. | Crédito, *m.* (credit).

grubstake [—steik] v. tr. Subvencionar a, ayudar a (a miner). || Conceder un crédito a (to give credit to).

grudge [grʌdʒ] n. Rencor, *m.*, resentimiento, *m.* || *To bear s.o. a grudge*, estar resentido con alguien, guardar rencor a alguien.

grudge [grʌdʒ] v. tr. Envidiar (to envy). || Dar a regañadientes (to give). || Ver con malos ojos (to resent).

grudgingly [grʌdʒiŋli] adv. A regañadientes.

gruel [gruəl] n. CULIN. Gachas, *f. pl.*

gruelling [—iŋ] adj. Penoso, sa; duro, ra (hard). || Agotador, ra (exhausting).

— N. Prueba (*f.*) dura. || Paliza, *f.* (beating).
gruesome [ˈgru:səm] adj. Espantoso, sa; horrible.
gruff [grʌf] adj. Ronco, ca (harsh). || Brusco, ca (blunt).
gruffness [—nis] n. Brusquedad, *f.*
grumble [ˈgrʌmbl] n. Queja, *f.* (complaint). || Rugido, *m.*, retumbo, *m.* (of a gun, thunder, etc.).
grumble [ˈgrʌmbl] v. tr. Decir refunfuñando.
— V. intr. Quejarse (*at, about*, de) [to complain]. || Refunfuñar (to moan). || Retumbar a lo lejos, rugir (gun, thunder).
grumbler [—ə*] n. Refunfuñador, ra; refunfuñón, ona.
grumbling [—iŋ] adj. Gruñón, ona; refunfuñón, ona.
grume [gru:m] n. Grumo, *m.*, cuajarón, *m.*, coágulo, *m.* (clot of blood).
grummet [ˈgrʌmet] n. Ojal, *m.*
grumous [ˈgru:məs] adj. Grumoso, sa.
grumpiness [grʌmpinis] n. Malhumor, *m.*, mal genio, *m.*
grumpish [ˈgrʌmpiʃ] or **grumpy** [ˈgrʌmpi] adj. Malhumorado, da; gruñón, ona.
grunt [grʌnt] n. Gruñido, *m.* (sound).
grunt [grʌnt] v. tr. Decir gruñendo.
— V. intr. Gruñir.
grunter [—ə*] n. FAM. Marrano, *m.* (pig). || FIG. Refunfuñón, ona (grumbler).
grunting [—iŋ] adj. Gruñidor, ra.
Gruyère [ˈgru:jɛə*] n. Gruyere, *m.* (cheese).
gryphon [ˈgrifən] n. MITH. Grifo, *m.*
G-string [ˈdʒi:striŋ] n. FAM. Taparrabo, *m.*(garment).
guacamole [ˌgwækəˈməuli] n. Guacamol, *m.*, guacamole, *m.*
guaco [ˈgwɑ:kəu] n. BOT. Guaco, *m.*
Guadaloupe [ˌgwɑ:dəˈlu:p] pr. n. GEOGR. Guadalupe, *f.* (island).
guaiacol [ˈgwaiəkəl] n. Guayacol, *m.*
guaiacum [ˈgwɑiəkəm] n. BOT. Guayacán, *m.* (tree). | Guayaco, *m.* (wood).
guama [ˈgwɑ:mə] n. BOT. Guamo, *m.*, guama, *f.* (tree). | Guama, *f.* (fruit).
guanaco [gwəˈnɑ:kəu] n. ZOOL. Guanaco, *m.*
Guanche [ˈgwæntʃ] adj./n. Guanche (first inhabitants of the Canary Islands).
guano [ˈgwɑ:nəu] n. Guano, *m.* (fertilizer).
guarani [ˌgwɑ:rəˈni:] adj./n. Guaraní.
guarantee [ˌgærənˈti:] n. Garantía, *f.* (pledge, promise). || COMM. Garantía, *f.*: *to give a six-month guarantee*, dar una garantía de seis meses. | Certificado (*m.*) de garantía (certificate). || JUR. Garantía, *f.*, fianza, *f.* (guaranty). | Persona (*f.*) garantizada. | Fiador, ra; garante, *m.* & *f.* (guarantor).
guarantee [ˌgærənˈti:] v. tr. Garantizar: *to guarantee a clock for a year*, garantizar un reloj por un año. || Garantizar, ser fiador de (to act as a guarantor for). || Garantizar, avalar (a bill). || Responder de (s.o.'s conduct). || Asegurar (to ensure).
guaranteed [—d] adj. Garantizado, da. || Asegurado, da.
guarantor [ˌgærənˈtɔ:*] n. Garante, *m.* & *f.*
guaranty [ˈgærənti] n. Fianza, *f.*, garantía, *f.*
guard [gɑ:d] n. Guardia, *f.* (a keeping watch, a ceremonial escort, a protective force, body of people set to keep watch). || Centinela, *m.*, guardia, *m.* (sentry). || Guardián, *m.*, guarda, *m.* (warder). || Jefe (*m.*) de tren (of train). || Salvaguardia, *f.*, protección, *f.* (safeguard). || Guarda, *f.*, guarnición, *f.*, guardamano, *m.* (of a sword). || SP. Guardia, *f.* (in boxing, fencing). | Defensa, *m.* (in basketball, American football). || TECH. Dispositivo (*m.*) protector *or* de seguridad (in machinery). || — Pl. Guardia, *f. sing.* (royal regiment). || — MIL. *Advance guard*, avanzada, *f.* || *Changing of the guard*, relevo (*m.*) de la guardia. || *Civil guard*, guardia civil. || SP. *Low guard*, guardia baja. || *New* o *relieving guard, old guard*, guardia entrante, saliente. || FIG. *To be off one's guard*, estar descuidado *or* desprevenido. || *To be on guard*, estar de guardia. || FIG. *To be on one's guard*, estar en guardia. || MIL. *To change the guard*, relevar la guardia. | *To come off guard*, salir de guardia. | *To go on guard*, entrar de guardia. || *To keep guard over*, vigilar. | *To mount guard*, montar la guardia, hacer guardia. || FIG. *To put o.s. on guard*, ponerse en guardia. | *To put s.o. on his guard*, poner en guardia a uno. || MIL. *To stand guard*, montar la guardia. || *Under guard*, a buen recaudo.
guard [gɑ:d] v. tr. Vigilar, custodiar: *to guard a prisoner*, vigilar a un prisionero. || Proteger, defender (to defend, to provide with a guard, protective device, etc.). || Escoltar (to escort). || Guardar: *to guard the gates of the city*, guardar las puertas de la ciudad.
— V. intr. *To guard against*, protegerse contra (to take precautions), guardarse: *guard against doing that*, guárdate de hacer eso; impedir, evitar (to prevent).
guard boat [—bəut] n. Patrullero, *m.*, guardacostas, *m.*
guard chain [—tʃein] n. Cadena (*f.*) de seguridad.
guarded [ˈgɑ:did] adj. Precavido, da; cauteloso, sa (cautious). || Protegido, da. || Custodiado, da.
guardedly [—li] adv. Cautelosamente, con cautela.
guardhouse [ˈgɑ:dhaus] n. Prisión (*f.*) militar (for military prisoners). || Cuerpo (*m.*) de guardia (for the guard and military police).
guardian [ˈgɑ:djən] n. Tutor, ra (of an orphan). || Guardián, *m.*, guarda, *m.* (custodian). || Conservador, ra (of a museum). || Guardián, *m.* (superior of a Franciscan convent). || *Guardian angel*, ángel (*m.*) de la Guarda, ángel custodio.
guardianship [—ʃip] n. Tutela, *f.* (legal responsibility of guardian). || Amparo, *m.*, protección, *f.* (protection). || Conservación, *f.* (of a museum).
guard iron [ˈgɑ:dˈaiən] n. Quitapiedras, *m. inv.* (on a train).
guard rail [ˈgɑ:dreil] n. Barandilla, *f.* (of staircase). || Contracarril, *m.* (of rails).
guardroom [ˈgɑ:drum] n. See GUARDHOUSE.
guardsman [ˈgɑ:dzmən] n. MIL. Guardia, *m.*
— OBSERV. El plural de *guardsman* es *guardsmen.*
Guatemala [ˌgwætiˈmɑ:lə] pr. n. GEOGR. Guatemala, *m.*
Guatemalan [—n] adj./n. Guatemalteco, ca.
guava [ˈgwɑ:və] n. Guayabo, *m.* (tree). || Guayaba, *f.* (fruit). || — *Guava grove*, guayabal, *m.* || *Guava jelly*, guayaba, *f.*
gubernatorial [ˌgu:bənəˈtɔriəl] adj. Gubernativo, va. || Del gobernador. || FAM. Paternal.
gudgeon [ˈgʌdʒən] n. Gobio, *m.* (fish). || TECH. Muñón, *m.*, gorrón, *m.* (of an axle). | Clavija, *f.* (peg). || MAR. Hembra (*f.*) del gorrón, muñonera, *f.* (of a rudder). || FAM. Tonto, ta; pánfilo, la (idiot). || AUT. *Gudgeon pin*, eje (*m.*) del pistón.
Guelders [ˈgeldəz] pr. n. GEOGR. Güeldres, *f.*
guerdon [ˈgə:dən] n. Galardón, *m.*, recompensa, *f.*
guerilla or **guerrilla** [gəˈrilə] n. Guerrillero, *m.* || — *Guerrilla band*, guerrilla, *f.* (group). || *Guerrilla fighter*, guerrillero, *m.* || *Guerrilla warfare*, guerrilla, *f.*, guerra (*f.*) de guerrillas.
Guernsey [ˈgə:nzi] pr. n. GEOGR. Guernesey.
guess [ges] n. Cálculo, *m.* (an estimate). || Conjetura, *f.*, suposición, *f.* (conjecture): *to make a guess at*, hacer suposiciones sobre. || Acierto, *m.*: *of easy guess*, de fácil acierto. || U. S. Opinión, *f.*, parecer, *m.*: *my guess is that*, mi parecer es que. || — *At a guess*, a primera vista. || *At a rough guess*, a ojo de buen cubero. || *I give you three guesses*, te doy tres oportunidades para acertar. || *It's my guess that*, a mí me parece que, yo creo que. || *To have* o *to make a guess*, intentar adivinar.
guess [ges] v. tr./intr. Adivinar: *I will never guess*, nunca lo adivinaré. || Acertar (to conjecture correctly). || Suponer (to suppose): *he guessed as much*, ya lo suponía; *I guessed her to be younger*, suponía que era más joven. || U. S. Pensar, creer, suponer: *I guess so*, así lo creo yo. || — *Guess who!*, ¡adivina quién soy! || *To guess at*, intentar adivinar. || *To guess right*, acertar. || *To keep s.o. guessing*, mantener a uno a la expectativa *or* en la incertidumbre *or* en suspenso.
guessing game [—ingeim] n. Acertijo, *m.*, adivinanza, *f.*
guesswork [—wə:k] n. Conjetura, *f.*, conjeturas, *f. pl.*: *it's all guesswork*, son puras conjeturas. || *By guesswork*, a ojo de buen cubero.
guest [gest] n. Invitado, da (who receives hospitality). || Huésped, da (at a hotel). || Visita, *f.* (visit). || BIOL. Parásito, *m.* || — *Be my guest*, yo invito. || *Guest of honour*, invitado de honor. || *Guest room*, cuarto (*m.*) de huéspedes. || *Paying guest*, huésped (*m.*) que paga una pensión.
guesthouse [—haus] n. Casa (*f.*) de huéspedes.
guff [gʌf] n. FAM. Cuento, *m.*: *that's a load of guff*, todo eso son cuentos.
guffaw [gʌˈfɔ:] n. Carcajada, *f.*, risotada, *f.*
guffaw [gʌˈfɔ:] v. intr. Reírse a carcajadas.
guggle [ˈgʌgl] v. intr. Borbotar (water).
Guiana [gaiˈænə] pr. n. GEOGR. Guayana, *f.*
guidance [ˈgaidəns] n. Conducción, *f.*, dirección, *f.*, guía, *f.* (act of guiding). || Consejo, *m.*, asesoramiento, *m.* (advice). || Gobierno, *m.* (leadership). || Orientación, *f.*: *vocational guidance*, orientación profesional. || *I am telling you this for your guidance*, le digo esto para su buen gobierno.
guide [gaid] n. Guía, *m.* & *f.* (person who guides). || Guía, *f.* (book of information). || Guía, *f.*, método (*m.*) para principiantes (instructions book). || Guía, *f.* (example). || Consejero, ra; guía, *m.* (adviser, principle governing behaviour): *let conscience be your guide*, que la conciencia sea tu consejera. || Exploradora, *f.* (girl guide). || TECH. Guía *f.*
guide [gaid] v. tr. Guiar: *to guide some tourists*, guiar a unos turistas. || Dirigir: *to guide a boat*, dirigir un barco; *to guide s.o. in his studies*, dirigir a uno en sus estudios. || Dirigir, gobernar (to govern). || Orientar (to advise). || AVIAT. Pilotar.
— V. intr. Hacer de guía (to act as a guide).
guidebook [—buk] n. Guía (*f.*) turística.
guided missile [—idˈmisail] n. Proyectil (*m.*) teledirigido.
guide line [—lain] n. Línea (*f.*) directiva, directiva, *f.*, directriz, *f.* (directive). || Principio, *m.* (principle). || Pauta, *f.* (model).
guidepost [—pəust] n. Poste (*m.*) indicador.
guide rope [—rəup] n. Cuerda (*f.*) guía (of a balloon).
guidon [ˈgaidən] n. MIL. Guión, *m.*, banderín, *m.* (pennant). || Portaguión, *m.* (standard bearer).
guild [gild] n. Gremio, *m.*, corporación, *f.* (association). || Guilda, *f.*
guilder [ˈgildə*] n. Florín, *m.*

guildhall [ˈgildˈhɔ:l] n. Lugar (*m.*) de reunión de un gremio. || Ayuntamiento, *m.* (town hall).
guile [gail] n. Engaño, *m.* (trickery). || Astucia, *f.* (wiliness).
guileful [ˈgailful] adj. Engañoso, sa (who tricks). || Astuto, ta (wily).
guileless [ˈgaillis] adj. Sin engaño (act). || Franco, ca; leal (frank). || Cándido, da; inocente (naïve).
guilelessness [—nis] n. Candidez, *f.*, candor, *m.*, inocencia, *f.* (innocence). || Franqueza, *f.* (frankness).
guillemot [ˈgilimɔt] n. Pájaro (*m.*) bobo (bird).
guillotine [ˌgiləˈti:n] n. Guillotina, *f.* (for beheading people, machine for cutting paper).
guillotine [ˌgiləˈti:n] v. tr. Guillotinar.
guillotining [—iŋ] n. Guillotinamiento, *m.*
guilt [gilt] n. Culpa, *f.* (the fact of having committed a legal or moral offence). || Culpabilidad, *f.*: *guilt feelings*, sentimiento de culpabilidad.
guiltiness [—inis] n. Culpabilidad, *f.*
guiltless [—lis] adj. Inocente. || FIG. Ignorante.
guiltlessness [—lisnis] n. Inocencia, *f.*
guilty [—i] adj. Culpable: *to plead guilty*, declararse culpable; *they found him guilty*, lo declararon culpable. || — *Not guilty*, soy inocente. || *To have a guilty conscience*, remorderle a uno la conciencia. || *To plead not guilty*, declararse inocente. || *Verdict of guilty*, sentencia (*f.*) de culpabilidad.
guinea [ˈgini] n. Guinea, *f.* (monetary unit).
Guinea [ˈgini] pr. n. GEOGR. Guinea, *f.*
guinea fowl [—faul] or **guinea hen** [—hen] n. ZOOL. Gallina (*f.*) de Guinea, pintada, *f.*
Guinean [ˈginiən] adj./n. Guineo, a.
Guinea pig [ˈginipig] n. ZOOL. Conejillo (*m.*) de Indias, cobaya, *f.*, cobayo, *m.* [*Amer.*, cuy, *m.*]. || FIG. Conejillo (*m.*) de Indias.
guipure [giˈpyr] n. Guipur, *m.*
guise [gaiz] n. Modo, *m.*, guisa, *f.*: *in this guise*, de ese modo. || Apariencia, *f.* (outward appearance). || Pretexto, *m.*: *under the guise of*, con el pretexto de, so pretexto de.
guitar [giˈtɑ:*] n. Guitarra, *f.* || *Guitar maker, guitar seller*, guitarrista, *m.*
— Adj. De guitarra: *guitar music*, música de guitarra.
guitarist [giˈtɑ:rist] n. Guitarrista, *m. & f.*
gulch [gʌlʃ] n. Barranco, *m.*
gulden [ˈguldən] n. Florín, *m.*
gules [gju:lz] n. HERALD. Gules, *m. pl.*
gulf [gʌlf] n. Golfo, *m.* (large bay). || FIG. Abismo, *m.* (huge gap).
Gulf Stream [—stri:m] pr. n. GEOGR. Corriente (*f.*) del Golfo.
gulfweed [—wi:d] n. BOT. Sargazo, *m.*
gull [gʌl] n. Gaviota, *f.* (bird). || FAM. Primo, ma; pánfilo, la (a dupe).
gull [gʌl] v. tr. Pegársela, engañar.
gullet [ˈgʌlit] n. ANAT. Esófago, *m.* || FAM. Garganta, *f.*, gaznate, *m.* (throat). || Canal, *m.* (channel). || Barranco, *m.*, hondonada, *f.* (gully).
gullibility [ˌgʌliˈbiliti] n. FAM. Credulidad, *f.*
gullible [ˈgʌləbl] adj. FAM. Crédulo, la; bobo, ba.
gully [ˈgʌli] n. Hondonada, *f.*, barranco, *m.* (ravine).
gully [ˈgʌli] v. tr. Formar barrancos en.
gulp [gʌlp] n. Trago, *m.* (drink): *at one gulp*, de un trago. || Bocado, *m.* (food). || FIG. Nudo (*m.*) en la garganta (of anxiety).
gulp [gʌlp] v. tr. Tragarse (to swallow). || *To gulp down*, reprimir, contener (one's rage, etc.), tragarse, echarse al coleto (a drink).
— V. intr. Tragar, engullir. || FIG. Tener un nudo en la garganta (to be anxious). || *To gulp for breath*, respirar hondo.
gum [gʌm] n. Goma, *f.* (natural substance or sth. similar). || Gomero, *m.*, árbol (*m.*) del que se saca la goma (gum tree). || Resina, *f.* (resin). || Caucho, *m.* (rubber). || Chicle, *m.* (chewing gum). || Pegamento, *m.*, goma, *f.* (glue to stick). || Legaña, *f.* (of the eyes). || ANAT. Encía, *f.* (of mouth). || — Pl. U. S. Chanclos (*m.*) de goma. || — FAM. *¡By gum!*, ¡caray! || *Gum arabic*, goma arábiga. || *Gum resin*, gomorresina, *f.* || *Gum tree*, gomero, *m.* || FAM. *Up a gum tree*, en un lío.
gum [gʌm] v. tr. Pegar con goma (to stick with gum). || Engomar (to smear with gum). || FIG. FAM. *To gum up*, paralizar, parar (to stop), estropear (to spoil).
— V. intr. Exudar goma (to exude gum). || Espesarse (to become gummy).
Gumbo [ˈgʌmbəu] n. Dialecto (*m.*) hablado en Luisiana.
gumboil [ˈgʌmbɔil] n. Flemón, *m.*
gumdrop [ˈgʌmdrɔp] n. U. S. Pastilla (*f.*) de goma.
gumma [ˈgʌmə] n. MED. Goma, *f.*
— OBSERV. El plural de *gumma* es *gummata*.
gummatous [ˈgʌmətəs] adj. MED. Gomoso, sa.
gumminess [ˈgʌminis] n. Gomosidad, *f.*, pegajosidad, *f.*, viscosidad, *f.*
gummy [ˈgʌmi] adj. Gomoso, sa (containing or like gum). || Pegajoso, sa (sticky). || Viscoso, sa (viscous). || Legañoso, sa (eyes). || Hinchado, da (ankle).
gumption [ˈgʌmpʃən] n. FAM. Sentido (*m.*) común, seso, *m.* (common sense). | Vigor, *m.*, brío, *m.*, energía, *f.* (drive). | Iniciativa, *f.* (initiative). | Gramática (*f.*) parda (skill).
gun [gʌn] n. Arma, *f.* (weapon). || Revólver, *m.* (revolver). || Pistola, *f.* (pistol). || Fusil, *m.*: *needle gun*, fusil de aguja. || Escopeta, *f.* (for hunting): *double-barrelled gun*, escopeta de dos cañones. || Rifle, *m.* (for big game). || Escopeta, *f.*, carabina, *f.*: *air gun*, escopeta de aire comprimido. || Ametralladora, *f.* (machine gun). || Cañón, *m.* (cannon). || Disparo, *m.* (shot). || Cañonazo, *m.* (discharge). || Cazador, *m.*, escopeta, *f.* (hunter): *a party of six guns*, un grupo de seis cazadores. || Pistolero, *m.* (killer). || Pistola, *f.* (for painting). || Inyector, *m.* (for lubricating). || — FAM. *Big gun*, pez gordo. || *Machine gun*, ametralladora. || *Six-gun salute*, salva de seis cañonazos. || *The guns*, la artillería: *antiaircraft guns*, artillería antiaérea. || *To bring the gun to the shoulder*, encararse el fusil, echarse el fusil a la cara. || FIG. *To go great guns*, avanzar a buen paso. | *To jump the gun*, adelantarse (to act before the proper time). | *To stick to one's guns*, mantenerse en sus trece.
gun [gʌn] v. tr. Disparar a (to shoot). || U. S. FAM. Acelerar a fondo (a car). || U. S. FAM. *To gun down*, matar [a tiros].
— V. intr. FAM. Acelerar a fondo (car). || Ir de caza (to go hunting). || *To gun for*, cazar (to hunt), andar a la caza de (to look for), perseguir (to aim at).
gun barrel [—ˌbærəl] n. Cañón (*m.*) de escopeta.
gunboat [—bəut] n. MAR. Cañonero, *m.*, lancha (*f.*) cañonera.
gun carriage [—ˌkæridʒ] n. Cureña, *f.*
gun case [—keis] n. Funda (*f.*) de escopeta.
guncotton [—ˌkɔtn] n. Algodón (*m.*) pólvora (celulose nitrate).
gun crew [—kru:] n. Dotación (*f.*) de una batería.
gun deck [—dek] n. Batería, *f.*, cubierta (*f.*) de batería.
gundog [—dɔg] n. Perro (*m.*) de caza.
gunfight [—ˌfait] n. Pelea (*f.*) a tiros, tiroteo, *m.*
gunfire [—faiə*] n. Fuego, *m.*, disparo, *m.* [de escopeta, pistola, fusil, cañón, etc.]. || MIL. Fuego (*m.*) de artillería, cañoneo, *m.* || Tiroteo, *m.* (shooting).
gun licence [—ˈlaisəns] n. Licencia (*f.*) de armas.
gunlock [—lɔk] n. Llave (*f.*) de fusil.
gunman [—mən] n. Pistolero, *m.* (gangster).
— OBSERV. El plural de *gunman* es *gunmen*.
gunmetal [ˌmetl] n. Bronce (*m.*) de cañón (variety of bronze). || Bronce (*m.*) industrial (used for belt buckles, toys, etc.). || Gris (*m.*) oscuro (colour).
gunnel [ˈgʌnl] n. MAR. Regala, *f.*, borda, *f.*
gunner [ˈgʌnə*] n. MIL. Artillero, *m.* || Arponero, *m.* (harpooner). || Cazador, *m.*, escopeta, *f.* (hunter).
gunnery [ˈgʌnəri] n. Artillería, *f.* (artillery).
gunny [gʌni] n. Yute, *m.* (jute). || Arpillera, *f.*, tela (*f.*) de saco (coarse cloth).
gunport [ˈgʌnpɔ:t] n. Porta, *f.*, cañonera, *f.*
gunpowder [ˈgʌnˌpaudə*] n. Pólvora, *f.*
gun room [ˈgʌnrum] n. MAR. Sala (*f.*) de suboficiales. || Armería, *f.*, sala (*f.*) de armas (room for sporting guns).
gunrunner [ˈgʌnˌrʌnə*] n. Traficante (*m.*) de armas.
gunrunning [—iŋ] n. Tráfico (*m.*) *or* contrabando (*m.*) de armas.
gunshot [ˈgʌnʃɔt] n. Disparo, *m.* (a shot). || Tiro, *m.*: *out of gunshot*, fuera de tiro. || Cañonazo, *m.* (of cannon). || *Within gunshot*, a tiro de fusil.
gun-shy [ˈgʌnʃai] adj. Asustadizo, za.
gunsmith [ˈgʌnsmiθ] n. Armero, *m.* || *Gunsmith's shop*, armería, *f.*
gunstock [ˈgʌnstɔk] n. Culata, *f.*
gunwale [ˈgʌnl] n. MAR. Regala, *f.*, borda, *f.*
gurgitation [ˌgə:dziˈteiʃən] n. Hervor, *m.*, ebullición, *f.* (of boiling water). || Burbujeo, *m.* (of cold water).
gurgle [ˈgə:gl] n. Borboteo, *m.* (of water). || Gorjeo, *m.* (of a child). || Murmullo, *m.* (of stream).
gurgle [ˈgə:gl] v. intr. Borbotear (water). || Gorjear (children).
gurnard [ˈgə:nəd] or **gurnet** [ˈgə:nit] n. Rubio, *m.* (fish).
gush [gʌʃ] n. Chorro, *m.* (outpour). || FIG. Efusión (*f.*) exagerada *or* excesiva (exaggerated display of feeling). | Torrente, *m.* (of words).
gush [gʌʃ] v. tr. Derramar. || FIG. Decir con excesiva efusión (to utter too effusively).
— V. intr. Salir a chorros *or* a borbotones, brotar (to flow out). || FIG. *To gush over*, hablar con excesiva efusión de.
gusher [—ə*] n. Pozo (*m.*) surtidor, pozo (*m.*) brotante [de petróleo]. || FIG. Persona (*f.*) muy efusiva *or* expansiva.
gushing [—iŋ] adj. Que brota, que sale a chorros. || FIG. Efusivo, va; expansivo, va (person).
gusset [ˈgʌsit] n. Cuchillo, *m.*, escudete, *m.* (in sewing). || ARCH. Cartabón, *m.*
gust [gʌst] n. Ráfaga, *f.*, racha, *f.* (of wind). || Bocanada, *f.* (of smoke, etc.). || Aguacero, *m.*, chaparrón, *m.* (of rain). || Explosión, *f.* (of noise). || Acceso, *m.*, arrebato, *m.*: *a gust of anger*, un acceso de cólera.
gustation [gʌsˈteiʃən] n. Gustación, *f.* (act of tasting). || Gusto, *m.* (sense of taste).
gustative [gʌsˈteitiv] adj. Gustativo, va.
gustily [ˈgʌstili] adv. En ráfagas. || FIG. Impetuosamente.
gustiness [ˈgʌstinis] n. Impetuosidad, *f.*
gusto [ˈgʌstəu] n. Placer, *m.*: *with gusto*, con placer. || Entusiasmo, *m.*

gusty [ˈgʌsti] adj. Que viene en ráfagas: *gusty rain*, lluvia que viene en ráfagas. || Ventoso, sa; borrascoso, sa: *a gusty day*, un día ventoso. || FIG. Impetuoso, sa.
gut [gʌt] n. ANAT. Intestino, *m.*, tripa, *f.* || Cuerda, *f.*, tripa, *f.* (used in musical instruments). || Sedal, *m.* (for fishing). || Paso (*m.*) estrecho (narrow passage of water). || — Pl. FAM. Tripas, *f.*, barriga, *f. sing.* (entrails). | Agallas, *f.*, energía, *f. sing.*, nervio, *m. sing.* (pluck and determination). | Fuerza, *f. sing.* (force).
— Adj. Fundamental, esencial.
gut [gʌt] v. tr. Destripar (to remove the entrails). || Limpiar (fishes). || Vaciar (to empty). || FIG. Resumir (a book). | Extraer lo esencial de. || *The fire gutted the house*, el fuego no dejó más que las paredes de la casa.
gutta [ˈgʌtə] n. ARCH. Gota.
— OBSERV. El plural de *gutta* es *guttas* o *guttae*.
gutta-percha [ˈgʌtəˈpəːtʃə] n. Gutapercha, *f.*
gutter [ˈgʌtə*] n. Canal, *m.*, canalón, *m.* (of a roof). || Arroyo, *m.*, cuneta, *f.* (of street). || Cuneta, *f.* (of roads). || FIG. Arroyo, *m.*: *to raise s.o. from the gutter*, sacar a alguien del arroyo. || Espacio (*m.*) en blanco entre los sellos (philately). || Ranura, *f.*, estría, *f.* (groove, channel).
gutter [ˈgʌtə*] v. tr. Poner canalones (in a house). || Abrir surcos en (the soil). || Acanalar (to groove).
— V. intr. Correr (water). || Derretirse (candles). || *To gutter out*, apagarse.
gutter press [—pres] n. Prensa (*f.*) sensacionalista.
guttersnipe [—snaip] n. Golfillo, *m.*, pilluelo, la.
guttural [ˈgʌtərəl] adj. Gutural.
— N. Gutural, *f.*
gutturalize [ˈgʌtərəlaiz] v. tr. Pronunciar guturalmente.
guy [gai] n. FAM. Tío, *m.*, tipo, *m.*, individuo, *m.*, sujeto, *m.*, chico, *m.* (fellow): *a great guy*, un tío formidable. | Mamarracho, *m.*, adefesio, *m.* (ridiculous person). || Viento, *m.*, tirante, *m.* (rope or chain).
guy [gai] v. tr. Sujetar con viento *or* tirante (to fasten with guys). || Remedar a, parodiar a (to parody). || Ridiculizar (to ridicule). || Tomar el pelo a (to tease).
Guy [gai] pr. n. Guido, *m.*
Guyana [gaiˈænə] pr. n. GEOGR. Guyana, *f.*
guzzle [ˈgʌzl] v. tr./intr. FAM. Soplarse (to drink greedily and rapidly). | Engullirse, tragarse, zamparse (to eat greedily and rapidly).
guzzler [ˈgʌzlə*] n. FAM. Bebedor, ra (drunkard). | Comilón, ona (glutton).
gybe [dʒaib] v. tr. MAR. Poner a la capa, poner en facha.
— V. intr. MAR. Ponerse a la capa, ponerse en facha.
gym [dʒim] n. Gimnasio, *m.* (gymnasium). || Gimnasia, *f.* (gymnastics). || *Gym shoes*, zapatos (*m.*) de tenis *or* de lona.
gymkhana [dʒimˈkɑːnə] n. Gymkhana, *f.*
gymnasium [dʒimˈneizjəm] n. SP. Gimnasio, *m.* || Instituto, *m.* (school in Germany).
— OBSERV. El plural de *gymnasium* es *gymnasia* o *gymnasiums*.
gymnast [ˈdʒimnæst] n. Gimnasta, *m.* & *f.*
gymnastic [dʒimˈnæstik] adj. Gimnástico, ca.
gymnastics [—s] n. Gimnasia, *f.*
gymnosperm [ˈdʒimnəˌspəːm] n. BOT. Gimnosperma, *f.* (seed plant).
gynaeceum [ˌgainiˈsiːəm] n. Gineceo, *m.*
— OBSERV. El plural de *gynaeceum* es *gynaecea*.
gynaecological (U. S. **gynecological**) [ˌgainikəˈlɔdʒikəl] adj. Ginecológico, ca.
gynaecologist (U. S. **gynecologist**) [ˌgainiˈkɔlədʒist] n. Ginecólogo. ga.
gynaecology (U. S. **ginecology**) [ˌgainiˈkɔlədʒi] n. Ginecología, *f.*
gynoecium (U. S. **gynecium**) [ˌgainiˈsiːəm] n. Gineceo, *m.*
— OBSERV. El plural es *gynoecia* y *gynecia*.
gyp [dʒip] n. U. S. FAM. Timo, *m.* (cheat). | Timador, ra (swindler). || Criado (*m.*) en la Universidad de Cambridge.
gyp [dʒip] v. tr./intr. U. S. FAM. Timar.
gypseous [ˈdʒipsiəs] adj. Yesoso, sa.
gypsum [ˈdʒipsəm] n. Yeso, *m.* || *Gypsum pit*, yesera, *f.*
gypsum [ˈdʒipsəm] v. tr. Enyesar.
gypsy [ˈdʒipsi] adj./n. Gitano, na (in Western Europe). || Zíngaro, ta (in Central Europe).
gypsy moth [—mɔθ] n. ZOOL. Lagarta, *f.*
gyrate [ˈdʒaiərit] v. intr. Girar.
gyration [ˌdʒaiəˈreiʃən] n. Giro, *m.*, vuelta, *f.*, rotación, *f.*
gyratory [ˈdʒaiərətəri] adj. Giratorio, ria.
gyre [ˈdʒaiə*] n. Rotación, *f.*
gyre [ˈdʒaiə*] v. intr. Girar, dar vueltas.
gyrfalcon [ˈdʒəːˌfɔːlkən] n. U. S. ZOOL. Gerifalte, *m.*
gyro [ˈdʒaiərəu] n. Giroscopio, *m.* (gyroscope). || Brújula (*f.*) giroscópica, girocompás, *m.*
gyrocompass [ˈdʒaiərəuˌkʌmpəs] n. Brújula (*f.*) giroscópica, girocompás, *m.*
gyropilot [ˈdʒaiərəuˈpailət] n. Piloto (*m.*) automático, giropiloto, *m.*
gyroplane [ˈdʒaiərəplein] n. Autogiro, *m.*
gyroscope [ˈgaiərəskəup] n. Giroscopio, *m.*
gyroscopic [ˌgaiərəsˈkɔpik] adj. Giroscópico, ca.
gyrostabilizer [ˌdʒaiərəuˈsteibilaizə*] n. Estabilizador (*m.*) giroscópico.
gyrostat [ˈgaiərəustæt] n. Giróstato, *m.* || Estabilizador (*m.*) giroscópico.

H

h [eitʃ] n. H, *f.* (letter of alphabet).
habeas corpus [ˈheibjesˈkɔːpəs] n. JUR. Hábeas corpus, *m.*
— OBSERV. El *hábeas corpus* es un principio destinado a evitar que se mantenga a un detenido en prisión preventiva sin que haya un motivo que lo justifique. El *writ of habeas corpus* estipula que los funcionarios que tienen a un detenido bajo su custodia deben llevarle ante los tribunales.
haberdasher [ˈhæbədæʃə*] n. Mercero, ra (dealer in small articles). || U. S. Camisero, ra (shirt dealer). | Dueño (*m.*) de una tienda de artículos para caballeros.
haberdashery [—ri] n. Mercería, *f.* (shop). || Artículos (*m. pl.*) de mercería (goods). || U. S. Camisería, *f.* (shop). | Ropa (*f.*) para caballeros (men's clothing).
habergeon [ˈhæbədʒən] n. Cota (*f.*) de mallas.
habiliments [həˈbilimәntz] pl. n. Ropa, *f. sing.*
habit [ˈhæbit] n. Costumbre, *f.*, hábito, *m.*: *to fall into the habit of*, coger la costumbre de. || Hábito, *m.* (monk's or nun's robe): *to take the habit*, tomar el hábito. || Amazona, *f.*, traje (*m.*) de montar (for riding sidesaddle). || Traje, *m.* (costume, dress). || Manera (*f.*) de ser (charasteristic condition of mind). || Constitución, *f.* (condition of body). || Manera (*f.*) de crecer. || — *By* o *from* o *out of habit*, por costumbre. || *Habit of mind*, manera (*f.*) de ver las cosas, carácter, *m.* || *To be in the habit of doing sth.*, acostumbrar *or* tener la costumbre de *or* soler hacer algo. || *To get into the habit of doing sth.*, acostumbrarse a hacer algo. || *To get out of the habit of doing sth.*, perder la costumbre de hacer algo. || *To kick the habit of*, quitarse de.
habit [ˈhæbit] v. tr. Vestir (to dress).
habitability [hæbitəˈbiliti] n. Habitabilidad, *f.*
habitable [ˈhæbitəbl] adj. Habitable.
— OBSERV. La palabra inglesa *habitable* se aplica sobre todo a las casas, mientras *inhabitable* se emplea particularmente para calificar los países y lugares.
habitableness [—nis] n. Habitabilidad, *f.*
habitant [ˈhæbitənt] n. Habitante, *m.* & *f.*
habitant or **habitan** [ˈhæbitɔ̃ːŋ] n. Canadiense (*m.*) francés.
habitat [ˈhæbitæt] n. Habitat, *m.*, hábitat, *m.*
habitation [ˌhæbiˈteiʃən] n. Habitación, *f.* (act of living in a place). || Morada, *f.* (dwelling).
habit-forming [ˈhæbitˌfɔːmiŋ] adj. Que crea hábito.
habitual [həˈbitjuəl] adj. Habitual, acostumbrado, da (usual, accustomed). || Inveterado, da; empedernido, da: *a habitual smoker*, un fumador empedernido.
habitually [—i] adv. Habitualmente (regularly). || Por costumbre (by habit).
habituate [həˈbitjueit] v. tr. Acostumbrar, habituar (to accustom). || U. S. FAM. Frecuentar, ir a menudo a (to go frequently).

habituation [hæbitju'eiʃən] n. Habituación, *f.*
habitué [hə'bitjuei] n. Cliente (*m.*) habitual (of a restaurant). || Asiduo, dua (of a club).
Habsburg [hapsbə:g] pr. n. HIST. Habsburgo.
hachure [hæ'ʃjuə*] n. Raya, *f.*
hachure [hæ'ʃjuə*] v. tr. Señalar *or* sombrear con rayas.
hacienda [,hæsi'endə] n. Hacienda, *f.*
hack [hæk] n. Penco, *m.*, jamelgo, *m.* (worn-out horse). || Caballo (*m.*) de alquiler (horse let out for hire). || Caballo (*m.*) de silla (saddle horse). || Coche (*m.*) de alquiler (coach). || FAM. Taxi, *m.* | Taxista, *m.* (driver). || Escritorzuelo, *m.* (bad writer). || Negro, *m.* (drudge). || Comedero, *m.* (for a hawk's meat). || SP. Puntapié, *m.* (kick). || Corte, *m.* (cut). || Mella, *f.* (notch). || Hachazo, *m.*, machetazo, *m.* (rough cut, sharp blow). || Hacha, *f.*, machete, *m.* (tool). || MIN. Pico, *m.* || Tos (*f.*) seca (dry cough). || Encella, *f.* (for drying cheese).
— Adj. Mercenario, ria (writer, work). || Trillado, da (hackneyed). || *Hack stand*, parada, *f.*
hack [hæk] v. tr. Cortar, acuchillar (to cut). || Cortar con hacha *or* con machete. || FIG. Usar a menudo (to employ often). || Alquilar (to hire). || SP. Dar un puntapié a. || FAM. Destrozar. || *To hack to pieces*, destrozar, hacer trizas, hacer pedazos.
— V. intr. Toser (to cough). || Montar a caballo (to ride for pleasure). || — *To hack at*, acuchillar (s.o.), hachear (sth.). || *To hack for*, ser el negro de (to be a writer's substitute).
hackamore ['hækəmɔ*] n. U. S. Jáquima, *f.*, cabestro, *m.* (halter).
hackberry ['hækberi] n. BOT. Almez, *m.* (tree or wood). || Almeza, *f.* (fruit).
hack hammer [hæk'hæmə*] n. Alcotana, *f.*, martillo (*m.*) para desbastar piedra.
hacking ['hækiŋ] adj. MED. Seco, ca (cough).
hackle ['hækl] n. Pluma (*f.*) del cuello (of a cock). || Pelo (*m.*) erizado (of a dog). || Mosca (*f.*) para pescar (in fishing). || Rastrillo, *m.* (for combing flax). || — Pl. Collar, *m. sing.* (of birds). || FAM. *With one's hackles up*, indignado, da; echando chispas.
hackle ['hækl] v. tr. Rastrillar (the flax). || Cortar (to hack). || FAM. Destrozar, mutilar.
hackman ['hækmən] n. Cochero, *m.* || FAM. Taxista, *m.*
— OBSERV. El plural de esta palabra es *hackmen*.
hackmatack ['hækmətæk] n. BOT. Alerce, *m.*
hackney ['hækni] n. Caballo (*m.*) de alquiler (hack). || Caballo (*m.*) de silla (saddle horse). || Coche (*m.*) de alquiler (coach).
— Adj. FIG. Trillado, da.
hackney carriage ['hækni'kæridʒ] or **hackney coach** [—kəutʃ] n. Coche (*m.*) de alquiler.
hackneyed ['hæknid] adj. Trillado, da: *a hackneyed theme*, un tema trillado. || Estereotipado, da: *a hackneyed phrase*, una expresión estereotipada.
hacksaw ['hæksɔ:] n. Sierra (*f.*) para metales.
hackwork ['hækwə:k] n. Trabajo (*m.*) comercializado.
had [hæd] pret. & p. p. See HAVE.
haddock ['hædək] n. Abadejo, *m.* (fish).
hade [heid] n. GEOL. Inclinación, *f.*, buzamiento, *m.*
hade [heid] v. intr. GEOL. Buzar.
Hades ['heidi:z] pr. n. Hades, *m.* (Pluto). || Infierno, *m.* (hell).
Hadrian ['heidriən] pr. n. Adriano, *m.*
haematic [hi:'mætik] adj. Hemático, ca.
haematin ['hi:mətin] n. Hematina, *f.*
haematite ['hemətait] n. MIN. Hematites, *f.*
haematocyte ['hemətəu,sait] n. Hematocito, *m.*
haematologist [hi:mə'tɔlədʒist] n. Hematólogo, *m.*
haematology [hi:mə'tɔlədʒi] n. MED. Hematología, *f.*
haematoma ['hi:mətəumə] n. MED. Hematoma, *m.*
— OBSERV. El plural es *haematomas* o *haematomata*.
haematosis [hi:mə'təusis] n. BIOL. Hematosis, *f.*
haematozoan [hi:mətəu'zəuən] or **haematozoon** [hi:mətəu'zəuɔn] n. ZOOL. Hematozoario, *m.*
— OBSERV. El plural es *haematozoa*.
haematuria [hi:mə'tjuəriə] n. MED. Hematuria, *f.*
haemocyte ['hi:məsait] n. Hematocito, *m.*
haemoglobin [hi:məu'gləubin] n. Hemoglobina, *f.*
haemolysis [hi:'mɔləsis] n. Hemólisis, *f.*
haemophilia [hi:məu'filiə] n. Hemofilia, *f.*
haemophiliac [—k] n. Hemofílico, ca.
haemophilic [hi:məu'filik] adj. Hemofílico, ca.
haemoptysis [hi:'mɔuptisis] n. MED. Hemoptisis, *f.*
haemorrhage ['hemərid3] n. MED. Hemorragia, *f.*
haemorrhagic [hemə'rædʒik] adj. MED. Hemorrágico, ca.
haemorrhoidal [hemə'rɔidəl] adj. MED. Hemorroidal.
haemorrhoids ['hemərɔidz] pl. n. MED. Hemorroides, *f.*, almorranas, *f.*
haemostatic [hi:mə'stætik] adj. MED. Hemostático, ca.
— N. MED. Hemostático, *m.*
haft [hɑ:ft] n. Mango, *m.* (of a knife). || Puño, *m.* (of a sword).
haft [hɑ:ft] v. tr. Poner mango a (a knife). || Poner puño a (a sword).
hag [hæg] n. Bruja, *f.* (ugly old woman).
haggard ['hægəd] adj. Ojeroso, sa (looking worn out). || Macilento, ta (very pale). || Extraviado, da (wild-eyed). || Zahareño, ña (hawk).
— N. Halcón (*m.*) zahareño.
haggis ['hægis] n. Plato (*m.*) típico escocés hecho con las asaduras del cordero.
haggish ['hægiʃ] adj. De bruja.
haggle ['hægl] n. Regateo, *m.*
haggle ['hægl] v. intr. Regatear. || *To haggle about* o *over*, regatear.
haggler ['hæglə*] n. Regateador, ra.
haggling ['hægliŋ] n. Regateo, *m.*
hagiographer [hægi'ɔgrəfə*] n. Hagiógrafo, *m.*
hagiographic [hægiə'græfik] adj. Hagiográfico, ca.
hagiography [hægi'ɔgrəfi] n. Hagiografía, *f.*
hagiology [hægi'ɔlədʒi] n. Hagiología, *f.*
hagridden ['hægrid'n] adj. Atormentado por las pesadillas. || FIG. Obsesionado, da.
Hague (The) [heig] pr. n. GEOGR. La Haya.
ha-ha [hɑ:'hɑ:] interj. ¡Ja, ja, ja!
haick or **haik** [haik] n. Almalafa, *f.*
hail [heil] n. Granizo, *m.* (frozen raindrops). || FIG. Lluvia, *f.*, granizada, *f.*: *a hail of arrows*, una lluvia de flechas. || Grito, *m.* (call). || Saludo, *m.* (salute). || *Within hail*, al alcance de la voz.
— Interj. ¡Hola! || REL. *Hail, Mary, full of grace*, Dios te salve, María, llena eres de gracia.
hail [heil] v. tr. Llamar: *to hail a person*, llamar a una persona; *to hail a taxi*, llamar un taxi. || Saludar (to salute). || Aclamar (to acclaim). || FIG. Acoger: *he hailed the news with joy*, acogió las noticias con alegría. || FIG. FAM. Lanzar una andanada de (blows, insults).
— V. intr. Granizar. || — FIG. *To hail down on*, llover sobre. || *To hail from*, proceder de, venir de (to come from), ser de (to be a native of).
hail-fellow or **hail-fellow-well-met** ['heil,feləu'wel'-met] adj. Simpático, ca.
Hail Mary ['heil'mɛəri] n. REL. Avemaría, *f.*
hailstone ['heilstəun] n. Granizo, *m.*, piedra, *f.*
hailstorm ['heilstɔ:m] n. Granizada, *f.*
hair [hɛə*] n. Pelo, *m.* (of human or animal body). || Pelo, *m.*, cabello, *m.* (on human head): *to have one's hair cut*, cortarse el pelo. || Crin, *f.*, cerda, *f.* (of horse's mane). || Cerda, *f.* (of pig). || BOT. Pelo, *m.*, vello, *m.*, pelusa, *f.*, pelusilla, *f.* || — *Against the hair*, a contrapelo. || *Head of hair*, pelo, *m.*, cabellera, *f.* || FAM. *Keep your hair on!*, ¡no te sulfures! | *Not to touch a hair on s.o.'s head*, no tocarle ni un pelo a alguien. | *Not to turn a hair*, no movérsele a uno un pelo. || FIG. *To a hair*, exactamente. || *To comb one's hair*, peinarse. || *To do one's hair*, peinarse, arreglarse el pelo. || U. S. FAM. *To get in one's hair*, ponerle a uno nervioso, atacar los nervios a uno. || *To have one's hair done*, ir a la peluquería. || *To let one's hair down*, dejarse el pelo suelto, soltarse el pelo (to undo one's hair), soltarse, el pelo (to be free in behaviour). || *To lose one's hair*, caérsele a uno el pelo. || FIG. *To make s.o.'s hair stand on end*, ponerle a uno los pelos de punta. || *To put up one's hair*, recogerse el pelo. || FIG. *To split hairs*, hilar muy fino. | *To tear each other's hair out*, tirarse de los pelos (to squabble). | *To tear one's hair*, tirarse de los pelos, mesarse los cabellos. || *White hair*, cana, *f.*, canas, *f. pl.*
hairband [—,bænd] n. Cinta, *f.*
hairbrained [—'breind] adj. FIG. Ligero de cascos, atolondrado, da (harebrained).
hairbreadth [—bredθ] n. FIG. Pelo, *m.* || — FIG. *By a hairbreadth*, por los pelos, por un pelo: *he escaped by a hairbreadth*, se libró por los pelos; por muy poco: *he lost the election by a hairbreadth*, perdió las elecciones por muy poco; un pelo, *he didn't depart by a hairbreadth from the instructions*, no se apartó un pelo de las instrucciones. | *To a hairbreadth*, muy: *accurate to a hairbreadth*, muy exacto. | *Within a hairbreadth*, a dos dedos, a dos pasos.
— Adj. *To have a hairbreadth escape*, escapar por los pelos, escapar por el canto de un duro.
hairbrush [—brʌʃ] n. Cepillo, *m.* [para el pelo].
haircloth [—klɔθ] n. Tela (*f.*) de crin (cloth). || REL. Cilicio, *m.* (hair shirt).
hair clip [—klip] n. Horquilla, *f.*
haircut [—kʌt] n. Corte (*m.*) de pelo. || *To have a haircut*, cortarse el pelo.
haircutter [—'kʌtə*] n. Peluquero, *m.*
haircutting [—,kʌtiŋ] n. Corte (*m.*) de pelo (haircut). || Peluquería, *f.*
hairdo [—du:] n. Peinado, *m.*
hairdresser [—,dresə*] n. Peluquero, ra.
hairdresser's [—,dresɔ:z] n. Peluquería, *f.*
hairdressing [—,dresiŋ] n. Peluquería, *f.* (work of a hairdresser). || Peinado, *m.* (hairdo).
hair dryer [—draiə*] n. Secador, *m.* [para el pelo].
hair dye [—dai] n. Tinte (*m.*) para el pelo.
hair grip [—grip] n. Horquilla, *f.*
hairiness [—inis] n. Pilosidad, *f.* || Abundancia (*f.*) de pelo.
hairless [—lis] adj. Sin pelo (animal). || Lampiño, ña (face). || Sin pelo, calvo, va (head).
hairline [—lain] n. Nacimiento (*m.*) del pelo (limit of hair growth). || Trazo, *m.* (of a letter). || Rayita, *f.* (thin line).
— Adj. Muy fino, na. || FIG. Muy pequeño, ña; sutil.
hair lock [—lɔk] n. Rizo (*m.*) de pelo.
hairnet [—net] n. Redecilla, *f.*
hairpiece [—pi:s] n. Postizo, *m.*

hairpin [—pin] n. Horquilla, *f.*
— Adj. *Hairpin bend*, curva muy cerrada.
hair-raiser [—ˌreizə*] n. Historia (*f.*) espeluznante.
hair-raising [—ˌreiziŋ] adj. Que pone los pelos de punta, espeluznante.
hair-remover [—riˈmu:və*] n. Depilatorio, *m.*
hairsbreadth [—zbredθ] adj./n. See HAIRBREADTH.
hair setting [—ˈsetiŋ] n. Marcado, *m.*
hair shirt [—ˈʃə:t] n. REL. Cilicio, *m.*
hair slide [—slaid] n. Pasador, *m.*
hairsplitting [—ˌsplitiŋ] n. Sutilezas, *f. pl.*
— Adj. Sutil (argument). || Quisquilloso, sa (person).
hair stroke [—strəuk] n. Perfil, *m.* (of a letter).
hairstyle [—stail] n. Peinado, *m.*
hairy [ˈhɛəri] adj. Peludo, da (covered with hair, like hair). || Melenudo, da (having more hair than normal). || FIG. Antiguo, gua (a joke, etc.).
Haiti [ˈheiti] pr. n. GEOGR. Haití, *m.*
Haitian [ˈheiʃjən] adj./n. Haitiano, na.
hake [heik] n. Merluza, *f.* (fish).
halation [həˈleiʃən] n. PHOT. Halo, *m.*
halberd [ˈhælbə:d] n. Alabarda, *f.*
halberdier [ˌhælbəˈdiə*] n. Alabardero, *m.*
halcyon [ˈhælsiən] n. Alción, *m.*
— Adj. Alciónico: *halcyon days*, días alciónicos.
hale [heil] adj. Sano, na; robusto, ta. || *To be hale and hearty*, estar más sano que una manzana, ser fuerte como un roble.
half [hɑ:f] adj. Medio, dia: *half an hour* o *a half hour*, media hora; *two and a half pints*, dos pintas y media. || Mediano, na: *half knowledge of the subject*, mediana idea del asunto. || A medias: *half owner*, propietario a medias. || — *Half a dozen*, media docena. || *Half ..., half ...*, mitad ..., mitad ...: *half man half beast*, mitad hombre, mitad animal.
— Adv. A medias: *to half do sth.*, hacer algo a medias. || Medio: *half asleep*, medio dormido; *half crying*, medio llorando. || — *Half as many, half as much*, la mitad. || *Half as much again*, la mitad más. || *He is half as big again as his brother*, tiene una vez y media la estatura de su hermano. || *It isn't half bad*, no está nada mal. || *It isn't half cold!*, ¡hace muchísimo frío! || *Not half*, no poco, mucho: *you liked it? — Not half!*, ¿te gustó? — ¡No poco!; muy: *she's not half pretty*, es muy mona. || *To be half...*, estar casi...: *I was half sure she'd come*, estaba casi seguro de que vendría.
— N. Mitad, *f.*: *half of the time he does nothing*, la mitad del tiempo no hace nada. || Parte, *f.*: *the larger half*, la parte más grande; *a good half*, una gran parte. || Medio, *m.*: *two and a half*, dos y medio. || Semestre, *m.* (of school year). || SP. Medio, *m.* (player): *left half*, medio izquierda. | Tiempo, *m.* (division of a match): *the first half*, el primer tiempo. | Campo, *m.* (of a sports pitch). || Media pinta, *f.*: *a half of bitter*, media pinta de cerveza. || Cuarto, *m.*: *a half of butter*, un cuarto de mantequilla. || — FIG. *Better half*, media naranja, cara mitad (wife). | *By half*, con mucho: *bigger by half*, con mucho más grande. || *By halves*, a medias. || *Half and half*, mitad y mitad. || *Half past ten* [U. S., *half after ten*], las diez y media. || *Outward half*, billete (*m.*) de ida. || *Return half*, billete (*m.*) de vuelta. || *To be too... by half*, pasarse de...: *he is too clever by half*, se pasa de listo. || *To cut in half* o *in halves*, cortar por la mitad. || *To go halves with*, ir a medias con. || *Too long by half*, demasiado largo. || *Two hours and a half*, dos horas y media.
— OBSERV. El plural de *half* es *halves*.
— Cuando *half* califica un sustantivo, el verbo concuerda con dicho sustantivo *(half the apple is bad, half the apples are bad)*. Si *half* se emplea solo y representa una gran cantidad, el verbo puede ir en plural *(half are sold)*.
half-a-crown [—əˈkraun] n. Media corona, *f.* (coin).
half-alive [—əˈlaiv] adj. Medio muerto, ta.
half-and-half [—ændhɑ:f] adj. Mitad y mitad.
— Adv. A medias.
halfback [—bæk] n. SP. Medio, *m.*
halfback line [—bæklain] n. SP. Línea (*f.*) media.
half-baked [—ˈbeikt] adj. FIG. Mal concebido, da; apresurado, da (poorly planned). | Disparatado, da; tonto, ta (foolish). || CULIN. Medio cocido, da.
half binding [—ˌbaindiŋ] n. Media pasta, *f.*
half blood [—blʌd] n. Mestizo, za.
half-blood [—blʌd] adj. Medio, dia: *half-blood sister*, media hermana.
half boot [—bu:t] n. Bota (*f.*) corta, bota (*f.*) de media caña.
half-bound [—baund] adj. Encuadernado en media pasta.
half-bred [—bred] adj. Mestizo, za.
half-breed [—bri:d] n. Mestizo, za.
half brother [—ˌbrʌðə*] n. Hermanastro, *m.*, medio hermano, *m.*
half-caste [—kɑ:st] adj./n. Mestizo, za.
half-closed [—kləuzd] adj. Entreabierto, ta.
half cock [—kɔk] n. *At half cock*, con el seguro echado (gun). || FIG. *To go off at half cock*, actuar con precipitación (to act to hastily).
half crown [—ˈkraun] n. Media corona, *f.* (two shillings and a half).
half-dead [—ded] adj. Medio muerto, ta.
half-dollar [—ˈdɔlə*] n. Medio dólar, *m.*
half-empty [—ˈempti] adj. Medio vacío, a.
half fare [—fɛə*] n. Medio billete, *m.*
half-full [—ful] adj. Medio lleno, na; a medio llenar.
halfhearted [—ˈhɑ:tid] adj. Que carece de entusiasmo, poco entusiasta.
halfheartedly [—ˈhɑ:tidli] adv. Sin entusiasmo.
half-holiday [—ˈhɔlədi] n. Medio día (*m.*) festivo.
half hour [—ˈauə*] n. Media hora, *f.*: *to be taken every half-hour*, para tomar cada media hora. || *The train leaves on the half-hour*, el tren sale a la media *or* cada media hora.
— Adj. De media hora: *half-hour journey*, viaje de media hora.
half-hourly [—ˈauəli] adv. Cada media hora.
— Adj. De cada media hora.
half-learned [—ˈlə:nd] adj. Semiculto, ta (word).
half-length [—leŋθ] adj. De medio cuerpo (portrait).
— N. SP. Medio cuerpo, *m.* || Busto, *m.* (portrait).
half-life [—laif] n. Período, *m.* (in nuclear reaction).
half-light [—lait] n. Primeras luces, *f. pl.*, amanecer, *m.* (of the dawn). || Media luz, *f.* (before darkness).
— Adj. A media luz.
half-mast [—ˈmɑ:st] n. *At half-mast*, a media asta.
half measures [—ˈmeʒə:z] pl. n. *To take half measures*, tomar medidas poco eficaces, aplicar paños calientes.
half-moon [—ˈmu:n] n. ASTR. Media luna, *f.* || Media luna, *f.* (of fingernails).
half mourning [—ˈmɔ:niŋ] n. Medio luto, *m.* (period). || Vestido (*m.*) de medio luto (costume).
half note [—ˈnəut] n. U. S. MUS. Blanca, *f.*
half-opened [—ˈəupənd] adj. Medio abierto, ta; entreabierto, ta.
half pay [—ˈpei] n. Media paga, *m.*, medio sueldo, *m.*
half-pay [—pei] adj. A media paga, a medio sueldo.
halfpenny [ˈheipni] n. Medio penique, *m.* (coin).
— OBSERV. El plural es *halfpence* o *halfpennies*.
half-price [ˈhɑ:fˈprais] adv. A mitad de precio.
half relief [—riˈli:f] n. ARTS. Medio relieve, *m.*
half-seas over [—si:zˈəuvə*] adj. FAM. Calamocano, na; achispado, da; entre Pinto y Valdemoro.
half sister [—ˌsistə*] n. Hermanastra, *f.*, media hermana, *f.*
half step [—step] n. U. S. MUS. Semitono, *m.*
half-timbered [—ˈtimbəd] adj. Con entramado de madera.
half time [—ˈtaim] n. SP. Descanso, *m.*
half-time [—ˈtaim] adj. De media jornada (work). || — *The half-time score*, el tanteo en el descanso. || *To work half-time*, trabajar media jornada.
half title [—ˈtaitl] n. PRINT. Anteportada, *f.*, portadilla, *f.* (of a book).
halftone [—təun] n. PRINT. Media tinta, *f.*, medio tono, *m.* || MUS. Semitono, *m.*
halftone [—təun] adj. PRINT. A media tinta.
half-truth [—tru:θ] n. Verdad (*f.*) a medias.
half-turn [—tə:n] n. Media vuelta, *f.*
halfway [—ˈwei] adj. Medio, dia; intermedio, dia: *halfway point*, punto medio. || Parcial (partial): *halfway measures*, medidas parciales.
— Adv. A medio camino, a mitad de camino: *halfway between two points*, a medio camino entre dos puntos; *halfway to Paris*, a mitad de camino de París. || — *Halfway up*, a media cuesta, en la mitad de la cuesta. | *To do halfway*, hacer a medias. || FIG. *To meet s.o. halfway*, partir la diferencia con uno (about a price), llegar a un arreglo con uno (arrangement).
half-wit [—wit] n. Tonto, ta; imbécil, *m. & f.*
half-witted [—ˈwitid] adj. Tonto, ta; imbécil.
half year [—ˈjə:*] n. Semestre, *m.*
half-yearly [—ˈjə:li] adj. Semestral.
— Adv. Semestralmente, cada seis meses.
halibut [ˈhælibət] n. Halibut, *m.* (fish).
halieutic [ˌhæliˈju:tik] adj. Haliéutico, ca.
halieutics [—s] n. Haliéutica, *f.*
hall [hɔ:l] n. Entrada, *f.*, vestíbulo, *m.*, "hall", *m.* (entrance room). || Sala, *f.* (in a castle, large building): *concert hall*, sala de conciertos. || Comedor, *m.* (dining hall in college, etc.). || Casa (*f.*) solariega (mansion). || Colegio (*m.*) mayor (college). || U. S. Pasillo, *m.*, corredor, *m.* (corridor). || — *City hall*, ayuntamiento, *m.* (building), municipalidad, *f.*, municipio, *m.* || *Dance hall*, sala (*f.*) de baile. || *Hall of fame*, galería (*f.*) de personajes (memorial). || *Town Hall*, ayuntamiento, *m.*
hallelujah [ˌhæliˈlu:jə] n. Aleluya, *m.* or *f.*
halliard [ˈhæljəd] n. MAR. Driza, *f.*
hallmark [ˈhɔ:lmɑ:k] n. Contraste, *m.* (official stamps of guarantee). || FIG. Sello, *m.*: *the hallmark of genius*, el sello del genio.
hallo [həˈləu] interj. See HULLO.
hallo [həˈləu] v. intr. Gritar.
halloo [həˈlu:] n. Grito, *m.*
— Interj. ¡Hala! (in hunting).
halloo [həˈlu:] v. intr. Gritar (to shout). || Llamar (to call).
hallow [ˈhæləu] v. tr. Santificar: *hallowed be Thy Name*, santificado sea Tu Nombre. || FIG. Venerar, reverenciar.
hallowed [ˈhæləud] adj. Santo, ta (ground).
Hallowe'en (U. S. **Halloween**) [ˈhæləuˈi:n] n. Víspera (*f.*) del Día de Todos los Santos.
hallucinate [həˈlu:sineit] v. tr. Alucinar.
— V. intr. Alucinarse.
hallucination [həˌlu:siˈneiʃən] n. Alucinación, *f.*
hallucinatory [həˌlu:siˈneiʃən] adj. Alucinante.

hallucinogen [hə'lu:sinədʒen] n. Alucinógeno, *m.*
hallucinogenic [hə'lu:sinədʒenik] adj. Alucinógeno, na.
hallux ['hælʌks] n. ANAT. Dedo (*m.*) gordo del pie.

— OBSERV. El plural de *hallux* es *halluces.*

hallway ['hɔ:lwei] n. U. S. Entrada, *f.*, vestíbulo, *m.*, "hall", *m.* (entrance room). | Pasillo, *m.*, corredor, *m.* (connecting passage).
halm [hα:m] n. See HAULM.
halo ['heiləu] n. ASTR. Halo, *m.* || REL. Aureola, *f.*, nimbo, *m.* || FIG. Halo, *m.*, aureola, *f.*
halo ['heiləu] v. tr. ASTR. Rodear con un halo. || REL. Aureolar, nimbar.
halogen ['hæləudʒən] n. CHEM. Halógeno, *m.*
halogenous [hə'lɔdʒinəs] adj. CHEM. Halógeno, na.
halography [hə'lɔgrəfi] n. CHEM. Halografía, *f.*
haloid ['hælɔid] adj. Haloideo, a.
— N. Haloideo, *m.*
halt [hɔ:lt] adj. (Ant.) Cojo, ja.
— N. Alto, *m.*, parada, *f.* (temporary stop). || Interrupción, *f.* || Parada, *f.*, apeadero, *m.* (small railway station). || (Ant.) Cojera, *f.* (lameness). | Lisiados, *m. pl.* (cripples). || — *Halt!*, ¡alto! || *To bring to a halt*, parar, detener. || *To call a halt*, mandar hacer alto. || FIG. *To call a halt to*, poner coto a. || *To come to a halt*, pararse.
halt [hɔ:lt] v. tr. Parar, detener (to stop sth. or s.o.). ||Interrumpir.
— V. intr. Pararse (to stop). || Hacer alto. || Interrumpirse. || Cojear (in walking). || FIG. *To halt between two opinions*, vacilar entre dos opiniones.
halter [—ə*] n. Cabestro, *m.*, ronzal, *m.*, jáquima, *f.* (of a horse). || Soga, *f.*, dogal, *m.* (for hanging criminals). || U. S. Blusa (*f.*) sin espalda (blouse).
halter [—ə*] v. tr. Poner el ronzal a, encabestrar (a horse). || Ahorcar (a criminal). || FIG. Poner trabas a (to hamper).
halting [—iŋ] adj. Vacilante (marked by hesitation). || Cojo, ja; defectuoso, sa (verse).
halve [hα:v] v. tr. Compartir (to share equally). || Partir en dos, partir por la mitad (to divide into two portions). || Reducir a la mitad (to lessen by half). || TECH. Machihembrar (in woodwork). || SP. Empatar.
halves [hα:vz] pl. n. See HALF.
halyard ['hæljəd] n. MAR. Driza, *f.*
ham [hæm] n. Jamón, *m.* (food): *ham sandwich*, bocadillo de jamón. || ANAT. Corva, *f.* (back of the thigh). || — Pl. FAM. Nalgas, *f.*, trasero, *m. sing.* || — FAM. *Ham actor*, comicastro, *m.*, mal actor, *m.* || *Radio ham*, radioaficionado, da.
ham [hæm] v. tr. FAM. Exagerar, interpretar de una manera exagerada (a part).
hamadryad [,hæmə'draiəd] n. ZOOL. Cinocéfalo, *m.* (baboon). | Cobra (*f.*) real (snake). || MYTH. Hamadría, *f.*, hamadríada, *f.*
Hamburg ['hæmbə:g] pr. n. GEOGR. Hamburgo.
hamburger ['hæmbə:gə*] n. Hamburguesa, *f.*
hamburg steak ['hæmbə:gsteik] or **hamburger steak** ['hæmbəgəsteik] n. Hamburguesa, *f.*
ham-fisted ['hæm'fistid] adj. Que tiene manazas. || FIG. Torpe (clumsy).
hamlet ['hæmlit] n. Aldea, *f.*, caserío, *m.*
hammer ['hæmə*] n. Martillo, *m.* (tool). || Macillo, *m.* (in a piano). || Percursor, *m.* (of a firearm). || Martillo, *m.* (the gavel of a judge, auctioneer). || Martinete, *m.* (drop hammer). || ELECTR. Vibrador (*m.*) automático (trembler). || ANAT. Martillo, *m.* (in the ear). || SP. Martillo, *m.*: *throwing the hammer*, lanzamiento del martillo. || — FIG. *Between the hammer and the anvil*, entre la espada y la pared. || *Blow of a hammer*, martillazo, *m.* || *The hammer and sickle*, la hoz y el martillo. || *To come under the hammer*, salir a subasta. || FIG. *To go at it hammer and tongs*, luchar con todas sus fuerzas *or* a brazo partido (fighting), echar el resto (working).
hammer ['hæmə*] v. tr. Martillar, martillear (to hit sth. with a hammer). || Batir: *to hammer iron*, batir el hierro. || Clavar (a nail, etc.). || COMM. Declarar insolvente (on the Stock Exchange). | Hacer bajar (prices). || — FIG. *To hammer a book, a film*, despedazar un libro, una película. | *To hammer an opponent*, machacar a un adversario (in boxing), dar una paliza a un adversario (to beat by a large margin). | *To hammer a point home*, insistir *or* hacer hincapié en un punto. || *To hammer into shape*, forjar a martillo (metals, etc.), poner a punto (a project). || FIG. *To hammer one's brains*, romperse la cabeza. | *To hammer sth. into s.o.*, meterle algo en la cabeza a uno.
— V. intr. Martillar.
— ***To hammer at***, aporrear (a door). || ***To hammer away***, trabajar con ahínco (*at*, en). | Insistir, hacer hincapié (*on*, en). || ***To hammer down***, remachar. || ***To hammer in***, clavar. || ***To hammer on*** aporrear: *to hammer on the door*, aporrear la puerta. || ***To hammer out***, extender bajo el martillo (metal, leather, etc.). | Inventar (an excuse). | Llegar a (an agreement, etc.).
hammerer ['hæmərə*] n. Martillador, *m.*
hammerhead [hæməhed] n. Cabeza (*f.*) de martillo (the head of a hammer). || ZOOL. Pez (*m.*) martillo. || U. S. FAM. Mentecato, ta (blockhead).
hammering [—riŋ] n. Martilleo, *m.* || MIL. Machaqueo, *m.*, martilleo, *m.*, bombardeo (*m.*) intensivo. || FAM. Paliza, *f.* (thrashing).
hammerlock [—lɔk] n. SP. Llave (*f.*) al brazo (in wrestling).
hammersmith ['hæməsmiθ] n. Martillador, *m.*
hammock ['hæmək] n. Hamaca, *f.* || MAR. Coy, *m.*
hamper ['hæmpə*] n. Cesta, *f.*, canasta, *f.* (large basket). || FIG. Obtáculo, *m.*, estorbo, *m.*
hamper ['hæmpə*] v. tr. Obstaculizar, estorbar, impedir, poner trabas a.
hamster ['hæmstə*] n. Hámster, *m.* (rodent).
hamstring ['hæmstriŋ] n. ANAT. Tendón (*m.*) de la corva.
hamstring ['hæmstriŋ] v. tr. Cortar el tendón de la corva, desjarretar (to sever the hamstring). || FIG. Paralizar, incapacitar (to cripple).
hand [hænd] n. Mano, *f.* (part of the body): *the right hand*, la mano derecha. || Manecilla, *f.*, mano, *f.* (of a clock). || Aguja, *f.* (of an instrument). || Escritura, *f.*, letra, *f.* (writing): *by the same hand*, con la misma letra. || Firma, *f.* (signature). || Aplausos, *m. pl.*, ovación, *f.* (applause): *the audience gave her a big hand*, el público le dio una gran ovación. || Mano, *f.* (for marriage): *to give one's hand to*, conceder su mano a. || Autoridad, *f.* (authority). || Palmo, *m.* (measure). || MAR. Marinero, *m.* | Tripulante, *m.* (on board ship). || Trabajador, *m.*, operario, *m.*, mano, *f.* (workman). || AGR. Peón, *m.* || Manojo, *m.* (of tobacco). || Mano, *f.*, racimo, *m.* (bunch): *a hand of bananas*, un racimo de plátanos. || Mano, *f.* (handstone for maize, cocoa, etc.). || Mano, *f.* (a round of cards): *one last hand!*, ¡la última mano! || Mano, *f.* (player). || Partida, *f.* (game). || Mano, *f.*, cartas, *f. pl.*: *I have a good hand*, tengo una buena mano. || FIG. Mano, *f*: *two portraits by the same hand*, dos retratos por la misma mano; *to have a good hand for painting*, tener buena mano para la pintura; *give her a hand*, échale una mano. || Influencia, *f.* || — Pl. MAR. Tripulación, *f. sing.* || — FAM. *A cool hand*, un fresco. || *All hands on deck!*, ¡toda la tripulación a cubierta! || *At close hand*, muy cerca, a mano. || *At first, at second hand*, de primera, de segunda mano. || *At hand*, a mano, muy cerca (within reach), muy cerca (very close in future time), listo, ta (ready). || *At the hands of*, por [obra de]. || *By* o *with a masterly hand*, con mano maestra. || *By hand*, a mano: *made by hand*, hecho a mano; *written by hand*, escrito a mano; con biberón (by feeding from a bottle), en mano: *to deliver sth. by hand*, entregar algo en mano; a fuerza de brazos (with the hands). || *By the hand*, de la mano. || FIG. *Clean hands*, manos limpias. || *From hand to hand*, de mano en mano. || FIG. *From hand to mouth*, al día: *to live from hand to mouth*, vivir al día. || COMM. *Goods left on our hands*, mercancías (*f. pl.*) que no se han vendido. || FIG. *Hand and foot*, de pies y manos. || *Hand in hand*, de la mano: *to walk hand in hand*, pasearse de la mano; cogidos de la mano: *we were sitting hand in hand*, estábamos sentados cogidos de la mano; de común acuerdo: *both countries will walk hand in hand*, los dos países actuarán de común acuerdo. || FIG. *Hand on heart*, poniéndose la mano en el pecho. | *Hand over fist*, rápidamente. || *Hands off!*, ¡las manos quietas!, ¡no toquen! || *Hands together*, con las manos juntas. || FIG. *Hands to the plough!*, ¡manos a la obra! || *Hands up!*, ¡arriba las manos!, ¡manos arriba! (raise both hands), ¡levante la mano! (raise one hand as in a vote). || *Hand to hand*, cuerpo a cuerpo. || FIG. *He can turn his hand to anything*, lo mismo sirve para un barrido que para un fregado. | *I had no hand in it*, no tengo nada que ver con este asunto. || *In hand*, que se está estudiando *or* discutiendo, que está entre manos: *the matter in hand*, el problema que se está estudiando; en la mano: *sword in hand*, con la espada en la mano; dominado, da (under control), entre manos (in progress), en reserva (in reserve), en efectivo, disponible: *money in hand*, dinero disponible. || *In one's own hand*, de su puño y letra, de su propia mano. || *In the hands of*, en manos de. || *Into s.o.'s own hands*, en propia mano. || FIG. *Iron hand in a velvet glove*, mano de hierro en guante de seda. || *Leading hand*, mano (in card games). || FIG. *Lost with all hands*, no se salvó nadie. | *My hands are tied*, tengo las manos atadas, estoy maniatado. | *Not to do a hand's turn*, estar mano sobre mano, no dar golpe. | *Not to lift a hand*, no mover un dedo. | *On all hands* o *on every hand*, por todas partes. || *On hand*, a mano (within reach), en reserva (in reserve), pendiente (unresolved). || *On hands and knees*, a gatas, a cuatro patas. || *On one's hands*, en manos de uno, a cargo de uno. || *On the left hand*, a la izquierda. || *On the one hand ... on the other*, por un lado ... por otro, por una parte ... por otra. || *On the right hand*, a la derecha. || *Out of hand*, en seguida (immediately), fuera de control (out of control). || *Out of one's hands*, fuera de su alcance. || *Situation well in hand*, situación (*f.*) que se ha conseguido dominar. || *Sleight of hand*, juego (*m.*) de manos. || *The children are on my hands all day*, los niños están conmigo todo el día. || *To ask for the hand of*, pedir la mano de (in marriage). || FIG. *To bear s.o. a hand*, echar una mano a uno. | *To be clay in the hands of*, ser un títere en manos de. | *To be free with one's hands*, tener las

manos largas, ser largo de manos. | *To be hand in glove together*, ser uña y carne (in intimate association), estar conchabados (in close cooperation). || *To be in good hands*, estar en buenas manos. || *To be near at hand*, estar muy cerca. || FIG. *To be s.o.'s right hand*, ser el brazo derecho de alguien. | *To be tied hand and foot*, estar atado de pies y manos. | *To bind hand and foot*, atar de pies y manos. | *To bite the hand that feeds one*, volverse en contra de su bienhechor, ser poco agradecido. || *To change hands*, cambiar de manos (sth. carried or held), cambiar de dueño (property, shop, etc.). || *To clap hands*, batir palmas. || *To come to hand*, llegar a su destino (a letter). || *To come to hands*, llegar a las manos. || FIG. *To dirty* o *to soil one's hands*, ensuciarse las manos. || *To fall into the hands of*, caer en las manos de. || *To force s.o.'s hand*, forzarle la mano a alguien. || *To get one's hand in*, adquirir práctica. || *To get out of hand*, desmandarse (persons). || *To get sth. off one's hands*, deshacerse de algo, quitarse algo de encima. || FIG. *To get* o *to have the upper hand*, llevar ventaja. | *To go hand in hand*, ir juntos. | *To grab a chance with both hands*, no dejar escapar una oportunidad. || FAM. *To grease s.o.'s hand*, untarle la mano a alguien. || *To hand*, a mano. || *To have a free hand*, tener campo libre, tener carta blanca. || *To have a hand in*, intervenir en, tomar parte en, tener participación en. || *To have in one's hand*, tener en sus manos. || FIG. *To have one's hands full*, estar muy ocupado: *I have my hands full with this new job*, estoy muy ocupado con este nuevo trabajo. | *To have s.o. eating out of one's hand*, poder manejar a alguien como se quiere. || *To have work on hand*, tener trabajo entre manos. || *To hold hands*, ir cogidos de la mano. || *To hold out* o *to offer one's hand*, tender la mano a. || *To join hands*, unirse. || *To join hands in marriage*, casarse. || *To keep one's hand in*, no perder la práctica (*at*, de). || *To keep one's hands off*, no tocar. || FIG. *To know sth. like the back of one's hand*, conocer algo como la palma de la mano. || *To lay hands on*, echar mano a (to take), tocar (to touch), ponerle la mano encima a, alzarle la mano a (to injure), imponer las manos a (in blessing, confirming, etc.), encontrar (to find). || *To leave in s.o.'s hands*, dejar en manos de uno. || *To lend a (helping) hand*, echar una mano a. || *To need hands*, estar falto de brazos *or* de mano de obra. || *To place o.s. in s.o.'s hands*, ponerse en manos de alguien. || *To play into s.o.'s hands*, hacerle el juego a alguien. || *To put into s.o.'s hand*, poner en manos de alguien. || FIG. *To put one's hand down*, echarse la mano al bolsillo. || *To put one's hand to*, emprender. || *To raise one's hand against s.o.*, alzarle *or* levantarle la mano a alguien. || *To rule with a heavy* o *hard hand*, gobernar con mano dura. || *To set one's hand to*, firmar (to sign), emprender (to begin). || *To shake hands*, dar la mano, estrechar la mano: *I shook hands with the President*, le di la mano al Presidente; *the President shook hands with me*, el Presidente me dio la mano; darse la mano: *they shook hands*, se dieron la mano. || FIG. *To show one's hand*, descubrir su juego, poner las cartas boca arriba. | *To stain one's hand with blood*, ensangrentarse las manos. || *To take a hand in*, intervenir en. || *To take in hand*, ocuparse de, encargarse de. || *To take one's life in one's hand*, jugarse la vida. || *To take s.o.'s hand*, coger la mano de alguien. || *To take sth. off s.o.'s hands*, quitarle a alguien algo. || *To take sth. on one's hands*, encargarse de algo. || *To take the law into one's own hands*, tomarse la justicia por su mano. || *To talk with one's hands*, hablar con las manos. || *To throw in one's hand*, tirar las cartas (in card games). || *To throw up one's hands*, echarse *or* llevarse las manos a la cabeza. || *To tie s.o.'s hands*, atar a uno de manos *or* las manos. || *To turn one's hand to*, dedicarse a. || *To wait on s.o. hand and foot*, ser el esclavo de alguien, desvivirse por alguien. || FIG. *To wash one's hands of*, lavarse las manos de. || *To win hands down*, ganar fácilmente. || *To write a good hand*, tener buena letra. || *We have five minutes in hand*, nos quedan cinco minutos. || *Vote by show of hands*, votación (*f.*) a mano alzada. || *With a firm hand*, con firmeza. || *With a heavy hand*, con mano dura. || *With high hand*, despóticamente. || *You couldn't see your hand in front of you*, no se veía absolutamente nada, no se veía la mano. || *Your letter of the 10th is to hand*, he recibido su carta del 10.

— Adj. De mano: *hand grenade*, granada de mano; *hand luggage*, equipaje de mano. || Hecho a mano (handmade).

hand [hænd] v. tr. Dar: *he handed her the ticket*, le dio el billete. || Alargar, dar: *will you hand me that book?*, ¿quiere alargarme este libro? || Ayudar a: *he handed her into the taxi*, le ayudó a subir al taxi; *he handed her out of the taxi*, le ayudó a salir del taxi. || MAR. Aferrar. || FAM. *To hand it to s.o.*, reconocer algo a alguien: *I've got to hand it to you*, tengo que reconocértelo.

— ***To hand about***, hacer circular, pasar de mano en mano. || ***To hand down***, transmitir: *songs handed down from generation to generation*, canciones transmitidas de generación en generación. | Ayudar a bajar (from a carriage). | Bajar (to pass down). | Anunciar (a sentence). || ***To hand in***, presentar (a resignation, etc.). | Entregar (to give). | Ayudar a entrar *or* a subir. || SP. ***To hand off***, apartar con la mano (in rugby). || ***To hand on***, transmitir (traditions). | Comunicar (news). | Pasar, dar (to give). || ***To hand out***, dar (to give). | Aplicar (a punishment, etc.). | Distribuir, repartir (to distribute). || ***To hand over***, entregar. | Transmitir (one's authority). | Ceder (one's property). || ***To hand round***, pasar de mano en mano, hacer circular.

handbag [—bæg] n. Bolso, *m.* [*Amer.*, saco, *m.*, cartera, *f.*].

handball [—bɔ:l] n. SP. Balonmano, *m.* (sport). | Pelota (*f.*) de balonmano (ball).

handbarrow [—ˈbærəu] n. Carretilla, *f.* (wheelbarrow). || Parihuelas, *f. pl.*, camilla, *f.*, andas, *f. pl.* (stretcher).

handbell [—bel] n. Campanilla, *f.*

handbill [—bil] n. Prospecto, *m.*

handbook [—buk] n. Guía, *f.* (guidebook). || Manual, *m.*, libro (*m.*) de referencias (reference book). || Libro (*m.*) de apuntes (book of a bookmaker).

hand brake [—breik] n. AUT. Freno (*m.*) de mano.

handcar [—kɑ:*] n. Vagoneta, *f.*, carretilla (*f.*) de servicio, zorrilla, *f.*

handcart [—kɑ:t] n. Carretilla, *f.*

handclasp [—klɑ:sp] n. Apretón (*m.*) de manos.

handcraft [—krɑ:ft] n. See HANDICRAFT.

handcuff [—kʌf] v. tr. Poner las esposas a, esposar.

handcuffs [—kʌfs] pl. n. Esposas, *f.*

handed [hændid] adj. De ... manos: *white-handed*, de manos blancas.

handful [—ful] n. Puñado, *m.* || FIG. Puñado, *m.*: *a handful of survivors*, un puñado de supervivientes. || FAM. *This child is a real handful*, este niño es una verdadera lata *or* un bicho malo.

hand glass [—glɑ:s] n. Espejo, (*m.*) de mano (mirror). || Lupa, *f.* (magnifying glass). || MAR. Reloj (*m.*) de arena (a quarter or half-minute sandglass).

handgrip [—grip] n. Mango, *m.* (of tennis racquet, golf club). || Puño, *m* (of motorcycle, bicycle). || Apretón (*m.*) de manos (handshake). || *To come to handgrips*, tener una agarrada, llegar a las manos.

handgun [—gʌn] n. Pistola, *f.*

handicap [ˈhændikæp] n. Desventaja, *f.*, "handicap", *m.* (disadvantage). || FIG. Obstáculo, *m.* (hindrance). || SP. "Handicap", *m.*

handicap [ˈhændikæp] v. tr. Perjudicar (to put at a disadvantage). || SP. Conceder un handicap a. || *To be handicapped*, estar en situación de inferioridad; tener desventajas; estar desfavorecido, da.

handicapped [—t] adj. MED. Subnormal.

handicraft [ˈhændikrɑ:ft] n. Artesanía, *f.* (occupation, art). || Habilidad (*f.*) manual (manual skill).

handicraftsman [—smən] n. Artesano, *m.*

— OBSERV. El plural de esta palabra es ***handicraftsmen***.

handily [ˈhændili] adv. Diestramente, hábilmente (in a handy way). || Convenientemente (conveniently). || A mano (near). || U. S. Con facilidad (easily).

handiness [ˈhændinis] n. Destreza, *f.*, habilidad, *f.* (skill). || Proximidad, *f.* (closeness). || Conveniencia, *f.*, comodidad, *f.* (convenience). || Manejabilidad, *f.*, lo manejable (of a ship, etc.).

handiwork [ˈhændiwə:k] n. Obra, *f.*: *this is some of John's handiwork*, ésta es obra de Juan. || Trabajo (*m.*) manual.

handkerchief [ˈhæŋkətʃif] n. Pañuelo, *m.*

handle [ˈhændl] n. Mango, *m.* (grip of a tool, weapon, utensil, etc.). || Asa, *f.* (of bag, basket, cup). || Puño, *m.* (of a bicycle, etc.). || Pomo, *m.* (of sword, stick, door knob). || Manilla, *f.*, manija, *f.*, tirador, *m.* (door lever). || Brazo, *m.*, palanca, *f.* (lever). || Tirador, *m.* (of a drawer). || Varal, *m.* (of handcart). || AUT. Manivela, *f.* || Manubrio, *m.* (of hurdy-gurdy). || FIG. Pretexto, *m.* (pretext). || FAM. Título, *m.* (title). || FIG. *To fly off the handle*, salir *or* salirse de sus casillas. | *To give handle to*, dar pie a, dar motivo a.

handle [ˈhændl] v. tr. Tocar: *please do not handle the goods*, por favor no toque la mercancía. || Manejar: *he can handle a saw*, sabe manejar una sierra. || Manipular: *to handle heavy pieces*, manipular piezas pesadas. || Dirigir, gobernar: *to handle a boat*, dirigir un barco. || Conducir [*Amer.*, manejar] (a car). || Controlar, dominar (to control): *the police could not handle the crowd*, la policía no podía controlar a la multitud. || Poder con, tener capacidad para: *the factory cannot handle the increase in demand*, la fábrica no puede con el aumento de la demanda. || Ocuparse de (to deal with). || Tratar: *I don't know how to handle this problem*, no sé cómo tratar este problema; *she is hard to handle*, es difícil de tratar. || Tratar en, comerciar en (to do business in). || Tener: *they don't handle that brand*, no tienen esta marca. || Manejar (business). || SP. Tocar con la mano (in football). || — *Handle with care*, frágil (inscription on a parcel). || FIG. *To handle with kid gloves*, tratar con muchos miramientos *or* con mucho tacto.

— V. intr. Manejarse. || Ser manejable: *this car handles well*, este coche es muy manejable.

handleable [ˈhændləbl] adj. Manejable.

handlebar [ˈhændlbɑ:*] n. Manillar, *m.*, guía, *f.* (of a bicycle).

— OBSERV. Esta palabra se emplea frecuentemente en plural.

handler [ˈhændlə*] n. COMM. Negociante, *m.*, tratante, *m.* || SP. Entrenador, ra.
handless [ˈhændlis] adj. Manco, ca. || FIG. Torpe (clumsy).
handling [ˈhændliŋ] n. Manejo, *m.* (of tools, etc.). || Manipulación, *f.*, manutención, *f.* (of goods). || Conducción, *f.* [*Amer.*, manejo, *m.*] (of a car). || Gobierno, *m.* (of a ship). || Manera (*f.*) de tratar (of a matter). || Trato, *m.* (of a person). || SP. Toque (*m.*) con la mano. || *Rough handling*, malos tratos.
handmade [ˈhændˈmeid] adj. Hecho a mano.
handmaid [ˈhændˈmeid] n. Criada, *f.*
hand-me-down [ˈhændmi:daun] adj. FAM. Heredado, da; de segunda mano, usado, da.
— Pl. n. FAM. Ropa (*f. sing.*) heredada *or* de segunda mano *or* usada.
handout [ˈhændaut] n. Prospecto, *m.*, folleto, *m.* (leaflet). || Octavilla, *f.* (political propaganda leaflet). || Comunicado (*m.*) de prensa (release). || Información, *f.* || U. S. Limosna, *f.* (given to a tramp).
handpick [ˈhændpik] v. tr. Escoger a dedo (people). || Escoger con sumo cuidado (things).
handrail [ˈhændreil] n. Pasamano, *m.*, barandilla, *f.*
handsaw [ˈhændsɔ:] n. Serrucho, *m.*, sierra (*f.*) de mano.
hands-down [ˈhændzdaun] adj. Fácil. || Indisputable, sin lugar a dudas.
handsel [ˈhænsəl] n. Aguinaldo, *m.* (New Year's gift). || Señal, *f.* (pledge).
handsel [ˈhænsəl] v. tr. Estrenar (to use for the first time). || Inaugurar (to inaugurate). || Dar un aguinaldo a (s.o.).
handset [ˈhændset] n. Microteléfono, *m.*, pesa, *f.*
handsewn [ˈhændsəun] adj. Cosido a mano.
handshake [ˈhændʃeik] n. Apretón (*m.*) de manos.
hands-off [ˈhændzɔf] adj. De no intervención.
handsome [ˈhændsəm] adj. Hermoso, sa; guapo, pa; bello, lla (women). || Apuesto, ta; guapo, pa (men). || Elegante (smart). || Considerable (large): *a handsome prize*, un premio considerable. || Muy bueno, na: *a handsome salary*, un salario muy bueno. || Generoso, sa (generous). || Grande: *a country house of handsome proportions*, una casa de campo de grandes proporciones. || *To do the handsome thing by s.o.*, portarse muy bien con alguien.
handsomely [—li] adv. Bien, elegantemente, con elegancia (smartly). || Bien, generosamente (generously).
handsomeness [—nis] n. Belleza, *f.* || Generosidad, *f.*
handspike [ˈhændspaik] n. MAR. Espeque, *m.* || Palanca, *f.* (lever).
handspring [ˈhændspriŋ] n. SP. Voltereta (*f.*) sobre las manos, salto (*m.*) mortal.
handstand [ˈhændstænd] n. SP. Pino, *m.*
handstone [ˈhændstəun] n. Mano, *f.* (for grinding maize, etc.).
hand-to-hand [ˈhændtuˈhænd] adj. Cuerpo a cuerpo.
— Adv. Cuerpo a cuerpo.
hand-to-mouth [ˈhændtuˈmauθ] adj. *To lead a hand-to-mouth existence*, vivir al día.
handwheel [ˈhændwi:l] n. Volante, *m.*
handwork [ˈhændwə:k] n. Trabajo (*m.*) hecho a mano.
handwoven [ˈhændˌwəuvən] adj. Tejido a mano.
handwrite [ˈhændˌrait] v. tr. Escribir a mano.
handwriting [—iŋ] n. Letra, *f.* (one person's style): *I recognize your handwriting*, conozco su letra. || Escritura, *f.* (writing done by hand).
— OBSERV. Esta palabra no lleva nunca el artículo *a*.
handwritten [ˈhændˌritn] adj. Escrito a mano: *a handwritten letter*, una carta escrita a mano.
handy [ˈhændi] adj. A mano, cercano, na (close at hand): *the shops are handy*, las tiendas están a mano. || Mañoso, sa (able to do small jobs). || Diestro, tra; hábil (dexterous). || Práctico, ca; cómodo, da (convenient). || Manejable (easily handled). || Útil (useful). || *To come in handy*, venir bien.
handyman [ˈhændimæn] n. Factótum, *m.* (man employed to do many jobs). || Hombre (*f.*) mañoso (skilful man).
— OBSERV. El plural es *handymen*.
hang [ˈhæŋ] n. Caída, *f.* (of garment). || Inclinación, *f.*, declive, *m.* (slope). || FAM. Comino, *m.*, bledo, *m.*: *I don't give a hang*, me importa un bledo. || FAM. *To get the hang of sth.*, cogerle el truco a algo (to get the knack), comprender *or* entender algo (to understand).
hang* [ˈhæŋ] v. tr. Colgar (to suspend, to fasten pictures): *to hang sth. on the wall*, colgar algo en la pared. || Adornar (to ornament): *she hung the room with pictures and drapes*, adornó el cuarto con cuadros y colgaduras. || Pegar, poner (wallpaper, posters, etc.). || Cubrir (to cover). || Ahorcar (to kill by suspending from the neck). || Manir (game or meat). || Bajar (one's head). || Hacer flotar (in the air). || — FAM. *Hang it!*, ¡por Dios! | *Hang you!*, ¡maldito seas! || *I'll be hanged if...*, que me ahorquen si ... || *To hang o.s.*, ahorcarse.
— V. intr. Colgar (to be suspended): *painting hanging on the wall*, cuadro colgado en la pared. || Caer (garments, curtains). || Inclinarse (to lean). || Ser ahorcado (a criminal). || Flotar (in the air). || Estar pendiente (to be pending). || — *To hang by a thread*, pender de un hilo. || *To hang heavy*, transcurrir lentamente (time). || *To leave a question hanging*, dejar pendiente una cuestión.
— FAM. ***To hang about*** o ***around***, vagar, haraganear, perder el tiempo (to loiter). | Andar rondando por (a place). | Andar rondando (s.o.). | Esperar (to wait). || ***To hang back***, quedarse atrás (to be reluctant to advance). | Vacilar (to hesitate). | Hacerse el remolón (to shirk). || ***To hang behind***, rezagarse. || ***To hang down***, caer, colgar (hair). | Inclinarse (tower). || ***To hang on***, mantenerse firme, resistir, aguantar (to resist). | Quedarse, permanecer (to remain). | Agarrarse (to hold on). | Depender de (to depend upon). | Estar pendiente de: *the people hung on his words*, la gente estaba pendiente de sus palabras. | — FAM. *Hang on!*, ¡espérate! (wait). | FAM. *To hang one on*, pegar un golpe a. | *To hang on to*, agarrarse a; pegarse a (to stick to). || ***To hang out***, tender, colgar (to put out washing). | Colgar fuera. | Sacar (the tongue). | Izar (a flag or signal). | Estar suspendido. | FAM. Vivir (to reside). | U. S. FAM. Frecuentar (to frequent). || ***To hang over***, estar suspendido sobre. | FIG. Cernerse sobre (to threaten). | U. S. Sobrevivir; estar pendiente (problem). || ***To hang together***, ser lógico (argument). | Permanecer unidos, ayudarse mutuamente (persons). || ***To hang up***, colgar (to suspend, to end a telephone conversation). | Cortar, apagar (TV). | FAM. Retrasar (to delay). | Aplazar (to postpone). | ***To hang upon***, estar pendiente de (one's words).
— OBSERV. El verbo *to hang* tiene un pretérito y un participio pasivo irregulares (***hung***) excepto cuando significa « ahorcar » en cuyo caso son regulares (***hanged***)
hangar [ˈhæŋə*] n. AVIAT. Hangar, *m.* || Cobertizo, *m.* (shed).
hangdog [ˈhæŋdɔg] adj. Avergonzado, da.
hanger [ˈhæŋə*] n. Gancho, *m.* (in general). || Percha, *f.* (clothes hanger). || Percha, *f.*, gancho, *m.* (for hats). || Alzapaño, *m.* (for curtains). || Llares, *m. pl.* (for pots). || Puñal, *m.* (dagger). || Verdugo, *m.* (hangman).
hanger-on [ˈhæŋərˈɔn] n. Lapa, *f.*, pegote, *m.* (person who attaches himself to another). || Gorrón, ona; parásito, *m.* (parasite).
hanging [ˈhæŋiŋ] adj. Colgante, pendiente (suspended). || Colgante (bridge, garden). || Patibulario, ria; lúgubre (look). || Feroz (judge). || FAM. Que merece la horca (matter). || *Hanging committee*, comité (*m.*) que selecciona las obras que se han de exponer.
— N. Colgamiento, *m.* (action of hanging). || Horca, *f.*, ejecución, (*f.*) en la horca (of a criminal): *to deserve hanging*, merecer la horca. || Colocación, *f.* (of bells, wallpaper). || Empapelado, *m.* (of a room). || — Pl. Colgaduras, *f.* (curtains).
hangman [ˈhæŋmən] n. Verdugo, *m.*
— OBSERV. El plural de esta palabra es *hangmen*.
hangnail [ˈhæŋneil] n. Padrastro, *m.*
hangout [ˈhæŋaut] n. FAM. Lugar (*m.*) de reunión habitual, cuartel (*m.*) general, guarida, *f.*
hangover [ˈhæŋˌəuvə*] n. FAM. Resaca, *f.* (after drinking). || Restos, *m. pl.* (remains).
hank [hæŋk] n. Madeja, *f.* (of wool). || Ovillo, *m.* (of cotton). || MAR. Anillo (*m.*) de una vela. || FIG. Madeja, *f.* (of hair).
hanker [ˈhæŋkə*] v. intr. *To hanker for* o *after*, anhelar, ansiar.
hankering [ˈhæŋkəriŋ] n. Anhelo, *m.* (strong desire). || Añoranza, *f.* (nostalgia).
hankie or **hanky** [ˈhæŋki] n. FAM. Pañuelo, *m.*
hanky-panky [ˈhæŋkiˈpæŋki] n. FAM. Trucos, *m. pl.* (tricks). | Trampa, *f.* (trickery, deception). | Camelo, *m.* (con).
Hansard [ˈhænsɑ:d] pr. n. Actas (*f. pl.*) oficiales de los debates parlamentarios.
hanse [hæns] n. Hansa, *f.*
hanseatic [ˌhænsiˈætik] adj. Hanseático, ca.
hansom [ˈhænsəm] n. Cabriolé, *m.*, coche (*m.*) de dos ruedas tirado por un caballo.
hap [hæp] n. Casualidad, *f.* (chance). || Destino, *m.*, suerte, *f.* (fortune).
hap [hæp] v. intr. Ocurrir por casualidad.
haphazard [ˈhæpˈhæzəd] adj. Fortuito, ta; casual.
— Adv. A la buena de Dios.
— N. Casualidad, *f.*
hapless [ˈhæplis] adj. Desgraciado, da; desventurado, da.
haplessness [—nis] n. Infortunio, *m.*, desventura, *f.*
ha'p'orth [ˈheipəθ] n. FAM. Medio penique, *m.*
— OBSERV. Esta palabra es la forma abreviada de *halfpennyworth*.
happen [ˈhæpən] v. intr. Suceder, ocurrir, pasar: *how did it happen?*, ¿cómo ocurrió?, ¿cómo sucedió?; *it happened in June*, pasó en junio; *if an accident happens*, si ocurre un accidente. || Producirse, ocurrir: *the accident happened at 12 o'clock*, el accidente se produjo a las 12. || Lograr: *how did you happen to find it?*, ¿cómo logró encontrarle? || — *Don't let this happen again*, que eso no vuelva a suceder. || *How does it happen that?*, ¿cómo puede ser que? || *If you happen to see him*, si por casualidad lo ves. || *I happened to be out*, dio la casualidad de que estaba fuera. || *It so happens that* o *as it happens*, da la casualidad de que. || *To happen on* o *upon*, dar con

(to find). || *Whatever happens* o *no matter what happens* o *happen what may*, pase lo que pase.
happening [—iŋ] n. Suceso, *m.*, acontecimiento, *m.* (event). || "Happening", *m.* [espectáculo artístico improvisado en el que participa el público].
happily [ˈhæpili] adv. Felizmente (in a happy way). || Afortunadamente (luckily). || *They lived happily ever after*, vivieron felices, comieron perdices y a mí no me dieron (in a fairy tale).
happiness [ˈhæpinis] n. Felicidad, *f.* || Alegría, *f.* (merriment). || Contento, *m.* (contentment). || Propiedad, *f.* (of a word, sentence).
happy [ˈhæpi] adj. Feliz: *she was happy with her husband*, era feliz con su marido; *he's a happy man*, es un hombre feliz; *a happy life*, una vida feliz. || Contento, ta: *he is happy in his work*, está contento con su trabajo. || Alegre: *a happy character*, un carácter alegre; *a happy tune*, una melodía alegre. || FAM. Alegre (tipsy). | Apropiado, da; acertado, da; feliz (appropriate). | — *Are you happy with the idea?*, ¿te parece bien la idea? || *Happy birthday!*, ¡felicidades!, ¡feliz cumpleaños! || *Happy ending*, final (*m.*) feliz, feliz desenlace, *m.* || *I am happy to see you*, me alegra verle, me alegro de verle. || *I am happy to tell you that*, tengo mucho gusto en decirle que. || *I am very happy for you*, me alegro mucho por ti. || *To be as happy as a lark*, estar más alegre que unas Pascuas.
happy-go-lucky [ˈhæpigəuˈlʌki] adj. Despreocupado, da. || *A happy-go-lucky type*, un viva la virgen.
Hapsburg [ˈhæpsbəːg] pr. n. HIST. Habsburgo.
hara-kiri [ˈhærəˈkiri] n. Haraquiri, *m.*
harangue [həˈræŋ] n. Arenga, *f.*
harangue [həˈræŋ] v. tr. Arengar.
harass [ˈhærəs] v. tr. Acosar, hostigar: *to harass s.o. with questions*, acosar a alguien a preguntas. || Agobiar: *he was harassed by the cares of a large family*, estaba agobiado por los cuidados de una gran familia. || Atormentar (to worry). || MIL. Hostilizar, hostigar. || *Harassed by doubts*, acosado por las dudas.
harassment [—mənt] n. Hostigamiento, *m.* (pestering). || Tormento, *m.* (worry). || MIL. Hostigamiento, *m.*
harbinger [ˈhɑːbindʒə*] n. Precursor, *m.* (person). || Presagio, *m.* (thing).
harbinger [ˈhɑːbindʒə*] v. tr. Anunciar, ser el precursor de.
harbour (U. S. **harbor**) [ˈhɑːbə*] n. Puerto, *m.* (port). || FIG. Puerto, *m.*, refugio, *m.*
harbour (U. S. **harbor**) [ˈhɑːbə*] v. tr. Encubrir (a criminal). || Hospedar (to lodge). || FIG. Abrigar (hopes). | Tener (suspicions). | Contener (to contain). || *To harbour a grudge*, guardar rencor.
— V. intr. Ponerse a cubierto, refugiarse.
harbourage (U. S. **harborage**) [—ridʒ] n. Refugio, *m.* || MAR. Fondeadero, *m.* (place). | Fondeo, *m.* (act).
harbour master (U. S. **harbor master**) [—ˌmɑːstə*] n. Capitán (*m.*) de puerto.
hard [hɑːd] adj. Duro, ra: *a hard egg*, un huevo duro; *a hard man*, un hombre duro; *hard climate*, clima duro. || Resistente (strong). || Difícil: *this question is hard to answer*, esta pregunta es difícil de contestar. || Arduo, dua; duro, ra: *hard work*, un trabajo duro. || Difícil, duro, ra: *a hard life*, una vida difícil. || Malo, la: *hard times*, malos tiempos; *hard luck*, mala suerte. || Severo, ra (*on*, *to*, *towards*, con): *a hard punishment*, un castigo severo; *a hard teacher*, un profesor severo. || Fuerte (blow). || Riguroso, sa (winter, weather). || Innegable, incontestable (undeniable): *hard facts*, hechos innegables. || Alcohólico, ca: *hard drinks*, bebidas alcohólicas. || Agraz, áspero, ra (wine). || Fermentado, da: *hard cider*, sidra fermentada. || De piedra: *a hard heart*, un corazón de piedra. || Duro, ra (voice, words). || Difícil (person): *he is hard to get on with*, es difícil llevarse bien con él. || Cruel (fate). || Apretado, da (knot). || GRAMM. Fuerte (consonants *g*, *c*, *s*). || Penetrante: *a hard look*, una mirada penetrante. || Firme (muscle). || Escleroso, sa (tissues). || MIL. Encarnizado, da: *hard fight*, lucha encarnizada. || SP. Reñido, da (match). || COMM. Sostenido, da (stock market). || — *A hard bargain*, un trato poco ventajoso. || *A hard drinker*, un gran bebedor. || *A hard worker*, una persona muy trabajadora. || *Hard and fast*, estricto, ta; inflexible (rule). || SP. *Hard court*, pista (*f.*) de tenis de cemento. || *Hard currency*, divisa fuerte. || *Hard feelings*, resentimiento, *m. sing.* || *Hard hat*, casco protector. || FIG. *Hard nut to crack*, hueso duro de roer. || *Hard of hearing*, duro de oído. || *Hard sell*, publicidad agresiva [hecha por un vendedor]. || *Hard to deal with*, de trato difícil. || *Hard water*, agua gorda *or* dura. || *It's hard work for him to*, le cuesta mucho trabajo. || *No hard feelings*, olvidémoslo. || *On the cold hard ground*, en el mismo suelo. || *To be as hard as nails*, see NAIL. || *To be hard on one's clothes*, gastar mucho la ropa. || *To have a hard time of it*, pasarlo mal. || *To make it hard for s.o.*, hacerle las cosas difíciles a uno. || *What hard luck!*, ¡qué mala suerte! || *You are too hard on him*, eres demasiado severo con él.
— Adv. Fuerte: *hit it hard*, dale fuerte; *it is raining hard*, está lloviendo fuerte. || Severamente, con severidad (severely). || Mucho: *to work hard*, trabajar mucho; *to drink hard*, beber mucho. || — *Hard by*, muy cerca. || *Hard come by*, difícilmente obtenido. || *Hard upon*, muy de cerca. || *To be freezing hard*, helar fuerte. || *To be hard at it*, trabajar mucho *or* con ahínco. || *To beg hard for sth.*, pedir algo con insistencia. || FAM. *To be hard up*, no tener un céntimo. || *To be hard upon s.o.'s heels*, ir pisando los talones a alguien. || *To die hard*, tardar en desaparecer (rumour), tener siete vidas como los gatos (person). || *To follow hard after*, seguir de cerca. || *To go hard with s.o.*, irle mal a alguien. || FIG. *To hit s.o. hard*, ser un golpe duro para alguien. || *To hold on hard*, agarrarse bien. || *To look hard*, mirar fijamente.
hard-bitten [ˈhɑːdˈbitn] adj. Tenaz, duro, ra (enduring).
hard-boiled [ˈhɑːdˈbɔild] adj. Duro, ra (egg). || FIG. Duro, ra.
hard cash [ˈhɑːdkæʃ] n. Dinero (*m.*) contante y sonante.
hard-drawn [ˈhɑːdˈdrɔːn] adj. Estirado en frío (metal).
harden [ˈhɑːdn] v. tr. Endurecer (to make hard). || MED. Endurecer (tissues). || FIG. Endurecer, insensibilizar (one's heart). | Acostumbrar, curtir (to inure). || TECH. Templar (steel). || — *To harden o.s. to the cold*, acostumbrarse al frío. || *To harden s.o. to war*, aguerrir a alguien.
— V. intr. Endurecerse (to become hard). || Subir (prices). || Acostumbrarse (to accustom o.s.). || Endurecerse (to become unfeeling).
hardener [—ə*] n. Sustancia (*f.*) que sirve para endurecer algo.
hardening [—iŋ] n. Endurecimiento, *m.* || Temple, *m.* (of steel). || FIG. Endurecimiento, *m.*
hard-featured [ˈhɑːdˈfiːtʃəd] n. De facciones duras.
hardfisted [ˈhɑːdˌfistid] adj. De manos callosas. || FIG. Mezquino, na; tacaño, ña (mean).
hard-fought [ˈhɑːdfɔːt] adj. Reñido, da.
hardhead [ˈhɑːdhed] adj. Terco, ca; testarudo, da (stubborn).
hardheaded [ˈhɑːdˈhedid] adj. Realista, práctico, ca. || Terco, ca; testarudo, da (stubborn).
hardheadedness [—nis] n. Terquedad, *f.*, testarudez, *f.* (stubbornness). || Realismo, *m.*
hardhearted [ˈhɑːdˈhɑːtid] adj. Sin corazón, insensible, duro de corazón.
hardheartedness [—nis] n. Dureza (*f.*) de corazón, falta (*f.*) de sensibilidad.
hardihood [ˈhɑːdihud] n. Osadía, *f.*, atrevimiento, *m.*, audacia, *f.* (boldness). || Descaro, *m.* (shamelessness).
hardily [ˈhɑːdili] adv. Osadamente, con atrevimiento *or* audacia. || Vigorosamente.
hardiness [ˈhɑːdinis] n. Vigor, *m.*, resistencia, *f.*, aguante, *m.* (strength). || FIG. Osadía, *f.*, atrevimiento, *m.*, audacia, *f.* (boldness).
hard labour (U. S. **hard labor**) [ˈhɑːd ˈleibə*] n. JUR. Trabajos (*m. pl.*) forzados *or* forzosos.
hardly [ˈhɑːdli] adv. Apenas, escasamente (scarcely). || Duramente (harshly). || Severamente (severely). || Difícilmente, con dificultad (not easily). || — *Hardly anyone*, casi nadie. || *Hardly ever*, casi nunca. || *He could hardly have said that*, es muy poco probable que haya dicho que. || *It can hardly be doubted that*, no cabe duda que, es de lo más probable que. || *You need hardly say*, huelga decir.
— Interj. ¡Qué va!
hardmouthed [ˈhɑːdmauðd] adj. Duro de boca: *hardmouthed horse*, caballo duro de boca.
hardness [ˈhɑːdnis] n. Dureza, *f.* (quality of not being soft). || Dificultad, *f.* (difficulty). || Rigor, *m.* (of winter). || Dureza, *f.*, gordura, *f.* (of water). || Severidad, *f.* (severity). || Insensibilidad, *f.* (of heart). || *Hardness of hearing*, dureza de oído.
hard pressed [ˈhɑːdprest] adj. Apremiado, da.
hards [hɑːdz] pl. n. Desechos (*m.*) de cáñamo *or* de lino.
hard-set [ˈhɑːdset] adj. Apurado, da (in trouble). || Que ha fraguado, endurecido, da (cement). || Empollado, da; incubado, da (egg).
hard-shell [ˈhɑːdʃel] adj. Que tiene un caparazón duro (mollusc). || FIG. Duro, ra; inflexible.
hardship [ˈhɑːdʃip] n. Dificultad, *f.*, apuro, *m.*: *I have suffered great hardships*, he pasado muchos apuros. || Dificultad, *f.* (difficulty).
hard-solder [ˈhɑːdˈsɔldə*] v. tr. TECH. Soldar con cobre.
hardtack [ˈhɑːdtæk] n. MAR. Galleta, *f.*
hardtop [ˈhɑːdtɔp] n. Descapotable (*m.*) con capota dura.
hardware [ˈhɑːdwεə*] n. Ferretería, *f.*, quincallería, *f.* (articles of metal). || MIL. Armas, *f. pl.* || TECH. "Hardware", *m.*, maquinaria, *f.*, equipos (*m. pl.*) y dispositivos [que integran una computadora]. || — *Hardware dealer*, ferretero, *m.*, quincallero, *m.* || *Hardware shop* o *store*, ferretería, *f.*, quincallería, *f.*
hard-won [ˈhɑːdwʌn] adj. Ganado a duras penas *or* con mucha dificultad.
hardwood [ˈhɑːdwud] n. Madera (*f.*) dura.
hard-working [ˈhɑːdˈwəːkiŋ] adj. Trabajador, ra.
hardy [ˈhɑːdi] adj. Robusto, ta. || BOT. Resistente. || FIG. Atrevido, da; audaz.
hare [hεə*] n. ZOOL. Liebre, *f.* || — FAM. *Mad as a March hare*, loco de atar *or* de remate *or* rematado, más loco que una cabra. | *To run with the hare and hunt with the hounds*, ponerle una vela a Dios y otra al diablo. | *To start a hare*, andarse con rodeos.
hare [hεə*] v. intr. Volar, correr muy de prisa.
hare and hounds [hεə* ænd haundz] n. See PAPER CHASE.
harebell [—bəl] n. BOT. Campánula, *f.*

harebrained [—breind] adj. Atolondrado, da; ligero de cascos.

harehound [—haund] n. Lebrel, *m.* (dog).

harelip [—ˈlip] n. Med. Labio (*m.*) leporino.

harelipped [ˈhɛəˈlipt] adj. Labihendido, da; de labio leporino.

harem [ˈhɛərəm] n. Harén, *m.*

hare's-foot trefoil [ˈhɛəzfut ˈtrefɔil] n. Bot. Pie (*m.*) de liebre.

haricot [ˈhærikəu] n. Bot. Judía, *f.* (bean). || Culin. Guiso (*m.*) de cordero con judías (stew).

hark [hɑ:k] v. tr. (Ant.). Escuchar.
— V. intr. (Ant.). Escuchar. || — Fig. *To hark back to*, volver a (to go back to), recordar (to remember). || *To hark to*, escuchar, prestar oído a.

harken [ˈhɑ:kən] v. tr. Escuchar.

harl or **harle** [hɑ:l] n. Hebra, *f.* (of flax, hemp). || Mosca, *f.* (in fishing).

harlequin [ˈkɑ:likwin] n. Arlequín, *m.*
— Adj. Abigarrado, da.

harlequinade [ˌhɑ:likwiˈneid] n. Arlequinada, *f.*, payasada, *f.*

harlot [ˈhɑ:lət] n. Ramera, *f.* (prostitute).

harlotry [—ri] n. Prostitución, *f.*

harm [hɑ:m] n. Daño, *m.*: *the bad weather has done a lot of harm to the crop*, el mal tiempo ha hecho mucho daño a la cosecha. || Perjuicio, *m.* || — *There is no harm in her*, no es una mala mujer. || *There is no harm in saying so*, no es malo decirlo, no hay ningún mal en decirlo. || *To be out of harm's way*, estar a salvo. || *To do harm to*, perjudicar a, hacer mal a. || *To keep out of harm's way*, mantenerse a salvo.

harm [hɑ:m] v. tr. Dañar, estropear (sth.). || Perjudicar (s.o., s.o.'s interest). || Hacer daño (to hurt physically).

harmful [—ful] adj. Perjudicial (*to*, para). || Dañino, na (pest, etc.). || Nocivo, va; dañino, na (thing). || Pernicioso, sa (person).

harmfulness [—fulnis] n. Maldad, *f.* (of a person). || Lo perjudicial. || Nocividad, *f.* (of a thing).

harmless [—lis] adj. Inofensivo, va.

harmlessly [—lisli] adv. Inocentemente.

harmlessness [—lisnis] n. Inocuidad, *f.* (of a beverage, etc.). || Inocencia, *f.*

harmonic [hɑ:ˈmɔnik] adj. Phys. Mus. Math. Armónico, ca.
— N. Armónico, *m.*

harmonica [hɑ:ˈmɔnikə] n. Mus. Armónica, *f.*

harmonics [hɑ:ˈmɔnikz] n. Mus. Armonía, *f.*

harmonious [hɑ:ˈməunjəs] adj. Armonioso, sa. || *To live in harmonious peace*, vivir en paz y armonía.

harmonist [ˈhɑ:mənist] n. Mus. Armonista, *m.*

harmonium [hɑ:ˈməunjəm] n. Mus. Armonio, *m.* (reed organ).

harmonization [ˌhɑ:mənaiˈzeiʃən] n. Mus. Armonización, *f.*

harmonize [ˈhɑ:mənaiz] v. tr./intr. Armonizar.

harmony [ˈhɑ:məni] n. Armonía, *f.*

harness [ˈhɑ:nis] n. Guarniciones, *f. pl.*, arreos, *m. pl.*, arneses, *m. pl.* (for draught animals). || Andadores, *m. pl.* (for children). || Hist. Arnés, *m.* || — *Harness maker*, guarnicionero, *m.*, talabartero, *m.* || Fig. *To be back in harness*, haber reanudado el trabajo. | *To die in harness*, morir con las botas puestas *or* al pie del cañón. | *To get back in harness*, reanudar el trabajo.

harness [ˈhɑ:nis] v. tr. Enjaezar, poner los arreos a (to put a harness on). || Enganchar: *to harness a horse to a carriage*, enganchar un caballo a un carro. || Aprovechar (a river, waterfall).

harp [hɑ:p] n. Mus. Arpa, *f.*

harp [hɑ:p] v. intr. Mus. Tocar el arpa. || — Fam. *To be always harping on the same string*, estar siempre con la misma cantinela. | *To harp on*, machacar.

harpist [ˈhɑ:pist] n. Mus. Arpista, *m. & f.*

harpoon [hɑ:ˈpu:n] n. Arpón, *m.*

harpoon [hɑ:ˈpu:n] v. tr. Arponear.

harpooner [—ə*] n. Arponero, *m.*

harpsichord [ˈhɑ:psikɔ:d] n. Mus. Clavicordio, *m.*, clave, *m.*, clavecín, *m.*

harpy [ˈhɑ:pi] n. Arpía, *f.* || Fig. Arpía, *f.*

harquebus [ˈhɑ:kwibəs] n. Arcabuz, *m.*

harquebusier [ˌha:kwibəˈsiə*] n. Arcabucero, *m.*

harridan [ˈhæridən] n. Fig. Bruja, *f.*, arpía, *f.*

harrier [ˈhæriə*] n. Zool. Especie (*f.*) de halcón (hawk). | Perro (*m.*) de caza (hound). || Sp. Corredor (*m.*) de cross-country.

harrow [ˈhærəu] n. Agr. Grada, *f.*

harrow [ˈhærəu] v. tr. Agr. Gradar. || Fig. Destrozar, partir (s.o.'s heart). | Atormentar (s.o.).

harrowing [—iŋ] adj. Desgarrador, ra; angustioso, sa.

harry [ˈhæri] v. tr. Acosar (to harass). || Asolar, arrasar (to ravage).

Harry [ˈhæri] pr. n. Enrique, *m.* || — Fam. *Old Harry*, Pedro Botero (the Devil). | *To play old Harry with*, fastidiar, estropear (to spoil), hacer pasarlas moradas (to pester).

harsh [hɑ:ʃ] adj. Áspero, ra (to the touch, to the taste). || Discordante (sound). || Duro, ra; severo, ra (severe). || Desabrido, da (character). || Violento, ta (contrast). || Chillón, ona (colour). || Muy duro, ra (words). || Áspero, ra (voice).

harshness [—nis] n. Aspereza, *f.* (to the touch, to the taste). || Discordancia, *f.* (of a sound). || Severidad, *f.* (severity). || Desabrimiento, *m.* (of character).

hart [hɑ:t] n. Zool. Ciervo, *m.*

hartshorn [—shɔ:n] n. Zool. Cuerno (*m.*) de ciervo. || Chem. Amoniaco, *m.*

harum-scarum [ˈhɛərəmˈskɛərəm] adj. Atolondrado, da.
— N. Atolondrado, da; cabeza (*f.*) de chorlito.

haruspex [həˈrʌspeks] n. Hist. Arúspice, *m.*
— Observ. El plural de *haruspex* es *haruspices*.

harvest [ˈhɑ:vist] n. Cosecha, *f.*, siega, *f.* (of cereals). || Recolección, *f.*, cosecha, *f.* (of vegetables). || Vendimia, *f.* (of grapes). || Cosecha, *f.* (yield of crops): *a good harvest*, una buena cosecha. || Fig. Cosecha, *f.* || *Harvest festival*, fiesta (*f.*) de la cosecha.

harvest [ˈhɑ:vist] v. tr. Cosechar, recoger.
— V. intr. Cosechar, hacer la cosecha.

harvest bug [—bʌg] n. Zool. Ácaro, *m.*

harvester [—ə*] n. Segador, ra; cosechador, ra (person). || Segadora, *f.* (machine).

harvester-thresher [—əθreʃə*] n. Segadora trilladora, *f.* (machine).

harvestman [—mæn] n. Agr. Segador, *m.* || Zool. Segador, *m.*
— Observ. El plural de esta palabra es *harvestmen*.

harvest time [—taim] n. Mies, *f.*, siega, *f.*

has [hæz] 3rd pers. sing. pres. indic. See have.

has-been [—bi:n] n. Fam. Persona (*f.*) acabada.

hash [hæʃ] n. Culin. Picadillo, *m.* || Fam. Estropicio, *m.* (mess). | Mezcolanza, *f.*, revoltillo, *m.*, lío, *m.* (mix-up). || — Fam. *To make a hash of*, estropear por completo. | *To settle s.o.'s hash*, ajustarle las cuentas a uno, cargarse a uno.

hash [hæʃ] v. tr. Culin. Picar. || Fam. Hacer un lío. || — U. S. Fam. *To hash out*, discutir a fondo. | *To hash up*, embrollar.

hasheesh [ˈhæʃiʃ] or **hashish** [ˈhæʃi:ʃ] n. Hachís, *m. inv.*

haslet [ˈheizlit] n. Culin. Asaduras, *f. pl.*

hasp [hɑ:sp] n. Pestillo, *m.* (of door). || Cierre, *m.* (of padlock). || Falleba, *f.* (of window). || Broche, *m.* (of books). || Madeja, *f.* (of thread).

hassle [ˈhæsəl] n. U. S. Fam. Follón, *m.*, jaleo, *m.* (heated discussion). | Pelea, *f.* (squabble).

hassock [ˈhæsək] n. Cojín, *m.* (cushion). || Mata (*f.*) de hierba (tuft of grass).

haste [heist] n. Prisa, *f.* || — *In haste*, de prisa, apresuradamente. || Fig. *More haste less speed*, vísteme despacio que tengo prisa. || *To make haste*, darse prisa, apresurarse.

haste [heist] v. intr. (Ant.). Apresurarse, darse prisa.

hasten [ˈheisn] v. tr. Apresurar, acelerar (sth.). || Dar prisa a (s.o.). || *To hasten one's steps*, apresurar el paso, apretar el paso.
— V. intr. Apresurarse, darse prisa. || — *To hasten away* o *off* o *out*, irse precipitadamente. || *To hasten back*, volver a toda prisa. || *To hasten in*, entrar a toda prisa. || *To hasten up*, llegar corriendo.

hastily [ˈheistli] adv. De prisa, apresuradamente (quickly). || Sin reflexionar, a la ligera (rashly).

hastiness [heistinis] n. Prisa, *f.*, rapidez, *f.* || Precipitación, *f.*

hasty [ˈheisti] adj. Apresurado, da (rash). || Hecho de prisa, precipitado, da (done with haste). || Rápido, da (quick). || Ligero, ra; irreflexivo, va: *it was a very hasty decision*, fue una decisión muy irreflexiva.

hat [hæt] n. Sombrero, *m*: *to put one's hat*, ponerse el sombrero; *with one's hat on*, con el sombrero puesto *or* en la cabeza. || — *Bowler hat*, sombrero hongo, bombín, *m.* || *Cardinal's hat*, capelo cardenalicio. || *Cocked hat*, sombrero de tres picos *or* de candil. || || *Crush hat*, sombrero de muelles. || *Felt hat*, sombrero flexible. || *Hat in hand*, humildemente. || *Hat shop*, sombrería, *f.* || Fig. *Hats off!*, ¡hay que descubrirse! | *I'll eat my hat if...*, que me ahorquen si... | *Keep it under your hat*, no diga nada de eso. | *My hat!*, ¡naranjas! || *Opera hat*, sombrero de muelles. || *Panama hat*, jipijapa, *m.* || *Soft hat*, sombrero flexible. || *Straw hat*, sombrero de paja. || *Three-cornered hat*, sombrero de tres picos. || *To pass the hat*, pasar la gorra (to collect). || *Top hat*, sombrero de copa. || Fig. *To take one's hat off to*, descubrirse ante. | *To talk through one's hat*, decir tonterías, disparatar, desbarrar (to talk nonsense). | *To throw one's hat in the ring*, echarse al ruedo.

hatband [—bænd] n. Cinta (*f.*) del sombrero.

hat block [—blɔk] n. Horma, *f.*

hatbox [—bɔks] n. Sombrerera, *f.*

hatch [hætʃ] n. Salida (*f.*) del huevo *or* del cascarón. || Pollada, *f.* (brood). || Ventanilla, *f.* (for serving). || Mar. Escotilla, *f.* | Trampa, *f.* (trapdoor). | Compuerta, *f.* (floodgate). || Rayado, *m.*, sombreado, *m.* (drawing). || Fam. *Down the hatch!*, ¡salud!

hatch [hætʃ] v. tr. Incubar, empollar (to incubate). || Hacer salir del cascarón (chickens). || Rayar, sombrear (to stripe with parallel lines). || Fig. Maquinar, idear, tramar (a plot).
— V. intr. Salir del cascarón *or* del huevo. || Fig. Madurar.

hatchel [ˈhætʃəl] n. Rastrillo, *m.*

hatchery [ˈhætʃəri] n. Criadero, *m.*

hatchet [ˈhætʃit] n. Hacha, *f.* || — *Hatchet face*, rostro afilado. || *To bury the hatchet*, enterrar el hacha de la guerra, hacer las paces. || *To dig up the hatchet*, desenterrar el hacha de la guerra.
hatchet-faced [—feist] adj. De facciones enjutas, de rostro afilado.
hatching [ˈhætʃiŋ] n. Incubación, *f.* (of eggs). || Salida (*f.*) del cascarón *or* del huevo (of chickens). || PRINT. Sombreado, *m.* || FIG. Maquinación, *f.*
hatchment [ˈhætʃmənt] n. HERALD. Escudo (*m.*) que lleva las armas de un caballero fallecido.
hatchway [ˈhætʃwei] n. MAR. Escotilla, *f.*
hate [heit] n. Odio, *m.*: *I could see hate in his eyes*, veía odio en su mirada.
hate [heit] v. tr. Odiar, aborrecer, detestar (to abhor): *I hate her*, la odio. || FIG. Odiar, detestar: *he hates to get up early*, odia levantarse temprano. | Sentir, lamentar (to regret): *I should hate to disappoint you*, lamentaría decepcionarle. || *He hates to be contradicted*, no soporta que le contradigan.
hateful [—ful] adj. Odioso, sa; aborrecible.
hatefulness [—fulnis] n. Lo odioso, carácter (*m.*) odioso.
hatless [ˈhætlis] adj. Sin sombrero.
hatpin [ˈhætpin] n. Alfiler (*m.*) de sombrero.
hatrack [ˈhætræk] n. Percha (*f.*) para sombreros.
hatred [ˈheitrid] n. Odio, *m.* (*for*, a), aborrecimiento, *m.* (*for*, de). || *Out of hatred for*, por odio a.
hatter [ˈhætə*] n. Sombrerero, ra. || FAM. *To be as mad as a hatter*, estar más loco que una cabra.
hauberk [ˈhɔːbəːk] n. Cota (*f.*) de mallas.
haughtiness [ˈhɔːtinis] n. Altanería, *f.*, altivez, *f.*, arrogancia, *f.*
haughty [ˈhɔːti] adj. Altanero, ra; altivo, va; arrogante.
haul [hɔːl] n. Tirón, *m.* (heavy pull). || Trayecto, *m.*, recorrido, *m.* (journey). || Redada, *f.* (in fishing). || Botín, *m.* (loot). || U. S. Camionaje, *m.*, transporte, *m.*, acarreo, *m.*
haul [hɔːl] v. tr. Arrastrar (to drag). || Acarrear (to transport by rail, road). || AUT. Remolcar (a car). || — *To haul down the flag*, arriar bandera (to lower the colours). || *To haul over the coals*, echar una bronca *or* un rapapolvo. || *To haul up*, izar.
— V. intr. Tirar de (to pull). || MAR. Halar.
haulage [—idʒ] n. Transporte, *m.*, acarreo, *m.*, camionaje, *m.*
hauler [ˈhɔːlə*] or **haulier** [ˈhɔːljə*] n. Transportista, *m.*
haulm [hɔːm] n. BOT. Rastrojo, *m.* (after harvesting). | Tallo, *m.* (stalk).
haunch [hɔːntʃ] n. ANAT. Cadera, *f.* || ARCH. Riñón (*m.*) de una bóveda. || CULIN. Pernil, *m.* || — ANAT. *Haunch bone*, hueso iliaco. || *To sit on one's haunches*, ponerse en cuclillas.
haunt [hɔːnt] n. Lugar (*m.*) frecuentado (*of*, por), lugar (*m.*) predilecto. || Guarida, *f.* (of animals, criminals, etc.).
haunt [hɔːnt] v. tr. Aparecer en (ghosts). || Frecuentar (to frequent). || Seguir, perseguir (to follow s.o. around). || Perseguir, obsesionar, atormentar (memories). || *To be haunted*, estar encantado.
haunter [—ə*] n. Asiduo, dua.
haunting [—iŋ] adj. Obsesionante.
hautbois or **hautboy** [ˈəubɔi] n. MUS. Oboe, *m.* || BOT. Fresón, *m.* (strawberry).
Havana [həˈvænə] pr. n. GEOGR. La Habana (city). || FAM. Habano, *m.* (cigar).
Havanan [—n] adj./n. Habanero, ra; habano, na.
have [hæv] n. Rico, *m.* || Timo, *m.* (swindle). || *The haves and the have-nots*, los ricos y los pobres.
have* [hæv] v. tr. Tener: *they have two cars*, tienen dos coches; *I have four brothers*, tengo cuatro hermanos; *he has good ideas*, tiene buenas ideas; *to have news, talks, a discussion, a quarrel, influenza*, tener noticias, conversaciones, una discusión, una riña, gripe. || Recibir, tener (to receive): *I had a letter from John today*, he recibido una carta de Juan esta mañana. || Llevar, tener: *the coat has no label*, el abrigo no lleva etiqueta. || Permitir: *I won't have it!*, ¡no lo permitiré!; *I won't have them do this*, no permitiré que hagan eso. || Decir: *the story has it that*, la historia dice que; *as Lorca has it*, como dice Lorca. || Tomar: *have a drink*, tome una copa; *have another biscuit*, tome otra galleta. || Tomar, coger: *I had my holidays in June*, cogí las vacaciones en junio. || Encontrar (to find): *I have no words to express my desperation*, no encuentro palabras para expresar mi desesperación. || Conseguir, encontrar: *it is to be had at the butcher's*, esto se consigue en la carnicería. || Saber: *I have it by heart*, lo sé de memoria. || Enterarse, saber: *I had it from the baker*, me enteré por el panadero. || Tener conocimientos de: *I have Chinese*, tengo conocimientos de chino. || Dar (to give): *let me have an answer*, dame una contestación. || Hacer: *to have a trip*, hacer un viaje. || Pasar (to spend): *to have a pleasant evening*, pasar una noche agradable; *to have a good time*, pasarlo bien. || Mandar: *have him cut the lawn*, mándale cortar el césped; *to have a dress made*, mandar hacer un traje; *to have sth. done*, mandar hacer algo. || Tener ganado: *now he has the game*, ahora tiene ganada la partida. || Tener agarrado: *his opponent had him by the neck*, su adversario le tenía agarrado por el cuello. || FAM. Engañar (to deceive): *I've been had* o *they had me*, me han engañado. | Entender (to understand): *do you have me?*, ¿me entiendes? || — *And what have you*, y qué sé yo (and so on). || *As luck would have it he arrived on time*, la suerte dispuso que llegara a tiempo. || *Have it your own way*, haga lo que quiera. || *He had his leg broken*, se rompió la pierna. || *He had his wallet stolen*, le robaron la cartera. || *I had better do it*, más vale que lo haga. || *I had rather do it*, preferiría hacerlo. || *I'll have you know*, para que sepa usted. || *I won't have it!*, ¡no me lo creo! || *I would have the government ban alcohol*, quisiera que el Gobierno prohibiese el alcohol. || *Let me have your book*, dame tu libro. || *Now I have you!*, ¡ya te tengo! (to catch). || *To have a baby*, tener un niño. || *To have a bath*, darse un baño, bañarse. || *To have a cigarette*, fumarse un cigarrillo. || *To have a game*, jugar *or* echar una partida. || *To have a haircut*, cortarse el pelo. || *To have a lesson*, dar clase. || *To have an operation*, operarse, sufrir una operación. || *To have a shave*, afeitarse. || *To have a shower*, ducharse. || *To have a try*, intentar. || *To have breakfast*, desayunar. || *To have dinner*, comer. || *To have done with*, haber acabado con. || *To have it*, ganar (to win), acertar (to guess), cobrar (to be punished, etc.). || *To have it that*, declarar, afirmar (to assert). || *To have lunch*, almorzar. || *To have sth. to do*, tener algo que hacer. || *To have to*, tener que, deber: *I have to go*, tengo que irme. || *To have to do with*, tener que ver con. || *To have trouble with*, tener problemas con. || *To let s.o. have it*, pegarle a alguien, darle [una paliza] a alguien (to hit), decirle a alguien cuatro verdades (to remonstrate). || *To let s.o. have sth.*, dejarle algo a alguien. || *What would you have me do?*, ¿qué quieres que haga? || *Will you have...?*, ¿quieres...? || *You've got me there*, aquí me has cogido.
— V. aux. Haber: *I have seen*, he visto; *I had gone*, había ido; *he has been speaking for two hours*, está hablando desde hace dos horas; *I have studied here for five months*, hace cinco meses que estudio aquí. || — *I have a brother*. — *So have I*, tengo un hermano. — Yo también. || *I haven't seen you for weeks*, hace semanas que no te veo, no te he visto desde hace semanas. || *It has grown*. — *So it has!*, ha crecido. — ¡Ya lo creo! || *To have just done*, acabar de hacer. || *You haven't washed*. — *I have!*, no te has lavado. — Sí. || *You've been drinking*. — *I haven't*, has bebido. — No.
— ***To have about***, llevar [consigo]. || ***To have against***, tener en contra. || ***To have at***, atacar. || ***To have back***, hacer volver (s.o.). | — *You can have it back tomorrow*, se lo devolverán mañana. || ***To have down***, tener apuntado (written down). | Hacer venir, invitar (invited). | Derribar (to knock down). || ***To have in***, hacer *or* dejar pasar (to show in). | Tener en casa (guests, workmen). | — *To have it in for s.o.*, tenerla tomada con alguien. | *To have it in one*, ser capaz de [hacer algo]. || ***To have on***, llevar, tener: *to have a coat on*, llevar un abrigo. | Poner en (to bet). | — *To have nothing on*, estar desnudo (to be naked), no tener nada sobre (to have no information about), no ser nada comparado con (to be nothing compared to), no tener nada que hacer (to have nothing to do). | FAM. *To have s.o. on*, tomar el pelo a alguien. | *To have sth. on*, estar vestido (to be dressed), tener algo sobre (to possess information), tener un compromiso (to have a prior engagement). || ***To have out***, hacer salir. | — *To have a tooth out*, arrancarse una muela, sacarse una muela. | FAM. *To have it out with*, poner las cosas en claro con. | *To have one's appendix out*, operarse de apendicitis. | *To have one's tonsils out*, operarse de amígdalas. || ***To have up***, hacer venir, invitar (guests). | Llevar ante los tribunales (for a crime, etc.). | Hacer levantarse (to make get up).

— OBSERV. Cuando el verbo *to have* significa "to possess" va seguido muy frecuentemente en el habla corriente por el participio pasivo "got" sin que sea modificado el sentido (*I have got a house*, tengo una casa).
— El pretérito y el participio pasivo de este verbo son irregulares (***had***) así como la tercera persona del singular del presente de indicativo (***has***).

haven [ˈheivn] n. MAR. Abrigo (*m.*) natural, abra, *f.* (small natural harbour). || FIG. Refugio, *m.* (shelter).
have-not [hævnɔt] n. Pobre, *m.*
haven't [ˈhævnt] contraction of *have not*.
haversack [ˈhævəsæk] n. Mochila, *f.*
having [ˈhæviŋ] n. Posesión, *f.* || — Pl. Haber, *m. sing.*, bienes, *m.*, fortuna, *f. sing.*
havoc [ˈhævək] n. Estragos, *m. pl.*: *to make havoc of* o *to play havoc with*, hacer estragos en.
haw [hɔː] n. ZOOL. Membrana (*f.*) nictitante. || BOT. Baya (*f.*) del espino (berry). | Espino, *m.* (hawthorn). || Vacilación (*f.*) al hablar, carraspeo, *m.*
— Interj. ¡Ria! (to horse).
Hawaii [hɑːˈwaiiː] pr. n. GEOGR. Hawai.
Hawaiian [hɑːˈwaiiən] adj./n. Hawaiano, na. || MUS. *Hawaiian guitar*, guitarra hawaiana.
haw-haw [ˈhɔːhɔː] n. Risa (*f.*) estúpida, carcajada, *f.*
hawk [hɔːk] n. Halcón, *m.* (bird). || Esparavel, *m.* (plasterer's). || Carraspeo, *m.* (cough). || FIG. Buitre, *m.* || — FIG. *Hawks and doves*, halcones y palomas. || *Hawk nose*, nariz aguileña.

hawk [hɔ:k] v. tr. Vender de puerta en puerta (to sell from door to door). || Pregonar, vender por las calles (to peddle in the streets by shouting). || — *To hawk about*, difundir, propalar (news). || *To hawk up*, expectorar, arrojar tosiendo (to cough up).
— V. intr. Carraspear (to cough). || Ser vendedor ambulante (to be a hawker). || SP. Cazar con halcón (in hunting).
hawker [—ə*] n. Vendedor ambulante (seller). || Cetrero, *m.*, halconero, *m.* (falconer).
hawk-eyed [—aid] adj. Con ojos de lince.
hawking [—iŋ] n. Halconería, *f.* (hunting). || MED. Carraspeo, *m.* || Venta (*f.*) ambulante.
hawkmoth [—mɔθ] n. ZOOL. Esfinge, *f.*
hawk-nosed [—nəuzd] adj. De nariz aguileña.
hawse [hɔ:z] n. MAR. Escobén, *m.* (hawsehole).
hawsehole [—həul] n. MAR. Escobén, *m.*
hawser [ˈhɔ:zə*] n. MAR. Guindaleza, *f.*
hawthorn [ˈhɔ:θɔ:n] n. BOT. Espino, *m.*
hay [hei] n. BOT. Heno, *m.*: *to make hay*, hacer heno. || — FIG. *Make hay while the sun shines*, a la ocasión la pintan calva. || FAM. *To hit the hay*, irse al catre, irse a la piltra (to go to bed). || FIG. *To make hay of sth.*, enredar algo (to mix up), echar algo abajo *or* por tierra (an argument).
hay [hei] v. tr. Secar [hierba] (to dry grass). || Echar forraje a (to feed).
— V. intr. Hacer heno, henificar.
haycock [—kɔk] n. Montón (*m.*) de heno, almiar, *m.*
hay fever [—ˌfi:və*] n. MED. Fiebre (*f.*) del heno.
hayfield [—fi:ld] n. Henar, *m.*
hayfork [—fɔ:k] n. AGR. Bieldo, *m.*
hayloft [—lɔft] n. Henil, *m.*
haymaking [—ˈmeikiŋ] n. AGR. Siega (*f.*) del heno, henificación, *f.*
hayrack [—ræk] n. Pesebre, *m.*
hayrick [—rik] n. Almiar, *m.*
hayseed [—si:d] n. U. S. FAM. Paleto, *m.*, cateto, *m.*
haystack [—stæk] n. Almiar, *m.* || FIG. *To look for a needle in a haystack*, buscar una aguja en un pajar.
haywire [ˈ—waiə*] adj. FAM. Estropeado, da (out of order). | Desorganizado, da (mixed-up). | Chalado, da; loco, ca (mad). || FAM. *To go haywire*, estropearse (machine, etc.), desorganizarse (plan, etc.), volverse loco (person).
— N. Alambre (*m.*) para atar el heno.
hazard [ˈhæzəd] n. Peligro, *m.*, riesgo, *m.* (risk): *to run the hazard*, correr el riesgo. || Azar, *m.* (chance). || SP. Servicio (*m.*) ganador (tennis). | Obstáculo, *m.* (golf). | Tronera, *f.* (billiards). || — *At all hazards*, cueste lo que cueste. || *At hazard*, en juego.
hazard [ˈhæzəd] v. tr. Arriesgar, poner en peligro (to endanger). || Aventurar (a guess).
hazardous [—əs] adj. Arriesgado, da; peligroso, sa; aventurado, da.
haze [heiz] n. Neblina, *f.* (of vapour). || FIG. Confusión, *f.*, vaguedad, *f.*
haze [heiz] v. tr. MAR. Agobiar de faenas. || U. S. Dar una novatada a (a new student).
hazel [ˈheizl] n. BOT. Avellano, *m.* (tree).
— Adj. De avellano. || *Hazel eyes*, ojos (*m.*) color de avellana.
hazelnut [—nʌt] n. Avellana, *f.* (fruit).
haziness [ˈheizinis] n. Nebulosidad, *f.* || FIG. Nebulosidad, *f.*, vaguedad, *f.*
hazy [ˈheizi] adj. Nebuloso, sa. || FIG. Nebuloso, sa; confuso, sa; vago, ga (vague, obscure). | Vago, ga (indefinite). || FAM. Achispado, da (tipsy). || FIG. *I'm hazy about Latin*, tengo unos conocimientos muy vagos de latín.
he [hi:] pron. Él: *I don't sing but he does*, no canto pero él sí. || *He who*, el que, quien: *he who believes in God*, el que crea en Dios.
— Adj. Macho: *he-goat*, macho cabrío.
— N. Macho, *m.* (animal). || Hombre, *m.*, varón, *m.* (man).
— OBSERV. A diferencia del pronombre *él*, el pronombre inglés *he* sólo se emplea para personas, no para cosas.
head [hed] n. Cabeza, *f.* (part of body): *my head hurts*, me duele la cabeza. || Cabeza, *f.* (of procession, axe, etc.): *I was at the head of the list*, estaba en cabeza de la lista. || Jefe, *m.*, cabeza, *m.* (chief): *head of the family*, cabeza de familia. || Director, ra (of school, etc.): *he was the head of the organization*, era el director de la organización. || Nacimiento, *m.*, cabecera, *f.* (of river). || Cabecera, *f.* (of bed, table). || Cabecero, *m.* (headboard of a bed). || Espuma, *f.* (of beer). || Nata, *f.* (of milk). || MIN. Frente, *m.* || Cara, *f.* (of a coin). || Punta, *f.* (of arrow, spear). || Cotillo, *m.* (of hammer). || Tapa, *f.* (of cask). || Cabeza, *f.* (of nail, pin): *nails with larger heads*, clavos con la cabeza más grande. || Puño, *m.* (of stick). || Proa, *f.* (of ship). || Altura (*f.*) de caída (of water). || Presión, *f.* (of steam). || Cabeza, *f.* (of bridge). || Parte (*f.*) superior (of column). || GEOGR. Punta, *f.* (headland). || Cabeza, *f.*, res, *f.* (of cattle). || Asta, *f.* (of deer). || Cogollo, *m.* (of cabbage). || Copa, *f.* (of tree). || Cabezuela, *f.* (of flowers). || Cabeza, *f.* (of asparagus, garlic). || Espiga, *f.* (of corn). || Culata, *f.* (of cylinder). || Cabeza, *f.*, persona, *f.*: *a dollar a head*, un dólar por cabeza. || Encabezamiento, *m.* (of a chapter). || Título, *m.* (on a newspaper). || Capítulo, *m.*, sección, *f.*, rúbrica, *f.* (section). || Punto, *m.* (point). || Principio, *m.*: *begin at the head of the page*, empiece por el principio de la página. || MUS. Parche, *m.* (of a drum). || Cabeza, *f.* (of tape recorder): *recording, playback, erasing head*, cabeza sonora, auditiva, supresora. || Cabezal, *m.* (of a lathe). || MIL. Ojiva, *f.*, cabeza, *f.* (of a missile). || MAR. Gratil, *m.* (of sails). || Cuerpo, *m.* (of bell). || Facilidad, *f.*, aptitud, *f.*, cabeza, *f.*: *a good head for figures*, una gran facilidad para los números. || Cabeza, *f.*, inteligencia, *f.*, (intelligence). || Punto (*m.*) decisivo *or* crítico, culminación, *f.*: *things are coming to a head*, las cosas llegan a un punto crítico. || U. S. FAM. Retrete, *m.* || — *At the head of*, a la cabeza de. || *By a head*, por una cabeza. || *Crowned head*, testa coronada. || *From head to foot*, de pies a cabeza, de arriba abajo. || *Head down*, con la cabeza baja. || *Head first*, de cabeza. || *Head of department*, jefe de servicio. || *Head of hair*, pelo, *m.*, cabellera, *f.* || *Head of state*, jefe de Estado. || *Head on*, de frente. || *Heads I win, tails you lose*, cara o cruz. || *Head wind*, viento (*m.*) en contra. || FIG. *He can do it standing on his head*, lo puede hacer con los ojos cerrados. || *He is a head taller than I*, me saca la cabeza. || FIG. *He is head and shoulders above me*, me aventaja en mucho. | *I can't make head or tail of this*, esto no tiene ni pies ni cabeza (I don't understand). | *Mary is head over heels in love with me*, María anda de cabeza por mí, María está locamente enamorada de mí. | *Not to lift one's head*, no levantar cabeza. | *On your own head be it*, ¡allá tú! | *Out of his own head*, de su propia cosecha. | *Over one's head*, fuera del alcance de uno (a subject), por encima de uno, sin avisar a uno. || *The lettuce is a shilling a head*, cada lechuga cuesta un chelín. || FIG. *They put their heads together*, se consultaron entre sí, cambiaron impresiones. | *To act* o *to go over s.o.'s head*, actuar a espaldas de alguien. | *To beat one's head against a brick wall*, darse de cabeza contra la pared. || *To be at the head of*, estar al frente de (troops), encabezar, estar al principio *or* en cabeza de (a list). || FIG. *To be hanging over one's head*, estar pendiente de un hilo. || FAM. *To be off* o *out of one's head*, estar loco, estar chalado, haber perdido el juicio *or* la cabeza. || FIG. *To be on s.o.'s head*, estar bajo la responsabilidad de uno. || FAM. *To be weak* o *soft in the head*, andar mal de la cabeza, estar mal de la cabeza. | *To bite s.o.'s head off*, echar una bronca a alguien. || FIG. *To bother one's head about*, preocuparse por. | *To bring sth. to a head*, llevar algo a un punto decisivo. | *To come into one's head*, pasarle a uno por la cabeza. || *To come to a head*, abrirse (abscess), llegar a un punto decisivo. || FAM. *To eat one's head off*, comer como una lima *or* como un sabañón. || FIG. *To enter s.o.'s head*, pasarle a uno por la cabeza. | *To gather head*, cobrar fuerzas. | *To get it into one's head to do*, metérsele a uno en la cabeza hacer. | *To get sth. through s.o.'s head*, meter algo en la cabeza de alguien. | *To give a horse its head*, dar rienda suelta a un caballo. | *To give s.o. his head*, dejar a alguien obrar a su antojo. | *To go head and shoulders into*, meterse de cabeza en. || *To go head over heels*, dar una voltereta (to somersault), caer patas arriba (to fall). || FAM. *To go off* o *out of one's head*, perder el juicio *or* la cabeza. || *To go straight out of s.o.'s head*, irsele a uno de la cabeza. || FIG. *To go to one's head*, subírsele a la cabeza. | *To hang* o *to hide one's head*, caérsele a uno la cara de vergüenza. || *To have a bad head*, tener dolor de cabeza. || FIG. *To have a good head on one's shoulders*, ser capaz *or* inteligente. | *To have one's head screwed on*, tener la cabeza en su sitio. | *To hit the nail on the head*, dar en el clavo, acertar. | *To keep one's head*, no perder la cabeza. | *To keep one's head above water*, mantenerse a flote. | *To knock on the head*, dar al traste con. | *To laugh one's head off*, reír a mandíbula batiente. | *To lay* o *to put heads together*, colaborar. | *To lose one's head*, perder la cabeza. | *To make head*, hacer progresos. | *To make heads turn*, hacer volver la cabeza, atraer mucho la atención. || *To nod one's head*, asentir con la cabeza. || *To put a price on s.o.'s head*, poner la cabeza de uno a precio. || FIG. *To put it into s.o.'s head*, metérselo en la cabeza a alguien. | *To put out of one's head*, quitarse de la cabeza, dejar de pensar en. || MATH. *To reckon in one's head*, calcular mentalmente. || *To shake one's head*, negar con la cabeza. || FIG. *To speak over the head of*, no ponerse al alcance de. || *To stand on one's head*, hacer el pino. || FIG. *To take it into one's head to do sth.*, metérsele a uno en la cabeza hacer algo. || FIG. *To talk one's head off*, hablar por los codos. || *To talk s.o.'s head off*, poner la cabeza bomba a alguien. || *To toss for sth. heads or tails*, echar algo a cara o cruz. || FIG. *To turn s.o.'s head*, subírsele a la cabeza a uno. | *Two heads are better than one*, cuatro ojos ven más que dos. | *Use your head*, reflexione un poco. | *We took it into our heads to*, se nos ocurrió.
— Adj. Principal. || Delantero, ra. || *Head post office*, casa (*f.*) de correos.
head [hed] v. tr. Encabezar: *to head a demonstration*, encabezar una manifestación; *his name heads the list*, su nombre encabeza la lista; *the date heads the letter*, la fecha encabeza la carta. || Ir en cabeza de (to precede). || Estar a la cabeza de: *the girl heads her class at school*, la muchacha está a la cabeza de su clase en la escuela. || Dirigir, estar a la cabeza de (a

firm, etc.). || Coronar: *the spire heads the tower*, la aguja corona la torre. || Titular (to entitle). || Desmochar (to cut the head off): *to head a tree*, desmochar un árbol. || Poner tapa a (a cask). || Conducir, llevar: *they headed the herd into a valley*, condujeron el ganado a un valle. || Bordear, dar la vuelta a (a cape, etc.). || SP. Dar un cabezazo a, cabecear (the ball). | Meter de cabeza (a goal). || — *To head back*, ojear (game), cortar la retirada a (the enemy). || *To head off*, cortar el paso a, interceptar el camino a (s.o.), desviar (a question), disuadir (from doing sth.). || MAR. *To head the ship for*, hacer rumbo a.

— V. intr. *To head for*, dirigirse hacia (to move forward), hacer rumbo a (a ship). || *To head for ruin*, ir a la ruina.

headache [—eik] n. Dolor (*m.*) de cabeza. || FIG. Quebradero (*m.*) de cabeza.

headband [—bænd] n. Cinta, *f.* (for the hair). || Casco, *m.* (of earphones). || PRINT. Cabecera, *f.*

headboard [—bɔ:d] n. Cabecero, *m.* (of a bed).

headcheese [—tʃi:z] n. U. S. Queso (*m.*) de cerdo.

headdress [—dres] n. Tocado, *m.*

headed [—id] adj. Con membrete (paper). || BOT. Repolludo, da (cabbage). || — *Black-headed*, de pelo negro (person), de cabeza negra (animal). || *Two-headed*, bicéfalo, la.

header [ə*] n. Salto (*m.*) de cabeza (dive headfirst). || Caída (*f.*) de cabeza (fall). || ARCH. Tizón, *m.* || SP. Cabezazo, *m.* (in football). || *To take a header*, caerse de cabeza.

headfirst [—'fə:st] adv. De cabeza.

headframe [—freim] n. Castillete (*m.*) de extracción (of a mine).

headgear [—giə*] n. Tocado, *m.* (headdress).

headhunter [—ˌhʌntə*] n. Cazador (*m.*) de cabezas.

heading [—iŋ] n. Encabezamiento, *m.*, título, *m.* (of a chapter). || Membrete, *m.* (of a letter). || Breve introducción, *f.* (introductory paragraph). || Rúbrica, *f.*, apartado, *m.* (section). || SP. Cabezazo, *m.* || MAR. AVIAT. Rumbo, *m.*, orientación, *f.*

head lamp [—læmp] n. AUT. Faro, *m.* || Farol, *m.* (of locomotive).

headland [—lænd] n. GEOGR. Punta, *f.*, promontorio, *m.*, cabo, *m.*

headless [—lis] adj. Sin cabeza (body, nail). || ZOOL. Acéfalo, la. || FIG. Sin cabeza, sin jefe. | Sin cabeza, tonto, ta (foolish).

headlight [—lait] n. AUT. Faro, *m.* || Farol, *m.* (of locomotive).

headline [—lain] n. Título, *m.* (in a book). || Titular, *m.* (in a newspaper). || MAR. Rebenque, *m.* || — *To hit the headlines*, ser pasto de la actualidad. || *To make the headlines*, estar en primera plana.

headlong [—lɔŋ] adj. De cabeza (with the head foremost). || Precipitado, da (hasty). || Impetuoso, sa (impetuous). || Escarpado, da (cliffs).

— Adv. De cabeza (headfirst). || Precipitadamente (hastily).

headman [—'mæn] n. Jefe, *m.*

— OBSERV. El plural de esta palabra es *headmen*.

headmaster [—'mɑ:stə*] n. Director, *m.*

headmistress [—'mistris] n. Directora, *f.*

headmost [—məust] adj. Primero, ra.

head-on [—'ɔn] adj./adv. De frente.

headphones [—fəunz] pl. n. Auriculares, *m.* [*Amer.*, audífonos, *m.*]

headpiece [—ˌpi:s] n. Yelmo, *m.* || PRINT. Cabecera, *f.*

headquarters [—'kwɔ:təz] pl. n. MIL. Cuartel (*m. sing.*) general. || Oficina (*f. sing.*) central (main office). || Sede, *f. sing.* (of an organization). || Domicilio (*m. sing.*) social (of a firm). || FIG. Centro (*m. sing.*) de operaciones, cuartel (*m. sing.*) general.

headrest [—rest] n. Cabecero, *m.*, cabezal, *m.*

headroom [—rum] n. Altura (*f.*) libre (under a bridge).

headset [—set] n. Auriculares, *m. pl.* [*Amer.*, audífonos, *m. pl.*].

headship [—ʃip] n. Dirección, *f.*

headshrinker [—ʃriŋkə*] n. Reductor (*m.*) de cabezas. || FAM. Psiquiatra, *m.*

headsman [—zmæn] n. Verdugo, *m.*

— OBSERV. El plural de esta palabra es *headsmen*.

headspring [—spriŋ] n. Fuente, *f.*, manantial, *m.* (of a river).

headstall [—stɔ:l] n. Jáquima, *f.*

headstock [—stɔk] n. TECH. Contrapunta, *f.*

headstone [—stəun] n. Lápida (*f.*) mortuoria (tombstone). || ARCH. Piedra (*f.*) angular.

headstream [—stri:m] n. Arroyo (*m.*) que constituye el nacimiento de un río.

headstrong [—strɔŋ] adj. Voluntario, ria; testarudo, da.

head voice [—vɔis] n. MUS. Falsete, *m.*

headwaiter [—weitə*] n. Jefe (*m.*) de comedor, « maître », *m.*

headwaters [—'wɔ:təz] pl. n. Cabecera, *f. sing.*

headway [—wei] n. Progreso, *m.* (progress). || Salida, *f.* (of a ship). || Altura (*f.*) libre (headroom). || *To make headway*, hacer progresos (to make progress), avanzar (to move forward).

headword [—wə:d] n. Encabezamiento, *m.*

headwork [—wə:k] n. Trabajo (*m.*) mental.

heady [—i] adj. Embriagador, ra (intoxicating). || Fuerte (wine). || Vertiginoso, sa: *the heady heights*, las alturas vertiginosas. || FIG. Impetuoso, sa. | Sensato, ta (judicious).

heal [hi:l] v. tr. Curar (a disease, a patient). || Cicatrizar, curar (a wound). || FIG. Curar, remediar. || FIG. *To heal the breach between two people*, reconciliar a dos personas.

— V. intr. Cicatrizarse (wounds). || Curarse, sanar (people). || FIG. Remediarse.

healable [—əbl] adj. Curable.

heal-all [—ɔ:l] n. Panacea, *f.*

healer [—ə*] n. Curador, ra.

healing [—iŋ] adj. Cicatrizante (ointment). || Curativo, va (remedy).

— N. Curación, *f.* (of disease). || Cicatrización, *f.* (of wound).

health [helθ] n. Salud, *f.* || Sanidad, *f.*: *public health*, sanidad pública. || — *Good health!*, ¡salud! || *Health certificate*, certificado médico. || *Health measures*, medidas sanitarias. || *Health officer*, inspector (*m.*) de sanidad. || *Health resort*, balneario, *m.* || *Ministry of Health*, Dirección (*f.*) General de Sanidad. || *To be in bad, in good health*, estar bien, mal de salud. || *To drink s.o.'s health*, beber a la salud de alguien. || *To your health!*, ¡a tu salud!

healthful [—ful] adj. Saludable, sano, na.

healthiness [—inis] n. Salubridad, *f.*

healthy [—i] adj. Sano, na (in good health). || Sano, na; saludable: *a healthy climate*, un clima sano. || Salubre (salubrious). || Considerable (part). || Favorable (impression). || Bueno, na: *healthy appetite*, buen apetito. || Sano, na (sound). || *To have a healthy look*, estar rebosante de salud.

heap [hi:p] n. Montón, *m.*: *a heap of rubbish*, un montón de basura; *a heap of troubles*, un montón de problemas. || — U. S. *A whole heap of*, un montón de, montones de. || *Heaps of*, un montón de, montones de. || FAM. *To be struck all of a heap*, quedarse pasmado.

heap [hi:p] v. tr. Amontonar. || Colmar, llenar (a dish). || FIG. Colmar de (praises, etc.). || — *A heaped spoonful*, una cucharada colmada. || *To heap up*, amontonar.

hear* [hiə*] v. tr. Oír: *he heard my voice*, oyó mi voz; *he heard me coming*, me oyó venir. || Escuchar: *she refused to hear me*, se negó a escucharme. || Recibir: *I can't hear you now*, no puedo recibirle ahora. || Tomar: *to hear a child's lesson*, tomar la lección a un niño. || Asistir a (lectures). || Saber, enterarse de (a piece of news). || JUR. Ver (a case). | Oír (a witness, defendant). || MUS. RAD. Escuchar. || — *I have heard he is ill*, me han dicho que está enfermo, he oído decir que está enfermo. || U. S. *I hear you talking*, estoy completamente de acuerdo con lo que Ud. dice. || *To be heard*, oírse. || *To hear confession*, confesar. || *To hear Mass*, oír misa. || *To hear out*, escuchar hasta el final.

— V. intr. Oír: *I can hear you, I'm not deaf*, le oigo, no soy sordo. || — *Hear, hear!*, ¡muy bien! || *He won't hear of it*, no quiere oír hablar de ello. || *Let me hear from you*, escríbame, déme noticias suyas. || *To hear about*, oír hablar de (to listen to), saber, enterarse de (to know). || *To hear from*, tener noticias de, saber: *I heard from her yesterday*, tuve noticias de ella ayer. || *To hear of*, tener noticias de (to learn of), saber, enterarse de (to be informed of), oír hablar de: *I never heard of such a thing*, nunca oí hablar de tal cosa. || FAM. *You will hear of it!*, ¡ya verás lo que es bueno!, ¡ya oirás hablar de esto!

— OBSERV. Pret. & p. p. ***heard***

heard [hə:d] pret. & p. p. See HEAR.

hearer ['hiərə*] n. Oyente, *m.* & *f.* || — Pl. Auditorio, *m. sing.*

hearing ['hiəriŋ] n. Oído, *m.* (sense). || Audición, *f.* (act of hearing): *the hearing of a sound*, la audición de un sonido. || JUR. Audición, *f.* (of witnesses). | Audiencia, *f.*, vista, *f.* (of a case). || MUS. Audición, *f.* || — *Hard of hearing*, duro de oído. || *In s.o.'s hearing*, en presencia de alguien. || *Out of hearing*, fuera del alcance del oído. || *To come to s.o.'s hearing*, llegar a oídos de alguien, llegar al conocimiento de uno. || *To give s.o. a fair hearing*, escuchar a alguien imparcialmente. || *To refuse s.o. a hearing*, negarse a escuchar a alguien. || *Within hearing*, al alcance del oído.

hearing aid [—eid] n. Aparato (*m.*) para sordos.

hearken ['hɑ:kən] v. intr. *To hearken to*, escuchar (to listen).

hearsay ['hiəsei] n. Rumor, *m.* || *To know sth. by hearsay* o *from hearsay*, saber algo de oídas.

hearse [hə:s] n. Coche (*m.*) fúnebre.

heart [hɑ:t] n. ANAT. Corazón, *m.*: *heart transplant*, transplante de corazón. || FIG. Corazón, *m.*: *she has a kind heart*, tiene buen corazón; *he went off with a heavy heart*, se fue con el corazón encogido. | Fondo, *m.* (of a matter). | Centro, *m.*, corazón, *m.* (of a place). | Centro, *m.*, casco, *m.*, corazón, *m.* (of a city). | Ánimo, *m.*, corazón, *m.* (courage). || Corazón, *m.* (of a fruit, etc.). || Cogollo, *m.* (of lettuce). || AGR. Estado, *m.* (of the soil). || — Pl. Corazones, *m.* (in cards): *the eight of hearts*, el ocho de corazones. | Copas, *f.* (in Spanish cards). || — *At heart*, en el fondo. || *By heart*, de memoria. || FIG. *Change of heart*, cambio (*m.*) de parecer. || FAM. *Dear heart!*, ¡amor mío! || *From one's heart*, de todo corazón. || *From* *the bottom of my heart*, de todo corazón. || *Have a heart!*, ¡ten piedad! || *Heart and soul*, con toda el alma, en cuerpo y alma. || MED. *Heart attack*, ataque (*m.*) al corazón. | *Heart disease*, enfermedad (*f.*) cardiaca *or* del corazón. | *Heart failure*, colapso, *m.* || *Heart of the matter*, meollo (*m.*) de la cuestión. || *Heart of oak*, valiente, *m.* || *Heart to heart*, franco, ca. || *In one's heart*, en el fondo [del corazón]. || *In one's heart of hearts*, en lo más recóndito de su corazón. || *In the heart of winter*, en pleno invierno. || *My heart missed*, se me encogió el corazón. || *My heart sank*, se me cayó el alma a los pies. || *Not to have the heart to do sth.*, no tener corazón *or* valor para hacer algo. || *Out of heart*, desanimado, da; descorazonado, da. || *Set your heart at rest*, no se preocupe, tranquilícese. || *To appeal to the heart*, hablar al corazón. || *To be good at heart*, tener buen corazón. || *To be in no heart for laughing*, no tener ganas de reír. || *To break s.o.'s heart*, partirle el corazón a uno. || *To cry one's heart out*, llorar a lágrima viva. || *To die of a broken heart*, morirse de pena. || *To do one's heart good*, alegrarle a uno. || *To eat one's heart out*, consumirse (with grief, remorse, etc.). || *To get straight to the heart of the matter*, ir al grano. || *To get to the heart of*, entrar en el fondo de. || *To give one's heart to*, dar su corazón a. || *To have a change of heart*, cambiar de opinión. || *To have a heart of gold*, tener un corazón que se sale del pecho, tener un corazón de oro. || *To have at heart*, tomar a pecho. || *To have heart trouble*, padecer del corazón. || *To have no heart*, no tener corazón. || *To have one's heart in one's boots*, estar con *or* tener el alma en un hilo. || *To have one's heart in one's mouth*, tener el alma en un hilo, tener el corazón en un puño. || *To have one's heart in one's work*, poner toda su alma en el trabajo. || *To have one's heart in the right place*, tener buen corazón. || *To lose heart*, descorazonarse, desanimarse. || *To lose one's heart to*, enamorarse de, dar su corazón a. || *To one's heart delight* o *content*, hasta quedarse satisfecho. || *To open one's heart to*, abrir su pecho a. || *To set one's heart on doing*, poner todo su afán en hacer. || *To take heart*, cobrar ánimo. || *To take sth. to heart*, tomar algo a pecho. || *To wear one's heart on one's sleeve*, llevar el corazón en la mano. || *To win s.o.'s heart*, enamorar a alguien. || *With all one's heart*, con toda su alma (to love), de todo corazón (to say). || *With half a heart*, sin entusiasmo. || *You're a man after my own heart*, eres un hombre de los que me gustan.

heartache [—eik] n. Angustia, *f.*, pesar, *m.*, pena, *f.*, congoja, *f.*

heartbeat [—bi:t] n. Latido (*m.*) del corazón.

heartbreak [—breik] n. Congoja, *f.*, angustia, *f.*

heartbreaking [—ˈbreikiŋ] adj. Desgarrador, ra; que parte el corazón.

heartbroken [ˌbrəukən] adj. *To be heartbroken*, tener el corazón destrozado *or* desgarrado (to be overwhelmed with grief). || *To be heartbroken about sth.*, sentir mucho algo, lamentar algo.

heartburn [—bə:n] n. MED. Acedía, *f.*

heartburning [—bə:niŋ] n. Envidia, *f.* (jealousy). || Rencor, *m.* (rancour). || Descontento *m.* (discontent).

hearten [ˈhɑ:tn] v. tr. Animar, alentar.

heartfelt [ˈhɑ:tfelt] adj. Sincero, ra; sentido, da.

hearth [—hɑ:θ] n. Hogar, *m.* || FIG. Hogar, *m.*: *without hearth or home*, sin casa ni hogar. || TECH. Crisol, *m.* (of blast furnace). | Solera, *f.* (of reverberatory furnace).

hearthstone [—stəun] n. Piedra (*f.*) de la chimenea. || Blanco (*m.*) de España (for cleaning). || U. S. Hogar, *m.* (home).

heartily [ˈhɑ:tili] adv. Cordialmente (warmly). || Sinceramente (sincerely). || De buena gana (to eat, to laugh). || Completamente (fully): *I heartily agree with you*, estoy completamente de acuerdo con Ud.

heartiness [ˈhɑ:tinis] n. Cordialidad, *f.* (warmth). || Sinceridad, *f.* (sincerity). || Entusiasmo, *m.* (enthusiasm). || Campechanía, *f.* (friendliness of a person).

heartless [ˈhɑ:tlis] adj. Despiadado, da; cruel, sin corazón, inhumano, na.

heartlessness [ˈhɑ:tlisnis] n. Crueldad, *f.*, inhumanidad, *f.*, falta (*f.*) de humanidad.

heartrending [ˈhɑ:tˌrendiŋ] adj. Desgarrador, ra: *a heartrending cry*, un grito desgarrador. || Conmovedor, ra (moving).

heart-searching [ˈhɑ:tˌsə:tʃiŋ] n. Examen (*m.*) de conciencia.

heartsease [ˈhɑ:tsi:z] n. BOT. Trinitaria, *f.* || FIG. Sosiego, *m.*, serenidad, *f.*

heartsick [ˈhɑ:tsik] adj. Desanimado, da. || FAM. *Heartsick lover*, enamorado perdido.

heartsickness [ˈhɑ:tsiknis] n. Desconsuelo, *m.*, descorazonamiento, *m.*

heartstrings [ˈhɑ:tstriŋz] pl. n. *To play on s.o.'s heartstrings*, tocarle la fibra sensible a uno.

heart-to-heart [ˈhɑ:təˈhɑ:t] adj. Franco, ca; sincero, ra (candid). || *To have a heart-to-heart talk with s.o.*, tener una conversación íntima con alguien.

heart-whole [ˈhɑ:thəul] adj. Libre (not in love). || Sincero, ra (sincere). || Que no ha perdido ánimo (undismayed).

heartwood [ˈhɑ:twud] n. BOT. Duramen, *m.*

hearty [ˈhɑ:ti] adj. Cordial (cordial): *a hearty welcome*, una cordial bienvenida. || Sincero, ra (sincere). || Campechano, na (good-hearted, cheerful). || Robusto, ta; sano, na (strong and healthy). || Fuerte, enérgico, ca (vigorous). || Abundante (meal). || Bueno, na (appetite). || Fértil (land). || FAM. *To be a hearty eater*, tener un buen saque.

— N. MAR. Compañero, *m.*

heat [hi:t] n. Calor, *m.*: *specific heat*, calor específico; *blistering heat*, calor abrasador. || Calefacción, *f.*: *the heat should be turned off*, habría que apagar la calefacción. || FIG. Calor, *m.*: *in the heat of the battle, of the argument*, en el calor de la batalla, de la discusión. | Pasión, *f.* (passion). || ZOOL. Celo, *m.*: *on heat*, en celo. || SP. Eliminatoria, *f.*, serie, *f.* || MED. Mancha (*f.*) roja (on the skin). || — *Dead heat*, empate, *m.* || FIG. *To get into a heat*, acalorarse. || *To heat sth. to red heat*, calentar algo al rojo, poner algo al rojo. || U. S. FAM. *To turn the heat on*, ejercer una presión sobre.

— Adj. De calor: *heat exchanger*, cambiador de calor; *heat wave*, ola de calor. || Térmico, ca: *heat energy*, energía térmica; *heat engine*, motor térmico. || — *Heat lightning*, fucilazo, *m.*, relámpago (*m.*) de calor. || *Heat rash*, sarpullido, *m.*

heat [hi:t] v. tr. Calentar. || FIG. Acalorar.

— V. intr. Calentarse. || FIG. Acalorarse.

heated [—id] adj. Acalorado, da (argument, etc.). || Caliente (air). || *To get heated*, acalorarse.

heater [—ə*] n. Calentador, *m.* (stove, furnace). || Radiador, *m.* (radiator). || ELECTR. Filamento, *m.* || U. S. POP. Revólver, *m.*, pistola, *f.* (pistol).

heath [hi:θ] n. BOT. Brezo, *m.* (plant). || Brezal, *m.* (land). || Terreno (*m.*) baldío (uncultivated land).

heathen [ˈhi:ðən] adj./n. Pagano, na. || FIG. Salvaje (ill-mannered person). || *The heathen*, los paganos.

heathendom [—dəm] n. Paganos, *m. pl.*

heathenish [ˈhi:ðəniʃ] adj. Pagano, na. || FIG. Bárbaro, ra; salvaje.

heathenism [ˈhi:ðənizəm] n. Paganismo, *m.* || FIG. Barbarie, *f.*

heathenize [ˈhi:ðənaiz] v. tr. Paganizar.

heather [ˈheðə*] n. BOT. Brezo, *m.*

heathery [—ri] or **heathy** [ˈhi:θi] adj. Cubierto de brezos.

heating [ˈhi:tiŋ] adj. De caldeo: *heating surface*, superficie de caldeo. || Calorífico, ca: *heating power*, potencia calorífica. || Calentador, ra (warming).

— N. Calefacción, *f.*: *central heating*, calefacción central. || Calentamiento, *m.*

heat-resistant [ˈhi:triˈzistənt] adj. Resistente al calor, calorífugo, ga.

heatstroke [ˈhi:tstrəuk] n. MED. Insolación, *f.*

heave [hi:v] n. Gran esfuerzo, *m.* [para levantar] (big effort). || Tirón, *m.* (pull). || Empujón, *m.* (push). || Movimiento, *m.*, agitación, *f.* (of waves). || Palpitación, *f.* (of the breast). || Náusea, *f.* (nausea). || GEOL. Desplazamiento (*m.*) lateral. || — Pl. VET. Huélfago, *m. sing.*

heave* [hi:v] v. tr. Tirar de (to pull). || Empujar (to push). || Levantar (to lift). || Exhalar (a sigh). || Arrojar, tirar, lanzar (to throw). || MAR. Levantar (the anchor). || GEOL. Desplazar lateralmente.

— V. intr. Subir y bajar (waves). || Levantarse (road). || Palpitar (breast). || Tener náuseas (to retch). || Jadear (to pant). || MAR. Virar. || — MAR. *To heave at*, halar de (a rope). | *To heave back*, soltar. | *To heave in sight*, aparecer. | *To heave off*, hacerse a la mar. | *To heave out*, largar las velas. | *To heave to*, ponerse al pairo, pairar.

— OBSERV. Cuando *to heave* significa "levantar, tirar, empujar, etc.", se aplica siempre a objetos pesados e indica la necesidad de un gran esfuerzo.
— Cuando tiene un sentido marítimo, *to heave* tiene un pretérito y un participio pasivo irregulares (**hove**).

heaven [ˈhevn] n. Cielo, *m.*: *to go to heaven*, ir al cielo. || FIG. Gloria, *f.* (sensation): *this is heaven*, esto es [la] gloria. | Paraíso, *m.* (place): *this place is heaven*, este sitio es el paraíso. || Dios, *m.*: *Heaven protect you!*, ¡que Dios le guarde! || — Pl. Cielo, *m. sing.* (sky): *the stars shone in the heavens*, las estrellas brillaban en el cielo. || — *By heaven!*, ¡cielos! || *For heaven's sake!*, ¡por amor de Dios!, ¡por Dios! || *Good heavens!*, ¡Dios mío!, ¡madre mía! || *Heaven forbid!*, ¡Dios me *or* te *or* le libre! || *Heaven knows*, sabe Dios, Dios es testigo. || *Thank Heaven!*, ¡gracias a Dios! || FIG. *To be in the seventh heaven*, estar en el séptimo cielo. | *To cry out to heaven*, clamar al cielo. | *To move heaven and earth*, mover cielo y tierra.

heavenly [—li] adj. Celestial. || FIG. Divino, na. || ASTR. Celeste: *heavenly body*, cuerpo celeste.

heaven-sent [—sent] adj. FIG. Llovido del cielo: *a heaven-sent opportunity*, una oportunidad llovida del cielo.

heavenward [—wəd] or **heavenwards** [—wədz] adv. Hacia el cielo.

heaver [ˈhi:və*] n. Cargador, *m.*, descargador, *m.*

heavily [ˈhevili] adv. Pesadamente (to walk, to fall). || Mucho: *to drink heavily*, beber mucho; *to lose heavily*, perder mucho. || Profundamente: *to sigh, to sleep heavily*, suspirar, dormir profundamente. || Con dificultad (to breathe, etc.). || *Heavily damaged*, muy estropeado.

heaviness [ˈhevinis] n. Pesadez, *f.* (of the body). || Peso, *m.* (of a burden). || Pesadez, *f.* (of a meal). || Peso, *m.* (of taxes). || — *Heaviness in the head,* cabeza pesada. || *Heaviness of heart,* tristeza, *f.*

heavy [ˈhevi] adj. Pesado, da: *a heavy suitcase,* una maleta pesada; *a heavy metal,* un metal pesado. || Fuerte (rain, emphasis, meal, scent, storm, waves, blow). || Grande (expense, loss, defeat). || Grueso, sa (line, scar, paper, cloth, cable, sea). || Pesado, da (head, eyes). || Cargado, da; pesado, da (atmosphere). || Pesado, da (weather). || Intenso, sa (electric current). || Espeso, sa; denso, sa (liquid). || Denso, sa (traffic, population). || Abundante (harvest). || Difícil, malo, la (surface): *it was heavy going,* el camino era difícil. || Encapotado, da (sky). || De peso (important). || Duro, ra (strict): *to rule with a heavy hand,* gobernar con mano dura. || Triste (sad). || Oprimido, da (heart). || Malo, la (humour). || Abatido, da; deprimido, da (depressed). || Torpe (clumsy). || Cansado, da (tired). || Profundo, da (sleep, silence, sigh). || Grave, grande (responsibility). || Difícil, penoso, sa (difficult). || Pesado, da (difficult to digest). || Pesado, da (tread). || Pesado, da; lento, ta (slow). || Arcilloso, sa (soil). || Pesado, da (road). || Empinado, da (gradient). || Pesado, da (boring). || Corpulento, ta (stout). || THEATR. Serio, ria (part). || MIL. Pesado, da; grueso, sa (artillery). | Graneado, da (fire). || SP. Pesado, da (weight). || MED. Bueno, na (cold). || CHEM. Pesado, da (hydrogen, oil). || — FIG. *A heavy burden,* una carga pesada. || *An engine which is heavy on petrol,* un motor que consume mucha gasolina. || *Heavy industry,* industria pesada. || PRINT. *Heavy type,* negrita, *f.* || *Heavy water,* agua pesada. || *Heavy with young,* grávida, preñada (animals). || *Is it heavy?,* ¿pesa mucho? || *The air was heavy with smoke,* el aire estaba cargado de humo. || *To be a heavy drinker, eater, smoker,* beber, comer, fumar mucho. || *We've had a heavy day,* hemos tenido un día muy cargado.
— Adv. See HEAVILY. || — *Time hangs heavy on his hands,* se le hace muy largo el tiempo. || *To hang heavy,* transcurrir lentamente (time). || *To lie heavy on one's conscience,* pesarle a uno en la conciencia.
— Pl. n. MIL. Artillería (*f. sing.*) pesada.

heavy-duty [—ˈdju:ti] adj. Para trabajos duros. || Para grandes cargas (lifting devices, etc.).

heavy-handed [—ˈhændid] adj. Severo, ra; autoritario, ria (domineering). || Torpe (clumsy).

heavyhearted [—ˈhɑ:tid] adj. Afligido, da; pesaroso, sa; con el corazón oprimido.

heavyset [—set] n. U. S. Rechoncho, cha (stocky).

heavyweight [—weit] n. SP. Peso (*m.*) pesado. || SP. *Light heavyweight,* peso semipesado.

hebdomadal [hebˈdɔmədl] adj. Semanal, hebdomadario, ria.

hebetate [ˈhebiteit] v. tr. Embrutecer.
— V. intr. Embrutecerse.

hebetude [ˈhebitju:d] n. Embrutecimiento, *m.*

Hebraic [hi:ˈbreiik] adj. Hebraico, ca.

Hebraism [ˈhi:breiizəm] n. Hebraísmo, *m.*

Hebraist [ˈhi:breiist] n. Hebraísta, *m. & f.*; hebraizante, *m. & f.*

Hebrew [ˈhi:bru:] adj. Hebreo, a.
— N. Hebreo, a (people). || Hebreo, *m.* (language).

Hebrides [ˈhebridi:z] pl. pr. n. GEOGR. Hébridas, *f.*

hecatomb [ˈhekətu:m] n. Hecatombe, *f.*

heck [hek] interj. FAM. See HELL.

heckle [ˈhekl] n. Rastrillo, *m.*

heckle [ˈhekl] v. tr. Interrumpir [a un orador] haciendo preguntas molestas. || Rastrillar (flax, hemp).

heckler [—ə*] n. Persona (*f.*) que interrumpe a un orador haciendo preguntas molestas.

hectare [ˈhektɑ:*] n. Hectárea, *f.*

hectic [ˈhektik] adj. Agitado, da; ajetreado, da: *a hectic day,* un día agitado; *a hectic life,* una vida ajetreada. || Febril: *hectic activity,* actividad febril. || MED. Héctico, ca; hético, ca; tísico, ca. || FAM. *Hectic confusion,* barullo, *m.*
— N. Fiebre (*f.*) héctica, tisis, *f.*

hectogramme (U. S. **hectogram**) [ˈhektəugræm] n. Hectogramo, *m.*

hectolitre (U. S. **hectoliter**) [ˈhektəuˌli:tə*] n. Hectolitro, *m.*

hectometre (U. S. **hectometer**) [ˈhektəuˌmi:tə*] n. Hectómetro, *m.*

hector [ˈhektə*] n. Matamoros, *m. inv.*

hector [ˈhektə*] v. tr. Intimidar [con bravatas].
— V. intr. Echar bravatas.

hectowatt [ˈhektəuwɔt] n. ELECTR. Hectovatio, *m.*

heddle [ˈhedəl] n. Lizo, *m.* (of a loom).

hedge [hedʒ] n. Seto, *m.*, seto (*m.*) vivo (of garden, field). || Hilera, *f.*, fila, *f.* (of police). || FIG. Barrera, *f.* (barrier). || *Quickset hedge,* seto vivo.

hedge [hedʒ] v. tr. Cercar (to enclose). || FIG. Proteger, guardar (to protect). | Protegerse contra (to protect o.s.). | Poner trabas a (to hinder). || Compensar (bet). || — *To hedge in,* cercar. || FIG. *To hedge in* o *about with,* rodear de. || *To hedge off,* separar con un seto.
— V. intr. FIG. Contestar con evasivas, salir por la tangente (to refuse to commit o.s.). | Parapetarse: *to hedge behind the rules,* parapetarse detrás de los reglamentos. || COMM. Hacer operaciones de bolsa compensatorias. || Hacer apuestas compensatorias.

hedgehog [—hɔg] n. ZOOL. Erizo, *m.* || MIL. Alambrada, *f.* (barbed wire).

hedgehop [—hɔp] v. intr. AVIAT. Volar bajo *or* en vuelo rasante.

hedgehopping [—ˈhɔpiŋ] n. AVIAT. Vuelo (*m.*) rasante.

hedgerow [—rəu] n. Seto, *m.*, seto (*m.*) vivo.

hedonic [hiˈdɔnik] adj. Hedonista.

hedonism [ˈhi:dəunizəm] n. Hedonismo, *m.*

hedonist [ˈhi:dəunist] n. Hedonista, *m. & f.*

hedonistic [hidɔˈnistik] adj. Hedonista.

heebie-jeebies [ˌhibiˈdʒibiz] pl. n. U. S. FAM. *To have the heebie-jeebies,* estar hecho un manojo de nervios.

heed [hi:d] n. Atención, *f.*: *pay* o *give* o *take heed to what he says,* presta atención a lo que dice. || Cuidado, *m.* (care): *take heed not to lose it,* ten cuidado de no perderlo. || — *To take heed of. s.o.'s advice,* tener en cuenta *or* tomar en consideración los consejos de alguien. || *To take no heed of,* no hacer caso de, no tener en cuenta.

heed [hi:d] v. tr. Tener en cuenta, hacer caso de (to take notice). || Prestar atención a (to pay attention to).

heedful [—ful] adj. Atento, ta (*of,* a) [attentive]. || Cuidadoso, sa (careful).

heedfulness [—fulnis] n. Cuidado, *m.*

heedless [—lis] adj. Desatento, ta (inattentive). Descuidado, da; despreocupado, da (careless). || *To be heedless of advice,* hacer caso omiso de los consejos.

heedlessly [—lisli] adv. A la ligera, con despreocupación.

heedlessness [—lisnis] n. Desatención, *f.* || Descuido, *m.*, despreocupación, *f.* (carelessness).

hee-haw [ˈhi:ˈhɔ:] n. Rebuzno, *m.* (of an ass). || FIG. FAM. Carcajada, *f.* (coarse laugh).

hee-haw [ˈhi:ˈhɔ:] v. intr. Rebuznar (an ass). || FIG. FAM. Reír a carcajadas (to laugh).

heel [hi:l] n. ANAT. Talón, *m.* || Talón, *m.* (of sock, stocking, shoe). || Tacón, *m.* (on sole of shoe): *high heels,* tacones altos. || FIG. Talón, *m.* [parte inferior y trasera de una cosa]. | Restos, *m. pl.* (remainder). | Pico, *m.* (crust of bread). || MUS. Talón, *m.* (of violin bow). || MAR. Escora, *f.* (list). | Talón, *m.* (of the keel). || U. S. FIG. FAM. Sinvergüenza, *m.* (cad). || — FIG. *Achilles' heel,* talón de Aquiles. || FIG. *Heels over head o head over heels,* patas arriba. | *To be at* o *on s.o.'s heels,* seguirle a uno de cerca, pisarle los talones a uno. || *To be down at heel,* tener el tacón gastado (shoe), estar desaliñado, estar mal vestido, estar desharrapado (s.o.). || FIG. *To be under the heel of the invader,* estar bajo el yugo del invasor. | *To bring s.o. to heel,* meter a alguien en cintura *or* en vereda, someter a alguien. || *To come to heel,* acudir [un perro cuando se le llama]. || FIG. *To cool* o *to kick one's heels,* hacer antesala (in a building), estar de plantón (waiting in the street). | *To follow close* o *to tread on s.o.'s heels,* pisarle los talones a uno. | *To kick up one's heels,* echar una cana al aire. | *To lay by the heels,* pillar, poner en chirona (to put in jail). | *To show a clean pair of heels* o *to take to one's heels,* poner pies en polvorosa. | *To turn on one's heel,* volver las espaldas, dar media vuelta.

heel [hi:l] v. tr. Poner tacón a (a shoe). || Remendar el talón de (a sock, stocking). || Poner espolones a (a cock). || SP. Talonar (a ball). || MAR. Inclinar. || FIG. Seguir de cerca, pisarle los talones a.
— V. intr. Seguir de cerca al amo (a dog). || Taconear (in dancing). || MAR. Escorar (to list).

heeled [—d] adj. De tacón (shoes). || U. S. FAM. *Well-heeled,* de mucho dinero (wealthy).

heeling [—iŋ] n. SP. Talonaje, *m.*

heelpiece [—pi:s] n. Tacón, *m.* (heel of a shoe). || Talón (*m.*) reforzado (of stocking).

heelpost [—pəust] n. Montante, *m.* (of a door).

heeltap [—tæp] n. Tapa (*f.*) de tacón (of a shoe). || Escurriduras, *f. pl.* (last drops of liquid).

heft [heft] n. U. S. FAM. Peso, *m.* (weight). | Mayor parte, *f.* (bulk).

heft [heft] v. tr. Levantar (to lift). || Sopesar (to test the weight of).

hefty [—i] adj. Pesado, da (heavy). || Robusto, ta; fornido, da (robust).

Hegelian [heiˈgi:ljən] adj./n. Hegeliano, na.

Hegelianism [heigi:ˈljənizəm] n. PHIL. Hegelianismo, *m.*

hegemony [hiˈgeməni] n. Hegemonía, *f.*

Hegira [ˈhedʒirə] n. Hégira, *f.*, héjira, *f.*

he-goat [ˈhi:ˈgəut] n. Macho cabrío, *m.*

heifer [ˈhefə*] n. Novilla, *f.*, vaquilla, *f.*

heigh! [hei] interj. ¡Oiga!, ¡oye!, ¡eh! (to s.o.). || ¡Ah! (of suprise).

heigh-ho! [ˈheiˈhəu] interj. ¡Ay!

height [hait] n. Altura, *f.*: *the height of a building,* la altura de un edificio; *height above sea level,* altura sobre el nivel del mar; *to be ten feet in height,* tener una altura de diez pies. || Estatura, *f.* (of people). || Altura, *f.* (natural elevation). || Colina, *f.*, cerro, *m.* (hill). || Montaña, *f.*, monte, *m.* (mountain). || Altura, *f.*, cima, *f.*, cumbre, *f.*: *the heights of the Himalayas,* las cimas del Himalaya. || FIG. Colmo, *m.*: *the height of stupidity,* el colmo de la tontería. | Cumbre, *f.*: *the height of one's career,* la cumbre de su carrera. | Punto (*m.*) culminante, culminación, *f.*: *it was at its height,* estaba en su punto culminante. | Lo más

recio, punto (*m.*) culminante: *at the height of the storm*, en lo más recio de la tormenta. || — *Height sickness*, vértigo, *m.* [*Amer.*, soroche, *m.*, puna, *f.*]. || FIG. *In the height of summer*, en pleno verano. | *It's the height of fashion*, es el último grito. || *To be afraid of heights*, tener vértigo. || *What height are you?*, ¿cuánto mides?, ¿qué estatura tienes?
heighten [—n] v. tr. Elevar, levantar, hacer más alto (wall, building). || FIG. Aumentar (one's enjoyment, etc.). | Realzar (to enhance).
— V. intr. Aumentar (to increase). || Intensificarse (to become more intense).
heightening [—niŋ] n. Elevación, *f.* (of a wall, etc.). || Aumento, *m.* (intensification).
heinous [ˈheinəs] adj. Atroz, nefando, da (crime).
heir [εə*] n. Heredero, *m.*: *to appoint s.o. as one's heir*, instituir heredero *or* por heredero a uno. || — JUR. *Heir apparent*, heredero forzoso. || *Heir at law*, heredero legítimo. || *Heir presumptive*, presunto heredero. || FIG. *The new government was heir to an economic crisis*, el nuevo gobierno heredó una crisis económica. || *To fall heir to a property*, heredar una propiedad.
heirdom [—dəm] n. JUR. Herencia, *f.* (inheritance). | Cualidad (*f.*) de heredero (heirship).
heiress [—ris] n. Heredera, *f.* || FIG. Soltera (*f.*) rica.
heirloom [—lu:m] n. Reliquia (*f.*) *or* joya de familia. || FIG. Herencia, *f.*
heirship [—ʃip] n. JUR. Cualidad (*f.*) de heredero.
Hejira [ˈhedʒirə] n. Hégira, *f.*, héjira, *f.*
held [held] pret. & p.p. See HOLD.
Helen [ˈhelin] pr. n. Helena, *f.*, Elena, *f.*
heliacal [hiˈlaiəkəl] adj. ASTR. Heliaco, ca.
helical [ˈhelikəl] adj. TECH. Helicoidal.
helices [ˈhelisi:z] pl. n. See HELIX.
helicoid [ˈhelikɔid] n. MATH. Helicoide, *m.*
— Adj. Helicoidal.
helicoidal [—əl] adj. Helicoidal.
helicon [ˈhelikən] n. MUS. Helicón, *m.*
helicopter [ˈhelikɔptə*] n. Helicóptero, *m.*
heliocentric [ˌhi:liəuˈsentrik] adj. ASTR. Heliocéntrico, ca.
heliochromy [ˌhi:liəuˈkrəumi] n. Heliocromía, *f.* (colour photography).
Heliogabalus [ˌhi:liəuˈgæbələs] pr. n. Heliogábalo, *m.*
heliograph [ˈhi:liəugrɑ:f] n. Heliógrafo, *m.*
heliograph [ˈhi:liəugrɑ:f] v. tr. Comunicar por heliógrafo (a message).
heliography [ˌhi:liˈɔgrəfi] n. Heliografía, *f.*
heliogravure [ˈhi:liəugrəˈvjuə*] n. Heliograbado, *m.*, huecograbado, *m.* (photoengraving).
heliometer [ˌhi:liˈɔmitə*] n. Heliómetro, *m.*
helioscope [ˈhi:ljəskəup] n. Helioscopio, *m.*
heliotherapy [ˈhi:liəuˈθerəpi] n. Helioterapia, *f.*
heliotrope [ˈheljətrəup] n. BOT. MIN. Heliotropo, *m.*
heliotropin [hi:ˈliɔtrəpin] n. CHEM. Heliotropina, *f.*
heliotropism [hi:ˈliɔtrəpizəm] n. Heliotropismo, *m.*
heliotypy [ˈhi:ljətaipi] n. Heliotipia, *f.* (process).
heliport [ˈhelipɔ:t] n. Helipuerto, *m.*
helium [ˈhi:ljəm] n. CHEM. Helio, *m.* || CHEM. *Helium nucleus*, helión, *m.*
helix [ˈhi:liks] n. ANAT. MATH. ZOOL. Hélice, *m.* || ARCH. Voluta, *f.*, espiral, *f.*

— OBSERV. El plural de la palabra inglesa es *helixes* o *helices*.

hell [hel] n. Infierno, *m.*: *sinners go to hell*, los pecadores van al infierno. || FIG. Garito, *m.* (gambling house). || — FIG. FAM. *A hell of a*, estupendo, da; macanudo, da (very good): *it was a hell of a (good) party*, ha sido un guateque estupendo; de mil demonios, fatal, malísimo, ma (very bad): *I've had a hell of a day at the office*, he pasado un día fatal en la oficina; de mil demonios, infernal: *a hell of a noise*, un ruido de mil demonios; excesivo, va: *to pay a hell of a price*, pagar un precio excesivo. | *A hell of a lot*, muchísimo. | *As... as hell*, muy...: *as fast as hell*, muy rápido. || FIG. *Come hell or high water*, pase lo que pase, contra viento y marea. || FIG. FAM. *Go to hell*, ¡vete al infierno!, ¡vete al diablo! || FIG. *It is better to reign in hell than to serve in heaven*, más vale ser cabeza de ratón que cola de león. | *Just for the hell of it*, por puro gusto. | *Like hell*, a demonios (to smell), como un negro (to work), como un descosido (to run). | *Like hell!*, ¡ni hablar! | *Oh hell!*, ¡demonio!, ¡caramba!, ¡caray! | *The hell of it is that*, lo peor del caso es que. | *The road to hell is paved with good intentions*, el camino del infierno está empedrado de buenas intenciones. | *Till hell freezes over*, cuando las ranas críen pelos. | *To be hell on*, ser malísimo para. | *To give s.o. hell*, hacerle a uno pasar las negras *or* pasarlas moradas. | *To go hell for leather*, ir como si se le llevara el diablo. | *To go through hell*, pasarlas moradas. || FIG. FAM. *To hell with...!*, fuera...! | *To hell with it!*, ¡qué diablos! | *To play hell with*, estropear, echar a perder (to ruin). | *To raise hell*, armar la de Dios es Cristo. | *What the hell...!*, ¡qué diablos...!, ¡qué demonios...! | *Who the hell?*, ¿quién diablos?
— Interj. ¡Demonio!, ¡caramba!
hell-bent [—bent] adj. U. S. FAM. Completamente decidido (*on*, a).
hellcat [—kæt] n. Arpía, *f.*, bruja, *f.*
hellebore [ˈhelibɔ:*] n. BOT. Eléboro, *m.* || BOT. *White hellebore*, vedegambre, *m.*
Hellene [ˈheli:n] n. Heleno, na.
Hellenic [heˈli:nik] adj. Helénico, ca; heleno, na.
Hellenism [ˈhelinizəm] n. Helenismo, *m.*
Hellenist [ˈhelinist] n. Helenista, *m.* & *f.*
Hellenistic [ˌheliˈnistik] adj. Helenista, helenístico, ca.
Hellenization [ˌhelənəˈzeiʃən] n. Helenización, *f.*
Hellenize [ˈhelinaiz] v. tr. Helenizar.
hellfire [ˈhelˈfaiə*] n. Fuego (*m.*) del infierno.
hellhound [ˈhelhaund] n. MYTH. Cancerbero, *m.* || FIG. Monstruo, *m.*
hellish [ˈheliʃ] adj. Infernal, diabólico, ca (infernal). || Horrible: *it was a hellish sight*, era un espectáculo horrible. || — FAM. *It was hellish cold*, hacía un frío de mil demonios. | *It was hellish difficult*, era tremendamente difícil.
hellishness [—nis] n. Maldad, *f.*
hello! [ˈheˈləu] interj. ¡Hola! (greeting). || ¡Oiga!, ¡oye!, (to call attention). || ¡Diga! (when answering telephone). || ¡Oiga! (when phoning somebody). || ¡Vaya! (surprise).
helm [helm] n. MAR. Timón, *m.*: *to be at the helm*, llevar el timón. || Yelmo, *m.* (helmet). || FIG. Timón, *m.*: *to take the helm*, empuñar el timón.
helm [helm] v. tr. Gobernar, dirigir.
helmet [ˈhelmit] n. Casco, *m.* (of soldier, fireman, etc.). || Escafandra, *f.* (of diver). || Careta, *f.* (of worker). || (Ant.). Yelmo, *m.*
helmeted [—id] adj. Con casco.
helminth [ˈhelminθ] n. ZOOL. Helminto, *m.*
helminthiasis [helminˈθaiəsis] n. MED. Helmintiasis, *f.*
helmsman [ˈhelmzmən] n. Timonel, *m.*, timonero, *m.*

— OBSERV. El plural de esta palabra es *helmsmen*.

helot [ˈhelət] n. Ilota, *m.* (Spartan serf).
helotism [—izəm] n. Ilotismo, *m.*
help [help] n. Ayuda, *f.*: *to ask for help*, pedir ayuda; *to give s.o. some help*, prestar ayuda a uno. || Socorro, *m.*, auxilio, *m.* (to s.o. in danger): *to shout for help*, pedir socorro a gritos; *to go to s.o.'s help*, prestar socorro a alguien. || Ayuda, *f.*: *my son is a great help to me*, mi hijo es una gran ayuda para mí. || Remedio, *m.*: *there's no help for it*, no hay más remedio. || Criado, da (servant). || Empleado, *m.* (employee). || Criados, *m. pl.* (servants). || Empleados, *m. pl.* (employees): *it's difficult to get help these days*, es difícil conseguir empleados en estos tiempos. || — *Can I be of any help?*, ¿le puedo ayudar? || *Daily help*, asistenta, *f.* || *Help!*, ¡socorro! || *Mother's help*, chica (*f.*) que cuida a los niños en una familia. || *Past help*, desahuciado, da; perdido, da. || *To come to s.o.'s help*, acudir en auxilio de uno. || *With the help of*, con la ayuda de.
help [help] v. tr. Ayudar: *will you help me with this problem?*, ¿me quiere ayudar con este problema? || Auxiliar, socorrer (a person in danger). || Aliviar (to relieve): *this will help the pain*, esto aliviará el dolor. || Evitar (to avoid): *we cannot help his going if he wants to*, no podemos evitar que se vaya si quiere; *things we cannot help*, cosas que no podemos evitar. | Servir (to serve): *to help s.o. to more meat*, servir más carne a uno. || Facilitar (to facilitate). || Fomentar (a scheme). || — *I can't help it*, no lo puedo remediar. || *I can't help wishing I'd known sooner*, la verdad es que me hubiera gustado saberlo antes. || *I (he, etc.) couldn't help laughing* o *I (he, etc.) couldn't help but laugh*, no pude (pudo, etc.) menos que reír. || *It can't be helped*, no hay más remedio, no se puede remediar. || *I won't be longer than I can help*, no tardaré más de lo necesario. || *Not if I can help it*, no si lo puedo evitar. || *So help me God!*, ¡bien lo sabe Dios! || *That didn't help matters much*, eso no sirvió de mucho. || *To help along*, ayudar (s.o.), fomentar (a scheme). || *To help down*, ayudar a bajar. || *To help o.s.*, servirse: *help yourself to cheese*, sírvete queso; mangar (to steal): *to help o.s. to s.o.'s wallet*, mangarle la cartera a uno. || *To help s.o. off with his coat*, ayudar a uno a quitarse el abrigo. || || *To help s.o. on with his coat*, ayudar a uno a ponerse el abrigo. || *To help s.o. out*, echarle una mano a uno, ayudar a uno (to lend a hand), ayudar a uno a salir (from a place), ayudar a uno a bajar (from a car). || *To help s.o. up*, ayudar a uno a levantarse *or* a subir.
helper [—ə*] n. Ayudante, *m*, auxiliar, *m.* & *f.*, asistente, *m.* || Colaborador, ra (collaborator).
helpful [—ful] adj. Útil (useful). || Provechoso, sa (beneficial). || Servicial (obliging). || Amable (kind).
helpfulness [—nis] n. Utilidad, *f.* (usefulness). || Amabilidad, *f.* (kindness).
helping [—iŋ] adj. *To lend s.o. a helping hand*, echarle una mano a alguien.
— Ayuda, *f.* (help). || Ración, *f.*, porción, *f.*, (portion). || Plato, *m.* (plate). || *Would you like a second helping?*, ¿quieres repetir?
helpless [—lis] adj. Desamparado, da; desvalido, da (unprotected): *a helpless orphan*, un huérfano desamparado. || Impotente, incapaz (powerless). || Incapaz, inútil (incapable): *this boy is completely helpless*, este chico es completamente incapaz. || Impotente, imposibilitado, da (an invalid). || *Helpless creature*, criatura indefensa.
helplessly [—lisli] adv. En vano, inútilmente. || Sin esperanza.

helplessness [—lisnis] n. Desamparo, *m.* || Impotencia, *f.* (powerlessness). || Incapacidad, *f.* (incapability).
helpmate [—meit] or **helpmeet** [—mi:t] n. Buen compañero, *m.*, buena compañera, *f.* (companion). || Esposo, sa (spouse).
helter-skelter [ˈheltəˈskeltə*] adj. Ajetreado, da: *a helter-skelter life*, una vida ajetreada. || *A helter-skelter flight*, una desbandada.
— Adv. Atropelladamente (to run, etc.). || A la desbandada (to flee). || En desorden (in random order).
— N. Tobogán, *m* (in a fair). || Barullo, *m.*, ajetreo, *m.* (confusion): *the helter-skelter of life today*, el barullo de la vida actual. || Desbandada, *f.* (confused hurry).
helve [helv] n. Mango, *m.* (handle). || FIG. *To throw helve after hatchet*, echar la soga tras el caldero.
Helvetia [helˈvi:ʃjə] pr. n. GEOGR. Helvecia, *f.*
Helvetian [—n] adj. Helvecio, cia; helvético, ca.
— N. Helvecio, cia.
Helvetic [helˈvetik] adj. Helvético, ca.
hem [hem] n. Dobladillo, *m.* (of garment). || FIG. Orilla, *f.*, borde, *m.* (edge).
— Interj. ¡Ejem!
hem [hem] v. tr. Hacer un dobladillo en. || FIG. *To hem in*, encerrar, rodear.
— V. intr. Carraspear (to clean one's throat). || FIG. *To hem and haw*, vacilar al hablar.
he-man [ˈhi:mæn] n. FAM. Machote, *m.*

— OBSERV. El plural de esta palabra es *he-men.*

hematic [hi:ˈmætik] adj. U. S. Hemático, ca.
hematin or **hematine** [ˈhi:mətin] n. U. S. Hematina, *f.* (haematin).
hematite [ˈhemətait] n. U. S. MIN. Hematites, *f.*
hematocyte [ˈhəmətəusait] n. U. S. Hematocito, *m.*
hematologist [hi:məˈtɔlədʒist] n. U. S. MED. Hematólogo, *m.*
hematology [hi:məˈtɔlədʒi] n. U. S. MED. Hematología, *f.*
hematoma [ˈhi:mətəumə] n. U. S. Hematoma, *m.*

— OBSERV. El plural de la palabra americana es *hematomas* o *hematomata.*

hematosis [hi:məˈtəusis] n. U. S. BIOL. Hematosis, *f.*
hematozoan or **hematozoon** [hi:mətəuˈzəuən] n. U. S. ZOOL. Hematozoario, *m.*

— OBSERV. El plural es *hematozoa.*

hematuria [hi:məˈturjə] n. U. S. MED. Hematuria, *f.*
hemeralopia [ˌheməraˈləupjə] n. MED. Nictalopía, *f.*
hemeralopic [ˌheməraˈləupik] adj. MED. Nictálope.
hemicycle [ˈhemiˌsaikl] n. Hemiciclo, *m.*
hemidemisemiquaver [ˈhemiˈdemiˈsemikˌweivə*] n. MUS. Semifusa, *f.*
hemihedral [ˌhemiˈhi:drəl] adj. Hemiedro, dra.
hemiplegia [ˌhemiˈpli:dʒə] n. MED. Hemiplejía, *f.*, hemiplejia, *f.*
hemiplegic [—ik] adj./n. Hemipléjico, ca.
hemiptera [heˈmiptərə] pl. n. ZOOL. Hemípteros, *m.*
hemipteran (U. S. **hemipteron**) [—n] n. ZOOL. Hemíptero, *m.*
hemipterous [—rəs] adj. Hemíptero, ra.
hemisphere [ˈhemisfiə*] n. Hemisferio, *m.* || FIG. Campo, *m.*, sector, *m.* (field).
hemispheric [ˌhemisˈferik] or **hemispherical** [—əl] adj. Hemisférico, ca.
hemistich [ˈhemistik] n. POET. Hemistiquio, *m.*
hemline [ˈhemlain] n. Bajo, *m.* (of a skirt). || *Hemlines have gone up this year*, los trajes son más cortos este año.
hemlock [ˈhemlɔk] n. BOT. Cicuta, *f.*
hemocyte [hi:məsait] n. U. S. Hematocito, *m.*
hemoglobin [hi:məuˈgləubin] n. U. S. Hemoglobina, *f.* (haemoglobin).
hemolysis [hi:ˈmɔləsis] n. U. S. Hemólisis, *f.*
hemophilia [hi:məuˈfiliə] n. U. S. Hemofilia, *f.*
hemophiliac [—k] n. U. S. Hemofílico, ca.
hemophilic [hi:məuˈfilik] adj. U. S. Hemofílico, ca.
hemoptysis [hi:ˈməuptisis] n. U. S. MED. Hemoptisis, *f.* (haemoptysis).
hemorrhage [ˈhemәridʒ] n. MED. Hemorragia, *f.*
hemorrhagic [—ik] adj. U. S. MED. Hemorrágico, ca.
hemorrhoidal [hemərɔidəl] adj. U. S. MED. Hemorroidal.
hemorrhoids [ˈhemərɔidz] pl. n. MED. Hemorroides, *f.*, almorranas, *f.*
hemostatic [hi:məˈstætik] adj. MED. Hemostático, ca.
— N. MED. Hemostático, *m.*
hemp [hemp] n. Cáñamo, *m.* (plant, fibre). || Hachís, *m.* (hashish). || Marihuana, *f.* (marijuana). || — *Field of hemp*, cañamar, *m.* || *Indian hemp*, hachís. || *Manila hemp*, cáñamo de Manila, abacá, *m.*
hempseed [—si:d] n. Cañamón, *m.*
hemstitch [hemstitʃ] n. Vainica, *f.* (sewing).
hemstitch [hemstitʃ] v. tr. Hacer vainica en.
hen [hen] n. Gallina, *f.* (chicken). || Hembra, *f.* (female bird). || FAM. Mujer, *f.* (woman). || — FAM. *Hen party*, reunión (*f.*) de mujeres. | *Old church hen*, rata (*f.*) de sacristía. | *Old hen*, viejarrona, *f.*
henbane [—bein] n. Beleño, *m.* (plant).
hence [hens] adv. De aquí a (from now): *two years hence*, de aquí a dos años. || Por lo tanto, de aquí (therefore): *hence the evils which plague us*, de aquí los males que venimos padeciendo. || De aquí (from this place): *three miles hence*, a tres millas de aquí. || De acá, de este bajo mundo (from this life).
— Interj. ¡Fuera de aquí!
henceforth [—ˈfɔ:θ] adv. De ahora en adelante.
henceforward [—ˈfɔ:wəd] adv. De ahora en adelante.
henchman [ˈhentʃmən] n. Hombre (*m.*) de confianza (trusted underling). || Secuaz, *m.* (follower). || Guardaespaldas, *m. inv.* (bodyguard). || U. S. Partidario, *m.* (supporter).

— OBSERV. El plural de esta palabra es *henchmen.*

hencoop [ˈhenku:p] n. Gallinero, *m.*
hendecagon [henˈdekəgən] n. Endecágono, *m.*
hendecagonal [hendeˈkægənəl] adj. Endecágono, na.
hendecasyllabic [hendekəsiˈlæbik] adj. Endecasílabo, ba.
hendecasyllable [ˈhendekəˌsiləbl] n. Endecasílabo, *m.*
henequen [ˈhenikən] n. BOT. Henequén, *m.*
henhouse [ˈhenˈhaus] n. Gallinero, *m.*
henna [ˈhenə] n. BOT. Alheña, *f.*
hennery [ˈhenəri] n. Corral, *m.* (poultry yard). || Gallinero, *m.* (henroost). || Granja (*f.*) avícola (poultry farm).
henpeck [ˈhenpek] v. tr. Dominar (one's husband).
henpecked [—t] adj. Dominado por su mujer.
henroost [ˈhenru:st] n. Gallinero, *m.*
henry [ˈhenri] n. ELECTR. Henrio, *m.* (unit).
Henry [ˈhenri] pr. n. Enrique, *m.*
hep [hep] adj. U. S. FAM. Enterado, da (well informed). | Moderno, na (modern). | Aficionado, da [al jazz].
hepatic [hiˈpætik] adj. Hepático, ca.
hepatica [hiˈpætikə] n. BOT. Hepática, *f.*
hepatitis [ˌhepəˈtaitis] n. MED. Hepatitis, *f.*
hepcat [ˈhepkæt] n. U. S. FAM. Aficionado (*m.*) a la música de jazz.
hepped up [ˈheptʌp] adj. FAM. Entusiasta.
heptachord [ˈheptəkɔ:d] n. MUS. Heptacordio, *m.*, heptacordo, *m.*
heptagon [ˈheptəgən] n. Heptágono, *m.*
heptagonal [hepˈtægənl] adj. Heptágono, na; heptagonal.
heptahedron [ˈheptəˈhedrən] n. MATH. Heptaedro, *m.*
heptameter [hepˈtæmitə*] n. Heptámetro, *m.* (verse).
heptarchy [hepˈtɑ:ki] n. Heptarquía, *f.*
heptasyllabic [ˈheptəsiˈlæbik] adj. Heptasílabo, ba.
heptasyllable [ˈheptəˈsiləbl] n. Heptasílabo, *m.*
her [hə:*] poss. adj. Su: *her mouth*, su boca; *her ears*, sus orejas. || De ella (to distinguish *her* from *his*): *is it her book or his?*, ¿es el libro de ella o de él?
— Pers. pron. of 3rd pers. f. sing. La (accusative): *I saw her yesterday*, la vi ayer; *he loves her*, la quiere. || Le (dative): *he gave her a pound*, le dio una libra; *he hit her*, le pegó. (See OBSERV). || Ella (after a preposition): *it is for her*, es para ella. || *To her who told you so*, a la que se lo dijo.

— OBSERV. The English possessive adjective is often translated by the definite article in Spanish (*he bit her hand*, le mordió la mano; *she took her gloves from her bag*, sacó los guantes del bolso).
— When the direct and indirect objects are both pronouns, the dative *le* becomes *se* and is placed before the accusative pronoun (*he gave it to her*, se lo dio; *give it to her*, dáselo).

Heracles [herəkli:z] pr. n. Heracles, *m.*
herald [ˈherəld] n. Heraldo, *m.* || FIG. Precursor, *m.*, anunciador, *m.* (forerunner).
herald [ˈherəld] v. tr. Anunciar.
heraldic [heˈrældik] adj. Heráldico, ca.
heraldist [ˈherəldist] n. Heraldista, *m.*, heráldico, *m.*
heraldry [ˈherəldri] n. Heráldica, *f.* (science). || Escudos (*m. pl.*) de armas (coats of arms). || *Book of heraldry*, libro (*m.*) de armas, armorial, *m.*
herb [hə:b] n. Hierba, *f.*: *medicinal herbs*, hierbas medicinales. || — Pl. CULIN. Finas (*f.*) hierbas.
herbaceous [hə:ˈbeiʃəs] adj. BOT. Herbáceo, a.
herbage [ˈhə:bidʒ] n. Herbaje, *m.* (herbaceous plants). || JUR. Herbaje, *m.*, derecho (*m.*) de pastoreo.
herbal [ˈhə:bəl] adj. Herbario, ria.
— N. Herbario, *m.* (book).
herbalist [ˈhə:bəlist] n. Herbolario, *m.*
herbarium [hə:ˈbɛəriəm] n. Herbario, *m.*

— OBSERV. El plural de *herbarium* es *herbaria* o *herbariums.*

Herbert [ˈhə:bət] pr. n. Herberto, *m.*
herbicide [ˈhə:bisaid] n. Herbicida, *m.*
herbivora [ˈhə:bəvərə] pl. n. ZOOL. Herbívoros, *m.*
herbivore [hə:ˈbivɔ:*] n. ZOOL. Herbívoro, ra.
herbivorous [hə:ˈbivərəs] adj. ZOOL. Herbívoro, ra.
herborist [ˈhə:bərist] n. Herbolario, *m.*
herborization [hə:bəraiˈzeiʃən] n. Herborización, *f.*
herborize [ˈhə:bəraiz] v. intr. Herborizar.
Herculean [ˌhə:kjuˈliən] adj. Hercúleo, a.
hercules [ˈhə:kjuli:z] n. FAM. Hércules, *m.* (strong man).
Hercules [ˈhə:kjuli:z] pr. n. Hércules, *m.*
Hercynian [hə:ˈsinjən] adj. GEOL. Herciniano, na.
herd [hə:d] n. Manada, *f.*, rebaño, *m.* (of animals). || Piara, *f.* (of pigs). || Pastor, *m.*; vaquero, *m.* (herdsman). || FIG. Manada, *f.*, multitud, *f.* (of people). || — FIG. *The common herd*, el vulgo, la masa. | *The herd instinct*, el instinto gregario.

herd [hə:d] v. tr. Guardar (to watch). || Reunir en manada (to round up). || Conducir [en manada] (to drive). || FIG. Apiñar, agrupar.

— V. intr. *To herd into a place*, entrar en manada en un sitio. || *To herd together*, reunirse *or* juntarse en manada (cattle), apiñarse (people). || *To herd with*, asociarse a.

herdbook [—buk] n. Libro (*m.*) genealógico de una raza bovina.

herdsman [—zmən] n. Pastor, *m.* (of sheep). || Vaquero, *m.* (of cattle).

— OBSERV. El plural de esta palabra es *herdsmen*.

here [hiə*] adv. Aquí: *here it is*, aquí está. || Aquí, acá: *come here*, ven aquí. || En este momento, ahora (at this moment). || En ese momento (at that moment). || De aquí: *I prefer this one here*, prefiero éste de aquí. || — *Are they here yet?*, ¿han llegado ya? || *Here and now*, ahora mismo. || *Here and there*, aquí y allá, acá y allá. || *Here below*, aquí abajo. || *Here goes!*, ¡vamos a ver! || *Here is, here are*, he aquí, aquí está, aquí estan. || *Here is your hat*, aquí está su sombrero, aquí tiene usted su sombrero. || *Here it goes!*, ¡ahí va! || *Here lies*, aquí yace. || *Here's to friendship!*, ¡brindemos por la amistad! || *Here she comes*, ya viene. || *Here, there and everywhere*, en todas partes. || *Here we are*, aquí estamos (upon arrival), ya está (that's it). || *Here you are!*, ¡aquí lo tiene! || *In here, please*, por aquí, por favor. || *Look here!*, ¡mire!, ¡oiga! || *Near here*, aquí cerca, por aquí. || FIG. *That's neither here nor there*, eso no tiene nada que ver, eso no viene al caso. || FAM. *This here book* o *this book here*, este libro. || *Up to here*, hasta aquí.

— Interj. ¡Presente! (present). || ¡Toma!: *here!, I don't need this*, ¡toma!, no lo necesito. || ¡Oiga!, ¡oye! (calling attention).

hereabout [—rə,baut] or **hereabouts** [—s] adv. Por aquí.

hereafter [—r'ɑ:ftə*] adv. De ahora en adelante (from now on). || En el futuro (in the future). || En la otra vida (in the after life). || Más adelante, a continuación (later in the book).

— N. Otra vida, *f.*, más allá, *m.* (after life). || Porvenir, *m.*, futuro, *m.* (future).

hereby [—'bai] adv. Por este medio (by this means). || Por la presente (in this document).

hereditable [hi'reditəbl] adj. Heredable.

hereditament [,heri'ditəmənt] n. JUR. Bienes (*m. pl.*) que pueden heredarse, herencia, *f.*

hereditary [hi'reditəri] adj. Hereditario, ria.

heredity [hi'rediti] n. BIOL. Herencia, *f.*

herein ['hiər'in] adv. En esto (in this). || En ésta (in letters). || Aquí mencionado, da (specified). || Aquí dentro (inside). || Sobre este punto (in this matter). || *The letter enclosed herein*, la carta adjunta.

hereinabove ['hiərinə,bʌv] adv. Más arriba.

hereinafter ['hiərin'ɑ:ftə*] adv. Más adelante, a continuación, más abajo.

hereinbefore ['hiərinbi'fɔ:*] adv. Arriba, más arriba.

hereinbelow ['hiərinbiləu] adv. Más abajo.

hereof [hiər'ɔv] adv. De esto (of this). || Su: *this box and the contents hereof*, esta caja y su contenido.

hereon [hiər'ɔn] adj. Sobre esto, acerca de esto.

heresiarch [he'ri:ziɑ:k] n. Heresiarca, *m.*

heresy ['herəsi] n. Herejía, *f.*

heretic ['herətik] n. Hereje, *m. & f.*

— Adj. Herético, ca.

heretical [hi'retikəl] adj. Herético, ca.

hereto ['hiə'tu:] adv. A esto. || *Affixed* o *annexed hereto*, adjunto, ta.

heretofore ['hiətu'fɔ:*] adv. Hasta ahora (until now). || Antes (formerly).

hereunder [hiər'ʌndə*] adv. Más abajo, más adelante, a continuación.

hereupon ['hiərə'pɔn] adv. En seguida (at once). || En esto (thereupon). || Sobre esto (upon this). || Por consiguiente (consequently).

herewith ['hiə'wið] adv. Adjunto, ta (enclosed).

heritable ['heritəbl] adj. JUR. Heredable (property). | Apto para heredar (person). || Hereditario, ria (disease, etc.).

heritage ['heritidʒ] n. JUR. Herencia, *f.* || FIG. Patrimonio, *m.*

heritor ['heritə*] n. Heredero, ra.

herl [hə:l] n. Mosca, *f.* (in fishing).

hermaphrodism [hə:mæ'frədizəm] n. Hermafroditismo, *m.*

hermaphrodite [hə:'mæfrədait] adj./n. Hermafrodita.

hermaphroditic [hə:,mæfrə'ditik] or **hermaphroditical** [—əl] adj. Hermafrodita.

hermaphroditism [—tizəm] n. Hermafroditismo, *m.*

hermeneutic [,hə:mən'ju:tik] or **hermeneutical** [—əl] adj. Hermenéutico, ca.

Hermes ['hə:mi:z] pr. n. Hermes, *m.*

hermetic [hə:'metik] or **hermetical** [—əl] adj. Hermético, ca.

hermetically [—əli] adv. Herméticamente.

hermeticism [hə:'metisizəm] or **hermetism** [hə:'metizəm] n. Hermetismo, *m.*

hermit ['hə:mit] n. Ermitaño, *m.*

hermitage ['hə:mitidʒ] n. Ermita, *f.*

hermit crab ['hə:mit'kræb] n. ZOOL. Ermitaño, *m.*, paguro, *m.*

hern [hə:n] n. ZOOL. Garza, *f.* (heron).

hernia ['hə:njə] n. MED. Hernia, *f.*

— OBSERV. El plural de *hernia* es *hernias* o *herniae*.

hernial [—l] adj. MED. Herniario, ria.

hero ['hiərəu] n. Héroe, *m.* (superman, warrior). || Héroe, *m.*, protagonista, *m.*, personaje (*m.*) principal (in a novel, etc.).

— OBSERV. El plural de *hero* es *heroes*.

Herod ['herəd] pr. n. Herodes, *m.*

Herodotus [he'rɔdətəs] pr. n. Herodoto, *m.*, Heródoto, *m.*

heroic [hi'rəuik] adj. Heroico, ca. || FIG. Heroico, ca (remedy, decision, verse, etc.). | Extremo, ma (measures). | Radical (medical treatment).

— N. Verso (*m.*) heroico, decasílabo, *m.* || — Pl. Grandilocuencia, *f. sing.*

heroical [—əl] adj. See HEROIC.

heroicomic [hə,reuikɔmik] adj. Heroicocómico, ca.

heroin ['herəuin] n. MED. Heroína, *f.*

heroine ['herəuin] n. Heroína, *f.* || Protagonista, *f.*, personaje (*m.*) principal (in a novel, etc.).

heroism ['herəuizəm] n. Heroísmo, *m.*

heron ['herən] n. Garza, *f.*, garza (*f.*) real (bird).

hero worship ['hiərəu'wə:ʃip] n. Veneración, *f.* || Culto (*m.*) a los héroes.

hero-worship ['hiərəu,wə:ʃip] v. tr. Rendir culto a, venerar.

herpes ['hə:pi:z] n. MED. Herpes, *m. pl.* or *f. pl.*, herpe, *m.* or *f.*

herpetic [hə:'petik] adj. MED. Herpético, ca.

herpetism [—izəm] n. MED. Herpetismo, *m.*

herpetology [,hə:pə'tɔlədʒi] n. Herpetología, *f.*

herring ['heriŋ] n. Arenque, *m.* (fish). || — CULIN. *Red herring*, arenque ahumado. || FAM. *Red herring*, pretexto (*m.*) para desviar la atención. | *To draw a red herring across the track*, desviar la atención, despistar.

herringbone [—bəun] adj. De espiga (cloth, clothes, etc.). || De espinapez (floors and walls). || *Herringbone stitch*, punto (*m.*) de escapulario.

— N. Espiga, *f.* (in cloth). || Espinapez, *f.* (in floors and walls).

hers [hə:z] poss. pron. Suyo, ya: *I didn't know the money was hers*, no sabía que el dinero era suyo. || El suyo, la suya: *of the two dresses I prefer hers*, de los dos vestidos prefiero el suyo. || De ella: *it is hers not his*, es de ella, no de él. | El de ella, la de ella: *this wallet is hers not his*, esta cartera es la de ella no la de él. || *Of hers*, suyo, ya: *a friend of hers*, un amigo suyo.

— OBSERV. When *suyo, suya*, which means both "his" and "hers", might result in ambiguity in Spanish, constructions with *de ella* may be used to avoid confusion.

— Téngase en cuenta que el pronombre posesivo *hers* se puede aplicar tanto a un objeto como a varios (*give me hers*; dame el suyo, dame los suyos).

herself [hə:'self] pers. pron. of 3rd pers. f. sing. Se (reflexive): *she washed herself*, se lavó. || Ella [misma], sí [misma] (after preposition): *she bought it for herself*, se lo compró para ella misma. || Ella misma (emphatic): *she didn't believe it until she had seen it herself*, no se lo creía hasta haberlo visto ella misma. || En persona (in person). || — *She did it all by herself*, lo hizo ella sola. || *She is not herself today*, no se siente bien hoy.

hertz [hə:ts] n. PHYS. Hertz, *m.*, hertzio, *m.*, hercio, *m.*

hertzian [—iən] adj. PHYS. Hertziano, na: *hertzian wave*, onda hertziana.

he's [hi:z] contraction of *he is* or *he has*.

hesitance ['hezitəns] or **hesitancy** [—i] n. Vacilación, *f.*, indecisión, *f.*, irresolución, *f.*: *he missed the opportunity because of his hesitancy*, perdió la oportunidad por culpa de su vacilación.

hesitant ['hezitənt] adj. Vacilante (speech, actions). || Vacilante, irresoluto, ta; indeciso, sa (character). || *A baby's first hesitant steps*, los primeros pasos titubeantes de un niño.

hesitantly [—li] adv. Con indecisión, con irresolución.

hesitate ['heziteit] v. intr. Vacilar: *he hesitated to take the first step*, vaciló en dar el primer paso; *I hesitate between the green one and the red one*, vacilo entre el verde y el rojo; *he didn't hesitate to ...*, no vaciló en ... || No decidirse: *I'm still hesitating about joining the expedition*, no me decido todavía a tomar parte en la expedición. || Vacilar, titubear (when speaking). || — *He hesitates at nothing*, no repara en nada, no se arredra por nada. || *Without hesitating*, sin vacilar.

hesitating [—iŋ] adj. Vacilante, indeciso, sa. || Poco seguro, ra.

hesitatingly [—iŋli] adv. Con indecisión, con irresolución.

hesitation [,hezi'teiʃən] n. Vacilación, *f.*, irresolución, *f.*, indecisión, *f.* (indecision). || Duda, *f.* (doubt). || *Without further hesitation*, sin vacilar más.

hesitative [,hezi'teitiv] adj. Vacilante, indeciso, sa.

Hesperian [hes'piəriən] adj. Occidental.

Hesperides [hes'peridi:z] pl. pr. n. MYTH. Hespérides, *f.* (nymphs).

hetaera [hi'tiərə] or **hetaira** [hi'tairə] n. Hetaira, *f.*, hetera, *f.*

— OBSERV. El plural de la palabra *hetaera* es *hetaerae* o *hetaeras* y el de la palabra *hetaira* es *hetairai* o *hetairas*.

heteroclite [ˈhetərəuklait] adj. Heteróclito, ta.
heterodox [ˈhetərəudɔks] adj. Heterodoxo, xa.
heterodoxy [—i] n. Heterodoxia, *f.*
heterodyne [ˈhetərəudain] adj. ELECTR. Heterodino, na.
— N. ELECTR. Heterodino, *m.*
heterogamous [ˌhetəˈrɔgəməs] adj. Heterógamo, ma.
heterogamy [ˌhetəˈrɔgəmi] n. Heterogamia, *f.*
heterogeneity [ˈhetərəudʒiˈni:iti] n. Heterogeneidad, *f.*
heterogeneous [ˈhetərəuˈdʒi:njəs] adj. Heterogéneo, a.
heterogenesis [ˌhetərəuˈdʒenisis] n. Heterogenia, *f.*
heteronomous [ˌhetəˈrɔnəməs] adj. Heterónomo, ma.
heteronomy [ˌhetəˈrɔnəmi] n. Heteronomía, *f.*
heterosexual [ˈhetərəuˈseksjuəl] adj./n. Heterosexual.
heuristic [hjuəˈristik] adj. Heurístico, ca.
— N. Heurística, *f.*
hevea [ˈhi:vi:ə] n. BOT. Hevea, *m.*
hew* [hju:] v. tr. Cortar (to cut). || Talar, cortar (trees). || Labrar, tallar (to shape). || — *To hew down*, talar. || *To hew out*, tallar (a statue), excavar (a hole), hacerse (a career).
— V. intr. Dar golpes con el hacha. || U. S. Conformarse (*to*, con).

— OBSERV. Pret. ***hewed;*** p. p. ***hewed, hewn.***

hewn [hju:n] p. p. See HEW.
hex [heks] n. Bruja, *f.* (witch). || Mal (*m.*) de ojo, maleficio, *m.* (jinx).
hex [heks] v. tr. Embrujar.
hexachord [ˈheksəkɔ:d] n. MUS. Hexacordo, *m.*
hexagon [ˈheksəgən] n. Hexágono, *m.*
hexagonal [hekˈsægənl] adj. Hexagonal.
hexahedral [ˈheksəˈhedrəl] adj. Hexaédrico, ca.
hexahedron [ˈheksəˈhedrən] n. Hexaedro, *m.*

— OBSERV. El plural de *hexahedron* es *hexahedrons* o *hexahedra.*

hexameter [hekˈsæmitə*] n. Hexámetro, *m.*
hexametrical [heksəˈmetrikəl] adj. Hexámetro, tra.
hey! [hei] interj. ¡Eh!, ¡oye!, ¡oiga!
heyday [ˈheidei] n. Auge, *m.*, apogeo, *m.*: *the heyday of the Empire*, el auge del Imperio. || Flor, *f.*: *heyday of youth, of life*, flor de la juventud, de la edad.
Hezekiah [ˌheziˈkaiə] pr. n. Ezequías, *m.*
hi [hai] interj. ¡Oye! || U. S. FAM. ¡Hola! (hullo).
hiatus [haiˈeitəs] n. GRAMM. Hiato, *m.* || FIG. Laguna, *f.* (gap).

— OBSERV. El plural de esta palabra es *hiatuses* o *hiatus.*

hibernal [haiˈbə:nl] adj. POET. Invernal, hibernal.
hibernate [ˈhaibəneit] v. intr. Hibernar (animals). || Invernar (people).
hibernating [—iŋ] adj. Hibernante (animals).
hibernation [ˌhaibəˈneiʃən] n. Hibernación, *f.* (of animals).
Hibernian [haiˈbə:njən] adj./n. POET. Irlandés, esa.
hibiscus [hiˈbiskəs] n. BOT. Hibisco, *m.*
hicatee [ˈhikəti:] n. ZOOL. Hicotea, *f.* (tortoise).
hiccup or **hiccough** [ˈhikʌp] n. Hipo, *m.* || *To have the hiccups*, tener hipo.
hiccup or **hiccough** [ˈhikʌp] v. intr. Hipar, tener hipo.
— V. tr. Decir [algo] hipando.
hick [hik] adj./n. U. S. Cateto, ta; paleto, ta.
hickory [ˈhikəri] n. BOT. Nogal (*m.*) americano.
hicotee [ˈhikəti:] n. ZOOL. Hicotea, *f.* (tortoise).
hid [hid] pret. & p. p. See HIDE.
hidalgo [hiˈdælgəu] n. Hidalgo, *m.*
hidden [ˈhidn] p. p. See HIDE.
— Adj. Escondido, da. || FIG. Oculto, ta: *his words had a hidden meaning*, sus palabras tenían un sentido oculto.
hide [haid] n. Puesto, *m.* (concealed place). || Piel, *f.* (animal skin). || Piel, *f.*, cuero, *m.* (tanned skin). || FAM. Pellejo, *m.* (of a person). || — FAM. *To have a thick hide*, ser un caradura. | *To save one's hide*, salvar el pellejo. | *To tan s.o.'s hide*, dar una paliza *or* zurrar la badana a alguien. | *We haven't seen hide nor hair of him*, no le hemos visto el pelo.
hide* [haid] v. tr. Esconder (*from*, de): *hidden treasure*, tesoro escondido; *where can we hide the presents?*, ¿dónde podemos esconder los regalos? || Ocultar (*from*, a): *to hide sth. from s.o.*, ocultar algo a alguien. || Ocultar, disimular: *to hide one's fears, ones thoughts*, ocultar sus temores, sus pensamientos. || Tapar, ocultar (to cover up): *to hide one's face in one's hands*, taparse la cara con las manos, ocultar el rostro entre las manos; *a cloud hid the sun*, una nube ocultaba el sol. || Encubrir: *to hide the truth, a criminal*, encubrir la verdad, a un criminal. || FAM. Dar una paliza (to thrash).
— V. intr. Esconderse ocultarse: *to hide under the bed*, esconderse debajo de la cama. || FIG. Ampararse: *he is hiding behind his authority*, se ampara en su autoridad. || *To hide out*, esconderse, estar escondido.

— OBSERV. Pret. ***hid;*** p. p. ***hidden, hid.***

hide-and-seek [ˈhaidˈnsi:k] n. Escondite, *m.* [*Amer.*, escondidas, *f. pl.*]: *to play hide-and-seek*, jugar al escondite.
hideaway [ˈhaidəˌwəi] n. Escondite, *m.*, escondrijo, *m.*
hidebound [ˈhaidbaund] adj. De miras estrechas (narrow-minded). || Chapado a la antigua (old-fashioned). || Conservador, ra (conservative). || Estrecho, cha (ideas). || Con la piel pegada a los huesos (cattle, etc.).
hideous [ˈhidiəs] adj. Horroroso, sa; horrible, espantoso, sa (ugly, frightful). || Repelente, repugnante (repugnant). || Monstruoso, sa (monstrous).
hideousness [—nis] n. Atrocidad, *f.*, horror, *m.* (of a crime). || Fealdad (*f.*) espantosa (of a person).
hideout [ˈhaidaut] n. Escondite, *m*, escondrijo, *m.*
hiding [ˈhaidiŋ] n. Ocultación, *f.*, disimulación, *f.* (of one's joy, etc.). || JUR. Encubrimiento, *m.* (of a criminal). || FAM. Paliza, *f.*: *to give s.o. a good hiding*, darle a uno una buena paliza. || — *To be in hiding*, estar escondido. || *To come out of hiding*, salir de su escondite. || *To go into hiding*, esconderse.
hiding place [—pleis] n. Escondite, *m.*
hie [hai] v. intr. POET. Ir de prisa.
hiemal [ˈhaiəməl] adj. Invernal.
hierarch [ˈhaiərɑ:k] n. Jerarca, *m.*
hierarchic [ˌhaiəˈrɑ:kik] or **hierarchical** [—əl] or **hierarchal** [ˌhaiəˈrɑ:kəl] adj. Jerárquico, ca.
hierarchization [ˈhaiərɑ:kaiˈzeiʃən] n. Jerarquización, *f.*
hierarchize [ˈhaiərɑ:kaiz] v. tr. Jerarquizar.
hierarchy [ˈhaiərɑ:ki] n. Jerarquía, *f.*
hieratic [ˌhaiəˈrætik] or **hieratical** [—əl] adj. Hierático, ca.
hieroglyph [ˈhaiərəuglif] n. Jeroglífico, *m.*
hieroglyphic [ˌhaiərəuˈglifik] adj. Jeroglífico, ca.
— Pl. n. Jeroglíficos, *m.*
Hieronymite [ˌhaiəˈrɔnimait] pr. n. REL. Jerónimo, *m.*
Hieronymus [ˌhaiəˈrɔniməs] pr. n. Jerónimo, *m.*
hierophant [ˈhaiərəufænt] n. Hierofanta, *m.*, hierofante, *m.*
hi-fi [ˈhaiˈfai] n. Alta (*f.*) fidelidad.
— Adj. De alta fidelidad.

— OBSERV. Esta palabra es la abreviatura de *high fidelity.*

higgle [ˈhigl] v. intr. Regatear.
higgledy-piggledy [ˈhigldiˈpigldi] adv. En desorden, a la buena de Dios.
— Adj. Desordenado, da (disorderly). || Revuelto, ta (in a mess).
high [hai] adj. Alto, ta (building, official, command, collar): *a high hill*, una colina alta; *High Commissioner*, Alto Comisario. || De alto, de altura: *the wall is six feet high*, la pared tiene seis pies de alto. || Alto, ta; elevado, da (price, percentage, wages, temperature, thoughts). || Elevado, da (language). || Grande (number, speed, altitude, hopes, respect). || Fuerte (wind, explosive). || Alto, ta; importante (post). || Mayor (altar, Mass, street). || Violento, ta; vehemente (passion). || Agudo, da (voice). || Alto, ta (musical note). || Culminante: *it was the high time of my life*, fue el período culminante de mi vida. || Superior (quality). || Pleno, na: *at high noon*, en pleno mediodía. || Crecido, da (river). || Brillante (polish, shine). || Pasado, da (foodstuffs). || Picante (sauce). || Manido, da (game). || Subido, da (colour). || Sumo (Pontiff). || Altanero, ra (manner). || ELECTR. Alto, ta (frequency). || PHYS. Alto, ta (pression). || GRAMM. Alto, ta: *High German*, alto alemán. || FAM. Achispado, da (drunk). || — MAR. *A high sea is running*, el mar está encrespado. || *High and dry*, en seco (boat), plantado, da (person). || *High and low*, de todas las clases (people). || FIG. *High and mighty*, engreído, da. || *High antiquity*, la antigüedad remota. || MED. *High blood pressure*, hipertensión (*f.*) arterial, presión alta. || MIL. *High command*, alto mando. || JUR. *High Court*, Tribunal Supremo. || *High day*, día (*m.*) de fiesta. || SP. *High diving*, salto (*m.*) de palanca. || *Highest bid*, mejor postura, *f.* (in auction). || *High fidelity*, alta fidelidad. || *High hand*, despotismo, *m.* || *High hat*, sombrero (*m.*) de copa (top hat). || FAM. *High jinks*, jolgorio, *m.*, juerga, *f.*, jarana, *f.*: *to be up to high jinks*, estar de jarana. || SP. *High jump*, salto (*m.*) de altura. || *High living*, vida regalada. || *High officials*, altos funcionarios. || *High priest*, sumo sacerdote. || *High relief*, alto relieve. || *High school*, instituto (*m.*) de segunda enseñanza. || *High sea* o *high seas*, alta mar. || *High society*, alta sociedad. || *High spirits*, alegría, *f.*, buen humor, *m.* || *High tea*, merienda cena, *f.* || MED. *High temperature* o *high fever*, fiebre (*f.*) fuerte. || *High tide*, see TIDE. || *High time*, see TIME. || JUR. *High treason*, alta traición. || *High water*, marea alta (sea), crecida, *f.* (river). || *How high is that wall?*, ¿cuál es la altura de esta pared?, ¿cuánto mide esta pared? || *In high places* o *circles*, en las altas esferas. || *In the highest sense of the word*, en toda la extensión de la palabra. || *On the high seas*, en alta mar. || *The Most High*, el Altísimo (God). || FIG. *To be high*, estar drogado. || *To be in high spirits*, estar de buen humor. || *To have a high opinion of s.o.*, tener buen concepto de alguien, tener en mucho a alguien. || *To have high words with s.o.*, tener unas palabras con alguien. || *To live the high life*, darse la gran vida. || *To set a high value on sth.*, dar un gran valor a algo. || *To speak of s.o. in high terms*, hablar en términos elogiosos de alguien, hablar muy bien de alguien. || *To the highest degree*, hasta el máximo. || *We have been friends since we were so high*, somos amigos desde niños.
— Adv. Alto: *to aim high*, apuntar alto. || Alto, a gran altura: *to fly high*, volar a gran altura. || Fuerte: *to blow high*, soplar fuerte; *to play* o *to stake high*,

jugar fuerte. || Muy bien: *high paid*, muy bien pagado. || — *Boats cannot sail very high up this river*, los barcos no pueden llegar muy arriba en este río. || *High above* o *high over sth.*, muy por encima de algo. || *How high?*, ¿hasta qué altura? (how far up), ¿cuánto? (price). || FIG. *To aim high*, picar muy alto. | *To climb* o *to rise high*, subir muy alto. || *To come high on a list*, estar al principio de una lista. || FIG. *To fly high*, picar muy alto. || *To fly 3000 metres high*, volar a una altura de 3000 metros. || *To go as high as*, llegar hasta. || *To go back high in the past*, volver muy atrás en el pasado. || *To run high*, ser alto (precios), ser numerosos: *accidents are running high this year*, son numerosos los accidentes este año; estar encrespado (the sea), estar crecido (river), estar acalorado (spirits), estar desencadenado (passions). || *To search high and low for sth.*, buscar algo por todas partes *or* de arriba abajo. || *To sing high*, cantar con voz aguda. || *Words ran high*, la discusión fue muy acalorada.

— N. Altura, *f.* || Extremo, *m.*, máximo, *m.* || Zona (*f.*) de alta presión. || U. S. FAM. Récord, *m.*, alto nivel, *m.* || U. S. AUT. Directa, *f.*, cuarta velocidad, *f.* || — *From on high*, de arriba. || *On high*, en las alturas, en el cielo.

highball [—bɔ:l] n. U. S. Whisky (*m.*) con agua *or* soda y hielo.

highborn [—bɔ:n] adj. Linajudo, da; de alta alcurnia.

highboy [—bɔi] n. Cómoda (*f.*) alta.

highbred [—ˈbred] adj. De abolengo.

highbrow [—brau] adj./n. Intelectual.

highchair [—tʃɛə*] n. Silla (*f.*) alta para niño.

high-class [—klɑ:s] adj. De categoría (classy). || De primera clase (first-class).

higher [—ə*] adj. Más alto, más alta (bigger). || Mayor (number, speed, altitude). || Superior: *higher vertebrate*, vertebrado superior; *higher mathematics*, matemáticas superiores; *higher education*, enseñanza superior.

highest [—əst] adj. Más alto. || Sumo, ma; supremo, ma (supreme). || Mayor, máximo, ma. || REL. *Glory to God in the highest*, Gloria a Dios en las alturas.

highfalutin [—fəˈlu:tin] or **highfaluting** [—fəˈlu:tiŋ] adj. Pomposo, sa (pompous). || Presumido, da (pretentious).

high-flown [—fləun] adj. Altisonante, rimbombante (words).

high-flying [—ˌflaiiŋ] adj. Ambicioso, sa (person). | Disparatado, da (hopes).

high-frequency [ˈ—fri:kwənsi] adj. ELECTR. De alta frecuencia.

high-grade [—greid] adj. De calidad superior. || *High-grade petrol*, gasolina (*f.*) plomo, supercarburante, *m.*

highhanded [—ˈhændid] adj. Arbitrario, ria (arbitrary). || Despótico, ca; tiránico, ca (overbearing).

high-hat [—ˈhæt] adj. U. S. FAM. Snob, esnob, presumido, da (stuck-up). | Engreído, da (arrogant).

— N. Snob, *m.* & *f.*, esnob, *m.* & *f.*

high-hat [—ˈhæt] v. tr. U. S. FAM. Desairar, tratar con desprecio.

high-heeled [—hi:ld] adj. De tacón alto (shoes).

highjack [—ˌdʒæk] v. tr. See HIJACK.

highjacker [—ˌdʒækə*] n. See HIJACKER.

highjacking [—ˌdʒækiŋ] n. See HIJACKING.

highland [—lənd] adj. Montañoso, sa (mountainous). || De las montañas, de las tierras altas (customs, etc.). || Montañés, esa (people).

— N. Tierras (*f. pl.*) altas, región (*f.*) montañosa, montañas, *f. pl.*

highlander [—ˈləndə*] n. Montañés, esa.

highlands [—ləndz] pl. n. Montañas, *f.*, tierras (*f.*) altas, región (*f. sing.*) montañosa.

Highlands [—ləndz] pl. pr. n. GEOGR. Región (*f. sing.*) montañosa de Escocia.

high-level [—ˈlevl] adj. De alto nivel.

highlight [—lait] n. ARTS. Toque (*m.*) de luz. || FIG. Punto (*m.*) *or* momento (*m.*) culminante, atracción (*f.*) principal (of a spectacle, etc.). | Característica (*f.*) notable, lo saliente (marking feature).

highlight [—lait] v. tr. ARTS. Poner los toques de luz. || FIG. Destacar, subrayar, hacer resaltar.

highly [—li] adv. Muy (very): *highly pleased*, muy contento. || Muy bien: *a highly paid position*, un puesto muy bien pagado. || Sumamente (extremely). || Favorablemente (favourably). || — *Highly bred*, de buena raza (animals). || *Highly coloured*, subido de color, de color subido. || *Highly placed*, muy bien situado. || *Highly seasoned*, muy picante || *Highly strung*, tenso, sa (nerves), hipertenso, sa; muy nervioso, sa (person). || *To speak highly of s.o.*, hablar muy bien de alguien. || *To think highly of s.o.*, tener en mucho a alguien.

high-minded [—ˈmaindid] adj. Magnánimo, ma. || Noble, de sentimientos elevados.

highness [—nis] n. Alteza, *f.* (prince, princess). || Altura, *f.*, nivel, *m.* (level). || Nobleza (*f.*) de sentimientos (of mind). || *His, Her* o *Your Highness*, Su Alteza.

high-octane [—ˈɔktein] adj. De gran índice de octano. || *High-octane gasoline*, gasolina (*f.*) plomo, supercarburante, *m.*

high-pitched [—ˈpitʃt] adj. Agudo, da (note, voice). || Empinado, da (roof). || Realzado, da; peraltado, da (arch). || FIG. Elevado, da.

high-powered [—ˈpauəd] adj. De gran potencia. || FIG. Dinámico, ca (person).

high-pressure [—ˈpreʃə*] adj. De alta presión. || FAM. Enérgico, ca (salesman).

high-pressure [—ˈpreʃə*] v. tr. FAM. Ejercer una presión sobre.

high-priced [—ˈpraist] adj. Muy caro, ra; de alto precio.

high-proof [—ˈpru:f] adj. Con mucho alcohol.

high-ranking [—ˈræŋkiŋ] adj. De alta graduación, superior (official). || De categoría.

highroad [—rəud] n. Carretera, *f.* (main road). || FIG. Camino (*m.*) real (shortest way).

high-sounding [—ˌsaundiŋ] adj. Altisonante.

high-speed [—spi:d] adj. De gran velocidad, rápido, da. || *High-speed steel*, acero rápido.

high-spirited [—ˈspiritid] adj. Animoso, sa (courageous). || Alegre (merry). || Fogoso, sa (horses).

high-strung [—ˈstrʌŋ] adj. Tenso, sa (nerves). || Hipertenso, sa; muy nervioso, sa (person).

high-tension [—ˈtenʃən] adj. ELECTR. De alta tensión.

high-test [—ˈtest] adj. *High-test fuel*, supercarburante, *m.*, gasolina (*f.*) plomo.

high-toned [—ˈtəund] adj. De mucha categoría. || Elegante (stylish). || FAM. Pretencioso, sa.

high-up [ˈhaiʌp] adj. FAM. Importante.

— N. FAM. Persona (*f.*) importante, personalidad, *f.*

highway [—wei] n. Carretera, *f.* || JUR. Vía (*f.*) pública. || U. S. Autopista, *f.* || — *Highway code*, código (*m.*) de la circulación. || *Highway robbery*, asalto, *m.*, atraco, *m.*

highwayman [—weimən] n. Salteador (*m.*) de caminos.

— OBSERV. El plural de esta palabra es *highwaymen*.

hijack [—ˌdʒæk] v. tr. Robar (goods in transit). || Asaltar, atracar (people). || Forzar, obligar (to oblige). || Secuestrar, desviar (aeroplanes).

hijacker [—ˌdʒækə*] n. Asaltador, ra. || Secuestrador, ra; pirata (*m.*) del aire (of aeroplanes).

hijacking [—ˌdʒækiŋ] n. Asalto, *m.* || Secuestro, *m.* (of aeroplanes).

hike [haik] n. Excursión (*f.*) a pie. || *To go on a hike*, hacer una excursión, ir de excursión.

hike [haik] v. intr. Ir de excursión (to go on a hike). || Ir andando, ir a pie (to go walking).

— V. tr. U. S. Aumentar (prices, production). || — FAM. *To hike it*, ir andando. || *To hike up*, subirse (one's trousers, etc.).

hiker [—ə*] n. Excursionista, *m.* & *f.*

hiking [—iŋ] n. Excursionismo, *m.*

hilarious [hiˈlɛəriəs] adj. Hilarante, divertidísimo, ma (funny). || Alegre (merry). || *Hilarious laughter*, carcajada, *f.*

hilarity [hiˈlæriti] n. Hilaridad, *f.*

hill [hil] n. Colina, *f.*, cerro, *m.*, otero, *m.* || Cuesta, *f.* (slope). || Montoncillo, *m.* (small heap). || — FAM. *To be over the hill*, tener muchos años (to be old). | *To go over the hill*, desertar (to desert), largarse (to escape). | *To take to the hills*, echarse al monte. | *Up hill and down dale*, por todos los lados.

hillbilly [—bili] n. Serrano, na; montañés, esa.

hillock [—lək] n. Altozano, *m.*, montecillo, *m.*

hillside [—ˈsaid] n. Ladera, *f.*

hilltop [—ˈtɔp] n. Cumbre (*f.*) de una colina.

hilly [—i] adj. Montuoso, sa; accidentado, da. || Con cuestas empinadas (road).

hilt [hilt] n. Puño, *m.*, empuñadura, *f.* (of dagger, sword). || FIG. *Up to the hilt*, hasta las cachas, hasta el cuello (to be involved), completamente, totalmente (to prove sth., to commit o.s.).

hilt [hilt] v. tr. Poner un puño *or* una empuñadura a.

him [him] pers. pron. of 3rd pers. m. sing. Lo, le (accusative): *I saw him go*, lo vi marcharse. (See OBSERV. under LE in Spanish-English section.) || Le (dative): *give him the book*, dale el libro; *who did that to him?*, ¿quién le ha hecho esto? (See OBSERV.) || Él (after a preposition): *it's for him*, es para él; *whom shall I give it to? Him or her?*, ¿a quién se lo doy? ¿A él o a ella? || *To him who*, al que.

— OBSERV. When the direct and indirect objects are both pronouns the dative *le* becomes *se* and is placed before the accusative pronoun (*he sold it to him*, se lo vendió; *give it to him*, dáselo.)

Himalayas [ˌhiməˈleiəz] pl. pr. n. GEOGR. Himalaya, *m. sing.*

himself [himˈself] pers. pron. of 3rd pers. m. sing. Se (reflexive): *he has hurt himself*, se ha hecho daño. || Él [mismo], sí [mismo]: *for himself*, para él. || Él mismo (emphatic): *if he hadn't said so himself*, si no lo hubiera dicho él mismo. || En persona (in person). || *He did it all by himself*, lo hizo él solo.

hind [haind] adj. Trasero, ra (back). || FIG. *To talk the hind leg off a donkey*, hablar por los codos.

— N. ZOOL. Cierva, *f.* (female deer). || Gañán, *m.*, mozo (*m.*) de labranza (farm worker).

— OBSERV. El comparativo del adjetivo *hind* es *hinder* y el superlativo *hindmost* o *hindermost*.

hinder [—ə*] adj. Trasero, ra.

hinder [—ə*] v. tr. Entorpecer, dificultar (to make difficult): *snow hinders the traffic*, la nieve entorpece la circulación. || Poner trabas a, obstaculizar (to

obstruct): *the break of the cease-fire hindered negotiations*, la ruptura del alto el fuego puso trabas a las negociaciones. || Estorbar (to get in the way). || Impedir (to prevent): *to hinder s.o. from doing sth.*, impedir a uno hacer algo, impedir a uno que haga algo.
— V. intr. Ser un estorbo.
hindermost [ˈhaindəməust] adj. See HINDMOST.
Hindi [ˈhindi:] n. Hindi, *m.*
hindmost [ˈhaindməust] adj. Trasero, ra; posterior (rear). || Último, ma (last). || *Hindmost part*, parte trasera *or* de atrás.
Hindoo [ˈhinˈdu:] adj./n. Hindú.
hindquarters [ˈhaindˈkwɔ:təz] pl. n. Cuartos (*m.*) traseros. || FIG. FAM. Trasero, *m. sing.*
hindrance [ˈhindrəns] n. Obstáculo, *m.*, estorbo, *m.* (*to*, para). || Impedimento, *m.* (prevention).
hindsight [ˈhaindsait] n. MIL. Alza, *f.* (of arms). || FIG. Percepción (*f.*) retrospectiva.
Hindu [ˈhinˈdu:] adj./n. Hindú.
Hinduism [ˈhinduizəm] n. Hinduismo, *m.*
Hindustan [ˌhinduˈstɑ:n] pr. n. GEOGR. Indostán, *m.*
Hindustani [ˌhinduˈstɑ:ni] adj. Indostanés, esa; indostano, na.
— N. Indostano, na; indostanés, esa. || Indostaní, *m.* (language).
hinge [hindʒ] m. TECH. Bisagra, *f.*, charnela, *f.* | Bisagra, *f.*, gozne, *m.* (of door). || ZOOL. Charnela, *f.* (of molluscs). || Fijasellos, *m. inv.* (for stamps). || FIG. Eje, *m.*, punto (*m.*) esencial.
hinge [hindʒ] v. intr. FIG. Depender: *his career hinges upon this speech*, su carrera depende de este discurso. || TECH. Girar (*on*, sobre).
— V. tr. Engoznar, poner bisagras.
hinged [—d] adj. De bisagra.
hinny [ˈhini] n. ZOOL. Burdégano, *m.*
hint [hint] n. Indirecta, *f.*: *I dropped him a hint*, le tiré una indirecta; *I think that was a hint for us to leave*, creo que eso fue una indirecta para que nos marcháramos. || Pista, *f.* (clue): *I can't guess it, give me a hint*, no lo puedo adivinar, dame una pista. || Consejo, *m.* (piece of advice). || Indicación, *f.*, indicio, *m.* (indication). || Idea, *f.*: *give me a hint as to how the novel ends*, dame una idea de cómo acaba la novela. || FIG. Pizca, *f.* (trace): *there is not a hint of malice in his words*, no hay ni una pizca de malicia en lo que dice. | Sombra, *f.*: *there is not a hint of truth in his story*, no hay una sombra de verdad en su historia. || — *A broad hint*, una insinuación muy clara. || *To take the hint*, darse por aludido (bad sense), aprovechar el consejo (to follow advice). || *To throw out a hint that*, dar a entender que, insinuar que.
hint [hint] v. tr. Dar a entender, insinuar.
— V. intr. Soltar indirectas. || *To hint at*, insinuar: *what are you hinting at?*, ¿qué estás insinuando?; aludir a, hacer alusión a: *he hinted at the possibility of*, aludió a la posibilidad de.
hinterland [ˈhintəlænd] n. Interior, *m.*
hip [hip] n. ANAT. Cadera, *f.*: *hip joint*, articulación de la cadera. | Perímetro (*m.*) de caderas (measurement). || BOT. Escaramujo, *m.* (fruit of rose). || ARCH. Lima (*f.*) tesa. || — *Hip bath*, baño (*m.*) de asiento. || ARCH. *Hip roof*, tejado (*m.*) de cuatro aguas. || FIG. *To have s.o. on the hip*, tener a uno acorralado. || *To sway one's hips*, contonearse.
— Interj. *Hip! hip! hurrah!*, ¡hurra!, ¡viva!
hipbone [ˈhipbəun] n. Cía, *f.*, hueso (*m.*) de la cadera.
Hipparchus [hiˈpɑ:kəs] pr. n. Hiparco, *m.*
hipped [hipt] adj. De cuatro aguas (roof). || FAM. Desanimado, da; triste (depressed). | Obsesionado, da (*on*, por).
hippie [ˈhipi] n. "Hippie", *m.* & *f.*, "hippy", *m.* & *f.*
hippo [ˈhipəu] n. FAM. Hipopótamo, *m.*
hippocampus [ˌhipəuˈkæmpəs] n. Hipocampo, *m.*, caballo (*m.*) marino.
— OBSERV. El plural de *hippocampus* es *hippocampi*.
Hippocrates [hiˈpɔkrəti:z] pr. n. Hipócrates, *m.*
Hippocratic [ˌhipəuˈkrætik] adj. Hipocrático, ca.
Hippocratism [ˌhipəuˈkrætizəm] n. Hipocratismo, *m.*
hippodrome [ˈhipədrəum] n. HIST. Hipódromo, *m.*
hippogriff or **hippogryph** [ˈhipəgrif] n. MYTH. Hipogrifo, *m.*
hippophagistical [hipɔfəˈdʒistikəl] adj. Hipofágico, ca.
hippophagous [hiˈpɔfəgəs] adj. Hipófago, ga; hipofágico, ca.
hippophagy [hiˈpɔfədʒi] n. Hipofagia, *f.*
hippopotamus [ˌhipəˈpɔtəməs] n. ZOOL. Hipopótamo, *m.*
— OBSERV. El plural es *hippopotamuses* o *hippopotami*.
hippy [ˈhipi] n. "Hippie", *m.* & *f.*, "hippy", *m.* & *f.*
hipster [ˈhipstə*] n. U. S. FAM. Joven (*m.*) excéntrico. | Músico (*m.*) de jazz.
hircine [ˈhə:sain] adj. Cabruno, na (goat-like).
hire [ˈhaiə*] n. Alquiler, *m.* (of house, etc.). || Sueldo, *m.* (wages). || Contratación, *f.* (engagement). || COMM. Interés, *m.* (of capital). || — *For hire*, de alquiler (house, television, etc.), libre (taxi). || *For hire*, se alquila (notice). || *Hire purchase*, compra (*f.*) a plazos: *to buy sth. on hire purchase*, comprar algo a plazos. || *On hire*, alquilado, da. || *To get a television on hire*, alquilar una televisión.
hire [ˈhaiə*] v. tr. Alquilar: *I should like to hire a television*, quisiera alquilar una televisión. || Contratar (a person): *we shall have to hire s.o. to do the job*, tendremos que contratar a alguien para que haga el trabajo. || *To hire out*, alquilar.
hired [—d] adj. De alquiler (carriage). || MIL. Mercenario, ria. || JUR. A sueldo, pagado, da (assassin).
hireling [—liŋ] n. Mercenario, *m.*
hirer [—ə*] n. Arrendador, ra.
hirsute [ˈhə:sju:t] adj. Hirsuto, ta.
his [hiz] poss. adj. Su (see OBSERV.): *his mouth*, su boca; *his ears*, sus orejas. || De él (to distinguish *his* from *her*): *is it his book or hers?*, ¿es el libro de él o de ella?
— Poss. pron. Suyo, suya (see OBSERV.): *I didn't know the money was his*, no sabía que el dinero era suyo. || El suyo, la suya: *of the two suits I prefer his*, de los dos trajes prefiero el suyo. || De él: *it is his, not hers*, es de él, no de ella. || El *or* la de él: *this wallet is his*, esta cartera es la de él. || *Of his*, suyo, ya: *a friend of his*, un amigo suyo.
— OBSERV. The English possessive adjective is often translated by the definite article in Spanish (*she bit his hand*, le mordió la mano; *with his hands in his pocket*, con las manos en el bolsillo).
— When *suyo, suya*, which means both "his" and "hers", might result in ambiguity in Spanish, constructions with *de él* may be used to avoid confusion.
— Téngase en cuenta que el pronombre posesivo *his* se puede aplicar tanto a un objeto como a varios (*give me his*, dame el suyo, dame los suyos).
Hispania [hisˈpænjə] pr. n. Hispania, *f.* (Roman name for Iberian Peninsula).
Hispanic [hisˈpænik] adj. Hispánico, ca.
Hispanicism [hisˈpænisizəm] n. Hispanismo, *m.*
Hispanicist [hisˈpænisist] n. Hispanista, *m.* & *f.*
hispanicize [hisˈpænisaiz] or **hispanize** [ˈhispənaiz] v. tr. Hispanizar.
hispanist [ˈhispənist] n. Hispanista, *m.* & *f.*
Hispano-America [hisˈpænəuəˈmerikə] pr. n. GEOGR. Hispanoamérica, *f.*
Hispano-American [—n] adj./n. Hispanoamericano, na.
Hispano-Americanism [—nizəm] n. Hispanoamericanismo, *m.*
Hispano-Americanist [—nist] n. Hispanoamericanista, *m.* & *f.*
Hispano-Arabic [hisˈpænəuˈærəbik] adj. Hispanoárabe.
Hispano-Jewish [hisˈpænəuˈdʒu:iʃ] adj. Hispanojudío, a.
Hispanophile [hisˈpænəufail] n. Hispanófilo, la.
Hispanophobe [hisˈpænəufəub] n. Hispanófobo, ba.
Hispanophobia [hispænəuˈfəubjə] n. Hispanofobia, *f.*
Hispanophobic [hispænəuˈfəubik] adj. Hispanófobo, ba.
hispid [ˈhispid] adj. Híspido, da.
hiss [his] n. Siseo, *m.* (to call attention). || Silbido, *m.* (of disapproval). || Silbido, *m.* (of air, steam, etc.). || Silbido, *m.* (of snake). || GRAMM. Letra (*f.*) sibilante. || — Pl. Silbidos, *m.*, silba, *f. sing.*, pita, *f. sing.*, abucheo, *m. sing.* (of disapproval).
hiss [his] v. tr. Silbar. || THEATR. Silbar, pitar, abuchear.
— V. intr. Silbar.
histamine [ˈhistəmi:n] n. BIOL. Histamina, *f.*
histological [ˌhistəˈlɔdʒikəl] adj. Histológico, ca.
histologist [hisˈtɔlədʒist] n. Histólogo, ga.
histology [hisˈtɔlədʒi] n. Histología, *f.*
historian [hisˈtɔ:riən] n. Historiador, ra.
historiated [histəˈrieitid] adj. Historiado, da (adorned): *historiated letter*, letra historiada.
historic [hisˈtɔrik] adj. Histórico, ca.
historical [—əl] adj. Histórico, ca: *a historical novel*, una novela histórica. || FAM. Memorable, histórico, ca (meeting). || GRAMM. *Historical present*, presente histórico.
historicity [histəˈrisiti] n. Historicidad, *f.*
historiographer [hisˌtɔ:riˈɔgrəfə*] n. Historiógrafo, fa.
historiography [hisˌtɔ:riˈɔgrəfi] n. Historiografía, *f.*
history [histəri] n. Historia, *f.*: *the history of literature, of aviation*, la historia de la literatura, de la aviación. || — REL. *Bible* o *sacred history*, Historia Sacra *or* Sagrada. || *Natural history*, historia natural. || FIG. *That's ancient history*, eso es cosa vieja. || *That's the way history is written!*, ¡así se escribe la historia. || *To go down in history*, pasar a la historia. || *To know the inner history of an affair*, conocer todos los pormenores de un asunto.
histrion [ˈhistriən] n. Histrión, *m.*
histrionic [ˌhistriˈɔnik] adj. Histriónico, ca.
histrionics [—s] pl. n. Histrionismo, *m. sing.* || FIG. Comedia, *f.*, teatro, *m.* (display of emotion).
hit [hit] n. Golpe, *m.*: *a hit on the head*, un golpe en la cabeza. || Tiro, *m.* (in sports): *what a good hit!*, ¡qué tiro más bueno! || Tiro (*m.*) certero, acierto, *m.* (when aiming at sth.). || MIL. Impacto, *m.* || FIG. Pulla, *f.* (sarcastic remark): *to have a hit at s.o.*, tirar una pulla a uno. | Ataque, *m.* (attack). | Éxito, *m.*, sensación, *f.* (success, sensation). | Acierto, *m.* (in guessing). || — *Direct hit*, impacto directo (of bomb, artillery, etc.), acierto, tiro certero. || *Hit or miss*, al azar, a la buena de Dios. || *Hit parade*, lista (*f.*) de éxitos. || *Hit record* o *song*, éxito, *m.* || *Lucky hit*,

golpe (*m.*) de suerte. || FAM. *Smash hit*, exitazo, *m.* || FIG. *That's a hit at you!*, ¡esto va por ti! || *The play was a big hit*, la obra tuvo mucho éxito. || *To be a hit*, ser un éxito, tener éxito (to be successful), dar en el blanco (to hit the target). || FIG. *To make a hit*, ser un éxito (to be a success), acertar (to hit the mark), dar el golpe (to make an impact). | *To make a hit with s.o.*, caerle en gracia a uno, caerle simpático a uno. || *To score* o *to make a hit*, dar en el blanco, acertar: *he made five hits*, dio cinco veces en el blanco. || FIG. *To take a hit at*, atacar.

hit* [hit] v. tr. Pegar a, golpear (to strike): *he hit me, mummy*, mamá, me ha pegado; *to hit hard*, pegar fuerte. || Dar en: *to hit the target*, dar en el blanco *or* en el objetivo; *he it the bottle with a stone*, dio en la botella con una piedra. || Dar: *I think I hit him*, creo que le he dado; *I've been hit!*, ¡me han dado! || Herir (to wound). || Chocar contra *or* con: *the car hit the wall, a stone*, el coche chocó contra el muro, con una piedra. || Darse: *he hit his head on the lamp*, se dio con la cabeza en la lámpara. || Azotar: *the gales which hit many cities*, las tempestades que azotaron muchas ciudades. || Alcanzar: *he was hit by two shots*, fue alcanzado por dos tiros. || Alcanzar, llegar a (a price, etc.). || Sobrecoger: *the panic which hit the population*, el pánico que sobrecogió a la población. || Dar, pegar, asestar (a blow): *she hit him a slap in the face*, le dio una bofetada en la cara. || Dar a: *to hit a nail with a hammer*, darle a un clavo con un martillo. || FIG. Atinar con, acertar (to guess). | Encontrar, dar con (to find). | Afectar: *his company was hard hit by the strike*, su compañía fue seriamente afectada por la huelga. | Herir (one's pride). | Tropezar con (difficulties). | Ganar (money). | Echarse en (bed, floor). || SP. Marcar: *he hit a six*, marcó un seis (in cricket). || U. S. FIG. Llegar a (to arrive at): *when we hit the motorway*, cuando llegamos a la autopista. || — FIG. FAM. *It hits you in the eye*, salta a la vista. || *Our ship hit stormy weather*, nuestro barco fue cogido por una tempestad. || FIG. *Then it hit me that*, de repente caí en la cuenta de que. | *To hit a man when he is down*, rematar a un hombre. || *To hit below the belt*, dar un golpe bajo. || *To hit home*, dar en el blanco (a blow, an insult). || FIG. *To hit it*, dar en el clavo. | *To hit it off with s.o.*, hacer buenas migas con alguien, llevarse bien con alguien. | *To hit one's fancy*, apetecer a uno. || *To hit s.o. back*, devolverle a uno los golpes. || FIG. *To hit s.o. off*, remedar *or* imitar a alguien (to imitate), captar el parecido de alguien (to portray well). || FAM. *To hit the bottle*, darle a la botella, darse a la bebida. || *To hit the brake, the accelerator*, darle al freno, al acelerador. || *To hit the mark*, dar en el clavo, acertar. || FIG. FAM. *To hit the nail on the head*, dar en el clavo. | *To hit the road*, irse, largarse. || FAM. *To hit the sack*, irse al catre. || U. S. FIG. *To hit the spot*, venirle muy bien a uno.

— V. intr. Dar, golpear: *his head hit against the wall*, su cabeza dio contra la pared. || Chocar: *the car hit against the kerb*, el coche chocó contra el borde de la acera. || U. S. Encenderse (cylinders). || — FIG. *Hit or miss*, a la buena de Dios, al azar. || MIL. *To hit and run*, atacar y retirarse. || *To hit at* o *to hit out at*, dar *or* asestar un golpe a (one blow), dar golpes a (several times), meterse con, tirar pullas a (to attack verbally). || *To hit back*, devolver los golpes. || FIG. *To hit on* o *upon*, dar en (the mark), dar con, encontrar: *to hit on the right word*, dar con la palabra adecuada; ocurrírsele [a uno]: *he hit on the idea that* o *of*, se le ocurrió la idea de que *or* de.

— OBSERV. Pret & p. p. ***hit***.

hit-and-run [ˈhitənˈrʌn] adj. Que causa un accidente y se da a la fuga (driver).

hitch [hitʃ] n. Obstáculo, *m.*, impedimento, *m.* (hindrance): *this was a serious hitch in the negotiations*, esto representaba un grave obstáculo para el buen desarrollo de las negociaciones. || Dificultad, *f.*, problema, *m.*, pega, *f.* (fam.): *there shouldn't be any hitch*, no tendría que haber ningún problema. || Tirón, *m.* (sharp pull). || Movimiento (*m.*) brusco (sudden movement). || Alto (*m.*) *or* parada repentina (stop). || Cojera, *f.* (limp). || MAR. Vuelta (*f.*) de cabo (knot). || U. S. MIL. Período (*m.*) militar. || — *If there is the slightest hitch*, si surge la menor dificultad. || RAD. *Technical hitch*, incidente técnico. || *Without a hitch*, sin problema alguno, sin ningún tropiezo.

hitch [hitʃ] v. tr. Atar, amarrar (to tie). || Atar: *to hitch a horse to a tree*, atar un caballo a un árbol. || Enganchar: *to hitch horses to a cart*, enganchar los caballos al carro; *to hitch a trailer to a car*, enganchar un remolque a un coche. || Uncir (oxen). || MAR. Amarrar. || Subirse (one's trousers, socks). || Remangarse, arremangarse (one's sleeves). || Apretarse (one's belt). || — FAM. *To get hitched*, casarse. || *To hitch a ride*, hacerse llevar en coche. || *To hitch one's chair to the table*, acercar a tirones la silla hacia la mesa.

— V. intr. Andar a trompicones (to walk haltingly). || Engancharse: *the trailer hitches on to the car*, el remolque se engancha al coche. || Engancharse (to get caught): *her skirt hitched on a nail*, su falda se enganchó en un clavo. || Hacer autostop (to hitchhike). || FAM. Llevarse bien (to get on well).

— OBSERV. El verbo transitivo *to hitch* se emplea frecuentemente con la proposición *up* sin que cambie el significado.

hitchhike [ˈhitʃhaik] v. intr. Hacer autostop.

hitchhiker [—ə*] n. Autostopista, *m.* & *f.*

hitchhiking [—iŋ] or **hitching** [ˈhitʃiŋ] n. Autostop, *m.*

hither [ˈhiðə*] adv. Aquí, acá (here). || *Hither and thither*, acá y acullá.

— Adj. Más cercano, na (nearest). || Este, esta (this).

hitherto [ˈhiðəˈtu:] adv. Hasta ahora. || Hacia acá.

hitherward [ˈhiðəˈwəd] adv. Por aquí, hacia aquí.

hitter [ˈhitə*] n. Golpeador, *m.* || *To be a good hitter*, pegar fuerte (in boxing), ser un buen bateador (in cricket, etc.).

Hittite [ˈhitait] adj./n. Hitita.

hive [haiv] n. Colmena, *f.* (for bees). || Enjambre, *m.* (swarm). || — Pl. MED. Urticaria, *f. sing.* || FIG. *A hive of industry*, una colmena humana.

hive [haiv] v. tr. Meter en la colmena, encorchar (bees). || Acopiar (honey). || FIG. Almacenar (goods). | Albergar (to lodge).

— V. intr. Vivir en una colmena (bees). || FIG. Vivir en comunidad (people). || *To hive off*, enjambrar.

ho [həu] interj. ¡Eh!, ¡oiga! (to call attention). || MAR. *Land ho!*, ¡tierra a la vista!

hoar [hɔ:*] adj. Cano, na (hair). || Blanco, ca (frost).

— N. Escarcha, *f.* (hoarfrost).

hoard [hɔ:d] n. Tesoro, *m.*: *a miser's hoard*, el tesoro de un avaro. || Provisión, *f.*: *a squirrel's hoard of nuts*, la provisión de nueces de una ardilla. || FIG. Colección, *f.*, repertorio, *m.*: *he has a hoard of anecdotes*, tiene un repertorio de anécdotas.

hoard [hɔ:d] v. tr. Acumular, amontonar: *to hoard supplies*, acumular provisiones. || Acaparar (sth. in short supply). || Atesorar (money).

hoarder [—ə*] n. Acaparador, ra.

hoarding [—iŋ] n. Acumulación, *f.*, amontonamiento, *m.* (of supplies). || Atesoramiento, *m.* (of money). || Acaparamiento, *m.* (of sth. in short supply). || Valla, *f.* (temporary fence). || Cartelera, *f.*, valla (*f.*) publicitaria (billboard).

hoarfrost [ˈhɔ:ˈfrɔst] n. Escarcha, *f.*

hoariness [ˈhɔ:rinis] n. Canicie, *f.* (of hair). || Blancura, *f.* (whiteness).

hoarse [hɔ:s] adj. Ronco, ca (husky). || — *To be hoarse*, tener la voz ronca. || *To shout o.s. hoarse*, enronquecer a fuerza de gritar, desgañitarse.

hoarsen [ˈhɔ:sn] v. tr. Enronquecer, poner ronco.

— V. intr. Enronquecerse, ponerse ronco.

hoarseness [—is] n. Ronquedad, *f.* (of a sound). || MED. Ronquera, *f.* (of voice).

hoary [ˈhɔ:ri] adj. Cano, na (hair). || Que tiene el pelo cano (person). || FIG. Viejo, ja (old).

hoax [həuks] n. Broma, *f.* [de mal gusto] (practical joke). || Bola, *f.* (lie). || Mistificación, *f.* (trick). || Engaño, *m.* (deceptive action). || *To play a hoax on s.o.*, engañar a alguien.

hoax [həuks] v. tr. Gastar una broma (to play a trick on). || Engañar (to deceive).

hob [hɔb] n. Repisa, *f.* (of a chimney). || Duende, *m.* (goblin). || TECH. Fresa, *f.* || Patín, *m.* (of a sledge). || — U. S. *To play hob with*, causar trastorno a, trastornar (to cause an upset), tomarse libertades con. | *To raise hob*, armar jaleo.

hobble [ˈhɔbl] n. Traba, *f.*, maniota, *f.* (fetter). || Cojera, *f.* (halting walk). || FIG. Traba, *f.*, obstáculo, *m.* (hindrance).

hobble [ˈhɔbl] v. tr. Trabar, manear (to join the legs of an animal). || Hacer cojear (to cripple). || FIG. Poner trabas a, obstaculizar.

— V. intr. Cojear (to limp).

hobbledehoy [ˈhɔbldiˈhɔi] n. Adolescente, *m.* (youth). || Zangolotino, *m.* (clumsy boy).

hobble skirt [ˈhɔblskə:t] n. Falda (*f.*) tubo.

hobby [ˈhɔbi] n. Pasatiempo (*m.*) favorito, afición, *f.* || ZOOL. Baharí, *m.*, tagarote, *m.* (hawk).

hobbyhorse [—hɔ:s] n. Caballito (*m.*) de juguete (a children's wooden horse). || Caballo (*m.*) mecedor (a rocking horse). || FIG. Caballo (*m.*) de batalla (favourite topic). || FIG. *To ride one's hobbyhorse*, estar siempre con la misma canción.

hobgoblin [ˈhɔbgɔblin] n. Duende, *m.* || FIG. Espantajo, *m.*

hobnail [ˈhɔbneil] n. Clavo, *m.*

hobnailed [—d] adj. Con clavos.

hobnob [ˈhɔbnɔb] v. intr. Codearse (to be on friendly terms): *to hobnob with the rich*, codearse con la gente rica. || Beber (to drink).

hobo [ˈhəubəu] n. U. S. Vagabundo, da (tramp). | Temporero, *m.* (a seasonal migratory worker).

hock [hɔk] n. Corvejón, *m.*, jarrete, *m.* (of animal's leg). || Vino (*m.*) del Rin. || — U. S. FAM. *Hock shop*, Monte (*m.*) de Piedad. | *In hock*, empeñado, da (in pawn).

hock [hɔk] v. tr. Desjarretar. || U. S. FAM. Empeñar (to pawn).

hockey [ˈhɔki] n. SP. Hockey, *m.*: *field hockey*, hockey sobre hierba; *ice hockey*, hockey sobre hielo; *hockey on skates*, hockey sobre ruedas *or* patines.

hocus [ˈhəukəs] v. tr. Engañar (to deceive). || Drogar (to drug s.o.). || Echar una droga en (a drink).

hocus-pocus [ˈhəukəsˈpəukəs] n. Pasapasa, *m.* (magic). || FIG. Trampa, *f.* (trickery). | Camelo, *m.*

(meaningless, distracting talk). | Truco, *m.* (trick).
— Interj. Abracadabra.

hocus-pocus [ˈhəukəsˈpəukəs] v. tr. Engañar (to trick).

hod [hɔd] n. Cuezo, *m.* (trough). || Capacho, *m.* (for carrying bricks). || Cubo (*m.*) para el carbón (coal scuttle).

hod carrier [—ˈkæriə*] n. Peón (*m.*) de albañil.

hodgepodge [ˈhɔdʒpɔdʒ] n. See HOTCHPOTCH.

hodman [ˈhɔdmən] n. Peón (*m.*) de albañil.
— OBSERV. El plural de esta palabra es *hodmen*.

hoe [həu] n. Azada, *f.*, azadón, *m.*

hoe [həu] v. tr. Azadonar (to dig). || Sachar (to weed). || FIG. *To have a long row to hoe*, tener tela para cortar.

hog [hɔg] n. ZOOL. Cerdo, *m.*, puerco, *m.*, marrano, *m.* [*Amer.*, chancho, *m.*] (pig). || FIG. FAM. Cerdo, *m.*, puerco, *m.*, marrano, *m.* [*Amer.*, chancho, *m.*] (greedy person). || — VET. *Hog cholera*, peste porcina. || FIG. FAM. *To go the whole hog*, llegar hasta el final (to finish what one has started), poner toda la carne en el asador (to commit o.s. entirely).

hog [hɔg] v. tr. Arquear. || FAM. Acaparar (to keep for o.s.).
— V. intr. Arquearse.

hogback [—bæk] n. Montaña (*f.*) escarpada [*Amer.*, cuchilla, *f.*].

hoggish [—iʃ] adj. Glotón, ona (greedy). || Guarro, ra (filthy).

hoggishness [—nis] n. Glotonería, *f.* (greediness). || Suciedad, *f.* (filthiness).

hogmanay [—mənei] n. Noche (*f.*) vieja, nochevieja, *f.* [en Escocia]. || Aguinaldo, *m.* (gift).

hogshead [—zhed] n. Pipa, *f.* (large cask). || Medida (*f.*) que equivale aproximadamente a 240 litros.

hog-tie [—tai] v. tr. Atar las cuatro patas de (an animal). || U. S. Trabar, poner trabas a (to hamper).

hogwash [—wɔʃ] n. Bazofia, *f.* (pigswill). || Desperdicios, *m. pl.* (leftovers). || U. S. Tonterías, *f. pl.*, disparates, *m. pl.*

hoi polloi [hɔiˈpɔlɔi] n. U. S. Masa, *f.*, masas, *f. pl.*, populacho, *m.* (common people).

hoist [hɔist] n. Levantamiento, *m.* (lifting). || Torno, *m.*, cabria, *f.* (lifting mechanism). || Montacargas, *m. inv.* (lift, elevator). || Grúa, *f.* (crane). || MAR. Guinda, *f.* (of mast). | Relinga, *f.* (of sail). || *To give s.o. a hoist*, aupar a alguien.

hoist [hɔist] v. tr. Izar (flag, sails). || Levantar (heavy things). || Subir: *to hoist the merchandise on to the boat*, subir las mercancías al barco. || MIN. Sacar (coal, etc.).

hoity-toity [ˈhɔitiˈtɔiti] adj. FAM. Presumido, da. || FAM. *To be hoity-toity*, darse pote.
— Interj. FAM. ¡Anda ya!

hold [həuld] n. Asidero, *m.*: *there were no holds on the rock face*, no había asideros en la roca. || Autoridad, *f.*, dominio, *m.* (control, authority). || MIL. Fortificación, *f.* || Prisión, *f.* (jail). || MUS. Calderón, *m.* || MAR. Bodega, *f.* (of ship). || SP. Llave, *f.*, presa, *f.* (in wrestling). || — *Catch hold!*, ¡toma! || *To catch* o *to grab* o *to grasp* o *to lay* o *to seize hold of*, coger, agarrar (to catch, to take, to pick up, etc.), agarrarse a (to hang on to). || *To gain a strong hold on* o *to gain a firm hold over*, apoderarse de (to take control of), llegar a dominar (a country). || *To get hold of*, coger, agarrar: *wait until I get hold of you*, espera a que te coja; encontrar (to find): *this stamp is hard to get hold of*, este sello es difícil de encontrar; conseguir (to obtain): *where dit you get hold of that?*, ¿dónde conseguiste esto?; apoderarse de (secret information, etc.), localizar (to get in touch with): *I'll try to get hold of her*, intentaré localizarla. || *To get hold of an idea*, ocurrírsele a uno una idea. || *To get hold on o.s.* dominarse. || *To have a firm hold on the situation*, dominar la situación. || *To have a hold on* o *over s.o.*, tener ascendiente sobre alguien. || *To keep a strong hold on*, controlar rigurosamente (prices, spending, etc.). || *To keep hold of*, no soltar: *I kept hold of the rope*, no solté la cuerda; agarrarse a (a railing), conservar a toda costa (privileges, etc.). || *To lose hold of*, soltar. || *To lose one's hold on*, perder su influencia sobre (to lose one's influence on). || *To relax one's hold*, aflojar la mano (to relax one's grip), abrir la mano (to become less strict). || *To take hold*, afianzarse. || *To take hold of*, coger, agarrar (to catch, to pick up, etc.), agarrarse a (to hang on to), apoderarse de (to take control of), dominar (to control).

hold* [həuld] v. tr. Tener: *he was holding the book in his hand*, tenía el libro en la mano. || Agarrar (to grasp). || Sujetar: *you hold the nail, the ladder for me*, sujéteme el clavo, la escalera. || Guardar (to keep). || Tener capacidad para, caber: *it holds five people*, tiene capacidad para cinco personas, caben cinco personas. || Mantener: *she held her head above the water*, mantuvo la cabeza fuera del agua; *to hold s.o.'s interest*, mantener el interés de uno. || Sostener (to keep from falling): *to hold the roof*, sostener el tejado. || Defender (opinion). || Reservar (room, tickets). || Ocupar, tener (a post). || Desempeñar (a function). || Ocupar (territory). || Tener (to possess): *to hold funds*, tener fondos. || Poseer (a title, medal, etc.). || Considerar: *I don't hold myself responsible*, no me considero responsable. || Tomar: *to hold s.o. to be a fool*, tomarle a uno por tonto. || Mantener, sostener: *he holds that it is possible*, mantiene que es posible. || Creer (to believe). || Hacer cumplir: *to hold one to his word*, hacer cumplir a uno su palabra. || Tener: *he holds funny ideas on the subject*, tiene ideas extrañas sobre el asunto. || Contener: *to hold one's breath*, contener la respiración. || JUR. Presidir: *a judge holds court*, un juez preside el tribunal. | Detener (to arrest). | Retener, tener: *to hold s.o. in the police station*, retener a uno en la comisaría. | Tener (a contract). || Celebrar (a meeting, a religious service). || Tener (a conversation). || MIL. Mantenerse en, retener (an occupied position). | Defender (one's own ground). || MUS. Sostener (a note). || SP. Tener (a record). || — *Hold it!*, ¡para!, ¡espera! || *Hold the line*, no cuelgue, no se retire (on the telephone). || *There is no holding him*, no hay quien le pare. || *To be held*, celebrarse, tener lugar (concert, meeting). || *To hold an inquiry*, hacer una encuesta. || *To hold a parley with s.o.*, parlamentar. || *To hold hands*, ir cogidos de la mano. || *To hold one's audience*, mantener la atención *or* el interés del público. || *To hold o.s. ready for*, estar listo *or* preparado para. || *To hold o.s still*, quedarse quieto. || *To hold o.s. upright*, mantenerse derecho. || *To hold s.o. hostage*, tener a uno como rehén. || *To hold s.o. in respect*, tener respeto a alguien. || *To hold s.o. prisoner*, tener preso a alguien. || *To hold s.o.'s hand*, cogerle la mano a alguien. || *To hold s.o. tight in one's arms*, estrechar a uno en sus brazos. || *To hold sth. cheap*, menospreciar algo. || *To hold sth. fast* o *tight*, sujetar *or* agarrar bien algo. || *To hold sth. in mind*, recordar algo. || *To hold sth. in position*, sujetar algo, mantener algo en posición. || *To hold the key to the puzzle*, tener la clave del enigma. || *To hold the road well*, tener buena adherencia *or* estabilidad, agarrarse bien (a car). || *What the future holds*, lo que nos reserva el futuro.
— V. intr. Mantenerse, sostenerse. || Agarrarse (to seize). || Pegarse (to adhere). || Ser válido, valer, seguir siendo válido (to be valid): *my offer still holds*, mi oferta es válida todavía. || Aguantar, resistir: *I don't know if the rope will hold*, no sé si la cuerda resistirá. || Resistir (not to give way). || Durar (to last): *my luck cannot hold for ever*, mi suerte no puede durar siempre. || *To hold good for*, valer para.
— **To hold back**, reprimir, contener (tears, emotions). | Contener (a crowd). | Retener (a person). | Guardar (to keep in reserve). | Ocultar (the truth): *you are not holding anything back from me?*, ¿no me estarás ocultando algo? | Vacilar (to hesitate). | Abstenerse, contenerse (to refrain). | — *To hold back for*, reservarse para. | *To hold back from doing sth.*, guardarse de hacer algo. || **To hold by**, pegarse a (to adhere). | Mantenerse fiel a (one's beliefs). | Mantenerse fiel a, aferrarse a (one's opinions). || **To hold down**, sujetar (a person on the ground, etc.). | Bajar (to lower). | Oprimir (to oppress). | — *To hold down a job*, conservar su puesto (to have a job), estar a la altura de su cargo (to be able to keep a job). || **To hold forth**, perorar (to talk at length). | Hablar detenidamente: *to hold forth on a subject*, hablar detenidamente de un tema. | Ofrecer (to offer). || **To hold in**, refrenar (a horse, one's passions). | Contener, reprimir (emotions). | — *To hold o.s. in*, contenerse, dominarse. || **To hold off**, sujetar (a dog, a person): *they had to hold him off to avoid a fight*, tuvieron que sujetarle para evitar una pelea. | Rechazar, resistir a (an attack). | Mantener a distancia (to keep s.o. away). | Contener (a crowd). | Aplazar (to postpone). | Esperar (to wait). | Mantenerse a distancia (to stay away). | Vacilar (to hesitate). | — *I hope the storm will hold off*, espero que no estalle la tormenta. | *The rain is holding off*, hasta ahora no llueve. || **To hold on**, sujetar: *this screw holds the propeller on*, este tornillo sujeta la hélice. | Agarrarse: *hold on tight*, agárrate bien; *hold on to my belt*, agárrate a mi cinturón. | Resistir, aguantar: *can you hold on another two days?*, ¿puede resistir dos días más? | Esperar (to wait). | — *Hold on!*, ¡no cuelgue!, no se retire (on the telephone). | *Hold on a moment*, espera un momento. | *To hold on to a post*, mantenerse en su puesto. || **To hold out**, tender, alargar (one's hand). | Ofrecer (to offer). | Dar (hopes). | Durar (to last). | Resistir: *how long can they hold out without food?*, ¿cuánto tiempo pueden resistir sin comer?; *to hold out against the enemy*, resistir al enemigo. | — *To hold out for*, insistir en. || **To hold over**, aplazar, diferir (to postpone). | Dejar [pendiente]: *let's hold this over until the next meeting*, dejemos esto hasta la próxima reunión. | Amenazar con (to threaten). | — *To be held over*, quedar pendiente. || **To hold to**, pegarse a (to stick). | Aferrarse a (one's opinion). | Mantenerse fiel a (a belief). || **To hold together**, sujetar, unir (various parts): *the two boards are held together by a nail*, las dos tablas de madera están unidas por un clavo. | Mantener unido: *a good leader holds the nation together*, un buen dirigente mantiene la nación unida. | Mantenerse unido (to stick together): *the government held together throughout the crisis*, el gobierno se mantuvo unido durante la crisis. | Poder sostenerse (an alibi). | Ser coherente (story). | Ir unido: *drink, poverty, crime, all these hold together*, la bebida, la miseria y el crimen, todo va unido. || **To hold up**, sostener, sujetar: *there is nothing holding the wall up*, no hay nada que sujete la pared. | Levantar (to lift up): *hold your hand, your head up*, levante la mano, la cabeza. | Poner:

to hold something up to the light, poner algo a contraluz; *to hold s.o. up as a model*, poner a alguien como ejemplo; *to hold s.o. up to ridicule*, poner a alguien en ridículo. | Estorbar, entorpecer: *roadworks hold up the traffic*, las obras entorpecen el tráfico. || Interrumpir (to interrupt). | Retrasar (to delay). | Suspender: *the trial was held up when the witness did not appear*, el juicio fue suspendido al no comparecer el testigo. | Suspender (payments). | Detener: *the train was held up for five minutes*, el tren fue detenido durante cinco minutos. | Asaltar, atracar (to attack, to rob). | Mantenerse en pie (to remain standing). | Seguir bueno (weather). | Durar (good weather). | Aguantar, resistir. || ***To hold with***, estar con, estar de parte de: *those who hold with me*, los que están conmigo *or* de mi parte. | Estar de acuerdo con (to agree with). | Aprobar: *I don't hold with such behaviour*, no apruebo esos modales.

— OBSERV. Pret. & p. p. **held**.

holdall [—ɔ:l] n. Bolsa (*f.*) de viaje (bag). || Maleta, *f.* (suitcase).

holdback [—bæk] n. Estorbo, *m.*, obstáculo, *m.* (obstacle). || Retención, *f.* (of salary). || Seguro, *m.* (lock).

holder [—ə*] n. Poseedor, ra: *the holder of the winning ticket*, el poseedor del billete premiado; *holder of the middleweight title*, poseedor del título de los pesos medios (in boxing). || Tenedor, *m.* (of bonds, etc.): *the holder of a bill of exchange*, el tenedor de una letra de cambio. || Portador, *m.* (bearer). || Arrendatario, ria (tenant). || Inquilino, na (of a flat). || Titular, *m.* & *f.* (of office, title, passport, etc.). || Soporte, *m.* (support). || Asidero, *m.* (handle). || Agarrador, *m.* (of an iron). || Receptáculo, *m.* (receptacle). || — *Cigarette holder*, boquilla, *f.* || *Curtain holder*, alzapaño, *m.* || SP. *Record holder*, plusmarquista, *m.* & *f.*, recordman, *m.*, recordwoman, *f.*

— OBSERV. Cuando la palabra *holder* se emplea en la formación de compuestos equivale frecuentemente al prefijo español *porta* (penholder, *portaplumas*).

holdfast [—fɑ:st] n. TECH. Grapa, *f.* || BOT. Zarcillo, *m.*

holding [—iŋ] n. Posesión, *f.* (possession). || Terreno, *m.*, propiedad, *f.* (piece of land). || Celebración, *f.* (of a session). || "Holding", *m.* (financial organization). || — Pl. COMM. Valores (*m.*) en cartera (shares, etc. in a company). || SP. *Holding is forbidden in boxing*, en boxeo está prohibido agarrarse.

holding company [—iŋ'kʌmpəni] n. COMM. "Holding", *m.*

holdover [—ˌəuvə*] n. U. S. Vestigio, *m.* (remnant). | Continuación, *f.* || SP. *There are three holdovers from last year's team playing*, quedan tres jugadores del equipo del año pasado.

holdup [—ʌp] n. Atraco (*m.*) a mano armada. || Interrupción, *f.* (of services). || Embotellamiento, *m.*, atasco, *m.* (traffic jam). || *Holdup man*, atracador, *m.*

hole [həul] n. Agujero, *m.*, boquete, *m.* (small hole, in clothes, etc.): *there's a hole in the bucket*, el cubo tiene un agujero; *to cut a hole in the ice*, hacer un agujero en el hielo. || Hoyo, *m.*: *to dig a hole*, cavar un hoyo. || Cavidad, *f.* (cavity). || Boquete, *m.*, agujero, *m.* (in wall). || Bache, *m.* (in roads). || Madriguera, *f.* (of rabbits). || Agujero, *m.*, ratonera, *f.* (of mice). || FIG. Poblacho, *m.* (town). | Cuchitril, *m.* (unpleasant house). | Apuro, *m.*, aprieto, *m.* (tight spot). || SP. Hoyo, *m.* (in golf): *hole in one*, hoyo en uno. || — FIG. *A hole to crawl out of*, una escapatoria. | *Money burns a hole in his pocket*, el dinero le quema en el bolsillo. | *The journey knocked a big hole in his finances*, el viaje mermó considerablemente sus finanzas. | *To knock holes in an argument*, echar abajo un argumento. | *To pick holes in*, see PICK. || *To wear into holes*, agujerearse.

hole [həul] v. tr. Agujerear (to make holes in). || Hacer un boquete *or* un agujero en (a wall). || Abrir, perforar (a tunnel). || SP. Meter en el hoyo (a ball).
— V. intr. SP. Meter la pelota en el hoyo (in golf). || FIG. FAM. *To hole up*, esconderse (to hide).

hole-and-corner ['həulənd'kɔ:nə*] adj. Clandestino, na; secreto, ta.

holey ['həuli] adj. Agujereado, da.

holiday ['hɔlidei] n. Fiesta, *f.*, día (*m.*) de fiesta, día (*m.*) festivo: *today is a holiday*, hoy es fiesta. || Vacaciones, *f. pl.*: *two weeks' holiday*, dos semanas de vacaciones; *to be on holiday*, estar de vacaciones. || — Pl. Vacaciones, *f.*: *summer holidays*, vacaciones de verano. || — *Holidays with pay*, vacaciones retribuidas *or* pagadas. || *Where did you spend your summer holidays?*, ¿dónde veraneaste?
— Adj. De fiesta (atmosphere, clothes). || De veraneo (place). || Alegre, festivo, va (spirit). || *Holiday season*, época (*f.*) de las vacaciones.

holiday ['hɔlidei] v. intr. Pasar las vacaciones. || Veranear (in summer).

holidaying [—iŋ] n. Vacaciones, *f. pl.* || Veraneo, *m.* (in summer).

holidaymaker [—ˌmeikə*] n. Persona (*f.*) que está de vacaciones. || Veraneante, *m.* & *f.* (in summer).

holily ['həulili] adv. Santamente.

holiness ['həulinis] n. Santidad, *f.* || *His Holiness Pope John XXIII*, Su Santidad el Papa Juan XXIII.

Holland ['hɔlənd] pr. n. GEOGR. Holanda, *f.*

Hollander [—ə*] n. Holandés, esa.

hollands [—z] n. Ginebra (*f.*) holandesa.

holler ['hɔlə*] v. tr./intr. FAM. Gritar (to shout).

hollow ['hɔləu] adj. Hueco, ca: *hollow tree*, árbol hueco; *hollow sound*, sonido hueco. || Ahuecado, da; cavernoso, sa (voice). || Hundido, da: *hollow eyes, cheeks*, ojos hundidos, mejillas hundidas. || Encajonado, da (road). || Vacío, a (stomach). || FIG. Vacío, a: *hollow promises*, promesas vacías. | Falso, sa (friendship). | Engañoso, sa (peace). | Vano, na (triumph).
— Adv. A hueco: *it sounds hollow*, suena a hueco. || FIG. FAM. Por completo: *to beat s.o. hollow*, derrotar por completo a alguien.
— N. Hueco, *m.*: *in the hollow of one's hand*, en el hueco de la mano. || Hondonada, *f.*: *a village situated in a hollow*, un pueblo situado en una hondonada. || Agujero, *m.* (hole). || Depresión, *f.* (depression).

hollow ['hɔləu] v. tr. *To hollow out*, ahuecar: *to hollow out a tree trunk*, ahuecar el tronco de un árbol; abrir, cavar: *to hollow a channel*, abrir un surco; cavar (the ground), vaciar (to empty): *to hollow out one half of a coconut shell*, vaciar la mitad de un coco; escotar (the neck of a dress).

hollow-eyed [—aid] adj. De ojos hundidos. || Ojeroso, sa (from sickness or fatigue).

hollowness [—nis] n. Cavidad, *f.* (hole). || FIG. Vaciedad, *f.* (of words, etc.). | Falsedad, *f.* (of friendship).

hollow ware [—wɛə*] n. Platos (*m. pl.*) y recipientes (*m. pl.*) hondos.

holly ['hɔli] n. BOT. Acebo, *m.*

hollyhock [—hɔk] n. Malva (*f.*) loca, malvarrosa, *f.* (plant, flower).

holm [həum] n. BOT. Encina, *f.* (oak). || Isleta, *f.* (islet). || Vega, *f.* (flat river bank). || BOT. *Holm oak*, encina, *f.*

holmium ['həulmjəm] n. CHEM. Holmio. *m.*

holocaust ['hɔləkɔ:st] n. Holocausto, *m.* (sacrifice). || Destrucción (*f.*) por el fuego.

holograph ['hɔləugrɑ:f] adj. Ológrafo, fa.
— N. Ológrafo, *m.*

holographic [hɔlə'græfik] or **holographical** [—əl] adj. Ológrafo, fa: *holographic will*, testamento ológrafo.

holohedral [ˌhɔləu'hi:drəl] adj. Holoédrico, ca.

holothurian [ˌhɔləu'θjuəriən] n. ZOOL. Holoturia, *f.*

holster ['həulstə*] n. Pistolera, *f.*, funda (*f.*) de pistola.

holt [hault] n. Bosquecillo, *m.* (copse). || Colina (*f.*) poblada de árboles, monte, *m.* (hill).

holus-bolus ['həuləs'bəuləs] adv. FAM. Completamente (altogether). | De un trago (to swallow).

holy ['həuli] adj. Santo, ta: *the holy Catholic Church*, la santa Iglesia católica; *Holy Sepulcher*, Santo Sepulcro; *Holy Week*, Semana Santa; *holy war*, guerra santa. || Sagrado, da: *Holy Family*, Sagrada Familia. || Sacro, cra: *the Holy Roman Empire*, el Sacro Imperio Romano. || Bendito, ta (bread, water).

Holy Alliance [—ə'laiəns] n. HIST. Santa Alianza, *f.*

Holy Bible [—'baibl] n. REL. Santa Biblia, *f.*

Holy City [—'siti] n. REL. Ciudad (*f.*) Santa (Rome, Jerusalem, etc.). || FIG. Cielo, *m.* (Heaven).

Holy Communion [—kə'mju:njən] n. REL. Sagrada Comunión, *f.*

holy day [—dei] n. Día (*m.*) de fiesta, fiesta, *f.*

Holy Face [—feis] n. REL. Santa Faz, *f.*

Holy Father [—'fɑ:ðə*] n. REL. Padre (*m.*) Santo, Santo Padre, *m.*

Holy Ghost [—gəust] n. REL. Espíritu (*m.*) Santo.

Holy Grail [—greil] n. REL. Santo Grial, *m.*

Holy Land [—lænd] n. REL. Tierra (*f.*) Santa.

Holy Office [—'ɔfis] n. Santo Oficio, *m.*

holy of holies [—ov'həuliz] n. Sanctasanctórum, *m.*

holy oil [—ɔil] n. REL. Santos Óleos, *m. pl.*

holy orders [—'ɔ:dəz] pl. n. REL. Órdenes (*f.*) sagradas. || *To take* o *to enter holy orders*, ordenarse (to be ordained).

Holy Scripture [—'skriptʃə*] n. REL. Sagrada Escritura, *f.*

Holy See [—si:] n. REL. Santa Sede, *f.*

Holy Spirit [—'spirit] n. REL. Espíritu (*m.*) Santo.

holystone [—stəun] n. MAR. Piedra (*f.*) arenisca que se usa para limpiar la cubierta de un barco.

holystone [—stəun] v. tr. MAR. Limpiar con piedra arenisca.

homage ['hɔmidʒ] n. Homenaje, *m.*: *to pay* or *to do homage to*, rendir homenaje a.

home [həum] n. Casa, *f.*: *at home*, en casa; *to leave home*, marcharse de casa. || Hogar, *m.*: *home, sweet home*, hogar, dulce hogar; *the comforts of home*, las comodidades del hogar. || Domicilio, *m.*: *the police searched his home*, la policía registró su domicilio; *goods delivered to your home*, servicio a domicilio. || Asilo, *m.*: *old people's home*, asilo de ancianos; *children's home*, asilo de niños. || Hogar, *m.* (institute): *soldier's home*, hogar del soldado. || FIG. Morada, *f.*: *one's last home*, su última morada; *my home is in Heaven*, mi morada está en el cielo. | Patria, *f.* (homeland). | Patria (*f.*) chica, ciudad (*f.*) natal (home town). | Tierra, *f.*: *Spain, the home of the orange*, España, la tierra de la naranja. | Cuna, *f.*: *the home of fine arts*, la cuna de las Bellas Artes. || BIOL. ZOOL. Habitat, *m.* (habitat). || Meta, *f.* (in games). || —

FIG. *A home from home*, una segunda casa. | *An Englishman's home is his castle*, cada uno es rey en su casa. || *At home and abroad*, dentro y fuera del país. || *East, west, home's best*, no hay nada como la casa de uno. || *Make yourself at home*, está usted en su casa. || *Maternity home*, casa de maternidad. || FIG. *Men make houses, but women make homes*, el hombre hace la casa, pero la mujer hace el hogar. || MED. *Rest home*, casa de reposo. || *There's no place like home*, no hay nada como la casa de uno. || *To be away from home*, estar fuera [de casa]. || FIG. *To be o to feel at home*, sentirse a gusto (with s.o.), estar en su elemento (to be in one's element), sentirse como en su casa (in s.o. else's house). || *To give s.o. a home*, darle un hogar a alguien. || *To have neither house nor home*, no tener ni casa ni hogar, no tener donde caerse muerto. || *To make one's home in London*, establecerse en Londres. || *To make o.s. at home*, sentirse como en su casa.

— Adj. Casero, ra: *home cooking*, cocina casera; *home remedy*, remedio casero. || Del hogar, hogareño, ña: *home comforts*, las comodidades del hogar. || De familia: *home life*, vida de familia. || Doméstico, ca: *my wife looks after home finances*, mi mujer se ocupa de la economía doméstica. || Natal, nativo, va: *home town*, ciudad natal. || Nacional: *home front*, frente nacional. || Interior, nacional: *home affairs*, asuntos interiores; *home politics*, política interior; *home market*, mercado nacional. || Del país: *home news*, noticias del país. || Metropolitano, na (population). || SP. De casa: *the home team*, el equipo de casa. | En casa: *to play a home game*, jugar un partido en casa. | De llegada (straight). || — *Home address*, domicilio, *m.*, dirección privada *or* particular. || *Home appliances*, aparatos electrodomésticos. || *Home economics*, economía doméstica. || *Home journey*, viaje (*m.*) de regreso *or* de vuelta, viaje (*m.*) a casa. || *Home Office*, Ministerio (*m.*) de Gobernación (in Spain), Ministerio (*m.*) del Interior (in other countries). || *Home port*, puerto (*m.*) de origen. || *Home Secretary*, Ministro (*m.*) de Gobernación (in Spain), Ministro (*m.*) del Interior (in other countries). || *Mental home*, casa de salud *or* de reposo. || FAM. *To give s.o. a few home truths*, cantarle *or* decirle cuatro verdades a uno, cantarle *or* decirle a uno las verdades del barquero.

— Adv. A casa (motion): *I'm going home*, voy a casa; *I don't like the people he brings home*, no me gusta la gente que trae a casa. || En casa (at home): *to stay home*, quedarse en casa. || A fondo: *to drive home*, meter a fondo. || En el blanco: *to hit home*, dar en el blanco. || — FIG. *It came home to him*, se dio perfecta cuenta de ello. || *Nothing to write home about*, nada del otro mundo. || *To be home*, estar de vuelta (after a journey), estar en casa, estar: *is John home?*, ¿está Juan? || FIG. *To bring sth. home to s.o.*, conseguir que alguien se dé perfecta cuenta de algo. || *To come home*, volver a casa (to one's house), volver a su país (to one's country). || *To drive a nail home*, remachar el clavo. || FIG. *To go home*, dar en el blanco (shot), causar impresión (speech, reproach). | *To push one's insults home*, poner a alguien de vuelta y media. || *To see o to take s.o. home*, acompañar a alguien. || *To send s.o. home from abroad*, repatriar a alguien. || *To strike home*, dar en el blanco.

home [həum] v. tr. Dirigir (missiles, etc.).

— V. intr. Volver a casa (pigeons). || *To home in on a target*, dirigirse hacia el blanco (missiles, etc.).

home-baked [—ˈbeikt] adj. Casero, ra; hecho en casa (cakes).

home-brewed [—ˈbru:d] adj. Casero, ra; hecho en casa.

homecoming [—ˌkʌmiŋ] n. Regreso, *m.*, regreso (*m.*) al hogar.

home fire [—ˈfaiə] n. Fuego (*m.*) del hogar. || FIG. *To keep the home fires burning*, hacer que todo siga marchando igual.

homegrown [—ˈgrəun] adj. De cosecha propia (from one's own land). || Del país (grown locally).

homeland [—lænd] n. Patria, *f.*, tierra (*f.*) natal.

homeless [—lis] adj. Sin casa ni hogar. || *Millions homeless*, millones de personas sin hogar.

homelife [—laif] n. Vida (*f.*) de familia.

homelike [—laik] adj. Íntimo, ma; hogareño, ña.

homeliness [—linis] n. Sencillez, *f.* (simplicity). || Intimidad, *f.* (privacy). || U. S. Fealdad, *f.* (ugliness).

home-loving [—lʌviŋ] adj. Hogareño, ña; casero, ra.

homely [—li] adj. Sencillo, lla; llano, na (simple). || Familiar (atmosphere, style). || Casero, ra; doméstico, ca (home). || Cómodo, da (comfortable). || Feúcho, cha (not attractive).

homemade [—ˈmeid] adj. Casero, ra (meals). || Hecho en casa, casero, ra; de fabricación casera.

homeopath [ˈhəumjəupæθ] n. MED. Homeópata, *m.*

homeopathic [ˌhəumjəuˈpæθik] adj. MED. Homeópata (doctor). | Homeopático, ca (medicine).

homeopathy [həumiˈɔpəθi] n. MED. Homeopatía, *f.*

homer [ˈhəumə*] n. Paloma (*f.*) mensajera (pigeon).

Homer [ˈhəumə*] pr. n. Homero, *m.*

Homeric [həuˈmerik] or **Homerical** [—əl] adj. Homérico, ca.

home rule [ˈhəumru:l] n. Autonomía, *f.*, gobierno (*m.*) autónomo.

home run [ˈhəumrʌn] n. U. S. SP. Carrera (*f.*) completa del bateador [U. S., jonrón, *m.*] (in baseball).

homesick [ˈhəumsik] adj. Nostálgico, ca. || *To be homesick*, tener morriña, sentir nostalgia, añorar.

homesickness [—nis] n. Nostalgia, *f.*, morriña, *f.*, añoranza, *f.*

homespun [ˈhəumspʌn] adj. Casero, ra; tejido en casa (cloth). || Sencillo, la; llano, na (unsophisticated).

— N. Tela (*f.*) tejida en casa (fabric).

homestead [ˈhəumsted] n. Granja, *f.* [*Amer.*, estancia, *f.*, hacienda, *f.*] (farm). || U. S. Heredad, *f.*

homestretch [ˈhəumstretʃ] n. U. S. SP. Recta (*f.*) final *or* de llegada (of a racecourse).

homeward [ˈhəumwəd] adj. De regreso, de vuelta (journey).

— Adv. Hacia casa (to one's house). || Hacia la patria (to one's country). || MAR. Rumbo a su puerto de origen. || *To be homeward bound*, volver a casa *or* a su patria.

homewards [—z] adv. Hacia casa (to one's house). || Hacia la patria (to one's country).

homework [ˈhəumwə:k] n. Deberes, *m. pl.*

homicidal [ˌhɔmiˈsaidl] adj. Homicida.

homicide [ˈhɔmisaid] n. Homicidio, *m.* (crime). || Homicida, *m. & f.* (criminal).

homily [ˈhɔmili] n. Homilía, *f.* || FIG. Sermón, *m.*, rapapolvo, *m.*

homing [ˈhəumiŋ] adj. TECH. *Homing head*, cabeza buscadora. | *Homing missile*, proyectil (*m.*) con cabeza buscadora. || ZOOL. *Homing pigeon*, paloma mensajera (bird).

— N. Dirección (*f.*) por radio.

hominy [ˈhɔmini] n. U. S. Maíz (*m.*) molido.

homocentre [ˈhəuməuˌsentə*] n. Homocentro, *m.*

homoeopath [ˈhəumjəupæθ] n. MED. Homeópata, *m.*

homoeopathic [ˌhəumjəuˈpæθik] adj. MED. Homeópata (doctor). | Homeopático, ca (medicine).

homoeopathy [ˌhəumiˈɔpəθi] n. MED. Homeopatía, *f.*

homogeneity [ˌhɔməudʒeˈni:iti] n. Homogeneidad, *f.*

homogeneous [ˌhɔməuˈdʒi:njəs] adj. Homogéneo, a.

homogenization [hɔməuˌdʒənaiˈzeiʃən] n. Homogeneización, *f.*

homogenize [həˈmɔdʒənaiz] v. tr. Homogeneizar.

homograph [ˈhɔməugrɑ:f] n. Homógrafo, *m.*

homographic [ˌhɔməuˈgræfik] adj. GRAMM. Homógrafo, fa.

homography [həˈmɔgrəfi] n. Homografía, *f.*

homologation [hɔmələˈgeiʃən] n. Homologación, *f.*

homologize [həuˈmɔlədʒaiz] v. intr. Corresponder (*with*, a).

— V. tr. Hacer corresponder.

homologous [həˈmɔləgəs] adj. CHEM. MATH. Homólogo, ga.

homologue (U. S. **homolog**) [ˈhɔmələg] n. BIOL. Elemento (*m.*) homólogo.

homology [həˈmɔlədʒi] n. Homología, *f.*

homonym [ˈhɔməunim] n. Homónimo, *m.*

homonymic [ˌhɔməˈnimik] or **homonymous** [ˌhɔˈmɔniməs] adj. Homónimo, ma.

homonymy [həˈmɔnimi] n. Homonimia, *f.*

homophone [ˈhɔməufəun] n. Homófono, *m.*

homophonic [ˌhɔməˈfɔnik] or **homophonous** [ˌhɔməˈfɔnəs] adj. Homófono, na.

homophony [həˈmɔfəni] n. Homofonía, *f.*

homosexual [ˈhəuməuˈseksjuəl] adj./n. Homosexual.

homosexuality [ˈhəuməuseksjuˈæliti] n. Homosexualidad, *f.*

homothetic [hɔməˈθetik] adj. MATH. Homotético, ca.

homunculus [həuˈmʌŋkjuləs] n. Homúnculo, *m.*

— OBSERV. El plural de *homunculus* es *homunculi*.

homy [ˈhəumi] adj. Íntimo, ma.

Honduran [hɔnˈdjuərən] adj./n. Hondureño, ña.

Honduras [hɔnˈdjuərəs] pr. n. GEOGR. Honduras, *f.*

hone [həun] n. Piedra (*f.*) de afilar.

hone [həun] v. tr. Afilar.

honest [ˈɔnist] adj. Honrado, da; recto, ta: *a thoroughly honest person*, una persona honrada de los pies a la cabeza; *an honest judge*, un juez recto. || Sincero, ra; franco, ca: *give me your honest opinion*, dame tu opinión sincera. || Honesto, ta (decent, chaste). || Razonable (reasonable). || Justo, ta; equitativo, va (fair). || — *By honest means*, en buena lid. || *I didn't do it, honest*, no lo he hecho yo, te lo prometo *or* te lo juro. || *The honest truth*, la pura verdad. || *To earn an honest living*, ganarse la vida honradamente.

honestly [—li] adv. Honradamente. || Sinceramente, francamente: *I honestly believed that*, creía sinceramente que. || Con toda sinceridad: *honestly, I can assure you*, con toda sinceridad le puedo asegurar. || — *Honestly!*, ¡hay que ver! || *Honestly?*, ¿de verdad? || *Honestly speaking*, con toda sinceridad.

honesty [—i] n. Honradez, *f.*, rectitud, *f.*: *to put honesty above everything*, poner la honradez por encima de todo. || Sinceridad, *f.* (sincerity). || Honestidad, *f.* (chastity).

honey [ˈhʌni] n. Miel, *f.*: *as sweet as honey*, tan dulce como la miel. || U. S. FAM. Cielo, *m.*, mi vida (term of endearment). || — U. S. FAM. *Hello, honey!*, ¡hola, guapa! | *That's a honey of a dress*, este traje es precioso. || FIG. *To be all sugar and honey o to be all honey*, ser todo miel.

honey [ˈhʌni] v. tr. Endulzar (to sweeten). || FIG. Halagar (to flatter).

honeybee [—bi:] n. Abeja, *f.* [doméstica].
honeycomb [—kəum] n. Panal, *m.* || FIG. Laberinto, *m.*: *the old part of the town is a honeycomb of narrow streets*, la parte antigua de la ciudad es un laberinto de callejuelas. || TECH. Sopladura, *f.* (in metal).
— Adj. TECH. En forma de panal. || *Honeycomb radiator*, radiador (*m.*) de rejilla.
honeycomb [—kəum] v. tr. Acribillar (to make holes in). || Carcomer, roer: *beams honeycombed by woodworm*, vigas roídas por la carcoma. || FIG. *Hills honeycombed with caves*, colinas llenas de cuevas.
honeydew [—dju:] n. Zumo (*m.*) dulce (of plants). | Melón (*m.*) dulce (melon).
honeyed [—d] adj. Endulzado con miel. || FIG. *Honeyed words*, palabras melosas.
honeymoon [—mu:n] n. Luna (*f.*) de miel, viaje (*m.*) de novios.
honeymoon [—mu:n] v. intr. Pasar la luna de miel, hacer su viaje de novios.
honeymooner [—mu:nə*] n. Recién casado, *m.*, recién casada, *f.*
honeysuckle [—ˌsʌkl] n. BOT. Madreselva, *f.*
honied [—d] adj. See HONEYED.
honk [hɔŋk] n. Graznido, *m.* (of goose). || Bocinazo, *m.* (of car horn).
honk [hɔŋk] v. intr. Graznar (a goose). || Tocar la bocina (with a horn).
honkie-tonk or **honky-tonk** [ˈhɔŋkitɔŋk] U. S. FAM. Garito, *m.*
honor [ˈɔnə*] n./v. tr. U. S. See HONOUR.
honorable [ˈɔnərəbl] adj. U. S. See HONOURABLE.
honorableness [—nis] n. U. S. See HONOURABLENESS.
honorarium [ˌɔnəˈrεəriəm] n. Honorarios, *m. pl.*

— OBSERV. El plural de *honorarium* es *honoraria* o *honorariums*.

honorary [ˈɔnərəri] adj. Honorario, ria; de honor: *honorary member*, miembro honorario. || Honorífico, ca (duties).
honorific [ˌɔnəˈrifik] adj. Honorífico, ca.
— N. Tratamiento (*m.*) honorífico.
honour [ˈɔnə*] (U. S. **honor**) n. Honor, *m.* (moral integrity, virtue): *a man of honour*, un hombre de honor; *his honour is at stake*, su honor está en juego; *your presence is an honour for me*, su presencia es un honor para mí. || Honra, *f.*, honor, *m.* (in the eyes of others): *to fight to defend one's honour*, luchar en defensa de su honra; *to lose one's honour*, perder la honra. || Orgullo, *m.*, honra, *f.*: *to be an honour to one's country*, ser el orgullo de su país. || Condecoración, *f.* (medal, decoration). || Señoría, *f.* (title): *Your Honour*, Su Señoría. || — Pl. Honores, *m.*: *with full military honours*, con todos los honores militares. || Licenciatura (*f. sing.*) superior (honours degree). || Cartas (*f.*) más altas [de los triunfos] (in cards). || FIG. Honores (*m.*) de la casa: *let me do the honours*, déjame que haga los honores de la casa. || — FIG. *A prophet is no honour in his own country*, nadie es profeta en su tierra. || *Field of honour*, campo (*m.*) del honor. || *Honour bright!*, ¡a fe mía! || *Honours degree*, licenciatura (*f.*) superior. || *Honours of war*, honores de la guerra. || FIG. *Honour to whom honour is due*, a tal señor, tal honor. || *In honour of*, en honor de. || *Last honours*, honras fúnebres. || *Legion of Honour*, Legión (*f.*) de Honor. || *On my honour!*, ¡palabra de honor! || *Point of honour*, amor propio. || FIG. *There is honour among thieves*, un lobo a otro no se muerden. || *To be in honour bound to*, *to be on one's honour to*, estar obligado por el honor a, estar moralmente obligado a. || FIG. *To carry off the honours*, llevarse la palma. || *To deem* o *to consider* o *to regard it an honour to*, tener a honra. || *To do honour to one's regiment*, ser un orgullo para su regimiento. || *To do* o *to pay honour to s.o.*, rendir honores a alguien. || *To have the honour to*, tener el honor de. || *To pass an examination with honours*, sacar un sobresaliente. || *To swear on one's honour*, jurar por su honor. || *Upon my honour!*, ¡por mi honor!, ¡palabra de honor! || *Word of honour*, palabra (*f.*) de honor.
honour (U. S. **honor**) [ˈɔnə*] v. tr. Honrar: *to honour God*, honrar a Dios; *to honour one's father and mother*, honrar padre y madre; *to honour with one's presence*, honrar con su presencia. || Honrar, hacer honor a (to be a credit to): *to honour one's family name*, hacer honor a su apellido. || Honrar, premiar (for one's services). || Rendir homenaje (to pay homage). || Cumplir con, hacer honor a (one's word). || Hacer honor a (one's signature). || Satisfacer, honrar, hacer honor a (one's debts). || COMM. Aceptar (a cheque).
honourable (U. S. **honorable**) [ˈɔnərəbl] adj. Honorable: *an honourable family*, una familia honorable. || Honrado, da (honest). || Honroso, sa (praiseworthy): *honourable actions*, acciones honrosas; *honourable feelings*, sentimientos honrosos; *an honourable treaty*, un tratado honroso. || — *Honourable mention*, mención honorífica. || *The Honourable member for*, el Ilustre representante de.
honourableness (U. S. **honorableness**) [—nis] n. Honorabilidad, *f.* || Honradez, *f.* (honesty).
honourably (U. S. **honorably**) [—i] adv. Honradamente, honorablemente, honrosamente.
hooch [hu:tʃ] n. U. S. FAM. Aguardiente, *m.*
hood [hud] n. Capucha, *f.* (attached to the collar of a garment). || Capirote, *m.* (pointed hat). || Muceta, *f.* (of academic gown). || Capota, *f.* (of car, pram). || Capirote, *m.* (of falcon). || ARCH. Campana, *f.* (of fireplace). | Sombrerete, *m.* (of chimney). || U. S. Capó, *m.* (bonnet of a car). || U. S. FAM. Rufián, *m.*, matón, *m.* (hoodlum). || *Little Red Riding Hood*, Caperucita Roja.
hood [hud] v. tr. Cubrir con una capucha *or* un capirote. || Encapirotar (a falcon). || Poner capota a (a car). || Tapar (to cover up).
hooded [—id] adj. Con capota (car, pram). || Con capucha (man). || Encapirotado, da (falcon). || ZOOL. Capuchino, na (of two different colours). | Moñudo, da (having a crest). || *Hooded snake*, cobra, *f.*
hoodlum [—ləm] n. Matón, *m.*, rufián, *m.*
hoodoo [ˈhu:du:] n. U. S. FAM. Vudú, *m.* (religion). | Aojo, *m.*, mal (*m.*) de ojo (evil spell). | Gafe, *m.* (jinx).
hoodoo [ˈhu:du:] v. tr. U. S. FAM. Echar mal de ojo a, aojar a (to put a curse on). | Traer mala suerte (to bring bad luck).
hoodwink [ˈhudwiŋk] v. tr. Vendar los ojos a (to blindfold). || Engañar (to deceive, to trick).
hooey [ˈhu:i] n. FAM. Tonterías, *f. pl.* (nonsense).
hoof [hu:f] n. Casco, *m.*, pezuña, *f.* || Pata, *f.* (foot). || — *Cattle on the hoof*, ganado (*m.*) en pie. || *Cloven hoof*, pata hendida.

— OBSERV. El plural es *hoofs* o *hooves*.

hoof [hu:f] v. tr. FAM. *To hoof it*, ir andando, ir en el coche de San Fernando (to walk), bailar (to dance).
hoofed [hu:ft] adj. Ungulado, da.
hook [huk] n. Gancho, *m.*, garfio, *m.* (for holding, for lifting). || Anzuelo, *m.* (in fishing): *baited hook*, anzuelo con cebo. || Aldabilla, *f.* (of door, window, etc.). || Percha, *f.* (for hanging clothes). || Corchete, *m.* (on a dress). || Garabato, *m.* (in butcher's shop). || AGR. Hoz, *f.* || SP. Gancho, *m.* (in boxing). || FIG. Recodo, *m.* (of river, road, etc.). | Punta, *f.* (headland). || — Pl. FAM. Garras, *f.* (hands). || — FIG. *By hook or by crook*, por las buenas o por las malas. || *Hooks and eyes*, corchetes, *m.* || AGR. *Manure hook*, horca (*f.*) para el estiércol. || *Meat hook*, garabato, *m.* || *Off the hook*, descolgado, da (telephone). || U. S. FIG. *On one's own hook*, por iniciativa propia (without getting advice), solo, la (by o.s.). || FIG. FAM. *To get s.o. off the hook*, sacar a uno de un apuro. | *To sling one's hook*, irse con la música a otra parte. | *To swallow a story hook, line and sinker*, tragarse el anzuelo, creérselo todo. || *To take the hook*, picar (fish), tragar el anzuelo (person).
hook [huk] v. tr. Enganchar (to fasten): *to hook a trailer to a car*, enganchar un remolque a un coche. || Colgar (to hang up). || Atar: *to hook a string round the handle of a door*, atar una cuerda al picaporte. || Pescar, coger (fish). || Poner: *to hook the bait to the line*, poner el cebo en el anzuelo. || Encorvar (to curve, to bend). || Dar forma de gancho a (to make into the form of a hook). || Abrochar (a dress, etc.). || Enganchar con el bichero (a boat). || Encornar (a bull). || FIG. Pescar: *to hook a new client*, pescar un nuevo cliente. || SP. Talonar (a ball in rugby). | Dar un gancho (in boxing). | Dar efecto a (the ball in baseball). || U. S. FAM. Birlar, robar (to steal). || — *Her dress got hooked on a nail*, su vestido se enganchó en un clavo. || *To hook arms*, agarrarse del brazo. || *To hook a rug*, hacer una alfombra de nudo. || *To hook in*, enganchar (a horse), poner entre corchetes (words), echar el guante a (to catch hold of). || U. S. FIG. FAM. *To hook it*, pirárselas, largarse. || *To hook on*, enganchar (to attach), colgar (to hang). || *To hook up*, abrochar (to fasten clothes), poner (curtains), enganchar (to attach), conectar (to connect), acoplar (to couple).
— V. intr. Engancharse: *the rope hooked on to the branch*, la cuerda se enganchó en la rama. || Torcer: *the road hooks round to the left*, la carretera tuerce a la izquierda. || SP. Dar un gancho (in boxing). || U. S. FIG. FAM. Largarse, pirárselas (to go). || — *To hook at*, dar cornadas, cornear (the bull). || *To hook on to*, pegarse a (a person). || *To hook up*, abrocharse.
hooka or **hookah** [ˈhukə] n. Narguile, *m.* (Oriental pipe).
hooked [hukt] adj. Ganchudo, da (hook-shaped): *a hooked nose*, una nariz ganchuda. || — *Hooked rug*, alfombra de nudo. || *Hooked on drugs*, adicto a las drogas. || *To get hooked on*, enviciarse en, aficionarse a.
hooker [hukə*] n. SP. Talonador, *m.* (in rugby). || MAR. Urca, *f.*
hookey [ˈhuki] n. FAM. *To play hookey*, hacer novillos.
hookup [ˈhukʌp] n. Red (*f.*) de circuitos (to make a radio, etc.). || Conexión, *f.* (connection). || Emisión (*f.*) transmitida a varios países [por Eurovisión o Mundovisión). || FAM. Alianza, *f.*
hookworm [ˈhukwə:m] n. ZOOL. Anquilostoma, *m.* || MED. Anquilostomiasis, *f.* (illness).
hooky [ˈhuki] n. *To play hooky*, hacer novillos.
hooligan [ˈhu:ligən] n. Gamberro, *m.*
hooliganism [huliˈgænizəm] n. Gamberrismo, *m.*
hoop [hu:p] n. Aro, *m.* (of skirt, child's toy). || Fleje, *m.* (of barrel). || Aro, *m.* (in croquet). || Llanta, *f.* (of a wheel). || *To trundle a hoop*, jugar al aro.

hoop [hu:p] v. intr. See WHOOP.
— V. tr. Enarcar (a cask).
hoopoe [ˈhu:pu:] n. Abubilla, *f.* (bird).
hoopskirt [ˈhu:pˌskə:t] n. Miriñaque, *m.*
hoosegow [ˈhusgau] n. U. S. FAM. Trena, *f.*, chirona, *f.* (gaol).
hoot [hu:t] n. Ululato, *m.* (of an owl). || Bocinazo, *m.* (of a car). || Toque (*m.*) de sirena (of boat, factory). || Silbato, *m.* (of a locomotive). || Grito, *m.* (shout). || — *A hoot of laughter*, una risotada. || FIG. *I don't care a hoot* o *two hoots*, no me importa un bledo *or* un pepino *or* un pito. || *This is not worth a hoot*, esto no vale un pito *or* un comino.
hoot [hu:t] v. intr. Ulular (owl). || Silbar (person). || Abuchear (to boo). || Dar un bocinazo, tocar la bocina (car). || Dar un toque de sirena (ship). || Pitar (siren). || Silbar (a train). || *To hoot with laughter*, carcajearse.
— V. tr. Abuchear, pitar, silbar (to boo).
hooter [—ə*] n. Sirena, *f.* (siren). || Bocina, *f.* (of a car).
hoove [hu:v] n. VET. Meteorismo, *m.*
hoover [—ə*] n. Aspiradora, *f.*
hoover [—ə*] v. tr. Pasar la aspiradora en.
hooves [hu:vz] pl. n. See HOOF.
hop [hɔp] n. BOT. Lúpulo, *m.* || Saltito, *m.*, salto, *m.*, brinco, *m.* (little jump). || Salto (*m.*) a la pata coja (on one foot). || Vuelo, *m.* (by plane). || Etapa, *f.* (stage of a journey). || FAM. Baile, *m.* (dance). | Estupefaciente, *m.* (narcotic). | Trola, *f.*, cuento, *m.* (lie). || — SP. *Hop, step and jump* o *hop, skip and jump*, triple salto. || FIG. FAM. *To catch s.o. on the hop*, pillar a alguien con las manos en la masa (to catch s.o. red-handed), coger desprevenido a alguien (to catch s.o. unawares).
hop [hɔp] v. intr. Saltar, brincar, dar un saltito *or* saltitos. || Ir a saltitos: *to hop along the street*, ir a saltitos por la calle. || Saltar a la pata coja (on one leg). || Saltar: *to hop out of bed*, saltar de la cama; *to hop over the fence*, saltar la valla. || Dar *or* pegar un salto: *hop across to the baker's for me*, pega un salto a la panadería por mí. || FAM. Bailar (to dance). || — FIG. *To hop from one thing to another*, pasar de una cosa a otra. || *To hop off*, largarse (to go away), bajar de un salto de (a bus, bicycle, etc.). || *To hop on*, montar de un salto en (a bicycle), subir a (a bus, train, etc.). || *To hop over to*, darse una vuelta por, pegar un salto a: *I think I'll hop over to London at the weekend*, este fin de semana creo que me daré una vuelta por Londres. || *To hop to it*, echar manos a la obra.
— V. tr. Saltar (to jump over). || U. S. Subir a, coger (a bus, etc.). || — FAM. *Hop it!*, ¡lárgate! || *To hop a train* o *to hop a ride in a train*, subirse en un tren en marcha para no pagar billete. || FAM. *To hop the twig*, estirar la pata (to die). | *To hop up*, drogar.
hope [həup] n. Esperanza, *f.*: *hope is my only consolation*, la esperanza es mi único consuelo; *new hopes for peace*, nuevas esperanzas de paz; *there is a hope of success*, hay esperanza de éxito. || Posibilidad, *f.* (chance). || — *As a last hope*, como última esperanza. || *In the hope of* o *that*, con la esperanza de *or* de que. || *Land of hope*, tierra (*f.*) de promisión. || *One should never lose hope*, la esperanza es lo último que se pierde. || FAM. *Some hopes!*, ¡espérate sentado! || *There is no hope for him*, no le queda ninguna esperanza. || *To be beyond hope*, ser un caso desesperado. || *To build up hopes*, hacerse ilusiones. || *To fulfil one's hopes*, llenar las esperanzas de uno. || *To give hope for* o *that*, dar esperanza de *or* de que. || *To have high hopes*, tener muchas esperanzas. || *To have hopes that*, tener esperanzas de que. || *To have little hope*, tener pocas esperanzas. || *To live in hope of sth.*, tener la esperanza de algo. || *To live on hope*, vivir de esperanzas. || *To place all one's hopes in s.o.*, poner todas sus esperanzas en alguien. || *We must hope against hope*, la esperanza es lo último que se pierde. || *Whilst there is life, there is hope*, mientras hay vida hay esperanza.
hope [həup] v. intr. Esperar: *I hope so*, espero que sí; *I hope not*, espero que no. || — *I should hope so!*, ¡eso espero! || *To hope for*, tener esperanzas de: *to be hoping for success*, tener esperanzas de éxito; contar con (to count on): *we are hoping for good weather*, contamos con el buen tiempo; esperar: *all we can do is to hope for a miracle*, todo lo que podemos hacer es esperar un milagro. || *To hope in*, confiar en.
— V. tr. Esperar: *I hope he will come*, espero que vendrá. || — *Hoping to hear from you*, en espera de sus gratas noticias (in letters). || *To hope to God that*, esperar en Dios que.
hope chest [—tʃest] n. U. S. FAM. Ajuar, *m.*
hopeful [—ful] adj. Esperanzador, ra; alentador, ra; prometedor, ra: *the situation seems hopeful*, la situación parece esperanzadora. || Optimista: *he is in a hopeful mood*, está de humor optimista. || Confiado, da (confident). || Que promete, prometedor, ra (promising). || *To be hopeful that*, tener muchas esperanzas de que.
— N. Promesa, *f.* (person).
hopefully [—fuli] adv. Con optimismo. || De un modo alentador *or* prometedor.
hopefulness [—fulnis] n. Optimismo, *m.* || Aspecto (*m.*) alentador *or* prometedor (of a situation).
hopeless [—lis] adj. Desesperado, da (case, state, etc.): *the situation seems hopeless*, la situación parece desesperada. || Imposible: *it's a hopeless job*, es un trabajo imposible. || MED. Desahuciado, da (an incurable person). || FAM. Inútil (useless). | Perdido, da: *a hopeless drunkard*, un borracho perdido. || *To give sth. up as hopeless*, dejar algo por imposible.
hopelessly [—lisli] adv. Sin esperanza, con desesperación. || Desesperadamente (in love). || *To be hopelessly drunk*, estar borracho perdido, estar completamente borracho.
hopelessness [—lisnis] n. Desesperación, *f.* || Inutilidad, *f.* (of an effort). || Estado (*m.*) desesperado (of incurable person, a situation).
hophead [ˈhɔphed] n. U. S. FAM. Drogadicto, ta; toxicómano, na.
hop-o'-my-thumb [ˈhɔpəmiˈθʌm] n. FAM. Enano, na (midget).
hopped up [ˈhɔptʌp] adj. U. S. FAM. Drogado, da. | Excitado, da (excited). | Arreglado, da (a car engine).
hopper [ˈhɔpə*] n. ZOOL. Insecto (*m.*) saltador. || TECH. Tolva, *f.* (of mill). | Tragante, *m.* (of furnace). || MAR. Gánguil, *m.* (boat). || FAM. Pulga, *f.* (flea). || *Hopper car*, vagón (*m.*) tolva.
hopping [ˈhɔpiŋ] adj. *He is hopping mad*, está que bota, está que trina (he is angry).
hopple [ˈhɔpl] n. Traba, *f.*, maniota, *f.* (rope).
hopple [ˈhɔpl] v. tr. Trabar, poner trabas (an animal).
hopscotch [ˈhɔpskɔtʃ] n. Infernáculo, *m.*, tejo, *m.* [*Amer.*, rayuela, *f.*] (game).
Horace [ˈhɔrəs] pr. n. Horacio, *m.*
horary [ˈhɔrəri] adj. Horario, ria.
horde [hɔ:d] n. Horda, *f.* || FIG. Multitud, *f.*
horizon [həˈraizn] n. Horizonte, *m.*: *on the horizon*, en el horizonte. || FIG. Horizonte, *m.*, perspectiva, *f.*
horizontal [ˌhɔriˈzɔntl] adj. Horizontal. || SP. *Horizontal bar*, barra fija.
— N. Horizontal, *f.* (line).
horizontality [ˌhɔrizɔnˈtæliti] n. Horizontalidad, *f.*
horizontally [ˌhɔriˈzɔntli] adv. Horizontalmente.
hormonal [ˈhɔ:ˈməunəl] adj. Hormonal.
hormone [ˈhɔ:məun] n. BIOL. Hormona, *f.*
horn [hɔ:n] n. Cuerno, *m.*, asta, *f.* (of bull, deer). || Asta, *f.*, cuerno, *m.* (substance): *a horn comb*, un peine de asta. || Cuerno, *m.* (of an insect, snail, the moon). || MUS. Trompa, *f.*, cuerno, *m.* || Bocina, *f.*, claxon, *m.* (of a car): *to blow the horn*, tocar la bocina. || Calzador, *m.* (for shoes). || Pabellón, *m.*, bocina, *f.* (of gramophone, loudspeaker). || Brazo, *m.* (of river). || Punta, *f.* (of anvil). || — MUS. *French horn*, trompa, *f.* || FIG. *Horn of plenty*, cuerno de la abundancia, cornucopia, *f.* || MUS. *Horn player*, trompa, *m.* || *Hunting horn*, cuerno de caza. || FIG. *On the horns of a dilemma*, entre la espada y la pared. | *To blow one's own horn*, echarse flores. | *To draw in one's horns*, bajársele a uno los humos, moderarse.
horn [hɔ:n] v. tr. Dar una cornada a, cornear.
— V. intr. *To horn in*, entrometerse (*on*, en).
hornbeam [ˈhɔ:nbi:m] n. BOT. Carpe, *m.*
hornblende [ˈhɔ:nblend] n. MIN. Hornablenda, *f.*
hornbook [ˈhɔ:nbuk] n. Abecedario, *m.*
horned [ˈhɔ:nid] adj. Con cuernos (animals). || — U. S. ZOOL. *Horned owl*, búho, *m.* || ZOOL. *Horned toad*, lagarto cornudo. | *Horned viper*, víbora cornuda.
hornet [ˈhɔ:nit] n. ZOOL. Avispón, *m.* (wasp). || — FAM. *To bring a hornet's nest about one's ears* o *to stir up a hornet's nest*, meterse en un avispero *or* en un lío.
hornless [ˈhɔ:nlis] adj. Mocho, cha; sin cuernos.
horn owl [ˈhɔ:naul] n. ZOOL. Búho, *m.*
hornpipe [ˈhɔ:npaip] n. MUS. Chirimía, *f.* (instrument). | Baile (*m.*) de marineros (dance).
horn-rimmed [ˈhɔ:nrimd] adj. De concha (glasses).
hornswoggle [ˈhɔ:nsˌwɔgl] v. tr. U. S. FAM. Embaucar, engañar (to hoax).
horny [ˈhɔ:ni] adj. Córneo, a (of or like horn). || Calloso, sa (hands). || Con cuernos (horned).
hologe [ˈhɔrəlɔdʒ] n. Reloj, *m.*
horologer [—ə*] or **horologist** [ist] n. Relojero, ra.
horoscope [ˈhɔrəskəup] n. Horóscopo, *m.*: *to cast a horoscope*, hacer un horóscopo.
horrendous [hɔˌrendəs] adj. Horrendo, da.
horrent [ˈhɔrənt] adj. Erizado, da. || Horrorizado, da.
horrible [ˈhɔrəbl] adj. Horrible, horroroso, sa; horrendo, da: *horrible weather*, un tiempo horroroso; *a horrible sight*, una visión horrible. || *Don't be horrible!*, ¡no seas antipático!
horribly [—i] adv. Horriblemente (in a horrible manner). || Terriblemente (to a horrible degree). || *It's horribly cold*, hace un frío espantoso.
horrid [ˈhɔrid] adj. Antipático, ca; odioso, sa (unkind). || Horrible, horroroso, sa (horrible). || Inaguantable, insoportable (a child). || *To be horrid to s.o.*, tratar muy mal a alguien.
horrific [hɔˈrifik] adj. Horrendo, da; horroroso, sa.
horrify [ˈhɔrifai] v. tr. Horrorizar. || *I was horrified at the idea*, me horrorizaba la idea.
horripilation [hɔripiˈleiʃən] n. Horripilación, *f.*
horror [ˈhɔrə*] n. Horror, *m.*, pavor, *m.* (fear): *pale with horror*, pálido de horror. || Horror, *m.*: *the horrors of war*, los horrores de la guerra. || Ansia, *f.*, angustia, *f.* (of death). || Diablo, *m.*: *this child is a horror*, este niño es un diablo. || — *Horror film*, película (*f.*) de miedo. || *It gives me the horrors*, me da horror. || *To have a horror of*, tener horror a. || *You horror!*, ¡antipático!

horror-stricken [—,strikən] adj. Horrorizado, da.
hors d'oeuvre [ɔ:ˈdə:vr] n. CULIN. Entremés, *m.*
— OBSERV. El plural de esta palabra es *hors d'œuvres.*
horse [hɔ:s] n. Caballo, *m.* (animal). || Caballete, *m.* (of a carpenter). || Potro, *m.* (in gymnastics). || MIL. Caballería, *f.* (cavalry). || Caballo, *m.* (in chess). || MAR. Marchapié, *m.* || FIG. FAM. Caballo, *m.* (heavy-featured person). || — *Cart horse*, caballo de tiro. || *Change of horse*, relevo, *m.* || FIG. *Don't look a gift horse in the mouth*, a caballo regalado no le mires el diente. || FIG. FAM. *Hold your horses!*, ¡no te sulfures! (control your temper), ¡echa el freno!, ¡para el carro! (not so fast). || MIL. *Horse soldier*, soldado (*m.*) de a caballo. || *Saddle horse*, caballo de montar *or* de silla. || SP. *Side* o *pommelled horse*, potro (*m.*) con arzón. || FIG. *That's a horse of a different colour*, eso es otro cantar, eso es harina de otro costal. | *To be flogging a dead horse*, azotar el aire. | *To be on* o *to get on one's high horse, to mount* o *to ride the high horse*, tener muchos humos, darse importancia *or* pisto *or* aires. | *To change horses in midstream*, efectuar un cambio a mitad de camino. | *To come down off one's high horse*, bajársele a uno los humos. | *To eat like a horse*, comer como un sabañón, comer como un regimiento. || *To get on* o *to mount a horse*, subir a *or* montar a caballo. || FIG. *To get sth. straight from the horse's mouth*, saber algo de buena tinta. || *To horse!*, ¡a caballo! || *To play the horses*, apostar en las carreras de caballos. | FIG. *White horses*, cabrillas, *f. pl.* (of waves). | *Wild horses could not drag it out of him*, no se puede sacárselo ni con tenazas. || *Wooden horse* (*of Troy*) o *Trojan horse*, caballo de Troya.
— Adj. De caballos (race). || Montado, da (artillery). || FIG. Basto, ta (coarse).
horse [hɔ:s] v. tr. Proveer de caballos. || FAM. Tomar el pelo a (to kid).
— V. intr. Estar salida (a mare). || U. S. *To horse around*, hacer el tonto, bromear.
horseback [—bæk] n. *On horseback*, a caballo.
horsebean [—bi:n] n. BOT. Haba (*f.*) panosa.
horse block [—blɔk] n. Montadero, *m.*
horse box [—bɔks] n. Vagón (*m.*) para transportar caballos (railway). || Furgón (*m.*) para el transporte de caballos (car).
horsebreaker [—,breikə*] n. Domador (*m.*) de caballos.
horse butcher's [—ˈbutʃə*] n. Expendeduría (*f.*) de carne de caballo, carnicería (*f.*) hipofágica.
horse chestnut [—ˈtʃesnʌt] n. BOT. Castaña (*f.*) de Indias (fruit). | Castaño (*m.*) de Indias (tree).
horsecloth [—klɔθ] n. Manta (*f.*) para caballos.
horsedealer [—,di:lə*] n. Chalán, *m.*, tratante (*m.*) de caballos.
horse doctor [—,dɔktə*] n. Veterinario, *m.* || FIG. FAM. Matasanos, *m. inv.* (doctor).
horse-drawn [—drɔ:n] adj. Tirado por caballos, de tracción de sangre.
horseflesh [—fleʃ] n. Carne (*f.*) de caballo. || Caballos, *m. pl.*: *a good judge of horseflesh*, un entendido en caballos.
horsefly [—flai] n. Tábano, *m.* (insect).
Horse Guards [—gɑ:dz] pl. n. Guardia (*f. sing.*) montada.
horsehair [—hεə*] n. Crin, *f.*
horselaugh [—lɑ:f] n. Carcajada, *f.*, risotada, *f.*
horseless [—lis] adj. Sin caballo. || *Horseless carriage*, automóvil, *m.*
horse mackerel [—ˈmækrəl] n. Jurel, *m.* (fish).
horseman [—mən] n. Jinete, *m.*, caballista, *m.* (rider).
— OBSERV. El plural de esta palabra es *horsemen.*
horsemanship [—mənʃip] n. Equitación, *f.*
horse opera [—ˈɔpərə] n. U. S. Película (*f.*) del Oeste.
horseplay [—plei] n. Payasadas, *f. pl.* || Pelea, *f.* (boisterous fun).
horse pond [—pɔnd] n. Abrevadero (*m.*) de caballos.
horsepower [—,pauə*] inv. n. Caballo (*m.*) de vapor, caballo, *m.*: *a four horsepower car*, un coche de cuatro caballos. || Potencia, *f.*: *brake horsepower*, potencia al freno. || COMM. *Treasury horsepower*, caballo fiscal.
horse racing [—ˈreisiŋ] n. Carreras (*f. pl.*) de caballos, hipismo, *m.*
horseradish [—,rædiʃ] n. Rábano (*m.*) picante.
horse's ass [—zæs] n. FAM. Burro, *m.*, necio, *m.*
horse sense [—sens] n. FIG. FAM. Sentido (*m.*) común.
horseshoe [—ʃu:] n. Herradura, *f.* || *Horseshoe arch*, arco (*m.*) de herradura.
horse show [—ʃəu] n. Concurso (*m.*) hípico.
horsetail [—teil] n. BOT. Cola (*f.*) de caballo.
horse thief [—θi:f] n. Cuatrero, *m.*
horse trade [—treid] n. Chalaneo, *m.*
horsewhip [—wip] n. Látigo, *m.*
horsewhip [—wip] v. tr. Dar latigazos a, azotar.
horsewoman [—,wumən] n. Caballista, *f.*, amazona, *f.*
— OBSERV. El plural de esta palabra es *horsewomen.*
horsiness [—inis] n. Afición (*f.*) a los caballos. || Aspecto (*m.*) caballuno.
horsy [—i] adj. Caballuno, na: *horsy features*, rasgos caballunos. || Hípico, ca. || Aficionado a los caballos y a las carreras. || *A horsy smell*, un olor a caballo.

hortative [ˈhɔ:tətiv] or **hortatory** [ˈhɔ:tətəri] adj. Exhortador, ra; exhortatorio, ria.
horticultural [,hɔ:tiˈkʌltʃərəl] adj. Hortícola.
horticulture [ˈhɔ:tikʌltʃə*] n. Horticultura, *f.*
horticulturist [,hɔ:tiˈkʌltʃərist] n. Horticultor, *m.*
hosanna [həuˈzænə] n. REL. Hosanna, *m.*
hose [həuz] n. Manguera, *f.*, manga, *f.* (flexible tube). || Medias, *f. pl.* (women's stockings). || Calcetines, *m. pl.* (socks). || (Ant.). Calzas, *f. pl.* (mediaeval tights).
— OBSERV. Esta palabra es invariable excepto cuando significa « manguera ».
hose [həuz] v. tr. Regar con una manga (to water). || Limpiar con una manga (to clean).
hosier [ˈhəuziə*] n. Calcetero, ra.
hosiery [—ri] n. Calcetería, *f.*, géneros (*m. pl.*) de punto (goods). || Medias (*f. pl.*) y calcetines (in a store).
hospice [ˈhɔspis] n. Hospicio, *m.*
hospitable [ˈhɔspitəbl] adj. Hospitalario, ria; acogedor, ra. || FIG. Abierto, ta; receptivo, va: *a person hospitable to new ideas*, unas persona abierta a las nuevas ideas.
hospitably [—i] adv. Con hospitalidad, de una manera hospitalaria.
hospital [ˈhɔspitl] n. MED. Hospital, *m.*: *hospital train*, tren hospital; *hospital ship*, buque hospital. || HIST. Hospicio, *m.* || — MIL. *Field hospital*, hospital de sangre. || *Maternity hospital*, casa (*f.*) de maternidad. || *Mental hospital*, manicomio, *m.*
hospitaler [—ə*] n. U. S. Capellán, *m.*
Hospitaler [—ə*] n. U. S. REL. Caballero (*m.*) hospitalario, hospitalario, *m.*
hospitality [,hɔspiˈtæliti] n. Hospitalidad, *f.*
hospitalization [,hɔspitəlaiˈzeiʃən] n. Hospitalización, *f.*
hospitalize [ˈhɔspitəlaiz] v. tr. Hospitalizar.
hospitaller [ˈhɔspitlə*] n. Capellán, *m.* (in a hospital).
Hospitaller [ˈhɔspitlə*] n. REL. Caballero (*m.*) hospitalario, hospitalario, *m.*
host [həust] n. Anfitrión, ona; huésped, da (at a meal, etc.). || BIOL. BOT. Huésped, *m.* (plant, animal). || Hostelero, *m.*, mesonero, *m.* (of an inn). || Multitud, *f.* (multitude). || Montón, *m.* (of ideas, etc.). || Hueste, *f.* (of angels, enemies). || Presentador, *m.* (in cabaret, etc.). || — *Host nation*, país organizador (of a competition, etc.). || FIG. *To reckon without one's host*, no contar con la huéspeda.
Host [həust] n. REL. Hostia, *f.* || *Lord God of Hosts*, Señor (*m.*) de los ejércitos.
hostage [ˈhɔstidʒ] n. Rehén, *m.*: *to hold hostage*, tener como rehén.
hostel [ˈhɔstəl] n. Residencia, *f.* (for students). || Albergue, *m.*: *youth hostel*, albergue juvenil. || Hotel, *m.*, parador, *m.*
hostelry [—ri] n. Hostal, *m.*
hostess [ˈhəustis] n. Anfitriona, *f.*, huéspeda, *f.* (at a meal, etc.). || Hostelera, *f.*, mesonera, *f.* (of an inn). || Azafata, *f.* (air hostess). || Presentadora, *f.* (in cabaret, etc.).
hostile [ˈhɔstail] adj. Hostil, enemigo, ga: *a hostile nation*, una nación hostil. || De hostilidad: *hostile act*, acto de hostilidad. || *To be hostile to*, estar en contra de (reform, etc.).
hostility [hɔsˈtiliti] n. Hostilidad, *f.* || — Pl. Hostilidades, *f.*: *to begin, to renew hostilities*, romper, reanudar las hostilidades.
hot [hɔt] adj. Caliente: *hot water*, agua caliente; *the radiator is hot*, el radiador está caliente. || Cálido, da; caluroso, sa (climate). || Caluroso, sa; de calor (day). || Abrasador, ra (sun). || CULIN. Picante (spicy). || Fuerte, subido, da (colours). || Fresco, ca; reciente (scent, trail). || ELECTR. De alta tensión (wire). || TECH. En caliente (working metals). | Radioactivo, va (radioactive). || FIG. Acalorado, da (argument). | Vivo, va (temper). | Muy discutido, da; controvertido, da (controversial). | Muy delicado, da (situation). | Peligroso, sa (dangerous). | Porfiado, da (pursuit). | Ardiente (follower, supporter). | Apasionado, da (passionate). | Feroz (battle). | Caliente (in children's games): *now you're hot*, caliente, caliente. || FIG. FAM. Robado, da (stolen). | Estupendo, da; extraordinario, ria (very good). || POP. Caliente.
— FIG. *A hot contest*, una lucha muy reñida. || *Boiling hot*, ardiendo, abrasando. || FIG. *Hot air*, música (*f.*) celestial, palabras (*f. pl.*) al aire. | *Hot and strong*, muy fuerte. | *Hot favourite*, gran favorito, *m.* (horse racing, etc.). | *Hot for*, ansioso de. | *Hot from London*, recién llegado de Londres. | *Hot line*, teléfono rojo (between Washington and Moscow). | *Hot music*, "swing", *m.* | *Hot news*, noticia (*f.*) bomba (big news), noticias (*f. pl.*) de última hora (latest news). | *Hot seat*, silla eléctrica (electric chair), apuro, *m.*, aprieto, *m.* (tight spot). | *Hot tip*, informe seguro. | *Hot words*, palabras (*f.*) mayores. | *Hot work*, trabajo duro. | *News hot from the press*, noticias (*f. pl.*) de última hora. | *Not so hot*, no tan bueno. || *To be hot*, tener calor (person): *I am very hot*, tengo mucho calor; hacer calor (weather): *it's very hot today*, hoy hace mucho calor; estar caliente (things): *the soup is very hot*, la sopa está muy caliente. || FIG. *To be hot on*, ser muy aficionado a (to be fond of), ser perito en (to be an expert on). | *To be hot on s.o.'s track* o *on s.o.'s trail*, seguir a alguien de cerca, estar sobre la pista de alguien. || FAM. *To be hot stuff*, ser cachondo, da (lecherous). || FIG. *To be hot stuff at*

geography, ser un hacha en geografía. | *To be hot stuff at tennis*, ser un as del tenis. | *To blow hot and cold*, see BLOW. | *To get all hot and bothered*, ponerse nervioso y colorado, sofocarse (to get flustered). || *To get hot*, acalorarse (angry person), calentarse (thing), empezar a hacer calor (weather). || FIG. *To get o.s. into hot water*, meterse en un aprieto *or* en un lío. | *To give it s.o. hot*, echar un rapapolvo a alguien. | *To have a hot temper*, tener un genio violento *or* fuerte *or* vivo. | *To make a place too hot for s.o.*, hacer que la situación sea inaguantable para alguien. | *To put s.o. in the hot sea*, ponerle a uno en un aprieto. || *White hot*, calentado al rojo blanco.
— Adv. Con calor. || Calurosamente. || Acaloradamente. || Ardientemente. || Vehementemente. || Apasionadamente. || Violentamente.

hot [hɔt] v. tr. FAM. Calentar.

hot baths [—bɑ:ðz] pl. n. Termas, *f.*

hotbed [—bed] n. Estercolero, *m.* (dunghill). || FIG. Semillero, *m.* (of vice, disease, etc.).

hot-blooded [—ˈblʌdid] adj. *To be hot-blooded*, tener la sangre caliente, ser muy apasionado.

hotchpotch [—ʃpɔtʃ] n. CULIN. Ropa (*f.*) vieja (stew). || FIG. Mezcolanza, *f.*, batiburrillo, *m.* (mixture).

hot dog [ˈhɔtˈdɔg] n. Perro (*m.*) caliente (sandwich).

hotel [həuˈtel] n. Hotel, *m.*: *at* o *in a hotel*, en un hotel.

hotelkeeper [—ˈki:pə*] n. Hotelero, ra.

hotfoot [ˈhɔtfut] adv. FAM. A toda prisa (very fast).

hotfoot [ˈhɔtfut] v. tr./intr. *To hotfoot it*, volar, ir corriendo (to go quickly).

hothead [ˈhɔthed] n. FAM. Impulsivo, va.

hotheaded [ˈhɔtˈhedid] adj. Impulsivo, va; impetuoso, sa (impetuous). || Enfadadizo, za (quick-tempered). || Exaltado, da (excitable).

hothouse [ˈhɔthaus] n. Invernadero, *m.* (for plants).

hotly [ˈhɔtli] adv. De cerca: *hotly pursued*, seguido de cerca. || Con pasión (fiercely). || Acaloradamente. || Violentamente.

hotness [ˈhɔtnis] n. Lo picante (of a spice). || FIG. Ardor, *m.* (of passions).

hot pants [ˈhɔtpænts] pl. n. Shorts, *m.*, pantalones (*m.*) cortos (garment).

hot plate [ˈhɔtpleit] n. Calientaplatos, *m. inv.* || Hornillo, *m.* (portable stove).

hot pot [ˈhɔtpɔt] n. CULIN. Estofado, *m.* (stewed meat and vegetables).

hot-press [ˈhɔtpres] n. TECH. Calandria, *f.*

hot-press [ˈhɔtpres] v. tr. TECH. Calandrar.

hot rod [ˈhɔtrɔd] n. U. S. FAM. Bólido, *m.* (fast car).

hotshot [hɔtʃɔt] adj. U. S. FAM. Brillante, de primera.

hot spot [ˈhɔtspɔt] n. FIG Situación (*f.*) crítica. | Sitio (*m.*) donde la situación es crítica. | Sala (*f.*) de fiestas (nightclub).

hot springs [ˈhɔtˈspriŋz] pl. n. Aguas (*f.*) termales.

Hottentot [ˈhɔtntɔt] adj./n. Hotentote, ta.

hot-water bottle [hɔtˈwɔ:tə,bɔtl] n. Bolsa (*f.*) de agua caliente.

hound [haund] n. Perro, *m.* [de caza], podenco, *m.* (hunting dog). || FIG. Canalla, *m.* || — *Pack of hounds*, jauría, *f.* || *To follow the hounds* o *to ride to hounds*, cazar con jauría.

hound [haund] v. tr. Acosar, perseguir (to harass, to pursue). || Cazar con perros. || Azuzar (a dog). || — *To hound s.o. down*, acosar a alguien. || *To hound s.o. on*, incitar a uno (*to*, a).

hound's tongue [ˈhaundz,tʌŋ] n. BOT. Cinoglosa, *f.*

hound's-tooth check [ˈhaundz,tu:θˈtʃek] n. U. S. Pata (*f.*) de gallo (fabric).

hour [auə*] n. Hora, *f.*: *there are sixty minutes in an hour*, hay sesenta minutos en una hora; *dinner hour*, la hora de comer; *at an early hour*, a una hora temprana; *at this hour he's usually having a nap*, a esta hora suele dormir la siesta; *the fateful hour*, la hora fatal. || FIG. Hora, *f.*, momento, *m.* || — Pl. Horario, *m. sing.*: *to keep reasonable hours*, respetar un horario razonable. || REL. Horas, *f.*
— *After hours*, fuera de horas. || *A good hour*, una hora larga (easily an hour). || *A hundred miles an hour*, cien millas por hora. || *An eight-hour day*, una jornada de ocho horas. || *An hour and a half*, una hora y media. || *A quarter of an hour*, un cuarto de hora. || *At all hours*, a todas horas. || *At an hour's notice*, con aviso previo de una hora. || *At the eleventh hour*, a última hora. || *By the hour*, por horas. || *Children's hour*, programa (*m.*) infantil (on the radio, etc.). || *Half an hour* o *half hour*, media hora. || FIG. *His hour has come*, ha llegado su hora. || *Hour by hour*, de hora en hora. || *Hour of truth*, hora de la verdad. || *Hours on end*, horas enteras. || *Office* o *business hours*, horas de oficina. || *Off-peak hour*, horas de menos afluencia *or* tráfico (transport), horas de menor consumo (gas, etc.). || *On the hour*, a la hora en punto. || *Peak hours*, horas de mayor consumo (gas, etc.), horas punta *or* de mayor afluencia (transport, etc.). || *Per hour*, por hora (speed, production, etc.), a la hora, por hora (wages). || *Rush hour*, hora de mayor afluencia, hora punta. || *Small hours*, altas horas. || *The news is broadcast on the hour and on the half hour*, dan las noticias a las horas y a las medias. || *The questions of the hour*, los problemas actuales. || *To keep good hours*, acostarse temprano. || *To keep late hours*, acostarse tarde, trasnochar. || *To keep regular hours*, llevar una vida ordenada. || *To strike the hour*, dar la hora. || *To take hours over sth.*, tardar horas en hacer algo. || *To work long hours*, trabajar muchas horas. || *Visiting hours*, horas de visita. || *Working hours*, horas de trabajo. || *Zero hour*, hora H.

hour circle [—ˈsə:kl] n. ASTR. Círculo (*m.*) horario.

hourglass [—glɑ:s] n. Reloj (*m.*) de arena.

hour hand [—hænd] n. Horario, *m.*, manecilla (*f.*) de las horas.

houri [ˈhuəri] n. Hurí, *f.*

hourly [ˈauə:li] adj. De cada hora. || Cada hora (trains, etc.): *there is an hourly train to London*, hay un tren para Londres cada hora. || Por hora (wage, output). || Incesante (continual). || *On an hourly basis*, por hora.
— Adv. Cada hora (every hour): *the medicine should be taken hourly*, se debe tomar el medicamento cada hora. || Por hora, por horas (to pay). || De un momento a otro (at any moment): *we're expecting news hourly*, esperamos noticias de un momento a otro.

house [haus] n. Casa, *f.*: *a three-story house*, una casa de tres pisos; *publishing house*, casa editorial. || Cámara, *f.* (of legislative body): *the House of Lords*, la Cámara de los Lores. || Colegio (*m.*) mayor (of students' residence). || Casa, *f.* (of a noble family): *the House of Bourbon*, la Casa de Borbón. || COMM. Casa, *f.* (commercial establishment). || THEATR. Sala, *f.* (theatre). | Público, *m.* (audience). || ASTR. Casa, *f.*
— THEATR. *A good house*, mucho público (a big audience), buen público (a good audience). || *At my house*, en casa, en mi casa. || *Country house*, casa de campo. || FIG. *Disorderly house*, see DISORDERLY. || *Doll's house*, casa de muñecas. || *Eating house*, restaurante, *m.* || *Fashion house*, casa de modas. || *From house to house*, de casa en casa. || *Full house*, [teatro] lleno (theatre), no hay localidades (notice outside theatre), full, *m.* (poker). || *Gambling house*, casa de juego. || *Have a drink on the house*, tómate una copa, invita *or* paga la casa. || *House of cards*, castillo (*m.*) de naipes. || *House of Commons*, Cámara de los Comunes. || *House of correction*, correccional, *m.*, reformatorio, *m.* || U. S. *House of Representatives*, Cámara de Representantes. || *Houses of Parliament*, Parlamento, *m. sing.* || *Lower House*, Cámara Baja. || *Mother house*, casa matriz. || *On the house*, regalo (*m.*) *or* cortesía (*f.*) de la casa. || *Out of house and home*, sin casa ni hogar, en la calle. || *Parents' house*, casa paterna. || *The House of God*, la casa de Dios. || THEATR. *To bring the house down*, ser un exitazo. || U. S. *To clean house*, hacer las labores domésticas. || FIG. *To get on like a house on fire*, llevarse de maravilla (to get on very well), progresar rápidamente (to progress). || *To keep house*, llevar la casa. || *To keep open house*, tener mesa franca *or* casa abierta. || *To keep to the house*, quedarse en casa. || *To make a House*, obtener el quórum. || *To move house*, mudarse. || *To run the house*, llevar la casa. || *To set up house*, poner casa. || *Upper House*, Senado, *m.*, Cámara Alta.

house [hauz] v. tr. Alojar: *the new wing will house fifty students*, la nueva ala podrá alojar a cincuenta estudiantes. || Albergar, alojar (to put up). || Dar alojamiento para (on a large scale): *to house immigrants*, dar alojamiento para los inmigrantes. || Almacenar (to store). || Entrojar (grain). || Poner a cubierto *or* al abrigo (to shelter). || Contener (to contain). || TECH. Encajar. || MAR. Calar (the mast). | Amainar (a sail). || Aparcar (a car).
— V. intr. Alojarse, vivir.

house agent [—,eidʒənt] n. Agente (*m.*) inmobiliario.

house arrest [—əˈrest] n. Arresto (*m.*) domiciliario.

houseboat [—bəut] n. Casa (*f.*) flotante.

housebreak [—breik] v. intr. Robar con fractura.
— V. tr. Enseñar (animals).

housebreaker [—ˈbreikə*] n. Ladrón, *m.*, atracador, *m.* (robber). || Demoledor de casas (who dismantles houses).

housebreaking [—ˈbreikiŋ] n. JUR. Allanamiento (*m.*) de morada. | Robo (*m.*) con fractura (robbery). || Demolición (*f.*) de un edificio.

houseclean [—kli:n] v. tr./intr. Limpiar [la casa], hacer la limpieza de [la casa]. || FIG. Limpiar.

housecleaning [—ˈkli:niŋ] n. Limpieza (*f.*) de la casa.

housecoat [—kəut] n. Bata, *f.*

housedress [—dres] n. Bata, *f.*

housefly [—flai] n. Mosca (*f.*) doméstica.

houseful [—ful] n. Casa (*f.*) llena (of guests, etc.).

household [—həuld] n. Casa, *f.*, familia, *f.*: *theirs is a happy household*, su casa es una casa feliz. || Casa, *f.*: *to look after the household*, ocuparse de la casa. || *The Royal Household*, la Corte.
— Adj. Casero, ra; doméstico, ca: *the household chores*, los quehaceres domésticos. || De la casa: *household expenses*, gastos de la casa. || Casero, ra: *household remedy*, remedio casero; *household bread*, pan casero. || Familiar, común (common). || Real (royal): *household troops*, guardia real. || — *Household gods*, dioses (*m.*) lares. || *Household word*, nombre muy conocido, palabra muy conocida.

householder [—ˈhəuldə*] n. Cabeza (*m.*) de familia (head of a family). || Dueño (*m.*) *or* dueña (*f.*) de una casa (owner). || Inquilino, na (tenant).

househunting [—ˈhʌntiŋ] n. Búsqueda (*f.*) de una casa.

housekeeper [—'ki:pə*] n. Ama (*f.*) de casa (housewife): *his wife is a good housekeeper*, su mujer es una buena ama de casa. || Ama (*f.*) de llaves (woman paid to run a home).
housekeeping [—'ki:piŋ] n. Gobierno (*m.*) de la casa (running of a house). || Quehaceres (*m. pl.*) domésticos (housework). || Dinero (*m.*) para gastos domésticos.
houseleek [—li:k] n. BOT. Siempreviva (*f.*) mayor.
houseline [—lain] n. MAR. Piola, *f.*
housemaid [—meid] n. Criada, *f.* [*Amer.*, mucama, *f.*] || MED. *Housemaid's knee*, higroma, *m.*, hidrartrosis, *f.*
house organ ['ɔ:gən] n. Publicación (*f.*) interna.
house painter [—'peintə*] n. Pintor (*m.*) de brocha gorda.
house party [—'pɑ:ti] n. Estancia (*f.*) en la casa de campo de un amigo (gathering). || Invitados, *m. pl.*, convidados, *m. pl.* (guests).
house physician [—fi'ziʃən] n. MED. Interno, *m.* (in a hospital).
houseroom [—rum] n. *I wouldn't give it houseroom*, no lo tendría en casa. || *There's houseroom for everybody*, hay sitio en casa para todos. || *To find houseroom for s.o.*, encontrar sitio en su casa para alguien.
house surgeon [—'sə:dʒən] n. MED. Cirujano (*m.*) interno (in a hospital).
house-to-house [—tə'haus] adj. De casa en casa (from house to house): *house-to-house inquiries*, investigaciones de casa en casa.
— Adv. De casa en casa.
housetop [—tɔp] n. Tejado, *m.* (roof). || FIG. *To claim sth. from the housetops*, gritar algo a los cuatro vientos, pregonar algo a voz en grito.
house-train [—trein] v. tr. Enseñar (an animal).
housewares [—wɛə:z] pl. n. Utensilios (*m.*) domésticos.
housewarming [—'wɔ:miŋ] n. Inauguración (*f.*) de una casa. || *To have a housewarming party*, inaugurar la casa.
housewife [—waif] n. Ama (*f.*) de casa. || Madre (*f.*) de familia (mother). || Sus labores, *f. pl.* (on official forms): *profession: housewife*, profesión: sus labores.
— OBSERV. El plural de esta palabra es *housewives*.
housewife ['hʌzif] n. Costurero, *m.* (sewing kit).
— OBSERV. El plural de esta palabra es *housewives*.
housewifery ['haus‚waifəri] n. Gobierno (*m.*) de la casa (housekeeping).
housework ['hauswə:k] n. Quehaceres (*m. pl.*) domésticos.
housing ['hausiŋ] n. Alojamiento, *m.* (accommodation). || Vivienda, *f.*: *Ministry of Housing*, Ministerio de la Vivienda; *housing shortage*, crisis de la vivienda; *housing plan*, proyecto relativo a la vivienda. || Casas, *f. pl.* (houses). || Almacenaje, *m.* (storage). || Entrojamiento, *m.* (of cereals). || Gualdrapa, *f.* (of a horse). || AUT. Cárter, *m.* || TECH. Bastidor, *m.* (of machine). || ARCH. Empotramiento, *m.* (of beams). || *Housing estate*, urbanización, *f.*
hove [həuv] pret. & p. p. MAR. See HEAVE.
hovel ['hɔvəl] n. Casucha, *f.*, cuchitril, *m.* (miserable dwelling). || Cobertizo, *m.* (shed).
hover ['hɔvə*] v. intr. Cernerse (eagle, helicopter). || Revolotear (bird, butterfly). || Quedarse suspendido *or* flotando en el aire (paper, leaves, embers). || FIG. Rondar: *he is always hovering around me*, está siempre rondando alrededor de mí. || — FIG. *A smile hovered over her lips*, esbozó una sonrisa. | *To hover over*, cernerse sobre (danger).
hovercraft [—krɑ:ft] n. Aerodeslizador, *m.*
how [hau] adv. Como: *do it how you like*, hazlo como quieras. || Cómo (in what way): *how did he do it?*, ¿cómo lo hizo?; *I don't know how to thank you*, no sé cómo agradecerle; *you should see how the children run*, hay que ver cómo corren los niños; *how he snores!*, ¡cómo ronca!; *how big is it?*, ¿cómo es de grande?; *how do you like your tea?*, ¿cómo quiere su té? || Cómo, qué tal: *how was the meal, the film?*, ¿qué tal estuvo la comida, la película?; *how do you find it?*, ¿qué tal lo encuentras? || Qué (in exclamations before an adjective or adverb): *how pretty she is!*, ¡qué guapa es! || Lo... que, cómo, cuán (to what extent): *you don't realize how difficult it is*, no te das cuenta de lo difícil que es *or* de cómo es de difícil *or* cuán difícil es. || Que (that): *I told him how I had spoken to you*, le dije que te había hablado. || A cuánto: *how did you buy it?*, ¿a cuánto lo compraste?; *how are fruits today?*, ¿a cuánto está la fruta hoy? || — *And how!*, ¡y cómo! || *How about?*, ¿qué te (le, os, etc.) parece si ...?: *how about going to the cinema?*, ¿qué te parece si vamos al cine?; y ... qué: *how about me?, you haven't given me anything*, ¿y yo qué?, a mí no me has dado nada. || *How are you?*, ¿cómo está usted?, ¿qué tal está Vd.? || *How can it be?*, ¿cómo puede ser? || *How can you!*, ¿no te da vergüenza? || *How come?*, ¿cómo es eso? || *How come...?*, ¿cómo es que...? || *How do you do?*, ¿cómo está usted? (how are you), encantado, da; mucho gusto (pleased to meet you). || *How early?*, ¿cuándo?, ¿a qué hora? || *How else?*, claro (of course), ¿de qué otra manera? (in what other way). || *How far?*, ¿a qué distancia? || *How glad I am!*, ¡cuánto me alegro! || *How is it that?*, ¿cómo es que? || *How is that?*, ¿cómo es eso? || *How is that for...?*, ¿qué te parece...? || *How kind of you!*, ¡es Ud. muy amable!, ¡qué amabilidad la suya! || *How late?*, ¿cuándo?, ¿a qué hora? || *How long?*, ¿cuánto tiempo?, ¿cuánto?: *how long will you be?*, ¿cuánto tiempo tardarás?; *how long is the film?*, ¿cuánto dura la película?; cómo ... de largo: *how long is the rope?*, ¿cómo es la cuerda de larga?; *how long do you want it?*, ¿cómo lo quieres de largo? || *How many?*, ¿cuántos, tas?: *how many times?*, ¿cuántas veces? || *How much?*, ¿cuánto, ta? || *How much is it?*, ¿cuánto vale? || *How now?*, ¿y entonces? || *How often?*, ¿cuántas veces? || *How old are you?*, ¿qué edad tienes?, ¿cuántos *or* qué años tienes? || *How on earth* o *how the devil* o *how the dickens?*, ¿cómo diablos?, ¿cómo demonios? || *How pleased I am to see you*, ¡cuánto me alegro de verle! || *How so?*, ¿cómo es eso? || *How soon can you come?*, ¿cuándo puedes venir? || *How sorry I am!*, ¡cuánto lo siento! || *That was how*, así fue como. || *To know how to do sth.*, saber hacer algo, saber cómo se hace algo. || *To learn how to do sth.*, aprender a hacer algo.
— N. Modo, *m.*, forma, *f.*, manera, *f.* || — *The hows and whys*, el cómo y el porqué. || *The how, the when and the wherefore*, todos los detalles.
howdah [—də] n. Silla (*f.*) de elefante.
howdy [—di] interj. ¡Hola!, ¿qué hay?
how-d'ye-do [—di'du:] n. FAM. Lío, *m.* (annoying situation).
however [hau'evə*] adv. Por ... que (with subjunctive): *however much I should like to*, por mucho que me guste; *however much you insist*, por más que te empeñes; *however cold it is*, por mucho frío que haga. || Como (with subjunctive): *do it however you can*, hazlo como puedas. || De cualquier manera que (with subjunctive): *however he may do it*, de cualquier manera que lo haga. || Cómo (how): *however did he manage it?*, ¿cómo lo consiguió? || Sin embargo, no obstante: *I do not, however, agree with the second method*, sin embargo no estoy de acuerdo con el segundo método. || — *However it may be* o *that may be*, sea lo que sea. || *However much he may admire you*, aunque le admire mucho. || *However you may decide*, decida lo que decida.
howitzer ['hauitsə*] n. MIL. Obús, *m.* (short cannon).
howl [haul] n. Aullido, *m.* (of dogs, wolves). || Rugido, *m.*, bramido, *m.* (of wind). || Alarido, *m.* (of pain). || Berrido, *m.* (of a crying child). || Gritos, *m. pl.*, abucheo, *m.* (hoot). || *Howl of laughter*, carcajada, *f.*
howl [haul] v. intr. Aullar (dogs, wolves). || Gritar, vociferar (crowds). || Dar alaridos: *to howl with pain*, dar alaridos de dolor. || Rugir, bramar (the wind). || Berrear (to cry like a child). || — *To howl with laughter*, reír a carcajadas. || *To howl with rage*, bufar de cólera.
— V. tr. Gritar. || *To howl a speaker down*, callar a un orador a gritos *or* abucheándole.
howler [—ə*] n. Plancha, *f.*, pifia, *f.*, error (*m.*) garrafal (bad mistake): *to make a howler*, tirarse una plancha, cometer una pifia, hacer una falta garrafal. || ZOOL. Aullador, *m.*, mono (*m.*) aullador (monkey).
howling [—iŋ] adj. Aullador, ra (that howls). || Rugiente (wind). || Furioso, sa (storm, etc.). || FAM. Garrafal (mistake). | Escandaloso, sa (injustice). | Clamoroso, sa (success). | Lúgubre (wilderness).
— N. Aullido, *m.* (of dog, etc.). || Alaridos, *m. pl.* (of pain). || Rugido, *m.*, bramido, *m.* (of wind).
howsoever [hausəu'evə*] adv. Comoquiera que, de cualquier manera que (in whatever way). || Por muy ... que (to whatever extent).
hoy [hɔi] interj. ¡Eh!
hoyden ['hɔidn] n. Marimacho, *m.*, machota, *f.* (tomboy).
hoydenish [—iʃ] adj. Poco femenino, na; hombruno, na.
hub [hʌb] n. Cubo, *m.* (of a wheel). || FIG. Centro, *m.*, eje, *m.*: *London is the hub of the financial world*, Londres es el eje del mundo financiero.
hubble-bubble ['hʌbl‚bʌbl] n. Narguile, *m.* (pipe). || Algarabía, *f.* (hubbub). || Borboteo, *m.* (gurgling).
hubbub ['hʌbʌb] n. Alboroto, *m.*, barullo, *m.*, jaleo, *m.* (tumult). || Vocerío, *m.*, algarabía, *f.* (of voices).
hubby ['hʌbi] n. FAM. Marido, *m.*
hubcap ['hʌbkæp] n. Tapacubos, *m. inv.* (of a car).
huckle ['hʌkl] n. ANAT. Cadera, *f.* (hip).
huckleberry ['hʌklberi] n. BOT. Arándano, *m.*
hucklebone ['hʌklbəun] n. ANAT. Cía, *f.*, hueso (*m.*) de la cadera (hipbone). || U. S. ANAT. Astrágalo, *m.*, taba, *f.* (knucklebone).
huckster ['hʌkstə*] n. Buhonero, *m.*, vendedor (*m.*) ambulante (pedlar). || FAM. Mercachifle, *m.* || U. S. FAM. Agente (*m.*) de publicidad (advertising man).
huckster ['hʌkstə*] v. intr. Regatear (to haggle).
— V. tr. Revender.
huddle ['hʌdl] n. Grupo, *m.* [apretado], turba, *f.*, tropel, *m.* (group): *a huddle of people sheltering from the rain*, un grupo de personas resguardándose de la lluvia. || Montón, *m.* (of things). || Confusión, *f.*, batiborrillo, *m.* (confusion, muddle). || U. S. *To go into a huddle*, conferenciar *or* discutir en secreto.
huddle [hʌdl] v. tr. Amontonar, apiñar (to bunch together). || — *To huddle on*, ponerse sin cuidado (one's clothes). || *To huddle o.s. up*, acurrucarse. || *To huddle over* o *through* o *up*, hacer de prisa y corriendo (a piece of work).

— V. intr. Amontonarse, apiñarse, apretarse unos contra otros. || *To huddle up*, acurrucarse.
hue [hju:] n. Tinte, *m.* (colour). || Matiz, *m.* (shade). || Vocerío, *m.* (in hunting). || Fig. Matiz, *m.* || — *Hue and cry*, protesta clamorosa, grito (*m.*) de indignación (protest), griterío, *m.* (shouting), persecución, *f.* (pursuit). || *To raise a hue and cry against*, protestar *or* gritar contra.
hued [—d] adj. Colorado, da. || — *Many-hued*, de muchos colores, multicolor. || *Yellow-hued*, de color amarillo.
huff [hʌf] n. Enfado, *m.*, enojo, *m.* (anger). || Mal humor, *m.* (bad temper). || Soplo, *m.* (in draughts). || — *To be in a huff*, estar enojado, haberse picado. || *To go off in a huff* o *to get into a huff*, picarse, amoscarse.
huff [hʌf] v. tr. Ofender, enojar, picar (to offend, to annoy). || Maltratar (to bully). || Comerse, soplar (a piece in draughts).
— V. intr. Picarse (to take offence). || Enojarse (to become angry). || Bufar, resoplar (to snort).
huffily [—ili] adv. De mal talante, de malhumor.
huffiness [—inis] n. Susceptibilidad, *f.* (touchiness). || Malhumor, *m.* (bad temper).
huffy [—i] adj. Enojadizo, za; enfadadizo, za; susceptible (touchy). || Enojado, da (angry). || *To be huffy about*, picarse por, enfadarse por.
hug [hʌg] n. Abrazo, *m*: *he gave her a hug*, le dio un abrazo.
hug [hʌg] v. tr. Abrazar (to embrace). || Ahogar, apretar (a bear). || Fig. Aferrarse a (an opinion). | Acariciar (an idea). || Arrimarse a, no apartarse de (the coast, a wall). || Ceñirse a, pegarse a: *to hug the kerb*, pegarse a la acera. || *To hug o.s.*, congratularse.
huge [hju:dʒ] adj. Enorme: *a huge animal*, un animal enorme. || Inmenso, sa; enorme: *a huge building*, un edificio inmenso. || Amplio, plia: *a huge collection of samples*, un amplio muestrario. || Altísimo, ma (prices). || Descomunal (colossal): *a man of huge physical strength*, un hombre de una fuerza descomunal.
hugely [—li] adv. Enormemente (to a huge extent). || Muchísimo (very much).
hugeness [—nis] n. Inmensidad, *f.*
hugger-mugger [ˈhʌgəˌmʌgə*] adj. (Ant.). Secreto, ta (secret). || Desordenado, da.
— Adv. (Ant.). En secreto (secretly). || Desordenadamente (in a disorderly fashion).
— N. Desorden, *m.*, confusión, *f.* (jumble). || (Ant.). Secreto, *m.* (secrecy): *in hugger-mugger*, en secreto.
Hugh [hju:] or **Hugo** [ˈhju:gəu] pr. n. Hugo, *m.*
Huguenot [ˈhju:gənɔt] adj./n. Hugonote, ta.
hulk [hʌlk] n. Casco, *m.* (hull of a ship). || Armatoste, *m.* (sth. or s.o. big and clumsy). || Carraca, *f.* (old boat).
hulking [—iŋ] adj. Grande y pesado, voluminoso, sa.
hull [hʌl] n. Mar. Casco, *m.* (of boat). || Aviat. Casco, *m.* || Bot. Cáscara, *f.* (shell). | Vaina, *f.* (pod). || Casquillo, *m.* (of a cartridge).
hull [hʌl] v. tr. Perforar el casco de [un barco] (with a torpedo, etc.). || Desvainar (peas). || Cascar (nuts). || Mondar (barley). || Descascarillar (oats).
hullabaloo [ˌhʌləbəˈlu:] n. Fam. Jaleo, *m.*, follón, *m.*, bullicio, *m.*, lío, *m.*
hullo [ˈhʌˈləu] interj. ¡Hola! (greeting). || ¡Diga! (answering the phone). || ¡Oiga! (calling by phone). || ¡Oiga!, ¡oye! (call). || ¡Vaya! (surprise).
hum [hʌm] n. Tarareo, *m.*, canturreo, *m.* (of a song). || Zumbido, *m.* (of bees, bombs, bullets, engine). || Murmullo, *m.* (murmur).
— Interj. ¡Ejem!
hum [hʌm] v. tr. Tararear, canturrear (a tune). || Arrullar (a child to sleep).
— V. intr. Tararear, canturrear: *he always hums when he is happy*, siempre tararea cuando está contento. || Zumbar (bees, bombs, bullets, engine). || Fig. Hervir (with activity). || Fam. Apestar (to smell bad). || — *Business is humming*, los negocios marchan bien. || *To hum and haw*, vacilar. || *To make things hum, to start things humming*, desplegar gran actividad, activar las cosas. || *Town humming with activity*, ciudad muy activa.
human [ˈhju:mən] adj. Humano, na: *human being*, ser humano; *human nature*, naturaleza humana.
— N. Humano, *m.*
humane [hju:ˈmein] adj. Humano, na: *he has a very humane relationship with his employees*, tiene un trato muy humano con sus empleados. || Humanístico, ca (of the humanities). || *Humane studies*, humanidades, *f.*
humaneness [—nis] n. Humanidad, *f.*, sentimientos (*m. pl.*) humanos.
humanism [ˈhju:mənizəm] n. Humanismo, *m.*
humanist [ˈhju:mənist] adj./n. Humanista.
humanistic [ˌhju:məˈnistik] adj. Humanístico, ca.
humanitarian [hju:ˌmæniˈtɛəriən] adj. Humanitario, ria.
— N. Filántropo, pa; persona (*f.*) humanitaria.
humanitarianism [—izəm] n. Humanitarismo, *m.*
humanity [hju:ˈmæniti] n. Humanidad, *f.*, género (*m.*) humano (mankind). || Naturaleza (*f.*) humana (human nature). || Humanidad, *f.* (kindness of heart). || — Pl. Humanidades, *f.*: *to study humanities*, estudiar humanidades.
humanization [ˌhju:mənaiˈzeiʃən] n. Humanización, *f.*
humanize [ˈhju:mənaiz] v. tr. Humanizar.
humankind [ˈhju:mənˈkaind] n. Humanidad, *f.*, género (*m.*) humano, especie (*f.*) humana.
humanly [ˈhju:mənli] adv. Humanamente.
humble [ˈhʌmbl] adj. Humilde: *my humble abode*, mi humilde morada; *in my humble opinion*, a mi humilde parecer. || — *Of humble birth*, de humilde cuna. || *Your humble servant*, su humilde servidor.
humble [ˈhʌmbl] v. tr. Humillar. || *To humble o.s.*, humillarse.
humble-bee [—bi:] n. Zool. Abejorro, *m.*
humbleness [—nis] n. Humildad, *f.*
humbling [—iŋ] adj. Humillante.
humbly [—i] adv. Humildemente, con humildad.
humbug [ˈhʌmbʌg] n. Bola, *f.*, embuste, *m.* (lie). || Engaño, *m.* (deceit). || Tonterías, *f. pl.*, disparates, *m. pl.* (nonsense). || Farsa, *f.* (farce). || Farsante, *m.* (person). || Caramelo (*m.*) de menta (sweet).
humbug [ˈhʌmbʌg] v. tr. Embaucar, engañar (to mislead).
humdinger [hʌmˈdiŋgə*] n. Fam. Maravilla, *f.*: *she's a humdinger of a girl*, es una maravilla de chica.
humdrum [ˈhʌmdrʌm] adj. Monótono, na (monotonous). || Rutinario, ria (routine). || Aburrido, da (boring). || Vulgar (commonplace).
— N. Monotonía, *f.* (monotony). || Rutina, *f.* (routine). || Pelma, *m.* & *f.* (person). || Lata, *f.*, pesadez, *f.* (nuisance).
humeral [ˈhju:mərəl] adj. Anat. Humeral.
— N. Rel. Humeral, *m.* (veil).
humerus [ˈhju:mərəs] n. Anat. Húmero, *m.* (bone).
— Observ. El plural de esta palabra es *humeri*.
humid [ˈhju:mid] adj. Húmedo, da.
humidification [ˌhju:midifiˈkeiʃən] n. Humedecimiento, *m.*
humidifier [—faiə*] adj. Humedecedor, ra.
— N. Humedecedor, *m.*
humidify [hju:ˈmidifai] v. tr. Humedecer.
humidity [hju:ˈmiditi] n. Humedad, *f.*
humidor [ˈhju:midɔ:*] n. Bote (*m.*) que mantiene húmedo el tabaco. || Humedecedor, *m.* (humidifier).
humiliate [hju:ˈmilieit] v. tr. Humillar.
humiliating [—iŋ] adj. Humillante.
humiliation [hju:ˌmiliˈeiʃən] n. Humillación, *f.*
humility [hju:ˈmiliti] n. Humildad, *f.*
humming [ˈhʌmiŋ] adj. Que zumba (bees, bombs, bullets, engine). || Fam. En pleno desarrollo, que funciona bien, que pita (affair). | Muy fuerte (blow).
— N. Tarareo, *m.*, canturreo, *m.* (of a tune). || Zumbido, *m.* (of bees, bombs, bullets, engine). || Murmullo, *m.* (murmur).
hummingbird [—bə:d] n. Colibrí, *m.*, pájaro (*m.*) mosca.
humming top [—tɔp] n. Peonza, *f.*, trompo, *m.*
hummock [ˈhʌmək] n. Morón, *m.*, montecillo, *m.* (of earth). || Montículo (*m.*) de hielo (of ice).
humor [ˈhju:mər] n. U. S. See humour.
humoral [—əl] adj. Anat. Humoral.
humoresque [ˌhju:məˈresk] n. Mus. Capricho, *m.*
humorist [ˈhju:mərist] n. Humorista, *m.* & *f.* (writer or teller of jokes). || Gracioso, sa (funny person). || Bromista, *m.* & *f.* (joker).
humoristic [ˌhju:məˈristik] adj. Humorístico, ca.
humorless [ˈhju:məlis] adj. U. S. See humourless.
humorous [ˈhju:mərəs] adj. Humorístico, ca; humorista (writer). || Gracioso, sa; divertido, da; chistoso, sa (person, remark, etc.).
humorously [—li] adv. Con gracia, humorísticamente. || Con tono jocoso, jocosamente.
humorousness [—nis] n. Humorismo, *m.*, gracia, *f.*
humour [ˈhju:mə*] n. Humor, *m.*: *sense of humour*, sentido del humor; *in a good humour*, de buen humor. || Gracia, *f.* (of a joke): *I don't see the humour of it*, no le veo la gracia. || Capricho, *m.* (whim). || Anat. Humor, *m.* (fluid): *aqueous, vitrous humor*, humor ácueo, vítreo. || — *Bad* o *ill humour*, malhumor, *m.*, mal humor. || *Out of humour*, de mal humor. || *To be in no humour for laughing*, no tener humor para reírse. || *To be lacking in humour*, no tener sentido del humor.
humour [ˈhju:mə*] v. tr. Seguir el humor a (to play s.o.'s game). || Complacer (to oblige, to please).
humourist [—rist] n. See humorist.
humourless [—lis] adj. Sin sentido del humor. || Que no tiene gracia (joke).
hump [hʌmp] n. Joroba, *f.*, corcova, *f.*, giba, *f.* (of person's back). || Joroba, *f.*, giba, *f.* (of camel). || Montecillo, *m.* (in the ground). || Fig. Malhumor, *m.*: *to have the hump*, estar de malhumor. | Nostalgia, *f.* || — Fig. *To be over the hump*, haber vencido una dificultad. | *To give s.o. the hump*, jorobar *or* fastidiar a uno.
hump [hʌmp] v. tr. Fig. Fam. Cargar con, llevar (to carry). || *To hump one's back*, encorvarse (person), arquear el lomo (cat).
— V. intr. U. S. Fam. Matarse (to exert o.s.). | Darse prisa (to hurry).
humpback [—bæk] n. Joroba, *f.*, corcova, *f.*, giba, *f.* (back). || Jorobado, da; corcovado, da (person).
humpbacked [—bækt] adj. Jorobado, da; corcovado, da.

humped [hʌmpt] adj. Jorobado, da; corcovado, da.
humph [hʌmf] interj. ¡Bah!
humpy [ˈhʌmpi] adj. Desigual (ground). || Jorobado, da (humpbacked).
humus [ˈhju:məs] n. AGR. Mantillo, *m.*, humus, *m.*
Hun [hʌn] n. HIST. Huno, *m.* || FAM. Alemán, ana.
hunch [hʌntʃ] n. Joroba, *f.*, giba, *f.*, corcova, *f.* (hump). || Trozo, *m.* (small piece). || FIG. Presentimiento, *m.*, idea, *f.*, corazonada, *f.*: *I've got a hunch he won't come*, tengo la idea de que no va a venir.
hunch [hʌntʃ] v. tr. *To hunch one's back*, encorvarse. || *To sit hunched up*, estar sentado con el cuerpo encorvado. || *With hunched shoulders*, con la cabeza muy metida entre los hombros.
— V. intr. U. S. Empujar (to shove, to jostle).
hunchback [—bæk] n. Jorobado, da; corcovado, da (person). || Joroba. *f.*, corcova, *f.*, giba, *f.* (hump).
hunchbacked [—bækt] adj. See HUMPBACKED.
hundred [ˈhʌndrəd] adj. Cien, ciento (see OBSERV.) || *The Hundred Years' War*, la Guerra de los Cien Años.
— N. Ciento, *m.*: *a hundred oysters*, un ciento de ostras. || Centenar, *m.*: *a hundred men*, un centenar de hombres; *by the hundred, by the hundreds, in hundreds*, por *or* a centenares. || Centena, *f.*: *hundreds of times*, centenas de veces. || HIST. División (*f.*) administrativa del condado. || — *A hundred miles away*, a cien leguas. || *A hundred miles per hour*, cien por hora. || FIG. *A hundred per cent*, cien por cien. | *A hundred times*, cientos de veces, un montón de veces. | *A hundred to one it will be a success*, apuesto a que va a ser un éxito. || *Five hundred*, quinientos, tas. || *Hundreds and thousands of people*, miles y miles de personas. || *In 1900 (nineteen hundred)*, en 1900 [mil novecientos]. || *Nine hundred*, novecientos, tas. || FIG. *Ninety times out of a hundred*, la mayoría de las veces, casi siempre. || *Not one in a hundred*, ni uno. || *One hundred*, cien, ciento. || *To get six hundred a year*, ganar seiscientas libras al año. || *To live to be a hundred*, llegar a los cien años. || *Two hundred*, doscientos, tas: *two hundred women*, doscientas mujeres. || *Two hundred and one*, doscientos uno.
— OBSERV. The form *ciento* is only used when the number stands alone or is followed by another number, by tens or by units (*ciento*, a hundred; *ciento cinco*, a hundred and five; *ciento treinta*, a hundred and thirty). It is automatically apocopated to the form *cien* when followed by a noun or by the numbers *mil, millón, billón*, etc. (*cien libros*, a hundred books; *cien casas*, a hundred houses; *cien mil hombres*, a hundred thousand men). Multiples of *ciento* are written as one word with plural form (*doscientos diez*, two hundred and ten; *página seiscientas dos*, page six hundred and two).
hundredfold [—fəuld] adj. Céntuplo, pla.
— N. Céntuplo, *m.* || — *To increase a hundredfold*, centuplicar, aumentar cien veces. || *To repay a hundredfold*, devolver ciento por uno.
hundredth [ˈhʌndrədθ] adj. Centésimo, ma (in a series). || Centésimo, ma; centavo, va (being one of 100 equal parts).
— N. Centésima parte, *f.*, centésimo, *m.*, centavo, *m.* (one of 100 parts). || Centésimo, ma (in hundredth position).
hundredweight [ˈhʌndrədweit] n. Quintal, *m.*
hung [hʌŋ] pret. & p. p. See HANG.
Hungarian [hʌŋˈgɛəriən] adj./n. Húngaro, ra.
Hungary [ˈhʌŋgəri] pr. n. GEOGR. Hungría, *f.*
hunger [ˈhʌŋgə*] n. Hambre, *f.* (craving for food): *to satisfy one's hunger*, aplacar el hambre. || FIG. Sed, *f.*: *hunger for adventure*, sed de aventuras. || — FIG. *Hunger is a poor adviser*, el hambre es mala consejera. | *Hunger is the best sauce*, a buen hambre no hay pan duro. | *Hunger sharpens the wit*, el hambre aguza el ingenio. || *Hunger strike*, huelga (*f.*) del hambre. || *To be weak from hunger*, estar muerto de hambre. || *To die from hunger*, morir *or* morirse de hambre. || *To stave off hunger*, engañar *or* matar el hambre.
hunger [ˈhʌŋgə*] v. intr. Tener hambre (to be hungry). || FIG. *To hunger after* o *for*, tener sed *or* hambre de.
— V. tr. Hacer pasar hambre.
hungrily [ˈhʌŋgrili] adv. Ávidamente. || Con ansia: *he looked hungrily at the cake*, miraba el pastel con ansia.
hungry [ˈhʌŋgri] adj. Hambriento, ta (feeling hunger). || De hambre: *hungry look*, cara de hambre. || FIG. Ávido, da; sediento, ta: *hungry for news*, ávido de noticias. || AGR. Pobre (land). || — *I am ravenously hungry* o *as hungry as a wolf* o *hungry enough to eat a horse*, tengo un hambre que no veo *or* un hambre canina. || *To be* o *to feel hungry*, tener hambre. || *To be very hungry*, tener mucha hambre. || *To go hungry*, pasar hambre. || *To look hungry*, tener cara de hambre. || *To make s.o. hungry*, darle hambre a uno.
hung up [hʌŋ ʌp] adj. FAM. Obsesionado, da.
hunk [hʌŋk] n. Trozo, *m.*, pedazo, *m.*: *a hunk of bread*, un trozo de pan.
hunkers [ˈhʌŋkəz] pl. n. *To be on one's hunkers*, estar en cuclillas.
hunks [hʌŋks] n. FAM. Avaro, *m.*, tacaño, *m.* (miser). || Persona (*f.*) de malhumor.
hunky [ˈhʌŋki] n. U. S. FAM. Inmigrante (*m.*) de Europa Central.
hunky-dory [—ˈdɔ:ri] adj. U. S. FAM. Muy bien.
Hunnish [ˈhʌniʃ] adj. De los hunos. || FAM. Bárbaro, ra.
hunt [hʌnt] n. Caza, *f.*, cacería, *f.*, partida (*f.*) de caza (of small game). || Cacería, *f.*, montería, *f.* (of big game). || Cazadores, *m. pl.* (huntsmen). || Búsqueda, *f.*, busca, *f.*: *the hunt for the criminal*, la búsqueda del criminal. || Persecución, *f.* (pursuit). || *To go on a hunt for*, ir en busca de, buscar.
hunt [hʌnt] v. tr. Perseguir (to pursue). || Cazar: *to hunt foxes, whales*, cazar zorros, ballenas. || Recorrer, cazar en: *to hunt an area for foxes*, recorrer una región en busca de zorros. || Cazar con (hounds). || Buscar (to search for). || — *To hunt down*, acorralar (to corner), dar con (to find). || *To hunt out*, echar (s.o.), conseguir encontrar (sth.), descubrir (truth). || *To hunt up*, encontrar (to find), buscar (to look for).
— V. intr. Cazar, ir de cacería (small game). || Ir de cacería *or* de montería (big game). || FIG. Buscar (to search). || — *To go hunting*, ir de caza *or* de cacería. || *To hunt about for*, buscar por todas partes. || *To hunt after* o *for*, buscar.
— OBSERV. En Inglaterra *to hunt* se suele emplear para la caza de pelo mientras *to shot* se aplica más generalmente a la caza de pluma. En cambio, en Estados Unidos, *to hunt* se usa para cualquier tipo de caza.
hunter [—ə*] n. Cazador, *m.* (someone who hunts). || Caballo (*m.*) de caza (horse). || Perro (*m.*) de caza (dog). || Saboneta, *f.* (watch). || FIG. Cazador, *m.*
hunting [ˈhʌntiŋ] n. Caza, *f.*, cacería, *f.* (small game). || Cacería, *f.*, montería, *f.* (big game). || FIG. Caza, *f.*
— Adj. De caza: *hunting knife*, cuchillo de caza.
hunting box [—bɔks] n. Pabellón (*m.*) de caza.
hunting dog [—dɔg] n. Perro (*m.*) de caza.
hunting field [—fi:ld] or **hunting ground** [—graund] n. Terreno (*m.*) de caza.
hunting horn [—hɔ:n] n. Cuerno, *m.*, trompa, *f.*
hunting lodge [—lɔdʒ] n. U. S. Pabellón (*m.*) de caza.
hunting watch [—ˈwɔtʃ] n. Saboneta, *f.* (watch).
huntress [ˈhʌntris] n. Cazadora, *f.*
huntsman [ˈhʌntsmən] n. Cazador, *m.* || Montero, *m.* (of big game).
— OBSERV. El plural de esta palabra es *huntsmen*.
hunt the slipper [hʌntðəˈslipə*] or **hunt the thimble** [hʌntðəˈθimbl] n. Zurriago (*m.*) escondido (game).
hurdle [ˈhə:dl] n. Valla, *f.* (fence). || SP. Valla, *f.* || FIG. Barrera, *f.*, obstáculo, *m.* || SP. *The one hundred metres hurdles*, los cien metros vallas.
hurdle [ˈhə:dl] v. tr. Vallar, cercar con vallas (to surround). || SP. Saltar (to jump). || FIG. Salvar, vencer (an obstacle).
— V. intr. Saltar vallas. || SP. Participar en una carrera de vallas.
hurdler [—ə*] n. SP. Corredor (*m.*) de vallas.
hurdle race [—reis] n. SP. Carrera (*f.*) de vallas, carrera (*f.*) de obstáculos.
hurdy-gurdy [ˈhə:diˌgə:di] n. MUS. Organillo, *m.* (barrel organ). || (Ant.). Zanfonía, *f.*
hurl [hə:l] n. Lanzamiento, *m.*, tiro, *m.*
hurl [hə:l] v. tr. Lanzar, arrojar (to throw). || Soltar (insults, etc.). || — *To hurl back*, rechazar. || *To hurl down*, derribar. || *To hurl o.s.*, lanzarse (into sth.). || *To hurl o.s. at sth.*, abalanzarse sobre algo. || *To hurl o.s. from*, tirarse de.
hurler [—ə*] n. Lanzador, *m.* (baseball).
hurly-burly [ˈhə:liˌbə:li] n. Barullo, *m.*, tumulto, *m.*, alboroto, *m.*
— Adj. Tumultuoso, sa; alborotado, da.
Huron [ˈhjuərən] adj./n Hurón, ona.
hurrah [huˈrɑ:] or **hurray** [huˈrei] interj. ¡Hurra! || *Hurrah for...!*, ¡viva...!
— N. Vítor, *m.*
hurrah [huˈrɑ:] v. tr. Vitorear, aclamar.
— V. intr. Dar vítores.
hurricane [ˈhʌrikən] n. Huracán, *m.*
hurricane deck [—dek] n. MAR. Cubierta (*f.*) superior.
hurricane lamp [—læmp] n. Farol, *m.*
hurried [ˈhʌrid] adj. Apresurado, da (done quickly). || Hecho de prisa (done quickly and badly). || Rápido, da (reading). || — *To have a hurried meal*, comer de prisa. || *We were hurried when we wrote this letter*, teníamos mucha prisa cuando escribimos esta carta.
hurriedly [—li] adv. Apresuradamente, precipitadamente. || *He left the room hurriedly*, salió corriendo de la habitación.
hurry [ˈhuri] n. Prisa, *f.* || Precipitación, *f.* (rush). || — *Are you in a hurry for this translation?*, ¿le corre prisa esta traducción? || *In a hurry*, de prisa: *he ate in a hurry*, comió de prisa; tan pronto: *I will not return in a hurry*, no voy a volver tan pronto. || *Is there any hurry?*, ¿corre prisa? || *There is no hurry*, no hay prisa. || *To be in a hurry*, tener prisa: *to be in a hurry to do sth.*, tener prisa por hacer algo. || *To be in no hurry*, no tener prisa. || *To leave in a hurry*, salir corriendo. || *What's your hurry?*, ¿por qué te das tanta prisa?, ¿qué prisa tienes?
hurry [ˈhʌri] v. tr. Dar prisa a (to make move quickly): *don't hurry me!*, ¡no me des prisa! || Hacer de prisa: *to hurry work*, hacer el trabajo de prisa. || Acelerar: *to hurry negotiations through*, acelerar la conclusión de las negociaciones. || Llevar a toda prisa: *I hurried her to the hospital*, le llevé al hospital a toda prisa. || — *To hurry s.o. into a car*, meter a alguien de prisa

en un coche. || *To hurry s.o. into doing sth.*, dar prisa a alguien para que haga algo.
— V. intr. Darse prisa, apresurarse: *don't hurry!*, ¡no te des prisa! || Ir *or* irse de prisa: *to hurry to a place*, ir de prisa a un sitio.
— **To hurry after,** correr detrás de. || **To hurry along,** Ir de prisa (to walk). | Pasar de prisa. | Acelerar (sth.). || Llevar *or* llevarse rápidamente (s.o.). || **To hurry away,** llevar *or* llevarse rápidamente (s.o.). | Irse corriendo, irse de prisa (to depart rapidly). || **To hurry back,** hacer volver rápidamente [a un sitio] (to bring back). | Volver rápidamente *or* corriendo (to come back). || **To hurry down,** hacer bajar rápidamente (to take down). | Bajar rápidamente *or* corriendo (to descend). || **To hurry in,** entrar corriendo. || **To hurry off,** llevar *or* llevarse rápidamente (s.o.). | Irse de prisa *or* corriendo. || **To hurry on,** dar prisa a (people). | Acelerar (things). | Apresurar *or* acelerar el paso (walking). || **To hurry out,** sacar rápidamente, hacer salir rápidamente (to make leave). | Salir corriendo *or* de prisa (to leave). || **To hurry over,** hacer de prisa y corriendo (a task). || **To hurry up,** apresurar. | Subir rápidamente *or* corriendo (to climb). | Darse prisa, apresurarse (to speed up). | — *Hurry up!*, ¡dese prisa!, ¡rápido!
hurry-scurry [—'skʌri] n. Precipitación, *f.*
— Adv. En desorden (in a disorderly manner). || Precipitadamente, atropelladamente (hurriedly).
hurry-scurry [—'skʌri] v. intr. Precipitarse.
hurst [hə:st] n. Colina, *f.* (hill). || Bosquecillo, *m.* (small wood). || Banco (*m.*) de arena (sandbank).
hurt [hə:t] n. Daño, *m.*, mal, *m.* (harm). || Herida, *f.* (wound). || FIG. Daño, *m.*, perjuicio, *m.* (damage). | Golpe, *m.* (to s.o.'s pride).
hurt* [hə:t] v. tr. Hacer daño, lastimar (to cause bodily injury). || Doler (to cause physical pain): *it hurts me*, me duele; *where does it hurt?*, ¿dónde le duele? || Herir (to wound). || SP. Lesionar (to injure). || Estropear, dañar: *the storm hurt his crop*, la tormenta ha dañado su cosecha. || Perjudicar: *to hurt s.o.'s interests*, perjudicar los intereses de uno. || Doler, herir (mental pain): *his words hurt me*, me han dolido sus palabras. || Ofender (to offend). || — FIG. *He wouldn't hurt a fly*, es incapaz de matar una mosca. || *To get hurt*, hacerse daño, lastimarse (to hurt o.s.), ser herido (to be wounded). || *To hurt one's leg*, lastimarse la pierna, hacerse daño en la pierna. || *To hurt o.s.*, hacerse daño, lastimarse. || *To hurt s.o.'s feelings*, ofenderle a uno.
— V. intr. Doler: *my head hurts*, me duele la cabeza. || Hacer daño. || Estropearse (to get spoiled). || *Nothing hurts like the truth* o *the truth always hurts*, sólo la verdad ofende.

— OBSERV. Pret. & p. p. **hurt.**

hurtful [—ful] adj. Dañoso, sa (harmful). || Nocivo, va (to the health). || Perjudicial (detrimental). || Hiriente (words, remark).
hurtfulness [—fulnis] n. Nocividad, *f.*
hurtle ['hə:tl] v. tr. Lanzar, arrojar (to hurl).
— V. intr. Lanzarse, precipitarse. || Caer violentamente (to fall). || — *To hurtle along*, ir como un rayo. || *To hurtle down*, caer estrepitosamente (rocks), llover (missiles). || *To hurtle past*, pasar como un rayo.
hurtless ['hə:tlis] adj. Inofensivo, va (harmless). || Ileso, sa; sano y salvo, sana y salva (unharmed). || Intacto, ta (intact).
husband ['hʌzbənd] n. Marido, *m.*, esposo, *m.*
husband ['hʌzbənd] v. tr. Ahorrar, economizar: *to husband one's resources*, ahorrar fondos. || Escatimar (one's strength). || FAM. Casar.
husbandman [—mən] n. Agricultor, *m.*, labrador, *m.*

— OBSERV. El plural de *husbandman* es *husbandmen.*

husbandry ['hʌzbəndri] n. AGR. Agricultura, *f.* || Ahorro, *m.* (saving). || Buen gobierno, *m.* (management). || *Animal husbandry*, cría (*f.*) de ganado, ganadería, *f.*
hush [hʌʃ] n. Silencio, *m.* (silence). || Quietud, *f.* (stillness): *the hush of the night*, la quietud de la noche.
— Interj. ¡Chitón!, ¡cállate!, ¡cállese!
hush [hʌʃ] v. tr. Callar, hacer callar (to make silent). || Calmar (to calm). || *To hush up*, echar tierra a (an affair), hacer callar (a person).
— V. intr. Callarse.
hushaby ['hʌʃəbai] interj. *Hushaby baby!*, ¡ea, mi niño!, ¡arrorró mi nene!
hush-hush ['hʌʃ'hʌʃ] adj. Muy secreto, muy secreta.
hush-hush ['hʌʃ'hʌʃ] v. tr. Hacer callar, callar.
hush money ['hʌʃ,mʌni] n. FAM. Mamela, *f.*, guante, *m.* (bribe).
husk [hʌsk] n. Cáscara, *f.* (of nuts, cereals, etc.). || Farfolla, *f.*, envoltura (*f.*) de la mazorca (of maize). || Vaina, *f.* (of peas and beans). || Pellejo, *m.* (of grapes). || Erizo, *m.* (of chestnut). || Binza, *f.*, tela, *f.* (of onion). || — Pl. Ahechaduras, *f.*
husk [hʌsk] v. tr. Descascarar (nuts, etc.). || Descascarar, descascarillar (cereals). || Pelar, desvainar, desgranar (peas and beans). || Pelar, mondar (chestnuts, onions). || Despellejar (grapes).
huskily ['hʌskili] adv. Con voz ronca.
huskiness ['hʌskinis] n. Ronquera, *f.*, enronquecimiento, *m.*
husky ['hʌski] adj. Con cáscara (nuts, cereals, etc.). || Con vaina (peas and beans). || Ronco, ca (voice). || U. S. FAM. Fuerte, fornido, da (strong).
— N. ZOOL. Perro (*m.*) esquimal. || Esquimal, *m.* & *f.* (Eskimo).
hussar [hu'zɑ:*] n. MIL. Húsar, *m.*
Hussite ['hʌsait] adj./n. HIST. Husita.
hussy ['hʌsi] n. FAM. Fresca *f.* (saucy girl). | Lagarta, *f.* (immoral woman).
hustings ['hʌstiŋz] pl. n. Elecciones, *f.* (election). || Tribuna (*f. sing.*) electoral (platform). || FIG. Tribuna, *f.*, plataforma, *f.*
hustle ['hʌsl] n. Prisa, *f.* (hurry). || Empujón, *m.* (shove). || Empuje, *m.* (energy). || Bullicio, *m.* (activity). || FAM. Estafa, *f.*, timo, *m.* (swindle). || — *The hustle and bustle of modern life*, el ajetreo de la vida moderna. || U. S. FAM. *To get a hustle on*, darse prisa.
hustle ['hʌsl] v. tr. Empujar: *they hustled him out of the station*, le empujaron fuera de la estación. || Sacudir (to shake). || Dar prisa a (to hurry s.o.). || Acelerar (sth.). || FAM. Robar (to steal). | Estafar, timar (to swindle). || — *He was hustled into agreement*, le obligaron a llegar rápidamente a un acuerdo. || *To hustle things on*, llevar las cosas a buen paso.
— V. intr. Abrirse paso a codazos (to push one's way): *he hustled through the crowd*, se abrió paso a codazos entre la muchedumbre. || Darse prisa, apresurarse (to hurry). || U. S. Ajetrearse, moverse (to bustle).
hustler [—ə*] n. FAM. Despabilado, da (energetic person). | Puta, *f.*, ramera, *f.* (whore).
hut [hʌt] n. Cabaña, *f.*, choza, *f.* (log cabin). || Cobertizo, *m.* (garden shed). || Casucha, *f.*, chabola, *f.* (small house, hovel). || MIL. Barraca, *f.* || *Mountain hut*, albergue (*m.*) de montaña.
hutch [hʌtʃ] n. Conejera, *f.* (cage). || MIN. Vagoneta, *f.* (truck). || Artesa, *f.* (trough). || Hucha, *f.*, arca, *f.* (large box). || FAM. Chabola, *f.*, casucha *f.* (hovel). || U. S. Aparador, *m.* (cupboard).
huzza [hu'zɑ:] interj. ¡Hurra!
— N. Vítor, *m.*, viva, *m.*
huzza [hu'zɑ:] v. tr. Vitorear, aclamar.
— V. intr. Dar vítores, dar vivas.
hyacinth ['haiəsinθ] n. Jacinto, *m.* (flower, gem).
hyaena [hai'i:nə] n. ZOOL. Hiena, *f.*
hyaline ['haiəlin] adj. Hialino, na.
— N. CHEM. Hialina, *f.* || Mar (*m.*) transparente (sea). || Cielo (*m.*) diáfano (sky).
hyalite ['haiəlait] n. MIN. Hialita, *f.*
hybrid ['haibrid] adj. Híbrido, da.
— N. Híbrido, *m.* || Mestizo, za (person).
hybridism ['haibridizəm] or **hybridity** ['haibriditi] n. Carácter (*m.*) híbrido, hibridismo, *m.*
hybridization [haibridai'zeiʃən] n. Hibridación, *f.*
hybridize ['haibridaiz] v. tr. Hibridizar.
hydatid ['haidətid] n. MED. Hidátide, *f.*
hydra ['haidrə] n. MYTH. ZOOL. Hidra, *f.*
hydracid [hai'dræsid] n. CHEM. Hidrácido, *m.*
hydrangea [hai'dreindʒə] n. BOT. Hortensia, *f.*
hydrant ['haidrənt] n. Boca (*f.*) de riego. || *Fire hydrant*, boca (*f.*) de incendio.
hydrargyriasis [haidrɑ:'dʒiriəzis] or **hydrargyrism** [haidrɑ:'dʒirizəm] n. MED. Hidrargirismo, *m.*
hydrargyrum [hai'drɑ:dʒirəm] n. CHEM. Hidrargiro, *m.*
hydrarthrosis [haidrɑ:'θrəuzis] n. MED. Hidrartrosis, *f.*
hydratable ['haidrətəbl] adj. CHEM. Hidratable.
hydrate ['haidreit] n. CHEM. Hidrato, *m.*
hydrate ['haidreit] v. tr. CHEM. Hidratar.
— V. intr. Hidratarse.
hydration [hai'dreiʃən] n. CHEM. Hidratación, *f.*
hydraulic [hai'drɔ:lik] or **hydraulical** [—əl] adj. Hidráulico, ca: *hydraulic brake, cement*, freno, cemento hidráulico; *hydraulic press*, prensa hidráulica; *hydraulic power*, fuerza hidráulica; *hydraulic jack*, gato hidráulico.
hydraulics [—s] n. Hidráulica, *f.* (science).
hydric ['haidrik] adj. Hídrico, ca.
hydride ['haidraid] n. CHEM. Hidruro, *m.*
hydro ['haidrəu] n. Estación (*f.*) termal, balneario, *m.*
hydrobromic [,haidrəu'brəumik] adj. CHEM. Bromhídrico, ca (acid).
hydrocarbon [,haidrəu'kɑ:bən] n. CHEM. Hidrocarburo, *m.*
hydrocarbonate [—eit] n. CHEM. Hidrocarbonato, *m.*
hydrocele ['haidrəusi:l] n. MED. Hidrocele, *f.*
hydrocephalic [,haidrəuse'fælik] adj./n. MED. Hidrocéfalo, la.
hydrocephalous [haidrəu'sefələs] adj. MED. Hidrocéfalo, la.
hydrocephalus ['haidrəu'sefələs] n. MED. Hidrocefalia, *f.*
hydrochloric ['haidrəu'klɔrik] adj. CHEM. Clorhídrico, ca.
hydrochloride ['haidrəu'klɔ:raid] n. CHEM. Clorhidrato, *m.*
hydrocyanic [,haidrəusai'ænik] adj. CHEM. Cianhídrico, ca.
hydrodynamic ['haidrəudai'næmik] or **hydrodynamical** [—ikəl] adj. Hidrodinámico, ca.
hydrodynamics [—s] n. Hidrodinámica, *f.* (science).
hydroelectric [,haidrəui'lektrik] adj. Hidroeléctrico, ca.
hydroelectricity ['haidrəuilek'trisiti] n. Hidroelectricidad, *f.*

hydrofluoric [ˈhaidrəufluˈɔrik] adj. Fluorhídrico, ca.
hydrofoil [ˈhaidrəfɔil] n. MAR. Patín, *m.* (fin). | Aerodeslizador, *m.* (craft).
hydrogel [ˈhaidrədʒel] n. CHEM. Hidrogel, *m.*
hydrogen [ˈhaidridʒən] n. CHEM. Hidrógeno, *m.*: *heavy hydrogen*, hidrógeno pesado. || — *Hidrogen bomb*, bomba (*f.*) de hidrógeno. || *Hydrogen chloride*, hidrocloruro, *m.*
hydrogenate [haiˈdrɔdʒineit] v. tr. Hidrogenar.
hydrogenation [ˌhaidrɔdʒəˈneiʃən] n. Hidrogenación, *f.*
hydrogenize [haiˈdrɔdʒinaiz] v. tr. Hidrogenar.
hydrogenous [haiˈdrɔdʒinəs] adj. Hidrogenado, da.
hydrogen peroxide [ˈhaidridʒən pəˈrɔksaid] n. CHEM. Agua (*f.*) oxigenada.
hydrographer [haiˈdrɔgrəfə*] n. Hidrógrafo, fa.
hydrographic [ˌhaidrəuˈgræfik] or **hydrographical** [—əl] adj. Hidrográfico, ca.
hydrography [haiˈdrɔgrəfi] n. Hidrografía, *f.*
hydrologic [haidrəˈlɔdʒik] or **hydrological** [—əl] adj. Hidrológico, ca.
hydrologist [haiˈdrɔlədʒist] n. Hidrólogo, *m.*
hydrology [haiˈdrɔlədʒi] n. Hidrología, *f.*
hydrolyse or **hydrolyze** [ˈhaidrəlaiz] v. tr. Hidrolizar.
hydrolysis [haiˈdrɔlisis] n. CHEM. Hidrólisis, *f.*

— OBSERV. El plural de *hydrolysis* es *hydrolyses*.

hydromechanical [ˌhaidrəumiˈkænikəl] adj. Hidromecánico, ca.
hydromechanics [ˌhaidrəumiˈkæniks] n. Hidromecánica, *f.*
hydromel [ˈhaidrəmel] n. Hidromel, *m.*, aguamiel, *m.*
hydrometer [haiˈdrɔmitə*] n. Hidrómetro, *m.*
hydrometric [ˌhaidrəuˈmetrik] or **hydrometrical** [—əl] adj. Hidrométrico, ca.
hydrometry [haiˈdrɔmitri] n. Hidrometría, *f.*
hydrophilic [ˌhaidrəuˈfilik] or **hydrophile** [ˈhaidrəufail] adj. Hidrófilo, la.
hydrophobe [ˌhaidrəuˈfəub] n. Hidrófobo, ba.
hydrophobia [ˌhaidrəuˈfəubjə] n. MED. Hidrofobia, *f.*
hydrophobic [ˌhaidrəuˈfəubik] adj. Hidrófobo, ba.
hydropic [haiˈdrɔpik] adj. MED. Hidrópico, ca.
hydroplane [ˈhaidrəuplein] n. AVIAT. Hidroavión, *m.*, hidroplano, *m.* (seaplane). || MAR. Hidroplano, *m.*
hydropneumatic [haidrənjuˈmætik] adj. Hidroneumático, ca.
hydropower [haidrəˈpauə*] n. Fuerza (*f.*) hidroeléctrica.
hydrops [ˈhaidrɔps] or **hydropsy** [—i] n. MED. Hidropesía, *f.*
hydroscope [ˈhaidrəskəup] n. Hidroscopio, *m.*
hydrosilicate [ˌhaidrəˈsilikeit] n. Hidrosilicato, *m.*
hydrosphere [ˈhaidrəsfiə] n. Hidrosfera, *f.*
hydrostatic [ˌhaidrəuˈstætik] adj. Hidrostático, ca.
hydrostatics [—s] n. Hidrostática, *f.*
hydrotherapeutic [ˈhaidrəˌθerəˈpju:tik] or **hydrotherapeutical** [—əl] adj. Hidroterápico, ca.
hydrotherapeutics [—s] n. Hidroterapia, *f.*
hydrotherapy [ˌhaidrəuˈθerəpi] n. Hidroterapia, *f.*
hydrous [ˈhaidrəs] adj. CHEM. Hidratado, da. || Acuoso, sa.
hydroxide [haiˈdrɔksaid] n. Hidróxido, *m.*
hydroxyl [haiˈdrɔksil] n. Hidroxilo, *m.*, oxhidrilo, *m.*
hydrozoan [ˌhaidrəˈzəuən] n. ZOOL. Hidrozoario, *m.*
hyena [haiˈi:nə] n. ZOOL. Hiena, *f.*
hyetograph [haiˈetəgrɑ:f] n. Mapa (*m.*) pluviométrico.
hygiene [ˈhaidʒi:n] n. Higiene, *f.* (system).
hygienic [haiˈdʒi:nik] or **hygienical** [—əl] adj. Higiénico, ca.
hygienics [—s] n. Higiene, *f.* (science).
hygienist [—ist] n. Higienista, *m.*
hygroma [ˈhaiˈgrəumə] n. MED. Higroma, *m.*
hygrometer [haiˈgrɔmitə*] n. Higrómetro, *m.*
hygrometric [ˌhaigrəuˈmetrik] or **hygrometrical** [—əl] adj. Higrométrico, ca.
hygrometry [haiˈgrɔmitri] n. Higrometría, *f.*
hygroscope [ˈhaigrəskəup] n. Higroscopio, *m.*
hygroscopic [—ik] adj. Higroscópico, ca.
hymen [ˈhaimen] n. ANAT. Himen, *m.* || Himeneo, *m.* (marriage).
hymenoptera [haimənˈɔptərə] pl. n. ZOOL. Himenópteros, *m.*
hymenopteran (U. S. **hymenopteron**) [haimenˈɔptərən] n. ZOOL. Himenóptero, *m.*
hymenopterous [haimenˈɔptərəs] adj. ZOOL. Himenóptero, ra.
hymn [him] n. Himno, *m.*
hymn [him] v. tr. Cantar alabanzas: *let us hymn God*, cantemos alabanzas al Señor.
— V. intr. Cantar himnos.
hymnal [ˈhimnəl] or **hymnbook** [ˈhimbuk] n. REL. Libro (*m.*) de himnos, himnario, *m.*
hymnody [ˈhimnəudi] n. Himnos, *m. pl.* (hymns).
hyoid [ˈhaiɔid] adj. ANAT. Hioides, hioideo, a.
— N. ANAT. Hioides, *m.*
hyperacidity [ˌhaipərəˈsiditi] n. MED. Hiperacidez, *f.*
hyperbaton [haiˈpə:bətɔn] n. GRAMM. Hipérbaton, *m.*

— OBSERV. El plural de la palabra inglesa es *hyperbatons* o *hyperbata*.

hyperbola [haiˈpə:bələ] n. MATH. Hipérbola, *f.*

— OBSERV. El plural de la palabra inglesa es *hyperbolas* o *hyperbolae*.

hyperbole [haiˈpə:bəli] n. GRAMM. Hipérbole, *f.*
hyperbolic [ˌhaipə:ˈbɔlik] or **hyperbolical** [—əl] adj. Hiperbólico, ca.
hyperboloid [haiˈpə:bəlɔid] n. MATH. Hiperboloide, *m.*
hyperborean [ˌhaipəbɔ:ˈriən] adj. Hiperbóreo, a; hiperboreal. || FAM. Del norte.
hyperchlorhydria [haipə:klɔ:ˈri:driə] n. MED. Hiperclorhidria, *f.*
hypercritical [ˈhaipəˈkritikəl] adj. Hipercrítico, ca.
hyperdulia [ˌhaipədju:ˈlaiə] n. REL. Hiperdulía, *f.*
hyperfocal [ˌhaipəˈfəukəl] adj. Hiperfocal: *hyperfocal distance*, distancia hiperfocal.
hypermetropia [ˌhaipəmiˈtrəupjə] n. MED. Hipermetropía, *f.* (longsightedness).
hypermetropic [ˌhaipəmiˈtrɔpik] adj. MED. Hipermétrope.
hypermnesia [haipə:mˈniziə] n. MED. Hipermnesia, *f.*
hypernervous [haipə:ˈnə:vəs] adj. Hipernervioso, sa.
hyperopia [ˌhaipəˈrəupjə] n. MED. Hipermetropía, *f.*
hyperopic [ˌhaipəˈrəupik] adj. MED. Hipermétrope.
hyperphysical [ˈhaipəˈfizikəl] adj. Sobrenatural.
hypersecretion [haipə:siˈkri:ʃən] n. MED. Hipersecreción, *f.*
hypersensitive [ˈhaipəˈsensitiv] adj. Hipersensible.
hypersensitivity [ˌhaipəsensiˈtiviti] n. Hipersensibilidad, *f.*
hypertension [ˌhaipəˈtenʃən] n. MED. Hipertensión, *f.*
hypertensive [ˈhaipəˈtensiv] adj. MED. Hipertenso, sa.
hyperthermia [haipə:ˈθə:mjə] n. Hipertermia, *f.*
hyperthyroidism [ˌhaipəˈθairɔidizəm] n. MED. Hipertiroidismo, *m.*
hypertonic [ˌhaipəˈtɔnik] adj. Hipertónico, ca.
hypertrophic [ˌhaipəˈtrəufik] adj. MED. Hipertrófico, ca.
hypertrophy [haiˈpə:trəfi] n. MED. Hipertrofia, *f.*
hypertrophy [haiˈpə:trəfi] v. intr. MED. Hipertrofiarse.
— V. tr. MED. Hipertrofiar.
hypervitaminosis [haipə:vitəmiˈnəusis] n. MED. Hipervitaminosis, *f.*

— OBSERV. El plural de *hypervitaminosis* es *hypervitaminoses*.

hyphen [ˈhaifən] n. Guion, *m.*
hyphen [ˈhaifən] or **hyphenate** [ˈhaifəneit] v. tr. Unir con guion, escribir con guion. || U. S. FAM. *Hyphenated American*, norteamericano de origen extranjero.
hypnosis [hipˈnəusis] n. Hipnosis, *f.*

— OBSERV. El plural de la palabra inglesa es *hypnoses*.

hypnotic [hipˈnɔtik] adj. Hipnótico, ca.
— N. Hipnótico, *m.* (drug). || Persona (*f.*) hipnotizada *or* fácil de hipnotizar (person).
hypnotism [ˈhipnətizəm] n. MED. Hipnotismo, *m.*
hypnotist [ˈhipnətist] n. MED. Hipnotizador, ra.
hypnotize [ˈhipnətaiz] v. tr. Hipnotizar.
hypnotizer [ˈhipnətaizə*] n. Hipnotizador, ra.
hypnotizing [—iŋ] adj. Hipnotizador, ra.
hypo [ˈhaipəu] n. CHEM. Hiposulfito (*m.*) sódico. || PHOT. Fijador, *m.* || U. S. FAM. Inyección, *f.* (injection). | Jeringa, *f.* (syringe).
hypocaust [ˈhaipəukɔ:st] n. Hipocausto, *m.*
hypocenter [haipəˈsentə*] n. Hipocentro, *m.*
hypochlorhydria [haipəklɔ:ˈri:driə] n. MED. Hipoclorhidria, *f.*
hypochlorite [haipəˈklɔ:rait] n. CHEM. Hipoclorito, *m.*
hypochlorous [ˌhaipəuˈklɔ:rəs] adj. Hipocloroso, sa.
hypochondria [ˌhaipəuˈkɔndriə] n. Hipocondría, *f.*
hypochondriac [ˌhaipəuˈkɔndriæk] adj./n. Hipocondriaco, ca; hipocondríaco, ca.
hypochondriasis [ˌhaipəukɔnˈdraiəsis] n. Hipocondría, *f.*
hypochondrium [ˌhaipəˈkɔndriəm] n. ANAT. Hipocondrio, *m.*

— OBSERV. El plural de la palabra *hypochondrium* es *hypochondria*.

hypocrisy [hiˈpɔkrəsi] n. Hipocresía, *f.*
hypocrite [ˈhipəkrit] n. Hipócrita, *m. & f.*
hypocritical [ˌhipəuˈkritikəl] adj. Hipócrita.
hypoderma [ˌhaipəuˈdə:mə] n. BOT. ZOOL. Hipodermis, *f.*
hypodermal [—əl] adj. Hipodérmico, ca.
hypodermic [—ik] adj. Hipodérmico, ca.
— N. MED. Jeringa (*f.*) hipodérmica (syringe). | Aguja (*f.*) hipodérmica (needle). | Inyección (*f.*) hipodérmica (injection).
hypodermis [ˌhaipəˈdə:mis] n. ANAT. Hipodermis, *f.*
hypogaeum [ˌhaipəˈdʒi:əm] n. Hipogeo, *m.*

— OBSERV. El plural de esta palabra es *hypogaea*.

hypogastric [ˌhaipəuˈgæstrik] adj. ANAT. Hipogástrico, ca.
hypogastrium [ˌhaipəuˈgæstriəm] n. ANAT. Hipogastrio, *m.*

— OBSERV. El plural de *hypogastrium* es *hypogastria*.

hypogeum [haipəˈdʒi:əm] n. Hipogeo, *m.*

— OBSERV. El plural de esta palabra es *hypogea*.

hypophysis [haiˈpɔfisis] n. ANAT. Hipófisis, *f.*

— OBSERV. El plural de *hypophysis* es *hypophyses*.

hypostyle [ˈhaipəustail] adj. ARCH. Hipóstilo, la.
hyposulphite (U. S. **hyposulfite**) [ˌhaipəuˈsʌlfait] n. CHEM. Hiposulfito, *m.*
hipotension [ˌhaipəuˈtenʃən] n. Hipotensión, *f.*
hypotensive [ˌhaipəuˈtensiv] adj. Hipotenso, sa.

hypotenuse or **hypothenuse** [hai'pɔtinju:z] n. MATH. Hipotenusa, *f.*
hypothalamus [ˌhaipəu'θæləməs] n. ANAT. Hipotálamo, *m.*
— OBSERV. El plural de *hypothalamus* es *hypothalami.*
hypothec [hai'pɔθek] n. JUR. Hipoteca, *f.*
hypothecary [hai'pɔθikəri] adj. JUR. Hipotecario, ria.
hypothecate [hai'pɔθikeit] v. tr. JUR. Hipotecar.
hypothermia [ˌhaipəu'θə:mjə] n. MED. Hipotermia, *f.*
hypothesis [hai'pɔθisis] n. Hipótesis, *f.*
— OBSERV. El plural de *hypothesis* es *hypotheses.*
hypothetic [ˌhaipəu'θetik] or **hypothetical** [—əl] adj. Hipotético, ca.
hypothyroidism [ˌhaipəu'θairɔidizəm] n. MED. Hipotiroidismo, *m.*
hypotonic [ˌhaipəu'tɔnik] adj. Hipotónico, ca.
hypsometer [hip'sɔmitə*] n. PHYS. Hipsómetro, *m.*
hypsometry [hip'sɔmitri] n. PHYS. Hipsometría, *f.*
hyssop ['hisəp] n. Hisopo, *m.*
hysteresis [ˌhistə'ri:sis] n. PHYS. Histéresis, *f.*
— OBSERV. El plural de esta palabra es *hystereses.*
hysteria [his'tiəriə] n. MED. Histeria, *f.*, histerismo, *m.* ‖ FAM. Ataque (*m.*) de nervios.
hysteric [his'terik] or **hysterical** [—əl] adj. Histérico, ca.
hysterics [—s] n. MED. Histerismo, *m.*, crisis (*f.*) de histeria. ‖ FAM. Ataque (*m.*) histérico, ataque (*m.*) de nervios. | Nerviosismo, *m.* ‖ *To go into hysterics,* ponerse histérico.

I

I [ai] n. I, *f.* (letter of the alphabet).
I [ai] n. PHIL. Yo, *m.*, ego, *m.*
— Adj. De doble T: *I beam,* viga de doble T.
— Pers. pron. Yo: *it is I,* soy yo; *shall I do it or will you?,* ¿lo hago yo o lo haces tú? ‖ *I am going to Madrid,* voy a Madrid.
— OBSERV. The English personal pronoun is not usually translated into Spanish unless emphasis is sought (*I find it difficult,* lo encuentro difícil *or* yo lo encuentro difícil; *I for one find it difficult,* yo lo encuentro difícil).
iamb ['aiæmb] n. POET. Yambo, *m.*
iambic [ai'æmbik] adj. POET. Yámbico, ca.
— N. POET. Yambo, *m.* (iambus). | Verso (*m.*) yámbico (verse).
iambus [ai'æmbəs] n. POET. Yambo, *m.*
— OBSERV. El plural de *iambus* es *iambi* o *iambuses.*
Iberia [ai'biəriə] pr. n. GEOGR. Iberia, *f.*
Iberian [—n] adj. Ibérico, ca (of the Iberian Peninsula). ‖ Ibero, ra (of ancient Iberia). ‖ GEOGR. *Iberian Peninsula,* Península Ibérica.
— N. Ibero, ra; ibérico, ca (a Spaniard or Portuguese). ‖ HIST. Ibero, ra. ‖ Lengua (*f.*) ibera (language).
ibex ['aibeks] n. ZOOL. Íbice, *m.*
— OBSERV. El plural de *ibex* es *ibexes* o *ibices.*
ibidem [i'baidem] lat. adv. Ibídem.
— OBSERV. Abbreviation : *ibid* o *ib* in both languages.
ibis ['aibis] n. ZOOL. Ibis, *m.*
— OBSERV. El plural en inglés es *ibises* o *ibis.*
Ibiza [i'vi:θæ] pr. n. GEOGR. Ibiza.
Ibizan [—n] adj./n. Ibicenco, ca.
icaco [i'kɑ:kə] n. BOT. Icaco, *m.*
Icarian [i'kɛəriən] adj. Icario, ria; icáreo, a.
Icarus ['aikərus] pr. n. MYTH. Ícaro, *m.*
ice [ais] n. Hielo, *m.* (solidified water): *blocks of ice,* hielo en barras; *ice cubes,* cubitos de hielo. ‖ Helado, *m.* (ice cream). ‖ Polo, *m.* (iced lolly). ‖ CULIN. Escarcha, *f.* (icing). ‖ FAM. Diamantes, *m. pl.* ‖ — *Carbonic ice,* hielo carbónico. ‖ CHEM. *Dry ice,* nieve carbónica. ‖ *Ice bag,* bolsa (*f.*) de hielo. ‖ FIG. *To break the ice,* romper el hielo. | *To cut no ice,* no tener importancia; no convencer. | *To have on ice,* tener en el bote *or* en el bolsillo. ‖ *To keep on ice,* conservar en hielo (food), tener en reserva (to keep handy), haber metido en chirona (to keep in jail). ‖ FIG. *To put on ice,* dejar para más tarde. | *To skate* o *to tread on thin ice,* pisar un terreno peligroso.
ice [ais] v. tr. Helar (to convert into ice). ‖ Enfriar, refrescar (to cool). | Alcorzar, escarchar, garapiñar (to cover with icing).
— V. intr. Helarse.
Ice Age [—eidʒ] n. GEOL. Período (*m.*) glaciar.
ice axe (U. S. **ice ax**) [—æks] n. SP. Pico (*m.*) de alpinista, piqueta, *f.*
iceberg [—bə:g] n. Iceberg, *m.* ‖ FIG. FAM. Témpano, *m.* (unemotional person).
iceblink [—bliŋk] n. Claridad (*f.*) en el horizonte producida por el reflejo de la luz sobre el hielo.
iceboat [—bəut] n. Trineo (*m.*) de vela [para deslizarse sobre el hielo]. ‖ Rompehielos, *m. inv.* (icebreaker).
icebound [—baund] adj. MAR. Detenido por el hielo, preso entre hielos: *an icebound ship,* un barco detenido por el hielo. ‖ Obstruido *or* bloqueado por el hielo: *an icebound harbour,* un puerto obstruido por el hielo.
icebox [—bɔks] n. Nevera, *f.*
icebreaker [—ˌbreikə*] n. MAR. Rompehielos, *m. inv.* (ship). ‖ Espolón, *m.* (of a pier).
ice bucket [—'bʌkit] n. Cubo (*m.*) con hielo para mantener frío el champán u otra bebida.
ice cap [—kæp] n. Casquete (*m.*) glaciar (in the poles). ‖ Helero, *m.*, glaciar, *m.* (glacier).
ice-cold [—kəuld] adj. Helado, da.
ice cream [—kri:m] n. Helado, *m.*
ice-cream cone [—'kri:mkəun] n. Helado (*m.*) de cucurucho (ice cream). ‖ Cucurucho (*m.*) de helado (cone-shaped wafer).
ice-cream parlor [—'kri:m'pɑ:lə*] n. U. S. Heladería, *f.*
ice-cream soda [—'kri:m'səudə] n. Soda (*f.*) mezclada con helado.
iced [—t] adj. Helado, da. ‖ Enfriado, da; refrescado, da. ‖ CULIN. Escarchado, da: *iced fruits,* fruta escarchada.
icefall [—fɔ:l] n. Cumbre (*f.*) del glaciar (steep part of glacier). ‖ Cascada (*f.*) helada (frozen waterfall).
ice fender [—'fendə*] n. MAR. Rompehielos, *m. inv.*
ice field [—fi:ld] n. Banquisa, *f.*, banco (*m.*) de hielo (sheet of floating ice). ‖ Helero, *m.* (ice cap).
ice floe [—fləu] n. Témpano (*m.*) de hielo.
ice foot [—fut] n. Faja (*f.*) costera de hielo.
ice hockey [—ˌhɔki] n. SP. Hockey (*m.*) sobre hielo.
ice house [—haus] n. Nevera, *f.* (where ice is stored). ‖ Fábrica (*f.*) de hielo.
Iceland [—lənd] pr. n. GEOGR. Islandia, *f.*
Icelander [—'ləndə*] n. Islandés, esa.
Icelandic [—'ləndik] adj. Islandés, esa.
— N. Islandés, *m.* (language).
iceman [—mæn] n. U. S. Fabricante (*m.*) de hielo (who makes ice). | Vendedor (*m.*) de hielo (who sells ice). | Repartidor (*m.*) de hielo (who delivers ice).
— OBSERV. El plural de esta palabra es *icemen.*
ice pack [—pæk] n. Banco (*m.*) de hielo. ‖ Bolsa (*f.*) de hielo (ice bag).
ice pail [—peil] n. Cubo (*m.*) para el hielo.
ice pick [—pik] n. Piqueta (*f.*) para romper hielo (mountaineer's tool). ‖ Punzón (*m.*) para romper hielo (kitchen implement).
ice point [—pɔint] n. Punto (*m.*) de congelación.
ice rink [—riŋk] n. Pista (*f.*) de patinaje.
ice sailing [—'seiliŋ] n. SP. Navegación (*f.*) a vela sobre hielo.
ice sheet [—ʃi:t] n. Casquete (*m.*) glaciar (in the poles). ‖ Helero, *m.*, glaciar, *m.* (glacier).
ice skate [—skeit] n. SP. Patín (*m.*) de cuchilla.
ice-skate [—skeit] v. intr. SP. Patinar sobre hielo.
ice skating [—'skeitiŋ] n. SP. Patinaje (*m.*) sobre hielo.
ice tray [—trei] n. Bandeja (*f.*) para los cubiletes *or* cubitos de hielo.
ichneumon [ik'nju:mən] n. ZOOL. Mangosta, *f.*, icneumón, *m.* (mangoose). | Icneumón, *m.* (fly).
ichor ['aikɔ:*] n. MED. Icor, *m.*
ichorous ['aikərəs] adj. MED. Icoroso, sa.
ichthyocolla ['ikθiəkəljə] n. Ictiocola, *f.*
ichthyol ['ikθiɔl] n. CHEM. Ictiol, *m.*
ichthyologist [ˌikθi'ɔlədʒist] n. Ictiólogo, *m.*
ichthyology [ˌikθi'ɔlədʒi] n. Ictiología, *f.*

ichthyophagist [,ikθi'ɔfədʒist] n. Ictiófago, ga.
ichthyophagous [,ikθi'ɔfəgəs] adj. Ictiófago, ga.
ichthyophagy [,ikθi'ɔfədʒi] n. Ictiofagia, *f.*
ichthyosaur [,ikθiə'sɔ:r] n. ZOOL. Ictiosauro, *m.*
icicle ['aisik'l] n. Carámbano, *m.*
icily ['aisili] adv. Fríamente, glacialmente.
iciness ['aisnis] n. Frialdad, *f.*
icing ['aisiŋ] n. CULIN. Glaseado, *m.*, escarchado, *m.* || AVIAT. Capa (*f.*) de escarcha. || MED. *Icing liver,* cirrosis hepática.
icing sugar [—'ʃugə*] n. Azúcar (*m.* & *f.*) en polvo.
icon ['aikɔn] n. REL. Icono, *m.*
iconoclasm [ai'kɔnəuklæzəm] n. REL. Iconoclasia, *f.*
iconoclast [ai'kɔnəuklæst] n. Iconoclasta, *m.* & *f.*
iconoclastic [ai,kɔnəu'klæstik] adj. Iconoclasta.
iconographer [,aikɔ'nɔgrəfə*] n. Iconógrafo, *m.*
iconographic [,aikɔnə'græfik] adj. Iconográfico, ca.
iconography [,aikɔ'nɔgrəfi] n. Iconografía, *f.*
iconolatry [ikɔ'nɔlətri] n. Iconolatría, *f.*
iconology [,ikɔ'nɔlədʒi] n. Iconología, *f.*
iconoscope [ai'kɔnəskəup] n. Iconoscopio, *m.*
icosahedron ['aikəsə'hedrən] n. MATH. Icosaedro, *m.* (solid figure).
icteric [ik'terik] adj. Ictérico, ca.
icterus ['iktərəs] n. MED. Ictericia, *f.*
ictus ['iktəs] n. MED. Ictus, *m.* (stroke). || GRAMM. Ictus, *m.* (stress).
icy ['aisi] adj. Helado, da (hand, foot). || Glacial (wind, room). || Cubierto de nieve *or* de hielo (mountain). || FIG. Glacial (look).
I'd [aid] contraction of *I had, I should, I would.*
idea ['aidiə] n. Idea, *f.*: *that's my idea of America,* ésa es mi idea de América; *have you any idea of the time?,* ¿tienes idea de la hora que es? || Intención, *f.* (intention). || Idea, *f.* (belief, outline, skill). || Plan, *m.*, proyecto, *m.* (plan). || — *Bright idea,* idea luminosa, idea genial. || *Central, fixed idea,* idea central, fija. || *No idea!,* ¡ni idea! || *Not to have the foggiest* o *slightest idea,* no tener la menor *or* la más mínima *or* la más remota idea. || *That's the idea!,* ¡exacto!, ¡eso es! || *The idea is to go tomorrow,* pensamos ir mañana. || *To be a good, a bad idea,* ser una buena, una mala idea. || *To form* o *to get an idea,* formarse una idea. || *To get an idea into one's head,* metérsele a uno una idea en la cabeza. || *To get an idea of sth.,* hacerse una idea de algo. || *To get used to the idea of,* hacerse a la idea de. || *To have no idea,* no tener ni idea. || *To put ideas into s.o.'s head,* meterle ideas en la cabeza a alguien. || FAM. *What's the big idea?,* ¿a qué viene eso? || *Whose idea was it?,* ¿a quién se le ocurrió?
ideal [ai'diəl] adj. Ideal: *the ideal woman,* la mujer ideal.
— N. Ideal, *m.* || *Man of ideal,* hombre de ideales.
idealism [—izəm] n. Idealismo, *m.*
idealist [—ist] n. Idealista, *m.* & *f.*
idealistic [—istik] adj. Idealista.
ideality [,aidi'æliti] n. Idealidad, *f.*
idealization [ai,diəlai'zeiʃən] n. Idealización, *f.*
idealize [ai'diəlaiz] v. tr. Idealizar.
idealizing [—iŋ] adj. Idealizador, ra.
ideally [ai'diəli] adv. Idealmente. || A las mil maravillas, perfectamente (perfectly).
ideate [ai'dieit] v. tr. Idear, concebir (to construct a mental image of). || Imaginar (to imagine).
idée fixe [i:'dei'fi:ks] n. Idea (*f.*) fija.
idem ['aidəm] adv. Ídem.
identical [ai'dentikəl] adj. Idéntico, ca. || FAM. *This is the identical spot where we stood yesterday,* éste es el mismo sitio donde estuvimos ayer.
identicalness [—nis] n. Identidad, *f.*
identifiable [ai'dentifaiəbl] adj. Identificable.
identification [ai,dentifi'keiʃən] n. Identificación, *f.* || — *Identification card,* tarjeta (*f.*) de identidad. || *Identification papers,* documentos (*m.*) de identidad. || *Identification tag,* placa (*f.*) de identificación.
identify [ai'dentifai] v. tr. Identificar. || *To identify o.s. with,* identificarse con.
identity [ai'dentiti] n. Identidad, *f.*: *identity card,* carnet *or* documento *or* tarjeta de identidad. || Identidad, *f.* (exact similarity). || *Mistaken identity,* identificación errónea.
ideogram ['idiəugræm] n. Ideograma, *m.*
ideograph ['idiəugrɑ:f] n. Ideograma, *m.*
ideologic [,aidi'ɔlədʒik] or **ideological** [—əl] adj. Ideológico, ca.
ideologist [,aidi'ɔlədʒist] n. Ideólogo, *m.*
ideology [,aidi'ɔlədʒi] n. Ideología, *f.*
ides [aidz] pl. n. Idus, *m.*, idos, *m.*
idiocy ['idiəsi] n. Idiotez, *f.*
idiom ['idiəm] n. Idioma, *m.*, lenguaje, *m.* (language of a community). || Modismo, *m.*, idiotismo, *m.*, locución, *f.* (expression). || Estilo, *m.* (writer's style).
idiomatic [,idiə'mætik] adj. Idiomático, ca.
idiopathy ['idiə,pæθi] n. Idiopatía, *f.*
idiosyncrasy [,idiə'siŋkrəsi] n. Idiosincrasia, *f.* || *Occupational idiosyncrasy,* deformación profesional.
idiosyncratic [,idiəsiŋ'krætik] adj. Idiosincrásico, ca.
idiot ['idiət] n. Tonto, ta; imbécil, *m.* & *f.*, idiota, *m.* & *f.* || — *To play the idiot,* hacerse el tonto. || *Village idiot,* tonto del pueblo. || FAM. *You idiot!,* ¡idiota!, ¡imbécil!
idiotic [,idi'ɔtik] adj. Idiota, imbécil, tonto, ta.
idiotism ['idiətizəm] n. U. S. Idiotez, *f.* (idiocy). || Idiotismo, *m.* (idiom).
idiotize ['idiətaiz] v. tr. Idiotizar.
idle ['aidl] adj. Perezoso, sa; holgazán, ana; vago, ga; gandul (unwilling to work). || Ocioso, sa (at leisure). || Parado, da; desocupado, da (out of work). || Infundado, da: *idle fears,* temores infundados. || Frívolo, la; fútil: *idle talk,* conversación frívola. || Vano, na; inútil (useless). || COMM. Improductivo, va (capital). || Parado, da (machine). || — *Idle moment,* momento (*m.*) de ocio. || TECH. *Idle wheel,* rueda intermedia. | *To run idle,* funcionar en vacío (machine, engine), girar loco (mechanism).
idle ['aidl] v. intr. Perder el tiempo (to waste time). || Estar ocioso (to be at leisure). || Holgazanear, gandulear (to be lazy). || Estar parado, estar desocupado (to be out of work). || TECH. Funcionar en vacío (engine, machine). | Girar loco (mechanism).
— V. tr. *To idle away,* perder, desperdiciar: *to idle away the morning,* perder la mañana.
idleness [—nis] n. Ociosidad, *f.* (leisure). || Holgazanería, *f.*, gandulería, *f.* (laziness). || Paro, *m.*, desocupación, *f.* (unemployment). || Inutilidad, *f.* (uselessness). || Futilidad, *f.* (futility).
idler [—ə*] n. Ocioso, sa; holgazán, ana; vago, ga; gandul (lazy person). || TECH. Polea (*f.*) loca (pulley). | Rueda (*f.*) intermedia (wheel).
idler pulley [—ə'puli] n. TECH. Polea (*f.*) loca.
idler wheel [—əwi:l] n. U. S. TECH. Rueda (*f.*) intermedia.
idly ['aidli] adv. Ociosamente (lazily). || Inútilmente (uselessly). || Distraídamente (absentmindedly).
idol ['aidl] n. Ídolo, *m.*
idolater [ai'dɔlətə*] n. Idólatra, *m.*
idolatress [ai'dɔlətris] n. Idólatra, *f.*
idolatrize [ai'dɔlətraiz] v. tr. Idolatrar.
idolatrous [ai'dɔlətrəs] adj. Idólatra (person). || Idolátrico, ca: *idolatrous cult,* culto idolátrico.
idolatry [ai'dɔlətri] n. Idolatría, *f.*
idolization [,aidəulai'zeiʃən] n. Idolatría, *f.*
idolize ['aidəlaiz] v. tr. Idolatrar.
idolizer [—ə*] n. Idólatra, *m.* & *f.*
idyll or **idyl** ['idil] n. Idilio, *m.*
idyllic [ai'dilik] adj. Idílico, ca.
idyllist ['aidilist] n. Autor (*m.*) de idilios.
i. e. ['ai'i:] abbrev. of *id est,* es decir, o sea.
if [if] conj. Si: *if it rains we will stay at home,* si llueve nos quedaremos en casa; *do you know if he's in?,* ¿sabes si está en casa? || Si bien, aunque: *he is kind, if a bit too impulsive,* es amable, aunque un poco impulsivo. || — *As if by chance,* como por casualidad. || *He's tall if anything,* es más bien alto. || *He is tired if anything,* quizás esté cansado. || *If and when I like,* si quiero y cuando quiera. || *If I were you,* yo en tu lugar, yo que tú. || *If not,* si no. || *If only to speak to him,* aunque sea sólo para hablarle. || *If only we had known!,* ¡si lo hubiésemos sabido!, ¡ojalá lo hubiésemos sabido! || *I'll go tomorrow, if at all,* iré mañana, si es que voy. || *I shouldn't wonder if it rains,* no me extrañaría que lloviera. || *If so,* si es así, de ser así.
— N. Condición, *f.* (condition). || Suposición, *f.*, hipótesis, *f.*, supuesto, *m.* (supposition). || *Ifs and buts,* pegas, *f.*
igloo (U. S. **iglu**) ['iglu:] n. Iglú, *m.*
Ignatius [ig'neiʃjəs] pr. n. Ignacio, *m.*
igneous ['igniəs] adj. Ígneo, a: *igneous rock,* roca ígnea.
ignis fatuus ['ignis'fætjuəs] n. Fuego (*m.*) fatuo.

— OBSERV. El plural de *ignis fatuus* es *ignes fatui.*

ignitable [ig'naitəbl] adj. Inflamable.
ignite [ig'nait] v. tr. Encender, prender fuego a.
— V. intr. Encenderse (to begin to burn).
igniter [ig'naitə*] or **ignitor** [ig'naitə*] n. Deflagrador, *m.*
ignitible [ig'naitibl] adj. Inflamable.
ignition [ig'niʃən] n. Ignición, *f.* (action). || Encendido, *m.* (in a car, a rocket). || *Ignition coil,* bobina (*f.*) de encendido.
ignition key [—ki:] n. Llave (*f.*) de contacto.
ignition point [—pɔint] n. Punto (*m.*) de combustión.
ignoble [ig'nəubl] adj. Innoble, vil.
ignobleness [—nis] n. Bajeza, *f.*
ignominious [,ignəu'miniəs] adj. Ignominioso, sa.
ignominy ['ignəmini] n. Ignominia, *f.*
ignoramus [,ignə'reiməs] n. Ignorante, *m.* & *f.*, inculto, ta.
ignorance ['ignərəns] n. Ignorancia, *f.*: *ignorance of the law is no excuse,* la ignorancia de la ley no exime su cumplimiento. || — *Through ignorance,* por ignorancia. || *To be in ignorance of,* ignorar, desconocer, no saber.
ignorant ['ignərənt] adj. Ignorante. || *To be ignorant of,* ignorar, no saber, desconocer.
ignorantism [—izəm] n. Ignorantismo, *m.*
ignore [ig'nɔ:*] v. tr. No hacer caso de, hacer caso omiso de: *he ignored their warnings,* no hizo caso de sus advertencias. || Pasar por alto (to leave out). || No hacer caso a (s.o.). || JUR. Sobreseer.
iguana [i'gwɑ:nə] n. ZOOL. Iguana, *f.*
iguanodon [i'gwɑ:nədɔn] n. ZOOL. Iguanodonte, *m.*
ikon ['aikən] n. Icono, *m.*
ileac ['ili:ək] or **ileal** ['ili:əl] adj. ANAT. Iliaco, ca; ilíaco, ca.
ileocecal ['iliəsi:kəl] adj. ANAT. Ileocecal.
ileum ['ili:əm] n. ANAT. Íleon, *m.*

ileus [ˈili:əs] n. MED. Íleo, *m.*
ilex [ˈaileks] n. BOT. Encina, *f.* (holm oak). | Acebo, *m.* (holly).
iliac [ˈiliæk] adj. ANAT. Iliaco, ca; ilíaco, ca.
Iliad [ˈiliəd] n. Ilíada, *f.*
ilium [ˈiliəm] n. ANAT. Ilion, *m.*

— OBSERV. El plural de *ilium* es *ilia.*

ilk [ilk] n. Índole, *f.*, clase, *f.* (sort): *of that ilk*, de esta índole.
I'll [ail] contraction of *I will* and *I shall.*
ill [il] adj. Enfermo, ma (sick): *seriously ill*, enfermo de gravedad, gravemente enfermo. || Malo, la (unfortunate): *ill news*, malas noticas. || Malo, la (causing harm): *ill turn*, mala jugada; *ill repute*, mala fama. || FIG. Enfermo, ma: *to make s.o. ill*, poner enfermo a uno. || — *To be taken ill* o *to fall ill*, caer enfermo, ponerse enfermo, enfermar. || *To feel ill*, encontrarse mal, sentirse mal.
— Adv. Mal (adversely). || Difícilmente. || — *Ill at ease*, molesto, ta (uncomfortable), inquieto, ta; intranquilo, la (anxious). || *To be ill spoken of*, tener mala fama. || *To take sth. ill*, tomar algo a mal. || *We can ill afford the time*, casi no tenemos tiempo. || *We can ill afford to refuse*, no podemos permitirnos el lujo de negarnos.
— N. Mal, *m.*, desgracia, *f.*, infortunio, *m.* (misfortune). || MED. Mal, *m.*
ill-advised [—ədˈwaizd] adj. Malaconsejado, da; imprudente (person). || Poco atinado, da (action).
illation [iˈleiʃən] n. Ilación, *f.*
illative [iˈleitiv] adj. GRAMM. Ilativo, va.
ill-behaved [ˈilbiˈheivd] adj. Mal educado, da; de malos modales.
ill-boding [ˈilˈbəudiŋ] adj. De mal agüero.
ill-bred [ˈilˈbred] adj. Mal educado, da.
ill-conditioned [ˈilkənˈdiʃənd] adj. En mal estado (thing). || Desabrido, da (person).
ill-considered [ˈilkənˈsidəd] adj. Poco estudiado, da; poco meditado, da (not properly considered). || Apresurado, da (hasty): *ill-considered measures*, medidas apresuradas. || Imprudente (unwise).
ill-defined [ˈildiˈfaind] adj. Mal definido, da.
illegal [iˈli:gəl] adj. Ilegal.
illegality [iliˈgæliti] n. Ilegalidad, *f.*
illegibility [iˌledʒiˈbiliti] n. Ilegibilidad, *f.*
illegible [iˈledʒəbl] adj. Ilegible: *illegible signature*, firma ilegible.
illegibly [iˈledʒəbli] adv. De una manera ilegible.
illegitimacy [ˌiliˈdʒitiməsi] n. Ilegitimidad, *f.*
illegitimate [ˌiliˈdʒitimit] adj. Ilegítimo, ma (bastard): *illegitimate son*, hijo ilegítimo. || Ilógico, ca (not logical). || Ilegítimo, ma (contrary to law).
illegitimate [ˌiliˈdʒitimeit] v. tr. Ilegitimar.
ill-fated [ˈilˈfeitid] adj. Desafortunado, da; desdichado, da (destined to have bad luck). || Fatal: *an ill-fated encounter*, un encuentro fatal.
ill-favoured (U. S. **ill-favored**) [ˈilˈfeivəd] adj. Feo, a; poco agraciado, da (ugly). || Desagradable (unpleasant).
ill-founded [ˈilˈfaundid] adj. Infundado, da; sin fundamento.
ill-gotten [ˈilˈgɔtn] adj. Mal adquirido, da; adquirido por medios ilícitos.
ill health [ˈilˈhelθ] n. Mala salud, *f.*
ill humour (U. S. **ill humor**) [ˈilˈhju:mə*] n. Mal genio, *m.*, malhumor, *m.*, mal humor, *m.*
ill-humoured (U. S. **ill-humored**) [—d] adj. Malhumorado, da.
illiberal [iˈlibərəl] adj. Falto de liberalidad. || Intolerante.
illicit [iˈlisit] adj. Ilícito, ta.
illicitness [—nis] n. Ilicitud, *f.*
illimitable [iˈlimitəbl] adj. Ilimitable. || Ilimitado, da; infinito, ta (having no limits).
illimited [iˈlimitid] adj. Ilimitado, da.
ill-informed [ˈilinˈfɔ:md] adj. Mal informado, da.
illiteracy [iˈlitərəsi] n. Analfabetismo, *m.* || Ignorancia, *f.*
illiterate [iˈlitərit] adj. Analfabeto, ta (unable to read or write). || Iletrado, da; inculto, ta (lacking culture). || Ignorante.
— N. Analfabeto, ta.
ill luck [ˈilˈlʌk] n. Mala suerte, *f.*, desgracia, *f.*
ill-mannered [ˈilˈmænəd] adj. Maleducado, da; mal educado, da.
ill nature [ˈilˈneitʃə*] n. Mal carácter, *m.* (unpleasant disposition). || Malevolencia, *f.* (wickedness).
ill-natured [—d] adj. De mal genio, malhumorado, da. || Malévolo, la (wicked).
illness [ˈilnis] n. Enfermedad, *f.*: *to recover from a long illness*, salir de una larga enfermedad.
illogical [iˈlɔdʒikəl] adj. Ilógico, ca.
illogicality [ˈilɔdʒiˈkæliti] n. Ilogismo, *m.*, falta (*f.*) de lógica.
illogicalness [iˈlɔdʒikəlnis] n. See ILLOGICALITY.
ill-omened [ˈilˈəumend] adj. De mal agüero.
ill-pleased [ˈilˈpli:zd] adj. Descontento, ta.
ill-starred [ˈilˈstɑ:d] adj. Desafortunado, da; desgraciado, da; malhadado, da (person). || Aciago, ga (day). || Fatal (ill-fated).
ill-suited [ˈilˈsju:təd] adj. Impropio, pia (not appropriate).
ill-tempered [ˈilˈtempəd] adj. De mal carácter, de mal genio (person). || Malhumorado, da (remark, etc.).
ill-timed [ˈilˈtaimd] adj. Inoportuno, na; intempestivo, va.
ill-treat [ˈilˈtri:t] v. tr. Maltratar.
ill-treatment [—mənt] n. Maltratamiento, *m.*, malos tratos, *m. pl.*
illuminance [iˈljuminəns] n. PHYS. Iluminancia, *f.*
illuminate [iˈljumineit] v. tr. Iluminar (to light up). || Aclarar: *to illuminate a problem*, aclarar un problema. || Iluminar (with colours, lights).
illuminated [iˈlju:mineitid] adj. Iluminado, da. || Luminoso, sa.
illuminati [iˌlu:miˈnɑ:ti] pl. n. Iluminados, *m.*
illuminating [iˈljumineitiŋ] n. See ILLUMINATION.
— Adj. De alumbrado: *illuminating gas*, gas de alumbrado. || Luminoso, sa: *illuminating power*, potencia luminosa. || Revelador, ra (remark, etc.). || Instructivo, va: *illuminating book*, libro instructivo.
illumination [iˌljumineiʃən] n. Iluminación, *f.*, alumbrado, *m.* (of buildings). || ARTS. Iluminación, *f.* || Aclaración, *f.* (of a problem). || Inspiracion, *f.* || PHYS. Iluminación, *f.*, iluminancia, *f.* || — Pl. Luces, *f.*, iluminación, *f. sing.*, iluminaciones, *f.*
illuminator [iˈljumineitə*] n. Iluminador, ra.
illumine [iˈljumin] v. tr. See ILLUMINATE.
illuminism [—izəm] n. Iluminismo, *m.*
illuminist [—ist] n. Iluminado, da.
ill-use [ˈilˈju:z] v. tr. Maltratar.
illusion [iˈlu:ʒən] n. Ilusión, *f.*: *optical illusion*, ilusión óptica.
illusionary [—əri] adj. Ilusorio, ria.
illusionism [iˈlu:ʒənizəm] n. Ilusionismo, *m.*
illusionist [iˈlu:ʒənist] n. Ilusionista, *m.* & *f.*
illusive [iˈlu:siv] adj. Ilusorio, ria.
illusory [iˈlu:səri] adj. Ilusorio, ria.
illustrate [ˈiləstreit] v. tr. Ilustrar (a book). || FIG. Ilustrar, aclarar (to clarify).
illustration [ˌiləsˈtreiʃən] n. Ilustración, *f.* (of a book). || FIG. Aclaración, *f.* (clearing up). | Ilustración, *f.*, ejemplo, *m.* (instance).
illustrative [ˈiləstreitiv] adj. Ilustrativo, va; aclaratorio, ria.
illustrator [ˈiləstreitə*] n. Ilustrador, ra.
illustrious [iˈlʌstriəs] adj. Ilustre.
ill will [ˈilˈwil] n. Mala voluntad, *f.* (unwillingness). || Rencor, *m.* (grudge).
I'm [aim] contraction of *I am.*
image [ˈimidʒ] n. Imagen, *f.* || FIG. Reputación, *f.*, fama, *f.* (reputation). || — *He is the living* o *spitting image of his father*, es el vivo retrato de su padre. || *Image maker*, imaginero, *m.* || *In one's own image*, a su imagen. || *Mirror image*, reflejo exacto. || *Poetic images*, imágenes poéticas. || FIG. *To have a bad image of s.o.*, tener mal concepto de alguien.
image [ˈimidʒ] v. tr. Reflejar (to reflect). || Imaginar (to imagine). || Representar (to represent). || Simbolizar (to symbolize).
imagery [ˈimidʒəri] n. Imágenes, *f. pl.* (figurative language). || Imaginaciones, *f. pl.* (things one imagines). || REL. Imágenes, *f. pl.* (images). | Imaginería, *f.* (art).
imaginable [iˈmædʒinəbl] adj. Imaginable. || *The fastest imaginable car*, el coche más veloz que uno se puede imaginar.
imaginary [iˈmædʒinəri] adj. Imaginario, ria.
imagination [iˌmædʒiˈneiʃən] n. Imaginación, *f.*: *don't let your imagination run away with you!*, ¡no se deje llevar por la imaginación! || Imaginación, *f.*, imaginativa, *f.*, inventiva, *f.* (power).
imaginative [iˈmædʒinətiv] adj. Imaginativo, va: *imaginative power*, facultad imaginativa.
imaginativeness [—nis] n. Imaginativa, *f.*, inventiva, *f.*, imaginación, *f.*
imagine [iˈmædʒin] v. tr. Imaginar (to conceive, to invent). || Figurarse, imaginarse, suponer (to suppose). || — *Don't imagine that...*, no te vayas a creer que... || *Imagine that!*, *just imagine!*, ¡imagínate!, ¡fíjate! || *Imagine that you are president*, imagínate que eres presidente.
imago [iˈmeigəu] n. PHIL. Imagen, *f.*

— OBSERV. El plural de la palabra inglesa *imago* es *imagines* o *imagos.*

imam or **imaum** [iˈmɑ:m] n. REL. Imán, *m.*
imamate [iˈmɑ:meit] n. REL. Imanato, *m.*
imbalance [imˈbæləns] n. Falta (*f.*) de equilibrio, desequilibrio, *m.*
imbecile [ˈimbisi:l] adj./n. Imbécil.
imbecility [ˌimbiˈsiliti] n. Imbecilidad, *f.*
imbed [imˈbed] v. tr. Empotrar, encajar.
imbibe [imˈbaib] v. tr. Embeber, absorber (to take in liquid). || Aspirar (air). || FIG. Impregnarse de, embeberse de, empaparse de *or* en (ideas, etc.). | Beber (to drink).
— V. intr. Beber.
imbibing [—iŋ] n. Imbibición, *f.*, absorción, *f.*
imbricate [ˈimbrikit] or **imbricated** [ˈimbrikeitid] adj. Imbricado, da.
imbricate [ˈimbrikeit] v. tr. Imbricar, traslapar.
— V. intr. Superponerse, traslaparse.
imbrication [imbriˈkeiʃən] n. Imbricación, *f.*, superposición, *f.*
imbroglio [imˈbrəuliəu] n. Embrollo, *m.*, lío, *m.*

imbrue [imˈbru:] v. tr. Bañar: *to imbrue sth. in blood*, bañar algo en sangre.

imbrute [imˈbru:t] v. tr. Embrutecer.
— V. intr. Embrutecerse.

imbue [imˈbju:] v. tr. Empapar (*with*, en) [with a liquid]. || Imbuir (*with*, de) [with emotions, etc.].

imitable [ˈimitəbl] adj. Imitable.

imitate [ˈimiteit] v. tr. Imitar.

imitating [—iŋ] adj. Imitador, ra.

imitation [ˌimiˈteiʃən] n. Imitación, *f.* || — *Beware of imitations*, desconfíe de las imitaciones. || *In imitation of*, a imitación de.
— Adj. De imitación, artificial, imitación: *imitation leather*, cuero artificial. || *Imitation jewelry*, joyas (*f. pl.*) de imitación, bisutería, *f.*

imitative [ˈimitətiv] adj. Imitativo, va.

imitator [ˈimiteitə*] n. Imitador, ra.

immaculate [iˈmækjulit] adj. Inmaculado, da; limpio, pia (very clear). || Perfecto, ta (perfect). || REL. Inmaculado, da; purísimo, ma. || REL. *The Immaculate Conception*, La Inmaculada Concepción.

immanence or **immanency** [ˈimənəns] n. Inmanencia, *f.*

immanent [ˈimənənt] adj. Inmanente.

immanentism [ˈimənənˌtizəm] n. Inmanentismo, *m.*

immaterial [ˌiməˈtiəriəl] adj. Inmaterial (having no substance). || Indiferente: *it's immaterial to me whether you go or stay*, me es indiferente que te vayas o que te quedes. || *That's immaterial*, no importa.

immaterialism [ˌiməˈtiəriəlizəm] n. PHIL. Inmaterialismo, *m.*

immateriality [ˈiməˌtiəriˈæliti] n. Inmaterialidad, *f.* || Insignificancia, *f.* (unimportance).

immature [ˌiməˈtjuə*] adj. BOT. Inmaduro, ra; no maduro, ra; verde. || Inmaduro, ra (person). || Juvenil (childish).

immaturity [ˌiməˈtjuəriti] n. Inmadurez, *f.*, falta (*f.*) de madurez.

immeasurability [iˌmeʒərəˈbiliti] n. Inconmensurabilidad, *f.*

immeasurable [iˈmeʒərəbl] adj. Inmensurable, inconmensurable.

immeasurableness [—nis] n. Inconmensurabilidad, *f.*

immediacy [iˈmi:djəsi] n. Inmediación, *f.*, proximidad, *f.* (proximity). || Urgencia, *f.* (urgency): *the immediacy of our needs*, la urgencia de nuestras necesidades. || Carácter (*m.*) inminente (of a danger).

immediate [iˈmi:djət] adj. Inmediato, ta: *immediate response*, respuesta inmediata. || PHIL. Intuitivo, va. || Cercano, na; próximo, ma (near): *immediate future*, futuro próximo. || Directo, ta (directly related). || Urgente. || — *Immediate danger*, peligro inminente. || *Immediate need*, primera necesidad. || *Immediate neighbourhood*, inmediaciones, *f. pl.* || *To take immediate action*, actuar inmediatamente.

immediately [—li] adv. Inmediatamente, en seguida (at once). || Directamente (directly). || Sin demora, sin retraso (without delay).
— Prep. Tan pronto como, en cuanto.

immedicable [iˈmedikəbl] adj. Irremediable, incurable.

immemorial [ˌimiˈmɔ:riəl] adj. Inmemorial. || *From time immemorial*, desde tiempo inmemorial.

immense [iˈmens] adj. Inmenso, sa; enorme. || FAM. Estupendo, da (very good).

immensely [—li] adv. Enormemente. || Muy (very). || FAM. Estupendamente.

immensity [—iti] n. Inmensidad, *f.* || FIG. Cosa (*f.*) enorme.

immensurable [—jə:rəbl] adj. Inmensurable.

immerge [iˈmə:dʒ] or **immerse** [iˈmə:s] v. tr. Sumergir, hundir (to dip): *to immerse one's feet in water*, sumergir los pies en el agua. || REL. Bautizar por inmersión. || FIG. Enfrascar, sumir: *to immerse o.s. in work*, enfrascarse en el trabajo. | Sumir, absorber: *he was immersed in thought*, estaba absorto en sus pensamientos.

immersion [iˈmə:ʃən] n. Inmersión, *f.* || *Immersion heater*, calentador (*m.*) de inmersión.

immesh [iˈmeʃ] v. tr. Enredar.

immethodical [imiˈθɔdikəl] adj. Sin método.

immigrant [ˈimigrənt] adj./n. Inmigrante, inmigrado, da.

immigrate [ˈimigreit] v. intr. Inmigrar.

immigration [ˌimiˈgreiʃən] n. Inmigración, *f.*

immigratory [ˈimigreitəri] adj. Inmigratorio, ria.

imminence [ˈiminəns] or **imminency** [—i] n. Inminencia, *f.*

imminent [ˈiminənt] adj. Inminente.

immitigable [iˈmitigəbəl] adj. Que no se puede mitigar.

immix [iˈmiks] v. tr. Mezclar.

immixture [iˈmikstʃə] n. Mezcla, *f.* (mixture). || FIG. Intromisión, *f.* (meddling).

immobile [iˈməubail] adj. Inmóvil (motionless). || Fijo, ja; inmutable (not changing).

immobility [ˌiməuˈbiliti] n. Inmovilidad, *f.* || Inmutabilidad, *f.*

immobilization [iˌməubilaiˈzeiʃən] n. Inmovilización, *f.*

immobilize [iˈməubilaiz] v. tr. Inmovilizar.

immoderate [iˈmɔdərit] adj. Inmoderado, da (beyond the proper limits). || Desmedido, da; desmesurado, da; excesivo, va (unreasonably large). || Descomunal: *immoderate appetite*, apetito descomunal.

immoderation [ˈiˌmɔdəˈreiʃən] n. Falta (*f.*) de moderación, exceso, *m.*

immodest [iˈmɔdist] adj. Inmodesto, ta (not humble). || Indecente, impúdico, ca (indecent). || Impudente, desvergonzado, da (bold).

immodesty [iˈmɔdisti] n. Inmodestia, *f.* (lack of modesty). || Impudicia, *f.*, impudor, *m.* (indecency). || Impudencia, *f.*, desvergüenza, *f.* (boldness).

immolate [ˈiməuleit] v. tr. Inmolar.

immolation [ˌiməuˈleiʃən] n. Inmolación, *f.*

immolator [ˈiməuleitə*] n. Inmolador, ra.

immoral [iˈmɔrəl] adj. Inmoral. || Disoluto, ta (life). || Vicioso, sa (vicious).

immoralism [iməˈrælizəm] n. Inmoralismo, *m.*

immoralist [iˈmɔrəlist] n. Inmoralista, *m.* & *f.*

immorality [iməˈræliti] n. Inmoralidad, *f.*

immortal [iˈmɔ:tl] adj. Inmortal. || FIG. Imperecedero, ra (memories, etc.).
— N. Inmortal, *m.* & *f.*

immortality [ˌimɔ:ˈtæliti] n. Inmortalidad, *f.*

immortalize [iˈmɔ:təlaiz] v. tr. Inmortalizar.

immortelle [ˌimɔ:ˈtel] n. BOT. Siempreviva, *f.*

immovability [iˌmu:vəˈbiliti] n. Inmovilidad, *f.* (immobility). || Inmutabilidad, *f.*, impasibilidad, *f.* (impassibility). || Inflexibilidad, *f.* (firmness). || Inamovilidad, *f.* (of a post).

immovable [iˈmu:vəbl] adj. Inmóvil. || Impasible, inmutable (unemotional). || Inflexible (steadfast). || Inamovible (post). || JUR. Inmueble. || REL. *Immovable feast*, fiesta fija.
— N. JUR. Bienes (*m. pl.*) raíces *or* inmuebles.

immune [iˈmju:n] adj. Inmune (*to*, a). || FIG. Exento, ta (*from*, de) [taxes].

immunity [iˈmju:niti] n. Inmunidad, *f.* (*to*, contra). || JUR. Exención, *f.* (*from*, de). || *Diplomatic, parliamentary immunity*, inmunidad diplomática, parlamentaria.

immunization [ˌimju:naiˈzeiʃən] n. Inmunización, *f.*

immunize [ˈimju:naiz] v. tr. Inmunizar.

immunogenic [ˌimju:nəuˈdʒenik] adj. Inmunizador, ra.

immunology [ˌimju:ˈnɔlədʒi] n. Inmunología, *f.*

immure [iˈmjuə*] v. tr. Emparedar (to shut up within walls). || Encerrar (to imprison).

immurement [—mənt] n. Emparedamiento, *m.*

immutability [iˌmju:təˈbiliti] n. Inmutabilidad, *f.*

immutable [iˈmju:təbl] adj. Inmutable.

imp [imp] n. Diablillo, *m.*, duendecillo, *m.*, trasgo. *m.* (young devil). || FAM. Pícaro, ra (mischievous person).

impact [ˈimpækt] n. Impacto, *m.*, choque, *m.* (shock). || Colisión, *f.*, choque, *m.* (collision). || FIG. Impacto, *m.*, efecto, *m.* (effect). | Repercusiones, *f. pl.*, consecuencias, *f. pl.* (consequences).

impact [imˈpækt] v. tr. Incrustar.

impair [imˈpɛə*] v. tr. Dañar, perjudicar, deteriorar.

impairment [—mənt] n. Deterioro, *m.*, daño, *m.*

impale [imˈpeil] v. tr. Empalar (as punishment). || Atravesar (with a sword, etc.).

impalement [—mənt] n. Empalamiento, *m.*

impalpability [imˌpælpəˈbiliti] n. Impalpabilidad, *f.*

impalpable [imˈpælpəbl] adj. Impalpable. || FIG. Intangible, impalpable.

imparadise [imˈpærədaiz] v. tr. Llevar al colmo de la felicidad, colmar de felicidad (a person). || Convertir en paraíso (a place).

imparity [imˈpæriti] n. Disparidad, *f.*

impark [imˈpɑ:k] v. tr. Acorralar, encerrar (animals). || Cercar, vallar (land).

impart [imˈpɑ:t] v. tr. Impartir, dar (to give). || Conceder (to grant). || Comunicar (to make known).

impartial [imˈpɑ:ʃəl] adj. Imparcial.

impartiality [ˈimˌpɑ:ʃiˈæliti] n. Imparcialidad, *f.*

impartible [imˈpɑ:təbl] adj. Indivisible (estate).

impartment [imˈpɑ:tmənt] n. Comunicación, *f.*, transmisión, *f.* (of news).

impassable [imˈpɑ:səbl] adj. Intransitable (street, corridor, roads). || Infranqueable (barrier).

impasse [æmˈpɑ:s] n. Callejón (*m.*) sin salida (street). || FIG. Callejón (*m.*) sin salida, atolladero, *m.*: *talks have reached an impasse*, las negociaciones están en un atolladero.

impassibility [ˈimˌpɑ:siˈbiliti] n. Impasibilidad, *f.*

impassible [imˈpæsibl] adj. Impasible.

impassion [imˈpæʃən] v. tr. Apasionar.

impassioned [—d] adj. Apasionado, da.

impassive [imˈpæsiv] adj. Impasible (not showing emotion). || Insensible.

impassiveness [—nis] or **impassivity** [—iti] n. Impasibilidad, *f.* || Insensibilidad, *f.*

impaste [imˈpeist] v. tr. ARTS. Empastar. || Convertir en pasta.

impasto [imˈpɑ:stəu] n. Empaste, *m.*

impatience [imˈpeiʃəns] n. Impaciencia, *f.*

impatient [imˈpeiʃənt] adj. Impaciente. || — *To be impatient of*, no soportar (to be unable to endure). || *To be impatient to do sth.*, tener muchos deseos de hacer algo, estar impaciente por hacer algo. || *To get impatient*, perder la paciencia. || *To make s.o. impatient*, impacientar a uno.

impavid [imˈpævid] adj. Impávido, da (fearless).

impawn [imˈpɔ:n] v. tr. Empeñar (to put in pawn). || FIG. Comprometer, arriesgar (to risk).

impeach [im'pi:tʃ] v. tr. JUR. Acusar (to charge with a crime). | Encausar, enjuiciar (to prosecute). | Recusar (evidence, a witness). || Poner en tela de juicio (to question): *to impeach the veracity of a statement*, poner en tela de juicio la veracidad de una declaración. || Censurar (s.o.'s conduct).
impeachable [—əbl] adj. JUR. Acusable (chargeable). | Recusable (evidence, a witness). || Controvertible, discutible (probity, veracity). || Censurable (conduct).
impeacher [—ə*] n. Denunciador, ra.
impeachment [—mənt] n. JUR. Acusación, *f.* (accusation). | Enjuiciamiento, *m.* (prosecution). | Recusación, *f.* (of evidence, a witness). || Puesta (*f.*) en tela de juicio (of s.o.'s veracity). || Censura, *f.* (of s.o.'s conduct).
impeccability [im,pekə'biliti] n. Impecabilidad, *f.*
impeccable [im'pekəbl] adj. Impecable.
impecuniosity [impi,kju:ni'ɔsiti] n. Falta (*f.*) de dinero, escasez (*f.*) de recursos, pobreza, *f.*
impecunious [,impi'kju:njəs] adj. Falto de dinero, sin dinero, pobre, indigente.
impedance [im'pi:dəns] n. ELECTR. Impedancia, *f.*
impede [im'pi:d] v. tr. Estorbar (to hinder): *to impede the traffic*, estorbar el tráfico. || *If you want to go on the stage I shall not impede you*, si quieres ser actor no te lo voy a impedir.
impediment [im'pedimənt] n. Estorbo, *m.* (hindrance). || Obstáculo, *m.*, impedimento, *m.* (obstacle). || Defecto (*m.*) del habla (speech defect). || JUR. Impedimento, *m.*: *diriment impediment*, impedimento dirimente.
impedimenta [im,pedi'mentə] pl. n. MIL. Impedimenta, *f. sing.* || FAM. Equipaje, *m. sing.*
impel [im'pel] v. tr. Impeler, impulsar (to drive forward). || Empujar (to push). || Mover (to move). || Mover, incitar, inducir (to urge): *what impelled him to do such a thing?*, ¿qué le incitó a hacer tal cosa? || Obligar (to compel): *I feel impelled to do it*, me veo obligado a hacerlo.
impellent [—ənt] adj. Impelente.
— M. Motor, *m.* || Fuerza (*f.*) impelente.
impeller [—ə*] n. TECH. Rueda (*f.*) motriz (wheel). | Rotor, *m.* || FIG. Instigador, ra.
impelling [—iŋ] adj. Impelente: *inpelling force*, fuerza impelente.
impend [im'pend] v. intr. Ser inminente, cernerse.
impendence [im'pendəns] n. Inminencia, *f.*
impendent [im'pendənt] or **impending** [im'pendiŋ] adj. Inminente (imminent): *an impending disaster*, un desastre inminente. || Próximo, ma (in the near future).
impenetrability [im,penitrə'biliti] n. Impenetrabilidad, *f.*
impenetrable [im'penitrəbl] adj. Impenetrable.
impenitence [im'penitəns] or **impenitency** [—i] n. Impenitencia, *f.*
impenitent [im'penitənt] adj. Impenitente.
imperative [im'perətiv] adj. Imperioso, sa (urgent): *imperative need*, necesidad imperiosa. || Imprescindible, indispensable (necessary). || Perentorio, ria; imperioso, sa (peremptory). || GRAMM. Imperativo, va: *the imperative mood*, el modo imperativo.
— N. GRAMM. Imperativo, *m.*
imperativeness [—nis] n. Urgencia, *f.*
imperatorial [im,perə'tɔ:riəl] adj. Imperatorio, ria.
imperceptibility ['impə,septə'biliti] n. Imperceptibilidad, *f.*
imperceptible [,impə'septəbl] adj. Imperceptible.
imperfect [im'pə:fikt] adj. Imperfecto, ta; defectuoso, sa (defective). || Incompleto, ta (incomplete). || GRAMM. Imperfecto.
— N. GRAMM. Imperfecto, *m.*, pretérito (*m.*) imperfecto.
imperfection [,impə'fekʃən] n. Imperfección, *f.* || Imperfección, *f.*, defecto, *m.* (defect).
imperforate [im'pə:fərit] adj. Sin perforaciones, sin dentado (stamp).
imperforation [im,pə:fə'reiʃən] n. Imperforación, *f.*
imperial [im'piəriəl] adj. Imperial: *imperial crown*, corona imperial. || FIG. Señorial.
— N. Perilla, *f.* (beard). || Imperial, *f.* (top deck of a coach). || *Imperial gallon*, galón inglés [4,543 litros].
imperialism [—izəm] n. Imperialismo, *m.*
imperialist [—ist] adj./n. Imperialista.
imperialistic [impiəriə'listik] adj. Imperialista.
imperil [im'peril] v. tr. Arriesgar, poner en peligro.
imperious [im'piəriəs] adj. Imperioso, sa (need). || Autoritario, ria (person).
imperiousness [—nis] n. Autoridad, *f.* || Arrogancia, *f.* || Urgencia, *f.*
imperishable [im'periʃəbl] adj. Imperecedero, ra.
imperium [im'piəriəm] n. Imperio, *m.*, poder (*m.*) absoluto (authority).
impermanence [im'pə:mənəns] n. Inestabilidad, *f.* || Temporalidad, *f.*
impermanent [im'pə:mənənt] adj. Inestable (unstable). || Temporal (temporary).
impermeability [im,pə:mjə'biliti] n. Impermeabilidad, *f.*
impermeable [im'pə:mjəbl] adj. Impermeable (*to*, a).
impermissible [impə:'misibl] adj. Inadmisible, intolerable.
impersonal [im'pə:snl] adj. Impersonal.
impersonality [im,pə:sə'næliti] n. Impersonalidad, *f.*
impersonate [im'pə:səneit] v. tr. Hacerse pasar por (to pretend to be s.o. else). || Imitar (to imitate in order to entertain). || Representar *or* interpretar el papel de (to act the part of). || FIG. Encarnar (to embody). | Personificar (to personify).
impersonation [im,pə:sə'neiʃən] n. Imitación, *f.* (as entertainment). || Interpretación, *f.* (of a part). || FIG. Encarnación, *f.* (embodiment). | Personificación, *f.* (personification).
impersonator [im'pə:səneitə*] n. Imitador, ra (entertainer). || Intérprete, *m.* & *f.* (actor).
impertinence [im'pə:tinəns] n. Impertinencia, *f.* (rudeness, rude act or remark). || Impertinencia, *f.*, improcedencia, *f.* (irrelevance). || Inoportunidad, *f.* (untimeliness). || *A piece of impertinence*, una impertinencia.
impertinent [im'pə:tinənt] adj. Impertinente (impudent): *he was impertinent to me*, fue impertinente conmigo. || Impertinente, improcedente (irrelevant). || Fuera de lugar, inoportuno, na (inappropriate).
impertinently [—li] adv. Con impertinencia.
imperturbability ['impə,tə:bə'biliti] n. Imperturbabilidad, *f.*
imperturbable [,impə'tə:bəbl] adj. Imperturbable, impertérrito, ta.
impervious [im'pə:vjəs] adj. Insensible (insensitive): *impervious to pain*, insensible al dolor; *impervious to criticism*, insensible a las críticas. || Impenetrable (impenetrable). || — *Impervious to water*, impermeable. || *To be impervious to reason*, no atender a razones.
imperviousness [—nis] n. Impenetrabilidad, *f.* || Insensibilidad, *f.* (insensitivity): *his imperviousness to criticism*, su insensibilidad a las críticas. || TECH. Impermeabilidad, *f.*
impetigo [,impi'taigəu] n. MED. Impétigo, *m.*
impetrate ['impətreit] v. tr. Impetrar: *to impetrate divine protection*, impetrar la protección divina.
impetration [impə'treiʃən] n. Impetración, *f.*
impetrating ['impətreitiŋ] adj. Impetrador, ra; impetrante.
impetrator ['impətreitə*] n. Impetrador, ra; impetrante, *m.* & *f.*
impetuosity [im,petju'ɔsiti] n. Impetuosidad, *f.*
impetuous [im'petjuəs] adj. Impetuoso, sa.
impetuousness [—nis] n. Impetuosidad, *f.*
impetus ['impitəs] n. Ímpetu, *m.* (force). || FIG. Impulso, *m.*: *the new treaty will give impetus to trade between the two countries*, el nuevo tratado dará un impulso al comercio entre los dos países. | Estímulo, *m.*, incentivo, *m.* (incentive).
impiety [im'paiəti] n. Impiedad, *f.*
impinge [im'pindʒ] v. intr. *To impinge on* o *against*, tropezar con, chocar con *or* contra. || *To impinge on* o *upon*, usurpar (to encroach upon), impresionar (to make an impression).
impingement [—mənt] n. Choque, *m.* (collision). || Impresión, *f.* (impression). || Intrusión, *f.*, usurpación, *f.* (encroachment).
impious ['impiəs] adj. Impío, a.
impish ['impiʃ] adj. Travieso, sa; pícaro, ra.
implacability [im,plækə'biliti] n. Implacabilidad, *f.*
implacable [im'plækəbl] adj. Implacable.
implant ['implα:nt] n. MED. Injerto, *m.*
implant [im'plα:nt] v. tr. Implantar (to plant deeply). || Inculcar (to instil firmly in the mind). || MED. Injertar, implantar.
implantation [,implα:n'teiʃən] n. Implantación, *f.*
implausible [im'plɔ:zəbl] adj. Inverosímil.
impledge [im'pledʒ] v. tr. Empeñar.
implement ['implimənt] n. Herramienta, *f.* (tool). || Utensilio, *m.* (utensil). || Instrumento, *m.* (instrument). || — *Farm implements*, aperos (*m.*) de labranza. || *Writing implements*, artículos (*m.*) *or* objetos (*m.*) de escritorio.
implement ['implimənt] v. tr. Llevar a cabo (to carry out). || Realizar, ejecutar (to execute). || Cumplir (a promise). || Aplicar (a law). || Poner en práctica *or* en ejecución (decisions, measures).
implementation [,implimen'teiʃən] n. Realización, *f.*, ejecución, *f.* (execution). || Aplicación, *f.* (of a law). || Puesta (*f.*) en práctica *or* en ejecución (of decisions, measures).
implicate ['implikeit] v. tr. Implicar (to imply). || || Comprometer, implicar, complicar (to involve): *he was implicated in the scandal*, fue comprometido en el escándalo.
implication [,impli'keiʃən] n. Implicación, *f.* (thing implied). || Complicidad, *f.*, implicación, *f.* (in a crime, etc.). || Repercusión, *f.*, consecuencia, *f.*, incidencia, *f.*: *one cannot tell what the implications of his action will be*, no se puede decir cuáles serán las consecuencias de su acción.
implicative [im'plikətiv] or **implicatory** [impli'keitəri] adj. Implicatorio, ria.
implicit [im'plisit] adj. Implícito, ta (understood though not stated). || Absoluto, ta (absolute).
implied [im'plaid] adj. Implícito, ta.
implore [im'plɔ:*] v. tr. Suplicar: *to implore s.o. to do sth.*, suplicar a uno que haga algo. || Implorar: *to implore forgiveness*, implorar perdón. || *I implore you!*, ¡se lo suplico!
imploring [—riŋ] adj. Suplicante.
imploringly [—riŋli] adv. De modo suplicante.

implosive [im'pləusiv] adj. GRAMM. Implosivo, va.

imply [im'plai] v. tr. Implicar, suponer (to involve): *this implies a great effort from us*, esto supone un gran esfuerzo por nuestra parte. || Presuponer, suponer (to presuppose). || Insinuar (to hint). || Dar a entender: *without actually saying so he implied that...*, sin llegar a decirlo dio a entender que... || Significar, querer decir (to mean).

impolicy [im'pɔlisi] n. Política (*f.*) poco hábil, mala política, *f.*, imprudencia, *f.*

impolite [,impə'lait] adj. Mal educado, da; descortés.

impolitely ['—li] adv. Con descortesía, descortésmente.

impoliteness [—nis] n. Mala educación, *f.*, descortesía, *f.*

impolitic [im'pɔlitik] adj. Impolítico, ca; imprudente.

imponderability [im,pɔndərə'biliti] n. Imponderabilidad, *f.*

imponderable [im'pɔndərəbl] adj. Imponderable.
— N. Imponderable, *m.*

import ['impɔ:t] n. COMM. Artículo (*m.*) importado, mercancía (*f.*) importada (sth. imported). | Importación, *f.*: *a rise in imports*, un aumento de las importaciones. || Significado, *m.*, sentido, *m.* (meaning). || Importancia, *f.* (importance). || — COMM. *Import duty*, derechos (*m. pl.*) de importación. || *Import licence*, permiso (*m.*) *or* licencia (*f.*) de importación. || *Import trade*, comercio (*m.*) de importación.

import [im'pɔ:t] v. tr. Importar (goods): *we import Spanish oranges into our country*, importamos naranjas españolas en nuestro país. || FIG. Introducir (ideas). | Implicar (to imply). | Significar, querer decir (to mean).
— V. intr. Importar, tener importancia (to matter).

importable [—əbl] adj. COMM. Importable.

importance [—əns] n. Importancia, *f.* || — *Of importance*, importante. || *Of the highest importance* o *of the first importance*, de mucha importancia, primordial. || FIG. *She is full of her own importance*, se da mucho tono. || *To be of importance*, tener importancia, ser importante.

important [—ənt] adj. Importante. || Engreído, da (conceited). || — *It's not important*, no importa, no tiene importancia. || *The important thing is...*, lo importante es... || *To try and look important*, darse mucho tono.

importantly [—əntli] adv. Dándose mucho tono (to speak).

importation [,impɔ:'teiʃən] n. Importación, *f.*

importer [im'pɔ:tə*] n. Importador, ra.

importing [im'pɔ:tiŋ] adj. Importador, ra: *importing country*, país importador.

importunate [im'pɔ:tjunit] or **importune** [im'pɔ:tju:n] adj. Importuno, na (annoyingly persistent). || Molesto, ta; pesado, da (bothersome).

importune [im'pɔ:tju:n] v. tr. Importunar (to annoy). || Molestar (to bother). || Hacer proposiciones deshonestas (said of a prostitute).

importunity [,impɔ:'tju:niti] n. Importunidad, *f.*

impose [im'pəuz] v. tr./intr. Imponer (conditions, a doctrine, etc.): *to impose one's ideas on s.o.*, imponer las ideas propias a otro. || COMM. Gravar con (a tax). || REL. PRINT. Imponer. || — *To impose on* o *upon*, engañar a (to cheat), abusar de, aprovecharse de (to take advantage of). || *To impose o.s.*, imponerse.

imposing [—iŋ] adj. Imponente, impresionante. || PRINT. *Imposing table*, platina, *f.*

imposition [,impə'ziʃən] n. Imposición, *f.*: *the imposition of certain conditions*, la imposición de ciertas condiciones. || Impuesto, *m.*, gravamen, *m.* (tax). || Abuso, *m.*: *it is an imposition to ask him for help*, es un abuso pedirle ayuda. || Castigo, *m.* (at school). || PRINT. Imposición, *f.* || FAM. Engaño, *m.* (deception). || — REL. *Imposition of hands*, imposición de manos. || *Would it be too much of an imposition to...?*, le resultaría muy molesto...?

impossibility [im,pɔsə'biliti] n. Imposibilidad, *f.* || Cosa (*f.*) imposible, imposible, *m.*: *to ask for impossibilities*, pedir imposibles.

impossible [im'pɔsəbl] adj. Imposible: *an impossible task*, una tarea imposible; *it is impossible for me to do it*, me es imposible hacerlo. || Inaceptable (unacceptable). || Insorportable, inaguantable (unbearable): *he's an impossible person!*, ¡es una persona inaguantable! || Intratable (difficult to get on with). || FIG. Ridículo, la: *an impossible hat*, un sombrero ridículo. || — *It's not impossible that*, es posible que. || *Lack of ammunition made attack impossible*, la falta de municiones imposibilitó el ataque. || *To do the impossible*, hacer lo imposible. || *Your decision makes it impossible for me to go*, su decisión me quita la posibilidad de ir, su decisión impide que vaya.

impossibleness [—nis] n. Imposibilidad, *f.*

impossibly [—i] adv. Imposiblemente. || — *It is impossibly expensive*, es carísimo, es de lo más caro. || *Not impossibly*, quizás.

impost ['impəust] n. COMM. Impuesto, *m.* (tax). | Derecho (*m.*) de aduana (customs duty). || ARCH. Imposta, *f.* || SP. Handicap, *m.*

impostor [im'pɔstə*] n. Impostor, ra.

imposture [im'pɔstʃə*] n. Impostura, *f.*, engaño, *m.*

impotence ['impətəns] or **impotency** [—i] n. Impotencia, *f.*

impotent ['impətənt] adj. Impotente.

impound [im'paund] v. tr. JUR. Confiscar, embargar (goods). || Meter en la perrera (dogs). || Poner en el depósito (cars). || Encerrar (to shut up). || U. S. Embalsar (water).

impoverish [im'pɔvəriʃ] v. tr. Empobrecer (people). || Agotar (land).

impoverishment [—mənt] n. Empobrecimiento, *m.* || AGR. Agotamiento, *m.*

impracticability [im,præktikə'biliti] n. Impracticabilidad, *f.*, imposibilidad, *f.* || Cosa (*f.*) impracticable *or* imposible.

impracticable [im'præktikəbl] adj. Impracticable, irrealizable, imposible de realizar (plan). || Intransitable (road). || Intratable (person).

impractical [im'præktikəl] adj. U. S. Poco práctico, ca (person, idea, etc.).

imprecate ['imprikeit] v. tr. Imprecar (evil). || Echar (curses). || Maldecir (to curse).

imprecation [,impri'keiʃən] n. Imprecación, *f.*

imprecatory ['imprikeitəri] adj. Imprecatorio, ria.

imprecise [impri'sais] adj. Impreciso, sa.

imprecision [impri'siʒən] n. Imprecisión, *f.*

impregnable [im'pregnəbl] adj. Inexpugnable (castle, fortification, etc.). || Invulnerable (position). || Impregnable (that can be impregnated). || FIG. Inquebrantable (belief).

impregnate [im'pregnit] adj. Embarazada, preñada (woman). || FIG. Impregnado, da.

impregnate ['impregneit] v. tr. BIOL. Fecundar. || Impregnar, empapar (to saturate). || FIG. Impregnar (to imbue).

impregnation [,impreg'neiʃən] n. Impregnación, *f.* || BIOL. Fecundación, *f.*

impresario [,impre'sɑ:riəu] n. THEATR. Empresario, *m.*

imprescriptibility [,impriskripti'biliti] n. Imprescriptibilidad, *f.*

imprescriptible [,impris'kriptəbl] adj. Imprescriptible.

impress ['impres] n. Impresión, *f.* || Sello, *m.*: *the printer's impress*, el sello del impresor. || FIG. Marca, *f.*, sello, *m.* (distinguishing mark). | Huella, *f.*, impresión, *f.* (an effect on the mind).

impress [im'pres] v. tr. Imprimir (to press a mark on sth.). || Estampar (a design, signature, etc.). || Sellar (to seal). || Imprimir (to print). || Grabar (upon s.o.'s mind). || FIG. Convencer de: *we tried to impress on him the importance of his work*, intentamos convencerle de la importancia de su trabajo. | Inculcar: *to impress an idea on s.o.*, inculcar una idea a alguien. || Impresionar: *he tried to impress me*, trató de impresionarme; *he is not easily impressed*, no se deja impresionar fácilmente. || MIL. Requisar. || — *He impressed me favourably*, me hizo *or* me causó buena impresión, me impresionó favorablemente. || *How did it impress you?*, ¿qué impresión le produjo? || *The incident impressed itself upon my mind*, el incidente se me quedó grabado en la memoria. || *The story deeply impressed us*, el relato nos causó una gran impresión, el relato nos impresionó mucho.
— V. intr. Hacer *or* causar [buena] impresión.

impressibility [im,presi'biliti] n. Impresionabilidad, *f.*

impressible [im'presəbl] adj. Imprimible, estampable (capable of being impressed). || Impresionable (impressionable).

impression [im'preʃən] n. Impresión, *f.* (an impressing or being impressed). || Señal, *f.*, huella, *f.*, marca, *f.* (mark). || PRINT. Ejemplar, *m.* (copy made from type). | Tirada, *f.* (group of copies). | Impresión, *f.* (printing). || Molde, *m.* (in dentistry). || FIG. Impresión, *f.*: *the film left me with an impression of sadness*, la película me dejó una impresión de tristeza; *to have the impression that*, tener la impresión de que; *to make a bad impression*, causar mala impresión. || — *To be under the impression that*, tener la impresión de que. || *To make an impression*, impresionar. || *To make an impression on* o *upon*, impresionar a. || *Your words make no impression on me*, tus palabras no me hacen el menor efecto *or* ningún efecto.

impressionability [im,preʃnə'biliti] n. Impresionabilidad, *f.*

impressionable [im'preʃnəbl] adj. Impresionable.

impressionism [im'preʃnizəm] n. ARTS. Impresionismo, *m.*

impressionist [im'preʃnist] adj./n. Impresionista.

impressionistic [im,preʃə'nistik] adj. Impresionista.

impressive [im'presiv] adj. Impresionante.

impressively [—li] adv. De forma *or* de modo impresionante.

impressiveness [—nis] n. Carácter (*m.*) impresionante, lo impresionante.

impressment [im'presmənt] n. Requisa, *f.*, requisición, *f.*

imprest ['imprest] n. Préstamo, *m.*, anticipo, *m.*

imprimatur [,impri'meitə*] n. Imprimátur, *m.*

imprint ['imprint] n. Impresión, *f.*, marca, *f.* (mark produced by pressure). || FIG. Sello, *m.*: *the work bore the imprint of his personality*, el trabajo llevaba el sello de su personalidad. || PRINT. Pie (*m.*) de imprenta (printer's mark).

imprint [im'print] v. tr. Imprimir. || Estampar (on cloth). || FIG. Grabar (on the mind).

imprison [im'prizn] v. tr. Encarcelar, aprisionar, poner en la cárcel.

imprisonment [—mənt] n. Encarcelamiento, *m.* (action). || Cárcel, *f.*, prisión, *f.*: *sentenced to five years' imprisonment*, condenado a cinco años de cárcel. || *False imprisonment*, detención (*f.*) ilegal.
improbability [im͵prɔbəˈbiliti] n. Improbabilidad, *f.* || Inverosimilitud, *f.*
improbable [imˈprɔbəbl] adj. Improbable (not probable). || Inverosímil (hard to believe). || *It seems improbable*, parece poco probable.
improbity [imˈprəubiti] n. Improbidad, *f.*
impromptu [imˈprɔmptju:] adj. Improvisado, da.
— Adv. Improvisadamente, sin preparación (without preparation). || De repente, de improviso (unexpectedly).
— N. Mus. Impromptu, *m.* || Improvisación, *f.*
improper [imˈprɔpə*] adj. Indecente, impropio, pia (indecent). || Indecoroso, sa (indecorous). || Impropio, pia; inadecuado, da (unfit). || Inexacto, ta (wrong). || Incorrecto, ta: *it would be improper to decline the invitation*, sería incorrecto rehusar la invitación. || MATH. *Improper fraction*, fracción impropia.
impropriate [imˈprəupriət] adj. Secularizado, da.
impropriate [imˈprəuprieit] v. tr. REL. Secularizar.
impropriation [im͵prəupriˈeiʃən] n. REL. Secularización, *f.*
impropriety [͵impr əˈpraiəti] n. Impropiedad, *f.* (of language). || Indecencia, *f.* (unseemliness). || Falta (*f.*) de decoro (indecorousness). || Incorrección, *f.*
improvable [imˈpru:vəbl] adj. Perfectible, mejorable.
improve [imˈpru:v] v. tr. Mejorar (to make better). || Perfeccionar: *to improve one's knowledge of Spanish*, perfeccionar sus conocimientos del español. || Favorecer: *that dress improves her greatly*, ese vestido le favorece mucho. || Hacer mejoras en: *to improve a property*, hacer mejoras en una propiedad. || AGR. Abonar. || Aumentar (production). || Aumentar el valor de (to increase the value of). || Cultivar (the mind). || Aprovechar (an opportunity). || TECH. Perfeccionar.
— V. intr. Mejorar, mejorarse: *do you think that his health has improved?*, ¿cree Ud. que su salud ha mejorado? || Perfeccionarse (knowledge). || Hacer progresos (to make progress). || Aumentar (production). || Subir, aumentar (prices). || — *To improve on* o *upon*, mejorar: *to improve on a translation*, mejorar una traducción. || *To improve on s.o's offer*, sobrepujar una oferta.
improvement [—mənt] n. Mejora, *f.*, mejoramiento, *m.* (a making better). || Progreso, *m.* (progress). || Aumento, *m.* (increase). || Ampliación, *f.* (enlargement). || Cultivo, *m.*, desarrollo, *m.* (of the mind). || Reforma, *f.*: *to make improvements in a house*, hacer reformas en una casa. || MED. Mejoría, *f.* || Aprovechamiento, *m.* (of the occasion). || TECH. Perfeccionamiento, *m.* || AGR. Abono, *m.* || — *To be open to improvement*, poderse mejorar. || *Your new house is a great improvement on the last one*, su nueva casa es mucho mejor que la anterior.
improver [imˈpru:və*] n. Aprendiz, *m.*
improvidence [imˈprɔvidəns] n. Imprevisión, *f.*
improvident [imˈprɔvidənt] adj. Imprevisor, ra (without foresight). || Gastador, ra (thriftless).
improving [imˈpru:viŋ] adj. FIG. Instructivo, va; edificante. || *The patient is improving*, el enfermo está mejor.
improvisation [ˈimprəvaiˈzeiʃən] n. Improvisación, *f.*
improvisator [ˈimprəvaiˈzeitə*] n. Improvisador, ra.
improvise [ˈimprəvaiz] v. tr./intr. Improvisar.
improviser [ˈimprəvaizə*] n. Improvisador, ra.
imprudence [imˈpru:dəns] n. Imprudencia, *f.*
imprudent [imˈpru:dənt] adj. Imprudente.
impubic [imˈpjubik] adj. Impúber.
impudence [ˈimpjudəns] n. Impudencia, *f.*, descaro, *m.*, desfachatez, *f.*, desvergüenza, *f.* (shamelessness). || Insolencia, *f.* (insolence).
impudent [ˈimpjudənt] adj. Impudente, desvergonzado, da; descarado, da (shameless). || Insolente.
impudicity [͵impjuˈdisiti] n. Impudicia, *f.*
impugn [imˈpju:n] v. tr. Impugnar.
impugnable [—əbl] adj. Impugnable.
impugnation [impəgˈneiʃən] n. Impugnación, *f.*
impugning [imˈpju:niŋ] adj. Impugnativo, va (challenging).
impugnment [imˈpju:nmənt] n. Impugnación, *f.*
impulse [ˈimpʌls] n. Impulso, *m.*: *his first impulse was to*, su primer impulso fue; *to yield to an impulse*, dejarse llevar por un impulso. || TECH. ELECTR. Impulso, *m.*, impulsión, *f.* || Impulso, *m.*, influjo, *m.* (in physiology). || — *I bought it on impulse*, lo compré sin reflexionar. || *Man of impulse*, hombre impulsivo. || *Nerve impulse*, influjo nervioso.
impulsion [imˈpʌlʃən] n. Impulsión, *f.*, impulso, *m.*
impulsive [imˈpʌlsiv] adj. Impulsivo, va.
impulsiveness [—nis] or **impulsivity** [—iti] n. Impulsividad, *f.*
impunity [imˈpju:niti] n. Impunidad, *f.*
impure [imˈpjuə*] adj. Impuro, ra.
impurity [—riti] n. Impureza, *f.*
imputability [im͵pju:təbiliti] n. Imputabilidad, *f.*
imputable [imˈpju:təbl] adj. Imputable, achacable.
imputation [͵impjuˈteiʃən] n. Imputación, *f.*
impute [imˈpju:t] v. tr. Imputar, atribuir, achacar.
imputer [—ə*] n. Imputador, ra.
imputrescibility [͵impjutresiˈbiliti] n. Imputrescibilidad, *f.*
imputrescible [͵impjuˈtresibl] adj. Imputrescible.
in [in] prep.

> **1.** Place. — **2.** Time. — **3.** Manner. — **4.** Weather. — **5.** Activity. — **6.** Meaning "relating to". — **7.** With verb. — **8.** After superlative. — **9.** Expressions.

1. PLACE. — En: *in France*, en Francia; *in Madrid*, en Madrid; *in the cage*, en la jaula; *in bed*, *in prison*, *in school*, en la cama, en la cárcel, en el colegio; *wounded in the shoulder*, herido en el hombro; *he had a stick in his hand*, tenía un palo en la mano. || De: *the furniture in the room*, los muebles del cuarto. || A: *to arrive in England*, llegar a Inglaterra; *in the distance*, a lo lejos; *in everybody's eyes*, a los ojos de todos; *throw it in the fire*, échalo al fuego. || Al, en: *to look at o.s. in the mirror*, mirarse en el espejo. || Con: *I can't go out in this heat*, no puedo salir con este calor; *she came in her new dress*, vino con el traje nuevo; *you look pretty in that dress*, está Ud. muy guapa con ese traje. || Por: *to walk in the street*, pasearse por la calle.
2. TIME. — En: *in 1970*, *in the year 1970*, en 1970, en el año 1970; *in the 19th century*, en el siglo XIX [diez y nueve]: *in winter*, *in September*, en invierno, en septiembre; *he did it in an hour*, lo hizo en una hora; *in my youth*, en mi juventud; *in my time*, en mis tiempos. || De: *at two o'clock in the afternoon*, a las dos de la tarde. || Por: *in the morning*, *in the afternoon*, *in the evening*, por la mañana, por la tarde, por la noche. || Dentro de: *he will be along in a while*, *in an hour*, estará aquí dentro de un rato, dentro de una hora. || Durante, de: *in the daytime*, durante el día, de día. || Durante, bajo: *in the reign of*, durante el reinado de. || — *Early in the morning*, de madrugada, por la mañana temprano. || *I haven't seen my cousin in years*, no veo a mi primo desde hace años, hace años que no veo a mi primo. || *In the thirties*, *in the twenties*, en los años treinta, en los años veinte. || *In time*, a tiempo. || *I was back in a month*, volví al cabo de un mes, volví al mes.
3. MANNER. — En: *in a loud*, *a low voice*, en voz alta, baja; *to write in verse*, escribir en verso; *he said it in English*, lo dijo en inglés; *in cash*, en metálico; *in these circumstances*, en estas circunstancias. || De: *in uniform*, de uniforme; *in wood*, de madera; *covered in mud*, cubierto de barro; *dressed in black*, vestido de negro; *in fashion*, de moda; *in civilian clothes*, de paisano; *in an amusing way*, de una manera graciosa; *in mourning*, de luto; *in good humour*, de buen humor. || A, con: *in ink*, a tinta. || A: *in hundreds*, *in dozens*, *in millions*, a cientos, a docenas, a millones. || Por: *in writing*, por escrito; *in alphabetical order*, por orden alfabético; *cut in half*, cortado por la mitad; *packed in dozens*, empaquetados por docenas. || Con: *in anger*, con ira; *people in good health*, gente con buena salud; *in all frankness*, con toda franqueza; *to speak in a raucous voice*, hablar con voz ronca. || — *Any man in his senses*, cualquiera que esté en su sano juicio, cualquier hombre sensato. || *In a big way*, a lo grande. || *In chains*, encadenado, da. || *In despair*, desesperado, da. || *In tears*, llorando. || *In the European fashion*, a la europea, al estilo europeo. || *She was in trousers*, llevaba pantalones. || *The girl in black*, la chica vestida de negro. || *To be in difficulties*, estar en un aprieto. || *To be in poor health*, estar mal de salud. || *To line up in fours*, formar en filas de a cuatro, alinearse de cuatro en fondo.
4. WEATHER. — A: *to sit in the sun*, sentarse al sol. || Bajo: *in the rain*, bajo la lluvia.
5. ACTIVITY. — En: *he is somebody in chemicals*, es una persona importante en la industria química; *the latest thing in shoes*, lo último en zapatos; *to be in the army*, estar en el ejército. || De: *to buy shares in a company*, comprar acciones de una compañía. || — *He is in the diamond business*, trabaja en el sector de los diamantes. || *He spends all his time in reading*, se pasa el tiempo leyendo. || *He travels in shoes*, es viajante de zapatos. || *Those in teaching*, los profesores, los que se dedican a la enseñanza. || *To engage in trade*, abrir *or* poner un negocio (to open a business), tener relaciones comerciales (to have commercial relations). || *To have shares in steel*, tener acciones de las acerías.
6. MEANING "RELATING TO". — De: *better in health*, mejor de salud; *blind in one eye*, ciego de un ojo; *a rise in prices*, una subida de precios; *five kilometres in length*, cinco kilómetros de largo; *lame in one foot*, cojo de un pie. || En: *he is very bad in Latin*, es muy malo en latín; *slow in acting*, lento en obrar; *to believe in God*, creer en Dios; *my trust in him will never die*, mi confianza en él nunca morirá. || Por: *to be interested in s.o.*, *in sth.*, interesarse por alguien, por algo. || — *A change in tactics*, un cambio de táctica. || *Long in the leg*, de piernas largas. || *To differ in opinion*, tener opiniones distintas. || *To differ in opinion with*, no compartir la opinión de. || *Short in height*, de baja estatura.
7. WITH VERB. — Al: *in crossing the street*, al cruzar la calle; *in saying this*, al decir esto; *in touring the world he matured a lot*, al dar la vuelta al mundo

adquirió mucha madurez; *in working so hard he lost his health*, al trabajar tanto perdió la salud. || Mientras (while).
8. AFTER SUPERLATIVE. — De: *the best in the world*, el mejor del mundo; *the biggest city in the world*, la ciudad más grande del mundo.
9. EXPRESSIONS. — *A chance in a million*, una oportunidad entre mil. || *A one in ten gradient*, una pendiente del diez por ciento. || *Four in ten*, cuatro de cada diez. || *In all*, en total. || *In fact*, de hecho, en realidad. || *In particular*, en particular. || *In that*, porque, ya que. || *The person in question*, la persona en cuestión. || *To have it in one to do sth.*, ser capaz de hacer algo.
— Adv. Dentro, adentro: *in here, in there*, aquí dentro, allí dentro; *in you go!*, ¡para dentro!, ¡vete para adentro! || — *All in*, todo incluido. || *Day in day out*, día tras día. || FAM. *He's in for it*, la va a pagar, se va a armar la gorda. | *He's in for trouble*, se la va a cargar. || *In and out*, entrando y saliendo. || *My luck is in*, estoy de suerte. || *On the way in*, al entrar. || *Oysters, asparragus are in*, es la temporada de las ostras, de los espárragos. || *The sun is in*, el sol se ha ido. || *To be all in*, estar rendido *or* agotado. || *To be in*, estar, estar en casa (at home): *is Fred in?*, ¿está Federico en casa?, ¿está Federico?; estar (at the office), estar en la cárcel (to be in prison), estar en el poder: *the Liberals are in*, los liberales están en el poder; estar de moda: *trousers are in this year*, este año están de moda los pantalones; estar recogido: *the potatoes are in*, las patatas están recogidas; haber llegado: *the train is in*, ha llegado el tren; batear (in cricket and baseball). || *To be in for*, ir a: *it looks like we are in for rain*, parece que va a llover; tomar parte en, participar en (a competition), ser candidato a (a post), presentarse a (an exam). || *To be in on*, estar enterado de, estar al tanto de. || *To be in on the secret*, estar en el secreto. || *To be in with s.o.*, estar en buenas relaciones con alguien (to be on good terms with s.o.), ser amigo de *or* tener amistad con alguien (to be friendly with s.o.), estar a favor de alguien (to be in s.o.'s favour). || *To feel all in*, estar rendido *or* agotado. || FAM. *To have it in for s.o.*, tenerla tomada con alguien. | *We're in for an unpleasant time*, vamos a pasar un momento desagradable. || FAM. *You don't know what you're in for*, no sabes la que te espera.
— Adj. De entrada: *the in door*, la puerta de entrada. || Interior, de adentro (inner). || De moda (fashionable). || Moderno, na (modern). || En el poder (party).
— N. *The ins*, los que están en el poder, los que mandan. || U. S. FAM. Influencia, *f.* || *The ins and outs*, los pormenores, los detalles.
— OBSERV. "*In*" se emplea frecuentemente después de varios verbos (to come, to get, to give, to go, etc.) cuyo sentido modifica. Por lo tanto, remitimos a cada uno de ellos para sus distintas traducciones.

inability [inə'biliti] n. Incapacidad, *f.*
inaccessibility ['inæk,sesə'biliti] n. Inaccesibilidad, *f.*
inaccessible [,inæk'sesəbl] adj. Inaccesible (place, height). || Inasequible (prices, etc.).
inaccuracy [in'ækjurəsi] n. Inexactitud, *f.* (lack of accuracy). || Equivocación, *f.*, error, *m.* (mistake).
inaccurate [in'ækjurit] adj. Inexacto, ta (not accurate). || Incorrecto, ta; erróneo, a (in error).
inaction [in'ækʃən] n. Inacción, *f.*
inactivate [in'æktiveit] v. tr. Volver inactivo.
inactive [in'æktiv] adj. Inactivo, va. || — MIL. *Inactive list*, escalafón (*m.*) de reserva. | *Inactive status*, situación (*f.*) de reserva.
inactivity [,inæk'tiviti] n. Inactividad, *f.* || Ociosidad, *f.* (idleness).
inadaptable [,inə'dæptəbl] adj. Inadaptable.
inadequacy [in'ædikwəsi] n. Inadecuación, *f.* (unsuitability). || Insuficiencia, *f.*
inadequate [in'ædikwit] adj. Inadecuado, da (unsuitable). || Insuficiente (insufficient).
inadmissibility ['inəd,misə'biliti] n. Inadmisibilidad, *f.* || JUR. Improcedencia, *f.*
inadmissible [,inəd'misəbl] adj. Inadmisible. || JUR. Improcedente.
inadvertence [,inəd'və:təns] n. Inadvertencia, *f.*
inadvertency [—i] n. Inadvertencia, *f.*
inadvertent [,inəd'və:tənt] adj. Inadvertido, da; descuidado, da (negligent). || Involuntario, ria (unintentional).
inadvertently [—li] adv. Por inadvertencia.
inadvisability [,inəd'vaizə'biliti] n. Inconveniencia, *f.*
inadvisable [,inəd'vaizəbl] adj. Poco aconsejable, desaconsejable, inconveniente.
inaesthetic [inis'θetik] adj. Inestético, ca.
inalienability [in,eiljənə'biliti] n. Inalienabilidad, *f.*
inalienable [in'eiljənəbl] adj. Inalienable.
inalterability [i,nɔ:ltərə'biliti] n. Inalterabilidad, *f.*
inalterable [i'nɔ:ltərəbl] adj. Inalterable.
inamorata [in,æmə'rɑ:tə] n. Enamorada, *f.*, amada, *f.*
inamorato [in,æmə'rɑ:təu] n. Enamorado, *m.*, amado, *m.* (male lover).
in-and-in ['inə'nin] adj./adv. Por consanguinidad.
inane [i'nein] adj. Inane, fútil (futile). || Necio, cia (silly). || Vacío, a (empty).
— N. Vacío, *m.*
inanimate [in'ænimit] adj. Inanimado, da.
inanition [,inə'niʃən] n. MED. Inanición, *f.*
inanity [i'næniti] n. Inanidad, *f.*, futilidad, *f.* (futility). || Necedad, *f.* (stupidity).
inappetence [i'næpitəns] or **inappetency** [—i] n. Inapetencia, *f.*
inappetent [i'næpitənt] adj. Inapetente.
inapplicability ['in,æplikə'biliti] n. Falta (*f.*) de aplicabilidad.
inapplicable [in'æplikəbl] adj. Inaplicable.
inapposite [in'æpəzit] adj. Inadecuado, da.
inappreciable [,inə'pri:ʃəbl] adj. Inapreciable, insignificante.
inappreciative [inə'pri:ʃiətiv] adj. Que no sabe apreciar.
inapprehensible [inæpri'hensibl] adj. Incomprensible.
inapprehension [inæpri'henʃən] n. Incomprensión, *f.*
inapproachability ['inə,prəutʃəbiliti] n. Inaccesibilidad, *f.*
inapproachable [,inə'prəutʃəbl] adj. Inaccesible.
inappropriate [,inə'prəupriit] adj. Impropio, pia; inadecuado, da (unsuitable). || Inconveniente (inconvenient). || Impropio, pia (word).
inappropriateness [—nis] n. Impropiedad, *f.*
inapt [in'æpt] adj. Inepto, ta; inhábil (lacking skill). || Torpe (awkward). || Inadecuado, da (inappropriate).
inaptitude [in'æptitju:d] n. Inaptitud, *f.*, ineptitud, *f.*, incapacidad, *f.*
inarch [in'ɑ:tʃ] v. tr. AGR. Injertar por aproximación.
inarm [in'ɑ:m] v. tr. Estrechar, abrazar (to embrace).
inarticulate [,inɑ:'tikjulit] adj. Inarticulado, da (sounds, speech). || Incapaz de expresarse (person). || *He was inarticulate with grief*, tenía la voz embargada por el dolor.
in articulo mortis [inɑ:'tikjulə'mɔ:tis] adv. In artículo mortis.
inartificial [inɑ:ti'fiʃəl] adj. Natural, sin artificio (unaffected). || Sin arte, poco artístico, ca (lacking art).
inartistic [,inɑ:'tistik] adj. Poco artístico, ca; sin arte.
inasmuch [inəz'mʌtʃ] adv. *Inasmuch as*, puesto que, visto que, en vista de que, ya que (since, because), en la medida en que (insofar as).
inattention [,inə'tenʃən] n. Falta (*f.*) de atención, inatención, *f.*, desatención, *f.*, distracción, *f.*
inattentive [,inə'tentiv] adj. Poco atento, ta; desatento, ta; distraído, da.
inattentively [—li] adv. Distraídamente.
inaudible [in'ɔ:dəbl] adj. Inaudible.
inaudibly [—i] adv. De modo inaudible. || *She said it almost inaudibly*, lo dijo de modo que apenas se oía.
inaugural [i'nɔ:gjurəl] adj. Inaugural.
— N. Discurso (*m.*) inaugural *or* de apertura (speech). || Inauguración, *f.* (ceremony).
inaugurate [i'nɔ:gjureit] v. tr. Dar posesión de un cargo a (an official). || Inaugurar (a new building, an exhibition, etc.). || Descubrir (a statue). || FIG. Inaugurar, introducir.
inauguration [i,nɔ:gju'reiʃən] n. Inauguración, *f.* (of a building, exhibition, etc.). || Investidura, *f.*, toma (*f.*) de posesión (of an official).
inaugurator [i'nɔ:gjureitə*] n. Inaugurador, ra.
inauspicious [,inɔ:s'piʃəs] adj. Desfavorable, poco propicio, cia.
inauspiciously [—li] adv. En condiciones desfavorables, bajo malos auspicios.
inbeing [in'bi:iŋ] n. Esencia, *f.*
in-between [inbi'twi:n] adj. Intermedio, dia.
inboard ['in'bɔ:d] adv./adj. MAR. Dentro del casco.
inborn ['in'bɔ:n] adj. Innato, ta. || MED. Congénito, ta.
inbreathe ['in'bri:ð] v. tr. Inspirar.
inbred ['inbred] adj. Procreado en consanguinidad, consanguíneo, a (animals). || Engendrado por endogamia (people). || Innato, ta (innate).
inbreed ['in'bri:d] v. tr. Procrear en consanguinidad (animals). || Engendrar por endogamia (people).
inbreeding [—iŋ] n. Endogamia, *f.* (of people). || Procreación (*f.*) en consanguinidad (of animals).
Inca ['iŋkə] n. Inca, *m.* & *f.*
— Adj. Incaico, ca; incásico, ca.
incalculable [in'kælkjuləbl] adj. Incalculable (countless). || Imprevisible (unpredictable).
Incan ['iŋkən] adj. Incaico, ca; incásico, ca.
incandesce [inkæn'des] v. intr. Ponerse incandescente.
incandescence ['inkæn'desns] n. Incandescencia, *f.*
incandescent ['inkæn'desnt] adj. Incandescente. || *Incandescent lamp*, lámpara (*f.*) incandescente *or* de incandescencia.
incantation [,inkæn'teiʃən] n. Conjuro, *m.* (spell).
incantatory [in'kæntə,tori] adj. Mágico, ca.
incapability [in,keipə'biliti] n. Incapacidad, *f.*
incapable [in'keipəbl] adj. Incapaz (not capable). || Incompetente. || JUR. Incapaz (person).
incapacious [inkə'peiʃəs] adj. Estrecho, cha (having little capacity). || (Ant.). Atrasado mental.
incapacitate [,inkə'pæsiteit] v. tr. Incapacitar (to make incapable): *incapacitated by illness*, incapacitado por la enfermedad. || SP. Descalificar. || JUR. Incapacitar.
incapacitation ['inkə,pæsi'teiʃən] n. JUR. Privación (*f.*) de capacidad.
incapacity [,inkə'pæsiti] n. Incapacidad, *f.*: *incapacity to govern*, incapacidad para governar; *legal incapacity*, incapacidad legal.
incarcerate [in'kɑ:səreit] v. tr. Encarcelar.
incarceration [in,kɑ:sə'reiʃən] n. Encarcelamiento, *m.*, encarcelación, *f.*

incarnadine [inˈkɑːnədain] adj. Encarnado, da.
— N. Encarnado, *m.* (colour).
incarnadine [inˈkɑːnədain] v. tr. Encarnar (to make flesh-coloured). ‖ Volver encarnado *or* rojo (to turn red).
incarnate [inˈkɑːnit] adj. Encarnado, da: *the incarnate God*, Dios encarnado. ‖ Encarnado, da (flesh-coloured). ‖ — *Beauty incarnate*, la encarnación de la belleza. ‖ *To become incarnate*, encarnar.
incarnate [ˈinkɑːneit] v. tr. Encarnar.
incarnation [ˌinkɑːˈneiʃən] n. Encarnación, *f.*
incase [inˈkeis] v. tr. See ENCASE.
incaution [inˈkɔːʃən] n. Descuido, *m.*, negligencia, *f.* (negligence). ‖ Imprudencia, *f.*
incautious [inˈkɔːʃəs] adj. Descuidado, da; negligente. ‖ Imprudente, incauto, ta (lacking in prudence).
incendiarism [inˈsendjərizəm] n. Incendio (*m.*) premeditado (crime of arson). ‖ Piromanía, *f.*
incendiary [inˈsendjəri] adj. Incendiario, ria.
— N. Incendiario, ria; pirómano, na (person). ‖ Bomba (*f.*) incendiaria (bomb). ‖ FIG. Agitador, ra.
incense [ˈinsens] n. Incienso, *m.* ‖ FIG. Incienso, *m.* (flattery).
incense [ˈinsens] v. tr. Incensar.
— V. intr. Quemar incienso.
incense [inˈsens] v. tr. Encolerizar, sulfurar, sacar de sus casillas (to anger).
incense bearer [—ˈbɛərə*] n. Turiferario, *m.*
incense boat [—bəut] n. Naveta, *f.*
incense burner [—ˈbəːnə*] n. Pebetero, *m.*
incensory [ˈinsensəri] n. Incensario, *m.*
incentive [inˈsentiv] adj. Estimulante.
— N. Incentivo, *m.*, estímulo, *m.*, aliciente, *m.*, acicate, *m.*: *an incentive to work*, un incentivo para trabajar.
incept [inˈsept] v. tr. BIOL. Ingerir. ‖ FIG. Empezar.
inception [inˈsepʃən] n. Principio, *m.*, comienzo, *m.* (origin). ‖ MED. Ingestión, *f.*
inceptive [inˈseptiv] adj. Inicial (initial). ‖ GRAMM. Incoativo, va.
— N. GRAMM. Verbo (*m.*) incoativo.
incertitude [inˈsəːtitjuːd] n. Incertidumbre, *f.*
incessancy [insesˈnsi] n. Continuidad, *f.*
incessant [inˈsesnt] adj. Incesante, continuo, nua; constante.
incessantly [—li] adv. Sin cesar, incesantemente, constantemente.
incest [ˈinsest] n. Incesto, *m.*
incestuous [inˈsestjuəs] adj. Incestuoso, sa.
inch [intʃ] n. Pulgada, *f.* [unidad de medida equivalente a 2,54 cm.] (measure). ‖ FIG. Pizca, *f.*: *he hasn't an inch of common sense*, no tiene ni pizca de sentido común. ‖ — FIG. *By inches*, poco a poco. | *Every inch a lady*, una señora de pies a cabeza. | *Give him an inch and he'll take a yard*, dale la mano y te cogerá el brazo. | *Inch by inch*, poco a poco (little by little), palmo a palmo (to gain ground, etc.). | *Not an inch of room was there*, no cabía un alfiler. | *They scoured every inch of the beach*, registraron la playa palmo a palmo *or* minuciosamente. | *To know every inch of*, conocer palmo a palmo. | *Within an inch of*, a dos pasos de.
inch [intʃ] v. tr. Hacer avanzar *or* retroceder poco a poco.
— V. intr. *To inch forward*, avanzar poco a poco.
inchoate [ˈinkəueit] adj. JUR. Incoado, da. ‖ Rudimentario, ria. ‖ Incipiente (initial).
inchoation [ˌinkəuˈeiʃən] n. Incoación, *f.*
inchoative [ˈinkəueitiv] adj. Incoativo, va.
— N. GRAMM. Verbo (*m.*) incoativo.
incidence [ˈinsidəns] n. PHYS. Incidencia, *f.*: *angle of incidence*, ángulo de incidencia. ‖ Frecuencia, *f.* (frecuency). ‖ FIG. Alcance, *m.* (reach). | Extensión, *f.* (of a disease). | Peso, *m.* (of a tax). | Efecto, *m.* (effect).
incident [ˈinsidənt] adj. Incidente. ‖ *Incident to*, que acompaña a, inherente a, propio de: *risks incident to a profession*, los riesgos que acompañan a una profesión.
— N. Incidente, *m.*: *a diplomatic incident*, un incidente diplomático. ‖ Incidentes, *m. pl.*: *the meeting took place without incident*, la reunión tuvo lugar sin incidentes; *a life full of incident*, una vida llena de incidentes. ‖ Episodio, *m.* (in a novel, play).
incidental [ˌinsiˈdentl] adj. Incidente: *incidental question*, cuestión incidente. ‖ Incidental: *incidental observation*, observación incidental. ‖ Imprevisto, ta; accesorio, ria (expense). ‖ De fondo (music). ‖ Fortuito, ta (casual). ‖ Secundario, ria (secondary). ‖ — *Incidental clause*, inciso, *m.* ‖ *Incidental to*, que acompaña a, inherente a, propio de: *the worries incidental to motherhood*, las preocupaciones propias de la maternidad.
— N. Elemento (*m.*) accesorio *or* secundario. ‖ — Pl. COMM. Imprevistos, *m.*
incidentally [—i] adv. A propósito, dicho sea de paso (by the way). ‖ Incidentemente.
incinerate [inˈsinəreit] v. tr. Incinerar (body). ‖ Quemar (rubbish).
incineration [inˌsinəˈreiʃən] n. Incineración, *f.*
incinerator [inˈsinəreitə*] n. Quemador (*m.*) *or* incinerador (*m.*) de basuras (for rubbish). ‖ Crematorio, *m.*, horno (*m.*) crematorio (crematorium).
incipience [inˈsipiəns] or **incipiency** [—i] n. Comienzo, *m.*, principio, *m.* (beginning).
incipient [inˈsipiənt] adj. Incipiente.
incise [inˈsaiz] v. tr. Cortar, hacer una incisión en (to make a cut in). ‖ Grabar (to engrave, to carve). ‖ MED. Sajar.
incision [inˈsiʒən] n. Incisión, *f.*
incisive [inˈsaisiv] adj. Incisivo, va; cortante, mordaz (tone, style). ‖ Incisivo, va; cortante (instrument). ‖ Penetrante (mind). ‖ Incisivo, va (tooth).
incisiveness [inˈsaisivnis] n. Mordacidad, *f.* (of words). ‖ Penetración, *f.* (of mind).
incisor [inˈsaizə*] n. Diente (*m.*) incisivo, incisivo, *m.*
incitation [ˌinsaiˈteiʃən] n. Incitación, *f.*
incite [inˈsait] v. tr. Incitar: *the soldier incited his comrades to rise against their officers*, el soldado incitó a sus compañeros a que se sublevaran contra sus oficiales. ‖ Provocar: *insults incite resentment*, los insultos provocan el resentimiento.
incitement [—mənt] n. Incitamiento, *m.*, incitación, *f.*: *incitement to crime*, incitación al crimen. ‖ Estímulo, *m.*, incentivo, *m.* (stimulus).
inciter [—ə*] n. Incitador, ra.
inciting [—iŋ] adj. Incitador, ra; incitante.
incivility [ˌinsiˈviliti] n. Descortesía, *f.*, incivilidad, *f.*
incivism [ˈinsivizm] n. Falta (*f.*) de civismo.
in-clearing [ˈinkliəriŋ] n. COMM. Cheques (*m. pl.*) recibidos por un banco a través de la cámara de compensación.
inclemency [inˈklemənsi] n. Inclemencia, *f.*
inclement [inˈklemənt] adj. Inclemente. ‖ Inclemente, riguroso, sa (weather).
inclinable [inˈklainəbl] adj. Propenso, sa; inclinado, da (*to*, a) [prone]. ‖ Que se puede inclinar (a table, stand, etc.).
inclination [inkliˈneiʃən] n. Inclinación, *f.*: *the inclination of a roof*, la inclinación de un tejado; *an inclination of the head*, una inclinación de la cabeza. ‖ Pendiente, *f.* (slope). ‖ FIG. Inclinación, *f.*, tendencia, *f.*, propensión, *f.* (leaning, tendency). ‖ — *He has an inclination to lie*, tiene tendencia a mentir. ‖ *He has an inclination towards women*, le gustan las mujeres. ‖ *My inclination is towards the second alternative*, prefiero la segunda solución.
incline [inˈklain] n. Pendiente, *f.*, cuesta, *f.* (slope).
incline [inˈklain] v. tr. Inclinar (to slope). ‖ FIG. Inclinar (to give a tendency to). | Inducir (to induce). ‖ — FIG. *I am inclined to believe him*, me inclino a creerle, estoy dispuesto a creerle. | *It is inclined to warp*, tiene tendencia a alabearse. | *They are that way inclined*, son así. | *To be well inclined towards s.o.*, estar bien dispuesto con alguien. | *To incline one's steps towards*, dirigir sus pasos hacia. | *When he feels that way inclined*, cuando le da la gana, cuando le apetece.
— V. intr. Inclinarse. ‖ MED. Tener propensión (*to*, a) [towards an illness]. ‖ *Green that inclines to blue*, verde que tira a azul.
inclined [—d] adj. Inclinado, da: *inclined plane*, plano inclinado.
inclining [—iŋ] adj. Inclinador, ra; inclinante.
— N. Inclinación, *f.* (slanting).
inclinometer [ˌinkliˈnɔmitə*] n. AVIAT. Clinómetro, *m.*
inclose [inˈkləuz] v. tr. See ENCLOSE.
inclosure [inˈkləuʒə*] n. See ENCLOSURE.
include [inˈkluːd] v. tr. Incluir: *to include an item in the bill*, incluir un artículo en la cuenta; *the price includes meals*, el precio incluye la comida. ‖ Adjuntar (in a letter). ‖ *I hope you don't include me in that remark*, espero que esta observación no va dirigida también a mí.
included [—id] adj. Incluido, da: *all* o *everything included*, todo incluido. ‖ Incluso, incluido, da: *all his property was sold, his house included*, se vendieron todos sus bienes, incluso su casa.
including [—iŋ] adj. Incluso, inclusive, con inclusión de. ‖ — *Everyone, including the President*, todos, incluso *or* inclusive el Presidente. ‖ *I have five including this one*, con éste tengo cinco. ‖ *Including service*, servicio comprendido *or* incluido.
inclusion [inˈkluːʒən] n. Inclusión, *f.*
inclusive [inˈkluːsiv] adj. Inclusivo, va. ‖ Inclusive: *pages ten to fifteen inclusive*, de la página diez a la quince inclusive. ‖ — *Inclusive of transport*, transporte incluido. ‖ *Inclusive terms*, precio (*m.*) todo incluido. ‖ *To be inclusive of*, incluir.
inclusively [—li] adv. Inclusive.
incoagulable [inkəˈægjuləbl] adj. Incoagulable.
incoercibility [inkəuəːsiˈbiliti] n. Incoercibilidad, *f.*
incoercible [inkəuˈəːsibl] adj. Incoercible.
incognito [inˈkɔgnitəu] adj. Incógnito, ta.
— Adv. De incógnito: *to travel incognito*, viajar de incógnito.
— N. Incógnito, *m.*: *to preserve one's incognito*, guardar el incógnito.
incognizance [inˈkɔgnizəns] n. Ignorancia, *f.*, desconocimiento, *m.*
incognizant [inˈkɔgnizənt] adj. Ignorante.
incoherence [ˌinkəuˈhiərəns] or **incoherency** [—i] n. Incoherencia, *f.*
incoherent [ˌinkəuˈhiərənt] adj. Incoherente.
incoherently [—li] adv. De modo incoherente.
incombustibility [ˈinkəmˌbʌstəˈbiliti] n. Incombustibilidad, *f.*

incombustible [ˌinkəmˈbʌstəbl] adj. Incombustible.
— N. Sustancia (*f.*) incombustible.

income [ˈinkʌm] n. Ingresos, *m. pl.*: *his income as a lawyer*, sus ingresos de abogado. || Renta, *f.* (private income). || Rédito, *m.* (interest). || *— Earned income*, ingresos profesionales. || *Gross income*, renta bruta. || *He cannot live on his income*, no puede vivir con su sueldo *or* con lo que gana. || *Income group* o *bracket*, categoría (*f.*) de contribuyentes. || *Income return*, declaración (*f.*) de impuestos. || *Income tax*, impuesto (*m.*) sobre la renta, impuesto (*m.*) de utilidades. || *National income*, renta nacional. || *Real income*, poder adquisitivo (purchasing power). || *To live on one's private income*, vivir de sus rentas.

incomer [ˈinˌkʌmə*] n. Inmigrante, *m.* & *f.* (immigrant). || Recién llegado, recién llegada (newcomer). || Intruso, sa (intruder).

incoming [ˈinˌkʌmiŋ] adj. Que entra, entrante. || Entrante: *the incoming year*, el año entrante. || Nuevo, va: *the incoming President*, el nuevo Presidente. || MAR. Ascendente (tide).
— N. Entrada, *f.* (entrance). || Llegada, *f.* (arrival). || — Pl. Ingresos, *m.*

incommensurability [ˈinkəˌmenʃərəˈbiliti] n. Inconmensurabilidad, *f.*

incommensurable [ˌinkəˈmenʃərəbl] adj. Inconmensurable.

incommensurate [ˌinkəˈmenʃərit] adj. Inconmensurable. || Desproporcionado, da (out of proportion).

incommode [ˌinkəˈməud] v. tr. Incomodar, molestar (to cause annoyance to). || Estorbar (to hinder).

incommodious [ˌinkəˈməudjəs] adj. Incómodo, da (uncomfortable).

incommodity [inkəˈmɔditi] n. Incomodidad, *f.*

incommunicability [inkəmjunikəˈbiliti] n. Incomunicabilidad, *f.*

incommunicable [ˌinkəˈmju:nikəbl] adj. Incomunicable.

incommunicado [ˈinkəmˌju:niˈkɑ:dəu] adj. Incomunicado, da.

incommunicative [inkəˈmju:nikeitiv] adj. Poco expansivo, va; reservado, da.

incommutability [ˌinkəmju:təˈbiliti] n. Inconmutabilidad, *f.*

incommutable [ˌinkəˈmju:təbl] adj. Inconmutable.

incompact [inkəmˈpækt] adj. No compacto, ta. || Blando, da (soft).

incomparability [inˌkɔmpərəˈbiliti] n. Excelencia, *f.*

incomparable [inˈkɔmpərəbl] adj. Incomparable.

incompassionate [inkəmˈpæʃənit] adj. Incompasivo, va.

incompatibility [ˈinkəmˌpætəˈbiliti] n. Incompatibilidad, *f.*

incompatible [ˌinkəmˈpætəbl] adj. Incompatible.

incompetence [inˈkɔmpitəns] or **incompetency** [—i] n. Incompetencia, *f.*

incompetent [inˈkɔmpitənt] adj./n. Incompetente.

incomplete [ˌinkəmˈpli:t] adj. Incompleto, ta. || Inacabado, da; sin terminar (unfinished). || Imperfecto, ta (not perfect).

incompleteness [ˌinkəmˈpli:tnis] or **incompletion** [ˌinkəmˈpli:ʃən] n. Estado (*m.*) incompleto. || *Due to the incompletion of the book*, puesto que el libro no está terminado.

incompliance [inkəmˈplaiəns] or **incompliancy** [—i] n. Inflexibilidad, *f.* || Desobediencia, *f.*

incompliant [inkəmˈplaiənt] adj. Inflexible. || Desobediente.

incomprehensibility [inˌkɔmprihensəˈbiliti] n. Incomprensibilidad, *f.*

incomprehensible [inˈkɔmpriˈhensəbl] adj. Incomprensible.

incomprehension [inkɔmpriˈhenʃən] n. Incomprensión, *f.*

incomprehensive [inkɔmpriˈhensiv] adj. Incomprensivo, va; poco comprensivo, va (understanding little). || Limitado, da (including little).

incompressibility [ˈinkəmˌpresəˈbiliti] n. Incompresibilidad, *f.*

incompressible [ˌinkəmˈpresəbl] adj. Incompresible, incomprimible.

incomputable [ˌinkəmˈpju:təbl] adj. Incalculable.

inconceivability [ˈinkənˌsi:vəˈbiliti] n. Lo inconcebible.

inconceivable [ˌinkənˈsi:vəbl] adj. Inconcebible.

inconciliable [ˌinkənˈsiljəbl] adj. Inconciliable (irreconcilable).

inconclusive [ˌinkənˈklu:siv] adj. Poco concluyente, poco convincente (not convincing). || No decisivo, va (indecisive).

incondensable [inkənˈdensəbl] adj. No condensable.

incondite [inˈkɔndit] adj. Mal construido, da (literary work). || Tosco, ca; basto, ta (coarse).

incongruence [inˈkɔŋgruəns] n. Incongruencia, *f.*

incongruent [inˈkɔŋgruənt] adj. Incongruente. || Inadecuado, da (inappropriate).

incongruity [ˌinkɔŋˈgru:iti] n. Incongruidad, *f.*, incongruencia, *f.* || Inadecuación, *f.*

incongruous [inˈkɔŋgruəs] adj. Incongruo, grua; incongruente. || Incompatible. || Inadecuado, da. || *Incongruous colours*, colores que no van uno con otro.

incongruousness [—nis] n. Incongruencia, *f.*

inconsequence [inˈkɔnsikwəns] n. Inconsecuencia, *f.*

inconsequent [inˈkɔnsikwənt] adj. Inconsecuente (mind). || Ilógico, ca (reasoning). || Inconexo, xa (ideas).

inconsequential [inkɔnseˈkwenʃəl] adj. De poca importancia, sin trascendencia, insignificante (unimportant). || Inconsecuente, ilógico, ca (inconsequent).

inconsiderable [ˌinkənˈsidərəbl] adj. Insignificante.

inconsiderate [ˌinkənˈsidərit] adj. Desconsiderado, da (without consideration for others). || Inconsiderado, da (thoughtless). || *That was inconsiderate of him!*, ¡qué falta de consideración por su parte!

inconsiderateness [ˌinkənˈsidəritnis] or **inconsideration** [ˈinkənˌsidəˈreiʃən] n. Inconsideración, *f.*, irreflexión, *f.* (thoughtlessness). || Falta (*f.*) de consideración (towards others).

inconsistency [ˌinkənˈsistənsi] n. Inconsistencia, *f.* (of a substance). || Inconsecuencia, *f.*, falta (*f.*) de lógica (inconsequence). || Contradicción, *f.*

inconsistent [ˌinkənˈsistənt] adj. Inconsistente (substance). || Inconsecuente, ilógico, ca (ideas, actions). || Contradictorio, ria. || *Inconsistent with*, que se contradice con, que no concuerda con, que contradice.

inconsolable [inkənˈsəuləbl] adj. Inconsolable, desconsolado, da (person). || Inconsolable (grief).

inconsonance [inˈkɔnsənəns] n. Desacuerdo, *m.*, discordancia, *f.*

inconsonant [inˈkɔnsənənt] adj. Discordante. || *To be inconsonant with*, no concordar con.

inconspicuous [ˌinkənˈspikjuəs] adj. Discreto, ta; que no llama la atención. || *I try to be as inconspicuous as possible*, procuro no llamar la atención.

inconstancy [inˈkɔnstənsi] n. Inconstancia, *f.* (fickleness). || Inestabilidad, *f.* (unsteadiness).

inconstant [inˈkɔnstənt] adj. Inconstante (fickle). || Inestable (unsteady).

inconstructible [inkənˈstrʌktibl] adj. Inconstruible.

inconsumable [inkənˈsju:məbl] adj. Incombustible (by fire). || COMM. No consumible.

incontestability [ˈinkənˌtestəˈbiliti] n. Incontestabilidad, *f.*

incontestable [ˌinkənˈtestəbl] adj. Incontestable, indiscutible, incontrovertible.

incontinence [inˈkɔntinəns] n. Incontinencia, *f.*

incontinent [inˈkɔntinənt] adj. Incontinente.

incontrovertible [ˈinkɔntrəˈvə:təbl] adj. Incontrovertible, indiscutible.

inconvenience [ˌinkənˈvi:njəns] n. Inconvenientes, *m. pl.*, molestia, *f.*: *the inconvenience of living in a small house*, los inconvenientes de vivir en una casa pequeña. || *I was put to great inconvenience by his late arrival*, me causó mucha molestia su llegada tardía.

inconvenience [ˌinkənˈvi:njəns] v. tr. Incomodar, molestar, causar molestia.

inconvenient [ˌinkənˈvi:njənt] adj. Incómodo, da (house). || Molesto, ta (person). || Inoportuno, na (time). || *If it is not inconvenient for you*, si no le sirve de molestia.

inconveniently [—li] adv. Inoportunamente, en un momento inoportuno (untimely). || De un modo incómodo (uncomfortably).

inconvertibility [inkənˌvə:tə biliti] n. No convertibilidad, *f.*

inconvertible [ˌinkənˈvə:təbl] adj. Inconvertible.

inconvincible [inkənˈvinsibl] adj. Imposible de convencer, inconvencible.

incoordinate [inkəˈɔ:dinit] adj. No coordinado, da.

incoordination [inkəˌɔ:diˈneiʃən] n. Incoordinación, *f.*, falta (*f.*) de coordinación.

incorporable [inˈkɔ:pərəbl] adj. Incorporable.

incorporate [inˈkɔ:pərit] adj. Incorporado, da (incorporated). || Incorpóreo, a (incorporeal).

incorporate [inˈkɔ:pəreit] v. tr. Incorporar, incluir: *to incorporate in* o *into*, incluir *or* incorporar en. || Contener (to contain). || Incorporar, admitir como miembro. || JUR. Constituir en sociedad (a firm).
— V. intr. Incorporarse. || Unirse (to join). || JUR. Constituirse en sociedad, formar una sociedad.

incorporated [—id] adj. Incorporado, da. || JUR. Constituido en sociedad.

incorporation [inˌkɔ:pəˈreiʃən] n. Incorporación, *f.* || Unión, *f.* || JUR. Constitución (*f.*) en sociedad (of a company).

incorporeal [ˌinkɔ:ˈpɔ:riəl] adj. Incorpóreo, a.

incorporeity [inˌkɔ:pɔ:ˈri:iti] n. Incorporeidad, *f.*

incorrect [ˌinkəˈrekt] adj. Incorrecto, ta (behaviour, style). || Inexacto, ta (statement). || Erróneo, a (views). || Inadecuado, da (clothes).

incorrectness [—nis] n. Incorrección, *f.* (of behaviour, style). || Inexactitud, *f.* (of statement). || Lo erróneo (of views).

incorrigibility [inˌkɔridʒəˈbiliti] n. Incorregibilidad, *f.*

incorrigible [inˈkɔridʒəbl] adj. Incorregible.

incorrodible [inkəˈrəudibl] adj. Inatacable (metal).

incorrupt [ˌinkəˈrʌpt] adj. Incorrupto, ta.

incorruptibility [ˈinkəˌrʌptəˈbiliti] n. Incorruptibilidad, *f.*

incorruptible [ˌinkəˈrʌptəbl] adj. Incorruptible.

increase [ˈinkri:s] n. Aumento, *m.*: *a fifty per cent increase*, un aumento del cincuenta por ciento; *an increase in production*, un aumento de la producción. || Aumento, *m.*, subida, *f.* (of prices). || *To be on the increase*, aumentar, ir creciendo.

increase [inˈkri:s] v. tr. Aumentar, incrementar: *to increase exports*, incrementar las exportaciones. || Aumentar (prices).
— V. intr. Aumentarse, aumentar. || Subir, aumentar (prices).
increasing [—iŋ] adj. Creciente.
increasingly [—iŋli] adv. Cada vez más: *this work gets increasingly difficult*, este trabajo se pone cada vez más difícil.
increate [inkriˈeit] adj. REL. Increado, da.
incredibility [in,krediˈbiliti] n. Incredibilidad, *f.*
incredible [inˈkredəbl] adj. Increíble.
incredulity [,inkriˈdju:liti] n. Incredulidad, *f.*
incredulous [inˈkredjuləs] adj. Incrédulo, la; descreído, da (person). || Incrédulo, la: *an incredulous look*, una mirada incrédula.
incredulously [—li] adv. Con incredulidad.
increment [ˈinkrimənt] n. Aumento, *m.*, incremento, *m.* (increase). || MATH. Incremento, *m.* || *Unearned increment*, plusvalía, *f.*
incriminate [inˈkrimineit] v. tr. Incriminar.
incrimination [in,krimiˈneiʃən] n. Incriminación, *f.*
incrust [inˈkrʌst] v. tr. Encostrar, incrustar (to cover with). || Incrustar (with gems, etc.).
incrustation [,inkrʌsˈteiʃən] n. Incrustación, *f.*
incubate [ˈinkjubeit] v. tr. Incubar. || Empollar, incubar (to sit on an egg).
— V. intr. Incubar.
incubation [,inkjuˈbeiʃən] n. Incubación, *f.*: *incubation period*, período de incubación.
incubative [ˈinkju,beitiv] adj. Incubador, ra.
incubator [ˈinkjubeitə*] n. Incubadora, *f.*
incudes [ˈiŋkju:di:z] pl. n. See INCUS.
inculcate [ˈinkʌlkeit] v. tr. Inculcar.
inculcation [,inkʌlˈkeiʃən] n. Inculcación, *f.*
inculcator [ˈinkʌlkeitə*] n. Inculcador, ra.
inculpability [in,kʌlpəˈbiliti] n. Inculpabilidad, *f.*
inculpable [inˈkʌlpəbl] adj. Inculpable.
inculpate [ˈinkʌlpeit] v. tr. Inculpar.
inculpation [,inkʌlˈpeʃən] n. Inculpación, *f.*
inculpatory [inˈkʌlpətəri] adj. Acusador, ra.
incumbency [inˈkʌmbənsi] n. Incumbencia, *f.*
incumbent [inˈkʌmbənt] adj. Apoyado, da. || *It is incumbent on you*, te incumbe a ti.
— N. REL. Beneficiado, *m.* || Titular, *m.* (of an office).
incunable [inˈkju:nəbl] n. Incunable, *m.*
incunabula [,inkjuˈnæbjulə] pl. n. Incunables, *m.*
incunabular [,inkjuˈnæbjulə*] adj. Incunable.
incunabulum [,inkjuˈnæbjuləm] n. Incunable, *m.*

— OBSERV. El plural de la palabra inglesa es *incunabula*.

incur [inˈkə:*] v. tr. Incurrir en: *to incur the king's disfavour, punishment, hatred*, incurrir en la desgracia del rey, en castigo, en odio. || Contraer (debt, obligation). || Sufrir (a loss). || Incurrir en (expenses).
incurability [in,kjuərəˈbiliti] n. Incurabilidad, *f.*
incurable [inˈkjuərəbl] adj. Incurable. || FIG. Irremediable.
— N. Enfermo (*m.*) incurable, incurable, *m.*
incuriosity [inkjuəriˈɔsiti] n. Falta (*f.*) de curiosidad, indiferencia, *f.*
incurious [inˈkjuəriəs] adj. Poco curioso, sa; indiferente.
incursion [inˈkə:ʃən] n. Incursión, *f.*
incursive [inˈkə:siv] adj. Agresor, ra; invasor, ra.
incurvate [ˈinkə:vit] adj. Encorvado, da.
incurvate [ˈinkə:veit] v. tr. Encorvar.
incurvation [,inkə:ˈveiʃən] n. Encorvamiento, *m.*, encorvadura, *f.*
incurve [ˈinˈkə:v] v. tr. Encorvar.
— V. intr. Encorvarse.
incus [ˈiŋkəs] n. ANAT. Yunque, *m.* (in the ear).

— OBSERV. El plural de *incus* es *incudes*.

indebted [inˈdetid] adj. Endeudado, da (*to*, con) [owing money]. || FIG. Agradecido, da (grateful): *she is very indebted to you*, le está muy agradecida.
indebtedness [—nis] n. Deuda, *f.* (debt). || FIG. Agradecimiento, *m.*
indecency [inˈdi:snsi] n. Indecencia, *f.*
indecent [inˈdi:snt] adj. Indecente, indecoroso, sa. || — JUR. *Indecent assault*, atentado (*m.*) contra el pudor. | *Indecent exposure*, exhibicionismo, *m.*
indeciduous [indiˈsidjuəs] adj. Perenne.
indecipherable [,indiˈsaifərəbl] adj. Indescifrable.
indecision [,indiˈsiʒən] n. Indecisión, *f.*, irresolución, *f.*
indecisive [,indiˈsaisiv] adj. Indeciso, sa; irresoluto, ta (person). || Que no resuelve nada (not conclusive).
indecisiveness [—nis] n. Indecisión, *f.*, irresolución, *f.*
indeclinable [,indiˈklainəbl] adj. Indeclinable.
indecorous [inˈdekərəs] adj. Indecoroso, sa; impropio, pia; incorrecto, ta.
indecorum [,indiˈkɔ:rəm] n. Indecoro, *m.*, falta (*f.*) de decoro.
indeed [inˈdi:d] adv. Efectivamente, en efecto: *indeed, he was the only one*, efectivamente, fue el único. || Realmente (really). || — *Did he indeed?*, ¿de verdad?, ¿de veras? || *Indeed?*, ¿de verdad?, ¿de veras? || *Thank you very much indeed*, muchísimas gracias. || *That's a gift indeed*, eso sí que es un regalo. || *Very glad indeed*, realmente muy contento. || *Yes indeed!*, ¡naturalmente!, ¡claro que sí!, ¡ya lo creo!
indefatigability [ˈindi,fætigəˈbiliti] n. Fuerzas (*f. pl.*) inagotables.
indefatigable [,indiˈfætigəbl] adj. Infatigable, incansable.
indefeasibility [ˈindi,fi:zəˈbiliti] n. Irrevocabilidad, *f.*
indefeasible [,indiˈfi:zəbl] adj. Irrevocable.
indefectibility [ˈindi,fektəˈbiliti] n. Indefectibilidad, *f.*
indefectible [,indiˈfektəbl] adj. Indefectible.
indefensible [,indiˈfensəbl] adj. Indefensible, indefendible. || Insostenible (theory). || Injustificable (unjustifiable).
indefinable [,indiˈfainəbl] adj. Indefinible.
indefinite [inˈdefinit] adj. Indefinido, da; impreciso, sa: *indefinite plans*, proyectos indefinidos. || Indefinido, da; indeterminado, da: *indefinite period*, período indeterminado. || GRAMM. Indefinido, da; indeterminado, da: *indefinite article, adjective, pronoun*, artículo, adjetivo, pronombre indefinido. | *Past indefinite*, pretérito indefinido. || *You're being very indefinite*, es muy impreciso *or* es muy vago lo que dices.
indehiscent [,indiˈhisənt] adj. BOT. Indehiscente.
indeliberation [ˈindi,libəˈreiʃən] n. Indeliberación, *f.*
indelibility [in,deliˈbiliti] n. Indelebilidad, *f.*
indelible [inˈdelibl] adj. Indeleble, imborrable.
indelicacy [inˈdelikəsi] n. Indelicadeza, *f.*, falta (*f.*) de delicadeza.
indelicate [inˈdelikit] adj. Indelicado, da; poco delicado, da.
indemnification [in,demniˈfikeiʃən] n. Indemnización, *f.*
indemnify [inˈdemnifai] v. tr. Asegurar (*against*, contra) [to secure]. || Indemnizar (to compensate).
indemnity [inˈdemniti] n. Indemnidad, *f.* (security). || Indemnización, *f.*, reparación, *f.*, compensación, *f.*
indemonstrable [inˈdemənstrəbl] adj. Indemostrable.
indent [ˈindent] n. Muesca, *f.* (notch). || Hendidura (*f.*) *or* quebradura (*f.*) de la costa (on the coastline). || COMM. Pedido, *m.* || Requisición, *f.*
indent [inˈdent] v. tr. Dentar, hacer muescas en (to notch). || Abollar (to dent). || PRINT. Sangrar. || JUR. Hacer por duplicado (to duplicate). | Cortar en dos partes [un documento]. || Pedir, hacer un pedido de (goods).
— V. intr. *To indent on s.o. for sth.*, pedir algo a alguien.
indentation [,indenˈteiʃən] n. Muesca, *f.* (notch). || Hendidura (*f.*) *or* quebradura (*f.*) en la costa. || PRINT. Sangría, *f.*
indention [inˈdenʃən] n. PRINT. Sangría, *f.*
indenture [inˈdentʃə*] n. Documento (*m.*) cortado en dos partes (divided document). || Contrato, *m.* (contract).
indenture [inˈdentʃə*] v. tr. Ligar por un contrato.
independence [,indiˈpendəns] n. Independencia, *f.*: *to gain independence*, conseguir la independencia.
independency [,indiˈpendənsi] n. Estado (*m.*) independiente (state). || Independencia, *f.* (independence).
independent [,indiˈpendənt] adj. Independiente. || — *To become independent of*, independizarse de. || *To be independent of*, no depender de.
— N. Independiente, *m.* & *f.*
indescribable [,indisˈkraibəbl] adj. Indescriptible.
indestructibility [ˈindis,trʌktəˈbiliti] n. Indestructibilidad, *f.*
indestructible [,indisˈtrʌktəbl] adj. Indestructible.
indeterminable [,indiˈtə:minəbl] adj. Indeterminable.
indeterminate [,indiˈtə:minit] adj. Indeterminado, da (not fixed). || Indefinido, da (undefined). || MATH. Indeterminado, da. || BOT. Racimoso, sa.
indetermination [ˈindi,tə:miˈneiʃən] n. Indeterminación, *f.*, indecisión, *f.*, irresolución, *f.*
indeterminism [,indiˈtə:minizəm] n. Indeterminismo, *m.* (theory).
indeterminist [,indiˈtə:minist] adj./n. Indeterminista.
indeterministic [,inditə:miˈnistik] adj. Indeterminista.
index [ˈindeks] n. Índice, *m.*, señal, *f.*, indicio, *m.*, prueba, *f.*: *the number of new cars is an index of prosperity*, el número de coches nuevos es un índice de prosperidad. || Índice, *m.* (forefinger). || Índice, *m.* (of a book). || Indicador, *m.* (of an instrument). || PRINT. Manecilla, *f.* || MATH. Exponente, *m.*, índice, *m.* || REL. Índice, *m.* || — *Index card*, ficha, *f.* || REL. *Index Expurgatorious*, Índice Expurgatorio. | *Index Librorum Prohibitorum*, Índice de libros prohibidos. || PHYS. *Index of refraction, refractive index*, índice de refracción. || *The cost-of-living index*, el índice del coste de la vida.

— OBSERV. El plural de la palabra *index* es *indexes* o *indices*.

index [ˈindeks] v. tr. Poner un índice a (a book). || Poner en el índice (an entry). || Clasificar (to file).
index finger [—ˈfiŋgə*] n. Dedo (*m.*) índice.
index number [—ˈnʌmbə*] n. Índice, *m.*, indicador, *m.* [de precios, etc.].
India [ˈindjə]-pr. n. GEOGR. India, *f.*

— OBSERV. The article must be used in Spanish with the name of this country.

India ink [—iŋk] n. Tinta (*f.*) china.
Indiaman [—mən] n. Barco (*m.*) que hace el servicio de las Indias Orientales.
Indian [—n] adj. Indio, dia.
— N. Indio, dia (person). || Indio, *m.* (language).
Indian club [—klʌb] n. SP. Maza (*f.*) de gimnasia.
Indian corn [—kɔ:n] n. BOT. Maíz, *m.*

Indian file [—fail] n. Fila (*f.*) india.
Indian giver [ˈgivə*] n. U. S. FAM. Persona (*f.*) que hace un regalo a otra y luego pide que le sea devuelto.
Indian hemp [—hemp] n. BOT. Cáñamo (*m.*) de la India.
Indian ink [—iŋk] n. Tinta (*f.*) china.
Indianism [—nizəm] n. Indianismo, *m.* || Indigenismo, *m.* (Latin-American politico-literary movement in favour of the Indians).
indianist [—ist] n. Indianista, *m.* & *f.*
Indian meal [—mi:l] n. Harina (*f.*) de maíz.
Indian millet [—ˈmilit] n. BOT. Alcandía, *f.*
Indian Ocean [—ˈəuʃən] pr. n. GEOGR. Océano (*m.*) Índico.
Indian reed [—ri:d] n. BOT. Cañacoro, *m.*
Indian summer [—sʌmə*] n. Veranillo (*m.*) de San Martín *or* del membrillo.
India paper [ˈindjəˈpeipə*] n. Papel (*m.*) de China.
India rubber [ˈindjəˈrʌbə*] n. Goma (*f.*) de borrar (rubber eraser). || Caucho, *m.* (natural rubber).
indicate [ˈindikeit] v. tr. Indicar, señalar (to point out, to show).
indication [ˌindiˈkeiʃən] n. Indicación, *f.*, señal, *f.* (sign). || Indicación, *f.*
indicative [inˈdikətiv] adj. Indicativo, va; indicador, ra (giving an indication). || GRAMM. Indicativo. || *To be indicative of*, indicar.
— N. GRAMM. Indicativo, *m.*
indicator [ˈindikeitə*] n. Indicador, *m.* || AUT. Indicador, *m.*, intermitente, *m.* || TECH. Indicador, *m.*
indices [ˈindisi:z] pl. n. See INDEX.
indict [inˈdait] v. tr. JUR. Acusar (*for*, de), procesar. || JUR. *To indict sth. as false*, tachar algo de falsedad.
indictable [—əbl] adj. Procesable.
indiction [inˈdikʃən] n. Indicción, *f.*
indictment [inˈdaitmənt] n. Acusación, *f.*: *bill of indictment*, acta de acusación.
Indies [ˈindiz] pl. n. GEOGR. Indias, *f.*: *the West Indies*, las Indias Occidentales; *the East Indies*, las Indias Orientales.
indifference [inˈdifrəns] n. Indiferencia, *f.* (*to*, ante) [lack of interest].
indifferent [inˈdifrənt] adj. Indiferente: *it is indifferent to him*, le es indiferente. || Insignificante, poco importante (insignificant). || FIG. Regular (neither good nor bad). || CHEM. Neutro, tra.
indifferentism [inˈdifrəntizəm] n. Indiferentismo, *m.*
indifferently [inˈdifrəntli] adv. Indiferentemente. || *He paints indifferently*, su pintura es muy regular.
indigence [ˈindidʒəns] n. Indigencia, *f.*
indigene [ˈindidʒi:n] n. Indígena, *m.* & *f.*
indigenous [inˈdidʒinəs] adj. Indígena, nativo, va.
indigent [ˈindidʒənt] adj. Indigente.
indigested [indiˈdʒestid] adj. Mal digerido, da (food). || Mal asimilado, da (knowledge). || Confuso, sa (text).
indigestibility [ˈindiˌdʒestəˈbiliti] n. Indigestibilidad, *f.*
indigestible [ˌindiˈdʒestəbl] adj. Indigesto, ta.
indigestion [ˌindiˈdʒestʃən] n. Indigestión, *f.*, empacho, *m.*: *to suffer from indigestion*, tener una indigestión.
indign [inˈdain] adj. Indigno, na.
indignant [inˈdignənt] adj. Indignado, da. || — *To get indignant*, indignarse. || *To make s.o. indignant*, indignar a uno.
indignantly [—li] adv. Con indignación.
indignation [ˌindigˈneiʃən] n. Indignación, *f.* || *Indignation meeting*, reunión (*f.*) de protesta.
indignity [inˈdigniti] n. Indignidad, *f.* (lack of dignity). || Ultraje, *m.*, afrenta, *f.* (outrage).
indigo [ˈindigəu] n. Índigo, *m.* (dye, plant). || Añil, *m.*, índigo, *m.* (colour).
— Adj. De color añil, añil.
indigo bird [—bə:d] or **indigo bunting** [—ˈbʌntiŋ] n. ZOOL. Azulejo, *m.*
indirect [ˌindiˈrekt] adj. Indirecto, ta (not direct). || FIG. Sucio, cia (dishonest). || — U. S. GRAMM. *Indirect discourse*, estilo indirecto. || *Indirect lighting*, luz indirecta. || GRAMM. *Indirect object*, complemento indirecto. | *Indirect speech*, estilo indirecto. || *Indirect tax*, impuesto indirecto.
indiscernible [ˌindiˈsə:nəbl] adj. Indiscernible, imperceptible.
indiscipline [inˈdisiplin] n. Indisciplina, *f.*
indiscreet [ˌindisˈkri:t] adj. Indiscreto, ta; imprudente.
indiscrete [ˌindisˈkri:t] adj. Homogéneo, a.
indiscretion [ˌindisˈkreʃən] n. Indiscreción, *f.*, imprudencia, *f.*
indiscriminate [ˌindisˈkriminit] adj. Indistinto, ta. || Sin criterio (person).
indiscriminately [—li] adv. Indistintamente. || Sin criterio.
indiscrimination [ˈindisˌkrimiˈneiʃən] n. Falta (*f.*) de criterio *or* de discriminación.
indispensable [ˌindisˈpensəbl] adj. Indispensable, imprescindible (essential). || Ineludible, obligatorio, ria (inevitable).
indispose [ˌindisˈpəuz] v. tr. Indisponer.
indisposed [—d] adj. Indispuesto, ta.
indisposition [ˌindispəˈziʃən] n. Indisposición, *f.* (slight illness). || Aversión, *f.* (disinclination).
indisputability [ˈindispju:təˈbiliti] n. Indisputabilidad, *f.*, incontestabilidad, *f.*
indisputable [ˈindisˈpju:təbl] adj. Indisputable, indiscutible, incontestable, incontrovertible.
indisputably [—i] adv. Incontestablemente, sin duda alguna.
indissolubility [ˈindiˌsɔljuˈbiliti] n. Indisolubilidad, *f.*
indissoluble [ˌindiˈsɔljubl] adj. Indisoluble.
indistinct [ˌindisˈtiŋkt] adj. Indistinto, ta; confuso, sa (not clear). || Indistinto, ta (not plainly defined).
indistinctive [ˌindisˈtiŋktiv] adj. Común y corriente.
indistinctness [ˌindisˈtiŋktnis] n. Falta (*f.*) de claridad.
indistinguishable [ˌindisˈtiŋgwiʃəbl] adj. Indistinguible (not easy to differentiate).
indite [inˈdait] v. tr. Redactar (text, letter). || Componer (verse).
inditement [—mənt] n. Redacción, *f.*, composición, *f.*
inditer [—ə*] n. Redactor, ra; escritor, ra.
indium [ˈindiəm] n. CHEM. Indio, *m.*
individual [ˌindiˈvidjuəl] adj. Individual (existing as a complete and separate entity). || Personal, particular, propio, pia: *a very individual style of dress*, un estilo de vestido muy personal; *their individual qualities*, sus cualidades particulares. || — *Add up the individual marks*, suma cada una de las notas. || *The guests all have individual telephones*, cada invitado tiene su priopio teléfono *or* su teléfono.
— N. Individuo, *m.* || *Private individual*, particular, *m.*
individualism [—izəm] n. Individualismo, *m.*
individualist [—ist] n. Individualista, *m.* & *f.*
individualistic [ˌindiˌvidjuəˈlistik] adj. Individualista.
individuality [ˌindiˌvidjuˈæliti] n. Individualidad, *f.* || Personalidad, *f.* (special characteristics).
individualization [ˌindiˌvidjuəlaiˈzeiʃən] n. Individualización, *f.*
individualize [ˌindiˈvidjuəlaiz] v. tr. Individualizar (to make individual). || Particularizar.
individually [ˌindiˈvidjuəli] adv. Individualmente. || Personalmente (personally).
individuate [indiˈvidjueit] v. tr. Individuar.
individuation [ˈindiˌvidjuˈeiʃən] n. Individuación, *f.*
indivisibility [ˈindiˌviziˈbiliti] n. Indivisibilidad, *f.*
indivisible [ˌindiˈvizəbl] adj. Indivisible.
indivision [indiˈviʒən] n. Indivisión, *f.*
Indochina [ˈindəuˈtʃainə] pr. n. GEOGR. Indochina, *f.*
Indochinese or **Indo-Chinese** [ˈindəutʃaiˈni:z] adj. Indochino, na.
— N. Indochino, na (person). || Indochino, *m.*, (language).
indocile [inˈdəusail] adj. Indócil.
indocility [ˌindəuˈsiliti] n. Indocilidad, *f.*
indoctrinate [inˈdɔktrineit] v. tr. Adoctrinar.
indoctrination [inˌdɔktriˈneiʃən] n. Adoctrinamiento, *m.*
Indo-European [ˈindəuˌjuərəˈpi:ən] adj./n. Indoeuropeo, a.
Indo-Germanic [ˈindəudʒə:ˈmænik] adj./n. Indogermánico, ca.
indolence [ˈindələns] n. Indolencia, *f.*
indolent [ˈindələnt] adj. Indolente (lazy). || Indoloro, ra (painless).
indomitable [inˈdɔmitəbl] adj. Indomable, indómito, ta.
Indonesia [ˌindəuˈni:zjə] pr. n. GEOGR. Indonesia, *f.*
Indonesian [—n] adj./n. Indonesio, sia.
indoor [ˈindɔ:*] adj. Interior: *indoor aerial*, antena interior. || — *Indoor activities*, actividades caseras. || *Indoor clothes*, traje (*m.*) de casa. || *Indoor games*, juegos (*m.*) de sociedad. || *Indoor lavatory*, retrete (*m.*) en la casa. || *Indoor life*, vida casera *or* de familia. || *Indoor sports*, deportes (*m.*) en sala. || *Indoor swimming pool*, piscina cubierta.
indoors [ˈinˈdɔ:z] adv. Dentro: *we'll be more comfortable indoors*, estaremos mejor dentro. || En casa: *to be, to stay in doors*, estar, quedarse en casa. || — *Indoors and outdoors*, dentro y fuera de la casa. || *Indoors it is decorated with red velvet*, el interior está decorado con terciopelo rojo. || *Let's go indoors, it's warmer*, entremos, que hace más calor dentro.
indophenol [indəˈfi:nɔl] n. CHEM. Indofenol, *m.*
indorse [inˈdɔ:s] v. tr. See ENDORSE.
indraught (U. S. **indraft**) [ˈindrɑ:ft] n. Corriente, *f.* || Aspiración (*f.*) de aire.
indubitable [inˈdju:bitəbl] adj. Indudable, indubitable.
indubitably [inˈdju:bitəbli] adv. Indudablemente, sin duda.
induce [inˈdju:s] v. tr. Inducir, persuadir (to convince): *I have induced him to accompany us*, le persuadí de que nos acompañara, le induje a que nos acompañara. || Causar, ocasionar, producir, provocar (to cause). || PHYS. Inducir. || (Ant.). Inducir (to infer).
inducement [—mənt] n. Incentivo, *m.*, estímulo, *m.*, aliciente, *m.* (incentive). || Atractivo, *m.* (attractiveness). || Móvil, *m.* (motive).
inducer [—ə*] n. Inducidor, ra; provocador, ra.
inducing [—iŋ] adj. Inducidor, ra; inductor, ra.
induct [inˈdʌkt] v. tr. Instalar (into a position, office). || Admitir (in a society). || Iniciar (to initiate). || PHYS. Inducir. || U. S. MIL. Incorporar a filas.
inductance [inˈdʌktəns] n. PHYS. Inductancia, *f.*
inductee [indʌkˈti:] n. MIL. Recluta, *m.*
inductile [inˈdʌktail] adj. PHYS. Indúctil, no dúctil. || FIG. Inflexible.
induction [inˈdʌkʃən] n. PHIL. ELECTR. Inducción, *f.* || TECH. Admisión, *f.* || Instalación, *f.* (installation).

|| Admisión, *f.* (in a society). || Iniciación, *f.* (initiation). || U. S. MIL. Incorporación, *f.*
induction coil [—kɔil] n. ELECTR. Bobina (*f.*) *or* carrete (*m.*) de inducción.
inductive [in'dʌktiv] adj. Inductivo, va (logic). || Inductor, ra (inducing). || ELECTR. Inductor, ra (of electric or magnetic induction). | Inductivo, va (of inductance).
inductively [—li] adv. Por inducción.
inductor [in'dʌktə*] n. ELECTR. CHEM. Inductor, *m.*
indue [in'dju:] v. tr. See ENDUE.
indulge [in'dʌldʒ] v. tr. Mimar, consentir (to pamper). || Consentir, ceder a (to comply with): *to indulge s.o.'s wishes*, consentir los caprichos de uno. || Dar rienda suelta a (to let loose): *to indulge one's anger*, dar rienda suelta a su cólera. || Complacer (a person). || COMM. Conceder un plazo a. || *To indulge o.s.*, darse gusto.
— V. intr. *I don't indulge*, no fumo (in smoking), no bebo (in drinking). || *To indulge in*, entregarse a (vice, pleasures, etc.), permitirse el lujo de, darse el gusto de.
indulgence [in'dʌldʒəns] n. Indulgencia, *f.*, complacencia, *f.* (pampering). || Tolerancia, *f.*, indulgencia, *f.* (tolerance, leniency). || Satisfacción, *f.* (of desire, etc.). || Exceso, *m.*, desenfreno, *m.* (self-indulgence). || Vicio, *m.* (a habit indulged in). || COMM. Moratoria, *f.* || REL. Indulgencia, *f.*
indulgence [in'dʌldʒəns] v. tr. Indulgenciar, conceder indulgencias a.
indulgent [in'dʌldʒənt] adj. Indulgente (*towards*, con).
indult [in'dʌlt] n. REL. Indulto, *m.*
indurate ['indjuəreit] v. tr. Endurecer. || FIG. Endurecer (feelings). || MED. Indurar.
— V. intr. Endurecerse. || MED. Indurarse. || FIG. Endurecerse.
induration [indjuə'reiʃən] n. Endurecimiento, *m.* || MED. Induración, *f.* || FIG. Endurecimiento, *m.*
Indus ['indəs] pr. n. GEOGR. Indo, *m.*
industrial [in'dʌstriəl] adj. Industrial. || — *Industrial accident*, accidente (*m.*) de trabajo. || *Industrial disease*, enfermedad (*f.*) profesional. || *Industrial relations*, relaciones (*f.*) profesionales.
— N. Industrial, *m.* || — Pl. Valores (*m.*) industriales.
industrialism [in'dʌstriəlizəm] n. Industrialismo, *m.*
industrialist [in'dʌstriəlist] n. Industrial, *m.*
industrialization [in,dʌstriəlai'zeiʃən] n. Industrialización, *f.*
industrialize [in'dʌstriəlaiz] v. tr. Industrializar.
industrious [in'dʌstriəs] adj. Trabajador, ra; industrioso, sa; laborioso, sa. || Estudioso, sa; aplicado, da (studious).
industriousness [—nis] n. Laboriosidad, *f.* || Aplicación, *f.*
industry ['indəstri] n. Industria, *f.*: *heavy industry*, industria pesada: *iron and steel industry*, industria siderúrgica. || Laboriosidad, *f.*, diligencia, *f.* (industriousness). || Aplicación, *f.* || *The tourist industry*, el turismo.
indwell ['in'dwel] v. tr. Residir en, morar en.
— V. intr. Residir, morar.
indweller [—ə*] n. Habitante, *m.* & *f.*, residente, *m.* & *f.*
inebriant [in'i:briənt] adj. Embriagador, ra; embriagante.
inebriate [i'ni:brieit] v. tr. Embriagar, emborrachar (to intoxicate). || FIG. Embriagar.
inebriate [i'ni:briit] adj. Ebrio, a; embriagado, da; borracho, cha.
— N. Borracho, cha.
inebriated [—id] adj. Ebrio, a; embriagado, da.
inebriation [i,ni:bri'eiʃən] n. Embriaguez, *f.*, ebriedad, *f.*
inebriety [,ini'braiəti] n. Embriaguez, *f.*, ebriedad, *f.*
inedible [in'edibl] adj. Incomible, incomestible.
inedited [in'editid] adj. Inédito, ta (unpublished).
ineducable [in'edjukəbl] adj. Ineducable.
ineffability [inefə'biliti] n. Inefabilidad, *f.*
ineffable [in'efəbl] adj. Inefable.
ineffaceable [,ini'feisəbl] adj. Indeleble, imborrable.
ineffective [,ini'fektiv] Ineficaz (without effect). || Inútil (useless). || Ineficaz (person). || *To prove ineffective*, no surtir efecto.
ineffectiveness [—nis] n. Ineficacia, *f.*
ineffectual [,ini'fektjuəl] adj. Ineficaz, inútil.
inefficacious [,inefi'keiʃəs] adj. Ineficaz.
inefficacy [in'efikəsi] n. Ineficacia, *f.*
inefficiency [ini'fiʃənsi] n. Ineficacia, *f.*, inutilidad, *f.* (of an act). || Incompetencia, *f.*, ineficacia, *f.* (of a person).
inefficient [,ini'fiʃənt] adj. Ineficaz, inútil (useless). || Ineficaz, incompetente.
inelastic [,ini'læstik] adj. No elástico, ca (not elastic). || FIG. Inflexible (not adaptable). | Fijo, ja (supply and demand).
inelasticity [,inilæs'tisiti] n. Falta (*f.*) de elasticidad. || FIG. Inflexibilidad, *f.*
inelegance [in'eligəns] n. Inelegancia, *f.*
inelegancy [in'eligənsi] n. Inelegancia, *f.*
inelegant [in'eligənt] adj. Poco elegante.
ineligibility [in,elidʒə'biliti] n. Inelegibilidad, *f.*
ineligible [in'elidʒəbl] adj. Inelegible (not eligible). || Inadecuado, da (unsuited). || No apto (for military service).
ineluctability [ine,lʌktə'biliti] n. Calidad (*f.*) de ineluctable, inevitabilidad, *f.*
ineluctable [ine'lʌktəbl] adj. Ineluctable, inevitable.
ineludible [inə'ludəbl] adj. Ineludible.
inept [i'nept] adj. Inepto, ta; incapaz (incompetent). || Inadecuado, da (unfit). || Inepto, ta; estúpido, da.
ineptitude [i'neptitju:d] n. Ineptitud, *f.*, incapacidad, *f.* (incompetence). || Inepcia, *f.*, necedad, *f.*, ineptitud, *f.* (inept action).
ineptness [i'neptnis] n. Ineptitud, *f.*, incapacidad, *f.*
inequality [,ini'kwɔliti] n. Desigualdad, *f.* (lack of equality). || Injusticia, *f.* (injustice). || Desigualdad, *f.* (unevenness). || ASTR. MATH. Desigualdad, *f.*
inequation [in'ikwei'ʃən] n. MATH. Inecuación, *f.*
inequitable [in'ekwitəbl] adj. Injusto, ta.
inequity [in'ekwiti] n. Injusticia, *f.*, falta (*f.*) de equidad.
ineradicable [ini'rædikəbl] adj. Inextirpable. || Indeleble (ineffaceable).
inerrability [inerə'biliti] n. Infalibilidad, *f.*
inerrable [i'nerəbl] adj. Infalible.
inert [i'nə:t] adj. Inerte. || FIG. Inerte. || *Inert gas*, gas (*m.*) inerte.
inertia [i'nə:ʃjə] n. Inercia, *f.*
inertial [i'nə:ʃjəl] adj. De inercia: *inertial force*, fuerza de inercia. || — *Inertial guidance*, dirección (*f.*) por inercia. || *Inertial mass*, masa inerte.
inertness [i'nə:tnis] n. Inercia, *f.*
inescapable [,inis'keipəbl] adj. Ineludible, inevitable.
inessential ['ini'senʃəl] adj. No esencial, accesorio, ria.
— N. Lo accesorio.
inestimable [in'estiməbl] adj. Inestimable.
inevitability [in,evitə'biliti] n. Inevitabilidad, *f.*
inevitable [in'evitəbl] adj. Inevitable, ineludible.
— N. Lo inevitable.
inexact [,inig'zækt] adj. Inexacto, ta.
inexactitude [,inig'zæktitju:d] n. Inexactitud, *f.*
inexactly [,inig'zæktli] adv. De modo inexacto.
inexcusable [,iniks'kju:zəbl] adj. Imperdonable, inexcusable.
inexecutable [in'eksikjutəbl] adj. Inejecutable.
inexecution [in,eksi'kju:ʃən] n. Inejecución, *f.*, incumplimiento, *m.*
inexhaustible [,inig'zɔ:stəbl] adj. Inagotable.
inexigible [ini'gzidʒibl] adj. Inexigible.
inexistent [inik'sistənt] adj. Inexistente.
inexorability [in,eksərə'biliti] n. Inexorabilidad, *f.*
inexorable [in'eksərəbl] adj. Inexorable.
inexpediency [,iniks'pi:djənsi] n. Inoportunidad, *f.*, inconveniencia, *f.*
inexpedient [,iniks'pi:djənt] adj. Inoportuno, na; inconveniente.
inexpensive [,iniks'pensiv] adj. Barato, ta; económico, ca; poco costoso, sa.
inexpensively [—li] adv. Barato, gastando poco dinero.
inexperience [,iniks'piəriəns] n. Inexperiencia, *f.*, falta (*f.*) de experiencia.
inexperienced [—t] adj. Inexperto, ta; sin experiencia.
inexpert [,ineks'pə:t] adj. Inexperto, ta.
inexpertness [—nis] n. Impericia, *f.*, inexperiencia, *f.*
inexpiable [in'ekspiəbl] adj. Inexpiable.
inexplainable [inəks'pleinəbl] adj. Inexplicable.
inexplicability [in,eksplikə'biliti] n. Carácter (*m.*) inexplicable.
inexplicable [in'eksplikəbl] adj. Inexplicable.
inexplicit [,iniks'plisit] adj. Poco explícito, ta.
inexpressibility [inikspresi'biliti] n. Inefabilidad, *f.*
inexpressible [iniks'presəbl] adj. Inexpresable, indecible, inefable.
inexpressive [,iniks'presiv] adj. Inexpresivo, va (devoid of expression): *an inexpressive style*, un estilo inexpresivo. || Reservado, da; callado, da (reserved).
inexpugnable [,iniks'pʌgnəbl] adj. Inexpugnable.
inextensible [,inik'stensəbl] adj. Inextensible.
in extenso [,inik'stensəu] adv. phr. In extenso.
inextinguishable [,iniks'tiŋwiʃəbl] adj. Inextinguible (passion, etc.). || Inapagable (fire, light, etc.).
inextirpable [iniks'tə:pəbl] adj. Inextirpable.
in extremis [iniks'treimis] adv. phr. In extremis.
inextricable [in'ekstrikəbl] adj. Inextricable.
infallibility [in,fælə'biliti] n. Infalibilidad, *f.*
infallible [in'fæləbl] adj. Infalible.
infamous ['infəməs] adj. De mala fama, infame (of ill repute). || Infame, odioso, sa (arousing horror). || JUR. Infame (crime, person). | Infamante (punishment).
infamously [—li] adv. De una manera infame.
infamy ['infəmi] n. Infamia, *f.*
infancy ['infənsi] n. Infancia, *f.*, niñez, *f.* || FIG. Principio, *m.*, infancia, *f.* || JUR. Minoría (*f.*) de edad, menor edad, *f.*
infant ['infənt] n. Niño, ña (very young child). || Párvulo, la (young pupil). || JUR. Menor (*m.* & *f.*) de edad (minor). || *The infant Jesus*, el niño Jesús.
— Adj. FIG. Naciente (industry, etc.). || De párvulos (school). || *Infant mortality rate*, mortalidad (*f.*) infantil.
infanta [in'fæntə] n. Infanta, *f.* (princess).
infante [in'fænti] n. Infante, *m.* (prince).
infanticidal [—saidəl] adj. Infanticida.
infanticide [in'fæntisaid] n. Infanticidio, *m.* (the killing of a child). || Infanticida, *m.* & *f.* (murderer).

infantile ['infəntail] adj. Infantil. || MED. *Infantile paralysis*, parálisis (*f.*) infantil.
infantilism [in'fæntilizəm] n. Infantilismo, *m.*
infantine ['infəntain] adj. Infantil, pueril.
infantry ['infəntri] n. MIL. Infantería, *f.*
infantryman [—mən] n. MIL. Soldado (*m.*) de infantería, infante, *m.*
— OBSERV. El plural de esta palabra es *infantrymen.*
infarct [in'fɑ:kt] n. MED. Infarto, *m.*: *infarct of the myocardium*, infarto del miocardio.
infatuate [in'fætjueit] v. tr. Atontar (to make foolish). || Enamorar locamente, chiflar (to inspire with foolish passion).
infatuated [—id] adj. *To be infatuated with*, estar encaprichado por (an idea), estar chiflado por *or* locamente enamorado de (a person).
infatuation [in,fætju'eiʃən] n. Enamoramiento, *m.*, encaprichamiento, *m.*
infeasible [in'fi:zibl] adj. No factible, imposible de hacer.
infect [in'fekt] v. tr. Infectar, inficionar: *to infect a wound*, infectar una herida. || Contaminar, contagiar (to contaminate). || FIG. Corromper. || FIG. *He infected everybody with his indignation*, contagió a todos su indignación.
infection [in'fekʃən] n. Infección, *f.* || Contaminación, *f.*, contagio, *m.*
infectious [in'fekʃəs] adj. Infeccioso, sa; contagioso, sa: *an infectious disease*, una enfermedad contagiosa. || FIG. *Infectious laughter*, risa contagiosa.
infectiousness [—nis] n. Contagiosidad, *f.*
infective [in'fektiv] adj. Infeccioso, sa.
infecund [in'fikʌnd] adj. Infecundo, da.
infecundity [,infi'kʌnditi] n. Infecundidad, *f.*
infelicitous [,infi'lisitəs] adj. Inapropriado, da; poco afortunado, da; desacertado, da (not appropriate). || Desgraciado. da (not happy).
infelicity [,infi'lisiti] n. Inoportunidad, *f.* (unsuitability). || Desacierto, *m.*, metedura (*f.*) de pata (blunder). || (Ant.) Desgracia, *f.*, infelicidad, *f.* (misfortune).
infer [in'fə:*] v. tr. Inferir, deducir (to deduce).
inferable [—rəbl] adj. Deducible.
inference ['infərəns] n. Inferencia, *f.*, deducción, *f.* || *By inference*, por deducción.
inferential [,infə'renʃəl] adj. Que se deduce, que se infiere.
inferior [in'fiəriə*] adj. Inferior, de poca calidad (of poor quality). || Inferior (of poorer quality, of lower rank or status). || Inferior (placed lower down).
— N. Inferior, *m.*
inferiority [in,fiəri'ɔriti] n. Inferioridad, *f.*: *inferiority complex*, complejo de inferioridad.
infernal [in fə:nl] adj. Infernal (of hell). || FAM. Infernal, endemoniado, da: *infernal noise*, ruido endemoniado. || — *Infernal machine*, máquina (*f.*) infernal. || FAM. *Why won't this infernal contraption work?*, ¿por qué no funciona este maldito cacharro?
infernally [in'fə:nli] adv. Terriblemente. || *It is infernally hot*, hace un calor de mil demonios.
inferno [in'fə:nəu] n. Infierno, *m.* (hell, or place resembling it). || FIG. Hoguera, *f.* (blazing building). | Llamas, *f. pl.*: *the girders melted in the inferno*, las vigas se derritieron entre las llamas. || *Dante's Inferno*, el Infierno de Dante.
infertile [in'fə:tail] adj. Estéril (land). || Infecundo, da; estéril (people).
infertility [infə:'tiliti] n. Esterilidad, *f.* (of land). || Infecundidad, *f.*, esterilidad, *f.* (of a person).
infest [in'fest] v. tr. Infestar, plagar.
infeudation [,infju'deiʃən] n. Enfeudación, *f.*
infidel ['infidəl] adj./n. Infiel, pagano, na.
infidelity [,infi'deliti] n. Infidelidad, *f.* || FIG. Deslealtad, *f.* (disloyalty).
infield [infi:ld] n. SP. Terreno (*m.*) central (ground near the wicket in cricket). | Jugadores (*m. pl.*) centrales (players in this area). | Cuadro (*m.*) interior (playing square in baseball). | Jugadores (*m. pl.*) del cuadro interior (players in this area). || Tierras (*f. pl.*) alrededor de una granja (lands near a farmhouse).
infielder [—ə*] n. SP. Jugador (*m.*) central (in cricket). | Jugador (*m.*) del cuadro interior (in baseball).
infighting ['infaitiŋ] n. SP. Lucha (*f.*) cuerpo a cuerpo (in boxing).
infiltrate ['infiltreit] n. MED. Infiltrado, *m.*
infiltrate ['infiltreit] v. intr. Infiltrarse (*into*, en).
— V. tr. Infiltrar. || Infiltrarse en: *to infiltrate an organization*, infiltrarse en una organización.
infiltration [,infil'treiʃən] n. Infiltración, *f.*
infinite ['infinit] adj. Infinito, ta. || — GRAMM. *Infinite verb*, forma sustantiva del verbo. || *To do infinite harm*, hacer muchísimo daño.
— N. Infinito, *m.*
infinitesimal [,infini'tesiməl] adj. Infinitesimal, infinitésimo, ma. || MATH. *Infinitesimal calculus*, cálculo (*m.*) infinitesimal.
— N. MATH. Cantidad (*f.*) infinitesimal.
infinitive [in'finitiv] adj. GRAMM. Infinitivo.
— N. GRAMM. Infinitivo, *m.*
infinitude [in'finitju:d] n. Infinitud, *f.*, infinidad, *f.*
infinity [in'finiti] n. Infinidad, *f.* (quality of being infinite, a large amount or quantity). || MATH. Infinito, *m.*
infirm [in'fə:m] adj. Enfermizo, za; débil (physically weak). || JUR. Nulo, la (document). || FIG. *Infirm of purpose*, indeciso, sa; irresoluto, ta.
infirm [in'fə:m] v. tr. Invalidar, infirmar.
infirmary [—əri] n. Enfermería, *f.* (of school, etc.). || Hospital, *m.*
infirmity [—iti] n. Enfermedad, *f.*, achaque, *m.* (illness). || Debilidad, *f.* (weakness). || FIG. Debilidad, *f.*, flaqueza, *f.*
infix ['infiks] n. GRAMM. Infijo, *m.*
infix ['infiks] v. tr. Inculcar (to instil). || Intercalar (to insert). || Fijar (to set in).
inflame [in'fleim] v. tr. Inflamar (to set on fire). || MED. Inflamar. || FIG. Avivar (passion). | Encender: *anger inflamed her cheeks*, la cólera encendía sus mejillas.
— V. intr. Inflamarse, encenderse (to catch fire). || MED. Inflamarse. || FIG. Inflamarse, acalorarse.
inflammability [in,flæmə'biliti] n. Inflamabilidad, *f.*
inflammable [in'flæməbl] adj. Inflamable (easily set on fire). || FIG. Irritable (easily angered or excited).
— N. Sustancia (*f.*) inflamable.
inflammation [,inflə'meiʃən] n. Inflamación, *f.* || MED. Inflamación, *f.* || FIG. Acaloramiento, *m.*
inflammatory [in'flæmətəri] adj. MED. Inflamatorio, ria. || FIG. Incendiario, ria (that stirs up feelings).
inflate [in'fleit] v. tr. Hinchar, inflar (to cause to swell with gas or air). || COMM. Provocar la inflación de. || *To inflate s.o. with pride*, llenar a uno de orgullo, engreír a alguien.
inflated [—id] adj. Hinchado, da; inflado, da (full of air or gas). || FIG. Pomposo, sa; rimbombante (language, style). | Henchido, da; engreído, da (elated with pride). || COMM. En situación inflacionista, inflacionario, ria. | Excesivo, va (prices).
inflation [in'fleiʃən] n. Inflado, *m.* (with air or gas). || Pomposidad, *f.*, rimbombancia, *f.* (of language). || COMM. Inflación, *f.*: *runaway inflation*, inflación galopante.
inflationary [in'fleiʃnəri] adj. Inflacionario, ria; inflacionista.
inflationism [in'fleiʃnizəm] n. Inflacionismo, *m.*
inflationist [in'fleiʃnist] n. Inflacionista, *m.* & *f.*
inflator [in'fleitə*] n. Bomba, *f.* [para hinchar neumáticos]. || Inflador, *m.*
inflect [in'flekt] v. tr. GRAMM. Declinar. | Conjugar. || Torcer, doblar (to bend). || MUS. Modular.
inflection [in'flekʃən] n. Inflexión, *f.*
inflexibility [in,fleksə'biliti] n. Inflexibilidad, *f.*
inflexible [in'fleksəbl] adj. Inflexible.
inflexion [in'flekʃən] n. Inflexión.
inflict [in'flikt] v. tr. Infligir, imponer (a punishment, penalty). || Dar, asestar (blow). || Hacer, causar (wounds, grief, harm). || *To inflict o.s. on s.o.*, imponer su presencia a alguien.
infliction [in'flikʃən] n. Imposición, *f.* (act of inflicting punishment). || Castigo, *m.* (punishment).
inflorescence [inflɔ'resəns] n. BOT. Florescencia, *f.*
inflow ['infləu] n. Afluencia, *f.*
influence ['influəns] n. Influencia, *f.* (*on*, *over*, sobre; *with*, con) [indirect power]. || ELECTR. Inducción, *f.* || — *A man of influence*, un hombre influyente. || *To be an influence*, tener influencia. || *To bring every influence to bear*, utilizar toda su influencia. || *To get sth. by influence*, conseguir algo por influencias. || *To have an influence over s.o.*, ejercer una influencia sobre uno. || FIG. *To have influence at court*, tener buenas aldabas. || *Under the influence of drink*, *of drugs*, bajo los efectos del alcohol, de las drogas.
influence ['influəns] v. tr. Influenciar (a person). || Influir en (a decision, etc.). || *He is easily influenced*, es influenciable.
influent ['influənt] adj. Afluente.
— N. Afluente, *m.*
influential [,influ'enʃəl] adj. Influyente.
influenza [,influ'enzə] n. MED. Gripe, *f.*
influenzal [—l] adj. MED. Gripal.
influx ['inflʌks] n. Entrada, *f.* (of liquid, gas, etc.). || Desembocadura, *f.* (of a river in the sea). || Afluencia, *f.*: *the influx of tourists*, la afluencia de turistas.
inform [in'fɔ:m] v. tr. Informar (*about*, sobre), poner al corriente (*about*, de) [to communicate information to]. || Informar, avisar (*of*, de) [to tell]. || Inspirar (to inspire). || (Ant.) Formar, moldear (the mind). || — *I am pleased to inform you that*, tengo el placer de comunicarle que. || || *To keep o.s. informed*, mantenerse al corriente. || *To keep s.o. informed*, tener a alguien al corriente.
— V. intr. *To inform against*, denunciar a, delatar a.
informal [in'fɔ:ml] adj. Sencillo, lla (person). || Sin cumplidos, entre amigos, sin etiqueta, sin ceremonia : *an informal dinner*, una cena entre amigos. || Familiar (tone). || No oficial, extraoficial, oficioso, sa (unofficial). || *Informal dress*, traje (*m.*) de calle.
informality [,infɔ:'mæliti] n. Sencillez, *f.* (of a person). || Carácter (*m.*) íntimo (intimacy). || Ausencia (*f.*) de ceremonia (of a dinner, etc.).
informally [in'fɔ:məli] adv. Sin ceremonia (without ceremony). || En tono de confianza (speaking). || Sencillamente (dressed). || Oficiosamente (unofficially).
informant [in'fɔ:mənt] n. Informante, *m.* & *f.*

information [ˌinfəˈmeiʃən] n. Información, *f.* (the communication of news, knowledge, etc.). || Datos, *m. pl.*, información, *f.*: *to have no information regarding*, no tener información sobre; *to feed a machine with information*, introducir información *or* datos en una máquina. || JUR. Denuncia, *f.*, acusación, *f.* (complaint or accusation). || Conocimientos, *m. pl.* (knowledge): *the information we have today about hormone behaviour*, los conocimientos que hoy tenemos sobre el comportamiento de las hormonas. || — *A piece of information*, una información, un dato. || *By way of information*, a título de información, a título informativo. || *Classified information*, información de difusión secreta *or* reservada. || *For your information*, para que lo sepa Ud., para su información. || *Information service*, servicio (*m.*) de información. || *To ask for information*, pedir informes *or* información. || *To give information to the police*, proporcionar información a la policía. || JUR. *To lay an information against s.o.*, denunciar *or* delatar a alguien.
information bureau [—bjuəˈrəu] n. Centro (*m.*) de informaciones.
information desk [—desk] n. Informaciones, *f. pl.*: *where is the information desk?*, ¿dónde están las informaciones?
informative [inˈfɔːmətiv] adj. Informativo, va.
informed [inˈfɔːmd] adj. Informado, da; al corriente, al tanto (having much information). || Culto, ta (having much education).
informer [inˈfɔːmə*] n. Denunciante, *m.* & *f.*, delator, ra. || Confidente, *m.* (of the police).
infraction [inˈfrækʃən] n. Infracción, *f.*
infractor [inˈfræktə*] n. Infractor, ra.
infra dig [ˈinfrəˈdig] adj. Indigno (*for*, de).
infrangible [inˈfrændʒibl] adj. Irrompible. || FIG. Inquebrantable.
infrared [ˈinfrəˈred] adj. Infrarrojo, ja.
— N. Infrarrojo, *m.*
infrasonic [ˈinfrəˈsɔnik] adj. *Infrasonic wave*, infrasonido, *m.*
infrastructure [ˈinfrəˌstrʌktʃə*] n. Infraestructura, *f.*
infrequency [inˈfriːkwənsi] n. Poca frecuencia, *f.*, rareza, *f.*
infrequent [inˈfriːkwənt] adj. Poco frecuente, infrecuente, raro, ra.
infrequently [—li] adv. Raramente, raras veces.
infringe [inˈfrindʒ] v. tr. Infringir, violar (law, etc.).
— V. intr. *To infringe on* o *upon*, usurpar (s.o.'s rights).
infringement [—mənt] n. Infracción, *f.*, violación, *f.* (of a law). || Usurpación, *f.* (encroachment).
infulae [ˈinfjuli] pl. n. Ínfulas, *f.*
infuriate [inˈfjuərieit] v. tr. Enfurecer, poner furioso (to make furious): *sometimes you infuriate me*, a veces me pones furioso. || Exasperar: *all this gossip infuriates me*, todo este chismorreo me exaspera.
infuriating [—iŋ] adj. Exasperante.
infuriation [inˌfjuəriˈeiʃən] n. Exasperación, *f.*, enfurecimiento, *m.*
infuse [inˈfjuːz] v. tr. FIG. Infundir (to instil). || Hacer una infusión de (to soak tea, etc.).
infusion [inˈfjuːʒən] n. Infusión, *f.*
infusoria [infjuːˈzɔːriə] pl. n. ZOOL. Infusorios, *m.*
ingathering [ˈinˌgæðəriŋ] n. Recolección, *f.*, recogida, *f.* (of harvest).
ingeminate [inˈdʒemineit] v. tr. Repetir, reiterar (to repeat).
ingemination [inˌdʒemiˈneiʃən] n. Repetición, *f.*, reiteración, *f.*
ingenious [inˈdʒiːnjəs] adj. Ingenioso, sa.
ingeniousness [—nis] n. Ingeniosidad, *f.*, ingenio, *m.*
ingénue [ˌɛ̃ːnʒeiˈnjuː] n. THEATR. Ingenua, *f.*
ingenuity [ˌindʒiˈnjuːiti] n. Ingeniosidad, *f.*, ingenio, *m.* (ingeniousness). || Cosa (*f.*) ingeniosa (ingenious device).
ingenuous [inˈdʒenjuəs] adj. Ingenuo, nua; cándido, da (naïve). || Franco, ca; sincero, ra (frank, candid).
ingenuousness [—nis] n. Ingenuidad, *f.*, candidez, *f.*, candor, *m.* (naïveness). || Franqueza, *f.*, sinceridad, *f.* (frankness).
ingest [inˈdʒest] v. tr. Ingerir.
ingestion [—ʃən] n. Ingestión, *f.*
ingle [ˈiŋgl] n. Fuego (*m.*) de chimenea, lumbre, *f.* (fire). || Hogar, *m.*, chimenea, *f.* (fireplace).
inglenook [—nuk] n. Rincón (*m.*) de la chimenea (chimney corner). || *In the inglenook*, junto a la chimenea, al amor de la lumbre.
inglorious [inˈglɔːriəs] adj. Vergonzoso, sa; ignominioso, sa (shameful). || Sin fama, desconocido, da (not famous).
in-goal [ˈinˌgəul] n. SP. Zona (*f.*) de meta (in rugby).
ingoing [ˈinˌgəuiŋ] adj. Entrante, que entra.
ingot [ˈingət] n. Lingote, *m.*, barra, *f.*: *gold ingots*, lingotes de oro, oro en barras; *ingot steel*, acero en lingotes. || Lingotera, *f.* (mould).
ingrain [ˈinˈgrein] v. tr. FIG. Inculcar (habits, tastes, etc.). || Teñir (to dye).
ingrain carpet [—ˈkɑːpit] n. Alfombra (*f.*) reversible.
ingrained [—d] adj. Inculcado, da. || Arraigado, da (firmly established).
ingrate [inˈgreit] adj./n. Ingrato, ta.
ingratiate [inˈgreiʃieit] v. tr. *To ingratiate o.s. with.*, congraciarse con.
ingratiating [—iŋ] adj. Zalamero, ra.
ingratitude [inˈgrætitjuːd] n. Ingratitud, *f.*
ingravescent [inˈgrævesənt] adj. MED. Que se agrava.
ingredient [inˈgriːdjənt] n. Ingrediente, *m.*
ingress [ˈingres] n. Acceso, *m.* (access, entrance). || Entrada, *f.*, ingreso, *m.* (going in).
ingrowing [ˈinˌgrəuiŋ] adj. Que crece hacia dentro. || *Ingrowing nail*, uñero, *m.*, uña encarnada.
ingrown [ˈingrəun] adj. Crecido hacia dentro. || FIG. Innato, ta. || *Ingrown nail*, uñero, *m.*, uña encarnada.
inguinal [ˈingwinl] adj. ANAT. Inguinal.
ingurgitate [inˈgəːdʒiteit] v. tr. Ingurgitar engullir
ingurgitation [ingəːdʒiˈteiʃən] n. Ingurgitación, *f*
inhabit [inˈhæbit] v. tr. Habitar (to occupy). || Vivir en (to live in).
inhabitable [—əbl] adj. Habitable.
inhabitancy [—ənsi] n. Residencia, *f.* (residence). || Domicilio, *m.* (home).
inhabitant [—ənt] n. Habitante, *m.*
inhabitation [inˌhæbiˈteiʃən] n. Habitación, *f.*
inhabited [inˈhæbitid] adj. Habitado, da; poblado, da.
inhalant [inˈheilənt] n. Medicamento (*m.*) para inhalación *or* para inhalar.
— Adj. Inhalador, ra; para inhalar.
inhalation [ˌinhəˈleiʃən] n. Inhalación, *f.*
inhale [inˈheil] v. tr. MED. Inhalar. || Aspirar, inhalar (air). || Tragar (tobacco smoke).
inhaler [—ə*] n. Inhalador, *m.*
inharmonic [inhɑːˈməunik] adj. Inarmónico, ca.
inharmonious [ˌinhɑːˈməunjəs] adj. Inarmónico, ca (sounds). || FIG. Falto de *or* sin armonía, poco armonioso, sa (colours, relations, etc.).
inharmoniousness [—nis] n. Disonancia, *f.*, discordancia, *f.*, falta (*f.*) de armonía.
inharmony [inhɑːˈməuni] n. Inarmonía, *f.*
inhere [inˈhiə*] v. intr. Ser inherente (*in*, a), ser propio (*in*, de).
inherence [inˈhiərəns] or **inherency** [—i] n. Inherencia, *f.*
inherent [inˈhiərənt] adj. Inherente (*in*, a), propio, pia (*in*, de), intrínseco, ca.
inherit [inˈherit] v. tr. Heredar (a fortune, a title).
— V. intr. Heredar.
inheritability [—əbiliti] n. Transmisibilidad, *f.* (of property, title). || Capacidad (*f.*) para heredar (of person).
inheritable [inˈheritəbl] adj. Transmisible (property, title). || Capaz de heredar, que puede heredar (person).
inheritance [inˈheritəns] n. Herencia, *f.*: *to receive an inheritance*, recibir una herencia. || Sucesión, *f.*: *intestate, testate inheritance*, sucesión intestada, testada. || FIG. MED. Herencia, *f.* || — *Inheritance tax*, impuesto (*m.*) sobre sucesiones. || *To come into an inheritance*, heredar.
inheritor [inˈheritə*] n. Heredero, *m.* (heir).
inheritress [inˈheritris] or **inheritrix** [inˈheritriks] n. Heredera, *f.* (heiress).
inhibit [inˈhibit] v. tr. Inhibir, reprimir (to restrain, to hold in check). || Impedir (to prevent).
inhibition [ˌinhiˈbiʃən] n. Inhibición, *f.*
inhibitor [inˈhibitə*] n. CHEM. Inhibidor, *m.*
inhibitory [inˈhibitəri] adj. Inhibitorio, ria.
inhospitable [inˈhɔspitəbl] adj. Inhóspito, ta (place). || Inhospitalario, ria (person).
inhospitality [ˈinˌhɔspiˈtæliti] n. Inhospitalidad, *f.*, falta (*f.*) de hospitalidad.
inhuman [inˈhjuːmən] adj. Inhumano, na (lacking human mercy). || Insensible, frío, a (insensitive). || Sobrehumano, na (superhuman).
inhumane [ˌinhjuˈmein] adj. Inhumano, na.
inhumanity [ˌinhjuːˈmæniti] n. Inhumanidad, *f.*
inhumation [ˌinhjuːˈmeiʃən] n. Inhumación, *f.*
inhume [inˈhjuːm] v. tr. Inhumar.
inimical [iˈnimikəl] adj. Hostil (hostile). || Contrario, ria; que va en contra de: *inimical to the national interest*, contrario al interés nacional.
inimically [—i] adv. Con hostilidad.
inimitable [iˈnimitəbl] adj. Inimitable.
iniquitous [iˈnikwitəs] adj. Inicuo, cua.
iniquity [iˈnikwiti] n. Iniquidad, *f.*
initial [iˈniʃəl] adj. Inicial, primero, ra (of or occurring at the beginning). || COMM. Inicial (capital).
— N. Inicial, *f.* (first letter). || Letra (*f.*) florida (large decorative letter). || — Pl. Iniciales, *f.* (of a name). || Siglas, *f.* (used as abbreviation): *I.L.O. are the initials of the International Labour Organization*, O.I.T. son las siglas de la Organización Internacional del Trabajo.
initial [iˈniʃəl] v. tr. Poner iniciales a, poner las iniciales a. || Firmar con las iniciales (to sign). || JUR. Rubricar (a document).
initially [—i] adv. Inicialmente, al principio.
initiate [iˈniʃieit] v. tr. Iniciar: *to initiate an investigation*, iniciar una investigación; *to initiate s.o. into a practice*, iniciar a uno en una práctica. || Entablar, iniciar (negotiations). || Entablar (proceedings). || Admitir (into a secret society).
initiate [iˈniʃiit] adj./n. Iniciado, da.
initiation [iˌniʃiˈeiʃən] n. Iniciación, *f.*, principio, *m.*, comienzo, *m.* (beginning). || Iniciación, *f.* (into a practice, a society).
initiative [iˈniʃiətiv] n. Iniciativa, *f.*: *to take the initiative*, tomar la iniciativa; *on one's own initiative*, por iniciativa propia.
— Adj. Preliminar.

initiator [iˈniʃieitə*] n. Iniciador, ra.
initiatory [iˈniʃiətəri] adj. Iniciador, ra. || Preliminar (preliminary). || De iniciación (ceremonies).
inject [inˈdʒekt] v. tr. Inyectar, poner una inyección de: *to inject penicillin*, inyectar penicilina. || Inyectar en, poner una inyección en: *to inject an infected tissue with a liquid*, inyectar un líquido en un tejido infectado. || Poner una inyección a (to administer an injection to). || TECH. Inyectar. || FIG. Introducir (to introduce into). | Infundir (enthusiasm, etc.).
injectable [—əbl] adj. Inyectable.
injection [inˈdʒekʃən] n. TECH. Inyección, *f.*: *injection feeding*, alimentación por inyección. || MED. Inyección, *f.*: *to put o.s. an injection*, ponerse una inyección.
injector [inˈdʒektə*] n. Inyector, *m.*
injudicious [ˌindʒuːˈdiʃəs] adj. Poco juicioso, sa; imprudente.
injunction [inˈdʒʌŋkʃən] n. Mandato, *m.*, orden, *f.* (command). || JUR. Requerimiento, *m.*, intimación, *f.* (summons). | Entredicho, *m.* (prohibition).
injure [ˈindʒə*] v. tr. Herir (to wound). || Lastimar, dañar, hacer daño (to hurt). || FIG. Herir (feelings). | Perjudicar (reputation, etc.). | Ofender (to offend). || Estropear (to spoil). || SP. Lesionar. || JUR. Causar perjuicio a. || — *He injured his leg*, se lesionó la pierna. || *The injured*, los heridos. || JUR. *The injured party*, la parte perjudicada.
injurious [inˈdʒuəriəs] adj. Injurioso, sa; ofensivo, va (offensive). || Nocivo, va; perjudicial (harmful).
injury [ˈindʒəri] n. Herida, *f.*, lesión, *f.* (physical damage). || Daño, *m.* (physical hurt). || Ofensa, *f.* (offensive treatment). || JUR. Perjuicio, *m.*, daño, *m.* || — *To do o.s. an injury*, hacerse daño, lastimarse. || *To the injury of*, en detrimento de, en perjuicio de.
injury time [—taim] n. SP. Descuento, *m.*
injustice [inˈdʒʌstis] n. Injusticia, *f.* || *To do s.o. an injustice*, hacerle una injusticia a alguien (to treat s.o. badly), juzgar mal a alguien, ser injusto con alguien (to misjudge s.o.).
ink [iŋk] n. Tinta, *f.* (for pen, of fish). || — *Indian* o *India ink*, tinta china. || *In ink*, con tinta. || *Invisible ink*, tinta simpática. || *Printer's ink*, tinta de imprenta.
ink [iŋk] v. tr. Entintar (a plate for engraving). || *To ink in* o *over*, marcar *or* repasar con tinta.
inker [—ə*] n. PRINT. Rodillo (*m.*) entintador.
inkhorn [—hɔːn] n. (Ant.). Tintero, *m.* [en forma de asta].
— Adj. Culto, ta: *inkhorn terms*, palabras cultas.
inking [—iŋ] n. PRINT. Entintado, *m.*
— Adj. PRINT. Entintador, ra.
inkling [—liŋ] n. Idea, *f.*: *I had no inkling that you were there*, no tenía ni idea de que estabas allí. || Impresión, *f.* (feeling, impression). || Algo, *m.*, tinte, *m.*: *there is an inkling of truth in what he says*, hay algo de verdad en lo que dice. || Indicio, *m.* (hint). || Sospecha, *f.* (suspicion). || *To have some inkling of*, tener cierta idea de *or* una ligera idea de.
ink pad [—pæd] n. Almohadilla, *f.*, tampón, *m.*
inkpot [—pɔt] n. Tintero, *m.*
inkslinger [—sliŋgə*] n. FAM. Chupatintas, *m. inv.*
inkstand [—stænd] n. Tintero (*m.*) de despacho.
inkwell [—wel] n. Tintero, *m.* [de pupitre].
inky [—i] adj. Manchado de tinta (stained with ink). || Parecido a la tinta (resembling ink). || Negro, gra (black).
inlaid [ˈinleid] pret. & p. p. See INLAY.
inland [—lənd] n. Interior, *m.* (interior of a country).
— Adj. Interior (away from the coast). || Interior, nacional (trade, post, etc.). || Nacional (produce). || Del interior (roads, town, etc.). || *Inland navigation*, navegación (*f.*) fluvial.
inland [inˈlænd] adv. Hacia el interior, tierra adentro.
inlander [ˈinləndə*] n. Habitante (*m.*) del interior.
Inland Revenue [ˈinləndˈrevinjuː] n. Contribuciones, *f. pl.*, (government income). || Hacienda, *f.*, fisco, *m.* (government department). || *Inland revenue stamp*, timbre fiscal.
Inland Sea [ˈinlənd ˌsiː] pr. n. GEOGR. Mar (*m.*) del Japón.
in-law [inˈlɔː] n. Pariente (*m.*) político. || — Pl. Familia (*f. sing.*) política.
inlay [ˈinlei] n. Incrustación, *f.* || Taracea, *f.* (with different coloured woods). || Damasquinado, *m.* (with gold or silver). || Empaste, *m.* (for a tooth).
inlay [ˈinˈlei] v. tr. Incrustar: *to inlay mother-of-pearl into wood*, incrustar nácar en madera. || Adornar con incrustaciones de: *to inlay a box with mother-of-pearl*, adornar una caja con incrustaciones de nácar. || Taracear, adornar con marquetería (with different coloured woods). || Damasquinar (with a decoration of gold or silver). || Montar (a picture). || *To inlay a floor with mosaic*, poner mosaicos en el suelo.
inlet [ˈinlet] n. Cala, *f.*, ensenada, *f.* (small bay). || Brazo (*m.*) de mar (narrow arm of sea). || Brazo, *m.* (of river). || TECH. Entrada, *f.*, admisión, *f.*: *inlet valve*, válvula de admisión.
inlier [ˈinlaiə*] n. GEOL. Afloramiento (*m.*) de rocas viejas rodeadas por otras más jóvenes.
inlying [ˈinlaiiŋ] adj. Del interior (inland).
inmate [ˈinmeit] n. Habitante, *m.* & *f.*, inquilino, na (occupant of a dwelling). || Internado, da (of a mental home, camp, etc.). || Enfermo, ma (in a hospital). || Preso, *m.*, presidiario, *m.* (prisoner).
inmost [ˈinməust] adj. Más íntimo, ma; más profundo, da; más secreto, ta (most private or secret). || Situado más adentro (room, etc.).
inn [in] n. Posada, *f.*, hostería, *f.*, mesón, *m.*, venta, *f.* (a type of hotel). || Taberna, *f.* (tavern). || *Inns of Court*, Colegio (*m.*) de abogados de Londres.
innards [ˈinəːdz] pl. n. FAM. Tripas, *f.*, entrañas, *f.* (entrails). || FIG. Entrañas, *f.*
innate [ˈiˈneit] adj. Innato, ta.
innavigable [iˈnævigəbl] adj. Innavegable.
inner [ˈinə*] adj. Interior: *inner court*, patio interior; *inner rooms*, habitaciones interiores; *inner dock*, dársena interior. || Interior, interno, na: *the inner part*, la parte interna. || FIG. Oculto, ta; secreto, ta (hidden): *the inner meaning*, el sentido oculto. | Interior: *inner life*, vida interior. | Íntimo, ma. || ANAT. *Inner ear*, oído interno.
— N. Primer espacio (*m.*) después de la diana (ring of a target). || Tiro (*m.*) que da en este espacio (shot).
innermost [—məust] adj. Más íntimo, ma; más profundo, da; más secreto, ta (most private or secret). || Situado más adentro: *the innermost room*, la habitación situada más adentro.
inner tube [—tjuːb] n. Cámara, *f.* (of tyre).
innervate [ˈinəːveit] v. tr. Inervar.
innervation [ˌinəːˈveiʃən] n. ANAT. Inervación, *f.*
innerve [iˈnəːv] v. tr. Inervar.
inning [ˈinin] n. SP. Entrada, *f.*, turno, *m.*
innings [—z] n. SP. Entrada, *f.*, turno, *m.* (in cricket, baseball). || FIG. *To have had a good innings*, haber tenido una vida larga y buena.

— OBSERV. Esta palabra se construye tanto con el singular como con el plural.

innkeeper [ˈinˌkiːpə*] n. Posadero, ra; mesonero, ra (of an hotel). || Tabernero, ra (of a tavern).
innocence [ˈinəsəns] n. Inocencia, *f.*: *in all innocence*, con toda inocencia.
innocent [ˈinəsnt] adj. Inocente (free from guilt or evil, naïve, harmless): *an innocent young girl*, una chica inocente; *an innocent joke*, una broma inocente. || Desprovisto, ta; sin: *a room innocent of furniture*, una habitación desprovista de muebles. || Autorizado, da (authorized).
— N. Inocente, *m.* & *f.*
Innocent [ˈinəsnt] pr. n. Inocencio, *m.*
innocuity [inɔˈkjuːiti] n. Inocuidad, *f.*
innocuous [iˈnɔkjuəs] adj Inocuo, cua; inofensivo, va.
innocuousness [—nis] n. Inocuidad, *f.*
innominate [iˈnɔminit] adj. Innominado, da: *innominate bone*, hueso innominado.
innovate [ˈinəuveit] v. tr./intr. Innovar.
innovation [ˌinəuˈveiʃən] n. Innovación, *f.*
innovative [ˈinəuveitiv] adj. Innovador, ra.
innovator [ˈinəuveitə*] n. Innovador, ra.
innovatory [ˈinəuveitəri] adj. Innovador, ra.
innoxious [iˈnɔkʃəs] adj. Inocuo, cua.
innoxiousness [—nis] n. Inocuidad, *f.*
innuendo [ˌinjuˈendəu] n. Indirecta, *f.*, insinuación, *f.* (malicious insinuation). || JUR. Insinuación, *f.*

— OBSERV. El plural de *innuendo* es *innuendoes*.

innumerability [iˌnjuːmərəˈbiliti] n. Innumerabilidad, *f.*
innumerable [iˈnjuːmərəbl] adj. Innumerable. || *There are innumerable difficulties*, hay muchísimas dificultades *or* una infinidad de dificultades *or* un sinnúmero de dificultades.
innutrition [ˌinjuˈtriʃən] n. MED. Desnutrición, *f.*
innutritious [ˌinjuˈtriʃəs] adj. Poco nutritivo, va (food).
inobservance [ˌinəbˈzəːvəns] or **inobservancy** [—i] n. Falta (*f.*) de atención, desatención, *f.*, descuido, *m.* (lack of attention). || Inobservancia, *f.* (of a law, custom, etc.). || Incumplimiento, *m.* (of a promise).
inobservant [ˌinəbˈzəːvənt] adj. Desatento, ta (inattentive). || Inobservante (of a law, custom).
inoculate [iˈnɔkjuleit] v. tr. MED. Inocular: *to inoculate s.o. with a virus*, inocular un virus a uno. || *To get inoculated*, vacunarse.
inoculation [iˌnɔkjuˈleiʃən] n. MED. Inoculación, *f.*
inodorous [inˈəudərəs] adj. Inodoro, ra.
inoffensive [ˌinəˈfensiv] adj. Inofensivo, va.
inofficious [ˌinəˈfiʃəs] adj. JUR. Inoficioso, sa.
inoperable [inˈɔpərəbl] adj. MED. Inoperable: *inoperable tumour*, tumor inoperable. || Impracticable (not practicable).
inoperative [inˈɔpərətiv] adj. Inoperante.
inopportune [inˈɔpətjuːn] adj. Inoportuno, na.
inopportuneness [—nis] n. Inoportunidad, *f.*
inordinacy [inˈɔːdinəsi] n. Desmesura, *f.*, exceso, *m.* (excess). || Desorden, *m.* (disorder).
inordinate [iˈnɔːdinit] adj. Desmesurado, da; excesivo, va (not within reasonable limits). || Desordenado, da (disorderly).
inorganic [ˌinɔːˈgænik] adj. Inorgánico, ca: *inorganic chemistry*, química inorgánica.
inorganization [inɔːgənaiˈzeiʃən] n. Falta (*f.*) de organización.
inosculate [iˈnɔskjuleit] v. tr. ANAT. Unir por anastomosis.
— V. intr. Anastomosarse.
inosculation [iˌnɔskjuleiʃən] n. ANAT. Anastomosis, *f.*
inoxidizable [inɔksiˈdaizəbl] adj. Inoxidable.

inpatient [ˈinˌpeiʃənt] n. Enfermo (*m.*) internado en un hospital.
in petto [inˈpetəu] adv. phr. In péctore.
input [ˈinput] n. Entrada, *f.* (terminal for the introduction of power or energy to a machine). || TECH. Energía (*f.*) de entrada (power or energy put into a machine). || "Input", *m.*, entrada, *f.* (information fed to computers). || COMM. Factor (*m.*) de producción [*Amer.*, insumo, *m.*].
inquest [ˈinkwest] n. Investigación, *f.*, encuesta, *f.*
inquietude [inˈkwaiitju:d] n. Desasosiego, *m.*, inquietud, *f.*
inquiline [ˈinkwilain] n. ZOOL. Inquilino, na.
inquire [inˈkwaiə*] v. tr. Informarse de, preguntar: *to inquire the price*, informarse del precio. || Preguntar: *to inquire sth. of s.o.*, preguntar algo a alguien; *to inquire a person's name*, preguntar el nombre de una persona.
— V. intr. Preguntar: "*how are you?*", *he inquired*, "¿cómo estás?" preguntó. || — *Inquire at number twenty*, razón: número veinte. || *Inquire within*, razón aquí.
— **To inquire about,** informarse de: *he inquired about the price*, se informó del precio. | Preguntar por: *your uncle inquired about you yesterday*, tu tío preguntó por ti ayer. | Pedir informes sobre (to make inquiries about). | Hacerse preguntas sobre: *people are beginning to inquire about his absence*, la gente empieza a hacerse preguntas sobre su ausencia. || **To inquire after,** preguntar por. || **To inquire for,** preguntar por. || **To inquire into,** investigar *or* hacer investigaciones sobre: *the police are inquiring into his sudden death*, la policía está haciendo investigaciones sobre su muerte repentina; *to inquire into s.o.'s private life*, hacer investigaciones sobre la vida privada de alguien. | Hacer una investigación sobre, estudiar, examinar (to make a study of).
inquirer [inˈkwaiərə*] n. El que pregunta, la que pregunta (s.o. who asks). || Investigador, ra (researcher).
inquiring [inˈkwaiəriŋ] adj. Curioso, sa. || Interrogativo, va; inquisitivo, va; inquisidor, ra (look).
inquiry [inˈkwaiəri] n. Pregunta, *f.* (question). || Investigación, *f.* (investigation, study of a particular subject): *to hold an inquiry into alcoholism*, hacer una investigación sobre el alcoholismo. || Encuesta, *f.*, investigación, *f.*, pesquisa, *f.* (police investigation): *to set up an inquiry*, hacer una encuesta. || Petición (*f.*) de información (request for information). || — *All inquiries to*, dirigirse a. || *Board of Inquiry*, Comisión (*f.*) de investigación. || *Expression of inquiry*, mirada interrogativa *or* inquisitiva *or* inquisidora. || *Inquiries*, información (sign). || *Inquiries at number twenty*, razón: número veinte. || *To make inquiries*, hacer investigaciones (*about*, sobre) [police], pedir informes *or* información (*about*, sobre) [to seek information]. || *Upon* o *on inquiry, he was told that...*, a su pregunta contestaron que...
inquiry agent [—ˈeidʒənt] n. Detective (*m.*) privado.
inquiry office [—ˈɔfis] n. Oficina (*f.*) de informaciones.
inquisition [ˌinkwiˈziʃən] n. Inquisición, *f.*, investigación, *f.* (close investigation). || *The Inquisition*, la Inquisición.
inquisitional [—l] adj. Inquisitorial.
inquisitive [inˈkwizitiv] adj. Preguntón, ona (prying). || Curioso, sa (interested, curious). || *Inquisitive look*, mirada inquisidora *or* inquisitiva.
inquisitively [—li] adv. Con curiosidad (curiously). || Indiscretamente (indiscreetly).
inquisitiveness [—nis] n. Curiosidad, *f.*
inquisitor [inˈkwizitə*] n. JUR. Investigador, *m.* || REL. Inquisidor, *m.*
inquisitorial [inˌkwiziˈtɔ:riəl] adj. Inquisitorial.
inroad [ˈinrəud] n. MIL. Incursión, *f.* (raid). || FIG. Intrusión, *f.* | Usurpación, *f.* (*into*, de) [encroachment]. || — FIG. FAM. *To make inroads on one's capital*, mermar su capital. | *To make inroads on s.o.'s time*, hacerle perder el tiempo a alguien.
inrush [ˈinrʌʃ] n. Irrupción, *f.* || Afluencia, *f.*: *inrush of tourists*, afluencia de turistas. || Entrada (*f.*) repentina (of air, fluid, etc.).
insalivate [inˈsæliveit] v. tr. BIOL. Insalivar.
insalivation [insæliˈveiʃən] n. BIOL. Insalivación, *f.*
insalubrious [ˌinsəˈlu:briəs] adj. Insalubre.
insalubrity [ˌinsəˈlu:briti] n. Insalubridad, *f.*
insane [inˈsein] adj. Loco, ca; demente (person). || FIG. Insensato, ta; loco, ca (action). || — *Insane asylum*, manicomio, *m.* || *The insane*, los locos. || *To drive s.o. insane*, volver loco a alguien.
insanitary [inˈsænitəri] adj. Insalubre, antihigiénico, ca; malsano, na.
insanity [inˈsæniti] n. Locura, *f.*, demencia, *f.* || JUR. Enajenación (*f.*) mental. || FIG. Locura, *f.*, insensatez, *f.* (foolish act): *pure insanity*, pura locura.
insatiability [inˌseiʃjəˈbiliti] n. Insaciabilidad, *f.*
insatiable [inˈseiʃjəbl] adj. Insaciable.
insatiate [inˈseiʃiit] adj. FIG. Insaciable (never satisfied).
inscribable [inˈskraibəbl] adj. MATH. Inscribible.
inscribe [inˈskraib] v. tr. Inscribir (to write, to enrol). || Grabar (to engrave). || Dedicar (to dedicate). || MATH. Inscribir. || COMM. Registrar (stock).
inscribed [—d] adj. Inscrito, ta. || COMM. Registrado, da (stock).
inscription [inˈskripʃən] n. Inscripción, *f.* || Dedicatoria, *f.* (in a book). || COMM. Registro, *m.* | Valores (*m. pl.*) registrados.
inscrutability [inˌskru:təˈbiliti] n. Inescrutabilidad, *f.*
inscrutable [inˈskru:təbl] adj. Inescrutable.
insect [ˈinsekt] n. Insecto, *m.* || FIG. Bicho, *m.*
insecticidal [inˈsektisaidl] adj. Insecticida.
insecticide [inˈsektisaid] n. Insecticida, *m.*
insectivora [inˈsektivərə] pl. n. Insectívoros, *m.*
insectivore [inˈsektivɔ:*] n. Insectívoro, *m.*
insectivorous [ˌinsekˈtivərəs] adj. Insectívoro, ra.
insecure [ˌinsiˈkjuə*] adj. Inseguro, ra (uncertain, unsure). || Poco seguro, ra: *the ice is insecure*, el hielo está poco seguro. || Inestable (unstable): *an insecure table*, una mesa inestable.
insecurity [—riti] n. Inseguridad, *f.*
inseminate [inˈseminit] v. tr. Inseminar.
insemination [inˌsemiˈneiʃən] n. Inseminación, *f.*: *artificial insemination*, inseminación articial.
insensate [inˈsenseit] adj. Insensato, ta (foolish). || Insensible (unfeeling).
insensibility [inˌsensiˈbiliti] n. Insensibilidad, *f.* || MED. Inconsciencia, *f.*
insensible [inˈsensəbl] adj. Insensible: *insensible to cold, to sorrow*, insensible al frío, al dolor. || Inconsciente (unaware): *insensible of the risk*, inconsciente del peligro. || Insensible, imperceptible (imperceptible). || MED. Inconsciente (unconscious). || *To drink o.s. insensible*, beber hasta perder el conocimiento.
insensitive [inˈsensitiv] adj. Insensible.
insensitiveness [—nis] or **insensitivity** [inˌsensəˈtiviti] n. Insensibilidad, *f.*
insentient [inˈsenʃənt] adj. Inconsciente.
inseparability [inˌsepərəˈbiliti] n. Inseparabilidad, *f.*
inseparable [inˈsepərəbl] adj. Inseparable: *inseparable friends*, amigos inseparables.
— Pl. n. Amigos (*m.*) inseparables (friends). || Cosas (*f.*) inseparables (things).
insert [ˈinsə:t] n. Encarte, *m.* (in a book, magazine, etc.). || Entredós, *m.* (in sewing).
insert [inˈsə:t] v. tr. Introducir: *to insert a key in the lock*, introducir una llave en la cerradura. || Introducir, insertar, incluir: *to insert a clause in a contract*, introducir una cláusula en un contrato. || Insertar (advertisement in a newspaper). || Intercalar (between pages).
insertable [—əbl] adj. Insertable, incluible.
inserted [inˈsə:tid] adj. BOT. ZOOL. Inserto, ta.
insertion [inˈsə:ʃən] n. Inserción, *f.* (an inserting, a thing inserted) || Encarte, *m.* (in a book, magazine). || Anuncio, *m.* (advertisement). || BOT. ANAT. Inserción, *f.* || Entredós, *m.* (band of lace or embroidery).
inset [ˈinset] n. Recuadro, *m.* (in a picture, map, etc.). || Encarte, *m.* (extra page of a book). || Entredós, *m.* (of material).
inset [ˈinˈset] v. tr. Insertar (to insert). || Encartar (in a book).

— OBSERV. El verbo *inset* no varía en el pretérito y en el participio pasivo (*inset*), excepto cuando significa "encartar" en cuyo caso se usa la forma *insetted*.

inshore [ˈinˈʃɔ:*] adj. Cercano a la orilla (near the shore). || Costero, ra (coastal).
— Adv. Hacia la orilla: *to drift inshore*, ser empujado hacia la orilla. || Cerca de la orilla (near the shore). || *To be inshore of sth.*, estar entre algo y la orilla.
inside [ˈinˈsaid] adj. Interior: *inside wall*, pared interior; *inside diameter*, diámetro interior; *inside pages of a paper*, páginas interiores de un periódico. || Confidencial, secreto, ta: *inside information*, información confidencial.
— Adv. Dentro, adentro: *wait inside*, espera dentro; *stay inside*, quédate adentro. || Para adentro, adentro (movement towards): *go inside*, vete para adentro. || Por dentro: *red outside, green inside*, rojo por fuera, verde por dentro. || Abajo (in a bus). || En la cárcel (in jail). || — FAM. *Inside of*, en menos de: *inside of a week*, en menos de una semana; dentro de (within). || *Please, step inside*, pase, for favor. || *To come inside*, entrar. || *To go inside*, entrar (to enter), ir a la cárcel (to go to jail).
— Prep. Dentro de.
— N. Interior, *m.* (interior). || Parte (*f.*) de adentro, parte (*f.*) interior (inner part of pavement, etc.). || Forro, *m.* (lining). || — Pl. FAM. Tripas, *f.* (stomach and intestines). || — *On the inside*, por dentro. || *To know the inside of an affair*, conocer las interioridades de un asunto. || *To overtake on the inside*, adelantar por la derecha (for those driving on the right), adelantar por la izquierda (for those driving on the left). || *To see sth. from the inside*, estudiar algo por dentro.
inside forward [ˈinsaidˈfɔ:wəd] n. SP. Interior, *m.*
inside job [inˈsaidʒɔb] n. FAM. Crimen (*m.*) cometido con la complicidad de una persona allegada a la víctima. || *This must be an inside job*, esto debe hacerlo alguien de la casa.
inside left [ˈinsaidˈleft] n. SP. Interior (*m.*) izquierda.
inside out [inˈsaidaut] adv. Al revés (the wrong way round). || — *To know sth. inside out*, conocer algo a fondo (to know thoroughly). || *To turn sth. inside out*, registrar de arriba abajo (to search), volver algo del revés (to put sth. the wrong way round).
insider [inˈsaidə*] n. Persona (*f.*) enterada.

inside right [ˈinsaidˈrait] n. SP. Interior (*m.*) derecha.
inside track [ˈinsaidˈtræk] n. SP. Pista (*f.*) interior. || FIG. Ventaja, *f.*
insidious [inˈsidiəs] adj. Insidioso, sa.
insidiousness [—nis] n. Insidia, *f.*
insight [ˈinsait] n. Perspicacia, *f.*, penetración, *f.* (perspicacity). || Idea, *f.*: *to get an insight into*, hacerse una idea de.
insignia [inˈsigniə] pl. n. Insignias, *f.*

— OBSERV. En Inglaterra *insignia* se considera como un sustantivo plural. En Estados Unidos se puede emplear como singular. En este último caso el plural es *insignias.*

insignificance [ˌinsigˈnifikəns] n. Insignificancia, *f.*
insignificant [ˌinsigˈnifikənt] adj. Insignificante.
insincere [ˌinsinˈsiə*] adj. Insincero, ra; poco sincero, ra (not sincere). || Hipócrita (hypocritical).
insincerity [ˌinsinˈseriti] n. Insinceridad, *f.*, falta (*f.*) de sinceridad. || Hipocresía, *f.*
insinuate [inˈsinjueit] v. tr. Insinuar. || — *To insinuate o.s. into*, insinuarse en. || *To insinuate that*, insinuar que, dar a entender que.
insinuating [—iŋ] adj. Insinuante.
insinuation [inˌsinjuˈeiʃən] n. Insinuación, *f.*
insinuative [inˌsinjuˈeitiv] adj. Insinuante.
insipid [inˈsipid] adj. Soso, sa; insípido, da (tasteless). || FIG. Soso, sa; insulso, sa (dull).
insipidity [ˌinsiˈpiditi] or **insipidness** [inˈsipidnis] n. Insipidez, *f.*, sosería, *f.* || FIG. Sosería, *f.*, insulsez, *f.*
insist [inˈsist] v. intr. Insistir, empeñarse: *if you insist, you will only make him angry*, si insistes sólo conseguirás que se enfade. || — *To insist on* o *upon doing sth.*, empeñarse en hacer algo, insistir en hacer algo. || *To insist on* o *upon sth.*, exigir algo, insistir en algo.
— V. tr. Insistir en: *he insists that it was so*, insiste en que fue así; *he insists that you apologize*, insiste en que pidas disculpas.
insistence [inˈsistəns] n. Insistencia, *f.*, empeño, *m.* || *He came at my insistence*, vino ante mi insistencia.
insistency [—i] n. Insistencia, *f.*, empeño, *m.*
insistent [inˈsistənt] adj. Insistente. || *They were most insistent that I bring you*, insistieron mucho en que te trajera.
insistently [—li] adv. Con insistencia, insistentemente.
in situ [inˈsitu] adv. phr. En el lugar de origen, en el sitio.
insobriety [insəuˈbraiəti] n. Intemperancia, *f.*
insofar [ˈinsəuˈfɑː] adv. *Insofar as*, en la medida en que.
insolate [ˈinsəleit] v. tr. Insolar.
insolation [ˌinsəuˈleiʃən] n. Insolación, *f.*
insole [ˈinsəul] n. Plantilla, *f.* (for shoes).
insolence [ˈinsələns] n. Insolencia, *f.*, descaro, *m.*
insolent [ˈinsələnt] adj. Insolente, descarado, da.
insolubility [inˌsɔljuˈbiliti] n. Insolubilidad, *f.*
insoluble [inˈsɔljubl] adj. Insoluble.
insolvable [inˈsɔlvəbl] adj. Insoluble.
insolvency [inˈsɔlvənsi] n. COMM. Insolvencia, *f.*
insolvent [inˈsɔlvənt] adj./n. COMM. Insolvente. || *To declare o.s. insolvent*, declararse en quiebra.
insomnia [inˈsɔmniə] n. MED. Insomnio, *m.*
insomniac [—k] n. Insomne, *m.* & *f.*
insomnious [—s] adj. Insomne (sleepless).
insomuch [ˌinsəuˈmʌtʃ] adv. *Insomuch as*, puesto que, ya que (since, because). || *Insomuch that*, hasta tal punto que.
insouciance [inˈsuːsjəns] n. Despreocupación, *f.*
insouciant [inˈsuːsjənt] adj. Despreocupado, da.
inspect [inˈspekt] v. tr. Inspeccionar, examinar, registrar. || MIL. Pasar revista a (troops).
inspection [inˈspekʃən] n. Inspección, *f.*, registro, *m.*, examen, *m.* || MIL. Revista, *f.*
inspector [inˈspektə*] n. Inspector, *m.*
inspectoral [inˈspektərəl] adj. De inspector.
inspectorate [inˈspektərit] n. Cargo (*m.*) de inspector (office). || Cuerpo (*m.*) de inspectores (staff of inspectors). || Distrito (*m.*) asignado a un inspector (district under an inspector).
inspectorship [inˈspektəʃip] n. Cargo (*m.*) de inspector.
inspiration [ˌinspəˈreiʃən] n. Inspiración, *f.* || Aspiración, *f.*, inspiración, *f.* (inhaling). || *His courageous behaviour was an inspiration for all of us*, su valor nos infundió ánimo a todos.
inspirational [ˌinspəˈreiʃənl] adj. Inspirador, ra (persons, etc.). || Inspirado, da (inspired).
inspiratory [inˈspaiərətəri] adj. ANAT. Inspirador, ra: *inspiratory muscles*, músculos inspiradores.
inspire [inˈspaiə*] v. tr. Inspirar (to give inspiration). || Sugerir, inspirar (to suggest). || Dar, infundir: *to inspire s.o. with fear*, infundir miedo a alguien. || Aspirar, inspirar (to inhale). || *To inspire s.o. to do sth.*, incitar a alguien a que haga algo.
— V. intr. Inspirar, aspirar.
inspired [—d] adj. Inspirado, da; de inspiración: *in an inspired moment*, en un momento de inspiración. || Genial: *his performance was absolutely inspired*, su actuación fue absolutamente genial.
inspirer [—rə*] n. Inspirador, ra.
inspiring [—riŋ] adj. Inspirador, ra.
inspirit [inˈspirit] v. tr. Alentar, animar.
inspiriting [—iŋ] adj. Alentador, ra; estimulante.
inspissate [inˈspiseit] v. tr. Espesar (to thicken). || Condensar (to condense).
— V. intr. Espesarse (to thicken). || Condensarse (to condense).
inspissation [inspiˈseiʃən] n. Espesamiento, *m.* (thickening). || Condensación, *f.* (condensation).
inst. [ˈinstənt] abbrev. of *instant*, del actual, del corriente: *the 9th inst.*, el nueve del corriente.
instability [ˌinstəˈbiliti] n. Inestablidad, *f.*, instabilidad, *f.* (lack of stability).
instable [insˈteibl] adj. Inestable, instable.
install [inˈstɔːl] v. tr. Instalar: *to install electricity*, instalar la electricidad; *they have installed a hundred poor families in the neighbourhood*, han instalado a cien familias pobres en el barrio. || *To install o.s.*, instalarse.
installation [ˌinstəˈleiʃən] n. Instalación, *f.*
instalment (U. S. **installment**) [inˈstɔːlmənt] n. Plazo, *m.* (of payment): *to pay by* o *in instalments*, pagar a plazos. || Fascículo, *m.* (of a book). || Instalación, *f.* (an installing). || — *Annual instalment*, anualidad, *f.* || *Instalment plan*, venta (*f.*) or compra (*f.*) a plazos. || *Monthly instalment*, mensualidad, *f.*
instance [ˈinstəns] n. Ejemplo, *m.* (example). || Caso, *m.* (case). || — *At the instance of*, a petición de. || JUR. *Court of first instance*, tribunal (*m.*) de primera instancia. || *For instance*, por ejemplo. || *In many instances*, en muchos casos. || *In that instance*, en ese caso. || *In the first instance*, en primer lugar.
instance [ˈinstəns] v. tr. Ilustrar: *he instanced his speech with several examples*, ilustró su discurso con varios ejemplos. || Citar como ejemplo (to quote).
instancy [—i] n. Inminencia, *f.* (of a danger). || Urgencia, *f.* (of a need). || Insistencia, *f.* (of a request).
instant [ˈinstənt] adj. Urgente (urgent). || Inminente (imminent). || Inmediato, ta (immediate). || Insistente (request). || Instantáneo, a (coffee, soup, etc.). || *Your letter of the 10th instant*, su carta del 10 del corriente *or* del actual.
— N. Instante, *m.*, momento, *m.*: *in an instant*, en un instante. || — *Come this instant*, ven ahora mismo. || *On the instant*, al instante, inmediatamente. || *The instant he arrived*, en cuanto llegó. || *The instant he arrives*, en cuanto llegue.
instantaneity [instæntəˈniːiti] n. Instantaneidad, *f.*
instantaneous [ˌinstənˈteinjəs] adj. Instantáneo, a.
instantly [ˈinstəntli] adv. Instantáneamente, al instante, inmediatamente.
instauration [instɔːˈreiʃən] n. Restauración, *f.*
instaurator [ˈinstɔːreitə*] n. Restaurador, *m.*
instead [inˈsted] adv. En su lugar. || — *Instead of*, en vez de, en lugar de. || *We did not go to Rome but to Venice instead*, en vez de ir a Roma fuimos a Venecia.
instep [ˈinstep] n. Empeine, *m.* (of human foot). || Caña, *f.* (of horse).
instigate [ˈinstigeit] v. tr. Instigar, incitar (s.o.). || Fomentar (rebellion, etc.).
instigating [—iŋ] adj. Instigador, ra.
instigation [ˌinstiˈgeiʃən] n. Instigación, *f.*: *at* o *on the instigation of*, a instigación de.
instigative [ˌinstiˈgeitiv] adj. Instigador, ra.
instigator [ˈinstigeitə*] n. Instigador, ra.
instil (U. S. **instill**) [inˈstil] v. tr. Instilar. || FIG. Infundir, inculcar (*into*, a) [ideas, etc.].
instinct [ˈinstiŋkt] n. Instinto, *m.*: *by instinct*, por instinto; *self-preservation instinct*, instinto de conservación; *maternal instinct*, instinto materno.
— Adj. *Instinct with*, lleno de.
instinctive [inˈstiŋktiv] adj. Instintivo, va.
institute [ˈinstitjuːt] n. Instituto, *m.* (research organization): *geographical institute*, instituto geográfico. || Asociación, *f.*, institución, *f.* (welfare organization). || Centro (*m.*) social (social centre). || U. S. Seminario, *m.* (seminar). || — Pl. JUR. Instituciones, *f.* || *The institutes of Justinian*, la Instituta.

— OBSERV. La palabra inglesa *institute* no tiene nunca el significado de "instituto de segunda enseñanza".

institute [ˈinstitjuːt] v. tr. Instituir, fundar, establecer (to found). || Iniciar, empezar (to begin). || Investir (to invest). || JUR. Entablar: *to institute proceedings*, entablar un proceso.
institution [ˌinstiˈtjuːʃən] n. Institución, *f.*: *welfare institution*, institución benéfica; *cricket is an English institution*, el criquet es una institución en Inglaterra. || Establecimiento, *m.*, creación, *f.*, institución, *f.*: *the institution of The National Health Service helped the poor*, la creación del Seguro de Enfermedad fue una ayuda para los pobres. || Asociación, *f.* (society). || Manicomio, *m.* (madhouse). || Hospicio, *f.* (for abandoned children). || Investidura, *f.* (investiture). || JUR. Iniciación, *f.* (of proceedings). || FAM. Institución, *f.* (familiar person): *he is a local institution*, es una institución local. || — Pl. JUR. Instituciones, *f.*
institutional [—l] adj. Institucional. || Con instituciones benéficas (religion). || U. S. De prestigio (publicity).
institutionalization [instiˈtjuːʃənəlaiˈzeiʃən] n. Institucionalización, *f.*
institutionalize [instiˈtjuːʃənəlaiz] v. tr. Institucionalizar. || FAM. Meter en una institución.
institutionary [instiˈtjuːʃənəri] adj. Institucional.
instruct [inˈstrʌkt] v. tr. Dar instrucciones a (to command formally, to advise, i.e. a jury). || Instruir (to teach). || Ordenar, mandar (to order). || Avisar (to notify). || — *The Committee had not been instructed*

to deal with this question, la Comisión no ha sido encargada de ocuparse de esta cuestión. || *To instruct s.o. in Latin*, enseñar latín a uno.
instruction [inˈstrʌkʃən] n. Instrucción, *f.*, enseñanza, *f.* (teaching). || — Pl. Instrucciones, *f.*: *instructions for use*, instrucciones para el uso; *to follow s.o.'s instructions perfectly*, seguir las instrucciones de alguien al pie de la letra. || — *On the instructions of*, por orden de, siguiendo las instrucciones de. || *To give driving instruction*, dar clases de conducir.
instructional [—l] adj. De instrucción.
instructive [inˈstrʌktiv] adj. Instructivo, va.
instructor [inˈstrʌktə*] n. Instructor, *m.* || Profesor, *m.* (teacher). || Maestro, *m.*: *fencing instructor*, maestro de esgrima. || MIL. Instructor, *m.* || SP. Instructor, *m.*, monitor, *m.* || U. S. Profesor (*m.*) auxiliar.
instructress [inˈstrʌktris] n. Profesora, *f.*
instrument [ˈinstrumənt] n. Instrumento, *m.* (tool, etc.). || FIG. AVIAT. MUS. JUR. Instrumento, *m.* || — Pl. MED. Instrumental, *m. sing.*: *a surgeon's instruments*, el instrumental de un cirujano. || — *Musical instrument*, instrumento músico. || *String, brass, percussion, wind instrument*, instrumento de cuerda, de metal, de percusión, de viento. || *To play an instrument*, tocar un instrumento.
instrument [ˈinstrumənt] v. tr. MUS. Instrumentar, orquestar.
instrumental [ˌinstruˈmentl] adj. Instrumental: *instrumental music*, música instrumental. || *To be instrumental in* o *to*, contribuir a.
instrumentalism [—lizəm] n. Instrumentalismo, *m.*
instrumentalist [ˌinstruˈmentəlist] n. MUS. Instrumentista, *m.* & *f.*
instrumentality [ˌinstrumenˈtæliti] n. *Through the instrumentality of*, por intermedio de, por mediación de (a person), por medio de (a thing).
instrumentation [ˌinstrumenˈteiʃən] n. MUS. Instrumentación, *f.* || Empleo (*m.*) de instrumentos.
instrument board [ˈinstrumənbɔ:d] n. Tablero (*m.*) de mandos, salpicadero, *m.* (of a car). || Tablero (*m.*) *or* cuadro (*m.*) de instrumentos (of an aircraft).
instrument flying [ˈinstruməntflaiiŋ] n. AVIAT. Vuelo (*m.*) con instrumentos.
instrument landing system [ˈinstruməntˈlændiŋ ˈsistim] n. AVIAT. Sistema (*m.*) de aterrizaje por instrumentos.
instrument panel [ˈinstruməntˈpænl] n. AVIAT. Tablero (*m.*) *or* cuadro (*m.*) de instrumentos. || AUT. Tablero (*m.*) de mandos, salpicadero, *m.*
insubmergible [ˌinsəbˈmə:dʒəbl] or **insubmersible** [insəbˈmə:səbl] adj. Insumergible.
insubordinate [ˌinsəˈbɔ:dinit] adj. Insubordinado, da.
insubordination [ˈinsəˌbɔ:diˈneiʃən] n. Insubordinación, *f.*
insubstantial [ˌinsəbˈstænʃəl] adj. Insubstancial (soul). || Inconsistente, flojo, ja (weak): *insubstantial arguments*, argumentos flojos. || Infundado, da (unreal): *insubstantial fears*, temores infundados. || Insignificante.
insubstantiality [insəbstænʃiˈæliti] n. Insubstancialidad, *f.* (of soul). || Poco peso, *m.*, inconsistencia, *f.* (weakness). || Falta (*f.*) de fundamento, irrealidad, *f.* (unreality).
insufferable [inˈsʌfərəbl] adj. Insufrible, inaguantable, insoportable (not to be tolerated).
insufferably [inˈsʌfərəbli] adv. De modo intolerable. || *Insufferably selfish*, de lo más egoísta.
insufficiency [ˌinsəˈfiʃənsi] n. Insuficiencia, *f.* (inadequacy). || Limitación, *f.*: *to know one's own insufficiencies*, conocer sus propias limitaciones. || MED. Insuficiencia, *f.*
insufficient [ˌinsəˈfiʃənt] adj. Insuficiente.
insufflate [ˈinsʌfleit] v. tr. Insuflar.
insufflation [insʌˈfleiʃən] n. Insuflación, *f.*
insufflator [ˈinsʌfleitə*] n. Insuflador, *m.*
insular [ˈinsjulə*] adj. Insular (inhabiting or forming an island). || FIG. Estrecho de miras (narrow-minded). | Aislado, da (insulated). || MED. Insular.
insularity [ˌinsjuˈlæriti] n. Insularidad, *f.* || FIG. Estrechez (*f.*) de miras.
insulate [ˈinsjuleit] v. tr. PHYS. Aislar. || FIG. Aislar, apartar (to isolate).
insulating [—iŋ] adj. Aislante, aislador, ra: *insulating tape*, cinta aislante.
insulation [ˌinsjuˈleiʃən] n. PHYS. Aislamiento, *m.* || FIG. Aislamiento, *m.*
insulator [ˈinsjuleitə*] n. Aislador, *m.*, aislante, *m.*
insulin [ˈinsjulin] n. Insulina, *f.*
insult [ˈinsʌlt] n. Insulto, *m.*, injuria, *f.* || U. S. MED. Trauma, *m.*
insult [inˈsʌlt] v. tr. Insultar, injuriar. || *To feel insulted*, ofenderse, sentirse ofendido.
insulter [—ə*] n. Insultador, ra.
insulting [—iŋ] adj. Insultante, ofensivo, va.
insuperable [inˈsju:pərəbl] adj. Insuperable.
insupportable [ˌinsəˈpɔ:təbl] adj. Insoportable, inaguantable (unbearable).
insuppressible [ˌinsəˈpresəbl] adj. Irreprimible.
insurable [inˈʃuərəbl] adj. Asegurable.
insurance [inˈʃuərəns] n. Seguro, *m.*: *insurance against theft*, seguro contra robo; *insurance on new cars is high*, el seguro de los coches nuevos es alto; *the insurance on this is five hundred pounds*, esto tiene un seguro de quinientas libras; *accident insurance*, seguro contra accidentes; *insurance policy*, póliza de seguro; *insurance premium*, prima de seguro. || — *Fire insurance*, seguro contra incendios. || *Fully comprehensive insurance*, seguro a todo riesgo. || *Insurance agent, broker, company*, agente, corredor, compañía de seguros. || *Life, mutual, third party insurance*, seguro de vida *or* sobre la vida, mutuo, contra terceros. || *National* o *social insurance*, seguros sociales. || *To take out an insurance*, hacerse un seguro.
insurant [ˈinʃuərənt] n. Asegurado, da.
insure [inˈʃuə*] v. tr. Asegurar.
— V. intr. Asegurarse.
insured [—d] adj./n. Asegurado, da.
insurer [—rə*] n. Asegurador, ra.
insurgence [inˈsə:dʒəns] n. Insurrección, *f.*, levantamiento, *m.*
insurgency [inˈsə:dʒənsi] n. Rebelión, *f.* || Insurrección, *f.*, levantamiento, *m.* (insurgence).
insurgent [inˈsə:dʒənt] adj./n. Insurrecto, ta; insurgente.
insurmountable [ˌinsəˈmauntəbl] adj. Insalvable (obstacle). || Insuperable (difficulty).
insurrection [ˌinsəˈrekʃən] n. Insurrección, *f.*
insurrectional [—l] adj. Insurreccional.
insurrectionary [—əri] adj. Insurreccional, insurrecto, ta; insurgente.
— N. Insurrecto, ta; insurgente, *m.* & *f.*
insurrectionist [—ist] n. Insurrecto, ta; insurgente, *m.* & *f.*
insusceptibility [ˈinsəˌseptəˈbiliti] n. Insensibilidad, *f.* || Falta (*f.*) de susceptibilidad.
insusceptible [ˌinsəˈseptəbl] adj. Insensible (not affected emotionally). || No susceptible (not sensitive).
inswinger [inˈswiŋə*] n. SP. Lanzamiento (*m.*) con efecto (in cricket).
intact [inˈtækt] adj. Intacto, ta.
intaglio [inˈtɑ:liəu] n. Talla, *f.* (engraved design). || Piedra (*f.*) preciosa grabada en hueco (gem). || *Intaglio engraving*, grabado (*m.*) en hueco, huecograbado, *m.*
intake [ˈinteik] n. Toma, *f.*, entrada, *f.* (of air). || Toma, *f.* (of water). || AUT. Entrada (*f.*) de aire (of a carburettor). | Admisión, *f.* | Válvula (*f.*) de admisión (entry for fuel, water, steam, etc.). || MIN. Pozo (*m.*) de ventilación. || Consumo, *m.* (thing taken in). || Aspiración, *f.* || Número (*m.*) de personas admitidas (in a college, club, etc.). || MIL. Reclutas, *m. pl.* || Menguado, *m.* (in knitting). || *Food intake*, ración, *f.*
intangibility [inˌtændʒəˈbiliti] n. Intangibilidad, *f.*
intangible [inˈtændʒəbl] adj. Intangible (not tangible).
— N. Cosa (*f.*) intangible.
intangibleness [—nis] n. Intangibilidad, *f.*
intarsia [inˈtɑ:siə] n. ARTS. Marquetería, *f.*, taracea, *f.*
integer [ˈintidʒə*] n. MATH. Entero, *m.*, número (*m.*) entero. || FIG. Totalidad, *f.*
integrable [ˈintigrəbl] adj. MATH. Integrable.
integral [ˈintigrəl] adj. Integrante: *an integral part of his studies*, una parte integrante de sus estudios; *a part integral with the whole*, una parte integrante del todo. || Integral, íntegro, gra (complete). || MATH. *Integral calculus*, cálculo (*m.*) integral.
— N. MATH. Integral, *f.*
integrality [inteˈgræliti] n. Integridad, *f.* (wholeness).
integrant [ˈintegrənt] adj. Integrante.
— N. Parte (*f.*) integrante, elemento, *m.*, componente, *m.* (component, part).
integrate [ˈintigreit] v. tr. Integrar.
— V. intr. Integrarse (*into*, en).
integration [ˌintiˈgreiʃən] n. Integración, *f.*
integrationist [ˌintiˈgræʃnist] n. Integracionista, *m.* & *f.* (s.o. in favour of integration).
integrative [ˈintigreitiv] adj. Integrador, ra.
integrator [ˈintigreitə*] n. Integrador, *m.*
integrity [inˈtegriti] n. Integridad, *f.* (probity, soundness). || Totalidad, *f.*, integridad, *f.* (wholeness).
intellect [ˈintilekt] n. Intelecto, *m.*, inteligencia, *f.* (intelligence). || FIG. Intelectual, *m.* & *f.* (person of superior reasoning power). | Intelectuales, *m. pl.*, intelectualidad, *f.* (intelligentsia).
intellection [intiˈlekʃən] n. Idea, *f.* (thought).
intellectual [ˌintiˈlektjuəl] adj./n. Intelectual.
intellectualism [ˌintiˈlektjuəlizəm] n. PHIL. Intelectualismo, *m.*
intellectualist [ˌintilekˈtjuəlist] adj./n. Intelectualista.
intellectualistic [—ik] adj. Intelectualista.
intellectuality [ˈintiˌlektjuˈæliti] n. Intelectualidad, *f.*
intellectualize [ˌintiˈlektjuəlaiz] v. tr. Intelectualizar.
intelligence [inˈtelidʒəns] n. Inteligencia, *f.*: *intelligence test*, test *or* prueba de inteligencia. || Noticia, *f.*, información, *f.* (news). || MIL. Información, *f.* (secret information). | Servicio (*m.*) de información (service). || — MIL. *Intelligence bureau* o *department*, servicio (*m.*) de información. | *Intelligence officer*, oficial (*m.*) del servicio de información. || *Intelligence quotient*, cociente (*m.*) intelectual *or* de inteligencia.
intelligencer [—ə*] n. Informador, ra (s.o. who brings news). || Espía, *m.* & *f.*, agente (*m.*) secreto (spy).
intelligent [inˈtelidʒənt] adj. Inteligente.
intelligential [inteliˈdʒenʃəl] adj. Intelectual.
intelligentsia [inˌteliˈdʒentsiə] n. Intelectualidad, *f.*, intelligentsia, *f.*

intelligibility [in,telidʒə'biliti] n. Inteligibilidad, *f.*
intelligible [in'telidʒəbl] adj. Inteligible.
intemperance [in'tempərəns] n. Intemperancia, *f.*, falta (*f.*) de moderación.
intemperate [in'tempərit] adj. Intemperante, inmoderado, da (person). || Excesivo, va (zeal). || Inclemente (climate). || Violento, ta (wind).
intend [in'tend] v. tr. Querer hacer: *I intended no harm*, no quería hacer daño. || Tener la intención *or* el propósito de: *I intend going*, tengo la intención de ir. || Querer decir (to mean). || — *I hope that remark was not intended for me*, espero que esta observación no iba dirigida a mí. || *To intend for*, destinar a: *this book is not intended for young girls*, este libro no está destinado a chicas jóvenes. || *To intend to*, tener la intención *or* el propósito de: *to intend to do sth.*, tener la intención de hacer algo; pretender, querer: *I intend to be obeyed*, pretendo que se me obedezca. || *We fully intend to continue*, tenemos la firme intención *or* el firme propósito de continuar.
intendance [—əns] n. Intendencia, *f.*
intendancy [—ənsi] n. Intendencia, *f.*
intendant [—ənt] n. Intendente, *m.*
intended [—id] adj. Proyectado, da (planned). || Deliberado, da; intencional (intentional). || Futuro, ra (husband, wife).
— N. Fam. Prometido, da; novio, via.
intendment [—mənt] n. Jur. Espíritu, *m.* (of a law, etc.).
intense [in'tens] adj. Intenso, sa; fuerte (heat, pain, colour). || Profundo, da (look). || Ardiente, apasionado, da (highly emotional). || Enorme, sumo, ma (interest, etc.). || Phot. Reforzado, da.
intensification [in,tensifi'keiʃən] n. Intensificación, *f.*
intensifier [in'tensifaiə*] n. Phot. Reforzador, *m.*
intensify [in'tensifai] v. tr. Intensificar (trade, pain, measures, etc.). || Aumentar (joy). || Phot. Reforzar.
— V. intr. Intensificarse || Aumentar.
intension [in'tenʃən] n. Phil. Comprensión, *f.* || Intensidad, *f.* (intensity). || Intensificación, *f.* (intensification). || Determinación, *f.*
intensity [in'tensiti] n. Intensidad, *f.*
intensive [in'tensiv] adj. Intensivo, va: *intensive course*, curso intensivo; *intensive cultivation* o *farming*, cultivo intensivo. || Profundo, da: *to make an intensive study of*, hacer un estudio profundo de. || Gramm. Intensivo, va (giving emphasis).
— N. Palabra (*f.*) intensiva.
intent [in'tent] adj. Atento, ta; profundo, da: *an intent gaze*, una mirada atenta. || Constante (application). || *Intent on* o *upon*, resuelto a, determinado a (with firm intention to), absorto en (engrossed in), atento a (with one's attention concentrated on).
— N. Intención, *f.*, propósito, *m.* || — *To all intents and purposes*, prácticamente. || *With malicious intent*, con fines delictivos *or* criminales.
intention [in'tenʃən] n. Intención, *f.*: *it is my intention to*, tengo la intención de; *first intention*, primera intención; *healing by first, second intention*, cura de *or* por primera, de *or* por segunda intención; *the intentions of a Mass*, las intenciones de una misa. || *I have no intention of going*, no tengo ninguna intención de ir, no me propongo ir.
intentional [—əl] adj. Intencional, deliberado, da.
intentionality [—əliti] n. Intencionalidad, *f.*
intentionally [—əli] adv. Intencionalmente, intencionadamente, a propósito, adrede.
intentioned [in'tenʃənd] adj. Intencionado, da.
intently [in'tentli] adv. Atentamente.
intentness [in'tentnis] n. Gran atención, *f.*, aplicación, *f.* (*on*, a).
inter [in'tə:*] v. tr. Enterrar (to bury).
interact ['intərækt] n. Theatr. Entreacto, *m.*
interact [,intər'ækt] v. intr. Actuar recíprocamente.
interaction [,intər'ækʃən] n. Interacción, *f.*, acción (*f.*) recíproca.
interactive [,intər'æktiv] adj. Recíproco, ca.
interallied ['intə:ə'laid] adj. Interaliado, da.
interamerican [intə:ə'merikən] adj. Interamericano, na.
interandean [intə:'ændi:n] adj. Interandino, na.
interbreed ['intə'bri:d] v. tr. Cruzar.
— V. intr. Cruzarse.
intercadence ['intə:'keidəns] n. Med. Intercadencia, *f.* (of pulse).
intercadent ['intə:'keidənt] adj. Med. Intercadente.
intercalary [in'tə:kələri] adj. Intercalar: *intercalary day*, día intercalar. || Bisiesto (year). || Intercalado, da (inserted).
intercalate [in'tə:kəleit] v. tr. Intercalar.
intercalation [in,tə:kə'leiʃən] n. Intercalación, *f.*
intercede [,intə:'si:d] v. intr. Interceder: *to intercede with s.o. for another*, interceder con *or* cerca de alguien por otro.
interceding [—iŋ] adj. Intercesor, ra.
interceder [—ə*] n. Intercesor, ra.
intercellular ['intə:'seljulə*] adj. Intercelular.
intercept [,intə:'sept] v. tr. Interceptar (a message). || Parar *or* detener en el camino (to stop s.o.). || Parar (s.o.'s escape). || Cortar (s.o.'s retreat). || Cortar (line, circuit). || Math. Cortar.
interception [,intə:'sepʃən] n. Intercepción, *f.*, interceptación, *f.* || Math. Intersección, *f.*
interceptive [,intə:'septiv] adj. Que intercepta.
interceptor [,intə'septə*] n. Aviat. Interceptador, *m.* || Persona (*f.*) que intercepta.
intercession [,intə'seʃən] n. Intercesión, *f.*
intercessor [,intə'sesə*] n. Intercesor, ra.
intercessory [,intə'sesəri] adj. Intercesor, ra.
interchange ['intə:'tʃeindʒ] n. Intercambio, *m.*: *interchange of letters*, intercambio de cartas. || Cambio, *m.*: *interchange of ideas*, cambio de impresiones. || Pasos (*m. pl.*) elevados a distintos niveles (of roads). || Alternación, *f.* (of day and night).
interchange [,intə:'tʃeindʒ] v. tr. Intercambiar, cambiar. || Alternar (to alternate).
interchangeable [,intə:'tʃeindʒəbl] adj. Intercambiable.
intercollegiate ['intə:kə'li:dʒiit] adj. Entre varios colegios *or* varias universidades.
intercolumnar [intə:kə'lʌmnə*] adj. Arch. Entre columnas.
intercolumniation [intə:kəlʌmni'eiʃən] n. Arch. Intercolumnio, *m.*
intercom ['intə:kɔm] n. Sistema (*m.*) de intercomunicación, intercomunicador, *m.* (of boats, etc.). || Interfono, *m.* (in factories, offices, etc.).
intercommunicate [,intə:kə'mju:nikeit] v. intr. Comunicarse, intercomunicarse.
intercommunication ['intə:kə,mju:ni'keiʃən] n. Intercomunicación, *f.*
interconnect [intə:kə'nekt] v. tr. Electr. Interconectar. || Conectar.
— V. intr. Conectar.
interconnected [—id] adj. Que se comunican (rooms). || Aviat. Conectado, da (rudders). || Ligado, da; íntimamente relacionado (facts).
interconnection or **interconnexion** ['intə:kə'nekʃən] n. Electr. Interconexión, *f.* || Conexión, *f.*
intercontinental ['intə:,konti'nentl] adj. Intercontinental.
intercostal [,intə:'kɔ:stl] adj. Anat. Intercostal.
intercourse ['intə:kɔ:s] n. Trato, *m.* (social dealings). || Relaciones, *f. pl.* (commercial, political dealings). || Intercambio, *m.* (interchange). || Contacto (*m.*) sexual (sexual union).
intercrop ['intə:'krɔp] v. intr. Agr. Alternar cultivos.
intercurrent ['intə:'kʌrənt] adj. Intercalado, da.
interdenominational ['intə:di,nɔmi'neiʃənl] adj. Entre varias confesiones *or* religiones.
interdental ['intə:'dentl] adj. Interdental.
interdepartmental ['intə:,di:pɑ:t'mentl] adj. Interdepartamental.
interdepend [,intə:di'pend] v. intr. Depender el uno del otro.
interdependence [,intə:di'pendəns] or **interdependency** [—i] n. Interdependencia, *f.*
interdependent [,intə:di'pendənt] adj. Interdependiente.
interdict ['intə:dikt] n. Rel. Interdicto, *m.*, entredicho, *m.* || Jur. Interdicto, *m.* || Interdicción, *f.*, prohibición, *f.*
interdict [,intə:'dikt] v. tr. Poner en entredicho. || Prohibir (to forbid).
interdiction [,intə:'dikʃən] n. Jur. Rel. Interdicto, *m.* || Interdicción, *f.*, prohibición, *f.*
interdictory [,intə:'diktəri] adj. Jur. Prohibitivo, va; prohibitorio, ria.
interdigital ['intə:'didʒitl] adj. Zool. Interdigital.
interest ['intrist] n. Interés, *m.*: *he looked at me with interest*, me miró con interés; *public interest*, interés público. || Beneficio, *m.*, provecho, *m.*: *in one's own interest*, en beneficio propio. || Comm. Interés, *m.*, participación, *f.* (participation). | Interés, *m.*, rédito, *m.* (on money lent): *to lend at interest*, prestar con interés; *a ten per cent interest*, un interés del *or* de un diez por ciento. || — Pl. Industria, *f. sing.*: *the steel interests*, la industria del acero, la industria siderúrgica. || Negocios, *m.*: *he has mining interests in South Africa*, tiene negocios en Sudáfrica relacionados con las minas. || — *Business interests*, los negocios, el mundo de los negocios. || *Compound interest*, interés compuesto. || *His main interest is music*, la música es lo que más le interesa. || *In the interest of peace*, en pro de la paz. || *It is not in your interest*, no va en beneficio suyo. || *Simple interest*, interés simple. || *The landed interests*, los terratenientes. || *To be of interest*, tener interés, ser interesante, interesar: *it is of no interest to me*, no me interesa. || *To have a controlling interest in a firm*, tener la mayor parte de las acciones de una compañía. || *To pay back with interest*, pagar con creces (figurative sense), pagar con interés (literal sense). || *To show an interest in*, mostrar interés en *or* por. || *To take an interest in*, tomarse interés por, interesarse por *or* en. || Comm. *To yield a high interest*, dar un interés elevado. || *Vested interest*, see VESTED.
interest ['intrist] v. tr. Interesar.
interested [—id] adj. Interesado, da: *the interested party*, la parte interesada. || *To be interested in sport*, interesarle a uno el deporte, interesarse en *or* por el deporte.
interesting [—iŋ] adj. Interesante. || Fig. *In an interesting condition*, en estado interesante (pregnant).
interface ['intə:feis] n. Superficie (*f.*) de contacto.
interfacial [,intə:'feiʃəl] adj. Math. Diedro (angle).

interfere [,intə'fiə*] v. intr. Entrometerse: *stop interfering!*, ¡deja de entrometerte! || PHYS. Interferir. || JUR. Reclamar la prioridad de un invento. || *To interfere with*, estorbar, dificultar (to hinder), tocar (to touch), estropear (to ruin), entrometerse *or* meterse en (other people's business), producir interferencias en (a radio), oponerse a, chocar con (interests).
interference [—rəns] n. Intromisión, *f.*, ingerencia, *f.* (the act of interfering). || SP. Obstrucción, *f.* || PHYS. Interferencia, *f.* || RAD. Parásitos, *m. pl.*, interferencias, *f. pl.*
interfering [,intə:'fiəriŋ] adj. Interferente. || Entrometido, da (person).
interfuse [,intə:'fju:z] v. tr. Mezclar.
— V. intr. Mezclarse, fundirse.
interfusion [,intə:'fju:ʒən] n. Mezcla, *f.* (mixing).
interglacial ['intə:'gleisjəl] adj. Interglacial.
intergovernmental ['intə:'gʌvən'mentl] adj. Intergubernamental.
interim ['intərim] n. Ínterin, *m.* (interval). || *In the interim*, en el ínterin, entretanto.
— Adj. Provisional, interino, na: *an interim decision*, una decisión provisional.
interior [in'tiəriə*] adj. Interior: *the interior market*, el mercado interior. || Interno, na (internal). || Profundo, da: *the interior meaning of the play*, el significado profundo de la obra. || — MATH. *Interior angle*, ángulo interno. || *Interior monologue*, monólogo (*m.*) interior.
— N. Interior, *m.*
interiority [intiə'riɔriti] n. Interioridad, *f.*
interjacent [intə:'dʒeisənt] adj. Interyacente.
interject [,intə:'dʒekt] v. tr. Interponer.
interjection [,intə:'dʒekʃən] n. GRAMM. Interjección, *f.* || Interposición, *f.*
interjectional [,intə:'dʒekʃənl] adj. Interjectivo, va.
interjectory [,intə:'dʒektəri] adj. Interpuesto, ta.
interlace [,intə:'leis] v. tr. Entrelazar (to cross things over and under). || Entremezclar (to mix).
— V. intr. Entrelazarse. || Entremezclarse.
interlacement [—mənt] n. Entrelazamiento, *m.*
interlacing [—iŋ] n. Entrelazamiento, *m.*
interlard [,intə:'lɑ:d] v. tr. Entreverar.
interleaf ['intəli:f] n. Página (*f.*) blanca intercalada.
interline [,intə:'lain] v. tr. Interlinear (to write between lines). || Entretelar (in sewing).
interlinear [,intə:'liniə*] adj. Interlineal.
interlineation ['intə:,lini'eiʃən] n. Interlineación, *f.*, interlineado, *m.*
interlining [,intə:'lainiŋ] n. Entretela, *f.* (in sewing). || Interlineado, *m.*, interlineación, *f.* (interlineation).
interlock [,intə:'lɔk] v. tr. Engranar (teeth of a mechanism). || Enganchar (to hook together). || Encajar (to insert). || Trabar, entrelazar (to connect).
— V. intr. Engranar. || Engancharse. || Encajar (to fit). || Trabarse, entrelazarse (to be connected).
interlocution [,intələu'kju:ʃən] n. Conversación, *f.*, interlocución, *f.*
interlocutor [,intə'lɔkjutə*] n. Interlocutor, ra.
interlocutory [—ri] adj. JUR. Interlocutorio, ria: *to award an interlocutory decree*, formar auto interlocutorio.
interlope [,intə:'ləup] v. intr. Entrometerse (to meddle). || Hacer negocios fraudulentos.
interloper ['intə:ləupə*] n. Intruso, sa (in s.o. else's property). || Entrometido, da (in s.o. else's affairs). || Traficante, *m.*
interloping [,intə:ləupiŋ] adj. Intérlope, fraudulento, ta.
interlude ['intəlu:d] n. MUS. Interludio, *m.* || THEATR. Entremés, *m.* (short play). | Entreacto, *m.* (entr'acte). || Intervalo, *m.* (interval).
intermarriage [,intə'mæridʒ] n. Matrimonio (*m.*) mixto (between different races, etc.). || Matrimonio (*m.*) entre consanguíneos (between close relations).
intermarry ['intə'mæri] v. intr. Casarse entre consanguíneos *or* entre parientes (between close relations). || Casarse [personas de distintas razas, etc.]. || *These tribes have intermarried for centuries*, estas tribus se han casado entre sí durante siglos.
intermaxillary [intə'mæk'siləri] adj. ANAT. Intermaxilar.
intermeddle [,intə'medl] v. tr. Intervenir, inmiscuirse, entremeterse, entrometerse (*with*, en).
intermeddling [—iŋ] n. Intervención, *f.*, intromisión, *f.*, entremetimiento, *m.*
intermediary [,intə'mi:djəri] adj. Intermediario, ria (acting between persons). || Intermedio, dia (intermediate).
— N. Intermediario, ria (mediator). || Etapa (*f.*) intermedia (phase).
intermediate [,intə'mi:djət] adj. Intermedio, dia.
— N. Intermediario, ria (mediator).
intermediate [,intə'mi:dieit] v. intr. Intermediar, mediar.
intermediation [,intə:mi'dieiʃən] n. Mediación, *f.*
intermediator [,intə:'mi:dieitə*] n. Intermediario, ria.
interment [in'tə:mənt] n. Entierro, *m.*
intermezzo [,intə'metsəu] n. MUS. Intermezzo, *m.*

— OBSERV. El plural de la palabra inglesa es *intermezzi* o *intermezzos*.

interminable [in'tə:minəbl] adj. Interminable.
intermingle [,intə:'miŋgl] v. tr. Entremezclar.
— V. int. Entremezclarse.
interministerial [,intə:minis'tiəriəl] adj. Interministerial.
intermission [,intə'miʃən] n. Intermisión, *f.*, interrupción, *f.* (interruption). || CINEM. Descanso, *m.* || THEATR. Entreacto, *m.*, descanso, *m.* || MED. Intermitencia, *f.*
intermissive [,intə'misiv] adj. Intermitente.
intermit [,intə:'mit] v. tr. Interrumpir.
— V. intr. Interrumpirse. || MED. Ser intermitente.
intermittence [,intə'mitəns] or **intermittency** [—i] n. Intermitencia, *f.*
intermittent [,intə'mitənt] adj. Intermitente. || — ELECTR. *Intermittent current*, corriente (*f.*) intermitente. || MED. *Intermittent fever*, fiebre (*f.*) intermitente.
intermix [,intə'miks] v. tr. Entremezclar.
— V. intr. Entremezclarse.
intermixture [,intə'mikstʃə*] n. Mezcla, *f.*
intermolecular [,intə:məu'lekjulə*] adj. Intermolecular.
intermuscular [,intə'mʌskjulə*] adj. ANAT. Intermuscular.
intern [,intə:n] n. MED. Interno, *m.*
intern [in'tə:n] v. tr. Internar.
— V. intr. Trabajar como interno.
internal [—l] adj. Interno, na: *internal injuries*, lesiones internas; *internal organs*, órganos internos. || Interior: *internal trade*, comercio interior. || Interno, na; intestino, na: *internal conflicts*, luchas intestinas. || Intrínseco, ca (intrinsic). || — MATH. *Internal angle*, ángulo interno. || *Internal medicine*, medicina interna. || U. S. *Internal Revenue*, rentas públicas.
— Pl. n. ANAT. Órganos (*m.*) internos. || FIG. Cualidades (*f.*) esenciales.
internal-combustion engine [in'tə:nlkəm'bʌstʃən 'endʒin] n. Motor (*m.*) de combustión interna.
internally [in'tə:nəli] adv. Interiormente. || MED. *Not to be used internally*, uso externo.
international [,intə'næʃənl] adj. Internacional. || — GEOGR. *International date line*, línea (*f.*) de cambio de fecha. || *International law*, derecho (*m.*) internacional.
— N. SP. Internacional, *m.* & *f.* (sportsman). | Partido (*m.*) internacional (match). || Internacional, *f.* (organization): *the First International*, la Primera Internacional.
Internationale [,intənæʃə'nɑ:l] n. Internacional, *f.* (hymn).
internationalism [,intə'næʃnəlizəm] n. Internacionalismo, *m.*
internationalist [,intə'næʃnəlist] n. Internacionalista, *m.* & *f.*
internationality [,intənæʃn'æliti] n. Internacionalidad, *f.*
internationalization ['intə,næʃnəlai'zeiʃən] n. Internacionalización, *f.*
internationalize [,intə'næʃnəlaiz] v. tr. Internacionalizar.
interne ['intə:n] n. See INTERN.
internecine [,intə'ni:sain] adj. De aniquilación mutua (mutually destructive): *internecine war*, guerra de aniquilación mutua. || Mortífero, ra (deadly).
internee [,intə:'ni:] n. Internado, da.
internist [in'tə:nist] n. MED. Internista, *m.* & *f.*, médico (*m.*) internista.
internment [in'tə:nmənt] n. MIL. Internamiento, *m.* || JUR. Internación, *f.*
internode ['intə:nəud] n. BOT. Entrenudo, *m.*
inter nos [intə:'nɔs] adv. phr. Entre nosotros.
internship ['intə:nʃip] n. U. S. Puesto (*m.*) de interno.
internuncio [,intə:'nʌnʃiəu] n. REL. Internuncio, *m.*
interoceanic ['intə:r,əuʃi'ænik] adj. Interoceánico, ca.
interosculate [,intə:'ɔskjuleit] v. intr. Entremezclarse, confundirse (to intermix). || BOL. Tener características comunes.
interpage [intə:'peidʒ] v. tr. Interpaginar.
interparietal [,intə:pə'raiitl] adj. ANAT. Interparietal.
interparliamentary ['intə:,pɑ:lə'mentəri] adj. Interparlamentario, ria.
interpellant [,intə:'pelənt] adj./n. Interpelador, ra; interpelante.
interpellate [in'tə:peleit] v. tr. Interpelar.
interpellation [in,tə:pe'leiʃən] n. Interpelación, *f.*
interpellator [in'tə:peleitə*] n. Interpelador, ra; interpelante, *m.* & *f.*
interpenetrate [,intə:'penitreit] v. tr. Penetrar.
— V. intr. Compenetrarse.
interpenetration ['intə:,peni'treiʃən] n. Compenetración, *f.* || Interpenetración, *f.*
interphone ['intə:fəun] n. Teléfono (*m.*) interior, interfono, *m.*
interplanetary [,intə'plænitəri] adj. Interplanetario, ria.
interplay ['intə'plei] n. Interacción, *f.*
interplay ['intə'plei] v. intr. Actuar recíprocamente.
interpolate [in'tə:pəuleit] v. tr. Interpolar.
interpolating [—iŋ] adj. Interpolador, ra.
interpolation [in,tə:pəu'leiʃən] n. Interpolación, *f.*
interpolator [in'tə:pəuleitə*] n. Interpolador, ra.
interposal [,intə:'pəuzl] n. Interposición, *f.* || Intervención, *f.*

interpose [ˌintəˈpəuz] v. tr. Interponer.
— V. intr. Interponerse (to come between). || Intervenir (to intervene). || Interrumpir (to interrupt).
interposed [—d] adj. Interpuesto, ta.
interposition [inˌtə:pəˈziʃən] n. Interposición, *f.*
interpret [inˈtə:prit] v. tr. Interpretar.
— V. intr. Hacer de intérprete (to act as an interpreter).
interpretable [—əbl] adj. Interpretable.
interpretation [inˌtə:priˈteiʃən] n. Interpretación, *f.*
interpretative [inˌtə:pritətiv] adj. Interpretativo, va.
interpreter [inˈtə:pritə*] n. Intérprete, *m.* & *f.*
interpretive [inˈtə:pritiv] adj. U. S. Interpretativo, va.
interprofessional [ˌintə:prəˈfeʃənl] adj. Interprofesional.
interregnum [ˌintəˈregnəm] n. Interregno, *m.*

— OBSERV. El plural de la palabra *interregnum* es *interregnums* o *interregna.*

interrelated [intə:riˈleitid] adj. Relacionado, da; estrechamente ligado, estrechamente vinculado.
interrelation [intə:riˈleiʃən] n. Correlación, *f.* || Relación, *f.*
interrogate [inˈterəugeit] v. tr. Interrogar.
interrogation [inˌterəuˈgeiʃən] n. Interrogatorio, *m.*: *a police interrogation,* un interrogatorio de la policía. || Interrogación, *f.* (question, questioning).
interrogative [ˌintəˈrɔgətiv] adj. Interrogativo, va: *interrogative sentence,* oración interrogativa. || Interrogador, ra: *an interrogative look,* una mirada interrogadora.
— N. Palabra (*f.*) *or* oración (*f.*) interrogativa.
interrogator [inˈterəugeitə*] n. Interrogador, ra.
interrogatory [ˌintəˈrɔgətəri] adj. Interrogador, ra.
— N. JUR. Interrogatorio, *m.*
interrupt [ˌintəˈrʌpt] v. tr. Interrumpir.
— V. intr. Interrumpir.
interrupter [—ə*] n. ELECTR. Interruptor, *m.*
interruption [ˌintəˈrʌpʃən] n. Interrupción, *f.*
interruptor [ˌintəˈrʌptə*] n. ELECTR. Interruptor, *m.*
intersect [ˌintəˈsekt] v. tr. Cruzar (to cross). || MATH. Cortar.
— V. intr. MATH. Intersecarse. || Cruzarse (roads).
intersection [—ʃən] n. Intersección, *f.* || Cruce, *m.* (crossroads).
intersession [ˈintəˌseʃən] n. U. S. Vacaciones (*f. pl.*) semestrales universitarias.
intersex [ˈintəseks] n. Individuo (*m.*) con características intersexuales.
intersexual [ˌintəˈseksjuəl] adj. Intersexual.
interspace [ˈintəˈspeis] n. Intervalo, *m.*, espacio (*m.*) intermedio.
interspace [ˈintəˈspeis] v. tr. Espaciar.
intersperse [ˌintəˈspə:s] v. tr. Esparcir, entremezclar: *daisies interspersed amongst the poppies,* margaritas esparcidas entre las amapolas. || Salpicar: *a field interspersed with poppies,* un campo salpicado de amapolas; *to intersperse a lecture with anecdotes,* salpicar de anécdotas una conferencia.
interspersion [ˌintəˈspə:ʃən] n. Mezcla, *f.*
interstate [intəˈsteit] adj. Entre estados.
interstellar [ˈintəˈstelə*] adj. Interestelar, intersideral.
interstice [inˈtə:stis] n. Intersticio, *m.*
interstitial [intəˈstiʃəl] adj. Intersticial.
intertrigo [ˌintəˈtraigəu] n. MED. Intertrigo, *m.*
intertropical [ˌintəˈtrɔpikəl] adj. Intertropical.
intertwine [ˌintəˈtwain] v. tr. Entrelazar.
— V. intr. Entrelazarse.
interurban [ˌintə:ˈə:bən] adj. Interurbano, na.
interval [ˈintəvəl] n. Intervalo, *m.* (period of time, space between two points). || Entreacto, *m.*, descanso, *m.* (in theatre). || Descanso, *m.* (in cinema, in sports events). || Descanso, *m.*, pausa, *f.* (short break). || MUS. Intervalo, *m.* || — *At intervals,* de vez en cuando, a intervalos (from time to time), de trecho en trecho, a intervalos (here and there). || *Bright intervals,* claros, *m.* (in meteorology).
intervene [ˌintəˈvi:n] v. intr. Intervenir, mediar: *to intervene in s.o.'s defence,* intervenir en defensa de alguien. || Ocurrir (to happen). || Transcurrir, mediar (time). || Mediar (distance). || *In the intervening days,* durante los días intermedios.
intervention [ˌintəˈvenʃən] n. Intervención, *f.*
interventionism [ˌintəˈvenʃənizəm] n. Intervencionismo, *m.*
interventionist [ˌintəˈvenʃənist] adj./n. Intervencionista.
interview [ˈintəvju:] n. Entrevista, *f.*, interviú, *f.*
interview [ˈintəvju:] v. tr. Entrevistar.
interviewer [—ə*] n. Entrevistador, ra.
interweave* [ˌintəˈwi:v] v. tr. Entretejer. || FIG. Entremezclar.
— V. intr. Entremezclarse.

— OBSERV. Pret. ***interwove;*** p. p. ***interwoven.***

interweaving [—iŋ] n. Entretejido, *m.*
interwove [ˌintəˈwəuv] pret. See INTERWEAVE.
interwoven [—ən] p. p. See INTERWEAVE.
intestacy [inˈtestəsi] n. JUR. Hecho (*m.*) de morir intestado. | Falta (*f.*) de testamento.
intestate [inˈtestit] adj./n. JUR. Intestado, da.
intestinal [inˈtestinl] adj. Intestinal. || U. S. *Intestinal fortitude,* valor, *m.*, estómago, *m.* (fam.).
intestine [inˈtestin] n. ANAT. Intestino, *m.*: *small, large intestine,* intestino delgado, grueso.
— Adj. Intestino, na: *intestine conflicts,* luchas intestinas.
intimacy [ˈintiməsi] n. Intimidad, *f.* (state of being intimate). || Relaciones (*f. pl.*) íntimas (sexual relations).
intimate [ˈintimit] adj. Íntimo, ma: *intimate friends,* amigos íntimos; *intimate feelings,* sentimientos íntimos. || Amoroso, sa (loving). || Personal: *an intimate style of writing,* un estilo personal. || Profundo, da: *intimate knowledge,* conocimiento profundo. || — *To become intimate with s.o.,* intimar con alguien. || *To be intimate with s.o.,* tener relaciones íntimas con alguien.
— N. Íntimo, *m.*
intimate [ˈintimeit] v. tr. Insinuar, dar a entender (to hint). || Anunciar, notificar (to announce).
intimating [ˈintimeitiŋ] adj. Intimatorio, ria.
intimation [ˌintiˈmeiʃən] n. Insinuación, *f.* (hint). || Indicio, *m.* (insight). || Indicación, *f.* (indication).
intimidate [inˈtimideit] v. tr. Intimidar.
intimidation [inˌtimiˈdeiʃən] n. Intimidación, *f.*
intimidator [inˈtimideitə*] n. Persona (*f.*) que intimida.
intimist [ˈintimist] adj./n. Intimista.
intimity [inˈtimiti] n. Intimidad, *f.*
intitule [inˈtitjul] v. tr. Titular (a legislative act).
into [ˈintu] prep. En: *to enter into,* entrar en; *to fall into enemy hands,* caer en manos del enemigo; *to come into contact with,* entrar en contacto con; *to change from one thing into another,* convertirse de una cosa en otra; *to fold into four,* doblar en cuatro. || A: *to open into the street,* dar a la calle; *to translate into French,* traducir al francés. || Hacia: *they went off into the setting sun,* se fueron hacia el sol poniente; *a journey into the future,* un viaje hacia el futuro. || Contra: *to crash into,* estrellarse contra. || Contra, con: *to bump into a tree,* tropezar contra un árbol; *to bump into an old friend,* tropezar con un viejo amigo. || Dentro: *get into the sack,* métete dentro del saco. || — *Three into twelve goes four,* doce entre tres son cuatro. || *To grow into a man,* hacerse un hombre. || *To work into the night,* trabajar hasta muy entrada la noche.

— OBSERV. La preposición "into" se emplea muy frecuentemente después de varios verbos (to come, to fall, to get, to go, etc.) cambiando su sentido. Por lo tanto remitimos a cada uno de ellos para sus distintas traducciones.

intolerability [inˌtɔlərəbiliti] n. Inadmisibilidad, *f.*
intolerable [inˈtɔlərəbl] adj. Intolerable, inadmisible.
intolerance [inˈtɔlərəns] n. Intolerancia, *f.*
intolerant [inˈtɔlərənt] adj./n. Intolerante (*of,* con, para).
intonate [ˈintəuneit] v. tr. See INTONE.
intonation [ˌintəuˈneiʃən] n. Entonación, *f.*
intone [inˈtəun] v. tr. Salmodiar (to chant). || Entonar (to sing the opening phrase of).
in toto [inˈtəuˈtəu] adv. En su totalidad.
intoxicant [inˈtɔksikənt] adj. Embriagador, ra.
— N. Bebida (*f.*) alcohólica (alcoholic drink). || Sustancia (*f.*) que embriaga (drug).
intoxicate [inˈtɔksikeit] v. tr. Embriagar, emborrachar (to make drunk). || MED. Intoxicar. || FIG. Embriagar (joy, etc.).
intoxicating [—iŋ] adj. Embriagador, ra.
intoxication [inˌtɔksiˈkeiʃən] n. Embriaguez, *f.*, borrachera, *f.* || MED. Intoxicación, *f.* || FIG. Embriaguez, *f.*
intracellular [ˌintrəˈseljulə*] adj. Intracelular.
intractability [inˌtræktəˈbiliti] n. Indocilidad, *f.* (of a person). || Insolubilidad, *f.* (of a problem). || Dificultad, *f.* (difficulty).
intractable [inˈtræktəbl] adj. Intratable (difficult to manage). || Indisciplinado, da (unruly). || Insoluble (problem). || TECH. Difícil de labrar. || MED. Incurable. || Incultivable (land).
intradermic [intrəˈdə:mik] adj. Intradérmico, ca.
intrados [inˈtreidɔs] n. ARCH. Intradós, *m.*
intramural [ˈintrəˈmjuərəl] adj. Situado intramuros.
intramurally [—i] adv. Intramuros.
intramuscular [ˈintrəˈmʌskjulə*] adj. Intramuscular: *intramuscular injection,* inyección intramuscular.
intransigence [inˈtrænsidʒəns] n. Intransigencia, *f.*
intransigency [—i] n. Intransigencia, *f.*
intransigent [inˈtrænsidʒənt] adj. Intransigente.
intransitive [inˈtrænsitiv] adj. Intransitivo, va.
— N. Intransitivo, *m.*
intransmissible [intrænsˈmisibl] adj. Intrasmisible.
intranuclear [intrəˈnju:kliə*] adj. PHYS. Intranuclear.
intrastate [ˌintrəˈsteit] adj. U. S. Interior.
intrauterine [intrəˈjutərain] adj. MED. Intrauterino, na.
intravenous [intrəˈvi:nəs] adj. Intravenoso, sa.
intravenously [—li] adv. Por vía intravenosa.
intreat [inˈtri:t] v. tr. Suplicar, implorar, rogar.
intrench [inˈtrentʃ] v. tr./intr. See ENTRENCH.
intrepid [inˈtrepid] adj. Intrépido, da.
intrepidity [intriˈpiditi] n. Intrepidez, *f.*
intricacy [ˈintrikəsi] n. Intrincamiento, *m.* || Dédalo, *m.*, laberinto, *m.* (of a town). || Complejidad, *f.* (of a problem).
intricate [ˈintrikit] adj. Intrincado, da. || Complejo, ja; complicado, da (problem).

intrigant [ˈintrigənt] n. Intrigante, *m.*
intrigante [intriˈgɑːnt] n. Intrigante, *f.*
intrigue [inˈtriːg] n. Intriga, *f.* (plot, etc.). || (Ant.) Relaciones (*f. pl.*) amorosas ilícitas.
intrigue [inˈtriːg] v. tr./intr. Intrigar: *she intrigues me*, me intriga; *they remained intriguing late into the night*, se quedaron intrigando hasta muy avanzada la noche.
intriguer [—ə*] n. Intrigante, *m.* & *f.*
intriguing [—iŋ] adj. Intrigante, enredador, ra (scheming). || Fascinante, misterioso, sa; curioso, sa; intrigante (fascinating).
intrinsic [inˈtrinsik] adj. Intrínseco, ca.
introduce [ˌintrəˈdjuːs] v. tr. Presentar: *may I introduce you to my wife?*, le presento a mi mujer; *to introduce s.o. into society*, presentar a alguien en sociedad. || Introducir: *to introduce a new fashion*, introducir una nueva moda; *to introduce one's products into foreign markets*, introducir sus productos en el mercado exterior; *to introduce s.o. into high society*, introducir a alguien en la alta sociedad. || Lanzar: *to introduce a new toothpaste*, lanzar una nueva pasta de dientes. || Iniciar: *to introduce s.o. to modern art*, iniciar a alguien en el arte moderno. || Introducir (to insert): *to introduce the key in the lock*, introducir la llave en la cerradura. || Presentar: *to introduce a bill before Parliament*, presentar un proyecto de ley ante el Parlamento. || Prologar (to preface a book). || — *He was introduced into a room*, lo hicieron entrar en una habitación. || *I was introduced into his presence*, me llevaron ante él. || *To introduce a question*, hacer una pregunta (to ask), abordar un tema (to bring a subject up).
introduction [ˌintrəˈdʌkʃən] n. Introducción, *f.* || Presentación, *f.* (of one person to another): *letter of introduction*, carta de presentación. || Introducción, *f.*, prólogo, *m.* (of a book). || Mus. Preludio, *m.*
introductive [ˌintrəˈdʌktiv] or **introductory** [ˌintrəˈdʌktəri] adj. Preliminar, introductorio, ria.
introit [ˈintrɔit] n. Rel. Introito, *m.*
intromission [ˌintrəuˈmiʃən] n. Introducción, *f.* (inserting). || Intromisión, *f.* (interference). || Admisión, *f.* (admission).
intromit [ˌintrəuˈmit] v. tr. Introducir, insertar (to put in). || Admitir.
introspect [ˌintrəuˈspekt] v. intr. Practicar la introspección.
introspection [ˌintrəuˈspekʃən] n. Introspección, *f.*
introspective [ˌintrəuˈspektiv] adj. Introspectivo, va.
introversion [ˌintrəuˈvəːʃən] n. Introversión, *f.*
introversive [ˌintrəuˈvəːsiv] adj. Introverso, sa.
introvert [ˈintrəuvəːt] adj./n. Introvertido, da.
introvert [ˌintrəuˈvəːt] v. tr. Volver hacia sí mismo (to direct upon o.s.). || Med. Invaginar.
introverted [—id] adj. Introvertido, da.
intrude [inˈtruːd] v. tr. Imponer (to force upon). || Meter por fuerza. || Geol. Introducir (to force between rock strata).
— V. intr. Entrometerse, inmiscuirse: *we were talking but he kept on intruding*, estábamos charlando, pero él seguía entrometiéndose. || Imponerse (to impose). || — *Am I intruding?*, ¿estorbo?, ¿molesto? || *To intrude upon*, interrumpir: *to intrude upon a conversation*, interrumpir una conversación; meterse en: *to intrude upon s.o.'s privacy*, meterse en la vida privada de alguien.
intruder [—ə*] n. Intruso, sa.
intrusion [inˈtruːʒən] n. Entremetimiento, *m.* (meddling). || Jur. Intrusión, *f.*, usurpación. *f.* || Geol Intrusión, *f.*
intrusive [inˈtruːsiv] adj. Intruso, sa.
intubate [ˈintjubeit] v. tr. Med. Intubar.
intubation [intjuˈbeiʃən] n. Med. Intubación, *f.*
intuit [inˈtjuːit] v. tr./intr. Intuir.
intuition [ˌintjuːˈiʃən] n. Intuición, *f.*
intuitional [ˌintjuːˈiʃənl] adj. Intuitivo, va.
intuitionism [ˌintjuːˈiʃənizəm] n. Intuicionismo, *m.*
intuitive [inˈtjuːitiv] adj. Intuitivo, va.
intuitiveness [—nis] n. Intuición, *f.*
intumesce [ˌintjuːˈmes] v. intr. Hincharse.
intumescence [—ns] n. Intumescencia, *f.*, tumefacción, *f.*, hinchazón, *f.*
intumescent [—nt] adj. Intumescente, tumefacto, ta; hinchado, da.
intussuscept [ˌintəssəˈsept] v. tr. Med. Invaginar.
inunction [inˈʌŋkʃən] n. Untura, *f.*, unción, *f.* (ointing). || Ungüento, *m.* (ointment).
inundable [iˈnʌndəbl] adj. Inundable (easily flooded).
inundate [ˈinʌndeit] v. tr. Inundar.
inundation [ˌinʌnˈdeiʃən] n. Inundación, *f.*
inurbane [ˌinəːˈbein] adj. Inurbano, na; descortés.
inurbanity [ˌinəːˈbæniti] n. Descortesía, *f.*
inure [iˈnjuə*] v. tr. Habituar, acostumbrar (to accustom). || Endurecer (to harden).
— V. intr. Jur. Entrar en vigor, aplicarse (to take effect).
inurement [—mənt] n. Hábito, *m.*, costumbre, *f.* (custom). || Endurecimiento, *m.* (hardening). || Jur. Entrada (*f.*) en vigor, aplicación, *f.*
inurn [inˈəːn] v. tr. Poner en una urna.
inutile [inˈjuːtail] adj. Inútil.
inutility [ˌinjuːˈtiliti] n. Inutilidad, *f.*
in vacuo [inˈvækjuəu] adv. En vacío.
invade [inˈveid] v. tr. Invadir (a country, region, etc.): *a city invaded by tourists*, una ciudad invadida por los turistas. || Meterse en: *to invade s.o.'s privacy*, meterse en la vida privada de alguien. || Usurpar (s.o.'s rights).
invader [—ə*] n. Invasor, ra.
invaginate [in vædʒineit] v. tr. Med. Invaginar.
— V. intr. Med. Invaginarse.
invagination [invædʒiˈneiʃən] n. Med. Invaginación, *f.*
invalid [ˈinvəliːd] adj. Inválido, da (disabled). || Enfermo, ma (sick). || Enfermizo, za (sickly). || Para enfermos (for sick people).
— N. Inválido, *m.*, persona (*f.*) inválida (incapacitated person). || Enfermo, ma (sick person).
invalid [inˈvælid] adj. Nulo, la: *an invalid contract*, un contrato nulo. || *To become invalid*, caducar.
invalid [ˌinvəˈliːd] v. tr. Dejar inválido (to disable). || Poner enfermo (to make sick). || *To invalid out*, dar de baja por invalidez (from military service).
— V. intr. Quedarse inválido. || Ponerse enfermo. || Darse de baja por invalidez.
invalidate [inˈvælideit] v. tr. Invalidad, anular.
invalidation [inˌvæliˈdeiʃən] n. Invalidación, *f.*, anulación, *f.*
invalidity [ˌinvəˈliditi] n. Med. Invalidez, *f.* (infirmity). | Enfermedad, *f.*, mala salud, *f.* (sickness). || Jur. Invalidez, *f.*, nulidad, *f.*
invaluable [inˈvæljuəbl] adj. Inestimable, inapreciable.
invar [inˈvɑː*] n. Invar, *m.* (metal).
invariability [inˌvɛəriəˈbiliti] n. Invariabilidad, *f.*
invariable [inˈvɛəriəbl] adj. Invariable.
invariably [inˈvɛəriəbli] adv. Invariablemente. || Siempre, constantemente (always).
invariant [inˈvɛəriənt] adj. Invariable, constante.
invasion [inˈveiʒən] n. Invasión, *f.* (an invading or being invaded). || Jur. Usurpación, *f.* (of s.o.'s rights). || Entremetimiento, *m.* (intrusion).
invasive [inˈveisiv] adj. Invasor, ra.
invective [inˈvektiv] n. Invectiva, *f.*: *to thunder invectives against s.o.*, fulminar invectivas contra alguien.
inveigh [inˈvei] v. intr. *To inveigh against*, lanzar invectivas contra, vituperar.
inveigle [inˈviːgl] v. tr. Embaucar, engatusar (to cajole): *he inveigled me into doing such a thing*, me embaucó para que hiciese tal cosa.
inveiglement [—mənt] n. Embaucamiento, *m.*, engatusamiento, *m.*
invent [inˈvent] v. tr. Inventar.
invention [inˈvenʃən] n. Invención, *f.*, invento, *m.* *of his own invention*, de su propia invención. || Inventiva, *f.* (inventiveness). || Mentira, *f.* (untrue story).
inventive [inˈventiv] adj. Inventivo, va.
inventiveness [—nis] n. Inventiva, *f.*
inventor [inˈventə*] n. Inventor, ra.
inventory [ˈinvəntri] n. Inventario, *m.* (itemized list). || Existencias, *f. pl.* (stock).
inventory [ˈinvəntri] v. tr. Inventariar, hacer un inventario de.
inverness [ˌinvəˈnis] n. Macfarlán, *m.*, macferlán, *m.*
inverse [ˈinˈvəːs] adj. Inverso, sa.
— N. Lo inverso (opposite). || Lo contrario, *m.* (contrary).
inversion [inˈvəːʃən] n. Inversión, *f.* (an inverting or sth. inverted). || Gramm. Inversión, *f.* || Math. Inversión, *f.* || Inversión, *f.* [sexual] (homosexuality).
inversive [inˈvəːsiv] adj. Inverso, sa.
invert [ˈinvəːt] n. Invertido, da.
— Adj. Invertido, da (sugar).
invert [inˈvəːt] v. tr. Invertir.
invertebrata [inˌvəːtiˈbrɑːtə] pl. n. Invertebrados, *m.*
invertebrate [inˈvəːtibrit] adj. Zool. Invertebrado, da.
— N. Zool. Invertebrado, *m.*
inverted commas [inˈvəːtidˈkɔməz] pl. n. Comillas, *f.*
invest [in vest] v. tr. Invertir: *to invest money in a business*, invertir dinero en un negocio. || Investir (to install in office). || Conferir [with a dignity, etc.]. || Envolver: *invested with an air of mystery*, envuelto en un aire de misterio. || Mil. Sitiar, cercar (to besiege).
— V. intr. Hacer una inversión, invertir dinero. || Fig. Fam. *To invest in*, comprarse: *I invested in a new dress yesterday*, ayer me compré un nuevo traje.
investigate [inˈvestigeit] v. tr. Investigar. || Examinar (to examine). || Estudiar (to study).
— V. intr. Hacer una investigación.
investigating [—iŋ] adj. Investigador, ra.
investigation [inˌvestiˈgeiʃən] n. Investigación, *f.* || Estudio, *m.* (study).
investigative [inˈvestigeitiv] adj. Investigador, ra.
investigator [inˈvestigeitə*] n. Investigador, ra.
investigatory [inˈvestigeitəri] adj. Investigador, ra.
investiture [inˈvestitʃə*] n. Investidura, *f.*
investment [inˈvestmənt] n. Inversión, *f.*: *a two hundred pound investment*, una inversión de doscientas libras. || Mil. Sitio, *m.*, cerco, *m.* || Jur. Rel. Investidura, *f.* (investiture). || — Pl. Inversiones, *f.* (money invested). || Valores (*m.*) en cartera (shares).
investor [inˈvestə*] n. Inversionista, *m.* & *f.*
inveteracy [inˈvetərəsi] n. Lo arraigado (of a habit). || Costumbre (*f.*) arraigada (long standing habit).
inveterate [inˈvetərit] adj. Inveterado, da; empedernido, da (smoker, etc.). || Arraigado, da (habit).
invidious [inˈvidiəs] adj. Odioso, sa (odious): *invidious comparisons*, comparaciones odiosas. || Que produce envidia (causing envy).
invigilate [inˈvidʒileit] v. tr. Vigilar [a los candidatos].
invigilator [—ə*] n. Vigilante, *m.*

invigorate [inˈvigəreit] v. tr. Vigorizar, dar vigor a, fortificar (to give vigour to). || Animar, estimular (to enliven).
invigorating [—iŋ] adj. Tónico, ca; que da vigor. || Estimulante.
invigoration [in,vigəˈreiʃən] n. Fortalecimiento, *m.*
invigorative [inˈvigərətiv] adj. Fortificante, tónico, ca.
invigorator [inˈvigə,reitə*] n. Tónico, *m.*
invincibility [in,vinsiˈbiliti] n. Invencibilidad, *f.*
invincible [inˈvinsəbl] adj. Invencible.
inviolability [in,vaiələˈbiliti] n. Inviolabilidad, *f.*
inviolable [inˈvaiələbl] adj. Inviolable.
inviolate [inˈvaiəlit] adj. Inviolado, da.
invisibility [in,vizəˈbiliti] n. Invisibilidad, *f.*
invisible [inˈvizəbl] adj. Invisible. || *Invisible ink*, tinta simpática.
— N. Lo invisible. || *The Invisible*, Dios (God), el mundo invisible (unseen world).
invitation [,inviˈteiʃən] n. Invitación, *f.*: *invitation card*, tarjeta de invitación.
invitatory [inˈvaitətəri] n. REL. Invitatorio, *m.* (in church services).
invite [inˈvait] n. FAM. Invitación, *f.*
invite [inˈvait] v. tr. Invitar, convidar: *to invite s.o. to dinner*, invitar a alguien a cenar. || Pedir, solicitar (to ask for). || Solicitar (questions, opinions). || Incitar (to incite). || Provocar (to cause): *his suggestion invited a lot of criticism*, su sugerencia provocó muchas críticas. || Buscarse: *to invite trouble*, buscarse problemas.
inviting [—iŋ] adj. Atractivo, va (attractive). || Tentador, ra (tempting). || Seductor, ra (seductive). || Provocativo, va (provocative). || Apetitoso, sa (food).
invitingly [—iŋli] adv. De forma atractiva *or* tentadora. || *The door was invitingly open*, la puerta abierta invitaba a entrar.
invocation [,invəuˈkeiʃən] n. Invocación, *f.* || *Under the invocation of*, bajo la advocación de.
invocatory [inˈvɔkətəri] adj. Invocatorio, ria.
invoice [ˈinvɔis] n. COMM. Factura, *f.*: *pro forma invoice*, factura pro forma. || — *As per invoice*, según factura. || *Invoice clerk*, facturador, ra. || *To make out an invoice*, extender una factura.
invoice [ˈinvɔis] v. tr. COMM. Facturar.
invoke [inˈvəuk] v. tr. Invocar (to appeal to in prayer). || Invocar (evil spirits). || Recurrir a, acogerse a, invocar (to fall back on): *he invoked his special powers to justify the action*, recurrió a sus poderes especiales para justificar su acción. || Suplicar, implorar (to implore). || Pedir (to ask for): *to invoke s.o.'s aid*, pedir la ayuda de alguien.
invoker [—ə*] n. Invocador, ra.
involucrate [,invəˈlu:krət] adj. Involucrado, da.
involuntarily [inˈvɔləntərili] adv. Sin querer, involuntariamente.
involuntary [inˈvɔləntəri] adj. Involuntario, ria.
involute [ˈinvəlu:t] n. MATH. Involuta, *f.*
— Adj. Enrevesado, da; complicado, da (involved). || Espiral, en espiral.
involution [,invəˈlu:ʃən] n. Complicación, *f.* (entanglement). || MATH. BIOL. MED. Involución, *f.*
involve [inˈvɔlv] v. tr. Concernir, atañer: *this problem involves us all*, este problema nos concierne a todos. || Afectar (to affect). || Suponer, implicar (to imply): *this job involves little work*, este empleo supone poco trabajo. || Acarrear, ocasionar (to entail). || Comprometer, complicar: *to involve s.o. in a theft*, comprometer a uno en un robo. || Mezclar, envolver, meter: *don't involve me in the argument*, no me mezcles a mí en la discusión. || Requerir, exigir (to require): *it involves a large labour force*, requiere un gran número de trabajadores. || Comprender (to include). || Enredar, complicar (to complicate). || (Ant.). Envolver (to wrap). || MATH. Elevar a cierta potencia. || — *A question of honour is involved*, el honor está en juego, se trata de una cuestión de honor. || *The forces involved*, las fuerzas en juego. || *Those involved*, los interesados. || *To be involved in*, estar metido *or* complicado en. || *To get involved in*, meterse en, enredarse en.
involved [—d] adj. Complicado, da; enrevesado, da. || See INVOLVE.
involvement [—mənt] n. Envolvimiento, *m.* (an involving). || Complicación, *f.*, enredo, *m.* (complicated state of affairs). || Compromiso, *m.* (in politics, etc.). || Participación, *f.*, implicación, *f.* (in a plot).
invulnerability [in,vʌlnərəˈbiliti] n. Invulnerabilidad, *f.*
invulnerable [inˈvʌlnərəbl] adj. Invulnerable.
inwall [ˈinwɔ:l] v. tr. U. S. Cercar con un muro.
inward [ˈinwəd] adj. Interior, interno, na: *inward peace*, paz interior. || Íntimo, ma: *inward thoughts*, pensamientos íntimos.
— Adv. Hacia dentro.
inward-flow [—fləu] adj. Centrípeto, ta.
inwardly [—li] adv. Interiormente. || *To laugh inwardly*, reír para sus adentros.
inwardness [—nis] n. Espiritualidad, *f.* (spirituality). || Esencia, *f.* (inner nature). || Sentido (*m.*) profundo (meaning).
inwards [ˈinwədz] adv. Hacia dentro.
— Pl. n. FAM. Tripas, *f.*, entrañas, *f.*
inweave* [ˈinˈwi:v] v. tr. Entretejer.
— OBSERV. Pret **inwove;** p. p. **inwoven.**
inwrap [ˈinræp] v. tr. Envolver.
inwrought [ˈinˈrɔ:t] adj. Bordado, da. || Incrustado, da (inlaid). || Entretejido, da (interwoven).
iodate [ˈaiəudeit] n. CHEM. Yodato, *m.*
iodate [ˈaiəudeit] v. tr. Tratar con iodo, yodar.
iodic [aiˈɔdik] adj. CHEM. Yódico, ca: *iodic acid*, ácido yódico.
iodide [ˈaiəudaid] n. CHEM. Yoduro, *m.*
iodine [ˈaiəudi:n] n. CHEM. Yodo, *m.*
iodism [ˈaiəudizəm] n. MED. Yodismo, *m.*
iodization [aiəudaiˈzeiʃən] n. Yoduración, *f.*
iodize [ˈaiəudaiz] v. tr. Yodar.
iodoform [aiˈɔdəfɔ:m] n. CHEM. Yodoformo, *m.*
ion [ˈaiən] n. CHEM. PHYS. Ion, *m.* || *Ion exchange*, intercambio (*m.*) de iones.
Ionia [aiˈəunjə] pr. n. GEOGR. Jonia, *f.*
Ionian [—n] adj./n. Jonio, nia; jónico, ca. || GEOGR. *Ionian Sea*, Mar Jónico.
ionic [aiˈɔnik] adj. CHEM. PHYS. Iónico, ca.
Ionic [aiˈɔnik] adj. Jónico, ca.
ionization [,aiənaiˈzeiʃən] n. CHEM. PHYS. Ionización, *f.*
ionize [ˈaiənaiz] v. tr. CHEM. PHYS. Ionizar.
— V. intr. CHEM. PHYS. Ionizarse.
ionosphere [aiˈɔnəsfiə*] n. Ionosfera, *f.*
iota [aiˈəutə] n. Iota, *f.* (letter of the Greek alphabet). || Pizca, *f.*, ápice, *m.* (a very small amount): *not an iota of truth*, ni una pizca de verdad.
IOU [ˈaiəuˈju:] n. Pagaré, *m.*
ipecac [ˈipikæk] n. BOT. Ipecacuana, *f.*
ipecacuanha [,ipikækjuˈænə] n. BOT. Ipecacuana, *f.*
ipso facto [ˈipsəuˈfæktəu] adv. phr. Ipso facto.
Irak [iˈrɑ:k] pr. n. GEOGR. Irak, *m.*, Iraq, *m.*
Iran [i:ˈrɑ:n] pr. n. GEOGR. Irán, *m.*
Iranian [iˈreinjən] adj. Iranio, nia; iraní.
— N. Iranio, nia; iraní, *m.* & *f.* (inhabitant of Iran). || Iranio, *m.* (language).
Iraq [iˈrɑ:k] pr. n. GEOGR. Irak, *m.*, Iraq, *m.*
Iraqi [—i] adj. Iraquí, iraqués, esa.
— N. Iraquí, *m.* & *f.*, iraqués, esa (inhabitant of Iraq). || Iraquí, *m.*, iraqués, *m.* (language).
Iraqian [—iən] adj./n. See IRAQI.
irascibility [i,ræsiˈbiliti] n. Irascibilidad, *f.*
irascible [iˈræsibl] adj. Irascible, colérico, ca.
irate [aiˈreit] adj. Airado, da; furioso, sa.
ire [ˈaiə*] n. Ira, *f.*, cólera, *f.*
ireful [—ful] adj. Iracundo, da.
Ireland [ˈaiələnd] pr. n. GEOGR. Irlanda, *f.* : *Northern Ireland*, Irlanda del Norte.
Irene [aiˈri:ni] pr. n. Irene, *f.*
irenic [—k] or **irenical** [—kəl] adj. REL. Pacífico, ca.
iridaceae [irideisi:i] pl. n. BOT. Iridáceas, *f.*
iridescence [iriˈdesns] n. Iridiscencia, *f.*, irisación, *f.*
iridescent [iriˈdesnt] adj. Iridiscente, irisado, da.
iridium [aiˈridiəm] n. CHEM. Iridio, *m.*
iris [ˈaiəris] n. ANAT. Iris, *m.* || BOT. Lirio, *m.* || Iris, *m.*, arco (*m.*) iris (rainbow).
— OBSERV. El plural de la palabra inglesa es *irises* o *irides.*
iris diaphragm [—ˈdaiəfræm] n. PHOT. Diafragma (*m.*) iris.
Irish [ˈaiəriʃ] adj. Irlandés, esa. || *Irish Free State*, Estado (*m.*) libre de Irlanda.
— N. Irlandés, *m.*, (language). || *The Irish*, los irlandeses.
Irish coffee [—ˈkɔfi] n. Café (*m.*) irlandés, café (*m.*) con whisky y nata.
Irishism [—izəm] n. Modismo (*m.*) irlandés.
Irishman [—mən] n. Irlandés, *m.*
— OBSERV. El plural de *Irishman* es *Irishmen.*
Irish potato [—pəˈteitəu] n. BOT. Patata (*f.*) blanca.
Irish Sea [—si:] pr. n. GEOGR. Mar (*m.*) de Irlanda.
Irish whiskey [—ˈwiski] n. Whisky (*m.*) irlandés.
Irishwoman [—,wumən] n. Irlandesa, *f.*
— OBSERV. El plural de *Irishwoman* es *Irishwomen.*
irk [ə:k] v. tr. Molestar, fastidiar.
irksome [—səm] adj. Molesto, da; fastidioso, sa.
irksomeness [—səmnis] n. Molestia, *f.*, fastidio, *f.*
iron [ˈaiən] n. MIN. Hierro, *m.* (metal): *red-hot iron*, hierro candente. || Plancha, *f.* (for pressing clothes). || Hierro (*m.*) candente (for branding). || SP. Palo (*m.*) de golf (golf club). || FIG. Hierro, *m.*, acero, *m.*: *a man of iron*, un hombre de hierro. || FAM. Revólver, *m.*, pistola, *f.* (firearm). || — Pl. Hierros, *m.*, grilletes, *m.*, grillos, *m.* (chains). || — *Cast iron*, hierro colado, arrabio, *m.*, fundición, *f.* || *Corrugated iron*, chapa ondulada. || *Curling iron*, tenacillas (*f. pl.*) de rizar, rizador (*m.*) para el pelo. || *In irons*, encadenado. || *Iron plate*, pletina, *f.* || *Merchant iron*, hierro comercial. || *Old iron*, chatarra, *f.*, hierro viejo. || *Pig iron*, arrabio, *m.*, hierro colado, hierro en lingotes. || *Round, soft iron*, hierro redondo, dulce. || *Square iron bar*, hierro cuadradillo *or* cuadrado. || FIG. *Strike while the iron is hot*, al hierro candente batir de repente. || FIG. *To have many irons in the fire*, tener muchas actividades (to be busy), tener muchos recursos (to be resourceful). | *Will of iron*, voluntad de hierro, voluntad férrea. || *Wrought iron*, hierro forjado.
iron [ˈaiən] v. tr. Planchar (to press). || Herrar (to guarnish with iron). || *To iron out*, planchar (a crease), hacer desaparecer, suprimir (to remove), allanar (difficulties).
— V. intr. Planchar.

Iron Age [—eidʒ] n. GEOL. Edad (*f.*) de hierro.
ironbound [—baund] adj. Zunchado, da (bound with iron). || Inflexible, férreo, a (inflexible). || Escabroso, sa (rocky).
ironclad [—klæd] adj. Acorazado, da (protected by iron plates). || U. S. Riguroso, sa (rigorous, strict).
— N. MAR. Acorazado, *m.*
Iron Curtain [—ˈkəːtn] n. FIG. Telón (*m.*) de acero.
ironer [ˈaiənə*] n. Planchador, ra.
iron foundry [ˌfaundri] n. Fundición (*f.*) de hierro.
iron grey [—ˈgrei] adj. Gris oscuro. || Entrecano, na (hair).
— N. Gris (*m.*) oscuro.
iron horse [—hɔːs] n. FAM. Locomotora, *f.* (locomotive). | Ferrocarril, *m.* (train).
ironic [airɔnik] or **ironical** [—əl] adj. Irónico, ca.
ironing [ˈaiəniŋ] n. Planchado, *m.* || *When I finish the ironing*, cuando termine de planchar.
ironing board [—bɔːd] n. Tabla (*f.*) *or* mesa (*f.*) de planchar.
ironist [ˈaiənist] n. Ironista, *m.* & *f.*
iron lung [ˈaiənlʌŋ] n. MED. Pulmón (*m.*) de acero.
ironmaster [—ˈmɑːstə*] n. Fabricante (*m.*) de hierro.
iron mold [—məuld] n. U. S. Mancha (*f.*) de tinta *or* de moho.
ironmonger [—ˌmʌŋgə*] n. Quincallero, *m.*, ferretero, *m.* (hardware dealer).
ironmongery [—ˌmʌŋgəri] n. Quincallería, *f.*, ferretería, *f.* (place). || Quincalla, *f.*, ferretería, *f.* (wares).
iron mould [—məuld] n. Mancha (*f.*) de tinta *or* de moho.
iron ore [—ɔ*] n. Mineral (*m.*) de hierro.
ironside [—said] n. Hombre (*m.*) valiente.
Ironsides [—saidz] pl. n. HIST. Caballería (*f. sing.*) de Cromwell en la guerra civil inglesa.
ironstone [—stəun] n. MIN. Mineral (*m.*) de hierro.
ironware [—wɛə*] n. Quincalla, *f.*, ferretería, *f.*
ironwood [—wud] n. BOT. Quiebrahacha, *m.*, jabí, *m.*
ironwork [—wəːk] n. Herrajes, *m. pl.*: *the ironwork on a trunk*, los herrajes de un baúl. || Carpintería (*f.*) metálica, armazón (*f.*) de hierro (iron framework).
ironworker [—wəːkə*] n. Herrero, *m.*
ironworks [—wəːks] n. Fundición (*f.*) de hierro (iron foundry). || Fábrica (*f.*) siderúrgica (iron and steel works).
irony [ˈaiəni] adj. De hierro.
irony [ˈaiərəni] n. Ironía, *f.* || *The irony is that...*, lo gracioso es que...
irradiance [iˈreidjəns] n. Irradiación, *f.*, radiación, *f.* || Resplandor, *m.* (brightness).
irradiant [iˈreidjənt] adj. Radiante. || Resplandeciente (brilliant).
irradiate [iˈreidieit] v. tr. Irradiar. || FIG. Iluminar.
— V. intr. Lucir, brillar.
irradiation [iˌreidiˈeiʃən] n. Irradiación, *f.*
irradiative [iˈreidiˌeitiv] adj. Radiante (irradiant). || FIG. Que ilumina (for the soul, etc.).
irrational [iˈræʃənl] adj. Irracional.
— N. MATH. Número (*m.*) irracional.
irrationalism [iˈræʃənəlizm] n. PHIL. Irracionalismo, *m.*
irrationalist [iˈræʃənəlist] adj./n. Irracionalista.
irrationality [iˈræʃəˈnæliti] n. Irracionalidad, *f.*, sinrazón, *f.* (quality). || Absurdo, *m.* (act).
irreceivability [iriˌsiːvəˈbiliti] n. Inadmisibilidad, *f.*
irreceivable [iriˈsiːvəbl] adj. JUR. Inadmisible.
irreclaimable [ˌiriˈkleiməbl] adj. Incorregible (person). || Incultivable (land).
irrecognizable [iˈrekəgnaizəbl] adj. Irreconocible.
irreconcilability [iˌrekənsailəbiliti] n. Imposibilidad (*f.*) de reconciliar (of enemies). || Incompatibilidad, *f.* (of opinions).
irreconcilable [iˈrekənsailəbl] adj. Irreconciliable (enemies). || Inconciliable, incompatible (ideas).
— N. Persona (*f.*) intransigente. || — Pl. Ideas (*f.*) inconciliables.
irrecoverable [ˌiriˈkʌvərəbl] adj. Irrecuperable (object). || Irrecuperable, incobrable (money). || FIG. Irremediable (loss).
irrecusable [iriˈkjuːzəbl] adj. Irrecusable.
irredeemable [ˌiriˈdiːməbl] adj. Irredimible (that cannot be bought back). || COMM. No amortizable (government loan or annuity). | Inconvertible (paper money). || FIG. Irremediable (without remedy). | Incorregible (incorrigible). | Irreparable (fault).
irredentism [ˌiriˈdentizəm] n. Irredentismo, *m.*
irredentist [ˌiriˈdentist] n. Irredentista, *m.* & *f.*
irreducibility [ˌiridjuːsiˈbiliti] n. Irreductibilidad, *f.*
irreducible [ˌiriˈdjuːsəbl] adj. Irreducible, irreductible.
irrefragability [iˌrefrægəˈbiliti] n. Incontestabilidad, *f.*, indiscutibilidad, *f.*
irrefragable [iˈrefrəgəbl] adj. Incontestable, indiscutible, irrefragable.
irrefrangible [ireˈfrændʒibl] adj. Inviolable (law).
irrefutable [iˈrefjutəbl] adj. Irrefutable, irrebatible.
irregular [iˈregjulə*] adj. Irregular: *irregular attendance, conduct*, asistencia, conducta irregular; *irregular verb*, verbo irregular. || Desigual (surface).
— N. MIL. Soldado (*m.*) irregular.
irregularity [iˌregjuˈlæriti] n. Irregularidad, *f.* || Desigualdad, *f.* (of a surface).
irrelevance [iˈrelivəns] or **irrelevancy** [—i] n. Falta (*f.*) de pertinencia, impertinencia, *f.* || Observación (*f.*) fuera de lugar (irrelevant remark). || JUR. Improcedencia, *f.*
irrelevant [iˈrelivənt] adj. Fuera de propósito, fuera de lugar (remark). || Impertinente, no pertinente (not to the point). || JUR. Improcedente. || *Questions that are irrelevant to the subject being discussed*, cuestiones que no tienen nada que ver con el tema discutido *or* ajenas al tema discutido.
irrelievable [iriˈliːvəbl] adj. Imposible de aplacar *or* de aliviar. || Irremediable.
irreligion [ˌiriˈlidʒən] n. Irreligión, *f.*
irreligious [ˌiriˈlidʒəs] adj. Irreligioso, sa.
irreligiousness [—nis] n. Irreligiosidad, *f.*
irremediable [ˌiriˈmiːdjəbl] adj. Irremediable.
irremissible [iriˈmisibl] adj. Irremisible (unpardonable). || Inevitable (unavoidable).
irremovability [ˈiriˌmuːvəˈbiliti] n. Inamovilidad, *f.* (of civil servant).
irremovable [iriˈmuːvəbl] adj. Inamovible. || Inmutable (immutable). || FIG. Invencible, insuperable (obstacle).
irreparable [iˈrepərəbl] adj. Irreparable (that cannot be repaired). || Irremediable (that cannot be remedied).
irreplaceable [ˌiriˈpleisəbl] adj. Irreemplazable, irremplazable, insustituible.
irreprehensible [ˌiripriˈhensəbl] adj. Irreprensible.
irrepressible [ˌiriˈpresəbl] adj. Incontenible: *irrepressible laughter*, risa incontenible. || Incontrolable.
irreproachable [ˌiriˈprəutʃəbl] adj. Irreprochable, intachable, irreprensible.
irresistibility [ˈiriˌzistəˈbiliti] n. Lo irresistible.
irresistible [ˌiriˈzistəbl] adj. Irresistible.
irresolute [iˈrezəluːt] adj. Irresoluto, ta; indeciso, sa.
irresolution [ˈiˌrezəˈluːʃən] or **irresoluteness** [iˈrezəluːtnis] n. Irresolución, *f.*, indecisión, *f.*
irresolvable [ˌiriˈzɔlvəbl] adj. Irresoluble, insoluble (unsolvable). || CHEM. Irreducible.
irrespective [ˌirisˈpektiv] adj. Desconsiderado, da. || *Irrespective of*, sin tomar en consideración, sin tener en cuenta.
irrespirable [iˈrespirəbl] adj. Irrespirable.
irresponsibility [ˈirisˌpɔnsəˈbiliti] n. Irreflexión, *f.*, irresponsabilidad, *f.*, falta (*f.*) de seriedad. || JUR. Irresponsabilidad, *f.*
irresponsible [ˌirisˈpɔnsəbl] adj. Irreflexivo, va; irresponsable; poco serio, ria. || JUR. Irresponsable.
irresponsive [ˌirisˈpɔnsiv] adj. Poco entusiasta, frío, a (not enthusiastic). || Insensible (insensitive): *irresponsive to entreaties*, insensible a las súplicas.
irresponsiveness [—nis] n. Frialdad, *f.*, insensibilidad, *f.* (insensitiveness).
irretentive [ˌiriˈtentiv] adj. *Irretentive memory*, mala memoria.
irretrievable [ˌiriˈtriːvəbl] adj. Irrecuperable. || Irreparable, irremediable (error).
irreverence [iˈrevərəns] n. Irreverencia, *f.*, falta (*f.*) de respeto.
irreverent [iˈrevərənt] adj. Irreverente, irrespetuoso, sa.
irreversibility [ˈiriˌvəːsəˈbiliti] n. Irreversibilidad, *f.* || Irrevocabilidad, *f.* (of a decision).
irreversible [ˌiriˈvəːsəbl] adj. Irreversible. || Irrevocable (decision).
irrevocability [iˌrevəkəˈbiliti] n. Irrevocabilidad, *f.*
irrevocable [iˈrevəkəbl] adj. Irrevocable.
irrigable [ˈirigəbl] adj. Irrigable. || *Irrigable lands*, tierras de regadío.
irrigate [ˈirigeit] v. tr. AGR. Irrigar, regar. || MED. Irrigar.
irrigation [ˌiriˈgeiʃən] n. AGR. Irrigación, *f.*, riego, *m.* || MED. Irrigación, *f.* || *Irrigation channel*, acequia, *f.*, canal (*m.*) de riego.
irrigator [ˈirigeitə*] n. AGR. Regador, ra (person). | Regadera, *f.* (implement). || MED. Irrigador, *m.*
irritability [ˌiritəˈbiliti] n. Irritabilidad, *f.*
irritable [ˈiritəbl] adj. Irritable.
irritably [—i] adv. Con tono malhumorado, de mal talante.
irritant [ˈiritənt] adj. Irritante.
— N. Agente (*m.*) irritante.
irritate [ˈiriteit] v. tr. MED. Irritar (organ, skin). | Enconar (wound). || FIG. Irritar, poner nervioso. || *To get irritated*, irritarse, ponerse nervioso.
irritating [—iŋ] adj. Irritante: *an irritating effect on the skin*, un efecto irritante en la piel. || Molesto, ta; enojoso, sa (annoying).
irritation [ˌiriˈteiʃən] n. Irritación, *f.*
irritative [ˈiriteitiv] adj. MED. Que irrita, irritante.
irrupt [iˈrʌpt] v. intr. Irrumpir (*into*, en).
irruption [iˈrʌpʃən] n. Irrupción, *f.*
is [iz] 3rd pers. sing. pres. indic. See BE.
Isaac [ˈaizək] pr. n. Isaac, *m.*
Isabel [ˈizəbel] or **Isabella** [izəˈbelə] pr. n. Isabel, *f.*
Isabelline [izəˈbelin] adj./n. Isabelino, na.
Isaiah [aiˈzaiə] pr. n. Isaías, *m.*
isba [ˈizbə] n. Isba, *f.*
ischemia [isˈkiːmiə] n. MED. Isquemia, *f.*
ischium [ˈiskiəm] n. ANAT. Isquion, *m.*

— OBSERV. El plural de la palabra inglesa es *ischia*.

Ishmael [ˈiʃmeiəl] pr. n. Ismael, *m.*
Ishmaelite [ˈiʃmiəlait] adj./n. Ismaelita.
Isidore [ˈizidɔː*] pr. n. Isidoro, *m.*, Isidro, *m.*
Isidorian [ˌiziˈdɔːriən] adj. Isidoriano, na.

isinglass [ˈaiziŋglɑ:s] n. Ictiocola, *f.*, cola (*f.*) de pescado (glue). || MIN. Mica, *f.* (mica).
Isis [ˈaisis] pr. n. Isis, *f.*
Islam [ˈizlɑ:m] n. Islam, *m.*
Islamic [izˈlæmik] adj. Islámico, ca.
Islamism [ˈizləmizəm] n. Islamismo, *m.*
Islamite [ˈizləmait] adj./n. Islamita.
islamization [izləmiˈzeiʃən] n. Islamización, *f.*
islamize [ˈizləmaiz] v. tr. Islamizar.
island [ˈailənd] n. Isla, *f.* (in the sea). || Isleta, *f.*, refugio, *m.* (traffic island). || MAR. Superestructura, *f.* (of an aircraft carrier). || *Small island*, isla pequeña, islote, *m.*
island [ˈailənd] v. tr. Aislar (to isolate). || Salpicar (to intersperse with).
islander [—ə*] n. Isleño, ña; insular, *m.* & *f.*
isle [ail] n. Islote, *m.*, isleta, *f.* (small island). || Isla, *f.*: *the Isle of Wight*, la Isla de Wight; *the British Isles*, las Islas Británicas.
islet [ˈailit] n. Islote, *m.*
ism [ˈizəm] n. FAM. Ismo, *m.* (theory).
isn't [ˈiznt] contraction of *is not*.
isobar [ˈaisəubɑ:*] n. Isobara, *f.*
isobaric [aisəˈbærik] adj. Isobárico, ca.
isochromatic [ˌaisəukrəuˈmætik] adj. Isocromático, ca.
isochronous [aiˈsɔkrənəs] adj. Isócrono, na.
isoclinal [aisəˈklainəl] adj. GEOL. Isoclinal. || Isoclino, na: *isoclinal line*, línea isoclina.
isocline [ˈaisəklain] n. GEOL. Pliegue (*m.*) isoclinal.
isogamous [aiˈsɔgəməs] adj. BIOL. Isógamo, ma.
isogamy [aiˈsɔgəmi] n. BIOL. Isogamia, *f.*
isogloss [ˈaisəuglɔs] n. Isoglosa, *f.*
isogonal [aiˈsɔgənəl] adj. Isógono, na.
isogonic [aisəˈgɔnik] adj. Isógono, na.
isolate [ˈaisəleit] v. tr. Aislar.
isolating [—iŋ] adj. Aislador, ra.
isolation [ˌaisəuˈleiʃən] n. Aislamiento, *m.*
isolationism [ˌaisəuˈleiʃnizəm] n. Aislacionismo, *m.*
isolationist [ˌaisəuˈleiʃnist] adj./n. Aislacionista.
isolator [ˈaisəleitə*] n. Aislante, *m.*, aislador, *m.*
isomer [ˈaisəmə*] n. Isómero, *m.*
isomeric [ˌaisəuˈmerik] adj. Isómero, ra.
isomerism [aiˈsɔmərizm] n. CHEM. Isomería, *f.*
isomerous [aiˈsɔmerəs] adj. Isómero, ra.
isometric [ˌaisəuˈmetrik] or **isometrical** [—əl] adj. Isométrico, ca.
isomorph [ˌaisəuˈmɔ:f] n. Cuerpo (*m.*) isomorfo.
isomorphic [—ik] adj. Isomorfo, fa.
isomorphism [—izəm] n. Isomorfismo, *m.*
isomorphous [—əs] adj. Isomorfo, fa.
isopod [ˈaisəpɔd] n. ZOOL. Isópodo, *m.* (crustacean).
— Adj. ZOOL. Isópodo, da.
isosceles [aiˈsɔsili:z] adj. MATH. Isósceles: *isosceles triangle*, triángulo isósceles.
isotherm [ˈaisəuθə:m] n. Isoterma, *f.*
isothermal [ˌaisəuˈθə:məl] adj. Isotermo, ma; isotérmico, ca.
isothermic [ˌaisəuˈθə:mik] adj. Isotérmico, ca.
isotonic [aisəuˈtɔnik] adj. PHYS. Isotónico, va; isótono, na.
isotonicity [aisəutəˈnisiti] n. PHYS. Isotonía, *f.*
isotope [ˈaisəutəup] n. CHEM. Isótopo, *m.*
isotopic [ˌaisəuˈtɔpik] adj. CHEM. Isotópico, ca.
isotopy [aiˈsɔtəpi] n. CHEM. Isotopía, *f.*
isotropic [aisəuˈtrɔpik] adj. BIOL. PHYS. Isótropo, pa.
isotropous [aiˈsɔtrəpəs] adj. BIOL. PHYS. Isótropo, pa.
isotropy [aiˈsɔtrəpi] n. BIOL. PHYS. Isotropía, *f.*
Israel [ˈizreiəl] pr. n. GEOGR. Israel, *m.*
Israeli [izˈreili] adj./n. Israelí.
Israelite [ˈizriəlait] adj./n. Israelita.
Israelitish [ˈizriəlaitiʃ] adj. Israelítico, ca.
issei [ˈiˈsei] n. U. S. Inmigrante (*m.*) japonés.

— OBSERV. El plural de *issei* es *issei* o *isseis*.

issuable [ˈiʃu:əbl] adj. JUR. En litigio.
issuant [ˈiʃuənt] adj. HERALD. Naciente, saliente.
issue [ˈiʃu:] n. Salida, *f.* (exit). || Derrame, *m.* (of a liquid). || Flujo, *m.*, desagüe, *m.*, salida, *f.* (of water). || Desembocadura, *f.* (of a river). || Emisión, *f.* (of shares, paper money, stamps, etc.). || Publicación, *f.* (publication). || Edición, *f.*, tirada, *f.* (edition). || Número, *m.* (copy): *back issue*, número atrasado. || Expedición, *f.* (of a passport). || Distribución, *f.*, reparto, *m.* (distribution). || Venta, *f.* (of tickets). || MED. Exutorio, *m.* (of ulcer, etc.). | Derrame, *m.* (of blood, etc.). || Resultado, *m.*, consecuencia, *f.* (outcome). || Cuestión, *f.*, punto, *m.*, problema, *m.* (question under discussion). || Asunto, *m.* (matter, affair). || JUR. Progenie, *f.*, prole, *f.*, descendencia, *f.* (offspring). || Beneficio, *m.* (profit). || — *At issue*, en discusión (point), en juego (interests), en litigio (legal matter), en desacuerdo (persons). || *In the issue*, finalmente, al final. || *Side issue*, cuestión secundaria. || *To avoid the issue*, andar con rodeos. || *To bring an affair to an issue*, llevar un asunto a un punto decisivo. || *To force the issue*, forzar una decisión. || *To join issue with*, discutir con (to discuss), estar en desacuerdo con (to disagree). || *To raise the issue of*, plantear el problema de. || *To take issue with*, estar en desacuerdo con.
issue [ˈiʃu:] v. intr. Salir (to come out). || Ser descendiente (*from*, de). || Resultar (to result). || — *To issue forth* o *out*, brotar (blood, liquid), salir (to come out). || *To issue from*, descender de, proceder de (a family), derivarse de, resultar de (a cause). || *To issue in*, llegar a, resultar en.
— V. tr. Publicar (to publish). || Distribuir, repartir [*to*, entre] (to distribute): *to issue children with milk*, repartir leche entre los miños. || Dar (to give). || Emitir, poner en circulación (shares, stamps, banknotes). || Promulgar (a decree). || Dar (an order). || Expedir (a certificate, passport, etc.). || Expender (tickets). || Extender (a cheque, a warrant). || Facilitar, dar (a licence). || Asignar, conceder (credits). || Conceder, otorgar (a loan). || Pronunciar (a verdict). || *When is the newspaper issued?*, ¿cuándo se publica el periódico?
issueless [—lis] adj. Sin descendencia (person). || Sin salida (street, etc.).
issuing [—iŋ] adj. Descendiente (*from*, de) [born]. || COMM. Emisor, ra: *issuing bank*, banco emisor.
Istanbul [ˌistænˈbu:l] pr. n. GEOGR. Estambul.
Isthmian [ˈisθmiən] adj. Ístmico, ca: *Isthmian games*, juegos ístmicos.
— N. Istmeño, na.
isthmus [ˈisməs] n. Istmo, *m.*

— OBSERV. El plural de la palabra inglesa es *isthmuses* o *isthmi*.

it [it] pron. Él, ella, ello (subject of verb, but generally omitted in Spanish): *where is the book? — It is here*, ¿dónde está el libro? — Está aquí. || Lo, la (accusative, usually placed before the verb, except after the infinite, the imperative and the gerund): *I saw it*, lo *or* la vi; *I believe it*, lo creo; *I want to see it*, quiero verlo, lo quiero ver; *look at it closely*, míralo de cerca. || Le (dative case): *give it a turn*, dale la vuelta. || Él, ella, ello (after prepositions): *we spoke about it*, hablamos de ello; *I'll see to it*, me ocuparé de ello. || — *I don't think it necessary to arrive early*, no considero que sea necesario llegar temprano. || *That's it!*, ¡eso es! (agreement), ¡ya está!, ¡está bien! (it's all right), ¡se acabó!, ¡hemos terminado! (on finishing sth.). || *That's just it*, ahí está. || *The worst of it is that...*, lo peor del caso es que... || *This is it!*, ¡ha llegado el momento!, ¡ha llegado la hora! || *What is it?*, ¿qué es eso? || *With it*, see WITH.
— N. Aquél, *m.*, atractivo, *m.*, no sé qué, *m.*: *she's got it*, tiene un no sé qué. || FAM. Vermut, *m.*: *gin and it*, vermut con ginebra. || — *He thinks he's it*, se lo tiene creído. || *You're it, I'm it*, tú te quedas, yo me quedo (playing tag).

— OBSERV. En muchas expresiones impersonales *it* no se traduce en español (*he considers it bad to kill*, considera que es malo matar; *how is it that you have such a big house?*, ¿cómo es que tiene Ud. una casa tan grande?; *I have heard it said that...*, he oído decir que...; *it is a long way to Madrid*, Madrid está muy lejos; *it's Peter*, soy Pedro; *it is not in me to do it*, no soy capaz de hacerlo, no es propio de mí hacer eso; *it is snowing*, está nevando; *it is said that ...*, se dice que ...; *it is six o'clock*, son las seis; *oh! it's you*, ¡ah! eres tú; *it is I* o *it is me*, soy yo).

Italian [iˈtæljən] adj. Italiano, na.
— N. Italiano, na (inhabitant of Italy). || Italiano, *m.* (language).
italianate [iˈtæljəneit] adj. De estilo italiano.
italianism [iˈtæljənizəm] n. Italianismo, *m.*
italianist [iˈtæljənist] n. Italianista, *m.* & *f.*
italianization [itæljənaiˈzeiʃən] n. Italianización, *f.*
italianize [iˈtæljənai:z] v. tr. Italianizar.
— V. intr. Italianizarse.
italic [iˈtælik] adj. PRINT. Bastardilla, cursiva.
— N. Bastardilla, *f.*, cursiva, *f.* || — Pl. Bastardilla, *f. sing*, cursiva, *f. sing.*
Italic [iˈtælik] adj. Itálico, ca.
italicize [iˈtælisaiz] v. tr. Escribir *or* imprimir en bastardilla *or* en cursiva. || Subrayar (to underline).
Italy [ˈitəli] pr. n. GEOGR. Italia, *f.*
itch [itʃ] n. MED. Picazón, *f.*, picor, *m.*, comezón, *f.* (sensation). || FIG. Prurito, *m.*, ganas, *f. pl.* (desire). || — MED. *The itch*, la sarna (scabies). || FIG. *To have an itch* o *the itch to*, estar impaciente por, tener el prurito de, tener muchas ganas de.
itch [itʃ] v. intr. Picar (to irritate): *my hand itches*, me pica la mano. || FIG. Anhelar (to long). || *To be itching to*, estar impaciente por, tener el prurito de, tener muchas ganas de.
itchiness [ˈitʃinis] n. Picazón, *f.*, comezón, *f.*, picor, *m.* (itch).
itching [ˈitʃiŋ] adj. MED. Que pica, que produce comezón. || Irresistible (desire). || — *Itching powder*, polvos (*m. pl.*) de picapica. || FIG. *To have an itching palm*, ser codicioso, sa.
— N. See ITCH.
itchy [ˈitʃi] adj. Picante. || *I have an itchy hand*, me pica la mano, siento comezón en la mano.
it'd [itd] contraction of *it would* and *it had*.
item [ˈaitəm] adv. Ítem, además.
— N. Artículo, *m.* (article). || THEATR. Número, *m.* (number). || Noticia, *f.*, suelto, *m.* (piece of news). || Detalle, *m.* (detail). || Punto, *m.* (on an agenda): *the first item on the agenda*, el primer punto del orden del día. || Punto, *m.* (point). || COMM. Partida, *f.*, asiento, *m.*
itemize [ˈaitəmaiz] v. tr. Detallar. || Especificar.
iterate [ˈitəreit] v. tr. Iterar, repetir, reiterar.
iteration [ˌitəˈreiʃən] n. Iteración, *f.*, repetición, *f.*, reiteración, *f.*

iterative [ˈitərətiv] adj. Iterativo, va; reiterativo, va. || GRAMM. Frecuentativo, va.
itineracy [iˈtinərəsi] or **itinerancy** [iˈtinərənsi] n. Carácter (*m.*) itinerante (itinerant nature). || Vida (*f.*) itinerante (itinerant life). || Cambio (*m.*) frecuente de residencia (change of residence).
itinerant [iˈtinərənt] adj. Itinerante, ambulante.
itinerary [aiˈtinərəri] n. Itinerario, *m.* (route). || Relación (*f.*) de un viaje (account). || Guía, *f.* (guidebook).
— Adj. Itinerario, ria.
itinerate [iˈtinəreit] v. intr. Viajar *or* desplazarse constantemente.
it'll [itl] contraction of *it will* and *it shall.*
its [its] poss. adj. Su, sus.

— OBSERV. The English possessive adjective is often translated by the definite article in Spanish (*its handle came off,* se le desprendió el asa; *when the lion leaves its den,* cuando el león sale de la leonera).

it's [its] contraction of *it has* and *it is.*
itself [itˈself] pron. Se: *the dog has hurt itself,* el perro se ha hecho daño. || [Él] mismo, [ella] misma, [ello] mismo: *the horse itself knows the way,* el caballo mismo sabe el camino; *it drank the water itself,* él mismo se bebió el agua. || Sí [mismo], sí [misma] (after preposition): *the speech was all right in itself,* el discurso en sí *or* en sí mismo estuvo bien. || Mismo, ma (emphasis): *Lewis spent the night in the palace itself,* Luis pasó la noche en el mismo palacio. || — *By itself,* solo, la: *the doll sits up by itself,* la muñeca se incorpora sola; aislado, da: *the house stands by itself,* la casa está aislada. || *He is kindness itself,* es la bondad misma, es la bondad personificada.
I've [aiv] contraction of *I have.*
ivied [ˈaivid] adj. Cubierto de hiedra.
ivory [ˈaivəri] n. Marfil, *m.* (substance). || Color (*m.*) marfil (colour). || — Pl. FAM. Teclas, *f.* (piano keys). | Dientes, *m.* (teeth). | Bolas, *f.* (in billiards). | Dados, *m.* (dice). || FAM. *To tickle the ivories,* tocar el piano.
— Adj. De marfil, marfileño, ña (of ivory). || De color marfil, marfileño, ña (ivory coloured). || Ebúrneo, a; de marfil, marfileño, ña (resembling ivory). || — *Ivory black,* negro (*m.*) de marfil. || BOT. *Ivory nut,* tagua, *f.,* marfil (*m.*) vegetal. | *Ivory palm,* tagua, *f.* || FIG. *Ivory tower,* torre (*f.*) de marfil.
Ivory Coast [—kəust] pr. n. GEOGR. Costa (*f.*) de Marfil.
ivy [ˈaivi] n. BOT. Hiedra, *f.,* yedra, *f.*
izard [ˈizəd] n. ZOOL. Gamuza, *f.,* rebeco, *m.*

J

j [dʒei] n. J, *f.* (letter): *a capital j,* una j mayúscula.
jab [dʒæb] n. Golpe (*m.*) seco (a blow, poke). || Pinchazo, *m.* (a stab). || Estocada, *f.* (with a sword). || Codazo, *m.* (with elbow). || FAM. Inyección, *f.,* pinchazo, *m.*
jab [dʒæb] v. tr. Pinchar: *he jabbed my finger with a needle,* me pinchó el dedo con una aguja. || Herir (with a sword, bayonet, etc.). || Dar un codazo a (with the elbow). || Dar un puñetazo a (with the fist). || Señalar: *he jabbed his finger at the headlines,* señaló los titulares con el dedo. || *To jab into,* clavar en, hundir en.
— V. intr. *To jab at s.o. with a knife,* intentar clavarle un cuchillo a alguien.
jabber [—ə*] n. Algarabía, *f.* (noise of many loud voices). || Farfulla, *f.,* chapurreo, *m.* (fast, unintelligible speech). || Charloteo, *m.,* cotorreo, *m.*
jabber [—ə*] v. tr. Farfullar, chapurrear. || Decir atropelladamente.
— V. intr. Farfullar, chapurrear (unintelligibly). || Charlotear, cotorrear (to chatter). || Hablar atropelladamente (to speak fast).
jabiru [ˈdʒæbiru:] n. ZOOL. Jabirú, *m.*
jaborandi [ˌdʒæbəˈrændi] n. BOT. Jaborandi, *m.* (bird)
jabot [ˈʒæbəu] n. Chorrera, *f.*
jacamar [ˈdzækəˌmɑ:] n. ZOOL. Jacamar, *m.,* jacamara, *f.*
jacaranda [ˌdʒækəˈrændə] n. BOT. Jacarandá, *f.*
jacinth [ˈdʒæsinθ] n. MIN. Jacinto, *m.* || Naranja, *m.* (colour).
jack [dʒæk] n. Gato, *m.* [*Amer.,* cric, *m.*] (a tool). || Sacabotas, *m. inv.* (bootjack). || MAR. Pabellón, *m.,* bandera (*f.*) de proa (national flag). | Marinero, *m.* (sailor). || Valet, *m.,* jota, *f.* (card). || Sota, *f.* (Spanish cards). || ELECTR. Enchufe (*m.*) hembra. || Lucio (*m.*) pequeño (fish). || Macho, *m.* (male of some animals). || SP. Boliche, *m.* (in bowls). || POP. Pasta, *f.* (money). || — Pl. Tabas, *f.,* cantillos, *m.*: *to play jacks,* jugar a las tabas.
jack [dʒæk] v. tr. Levantar con el gato: *we jacked up the car,* levantamos el coche con el gato. || Aumentar, subir (to raise): *to jack up prices,* aumentar los precios.
Jack [dʒæk] pr. n. Juan, *m.,* Juanito, *m.* || — FIG. *Before you could say Jack Robinson,* en un decir Jesús. | *Every Jack has his Jill,* cada oveja con su pareja. | *Every man Jack,* cada quisque. | *I'm all right, Jack,* ande yo caliente y ríase la gente.
jack-a-dandy [ˈdʒækəˈdændi] n. Dandy, *m.*
jackal [ˈdʒækɔ:l] n. ZOOL. Chacal, *m.*
jackanapes [ˈdʒækəneips] n. Mequetrefe, *m.* (conceited boy). || Mono *m.* (monkey). || Diablillo, *m.* (naughty child).
jackass [ˈdʒækæs] n. Burro, *m.,* asno, *m.* || FIG. Burro, *m.* (foolish person).
jackboot [ˈdʒækbu:t] n. Bota (*f.*) alta.
jackdaw [ˈdʒækdɔ:] n. ZOOL. Chova, *f.* (bird).
jacket [ˈdʒækit] n. Chaqueta, *f.,* americana, *f.* [*Amer.,* saco, *m.*] (of man's suit). || Chaqueta, *f.* (of a woman's suit, of pyjamas, etc.). || Sobrecubierta, *f.* (of a book). || Forro, *m.* (of a record). || Carpeta, *f.* (file). || Camisa, *f.* (casing for tubes, cylinders, pipes). || Casquillo, *m.* (of a bullet). || Cáscara, *f.* (of a fruit). || Piel, *f.* (of potatoes). || — FIG. FAM. *To dust s.o.'s jacket,* sacudirle el polvo a uno. || *Strait jacket,* camisa (*f.*) de fuerza.
jacket [ˈdʒækit] v. tr. Cubrir.
Jack Frost [ˈdʒækˈfrɔst] n. Helada, *f.* (freeze). || Escarcha, *f.* (frost). || Invierno, *m.* (winter). || Tiempo (*m.*) frío (cold weather).
jack-in-office [ˈdʒækinˈɔfis] n. Funcionario (*m.*) meticuloso.
jack-in-the-box [ˈdʒækinðəbɔks] n. Caja (*f.*) sorpresa.

— OBSERV. El plural de la palabra *jack-in-the-box* es *jacks-in-the-box* o *jack-in-the-boxes.*

Jack Ketch [ˈdʒækˈketʃ] n. Verdugo, *m.*
jackknife [ˈdʒæknaif] n. Navaja, *f.* (a knife). || SP. Salto (*m.*) de la carpa (a dive).
jackknife [ˈdʒæknaif] v. intr. Hacer el salto de la carpa (to dive). || Colear [un camión articulado] (a lorry).
jack mackerel [ˈdʒækˈmækrəl] n. Jurel, *m.* (fish).
jack-of-all-trades [ˈdʒækəvˈɔ:ltreidz] n. Persona (*f.*) apañada *or* mañosa (skilful person). || Factótum, *m.* (factotum). || *Jack-of-all-trades, master of none,* hombre de muchos oficios, maestro de ninguno.
jack-o'lantern [ˈdʒækəuˌlæntən] n. Fuego (*m.*) fatuo (will o'the wisp). || Linterna (*f.*) hecha con una calabaza (pumpkin lamp).
jack plane [ˈdʒækplein] n. TECH. Garlopa, *f.*
jackpot [ˈdʒækpɔt] n. Premio (*m.*) gordo (main prize). || Bote, *m.* (cards). || *To hit the jackpot,* dar en el blanco (to be successful), sacar el premio gordo, tocarle a uno el premio gordo.
jack-pudding [ˈdʒækˈpudiŋ] n. Payaso, *m.,* bufón, *m.*
jackrabbit [ˈdʒækˌræbit] n. Liebre (*f.*) americana.
jackstone [ˈdʒækstəun] n. U. S. Taba, *f.,* cantillo, *m.* || — Pl. U. S. Tabas, *f.,* cantillos, *m.*
jackstraw [ˈdʒækstrɔ:] n. Palillo, *m.* || FIG. Muñeco (*m.*) de paja. || — Pl. Palillos, *m.*
Jack-tar [ˈdʒækˈtɑ:*] FAM. Marinero, *m.*
Jacob [ˈdʒeikəb] pr. n. Jacob, *m.*
Jacobean [ˌdʒækəˈbi:ən] adj. De la época de Jacobo I, jacobino, na.
Jacobin [ˈdʒækəubin] adj./n. Jacobino, na.
Jacobinism [—izəm] n. Jacobinismo, *m.*
Jacobite [ˈdʒækəbait] n. Jacobita, *m.* & *f.*
Jacobitical [ˌdʒækəˈbitikəl] adj. Jacobita.
jactation [ˌdʒækˈteiʃən] n. Jactancia, *f.* (a boast). || MED. Agitación, *f.*
jactitation [ˈdʒæktiˈteiʃən] n. MED. Agitación, *f.* || JUR. Impostura, *f.*
jade [dʒeid] n. MIN. Jade, *m.* || Color (*m.*) jade (colour). || FAM. Jamelgo, *m.,* penco, *m.* (horse). | Mujerzuela, *f.* (woman).
jaded [—id] adj. Harto, ta; ahíto, ta (satiated). || Agotado, da; reventado, da (tired out).

jag [dʒæg] m. Mella, *f.* (of a break). || Siete, *m.* (of a tear). || Diente, *m.* (tooth of saw). || Punta, *f.* (sharp projection). || FAM. Juerga, *f.* (spree). || FAM. *To have a jag on*, estar trompa *or* borracho [*Amer.*, estar mamado].
jag [dʒæg] v. tr. Dentar (edge of cloth). || Mellar (a knife edge).
jagged [—id] adj. Dentado, da. || Mellado, da. || Serrado, da (serrated).
jaggery [ˈdʒægəri] n. Azúcar (*m.*) de palmera.
jaggy [ˈdʒægi] adj. See JAGGED.
jaguar [ˈdʒægjuə*] n. ZOOL. Jaguar, *m.*
jai alai [ˈhailai] n. SP. Jai alai, *m.*, pelota (*f.*) vasca.
jail [dʒeil] n. Cárcel, *f.*: *to go to jail*, ir a la cárcel; *to be in jail*, estar en la cárcel. || Prisión, *f.*, cárcel, *f.*: *sentenced to 10 years' jail*, condenado a diez años de prisión.
jail [dʒeil] v. tr. Encarcelar.
jailbird [—bəːd] n. Presidiario (*m.*) reincidente, preso (*m.*) reincidente.
jailbreak [—breik] n. Evasión, *f.*, fuga, *f.*
jailer or **jailor** [—ə*] n. Carcelero, *m.*
Jakarta [dʒəˈkɑːtə] pr. n. GEOGR. Yakarta.
jalap [ˈdʒæləp] n. BOT. Jalapa, *f.*
Jalapan [ˈdʒæləpən] adj./n. Jalapeño, ña.
jalopy or **jaloppy** [dʒəˈlɔpiː] n. FAM. Cafetera, *f.*, cacharro, *m.* (car). | Cacharro, *m.* (plane).
jalousie [ˈʒæluziː] n. Celosía, *f.* (blind).
jam [dʒæm] n. Mermelada, *f.* (food): *bread and jam*, pan con mermelada. || Atasco, *m.* (a blockage). || Agolpamiento, *m.* (of people). || Machucamiento, *m.* (crushing). || Embotellamiento, *m.*, atasco, *m.*: *the traffic jam was a mile long*, el embotellamiento del tráfico se extendía sobre una milla. || Barrera, *f.* (of ice in a river). || FAM. Apuro, *m.*, lío, *m.* (difficult situation): *to be in a jam*, estar en un apuro; *to get into a jam*, meterse en un lío; *to get out of a jam*, salir de un apuro. || FAM. *What do you want?, jam on it?*, ¿qué quieres encima? ¿que te lo traiga en bandeja de plata?
jam [dʒæm] v. tr. Meter a la fuerza (to force to enter): *he jammed the coin into the slot*, metió a la fuerza la moneda en la ranura. || Pillar (to catch): *to jam one's fingers in a door*, pillarse los dedos en una puerta. || Apretar, apiñar (to squash): *to jam people against a wall*, apretar a la gente contra un muro. || Atestar, atiborrar: *the room was jammed with people*, el cuarto estaba atestado de gente. || Llenar hasta los topes (to fill to the brim). || Atorar, atascar (to clog): *rubbish jammed the pipes*, la basura atoró la tubería. || Bloquear (to block). || Atascar (a nut, a moving part). || Causar un embotellamiento de: *the demonstration jammed the traffic*, la manifestación causó el embotellamiento del tráfico. || RAD. Interferir (radio signals). | Causar interferencia en (to cause interference). || — *To jam on one's hat*, encasquetarse el sombrero. || *To jam on the brakes*, frenar en seco, dar un frenazo. || *To jam the door shut*, atrancar la puerta. || *We can't jam any more in*, ya no caben más cosas.
— V. intr. Atrancarse (to become fixed or wedged): *the door has jammed*, se ha atrancado la puerta. || Atascarse, atorarse (to get clogged). || Encasquillarse (a firearm). || Agarrotarse (brakes).
Jamaica [dʒəˈmeikə] pr. n. GEOGR. Jamaica, *f.*
Jamaican [—n] adj./n. Jamaicano, na.
jamboree [ˌdʒæmbəˈriː] n. Jamboree, *m.*, reunión (*f.*) internacional de exploradores. || FAM. Juerga, *f.* (spree).
James [dʒeimz] pr. n. Jaime, *m.*, Jacobo, *m.*, Diego, *m.*, Santiago, *m.*
— OBSERV. *Jacobo* is used specifically for the king of Scotland. *Jaime* is used above all in Aragon, Valencia, Catalonia and the Balearic Islands.
jamming [ˈdʒæmiŋ] n. Atascamiento, *m.*, atrancamiento, *m.* || RAD. Interferencia, *f.*
jam session [—ˈseʃən] n. MUS. Concierto (*m.*) de jazz improvisado.
Jane [dʒein] pr. n. Juana, *f.* || *To be a plain Jane*, tener poco atractivo, ser del montón.
jangle [ˈdʒæŋgl] n. Ruido (*m.*) de chatarra (metallic noise). || Cascabeleo, *m.* (of small bells), cencerreo, *m.* (of cow bells). || Riña, *f.* (quarrel). || Parloteo, *m.* (chattering).
jangle [ˈdʒæŋgl] v. tr. Hacer sonar.
— V. intr. Hacer un ruido de chatarra (tins, etc.). || Cencerrear (bells). || Reñir, discutir (to bicker).
janissary [ˈdʒænisəri] n. MIL. Jenízaro, *m.*
janitor [ˈdʒænitə*] n. Portero, *m.*
janitress [ˈdʒænitris] n. Portera, *f.*
Janizary [ˈdʒænisəri] n. MIL. Jenízaro, *m.*
Jansenism [ˈdʒænsnizəm] n. REL. Jansenismo, *m.*
Jansenist [ˈdʒænsnist] adj./n. Jansenista.
Jansenistic [dʒænsnistik] adj. Jansenista.
January [ˈdʒænjuəri] n. Enero, *m.*
Jap [dʒæp] adj./n. FAM. Japonés, esa.
japan [dʒəˈpæn] n. Laca (*f.*) de China, laca (*f.*) de Japón.
japan [dʒəˈpæn] v. tr. Barnizar con laca de China *or* de Japón.
Japan [dʒəˈpæn] pr. n. GEOGR. Japón, *m.*
Japanese [ˌdʒæpəˈniːz] adj. Japonés, esa.
— N. Japonés, esa (inhabitant). || Japonés, *m.* (language). || *The Japanese*, los japoneses.
jape [dʒeip] n. Broma, *f.*
jape [dʒeip] v. intr. Bromear.
japonica [dʒəˈpɔnikə] n. BOT. Membrillo (*m.*) japonés.
jar [dʒɑː*] n. Tarro, *m.* (jam pot). || Tinaja, *f.* (a large earthenware pot). || Cántaro, *m.* (water picher). || Jarra, *f.* (jug). || Vasija, *f.* (recipient, vessel). || Choque, *m.*, sacudida, *f.* (an impact). || Sonido (*m.*) discordante (discordant sound). || FIG. Conflicto, *m.* (conflict). | Choque, *m.*, golpe, *m.* (blow, shock). || — *Leyden jar*, botella (*f.*) de Leyden. || *On the jar*, entreabierto, ta; entornado, da.
jar [dʒɑː*] v. tr. Sacudir (to shake). || Mover (to move). || Lastimar (sounds): *to jar one's ears*, lastimar los oídos de uno. || Herir (feelings). || Irritar (the nerves).
— V. intr. Chirriar (harsh sounds). || Desentonar, sonar mal (music). || Chocar (colours). || Sacudirse, vibrar (to shake). || FIG. Reñir (to argue). || — *To jar on*, chocar contra. || FIG. *To jar on* o *upon*, irritar, molestar. | *To jar on s.o.'s nerves*, ponerle a uno los nervios de punta. | *To jar with*, no concordar con.
jardinière [ˌʒɑːdiˈnjeə*] n. Jardinera, *f.* (box for plant pots). || Macetón, *m.* (ornamental plant pot). || CULIN. Menestra, *f.*
jargon [ˈdʒɑːgən] n. Jerga, *f.*: *medical jargon*, jerga médica. || Jerigonza, *f.*, galimatías, *m.* (gibberish).
jargonistic [ˌdʒɑːgəˈnistik] adj. Jergal.
jarring [ˈdʒɑːriŋ] adj. Que chocan (colours). || Discordante (sound). || FIG. Discorde (opinion, etc.).
jarvey [ˈdʒɑːvi] n. FAM. Cochero, *m.*
jasmin or **jasmine** [ˈdʒæsmin] n. BOT. Jazmín, *m.*
jasper [ˈdʒæspə*] n. MIN. Jaspe, *m.*
jaundice [ˈdʒɔːndis] n. MED. Ictericia, *f.* || FIG. Celos, *m. pl.*, envidia, *f.* (envy).
jaundice [ˈdʒɔːndis] v. tr. MED. Dar ictericia a. || FIG. Dar envidia *or* celos a.
jaundiced [—t] adj. MED. Ictérico, ca. || Cetrino, na; amarillo, lla (yellow). || FIG. Amargado, da (embittered). | Envidioso, sa (envious).
jaunt [dʒɔːnt] n. Paseo, *m.*, excursión (*f.*) corta.
jaunt [dʒɔːnt] v. intr. Ir de paseo.
jauntiness [—inis] n. Viveza, *f.* (liveliness). || Desenvoltura, *f.* (self-confidence). || Garbo, *m.* (grace).
jaunty [—i] adj. Vivaz (lively). || Desenvuelto, ta (free and easy): *jaunty manner*, aire desenvuelto. || Garboso, sa (graceful).
Java [ˈdʒɑːvə] pr. n. GEOGR. Java.
Javan [—n] or **Javanese** [ˌdʒɑːvəˈniːz] adj./n. Javanés, esa.
javelin [ˈdʒævlin] n. (Ant.). Venablo, *m.* (weapon). || SP. Jabalina, *f.*: *throwing the javelin*, lanzamiento de la jabalina.
jaw [dʒɔː] n. ANAT. Mandíbula, *f.* (of person). || ZOOL. Quijada, *f.* (of animal). || TECH. Mordaza, *f.*, mandíbula, *f.* (of vice, pliers, pincers). || Embocadura, *f.* (of a channel). || FAM. Charla, *f.* (chat). || Ola, *f.* (wave). || Mar, *m.* (sea). || — Pl. Boca, *f. sing.*, fauces, *f.* || — FAM. *Hold your jaw!*, ¡cierra el pico!, ¡cállate! | *It's a lot of jaw*, todo son palabras. || *Jaw clutch*, embrague (*m.*) de mordaza. || *Jaw coupling*, acoplamiento dentado. || FIG. *The jaws of death*, la boca del lobo (great danger).
jaw [dʒɔː] v. tr. Regañar, echar una bronca a (to scold).
— V. intr. Hablar por los codos (to talk and talk). || Charlar (to chat).
jawbone [—bəun] n. ANAT. Mandíbula, *f.*, maxilar, *m.* (of people). || Quijada, *f.* (of animals).
jawbreaker [—ˌbreikə*] n. FAM. Trabalenguas, *m. inv.* (tongue twister). | Caramelo (*m.*) de goma (sweet). || Triturador, *m.* (of stones, etc.).
jay [dʒei] n. Arrendajo, *m.* (bird). || FIG. Cotorra, *f.* (chatterbox). | Tonto, ta (fool).
jaywalk [—wɔːk] v. intr. Cruzar la calle imprudentemente.
jaywalker [—ˈwɔːkə*] n. Peatón (*m.*) imprudente.
jazz [dʒæz] n. MUS. Jazz, *m.* || FAM. Palabrería, *f.* (hot air).
— Adj. De jazz.
jazz [dʒæz] v. tr. Arreglar para jazz. || FIG. *To jazz up*, alegrar, animar.
— V. intr. Tocar jazz (to play jazz). || Bailar jazz (to dance jazz).
jazz band [—bænd] n. MUS. Orquesta (*f.*) de jazz.
jazzman [—mæn] n. Músico (*m.*) de jazz.
— OBSERV. El plural de *jazzman* es *jazzmen*.
jazzy [—i] adj. MUS. De jazz. | Animado, da (lively). | Sincopado, da (syncopated). || De colores chillones, llamativo, va (brightly coloured).
jealous [ˈdʒeləs] adj. Celoso, sa: *jealous of one's rights*, celoso de sus derechos; *a jealous husband*, un marido celoso. || Envidioso, sa (envious, resentful). || *To be jealous of*, tener celos de, estar celoso de.
jealousy [ˈdʒeləsi] n. Celos, *m. pl.* || Envidia, *f.* (envy).
Jean [dʒiːn] pr. n. Juana, *f.*
jeans [dʒiːnz] pl. n. Pantalones (*m.*) vaqueros (trousers). || Mono, *m. sing.* (overalls).
jeep [dʒiːp] n. MIL. Jeep, *m.*, todo terreno, *m.* [*Amer.*, coche campero, *m.*].
jeer [dʒiə*] n. Mofa, *f.*, burla, *f.*, escarnio, *m.* (mockery). || Abucheo, *m.* (boo). || — Pl. MAR. Drizas, *f.* (rigging).
jeer [dʒiə*] v. tr. Mofarse de, burlarse de (to mock). || Abuchear (to boo). || Insultar (to insult).
— V. intr. Mofarse, burlarse. || *To jeer at*, mofarse de,

burlarse de, hacer escarnio de (to mock), abuchear a (to boo), insultar a (to insult).
jeering [—riŋ] adj. Burlón, ona: *a jeering smile*, una sonrisa burlona.
— N. Abucheo, *m.* (booing). || Burla, *f.*, mofa, *f.*, escarnio, *m.* (mockery). || Insultos, *m. pl.* (insults).
jehad [dʒiˈhɑ:d] n. REL. Guerra (*f.*) santa.
Jehoshaphat [dʒiˈhɔʃəfæt] pr. n. GEOGR. Josafat.
Jehovah [dʒiˈhəuvə] pr. n. REL. Jehová, *m.*
Jehovah's Witness [—zˈwitnis] pr. n. REL. Testigo (*m.*) de Jehová.
jejune [dʒiˈdʒu:n] adj. Árido, da; seco, ca (dry). || Aburrido, da; sin interés (lacking interest). || U. S. Inmaduro, ra.
jejuneness [—nis] n. Aridez, *f.* (dryness). || FIG. Falta (*f.*) de interés (lack of interest). | Aridez, *f.* (of style). || U. S. Inmadurez, *f.*
jejunum [—əm] n. ANAT. Yeyuno, *m.*

— OBSERV. El plural de *jejunum* es *jejuna*.

jell [dʒel] v. tr. FIG. Moldear, dar forma (to cause to take shape).
— V. intr. Cuajar. || FIG. Tomar forma, cristalizarse (to take shape).
jellify [ˈdʒelifai] v. tr. Convertir en gelatina.
jelly [ˈdʒeli] n. CULIN. Gelatina, *f.* (gelatinous food). || Jalea, *f.*: *citron jelly*, jalea de cidra. || — *Jelly baby*, muñeco (*m.*) de caramelo. || *Petroleum jelly*, vaselina, *f.* || *To pound into a jelly*, hacer trizas *or* papilla.
jellyfish [—fiʃ] n. ZOOL. Medusa, *f.* || FAM. Calzonazos, *m. inv.* (man).
jemmy [ˈdʒemi] n. Palanqueta, *f.*, ganzúa, *f.* (tool). || CULIN. Cabeza (*f.*) de cordero (sheep's head).
Jennerian [dʒeˈni:əriən] adj. Jenneriano, na.
jenny [ˈdʒeni] n. Hembra, *f.* (female animal). || Burra, *f.* (female ass). || TECH. Máquina (*f.*) de hilar.
jeopardize [ˈdʒepədaiz] v. tr. Arriesgar, poner en peligro (to endanger). || Comprometer.
jeopardy [ˈdʒepədi] n. Riesgo, *m.*, peligro, *m.* || *To be in jeopardy*, estar en peligro.
jerboa [dʒə:ˈbəuə] n. ZOOL. Jerbo, *m.*, gerbo, *m.*
jeremiad [ˌdʒeriˈmaiəd] n. Jeremiada, *f.* (lamentation).
Jeremiah [ˌdʒeriˈmaiə] pr. n. Jeremías, *m.*
Jericho [ˈdʒerikəu] pr. n. GEOGR. Jericó.
jerk [dʒə:k] n. Sacudida, *f.* (sudden movement): *by jerks*, a sacudidas. || Tirón, *m.* (sudden pull). || Empujón, *m.* (shove). || Espasmo, *m.* (reflex action). || CULIN. Cecina, *f.* [*Amer.*, charqui, *m.*] (dry meat). || U. S. FAM. Idiota, *m.* & *f.* (idiot). | Pelmazo, za; latoso, sa (nuisance). || — FAM. *Physical jerks*, ejercicios físicos. || *Put a jerk in it!*, ¡ánimo!, ¡date prisa! || *To have the jerks*, tener el baile de San Vito (illness), tener hormiguillo.
jerk [dʒə:k] v. tr. Mover a tirones (to move by tugging). || Sacudir, dar una sacudida a (to shake). || Lanzar bruscamente (to throw). || Dar un tirón a (to give a sharp pull). || Acecinar [*Amer.*, charquear], curar al sol (to cure meat). || — *Jerked meat*, cecina, *f.* [*Amer.*, charqui, *m.*]. || *To jerk o.s. free*, librarse de un tirón. || *To jerk sth. off*, quitar algo de un tirón. || *To jerk sth. out*, decir algo a trompicones (to say), sacar algo de un tirón (to take out).
— V. intr. Moverse a trompicones (to move in stops and starts). || *The door jerked open*, la puerta se abrió de golpe.
jerkin [ˈdʒə:kin] n. (Ant.). Jubón, *m.*, justillo, *m.*
jerkwater [ˈdʒə:kˌwɔ:tə*] adj. U. S. FAM. De poca monta (poor, trivial). || *A jerkwater town*, un pueblecito perdido.
jerky [ˈdʒə:ki] adj. Espasmódico, ca. || Desigual (road). || Que traquetea (car).
— N. Cecina, *f.*, tasajo, *m.* [*Amer.*, charqui, *m.*] (dry meat).
jeroboam [ˌdʒerəˈbəuəm] n. Botella (*f.*) grande.
Jerome [dʒəˈrəum] pr. n. Jerónimo, *m.*
jerrican [ˈdʒerikæn] n. Bidón, *m.*
jerry [ˈdʒeri] n. FAM. Orinal, *m.* (chamber pot). || MIL. FAM. Soldado (*m.*) alemán.
— Adj. De mala calidad.
jerry-builder [—ˌbildə*] n. Constructor (*m.*) malo.
jerry-building [—ˌbildiŋ] n. Construcción (*f.*) de baja calidad, mala construcción, *f.*
jerry-built [—bilt] adj. Construido con materiales de mala calidad, mal construido, da.
jerry can [—kæn] n. Bidón, *m.*
jerrymander [—ˌmændə*] v. tr. See GERRYMANDER.
jersey [ˈdʒə:zi] n. Jersey, *m.* (garment). || Tejido (*m.*) de punto (material).
Jerusalem [dʒəˈru:sələm] pr. n. Jerusalén.
Jerusalem artichoke [—ˈɑ:titʃəuk] n. Aguaturma, *f.*, pataca, *f.*
jess or **jesse** [dʒes] n. U. S. Pihuela, *f.*
jessamine [ˈdʒesəmin] n. BOT. Jazmín, *m.* (jasmine).
jest [dʒest] n. Broma, *f.*, burla, *f.*, mofa, *f.* (mocking). || Chiste, *m.* (joke). || Hazmerreír, *m.* (laughingstock). || *In jest*, en broma.
jest [dʒest] v. intr. Bromear (to speak jokingly). || Mofarse, burlarse (*about*, de) [to speak tauntingly].
jester [—ə*] n. Bromista, *m.* & *f.* (person who jests). || (Ant.). Bufón, *m.* (buffoon).
jesting [—iŋ] adj. Guasón, ona.
— N. Chistes, *m. pl.* (jokes). || Bromas, *f. pl.* (practical jokes).
Jesuit [ˈdʒezjuit] adj./n. REL. Jesuita, *m.*
Jesuitic [ˌdʒezjuˈitik] or **Jesuitical** [—əl] adj. REL. Jesuítico, ca.
Jesuitism [ˈdʒezjuitizəm] n. Jesuitismo, *m.*
Jesus [ˈdʒi:zəs] pr. n. REL. Jesús, *m.* || — REL. *Jesus Christ*, Jesucristo, *m.* || *Society of Jesus*, Compañía (*f.*) de Jesús.
jet [dʒet] n. Chorro, *m.* (of water, steam, blood, etc.). || Surtidor, *m.* (pipe). || Surtidor, *m.*, pulverizador, *m.*, chicler, *m.* (of the carburetter). || Llama, *f.* (flame). || Mechero, *m.* (gas burner). || AVIAT. Avión (*m.*) de reacción, reactor, *m.* (plane). | Reactor, *m.* (engine). || MIN. Azabache, *m.* (black mineral).
jet [dʒet] v. tr. Lanzar en chorro.
— V. intr. Salir a chorros. || Volar en avión de reacción.
jet-black [—blæk] adj. Negro como el azabache.
jet engine [—ˈendʒin] n. AVIAT. Reactor, *m.*
jet fighter [—ˈfaitə*] n. AVIAT. Avión (*m.*) de caza de reacción.
jetliner [—ˈlainə*] n. Avión (*m.*) de reacción, reactor, *m.* [de pasajeros].
jet plane [—plein] n. AVIAT. Avión (*m.*) de reacción, reactor, *m.*
jet-propelled [—prəˈpeld] adj. De propulsión a chorro, de reacción.
jet propulsion [—prəˈpʌlʃən] n. Propulsión (*f.*) a chorro.
jet-propulsion [—prəˈpʌlʃən] adj. De propulsión a chorro, de reacción.
jetsam [—səm] n. MAR. Echazón, *f.*, carga (*f.*) arrojada al mar. || FIG. Desecho, *m.*
jet sprayer [—ˌspreiə*] n. Pulverizador, *m.*
jet stream [—stri:m] n. Corriente (*f.*) en chorro (in meteorology). || Chorro, *m.* (of a jet).
jettison [ˈdʒetisn] n. MAR. Echazón, *f.* (action).
jettison [ˈdʒetisn] v. tr. MAR. Echar [la carga] al mar. || FIG. Deshacerse de (to get rid of).
jetty [ˈdʒeti] n. Malecón, *m.*, muelle, *m.*, escollera, *f.*
— Adj. Negro como el azabache.
Jew [dʒu:] n. Judío, a.
jewel [ˈdʒu:əl] n. Joya, *f.*, alhaja, *f.* (bracelet, ring, etc.). || Piedra (*f.*) preciosa (precious stone). || Rubí, *m.* (in a watch): *a watch with 21 jewels*, un reloj de 21 rubíes. || FIG. Joya, *f.*, perla, *f.* (person). || *Jewel case* o *jewel box*, joyero, *m.*
jewel [ˈdʒu:əl] v. tr. Alhajar, enjoyar.
jeweled (U. S. **jewelled**) [—d] adj. Alhajado, da; enjoyado, da (person, dress). || Adornado con piedras preciosas (object). || Con rubíes (watch).
jeweller (U. S. **jeweler**) [—ə*] n. Joyero, *m.* || *Jeweller's* o *jeweler's*, joyería, *f.*
jewellery [U. S. **jewelery**) [ˈdʒu:əlri] n. Joyería, *f.* (shop). || Joyas, *f. pl.*, alhajas, *f. pl.* (jewels).
Jewess [ˈdʒu:is] n. Judía, *f.*
Jewish [ˈdʒu:iʃ] adj. Judío, a.
Jewishness [ˈdʒu:iʃnis] n. Judaísmo, *m.*
Jewry [ˈdʒuəri] n. Pueblo (*m.*) judío (the Jewish people). || (Ant.). Judería, *f.* (district).
jew's-harp or **jews'-harp** [ˈdʒu:zˈhɑ:p] n. MUS. Birimbao, *m.*, guimbarda, *f.*
jib [dʒib] n. MAR. Foque, *m.* (sail). || TECH. Aguilón, *m.* (of crane).
jib or **jibb** [dʒib] v. tr. MAR. Poner a la capa (to gybe).
— V. intr. Plantarse (a horse). || Resistirse (a person). || *To jib at sth.*, resistirse *or* oponerse a algo.
jibboom [ˈdʒibˈbu:m] n. MAR. Botalón, *m.*
jibe [dʒaib] v. intr. U. S. Concordar, estar de acuerdo.
jibe [dʒaib] n. See GIBE.
jibe [dʒaib] v. tr./intr. MAR. See GYBE.
jiffy [ˈdʒifi] n. FAM. Momento, *m.* || FAM. *It was done in a jiffy*, lo hizo en un decir Jesús *or* en un santiamén *or* en un periquete.
jig [dʒig] n. Giga, *f.* (dance and its music). || TECH. Gálibo, *m.*, calibre, *m.*, plantilla, *f.* (gauge). || MIN. Criba, *f.* || Anzuelo (*m.*) de cuchara (hook). || FIG. FAM. *The jig is up*, todo se acabó.
jig [dʒig] v. tr. MIN. Separar por vibración y lavado, cribar (ore). || TECH. Pasar por la plantilla (a part).
— V. intr. Bailar la giga (to dance). || Andar a saltitos (to move with little jumps). || Dar saltitos (to jump up and down). || *He keeps jigging up and down*, no puede estarse quieto.
jigger [ˈdʒigə*] n. Bailarín (*m.*) de giga (dancer). || ELECTR. Transformador, *m.* || MIN. Criba, *f.* || MAR. Balandra, *f.* (boat). | Palo (*m.*) de mesana, contramesana, *f.* (mast). | Anzuelo (*m.*) de cuchara (hook). || SP. Apoyo, *m.* (in billiard). || ZOOL. Nigua, *f.* (chigoe). || FAM. Chisme, *m.*, artefacto, *m.* || U. S. Medida (*f.*) para líquidos (for drinks).
jiggered [ˈdʒigəd] adj. FAM. *I'm jiggered if*, que me lleven los demonios si. | *Well I'm jiggered!*, ¡vaya por Dios!
jiggermast [ˈdʒigəˌmɑ:st] n. MAR. Contramesana, *f.*, palo (*m.*) de mesana.
jiggery-pokery [ˈdʒigəriˈpəukəri] n. FAM. Trampa, *f.*
jiggle [ˈdʒigl] v. intr. Menearse, zangolotearse.
— V. tr. Menear, zangolotear.
jigsaw [ˈdʒigsɔ:] n. TECH. Sierra (*f.*) de vaivén (saw). || Rompecabezas, *m. inv.* (puzzle). || *Jigsaw puzzle*, rompecabezas.
jihad [dʒiˈhɑ:d] n. REL. Guerra (*f.*) santa.
jilt [dʒilt] v. tr. Dejar plantado a (a fiancé). || Dar calabazas a (to reject a suitor).

Jim [dʒim] pr. n. Santiago, *m.*, Santi, *m.* || *Jim Crow*, negro, *m.* (negro), discriminación (*f.*) racial (discrimination).
jimjams [ˈdʒimdʒæmz] pl. n. U. S. FAM. Delírium tremens, *m.*
jimmy [ˈdʒimi] n. Ganzúa, *f.*, palanqueta, *f.*
jimmy [ˈdʒimi] v. tr. Forzar [con una ganzúa].
jimsonweed [ˈdʒimsən,wi:d] n. BOT. Estramonio, *m.*
jingle [ˈdʒiŋgl] n. Cascabeleo, *m.*, tintineo, *m.* (sound of bells). || Tintineo, *m.*, sonido, *m.* (of glassware, of coins, etc.). || Cascabel, *m.* (of tambourine). || Rima (*f.*) infantil (childish rhyme). || Canción, *f.*, copla, *f.* (song). || Anuncio (*m.*) comercial cantado (advertisement).
jingle [ˈdʒiŋgl] v. intr. Cascabelear (bells). || Tintinear, sonar (glasses, coins, etc.).
— V. tr. Hacer cascabelear, sonar (bells). || Agitar (keys, coins).
jingly [ˈdʒiŋgli] adj. Que tintinea. || Metálico, ca (sound).
jingo [ˈdʒiŋgəu] adj./n. Jingoísta, patriotero, ra. || *By jingo!*, ¡caramba!
jingoism [—izəm] n. Jingoísmo, *m.*, patriotería, *f.*
jingoist [—ist] n. Jingoísta, *m.* & *f.*, patriotero, ra.
jingoistic [dʒiŋgəuˈistik] adj. Jingoísta, patriotero, ra.
jinks [dʒiŋks] pl. n. Jolgorio, *m. sing.*, juerga, *f. sing.*: *the girls were up to (high) jinks in the dormitory*, las niñas estaban de jolgorio en el dormitorio.
jinn [dʒin] n. Genio, *m.*
jinx [dʒiŋks] n. FAM. Gafe, *m.*, cenizo, *m.* (person). | Maleficio, *m.* (spell): *to break the jinx*, romper el maleficio. | Cenizo, *m.*, mala suerte, *f.* (bad luck). || — FAM. *This car is a jinx*, este coche trae mala suerte. | *To put a jinx on*, echar mal de ojo a.
jinx [dʒiŋks] v. tr. FAM. Traer mala suerte a.
jipijapa [hi:pi:ˈhα:pə] n. Jipijapa, *m.* (hat).
jitney [ˈdʒitni] n. U. S. FAM. Moneda (*f.*) de cinco centavos (coin). | Colectivo, *m.* (bus, car).
jitter [ˈdʒitə*] v. intr. FAM. Temblar de miedo, tener mieditis.
jitters [ˈdʒitəz] pl. n. FAM. Nervios, *m.*, miedo, *m.*, canguelo, *m.*, mieditis, *f.* || — FAM. *To give s.o. the jitters*, darle miedo a alguien. | *To have the jitters*, tener miedo *or* mieditis, tener canguelo.
jittery [ˈdʒitəri] adj. FAM. *To be jittery*, tener canguelo. | *To get jittery*, entrarle miedo a uno.
Jivaro [ˈhi:vərəu] n. Jíbaro, ra.
Jivaroan [—ən] adj. Jíbaro, ra.
jive [dʒaiv] n. MUS. "Swing", *m.* || U. S. FAM. "Argot", *m.*, jerga, *f.* (slang).
jive [dʒaiv] v. intr. Bailar el "swing". || U. S. FAM. Burlarse.
Joachim [ˈdʒəuəkim] pr. n. Joaquín, *m.*
Joan [dʒəun] pr. n. Juana, *f.* || *Joan of Arc*, Juana de Arco.
job [dʒɔb] n. Trabajo, *m.* (work): *I've got a job for you*, tengo un trabajo para ti. || Trabajo, *m.*, empleo, *m.*: *to look for a job*, buscar un empleo, buscar trabajo. || Cometido, *m.*, función, *f.*: *his job is to file them*, su cometido es archivarlos. || Asunto, *m.* (affair). || FAM. Chanchullo, *m.* (dishonest practice). | Golpe, *m.* (robbery). || Destajo, *m.* (piecework): *to work by the job*, trabajar a destajo. || Pinchazo, *m.* (jab). || — FIG. *A bad job*, un mal asunto (bad state of affairs). || *And a good job too!*, ¡menos mal! || *I had a job to do it*, me costó trabajo hacerlo. || *It's not my job!*, ¡eso no es cosa mía! || *Just the job!*, ¡justo lo que nos hacía falta!, ¡estupendo! || *That car is just the job*, ese coche es exactamente lo que buscaba. || *To be on the job*, estar trabajando. || *To be out of a job*, estar sin trabajo, estar parado. || *To create jobs*, crear puestos de trabajo. || FAM. *To do a job on s.o.*, perjudicar mucho a alguien. || *To fall down on the job*, no estar a la altura del trabajo, fallar en el trabajo. || *To know one's job*, saber *or* conocer su oficio. || *To lose one's job*, perder su trabajo. || *To make a good job of sth.*, hacer algo bien. || *To make the best of a bad job*, poner a mal tiempo buena cara. || *To throw it in as a bad job*, darse por vencido. || *What a good job he was there!*, ¡menos mal que estaba allí!
— Adj. A destajo, a tanto alzado (by the piece). || Laboral, del trabajo (labour). || Alquilado, da (rent).
job [dʒɔb] v. tr. Dar [trabajo] a tanto alzado *or* a destajo (to give work to s.o. else). || Comprar y vender como intermediario (as a middleman). || Comprar y vender [acciones] (on Stock Exchange). || Meter: *he jobbed his son into the post*, metió a su hijo en el puesto. || Alquilar (horses, carriages). || Pinchar (to jab).
— V. intr. Trabajar a destajo (to work by the job). || Trabajar como corredor (as an agent). || U. S. Trabajar de vez en cuando (to do casual jobs).
Job [dʒəub] pr. n. Job, *m.*
jobber [dʒɔbə*] n. Intermediario, *m.* (middleman). || COMM. Corredor (*m.*) de Bolsa (middleman on the Stock Exchange). | Agiotista, *m.* (speculator). || Trabajador (*m.*) a destajo (pieceworker). || FAM. Chanchullero, *m.* (corrupt person).
jobbery [—əri] n. Chanchullos, *m. pl.*, intrigas, *f. pl.* (underhand business). || *A piece of jobbery*, un chanchullo, una intriga.
jobbing printer [ˈdʒɔbiŋˈprintə*] n. PRINT. Impresor (*m.*) de circulares, prospectos, etc. [y no de libros y revistas].
jobless [ˈdʒɔblis] adj. Sin trabajo.
job lot [ˈdʒɔblɔt] n. Partida (*f.*) de artículos vendidos a bajo precio (lot of cheap goods). || Surtido, *m.* (set of goods).
job printer [dʒɔbˈprintə*] n. U. S. See JOBBING PRINTER.
jockey [ˈdʒɔki] n. Jinete, *m.*, "jockey", *m.*
jockey [ˈdʒɔki] v. tr. Embaucar (to deceive). || Manejar (to handle). || Montar (a horse). || — *To jockey s.o. into doing sth.*, persuadirle a alguien a que haga algo. || *To jockey s.o. out of sth.*, quitar algo a alguien con artimañas.
— V. intr. Maniobrar.
jockstrap [ˈdʒɔkstræp] n. Suspensorio, *m.*
jocose [dʒəˈkəus] adj. Jocoso, sa; gracioso, sa; divertido, da (amusing): *jocose remarks*, observaciones jocosas. || Burlón, ona; bromista (full of jokes). || Alegre (happy).
jocosity [dʒəuˈkɔsiti] n. Jocosidad, *f.*
jocular [ˈdʒɔkjulə*] adj. See JOCOSE.
jocularity [,dʒɔkjuˈlæriti] n. Jocosidad, *f.*
jocund [ˈdʒɔkənd] adj. Jocoso, sa (inspiring laughter). || Jocundo, da; jovial (cheerful).
jocundity [dʒəuˈkʌnditi] n. Jocundidad, *f.*, jovialidad, *f.* (cheerfulness).
jodhpurs [ˈdʒɔdpuəz] pl. n. Pantalones (*m.*) de montar.
jog [dʒɔg] n. Empujón, *m.*, sacudida, *f.* (little push). || Codazo, *m.* (blow with the elbow). || Trote (*m.*) corto (slow run). || FIG. Estímulo, *m.* || U. S. Saliente, *m.* (on a wall). || FIG. *To give s.o.'s memory a jog*, refrescarle la memoria a uno.
jog [dʒɔg] v. tr. Dar un empujón a (to give a slight push). || Refrescar [la memoria] (memory). || Sacudir (to shake). || *To jog s.o.'s elbow*, darle ligeramente en el codo a uno.
— V. intr. *To jog along*, ir tranquilamente (to go peacefully along), andar con un traqueteo (a horse-drawn coach), andar a trote corto *or* a paso lento (horse), avanzar poco a poco (to progress slowly), ir tirando (to manage).
joggle [ˈdʒɔgl] n. TECH. Lengüeta, *f.*, espiga, *f.*, barbilla, *f.* || Sacudida (*f.*) ligera (a shake).
joggle [ˈdʒɔgl] v. tr. Menear (to jiggle). || Mover (to move). || TECH. Ensamblar (to join wood).
— V. intr. Menearse (to jiggle). || *To joggle along*, andar con un traqueteo (an old car, carriage, etc.).
jogtrot [ˈdʒɔgˈtrɔt] n. Trote (*m.*) corto (of horses): *at a jogtrot*, a trote corto. || FIG. Rutina, *f.* (routine).
john [dʒɔn] n. U. S. FAM. Retrete, *m.* [*Amer.*, inodoro, *m.*, baño, *m.*] (lavatory).
John [dʒɔn] pr. n. Juan, *m.* || — FAM. *John Barleycorn*, licor, *m.* || *John Bull*, héroe (*m.*) de una novela que personifica a Inglaterra. || U. S. *John Doe*, Fulano (*m.*) de Tal. || *John the Baptist*, San Juan Bautista.
John dory [—ˈdɔri] n. Pez (*m.*) de san Pedro.
Johnny [ˈdʒɔni] pr. n. Juanito, *m.* || FAM. Sujeto, *m.*, individuo, *m.*, tipo, *m.* (person).
johnnycake [—keik] n. U. S. Pan (*m.*) *or* torta (*f.*) de maíz.
join [dʒɔin] n. Juntura, *f.*, unión, *f.* || Costura, *f.* (seam).
join [dʒɔin] v. tr. Juntar, unir: *to join two things together*, juntar dos cosas; *to join the tables*, juntar las mesas. || Unir: *to join two people in matrimony*, unir a dos personas en matrimonio; *a line joins two points*, una línea une dos puntos. || Ir a dar a, empalmar con: *the path which joins the road*, el camino que va a dar a la carretera. || Hacer frontera con, lindar con: *the United States of America joins Canada in the north*, los Estados Unidos de América hacen frontera con Canadá por el norte. || Reunirse con, juntarse con: *to join one's friends*, reunirse con sus amigos. || Entrar en, ingresar en: *he joined the company last year*, entró en la empresa el año pasado. || Afiliarse a (a party). || MIL. Incorporarse a (one's unit). | Alistarse en (the army). || Hacerse socio de (to become a member of a club). || TECH. Ensamblar, unir (two pieces). || — *He will be joining us next week*, llegará la semana que viene. || *To join end to end*, unir por la punta. || *To join battle*, trabar batalla. || *To join forces with s.o.*, unirse con alguien. || FIG. *To join hands*, darse la mano (to shake hands), asociarse. || MAR. *To join one's ship*, regresar a bordo. || *To join s.o. in a glass of cognac*, tomar una copa de coñac con alguien. || *To join together in wishing s.o....*, unirse todos para desearle a alguien... || *To join with s.o. in an opinion*, compartir con alguien una opinión, hacerse eco de la opinión de alguien. || *Will you join us for dinner?*, ¿quieren cenar con nosotros?
— V. intr. Unirse (to become united). || Empalmar (lines). || Confluir (rivers). || Hacerse socio (of a club or society). || MIL. Alistarse (in the army).
— **To join in**, tomar parte en, participar en (to take part): *everybody joined in the argument*, todos participaron en la discusión. | Intervenir en (a debate, discussion). | Ponerse [todos] a...: *everybody joined in the applause, in the singing*, todos se pusieron a aplaudir, a cantar. || **To join up**, alistarse (in the army). | Juntar (two things). | Unirse (two roads, etc.). | Reunirse (people).
joinder [ˈdʒɔində*] n. Reunión, *f.*, unión, *f.*
joiner [ˈdʒɔinə*] n. Carpintero, *m.*, ebanista, *m.*
joinery [ˈdʒɔinəri] n. Carpintería, *f.*, ebanistería, *f.*

joining [ˈdʒɔiniŋ] n. Unión, *f.* || Bisagra, *f.* (of a door).
joint [dʒɔint] adj. Unido, da. || Colectivo, va; combinado, da; en común (collective, combined): *joint effort*, esfuerzo colectivo. || Conjunto, ta: *joint naval exercises*, maniobras navales conjuntas; *joint declaration*, declaración conjunta. || Mutuo, tua (agreement). || Solidario, ria (responsibility). || COMM. Conjunto, ta (account). || — *Joint author*, coautor, *m.* || *Joint commission, joint committee*, comisión mixta, comisión conjunta, comisión paritaria. || *Joint estate*, copropiedad, *f.* || *Joint guardian*, cotutor, *m.* || *Joint heir*, coheredero, *m.* || *Joint manager*, codirector, ra. || *Joint owner*, copropietario, ria. || *Joint ownership*, copropiedad, *f.* || *Joint partner*, copartícipe, *m.* & *f.* || *Joint stock*, capital (*m.*) social.
— N. Juntura, *f.*, unión, *f.*, junta, *f.* (join). || Ensambladura, *f.* (in wood). || TECH. Articulación, *f.* || ANAT. Articulación, *f.* || BOT. Nudo, *m.* || GEOL. Grieta, *f.* || CULIN. Corte (*m.*) para asar (meat for roasting). | Asado, *m.* (roast meat). || Bisagra, *f.* (of a door). || FAM. Antro, *m.* (place). | Porro, *m.* (marijuana). || — *Gambling joint*, garito, *m.* || *Hinged joint*, articulación, *f.* || FIG. *Joint in the harness*, punto débil *or* flaco *or* vulnerable. || *Out of joint*, dislocado, da (dislocated), descentrado, da (disordered). || *Rheumatism of the joints*, reúma (*m.*) articular. || *To come out of joint*, dislocarse. || *To put out of joint*, dislocar, desencajar. || TECH. *Universal joint*, junta cardán *or* universal. || *To throw out of joint*, dislocarse (a bone).
joint [dʒɔint] v. tr. Juntar, unir (to join). || Ensamblar (to join wood). || Descuartizar (animals into joints). || Articular.
jointed [ˈdʒɔintid] adj. Articulado, da. || Desmontable (fishing rod). || BOT. Nudoso, sa.
jointer [ˈdʒɔintə*] n. Garlopa, *f.* (plane).
jointly [dʒɔintli] adv. Conjuntamente, en común.
jointress [—ris] n. Viuda (*f.*) usufructuaria.
joint-stock company [—ˈstok,kʌmpəni] n. COMM. Sociedad (*f.*) anónima.
jointure [ˈdʒɔintʃə*] n. JUR. Viudedad, *f.*
joist [ˈdʒɔist] n. ARCH. Vigueta, *f.*
joke [dʒəuk] n. Chiste, *m.* (funny story): *he told me a joke*, me contó un chiste. || Broma, *f.* (funny situation, prank): *he must have his little joke*, le encanta gastar bromas; *I can take a joke*, yo sé tomar las bromas; *it is no joke*, no es broma; *practical joke*, broma pesada. || Hazmerreír, *m.*: *he's the joke of the office*, es el hazmerreír del despacho. || Payaso, sa; bufón, ona (buffoon). || — *As a joke*, en broma, bromeando. || *I did it for a joke*, lo hice en broma. || *I don't see the joke*, no le veo la gracia. || *It's no joke working with him*, no tiene ninguna gracia trabajar con él. || *To crack a joke*, hacer un chiste (to say sth. witty), contar un chiste (to tell a funny story). || *The joke is that*, lo gracioso es que. || *The joke was on him*, fue él quien pagó la broma, él fue la víctima de la broma. || *To know how to take a joke*, saber tomar las bromas. || *To make a joke of everything*, no tomar nada en serio, tomar todo en broma. || *To play a (practical) joke on s.o.*, gastarle una broma a alguien. || *To take as a joke*, tomar en broma.
joke [dʒəuk] v. intr. Bromear: *he is joking*, está bromeando. || Contar chistes (to tell jokes). || — *And he wasn't joking*, y hablaba en serio, y no era broma. || *Joking apart*, hablando en serio, bromas aparte. || *To be in a joking mood*, estar de broma. || *To joke about sth.*, bromear sobre algo. || *You must be joking!*, ¡no hablarás en serio!
— V. tr. Dar una broma a, gastar bromas a.
joker [—ə*] n. Bromista, *m.* & *f.* (s.o. who jokes a lot). || Chistoso, sa (wit). || Payaso, sa; bufón, ona (buffoon). || Comodín, *m.* (in a pack of cards). || FAM. Tipo, *m.*, individuo, *m.*, sujeto, *m.* (bloke): *what's that joker doing here?*, ¿qué hace este tipo aquí? || U. S. Disposición (*f.*) engañosa (in a legal document).
joking [—iŋ] adj. Humorístico, ca; gracioso, sa.
— N. Bromas, *f. pl.* || Chistes, *m. pl.*
jokingly [—iŋli] adv. En broma.
jollification [,dʒɔlifiˈkeiʃən] n. FAM. Jolgorio, *m.*
jollify [ˈdʒɔlifai] v. intr. FAM. Pasarlo en grande.
jolliness [ˈdʒɔlinis] n. Jovialidad, *f.*
jollity [ˈdʒɔliti] n. Jovialidad, *f.* (joviality). || Alegría, *f.*, regocijo, *m.* (gaiety). || Jolgorio, *m.* (merrymaking).
jolly [ˈdʒɔli] adj. Jovial, alegre (jovial): *a jolly fellow*, un tipo jovial. || FAM. Divertido, da (amusing). | Piripi (a little drunk): *to get jolly*, ponerse piripi. | Bueno, na (used intensively): *a jolly mess*, un buen lío. || Bonito, ta (pretty). || — FAM. *He gave her a jolly hiding*, le dio una buena tunda. | *It's a jolly shame*, es una verdadera vergüenza. | *Jolly fool*, tonto (*m.*) de remate. || *The jolly God*, Baco. || FAM. *To have a jolly time*, pasarlo en grande. | *To make a jolly din*, armar mucho jaleo.
— Adv. FAM. Muy, la mar de (very): *jolly tired*, muy cansado. || — *A jolly good hiding*, una buena tunda. || *He's jolly well right*, tiene toda la razón. || *I'll do what I jolly well like*, haré lo que me dé la gana. || *Jolly good!*, ¡estupendo! || *Take jolly good care of her*, cuídala muy bien.
jolly [ˈdʒɔli] v. tr. Convencer: *to jolly s.o. into doing sth.*, convencer a uno para que haga algo. || Seguirle el humor a (to humour). || Animar (to encourage).
— V. intr. Burlarse.
jolly boat [—bəut] n. MAR. Bote, *m.*, esquife, *m.*
Jolly Roger [—ˈrɔdʒə*] n. (Ant.). Pabellón (*m.*) pirata, bandera (*f.*) negra (flag).
jolt [dʒəult] n. Sacudida, *f.* (jerk): *the car gave a jolt*, el coche dio una sacudida. || Choque, *m.* (bump): *the jolt of the car against the kerb*, el choque del coche contra el borde de la acera. || FIG. Susto, *m.* (fright): *it gave me quite a jolt*, ¡menudo susto me dio! || — *The car stopped with a jolt*, el coche se paró en seco. || FIG. *The news of his death was a jolt for her*, la noticia de su muerte le impresionó mucho.
jolt [dʒəult] v. tr. Sacudir (to shake). || Dar un empujón *or* una sacudida a (to give a shove). || — *He jolted the glass out of my hand*, me dio un empujón que me hizo soltar el vaso. || *To jolt s.o. back to reality*, hacer que uno vuelva bruscamente a la realidad.
— V. intr. Moverse a sacudidas (to move jerkily). || Traquetear (vehicle). || *To jolt along*, avanzar dando tumbos.
jolting [—iŋ] n. Traqueteo, *m.* (of a car, etc.).
Jonah [ˈdʒəunə] pr. n. Jonás, *m.* || FIG. Gafe, *m.* (jinx).
Jonathan [ˈdʒɔnəθən] pr. n. Jonatás, *m.*, Jonatán, *m.*
jongleur [ʒɔ̃:ŋˈglə:*] n. (Ant.). Juglar, *m.*
jonnycake [ˈdʒɔnikeik] n. See JOHNNYCAKE.
jonquil [ˈdʒɔŋkwil] n. BOT. Junquillo, *m.*
Jordan [ˈdʒɔ:dn] pr. n. GEOGR. Jordán, *m.* (river). | Jordania, *f.* (country).
Jordan [ˈdʒɔ:dn] or **Jordanian** [dʒɔ:ˈdeinjən] adj./n. Jordano, na.
jorum [ˈdʒɔ:rəm] n. Tazón, *m.*
Joseph [ˈdʒəuzif] pr. n. José, *m.*
Josephine [ˈdʒəuzifi:n] pr. n. Josefina, *f.*
josh [dʒɔʃ] n. Broma, *f.*
josh [dʒɔʃ] v. tr. U. S. FAM. Tomar el pelo a (to tease): *stop joshing him*, deja de tomarle el pelo.
— V. intr. U. S. FAM. Bromear, estar de broma.
Joshua [ˈdʒɔʃwə] pr. n. Josué, *m.*
joss [dʒɔs] n. REL. Ídolo (*m.*) chino.
joss house [—haus] n. REL. Templo (*m.*) chino.
joss stick [—stik] n. Pebete, *m.*
jostle [ˈdʒɔsl] n. Empujones, *m. pl.* (shoving).
jostle [ˈdʒɔsl] v. tr. Empujar, dar empujones a (to push). || *To jostle one's way through the crowd*, abrirse paso a codazos entre la multitud.
— V. intr. Codear (to elbow). || Empujar, dar empujones (to push). || Abrirse paso a empujones: *to jostle for tickets*, abrirse paso a empujones para ir a comprar billetes. || — *To jostle against*, chocar contra. || *To jostle with*, — mezclarse con.
jot [dʒɔt] n. Jota, *f.*: *I don't understand a jot*, no entiendo ni jota; *not a jot*, ni jota. || Pizca, *f.*, poco, *m.* (tiny amount). || *I don't care a jot*, me importa poco.
jot [dʒɔt] v. tr. *To jot down*, tomar nota de, anotar, apuntar: *jot it down*, apúntalo.
jotter [—ə*] n. Bloc, *m.* (notepad).
jotting [—iŋ] n. Apunte, *m.*, nota, *f.*
joule [dʒu:l] n. PHYS. Julio, *m.*, joule, *m.*
journal [ˈdʒə:nl] n. Diario, *m.* (daily record, diary). || Periódico, *m.* (newspaper). || Revista, *f.* (magazine). || COMM. Diario, *m.* (in bookkeeping). || Boletín, *m.* (of a club, learned society, etc.). || MAR. Diario (*m.*) de a bordo. || TECH. Gorrón, *m.*, muñón, *m.*
journal box [—bɔks] n. TECH. Cojinete, *m.* (bearing).
journalese [dʒə:nəˈli:z] n. Lenguaje (*m.*) periodístico.
journalism [ˈdʒə:nəlizəm] n. Periodismo, *m.*
journalist [ˈdʒə:nəlist] n. Periodista, *m.* & *f.*
journalistic [,dʒə:nəˈlistik] adj. Periodístico, ca.
journalize [ˈdʒə:nəlaiz] v. tr. Contabilizar (in bookkeeping). || Apuntar en un diario.
— V. intr. Escribir un diario (to keep a diary).
journey [ˈdʒə:ni] n. Viaje, *m.*: *a long journey*, un viaje largo; *outward, return journey*, viaje de ida, de vuelta; *four journeys to the kitchen*, cuatro viajes a la cocina; *I was on a journey*, estaba de viaje. || — *Have a nice journey!*, ¡buen viaje! || *To go on a journey*, ir de viaje. || FIG. FAM. *To go on one's last journey*, irse al otro mundo, irse al otro barrio (to die).
journey [ˈdʒə:ni] v. intr. Viajar.
journeyman [ˈdʒə:nimən] n. Oficial, *m.* (qualified worker).

— OBSERV. El plural de *journeyman* es *journeymen*.

journeywork [ˈdʒə:niwə:k] n. Trabajo (*m.*) realizado por un oficial. || FIG. Trabajo (*m.*) rutinaro.
joust [dʒaust] n. (Ant.) Justa, *f.*, torneo, *m.*
joust [dʒaust] v. intr. (Ant.). Participar en una justa.
Jove [dʒəuv] pr. n. MYTH. Júpiter, *m.* || *By Jove!*, ¡por Júpiter!, ¡por Dios!
jovial [ˈdʒəuvjəl] adj. Jovial.
joviality [,dʒəuviˈæliti] n. Jovialidad, *f.*
Jovian [ˈdʒəuvjən] adj. Joviano, na.
jowl [dʒaul] n. Papada, *f.* (fleshy part under the jaw). || Mandíbula, *f.* (jawbone of people). || Quijada, *f.* (jawbone of animals). || Mejilla, *f.*, carrillo, *m.* (cheek). || ZOOL. Papada, *f.* (of oxen). | Barba, *f.* (of birds). || FIG. *Cheek by jowl*, cara a cara.
joy [dʒɔi] n. Alegría, *f.*, júbilo, *m.* (great gladness). || Deleite, *m.*, placer, *m.* (pleasure). || — *Her voice was a joy to the ear*, su voz era un regalo para el oído. || *It is a joy to hear her*, da gusto oírla *or* escucharla, es un placer escucharla. || *It's a joy to see*, da gusto verlo. || *I wish you joy*, le doy la enhorabuena (congratulations), le deseo suerte (good luck). || *She is her mother's joy*, es la alegría de su madre. || *The joys of country life*, los placeres de la vida en el campo. || *To beam*

with joy, estar radiante de alegría. || *To be beside o.s. with joy*, estar loco de alegría. || *To jump for joy*, saltar de alegría.
joyful [—ful] adj. Alegre, contento, ta.
joyfulness [—fulnis] n. Alegría, *f.*, gozo, *m.*
joyless [ˈdʒɔilis] adj. Triste, sin alegría.
joylessness [ˈdʒɔilisnis] n. Tristeza, *f.*
joyous [ˈdʒɔiəs] adj. Alegre, gozoso, sa (happy). || *A joyous event*, un feliz acontecimiento.
joyride [ˈdʒɔiraid] n. FAM. Paseo (*m.*) en coche [sin autorización].
joy stick [ˈdʒɔistik] n. AVIAT. FAM. Palanca (*f.*) de mando.
jubbah (U. S. **jubba**) [ˈdʒəbə] n. Aljuba, *f.*
jubilance [ˈdʒu:biləns] n. Júbilo, *m.*, alborozo, *m.*
jubilant [ˈdʒu:bilənt] adj. Jubiloso, sa; alborozado, da.
jubilate [ˈdʒu:bileit] v. intr. Exultar de alegría.
jubilation [ˌdʒu:biˈleiʃən] n. Júbilo, *m.*, regocijo, *m.*, alborozo, *m.*
jubilee [ˈdʒu:bili:] n. Quincuagésimo aniversario, *m.* (fiftieth anniversary). || Aniversario, *m.* (anniversary). || HIST. REL. Jubileo, *m.* || Júbilo, *m* (jubilation).
— Adj. Jubilar.
Judaea [dʒu:ˈdiə] pr. n. GEOGR. Judea, *f.*
Judaeo-Christian [dʒu:ˈdiəuˈkristjən] adj./n. Judeocristiano, na.
Judaeo-German [—ˈdʒə:mən] n. Judeoalemán, *m.*
Judaeo-Spanish [—ˈspæniʃ] adj./n. Judeoespañol.
Judah [ˈdʒu:də] pr. n. Judá, *m.*
Judaic [dʒuˈdeiik] adj. Judaico, ca.
Judaical [—əl] adj. Judaico, ca.
Judaism [ˈdʒu:deiizəm] n. REL. Judaísmo, *m.*
Judaist [ˈdʒu:deiist] n. Judaizante, *m.* & *f.*
Judaize [ˈdʒu:deiaiz] v. tr. Convertir al judaísmo.
— V. intr. Judaizar.
Judaizer [—ə*] n. Judaizante, *m.* & *f.*
Judas [ˈdʒu:dəs] pr. n. Judas. || FIG. Judas, *m.* (traitor). || *Judas Iscariot*, Judas Iscariote.
judas hole [—həul] n. Mirilla, *f.*
Judas tree [—tri:] n. BOT. Ciclamor, *m.*
Judea [dʒu:ˈdiə] pr. n. GEOGR. Judea, *f.*
judge [dʒʌdʒ] n. JUR. Juez, *m.*: *judge of the court of first instance*, juez de primera instancia. || Juez, *m.* (in a competition). || Árbitro, *m.* (in a dispute). || SP. Juez, *m.*: *the line judges*, los jueces de línea. || Entendido, da; conocedor, ra: *a good judge of music*, un entendido en música. || — *I am a poor judge of music*, no entiendo de música. || *Judge advocate*, auditor (*m.*) militar. || *The Divine Judge*, el Juez Supremo. || *To be a poor judge of character*, no saber juzgar a la gente. || *To be no judge of*, no poder juzgar.
Judge [dʒʌdʒ] n. Juez, *m.* (in Jewish history). || *The Book of Judges*, el libro de los Jueces.
judge [dʒʌdʒ] v. tr. JUR. Juzgar: *to judge a case*, juzgar un caso. | Declarar: *they judged him guilty*, le declararon culpable. || SP. Arbitrar. | Juzgar (in a competition). || Considerar, estimar, juzgar (to consider): *it has been judged necessary*, se ha juzgado necesario. || Calcular, evaluar: *he judged the distance well*, calculó bien la distancia. || — *It is difficult* o *hard to judge*, es difícil de juzgar. || FIG. *One can't judge a book by its cover*, no se puede juzgar por las apariencias.
— V. intr. Opinar, formarse una opinión (to arrive at an opinion). || Juzgar: *don't judge too hastily*, no juzgues apresuradamente. || Ser juez, juzgar, actuar como juez (to act as a deciding body). || — *How did the jury judge?*, ¿cuál ha sido el veredicto del jurado? || *Judging by* o *from the weight of it*, a juzgar por el peso. || *One cannot judge by appearances*, no se puede juzgar por las apariencias. || *To judge well, ill of s.o.*, tener una buena, una mala opinión de alguien.
judgement [ˈdʒʌdʒmənt] n. See JUDGMENT.
Judges [ˈdʒʌdʒiz] n. REL. Libro (*m.*) de los Jueces.
judgeship [—ʃip] n. Judicatura, *f.*, magistratura, *f.*
judgment or **judgement** [ˈdʒʌdʒmənt] n. JUR. Juicio, *m.* (trial). | Sentencia, *f.*, fallo, *m.* (legal sentence): *judgment by default*, sentencia en rebeldía. || Juicio, *m.*: *a man of sound judgment*, un hombre de mucho juicio. || Opinión, *f.* (opinion): *in your judgment*, en su opinión. || REL. Juicio, *m.*: *Last Judgment*, Juicio Final; *Judgment Day*, Día del Juicio. || Apreciación, *f.*: *an error of judgment*, un error de apreciación. || — *In the judgment of many*, para muchos, a los ojos de muchos. || FAM. *It's a judgment on you*, es un castigo de Dios. || *Judgment seat*, tribunal, *m.* || *Sense of judgment*, juicio. || *To form a judgment on sth.*, formarse una opinión sobre algo. || *To give one's judgment on sth.*, dar su opinión sobre algo. || *To make a judgment about sth.*, emitir un juicio sobre algo. || *To pass judgment*, pronunciar una sentencia (in court), juzgar (to judge). || *To the best of my judgment*, por lo que puedo juzgar, según mi entender.
judicature [ˈdʒu:dikətʃə*] n. JUR. Judicatura, *f.* (administration, body of judges). | Juzgado, *m.*, tribunal, *m.* (a law court).
judicial [dʒu:ˈdiʃəl] adj. JUR. Judicial: *judicial powers*, poderes judiciales. | Legal: *judicial separation*, separación legal. || Sensato, ta; juicioso, sa (judicious). || Imparcial (unbiased). || *Judicial faculty*, sentido crítico, discernimiento, *m.*
judiciary [dʒuˈdiʃiəri] n. JUR. Magistratura, *f.* (the apparatus of law and its administrators). || Poder (*m.*) judicial: *the legislative, the executive and the judiciary*, el poder legislativo, ejecutivo y judicial.
— Adj. Judicial.
judicious [dʒuˈdiʃəs] adj. Juicioso, sa; sensato, ta.
judiciousness [—nis] n. Sensatez, *f.*, juicio, *m.*, buen sentido, *m.*
Judith [ˈdʒu:diθ] pr. n. Judit, *f.*
judo [ˈdʒu:dəu] n. SP. Judo, *m.*
judoka [ˈdʒu:dəukə] n. Judoka, *m.*
jug [dʒʌg] n. Jarra, *f.* (for water, beer, etc.). || FAM. Chirona, *f.*, trena, *f.* (prison): *to be in the jug*, estar en la trena, estar en chirona.
jug [dʒʌg] v. tr. CULIN. Estofar. || FAM. Encarcelar, meter en chirona. || *Jugged hare*, encebollado (*m.*) de liebre.
juggernaut [ˈdʒʌgənɔ:t] n. Monstruo (*m.*) que destruye a los hombres. || Fuerza (*f.*) irresistible.
juggle [ˈdʒʌgl] n. Juegos (*m. pl.*) malabares (tricks of dexterity). || Juego (*m.*) de manos (magic trick). || FIG. Timo, *m.* (swindle). | Truco, *m.*, treta, *f.*, trampa, *f.* (trick).
juggle [ˈdʒʌgl] v. intr. Hacer juegos malabares (to perform tricks of dexterity). || Hacer juegos de manos (a magician). || — *To juggle s.o. out of*, quitar engañosamente a alguien. || *To juggle with*, hacer juegos malabares con (in a circus, etc.), dar vueltas a (ideas), hacer malabarismos con: *to juggle skilfully with numbers*, hacer malabarismos con los números; falsificar, hacer trampas con (to falsify, to manipulate).
— V. tr. Hacer juegos malabares con (to perform tricks of dexterity with). || FIG. Falsear, falsificar (to falsify). | Embaucar (to cheat). || *To juggle away*, escamotar, escamotear (to make vanish).
juggler [—ə*] n. Malabarista, *m.* & *f.* || Prestidigitador, *m.*, ilusionista, *m.* & *f.* (magician).
jugglery [ˈdʒʌgləri] or **juggling** [ˈdʒʌgliŋ] n. Juegos (*m. pl.*) malabares (tricks of dexterity). || Juegos (*m. pl.*) de manos, prestidigitación, *f.* (magic trick). || FIG. Timo, *m.*, fraude, *m.* (swindle). | Trampas, *f. pl.* (tricks). | Manipulación, *f.* (manipulation). | Falsificación, *f.* (falsification).
jughead [ˈdʒʌghed] n. FAM. Testarudo, da; cabezota, *m.* & *f.* (stubborn). | Mentecato, ta (idiot).
Jugoslav [ˈju:gəuˈslɑ:v] adj./n. Yugoslavo, va.
Jugoslavia [ˈju:gəuˈslɑ:vjə] pr. n. Yugoslavia, *f.*
Jugoslavian [—n] adj. Yugoslavo, va.
Jugoslavic [—vik] adj. Yugoslavo, va.
jugular [ˈdʒʌgjulə*] adj. ANAT. Yugular: *jugular vein*, vena yugular.
— N. Yugular, *f.* (vein).
jugulate [ˈdʒʌgjuleit] v. tr. Degollar. || FIG. Detener (a disease, an epidemic).
juice [dʒu:s] n. Jugo, *m.* (fluid). || Jugo, *m.* (of meat). || Zumo, *m.*, jugo, *m.* (of fruits, etc.). || FAM. Lo picante (of a story). | Gasolina, *f.* (petrol). | Corriente, *f.* (electricity). || *Gastric juice*, jugo gástrico.
juiciness [ˈdʒu:sinis] n. Jugosidad, *f.* || FAM. Lo picante.
juicy [ˈdʒu:si] adj. Jugoso, sa (rich in juice): *a juicy orange*, una naranja jugosa. || FAM. Sustancioso, sa (profitable): *juicy profits*, beneficios sustanciosos. | Picante, sabroso, sa (racy): *a juicy story*, una historia picante.
jujitsu [dʒu:ˈdʒitsu:] n. Jiu-jitsu, *m.*
juju [ˈdʒu:dʒu:] n. Grisgrís, *m.*, talismán, *m.*
jujube [ˈdʒu:dʒu:b] n. BOT. Azufaifa, *f.* (fruit). | Azufaifo, *m.* (plant). || Pastilla (*f.*) de azufaifa (sweet).
jujutsu [dʒu:ˈdʒutsu:] n. Jiu-jitsu, *m.*
jukebox [ˈdʒu:kbɔks] n. Máquina (*f.*) de discos.
julep [ˈdʒu:lep] n. Julepe, *m.* (drink).
Jules [ˈdʒu:lz] pr. n. Julio, *m.*
Julian [dʒu:ljən] pr. n. Julián, *m.* || Juliano, *m.* (Roman emperor).
— Adj. Juliano, na: *Julian calendar*, calendario juliano.
Juliana [ˌdʒu:liˈɑ:nə] pr. n. Juliana, *f.*
julienne [ˌdʒu:liˈen] n. Juliana, *f.*, sopa, (*f.*) juliana.
Juliet [ˈdʒu:ljət] pr. n. Julieta, *f.*
July [dʒuˈlai] n. Julio, *m.*: *on the nineteenth of July 1982*, el 19 [diez y nueve] de julio de 1982.
jumble [ˈdʒʌmbl] n. Revoltijo, *m.*, embrollo, *m.*, confusión, *f.*, mezcolanza, *f.* (confused collection). || FIG. Confusión, *f.* (mental). || — *A jumble of books*, un montón de libros revueltos. || *To get into a jumble*, hacerse un lío, embrollarse.
jumble [ˈdʒʌmbl] v. tr. Embrollar, confundir (to confuse). || Mezclar (to mix). || *Jumbled papers*, papeles revueltos.
jumble sale [—seil] n. Venta (*f.*) por liquidación (clearance sale). || Venta (*f.*) de caridad.
jumbo [ˈdʒʌmbəu] adj. Muy grande, enorme, colosal, gigantesco, ca (very big). || *Jumbo jet*, jumbo, *m.*, avión (*m.*) de reacción de gran capacidad.
— N. Coloso, *m.* (big animal). || FAM. Elefante, *m.*
jump [dʒʌmp] n. Salto, *m.*: *with a jump he avoided the puddle*, salvó el charco de un salto *or* dando un salto; *it was a difficult jump, but he made it*, era un salto difícil, pero logró darlo. || Aumento (*m.*) grande, salto, *m.* (of prices). || Salto, *m.* (short trip). || Sobresalto, *m.* (of surprise). || Acción (*f.*) de comer [en damas] (in draughts). || SP. Obstáculo, *m.* (in a race). | Salto, *m.*: *high jump*, salto de altura; *long jump*, salto de longitud; *to take a jump*, dar un salto (a

horse). || — FIG. *Now he is in for the high jump!*, ¡ahora se va a enterar! || *There has been a big jump in sales*, las ventas han experimentado un aumento muy grande. || *To be one jump ahead of s.o.*, llevar ventaja a alguien. || *To give a jump*, dar un salto. || *To give s.o. a jump*, dar un susto a alguien. || *To have the jump on s.o.*, llevar ventaja a alguien. || *To take a running jump at*, coger impulso para saltar.

jump [dʒʌmp] v. intr. Saltar: *he hurt his leg when he jumped*, se hizo daño en la pierna al saltar. || Tirarse, saltar (from a height). || Botar, rebotar (to bounce). || Sobresaltarse (to start): *she jumped when I called her*, se sobresaltó cuando le llamé. || Dar un salto: *the cost of living, the temperature jumped*, el coste de la vida, la temperatura dio un salto. || Comerse una ficha [en damas] (in draughts). || — FIG. *And jump to it!*, ¡y hazlo volando!, !rápido! || *He jumped on the bus*, subió de un salto al autobús. || FIG. *I nearly jumped out of my skin!*, ¡qué susto me pegué! | *I was criticizing her and John jumped down my throat*, estaba criticándola y Juan se puso furioso. || *To jump about*, dar saltos, brincar, saltar. || *To jump across* o *over sth.*, salvar *or* cruzar algo de un salto. || *To jump ahead*, ponerse el primero de un salto. || *To jump at a chance*, aprovechar una oportunidad. || *To jump at s.o.*, echarse encima de alguien. || *To jump back*, dar un salto atrás. || *To jump down*, bajar de un salto. || *To jump for joy*, saltar de alegría. || FIG. *To jump from one thing to another*, saltar de un tema a otro. || *To jump in*, saltar a, subir de un salto a (car), saltar a (water). || FIG. *To jump in at the deep end*, coger el toro por los cuernos. || *To jump in the water*, tirarse al agua. || FIG. *To jump on s.o.*, echarse encima de alguien. || *To jump out from behind*, salir de repente de detrás de. || *To jump out of* o *to jump from*, saltar de. || *To jump to conclusions*, sacar conclusiones precipitadas. || *To jump up*, levantarse de golpe *or* de un salto. || *To jump with*, concordar con, coincidir con. || *To make s.o. jump*, sobresaltar a uno.

— V. tr. Saltar, salvar (to cross by leaping): *he jumped the wall*, saltó el muro. || SP. Hacer saltar: *he jumped the horse over the fence*, hizo saltar la valla al caballo. | Presentar en un concurso (to present in a competition). | Levantar (game). || Saltarse (to miss out): *you jumped a few details*, se saltó algunos detalles. || Usurpar (to usurp). || Comer (in draughts): *he jumped my king*, me comió la dama. || FAM. Agredir, atacar (to attack). | Escapar de, fugarse de (a prison). | Largarse de (a town). || — *To jump a bid*, marcar más alto (in bridge). || *To jump a claim*, usurpar una concesión minera. || *To jump a queue*, colarse. || U. S. FAM. *To jump a train*, subirse a un tren en marcha para no pagar billete. || FAM. *To jump the lights*, saltarse el semáforo. || *To jump the rails* o *the tracks*, descarrilar, salirse de las vías.

jumper [ˈdʒʌmpə*] n. Saltador, ra (s.o. who jumps). || ELECTR. Cable (*m.*) de conexión. || MIN. Barrena, *f.* || Jersey, *m.* [cerrado] (pullover). || U. S. Vestido (*m.*) sin mangas (dress). | Pelele, *m.* (rompers). | Mono, *m.* (for workmen).

jumpiness [ˈdʒʌmpinis] n. Nerviosismo, *m.*

jumping [ˈdʒʌmpiŋ] n. SP. Pruebas (*f. pl.*) de saltos (in athletics). || *Show jumping*, concurso hípico.

jumping bean [—bi:n] n. BOT. Judía (*f.*) saltadora [*Amer.*, frijol *or* poroto saltador].

jumping jack [—djæk] n. Buscapiés, *m. inv.* (firework). || Pelele, *m.* (child's toy).

jumping-off place [—ˈɔ:fpleis] n. Lugar (*m.*) remoto. || FIG. Situación (*f.*) extrema.

jump-off [ˈdʒʌmpɔf] n. Salida, *f.* (in a race).

jump rope [ˈdʒʌmprəup] n. U. S. Saltador, *m.*, comba, *f.* (skipping rope).

jump seat [ˈdʒʌmpsi:t] n. Traspuntín, *m.*, traspontín, *m.* (in a car).

jump suit [ˈdʒʌmpsju:t] n. Mono, *m.* (garment).

jumpy [ˈdʒʌmpi] adj. Nervioso, sa (nervous). || Asustadizo, za (easily frightened). || Que traquetea (train, etc.). || Cortado, da (style).

juncaceae [dʒʌŋˈkeisi:i] pl. n. BOT. Juncáceas, *f.*

junction [ˈdʒʌŋkʃən] n. Empalme, *m.* (of railway). || Estación (*f.*) de empalme (railway station). || Unión, *f.*, juntura, *f.* (join). || Cruce, *m.* (of roads). || ELECTR. Empalme, *m.* || Confluencia, *f.* (of rivers).

junction box [—bɔks] n. ELECTR. Caja (*f.*) de empalme.

juncture [ˈdʒʌŋktʃə*] n. Unión, *f.*, juntura, *f.* (join). || ANAT. Coyuntura, *f.* || Confluencia, *f.* (of rivers). || Momento, *m.* (moment). || Coyuntura, *f.* (time with relation to circumstances): *at this juncture*, en esta coyuntura.

June [dʒu:n] n. Junio, *m.*: *on the fourth of June 1901*, el cuatro de junio de 1901.

June beetle [—ˈbi:tl] n. U. S. ZOOL. Escarabajo, *m.*

June bug [—bʌg] n. U. S. ZOOL. Escarabajo, *m.*

jungle [ˈdʒʌŋgl] n. Selva, *f.*, jungla, *f.*: *tropical jungle*, selva tropical. || FIG. Maraña, *f.* (tangle, jumble). | Laberinto, *m.* (maze). || FIG. *The concrete jungle*, el mundo de hormigón, el universo de hormigón.

junior [ˈdʒu:njə*] adj. Hijo: *John Brown junior*, John Brown hijo. || Subalterno, na; inferior (lower in grade): *junior officer*, oficial subalterno. || Más nuevo, va; más reciente (more recent): *their club is two years junior to ours*, su club es dos años más reciente que el nuestro. || De menor antigüedad: *the junior members of the committee*, los miembros de menor antigüedad de la comisión. || Más joven, menor (younger). || SP. Juvenil: *the junior team*, el equipo juvenil. || U. S. De penúltimo año.

— N. Subalterno, na (lower in grade). || Menor, *m.* & *f.* (younger person). || Jovencito, *m.*: *come here, Junior*, ven aquí, jovencito. || U. S. Estudiante (*m.* & *f.*) de penúltimo año (student). || Pequeño, ña (in school): *the seniors and the juniors*, los mayores y los pequeños. || SP. Juvenil, *m.* & *f.* || — *She is two years my junior*, le llevo dos años, es dos años más joven que yo. || SP. *To play for the juniors*, jugar en el equipo juvenil.

junior college [—ˈkɔlidʒ] n. U. S. Colegio (*m.*) universitario para los dos primeros años.

juniper [ˈdʒu:nipə*] n. BOT. Enebro, *m.*

junk [dʒʌŋk] n. MAR. Junco, *m.* (eastern vessel). | Cuerda (*f.*) gastada (old rope). | Cecina, *f.* (meat). || FAM. Sandeces, *f. pl.* (nonsense). | Trastos (*m. pl.*) viejos (useless objects). | Chatarra, *f.* (old iron, metal). || — FAM. *He talks a lot of junk*, no dice más que tonterías. | *The book is a load of junk*, el libro es una porquería. | *Where did you buy this junk?*, ¿dónde compraste esta porquería *or* estas porquerías?

junk [dʒʌŋk] v. tr. U. S. Desechar, tirar a la basura. | Hacer chatarra.

junket [ˈdʒʌŋkit] n. Dulce (*m.*) de leche cuajada (sweet). || U. S. Excursión, *f.* (excursion). | Viaje, *m.* (journey). | Fiesta, *f.* (party).

junket [ˈdʒʌŋkit] v. intr. U. S. Ir de excursión (to go on an excursion).

junk heap [dʒʌŋkhi:p] n. Vertedero, *m.*

junkie [ˈdʒʌŋki] n. FAM. Toxicómano, na; drogadicto, ta.

junkman [ˈdʒʌŋkmən] or **junk merchant** [ˈdʒʌŋkˌmə:tʃənt] n. Trapero, *m.*

— OBSERV. El plural de *junkman* es *junkmen*

junk market [ˈdʒʌŋkmɑ:kit] n. Rastro, *m.*, mercado (*m.*) de objetos de lance.

junkshop [ˈdʒʌŋkʃɔp] n. Baratillo, *m.*

junkyard [ˈdʒʌŋkjɑ:d] n. Depósito (*m.*) de chatarra.

junta [ˈdʒʌntə] n. HIST. Junta, *f.*

junto [ˈdʒʌntə] n. Facción, *f.*

Jupiter [ˈdʒu:pitə*] pr. n. MYTH. Júpiter, *m.*

jural [ˈdʒuərəl] adj. Jurídico, ca; legal.

Jurassic [dʒuˈræsik] adj. GEOL. Jurásico, ca.

— N. GEOL. Período (*m.*) jurásico, jurásico, *m.*

jurat [ˈdʒuəræt] n. Escritura (*f.*) notarial.

juratory [ˈdʒuərətəri] adj. JUR. Bajo juramento (declaration). | Jurado, da (obligation).

jurel [huˈrel] n. ZOOL. Jurel, *m.* (fish).

juridic [dʒuəˈridik] adj. Jurídico, ca.

juridical [—əl] adj. Jurídico, ca.

jurisconsult [ˈdʒuəriskənˌsʌlt] n. Jurisconsulto, *m.*

jurisdiction [ˌdʒuərisˈdikʃən] n. Jurisdicción, *f.* || *To fall* o *to come under s.o.'s jurisdiction*, caer bajo la jurisdicción de uno, ser de la competencia de uno.

jurisdictional [—əl] adj. Jurisdiccional.

jurisprudence [ˈdʒuərisˌpru:dəns] n. Jurisprudencia, *f.* || *Medical jurisprudence*, medicina (*f.*) legal.

jurisprudent [ˈdʒuərisˌpru:dənt] n. Jurisperito, *m.*

jurist [ˈdʒuərist] n. Jurista, *m.* & *f.*

juristic [dʒuəˈristik] adj. Jurídico, ca.

juristical [—əl] adj. Jurídico, ca.

juror [ˈdʒuərə*] n. Jurado, da (person).

jury [ˈdʒuəri] n. Jurado, *m.*: *to sit on the jury*, ser miembro del jurado. || Tribunal, *m.* (for exams).

jury box [—bɔks] n. Tribuna (*f.*) *or* banco (*m.*) del jurado.

juryman [—mən] n. Miembro (*m.*) de un jurado, jurado, *m.*

— OBSERV. El plural de *juryman* es *jurymen*.

jurymast [—mɑ:st] n. MAR. Bandola, *f.*

jury rig [—rig] n. MAR. Aparejo (*m.*) provisional.

jurywoman [—ˈwumən] n. Jurado, *m.*

— OBSERV. El plural de *jurywoman* es *jurywomen*.

jussive [ˈdʒʌsiv] adj. GRAMM. Imperativo, va.

— N. GRAMM. Imperativo, *m.*

just [dʒʌst] adj. Justo, ta (fair, deserved, honest): *a just decision*, una decisión justa; *a just price, man* un precio, un hombre justo. || Justificado, da; fundado, da; justo, ta (well-founded, justified): *just grounds for complaint*, motivo justificado de queja. || Exacto, ta; justo, ta (accurate). || — *As is just*, como es justo. || *To get one's just reward* o *deserts*, recibir su merecido. || *To plead for a just cause*, abogar por una causa justa.

— Pl. n. *The just*, los justos: *to sleep the sleep of the just*, dormir el sueño de los justos.

— Adv. Justo: *just in front, behind, opposite*, justo delante, detrás, en frente; *just enough*, justo lo suficiente. || Justamente, justo: *I was just calling you when you arrived*, te estaba llamando justamente cuando llegaste. || Exactamente, precisamente: *it's just what I expected*, es exactamente lo que esperaba; *it's just a year ago that*, hace un año exactamente que; *just what did he say?*, ¿qué dijo exactamente?; *that's just what I mean*, es precisamente lo que quiero decir; *just how much I couldn't say*, no te podría decir exactamente cuánto; *he does just as he pleases*, hace exactamente lo que le da la gana. || En punto, justo (with time): *it was just two o'clock*, eran justo las dos, eran las dos en punto. || Sólo, solamente, no... más que: *there is just one left*, sólo queda uno, no queda más que uno; *it's just the postman*, no es más que el cartero; *but he's just a corporal*, pero es solamente un cabo; *it'll just take me a moment*, sólo tardaré un momento. || Sólo, solamente, nada más: *just once*, una vez nada más; *just a little*, un poquito nada más; *just you and I*, tú y yo nada más. || Ahora mismo (now): *I'm just leaving*, salgo ahora mismo; *it's just starting to rain*, ahora mismo empieza a llover; *the train is just arriving*, el tren está llegando ahora mismo. || Sencillamente (simply): *I just refused*, me negué sencillamente; *just tell him to leave you alone*, dile sencillamente que te deje en paz. || Francamente, sencillamente: *it's just incredible*, es francamente increíble; *it was just wonderful, perfect*, fue sencillamente maravilloso, perfecto. || Recién (newly): *those just arrived*, los recién llegados; *a record just out*, un disco recién salido. || De pronto (suddenly): *he just arrived without warning*, llegó de pronto sin avisar. || Mismo: *just here*, aquí mismo; *just by the door*, al lado mismo de la puerta. || — *A book which just came out*, un libro recién publicado *or* que acaba de publicarse. || *He had just arrived*, acababa de llegar. || *He has just left school*, acaba de terminar el colegio *or* los estudios secundarios. || *He only just escaped drowning*, por poco se ahoga. || *He only just managed to reach the top*, llegó con mucha dificultad a la cima. || *I just can't understand her*, no la llego a comprender. || *I just missed the train*, perdí el tren por muy poco. || *I'm just starving*, me muero de hambre. || *I only just caught the bus*, cogí el autobús por los pelos. || *I only just finished in time*, terminé justo a tiempo. || *It's just as good*, es lo mismo. || *It's just as well you were there*, menos mal que estabas allí. || *It would be just as well for you to reconsider*, más vale que lo vuelvas a pensar. || *I've got just enough to live on*, tengo justo lo suficiente para vivir. || *Just about*, poco más o menos: *there were just about a hundred people there*, había cien personas poco más o menos; por: *I lost it just about here*, lo perdí por aquí; a punto de: *they were just about to leave*, estaban a punto de marcharse; justo: *I had just about enough*, tenía justo lo suficiente; ya: *I'm just about fed up with it*, ya estoy harto. || *Just a moment*, un momento. || *Just as*, nada más, justo al: *just as we left it started raining*, nada más salir nosotros *or* justo al salir nosotros se puso a llover; tal como, tal y como: *we found everything just as we had left it*, encontramos todo tal y como lo habíamos dejado; *come just as you are*, ven tal y como estás; justo cuando, justo en el momento en que: *they arrived just as the fight started*, llegaron justo en el momento en que empezó la pelea; *it happened just as you called*, ocurrió justo en el momento en que llamaste. || *Just as I thought*, ya me lo figuraba, lo que me figuraba. || *Just as you please*, como usted quiera. || *Just before, after*, justo antes, después. || *Just here*, aquí mismo, aquí. || *Just imagine!* o *just think!*, ¡fíjate!, ¡imagínate! || *Just let me see him!*, ¡como lo vea! || *Just listen*, escucha un momento. || *Just now*, actualmente: *business is bad just now*, los negocios van mal actualmente; en este momento, ahora mismo: *I'm busy just now*, estoy ocupado en este momento; hace un momento: *he came just now*, vino hace un momento. || FAM. *Just shut up about it, will you?*, cállate ya, ¿quieres? || *Just taste this*, prueba un poco de esto. || *Just then*, en ese momento, en ese mismo momento. || *Just the same*, see SAME. || *Just this once*, por una vez. || *Not just yet*, todavía no. || *She dances just as well as you*, ella baila tan bien como tú. || *She's just a child*, no es más que una niña. || *That's just it!*, ¡ahí está! || *That's just too bad*, ¡qué lástima!, ¡qué pena! || *The car just missed him*, casi le atropelló el coche. || *To do sth. just as a joke*, hacer algo en plan de broma. || *To do sth. just for a laugh*, hacer algo en plan de broma *or* para divertirse. || *We were just discussing that*, precisamente estábamos hablando de eso. || FAM. *Won't o wouldn't I just!* o *don't I just!*, ¡ya lo creo! || *You just missed him*, acaba de marcharse. || *You just missed the bull's-eye*, poco te faltó para dar en el blanco. || *You're just in time to see the show*, llegas justo a tiempo *or* llegas a punto para ver el espectáculo.

justice [ˈdʒʌstis] n. Justicia, *f.* (equity): *I doubt the justice of the decision*, dudo de la justicia de la decisión. || JUR. Justicia, *f.* (administration of law): *the forces of justice*, las fuerzas de la justicia; *justice has been done*, se ha hecho justicia. | Juez, *m.* (judge): *justice of the peace*, juez de paz. || — *In justice to*, para ser justo con. || *Let justice be done*, que la justicia se cumpla. || *Mr. Justice Brown*, el magistrado señor Brown. || *The dress does not do her justice*, el traje no le favorece. || *Their marks didn't do them justice*, merecían una nota más alta. || *The photo doesn't do you justice*, no estás favorecido *or* no has salido bien en la foto. || *To administer justice*, administrar [la] justicia. || *To bring s.o. to justice*, llevar a uno ante la justicia *or* ante los tribunales. || *To demand justice*, pedir justicia. || *To do a meal justice*, hacer honor a la comida. || *To do s.o. justice*, hacer justicia a (a criminal, etc.). || *To do o.s. justice*, quedar bien.

justiceship [—ʃip] n. Judicatura, *f.*

justiciable [dʒʌsˈtiʃiəbl] adj. Justiciable.

justiciar [dʒʌsˈtiʃiɑ:*] n. HIST. Justicia (*m.*) mayor.

justiciary [dʒʌsˈtiʃiəri] n. HIST. Justicia (*m.*) mayor.

justifiable [ˈdʒʌstifaiəbl] adj. Justificable.

justification [ˌdʒʌstifiˈkeiʃən] n. Justificación, *f.* || PRINT. Justificación, *f.*

justificative [ˈdʒʌstifikeitiv] adj. Justificativo, va.

justificatory [ˈdʒʌstifikeitəri] adj. Justificador, ra.

justify [ˈdʒʌstifai] v. tr. Justificar: *the end justifies the means*, el fin justifica los medios. || PRINT. Justificar. || — *Am I justified in refusing?*, ¿tengo razón en negarme? || *To justify o.s.*, justificarse.

Justinian [dʒʌsˈtiniən] pr. n. Justiniano, *m.*

justly [ˈdʒʌstli] adv. Con justicia, justamente (fairly). || Con razón: *she justly remarked that*, con razón observó que.

justness [ˈdʒʌstnis] n. Justicia, *f.* || Rectitud, *f.* || Exactitud, *f.* (of a remark, etc.).

jut [dʒʌt] n. ARCH. Salidizo, *m.*, saliente, *m.* || Saliente, *m.* (of rock).

jut [dʒʌt] v. intr. Sobresalir. || *To jut out*, sobresalir.

jute [dʒu:t] n. BOT. Yute, *m.*

juvenile [ˈdʒu:vinail] adj. Juvenil: *juvenile delinquency*, delincuencia juvenil; *juvenile behaviour*, comportamiento juvenil. || Infantil (childish). || De menores (for the young): *juvenile court*, tribunal de menores.
— N. Joven, *m.* & *f.*, menor, *m.* & *f.*, adolescente, *m.* & *f.* (young person). || Publicación (*f.*) juvenil, libro (*m.*) para niños (book for young people). || U. S. Galán (*m.*) joven (in a play).

juvenile lead [—li:d] n. THEATR. Papel (*m.*) de galán joven (part). | Galán (*m.*) joven (actor).

juvenilia [ˌdʒu:viˈnilјə] pl. n. Obras (*f.*) de juventud.

juvenility [ˌdʒu:viˈniliti] n. Juventud, *f.*

juxtalinear [ˌdʒʌkstəˈliniə*] adj. Yuxtalineal.

juxtapose [ˈdʒʌkstəpəuz] v. tr. Yuxtaponer.

juxtaposition [ˌdʒʌkstəpəˈziʃən] n. Yuxtaposición, *f.*

K

k [kei] n. K, *f.* (letter): *a small, capital k*, una k minúscula, mayúscula.

Kabyle [kəˈbail] n. Cabila, *m.* & *f.*

kadi [ˈkɑ:di] n. REL. Cadí, *m.*

kaftan [ˈkæftən] n. Caftán, *m.*

kainite [ˈkainait] n. CHEM. Kainita, *f.*

kaiser [ˈkaizə*] n. Káiser, *m.*

kaki [ˈkɑ:ki] n. BOT. Caqui, *m.*, kaki, *m.* (Japanese persimmon).

kale [keil] n. BOT. Col (*f.*) rizada. || U. S. FAM. Pasta, *f.* [*Amer.*, plata, *f.*] (money).

kaleidoscope [kəˈlaidəskəup] n. Calidoscopio, *m.*, caleidoscopio, *m.*

kaleidoscopic [kəˌlaidəˈskɔpik] adj. Calidoscópico, ca; caleidoscópico, ca.

kalends [ˈkælendz] pl. n. HIST. Calendas, *f.*

Kalmuck [ˈkælmək] adj./n. Calmuco, ca.

kamikaze [ˌkɑ:miˈkɑ:zi:] n. Kamikase, *m.*

Kanaka [ˈkænəkə] n. Canaco, ca.

kangaroo [ˌkæŋgəˈru:] n. ZOOL. Canguro, *m.*

kangaroo court [—kɔ:t] n. U. S. Tribunal (*m.*) desautorizado.

Kantian [ˈkæntiən] adj./n. PHIL. Kantiano, na.

Kantianism [—izəm] n. Kantismo, *m.*
kaolin (U. S. **kaoline**) [ˈkeiəlin] n. MIN. Caolín, *m.*
kapok [ˈkeipɔk] n. BOT. Kapok, *m.*, capoc, *m.*, miraguano, *m.* (fibre).
kapok tree [—tri:] n. BOT. Kapok, *m.*, capok, *m.*, miraguano, *m.* (tree).
kappa [ˈkæpə] n. Kappa, *f.* (Greek letter).
karakul [ˌkɑːrɑːˈkʌl] n. ZOOL. Caracul, *m.* (sheep). || Astracán, *m.* (fur).
karat [ˈkærət] n. Quilate, *m.*: *18 karat gold*, oro de 18 quilates.
karate [kəˈrɑːti] n. SP. Karate, *m.*
karting [ˈkɑːtiŋ] n. SP. Carrera (*f.*) de karts, karting, *m.*
karyoplasm [ˈkæriəˌplæzəm] n. BIOL. Carioplasma, *m.* (nuclear protoplasm).
Kashmir [ˈkæʃmiə*] pr. n. GEOGR. Cachemira, *f.*
katabolic [ˌkætəˈbɔlik] adj. Catabólico, ca.
katabolism [kəˈtæbəlizəm] n. Catabolismo, *m.*
Katanganese [kæˌtæŋgəˈni:z] adj./s. Katangueño, ña.
katharsis [kəˈθɑːsis] n. Catarsis, *f.*
Katherine [ˈkæθərin] or **Kathleen** [ˈkæθli:n] pr. n. Catalina, *f.*
katydid [ˈkeitidid] n. ZOOL. Saltamontes, *m. inv.*
kauri [ˈkauri] n. BOT. Pino (*m.*) de Nueva Zelanda.
kayak [ˈkaiæk] n. Kayac, *m.*
kebab [kəˈbæb] n. Pincho, *m.*, broqueta, *f.*, brocheta, *f.*
kedge [kedʒ] n. MAR. Anclote, *m.*
kedge [kedʒ] v. tr. MAR. Espiar por un anclote.
keel [ki:l] n. MAR. AVIAT. ZOOL. Quilla, *f.* || MAR. Barco, *m.* (boat). | Chalana, *f.* (long, flat boat). || — MAR. *Bilge keel*, quilla de balance. || *To be on an even keel*, no tener diferencia de calado (a ship), estar en equilibrio (to be well balanced).
keel [ki:l] v. tr. MAR. Dar de quilla: *to keel a boat*, dar de quilla a un barco.
— V. intr. MAR. Zozobrar, volcar. || *To keel over*, zozobrar (a boat), volcarse (a thing), desplomarse (a person).
keelhaul [—hɔ:l] v. tr. HIST. Pasar por debajo de la quilla (as punishment).
keelson [ˈkelsn] n. MAR. Sobrequilla, *f.*
keen [ki:n] adj. Afilado, da (sharp): *a keen blade*, una hoja afilada. || Agudo, da: *a keen mind*, una mente aguda; *keen eyesight*, vista aguda; *a keen sense of humour*, un sentido agudo del humor. || Agudo, da (pain). || Fino, na: *a very keen ear*, un oído muy fino. || Penetrante: *a keen stare*, una mirada penetrante; *a keen wind*, un viento penetrante. || Fuerte, vivo, va; intenso, sa (feelings): *a keen desire*, un vivo deseo. || Vivo, va; profundo, da: *a keen interest*, un vivo interés. || Concienzudo, da (conscientious). || Entusiasta (enthusiastic). || Cortante (cold). || Deseoso, sa; ansioso, sa (greedy): *keen to arrive at the truth*, deseoso de llegar a la verdad. || Competitivo, va (prices). || Fuerte (competition). || — *To be a keen cyclist*, ser muy aficionado al ciclismo. || *To be keen on*, gustarle a uno: *I'm keen on that girl*, me gusta esta chica; *I'm keen on Beethoven*, me gusta Beethoven; *I'm not keen on custard*, no me gustan las natillas; ser aficionado a: *he's keen on football*, es aficionado al fútbol. || *To be keen to do sth.*, tener muchas ganas de hacer algo, tener un vivo deseo de hacer algo. || *To have a keen appetite*, tener buen apetito. || *Try to seem keen*, intenta demostrar un poco de entusiasmo. || *We're not all that keen to go*, no nos entusiasma la idea de ir.
— N. Lamento (*m.*) fúnebre [con que se acompaña en Irlanda la muerte de una persona].
keen [ki:n] v. intr. Cantar un lamento fúnebre.
keenly [—li] adv. Con entusiasmo: *the match was keenly fought*, el partido se jugó con entusiasmo. || Profundamente, vivamente: *keenly interested in*, profundamente interesado por; *keenly affected*, profundamente afectado. || Fijamente: *he looked at her keenly*, la miró fijamente. || — *A keenly disputed point*, un punto muy controvertido. || *To listen keenly*, escuchar con mucha atención.
keenness [—nis] n. Lo afilado, lo cortante (of a knife blade). || Rigor, *m.* (of the cold). || Agudeza, *f.* (of mind, sight). || Profundidad, *f.*, intensidad, *f.* (of emotion). || Finura, *f.* (of sense of smell, hearing). || Entusiasmo, *m.* (enthusiasm): *keenness to do sth.*, entusiasmo por hacer algo. || Deseo, *m.* (desire). || *The keenness of the wind*, el viento penetrante.
keep [ki:p] n. HIST. Torre (*f.*) del homenaje (of a castle). || Sustento, *m.*: *to earn one's keep*, ganarse el sustento. || Subsistencia, *f.* (maintenance). || — *For keeps*, para siempre (for ever). || *He's not worth his keep*, no sirve para nada. || *It's yours for keeps*, te lo puedes quedar. || *To play for keeps*, jugar de veras.
keep* [ki:p] v. tr. Guardar: *I am keeping old newspapers*, estoy guardando periódicos viejos; *to keep silence*, guardar silencio; *to keep a secret*, guardar un secreto; *keep it till I come back*, guárdalo hasta que yo vuelva; *keep me a place in the queue*, guárdame un sitio en la cola; *to keep the commandments*, guardar los mandamientos. || Quedarse: *I lent him my book and he kept it*, le presté mi libro y se quedó con él. || Mantener: *to keep a family*, mantener una familia; *to keep order*, mantener el orden; *to keep a car in good condition*, mantener un coche en buenas condiciones; *to keep one's composure*, mantener la compostura; *to keep a door open*, mantener una puerta abierta. || Reservar, guardar: *I keep this whisky for special friends*, este whisky lo reservo para amigos especiales. || Tener: *it keeps me very busy*, me tiene muy ocupado; *to keep an open mind*, tener amplitud de ideas; *to keep s.o. in prison*, tener a alguien en la cárcel; *to keep the workers happy*, tener a los trabajadores contentos. || Hacer (to make): *to keep s.o. working*, hacer trabajar a uno; *he kept me waiting*, me hizo esperar; *she keeps him very happy*, le hace muy feliz. || Observar: *to keep the law*, observar la ley. || Cumplir: *to keep a promise*, cumplir una promesa. || Acudir a: *to keep an appointment*, acudir a una cita. || Tener: *to keep a maid, a shop*, tener criada, una tienda. || Criar (to raise livestock). || Llevar: *to keep accounts*, llevar la contabilidad *or* las cuentas. || Entretener, detener, retener: *can I keep you for a few minutes?*, ¿le puedo entretener unos minutos?; *what kept you?*, ¿qué te entretuvo?; *to keep s.o. to dinner*, retener a alguien a cenar. || Conservar, mantener: *keep it warm*, consérvalo caliente. || Contener, dominar: *to keep one's temper*, contener el malhumor. || Cuidar: *to keep s.o.'s dog whilst he is away*, cuidar el perro de alguien mientras está de viaje. || Seguir (a track, way, direction). || Quedarse en: *he kept his house*, se quedó en casa; *she keeps her room*, se queda en su cuarto. || Celebrar (to celebrate): *to keep a feast*, celebrar una fiesta. || Defender: *to keep goal*, defender la portería. || Salvar (to save): *to keep s.o. from despair*, salvar a alguien de la desesperación. || — *God keep you!*, ¡Dios le guarde! || *He can't keep a job*, no puede quedarse en ningún trabajo. || *Keep it out of harm's way*, guárdalo en un sitio seguro. || FAM. *Keep it under your hat*, no se lo digas a nadie. || *Keep the change*, quédese con la vuelta. || *Keep your hands to yourself!*, ¡las manos quietas! || *Keep your town tidy*, mantenga limpia la ciudad. || *This shop doesn't keep snails*, en esta tienda no se venden caracoles. || *To keep a diary*, escribir *or* llevar un diario. || *To keep a little money by*, tener un poco de dinero apartado. || *To keep a note of*, apuntar. || *To keep boarders*, tener huéspedes. || *To keep company*, acompañar. || *To keep going*, mantener: *he managed to keep the firm going*, consiguió mantener la empresa; mantener con vida: *the doctors kept him going*, los médicos le mantuvieron con vida; hacer funcionar (a machine, motor, etc.), mantener (to maintain), hacer durar (to make last). || *To keep one's distance*, guardar las distancias. || *To keep one's seat*, permanecer sentado (audience, etc.), conservar el escaño (in an election). || *To keep one's word*, cumplir su palabra. || *To keep s.o. amused*, entretener a alguien. || *To keep s.o. quiet*, hacer callar a alguien. || *To keep s.o. somewhere*, no dejar a alguien salir de un sitio, tener a alguien encerrado en un sitio. || *To keep sth. dry*, impedir que se moje algo. || *To keep to o.s.*, guardarse: *he kept the secret to himself*, se guardó el secreto. || *To keep under lock and key*, guardar bajo siete llaves, guardar bajo llave.
— V. intr. Seguir, continuar (to continue): *to keep singing*, seguir cantando; *keep on this path*, siga por este camino. || Conservarse: *wine doesn't keep once the bottle is opened*, el vino no se conserva una vez abierta la botella. || Mantenerse: *he keeps in good health*, se mantiene en buena salud. || Permanecer, seguir siendo (to remain): *to keep faithful to one's wife*, seguir siendo fiel a su mujer. || Quedarse: *to keep in bed*, quedarse en cama. || No dejar de (to do sth. persistently): *he keeps asking me the time*, no deja de preguntarme la hora. || Estarse, quedarse: *keep still!*, ¡estate quieto! || Esperar (to wait): *that can keep till later*, eso puede esperar hasta más tarde. || Vivir (to lodge). || — *How are you keeping?*, ¿qué tal estás?, ¿cómo estás? || *To keep clear of*, evitar, evitar todo contacto con. || *To keep cool*, see COOL. || *To keep going*, seguir (to persevere with an action): *you keep going until you come to a church*, siga usted hasta llegar a una iglesia; *he kept going until she was exhausted*, siguió hasta agotarla; seguir viviendo *or* con vida (to stay alive), ir tirando (to manage), seguir funcionando (a machine), continuar (to continue), durar (to last). || *To keep quiet* o *silent about*, guardar silencio sobre. || *To keep right*, circular por la derecha, ceñirse a la derecha. || *To keep well*, estar bien de salud.
— ***To keep at***, seguir con: *to keep at work*, seguir con su trabajo. | U. S. Importunar (to nag). | — *Keep at it!*, ¡ánimo! | *To keep at it*, perseverar (to make an effort), insistir (to insist). || ***To keep away***, mantener a distancia (to stop from coming nearer): *to keep the photographers away*, mantener a distancia a los fotógrafos. | Mantenerse a distancia (to stay at a distance). | Alejar (to ward off): *to keep the devil away*, alejar al demonio. | No ir (not to go). | Impedir (to prevent). | — *Keep away!*, ¡no te acerques! | *To keep away from*, no acercarse a (not to go near), evitar (to avoid), mantener alejado de (to prevent from going near). | *To keep medicines away from children*, poner las medicinas fuera del alcance de los niños. | *You keep away from here in the future*, no vuelvas nunca más por aquí. || ***To keep back***, contener: *the police kept back the crowd*, la policía contuvo a la multitud; *to keep back one's tears*, contener el llanto. | No acercarse, mantenerse a distancia: *the crowd kept back*, la gente no se acercó. | Ocultar: *he kept some of the facts back*, ocultó algunos hechos. | Quedarse con: *I've kept back half of your money*, me he quedado

con la mitad de su dinero. | Retrasar (to delay). || **To keep down,** contener (a rebellion). | Oprimir (people). | Mantenerse agachado (to avoid being spotted). | Mantener bajo (temperature, price). | — *Keep your head down*, no levantes la cabeza. || **To keep from,** impedir: *they kept me from going out*, me impidieron salir. | Evitar (to avoid). | Mantener alejado de (to prevent from approaching). | Ocultar: *he kept the facts from me*, me ocultó los hechos. | Abstenerse de (to refrain from). | — *He kept me from being too bored*, consiguió que no me aburriese demasiado. | *I do it to keep from putting on weight*, lo hago para no engordar. || **To keep in,** disimular: *he kept in his sadness*, disimuló su tristeza. | Quedarse en casa, no salir (to stay indoors). | Impedir salir, no dejar salir (to prevent from going out). | Castigar a salir más tarde [del colegio] (school punishment). | Mantener encendido, no dejar que se apague (a fire). | *To keep in mind*, see MIND. | *To keep in with s.o.*, mantenerse en buenos términos con alguien. || **To keep off,** mantenerse lejos *or* a distancia [de] (to stay away from). | Mantener a distancia (to hold at a distance). | Alejar (to ward off). | Cerrar el paso a (to put a stop to). | — *If the rain keeps off*, si no llueve. | *Keep off the grass*, prohibido pisar el césped. | *Keep the dog off*, no suelte al perro. | *Keep your hands off!*, ¡no toques! | *Private property, keep off*, propiedad privada, prohibido el paso. | *To keep off a subject*, evitar un tema, no mencionar un tema. | *To keep the sun, the rain off sth.*, resguardar algo del sol, de la lluvia. || **To keep on,** no quitarse: *keep your coat on*, no te quites el abrigo. | Seguir: *to keep on dancing*, seguir bailando; *to keep on with sth.*, seguir con algo. | No dejar de: *he keeps on asking me*, no deja de preguntarme. | Insistir: *don't keep on!*, ¡no insistas! | No despedir, quedarse con (a servant). | No apagar (lights). | — *To keep on at s.o.*, estar siempre encima de alguien. || **To keep out,** no entrar, quedarse fuera. | No dejar entrar, no admitir (not to admit). | No meterse (not to get involved in): *I'm keeping out of this*, yo no me meto en eso; *to keep out of trouble*, no meterse en líos. | — *Keep out*, prohibida la entrada (sign). | *This coat will keep the cold out*, este abrigo te resguardará del frío. || **To keep to,** quedarse en: *to keep to the house*, quedarse en la casa. | Limitarse a (to restrict o.s. to). | Cumplir con (a promise). | Seguir (a direction). | — *He should keep to swimming*, debería dedicarse a la natación. | *To keep o.s. to o.s.*, vivir apartado. | *To keep s.o. to his word*, cogerle a uno la palabra. | *To keep sth to o.s.*, negarse a compartir algo. | *To keep to one's bed*, guardar cama. | *To keep to the left*, circular por la izquierda, ceñirse a la izquierda. | *To keep to the original plan*, seguir el proyecto original. || **To keep together,** poner juntos: *keep all the relevant papers together*, ponga juntos todos los documentos pertinentes. | Mantenerse unidos. | — *Only the children keep their marriage together*, sólo siguen juntos por los niños. | *Please keep together*, no se separen. | *Put some string round it to keep it together*, sujétalo con una cuerda. || **To keep under,** dominar (one's passions). | Someter oprimir (people). || **To keep up,** levantar: *keep your spirits up*, levanta el ánimo. | Continuar, seguir: *the rain kept up all day*, la lluvia continuó todo el día. | Tener en vela: *the baby kept me up all night*, el niño me tuvo en vela toda la noche. | No retrasarse en, no quedarse atrás en: *to keep up the payments*, no retrasarse en el pago. | Seguir con: *I want to keep up my French*, quiero seguir con el francés. | Mantener: *to keep up a property, a motor, traditions*, mantener una propiedad, un motor, las tradiciones. | Sostener: *this keeps the ceiling up*, esto sostiene el techo. | Sujetar: *my belt keeps my trousers up*, el cinturón me sujeta los pantalones. | Mantener alto (a price), | FAM. Alojar (to lodge). | — *He'll never keep it up*, no podrá resistir *o* aguantar. | *I hope I'm not keeping you up*, espero que no le estoy entreteniendo demasiado. | *Keep it up!*, ¡sigue! | *To keep up appearances*, guardar las apariencias. | *To keep up with*, seguir: *it is difficult to keep up with the class*, es difícil seguir la clase. | Mantenerse al ritmo de: *he couldn't keep up with me*, no podía mantenerse a mi ritmo. | *To keep up with one's work*, tener el trabajo al día. | *To keep up with the Joneses*, achantar a los vecinos. | *To keep up with the times*, ser muy de su época.

— OBSERV. Pret. & p. p. **kept.**

keeper [—ə*] n. Guarda, *m.* (guard). || Dueño, ña (of a shop, boardinghouse). || Guardarbosque, *m.* (gamekeeper). || Guarda, *m.*, guardián, *m.* (of zoo). || Carcelero, *m.* (of a jail). || Loquero, *m.* (of asylum). || Conservador, ra (in museum, etc.). || Archivero, *m.* (in records office). || ELECTR. Armadura, *f.* || Pestillo, *m.* (small latch). || Seguro, *m.* (safety latch). || *These apples are good keepers*, estas manzanas se conservan muy bien.

keeping [—iŋ] n. Cargo, *m.*, cuidado, *m.* (care): *in s.o.'s keeping*, al cuidado de alguien. || Observación, *f.*, cumplimiento, *m.* (of the law). || Mantenimiento, *m.*, conservación, *f.* (upkeep). || — *In keeping with*, de acuerdo con. || *In safe keeping*, en buenas manos, en lugar seguro. || *Out of keeping with*, no de acuerdo con: *his behaviour is out of keeping with his profession*, su comportamiento no está de acuerdo con su profesión. || *Wine improves with keeping*, el vino mejora con el tiempo.

keepsake [—seik] n. Recuerdo, *m.*

kefir [keˈfiːə*] n. Kéfir, *m.*

keg [keg] n. Barril, *m.*, cuñete, *m.*

kelp [kelp] n. BOT. Varec, *m.*, alga (*f.*) marina.

kelson [ˈkelsn] n. MAR. Sobrequilla, *f.*

kelt [kelt] n. ZOOL. Salmón (*m.*) zancado.

Kelt [kelt] n. Celta, *m.* & *f.* (Celt).

Keltic [—ik] adj. Celta (Celtic).

— N. Celta, *m.* (language).

ken [ken] n. Vista, *f.* (sight). || *Beyond my ken*, fuera de mis conocimientos *or* de mi alcance.

ken [ken] v. tr. Saber (to have knowledge of). || Comprender (to understand). || Conocer (to be acquainted with). || Reconocer (to recognize).

kennel [kenl] n. Caseta (*f.*) para el perro (for a dog). || — Pl. Perrera, *f. sing.* (place where dogs are kept). || Jauría, *f.* (pack of dogs).

kennel [ˈkenl] v. tr. Poner en la perrera.

kenotron [ˈkenəˌtrɔn] n. Kenotrón, *m.*

kepi [ˈkeipi] n. Quepis, *m.* (cap).

kept [kept] pret. & p. p. See KEEP. || *Kept woman*, mujer mantenida.

keratin [ˈkerətin] n. Queratina, *f.*

kerb [kəːb] n. Bordillo, *m.* (of the pavement). || Brocal, *m.* (of a well).

kerbstone [ˈkəːbstəun] n. Piedra (*f.*) del bordillo.

kerchief [ˈkəːtʃif] n. Pañuelo (*m.*) de cabeza.

kerf [kəːf] n. Corte, *m.*

kermes [ˈkəːmiz] n. Quermes, *m.* (of an insect). || BOT. Coscoja, *f.*

kermes oak [—ˈəuk] n. BOT. Coscoja, *f.*

kermess or **kermis** [ˈkəːmis] n. Kermesse, *f.*, quermese, *f.*, verbena, *f.*

kernel [ˈkəːnl] n. FIG. Meollo, *m.*, núcleo, *m.*, médula, *f.* (centre of argument, etc.). || Pepita, *f.* (of a fruit). || Grano, *f.* (of wheat).

kerosene or **kerosine** [ˈkerəsiːn] n. Queroseno, *m.*

kerseymere [ˈkəːzimiə*] n. Cachemira, *f.* (cloth).

kestrel [ˈkestrəl] n. Cernícalo, *m.* (bird).

ketch [ketʃ] n. MAR. Queche, *m.*

ketchup [ˈketʃəp] n. Salsa (*f.*) de tomate.

ketone [ˈkiːtəun] n. CHEM. Acetona, *f.*

kettle [ˈketl] n. Hervidor, *m.* [en forma de tetera] (for boiling water). || U. S. Olla, *f.* (large pot). || — FIG. *That's a different kettle of fish*, eso es harina de otro costal. | *To get into a fine kettle of fish*, meterse en un berenjenal.

kettledrum [—drʌm] n. MUS. Timbal, *m.*

kettledrummer [—ˌdrʌmə*] n. MUS. Timbalero, *m.*

kevel [ˈkevl] n. MAR. Cornamusa, *f.*

key [kiː] n. Llave, *f.* (for a lock, for clockwork). || Clave, *f.* (of a code, map, diagram, etc.). || TECH. Chaveta, *f.*, clavija, *f.* (pin, wedge in metalwork). | Espiga, *f.*, clavija, *f.* (in woodwork). | Cuña, *f.* (wedge for a stretch frame). || ARCH. Clave, *f.* (keystone). || MUS. Tono, *m.*: *major key*, tono mayor. | Tecla, *f.* (of a piano). | Llave, *f.*, pistón, *m.* (of wind instruments). || Tecla, *f.* (of a typewriter): *back space key*, tecla de retroceso. || FIG. Llave, *f.*: *that port is the key to the country*, ese puerto es la llave del país. | Clave, *f.*: *the key to the problem, to the puzzle*, la clave del problema, del enigma. || Clave, *f.* (book of answers). || ELECTR. Llave, *f.*, conmutador, *m.* (switch which opens or cuts a circuit). | Manipulador, *m.* (of a telegraph). || GEOGR. Cayo, *m.*, isleta, *f.* (reef or low island). || FIG. Tono, *m.*: *speaking in a plaintive key*, hablando en tono lastimero. || — *Master key*, llave maestra. || MUS. *Off key* o *out of key*, desafinado, da (out of tune). || *Skeleton key*, ganzúa, *f.* || MUS. *To be in key*, llevar el tono, estar afinado. | *To play, to sing out of key*, desafinar. || FIG. *To touch the right key*, tocar la cuerda sensible (to find s.o.'s soft spot).

— Adj. Clave (essential): *key industry*, industria clave; *key position*, posición clave.

key [kiː] v. tr. TECH. Calzar con chavetas (metalwork). | Acuñar (to tighten a stretch frame). || MUS. Afinar (to tune up). || FIG. Poner a tono con (to harmonize with). || FIG. *To key up*, emocionar, excitar.

keyboard [—bɔːd] n. Teclado, *m.* (of a piano, typewriter, etc.).

keyhole [—həul] n. Ojo (*m.*) de la cerradura.

keyman [—mæn] n. Hombre (*m.*) clave.

— OBSERV. El plural es *keymen* (hombres clave).

keynote [—nəut] n. MUS. Nota (*f.*) tónica, tónica, *f.* || FIG. Piedra (*f.*) angular, idea (*f.*) fundamental. || FIG. *Keynote address*, discurso (*m.*) inaugural, discurso (*m.*) de apertura.

key punch [—pʌntʃ] n. Perforadora, *f.* (for computers).

key ring [—riŋ] n. Llavero, *m.*

key signature [—ˈsignitʃə*] n. MUS. Armadura, *f.*

keystone [—stəun] n. ARCH. Clave, *f.* || FIG. Piedra (*f.*) angular.

Key West [—ˈwest] pr. n. GEOGR. Cayo (*m.*) Hueso.

khaki [ˈkɑːki] n. Caqui, *m.* (colour). || Tela (*f.*) caqui (cloth).

— Adj. Caqui, *inv.*

khan [kɑːn] n. Kan, *m.* (title). || Mesón, *m.* (inn).

khanate [ˈkɑːneit] n. Kanato, *m.*

Khartoum [kɑːˈtuːm] pr. n. GEOGR. Jartum.

khedive [keˈdiːv] n. Jedive, *m.*

kibbutz [kiˈbuts] n. Kibutz, *m.*

— OBSERV. El plural de *kibbutz* es *kibbutzim*.

kibitzer [ˈkibətsə*] n. FAM. Mirón, ona.

kibosh [ˈkaibɔʃ] n. FAM. Tonterías, *f. pl.* || *To put the kibosh on sth.*, poner término a algo.

kick [kik] n. Patada, *f.*, puntapié, *m.* (act or instance of kicking): *to give s.o. a kick in the pants*, darle a uno una patada en el trasero. || Coz, *f.* (of an animal). || Retroceso, *m.*, culatazo, *m.* (recoil of a firearm). || FIG. Fuerza, *f.* (energy). || SP. Tiro, *m.* (in football): *a kick at goal*, un tiro a gol. | Golpe, *m.*: *free kick*, golpe franco. | Patada, *f.* (in rugby). | Piernas, *f. pl.*, movimiento (*m.*) de las piernas (in swimming): *you must improve your kick*, tienes que mejorar el movimiento de las piernas. || — FAM. *Not to get a kick out of sth.*, no encontrar la gracia a algo. || SP. *To be* o *to have a good kick*, tener buen tiro (in football), tener buena patada (in rugby). || FAM. *To do sth. for kicks*, hacer algo porque le hace gracia a uno, hacer algo para divertirse. | *To get a kick out of sth.*, encontrar placer en algo. | *To have a kick*, ser muy fuerte, ser tónico, ca: *this drink has a kick in it*, esta bebida es tónica.

kick [kik] v. tr. Dar un puntapié a, dar una patada a (a person or object). || Dar una coz a (animals). || Dar culatazo en (a firearm). || SP. Marcar, meter (to score): *to kick a goal, a penalty*, marcar un gol, un penalty. | Pasar [de una patada]: *he kicked the ball to me*, me pasó la pelota. || Mandar de una patada: *he kicked the bottle across the room*, de una patada mandó la botella al otro lado de la habitación. || Dar patadas a: *he walked down the road kicking a ball*, bajó la calle dando patadas a una pelota. || Mover: *to kick one's legs*, mover las piernas. || FAM. Librarse de (to get rid of). || — FIG. *He could have kicked himself*, se comió los puños de rabia, se dio de cabeza contra la pared. || *To kick a man when he's down*, dar patadas a un hombre cuando ya está en el suelo (real sense), dar la puntilla (figurative sense). || FIG. *To kick one's heels*, estar de plantón. | *To kick s.o. upstairs*, deshacerse de alguien dándole un puesto honorífico. | *To kick the bucket*, estirar la pata, hincar el pico (to die).

— V. intr. Dar patadas, dar puntapiés (to strike out with the foot). || Dar coces (animals). || Dar culatazo, retroceder (to recoil, of a firearm). || SP. Mover las piernas (in swimming). | Chutar (in football). || FIG. Protestar mucho. || — FIG. FAM. *To be alive and kicking*, estar vivito y coleando. | *To be still kicking*, no haber abandonado la lucha.

— **To kick against,** oponerse a. || **To kick around** o **about,** dar patadas a (a ball). | Tratar a patadas, dar malos tratos a (a person). | Andar rodando (to hang about). | Dar vueltas a (an idea, a project, etc.). | — *It's kicking around here somewhere*, está rodando por aquí. || **To kick aside,** apartar con una patada. || **To kick back,** devolver (a football). | Retroceder (a crank). | Dar culatazo (a gun). | FIG. Devolver golpe por golpe (to strike back). || **To kick down,** derribar. || **To kick in,** derribar a patadas (a door). | Tirar de una patada: *he kicked her in the river*, le tiró de una patada al agua. | FAM. Estirar la pata (to die). || **To kick off,** empezar: *to kick off a party with a song*, empezar una fiesta cantando. | Hacer el saque de centro (in sports). | U. S. FAM. Estirar la pata (to die). || **To kick out,** echar a patadas, poner de patitas en la calle: *they kicked him out of the bar*, le echaron a patadas del bar. | Dar patadas, dar puntapiés (to strike out with the foot). | Dar coces (an animal). || **To kick over,** tirar de una patada. || **To kick up,** levantar (dust). | Ponerse furioso (to get angry). | Subir, aumentar (prices, etc.). | FAM. *To kick up a dust* o *a row*, armar un escándalo; *to kick up a fuss*, armar un escándalo, armar un follón; *to kick up one's heels*, echar una cana al aire.

kickback [—bæk] n. Retroceso, *m.*, culatazo, *m.* (of firearm). || U. S. Comisión, *f.* (money). | Reacción, *f.* (of a person).

kicker [—ə*] n. SP. Chutador, *m.* || Coceador, ra [*Amer.*, pateador, ra]. || FIG. FAM. *To be a kicker*, tener agallas (to be a fighter).

kickoff [—ˈɔf] n. SP. Saque (*m.*) del centro. || FIG. FAM. Principio, *m.*, comienzo, *m.* || FIG. FAM. *For a kickoff*, para empezar.

kickshaw [—ʃɔ:] n. FAM. Golosina, *f.* (tidbit). | Fruslería, *f.* (trinket).

kickstand [—stænd] n. Soporte, *m.* (on bikes, motorcycles).

kick starter [—ˈstɑ:tə*] n. Arranque, *m.*, pedal (*m.*) de arranque.

kid [kid] n. ZOOL. Cabrito, *m.* || Cabritilla, *f.* (skin): *kid gloves*, guantes de cabritilla. || Cría, *f.* (young of various animals). || Niño, ña; crío, cría (child, young person). || — FIG. *To handle with kid gloves*, tratar con guante blanco. | *Kid stuff* o *kid's stuff*, cosas (*f. pl.*) de niños (childish), facilísimo, tirado (very easy): *it's kid's stuff*, está tirado, es facilísimo.

kid [kid] v. tr. FAM. Meter la trola de: *David kidded me that he'd broken his arm*, David me metió la trola de que se había roto el brazo. | Tomar el pelo a: *stop kidding me*, deja de tomarme el pelo. || *To kid o.s. that*, hacerse la ilusión de que.

— V. intr. Bromear. || Parir (a goat). || — *¿Are you kidding?*, ¿en serio? || *He was only kidding*, estaba bromeando, lo decía en broma. || *No kidding!*, ¡no me digas! || *You're kidding!*, ¡no me digas!, ¡no estarás hablando en serio!

kidder [—ə*] n. Bromista, *m.* & *f.*

kiddy [ˈkidi] n. Crío, cría (child).

kidnap [ˈkidnæp] v. tr. Raptar, secuestrar.

kidnapper [—ə*] n. Raptor, ra; secuestrador, ra.

kidnapping [—iŋ] n. Rapto, *m.*, secuestro, *m.*

kidney [ˈkidni] n. ANAT. Riñón, *m.* || FIG. Índole, *f.* || CULIN. Riñón, *m.*

kidney bean [—bi:n] n. Judía, *f.*, alubia, *f.* [*Amer.*, frijol, *m.*, poroto, *m.*] (bean). || U. S. Alubia (*f.*) pinta.

kidney machine [—məˈʃi:n] n. MED. Riñón (*m.*) artificial.

kidney stone [—stəun] n. MED. Cálculo (*m.*) renal.

kidskin [ˈkidskin] n. Cabritilla, *f.*

kier [kiə*] n. TECH. Autoclave (*m.*) para blanquear.

kieselguhr or **kieselgur** [ˈki:zəlgu:ə] n. MIN. Kieselgur, *m.*

kieserite [ˈki:zəˌrait] n. MIN. Kieserita, *f.*

kif [kif] n. Kif, *m.*

kilderkin [ˈkildəkin] n. Pequeño barril, *m.*

kill [kil] n. Muerte, *f.* (in hunting, bullfighting). || Caza, *f.*, cacería, *f.* (the animals killed in a hunt).

kill [kil] v. tr. Matar: *the dog was killed by a car*, el perro fue matado por un coche; *he killed his wife's lover*, mató al amante de su mujer. || FIG. Echar abajo: *to kill a bill*, echar abajo un proyecto de ley. | Acabar con, arruinar: *this has killed my hopes*, esto ha acabado con mis esperanzas. | Amortiguar (sound). | Matar, acabar con: *this work is killing me*, este trabajo me está matando, este trabajo acabará conmigo. | Hacer morir de risa: *that joke killed me*, ese chiste me hizo morir de risa. | Hundir (a boat). || FIG. FAM. Apagar, parar (a motor). || SP. Parar (in football). || Sacrificar, matar (to slaughter animals). || FIG. Suprimir (to prevent publication of). || — FIG. *The suspense was killing me*, el suspenso me tenía en vilo. | *This will kill you!*, ¡te vas a morir de risa! || *To kill off*, exterminar. || *To kill o.s.*, matarse. || FIG. *To kill the flavour of sth.*, quitar el sabor de algo. | *To kill time*, matar el tiempo. | *To kill two birds with one stone*, matar dos pájaros de un tiro.

— V. intr. Matar (to destroy life). || FIG. *To be dressed to kill*, estar de punta en blanco *or* de tiros largos.

killer [—ə*] n. Asesino, na (one who kills). || — *This disease is a killer*, esta enfermedad es mortal. || FAM. *This joke is a killer*, este chiste es para morirse de risa.

killer whale [ˈkiləˈweil] n. ZOOL. Orca, *f.*

killick [ˈkilik] n. Piedra (*f.*) que sirve de ancla.

killing [ˈkiliŋ] adj. Mortal (mortal). || Asesino, na (murderous). || FAM. Agotador, ra; matador, ra (exhausting). | Para morirse de risa (irresistibly funny). | Asesino, na (fierce): *a killing glance*, una mirada asesina.

— N. Asesinato, *m.* (murder). || Matanza, *f.* (slaughter, massacre). || U. S. FAM. Buena operación, *f.*, éxito, *m.* (financial coup).

killjoy [ˈkildʒɔi] n. Aguafiestas, *m.* & *f. inv.*

kill-or-cure [ˈkilɔ:ˈkjuə*] adj. FAM. De caballo (remedy).

kiln [kiln] n. Horno, *m.*

kiln-dry [—drai] v. tr. Secar al horno.

kilo [ˈki:ləu] n. Kilo, *m.*

kilocalorie [ˈki:ləuˌkæləri] n. Kilocaloría, *f.*

kilocycle [ˈki:ləuˌsaikl] n. Kilociclo, *m.*

kilogram, kilogramme [ˈkiləugræm] n. Kilogramo, *m.*

kilogram calorie [—ˈkæləri] n. Kilocaloría, *f.*

kilogram-metre (U. S. **kilogram-meter**) [ˈkiləugræˌmi:tə*] n. Kilográmetro, *m.*

kilojoule [ˈki:ləudʒu:l] n. Kilojulio, *m.*

kilolitre (U. S. **kiloliter**) [ˈki:ləuˌli:tə*] n. Kilolitro, *m.*

kilometre (U. S. **kilometer**) [ˈkiləuˌmi:tə*] n. Kilómetro, *m.*

kilometric [ˈkiləuˌmetrik] adj. Kilométrico, ca.

kiloton [ˈki:ləutʌn] n. Kilotón, *m.* (en física nuclear).

kilovolt [ˈki:ləuvəult] n. Kilovoltio, *m.*

kilowatt [ˈkiləuwɔt] n. Kilovatio, *m.*

kilowatt-hour [—ˈauə*] n. Kilovatio-hora, *m.*

kilt [kilt] n. Falda (*f.*) escocesa, "kilt", *m.*

kilt [kilt] v. tr. Plegar (to pleat).

kimono [kiˈməunəu] n. Kimono, *m.*, quimono, *m.*

kin [kin] n. Parientes, *m. pl.*, familia, *f.* (relatives). || *Next of kin*, pariente más cercano *or* parientes más cercanos.

— Adj. Emparentado, da (kindred).

kinaesthesia [ˌkainisˈθi:zjə] n. Cinestesia, *f.*

kinaesthesis or **kinesthesis** [ˌkainisˈθi:sis] n. Cinestesia, *f.*

kind [kaind] adj. Amable, amistoso, sa (friendly, helpful): *kind words*, palabras amables. || Bueno, na; cariñoso, sa: *kind to animals*, cariñoso con los animales. || Amable, bondadoso, sa (well-disposed): *kind to his servants*, amable con sus sirvientes. || Comprensivo, va (understanding). || Favorable (favourable). || Benigno, na: *a kind climate*, un clima benigno. || Bueno, na (beneficial): *kind to the skin*, bueno para el cutis. || — *Be so kind as to*, sea tan amable de, tenga la bondad de. || *It is very kind of you*, es muy amable de su parte. || *Kind regards*, muchos recuerdos. || *That wasn't very kind of them*, no fue muy simpático de su parte. || *The critics were not kind to his book*, los críticos han sido bastante duros con su libro.

|| *They were kind enough to*, tuvieron la amabilidad de. || *Would you be so kind as to?*, ¿me haría Ud. el favor de?, ¿tendría Ud. la bondad de?
— N. Clase, *f.*, tipo, *m.*: *a different kind of wine*, una clase diferente de vino. || Tipo, *m.*: *what kind of car do you drive?*, ¿qué tipo de coche conduces? || Clase, *f.*, tipo, *m.*: *I am not that kind of person*, no soy de esa clase de personas. || Índole, *f.*, carácter, *m.*: *they are different in kind*, son de distinta índole. || Cantidad, *f.*: *I haven't got that kind of money*, no tengo esa cantidad de dinero. || Especie, *f.*: *a kind of grey*, una especie de gris. || Género, *m.*, especie, *f.*: *other animals of their kind*, otros animales de su misma especie; *human kind*, especie humana. || REL. Especie, *f.* (for Communion). || — *A kind of*, cierto, ta: *there is a kind of harmony*, hay una cierta armonía. || *In a kind of way*, en cierta manera. || *In kind*, en especie: *payment in kind*, pago en especie. || *Nothing of the kind*, nada por el estilo. || *Of a kind*, de la misma especie *or* clase (belonging to the same group), una especie de: *coffee of a kind*, una especie de café. || *Of all kinds*, de todas clases, toda clase de: *food of all kinds*, toda clase de comida. || *Of the kind*, parecido, casi igual, por el estilo: *he has sth. of the kind*, tiene algo parecido. || *They are the kind who don't care*, son de los que no se preocupan. || *They are two of a kind*, son tal para cual. || FIG. *To repay in kind*, pagar con la misma moneda.
— Adv. FAM. *I kind of liked her*, en cierta manera la quería. | *I'm kind of tired*, estoy como *or* algo cansado. | *It's kind of round*, es como redondo. | *I've kind of got a headache*, tengo una especie de dolor de cabeza, tengo como un dolor de cabeza.

kindergarten [ˈkində,gɑ:tn] n. Jardín (*m.*) de la infancia, colegio (*m.*) de párvulos, "kindergarten", *m.* (school for young children).

kindhearted [ˈkaindˈhɑ:tid] adj. Bondadoso, sa; de buen corazón.

kindheartedness [—nis] n. Bondad, *f.*, buen corazón, *m.* (kindness).

kindle [ˈkindl] v. tr. Encender. || FIG. Encender, atizar, provocar: *to kindle anger, passion*, encender la ira, la pasión. | Despertar (interest, suspicions).
— V. intr. Encenderse. || FIG. Inflamarse.

kindliness [ˈkaindlinis] n. Bondad, *f.*, amabilidad, *f.* (goodness). || Benignidad, *f.* (of climate).

KINSHIP — PARENTESCO, *m.*

I. The family. — La familia.

relations, relatives, kinfolk, kin	parientes *m.*
my family *o* people	los míos, mi familia *f.*
next of kin	pariente (*m. sing.*) más cercano, parientes (*m. pl.*) más cercanos
family life	vida (*f.*) familiar
caste	casta *f.*
tribe	tribu *f.*
clan	clan *m.*
dynasty	dinastía *f.*
race, breed	raza *f.*
stock	estirpe *f.*
lineage	linaje *m.*
origin	origen *m.*
ancestry	ascendencia *f.*
ancestors, forebears, forefathers	antepasados *m.*
extraction	extracción *f.*, origen *m.*
descent, offspring	descendencia *f.*
descendants	descendientes *m.*
progeny, issue	progenie *f.*, prole *f.*
succession	sucesión *f.*
consanguinity, blood relationship	consanguinidad *f.*
affinity	afinidad *f.*
kinsmen by blood, by affinity	parientes (*m.*) consanguíneos, por afinidad
blood	sangre *f.*
generation	generación *f.*
branch	rama *f.*
family tree	árbol (*m.*) genealógico
of noble birth	de noble alcurnia
of humble birth	de humilde cuna

II. Parents and children. — Padres (*m.*) e hijos, *m.*

marriage	matrimonio *m.*
couple	pareja *f.*
husband	marido *m.*, esposo *m.*
foster parents	padres (*m.*) adoptivos
progenitor	progenitor *m.*
patriarch	patriarca *m.*
head of the family *o* of the household	cabeza (*m.*) de familia
father	padre *m.*
family man	padre (*m.*) de familia
papa, dad	papá, papi
daddy	papaíto
foster *o* adoptive father	padre (*m.*) adoptivo
father-in-law	suegro *m.*, padre (*m.*) político
stepfather	padrastro *m.*
godfather	padrino *m.*
mother	madre *f.*
mama, mum, ma	mamá *f.*, mama *f.*
mummy	mamaíta *f.*
wife	mujer *f.*, esposa *f.*
better half (fam.)	media naranja *f.*
foster *o* adoptive mother	madre (*f.*) adoptiva
stepmother	madrastra *f.*
godmother	madrina *f.*
mother-in-law	suegra *f.*, madre (*f.*) política
son	hijo *m.*
daughter	hija *f.*
child	niño *m.*, hijo *m.*; niña *f.*, hija *f.*
children	hijos *m.*, niños *m.*
legitimate child	hijo (*m.*) legítimo
natural child	hijo (*m.*) natural
bastard child	hijo (*m.*) bastardo
illegitimate child	hijo (*m*) ilegítimo
adulterine child	hijo (*m.*) adulterino
adopted *o* foster child	hijo (*m.*) adoptivo
stepson, stepchild	hijastro *m.*
stepdaughter, stepchild	hijastra *f.*
son-in-law	yerno *m.*, hijo (*m.*) político
daughter-in-law	nuera *f.*, hija (*f.*) política
only child	hijo (*m.*) único
first-born	primogénito *m.*
second-born	segundogénito *m.*
second son	segundón *m.*
youngest, youngest child	benjamín *m.*, hijo (*m.*) menor
eldest child	hijo (*m.*) mayor
godchild, godson	ahijado *m.*
goddaughter	ahijada *f.*
dauphin	delfín *m.*
heir	heredero *m.*
orphan	huérfano *m.*, huérfana *f.*
foundling	expósito *m.*, expósita *f.*

III. Other relatives. — Otros parientes, *m.*

brother	hermano *m.*
sister	hermana *f.*
full brother, brother-german	hermano (*m.*) carnal
full sister, sister-german	hermana (*f.*) carnal
half brother	medio hermano *m.*
half sister	media hermana *f.*
stepbrother	hermanastro *m.*
stepsister	hermanastra *f.*
foster brother	hermano (*m.*) de leche
uterine brother	hermano (*m.*) de madre *or* uterino
twin brother	mellizo *m.*, gemelo *m.*
brother-in-law	cuñado *m.*, hermano (*m.*) político
sister-in-law	cuñada *f.*, hermana (*f.*) política
brother of one's brother-in-law *or* sister-in-law	concuñado *m.*
brotherhood	hermandad *f.*
brotherly love	amor (*m.*) fraternal
fraternity	fraternidad *f.*
confraternity	confraternidad *f.*
grandparents	abuelos *m.*
grandfather	abuelo *m.*
grandad, grandpa	abuelito *m.*
grandmother	abuela *f.*
granny, gran, nanny, grandma	abuelita *f.*
step-grandfather	abuelastro *m.*
step-grandmother	abuelastra *f.*
great-grandfather	bisabuelo *m.*
great-grandmother	bisabuela *f.*
great-great-grandfather	tatarabuelo *m.*
great-great-grandmother	tatarabuela *f.*
grandchildren	nietos *m.*
grandson	nieto *m.*
granddaughter	nieta *f.*
great-grandson	bisnieto *m.*, biznieto *m.*
great-granddaughter	bisnieta *f.*, biznieta *f.*
great-great-grandson	tataranieto *m.*
great-great-granddaughter	tataranieta *f.*
uncle	tío *m.*
aunt	tía *f.*
aunty, auntie	tita *f.*
my uncle on my mother's side	mi tío (*m.*) materno
great-uncle, granduncle	tío (*m.*) abuelo
great-aunt, grandaunt	tía (*f.*) abuela
nephew	sobrino *m.*
niece	sobrina *f.*
great-nephew	sobrino (*m.*) nieto
great-niece	sobrina (*f.*) nieta
cousin	primo *m.*, prima *f.*
cousin-in-law	primo (*m.*) político, prima (*f.*) política
first cousin	primo (*m.*) carnal *or* hermano, prima (*f.*) carnal *or* hermana
second cousin	primo (*m.*) segundo, prima (*f.*) segunda
first cousin once removed	tío (*m.*) segundo (uncle), sobrino (*m.*) segundo (nephew), tía (*f.*) segunda (aunt), sobrina (*f.*) segunda (niece).
distant cousin	primo (*m.*) lejano, prima (*f.*) lejana

kindling [ˈkindliŋ] n. Encendimiento, *m.* (act of lighting). || Leña, *f.*, astillas, *f. pl.* (firewood). || FIG. Encendimiento, *m.* (of passion, etc.).
kindly [ˈkaindli] adj. Amable, bondadoso, sa (person). || Amable, cariñoso, sa (remark). || Agradable (place). || Benigno, na (climate). || Favorable (wind).
— Adv. Amablemente (nicely). || Bondadosamente (gently). || Por favor: *kindly come this way*, venga por aquí, por favor. || — *To take kindly to*, aceptar gustoso. || *To take sth. kindly*, tomar algo bien, apreciar algo.
kindness [ˈkaindnis] n. Amabilidad, *f.*, bondad, *f.* (*to*, con) [quality of being kind]: *he had the kindness to bring me flowers*, tuvo la amabilidad de traerme flores. || Buen trato, *m.* (*to*, de) [animals]. || Atención, *f.*, consideración, *f.* (consideration). || — *To do s.o. a kindness*, hacerle un favor a alguien, tener una amabilidad con alguien. || *To show kindness to s.o.*, mostrarse amable con alguien.
kindred [ˈkindrid] adj. Emparentado, da (related by blood). || De tronco común (of common origin): *kindred languages*, idiomas de tronco común. || Similar, semejante, afín (similar). || *Kindred spirits*, almas gemelas.
— N. Parientes, *m. pl.* (kin). || Parentesco, *m.* (kinship).
kine [kain] pl. n. (Ant.) Vacas, *f.* (cows). || Ganado, *m. sing.* (cattle).
— OBSERV. La palabra *kine* es el plural antiguo de *cow.*
kinematic [ˌkainiˈmætik] adj. Cinemático, ca.
kinematics [—s] n. Cinemática, *f.*
kinematograph [ˌkainiˈmætəugrɑ:f] n. Cinematógrafo, *m.*
kinescope [ˈkinəskəup] n. Cinescopio, *m.*
kinesitherapy [kinisiˈθerəpi] n. Kinesiterapia, *f.*
kinesthesia [ˌkainisˈθi:zjə] n. Cinestesia, *f.*
kinesthesis [ˌkainisˈθi:sis] n. Cinestesia, *f.*

— OBSERV. El plural de *kinesthesis* es *kinestheses.*

kinetic [kaiˈnetik] adj. Cinético, ca. || *Kinetic energy*, energía cinética.
kinetics [—s] n. Cinética, *f.*
kinfolk [ˈkinfəuk] pl. n. U. S. (Ant.). Parientes, *m.*
king [kiŋ] n. Rey, *m.*: *King Charles*, el rey Carlos; *the lion is the king of the jungle*, el león es el rey de la selva; *the king of Spanish football*, el rey del fútbol español. || Rey, *m.* (in chess, card games). || Dama, *f.* (in draughts). || — *Book of Kings*, libro (*m.*) de los Reyes. || *King of kings*, Rey de reyes. || *King of Rome*, Rey de Roma. || *The Sun king*, el rey Sol. || *The three Kings*, los Reyes Magos. || *To live, to treat like a king*, vivir, tratar a cuerpo de rey.
kingbolt [—bəult] n. TECH. Clavija (*f.*) maestra, pivote (*m.*) central.
king cobra [—ˈkəubrə] n. ZOOL. Cobra (*f.*) real.
kingcup [ˈkiŋkʌp] n. BOT. Botón (*m.*) de oro.
kingdom [—dəm] n. Reino, *m.* || — FAM. *Kingdom come*, el otro mundo: *to blast s.o. to kingdom come*, enviar a alguien al otro mundo. || *The animal kingdom*, el reino animal. || *The plant kingdom*, el reino vegetal. || FAM. *Till kingdom come*, hasta el Día del Juicio.
kingfisher [—ˌfiʃə*] n. Martín (*m.*) pescador (bird).
kinglet [—lit] n. Reyezuelo, *m.*
kingly [—li] adj. Real.
king of arms [—əvˈɑ:mz] n. Rey (*m.*) de armas.
kingpin [—pin] n. Bolo (*m.*) central (in bowling). || TECH. Clavija (*f.*) maestra, pivote (*m.*) central. || FIG. Persona (*f.*) clave (key person). | Alma, *f.* (of a team). | Piedra (*f.*) angular (essential thing).
king post [—pəust] n. ARCH. Pendolón, *m.*
Kings [—z] n. REL. Libro (*m.*) de los Reyes (in the Bible).
King's Bench [—zˈbentʃ] n. HIST. JUR. Tribunal (*m.*) Supremo.
king's bishop [—zˈbiʃəp] n. Alfil rey, *m.*
king's evil [—zˈi:vl] n. Escrófula, *f.*
kingship [—ʃip] n. Realeza, *f.*, majestad, *f.* (royalty). || Monarquía, *f.* (monarchy). || Trono, *m.* (throne).
king-size [—saiz] adj. Enorme. gigante (huge). || *King-size cigarettes*, cigarrillos largos.
kink [kiŋk] n. Retorcimiento, *m.* (twist or loop in a cable, pipe, etc.). || Rizo, *m.* (in hair). || Arruga, *f.*, pliegue, *m.* (crease, fold). || MED. Tortícolis, *f. inv.* || FAM. Chifladura, *f.*, manía, *f.* (mental twist). | Fallo, *m.*, defecto, *m.* (defect).
kink [kiŋk] v. tr. Retorcer (to twist).
— V. intr. Retorcerse. || Ensortijarse, rizarse (hair).
kinky [kiŋki] adj. Retorcido, da (twisted). || Ensortijado, da; rizado, da (curly). || FAM. Chiflado, da (crazy). | Extraño, ña; raro, ra (strange).
kino [ˈki:nəu] n. Quino, *m.*
kinsfolk [ˈkiŋzfəuk] pl. n. Parientes, *m.*
kinship [ˈkiŋʃip] n. Parentesco, *m.* (family relationship). || Afinidad, *f.* (similarity).
kinsman [ˈkiŋzmən] n. Pariente, *m.*

— OBSERV. El plural de *kinsman* es *kinsmen.*

kinswoman [ˈkinzˌwumən] n. Parienta. *f.*

— OBSERV. El plural de *kinswoman* es *kinswomen.*

kiosk [kiˈɔsk] n. Quiosco, *m.*, kiosco, *m.*
kip [kip] n. Piel (*f.*) de cordero *or* de becerro (animal hide). || FAM. Catre, *m.*, piltra, *f.* (bed). | Pensión, *f.* (boardinghouse). | Alojamiento, *m.* (lodging). || — FAM. *To have a kip*, echar una cabezada. | *You ought to get some kip*, deberías domir un poco *or* echar una cabezada.
kip [kip] v. intr. Dormir: *he's kipping*, está durmiendo.
kipper [—ə*] n. Arenque (*m.*) *or* salmón (*m.*) ahumado y salado.
kipper [—ə*] v. tr. Curar, ahumar.
kirk [kə:k] n. Iglesia, *f.* || *The Kirk*, la Iglesia [Presbiteriana] de Escocia.
kirsch [kiəʃ] n. Kirsch, *m.*
kismet [ˈkismet] n. Destino, *m.*
kiss [kis] n. Beso, *m.*: *give me a kiss*, dame un beso. || Roce, *m.* (light touch). || Merengue, *m.* (sweet). || — *The kiss of life*, respiración (*f.*) boca a boca. || *To blow s.o. a kiss*, enviar un beso a alguien.
kiss [kis] v. tr. Besar: *to kiss the hand*, besar la mano. || Rozar (to touch lightly). || — *To kiss away*, hacer olvidar con besos. || *To kiss s.o. goodbye*, dar un beso de despedida a alguien. || FIG. *To kiss sth. goodbye*, despedirse de algo, decir adiós a algo. | *To kiss the ground*, besar el suelo.
— V. intr. Besarse. || Rozarse (balls in billiards). || *They kissed*, se besaron, se dieron un beso.
kiss-curl [—kə:l] n. Caracol, *m.* (of hair).
kisser [—ə*] n. FAM. Besucón, ona (person). | Morro, *m.*, boca, *f.* (mouth). | Jeta, *f.* (face).
kissproof [—pru:f] adj. Indeleble (lipstick).
kit [kit] n. Herramientas, *f. pl.* (tools): *a plumber's kit*, las herramientas del fontanero. || Caja (*f.*) de las herramientas (box). || Botiquín, *m.* (first-aid). || MIL. SP. Equipo, *m.* || Equipaje, *m.*, equipo, *m.* (equipment, gear). || Grupo, *m.*, conjunto, *m.* (group). || Maqueta, *f.* (toy model to be assembled). || Avíos, *m. pl.*: *washing kit*, avíos de aseo; *shoe cleaning kit*, avíos de limpiar zapatos. || Conjunto (*m.*) de piezas [para montar un coche *or* una radio, etc.]. || FAM. *The whole kit and caboodle*, toda la pesca.
kit [kit] v. tr. Equipar. || *To kit out*, equipar.
kit bag [—bæg] n. Macuto, *m.* (knapsack). || Bolsa, *f.* (canvas bag).
kitchen [kitʃin] n. Cocina, *f.*
kitchen boy [—bɔi] n. Pinche, *m.*
kitchener [—ə*] n. Cocinero, *m.*
kitchenette [ˌkitʃiˈnet] n. Cocina (*f.*) pequeña.
kitchen garden [ˈkitʃinˈgɑ:dn] n. Huerto, *m.*
kitchen maid [ˈkitʃinmeid] n. Ayudanta (*f.*) de cocinera.
kitchen police [ˈkitʃinpəˈli:s] n. U. S. MIL. Servicio (*m.*) de cocina.
kitchen range [ˈkitʃinreindʒ] n. Cocina (*f.*) económica.
kitchen sink [ˈkitʃinˈsiŋk] n. Fregadero, *m.*, pila (*f.*) de cocina.
kitchen-sink drama [—ˈdrɑ:mə] n. THEATR. Comedia (*f.*) de costumbres.
kitchenware [ˈkitʃinwɛə*] n. Utensilios (*m. pl.*) de cocina, batería (*f.*) de cocina.
kite [kait] n. ZOOL. Milano, *m.* (bird). || Cometa, *f.* (toy). || COMM. Cheque (*m.*) sin fondos. || — Pl. MAR. Sobrejuanete, *m. sing.* || FIG. *To fly a kite*, lanzar una idea para tantear el terreno.
kith [kiθ] n. Amigos, *m. pl.* (friends). || *Kith and kin*, parientes y amigos.
kit inspection [kit inˈspekʃən] n. Revista, *f.*
kitten [ˈkitn] n. Gatito, *m.* || — FAM. *She'll have kittens!*, ¡le dará un ataque! | *We almost had kittens!*, ¡casi nos morimos del susto!
kitten [ˈkitn] v. intr. Parir (a cat).
kittenish [—iʃ] adj. Coquetón, ona.
kittiwake [ˈkitiweik] n. ZOOL. Gaviota, *f.* (sea gull).
kitty [ˈkiti] n. Plato, *m.*, platillo, *m.*, bote, *m.* (into which each player puts a stake). || FAM. Fondo (*m.*) común, reserva, *f.* (of money, goods, etc.). | Gatito, *m.* (kitten).
kiwi [ˈki:wi] n. ZOOL. Kiwi, *m.* (bird).
klaxon [ˈklæksn] n. Claxon, *m.*, klaxon, *m.*
kleptomania [ˌkleptəuˈmeinjə] n. Cleptomanía, *f.*
kleptomaniac [ˌkleptəuˈmeiniæk] n. Cleptómano, na.
knack [næk] n. Facilidad, *f.*: *a knack for remembering names*, facilidad para recordar nombres. || Tranquillo, *m.*, truco, *m.*: *it's easy once you get the knack*, es fácil una vez que le coges el tranquillo. || Habilidad, *f.*, maña, *f.*: *to have the knack of doing sth.*, tener maña para hacer algo. || Don, *m.*: *to have the knack of doing the right thing*, tener el don de hacer lo que se debe.
knacker [—ə*] n. Matarife, *m.*, descuartizador, *m.* (for horses). || Desguazador, *m.* (for cars, etc.).
knag [næg] n. Nudo, *m.* (in wood).
knap [næp] v. tr. Golpear (to knock). || Picar (stones). || Mordisquear (to bite).
knapsack [—sæk] n. Mochila, *f.*
knar [nɑ:*] n. Nudo, *m.* (in wood).
knave [neiv] n. Bribón, *m.*, granuja, *m.*, bellaco, *m.* (rogue). || Sota, *f.* (in Spanish cards). || Jota, *f.* (in international cards).
knavery [ˈneivəri] n. Bribonada, *f.*, bribonería, *f.*, bellaquería, *f.*, picardía, *f.*
knavish [ˈneiviʃ] adj. Bribón, ona; bellaco, ca; picaresco, ca (roguish).
knead [ni:d] v. tr. Amasar (dough, clay). || Dar masaje a (to massage). || FIG. Formar, moldear (to shape).
kneading trough [—iŋtrɔf] n. Artesa, *f.*, amasadera, *f.*
knee [ni:] n. ANAT. Rodilla, *f.*: *he was on his knees*, estaba de rodillas; *down on one's knees*, de rodillas;

to bend o *to bow the knee*, doblar la rodilla. || TECH. Codo, *m.* || Rodillera, *f.* (part of a garment that covers the knee). || — *To bring s.o. to his knees*, poner a alguien de rodillas. || *To go down on one's knees*, arrodillarse. || *To go down on one's knees to s.o.*, suplicar a alguien de rodillas.

knee [ni:] v. tr. Dar con la rodilla a.

knee breeches [—ˌbritʃiz] pl. n. Calzón (*m. sing.*) corto.

kneecap [—kæp] n. ANAT. Rótula, *f.*

knee-deep [—di:p] adj. *The water was knee-deep*, el agua llegaba hasta las rodillas. || *To be knee-deep in water*, estar metido en el agua hasta las rodillas.

knee-high [—hai] adj. *The grass was knee-high*, la hierba llegaba hasta las rodillas.

kneehole desk [ˈni:həulˈdesk] n. Mesa (*f.*) con un hueco para meter las rodillas, mesa (*f.*) de despacho.

knee jerk [ˈni:dʒə:k] n. Reflejo (*m.*) rotuliano *or* de la rótula.

knee joint [ˈni:dʒɔint] n. ANAT. Articulación (*f.*) de la rodilla. || TECH. Junta (*f.*) articulada.

kneel* [ni:l] v. intr. Arrodillarse. || — *To be kneeling*, estar de rodillas. || *To kneel down*, ponerse de rodillas, arrodillarse.

— OBSERV. Pret. & p. p. ***knelt, kneeled.***

kneeling chair [ˈni:liŋtʃɛə*] n. REL. Reclinatorio, *m.*

kneepad [ˈni:pæd] n. Rodillera, *f.*

kneepan [ˈni:pæn] n. ANAT. Rótula, *f.*

knell [nel] n. Toque (*m.*) de difuntos, tañido (*m.*) fúnebre. || FIG. Fin, *m.* (end): *to sound the knell of*, anunciar el fin de.

knelt [nelt] pret. & p. p. See KNEEL.

knew [nju:] pret. See KNOW.

knickerbockers [ˈnikəbɔkəz] pl. n. Bombachos, *m.* (trousers).

knickers [ˈnikəz] pl. n. Bragas, *f.* (women's panties). || Bombachos, *m.* (knickerbockers).

knickknack [ˈniknæk] n. Chuchería, *f.*

knife [naif] n. Cuchillo, *m.* (cutting instrument): *bread, butter knife*, cuchillo para el pan, para la mantequilla. || Navaja, *f.* (with folding blade). || Cuchilla, *f.* (cutting blade in a machine). || MED. Bisturí, *m.* (scalpel). || — *Knife and fork*, cubierto, *m.* (cutlery). || *To get one's knife into s.o.*, tener rabia *or* manía a alguien.

— OBSERV. El plural de *knife* es *knives.*

knife [naif] v. tr. Cortar con cuchillo (to cut with a knife). || Apuñalar (to stab). || U. S. FIG. Dar una puñalada trapera a (to stab s.o. in the back).

knife-edge [—edʒ] n. Filo, *m.* || FIG. *To be balancing on a knife-edge*, estar pendiente de un hilo.

knife grinder [—ˌgraində*] n. Afilador, *m.*

knife switch [—switʃ] n. ELECTR. Interruptor (*m.*) de cuchilla.

knight [nait] n. Caballero, *m.: the knights of the Round Table*, los caballeros de la Tabla Redonda. || Caballo, *m.* (in chess).

knight [nait] v. tr. Armar caballero. || FIG. Conceder el título de "Sir" a.

knight-errant [—ˈerənt] n. Caballero (*m.*) andante. || FIG. Don Quijote, *m.* (defender of just causes).

— OBSERV. El plural de *knight-errant* es *knights-errant.*

knight-errantry [—ˈerəntri] n. Caballería (*f.*) errante. || FIG. Quijotismo, *m.* (defence of just causes).

knighthood [—hud] n. Caballería, *f.* (knights). || Título (*m.*) de caballero (rank). || FIG. Título (*m.*) de "Sir".

knightly [—li] adj. Caballeresco, ca: *knightly deeds*, hazañas caballerescas.

Knight Templer [—ˈtemplə*] n. Templario, *m.*

knit [nit] n. Punto, *m.* (a stitch in knitting). || *Knit goods*, géneros (*m.*) de punto.

knit* [nit] v. tr. Tejer: *to knit a dress*, tejer un traje. || Juntar, unir (to join together). || — *To knit one's brows*, fruncir el ceño *or* el entrecejo. || FIG. *To knit up*, poner punto final a.

— V. intr. Hacer punto [*Amer.*, hacer malla, tejer, tricotar]: *Elena likes knitting*, a Elena le gusta hacer punto. || Unirse, soldarse (to unite). || Soldarse (bones).

— OBSERV. Pret. & p. p. ***knit, knitted.***

knitter [—ə*] n. Persona (*f.*) que hace punto.

knitting [—iŋ] n. Tejido (*m.*) de punto (cloth). || Punto (*m.*) de aguja, labor (*f.*) de punto (process). || *I must do some knitting*, tengo que hacer punto.

knitting machine [ˈnitiŋməˌʃi:n] n. Máquina (*f.*) de hacer punto, tricotosa, *f.*

knitting needle [ˈnitiŋˌni:dl] n. Aguja (*f.*) de hacer punto [*Amer.*, aguja de tejer].

knitwear [ˈnitwɛə*] n. Artículos (*m. pl.*) *or* géneros (*m. pl.*) de punto.

knives [naivz] pl. n. See KNIFE.

knob [nɔb] n. Bulto, *m.*, protuberancia, *f.* (protuberance). || Tirador, *m.* (of a drawer). || Botón, *m.* (of a radio). || Nudo, *m.* (on a tree). || Pomo, *m.* (of a door, stick, sword). || Terrón, *m.: sugar knob*, terrón de azúcar. || Pedazo, *m.* (of butter, coal). || U. S. Loma, *f.*, montículo, *m.* (hillock).

knobble [nɔbl] n. Bulto (*m.*) pequeño.

knobbly [ˈnɔbli] or **knobby** [ˈnɔbi] adj. Nudoso, sa: *knobbly tree*, árbol nudoso. || Lleno de bultos (covered with knobs).

knobkerrie [ˈnɔbkeri] n. Clava, *f.* (club).

knock [nɔk] n. Golpe, *m.*, llamada, *f.*, toque, *m.* (at the door). || Golpe, *m.*, choque, *m.* || FIG. Revés, *m.*, golpe *m.* (of bad luck or misfortune). || TECH. Picado, *m.*, golpeteo, *m.* (in motor). || FIG. FAM. Crítica, *f.* (criticism): *a knock at the monarchy*, una crítica de la monarquía. || — *There was a knock at the door*, llamaron a la puerta. || *To get a knock on the head*, recibir un golpe en la cabeza. || FIG. *To take a hard knock*, sufrir un gran revés, recibir un golpe duro.

knock [nɔk] v. tr. Golpear, pegar (to hit). || Chocar contra (to collide with). || FAM. Meterse con (to find fault with). | Poner por los suelos, dar un palo a (to criticize). || — FIG. *Our plans have been knocked on the head*, han dado al traste con nuestros planes. || *To knock a hole in sth.*, hacer *or* abrir un agujero en algo. || *To knock sth. flying*, enviar algo por los aires. || FIG. *To knock one's head against a brick wall*, darse de cabeza contra la pared (in anger). || *To knock one's head on the luggage rack*, dar con la cabeza en la redecilla. || *To knock the bottom out of*, quitar el fondo de (a box), acabar con (to destroy), ser el fin de: *the accident knocked the bottom out of his world*, el accidente fue el fin del mundo para él. || *To knock to pieces*, hacer pedazos.

— V. intr. Golpear. || Llamar: *to knock at the door*, llamar a la puerta. || Picar (a motor). || FAM. Criticar. || FAM. *He's knocking on seventy*, va para los setenta (age).

— ***To knock about,*** maltratar (to subject to rough treatment). | Golpear (to hit). | Zarandear, zamarrear (in a crowd). | Rodar: *they knock about the streets all day*, pasan el día rodando por las calles. || ***To knock against,*** dar contra. || ***To knock back,*** beber [de un trago] (to drink). || ***To knock down,*** atropellar (a person). | Derribar (an object). | Tirar (to make fall). | Rebajar (the price). | Adjudicar (in an auction): *it was knocked down to him for 500 pounds*, le ha sido adjudicado en 500 libras. || ***To knock in,*** hacer entrar a golpes. | Clavar (a nail). | Abollar (to dent). | Aplastar: *to knock s.o.'s head in*, aplastar la cabeza a alguien. | Derribar (a door). || ***To knock into,*** hacer entrar a golpes. | Chocar con. || ***To knock off,*** tirar: *to knock sth. off the table*, tirar algo de la mesa. | Romper (to break off). | Hacer saltar a golpes. | Rebajar en: *to knock one pound off an article*, rebajar un artículo en una libra. | Bajar en, mejorar en: *to knock two seconds off the world record*, bajar el récord mundial en dos segundos. | Despachar (to do sth. hurriedly). | Poner fin a (to finish). | Terminar: *the men knock off at six*, los trabajadores terminan a las seis. | FAM. Birlar, mangar (to steal), detener (to arrest), cargarse, liquidar (to kill). | — *Knock it off!*, ¡basta ya! || FIG. *To knock s.o.'s head off*, pegar una buena paliza a uno. || ***To knock out,*** vaciar: *to knock out a pipe*, vaciar una pipa. | Dejar K.O., noquear, dejar fuera de combate (in boxing). | Dejar sin conocimiento (to make unconscious). | SP. Eliminar (to eliminate). | Quitar (to remove). | Partirse: *to knock two teeth out*, partirse dos dientes. | FAM. Dejar pasmado (to amaze). || ***To knock over,*** tirar (a glass, etc.). || Atropellar (a pedestrian). || ***To knock together,*** golpear (to strike). | Golpearse (to hit each other). | Hacer de prisa y corriendo (to make hurriedly). || ***To knock up,*** despertar (to awaken). | Construir precipitadamente (a house). | Hacer de prisa y corriendo (to make quickly). | Marcar (in cricket). | Pelotear (in tennis). | Reventar, derrengar (to exhaust). | POP. Dejar embarazada. | — *To knock up against*, tropezar con (difficulties, people).

knockabout [—əbaut] adj. De diario (clothes). || De risa (a play). || Bullicioso, sa (boisterous).

— N. Yate (*m.*) pequeño (yacht). || *To have a knockabout with a ball*, jugar con un balón, dar patadas a un balón.

knockdown [—ˈdaun] adj. Que derriba (a blow). || U. S. Desmontable: *knockdown table*, mesa desmontable. || *Knockdown price*, precio (*m.*) de saldo.

— N. SP. Caída, *f.* (in boxing). || Golpe (*m.*) muy fuerte.

knocker [—ə*] n. Aldaba, *f.*, aldabón, *m.* (of door). || FAM. Criticón, ona (faultfinder).

knocking [—iŋ] n. Golpeo, *m.*, golpeteo, *m.* || Golpes, *m. pl.: we heard a knocking at the door*, oímos golpes en la puerta.

knock-kneed [ni:d] adj. Patizambo, ba; zambo, ba.

knockout [—aut] n. SP. "Knock out", *m.*, K.O., *m.*, fuera de combate, *m.* (boxing). || FIG. Maravilla, *f.: she is a knockout*, es una maravilla.

— Adj. FAM. Maravilloso, sa (marvellous). || Que deja sin conocimiento (a blow). || Que pone fuera de combate, que noquea (in boxing). || SP. FAM. *Knockout drops*, narcótico, *m. sing.*

knockup [—ʌp] n. SP. Peloteo, *m.* (in tennis). || *To have a knockup*, pelotear.

knoll [nəul] n. Loma, *f.*, montículo, *m.*

knot [nɔt] n. Nudo, *m.: he tied a knot*, hizo un nudo. || Lazo, *m.* (ornamental ribbon). || MIL. Galón, *m.* || Grupo, *m.* (a group): *a knot of people*, un grupo de personas. || MED. Haz, *m.* (of nerves). || BOT. Nudo, *m.*, nudosidad, *f.* || MAR. Nudo, *m.* || FIG. Nudo, *m.* (of problem, question). | Vínculo, *m.*, lazo, *m.* (of marriage). || — *Knot of hair*, enmarañamiento (*m.*) del pelo (tangle), moño, *m.* (bun). || FIG. *To get tied up in knots*, enmarañarse, enredarse, liarse. || MAR. *To make ten knots*, hacer diez nudos. || *To tie a knot in one's handkerchief*, hacer un nudo en el pañuelo. || FIG. *To tie the knot*, echar las bendiciones. || *To untie a knot*, deshacer *or* desatar un nudo.

knot [nɔt] v. tr. Atar con un nudo (to tie with a knot). || Anudar: *he knotted the rope*, anudó la cuerda. || Enmarañar, enredar, liar (to tangle). || Fruncir (the eyebrows).
— V. intr. Anudarse. || Enredarse (to get tangled). || Agruparse (to crowd).

knotgrass [—grɑ:s] n. BOT. Centinodia, *f.*

knothole [—həul] n. Hueco (*m.*) que queda en la madera al desprenderse un nudo.

knotty [—i] adj. Nudoso, sa (having knots). || FIG. Espinoso, sa; intrincado, da (hard to solve).

knout [naut] n. Knut, *m.* (whip).

knout [naut] v. tr. Azotar con un knut.

know [nəu] n. *To be in the know*, estar enterado, estar al tanto.

know* [nəu] v. tr. Saber: *he knows how to swim*, sabe nadar; *he knows French*, sabe francés; *I don't know how you do it*, no sé cómo lo haces; *I know it by heart*, lo sé de memoria; *I always knew that it would happen*, ya sabía yo que sucedería; *to know one for what one is*, saber muy bien lo que es uno; *not to want to know anything*, no querer saber nada. || Conocer (acquaintance): *do you know my father?*, ¿conoces a mi padre?; *do you know Athens?*, ¿conoces Atenas?; *to know poverty*, conocer la miseria; *he knows me by sight*, me conoce de vista. || Reconocer (recognize): *I knew him from o by his voice*, le reconocí por la voz. || Distinguir: *to know truth from falsehood*, distinguir la verdad de la mentira; *I know one from another*, distingo uno de otro. || Ver: *she had never been known to weep*, nunca se le había visto llorar; *I've never known anyone to lie like he does*, nunca he visto a uno que mienta tanto como él. || — *As is well known*, como es sabido. || *Be it known that*, se da a conocer que. || *Don't I know it!*, ¡y usted que lo diga! || FIG. *Everyone knows on which side his bread is buttered*, cada uno sabe dónde le aprieta el zapato. || *He is known to be weak*, se sabe que es débil. || *He knows everything*, se lo sabe todo, sabe todo. || *I knew him for a Spaniard*, le tomaba por español. || *It is a known fact that o it is known that*, se sabe que. || *Not to know anything about anything*, no saber nada de nada. || FIG. *Not to know s.o. from Adam*, no conocer a uno ni por asomo. || *Not to know the first thing about sth.*, no saber ni jota de algo. || *Not to know what to do with o.s.*, no saber dónde meterse. || *She knows all about cars*, entiende mucho de coches. || *There's no knowing*, no se puede saber. || *To be known as o to be known to be*, ser conocido como (reputation), ser conocido por el nombre de (name). || *To be worth knowing*, ser digno de saberse (a fact), valer la pena de ser conocido (place, person). || *To get to know s.o.*, conocer: *when you get to know each other a bit better*, cuando os conozcáis un poco mejor. || *To get to know sth.*, enterarse de algo (to be informed), conocer: *to get to know a country*, conocer un país. || FIG. *To know all the tricks of the trade*, conocer muy bien el percal *or* el paño *or* el asunto. || *To know a thing or two*, saber algo, conocer cuatro cosas. || FIG. *To know a woman*, conocer a una mujer (in the biblical sense). || *To know each other*, conocerse. || *To know for sure*, estar seguro de, saber a punto fijo. || FIG. *To know how many beans make five*, saber cuántas son cinco. || *To know how to do sth.*, saber hacer algo. || *To know how to get by*, saber arreglárselas. || *To know more than one says*, saber más de lo que uno dice. || *To know one's own mind*, saber lo que se quiere. || *To know one's own weaknesses*, saber dónde le aprieta el zapato a uno, conocer sus propios defectos. || *To know one to be a good teacher*, saber que uno es un buen profesor. || *To know only too well that*, saber de sobra que. || *To know o.s.*, conocerse a sí mismo. || FIG. *To know s.o. inside out*, conocer el pie que calza uno. | *To know sth. backwards*, saber algo al dedillo *or* como el padre nuestro. || *To know sth. like the back of one's hand*, conocer algo como la palma de la mano. || *To know too much*, saber más de la cuenta. || *To know what's what*, saber cuántas son cinco. || *To let s.o. know sth.*, avisar algo a alguien, dar a conocer algo a alguien. || *To make it known to s.o. that*, dar a conocer a alguien que, informar a alguien de que. || *To make o.s. known*, darse a conocer. || *What do you know?*, ¿tú qué sabes? || *Without his (my, etc.) knowing it*, sin saberlo él (yo, etc.). || *You don't know what you're letting yourself in for*, no sabes dónde te metes. || *You wouldn't know him from a Frenchman*, se lo tomaría por un francés.
— V. intr. Saber: *as far as I know!*, ¡que yo sepa! || — *Do you know about Peter?*, ¿sabes lo de Pedro? || *Goodness knows! o God only knows!*, ¡sabe Dios!, ¡vete a saber! || *He's not young, you know*, no te creas que es joven. || *How should I know!*, ¡yo qué sé!, ¡qué sé yo! || *I don't know about you, but I'm leaving*, no sé lo que vas a hacer tú, pero yo me voy. || *If only I'd known!*, de haberlo sabido antes. || *I know!*, ¡ya lo sé! || *I know better than anyone!*, ¡lo sé mejor que nadie! || *I ought to know!*, ¡lo sabré yo! || *So now you know!*, ¡conque ya lo sabes! || *They didn't want to know*, no quisieron saber nada. || *Three hours is a long time, you know*, tres horas son muchas ¿sabes? || *To know about*, entender de (to have a knowledge of), saber: *I didn't know about that*, eso no lo sabía. || *To know better than to*, saber que no se debe: *I know better than to play with fire*, sé que no se debe jugar con fuego; guardarse de: *he knew better than to believe them*, se guardó de creerlos. || *To know of*, saber de: *I know of s.o. who can help you*, sé de alguien que te puede ayudar. || FIG. *To know where the shoe pinches*, saber uno dónde le aprieta el zapato. || *To let s.o. know of sth.*, informar a alguien de algo. || *Who knows?*, ¿quién sabe?, ¡vete a saber! || *You know best*, usted lo sabe mejor que nadie. || *You ought to know better!*, ¡ya tenías que saber esas cosas!

— OBSERV. Pret. ***knew;*** p. p. ***known.***

knowable [—əbl] adj. Conocible.

know-all [—ɔ:l] n. Sabelotodo, *m.* & *f.*, sabihondo, da (pedant).

know-how [—hau] n. Habilidad, *f.*, destreza, *f.* (skill). || Conocimientos, *m. pl.* (knowledge): *scientific know-how*, conocimientos científicos.

knowing [—iŋ] adj. Astuto, ta; sagaz (shrewd). || Deliberado, da (deliberate). || Instruido, da; culto, ta (educated). || De complicidad, de entendimiento (glance, wink).
— N. Conocimiento, *m.*

knowingly [—iŋli] adv. Astutamente, sagazmente. || A sabiendas, deliberadamente: *he started the fire knowingly*, provocó el incendio deliberadamente.

know-it-all [—itɔ:l] n. U. S. FAM. Sabelotodo, *m.* & *f.*, sabihondo, da.

knowledge [ˈnɔlidʒ] n. Conocimiento, *m.*: *intuitive knowledge*, conocimiento intuitivo. || Conocimientos, *m. pl.*, saber, *m.*: *to apply one's knowledge*, aplicar sus conocimientos. || — *A little knowledge is a dangerous thing*, es mejor no saber nada que saber poco. || *A working knowledge of French*, conocimientos sólidos de francés. || *I had no knowledge of it*, no tenía conocimiento de ello, no sabía nada de ello. || *It has come to my knowledge*, me enteré, ha llegado a mi conocimiento. || *It is common knowledge that*, es del dominio público que (a piece of news), todo el mundo sabe que (everybody knows that). || *Knowledge is power*, saber es poder. || *Not to my knowledge*, que yo sepa no. || *To have a thorough knowledge of*, conocer a fondo, dominar. || *To my knowledge*, que yo sepa. || *With full knowledge of the facts*, con conocimiento de causa. || *Without my knowledge*, sin saberlo yo.

knowledgeable [—əbl] adj. Informado, da (informed). || Erudito, ta (erudite). || *He is knowledgeable about Spanish art*, sabe mucho de arte español.

known [nəun] p. p. See KNOW.

know-nothing [—ˈnʌθiŋ] n. Ignorante, *m.* & *f.*

knuckle [nʌkl] n. ANAT. Nudillo, *m.* (of finger). || Jarrete, *m.* (of an animal). || CULIN. Jarrete, *m.*: *knuckle of pork*, jarrete de cerdo. || TECH. Junta (*f.*) articulada. || — Pl. Llave (*f. sing.*) inglesa, manopla, *f. sing.* || — FIG. *Near the knuckle*, rayando en la indecencia. || *To rap s.o.'s knuckles*, pegar en los nudillos a alguien.

knuckle [nʌkl] v. tr. Golpear con los nudillos.
— V. intr. *To knuckle down to*, ponerse seriamente a [hacer]. || *To knuckle under*, pasar por el aro, someterse.

knucklebone [—bəun] n. ANAT. Nudillo, *m.* (of people). || Taba, *f.* (of animals). || — Pl. Tabas, *f.* (game).

knuckle-duster [ˌdʌstə*] n. Manopla, *f.*, llave (*f.*) inglesa.

knur [nə:*] n. BOT. Nudo, *m.* (in tree trunks).

knurl [nə:rl] n. BOT. Nudo, *m.* || Grafilado, *m.* (in metalwork).

knurled [nə:rld] adj. Nudoso, sa (tree trunk). || Grafilado, da (coin, etc.).

koala [kəuˈɑ:lə] n. ZOOL. Koala, *m.*

Kodiak bear [ˈkəudiækbeə*] n. ZOOL. Oso (*m.*) americano.

kohlrabi [kəulˈrɑ:bi] n. BOT. Colinabo, *m.*

kola nut [ˈkəulənʌt] n. BOT. Nuez (*f.*) de cola.

kola tree [ˈkəulətri:] n. BOT. Cola, *f.*

kolinsky [kəˈlinski] n. ZOOL. Visón (*m.*) de Siberia.

kolkhoz [kɔlˈkɔz] n. Koljoz, *m.*, granja (*f.*) colectiva (in U.S.S.R.)

— OBSERV. El plural de *kolkhoz* es *kolkhozy* o *kolkhozes.*

kopeck [ˈkəupek] n. Copec, *m.*, kopek, *m.* (currency).

Koran [kɔˈrɑ:n] pr. n. REL. Corán, *m.*, Alcorán, *m.*

Koranic [—ik] adj. Coránico, ca.

Korea [kəˈriə] pr. n. GEOGR. Corea, *f.*

Korean [kəˈriən] adj./n. Coreano, na.

koruna [ˈkɔ:rənɑ:] n. Corona (*f.*) checa (currency).

— OBSERV. El plural es *koruny* o *korunas.*

kosher [ˈkəuʃə*] adj. Permitido por la religión judía (food). || *Kosher butcher*, carnicero (*m.*) que vende carne preparada para los judíos.

koumiss [ˈku:mis] n. Kumis, *m.* (drink).

kowtow [ˈkauˈtau] n. Reverencia (*f.*) china.

kowtow [ˈkauˈtau] v. intr. Hacer una reverencia china [arrodillarse y tocar el suelo con la frente]. || FIG. Demostrar sumo respeto. || *To kowtow to s.o.*, humillarse ante alguien.

kraft [krɑ:ft] n. Kraft, *m.*, papel (*m.*) de envolver.

krater [ˈkreitə*] n. Crátera, *f.* (vase).

kris [kri:s] n. Puñal (*m.*) malayo, cris, *m.*
krona [ˈkru:næ] n. Corona (*f.*) sueca (currency).
— OBSERV. El plural de *krona* es *kronor*.
krone [ˈkrəunə] n. Corona (*f.*) danesa o noruega (currency).
— OBSERV. El plural de *krone* es *kroner*.
krypton [ˈkriptən] n. CHEM. Criptón, *m.*
kudos [ˈkju:dɔs] n. Prestigio, *m.*, gloria, *f.*, fama, *f.*
kulak [ˈkju:læk] n. Kulak, *m.*
kumiss [ˈku:mis] n. Kumis, *m.* (drink).
kümmel [ˈkuməl] n. Cúmel, *m.*, kummel, *m.* (liquor).
Kurd [kə:d] or **Kurdish** [—iʃ] adj./n. Curdo, da; kurdo, da.
kyphosis [kaiˈfəusis] n. MED. Cifosis, *f.*
Kyrie eleison [kirieieˈleisˈn] n. REL. Kirieeleisón, *m.*

L

l [el] n. L, *f.* (letter of alphabet). || Libra, *f.* (pound). || *L plate*, placa obligatoria que lleva en el coche el aprendiz de conductor o la autoescuela.
— Adj. En forma de L.
la [lɑ:] n. MUS. La, *m.* (fixed notation). | Superdominante, *f.* (movable notation).
lab [læb] n. FAM. Laboratorio, *m.*
labefaction [ˌlæbiˈfækʃən] n. Decrepitud, *f.*
label [ˈleibl] n. Etiqueta, *f.* (tag). || Etiqueta, *f.*, rótulo, *m.*, membrete, *m.*, marbete, *m.* (on merchandise). || Letrero, *m.* (notice). || Tejuelo, *m.* (on the spine of a book). || Cinta, *f.* (ribbon to hold the seal). || FIG. Etiqueta, *f.*: *political labels*, etiquetas políticas. | Designación, *f.*, calificación, *f.* || FAM. Apodo, *m.* (nickname). || ARCH. Goterón, *m.* || HERALD. Lambel, *m.*
label [ˈleibl] v. tr. Poner etiqueta a, etiquetar (to attach a label). || Rotular, poner un letrero a. || Facturar (luggage). || FAM. Apodar (to nickname). || FIG. Clasificar. | Calificar. || CHEM. Marcar.
labelling (U. S. **labeling**) [—iŋ] n. Etiquetado, *m.* || FIG. Clasificación, *f.* | Calificación, *f.*, designación, *f.*
labia [ˈleibiə] pl. n. See LABIUM.
labial [ˈleibjəl] adj. Labial.
— N. GRAMM. Labial, *f.* || MUS. Caño (*m.*) de boca (of an organ).
labialization [ˌleibiəlaiˈzeiʃən] n. Labialización, *f.*
labialize [ˈleibiəlaiz] v. tr. Labializar.
labiate [ˈleibiət] adj. BOT. Labiado, da.
— N. BOT. Labiada, *f.*
labiodental [ˈleibiəuˈdentl] adj. GRAMM. Labiodental.
— N. GRAMM. Labiodental, *f.*
labiovelar [ˈleibiəuˈvi:lə] adj. GRAMM. Labiovelar.
— N. GRAMM. Labiovelar, *f.*
labium [ˈleibiəm] n. BOT. Labio, *m.* || — Pl. ANAT. Labios, *m.* (of vulva).
— OBSERV. El plural de esta palabra es *labia*.
labor [ˈleibə*] n. U. S. See LABOUR. || — *Labor union*, sindicato, *m.* (trade union). | *Labor unionist*, sindicalista, *m.* & *f.* (trade unionist).
laboratory [ləˈbɔrətəri] n. Laboratorio, *m.*
labored [ˈleibəd] adj. U. S. See LABOURED.
laborer [ˈleibərə*] n. U. S. See LABOURER.
laboring [ˈleibəriŋ] adj./n. U. S. See LABOURING.
laborious [ləˈbɔ:riəs] adj. Laborioso, sa; penoso, sa; difícil (involving hard work): *a laborious task*, una tarea penosa. || Trabajador, ra; laborioso, sa (hardworking).
laboriousness [—nis] n. Laboriosidad, *f.* (of a person). || Dificultad, *f.*: *the laboriousness of a task*, la dificultad de una tarea.
laborite [ˈleibərait] n. U. S. See LABOURITE.
laborsaving [ˈleibə*ˌseiviŋ] adj./n. U. S. See LABOURSAVING.
labour [ˈleibə*] n. Trabajo, *m.* (work): *manual labour*, trabajo manual. || Labor, *f.*, tarea, *f.* (task). || Faena, *f.* (hard task). || Esfuerzo, *m.*, esfuerzos, *m. pl.*, trabajo, *m.* (effort): *lost labour*, trabajo en vano; *after much labour*, tras grandes esfuerzos. || MED. Parto, *m.* (childbirth): *to be in labour*, estar de parto. | Dolores (*m. pl.*) del parto (pains). || Mano (*f.*) de obra, trabajadores, *m. pl.* (manpower): *labour shortage*, falta de mano de obra. || Obreros, *m. pl.*, clase (*f.*) obrera, (the workers). || Laborismo, *m.*, partido (*m.*) laborista (party). || — *Hard labour*, trabajos forzados *or* forzosos. || *International Labour Office*, Oficina (*f.*) Internacional del Trabajo. || *International Labour Organization*, Organización (*f.*) Internacional del Trabajo. || FIG. *Labour of love*, trabajo desinteresado, trabajo hecho por amor al arte (without payment), trabajo agradable (pleasant). || *Ministry of Labour*, Ministerio (*m.*) del Trabajo. || *Skilled labour*, mano de obra especializada. || *The Herculean labours*, los trabajos de Hércules.
— Adj. Laborista: *Labour Party*, Partido laborista. || Laboral: *labour dispute*, conflicto laboral; *labour relations*, relaciones laborales. || Obrero, ra: *labour movement*, movimiento obrero. || De la mano de obra: *labour cost*, coste de la mano de obra. || De trabajo: *labour camp*, campo de trabajo. || — *Labour Day*, Día (*m.*) del Trabajo. || *Labour exchange*, Bolsa (*f.*) de Trabajo. || *Labour force*, mano (*f.*) de obra. || *Labour market*, mercado (*m.*) del trabajo.
labour [ˈleibə*] v. intr. Trabajar (to work): *I was labouring under difficulties*, estuve trabajando en condiciones difíciles. || Esforzarse, hacer esfuerzos, afanarse (to dedicate o.s. diligently): *to labour for*, afanarse por. || Desplazarse penosamente, moverse con dificultad, avanzar difícilmente (to move very slowly). || Estar de parto (a woman). || MAR. Balancear y cabecear (a ship). || — *The engine is beginning to labour*, el motor empieza a funcionar con dificultad. || *To labour under*, ser víctima de. || *To labour under a delusion*, estar engañado *or* equivocado (to be wrong). || *To labour up the hill*, subir con dificultad la pendiente.
— V. tr. Insistir en, machacar en: *to labour a point*, insistir en un punto; *you needn't labour the point*, no hace falta que insistas en esto. || Pulir, trabajar (one's style). || AGR. Labrar.
laboured [—d] adj. Forzado, da; pesado, da (style). || Penoso, sa; dificultoso, sa (movement). || Dificultoso, sa; penoso, sa; fatigoso, sa (respiration).
labourer [—rə*] n. Trabajador, *m.*, obrero, *m.* (worker). || Jornalero, *m.* (day worker). || Peón, *m.* (unskilled worker): *bricklayer's labourer*, peón de albañil. || AGR. Bracero, *m.*, peón, *m.*, labriego, *m.* (farm worker).
labouring [—riŋ] n. Trabajo (*m.*) manual, labor, *f.*
— Adj. Obrero, ra (class). || Laborable (day). || Jadeante (breast). || Anhelante (soul).
labourite [ˈleibərait] n. Laborista, *m.* & *f.*
laboursaving [ˈleibəˌseiviŋ] adj. Que ahorra trabajo. || Que economiza mano de obra.
— N. Economía (*f.*) de trabajo *or* de mano de obra.
labradorite [ˈlæbrədorait] n. MIN. Labradorita, *f.*
labret [ˈleibrit] n. Adorno (*m.*) de piedra, de hueso o de concha que se colocan en el labio ciertas tribus primitivas.
labrum [ˈleibrəm] n. Labio, *m.* (lip). || ZOOL. Labro, *m.*
— OBSERV. El plural de *labrum* es *labra*.
laburnum [ləˈbə:nəm] n. BOT. Codeso, *m.*
labyrinth [ˈlæbərinθ] n. Laberinto, *m.*
labyrinthian [ˌlæbəˈrinθiən] or **labyrinthine** [ˌlæbəˈrinθain] adj. Laberíntico, ca.
lac [læk] n. Laca, *f.*
laccolite [ˈlækəlait] or **laccolith** [ˈlækəliθ] n. GEOL. Lacolito, *m.*
lace [leis] n. Encaje, *m.* (fabric). || Cinta, *f.* (ribbon). || Galón, *m.*, trencilla, *f.* (braid). || Galón, *m.* (of gold, silver). || Cordón, *m.* (of shoes, etc.). || — *Bobbin lace*, encaje de bolillos. || *Lace curtains*, visillos, *m.*
lace [leis] v. tr. Atar (shoes, corset). || Adornar con encajes (to adorn with lace). || Poner una cinta *or* un cordón a (to put a ribbon or lace on). || Ajustar el corsé a (body). || Entrelazar (to interlace). || Rayar (to streak). || FAM. Dar una paliza a (to beat). | Rociar, echar (a drink): *he likes to lace his coffee with brandy*, le gusta rociar el café con coñac, le gusta echar coñac al café.
— V. intr. Atarse con cordones *or* cintas. || FAM. *To lace into s.o.*, ponerle verde a uno.
Lacedaemon [ˌlæsiˈdi:mən] pr. n. GEOGR. Lacedemonia, *f.*
lace glass [ˈleisglɑ:s] n. Vidrio (*m.*) afiligranado.
lace maker [ˈleisˌmeikə*] n. Encajero, ra.
lace pillow [ˈleisˈpiləu] n. Cojín, *m.*, almohadilla, *f.*

lacerate [ˈlæsəreit] v. tr. Lacerar (to tear). || FIG. Herir (feelings).
lacerate [ˈlæsərit] or **lacerated** [ˈlæsəreitid] adj. Lacerado, da.
laceration [ˌlæsəˈreiʃən] n. Laceración, *f.* || MED. Desgarrón, *m.*
lacework [ˈleiswə:k] n. Encajes, *m. pl.* (lace). || Pasamanería, *f.* (trimmings).
laches [ˈleitʃiz] n. JUR. Negligencia, *f.*
lachryma christi [ˈlækriməˈkristi] n. Lácrima christi, *m.* (wine).
lachrymal [ˈlækriməl] adj. ANAT. Lagrimal, lacrimal. || Lacrimatorio (vase).
— N. Lacrimatorio, *m.* (vase).
lachrymator [ˈlækrimeitə*] n. Gas (*m.*) lacrimógeno (tear gas).
lachrymatory [ˈlækrimətəri] adj. Lacrimatorio (vase). || Lacrimógeno, na (producing tears).
— N. Vaso (*m.*) lacrimatorio.
lachrymose [ˈlækriməus] adj. Lloroso, sa; llorón, ona; lagrimoso, sa; lacrimoso, sa.
lacing [ˈleisiŋ] n. Atadura, *f.* (act). || Cordón, *m.* (shoelace). || Galón, *m.* (of gold, silver). || FAM. Paliza, *f.* (thrashing).
lack [læk] n. Falta, *f.*, carencia, *f.*, escasez, *f.* (shortage): *lack of cereals*, carencia de cereales. || Falta, *f.* (absence): *lack of judgment*, falta de juicio. || Necesidad, *f.* (necessity). || — *For lack of*, por falta de, a falta de. || *There is no lack of examples*, no faltan ejemplos, hay bastantes ejemplos. || *Through lack of*, por falta de, a falta de. || *To supply the lack*, proporcionar lo que falta.
lack [læk] v. tr. Carecer de, faltarle a uno, no tener: *to lack money*, carecer de dinero; *he lacks authority*, carece de autoridad; *he lacks experience*, le falta experiencia, no tiene experiencia. || Necesitar (to need): *what is it that I lack*, ¿qué es lo que necesito?
— V. intr. Faltar: *money is lacking for the plan*, falta dinero para el proyecto. || *To be lacking in*, faltarle a uno, carecer de: *he is lacking in courage*, carece de valor, le falta valor.
lackadaisical [ˌlækəˈdeizikəl] adj. Tardo, da; lento, ta (slow). || Apático, ca; indolente (listless). || Descuidado, da (careless). || Poco enérgico, ca; lánguido, da (weak). || Vago, ga; perezoso, sa (lazy). || Distraído, da (dreamy). || Afectado, da (affected).
lackaday [ˈlækədei] interj. ¡Ay!
lackey [ˈlæki] n. Lacayo, *m.* (servant). || FIG. Lacayo, *m.*
lacking [ˈlækiŋ] adj. *Lacking in*, sin: *lacking in meaning*, sin sentido. || *She is lacking in courage*, le falta valor, carece de valor. || *Subject on which books are lacking*, tema sobre el cual no hay libros.
lacklustre (U. S. **lackluster**) [ˈlækˌlʌstə*] adj. Sin brillo, sin vida, apagado, da (dull). || Soso, sa (colourless).
Laconia [ləˈkəunjə] pr. n. GEOGR. Laconia, *f.*
laconic [ləˈkɔnik] adj. Lacónico, ca.
laconicism [ləˈkɔnisizəm] or **laconism** [ˈlækənizəm] n. Laconismo, *m.*
lacquer [ˈlækə*] n. Laca, *f.* (hair spray, varnish, ware coated with this varnish). || Pintura (*f.*) al duco, pintura (*f.*) esmalte (hard gloss paint).
lacquer [ˈlækə*] v. tr. Pintar con laca, dar laca, laquear (to coat with varnish). || Echar laca a, poner laca en (to spray hair). || Pintar al duco.
lacquey [ˈlæki] n. Lacayo, *m.*
lacrima christi [ˈlækriməˈkristi] n. Lácrima christi, *m.* (wine).
lacrimal [ˈlækriməl] adj./n. See LACHRYMAL.
lacrimation [ˌlækriˈmeiʃən] n. Lágrimas, *f. pl.*
lacrimator [ˈlækrimeitə*] n. Gas (*m.*) lacrimógeno (tear gas).
lacrimatory [ˈlækrimətəri] adj./n. See LACHRYMATORY.
lacrimose [ˈlækriməus] adj. Lloroso, sa; llorón, ona; lagrimoso, sa; lacrimoso, sa.
lacrosse [ləˈkrɔs] n. Juego (*m.*) parecido a la vilorta.
lactary [ˈlæktəri] adj. Lácteo, a.
— N. U. S. Lechería, *f.* (dairy).
lactase [ˈlækteis] n. CHEM. Lactasa, *f.*
lactate [ˈlækteit] n. CHEM. Lactato, *m.*
lactate [ˈlækteit] v. intr. Secretar leche (to secrete milk). || Lactar (to suckle young).
lactation [lækˈteiʃən] n. Lactancia, *f.* (suckling). || Secreción (*f.*) de leche.
lacteal [ˈlæktiəl] adj. Lácteo, a: *lacteal fever*, fiebre láctea. || ANAT. Lácteo, a; quilífero, ra.
— N. ANAT. Vaso (*m.*) lácteo *or* quilífero.
lacteous [ˈlæktiəs] adj. Lácteo, a; lechoso, sa.
lactescent [lækˈtesənt] adj. Lactescente.
lactic [ˈlæktik] adj. Láctico, ca: *lactic acid*, ácido láctico.
lactiferous [lækˈtifərəs] adj. Lactífero, ra.
lactone [ˈlæktəun] n. CHEM. Lactona, *f.*
lactose [ˈlæktəus] n. CHEM. Lactosa, *f.*
lacuna [ləˈkju:nə] n. Laguna, *f.* (break in continuity). || BIOL. Laguna, *f.*

— OBSERV. El plural de *lacuna* es *lacunae* o *lacunas*.

lacunar [ləˈkju:nə*] n. ARCH. Artesón, *m.*, lagunar, *m.*
lacustrine [ləˈkʌstrain] adj. Lacustre.
lacy [ˈleisi] adj. De encaje. || Parecido al encaje. || FIG. Fino, na.
lad [læd] n. Chaval, *m.*, chico, *m.*, muchacho, *m.* (boy). || Mozo (*m.*) de cuadra (stableboy). || — *He's a bit of a lad!*, ¡qué tío! || *The lads*, los amigos.
ladder [ˈlædə*] n. Escalera (*f.*) de mano, escala, *f.* (for climbing). || Escala, *f.* (of rope). || FIG. Escalón, *m.*, peldaño, *m.*: *on the ladder to success*, en los peldaños del éxito. | Escala, *f.*, jerarquía, *f.*: *the social ladder*, la escala social. | Escala, *f.* (of salaries). | Carrera, *f.*, carrerilla, *f.* (in a stocking): *to make a ladder in*, hacerse una carrerilla en. || — MAR. *Accomodation ladder*, escala real. || FIG. *At the top of the ladder*, en la cumbre. || *Rope ladder*, escala de cuerda.
ladder [ˈlædə*] v. tr. Hacerse una carrera *or* una carrerilla en [una media].
— V. intr. Correrse.
ladder-back [—bæk] adj. Con respaldo de barrotes horizontales (chair back).
ladderless [—lis] adj. Indesmallable.
ladder mender [—ˌmendə*] n. Zurcidora, *f.* (person). || Máquina (*f.*) para coger puntos en las medias (tool).
ladderproof [—pru:f] adj. Indesmallable.
ladder stitch [—stitʃ] n. Calado, *m.* (in embroidery).
ladder truck [—trʌk] n. U. S. Coche (*m.*) de bomberos con escalera.
laddie [ˈlædi] n. See LAD.
lade* [leid] v. tr. MAR. Cargar (to load). | Embarcar (to take on board).

— OBSERV. Pret. ***laded;*** p. p. ***laden.***

laden [leidn] p. p. See LADE.
— Adj. Cargado, da (*with*, de) [loaded]. || FIG. Agobiado, da.
la-di-da [ˈlɑ:diˈdɑ:] adj. FAM. Afectado, da; presuntuoso, sa; presumido, da.
ladies [ˈleidiz] pl. n. See LADY.
Ladin [ləˈdi:n] n. Ladino, *m.* (language).
lading [ˈleidiŋ] n. MAR. Cargamento, *m.*, flete, *m.* || MAR. *Bill of lading*, conocimiento (*m.*) de embarque.
Ladino [ləˈdi:nəu] n. Ladino, *m.* [lenguaje judeo-español].
ladle [ˈleidl] n. Cucharón, *m.* (for serving). || Cazo, *m.* (for kitchen). || TECH. Caldero (*m.*) de colada.
ladle [ˈleidl] v. tr. Servir [con cucharón] (to serve). || FIG. Repartir: *he ladled out compliments to everybody*, repartió cumplidos a todos. || TECH. Colar.
ladleful [ˈleidlful] n. Cucharón, *m.*
lady [ˈleidi] n. Señora, *f.*: *act like a lady*, pórtese como una señora. || — Pl. Servicios (*m.*) de señoras, aseos (*m.*) de señoras (toilet): *where is the ladies?*, ¿dónde están los servicios de señoras? || Señoras, *f.* (sign on door). || — *A perfect lady*, toda una señora. || *First Lady*, primera dama. || *His good lady*, su mujer, su señora. || *His young lady*, su novia. || *How is your good lady?*, ¿cómo está su señora? || *Ladies and Gentlemen*, señoras y señores, señoras y caballeros. || *Lady of loose living*, mujer (*f.*) de la vida, mujer (*f.*) de vida airada. || *Lady of the house*, señora de la casa. || REL. *Our Lady*, Nuestra Señora. || FIG. *Painted lady*, fulana, *f.* || *Young lady*, señorita, *f.*
— Adj. *Ladies' hairdresser's*, peluquería (*f.*) de señoras. || *Ladies' man* o *lady's man*, hombre mujeriego. || *Lady chapel*, capilla (*f.*) de la Virgen. || *Lady Day*, Anunciación, *f.* || *Lady doctor*, médica, *f.*, doctora, *f.* || *Lady dog*, perra, *f.* || *Lady help*, asistenta, *f.* || *Lady lawyer*, abogada, *f.* || *Lady mayoress*, alcaldesa, *f.*

— OBSERV. *Lady* se emplea también como título nobiliario (duquesas, condesas, etc.).

ladybird [ˈleidibə:d] (U. S. **ladybug**) [ˈleidibʌg] n. ZOOL. Mariquita, *f.*
ladyfinger [ˈleidiˌfiŋgə*] n. CULIN. Lengua (*f.*) de gato (biscuit).
lady-in-waiting [ˈleidiinˈweitiŋ] n. Dama (*f.*) de honor, azafata, *f.*

— OBSERV. El plural es *ladies-in-waiting*.

lady-killer [ˈleidiˌkilə*] n. FAM. Castigador, *m.*, ladrón (*m.*) de corazones, tenorio, *m.*
ladylike [ˈleidilaik] adj. Elegante, fino, na; distinguido, da. || FAM. Afeminado, da (effeminate).
ladylove [ˈleidilʌv] n. Amada, *f.* (sweetheart).
lady's companion [ˈleidizkəmˈpænjən] n. Señora (*f.*) de compañía.
Ladyship [ˈleidiʃip] n. *Your Ladyship*, su señoría.
lady's maid [ˈleidizmeid] n. Doncella, *f.*
lag [læg] n. Revestimiento (*m.*) calorífugo *or* termoaislante (lagging). || Intervalo, *m.* (length of time between two events). || Retraso, *m.* (delay). || ELECTR. Retardo, *m.* || Listón, *m.* (strip, lath). || FAM. Presidiario, *m.* (convict). | Condena, *f.* (sentence).
lag [læg] v. tr. Poner un revestimiento termoaislante *or* calorífugo a (to cover with lagging). || Revestir, cubrir (to cover). || FAM. Encarcelar (to jail).
— V. intr. Retrasarse (to be behind time). || Rezagarse, quedarse atrás (walking). || *To lag behind*, estar retrasado, estar rezagado, tener retraso.
lagan [ˈlægən] n. MAR. Mercancías (*f. pl.*) arrojadas al mar y marcadas con una boya para poder ser recogidas.
lager [ˈlɑ:gə*] n. Cerveza (*f.*) dorada.
laggard [ˈlægəd] adj. Rezagado, da (who lags behind). || Tardo, da; lento, ta (sluggish). || Remolón, ona; vago, ga (lazy).

— N. Vago, ga; remolón, ona (lazy). || Rezagado, da; retrasado, da (loiterer).
lagger [ˈlægə*] n. Vago, ga; remolón, ona (lazy). || Rezagado, da; retrasado, da (loiterer).
lagging [ˈlægiŋ] n. Revestimiento (*m.*) calorífugo *or* termoaislante (covering to reduce heat loss). || Revestimiento, *m.*, forro, *m.* (covering). || Retraso, *m.* (time lag).
— Adj. Retrasado, da; rezagado, da.
lagoon [ləˈgu:n] n. Laguna, *f.*
laic [ˈleiik] adj./n. Laico, ca; seglar.
laical [—əl] adj. Laico, ca.
laicism [ˈleiisizəm] n. Laicismo, *m.*
laicization [ˌleiisaiˈzeiʃən] n. Laicización, *f.* [*Amer.*, laicalización, *f.*].
laicize [ˈleiisaiz] v. tr. Laicizar, dar carácter laico a [*Amer.*, laicalizar].
laid [leid] pret. & p. p. See LAY.
laid paper [—ˈpeipə*] n. Papel (*m.*) vergé.
lain [lein] p. p. See LIE (meaning "echarse").
lair [lɛə*] n. Guarida, *f.* (of wild animals). || FIG. Guarida, *f.*
lair [lɛə*] v. intr. Recogerse en su guarida.
laird [lɛəd] n. Terrateniente, *m.* (Scottish landlord).
laisser-faire or **laissez-faire** [ˈleiseiˈfɛə*] n. Liberalismo, *m.*
laity [ˈleiiti] n. Laicado, *m.*, seglares, *m. pl.* || FIG. Profanos, *m. pl.*, legos, *m. pl.*
lake [leik] n. GEOGR. Lago, *m.* || Laca, *f.* (dye). || *Ornamental lake*, estanque, *m.*
— Adj. Lacustre, de lago: *lake plant*, planta lacustre. || *The Lake District*, la Región de los Lagos (in England).
lake dweller [—ˌdwelə*] n. Habitante (*m.* & *f.*) de una vivienda lacustre.
lake dwelling [—ˌdweliŋ] n. Vivienda (*f.*) lacustre.
Lake poet [—ˌpəuit] n. Lakista, *m.* & *f.*
Lake school [—sku:l] n. Lakismo, *m.*
lallation [læˈleiʃən] n. Lambdacismo, *m.*
lam [læm] n. U. S. FAM. Huida, *f.* || U. S. FAM. *To take it on the lam*, tomar las de Villadiego, largarse.
lam [læm] v. tr. FAM. Dar una paliza.
— V. intr. U. S. FAM. Huir.
lama [ˈlɑ:mə] n. Lama, *m.* (priest).
Lamaism [ˈlɑ:məizəm] n. REL. Lamaísmo, *m.*
Lamaist [ˈlɑ:məist] adj./n. REL. Lamaísta.
Lamaistic [lɑ:məˈistik] adj. REL. Lamaísta.
lamasery [ˈlɑ:məsəri] n. REL. Lamasería, *f.*
lamb [læm] n. Cordero, *m.* (animal and meat). || Piel (*f.*) de cordero, cordero, *m.* (lambskin). || FIG. Cordero, *m.* (mild person). | Cielo, *m.* (good lovable person). || — *Lamb chop*, chuleta (*f.*) de cordero. || *The Lamb of God*, el Cordero de Dios.
lamb [læm] v. tr./intr. Parir [la oveja].
lambast or **lambaste** [læmˈbeist] v. tr. Dar una paliza (to thrash). || Poner como un trapo (to scold).
lambda [ˈlæmdə] n. Lambda, *f.* (Greek letter).
lambdacism [ˈlæmdəsizəm] n. Lambdacismo, *m.*
lambency [ˈlæmbənsi] n. Palidez, *f.* (paleness). || Vacilación, *f.* (movement).
lambent [ˈlæmbənt] n. Macilento, ta; pálido, da (softly glowing). || Vacilante (dancing, flickering). || FIG. Brillante (humour, eyes, etc.).
lambkin [ˈlæmkin] n. Corderito, *m.*, corderillo, *m.* || FAM. Cielo, *m.*
lamblike [ˈlæmlaik] adj. Manso como un cordero.
lambskin [ˈlæmskin] n. Piel (*f.*) de cordero, cordero, *m.* (skin, fur).
lamb's wool [ˈlæmzwul] n. Lana (*f.*) de cordero.
lame [leim] adj. Cojo, ja (unable to walk, run, etc.): *a lame woman*, una mujer coja; *he was lame*, era cojo; *I am lame today*, estoy cojo hoy. || Lisiado, da (injured in the foot or leg). || FIG. Poco convincente, débil, malo, la: *a lame excuse*, una excusa mala. | Flojo, ja (an argument). | Cojo, ja: *a lame verse*, un verso cojo. || — U. S. *A lame back*, dolor (*m.*) de espalda. || *Lame person*, cojo, ja. || *To go lame*, empezar a cojear. || *To walk lame*, cojear. || *You are lame in one foot*, cojeas de un pie.
— N. Hoja, *f.* (of metal).
lame [leim] v. tr. Dejar cojo (to cause to limp). || Lisiar (to injure). || Incapacitar (to render unfit).
lamé [ˈlɑ:mei] n. Lamé, *m.*
lame duck [ˈleimˈdʌk] n. Incapaz, *m.* & *f.* (ineffectual person). || Cosa (*f.*) inútil (useless thing). || Persona (*f.*) incapacitada (physically handicapped person). || Especulador (*m.*) insolvente (insolvent speculator). || U. S. FAM. Cesante, *m.*, funcionario (*m.*) cesante (official). | Diputado (*m.*) no reelegido (congressman).
lamella [ləˈmelə] n. ANAT. Laminilla, *f.*, lámina, *f.* || BOT. Laminilla, *f.*
— OBSERV. El plural es *lamellae* o *lamellas*.
lamellar [ləˈmelə*] adj. Laminar, laminoso, sa.
lamellate or **lamellated** [ˈlæməleit] adj. Laminoso, sa.
lamellibranch [ləˈmeliˌbræŋk] n. ZOOL. Lamelibranquio, *m.*
— OBSERV. El plural de esta palabra es *lamellibranchia*.
lamellicorn [ləˈmeliˌkɔ:n] adj. ZOOL. Lamelicornio.
— N. ZOOL. Lamelicornio, *m.*
— OBSERV. El plural de esta palabra es *lamellicornia*.
lamellirostres [ləˌmeliˈrɔstriz] pl. n. Lamelirrostros, *m.* (birds).
lamely [ˈleimli] adj. Cojeando, renqueando (to walk). || FIG. Con poca convicción (when arguing).
lameness [ˈleimnis] n. Cojera, *f.* || FIG. Debilidad, *f.*, flojedad, *f.* (weakness). | Falta (*f.*) de convicción (in arguing).
lament [ləˈment] n. Lamento, *m.* (of grief). || Queja, *f.* (complaint). || MUS. Endecha, *f.*
lament [ləˈment] v. intr. *To lament for* o *over*, lamentarse por *or* de (to feel great sorrow), llorar (to show great sorrow): *to lament for a friend*, llorar a un amigo.
— V. tr. Lamentar, llorar (to mourn): *he laments the death of his friend*, llora la muerte de su amigo. || Sentir, lamentar, lamentarse de (to regret deeply): *to lament having done sth.*, sentir haber hecho algo. || *It is much to be lamented that*, es de lamentar que.
lamentable [ˈlæməntəbl] adj. Lamentable (pitiable): *he is in a lamentable state*, está en un estado lamentable. || Lastimero, ra (mournful).
lamentation [ˌlæmenˈteiʃən] n. Lamentación, *f.* (lamenting). || Lamento, *m.* (lament).
lamented [ləˈmentid] adj. Llorado, da (dead person).
lamenting [ləˈmentiŋ] n. Lamentación, *f.*
lamina [ˈlæminə] n. Hoja, *f.* (of metal). || BOT. Lámina, *f.* || ANAT. Laminilla, *f.*, lámina, *f.*
— OBSERV. El plural de la palabra inglesa *lamina* es *laminae* o *laminas*.
laminable [ˈlæminəbl] adj. Laminable.
laminal [ˈlæminəl] or **laminar** [ˈlæminə*] adj. Laminar: *laminar structure*, estructura laminar.
laminate [ˈlæminət] adj. Laminado, da.
— N. Laminado, *m.*
laminate [ˈlæmineit] v. tr. Laminar (to roll). || Dividir en láminas (to split into thin plates). || Contrachapar, contrachapear (to unite superimposed layers).
— V. intr. Dividirse en láminas, estratificarse.
laminated [—id] adj. Laminado, da. || Hojoso, sa (sheet). || Contrachapado, da (wood).
lamination [ˌlæmiˈneiʃən] n. Laminación, *f.*, laminado, *m.*
laminose [ˈlæminəus] or **laminous** [ˈlæminəs] adj. Laminoso, sa.
Lammas [ˈlæməs] n. *Lammas Day*, primero (*m.*) de agosto.
lammergeyer (U. S. **lammergeier**) [ˈlæməgaiə*] n. ZOOL. Quebrantahuesos, *m. inv.*
lamp [læmp] n. Lámpara, *f.*: *electric, gas, oil lamp*, lámpara eléctrica, de gas, de aceite; *lamp bracket*, brazo de lámpara. || Farol, *m.*, farola, *f.* (in the street). || Faro, *m.* (of cars, etc.): *rear lamp*, faro trasero. || MAR. Luz (*f.*) de navegación. || Linterna, *f.* (pocket torch). || ELECTR. Bombilla, *f.* (bulb). || — Pl. FAM. Luceros, *m.*, sacáis, *m.*, pajarillas, *f.* (eyes). || — *Arc lamp*, lámpara de arco. || *Bracket* o *wall lamp*, aplique, *m.* || *Hanging lamp*, lámpara suspendida. || *Incandescent lamp*, lámpara de incandescencia *or* incandescente. || *Infrared lamp*, lámpara de rayos infrarrojos. || *Mercury vapour lamp*, lámpara de vapor de mercurio. || *Miner's* o *safety lamp*, lámpara de minero *o* de seguridad. || *Pocket lamp*, linterna, *f.* || *Reading lamp*, lámpara para la mesilla de noche. || *Spirit lamp*, lámpara de alcohol. || *Sun-ray lamp*, lámpara solar. || *Ultraviolet lamp*, lámpara de rayos ultravioletas.
lamp [læmp] v. tr. Poner lámparas. || Iluminar. || U. S. FAM. Echar el ojo a.
lampblack [—blæk] n. Negro (*m.*) de humo.
lamp chimney [—ˌtʃimni] n. Tubo (*m.*) de cristal de lámpara.
lamp dealer [—ˌdi:lə*] n. Lamparero, *m.*
lamp holder [—ˌhəuldə*] n. Casquillo, *m.*, portalámparas, *m. inv.*
lampion [ˈlæmpiən] n. Farolillo, *m.*
lamplight [ˈlæmplait] n. Luz (*f.*) de la lámpara: *by lamplight*, a la luz de la lámpara. || Luz (*f.*) de un farol (in the street).
lamplighter [—ə*] n. Farolero, *m.*
lamp maker [ˈlæmpˌmeikə*] n. Lamparero, *m.*
lamp oil [ˈlæmpɔil] n. Aceite (*m.*) lampante. || Petróleo (*m.*) lampante.
lampoon [læmˈpu:n] n. Pasquín, *m.*, libelo, *m.* (piece of satirical writing).
lampoon [læmˈpu:n] v. tr. Escribir pasquines contra, satirizar.
lamppost [ˈlæmppəust] n. Poste (*m.*) de alumbrado (post). || Farol, *m.*, farola, *f.* (streetlight).
lamprey [ˈlæmpri] n. ZOOL. Lamprea, *f.* (fish).
lampshade [ˈlæmpʃeid] n. Pantalla, *f.*
lanate [ˈleineit] adj. BOT. Velloso, sa; lanado, da.
Lancashire [ˈlæŋkəʃiə*] pr. n. GEOGR. Lancaster (county).
Lancaster [ˈlæŋkəstə*] pr. n. Lancaster.
lance [lɑ:ns] n. Lanza, *f.* (weapon). || Lancero, *m.* (soldier). || Arpón, *m.* (for fishing). || MED. Lanceta, *f.* || Lanza, *f.* (of a hosepipe). || U. S. ZOOL. Amodita, *f.* (launce). || *Lance head*, moharra, *f.*, punta (*f.*) de la lanza.
lance [lɑ:ns] v. tr. Lancear (to pierce with a lance). || MED. Abrir [con una lanceta].
lance corporal [—ˈkɔ:pərəl] n. MIL. Cabo (*m.*) interino.
lancelet [ˈlɑ:nslət] n. Anfioxo, *m.* (marine animal).
Lancelot [ˈlɑ:nslət] pr. n. Lancelote, *m.*, Lanzarote, *m.*
lanceolar [ˈlɑ:nsiələ*] or **lanceolate** [ˈlɑ:nsiələt] adj. ARCH. BOT. Lanceolado, da.

lancer [ˈlɑ:nsə*] n. MIL. Lancero, *m.* || — Pl. Lanceros, *m.* (dance).
lance sergeant [ˈlɑn:sˈsɑ:dʒənt] n. MIL. Sargento (*m.*) interino.
lancet [ˈlɑ:nsit] n. MED. Lanceta, *f.* || ARCH. Ojiva, *f.* || — *Lancet arch*, arco apuntado. || *Lancet window*, ventana (*f.*) ojival.
lanciform [ˈlɑ:nsifɔ:m] adj. Lanciforme.
lancinate [ˈlɑ:nsineit] v. intr. Lancinar, dar punzadas.
lancinating [—iŋ] adj. Punzante, lancinante.
lancination [ˌlɑ:nsiˈneiʃən] n. Punzada, *f.*
land [lænd] n. Tierra, *f.*: *to travel over land and sea*, viajar por tierra y por mar; *to sight land*, divisar tierra. || País, *m.*, tierra, *f* (country, state). || País, *m.*, pueblo, *m.* (people). || Tierra, *f.*: *the land here is good for farming*, la tierra aquí es buena para el cultivo. || Suelo, *m.*, tierra, *f.* (soil): *poor land*, suelo pobre. || Campo, *m.*: *I want to get back to the land*, deseo volver al campo. || Tierras, *f. pl.*, finca, *f.* [*Amer.*, estancia, *f.*, hacienda, *f.*] (of an owner): *he has 1 000 hectares of land*, tiene 1 000 hectáreas de tierras, tiene una finca de 1 000 hectáreas. || JUR. Bienes (*m. pl.*) raíces. || Zona, *f.* (area): *forest land*, zona forestal. || TECH. Parte (*f.*) plana entre las estrías (of a rifle, etc.). || — AGR. *Arable land*, tierra de cultivo. || *By land*, por tierra. || *Drift from the land*, éxodo (*m.*) rural, abandono (*m.*) del campo. || *Dry land*, tierra firme (opposed to sea), tierra de secano (in agriculture). || *Flight from land*, éxodo (*m.*) rural, despoblación (*f.*) del campo. || *Irrigated land*, tierra de regadío. || *Land ho!*, ¡tierra! || FIG. *Land of milk and honey*, tierra de Jauja, paraíso (*m.*) terrenal. | *Land of nod*, sueño, *m.* | *Land of plenty*, tierra de abundancia. || *Native land*, tierra *or* país natal, patria, *f.* || MIL. *No man's land*, tierra de nadie. || *On land*, en tierra. || *Piece of land*, terreno, *m.* || *Promised land* o *land of promise*, tierra de promisión. || *To make land*, llegar a tierra (ship), aterrizar, tomar tierra (aircraft). || *To see how the land lies*, tantear el terreno (before taking action). || *Tract of land*, terreno, *m.*
— Adj. Terrestre: *land defenses*, defensas terrestres. || De tierra: *land breeze*, viento de tierra. || Agrario, ria: *land reform*, reforma agraria.
land [lænd] v. tr. Hacer aterrizar (a plane). || Desembarcar (to disembark). || Descargar (goods). || Dejar (to drop). || Sacar (to bring a fish to shore). || Hacer llegar: *to land a golf ball next to the hole*, hacer llegar una pelota de golf junto al hoyo. || FIG. Asestar, dar (a blow). | Conseguir, lograr (a good job, contract, prize, etc.). | Meter: *to land somebody in trouble*, meter a alguien en un lío. | Llevar: *his crime landed him in prison*, su crimen le llevó a la cárcel. || FAM. *To get landed with*, tener que cargar con.
— V. intr. Aterrizar (a plane on land). || Amerizar, amarar (on the sea). || Alunizar (on the moon). || Posarse (birds, etc.). || Desembarcar (to disembark). || Llegar (to arrive). || MAR. Atracar, arribar (to reach port). || Caer: *I jumped off the wall and landed badly*, salté del muro y caí mal. || Dar (to hit): *the dart landed on the target*, la flecha dio en el blanco. || — FIG. *To land on*, caer encima: *he landed on me unexpectedly*, me cayó encima sin avisar. || *To land on one's feet*, caer de pie (from a fall), salir adelante (to emerge safely from a situation). || *To land on one's head*, caer de cabeza. || *To land up somewhere*, ir a parar a cierto sitio.
land agent [—ˌeidʒənt] n. Administrador, *m.* (manager of an estate). || Corredor (*m.*) de fincas (seller).
landau [—ɔ:] n. Landó, *m.* (carriage). || Coche (*m.*) descapotable (car).
landaulet [—ɔ:ˈlet] n. Landó (*m.*) pequeño (carriage). || Coche (*m.*) descapotable (car).
land bank [—bæŋk] n. Banco (*m.*) hipotecario.
land crab [—kræb] n. ZOOL. Cangrejo (*m.*) de tierra.
landed [—id] adj. Hacendado, da; terrateniente, que tiene tierras (owning land). || Que consiste en tierras (consisting of land). || — *Landed gentry*, terratenientes, *m. pl.* || *Landed property*, bienes (*m. pl.*) raíces. || *Loan on landed property*, crédito hipotecario.
landfall [—fɔ:l] n. MAR. Recalada, *f.* (sighting of land). | Arribada, *f.* (arrival at land). || AVIAT. Vista (*f.*) de tierra. | Aterrizaje, *m.* (landing).
land forces [—fɔ:siz] pl. n. MIL. Fuerzas (*f.*) terrestres, ejército (*m. sing.*) de tierra.
land grant [—grɑ:nt] n. Concesión (*f.*) de terrenos *or* de tierras.
landgrave [—greiv] n. Landgrave, *m.*
landgraviate [—ˈgreiviət] n. Landgraviato, *m.*
landholder [—ˌhəuldə*] n. Terrateniente, *m.* & *f.*
landholding [—ˌhəuldiŋ] n. Tenencia (*f.*) de tierras, posesión (*f.*) de tierras.
landing [ˈlændiŋ] n. Desembarco, *m.* (of passengers, troops). || Desembarque, *m.* (of cargo). || AVIAT. Aterrizaje, *m.* (of a plane on land): *emergency* o *forced landing*, aterrizaje forzoso. | Amerizaje, *m.*, amaraje, *m.* (of a plane on the sea). || Alunizaje, *m.* (on moon). || Desembarcadero, *m.* (jetty). || Descansillo, *m.*, rellano, *m.* (of a staircase).
landing barge [—bɑ:dʒ] n. MIL. Lancha (*f.*) de desembarco.
landing carriage [—ˈkæridʒ] n. Tren (*m.*) de aterrizaje.
landing craft [—krɑ:ft] n. MIL. Lancha (*f.*) de desembarco.
landing deck [—dek] n. Cubierta (*f.*) de aterrizaje (of an aircraft carrier).
landing field [—fi:ld] n. AVIAT. Campo (*m.*) de aterrizaje.
landing force [—fɔ:s] n. Cuerpo (*m.*) expedicionario.
landing gear [—giə*] n. AVIAT. Tren (*m.*) de aterrizaje.
landing ground [—graund] n. AVIAT. Campo (*m.*) de aterrizaje.
landing net [—net] n. Salabardo, *m.*, manguilla, *f.*, sacadera, *f.*
landing party [—ˌpɑ:ti] n. MIL. Destacamento (*m.*) de desembarco.
landing stage [—steidʒ] n. MAR. Desembarcadero, *m.*
landing strip [—strip] n. AVIAT. Pista (*f.*) de aterrizaje.
landlady [ˈlændˌleidi] n. Patrona, *f.*, dueña, *f.* (of boardinghouse). || Propietaria, *f.* (of land). || Propietaria, *f.*, casera, *f.* (of a rented house).
landless [ˈlændlis] adj. Sin tierras.
landlocked [ˈlændlɔkt] adj. Cercado *or* rodeado de tierra: *a landlocked bay*, una bahía rodeada de tierra. || Que no tiene acceso al mar: *a landlocked country*, un país que no tiene acceso al mar.
landlord [ˈlændlɔ:d] n. Patrón, *m.*, dueño, *m.* (of a pub, a boardinghouse). || Propietario, *m.* (of land). || Propietario, *m.*, casero, *m.* (of a rented house).
landlordism [—izəm] n. Sistema (*m.*) de arrendamiento de tierras.
landlubber [ˈlændˌlʌbə*] n. FAM. Marinero (*m.*) de agua dulce.
landmark [ˈlændmɑ:k] n. Señal, *f.* (mark). || Mojón, *m.* (for marking a route or boundary). || MAR. Marca, *f.*, señal, *f.* || FIG. Hito, *m.*, acontecimiento (*m.*) decisivo.
land mine [ˈlændmain] n. MIL. Mina (*f.*) terrestre.
land office [ˈlændˌɔfis] n. Oficina (*f.*) del catastro.
land-office business [—ˈbiznis] n. U. S. FIG. Negocio (*m.*) magnífico.
landowner [ˈlændˌəunə*] n. Terrateniente, *m.* & *f.*, propietario, ria.
landownership [—ʃip] n. Posesión (*f.*) de tierras, tenencia (*f.*) de tierras.
land-poor [ˈlændpuə*] adj. Que no puede explotar sus tierras por falta de recursos.
land power [ˈlændˌpauə*] n. Potencia (*f.*) militar terrestre.
land reclamation [ˈlændˌrekləˈmeiʃən] n. Tierra (*f.*) ganada al mar (creation of land). || Puesta (*f.*) en cultivo de las tierras, aprovechamiento (*m.*) de las tierras (improvement of land).
land register [ˈlændˌredʒistə*] n. Registro (*m.*) de la propiedad.
landscape [ˈlændskeip] n. Paisaje, *m.* || — *Landscape architect*, arquitecto (*m.*) paisajista. || *Landscape architecture*, profesión (*f.*) de arquitecto paisajista. || *Lanscape gardener*, jardinero (*m.*) paisajista. || *Landscape gardening*, profesión (*f.*) de jardinero paisajista. || *Landscape painter*, paisajista, *m.* & *f.*
landscape [ˈlændskeip] v.tr. Ajardinar.
landscapist [—ist] n. Paisajista, *m.* & *f.* (painter).
land settlement [ˈlændˈsetlmənt] n. Colonización, *f.*
landslide [ˈlændslaid] n. Corrimiento (*m.*) *or* desprendimiento (*m.*) de tierras. || FIG. Triunfo (*m.*) electoral aplastante.
landslip [ˈlændslip] n. Corrimiento (*m.*) *or* desprendimiento (*m.*) de tierras.
landsman [ˈlændzmən] n. Hombre (*m.*) que vive en la tierra. || FIG. Marinero (*m.*) inexperto, marinero (*m.*) de agua dulce.
— OBSERV. El plural de esta palabra es *landsmen*.
land survey [ˈlændˈsə:vei] or **land surveying** [—iŋ] n. Agrimensura, *f.*, topografía, *f.*
land surveyor [ˈlændsəˈveiə*] n. Agrimensor, *m.*
land tax [ˈlændtæks] n. Impuesto (*m.*) territorial.
land tenure [ˈlændˈtenjuə*] n. Régimen (*m.*) de la propiedad agrícola.
land use [ˈlændju:s] or **land utilization** [ˈlændˌju:tilaiˈzeiʃən] n. Explotación (*f.*) del suelo.
landward [ˈlændwəd] adj. Más cerca de la tierra.
— Adv. Hacia la tierra.
landwards [ˈlændwədz] adv. Hacia la tierra.
lane [lein] n. Camino, *m.* (in the country). || Callejuela, *f.*, callejón, *m.* (in the town). || Carril, *m.*, vía, *f.*, banda, *f.* (of a motorway). || Calle, *f.* (rows of people): *to form a lane*, hacer calle. || MAR. AVIAT. Ruta, *f.* || SP. Calle, *f.* (in athletics, swimming). | Pista, *f.* (in bowling).
lang syne or **langsyne** [læŋˈsain] adv. Antaño. || *Auld lang syne*, tiempos (*m. pl.*) de antaño, tiempos remotos.
language [ˈlæŋgwidʒ] n. Lenguaje, *m.* (faculty, mode, style of speech): *language is man's method of communication*, el lenguaje es el medio de comunicación del hombre; *don't use that language with me*, no uses ese lenguaje conmigo; *scientific language*, lenguaje científico. || Lengua, *f.*, idioma, *m.* (of a country): *he speaks three languages*, habla tres idiomas. || — *Agglutinative language*, lengua aglutinante. || *Bad language*, palabrotas, *f. pl.* || *Dead language*, lengua muerta. || *He uses bad language* o *his language is very bad*, es muy mal hablado. || *Living language*, lengua viva. || *Modern languages*, lenguas modernas. || *Native language*, lengua materna *or* nativa. || *Strong language*, palabras mayores *or* fuertes.

— Adj. De idiomas: *language school, teacher*, escuela, profesor de idiomas.
langue d'oc [lãgdɔk] n. Lengua (*f.*) de oc.
langue d'oil [lãgdɔil] n. Lengua (*f.*) de oíl.
languid [ˈlæŋgwid] adj. Lánguido, da.
languidness [—nis] n. Languidez, *f.*
languish [ˈlæŋgwiʃ] v. intr. Languidecer (to become languid). || FIG. Consumirse (in prison). | Decaer (interest). | Languidecer (conversation). | Echar una mirada lánguida [para ganarse la simpatía]. || *To languish for*, consumirse por (to pine for).
languishing [—iŋ] adj. Que va decayendo (interest). || Lánguido, da (look, eyes). || Que se consume (lover).
languishment [—mənt] n. Languidez, *f.* || MED. Postración, *f.* || FIG. Mirada (*f.*) lánguida.
languor [ˈlæŋgə*] n. Languidez, *f.*
languorous [—rəs] adj. Lánguido, da.
laniary [ˈlænjəri] adj. Canino (tooth).
— N. Canino, *m.*, diente (*m.*) canino.
laniferous [ləˈnifərəs] or **lanigerous** [ləˈnidʒərəs] adj. ZOOL. Lanífero, ra.
lank [læŋk] adj. Larguirucho, cha: desgarbado, da; desmadejado, da (tall and thin). || Flaco, ca; seco, ca (thin). || Lacio, cia (hair). || Hundido, da (cheeks).
lankiness [—inis] n. Flacura, *f.* (thinness). || Desmadejamiento, *m.* (gawkiness).
lanky [—i] adj. Larguirucho, cha (tall and thin). Desgarbado, da; desmadejado, da (gawky).
lanolin [ˈlænəuli:n] or **lanoline** [ˈlænəuli:n] n. Lanolina, *f.*
lansquenet [ˈlɑ:nskənet] n. HIST. Lansquenete, *m.*
lantern [ˈlæntən] n. Farol, *m.*, linterna, *f.* (portable light). || ARCH. Linterna, *f.* || MAR. Linterna, *f.* (of lighthouse). | Fanal, *m.*, farol, *m.* (in a ship). || Linterna (*f.*) mágica (magic lantern). || — *Chinese lantern*, farolillo, *m.* || *Lantern lecture*, conferencia (*f.*) con proyecciones.
lantern fly [—flai] n. Cocuyo, *m.* (insect).
lantern-jawed [—ˈdʒɔ:d] adj. FAM. Chupado de cara.
lantern pinion [—ˈpinjən] n. Linterna, *f.*
lantern slide [—slaid] n. Diapositiva, *f.*
lantern wheel [—wi:l] n. Linterna, *f.*
lanthanum [ˈlænθənəm] n. CHEM. Lantano, *m.*
lanuginous [ləˈnju:dʒinəs] adj. Lanuginoso, sa.
lanyard [ˈlænjəd] n. MAR. Acollador, *m.*
Laodicea [ˌleiəudiˈsiə] pr. n. GEOGR. Laodicea, *f.*
Laos [lauz] pr. n. GEOGR. Laos, *m.*
Laotian [ˈlauʃiən] adj./n. Laosiano, na.
lap [læp] n. Rodillas, *f. pl.*, regazo, *m.*: *she was sitting with the child on her lap*, estaba sentada con el niño en sus rodillas. || Faldón, *m.* (of a coat). || Regazo, *m.* (of an apron, etc.). || GEOGR. Depresión, *f.* (of a valley). || ARCH. Revestimiento, *m.* || ELECTR. Aislante, *m.* || Chapoteo, *m.*: *the lap of the water on the shore*, el chapoteo del agua contra la orilla. || Lametón, *m.*, lengüetada, *f.* (of a dog drinking). || TECH. Rueda (*f.*) de pulir, bruñidor, *m.* (polishing disk). || SP. Vuelta, *f.*: *lap of honour*, vuelta de honor; *four laps of the track*, cuatro vueltas a la pista. || ANAT. Lóbulo, *m.* (of ear). || Vuelta, *f.* (part which overlaps). || Imbricación, *f.* (of tiles). || FIG. Etapa, *f.* (stage): *the last lap of a journey*, la etapa final de un viaje. | Seno, *m.* (bosom). || — FIG. *It dropped into my lap*, me llegó a las manos. | *It is in the lap of the gods*, está en manos de Dios. | *To live in the lap of luxury*, vivir *or* nadar en la abundancia.
lap [læp] v. intr. Chapotear (water). || Dar lengüetadas (a dog). || Imbricarse, traslaparse (to overlap). || SP. Dar una vuelta. || *To lap over*, sobresalir (to project), imbricarse, traslaparse (to overlap).
— V. tr. Beber a lengüetadas (animals): *the cat was lapping its milk*, el gato bebía su leche a lengüetadas. || Chocar suavemente contra, lamer: *the waves lapped the side of the boat*, las olas chocaban suavemente contra el borde del barco. || Doblar (to fold). || Traslapar, solapar, imbricar (tiles, etc.). || Empalmar a media madera (to join by overlapping). || TECH. Pulir (to polish). | Esmerilar (metal). || ELECTR. Enfundar, revestir, forrar. || Envolver (to wrap). || SP. Sacar una vuelta de ventaja, adelantar: *to lap s.o. twice*, adelantar a alguien dos veces. | Dar una vuelta a (a track or course). || FIG. *To lap up*, beber a lengüetadas (animals), sorber (to drink quickly and noisily), disfrutar con (to enjoy), tragarse (to believe).
lapdog [ˈlæpdɔg] n. ZOOL. Perro (*m.*) faldero.
lapel [ləˈpel] n. Solapa, *f.* (of coat, etc.).
lapful [ˈlæpful] n. *He had a lapful of books*, tenía un montón de libros en las rodillas.
lapidary [ˈlæpidəri] adj. Lapidario, ria.
— N. Lapidario, *m.*
lapidate [ˈlæpideit] v. tr. Lapidar.
lapidation [ˌlæpiˈdeiʃən] n. Lapidación, *f.* (stoning).
lapidification [ˌlæpidifiˈkeiʃən] n. Lapidificación, *f.*, petrificación, *f.*
lapidify [læˈpidifai] v. tr. Lapidificar, petrificar.
— V. intr. Lapidificarse, petrificarse.
lapilli [ləˈpilai] pl. n. GEOL. Lapilli, *m.*
lapis lazuli [ˌlæpisˈlæzjulai] n. MIN. Lapislázuli, *m.* || Azul (*m.*) de ultramar (colour).
lap joint [ˈlæpdʒɔint] n. Empalme (*m.*) a media madera.
lap-joint [ˈlæpdʒɔint] v. tr. Empalmar a media madera.
Lapland [ˈlæplænd] pr. n. GEOGR. Laponia, *f.*
Laplander [—ə*] n. Lapón, ona.
Lapp [læp] adj./n. Lapón, ona. || — N. Lapón, *m.* (language).
lappet [ˈlæpit] n. Orejera, *f.* (of cap). || Caída, *f.*, (of lady's headdress). || Faldón, *m.* (of garment). || Solapa, *f.* (of pocket). || Pliegue, *m.*, doblez, *f.* (of clothing). || Lóbulo, *m.* (of the ear). || Pliegue, *m.* (of a membrane). || Moco, *m.*, carúncula, *f.* (of a turkey cock). || Escudo, *m.* (of a keyhole).
lapping [ˈlæpiŋ] n. Chapoteo, *m.* (of water).
lap robe [ˈlæpˈrəub] n. Manta (*f.*) de viaje (heavy blanket).
lapse [læps] n. Lapso, *m.*, período, *m.* (period): *a short lapse of time*, un breve lapso de tiempo. || Transcurso, *m.*: *the lapse of time*, el transcurso del tiempo. || Fallo, *m.*: *a memory lapse*, un fallo de memoria. || Lapso, *m.*, lapsus, *m.* (mistake when speaking). || Equivocación, *f.*, error, *m.* (mistake). || Desliz, *m.*, falta, *f.*, error, *m.* (moral mistake). || Caída, *f.*: *lapse into heresy*, caída en la herejía. || Caída (*f.*) en desuso (falling into desuse). || Derogación, *f.* (of one's principles). || JUR. Caducidad, *f.* (of laws). | Prescripción, *f.* (of rights). || — *Lapse from one's duty*, falta a su deber. || *Lapse of the pen*, lapsus cálami. || *Lapse of the tongue*, lapsus linguae.
lapse [læps] v. intr. Transcurrir, pasar (time). || JUR. Caducar. || Caer, incurrir: *to lapse into bad habits*, incurrir en malas costumbres. || Caer en el error, equivocarse (to err). || Cometer un desliz (morally). || Faltar: *to lapse from duty*, faltar a su deber. || Recaer, reincidir (to relapse). || Recurrir: *to lapse into one's own language*, recurrir a su propia lengua. || Desaparecer (to cease to be). || Caer en desuso (habits, customs). || — *To lapse into silence*, quedarse callado, no decir palabra. || *To lapse into unconsciousness*, perder el conocimiento.
lapsed [—t] adj. REL. Lapso, sa. || JUR. Caducado, da.
lapstrake [ˈlæpstreik] or **lapstreak** [ˈlæpstri:k] adj. De tingladillo.
— N. Barco (*m.*) de tingladillo.
lapwing [ˈlæpwiŋ] n. ZOOL. Avefría, *f.*
lar [lɑ:*] n. Lar, *m.* || — Pl. Dioses lares.
— OBSERV. El plural de esta palabra es *lares* tanto en inglés como en español.
larboard [ˈlɑ:bəd] adj. MAR. De babor.
— Adv. A babor.
— N. Babor, *m.*
larcener [ˈlɑ:sinə*] or **larcenist** [ˈlɑ:sinist] n. Ratero, *m.* (thief).
larcenous [ˈlɑ:sinəs] adj. Culpable de robo *or* de hurto (person). || *Larcenous action*, robo, *m.*
larceny [ˈlɑ:səni] n. Ratería, *f.*, hurto, *m.*, robo, *m.*, latrocinio, *m.* || *Petty larceny*, robo de menor cuantía, hurto, ratería.
larch [lɑ:tʃ] n. BOT. Alerce, *m.*
lard [lɑ:d] n. CULIN. Manteca (*f.*) de cerdo.
lard [lɑ:d] v. tr. CULIN. Mechar, lardar. || FIG. Entreverar, sembrar [*with*, de] (a speech, a text).
larder [ˈlɑ:də*] n. Despensa, *f.* (pantry).
lardon [ˈlɑ:dən] or **lardoon** [lɑ:ˈdu:n] n. CULIN. Mecha, *f.*, lonja (*f.*) de tocino.
lardy [ˈlɑ:di] adj. Mantecoso, sa.
lardy-dardy [—ˈdɑ:di] adj. FAM. Presuntuoso, sa.
large [lɑ:dʒ] adj. Grande: *a large farm*, una finca grande. || Grande, abundante, copioso, sa (meal). || Grande, importante: *a large sum of money*, una gran cantidad de dinero; *a large company*, una sociedad importante. || Grande, voluminoso, sa (parcel). || Grande, numeroso, sa (family). || Amplio, plia: *to have large views*, tener miras amplias. || Liberal, espléndido, da (generous). || Amplio, plia; extenso, sa (powers). || Grande (size of clothes). || MAR. Favorable (wind). || — *As large as life*, de tamaño natural (life-size), en persona (in person). || *On a large scale*, en gran escala. || *To a large extent*, en gran parte.
— Adv. MAR. Con viento a la cuadra. || — *At large*, en libertad, libre, suelto, ta: *the fugitive is still at large*, el fugitivo está aún en libertad; en general: *the public at large*, el público en general; extensamente, largamente: *to speak at large*, hablar extensamente. || U. S. *Congressman-at-large*, diputado (*m.*) que representa una región entera.
large-handed [—ˈhændid] adj. De manos grandes. || FIG. Dadivoso, sa; generoso, sa; espléndido, da (generous).
large-hearted [—ˈhɑ:tid] adj. Dadivoso, sa; desprendido, da; magnánimo, ma (generous).
large-heartedness [—ˈhɑ:tidnis] n. Largueza, *f.*, generosidad, *f.*, magnanimidad, *f.*
large intestine [—inˈte stin]n. ANAT. Intestino (*m.*) grueso.
largely [ˈlɑ:dʒli] adv. En gran parte (mainly). || Considerablemente, ampliamente (much). || Generosamente (generously). || *Largely sufficient*, más que suficiente.
large-minded [ˈlɑ:dʒˈmaindid] adj. Tolerante, de ideas *or* miras amplias.
large-mindedness [—nis] n. Amplitud (*f.*) de ideas *or* de miras.
largeness [ˈlɑ:dʒnis] n. Tamaño, *m.* (in space). || Grosor, *m.* (in mass). || FIG. Amplitud, *f.* (of mind). | Magnitud, *f.*
larger [ˈlɑ:dʒə*] comp. adj. Más grande, mayor.

large-scale [ˈlɑːdʒskeil] adj. En gran escala.
large-sized [ˈlɑːdʒsaizd] adj. De gran tamaño.
largess or **largesse** [lɑːˈdʒes] n. Dádiva, *f.* (gift). || Largueza, *f.*, generosidad, *f.* (generosity).
larghetto [lɑːˈgetəu] adv. MUS. Larghetto.
— N. MUS. Larghetto, *m.*
largish [lɑːdʒiʃ] adj. Bastante largo, ga; más bien largo, ga.
largo [ˈlɑːgəu] adv. MUS. Largo.
— N. MUS. Largo, *m.*
lariat [ˈlæriət] n. Lazo, *m.* (lasso). || Cabestro, *m.* (for picketing horses).
lark [lɑːk] n. ZOOL. Alondra, *f.* (bird). || FAM. Broma, *f.* (joke): *to have a lark with s.o.*, gastar una broma a uno; *this wedding lark cost me a fortune*, la broma de la boda me costó un dineral. | Travesura, *f.* (mischievous action). | Juerga, *f.*, parranda, *f.* (binge, spree): *what a lark we had!*, ¡qué juerga nos corrimos!; *to go on a lark*, irse de juerga. || — FAM. *To do sth. for a lark*, hacer algo para divertirse. | *To get up with the lark*, levantarse con el alba *or* con las gallinas. | *What a lark!*, ¡qué divertido!
lark [lɑːk] v. intr. FAM. Andar de juerga. | Divertirse (to amuse o.s.). || — FAM. *Stop larking about!*, ¡déjate de tonterías *or* de sandeces *or* de bromas! | *To lark about*, hacer el tonto. | *To lark about with sth.*, juguetear con algo.
larkspur [—spəː*] n. BOT. Espuela (*f.*) de caballero.
larky [ˈlɑːki] adj. FAM. Bromista.
larrikin [ˈlærikin] n. FAM. Golfo, *m.*, gamberro, *m.*
larrup [ˈlærəp] v. tr. Dar una paliza a.
larva [ˈlɑːvə] n. ZOOL. Larva, *f.*

— OBSERV. El plural de la palabra inglesa es *larvae*.

larval [—l] adj. ZOOL. Larval. || MED. Larvado, da.
larvicolous [lɑːˈvikələs] adj. Larvícola.
laryngeal [ˌlærinˈdʒiːəl] adj. Laríngeo, a.
laryngectomy [ˌlærinˈdʒektəmi] n. MED. Laringectomía, *f.*
laryngitis [ˌlærinˈdʒaitis] inv. n. MED. Laringitis, *f.*
laryngologist [ˌlæriŋˈgɔlədʒist] n. MED. Laringólogo, *m.* (specialist).
laryngology [læriŋˈgɔlədzi] n. Laringología, *f.*
laryngoscope [ləˈriŋgəskəup] n. MED. Laringoscopio, *m.* (instrument for examining the larynx).
laryngoscopy [ˌlæriŋˈgɔskəpi] n. MED. Laringoscopia, *f.*
laryngotomy [ˌlæriŋˈgɔtəmi] n. MED. Laringotomía, *f.*
larynx [ˈlæriŋks] n. ANAT. Laringe, *f.*

— OBSERV. El plural de la palabra inglesa es *larynges* o *larynxes*.

lascivious [ləˈsiviəs] adj. Lascivo, va; lujurioso, sa.
lasciviousness [—nis] n. Lascivia, *f.*, lujuria, *f.*
laser [leizə*] n. Laser, *m.*: *laser beam*, rayo laser.
lash [læʃ] n. Tralla, *f.* (striking part of whip). || Latigazo, *m.*, azote, *m.* (blow with the whip). || Azote, *m.* (punishment). || FIG. Coletazo, *m.* (of a tail). | Azote, *m.* (of wind). | Embate, *m.* (of waves). || ANAT. Pestaña, *f.* (eyelash). || MAR. Amarra, *f.* (rope). || FIG. Aguijonamiento, *m.*, incitación, *f.* (of desire). | Sarcasmo, *m.*, pulla, *f.* (remark).
lash [læʃ] v. tr. Azotar a, dar latigazos a (to whip). || Azotar: *the waves lashed the rocks*, las olas azotaban las rocas; *the rain lashed the windows*, la lluvia azotaba los cristales. || Sacudir: *the wind lashed the trees*, el viento sacudía los árboles. || FIG. Incitar (to excite). | Atacar violentamente, fustigar (when speaking). || Atar (to bind). || MAR. Amarrar, trincar. || — *To lash its tail*, dar coletazos. || *To lash o.s. into a fury*, ponerse furioso.
— V. intr. Dar coletazos, agitarse (tail). || Azotar el aire (swords, etc.).
— **To lash against**, azotar (wind, rain). || **To lash down**, caer con fuerza (rain, hail). | Sujetar, atar firmemente (to bind). || **To lash on**, hacer andar a latigazos. || **To lash out**, dar una coz, dar coces (a horse, etc.). | Repartir golpes a diestro y siniestro (a person with his fists). | Estallar (with anger). | Gastar (money). | — *To lash out at*, dar un latigazo a (a horse), lanzar una indirecta a, tirar una pulla a (to criticize).
lashing [—iŋ] n. Azotaina, *f.*, azotes, *m. pl.*, flagelación, *f.* (whipping). || Azotes, *m. pl.* (of rain). || FIG. Bronca, *f.* (scolding). || Ligadura, *f.*, atadura, *f.* (tying). || MAR. Amarra, *f.*, trinca, *f.* (rope). || — Pl. FAM. Montones, *m.*: *lashings of cream*, montones de nata.
lass [læs] n. Muchacha, *f.*, chica, *f.* (young girl). || Novia, *f.* (sweetheart).
lassie [ˈlæsi] n. Muchacha, *f.*, chica, *f.*
lassitude [ˈlæsitjuːd] n. Lasitud, *f.*, cansancio, *m.*
lasso [læˈsuː] n. Lazo, *m.*
lasso [læˈsuː] v. tr. Coger con el lazo.
lassoer [—ə*] n. Laceador, *m.*
last [lɑːst] adj. Último, ma: *the last time*, la última vez; *the last row*, la última fila; *his last three books*, sus tres últimos libros; *you are my last hope*, eres mi última esperanza; *the last Saturday of the year*, el último sábado del año; *he is the last person I would have suspected it from*, es la última persona a quien hubiera sospechado; *my last offer*, mi última oferta. || Último, ma; final: *the last stage*, la etapa final; *the last match of the season*, el partido final de la temporada. || Pasado, da: *last month*, el mes pasado; *last Saturday*, el sábado pasado; *on Saturday last*, el sábado pasado. || Sumo, ma; extremo, ma (greatest). || — *Before last*, penúltimo, ma: *the house before last*, la penúltima casa; antepasado, da: *the week before last*, la semana antepasada. || *Every last one*, todos y cada uno. || *I haven't seen him these last two years*, hace dos años que no le veo. || *Last but not least* o *by no means least*, el último en orden aunque no en importancia. || *Last but one*, penúltimo, ma: *the last house but one*, la penúltima casa. || *Last honours*, honras (*f.*) fúnebres. || *Last night*, anoche, ayer por la noche (yesterday), último día, última función *or* representación (of a play), último día (of a film). || *Last November*, el mes de noviembre pasado. || *Last thing at night*, al final del día. || *That's the last thing that's worrying me*, es lo que menos me preocupa. || *The Last Judgment*, el Juicio Final. || FIG. *The last thing* o *the last word in hats*, el último grito en sombreros. || *The night before last*, antes de anoche, anteanoche. || *This day last week*, hace exactamente una semana. || *To be the last* o *the last one* o *the last person to do sth.*, ser el último en hacer algo. || *To have the last word*, tener la última palabra. || *To pay one's last respects*, rendir el último homenaje.
— Adv. El último, la última, lo último: *we'll do this last*, haremos esto lo último; *they arrived last*, ellos llegaron los últimos. || El último, la última, en último lugar, en la última posición (in a competition or race). || Por última vez, la última vez: *we last saw him in Paris*, la última vez le vimos en París; *when did it last happen?*, ¿cuándo ocurrió por última vez? || En último lugar (at the end). || Por último, finalmente: *and last we'll go to the cinema*, y por último iremos al cine.
— N. Último, ma: *who is the last in the queue?*, ¿quién es el último de la cola? || Lo que queda, el resto: *would anyone like the last of the cheese?*, ¿quiere alguien el resto del queso? || Final, *m.*, fin, *m.*: *to be true to the last*, ser fiel hasta el final. || Último día, *m.*: *the last of the month*, el último día del mes. || Anterior, *m.* & *f.*: *that apple was better than the last*, esa manzana era mejor que la anterior. || Unidad (*f.*) de peso y de capacidad (measure). || Horma, *f.* (for shoes). || COMM. Última, *f.* (letter): *in my last*, en mi última. || — *At last*, por fin. || *At long last*, por fin, al fin y al cabo. || FIG. *Stick to your last!*, ¡zapatero, a tus zapatos! || *The last of the apples*, la última manzana. || FIG. *To be near one's last*, estar en las últimas. | *To breathe one's last*, exhalar el último suspiro. || *To have seen the last of s.o.*, haber visto a alguien por última vez. || *To speak one's last*, pronunciar su última palabra. || *You haven't heard the last of this*, volverás a oír hablar del asunto. || *You haven't seen the last of me*, volverás a verme.
last [lɑːst] v. intr. Durar: *his illness lasted a week*, su enfermedad duró una semana; *this coat has lasted a long time*, este abrigo ha durado mucho tiempo. || Permanecer: *his memory will last*, permanecerá su recuerdo. || Aguantar, resistir: *I can't last much longer*, no puedo aguantar mucho más. || Llegarle a uno, alcanzar: *I don't think my money will last*, no creo que me llegue el dinero. || Conservarse (a custom, etc.). || — *Made to last*, duradero, ra. || *This is too good to last*, esto es demasiado bueno para que dure. || *To last out*, resistir (to survive), llegarle a uno, alcanzar: *will the food last out till the end of the week?*, ¿nos llegará la comida hasta el final de la semana?
— V. tr. Durar: *those shoes didn't last you long*, estos zapatos no te han durado mucho tiempo. || *To last out*, aguantar, resistir: *my coat will not last the winter out*, mi abrigo no aguantará todo el invierno; sobrevivir a (to outlive): *he lasted the war out*, sobrevivió a la guerra.
last-ditch [—ditʃ] adj. FIG. Último, ma; desesperado, da: *a last-ditch effort*, un último esfuerzo. | Hasta el extremo (resistance, etc.).
lastex [ˈlæsteks] n. Lástex, *m.* (trademark).
lasting [ˈlɑːstiŋ] adj. Duradero, ra: *a lasting peace*, una paz duradera. || Resistente (strong). || Constante (fear, etc.). || Profundo, da: *it created a lasting impression on me*, me produjo una profunda impresión.
— N. Tela (*f.*) fuerte. || FIG. Resistencia, *f.*
lastingness [—nis] n. Durabilidad, *f.*, permanencia, *f.*
lastly [ˈlɑːstli] adv. Por último, finalmente.
last-minute [ˈlɑːstˈminit] adj. De última hora (news, decision, etc.).
last name [ˈlɑːstˈneim] n. Apellido, *m.*
last offices [ˈlɑːstˈɔfisiz] pl. n. REL. Oficio (*m. sing.*) de difuntos.
last quarter [ˈlɑːstˈkwɔːtə*] n. Cuarto (*m.*) menguante (of the moon).
last sleep [ˈlɑːstˈsliːp] n. Último sueño, *m.* (death).
last straw [ˈlɑːstˈstrɔː] n. FIG. Colmo, *m.*, acabóse, *m.* || FIG. *It's the last straw*, es el colmo, es la última gota que hace rebasar la copa, es el acabóse.
Last Supper [ˈlɑːstˈsʌpə*] n. REL. Última Cena, *f.*
latch [lætʃ] n. Picaporte, *m.*, pestillo, *m.* (of a door). || Pestillo, *m.* [de golpe] (of window). || — *On the latch*, cerrado con picaporte. || *To drop the latch*, correr *or* echar el pestillo.
latch [lætʃ] v. tr. Cerrar [con picaporte].
— V. intr. *To latch on to*, pegarse a (a person), darse cuenta de (a fact), agarrarse a (to grasp).
latchet [ˈlætʃit] n. Cordón (*m.*) del zapato.
latchkey [ˈlætʃkiː] n. Llave, *f.* (de picaporte).

late [leit] adj. Tardío, a: *his late arrival*, su llegada tardía; *late middle English*, inglés medio tardío; *it is a late summer*, es un verano tardío. || Último, ma (last): *in the late war*, en la última guerra; *in the late years*, en los últimos años. || Reciente (recent). || Retrasado, da (delayed). || Atrasado, da (delivery). || GRAMM. Tardío (Latin). || De fines de: *a late 16th century church*, una iglesia de fines del siglo XVI. || Ex, antiguo, gua (former): *the late Foreign Minister*, el ex ministro de Asuntos Exteriores. || Fallecido, da; difunto, ta: *my late husband*, mi difunto marido. || Avanzado, da (age, hour, season): *at a late hour*, a una hora avanzada. || — *A late party*, una reunión que acaba tarde. || *He is late*, ya tenía que estar aquí (before arriving), ha llegado tarde (upon arriving). || *In the late afternoon*, hacia el final de la tarde. || *In the late nineteenth century*, a fines *or* a finales del siglo diez y nueve. || *It is late*, es tarde. || *It is too late*, es demasiado tarde. || *I was late in coming*, llegué tarde. || *Of late years*, en estos últimos años. || U. S. *The late late show*, la película nocturna [en la televisión]. || *The late show*, la última función. || *To be late*, llegar tarde (a person), llevar retraso (a train, etc.), tardar: *he was late in going to bed*, tardó en acostarse; caer tarde (feast, event). || *To get* o *to grow late*, hacerse tarde: *it's getting late*, se está haciendo tarde. || *To make s.o. late*, retrasar a uno, hacer llegar tarde a uno, entretener a uno.
— Adv. Tarde: *to arrive late*, llegar tarde; *very late in the night*, muy tarde por la noche. || Con retraso (after the appointed time). || Tardíamente, tarde (too late). || Recientemente (recently). || Anteriormente: *late of York*, anteriormente domiciliado en York. || — *As late as*, todavía en: *this custom existed as late as last century*, esta costumbre existía todavía en el siglo pasado; hasta (until). || *As late as yesterday*, no más tarde que ayer, ayer mismo. || *Better late than never*, más vale tarde que nunca. || *Late in*, hacia fines de: *late in the year*, hacia fines de año. || *Late in life*, a una edad avanzada. || *Late in the afternoon*, a última hora de la tarde. || FIG. *Late in the day*, tarde. || *Late in years*, de edad avanzada. || *Late last century*, hacia fines del siglo pasado. || *Late of Oxford*, antiguo de Oxford. || *Of late*, últimamente, recientemente. || *To arrive ten minutes late*, llegar con diez minutos de retraso. || *To keep s.o. late*, entretener a alguien hasta muy tarde. || *To stay up late*, quedarse levantado hasta muy tarde.

latecomer [—ˈkʌmə*] n. Rezagado, da (who lags behind). || Retrasado, da; persona (*f.*) que llega tarde (who arrives late). || Recién llegado, recién llegada, nuevo, va (newcomer).

lateen [ləˈti:n] adj. MAR. Latina (sail).
— N. MAR. Vela (*f.*) latina. || *Lateen yard*, entena, *f.*

lately [ˈleitli] adv. Últimamente, recientemente. || Hace poco: *until lately*, hasta hace poco.

laten [ˈleitən] v. intr. Hacerse tarde.

latency [—si] n. Estado (*m.*) latente.

lateness [ˈleitnis] n. Retraso, *m.* (of train, person's arrival, etc.). || Llegada (*f.*) tardía (of a person). || Lo avanzado (of the hour). || Fecha (*f.*) reciente (of an event). || *Lateness will be punished*, será castigado el que llegue tarde.

latent [ˈleitənt] adj. Latente: *latent heat*, calor latente; *in a latent state*, en estado latente. || Oculto, ta (defect, qualities).

later [ˈleitə*] comp. adj. See LATE. || Posterior: *his later works*, sus obras posteriores; *a later date*, una fecha posterior. || Último, ma (last). || Más reciente: *this picture is later than the other*, este cuadro es más reciente que el otro.
— Comp. adv. See LATE. || Después, más tarde: *three years later*, tres años después. || — *Later on*, más tarde, después. || *No later than yesterday*, ayer mismo, no más tarde que ayer. || *See you later*, hasta luego, hasta pronto.

lateral [ˈlætərəl] adj. Lateral.

laterally [—i] adv. Lateralmente.

Lateran [ˈlætərən] adj. REL. Lateranense.
— N. REL. Letrán, *m.*

latest [ˈleitist] superl. adj. See LATE. || Último, ma: *the latest news*, las últimas noticias. || Más reciente (recent). || *The latest thing in hats*, el último grito en sombreros.
— Superl. adv. See LATE.
— N. Última noticia, *f.* (latest news): *have you heard the latest?*, ¿has oído la última noticia? || Lo último. || — *At the latest*, a más tardar. || *The latest that suits me is*, lo más tarde que me conviene es. || *The very latest*, el último grito (in fashion).

latex [ˈleiteks] n. BOT. Látex, *m.*

— OBSERV. El plural de *latex* es *latices* o *latexes*.

lath [lɑ:θ] n. Listón, *m.* || FAM. *As thin as a lath*, como un fideo.

lath [lɑ:θ] v. tr. Listonar.

lathe [leið] n. Torno, *m.* (for pottery). || Torno, *m.* (machine tool).

lathe [leið] v. tr. Tornear.

lathe operator [—ˈɔpəreitə*] n. Tornero, *m.*

lather [ˈlɑ:ðə*] n. Espuma, *f.* (of soap, etc.). || Sudor, *m.* (on a horse).

lather [ˈlɑ:ðə*] v. intr. Hacer espuma (soap). || Estar cubierto de sudor (of sweat).
— V. tr. Enjabonar (with soap). || FAM. Dar una paliza, zurrar (to thrash).

lather [ˈleiðə*] n. Tornero, *m.* (of machine tool). || Alfarero, *m.* (in pottery).

lathery [ˈlɑ:ðəri] adj. Espumoso, sa (liquid). || Lleno de espuma (chin). || Sudoroso, sa (covered in sweat).

lathing [ˈlɑ:θiŋ] n. Enlistonado, *m.*, listonado, *m.* (lathwork). || Listones, *m. pl.*

lathwork [ˈlɑ:θwə:k] n. Enlistonado, *m.*, listonado, *m.*

latices [ˈlætisi:z] pl. n. See LATEX.

latifundium [lætiˈfʌndiəm] n. Latifundio, *m.*

— OBSERV. El plural de la palabra inglesa es *latifundia*.

Latin [ˈlætin] adj. Latino, na.
— N. Latino, na (person). || Latín, *m.* (language): *Low Latin*, bajo latín; *Vulgar Latin*, latín vulgar *or* rústico. || FAM. *Dog Latin*, latín de cocina *or* macarrónico.

Latin America [—əˈmerikə] pr. n. GEOGR. América Latina, *f.*, Latinoamérica, *f.*

Latin American [—əˈmerikən] n. Latinoamericano, na.

Latin-American [—əˈmerikən] adj. Latinoamericano, na.

— OBSERV. *Latinoamericano* is the term used by Latin Americans. In Spain *hispanoamericano* and *iberoamericano* are more commonly used.

Latinism [ˈlætinizəm] n. Latinismo, *m.*

Latinist [ˈlætinist] n. Latinista, *m.* & *f.*

Latinity [ləˈtiniti] n. Latinidad, *f.*

Latinization [ˌlætiniˈzeiʃən] n. Latinización, *f.*

Latinize [ˈlætinaiz] v. tr./intr. Latinizar.

latish [ˈleitiʃ] adj. Un poco tardío.
— Adv. Un poco tarde.

latitude [ˈlætitju:d] n. Latitud, *f.* || FIG. Latitud, *f.*, amplitud, *f.*, libertad, *f.* (freedom to act).

latitudinal [ˌlætiˈtju:dinl] adj. Latitudinal, transversal.

latitudinarian [ˈlætiˌtju:diˈnɛəriən] adj./n. Latitudinario, ria.

latitudinarianism [—izəm] n. Latitudinarismo, *m.*

Latium [ˈleiʃjəm] pr. n. GEOGR. Lacio, *m.*

Latona [ləˈtəunə] pr. n. MYTH. Latona, *f.*

latria [ləˈtraiə] n. REL. Latría, *f.*

latrine [ləˈtri:n] n. Letrina, *f.*, retrete, *m.*

latten [ˈlætn] n. Latón, *m.* (brass alloy). || Hojalata, *f.* (tin).

latter [ˈlætə*] adj. Segundo, da; último, ma: *the latter half of the week*, la segunta mitad de la semana. || Último, ma; más reciente: *his latter works*, sus últimas obras.
— Pron. Éste, ésta: *the former ... the latter...*, aquél ... éste.

latter-day [—dei] adj. Moderno, na; reciente, de nuestros días.

Latter-day Saint [—deiseint] n. REL. Santo (*m.*) del último día, mormón, ona.

latterly [ˈlætə:li] adv. Últimamente, recientemente (recently). || Después, más tarde (after).

lattice [ˈlætis] n. Celosía, *f.*, enrejado, *m.* || HERALD. Celosía, *f.* || PHYS. Retículo, *m.* (of a reactor).
— Adj. Enrejado, da (door). || De celosía (girder, etc.). || De celosía, enrejado, da (window).

lattice [ˈlætis] v. tr. Enrejar, poner celosía a.

latticed [—t] adj. Enrejado, da; con celosía.

latticework [—wə:k] n. Celosía, *f.*, enrejado, *m.*

Latvia [ˈlætviə] pr. n. GEOGR. Letonia, *f.*

Latvian [—n] adj./n. Letón, ona. || — N. Letón *m.* (language).

laud [lɔ:d] n. Alabanza, *f.* (praise). || — Pl. REL. Laudes, *f.*

laud [lɔ:d] v. tr. Alabar, elogiar, encomiar.

laudability [ˌlɔ:dəˈbiliti] n. Lo encomiable, lo elogiable.

laudable [ˈlɔ:dəbl] adj. Laudable, loable.

laudanum [ˈlɔdnəm] n. Láudano, *m.*

laudation [lɔ:ˈdeiʃən] n. Alabanza, *f.*

laudative [ˈlɔ:dətiv] or **laudatory** [ˈlɔ:dətəri] adj. Laudatorio, ria; elogioso, sa; encomiástico, ca.

laugh [lɑ:f] n. Risa, *f.* (expression of amusement): *mocking laugh*, risa burlona. || Broma, *f.* (joke). || — *A loud laugh*, una carcajada, una risotada. || *Good for a laugh*, divertido, da. || *He is a good laugh*, es un tipo gracioso. || *Just for a laugh* o *for laughs*, sólo para divertirse. || *To give a forced laugh* o *to force a laugh*, reír de dientes afuera, reír con risa de conejo. || *To have the last laugh*, ser el que ríe el último. || *To raise a laugh*, causar risa. || *We had a good laugh the other day*, nos reímos mucho el otro día. || *What a laugh!*, ¡qué risa!

laugh [lɑ:f] v. intr. Reír, reírse: *to start laughing*, echarse a reír. || — *He who laughs last laughs longest* o *he laughs best who laughs last*, quien ríe el último ríe mejor, al freír será el reír. || *To burst out laughing*, soltar la carcajada, echarse a reír a carcajadas. || *To die laughing*, morirse de risa. || *To laugh about* o *over*, reírse de. || *To laugh at*, reírse de: *to laugh at s.o.*, reírse de uno. || *To laugh heartily*, reír con ganas. || *To laugh in s.o.'s face*, reírse de uno en su cara *or* en sus barbas. || FIG. *To laugh on the other* o *the wrong side of one's face*, llorar. || *To laugh out loud*, reírse a carcajadas. || FIG. *To laugh s.o. out of court*, poner a alguien en ridículo. || *To laugh until one's sides ache*, reir a mandibula batiente. || *To laugh up one's sleeve* or *to o.s.*, reírse para su capote *or* para su sayo *or* para su coleto *or* para sus adentros *or* a solas *or* por lo bajo. || *To make one laugh*, dar risa. || *To make s.o. laugh on the other* o *on the wrong side of his face*, quitarle a uno las ganas de reír. || *To split one's sides laughing*, partirse de risa.

— V. tr. Decir riendo. || — *They laughed their approval*, aprobaron riendo. || *To laugh away*, tomar a risa. || *To laugh away the time with jokes*, matar el tiempo contando chistes. || *To laugh down*, ridiculizar. || *To laugh off*, tomar a risa. || *We laughed him out of his bad humour*, le hicimos reír tanto que se puso de buen humor.

laughable [—əbl] adj. Ridículo, la; absurdo, da. || Irrisorio, ria: *a laughable offer*, una oferta irrisoria. || *To be laughable*, dar que reír, ser de risa.

laughing [—iŋ] adj. Risueño, ña: *laughing eyes*, ojos risueños; *a laughing fountain*, una fuente risueña. || — *It's no laughing matter*, no es cosa de risa. || *Laughing gas*, gas (*m.*) hilarante. || *To have a laughing fit*, tener un ataque de risa.

— N. Risas, *f. pl.*

laughingly [—li] adv. Riendo.

laughingstock [ˈlɑːfiŋstɔk] n. Hazmerreír, *m. inv.*: *to be the laughingstock of everyone*, ser el hazmerreír de todo el mundo.

laughter [ˈlɑːftə*] n. Risa, *f.*, risas, *f. pl.*, carcajadas, *f. pl.*: *the laughter of the audience*, las risas del público. || — *Roar* o *peals of laughter*, carcajadas. || *To burst into laughter*, soltar la carcajada. || *Uncontrollable laughter*, risa nerviosa.

launce [lɑːns] n. Amodita, *f.* (sea fish).

Launcelot [ˈlɑːnslət] pr. n. Lancelote, *m.*, Lanzarote, *m.* (Lancelot).

launch [lɔːntʃ] n. Lancha, *f.* (craft): *motor launch*, lancha motora. || Botadura, *f.* (launching).

launch [lɔːntʃ] v. tr. Botar (a ship). || Lanzar (a missile, an actor, a new product). || Echar al mar, sacar al mar (a lifeboat). || Crear, fundar (a new company). || Estrenar (play, film). || Emprender (a project, an attack). || Emitir (to emit, to issue). || Lanzar (to throw). || FAM. *To launch into eternity*, mandar al otro mundo.

— V. intr. Lanzarse. || — *To launch forth* o *into*, lanzarse en (explanations). || *To launch out on*, lanzarse en, emprender (an enterprise).

launcher [—ə*] n. Lanzador, *m.* || — MIL. *Grenade launcher*, lanzagranadas, *m. inv.* | *Rocket launcher*, lanzacohetes, *m. inv.*

launching [—iŋ] n. Lanzamiento, *m.* (of a missile, a probe). || Botadura, *f.* (of a ship). || Estreno, *m.* (of play, film). || Lanzamiento, *m.* (of a campaign, etc.). || Iniciación, *f.* (beginning). || Fundación, *f.*, creación, *f.* (foundation). || Puesta (*f.*) en servicio (making operational). || — *Launching pad*, plataforma (*f.*) de lanzamiento. || *Launching ramp*, rampa (*f.*) de lanzamiento. || *Launching site*, rampa (*f.*) de lanzamiento.

launder [ˈlɔːndə*] n. MIN. Reguera (*f.*) de la colada.

launder [ˈlɔːndə*] v. tr. Lavar (to wash). || Lavar y planchar (to wash and iron).

— V. intr. Lavar la ropa (to wash). || Resistir el lavado (to bear washing).

launderer [—rə*] n. Lavandero, *m.*

launderette [ˌlɔːndəˈret] n. Lavandería (*f.*) automática.

laundress [ˈlɔːndris] n. Lavandera, *f.*

laundromat [ˈlɔːndrəˈmæt] n. U. S. Lavandería (*f.*) automática.

laundry [ˈlɔːndri] n. Lavandería, *f.* (place). || Ropa (*f.*) sucia (dirty clothes). || Ropa (*f.*) limpia (clean clothes). || *Laundry basket*, cesto (*m.*) de la ropa sucia.

laundryman [—mæn] n. Lavandero, *m.*

— OBSERV. El plural de esta palabra es *laundrymen*.

laundrywoman [—ˈwumən] n. Lavandera, *f.*

— OBSERV. El plural de esta palabra es *laundrywomen*.

laureate [ˈlɔːriit] adj./n Laureado, da.

laurel [ˈlɔrəl] n. BOT. Laurel, *m.* || U. S. BOT. Rododendro, *m.* | Azalea, *f.* || — Pl. FIG. Laureles, *m.* (award): *laden with laurels*, cargado de laureles. || — BOT. *Cherry laurel*, laurel cerezo *or* real. || FIG. *To cast a stain on one's laurels*, mancillar sus laureles. | *To look to one's laurels*, no dormirse en los laureles. | *To rest on one's laurels*, dormirse en los laureles. | *To win laurels*, cosechar *or* conquistar laureles.

laurel [ˈlɔrəl] v. tr. Laurear.

Laurence [ˈlɔrəns] pr. n. Lorenzo, *m.*

lav [læv] n. FAM. See LAVATORY.

lava [ˈlɑːvə] n. Lava, *f.* (of a volcano): *lava flows*, torrentes de lava.

lavabo [ləˈveibəu] n. REL. Lavatorio, *m.*, lavabo, *m.*

lavage [læˈvɑːʒ] n. MED. Lavado, *m.* (of stomach, etc.).

lavaret [ˈlævəret] n. Farra, *f.* (fish).

lavatory [ˈlævətəri] n. Retrete, *m.* (a water closet). || U. S. Lavabo, *m.*, servicios, *m. pl.*, cuarto (*m.*) de aseo (washroom). || *Public lavatory*, servicios [públicos].

lave [leiv] v. tr. Lavar (to wash). || Bañar (river, sea).

lavender [ˈlævində*] n. BOT. Espliego, *m.*, lavanda, *f.*, alhucema, *f.* || Azul, *m.*, color (*m.*) de lavanda (colour). || *Lavender water*, lavanda, *f.*

— Adj. Azul, [de] color de lavanda.

lavish [ˈlæviʃ] adj. Pródigo, ga; generoso, sa (generous): *to be lavish of*, ser pródigo de. || Abundante, profuso, sa (abundant). || Lujoso, sa (luxurious). || Desconsiderado, da; desmesurado, da (disproportionate). || *To be lavish with one's money*, no escatimar gastos, despilfarrar el dinero.

lavish [ˈlæviʃ] v. tr. Prodigar.

lavishly [—li] adv. Generosamente (generously). || Profusamente, con profusión (abundantly). || Lujosamente (luxuriously).

lavishness [—nis] n. Prodigalidad, *f.*, generosidad, *f.* (generosity). || Abundancia, *f.*, profusión, *f.* (abundance). || Lujo, *m.* (luxury).

law [lɔː] n. JUR. Ley, *f.* (governing customs): *to break the law*, quebrantar la ley; *law in force*, ley vigente. | Derecho, *m.*: *administrative, canon, civil, commercial, constitutional, common* o *consuetudinary* o *customary, criminal, international, maritime law*, derecho administrativo, canónico, civil, mercantil [*Amer.*, comercial], político, consuetudinario, penal, internacional, marítimo. | Derecho, *m.*, leyes, *f. pl.* (study): *to read law*, estudiar derecho *or* leyes. | Ley, *f.* (bill in Parliament). | Lo contencioso: *law department*, servicio de lo contencioso. | Jurisprudencia, *f.* (jurisprudence). || Ley, *f.*: *the law of gravitation*, la ley de la gravedad; *the law of supply and demand*, la ley de la oferta y la demanda. || SP. Regla, *f.*, ley, *f.*: *the offside law*, la regla del fuera de juego. || FAM. Policía, *f.* || — *According to law*, según la ley. || *As the law at present stands*, según la legislación vigente. || *By law*, según la ley. || *Custom has the force of law*, la costumbre hace ley *or* tiene fuerza de ley. || *His word is law*, su palabra es ley, lo que dice va a misa (fam.). || JUR. *Ignorance of the law is no excuse*, la ignorancia de la ley no excusa su cumplimiento. || *In law*, según la ley. || *Law and order*, orden público. || *Law of contradiction*, principio (*m.*) de la contradicción. || *Law of mass action*, ley de la acción de las masas. || *Law of nature*, ley natural. || PHYS. *Law of reflection, of refraction*, ley de la reflexión, de la refracción. || *Law of the jungle*, ley de la selva. || *Law of thermodynamics*, principios termodinámicos. || *Laws are made to be broken*, hecha la ley, hecha la trampa. || *Law school*, facultad (*f.*) de derecho. || JUR. *Martial law*, ley marcial. | *Officer of the law*, representante (*m.*) de la ley. || *One law for o.s. and one for everyone else* or *one law for the rich another for the poor*, la ley del embudo. || JUR. *Prohibition law*, ley seca. | *Salic law*, ley sálica. || *The forces of law and order*, las fuerzas del orden. || REL. *The Law*, la Ley [de Moisés]. || FIG. *The strong man is a law unto himself*, allá van las leyes do *or* donde quieren reyes. || *To be above the law*, estar por encima de la ley. || FIG. *To be a law unto o.s.*, dictar sus propias leyes. || JUR. *To be at law*, estar en pleito. | *To be outside the law*, estar fuera de la ley. | *To come under the law*, estar condenado por la ley. | *To go to law*, recurrir a la justicia, poner pleito. | *To have force of law*, tener fuerza de ley. | *To have the law on s.o.*, llevar ante los tribunales a alguien, poner pleito a alguien. || *To keep within the law*, obrar legalmente. || *To lay down the law*, dictar la ley. || JUR. *To practise law*, ejercer la profesión de abogado. || *To take the law into one's own hands*, tomarse la justicia por su mano. || JUR. *To take to law*, citar ante la justicia, llevar ante los tribunales.

— Adj. Jurídico, ca: *law term*, término jurídico. || Legal.

law-abiding [—əˌbaidiŋ] adj. Observante de la ley, respetuoso de las leyes.

law adviser [—ədˌvaizə*] n. Asesor (*m.*) jurídico.

lawbreaker [—ˌbreikə*] n. Infractor (*m.*) de la ley, violador (*m.*) de la ley.

lawbreaking [—ˌbreikiŋ] n. Violación (*f.*) de la ley.

lawcourt [—kɔːt] n. Tribunal (*m.*) de justicia.

lawful [—ful] adj. Legal (in accordance with the law). || Lícito, ta (permitted by law). || Legítimo, ma (recognized by law). || Válido, da (contract). || Justo, ta (just). || *Lawful day*, día (*m.*) hábil.

lawfulness [—fulnis] n. Legalidad, *f.* || Legitimidad, *f.* (legitimacy).

lawgiver [—ˌgivə*] n. Legislador, ra.

law Latin [—ˈlætin] n. Latín (*m.*) macarrónico.

lawless [—lis] adj. Ilegal, ilícito, ta (illegal). || Sin leyes (without law). || Ingobernable, desordenado, da (unorderly). || Anárquico, ca.

lawlessness [—lisnis] n. Anarquía, *f.* || Desorden, *m.*, licencia, *f.*

lawmaker [—ˌmeikə*] n. Legislador, ra.

lawmaking [—ˌmeikiŋ] n. Elaboración (*f.*) de las leyes.

— Adj. Legislativo, va.

law merchant [—ˈməːtʃənt] n. Derecho (*m.*) mercantil [*Amer.*, derecho (*m.*) comercial].

lawn [lɔːn] n. Césped, *m.* (grass). || Linón, *m.* (fabric).

lawn mower [—ˌməuə*] n. Cortacéspedes, *m. inv.*

lawn tennis [—ˈtenis] n. SP. Tenis (*m.*) sobre hierba.

law officer [ˈlɔːˌɔfisə*] n. JUR. Consejero (*m.*) jurídico [de la Corona].

Lawrence [ˈlɔrəns] pr. n. Lorenzo, *m.*

lawrencium [lɔˈrensjəm] n. CHEM. Laurencio, *m.*

lawsuit [ˈlɔːsjuːt] n. JUR. Pleito, *m.*, juicio, *m.*, proceso, *m.* (case presented before a civil court).

lawyer [ˈlɔːjə*] n. Jurista, *m.* & *f.* (legal expert). || U. S. Abogado, *m.*

— Observ. En inglés la palabra *lawyer* se aplica a cualquier jurista que esté autorizado a asesorar a sus clientes en cuestiones jurídicas. Por lo tanto puede designar tanto a un procurador de los tribunales como a un abogado.

lax [læks] adj. Flojo, ja (untensed). || Elástico, ca (conscience). || Laxo, xa; relajado, da (discipline, morals). || Negligente, descuidado, da (negligent). || Vago, ga; confuso, sa (ideas). || Med. Flojo, ja; suelto, ta (bowels). || Flojo, ja; fláccido, da; flácido, da (flesh).

laxation [læk'seiʃən] n. Laxación, *f.*, laxamiento, *m.* relajamiento, *m.*

laxative ['læksətiv] adj. Laxante.
— N. Med. Laxante, *m.*

laxism ['læksizəm] n. Laxismo, *m.*

laxity ['læksiti] or **laxness** ['læksnəs] n. Laxitud, *f.* (looseness). || Flojedad, *f.* (of a rope). || Flaccidez, *f.*, flacidez, *f.* (of flesh). || Elasticidad, *f.* (of conscience). || Relajamiento, *m.* (of discipline, morals). || Negligencia, *f.*, descuido, *m.* (negligence).

lay [lei] adj. Laico, ca; seglar: *a lay preacher*, un predicador seglar. || Profano, na; lego, ga (not expert). || Rel. Lego, ga: *lay brother*, hermano lego; *lay sister*, hermana lega.
— N. Lay, *m.*, endecha, *f.* (song, poem). || Configuración, *f.* (nature of land). || Orientación, *f.* || Situación, *f.*, disposición, *f.* (situation). || Ocupación, *f.* || Guarida, *f.* (animal lie). || — *Hen in lay*, gallina ponedora. || Pop. *She is an easy lay*, es una mujer fácil. || *To come into lay*, empezar a poner huevos. || *To go out of lay*, dejar de poner huevos. || Fig. *To study the lay of the land*, estudiar el terreno.

lay* [lei] v. tr. Poner, colocar (to place): *to lay a carpet, bricks*, poner una alfombra, ladrillos. || Disponer (to arrange). || Poner: *to lay the table, the tablecloth*, poner la mesa, el mantel. || Tender (pipe line, cable, railway line). || Preparar (fire). || Cubrir (to cover). || Echar (foundations). || Derribar, tirar al suelo (to knock s.o. down). || Derribar (to flatten). || Echar abajo (to destroy). || Alisar (to smooth). || Asentar (dust). || Calmar (wind). || Acostar (to put to bed): *to lay a child on a sofa*, acostar a un niño en un sofá. || Presentar, exponer (facts). || Presentar, formular (a claim). || Valorar (damages). || Echar (the blame). || Hacer (an accusation). || Dar (an information). || Dar (*on, upon*, a) [importance]. || Atribuir (a responsibility). || Formar, hacer (a plan). || Urdir, tramar (a plot). || Poner, imponer (a fine, tax, etc.). || Situar (a play, etc.). || Aquietar, calmar, acallar (fears). || Conjurar (ghost). || Sp. Hacer (a bet). | Apostar por (a horse, etc.). | Apostar (a sum). || Agr. Encamar (corn). | Poner (eggs). || Mil. Apuntar (to aim a gun). | Tender (a trap, an ambush). || Mar. Trazar, marcar (the course). | Corchar (a rope). | Sembrar (a mine). || Fam. Acostarse con. || — *The story is laid in Spain*, la historia se sitúa en España. || *To lay an axe to a tree*, dar un hachazo a un árbol. || *To lay bare*, poner al descubierto. || *To lay eyes on*, ver: *I haven't laid eyes on him for ten years*, hace diez años que no le he visto; mirar (to look at). || *To lay flat*, arrasar: *to lay a town flat*, arrasar una ciudad; extender: *to lay sth. flat on the table*, extender algo sobre la mesa. || *To lay hands on*, see HAND. || *To lay hold of*, agarrar. || *To lay low*, see LOW. || *To lay open*, see OPEN. || *To lay siege to*, asediar, poner sitio a, sitiar. || Fig. *To lay to rest*, enterrar. || *To lay waste*, devastar, asolar.
— V. intr. Poner huevos (a hen). || Estar, estar situado (to be situated). || Poner la mesa: *lay for five*, pon la mesa para cinco. || Apostar (to bet).
— ***To lay about***, repartir golpes a diestro y siniestro. || ***To lay aside***, dejar a un lado (sth. that is unwanted). | Guardar (to save). | Dejar de lado (scruples, prejudices). || ***To lay away***, guardar (to store). || ***To lay before***, presentar, exponer: *he laid the problem before me*, me presentó el problema; someter: *to lay a bill before Parliament*, someter un proyecto de ley al Parlamento. || ***To lay by***, guardar (to save). || ***To lay down***, deponer, rendir (arms). | Dejar, soltar (a burden). | Dejar a un lado (pen, tools). | Dar, ofrendar, sacrificar: *he laid down his life*, dio su vida. | Imponer, fijar, poner (conditions). | Establecer, dictar (a rule). | Sentar, formular (a principle). | Sentar, establecer (a precedent). | Sostener (an opinion). | Afirmar: *he laid down the fact that he disagreed*, afirmó que no estaba de acuerdo. | Guardar (to save). | Poner en el suelo (to put on the ground). | Acostar (to put to bed). | Echarse *or* tumbarse en el suelo (o.s.). | Apostar (to bet). | Conservar (wine). | Trazar, proyectar, fijar (a plan). | Cubrir (a surface). | Mar. Poner en un dique seco *or* en los astilleros (a ship). | Hacer el tendido de, tender (a railway). | Levantar, trazar (a map). | Dimitir (one's office). | Poner en el tapete (cards). || ***To lay in***, proveerse de, abastecerse de (to provide o.s. with). | Ahorrar (to save). | Acumular (to amass). | Comprar (to buy). || ***To lay into*** dar una paliza a (to thrash). || ***To lay off***, despedir (to dismiss). | Dejar de: *to lay off smoking*, dejar de fumar. | Dejar de utilizar (a machine). | Dejar de trabajar (to stop working). | Trazar (a line). | Extender (paint). | Mar. Alejarse. | Fam. Dejar en paz (to leave alone). | — *Lay off it!*, ¡ya está bien! || ***To lay on***, proveer de (to provide). | Instalar, poner (to install). | Conectar (to connect). | Dar, asestar, propinar (blows). | Pegar (to beat). | Imponer (taxes). | Rel. Imponer (hands). | Atacar (to attack). | Aplicar (paint). | — Fam. *To lay it on thick*, recargar *or* cargar las tintas, exagerar (to exaggerate), adular (to flatter). | *To lay one's hopes on*, cifrar sus esperanzas en. || ***To lay out***, presentar (to present): *he laid out the facts to us*, nos presentó los hechos. | Invertir, emplear (to invest money). | Desembolsar (to spend money). | Tender, extender (to stretch out). | Estirar, alargar (cable). | Exponer (to exhibit for people to see). | Trazar, levantar (a map, plan). | Disponer (to arrange in a certain order). | Servir (a meal). | Acondicionar (a mine). | Mil. Levantar (a camp). | Trazar, construir (a road). | Amortajar, preparar [un cadáver] para un entierro (a corpse). | Fam. Liquidar, cargarse, matar (to kill). | Fam. Poner fuera de combate (to knock out), hacer besar la lona (to floor a boxer). | — *To lay o.s. out*, hacer todo lo posible. || ***To lay over***, diferir (to postpone). | Parar (to stop over). || Mar. ***To lay to***, pairar. || ***To lay up***, encerrar en el garaje (a car). | Desarmar (a warship). | Atracar (a boat). | Dejar de lado (to leave aside). | Obligar a guardar cama (to confine to bed). | Enfermar (to make ill). | Guardar, almacenar (to store). | Ahorrar (to save). | Acumular, amasar (to amass). | Fig. Prepararse (troubles). | — *To be laid up*, guardar cama.

— Observ. Pret. & p. p. ***laid***.

lay [lei] pret. See LIE (meaning "echarse", etc.).

layabout [—əbaut] n. Holgazán, ana; vago, ga.

lay-by [—bai] n. Área (*f.*) de aparcamiento (on motorway). || Apartadero, *m.* (railways). || Fam. Ahorros, *m. pl.* (savings).

lay days [—'deiz] pl. n. Mar. Días (*m.*) de estadía.

layer [—ə*] n. Capa, *f.*: *layer of cream, of paint*, capa de nata, de pintura. || Capa, *f.*, lámina, *f.* (of wood, metal). || Geol. Estrato, *m.* || Gallina (*f.*) ponedora (hen). || Agr. Acodo, *m.*, mugrón, *m.* (shoot). || Ostral, *m.* (oyster bed). || Mil. Apuntador, *m.* (who lays guns). || Instalador, *m.* (who lays pipes, railway lines).

layer ['leiə*] v. tr. Agr. Acodar (a rose tree).
— V. intr. Agr. Encamarse (corn).

layerage [—ridʒ] or **layering** [—riŋ] n. Agr. Acodadura, *f.*

layette [lei'et] n. Canastilla, *f.*, ajuar (*m.*) de niño.

lay figure ['lei'figə*] n. Maniquí, *m.* & *f.* (model). || Fig. Pelele, *m.*, fantoche, *m.*

laying ['leiŋ] n. Colocación, *f.*, instalación, *f.* (placing). || Tendido, *m.* (of pipe, cable). || Puntería, *f.* (of a gun). || Puesta, *f.* (of an egg).

laying down [—'daun] n. Colocación, *f.* (placing). || Establecimiento, *m.*, asentamiento, *m.* (of a principle). || Fijación, *f.*, imposición, *f.* (of conditions). || Formulación, *f.* (of a doctrine). || Tendido, *m.* (of pipe, cable, railway). || Levantamiento, *m.*, trazado, *m.* (of a map). || Dimisión, *f.* (of one's office). || Sacrificio, *m.* (of one's life). || Mar. Colocación, (*f.*) en el dique.

laying in [—'in] n. Almacenamiento, *m.*

laying on [—'ɔn] n. Imposición, *f.* (of taxes, of hands). || Colocación, *f.*, instalación, *f.* (of gas, water). || Aplicación, *f.* (of paint).

laying out [—'aut] n. Disposición, *f.* (arrangement). || Presentación, *f.*, exposición, *f.* (exhibition). || Presentación, *f.* (of proof). || Trazado, *m.* (of a map, plan). || Mil. Levantamiento, *m.* (of a camp). || Amortajamiento, *m.* (of a corpse). || Inversión, *f.* (investment). || Gasto, *m.*, desembolso, *m.* (of money). || Fam. Liquidación, *f.* (elimination). | Puesta (*f.*) fuera de combate (of a boxer). || Print. Composición, *f.*

laying up [—'ʌp] n. Desarme, *m.* (of a warship). || Atraque, *m.* (of a boat). || Encierro (*m.*) en un garaje (of a car). || Acumulación, *f.* (of money). || Preparación, *f.* (of troubles).

layman ['leimən] n. Seglar, *m.*, lego, *m.*, laico, *m.* || Fig. Lego, *m.*, profano, *m.*
— Observ. El plural de esta palabra es *laymen*.

layoff ['leiɔf] n. Paro (*m.*) involuntario *or* forzoso (unemployment). || Despido, *m.* (dismissal). || Cierre, *m.* (closing).

layout ['leiaut] n. See LAYING OUT.

layover ['leiəuvə*] n. Escala, *f.* (travelling by plane, boat). || Parada, *f.* (travelling by train, car).

lay reader ['lei'ri:də*] n. Rel. Lego (*m.*) autorizado a dirigir oficios religiosos.

lazar ['læzə*] n. Leproso, *m.* || *Lazar house*, leprosería, *f.*

lazaret [ˌlæzə'ret] or **lazaretto** [—əu] n. Lazareto, *m.*

Lazarist ['læzərist] n. Rel. Lazarista, *m.*

Lazarus ['læzərəs] pr. n. Lázaro, *m.*

laze [leiz] n. Descanso, *m.* || *To have a laze*, holgazanear (to be idle), descansar (to rest).

laze [leiz] v. intr. Holgazanear (to be idle). || Descansar, no hacer nada (to rest).
— V. tr. *To laze away*, desperdiciar, perder [el tiempo].

lazily [—ili] adv. Perezosamente (idly). || Lentamente (slowly).

laziness [—inis] n. Pereza, *f.*, holgazanería, *f.*

lazulite ['læzjulait] n. Min. Lazulita, *f.*

lazy ['leizi] adj. Perezoso, sa; holgazán, ana; vago, ga (idle). || Lento, ta (slow): *lazy pace*, paso lento. || De pereza: *lazy days*, días de pereza.

lazybones [—ˌbəunz] n. FAM. Gandul, la; vago, ga; holgazán, ana.
lazy Susan [—ˈsu:zn] n. U. S. Bandeja (*f.*) giratoria para servir la comida en la mesa.
lea [li:] n. Prado, *m.* || Ovillo, *m.*, madeja, *f.* (of yarn).
leach [li:tʃ] n. Sustancia (*f.*) para lixiviar (substance). || Lixiviación, *f.* (leaching).
leach [li:tʃ] v. tr. Lixiviar. || *To leach away* o *out*, extraer por lixiviación.
leaching [—iŋ] n. Lixiviación, *f.*
lead [li:d] n. Correa, *f.* (for dog). || Traílla, *f.* (for hunting dog). || THEATR. Primer papel, *m.* (role): *she has the lead in this play*, tiene el primer papel en esta obra de teatro. | Primer actor, *m.* (male actor). | Primera actriz, *f.* (female actor). || MUS. Tema (*m.*) principal. || GEOL. Pasadizo, *m.* (in ice field). || MIN. Filón, *m.*, veta, *f.* || TECH. Avance, *m.* (mechanics). | Acequia, *f.* (irrigation canal). | Caz, *m.* (of a mill). || ELECTR. Cable, *m.* || Mano, *f.* (in cards): *it's my lead*, soy mano, es mi mano. || SP. Golpe (*m.*) inicial (in boxing). || Pista, *f.*, indicación, *f.* (clue): *he gave me a good lead to find a job*, me dio una buena indicación para encontrar una colocación. || Introducción, *f.* (of a newspaper article). || Noticia (*f.*) más importante (important piece of news). || Dirección, *f.*, mando, *m.* (direction). || Supremacía, *f.* (supremacy). || Ejemplo, *m.*: *to follow s.o.'s lead*, seguir el ejemplo de alguien. || Iniciativa, *f.* (initiative). || Ventaja, *f.*: *to have a lead of two kilometres*, llevar una ventaja de dos kilómetros. || Primer lugar, *m.*, cabeza, *f.*: *to be in* o *to have the lead*, ir en primer lugar *or* en cabeza. || — *To give s.o. a lead*, guiar a uno, orientar a uno. || *To give the lead*, dar el tono. || *To return the lead*, volver a jugar una carta del mismo palo (in cards). || *To take the lead*, ponerse a la cabeza (of a procession), desempeñar el primer papel (in a play), llevar la batuta (the command), tomar la delantera (in a race): *he took the lead over me*, me tomó la delantera.
lead* [li:d] v. tr. Llevar, conducir: *this road leads you to London*, esta carretera le lleva a Londres; *he led the police to the hideout*, condujo a la policía al escondrijo; *lead me to him*, lléveme a verlo; *what led me to Paris?*, ¿qué me llevó a París?; *his discovery led him to the solution of the mystery*, su descubrimiento le condujo a la solución del misterio. || Inducir a, llevar a, hacer: *what lead you to study Chinese?*, ¿qué le indujo a estudiar chino?; *what lead you to believe that?*, ¿qué te hizo creer eso? || Inducir: *he led me into error*, me indujo a error. || Guiar (to guide). || Remitir: *each reference led him to another*, cada referencia le remitía a otra. || Canalizar, encauzar (to channel). || MUS. Dirigir (an orchestra). | Ser primer violín (to play first violin). || Ir a la cabeza de (a race). || Encabezar, ir a la cabeza de (a procession). || Encabezar (a movement, an organization). || Dirigir (a country, a team, an expedition). || Estar a la cabeza de: *this country leads the world in agriculture*, este país está a la cabeza del mundo en agricultura. || Llevar la delantera a: *Peter led the field during the first half of the race*, Pedro llevó la delantera a los demás corredores durante la primera mitad de la carrera. || Llevar una ventaja *or* un adelanto de: *he led me by one hour*, me llevaba una ventaja de una hora. || Llevar: *to lead s.o. into evil ways*, llevar a alguien por mal camino. || Ganar a: *England is leading Spain, two one*, Inglaterra gana a España dos a uno. || Salir con (in cards). || Llevar (a life): *he led a dog's life*, llevaba una vida de perros. || Apuntar delante de [la pieza] (in shooting). || — *She led him a hard life*, le hizo llevar una vida imposible. || *To be easily led*, ser muy influenciable. || *To be led to the conclusion that*, llegar a la conclusión de que. || FIG. *To lead s.o. on a wild goose chase* o *to lead s.o. a merry dance*, mandar a alguien de la ceca a la meca, traerle a uno al retortero. || *To lead s.o. out to dance*, sacar a alguien a bailar. || *To lead s.o. to Christ*, convertir a alguien a la fe de Cristo. || FIG. *To lead s.o. up the garden path*, hacer tragar el anzuelo a alguien. || *To lead the field*, ir el primero, estar en cabeza (to be first), ganar (to win). || *To lead the way*, ir el primero, ir en cabeza (to go first), enseñar el camino (to show the way), dar el ejemplo (to set an example).
— V. intr. Ir delante (to go first). || Ir a la cabeza, ir en primer lugar (in a procession, race). || Ponerse delante (to go in front). || Ir, conducir, llevar (to be a way to): *this road leads to London*, esta carretera va a Londres. || Producir, causar. || Conducir: *the information led to his arrest*, la información condujo a su detención. || Ser el jefe, tener el mando, mandar (to be in command). || Dirigir (to direct). || Salir (in cards). || SP. Iniciar (in boxing). | Ir en cabeza (in a race). | Ganar, ir ganando: *Scotland is leading two nil*, Escocia gana dos a cero; *to be leading two sets to one*, ganar dos juegos a uno. || — *To lead for the defence*, ser el abogado principal de la defensa. || *To lead to nothing*, no llevar a nada *or* a ninguna parte.
— ***To lead astray***, llevar por mal camino. || ***To lead away***, llevar (to take away). | FIG. Apartar (to keep away from). || ***To lead back***, volver a llevar: *lead the horse back to the stable*, vuelve a llevar el caballo a la cuadra. | — *This road leads back to London*, por esta carretera se vuelve a Londres. || ***To lead in***, hacer entrar en (to bring in). | ELECTR. Traer (current). || ***To lead off***, empezar (to start). | Abrir (the conversation). | Entablar (negotiations). | SP. Abrir el juego. | Salir (cards). | Salir de: *the street leads off the main road*, la calle sale de la carretera principal. | Comunicar con: *the room leads off the kitchen*, la habitación comunica con la cocina. | Llevarse (to take away). || ***To lead on***, llevar, conducir (to take forward). | Seducir a (to seduce). | Animar a, incitar a (to encourage). | FIG. Engañar (to deceive). | *To lead s.o. on to believe that*, hacer creer a alguien que. || ***To lead up to***, llevar a, conducir a (to cause). | Preparar el terreno para (to prepare the way for). | — *What are you leading up to?*, ¿a dónde quiere Ud. llegar?

— OBSERV. Pret. & p. p. ***led***.

lead [led] n. Plomo, *m.* (metal and objects made of it). || Mina, *f.* (of a pencil). || MAR. Sonda, *f.*, escandallo, *m.* || PRINT. Regleta, *f.* || Plomo, *m.*, tiras (*f. pl.*) de plomo (in window). || — FIG. *It is as heavy as lead*, pesa más que el plomo. || *Red lead*, minio, *m.* (paint). || FAM. *To fill s.o. full of lead*, acribillar a uno a balazos. | *To swing the lead*, hacerse el remolón. || *White lead*, albayalde, *m.*
lead [led] v. tr. Forrar con plomo (to line). || Cubrir con plomo (to cover). || Emplomar (a window). || PRINT. Regletear, interlinear, espaciar.
leaden [ˈledn] adj. De plomo, plúmbeo, a (of lead). || Plomizo, za (colour). || FIG. De plomo, pesado, da (dull). | Desanimado, da (depressed). || — *A leaden sky*, un cielo grisáceo *or* plomizo. || *A leaden weight*, un peso enorme. || *His pace was leaden*, andaba con paso pesado.
leader [ˈli:də*] n. Guía, *m.* & *f.* (guide). || Jefe, *m.* & *f.*, dirigente, *m.* & *f.* (who organizes or directs). || Cabecilla, *m.* (of thieves, a gang, rebels). || Jefe, *m.*, líder, *m.* (in politics). || Caudillo, *m.* (of military forces). || Conductor, *m.* (of masses). || Primero, ra (first person of a moving group). || JUR. Abogado (*m.*) principal. || MUS. Primer violín, *m.* (first violin). | Director, *m.* (of a band). || Editorial, *m.*, artículo (*m.*) de fondo (in newspapers). || TECH. Conducto, *m.* || MIN. Filón, *m.* || Guía, *f.*, caballo (*m.*) delantero (in a team of horses). || COMM. Artículo (*m.*) de reclamo. || BOT. Brote (*m.*) terminal. || Sotileza, *f.* (of a fishing line). || SP. Líder, *m.* || — Pl. PRINT. Puntos (*m.*) conductores para guiar la vista. || *He's a born leader*, nació para mandar.
leadership [—ʃip] n. Dirección, *f.*, mando, *m.*: *to have powers of leadership*, tener dotes de mando; *under the leadership of*, bajo la dirección de; *to take over the leadership*, tomar el mando. || Jefatura, *f.*, liderato, *m.*, liderazgo, *m.* (in politics). || Caudillaje, *m.* (of military forces).
lead-in [ˈli:dˈin] n. RAD. Bajada (*f.*) de antena. || Introducción, *f.*, entrada, *f.* (introduction).
— Adj. ELECTR. De entrada.
leading [li:diŋ] adj. Que va a la cabeza, que va en cabeza, que encabeza: *the leading car of a race*, el coche que va a la cabeza de la carrera *or* que encabeza la carrera. || Primero, ra: *the leading runners are now in sight*, los primeros corredores están a la vista ahora. || TECH. Conductor, ra (wire). || MAR. Que impulsa (wind). || AUT. Delantero, ra: *leading axle*, eje delantero. || AVIAT. De ataque: *leading edge*, borde de ataque. || COMM. De propaganda, de reclamo (goods). || MIL. De vanguardia: *leading column*, columna de vanguardia. || FIG. Dominante (idea). | Notable, destacado, da; eminente, importante (people). || JUR. Que sienta jurisprudencia (case). | Principal (counsel). || Primero, ra; principal (character, part in theatre). || — *Leading article*, artículo (*m.*) de fondo, editorial, *m.* || THEATR. *Leading lady*, primera dama, primera actriz. || *Leading man*, primer galán, primer actor (theatre), jefe, *m.*, dirigente, *m.* (chief). || *Leading note* o *tone*, nota (*f.*) sensible. || *Leading power*, fuerza (*f.*) motriz. || *Leading question*, pregunta (*f.*) hecha de tal manera que sugiere la respuesta deseada. || *Leading strings*, andadores, *m.*
— N. Conducción, *f.* || Dirección, *f.* (of a company, etc.). || Mando, *m.* (command).
leading [ˈlediŋ] n. Emplomado, *m.*
lead line [ˈledˌlain] n. MAR. Sonda, *f.*
leadoff [ˈli:dˈɔf] n. U. S. Comienzo, *m.*, principio, *m.*
lead pencil [ˈledˈpensl] n. Lápiz (*m.*) de mina, lapicero, *m.*
lead poisoning [ˈled pɔizniŋ] n. MED. Saturnismo, *m.*
leadsman [ˈledzmən] n. MAR. Sondeador, *m.*

— OBSERV. El plural de *leadsman* es *leadsmen*.

leaf [li:f] n. BOT. Hoja, *f.* (of tree, stem): *deciduous leaf*, hoja caduca; *dead leaf*, hoja seca; *to come into leaf*, echar hojas. | Pétalo, *m.* (of flower). || Hoja, *f.* (of paper). || Página, *f.* (of a book). || Hoja (*f.*) abatible (of table). || Hoja, *f.*, batiente, *m.* (of door, shutter, etc.). || Lonja, *f.* (of bacon). || TECH. Hoja, *f.* (of spring, metals). || — *A tree in leaf*, un árbol con hojas *or* cubierto de hojas. || *Gold leaf*, pan (*m.*) de oro, oro batido. || *Leaf bud*, yema, *f.* [de un árbol]. || *Leaf tobacco*, tabaco (*m.*) en rama. || *Loose* o *mobile leaf*, hoja suelta *or* volante. || *Tea leaves*, posos, *m.* (dregs), hojas de té (of the plant). || FIG. *To shake like a leaf*, temblar como un azogado. | *To take a leaf out of s.o.'s book*, seguir el ejemplo *or* tomar ejemplo de alguien. | *To turn over a new leaf*, hacer borrón y cuenta nueva, volver la hoja, empezar nueva vida.

— OBSERV. El plural de *leaf* es *leaves*.

leaf [li:f] v. tr. *To leaf through a book*, hojear un libro.
— V. intr. Echar hojas.
leafage [—idʒ] n. BOT. Follaje, *m.*, fronda, *f.*
leafless [—lis] adj. Deshojado, da; sin hojas.
leaflet [—lit] n. Folleto, *m.* (pamphlet). || Prospecto, *m.* (publicity sheet). || BOT. Foliolo, *m.*, hojuela, *f.* || *Propaganda leaflet*, octavilla, *f.* (single sheet), folleto (*m.*) de propaganda (booklet).
leaf mould (U. S. **leaf mold**) [—məuld] n. AGR. Mantillo, *m.*
leaf spring [—spriŋ] n. TECH. Ballesta, *f.*
leafstalk [—stɔ:k] n. BOT. Pecíolo, *m.*
leafy [—i] adj. Frondoso, sa.
league [li:g] n. Liga, *f.* (sporting). || Asociación, *f.* (political association). || Liga, *f.* (alliance). || Legua, *f.* (measure of distance). || — *Hanseatic League*, Liga Hanseática. || *Holy League*, Santa Liga. || *League of Nations*, Sociedad (*f.*) de Naciones. || *To be in league with s.o.*, estar asociado con alguien (in business), estar conchabado con alguien (secret agreement). || *To form a league against*, aliarse contra.
league [li:g] v. intr. *To league together*, unirse, aliarse, coligarse.
— V. tr. Unir, aliar.
leaguer [—ə*] n. Miembro (*m.*) de una liga.
leak [li:k] n. Vía (*f.*) de agua (in a boat): *the boat has a leak*, el buque tiene una vía de agua. || Gotera, *f.*: *there is a leak in the roof*, hay una gotera en el tejado. || Agujero, *m.* (hole). || Escape, *m.*, salida, *f.*, pérdida, *f.*, fuga, *f.* (of gas or liquid). || Pérdida, *f.* (loss). || FIG. Fuga, *f.* (of money). | Filtración, *f.* (of secret information). || *To spring a leak*, empezar a hacer agua, hacerse una vía de agua (a boat), tener un escape (a pipe).
leak [li:k] v. intr. Hacer agua (a boat). || Salirse (a container): *the pot is leaking*, la olla se sale. || Tener un escape, perder (a pipe). || Gotear (a roof). || Hacer agua, dejar entrar el agua (shoes). || Salirse (liquid). || Salirse, escaparse (gas). || FIG. Filtrarse (información). || *To leak out*, trascender (news), filtrarse (secret information), descubrirse (to be discovered).
— V. tr. Dejar salir, dejar escapar (liquid, gas). || Rezumar (to exude): *to leak water*, rezumar agua. || FIG. Pasar: *to leak information to the enemy*, pasar información al enemigo.
leakage [—idʒ] n. See LEAK. || ELECTR. *Earth leakage*, pérdida (*f.*) a tierra.
leakproof [—pru:f] adj. Estanco, ca; hermético, ca.
leaky [—i] adj. Que hace agua, que tiene vías de agua (boat). || Que deja entrar el agua (shoe). || Que tiene goteras (roof). || Agujereado, da (with holes). || Que tiene escapes, que se sale (container, pipe). || FIG. Que tiene fallos, que falla (memory). | Indiscreto, ta (person).
lean [li:n] adj. Magro, gra; sin grasa (meat). || Flaco, ca; delgado, da (person). || Enjuto, ta (face). || Frugal (diet). || Pobre (soil). || Malo, la; escaso, sa (crop). || Malo, la: *a lean year for farmers*, un mal año para los labradores. || — *Lean years*, años (*m. pl.*) de escasez, vacas flacas. || *To grow lean*, enflaquecer.
— N. Carne (*f.*) magra, carne (*f.*) sin grasa, magro, *m.* (meat). || Inclinación, *f.* (of a wall, etc.). || *On the lean*, inclinado, da.
lean* [li:n] v. intr. Inclinarse, ladearse: *the lamppost leans dangerously*, el farol se inclina peligrosamente. || FIG. Inclinarse: *he leans towards communism*, se inclina hacia el comunismo. || — *Do not lean out of the window*, prohibido asomarse al exterior (in trains). || *To lean against* o *to lean back against*, apoyarse en *or* contra. || *To lean back in a chair*, reclinarse *or* respaldarse en una silla. || *To lean forward*, inclinarse. || *To lean on*, apoyarse en: *to lean on the table*, apoyarse en la mesa. || FIG. *To lean on s.o.*, presionar a uno. | *To lean on s.o. for support*, contar con el apoyo de uno. || *To lean out of*, asomarse a: *to lean out of the window*, asomarse a la ventana. || FIG. *To lean over backwards to*, no escatimar esfuerzos para. || *To lean over s.o.*, inclinarse sobre uno. || *To lean to*, inclinarse hacia *or* a.
— V. tr. Inclinar (to incline). || Apoyar, poner: *lean it against the wall for a moment*, apóyalo contra la pared un minuto; *lean your head on my shoulder*, apoya la cabeza en mi hombro. || *To lean one's elbows on the table*, acodarse en la mesa, apoyar los codos en la mesa. || *To lean one's head back*, echar la cabeza hacia atrás.

— OBSERV. Pret. & p. p. ***leaned, leant.***

leaning [—iŋ] n. Inclinación, *f.* || FIG. Inclinación, *f.*, propensión, *f.* (sympathy). | Predilección, *f.* [*to, towards*, por] (liking). | Tendencia, *f.* (tendency).
— Adj. Inclinado, da: *the leaning tower of Pisa*, la torre inclinada de Pisa.
leanness [—nis] n. Flaqueza, *f.*, delgadez, *f.* (of a person). || Magrez, *f.* (of meat). || FIG. Escasez, *f.*, carestía, *f.* (shortage).
leant [lent] pret. & p. p. See LEAN.
lean-to [ˈli:ntu:] n. Cobertizo, *m.*
— Adj. De una sola vertiente (roof).
— OBSERV. El plural de esta palabra es *lean-tos*.

leap [li:p] n. Salto, *m.*, brinco, *m.* (jump): *he cleared the stream with one leap*, cruzó el arroyo de un salto. || Obstáculo (*m.*) que hay que salvar (obstacle). || FIG. Salto, *m.*, paso, *m.*: *a great leap forwards*, un gran paso hacia adelante. | Cambio, *m.* (change). | Vuelco, *m.*: *his heart gave a leap*, el corazón le dio un vuelco. || — FIG. *A leap in the dark*, un salto en el vacío. | *By leaps and bounds*, a pasos agigantados. || *Leap day*, día (*m.*) intercalar (29th of February). || *Leap year*, año bisiesto.
leap* [li:p] v. intr. Saltar (to jump). || Dar un salto (to give a jump). || Echarse, lanzarse: *she leapt into his arms*, se echó en sus brazos. || Dar un vuelco (the heart). || — *To leap about*, dar saltos. || *To leap at*, saltarle [a uno] encima (s.o.), no dejar escapar, aprovechar (an offer, an opportunity). || *To leap down*, bajar de un salto. || *To leap for joy*, dar botes *or* saltos de alegría. || *To leap off*, bajar de un salto de. || *To leap on to*, subir de un salto a. || *To leap out of*, saltar de. || *To leap over*, saltar por encima de, salvar de un salto. || *To leap to one's feet*, ponerse de pie de un salto. || *To leap up*, pegar un salto, saltar (a person), elevarse, brotar (a flame).
— V. tr. Saltar por encima de, salvar de un salto (to jump over). || Hacer saltar (a horse).

— OBSERV. Pret. & p. p. ***leaped, leapt.***

leaper [—ə*] n. Saltador, ra.
leapfrog [—frɔg] n. Pídola, *f.*, piola, *f.*: *to play leapfrog*, jugar a la pídola.
leapfrog [—frɔg] v. intr. Jugar a la pídola.
— V. tr. Saltar por encima de (to jump over).
leaping [—iŋ] adj. Saltador, ra.
— N. Salto, *m.*
leapt [lept] pret. & p. p. See LEAP.
learn* [lə:n] v. tr. Aprender: *to learn to swim*, aprender a nadar; *how long have you been learning Spanish?*, ¿cuánto tiempo llevas aprendiendo español? || Instruirse [*about*, en] (to instruct o.s.). || Enterarse de, saber (to find out about): *I have not yet learned if everything went right*, no sé todavía si todo ha ido bien. || — *To learn by heart*, aprender de memoria. || *To learn how to do sth.*, aprender a hacer algo. || *To learn one's lesson*, aprenderse la lección; escarmentar. || *To learn sth. up*, esforzarse por aprender algo.
— V. intr. Aprender. || — *I have learnt better since then*, ahora me sé la lección. || *It's never too late to learn*, cada día se aprende algo nuevo. || *To learn from experience*, aprender por experiencia. || *To learn from one's mistakes*, aprender por experiencia. || *To learn from other people's mistakes*, escarmentar en cabeza ajena. || *To learn of*, enterarse de, saber (to find out about), saber de, conocer: *have you learnt of any good restaurant around here?*, ¿conoce algún buen restaurante por aquí?

— OBSERV. Pret. & p. p. ***learned, learnt.***

learned [—id] adj. Instruido, da; culto, ta (educated). || Sabio, bia (wise). || Erudito, ta (erudite). || Docto, ta (form of address): *my learned friend*, mi docto colega. || Liberal (profession). || Cultural (society). || *Learned word*, palabra culta.
learner [ˈlə:nə*] n. Principiante, *m.* & *f.* (beginner). || Aprendiz, za (apprentice, driver). || Estudiante, *m.* & *f.* (student). || *To be a quick learner*, aprender rápidamente.
learner driver [ˈlə:nə* ˈdraivə*] n. Conductor (*m.*) principiante, aprendiz (*m.*) de conductor, aprendiza (*f.*) de conductora.
learning [ˈlə:niŋ] n. Saber, *m.*, erudición, *f.*, conocimientos, *m. pl.*, conocimiento, *m.* (knowledge): *a man of great learning*, un hombre de gran saber. || Estudio, *m.* (study). || *Seat of learning*, centro (*m.*) de estudios.
learnt [lə:nt] pret. & p. p. See LEARN.
lease [li:s] n. JUR. Arrendamiento, *m.*, arriendo, *m.* (contract). | Contrato (*m.*) de arrendamiento (document when leasing land). | Contrato (*m.*) de inquilinato *or* de alquiler (document when leasing a house, etc.). | Período (*m.*) de arrendamiento (period). || — FIG. *To give s.o. a new lease of life*, dar nuevas fuerzas a uno. || *To let out on lease*, dar en arriendo, arrendar. || FIG. *To take on a new lease of life*, empezar una nueva vida. || *To take on lease*, tomar en arrendamiento *or* en arriendo, arrendar.
lease [li:s] v. tr. JUR. Arrendar, dar *o* ceder en arriendo (to let out). | Arrendar, tomar en arriendo (to take on lease). | Alquilar (to rent, to hire).
leasehold [—həuld] adj. Arrendado, da; en arriendo.
— N. JUR. Propiedad (*f.*) *or* casa (*f.*) arrendada (property). | Arrendamiento, *m.* (right of holding property).
leaseholder [—həuldə*] n. Arrendatario, ria.
lease-lend [— lend] n. Préstamo (*m.*) y arriendo.
leash [li:ʃ] n. Correa, *f.* (for dogs, etc.). || Traílla, *f.* (for hunting dogs). || Pihuela, *f.* (for a hawk). || — *The dog is on the leash*, el perro está atado. || FIG. *To hold in leash*, mantener a raya, dominar. | *To strain at the leash*, procurar sacudir el yugo.
leash [li:ʃ] v. tr. Atar (to tie up). || Poner la correa a (a dog). || Atraillar, poner la traílla a (hunting dogs).
leasing [ˈli:siŋ] n. Arrendamiento, *m.*, alquiler, *m.* || "Leasing", *m.* [arrendamiento con opción de compra].

least [li:st] adj. Menor, [más] mínimo, ma; más pequeño, ña: *he hasn't got the least chance*, no tiene la más mínima posibilidad; *the least offence is heavily punished*, el menor delito es severamente castigado; *the least noise startles her*, el ruido más pequeño le asusta. || Menor (smallest in size, amount, importance, age). || — *Not the least bit*, en absoluto: *I am not the least bit annoyed*, no estoy enfadado en absoluto. || MATH. *The least common multiple*, el mínimo común múltiplo.
— N. Lo menos: *that is the least you could do*, eso es lo menos que podrías hacer. || El menor, la menor, el más pequeño, la más pequeña: *that is the least of my problems*, ése es el menor de mis problemas. || — *At least*, por lo menos: *he is at least 40*, tiene por lo menos 40 años; por lo menos, al menos: *you could at least say thank you*, al menos podrías dar las gracias. || *At the very least*, como mínimo. || *In the least*, en lo más mínimo. || *Not in the least*, nada, en absoluto: *it does not matter in the least*, no importa en absoluto. || *That's the least of my worries*, esto es lo que menos me preocupa. || *To say the least*, para no decir otra cosa peor.
— Adv. Menos: *the least possible*, lo menos posible; *I am the least able to do it*, yo soy el que menos puede hacerlo; *the least happy*, el menos contento. || — *He least of all*, él menos que nadie. || *Least of all*, sobre todo, y menos que a nadie: *don't tell anyone, least of all your mother*, no se lo digas a nadie, sobre todo a tu madre; menos: *he deserves it least of all*, él es el que menos se lo merece. || *Least of all would I want to criticize you*, no tengo la más mínima intención de criticarle.

leastways [—weiz] or **leastwise** [—waiz] adv. Por lo menos (at least).

leat [li:t] n. Saetín, *m.* (of a mill).

leather [ˈleðə*] n. Piel, *f.*, cuero, *m.*: *a leather coat, belt*, un abrigo, un cinturón de cuero; *leather gloves, bags*, guantes, bolsos de piel. || Gamuza, *f.* (for washing cars, windows, etc.). || SP. FAM. Cuero, *m.*, pelota, *f.* (ball). || — *Fancy leather goods*, tafiletería, *f.*, marroquinería, *f.* || *Leather bottle*, bota, *f.*, odre, *m.* || *Patent leather*, charol, *m.*
— Adj. De cuero, de piel: *leather case*, estuche de cuero.

leather [ˈleðə*] v. tr. Cubrir con cuero (to cover with leather). || FAM. Zurrar (to tan s.o.'s hide).

leatherback [—bæk] n. ZOOL. Laúd, *m.* (marine turtle).

leather-bound [—baund] adj. Encuadernado en cuero.

leather dresser [—ˈdresə*] n. Curtidor (*m.*) de pieles.

leather dressing [—ˈdresiŋ] n. Curtido (*m.*) de pieles.

leatherette [ˌleðəˈret] n. Similicuero, *m.* (imitation leather).

leathern [ˈleðə:n] adj. De cuero (of leather). || Parecido al cuero (like leather).

leatherneck [ˈleðənek] n. U. S. FAM. Soldado (*m.*) de infantería de marina.

leatheroid [ˈleðərɔid] n. Similicuero, *m.*, cuero (*m.*) artificial.

leathery [ˈleðəri] adj. Parecido al cuero (like leather). || FIG. Correoso, sa (meat). | Curtido, da (skin).

leave [li:v] n. Permiso, *m.* (permission): *to beg leave to*, pedir permiso para; *by your leave*, con su permiso. || MIL. Permiso, *m.*, licencia, *f.*: *to be on leave*, estar de permiso. || — *Leave of absence*, permiso para ausentarse. || *On ticket of leave*, en libertad condicional. || FIG. *To have taken leave of one's senses*, haber perdido la cabeza. | *To take French leave*, despedirse a la francesa. || *To take leave of s.o.* o *to take one's leave of s.o.*, despedirse de alguien. || FIG. *Without so much as a by your leave*, sin pedir permiso

leave* [li:v] v. intr. Irse, marcharse: *he is leaving tomorrow*, se va mañana. || Salir: *he is leaving for Madrid*, sale para Madrid; *the train is leaving*, el tren sale.
— V. tr. Dejarse (to forget): *he left his lighter in the bar*, se dejó el encendedor en el bar. || Dejar: *to leave a tip*, dejar una propina; *to leave things lying about*, dejar las cosas desparramadas; *leave what you don't like*, deja lo que no te guste; *I leave it to your sense of fairness*, lo dejo a su sentido de la justicia; *leave it until tomorrow*, déjalo para mañana; *leave the door open*, deja la puerta abierta; *let's leave it at that*, dejemos las cosas así, dejémoslo así; *she left a note for him*, le dejó una nota. || Salir de (to go out of): *he left the cinema*, salió del cine. || Dejar: *I must leave you*, debo dejaros. || Marcharse de, irse de (home, job). || Dejar, abandonar: *to leave one's wife*, abandonar a su mujer. || JUR. Legar, dejar (in a will). || — *I leave it to you*, lo dejo en sus manos. || *Leave me alone!*, ¡déjame en paz! || *Leave that radio alone*, deja de tocar la radio. || *Leave your nails alone*, deja de morderte las uñas. || *Take it or leave it*, lo toma o lo deja. || *To be left*, quedar (to remain): *how many are there left?*, ¿cuántos quedan?; quedarse (s.o.). || *To have left*, quedarle a uno: *I have four left*, me quedan cuatro. || *To leave be*, dejar en paz (to stop annoying). || *To leave go* o *to leave hold of*, soltar. || *To leave much to be desired*, dejar mucho que desear. || *To leave room for*, dejar sitio para (physically), dejar lugar para *or* a (hope, doubt). || *To leave school*, salir del colegio: *what time do you leave school in the afternoon?*, ¿a qué hora sales del colegio por la tarde?; dejar de ir al colegio: *some people leave school at 16*, algunos dejan de ir al colegio a los 16 años; dejar el colegio, salirse del colegio: *his father's death forced him to leave school*, la muerte de su padre le obligó a salirse del colegio. || *To leave the road*, salirse de la carretera. || *To leave the table*, levantarse de la mesa. || *To leave the track* o *the rails*, salirse de la vía, descarrilar. || *To leave to chance*, dejar a la suerte, dejar en manos del destino. || *To leave undone*, no hacer; no terminar. || MATH. *Two from six leaves four*, seis menos dos son cuatro.
— ***To leave about***, dejar tirado, dejar rodando, no dejar en su sitio: *why do you always leave your clothes about?*, ¿por qué deja siempre la ropa tirada? | Dejar por medio: *you shouldn't leave so much money about*, no debería dejar tanto dinero por medio. || ***To leave aside***, omitir, dejar de lado, prescindir de (to omit). | Olvidar (to forget). || ***To leave behind***, dejar atrás: *slow down, you are leaving me behind*, ve más despacio, me estás dejando atrás. | Olvidarse, dejarse: *wait, I've left my umbrella behind*, espera, que me he olvidado el paraguas. | Dejar: *this leaves a nasty smell behind*, esto deja mal olor. || ***To leave off***, dejar de: *to leave off smoking*, dejar de fumar. | No ponerse: *leave your coat off*, no te pongas el abrigo. | Pararse (rain). | Acabar: *where did we leave off?*, ¿dónde acabamos? || ***To leave out***, omitir, saltarse (to omit). | Dejar fuera (washing, etc.). | Dejar a mano: *I'll leave the records out for you*, te dejaré los discos a mano. | Excluir (to exclude). || ***To leave over***, dejar, aplazar (to postpone). | — *To be left over*, sobrar (to be over): *there are ten left over*, sobran diez.

— OBSERV. Pret. & p. p. ***left***.

leave [li:v] v. intr. Echar hojas.

leaved [li:vd] adj. Cubierto de hojas (in leaf). || De hojas (door). || Con largueros (table).

leaven [ˈlevn] n. Levadura, *f.* || FIG. Estímulo, *m.* (stimulus). | Fermento, *m.*, germen, *m.*

leaven [ˈlevn] v. tr. Leudar (dough). || FIG. Impregnar (*with*, de) [to spread through]. | Transformar, modificar (to change).

leavening [—iŋ] n. Fermentación, *f.* || Levadura, *f.* (leaven).

leaves [li:vz] pl. n. See LEAF.

leave-taking [li:vˈteikiŋ] n. Despedida, *f.*

leaving [ˈli:viŋ] n. Salida, *f.* (departure). || — Pl. Restos, *m.*, sobras, *f.*

Lebanese [ˌlebəˈni:z] adj./n. Libanés, esa.

Lebanon [ˈlebənən] pr. n. GEOGR. Líbano, *m.*

lecher [ˈletʃə*] n. Lascivo, va; libertino, na.

lecherous [ˈletʃərəs] adj. Lascivo, va; libertino, na; lujurioso, sa.

lechery [ˈletʃəri] n. Lascivia, *f.*, lujuria, *f.*, libertinaje, *m.* (lewdness).

lectern [ˈlektə:n] n. Atril, *m.*, facistol, *m.*

lection [ˈlekʃən] n. REL. Lección, *f.*

lector [ˈlektɔ:*] n. REL. Lector, *m.*

lectorate [ˈlektəreit] n. REL. Lectorado, *m.*

lecture [ˈlektʃə*] n. Conferencia, *f.*: *lecture room*, sala de conferencias; *a lecture on birth control*, una conferencia sobre la regulación de nacimientos. || Clase, *f.*, curso, *m.* (in University): *to attend lectures on*, dar clases de, seguir un curso de. || FIG. Sermón, *m.*, reprimenda, *f.* (reprimand): *to read s.o. a lecture*, echar un sermón a uno.

lecture [ˈlektʃə*] v. intr. Dar una conferencia: *to lecture on space travel*, dar una conferencia sobre viajes espaciales. || Dar conferencias (to give lectures). || Dar clase *or* clases (in University). || Hablar (to speak): *I haven't heard anyone lecture so well*, nunca oí hablar a nadie tan bien.
— V. tr. Dar una conferencia *or* conferencias a. || Dar clase *or* clases a (in University). || FIG. Sermonear a, echar un sermón *or* una reprimenda a (to reprimand).

lecture hall [—hɔ:l] n. Aula, *f.* (classroom). || Sala (*f.*) de conferencias.

lecturer [—rə*] n. Profesor, ra (in University): *assistant lecturer*, profesor adjunto. || Conferenciante, *m.* & *f.* [*Amer.*, conferencista, *m.* & *f.*] (who gives lectures).

lectureship [—ʃip] n. Cargo (*m.*) de profesor, cátedra, *f.* (in a college or university).

led [led] pret. & p. p. See LEAD.

ledge [ledʒ] n. Saliente, *m.* (part which juts out). || Repisa, *f.*, anaquel, *m.* (shelf). || Antepecho, *m.* (of a window). || ARCH. Cornisa, *f.* (cornice). || MIN. Vena, *f.*, veta, *f.* (stratum rich in ore). || Banco (*m.*) de arrecifes (reef).

ledger [—ə*] n. COMM. Libro (*m.*) mayor (in book-keeping). || Lápida (*f.*) sepulcral (tombstone). || Travesaño (*m.*) de andamio (of a scaffold).

ledger line [—lain] n. MUS. Línea (*f.*) suplementaria.

ledger paper [—ˈpeipə*] n. Papel (*m.*) de cuentas.

lee [li:] adj. MAR. De sotavento, a sotavento.
— N. MAR. Sotavento, *m.* || FIG. Abrigo, *m.* (shelter): *in the lee of*, al abrigo de.

lee board [—bɔ:d] n. MAR. Orza (*f.*) de deriva.

leech [li:tʃ] n. Sanguijuela, *f.* (animal). || FIG. Parásito, *m.*, sanguijuela, *f.* (parasite). | Lapa, *f.* (clinging person). || MAR. Grátil, *m.*, gratil, *m.* (of a sail). || (Ant.). Médico, *m.*

leek [li:k] n. BOT. Puerro, *m.*

leer [liə*] n. Mirada (*f.*) de reojo lasciva (of lust). || Mirada (*f.*) de soslayo maliciosa (malicious).

leer [liə*] v. intr. Echar una mirada de soslayo *or* de reojo, mirar de soslayo *or* de reojo [de manera lasciva o maliciosa].

leering [—riŋ] adj. De reojo, de soslayo (glance). || Lascivo, va; impúdico, ca (lustful).

leery [—ri] adj. U. S. Suspicaz; receloso, sa (suspicious). | Malicioso, sa; astuto, ta (knowing).

lees [li:z] pl. n. Heces, *f.*, poso, *m. sing.* (dregs). || FIG. Hez, *f. sing.* (of society). || FIG. *To drain* o *to drink the cup to the lees*, apurar el cáliz hasta las heces.

lee side [ˈli:said] n. MAR. Banda (*f.*) de sotavento, sotavento, *m.*

leeward [ˈli:wəd] adj. MAR. De sotavento, a sotavento.
— Adv. MAR. A sotavento.
— N. MAR. Sotavento, *m.*

Leeward Islands [—ˈailəndz] pl. pr. n. GEOGR. Islas (*f.*) de Sotavento.

leeway [ˈli:wei] n. MAR. AVIAT. Deriva, *f.* (drift). || FIG. Atraso, *m.*, atrasos, *m. pl.*: *to have a lot of leeway to make up*, tener muchos atrasos que recuperar. | Campo, *m.*, libertad, *f.* (for action). | Margen, *m.* (spare time, spare money). || MAR. *To make leeway*, abatir, derivar.

left [left] pret. & p. p. See LEAVE.

left [left] adj. Izquierdo, da: *the left bank of the river*, la orilla izquierda del río; *the left hand*, la mano izquierda; *the left side*, el lado izquierdo. || Izquierdista, de izquierdas (in politics). || *Left hook*, gancho (*m.*) de izquierda (in boxing).
— Adv. A *or* hacia la izquierda: *to turn left*, torcer a la izquierda.
— N. Izquierda, *f.*: *to turn to the left*, torcer a la izquierda; *on your left*, a su izquierda. || Mano (*f.*) izquierda, izquierda, *f.*, zurda, *f.* (left hand). || Pie (*m.*) izquierdo (left foot). || Directo (*m.*) de izquierda, izquierdazo, *m.* (in boxing). || Izquierda, *f.* (in politics). || *On the left*, a la izquierda: *a little further down on the left*, un poco más abajo a la izquierda; por la izquierda: *to drive on the left*, conducir por la izquierda.

left-hand [—hænd] adj. Izquierdo, da; de la izquierda. || — *Left-hand drive*, conducción (*f.*) a la izquierda. || *Left-hand side*, izquierda, *f.*, lado izquierdo.

left-handed [—ˈhændid] adj. Zurdo, da; zocato, ta (person). || Para zurdos: *left-handed golf club*, palo de golf para zurdos. || FIG. Torpe, desmañado, da (clumsy). | Ambiguo, gua; equívoco, ca (compliments). || FIG. *Left-handed marriage*, matrimonio por detrás de la iglesia.
— Adv. Con la mano izquierda.

left-hander [—ˈhændə*] n. Zurdo, da; zocato, ta (left-handed person). || Directo (*m.*) de izquierda, izquierdazo, *m.* (blow with the left hand).

Leftism [ˈleftizəm] n. Izquierdismo, *m.*

Leftist [ˈleftist] adj. Izquierdista, de izquierdas.
— N. Izquierdista, *m.* & *f.*

left luggage [ˈleftˈlʌgidʒ] n. Equipaje (*m.*) en consigna.

left-luggage office [ˈleftˈlʌgidʒ,ɔfis] n. Consigna, *f.*

leftover [ˈleft,əuvə:*] adj. Restante, sobrante.

leftovers [—z] pl. n. Sobras, *f.*, restos, *m.*

leftward [ˈleftwəd] adj./adv. Hacia la izquierda.

left wing [ˈleftˈwiŋ] n. Izquierda, *f.* (in politics). || SP. Extremo (*m.*) izquierda (in football, hockey). | Ala (*f.*) izquierda (in rugby).

left-wing [ˈleftˈwiŋ] adj. Izquierdista, de izquierdas: *left-wing policy*, política izquierdista.

left winger [—ə*] n. Izquierdista, *m.* & *f.* (in politics). || SP. Extremo (*m.*) izquierda (in football, hockey). | Ala (*f.*) izquierda (in rugby).

lefty [ˈlefti] n. FAM. Izquierdista, *m.* & *f.* (in politics). | Zurdo, da; zocato, ta (left-handed person).

leg [leg] n. Pierna, *f.* (of a person). || Pata, *f.* (of animals, etc.). || Pata, *f.*, pie, *m.* (of furniture). || Soporte, *m.* (support). || Pernera, *f.* (of trousers). || Caña, *f.* (of boots). || CULIN. Pierna, *f.* (joint): *a leg of lamb*, una pierna de cordero. | Muslo, *m.* (of chicken). | Anca, *f.* (of frogs). | Pernil, *m.* (of venison, pork). || Pierna, *f.* (of compass, triangle, etc.). || Cateto, *m.* (of right-angled triangle). || Etapa, *f.* (stage of a journey, race). || MAR. Trayecto, *m.* (distance covered). | Bordada, *f.* (in sailing). || — SP. *Leg before wicket*, eliminación (*f.*) del bateador por obstrucción de la pelota con la pierna. || *Leg of pork*, jamón, *m.* || FIG. *Not to have a leg to stand on*, carecer de fundamento, no tener en qué apoyarse. | *To be on one's* [o *its*] *last legs*, estar dando las diez de últimas, estar en las últimas. | *To find one's legs*, recobrarse, levantarse (after a setback), establecerse (to establish o.s.). || *To give s.o. a leg up*, ayudar a alguien a subir (to get on a horse, etc.), echar una mano a alguien (to help). || FIG. *To have been on one's legs all day*, no haberse sentado en todo el día, no haber tenido un momento de respiro en todo el día. | *To have the legs of s.o.*, correr más rápido que alguien. | *To keep one's legs*, mantenerse de pie. | *To pull s.o.'s leg*, tomarle el pelo a uno. | *To run as fast as one's legs will carry one*, correr a toda mecha *or* a todo gas. | *To set s.o. on his legs*, ayudar a alguien a levantar cabeza. || FIG. FAM. *To shake a leg*, darse prisa, volar (to hurry up), mover el esqueleto, bailar (to dance). | *To show a leg*, levantarse de la cama. || FIG. *To stand on one's own legs*, valerse por sí mismo. | *To stretch one's legs*, estirar las piernas (to take a walk). | *To take to one's legs*, poner pies en polvorosa. | *To walk s.o. off his legs*, dejar agotado a alguien. || *Wooden leg*, pata de palo.

leg [leg] v. tr. *To leg it*, ir a pie, ir a pata, ir andando (to walk), largarse (to run).

legacy [ˈlegəsi] n. Legado, *m.*, herencia, *f.* || FIG. Patrimonio, *m.*, herencia, *f.*

legal [ˈli:gəl] adj. Jurídico, ca: *legal procedure*, procedimientos jurídicos. || Legal (in accordance with the law). || Lícito, ta (permitted by law). || Legítimo, ma (recognized by law). || Civil (year). || — JUR. *Legal adviser*, asesor jurídico. | *Legal age*, mayoría (*f.*) de edad. | *Legal aid*, abogacía (*f.*) de pobres. | *Legal costs*, costas, *f.* | *Legal document*, acta legalizada. | *Legal entity*, persona jurídica. | *Legal expert*, asesor jurídico. | *Legal holiday*, fiesta (*f.*) legal. | *Legal profession*, abogacía, *f.* | *Legal responsibility*, responsabilidad (*f.*) civil. | *Legal status* o *capacity*, personalidad jurídica. | *Legal tender*, moneda (*f.*) de curso legal (currency). | *Of legal age*, mayor de edad. | *To take legal action against s.o.*, entablar un pleito contra alguien.

legalism [—izəm] n. Legalismo, *m.*

legalist [—ist] n. Legalista, *m.* & *f.*

legalistic [ˈli:gəˈlistik] adj. Legalista.

legality [liˈgæliti] n. Legalidad, *f.* || — Pl. Trámites (*m.*) jurídicos (legal formalities).

legalizable [ˈli:gəlaizəbl] adj. Legalizable.

legalization [,li:gəlaiˈzeiʃən] n. Legalización, *f.*

legalize [ˈli:gəlaiz] v. tr. Legalizar.

legally [ˈli:gəli] adv. Legalmente.

legate [ˈlegit] n. Legado, *m.*

legate [liˈgeit] v. tr. Legar.

legatee [,legəˈti:] n. JUR. Legatario, ria.

legateship [ˈlegitʃip] n. Legacía, *f.*

legatine [ˈlegətain] adj. De un legado.

legation [liˈgeiʃən] n. Legación, *f.*

legator [liˈgeitə*] n. JUR. Testador, ra.

legend [ˈledʒənd] n. Leyenda, *f.* (story). || Pie, *m.* (of a cartoon). || Clave, *f.*, signos, *m. pl.* (of a map). || Inscripción, *f.* || *Black legend*, leyenda negra.

legendary [ˈledʒəndəri] adj. Legendario, ria.

legerdemain [ˈledʒədəˈmein] n. Juego (*m.*) de manos, prestidigitación, *f.* (conjuring). || Truco, *m.* (trick).

legged [legd] adj. De piernas (people): *long-legged*, de piernas largas. || De patas (animals, furniture, etc.): *round-legged*, de pata redonda.

leggings [ˈleginz] pl. n. Polainas, *f.*

leg guards [leggɑ:dz] pl. n. Defensas, *f.* (on motorbike). || SP. Espinilleras, *f.*

leggy [ˈlegi] adj. Zanquilargo, ga; patilargo, ga.

leghorn [ˈleghɔ:n] n. Paja (*f.*) italiana (straw). || Sombrero (*m.*) de paja italiana (hat). || Gallina (*f.*) leghorn, leghorn, *f.* (hen).

Leghorn [ˈlegˈhɔ:n] pr. n. GEOGR. Liorna.

legibility [,ledʒiˈbiliti] n. Legibilidad, *f.*

legible [ˈledʒəbl] adj. Legible.

legion [ˈli:dʒən] n. Legión, *f.*: *the Foreign Legion*, la Legión Extranjera. || FIG. Legión, *f.* (great number). || *Legion of Honour*, Legión de Honor.

legionary [—əri] adj. Legionario, ria; de la legión.
— N. Legionario, *m.*

legionnaire [,li:dʒəˈnεə*] n. U. S. MIL. Legionario, *m.*

legislate [ˈledʒisleit] v. intr. JUR. Legislar.
— V. tr. Establecer por ley.

legislation [,ledʒisˈleiʃən] n. JUR. Legislación, *f.*

legislative [ˈledʒislətiv] adj. JUR. Legislativo, va: *legislative assembly*, asamblea legislativa.
— N. Cuerpo (*m.*) legislativo.

legislator [ˈledʒis,leitə*] n. JUR. Legislador, *m.*

legislature [ˈledʒis,leitʃə*] n. JUR. Legislatura, *f.* || Cuerpo (*m.*) legislativo (lawmaking body).

legist [ˈli:dʒist] n. JUR. Legista, *m.*

legitimacy [liˈdʒitiməsi] n. Legitimidad, *f.*

legitimate [liˈdʒitimit] adj. Legítimo, ma (claim, child, king, etc.). || Válido, da; justo, ta: *a legitimate argument*, un argumento válido. || Auténtico, ca (theatre, music).

legitimate [liˈdʒitimeit] v. tr. Legitimar.

legitimation [li,dʒitiˈmeiʃən] n. JUR. Legitimación, *f.*

legitimism [liˈdʒitimizəm] n. Legitimismo, *m.*

legitimist [liˈdʒitimist] adj./n. Legitimista.

legitimization [,lidʒitimiˈzeiʃən] n. Legitimación, *f.*

legitimize [liˈdʒitimaiz] v. tr. Legitimar.

legless [ˈleglis] adj. Sin piernas (person). || Sin patas (furniture, animal).

leg-of-mutton [ˈlegəvˈmʌtn] adj. De jamón (sleeve). || MAR. Triangular (sail).

leg-pull [ˈlegpul] n. FAM. Tomadura (*f.*) de pelo, broma, *f.*

leg-puller [—ə*] n. FAM. Bromista, *m.* & *f.*

legroom [ˈlegru:m] n. Sitio (*m.*) para las piernas.

legume [ˈlegju:m] n. BOT. Legumbre, *f.*

leguminous [leˈgju:minəs] adj. Leguminoso, sa.

leister [ˈli:stə*] n. Arpón (*m.*) de tres púas.

leisure [ˈleʒə*] n. Ocio, *m.*: *a life of leisure*, una vida de ocio. || Tiempo (*m.*) libre (free time): *I have the leisure to do it*, tengo tiempo libre para hacerlo. ||

— *At leisure*, desocupado, da; libre: *he is at leisure*, está desocupado; con tiempo, con tranquilidad, sin prisa (peacefully). || *At one's leisure*, en sus momentos de ocio, en sus ratos libres (in one's spare time), cuando uno tenga tiempo *or* un rato: *do it at your leisure*, hazlo cuando tengas tiempo. || *Leisure occupation*, pasatiempo, *m.* || *Leisure time*, tiempo libre, ratos (*m. pl.*) libres, momentos (*m. pl.*) de ocio.

leisured [—d] adj. Desocupado, da; ocioso, sa (not occupied). || Pausado, da; sin prisa (unhurried).

leisurely [—li] adj. Pausado, da; sin prisa.
— Adv. Sin prisa, despacio.

leitmotiv or **leitmotif** [ˈlaitməuˌti:f] n. Leitmotiv, *m.*, tema (*m.*) central.

lemma [ˈlemə] n. Lema, *m.* (in logic and mathematics).

— Observ. El plural de la palabra inglesa *lemma* es *lemmata* o *lemmas.*

lemming [ˈlemiŋ] n. Zool. Lemming, *m.*, ratón (*m.*) campestre.

lemnaceae [lemˈneisii] pl. n. Lemnáceas, *f.*

lemniscus [lemˈniskəs] n. Anat. Lemnisco, *m.*

— Observ. El plural de la palabra inglesa es *lemnisci.*

lemon [ˈlemən] n. Bot. Limonero, *m.* (tree). | Limón, *m.* (fruit): *lemon juice*, zumo de limón. || Amarillo (*m.*) limón (colour). || U. S. Fam. Primo, ma; lila, *m.* & *f.* (twit). || — *Lemon balm*, toronjil, *m.* || *Lemon drop*, caramelo (*m.*) *or* pastilla (*f.*) de limón. || *Lemon grove*, limonar, *m.* || *Lemon squash*, zumo (*m.*) de limón. || *Lemon squeezer*, exprimelimones, *m. inv.*, exprimidor, *m.*
— Adj. Amarillo limón, cetrino, na.

lemonade [ˌleməˈneid] n. Limonada, *f.*, limón (*m.*) natural (lemon drink). || Gaseosa, *f.* (fizzy drink).

lempira [lemˈpiræ] n. Lempira, *m.* (monetary unit of Honduras).

lemur [ˈli:mə*] n. Zool. Lémur, *m.*

lemures [ˈlemjuəri:z] pl. n. Myth. Lémures, *m.*

lend* [lend] v. tr. Prestar: *can you lend me ten pounds?*, ¿me puede prestar diez libras? || Fig. Dar, conferir: *to lend a touch of gaiety*, dar una nota de alegría. || — Fig. *To lend a hand*, echar una mano. || *To lend o.s. to*, prestarse a: *the sentence lends itself to several interpretations*, la frase se presta a varias interpretaciones.
— V. intr. Prestar dinero.

— Observ. Pret. & p. p. **lent**.

lender [—ə*] n. Prestamista, *m.* & *f.* (professional). || Prestador, ra (accidental).

lending [—iŋ] n. Préstamo, *m.*, otorgamiento (*m.*) de un préstamo. || *Lending library*, biblioteca (*f.*) de préstamo.

lend-lease [—ˈli:s] n. Préstamo (*m.*) y arriendo. || *Lend-Lease Act*, ley (*f.*) de préstamo y arriendo.

length [leŋθ] n. Longitud, *f.*, largo, *m.*: *length over all*, longitud total; *seven metres in length*, siete metros de largo *or* de longitud; *the length of a football field*, la longitud de un campo de fútbol; *the length of a skirt*, la longitud de una falda. || Largo, *m.*: *three lengths of material*, tres largos de tela; *ten lengths of the swimming pool*, diez largos de la piscina. || Longitud, *f.* (of a story, joke). || Lo largo, longitud, *f.* (of parts of the body). || Largo, *m.* (of hair). || Duración, *f.* (of time): *the length of a film*, la duración de una película. || Extensión, *f.* (extension): *the length of a letter*, la extensión de una carta. || Espacio, *m.* (space). || Distancia, *f.* (distance). || Tramo, *m.* (part of a road, track, etc.). || Recorrido, *m.* (of route). || Pedazo, *m.*, trozo, *m.* (piece). || Gramm. Cantidad, *f.* (amount of stress). || Mar. Eslora, *f.*, largo, *m.* (of a boat). || Sp. Largo, *m.* (length of a bicycle). | Cuerpo, *m.* (in swimming and horse racing): *to win by a length*, ganar por un cuerpo. || — *Along the whole length of*, a lo largo de todo. || *At full length*, a todo lo largo (to lie), con todo detalle (to explain). || *At great length*, con muchos detalles. || *At length*, finalmente, por fin (at last), con todo detalle: *to explain at length*, explicar con todo detalle. || *Focal length*, distancia focal. || *For what length of time?*, ¿durante cuánto tiempo? || *Some length of time*, algún tiempo, bastante tiempo. || *The length and breadth of*, todo, da; entero, ra: *over the length and breadth of the country*, por el país entero. || *The length of time required to do sth.*, el tiempo requerido para hacer algo. || *To fall full length*, caer cuan largo es uno. || Fig. *To go to any lengths*, ser capaz de hacer cualquier cosa. | *To go to great lengths*, hacer un gran esfuerzo. | *To go to the length of*, llegar hasta el extremo de. | *To keep at arm's length*, mantener a distancia. | *To measure one's length on the floor*, medir el suelo (to fall down). || *To walk the length of*, recorrer: *we walked the whole length of the train*, recorrimos todo el tren. || *What length is it?*, ¿cuánto mide?, ¿cuánto tiene de largo?

lengthen [ˈleŋθən] v. intr. Alargarse, prolongarse. || Crecer (days)
— V. tr. Alargar: *to lengthen a dress*, alargar un vestido. || Alargar, prolongar (time).

lengthening [—iŋ] n. Alargamiento, *m.* || Prolongación, *f.* (of time).

lengthily [ˈleŋθili] adv. Largamente, extensamente.

lengthiness [ˈleŋθinis] n. Duración (*f.*) excesiva, prolijidad, *f.* (of a speech).

lengthways [ˈleŋθweiz] adv. Longitudinalmente, a lo largo. || *To measure sth. lengthways*, medir el largo de algo.

lengthwise [ˈleŋθwaiz] adv. Longitudinalmente, a lo largo.
— Adj. Longitudinal.

lengthy [ˈleŋθi] adj. Largo, ga (in distance). || Largo, ga; prolongado, da (in time). || Fam. Larguísimo, ma; demasiado largo, ga: *a lengthy journey*, un viaje larguísimo.

lenience [ˈli:njəns] or **leniency** [—i] n. Clemencia, *f.*, indulgencia, *f.*, poca severidad, *f.*

lenient [ˈli:njənt] adj. Clemente, indulgente, poco severo, ra.

Leninism [ˈleninizəm] n. Leninismo, *m.*

Leninist [ˈleninist] or **Leninite** [ˈleninait] adj./n. Leninista.

lenitive [ˈlenitiv] adj. Lenitivo, va.
— N. Med. Lenitivo, *m.* || Fig. Lenitivo, *m.*

lenity [ˈleniti] n. Lenidad, *f.*, poca severidad, *f.*, indulgencia, *f.*

lens [lenz] n. Phys. Lente, *f.*: *magnifying lens*, lente de aumento. || Lupa, *f.* (magnifying glass). || Phot. Objetivo, *m.* || Anat. Cristalino, *m.* || *Contact lens*, lente de contacto, lentilla, *f.*

— Observ. El plural de *lens* es *lenses.*

Lent [lent] n. Rel. Cuaresma, *f.*

lent [lent] pret. & p. p. See lend.

Lenten [ˈlentən] adj. Cuaresmal, de Cuaresma. || Fig. Escaso, sa; pobre (meager). | Sin carne (meatless).

lenticular [lenˈtikjulə*] adj. Lenticular.

lentil [ˈlentil] n. Bot. Lenteja, *f.*

lentiscus [lenˈtiskəs] or **lentisk** [ˈlentisk] n. Bot. Lentisco, *m.*

Leo [ˈli:əu] pr. n. León, *m.* (Christian name). || Astr. Leo, *m.*, León, *m.*

leonine [ˈli:əunain] adj. Leonino, na.

leopard [ˈlepəd] n. Zool. Leopardo, *m.* || Herald. León (*m.*) rampante. || Fig. *The leopard cannot change his spots*, genio y figura hasta la sepultura.

leopardess [—is] n. Zool. Leopardo (*m.*) hembra.

leotard [ˈliətɑ:d] n. Leotardo, *m.*

leper [ˈlepə*] n. Leproso, sa. || *Leper colony*, leprosería, *f.*

lepidopteran [ˌlepiˈdɔptərən] adj. Zool. Lepidóptero, ra.

lepidopteran or **lepidopteron** [ˌlepiˈdɔptərən] n. Zool. Lepidóptero, *m.*

— Observ. El plural de la palabra inglesa *lepidopteron* es *lepidoptera.*

lepidopterous [lepidɔptərəs] adj. Zool. Lepidóptero, ra.

leporine [ˈlepərain] adj. Leporino, na.

leprechaun [ˈleprəkɔ:n] n. Myth. Duende, *m.*, gnomo, *m.* [irlandés].

leprosarium [ˌleprəˈsɛəriəm] n. Leprosería, *f.*

leprosy [ˈleprəsi] n. Med. Lepra, *f.*

leprous [ˈleprəs] adj. Leproso, sa. || Fig. Desconchado, da (walls).

Lerna [ˈlə:nə] pr. n. Lerna.

Lernaean [ˈlə:ˈni:ən] adj. Myth. *Lernaean hydra*, hidra (*f.*) de Lerna.

Lesbian [ˈlezbiən] adj./n. Lesbiano, na; lesbio, bia. || — N. Lesbiana, *f.* (homosexual woman).

Lesbianism [ˈlezbiənizəm] n. Lesbianismo, *m.*

Lesbos [ˈlezbɔs] pr. n. Geogr. Lesbos.

lese majesty [ˈli:zˈmædʒisti] n. Jur. Crimen (*m.*) de lesa majestad.

lesion [ˈli:ʒən] n. Lesión, *f.*

less [les] adj. Menos: *he has less money than I*, tiene menos dinero que yo; *no less than three members*, no menos de tres miembros; *to spend less money*, gastar menos dinero; *less customers than the year before*, menos clientes que el año anterior; *ten shillings is less than a pound*, diez chelines son menos que una libra. || Inferior, menor: *the price is less than last year's*, el precio es inferior al *or* menor que el del año pasado; *5 is less than 7*, cinco es inferior a siete; *speeds less than 90 k.p.h.*, velocidades inferiores a noventa km/h. || Menor: *the danger is less now*, el peligro es menor ahora. || — *In less than no time*, en un abrir y cerrar de ojos, en menos de nada. || *It's nothing less than terrifying*, es francamente espantoso. || *It was nobody less than the King!* o *no less a person than the King!*, ¡era nada menos que el rey!, ¡era el mismísimo rey. || *Less of it!*, ¡ya está bien! || *No less than*, por lo menos (at least): *there were no less than 10 000 people*, había por lo menos 10 000 personas; nada menos que (as much as): *he earns no less than a million a year*, gana nada menos que un millón al año. || *Nothing less than*, nada menos que. || *Saint James the Less*, Santiago el Menor. || *That was given me by the King, no less*, eso me lo dio el mismo rey. || *The answer was sth. less* o *somewhat less than polite*, la contestación no fue nada cortés. || *To be nothing less than*, ser un verdadero: *it is nothing less than a crime*, es un verdadero crimen.
— Adv. Menos: *my head aches less now*, ahora me duele menos la cabeza; *he is less happy*, está menos alegre; *this is worth less than the other*, éste vale menos que el otro; *it is worth less than 100 pesetas*, vale

menos de 100 pesetas; *it is worth 100 pesetas less*, vale 100 pesetas menos; *some of his less known works*, algunas de sus obras menos conocidas; *if we were one man less*, si fuéramos uno menos; *not a penny less*, ni un penique menos; *he spoke less than I expected*, habló menos de lo que yo me esperaba. || — *Even less*, aun menos. || *I was less offended than angry*, me enfadé más que me ofendí. || *Less and less*, cada vez menos. || *Less than*, ni mucho menos: *to be less than easy*, no ser fácil ni mucho menos. || *More or less*, más o menos: *more or less easy*, más o menos fácil. || *None the less*, sin embargo, a pesar de todo: *none the less he is a good runner*, sin embargo es un buen corredor. || *So much the less*, tanto menos. || *Still less*, todavía menos. || *The less... the less*, mientras menos... menos, cuanto menos... menos: *the less you read, the less you learn*, cuanto menos lees menos aprendes. || *The less you think of it the better*, cuanto menos lo pienses mejor. || *To grow less*, disminuir.

— Prep. Menos: *1 000 francs less certain deductions*, 1 000 francos menos ciertos descuentos; *a year less a week*, un año menos una semana; *seven less five is two*, siete menos cinco son dos.

— N. Menor, *m.* & *f.*: *of the two evils it is the less*, de los dos males es el menor. || Menos: *less was given than should have been*, dieron menos de lo que se debía; *people have died for less*, hay quien ha muerto por menos.

lessee [leˈsiː] n. JUR. Inquilino, na (of a house). | Arrendatario, ria (of lands).

lessen [ˈlesn] v. tr. Disminuir, reducir.

— V. intr. Disminuir, reducirse.

lessening [—iŋ] n. Disminución, *f.*, reducción, *f.*

lesser [ˈlesə*] comp. adj. Menor: *the lesser evil*, el mal menor. || Menor, más pequeño, ña: *the lesser half*, la mitad más pequeña. || De menos categoría: *one of the lesser officials*, uno de los funcionarios de menos categoría. || *Lesser Antilles*, Antillas (*f.*) Menores.

lesson [ˈlesn] n. Lección, *f.*: *to recite a lesson*, dar la lección. || Clase, *f.*: *to give Spanish lessons* o *lessons in Spanish*, dar clases de español. || Lectura, *f.*, lección, *f.* (Bible reading). || — FIG. *Let that be a lesson to you*, que eso te sirva de lección. | *Now I'm going to teach them a lesson*, ahora les voy a dar una lección. | *To learn one's lesson*, escarmentar. || *To make a child say his lesson*, tomarle la lección a un niño. || *To take Spanish lessons*, dar clases de español.

lesson [ˈlesn] v. tr. Dar una lección a.

lessor [leˈsɔː*] n. JUR. Arrendador, ra.

lest [lest] conj. Por miedo a que, por temor a que (for fear that): *I didn't do it lest he should beat me*, no lo hice por miedo a que me pegase. || Para que no: *they kept quiet lest he should wake up*, se callaron para que no se despertase. || Para no (followed by the infinitive): *they did not come lest they should disturb you*, no vinieron para no molestarle. || Que (after verbs of fearing): *he was anxious lest I should miss the train*, temía que yo perdiese el tren.

— OBSERV. *Para no* can only be used to translate *lest* when the subject of the two clauses is the same.

let [let] n. Alquiler, *m.* (renting of a house). || Arrendamiento, *m.*, arriendo, *m.* (renting of land). || Obstáculo, *m.*, traba, *f.* (hindrance). || SP. Let, *m.*, servicio (*m.*) nulo (tennis, etc.). || *Without let or hindrance*, sin estorbo ni obstáculo.

— OBSERV. The term "net" is sometimes used incorrectly in Spanish for "let".

let* [let] v. tr. Dejar, permitir: *he let me do it*, me dejó hacerlo; *let me see your injury*, déjame ver tu herida; *will you let me give you a piece of advice?*, ¿me permite que le dé un consejo? || Alquilar (to rent a house). || Arrendar (to rent land). || — *He doesn't speak French, let alone Chinese*, no habla francés y aun menos chino. || *House to let*, se alquila (inscription). || *I didn't even see him, let alone speak to him*, ni siquiera le vi. ¿cómo iba a hablarle? || *To let alone* o *to let be*, dejar en paz, dejar tranquilo. || MED. *To let blood*, sangrar, hacer una sangría. || *To let fall*, soltar, dejar caer (to drop), echar, decir, soltar: *to let fall a hint*, soltar una indirecta; soltar: *he let fall a few oaths*, soltó unos tacos; trazar: *to let fall a perpendicular*, trazar una perpendicular. || *To let fly*, see FLY. || *To let go*, soltar (to release), dejar en libertad (to set free), fondear, anclar (to drop anchor). || *To let go of*, soltar. || *To let know*, avisar: *let me know if anyone calls*, avísame si llama alguien; dar a conocer, informar (to inform). || *To let loose*, see LOOSE. || *To let o.s.*, dejarse: *to let o.s. be caught*, dejarse coger; *to let o.s. be seen*, dejarse ver. || *To let o.s. go*, dejarse llevar, abandonarse (to lose one's inhibitions), abandonarse, dejarse, descuidarse (to cease to have pride in o.s.). || *To let o.s. go on a subject*, dejarse llevar por un tema. || *To let slip*, dejar pasar (an opportunity), revelar (a secret). || *To let well alone* o *well enough alone*, dejar [una cosa] como está. || *Well, let it go at that*, dejémoslo así. || *Without letting any blood*, sin derramamiento de sangre.

— V. intr. Alquilarse (house). || Arrendarse (land). || *To let*, se alquila (inscription).

— **To let by,** dejar pasar. || **To let down,** bajar: *to let a basket down on a rope*, bajar una cesta con una cuerda. | Descender, bajar (s.o.). | Fallar: *the car, the weather let us down*, el coche, el tiempo nos falló. | Alargar (to lengthen). | Soltarse (hair). | Desinflar, deshinchar (to deflate). | Aflojar (a spring). | FIG. Defraudar (to deceive), fallar: *he let me down*, me falló; abandonar (a friend). | — FIG. *To be let down*, llevarse un chasco. | FIG. *To let one's hair down*, soltarse el pelo. | FIG. *To let o.s. down*, no estar a la altura de sus compromisos. | *To let o.s. down by a rope*, descolgarse *or* bajar por una cuerda. | *To let s.o. down gently*, ser indulgente con alguien. || **To let in,** dejar entrar: *they let me in*, me dejaron entrar; *a hole that lets the cold in*, un agujero que deja entrar el frío. | Hacer entrar, dejar entrar: *when he came I let him in*, cuando vino le dejé entrar. | Abrir: *it was his mother who let me in*, fue su madre quien me abrió. | Permitir, dar paso a: *these measures will let in too many excuses*, estas medidas permitirán demasiadas excusas. | Estafar, timar (to swindle). | Engañar (to mislead). | Encajar (to insert). || — *I got let in for 500 pesetas*, tuve que pagar 500 pesetas. | *Let him in!*, ¡dile que entre! | *To let o.s. in*, abrir la puerta. | *To let o.s. in for*, meterse en: *to let o.s. in for trouble*, meterse en un lío; comprometerse a: *to let o.s. in for a speech*, comprometerse a hacer un discurso. | *To let s.o. in for difficulties*, crearle problemas a alguien, ocasionarle dificultades a alguien. | *To let s.o. in on a secret*, revelar un secreto a alguien. || **To let into,** empotrar: *to let a cupboard into a wall*, empotrar un armario en una pared. | Abrir: *to let a door into a wall*, abrir una puerta en una pared. | Revelar (a secret). | Dejar entrar en (to allow to enter): *he let me into his house*, me dejó entrar en su casa. | — FAM. *To let into s.o.*, atacar a alguien, arremeter contra alguien. || **To let off,** dispensar de (to exempt). | Perdonar (to forgive). | Disparar (a gun). | Tirar (a rocket). | Hacer explotar (a bomb). | Hacer estallar (firework). | Aflojar (a spring). | Dejar salir (the steam). | Emitir (to emit, to give off). | Alquilar (to hire). | — *To be let off with a light sentence*, sacar una condena muy leve. | *To be let off with a warning*, escapar con una amonestación. | FIG. *To let off steam*, desfogarse. || **To let on,** decir: *don't let on!*, ¡no lo digas!; *don't let on that it was me*, no digas que he sido yo. | Fingirse, hacerse: *he let on that he was dead*, se hizo el muerto. | Fingir: *he let on that his father was rich*, fingió que su padre era rico. | Hacerse pasar por: *he let on that he was a policeman*, se hizo pasar por un policía. | — *He never let on that he was angry*, disimuló su enfado. | *To let on about*, revelar. || **To let out,** poner en libertad, dejar salir (to set free). | Ensanchar (a garment). | Revelar, divulgar (a secret). | Dejar apagarse (a fire). | Soltar (a scream, a yell). | Dejar salir (air from a tyre). | Aflojar (to loosen). | Acompañar a la puerta (person who is leaving). | Alquilar (to rent a house). | Arrendar (to rent land). | MAR. Largar (sails). | U. S. Repartir [trabajo] (to portion out work), conceder [un contrato] (to assign a contract). | — *To let out a contract to s.o.*, contratar a alguien. | FIG. *To let out at s.o.*, decirle a uno cuatro verdades. | *To let out at s.o. with one's fist*, soltar un puñetazo a alguien. || **To let through,** dejar pasar (to allow to pass). || **To let up,** disminuir (to lessen). | Moderarse (to become moderate). | Dejar de trabajar (to stop working). | Aflojar, disminuir los esfuerzos (to slacken). | — *To let up on*, ser menos exigente con. | *When the rain lets up*, cuando llueva menos.

— V. aux. (1st and 3rd pers. of imperative). *Let everyone know*, que todos sepan. || *Let him live*, que viva. || *Let's get out of here!*, ¡vayámonos de aquí! || *Let's go!*, ¡vamos!, ¡vámonos!, ¡vayámonos! || *Let's not be silly*, no seas idiota, no hagamos el tonto. || *Let's not lose our heads*, no perdamos la cabeza. || *Let's see*, a ver, veamos: *let's see what you've done wrong*, a ver lo que has hecho mal. || *Let there be light*, hágase la luz. || *Let us sing*, cantemos. || *Let X be equal to Y*, supongamos que X es igual a Y.

— OBSERV. Pret. & p. p. *let*.

letdown [—ˈdaun] n. Decepción, *f.*, desilusión, *f.*, chasco, *m.* (disappointment). || Disminución, *f.*

lethal [ˈliːθəl] adj. Mortífero, ra: *a lethal weapon*, un arma mortífera. || Mortal: *a lethal dose*, una dosis mortal; *a lethal wound*, una herida mortal. || MED. Letal.

lethargic [leˈθɑːdʒik] adj. Letárgico, ca.

lethargically [—əli] adv. Letárgicamente.

lethargize [ˈleθəːdʒaiz] v. tr. Aletargar.

lethargy [ˈleθədʒi] n. Letargo, *m.*

let's [lets] contraction of *let us*.

Lett [let] n. Letón, ona.

letter [ˈletə*] n. Letra, *f.*: *the letter "f"*, la letra "f". || Carta, *f.*: *to write s.o. a letter*, escribirle una carta a alguien; *covering letter*, carta adjunta; *registered letter*, carta certificada. || PRINT. Tipo, *m.*, carácter, *m.*, letra, *f.* (type). || FIG. Letra, *f.* (literal meaning). || — Pl. Letras, *f.* (literature): *a man of letters*, un hombre de letras. || — *Block letters*, letras de molde. || *By letter post*, como carta. || *Capital letter*, mayúscula, *f.* || PRINT. *Compound letter*, signo (*m.*) doble. || *Cursive letter*, letra cursiva. || *Dead letter*, letra muerta. || *Dominical letter*, letra dominical. || *Italic letters*, letra bastardilla. || *Letter of advice*, aviso, *m.*, notificación, *f.* || *Letter of attorney*, poder, *m.* || *Letter of condolence*, carta de pésame. || *Letter* o *letters of* *credence, letters credential, credential letters,* cartas credenciales. || COMM. *Letter of credit,* carta de crédito. || *Letter of dismissal,* carta de despido. || *Letter of introduction,* carta de presentación *or* de recomendación. || MAR. *Letter* o *letters of marque,* patente (*f.*) de corso. || *Letter of sponsorship,* carta de llamada. || *Letters patent of nobility,* ejecutoria, *f. sing.* || *Love letter,* carta de amor. || *Open letter,* carta abierta. || *Small capital letter,* letra versalita. || *Small letter,* minúscula, *f.* || *To the letter,* al pie de la letra: *to carry out instructions to the letter,* cumplir las instrucciones al pie de la letra.

letter [ˈletə*] v. tr. Rotular (to inscribe). || PRINT. Imprimir *or* estampar con letras (to impress letters). || Poner un título a (a book).

letter [ˈletə*] n. Alquilador, ra.

letter book [—buk] n. Libro (*m.*) copiador.

letter box [—bɔks] n. Buzón, *m.*

lettercard [—kɑ:d] n. Billete (*m.*) postal.

letter carrier [—ˌkæriə*] n. U. S. Cartero, *m.* (postman).

lettered [—d] adj. Rotulado, da. || Estampado *or* marcado con letras (marked with letters). || Culto, ta (cultured). || Letrado, da; erudito, ta (learned).

letterer [—rə*] n. Rotulador, *m.*

letter file [—fail] n. Carpeta, *f.*

letterhead [—hed] n. Membrete, *m.* (heading). || Papel (*m.*) con membrete (headed paper).

lettering [—riŋ] n. Rotulado, *m.*, rotulación, *f.* (act of making letters). || Letras, *f. pl.*, rótulo, *m.*, inscripción, *f.*

letter-lock [—lɔk] n. Candado (*m.*) de combinación.

letter opener [—ˌəupənə*] n. Abrecartas, *m. inv.*

letter paper [—ˌpeipə*] n. Papel (*m.*) de escribir.

letter-perfect [—ˈpə:fikt] adj. Al pie de la letra: *he knows his part letter-perfect,* sabe su papel al pie de la letra. || Exacto, ta (correct).

letter press [—pres] n. Prensa (*f.*) de copiar.

letterpress [—pres] n. PRINT. Texto (*m.*) impreso (printed text). | Impresión (*f.*) tipográfica (printing).

letter scales [—skeilz] pl. n. Pesacartas, *m. inv.*

letters rogatory [ˈletə*zˈrɔgətəri] pl. n. JUR. Exhorto, *m. sing.*

letter writer [ˈletəˌraitə*] n. Manual (*m.*) de correspondencia (book). || El que escribe cartas, escritor (*m.*) de cartas (person).

Lettic [ˈletik] or **Lettish** [ˈletiʃ] adj. Letón, ona.

— N. Letón, *m.* (language).

letting [ˈletiŋ] n. Arrendamiento, *m.*

lettre de cachet [letrədəkæʃei] n. HIST. Carta (*f.*) cerrada con el sello real que exigía el encarcelamiento o destierro de una persona.

lettuce [ˈletis] n. BOT. Lechuga, *f.* || U. S. FAM. Pasta, *f.* (money).

letup [ˈletʌp] n. Descanso, *m.*, tregua, *f.* (rest). || Interrupción, *f.* || Moderación, *f.* (moderation). || Reducción, *f.*, disminución, *f.* (reduction).

leucaemia (U. S. **leucemia**) [ljuˈki:miə] n. MED. Leucemia, *f.*

leucaemic (U. S. **leucemic**) [ljuˈki:mik] adj. MED. Leucémico, ca.

leucoblast [ˈlju:kəblæst] n. BIOL. Leucoblasto, *m.*

leucocyte [ˈlju:kəusait] n. BIOL. Leucocito, *m.*

leucocytosis [ˌlju:kəusaiˈtəusis] n. MED. Leucocitosis, *f. inv.*

leucoma [lju:ˈkəumə] n. MED. Leucoma, *m.*

leucoplast [ˈlju:kəplæst] n. BOT. Leucoplasto, *m.*

leucorrhoea [ˌlju:kəˈri:ə] n. MED. Leucorrea, *f.*

leucosis [lju:ˈkəusis] n. MED. Leucosis, *f.*

leud [lju:d] n. HIST. Leude, *m.*

leukaemia (U. S. **leukemia**) [lju:ˈki:miə] n. MED. Leucemia, *f.*

leukaemic (U. S. **leukemic**) [lju:ˈki:mik] adj. MED. Leucémico, ca.

leukoblast [ˈlju:kəblæst] n. U. S. BIOL. Leucoblasto, *m.*

leukocyte [ˈlju:kəusait] n. U. S. BIOL. Leucocito, *m.*

leukocytosis [ˌlju:kəusaiˈtəusis] n. U. S. MED. Leucocitosis, *f. inv.*

leukoma [lju:ˈkəumə] n. U. S. MED. Leucoma, *m.*

leukorrhea [ˌlju:kəˈri:ə] n. U. S. MED. Leucorrea, *f.*

leukosis [lju:ˈkəusis] n. U. S. MED. Leucosis, *f.*

Levant [liˈvænt] pr. n. Levante, *m.*

levanter [—ə*] n. Viento (*m.*) de Levante (wind).

Levantine [ˈlevəntain] adj./n. Levantino, na.

levator [liˈveitə*] n. ANAT. Elevador, *m.*

— OBSERV. El plural de *levator* es *levatores.*

levee [ˈlevi] n. HIST. Recepción (*f.*) dada por un rey al principio de la tarde o cuando se levanta por la mañana (reception). || U. S. Dique, *m.* (dike). | Malecón, *m.* (jetty). | Recepción, *f.* (held by an high official).

level [ˈlevl] adj. Horizontal (horizontal). || A nivel (even). || Llano, na; plano, na (flat). || Raso, sa: *level spoonful,* cucharada rasa. || Igual (equal). || Igualado, da (of two moving objects): *they were level until the last straight,* estaban igualados hasta la recta final. || Estable (stable): *a level temperature,* una temperatura estable. || Uniforme: *a level tone,* un tono uniforme. || Sin emoción, tranquilo, la: *a level voice,* una voz sin emoción. || Ecuánime (equable). || Ordenado, da: *a level life,* una vida ordenada. || Flemático, ca: *the Englishman is very level,* el inglés es muy flemático. || Penetrante: *a level look,* una mirada penetrante. || PHYS. Equipotencial (equipotential). || — *Dead level,* al mismo nivel (objects), completamente igualados (moving objects, people). || *Level with,* al nivel de. || *Level with the ground,* a ras de tierra, a flor de tierra. || *One's level best,* todo lo posible, el máximo. || *To be level with,* estar a la misma altura *or* al mismo nivel que. || *To draw level with,* igualar.

— Adv. A nivel. || Horizontalmente (horizontally).

— N. Nivel, *m.* (instrument): *spirit level,* nivel de burbuja. || Nivel, *m.*: *sea level,* nivel del mar; *water level,* nivel del agua; *at ministerial level,* al nivel ministerial; *the general level is very high,* el nivel general es muy alto; *level of language,* nivel de lenguaje. || Altura, *f.*, nivel, *m.*: *to come down to s.o.'s level,* ponerse a la altura de alguien; *at shoulder level,* a la altura del hombro; *to be on the same level,* estar a la misma altura; *difference of level,* diferencia de nivel. || Índice, *m.*: *the alcohol level in the blood,* el índice de alcohol en la sangre; *intelligence level,* índice de inteligencia. || Línea (*f.*) visual (of a gun). || Llano, *m.*, superficie (*f.*) llana, llanura, *f.* (flat place). || — *At eye level,* a la altura del ojo. || *At ground level,* a ras de tierra. || *Noise level,* intensidad (*f.*) del ruido. || *On a level with,* al nivel de, a la misma altura que (at the same height as), equiparable con, parangonable con, comparable con (comparable with). || *On the level,* honrado, da; serio, ria (person, offer, etc.), en serio: *to tell s.o. sth. on the level,* decirle algo a alguien en serio. || *Out of level,* desnivelado, da. || *To find one's own level,* encontrar su sitio en la sociedad. || *To take a level,* nivelar (in topography).

level [ˈlevl] v. tr. Nivelar, allanar, aplanar (to make flat). || Nivelar (in surveying). || Arrasar (to raze): *the school was levelled by the hurricane,* el huracán arrasó el colegio. || Apuntar (to aim a weapon). || FIG. Dirigir (an accusation). | Igualar, nivelar (to make equal). || — *To level away,* nivelar, allanar. || *To level down,* rebajar al mismo nivel, igualar. || *To level up,* elevar al mismo nivel, igualar.

— V. intr. Nivelarse (to become balanced). || Estabilizarse (prices). || *To level off* o *out,* nivelarse (to become balanced), estabilizarse (prices), ponerse en una trayectoria horizontal [antes de aterrizar] (an aircraft).

level crossing [—ˈkrɔsiŋ] n. Paso (*m.*) a nivel.

leveler [—ə*] n. U. S. Nivelador, ra.

level-headed [—ˈhedid] adj. Sensato, ta; juicioso, sa.

leveling [—iŋ] n. U. S. See LEVELLING.

leveller [—ə*] n. Nivelador, ra.

levelling [—iŋ] n. Nivelación, *f.* (topography). || Aplanamiento, *m.*, allanamiento, *m.* (flattening).

levelling rod (U. S. **leveling rod**) [ˈlevliŋ rɔd] or **levelling staff** (U. S. **leveling staff**) [ˈlevliŋ stɑ:f] n. Jalón, *m.*, mira, *f.*

lever [ˈli:və*] n. Palanca, *f.* || FIG. Apoyo, *m.*, palanca, *f.* (influence).

lever [ˈli:və*] v. tr. Apalancar. || *To lever up,* levantar con una palanca.

leverage [—ridʒ] n. Apalancamiento, *m.* || Fuerza (*f.*) de la palanca. || FIG. Influencia, *f.* | Ventaja, *f.*

leveret [levərit] n. ZOOL. Lebrato, *m.*

leviable [ˈleviəbl] adj. Percibible, recaudable (tax). || Imponible (person).

Leviathan [liˈvaiəθən] pr. n. REL. Leviatán, *m.*

levigation [ˌleviˈgeiʃən] n. Levigación, *f.*

levitate [ˈleviteit] v. tr. Elevar *or* mantener en el aire por levitación.

— V. intr. Elevarse *or* mantenerse en el aire por levitación.

levitation [ˌleviˈteiʃən] n. Levitación, *f.*

Levite [ˈli:vait] n. REL. Levita, *m.*

Levitical [liˈvitikəl] adj. REL. Levítico, ca.

Leviticus [liˈvitikəs] pr. n. REL. Levítico, *m.*

levity [ˈleviti] n. Ligereza, *f.*

levy [ˈlevi] n. Exacción, *f.* (imposing of a tax). || Recaudación, *f.*, percepción, *f.* (collecting of a tax). || Impuesto, *f.* (amount paid). || Sobretasa, *f.* (surcharge). || MIL. Leva, *f.* (recruitment). || JUR. Embargo, *m.* (of property, etc.).

levy [ˈlevi] v. tr. Exigir (to exact taxes). || Recaudar, percibir (to collect taxes). || Imponer (a fine). || MIL. Reclutar, hacer una leva de (soldiers). || JUR. Embargar (to seize property). || — *To levy a duty on sth.,* gravar algo con un impuesto. || *To levy war on,* hacer la guerra a.

— V. intr. JUR. Imponer un embargo.

levy in mass [—inˈmæs] n. Movilización (*f.*) general.

lewd [lu:d] adj. Lascivo, va; lúbrico, ca (lascivious). || Indecente, obsceno, na (indecent).

lewdness [—nis] n. Lascivia, *f.*, lubricidad, *f.* (lasciviousness). || Obscenidad, *f.*

Lewis [ˈlu:is] pr. n. Luis, *m.* || MIL. *Lewis gun,* ametralladora, *f.*

lexical [ˈleksikəl] adj. Léxico, ca; lexicológico, ca.

lexicographer [ˌleksiˈkɔgrəfə*] n. Lexicógrafo, fa.

lexicographic [ˌleksikəuˈgræfik] or **lexicographical** [—əl] adj. Lexicográfico, ca.

lexicography [ˌleksiˈkɔgrəfi] n. Lexicografía, *f.*

lexicologic [ˌleksikəuˈlɔdʒik] or **lexicological** [—əl] adj. Lexicológico, ca.

lexicologist [ˌleksiˈkɔlədʒist] n. Lexicólogo, ga.

lexicology [ˌleksiˈkɔlədʒi] n. Lexicología, *f.*

lexicon [ˈleksikən] n. Léxico, *m.*

Leyden [ˈlaidn] pr. n. GEOGR. Leyden. || *Leyden jar,* botella (*f.*) de Leyden.

liability [ˌlaiəˈbiliti] n. Responsabilidad, *f.* (legal responsibility). || Sujeción, *f.*: *liability to duties*, sujeción a impuestos. || Tendencia, *f.* (propensity): *liability to catch cold*, tendencia a constiparse; *liability to explode*, tendencia a explotar. || Probabilidad, *f.* (probability). || Inconveniente, *m.* (drawback): *owning a car can be a liability*, tener un coche puede ser un inconveniente. || Estorbo, *m.* (nuisance). || — Pl. COMM. Pasivo, *m. sing.*, debe, *m. sing.*: *assets and liabilities*, el activo y el pasivo, el debe y el haber. | Deudas, *f.* (debts): *he met his liabilities*, satisfizo sus deudas. | Compromisos, *m.* (obligations). || — *Liability insurance*, seguro (*m.*) de responsabilidad civil. || *Limited-liability company*, sociedad [de responsabilidad] limitada.

liable [ˈlaiəbl] adj. JUR. Responsable: *to be liable for s.o.'s debts*, ser responsable de las deudas de alguien. || Sujeto, ta; sometido, da: *liable to duties*, sujeto a impuestos. || Expuesto, ta: *liable to a fine*, expuesto a una multa; *liable to a good hiding*, expuesto a una buena paliza. || Susceptible de: *liable to change*, susceptible de cambio. || Propenso, sa: *liable to catch cold*, propenso a constiparse. || Capaz: *she is liable to change her mind*, es capaz de cambiar de opinión. || — *To be liable for military service*, estar obligado a hacer el servicio militar. || *To be liable to snow*, ser probable que nieve. || U. S. *We are liable to be in Seattle next month*, puede ser que *or* es probable que estemos en Seattle el mes que viene.

liaise [liˈeiz] v. intr. MIL. Establecer el enlace.

liaison [liˈeizɔ̃] n. MIL. Enlace, *m.* || Coordinación, *f.*, enlace, *m.* (coordination). || GRAMM. Enlace, *m.* (between words). || Aventura, *f.* (love affair). || MIL. *Liaison officer*, oficial (*m.*) de enlace.

liana [liˈɑːnə] or **liane** [liˈaːn] n. BOT. Bejuco, *m.*, liana, *f.*

liar [ˈlaiə*] n. Mentiroso, sa; embustero, ra.

Lias [ˈlaiəs] n. GEOL. Lías, *m.*, liásico, *m.*

Liassic [laiˈæsik] adj. GEOL. Liásico, ca.

libation [laiˈbeiʃən] n. Libación, *f.*

libel [ˈlaibəl] n. Escrito (*m.*) difamatorio, libelo, *m.* (published statement). || Difamación, *f.* (act of publishing such a statement): *libel suit*, pleito por difamación. || FIG. Calumnia, *f.* (slander).

libel [ˈlaibəl] v. tr. Difamar [por escrito] (to publish a libel about). || FIG. Calumniar (to slander).

libeller (U. S. **libeler**) [—ə*] or **libellist** (U. S. **libelist**) [—ist] n. JUR. Libelista, *m.* & *f.* || Difamador, ra (defamer). || Calumniador, ra (slanderer).

libellous (U. S. **libelous**) [ˈlaibləs] adj. Difamatorio, ria. || Calumnioso, sa.

libellula [liˈbeljulə] n. Libélula, *f.* (insect).

liber [ˈlaibə*] n. Registro, *m.* (book). || BOT. Líber, *m.*

liberal [ˈlibərəl] adj. Liberal. || Libre: *a liberal interpretation of the rules*, una libre interpretación de las reglas. || Generoso, sa; liberal (generous): *a liberal reward*, una recompensa generosa. || — *Liberal arts*, artes (*f.*) liberales. || *Liberal education*, educación (*f.*) humanista. || *Liberal ideas*, ideas (*f.*) liberales. || *The Liberal Party*, el Partido liberal.

— N. Liberal, *m.* & *f.* || *The Liberals*, los liberales (political party).

liberalism [ˈlibərəlizəm] n. Liberalismo, *m.*

liberality [ˌlibəˈræliti] n. Liberalidad, *f.* || Amplitud (*f.*) de miras (broad-mindedness).

liberalization [ˌlibərəlaiˈzeiʃən] n. Liberalización, *f.*

liberalize [ˈlibərəlaiz] v. tr. Liberalizar.

— V. intr. Liberalizarse.

liberally [ˈlibərəli] adv. Liberalmente. || Liberalmente, generosamente (generously). || Libremente (to translate, etc.).

liberal-minded [ˈlibərəlˈmaindid] adj. Amplio, plia (ideas). || Tolerante (conscience). || Liberal (person).

liberal-mindedness [ˈlibərəlˈmaindidnis] n. Amplitud (*f.*) de miras (broad-mindedness). || Tolerancia, *f.* (tolerance).

liberate [ˈlibəreit] v. tr. Liberar, libertar (to free). || Poner en libertad (a prisoner). || Liberar (a country). || Librar (from obligations). || CHEM. Desprender, liberar (to give off a gas).

liberating [—iŋ] adj. Liberador, ra.

liberation [ˌlibəˈreiʃən] n. Liberación, *f.* || CHEM. Desprendimiento, *m.*, liberación, *f.* (of gas).

liberator [ˈlibəreitə*] n. Libertador, ra; liberador, ra.

liberatory [ˈlibərətəri] adj. Liberatorio, ria.

Liberia [laiˈbiəriə] pr. n. GEOGR. Liberia, *f.*

Liberian [—n] adj./n. Liberiano, na.

libertarian [ˌlibərˈtɛəriən] adj./n. Libertario, ria.

libertinage [ˈlibətinidʒ] n. Libertinaje, *m.*

libertine [ˈlibətain] adj./n. Libertino, na.

libertinism [ˈlibətinizəm] n. Libertinaje, *m.*

liberty [ˈlibəti] n. Libertad, *f.*: *liberty of action, of thought*, libertad de acción, de pensamiento. || MAR. Licencia, *f.*, permiso, *m.* (leave). || FAM. Libertad, *f.*, confianza, *f.* (familiarity). || Privilegio, *m.* || — *Liberty boat*, barco (*m.*) de los marineros que están de permiso. || *Liberty cap*, gorro frigio. || U. S. *Liberty Ship*, barco (*m.*) mercante. || *To be at liberty*, estar en libertad (to be free), estar libre, estar desocupado (to be at leisure), estar autorizado, tener derecho: *not to be at liberty to disclose sth.*, no estar autorizado a revelar una cosa. || *To pledge one's liberty*, hipotecar la libertad. || *To set at liberty*, poner en libertad. || *To take liberties*, tomarse libertades. || *To take the liberty of* o *to*, tomarse la libertad de.

libidinal [liˈbidinəl] or **libidinous** [liˈbidinəs] adj. Libidinoso, sa.

libido [liˈbiːdəu] n. Libido, *f.*

Libra [ˈlaibrə] pr. n. ASTR. Libra, *f.*

librarian [laiˈbrɛəriən] n. Bibliotecario, ria.

librarianship [—ʃip] n. Cargo (*m.*) de bibliotecario.

library [ˈlaibrəri] n. Biblioteca, *f.*: *reference, lending, public library*, biblioteca de consulta, de préstamo, pública; *circulating* o *mobile library*, biblioteca circulante. || *Newspaper library*, hemeroteca, *f.*

librate [ˈlaibreit] v. intr. Balancearse, oscilar.

libratory [ˈlaibrəˌtəri] adj. Que se balancea, oscilatorio, ria.

librettist [liˈbretist] MUS. Libretista, *m.* & *f.*

libretto [liˈbretəu] n. MUS. Libreto, *m.*

— OBSERV. El plural de la palabra inglesa es *librettos* o *libretti*.

Libya [ˈlibiə] pr. n. GEOGR. Libia, *f.*

Libyan [—n] adj./n. Libio, bia.

lice [lais] pl. n. See LOUSE.

licence (U. S. **license**) [ˈlaisəns] n. Licencia, *f.*, permiso, *m.*: *hunting, fishing licence*, licencia de caza, de pesca; *export licence*, licencia de exportación. || Autorización, *f.* (authorization). || Carnet, *m.*, permiso, *m.*: *driving licence*, carnet de conducir, permiso de conducción. || Licencia, *f.*: *poetic licence*, licencia poética. || Libertad, *f.* (freedom): *he was allowed some licence in interpreting the play*, le fue concedida cierta libertad en la interpretación de la obra. || Licencia, *f.*, libertinaje, *m.* (socially undesirable behaviour). || — *Licence number*, matrícula, *f.*, número (*m.*) de matrícula. || *Licence plate*, placa (*f.*) de matrícula, matrícula, *f.* || *Licence tax*, impuesto (*m.*) sobre patente. || *Road tax licence*, impuesto (*m.*) de circulación.

licence or **license** [ˈlaisəns] v. tr. Conceder una licencia *or* un permiso a. || Autorizar: *licenced to sell*, autorizado para vender. || Permitir (to permit). || *Licensed premises*, establecimiento autorizado para vender bebidas alcohólicas.

licencee [ˌlaisənˈsiː] n. See LICENSEE.

license [ˈlaisəns] n./v. tr. See LICENCE.

licensee [ˌlaisənˈsiː] n. Persona (*f.*) que tiene un permiso *or* una licencia, concesionario, *m.* || Persona (*f.*) autorizada para vender bebidas alcohólicas.

licenser [ˈlaisənsə*] n. Persona (*f.*) que concede un permiso *or* una licencia.

licentiate [laiˈsenʃiit] n. Licenciado, da.

licentious [laiˈsenʃəs] adj. Licencioso, sa.

licentiousness [—nis] n. Libertinaje, *m.*, licencia, *f.*

lichen [ˈlaikən] n. BOT. Liquen, *m.*

lich-gate [litʃgeit] n. Entrada (*f.*) de cementerio.

licit [ˈlisit] adj. Lícito, ta.

licitness [—nis] n. Licitud, *f.*

lick [lik] n. Lamedura, *f.*, lamido, *m.*, lengüetazo, *m.*, lengüetada, *f.* (the act of licking). || Mano, *f.* (light coating): *a lick of paint*, una mano de pintura. || Salina, *f.* (salt lick). || FAM. Poco, *m.* (little). | Golpe, *m.* (blow). || — FAM. *He won't do a lick of work*, no dará ni golpe. | *To give o.s. a lick and a promise*, lavarse rápidamente. | *To go at a great* o *at full lick*, ir a todo gas.

lick [lik] v. tr. Lamer: *he licked the ice cream*, lamió el helado. || Acariciar: *the waves licked the beach*, las olas acariciaban la playa. || FAM. Dar una paliza a (to beat). || — *To lick clean*, lamer. || FIG. *To lick into shape*, see SHAPE. || *To lick off*, quitar de un lametazo. || FIG. FAM. *To lick one's chops* o *one's lips*, relamerse. | *To lick s.o.'s shoes* o *boots* o *to lick up to s.o.*, hacer la pelotilla a alguien, dar coba a alguien. | *To lick the dust*, morder el polvo. || *To lick up*, beber a lengüetadas.

lickerish [—əriʃ] adj. Ávido, da (eager). || Goloso, sa (greedy). || Lascivo, va (lecherous). || Apetitoso, sa (appetizing).

lickety-split [ˌlikətiˈsplit] adv. FAM. A todo gas, a toda mecha.

licking [likiŋ] n. Lamido, *m.* (act of one who licks). || FIG. FAM. Paliza, *f.*: *to give s.o. a licking*, dar una paliza a alguien. || FIG. FAM. *Licking up*, pelotilla, *f.*, coba, *f.*

lickspittle [ˈlikspitl] n. FAM. Pelotillero, ra; cobista, *m.* & *f.*

licorice [ˈlikəris] n. Regaliz, *m.*

lictor [ˈliktə*] n. HIST. Lictor, *m.*

lid [lid] n. Tapa, *f.*, tapadera, *f.* (cover). || FAM. Güito, *m.* (hat). || ANAT. Párpado, *m.* (of the eye). || BOT. Opérculo, *m.* || — FAM. *To flip one's lid*, volverse loco. | *To flip one's lid for* o *over*, chiflarse por, volverse loco por. | *To put the lid on*, rematar.

lie [lai] n. Mentira, *f.*, embuste, *m.* || — *It's a pack of lies*, es una sarta de mentiras. || *Lie detector*, detector (*m.*) de mentiras. || *One lie makes many*, de una mentira nacen ciento. || *To act a lie*, actuar con falsedad. || *To give the lie to*, demostrar que [algo] es falso (to prove false), dar el mentís a (person), desmentir (a report). || *To tell a lie*, decir una mentira, mentir. || *White lie*, mentira piadosa.

lie [lai] v. intr. Mentir. || *To lie o.s. out of a scrape*, conseguir salir de un apuro por medio de mentiras.

lie [lai] n. Posición, *f.*, situación, *f.* (place). || Dirección, *f.*, orientación, *f.* (direction). || Configuración, *f.* (nature). || Guarida, *f.* (of a wild animal). || — FIG. *The lie of the land*, el estado de las cosas. | *To study the lie of the land*, estudiar el terreno.

lie* [lai] v. intr. Echarse, acostarse, tumbarse, tenderse (to assume a horizontal posture): *to lie on the floor*, echarse en el suelo. || Estar tendido, estar echado, estar acostado, estar tumbado (to be in a horizontal posture): *he was lying on the floor*, estaba tumbado en el suelo. || Estar acostado, dormir (to sleep). || Estar: *he lay dead on the ground*, estaba muerto en el suelo; *to lie hidden*, estar escondido; *to lie resting*, estar descansando; *the difference lies in the fact that*, la diferencia está en el hecho de que. || Estar, estar situado: *the town lies to the south*, la ciudad está al sur; *his grave lies over the hill*, su tumba está situada al otro lado de la colina. || Yacer, reposar, estar enterrado (the dead): *here lies Snow White*, aquí yace Blancanieves. || Quedarse (to remain): *to lie still*, quedarse inmóvil; *to lie in bed*, quedarse en la cama. || Estribar, radicar, residir: *you know where your interest lies*, ya sabes donde radica tu interés. || Extenderse: *a pall of smoke lies over the town*, una capa de humo se extiende sobre la ciudad; *the town lay before us*, la ciudad se extendía ante nosotros. || Depender: *the decision lies with you*, la decisión depende de ti. || Pertenecer, incumbir (to concern). || Cuajar (snow). || Estar depositado (money). || MIL. Acampar. || MAR. Estar anclado (to be at anchor). || JUR. Ser admisible *or* procedente. || — *The fault lies with him*, la culpa es suya. || *The route lay across a desert*, el camino atravesaba un desierto. || *The water lay two metres deep*, había dos metros de agua. || *To lie asleep*, estar durmiendo. || *To lie heavy on the conscience*, pesar en la conciencia. || *To lie idle*, estar parado (factory). || *To lie in ruins*, estar en ruinas. || *To lie in state*, estar de cuerpo presente. || *To lie under a charge of*, estar bajo la acusación de. || *To lie under obligation to*, tener la obligación de. || *To lie with a woman*, conocer mujer.
— ***To lie about***, estar tirado, estar rodando: *her clothes were lying about all over the room*, su ropa estaba tirada por toda la habitación. | — *Books were lying about everywhere*, había libros por todas partes. | *It's lying about here somewhere*, anda rodando por aquí. | *We lay about in the sun all day*, pasamos el día tumbados al sol. || ***To lie back***, recostarse (in an armchair, etc.). | Estar retranqueado, da (house). || ***To lie by***, estar sin utilizar (to be unused). | Descansar, pararse (to rest). | Estar a mano, estar cerca (to be near). || ***To lie down***, acostarse, tenderse, tumbarse, echarse : *to lie down on the floor*, tenderse en el suelo; *why don't you lie down for a while?*, ¿por qué no te echas un rato? | Estar acostado *or* tendido *or* echado *or* tumbado (state). | — *Lie down!*, ¡échate! (to a dog). | *To lie down under an insult*, aguantar un insulto. | *To take sth. lying down*, aguantar algo sin chistar. || ***To lie in***, estar de parto (to be confined due to childbirth). | Quedarse en la cama (to stay in bed). || ***To lie off***, mantenerse a distancia (boats). | Reservarse (for later on). | Descansar (to rest from work). || ***To lie over***, aplazarse, quedar aplazado (to be postponed). | *It can lie over*, nada se pierde con esperar. || ***To lie to***, pairar, estar al pairo (a ship). || ***To lie up***, estar sin utilizar (a vehicle). | Desarmar (a ship). | Guardar cama (during an illness). | Esconderse (to hide). | Descansar (to rest).

— OBSERV. Pret. ***lay***; p. p. ***lain***.

lie-abed [—əbed] n. FAM. Remolón, ona; perezoso, sa.

lied [li:t] n. MUS. Lied, *m.*

— OBSERV. El plural es *lieder* en ambos idiomas.

lief [li:f] adv. *I had as lief* o *I would as lief go as stay*, me da igual irme que quedarme. || *I would as lief have died*, hubiera preferido morir.

liege [li:dʒ] adj. HIST. Ligio (subject). | Feudal (lord). — N. HIST. Señor (*m.*) feudal (lord). | Vasallo, *m.* (vassal).

liegeman [ˈli:dʒmæn] n. HIST. Vasallo, *m.*

— OBSERV. El plural de *liegeman* es *liegemen*.

lien [liən] n. JUR. Carga, *f.*, gravamen, *m.* (encumbrance). | Derecho (*m.*) de retención (on a property).

lierne [liˈə:n] n. ARCH. Nervio (*m.*) secundario [de una bóveda].

lieu [lju:] n. Lugar, *m.* || *In lieu of*, en vez de, en lugar de.

lieutenancy [lefˈtenənsi] n. Lugartenencia, *f.* || MIL. Tenientazgo, *m.*

lieutenant [lefˈtenənt] n. Lugarteniente, *m.* (deputy). || MIL. Teniente, *m.* || MAR. Alférez (*m.*) de navío. || — MIL. *Lieutenant colonel*, teniente coronel. || MAR. *Lieutenant commander*, capitán (*m.*) de corbeta. || MIL. *Lieutenant general*, teniente general. || *Lieutenant governor*, vicegobernador, *m.* || U. S. MAR. *Lieutenant junior grade*, alférez de navío. || MIL. *Second lieutenant*, subteniente, *m.*

life [laif] n. Vida, *f.*: *life and death*, vida y muerte; *expectation of life*, esperanza de vida; *she has lived all her life in Dublin*, ha vivido toda su vida en Dublín; *city, home, family, private life*, vida de ciudad, casera, de familia, privada *or* íntima; *bird life*, la vida de los pájaros; *is there life on Mars?*, ¿hay vida en Marte? || Duración, *f.*, vida, *f.* (of a carpet, light bulb, etc.). || Biografía, *f.*, vida, *f.*: *he is writing the life of Disraeli*, está escribiendo la biografía de Disraeli. || Vida, *f.*, alma, *f.*, animación, *f.* (at a party). || Vida, *f.*, vitalidad, *f.*: *full of life*, lleno de vida. || Vigencia, *f.* (validity). || JUR. Cadena (*f.*) perpetua (life imprisonment). || Víctima, *f.* (being): *how many lives were lost?*, ¿cuántas víctimas hubo?; *no lives were lost*, no hubo víctimas. || — *A matter of life and death*, una cuestión de vida o muerte. || *Animal life*, los animales: *there is not much animal life here*, aquí no hay muchos animales; la vida animal: *animal or plant life*, la vida animal o vegetal. || *As large as life*, de tamaño natural (life-size): *a statue as large as life*, una estatua de tamaño natural; en persona (in person). || *At my time of life*, a mi edad. || *Early life*, juventud, *f.*, años (*m. pl.*) juveniles. || *Eternal life*, vida eterna. || *For dear life*, desesperadamente: *he ran for dear life*, corrió desesperadamente. || *For life*, de por vida. || *For one's life*, desesperadamente. || *From life*, del natural (painting). || *How's life?*, ¿cómo va la vida?, ¿qué cuentas? || *I can't for the life of me remember his name*, por mucho que lo intente no puedo acordarme de su nombre. || *I wouldn't go there for the life of me*, no iría allí por nada en el mundo. || *Later life*, los últimos años. || *Low life*, hampa, *f.* || *My life!*, ¡Dios mío! || *Never in my life have I seen such a thing*, en mi vida he visto tal cosa. || *Not on your life!*, ¡ni hablar! || *One's whole life through*, durante toda su vida. || *Run for your life!*, ¡sálvese quien pueda! || ARTS. *Still life*, bodegón, *m.*, naturaleza muerta. || *Such is life!*, ¡así es la vida! || *That's life!*, ¡son cosas de la vida!, ¡la vida es así! || *The cat has nine lives*, el gato tiene siete vidas. || *The good life*, la buena vida. || *The high life*, la alta sociedad. || *The life and soul of the party*, el alma de la fiesta. || *This is the life!*, ¡eso es vida! || *To bear a charmed life*, escaparse por milagro de todos los peligros. || *To begin life as a carpenter*, empezar de carpintero. || *To bring (back) to life*, reanimar, resucitar. || *To come to life*, resucitar (to resuscitate, to wake up), recobrar el conocimiento, volver en sí (to regain consciousness). || *To depart this life*, partir de esta vida. || *To escape with one's life from an accident*, escaparse con vida de un accidente. || *To have seen life*, haber vivido mucho. || FAM. *To have the time of one's life*, pasárselo en grande. || *To lay down one's life*, dar *or* ofrendar *or* sacrificar la vida. || *To lead a dog's life*, llevar una vida de perros. || *To live the life of Riley*, darse buena vida. || *To pay with one's life*, pagar con la vida. || *To put new life into sth.*, dar vida a algo, infundir nueva vida a algo. || *To see life*, ver mundo. || *To sell one's life dearly*, vender cara la vida. || *To send s.o. to prison for life*, mandarle a uno a la cárcel para toda su vida. || *To take one's life in one's hands*, jugarse la vida. || *To take one's own life*, quitarse la vida, atentar contra su vida. || *To take s.o.'s life*, quitar la vida a uno. || *True to life*, conforme a la realidad. || *What a life!*, ¡qué vida ésta!, ¡qué vida! || *With all the pleasure in life*, con muchísimo gusto.
— Adj. De la vida. || Vitalicio, cia (annuity, etc.). || Vital: *life force*, fuerza vital.

— OBSERV. El plural de *life* es *lives*.

life-and-death [—ənˌdeθ] adj. FIG. Encarnizado, da; a vida y muerte: *a life-and-death struggle*, una lucha encarnizada *or* a vida y muerte.

life annuity [—əˈnjuiti] n. JUR. Renta (*f.*) vitalicia, vitalicio, *m.*

life belt [—belt] n. Cinturón (*m.*) salvavidas.

lifeblood [—blʌd] n. Sangre, *f.* (blood). || Alma, *f.*, nervio, *m.*, parte (*f.*) vital (sth. of vital importance).

lifeboat [—bəut] n. Bote (*m.*) salvavidas, lancha (*f.*) de salvamento.

life buoy [—bɔi] n. Boya (*f.*) salvavidas.

life cycle [—ˈsaikl] n. Ciclo (*m.*) vital.

life expectancy [—iksˈpektənsi] n. Esperanza (*f.*) de vida.

life-giving [—ˌgiviŋ] adj. Vivificante, que da vida.

lifeguard [—gɑ:d] n. Bañero, *m.* (on beach, in swimming pool).

Life Guards [—gɑ:dz] pl. n. Regimiento (*m. sing.*) de caballería al servicio del soberano británico.

life history [—ˈhistəri] n. Ciclo (*m.*) biológico.

life imprisonment [—imˈpriznmənt] n. Cadena (*f.*) perpetua.

life insurance [—inˈʃuərəns] n. Seguro (*m.*) de vida.

life interest [—ˈintrist] n. Vitalicio, *m.*

life jacket [—ˌdʒækit] n. Chaleco (*m.*) salvavidas.

lifeless [—lis] adj. Sin vida, muerto, ta. || FIG. Flojo, ja; soso, sa (dull). | Sin vida, sin animación.

lifelessness [—lisnis] n. Falta (*f.*) de vida.

lifelike [—laik] adj. Que parece vivo (that seems alive). || Natural (that is well reproduced). || Parecido, da; que está hablando (portrait).

lifeline [—lain] n. Cuerda (*f.*) de salvamento (for sea rescue). || Cordel (*m.*) de señales (of a diver). || FIG. Cordón (*m.*) umbilical (vital supply line). | Línea (*f.*) de la vida (in palmistry).

lifelong [—lɔŋ] adj. De toda la vida, de siempre.

life member [—ˈmembə*] n. Miembro (*m.*) vitalicio.

life preserver [—priˌzə:və*] n. Salvavidas, *m. inv.* (buoy, jacket). || Vergajo, *m.* (for self-defence).

lifer [—ə*] n. FAM. Condenado (*m.*) a cadena perpetua (prisoner). | Condena (*f.*) a cadena perpetua (sentence).

life raft [—rɑ:ft] n. Balsa (*f.*) salvavidas.
lifesaver [—ˌseivə*] n. Bañero, *m.* (lifeguard). || FIG. Salvación, *f.*
lifesaving [—ˌseiviŋ] n. Salvamento (*m.*) y socorrismo. || *Lifesaving jacket*, chaleco (*m.*) salvavidas.
life-size [—ˈsaiz] or **life-sized** [—ˈsaizd] adj. De tamaño natural.
life span [—spæn] n. Vida, *f.*
life table [—ˌteibl] n. Tabla (*f.*) de mortalidad.
lifetime [—taim] n. Vida, *f.*: *the lifetime of sth.*, la vida de algo; *in my lifetime*, en mi vida. || — *The chance of a lifetime* (*for you*), la ocasión de tu vida. || *The work of a lifetime*, el trabajo de toda una vida.
— Adj. De toda una vida.
life vest [—vest] n. Chaleco (*m.*) salvavidas.
lifework [—ˈwə:k] n. Trabajo (*m.*) de la vida [de alguien]: *his lifework*, el trabajo de su vida.
lift [lift] n. Elevación, *f.*, levantamiento, *m.*, alzamiento, *m.* (act of lifting). || Empuje, *m.* (upward support). || Levantamiento, *m.* (of a weight). || Elevación, *f.* (in the ground). || Ascensión, *f.* (upward movement). || Agitación, *f.*, levantamiento, *m.* (of the waves). || Diferencia (*f.*) de nivel (of level). || Altura (*f.*) de elevación (of a crane, etc.). || Porte, *m.* (of s.o.'s head). || AVIAT. Fuerza (*f.*) de ascensión. | Empuje, *m.* (that raises an aircraft). | Sustentación, *f.*, fuerza (*f.*) de sustentación. | Puente (*m.*) aéreo (airlift). || Ascensor, *m.* [*Amer.*, elevador, *m.*] (elevator). || Montacargas, *m. inv.* (hoist). || Carga, *f.* (load that is lifted). || TECH. Gato, *m.*, levantacoches, *m. inv.* (jack). | Carrera, *f.* (of a valve). || MAR. Amantillo, *m.* || Escalón, *m.* (section in a mine). || Tapa, *f.* (in the heel of a shoe). || FIG. Exaltación, *f.* (of mind). || — *I got a lift from Madrid to Seville*, me cogió un coche de Madrid a Sevilla. || *To give s.o. a lift*, llevar en coche: *give me a lift to the next town*, lléveme en coche hasta la próxima ciudad; reanimar, levantar la moral *or* el ánimo: *your letter gave me a lift*, su carta me reanimó mucho. || *To give s.o. a lift with sth.*, echar una mano a alguien, ayudar: *can you give me a lift with that suitcase?*, ¿puede echarme una mano para llevar esta maleta?
lift [lift] v. tr. Levantar: *he can lift 200 kilos*, levanta 200 kilos. || Levantar, elevar, alzar: *the crane lifted the load*, la grúa levantó la carga. || Coger (to pick up). || Levantar en brazos (a child). || Quitarse (a hat). || Levantar, elevar, subir (one's eye, arm). || Alzar, levantar, erguir (a spire). || Izar (the flag). || Subir (to raise to a specified place): *it lifted the load to the third floor*, subió la carga hasta el tercer piso. || Levantar, suprimir (an embargo, restrictions, etc.). || Levantar (blockade). || Levantar, alzar (siege). || AGR. Arrancar (potatoes). | Desplantar (seedlings). || Transportar (by plane). || Transportar por puente aéreo (to transport by airlift). || MIL. Alargar (the fire). || MED. Hacer el estirado de la piel (s.o.'s face). || FIG. Exaltar, elevar (heart, mind). | Elevar (in rank, dignity). || FAM. Robar, mangar, birlar (to steal). | Copiar (to plagiarize). | Llevarse, ganarse: *they lifted all the prizes*, se llevaron todos los premios. || U. S. Cancelar, redimir (a mortgage). || — *He doesn't lift a finger to help*, no mueve un dedo para ayudar. || *She has had her face lifted*, le han estirado la piel [de la cara]. || *To lift down*, bajar. || *To lift one's hand against*, levantar la mano contra. || *To lift one's voice against*, levantar *or* alzar la voz contra. || *To lift up*, levantar (to raise off a surface), dar: *can you lift me up that box?*, ¿me das esa caja?; levantar, alzar (one's head, voice).
— V. intr. Elevarse (to go up). || Levantarse: *the nose of the plane lifted*, el morro del avión se levantó. || Disiparse (fog, gloom). || Alabearse (the floor). || Aparecer (land). || AVIAT. Despegar.
lift attendant [—əˌtendənt] n. Ascensorista, *m. & f.*
lift boy [—bɔi] n. Ascensorista, *m.*
lifting [—iŋ] n. Levantamiento, *m.* (of a weight). || AVIAT. Sustentación, *f.*: *lifting force*, fuerza de sustentación.
lifting gear [—giə*] n. Torno (*m.*) elevador.
lifting jack [—dʒæk] n. TECH. Gato, *m.*
liftman [—mæn] n. Ascensorista, *m.*
— OBSERV. El plural de *liftman* es *liftmen*.
lift-off [—ɔf] n. Despegue, *m.* (of a plane or rocket).
lift pump [—pʌmp] n. Bomba (*f.*) aspirante.
lift shaft [—ʃɑ:ft] n. Caja (*f.*) del ascensor, hueco (*m.*) del ascensor.
lift-up [—ʌp] adj. Abatible (seat).
lift valve [—vælv] n. Válvula (*f.*) de movimiento vertical.
ligament [ˈligəmənt] n. ANAT. Ligamento, *m.*
ligamental [ˌligəˈmentl] or **ligamentary** [ˌligəˈmentəri] or **ligamentous** [ˌligəˈmentəs] adj. ANAT. Ligamentoso, sa.
ligate [ˈlaigeit] v. tr. MED. Ligar, hacer una ligadura a.
ligation [laiˈgeiʃən] n. Ligación, *f.* || MED. Ligadura, *f.*
ligature [ˈligətʃuə*] n. Ligadura, *f.* || PRINT. Ligado, *m.* || MUS. Ligado, *m.*, ligadura, *f.*
ligature [ˈligətʃuə*] v. tr. Ligar, atar. || MED. Ligar, hacer una ligadura a.
light [lait] adj. Ligero, ra; liviano, na (See OBSERV.) [burden, material, meal, food, wine, coffee, sleep]. || Fino, na (rain). || Ligero, ra: *to walk with a light step*, andar con paso ligero. || Suave (wind, breeze). || De poco peso, ligero, ra (not heavy). || No muy fuerte (tax). || De poca monta, poco, ca (expenses). || Suave: *light grade*, pendiente suave. || Ligero, ra; despreocupado, da (spirits). || Ligero, ra (conduct): *a light woman*, una mujer ligera. || Leve (wound, punishment, error). || Ligero, ra (music, comedy, reading). || Alegre, contento, ta: *a light heart*, un corazón alegre. || Débil (sound). || Ligero, ra: *a light blow*, un golpe ligero. || Fácil, ligero, ra: *light work*, trabajo fácil. || Ligero, ra (soil). || Delicado, da (hand, touch). || Vacío, a (purse). || MIL. Ligero, ra (artillery, infantry, tanks). | De pequeño calibre (gun). || MAR. En lastre. || Vacío, a; sin carga (train). || De vía estrecha (railway). || TECH. Ligero, ra: *a light metal*, un metal ligero. | Feble, falto de peso (coin). || Falto de peso (underweight). || GRAMM. Débil. || Luminoso, sa: *light image*, imagen luminosa; *light ray*, rayo luminoso. || Claro, ra: *light blue*, azul claro; *a light room*, una habitación clara; *light eyes*, ojos claros. || Rubio, bia (hair). || Blanco, ca (skin): *light complexion*, tez blanca. || — *A light sleeper*, una persona que tiene un sueño ligero. || *As light as a feather*, tan ligero como una pluma. || *Light in the head*, ligero de cascos. || *To be light on one's feet*, ser ligero de pies, andar con mucha agilidad. || *To get light*, amanecer. || *To grow light*, clarear, hacerse de día. || *To make light of*, no tomar en serio, hacer poco caso de. || *To make light work of*, hacer con facilidad (to accomplish with ease), vencer con facilidad a (to defeat with ease). || *With a light heart*, contento, ta.
— Adv. *To travel light*, viajar con poco equipaje.
— OBSERV. The word *liviano* is used mainly in Latin America.
light* [lait] v. intr. Bajar. || — *To light into*, atacar. || *To light on* o *upon*, posarse: *a fly lighted on his nose*, una mosca se le posó en la nariz; tropezar con (to meet, to find). || FAM. *To light out*, largarse, irse.
— OBSERV. Pret. & p. p. **lighted, lit.**
light [lait] n. Luz, *f.*: *light and dark*, luz y oscuridad; *light and shade*, luz y sombra; *the light of day*, la luz del día; *the light of reason*, la luz de la razón. || Luz, *f.*: *electric light*, luz eléctrica; *turn on the light*, enciende la luz; *black light*, luz negra. || Lámpara, *f.*, luz, *f.* (lamp): *overhead light*, lámpara de techo. || Vela, *f.* (candle). || Linterna, *f.* (lantern). || Farol, *m.* (streetlight). || Faro, *m.* (lighthouse). || AUT. Faro, *m.* (headlight). | Luz, *f.*: *the lights on this car don't work*, las luces de este coche no funcionan. || Fuego, *m.*, lumbre, *f.* (flame): *have you got a light?*, ¿tiene fuego? || Brillo, *m.*: *the light in her eyes*, el brillo de sus ojos. || Día, *m.* (daylight): *it is light*, es de día. || Disco, *m.*, luz, *f.*, semáforo, *m.* (in the street): *red light*, disco rojo. || ARCH. Luz, *f.*, lumbrera, *f.* (window). | Cristal, *m.*, vidrio, *m.* (of a leaded window). || ARTS. Luz, *f.* (in painting). || FIG. Aspecto, *m.*, apariencia, *f.* (aspect): *I see things in a new light*, veo las cosas bajo otro aspecto. | Lumbrera, *f.* (outstanding person). || — Pl. Luces, *f.*: *city lights*, las luces de la ciudad. || Semáforos, *m.*, luces (*f.*) de tráfico (traffic lights). || Iluminaciones, *f.*, iluminación, *f. sing.*: *Christmas lights*, la iluminación de Navidad. || Candilejas, *f.* (of the stage). || FIG. Luces, *f.* (intelligence, culture). || — *According to one's lights*, según lo que uno sabe. || *Advertising lights*, letreros luminosos. || *Against the light*, a trasluz (to look at sth.), a contraluz (photography). || FIG. *A shining light*, una lumbrera. || *At first light*, al rayar la luz del día, a primera luz. || *Bengala light*, bengala, *f.* || *By the light of*, a la luz de. || *Driving lights*, luces de carretera. || *In the light of*, a la luz de: *in the light of recent information*, a la luz de las noticias recientes. || *In this light*, desde este punto de vista. || *Leading light*, figura (*f.*) principal. || *Let there be light!*, ¡hágase la luz! || *Lights out!*, ¡apaguen! || *Northern lights*, aurora (*f.*) boreal. || *Parking light*, luz de estacionamiento. || *Pavement light*, cristal, *m.* || *Pilot* o *warning light*, piloto, *m.* || *Point of light*, punto luminoso. || AUT. *Rear* o *tail lights*, pilotos, *m.*, luces posteriores. || *This room has a poor light*, esta habitación tiene poca luz. || SP. *To appeal against the light*, pedir la suspensión de un partido por falta de luz. || FIG. *To appear in one's true light*, mostrarse como se es. || *To be in one's own light*, estar en la sombra. || *To be light*, hacerse de día. || FIG. *To bring sth. to light*, sacar algo a luz, revelar algo. | *To cast* o *to throw* o *to shed light on sth.*, aclarar algo, arrojar luz sobre algo. | *To come to light*, salir a luz. | *To give s.o. the green light*, dar la luz verde a alguien. | *To portray s.o. in a favourable light*, mostrar el lado bueno de alguien. || *To put a light to*, encender. || *To see one's name in lights*, ver su nombre en los carteles. || FIG. *To see the light*, nacer, ver la luz (to be born), salir a luz (work), ver claramente las cosas (to understand), convertirse (to be converted). || *To set light to sth.*, prender fuego a algo, encender algo. || *To shine a light on sth.*, enfocar algo. || *To show s.o. a light*, iluminar a alguien. || *To stand in s.o.'s light*, quitarle la luz a alguien. || *To strike a light*, encender una cerilla *or* un fósforo.
light* [lait] v. tr. Encender: *to light a lamp, a cigarette, a fire*, encender una lámpara, un cigarrillo, un fuego. || Iluminar, alumbrar: *to light the way for s.o.*, iluminar el camino a alguien; *to light a building*, iluminar un edificio; *to light the streets*, iluminar las calles. || FIG.

Iluminar (s.o.'s eyes, face). || *To light up*, iluminar.
— V. intr. Encenderse: *the fire wouldn't light*, el fuego no se encendía. || Encender, encenderse (a lamp, etc.). || FIG. Iluminarse (eyes, face). || *To light up*, iluminarse (to become illuminated): *the house lit up*, la casa se iluminó; *her face lit up*, se le iluminó la cara; encender un cigarrillo (to begin to smoke).

— OBSERV. Pret. & p. p. **lighted, lit.**

light-armed [—'ɑ:md] adj. MIL. Con armas ligeras.
light bulb [—bʌlb] n. Bombilla, *f.*
light buoy [—bɔi] n. Boya (*f.*) luminosa.
lighten [—n] v. tr. Aligerar: *to lighten the load*, aligerar la carga. || Alijar (to unload): *to lighten a ship*, alijar un barco. || Aliviar (to relieve): *to lighten a sorrow*, aliviar una pena. || Amenizar (to make more amusing). || Iluminar: *the sun lightened the room*, el sol iluminó la habitación. || Aclarar: *to lighten a colour*, aclarar un color. || FIG. Iluminar (s.o.'s face).
— V. intr. Aligerarse, hacerse más ligero (to become lighter). || Aliviarse (sorrow). || Iluminarse, alegrarse (to become brighter). || Clarear (to grow light). || Aclararse, despejarse (sky). || Relampaguear (to flash): *it's lightening again*, vuelve a relampaguear.
lightening [—niŋ] n. Aligeramiento, *m.* (of a load). || Alivio, *m.* (relief). || Iluminación, *f.* (brightening). || Aclaramiento, *m.* (of the weather).
lighter [—ə*] n. Encendedor, *m.*, mechero, *m.* (for cigarettes). || Encendedor, ra (person). || TECH. Encendedor, *m.* || MAR. Barcaza, *f.*, gabarra, *f.*
lighter [—ə*] v. tr. Transportar en barcaza *or* en gabarra.
lighterage [—əridʒ] n. Transporte (*m.*) por medio de barcazas (transportation by lighter). || Coste (*m.*) del transporte en barcazas (cost).
lighterman [—əmən] n. Gabarrero, *m.*

— OBSERV. El plural de esta palabra es *lightermen*.

light-fingered [—,fiŋgəd] adj. FIG. Largo *or* listo de manos.
light-footed [—'futid] adj. De paso ligero, ligero de pies.
light-haired [—'hɛəd] adj. Rubio, bia.
light-headed [—'hedid] adj. Mareado, da (from drink). || Delirante (delirious). || Casquivano, na; ligero de cascos (scatterbrained).
lighthearted [—'hɑ:tid] adj. Alegre, contento, ta (gay). || Sin preocupaciones, despreocupado, da (free from care).
light heavyweight [—'heviweit] n. SP. Peso (*m.*) semipesado.
light horse [—'hɔ:s] n. MIL. Caballería (*f.*) ligera.
light-horseman [—'hɔ:smən] n. MIL. Soldado (*m.*) de caballería ligera.

— OBSERV. El plural de esta palabra es *light-horsemen*.

lighthouse [—haus] n. Faro, *m.* || *Lighthouse lamp*, fanal, *m.*
lighthouse keeper [—haus,ki:pə*] n. Torrero, *m.*
lighting [—iŋ] n. Alumbrado, *m.* (system). || Iluminación, *f.* (act of illuminating). || Encendido, *m.* (of a fire). || Luz, *f.* (of a picture). || — *Direct lighting*, alumbrado directo. || *Lighting effects*, efectos luminosos. || *Lighting engineer*, luminotécnico, *m.*, técnico (*m.*) en iluminación, ingeniero (*m.*) de luces. || *Lighting engineering*, luminotecnia, *f.* || *Street lighting*, alumbrado público.
lightly [—li] adv. Ligeramente (gently, to a small degree). || Con paso ligero (with a light step): *she walked lightly*, andaba con paso ligero. || A la ligera: *to take sth. lightly*, tomar algo a la ligera. || Alegremente (cheerfully). || Levemente (wounded). || *Lightly clad*, vestido con muy poca ropa.
light meter [—,mi:tə*] n. PHOT. Exposímetro, *m.*, fotómetro, *m.*
light-minded [—'maindid] adj. Frívolo, la; ligero de cascos.
lightness [—nis] n. Ligereza, *f.*, poco peso, *m.* (quality of being by no means heavy). || Carácter (*m.*) leve, levedad, *f.* (of a wound). || Facilidad, *f.* (easiness). || Agilidad, *f.*, ligereza, *f.* (agility). || Ligereza, *f.* (fickleness). || Luminosidad, *f.*, claridad, *f.* (degree of illumination). || Claridad, *f.* (of a colour).
lightning ['laitniŋ] n. Relámpago, *m.* (flash). || Rayo, *m.* (stroke): *lightning hit the church tower*, cayó un rayo en el campanario de la iglesia. || FIG. *As quick as lightning*, como un rayo.
— Adj. Relámpago: *a lightning visit*, una visita relámpago.
lightning arrester [—ə,restə*] n. Pararrayos, *m. inv.*
lightning bug [—bʌg] n. ZOOL. Luciérnaga, *f.*
lightning conductor [—kən,dʌktə*] n. Pararrayos, *m. inv.*
lightning rod [—rɔd] n. U. S. Pararrayos, *m. inv.*
light-o'-love ['laitəlʌv] n. Mujer (*f.*) ligera.
light opera ['lait'ɔpərə] n. Opereta, *f.*
light quantum ['lait'kwɔntəm] n. PHYS. Fotón, *m.*
lights [laits] pl. n. Bofes, *m.* (of slaughtered cattle).
light shell ['laitʃel] n. Proyectil (*m.*) luminoso.
lightship ['laitʃip] n. MAR. Buque (*m.*) faro.
light show ['laitʃəu] n. Juego (*m.*) de luces.
lightsome ['laitsəm] adj. Luminoso, sa; claro, ra (full of light). || Gracioso, sa (graceful). || Ágil (nimble). || Alegre (cheerful). || Frívolo, la (frivolous).
light source [laitsɔ:s] n. Fuente (*f.*) luminosa.
lights-out ['laitsaut] n. MIL. Retreta, *f.* || *Lights-out is at ten o'clock*, las luces se apagan a las diez.
light spot ['laitspɔt] n. Punto (*m.*) luminoso.
light wave ['laitweiv] n. Onda (*f.*) luminosa.
lightweight ['laitweit] adj. Ligero, ra; de poco peso.
— N. SP. Peso (*m.*) ligero (boxer). || U. S. FAM. Persona (*f.*) de poco peso *or* de poca entidad.
lightwood ['laitwud] n. Madera (*f.*) resinosa que se enciende fácilmente.
light-year ['laitjə:*] n. ASTR. Año (*m.*) luz, año (*m.*) de luz.
lignaloe [lai'næləu] n. Áloe, *m.* (drug).
ligneous ['ligniəs] adj. Leñoso, sa.
lignification [,lignifi'keiʃən] n. BOT. Lignificación, *f.*
lignify ['lignifai] v. intr. BOT. Lignificarse.
— V. tr. BOT. Convertir en madera.
lignite ['lignait] n. MIN. Lignito, *m.*
lignum vitae ['lignəm'vaiti:] n. BOT. Guayaco, *m.* (tree). | Palo (*m.*) santo (wood).
Ligures [li'gjuəri:z] pl. n. HIST. Ligures, *m.*
Liguria [li'gjuəriə] pr. n. GEOGR. Liguria, *f.*
Ligurian [—n] adj./n. Ligur.
likable ['laikəbl] adj. Amable, agradable, simpático, ca (person). || Agradable, grato, ta (thing).
likableness [—nis] n. Simpatía, *f.*, amabilidad, *f.*
like [laik] adj. Parecido, da; semejante, similar: *two like cases*, dos casos parecidos; *two people of like tastes*, dos personas de gustos similares. || Igual, equivalente: *like poles*, polos iguales. || Mismo, ma: *the like period last year*, la misma época del año pasado. || Análogo, ga: *cholera and other like illnesses*, el cólera y otras enfermedades análogas. || — *Like father like son*, de tal palo tal astilla. || *Something like twenty pounds*, unas veinte libras, algo así como veinte libras. || *They are as like as two peas*, se parecen como dos gotas de agua. || *To be like to*, ser probable que: *it is like to give us trouble*, es probable que nos cause problemas; ser capaz de: *he is like to come at any moment*, es capaz de venir a cualquier momento.
— Prep. Como: *there is nothing like swimming*, no hay nada como nadar; *to fight like a man*, luchar como un hombre; *to run like a hare*, correr como una liebre. || Igual que, del mismo modo que, como: *you think like my father*, piensas igual que mi padre; *he treated me like a brother*, me trataba como a un hermano. || Como, igual que: *a car like mine*, un coche igual que el mío; *eyes like diamonds*, ojos como diamantes. || — *I never saw anything like it*, nunca he visto cosa igual. || *It's not like him to do that*, no es de él hacer eso, no es propio de él hacer eso. || *It looks like a fine day tomorrow*, parece que mañana hará buen tiempo. || *Like that*, así: *I can't do it like that*, no lo puedo hacer así; *Spaniards are like that*, los españoles son así; como ése, como ésa: *I want a skirt like that*, quiero una falda como ésa. || *That's just like him!*, ¡eso es muy de él!, ¡es muy propio de él! || *That's more like it!*, ¡eso está mejor! || *To be like*, parecerse a (to resemble): *they are very much like their mother*, se parecen mucho a su madre. || *To be nothing like so rich*, estar lejos de ser tan rico. || *To be nothing like as happy as s.o. else*, no estar, ni mucho menos, tan contento como otro. || *To feel like*, see FEEL. || *To look like*, see LOOK. || *What does she sing like?*, ¿qué tal canta?, ¿cómo canta? || *What is she like?*, ¿qué tal es?, ¿cómo es? || *Who is she like?*, ¿a quién se parece? || *You are like a brother to me*, eres como un hermano para mí.
— Adv. *As like as not* o *like as not* o *like enough* o *very like*, probablemente, a lo mejor. || FAM. *It's like big*, es más bien grande, es como grande. || *It's nothing like*, no se parece en nada.
— Conj. FAM. Como: *do it like he does*, hazlo como él; *it was like when you were at home*, era como cuando estabas en casa.
— N. Igual, *m.* & *f.*, semejante, *m.* & *f.*: *we shall never see her like again*, nunca volveremos a ver una igual. || — Pl. Gustos, *m.* || — *And the like*, y cosas por el estilo. || *I have my likes and dislikes*, tengo mis preferencias. || *The likes of*, personas como: *it is not for the likes of you*, no es para personas como tú. || *To do the like*, hacer lo mismo.

— OBSERV. Like se emplea como sufijo y significa entonces « parecido a », « propio de », etc. : *woodlike*, parecido a la madera; *childlike*, propio de un niño; *to behave in an adultlike fashion*, comportarse como un adulto.

like [laik] v. tr./intr. Gustarle [a uno]: *do you like tea?*, ¿le gusta el té?; *how do you like your tea?*, ¿cómo le gusta el té?; *I like flamenco*, a mí me gusta el flamenco; *I like reading*, me gusta leer. || Gustarle [a uno], tenerle simpatía (friends and acquaintances): *I like Charles*, le tengo simpatía a Carlos, me gusta Carlos. || Querer a (close friends): *I like my parents*, quiero a mis padres. || Querer (to wish): *I don't like to interrupt*, no quiero interrumpir; *you can say what you like*, puede decir lo que quiera; *as you like*, como quiera; *when you like*, cuando quiera; *would you like another cup of tea?*, ¿quiere otra taza de té? || Gustarle [a uno]: *I should like to talk to you*, me gustaría hablar con Ud.; *would you like to go tomorrow?*, ¿le gustaría ir mañana?; *I like you to be near me*, me gusta que esté cerca de mí. || — *As much as (ever) you like*, todo lo que quiera. || *How do you like my article?*, ¿qué le parece mi artículo? || *If* *you like*, si quiere. || *I like milk but milk doesn't like me*, me gusta la leche pero me sienta mal. || FIG. *I like that!*, ¡qué bien!, ¡estupendo! || *I would like a dozen eggs, please*, quisiera una docena de huevos, por favor. || *This plant likes sunshine*, le sienta bien el sol a esta planta. || *To do what one likes with sth.*, hacer lo que uno quiere con algo. || *To like best*, gustarle más [a uno]. || *To like better*, preferir. || *What would you like to drink?*, ¿qué quiere beber? || *Whether you like it or not*, le guste o no le guste, quiera o no quiera. || *Would you like to do me a favour?*, ¿quiere hacerme un favor? || *Would you like to go for a walk?*, ¿le apetece dar un paseo?, ¿le gustaría dar un paseo?

likeable [—əbl] adj. Amable, agradable, simpático, ca (person). || Agradable, grato, ta (thing).

likeableness [—əblnis] n. Simpatía, *f.*, amabilidad, *f.*

likehood [—lihud] or **likeliness** [—linis] n. Posibilidad, *f.*: *there is little likelihood of*, hay poca posibilidad de. || Probabilidad, *f.* (probability): *in all likelihood*, con toda probabilidad. || Verosimilitud, *f.* (credibility).

likely [—li] adj. Probable (probable). || Posible (possible). || Plausible, verosímil (plausible). || Apropiado, da (suitable): *what is the likeliest moment to find you at home?*, ¿cuál es el momento más apropiado para encontrarle en casa? || Prometedor, ra (promising): *a likely lad*, un joven prometedor. || — *It is likely to be wet*, es probable que esté húmedo. || FIG. *That's a likely story!*, ¡puro cuento! || *They are likely to cause trouble afterwards*, puede ser que *or* es probable que ocasionen problemas después. || *To be not likely that*, ser poco probable que: *it is not likely that it will rain*, es poco probable que llueva. || *Where are you likely to be this evening?*, ¿dónde piensas estar esta noche?

— Adv. Probablemente. || — *As likely as not* o *likely as not*, probablemente, a lo mejor. || *Likely enough*, probablemente.

like-minded [— maindid] adj. De la misma opinión.

liken [—ən] v. tr. Comparar [*with*, *to*, con].

likeness [—nis] n. Semejanza, *f.*, parecido, *m.* (similarity). || Retrato, *m.* (portrait). || Verosimilitud, *f.* (credibility). || Forma, *f.*, apariencia, *f.*: *in the likeness of*, bajo la forma de. || — *Family likeness*, parecido de familia. || *The picture is a good likeness*, el retrato se parece mucho *or* está muy conseguido. || *To catch the likeness*, coger el parecido.

likewise [—waiz] adv. Del mismo modo, lo mismo, igualmente (the same way). || También, asimismo (also). || Además (moreover). || *To do likewise*, hacer lo mismo.

liking [—iŋ] n. Cariño, *m.*, simpatía, *f.* (for a person): *I took a liking to him*, le cogí simpatía, le tomé cariño. || Afición, *f.*, gusto, *m.* (for a thing). || Preferencia, *f.*, predilección, *f.* (preference). || — *He took a liking to it*, le cogió gusto. || *To have a liking for*, ser aficionado a (sth.), tener simpatía a (s.o.). || *To one's liking*, del gusto *or* del agrado de uno.

lilac [ˈlailək] n. BOT. Lila, *f.* || Lila, *m.* (colour).

— Adj. De color lila, lila.

liliaceae [ˌliliˈeiʃii] pl. n. BOT. Liliáceas, *f.*

liliaceous [liliˈeiʃəs] adj. BOT. Liliáceo, a.

Lilliput [ˈlilipʌt] pr. n. Liliput.

Lilliputian [ˌliliˈpju:ʃjən] adj./n. Liliputiense.

lilt [lilt] n. Canción (*f.*) alegre (song). || Deje, *m.* (singsong accent). || Balanceo, *m.* (light swaying). || Ritmo, *m.*, cadencia, *f.* (rhythm).

lilt [lilt] v. tr./intr. Cantar melodiosamente.

lily [ˈlili] n. Azucena, *f.* (flower). || HERALD. Flor (*f.*) de lis. || — BOT. *Calla lily*, cala, *f.*, lirio (*m.*) de agua. | *Lily of the valley*, lirio (*m.*) de los valles, muguete, *m.* | *Water lily*, nenúfar, *m.* | *White lily*, lirio blanco, azucena.

— Adj. Blanco como la azucena *or* como la nieve (white). || Inocente, puro, ra (pure).

lily-livered [—ˈlivəd] adj. Cobarde, miedoso, sa.

lily pad [—pæd] n. BOT. Hoja (*f.*) de nenúfar.

lily-white [—wait] adj. Blanco como la azucena *or* como la nieve. || FIG. Inocente, puro, ra (innocent).

Lima [ˈli:mə. US. ˈlaimə] pr. n. GEOGR. Lima.

Lima bean [—bi:n] n. BOT. Fríjol, *m.*, frijol, *m.*

limb [lim] n. ANAT. Miembro, *m.* || BOT. Rama, *f.* (branch of a tree). | Limbo, *m.* (of a petal). || Brazo, *m.* (of a cross). || Estribación, *f.* (of a mountain). || GRAMM. Período, *m.* (of a sentence). || ASTR. MATH. Limbo, *m.* || FAM. Representante, *m.* (of the law, etc.). | Chiquillo (*m.*) travieso, golfillo, *m.* (child). || — FIG. *Out on a limb*, en una situación precaria. || *To tear limb from limb*, despedazar.

limb [lim] v. tr. Desmembrar (a person). || Despedazar (an animal). || Podar (a tree).

limbed [—d] adj. De miembros: *strong-limbed*, de miembros fuertes.

limber [—bə*] adj. Flexible (thing). || Ágil (person).

— N. MIL. Armón, *m.* (of a gun carriage). || — Pl. MAR. Imbornales (*m.*) de cuaderna.

limber [—bə*] v. tr. Enganchar el armón a. || *To limber up*, volver ágil *or* flexible.

— V. intr. *To limber up*, hacer ejercicios de precalentamiento (an athlete), prepararse.

limbless [—lis] adj. Falto de un brazo *or* una pierna, tullido, da.

limbo [ˈlimbəu] n. REL. Limbo, *m.* || FIG. Olvido, *m.* (oblivion). | Mazmorra, *f.*, cárcel, *f.* (prison).

lime [laim] n. CHEM. Cal, *f.*: *lime cast*, enlucido con cal; *slaked lime*, cal muerta. || Liga, *f.* (birdlime). || BOT. Limero, *m.*, lima, *f.* (tree). | Lima, *f.* (fruit). | Tilo, *m.* (linden tree).

lime [laim] v. tr. Encalar (to spread lime over). || AGR. Abonar con cal. || Apelambrar (hides). || Untar con liga (to smear with birdlime). || Coger con liga (birds).

limeburner [—ˈbə:nə*] n. Calero, *m.*

limekiln [—kiln] n. Calera, *f.*, horno (*m.*) de cal.

limelight [—lait] n. THEATR. Foco, *m.*, proyector, *m.* || Luz (*f.*) de calcio. || — Pl. Candilejas, *f.* (footlights). || FIG. *To be in the limelight*, estar en el candelero, estar en la primera plana de la actualidad.

limen [ˈlaimən] n. Umbral, *m.*

limerick [ˈlimərik] n. Quintilla (*f.*) humorística.

limestone [ˈlaimstəun] n. Piedra (*f.*) caliza, caliza, *f.*

lime tree [ˈlaimtri:] n. BOT. Tilo, *m.*

lime-twig [ˈlaimtwig] n. Vareta, *f.*

limewash [ˈlaimwɔʃ] n. Lechada (*f.*) de cal.

limewater [ˈlaimˌwɔ:tə*] n. Agua (*f.*) de cal.

limey [ˈlaimi] n. FAM. Inglés, esa.

liminal [ˈliminl] adj. Liminal.

liminary [ˈliminəri] adj. Liminar (introductory).

limit [ˈlimit] n. Límite, *m.*: *the limits of his knowledge*, los límites de sus conocimientos; *speed limit*, límite de velocidad. || Máximo, *m.* (maximum). || Mínimo, *m.* (minimum). || MATH. Límite, *m.* || — *Age limit*, edad máxima. || *He o that is the limit!*, ¡es el colmo! || *To know no limits*, ser infinito, no tener límites. || *Within limits*, dentro de ciertos límites. || *Within the limits of the city*, dentro de la ciudad. || *Without limit*, sin límite, ilimitado, da.

limit [ˈlimit] v. tr. Limitar: *I have to limit my expenses*, tengo que limitar mis gastos. || *To limit o.s. to*, limitarse a.

limitary [—əri] adj. Limitador, ra (restrictive). || Limitado, da (limited). || Limítrofe (bordering).

limitation [ˌlimiˈteiʃən] n. Limitación, *f.* || Limitación, *f.*, restricción, *f.* || JUR. Prescripción, *f.*

limitative [ˌlimiˈteitiv] adj. Limitativo, va. || *Clause limitative*, cláusula restrictiva.

limited [ˈlimitid] adj. Limitado, da: *limited knowledge*, conocimientos limitados. || Escaso, sa; reducido, da (small). || — COMM. *Limited company* o *limited-liability company*, sociedad [de responsabilidad] limitada. || *Limited edition*, tirada (*f.*) de un número reducido de ejemplares. || *Limited mobilization*, movilización (*f.*) parcial. || *Limited monarchy*, monarquía (*f.*) constitucional. || *Limited partnership*, sociedad (*f.*) en comandita.

limiting [ˈlimitiŋ] adj. Restrictivo, va. || GRAMM. Determinativo, va.

limitless [ˈlimitlis] adj. Ilimitado, da; sin límites.

limn [lim] v. tr. Pintar (to paint, to draw). || Retratar, pintar (to portray in words).

limner [—nə*] n. Pintor, ra.

limnology [limˈnɔlədʒi] n. Limnología, *f.*

limonite [ˈlaimənait] n. MIN. Limonita, *f.*

limousine [ˈlimu:zi:n] n. Limusina, *f.* (car).

limp [limp] adj. Fláccido, da; flácido, da; blando, da; fofo, fa (floppy). || Débil (weak). || Debilitado, da: *limp with the heat*, debilitado por el calor. || Poco enérgico, ca (lacking energy). || Blandengue (lacking firmness). || Desmayado, da (voice). || TECH. Flexible (bookbinding). || FIG. *As limp as a rag*, como un trapo.

— N. Cojera, *f.*: *a slight limp*, una ligera cojera. || *To walk with a limp*, cojear.

limp [limp] v. intr. Cojear. || POET. Cojear (verse). || — *He limped off*, se marchó cojeando. || FIG. *The ships limped into harbour*, los barcos llegaron con dificultad al puerto.

limpet [ˈlimpit] n. ZOOL. Lapa, *f.* (shellfish). || FIG. Lapa, *f.* || MIL. *Limpet mine*, mina (*f.*) que se coloca en el casco de un barco.

limpid [ˈlimpid] adj. Límpido, da; claro, ra.

limpidity [limˈpiditi] n. Limpidez, *f.*, claridad, *f.*

limpness [ˈlimpnis] n. Flojedad, *f.*

limy [ˈlaimi] adj. Calizo, za (of caustic lime). || Untado de liga (with birdlime). || Pegajoso, sa (sticky).

linaceae [laiˈneisii:] pl. n. BOT. Lináceas, *f.*

linaceous [laiˈneiʃəs] adj. Lináceo, a.

linage [ˈlainidʒ] n. Número (*m.*) de líneas (number of lines). || Pago (*m.*) por líneas (payment).

linchpin [ˈlintʃpin] n. TECH. Pezonera, *f.* (of an axle). || FIG. Lo esencial, parte esencial (vital part). | Eje, *m.*: *he is the linchpin of the organization*, es el eje de la organización.

linden [ˈlindən] n. BOT. Tilo, *m.* (tree). | Tila, *f.* (infusion). || Madera (*f.*) de tilo (wood).

line [lain] n. Línea, *f.*, trazo, *m.*, raya, *f.* (by a pencil, pen). || Línea, *f.*, renglón, *m.* (of writing). || MUS. Línea, *f.* [del pentagrama]. || MATH. Línea, *f.*: *straight line*, línea recta. || Línea, *f.*, contorno, *m.* (outline). || Línea, *f.* (of the hand). || Línea, *f.*, rasgo, *m.* (feature). || Arruga, *f.* (wrinkle). || Fila, *f.* (row): *in a line*, en fila; *in line*, en filas. || Línea, *f.*, hilera, *f.* (of trees). || Fila, *f.* (of parked cars). || Cola, *f.* (of traffic, people). || Serie, *f.*, sucesión, *f.* (series). || Verso, *m.* (verse). || Líneas, *f. pl.*, letras, *f. pl.* (brief letter): *drop me a line*, escríbeme cuatro letras, ponme unas líneas. || Línea, *f.*, corte, *m.* (of a dress). || Línea, *f.* (of a vehicle). || Línea, *f.* (telephone). || Línea, *f.*, conferencia, *f.* (speaking on the telephone). || ELECTR. Línea, *f.*: *high-tension line*, línea de alta tensión. | Cable, *m.* (wire). | Cordón, *m.*, flexible, *m.* (flex). || Cuerda, *f.* (rope). || Línea, *f.* (rail). || Vía, *f.* (track): *down, up line*, vía descendente, ascendente. || AVIAT. Línea, *f.* || Línea, *f.*: *bus line*, línea de autobuses. || Vía, *f.*: *lines of communication*, vías de comunicación. || Línea, *f.* (in factory): *assembly line*, línea de montaje. || ARCH. Cordel, *m.*: *in the straight line*, tirado a cordel. | Alineación, *f.* (of a street): *building line*, alineación de los edificios. | Tubería, *f.*, cañería, *f.* (pipe). | Gola, *f.*, cimacio, *m.* (cyma). || PHYS. Raya, *f.* (of the spectrum). | Línea, *f.* (of television). || MAR. Cabo, *m.* (cord). | Línea, *f.*: *ship of the line*, barco de línea. | Compañía, *f.*: *shipping line*, compañía naviera. | Sedal, *m.*, cuerda, *f.* (for fishing). || MIL. Línea, *f.*: *front line*, primera línea; *line of battle*, línea de batalla. || Límite, *m.*: *to draw the line*, marcar *or* trazar el límite; *State line*, límite de un Estado. || SP. Raya, *f.* (on a court). | Línea, *f.*: *goal line*, línea de meta; *forward line*, línea delantera. || GEOGR. Ecuador, *m.* || COMM. Artículo, *m.* (article). | Surtido, *m.* (range of goods). || FIG. Línea, *f.* (of conduct). | Directiva, *f.*: *to work on the lines of*, trabajar siguiendo las directivas de. | Postura, *f.*, actitud, *f.* (position). | Especialidad, *f.*, rama, *f.* (department of activity): *that's not in my line*, eso no es de mi especialidad. | Ramo, *m.*: *in the building line*, en el ramo de la construcción. | Línea, *f.*: *the party line*, la línea del partido. | Límite, *m.*, límites, *m. pl.*: *one must draw the line somewhere*, hay que fijar ciertos límites. | Familia, *f.*: *he comes of a good line*, procede de buena familia. | Línea, *f.*, linaje, *m.* (of descent). | Línea, *f.*: *we are descended in direct line from*, descendemos en línea directa de. | Pista, *f.*, indicación, *f.* (clue): *to give a line on*, poner sobre la pista de, dar una indicación sobre. | Cuento, *m.* (patter). || — Pl. FAM. Partida (*f. sing.*) de matrimonio. | Destino, *m. sing.* (destiny). || Papel, *m. sing.* (actor's part). || — *All along the line*, en toda la línea. || *Along the lines of*, de acuerdo con. || *Along these lines*, de esta manera. || *Demarcation line*, línea de demarcación. || *Dotted line*, línea de puntos. || FIG. *Hard lines!*, ¡mala suerte! || *He is in line for promotion*, va a ser ascendido. || *He is in line for trouble!*, ¡va a tener problemas!, ¡se puede preparar! || *Hold the line!*, ¡no cuelgue!, ¡no se retire! || FIG. *Hot line*, teléfono rojo. || *It is more in my line*, me va mejor. || MAR. *Line abreast*, línea de frente. | *Line astern*, uno detrás de otro, en fila india. || *Line of fire*, línea de fuego *or* de tiro. || *Line of force*, línea de fuerza. || FIG. *Line of least resistance*, ley (*f.*) del mínimo esfuerzo. || *Line of route*, itinerario, *m.* || *Line of thought*, hilo (*m.*) del pensamiento. || *Line of vision*, visual, *f.* || *Next* o *new line*, punto y aparte (in dictation). || *Of the male line*, de la línea masculina. || *On the following lines*, de la manera siguiente. || *On the line of*, en la línea de. || MAR. *Plimsoll line*, línea de máxima carga. || *Royal line*, familia real. || *Sth. along these lines*, algo por el estilo. || *To be in line with*, estar de acuerdo con. || *To be on the right lines*, ir por buen camino. || *To be out of line with*, no estar de acuerdo con. || *To bring into line*, alinear (to line up), poner al día (to bring up to date), poner de acuerdo (to make agree), llamar al orden (to bring under control). || FIG. *To come into line with*, conformarse con la opinión de. | *To draw the line at*, no ir más allá de. || *To fall into line*, alinearse. || FIG. *To fall into line with*, conformarse con (s.o.'s ideas), conformarse con las ideas de (s.o.). | *To get a line on*, obtener información sobre, informarse sobre. | *To give s.o. line enough*, soltar la rienda a alguien. | *To have a good line*, tener mucha labia. | *To have a line on*, tener una idea de (idea), tener información sobre (information). | *To hold the line*, aguantar. | *To keep one's men in line*, mantener la disciplina entre sus hombres. | *To know where to draw the line*, saber dónde pararse. || *To lay down the broad lines of*, trazar las grandes líneas de. || FIG. *To lay on the line*, dar (sum of money). || *To leave the lines*, descarrilar (train). || *To read between the lines*, leer entre líneas. || FAM. *To shoot a line*, darse postín *or* bombo. || FIG. *To sign on the dotted line*, aprobar a ciegas. || *To stand in line*, hacer cola. || FIG. *To step out of line*, salir de las reglas. || *To toe the line*, pisar la línea (in a race), conformarse (to conform). || FIG. *To toe the party line*, seguir la línea del partido. | *What line are you in?*, *¿what's your line?*, ¿a qué se dedica Ud.?

line [lain] v. tr. Rayar (to cover with lines): *lined paper*, papel rayado. || Alinearse por (to stand in a line along). || Bordear: *road lined with poplars*, carretera bordeada de álamos. || Surcar, arrugar (to wrinkle). || Surcar (a field). || Forrar (to provide with an inner layer): *she lined her coat with silk*, forró su abrigo con seda. || Forrar (in bookbinding). || TECH. Revestir. | Entibar (a well). | Guarnecer (brakes). | Encamisar (a gun). || MAR. Reforzar (sails). || Llenar, cubrir (to cover). || — FAM. *To line one's pockets*, forrarse, llenarse los bolsillos (to make money). | *To line one's stomach*, hartarse, ponerse como el quico. || *To line up*, alinear, poner en fila (to arrange in a line).

— V. intr. *To line up*, alinearse, ponerse en fila (people), hacer cola (to queue), formarse (troops, teams).

lineage [ˈlaiˈnidʒ] n. See LINAGE.

lineage [ˈliniidʒ] n. Linaje, *m.*

lineal [ˈliniəl] adj. Lineal (linear). || En línea directa (descent).

lineally [—i] adv. En línea directa.

lineament [ˈliniəmənt] n. Lineamiento, *m.*, lineamento, *m.* || — Pl. Rasgos, *m.*, facciones, *f.* (facial features).

linear [ˈliniə] adj. Lineal. || — TECH. *Linear accelerator*, acelerador (*m.*) lineal. || MATH. *Linear equation*, ecuación (*f.*) lineal *or* de primer grado. || *Linear measure*, medida (*f.*) de longitud. || *Linear perspective*, perspectiva (*f.*) lineal.

lineation [ˌliniˈeiʃən] n. Líneas, *f. pl.* || Trazado, *m.*

line drawing [ˈlainˈdrɔːiŋ] n. Dibujo (*m.*) lineal.

line engraving [ˈlaininˈgreiviŋ] n. ARTS. Grabado (*m.*) en dulce, grabado (*m.*) con buril.

line fishing [ˈlainˌfiʃiŋ] n. Pesca (*f.*) con caña.

lineman [ˈlainmən] n. ELECTR. Instalador (*m.*) de líneas. || Guardavía, *m.* (railway).

— OBSERV. El plural de esta palabra es *linemen*.

linen [ˈlinin] n. Hilo, *m.*, lino, *m.* (textile). || Mantelería, *f.* (of table). || Ropa, *f.*: *clean, dirty linen*, ropa limpia, sucia. || Ropa (*f.*) blanca (of the house). || Ropa (*f.*) interior (underclothes). || Ropa (*f.*) de cama (bed linen). || — FIG. *Don't wash your dirty linen in public*, los trapos sucios se lavan en casa. || *Linen basket*, canasta (*f.*) or cesto (*m.*) de la ropa. || *Linen closet*, *linen cupboard*, armario (*m.*) de la ropa. || *Linen clothes* o *drapery*, lencería, *f.* || *Linen room*, lencería, *f.*

— Adj. De hilo, de lino: *linen cloth*, tela de hilo.

linendraper [—ˌdreipə*] n. Lencero, ra. || *Linendraper's*, lencería, *f.*

line-out [ˈlainaut] n. SP. Saque (*m.*) de banda.

liner [ˈlainə*] n. Transatlántico, *m.* (ship). || AVIAT. Avión (*m.*) de línea. || TECH. Forro, *m.*, revestimiento, *m.* (lining). | Camisa, *f.* (of a cylinder).

linesman [ˈlainzmən] n. SP. Juez (*m.*) de línea, juez (*m.*) de banda. || Guardavía, *m.* (on railway). || MIL. Soldado (*m.*) de línea. || U. S. ELECTR. Instalador (*m.*) de líneas.

— OBSERV. El plural de *linesman* es *linesmen*.

line spacer [ˈlainˌspeisə*] n. Interlineador, *m.* (of a typewriter).

lineup [ˈlainʌp] n. SP. Alineación, *f.*, formación, *f.* (football, rugby). || Hilera (*f.*) de personas (file).

ling [liŋ] n. Bacalao, *m.*, abadejo, *m.* (fish). || BOT. Brezo, *m.*

linger [ˈliŋgə*] v. intr. Rezagarse (to dawdle, to lag behind). || Callejear, vagabundear (to loiter). || Persistir, subsistir (use, hope, doubts, etc.). || Tardar: *to linger to go*, tardar en ir. || Quedarse (to stay). || Tardar en morirse. || Hacerse largo (to be too long): *the film lingers*, la película se hace larga. || — *To linger on* o *upon*, dilatarse en (to expatiate). || *To linger over*, no darse prisa en hacer, tardar en hacer: *to linger over a job*, tardar en hacer un trabajo; dilatarse en (to expatiate). || *To linger over a meal*, tardar en comer.

— V. tr. *To linger away*, perder (one's time). || *To linger out one's life*, arrastrar su vida.

lingerer [—rə*] n. Rezagado, da.

lingerie [ˈlɛ̃ʒəri] n. Ropa (*f.*) interior, ropa (*f.*) blanca (women's).

lingering [ˈliŋgəriŋ] adj. Lento, ta (death). || Persistente (doubt, smell). || Fijo, ja (look). || MED. Crónico, ca (disease).

lingo [ˈliŋgəu] n. FAM. Lengua, *f.*, idioma, *m.* (language). | Jerga, *f.* (jargon).

— OBSERV. El plural de esta palabra es *lingoes*.

lingua [ˈliŋgwə] n. Lengua, *f.*

— OBSERV. El plural de *lingua* es *linguae*.

lingual [ˈliŋgwəl] adj. Lingual (like or near the tongue). || GRAMM. Lingual.

— N. GRAMM. Lingual, *f.*

linguiform [ˈliŋgwiˌfɔːm] adj. En forma de lengua, lingüiforme.

linguist [ˈliŋgwist] n. Lingüista, *m.* & *f.* (specialist in linguistics). || Polígloto, ta (polyglot).

linguistic [liŋˈgwistik] adj. Lingüístico, ca.

linguistics [—s] n. Lingüística, *f.*

lingulate [ˈliŋgjəleit] adj. En forma de lengua, lingüiforme.

liniment [ˈlinimənt] n. Linimento, *m.*

lining [ˈlainiŋ] n. Forro, *m.* (of clothes). || TECH. Revestimiento, *m.*, forro, *m.* | Guarnición, *f.*, forro, *m.* (of brakes). || Forro, *m.* (in bookbinding). || MIN. Entibación, *f.*, entibado, *m.*

link [liŋk] n. Eslabón, *m.* (of a chain). || FIG. Vínculo, *m.*, lazo, *m.*: *the child was the only link between them*, el niño era el único vínculo existente entre ellos; *the links of friendship*, los lazos de la amistad. | Relación, *f.* (relationship, connection). || Malla, *f.* (of knitting). || Enlace, *m.*: *a rail link*, un enlace ferroviario. || TECH. Vástago, *m.* || AUT. Biela (*f.*) de acoplamiento. || Antorcha, *f.* (torch). || — Pl. Gemelos, *m.* (cuff links). || — FIG. *Missing link*, eslabón perdido. | *Weak link*, punto flaco.

link [liŋk] v. tr. Unir, enlazar (to join). || Acoplar (trains, spaceships). || FIG. Vincular, unir. || Conectar [*to*, con] (by telephone). || — *This is linked to what I said earlier*, eso está relacionado con lo que dije anteriormente. || *To link arms*, cogerse del brazo, darse el brazo. || *To link together*, unir.

— V. intr. Unirse, enlazarse. || Empalmar (two trains). || Acoplarse (to couple). || FIG. Unirse. || — *To link on to*, unirse a. || *To link together*, unirse.

— OBSERV. *To link* va seguido frecuentemente por *up* sin que cambie su sentido.

linkage [ˈliŋkidʒ] n. Enlace, *m.* || Unión, *f.* || Conexión, *f.* (telephone). || Eslabonamiento, *m.*, encadenamiento, *m.* (of facts). || Articulación, *f.* (joint). || Acoplamiento, *m.* (coupling). || BIOL. CHEM. Enlace, *m.* || TECH. Varillaje, *m.* || FIG. Vinculación, *f.*

linking [ˈliŋkiŋ] n. Unión, *f.* || Enlace, *m.* || Encadenamiento, *m.*, eslabonamiento, *m.* (of facts). || Acoplamiento, *m.* (coupling). || Articulación, *f.* (joint). || FIG. Vinculación, *f.*

links [liŋks] pl. n. SP. Campo (*m. sing.*) de golf. || Terreno (*m. sing.*) arenoso (sandy ground).

Link trainer [ˈliŋkˈtreinə*] n. Simulador (*m.*) de vuelo.

linkup [ˈliŋkʌp] n. Conexión, *f.* (by telephone). || Encuentro, *m.* (meeting of people, chiefs, etc.). || Unión, *f.* (of approaching forces). || Acoplamiento, *m.* (of spacecraft).

linnet [ˈlinit] n. Pardillo, *m.* (bird).

lino [ˈlainəu] n. Linóleo, *m.* (linoleum). || PRINT. Linotipia, *f.*

linocut [ˈlainəukʌt] n. Estampa (*f.*) impresa en linóleo.

linoleum [liˈnəuljəm] n. Linóleo, *m.*

linotype [ˈlainəutaip] n. PRINT. Linotipia, *f.* || *Linotype operator*, linotipista, *m.* & *f.*

linotyper [—ə*] or **lynotypist** [—ist] n. PRINT. Linotipista, *m.* & *f.*

linseed [ˈlinsi:d] n. Linaza, *f.*: *linseed meal*, harina de linaza; *linseed oil*, aceite de linaza.

linstock [ˈlinstɔk] n. (Ant.). Botafuego, *m.*

lint [lint] n. Hilas, *f. pl.* (for bandaging). || Pelusa, *f.* (fluff).

lintel [ˈlintl] n. ARCH. Dintel, *m.* (of doors).

linter [ˈlintə*] n. U. S. Desfibradora (*f.*) de algodón. || — Pl. Borra, *f. sing.*

lion [ˈlaiən] n. ZOOL. León, *m.* || Celebridad, *f.*, persona (*f.*) famosa (celebrity). || FIG. León, *m.* (brave man). || HERALD. León, *m.* || — ZOOL. *Sea lion*, león marino. || FIG. *The lion's share*, la parte del león, la mejor tajada. | *To put one's head in the lion's mouth*, meterse en la boca del lobo.

Lion [ˈlaiən] n. ASTR. Leo, *m.*, León, *m.*

lioness [—is] n. ZOOL. Leona, *f.*

lionet [—et] n. ZOOL. Cachorro (*m.*) de león.

lionhearted [—ˌhɑ:tid] adj. Valiente.

lionize [—aiz] v. tr. Agasajar mucho a, poner en primer plano a.

lip [lip] n. Labio, *m.* (of mouth, wound): *lower, upper lip*, labio inferior, superior. || Belfo, *m.*, morro, *m.*, labio, *m.* (of an animal). || Pico, *m.* (of a jug). || Borde, *m.* (of a cup). || Boquilla, *f.* (of a wind instrument). || Saliente, *m.*, reborde, *m.* (protuberance). || FAM. Impertinencia, *f.*, insolencia, *f.* (impertinence). || — FAM. *None of your lip!*, ¡no te insolentes!, ¡no seas descarado. || FIG. *To bite one's lip*, morderse los labios. | *To hang on s.o.'s lips*, estar pendiente de los labios *or* de las palabras de alguien. | *To keep a stiff upper lip*, poner a mal tiempo buena cara. | *To lick* o *to smack one's lips*, relamerse. | *To open one's lips*, despegar los labios. | *To screw up one's lips*, apretar los labios. | *To seal s.o.'s lips*, sellarle a uno los labios.

— Adj. GRAMM. Labial: *lip consonant*, consonante labial. || FIG. Falso, sa; hipócrita.

lip [lip] v. tr. Mojar los labios en (a cup). || Bañar (the coast). || Llevar a la boca, embocar (p. us.) [a trumpet, etc.] || Besar (to kiss). || FIG. Decir con la boca chiquita.

lipase [ˈlaipeis] n. BIOL. Lipasa, *f.*

lipid [ˈlipaid, US. ˈlipid] or **lipide** [ˈlipaid] n. Lípido, *m.*

lipoid [ˈlipɔid] adj. Lipoideo, a.

— N. Lipoide, *m.*

lipoma [liˈpəumə] n. MED. Lipoma, *m.*

— OBSERV. El plural de la palabra inglesa es *lipomata* o *lipomas*.

lipped [lipt] adj. De labios (person): *thin-lipped*, de labios finos. || Con pico (pitcher).

lip-read* [ˈlipri:d] v. tr./intr. Leer en los labios, interpretar por el movimiento de los labios.

— OBSERV. Pret. & p. p. ***lip-read***.

lip-reader [ˈlipˌri:də*] n. Persona (*f.*) que comprende por el movimiento de los labios.

lipreading [ˈlipˌri:diŋ] n. Comprensión (*f.*) del lenguaje hablado mediante la observación del movimiento de los labios.

lipsalve [ˈlipsɑ:v] n. MED. Pomada (*f.*) rosada. || FIG. Coba, *f.* (flattering).

lip service [ˈlipˌsə:vis] n. Jarabe (*m.*) de pico, palabras, *f. pl.* || FIG. *To pay lip service to*, hablar de boquilla de; fingir estar de acuerdo con.

lipstick [ˈlipstik] n. Barra (*f.*) de labios, lápiz (*m.*) de labios.

liquate [ˈlaikweit] v. tr. Licuar.

liquating [—iŋ] adj. Licuante, de licuación.

liquation [likˈweiʃən] n. Licuación, *f.*

liquefaction [ˌlikwiˈfækʃən] n. Licuefacción, *f.*

liquefacient [ˌlikwiˈfæʃənt] or **liquefactive** [ˌlikwiˈfæktiv] adj. Licuefactivo, va.

liquefiable [ˈlikwifaiəbl] adj. Licuable, licuefactible.

liquefier [ˈlikwifaiə*] n. Aparato (*m.*) de licuefacción, licuador, *m.*

liquefy [ˈlikwifai] v. tr. Licuar, licuefacer.

— V. intr. Licuarse.

liquefying [—iŋ] adj. Licuante.

liquescent [likˈwesənt] adj. Licuescente.

liqueur [liˈkjuə*] n. Licor, *m.* || — *Liqueur brandy*, coñac fino. || *Liqueur wine*, vino licoroso.

liquid [ˈlikwid] adj. Líquido, da (fluid). || Para líquidos (measure). || Claro, ra; transparente, puro, ra (clear, transparent). || MUS. Claro, ra (sound). || GRAMM. Líquido, da. || COMM. Líquido, da: *liquid cash*, dinero líquido; *liquid debt*, deuda líquida. || — *Liquid air*, aire líquido. || COMM. *Liquid assets*, activo [líquido].

— N. Líquido, *m.* || GRAMM. Consonante (*f.*) líquida.

liquidambar [ˌlikwiˈdæmbə*] n. BOT. Liquidámbar, *m.*

liquidatable [ˈlikwideitəbl] adj. Liquidable.

liquidate [ˈlikwideit] v. tr. COMM. Liquidar, saldar (a debt). | Liquidar (a business). || FIG. Liquidar (to get rid of, to kill).

liquidating [—iŋ] adj. Liquidador, ra.

liquidation [ˌlikwiˈdeiʃən] n. Liquidación, *f.* (of a debt, business, enemies): *to go into liquidation*, entrar en liquidación.

liquidator [ˈlikwideitə*] n. COMM. Liquidador, ra.

liquid crystal [ˈlikwidˈkristl] n. Cristal (*m.*) líquido.

liquid fire [ˈlikwidˈfaiə*] n. MIL. Líquido (*m.*) incendiario.

liquidity [likwiditi] n. Liquidez, *f.*, fluidez, *f.*

liquidize [ˈlikwidaiz] v. tr. Liquidar, licuar.

— V. intr. Liquidarse, licuarse.

liquidness [ˈlikwidnis] n. Liquidez, *f.*, fluidez, *f.*

liquor [ˈlikə*] n. Bebida (*f.*) alcohólica: *liquor trade*, comercio de bebidas alcohólicas. || Licor, *m.* (in chemistry, pharmacy). || Jugo, *m.*, salsa, *f.* (of meat). || FIG. FAM. *To be in liquor* o *to be the worse for liquor*, haber bebido más de la cuenta, estar borracho.

liquor [ˈlikə*] v. tr. FAM. *To liquor s.o. up*, emborrachar a uno.

— V. intr. FAM. *To liquor up*, beber, empinar el codo.

liquor cabinet [—ˌkæbinit] n. Licorera, *f.*

liquorice [ˈlikəris] n. BOT. Regaliz, *m.*

lira [ˈliərə] n. Lira, *f.*

— OBSERV. El plural de la palabra inglesa es *lire* o *liras*.

Lisbon [ˈlizbən] pr. n. GEOGR. Lisboa.

lisle [lail] n. Hilo (*m.*) de Escocia.

lisp [lisp] n. Ceceo, *m* (speech defect). || Balbuceo, *m.* (of a child). || FIG. Murmullo, *m.*, susurro, *m.* (of stream, leaves). || *To speak with a lisp* o *to have a lisp*, cecear.

lisp [lisp] v. tr. Decir ceceando.

— V. intr. Cecear. || Balbucear, balbucir (a child).

lisping [—iŋ] adj. Que cecea. || Balbuciente (a child). || FIG. Murmurador, ra.

lissom (U. S. **lissome**) [ˈlisəm] adj. Ágil (nimble). || Flexible.

list [list] n. Orillo, *m.*, orilla, *f.* (of cloth). || Lista, *f.*, raya, *f.* (stripe). || Listón, *m.* (of wood). || Lista, *f.* (enumeration): *price list*, lista de precios. || Escalafón, *m.* (of officials). || Catálogo, *m.* (catalogue). || MAR. Escora, *f.* || Inclinación, *f.* || — Pl. Liza, *f. sing.*, palestra, *f.*: *he entered the lists*, salió a la palestra. || — *Casualty list*, lista de bajas. || *Honours* o *prize list*, lista de premios. || MIL. *On the active list*, en activo. || *Waiting list*, lista de espera. || *Wine list*, carta (*f.*) de vinos.

list [list] v. tr. Hacer una lista de (to make a list of): *I listed all my records*, hice una lista de todos mis discos. || Poner en una lista, inscribir (to put on a list). || Enumerar (to enumerate). || COMM. Cotizar. || Poner un orillo a (a cloth). || *It is not listed*, no está en la lista, no figura en la lista.

— V. intr. MAR. Escorar. || MIL. Alistarse. || (Ant.) Querer (to wish).

listel [ˈlistl] n. ARCH. Listón, *m.*, listel, *m.*

listen [ˈlisn] v. intr. Escuchar, oír: *listen to me instead of gazing out of the window*, escúchame en vez de mirar por la ventana. || Prestar atención (to pay attention). || — *Not to listen to reason*, no atender a razones. || *To listen for*, estar atento a. || *To listen in*, escuchar la radio. || *To listen in to*, escuchar (radio programme), escuchar [a hurtadillas] (telephone conversation).

listen [ˈlisn] n. *To be on the listen*, estar a la escucha, escuchar. || *To have a listen*, escuchar.

listener [ˈlisnə*] n. Oyente, *m.* & *f.* || Radioyente, *m.* & *f.*, radioescucha, *m.* & *f.* (to the radio). || *To be a good listener*, saber escuchar.

listening [ˈlisniŋ] n. Escucha, *f.* || MIL. *Listening post*, puesto (*m.*) de escucha.

listing [ˈlistiŋ] n. Inscripción (*f.*) en una lista.

listless [ˈlistlis] adj. Decaído, da (lacking energy). || Indiferente, apático, ca (uninterested).

listlessness [—nis] n. Apatía, *f.*, inercia, *f.*, indiferencia, *f.*

list price [ˈlistprais] n. Precio (*m.*) de catálogo.

lit [lit] pret. & p. p. See LIGHT.

litany [ˈlitəni] n. REL. Letanía, *f.*

liter [ˈli:tə*] n. U. S. Litro, *m.*

literacy [ˈlitərəsi] n. Capacidad (*f.*) de leer y escribir. || *Literacy campaign*, campaña (*f.*) de alfabetización.

literal [ˈlitərəl] adj. Literal: *in the literal sense of the word*, en el sentido literal de la palabra; *literal*

translation, traducción literal. || Prosaico, ca (prosaic). || Crudo, da; sin disimulo (truth). || *Literal error*, errata, *f.*
— N. PRINT. Errata, *f.*
literalism [ˈlitərəlizəm] n. Carácter (*m.*) literal (literal interpretation). || Realismo, *m.* (realism).
literalize [ˈlitərəlaiz] v. tr. Tomar literalmente (to interpret). || Traducir literalmente (to translate).
literally [ˈlitərəli] adv. Literalmente, al pie de la letra: *he translates literally*, traduce literalmente. || Literalmente, verdaderamente (really).
literary [ˈlitərəri] adj. Literario, ria: *literary criticism*, crítica literaria. || — *Literary man*, hombre (*m.*) de letras, literato, *m.* || *Literary property*, propiedad literaria.
literate [ˈlitərit] adj. Letrado, da (erudite). || Que sabe leer y escribir (able to read and write).
— N. Persona (*f.*) letrada. || Persona (*f.*) que sabe leer y escribir.
literati [ˌlitəˈrɑːtiː] pl. n. Literatos, *m.*, hombres (*m.*) de letras.
literatim [ˌlitəˈrɑːtim] adv. Literalmente, al pie de la letra.
literature [ˈlitəritʃə*] n. Literatura, *f.*: *English literature*, literatura inglesa. || Profesión (*f.*) de escritor. || Obras (*f. pl.*) literarias (literary works). || Información, *f.*, folletos (*m. pl.*) publicitarios (printed matter). || Documentación, *f.* (on a subject).
lithe [laið] adj. Ágil (nimble). || Flexible.
litheness [—nis] n. Agilidad, *f.* (nimbleness). || Flexibilidad, *f.*
lithesome [—səm] adj. Ágil (nimble). || Flexible.
lithic [ˈliθik] adj. Lítico, ca.
lithium [ˈliθiəm] n. Litio, *m.* (metal).
lithochromy [ˌliθəˈkrəumi] n. Litocromía, *f.*
lithograph [ˈliθəugrɑːf] n. Litografía, *f.*
lithograph [ˈliθəugrɑːf] v. tr. Litografiar.
lithographer [liˈθɔgrəfə*] n. Litógrafo, *m.*
lithographic [ˌliθəuˈgræfik] adj. Litográfico, ca.
lithography [liˈθɔgrəfi] n. Litografía, *f.*
lithophagous [liˈθɔfəgəs] adj. ZOOL. Litófago, ga.
lithophyte [ˈliθəfait] n. BOT. Litófito, *m.*
lithoprint [ˈliθəuprint] v. tr. Litografiar.
lithosphere [ˈliθəusfiə*] n. GEOL. Litosfera, *f.*
lithotypography [ˌliθəutaiˈpɔgrəfi] n. Litotipografía, *f.*
Lithuania [ˌliθjuːˈeinjə] pr. n. GEOGR. Lituania, *f.*
Lithuanian [—n] adj. Lituano, na.
— N. Lituano, na (person). || Lituano, *m.* (language).
litigant [ˈlitigənt] adj./n. Litigante, pleiteante.
litigate [ˈlitigeit] v. tr. Litigar sobre, pleitear sobre.
— V. intr. Litigar.
litigation [ˌlitiˈgeiʃən] n. Litigio, *m.*, pleito, *m.*
litigious [liˈtidʒəs] adj. Litigioso, sa (point). || Pleitista (person).
litmus [ˈlitməs] n. Tornasol, *m.* || *Litmus paper*, papel (*m.*) de tornasol.
litotes [ˈlaitəutiːz] inv. n. Lítote, *f.*
litre [ˈliːtə*] n. Litro, *m.*
litter [ˈlitə*] n. Basura, *f.* (rubbish). || Papeles, *m. pl.* (scraps of paper). || Desorden, *m.* (disorder): *in a litter*, en desorden. || Camada, *f.* (offspring of animals). || Cama (*f.*) de paja, pajaza, *f.* (for animals). || Estiércol, *m.* (manure). || Mantillo, *m.* (humus). || Camilla, *f.* (a stretcher). || Litera, *f.* (ancient carriage).
litter [ˈlitə*] v. tr. Ensuciar: *papers littered the street*, unos papeles ensuciaban la calle. || Esparcir (to scatter). || Cubrir: *the wreckage of the plane littered the mountainside*, los restos del avión cubrían la ladera de la montaña. || Llenar: *he littered the room with chairs*, llenó la habitación de sillas. || Desordenar (to jumble). || Andar rodando por, estar esparcido por: *several books littered the table*, varios libros andaban rodando por la mesa. || Preparar una cama de paja a (to bed down). || Parir (to give birth to).
— V. intr. Parir (animals).
litterateur [ˈlitərəˈtəː*] n. Hombre (*m.*) de letras (literary man).
litter basket [ˈlitə*ˌbɑːskit] n. Papelera, *f.*
litterbug [—bʌg] n. Persona (*f.*) que tira papeles usados en la vía pública.
little [ˈlitl] adj. Pequeño, ña (small in size, stature, number): *little hands*, manos pequeñas; *a little person*, una persona pequeña; *a little child*, un niño pequeño; *a little herd*, un rebaño pequeño. || Poco, ca (small in degree, quantity): *we had little difficulty*, tuvimos poca dificultad; *of little importance*, de poca importancia; *we have little time left*, nos queda poco tiempo; *there is little space*, hay poco sitio; *a little money*, un poco de dinero; *a little water*, un poco de agua. || Pequeño, ña; poco, ca; corto, ta (in distance, duration). || Poco, ca (in force). || Estrecho, cha: *little minds*, mentes estrechas. || REL. Menor (hours, office). || ASTR. Menor (Bear). || — *A little kindness*, un poco de amabilidad. || *A little while*, un rato. || *A nice little house*, una casita muy mona. || *Has Johnny hurt his little arm?*, ¿te duele el bracito Juan? || *Little finger*, dedo (*m.*) meñique. || *Little if any o little or no*, muy poco. || *Little toe*, dedo pequeño del pie. || *My little man*, hijo mío. || *Poor little boy*, pobrecito. || *The little ones*, los pequeños. || *The little people*, los duendes. || *With no little fear*, con bastante miedo.
— N. Poco, *m.*: *give me a little*, dame un poco; *he did little to help*, hizo poco para ayudar. || Lo poco: *they took the little that I had*, me robaron lo poco que tenía; *the little that I could do*, lo poco que podía hacer. || — *After a little*, al poco tiempo. || *A little*, un rato, un poco (time): *stay a little*, quédate un rato; un poco (distance): *go down the road a little*, baja la calle un poco; algo, un poco: *a little better*, algo mejor. || *Every little helps*, muchos pocos hacen un mucho. || *For a little*, un poco, un rato. || *In little*, en pequeño. || *Little by little*, poco a poco. || *Little or nothing*, poco o nada, casi nada. || *Not a little*, mucho, no poco (amount), muy (degree). || *To make little of*, see MAKE. || *To think little of*, tener en poco, tener mala opinión de (to think badly of), dar poca importancia a, hacer poco caso de (to pay little attention to), no dudar en (not to hesitate). || *Wait a little!*, ¡espera un momento! || *We had little to do with it*, poco tuvimos que ver en aquello.
— Adv. Poco: *she dances little*, baila poco; *I see him very little*, le veo muy poco; *a little more than five years ago*, hace poco más de cinco años; *little known*, poco conocido. || — *As little as possible*, lo menos posible. || *Little did he know that*, no tenía la menor idea de que.
littleness [—nis] n. Pequeñez, *f.* || FIG. Pequeñez, *f.*, mezquindad, *f.*
little theater [—ˈθiətə*] n. Teatro (*m.*) experimental.
littoral [ˈlitərəl] adj. GEOGR. Litoral.
— N. GEOGR. Litoral, *m.*
lit up [ˈlitˈʌp] adj. FAM. Achispado, da; alegre.
liturgical [liˈtəːdʒikəl] adj. REL. Litúrgico, ca.
liturgics [liˈtəːdʒiks] n. REL. Liturgia, *f.*
liturgy [ˈlitəːdʒi] n. REL. Liturgia, *f.*
livable [ˈlivəbl] adj. Habitable: *a very livable house*, una casa muy habitable. || Llevadero, ra: *a livable life*, una vida llevadera. || *He's very livable with*, es muy fácil vivir con él.
live [laiv] adj. Vivo, va (living): *is that a live snake?*, ¿está viva esta serpiente? || Vivo, va; activo, va (lively). || Encendido, da; en ascuas (coal). || Encendido, da (match, fire). || Vivo, va (colour). || De actualidad, de interés actual, candente (question). || ELECTR. Con corriente, cargado, da (conductor, wire). || En directo (broadcast). || Motor, ra (axle). || Sin explotar, cargado, da: *a live bomb*, una bomba sin explotar. || Cargado, da (cartridge). || Útil: *live weight*, carga útil. || En vivo (animal weight). || — *A real live cowboy*, un vaquero de verdad, un vaquero en carne y hueso. || *Live coals*, ascuas, *f.*
live [liv] v. tr. Vivir, llevar, tener: *to live a wonderful life*, llevar una vida maravillosa. || Vivir, tener (an experience). || — *To live a lie*, vivir en la mentira. || *To live a part*, identificarse con un personaje. || *To live it up*, echar una cana al aire, pegarse la vida padre.
— V. intr. Vivir: *to live well*, vivir bien; *to live together*, vivir juntos. || Permanecer: *his name will live*, su nombre permanecerá. || — *As long as I live*, mientras viva. || *As ye live so shall ye die*, quien mal anda mal acaba. || *Long live the queen!*, ¡viva la reina! || *The times we live in*, en los tiempos en que vivimos. || *They all lived happily ever after*, vivieron felices, comieron perdices y a mí no me dieron (in tales). || *To live and learn*, vivir para ver. || *To live and let live*, vivir y dejar vivir. || *To live from one day to the next*, vivir al día. || *To live like a king*, vivir como un rey, vivir a cuerpo de rey, vivir como un pachá.
— **To live by,** vivir de: *he lives by his pen*, vive de su pluma. || **To live down,** conseguir que se olvide. || **To live in,** ser interno (at school, etc.). | Vivir en (a house, town). | Vivir en la casa (a maid, etc.). || **To live off,** vivir de. || **To live on,** seguir viviendo. | Perdurar: *his memory lives on*, su memoria perdura. || **To live on** o **upon,** vivir [de]: *what does she live on?*, ¿de qué vive?; *he lives on charity*, vive de limosna; *I don't earn enough to live on*, no gano bastante para vivir; *to live on hope*, vivir de esperanzas; vivir a expensas de: *he still lives on his parents*, vive todavía a expensas de sus padres; vivir con: *he lives on twenty pounds a month*, vive con veinte libras al mes. || **To live out,** acabar: *he lived out his days in exile*, acabó sus días en el exilio. | No vivir en la casa (maid, etc.). | Ser externo: *as a student I lived out*, cuando era estudiante era externo. | — *She won't live out the week*, no acabará la semana con vida. || **To live through,** sobrevivir a (a war). | Vivir (an experience): *I lived through all these events*, viví todos estos acontecimientos. || **To live up to,** cumplir con: *he lived up to his promise*, cumplió con su promesa. | Vivir según: *he lives up to his income*, vive según sus ingresos. | Vivir de acuerdo con: *he lived up to his principles*, vivió de acuerdo con sus principios.
liveable [ˈlivəbl] adj. See LIVABLE.
lived [livd] adj. *Short-lived*, de corta vida, de breve vida.
livelihood [ˈlaivlihud] n. Sustento, *m.* (subsistence). || — *To earn a livelihood*, ganarse la vida *or* el sustento. || *To earn an honest livelihood*, ganarse honradamente la vida.
liveliness [ˈlaivlinis] n. Viveza, *f.*, vivacidad, *f.*, vida, *f.* (briskness). || Animación, *f.*, vida, *f.* (activity).
live load [ˈlaivləud] n. Carga (*f.*) móvil.
livelong [ˈlivlɔŋ] adj. Entero, ra; todo, da. || *All the livelong day*, todo el santo día.

lively [ˈlaivli] adj. Vivo, va (vivacious). || Activo, va (active). || Enérgico, ca (forceful). || Gráfico, ca (graphic). || Realista (realistic). || Animado, da (party, debate). || Alegre (tune). || Rápido, da (pace, pitch). || Agudo, da (intense): *a lively sense of humour*, un sentido agudo del humor. || Vivo, va; grande (interest). || Vivo, va (bright, lucid, fresh): *lively colours*, colores vivos. || AUT. Que responde bien: *I've got a lively car*, tengo un coche que responde bien. || — *To make things lively for s.o.*, complicar la vida a alguien. || *To take a lively interest in sth.*, interesarse vivamente en algo.
liven [laivn] v. tr. *To liven up*, animar.
— V. intr. *To liven up*, animarse.
live oak [ˈlaiv əuk] n. BOT. Roble, *m.*
liver [ˈlivə*] n. ANAT. Hígado, *m.*: *liver complaint*, enfermedad del hígado. || CULIN. Hígado, *m.* || — FAM. *Fast* o *loose liver*, vividor, ra; juerguista, *m.* & *f.* | *Good liver*, persona (*f.*) que se da buena vida.
liveried [ˈlivərid] adj. Que lleva librea.
liverish [ˈlivəriʃ] adj. Que padece del hígado, hepático, ca (having liver disorder). || *To feel liverish*, estar pachucho, no encontrarse bien.
liverwort [ˈlivəwəːt] n. BOT. Hepática, *f.*
livery [ˈlivəri] n. Librea, *f.* (dress, costume of a servant). || Cuadra (*f.*) de caballos de alquiler (stable). || JUR. Entrega, *f.* (of property). || JUR. *Livery of seisin*, toma (*f.*) de posesión.
livery company [—ˌkʌmpəni] n. Gremio (*m.*) de la ciudad de Londres.
liveryman [—mən] n. Miembro (*m.*) de un gremio de la ciudad de Londres. || Propietario (*m.*) de caballos de alquiler *or* de carruajes de alquiler.

— OBSERV. El plural de *liveryman* es *liverymen.*

livery stable [—ˌsteibl] n. Cuadra (*f.*) de caballos de alquiler.
lives [laivz] pl. n. See LIFE.
livestock [ˈlaivstɔk] n. Ganado, *m.* (cattle). || Ganadería, *f.* (stock farming).
live wire [ˈlaivˌwaiə*] n. ELECTR. Alambre (*m.*) con corriente *or* cargado. || FIG. Persona (*f.*) enérgica.
livid [ˈlivid] adj. Plomizo, za (lead-coloured). || Lívido, da (discoloured). || FAM. Furioso, sa (angry).
lividity [liˈviditi] or **lividness** [ˈlividnis] n. Lividez, *f.*
living [ˈliviŋ] adj. Vivo, va; viviente (having life): *living beings*, seres vivientes. || Viviente, contemporáneo, a: *the greatest living sculptor*, el mejor escultor viviente. || Lleno de vida (image, style, picture). || Vivo, va: *she is the living image of her mother*, es el vivo retrato de su madre. || De vida: *living conditions*, condiciones de vida. || Vivo, va (water, force). || De mantenimiento (expenses). || Suficiente para vivir: *living wage*, sueldo suficiente para vivir. || — *Living death*, muerte (*f.*) en vida. || *Living language*, lengua viva. || *Living or dead*, muerto o vivo. || *No living man could do better*, nadie lo haría mejor. || *Not a living soul*, ni un alma.
— N. Vivos, *m. pl.*: *the living and the dead*, los vivos y los muertos. || Vida, *f.*: *to earn one's living*, ganarse la vida; *his living alone made him sad*, su vida solitaria le entristecía; *clean living*, vida ordenada; *loose living*, vida disoluta. || REL. Beneficio, *m.* || — *They make a bare living*, ganan lo justo para vivir. || *To make a living*, ganarse la vida. || *To make a living for s.o.*, mantener a alguien. || *To work for one's living*, ganarse la vida trabajando.
living allowance [—əˈlauəns] n. Dietas, *f. pl.*
living death [—deθ] n. Muerte (*f*) en vida.
living quarters [—ˈkwɔːtəz] pl. n. Alojamiento, *m. sing.*, residencia, *f. sing.*
living room [—rum] n. Cuarto (*m.*) de estar, sala (*f.*) de estar.
living space [—speis] n. Espacio (*m.*) vital.
lixiviate [likˈsivieit] v. tr. Lixiviar.
lixiviation [likˌsiviˈeiʃən] n. Lixiviación, *f.*
lizard [ˈlizəd] n. ZOOL. Lagarto, *m.* (big), lagartija, *f.* (small).
llama [ˈlɑːmə] n. ZOOL. Llama, *f.*
llanos [ˈlɑːnəus] pl. n. GEOGR. Llanos, *m.*
lo [ləu] interj. ¡He aquí! || *Lo and behold there he was!*, ¡y allí estaba!
loach [ləutʃ] n. ZOOL. Locha, *f.* (fish).
load [ləud] n. Carga, *f.* (burden). || Cabida, *f.*: *this washing machine takes a load of six pounds*, esta lavadora tiene una cabida de seis libras. || Peso, *m.* (weight). || Cargamento, *m.*, carga, *f.* (of vehicles, animals). || Carretada, *f.* (cartful). || MIL. Carga, *f.* (of a gun). || TECH. Carga, *f.* | Rendimiento, *m.* (of an engine): *at full load*, con pleno rendimiento. | Resistencia, *f.* || ELECTR. Carga, *f.* || FIG. Peso, *m.*: *you have taken a load off my mind*, me has quitado un peso de encima. || — Pl. FAM. Cantidades, *f.*, montones, *m.*: *loads of money*, cantidades de dinero. || — *Dead load*, peso muerto. || FAM. *Get a load of this!*, ¡mira esto! | *It's a load of rubbish*, es una porquería, no vale absolutamente nada. || *Peak load*, carga máxima. || *Useful load*, carga útil.
load [ləud] v. tr. Cargar: *to load coal on a lorry*, cargar carbón en un camión. || Hacer más pesado (to make heavier). || Cargar: *to load the dice*, cargar los dados. || MIL. Cargar: *to load a rifle*, cargar un fusil. || Cargar (wine). || ELECTR. Cargar. || Poner, cargar con: *to load a film in a camera*, poner un rollo en una cámara, cargar una cámara con un rollo. || Recargar (an insurance premium). || FIG. Agobiar: *to be loaded with debts*, estar agobiado de deudas. | Colmar, llenar [*with*, de] (honours). | Acompañar: *he loaded his arguments with examples*, acompañó sus argumentos con ejemplos. || — *Everything was loaded against him*, todo iba en contra suya. || *To load o.s. with*, cargarse de *or* con.
— V. intr. Cargar. || Tomar carga (to take a load on). || Cargarse: *how does this gun load?*, ¿cómo se carga este fusil? || Cargarse (a camera).
load displacement [—disˈpleismənt] n. MAR. Desplazamiento (*m.*) [del buque] con carga.
loaded [—id] adj. Cargado, da (animal, vehicle, dice, camera, gun, etc.). || *To be loaded*, estar cargado, estar tajado (drunk), estar forrado de dinero (rich).
loader [—ə*] n. Cargador, *m.* (person). || Cargadora, *f.* (machine).
load factor [—ˌfæktə*] n. Coeficiente (*m.*) de carga.
loading [—iŋ] n. Carga, *f.* (of goods): *loading and unloading*, carga y descarga. || Sobreprima, *f.* (insurance).
— Adj. De carga.
load line [—lain] n. MAR. Línea (*f.*) de flotación [del buque con carga].
loadstar [—stɑː*] n. See LODESTAR.
loadstone [—stəun] n. See LODESTONE.
loaf [ləuf] n. Pan, *m.* (bread). || Barra, *f.* (French bread). || Pan (*m.*) de azúcar (of sugar). || Callejeo, *m.* (wandering). || — FIG. *Half a loaf is better than none*, mejor que nada, menos da una piedra. || FAM. *Use your loaf*, piensa con la cabeza.

— OBSERV. El plural de *loaf* es *loaves.*

loaf [ləuf] v. tr. Pasar [el tiempo] ociosamente.
— V. intr. Holgazanear: *I spent the whole day loafing*, me pasé el día holgazaneando. || *To loaf about* o *around*, callejear (along the streets), holgazanear (to laze).
loafer [—ə*] n. Holgazán, ana (lazy person). || Azotacalles, *m. inv.* (on the street). || U. S. Mocasín, *m.* (shoes).
loam [ləum] n. Marga, *f.* (rich soil of clay and sand). || Mezcla (*f.*) de barro y arcilla (for making bricks, moulds, etc.). || ARCH. Adobe, *m.* || AGR. Mantillo, *m.*
loan [ləun] n. Préstamo, *m.* (sth. lent): *loan on trust*, préstamo de honor. || COMM. Empréstito, *m.* (of the State): *government loan*, empréstito del Estado; *a loan at 3 % interest*, un empréstito al 3 %. || Palabra (*f.*) tomada de otra lengua (loanword). || — *On loan*, prestado, da. || *To ask for the loan of*, pedir prestado. || *To issue a loan*, conceder un préstamo (s.o.), hacer un empréstito (the State). || *To raise* o *to float a loan*, emitir *or* lanzar un emprésito.
loan [ləun] v. tr. Prestar.
loan office [—ˈɔfis] n. Casa (*f.*) de préstamos.
loan shark [—ʃɑːk] n. FAM. Usurero, *m.*
loanword [—wəːd] n. Palabra (*f.*) tomada de otra lengua.
loath [ləuθ] adj. Reacio, cia. || — *Nothing loath*, de buena gana. || *To be loath to*, ser reacio a, estar poco dispuesto a.
loathe [ləuð] v. tr. Aborrecer, odiar: *I loathe vice*, aborrezco el vicio; *to loathe doing sth.*, aborrecer hacer algo.
loathing [—iŋ] n. Aborrecimiento, *m.* (*of*, de), odio, *m.* (*of*, a), aversión (*of*, por, a) [of s.o.]. || Repugnancia, *f.*, asco, *m.*, aversión, *f.* (*of*, a) [of sth.]. || *It fills me with loathing*, me asquea, me repugna.
loathsome [—səm] adj. Repugnante, asqueroso, sa (disgusting). || Odioso, sa (hateful).
loathsomeness [—səmnis] n. Lo odioso. || Lo repugnante, lo asqueroso.
loaves [ləuvz] pl. n. See LOAF.
lob [lɔb] n. Volea (*f.*) alta, "lob", *m.* (in tennis).
lob [lɔb] v. tr. SP. Lanzar [la pelota] por debajo del brazo (in cricket). | Volear, lanzar [la pelota] voleada (in tennis). | Bombear (in football). || FAM. Tirar, dar: *lob it to me, will you?*, tíramelo.
— V. intr. Andar con dificultad (to walk). || SP. Lanzar la pelota voleada.
lobar [ˈləubə*] adj. Lobular.
lobate [ˈləubeit] adj. BOT. Lobulado, da.
lobby [ˈlɔbi] n. Pasillo, *m.* (corridor). || Antecámara, *f.* (anteroom). || Sala (*f.*) de espera (waiting room). || Vestíbulo, *m.* (vestibule). || Pasillo (*m.*) de una cámara legislativa (in a legislative building). || Grupo, *m.*, grupo (*m.*) de presión: *the industrial reform lobby*, el grupo a favor de la reforma industrial.
lobby [ˈlɔbi] v. tr. Hacer aprobar [a bill] por medio de presiones. || Ejercer presiones sobre.
— V. intr. Ejercer presiones, cabildear.
lobbying [—iŋ] n. Presiones, *f. pl.*, cabildeo, *m.*
lobbyism [—izəm] n. Presiones, *f. pl.*, cabildeo, *m.*
lobbyist [—ist] n. El que ejerce presiones, cabildero, *m.*
lobe [ləub] n. Lóbulo, *m.*
lobectomy [ləuˈbektəmi] n. MED. Lobectomía, *f.*
lobed [ləubd] adj. Lobulado, da.
lobotomy [ləuˈbɔtəmi] n. MED. Lobotomía, *f.*
lobscouse [ˈlɔbskaus] n. Guisado, *m.*, guiso, *m.*
lobster [ˈlɔbstə*] n. ZOOL. Langosta, *f.* | Bogavante, *m.* (with claws). || *Spiny lobster*, langosta, *f.*
lobster boat [—bəut] n. MAR. Langostero, *m.*

lobster pot [—pɔt] n. MAR. Nasa, *f.*
lobular [ˈlɔbjulə*] or **lobulate** [ˈlɔbjulit] adj. Lobular, lobulado, da.
lobule [ˈlɔbjuːl] n. Lóbulo, *m.*
local [ˈləukəl] adj. Local (restricted to a particular place): *local customs*, costumbres locales; *local colour*, color local. || Limitado, da; restringido, da (outlook). || Ciudad, interior (on a letter). || Urbano, na: *local telephone service*, servicio telefónico urbano. || Del barrio (doctor). || Pueblerino, na: *local quarrels*, luchas pueblerinas. || Vecinal: *local road*, camino vecinal. || De cercanías (trains). || De línea (bus). || Local (authority, team, agent, dealer, radio station). || MED. Local (anaesthetic). | Externo, na (remedy). || GRAMM. De lugar (adverb). || — *A local man*, un hombre de aquí. || *Local government*, gobierno (*m.*) municipal. || *Local option*, derecho (*m.*) concedido a una región de determinar si una ley es aplicable o no en su territorio. || *Local time*, hora (*f.*) local.
— N. Tren (*m.*) de cercanías (train). || Autobús (*m.*) de línea (bus). || Informaciones (*f. pl.*) locales (news). || Equipo (*m.*) local (team). || COMM. Agente (*m.*) local. || FAM. Bar (*m.*) del barrio (pub). || Escenario, *m.* (of events). || Sello (*m.*) de correos válido únicamente en cierta área (stamp). || Examen (*m.*) regional (examination). || Indígena, *m.* & *f.*, nativo, va (person). || U. S. Sección (*f.*) local (of an organization). || *The locals are very friendly*, los vecinos de esta población son muy simpáticos, la gente del lugar es muy simpática.
locale [ləuˈkɑːl] n. Lugar, *m.* (place). || Escenario, *m.* (of events).
localism [ˈləukəlizəm] n. Localismo, *m.* || Provincialismo, *m.*, regionalismo, *m.* (word, etc.). || Mentalidad (*f.*) pueblerina, espíritu (*m.*) localista (interest in local affairs).
locality [ləuˈkæliti] n. Localidad, *f.* (neighbourhood). || Sitio, *m.*, lugar, *m.* (place). || Región, *f.* || Situación, *f.*, lugar, *m.* (situation). || Orientación, *f.*: *poor sense of locality*, mal sentido de la orientación. || Residencia, *f.*, domicilio, *m.*: *I don't know his present locality*, no conozco su residencia actual.
localizable [ˌləukəˈlaizeibl] adj. Localizable.
localization [ˌləukəlaiˈzeiʃən] n. Localización, *f.*
localize [ˈləukəlaiz] v. tr. Localizar.
locally [ˈləukəli] adv. Localmente. || En la localidad, en el lugar, en la región. || En el sitio: *staff engaged locally*, personal contratado en el sitio.
locate [ləuˈkeit] v. tr. Localizar (to look for and discover): *they have located the thief*, han localizado al ladrón. || Encontrar, hallar (to find): *can you locate the town on this map?*, ¿puede encontrar la ciudad en este mapa? || Situar [*Amer.*, ubicar] (to situate): *where is your house located?*, ¿dónde está situada su casa? || *To be located somewhere*, estar domiciliado en algún sitio (people).
— V. intr. U. S. Establecerse.
locating [—iŋ] n. See LOCATION.
location [ləuˈkeiʃən] n. Localización, *f.* (finding). || Situación, *f.*, sitio, *m.*, posición, *f.* (place). [*Amer.*, ubicación, *f.*] || Colocación, *f.* [*Amer.*, ubicación, *f.*] (placing). || CINEM. Exteriores, *m. pl.* || U. S. MIN. Concesión, *f.* || CINEM. *To film on location in Spain*, rodar en España.
locative [ˈlɔkətiv] adj. GRAMM. Locativo, va.
— N. GRAMM. Locativo, *m.*
loch [lɔk] n. Lago, *m.* (lake). || Ría, *f.* (estuary).
loci [ˈləusai] pl. n. See LOCUS.
lock [lɔk] n. Mecha, *f.*, mechón, *m.* (curl of hair). || Vedija, *f.*, vellón, *m.* (of wool). || Copo, *m.* (of cotton). || Cerradura, *f.* (on door, box, drawer, etc.): *he cut a hole in the door for the lock*, hizo un agujero en la puerta para la cerradura. || Candado, *m.* (for a bicycle, trunk, etc.). || Cerrojo, *m.* (bolt). || SP. Llave, *f.* (in wrestling). || Llave, *f.* (of a firearm). || TECH. Tope, *m.*, retén, *m.* (blocking device). || Esclusa, *f.* (on a canal). || Esclusa (*f.*) de aire (on submarines, spacecrafts, etc.). || AUT. Ángulo (*m.*) de giro. || FIG. Embotellamiento, *m.*, atasco, *m.* (traffic jam). | Callejón (*m.*) sin salida (deadlock). || — Pl. Cabellera, *f. sing.* (hair). || — FIG. *Lock, stock and barrel*, completamente, por completo. || *Under lock and key*, bajo siete llaves, bajo llave.
lock [lɔk] v. tr. Cerrar con llave (to fasten). || Encerrar (to shut in): *lock these prisoners in their cells*, encierre a esos prisioneros en sus celdas. || Juntar, unir (to fit parts tightly together). || TECH. Bloquear, trabar. || Enclavar (railway points, signals). || Enredar: *they locked their horns*, se enredaron los cuernos. || PRINT. Ajustar. || Hacer pasar por una esclusa (a boat). || — *To be locked in each other's arms*, estar estrechamente abrazados, estar unidos en un abrazo. || *To be locked in mortal combat*, estar enzarzados en una batalla mortal. || *To lock one's arms around s.o.'s neck*, echar los brazos al cuello de uno.
— V. intr. Cerrarse con llave (to shut with a key). || Unirse, juntarse (to fit tightly together). || Pasar por esclusas (a boat). || Bloquearse (mechanism).
— ***To lock away***, guardar bajo llave. || ***To lock in***, encerrar. || ***To lock into***, engranarse en. || ***To lock out***, dejar fuera a, cerrar la puerta a (to prevent from entering). | Declarar el cierre patronal *or* el "lock-out" (in a factory).|| ***To lock up***, cerrar: *to lock up the house*, cerrar la casa. | Dejar bajo llave: *to lock up money*, dejar dinero bajo llave. | Encarcelar (to imprison). | Encerrar (to shut in). | COMM. Inmovilizar, bloquear (capital). | Concluir, terminar (a stock).
lockage [—idʒ] n. Cierre (*m.*) con esclusas, sistema (*m.*) de esclusas (lock system). || Paso (*m.*) de un barco por una esclusa. || Peaje (*m.*) para pasar por una esclusa (toll).
lock bolt [—bəult] n. Pestillo, *m.*
lock chamber [—ˌtʃeimbə*] n. MAR. Esclusa, *f.*
locker [—ə*] n. Casillero, *m.* (shelf with pigeonholes). || Armario, *m.* (cupboard). || Cajón, *m.* [*Amer.*, gaveta, *f.*] (drawer). || MAR. Pañol, *m.* (storeroom). | Cajón, *m.* || U. S. Cámara (*f.*) frigorífica.
locker room [—ərum] n. Vestuario (*m.*) con casilleros *or* armarios.
locket [—it] n. Relicario, *m.* (for any souvenir). || Guardapelo, *m.* (for a lock of hair).
locking [—iŋ] n. Cierre (*m.*) con llave. || TECH. Bloqueo, *m.* (jam). || See LOCKAGE.
— Adj. De fijación.
lockjaw [—dʒɔː] n. MED. Trismo, *m.*
lockkeeper [—ˌkiːpə*] n. Esclusero, *m.*
locknut [—nʌt] n. TECH. Contratuerca, *f.*
lockout [—aut] n. Cierre (*m.*) patronal, "lock-out", *m.*
locksman [—smən] n. Esclusero, *m.*

— OBSERV. El plural de *locksman* es *locksmen*.

locksmith [—smiθ] n. Cerrajero, *m.*
lockstitch [—stitʃ] n. Punto (*m.*) de cadeneta.
lockup [—ʌp] n. Encierro, *m.* (of a person). || Cierre (*m.*) de una puerta (of a house). || FAM. Calabozo, *m.* (prison cell). | Cárcel, *f.*, jaula, *f.*, chirona, *f.* (prison building). || Garaje, *m.*, jaula, *f.* (garage). || Almacén, *m.* (shop). || COMM. Inmovilización, *f.* (of capital).
lock-up [—ʌp] adj. Con cerradura (desk, etc.).
loco [ˈləukəu] n. BOT. Especie (*f.*) de astrágalo. || FAM. Locomotora, *f.*, máquina, *f.* (locomotive).
— Adj. U. S. FAM. Loco, ca; chiflado, da (crazy).
locomobile [ˈləukəˌməubil] adj. Locomovible, locomóvil.
locomotion [ˌləukəˈməuʃən] n. Locomoción, *f.*
locomotive [ˈləukəˌməutiv] n. Locomotora, *f.*
— Adj. Locomotor, ra.
locomotor [ˌləukəˈməutə*] adj. Locomotor, ra. || MED. *Locomotor ataxy*, ataxia locomotriz.
locoweed [ˈləukəuˌwiːd] n. BOT. Especie (*f.*) de astrágalo.
locum (tenens) [ˈləukəmˈtiːnenz] n. Interino, na; suplente, *m.* & *f.*
locus [ˈləukəs] n. MATH. Lugar (*m.*) geométrico. || BIOL. Posición, *f.* [de un gene]. || Situación, *f.*, sitio, *m.*, lugar, *m.* (exact place of sth.). || Teatro, *m.*, escenario, *m.* (of a crime).

— OBSERV. El plural de *locus* es *loci*.

locust [ˈləukəst] n. ZOOL. Langosta, *f.* (cricket). | Cigarra, *f.* (cicada). || BOT. Algarroba, *f.* (fruit). || — BOT. *Locust bean*, algarroba, *f.* | *Locust tree*, algarrobo, *m.*
locution [ləuˈkjuːʃən] n. Locución, *f.*
locutory [ˈlɔkjutəri] n. Locutorio, *m.* (visiting room).
lode [ləud] n. MIN. Veta, *f.*, filón, *m.*
loden [ˈləudn] n. Loden, *m.* (material).
lodestar [ˈləudstɑː*] n. Estrella (*f.*) polar (star). || FIG. Norte, *m.*, guía, *m.*
lodestone [ˈləudstəun] n. Magnetita, *f.*, piedra (*f.*) imán.
lodge [lɔdʒ] n. Casa (*f.*) del guarda (of a caretaker). || Portería, *f.* (porter's house). || Pabellón, *m.*: *a hunting* o *a shooting lodge*, un pabellón de caza. || Posada, *f.* (inn). || Logia, *f.* (Masonic). || Madriguera, *f.* (of beavers, otters). || Tienda, *f.* [de indio] (tepee).
lodge [lɔdʒ] v. tr. Alojar, hospedar: *she lodges students in her house*, aloja estudiantes en su casa. || Albergar: *the house lodges three of us*, la casa alberga a tres de nosotros. || Encajar (to wedge). || Colocar (to place). || Contener (to contain). || Clavar (an arrow, a sword). || Alojar, meter (a bullet): *he lodged a bullet in my arm*, me metió una bala en el brazo. || Plantar (a blow). || Depositar (to deposit): *I lodged my money in the bank*, he depositado mi dinero en el banco. || Conferir (to vest). || Meter (an idea). || Presentar (a proof, a complaint). || Interponer (an appeal). || AGR. Encamar. || *To lodge in a gaol*, meter en la cárcel.
— V. intr. Alojarse, hospedarse (to live). || Alojarse, meterse: *the bullet lodged in his head*, la bala se alojó en su cabeza. || Clavarse (knife, arrow). || AGR. Encamarse.
lodgement [—mənt] n. See LODGMENT.
lodger [—ə*] n. Huésped, da (in a boardinghouse). || Inquilino, na (in a rented house).
lodging [—iŋ] n. Pensión, *f.*: *board and lodging*, pensión completa. || Alojamiento, *m.* (act). || MIL. Alojamiento, *m.* (of troops). || JUR. Presentación, *f.* (of complaint). || Depósito, *m.* (of money). || — Pl. Habitación, *f.*, habitaciones, *f. pl.* || — *Lodging house*, casa (*f.*) de huéspedes. || *To take lodgings*, alojarse.
lodgment [—mənt] n. MIL. Posición (*f.*) firme (foothold). || JUR. Depósito (*m.*) de dinero. || Depósito, *m.* (an accumulation of sth.). || Alojamiento, *m.* (of guests). || Pensión, *f.*, alojamiento, *m.* (house).
loess [ˈləuis] n. Loess, *m.*

— OBSERV. Esta palabra es invariable en ambos idiomas.

loft [lɔft] n. Desván, *m.* (attic). || Pajar, *m.* (for hay). || Palomar, *m.* (dovecote). || Galería, *f.*, triforio, *m.* (of a church). || SP. Inclinación, *f.* (of a golf club). | Golpe (*m.*) alto. || U. S. Piso (*m.*) alto (in a warehouse).

loft [lɔft] v. tr. SP. Lanzar [la pelota] en alto.

lofter [—ə*] n. SP. Palo (*m.*) de golf [para lanzar la pelota en alto].

loftily [—ili] adv. En alto. || FIG. Con arrogancia, con altanería (haughtily).

loftiness [—inis] n. Altura, *f.* (height). || FIG. Arrogancia, *f.*, altanería, *f.* (haughtiness). | Elevación, *f.*, nobleza, *f.* (of principles, sentiments). | Elevación, *f.* (of style).

lofty [—i] adj. Alto, ta (high). || FIG. Arrogante, altanero, ra; altivo, va (haughty). | Elevado, da; noble (principles, sentiments). | Elevado, da (style).

log [lɔg] n. Tronco, *m.* (large section of tree). || Leño, *m.*, tronco, *m.* (used for fuel). || AVIAT. Diario (*m.*) de vuelo. || MAR. Corredera, *f.* (speed gauge). | Cuaderno (*m.*) de bitácora, libro (*m.*) de navegación, diario (*m.*) de a bordo (book). || Diario, *m.* (on a journey, etc.). || MATH. Logaritmo, *m.* || — FIG. *As easy as falling off a log*, más fácil que beber un vaso de agua, tirado, da. | *To sleep like a log*, dormir como un tronco.

log [lɔg] v. tr. Cortar (trees). || Anotar, apuntar (to record). || MAR. Navegar a (to sail at). | Anotar en el cuaderno de bitácora. || — *He has logged two thousand flying hours*, tiene dos mil horas de vuelo. || *He logged one hundred kilometres yesterday*, ayer recorrió cien kilómetros. || *To log a piece of forest*, cortar los árboles de una parte de un bosque.

— V. intr. Cortar y transportar árboles.

loganberry [ˈləugənbəri] n. BOT. Frambueso, *m.* (bush). | Frambuesa, *f.* (fruit).

logarithm [ˈlɔgəriðəm] n. Logaritmo, *m.* || *Logarithm table*, tabla (*f.*) de logaritmos.

logarithmic [ˌlɔgəˈriðmik] adj. Logarítmico, ca.

logarithmically [—əli] adv. Por logaritmos.

logbook [ˈlɔgbuk] n. MAR. Cuaderno (*m.*) de bitácora, libro (*m.*) de navegación, diario (*m.*) de a bordo. || AVIAT. Diario (*m.*) de vuelo. || Diario, *m.* (on a journey, etc.). || Cuaderno (*m.*) de trabajo (of workmen). || RAD. Libro (*m.*) de escucha.

log cabin [ˈlɔgˌkæbin] n. Cabaña (*f.*) de troncos.

log chip [ˈlɔgˌtʃip] n. MAR. Barquilla (*f.*) de la corredera, guindola, *f.*

loge [ləuʒ] n. U. S. THEATR. Palco, *m.*

logger [ˈlɔgə*] n. Leñador, *m.* (woodcutter). || Maderero, *m.*, negociante (*m.*) en maderas.

loggerhead [ˈlɔgəhed] n. TECH. Instrumento (*m.*) de hierro para calentar brea. || ZOOL. Tortuga (*f.*) marina (turtle). || FIG. *To be at loggerheads*, estar a mal *or* disgustado *or* a matar.

loggia [ˈlɔdʒə] n. ARCH. Logia, *f.*

logging [ˈlɔgiŋ] n. Explotación (*f.*) forestal. || Transporte (*m.*) de troncos.

log hut [ˈlɔghʌt] n. Cabaña (*f.*) de troncos.

logic [ˈlɔdʒik] n. Lógica, *f.* || *In logic*, lógicamente.

logical [—əl] adj. Lógico, ca.

logician [ləuˈdʒiʃən] n. Lógico, ca.

logistic [ləuˈdʒistik] adj. Logístico, ca.

logistician [ˌlɔdʒisˈtiʃən] n. Logístico, *m.*

logistics [ləuˈdʒistik] n. Logística, *f.*

log line [ˈlɔglain] n. MAR. Cordel (*m.*) de la corredera.

logogram [ˈlɔgəugræm] n. Signo (*m.*) taquigráfico.

logographer [ləuˈgɔgrəfə*] n. Logógrafo, *m.*

logogriph [ˈlɔgəugrif] n. Logogrifo, *m.*

logomachy [lɔˈgɔməki] n. Logomaquia, *f.*

logos [ˈlɔgɔs] n. PHIL. Logos, *m.* || REL. Verbo, *m.* (Jesus).

logroll [ˈlɔgrəul] v. tr. U. S. Conseguir la aprobación de [una ley]. | Conducir en armadías (logs).

— V. intr. U. S. Prestarse una ayuda recíproca [en las votaciones].

logrolling [—iŋ] n. Publicidad (*f.*) mutua entre dos escritores. || U. S. Transporte (*m.*) de troncos en armadía (transport of timber). | Intercambio (*m.*) de favores políticos (arrangement between legislators to get their own projects carried out).

log ship [ˈlɔgʃip] n. MAR. Barquilla (*f.*) de la corredera, guindola, *f.*

logwood [ˈlɔgwud] n. BOT. Palo (*m.*) campeche.

logy [ˈləugi] adj. U. S. Torpe.

loin [lɔin] n. ANAT. Lomo, *m.* || Ijada, *f.*, ijar, *m.* (of animals). || CULIN. Solomillo, *m.* (of beef). | Lomo, *m.* (of pork, veal). || FIG. *To gird up one's loins*, prepararse para la lucha.

loincloth [ˈlɔinklɔθ] n. Taparrabo, *m.*

loiter [ˈlɔitə*] v. intr. Callejear (to hang about). || Retrasarse, rezagarse (to lag behind). || Holgazanear (to idle). || Perder el tiempo (to waste time). || Entretenerse: *don't loiter on the way*, no te entretengas por el camino. || JUR. Merodear: *to loiter with intent*, merodear con fines criminales.

— V. tr. *To loiter away*, perder (time).

loiterer [—rə*] n. Paseante (*m.* & *f.*) ocioso, azotacalles, *m.* & *f. inv.* || JUR. Merodeador, ra.

loll [lɔl] v. intr. Colgar (to hang). || Echarse (to lie). || Repantigarse (to slouch). || — *To loll about*, no dar golpe (to do nothing), repantigarse (to slouch). || *To loll against* o *back on*, recostarse en, apoyarse en. || *To loll out*, colgar (to hang).

— V. tr. Dejar colgar.

lollipop [ˈlɔlipɔp] n. Chupón, *m.*, pirulí, *m.* [*Amer.*, chupete, *m.*] (sweet). || Polo, *m.* (iced).

lollop [ˈlɔləp] v. intr. FAM. Moverse torpemente.

lolly [ˈlɔli] n. FAM. Chupón, *m.*, pirulí, *m.* [*Amer.*, chupete, *m.*]. | Polo, *m.* (iced). || POP. Pasta, *f.*, parné, *m.* (money).

lollypop [ˈlɔlipɔp] n. U. S. Chupón, *m.*, pirulí, *m.* [*Amer.*, chupete, *m.*] | Polo, *m.* (iced).

lombard [ˈlɔmbəd] n. MIL. Lombarda, *f.* (cannon).

Lombardy [ˈlɔmbədi] pr. n. GEOGR. Lombardía, *f.*

London [ˈlʌndən] pr. n. GEOGR. Londres.

— Adj. Londinense, de Londres.

Londoner [—ə*] n. Londinense, *m.* & *f.*

lone [ləun] adj. Solitario, ria (single, alone). || Solo, la (on one's own). || Aislado, da (isolated): *a lone place*, un sitio aislado. || Desierto, ta (deserted). || — FIG. *A lone wolf*, una persona solitaria. || *To play a lone hand*, actuar solo.

loneliness [—linis] n. Soledad, *f.* || Aislamiento, *m.* (isolation).

lonely [—li] adj. Solo, la (solitary): *I feel very lonely*, me siento muy solo. || Aislado, da (isolated). || Solitario, ria (without companions): *he lives a lonely life*, lleva una vida solitaria. || Solitario, ria; poco frecuentado, da (unfrequented): *this must be a lonely place in winter*, esto tiene que ser un lugar solitario en invierno.

loner [—ə*] n. Solitario, ria.

lonesome [—səm] adj. Solo, la (lonely). || Solitario, ria (solitary). || Aislado, da (isolated). || *On one's lonesome*, solo, la.

lonesomeness [—səmnis] n. See LONELINESS.

long [lɔŋ] adj. Largo, ga: *a long road*, una carretera larga; *the long side of the room*, la parte larga de la habitación; *a long life*, una vida larga; *two long miles*, dos millas largas. || Mucho, cha: *a long time*, mucho tiempo. || De largo, de longitud: *two feet long*, dos pies de largo. || De longitud (measure). || Bueno, na: *a long memory*, una buena memoria. || Fuerte, largo, ga (suit in cards). || Grande (figure). || Elevado, da; alto, ta; grande (price). || De largo alcance (far-reaching). || Viejo, ja: *a long friendship*, una vieja amistad. || De cuerpo entero (mirror). || Alto, ta (tall). || GRAMM. Largo, ga (vowel). || RAD. Largo, ga (wave). || — *A long face*, una cara larga. || *A long time ago*, hace mucho tiempo. || *As long as your arm*, larguísimo, ma. || *At long last*, see LAST. || *How long is it?*, ¿qué longitud tiene? (distance), ¿cuánto tiempo dura? (time). || *In the long run*, a la larga. || *It is a long time since I saw you*, hace mucho tiempo que no te he visto. || *It's a long way to*, hay una gran distancia a. || *It will take a long time*, tardará mucho, necesitará mucho tiempo. || FIG. *Long home*, última morada. || *Long in the leg*, de piernas largas. || *Long odds*, apuesta arriesgada. || MIL. *Long service*, alistamiento (*m.*) a largo plazo. || *Long shot*, plano largo (of film), posibilidad remota (possibility), apuesta arriesgada (bet). || FIG. *Not by a long shot*, ni mucho menos. || *Of long standing*, de larga duración. || FIG. *The long arm of the law*, el brazo de la justicia. || *They are a long time in coming*, tardan mucho en llegar. || *This play is two hours long*, esta obra de teatro dura dos horas. || *To be long in getting ready*, tardar mucho en prepararse. || FAM. *To be long in the tooth*, tener ya muchos años. || *To be long of*, tener muchas reservas de. || *To be long on practical experience*, tener mucha experiencia práctica. || *To get* o *to grow longer*, alargarse. || FIG. *To have a face as long as a mile*, llegarle a uno la cara a los pies. | *To have a long head*, tener vista, tener buen olfato. | *To have a long tongue*, tener la lengua suelta. | *To make a long nose*, hacer un palmo de narices. | *To pull a long face*, poner cara larga.

— N. Mucho tiempo, *m.*: *not for long*, no por mucho tiempo. || GRAMM. Larga, *f.* (syllable). || — Pl. Pantalones (*m.*) largos (trousers). || — *Before long*, en breve, dentro de poco, muy pronto. || *The long and the short of the matter*, los pormenores del asunto, el asunto con todos los detalles. || *The long and the short of the matter is*, en resumidas cuentas. || *To take long*, tomar mucho tiempo, tardar. || *Will you be there for long?*, ¿vas a quedarte allí mucho tiempo?

— Adv. [Durante] mucho tiempo (for a long time). || — *All day long*, [durante] todo el día, el día entero. || *As long as*, mientras: *I am not going out as long as it is raining*, mientras llueva no saldré; hasta donde: *as long as the eye can see*, hasta donde alcanza la vista; tanto como, todo el tiempo que: *keep it as long as you like*, quédatelo todo el tiempo que quieras; con tal que (provided that). || *Dont be long!*, ¡no tardes mucho!, ¡vuelve pronto! || FIG. *He is not long for this world*, le queda poco. || *How long?*, ¿cuánto tiempo? || *Long ago* o *since*, hace mucho tiempo. || *Long before he arrived*, mucho antes de que llegase. || *Long before now*, hace mucho tiempo. || *Long live the King!*, ¡viva el Rey! || *Not long ago* o *since*, hace poco. || *Not long before*, poco tiempo antes. || *Not to live long*, morir pronto. || FAM. *So long!*, ¡hasta luego!, ¡hasta pronto! || *So long as*, con tal que (provided that). || COMM. *To lend long*, prestar a largo plazo. || *To live long*, vivir mucho. || *To speak long about*, hablar largamente *or* mucho tiempo de. || *We shan't be long*, en seguida acabamos, no tardaremos mucho.

long [lɔŋ] v. intr. *To long for*, desear con ansia, anhelar. || *To long to*, anhelar, desear ardientemente, tener muchas ganas de.
longanimity [—gəˈnimiti] n. Longanimidad, *f.*
long-armed [—ɑ:md] adj. De brazos largos.
longbill [—bil] n. Agachadiza, *f.* (bird).
longboat [—bəut] n. MAR. Chalupa, *f.*, lancha, *f.*
longbow [—bəu] n. Arco, *m.* || FAM. *To draw the longbow*, decir cuchufletas.
longcloth [—klɔθ] n. Percal, *m.* (material). || — Pl. Pañales, *m.*
long-dated [—ˈdeitid] adj. A largo plazo.
long distance [—ˈdistəns] n. Conferencia, *f.* [interurbana].
long-distance [—ˈdistəns] adj. De larga distancia. || Interurbano, na: *a long-distance telephone call*, una conferencia interurbana. || *Long-distance runner*, corredor (*m.*) de fondo, fondista, *m.*
long-drawn-out [—drɔ:nˈaut] adj. Muy prolongado, da; interminable (sigh). || FIG. Interminable.
longe [lʌndʒ] n. See LUNGE.
longe [lʌndʒ] v. tr. Domar, amaestrar.
long-eared [ˈlɔŋiəd] adj. De orejas largas. || ZOOL. *Long-eared bat*, orejudo, *m.*
longed-for [ˈlɔŋdfɔ:*] adj. Ansiado, da; deseado ardientemente.
longer [ˈlɔŋgə*] comp. adv. Más tiempo. || Más: *ten hours longer*, diez horas más; *to live longer than*, vivir más que. || — *How much longer?*, ¿hasta cuándo? || *No longer*, ya no: *he is no longer a minister*, ya no es ministro.
— Comp. adj. See LONG.
longeron [ˈlɔndʒərən] n. AVIAT. Larguero, *m.*
longevity [lɔnˈdʒeviti] n. Longevidad, *f.*
longevous [lɔnˈdʒi:vəs] adj. Longevo, va.
long-faced [ˈlɔŋˈfeist] adj. Descontento, ta.
long green [ˈlɔŋˈgri:n] n. U. S. FAM. Billete, *m.*
longhair [ˈlɔŋhɛə*] adj./n. FAM. Intelectual.
long-haired [lɔŋˈhəd] adj. De pelo largo.
longhand [ˈlɔŋhænd] n. Escritura (*f.*) normal.
long-headed [ˈlɔŋˈhedid] adj. Dolicocéfalo, la. || FAM. *To be long-headed*, tener buen olfato.
long hop [ˈlɔŋhɔp] n. SP. Tiro (*m.*) corto (in cricket).
longhouse [ˈlɔŋhaus] n. Casa (*f.*) comunal.
long hundredweight [ˈlɔŋˈhʌndrədweit] n. Unidad (*f.*) de medida que equivale a 112 libras.
longing [ˈlɔniŋ] adj. Anhelante, ansioso, sa; impaciente.
— N. Anhelo, *m.*, deseo, *m.*, ansia, *f.* (desire). || Nostalgia, *f.*, añoranza, *f.* (nostalgia). || Antojo, *m.* (of pregnant woman). || *Sexual longing*, apetito (*m.*) sexual.
longingly [—li] adv. Con ansia.
longish [ˈlɔniʃ] adj. Bastante largo, más bien largo.
longitude [ˈlɔndʒitju:d] n. Longitud, *f.*
longitudinal [ˌlɔndʒiˈtju:dinl] adj. Longitudinal.
long johns [ˈlɔŋˈdʒɔnz] pl. n. FAM. Calzones (*m.*) largos.
long jump [ˈlɔŋdʒʌmp] n. SP. Salto (*m.*) de longitud.
long-legged [ˈlɔŋlegd] adj. De piernas largas, zanquilargo, ga.
long-lived [ˈlɔŋˈlivd] adj. De larga vida, longevo, va (people). || Duradero, ra (things). || FIG. Persistente (error).
long-necked [ˈlɔŋnekt] adj. De cuello largo, largo de cuello.
long off [ˈlɔŋˈɔf] n. SP. Jugador (*m.*) a la derecha del bateador (in cricket).
long on [ˈlɔŋˈɔn] n. SP. Jugador (*m.*) a la izquierda del bateador (in cricket).
long play [ˈlɔŋˈplei] n. Disco (*m.*) de larga duración, microsurco, *m.*
long-playing [ˈlɔŋˈpleiiŋ] adj. De larga duración: *a long-playing record*, un disco de larga duración.
long primer [ˈlɔŋˈpraimə*] n. PRINT. Entredós, *m.*
long-range [ˈlɔŋˈreindʒ] adj. MIL. De largo alcance. || De larga distancia, transcontinental (plane, etc.). || De mucho alcance (plan, etc.).
longshanks [ˈlɔŋʃæŋks] n. ZOOL. Zancuda, *f.* (bird).
long-shaped [ˈlɔŋʃeipt] adj. Largo, ga (face).
longshore [ˈlɔŋʃɔ:*] adj. MAR. Costero, ra.
longshoreman [—mən] n. MAR. Estibador, *m.*, cargador *or* descargador de muelle.

— OBSERV. El plural de *longshoreman* es *longshoremen*.

long sight [ˈlɔŋˈsait] n. Buena vista, *f.* || FIG. Perspicacia, *f.*, previsión, *f.*
longsighted [ˈlɔŋˈsaitid] adj. MED. Présbita. || FIG. Previsor, ra; perspicaz.
longsightedness [—nis] n. MED. Presbicia, *f.* || FIG. Previsión, *f.*, perspicacia, *f.*
long-sleeved [ˈlɔŋˈsli:vd] adj. De mangas largas.
longsome [ˈlɔŋsəm] adj. Larguísimo, ma.
long-spun [ˈlɔŋspʌn] adj. Interminable.
long-standing [ˈlɔŋˈstændiŋ] adj. Antiguo, gua; viejo, ja; de muchos años.
long stop [ˈlɔŋstɔp] n. SP. Jugador (*m.*) detrás del guardameta (in cricket).
long-suffering [ˈlɔŋˈsʌfəriŋ] adj. Sufrido, da; resignado, da; paciente.
— N. Paciencia, *f.*, resignación, *f.*
long suit [ˈlɔŋsju:t] n. Palo (*m.*) fuerte (in cards). || FIG. Especialidad, *f.*, punto (*m.*) fuerte.
long-term [ˈlɔŋˈtə:m] adj. A largo plazo: *a long-term credit*, un crédito a largo plazo.
long ton [ˈlɔŋˈtən] n. Tonelada (*f.*) inglesa, tonelada (*f.*) larga [1,016 toneladas métricas].
long-tongued [ˈlɔŋˈtʌŋd] adj. Que tiene la lengua suelta, parlanchín, ina (talkative). || Chismoso, sa (gossipy).
long-wave [ˈlɔŋˈweiv] adj. RAD. De onda larga.
longways [ˈlɔŋweiz] or **longwise** [ˈlɔŋwaiz] adv. A lo largo, longitudinalmente.
long-winded [ˈlɔŋˈwindid] adj. Prolijo, ja (person). || Interminable (story).
loo [lu:] n. FAM. Retrete, *m.*
looby [ˈlu:bi] n. Patán, *m.*
loofah [ˈlu:fɑ:] n. Esponja (*f.*) vegetal (sponge).
look [luk] n. Mirada, *f.* (glance): *to have a look at*, echar una mirada a. || Ojeada, *f.*: *take a look at this report*, échele una ojeada a este informe. || Aspecto, *m.*, apariencia, *f.*, apariencias, *f. pl.* (appearance): *by the look of it*, según las apariencias; *by the look of her*, a juzgar por su aspecto. || Criterio, *m.*, manera (*f.*) de ver, punto (*m.*) de vista (viewpoint). || — Pl. Belleza, *f. sing.* || — *By the look of things*, según parece. || *Do you want a look?*, ¿quieren verlo? || *Good looks*, belleza, *f.* || *Have a look!*, ¡mire! || *He gave me a severe look*, me echó una mirada severa. || *I don't like the look of things*, no me gusta el aspecto de las cosas, estas cosas me dan mala espina (fam.). || *I don't like her looks* o *the look of her*, no me gusta. || *Let me* o *let's have a look!*, ¡déjeme ver! || *New look*, nueva moda, nuevo estilo (fashion), nuevo aspecto (aspect). || *Odd look*, mirada de extrañeza, mirada extraña. || *She has her mother's looks*, se parece a su madre, tiene cierto parecido con su madre. || *The portrait has a look of your mother*, el retrato se parece bastante a su madre. || *To give a look*, mirar. || *To have* o *to take a look at*, mirar, echar un vistazo *or* una mirada a. || *To have a look for*, buscar. || *To have a look round*, recorrer con la mirada (to scan), visitar (to visit), inspeccionar (to inspect). || *To have a quick look at*, dar *or* echar un vistazo a. || *To have good looks*, ser guapo, pa. || *To have looks and youth*, ser guapo y joven. || *To judge by looks*, juzgar por las apariencias. || *To take a good* o *a long look at*, mirar bien, mirar cuidadosamente. || *To take a long hard look before doing it*, pensarlo bien antes de hacerlo.
look [luk] v. intr. Mirar: *we looked but couldn't find it*, miramos pero no lo pudimos encontrar. || Estar: *how pretty you look!*, ¡qué guapa estás! || Parecer: *he looks ill*, parece enfermo; *everything looks all right to me*, todo me parece muy bien; *he looked about to die*, parecía que estaba a punto de morirse; *it looks as if there is going to be a strike*, parece que va a haber una huelga. || Fijarse: *look and see how clever she is*, fíjate y verás qué lista es. || Mirar, tener cuidado: *look where you put your feet*, ten cuidado donde pones los pies. || Estar orientado hacia, mirar a, dar a (to face). || — *He did look a fool*, hizo el ridículo, quedó en ridículo. || *How does her hat look?*, ¿qué tal le sienta *or* le va el sombrero? || *How does it look?*, ¿qué le parece? || *Just look!*, ¡mira! || *Look alive!*, ¡muévete!, ¡menéate! || FIG. *Look before you leap*, antes de que te cases mira lo que haces. || *Look here!*, ¡oye!, ¡mira! || *Look sharp!*, ¡date prisa!, ¡pronto!, ¡rápido! || *Look who is talking!*, ¡mira quién habla! || *Look you!*, ¡oye tú! || *To look alike*, parecerse. || *To look like*, parecerse a: *he looks like his mother*, se parece a su madre; parecer que: *it looks like snow*, parece que va a nevar; parecer: *it looks like glass*, parece cristal. || *To look well*, tener buena cara (person), tener buen aspecto (thing). || *To look well on s.o.*, quedarle bien a uno (a garment).
— V. tr. Mirar (to regard intensely, to examine). || Expresar con la mirada *or* con los ojos (a feeling): *he looks his despair*, expresa con los ojos su desesperación. || Parecer: *he looks a thief*, parece un ladrón. || Representar: *he looks his age*, representa su edad. || — *He looks sadness itself*, es la viva imagen de la tristeza. || *Not to look o.s.*, no tener buena cara: *he doesn't look himself today*, hoy no tiene buena cara. || *To look the other way*, mirar para el otro lado. || *To look the part*, encajar muy bien en el papel. || *You don't look your usual self today*, hoy te encuentro cambiado.
— ***To look about***, mirar alrededor de, echar una mirada alrededor de: *to look about one*, mirar a su alrededor. | — *To look about for*, buscar [con los ojos]. || ***To look after***, cuidar de, cuidar a, ocuparse de (to take care of). | Encargarse de, ocuparse de (to attend to). | Vigilar (to watch over). || ***To look ahead***, mirar hacia adelante (while driving, etc.). | Mirar el porvenir, mirar el futuro. || ***To look around***, echar una mirada alrededor. || ***To look at***, mirar: *don't look at me like that*, no me mires así. | Considerar (to consider). | Examinar (to examine). | Mirar, enfocar (a situation). | — *Fair to look at*, agradable a la vista. | *He wouldn't look at it*, no quiso ni verlo. | *To look at her, you wouldn't know she was ill*, por su aspecto no dirías que está enferma, al verla no te creerías que está enferma. || ***To look away***, apartar la mirada. || ***To look back***, mirar hacia atrás: *he looked back as he left*, miró hacia atrás al irse. | FIG. Volverse atrás: *you can't look back at this stage of the work*, no se puede volver atrás en esta etapa del trabajo.

| Fig. Volver: *I'll look back later*, volveré más tarde. | — *He never looked back after his first sale*, no dejó de prosperar después de su primera venta. | *To look back on*, recordar. || **To look down,** recorrer con la mirada (to scan). | Bajar la mirada, bajar los ojos (to lower one's eyes). | Bajar (price). | — *To look down on* o *upon*, mirar por encima del hombro, mirar despectivamente (to disdain), dominar (to dominate): *the tower looks down on the valley*, la torre domina el valle. || **To look for,** buscar (to search): *we are looking for a flat*, estamos buscando un piso; *go and look for your book*, ve a buscar tu libro. | Esperar (to expect). || **To look forward,** considerar el futuro. | — *To look forward to*, esperar [con ansia]: *I look forward to seeing you again*, espero volverle a ver. || **To look in,** mirar la televisión (to watch television). | Hacer una visita rápida (to visit). | — *To look in at the window*, mirar por la ventana. | *To look in on s.o.*, pasar por casa de alguien (to call). || **To look into,** recorrer, hojear (a book). | Examinar, estudiar (a question): *I'll look into the matter*, estudiaré el asunto. || **To look on,** mirar. | Considerar: *he looks on her as a daughter*, la considera como a una hija. | Dar a (to command a view). || **To look out,** mirar fuera. | Escoger (to choose). | Buscar (to search): *look out some clothes*, busca algunos vestidos. | Tener cuidado (to be careful). | — *Look out!*, ¡cuidado! | *To look out for*, tener cuidado con (to be careful), estar atento a (to pay attention to), esperar (to wait), vigilar (to keep an eye on), acechar (to watch). | *To look out of*, asomarse a, mirar por (the window). | *To look out onto* o *over*, dar a: *my window looks out over the street*, mi ventana da a la calle; tener vistas a, dar a. || **To look over,** mirar por encima, echar un vistazo a, echar una ojeada a (to look at superficially): *I looked over the document*, miré el documento por encima, eché un vistazo al documento. | Revisar (to check). | Inspeccionar, registrar (a place). | — *To look sth. all over*, mirar algo por los cuatro costados. || **To look round,** mirar alrededor (around one). | Volver la cabeza (to turn round). | Inspeccionar (to visit, to inspect). | — *To look round for*, buscar. || **To look through,** echar un vistazo: *to look through a list*, echar un vistazo a una lista. | Mirar por: *he looked through the window*, miró por la ventana. | Mirar sin ver: *he looked right through me*, me miró sin verme. | Registrar (to search). | Hojear (a book). | Examinar cuidadosamente (to examine carefully). || **To look to,** mirar a, dar a: *building that looks to the south*, edificio que da al sur. | Buscar, recurrir a: *I always looked to my father for help*, siempre buscaba la ayuda de mi padre. | Contar con (to count on): *to look to s.o. to*, contar con alguien para. | Cuidar de, velar por (to take care of). | Ocuparse de (to attend to). | Tender a (to tend to). || **To look up,** ponerse mejor, mejorar: *things are looking up*, las cosas se están poniendo mejor. | Mirar para arriba, levantar los ojos (to gaze upwards). | Consultar (a list). | Buscar, mirar: *I have to look this word up in a dictionary*, tengo que buscar esta palabra en un diccionario. | Venir a ver, venir a visitar (to come and see): *look me up when you come back*, ven a verme cuando vuelvas. | Ir a ver, ir a visitar (to go and see). | — *To look s.o. up and down*, mirar a alguien de arriba abajo. | *To look up to*, respetar, apreciar. || **To look upon,** mirar, considerar.

looked-for [ˈluktfɔ:*] adj. Esperado, da.

looker [ˈlukə*] n. Espectador, ra. || U. S. Fam. Guapa, *f.*

looker-on [ˈlukərˈɔn] n. Espectador, ra.

— Observ. El plural de *looker-on* es *lookers-on*.

look-in [ˈlukin] n. Visita (*f.*) rápida (quick visit): *I gave her a look-in*, le hice una visita rápida.

looking [ˈlukiŋ] adj. *A queer-looking person*, una persona extraña.

— Observ. Este adjetivo va siempre precedido por otro del cual se separa por un guión.

looking glass [—glɑ:s] n. Espejo, *m.* (mirror).

lookout [ˈlukˈaut] n. Guardia, *f.* (action of keeping watch). || Mil. Centinela, *m.* (man). | Mirador, *m.*, atalaya, *f.* (post for a guard). | Vigilancia, *f.* (vigilance). || Mar. Vigía, *m.* (man). | Puesto (*m.*) del vigía (post). || Fam. Panorama, *m.*, perspectiva, *f.* (prospect). | Asunto, *m.*: *if he wants to go, that's his lookout*, si quiere ir, es asunto suyo. || — *To be on the lookout for*, estar al acecho de. || *To keep a lookout*, estar ojo avizor.

look-see [ˈluksi:] n. Vistazo, *m.*, ojeada, *f.*

loom [lu:m] n. Tech. Telar, *m.* (for textiles). || Mar. Guión, *m.* (of an oar). || Somorgujo, *m.* (bird). || Silueta (*f.*) borrosa (indistinct outline). || Aparación, *f.* (appearance).

loom [lu:m] v. intr. Dibujarse, perfilarse (to appear in silhouette). || Surgir, aparecer (to arise). || Surgir amenazadoramente (to threaten). || — *To loom large*, cobrar mucha importancia. || *To loom up out of* o *to loom up from*, surgir de.

loon [lu:n] n. Somorgujo, *m.* (bird). || Bobo, ba (simpleton).

loony [—i] adj. Fam. Chiflado, da; chalado, da (crazy). || Fam. *Loony bin*, casa (*f.*) de locos.

loop [lu:p] n. Lazo, *m.*, lazada, *f.*: *a loop in a rope*, un lazo en una cuerda. || Sinuosidad, *f.*, curva, *f.* (of a river, road). || Espira, *f.* (of a spiral). || Presilla, *f.* (for a button, of a belt). || Apartadero, *m.* (in a railway line). || Phys. Antinodo, *m.* || Electr. Circuito (*m.*) cerrado. || Aviat. Rizo, *m.* (in aerobatics): *to loop the loop*, rizar el rizo. || Sp. Bucle, *m.* (ice skating). || U. S. *To knock* o *to throw for a loop*, asombrar, desconcertar (to throw into bewilderment), trastornar, descomponer (to upset).

loop [lu:p] v. tr. Hacer un lazo en (a rope). || Arrollar, enroscar (to roll). || Asegurar con presilla (a button). || Atar con un lazo (to fasten). || Aviat. Rizar: *to loop the loop*, rizar el rizo. || — *To loop back*, recoger con un alzapaño (drapery). || *To loop up*, recoger.

— V. intr. Serpentear (to move in loops). || Hacer un lazo (a rope). || Aviat. Hacer un rizo.

looper [—ə*] n. Zool. Oruga (*f.*) geómetra [*Amer.*, oruga (*f.*) medidora].

loophole [—həul] n. Mil. Aspillera, *f.*, tronera, *f.* (of a castle). || Fig. Escapatoria, *f.*, evasiva, *f.*, pretexto, *m.*

loophole [—həul] v. tr. Mil. Hacer aspilleras *or* troneras en.

loop stitch [—stitʃ] n. Punto (*m.*) de cadeneta.

loopy [—i] adj. Fam. Turulato, ta (slightly crazy).

loose [lu:s] adj. Holgado, da (not fitting tightly): *a loose coat*, un abrigo holgado. || Suelto, ta: *loose papers*, papeles sueltos; *the sheep roamed loose on the hill*, las ovejas andaban sueltas por la colina; *loose rein*, rienda suelta. || Flojo, ja (knot, texture, screw). || Suelto, ta (hair). || Desatado, da (untied). || Flojo, ja: *there's a loose button on my shirt*, tengo un botón flojo en la camisa; *loose bandage*, venda floja. || Poco firme (earth). || Fig. Vago, ga; poco preciso, sa; poco exacto, ta: *a loose definition*, una definición poco exacta. | Libre: *a loose translation*, una traducción libre. | Relajado, da: *loose morals*, moralidad relajada. | Licencioso, sa; disoluto, ta (life). | Fácil (woman). | Desatado, da; suelto, ta: *loose tongue*, lengua desatada. | Sin ilación, inconexo, xa (ideas). | Deshilvanado, da (style). | Soez, grosero, ra (talk). || Med. Que se mueve (tooth). | Fofo, fa; fláccido, da; flácido, da (skin). | Suelto, ta (bowels). || Mil. Disperso, sa (order). || Sp. Abierto, ta (in rugby). | Flojo, ja (fielding in cricket). || Comm. A granel, suelto, ta (goods): *do you sell coffee in packages or loose?*, ¿vende el café en paquetes o suelto? || Tech. Desmontable (plant). | Flojo, ja (rope). | Loco, ca (wheel). || Chem. Libre. || Electr. Desconectado, da. || — Sp. *A loose ball*, una pelota suelta. || *Loose change* o *loose cash*, suelto, *m.*, dinero suelto. || Tech. *Loose pulley*, polea loca. || *Of loose build*, desgarbado, da; desgalichado, da. || *That man is a loose character*, aquel hombre es un perdido. || *To break* o *to get loose*, escaparse. || *To cast loose*, soltar. || *To come* o *to get* o *to work loose*, desatarse, aflojarse (knot, rope), desprenderse (part). || *To cut loose*, soltar: *to cut a rope loose*, soltar una cuerda; soltar las amarras (boat), liberarse (to free o.s. from domination), pasárselo en grande (to enjoy o.s.), soltarse el pelo (to drop all restraint). || *To cut loose from*, independizarse de. || *To give s.o. a loose rein*, dar a alguien rienda suelta. || *To hang loose*, estar colgando, colgar. || Fam. *To have a loose tongue*, írsele a uno la lengua, no poder callarse, tener la lengua suelta. | *To have a screw loose*, faltarle a uno un tornillo. || Fig. *To let loose*, dar rienda suelta a: *he let loose his anger*, dio rienda suelta a su cólera; enfadarse, echar una bronca: *he let loose at her*, se enfadó con ella; írsele a uno la lengua (to speak harshly), soltar (abuse). || *To let* o *to set loose*, poner en libertad, soltar (person), soltar (animal).

— N. Sp. Juego (*m.*) abierto (in rugby). || — *On the loose*, en libertad (free), suelto, ta (uncontrolled). || *To be* o *to go on the loose*, irse de juerga *or* de parranda.

loose [lu:s] v. tr. Poner en libertad, soltar (to set free). || Desatar (to untie). || Soltar (to unfasten). || Aflojar (screw, knot). || Soltar (hair). || Fig. Soltar, desatar (tongue). | Desencadenar, desatar (passions). || Mar. Largar, soltar. || Rel. Absolver. || — *To loose hold of*, soltar. || *To loose off*, disparar.

— V. intr. *To loose off*, disparar.

loose end [—end] n. Extremo (*m.*) suelto (sth. hanging free). || Fig. Cabo (*m.*) suelto (sth. still to be done). || — Fig. *At a loose end*, desocupado, da. | *At loose ends*, en desorden. | *To tie up the loose ends*, no dejar cabo suelto, atar cabos.

loose-fitting [—ˈfitiŋ] adj. Suelto, ta.

loose-jointed [—ˈdʒɔintid] adj. Desvencijado, da (thing). || Desgarbado, da; desgalichado, da (person).

loose-leaf [—li:f] adj. De hojas sueltas.

loose-living [—liviŋ] adj. De vida alegre.

loosely [—li] adv. Aproximadamente (approximately). || Holgadamente (amply). || Sin apretar (not tight). || Licenciosamente, disolutamente (immorally). || Imprecisamente, vagamente (imprecisely).

loosen [—n] v. tr. Aflojar, soltar (to slacken): *to loosen a screw, a knot*, aflojar un tornillo, un nudo. || Desatar, soltar, deshacer (to untie). || Fig. Soltar, desatar: *drink loosened his tongue*, la bebida le desató la lengua. || Aliviar, descargar (the bowels). || Relajar: *to loosen discipline*, relajar la disciplina. || Agr. Mullir (soil). || Sp. *To loosen up*, desentumecer (muscles).

— V. intr. Desatarse. || Soltarse, aflojarse. || Med. Aliviarse, descargarse (the bowels). || — *My cough has loosened up*, se me ha aliviado la tos. || SP. *To loosen up*, calentarse.

looseness [—nis] n. Relajamiento, *m.* (of morals, discipline). || Aflojamiento, *m.* (of a rope, screw). || Holgura, *f.* (of a coat, of a part). || Friabilidad, *f.*, falta (*f.*) de firmeza (of soil). || MED. Soltura (*f.*) de vientre (of bowels). | Flacidez, *f.*, flaccidez, *f.* (of skin). | Movilidad, *f.* (of a tooth). || FIG. Imprecisión, *f.*, vaguedad, *f.* falta (*f.*) de precisión (vagueness).

loose-tongued [—ˈtʌŋd] adj. Que tiene la lengua suelta.

loot [lu:t] n. Botín, *m.*, presa, *f.* (booty). || FAM. Ganancias, *f. pl.* (earnings). | Pasta, *f.* (money).

loot [lu:t] v. tr. Saquear (to pillage). || Llevar como botín (to carry off).
— V. intr. Entregarse al saqueo.

looter [—ə*] n. Saqueador, ra.

looting [—iŋ] n. Saqueo, *m.*

lop [lɔp] n. Recortes, *m. pl.* (cuttings of trees). || Chapoteo, *m.* (of waves).

lop [lɔp] v. tr. Cortar (branches from a tree). || Podar (a tree). || *To lop off*, cortar (to cut), llevarse: *taxes lop off half his salary*, los impuestos se llevan la mitad de su salario; cercenar (to reduce).
— V. intr. Caer (ears). || Colgar (to hang). || Saltar (to bound). || Chapotear (waves). || *To lop down in*, dejarse caer en (an armchair).

lope [ləup] n. Paso (*m.*) largo.

lope [ləup] v. intr. Andar con paso largo. || Andar muy de prisa (to walk quickly). || — ***To lope along***, andar *or* correr con paso largo. || ***To lope away*** o ***off***, alejarse con paso largo.

lop-eared [ˈlɔpiəd] adj. De orejas gachas, de orejas caídas.

lopsided [ˈlɔpˈsaidid] adj. Ladeado, da; torcido, da (drooping at one side). || Cojo, ja (table, chair). || Desproporcionado, da (unsymmetrical). || Desequilibrado, da (unbalanced). || MAR. Escorado, da (ship).

lopsidedly [—li] adv. De soslayo.

loquacious [ləuˈkweiʃəs] adj. Locuaz.

loquaciousness [—nis] n. Locuacidad, *f.*

loquacity [ləuˈkwæsiti] n. Locuacidad, *f.*

loquat [ˈləukwæt] n. BOT. Níspero (*m.*) del Japón.

loran [ˈlɔ:ræn] n. RAD. AVIAT. Loran, *m.* (Long Range Navigation).

lord [lɔ:d] n. Lord, *m.* (title): *House of Lords*, Cámara de los Lores. || Señor, *m.* (ruler, feudal estate owner). || REL. Señor, *m.* || Magnate, *m.*: *the cotton lords*, los magnates del algodón. || — FAM. *Drunk as a lord*, borracho como una cuba. || *Good Lord!*, ¡Dios mío! || *Lord and master*, dueño (*m.*) y señor. || REL. *Lord of Hosts*, Señor de los Ejércitos. || *Lord of the manor*, señor feudal. || *My lord*, su Ilustrísima (bishop), su señoría (judge), mi señor (noble). || *Our Lord*, Nuestro Señor. || REL. *The Lord*, el Señor. || *The Lords*, la Cámara de los Lores. || *To live like a lord*, vivir como un señor.
— OBSERV. El título de *Lord* se concede a los duques, marqueses, condes, vizcondes y barones ingleses (en este caso antecede directamente al apellido: *the Earl of Leicester* tiene el título de *Lord Leicester*), a los hijos menores de los duques y marqueses (en cuyo caso antecede al nombre y apellido) y a ciertos dignatarios como el *Lord Mayor* (alcalde).

lord [lɔ:d] v. intr. *To lord it*, dárselas de gran señor. || *To lord it over s.o.*, dominar a alguien, tratar despóticamente a alguien.

lord lieutenant [—lefˈtenənt] n. Gobernador, *m.* (of a county). || HIST. Virrey, *m.* (in Ireland).
— OBSERV. El plural de esta palabra es *lords lieutenant* o *lord lieutenants*.

lordliness [—linis] n. Carácter (*m.*) señorial, señorío, *m.* | Altivez, *f.*, arrogancia, *f.* (arrogance).

lordling [—liŋ] n. Hidalgüelo, *m.*, hidalgo (*m.*) de gotera. || FAM. Señorito, *m.*

lordly [—li] adj. Señorial (magnificent). || Noble. || Arrogante, altivo, va (haughty). || *To put on a lordly air*, dárselas de gran señor.

Lord Mayor [—ˈmɛə*] n. Alcalde, *m.*

Lord Privy Seal [—ˈprivisi:l] n. Guardasellos, *m. inv.*

Lord's day [ˈlɔ:dzˈdei] n. REL. Día (*m.*) del Señor.

lordship [ˈlɔ:dʃip] n. Señorío, *m.*, señoría, *f.* (dignity). || Señorío, *m.* (lands or estate). || Señorío, *m.* (authority). || *His Lordship*, Su Señoría.

Lord's Prayer [ˈlɔ:dz prɛə*] n. Padrenuestro, *m.*

lore [lɔ:*] n. Ciencia, *f.*, saber, *m.* (knowledge). || *The local lore*, la tradición local.

lorgnette [lɔ:ˈnjet] n. Impertinentes, *m. pl.* (eyeglasses). || Gemelos, *m. pl.* (opera glasses).

lorica [ləˈraikə] n. Loriga, *f.* (coat of mail).

lorn [lɔ:n] adj. (Ant.). Solitario, ria.

lorry [ˈlɔri] n. Camión, *m.* (truck). || Batea, *f.* (railway carriage). || *Lorry driver*, camionero, *m.*

lose* [lu:z] v. tr. Perder: *to lose a leg*, perder una pierna; *he lost his son*, perdió a su hijo; *to lose an opportunity*, perder una oportunidad; *he lost the train*, perdió el tren; *to lose a match, a battle*, perder un partido, una batalla; *all is lost*, todo está perdido; *the horse lost the race*, el caballo perdió la carrera; *he lost no time in telling us*, no perdió tiempo en decírnoslo, *we lost the thread of the conversation*, perdimos el hilo de la conversación; *she lost most of the sermon*, perdió la mayor parte del sermón. || No poder salvar la vida de (a patient). || Hacer perder, costar: *her rudeness lost her the job*, su grosería le costó el trabajo. || Atrasar: *my watch loses ten minutes a day*, mi reloj atrasa diez minutos por día. || — *Get lost!*, ¡vete al diablo! || *I'm lost without her*, estoy perdido sin ella. || *Not to lose a word of*, no perderse una palabra de. || *Sarcasm is lost on her*, el sarcasmo no le hace ningún efecto. || *She has not lost by it*, no ha perdido nada con eso. || *The joke, the music is lost on me*, no entiendo el chiste, la música. || *The motion is lost*, la moción queda rechazada. || MAR. *To be lost at sea*, morir ahogado (people), perderse en el mar, hundirse (boat). || *To be lost in amazement*, quedarse asombrado. || *To be lost in thought*, estar ensimismado *or* absorto en sus pensamientos. || *To get lost*, perderse. || *To give up for lost*, dar por perdido. || *To look lost*, parecer perdido. || *To lose ground*, perder terreno. || *To lose heart*, see HEART. || *To lose interest*, perder interés. || *To lose one's head*, perder la cabeza. || *To lose one's mind*, perder la razón *or* el juicio. || *To lose one's temper*, perder los estribos. || *To lose one's voice*, perder la voz, quedarse afónico. || *To lose one's way*, perderse, extraviarse [en el camino]. || *To lose o.s.*, perderse (on one's way), perderse, perder el hilo (in speaking, reading). || *To lose o.s. in thought*, ensimismarse, abstraerse. || *To lose sight of*, perder de vista. || *To lose weight*, perder peso, adelgazar. || *To stand to lose nothing*, no tener nada que perder.
— V. intr. Perder (to fail to win, to suffer loss): *to lose heavily*, perder estrepitosamente. || Atrasar: *my watch is losing*, mi reloj atrasa. || *To lose out*, salir perdiendo, perder.
— OBSERV. Pret & p. p. **lost**.

loser [—ə*] n. Perdedor, ra. || — *To be a bad loser*, no saber perder. || *To be a good loser*, saber perder. || *To be a loser*, sufrir *or* tener una pérdida (to suffer a loss), salir siempre perdiendo (to lose always). || *To come off the loser*, salir perdiendo.

losing [—iŋ] adj. Vencido, da; derrotado, da (team). || No agraciado, no premiado (number in a lottery). || Que deja pérdidas (business). || Con pérdida (bargain). || Perdedor, ra (card, etc.). || Perdido de antemano (game). || Malo, la; desventajoso, sa (proposition).
— N. Pérdida, *f.*

loss [lɔs] n. Pérdida, *f.* (a losing): *he met with a loss*, sufrió una pérdida. || Daño, *m.* (damage). || MED. Pérdida, *f.* (of blood, sight, etc.). || Derrota, *f.* (defeat). || COMM. Pérdida, *f.*: *to sell at a loss*, vender con pérdida. || PHYS. Pérdida, *f.* (of heat). || TECH. Pérdida, *f.* (energy wasted in a machine). || — Pl. Pérdidas, *f.* (of money). || MIL. Bajas, *f.* || — FIG. *At a loss for an answer*, sin saber qué contestar. || *Dead loss*, see DEAD. || *It's his loss*, es él quien pierde. || *Loss in transit*, objeto perdido durante el transporte. || *Loss of life*, víctimas, *f. pl.*: *there was no loss of life in the accident*, en el accidente no hubo víctimas. || *Loss of memory*, pérdida de memoria, amnesia, *f.* || *To be at a loss*, estar perdido, estar desorientado. || *To be at a loss for words*, no encontrar palabras con que expresarse. || *To be at a loss to do sth.*, no saber cómo hacer algo.

loss leader [—ˌli:də*] n. Artículo (*m.*) de lanzamiento.

lost [lɔst] pret. & p. p. See LOSE.
— Adj. Perdido, da: *lost property*, objetos perdidos; *many lost hours*, muchas horas perdidas; *a lost opportunity*, una oportunidad perdida; *twenty matches lost*, veinte partidos perdidos; *he's lost without his glasses*, está perdido sin las gafas. || Perdido, da; condenado, da: *a lost soul*, un alma perdida. || Insensible (*to*, a) [insensible]. || Absorto, ta; ensimismado, da (engrossed). || — *Lost and found* o *lost property office*, depósito (*m.*) de objetos perdidos. || || *Lost cause*, causa perdida. || FIG. *Lost to*, perdido para. | *Lost to the world*, absorto, ta; en otro mundo.

lot [lɔt] n. Porción, *f.*, parte, *f.*, lote, *m.* (portion). || Lote, *m.* (at auction). || Lote, *m.*, partida, *f.* (set of articles for sale). || Parcela, *f.* (of ground). || Solar, *m.*, terreno, *m.* (plot in town). || Destino, *m.*, suerte, *f.* (destiny, fate): *it's the common lot*, es el destino de todos. || Sorteo, *m.* (draw in lottery). || FAM. Panda, *f.*: *they are a lot of criminals*, son una panda de criminales. | Gente, *f.*: *the wife's parents are a queer lot*, los padres de mi mujer son gente muy rara. | Tipo, *m.*, individuo, *m.*, tío, *m.* (individual): *a dangerous lot*, un tipo peligroso. | Grupo, *m.*: *a fine lot of people*, un grupo de gente simpática. | Colección, *f.*: *a fine lot of books*, una buena colección de libros. | Serie, *f.* (series). || — FAM. *A bad lot*, una mala persona. | *A fat lot of good he is!*, ¡no sirve para nada! || *A lot*, cantidad: *what a lot of money!*, ¡qué cantidad de dinero!; mucho, mucha: *a lot of luck*, mucha suerte; *thanks a lot*, muchas gracias; mucho: *I write a lot*, escribo mucho; *he is a lot better today*, está mucho mejor hoy. || *An awful lot*, una barbaridad. || *By lots*, por sorteo. || *In one lot*, en bloque. || *Lots*, cantidades, mucho, mucha. || *Lots of*, cantidades de, mucho, mucha: *lots of money*, cantidades de dinero; mucho, mucha: *lots of love*, mucho cariño. || *Quite a lot of*, bastante: *quite a lot of books*, bastantes libros. || *Such a lot*, tanto, ta: *such a lot of lamps*, tantas lámparas. || *The lot*, todo, la totalidad: *that's the lot*, eso es todo; *he got the lot*, se lo llevó todo. || *The whole lot of* *them*, todos ellos. || *To cast in one's lot with*, probar fortuna con. || *To cast* o *to draw lots*, echarlo a suertes, echar suertes. || *To cast* o *to draw lots for sth.*, sortear algo, echar algo a suertes. || *To fall to s.o.'s.lot*, caerle a uno en suerte; incumbirle a uno. || *To throw in one's lot with s.o.*, compartir la suerte de alguien. || *What a lot of!*, ¡cuánto!, ¡cuánta!, ¡cuántos!, ¡cuántas!: *what a lot of people!*, ¡cuánta gente!

lot [lɔt] v. tr. Repartir en lotes (to divide).
— V. intr. U. S. Echar suertes.

loth [ləuθ] adj. See LOATH.

lotion [ˈləuʃən] n. Loción, *f.*

lottery [ˈlɔtəri] n. Lotería, *f.*

lotto [ˈlɔtəu] n. Lotería, *f.* (game).

lotus [ˈləutəs] n. BOT. Loto, *m.*

lotus-eater [—ˌi:tə*] n. FIG. Soñador, ra.

loud [laud] adj. Alto, ta; fuerte: *a loud voice*, una voz fuerte; *the music is too loud*, la música está demasiado alta. || Fuerte, grande: *a loud noise*, un ruido fuerte. || Ruidoso, sa (noisy): *a loud district*, un barrio ruidoso. || Estrepitoso, sa (laugh). || Clamoroso, sa (applause). || Sonoro, ra (bell). || Categórico, ca; rotundo, da (denial). || Flagrante, patente (lie). || Chillón, ona; llamativo, va: *loud colours*, colores chillones; *a loud shirt*, una camisa llamativa. || Cursi, de mal gusto (in bad taste). || Vulgar (unrefined behaviour, person). || — *In a loud voice*, en voz alta. || *To be loud in one's admiration*, manifestar calurosamente su admiración. || *To be loud in one's complaints*, quejarse a voz en grito. || *To be loud in one's praises of*, cantar las alabanzas de.
— Adv. Alto: *to speak loud*, hablar alto. || Fuerte: *a loud ticking clock*, un reloj que suena fuerte. || Ruidosamente (noisily). || Estrepitosamente (to laugh). || *To say sth. out loud*, decir algo en voz alta.

louden [ˈlaudn] v. tr. Intensificar.
— V. intr. Intensificarse.

loud-hailer [ˈlaudˈheilə*] n. Megáfono, *m.*

loudly [ˈlaudli] adv. En voz alta: *to talk loudly*, hablar en voz alta. || Ruidosamente (noisily). || Estrepitosamente (to laugh). || A voz en grito (to shout).

loudmouth [ˈlaudˈmauð] n. FAM. Gritón, ona (who shouts). | Fanfarrón, ona (braggart).

loudmouthed [ˈlaudˈmauðd] adj. FAM. Gritón, ona (shouting). | Fanfarrón, ona (boastful).

loudness [ˈlaudnis] n. Fuerza, *f.*, intensidad, *f.* (of a noise). || Sonoridad, *f.* (sonority). || Lo chillón (of a dress). || Vulgaridad, *f.* (of behaviour).

loudspeaker [ˈlaudˈspi:kə*] n. Altavoz, *m.* [*Amer.*, altoparlante, *m.*].

lough [lɔk] n. Lago, *m.* (lake). || Ría, *f.* (an arm of the sea).

louis [ˈlu:i] or **louis d'or** [—ˈdɔ:*] n. Luis, *m.* (coin).

Louis [ˈlu:i] pr. n. Luis, *m.*

Louisa [lu:ˈi:zə] or **Louise** [luˈi:z] pr. n. Luisa, *f.*

Louisiana [lu:ˌi:ziˈænə] pr. n. GEOGR. Luisiana, *f.*

lounge [laundʒ] n. Salón, *m.* (sitting room). || Salón, *m.* (in hotel, club, bar, etc.). || Sofá, *m.* (long sofa).

lounge [laundʒ] v. intr. Repantigarse (to sit or stand in a lazy manner). | Vagar, gandulear (to saunter idly). || — *To lounge about* o *around*, repantigarse (to sit in a lazy manner), holgazanear, gandulear (to do nothing).
— V. tr. *To lounge away*, malgastar, desperdiciar, perder ganduleando (time).

lounge car [—kɑ:*] n. U. S. Coche (*m.*) salón.

lounge chair [—tʃεə*] n. Tumbona, *f.*

lounger [—ə*] n. Gandul, la; haragán, ana (idler). || Azotacalles, *m.* & *f.* *inv.* (who roams the streets).

lounge suit [ˈlaundzˈsu:t] n. Traje (*m.*) de calle.

lour [ˈlauə*] n. Ceño, *m.*, entrecejo, *m.* (of a person). || Encapotamiento, *m.* (of the sky).

lour [ˈlauə*] v. intr. Fruncir el ceño *or* el entrecejo (to scowl). || FIG. Amenazar: *the clouds loured on the horizon*, las nubes amenazaban en el horizonte. | Encapotarse (the sky).

louse [laus] n. Piojo, *m.* (insect). || FIG. Canalla, *m.* & *f.*, sinvergüenza, *m.* & *f.*
— OBSERV. El plural de *louse* es *lice* cuando se trata del insecto y *louses* en el sentido figurado.

louse [lauz] v. tr. FAM. *To louse sth. up*, echar algo a perder.

lousy [—i] adj. Piojoso, sa (infested with lice). || FAM. Fatal, malísimo, ma: *the weather is lousy*, hace un tiempo fatal. || — FAM. *A lousy trick*, una cochinada. | *To be lousy with*, estar plagado de: *the place was lousy with detectives*, el sitio estaba plagado de detectives; estar forrado de: *he is lousy with money*, está forrado de dinero.

lout [laut] n. Bruto, *m.*, patán, *m.* (rough fellow).

loutish [—iʃ] adj. Bruto, ta; palurdo, da (boorish).

loutishness [—nis] n. Patanería, *f.*

Louvain [ˈlu:vɛ̃:ŋ] pr. n. GEOGR. Lovaina.

louver [ˈlu:və*] n. Persiana, *f.* (blind, moveable arrangement of slats for ventilation). || Respiradero, *m.* (fixed arrangement of slats for ventilation). || Lumbrera, *f.* (in medieval architecture). || Listón, *m.* (long slat). || Tablilla, *f.* (small slat). || AUT. Rejilla (*f.*) de ventilación.

louver board [—bɔ:d] n. Tablilla, *f.*

louvered [—d] adj. De tablillas.

louvre [ˈlu:və*] n. See LOUVER.

lovable [ˈlʌvəbl] adj. Adorable, encantador, ra.

love [lʌv] n. Amor, *m.*: *his love for his wife*, su amor por su mujer; *she was the love of his life*, ella era el amor de su vida; *mother love*, amor materno; *love for thy neighbour*, amor al prójimo; *love of money*, amor al dinero. || Amor, *m.* (loved person): *an old love of his*, un viejo amor suyo. || Cariño, *m.*, afecto, *m.* (affection). || Pasión, *f.*, afición, *f.*: *his love for cricket*, su pasión por el cricket, su afición al cricket. || Amorcillo, *m.* (Cupid). || Encanto, *m.* (lovable person): *your child is a love*, su niño es un encanto. || SP. Nada, cero (in tennis): *love, fifteen*, nada a quince; *fourty love*, cuarenta a cero. || — *A labour of love*, see LABOUR. || FAM. *Cupboard love*, amor interesado. || *For love*, por amor (lovingly): *he did it for love*, lo hizo por amor; gratis (free). || *For the love of*, por el amor de. || *For the love of God!*, ¡por Dios!, ¡por el amor de Dios! || *For the love of it*, por amor al arte: *to do sth. for the love of it*, hacer algo por amor al arte. || FAM. *For the love of Mike!*, ¡Por Dios!, ¡por el amor de Dios! || *Give my love to your parents*, dale recuerdos a tus padres. || *He is a little love*, es un cielo. || *In love with*, enamorado de. || *Love*, un abrazo (in letters). || *Love at first sight*, flechazo, *m.* || FAM. *Love in a cottage*, contigo pan y cebolla. || *Love is blind*, el amor es ciego. || *Love letter*, carta (*f.*) de amor. || *My love*, mi amor, amor mío. || *Neither for love nor money* o *not for love nor money*, por nada del mundo, por nada en el mundo, por todo el oro del mundo: *I wouldn't do it for love nor money*, no lo haría por todo el oro del mundo. || *There is no love lost between them*, no se aprecian. || *To be in love*, estar enamorado. || *To fall in love with*, enamorarse de. || *To make love to*, hacer la corte a, hacer el amor a (to court), hacer el amor con (to have sexual intercourse). || *To marry for love*, casarse por amor. || *To send one's love to s.o.*, enviar cariñosos saludos a. || *To work for love*, trabajar para el obispo *or* para el rey de Roma. || *With much love*, con todo el cariño de (in letters). || *With my love*, abrazos, *m. pl.* (in letters).

love [lʌv] v. tr. Querer, amar (to feel love for s.o.): *he loves his parents*, quiere a sus padres. || Tener cariño a (to feel affectionate). || Ser muy aficionado a: *he loves tennis*, es muy aficionado al tenis. || Gustarle [a uno] muchísimo, encantarle [a uno]: *I should love to go with you*, me gustaría muchísimo ir contigo; *I love cakes*, me gustan muchísimo los pasteles; *I love cooking*, me encanta guisar; *I love this book*, me encanta este libro. || — *He loves me, he loves me not*, me quiere, no me quiere (pulling petals off a daisy). || *I'd love to!*, ¡con mucho gusto! || *Love me, love my dog*, quien quiere a Beltrán, quiere a su can.
— V. intr. Estar enamorado, querer.

loveable [ˈlʌvəbl] adj. Adorable, encantador, ra.

love affair [ˈlʌvəˌfεə*] n. Amores, *m. pl.*, amorío, *m.* (romance). || Aventura, *f.*, intriga (*f.*) amorosa (intrigue).

love apple [ˈlʌvˌæpl] n. Tomate, *m.*

lovebird [ˈlʌvbə:d] n. ZOOL. Periquito, *m.* || — Pl. FIG. Tórtolos, *m.* (people in love).

love child [ˈlʌvtʃaild] n. Hijo (*m.*) natural, hijo (*m.*) del amor.
— OBSERV. El plural de *love child* es *love children*.

love feast [ˈlʌvfi:st] n. REL. Ágape, *m.*

love-in-a-mist [ˈlʌvnəˈmist] n. BOT. Arañuela, *f.*

love knot [ˈlʌvnɔt] n. Lacito, *m.*

loveless [ˈlʌvlis] adj. Sin amor: *loveless marriage*, matrimonio sin amor.

loveliness [ˈlʌvlinis] n. Encanto, *m.*, belleza, *f.*

lovelock [ˈlʌvlɔk] n. Caracol, *m.*, rizo (*m.*) en la sien.

lovelorn [ˈlʌvlɔ:n] adj. Abandonado por su amor (forsaken). || Herido de amor, suspirando de amor (languishing).

lovely [ˈlʌvli] adj. Encantador, ra (lovable): *her grandmother is a lovely person*, su abuela es una persona encantadora. || Precioso, sa; bonito, ta [*Amer.*, lindo, da] (beautiful): *isn't it lovely?*, ¡qué bonito! || Hermoso, sa; precioso, sa; bello, lla [*Amer.*, lindo, da] (attractive). || Delicioso, sa (delightful). || *To have a lovely time*, pasarlo maravillosamente, pasarlo muy bien.
— N. Belleza, *f.*

lovemaking [ˈlʌvˌmeikiŋ] n. Galanteo, *m.* (courting). || Relaciones (*f. pl.*) sexuales (sexual intercourse).

love match [ˈlʌvmætʃ] n. Matrimonio (*m.*) de amor.

love-potion [ˈlʌvˈpəuʃən] n. Filtro (*m.*) de amor.

lover [ˈlʌvə*] n. Amante, *m.* & *f.* || Novio, *m.* (boyfriend). || Novia, *f.* (girlfriend). || Amante, *m.* & *f.*, aficionado, da; amigo, ga: *he is a lover of good music*, es un amante de la buena música, es un aficionado a la buena música, es amigo de la buena música.

love seat [ˈlʌvsi:t] n. Confidente, *m.* (couch).

lovesick [ˈlʌvsik] adj. Enfermo de amor.

lovesickness [—nis] n. Mal (*m.*) de amores.

love song [ˈlʌvsɔŋ] n. MUS. Romanza, *f.*, canción (*f.*) de amor.

love token [ˈlʌvˌtəukən] n. Prueba (*f.*) de amor, prenda (*f.*) de amor.

loving [ˈlʌviŋ] adj. Cariñoso, sa (affectionate): *a loving son*, un hijo cariñoso. || Amoroso, sa (feeling or expressing love): *a loving look*, una mirada amorosa. || Aficionado, da (fond of). || *A loving friend*, un fiel amigo.

loving cup [—kʌp] n. Copa (*f.*) de la amistad.

loving-kindness [—ˈkaindnis] n. Bondad, *f.*
lovingly [—li] adv. Cariñosamente, con cariño (affectionately). || Amorosamente (amorously): *he looked at her lovingly*, la miró amorosamente.
lovingness [—nis] n. Cariño, *m.*
low [ləu] adj. Bajo, ja (in degree, height, intensity, sonority, cost, price, value, wages, speed): *low intelligence*, inteligencia baja; *low land*, tierra baja; *low number*, número bajo; *low price*, precio bajo; *in a low voice*, en voz baja; *low temperatures*, temperaturas bajas. || Estrecho, cha; poco, ca: *he has a low forehead*, tiene poca frente, tiene una frente estrecha. || Escotado, da (dress, neckline). || Pequeño, ña; bajo, ja; reducido, da (small): *profits have been low*, los beneficios han sido pequeños. || Escaso, sa: *supplies are low*, los abastecimientos son escasos; *we are low on petrol*, estamos escasos de gasolina. || Poco ca; poco numeroso, sa: *losses were low in the battle*, las bajas fueron pocas en la batalla. || Bajo, ja; poco profundo, da (shallow). || Profundo, da: *a low bow*, una reverencia profunda. || Grosero, ra; vulgar: *a low remark*, una observación grosera. || Vil (mean). || Malo, la: *low company*, malas compañías; *a low opinion*, mala opinión; *a low trick*, una mala jugada. || Humilde (birth, rank): *I am not ashamed of my low birth*, no me avergüenzo de mi humilde cuna. || Deprimido, da; abatido, da (depressed): *to feel low*, estar deprimido. || Desanimado, da; desalentado, da (downhearted). || Débil (weak): *a low moan was heard*, se oyó un débil quejido. || REL. Rezada (Mass). || GEOGR. MAR. Bajo, ja. || MED. Bajo, ja (blood pressure). || BIOL. Primitivo, va. || Tenue, bajo, ja (light). || CULIN. Lento, ta (fire). || MUS. Grave, bajo, ja. || Bajo (Latin, German). || — *To be in low spirits*, estar desanimado. || *To get low*, empezar a escasear. || *To lay low*, derribar (to overthrow), postrar [en cama] (to make bedridden). || *To lie low*, permanecer escondido (to keep hidden), mantenerse quieto (to keep quiet).
— Adv. Bajo: *to fly low*, volar bajo; *to speak, to sing low*, hablar, cantar bajo. || Profundamente: *to bow low*, inclinarse profundamente. || Poco: *to play low*, jugar poco; *to bet low*, apostar poco. || Barato, ta (cheap): *to be sold low*, venderse barato. || Recientemente (recently). || — *Cut low*, [muy] escotado, da (dress). || *Lowest paid workers*, los obreros peor pagados. || FIG. *To fall as low as to*, caer en una bajeza tal que. | *To fall low*, caer muy bajo. || MED. *To feed low*, ponerse a dieta. || *To hit low*, dar un golpe bajo.
— N. AUT. Primera, *f.* (first gear): *put the car in low*, ponga el coche en primera. || Área (*f.*) de baja presión, depresión, *f.* (in meteorology). || FIG. Lo más bajo, punto (*m.*) más bajo (low level). || FAM. *To be at an all-time low*, estar más bajo que nunca.
low [ləu] n. Mugido, *m.* (moo of a cow).
low [ləu] v. intr. Mugir (a cow).
low-altitude [—ˈæltitjud] adj. A poca altura.
lowborn [—ˈbɔ:n] adj. De familia humilde, de humilde cuna, de origen modesto.
lowboy [—bɔi] n. U. S. Cómoda, *f.*
lowbred [—bred] adj. Mal educado, da; malcriado, da.
lowbrow [—brau] n. Persona (*f.*) de poca cultura, ignorante, *m.* & *f.*
— Adj. De poca cultura, ignorante.
Low Church [—ˈtʃə:tʃ] n. Iglesia (*f.*) anglicana que no da mucha importancia a los ritos y al dogma.
low-class [—klɑ:s] adj. De clase baja, de clase humilde.
low comedy [—ˈkɔmidi] n. Farsa, *f.*
low-cost [—ˈkɔst] adj. Económico, ca; barato, ta.
Low Countries [—ˈkʌntriz] pl. pr. n. GEOGR. Países (*m.*) Bajos.
low-cut [—kʌt] adj. [Muy] escotado, da (dress).
low-down [—daun] adj. FAM. Vil, bajo, ja.
lowdown [—daun] n. FAM. *To give s.o. the lowdown*, dar informes confidenciales a alguien (to inform), decir la verdad a alguien (to tell the truth).
lower [—ə*] comp. adj. Más bajo. || Inferior: *the lower jaw*, la mandíbula inferior. || Bajo, ja. || Reciente (recent). || See LOW.
— Comp. adv. Más bajo. || See LOW.
lower [—ə*] v. tr. Bajar. || Bajar (the voice). || Lanzar (lifeboats). || Arriar (flag, sails). || Reducir, disminuir, bajar, aminorar (to reduce). || Rebajar, bajar (price). || Debilitar (to weaken). || FIG. Rebajar, humillar. || FIG. *To lower o.s.*, rebajarse.
— V. intr. Bajar.
lower [ˈlauə*] n./v. intr. See LOUR.
lowercase [ˈlauəkeis] n. PRINT. Caja (*f.*) baja.
lower class [ˈlauəˌklɑ:s] n. Clase (*f.*) baja.
lower-class [ˈlauəˌklɑ:s] adj. De clase baja.
Lower House [ˈlauəˌhaus] n. Cámara (*f.*) Baja.
lowering [ˈlauəriŋ] adj. Amenazador, ra (weather). || Ceñudo, da; con el entrecejo fruncido (person). || Encapotado, da; cubierto, ta (sky).
lowermost [ˈlauəməust] adj. Más bajo, ja.
lowest [ˈləuist] superl. adj. Más bajo, ja: *the lowest score*, la puntuación más baja. || Mínimo, ma: *lowest price*, precio mínimo. || MATH. *Lowest common denominator, multiple*, mínimo común denominador, múltiplo.
— N. Mínimo, *m.*: *at the lowest*, como mínimo; *prices are at their lowest*, los precios han bajado al mínimo. || *The lowest of the low*, de lo peor que hay.
low frequency [—ˈfri:kwənsi] n. Baja frecuencia, *f.*
low-frequency [ˈləuˈfri:kwənsi] adj. De baja frecuencia.
low gear [ˈləuˈgiə*] n. AUT. Primera velocidad, *f.*, primera, *f.*: *the car was in low gear*, el coche estaba en primera.
low-grade [ˈləuˈgreid] adj. De baja calidad.
low-heeled [ˈləuˈhi:ld] adj. Con tacones bajos.
lowing [ˈləuiŋ] n. Mugidos, *m. pl.* (of a cow).
lowland [ˈləulənd] n. Tierra (*f.*) baja. || — Pl. *The Lowlands*, la Baja Escocia.
— Adj. De tierra baja. || De la Baja Escocia.
lowlander [—ə*] n. Habitante (*m.* & *f.*) de tierra baja. || Habitante (*m.* & *f.*) de la Baja Escocia.
low-level [ˈləuˈlevl] adj. De bajo nivel. || De grado inferior, subalterno, na (staff).
lowliness [ˈləulinis] n. Humildad, *f.*, modestia, *f.* (humbleness).
lowly [ˈləuli] adj. Humilde, modesto, ta (humble). || Inferior.
— Adv. Humildemente.
low-lying [ˈləuˈlaiiŋ] adj. Bajo, ja.
low-minded [ˈləuˈmaindid] adj. Vulgar, chabacano, na.
low-necked [ˈləuˈnekt] adj. Escotado, da (dress).
lowness [ˈləunis] n. Falta (*f.*) de altura, poca altura, *f.* (lack of height). || Poca estatura, *f.* (in stature). || FIG. Bajeza, *f.* (meanness). | Humildad, *f.*, condición (*f.*) modesta (humbleness). | Desánimo, *m.*, desaliento, *m.* (discouragement). || Baratura, *f.*, lo barato (of price). || Gravedad, *f.* (of voice).
low-pitched [ˈləuˈpitʃt] adj. MUS. Bajo, ja; grave (voice). || ARCH. Poco inclinado, da (roof). | De techo bajo (room). || FIG. Poco elevado, da (ideals).
low pressure [ˈləuˈpreʃə*] n. Baja presión, *f.*
low-pressure [ˈləuˈpreʃə*] adj. De baja presión.
low-priced [ˈləuˈpraist] adj. Barato, ta (cheap).
low relief [ˈləuriˈli:f] n. ARTS. Bajorrelieve, *m.*, bajo relieve, *m.*
low-spirited [ˈləuˈspiritid] adj. Deprimido, da; desanimado, da.
Low Sunday [ˈləuˈsʌndi] n. Domingo (*m.*) de Cuasimodo.
low-tension [ˈləuˈtenʃən] adj. De baja tensión, de bajo voltaje.
low tide [ˈləuˈtaid] n. Marea (*f.*) baja, bajamar, *f.*
low water [ˈləuˈwɔ:tə*] n. Marea (*f.*) baja, bajamar, *f.* || FIG. Decadencia, *f.* (decline). || FIG. *To be in low water*, estar apurado.
low-water mark [—mɑ:k] n. Estiaje, *m.*
lox [lɔks] n. CULIN. Salmón (*m.*) ahumado. || Oxígeno (*m.*) líquido.
loyal [ˈlɔiəl] adj. Leal (true to one's ruler): *loyal subjects*, súbditos leales. || Fiel (faithful): *loyal supporters*, fieles partidarios.
loyalism [—izəm] n. Lealtad, *f.*, fidelidad, *f.*
loyalist [—ist] n. Leal, *m.* & *f.* || Legitimista, *m.* & *f.* (in England).
loyalty [ˈlɔiəlti] n. Lealtad, *f.*, fidelidad, *f.* (to a king). || Fidelidad, *f.* (to a person, cause, etc.).
lozenge [ˈlɔzindʒ] n. Rombo, *m.* (four-sided figure). || Pastilla, *f.*, tableta, *f.* (medicinal sweet). || HERALD. Losange, *m.*
LP [ˈelˈpi:] adj. De larga duración.
— N. Disco (*m.*) de larga duración, microsurco, *m.* (record).
— OBSERV. L. P. son las iniciales de *long-playing*.
lubber [ˈlʌbə*] n. Marinero (*m.*) de agua dulce (landlubber). || Palurdo, *m.* (clumsy person).
lubberliness [—linis] n. Torpeza, *f.*
lubberly [—li] adj. Palurdo, da; torpe.
— Adv. Torpemente.
lubricant [ˈlu:brikənt] n. Lubricante, *m.*, lubrificante, *m.* (grease, oil, etc.).
— Adj. Lubricante, lubrificante.
lubricate [ˈlu:brikeit] v. tr. Lubricar, lubrificar. || FAM. *Lubricated*, tajado, da (drunk).
lubricating [—iŋ] adj. Lubricante, lubrificante.
lubrication [ˌlu:briˈkeiʃən] n. Lubricación, *f.*, lubrificación, *f.*, engrase, *m.*
lubricator [ˈlu:brikeitə*] n. Lubricante, *m.*, lubrificante, *m.* (lubricant).
lubricity [lu:ˈbrisiti] n. Lubricidad, *f.* (slipperiness). || FIG. Lubricidad, *f.* (lewdness). | Duplicidad, *f.*, carácter (*m.*) esquivo (trickiness).
lubricous [ˈlu:brikəs] adj. Lúbrico, ca; resbaladizo, za (slippery). || FIG. Lúbrico, ca (lewd). | Huidizo, za; esquivo, va (tricky).
luce [ˈlu:s] n. Lucio, *m.* (fish).
lucency [ˈlu:snsi] n. Claridad, *f.*, luminosidad, *f.*
lucent [ˈlu:snt] adj. Luminoso, sa (luminous). || Translúcido, da; transparente (transparent).
lucern or **lucerne** [lu:ˈsə:n] n. BOT. Alfalfa, *f.*
lucid [ˈlu:sid] adj. Claro, ra; lúcido, da; resplandeciente (clear). || MED. Lúcido, da: *a lucid interval*, un intervalo lúcido. || FIG. Lúcido, da (mind). | Claro, ra (style, speech).
lucidity [lu:ˈsiditi] n. Lucidez, *f.*, brillantez, *f.*, claridad, *f.* (clarity). || FIG. Lucidez, *f.* (of thinking). | Claridad, *f.* (of style, speech). || MED. Lucidez, *f.*
lucidness [ˈlu:sidnis] n. Lucidez, *f.*

lucifer [ˈlu:sifə*] n. Fósforo, *m.* (match).
Lucifer [ˈlu:sifə*] pr. n. REL. Lucifer, *m.* || ASTR. Venus, *m.*, Lucífero, *m.*, Lucifer, *m.*
luciferous [lu:ˈsifərəs] adj. Lucífero, ra.
luck [lʌk] n. Suerte, *f.* (good fortune): *to wish s.o. luck*, desearle a uno suerte. || Destino, *m.*, suerte, *f.* (fate). || — *As luck would have it*, el azar *or* la suerte quiso que. || *A stroke of luck*, una suerte, un golpe de suerte, un momento de suerte. || *Beginner's luck*, suerte del principiante. || *Better luck next time*, otra vez será. || *Good luck!*, ¡buena suerte!, ¡suerte! || *Good luck to you!*, ¡que tengas suerte! || *Hard* o *bad luck*, mala suerte. || *Here's luck!*, ¡mucha suerte! || *Just my luck!*, ¡mi mala suerte de siempre!, ¡qué mala suerte la mía! || *Luck is blind*, la suerte es ciega. || *No such luck!*, ¡ojalá! || *That's your hard luck!*, ¡peor para ti!, ¡allá tú! || *The best of luck!*, ¡que tengas mucha suerte! || *The luck has turned*, la suerte ha cambiado. || *To be in luck*, estar de *or* con suerte. || *To be out of luck* o *to be down on one's luck*, no tener suerte, estar de mala suerte, estar de malas. || *To bring bad luck*, traer *or* dar mala suerte. || *To do sth. trusting to luck*, hacer algo confiando en la suerte. || *To have the luck of the devil*, tener una suerte de mil demonios. || *To keep sth. for luck*, conservar algo pensando que puede traer suerte. || *To push one's luck*, tentar la suerte. || *To trust to luck that*, confiar que. || *To try one's luck*, probar fortuna. || FAM. *What rotten luck!*, ¡qué suerte más negra *or* más perra! || *With a bit of luck* o *with any luck*, con un poco de suerte. || *Worse luck*, mala suerte: *I can't go out, worse luck!*, no puedo salir, ¡mala suerte!
luckily [—ili] adv. Por suerte, afortunadamente, por fortuna.
luckiness [—inis] n. Suerte, *f.*, fortuna, *f.*
luckless [—lis] adj. Desafortunado, da.
lucky [—i] adj. Afortunado, da: *a lucky event*, un acontecimiento afortunado. || Afortunado, da; con suerte: *a lucky person*, una persona con suerte; *lucky in love*, afortunado en amores. || Que trae suerte (charm, etc.). || Oportuno, na: *he came at a lucky moment*, llegó en un momento oportuno. || Propicio, cia (hour). || Favorable, de buen agüero (day). || — *How lucky!*, ¡qué suerte! || *It was lucky for you that...*, menos mal que... || *Lucky dip*, caja (*f.*) de las sorpresas. || *Lucky strike*, suerte. || *Thank your lucky stars!*, ¡bendice tu buena estrella! || *Third time lucky*, a la tercera va la vencida. || *To be a lucky sort*, tener mucha suerte. || *To be born lucky* o *under a lucky star*, haber nacido con buena estrella. || *To be lucky enough to*, tener la suerte de. || *To be lucky in that ...*, tener la suerte de que ... || *To be lucky to*, tener la suerte de.
lucrative [ˈlu:krətiv] adj. Lucrativo, va.
lucre [ˈlu:kə*] n. Lucro, *m.* || *Filthy lucre*, el vil metal.
Lucretia [lu:ˈkri:ʃjə] pr. n. Lucrecia, *f.*
Lucretius [lu:ˈkri:ʃjəs] pr. n. HIST. Lucrecio, *m.*
lucubrate [ˈlu:kjubreit] v. intr. Lucubrar, elucubrar.
lucubration [ˌlu:kjuˈbreiʃən] n. Lucubración, *f.*, elucubración, *f.*
ludicrous [ˈlu:dikrəs] adj. Absurdo, da; ridículo, la; grotesco, ca.
ludicrousness [—nis] n. Ridículez, *f.*, lo ridículo, lo absurdo, lo grotesco.
ludo [ˈlu:dəu] n. Parchís, *m.*, parchesi, *m.*
luff [lʌf] n. MAR. Orza, *f.*
luff [lʌf] v. intr. MAR. Orzar.
luffa [ˈlʌfə] n. U. S. Estropajo, *m.*
lug [lʌg] n. MAR. Vela (*f.*) al tercio (lugsail). || Agarradero, *m.* [*Amer.*, agarradera, *f.*] (handle). || Asa, *f.* (of a casserole). || TECH. Espiga, *f.*, saliente, *m.* (spike). || ELECTR. Lengüeta (*f.*) de conexión (for soldering wires). || Tirón, *m.* (a tug, pull). || Orejera, *f.* (of a cap). || ZOOL. Arenícola, *f.*, gusano, *m.* (lugworm). || FAM. Oreja, *f.* (ear).
lug [lʌg] v. tr. Arrastrar (to drag). || — *To lug sth. about*, cargar con algo. || *To lug in a subject*, sacar un tema a colación. || *To lug s.o. off*, llevarse a alguien.
— V. intr. Arrastrar.
luge [lu:dʒ] n. SP. Trineo, *m.* (sledge).
luggage [ˈlʌgidʒ] inv. n. Equipaje, *m.* (baggage). || Maletas, *f. pl.* (suitcases and trunks). || *Luggage in advance*, equipaje facturado.
luggage boot [—bu:t] n. AUT. Maleta, *f.*, maletero, *m.*
luggage carrier [—ˌkæriə*] n. Portaequipajes, *m. inv.*
luggage porter [—ˌpɔ:tə*] n. Mozo (*m.*) de equipajes.
luggage rack [—ræk] n. AUT. Portaequipajes, *m. inv.*, baca, *f.* || Redecilla, *f.* (in a train, a coach, a plane).
luggage trolley [—ˌtrɔli] n. Carretilla, *f.*
luggage van [—væn] n. Furgón (*m.*) de equipajes.
lugger [ˈlʌgə*] n. MAR. Lugre, *m.* (ship).
lugsail [ˈlʌgseil] n. MAR. Vela (*f.*) al tercio.
lugubrious [lu:ˈgu:briəs] adj. Lúgubre, lóbrego, ga; tétrico, ca.
lugworm [ˈlʌgwə:m] n. ZOOL. Arenícola, *f.*, gusano, *m.*
Luke [lu:k] pr. n. Lucas, *m.* || *The Gospel according to St Luke*, el Evangelio según San Lucas.
lukewarm [—wɔ:m] adj. Tibio, bia; templado, da (tepid). || FIG. Tibio, bia; poco entusiasta (half-hearted).
lukewarmness [—wɔ:mnis] n. Tibieza, *f.*
lull [lʌl] n. Calma, *f.*, recalmón, *m.* (in storm, wind). || FIG. Tregua, *f.*, momento (*m.*) de calma, pausa, *f.*, respiro, *m.* (truce).
lull [lʌl] v. tr. Calmar, sosegar (to calm, to soothe). || MAR. Calmar (sea, wind). || Acallar (to quiet). || *To lull to sleep*, arrullar, adormecer (to send to sleep), mecer, acunar (to rock).
— V. intr. Calmarse (to become less intense). || Amainar, encalmarse (wind, storm). || Calmarse (sea).
lullaby [ˈlʌləbai] n. Canción (*f.*) de cuna, nana, *f.*
lullaby [ˈlʌləbai] v. tr. Arrullar, acunar.
lumbago [lʌmˈbeigəu] n. MED. Lumbago, *m.*
lumbar [ˈlʌmbə*] adj. ANAT. Lumbar.
lumber [ˈlʌmbə*] n. Trastos (*m. pl.*) viejos (junk). || Maderos, *m. pl.*, madera, *f.* (wood).
lumber [ˈlʌmbə*] v. tr. Abarrotar, atestar, cargar: *the room was lumbered with old furniture*, la habitación estaba abarrotada de muebles viejos. || Amontonar (to pile up). || Talar (to fell timber). || — FIG. *To lumber s.o. with sth.*, hacer que alguien cargue con algo. || *To lumber together*, amontonar.
— V. intr. Talar, cortar madera (to fell timber). || Moverse *or* andar pesadamente (to move clumsily).
lumberer [—rə*] n. Leñador, *m.* (woodcutter). || FIG. Torpe.
lumbering [—riŋ] adj. Torpe, pesado, da (moving heavily). || Pesado, da (heavy).
— N. Explotación (*f.*) forestal (timber industry).
lumberjack [ˈlʌmbədʒæk] n. Leñador, *m.* (woodcutter).
lumberman [ˈlʌmbəmən] n. Leñador, *m.* (woodcutter). || Maderero, *m.* negociante (*m.*) en maderas (who deals in timber).
— OBSERV. El plural de *lumberman* es *lumbermen.*
lumber mill [ˈlʌmbəmil] n. Aserradero, *m.*
lumber room [ˈlʌmbərum] n. Cuarto (*m.*) trastero, cuarto (*m.*) de los trastos.
lumber trade [ˈlʌmbətreid] n. Industria (*f.*) maderera.
lumberyard [ˈlʌmbəjɑ:d] n. Almacén (*m.*) *or* depósito (*m.*) de madera.
lumen [ˈlumən] n. Lumen, *m.* [unidad de flujo luminoso] (measure of light). || ANAT. Abertura, *f.*
— OBSERV. El plural de la palabra inglesa es *lumina* o *lumens.*
luminary [ˈlu:minəri] n. ASTR. Luminar, *m.*, cuerpo (*m.*) luminoso. || FIG. Lumbrera, *f.* (outstanding person).
luminescence [ˌlu:miˈnesns] n. PHYS. Luminiscencia, *f.*, luminescencia, *f.*
luminescent [ˌlu:miˈnesnt] adj. PHYS. Luminiscente, luminescente.
luminiferous [ˌlu:miˈnifərəs] adj. Luminoso, sa.
luminosity [ˌlu:miˈnɔsiti] n. Luminosidad, *f.*
luminous [ˈlu:minəs] adj. Luminoso, sa: *luminous flux*, flujo luminoso. || *Luminous energy*, energía (*f.*) radiante.
luminousness [—nis] n. Luminosidad, *f.*
lummox [ˈlʌməks] n. U. S. FAM. Ganso, *m.*, tonto, *m.*
lummy [ˈlʌmi] interj. FAM. ¡Caray!
lump [lʌmp] n. Trozo, *m.*, pedazo, *m.*: *a lump of coal*, un trozo de carbón. || Terrón, *m.* (of sugar, earth). || Bloque, *m.* (of stone). || Grumo, *m.* (in cooking). || Masa, *f.*, montón, *m.* (mass). || Pella, *f.*: *a lump of clay*, una pella de arcilla. || Protuberancia, *f.*, bulto, *m.* (swelling). || MED. Chichón, *m.* (bruise). || FIG. Nudo, *m.*: *to have a lump in one's throat*, tener un nudo en la garganta. | Conjunto, *m.*, masa, *f.*, totalidad, *f.* (whole). || FIG. FAM. Pelmazo, za; pelma, *m.* & *f.* (bore): *he is a lump*, es un pelmazo. | Imbécil, *m.* & *f.*, bobo, ba (fool).
lump [lʌmp] v. tr. Amontonar (to put together). || Agrupar (to treat alike). || FAM. Aguantar (to bear): *you'll just have to lump it*, tendrás que aguantarte.
— V. intr. Hacerse grumos (in cooking). || Apelmazarse (clay). || Aterronarse (earth, etc.). || *To lump about* o *along*, andar *or* moverse pesadamente.
lumper [—ə*] n. MAR. Cargador, *m.*, descargador, *m.*, estibador, *m.* (docker).
lumpish [—iʃ] adj. FAM. Bobalicón, ona (stupid). | Torpe (clumsy). | Pesado, da (heavy, boring).
lumpishness [—iʃnis] n. FAM. Necedad, *f.* (stupidity). | Torpeza, *f.* (clumsiness). | Pesadez, *f.* (bore).
lump sugar [—ˈʃugə*] n. Azúcar (*m.*) en terrones *or* de cortadillo.
lump sum [—ˈsʌm] n. Cantidad (*f.*) total, suma (*f.*) global (total amount). || Precio (*m.*) a tanto alzado (overall estimate).
lumpy [—i] adj. Apelmazado, da (clay). || Aterronado, da (earth). || En terrones (sugar). || Grumoso, sa (sauce, food). || Granuloso, sa (skin). || Con chichones (with bruises). || Cubierto de protuberancias *or* bultos (surface). || Picado, da (sea). || Lleno de bultos (bed). || Torpe (clumsy).
lunacy [ˈlu:nəsi] n. Locura, *f.* || *It's sheer lunacy!*, ¡es una locura!, ¡es un disparate!
lunar [ˈlu:nə*] adj. Lunar.
lunar landing [ˈlu:nə*ˈlændiŋ] n. Alunizaje, *m.*, aterrizaje (*m.*) en la luna.
lunar month [ˈlu:nə*ˈmʌnθ] n. Mes (*m.*) lunar.
lunar year [ˈlu:nə*jə:*] n. Año (*m.*) lunar.
lunate [ˈlu:neit] adj. Lunado, da; en forma de media luna.
lunatic [ˈlu:nətik] adj. Loco, ca (insane). || Lunático, ca (whimsical). || Descabellado, da: *a lunatic plan*, un proyecto descabellado.
— N. Loco, ca.

lunatic asylum [—ə'sailəm] n. Manicomio, *m.*
lunatic fringe [—frindʒ] n. Extremistas, *m. pl.*, fanáticos, *m. pl.*
lunation [lu:'neiʃən] n. ASTR. Lunación, *f.*
lunch [lʌntʃ] n. Almuerzo, *m.* (midday meal). || U. S. Refrigerio, *m.*, bocado, *m.* (snack). || — *Buffet lunch*, lunch, *m.* || *Lunch hour*, hora (*f.*) de comer. || *To have o to take lunch*, almorzar, comer.
lunch [lʌntʃ] v. intr. Almorzar.
— V. tr. Convidar a almorzar a.
lunch basket [—,bα:skit] n. Cesta (*f.*) de la comida.
lunch counter [—,kauntə*] n. Cafetería, *f.*, snack-bar, *m.*
luncheon ['lʌntʃən] n. See LUNCH.
luncheon basket [—,bα:skit] n. Cesta (*f.*) de la comida.
luncheonette [,lʌnʃən'et] n. U. S. Cafetería, *f.*, snack-bar, *m.*
luncher ['lʌntʃə*] n. Persona (*f.*) que almuerza.
lunchroom ['lʌntʃrum] n. U. S. Restaurante (*m.*) pequeño.
lunchtime ['lʌntʃtaim] n. Hora (*f.*) de comer, hora (*f.*) del almuerzo.
lune [lu:n] n. MATH. Lúnula, *f.*
lunes [—z] pl. n. Ataques (*m.*) de locura.
lunette [lu:'net] n. ARCH. Luneto, *m.* || MIL. Luneta, *f.*
lung [lʌŋ] n. ANAT. Pulmón, *m.*: *iron lung*, pulmón de acero; *lung cancer*, cáncer del pulmón. || FIG. *To shout at the top of one's lungs*, gritar a voz en cuello *or* a voz en grito *or* con todas las fuerzas de los pulmones.
lunge [lʌndʒ] n. Embestida, *f.*, arremetida, *f.* (sudden forward movement). || SP. Estocada, *f.* (in fencing). || Ronzal, *m.*, cabestro, *m.* (rope for training horses).
lunge [lʌndʒ] v. tr. Domar, amaestrar (to train horses).
— V. intr. Lanzarse, arremeter, embestir (to move forwards suddenly). || SP. Atacar, tirarse a fondo (in fencing). || *To lunge (out) at*, arremeter contra.
lunger ['lʌŋə*] n. U. S. FAM. Tísico, ca.
lunula ['lu:njulə] n. MATH. Lúnula, *f.* || Lúnula, *f.*, blanco (*m.*) de las uñas (of nails).

— OBSERV. El plural de la palabra inglesa es *lunulae*.

lunule ['lu:nju:l] n. Lúnula, *f.*, blanco (*m.*) de las uñas.
Lupercalia [,lu:pə:'keiljə] pl. n. Lupercales, *f.*
lupin (U. S. **lupine**) ['lu:pin] n. BOT. Altramuz, *m.*, lupino, *m.*
lurch [lə:tʃ] n. Guiñada, *f.*, bandazo, *m.* (of a boat). || Bandazo, *m.* (of a vehicle, person, moving object). || Sacudida, *f.* (jolt). || FAM. *To leave s.o. in the lurch*, dejar a alguien en la estacada.
lurch [lə:tʃ] v. intr. Dar bandazos, guiñar (boat). || Dar bandazos (vehicle, person). || Dar sacudidas (to jolt). || *To lurch along*, ir dando bandazos (vehicle), ir tambaleándose, ir dando bandazos (drunkard).
lurcher [—ə*] n. Ratero, ra; mangante, *m.* & *f.*, ladronzuelo, la (thief). || Cazador (*m.*) furtivo (poacher). || Perro (*m.*) de cazador furtivo (dog).
lure [ljuə*] n. Señuelo, *m.* (in falconry). || Cebo, *m.* (device to attract animals). || FIG. Señuelo, *m.*, añagaza, *f.* (bait). | Aliciente, *m.*, atractivo, *m.* (incentive): *the lure of adventure*, el aliciente de la aventura. | Atractivo, *m.*, encanto, *m.*: *the lures of a woman*, los encantos de una mujer.
lure [ljuə*] v. tr. Engañar con el señuelo (in falconry). || FIG. Atraer. || — *To lure s.o. away from*, apartar a uno de. || *To lure s.o. into a trap*, hacer que alguien caiga en una trampa. || *To lure s.o. into doing sth.*, convencer a alguien de que haga algo.
lurid ['ljuərid] adj. Espeluznante (violent and shocking). || Sensacionalista, sensacional. || Lívido, da; pálido, da (pale, ashen). || Chillón, ona; llamativo, va (gaudy).
lurk [lə:k] v. intr. Estar escondido, esconderse (to be hidden). || Estar al acecho (to lie in wait). || FIG. Rondar (to be constantly present): *the suspicion lurked in her mind*, la sospecha rondaba por su mente.
lurker [—ə*] n. Persona (*f.*) que está al acecho. || Espía, *m.* (spy).
lurking [—iŋ] adj. Oculto, ta; vago, ga. || *Lurking place*, escondite, *m.* (hiding place), puesto, *m.* (of hunter).
luscious ['lʌʃəs] adj. Exquisito, ta; delicioso, sa (smells, tastes, etc.). || Exquisito, ta (colours). || Apetitoso, sa (woman). || Voluptuoso, sa (impressions, feelings). || Dulzón, ona (sickeningly sweet). || Empalagoso, sa (style).
lusciousness [—nis] n. Exquisitez, *f.* || Voluptuosidad, *f.* (voluptuousness).
lush [lʌʃ] adj. Exuberante, lujuriante (vegetation). || Verde (grass). || FIG. Exuberante, florido, da (writing).
— N. FAM. Borracho, cha (drunkard).
lushy [—i] adj. FAM. Tajado, da (drunk).
Lusiads (the) ['lu:siædz] pl. pr. n. Los Lusiadas.
Lusitania [,lu:si'teinjə] pr. n. GEOGR. Lusitania, *f.*
Lusitanian [—n] adj./n. Lusitano, na.
lust [lʌst] n. Lujuria, *f.*, lascivia, *f.* (sexual desire). || Ansia, *f.*, anhelo, *m.*, apetito, *m.*, gran deseo, *m.* (great desire). || REL. Concupiscencia, *f.*
lust [lʌst] v. intr. *To lust for o after*, codiciar (sth.), desear (s.o.).
luster [—ə*] n./v. tr. U. S. See LUSTRE.
lusterless [—əlis] adj. U. S. See LUSTRELESS.
lusterware [—əwεə*] n. U. S. See LUSTREWARE.
lustful [—ful] adj. Lujurioso, sa; lascivo, va; lúbrico, ca; libidinoso, sa (person). || Lleno de deseo (look).
lustfulness [—fulnis] n. Lujuria, *f.*, lascivia, *f.*
lustily [—ili] adv. Fuertemente.
lustiness [—inis] n. Fuerza, *f.*, vigor, *m.*
lustrate ['lʌstreit] v. tr. Purificar, lustrar.
lustration [lʌs'treiʃən] n. Purificación, *f.*, lustración, *f.*
lustre ['lʌstə*] n. Lustre, *m.* (gloss). || Brillo, *m.* (radiance, brightness). || Lustre, *m.*, brillo, *m.* (on a cloth). || Aguas, *f. pl.* (of a diamond). || Colgante, *m.* (glass pendant). || Araña, *f.* (chandelier hung with pendants). || Barniz (*m.*) vítreo, vidriado, *m.* (on pottery). || Cerámica (*f.*) *or* loza (*f.*) vidriada, cerámica (*f.*) decorada con reflejos metálicos (lustreware). || FIG. Lustre, *m.* (renown, distinction). || Lustrina, *f.* (fabric). || Lustro, *m.* (period of five years).
lustre ['lʌstə*] v. tr. Lustrar, dar brillo. || Lustrar (cloth). || Vidriar (pottery).
lustreless [—lis] adj. Sin brillo, deslustrado, da.
lustreware [—wεə*] n. Cerámica (*f.*) *or* loza (*f.*) vidriada, cerámica (*f.*) decorada con reflejos metálicos.
lustring ['lʌstriŋ] n. Lustrina, *f.*
lustrous ['lʌstrəs] adj. Brillante.
lustrum ['lʌstrəm] n. Lustro, *m.* (five years).

— OBSERV. El plural de la palabra inglesa es *lustra* o *lustrums*.

lusty ['lʌsti] adj. Fuerte, robusto, ta (person). || Fuerte (shout).
lutanist ['lu:tənist] n. Tañedor (*m.*) de laúd.
lute [lu:t] n. Zulaque, *m.* (cement for pipes). || MUS. Laúd, *m.*
lute [lu:t] v. tr. Zulacar, tapar con zulaque.
lutein ['lju:tiin] n. Luteína, *f.*
luteous ['lju:tiəs] adj. Lúteo, a; amarillento, ta.
lute player ['lu:t,pleiə*] n. Tañedor (*m.*) de laúd.
lutestring ['lju:tstriŋ] n. Lustrina, *f.*
Lutetia [lu'ti:ʃjə] pr. n. HIST. Lutecia, *f.*
lutetium [lu'tiʃiəm] n. Lutecio, *m.* (metal).
Luther ['lu:θə*] pr. n. Lutero, *m.*
Lutheran [—rən] adj./n. Luterano, na.
Lutheranism [—rənizəm] n. Luteranismo, *m.*
lutist ['lu:tist] n. Tañedor (*m.*) de laúd (player). || Fabricante (*m.*) de laúdes (maker).
lux [lʌks] n. PHYS. Lux, *m.*

— OBSERV. El plural de la palabra inglesa *lux* es *lux* o *luxes*.

luxate ['lʌkseit] v. tr. Dislocar, producir una luxación en.
luxation [lʌk'seiʃən] n. MED. Luxación, *f.*
luxe [luks] n. Lujo, *m.* || *De luxe*, de lujo.
Luxembourg or **Luxemburg** ['lʌksəmbə:g] pr. n. GEOGR. Luxemburgo, *m.*
Luxembourger or **Luxemburger** [—ə*] n. Luxemburgués, esa.
Luxembourgian or **Luxemburgian** [—iən] adj. Luxemburgués, esa.
luxuriance [lʌg'zjuəriəns] n. Exuberancia, *f.*
luxuriant [lʌg'zjuəriənt] adj. Exuberante.
luxuriate [lʌg'zjuərieit] v. intr. Disfrutar [*in*, de, con], deleitarse [*in*, con] (to revel in, to enjoy). || Crecer exuberantemente *or* con profusión (vegetation).
luxurious [lʌg'zjuəriəs] adj. Lujoso, sa (sumptuous): *a luxurious flat*, un piso lujoso. || Fastuoso, sa: *a luxurious life*, una vida fastuosa. || Voluptuoso, sa: *a luxurious sense of well-being*, un sentido voluptuoso del bienestar. || Sensual.
luxuriousness [—nis] n. Lujo, *m.*
luxury ['lʌkʃəri] n. Lujo, *m.*: *a life of luxury*, una vida de lujo; *the luxury of having two cars*, el lujo de tener dos coches. || Placer, *m.*, gusto, *m.*: *what a luxury to be able to rest at last!*, ¡qué gusto poder descansar por fin! || — *Luxury car, flat*, coche, piso de lujo. || *Luxury tax, article*, impuesto, artículo de lujo. || *Luxury trade*, comercio (*m.*) de artículos de lujo. || *To live in luxury*, vivir espléndidamente.
lycanthrope ['laikənθrəup] n. MED. Licántropo, *m.*
lyceum [lai'siəm] pr. n. Liceo, *m.* (at Athens). || Auditorio, *m.*, sala (*f.*) de conferencias (lecture hall). || Ateneo, *m.* (organization providing lectures, etc.).
lych-gate ['litʃgeit] n. ARCH. Entrada (*f.*) de cementerio.
lye [lai] n. CHEM. Lejía, *f.*
lying [—iŋ] adj. Mentiroso, sa (telling untruths). || Falso, sa (not true). || Tendido, da; echado, da (laid down). || Situado, da (situated).
— N. Mentira, *f.* (the telling of lies). || Mentiras, *f. pl.* (lies). || Lecho, *m.*, cama, *f.* (bed). || Descanso, *m.*, reposo, *m.* (rest).
lying-in [—iŋ'in] n. MED. Parto, *m.* || *Lying-in hospital*, maternidad, *f.*
lymph [limf] n. ANAT. Linfa, *f.* || *Lymph gland o node*, ganglio linfático.
lymphangitis [limfæn'dʒaitis] n. MED. Linfangitis, *f.*
lymphatic [lim'fætik] adj. Linfático, ca.
— N. Vaso (*m.*) linfático.
lymphatism [lim'fætizəm] n. MED. Linfatismo, *m.*
lymphocyte ['limfəsait] n. ANAT. Linfocito, *m.*
lymphocytosis [,limfəsai'təsis] n. Linfocitosis, *f.*
lymphoid ['limfɔid] adj. Linfoide.
lyncean [lin'siən] adj. De lince (eye). || Con ojos de lince (person).
lynch [lintʃ] v. tr. Linchar.
lynching [—iŋ] n. Linchamiento, *m.*
lynx [liŋks] n. ZOOL. Lince, *m.*

— OBSERV. El plural de esta palabra es *lynxes* o *lynx*.

lynx-eyed [—aid] adj. Con ojos de lince.
lyophilize [lai'ɔfəlaiz] v. tr. Liofilizar.
Lyra ['laiərə] pr. n. ASTR. Lira, *f.*
lyre ['laiə*] n. MUS. Lira, *f.*
lyrebird [—bə:d] n. Ave (*f.*) lira, menura, *m.* (bird).
lyric ['lirik] adj. Lírico, ca.
— N. Poema (*m.*) lírico (lyric poem). || — Pl. Poesía (*f. sing.*) lírica, lírica, *f. sing.* (genre). || Letra, *f. sing.* (words of a song).
lyrical [—əl] adj. Lírico, ca. || FIG. *To get lyrical about sth.*, entusiasmarse por algo.
lyrically [—əli] adv. Líricamente. || FIG. Entusiásticamente, con entusiasmo.
lyricism ['lirisizəm] n. Lirismo, *m.*
lyricist ['lirisist] n. Lírico, *m.* (poet). || Autor (*m.*) de la letra de una canción (song writer).
lyrist ['laiərist] n. Lírico, *m.* (lyric poet). || MUS. Tañedor (*m.*) de lira.
Lysistrata [lai'sistrətə] pr. n. Lisístrata, *f.*

M

m [em] n. M, *f.* (letter).
ma [mɑ:] n. FAM. Mamá, *f.*
ma'am [mæm, mɑ:m] n. Señora, *f.*
— OBSERV. Esta palabra es una forma abreviada de *madam* que se utiliza para dirigirse ya a la reina o a una princesa, ya a una mujer en señal de cortesía.
mac [mæk] n. FAM. Impermeable, *m.* (mackintosh).
macabre (U. S. **macaber**) [mə'kɑ:br] adj. Macabro, bra: *danse macabre*, danza macabra.
macaco [mə'kɑ:kəu] n. ZOOL. Ayeaye, *m.* (lemur). | Macaco, *m.* (macaque).
macadam [mə'kædəm] n. Macadán, *m.*, macadam, *m.*
macaque [mə'kɑ:k] n. Macaco, *m.* (monkey).
macaroni [,mækə'rəuni] n. Macarrones *m. pl.* (pasta). || FIG. Petimetre, *m.* (dandy). || FAM. Italiano, na.
macaronic [,mækə'rɔnik] adj. Macarrónico, ca.
— Pl. n. Versos (*m.*) macarrónicos.
macaroon [,mækə'ru:n] n. Macarrón, *m.*, mostachón, *m.* (cake).
macaw [mə'kɔ:] n. Ara, *m.* (parrot).
Maccabee ['mækəbi:] pr. n. Macabeo, *m.*
mace [meis] n. Maza, *f.* (club, ornamental staff of office). || Macero, *m.* (mace-bearer).
mace-bearer [—,bɛərə*] n. Macero, *m.*
macedoine [mæsei'dwɑ:n] n. Macedonia, *f.* (dish).
Macedonia [,mæsi'dəunjə] pr. n. GEOGR. Macedonia, *f.*
Macedonian [—n] adj./n. Macedónico, ca; macedonio, nia.
macer ['meisə*] n. Macero, *m.* (mace-bearer).
macerate ['mæsəreit] v. tr. Macerar.
— V. intr. Macerar, macerarse.
maceration [,mæsə'reiʃən] n. Maceración, *f.*, maceramiento, *m.*
macerator ['mæsəreitə*] n. Macerador, *m.*
Macfarlane [mək'fɑ:lən] n. Macfarlán, *m.*, macferlán, *m.* (overcoat).
Mach [mæk] n. PHYS. Mach, *m.* (number).
machete [mə'tʃeiti] n. Machete, *m.*
Machiavelli [,mækiə'veli] pr. n. Maquiavelo, *m.*
Machiavellian [,mækiə'veliən] adj. Maquiavélico, ca.
Machiavellianism [,mækiə'veliənizəm] or **Machiavellism** [,mækiə'velizəm] n. Maquiavelismo, *m.*
machicolated [mæ'tʃikəuleitid] adj. ARCH. Con matacanes.
machicolation [mæ,tʃikəu'leiʃən] n. ARCH. Matacán, *m.* (of a castle).
machinate ['mækineit] v. tr. Maquinar, complotar.
machination [,mæki'neiʃən] n. Maquinación, *f.*, intriga, *f.*
machinator ['mækineitə*] n. Maquinador, ra; intrigante, *m.* & *f.*
machine [mə'ʃi:n] n. Máquina, *f.*: *sewing, washing, adding machine*, máquina de coser, de lavar, de sumar. || FIG. Máquina, *f.* (person). | Máquina, *f.*, maquinaria, *f.* (machinery): *the political machine*, la maquinaria política. | Bicicleta, *f.*, máquina, *f.* (bicycle). | Moto, *f.* (motorcycle). | Coche, *m.*, máquina, *f.* (car). | Avión, *m.*, aparato, *m.* (aeroplane). || THEATR. Tramoya, *f.* || U. S. Bomba (*f.*) de incendios (fire pump). || — *Accounting machine*, máquina contabilizadora, máquina contable. || *Calculating machine*, máquina de calcular. || *Copying machine*, copiadora, *f.* || *Fruit o slot machine*, máquina tragaperras. || *Infernal machine*, máquina infernal. || *Reaping machine*, segadora, *f.*
— Adj. A máquina: *machine wound*, enrollado a máquina. || Mecánico, ca: *machine winding*, enrollamiento mecánico.
machine [mə'ʃi:n] v. tr. TECH. Mecanizar, trabajar con máquina herramienta. || Coser a máquina (to sew).
machine gun [—gʌn] n. MIL. Ametralladora, *f.*
machine-gun [—gʌn] v. tr. Ametrallar.
machine gunner [—,gʌnə*] n. MIL. Ametrallador, *m.*
machine-made [—meid] adj. Hecho a máquina.
machinery [mə'ʃi:nəri] n. Maquinaria, *f.* (machines): *agricultural machinery*, maquinaria agrícola. || Mecanismo, *m.* (mechanism). || FIG. Mecanismo, *m.*, maquinaria, *f.*: *administrative machinery*, el mecanismo administrativo. || THEATR. Tramoya, *f.*
machine shop [mə'ʃi:nʃɔp] n. Taller (*m.*) de construcción y de reparación de máquinas.
machine tool [mə'ʃi:ntu:l] n. Máquina (*f.*) herramienta.
machining [mə'ʃi:niŋ] n. TECH. Mecanizado, *m.* || Costura (*f.*) a máquina (swing).
machinist [mə'ʃi:nist] n. Mecánico, *m.* (who repairs). || Maquinista, *m.* (who operates). || Maquinista, *f.* (sewing machine operator). || THEATR. Tramoyista, *m.*, maquinista, *m.*
mack [mæk] n. FAM. Impermeable, *m.* (raincoat).
mackerel ['mækrəl] n. Caballa, *f.* (fish).
— Adj. Aborregado, da (sky).
mackintosh ['mækintɔʃ] n. Impermeable, *m.* (raincoat). || Gabardina, *f.* (cloth).
mackle or **macle** ['mækl] n. PRINT. Mácula, *f.*, maculatura, *f.*
mackle or **macle** ['mækl] v. tr. PRINT. Macular.
macle ['mækl] n. MIN. Macla, *f.* (twinned crystal).
macramé (U. S. **macrame**) [mə'krɑ:mi] n. Agremán, *m.* (lace, trimming).
macrobiotic [,mækrəbai'ɔtik] adj. Macrobiótico, ca.
macrobiotics [—s] n. Macrobiótica, *f.*
macrocephalic [,mækrəuse'fælik] or **macrocephalous** [,mækrəu'sefələs] adj. MED. Macrocéfalo, la.
macrocephaly [,mækrəu'sefəli] n. Macrocefalia, *f.*
macrocosm ['mækrəukɔzəm] n. Macrocosmo, *m.*
macrocyte ['mækrəu,sait] n. BIOL. Macrocito, *m.*
macrodactyl [mækrəu'dæktil] adj. Macrodáctilo, la.
macrogamete [,mækrəu'gæmi:t] n. BIOL. Macrogameto, *m.*
macromolecular [,mækrəuməu'lekjulə*] adj. Macromolecular.
macromolecule [,mækrəu'mɔlikju:l] n. Macromolécula, *f.*
macrophage [,mækrə'feidʒ] n. Macrófago, *m.*
macrophagic [,mækrə'fædʒik] adj. Macrófago, ga.
macrophotography [,mækrəufə'tɔgrəfi] n. Macrofotografía, *f.*
macropodid [mæ'krɔpədid] adj. Macrópodo, da.
— N. Macrópodo, *m.*
macroscopic [,mækrəu'skɔpik] adj. Macroscópico, ca.
macrosporange [,mækrəu'spɔrændʒ] n. BOT. Macrosporangio, *m.*
macrospore ['mækrəu,spɔ:] n. BOT. Macrospora, *f.*
macrural [mə'kru:rəl] adj. Macruro, ra.
macruran [mə'kruərən] adj. Macruro, ra.
— N. Macruro, *m.*
macula ['mækjulə] or **macule** ['mækju:l] n. MED. Mácula, *f.* || Mancha, *f.*, mácula, *f.* (on the sun, moon). || ANAT. *Macula lutea*, mácula, *f.* (of the eye).
— OBSERV. El plural de la palabra inglesa es *maculae*.
maculate ['mækjuleit] v. tr. Macular. || Manchar (to stain). || FIG. Manchar, mancillar (honour, etc.).
maculation [,mækju'leiʃən] n. Mácula, *f.* (spot, stain). || FIG. Mancha, *f.*, mancilla, *f.*
mad [mæd] adj. Loco, ca (insane): *he is mad*, está loco. || Loco, ca; insensato, ta (foolish): *a mad idea*, una idea insensata. || FIG. Furioso, sa: *he was mad at o with her*, estaba furioso con *or* contra ella. || Loco, ca (compass). || Rabioso, sa (dog). || — FAM. *As mad as a hatter o as a March hare o as they come*, loco de atar *or* de remate *or* rematado, más loco que una cabra. || FIG. *Like mad*, como un loco: *to run like mad*, correr como un loco; muchísimo (a lot). | *Mad with fear*,

muerto de miedo. || *Raving mad* o *stark mad*, loco furioso, loco perdido. || *That was a mad thing to do*, fue una locura. || FIG. *To be mad keen on doing sth.*, estar loco por hacer algo. | *To be mad on* o *about*, estar loco por. | *To be mad with joy*, estar loco de alegría. | *To drive s.o. mad*, volverle loco a uno. | *To get mad*, ponerse furioso, enfadarse. || *To go mad*, enloquecer, volverse loco. || FIG. *To make mad*, enfurecer, poner furioso.

Madagascan [ˌmædəˈgæskən] adj./n. Malgache.

Madagascar [ˌmædəˈgæskə*] pr. n. Madagascar.

madam [ˈmædəm] n. Señora, *f.* (polite title). || Patrona, *f.* (of a brothel). || FIG. *To be a bit of a madam*, tener muchos humos.

— OBSERV. El plural de *madam* es *mesdames* cuando se emplea como tratamiento de cortesía y *madams* si significa « patrona ». Esta palabra no va nunca seguida por el apellido.

Madame [ˈmædəm] n. Señora, *f.*

— OBSERV. El plural de este palabra es *Mesdames*.

madcap [ˈmædkæp] adj. Atolondrado, da; sin seso.
— N. Cabeza (*f.*) de chorlito, locuelo, la.

madden [ˈmædn] v. tr. Enloquecer, volver loco (to make insane). || FIG. Volver loco. || *It is maddening*, es para volverse loco.
— V. intr. Enloquecer, volverse loco. || FIG. Volverse loco.

maddening [—iŋ] adj. Enloquecedor, ra. || Exasperante (infuriating). || *It is maddening*, es para volverse loco.

madder [ˈmædə*] n. Rubia, *f.* (plant).

madding [ˈmædiŋ] adj. Enloquecido, da (frenzied). || *To live far from the madding crowd*, vivir lejos del mundanal ruido.

made [meid] p. p. & pret. See MAKE.

madeira [məˈdiərə] n. Madera, *m.* (wine).

Madeira [məˈdiərə] pr. n. GEOGR. Madera, *f.* (island).

made-to-order [ˈmeidtu:ˈɔːdə*] adj. Hecho a la medida.

made-up [ˈmeidʌp] adj. Inventado, da; ficticio, cia (fictitious): *a made-up story*, una historia inventada. || Compuesto, ta (put together): *a made-up page*, una página compuesta. || Maquillado, da (face). || Pintado, da (lips).

madhouse [ˈmædhaus] n. Manicomio, *m.* (mental hospital). || FIG. Casa (*f.*) de locos.

madly [ˈmædli] adv. Locamente. || Como un loco: *to shout madly*, gritar como un loco. || FIG. Terriblemente (extremely): *madly jealous*, terriblemente envidioso. || *To be madly in love with*, estar locamente enamorado de.

madman [ˈmædmən] n. Loco, *m.*

— OBSERV. El plural de *madman* es *madmen*.

madness [ˈmædnis] n. Locura, *f.* (insanity). || Furia, *f.*, rabia, *f.* (rage). || Rabia, *f.* (of dogs).

Madonna [məˈdɔnə] n. REL. Madona, *f.*

madras [məˈdrɑːs] n. Madrás, *m.* (fabric).

madreporaria [ˌmædripɔːˈrɛəriə] pl. n. ZOOL. Madreporarios, *m.*

madrepore [ˌmædripɔː*] n. ZOOL. Madrépora, *f.*

madreporite [mædri pɔːrait] n. Madreporita, *f.*

Madrid [məˈdrid] pr. n. GEOGR. Madrid.

madrigal [ˈmædrigəl] n. Madrigal, *m.*

madrigalian [mædriˈgeiliən] adj. Madrigalesco, ca.

Madrilenian [mædriˈliːniən] adj./n. Madrileño, ña.

madrona [məˈdrəunə] n. BOT. Madroño, *m.*

madwoman [ˈmædwumən] n. Loca, *f.*

— OBSERV. El plural es *madwomen*.

Maecenas [miˈsiːnæs] n. Mecenas, *m.*

maecenatism [miˈsiːnætizəm] n. Mecenazgo, *m.*

maelstrom [ˈmeilstrəum] n. Maelstrom, *m.* (whirlpool). || FIG. Torbellino, *m.*, remolino, *m.*

maenad [ˈmiːnæd] n. MYTH. Ménade, *f.* (bacchante).

— OBSERV. El plural de *maenad* es *maenads* o *maenades*.

maestoso [ˌmɑːesˈtəuzəu] adv. MUS. Maestoso.

maestro [mɑːˈestrəu] n. MUS. Maestro, *m.*

— OBSERV. El plural de la palabra inglesa *maestro* es *maestros* o *maestri*.

Mae West [ˈmeiˈwest] n. Chaleco (*m.*) salvavidas.

maffia or **mafia** [ˈmɑːfjə] n. Mafia, *f.*, maffia, *f.*

mafioso [ˌmɑfiˈəuzəu] n. Mafioso, *m.*

— OBSERV. El plural de *mafioso* es *mafiosi*.

mag [mæg] n. FAM. Revista, *f.* (magazine).

magazine [ˌmægəˈziːn] n. Revista, *f.* (publication). || Almacén, *m.* (warehouse). || Polvorín, *m.* (for explosives). || Pañol (*m.*) de municiones (of a warship). || Recámara, *f.* (of a rifle). || Carga, *f.* (of a camera). || *Magazine gun*, fusil (*m.*) de repetición.

magazinist [—ist] n. Colaborador (*m.*) de una revista.

Magdalen or **Magdalene** [ˈmægdəlin] pr. n. Magdalena, *f.*

Magdalenian [ˌmægdəˈliːnjən] adj. Magdaleniense.
— N. Magdalieniense, *m.*

Magellan [məˈgelən] pr. n. Magallanes. || *Strait of Magellan*, estrecho (*m.*) de Magallanes.

magenta [məˈdʒentə] adj. Magenta.

maggot [ˈmægət] n. Gusano, *m.*, cresa, *f.* (larva). || FIG. Capricho, *m.*, antojo, *m.* (whim).

maggoty [—i] adj. Agusanado, da. || FIG. Caprichoso, sa; antojadizo, za.

Magi [ˈmeidʒai] pl. n. *The three Magi*, los tres Reyes Magos.

Magian [ˈmeigiən] adj. Mago, ga.

magic [ˈmædʒik] adj. Mágico, ca: *magic power*, poder mágico; *magic lantern*, linterna mágica. || *Magic wand*, varita (*f.*) de las virtudes, varita mágica.
— N. Magia, *f.*: *white, black magic*, magia blanca, negra. || FIG. Magia, *f.* (charm). || *By magic* o *as if by magic*, por arte de magia, como por encanto.

magical [—əl] adj. Mágico, ca.

magically [—əli] adv. Por arte de magia.

magician [məˈdʒiʃən] n. Mago, *m.* (wizard). || Hechicero, *m.* (of a tribe). || Ilusionista, *m.* & *f.* (in a theatre).

magisterial [ˌmædʒisˈtiəriəl] adj. Magistral (of a master). || Autoritario, ria (authoritative). || Magistral (with masterly skill). || De magistrado (of a magistrate). || *With a magisterial tone*, en tono magistral.

magistracy [ˈmædʒistrəsi] n. Magistratura, *f.*

magistral [məˈdʒistrəl] adj. Magistral.

magistrate [ˈmædʒistreit] n. Magistrado, *m.* (judicial officer). || Juez (*m.*) municipal (judge). || *Examining magistrate*, juez de instrucción.

magistrature [ˈmædʒistrəˌtjuə*] n. Magistratura, *f.*

magma [ˈmægmə] n. Magma, *m.*

— OBSERV. El plural de la palabra inglesa *magma* es *magmata* o *magmas*.

Magna Carta or **Magna Charta** [ˈmægnəˈkɑːtə] pr. n. Carta (*f.*) Magna.

— OBSERV. *La Carta Magna*, que garantizaba las libertades civiles y políticas del pueblo inglés, fue concedida por el rey Juan Sin Tierra el 15 de junio de 1215.

Magna Graecia [ˈmægnəˈgriːʃiːə] pr. n. Magna Grecia, *f.*

magnanimity [ˌmægnəˈnimiti] n. Magnanimidad, *f.*

magnanimous [mægˈnæniməs] adj. Magnánimo, ma.

magnate [ˈmægneit] n. Magnate, *m.*

magnesia [mægˈniːʃə] n. CHEM. Magnesia, *f.*

magnesian [—n] adj. CHEM. Magnesiano, na.

magnesic [mægˈniːsik] adj. CHEM. Magnésico, ca.

magnesiferous [mægniːˈsifərəs] adj. Magnesífero, ra.

magnesite [ˈmægnisait] n. MIN. Magnesita, *f.*

magnesium [mægˈniːzjəm] n. CHEM. Magnesio, *m.*

magnet [ˈmægnit] n. Imán, *m.*

magnetic [mægˈnetik] adj. Magnético, ca: *magnetic equator, field, pole*, ecuador, campo, polo magnético; *magnetic induction, mine, needle, storm*, inducción, mina, aguja, tempestad magnética. || Magnetofónico, ca; magnético, ca: *magnetic tape*, cinta magnetofónica; *magnetic recording*, grabación magnética. || FIG. Atractivo, va (person, look).

magnetic compass [—ˈkʌmpəs] n. Brújula, *f.*

magnetic recorder [—riˈkɔːdə*] n. Magnetófono, *m.* [*Amer.*, grabadora, *f.*]

magnetics [—s] n. Magnetismo, *m.* (science).

magnetism [ˈmægnitizəm] n. Magnetismo, *m.* || FIG. Magnetismo, *m.*, atractivo, *m.* (charm).

magnetite [ˈmægnətait] n. MIN. Magnetita, *f.*

magnetizable [ˈmægnitaizəbl] adj. Magnetizable.

magnetization [ˌmægnitaiˈzeiʃən] n. Magnetización, *f.*, imantación, *f.*, imanación, *f.*

magnetize [ˌmægnitaiz] v. tr. Magnetizar. || Imantar, imanar, magnetizar: *to magnetize a needle*, imantar una aguja. || FIG. Magnetizar, atraer.

magneto [mægˈniːtəu] n. Magneto, *f.*

magnetoelectric [ˌmægniːtəuiˈlektrik] adj. Magnetoeléctrico, ca.

magnetometer [ˌmægnəˈtɔmitə*] n. PHYS. Magnetómetro, *m.*

magnetophone [mægˈnitəˌfəun] n. Magnetófono, *m.* [*Amer.*, grabadora, *f.*]

magnetoscope [mægˈnitəˌskəup] n. PHYS. Magnetoscopio, *m.*

magnetron [ˈmægnitrɔn] n. TECH. Magnetrón, *m.*

magnific [mægˈnifik] or **magnifical** [—əl] adj. Magnífico, ca.

Magnificat [mægˈnifikæt] n. REL Magníficat, *m.*

magnification [ˌmægnifiˈkeiʃən] n. PHYS. Aumento, *m.*, ampliación, *f.* || FIG. Enaltecimiento, *m.*, glorificación, *f.* (glorification). | Exageración, *f.*, (exaggeration).

magnificence [mægˈnifisns] n. Magnificencia, *f.*

magnificent [mægˈnifisnt] adj. Magnífico, ca.

magnifier [ˈmægnifaiə*] n. PHYS. Lupa, *f.*, lente (*f.*) de aumento (magnifying glass). || FIG. Exagerado, da.

magnify [ˈmægnifai] v. tr. Aumentar (to increase). || FIG. Exagerar: *he is inclined to magnify the difficulties*, tiene tendencia a exagerar las dificultades. | Enaltecer, exaltar, glorificar (to glorify). | Magnificar (God). || PHYS. Aumentar, ampliar (an image). | Amplificar (a sound).

magnifying [—iŋ] adj. PHYS. De aumento. || — *Magnifying glass*, lente (*f.*) de aumento, lupa, *f.* || *Magnifying power*, aumento, *m.* (magnification).

magniloquence [mægˈniləukwəns] n. Grandilocuencia, *f.*

magniloquent [mægˈniləukwənt] adj. Grandilocuente (ostentatious).

magnitude [ˈmægnitjuːd] n. Magnitud, *f.* || FIG. Magnitud, *f.*, envergadura, *f.*: *a project of great magnitude*, un proyecto de gran magnitud *or* de mucha envergadura. || Volumen, *m.* (of sound). || ASTR. MATH. Magnitud, *f.*

magnolia [mæg'nəuljə] n. BOT. Magnolio, *m.*, magnolia, *f.* (tree). | Magnolia, *f.* (flower).
magnoliaceae [mægnəul'jəsii] pl. n. BOT. Magnoliáceas, *f.*
magnum ['mægnəm] n. Botella (*f.*) de dos litros.
magnum opus [—'əupəs] n. Obra (*f.*) maestra (masterpiece).
magpie ['mægpai] n. Urraca, *f.* (bird). || FIG. Cotorra, *f.* (chatterbox).
maguey ['mægwei] n. BOT. Maguey, *m.*, pita, *f.*
magus ['meigəs] n. Mago, *m.* (Zoroastrian priest). || REL. Rey (*m.*) Mago. || *Simon Magus,* Simón Mago.
— OBSERV. El plural de la palabra inglesa es *magi.*
Magyar ['mægjɑ:*] adj./n. Magiar (Hungarian).
maharaja or **maharajah** [,mɑ:hə'rɑ:dʒə] n. Maharajá, *m.* (Hindu prince).
maharanee or **maharani** [,mɑ:hə'rɑ:ni:] n. Maharani, *f.* (wife of a maharaja).
mahatma [mə'hɑ:tmə] n. Mahatma, *m.*
Mahdi ['mɑ:di] n. Profeta, *m.* (Moslem prophet).
mahlstick ['mɔ:lstik] n. ARTS. Tiento, *m.* (maulstick).
mahogany [mə'hɔgəni] n. Caoba, *f.* (tree, wood).
— Adj. De caoba: *mahogany table,* mesa de caoba. || Caoba (colour).
Mahomet [mə'hɔmit] pr. n. Mahoma, *m.*
Mahometan [mə'hɔmitən] adj./n. Mahometano, na.
mahout [mə'haut] n. Cornaca, *m.* (elephant driver).
maid [meid] n. Criada, *f.* [*Amer.*, mucama, *f.*] (servant). || Camarera, *f.* (in a hotel). || Doncella, *f.* (virgin, young girl). || — *Lady's maid,* doncella, *f.* || *Maid of all work,* criada para todo. || *Maid of honour,* dama (*f.*) de honor. || *Old maid,* solterona, *f.* || HIST. *The maid of Orléans,* la Doncella de Orleáns (Joan of Arc).
maiden ['meidn] n. Doncella, *f.* (girl, virgin). || Guillotina, *f.*
— Adj. Virgen, virginal (virgin). || Soltera (unmarried). || De soltera: *maiden name,* apellido de soltera. || Primero, ra: *maiden trip,* primer viaje. || Inaugural: *maiden speech,* discurso inaugural. || SP. Que no ha ganado ninguna carrera (horse).
maidenhair [—hεə*] n. BOT. Culantrillo, *m.*
maidenhead [—hed] n. Virginidad, *f.* (quality). || ANAT. Himen, *m.*
maidenhood [—hud] n. Soltería, *f.* || Virginidad, *f.*
maidenly [—li] adj. Virginal. || Recatado, da; modesto, ta (modest).
— Adv. Recatadamente, modestamente.
maid-in-waiting ['meidin'weitiŋ] n. Dama (*f.*) de compañía.
— OBSERV. El plural es *maids-in-waiting.*
maidservant ['meid,sə:vənt] n. Criada, *f.*, sirvienta, *f.* [*Amer.*, mucama, *f.*].
maieutics [mei'ju:tiks] n. Mayéutica, *f.*
mail [meil] n. Correo, *m.*: *air mail,* correo aéreo; *the morning mail,* el correo de la mañana; *by return mail,* a vuelta de correo. || Correspondencia, *f.*: *to do one's mail,* escribir la correspondencia. || Cartas, *f. pl.*: *I got a lot of mail this morning,* he recibido un montón de cartas esta mañana. || Correo, *m.* (train, boat). || Cota (*f.*) de mallas (armour). || Caparazón, *m.* (of turtles, lobsters, etc.). || *Royal Mail,* Correos, Servicio (*m.*) de Correos.
— Adj. Postal: *mail plane,* avión postal. || De correo.
mail [meil] v. tr. Mandar por correo (to send). || Echar al correo (in a letter box).
mailbag [—bæg] n. Saca (*f.*) de correspondencia.
mailboat [—bəut] n. Buque (*m.*) correo.
mailbox or **mail box** [—bɔks] n. Buzón, *m.*
mail car [—kɑ:*] n. Coche (*m.*) de correos, furgón (*m.*) *or* vagón (*m.*) postal.
mail coach [—'kəutʃ] n. Diligencia, *f.* || Coche (*m.*) de correos, furgón (*m.*) *or* vagón (*m.*) postal (mail car).
mailing list [—iŋlist] n. Lista (*f.*) de personas a quienes se mandan propaganda o documentos.
mailman [—mən] n. U. S. Cartero, *m.* (postman).
— OBSERV. El plural de *mailman* es *mailmen.*
mail order [—,ɔ:də*] n. Pedido (*m.*) hecho por correo.
mail train [—trein] n. Tren (*m.*) correo.
mail van [—væn] n. Furgoneta (*f.*) postal (lorry). || Furgón (*m.*) *or* vagón (*m.*) postal (in railways).
maim [meim] v. tr. Mutilar, tullir, lisiar (a limb). || FIG. Mutilar (a text).
main [mein] adj. Principal: *the main problems,* los problemas principales. || Mayor: *main street,* calle mayor. || General, de primer orden: *main road* o *highway,* carretera general. || Principal (floor). || MAR. Mayor (mast, sail). | Principal: *main deck,* cubierta principal. | Maestro, tra: *main frame,* cuaderna maestra. || AVIAT. De sustentación (wing). || Principal (railway line). || GRAMM. Principal (clause). || Fuerte: *main course* o *main dish,* plato fuerte. || — *By main force,* a viva fuerza. || *Main body,* grueso, *m.* (of an army). || *Main office,* oficina (*f.*) central. || *Main sewer,* colector, *m.* || *Main shaft,* árbol (*m.*) de transmisión (of a car). || *The main thing,* lo principal, lo esencial. || *To look to the main chance,* velar por su propio interés.
— N. Parte (*f.*) principal *or* fundamental. || Cañería (*f.*) principal (principal pipe system). || Colector, *m.* (sewer). || ELECTR. Cable (*m.*) principal (main cable). || Línea (*f.*) principal (railways). || Pelea (*f.*) de gallos (cockfight). || POET. Alta mar, *f.* (high sea). | Palo (*m.*) mayor (mainmast). | Vela (*f.*) mayor (sail). || — *In the main,* por lo general, en general. || ELECTR. *The mains,* la red eléctrica. | *To plug sth. into the mains,* enchufar algo. | *To run off the mains,* funcionar con electricidad. || *With might and main,* con todas sus fuerzas.
Main [main] pr. n. GEOGR. Meno, *m.*
mainland ['meinlənd] n. Continente, *m.*, tierra (*f.*) firme.
mainly ['meinli] adv. Principalmente, sobre todo, especialmente.
mainmast ['meinmɑ:st] n. MAR. Palo (*m.*) mayor.
mainsail ['meinseil] n. MAR. Vela (*f.*) mayor.
mainsheet ['mainʃi:t] n. MAR. Escota (*f.*) mayor.
mainspring ['mainspriŋ] n. Muelle (*m.*) real (of a clock). || FIG. Causa (*f.*) principal, móvil (*m.*) esencial.
mainstay ['meinstei] n. MAR. Estay (*m.*) mayor. || FIG. Fundamento, *m.*, sostén, *m.*, punto (*m.*) de apoyo, pilar: *the mainstays of religion,* los fundamentos de la religión.
mainstream ['mainstri:m] n. Corriente (*f.*) principal.
maintain [mein'tein] v. tr. Mantener, conservar, cuidar (sth. unimpaired). || Mantener (speed). || Alimentar, mantener (fire). || Mantener, sustentar (a family, etc.). || Mantener, sostener (relations, correspondance, conversation). || Mantener (friendship). || Guardar (advantage, silence). || Conservar, mantenerse en (one's post). || Mantener, sostener (an opinion, one's reputation): *he maintains that he is innocent,* sostiene que es inocente. || JUR. Defender (a cause, one's rights). | Mantener (order). || MIL. Sostener (a siege). || FIG. *To maintain one's ground,* mantenerse en sus trece.
maintenance ['meintənəns] n. Conservación, *f.*, mantenimiento, *m.*, entretenimiento, *m.*, cuidado, *m.* (of sth. unimpaired): *maintenance costs,* gastos de mantenimiento. || Mantenimiento, *m.* (of order, peace, family, etc.). || Defensa, *f.*, mantenimiento, *m.* (of one's rights). || — *In maintenance of,* en apoyo de. || *Maintenance allowance,* pensión alimenticia.
maintop ['meintɔp] n. MAR. Cofa (*f.*) mayor.
main-topgallant mast [—'gæləntmɑ:st] n. MAR. Mastelerillo (*m.*) de juanete mayor.
main-topgallant sail [—'gæləntseil] n. MAR. Juanete (*m.*) mayor.
main-topmast [—mɑ:st] n. MAR. Mastelero (*m.*) de gavia *or* mayor.
main-topsail [—seil] n. MAR. Gavia, *f.*
main yard ['meinjɑ:d] n. MAR. Verga (*f.*) mayor.
Mainz [maintz] pr. n. GEOGR. Maguncia.
maisonette [,meizə'net] n. Dúplex, *m.* (two-storey flat). || Casita, *f.* (small house).
maitre d'hôtel ['metrədəu'tel] n. Jefe (*m.*) de comedor (headwaiter). || Mayordomo, *m.* (of a large household).
maize [meiz] n. BOT. Maíz, *m.*: *toasted maize,* maíz tostado. || *Maize field,* maizal, *m.*
majestic [mə'dʒestik]or **majestical** [—əl] adj. Majestuoso, sa.
majesty ['mædʒisti] n. Majestad, *f.* || — *God, the Divine Majesty,* Su Divina Majestad. || *Her Majesty the Queen,* Su Graciosa Majestad. || *His Catholic Majesty,* Su Majestad Católica (King of France). || *His Christian Majesty,* Su Majestad Cristianísima (King of Spain). || *His* o *Her* o *Your Majesty,* Su Majestad.
majolica [mə'jɔlikə] n. Mayólica, *f.*
major ['meidʒə*] adj. Mayor: *the major part,* la mayor parte. || Importante (of great magnitude). || Principal (main). || Grave (illness, wound). || JUR. Mayor de edad. || MUS. PHIL. Mayor. || Prioritario, ria (road). || REL. Mayor (orders). || U. S. De la especialidad, de especialización (academic subject, field). || — MIL. *Major general,* general (*m.*) de división. || *Major party,* partido mayoritario. || *Major suit,* palo (*m.*) mayor (cards).
— N. JUR. Persona (*f.*) mayor de edad, mayor (*m.* & *f.*) de edad. || PHIL. Mayor, *f.* (premise). || MIL. Comandante, *m.* || U. S. Especialidad, *f.* (of studies).
major ['meidʒə*] v. intr. U. S. Especializarse (in education): *to major in Spanish,* especializarse en español.
Majorca [mə'dʒɔ:kə] pr. n. GEOGR. Mallorca.
Majorcan [—n] adj./n. Mallorquín, ina.
majordomo ['meidʒə'dəuməu] n. Mayordomo, *m.*
majority [mə'dʒɔriti] n. Mayoría, *f.*: *the majority were happy,* la mayoría estaba contenta; *a majority of three,* tres votos de mayoría; *overwhelming majority,* mayoría abrumadora. || Mayoría, *f.*, mayor parte, *f.*: *the majority of the participants,* la mayor parte de los participantes. || JUR. Mayoría, *f.*, mayoría (*f.*) de edad (full legal age). || MIL. Grado (*m.*) de comandante. || *The silent majority,* la mayoría silenciosa.
make [meik] n. Marca, *f.* (provenance of manufacture): *he knows all the makes of French cars,* conoce todas las marcas de los coches franceses. || Hechura, *f.*: *she does not like the make of the coat,* no le gusta la hechura del abrigo. || Forma, *f.* (of an object). || Fabricación, *f.* (manufacture): *of Spanish make,* de fabricación española. || Estatura, *f.* (of a person). || CULIN. Confección, *f.* || ELECTR. Cierre, *m.* || FIG. Calidad, *f.* (quality of personality). || FIG. FAM. *To be on*

the make, intentar prosperar por todos los medios (businessman), buscar aventuras galantes, intentar conquistar a una mujer (man).

make* [meik] v. tr. Hacer: *to make impossible*, hacer imposible; *to make a noise*, hacer ruido; *to make a journey*, hacer un viaje; *to make a machine work*, hacer funcionar una máquina; *to make the bed*, hacer la cama; *bread is made of wheat*, el pan está hecho con trigo; *to make an effort*, hacer un esfuerzo. || Hacer, fabricar: *to make barrels*, hacer barriles; *to make a machine*, fabricar una máquina. || Hacer (remark, statement, proposal, offer). || Hacer (to total): *that makes 50*, esto hace 50. || Hacer, preparar: *to make a meal, tea*, hacer una comida, té. || Hacer, elaborar: *to make plans*, hacer planes. || Hacer, confeccionar (clothes). || Hacer, crear (to create): *God made man*, Dios hizo al hombre. || Hacer, nombrar: *they made him their president*, le hicieron presidente; *to make s.o. one's heir*, hacerle a alguien heredero. || Hacer: *to make s.o. a knight, an earl*, hacer a alguien caballero, conde. || Hacer, componer: *to make an opera*, hacer una ópera. || Hacer, obligar (to compel): *she was made to stop*, le hicieron detenerse. || Tomar (decision). || Cometer, hacer (error): *he made a mistake*, cometió una falta. || Efectuar (payment). || Dar: *to make an appointment with*, dar cita a. || Pronunciar, hacer (speech). || Celebrar, concertar (agreement). || Presentar (excuse). || Hacer de: *to make one's son a doctor*, hacer de su hijo un médico. || Convertir, transformar (*into*, en). || Ser: *he will make a good doctor*, será un buen médico; *this makes the third time*, es la tercera vez. || Ser, hacer, equivaler, ser equivalente *or* igual a: *two halves make a whole*, dos mitades hacen un entero; *five and five make ten*, cinco y cinco son diez. || Poner, volver: *to make s.o. sad*, ponerle a uno triste. || Hacer, poner: *that will make her happy*, eso la hará feliz. || Sacar (conclusion). || Pensar, deducir (to infer): *what does he make of that?*, ¿qué piensa de eso? || Servir de: *this stone will make a good hammer for me*, esta piedra me servirá perfectamente de martillo. || Servir para hacer: *silk makes elegant clothes*, la seda sirve para hacer trajes elegantes. || Hacer: *to make many friends*, hacer muchos amigos. || Recorrer, hacer (distance): *to make 60 miles in a day*, recorrer sesenta millas en un día. || Visitar (a place during a journey). || Llegar a: *will they make the finals?*, ¿llegarán a la final? || Sacar: *to make a profit*, sacar un beneficio. || Sacar, ganar (to earn): *he makes two thousand pounds a year*, gana dos mil libras por año. || Alcanzar, conseguir: *to make a high score*, alcanzar un tanteo elevado. || Intentar (to try): *he made to run but he couldn't*, intentó correr pero no pudo. || Calcular (to evaluate): *he made the distance about forty miles*, calculó la distancia en cuarenta millas aproximadamente. || Creer, imaginarse (to believe): *he is not so bad as you make him*, no es tan malo como te lo imaginas. || Poner (to say): *let's make it ten pounds, 3 o'clock*, pongamos diez libras, las tres. || Establecer como: *to make a rule that*, establecer como principio que. || Hacer famoso a, dar fama a: *the cotton trade is what made Manchester*, el comercio del algodón es lo que hizo a Manchester famoso. || Causar (to provoke): *to make trouble*, causar problemas. || Hacer de (to represent). || Ganar (a trick in cards). || Barajar (to shuffle cards). || GRAMM. Ser: *"to see" in the past tense makes "saw"*, el pretérito de "to see" es "saw"; *"mouse" makes "mice" in the plural*, el plural de "mouse" es "mice". || MIL. Hacer (peace, war). || Navegar a (knots). || Llegar a, alcanzar (land). || Divisar (to perceive). || Navegar con: *the ship made bad weather*, el barco navegó con mal tiempo. || Hacerse a: *to make sail*, hacerse a la vela. || ELECTR. Cerrar (a circuit). | Establecer (a contact). || SP. Entrar en: *to make the team*, entrar en el equipo. || U. S. FAM. Seducir (a girl). | Birlar (to steal). || — *He is a made man*, tiene un porvenir asegurado. || FAM. *He's as cute as they make 'em*, es de lo más astuto que hay. || *I don't know what to make of it*, no lo acabo de entender. || *Made in Spain*, hecho en España, de fabricación española. || *Make believe*, supongamos que, pongamos que (in games). || *To be made for*, estar hecho para: *you are made for this kind of thing*, estás hecho para esta clase de cosas. || *To be made of*, estar hecho con, ser de: *it is made of silver*, es de plata. || *To make a bid*, see BID. || FAM. *To make a bit on the side*, ganar algún dinero más. || FIG. *To make a break with s.o.*, reñir con alguien. || *To make a change*, cambiar. || JUR. *To make a complaint*, presentar una demanda. || *To make faces*, hacer muecas. || *To make a fool of o.s.*, hacer el ridículo, ridiculizarse. || *To make a fortune*, hacerse rico. || *To make a habit of*, acostumbrar, tener la costumbre de. || *To make a living*, ganarse la vida. || *To make a name*, hacerse un nombre. || PHOT. *To make a print*, hacer una copia. || *To make a record*, establecer un récord. || *To make a start*, empezar. || *To make available to*, poner a la disposición de. || *To make believe*, fingir. || *To make clear*, poner en claro. || *To make default*, faltar. || *To make do with sth.*, arreglárselas con algo. || *To make fast*, asegurar (to fasten). || *To make fire*, encender un fuego (to light a fire). || *To make friends with*, trabar amistad con, hacerse amigo de (to become friends), hacer las paces con, reconciliarse con (to become reconciled). || *To make fun of*, reírse de. || *To make good time*, ganar tiempo: *I can make good time on this road*, puedo ganar tiempo por esta carretera. || *To make haste*, darse prisa, apresurarse. || *To make it*, aguantar (to endure), llegar (to arrive), tener éxito (to succeed), conseguir lo deseado (to obtain). || FAM. *To make it with s.o.*, conseguir acostarse con alguien. || *To make known*, dar a conocer. || *To make life impossible for s.o.*, hacerle la vida imposible a uno. || *To make little of*, hacer caso omiso de, hacer poco caso de (to pay no attention to), sacar poco provecho de (to get little benefit from). || *To make love*, hacer el amor. || *To make much of*, dar mucha importancia a (to attach importance to), sacar mucho provecho de (to benefit by), tratar muy bien a (a person). || *To make one's contract*, cumplir un contrato (in card games). || *To make one's way*, abrirse paso (to open a path), salir bien (to come out all right), progresar, adelantar (to make progress). || *To make or break, to make or mar*, hacer la fortuna o ser la ruina de. || *To make peace*, hacer las paces. || *To make o.s. an authority*, llegar a ser una autoridad. || *To make o.s. a reputation*, cobrar buena fama, adquirir fama, hacerse famoso. || *To make o.s. indispensable*, hacerse indispensable. || *To make o.s. sick*, ponerse enfermo. || *To make o.s. uneasy*, preocuparse. || *To make people respect one*, hacerse respetar. || *To make pleasant reading*, ser agradable de leer. || *To make port*, llegar a buen puerto. || *To make room*, dejar sitio. || *To make sail*, zarpar. || *To make sense*, tener sentido. || *To make s.o. ashamed*, darle vergüenza a uno. || *To make s.o. hungry*, darle hambre a uno. || *To make s.o. laugh*, darle risa a uno, hacerle gracia a uno. || *To make s.o. sleepy*, darle sueño a uno. || *To make s.o. wonder* o *think*, darle que pensar a uno. || *To make sth. ready*, preparar algo. || *To make strong*, fortalecer. || *To make the best of*, sacar el mejor partido de. || *To make the most of it*, sacar el mayor partido *or* el mayor provecho de ello, aprovecharlo al máximo. || *To make the train*, coger el tren, alcanzar el tren. || *To make time*, ganar tiempo. || *To make use of*, hacer uso de, utilizar, servirse de, emplear. || *To make war*, hacer la guerra. || FAM. *To show what one is made of*, mostrar de lo que uno es capaz, revelar lo que uno lleva dentro. || *What do you make of it?*, ¿qué le parece? || *What do you make of this book, of this girl?*, ¿qué le parece este libro, esta chica? || *What do you make the time?*, ¿qué hora es?, ¿qué hora tienes?

— V. intr. Ir, dirigirse (*for, towards*, a, hacia) [to go]. || Abalanzarse (*at*, sobre) [to attack]. || Disponerse a: *she made to go*, se dispuso a salir. || Mostrarse (to prove to be). || Formarse (ice, flood, etc.). || MAR. Subir (tide). || — *To make against*, perjudicar, ser dañino *or* nocivo para (to be harmful): || ELECTR. *To make and break*, encenderse y apagarse. || *To make as if* o *as though*, simular que, fingir que, hacer el paripé de. || *To make certain of*, asegurarse de. || U. S. *To make like*, imitar, hacer como. || *To make merry*, divertirse. || *To make ready*, prepararse. || *To make so bold as to*, ser tan atrevido como para. || *To make sure of*, asegurarse de (to find out about).

— **To make after,** perseguir (to chase, to follow). || **To make at,** atacar a. || **To make away,** irse (to go). | — *To make away with*, llevarse, alzarse con (to steal), despilfarrar (fortune), suprimir, eliminar (to kill), destruir, hacer desaparecer (to get rid of). | *To make away with o.s.*, suicidarse (to kill o.s.). || **To make down,** achicar (a dress). || **To make for,** ir hacia *or* a, dirigirse hacia (to go). | Contribuir a *or* servir para crear: *it makes for difficulties*, contribuye a crear dificultades. || **To make into,** convertir en, transformar en. || **To make off,** irse, largarse (to go away). | — *To make off with*, arramblar con, alzarse con, llevarse (to steal). || **To make out,** hacer (list). | Extender (check, document). | Redactar (report). | Rellenar, llenar (a form). | Distinguir, divisar, vislumbrar (to perceive). | Descifrar (writing). | Comprender, [acabar de] entender (to understand): *I can't make it out*, no lo entiendo. | Creer, imaginarse (to believe): *he is not such a fool as people make out*, no es tan tonto como se imagina la gente. | Considerar (to regard). | Pretender, dar a entender (to claim): *to make out that*, pretender que. | Llegar a [una conclusión]: *how did you make that out?*, ¿cómo llegó a esta conclusión? | U. S. FAM. Arreglárselas: *don't worry, I'll make out*, no se preocupe, me las arreglaré. | Ir tirando (to get by). | Salir (to come out). | — *How did you make out in that matter?*, ¿cómo le fue en ese asunto? | *To make s.o. out to be a liar*, decir que alguien es un embustero. || **To make over,** ceder, traspasar (to hand over). | U. S. Arreglar (dress, house). || **To make up,** inventar (story). | Completar, suplir (sth. lacking). | Maquillar (to apply cosmetics to s.o.). | Maquillarse, pintarse (one's face). | Preparar (a prescription). | Confeccionar, hacer (dress). | Montar (to assemble). | Hacer (parcel, list, balance). | Envolver, empaquetar (goods into a parcel). | Constituir, componer (to constitute). | Reunir (to gather). | Echar carbón a (a fire). | Arreglar, concertar (a marriage, pact). | Compaginar, confeccionar (page). | Recuperar, compensar: *to make up lost time by extra work*, recuperar el tiempo perdido haciendo horas extraordinarias. | Compensar (a loss). | Recuperar (lost ground). | Colmar (a deficit). | Pagar (to pay). | Hacer las paces, reconciliarse: *I don't think they'll make up*, no creo que vayan a reconciliarse. | U. S. Repetir (an academic course, an examination). | — *The standing committee is made up of five persons*, la comisión permanente está integrada *or* constituida por cinco personas. | *To make it up again*, hacer las paces, reconciliarse. | *To make it up to s.o. for sth.*, indemnizar a alguien por algo. | *To make up a quarrel*, hacer las paces, reconciliarse. | *To make up for*, recuperar (to recover), compensar (to compensate), enmendar (one's faults), suplir (sth. lacking). | *To make up one's mind*, decidirse. | *To make up to s.o.*, acercarse a alguien (to come near), halagar a alguien (to flatter).

— OBSERV. Pret. & p. p. *made*.

make and break [—əndbreik] n. ELECTR. Interruptor (*m.*) automático.

make-believe [—biˌli:v] n. Simulación, *f.*, fingimiento, *m.* (pretence). || — *All this cordiality is but make-believe*, toda esta cordialidad es pura comedia. || *A world of make-believe*, un mundo de ensueño.
— Adj. Fingido, da; simulado, da. || De mentirijillas: *make-believe soldiers*, soldados de mentirijillas.

make-do [—du:] adj. Improvisado, da.
— N. Improvisación, *f.*

make-peace [—pi:s] n. Mediador, *m.*, pacificador, *m.*

maker [—ə*] n. Fabricante, *m.* (manufacturer). || Constructor, *m.* (of machine). || JUR. Firmante, *m.* || Autor, ra (of a book). || REL. *The Maker*, El Hacedor, El Creador (God).

makeshift [—ʃift] n. Expediente, *m.*, arreglo (*m.*) provisional.
— Adj. Provisional (temporary). || Improvisado, da: *a makeshift dinner*, una cena improvisada.

makeup [—ʌp] n. Construcción, *f.*, composición, *f.* (of several parts). || Estructura, *f.* (structure). || Carácter, *m.*, temperamento, *m.* (nature): *stolid makeup*, carácter impasible. || Maquillaje, *m.* (beauty products and art of applying them). || Confección, *f.* (of clothes). || PRINT. Compaginación, *f.*, confección, *f.*, ajuste, *m.* || FAM. Cuento, *m.*, historia (*f.*) inventada (story). || — *Makeup assistant*, maquillador, ra. || *Makeup base*, maquillaje de fondo. || *Makeup girl*, maquilladora, *f.*

makeweight [—weit] n. Complemento, *m.* [de peso]. || FIG. Tapaagujeros, *m. inv.*, comodín, *m.* (person). | Relleno, *m.* (padding).

making [ˈmeikiŋ] n. Fabricación, *f.* (manufacture). || Construcción, *f.* (of a bridge). || Confección, *f.* (of clothes). || Preparación, *f.* (of meals). || Preparación, *f.*, formación, *f.* (training). || Composición, *f.* (of a poem). || Creación, *f.* (of the world, of a post). || Hechura, *f.* (shape). || — Pl. Cualidades, *f.*, madera, *f. sing.*: *he has the makings of a leader*, tiene las cualidades de un jefe, tiene madera de jefe. || Ganancias, *f.* (earnings). || — *Revolution in the making*, revolución (*f.*) en potencia. || *That's history in the making*, son acontecimientos históricos *or* que pasarán a la historia. || *The marriage was none of her making*, no era responsable del matrimonio. || *The skirt was of her own making*, la falda era obra suya. || *To be still in the making*, estar haciéndose. || *To be the making of s.o.*, ser la causa del éxito *or* del triunfo *or* de la fortuna de alguien (to cause the success of), formar a alguien: *this failure was the making of him*, este fracaso le ha formado.

making-up [—ˈʌp] n. Maquillaje, *m.*

Malacca [məˈlækə] pr. n. GEOGR. Malaca.

malachite [ˈmæləkait] n. MIN. Malaquita, *f.*

malacopterygian [mæləkɔptəˈridʒiən] adj. Malacopterigio, gia.
— N. Malacopterigio, *m.*

maladjusted [ˈmæləˈdʒʌstid] adj. TECH. Mal ajustado, da. || FIG. Inadaptado, da.

maladjustment [ˈmæləˈdʒʌstmənt] n. TECH. Mal ajuste, *m.* || FIG. Inadaptación, *f.*

maladminister [ˈmælədˈministə*] v. tr. U. S. Administrar mal.

maladministration [ˈmælədˌminisˈtreiʃən] n. Mala administración, *f.*

maladroit [ˈmæləˈdrɔit] adj. Torpe.

maladroitness [—nis] n. Torpeza, *f.*

malady [ˈmælədi] n. MED. Enfermedad, *f.* (disease).

Malaga [ˈmæləgə] n. Málaga, *m.* (wine).

Málaga [ˈmæləgə] pr. n. GEOGR. Málaga.

Malagasy [ˌmæləˈgæsi] adj./n. Malgache.

malaguena [ˌmæləˈgeinjə] n. Malagueña, *f.*

malaise [mæˈleiz] n. Malestar, *m.*

malapropism [ˈmæləprɔpizəm] n. Barbarismo, *m.*

malapropos [ˈmælˈæprəpəu] adj. Inoportuno, na.
— Adv. Inoportunamente.

malar [ˈmeilə*] adj. ANAT. Malar. || *Malar bone*, malar, *m.*, pómulo, *m.*
— N. ANAT. Malar, *m.*, pómulo, *m.*

malaria [məˈlɛəriə] n. MED. Malaria, *f.*, paludismo, *m.*

malarial [—l] or **malarian** [—n] or **malarious** [—s] adj. Palúdico, ca (fever). || De la malaria, del paludismo (mosquito).

malaxate [ˈmælәkseit] v. tr. Malaxar, amasar.

malaxation [ˌmæləkˈseiʃən] n. Malaxación, *f.*, amasamiento, *m.*

Malay [məˈlei] or **Malayan** [—ən] adj./n. Malayo, ya.

Malaysia [məˈleiziə] pr. n. GEOGR. Malasia, *f.*, Malaysia, *f.*

Malaysian [—n] adj./n. Malasio, sia.

malcontent [ˈmælkənˌtent] adj./n. Descontento, ta.

Maldive Islands [ˈmɔ:ldivˈailəndz] pl. pr. n. GEOGR. Islas (*f.*) Maldivas.

male [meil] adj. BOT. ZOOL. Macho: *male panther*, pantera macho; *male fern*, helecho macho. || Varón: *male issue*, hijos varones; *male child*, hijo varón. || Masculino, na: *male sex*, sexo masculino. || De hombres: *male ward in a hospital*, sala de hombres en un hospital. || Viril, varonil (manly). || TECH. Macho. || TECH. *Male screw*, tornillo, *m.*
— N. BOT. ZOOL. Macho, *m.* || Varón, *m.* (person).

malediction [ˌmæliˈdikʃən] n. Maldición, *f.*

malefaction [ˌmæliˈfækʃən] n. Mala acción, *f.*, fechoría, *f.*

malefactor [ˈmælifæktə*] n. Malhechor, ra.

malefic [məˈlefik] adj. Maléfico, ca.

maleficence [məˈlefisns] n. Maleficencia, *f.*

maleficent [məˈlefisnt] adj. Maléfico, ca (malefic). || Perjudicial (harmful). || Criminal.

malevolence [məˈlevələns] n. Malevolencia, *f.*

malevolent [məˈlevələnt] adj. Malévolo, la.

malevolently [—li] adv. Malévolamente, con malevolencia.

malfeasance [mælˈfi:zəns] n. JUR. Hecho (*m.*) delictivo.

malformation [ˈmælfɔ:ˈmeiʃən] n. Malformación, *f.*

malfunction [ˈmælˈfʌnkʃən] n. Funcionamiento (*m.*) defectuoso.

malic [ˈmælik] adj. Málico, ca (acid).

malice [ˈmælis] n. Maldad, *f.* (ill will). || Rencor, *m.* (*to, towards*, a) [grudge]: *I bear her no malice*, no le guardo rencor. || JUR. Intención (*f.*) delictuosa. || *Malice aforethought*, premeditación, *f.*

malicious [məˈliʃəs] adj. Malo, la; malévolo, la (wicked). || Rencoroso, sa (rancorous). || JUR. Delictuoso, sa; delictivo, va (intent). | Delictivo, va (act). || JUR. *Malicious damage*, daño doloso.

maliciously [—li] n. Con maldad. || Por rencor, rencorosamente. || JUR. Con premeditación.

maliciousness [—nis] n. Malicia, *f.*, mala intención, *f.*

malign [məˈlain] adj. Maligno, na; malévolo, la (malevolent). || Perjudicial, pernicioso, sa: *a malign influence*, una influencia perjudicial. || MED. Maligno, na.

malign [məˈlain] v. tr. Calumniar, difamar (to slander). || Hablar mal de (to speak evil of).

malignancy [məˈlignənsi] n. Malignidad, *f.*, maldad, *f.*, malevolencia, *f.* || MED. Malignidad, *f.*

malignant [məˈlignənt] adj. Malvado, da; malo, la (person). || Perjudicial (harmful). || MED. Maligno, na.

malignity [məˈligniti] n. See MALIGNANCY.

Malines [mæˈli:n] pr. n. GEOGR. Malinas.

malinger [məˈlingə*] v. intr. Fingirse enfermo [para no trabajar o eludir una responsabilidad].

malingerer [—rə*] n. Enfermo (*m.*) fingido, enferma (*f.*) fingida, remolón, ona; simulador, ra.

malingering [—riŋ] n. Remolonería, *f.*, simulación, *f.*

mall [mɔ:l] n. Paseo, *m.* (avenue). || Mazo, *m.*, mallo, *m.* (hammer). || Mallo, *m.* (game).

mallard [ˈmæləd] n. Lavanco, *m.*, pato (*m.*) silvestre (duck).

malleability [ˌmæliəˈbiliti] n. Maleabilidad, *f.*

malleable [ˈmæliəbl] adj. Maleable.

malleolus [məˈli:ələs] n. ANAT. Maléolo, *m.*

— OBSERV. El plural es *malleoli*.

mallet [ˈmælit] n. Mazo, *m.*

malleus [ˈmæliəs] n. ANAT. Martillo, *m.* (of the ear).

— OBSERV. El plural es *mallei*.

mallow [ˈmæləu] n. BOT. Malva, *f.* || BOT. *Rose mallow*, malvarrosa, *f.*

malmsey [ˈmɑ:mzi] n. Malvasía, *f.* (wine).

malnutrition [ˈmælnju:ˈtriʃən] n. Desnutrición, *f.*

malodorous [mæˈləudərəs] adj. Maloliente.

malpractice [ˈmælˈpræktis] n. JUR. Negligencia, *f.*, incuria, *f.* (negligence). | Procedimientos (*m. pl.*) ilegales *or* desleales, hecho (*m.*) delictivo.

malt [mɔ:lt] n. Malta, *f.* (grain). || — *Malt liquor*, cerveza, *f.* || *Malt sugar*, maltosa, *f.*

malt [mɔ:lt] v. tr. Maltear: *malted milk*, leche malteada.

Malta [ˈmɔ:ltə] pr. n. GEOGR. Malta: *Knight of Malta*, caballero de Malta.

maltase [ˈmɔ:lteis] n. Maltasa, *f.*

Maltese [ˈmɔ:lˈti:z] adj./n. Maltés, esa. || *Maltese cross*, cruz de Malta.

malthouse [ˈmɔ:lthaus] n. Maltería, *f.*, fábrica (*f.*) de malta.

Malthusian [mælˈθju:zjən] adj./n. Maltusiano, na.

Malthusianism [—izəm] n. Maltusianismo, *m.*

malting [ˈmɔ:ltiŋ] n. Malteado, *m.*, maltaje, *m.*

maltose [ˈmɔ:ltəus] n. CHEM. Maltosa, *f.*

maltreat [mælˈtri:t] v. tr. Maltratar.

maltreatment [—mənt] n. Malos tratos, *m. pl.*, maltratamiento, *m.*, maltrato, *m.*

malvaceae [mælˈveisii:] pl. n. BOT. Malváceas, *f.*

malvasia [ˌmælvəˈsiə] n. Malvasía, *f.* (grape).

malversation [ˌmælvə:ˈseiʃən] n. JUR. Malversación, *f.*

mama [məˈmɑ:] n. FAM. Mamá, *f.*

Mameluke [ˈmæmilu:k] n. Mameluco, *m.*

mamilla [mæˈmilə] n. ANAT. Pezón, *m.*

— OBSERV. El plural de *mamilla* es *mamillae*.

mamillary [ˈmæmiləri] adj. ANAT. Mamilar.

mamma [məˈmɑ:] n. FAM. Mamá, *f.*
mamma [ˈmæmə] n. ANAT. Mama, *f.*, teta, *f.*
— OBSERV. El plural es *mammae.*
mammal [ˈmæməl] n. ZOOL. Mamífero, *m.*
mammalia [mæˈmeiljə] n. ZOOL. Mamíferos, *m. pl.* (class).
mammalian [—n] adj. ZOOL. Mamífero, ra.
— N. Mamífero, *m.*
mammary [ˈmæməri] adj. ANAT. Mamario, ria.
mammiferous [mæˈmifərəs] adj. ZOOL. Mamífero, ra.
mammilla [mæˈmilə] n. ANAT. Pezón, *m.*
— OBSERV. El plural de *mammila* es *mammilae.*
mammillary [ˈmæmiləri] adj. ANAT. Mamilar.
mammoth [ˈmæməθ] n. Mamut, *m.*
— Adj. Descomunal: *mammoth sale*, venta descomunal. || Gigante, ta: *a mammoth coach*, un autocar gigante.
mammy [ˈmæmi] n. Mamá, *f.*, mamaíta, *f.* || U. S. Niñera (*f.*) negra.
man [mæn] n. Hombre, *m.*, ser (*m.*) humano, persona, *f.* (human being). || Humanidad, *f.*, hombre, *m.*, género (*m.*) humano (human race). || Hombre, *m.* (adult male): *how many men are there here?*, ¿cuántos hombres hay aquí?; *men and women*, hombres y mujeres. || Varón, *m.* (male). || Uno: *a man must live*, uno tiene que vivir. || Criado, *m.*, sirviente, *m.* (valet). || MAR. Ordenanza, *m.* (orderly). | Marinero, *m.* (sailor). || MIL. Ordenanza, *m.* (orderly). | Soldado, *m.* (soldier). || TECH. Obrero, *m.* (workman). || COMM. Empleado, *m.* (employee). | Mozo, *m.* (boy). || SP. Ficha, *f.* (in draughts). | Pieza, *f.* (in chess). | Jugador, *m.* (player). || JUR. Ciudadano, *m.* (citizen). | Habitante, *m.* (inhabitant). || FAM. Hombre, *m.*, marido, *m.* (husband). | Hombre, *m.*, amante, *m.* (lover). || Estudiante, *m.*: *he's an Oxford man*, es un estudiante de Oxford. || Vendedor, *m.*: *here comes the newspaper man*, ahí viene el vendedor de periódicos. || — *All good men and true*, todos los que tienen derecho a llamarse hombres. || *All to a man*, todos sin exceptuar a nadie. || *A man is as old as he feels*, uno no tiene más edad que la que representa. || *A man of the world*, un hombre de mundo. || *An old man*, un anciano, un viejo. || *Any man*, cualquier hombre, cualquiera. || *As one man*, como un solo hombre, unánimemente. || *Best man*, padrino (*m.*) del novio. || *Between man and man*, de hombre a hombre. || *Every man*, todo el mundo. || *Every man for himself!*, ¡sálvese quien pueda! || *Family man*, padre de familia (father), hombre casero (devoted to his home). || *Good man!*, ¡muy bien! || *Great man*, gran hombre. || *He is a Manchester man*, es de Manchester. || *He is quite a little man already*, está ya hecho un hombre. || *He is the man for me*, es mi tipo de hombre (for a woman), es el hombre que necesito (for a job). || *He seems to be the very man for the job*, parece ser la persona más adecuada para este trabajo. || *I am your man*, soy el hombre que usted necesita, soy su hombre. || *I have lived here man and boy for forty years*, vivo aquí desde mi más tierna infancia, es decir desde hace cuarenta años. || *In the face of all men*, abiertamente, a la vista de todos. || *It is not fit for man or beast*, no hay quien se lo trague (food). || *Like a man*, como un hombre. || FAM. *Man!*, ¡hombre!: *come here, man!*, ¡ven aquí, hombre! || *Man for man the teams were matched*, hombre por hombre, los equipos estaban igualados. || FIG. *Man Friday*, factótum, *m.* || *Man of his word*, hombre de palabra. || *Man of letters*, hombre de letras, literato, *m.* || *Man of means* o *of property*, hombre muy rico. || *Man of straw*, testaferro, *m.*, hombre de paja. || *Man proposes, God disposes*, el hombre propone y Dios dispone. || *Man servant*, criado, sirviente. || *Man shall not live on bread alone*, no sólo de pan vive el hombre. || *Man trap*, cepo, *m.* || *Men say that*, dicen que, se dice que. || *Men's room*, servicios (*m. pl.*) para caballeros. || *My good man*, buen hombre: *here, my good man!*, ¡tenga, buen hombre! || *My little man*, hijo mío. || FAM. *My old man*, mi padre (father), mi marido (my husband). || *My young man*, mi novio. || *No man*, nadie. || *No man can serve two masters*, no se puede servir a Dios y al diablo. || *No man's land*, tierra (*f.*) de nadie. || FAM. *Old man*, hombre: *good-bye, old man*, adiós, hombre. || *Old man of the sea*, viejo lobo de mar. || *Red man*, piel (*m.*) roja. || *Sandwich man*, hombre anuncio. || *That man Smith*, ese Smith. || *The average man*, el hombre medio. || *The man in the street*, el hombre de la calle. || *The man of the moment* o *of the day*, el hombre del día. || *The old man*, el jefe (the boss), el director [de una escuela, de un colegio] (the headmaster). || *The rights of man*, los derechos del hombre. || *They were slain to a man*, mataron hasta el último, murieron todos. || *To be one's own man*, ser dueño de sí mismo, hacer lo que uno quiere. || *To fight man to man*, luchar cuerpo a cuerpo. || *To live as man and wife*, vivir como marido y mujer. || *To make a man of*, hacer un hombre: *the army will make a man of him*, el ejército le hará un hombre. || *To talk man to man*, hablar de hombre a hombre. || *What are you, man or mouse?*, ¿eres hombre o no? || *Young man*, joven, *m.*
— OBSERV. El plural de *man* es *men.*
man [mæn] v. tr. MIL. Guarnecer [de hombres] (to place men on). | Servir (a gun, post). | Armar (a battery). || MAR. AVIAT. Tripular (to crew). || Contratar personal para (a factory). || — *Manned flight*, vuelo tripulado. || *Man the pumps!*, ¡todos a las bombas!
man-about-town [—əˌbautˈtaun] n. Hombre (*m.*) de mundo.
— OBSERV. El plural es *men-about-town.*
manacle [ˈmænəkl] n. Manilla, *f.* || — Pl. Esposas, *f.* (handcuffs).
manacle [ˈmænəkl] v. tr. Esposar, poner esposas. || FIG. Estorbar (to hamper).
manage [ˈmænidʒ] v. tr. Manejar (tool, instrument). || Conducir, llevar [*Amer.*, manejar] (a car). || Gobernar (a ship). || Conducir, dirigir (an undertaking). || Dirigir, llevar: *to manage the affairs of the nation*, dirigir los asuntos del país. || Administrar, dirigir, llevar (an affair, a company, a bank, etc.): *to manage a hotel*, llevar un hotel. || Administrar (property). || Llevar (affairs, a person): *he manages his own affairs*, lleva él mismo sus negocios. || Domar (an animal). || Dominar (to dominate): *to manage one's husband*, dominar a su marido. || Conseguir, arreglárselas: *he managed to do it*, consiguió hacerlo, se las arregló para hacerlo; *he managed to see the president*, se las arregló para ver al presidente. || Hacer (a piece of work): *he managed it very cleverly*, lo ha hecho de una manera muy inteligente. || Poder comer *or* beber: *I could manage a bit more of lamb*, podría comer un poco más de cordero. || Querer: *can you manage another drink?*, ¿quieres otra copa? || FIG. Manejar (s.o.) || — *Can you manage ten o'clock?*, ¿puedes venir a las diez? || *Fifty pounds is the most that I can manage*, no puedo darle más de cincuenta libras. || *I can't quite manage to do it*, no puedo hacerlo.
— V. intr. Arreglárselas: *how do you manage alone?*, ¿cómo te las arreglas solo? || Llevar *or* dirigir los negocios (to direct business). || FAM. Conseguir su objetivo, lograr su propósito. || — *How does he sing? — He manages*, ¿ qué tal canta? — Se defiende. || *How will you do it? — I'll manage*, ¿cómo lo harás? — Me las arreglaré. || *Manage the best you can*, arreglátelas como puedas. || *To manage without sth., without s.o.*, prescindir de algo, de alguien.
manageability [ˌmænidʒəˈbiliti] n. Manejabilidad, *f.* (of tool). || Docilidad, *f.* (of person, animal). || Flexibilidad, *f.*
manageable [ˈmænidʒəbl] adj. Manejable (tool). || Dócil (person, animal). || Factible (undertaking).
manageableness [—nis] n. See MANAGEABILITY.
management [ˈmænidʒmənt] n. Dirección, *f.*, administración, *f.*, gestión, *f.* (administration). || Dirección, *f.*, consejo (*m.*) de administración, junta (*f.*) directiva (board of directors). || Habilidad, *f.* (skill). || Manejo, *m.* (of tools, persons).
manager [ˈmænidʒə*] n. Director, *m.*, gerente, *m.* (in business): *sales manager*, director de ventas. || Administrador, *m.* (of an estate). || Empresario, *m.*, apoderado, *m.* (of artists, sportsmen). || Manager, *m.* (of boxers). || Jefe, *m.*: *departmental manager*, jefe de servicio. || U. S. Jefe, *m.* (of a political party). || — *Business manager*, director comercial. || *His wife is a good manager*, su mujer es una buena administradora (in the home).
manageress [ˈmænidʒəˈres] n. Directora, *f.*, administradora, *f.*
managerial [ˌmænəˈdʒiəriəl] adj. Directivo, va; directorial, administrativo, va. || *Managerial staff*, personal (*m.*) dirigente, ejecutivos, *m. pl.*
managership [ˈmænidʒəʃip] n. Dirección, *f.*, administración, *f.*, gestión, *f.*
managing [ˈmænidʒiŋ] adj. Gerente: *managing director*, director gerente. || FIG. Mandón, ona.
— N. See MANAGEMENT.
man-at-arms [ˈmænətˈɑ:mz] n. Hombre (*m.*) de armas.
— OBSERV. El plural es *men-at-arms.*
manatee [ˌmænəˈti:] m. ZOOL. Manatí, *m.* (mammal).
manchineel [ˌmæntʃiˈni:l] n. Manzanillo, *m.* (tree).
Manchu [mænˈtʃu:] adj./n. Manchú, úa.
Manchurian [—n] adj./n. Manchú, úa.
manciple [ˈmænsipl] n. Ecónomo, *m.* (of a college).
Mancunian [mæŋˈkju:njən] adj. De Manchester.
— N. Persona (*f.*) de Manchester.
mandamus [mænˈdeiməs] n. JUR. Mandamiento (*m.*) judicial.
mandarin [ˈmændərin] n. Mandarín, *m.* (in China). || BOT. Mandarina, *f.* (fruit). | Mandarino, *m.*, mandarinero, *m.* (tree).
— Adj. Mandarino, na.
mandatary [ˈmændətəri] n. Mandatario, *m.*
mandate [ˈmændeit] n. JUR. Mandato, *m.* (given to a representative). | Mandamiento (*m.*) judicial, orden, *f.* (order). | Mandato, *m.* (over a territory). | Territorio (*m.*) bajo fideicomiso *or* mandato (mandated territory).
mandate [ˈmændeit] v. tr. Poner bajo el mandato (*to*, de): *New Guinea was mandated to Australia*, Nueva Guinea fue puesta bajo el mandato de Australia.
mandated [—id] adj. Bajo mandato, bajo fideicomiso: *mandated territory*, territorio bajo mandato.
mandator [mænˈdeitə*] n. JUR. Mandante, *m.*

mandatory [ˈmændətəri] adj. Obligatorio, ria (compulsory). || *Mandatory writ*, mandamiento (*m.*) judicial.
— N. Mandatario, *m.*
mandible [ˈmændibl] n. Mandíbula, *f.*
Mandingo [mænˈdingəu] n. Mandingo, *m.* (people of Africa).
mandola [mænˈdəulə] n. MUS. Mandora, *f.*
mandolin or **mandoline** [ˈmændəlin] n. MUS. Mandolina, *f.*
mandragora [mænˈdrægərə] or **mandrake** [ˈmændreik] n. BOT. Mandrágora, *f.* (plant).
mandrel [ˈmændrəl] or **mandril** [ˈmændril] n. TECH. Mandril, *m.*
mandrill [ˈmændril] n. Mandril, *m.* (monkey).
manducate [ˈmændjukeit] v. tr. Masticar (to chew).
manducation [mændjuˈkeiʃən] n. Masticación, *f.*
mane [mein] n. Crin, *f.*, crines, *f. pl.* (of horse). || Melena, *f.* (of lion, person).
man-eater [ˈmænˌi:tə*] n. Antropófago, *m.*, caníbal, *m.* (person). || Animal (*m.*) que come carne humana.
man-eating [ˈmænˌi:tiŋ] adj. Antropófago, ga; caníbal (person). || Que come carne humana (animal).
manège [mæˈneiʒ] n. Equitación, *f.* (horsemanship). || Picadero, *m.* (riding school).
manes [ˈmɑ:neiz] pl. n. Manes, *m.* (the souls of the dead).
maneuver [məˈnu:və*] n. /v. tr./intr. U. S. See MANOEUVRE.
maneuverability [məˌnu:vrəˈbiliti] n. U. S. See MANOEUVRABILITY.
maneuverable [məˈnuvərəbl] adj. U. S. Manejable, maniobrable.
manful [ˈmænful] adj. Valiente (brave). || Resuelto, decidido (resolute). || Varonil (manly).
manfulness [—nis] n. Valentía, *f.* (bavery). || Resolución, *f.* (determination). || Virilidad, *f.*, hombría, *f.* (manliness).
manganate [ˈmæŋgənət] n. CHEM. Manganato, *m.*
manganese [ˌmæŋgəˈni:z] n. CHEM. Manganeso, *m.* || CHEM. *Manganese dioxide*, manganesa, *f.*, manganesia, *f.*
manganesian [—iən] adj. Manganésico, ca.
manganic [mæŋˈgænik] adj. Mangánico (acid).
manganite [ˈmæŋgənait] n. Manganita, *f.*
manganous [ˈmæŋgənəs] adj. Manganésico, ca; manganoso, sa.
mange [meindʒ] n. MED. Sarna, *f.* (skin disease).
mangel-wurzel [ˈmæŋglˈwə:zl] n. BOT. Remolacha (*f.*) forrajera (beet).
manger [ˈmeindʒə*] n. Pesebre, *m.*
mangle [ˈmæŋgl] n. Máquina (*f.*) de planchar (to press). || Escurridor, *m.* (to squeeze out water).
mangle [ˈmæŋgl] v. tr. Planchar con máquina (to press). || Destrozar, despedazar (to hack, to cut). || FIG. Deformar (a word). | Mutilar (a text). || FAM. Destrozar (in performing).
mango [ˈmæŋgəu] n. BOT. Mango, *m.* (tree, fruit).

— OBSERV. El plural de la palabra inglesa *mango* es *mangoes* o *mangos.*

mangold [ˈmæŋgəld] or **mangold-wurzel** [—ˈwə:zl] n. BOT. Remolacha (*f.*) forrajera (beet).
mangosteen [ˈmæŋgəusti:n] n. BOT. Mangostán, *m.* (tree, fruit).
mangrove [ˈmæŋgrəuv] n. BOT. Mangle, *m.* (tree). || *Mangrove swamp*, manglar, *m.*
mangy [ˈmeindʒi] adj. MED. Sarnoso, sa (with mange). || FAM. Asqueroso, sa (shabby). || FAM. *Mangy trick*, mala jugada, cochinada, *f.*
manhandle [ˈmænˌhændl] v. tr. TECH. Manipular (to move by manual force). || FAM. Maltratar, tratar duramente: *the police began manhandling the demonstrators*, la policía empezó a maltratar a los manifestantes.
manhole [ˈmænhəul] n. Registro, *m.*, boca, *f.* [de acceso].
manhood [ˈmænhud] n. Hombres, *m. pl.* (men). || Virilidad, *f.*, edad (*f.*) viril, madurez, *f.* (state). || Hombría, *f.*, virilidad, *f.* (manly qualities).
man-hour [ˈmænˌauə*] n. Trabajo (*m.*) realizado por un hombre en una hora.
manhunt [ˈmænhʌnt] n. Caza (*f.*) del hombre.
mania [ˈmeinjə] n. Manía, *f.*: *persecution mania*, manía persecutoria; *to have a mania for*, tener la manía de.
maniac [ˈmeiniæk] adj./n. Maniaco, ca. || FIG. Fanático, ca.
maniacal [məˈnaiəkəl] adj. Maniaco, ca.
manic [ˈmænik] adj. Maniaco, ca. || *Manic-depressive psychosis*, manía depresiva.
Manichaean or **Manichean** [ˌmæniˈki:ən] adj./n. Maniqueo, a.
Manichaeism or **Manicheism** [ˌmæniˈki:izəm] n. Maniqueísmo, *m.*
manicure [ˈmænikjuə*] n. Manicura, *f.* (care): *to give s.o. a manicure*, hacerle a uno la manicura. || Manicuro, ra (manicurist).
manicure [ˈmænikjuə*] v. tr. Hacer la manicura a (s.o.). || Arreglar (nails).
manicurist [—ist] n. Manicuro, ra.
manifest [ˈmænifest] adj. Manifiesto, ta; evidente.
— N. MAR. Manifiesto, *m.* (list of a ship's cargo).
manifest [ˈmænifest] v. tr. Manifestar. || MAR. Registrar en un manifiesto.
manifestant [mæniˈfestənt] n. U. S. Manifestante, *m.* & *f.* (demonstrator).
manifestation [ˌmænifesˈteiʃən] n. Manifestación, *f.*
manifesto [ˌmæniˈfestəu] n. Manifiesto, *m.*

— OBSERV. El plural es *manifestoes* o *manifestos.*

manifold [ˈmænifəuld] adj. Multicopista: *manifold writer*, máquina multicopista. || FIG. Múltiple, numeroso, sa (numerous). | Variado, da; diverso, sa (varied). | Consumado, da; notorio, ria (thief, liar, etc.).
— N. Copia (*f.*) hecha con multicopista. || Colector, *m.* (pipe). || MATH. Multiplicidad, *f.* || PHIL. Diversidad, *f.*
manifold [ˈmænifəuld] v. tr. Tirar *or* hacer con multicopista, multicopiar (documents). || Multiplicar.
manifolder [—ə*] n. Multicopista, *f.*, máquina (*f.*) multicopista.
manikin [ˈmænikin] n. Maniquí, *m.* (of taylors, etc.). || Maniquí, *f.*, modelo, *f.* (of fashion). || FIG. Enano, *m.*, retaco, *m.* (tiny man).
Manila [məˈnilə] pr. n. GEOGR. Manila.
Manila or **Manilla** [məˈnilə] n. Manila, *m.* (cigar). || — *Manila hemp*, cáñamo (*m.*) de Manila, abacá, *m.* || *Manila paper*, papel (*m.*) de pruebas.
manille [məˈnil] n. Malilla, *f.* (in cards).
manioc [ˈmæniɔk] n. BOT. Mandioca, *f.*, yuca, *f.*
maniple [ˈmænipl] n. REL. Manípulo, *m.*
manipulate [məˈnipjuleit] v. tr. Manipular, manejar (to handle). || Accionar (a lever, a knob, etc.). || Falsear, amañar (election results, etc.). || Influir en (the market).
manipulation [məˌnipjuˈleiʃən] n. Manipulación, *f.*, manejo, *m.* || Falseamiento, *m.*, amaño, *m.* (falsification).
manipulator [məˈnipjuleitə*] n. Manipulador, *m.*
manitou [ˈmænitu:] n. Manitú, *m.*
mankind [mænˈkaind] n. Humanidad, *f.*, género (*m.*) humano (the human race). || Hombres, *m. pl.* (men).
manlike [ˈmænlaik] adj. Varonil, masculino, na (of a man). || De hombre, hombruno, na (resembling a man). || Hombruna (woman).
manliness [ˈmænlinis] n. Virilidad, *f.*, masculinidad, *f.*, hombría, *f.*
manly [ˈmænli] adj. Varonil, viril (virile). | De hombres, masculino, na: *manly sports*, deportes de hombres.
man-made [ˈmænmeid] adj. Hecho por la mano del hombre, artificial.
manna [ˈmænə] n. Maná, *m.* (godsend). || BOT. Maná, *m.* (of trees). || FIG. *Like manna from heaven*, como maná llovido del cielo.
manned [mænd] adj. Tripulado, da.
mannequin [ˈmænikin] n. See MANIKIN.
manner [ˈmænə*] n. Manera, *f.*, modo, *m.*: *I don't like his manner of talking*, no me gusta su manera de hablar. || Modo, *m.*, forma, *f.*, manera, *f.* (of payment). || Clase, *f.* (kind): *all manner of things*, toda clase de cosas. || Comportamiento, *m.*, modo (*m.*) de ser *or* de portarse (behaviour). || Aire, *m.*: *his easy manner*, su aire desenvuelto. || ARTS. Estilo, *m.*, manera, *f.* || — Pl. Modales, *m.*: *distinguished manners*, modales distinguidos. || Educación, *f. sing.*: *it is bad manners to interrupt*, es de mala educación interrumpir; *lack of manners*, falta de educación. || Costumbres, *f.*: *comedy of manners*, comedia de costumbres. || — *Adverb of manner*, adverbio de modo. || *After the manner of*, a la manera de. || *After this manner*, de esta manera. || *As if to the manner born*, como si estuviese acostumbrado desde la cuna. || *By no manner of means*, de ninguna manera *or* forma, de ningún modo. || *Don't forget your manners!*, ¡conserve los buenos modales! || *In a manner*, en cierto modo, en cierto sentido. || *In a manner of speaking*, como si dijéramos, por decirlo así. || *In like manner*, de la misma manera. || *In such a manner that*, de tal manera que. || *In the same manner as*, del mismo modo que. || *In this manner*, de esta manera. || *It's a manner of speaking*, es un decir. || *Road manners*, conportamiento en la carretera. || *Where are your manners?*, ¡vaya modales!
mannered [ˈmænəd] adj. De modales: *a well-mannered person*, una persona de buenos modales. || Amanerado, da: *a mannered style of writing*, un estilo amanerado.
mannerism [ˈmænərizəm] n. Amaneramiento, *m.* (affectation). || ARTS. Manierismo, *m.* || Peculiaridad, *f.*
mannerist [ˈmænərist] n. Manierista, *m.* & *f.*
manneristic [mænəˈristik] adj. Amanerado, da (affected). || ARTS. Manierista.
mannerless [ˈmænəlis] adj. Sin educación, de malos modales, maleducado, da.
mannerliness [ˈmænəlinis] n. Cortesía, *f.*, buenos modales, *m. pl.*, buena educación, *f.*
mannerly [ˈmænəli] adj. Cortés, bien educado, da; de buenos modales.
mannikin [ˈmænikin] n. See MANIKIN.
mannish [ˈmæniʃ] adj. Hombruna, viril (woman). || Masculino, na (dress).
mannishness [—nis] n. Aspecto (*m.*) hombruno, masculinidad, *f.*
manoeuvrability [məˌnu:vrəˈbiliti] n. Manejo, *m.*, maniobrabilidad, *f.*, manejabilidad, *f.*
manoeuvrable [məˈnu:vrəbl] adj. Manejable, maniobrable.

manoeuvre [mə'nu:və*] n. Maniobra, *f.*
manoeuvre [mə'nu:və*] v. tr. MIL. MAR. Hacer maniobrar. || FIG. Maniobrar, manejar (s.o.). | Maquinar, tramar (sth.). || — FIG. *To manoeuvre a friend into a good job*, arreglárselas hábilmente para conseguir un buen puesto a un amigo. || *To manoeuvre sth. into position*, poner algo en posición.
— V. intr. MIL. MAR. Maniobrar. || FIG. Maniobrar.
man-of-war ['mænəv'wɔ:*] n. MAR. Buque (*m.*) de guerra.
— OBSERV. El plural de esta palabra es *men-of-war*.
manometer [mə'nɔmitə*] n. Manómetro, *m.*
manor ['mænə*] n. Señorío, *m.*, feudo, *m.* (under the feudal system). || *Manor house*, casa solariega.
manorial [mə'nɔ:riəl] adj. Señorial, feudal (constituting a manor). || Solariego, ga (house).
manpower ['mænpauə*] n. TECH. Mano (*f.*) de obra. || MIL. Soldados, *m. pl.* || Hombres, *m. pl.* (men).
manrope ['mænrəup] n. MAR. Barandilla, *f.*
mansard ['mænsɑ:d] n. Tejado (*m.*) abuhardillado (roof). || Buhardilla, *f.* (garret).
manse [mæns] n. Casa (*f.*) de un pastor protestante.
manservant ['mæn,sə:vənt] n. Criado, *m.*, sirviente, *m.* [*Amer.*, mucamo, *m.*].
— OBSERV. El plural de esta palabra es *menservants*.
mansion ['mænʃən] n. Casa (*f.*) solariega (manor house). || Gran casa (*f.*) de campo (in the country). || Palacete, *m.*, hotelito, *m.* (in town). || — Pl. Casa (*f. sing.*) de vecindad, casa (*f.*) de vecinos (apartment house). || *Mansion House*, casa consistorial del alcalde de Londres.
man-size ['mænsaiz] or **man-sized** [—d] adj. De hombres, para hombres: *a man-size job*, un trabajo de hombres. || Muy grande (very big).
manslaughter ['mæn,slɔ:tə*] n. JUR. Homicidio (*m.*) involuntario.
manslayer ['mæn,sleiə*] n. JUR. Homicida, *m.* & *f.*
mantel ['mæntl] n. Manto, *m.* (of a fireplace).
mantelet ['mæntlit] n. Mantelete, *m.* (shelter). || Esclavina, *f.* (short cape). || Pantalla (*f.*) contra balas (screen).
mantelpiece ['mæntlpi:s] n. Manto, *m.* (mantel). || Repisa (*f.*) de chimenea (mantelshelf). || Chimenea, *f.* (fireplace).
mantelshelf ['mæntlʃelf] n. Repisa (*f.*) de chimena.
— OBSERV. El plural de *mantelshelf* es *mantelshelves*.
mantilla [mæn'tilə] n. Mantilla, *f.*
mantis ['mæntis] n. ZOOL. *Mantis prawn* o *shrimp*, esquila, *f.*, camarón, *m.* | *Praying mantis*, santateresa, *f.*, predicador, *m.* (insect).
— OBSERV. El plural es *mantises* o *mantes*.
mantissa [mæn'tisə] n. Mantisa, *f.* (of a logarithm).
mantle ['mæntl] n. Capa, *f.*, manto, *m.* (sleeveless cloak). || FIG. Manto, *m.*: *under the mantle of night*, bajo el manto de la noche. || TECH. Camisa (*f.*) exterior (of a furnace). | Manguito, *m.* (incandescent device). || Manto, *m.* (of molluscs). || ARCH. Paramento, *m.*
mantle ['mæntl] v. tr. Cubrir con un manto. || FIG. Cubrir (to cover). | Ocultar, tapar (to conceal).
— V. intr. Hacer espuma, cubrirse de espuma (liquid). || FIG. Enrojecerse, ruborizarse (to blush). | Subirse (blood).
mantlet ['mæntlit] n. See MANTELET.
mantrap ['mæntræp] n. Trampa, *f.*
manual ['mænjuəl] adj. Manual: *manual work* o *labour*, trabajo manual. || — *Manual alphabet*, alfabeto (*m.*) de sordomudos. || MIL. *Manual exercise*, instrucción (*f.*) con armas.
— N. Manual, *m.* (book). || MUS. Teclado (*m.*) de un órgano.
manually [—li] adv. A mano, manualmente.
manufactory [,mænju'fæktəri] n. Manufactura, *f.*, fábrica, *f.*
manufacturable [,mænju'fæktʃərəbl] adj. Manufacturable.
manufacture [,mænju'fæktʃə*] n. Fabricación, *f.* (act). || Producto (*m.*) manufacturado (product).
manufacture [,mænju'fæktʃə*] v. tr. Fabricar, manufacturar. || Confeccionar (clothes). || FIG. Fabricar en serie (art, literature). | Fabricar, inventar, forjar (a story).
manufacturer [—rə*] n. Fabricante, *m.*: *boiler manufacturer*, fabricante de calderas. || Industrial, *m.* || FIG. Autor, ra.
manufacturing [—riŋ] adj. Industrial, fabril, manufacturero, ra.
— N. Fabricación, *f.* || Confección, *f.* (of clothes).
manumission [,mænju'miʃən] n. JUR. Manumisión, *f.*
manumit [,mænju'mit] v. tr. Emancipar, libertar, manumitir (slaves).
manure [mə'njuə*] n. AGR. Abono, *m.*, estiércol, *m.* || *Manure heap*, estercolero, *m.*
manure [mə'njuə*] v. tr. Abonar, estercolar.
manuscript ['mænjuskript] adj. Manuscrito, ta (written by hand).
— N. Manuscrito, *m.* (document written by hand). || Original, *m.* (typewritten document).
Manx [mæŋks] adj. De la isla de Man. || Sin cola (cat).
— N. Lengua (*f.*) hablada en la isla de Man. || *The Manx*, los habitantes de la isla de Man.
Manxman [—mən] n. Natural (*m.*) de la isla de Man.
— OBSERV. El plural de *Manxman* es *Manxmen*.
many ['meni] adj. Muchos, muchas (with plural terms): *he has been here many times*, ha estado aquí muchas veces; *many of us*, muchos de nosotros. || Mucho, mucha (with collective nouns): *many people*, mucha gente. || — *A great many people*, un gran número de personas, muchísima gente. || *As many as*, hasta, no menos de: *as many as ten saw it*, hasta diez lo vieron; tantos *or* tantas como: *as many as you want*, tantos como quieras; cuantos, cuantas: *to as many as are present I would say*, a cuantos están presentes afirmo que. || *As many...as*, tantos *or* tantas... como: *as many times as you*, tantas veces como tú; *I have as many books as you*, tengo tantos libros como tú. || *Ever so many times*, no sé cuántas veces. || *For many years*, durante muchos años. || *How many?*, ¿cuántos?, ¿cuántas?: *how many are there?*, ¿cuántos hay? || *In as many*, en el mismo número de: *they have had ten children in as many years*, han tenido diez hijos en el mismo número de años. || *Many a man*, más de uno. || *Many a time*, más de una vez, muchas veces: *he has been here many a time*, ha estado aquí más de una vez. || *Many is the time*, más de una vez. || *Not very many*, no muchos, no muchas. || *Of many kinds*, de muchas clases. || *One too many*, uno de más, uno de sobra: *one card too many*, una carta de más. || *So many*, tantos, tantas: *so many men, so many minds*, tantos hombres, tantos pareceres. || *They were so many*, eran tantos, eran tantas. || *Too many*, demasiado, da: *too many flowers*, demasiadas flores. || *Twice as many*, dos veces más, el doble. || *You are none too many to*, ninguno de ustedes sobra para.
— Pron. Muchos, muchas.
— N. Mayoría, *f.*: *the will of the many*, la voluntad de la mayoría. || *A good* or *a great many*, muchísimos, mas; un gran número.
— OBSERV. El comparativo de *many* es *more* y el superlativo *most*.
many-coloured [—'kʌləd] adj. Multicolor.
manyfold [—'fəuld] adv. Muchas veces.
— Adj. See MANIFOLD.
manyplies [—plaiz] n. ZOOL. Libro, *m.* (omasum).
many-sided [—'saidid] adj. De muchos lados. || FIG. Complejo, ja (question). | Polifacético, ca; diverso, sa; variado, da (talent).
many-sidedness [—'saididnis] n. FIG. Complejidad, *f.* (of a question). | Diversidad, *f.*, variedad, *f.* (of a talent).
manzanilla [,mænzə'nilə] n. Manzanilla, *f.* (wine). || Manzanillo, *m.* (tree).
Maoism ['mæuizəm] n. Maoísmo, *m.*
Maoist ['mæuist] adj./n. Maoísta.
Maori ['mauri] adj./n. Maorí.
map [mæp] n. Mapa, *m.*: *blank* o *outline* o *skeleton map*, mapa mudo; *to draw up a map*, levantar un mapa; *relief map*, mapa en relieve. || Plano, *m.*: *map of a town*, plano de una ciudad. || Carta, *f.* (chart). || U. S. POP. Jeta, *f.*, hocico, *m.* (mug). || — *Map of the world*, mapamundi, *m.* || FAM. *Off the map*, en el otro mundo, donde Cristo dio las tres voces (place), que no es de actualidad (question). | *To disappear from the map*, desaparecer del mapa. | *To put on the map*, poner en el primer plano de la actualidad. | *To wipe off the map*, hacer desaparecer del mapa (to destroy).
map [mæp] v. tr. Levantar un mapa de (to make a map). || Indicar en el mapa (to represent on a map). || Trazar, dibujar (a plan). || FIG. *To map out*, proyectar, planear, organizar: *he mapped out his holidays*, planeó sus vacaciones.
maple ['meipl] n. BOT. Arce, *m.* (tree, wood): *maple sugar, syrup*, azúcar, jarabe de arce.
map maker ['mæp,meikə*] n. Cartógrafo, fa.
map making [—iŋ] n. Cartografía, *f.*
mapping ['mæpiŋ] n. Cartografía, *f.* || Levantamiento (*m.*) de planos.
maquette [mæ'ket] n. Maqueta, *f.*
maquis ['mæki:] n. Monte (*m.*) bajo, soto, *m.* (copse). || Resistencia (*f.*) de los franceses contra los alemanes en la segunda guerra mundial.
mar [mɑ:*] v. tr. Estropear, echar a perder (to damage). || Desfigurar (s.o.). || — *To mar one's enjoyment*, aguarle la fiesta a uno. || *To mar one's joy*, entristecer a uno.
marabou or **marabout** ['mærəbu:] n. Marabú, *m.*
marabout ['mærəbu:] n. Morabito, *m.* (Moslem hermit).
maraca [mə'rɑ:kə] n. MUS. Maraca, *f.* (percussion instrument).
maraschino [,mærəs'ki:nəu] n. Marrasquino, *m.* (liqueur).
marasmus [mə'ræzməs] n. MED. Marasmo, *m.*
— OBSERV. *Marasmus* no tiene el sentido figurado y familiar que tiene « marasmo » en español (falta de energía, estancamiento).
marathon ['mærəθən] n. Maratón, *m.* (race).
maraud [mə'rɔ:d] v. intr. Merodear.
marauder [—ə*] n. Merodeador, ra.
marauding [—iŋ] adj. Merodeador, ra.
— M. Merodeo, *m.*
maravedi [,mærə'veidi] n. Maravedí, *m.* (coin).

marble [ˈmɑ:bl] n. Mármol, *m.* (statue, stone): *sculpted in marble*, esculpido en mármol. || Canica, *f.*, bola, *f.* (ball): *to play marbles*, jugar a las canicas.
— Adj. De mármol: *marble pavement*, enlosado de mármol. || Del mármol: *marble industry*, industria del mármol. || Marmóreo, a; de mármol (whiteness).
marble [ˈmɑ:bl] v. tr. Jaspear, vetear.
marble cutter [—ˌkʌtə*] n. Marmolista, *m.* (worker). || *Marble-cutter's workshop*, marmolería, *f.*
marbleize [ˈmɑ:blaiz] v. tr. U. S. Jaspear, vetear (to marble).
marblework [ˈmɑ:blˈwə:k] n. Marmolería, *f.*
marbling [ˈmɑ:bliŋ] n. Jaspeado, *m.*, veteado, *m.*
marbly [ˈmɑ:bli] adj. Jaspeado, da; veteado, da.
marc [mɑ:k] n. Orujo, *m.*
marcasite [ˈmɑ:kəsait] n. Marcasita, *f.* (pyrite).
march [mɑ:tʃ] n. Marcha, *f.*: *on the march*, en marcha; *to organize a protest march*, organizar una marcha de protesta. || Paso, *m.*: *double march*, paso gimnástico. || MUS. Marcha, *f.*: *wedding march*, marcha nupcial. || FIG. Marcha, *f.*, adelanto, *m.*, progreso, *m.* (progress). || HIST. Marca, *f.* (border territory). || — *Day's march*, etapa, *f.* || *Forced march*, marcha forzada. || FAM. *To steal a march on*, aventajar a, tomar la delantera a, ganar por la mano a.
march [mɑ:tʃ] v. intr. Marchar, caminar (to walk). || Desfilar (in a procession). || MIL. Hacer una marcha. || FIG. Avanzar, progresar (to advance). || — MIL. *Forward march!* o *quick march!*, ¡de frente!, ¡ar! || *To march away* o *off*, irse. || *To march in*, entrar. || *To march on*, seguir su camino; pasar: *time marches on*, el tiempo pasa. || *To march out*, salir. || MIL. *To march past* o *by*, desfilar. || *To march upon* o *with*, lindar con (territory).
— V. tr. MIL. Hacer marchar, hacer efectuar una marcha. || Llevar andado, marchar (a distance). || *To march s.o. off*, llevarse a uno.
March [mɑ:tʃ] n. Marzo, *m.*: *5th March 1983*, el 5 de marzo de 1983.
marching orders [ˈmɑ:tʃiŋˌɔ:dəz] pl. n. MIL. Orden (*f. sing.*) de ponerse en marcha. || FIG. Despido, *m. sing.* (dismissal). || FIG. *To give s.o. his marching orders*, despedir a uno.
marchioness [ˈmɑ:ʃənis] n. Marquesa, *f.*
marchland [ˈmɑ:tʃlənd] n. Región (*f.*) fronteriza, marca, *f.*
marchpane [ˈmɑ:tʃpein] n. CULIN. Mazapán, *m.*
march-past [ˈmɑ:tʃˈpɑ:st] n. Desfile, *m.*
marconigram [mɑ:ˈkəunigræm] n. Radiograma, *m.*
Marcus [ˈmɑ:kəs] pr. n. Marco, *m.* || *Marcus Aurelius*, Marco Aurelio.
Mardi Gras [ˈmɑ:diˈgrɑ:] n. Martes (*m.*) de Carnaval.
mare [mɛə*] n. Yegua, *f.* (female horse).
mare's nest [ˈmɛəznest] n. FAM. Parto (*m.*) de los montes, descubrimiento (*m.*) ilusorio (worthless discovery). | Engaño, *m.* (hoax).
mare's tail [ˈmɛəzteil] n. BOT. Cola (*f.*) de caballo (aquatic plant). || Cirro, *m.* (cloud).
Margaret [ˈmɑ:gərit] pr. n. Margarita, *f.*
margarine [ˌmɑ:dʒəˈri:n] n. Margarina, *f.*
margarite [ˈmɑ:gəˌrait] n. Margarita, *f.* (pearl).
marge [mɑ:dʒ] n. FAM. Margarina, *f.* (margarine).
margin [ˈmɑ:dʒin] n. Margen, *f.* (of a river). || Lindero, *m.*, linde, *f.* (of a wood). || Margen, *m.*: *in the margin*, al margen; *bottom, head margin*, margen inferior, superior; *the margin of a page*, el margen de una página; *profit margin*, margen de beneficio; *safety margin*, margen de seguridad. || Provisión, *f.*, reserva, *f.* (reserve). || Cobertura, *f.* (in finance). || FIG. Límite, *m.*, margen, *m.* (limit). || — *By a narrow margin*, por un escaso margen. || *To allow s.o. some margin*, dejarle margen a uno.
margin [ˈmɑ:dʒin] v. tr. Dejar un margen a (page). || Poner al margen (notes). || Hacer una reserva de, tener una cobertura de (in finance).
marginal [—əl] adj. Marginal (note, profits). || PHYS. Periférico, ca (rays). || — *Marginal case*, caso (*m.*) marginal, caso (*m.*) límite. || *Marginal stop*, tecla (*f.*) marginal.
marginalia [ˌmɑ:dʒiˈneiljə] pl. n. Notas (*f.*) marginales.
marginalism [ˈmɑ:dʒinəlˌizəm] n. Marginalismo, *m.*
marginate [ˈmɑ:dʒineit] v. tr. Marginar.
margrave [ˈmɑ:greiv] n. Margrave, *m.*
margraviate [mɑ:ˈgreiviit] n. Margraviato, *m.*
margravine [ˈmɑ:grəvi:n] n. Mujer (*f.*) del margrave.
marguerite [ˌmɑ:gəˈri:t] n. Margarita, *f.* (daisy).
Marguerite [ˌmɑ:gəˈri:t] pr. n. Margarita, *f.*
Maria [məˈri:ə] pr. n. María, *f.* || FAM. *Black Maria*, coche (*m.*) celular.
Marian [ˈmɛəriən] adj. Mariano, na; marial (of the Virgin Mary).
Mariana [ˌmɛəriˈænə] pr. n. GEOGR. *Mariana Islands*, islas Marianas.
marianism [ˈmɛəriənizəm] n. Marianismo, *m.*
marianist [ˈmɛəriənist] adj./n. Marianista.
marigold [ˈmærigəuld] n. BOT. Maravilla, *f.*, caléndula, *f.*
marigraph [ˈmærigræf] n. Mareógrafo, *m.*
marijuana [ˌmæriˈhwɑ:nə] n. Marihuana, *f.*, marijuana, *f.*
marimba [məˈrimbə] n. MUS. Marimba, *f.*
marina [məˈri:nə] n. U. S. Puerto (*m.*) deportivo.
marinade [ˌmæriˈneid] n. CULIN. Adobo, *m.*, escabeche, *m.* (for meat). | Escabeche, *m.* (for fish).
marinade [ˌmæriˈneid] or **marinate** [ˈmærineit] v. tr. CULIN. Adobar, escabechar (meat). | Escabechar, marinar (fish).
marine [məˈri:n] adj. MAR. Marino, na: *marine life*, vida marina. | Naval (forces, engineer). | De marina (infantry). | Marítimo, ma (insurance). | Náutico, ca (chart).
— N. Soldado (*m.*) de infantería de marina. || Marina, *f.*: *the merchant marine*, la marina mercante. || Marina, *f.* (painting). || — Pl. Infantería (*f. sing.*) de marina. || FAM. *Tell that to the marines!*, ¡cuéntaselo a tu abuela!
mariner [ˈmærinə*] n. Marinero, *m.*, marino, *m.*
marinism [məˈri:nizəm] n. Marinismo, *m.*
marionette [ˌmæriəˈnet] n. Marioneta, *f.*, títere, *m.*
Marist [ˈmɛərist] adj./n. REL. Marista.
marital [ˈmæritl] adj. Marital. || Matrimonial. || *Marital status*, estado (*m.*) civil.
maritime [ˈmæritaim] adj. Marítimo, ma
marjoram [ˈmɑ:dʒərəm] n. BOT. Mejorana, *f.*
mark [mɑ:k] n. Huella, *f.* (trace): *the tyres left marks on the road*, los neumáticos dejaron huellas en la carretera; *marks of old age*, huellas de la vejez. || Signo, *m.* (sign): *his business shows all the marks of success*, su negocio presenta todos los signos de prosperidad. || Signo, *m.*, señal, *f.*: *as a mark of my esteem*, en señal de mi aprecio. || Señal, *f.*: *it is a mark of good weather*, es señal de buen tiempo. || Marca, *f.* (brand, trademark). || Marca, *f.*, etiqueta, *f.* (label). || Huella, *f.*, señal, *f.*: *marks of a blow*, las huellas de un golpe. || Signo, *m.*, cruz, *f.*: *he cannot write, he makes his mark*, no sabe escribir, firma con un signo. || Mancha, *f.* (stain). || Prueba, *f.*, testimonio, *m.*: *marks of friendship*, pruebas de amistad. || Sello, *m.*: *his works bear his mark*, sus obras llevan su sello. || Signo, *m.*: *punctuation marks*, signos de puntuación; *exclamation mark*, signo de admiración; *question mark*, signo de interrogación. || Llamada, *f.* (asterisk, etc.). || Nota, *f.* (in an examination): *he had a bad mark*, tuvo una mala nota. || Puntuación, *f.*: *what marks did you get?*, ¿qué puntuación sacó? || Cotización, *f.* (stock exchange). || Punto, *m.*: *reference mark*, punto de referencia. || SP. Línea (*f.*) de partida (in a race). | Tanto, *m.* (point of a score). || Objetivo, *m.*, meta, *f.*, blanco, *m.* (target, aim): *to hit the mark*, alcanzar el objetivo. || MAR. Señal, *f.* [de boya o de baliza] (on buoy). || ANAT. Boca (*f.*) del estómago (pit of the stomach). || Boliche, *m.* (bowls). || Nivel, *m.* (level): *water mark*, nivel de agua. || Marco, *m.* (German money). || Picadura, *f.* (of smallpox). || FIG. Nivel, *m.* (standard). || — FIG. *A man of mark*, una persona notable *or* relevante. | *Beside the mark*, fuera de lugar. | *Beyond the mark*, fuera de todo límite. || FAM. *Easy mark*, primo, ma; tonto, ta. || SP. *On your marks!, get set!, go!*, ¡preparados!, ¡listos!, ¡ya! || *Printer's mark*, pie (*m.*) de imprenta. || FIG. *To be near, over, under, wide of the mark*, estar cerca de, por encima de, por debajo de, lejos de la verdad *or* de la realidad. || *To be quick, slow off the mark*, arrancar rápidamente, lentamente (motor), ser rápido, lento (person). || FIG. *To be up to the mark*, estar a la altura (in ability), estar en perfecto estado de salud (in health), estar en forma (on form). | *To come up to the mark*, estar a la altura. || *To fall o to go wide of the mark*, no dar en el blanco (a shot). || FIG. *To hit the mark*, dar en el clavo, acertar. | *To leave one's mark*, dejar su huella. | *To make one's mark*, distinguirse, señalarse. || *To miss the mark*, no dar en el blanco.
mark [mɑ:k] v. tr. Marcar (clothes). || Señalar, indicar (a passage). || Señalar, marcar: *to mark the place with a cross*, señalar el sitio con una cruz. || Poner, señalar [el precio de]: *to mark (the price of) an article*, poner el precio a un artículo. || Poner la marca *or* la etiqueta a (to label). || Señalar: *this event marked the beginning of the revolution*, este suceso señaló el comienzo de la revolución. || Poner una nota, calificar, puntuar: *to mark an exercise*, poner una nota a un ejercicio. || Picar: *his face was marked by smallpox*, tenía la cara picada de viruelas. || Señalar (with a blow). || Indicar, revelar, mostrar: *his silence marked his anger*, su silencio indicaba su enfado. || COMM. Cotizar (stock exchange). || SP. Marcar (to watch a player, to indicate the score): *to mark an opposing player*, marcar a un jugador contrario. || MUS. Llevar, marcar: *to mark the rhythm*, llevar el compás. || Caracterizar: *the friendship which has marked our relations*, la amistad que ha caracterizado nuestras relaciones. || Distinguir, señalar: *the qualities which mark a leader*, las cualidades que distinguen a un dirigente. || Observar: *I marked her closely*, la observé atentamente. || Darse cuenta, observar: *mark that there is a difference*, dese cuenta de que hay una diferencia. || Prestar atención a, fijarse en, escuchar: *mark my words*, fíjese en mis palabras. || Marcar (cards). || — *Mark you, he did say he might be late*, cuidado, que dijo que a lo mejor llegaría tarde. || *To mark down*, rebajar (the price), apuntar, señalar: *he has marked down the items he wants*, ha señalado los artículos que quiere. || *To mark off*, delimitar (to indicate the limit), amojonar, jalonar (a road). || *To mark out*, trazar (boundaries), amojonar, jalonar (field). || *To mark s.o. off* o *out from*, distinguir a uno de. || *To mark s.o. out for*, escoger *or* señalar a uno para, destinar a uno a. || *To mark time*, see TIME. || *To mark up*, aumentar (prices).

— V. intr. Sp. Marcar.
Mark [mɑ:k] pr. n. Marcos, *m.* || *Mark Antony*, Marco Antonio.
markdown [—daun] n. Rebaja, *f.*, disminución, *f.* (of price).
marked [—t] adj. Marcado, da. || Acusado, da; acentuado, da; pronunciado, da: *a marked difference*, una diferencia pronunciada. || Apreciable, notable, sensible: *marked improvement*, mejora apreciable. || Destacado, da (enjoying notoriety). || Fichado, da (regarded with suspicion).
marker [—ə*] n. Marcador, *m.*
market [—it] n. Mercado, *m.* (place): *fish market*, mercado de pescado; *Sunday is market day*, el domingo hay mercado; *to go to market*, ir al mercado. || Salida, *f.*, mercado, *m.* (demand): *how is the market for this product?*, ¿qué salida tiene este producto? || Mercado, *m.* (sale): *open, unofficial market*, mercado libre, paralelo; *foreign exchange market*, mercado de cambios. || Bolsa, *f.* (stock exchange). || Mercado, *m.* (region): *the American market*, el mercado americano. || Fig. Tráfico, *m.* || — *At market price*, al precio del mercado. || *Black market*, mercado negro, estraperlo, *m.* || *Buyer's market*, mercado favorable al comprador. || *Common Market*, Mercado Común. || *Home market*, mercado interior *or* nacional. || *Into* o *on the market*, en venta, en el mercado. || *Market price*, precio (*m.*) de mercado *or* corriente. || *Market value*, valor (*m.*) comercial. || *Overseas market*, mercado exterior. || *Ready market*, fácil venta, *f.*, fácil salida. || *Seller's market*, mercado favorable al vendedor. || *Steady, quiet market*, mercado sostenido, encalmado. || *Stock market*, Bolsa, *f.*, mercado de valores. || *There is a good market for*, hay mucho mercado para, hay una gran demanda de. || *To be in the market for*, ser comprador de, estar dispuesto a comprar. || *To come into the market*, ponerse en venta, salir al mercado. || *To corner the market in*, acaparar el mercado de. || *To flood the market with*, inundar el mercado de. || *To make a market for*, crear un mercado para. || Fig. *To make a market of*, malvender. || *To play the market*, jugar a la Bolsa. || *To put on the market*, poner en venta, sacar al mercado. || *World market*, mercado mundial.
market [—it] v. tr. Poner en venta *or* a la venta, vender (to sell). || Comercializar.
— V. intr. Hacer la compra, ir al mercado (for provisions).
marketable [—itəbl] adj. De fácil venta, vendible. || Comercial.
marketeer [ˌmɑ:kiˈti:ə*] or **marketer** [ˌmɑ:kitə*] n. Vendedor, ra (market dealer, seller). || Partidario (*m.*) del Mercado Común. || *Black marketeer*, estraperlista, *m.* & *f.*
market garden [ˈmɑ:kitˌgɑ:dn] n. Huerto, *m.* (small), huerta, *f.* (large).
market gardener [—ə*] n. Hortelano, *m.*
market gardening [—iŋ] n. Cultivo (*m.*) de hortalizas.
market-gardening [—iŋ] adj. Hortelano, na: *a market-gardening region*, una región hortelana.
marketing [ˈmɑ:kitiŋ] n. Estudio (*m.*) *or* investigación (*f.*) de mercados (market research). || Comercialización, *f.* (of goods).
market order [ˈmɑ:kitˌɔ:də*] n. Orden (*f.*) de compra (to buy). || Orden (*f.*) de venta (to sell).
marketplace [ˈmɑ:kitpleis] n. Mercado, *m.*, plaza, *f.* [del mercado].
market research [ˈmɑ:kitriˈsə:tʃ] n. Estudio (*m.*) de mercados, investigación (*f.*) de mercados.
market town [ˈmɑ:kittaun] n. Mercado, *m.*, población (*f.*) con mercado.
marking [ˈmɑ:kiŋ] n. Marca, *f.*, señal, *f.* (mark). || Marcado, *m.* || Sp. Marcaje, *m.* || Cotización, *f.* (stock exchange) || Pinta, *f.* (on animals, etc.). || Nota, *f.*, calificación, *f.* (at school).
marking gauge [—ˌgeidʒ] n. Gramil, *m.*
marksman [ˈmɑ:ksmən] n. Tirador, *m.*

— Observ. El plural de *marksman* es *marksmen*.

marksmanship [—ʃip] n. Puntería (*f.*) excelente.
markup [ˈmɑ:kʌp] n. Subida, *f.*, alza, *f.*, aumento, *m.* (of prices). || Margen (*m.*) de beneficio (profit margin).
marl [mɑ:l] n. Marga, *f.*
marl [mɑ:l] v. tr. Margar, abonar con marga.
marlinespike or **marlinspike** [ˈmɑ:linˌspaik] n. Mar. Pasador, *m.*
marlpit [ˈmɑ:lpit] n. Margal, *m.*, marguera, *f.*
marmalade [ˈmɑ:məleid] n. Mermelada (*f.*) de naranja amarga.
marmoreal [ˌmɑ:ˈmɔ:rjəl] adj. Marmóreo, a.
marmoset [ˈmɑ:məuzet] n. Tití, *m.* (monkey).
marmot [ˈmɑ:mət] n. Zool. Marmota, *f.*
Maronite [ˈmærənait] adj./n. Maronita.
maroon [məˈru:n] adj. Castaño, ña.
— N. Castaño, *m.* (colour). || Petardo, *m.* (firework). || Cimarrón, *m.* (slave). || Mar. Persona (*f.*) abandonada en una isla desierta.
maroon [məˈru:n] v. tr. Mar. Abandonar en una isla desierta. || Fig. Aislar.
marque [mɑ:k] n. Patente (*f.*) de corso.
marquee [mɑ:ˈki:] n. Gran tienda (*f.*) de campaña (tent). || U. S. Marquesina, *f.* (rooflike projection).
marquess [ˈmɑ:kwis] n. Marqués, *m.*
marquessate [ˈmɑ:kwizit] n. Marquesado, *m.* (dignity, territory).
marquetry or **marqueterie** [ˈmɑ:kitri] n. Marquetería, *f.*, taracea, *f.*
marquis [ˈmɑ:kwis] n. Marqués, *m.*
marquisate [ˈmɑ:kwizit] n. Marquesado, *m.*
marquise [mɑ:ˈki:z] n. Marquesa, *f.* (title). || Lanzadera, *f.* (ring). || Fig. *To put on airs like a marquise*, dárselas de marquesa.

— Observ. Este título nobiliario sólo se aplica a las personas que no son inglesas. A estas últimas se les llama *marchioness*.

marriage [ˈmæridʒ] n. Matrimonio, *m.*: *to take in marriage* o *to contract marriage with*, contraer matrimonio con; *marriage of convenience*, matrimonio de conveniencia *or* de interés; *civil marriage*, matrimonio civil. || Boda, *f.*, casamiento, *m.* (ceremony). || Tute, *m.* (at cards). || Fig. Unión, *f.*, asociación, *f.* (intimate union). || — *By marriage*, político (family): *uncle by marriage*, tío político. || *Marriage by proxy*, matrimonio por poderes. || *Marriage lines* o *certificate of marriage*, partida (*f.*) de matrimonio. || Fam. *Marriage over the broomstick*, matrimonio por detrás de la iglesia. || *Marriage portion*, dote, *f.* || *Non-consummated marriage*, matrimonio rato.
marriageable [—əbl] adj. Casadero, ra; en edad de casarse. || Núbil (age).
married [ˈmærid] adj. Casado, da: *to be married*, estar casado. || De casados, conyugal: *married life*, vida de casados. || Matrimonial: *married state*, estado matrimonial. || — *Married couple*, matrimonio, *m.* || *Married name*, apellido (*m.*) de casada. || *To get married to*, casarse con.
marron glacé [ˈmærənˈglæsei] n. Castaña (*f.*) confitada, "marron (*m.*) glacé".
marrow [ˈmærəu] n. Med. Médula, *f.*: *spinal marrow*, médula espinal. || Culin. Tuétano, *m.* || Fig. Meollo, *m.* (essential part). || — Fig. *To the marrow*, hasta los tuétanos. || *Vegetable marrow*, calabacín, *m.*
marrowbone [—bəun] n. Culin. Hueso (*m.*) con tuétano. || Fam. *On your marrowbones!*, ¡de rodillas!
marrowfat [—fæt] n. Guisante (*m.*) de semilla grande.
marrowless [—lis] adj. Culin. Sin tuétano. || Fig. Poco enérgico, ca; sin nervio.
marry [ˈmæri] v. tr. Casar (to join in marriage): *they were married by the bishop*, los casó el obispo. || Casarse con, casar con (to get married): *he married her last month*, se casó con ella el mes pasado. || Casar: *he married his daughter last month*, casó a su hija el mes pasado; *he married his daughter to a foreigner*, casó a su hija con un extranjero. || Fig. Unir (to join closely). || — *They married each other*, se casaron [los dos]. || Fam. *To marry money*, casarse por interés. || *To marry off*, casar.
— V. intr. Casarse. || — *To marry a second time*, volver a casarse, casarse en segundas nupcias. || *To marry beneath one*, malcasarse. || *To marry into*, emparentar con.
Mars [mɑ:z] pr. n. Marte, *m.* (god, planet).
Marseilles [mɑ:ˈseilz] pr. n. Geogr. Marsella.
marsh [mɑ:ʃ] n. Zona (*f.*) pantanosa, pantano, *m.* (bog). || Marisma, *f.* (near the sea or a river).
— Adj. Pantanoso, sa.
marshal [—əl] n. Mil. Mariscal, *m.* | Comandante (*m.*) supremo, jefe (*m.*) supremo. || Maestro (*m.*) de ceremonias (master of ceremonies). || U. S. Jefe (*m.*) de policía (sheriff). | Oficial (*m.*) de justicia. | Jefe (*m.*) de bomberos.
marshal [—əl] v. tr. Formar (troops). || Poner en orden, ordenar (to arrange in order).
marshalling yard (U. S. **marshaling yard**) [—əliŋjɑ:d] n. Estación (*f.*) de apartado *or* de clasificación (railway).
marshalship [—əlʃip] n. Mariscalato, *m.*, mariscalía, *f.* (rank, position).
marsh fever [—ˈfi:və*] n. Med. Paludismo, *m.*, fiebre (*f.*) palúdica, malaria, *f.*
marsh gas [—gæs] n. Gas (*m.*) de los pantanos, metano, *m.*
marsh hen [—hen] n. Zool. Polla (*f.*) de agua.
marshmallow [—ˈmæləu] n. Bot. Malvavisco, *m.* || Culin. Melcocha, *f.*
marsh marygold [—ˈmærigəuld] n. Bot. Calta, *f.*
marshy [—i] adj. Pantanoso, sa.
marsupial [mɑ:ˈsju:pjəl] adj. Marsupial.
— N. Marsupial, *m.*
mart [mɑ:t] n. Centro (*m.*) comercial (trading centre). || Martillo, *m.* (for auction sale).
marten [ˈmɑ:tin] n. Zool. Marta, *f.*
martial [ˈmɑ:ʃəl] adj. Marcial: *martial law*, ley marcial. || Bélico, ca (war-minded). || Militar: *martial songs*, canciones militares.
Martian [ˈmɑ:ʃjən] adj./n. Marciano, na.
martin [ˈmɑ:tin] n. Vencejo, *m.*, avión, *m.* (bird).
Martin [ˈmɑ:tin] pr. n. Martín, *m.*
martinet [ˌmɑ:tiˈnet] n. Jefe (*m.*) muy autoritario, ordenancista, *m.*, sargento, *m.*
martingale [ˈmɑ:tiŋgeil] n. Gamarra, *f.*, amarra, *f.* (of a horse). || Mar. Moco (*m.*) del bauprés. || Martingala, *f.*, combinación, *f.* (in gambling).
Martinique [ˌmɑ:tiˈni:k] pr. n. Geogr. La Martinica.
Martinmas [ˈmɑ:tinməs] n. Día (*m.*) de San Martín (11th November).

martlet [ˈmɑːtlit] n. ZOOL. Vencejo, *m.*, avión, *m.* (martin).
martyr [ˈmɑːtə*] n. Mártir, *m.* & *f.* || — FIG. *To be a martyr to*, ser víctima de, padecer, estar aquejado de (an illness). | *To make a martyr of o.s.*, dárselas de mártir.
martyr [ˈmɑːtə*] v. tr. Martirizar.
martyrdom [—dəm] n. Martirio, *m.*
martyrize [ˈmɑːtəraiz] v. tr. Martirizar.
martyrology [ˌmɑːtəˈrɔlədʒi] n. Martirologio, *m.*
martyry [ˈmɑːtiri] n. Santuario (*m.*) en honor a un mártir.
marvel [ˈmɑːvəl] n. Maravilla, *f.*: *to work marvels*, hacer maravillas; *what a marvel!*, ¡qué maravilla! || *It's a marvel to me that*, me maravilla que.
marvel [ˈmɑːvəl] v. intr. Maravillarse, asombrarse: *I marvel at his patience*, me maravillo con su paciencia; *I marvel that you should remain so calm*, me maravilla que se quede tan tranquilo.
marvellous (U. S. **marvelous**) [—əs] adj. Maravilloso, sa. || FIG. *Isn't it marvellous?*, ¡qué bien!
marvel-of-Peru [—əvpəˈruː] n. BOT. Dondiego, *m.*, maravilla, *f.*
Marxian [ˈmɑːksjən] adj./n. Marxista.
Marxism [ˈmɑːksizəm] n. Marxismo, *m.*: *Marxism-Leninism*, marxismo-leninismo.
Marxist [ˈmɑːksist] adj./n. Marxista.
Mary [ˈmɛəri] pr. n. María, *f.* || FAM. *Bloody Mary*, vodka (*m.*) con jugo de tomate.
marzipan [ˌmɑːziˈpæn] n. Mazapán, *m.* (sweet).
mascara [mæsˈkɑːrə] n. Rimel, *m.*
mascle [ˈmɑːskl] n. HERALD. Macla, *f.*
mascot [ˈmæskət] n. Mascota, *f.*
masculine [ˈmæskjulin] adj. Masculino, na. || *Masculine rhyme*, rima asonantada.
— N. Masculino, *m.* (gender).
masculinity [ˌmæskjuˈliniti] n. Masculinidad, *f.*
maser [meizə*] n. PHYS. Maser, *m.*
mash [mæʃ] n. CULIN. Puré (*m.*) de patatas. || AGR. Afrecho (*m.*) remojado (animal food). || Malta (*f.*) remojada (in brewing). || Mezcla, *f.* (mixture). || FIG. Papilla, *f.*: *to reduce sth. to mash*, hacer algo papilla. || FAM. *To have a mash on s.o.*, estar encaprichado por alguien.
mash [mæʃ] v. tr. Triturar (to grind). || Machacar (to crush). || Mezclar (to mix). || — *Mashed potatoes*, puré (*m.*) de patatas. || FAM. *To be mashed on s.o.*, estar encaprichado por alguien. || *To mash potatoes*, hacer un puré de patatas.
masher [—ə*] n. FAM. Seductor, *m.*
mask [mɑːsk] n. Máscara, *f.*, careta, *f.* (covering, disguise): *carnival mask*, máscara de carnaval. || Enmascarado, da (person). || Máscara, *f.*: *gas mask*, máscara antigás. || Mascarilla, *f.*: *oxygen mask*, mascarilla de oxígeno; *death mask*, mascarilla mortuoria. || ARCH. Mascarón, *m.* || PHOT. Ocultador, *m.* || — FIG. *To throw off the mask*, quitarse la máscara. | *Under the mask of*, bajo el disfraz de.
mask [mɑːsk] v. tr. Enmascarar. || FIG. Ocultar, disfrazar, disimular. || PHOT. Ocultar, poner un ocultador a. || MIL. Camuflar (a battery). || MED. Poner una mascarilla a. || *To mask one's face*, enmascararse, ponerse una careta.
masked ball [ˈmɑːsktˈbɔːl] n. Baile (*m.*) de disfraces *or* de máscaras.
masker [ˈmɑːskə*] n. Máscara, *f.*, enmascarado, da.
masochism [ˈmæsəukizəm] n. Masoquismo, *m.*
masochist [ˈmæsəukist] n. Masoquista, *m.* & *f.*
masochistic [ˌmæsəuˈkistik] adj. Masoquista.
mason [ˈmeisn] n. Albañil, *m.* (in building industry). || Cantero, *m.* (stonemason).
Mason [ˈmeisn] n. Masón, *m.* (Freemason).
mason [ˈmeisn] v. tr. Mampostear, construir con mampostería.
mason bee [ˈmeisnˌbiː] n. Abeja (*f.*) albañila.
Masonic [məˈsɔnik] adj. Masónico, ca: *Masonic lodge*, logia masónica.
masonry [ˈmeisnri] n. Albañilería, *f.* (trade of a mason). || Fábrica, *f.*, mampostería, *f.*, obra (*f.*) de albañilería (brickwork, stonework).
Masonry [ˈmeisnri] n. Masonería, *f.* (Freemasonry).
masque [mɑːsk] n. THEATR. Mascarada, *f.*
masquerade [ˌmæskəˈreid] n. Mascarada, *f.*, baile (*m.*) de máscaras (ball). || Disfraz, *m.* (costume). || FIG. Farsa, *f.*, mascarada, *f.*
masquerade [ˌmæskəˈreid] v. intr. Disfrazarse (to put on a disguise): *a prince who masquerades as a peasant*, un príncipe que se disfraza de campesino. || Hacerse pasar (*as*, por) [to pretend to be].
mass [mæs] n. PHYS. Masa, *f.*: *the mass of a solid*, la masa de un cuerpo sólido; *critical mass*, masa crítica. || Masa, *f.*: *the lake became a mass of ice*, el lago se convirtió en una masa de hielo. || FIG. Montón, *m.*, cantidad, *f.*: *masses of money*, cantidades de dinero. || Mayoría, *f.*, mayor parte, *f.*: *the mass of Englishmen*, la mayoría de los ingleses. || — FIG. *He was a mass of bruises*, era un puro cardenal. || *In the mass*, en conjunto. || *Mass executions*, ejecuciones en masa. || *The masses*, la masa, las masas. || FIG. *To be a mass of nerves*, ser un manojo de nervios.
Mass [mæs] n. REL. Misa, *f.* || — *Black Mass*, misa negra. || *High Mass*, misa mayor. || *Low Mass*, misa rezada. || *Mass for the dead*, misa de difuntos. || *Midnight Mass*, misa del gallo. || *Morning Mass*, misa del alba. || *Outdoor Mass*, misa de campaña. || *Pontifical Mass*, misa pontifical. || *Requiem* o *funeral Mass*, misa de cuerpo presente. || *Sung Mass*, misa cantada. || *To attend Mass*, ir a misa (to go), oír misa (to hear). || *To go to Mass*, ir a misa. || *To hear Mass*, oír misa. || *To ring for Mass*, tocar a misa. || *To say Mass*, decir misa. || *To serve at Mass*, ayudar a misa. || *To sing* o *to say one's first Mass*, cantar misa (a newly-ordained priest).
mass [mæs] v. tr. Reunir en masa, agrupar. || MIL. Concentrar (troops).
— V. intr. Reunirse en masa, agruparse, congregarse. || MIL. Concentrarse (troops).
massacre [ˈmæsəkə*] n. Matanza, *f.* [*Amer.*, masacre, *f.*] (killing).
massacre [ˈmæsəkə*] v. tr. Matar en masa, hacer una matanza de.
massage [ˈmæsɑːʒ] n. Masaje, *m.*
massage [ˈmæsɑːʒ] v. tr. Dar masajes a.
massé [mæˈsei] n. SP. Massé, *m.* (billiard).
masseter [mæˈsiːtə] n. ANAT. Masetero, *m.*
masseur [mæˈsəː*] n. Masajista, *m.*
masseuse [mæˈsəːz] n. Masajista, *f.*
massif [ˈmæsiːf] n. GEOGR. Macizo, *m.*
massing [ˈmæsiŋ] n. Congregación, *f.* (of persons). || Amontonamiento, *m.* (of things). || MIL. Concentración, *f.* (of troops).
massive [ˈmæsiv] adj. Macizo, za (weighty). || Masivo, va: *a massive price increase*, un aumento masivo de precio. || Macizo, za (gold, silver). || Imponente (large and imposing).
massiveness [—nis] n. Lo macizo, macicez, *f.*
mass media [ˈmæsˈmiːdiə] n. Medios (*m. pl.*) informativos, medios (*m. pl.*) de comunicación de masa (press, radio, etc.).
mass meeting [ˈmæsˈmiːtiŋ] n. Mitin (*m.*) popular.
mass-produce [ˈmæsprəˌdjuːs] v. tr. Fabricar en serie.
mass production [ˈmæsprəˌdʌkʃən] n. Fabricación (*f.*) en serie.
massy [ˈmæsi] adj. Macizo, za.
mast [mɑːst] n. MAR. Palo, *m.*, mástil, *m.* || RAD. Poste, *m.* (post). || TECH. Torre, *f.* || AGR. Bellota, *f.* || — MAR. *Fore-topgallant mast*, mastelerillo (*m.*) de juanete de proa. | *Main-topgallant mast*, mastelerillo (*m.*) de juanete mayor. | *Mizzen-topgallant mast*, mastelero (*m.*) de perico. | *Topgallant mast*, masterillo, *m.* | *To sail before the mast*, servir como marinero.
mast [mɑːst] v. tr. MAR. Arbolar.
mastaba [ˈmæstəbə] n. Mastaba, *f.* (tomb).
master [ˈmɑːstə*] n. Amo, *m.* (of animals, slaves). || Señor, *m.* (of household): *the master of the house*, el señor de la casa. || Jefe, *m.*, patrón, *m.* (of workmen). || Dueño, *m.* (owner). || Maestre, *m.* (of a military order). || Maestro, *m.* (in primary school). || Profesor, *m.* (in secondary school). || Director, *m.* (head of a college). || Licenciado, da (University graduate): *Master of Arts*, licenciado en Letras; *master of sciences*, licenciado en ciencias. (See OBSERV.) || MAR. Capitán, *m.* (of ship). | Patrón, *m.* (of boat). || ARTS. Maestro, *m.* || Maestro, *m.* (in chess). || — *Fencing master*, maestro de armas. || FIG. *He's met his master*, ha dado con la horma de su zapato. | *I am the master now*, ahora mando yo. | *Like master like man*, de tal palo tal astilla. || *Master John Smith*, Señor Don John Smith. || *Master of ceremonies*, maestro de ceremonias (at a formal event), presentador, *m.* (of a show). || *The young master*, el señorito. || *To be a master of*, dominar. || *To be a past master at sth.*, ser experto *or* maestro en algo. || *To be master in one's own house*, mandar en su propia casa. || *To be master of the situation*, ser dueño de la situación. || *To be one's own master*, no depender de nadie. || *To make o.s. master of a situation*, llegar a dominar una situación.
— Adj. Maestro, tra: *master key*, llave maestra. || Principal: *master joint*, junta principal. || Directivo, va; rector, ra (idea). || Original (print, record). || Dominante (passion).

— OBSERV. No hay equivalencia exacta entre los títulos otorgados por las universidades de lengua española y las de gran Bretaña o Estados Unidos. El grado de *Master* se encuentra entre el de licenciado y el de doctor.

master [ˈmɑːstə*] v. tr. Dominar: *to master one's passions*, dominar las pasiones; *to master one's opponent*, dominar a su adversario. || Domar (a horse). || Superar, vencer (difficulties). || Dominar, llegar a ser experto en: *to master a language*, dominar un idioma.
master-at-arms [—rəˈtɑːms] n. MAR. Sargento (*m.*) de marina.

— OBSERV. El plural es *masters-at-arms*.

master builder [—bildə] n. Maestro (*m.*) de obras.
masterful [—ful] adj. Dominante, autoritario, ria (domineering). || Magistral (showing mastery): *a masterful speech*, un discurso magistral.
master hand [—hænd] n. Maestro, tra; experto, ta (expert). || Maestría, *f.* (great skill).
masterliness [—linis] n. Maestría, *f.*
masterly [—li] adj. Magistral, genial: *masterly work*, obra genial. || Maestro, tra: *masterly stroke*, golpe maestro. || *In a masterly manner*, de mano maestra.
master mason [—meisn] n. Maestro (*m.*) de albañilería.

mastermind [—ˌmaind] n. Cerebro, *m.* (person with superior brains).
mastermind [—ˌmaind] v. tr. Ser el cerebro de.
masterpiece [—pi:s] n. Obra (*f.*) maestra.
master's [—z] or **master's degree** [—zdiˈgri:] n. Título (*m.*) universitario entre la licenciatura y el doctorado.
master sergeant [—sɑ:dʒənt] n. MIL. Sargento (*m.*) mayor.
mastership [—ʃip] n. Magisterio, *m.* (position of a schoolmaster). || Maestría, *f.* (ability). || Autoridad, *f.* (dominion). || Dominio, *m.* (of a subject).
masterstroke [—strəuk] n. Golpe (*m.*) maestro.
mastery [—ri] n. Dominio, *m.* (control). || Supremacía, *f.*, superioridad, *f.*, dominio, *m.* (supremacy). || Maestría, *f.* (skill). || *To gain the mastery over*, llegar a dominar.
masthead [ˈmɑ:sthed] n. MAR. Tope, *m.* (highest part of a ship's mast). | Vigía, *m.* (lookout).
masthead [ˈmɑ:sthed] v. tr. MAR. Mandar [a alguien] al tope del palo (a sailor). | Izar (a flag, etc.).
mastic [ˈmæstik] n. Almáciga, *f.* (resin). || BOT. Lentisco, *m.* (tree). || Masilla, *f.* (cement).
masticate [ˈmæstikeit] v. tr. Masticar.
mastication [ˌmæstiˈkeiʃən] n. Masticación, *f.*
masticator [ˈmæstikeitə*] n. Masticador, *m.*
masticatory [ˈmæstikətəri] adj. Masticador, ra; masticatorio, ria.
— N. Masticatorio, *m.*
mastiff [ˈmæstif] n. Mastín, *m.* (dog).
mastitis [mæsˈtaitis] n. MED. Mastitis, *f.*
mastodon [ˈmæstədɔn] n. Mastodonte, *m.*
mastoid [ˈmæstɔid] adj. Mastoideo, a; mastoides. — N. ANAT. Mastoides, *f.*
mastoiditis [ˌmæstɔiˈdaitis] n. MED. Mastoiditis, *f.*
masturbate [ˈmæstə:ˌbeit] v. tr. Masturbar.
— V. intr. Masturbarse.
masturbation [ˌmæstə:ˈbeiʃən] n. Masturbación, *f.*
mat [mæt] n. Estera, *f.* (floor covering). || Felpudo, *m.*, esterilla, *f.* (behind a door). || Salvamanteles, *m. inv.* (table cover). || Tapete, *m.* (under vases, etc.). || Greña, *f.*: *a mat of hair*, una greña de pelo. || MAR. Pallete, *m.* || SP. Colchoneta, *f.* (in gymnastics). || FIG. Maraña, *f.*
mat [mæt] v. tr. Esterar (to cover with mats). || Enredar, enmarañar (to entangle).
— V. intr. Enredarse, enmarañarse (to get entangled).
mat or **matt** [mæt] n. U. S. Orla, *f.* (of a picture). || Superficie (*f.*) mate (of metals). || PRINT. Matriz, *f.*
— Adj. Mate.
mat or **matt** [mæt] v. tr. Deslustrar, poner mate (metal). || Esmerilar (glass).
matador [ˈmætədɔ:*] n. Matador, *m.*, diestro, *m.*
match [mætʃ] n. Igual, *m.* (person or thing equal to another). || Pareja, *f.*: *they are a good match*, hacen una buena pareja. || Matrimonio, *m.* (a marriage). || Partido, *m.* (mate): *he is a good match*, es un buen partido. || SP. Partido, *m.* (of football, tennis). | Combate, *m.* (in boxing). | Encuentro, *m.*, competición, *f.*: *an athletics match*, un encuentro de atletismo. || Fósforo, *m.*, cerilla, *f.*: *a box of matches*, una caja de fósforos. || MIL. Mecha, *f.* || — SP. *Deciding, return match*, partido de desempate, de vuelta. || *To be a bad match*, no hacer juego. || *To be a good match*, hacer juego: *her hat and shoes are a good match*, su sombrero y sus zapatos hacen juego, su sombrero hace juego con sus zapatos. || *To be a match for s.o.*, poder competir con uno. || FIG. *To be more than a match for s.o.*, darle ciento y raya a uno. | *To make a match of it*, casarse. | *To meet one's match*, encontrar la horma de su zapato. || *Wax match*, cerilla, *f.*
match [mætʃ] v. tr. Enfrentar (to bring into competition): *to match s.o. against s.o.*, enfrentar a una persona con otra. || Igualar, equiparar (to equal). || Casar, combinar (colours). || Parear, emparejar (gloves). || Hacer juego con: *the carpet should match the curtains*, la alfombra tendría que hacer juego con las cortinas. || Corresponder a: *his actions don't match his ideas*, sus acciones no corresponden a sus ideas. || Rivalizar con, competir con (to compete): *no one can match him in archery*, nadie puede rivalizar con él en el tiro al arco. || Encajar (to fit). || Casar, unir (to marry). || U. S. Echar al aire (to toss). || — U. S. *I'll match you to see who goes first*, echaremos a suertes quién va el primero. || *To be well matched*, hacer una buena pareja (married people), ser muy iguales (opponents).
— V. intr. Hacer juego: *ribbons that do not match with the dress*, cintas que no hacen juego con el vestido.
matchbox [—bɔks] n. Caja (*f.*) de fósforos *or* de cerillas.
matchet [—it] n. Machete, *m.*
matching [—iŋ] adj. Que hace juego.
— N. Combinación, *f.* (of colours).
matchless [—lis] adj. Incomparable, sin igual, sin par (having no equal).
matchmaker [—ˌmeikə*] n. Casamentero, ra (who arranges marriages). || Fabricante (*m.*) de fósforos (who makes matches). || SP. Organizador, ra.
matchmaking [—ˌmeikiŋ] n. Afición (*f.*) a casar a los demás. || Fabricación (*f.*) de fósforos. || Organización (*f.*) de encuentros deportivos.
matchmark [—mɑ:k] n. Señal, *f.* (on machine parts).
match point [—ˈpɔint] n. SP. Última jugada, *f.*, punto (*m.*) decisivo.
matchwood [—wud] n. Madera (*f.*) para fósforos. || Astillas, *f. pl.* (splinters). || FIG. *To make matchwood of*, hacer trizas.
mate [meit] n. Compañero, ra; camarada, *m.* & *f.* (companion, fellow worker). || Amigo, ga (friend). || Cónyuge, *m.* & *f.*, compañero, ra (spouse). || ZOOL. Macho, *m.*, hembra, *f.* (of animals). || Piloto, *m.* (on a merchant ship). || Ayudante, *m.*: *carpenter's mate*, ayudante de carpintero. || Mate, *m.* (in chess).
mate [meit] v. tr. Dar jaque mate a (in chess). || Aparear, acoplar (animals, birds). || Casar (to marry). || FIG. Hermanar, emparejar.
— V. intr. Acoplarse (animals). || Casarse (to get married). || *Mate!*, ¡jaque mate! (in chess).
maté [ˈmætei] n. Mate, *m.* (plant, tea).
mateless [ˈmeitlis] adj. Solo, la.
matelote [mætˈlɔut] n. CULIN. Guiso (*m.*) de pescado.
mater [ˈmeitə*] n. FAM. Madre, *f.* || ANAT. *Dura mater*, duramáter, *f.*, duramadre, *f.* | *Pia mater*, piamáter, *f.*, piamadre, *f.*
material [məˈtiəriəl] adj. Material (physical): *material necessities*, necesidades materiales. || Materialista: *material point of view*, punto de vista materialista. || Esencial, fundamental (essential): *material facts*, hechos fundamentales. || Profundo, da (change). || Grande, enorme (service). || JUR. Pertinente.
— N. Material, *m.*: *heatproof material*, material refractario. || Tela, *f.*, tejido, *m.* (cloth). || PHYS. Materia, *f.*: *fissionable material*, materia escindible *or* fisible. || MIL. Material: *war material*, material de guerra. || — Pl. Materiales, *m.*: *building materials*, materiales de construcción. || Material, *m. sing.*: *teaching materials*, material escolar. || Artículos, *m.*, objetos, *m.*: *office materials*, artículos de escritorio. || FIG. Hechos, *m.*, datos, *m.*, elementos, *m.* (facts). || — *Advertising material*, material de publicidad. || *Raw material*, materia prima.
materialism [məˈtiəriəlizəm] n. Materialismo, *m.*
materialist [məˈtiəriəlist] adj./n. Materialista.
materialistic [məˌtiəriəˈlistik] adj. Materialista.
materiality [məˌtiəriˈæliti] n. Materialidad, *f.* (being material). || JUR. Importancia, *f.* (importance).
materialization [məˌtiəriəlaiˈzeiʃən] n. Materialización, *f.* (apparition). || Realización, *f.* (realization).
materialize [məˈtiəriəlaiz] v. tr. Realizar, hacer realidad, materializar (plans). || Materializar (a spirit).
— V. intr. Realizarse, concretarse: *his plans never materialized*, sus planes no se realizaron. || Concretarse (ideas). || Materializarse (to appear).
materiel [məˌtiəriˈel] n. MIL. Material, *m.*
maternal [məˈtə:nl] adj. Maternal: *maternal instincts*, instintos maternales. || Materno, na: *maternal uncle*, tío materno.
maternity [məˈtə:niti] n. Maternidad, *f.* || — *Maternity belt*, faja (*f.*) de embarazo. || *Maternity dress*, vestido (*m.*) de maternidad. || *Maternity hospital*, casa (*f.*) de maternidad.
matey [ˈmeiti] adj. Simpático, ca (friendly). || *To get matey with s.o.*, hacerse amigo de alguien.
math [mæθ] n. U. S. FAM. Matemáticas, *f. pl.*
mathematical [ˌmæθiˈmætikəl] adj. Matemático, ca.
mathematically [—i] adv. Matemáticamente. || FIG. Por A más B (to prove).
mathematician [ˌmæθiməˈtiʃən] n. Matemático, ca.
mathematics [ˌmæθiˈmætiks] n. Matemáticas, *f. pl.*: *pure, applied mathematics*, matemáticas puras, aplicadas.
maths [mæθs] pl. n. FAM. Matemáticas, *f.*
matinal [ˈmætənəl] adj. Matinal.
matinée (U. S. **matinee**) [ˈmætinei] n. Primera sesión, *f.* (cinema). || Función (*f.*) de la tarde (theatre). || FAM. *Matinée idol*, ídolo (*m.*) del público.
mating [ˈmeitiŋ] n. Unión, *f.* (of persons). || Acoplamiento, *m.*, apareamiento, *m.* (of animals).
matins [ˈmætins] pl. n. REL. Maitines, *m.*
matrass [ˈmætrəs] n. CHEM. Matraz, *m.*
matriarch [ˈmeitriɑ:k] n. Mujer (*f.*) que manda [en su familia o tribu].
matriarchal [—əl] adj. Matriarcal.
matriarchate [—eit] n. Matriarcado, *m.*
matriarchy [—i] n. Matriarcado, *m.*
matrices [ˈmeitrisi:z] pl. n. Matrices, *f.*
matricidal [ˈmeitrisaidəl] adj. Matricida.
matricide [ˈmeitrisaid] n. Matricidio, *m.* (murder). || Matricida, *m.* & *f.* (murderer).
matriculate [məˈtrikjuleit] v. tr. Matricular.
— V. intr. Matricularse.
matriculation [məˌtrikjuˈleiʃən] n. Matrícula, *f.*, matriculación, *f.* (inscription). || Examen (*m.*) de ingreso (exam).
matrilineal [ˌmeitriˈlinjəl] adj. Por línea materna.
matrimonial [ˌmætriˈməunjəl] adj. Matrimonial.
matrimony [ˈmætriməni] n. Matrimonio, *m.* (wedding). || Vida (*f.*) conyugal (married life).
matrix [ˈmeitriks] n. TECH. Matriz, *f.* (mould). || GEOL. MATH. Matriz, *f.* || ANAT. Matriz, *f.*

— OBSERV. El plural de *matrix* es *matrices.*

matron [ˈmeitrən] n. Matrona, *f.* (elderly lady). || Enfermera (*f.*) jefe (in hospital). || Matrona, *f.* (prison guard). || Ama (*f.*) de llaves (in schools). || *Matron of honour*, dama (*f.*) de honor.

MATHS AND PHYSICS — MATEMÁTICAS (*f. pl.*) Y FÍSICA, *f.*

I. Mathematics. — Matemáticas, *f. pl.*

theorem	teorema *m.*
arithmetic	aritmética *f.*
calculation	cálculo *m.*
operation	operación *f.*
addition	suma *f.*, adición *f.*
sum	total *m.*, suma *f.*
2 plus 1 equals 3	dos más uno son tres
addend	sumando *m.*
plus, minus sign	signo (*m.*) más, menos
subtraction	resta *f.*, sustracción *f.*
4 minus 2 equals 2	cuatro menos dos son dos
remainder	resto *m.*
multiplication	multiplicación *f.*
multiplicand	multiplicando *m.*
multiplier	multiplicador *m.*
4 multiplied by 5, 4 times 5	4 multiplicado por 5
product	producto *m.*
division; divisor	división *f.*; divisor *m.*
dividend	dividendo *m.*
decimal point	coma *f.*
nought point four	cero coma cuatro, cero con cuatro
fraction	fracción *f.*, quebrado *m.*
ratio; proportion	razón *f.*; proporción *f.*
numerator	numerador *m.*
common denominator	común denominador *m.*
exponent	exponente *m.*
differential calculus	cálculo (*m.*) diferencial
integral calculus	cálculo (*m.*) integral
slide rule	regla (*f.*) de cálculo
function; derivative	función *f.*; derivada *f.*
power	potencia *f.*
to raise to the power of five	elevar a la quinta potencia
x squared	x al cuadrado
cube; three cubed	cubo *m.*; tres al cubo
to the fourth power *o* the power of four	elevado a cuatro *or* a la cuarta potencia
square, cube root	raíz (*f.*) cuadrada, cúbica
rule of three	regla (*f.*) de tres
logarithm	logaritmo *m.*
logarithm table	tabla (*f.*) de logaritmos
algebra	álgebra *f.*
equation	ecuación *f.*
unknown	incógnita *f.*
simple, quadratic, cubic equation	ecuación (*f.*) de primer, de segundo, de tercer grado
plane, solid, descriptive geometry	geometría (*f.*) plana, sólida, descriptiva
space	espacio *m.*
area	superficie *f.*, área *f.*
line; point	línea *f.*; punto *m.*
point	punto *m.*
circle	círculo *m.*
centre [U.S., center]	centro *m.*
circumference	circunferencia *f.*
arc; radius	arco *m.*; radio *m.*
diameter	diámetro *m.*
degree	grado *m.*
parallel	paralelo *m.*
polygon	polígono *m.*
equilateral, isosceles, scalene, right-angled triangle	triángulo (*m.*) equilátero, isósceles, escaleno, rectángulo
base; side	base *f.*; lado *m.*
hypothenuse	hipotenusa *f.*
quadrilateral	cuadrilátero *m.*
rectangle; square	rectángulo *m.*; cuadrado *m.*
trapezium	trapecio *m.*
rhomb, rhombus	rombo *m.*
ellipse	elipse *f.*
acute, right, obtuse angle	ángulo (*m.*) agudo, recto, obtuso
cube	cubo *m.*
sphere; cylinder	esfera *f.*; cilindro *m.*
cone	cono *m.*
pyramid; prism	pirámide *f.*; prisma *m.*
frustum	tronco *m.*
opposite	opuesto, ta
similar	semejante
rectangular, right-angled	rectangular
equidistant	equidistante
infinity	infinito *m.*

II. Mechanics. — Mecánica, *f.*

matter	materia *f.*
energy	energía *f.*
vacuum	vacío *m.*
liquid; solid; fluid	líquido *m.*; sólido *m.*; fluido *m.*
body; mass	cuerpo *m.*; masa *f.*
weight; density	peso *m.*; densidad *f.*
specific gravity	peso (*m.*) específico
gravity	gravedad *f.*
velocity	velocidad *f.*
kinetic energy	energía (*f.*) cinética
intensity	intensidad *f.*
friction	fricción *f.*
pressure	presión *f.*
to exert a force	ejercer una fuerza
vector	vector *m.*
work	trabajo *m.*
temperature; heat	temperatura *f.*; calor *m.*
conduction	conducción *f.*
conductor	conductor *m.*
radiation	radiación *f.*
expansion	expansión *f.* (of gas), dilatación *f.* (of metal)
quantum theory	teoría (*f.*) de los quanta *or* de los cuanta *or* cuántica
dynamics; kinematics	dinámica *f.*; cinemática *f.*
kinetics; statics	cinética *f.*; estática *f.*
torque	momento (*m.*) de torsión
axis of rotation	eje (*m.*) de rotación
moment of inertia	momento (*m.*) de inercia

III. Optics. — Óptica, *f.*

light; ray	luz *f.*; rayo *m.*
source	fuente *f.*
beam	haz *m.* (parallel rays)
diffraction	difracción *f.*
reflection; refraction	reflexión *f.*; refracción *f.*
incident ray	rayo (*m.*) incidente
angle of incidence	ángulo (*m.*) de incidencia
refractive index	índice (*m.*) de refracción
lens; image; focus	lente *f.*; imagen *f.*; foco *m.*
focal point	punto (*m.*) focal
focal length	distancia (*f.*) focal
convergent; divergent	convergente; divergente
concave; convex	cóncavo, va; convexo, xa
biconcave, concavo-concave	bicóncavo, va
biconvex, convexo-convex	biconvexo, xa
mirror	espejo *m.*

IV. Magnetics. — Magnetismo, *m.*

magnetism	magnetismo *m.*
magnetic field, flux	campo (*m.*), flujo (*m.*) magnético
magnetic induction	inducción (*f.*) magnética
magnet	imán *m.*
electromagnet	electroimán *m.*
electromagnetic	electromagnético, ca
pole	polo *m.*
coil	bobina *f.*, carrete *m.*

V. Electricity. — Electricidad, *f.*

electric current	corriente (*f.*) eléctrica
electron; proton	electrón *m.*; protón *m.*
positron	positrón *m.*
charge	carga *f.*
positive; negative	positivo, va; negativo, va
electromotive force	fuerza (*f.*) electromotriz
electrode	electrodo *m.*
anode; cathode	ánodo *m.*; cátodo *m.*
electropositive	electropositivo, va
electronegative	electronegativo, va

matronly [—li] adj. De matrona. || FIG. Maduro, ra; de edad.

matt or **matte** [mæt] n./adj./v. tr. See MAT.

matte [mæt] n. TECH. Mata, *f.*

matted [ˈmætəd] adj. Enmarañado, da.

matter [ˈmætə*] n. Materia, *f.*: *mind and matter*, el espíritu y la materia. || Materia, *f.*, sustancia, *f.*: *colouring matter*, materia colorante. || Importancia, *f.* (importance): *it makes no matter*, no tiene importancia. || Asunto, *m.*, cuestión, *f.*: *a matter requiring attention*, un asunto que requiere atención; *it's a matter of great concern to me*, es una cuestión que me preocupa mucho. || Tema, *m.* (of a speech). || Cuestión, *f.*: *it's a matter of taste*, es cuestión de gustos. || MED. Pus, *m.*, materia, *f.* || PHYS. JUR. Materia, *f.* || PRINT. Plomo, *m.* (type). | Material, *m.* || — *As a matter of fact*, en realidad. || *As if nothing was the matter*, como si nada, como si tal cosa. || *As matters stand*, tal y como están las cosas. || *Business matters*, negocios, *m. pl.* || *Form and matter*, forma (*f.*) y fondo. || *For that matter*, respecto a eso. || *Grey matter*, materia gris. || *In all matters of*, en todo lo que se refiere a. || *In the matter of*, en cuanto a, en materia de. || *In this matter*, al respecto. || *It's an easy matter*, es fácil. || *It's no great matter*, no importa, es poca cosa. || *It will be a matter of ten days*, será cosa de diez días. || *Matter of conscience*, caso (*m.*) de conciencia. || *Matter of course*, cosa (*f.*) normal, cosa que cae de su peso. || *Matter of fact*, cuestión de hecho. || *Matter of form*, cuestión de forma. || *Matter of history*, hecho histórico. || *Matter of law*, cuestión de derecho. || *Matter of state*, asunto de Estado. || *No matter*, no importa. || *No matter how fast you run*, por mucho que corras. || *No matter how well you do it*, por muy bien que lo hagas. || *Nothing's the matter*, no pasa nada. || *On the matter*, al respecto, sobre eso. || *Printed matter*, impresos, *m. pl.* || *Something must be the matter*, debe de pasar algo. || *That's quite another matter*, eso es harina de otro costal. || *There's sth. the matter*, pasa algo. || *There's sth. the matter with him*, algo le pasa. || *To carry matters too far*, llevar las cosas demasiado lejos. || *To go into the matter*, entrar en materia. || *What matter!*, ¡qué más da!, ¡qué importa! || *What's the matter?*, ¿qué pasa?, ¿qué ocurre? || *What's the matter with going home?*, ¿qué inconveniente hay

en ir a casa? || *What's the matter with you?*, ¿qué te pasa?, ¿qué te ocurre?
matter [ˈmætə*] v. intr. Importar: *it doesn't matter*, no importa; *what does it matter to him?*, ¿qué le importa? || MED. Supurar (to suppurate).
matterful [—ful] adj. Sustancial (book).
matter-of-course [—əvˈkɔːs] adj. Natural (manner). || Que cae de su peso (words). || Normal.
matter-of-fact [—əvˈfækt] adj. Prosaico, ca (prosaic). || Práctico, ca (practical). || Realista (sticking to facts).
Matthew [ˈmæθjuː] pr. n. Mateo, *m.* || REL. *The Gospel according to St. Matthew*, el Evangelio según San Mateo.
matting [ˈmætiŋ] n. Deslustrado, *m.* (dulling). || Superficie (*f.*) mate (dull surface). || Orla, *f.*, marco, *m.* (of a painting). || Estera, *f.* (floor covering). || Enmarañamiento, *m.* (tangle).
mattock [ˈmætək] n. Pico, *m.*, azadón, *m.*
mattrass [ˈmætrəs] n. CHEM. Matraz, *m.* (rounded glass container).
mattress [ˈmætris] n. Colchón, *m.* (for a bed): *wool mattress*, colchón de lana. || Somier, *m.*: *wire mattress*, somier metálico.
maturate [ˈmætjureit] v. intr. Madurar.
maturation [mætjuˈreiʃən] n. Maduración, *f.*
mature [məˈtjuə*] adj. Maduro, ra: *a mature person*, una persona madura; *a mature fruit*, una fruta madura. || Madurado, da; pensado, da: *a mature decision*, una decisión madurada. || Largo, ga: *after mature deliberations*, después de largas deliberaciones. || COMM. Vencido, da (in finance).
mature [məˈtjuə*] v. tr. Madurar.
— V. intr. Madurar. || COMM. Vencer.
maturing [—riŋ] n. Maduramiento, *m.*
maturity [—riti] n. AGR. FIG. Madurez, *f.* || COMM. Vencimiento, *m.*
matutinal [ˌmætjuːˈtainl] adj. Matutino, na.
maud [mɔːd] n. Manta (*f.*) escocesa.
maudlin [—lin] adj. Llorón, ona: *maudlin voice*, voz llorona. || Sensiblero, ra (weakly sentimental).
maul [mɔːl] n. Mazo, *m.*
maul [mɔːl] v. tr. Herir gravemente (to injure). || Maltratar (to treat roughly). || Vapulear, apalear (to beat). || FIG. Vapulear, dar un palo (to criticize). || FAM. Manosear (to paw). || U. S. Partir con un mazo (wood).
maulstick [—stik] n. ARTS. Tiento, *m.*
maunder [ˈmɔːndə*] v. intr. Divagar (to drivel). || Vagar, errar (to wander).
Maundy [ˈmɔːndi] pr. n. REL. Lavatorio, *m.* || — *Maundy money*, limosna (*f.*) que se da el Jueves Santo. || *Maundy Thursday*, Jueves Santo.
Maurice [ˈmɔris] pr. n. Mauricio, *m.*
Mauritania [ˌmɔriˈteinjə] pr. n. GEOGR. Mauritania, *f.*
Mauritanian [—n] adj./n. Mauritano, na.
Mauritius [məˈriʃəs] pr. n. GEOGR. Mauricio (island).
mauser [ˈmauzə*] n. MIL. Máuser, *m.* (gun).
mausoleum [ˌmɔːsəˈliəm] n. Mausoleo, *m.*

— OBSERV. El plural es *mausoleums* o *mausolea*.

mauve [məuv] n. Malva, *m.*
— Adj. Malva.
maverick [ˈmævrik] n. U. S. FAM. Inconformista, *m.* & *f.* (nonconformist). | Disidente, *m.* & *f.* (of a political party). | Res (*f.*) sin marcar (animal).
mavis [ˈmeivis] n. Tordo, *m.*, zorzal, *m.* (bird).
maw [mɔː] n. ZOOL. Cuajar, *m.* (of a ruminant). | Buche, *m.* (of a granivorous bird). | Fauces, *f. pl.* (of lions). || FAM. *To fill one's maw*, llenarse el buche.
mawkish [—kiʃ] adj. Sensiblero, ra (weakly sentimental). || Empalagoso, sa (cloingly sentimental).
mawkishness [—kiʃnis] n. Sensiblería, *f.* || Lo empalagoso.
maxilla [mækˈsilə] n. ANAT. Maxilar (*m.*) superior.

— OBSERV. El plural de la palabra inglesa *maxilla* es *maxillae* o *maxillas*.

maxillary [—əri] adj. ANAT. Maxilar.
— N. Maxilar, *m.* (bone).
maxim [ˈmæksim] n. Máxima, *f.*
maximal [—əl] adj. Máximo, ma.
maximize [ˈmæksimaiz] v. tr. Llevar al máximo.
maximum [ˈmæksiməm] n. Máximo, *m.*: *law of maxima*, ley de los máximos; *production reached a maximum*, la producción llegó al máximo. || *To the maximum*, al máximo.
— Adj. Máximo, ma: *maximum temperature*, temperatura máxima.

— OBSERV. El plural de *maximum* es *maxima* o *maximums*.

maxiskirt [ˈmæksiˌskəːt] n. Maxifalda, *f.*
maxwell [ˈmækswəl] n. PHYS. Maxvelio, *m.*, maxwell, *m.* (electromagnetic unit).
May [mei] n. Mayo, *m.*: *first of May*, primero de mayo.
may [mei] n. BOT. Flor (*f.*) del espino (flower of the hawthorn). | Espino, *m.* (hawthorn).
may* [mei] v. auxil. Poder (permission): *you may go now*, se puede ir ahora. || Poder, ser posible (probability): *you may be right*, puede que tengas razón; *it may snow*, es posible que nieve. || Poder (possibility): *he works so that he may eat*, trabaja para poder comer. || — *As you might expect*, como era de esperar. || *Be that as it may*, sea como sea, sea como fuere. || *Come what may*, pase lo que pase. || *How many may you be?*, ¿cuántos van a ser? || *How old may o might she be?*, ¿qué edad puede tener? || *If I may*, si me lo permite. || *If I may say so*, si se me permite. || *I hope it may be true*, espero que sea verdad. || *It may o might be that*, puede ser que *or* podría ser que. || *It may not be true*, puede ser que no sea verdad. || *May he rest in peace!*, ¡que en paz descanse! || *May I?*, ¿se permite? || *May I come in?* — *You may*, ¿puedo pasar? — Sí, por supuesto. || *May I have the pleasure of this dance?*, ¿quiere Ud. concederme este baile? || *May they both be happy!*, ¡ojalá sean felices! || *Might it not be well to warn him?*, ¿no estaría bien que le avisáramos? || *Run as he might he could not overtake me*, por mucho que corrió no me pudo adelantar. || *That's as may be*, puede ser, puede que sea así. || *We may as well stay here*, más vale que nos quedemos aquí. || *Whatever you may say*, por más que diga. || *Will you go?* — *I may*, ¿vas a ir? — Quizás *or* puede ser. || *You might open the window!*, ¡podrías abrir la ventana!

— OBSERV. La contracción de la forma negativa *may not* es *mayn't*. El pretérito de *may* es **might**.

Maya [ˈmæijə] n. Maya, *m.* & *f.* (person). || Maya, *m.* (language).
Mayan [—n] adj./n. Maya.
maybe [ˈmeibiː] adv. Quizá, quizás, tal vez.
May Day [ˈmeidei] n. Primero (*m.*) de Mayo.
Mayday [ˈmeidei] n. Señal (*f.*) de socorro, S.O.S., *m.*
mayflower [ˈmeiˌflauə*] n. BOT. Espino, *m.*
mayfly [ˈmeiflai] n. ZOOL. Cachipolla, *f.*, efímera, *f.*
mayhem [ˈmeihem] n. JUR. Mutilación (*f.*) criminal.
maying [ˈmeiiŋ] n. Celebración (*f.*) del primero de mayo.
mayn't [meint] contraction of *may not*. See MAY.
mayonnaise [ˌmeiəˈneiz] n. CULIN. Mayonesa, *f.*, salsa (*f.*) mahonesa.
mayor [mɛə*] n. Alcalde, *m.* || *Mayor of the palace*, mayordomo (*m.*) de palacio.
mayoralty [ˈmɛərəlti] n. Alcaldía, *f.* (office and term).
mayoress [ˈmɛəris] n. Alcaldesa, *f.*
maypole [ˈmeipəul] n. Mayo, *m.* (pole). || FAM. Zangolotino, *m.*, espingarda, *f.* (tall person).
Mazdaism [ˈmæzdəizəm] n. REL. Mazdeísmo, *m.*
maze [meiz] n. Laberinto, *m.* || FIG. *To be in a maze*, estar perplejo.
maze [meiz] v. tr. Dejar perplejo.
mazer [ˈmeizə*] n. Escudilla, *f.* (drinking bowl).
mazurka [məˈzəːkə] n. MUS. Mazurca, *f.*
mazy [ˈmeizi] adj. Laberíntico, ca. || FIG. Perplejo, ja (person). | Intrincado, da; enmarañado, da (things).
me [miː] pron. Me: *he looked at me*, me miró. || Mí (after preposition): *he came to me*, vino hacia mí; *it's for me*, es para mí. || — *Ah me!*, ¡pobre de mí! || FAM. *It's me*, soy yo. || *With me*, conmigo.
mead [miːd] n. Aguamiel, *f.*, hidromel, *m.* || (Ant.). Prado, *m.*, pradera, *f.* (meadow).
meadow [ˈmedəu] n. Prado, *m.*, pradera, *f.*
meadowsweet [—swiːt] n. BOT. Reina (*f.*) de los prados.
meadowy [—i] adj. Herboso, sa (grassy).
meagre (U. S. **meager**) [ˈmiːgə*] adj. FIG. Exiguo, gua; escaso, sa: *meagre rewards*, exigua recompensa. | Pobre: *a meagre supper*, una cena pobre. | Seco, ca; mediocre (style). | Poco, ca (clothing). || Flaco, ca (thin).
meagreness (U. S. **meagerness**) [—nis] n. Flaqueza, *f.* (thinness). || FIG. Escasez, *f.*
meal [miːl] n. Harina, *f.* (of grain). || Comida, *f.* (food). || *To make a meal of*, comer.
mealie [—i] n. BOT. Maíz, *m.*
mealtime [—taim] n. Hora (*f.*) de comer.
mealworm [—wəːm] n. ZOOL. Gusano (*m.*) de la harina.
mealy [—i] adj. Harinoso, sa (farinaceous). || Descolorido, da; pálido, da (complexion). || Enharinado, da (covered with meal). || Empolvado, da (covered with powder). || Salpicado, da (spotted with a colour). || FAM. Meloso, sa; camandulero, ra (mealymouthed).
mealymouthed [—imauðd] adj. FAM. Camandulero, ra; meloso, sa.
mean [miːn] adj. Medio, dia (average): *mean temperature*, temperatura media. || Mediano, na (quality). || Inferior, mediocre (inferior). || Humilde, pobre (humble). || Tacaño, ña; agarrado, da (stingy). || Mezquino, na (petty): *it's mean of him*, es mezquino de su parte. | Ruin, vil, despreciable: *mean character*, carácter ruin. || Malo, la (bad): *mean opinion*, mala opinión. | Malo, la (unkind). || Avergonzado, da (ashamed). || U. S. Desagradable, pajolero, ra: *mean job*, trabajo pajolero. | Muy malo: *mean weather*, tiempo muy malo. || — *Mean trick*, mala jugada. || *She is no mean cook*, es una cocinera excelente. || U. S. *To feel mean*, encontrarse mal.
— N. Promedio, *m.* (average). || MATH. Media, *f.*: *mean proportional*, media proporcional. || Término (*m.*) medio (middle term). || — Pl. Medios, *m.*, medio, *m. sing.*: *by what means did you get it?*, ¿con qué medios lo conseguiste? || Medio, *m. sing.*, manera, *f. sing.*: *I must find means to do it*, tengo que encontrar la manera de hacerlo. || Medios, *m.*, recursos, *m.*: *economic means*, medios económicos. || Medios, *m.* (of production, transport). || — *A man of means*, un hombre adinerado. || *By all manner of means*, por todos los medios, de todos modos. || *By all means!*, ¡no fal-

taba más!, ¡naturalmente!, ¡por supuesto! || *By all means come when you like*, venga por supuesto cuando quiera, por favor venga cuando quiera. || *By any means*, de cualquier modo. || *By fair means or foul*, por las buenas o por las malas. || *By means of*, por medio de, mediante. || *By no means*, de ningún modo, de ninguna manera (certainly not), nada (far from): *he is by no means a scholar*, no es nada erudito. || *Golden mean*, justo medio. || *The end justifies the means*, el fin justifica los medios. || *To live beyond one's means*, gastar más de lo que se tiene, vivir por encima de sus posibilidades.

mean* [mi:n] v. tr. Tener la intención de, querer: *she didn't mean to force you*, no tenía la intención de forzarte. || Pensar, tener la intención de (to intend): *what do you mean to do?*, ¿qué piensas hacer? || Destinar: *this remark was meant to offend him*, esta observación estaba destinada a molestarle. || Dirigir: *that remark was meant for you*, esta observación estaba dirigida contra usted. || Querer: *I mean you to speak*, quiero que hable. || Significar (to signify, to denote): *the Spanish word "mesa" means "table"*, la palabra española "mesa" significa "table"; *it doesn't mean much*, no significa gran cosa; *I can't tell you what it has meant to me*, no puedo decirle lo que ha significado para mí. || Querer decir: *what do you mean by that?*, ¿qué quieres decir con eso? || Aludir a, referirse a (to refer to): *do you mean him?*, ¿se refiere usted a él? || Suponer, implicar (to involve). || — *He meant it for a joke*, lo dijo en broma. || *This term doesn't mean anything to me*, este término no me suena. || *To be meant for*, servir para (to be for), nacer para (vocation), estar dirigido a (remarks). || *To mean business*, hablar *or* actuar en serio. || *To mean it*, decirlo en serio: *I'm sure you don't mean it*, estoy seguro de que no lo dices en serio. || *To mean well* o *no harm*, tener buenas intenciones. || *Without meaning it*, sin querer.

— OBSERV. Pret. & p. p. ***meant***.

meander [mi'ændə*] n. Meandro, *m.* (of a river). || ARCH. Meandro, *m.* (in Greek ornament). || — Pl. FIG. Meandros, *m.*

meander [mi'ændə*] v. intr. Serpentear (a river). || Vagar, errar (to wander).

meandrous [mi'ændrəs] adj. Sinuoso, sa.

meaning ['mi:niŋ] n. Significado, *m.*, sentido, *m.*: *I don't know the meaning of this word*, no conozco el sentido de esta palabra. || Acepción, *f.*, sentido, *m.*: *the first meaning of a word*, la primera acepción de una palabra. || Intención, *f.*, propósito, *m.* (purpose). || FIG. Significación, *f.* (importance). || — *Double meaning*, doble sentido. || *What's the meaning of?*, ¿qué significa?, ¿qué quiere decir?

— Adj. Significativo, va (expressive): *a meaning smile*, una sonrisa significativa. || Intencionado, da: *well-meaning words*, unas palabras bien intencionadas.

meaningful [—ful] adj. Significativo, va.

meaningless [—lis] adj. Sin sentido, que carece de sentido.

meanness ['mi:nnis] n. Mezquindad, *f.* || Tacañería, *f.* (stinginess). || Humildad, *f.* (humbleness). || Mediocridad, *f.* (mediocrity). || Maldad, *f.* (evil). || Bajeza, *f.*, vileza, *f.* (low character).

means [mi:nz] n. Medio, *m.*: *a means of transport*, un medio de transporte.

meant [ment] pret. & p. p. See MEAN.

meantime ['mi:n'taim] or **meanwhile** ['mi:n'wail] adv. Mientras tanto, entretanto.

— M. *In the meantime*, mientras tanto, entretanto.

measles ['mi:zlz] n. MED. Sarampión, *m.* || VET. Cisticercosis (*f.*) muscular (in pigs). || MED. *German measles*, rubéola, *f.*

measly ['mi:zli] adj. FAM. Ínfimo, ma (very small). || MED. Que tiene sarampión (infected with measles).

measurability [,meʒərə'biliti] n. Mensurabilidad, *f.*

measurable ['meʒərəbl] adj. Mensurable, medible.

measurably [—i] adv. Sensiblemente.

measure ['meʒə*] n. Medida, *f.*: *measure of length*, medida de longitud; *square, cubic measure*, medida de superficie, de volumen; *full measure*, medida exacta. || Medida, *f.* (in dressmaking). || Metro, *m.* (tape measure, yardstick). || JUR. Medida, *f.*: *to take drastic measures*, tomar medidas drásticas. | Proyecto (*m.*) de ley (bill). | Ley, *f.* (act). || FIG. Moderación, *f.*, mesura, *f.* || TECH. Justificación, *f.*, anchura, *f.*, ancho, *m.* (in printing). || MUS. Compás, *m.* || CHEM. Probeta (*f.*) graduada (utensil). || MATH. Divisor, *m.* || POET. Metro, *m.*, medida, *f.* || — Pl. GEOL. Yacimiento, *m. sing.* || — *Beyond* o *out of measure*, excesivamente (exceedingly). || *For good measure*, por añadidura. || *In a large measure*, en gran parte. || *In a measure*, hasta cierto punto, en cierto modo. || *In due measure*, con mesura. || *In great measure*, en gran parte. || *In some measure*, hasta cierto punto. || *Made to measure*, hecho a la medida. || *Sense of measure*, mesura, ponderación, *f.* || FIG. *To give one's measure*, mostrar de lo que uno es capaz. | *To set measures to*, poner coto a. || *To take s.o.'s measure*, tomarle a unos las medidas. || FIG. *To take the measure of*, calibrar.

measure ['meʒə*] v. tr. Medir: *he measured the table*, midió la mesa; *to measure in litres*, medir por litros; *thermometers measure temperature*, los termómetros miden la temperatura. || Tomar las medidas (in dressmaking): *they measured him for a suit*, le tomaron las medidas para un traje. || Medir la estatura de (s.o.). || FIG. Pesar, medir (words). | Sopesar, ponderar (acts). || — FIG. *He measured his length*, midió el suelo, se cayó cuan largo era. || *To measure off*, medir (fabric). || *To measure one's strength* o *o.s. against*, competir con, medirse con. || *To measure out*, medir (a specified length), repartir (to distribute). || *To measure up*, medir (wood).

— V. intr. Medir: *it measures two feet and a half*, mide dos pies y medio. || *To measure up to*, estar a la altura de.

measured [—d] adj. Medido, da (space, time). || Acompasado, da (tread). || Moderado, da; comedido, da; mesurado, da (language). || Prudente (statement). || *With measured steps*, con pasos contados.

measureless [—lis] adj. Sin medida, inmensurable, inconmensurable, inmenso, sa.

measurement [—mənt] n. Medida, *f.*, medición, *f.* (action). || Medida, *f.* (dimension, length). || COMM. Dimensiones, *f. pl.* (of goods). || — Pl. Medidas, *f.* (in dressmaking).

measurer [—rə*] n. Medidor, *m.*

measuring [—riŋ] n. Medición, *f.*, medida, *f.*

measuring chain [—riŋtʃein] n. Cadena (*f.*) de agrimensor.

measuring cup [—riŋ,kʌp] n. Vaso (*m.*) graduado.

measuring tape [—riŋ,teip] n. Cinta (*f.*) métrica.

measuring worm [—riŋ,wə:m] n. ZOOL. Oruga (*f.*) geómetra *or* medidora.

meat [mi:t] n. CULIN. Carne, *f.* (flesh). || Comida, *f.* (food, meal). || FIG. Meollo, *m.*, sustancia, *f.* (the essence, main part). | Materia, *f.* (for reflexion). || — *Cold meat*, fiambre, *m.* || FIG. *It was meat and drink to them*, disfrutaron con ello. | *One man's meat is another man's poison*, lo que es bueno para uno no lo es para todos.

meatball [—bɔ:l] n. Albóndiga, *f.*

meat fly [—flai] n. ZOOL. Moscarda, *f.*, moscón, *m.*

meat grinder [—,graində*] n. Máquina (*f.*) de picar carne.

meat hook [—huk] n. Gancho, *m.*, garabato, *m.*

meatless [—lis] adj. Sin carne. || REL. De vigilia (day).

meatman [—mən] n. U. S. Carnicero, *m.*

— OBSERV. El plural es *meatmen*.

meat pie [—'pai] n. Empanada, *f.*, pastel (*m.*) de carne.

meat safe [—seif] n. Fresquera, *f.*

meatus [mi'eitəs] n. ANAT. Meato, *m.*

— OBSERV. El plural de *meatus* es *meatus* o *meatuses*.

meaty ['mi:ti] adj. Carnoso, sa (fleshy). || Lleno de carne (full of meat). || FIG. Jugoso, sa; sustancioso, sa (full of substance).

Mecca ['mekə] pr. n. REL. La Meca, *f.* || FIG. Lugar (*m.*) predilecto, la meca, *f.*

— OBSERV. Esta palabra no va nunca precedida por el artículo en inglés.

Meccan [—n] adj./n. Mecano, na (from Mecca).

meccano [mi'kɑ:nəu] n. Mecano, *m.* (toy).

mechanic [mi'kænik] n. Mecánico, *m.*

mechanical [—əl] adj. Mecánico, ca (art, power, civilization, engineer). || FIG. Mecánico, ca; maquinal. || *Mechanical drawing*, dibujo (*m.*) industrial.

mechanics [—s] n. PHYS. Mecánica, *f.*: *wave mechanics*, mecánica ondulatoria. || FIG. Mecanismo, *m.*

mechanism ['mekənizəm] n. TECH. FIG. Mecanismo, *m.*: *firing, ejector mechanism*, mecanismo de disparo, de expulsión. || MUS. Técnica, *f.*

mechanist ['mekənist] n. Mecánico, *m.*

mechanistic [mekə'nistik] adj. Mecánico, ca.

mechanization [,mekənai'zeiʃən] n. Mecanización, *f.*

mechanize ['mekənaiz] v. tr. Mecanizar: *mechanized accountancy*, contabilidad mecanizada. || AGR. *Mechanized farming*, motocultivo, *m.*

mechanotherapy [,mekənə'θerəpi] n. MED. Mecanoterapia, *f.*

Mechlin ['meklin] pr. n. GEOGR. Malinas. || *Mechlin lace*, encaje (*m.*) de Malinas, malinas, *f.*

meconium [mi'kəuniəm] n. BIOL. Meconio, *m.*

medal ['medl] n. Medalla, *f.*: *to award s.o. a medal*, conceder una medalla a uno.

medal ['medl] v. tr. Condecorar, poner una medalla.

medalist ['medlist] n. U. S. See MEDALLIST.

medallion [mi'dæljən] n. Medallón, *m.*

medallist ['medlist] n. Medallista, *m.* & *f.* (engraver). || Galardonado *or* premiado con una medalla (recipient of a medal): *gold medallist*, galardonado con una medalla de oro. || Campeón, ona (champion). || Condecorado con una medalla (decorated with a medal).

meddle ['medl] v. intr. *To meddle in*, meterse en, entrometerse en, entremeterse en. || *To meddle with*, meterse en (to interfere), toquetear (to tamper).

meddler [—ə*] n. Entrometido, da; entremetido, da.

meddlesome [—səm] adj. Entrometido, da; entremetido, da.

meddlesomeness [—səmnis] n. Intromisión, *f.*, entrometimiento, *m.*, entremetimiento, *m.*

meddling [—iŋ] adj. Entrometido, da; entremetido, da.

— N. Intromisión, *f.*, entrometimiento, *m.*, entremetimiento, *m.*

Mede [mi:d] n. HIST. Medo, da.
Media [ˈmediə] pr. n. HIST. Media, *f.*
media pl. n. See MEDIUM.
mediaeval [ˌmediˈi:vəl] adj. Medieval.
mediaevalism [—izəm] n. Medievalismo, *m.*
mediaevalist [—ist] n. Medievalista, *m.* & *f.*
medial [ˈmi:djəl] adj. Intermedio, dia; central (in the middle). || Medio, dia (average).
median [ˈmi:djən] adj. Mediano, na
— N. MATH. Mediana, *f.* (line). | Valor (*m.*) mediano (quantity).
Median [ˈmi:djən] adj./n. Medo, da.
mediate [ˈmi:diit] adj. Mediato, ta.
mediate [ˈmi:dieit] v. tr. Ser mediador en, servir de intermediario para llegar a: *to mediate an agreement*, servir de intermediario para llegar a un acuerdo. || Transmitir, comunicar (to convey).
— V. intr. Mediar: *to mediate between two enemies*, mediar entre dos enemigos; *to mediate in an affair*, mediar en un asunto.
mediating [—iŋ] adj. Mediador, ra.
mediation [ˌmi:diˈeiʃən] n. Mediación, *f.*
mediative [ˌmi:diətiv] adj. Mediador, ra.
mediatize [ˈmi:diətaiz] v. tr. Mediatizar.
mediator [ˈmi:dieitə*] n. Mediador, ra.
mediatory [ˈmi:diətəri] adj. Mediador, ra.
mediatress [ˈmi:diətrəs] or **mediatrix** [ˈmi:diətrix] n. Mediadora, *f.*
medic [ˈmedik] n. FAM. Médico, ca (doctor). | Estudiante (*m.*) de medicina (student).
medicable [—əbl] adj. Curable.
medical [—əl] adj. Médico, ca: *medical attention*, asistencia médica; *medical treatment*, tratamiento médico. || De medicina (book, school, student). || — *Medical adviser*, consejero médico. || *Medical consultant*, médico consultor *or* de apelación *or* de consulta. || *Medical corps*, servicio (*m.*) de sanidad. || *Medical examination*, reconocimiento médico. || U. S. *Medical examiner*, médico (*m.*) forense. || *Medical jurisprudence*, medicina (*f.*) legal *or* forense. || *Medical kit*, botiquín, *m.* || *Medical man*, médico, *m.* || MIL. *Medical officer*, médico (*m.*) militar *or* castrense. || *Medical school*, Facultad (*f.*) de Medicina. || *Medical staff*, cuadro médico *or* facultativo.
— N. FAM. Reconocimiento (*m.*) médico.
medicament [meˈdikəmənt] n. Medicamento, *m.*, medicina, *f.*
medicaster [ˈmedikæstə*] n. Medicastro, *m.*, medicucho, *m.*
medicate [ˈmedikeit] v. tr. Medicinar (s.o.).
medicated [—id] adj. Hidrófilo (cotton). || Medicinal (soap, water).
medication [ˌmediˈkeiʃən] n. Medicación, *f.*
medicinal [meˈdisinl] adj. Medicinal.
medicine [ˈmedsin] n. MED. Medicina, *f.* (art, science): *forensic medicine*, medicina forense *or* legal. || Medicina, *f.*, medicamento, *m.* (drug). || Rito (*m.*) *or* objeto (*m.*) mágico (among savages). || FAM. Purga, *f.* || — *Patent medicine*, especifico, *m.* || FIG. *To give s.o. a taste of his own medicine*, pagarle a uno con la misma moneda. | *To take one's medicine*, cargar con las consecuencias.
medicine [ˈmedsin] v. tr. Medicinar, tratar.
medicine ball [—bɔ:l] n. Balón (*m.*) medicinal (heavy stuffed leather ball).
medicine cabinet [—ˈkæbinit] or **medicine chest** [—tʃest] or **medicine cupboard** [—ˌkʌbəd] n. Botiquín, *m.*
medicine man [—mæn] n. Hechicero, *m.* (priestly healer or sorcerer).

— OBSERV. El plural de *medicine man* es *medicine men*.

medico [ˈmedikəu] n. FAM. Médico, *m.* (doctor). | Estudiante (*m.*) de medicina (student).
medico-legal [—ˈli:gəl] adj. Medicolegal.
medieval [ˌmediˈi:vəl] adj. Medieval.
medievalism [—izəm] n. Medievalismo, *m.*
medievalist [—ist] n. Medievalista, *m.* & *f.*
mediocre [ˌmi:diˈəukə*] adj. Mediocre, mediano, na.
mediocrity [ˌmi:diˈɔkriti] n. Mediocridad, *f.*, mediania, *f.* (quality). || Mediocridad, *f.* (person).
meditate [ˈmediteit] v. tr. Meditar: *to meditate a speech*, meditar un discurso. || Planear: *to meditate an incursion*, planear una incursión.
— V. intr. Meditar. || *To meditate on* o *upon*, reflexionar sobre.
meditation [ˌmediˈteiʃən] n. Meditación, *f.*
meditative [ˈmeditətiv] adj. Meditabundo, da.
meditatively [ˈmeditətivli] adv. Con aire meditabundo.
meditator [ˈmediteitə*] n. Pensador, *m.*
Mediterranean [ˌmeditəˈreinjən] adj. Mediterráneo, a: *Mediterranean climate*, clima mediterráneo; *Mediterranean Sea*, Mar Mediterráneo.
— N. GEOGR. Mediterráneo, *m.*
medium [ˈmi:djəm] adj. Mediano, na (height, quality). || RAD. Medio, dia (wave). || CULIN. Medio hecho. || — SP. *Medium distance race*, carrera (*f.*) de medio fondo.
— N. Instrumento, *m.*, medio, *m.* (means). || Término (*m.*) medio (middle quality). || Medio (*m.*) ambiente (environment). || Médium, *m.* & *f.* (spiritualism). || PHYS. BIOL. Medio, *m.* || ARTS. Medio (*m.*) de expresión. || CHEM. Caldo (*m.*) de cultivo (for culture growth). | Agente, *m.* (liquid for suspending pigment). || — Pl. Medios, *m.* [de información]: *advertising media*, medios de publicidad. || — *Happy medium*, justo medio. || COMM. *Medium of exchange*, instrumento *or* medio de cambio. || *Through the medium of*, por medio de.

— OBSERV. El plural de *medium* es *mediums* o *media*.

medium-fine [—fain] adj. Entrefino, na; semifino, na.
medium-hault [—hɔ:l] adj. De distancias medias, continental (aircraft).
medium-sized [—saizd] adj. Mediano, na; de tamaño mediano.
medlar [ˈmedlə*] n. Níspero, *m.* (tree, fruit).
medley [ˈmedli] n. Mezcla, *f.*, mezcolanza, *f.* (mixture). || Miscelánea, *f.* (miscellany). || Confusión, *f.*: *a medley of voices*, una confusión de voces. || MUS. Popurrí, *m.*
— Adj. Mezclado, da (mixed). || Heteróclito, ta (motley). || SP. *Medley relay* o *race*, relevo (*m.*) estilos.
medulla [məˈdʌlə] n. ANAT. BOT. Médula, *f.*: *medulla spinalis*, médula espinal; *medulla oblongata*, médula oblonga.

— OBSERV. El plural de *medulla* es *medullas* o *medullae*.

medullary [—ri] adj. ANAT. BOT. Medular.
medusa [miˈdju:zə] n. (Ant.). Medusa, *f.* (jellyfish).

— OBSERV. El plural de la palabra inglesa *medusa* es *medusae*.

Medusa [miˈdju:zə] n. MYTH. Medusa, *f.*
meed [mi:d] n. Recompensa, *f.* (reward).
meek [mi:k] adj. Dócil, manso, sa (mild). || *As meek as a lamb*, manso como un cordero.
meekness [—nis] n. Docilidad, *f.*, mansedumbre, *f.*
meerschaum [ˈmiəʃəm] n. Espuma (*f.*) de mar (mineral). || Pipa (*f.*) de espuma de mar (pipe).
meet [mi:t] n. Reunión, *f.* (meeting). || Partida (*f.*) de caza (hunt). || SP. Encuentro, *m.*
— Adj. Conveniente (fitting): *it is meet that you go*, es conveniente que vaya.
meet* [mi:t] v. tr. Encontrar, encontrarse a *or* con (to come upon): *to meet s.o. in the street*, encontrarse a uno en la calle. || Entrevistarse con: *the minister will meet his colleague tomorrow*, el ministro se entrevistará con su colega mañana. || Encontrar, tropezar con, encontrarse con: *to meet a problem*, tropezar con un problema. || Ver (to see): *I hope to meet her tomorrow*, espero verla mañana. || Conocer: *I met my wife in Paris*, conocí a mi mujer en París; *I am very pleased to meet you*, estoy encantado de conocerle. || Enfrentarse con: *to meet the enemy*, enfrentarse con el enemigo; *he will meet him in the semifinals*, se enfrentará con él en las semifinales; *to meet a danger*, *a difficulty*, enfrentarse con un peligro, con una dificultad. || Recibir, ir a recibir, ir a buscar: *to meet s.o. at the station*, recibir a alguien en la estación. || Cruzarse con (to come across): *here the road meets the railway*, la carretera se cruza aquí con la vía férrea; *to meet another car*, cruzarse con otro coche. || Confluir con (two rivers). || Desembocar en (streets). || Unirse con: *this road meets the main road a mile from here*, esta carretera se une con la carretera general a una milla de aquí. || Empalmar con, enlazar con: *this flight meets all trains*, este vuelo empalma con todos los trenes. || Satisfacer (demand, need): *it does not meet my desires*, esto no satisface mis deseos; *production can't meet demand*, la producción no puede satisfacer la demanda. || Hacer honor a, cumplir con: *to meet an engagement*, hacer honor a un compromiso. || Cumplir con, satisfacer, llenar: *to meet all the requirements*, satisfacer todos los requisitos. || Cumplir con (obligations). || Conformarse con, acceder a (claims). || Costear, hacer frente a, sufragar, correr con: *I can meet all the expenses*, puedo costear todos los gastos. || Pagar (a bill). || Pagar, satisfacer (debt). || Cubrir (deficit). || Llegar a: *a noise met my ear*, un ruido llegó a mis oídos. || Mirar: *she dared not meet my eye*, no se atrevía a mirarme a los ojos. || Coger, tomar (the bus). || Recibir (a reward). || Responder a (an objection). || — *Meet Mr Warham*, le presento al Señor Warham. || *Pleased to meet you!*, ¡mucho gusto!, ¡encantado de conocerle! || *There is more to it than meets the eye*, hay más de lo que parece a primera vista, aquí hay gato encerrado. || *To arrange to meet s.o.*, dar cita a uno, citar a uno. || *To meet one's death*, encontrar la muerte, morir. || FIG. *To meet s.o. halfway*, llegar a un arreglo con alguien. || *To meet s.o.'s eye*, tropezar con la mirada de alguien. || *To meet the case*, convenir, ser apropiado. || *To meet the eye*, saltar a la vista.
— V. intr. Encontrarse, verse: *they met in Salford*, se vieron en Salford; *when shall we meet again?*, ¿cuándo nos veremos otra vez? || Conocerse (to become acquainted): *we met yesterday*, nos conocimos ayer. || Reunirse: *the assembly meets in London*, la asamblea se reúne en Londres. || Unirse (to join): *four lines that meet*, cuatro líneas que se unen. || Confluir: *the rivers meet outside the city*, los ríos confluyen en las afueras de la ciudad. || Enfrentarse: *the finalists meet tomorrow*, los finalistas se enfrentan mañana. || Cruzarse: *our eyes met*, nuestras miradas se cruzaron. || — *Extremes meet*, los extremos se tocan. || *To arrange to meet*, citarse, darse cita. || *To*

meet up with, encontrar. || *To meet with*, encontrar, encontrarse con (to encounter), tener (to have), recibir (a refusal), sufrir, experimentar (a loss), sufrir (accident), encontrar (violent death). || *Until we meet again!*, ¡hasta la vista!
— OBSERV. Pret. & p. p. **met.**

meeting [—iŋ] n. Encuentro, *m.* (coming together). || Reunión, *f.*: *a committee meeting*, la reunión de una comisión. || Reunión, *f.*, mitin, *m.* (political). || Sesión, *f.* (of an assembly): *open meeting*, sesión pública; *to open the meeting*, abrir la sesión; *to adjourn* o *to close the meeting*, levantar la sesión; *opening, plenary meeting*, sesión de apertura, plenaria. || Entrevista, *f.*: *the two ministers will have an official meeting tomorrow*, los dos ministros celebrarán una entrevista mañana. || Cita, *f.*: *I had a meeting with the director*, tuve una cita con el director. || Duelo, *m.*, desafío, *m.* (duel). || Confluencia, *f.* (of two rivers). || Empalme, *m.* (of roads). || SP. Reunión (*f.*) hípica. | Encuentro (*m.*) deportivo. || — *The meeting is open* o *is declared open*, se abre la sesión. || *To address the meeting*, tomar la palabra. || *To hold a meeting*, celebrar una sesión *or* una reunión.

meetinghouse [ˈmi:tiŋhaus] n. REL. Templo, *m.*

meeting place [ˈmi:tiŋpleis] n. Lugar (*m.*) de reunión, punto (*m.*) de reunión.

megacephalic [ˌmegəseˈfælik] or **megacephalous** [ˌmegəˈsefələs] adj. Megacéfalo, la.

megacycle [ˈmegəˌsaikl] n. Megaciclo, *m.*

megalith [ˈmegəliθ] n. Megalito, *m.*

megalithic [ˌmegəˈliθik] adj. Megalítico, ca.

megalocephalic [ˌmegələuseˈfælik] or **megalocephalous** [ˌmegələuˈsefələs] adj. Megalocéfalo, la.

megalomania [ˈmegələuˈmeinjə] n. Megalomanía, *f.*

megalomaniac [ˈmegələuˈmeiniæk] adj./n. Megalómano, na.

megaphone [ˈmegəfəun] n. Megáfono, *m.*

megathere [ˈmegəθiə] n. Megaterio, *m.* (fossil).

megaton [ˈmegətʌn] n. PHYS. Megatón, *m.*

megavolt [ˈmegəvəult] n. PHYS. Megavoltio, *m.*

megawatt [ˈmegəwɔt] n. PHYS. Megavatio, *m.*

megohm [ˈmegəum] n. PHYS. Megohmio, *m.*

megrim [ˈmi:grim] n. MED. Jaqueca, *f.* (migraine). || Vértigo, *m.* (in horses). || FIG. Capricho, *m.* (whim). || — Pl. FAM. Moral (*f. sing.*) baja (low spirits).

meharist or **mehariste** [məˈheirist] n. Meharista, *m.*

meiosis [maiˈəusis] n. BIOL. Meiosis, *f.*

Meknès [mekˈnes] pr. n. GEOGR. Mequínez, *m.*

melancholia [ˌmelənˈkəuljə] n. MED. Melancolía, *f.*

melancholiac [ˌmelənˈkəuljək] adj./n. MED. Melancólico, ca.

melancholic [ˌmelənˈkɔlik] adj. Melancólico, ca.

melancholy [ˈmelənkəli] adj. Melancólico, ca: *to make s.o. melancholy*, volver melancólico a uno. || Deprimente, triste (saddening).
— N. Melancolía, *f.*

Melanesia [ˌmeləˈni:zjə] pr. n. GEOGR. Melanesia, *f.*

Melanesian [—n] adj./n. Melanesio, sia.

mélange [meiˈlɑ̃:nʒ] n. Mezcla, *f.*, mezcolanza, *f.*

melba toast [ˈmelbəˈteust] n. U. S. Pan (*m.*) tostado.

Melchior [ˈmelkiɔ:*] pr. n. Melchor, *m.*

meld [meld] v. tr. Cantar, declarar, anunciar (in card games).

mêlée (U. S. **melee**) [ˈmelei] n. Pelea (*f.*) confusa, refriega, *f.* || Lucha, *f.*, conflicto, *m.* (conflict). || Confusión, *f.*

meliorate [ˈmi:liəreit] v. tr./intr. Mejorar.

melioration [ˌmi:liəˈreiʃən] n. Mejora, *f.*, mejoramiento, *m.*

melissa [meˈlisə] n. BOT. Toronjil, *m.*

melliferous [meˈlifərəs] adj. Melífero, ra.

mellifluous [meˈlifluəs] adj. Melifluo, flua: *mellifluous words*, palabras melifluas.

mellow [ˈmeləu] adj. Suave (voice). || Melodioso, sa (instrument). || Suave (colour, light). || Tierno, na (soft). || Maduro, ra (fruit). || Añejo, ja (wine). || Maduro, ra (character). || FAM. Achispado, da (tipsy). || AGR. Mollar (soil).

mellow [ˈmeləu] v. tr. Madurar (people, fruit). || Suavizar (voice, colour, wine). || AGR. Mullir (soil).
— V. intr. Madurar (people, fruit). || Suavizarse (voice, colour, wine).

mellowing [—iŋ] n. Maduración, *f.* (of people, fruit). || Suavización, *f.* (of voice, colour, wine). || AGR. Mullidura, *f.*

mellowness [—nis] n. Madurez, *f.* (of people, fruit). || AGR. Riqueza, *f.* || Suavidad, *f.* (of voice, colour, wine). || Lo melodioso (of an instrument).

melodic [miˈlɔdik] adj. MUS. Melódico, ca.

melodious [miˈləudjəs] adj. MUS. Melodioso, sa.

melodiousness [—nis] n. Lo melodioso (of an instrument). || Melodía, *f.*, armonía, *f.* (of music).

melodist [ˈmelədist] n. MUS. Melodista, *m.*, compositor (*m.*) de melodías.

melodize [—ˈdaiz] v. tr. Poner música a.

melodrama [ˈmeləuˌdrɑ:mə] n. Melodrama, *m.*

melodramatic [ˌmeləudrəˈmætik] adj. Melodramático, ca.

melodramatically [—əli] adv. Melodramáticamente.

melodramatize [ˌmeləuˈdræmətaiz] v. tr. Melodramatizar.

melody [ˈmelədi] n. MUS. Melodía, *f.* || *Melody writer*, melodista, *m.*, compositor (*m.*) de melodías.

melomane [ˈmeləmein] adj. Melómano, na.

melomania [meləˈmeiniə] n. Melomanía, *f.*

melomaniac [meləˈmeiniæk] n. Melómano, na.

melon [ˈmelən] n. BOT. Melón, *m.* (muskmelon). | Sandía, *f.* (watermelon). || U. S. FAM. Ganancias, *f. pl.* (profit). || — *Melon patch*, melonar, *m.* || U. S. FAM. *To cut a melon*, repartir el bacalao.

melopoeia [ˌmeləˈpijə] n. MUS. Melopea, *f.*

melt [melt] n. Colada, *f.* (molten metal). || Fundición, *f.* (melting). || Fusión, *f.*, derretimiento, *m.* (liquefaction).

melt [melt] v. tr. Derretir (to make liquid): *the sun melts the snow*, el sol derrite la nieve. || Fundir (metals). || Disolver (to dissolve). || Mezclar, combinar (to mix). || FIG. Ablandar. || *To melt down*, fundir.
— V. intr. Derretirse (to become liquid). || Disolverse (to dissolve). || Fundirse (metals). || FIG. Derretirse, ablandarse (to be moved). || — FIG. *Butter wouldn't melt in his mouth*, parece que no ha roto un plato en su vida. | *Money melts in his hands*, parece que tiene un boquete en la mano. || *To melt away*, derretirse (snow), fundirse (metal), desvanecerse (confidence), desaparecer (money, person), disiparse (crowd). || *To melt in one's mouth*, derretirse en la boca. || *To melt into*, fundirse en (colours), desaparecer en (to disappear), deshacerse en: *he melted into tears*, se deshizo en lágrimas; confundirse en (distance), mezclarse con (to mix).

melting [—iŋ] n. Fundición, *f.*, fusión, *f.* (of metal). || Derretimiento, *m.*, fusión, *f.* (thawing). || Disolución, *f.* (dissolution).
— Adj. Que se derrite (butter, snow). || Que se funde (metal). || FIG. Enternecedor, ra. || *Melting point*, punto (*m.*) de fusión.

melting pot [—iŋpɔt] n. Crisol, *m.* (crucible). || FIG. Crisol, *m.* (country). | Amalgama (*f.*) de gente (mixed society). || FIG. *To put everything back into the melting pot*, volver a ponerlo todo en tela de juicio.

melton [—ən] n. Muletón, *m.*

meltwater [—ˌwɔ:tə*] n. Aguanieve, *f.*

member [ˈmembə*] n. Miembro, *m.* (person): *a member of the family*, un miembro de la familia. || ANAT. Miembro, *m.* || Miembro, *m.*, socio, *m.* (of a society). || Diputado, *m.* (of Parliament). || MATH. GRAMM. Miembro, *m.* || — *Full-fledged member*, miembro de pleno derecho. || *Life member*, miembro vitalicio. || ANAT. *Male member*, miembro viril. || *Member of Parliament*, diputado, *m.*, miembro del Parlamento (in general), procurador (*m.*) en Cortes (in Spain). || "*Members only*", "sólo para socios". || *Ordinary member of the public*, persona (*f.*) cualquiera, ciudadano, *m.*
— Adj. Miembro: *member state*, Estado miembro.

membership [—ʃip] n. Calidad (*f.*) de miembro. || Calidad (*f.*) de socio. || Número (*m.*) de socios *or* miembros (members). || Ingreso, *m.*: *to apply for membership of the United Nations*, pedir su ingreso en las Naciones Unidas. || — *Membership dues*, cuota (*f.*) de socio. || *Membership is obligatory*, es obligatorio ser miembro. || *To acquire membership*, hacerse miembro *or* socio.

membrane [ˈmembrein] n. Membrana, *f.* (thin tissue).

membranous [memˈbreinəs] adj. Membranoso, sa.

memento [miˈmentəu] n. Recuerdo, *m.* (reminder). || REL. Memento, *m.*

— OBSERV. El plural de la palabra inglesa *memento* es *mementoes* o *mementos.*

memo [ˈmeməu] n. FAM. See MEMORANDUM.

memo book [—buk] n. Agenda, *f.*

memoir [ˈmemwɑ:*] n. Memoria, *f.* || Biografía, *f.*, reseña (*f.*) biográfica (biography). || Nota (*f.*) necrológica (obituary). || — Pl. Memorias, *f.*

memorabilia [ˌmeməraˈbiliə] pl. n. Acontecimientos (*m.*) memorables (events). || Recuerdos, *m.* (things).

memorable [ˈmemərəbl] adj. Memorable.

memorandum [ˌmeməˈrændəm] n. Memorándum, *m.*

— OBSERV. El plural de la palabra inglesa *memorandum* es *memorandums* o *memoranda.*

memorial [miˈmɔ:riəl] adj. Conmemorativo, va (festival, monument). || *Memorial faculty*, facultad (*f.*) de recordar.
— N. Monumento (*m.*) conmemorativo (monument). || Memorial, *m.* (petition). || Recuerdo, *m.* (reminder). || — U.S. *Memorial Day*, Día (*m.*) de conmemoración de los Caídos. || *War memorial*, monumento (*m.*) a los Caídos.

memorialist [—ist] n. Memorialista, *m.*, escritor (*m.*) de memorias.

memorialize [miˈmɔ:riəlaiz] v. tr. Conmemorar (to commemorate). || Solicitar por medio de un memorial (to petition).

memorization [ˌmeməraiˈzeiʃən] or **memorizing** [ˌmeməraiziŋ] n. Memorización, *f.*

memorize [ˈmeməraiz] v. tr. Memorizar, aprender de memoria.

memory [ˈmeməri] n. Memoria, *f.*: *I have a good memory*, tengo buena memoria; *to lose one's memory*, perder la memoria; *it slipped my memory*, se me fue de la memoria. || Recuerdo, *m.*: *memories of childhood*, recuerdos de la infancia; *of happy memory*, de feliz recuerdo. || Memoria, *f.* (of a computer). || — *From memory*, de memoria. || *If my memory serves me*, si mal no recuerdo, si la memoria no me falla. || *In memory* o *to the memory of*, en memoria de. || *Memory* *book*, álbum (*m.*) de recuerdos (scrapbook), álbum (*m.*) de firmas (autograph book). || *To bring away a pleasant memory of*, guardar *or* conservar un recuerdo agradable de. || *To call to memory*, recordar. || *To commit to memory*, aprender de memoria. || *To erase from one's memory*, borrar de la memoria. || *To have a memory like a sieve*, tener una memoria como un colador. || *To keep s.o.'s memory alive*, conservar el recuerdo de alguien. || *To the best of my memory*, que yo recuerde. || *Within living memory*, que se recuerda: *it's the coldest winter within living memory*, es el invierno más frío que se recuerda. || *Within my memory*, que yo recuerde.

Memphite [ˈmemfait] adj./n. Menfita.

men [men] pl. n. See MAN.

menace [ˈmenəs] n. Amenaza, *f.* (threat). || FAM. Pesado, da (nuisance).

menace [ˈmenəs] v. tr./intr. Amenazar.

menacing [—iŋ] adj. Amenazador, ra.

ménage [meˈnɑːʒ] n. Casa, *f.* (household). || Economía (*f.*) doméstica.

menagerie [miˈnædʒəri] n. Casa (*f.*) de fieras.

mend [mend] n. Reparación, *f.* (in roads, china, etc.). || Remiendo, *m.* (patch). || Zurcido, *m.* (darn). || Mejoría, *f.* (improvement). || FIG. *To be on the mend*, estar mejorando.

mend [mend] v. tr. Remendar: *to mend a jacket, shoes*, remendar una chaqueta, unos zapatos. || Zurcir (to darn). || Arreglar, reparar (roads). || Lañar, remendar (china). || Echar carbón a (fire). || Enmendar, corregir (to correct). || Mejorar (to improve): *to mend matters*, mejorar las cosas. || Arreglar: *now we must try and mend the situation*, ahora tenemos que intentar arreglar la situación. || — FIG. *To mend one's pace*, apresurar el paso. | *To mend one's ways*, enmendarse.
— V. intr. Mejorar, mejorarse (from an illness). || FIG. Enmendarse.

mendacious [menˈdeiʃəs] adj. Mendaz, mentiroso, sa.

mendacity [menˈdæsiti] n. Mendacidad, *f.* (quality or state of being mendacious). || Mentira, *f.*, embuste, *m.* (lie).

mendelevium [ˌmendəˈliːvjəm] n. CHEM. Mendelevio, *m.* (radioactive element).

Mendelian [menˈdiːliən] adj. Mendeliano, na.

Mendelianism [—izəm] or **Mendelism** [ˈmendəlizəm] n. Mendelismo, *m.*

mendicancy [ˈmendikənsi] n. Mendicidad, *f.*

mendicant [ˈmendikənt] adj./n. Mendicante, mendigo, ga. || REL. Mendicante: *the mendicant orders*, las órdenes mendicantes.

mendicity [menˈdisiti] n. Mendicidad, *f.*

mending [ˈmendiŋ] n. Reparación, *f.*, arreglo, *m.* (repair). || Zurcido, *m.* (darning). || Ropa (*f.*) por zurcir (clothes).

menfolk [ˈmenfəulk] pl. n. Hombres, *m.*

menhir [ˈmenhiə*] n. Menhir, *m.*

menial [ˈmiːnjəl] adj. Doméstico, ca (suited for a servant). || Bajo, ja (low, mean).
— N. Criado, da (domestic servant). || FIG. Lacayo, *m.* (servile person).

meningeal [məˈnindʒjəl] adj. Meníngeo, a.

meninges [məˈnindʒiːz] pl. n. Meninges, *f.*

meningitis [ˌmeninˈdʒaitis] n. MED. Meningitis, *f.*

— OBSERV. El plural de la palabra inglesa *meningitis* es *meningitides*.

meningococcus [məˌniŋgəuˈkɔkəs] n. MED. Meningococo, *m.*

— OBSERV. El plural es *meningococci*.

meninx [ˈmiːniŋks] n. Meninge, *f.*

— OBSERV. El plural de *meninx* es *meninges*.

menippean [meˈnipiən] adj. Menipeo, a.

meniscus [məˈniskəs] n. Menisco, *m.*

— OBSERV. El plural es *menisci* o *meniscuses*.

Mennonite [ˈmenənait] n. Menonita, *m.*

menopausal [menəuˈpɔːzəl] adj. Menopáusico, ca.

menopause [ˈmenəupɔːz] n. MED. Menopausia, *f.*

Menorca [meˈnɔrkəː] pr. n. GEOGR. Menorca.

menorrhagia [menəˈreidʒiə] n. MED. Menorragia, *f.*

menorrhoea [menəˈriːə] n. Menorrea, *f.*

menses [ˈmensiːz] pl. n. MED. Menstruo, *m. sing.*, reglas, *f.*, menstruación, *f. sing.*

Menshevik [ˈmenʃəvik] n. Menchevique, *m.*

— OBSERV. El plural es *Mensheviki* o *Mensheviks*.

menstrual [ˈmenstruəl] adj. MED. Menstrual: *menstrual cycle*, ciclo menstrual. || Mensual (monthly).

menstruate [ˈmenstrueit] v. intr. MED. Menstruar.

menstruation [ˌmenstruˈeiʃən] n. Menstruación, *f.*

mensurability [ˌmenʃurəˈbiliti] n. Mensurabilidad, *f.*

mensurable [ˈmenʃurəbl] adj. Mensurable, medible.

mensuration [ˌmensjuəˈreiʃən] n. Medida, *f.*, medición, *f.*

mental [ˈmentl] adj. Mental (of the mind): *mental faculties*, facultades mentales; *mental patient*, enfermo mental. || Psiquiátrico, ca: *mental hospital*, hospital psiquiátrico. || De las enfermedades mentales (specialist). || Del mentón (of the chin). || FAM. Chiflado, da; chalado, da (crazy): *she must be a bit mental*, debe de estar un poco chalada. || — *Mental age*, edad (*f.*) mental. || *Mental arithmetic*, cálculo (*m.*) mental. || *Mental deficiency*, deficiencia (*f.*) mental. || *Mental derangement*, alienación (*f.*) mental. || *Mental reservation*, reserva (*f.*) mental. || *Mental retardation*, retraso (*m.*) mental. || *Mental telepathy*, transmisión (*f.*) del pensamiento. || *Mental test*, prueba (*f.*) de inteligencia.

mentality [menˈtæliti] n. Mentalidad, *f.*: *sometimes it is difficult to understand the Spanish mentality*, a veces resulta difícil comprender la mentalidad española; *what a mentality!*, ¡vaya mentalidad!

menthol [ˈmenθɔl] n. CHEM. Mentol, *m.* || *Menthol cigarettes*, cigarrillos mentolados.

mentholated [—eitid] adj. Mentolado, da.

mention [ˈmenʃən] n. Mención, *f.*: *honourable mention*, mención honorífica. || *To make mention of*, hacer mención de, mencionar.

mention [ˈmenʃən] v. tr. Mencionar, hablar de, aludir a: *I avoided mentioning his divorce*, evité hablar de su divorcio. || Mencionar: *I don't want to mention his name*, no quiero mencionar su nombre. || Citar: *he was mentioned in the dispatches*, fue citado en la orden del día. || JUR. Mencionar (in a will) .|| — *Don't mention it*, no lo menciones, no hables de eso (don't speak about it), de nada, no hay de qué (thanks are unnecessary), no hay de qué (apology is unnecessary). || *I'll mention it when I see him*, se lo diré cuando lo vea. || *I need hardly mention that*, huelga decir que. || *Not to mention*, sin mencionar, por no decir nada de, además de. || *Not worth mentioning*, sin importancia. || *To make mention of*, hacer mención de. || *Too numerous to mention*, demasiado numerosos para citarlos aquí.

mentor [ˈmentɔː*] n. Mentor, *m.*

menu [ˈmenjuː] n. Carta, *f.*, lista (*f.*) de platos (a la carte). || Menú, *m.*, minuta, *f.* (fixed meal). || FIG. *What's on the menu?*, ¿qué hay de comer?

meow [miːˈau] n. Maullido, *m.* (sound made by a cat). || Miau, *m.* (onomatopoeia).

meow [miːˈau] v. intr. Maullar.

Mephistophelean or **Mephistophelian** [ˌmefistəˈfiːljən] adj. Mefistofélico, ca.

Mephistopheles [ˌmefisˈtɔfiliːz] pr. n. Mefistófeles, *m.*

mephitic [meˈfitik] adj. Mefítico, ca.

mephitis [meˈfaitis] n. Vapor (*m.*) *or* olor (*m.*) fétido, emanación (*f.*) mefítica.

mercantile [ˈməːkəntail] adj. Mercantil, comercial: *mercantile operation*, operación mercantil. || Comercial (affairs, nation, establishment). || JUR. Mercantil. || MAR. *Mercantile marine*, marina (*f.*) mercante.

mercantilism [ˈməːkəntilizəm] n. Mercantilismo, *m.*

mercantilist [ˈməːkəntilist] n. Mercantilista, *m.* & *f.*

mercedarian [ˌməːsəˈdærjən] n. Mercedario, ria (monk, nun).

mercenary [ˈməːsinəri] adj. Mercenario, ria. || *I have a purely mercenary interest in the matter*, mi interés en el asunto es puramente material.
— N. Mercenario, *m.*

mercer [ˈməːsə*] n. (Ant.). Mercero, ra.

mercerize [ˈməːsəraiz] v. intr. Mercerizar.

mercery [ˈməːsəri] n. Comercio (*m.*) de tejidos de seda (trade). || Tejidos (*m. pl.*) de seda (goods). || Mercería, *f.* (haberdashery).

merchandise [ˈməːtʃəndaiz] n. Mercancías, *f. pl.* [*Amer.*, mercaderías, *f. pl.*].

merchandise [ˈməːtʃəndaiz] v. tr. Comercializar. || Comerciar con *or* en.
— V. intr. Comerciar, negociar.

merchant [ˈməːtʃənt] n. Comerciante, *m.* & *f.*, negociante, *m.* & *f.* (person who directs large-scale trade): *grain merchant*, negociante en granos. || U. S. Comerciante (*m.*) al por menor, detallista, *m.* & *f.*, minorista, *m.* & *f.* (retailer). | Tendero, ra; vendedor, ra (shopkeeper). || Mercader, *m.*: *the Merchant of Venice*, el Mercader de Venecia.
— Adj. Mercante: *merchant marine* o *navy*, marina mercante. || Comercial. || Mercantil: *Law merchant*, derecho mercantil.

merchantable [—əbəl] adj. Comerciable.

merchantman [—mən] n. MAR. Buque (*m.*) mercante.

— OBSERV. El plural es *merchantmen*.

merciful [ˈməːsiful] adj. Clemente, compasivo, va; misericordioso, sa.

mercifulness [—nis] n. Clemencia, *f.*, compasión, *f.*, misericordia, *f.*

merciless [ˈməːsilis] adj. Despiadado, da; sin piedad.

mercilessness [—nis] n. Falta (*f.*) de compasión, crueldad, *f.*

mercurial [məːˈkjuəriəl] adj. CHEM. Mercurial, mercúrico, ca. || Mercurial (pertaining to the god or planet). || FIG. Vivo, va (lively). | Despierto, ta; despabilado, da (quick-witted). | Cambiadizo, za; voluble, versátil (changeable).

mercurialism [—iʒəm] n. MED. Hidrargirismo, *m.*

mercuriality [—iti] n. Viveza, *f.* (liveliness). || Inconstancia, *f.*, carácter (*m.*) cambiadizo.

mercuric [məːˈkjuərik] adj. Mercúrico, ca. || — CHEM. *Mercuric chloride*, cloruro (*m.*) de mercurio. | *Mercuric sulphide*, sulfuro (*m.*) de mercurio.

mercurochrome [məːˈkjuərəuˌkrəum] n. Mercurocromo, *m.*

mercurous [ˈməːkjurəs] adj. CHEM. Mercurioso.

mercury [ˈməːkjuri] n. CHEM. Mercurio, *m.*, azogue, *m.* || — *Mercury arc*, arco (*m.*) de mercurio. || *Mercury barometer*, barómetro (*m.*) de mercurio. || *Mercury chloride*, cloruro (*m.*) de mercurio. || *Mercury-vapour lamp*, lámpara (*f.*) de vapor de mercurio.

Mercury [ˈmə:kjuri] pr. n. Mercurio, *m.* (planet, god).
mercy [ˈmə:si] n. Misericordia, *f.*, clemencia, *f.*, compasión, *f.*: *to beg for mercy*, pedir clemencia. || Suerte, *f.*: *it's a mercy that the doctor arrived in time*, es una suerte que el médico llegara a tiempo. || Merced, *f.*: *at the mercy of*, a merced de. || — *For mercy's sake!*, ¡por piedad! || *I must be thankful for small mercies*, algo tengo que agradecer. || *To have mercy on s.o.*, tener compasión de uno. || FIG. *To leave to the tender mercies of s.o.*, dejar en las manos poco compasivas de alguien. || *To show no mercy to s.o.*, no tener la menor compasión de. || *To throw o.s. on s.o.'s mercy*, abandonarse a la merced de uno. || *Without mercy*, sin piedad, despiadadamente. || *Works of mercy*, obras (*f.*) de caridad.
mercy killing [—ˈkiliŋ] n. Eutanasia, *f.*
mere [miə*] adj. Mero, ra; simple, puro, ra: *mere foolishness*, una simple tontería. || — *A mere glance*, una simple ojeada. || *It's mere trifle*, es una nadería *or* una fruslería. || *It's mere talk*, es pura palabrería. || *She's a mere child*, no es más que una niña, es solamente una niña.
— N. Estanque, *m.* (pond). || Lago, *m.* (lake). || Pantano, *m.* (marsh).
merely [—li] adv. Meramente, simplemente, solamente: *they are not opposite, but merely different*, no son opuestos sino simplemente diferentes. || Sólo, solamente: *I merely asked his name*, sólo pregunté su nombre. || *She merely smiled*, se limitó simplemente a sonreír.
meretricious [ˌmeriˈtriʃəs] adj. De oropel (superficially attractive). || Engañoso, sa (fallacious). || Ampuloso, sa; enfático, ca (style).
meretrix [ˈmeritrix] n. (Ant.). Meretriz, *f.*
merganser [mə:ˈgænsə*] n. Mergo, *m.* (bird).
merge [mə:dʒ] v. tr. Unir (to join). || Fusionar (companies, political parties, etc.). || Fundir (colours).
— V. intr. Unirse (to join together). || Fusionarse: *the three parties have merged*, los tres partidos se han fusionado. || Fundirse: *the green merges into the yellow*, el verde se funde en el amarillo. || *Motorways merge*, empalme (*m.*) de autopistas.
mergence [—əns] n. Fusión, *f.* || Unión, *f.*
merger [—ə*] n. Unión, *f.* (joining). || Fusión, *f.* (of companies, parties).
meridian [məˈridiən] adj. Meridiano, na. || FIG. Máximo, ma.
— N. ASTR. GEOGR. Meridiano, *m.* || FIG. Cenit, *m.*, apogeo, *m.*
meridional [məˈridiənl] adj. Meridional, del sur.
— N. Meridional, *m.* & *f.*
meringue [məˈræŋ] n. CULIN. Merengue, *m.*
merino [məˈri:nəu] adj. Merino, na.
— N. Merino, *m.* (sheep).
merit [ˈmerit] n. Mérito, *m.*: *to treat everyone according to their merits*, tratar a cada uno según sus méritos; *a work of little merit*, una obra de poco mérito. || Cualidad, *f.*: *patience is one of his greatest merits*, la paciencia es una de sus mayores cualidades. || — Pl. JUR. Fondo, *m. sing.*: *to judge the merits of a case*, juzgar el fondo de un caso.
merit [ˈmerit] v. tr. Merecer, ser digno de (to deserve): *he doesn't merit your friendship* no merece tu amistad.
— V. intr. Hacer méritos.
meritorious [ˌmeriˈtɔ:riəs] adj. Meritorio, ria; que tiene mérito.
merlin [ˈmə:lin] n. Esmerejón, *m.* (bird).
Merlin [ˈmə:lin] pr. n. Merlín, *m.*
mermaid [ˈmə:meid] n. Sirena, *f.*
merman [ˈmə:mæn] n. Tritón, *m.*

— OBSERV. El plural de esta palabra es *mermen*.

Merovaeous or **Meroveous** [merəˈvi:əs] pr. n. Meroveo, *m.*
Merovingian [ˌmerəuˈvindʒiən] adj./n. HIST. Merovingio, gia.
merriment [ˈmerimənt] n. Alegría, *f.*, júbilo, *m.* (gaiety). || Risas, *f. pl.* (laughter). || Fiesta, *f.* (festivity). || Diversión, *f.* (entertainment). || *There is no cause for merriment*, no tiene ninguna gracia, no hay por qué alegrarse.
merriness [ˈmerinis] n. Alegría, *f.*, regocijo, *m.*
merry [ˈmeri] adj. Alegre: *he has a merry disposition*, tiene un carácter alegre. || Divertido, da; gracioso, sa: *a merry joke*, un chiste gracioso. || Achispado, da (slightly drunk). || — *Merry Christmas*, Felices Pascuas, Felices Navidades. || *The more the merrier*, cuantos más mejor. || *To make merry*, pasarlo bien, divertirse. || *To make merry over*, burlarse de, reírse de.
Merry-Andrew [—ˈændru:] n. Payaso, *m.*
merry-go-round [—gəuˌraund] n. Tiovivo, *m.*
merrymaker [—ˌmeikə*] n. Juerguista, *m.* & *f.*, parrandero, ra.
merrymaking [—ˌmeikiŋ] n. Diversión, *f.*, fiestas, *f. pl.*
— Adj. Alegre, festivo, va.
merrythought [—θɔ:t] n. Espoleta, *f.* (wishbone).
mésalliance [meˈzæliəns] n. Casamiento (*m.*) desigual, mal casamiento, *m.*
mescal [ˈmeskæl] n. BOT. Mezcal, *m.*
mescaline [ˈmeskəˌli:n] n. CHEM. Mezcalina, *f.*
mesdames [ˈmeidæm] pl. n. Señoras, *f.*
meseems [miˈsi:mz] v. impers. (Ant.) Me parece.

mesencephalon [ˌmesenˈkefəˌlɔn] n. ANAT. Mesencéfalo, *m.*
mesentery [ˈmezəntəri] n. ANAT. Mesenterio, *m.*
mesh [meʃ] n. Malla, *f.*: *fine mesh stocking*, medias de malla fina. || FIG. Red, *f.*: *caught up in a mesh of intrigue*, enmarañado en una red de intrigas. || Engranaje, *m.* (of gears). || — Pl. FIG. Red, *f. sing.* || — TECH. *In mesh*, engranado, da. || *Wire mesh*, tela metálica.
mesh [meʃ] v. tr. Coger con red. || TECH. Engranar (to engage). || Encajar bien (to fit).
— V. intr. Cogerse en la red, enredarse. || TECH. Engranar (to engage). || Encajar (to fit).
meshwork [—wə:k] n. Red. *f.* (network).
mesial [ˈmi:zjəl] adj. BIOL. Mediano, na.
mesmerist [ˈmezmərist] n. Hipnotizador, ra.
mesmerize [ˈmezməraiz] v. tr. Hipnotizar.
mesne [mi:n] adj. JUR. Intermediario, ria.
mesoblast [ˈmesəuˌblɑ:st] n. BIOL. Mesoblasto, *m.*
mesocarp [ˈmesəuˌkɑ:p] n. BOT. Mesocarpo, *m.*, mesocarpio, *m.*
mesocephalic [ˌmesəusəˈfælik] adj. ANAT. Mesocéfalo, la.
mesoderm [ˈmesəuˌdə:m] n. BIOL. Mesodermo, *m.*
Mesolithic [ˌmesəuˈliθik] adj. GEOL. Mesolítico, ca.
— N. GEOL. Mesolítico, *m.*
meson [ˈmi:zɔn] n. PHYS. Mesón, *m.*
Mesopotamia [ˌmesəpəˈteimjə] pr. n. GEOGR. Mesopotamia, *f.*
Mesopotamian [—n] adj./n. Mesopotámico, ca.
mesosphere [ˈmesəusfiə*] n. Mesosfera, *f.*
mesothelium [ˌmesəuˈθi:liəm] n. BIOL. Mesotelio, *m.*

— OBSERV. El plural de *mesothelium* es *mesothelia*.

mesothorax [ˌmesəuˈθɔ:ræks] n. ANAT. Mesotórax, *m.*

—OBSERV. El plural es *mesothoraxes* o *mesothoraces*.

mesotron [ˈmesəutrɔn] n. PHYS. Mesotrón, *m.*
Mesozoic [ˌmesəuˈzəuik] adj. GEOL. Mesozoico, ca.
mess [mes] n. Porquería, *f.*, asquerosidad, *f.*, suciedad, *f.* (dirt). || Porquería, *f.*: *the cat has made a mess on the floor*, el gato ha hecho una porquería en el suelo. || Confusión, *f.*, desorden, *m.* (disorderly state of things): *the room is in a mess*, la habitación está en desorden. || Revoltijo, *m.*, follón, *m.* (disorderly things): *the filing cabinet is a mess*, el fichero está hecho un revoltijo. || Lío, *m.*, follón, *m.* (awkward or confused situation): *his personal life is a mess*, su vida privada es un lío; *to get into a mess*, meterse en un lío; *to get out of a mess*, salir de un lío. || Lío, *m.* (mental): *when I try to speak French I get into an awful mess*, cuando intento hablar francés me armo un lío tremendo. || (Ant.). Ración, *f.*, plato, *m.* (portion of food): *mess of pottage*, plato de lentejas. || MIL. Rancho, *m.* (for soldiers). | Comida, *f.* (officers' food). | Comedor (*m.*) de la tropa (place where meals are taken). || Comida, *f.* (for dogs). || — MIL. *Mess hall*, comedor, *m.* | *Mess tin*, escudilla, *f.* | *Officers' mess*, imperio (*m.*) de oficiales. || *To be in a mess*, estar revuelto *or* desordenado (disorderly), estar metido en un lío (in an awkward situation), estar hecho un lío (confused). || *To make a mess of*, desordenar (to disarrange), ensuciar (to dirty), hacer con los pies (a job), echar a perder (one's life). || *What a mess!*, ¡qué asco!, ¡qué porquería! (something dirty), ¡qué lío!, ¡qué follón! (situation).
mess [mes] v. tr. MIL. Dar el rancho a (to supply with meals). || — *To mess* o *to mess up*, ensuciar (to dirty), desordenar (to disarrange), despeinar (hair), estropear, echar a perder (to spoil). || *To mess s.o. about*, fastidiarle a uno.
— V. intr. MIL. Comer el rancho. || — FAM. *Stop messing about!*, ¡déjate de tonterías! || *To mess about* o *around*, no hacer nada de particular, hacer esto y lo otro: *I spend the weekends messing about in the garden*, paso los fines de semana haciendo esto y lo otro en el jardín. || *To mess about with* o *around with*, entretenerse con: *he likes messing about with cars*, le gusta entretenerse con coches; enredar con: *stop messing around with that gun*, deja de enredar con ese fusil. || *To mess around with s.o. else's wife*, tener un lío con la mujer de otro. || *To mess in* o *with*, entrometerse *or* meterse en.
message [ˈmesidʒ] n. Recado, *m.* (non-official communication from person to person): *may I leave a message?*, ¿puedo dejar un recado? || Encargo, *m.*, recado, *m.* (errand): *to run messages*, hacer los encargos. || Mensaje, *m.* (official or important communication, teaching): *the Gospels are the message of Christ*, los Evangelios son el mensaje de Cristo; *a film with a message for modern youth*, una película con un mensaje para la juventud actual. || FAM. *To get the message*, comprender, caer en la cuenta.
message [ˈmesidʒ] v. tr. Mandar por intermedio de un recadero. || Transmitir por medio de señales.
Messalina [mesəˈlainə] pr. n. Mesalina, *f.*
messenger [ˈmesindʒə*] n. Mensajero, ra: *a messenger of the gods*, un mensajero de los dioses. || Recadero, ra (in an office, bank). || MAR. Virador, *m.* (of a capstan).
Messiah [miˈsaiə] n. Mesías, *m.*
messianic [ˌmesiˈænik] adj. Mesiánico, ca.
Messianism [meˈsaiənizəm] n. Mesianismo, *m.*
messieurs [ˈmesəz] pl. n. Señores, *m.*
messiness [ˈmesinis] n. Desorden, *m.* (disorder). || Suciedad, *f.* (dirtiness).

messmate [ˈmesmeit] n. Compañero (*m.*) de rancho.
Messrs. [ˈmesəz] pl. n. Sres. (abbreviation).
messuage [ˈmeswidʒ] n. JUR. Casa (*f.*) con sus dependencias y tierras.
mess-up [ˈmesʌp] n. FAM. Lío, *m.*, follón, *m.* (confusion): *the ceremony was an awful mess-up*, el acto fue un lío espantoso.
messy [ˈmesi] adj. Desordenado, da; en desorden (disorganized). || Sucio, cia (dirty): *the inside of the car is messy*, el interior del coche está sucio. || Confuso, sa (confused). || Lioso, sa: *a very messy affair*, un asunto muy lioso. || *Prawns are very messy to peel*, las gambas ensucian mucho al pelarlas.
mestiza [mesˈti:zə] n. Mestiza, *f.*
mestization [mestiˈzeiʃən] n. Mestizaje, *m.*
mestizo [mesˈti:zəu] n. Mestizo, za.
met [met] pret & p. p. See MEET.
metabolic [ˌmetəˈbɔlik] adj. Metabólico, ca.
metabolism [meˈtæbəlizəm] n. BIOL. Metabolismo, *m.*
metacarpal [ˌmetəˈkɑ:pl] adj. Metacarpiano, na.
— N. Hueso (*m.*) metacarpiano.
metacarpus [ˌmetəˈkɑ:pəs] n. ANAT. Metacarpo, *m.*
metal [ˈmetl] n. Metal, *m.*: *metal engraver*, grabador en metal. || Grava, *f.* (for surfacing roads). || Balasto, *m.* (of railways). || Vidrio (*m.*) fundido (molten glass). || Plomo, *m.* (printing types). || (Ant.). FIG. See METTLE. || HERALD. Metal, *m.* || — Pl. Rieles, *m.*, railes, *m.* (rails of a railway line). || — *Precious metals*, metales preciosos. || *Sheet metal*, lámina (*f.*) de metal.
metal [ˈmetl] v. tr. Cubrir con metal (to cover with metal). || Cubrir con grava (to surface a road with metal).
metaldehyde [meˈtældihaid] n. CHEM. Metaldehído, *m.*
metaling [ˈmetliŋ] n. Firme, *m.* (of a road).
metallic [miˈtælik] adj. Metálico, ca.
metalliferous [ˌmetəˈlifərəs] adj. Metalífero, ra.
metalling [ˈmetliŋ] n. Firme, *m.* (of a road).
metallization (U. S. **metalization**) [metəlaiˈzeiʃən] n. Metalización, *f.*
metallize (U. S. **metalize**) [ˈmetəlaiz] v. tr. Metalizar (a surface). || Vulcanizar (rubber).
metalloid [ˈmetəlɔid] n. Metaloide, *m.*
metallurgic [metəˈlə:dʒik] adj. Metalúrgico, ca.
metallurgical [—əl] adj. Metalúrgico, ca.
metallurgist [meˈtælədʒist] n. Metalúrgico, *m.*
metallurgy [meˈtælədʒi] n. Metalurgia, *f.*
metalwork [ˈmetəlwə:k] n. Metalistería, *f.*, trabajo (*m.*) del metal (craft). || Objetos (*m. pl.*) de metal.
metalworking [—iŋ] n. Metalistería, *f.*, trabajo (*m.*) del metal.
metamorphic [ˌmetəˈmɔ:fik] adj. Metamórfico, ca.
metamorphism [ˌmetəˈmɔ:fizəm] n. GEOL. Metamorfismo, *m.* || Metamorfosis, *f.* (metamorphosis).
metamorphose [ˌmetəˈmɔ:fəuz] v. tr. Metamorfosear, transformar.
— V. intr. Metamorfosearse, transformarse [*into, to*, en].
metamorphosis [ˌmetəˈmɔ:fəsis] n. BIOL. Metamorfosis, *f.* || Transformación, *f.*, metamorfosis, *f.* (change of character, form, etc.).
— OBSERV. El plural de *metamorphosis* es *metamorphoses.*
metaphase [ˈmetəfeiz] n. BIOL. Metafase, *f.*
metaphor [ˈmetəfə*] n. Metáfora, *f.*
metaphoric [ˌmetəˈfɔrik] or **metaphorical** [—əl] adj. Metafórico, ca.
metaphorize [ˈmetəfəraiz] v. tr. Metaforizar.
metaphrase [ˈmetəfreiz] n. Traducción (*f.*) literal.
metaphrase [ˈmetəfreiz] v. tr. Traducir literalmente.
metaphrastic [metəˈfræstik] adj. Literal.
metaphysical [ˌmetəˈfizikəl] adj. Metafísico, ca.
metaphysician [ˌmetəfiˈziʃən] n. Metafísico, *m.*
metaphysics [ˌmetəˈfiziks] n. Metafísica, *f.*
metaplasm [ˈmetəplæzəm] n. GRAMM. Metaplasmo, *m.*
metapsychic [metəˈsaikik] or **metapsychical** [—əl] adj. Metapsíquico, ca.
metapsychology [ˌmetəsaiˈkɔlədʒi] n. Metapsíquica, *f.*
metastasis [meˈtæstisis] n. Metástasis, *f.*
— OBSERV. El plural de la palabra inglesa es *metastases.*
metatarsal [ˌmetəˈtɑ:səl] adj. ANAT. Metatarsiano, na.
metatarsus [ˌmetəˈtɑ:sis] n. ANAT. Metatarso, *m.*
— OBSERV. El plural de *metatarsus* es *metatarsi.*
metathesis [meˈtæθəsis] n. GRAMM. Metátesis, *f.*
— OBSERV. El plural de *metathesis* es *metatheses.*
metathorax [ˌmetəˈθɔ:ræks] n. ZOOL. Metatórax, *m.*
métayer [ˈmetəiei] n. AGR. Aparcero, *m.*
metazoan [ˌmetəˈzəuən] adj. ZOOL. Metazoario, ria.
— N. Metazoario, *m.*, metazoo, *m.*
mete [mi:t] v. tr. Medir. || — *To mete out*, repartir, distribuir. || *To mete out punishment*, dar un castigo.
metempsychosis [ˌmetempsiˈkəusis] n. Metempsicosis, *f.*
— OBSERV. El plural de *metempsychosis* es *metempsychoses.*
meteor [ˈmi:tjə*] n. Meteoro, *m.*
meteoric [ˌmi:tiˈɔrik] adj. Meteórico, ca. || U. S. Atmosférico, ca (phenomenon). || FIG. Meteórico, ca; fugaz, rápido, da.
meteorism [ˈmi:tjərizəm] n. Meteorismo, *m.*
meteorite [ˈmi:tjərait] n. Meteorito, *m.*
meteoroid [ˈmi:tjərɔid] n. Meteorito, *m.*
meteorologic [ˌmi:tjərəˈlɔdʒik] or **meteorological** [—əl] adj. Meteorológico, ca.
meteorologist [ˌmi:tjəˈrɔlədʒist] n. Meteorólogo, ga; meteorologista, *m.* & *f.*
meteorology [ˌmi:tjəˈrɔlədʒi] n. Meteorología, *f.*
meter [ˈmi:tə*] n. Contador, *m.* (instrument). || U. S. See METRE.
meter [ˈmi:tə*] v. tr. Medir [con contador]. || U. S. Franquear [sellos] (to frank mail).
meterage [—ridʒ] n. Medición (*f.*) con contador.
methane [ˈmi:θein] n. CHEM. Metano, *m.*
methanol [ˈmi:θənɔl] n. CHEM. Metanol, *m.*, alcohol (*m.*) metílico.
methinks [miˈθiŋks] v. impers. Me parece, creo.
— OBSERV. El pret. es ***methought.***
method [ˈmeθəd] n. Método, *m.* [*of*, para]. || Manera, *f.*, modo, *m.* (of payment). || Procedimiento, *m.* (means). || JUR. Modalidad, *f.* (of application). || FIG. *There's method in his madness*, es menos loco de lo que parece.
methodic [miˈθɔdik] or **methodical** [—əl] adj. Metódico, ca.
Methodism [ˈmeθədizəm] n. REL. Metodismo, *m.*
Methodist [ˈmeθədist] adj./n. REL. Metodista.
methodize [ˈmeθədaiz] v. tr. Metodizar, sistematizar.
methodological [ˌmeθədəˈlɔdʒikəl] adj. Metodológico, ca.
methodology [ˌmeθəˈdɔlədʒi] n. Metodología, *f.*
methought [miˈθɔ:t] pret. See METHINKS.
Methuselah [miˈθju:zələ] pr. n. Matusalén, *m.* || FIG. *As old as Methuselah*, más viejo que Matusalén.
methyl [ˈmeθil] n. CHEM. Metilo, *m.* || *Methyl alcohol*, alcohol metílico, metanol, *m.*
methylate [ˈmeθileit] v. tr. Desnaturalizar, mezclar con metanol. || *Methylated spirit*, alcohol desnaturalizado.
methylene [ˈmeθili:n] n. CHEM. Metileno, *m.* || *Methylene blue*, azul (*m.*) de metileno.
methylic [meˈθilik] adj. Metílico, ca.
meticulosity [meˌtikjuˈlɔsiti] n. Meticulosidad, *f.*
meticulous [miˈtikjuləs] adj. Meticuloso, sa.
meticulousness [—nis] n. Meticulosidad, *f.*
métier [ˈmeitjei] n. Oficio, *m.*, profesión, *f.* || Especialidad, *f.*
métis or **metis** [ˈmeitis] n. Mestizo, za.
metol [ˈmetɔl] n. CHEM. Metol, *m.*
metonymical [metəˈnimikəl] adj. Metonímico, ca.
metonymy [miˈtɔnimi] n. Metonimia, *f.*
metope [ˈmetəup] n. ARCH. Metopa, *f.*
metre [ˈmi:tə*] n. Metro, *m.* (measure, rhythmic pattern): *square, cubic metre*, metro cuadrado, cúbico; *to measure in metres*, medir por metros.
metric [ˈmetrik] adj. Métrico, ca: *metric ton*, tonelada métrica. || *Metric system*, sistema métrico.
metrical [—əl] adj. Métrico, ca.
metrics [—s] n. POET. Métrica, *f.*
metrification [ˌmetrifiˈkeiʃən] n. Metrificación, *f.*
metrify [ˈmetrifai] v. tr. Metrificar.
metrist [ˈmetrist] n. Versificador, ra; metrificador, ra.
metritis [meˈtraitis] n. MED. Metritis, *f.*
metrology [meˈtrɔlədʒi] n. Metrología, *f.*
metronome [ˈmetrənəum] n. Metrónomo, *m.*
metronymic [ˌmetrəˈnimik] adj. Del apellido materno.
— N. Apellido (*m.*) materno.
metropolis [miˈtrɔpəlis] n. Metrópoli, *f.*
metropolitan [ˌmetrəˈpɔlitən] adj. Metropolitano, na.
— N. REL. Metropolitano, *m.*
mettle [ˈmetl] n. Ánimo, *m.*, valor, *m.*, temple, *m.* || — FIG. *To be on one's mettle*, estar dispuesto a mostrar su valor. | *To put s.o. on his mettle*, picar a uno en su amor propio. | *To show one's mettle*, mostrar lo que uno vale, mostrar su valor.
mettlesome [—səm] adj. Ardiente, fogoso, sa; animoso, sa; valiente.
Meuse [mə:z] pr. n. GEOGR. Mosa, *m.*
mew [mju:] n. Maullido, *m.* (noise made by a cat). || Miau (onomatopoeia). || Grito, *m.* (noise of a gull). || ZOOL. Gaviota, *f.* (gull). || Jaula, *f.* (cage).
mew [mju:] v. intr. Maullar (a cat). || Gritar (a gull). || Mudar (to moult).
— V. tr. Enjaular (to put in a cage).
mewing [—iŋ] n. Maullido, *m.* (of a cat). || Muda, *f.* (moulting).
mewl [mju:l] v. intr. Lloriquear (to whimper). || Maullar (a cat).
mews [mju:z] n. Caballerizas, *f. pl.* (stables). || Callejuela, *f.* (back street).
Mexican [ˈmeksikən] adj./n. Mejicano, na; mexicano, na.
Mexicanism [meksiˈkænizəm] n. Mejicanismo, *m.*, mexicanismo, *m.*
Mexico [ˈmeksikəu] pr. n. GEOGR. Méjico, México. || — *Mexico City*, Méjico *or* México [capital]. || *Gulf of Mexico*, golfo (*m.*) de Méjico *or* de México.
— OBSERV. See MÉXICO (Spanish-English part).
mezzanine [ˈmetsəni:n] n. Entresuelo, *m.* (storey between two main ones). || U. S. Entresuelo, *m.*
mi [mi:] n. MUS. Mi, *m.*
miaow [mi:ˈau] n. Maullido, *m.* (sound made by a cat). || Miau, *m.* (onomatopoeïa).
miaow [mi:ˈau] v. intr. Maullar.
miasma [miˈæzmə] n. Miasma, *m.*

— OBSERV. El plural de la palabra inglesa *miasma* es *miasmas* o *miasmata.* El género de la palabra española « miasma » es masculino aunque se usa a menudo el femenino erróneamente.

miaul [mi'aul] v. intr. Maullar.
mica ['maikə] n. MIN. Mica, *f.*
micaceous [mai'keiʃəs] adj. Micáceo, a.
mice [mais] pl. n. See MOUSE.
micelle [mi'sel] n. BIOL. CHEM. Micela, *f.*
Michael ['maikl] pr. n. Miguel, *m.*
Michaelmas ['miklməs] n. Día (*m.*) de San Miguel (29th September).
Michelangelo [,maikəl'ændʒiləu] pr. n. Miguel Ángel, *m.*
mickey ['miki] n. FAM. *To take the mickey out of,* tomar el pelo a.
mickle ['mikl] n. *Many a little makes a mickle,* muchos pocos hacen un mucho.
microampere [,maikrə'æmpεə*] n. ELECTR. Microamperio, *m.*
microanalysis [,maikrəuə'nælisis] n. CHEM. Microanálisis, *m.*
microbe ['maikrəub] n. Microbio, *m.*
microbial [mai'krəubiəl] or **microbic** [mai'krəubik] adj. Microbiano, na.
microbicidal [mai'krəubəsaidəl] adj. Microbicida.
microbicide [mai'krəubəsaid] n. Microbicida, *m.*
microbiology [,maikrəubai'ɔlədʒi] n. Microbiología, *f.*
microcephalic ['maikrəusə'fælik] or **microcephalous** ['maikrəu'sefələs] adj. Microcéfalo, la.
microcephaly [,maikrəu'sefəli] n. Microcefalia, *f.*
microclimate ['maikrəu,klaimit] n. Microclima, *m.*
microcosm ['maikrəukɔzəm] n. Microcosmo, *m.*
microcosmic ['maikrəu,kɔzmik] adj. Microcósmico, ca.
microfarad [,maikrəu'færəd] n. PHYS. Microfaradio, *m.*
microfilm ['maikrəufilm] n. Microfilm, *m.*, microfilme, *m.* (very small photographic film).
microfilm ['maikrəufilm] v. tr. Microfilmar.
micrography [mai'krɔgrəfi] n. Micrografía, *f.*
microgroove ['maikrəugru:v] n. Microsurco, *m.*
microhm ['maikrəum] n. ELECTR. Microhmio, *m.*, microhm, *m.*
micrometer [mai'krɔmitə*] n. Micrómetro, *m.*
micrometric [maikrə'metrik] or **micrometrical** [—əl] adj. Micrométrico, ca.
micron ['maikrən] n. Micra, *f.*, micrón, *m.*

— OBSERV. El plural de la palabra inglesa es *microns* o *micra.*

Micronesia [,maikrəu'ni:ʃiə] pr. n. GEOGR. Micronesia, *f.*
Micronesian [—n] adj. Micronesio, sia.
— N. Micronesio, sia (person). || Micronesio, *m.* (language).
microorganism ['maikrəu'ɔ:gənizəm] n. Microorganismo, *m.*
microphone ['maikrəfəun] n. Micrófono, *m.*: *to speak through* o *over the microphone,* hablar por el micrófono.
microphotograph ['maikrəu'fəutəgrɑ:f] n. Microfotografía, *f.*
microphotography [,maikrəufə'tɔgrəfi] n. Microfotografía, *f.*
microphysics [,maikrəu'fiziks] n. Microfísica, *f.*
microscope ['maikrəskəup] n. Microscopio, *m.*: *electron microscope,* microscopio electrónico.
microscopic [,maikrəs'kɔpik] or **microscopical** [—əl] adj. Microscópico, ca.
microscopy [mai'krɔskəpi] n. Microscopia, *f.*
microsecond [,maikrəu'sekənd] n. Microsegundo, *m.*
microtherm ['maikrəθə:m] n. Microtermia, *f.*
microwave ['maikrəweiv] n. Onda (*f.*) ultracorta, microonda, *f.*
micturate ['miktjureit] v. intr. Orinar.
micturition [,miktju'riʃən] n. Micción, *f.*
mid [mid] adj. Medio, dia: *the mid afternoon break,* el descanso de media tarde; *in mid journey,* a medio camino; *in mid course,* a media carrera. || GRAMM. Intermedio, dia (vowel). || — *From mid March to mid August,* de mediados de marzo a mediados de agosto. || *In mid air,* entre cielo y tierra, en pleno aire. || *In mid ocean,* en medio del océano.
— Prep. En medio de, entre.

— OBSERV. La palabra *mid* se emplea generalmente en la composición de palabras compuestas como *midday, midnight,* etc.

midbrain [—brein] n. ANAT. Mesencéfalo, *m.*, cerebro (*m.*) medio.
midday [—dei] n. Mediodía, *m.*
— Adj. Del mediodía.
midden [—n] n. Yacimiento (*m.*) arqueológico. || AGR. Muladar, *m.*, estercolero, *m.* (dunghill).
middle [—l] adj. Central, de en medio: *you have to go through the middle door,* tienes que pasar por la puerta de en medio; *middle axle,* eje central. || Intermedio, dia (intermediate). || Mediano, na (middling). || Medio, dia: *of middle height,* de estatura media. || Mediano, na: *middle age,* edad mediana. || ARCH. Medianero, ra (wall). || SP. Medio (weight). || Medio, dia (voice).
— N. Medio, *m.*, mitad, *f.*: *in the middle of the night, of the road,* en medio de la noche, de la calle. || Centro, *m.*: *right in the middle of the target,* en el mismo centro del blanco. || Mitad, *f.*: *cut it down the middle,* córtalo por la mitad. || FAM. Cintura, *f.* (waist): *round the middle,* alrededor de la cintura. || — *In the middle of,* en el centro de, en medio de (in the centre), en pleno: *in the middle of one's work,* en pleno trabajo. || *In the middle of August,* a mediados de agosto. || FAM. *In the middle of nowhere,* en el quinto pino (very far). || *In the very middle of,* en pleno centro de (just in the centre), en medio de: *in the very middle of the night,* en medio de la noche. || *They are in the middle of dinner,* están cenando.
middle ['midl] v. tr. Centrar. || MAR. Doblar en dos. || SP. Centrar.
middle-aged [—'eidʒd] adj. De mediana edad.
Middle Ages [—'eidʒiz] pl. pr. n. Edad (*f. sing*) Media.
middlebrow [—brau] adj. De cultura mediana.
middle class [—'klɑ:s] n. Clase (*f.*) media. || Burguesía, *f.* (bourgeoisie).
middle-class [—klɑ:s] adj. De la clase media. || Burgués, esa (bourgeois).
middle distance [—'distəns] n. ARTS. Segundo término, *m.*, segundo plano, *m.* || SP. Medio fondo, *m.*
middle ear [—iə*] n. ANAT. Oído (*m.*) medio.
Middle East [—'i:st] pr. n. GEOGR. Oriente (*m.*) Medio.
Middle English [—'iŋgliʃ] n. Inglés (*m.*) hablado entre los siglos XII y XV.
middle finger [—'fiŋgə*] n. Dedo (*m.*) medio *or* del corazón.
middleman [—mæn] n. COMM. Intermediario, *m.* || FAM. Alcahuete, *m.* (pimp).

— OBSERV. El plural de esta palabra es *middlemen.*

middlemost [—məust] adj. Central.
middle of the road [—əvðə'rəud] n. Política (*f.*) moderada *or* centrista.
middle-of-the-road [—əvðə'rəud] adj. Centrista, moderado, da (policy).
middle-sized [—'saizd] adj. De tamaño mediano (thing). || De mediana estatura (person).
middle term [—'tə:m] n. Término (*m.*) medio.
middleweight [—weit] n. SP. Peso (*m.*) medio.
middling ['midliŋ] adj. Mediano, na; regular.
— Pl. n. AGR. Acemite, *m. sing.* || COMM. Productos (*m.*) de calidad media.
— Adv. Regular. || *Middling good,* medianamente bueno, regular.
middy ['midi] n. FAM. Guardiamarina, *m.*, guardia (*m.*) marina (midshipman). || U. S. Marinera, *f.* (blouse). || U. S. *Middy blouse,* marinera, *f.*
midge [midʒ] n. Mosca (*f.*) enana.
midget ['midʒit] n. Enano, na (dwarf).
— Adj. Pequeñísimo, ma; en miniatura. || *Midget submarine,* submarino (*m.*) de bolsillo.
Midianite ['midiənait] n. REL. Madianita, *m.*
midland ['midlənd] adj. De tierra adentro, del interior.
— N. Región (*f.*) central. || *The Midlands,* región (*f.*) central de Inglaterra.
midmost ['midməust] adj. Central, en pleno centro.
— Adv. En pleno centro.
— N. Centro, *m.*
midnight ['midnait] adj. De medianoche: *midnight sun,* sol de medianoche. || — *Midnight mass,* misa (*f.*) del gallo. || FAM. *To burn the midnight oil,* quemarse las pestañas.
— N. Medianoche, *f.*
midrib ['midrib] n. BOT. Nervio (*m.*) central (of a leaf).
midriff ['midrif] n. ANAT. Diafragma, *m.* || Traje (*m.*) de dos piezas (woman's garment).
midsection ['mid'sekʃən] n. Sección (*f.*) media.
midship ['midʃip] adj. MAR. En medio del barco. || — *Midship frame,* cuaderna maestra. || *Midship gangway,* crujía, *f.*
midshipman ['midʃipmən] n. MAR. Guardiamarina, *m.*, guardia (*m.*) marina.

— OBSERV. El plural de *midshipman* es *midshipmen.*

midships ['midʃips] adv. MAR. En medio del barco.
midst [midst] n. *In our midst,* entre nosotros. || *In the midst of,* en medio de (in the middle of), en pleno: *in the midst of winter,* en pleno invierno.
— Prep. Entre.
midstream ['midstri:m] n. Medio (*m.*) del río. || FAM. *To change horses in midstream,* cambiar de camisa.
midsummer ['mid,sʌmə*] n. Pleno verano, *m.* (middle of the summer). || Solsticio (*m.*) de verano (period of the summer solstice). || — *A Midsummer Night's Dream,* el sueño de una noche de verano. || *Midsummer Day,* el día de San Juan (24th of June).
midterm ['midtə:m] n. Mitad (*f.*) del trimestre (of a school term). || Mitad (*f.*) del mandato (of a term of office). || U. S. FAM. Examen (*m.*) parcial a mitad del trimestre.
midway ['mid'wei] adj./adv. A medio camino, a mitad del camino.
— N. U. S. Avenida (*f.*) central (of a fair).
midweek ['midwi:k] adj./adv. Entre semana.
— N. Medio (*m.*) *or* mitad (*f.*) de la semana.
midweekly ['mid,wi:kli] adv. A mediados de cada semana.
midwife ['midwaif] n. Comadrona, *f.*, partera, *f.*

— OBSERV. El plural de *midwife* es *midwives.*

midwifery ['midwifəri] n. Obstetricia, *f.*
midwinter ['mid'wintə*] n. Pleno invierno, *m.* || Solsticio (*m.*) de invierno (solstice).

midyear [ˈmidjə:*] n. Mediados *or* mitad (*f.*) del año. || U. S. FAM. Examen (*m.*) parcial a mitad de curso, examen (*m.*) semestral.
— Adj. Semestral.
mien [mi:n] n. Semblante, *m.*, aire, *m.* (face). || Aspecto, *m.* (aspect). || Porte, *m.* (bearing).
miff [mif] n. U. S. FAM. Disgusto, *m.*
miff [mif] v. tr. U. S. FAM. Ofender, disgustar.
might [mait] n. Fuerza, *f.*, poder, *m.* (strength). || *With all one's might* o *with might and main*, con todas sus fuerzas.
might [mait] pret. See MAY.
might-have-been [—hævˌbi:n] n. Lo que hubiera podido suceder (event). || Fracasado, da (person).
mightily [—ili] adv. Con fuerza, poderosamente. || FAM. Sumamente, extremadamente (extremely).
mightiness [—inis] n. Fuerza, *f.*, poder, *m.*, poderío, *m.*
mighty [ˈmaiti] adj. Fuerte (strong). || Poderoso, sa (powerful): *a mighty country*, un país poderoso. || Extraordinario, ria: *he made a mighty effort*, hizo un esfuerzo extraordinario. || Enorme (great).
— Adv. FAM. Muy: *a mighty big man*, un hombre muy grande. || *To be mighty sorry*, sentirlo enormemente.
mignonette [ˌminjəˈnet] n. BOT. Reseda, *f.*
migraine [ˈmi:grein] n. MED. Jaqueca, *f.*
migrant [ˈmaigrənt] adj. Migratorio, ria.
— N. Trabajador (*m.*) que se traslada de un sitio a otro. || Ave (*f.*) migratoria (bird).
migrate [maiˈgreit] v. intr. Emigrar (people, animals, plants). || CHEM. Desplazarse (atoms, ions, etc.).
migrating [—iŋ] adj. Migratorio, ria.
migration [maiˈgreiʃən] n. Migración, *f.* (of people, animals, etc.). || CHEM. Migración, *f.*
migratory [ˈmaigrətəri] adj. Migratorio, ria. || Nómada.
mihrab [ˈmirab] n. Mihrab, *m.* (of a mosque).
mikado [miˈkɑ:dəu] n. Micado, *m.*
mike [maik] n. FAM. Micro, *m.*
Mike [maik] pr. n. FAM. Miguelín, *m.*, Miguelito, *m.* || *For the love of Mike!*, see LOVE.
mil [mil] n. Milésima (*f.*) de pulgada.
milady [miˈleidi] n. Miladi, *f.*
milage [ˈmailidʒ] n. See MILEAGE.
Milan [miˈlæn] pr. n. GEOGR. Milán.
Milanese [ˌmiləˈni:z] adj./n. Milanés, esa. || HIST. Milanesado, *m.*
milch [miltʃ] adj. Lechero, ra: *milch cow*, vaca lechera.
mild [maild] adj. Poco riguroso, sa; poco severo, ra (punishment, rule). || Templado, da; benigno, na (climate, weather). || Suave (wind). || Bondadoso, sa; dulce, apacible (person, character). || Dulce (look). || Suave (slope). || Flojo, ja (food, drink). || Suave (tobacco, cheese, medicine). || Benigno, na (disease, illness). || Dulce (steel). || *Mild success*, éxito (*m.*) de prestigio.
milden [ˈmaildən] v. tr. Suavizar.
— V. intr. Suavizarse.
mildew [ˈmildju:] n. Moho, *m.* || Mancha (*f.*) de humedad (stain). || AGR. Añublo, *m.*, tizón, *m.* (on plants). | Mildiu, *m.*, mildeu, *m.* (on vine).
mildew [ˈmildju:] v. tr. Enmohecer. || Manchar de humedad (to stain). || AGR. Atizonar, añublar (plants). | Atacar de mildiu (vine).
— V. intr. Enmohecerse. || Mancharse de humedad. || AGR. Atizonarse, añublarse (plants). | Estar atacado de mildiu (vine).
mildewy [—i] adj. Mohoso, sa. || Manchado de humedad. || AGR. Atizonado, da; añublado, da (plant). | Atacado de mildiu (vine).
mildly [ˈmaildli] adv. Suavemente (softly). || Ligeramente (lightly, slightly). || *To put it mildly*, para no decir más.
mildness [ˈmaildnis] n. Poca severidad, *f.* (of punishment). || Benignidad, *f.* (of climate, illness). || Dulzura, *f.*, suavidad, *f.* (of a person). || Bondad, *f.*, afabilidad, *f.* (of character). || Dulzura, *f.* (of a look). || Suavidad, *f.* (of tobacco, slope, etc.).
mile [mail] n. Milla, *f.* [unidad de medida que equivale a 1 609 m]. || MAR. Milla, *f.* [unidad de medida que equivale a 1 852 m]. || — *It is miles away*, está muy lejos. || FIG. *It stands out a mile*, se ve a la legua. || *I walked miles*, anduve kilómetros y kilómetros. || FIG. *You are miles out* o *off*, estás lejos de la cuenta (you are very much mistaken).
mileage [ˈmailidʒ] n. Distancia (*f.*) en millas (distance from one place to another). || Recorrido (*m.*) en millas (distance travelled). || Gastos (*m. pl.*) de viaje por millas recorridas (travel allowance per mile). || Coste (*m.*) de transporte por milla (transport cost per mile). || Kilometraje, *m.*, kilómetros, *m. pl.*: *what is the mileage of this car?*, ¿qué kilometraje tiene este coche?, ¿cuántos kilómetros ha recorrido este coche? || — *Mileage indicator*, cuentakilómetros, *m. inv.* || *Mileage ticket*, billete kilométrico de ferrocarril.

— OBSERV. The word *kilometraje* refers to the number of kilometres travelled.

milepost [ˈmailpəust] n. Mojón, *m.* [kilométrico].
miler [ˈmailə*] n. SP. Corredor (*m.*) de la milla (runner). || Caballo (*m.*) cuya especialidad es correr la milla.
milestone [ˈmailstəun] n. Mojón, *m.* [kilométrico]. || FIG. Jalón, *m.*, hito, *m.* (in s.o.'s life).
milfoil [ˈmilfɔil] n. BOT. Milenrama, *f.*
miliaria [miliˈɛəriə] n. MED. Fiebre (*f.*) miliar.
miliary [ˈmiliəri] adj. MED. Miliar: *miliary fever*, fiebre miliar.
milieu [ˈmi:ljə:] n. Medio ambiente, *m.*, entorno, *m.* (environment).
militancy [ˈmilitənsi] n. Belicosidad, *f.*, combatividad, *f.* (fighting spirit). || Actividad (*f.*) de un militante (in politics).
militant [ˈmilitənt] adj. Combatiente (engaged in fighting). || Belicoso, sa (aggressive). || Militante: *a militant socialist*, un socialista militante. || REL. Militante.
— N. Militante, *m.* & *f.*
militarism [ˈmilitərizəm] n. Militarismo, *m.*
militarist [ˈmilitərist] adj./n. Militarista.
militaristic [ˌmilitəˈristik] adj. Militarista.
militarization [ˈmilitəraiˈzeiʃən] n. Militarización, *f.*
militarize [ˈmilitəraiz] v. tr. Militarizar.
military [ˈmilitəri] adj. Militar: *military academy*, academia militar; *military attaché*, agregado militar; *military service*, servicio militar; *military training*, instrucción militar. || — *Military government*, gobierno (*m.*) militar. || *Military law*, código (*m.*) militar. || *Military man*, militar, *m.* || *Military police*, policía (*f.*) militar. || *Military record*, cartilla (*f.*) militar. || *The military*, los militares.
militate [ˈmiliteit] v. intr. Militar: *much evidence militates in his favour*, militan muchas pruebas en su favor.
militia [miˈliʃə] n. Milicia, *f.*
militiaman [—mən] n. Miliciano, *m.*

— OBSERV. El plural de *militiaman* es *militiamen*.

milk [milk] n. Leche, *f.* || — *Coconut milk*, leche de coco. || FIG. *It is no use crying over spilt milk*, a lo hecho, pecho. || *Milk chocolate*, chocolate (*m.*) con leche. || *Milk diet*, dieta láctea. || *Powdered milk*, leche en polvo. || *Skim milk*, leche desnatada. || FIG. *The milk of human kindness*, la amabilidad personificada.
milk [milk] v. tr. Ordeñar (an animal). || Sacar (juice, sap). || FIG. Exprimir (to exploit in order to get money from). | Sacar a (to get from). | Chupar: *they are milking me of my money*, me están chupando el dinero.
— V. intr. Dar leche.
milk-and-water [—ənˈwɔ:tə*] adj. Insulso, sa; insípido, da; soso, sa.
milk bar [—bɑ:*] n. Cafetería, *f.*
milk can [—kæn] n. Cántara (*f.*) *or* cántaro (*m.*) de leche, lechera, *f.*
milk churn [ˈmilktʃə:n] n. Lechera, *f.*, cántaro (*m.*) *or* cántara (*f.*) de leche.
milker [—ə*] n. Ordeñador, ra (person who milks). || Ordeñadora, *f.*, máquina (*f.*) de ordeñar (machine). || Vaca (*f.*) lechera (milch cow).
milk fever [—ˌfi:və*] n. MED. VET. Fiebre (*f.*) láctea.
milk-float [—fləut] n. Carro (*m.*) de la leche.
milkiness [—inis] n. Aspecto (*m.*) lechoso (appearance). || Color (*m.*) lechoso (colour).
milking [—iŋ] adj. Lechero, ra. || *Milking machine*, ordeñadora mecánica.
— N. Ordeño, *m.*
milk-livered [—ˌlivəd] adj. FAM. Que tiene sangre de horchata, cobarde.
milkmaid [—meid] n. Mujer (*f.*) que trabaja en una lechería, lechera, *f.* (dairymaid). || Ordeñadora, *f.* (who milks cows).
milkman [—mən] n. Lechero, *m.* (who sells milk). || Repartidor (*m.*) de la leche, lechero, *m.* (who delivers milk).

— OBSERV. El plural de *milkman* es *milkmen*.

milk of lime [—əvˈlaim] n. Lechada (*f.*) de cal.
milk of magnesia [—əvmægˈni:ʃə] n. Leche (*f.*) de magnesia.
milk pail [—peil] n. Ordeñadero, *m.*
milk shake [—ˈʃeik] n. Batido (*m.*) de leche [*Amer.*, leche (*f.*) malteada].
milksop [—sɔp] n. FAM. Persona (*f.*) que tiene sangre de horchata (person without spirit). | Gallina, *m.* (coward). | Marica, *m.* (effeminate man).
milk sugar [—ˈʃugə*] n. Lactosa, *f.*
milk toast [—təust] n. CULIN. Torrija, *f.*
milk tooth [—tu:θ] n. Diente (*m.*) de leche.

— OBSERV. El plural de *milk tooth* es *milk teeth*.

milkweed [—wi:d] n. BOT. Algodoncillo, *m.*
milk-white [—ˌwait] adj. Lechoso, sa; blanco como la leche.
milky [—i] adj. Lechoso, sa. || FIG. Timorato, ta (timid).
Milky Way [ˈmilkiˈwei] pr. n. ASTR. Vía (*f.*) Láctea.
mill [mil] n. Molino, *m.* (for grain, flour). || Molinillo, *m.* (grinder for coffee, pepper). || Pasapuré, *m.* (for vegetables). || Fábrica, *f.* (factory): *textile mill*, fábrica de tejidos. || Papelera, *f.*, fábrica (*f.*) de papel (for paper). || Serrería, *f.*, aserradero, *m.* (for sawing wood). || Prensa, *f.* (for stamping). || Prensa (*f.*) de acuñar monedas (for coins). || Taller, *m.* (in general, a small manufacturing works). || Fresa, *f.* (cutter). || Laminador, *m.*, laminadora, *f.* (rolling mill). || U. S. Milésima (*f.*) parte de un dólar. || — *Spinning mill*, fábrica de hilados, hilandería, *f.* || FAM. *To go through*

the mill, pasarlas negras *or* moradas. | *To put s.o. through the mill*, someter a alguien a duras pruebas.

mill [mil] v. tr. Moler (grain, beans, coffee, pepper, etc.). || Batir (cream). || Hacer puré (vegetables). || Abatanar (textiles). || Acordonar (to cut grooves on a coin). || TECH. Pulir (to polish). | Laminar (with a rolling mill). | Fresar, avellanar (gears). || MIN. Machacar, triturar (ore). || FAM. Pegar, moler a golpes (to beat).
— V. intr. Arremolinarse, apiñarse (to crowd around). || FAM. Pegar, pegarse.

millboard [—bɔ:d] n. Cartón (*m.*) piedra.

millcourse [—kɔ:s] n. Saetín, *m.*, caz, *m.*

milldam [—dæm] n. Presa (*f.*) de molino.

millenary [miˊlenəri] adj. Milenario, ria.
— N. Milenario, *m.* (a thousandth anniversary). || Milenio, *m.*, milenario, *m.* (millennium).

millennial [miˊleniəl] adj. Milenario, ria.

millennium [miˊleniəm] n. Milenio, *m.*, milenario, *m.* (a thousand years). || FIG. Edad (*f.*) de oro.

— OBSERV. El plural de *millennium* es *millenniums* o *millennia*.

millepede [ˊmilipi:d] n. ZOOL. Milpiés, *m. inv.*

miller [ˊmilə*] n. Molinero, ra. || Harinero, *m.* (of power-driven mill). || TECH. Fresadora, *f.*, máquina (*f.*) fresadora (machine). | Fresador, *m.* (person). || ZOOL. Mariposa, *f.*

miller's thumb [—zˊθʌm] n. ZOOL. Coto, *m.* (fish).

millesimal [miˊlesiməl] adj. Milésimo, ma.

millet [ˊmilit] n. BOT. Mijo, *m.*

mill hand [ˊmilhænd] n. Obrero, ra.

mill hopper [ˊmilˊhɔpə*] n. Tolva, *f.*

milliammeter [ˊmiliˊæmitə*] n. ELECTR. Miliamperímetro, *m.*

milliampere [miliˊæmpɛə*] n. ELECTR. Miliamperio, *m.* (one thousandth of an ampere).

milliard [ˊmiljɑ:d] n. Mil millones, *m. pl.*

milliary [ˊmiliəri] adj. Miliar.

millibar [ˊmilibɑ:*] n. PHYS. Milibar, *m.*

millicurie [ˊmili,kjuəri] n. PHYS. Milicurie, *m.*

millier [milˊjei] n. Tonelada (*f.*) métrica.

milligram or **milligramme** [ˊmiligræm] n. Miligramo, *m.*

millilitre (U. S. **milliliter**) [ˊmili,li:tə*] n. Mililitro, *m.* (one thousandth of a litre).

millimetre (U. S. **millimeter**) [ˊmili,mi:tə*] n. Milímetro, *m.*

millimetric [,miliˊmetrik] adj. Milimétrico, ca.

millimicron [ˊmili,maikrɔn] n. Milimicrón, *m.*, milimicra, *f.*

milliner [ˊmilinə*] n. Sombrerero, ra. || *Milliner's*, tienda (*f.*) de sombreros, sombrerería, *f.*

millinery [ˊmilinəri] n. Sombrerería, *f.* (milliner's work or business). || Sombreros (*m. pl.*) de señora (women's hats).

milling [ˊmiliŋ] n. Molienda, *f.* (act). || Fábrica (*f.*) de harina (flour factory). || Almacén (*m.*) de harina (warehouse). || Enfurtido, *m.*, batanadura, *f.* (of cloth). || Fresado, *m.* (of gears). || Trituración, *f.* (of ore). || Cordoncillo, *m.* (of coin). || — *Milling cutter*, fresa, *f.* || *Milling machine*, fresadora, *f.*

million [ˊmiljən] n. Millón, *m.* || — *A million dollar cheque*, un cheque de un millón de dólares. || *By the million* o *in millions*, a millones, por millones. || *Millions of*, millones de. || *One million pounds*, un millón de libras. || U. S. *To feel like a million*, estar en plena forma. || *Two million pesetas*, dos millones de pesetas. || FIG. *You are one in a million*, eres un mirlo blanco. | *You look like a million*, estás guapísima.

millionaire [,miljəˊnɛə*] n. Millonario, ria.

millionfold [ˊmiljən,fəuld] adj. Multiplicado por un millón.
— Adv. Un millón de veces.

millionth [ˊmiljənθ] adj./n. Millonésimo, ma.

millipede [ˊmilipi:d] n. ZOOL. Milpiés, *m. inv.*

millitherm [ˊmiliθə:m] n. PHYS. Militermia, *f.*

millivolt [ˊmilivəult] n. PHYS. Milivoltio, *m.*

milliwatt [ˊmiliwɔt] n. PHYS. Milivatio, *m.*

millowner [ˊmil,əunə*] n. Industrial, *m.*, propietario (*m.*) de una fábrica.

millpond [ˊmilpɔnd] n. Represa (*f.*) de molino.

millrace [ˊmilreis] n. Saetín, *m.*, caz, *m.*

millstone [ˊmilstəun] n. Muela, *f.*, piedra (*f.*) de molino. || FIG. *It's a millstone round his neck*, lleva una cruz a cuestas.

millstream [ˊmilstri:m] n. Agua (*f.*) que pasa por el saetín.

mill wheel [ˊmilwi:l] n. Rueda (*f.*) de molino.

millwright [ˊmilrait] n. Constructor (*m.*) de molinos.

milord [miˊlɔ:d] n. Milord, *m.*

milt [milt] n. Lecha, *f.*, lechaza, *f.* (of fish).

milt [milt] v. tr. ZOOL. Fecundar [las huevas].

milter [ˊmiltə*] n. Pez (*m.*) macho [en el tiempo de la freza].

mime [maim] n. Mimo, *m.*, pantomima, *f.* (entertainment). || Mimo, *m.* (actor). || Payaso, *m.* (clown).

mime [maim] v. tr. Imitar, remedar.
— V. intr. Actuar de mimo.

mimeograph [ˊmimiəgrɑ:f] n. Multicopista, *f.* [*Amer.*, mimeógrafo, *m.*] (machine). || Copia (*f.*) a multicopista (copy).

mimeograph [ˊmimiəgrɑ:f] v. tr. Tirar a multicopista, sacar copias de [en la multicopista], reproducir en la multicopista [*Amer.*, mimeografiar].

mimeographing [—iŋ] n. Reproducción (*f.*) de documentos [*Amer.*, mimeografía, *f.*].

mimesis [miˊmi:sis] n. Mimetismo, *m.*

mimetic [miˊmetik] adj. Mimético, ca. || FIG. Imitativo, va.

mimetism [miˊmetizəm] n. Mimetismo, *m.*

mimic [ˊmimik] adj. Mímico, ca; imitativo, va. || Fingido, da; ficticio, cia; simulado, da (pretended). || *Mimic art*, mímica, *f.*
— N. Mimo, *m.* (mime). || Imitador, ra (imitator).

mimic [ˊmimik] v. tr. Imitar, remedar (to imitate).
— OBSERV. Pret. & p. p. ***mimicked***.

mimicry [ˊmimikri] n. Mímica, *f.* (art). || Imitación, *f.*, remedo, *m.* (imitation). || ZOOL. BOT. Mimetismo, *m.*

mimographer [maiˊmɔgrəfə*] n. Mimógrafo, *m.*

mimosa [miˊməuzə] n. BOT. Mimosa, *f.*

minacious [miˊneiʃəs] adj. Amenazador, ra; amenazante.

minaret [ˊminəret] n. Alminar, *m.*, minarete, *m.*

minatory [ˊminətəri] adj. Amenazador, ra; amenazante. || JUR. Conminatorio, ria.

mince [mins] n. Carne (*f.*) picada (minced meat). || *Mince pie*, bizcocho (*m.*) con frutas picadas.

mince [mins] v. tr. Picar (meat). || Desmenuzar. || FIG. *Not to mince matters* o *not to mince one's words*, no tener pelos en la lengua, no andar con rodeos.
— V. intr. Andar con pasos medidos (to walk). || Hablar remilgadamente (to speak).

mincemeat [ˊminsmi:t] n. Carne (*f.*) picada (meat). || Conserva (*f.*) de fruta picada y especias. || FIG. *To make mincemeat of*, hacer trizas *or* picadillo a (a person), echar abajo (an argument).

mincer [ˊminsə*] n. Máquina (*f.*) de picar carne.

mincing [ˊminsiŋ] adj. Melindroso, sa; remilgado, da. || *Mincing machine*, máquina (*f.*) de picar carne.

mind [maind] n. Mente, *f.* (seat of consciousness): *conscious mind*, mente consciente. || Inteligencia, *f.* (intelligence): *he has a very quick mind*, tiene una inteligencia muy viva. || Opinión, *f.*, parecer, *m.* (opinion): *they were of the same mind*, eran de la misma opinión. || Cabeza, *f.*: *he got that idea fixed in his mind*, se metió esa idea en la cabeza; *he can't get it out of his mind*, no se lo puede quitar de la cabeza. || Cerebro, *m.*: *he is one of the great minds of the century*, es uno de los grandes cerebros del siglo. || Mentalidad, *f.* (mentality): *a liberal mind*, una mentalidad liberal. || Juicio, *m.* (sanity): *in one's right mind*, en su sano juicio. || Intención, *f.*, mente, *f.* (intention): *nothing is further from my mind*, no hay nada más lejos de mi intención; *it's not in my mind to*, no está en mi mente. || Pensamiento, *m.*, idea, *f.* (idea). || Espíritu, *m.*, alma, *f.* (soul): *peace of mind*, tranquilidad de espíritu. || Memoria, *f.* (memory). || — *He had no mind to do it*, no tenía intención de hacerlo. || *Mind's eye*, imaginación, *f.* || *My mind is made up*, he tomado mi decisión. || *Not to be clear in one's mind about*, no acordarse bien de (not to remember), no ver claramente (to be confused). || *Of unsound mind*, que no está en su sano juicio. || *Sound in mind*, cuerdo, da. || *State of mind*, estado (*m.*) de ánimo. || *The mind boggles*, uno puede imaginarse cualquier cosa. || *To bear in mind*, recordar (to remember), tener en cuenta, tener presente (to take into account): *bearing that in mind*, teniéndolo en cuenta. || *To be of a mind*, estar de acuerdo. || *To be of a mind to do sth.*, estar dispuesto a hacer algo. || *To be of sound mind*, estar en su sano juicio. || *To be in two minds*, estar indeciso, dudar. || *To be out of one's mind*, estar fuera de juicio, haber perdido el juicio. || *To be to one's mind*, gustar a uno (to be to one's liking). || *To be uneasy in one's mind*, no estar tranquilo. || *To bring one's mind to bear on sth.*, examinar algo. || *To bring to mind*, recordar. || *To call to mind*, acordarse de, recordar (to remember): *I cannot call it to mind*, no me puedo acordar de ello; recordar, traer a la memoria *or* a la mente (to remind): *that calls to mind a story I know*, esto me trae a la memoria una historia que conozco. || *To change one's mind*, cambiar *or* mudar de opinión (way of thinking), cambiar de idea *or* de intención (idea). || *To come to s.o.'s mind* o *to enter s.o.'s mind*, ocurrírsele a uno, venir a la mente de uno. || *To cross one's mind*, pasarle por la cabeza a uno. || *To give one's mind to sth.*, prestar atención a algo (to pay attention), dedicarse a algo (to dedicate o.s.). || *To give s.o. a piece* o *a bit of one's mind*, decir a alguien cuatro verdades *or* las verdades del barquero. || *To go* o *to pass out of mind*, olvidarse, caer en el olvido. || *To go out of one's mind*, perder el juicio. || *To have a good mind* o *a mind* o *a great mind to do sth.*, tener [muchas] ganas de hacer algo. || *To have half a mind to do sth.*, tener ciertas ganas de hacer algo. || *To have it in mind to do sth.*, tener la intención de hacer algo, pensar hacer algo. || *To have set one's mind on doing sth.*, estar resuelto a hacer algo. || *To have sth.* o *s.o. in mind*, pensar en algo *or* en alguien: *have you anyone in mind for the job?*, ¿ha pensado en alguien para ese trabajo? || *To have sth. on one's mind*, tener algo en la conciencia (to have sth. on one's conscience), estar pensando constantemente en algo, estar preocupado por algo (to worry about sth.). || *To keep an open mind*, tener amplitud de ideas. || *To keep in mind*, acordarse de, recordar (to remember), tener en cuenta, tener presente (to take into account). || *To keep one's mind on*, prestar atención a. || *To know one's mind*, saber lo que uno quiere: *he doesn't even know his own mind*, ni siquiera sabe lo que quiere. || *To lose one's mind*, perder la cabeza *or* el juicio. || *To make up one's mind*, decidirse: *come, make up your mind!*, ¡venga, decídase! || *To my mind*, a mi parecer, en mi opinión, a mi modo de ver: *that, to my mind, is excellent advice*, eso, a mi parecer, es un consejo excelente. || *To put s.o. in mind of*, recordar a alguien: *she puts me in mind of her mother*, me recuerda a su madre. || *To put s.o. in the mind for doing sth.*, dar a alguien ganas de hacer algo. || *To put sth. from* o *out of one's mind*, olvidarse de algo. || *To read s.o.'s mind*, adivinar el pensamiento de alguien. || *To set one's mind on*, estar resuelto a: *I have my mind set on going shopping today*, estoy resuelto a ir de compras hoy. || *To set one's mind on sth.*, estar resuelto a conseguir algo. || *To slip s.o.'s mind*, írsele completamente de la cabeza a uno *or* de la memoria, olvidársele [a uno]: *his name has slipped my mind*, se me ha olvidado su nombre. || *To speak one's mind*, decir lo que uno piensa, hablar sin rodeos. || *To take a great weight off s.o.'s mind*, quitarle a alguien un peso de encima. || *To take s.o.'s mind off sth.*, distraer a alguien de algo (to distract), quitar a alguien algo de la cabeza (to make s.o. forget sth.). || *To tell s.o. one's mind*, decir a alguien lo que uno piensa. || *Turn of mind*, espíritu, mentalidad. || *With an open mind*, con amplitud de ideas. || *With one mind*, por unanimidad, unánimemente.

mind [maind] v. tr. Cuidar (to take care of): *to mind the baby*, cuidar al niño. || Tener cuidado (to be careful): *mind how you cross the street*, ten cuidado al cruzar la calle. || Vigilar, cuidar (to guard). || Procurar: *mind you're not late*, procure no llegar tarde. || Prestar atención a, hacer caso de (to pay attention): *never mind what he says*, no hagas caso de lo que dice. || Hacer caso a (to listen to): *if you had minded me*, si me hubieras hecho caso. || Cumplir (rules). || Preocuparse por *or* de (to worry about): *don't mind the weather*, no te preocupes por el tiempo; *don't mind what people say*, no te preocupes de lo que diga la gente. || Pensar en, acordarse de (not to forget): *mind you phone him*, acuérdese de telefonearle. || — *Do you mind if I open the window?*, ¿le importa que abra la ventana? || *Do you mind my smoking?*, ¿le importa que fume? || *I don't mind the cold*, a mí no me importa *or* no me molesta el frío. || *I don't mind trying*, lo puedo intentar. || *I shouldn't mind a cup of tea*, me gustaría tomarme una taza de té. || *Mind my words!*, ¡presta atención a lo que te digo! || *Mind out*, ¡cuidado! || *Mind the paint!*, ¡cuidado con la pintura! || *Mind what you are doing!*, ¡cuidado con lo que haces! || *Mind you*, en realidad, la verdad es que: *mind you, it was not his fault*, en realidad no era culpa suya. || *Mind you don't fall!*, ¡ten cuidado de no caerte! || *Mind your language!*, ¡cuidado con lo que dices! || FAM. *Mind your own business*, no te metas en lo que no te importa. || *Mind yourself*, ten cuidado con lo que haces. || *Never mind him*, no le hagas caso (take no notice of him), no te preocupes por él (don't worry about him). || *Never mind that*, no te preocupes por eso. || FAM. *Never you mind!*, ¿y a ti qué te importa? || *Would you mind shutting the door?*, ¿le importaría cerrar la puerta? || *You don't mind my smoking, do you?*, no le importa que fume, ¿verdad?

— V. intr. Preocuparse: *don't mind about the gossip*, no se preocupe de las habladurías. || — FAM. *Do you mind!*, ¡vaya!, ¡por Dios! || *I don't mind*, no me importa, me da igual. || *If no one minds I will close the window*, si no le importa a nadie voy a cerrar la ventana. || *If you don't mind*, si no le importa, si le parece. || *Mind and do not be late*, procure no llegar tarde. || *Never mind*, no se preocupe (don't worry), no importa, da igual (it doesn't matter). || *Would you like a glass of wine? — I don't mind*, ¿quieres un vaso de vino? — Sí, con mucho gusto.

mind cure [—ˌkjuə*] n. Psicoterapia, *f.*

minded [—id] adj. Dispuesto, ta: *she is not minded to do it*, no está dispuesta a hacerlo. || — *He is commercially minded*, tiene una mentalidad mercantil. || *If you are so minded*, si le apetece, si quiere. || *Weak-minded*, pobre de espíritu.

mindful [—ful] adj. Cuidadoso, sa; atento, ta. || — *To be mindful of others*, pensar en los demás. || *To be mindful of sth.*, tener algo presente *or* en cuenta. || *To be mindful to do sth.*, no olvidar hacer algo.

mindless [—lis] adj. Sin inteligencia, estúpido, da (senseless). || Despreocupado, da (careless). || — *To be mindless of danger*, ser inconsciente del peligro. || *To be mindless of one's health*, no preocuparse por su salud. || *To be mindless of s.o.'s generosity*, no acordarse de la generosidad de alguien.

mind picture [—ˌpiktʃə*] n. Representación (*f.*) mental.

mind reader [—ˌri:də*] n. Adivinador (*m.*) de los pensamientos.

mind reading [—ˌri:diŋ] n. Lectura (*f.*) *or* adivinación (*f.*) de los pensamientos.

mine [main] poss. pron. [El] mío, [la] mía, [los] míos, [las] mías, [lo] mío: *this book is mine*, este libro es mío, este libro es el mío; *these are mine*, éstos son míos, éstos son los míos; *that's mine*, eso es mío. || Mío, mía: *the fault is mine*, la culpa es mía. || El mío, la mía: *give me mine*, dame el mío. || *Of mine*, mío, mía: *a friend of mine*, un amigo mío.

— OBSERV. Téngase en cuenta que el pronombre posesivo *mine* se puede aplicar tanto a un objeto como a varios (*give me mine*, dame el mío, dame los míos).

mine [main] n. MIN. MIL. MAR. Mina, *f.* || FIG. Mina, *f.*: *a mine of information*, una mina de información. || — MIL. *Antitank, delayed-action, antipersonnel, floating, submarine mine*, mina anticarro, de acción retardada, contra personal, flotante, submarina. || MIN. *Coal mine*, mina de carbón. || MIL. *Land mine*, mina terrestre. || MIL. *To lay a mine*, poner una mina. | *To lay mines*, fondear minas (in the sea), sembrar minas (in the ground).

mine [main] v. tr. Minar, socavar (the earth). || Cavar (a hole). || Extraer (minerals). || Explotar (a mine). || MIL. MAR. Poner *or* sembrar *or* fondear minas en, minar (to lay mines). | Volar *or* destruir con minas (to blow up). || FIG. Minar (to undermine).

— V. intr. Cavar una mina (to dig a mine). || Extraer minerales. || Poner *or* sembrar *or* fondear minas (to lay mines). || Trabajar en las minas *or* en la minería.

mine detector [—diˈtektə*] n. MIL. MAR. Detector (*m.*) de minas.

minefield [—fi:ld] n. MIL. Campo (*m.*) de minas, campo (*m.*) minado.

minelayer [—ˌleiə*] n. Minador, *m.* (ship).

mine laying [—ˌleiiŋ] n. Minado, *m.*

miner [—ə*] n. MIN. Minero, *m.* || MIL. Minador, *m.*, zapador, *m.*

mineral [ˈminərəl] adj. Mineral: *mineral water*, agua mineral; *mineral oil*, aceite mineral. || Minero, ra: *mineral deposit*, yacimiento minero; *mineral belt*, zona minera.

— N. Mineral, *m.*

mineralization [ˌminərəlaiˈzeiʃən] n. Mineralización, *f.*

mineralize [ˈminərəlaiz] v. tr. Mineralizar.

mineralogical [ˌminərəˈlɔdʒikəl] adj. Mineralógico, ca.

mineralogist [ˌminəˈrælədʒist] n. MIN. Mineralogista, *m.* & *f.*

mineralogy [ˌminəˈrælədʒi] n. Mineralogía, *f.*

Minerva [miˈnə:və] n. MYTH. Minerva, *f.*

mine shaft [mainʃɑ:ft] n. Pozo (*m.*) de extracción.

minestrone [ˌminesˈtrəuni] n. Sopa (*f.*) de verduras, sopa (*f.*) milanesa.

minesweeper [ˈmainˌswi:pə*] n. MAR. Dragaminas, *m. inv.*

minesweeping [—ˌswi:piŋ] n. MAR. Dragado (*m.*) de minas, rastreo (*m.*) de minas.

mine thrower [—ˌθrəuə*] n. MIL. Lanzaminas, *m. inv.*

minever [ˈminivə*] n. Armiño, *m.*

mingle [ˈmiŋgl] v. tr. Mezclar.

— V. intr. Mezclarse: *the water mingled with the ink*, el agua se mezcló con la tinta. || Confundirse: *his voice mingled with mine in song*, su voz se confundía con la mía en el canto. || Mezclarse: *he mingles with a bad crowd*, se mezcla con mala gente.

mingy [ˈmindʒi] adj. FAM. Tacaño, ña; cicatero, ra; mezquino, na (stingy).

miniature [ˈminjətʃə*] adj. Miniatura, en miniatura: *miniature train*, tren miniatura. || FAM. Diminuto, ta; pequeñísimo, ma (very small). || — *Miniature golf*, minigolf, *m.* || *Miniature model*, maqueta, *f.* || *Miniature painter*, miniaturista, *m.* & *f.*

— N. Miniatura, *f.* || *In miniature*, en miniatura.

miniaturist [ˈminjətjuərist] n. Miniaturista, *m.* & *f.*

miniaturization [ˌminjətjəraiˈzeiʃən] n. Miniaturización *f.*

miniaturize [ˈminjətjuəraiz] v. tr. Miniaturizar.

minibus [ˈminibʌs] n. Microbús, *m.*

minicab [ˈminikæb] n. Microtaxi, *m.*

minim [ˈminim] n. CHEM. Gota, *f.* (drop). || MUS. Mínima, *f.*, blanca, *f.* || REL. Mínimo, *m.* || Palo, *m.*, trazo, *m.* (in writing). || Pizca, *f.* (small portion).

minimal [ˈminiml] adj. Mínimo, ma.

minimize [ˈminimaiz] v. tr. Minimizar, reducir al mínimo, empequeñecer (to reduce to a minimum). || FIG. Menospreciar, minimizar (to underestimate).

minimum [ˈminiməm] adj. Mínimo, ma: *the minimum temperature*, la temperatura mínima.

— N. Mínimo, *m.*, mínimum, *m.*: *to reduce to a minimum*, reducir al mínimo. || *Keep expenses to a minimum*, gaste lo menos posible *or* el mínimo.

— OBSERV. El plural de *minimum* es *minimums* o *minima*.

minimum wage [—ˈweidʒ] n. Salario (*m.*) mínimo (legally fixed wage). || Mínimo (*m.*) vital (living wage).

mining [ˈmainiŋ] n. Minería, *f.* (work). || MIL. Minado, *m.* (mine laying).

— Adj. Minero, ra: *mining zone*, zona minera. || MIL. Minador, ra. || De minas: *mining engineer*, ingeniero de minas.

minion [ˈminjən] n. Favorito, ta; valido, *m.* (of the king). || Favorito, ta; predilecto, ta (favourite). || Secuaz, *m.* (servile follower). || FAM. Enchufado, da; paniaguado, da (of the government). || Miñona, *f.* (letter in printing). || FAM. *Minion of the law*, poli, *m.*

miniskirt [ˈminiskə:t] n. Minifalda, *f.*

MINING — MINERÍA, *f.*

I. General terms. — Términos (*m.*) generales.

bed, deposit, field	yacimiento *m.*
outcrop	afloramiento *m.*
fault	falla *f.*
vein, sean, lode	filón *m.*, veta *f.*, vena *f.*, criadero *m.*
gold reef	filón (*m.*) aurífero
pocket	bolsa *f.*
reservoir	depósito *m.*
trap	trampa *f.*
water table	capa (*f.*) de agua *or* acuífera
mine	mina *f.*
stratum, layer	banco *m.*, estrato *m.*, capa *f.*
quarry	cantera *f.*
clay pit	cantera (*f.*) de arcilla
peat bog	turbera *f.*
gold nugget	pepita (*f.*) de oro
gangue	ganga *f.*
prospector	prospector *m.* [*Amer.*, cateador *m.*]
prospecting	prospección *f.*, exploración *f.*
boring, drilling	sondeo *m.*, perforación *f.*
auger, drill	sonda *f.*, barrena *f.*
excavation	excavación *f.*
quarrying, extraction	extracción *f.*
borer, drill, drilling machine	perforadora *f.*
stonemason	cantero *m.*
stonecutter	picapedrero *m.*
miner	minero *m.*
mining engineer	ingeniero (*m.*) de minas
pan	batea *f.*

II. Minerals. — Minerales, *m.*

iron ore	mineral (*m.*) de hierro
crystal	cristal *m.*
rock	roca *f.*
stone	piedra *f.*
coal	carbón *m.*, hulla *f.*
anthracite	antracita *f.*
coke	coque *m.*
oil	petróleo *m.*
lignite	lignito *m.*
peat	turba *f.*
marl, loam	marga *f.*
sandstone	piedra (*f.*) arenisca
granite	granito *m.*
slate	pizarra *f.*
clay	arcilla *f.*
marble	mármol *m.*
gravel	gravilla *f.*
chalk	creta *f.*
quartz	cuarzo *m.*
gypsum	yeso *m.*

III. Coal mining. — Explotación (*f.*) del carbón.

coal field	cuenca (*f.*) carbonífera, yacimiento (*m.*) de carbón
coal mine, colliery	mina (*f.*) de carbón
opencast working	explotación (*f.*) a cielo abierto
level	piso *m.*
working face	frente (*m.*) de corte
winding *o* hoisting shaft	pozo (*m.*) de extracción
ventilation shaft	pozo (*m.*) de ventilación
pithead, mine entrance	bocamina *f.*
gallery	galería *f.*
timbering, shoring	entibado *m.*, entibación *f.*
prop, shore	entibo *m.*, puntal *m.*
lining, planking	encofrado *m.*
air vent	respiradero *m.*
truck	vagoneta *f.*
slag	escoria *f.*
slag heap	escorial *m.*, escombrera *f.*
tip	escombrera *f.*
collier, coal miner	minero (*m.*) de carbón
pick	pico *m.*
shovel	pala *f.*
wedge	cuño *m.*
jumper	barrena *f.*
explosive	explosivo *m.*
charge	barreno *m.*
blast hole	barreno *m.*
undercutter	rozadora *f.*
miner's *o* safety lamp	lámpara (*f.*) de minero *or* de seguridad
fire damp explosion	explosión (*f.*) de grisú
cave-in	derrumbamiento *m.*
landslide	desprendimiento (*m.*) de tierra
flooding	inundación *f.*
asphyxia, suffocation, gassing	asfixia *f.*

IV. Oil — Petróleo, *m.*

oil field	yacimiento (*m.*) petrolífero
wildcat	sondeo (*m.*) de exploración
percussive drilling	perforación (*f.*) por percusión
rotary drilling	perforación (*f.*) rotatoria *or* por rotación
offshore drilling	perforación (*f.*) submarina
well	pozo *m.*
derrick	torre (*f.*) de perforación, derrick *m.*
Christmas tree	árbol (*m.*) de Navidad
crown block	caballete (*m.*) portapoleas
travelling block	polea (*f.*) móvil
drill pipe *o* stem	vástago (*m.*) de perforación
drill bit	trépano *m.*
roller bit	trépano (*m.*) de rodillos
diamond bit	trépano (*m.*) de diamantes
swivel	cabeza (*f.*) de inyección de lodo
turntable, rotary table	mesa (*f.*) giratoria
pumping station	estación (*f.*) de bombeo
sampling	muestreo *m.*
sample	muestra *f.*
core sample	testigo (*m.*) de sondeo
storage tank	tanque (*m.*) de almacenamiento
pipeline	oleoducto *m.*
pipe laying	tendido (*m.*) de oleoductos
oil tanker	petrolero *m.*, buque (*m.*) aljibe
tank car, tanker	vagón (*m.*) cisterna
tank truck, tanker	camión (*m.*) cisterna
refining	refinación *f.*, refinado *m.*, refino *m.*
refinery	refinería *f.*
cracking	cracking *m.*, craqueo *m.*
separation	separación *f.*
fractionating tower	torre (*f.*) de fraccionamiento
fractional distillation	destilación (*f.*) fraccionada
distillation column	columna (*f.*) de destilación
polymerizing, polymerization	polimerización *f.*
reforming	reformación *f.*
purification	purificación *f.*
hydrocarbon	hidrocarburo *m.*
crude oil	petróleo (*m.*) crudo, petróleo (*m.*) bruto, crudo *m.*
petrol [U. S., gasoline]	gasolina *f.* [*Amer.*, nafta *f.*]
octane number	índice (*m.*) de octano
paraffin	parafina *f.*
kerosene	queroseno *m.*
gas oil	gas-oil *m.*, gasoil *m.*
lubricating oil	aceite (*m.*) lubricante
asphalt	betún *m.*
benzene	benceno *m.*
fuel	combustible *m.*, carburante *m.*
natural gas	gas (*m.*) natural
olefin	olefina *f.*
petrochemicals	productos (*m.*) petroquímicos
high-grade *o* high-octane petrol	supercarburante *m.*

minister [ˈministə*] n. Ministro, *m.*: *Minister of Finance*, ministro de Hacienda; *Minister of Labour*, ministro de Trabajo; *Minister plenipotentiary*, ministro plenipotenciario; *minister of religion*, ministro de la Iglesia; *minister without portfolio*, ministro sin cartera; *Prime Minister*, primer ministro; *Minister of Education*, ministro de Educación; *Minister of Health*, ministro de Sanidad. || REL. Pastor, *m.* (protestant clergyman).

minister [ˈministə*] v. intr. *To minister to*, atender a: *to minister to the needs of the poor*, atender a las necesidades de los pobres; ayudar a, contribuir a (to help), servir en (a parish).
— V. tr. Administrar (a sacrament). || Suministrar (to provide).

ministerial [ˌminisˈtiəriəl] adj. Ministerial (of ministry). || Gubernamental (of government). || REL. Pastoral. || *To be ministerial to*, servir para, contribuir a.

ministration [ˌminisˈtreiʃən] n. Ayuda, *f.*, servicio, *m.* (help). || REL. Ministerio, *m.*

ministry [ˈministri] n. Ministerio, *m.* || REL. Sacerdocio, *m.* | Clero, *m.* (clergy). || — *Ministry of Education*, Ministerio de Educación. || *Ministry of Finance*, Ministerio de Hacienda. || *Ministry of Foreign Affairs*, Ministerio de Asuntos Exteriores [*Amer.*, Ministerio de Relaciones Exteriores]. || *Ministry of Housing*, Ministerio de la Vivienda. || *Ministry of Labour*, Ministerio de Trabajo. || *Ministry of Public Works*, Ministerio de Obras Públicas. || *Ministry of the Interior*, Ministerio de la Gobernación (in Spain), Ministerio del Interior (in other countries).

minium [ˈminiəm] n. CHEM. Minio, *m.*

miniver [ˈminivə*] n. Armiño, *m.* (ermine).

mink [miŋk] n. Visón, *m.* (animal, fur).

minnesinger [ˈminiˌsiŋə*] n. HIST. Trovador (*m.*) alemán, minnesinger, *m.*

minnow [ˈminəu] n. Pececillo, *m.*

minor [ˈmainə*] adj. Menor, más pequeño, ña (smaller, junior). || Menor de edad (younger than legal age). || GEOGR. PHIL. REL. Menor: *minor orders*, órdenes menores. || Secundario, ria (secondary). || Menudo, da (small): *minor expenses*, gastos menudos. || Sin importancia, de poca importancia, nimio, mia: *a minor detail*, un detalle sin importancia. || Poco, ca: *of minor interest*, de poco interés. || MUS. Menor:

E minor, mi menor; *minor key*, tono menor. || Minoritario, ria (party).
— N. Menor (*m.* & *f.*) de edad. || Mus. Tono (*m.*) menor (key). || Phil. Menor, *f.* || Rel. Hermano (*m.*) menor. || U. S. Asignatura (*f.*) secundaria (academic subject).
minor [ˈmainə*] v. intr. U. S. Estudiar como asignatura secundaria: *to minor in Basque*, estudiar el vasco como asignatura secundaria.
Minorca [miˈnɔːkə] pr. n. Geogr. Menorca.
Minorcan [—n] adj./n. Menorquín, ina.
Minorite [ˈmainərait] n. Rel. Fraile (*m.*) franciscano, menor, *m.*
minority [maiˈnɔriti] n. Minoría, *f.* (less than half). || Minoría, *f.*, menor edad, *f.* (of age). || Minoría, *f.* (small group): *England is Protestant but with a Catholic minority*, Inglaterra es protestante con una minoría católica. || *A minority government*, un gobierno minoritario.
Minotaur [ˈmainətɔː*] n. Myth. Minotauro, *m.*
minster [ˈminstə*] n. Rel. Catedral, *f.* (cathedral). | Iglesia (*f.*) de un monasterio (monastery church).
minstrel [ˈminstrəl] n. Trovador, *m.*, juglar, *m.* || Fig. Poeta, *m.* | Músico, *m.* || U. S. Artista (*m.*) que parodia a los negros cantando o contando chistes.
minstrelsy [—si] n. Canto (*m.*) de trovador *or* de juglar (song). || Arte (*m.*) del trovador *or* del juglar, juglaría, *f.* (art). || Grupo (*m.*) de trovadores *or* juglares (group). || Mester (*m.*) de juglaría (poetry).
mint [mint] adj. Nuevo, va (not marred). || De menta: *mint sauce*, salsa de menta. || *In mint condition*, como nuevo.
— N. Bot. Menta, *f.*, hierbabuena, *f.* || Menta, *f.* (peppermint). || Pastilla (*f.*) *or* caramelo (*m.*) de menta (sweet). || Casa (*f.*) de la moneda, ceca, *f.* (ant.) [where coins are made]. || Fig. Mina, *f.*: *a mint of ideas*, una mina de ideas. || Fam. *To spend a mint*, gastar un dineral *or* una fortuna.
mint [mint] v. tr. Acuñar: *to mint money*, acuñar dinero. || Fig. Forjar, idear, inventar (to make up, to fabricate). | Acuñar (a word).
mintage [ˈmintidʒ] n. Acuñación, *f.* (act of minting). || Moneda (*f.*) acuñada (minted money). || Cuño, *m.*, sello, *m.* (stamp on a coin). || Fig. Invención, *f.*, creación, *f.* | Acuñación, *f.* (of a word).
minter [ˈmintə*] n. Monedero, *m.*, acuñador, *m.*
minuend [ˈminjuend] n. Math. Minuendo, *m.*
minuet [minjuˈet] n. Mus. Minué, *m.*
minus [ˈmainəs] adj. Negativo, va: *a minus quantity*, una cantidad negativa; *a minus number*, un número negativo. || De sustracción, menos: *minus sign*, signo menos *or* de sustracción. || — Fig. Fam. *A minus quantity*, una cantidad despreciable. | *He is a minus quantity*, es un cero a la izquierda. || *Minus difference*, diferencia (*f.*) en menos.
— N. Cantidad (*f.*) negativa (negative quantity). || Menos, *m.*, signo (*m.*) menos, signo (*m.*) de sustracción *or* de resta (mathematical sign).
— Prep. Menos: *seven minus five*, siete menos cinco. || Fam. Sin: *he came back minus his hat*, volvió sin sombrero. || *Minus zero temperature*, temperatura (*f.*) bajo cero.
minuscule [ˈminəskjuːl] adj. Minúsculo, la.
— N. Minúscula, *f.* (letter).
minute [maiˈnjuːt] adj. Menudo, da; diminuto, ta; muy pequeño, ña (small). || Minucioso, sa; detallado, da (precise): *he gave us a minute account of what had happened*, nos hizo una relación detallada de lo que había ocurrido. || Insignificante, ínfimo, ma; nimio, mia (of little importance).
minute [ˈminit] n. Minuto, *m.* (time, section of a degree). || Fig. Minuto, *m.*, momento, *m.*, instante, *m.* (a moment): *he will come in a minute*, vendrá dentro de un momento; *wait a minute*, espera un momento. || Nota, *f.*, minuta, *f.* (note). || — Pl. Actas, *f.*, acta, *f. sing.* (of a meeting): *to keep o to draw up the minutes*, preparar *or* redactar las actas; *to place on record in the minutes*, hacer constar en las actas. || — *At the last minute*, a última hora. || *Come at 9 o'clock to the minute*, ven a las 9 en punto. | *I'll do it in a minute*, lo haré en un minuto. || *I was expecting him any minute*, le esperaba de un momento a otro. || *Just a minute!*, ¡un momento! || *The minute (that)*, en el momento en que. || *This very minute*, al momento, ahora mismo. || *Up to the minute news*, noticias (*f. pl.*) de última hora. || *Up to the minute style*, último grito, última moda.
minute [ˈminit] v. tr. Anotar, apuntar, tomar nota de (to take note). || Minutar (contracts). || Levantar acta de (of a meeting). || Cronometrar (a race).
minute book [—buk] n. Libro (*m.*) de actas. || Jur. Minutario, *m.*
minute gun [—gʌn] n. Cañón (*m.*) de salvas.
minute hand [—hænd] n. Minutero, *m.*
minutely [—li] adj./adv. A cada minuto.
minutely [maiˈnjutli] adv. Detalladamente, minuciosamente.
minuteman [ˈminitmən] n. U. S. Miliciano, *m.* [durante la Guerra de Independencia].

— Observ. El plural de esta palabra es *minutemen*.

minuteness [maiˈnjutnis] n. Minuciosidad, *f.* || Pequeñez, *f.* (smallness).
minutiae [maiˈnjuːʃiiː] pl. n. Pequeños detalles, *m.*, minucias, *f.*
minx [minks] n. Fam. Fresca, *f.* || Fam. *A sly minx*, una lagarta.
Miocene [ˈmaiəusiːn] adj. Geol. Mioceno.
— N. Geol. Mioceno, *m.*
miracle [ˈmirəkl] n. Milagro, *m.*: *Jesus's first miracle was the changing of water into wine*, el primer milagro de Jesús fue la conversión del agua en vino. || Fig. Milagro, *m.*, prodigio *m.* || — *By a miracle*, de milagro, por milagro. || *Miracle play*, milagro, *m.*, auto (*m.*) sacramental.
miraculous [miˈrækjuləs] adj. Milagroso, sa (supernatural). || Fig. Milagroso, sa; prodigioso, sa; maravilloso, sa.
mirador [ˌmirəˈdɔ] n. Mirador, *m.*
mirage [ˈmirɑːʒ] n. Espejismo, *m.* (natural phenomenon). || Fig. Espejismo, *m.* (illusion).
mire [ˈmaiə*] n. Fango, *m.*, lodo, *m.*, cieno, *m.* (mud). || Lodazal, *m.*, ciénaga, *f.* (muddy place).
mire [maiə*] v. tr. Enlodazar, encenagar (to cover with mud). || Atascar, empantanar (to bog down). || Manchar de barro, salpicar de barro (to soil).
— V. intr. Atascarse, empantanarse (to stick in mud).
mirk [məːk] n. See murk.
mirkiness [—inis] n. See murkiness.
mirky [—i] adj. Oscuro, ra; lóbrego, ga; tenebroso, sa.
mirror [ˈmirə*] n. Espejo, *m.* || Fig. Espejo, *m.*, reflejo, *m.* (representation): *his novel is a mirror of today's society*, su novela es un espejo de la sociedad de hoy. | Modelo, *m.*, ejemplo, *m.* (model). || Retrovisor, *m.* (on a car).
mirror [ˈmirə*] v. tr. Reflejar. || *Life is mirrored in his book*, la vida se refleja en su libro.
mirth [məːθ] n. Alegría, *f.*, júbilo, *m.* (glee). || Hilaridad, *f.* (hilarity). || Risas, *f. pl.*, carcajadas, *f. pl.* (laughter).
mirthful [—ful] adj. Alegre, risueño, ña (merry).
mirthless [—lis] adj. Triste, sin alegría.
miry [ˈmaiəri] adj. Fangoso, sa; lodoso, sa; cenagoso, sa (muddy). || Sucio, cia (dirty).
misadventure [ˈmisədˈventʃə*] n. Desgracia, *f.* (misfortune). || Accidente, *m.* (accident). || Contratiempo, *m.* (mishap). || *Death by misadventure*, muerte accidental.
misadvise [ˈmisədˈvaiz] v. tr. Aconsejar mal, dar malos consejos a.
misalliance [ˈmisəˈlaiəns] n. Casamiento (*m.*) desigual, mal casamiento, *m.* || Fig. Unión (*m.*) or asociación desacertada.
misanthrope [ˈmizənθrəup] n. Misántropo, *m.*
misanthropic [ˌmizənˈθrɔpik] adj. Misantrópico, ca.
misanthropist [miˈzænθrəpist] n. Misántropo, *m.*
misanthropy [miˈzænθrəpi] n. Misantropía, *f.*
misapplication [ˈmisˌæpliˈkeiʃən] n. Uso (*m.*) indebido (ill use). || Mala aplicación, *f.* || Malversación, *f.* (of funds).
misapply [ˈmisəˈplai] v. tr. Usar indebidamente. || Aplicar mal. || Malgastar: *to misapply one's efforts*, malgastar los esfuerzos. || Malversar (funds).
misapprehend [ˈmisˌæpriˈhend] v. tr. Comprender mal. || Interpretar mal.
misapprehension [ˈmisˌæpriˈhenʃən] n. Malentendido, *m.*, equivocación, *f.* || Mala interpretación, *f.*: *misapprehension of the facts*, mala interpretación de los hechos. || — *To be under a misapprehension*, estar equivocado. || *To be under the misapprehension that*, creer erróneamente que, creer equivocadamente que.
misappropriate [ˈmisəˈprəuprieit] n. Malversar, desfalcar (to embezzle). || Hacer mal uso de (to appropriate to a bad use).
misappropriation [ˈmisəˌprəupriˈeiʃən] n. Malversación, *f.*, desfalco, *m.* (embezzlement). || Mal uso, *m.* (bad use).
misbecame [ˈmisbiˈkeim] pret. See misbecome.
misbecome* [ˈmisbiˈkʌm] v. tr. No ir, ir mal, no convenir: *it misbecomes him to criticize*, no le va el criticar.

— Observ. Pret. **misbecame**; p. p. **misbecome**.

misbecoming [—iŋ] adj. Impropio, pia (*to*, de).
misbegotten [ˈmisbiˌgɔtn] adj. Ilegítimo, ma; bastardo, da (child). || Extravagante, descabellado, da; estrafalario, ria: *another of his misbegotten plans*, otro de sus proyectos descabellados.
misbehave [ˈmisbiˈheiv] v. intr. Portarse mal, comportarse mal (to behave badly). || Ser malo (a child).
misbehaviour (U. S. **misbehavior**) [ˈmisbiˈheivjə*] n. Mala conducta, *f.*, mal comportamiento, *m.*
misbelief [ˈmisbiˈliːf] n. Rel. Herejía, *f.*, falsa creencia, *f.*, creencia (*f.*) errónea (wrong belief). || Opinión (*f.*) errónea, error, *m.* (mistaken opinion).
misbeliever [ˈmisbiˈliːvə*] n. Rel. Hereje, *m.* & *f.*, incrédulo, la.
miscalculate [ˈmisˈkælkjuleit] v. tr./intr. Calcular mal.
miscalculation [ˈmisˌkælkjuˈleiʃən] n. Cálculo (*m.*) erróneo, error (*m.*) de cálculo. || Fig. Desacierto, *m.*, equivocación, *f.*, error, *m.*
miscall [ˈmisˈkɔːl] v. tr. Llamar equivocadamente, llamar erróneamente: *he was miscalled "the champion"*, era llamado erróneamente "el campeón". || Fam. Insultar.
miscarriage [misˈkæridʒ] n. Med. Aborto, *m.* || Error, *m.*: *a miscarriage of justice*, un error judicial. || Extravío, *m.*, pérdida, *f.* (of a letter). || Fig. Fracaso, *m.* (failure).

miscarry [misˈkæri] v. intr. MED. Abortar. || Extraviarse, perderse (a letter). || FIG. Fracasar (to fail).
miscast* [misˈkɑːst] v. tr. Dar un papel poco apropiado a (an actor). || Distribuir mal los papeles en [una obra de teatro] (a play). || Sumar mal (to add up badly).

— OBSERV. Pret. & p. p. ***miscast.***

miscegenation [ˌmisidʒiˈneiʃən] n. Cruce (*m.*) de razas, mestizaje, *m.*
miscellanea [ˌmisiˈleinjə] pl. n. Miscelánea, *f. sing.* (literary miscellany).
miscellaneous [ˌmisiˈleinjəs] adj. Variado, da; vario, ria; diverso, sa (news). || Ecléctico, ca (writer).
miscellany [miˈseləni] n. Miscelánea, *f.*, mezcla, *f.*
mischance [misˈtʃɑːns] n. Mala suerte, *f.*, infortunio, *m.*, desgracia, *f.* || *By some mischance*, por desgracia.
mischief [ˈmistʃif] n. Travesura, *f.*, diablura, *f.* (of a child). || Daño, *m.*, perjuicio, *m.* (harm): *to do s.o. a mischief*, causar un daño a alguien. || Maldad, *f.*, mala intención, *f.* (evil): *there is no mischief in him*, no tiene ninguna maldad. || Discordia, *f.* (discord): *to make mischief between*, sembrar la discordia entre. || Pícaro, ra; diablillo, lla (mischievous child). || — *The mischief of it is that*, lo malo de esto es que. || *To be up to (some) mischief*, estar pensando en hacer de las suyas. || *To get into mischief*, hacer tonterías. || *To keep s.o. out of mischief*, impedir a alguien que haga tonterías *or* disparates.
mischief-maker [—ˌmeikə*] n. Lioso, sa; persona (*f.*) enredadora.
mischievous [ˈmistʃivəs] adj. Travieso, sa (child). || Malo, la (wicked). || Lioso, sa; enredador, ra (troublemaking). || Nocivo, va; dañino, na (harmful). || Perjudicial (damaging). || Malicioso, sa (look).
mischievousness [—nis] n. Picardía, *f.* (of a child). || Travesura, *f.* (prank). || Maldad, *f.* (wickedness).
miscible [ˈmisibl] adj. Miscible, mezclable.
miscolour (U. S. **miscolor**) [misˈkʌlə*] v. tr. Deformar, desnaturalizar, respresentar bajo un aspecto engañoso: *to miscolour the facts*, deformar los hechos.
misconceive [ˈmiskənˈsiːv] v. intr. Tener un concepto erróneo (*of*, de).
— V. tr. Comprender *or* interpretar mal.
misconception [ˈmiskənˈsepʃən] n. Concepto (*m.*) erróneo, concepto (*m.*) falso, idea (*f.*) falsa. || Equivocación, *f.*, malentendido, *m.* (misunderstanding).
misconduct [misˈkɔndʌkt] n. Mala conducta, *f.* (misbehaviour). || Mala administración, *f.* (mismanagement). || JUR. Adulterio, *m.* (adultery).
misconduct [ˈmiskənˈdʌkt] v. tr. Administrar *or* dirigir mal (to mismanage). || *To misconduct o.s.*, portarse mal.
misconstruction [ˈmiskənsˈtrʌkʃən] n. Mala interpretación, *f.*
misconstrue [ˈmiskənˈstruː] v. tr. Interpretar mal.
miscount [ˈmisˈkaunt] n. Error (*m.*) de cálculo, cálculo (*m.*) erróneo.
miscount [misˈkaunt] v. intr. Calcular mal, equivocarse en la cuenta.
— V. tr. Calcular mal.
miscreant [ˈmiskriənt] adj. Bellaco, ca (villainous). || Infiel, herético, ca.
— N. Bellaco, ca (villain). || Infiel, *m.* & *f.*, hereje, *m.* & *f.*
miscreate [ˈmiskriˈeit] or **miscreated** [—id] adj. Contrahecho, cha.
miscue [ˈmisˈkjuː] n. Pifia, *f.* (in billiards).
miscue [ˈmisˈkjuː] v. intr. Pifiar (in billiards). || THEATR. Equivocarse.
misdeal [ˈmisˈdiːl] n. Error (*m.*) en el reparto de las cartas.
misdeal* [ˈmisˈdiːl] v. tr./intr. Repartir mal.

— OBSERV. Pret. & p. p. ***misdealt.***

misdealt [ˈmisˈdelt] pret. & p. p. See MISDEAL.
misdeed [ˈmisˈdiːd] n. Delito, *m.* (crime). || Fechoría, *f.* (villainy).
misdemean [ˌmisdiˈmiːn] v. intr. Portarse mal.
misdemeanant [—ənt] n. JUR. Delincuente, *m.* & *f.*
misdemeanour (U. S. **misdemeanor**) [ˌmisdiˈmiːnə*] n. JUR. Infracción, *f.*, delito (*m.*) menor. || FIG. Fechoría, *f.* (misdeed). | Mala conducta, *f.* (bad behaviour).
misdirect [ˈmisdiˈrekt] v. tr. Dirigir mal (to give wrong directions). || Poner mal las señas en (a letter). || JUR. Instruir mal [al jurado] (a jury). || Dirigir mal (to aim badly).
misdirection [ˈmisdiˈrekʃən] n. Dirección (*f.*) errónea, mala dirección, *f.* (in a letter). || Información (*f.*) errónea (wrong information). || JUR. Malas instrucciones, *f. pl.* [al jurado] (of the jury).
misdoing [ˈmisˈduːiŋ] n. Delito, *m.* (crime). || Fechoría, *f.* mala acción, *f.* (villainy). || Falta, *f.* (fault).
misdoubt [ˈmisˈdaut] v. tr. Dudar (to have doubt about). || Sospechar (to suspect).
mise [miːz] n. Acuerdo, *m.* (agreement).
miser [ˈmaizə*] n. Avaro, ra.
miserable [ˈmizərəbl] adj. Desgraciado, da; desdichado, da (unfortunate): *I have never seen a man so miserable*, nunca vi a un hombre tan desgraciado. || Triste (sad). || Fatal, mal (sick): *I feel miserable*, me encuentro fatal. || Desagradable (disagreeable). || Miserable (wretched). || De pena (distressing). || Deplorable, lamentable (deplorable). || Vil, despreciable (contemptible). || Sin valor (valueless). || Indecente, miserable: *a miserable salary*, un sueldo miserable. || Malo, la: *miserable weather*, mal tiempo. || Miserable: *after four years he had saved a miserable twenty pounds*, al cabo de cuatro años sólo había ahorrado veinte miserables libras.
miserere [mizəˈriəri] n. REL. MUS. Miserere, *m.* (psalm).
misericord (U. S. **misericorde**) [miˈzerikɔːd] n. Relajación (*f.*) de las reglas monásticas. || Refectorio, *m.* [donde las reglas del ayuno son menos severas] (refectory). || Puñal, *m.*, misericordia, *f.* (dagger). || Misericordia, *f.*, coma, *f.* (seat).

— OBSERV. Esta palabra no tiene nunca el sentido de « compasión » o « perdón » que se traducen por *mercy.*

miserliness [ˈmaizəlinis] n. Avaricia, *f.*, mezquindad, *f.*, tacañería, *f.*
miserly [ˈmaizəli] adj. Mezquino, na, avaro, ra; tacaño, ña; avariento, ta.
misery [ˈmizəri] n. Miseria, *f.*, pobreza, *f.* (poverty). || Desgracia, *f.* (misfortune). || Tristeza, *f.*, pena, *f.* (sadness). || Desgracia, *f.*, infelicidad, *f.* (unhappiness). || Sufrimiento, *m.*, dolor, *m.* (pain). || Sufrimiento, *m.*, aflicción, *f.* (affliction). || — FAM. *She makes my life a misery*, me amarga la vida. || *To put a horse out of its misery*, rematar un caballo.
misestimate [misˈestimeit] n. Cálculo (*m.*) erróneo, estimación (*f.*) errónea.
misestimate [misˈestimeit] v. tr. Calcular mal, estimar erróneamente.
misfeasance [misˈfiːzəns] n. JUR. Abuso (*m.*) de autoridad.
misfire [ˈmisˈfaiə*] n. Fallo (*m.*) de tiro (of a gun). || Fallo (*m.*) de encendido (of a motor).
misfire [ˈmisˈfaiə*] v. intr. Fallar (a gun). || Tener fallos, fallar (a car). || FAM. No tener éxito, fallar: *the joke misfired*, el chiste no tuvo éxito.
misfit [ˈmisfit] n. Inadaptado, da (person). || Traje (*m.*) que no cae bien (suit).
misfortune [misˈfɔːtʃən] n. Desgracia, *f.*, infortunio, *m.*, desdicha, *f.* (ill fortune): *he had the misfortune to be blind*, tuvo la desgracia de ser ciego; *companion in misfortune*, compañero de infortunio. || Desgracia, *f.* (mishap).
misgave [ˈmisˈgeiv] pret. See MISGIVE.
misgive* [ˈmisˈgiv] v. tr. Hacer dudar (to cause doubt). || Hacer sospechar (to cause suspicion). || Hacer temer (to cause fear). || *My heart misgives me that*, tengo el presentimiento de que.

— OBSERV. Pret. ***misgave;*** p. p. ***misgiven.***

misgiven [ˈmisˈgivn] p. p. See MISGIVE.
misgiving [—iŋ] n. Duda, *f.*, recelo, *m.* (mistrust): *with some misgiving*, con cierto recelo. || Inquietud, *f.*, aprensión, *f.*, presentimiento, *m.*
misgovern [ˈmisˈgʌvən] v. tr. Gobernar mal (a country). || Administrar mal (a business).
misgovernment [—mənt] n. Mal gobierno, *m.*, desgobierno, *m.* (of a country). || Mala administración, *f.* (of a business).
misguidance [ˈmisˈgaidəns] n. Mala dirección, *f.* || Mala orientación, *f.* || Malos consejos, *m. pl.* (bad advice).
misguide [ˈmisˈgaid] v. tr. Dirigir mal (to direct badly). || Orientar mal (to guide badly). || Aconsejar mal (to advise badly). || Descaminar (to mislead).
misguided [—d] adj. Mal aconsejado, da (badly advised). || Descaminado, da (mislead). || Poco afortunado, da (attempt, conduct).
mishandle [ˈmisˈhændl] v. tr. Tratar mal, maltratar. || Manejar mal (to handle badly). || Llevar mal, tratar mal (a matter).
mishap [ˈmishæp] n. Contratiempo, *m.*, accidente, *m.*, desgracia, *f.*
mishear* [ˈmishiə*] v. tr. Oír mal.

— OBSERV. Pret. & p. p. ***misheard.***

misheard [ˈmisˈhəːd] pret. & p. p. See MISHEAR.
mishmash [ˈmiʃmæʃ] n. Mezcla, *f.*, revoltijo, *m.*
misinform [ˈmisinˈfɔːm] v. tr. Informar mal.
misinformation [misinfɔːˈmeiʃən] n. Información (*f.*) errónea.
misinterpret [ˈmisinˈtəːprit] v. tr. Interpretar mal.
misinterpretation [ˈmisinˌtəːpriˈteiʃən] n. Interpretación (*f.*) errónea, mala interpretación, *f.*
misjudge [ˈmisˈdʒʌdʒ] v. tr./intr. Juzgar mal.
misjudgment or **misjudgement** [—mənt] n. Juicio (*m.*) equivocado, estimación (*f.*) errónea.
mislaid [misˈleid] pret. & p. p. See MISLAY.
mislay* [misˈlei] v. tr. Extraviar, perder.

— OBSERV. Pret. & p. p. ***mislaid.***

mislead* [misˈliːd] v. tr. Engañar (to deceive). || Equivocar, descaminar (to lead into error). || Descarriar, corromper (to corrupt).

— OBSERV. Pret. & p. p. ***misled.***

misleading [—iŋ] adj. Engañoso, sa.
misled [misˈled] pret. & p. p. See MISLEAD.
mismanage [ˈmisˈmænidʒ] v. tr. Dirigir mal, administrar mal.
mismanagement [—mənt] n. Mala dirección, *f.*, mala administración, *f.*

mismatch [ˈmisˈmætʃ] v. tr. Emparejar mal.
misname [ˈmisˈneim] v. tr. Dar un nombre equivocado a, llamar equivocadamente.
misnomer [ˈmisˈnəumə*] n. Nombre (*m.*) equivocado. || Nombre (*m.*) inapropiado. || JUR. Error (*m.*) en el nombre.
misogamy [miˈsɔgəmi] n. Misogamia, *f.*
misogynist [maiˈsɔdʒinist] n. Misógino, *m.*
misogynous [maiˈsɔdʒinəs] adj. Misógino, na.
misogyny [maiˈsɔdʒini] n. Misoginia, *f.*
misplace [ˈmisˈpleis] v. tr. Colocar mal *or* fuera de su lugar. || Extraviar, perder (to lose). || Colocar mal (an accent). || FIG. Dar indebidamente *or* inmerecidamente (one's affection, confidence).
misplaced [—t] adj. Mal colocado, da. || Extraviado, da; perdido, da (lost). || Fuera de lugar, impropio, pia (word). || Inmerecido, da (affection).
misplacement [—mənt] n. Mala colocación, *f.*, colocación (*f.*) fuera de lugar. || Extravío, *m.* (loss).
misprint [ˈmisˈprint] n. Errata, *f.*, error (*m.*) de imprenta, falta (*f.*) tipográfica.
misprint [ˈmisˈprint] v. tr. Imprimir mal.
misprision [misˈpriʒən] n. JUR. Ocultación, *f.*, encubrimiento, *m.* (of a crime).
mispronounce [ˈmisprəˈnauns] v. tr. Pronunciar mal.
mispronunciation [ˈmisprəˌnʌnsiˈeiʃən] n. Mala pronunciación, *f.*
misquotation [ˈmiskwəuˈteiʃən] n. Cita (*f.*) errónea.
misquote [ˈmisˈkwəut] v. tr. Citar incorrectamente.
misread* [ˈmisˈri:d] v. tr. Leer mal (to read badly). || Interpretar mal (to interpret badly).
— OBSERV. Pret. & p. p. ***misread*** [ˈmisˈred].
misremember [ˈmisriˈmembə*] v. tr. Acordarse mal de, recordar mal.
misrepresent [ˈmisˌrepriˈzent] v. tr. Representar mal. || Desnaturalizar, desfigurar, desvirtuar (to distort).
misrepresentation [ˈmisˌreprizenˈteiʃən] n. Representación (*f.*) falsa. || Desnaturalización, *f.*, desfiguración, *f.* (of a fact).
misrule [ˈmisˈru:l] n. Mala administración, *f.*, mal gobierno, *m.* (misgovernment). || Desorden, *m.* (disorder).
misrule [ˈmisˈru:l] v. tr. Gobernar mal.
miss [mis] n. Señorita, *f.*: *Miss Jones*, la señorita Jones; *good morning, Miss*, buenos días, señorita. || *Miss World*, Miss Mundo.
miss [mis] n. Tiro (*m.*) errado, fallo, *m.* (shot). || Fracaso, *m.*, fallo, *m.* (failure). || — FIG. *A miss is as good as a mile*, por un clavo se pierde una herradura. || *To give a miss*, prescindir de: *I can give tobacco a miss*, puedo prescindir del tabaco; no asistir a (a conference, etc.), no visitar (a monument). || *To score a near miss*, acercarse al blanco.
miss [mis] v. tr. No dar en: *to miss the target*, no dar en el blanco. || Errar, fallar: *he missed his shot*, erró el tiro. || Perder: *to miss the train*, perder el tren. || Perder, dejar pasar, desperdiciar: *to miss an opportunity*, dejar pasar una oportunidad. || Notar la ausencia de (to note the absence of): *we missed him yesterday*, notamos su ausencia ayer. || Echar de menos: *I miss you very much*, te echo mucho de menos. || No conseguir, no alcanzar, fallar (one's aim). || Faltar a: *to miss class, an appointment*, faltar a clase, a una cita. || No asistir a, no acudir a (a meeting). || Dejar de encontrar: *you can't miss my house*, no puede dejar de encontrar mi casa. || Perderse en, equivocarse de (one's way). || Perderse: *I mustn't miss this play*, no debo perderme esta comedia. || No encontrar: *I missed her at the hotel*, no la encontré en el hotel. || Saltarse: *to miss a page*, saltarse una página. || Omitir (to omit). || Perder: *I missed my lighter in the underground*, perdí mi encendedor en el metro. || No entender, no comprender: *to miss a joke*, no entender un chiste. || No acertar: *to miss the solution*, no acertar la solución. || — *I missed what you said*, se me escapó lo que dijiste. || *It just missed me*, por poco me dio. || *The bullet just missed me*, la bala me pasó rozando. || *To miss one's footing*, perder pie. || *To miss out*, perder (to let go by), saltar, omitir (to omit). || FAM. *To miss the boat*, perder el tren, perder la oportunidad. || *To miss the mark*, no dar en el blanco. || *To miss the point*, no comprender. || *You are much missed*, se te echa mucho de menos. || *You did not miss much*, no te perdiste gran cosa. || *You just missed going to prison*, por poco te metían en la cárcel.
— V. intr. Errar *or* fallar el tiro. || No dar en el blanco. || Fallar, tener fallos (a motor). || Faltar: *you have never missed*, nunca has faltado; *is anything missing?*, ¿falta algo? || Fallar: *it can't miss!*, ¡es imposible que falle!
missal [ˈmisəl] n. REL. Misal, *m.*
missel thrush [—θrʌʃ] n. ZOOL. Cagaaceite, *m.*, tordo (*m.*) mayor (bird).
misshapen [ˈmisˈʃeipən] adj. Deformado, da (hat). || Deforme, contrahecho, cha (person).
missile [ˈmisail] n. Proyectil, *m.*, cohete, *m.*, misil, *m.*: *guided missile*, proyectil teledirigido. || Arma (*f.*) arrojadiza.
— Adj. Arrojadizo, za (weapon).
missing [ˈmisiŋ] adj. Perdido, da (lost). || Ausente (absent): *four pupils are missing*, cuatro alumnos están ausentes. || Desaparecido, da (disappeared). || Que falta (lacking). || — *Number of dead and missing*, número de muertos y desaparecidos. || *To be missing*, faltar: *how many are missing?*, ¿cuántos faltan?; no haber vuelto, haber desaparecido: *four planes are missing*, cuatro aviones no han vuelto.
mission [ˈmiʃən] n. Misión, *f.*: *to carry out a mission*, cumplir una misión. || REL. Misión, *f.* || U. S. Embajada, *f.* (embassy). || — *Goodwill mission*, misión de buena voluntad. || *Trade mission*, misión comercial.
missionary [ˈmiʃnəri] adj. Misional, misionero, ra.
— N. REL. Misionero, ra.
missioner [ˈmiʃnə*] n. Misionero, ra.
missis [ˈmisiz] n. FAM. Señora, *f.* (used by servants). | Parienta, *f.* (the wife).
Mississipi [ˌmisiˈsipi] pr. n. GEOGR. Misisipí, *m.*
missive [ˈmisiv] n. Misiva, *f.* (letter).
Missouri [miˈzuəri] pr. n. GEOGR. Misuri, *m.*
misspell* [ˈmisˈspel] v. tr. Escribir mal, ortografiar mal.
— OBSERV. Pret. & p. p. ***misspelt.***
misspelling [—iŋ] n. Falta (*f.*) de ortografía.
misspelt [ˈmisˈspelt] pret. & p. p. See MISSPELL.
misspend* [ˈmisˈspend] v. tr. Gastar mal, malgastar (money). || Desperdiciar, perder (one's time).
— OBSERV. Pret. & p. p. ***misspent.***
misstate [ˈmisˈsteit] v. tr. Exponer mal (to state incorrectly). || Desnaturalizar (to distort).
misstatement [—mənt] n. Afirmación (*f.*) *or* declaración (*f.*) errónea (incorrect statement). || Error, *m.*
misstep [ˈmisˈstep] n. Paso (*m.*) en falso, tropezón, *m.*, traspié, *m.* || FIG. Desliz, *m.*
missus [ˈmisəs] n. FAM. See MISSIS.
missy [ˈmisi] n. U. S. Señorita, *f.*
mist [mist] n. Niebla, *f.*, neblina, *f.* (fog). || Bruma, *f.* (at sea). || Calina, *f.* (haze). || Vaho, *m.* (of glasses). || FIG. Velo, *m.*: *a mist of tears*, un velo de lágrimas. || — *Scotch mist*, llovizna, *f.* || FIG. *The mist of time*, la noche de los tiempos.
mist [mist] v. tr. Cubrir de niebla. || Empañar (a mirror, the eyes).
— V. intr. Cubrirse de niebla. || Empañarse.
mistakable [misˈteikəbl] adj. Que puede confundirse: *the two boys are easily mistakable*, los dos chicos se pueden confundir fácilmente. || Ambiguo, gua; equívoco, ca (ambiguous).
mistake [misˈteik] n. Equivocación, *f.*, error, *m.*: *he made the mistake of*, cometió el error de; *I acknowledged my mistake*, confesé mi equivocación. || GRAMM. Falta, *f.*: *spelling mistake*, falta de ortografía. || — *And no mistake!*, ¡sin duda alguna!, ¡ciertamente!, ¡ya lo creo! || *By mistake*, sin querer (unintentionally), por equivocación. || *Let there be no mistake* o *make no mistake about it*, que quede bien claro. || *Sorry, my mistake*, lo siento, ha sido culpa mía. || *To make a mistake*, equivocarse, cometer un error.
mistake* [misˈteik] v. tr. Entender *or* interpretar mal (to misunderstand): *you mistook my words*, interpretaste mal mis palabras. || Equivocarse en, confundirse respecto a (to be wrong). || Equivocarse de (one's way). || — *There is no mistaking his voice*, su voz es inconfundible. || *To mistake s.o. for*, tomar a alguien por, confundir a alguien con.
— V. intr. Equivocarse.
— OBSERV. Pret. ***mistook;*** p. p. ***mistaken.***
mistaken [—ən] p. p. See MISTAKE.
— Adj. Equivocado, da (wrong): *you are mistaken*, estás equivocado. || Erróneo, a; inexacto, ta (inexact): *a mistaken declaration*, una declaración inexacta. || Mal comprendido, da; mal interpretado, da (word). || — *If I am not mistaken*, si no me equivoco. || *Mistaken ideas*, ideas falsas. || *Mistaken identity*, identificación errónea. || *To be mistaken about* o *as to*, estar equivocado *or* equivocarse acerca de *or* en cuanto a. || *You are mistaken in thinking that*, te engañas si piensas que, estás equivocado al pensar que.
Mister [ˈmistə*] n. Señor, *m.*: *good morning, Mister Jones*, buenos días, señor Jones. || FAM. Señor, *m.*: *give us a shilling, Mister*, me da un chelín, señor.
mistime [ˈmisˈtaim] v. tr. Hacer *or* decir a destiempo. || Calcular mal el momento de: *they mistimed the strike*, calcularon mal el momento de la huelga. || — *To mistime an answer*, contestar a destiempo. || *To nistime an entry*, entrar a destiempo.
mistiness [ˈmistinis] n. Estado (*m.*) brumoso, nebulosidad, *f.*
mistle thrush [ˈmisəlθrʌʃ] n. U. S. ZOOL. Cagaaceite, *m.*, tordo (*m.*) mayor (bird).
mistletoe [ˈmisltəu] n. BOT. Muérdago, *m.* (plant).
mistook [misˈtuk] pret. See MISTAKE.
mistral [ˈmistrəl] n. Mistral, *m.* (wind).
mistranslate [ˈmistrænsˈleit] v. tr. Traducir mal.
mistranslation [ˈmistrænsˈleiʃən] n. Mala traducción, *f.*, traducción (*f.*) errónea.
mistreat [ˈmisˈtri:t] v. tr. Maltratar, tratar mal.
mistreatment [—mənt] n. Trato (*m.*) malo, malos tratos, *m. pl.*, maltrato, *m.*
mistress [ˈmistris] n. Amante, *f.*, querida, *f.* (lover): *she was the king's mistress*, era la amante del rey. || Señora, *f.*: *the mistress of the house*, la señora de la casa. || Dueña, *f.*: *the dog's mistress*, la dueña del perro. || Profesora, *f.*: *the French mistress*, la profesora

de francés. || — *Mistress Jones*, la señora Jones. || *Mistress Mary*, Doña María. || *School mistress*, maestra (*f.*) de escuela. || *She is a mistress in the art of cookery*, es una experta en el arte de cocinar. || *She was mistress of the situation*, era dueña de *or* dominaba la situación.

mistrial [ˈmisˈtraiəl] n. JUR. Juicio que se declara nulo [por falta de unanimidad del jurado o por error de procedimiento].

mistrust [ˈmisˈtrʌst] n. Recelo, *m.* (suspicion). || Desconfianza, *f.* (lack of confidence).

mistrust [ˈmisˈtrʌst] v. tr. Recelar de, desconfiar de (to regard with suspicion): *I mistrust him*, desconfío de él. || Dudar de, no tener confianza en (to feel no confidence in): *he mistrusts his own capacities*, no tiene confianza en sus propias posibilidades.

mistrustful [—ful] adj. Receloso, sa; desconfiado, da.

misty [ˈmisti] adj. De niebla: *a misty day*, un día de niebla. || Brumoso, sa (in the sea). || FIG. Vago, ga; confuso, sa; nebuloso, sa (vague). || Empañado, da: *misty glass*, cristal empañado; *misty eyes*, la mirada empañada.

misunderstand* [ˈmisʌndəˈstænd] v. tr. Comprender *or* entender mal. || Interpretar mal. || *He misunderstood you*, no comprendió lo que le dijo.

— OBSERV. Pret. & p. p. ***misunderstood***.

misunderstanding [—iŋ] n. Error, *m.*, equivocación, *f.*, equívoco, *m.*, malentendido, *m.* (mistake): *there must be some misunderstanding*, debe de haber alguna equivocación. || Desavenencia, *f.*, desacuerdo, *m.* (dissension). || Concepto (*m.*) erróneo.

misunderstood [ˈmisʌndəˈstud] pret. & p. p. See MISUNDERSTAND.

— Adj. Mal comprendido, da; mal intepretado, da (thing). || Incomprendido, da (person).

misusage [ˈmisˈjuːsidʒ] n. See MISUSE.

misuse [ˈmisˈjuːs] n. Mal uso, *m.*, uso (*m.*) incorrecto (of words). || Maltrato, *m.* (ill treatment). || Mal empleo, *m.*, mal manejo, *m.* (of a machine, etc.). || JUR. Abuso, *m.*: *misuse of authority*, abuso de autoridad. || JUR. *Fraudulent misuse of funds*, malversación de fondos (embezzlement).

misuse [ˈmisˈjuːz] v. tr. Emplear mal (words, etc.). || Maltratar, tratar mal (to mistreat). || Manejar *or* emplear mal (a machine, etc.). || JUR. Abusar de, hacer mal uso de. | Malversar (funds).

mite [mait] n. Arador, *m.*, acárido, *m.* (insect). || REL. Ardite, *m.* (coin of very little value). || FIG. Pizca, *f.* (small quantity). | Chiquillo, lla (child). | Óbolo, *m.* (small contribution). || FIG. *It's a mite heavy*, es algo pesado.

miter [ˈmaitə*] n./v. tr. U. S. See MITRE.

miter box [—bɔks] n. U. S. Caja (*f.*) de ingletes.

mitered [—d] adj. U. S. Mitrado, da.

miter joint [—dʒɔint] n. U. S. Inglete, *m.*

Mithridates [ˌmiθriˈdeitiːz] pr. n. HIST. Mitrídates, *m.*

mithridatism [ˌmiθriˈdeitizəm] n. Mitridatismo, *m.*

mitigate [ˈmitigeit] v. tr. Mitigar, aliviar (a penalty). || Aligerar, aliviar (burden). || Temperar, templar, suavizar (climate). || Aliviar, hacer llevadero (pain, sorrow). || Atenuar (a fault). || Calmar, aplacar, moderar (wrath).

mitigation [ˌmitiˈgeiʃən] n. Mitigación, *f.*, alivio, *m.* (of a penalty). || Aligeramiento, *m.*, alivio, *m.* (of a burden). || Atenuación, *f.* (of a fault). || Alivio, *m.* (of a pain, sorrow). || Aplacamiento, *m.*, moderación, *f.* (of wrath).

mitigative [ˈmitəˌgeitiv] adj. Mitigante.

mitigator [ˈmitigeitə*] n. Mitigador, ra

mitigatory [ˈmitigətəri] adj. Mitigador, ra; mitigante.

mitosis [miˈtəusis] n. BIOL. Mitosis, *f.*

mitral [ˈmaitrəl] adj. Mitral. || ANAT. *Mitral valve*, válvula (*f.*) mitral.

mitre [ˈmaitə*] n. REL. Mitra, *f.* (headdress). || Inglete, *m.* (in carpentry).

mitre [ˈmaitə*] v. tr. Unir con ingletes. || REL. Conferir la mitra a.

mitre box [—bɔks] n. Caja (*f.*) de ingletes.

mitred [—d] adj. Mitrado, da: *mitred abbot*, abad mitrado.

mitre joint [—dʒɔint] n. Inglete, *m.*

mitt [mit] n. Mitón, *m.* (fingerless glove). || Guante, *m.* (glove). || FAM. Puño, *m.* (fist). | Mano, *f.* (hand).

mitten [ˈmitn] n. Manopla, *f.* (glove with single division for fingers). || Mitón, *m.* (mitt). || FAM. Guante, *m.* (glove). || FIG. *To give s.o. the mitten*, dar calabazas a uno.

mittimus [ˈmitimʌs] n. JUR. Orden (*f.*) de detención, auto (*m.*) de prisión.

mix [miks] n. Mezcla, *f.*

mix [miks] v. tr. Mezclar (to bring together several ingredients). || Amasar (flour, plaster, cement, etc.). || Preparar (drinks). || Aliñar, aderezar (to prepare a salad). || Mover (to turn over a salad). || Hacer (a mayonnaise). || FIG. Combinar, compaginar: *to mix business with pleasure*, combinar los negocios con el placer. | Reunir: *the party mixed old and young people*, la fiesta reunió a ancianos y jóvenes. || — *I don't want to get mixed up in it*, no quiero meterme en eso, no quiero estar comprometido en eso. || *To get all mixed up*, hacerse un lío. || FAM. *To mix it*, llegar a las manos. || *To mix up*, mezclar (to give a mix), confundir: *he mixed me up with Peter*, me confundió con Pedro; meter, complicar, implicar, comprometer (in an affair).

— V. intr. Mezclarse (to become mixed). || Asociarse (to associate). || Mezclarse, frecuentar, alternar: *he mixes with a bad crowd*, se mezcla con mala gente. || *He doesn't mix well*, no se lleva bien con la gente.

mixable [ˈmiksəbl] adj. Mezclable.

mixed [mikst] adj. Mezclado, da (blended). || Mixto, ta: *mixed school*, escuela mixta. || Variado, da (varied). || BOT. Mezclado, da. || Surtido, da; variado, da (sweets). || AGR. Mixto, ta: *mixed fertilizers*, abonos mixtos. || — SP. *Mixed doubles*, mixtos, *m.*, doble mixto, *m. sing.* || *Mixed feelings*, sentimientos contradictorios. || *Mixed ice*, helado (*m.*) de varios gustos. || *Mixed salad*, ensalada mixta.

mixed-up [—ʌp] adj. Mezclado, da. || Confuso, sa (confused). || Revuelto, ta (in disorder). || FIG. Confuso, sa.

mixer [ˈmiksə*] n. Mezcladora, *f.* || Hormigonera, *f.*, mezcladora, *f.* (of mortar). || CULIN. Batidora, *f.* || ELECTR. Mezclador, *m.* [de sonidos] (of sound). || CINEM. Operador (*m.*) de sonido. || FAM. Persona (*f.*) sociable (sociable person). || FAM. *To be a good mixer*, tener don de gentes, ser sociable.

mixing [ˈmiksiŋ] n. Mezcla, *f.*

mixture [ˈmikstʃə*] n. Mezcla, *f.* || MED. Mixtura, *f.* || CHEM. Mezcla, *f.* || Tela (*f.*) de mezclilla (fabric).

mix-up [ˈmiksˈʌp] n. FAM. Lío, *m.*, enredo, *m.*, confusión, *f.* (confusion). | Pelea, *f.* (fight).

mizen or **mizzen** [ˈmizn] n. MAR. Artimón, *m.*, mesana, *f.* (sail). | Palo (*m.*) de mesana (mast).

mizenmast or **mizzenmast** [—mɑːst] n. MAR. Palo (*m.*) de mesana.

mizzen-topgallant mast [—tɔpˈgæləntmɑːst] n. MAR. Mastelero (*m.*) de perico.

mizzen-topmast or **mizzen-topmast** [—ˈtɔpmɑːst] n. MAR. Mastelero (*m.*) de sobremesana.

mizzen-topsail [—ˈtɔpseil] n. MAR. Sobremesana, *f.*

mizzle [ˈmizl] n. Llovizna, *f.*

mizzle [ˈmizl] v. impers. Lloviznar (to drizzle).

— V. intr. FAM. Largarse (to go).

mnemonic [niˈmɔnik] adj. Mnemotécnico, ca; nemotécnico, ca.

mnemonics [—s] n. Mnemotecnia, *f.*, mnemotécnica, *f.*, nemotecnia, *f.*

Moabite [ˈməuəbait] adj./n. Moabita.

moan [məun] n. Gemido, *m.*, quejido, *m.*, lamento, *m.* (sound). || Queja, *f.* (complaint). || *To have a moan about sth.*, quejarse de algo.

moan [məun] v. intr. Gemir (to groan). || Quejarse, lamentarse (*about*, de) [to complain].

— V. tr. Decir gimiendo (to groan). || Llorar (a dead person). || Deplorar, lamentar (one's fate).

moaning [—iŋ] adj. Que gime (groaning). || Quejoso, sa (complaining).

— N. Gemido, *m.* (sound). || Queja, *f.* (complaint).

moat [məut] n. Foso, *m.* (of a castle).

moated [—id] adj. Con foso, rodeado con un foso.

mob [mɔb] n. Multitud, *f.*, muchedumbre, *f.* (crowd). || Tropel, *m.*, turba, *f.* (unruly crowd). || Pandilla, *f.* (gang). || Clase (*f.*) baja (low class). || Populacho, *m.*, masa, *f.* (masses). || Gentuza, *f.*, chusma, *f.* (rabble). || Bandada, *f.* (of birds). || — *Mob law*, ley (*f.*) de Lynch. || *To join the mob*, echarse a la calle.

mob [mɔb] v. tr. Asaltar, atropellar, acosar (to attack in masses). || Acosar, rodear: *the bullfighter was mobbed by his fans*, el torero fue rodeado por los aficionados. || Atestar: *the streets were mobbed with people*, las calles estaban atestadas de gente.

— V. intr. Agruparse, aglomerarse, apiñarse.

mobcap [—kæp] n. Cofia, *f.* (hat).

mobile [ˈməubail] adj. Móvil, movible. || Transportable, portátil (portable). || Ambulante (itinerant). || Orientable (antenna). || Móvil (facial expressions). || FIG. Voluble, cambiadizo, za (character). || FAM. *When we are mobile again*, cuando estemos de nuevo motorizados.

— N. ARTS. Móvil, *m.*

mobility [məuˈbiliti] n. Movilidad, *f.* || FIG. Volubilidad, *f.*

mobilizable [məubiˈlaizəbl] adj. Movilizable.

mobilization [ˌməubilaiˈzeiʃən] n. Movilización, *f.*

mobilize [ˈməubilaiz] v. tr. Movilizar.

mobster [ˈmɔbstə*] n. U. S. FAM. Gángster, *m.*

moccasin [ˈmɔkəsin] n. Mocasín, *m.* (shoe). || ZOOL. Mocasín, *m.* (snake).

mocha [ˈmɔkə] n. Moca, *m.* (coffee).

mock [mɔk] adj. Simulado, da; fingido, da (sham): *mock laugh*, risa fingida. || Falso, sa: *mock modesty*, falsa modestia. || Imitado, da (imitated). || Burlesco, ca; cómico, ca (burlesque). || COMM. De imitación, artificial: *mock bronze*, bronce de imitación. || — *Mock battle*, simulacro (*m.*) de combate. || *Mock jewelry*, joyas (*f. pl.*) de imitación, bisutería, *f.*

— N. Mofa, *f.*, burla, *f.* (sneer). || Hazmerreír, *m.* (laughingstock). || Simulacro, *m.* (simulacrum). || *To make a mock of sth.*, ridiculizar algo, hacer mofa de algo.

mock [mɔk] v. tr. Burlarse de, mofarse de, reírse de (to scoff at): *the other children mocked him*, los demás chicos se rieron de él. || Ridiculizar (to ridicule). || Frustrar (to thwart, to frustrate). || Remedar, imitar a (to mimic). || Defraudar (to deceive). || Burlar (the law).

— V. intr. Burlarse, reírse: *to mock at*, burlarse de.

mocker [—ə*] n. Mofador, ra; burlón, ona.

mockery [ˈmɔkəri] n. Burla, *f.*, mofa, *f.* (sneer). || Hazmerreír, *m.* (laughingstock). || Parodia, *f.*, simulacro, *m.*: *a mockery of the truth*, una parodia de la verdad. || Imitación, *f.*, remedo, *m.* (imitation). || *To make a mockery of*, ridiculizar.

mock-heroic [ˈmɔkhiˈrəuik] adj. Heroicoburlesco, ca; heroicocómico, ca.

mocking [ˈmɔkiŋ] adj. Burlón, ona; mofador, ra.

— N. Burla, *f.*, mofa, *f.* (mockery).

mockingbird [—bəːd] n. ZOOL. Sinsonte, *m.*

mock orange [ˈmɔkˈɔrindʒ] n. BOT. Jeringuilla, *f.*

mock-up [ˈmɔkʌp] n. Maqueta, *f.*, modelo (*m.*) a escala.

modal [ˈməudl] adj. GRAMM. MUS. PHIL. JUR. Modal.

modality [məuˈdæliti] n. Modalidad, *f.*

mode [məud] n. Modo, *m.*, manera, *f.*, forma, *f.* (manner): *a mode of life*, una manera de vivir. || Moda, *f.* (fashion). || MUS. PHIL. GRAMM. Modo, *m.*

model [ˈmɔdl] n. Maqueta, *f.* (of a monument, statue, etc.). || Modelo, *m.* (of a car, etc.). || FIG. Modelo, *m.*, dechado, *m.*, ejemplo, *m.* (example): *he is a model of virtue*, es un dechado de virtudes. || Modelo, *m.* & *f.* (for pictures). || Maniquí, *m.*, modelo, *m.* & *f.* (who demonstrates clothes). || Patrón, *m.*, modelo, *m.* (pattern) [in dressmaking]. || MAR. Gálibo, *m.*, vitola, *f.* || *Scale model*, maqueta.

— Adj. Ejemplar, modelo: *a model student*, un estudiante ejemplar; *Carmen is a model wife*, Carmen es una esposa modelo. || Modelo: *a model house*, una casa modelo; *model company*, empresa modelo. || En miniatura, de tamaño reducido (railway, car, plane). || *Model maker*, modelista, *m.* & *f.* (designer), maquetista, *m.* & *f.* (of a scale model).

model [ˈmɔdl] v. tr. Modelar: *to model clay, a bust*, modelar arcilla, un busto. || || Construir [a imitación de]: *to model a house after* o *on* o *upon a castle*, construir una casa a imitación de un castillo. || Presentar (a dress). || — *His work is modelled on Shakespeare*, su obra está inspirada en Shakespeare. || *To model o.s. on s.o.*, seguir el modelo *or* el ejemplo de alguien.

— V. intr. Modelar (to make a model). || Modelarse: *clay models well*, la arcilla se modela bien. || Posar (for an artist). || Pasar modelos, ser modelo, ser maniquí (for clothes).

modeller (U. S. **modeler**) [ˈmɔdlə*] n. Modelador, ra; modelista, *m.* & *f.*

modelling (U. S. **modeling**) [ˈmɔdliŋ] n. Modelado, *m.* || Profesión (*f.*) de modelo *or* maniquí. || Creación (*f.*) de modelos.

moderate [ˈmɔdərit] adj. Moderado, da; comedido, sa; mesurado, da (not extreme). || Razonable, módico, ca; moderado, da (reasonable): *moderate prices*, precios módicos. || Regular, mediano, na; mediocre (average): *moderate skill*, habilidad mediocre.

— N. Moderado, da.

moderate [ˈmɔdəreit] v. tr. Moderar: *you have to moderate your enthusiasm*, tiene que moderar su entusiasmo. || Aplacar (s.o.'s anger). || Presidir [una asamblea] (to preside over).

— V. intr. Moderarse (to become less extreme). || Amainar (the wind). || Presidir una asamblea (to preside). || Arbitrar, servir de moderador (to act as a moderator).

moderating [ˈmɔdəreitiŋ] adj. Moderador, ra.

moderation [ˌmɔdəˈreiʃən] n. Moderación, *f.*: *in* o *with moderation*, con moderación.

moderator [ˈmɔdəreitə*] n. Mediador, ra; árbitro, *m.*, moderador, ra (mediator). || Presidente (*m.*) del tribunal de exámenes (in a university). || PHYS. Moderador, *m.*

modern [ˈmɔdən] adj. Moderno, na.

— N. Persona (*f.*) moderna, moderno, na.

modernism [—izəm] n. Modernismo, *m.*

modernist [—ist] adj./n. Modernista.

modernistic [mɔdəˈnistik] adj. Modernista.

modernity [mɔˈdəːniti] n. Modernidad, *f.*, modernismo, *m.*

modernization [ˌmɔdənaiˈzeiʃən] n. Modernización, *f.*

modernize [ˈmɔdənaiz] v. tr. Modernizar.

modest [ˈmɔdist] adj. Modesto, ta; humilde (not conceited). || Púdico, ca; modesto, ta; recatado, da (decent, reserved): *a modest woman*, una mujer recatada. || Moderado, da; discreto, ta: *a modest success*, un éxito discreto. || Módico, ca: *a modest wage*, un sueldo módico.

modesty [—i] n. Modestia, *f.*, humildad, *f.* (humility). || Modestia, *f.*, recato, *m.*, pudor, *m.* (sense of decency). || Moderación, *f.* (moderation). || Modicidad, *f.* (of expenses, etc.).

modicum [ˈmɔdikəm] n. Pequeña cantidad, *f.*, pizca, *f.*

modifiable [ˈmɔdifaiəbl] adj. Modificable.

modification [ˌmɔdiˈfiˈkeiʃən] n. Modificación, *f.*

modificatory [ˈmɔdifikeitəri] adj. Modificador, ra.

modifier [ˈmɔdifaiə*] n. Modificador, ra (person). || GRAMM. Calificativo, *m.*

modify [ˈmɔdifai] v. tr. Modificar. || JUR. Atenuar.

— V. intr. Modificarse.

modillion [məuˈdiljən] n. ARCH. Modillón, *m.*

modish [ˈməudiʃ] adj. De moda.

modishly [—li] adv. Elegantemente, a la moda.

modiste [məuˈdiːst] n. Modisto, ta (dressmaker). || Sombrerero, ra (milliner).

modulate [ˈmɔdjuleit] v. tr. Modular (voice, sound). || Adaptar (*to*, a).

— V. intr. MUS. RAD. Modular.

modulation [ˌmɔdjuˈleiʃən] n. Modulación, *f.* || *Frequency modulation*, modulación de frecuencia, frecuencia modulada.

modulator [ˈmɔdjuleitə*] n. Modulador, *m.*

module [ˈmɔdjul] n. Módulo, *m.*

modulus [ˈmɔdjuləs] n. Módulo, *m.*, coeficiente, *m.* || *Modulus of elasticity*, módulo de elasticidad.

— OBSERV. El plural de *modulus* es *moduli*.

modus operandi [ˈmɔdəsˌɔpəˈrændiː] n. Procedimiento, *m.*

modus vivendi [ˈmɔdəsviˈvendi] n. Modus vivendi, *m.*

mofette or **moffette** [məuˈfet] n. GEOL. Mofeta, *f.*

Mogul [məuˈgʌl] adj./n. Mogol, la; mongol, la. || U. S. FAM. Magnate, *m.* (important person).

mohair [ˈməuhεə*] n. Mohair, *m.*

Mohammed [məuˈhæmed] pr. n. REL. Mahoma, *m.*

Mohammedan [məuˈhæmidən] adj./n. REL. Mahometano, na.

Mohammedanism [—izəm] n. REL. Mahometismo, *m.*

Mohican [ˈməuikən] adj./n. Mohicano, na.

moiety [ˈmɔiəti] n. Mitad, *f.* (half). || Parte, *f.*, porción, *f.* (share).

moil [mɔil] n. Trabajo (*m.*) penoso.

moil [mɔil] v. intr. Trabajar duramente, afanarse.

moiré [ˈmwɑːrei] n. Muaré, *m.*, moaré, *m.* (fabric).

moist [mɔist] adj. Húmedo, da: *a moist climate*, un clima húmedo; *eyes moist with tears*, ojos húmedos de lágrimas. || Mojado, da (wet).

moisten [ˈmɔisn] v. tr. Humedecer, mojar. || Humedecer (the skin).

— V. intr. Humedecerse, mojarse.

moistness [ˈmɔistnis] n. Humedad, *f.*

moisture [ˈmɔistʃə*] n. Humedad, *f.* (dampness). || Vaho, *m.*, empañamiento, *m.* (of mirror).

moisturize [—raiz] v. tr. Humedecer. || *Moisturizing cream*, crema (*f.*) hidratante.

moke [məuk] n. ZOOL. Burro, *m.*, asno, *m.* (donkey).

mol [məul] n. CHEM. Mol, *m.*

molar [ˈməulə*] n. Muela, *f.*, molar, *m.* (tooth).

— Adj. Molar.

molasses [məuˈlæsiz] n. Melaza, *f.* (treacle).

mold [məuld] n./v. tr/intr. U. S. See MOULD.

moldable [—əbl] adj. U. S. Moldeable.

moldboard [ˈməuldˌbɔːd] n. U. S. See MOULDBOARD.

molder [ˈməuldə*] n. U. S. Moldeador, ra.

molder [ˈməuldə*] v. intr. U. S. Desmoronarse.

moldiness [ˈməuldinis] n. U. S. Enmohecimiento, *m.*, estado (*m.*) mohoso.

molding [ˈməuldiŋ] n. U. S. See MOULDING.

moldy [ˈməuldi] adj. U. S. See MOULDY.

mole [məul] n. Topo, *m.* (animal). || Lunar, *m.* (on skin): *she has a mole on her face*, tiene un lunar en la cara. || Malecón, *m.* (jetty, breakwater). || Muelle, *m.* (harbour). || CHEM. Mol, *m.* || ZOOL. *Mole cricket*, grillo (*m.*) cebollero *or* real.

molecular [məuˈlekjulə*] adj. Molecular: *molecular mass*, masa molecular; *molecular weight*, peso molecular.

molecule [ˈmɔlikjuːl] n. Molécula, *f.*: *gram molecule*, molécula gramo.

molehill [ˈməulhil] n. Topera, *f.*

moleskin [ˈməulskin] n. Molesquín, *m.* (fabric). || — Pl. Pantalones (*m.*) de molesquín (trousers).

molest [məuˈlest] v. tr. Importunar, molestar.

molestation [ˌməulesˈteiʃən] n. Molestia, *f.*, importunidad, *f.*

moll [mɔl] n. POP. Amiga, *f.* (girlfriend). | Prostituta, *f.*

mollification [ˌmɔlifiˈkeiʃən] n. Aplacamiento, *m.*, apaciguamiento, *m.*

mollify [ˈmɔlifai] v. tr. Aplacar, apaciguar.

mollusc [ˈmɔləsk] n. ZOOL. Molusco, *m.*

mollusk [ˈmɔləsk] n. U. S. ZOOL. Molusco, *m.*

mollycoddle [ˈmɔlikɔdl] n. FAM. Niño (*m.*) mimado (spoilt boy). | Gallina, *m.* (coward). | Marica, *m.* (effeminate man).

mollycoddle [ˈmɔlikɔdl] v. tr. FAM. Mimar.

Molotov cocktail [ˈmɔlətɔvˈkɔkteil] n. Cóctel (*m.*) Molotov.

molt [məult] n./v. tr./intr. U. S. See MOULT.

molten [ˈməultən] adj. Fundido, da; derretido, da. || *Molten lava*, lava líquida.

molybdenum [mɔˈlibdinəm] n. CHEM. Molibdeno, *m.*

mom [mɔm] n. FAM. Mamá, *f.*, mamaíta, *f.*

moment [ˈməumənt] n. Momento, *m.*: *wait a moment*, espérate un momento; *when the moment came to do it*, cuando llegó el momento de hacerlo. || Importancia, *f.* (importance): *of great moment*, de gran importancia. || PHYS. Momento, *m.*: *moment of inertia*, momento de inercia. || — *A few moments later*, momentos después. || *At any moment*, de un momento a otro. || *At that moment*, en aquel momento. || *At the moment*, de momento, ahora. || *At the very moment when*, en el momento en que. || *At this moment*, en este momento. || *Crucial, fatal, psychological moment*, momento crucial, fatídico,psicológico. || *Every moment*, a cada momento. || *For the moment*, por el momento || *From that moment*, desde ese momento, a partir de ese momento. || *From the moment when*, desde el momento en que. || *In a moment*, dentro de un momento. || *Just a moment!*, ¡un momento! || *Last moments*, últimos momentos. || *Not a moment ago*, hace un momento. || *Not for a moment*, en absoluto. || *This moment*, ahora mismo. || *To be the man of the moment*, ser el hombre del momento. || *To have one's (good) moments*, tener buenos momentos.

momenta [məuˈməntə] pl. n. See MOMENTUM.

momentarily [ˈməuməntərili] adv. Momentáneamente (for a short moment). || De un momento a otro (at any moment).

momentariness [ˈməuməntərinis] n. Carácter (*m.*) momentáneo, poca duración, *f.*

momentary [ˈməuməntəri] adj. Momentáneo, a; pasajero, ra.

momently [ˈməuməntli] adv. A cada momento (every moment). || Momentáneamente (momentarily). || De un momento a otro (at any moment). || Durante unos momentos (for a short while).

momentous [məuˈmentəs] adj. De gran importancia, trascendental.

momentousness [—nis] n. Gran importancia, *f.*, trascendencia, *f.*

momentum [məuˈmentəm] n. PHYS. Momento, *m.* || Ímpetu, *m.*, velocidad, *f.* (speed): *to gather momentum*, adquirir velocidad. || Impulso, *m.*

— OBSERV. El plural de *momentum* es *momentums* o *momenta*.

monachal or **monacal** [ˈmɔnəkəl] adj. Monástico, ca; monacal.

monachism [ˈmɔnəkizəm] n. Monacato, *m.*

monad [ˈmɔnæd] n. Mónada, *f.*

monadism [ˈmɔnædizəm] n. Monadismo, *m.*

monarch [ˈmɔnək] n. Monarca, *m.* (king).

monarchal [mɔˈnɑːkəl] or **monarchial** [mɔˈnɑːkjəl] adj. Monárquico, ca.

monarchic [mɔˈnɑːkik] or **monarchical** [—əl] adj. Monárquico, ca.

monarchism [ˈmɔnəkizəm] n. Monarquismo, *m.*

monarchist [ˈmɔnəkist] adj./n. Monárquico, ca.

monarchistic [ˈmɔnəˈkistik] adj. Monárquico, ca.

monarchy [ˈmɔnəki] n. Monarquía, *f.*

monastery [ˈmɔnəstəri] n. Monasterio, *m.*

monastic [məˈnæstik] adj. Monacal, monástico, ca.
— N. Monje, *m.* (monk).

monasticism [məˈnæstisizəm] n. Monacato, *m.*

Monday [ˈmʌndi] n. Lunes, *m.*: *I shall come on Monday morning*, vendré el lunes por la mañana; *last Monday*, el lunes pasado; *next Monday*, el lunes que viene.

Monegasque [ˈmonigæsk] adj./n. Monegasco, ca.

monetary [ˈmʌnitəri] adj. Monetario, ria.

monetization [ˌmʌnitaiˈzeiʃən] n. Monetización, *f.*

monetize [ˈmʌnitaiz] v. tr. Monetizar.

money [ˈmʌni] n. Dinero, *m.*: *minted money*, dinero acuñado. || — Pl. Fondos, *m.*, dinero, *m. sing.*: *public moneys*, fondos públicos. || Cantidades (*f.*) de dinero. || — *Counterfeit money*, moneda falsa. || FAM. *For my money he's drunk!*, ¿a que está borracho? | *It's money for jam* o *for old rope*, es una ganga. | *Money burns a hole in his pocket*, el dinero le quema en el bolsillo. | *Money does not grow on trees*, el dinero no nace en macetas, no se atan los perros con longanizas. || *Money in hand*, dinero disponible. || FIG. *Money is welcome though it comes in a dirty clout*, el dinero no tiene olor. | *Money makes money*, el dinero llama al dinero. || *Money matters*, asuntos económicos. || *Money of account*, moneda de cuenta, moneda imaginaria. || *Money payment*, pago (*m.*) en metálico, pago (*m.*) en numerario. || *Money's worth*, valor (*m.*) en metálico. || FIG. *Money talks*, poderoso caballero es don Dinero. || *Paper money*, papel (*m*). moneda. || *Pocket money*, dinero para gastos menudos *or* de bolsillo. || *Ready money*, dinero líquido. || *There is good money in business*, se puede sacar mucho dinero de los negocios. || *There is money in it*, se le puede sacar mucho dinero, es un buen negocio. || FIG. *Time is money*, el tiempo es oro. | *To be in the money*, ser rico. | *To be made of money* o *to be rolling in money*, estar nadando en dinero, ser millonario. || *To be short of money*, andar escaso de dinero. || FAM. *To bring in big money*, ganar el dinero a espuertas, ganar más dinero que un torero. || *To coin money*, acuñar moneda (to make coins), forrarse de dinero (to earn much money). || *To come into money*, heredar dinero. || FIG. FAM. *To cost a mint of money*, costar un dineral *or* una fortuna. || *To do sth. for money*, hacer algo por dinero. || FIG. *To give s.o. a run for his money*, hacer pasar un mal rato a alguien (to give a bad time), permitir a alguien que le saque jugo al dinero (to give good value). | *To have money to burn*, estar forrado, nadar en dinero *or* en la abundancia. || *To make money*, hacer dinero (a person), dar dinero (a business): || *To make tons of money*, ganar dinero a espuertas. || *To marry money*, casarse por interés. || *To mint money*, acuñar *or* labrar *or* batir moneda. || *To part with one's money*, desembolsar dinero. || *To put money into*, colocar *or* invertir dinero en. || *To put money on*, apostar a (to bet). || FIG. *To spend money like water* o *to throw money down the drain*, tirar el dinero por la ventana. | *We got our money's worth*, le sacamos jugo al dinero. || *With my own money*, con mi dinero. || *Your money or your life!*, ¡la bolsa o la vida!

— OBSERV. El plural de la palabra *money* es *monies* o *moneys*.

moneybag [—bæg] n. Cartera, *f.*, monedero, *m.*

moneybags [—bægz] n. FAM. Ricachón, ona (rich person). | Dineral, *m.*, fortuna, *f.* (wealth).

money box [—bɔks] n. Hucha, *f.*, alcancía, *f.*

money changer [—ˌtʃeindʒə*] n. Cambista, *m.* & *f.*

moneyed [—d] adj. Rico, ca; adinerado, da.

moneygrubber [—ˌgrʌbə*] n. Avaro, ra.

moneylender [—ˌlendə*] n. Prestamista, *m.* & *f.*

moneyless [—lis] adj. Sin dinero, pobre.

moneymaker [—ˌmeikə*] n. Amasador (*m.*) de dinero (person). || Fuente (*f.*) *or* mina (*f.*) de dinero (thing).

moneymaking [—ˌmeikiŋ] adj. Rentable, productivo, va (business). || Que saca dinero de todo (person).
— N. Ganancia, *f.*

money market [—ˌmɑːkit] n. Mercado (*m.*) de valores, bolsa, *f.*

money-minded [—ˌmaindid] adj. Interesado, da.

money order [—ˌɔːdə*] n. Giro (*m.*) postal.

monger [ˈmʌŋgə*] n. COMM. Traficante, *m.*, negociante, *m.*, vendedor, ra.

— OBSERV. *Monger* se emplea sobre todo en palabras compuestas (*ironmonger*, ferretero: *fishmonger*, vendedor de pescado, pescadero).

Mongol [ˈmɔŋgɔl] adj./n. Mongol, la; mogol, la (Mogul).

Mongolia [mɔŋˈgəuljə] pr. n. GEOGR. Mongolia, *f.*

Mongolian [—n] adj. Mongol, la (of Mongolia). || MED. Mongólico, ca.
— N. Mongol, la (inhabitant of Mongolia). || Mongol *m.* (language).

Mongolic [mɔŋˈgəulik] adj. Mongólico, ca.
— N. Mongol, *m.* (language).

Mongolism [ˈmɔŋgəlizəm] n. MED. Mongolismo, *m.*

Mongoloid [ˈmɔŋgəlɔid] adj./n. Mongoloide.

mongoose [ˈmɔŋguːs] n. ZOOL. Mangosta, *f.*

mongrel [ˈmʌŋgrəl] n. Perro (*m.*) mestizo *or* cruzado || Mestizo, za (person).
— Adj. Mestizo, za.

monies [ˈmʌniz] pl. n. See MONEY.

monism [ˈmɔnizəm] n. PHIL. Monismo, *m.*

monition [məuˈniʃən] n. Admonición, *f.*, advertencia *f.* || JUR. Citación, *f.*

monitor [ˈmɔnitə*] n. Monitor, *m.*, instructor, *m.* || Alumno (*m.*) encargado de mantener la disciplina (in school). || RAD. Radioescucha, *m.* (a person). | Monitor, *m.*, receptor (*m.*) de control (apparatus). || MAR. Monitor, *m.* || ZOOL. Varano, *m.*

monitor [ˈmɔnitə*] v. tr. Controlar, comprobar (to check). || Escuchar, oír (to listen). || PHYS. Determinar [la contaminación radioactiva de].

monitoring [mɔniˈtɔriŋ] n. RAD. Control, *m.* | Servicio (*m.*) de escucha.

monitor room [ˈmɔnitərum] n. Cabina (*f.*) de escucha. || Cabina (*f.*) de control.

monk [mʌŋk] n. REL. Monje, *m.*

monkery [—əri] n. FAM. Monasterio, *m.* (monastery). | Vida (*f.*) monástica.

monkey [ˈmʌŋki] n. ZOOL. Mono, *m.* (ape), mona, *f.* (female ape). || FIG. FAM. Diablillo, *m.*, mico, *m.* (child). || TECH. Maza, *f.* (hammer). | Bigotera, *f.* (of a blast furnace). || FAM. Quinientas libras, *f. pl.* | U. S. Quinientos dólares, *m. pl.* || FAM. *To make a monkey out of s.o.*, tomar el pelo a alguien (to pull s.o.'s leg), ridiculizar a alguien (to make a fool of).

monkey [ˈmʌŋki] v. intr. FAM. Hacer tonterías *or* payasadas (to play the fool). || — FAM. *To monkey about*, entretenerse, perder el tiempo. | *To monkey about with*, enredar *or* jugar con (to play with), manosear (to finger), meterse con (a person).
— V. tr. Remedar, imitar.

monkey bread [—bred] n. BOT. Pan (*m.*) de mono, fruto (*m.*) del baobab (fruit). | Baobab, *m.* (tree).

monkey business [—ˌbiznis] n. FAM. Diablura, *f.*, travesura, *f.* (mischief). | Tejemanejes, *m. pl.*, trampas, *f. pl.* (trickery).

monkey jacket [—ˌdʒækit] n. Chaqueta (*f.*) corta (short dress jacket).

monkey-like [—laik] adj. De mono, simiesco, ca.

monkey-nut [—nʌt] n. Cacahuete, *m.* [*Amer.*, maní, *m.*] (groundnut).

monkeyshines [—ʃainz] pl. n. U. S. FAM. Diabluras, *f.*, travesuras, *f.* (mischief).

monkey suit [—sjuːt] n. Uniforme, *m.* || Traje (*m.*) de etiqueta (man's dress suit).

monkey tricks [—triks] pl. n. Diabluras, *f.*, travesuras, *f.* (mischief).

monkey wrench [—rentʃ] n. TECH. Llave (*f.*) inglesa, llave (*f.*) de cremallera.

monkhood [ˈmʌnkhud] n. Monacato, *m.*

monkish [ˈmʌŋkiʃ] adj. Frailuno, na; monacal, monástico, ca.

monoacid [ˈmɔnəuˈæsid] adj. CHEM. Monoácido, da
— N. CHEM. Monoácido, *m.*

monobasic [ˈmɔnəˈbeisik] adj. Monobásico, ca.

monobloc [ˈmɔnəblɔk] adj. Monobloque.

monochord [ˈmɔnəkɔːd] n. MUS. Monocordio, *m.*

monochromatic [ˈmɔnəkrəuˈmætik] adj. Monocromático, ca.
monochrome [ˈmɔnəkrəum] adj. Monocromo, ma; de un solo color.
— N. Monocromo, *m.*
monochromy [—i] n. Monocromía, *f.*
monocle [ˈmɔnəkl] n. Monóculo, *m.*
monocoque [ˈmɔnəkɔk] adj. Monocasco.
monocotyledon [ˈmɔnə,kɔtiˈli:dən] n. BOT. Monocotiledóneo, *m.*
monocotyledonous [ˈmɔnəkɔtiˈli:dənəs] adj. BOT. Monocotiledóneo, a.
monocracy [mɔˈnɔkrəsi] n. Autocracia, *f.*
monoculture [ˈmɔnə,kʌltʃə*] n. Monocultivo, *m.*
monody [ˈmɔnədi] n. MUS. Monodia, *f.* (single voice ode). | Treno, *m.* (threnody).
monogamist [mɔˈnɔgəmist] n. Monógamo, ma.
monogamous [mɔˈnɔgəməs] adj. Monógamo, ma.
monogamy [mɔˈnɔgəmi] n. Monogamia, *f.*
monogram [ˈmɔnəgræm] n. Monograma, *m.*
monograph [ˈmɔnəgrɑ:f] n. Monografía, *f.*
monographic [,mɔnəˈgræfik] adj. Monográfico, ca.
monolingual [,mɔnəˈlingwəl] adj. Monolingüe.
monolith [ˈmɔnəuliθ] n. Monolito, *m.*
monolithic [,mɔnəuˈliθik] adj. Monolítico, ca.
monolog [ˈmɔnəlɔg] n. U. S. Monólogo, *m.*
monologize [mɔˈnɔlədʒaiz] v. intr. Monologar.
monologue [ˈmɔnəlɔg] n. Monólogo, *m.*
monomania [ˈmɔnəuˈmeinjə] n. Monomanía, *f.*
monomaniac [ˈmɔnəuˈmeiniæk] n. Monomaníaco, ca.
monomaniacal [ˈmɔnəuˈmeiniækəl] adj. Monomaníaco, ca; monomaniático, ca.
monometallic [,mɔnəumeˈtælik] adj. Monometalista.
monometallism [,mɔnəuˈmetælizəm] n. Monometalismo, *m.*
monometallist [,mɔnəuˈmetəlist] n. Monometalista, *m.* & *f.*
monomial [məˈnəumiəl] n. MATH. Monomio, *m.*
mononuclear [,mɔnəuˈnju:kliə*] adj. Mononuclear.
mononucleosis [ˈmɔnəu,nu:kliˈəusis] n. MED. Mononucleosis, *f.*
monophase [ˈmɔnəfeiz] adj. ELECTR. Monofásico, ca.
Monophysite [məˈnɔfə,sait] n. Monofisita, *m.*
Monophysitic [mə,nɔfiˈsitik] adj. Monofisita.
Monophysitism [məˈnɔfi,saitizəm] n. Monofisismo, *m.*
monoplane [ˈmɔnəplein] n. Monoplano, *m.*
monopolist [məˈnɔpəlist] n. Monopolizador, ra.
monopolistic [mə,nɔpəˈlistik] adj. Monopolizador, ra.
monopolization [mə,nɔpəlaiˈzeiʃən] n. Monopolización, *f.*
monopolize [məˈnɔpəlaiz] v. tr. Monopolizar.
monopolizer [—ə*] n. Monopolizador, ra.
monopolizing [—iŋ] adj. Monopolizador, ra.
monopoly [məˈnɔpəli] n. Monopolio, *m.*
monorail [ˈmɔnəureil] adj. Monocarril, monorriel.
— N. Monocarril, *m.*, monorriel, *m.*
monosaccharide [ˈmɔnəu,sækəraid] n. CHEM. Monosacárido, *m.*
monosyllabic [ˈmɔnəusiˈlæbik] adj. Monosílabo, ba (word). || Monosilábico, ca (language).
monosyllable [ˈmɔnə,siləbl] n. Monosílabo, *m.*
monotheism [ˈmɔnəuθi:,izəm] n. REL. Monoteísmo, *m.*
monotheist [ˈmɔnəuθi:ist] n. REL. Monoteísta, *m.* & *f.*
monotheistic [ˈmɔnəuθi:istik] adj. REL. Monoteísta.
monotone [ˈmɔnətəun] adj. Monótono, na.
— N. Monotonía, *f.* || *In a monotone*, con una voz monótona, con monotonía.
monotonous [məˈnɔtnəs] adj. Monótono, na.
monotony [məˈnɔtni] n. Monotonía, *f.*
monotremata [,mɔnəuˈtri:mətə] pl. n. ZOOL. Monotremas, *m.*
monotype [ˈmɔnəutaip] n. PRINT. Monotipo, *m.* (machine). | Monotipia, *f.* (process).
monovalent [ˈmɔnəu,veilənt] adj. Monovalente.
— N. Monovalente, *m.*
Monseigneur or **Monsignor** [mɔnˈsi:njə*] n. Monseñor, *m.*
monsoon [mɔnˈsu:n] n. Monzón, *m.* (wind).
monster [ˈmɔnstə*] n. Monstruo, *m.*
— Adj. Monstruoso, sa.
monstrance [ˈmɔnstrəns] n. Custodia, *f.*
monstrosity [mɔnsˈtrɔsiti] n. Monstruosidad, *f.*
monstrous [ˈmɔnstrəs] adj. Monstruoso, sa.
monstrousness [—nis] n. Monstruosidad, *f.*
montage [mɔnˈtɑ:ʒ] n. Montaje, *m.*
Montagues [ˈmɔntəgju:z] pl. pr. n. Montescos, *m.*
monteith [mɔnˈti:θ] n. Ponchera (*f.*) de plata.
Montevidean [,mɔntiviˈdeiən] adj./n. Montevideano, na.
Montevideo [,mɔntiviˈdeiəu] pr. n. GEOGR. Montevideo.
month [mʌnθ] n. Mes, *m.*: *a hundred pounds a month*, cien libras al *or* por mes. || — *Calendar month*, mes civil. || *Current month*, mes corriente. || FIG. *It will take you a month of Sundays*, tardará siglos en hacerlo, tardará una eternidad en hacerlo. || *Last month*, el mes pasado. || *Lunar month*, mes lunar. || *Month's pay*, sueldo (*m.*) mensual, mensualidad, *f.* || FIG. *Never in a month of Sundays*, nunca. || *To go on for months*, durar meses y meses, durar meses.
monthly [—li] adj. Mensual: *monthly wage*, salario mensual. || *Monthly instalment* o *monthly payment*, mensualidad, *f.*
— Adv. Mensualmente, una vez al mes, todos los meses. || Mensualmente, por meses: *they pay him monthly*, le pagan por meses.
— N. Mensual, *m.*, revista (*f.*) mensual (publication). || — Pl. MED. FAM. Mes, *m. sing.* (menses).
monticule [ˈmɔntikjul] n. Montículo, *m.*
monument [ˈmɔnjumənt] n. Monumento, *m.* (building, memorial, work). || U. S. Mojón, *m.* (boundary mark).
monumental [,mɔnjuˈmentl] adj. Monumental. || FIG. Monumental, enorme (stupidity). | Monumental (literary work). | Garrafal (mistake).
monumentalize [,mɔnjuˈmentəlaiz] v. tr. Conmemorar con un monumento.
moo [mu:] n. Mugido, *m.* (of a cow).
moo [mu:] v. intr. Mugir.
mooch [mu:tʃ] v. intr. Vagar, haraganear (to idle). || U. S. FAM. Gorronear (to cadge).
— V. tr. U. S. FAM. Dar un sablazo: *he mooched ten dollars off me*, me dio un sablazo de diez dólares. | Birlar (to steal).
moocher [—ə*] n. U. S. FAM. Gorrón, *m.*, parásito, *m.* (parasite). | Sablista, *m.* (sponger).
mood [mu:d] n. Humor, *m.*: *to be, to put in a bad mood*, estar, poner de mal humor. || GRAMM. PHIL. Modo, *m.* || — Pl. Mal humor, *m. sing.*, malhumor, *m. sing.*, momentos (*m.*) de mal humor (bad mood). || Caprichos, *m.* (whims). || — *I am not in the mood*, no me apetece. || *I am not in the mood for*, no estoy para, no tengo ganas de. || *To be in the mood for*, estar de humor para, tener ganas de.
moodily [—ili] adv. Malhumoradamente. || Caprichosamente.
moodiness [—inis] n. Malhumor, *m.*, mal humor, *m.* (bad mood). || Tristeza, *f.*, melancolía, *f.* (sadness). || Humor (*m.*) cambiadizo (instability). || Caprichos, *m. pl.* (whims).
moody [—i] adj. Malhumorado, da (bad-tempered). || Triste, melancólico, ca; taciturno, na (sad). || De humor cambiadizo (fickle). || Caprichoso, sa (whimsical).
moon [mu:n] adj. Lunar: *moon capsule*, cápsula lunar.
— N. Luna, *f.*: *full moon*, luna llena; *new moon*, luna nueva; *crescent moon*, media luna. || ASTR. Lunación, *f.* || FIG. Mes, *m.* (month). || — *April moon*, luna de abril. || FIG. *Many moons ago*, hace muchas lunas *or* mucho tiempo. | *Once in a blue moon*, de Pascuas a Ramos, de higos a brevas. | *To ask for the moon*, pedir la luna. | *To bark* o *to bay at the moon*, ladrar a la luna. | *To promise the moon*, prometer la luna *or* el oro y el moro. || *Waning moon*, luna menguante. || *Waxing moon*, luna creciente.
moon [mu:n] v. intr. Mirar a las musarañas, estar en la Luna.
— V. tr. *To moon one's time away*, pasarse el tiempo mirando a las musarañas.
moonbeam [—bi:m] n. Rayo (*m.*) de luna.
moon blindness [—ˈblaindnis] n. Ceguera (*f.*) nocturna.
mooncalf [—kɑ:f] n. Idiota, *m.* & *f.*
moonfaced [—feist] adj. De cara redonda.
moonfish [—fiʃ] n. ZOOL. Pez (*m.*) luna.
moonish [—iʃ] adj. Variable (changeable). || Caprichoso, sa (capricious).
moonless [—lis] adj. Sin luna.
moonlight [—lait] n. Claro (*m.*) de luna, luz (*f.*) de la luna: *by moonlight, in the moonlight*, a la luz de la luna, con el claro de luna. || — *It was moonlight*, había luna. || FAM. *To do a moonlight flit*, see FLIT.
moonlighting [—laitiŋ] n. Pluriempleo, *m.*
moonlit [—lit] adj. Iluminado por la luna. || De luna (night).
moonrise [—raiz] n. Salida (*f.*) de la luna.
moonscape [—skeip] n. Paisaje (*m.*) lunar.
moonset [—set] n. Puesta (*f.*) de la luna.
moonshine [—ʃain] n. Claro (*m.*) de luna, luz (*f.*) de la luna (moonlight). || FAM. Pamplinas, *f. pl.* (nonsense). || U. S. FAM. Alcohol (*m.*) ilegalmente destilado. || FAM. *That's just moonshine*, eso es música celestial, no son más que pamplinas.
moonshiner [—,ʃainə*] n. U. S. FAM. Destilador (*m.*) ilegal de alcohol. | Contrabandista (*m.*) de alcohol.
moonstone [—stəun] n. Piedra (*f.*) de la luna.
moonstruck [—strʌk] adj. Lunático, ca; chiflado, da (mentally deranged). || Turulato, ta (flabbergasted).
moony [—i] adj. De la luna. || Parecido a la luna (moonlike). || Semilunar (crescent-shaped). || Distraído, da; en la luna (absentminded). || Soñador, ra (dreamy).
moor [muə*] n. Páramo, *m.*, brezal, *m.* (heath). || Terreno (*m.*) pantanoso (marsh). || Coto (*m.*) de caza (game preserve).
moor [muə*] v. tr. MAR. Amarrar (with cables or chains). | Anclar (with an anchor).
— V. intr. MAR. Echar las amarras. | Echar el ancla.
Moor [muə*] n. Moro, ra.
moorage [—ridʒ] n. MAR. Amarradura, *f.*, amarre, *m.* (action). | Amarradero, *m.* (place). | Amarraje, *m.* (charge).
moorcock [—kɔk] n. ZOOL. Lagópedo (*m.*) de Escocia.
moorhen [—hen] n. ZOOL. Polla (*f.*) de agua (gallinule). | Hembra (*f.*) del lagópedo de Escocia (female of the red grouse).

mooring [—riŋ] n. MAR. Amarradura, *f.*, amarre, *m.* || — Pl. MAR. Amarras, *f.* (cables). || Amarradero, *m. sing.* (place).
Moorish [—riʃ] adj. Moro, ra; morisco, ca. || Árabe (architecture). || *Moorish district*, morería, *f.*
moorland [—lənd] n. Páramo, *m.*
moose [mu:s] n. ZOOL. Alce, *m.*, anta, *f.*
moot [mu:t] adj. Discutible (point).
— N. Asamblea (*f.*) de ciudadanos (assembly). || JUR. Debate, *m.*
moot [mu:t] v. tr. Discutir, debatir (a point). || Someter a discusión (an idea).
mop [mɔp] n. Fregona, *f.* (for washing floors). || Mueca, *f.* (grimace). || MAR. Lampazo, *m.* || FAM. Greñas, *f. pl.*, pelambrera, *f.* (hair). || FAM. *Mrs. Mop*, la asistenta.
mop [mɔp] v. tr. Fregar (a floor). || Enjugarse, secarse (one's brow). || MAR. Fregar con lampazo. || *To mop up*, secar, limpiar (spilt liquids, etc.), dar una paliza a (to defeat), acabar con (the enemy, etc.), limpiar (territory), beberse (to drink up), llevarse (profits).
— V. intr. Hacer muecas (to grimace).
mope [məup] n. Melancólico, ca (person). || — Pl. Melancolía, *f. sing.*, moral (*f. sing.*) baja, abatimiento, *m. sing.* (low spirits).
mope [məup] v. intr. Estar abatido, tener ideas negras.
moped [ˈməuped] n. Ciclomotor, *m.*
mopish [ˈməupiʃ] adj. Abatido, da; alicaído, da; melancólico, ca.
mopishness [ˈməupiʃnis] n. Abatimiento, *m.*, decaimiento, *m.*, depresión, *f.*, melancolía, *f.* || Desaliento, *m.*, descorazonamiento, *m.* (discouragement).
mop-up [ˈmɔpʌp] n. MIL. FAM. Limpieza, *f.*
moquette [mɔˈket] n. Moqueta, *f.*
moraine [mɔˈrein] n. GEOL. Morrena, *f.*, morena, *f.*
moral [ˈmɔrəl] adj. Moral: *a moral problem*, un problema moral. || Con moralidad, honrado, da; recto, ta (man). || Virtuoso, sa; decente (woman). || Moral: *moral law, obligation*, ley, obligación moral; *moral victory*, victoria moral; *moral support*, apoyo moral. || De moral (book).
— N. Moraleja, *f.*: *the moral of a tale*, la moraleja de un cuento; *he drew a moral from*, sacó una moraleja de. || — Pl. Moral, *f. sing.* (principles of conduct). || Moralidad, *f. sing.*: *a man with no morals*, un hombre sin moralidad. || *Loose morals*, costumbres relajadas.
morale [mɔˈrɑ:l] n. Moral, *f.*, estado (*m.*) de ánimo: *our morale is high*, nuestra moral es alta. || *To undermine the morale of*, desmoralizar a.
moralism [ˈmɔrəlizəm] n. Moralismo, *m.*
moralist [ˈmɔrəlist] n. Moralista, *m.* & *f.* (student, writer). || Moralizador, ra (person who moralizes). || Persona (*f.*) con moralidad, persona (*f.*) honrada.
moralistic [mɔrəˈlistik] adj. Moralizador, ra.
morality [məˈræliti] n. Moralidad, *f.* (rightness). || Moral, *f.* (ethics). || Precepto (*m.*) moral.
morality play [—plei] n. Moralidad, *f.*
moralization [ˌmɔrəlaiˈzeiʃən] n. Moralización, *f.*
moralize [ˈmɔrəlaiz] v. intr. Moralizar.
— V. tr. Sacar la moraleja de (a fable). || Interpretar según la moral (an event). || Moralizar (s.o.).
moralizer [—ə*] n. Moralizador, ra.
moral philosophy [ˈmɔrəlfiˈlɔsəfi] n. Moral, *f.*, ética, *f.*
morass [məˈræs] n. Pantano, *m.*, marisma, *f.* (marsh). || FIG. Lío, *m.*, embrollo, *m.*
moratorium [ˌmɔrəˈtɔ:riəm] n. JUR. Moratoria, *f.*

— OBSERV. El plural de *moratorium* es *moratoria* o *moratoriums*.

moratory [ˈmɔrətəri] adj. Moratorio, ria.
moray [məˈrei] n. Morena, *f.* (fish).
morbid [ˈmɔ:bid] adj. MED. Patológico, ca (anatomy). | Mórbido, da: *morbid state*, estado mórbido. || Malsano, na; enfermizo, za; morboso, sa (mind). || Morboso, sa (gruesome): *the morbid details*, los detalles morbosos. || Malsano, na (curiosity). || Pesimista (depressed).
morbidity [mɔ:ˈbiditi] or **morbidness** [ˈmɔ:bidnis] n. Morbosidad, *f.* (incidence of disease, gruesomeness). || Morbosidad, *f.*, lo malsano, lo enfermizo (of mind). || Pesimismo, *m.* (depression).
mordacious [mɔ:ˈdeiʃəs] adj. Mordaz, cáustico, ca: *mordacious speech*, discurso mordaz.
mordacity [mɔ:ˈdæsiti] n. Mordacidad, *f.*, causticidad, *f.* (causticity).
mordancy [ˈmɔ:dənsi] n. Mordacidad, *f.*, causticidad, *f.*
mordant [ˈmɔ:dənt] adj. Mordiente (acids). || Mordaz, cáustico, ca (speech).
— N. TECH. Mordiente, *m.*
more [mɔ:*] adj. Más: *would you like some more wine?*, ¿quieres más vino?; *a few more days*, unos días más; *he has more books than I*, tiene más libros que yo; *to spend more money*, gastar más dinero; *more than one pound*, más de una libra. || Superior: *the price is more than last year's*, el precio es superior al del año pasado; *speeds of more than 100 k.p.h.*, velocidades superiores a 100 km/h. || Mayor: *the danger is more than it was*, el peligro es mayor de lo que era. || — *No more nonsense!*, ¡basta de tonterías! || *Without more ado*, sin más ni más.
— Adv. Más: *you must eat more*, tienes que comer más; *this is far more serious*, esto es mucho más grave; *some of Picasso's more famous pictures*, algunos de los cuadros más famosos de Picasso; *this is worth more than the other*, éste vale más que el otro; *it is worth more than 100 dollars*, vale más de 100 dólares; *it is worth 100 dollars more*, vale cien dólares más; *if we were one man more*, si fuéramos uno más; *not a penny more*, ni un penique más. || Más, más bien: *Is it a story? — No, it's more a play*, ¿es una novela? — No, es más bien una obra de teatro. || — *All the more*, aun más. || *All the more... since* o *because*, tanto más... cuanto que. || *If it happens any more*, si vuelve a ocurrir. || *I won't do it any more*, no lo haré más. || *More and more*, cada vez más, más y más: *he was getting more and more angry*, se estaba enfadando cada vez más. || *More or less*, más o menos. || *More than ever*, más que nunca. || *Neither more nor less*, ni más ni menos. || *Never more*, nunca más. || *No more no less*, ni más ni menos. || *Once more*, una vez más, otra vez, de nuevo. || *Still more*, más aún, todavía más. || *That is not done any more*, eso ya no se hace. || *That's more like it!*, ¡eso está mejor! || *The more*, más aún: *I was the more happy because*, me alegré más aún porque. || *The more..., the less*, cuanto más..., menos. || *The more..., the more*, cuanto más..., más: *the more you read, the more you learn*, cuanto más lees, más aprendes. || *There's not much more to go*, ya nos queda poco por hacer. || *To be more offended than angry*, ofenderse más que enfadarse. || *To be more than*, ser *or* estar más que: *I'm more than happy, I'm delighted*, estoy más que contento, estoy encantado. || *To be no more*, haber dejado de existir (to exist no longer), haber fallecido (to be dead). || *To have more than achieved sth.*, haber cumplido algo con creces.
— N. Más: *Peter asked for more*, Pedro pidio más; *more than expected*, más de lo esperado; *would you like some more?*, ¿quieres más? || — *And what is more*, y lo que es más, y además. || *I hope to see more of you*, espero volverle a ver (to meet again), espero verle más a menudo (to meet more often). || *Many failed but more succeeded*, muchos fracasaron pero más aún triunfaron. || *Much of his work is good, but more is terrible*, gran parte de su obra es buena, pero la mayor parte es infame. || *That's more than enough*, es más que suficiente. || *The more the merrier*, cuanto más mejor. || *To be no more than*, no ser más que: *he is no more than a child*, no es más que un niño.
morel [mɔˈrel] n. BOT. Cagarria, *f.*, morilla, *f.* (mushroom). | Hierba (*f.*) mora (nightshade).
morello [məˈreləu] n. BOT. Guinda, *f.* (cherry).
moreover [mɔ:ˈrəuvə*] adj. Además, por otra parte.
mores [ˈmɔ:riz] pl. n. Costumbres, *f.*, usos, *m.*, tradiciones, *f.*
Moresque [mɔ:ˈresk] adj. Árabe (art, architecture).
morganatic [ˌmɔ:gəˈnætik] adj. Morganático, ca.
morgue [mɔ:g] n. Depósito (*m.*) de cadáveres (mortuary). || U. S. Archivos, *m. pl.* (of a newspaper).
moribund [ˈmɔribʌnd] adj. Moribundo, da.
morion [ˈmɔ:riən] n. Morrión, *m.*
Morisco [məuˈriskəu] adj./n. Morisco, ca.

— OBSERV. El plural de la palabra inglesa es *Moriscos* o *Moriscoes*.

Mormon [ˈmɔ:mən] adj. REL. Mormónico, ca.
— N. REL. Mormón, ona.
Mormonism [—izəm] n. REL. Mormonismo, *m.*
morn [mɔ:n] n. POET. Mañana, *f.* (morning). | Alborada, *f.* (dawn).
morning [ˈmɔ:niŋ] adj. Matutino, na; de la mañana (breeze). || Del alba (star). || *Morning paper*, diario (*m.*) de la mañana.
— N. Mañana, *f.*: *in the morning*, por la mañana; *the following morning*, a la mañana siguiente; *at six o'clock in the morning*, a las seis de la mañana; *all the morning*, la mañana entera, toda la mañana; *tomorrow morning*, mañana por la mañana; *this morning*, esta mañana. || FIG. Comienzo, *m.* (beginning). || — *First thing in the morning*, por la mañana a primera hora. || *Good morning*, buenos días. || *In the grey of the morning*, al rayar el día, al despuntar el alba, de madrugada. || *Morning, noon and night*, mañana, tarde y noche. || FIG. *The morning after*, la mañana después de una borrachera. || *To get up early in the morning*, madrugar, levantarse temprano.
morning coat [—ˈkəut] n. Chaqué, *m.*
morning glory [—ˈglɔri] n. BOT. Maravilla, *f.*, dondiego (*m.*) de día.
mornings [—z] adv. Por la mañana.
morning sickness [—ˈsiknis] n. Náuseas, *f. pl.* [que se sienten por la mañana].
morning star [—ˈstɑ:*] n. Lucero (*m.*) del alba.
Moroccan [məˈrɔkən] adj./n. Marroquí.
morocco [məˈrɔkəu] n. Marroquí, *m.*, tafilete, *m.* (leather).
Morocco [məˈrɔkəu] pr. n. GEOGR. Marruecos.
moron [ˈmɔ:rɔn] n. MED. Retrasado (*m.*) mental (subnormal). || FAM. Imbécil, *m.* & *f.*, idiota, *m.* & *f.* (stupid).
moronic [məˈrɔnik] adj. MED. Retrasado mental. || FAM. Idiota.
morose [məˈraus] adj. Malhumorado, da; taciturno, na (gloomy).
moroseness [—nis] n. Taciturnidad, *f.*, malhumor, *m.*
morpheme [ˈmɔ:fi:m] n. GRAMM. Morfema, *m.*
Morpheus [ˈmɔ:fju:s] pr. n. MYTH. Morfeo, *m.*

morphia [ˈmɔːfjə] n. CHEM. Morfina, *f.*
morphine [ˈmɔːfiːn] n. CHEM. Morfina, *f.* || *Morphine addict*, morfinómano, na.
morphinism [—izəm] n. Morfinismo, *m.* (diseased condition). || Morfinomanía, *f.* (addiction).
morphinomaniac [mɔːfinəˈmeiniæk] n. MED. Morfinómano, na.
morphologic [ˌmɔːfəˈlɔdʒik] or **morphological** [—əl] adj. Morfológico, ca.
morphologist [mɔːˈfɔlədʒist] n. Experto (*m.*) en morfología.
morphology [mɔːˈfɔlədʒi] n. Morfología, *f.*
morphosis [mɔːˈfəusis] n. BIOL. Morfosis, *f.*

— OBSERV. El plural de *morphosis* es *morphoses*.

morrow [ˈmɔrəu] n. Día (*m.*) siguiente. || FIG. Porvenir, *m.*, futuro, *m.* || *On the morrow*, al día siguiente, el día después.
Morse code [mɔːsˈkəud] n. Morse, *m.*, alfabeto (*m.*) Morse.
morsel [ˈmɔːsəl] n. Bocado, *m.* (mouthful). || Pedazo, *m.* (a piece). || Poco, *m.*: *they gave us a morsel to eat*, nos dieron un poco de comer. || *Choice morsel*, bocado de cardenal.
mort [mɔːt] n. Toque (*m.*) de muerte (in hunting).
mortadella [ˌmɔːtəˈdelə] n. Mortadela, *f.*
mortal [ˈmɔːtl] adj. Mortal: *man is mortal*, el hombre es mortal; *mortal combat*, combate mortal; *mortal hatred*, odio mortal; *mortal agony*, agonía mortal; *mortal wound*, herida mortal; *mortal sin*, pecado mortal; *mortal remains*, restos mortales. || Humano, na (of a man). || FIG. Mortal (tedious): *the film was mortal*, la película era mortal. | Terrible (extreme): *mortal fear*, miedo terrible. || FIG. *It's no mortal good to anyone*, no es nada bueno para nadie.
— N. Mortal, *m.*, ser (*m.*) mortal: *a happy mortal*, un feliz mortal. || FAM. Individuo, *m.*, tipo, *m.*
mortality [mɔːˈtæliti] n. Mortalidad, *f.* (mortal nature, death rate): *infantile mortality*, mortalidad infantil. || Mortandad, *f.* (death): *heavy mortality*, gran mortandad. || Mortales, *m. pl.*, humanidad, *f.* (mankind). || *Mortality tables*, tablas (*f.*) de mortalidad.
mortally [ˈmɔːtəli] adv. Mortalmente: *mortally wounded*, mortalmente herido. || FIG. Mortalmente (grievously). | Terriblemente (very).
mortar [ˈmɔːtə*] n. Mortero, *m.*, almirez, *m.* (recipient). || Mortero, *m.*, argamasa, *f.* (building material). || MIL. Mortero, *m.*
mortar [ˈmɔːtə*] v. tr. Argamasar (in building). || MIL. Bombardear con morteros.
mortarboard [ˈmɔːtəbɔːd] n. Birrete, *m.* (hat). || Esparavel, *m.* (in building).
mortgage [ˈmɔːgidʒ] n. Hipoteca, *f.*: *to raise a mortgage*, hacer una hipoteca; *to pay off a mortgage*, levantar una hipoteca. || — *Mortgage bank*, banco hipotecario. || *Mortgage credit, deed, loan*, crédito, contrato, préstamo hipotecario.
mortgage [ˈmɔːgidʒ] v. tr. Hipotecar (property). || FIG. Hipotecar, empeñar: *to mortgage one's independence*, hipotecar su independencia.
mortgageable [—əbl] adj. Hipotecable.
mortgagee [ˌmɔːgəˈdʒiː] n. Acreedor (*m.*) hipotecario.
mortgager or **mortgagor** [ˌmɔːgəˈdʒɔː*] n. Deudor (*m.*) hipotecario.
mortice [ˈmɔːtis] n./v. tr. See MORTISE.
mortician [mɔːˈtiʃən] n. Empresario (*m.*) de pompas fúnebres (undertaker).
mortification [ˌmɔːtifiˈkeiʃən] n. Mortificación, *f.* || MED. Gangrena, *f.*
mortify [ˈmɔːtifai] v. tr. Mortificar. || MED. Gangrenar.
— V. intr. Mortificarse. || MED. Gangrenarse.
mortifying [—iŋ] adj. Mortificador, ra; mortificante.
mortise [ˈmɔːtis] n. Muesca, *f.*, mortaja, *f.*, escopleadura, *f.* || *Mortise gauge*, gramil, *m.*
mortise [ˈmɔːtis] v. tr. Escoplear, hacer muesca en (to cut a mortise in). || Ensamblar a espiga (to fasten).
mortmain [ˈmɔːtmein] n. JUR. Manos (*f. pl.*) muertas.
mortuary [ˈmɔːtjuəri] adj. Mortuorio, ria.
— N. Depósito (*m.*) de cadáveres (morgue).
mosaic [məuˈzeiik] adj. De mosaico: *mosaic floor*, suelo de mosaico.
— N. Mosaico, *m.* (floor, wall, etc.). || AVIAT. Aerofotografía, *f.* || FIG. Mosaico, *m.*
Mosaic [məuˈzeiik] adj. Mosaico, ca (of Moses).
Mosaism [məuˈzeizəm] n. Mosaísmo, *m.*
Moscow [ˈmɔskəu] pr. n. GEOGR. Moscú.
Moses [ˈməuziz] pr. n. Moisés, *m.* || *Moses basket*, moisés, *m.* (of a baby).
mosey [ˈməuzi] v. intr. U. S. Deambular (to stroll). | Irse (to go away).
Moslem [ˈmɔzlem] adj./n. Musulmán, ana.
Moslemism [—izəm] n. Religión (*f.*) musulmana.
mosque [mɔsk] n. Mezquita, *f.*
mosquito [məsˈkiːtəu] n. Mosquito, *m.* (insect): *mosquito bite*, picadura de mosquito.

— OBSERV. El plural de la palabra inglesa *mosquito* es *mosquitoes* o *mosquitos*.

mosquito boat [—bəut] n. Lancha (*f.*) torpedera.
mosquito curtain [—ˌkəːtn] or **mosquito net** [—net] n. Mosquitero, *m.*
moss [mɔs] n. BOT. Musgo, *m.* || Pantano, *m.* (bog).
moss [mɔs] v. tr. Cubrir con musgo.
mossback [—bæk] n. U. S. FAM. Retrógado, da.
moss-grown [—grəun] adj. Musgoso, sa (covered with moss). || FAM. Anticuado, da.
moss-trooper [—ˈtruːpə*] n. Bandido, *m.*, bandolero, *m.* (Royalist freebooter).
mossy [ˈmɔsi] adj. Cubierto de musgo, musgoso, sa.
most [məust] adj. Más: *who has most books?*, ¿quién tiene más libros?; *they are the most beautiful girls I've ever seen*, son las chicas más guapas que he visto en mi vida. || La mayoría de, la mayor parte de: *in most cases*, en la mayoría de los casos; *most people like the sun*, a la mayoría de la gente le gusta el sol. || *For the most part*, en su mayor parte; por lo general (generally).
— Adv. Más: *he is the most intelligent*, es el más inteligente; *which do you like most?*, ¿cuál es el que más te gusta? || De lo más, sumamente, muy (very): *the play was most amusing*, la obra fue de lo más entretenida. || U. S. FAM. Casi (almost). || — *Most likely*, muy probablemente. || *Most of all*, sobre todo.
— N. La mayoría: *most were in agreement*, la mayoría estaba de acuerdo. || La mayor parte: *most of the country is forest*, la mayor parte del país es bosque. || Lo máximo, lo más: *that's the most I can pay*, esto es lo máximo que puedo pagar. || — *At most* o *at the most*, a lo más, a lo sumo, como máximo. || *The very most*, lo más que. || *To make the most of*, sacar el mayor provecho de *or* el mayor partido de, aprovechar al máximo.

— OBSERV. *Most* se emplea en la formación del superlativo de los adjetivos polisílabos y del superlativo relativo. Se utiliza igualmente como superlativo de *much* y de *many*. Sin embargo *most* no debe emplearse cuando existe una comparación entre dos elementos, así no hay que decir *of those two men, John is the most intelligent* sino *the more intelligent*.

Most High [—hai] n. Altísimo, *m.* (God).
mostly [—li] adv. Principalmente, sobre todo (chiefly): *they are found mostly in the South*, se encuentran principalmente en el Sur. || La mayoría de las veces, casi siempre, generalmente (in the main). || En su mayor parte (for the most part).
mot [məu] n. Ocurrencia, *f.*, agudeza, *f.* (witticism). || *Mot juste*, palabra adecuada.
mote [məut] n. Mota, *f.* (spot, speck). || FIG. *To see the mote in another's eye and not the beam in one's own*, ver la paja en el ojo ajeno y no la viga en el propio.
motel [məuˈtel] n. Motel, *m.*
motet [məuˈtet] n. MUS. Motete, *m.*
moth [mɔθ] n. ZOOL. Mariposa, *f.* [nocturna]. | Polilla, *f.* (in clothes).
mothball [—bɔːl] n. Bola (*f.*) de naftalina.
moth-eaten [—ˌiːtn] adj. Apolillado, da. || FIG. Anticuado, da (outdated).
mother [ˈmʌðə*] n. Madre, *f.* (parent). || REL. Madre, *f.* || CULIN. Madre, *f.*: *mother of vinegar*, madre del vinagre. || FIG. Madre: *Greece, mother of democracy*, Grecia, madre de la democracia. || — *Every mother's son*, todo quisque, todo hijo de vecino. || *Foster mother*, madre adoptiva. || *Queen Mother*, reina madre.
— Adj. Materno, na (love). || Madre (country). || Matriz (church). || Materno, na (tongue).
mother [ˈmʌðə*] v. tr. Dar a luz a (to give birth). || Servir de madre a (to act as mother). || FIG. Concebir. | Reconocerse autor de. || Cuidar como una madre, cuidar como a un hijo (to care for). || Mimar (to spoil).
Mother Church [—ˈtʃəːtʃ] n. REL. Santa Madre Iglesia, *f.*
mother country [—ˌkʌntri] n. Madre patria, *f.*
motherhood [—hud] n. Maternidad, *f.*
mother-in-law [—inlɔː] n. Suegra, *f.*, madre (*f.*) política.

— OBSERV. El plural de *mother-in-law* es *mothers-in-law*.

motherland [—lænd] n. Madre patria, *f.*
motherless [—lis] adj. Huérfano de madre, sin madre.
motherliness [—linis] n. Cariño (*m.*) maternal, sentimientos (*m. pl.*) maternales.
motherly [—li] adj. Maternal.
— Adv. Maternalmente.
mother-of-pearl [—əvˈpəːl] adj. Nacarado, da.
— N. Madreperla, *f.*, nácar, *m.*
mother's boy [ˈmʌðəzbɔi] n. Hijo (*m.*) de su mamá.
Mother's Day [ˈmʌðəzdei] n. Día (*f.*) de la Madre.
mother ship [ˈmʌðəʃip] n. Buque (*m.*) nodriza.
mother superior [—sjuˈpiəriə*] n. Superiora, *f.*, madre (*f.*) superiora.
mother-to-be [ˈmʌðətəˈbiː] n. Futura madre, *f.*
mother tongue [—tʌŋ] n. Lengua (*f.*) materna (native language). || Lengua (*f.*) madre (from which others are derived).
mother wit [—ˈwit] n. Sentido (*m.*) común.
moth hole [ˈmɔθhəul] n. Picadura (*f.*) de polilla.
moth killer [ˈmɔθˌkilə*] n. Matapolillas, *m. inv.*
mothy [ˈmɔθi] adj. Lleno de polillas (infested with moths). || Apolillado, da (moth-eaten).
motif [məuˈtiːf] n. MUS. ARTS. Motivo, *m.* || Tema, *m.* (main subject).
motile [ˈməutail] adj. BIOL. Movible, móvil.
motility [məuˈtiliti] n. BIOL. Motilidad, *f.*, movilidad, *f.*
motion [ˈməuʃən] n. Movimiento, *m.*: *all her motions are clumsy*, todos sus movimientos son torpes. || Señas, *f. pl.*, gesto, *m.*, señal, *f.* (signal): *to make motion to*, hacer señas a. || Ademán, *m.*: *he made*

motion to get up, hizo ademán de levantarse. || Marcha, *f.*: *to be in motion*, estar en marcha; *to set in motion*, poner en marcha. || Movimiento, *m.* (of a clock). || Mecanismo, *m.* (of a machine). || Moción, *f.* (in an assembly): *censure motion*, moción de censura; *to second a motion*, apoyar una moción; *the motion is carried by 20 votes to 7 with 3 abstentions*, queda aprobada la moción por 20 votos a favor, 7 en contra y 3 abstenciones; *the motion is rejected* o *lost*, se rechaza la moción. || MUS. Cambio (*m.*) de tono. || MED. Deposición, *f.*, evacuación (*f.*) del vientre, deyección, *f.* || JUR. Pedimento, *m.* || — PHYS. *In motion*, en movimiento. || *Motion camera*, cámara (*f.*) tomavistas. || *Motion picture*, película, *f.* || *Motion pictures*, cine, *m.* || *Perpetual motion*, movimiento perpetuo. || *Substantive motion*, moción sobre el fondo de la cuestión. || *To bring forward a motion*, presentar una moción. || *To carry a motion*, aprobar una moción. || *To declare a motion receivable*, declarar una moción admisible. || *To go through the motions*, hacer algo como es debido. || *To table a motion*, presentar una moción (to propose), aplazar una moción sine die (to postpone). || *To vote on a motion*, votar una moción. || *Would this motion be in order?*, ¿se puede aceptar esta moción?

motion [ˈməuʃən] v. tr. Indicar con la mano: *he motioned me to come forward*, me indicó con la mano que avanzara.

— V. intr. Hacer señas *or* una señal.

motionless [—lis] adj. Inmóvil. || *To remain motionless*, no moverse, permanecer inmóvil.

motionlessness [—lisnis] n. Inmovilidad, *f.*

motivate [ˈməutiveit] v. tr. Motivar.

motivation [ˌməutiˈveiʃən] n. Motivo, *m.*, motivación, *f.*

motive [ˈməutiv] adj. Motor, motriz: *motive power*, fuerza motriz. || PHYS. Cinético, ca (energy).

— N. Motivo, *m.* (reason): *hidden motives*, motivos ocultos. || Móvil, *m.*: *the motive of a crime*, el móvil de un crimen. || ARTS. Motivo, *m.* || *Profit motive*, afán (*m.*) de lucro.

motive [ˈməutiv] v. tr. Motivar.

motivity [məuˈtiviti] n. Movilidad, *f.* || TECH. Energía (*f.*) cinética. | Fuerza (*f.*) motriz (motive power).

motley [ˈmɔtli] adj. Abigarrado, da; multicolor: *a motley crowd*, una multitud abigarrada. || Vario, ria; variado, da; diversificado, da (heterogeneous).

— N. Botarga, *f.* (costume). || Mezcla (*f.*) abigarrada de colores. || FIG. Revoltijo, *m.*, mezcolanza, *f.* (incongruous mixture).

moto-cross [ˈməutəkrɔs] n. Motocross, *m.*

motor [ˈməutə*] n. Motor, *m.*: *electric motor*, motor eléctrico. || Coche, *m.*, automóvil, *m.* (car). || — Pl. Acciones, *f.* [de fábricas de automóviles] (securities).

— Adj. Motor, motriz. || De motor, impulsado por un motor (motor-driven). || ANAT. Motor, ra.

motor [ˈməutə*] v. intr. Ir *or* viajar en coche.

motor bicycle [—ˌbaisikl] n. Motocicleta, *f.* || U. S. Velomotor, *m.*

motorbike [—baik] n. Motocicleta, *f.*, moto, *f.* || U. S. Velomotor, *m.*

motorboat [—bəut] n. Motora, *f.*, lancha (*f.*) motora.

motor bus [—bʌs] n. Autobús, *m.*

motorcade [—keid] n. Caravana (*f.*) *or* desfile (*m.*) de automóviles.

motorcar [—kɑ:*] n. Automóvil, *m.*, coche, *m.* (car).

motor coach [—kəutʃ] n. Autocar, *m.*

motorcycle [—ˌsaikl] n. Motocicleta, *f.*, moto, *f.*

motorcycle [—ˌsaikl] v. intr. Ir en motocicleta.

motorcycling [—ˌsaikliŋ] n. Motorismo, *m.*, motociclismo, *m.*

motorcyclist [—ˌsaiklist] n. Motorista, *m.* & *f.*, motociclista, *m.* & *f.*

motor-driven [—drivn] adj. Impulsado por un motor.

motordrome [—drəum] n. Autódromo, *m.*

motor fuel [—fjuəl] n. Carburante, *m.*

motor generator [—ˈdʒenəreitə*] n. ELECTR. Grupo (*m.*) convertidor.

motoring [—riŋ] n. Automovilismo, *m.* || *School of motoring* o *motoring school*, autoescuela, *f.*

— Adj. De automóvil, automovilístico, ca.

motorist [—rist] n. Automovilista, *m.* & *f.* || Conductor, ra (driver). || *Racing motorist*, corredor (*m.*) de coches.

motorization [ˌməutəraiˈzeiʃən] n. Motorización, *f.*

motorize [ˈməutəraiz] v. tr. Motorizar.

motorized [—d] adj. Motorizado, da. || *Motorized farming*, motocultivo, *m.*

motor launch [ˈməutəlɔ:ntʃ] n. Lancha (*f.*) motora.

motorless [ˈməutəlis] adj. Sin motor (plane).

motor lorry [ˈməutəˌlɔri] n. Camión, *m.*

motorman [ˈməutəmən] n. U. S. Conductor, *m.*, maquinista, *m.* (of trains). | Conductor, *m.* (of tram).

— OBSERV. El plural de *motorman* es *motormen*.

motor propellor [ˈməutəprəˈpelə*] n. TECH. Motopropulsor, *m.*

motor pump [ˈməutəpʌmp] n. Motobomba, *f.*

motor sailer [ˈməutəˌseilə*] n. Motovelero, *m.*

motor scooter [ˈməutəˌsku:tə*] n. Scooter, *m.*

motor scythe [ˈməutəsaið] n. AGR. Motosegadora, *f.*

motor ship [ˈməutəʃip] n. Motonave, *f.*

motor show [ˈməutəʃəu] n. Salón (*m.*) del automóvil.

motor tractor [ˈməutəˈtræktə*] n. Mototractor, *m.*

motor truck [ˈməutətrʌk] n. U. S. Camión, *m.*

motorway [ˈməutəwei] n. Autopista, *f.*

mottle [ˈmɔtl] n. Mancha (*f.*) *or* veta (*f.*) de color (spot). || Superficie (*f.*) abigarrada.

mottle [ˈmɔtl] v. tr. Abigarrar. || Motear, jaspear.

mottled [—d] adj. Abigarrado, da. || Veteado, da; jaspeado, da (grained). || De mezclilla, de varios colores (cloth). || Con manchas (skin). || Moteado, da (animal).

motto [ˈmɔtəu] n. Lema, *m.* || HERALD. Divisa, *f.*, lema, *m.* || Epígrafe, *m.* (in a literary work). || MUS. Tema, motivo, *m.* || Consigna, *f.*, santo y seña, *m.* (watchword). || Máxima, *f.* (maxim).

— OBSERV. El plural de *motto* es *mottoes* o *mottos*.

moue [mu:] n. Mueca, *f.*

mouflon or **moufflon** [ˈmu:flɔn] n. Musmón, *m.* (animal).

mouillé [mu:iˈjei] adj. GRAMM. Palatalizado, da; palatal.

moujik [ˈmu:ʒik] n. Mujic, *m.*

moulage [ˈmu:lɑ:ʒ] n. Molde, *m.* (plaster mould).

mould [məuld] n. Molde, *m.* (hollow container). || Pieza (*f.*) moldeada. || CULIN. Molde, *m.* || ARCH. Moldura, *f.* || Matriz, *f.* (in printing). || MAR. Gálibo, *m.*, vitola, *f.* || Molelo, *m.*, patrón, *m.*, plantilla, *f.* (pattern). || Forma, *f.* (shape). || FIG. Temple, *m.*, carácter, *m.*: *a man cast in a heroic mould*, un hombre de temple heroico. || AGR. Mantillo, *m.* (vegetable matter). || Moho, *m.* (fungus). || ANAT. Fontanela, *f.* || FIG. *Cast in the same mould*, cortado con el mismo patrón.

mould [məuld] v. tr. Moldear (to shape). || Moldear, vaciar (statues). || Ceñir: *dress which moulds the body*, traje que ciñe el cuerpo. || FIG. Formar, moldear (one's character). | Amoldar [*on*, a, según] (to adapt). || ARCH. Moldurar. || FIG. *To mould o.s. on s.o.*, tomar como modelo a alguien.

— V. intr. Enmohecerse (to go mouldy).

mouldable [—əbl] adj. Moldeable.

mouldboard [—bɔ:d] n. Vertedera (*f.*) del arado.

moulder [—ə*] n. Moldeador, ra.

moulder [—ə*] v. intr. Desmoronarse.

mouldiness [—inis] n. Enmohecimiento, *m.*, estado (*m.*) mohoso.

moulding [—iŋ] n. Moldeado, *m.*, moldeamiento, *m.* (action). || Vaciado, *m.* (of statues). || ARCH. Moldura, *f.* || ELECTR. Junquillo, *m.*, moldura, *f.* || FIG. Formación, *f.* (formation).

mouldy [—i] adj. Mohoso, sa; enmohecido, da (covered with mould). || FAM. Anticuado, da (old-fashioned). | Aburrido, da (boring). | Fatal (very bad). | Cochino, na (disreputable).

moult [məult] n. Muda, *f.*

moult [məult] v. tr. Mudar.

— V. intr. Mudar la piel (a snake) *or* las plumas (a bird).

mound [maund] n. Montón, *m.* (heap). || Montículo, *m.* (small hill). || Terraplén, *m.* (artificial bank of earth). || Túmulo, *m.* (over a grave). || HERALD. Globo, *m.*, mundo, *m.* || U. S. SP. Elevación, *f.*, altura, *f.*, montículo, *m.* [donde se pone el lanzador en béisbol].

mound [maund] v. tr. Amontonar (to heap up). || Terraplenar (to build up a bank).

mount [maunt] n. GEOGR. Monte, *m.* (mountain). || Montículo, *m.* (hillock). || Montura, *f.*, cabalgadura, *f.* (horse). || Engaste, *m.*, montura, *f.* (of jewels). || Soporte, *m.*, base, *f.* (support, base). || Fondo, *m.* (of a drawing, etc.). || Borde *m.* (of photo). || Portaobjeto, *m.* (of a microscope). || Fijasellos, *m. inv.* (for stamps). || MIL. Cureña, *f.* (of cannon).

mount [maunt] v. intr. Subir (to climb). || Montar a caballo (on a horse). || Aumentar (to increase). || *To mount up to*, elevarse hasta.

— V. tr. Subir (to climb). || Subir a (a table, a throne). || Montar a, subirse a (a horse). || Subir a, montar en (bicycle). || Proveer de caballo *or* caballos (to equip with horses). || Ayudar a subir a caballo. || Montar, armar (an engine). || Montar (a picture, statue, play, exhibition, etc.). || Engastar, montar (a jewel). || Fijar, pegar (stamps). || MAR. MIL. Montar (guns). | Estar armado con (to be armed with). || — MIL. *To mount an offensive*, lanzar *or* efectuar una ofensiva. || *To mount the guard*, montar la guardia.

mountain [ˈmauntin] n. Montaña, *f.* || FIG. Montón, *m.*: *a mountain of debts*, un montón de deudas. || FIG. *To make a mountain out of a molehill*, hacerse de todo una montaña.

— Adj. Montañoso, sa (mountainous). || Montañés, esa (people, costumes). || De montaña: *mountain artillery*, artillería de montaña.

mountain ash [—ˈæʃ] n. BOT. Serbal, *m.*

mountain cat [—kæt] n. ZOOL. Puma, *m.* (cougar). | Lince, *m.* | Gato (*m.*) montés (wildcat).

mountain chain [—tʃein] n. Cordillera, *f.*, sierra, *f.*

mountain climber [—ˌklaimə*] n. Montañero, ra; alpinista, *m.* & *f.* [*Amer.*, andinista, *m.* & *f.*].

mountain climbing [—ˌklaimiŋ] n. Montañismo, *m.*, alpinismo, *m.* [*Amer.*, andinismo, *m.*]

mountain dew [—ˈdju:] n. FAM. Whisky, *m.* [de contrabando].

mountain dweller [—ˌdwelə*] n. Montañés, esa.

mountaineer [ˌmaunti'niə*] n. Montañero, ra; alpinista, *m.* & *f.* [*Amer.*, andinista, *m.* & *f.*] (mountain climber). || Montañés, esa; serrano, na (dweller).
mountaineer [ˌmaunti'niə*] v. intr. Hacer alpinismo, escalar montañas.
mountaineering [—riŋ] n. Montañismo, *m.*, alpinismo, *m.* [*Amer.*, andinismo, *m.*] || *Mountaineering school*, escuela (*f.*) de montañismo.
mountain goat [—gəut] n. ZOOL. Cabra (*f.*) de las Montañas Rocosas.
mountain lion [—'laiən] n. ZOOL. Puma, *m.*
mountainous ['mauntinəs] adj. Montañoso, sa. || FIG. Enorme, monumental.
mountain range ['mauntinreindʒ] n. Cordillera, *f.*, sierra, *f.*
mountain sheep [—ʃi:p] n. ZOOL. Musmón (*m.*) de las Montañas Rocosas.
mountain sickness [—'siknis] n. Mal (*m.*) de montaña [*Amer.*, soroche, *m.*, puna, *f.*]
mountainside ['mauntinˌsaid] n. Falda (*f.*) *or* ladera (*f.*) de montaña.
mountaintop ['mauntinˌtɔp] n. Cumbre (*f.*) *or* cima (*f.*) de una montaña.
mountebank ['mauntibæŋk] n. Saltimbanqui, *m.* || FIG. Charlatán, *m.* (quack).
mounted police ['məuntidpə'lis] n. Policía (*m.*) montada.
mounter ['mauntə*] n. Montador, ra.
Mountie ['maunti] n. FAM. Miembro (*m.*) de la policía montada canadiense.
mounting ['mauntiŋ] n. Subida, *f.* (climbing). || Engaste, *m.*, montura, *f.* (of jewels). || Fondo, *m.* (of drawing, etc.). || Soporte, *m.*, base, *m.* (support). || THEATR. CINEM. Montaje, *m.* || TECH. Montaje, *m.*
mounting block [—blɔk] n. Montador, *m.*
Mounty ['maunti] n. FAM. Miembro (*m.*) de la policía montada canadiense.
mourn ['mɔ:n] v. tr. Llorar [la muerte de]. || Lamentar (to lament). || Llevar luto por (to wear mourning for).
— V. intr. Estar de luto (to be in mourning). || Lamentarse. || *To mourn for*, llorar la muerte de (the death of), deplorar, lamentar (a loss).
mourner [—ə*] n. Persona (*f.*) que está de luto (person in mourning). || Acompañante, *m.* & *f.*, doliente, *m.* & *f.* (at a funeral). || Plañidera, *f.* (hired mourner). || *Chief mourner*, el que preside un entierro.
mournful [—ful] adj. Triste, lúgubre (sad). || Afligido, da (grieved).
mournfulness [—fulnis] n. Tristeza, *f.*
mourning [—iŋ] n. Luto, *m.*, duelo, *m.* (period). || Luto, *m.* (clothes). || Aflicción, *f.*, tristeza, *f.* (sadness). || — *Deep mourning*, luto riguroso. || *Half mourning*, medio luto. || *House of mourning*, casa mortuoria. || *Mourning band*, brazalete, *m.* || *Mourning dress*, traje (*m.*) de luto. || *To be in mourning*, estar de luto. || *To be in mourning for*, llevar luto por. || *To come out of deep mourning*, aliviar el luto. || *To come out of mourning*, dejar *or* quitarse el luto. || *To go into mourning*, ponerse *or* vestirse de luto.
— Adj. De luto.
mouse [maus] n. ZOOL. Ratón, *m.* || FIG. Tímido, da (shy person). | Cobarde, *m.* & *f.* (coward). || MAR. Trinca, *f.* (of a hook). || Barrilete, *m.* (knot). || U. S. FAM. Ojo (*m.*) a la funerala.

— OBSERV. El plural de *mouse* es *mice*.

mouse [maus] v. intr. Cazar ratones. || FAM. *To mouse about*, fisgar.
mouse-ear [—iə*] n. BOT. Oreja (*f.*) de ratón.
mousehole [—həul] n. Ratonera, *f.*
mouser ['mauzə*] n. Gato (*m.*) cazador de ratones.
mousetrap ['maustræp] n. Ratonera, *f.*
mousey ['mausi] adj. See MOUSY.
mousse [mu:s] n. CULIN. Crema (*f.*) batida: *chocolate mousse*, crema batida de chocolate.
moustache [məs'tɑ:ʃ] n. Bigote, *m.*, bigotes, *m. pl.*
Mousterian [ˌmu:s'tiəriən] adj. GEOL. Musteriense.
mousy ['mausi] adj. Ratonesco, ca; ratonil. || Lleno de ratones (infested with mice). || FAM. Pardusco, ca (colour). || FIG. Tímido, da (shy). | Silencioso, sa (quiet).
mouth [mauθ] n. ANAT. Boca, *f.*: *I've got a bad taste in my mouth*, tengo mal sabor de boca. || Abertura, *f.* (of a tube, etc.). || Desembocadura, *f.*, bocas, *f. pl.* (of a river). || Entrada, *f.*: *he stopped at the mouth of the cave*, se detuvo a la entrada de la cueva. || MUS. Boquilla, *f.*, boca, *f.* (of an instrument). || Boca, *f.*, abertura, *f.* (of an oven, sewer, well, etc.). || Boca, *f.* (of a pitcher, a volcano). || Tragante, *m.* (of a blast furnace). || Gollete, *m.* (of a bottle). || Mueca, *f.*, gesto, *m.* (grimace). || — FIG. *By word of mouth*, de viva voz. | *From mouth to mouth*, de boca en boca. | *I've got seven mouths to feed*, tengo siete bocas que alimentar. | *Never look a gift horse in the mouth*, a caballo regalado no le mires el diente. | *Not to open one's mouth*, no abrir *or* no descoser la boca. || FAM. *Shut your mouth!*, ¡a callarse la boca! || FIG. *To be down in the mouth*, estar deprimido, estar cariacontecido *or* cabizbajo. | *To foam at the mouth*, echar espumarajos por la boca (with anger). | *To get sth. straight from the horse's mouth*, saber algo de buena tinta. | *To give mouth to*, expresar. || FAM. *To have a big mouth*, ser un bocazas. || FIG. *To keep one's mouth shut*, no decir esta boca es mía. | *To live from hand to mouth*, vivir al día. | *To look down in the mouth*, estar con la cara larga. | *To make one's mouth water*, hacérsele [a uno] la boca agua. | *To put words into s.o.'s mouth*, poner palabras en boca de uno. | *To shoot one's mouth off*, hablar más de la cuenta. | *To stop s.o.'s mouth*, cerrar el pico a uno. | *To take the words right out of s.o.'s mouth*, quitarle a uno las palabras de la boca.
mouth [mauð] v. tr. Articular (to form with the lips). || Pronunciar con afectación (to say in an affected manner). || Proferir (insults). || Acostumbrar al bocado (a horse). || Tomar *or* coger en la boca (to take into the mouth).
— V. intr. Hablar con rimbombancia. || Hacer una mueca (to grimace).
mouth-filling ['mauθˌfiliŋ] adj. Rimbombante (bombastic).
mouthful ['mauθful] n. Bocado, *m.* (eating). || Bocanada, *f.* (of air, smoke, etc.). || U. S. FAM. *You've said a mouthful!*, ¡así se habla!, ¡muy bien dicho!
mouth organ ['mauθˌɔ:gən] n. MUS. Armónica, *f.*
mouthpiece ['mauθpi:s] n. MUS. Boquilla, *f.* || Micrófono, *m.* (of a telephone). || Boquilla, *f.* (of a pipe). || FIG. Portavoz, *m.* [*Amer.*, vocero, *m*] (spokesman).
mouth-to-mouth respiration ['mauθtə'mauθˌrespə'reiʃən] n. Boca a boca, *m.*
mouthwash ['mauθwɔʃ] n. Enjuague, *m.*
mouth-watering ['mauθˌwɔ:təriŋ] adj. Muy apetitoso, sa; que hace la boca agua.
mouthy ['mauði] adj. Rimbombante (bombastic).
movability [ˌmu:və'biliti] or **movableness** ['mu:vəblnis] n. Movilidad, *f.*
movable ['mu:vəbl] adj. Movible, móvil. || Móvil: *movable feast*, fiesta móvil. || Desmontable (detachable). || JUR. Mobiliario, ria (effects). | Mueble (property).
— Pl. n. Muebles, *m.* (furniture). || JUR. Bienes (*m.*) muebles.
move [mu:v] n. FIG. Paso, *m.*: *he made the first move towards peace*, dio el primer paso hacia la paz; *false move*, paso en falso. | Marcha, *f.*: *Mexico is a nation on the move*, México es una nación en marcha. | Medida, *f.*, gestión, *f.*, acción, *f.*: *that was a wasted move*, fue una gestión inútil. | Maniobra, *f.* (manoeuvre). || Movimiento, *m.* (movement): *she made a move towards the door*, hizo un movimiento hacia la puerta. || Mudanza, *f.* (of house). || Traslado, *m.* (of person). || Jugada, *f.* (in chess, etc.): *mate in four moves*, mate en cuatro jugadas. || Turno, *m.*, vez, *f.* (turn). || — *A wise move*, una buena jugada, una buena maniobra. || *Don't make a move!*, ¡no se mueva! || FAM. *Get a move on!*, ¡date prisa!, ¡apresúrate! (be quick), ¡menéate!, ¡muévete! (do sth.) || *It is your move*, tú juegas, te toca a ti. || FAM. *To be always on the move*, no parar ni un momento, estar siempre moviéndose. || *To be on the move*, estar de acá para allá (to be moving), estar en camino (on the way), estar en movimiento (in motion), estar de viaje (travelling). || *To be up to every move*, sabérselas todas. || *To get a move on*, darse prisa, apresurarse. || *To have been on the move all day*, no haber parado en todo el día. || *To have first move*, salir (in games). || FIG. *To know every move in the game*, sabérselas todas. || *To make a move*, dar un paso (to take a step), tomar medidas (to take action), ponerse en marcha (to get started), irse (to go), levantarse (to stand up), jugar, hacer una jugada (in games). || FAM. *To make s.o. get a move on*, dar *or* meter prisa a uno. | *We must be on the move*, hay que irse. || *What's the next move?*, ¿qué hacemos ahora? || *Whose move is it?*, ¿quién juega?, ¿a quién le toca?
move [mu:v] v. tr. Cambiar de: *to move one's position*, cambiar de lugar; *he moved his job*, cambió de empleo. || Cambiar de sitio, trasladar: *let's move the table*, vamos a cambiar la mesa de sitio. || Mudarse de: *to move house*, mudarse de casa. || Mover, menear (head, arm, etc.). || Mover: *the wind moved the leaves*, el viento movía las hojas. || Trasladar (from one place to another). || Transportar (to transport). || Trasladar: *to move an official*, trasladar a un funcionario. || Mover, poner en movimiento *or* en marcha (to set in motion). | Poner en marcha *or* en funcionamiento (to switch on). || Mover, accionar: *moved by electricity*, accionado eléctricamente. || Remover (to stir up). || Sacudir, menear (to shake). || Mover, jugar (in chess, etc.): *he moved a piece*, movió una pieza. || Propulsar, impeler (to propel). || Mover a, incitar a, inducir a: *he moved me to speak*, me indujo a que hablara. || Emocionar, conmover, afectar: *these demonstrations move me very little*, esas demostraciones me conmueven muy poco; *much moved by the news*, muy afectado por las noticias. || Hacer cambiar de parecer: *nothing will move me*, nada me hará cambiar de parecer. || Proponer: *I move that the meeting be postponed*, propongo que se aplazca la reunión. || COMM. Vender. || Exonerar (the bowels). || — *Easily moved*, muy emocionable. || *Moved with anger*, movido por la cólera. || FIG. *Not to move hand or foot*, no moverse, no mover un dedo. || *To move a proposal*, hacer *or* formular una propuesta. || FIG. *To move s.o.'s heart*, conmover el corazón de alguien. || *To*

move s.o. to anger, provocar la cólera de uno. || *To move s.o. to laughter*, hacer reír a alguien. || *To move s.o. to pity*, mover a uno a compasión. || *To move s.o. to tears*, hacer llorar a uno. || *When the spirit moves one*, cuando le venga a uno en gana.

— V. intr. Moverse: *don't move!*, ¡no te muevas!; *I can't move*, no puedo moverme; *stop moving*, deja de moverte; *the Earth moves round the Sun*, la Tierra se mueve alrededor del Sol. || Trasladarse (from one place to another). || Cambiarse: *I am going to move to another seat*, me voy a cambiar de sitio. || Andar (to walk). || Estar en movimiento (to be moving). || Circular: *the crowd moving in the street*, la muchedumbre que circula por la calle. || *Ir: to move at high speed*, ir a gran velocidad; *things are moving slowly*, las cosas van lentamente. || Irse, marcharse (to go): *it is time we were moving*, ya es hora de marcharnos. || Cubrir, hacer: *I moved 600 kilometres that day*, hice seiscientos kilómetros aquel día. || Mudarse: *last year we moved into town*, el año pasado nos mudamos a la ciudad. || Mudar de casa (to move house). || Hacer una jugada, jugar (in games). || Tocar jugar, jugar: *who moves next?*, ¿a quién le toca jugar ahora?, ¿quién juega ahora? || Moverse (chess pieces). || Moverse, menearse (to shake). || Hacer progresos, adelantar (to progress). || Dar un paso (to take steps). || Hacer gestiones, tomar medidas (to take action). || Ponerse en marcha (to start up). || Funcionar: *this machine moves by hand*, esta máquina funciona a mano. || Venderse bien (to sell well). || — *Keep moving!*, ¡circulen! || *This article is not moving*, este artículo tiene mala salida *or* es de difícil venta. || *To keep the traffic moving*, mantener una circulación fluida. || *To move for*, proponer: *I move for a postponement of the meeting*, propongo un aplazamiento de la reunión. || *To move freely*, tener juego *or* holgura (a part). || *To move one step*, dar un paso.

— **To move about,** cambiar de sitio: *when I arrived they were moving the furniture about*, cuando llegué estaban cambiando los muebles de sitio. | Moverse (to be in motion). | Ir y venir (to come and go). | — *To move about freely*, circular libremente. || **To move along,** hacer circular. | Circular: *move along!*, ¡circulen! | Avanzar (to go forward). || **To move aside,** poner a un lado (sth.). | Ponerse a un lado. || **To move away,** alejar, apartar (sth.). | Alejarse, apartarse. || **To move back,** hacer retroceder. | Retroceder (to go backwards). | Echarse para atrás (to stand back). || **To move down,** bajar. || **To move forward,** avanzar. | Hacer avanzar, hacer progresar (to help progress). | Adelantar (a meeting). || **To move in,** instalarse (into a house). | Entrar (to enter). | — *To move in high society*, alternar con la alta sociedad. || **To move off,** alejarse (to go away). | Ponerse en camino (to set off). | Irse (to go). | Salir (a train). || **To move on,** hacer circular (a crowd). | Circular: *to make the crowd move on*, hacer circular la muchedumbre; *move on!*, ¡circulen! | Seguir su camino (to continue on one's way). | Avanzar (to go forward). | Pasar, transcurrir (the time). | Irse, marcharse (to go). || **To move out,** sacar (to take out). | Echar (to throw out). | Mudar (furniture). | Irse (to leave). | Mudarse, mudar de casa (to change one's residence). || **To move up,** subir (to make go up). | Correr (to take out of the way). | Adelantar (a date). | Subir (to go up). | Correrse (to make room). | Ser ascendido (to be promoted). | — *To be moved up*, cambiarse a la clase superior (in school).

moveability [ˌmu:vəˈbiliti] or **moveableness** [ˈmu:vəblnis] n. Movilidad, *f.*

moveable [ˈmu:vəbl] adj. See MOVABLE.

movement [ˈmu:vmənt] n. Movimiento, *m.*: *the movement of the waves*, el movimiento de las olas; *the separatist movement*, el movimiento separatista. || Gesto, *m.*, ademán, *m.* (gesture): *he made a movement of impatience*, hizo un gesto de impaciencia. || Acto, *m.*, acción, *f.* (act). || Impulso, *m.* (impulse). || Arrebato, *m.* (of anger). || Tendencia, *f.* (trend). || Transporte, *m.* (transport). || Traslado, *m.* (of goods, of an official). || Movimiento, *m.* (of a person). || Tráfico, *m.*, movimiento, *m.* (of ships, etc.). || Tráfico, *m.*, circulación, *f.* (of cars). || MAR. MIL. Maniobra, *f.* | Movimiento, *m.* || MUS. Movimiento, *m.* (division of a work). | Tiempo, *m.* (tempo). || TECH. Mecanismo, *m.* | Marcha, *f.*, funcionamiento, *m.* (working). | Juego, *m.*, holgura, *f.* (of a part). || COMM. Actividad, *f.* (activity). | Variación, *f.* (of price). || MED. Evacuación, *f.* [del vientre] (of the bowels). || — Pl. Actividades, *f.*, idas (*f.*) y venidas. || *Upward movement*, movimiento ascendente.

mover [ˈmu:və*] n. Motor, *m.* (moving force). || Autor, ra (of a motion). || Inspirador, ra; instigador, ra (of a plot, etc.). || U. S. Mozo (*m.*) de mudanzas (of furniture).

movie [ˈmu:vi] n. U. S. Película, *f.* (film). | Cine, *m.* (cinema). || — Pl. U. S. Cine, *m. sing.*: *to go to the movies*, ir al cine.

movie camera [—ˌkæmərə] n. Cámara, *f.*, tomavistas, *m. inv.*

moviegoer [—ˌgəuə*] n. U. S. Aficionado (*m.*) al cine, aficionada (*f.*) al cine.

movie house [—haus] n. U. S. Cine, *m.*

movie star [—stɑ:*] n. U. S. Estrella (*f.*) de cine.

moving [ˈmu:viŋ] adj. Móvil: *a moving target*, un blanco móvil. || En movimiento (in motion). || En marcha: *moving tram*, tranvía en marcha. || Motriz (force). || Motor, ra (driving). || Mecánico, ca (staircase). || FIG. Conmovedor, ra: *a moving story*, una historia conmovedora.

— N. Movimiento, *m.* (movement). || Traslado, *m.* || Mudanza, *f.* (of house).

moving picture [—ˈpiktʃə*] n. Película, *f.* [cinematográfica].

moving sidewalk [—ˈsaidwɔ:k] n. U. S. Pasillo (*m.*) rodante.

moving staircase [—ˈsteəkeis] or **moving stairway** [—ˈsteəwei] n. Escalera (*f.*) mecánica.

moving van [—væn] n. Camión (*m.*) de mudanzas.

mow [məu] n. U. S. Granero, *m.*, henil, *m.* (barn). | Montón (*m.*) de heno *or* de gavillas (heap of hay).

mow* [məu] v. tr. Segar, cortar (grass). || Segar (corn). || FIG. Segar. || FIG. *They mowed down the enemy with a machine gun*, barrieron al enemigo con una ametralladora.

— OBSERV. Pret. **mowed;** p. p. **mown, mowed.**

mower [—ə*] n. Cortacéspedes, *m. inv.* (for a garden). || AGR. Segadora, *f.* (machine). | Segador, ra (person).

mowing [—iŋ] n. Siega, *f.* (reaping). || Corte, *m.* (in the garden). || *Mowing machine*, segadora, *f.* (for corn), cortacéspedes, *m. inv.* (for a garden).

mown [məun] p. p. See MOW.

Mozarab [məuˈzærəb] n. Mozárabe, *m.* & *f.*

Mozarabic [məuˈzærəbik] adj. Mozárabe.

mozzetta or **mozetta** [məuˈzetə] n. Muceta, *f.* (short cape).

M.P. [ˈemˈpi:] abbrev. Miembro (*m.*) del Parlamento, diputado, *m.* (Member of Parliament). || Policía (*f.*) Militar (Military Police). || Policía (*f.*) Montada (Mounted Police).

Mr [ˈmistə*] abbrev. of *Mister*, Sr., señor.

Mrs [ˈmisiz] abbrev. of *Mistress*, Sra., señora.

mu [mju:] n. My, *f.* (Greek letter).

much [mʌtʃ] adj. Mucho, cha: *much attention*, mucha atención. || — *As much courage as*, tanto valor como. || *How much*, cuánto, ta: *how much wine shall I buy?*, ¿cuánto vino compro?; *when I think how much time I waste*, al pensar cuánto tiempo pierdo. || *I don't eat very much fruit*, no como mucha fruta. || *So much*, tanto, ta: *so much money*, tanto dinero. || *Too much*, demasiado, da: *too much wine*, demasiado vino. || *Twice as much water*, el doble de agua.

— Adv. Mucho: *do you drink much?*, ¿bebes mucho?; *much better*, mucho mejor; *it doesn't matter much*, no importa mucho; *much more*, mucho más. || Muy (before a past participle): *much annoyed*, muy enfadado. || Con mucho: *it much exceeds my expectations*, sobrepasa con mucho mis esperanzas. || — *As much as*, tanto como: *it is as much your fault as mine*, es tanto su culpa como la mía; todo lo que, cuanto: *do as much as you can*, haz todo lo que puedas. || *As much as to say...*, como si dijera... || *Ever so much*, muchísimo: *ever so much more intelligent*, muchísimo más inteligente. || *However much*, por mucho que. || *How much?*, ¿cuánto?: *how much is it?*, ¿cuánto vale? || *I don't want two, much less five*, no quiero dos y menos aún cinco. || *It's as much as I can do to remain awaken*, apenas puedo quedarme despierto. || *It was as much as I could do not to laugh*, poco faltó para que me riese. || *Much as I should like*, por mucho *or* por más que yo quisiera. || *Much the largest*, el más grande con mucho. || *Much the same*, poco más o menos lo mismo. || *Much the same age*, más o menos de la misma edad. || *Much to my surprise*, con gran sorpresa mía. || *Not much*, no mucho, poco. || FAM. *Not much!*, ¡ya lo creo!, ¡y cómo! (and how), ¡esto te lo crees tú! (I don't believe you). || *Not so much as*, ni siquiera (not even). || *Not so much... as*, no... sino más bien. || *So much*, see so. || *Thank you very much*, muchas gracias. || FAM. *That's too much of a good thing!*, ¡eso es demasiado! || *Too much*, demasiado: *it costs too much*, cuesta demasiado; de más: *she gave me ten pounds too much*, me dio diez libras de más. || *Very much*, muchísimo: *I like it very much*, me gusta muchísimo; *very much better*, muchísimo mejor; muy: *I am very much pleased*, estoy muy contento. || *You can't have too much of a good thing*, lo que abunda no daña.

— N. Mucho: *much remains to be done*, queda mucho por hacer; *there is not much to see*, no hay mucho que ver. || Gran parte, *f.*: *much of the land was flooded*, se inundó gran parte del terreno. || — *As much*, tanto: *as much again*, otro tanto; otro tanto: *can you do as much?*, ¿puede hacer otro tanto? || *Do you see much of one another?*, ¿os veis a menudo? || *Half as much again*, la mitad más. || *He's not much of a sportsman*, dista mucho de ser un deportista, le falta mucho para ser un deportista, es un deportista de poca entidad *or* de poca categoría. || *I don't think much of it*, no me parece gran cosa, en mi opinión no vale gran cosa. || *I thought as much*, ya me lo figuraba, ya me lo imaginaba. || FAM. *It is not up to much*, no vale mucho. || *I will say this much for him*, diré esto en su favor. || *There is not much in him*, no vale mucho. || *There is not much of it*, no hay mucho. || *This, that much*, tanto como esto, tanto como eso. || *To make much of*, see MAKE.

muchness [—nis] n. Magnitud, *f.* || FAM. *It's much of a muchness*, viene a ser lo mismo, es poco más o menos lo mismo.
mucillage [ˈmju:silidʒ] n. BOT. Mucílago, *m.* || U. S. Goma (*f.*) de pegar (adhesive).
mucilaginous [ˌmju:siˈlædʒinəs] adj. Mucilaginoso, sa.
muck [mʌk] n. Estiércol, *m.* (manure). || U. S. Mantillo, *m.* (fertile soil). || Suciedad, *f.* (dirt). || Lodo, *m.* (mud). || FAM. Porquería, *f.*, basura, *f.* || — *It was in a muck*, estaba asqueroso *or* sucio. || FAM. *To make a muck up of*, echar a perder.
muck [mʌk] v. tr. Estercolar (to manure). || FAM. Ensuciar (to dirty). | Echar a perder (to spoil). || — FAM. *To muck about*, fastidiar (s.o.). | *To muck out*, limpiar. | *To muck up*, ensuciar (to dirty), echar a perder (to spoil).
— V. intr. FAM. *To muck about*, perder el tiempo. | *To muck about with*, manosear, juguetear con (to handle), entretenerse con (to amuse o.s.), estropear, echar a perder (to ruin). | *To muck in with*, compartir un alojamiento con.
mucker [—ə*] n. Patán, *m.* (coarse person). || Persona (*f.*) soez (vulgar person). || Porrazo, *m.*, caída, *f.* (cropper). || *To come a mucker*, darse un porrazo, caerse.
muckiness [—inis] n. Suciedad, *f.*, asquerosidad, *f.*
muckrake [ˈmʌkreik] v. intr. Descubrir *or* revelar escándalos.
muckraker [—ə*] n. Revelador (*m.*) de escándalos.
muckworm [ˈmʌkwə:m] n. Gusano (*m.*) del estiércol. || FIG. Avaro, ra (miser).
mucky [ˈmʌki] adj. Asqueroso, sa; sucio, cia; puerco, ca. || *To get mucky*, ensuciar.
mucosa [mju:ˈkəusə] n. ANAT. Mucosa, *f.*

— OBSERV. El plural de la palabra inglesa *mucosa* es *mucosae, mucosa* o *mucosas*.

mucosity [mju:ˈkɔsiti] n. Mucosidad, *f.*
mucous [ˈmju:kəs] adj. Mucoso, sa. || *Mucous membrane*, mucosa, *f.*
mucus [ˈmju:kəs] n. Mucosidad, *f.*, moco, *m.*
mud [mʌd] n. Barro, *m.*, lodo, *m.* || Fango, *m.* (thick mud). || Cieno, *m.*, limo, *m.* (in a river). || Lodo, *m.* (in drilling). || ARCH. Adobe, *m.* || FIG. Cieno, *m.*, lodo, *m.*, fango, *m.* (dirt). || — FIG. *His name is mud*, tiene muy mala fama. || *Mud hut*, cabaña (*f.*) de barro. || *To get stuck in the mud*, empantanarse, atascarse en el fango (cart), embarrancarse (ship). || FIG. *To sling* o *to throw* o *to fling mud at s.o.*, calumniar a alguien, arrastrar a alguien por los suelos.
mud bath [—bɑ:θ] n. Baño (*m.*) de lodo.
muddiness [—inis] n. Fangosidad, *f.* (of the ground). || Turbiedad, *f.* (of a liquid). || FIG. Confusión, *f.*
muddle [ˈmʌdl] n. Confusión, *f.*, embrollo, *m.* (mental confusion). || Desorden, *m.* (disorder). || Revoltijo, *m.*, follón, *m.*: *a muddle of papers*, un revoltijo de papeles. || Embrollo, *m.*, lío, *m.* (mix-up): *what a muddle!*, ¡qué lío! || — *He was all in a muddle*, estaba hecho un lío. || *It was a dreadful muddle*, era un lío espantoso. || *To get into a muddle*, embrollarse, enredarse, armarse un lío.
muddle [ˈmʌdl] v. tr. Confundir, embrollar. || Dejar confuso *or* perplejo, aturdir (to daze). || Embotar (with drink). || Formar un lío con, enredar (to make a mess of). || *To get muddled*, armarse un lío.
— V. intr. Obrar confusamente *or* sin ton ni son. || *To muddle through*, salir del paso, arreglárselas.
muddlehead [—hed] n. Lioso, sa; persona (*f.*) que lo enreda todo.
muddleheaded [—ˌhedid] adj. Atontado, da; lioso, sa; despistado, da (person). || Confuso, sa (ideas).
muddler [ˈmʌdlə*] n. Lioso, sa; persona (*f.*) que lo enreda todo. || Varilla (*f.*) para mezclar cócteles.
muddy [ˈmʌdi] adj. Fangoso, sa; lleno de barro *or* de lodo: *a muddy path*, un sendero fangoso. || Con cieno, cenagoso, sa (river). || Lleno de barro: *your clothes are all muddy*, tu ropa está llena de barro. || Turbio, bia (liquid). || Macilento, ta (light). || Terroso, sa (complexion). || Oscuro, ra (dark). || Turbio, bia; confuso, sa (ideas).
muddy [ˈmʌdi] v. tr. Manchar de barro. || Enturbiar (a liquid). || Poner de color terroso (the complexion). || Turbar (one's mind).
— V. intr. Enturbiarse (a liquid).
Mudejar [mu:ˈdehɑ*] adj./n. Mudéjar.
mud flat [ˈmʌdflæt] n. Marisma, *f.*, terreno (*m.*) bajo que se inunda con la marea alta.
mudguard [ˈmʌdgɑ:d] n. Guardabarros, *m. inv.* (of a motorcycle, etc.). || Guardabarros, *m. inv.*, aleta, *f.* (of a car).
mudlark [ˈmʌdlɑ:k] n. FAM. Galopín, *m.* (child).
mudpack [ˈmʌdpæk] n. Mascarilla, *f.*
mudslinger [ˈmʌdˌsliŋgə*] n. Calumniador, ra.
mudslinging [ˈmʌdˌsliŋiŋ] n. Calumnia, *f.*, ataque (*m.*) calumnioso.
mud wall [ˈmʌdˈwɔ:l] n. Tapia, *f.*
muezzin [muˈezin] n. Almuecín, *m.*, almuédano, *m.*, muecín, *m.*
muff [mʌf] n. Manguito, *m.* (for the hands). || SP. Mala jugada, *f.*, fallo, *m.* || FAM. Chapucería, *f.* (sth. badly done). | Zopenco, ca (person).
muff [mʌf] v. tr. SP. Dejar escapar (the ball). | Fallar, errar (a shot). || Desperdiciar, perder (a chance). || *To muff an interview*, hacer mal una entrevista.
muffin [ˈmʌfin] n. CULIN. Mollete, *m.*, panecillo, *m.*
muffle [ˈmʌfl] n. Hocico, *m.*, morro, *m.* (of a cow). || Guante, *m.* (glove). || Sordina, *f.* (of a piano). || TECH. Mufla, *f.* (in a furnace).
muffle [ˈmʌfl] v. tr. Tapar: *to muffle one's throat*, taparse la garganta. || Amortiguar (a sound). || Enfundar (to put a cover on). || Tapar la cara *or* la boca a (to prevent from seeing or speaking). || *To muffle up*, embozar (with a cloak).
muffler [—ə*] n. Bufanda, *f.* (scarf). || MUS. Sordina, *f.* || AUT. Silenciador, *m.* (of exhaust pipe).
mufti [ˈmʌfti] n. REL. Muftí, *m.* || Traje (*m.*) de paisano (civil dress). || *In mufti*, vestido de paisano.
mug [mʌg] n. Tazón, *m.* (cup). || Jarra, *f.* (of beer). || Vaso, *m.* (for toothbrush). || FAM. Jeta, *f.*, hocico, *m.* (face). | Primo, ma (dupe). || U. S. FAM. Rufián, *m.*
mug [mʌg] v. tr. U. S. Atacar, asaltar (to attack). | Fotografiar (to photograph).
— V. intr. FAM. Exagerar los gestos (an actor). || FAM. *To mug up*, empollar (to study).
mugginess [—inis] n. Bochorno, *m.* (of weather).
mugging [—iŋ] n. FAM. Asalto, *m.*, ataque, *m.*
muggins [ˈmʌginz] inv. n. FAM. Primo, ma; tonto, ta.
muggy [ˈmʌgi] adj. Bochornoso, sa (weather).
mugwump [ˈmʌgwʌmp] n. U. S. Independiente, *m.* (in politics).
Muhammad [mʌˈhæmed] pr. n. Mahoma, *m.*
Muhammadan [mʌˈhæmidən] adj./n. Mahometano, na.
Muhammadanism [—izəm] n. REL. Mahometismo, *m.* (Islam).
mujik [ˈmu:ʒik] n. Mujic, *m.*
mulatto [mjuˈlætəu] adj./n. Mulato, ta.

— OBSERV. El plural de *mulatto* es *mulattoes*.

mulattress [mjuˈlætris] n. Mulata, *f.*
mulberry [ˈmʌlbəri] n. BOT. Mora, *f.* (berry). | Morera, *f.*, moral, *m.* (tree). || Color (*m.*) morado (colour). || — *Mulberry field*, moreral, *m.* || *Mulberry tree*, morera, *f.*, moral, *m.*
mulch [mʌltʃ] n. AGR. Pajote, *m.*
mulch [mʌltʃ] v. tr. AGR. Cubrir con pajote.
mulct [mʌlkt] n. Multa, *f.*
mulct [mʌlkt] v. tr. Multar. || FIG. Sacar (money, etc.).
mule [mju:l] n. Babucha, *f.* (slipper). || ZOOL. Mulo, *m.* (male). | Mula, *f.* (female). || FIG. Testarudo, da; mula, *f.*: *as stubborn as a mule*, testarudo como una mula. || BIOL. Híbrido (*m.*) estéril. || TECH. Máquina (*f.*) de hilar (spinning machine).
— Adj. Mular, mulero, ra.
mule jenny [—ˈdʒeni] n. TECH. Máquina (*f.*) de hilar.
mule skinner [—ˌskinə*] n. U. S. FAM. Mulero, *m.*, muletero, *m.*, arriero, *m.*
muleteer [ˌmju:liˈtiə*] n. Mulero, *m.*, muletero, *m.*, arriero, *m.*
mule track [ˈmju:ltræk] n. Camino (*m.*) de herradura.
mulish [ˈmju:liʃ] adj. Testaruro, da; terco, ca (stubborn).
mulishness [—nis] n. Testarudez, *f.*, terquedad, *f.*
mull [mʌl] n. Muselina (*f.*) fina.
mull [mʌl] v. tr./intr. Calentar con especias (to heat and spice). || FAM. *To mull over*, reflexionar sobre, rumiar sobre.
mullein [ˈmʌlin] n. BOT. Gordolobo, *m.*
muller [ˈmʌlə*] n. Moleta, *f.*
mullet [ˈmʌlit] n. Mújol, *m.* (fish). || *Red mullet*, salmonete, *m.* (fish).
mulligan [ˈmʌligən] n. U. S. FAM. Guisado, *m.*, guiso, *m.*
mullion [ˈmʌliən] n. ARCH. Parteluz, *m.*, mainel, *m.*
mullion [ˈmʌliən] v. tr. Dividir con parteluces *or* maineles.
multicellular [ˌmʌltiˈseljulə*] adj. BIOL. Multicelular, pluricelular.
multichannel [ˈmʌltiˈtʃænl] adj. De varios canales (television).
multicoloured (U. S. **multicolored**) [ˌmʌltiˈkʌləd] adj. Multicolor, policromo, ma.
multifarious [ˌmʌltiˈfɛəriəs] adj. Múltiple, vario, ria; diverso, sa; variado, da.
multifariousness [—nis] n. Multiplicidad, *f.*, diversidad, *f.*, variedad, *f.*
multifold [ˈmʌltiˌfəuld] adj. Múltiple.
multiform [ˈmʌltifɔ:m] adj. Multiforme.
multilateral [ˈmʌltiˈlætərəl] adj. Multilateral.
multilingual [ˌmʌltiˈliŋgwəl] adj. Poligloto, ta; polígloto, ta (person). || Plurilingüe (text, etc.).
multimillionaire [ˈmʌltimiljəˈnɛə*] adj./n. Multimillonario, ria.
multinational [ˌmʌltiˈnæʃənl] adj. Multinacional.
multinomial [ˌmʌltiˈnəumiəl] adj. Polinómico, ca.
— N. Polinomio, *m.*
multipara [mʌlˈtipərə] n. Multípara, *f.*

— OBSERV. El plural de la palabra inglesa es *multiparae*.

multiparous [mʌlˈtipərəs] adj. Multíparo, ra.
multiphase [ˈmʌltifeiz] adj. ELECTR. Polifásico, ca.
multiplane [ˈmʌltiplein] n. AVIAT. Multiplano, *m.*
multiple [ˈmʌltipl] adj. Múltiple. || MATH. Múltiplo, pla. || ELECTR. En paralelo (connection). || AGR. De varias rejas (plough). || COMM. *Multiple shop* o *store*, sucursal, *f.* [de una cadena de establecimientos].
— N. MATH. Múltiplo, *m.*

multiple-choice [—tʃɔis] adj. *Multiple-choice exam*, examen (*m.*) en el que las preguntas van seguidas de varias contestaciones entre las cuales se encuentra la solución exacta. || *Multiple-choice question*, pregunta (*f.*) que va seguida de varias contestaciones entre las cuales está incluida la solución exacta.
multiple sclerosis [—skliə'rəusis] n. MED. Esclerosis (*f.*) en placas.
multiplex ['mʌltipleks] adj. Múltiple (manifold). || ELECTR. Múltiplex.
multiplex ['mʌlti'pleks] v. tr. Transmitir por sistema múltiplex.
multiplexer [—ə] n. Multiplexor, *m.*
multipliable ['mʌltiplaiəbl] or **multiplicable** ['mʌltiplikəbl] adj. Multiplicable.
multiplicand [,mʌltiplikænd] n. Multiplicando, *m.*
multiplication [,mʌltipli'keiʃən] n. Multiplicación, *f.* || *Multiplication table*, tabla (*f.*) de multiplicar.
multiplicative [,mʌlti'plikətiv] adj. Multiplicativo, va.
multiplicity [,mʌltiplisiti] n. Multiplicidad, *f.*
multiplier ['mʌltiplaiə*] n. Multiplicador, *m.*
multiply ['mʌltiplai] v. tr. Multiplicar.
— V. intr. Multiplicarse.
multiplying ['mʌltiplaiiŋ] adj. Multiplicador, ra.
multitude ['mʌltitju:d] n. Multitud, *f.*, muchedumbre, *f.* (of persons). || Multitud, *f.*, infinidad, *f.* (of things). || — *For a multitude of motives*, por múltiples motivos. || *The multitude*, la masa.
multitudinous [,mʌlti'tju:dinəs] adj. Multitudinario, ria. || Muy numeroso, sa.
multivalence [,mʌlti'veiləns] n. Polivalencia, *f.*
multivalent [,mʌlti'veilənt] adj. Polivalente.
multure ['mʌltjə*] n. Maquila, *f.*
mum [mʌm] interj. ¡Chitón! || *Mum's the word!*, ¡punto en boca!
— Adj. Silencioso, sa. || *To keep mum*, mantenerse callado, no decir esta boca es mía, guardar silencio.
mum [mʌm] n. FAM. Mamá, *f.* (mother). || U. S. BOT. Crisantemo, *m.* || Cerveza (*f.*) fuerte (beer).
mum [mʌm] v. intr. Disfrazarse.
mumble ['mʌmbl] n. Refunfuño, *m.* || *To say in a mumble*, decir entre dientes.
mumble ['mʌmbl] v. tr./intr. Mascullar, decir *or* hablar entre dientes (to speak indistinctly).
mumbling [—iŋ] adj. *To say sth. in a mumbling voice*, decir algo entre dientes.
— N. *Stop that mumbling!*, ¡habla claro! (speak clearly), ¡silencio!
mumbo jumbo ['mʌmbəu'dʒʌmbəu] n. Fetiche, *m.* (fetish). || Conjuro, *m.* (spell). || Farsa, *f.*, comedia, *f.* (sham). || Galimatías, *m.* (gibberish).
mummer ['mʌmə*] n. Mimo, *m.* (in a pantomime). || Máscara, *m.* & *f.*, enmascarado, da (masked person).
mummery [—ri] n. Mascarada, *f.*, farsa, *f.* (mascarade). || THEATR. Pantomima, *f.*
mummification [,mʌmifi'keiʃən] n. Momificación, *f*
mummify ['mʌmifai] v. tr. Momificar.
— V. intr. Momificarse.
mummy ['mʌmi] n. Mamá, *f.* (mother). || Momia, *f.* (preserved body).
mummy ['mʌmi] v. tr. Momificar.
mummy cloth [—klɔθ] n. Venda, *f.*
mumpish ['mʌmpiʃ] adj. Malhumorado, da; desabrido, da.
mumps [mʌmps] pl. n. MED. Paperas, *f.*
munch [mʌntʃ] v. tr./intr. Mascar, ronzar.
mundane ['mʌndein] adj. Mundano, na (worldly). || Terrestre, terrenal (earthly).
mungo ['mʌŋgəu] n. Lana (*f.*) de baja calidad.
municipal [mju:'nisipəl] adj. Municipal. || *Municipal council*, concejo (*m.*) municipal.
municipality [mju:,nisi'pæliti] n. Municipio, *m.*
municipalization [mju:,nisipəlai'zeiʃən] n. Municipalización, *f.*
municipalize [mju:'nisipəlaiz] v. tr. Municipalizar.
munificence [mju:'nifisns] n. Munificencia, *f.*, generosidad, *f.*, liberalidad, *f.*
munificent [mju:'nifisnt] adj. Munificente, munífico ca; generoso, sa; liberal.
munificently [—li] adv. Con munificencia.
muniments ['mju:nimənts] pl. n. JUR. Documentos, *m.*
munitions [mju:'niʃənz] pl. n. MIL. Municiones, *f.*
munition [mju:'niʃən] v. tr. Amunicionar.
muraena [mju'ri:nə] n. Morena, *f.* (fish).
mural ['mjuərəl] adj. Mural: *mural painting*, pintura mural.
— N. ARTS. Mural, *m.*, pintura (*f.*) mural, fresco, *m.*
muralist [—ist] n. Pintor (*m.*) de murales.
murder ['mə:də*] n. JUR. Asesinato, *m.*, homicidio, *m.* (killing as a crime): *premeditated murder* o *murder in the first degree*, homicidio premeditado. || FIG. Asesinato, *m.*: *war is mass murder*, la guerra es un asesinato en masa. || FAM. Cosa (*f.*) espantosa *or* horrible. || — FAM. *It was murder crossing the mountain*, fue matador cruzar la montaña. || *To commit murder*, cometer un asesinato. || FIG. *To cry blue murder*, protestar enérgicamente, poner el grito en el cielo. | *To go through murder*, pasar las de Caín.
murder ['mə:də*] v. tr. Asesinar (to kill unlawfully). || Matar, asesinar: *the bombing murdered most of the civilian population*, el bombardeo mató a la mayoría de la población civil. || FIG. Destrozar, interpretar *or* ejecutar desastrosamente: *to murder a sonata*, interpretar desastrosamente una sonata. | Desfigurar, deformar (a quotation). | Chapurrear, hablar mal (a foreign language). | Degollar (a play).
— V. intr. Cometer un asesinato.
murderer [—rə*] n. Asesino, *m.*
murderess ['mə:dəris] n. Asesina, *f.*
murderous ['mə:dərəs] adj. Asesino, na; homicida. || *Murderous weapon*, arma mortífera.
murex ['mjuəreks] n. ZOOL. Múrice, *m.*, múrex, *m.*
— OBSERV. El plural de *murex* es *murices* o *murexes*.
murk [mə:k] or **murkiness** [—inis] n. Oscuridad, *f.*, tinieblas, *f. pl.*, lobreguez, *f.*
murky [—i] adj. Oscuro, ra; lóbrego, ga.
murmur ['mə:mə*] n. Murmullo, *m.* (of voice, river, etc.). || Susurro, *m.*, murmullo, *m.* (of wind). || Murmullo, *m.*, queja, *f.* (of disapproval). || MED. Soplo (*m.*) cardiaco (of the heart).
murmur ['mə:mə*] v. intr. Murmurar. || *To murmur against s.o.*, murmurar de alguien.
— V. tr. Murmurar.
murmuring [—iŋ] adj. Murmurador, ra; murmurante.
murphy ['mə:fi] n. FAM. Papa, *f.* (potato).
Murphy bed [—bed] n. Cama (*f.*) empotrada.
murrain ['mʌrin] n. VET. Epizootia, *f.*
muscadel [mʌskə'del] n. Moscatel, *m.* (wine).
muscadine ['mʌskədain] n. BOT. Uva (*f.*) moscatel, moscatel, *m.*
muscat ['mʌskət] n. BOT. Uva (*f.*) moscatel, moscatel, *m.* (grape).
muscatel [,mʌskə'tel] n. Moscatel, *m.* (wine).
muscle ['mʌsl] n. ANAT. Músculo, *m.* || — *He has a lot of muscle*, tiene muchos músculos. || FAM. *Not to move a muscle*, no inmutarse, permanecer impasible.
muscle ['mʌsl] v. intr. FAM. *To muscle in*, meterse [por fuerza] en.
muscle-bound [—baund] adj. Con los músculos agarrotados.
muscovado [,mʌskə'vɑ:də] n. Azúcar (*f.*) mascabada (unrefined sugar).
muscovite ['mʌskəuvait] n. MIN. Mica, *f.*
Muscovite ['mʌskəuvait] adj./n. Moscovita.
Muscovy ['mʌskəuvi] pr. n. GEOGR. Moscovia, *f.*
muscular ['mʌskjulə*] adj. Muscular: *muscular tissue*, tejido muscular. || Musculoso, sa (having strong muscles).
muscularity [,mʌskju'læriti] n. Musculatura, *f.*
musculature ['mʌskjulətʃuə] n. Musculatura, *f.*
muse [mju:z] n. Meditación, *f.* (meditation). || Musa, *f.* (source of inspiration).
muse [mju:z] v.tr./intr. Meditar, reflexionar (to ponder). || Contemplar (to watch). || Decir pensativamente (to say).
Muse [mju:z] pr. n. MYTH. Musa, *f.*
musette [mju'zet] n. MUS. Gaita, *f.*, cornamusa, *f.* (bagpipe).
musette bag [—bæg] n. MIL. Mochila, *f.*
museum [mju'ziəm] n. Museo, *m.*: *the Prado Museum*, el Museo del Prado.
museum piece [—pi:s] n. Pieza (*f.*) de museo. || FAM. Pieza (*f.*) de museo (person).
mush [mʌʃ] n. Gachas, *f. pl.* (porridge). || RAD. Interferencia, *f.* || FAM. Lío, *m.*, confusión, *f.* (mess). | Majaderías, *f. pl.*, pamplinas, *f. pl.* (silly things). | Sensiblería, *f.*, sentimentalismo, *m.* (maudlin sentimentality). || Viaje (*m.*) en trineo por la nieve (journey across snow).
— Interj. ¡Arre!
mush [mʌʃ] v. intr. Viajar en trineo.
mushroom [—rum] n. BOT. Seta, *f.*, hongo, *m.* || CULIN. Champiñón, *m.*, seta, *f.*
— Adj. De champiñones: *mushroom salad*, ensalada de champiñones. || En forma de hongo (like a mushroom in shape). || FIG. De crecimiento rápido (town). || TECH. De campana (insulator). || — *Mushroom cloud*, hongo atómico. || *To grow* o *to spring up like mushrooms*, crecer como hongos.
mushroom [—rum] v. intr. Crecer como hongos (to grow quickly). || Esparcirse (smoke, a cloud, etc.). || Tomar la forma de un hongo (to resemble a mushroom). || Recoger setas (to pick mushrooms). || FIG. *To mushroom into*, convertirse en poco tiempo en.
mushy [—i] adj. Blando, da; mollar (soft). || Empapado, da (ground). || Blando, da; en papilla (food). || FAM. Sentimentaloide. || RAD. Con interferencias.
music ['mju:zik] n. Música, *f.*: *chamber, instrumental, sacred, vocal, background music*, música de cámara, instrumental, sacra, vocal, de fondo. || Partitura, *f.* (score). || — FIG. *To face the music*, afrontar las consecuencias. || *To set a poem to music*, poner música a un poema.
musical [—əl] adj. De música: *musical box*, caja de música. || Musical (ear, evening). || De música, músico, ca (instrument). || De músicos: *Bach was a member of a musical family*, Bach pertenecía a una familia de músicos. || Aficionado a la música: *my family is very musical*, mi familia es muy aficionada a la música. || Armonioso, sa; melodioso, sa (sound, voice, verse). || *Musical comedy*, comedia (*f.*) musical.
— N. Comedia (*f.*) musical.
musicale [,mju:zi'kæl] n. U. S. MUS. Velada (*f.*) musical.

musicality [—iti] or **musicalness** [—nis] n. Musicalidad, *f.*
music book [ˈmju:zikbuk] n. Libro (*m.*) de música.
music box [—bɔks] n. Caja (*f.*) de música.
music hall [ˈmju:zikhɔ:l] n. Teatro (*m.*) de variedades, music-hall, *m.* || U. S. Sala (*f.*) de conciertos (for musical productions).
musician [mju:ˈziʃən] n. Músico, ca.
music lover [ˈmju:zik,lʌvə*] n. Melómano, na.
musicographer [,mju:ziˈkɔgrəfə*] n. Musicógrafo, fa.
musicologist [,mju:ziˈkɔlədʒist] n. Musicólogo, ga.
musicology [,mju:ziˈkɔlədʒi] n. Musicología, *f.*
music paper [ˈmju:zik,peipə*] n. Papel (*m.*) pautado.
music stand [ˈmju:zikstænd] n. Atril, *m.*
music stool [ˈmju:zikstu:l] n. Taburete (*m.*) de piano.
musing [ˈmju:ziŋ] adj. Meditativo, va; pensativo, va.
— N. Meditación, *f.*
musk [mʌsk] n. Almizcle, *m.* || Zool. *Musk deer*, almizclero, *m.*
muskeg [ˈmʌskeg] n. Terreno (*m.*) pantanoso.
muskellunge [ˈmʌskə,lʌndʒ] n. Sollo, *m.* (fish).
musket [ˈmʌskit] n. Mosquete, *m.*
musketeer [,mʌskiˈtiə*] n. Mosquetero, *m.*
musketoon [,mʌskiˈtu:n] n. Mosquetón, *m.*
musketry [ˈmʌskitri] n. Mosquetería, *f.* (musketeers). || Mosquetes, *m. pl.* (muskets). || Fusilería, *f.* (firing).
muskmelon [ˈmʌsk,melən] n. Bot. Melón, *m.*
muskrat [ˈmʌskræt] n. Zool. Ratón (*m.*) almizclero.
musk rose [ˈmʌskrəuz] n. Bot. Rosa (*f.*) almizcleña.
musky [ˈmʌski] adj. Almizclero, ra; almizcleño, ña.
Muslim [ˈmuslim] adj./n. Musulmán, ana.
muslin [ˈmʌzlin] n. Muselina, *f.* || *Cambric muslin*, percal, *m.*
musquash [ˈmʌskwɔʃ] n. Zool. Ratón (*m.*) amizclero.
muss [mʌs] n. U. S. Fam. Desorden, *m.* (disorder). | Riña, *f.* (squabble).
muss [mʌs] v. tr. U. S. Fam. Desordenar. | Arrugar, chafar (dress). || *To muss s.o.'s hair up*, despeinar a uno.
mussel [ˈmʌsl] n. Mejillón, *m.* (mollusc).
Mussulman [ˈmʌslmən] adj./n. Musulmán, ana.
mussy [ˈmʌsi] adh. U. S. Fam. Desordenado, da (disorganized). | Sucio, cia (dirty). | Arrugado, da (rumpled).
must [mʌst] n. Moho, *m.* (mould). || Mosto, *m.* (of grapes). || See MUSTH.
must [mʌst] v. aux. Deber, tener que (expressing obligation): *this is what he must do*, esto es lo que debe hacer; *you must respect your father's wishes*, debes respetar la voluntad de tu padre; *man must eat to live*, el hombre tiene que comer para vivir. || Deber de (expressing supposition): *it must be your sister*, debe de ser tu hermana; *her name is Pilar, so she must be Spanish*, se llama Pilar, por lo tanto debe de ser española; *he said that he must have made a mistake*, dijo que debía de haber cometido un error. || Tener que (expressing fatality): *why must it always rain on Sundays?*, ¿por qué tiene que llover todos los domingos?; *why must he always be talking?*, ¿por qué tiene que estar siempre hablando? || Tener que (expressing invitation, recommendation): *you must come to visit us*, tienes que venir a vernos; *you must get to know him*, tienes que conocerle. || — *It must be*, es más que probable, seguramente. || *One must be careful*, hay que tener cuidado.

— Observ. *Must* se emplea siempre en el presente, incluso cuando se refiere al pasado (*I told him what he must do*, le dije lo que debía hacer).

must [mʌst] n. Cosa (*f.*) indispensable, imperativo, *m.*, necesidad, *f.*: *it is an absolute must*, es de absoluta necesidad. || *This film, this book is a must*, no deje de ver esta película, de leer este libro; es imprescindible ver esta película, leer este libro.
mustache [məsˈtɑ:ʃ] n. Bigote, *m.*, bigotes, *m. pl.*
mustachios [mʌsˈtæʃiəuz] pl. n. Bigote, *m. sing.*, bigotes, *m.*
mustang [ˈmʌstæŋ] n. Zool. Mustang, *m.*, mustango, *m.* (horse).
mustard [ˈmʌstəd] n. Mostaza, *f.*
mustard gas [—gæs] n. Gas (*m.*) mostaza, yperita, *f.*
mustard oil [—ɔil] n. Aceite (*m.*) de mostaza.
mustard plaster [—,plɑ:stə*] n. Cataplasma (*f.*) de mostaza, sinapismo, *m.*
mustard-seed shot [—si:dˈʃɔt] n. Mostacilla, *f.*
muster [ˈmʌstə*] n. Mil. Revista, *f.* (inspection). || Reunión, *f.* (meeting). || Asamblea, *f.* (assembly). || — *Muster roll*, lista (*f.*) de revista (of troops), rol (*m.*) de la tripulación (of crew). || Fig. *To pass muster*, ser aceptable.
muster [ˈmʌstə*] v. tr. Mil. Formar. || Reunir (to gather). || — U. S. Mil. *To muster in*, enrolar, alistar. | *To muster out*, licenciar, dar de baja. || *To muster up*, cobrar (strength). || *To muster up one's courage*, revestirse *or* armarse de valor.
— V. intr. Reunirse (to gather together).
musth [mʌst] n. Celo, *m.* (of an elephant, etc.): *on o in musth*, en celo.
mustiness [ˈmʌstinis] n. Olor (*m.*) a cerrado *or* a humedad (smell).
musty [ˈmʌsti] adj. Mohoso, sa (mouldy). || Que huele a cerrado *or* a humedad. || Fig. Anticuado, da; viejo, ja; pasado de moda (old-fashioned). || *It smells musty here*, aquí huele a cerrado *or* a humedad.
mutability [,mju:təˈbiliti] n. Mutabilidad, *f.* || Inconstancia, *f.* (fickleness).
mutable [ˈmju:təbl] adj. Mudable, variable. || Cambiadizo, za; inconstante (fickle).
mutant [ˈmju:tənt] adj./n. Biol. Mutante.
mutate [mju:ˈteit] v. tr. Mudar, cambiar, transformar.
— V. intr. Experimentar un cambio, cambiar, transformarse.
mutation [mjuˈteiʃən] n. Mutación, *f.*
mute [mju:t] adj. Mudo, da (unable to speak, speechless). || Gramm. Mudo, da (letter). || Jur. *To stand mute*, negarse a responder al interrogatorio del tribunal.
— N. Mudo, da (person who cannot speak). || Gramm. Letra (*f.*) muda. || Mus. Sordina, *f.*
mute [mju:t] v. tr. Apagar, amortiguar, ensordecer (to deaden a sound). || Mus. Poner sordina a.
muted [—id] adj. Sordo, da (noise).
muteness [—nis] n. Mutismo, *m.* (silence). || Med. Mudez, *f.*
mutilate [ˈmju:tileit] v. tr. Mutilar.
mutilation [,mju:tiˈleiʃən] n. Mutilación, *f.*
mutilator [ˈmju:tileitə*] n. Mutilador, ra.
mutineer [,mju:tiˈniə*] n. Amotinador, *m.*, amotinado, *m.*, rebelde, *m.*
mutinous [ˈmju:tinəs] adj. Amotinado, da; sedicioso, sa (crew, sailor). || Fig. Rebelde.
mutinously [—li] adv. Sediciosamente.
mutiny [ˈmju:tini] n. Motín, *m.*, rebelión, *f.*, sedición, *f.*
mutiny [ˈmju:tini] v. intr. Amotinarse, sublevarse, rebelarse.
mutism [ˈmju:tizəm] n. Mudez, *f.*, mutismo, *m.*
mutt [mʌt] n. Fam. Perro (*m.*) mestizo (mongrel). | Bobo, ba; tonto, ta (stupid person).
mutter [ˈmʌtə*] n. Murmullo, *m.* (murmur). || Refunfuño, *m.* (grumbling).
mutter [ˈmʌtə*] v. tr. Murmurar, decir entre dientes. || Refunfuñar (angrily).
— V. intr. Murmurar, hablar entre dientes. || Refunfuñar (angrily). || Quejarse (to complain): *he's always muttering about sth.*, siempre se está quejando de algo.
muttering [—riŋ] n. Refunfuño, *m.*
mutton [ˈmʌtn] n. Cordero, *m.*: *leg, shoulder of mutton*, pierna, espaldilla de cordero. || Fig. *Mutton dressed as lamb*, vejestorio emperifollado.
mutton chop [—ˈtʃɔp] n. Chuleta (*f.*) de cordero.
muttonchops [—ˈtʃɔps] pl. n. Patillas, *f.* (side whiskers).
muttonhead [—hed] n. Fam. Bobo, ba.
mutual [ˈmju:tʃuəl] adj. Mutuo, tua: *mutual insurance*, seguros mutuos. || Mutuo, tua; recíproco, ca: *mutual admiration*, admiración mutua. || Fam. Común (common): *by mutual consent*, de común acuerdo. || — *Mutual aid*, ayuda mutua. || *Mutual benefit society*, mutualidad, *f.*, mutua, *f.*, mutual, *f.*
mutualism [ˈmju:tjuəlizəm] n. Mutualismo, *m.*
mutualist [ˈmju:tjuəlist] n. Mutualista, *m.* & *f.*
mutualistic [,mjutjuəˈlistik] adj. Mutualista.
mutuality [,mju:tjuˈæliti] n. Mutualidad, *f.* || Reciprocidad, *f.*
mutule [ˈmju:tju:l] n. Arch. Mútulo, *m.*
muzhik or **muzjik** [ˈmu:ʒik] n. Mujic, *m.*
muzziness [mʌzinis] n. Atontamiento, *m.* (from drinking). || Borrosidad, *f.* (of sight, ideas).
muzzle [ˈmʌzl] n. Hocico, *m.*, morro, *m.* (part of animal's head). || Bozal, *m.* (to prevent an animal from biting). || Boca, *f.* (of a weapon).
muzzle [ˈmʌzl] v. tr. Abozalar, poner bozal a (a dog, etc.). || Fig. Amordazar.
muzzle-loader [—,ləudə*] n. Mil. Arma (*f.*) que se carga por la boca.
muzzle velocity [—viˈlɔsiti] n. Mil. Velocidad (*f.*) inicial (of a shell).
muzzy [ˈmʌzi] adj. Atontado, da (with drink). || Borroso, sa (ideas, vision). || Deprimente (day).
my [mai] poss. adj. Mi: *my book*, mi libro; *my friends*, mis amigos. || Mío, mía: *listen, my sons*, escuchadme, hijos míos. || Fam. *My!*, ¡madre mía!

— Observ. The English possessive adjective is often translated by the definite article in Spanish (*I took my gloves from my bag*, saqué los guantes del bolso).

myalgia [maiˈældʒə] n. Med. Mialgia, *f.*
mycelium [maiˈsi:liəm] n. Bot. Micelio, *m.*

— Observ. El plural de *mycelium* es *mycelia*.

Mycenae [maiˈsi:ni] pr. n. Micenas (in Greece).
mycosis [maiˈkausis] n. Med. Micosis, *f.*

— Observ. El plural de la palabra inglesa es *mycoses*.

mydriasis [miˈdraiəsis] n. Med. Midriasis, *f.*
myelin or **myeline** [ˈmaiəlin] n. Mielina, *f.*
myelitis [,maiəˈlaitis] n. Med. Mielitis, *f.*
mygale [ˈmigəli] n. Migala, *f.* (spider).
myocarditis [,maiəkɑ:ˈdaitis] n. Med. Miocarditis, *f.*
myocardium [,maiəˈkɑ:diəm] n. Anat. Miocardio, *m.*

— Observ. El plural de *myocardium* es *myocardia*.

myograph [ˈmaiəgræf] n. Med. Miógrafo, *m.*
myoma [maiˈəumə] n. Med. Mioma, *m.*

— Observ. El plural de la palabra inglesa es *myomata* o *myomas*.

myope [ˈmaiəup] n. Med. Miope, *m.* & *f.*
myopia [maiˈəupjə] n. Med. Miopía, *f.*

myopic [mai'ɔpik] adj. MED. Miope.
myosotis [,maiəu'səutis] n. BOT. Miosota, *f.*, raspilla, *f.*
myriad ['miriəd] adj. Innumerable (countless).
— N. Miríada, *f.*
myriagramme or **myriagram** ['miriəgræm] n. Miriagramo, *m.*
myriametre (U. S. **myriameter**) ['miriəmitə*] n. Miriámetro, *m.*
myriapod or **myriopod** ['miriəpɔd] adj. ZOOL. Miriápodo, da.
— N. ZOOL. Miriápodo, *m.*
myrmidon ['mə:midən] n. Secuaz, *m.* (loyal follower). || Esbirro, *m.* (subordinate). || Asesino (*m.*) a sueldo (hired killer).
myrrh [mə:*] n. Mirra, *f.*
myrtaceae [mə:'teisii:] pl. n. BOT. Mirtáceas, *f.*
myrtle ['mə:tl] n. BOT. Arrayán, *m.*, mirto, *m.*
myself [mai'self] pron. Yo mismo, yo misma (emphatic): *I gave him the money myself*, le di el dinero yo mismo. || Me (reflexive): *I hurt myself*, me he hecho daño. || Mí [mismo], mí [misma] (after preposition): *I didn't buy it for myself*, no lo compré para mí. || — *I am sorry I blew up, I am not myself lately*, discúlpeme por haberme puesto furioso, no soy el mismo últimamente. || *I did it by myself*, lo hice [completamente] solo. || *I stayed by myself all morning*, me quedé [completamente] solo toda la mañana.
mysterious [mis'tiəriəs] adj. Misterioso, sa. || *To act in a mysterious manner*, andar con misterios, hacer misterios, ser muy misterioso.
mysteriousness [—nis] n. Misterio, *m.*, carácter (*m.*) misterioso.
mystery ['mistəri] n. Misterio, *m.* || Enigma, *m.* || REL. Misterio, *m.* || Auto (*m.*) sacramental, misterio, *m.* (medieval religious drama). || — *Mystery man*, hombre misterioso. || *Mystery novel*, novela policiaca. || *Wrapped in mystery*, misterioso, sa.
mystic ['mistik] adj. Esotérico, ca (rites). || Mágico, ca (formula). || Oculto, ta (power). || Sobrenatural (truth). || Misterioso, sa; enigmático, ca (mysterious). || REL. Místico, ca.
— N. Iniciado, da. || REL. Místico, ca.
mystical [—əl] adj. Místico, ca. || *Mystical theology*, mística, *f.*
mysticism ['mistisizəm] n. Misticismo, *m.* || Mística, *f.* (literary genre).
mystification [,mistifi'keiʃən] n. Mistificación, *f.*, engaño, *m.* (deceit). || Complejidad, *f.*, misterio, *m.*, oscuridad, *f.* (of a question). || Perplejidad, *f.*, confusión, *f.* (perplexity).
mystify ['mistifai] v. tr. Engañar (to deceive). || Desconcertar, dejar perplejo (to disconcert). || Desorientar, despistar (to confuse). || Llenar de misterio, oscurecer, complicar, enmarañar (a question).
mystique [mis'ti:k] n. Mística, *f.* || Misterio, *m.* (mystery).
myth [miθ] n. Mito, *m.*
mythic [—ik] or **mythical** [—ikəl] adj. Mítico, ca.
mythicize ['miθəsaiz] v. tr. Dar un sentido mítico a.
mythologer [mi'θɔlədʒə*] n. Mitólogo, *m.*
mythological [,miθə'lɔdʒikəl] adj. Mitológico, ca.
mythologist [mi'θɔlədʒist] n. Mitólogo, *m.*
mythology [mi'θɔlədʒi] n. Mitología, *f.*
mythomania [,miθəu'meiniə] n. Mitomanía, *f.*
mythomaniac [,miθəu'meiniæk] adj./n. Mitómano, na.
myxomatosis [,miksəumə'təusis] n. Mixomatosis, *f.*
myxomycetes [,miksə'maisi:ti:z] pl. n. BOT. Mixomicetos, *m.*

N

n [en] n. N, *f.* (letter). || FIG. *It's the nth. time I've told you*, es la enésima vez que te lo digo.
nab [næb] v. tr. FAM. Coger, pescar (s.o.). | Coger, mangar, birlar (sth.).
nabob ['neibɔb] n. Nabab, *m.*
nacelle [næ'sel] n. AVIAT. Barquilla, *f.*
nacre ['neikə*] n. Nácar, *m.*
nacreous ['neikriəs] or **nacred** ['neikəd] adj. Nacarado, da; anacarado, da.
nadir ['neidiə*] n. ASTR. Nadir, *m.* || FIG. Punto (*m.*) más bajo.
naevus ['ni:vəs] n. Nevo, *m.*

— OBSERV. El plural de *naevus* es *naevi.*

nag [næg] n. Rocín, *m.* (old horse). || Regañón, ona; quejica, *m.* & *f.* (complainer). || Quejas, *f. pl.* (complaints).
nag [næg] v. tr. Regañar, reñir (to tell off). || FIG. Remorder (the conscience). | Fastidiar, molestar (to annoy). | Machacar (to bother insistently). | Asaltar: *I was nagged by doubts*, me asaltaron las dudas.
— V. intr. Regañar, reñir (to tell off). || Quejarse (to complain). || Criticar (to criticize). || Gritar (to shout). || *To nag at*, molestar, fastidiar.
nagger [—ə*] n. Regañón, ona; criticón, ona (faultfinding person). || Quejica, *m.* & *f.* (complaining person).
nagging [—iŋ] adj. Regañón, ona; criticón, ona (faultfinding). || Quejica (complaining). || FIG. Continuo, nua; persistente (constant). | Punzante, lancinante (pain).
— N. Quejas, *f. pl.*
naiad ['naiæd] n. Náyade, *f.*

— OBSERV. El plural es *naiads* o *naiades.*

nail [neil] n. Uña, *f.* (of the finger, toe). || Garra, *f.* (claw). || Clavo, *m.* (metal spike). || — *To bang a nail in*, clavar un clavo. || FIG. *To be as hard as nails*, ser muy resistente (to be resistant), tener un corazón de piedra (to be hardhearted). || *To bite one's nails*, comerse *or* morderse las uñas. || *To drive a nail home*, remachar un clavo (to bang in), remachar el clavo (to insist). || FIG. *To fight tooth and nail*, see TOOTH. | *To hit the nail on the head*, dar en el clavo, acertar. | *To pay on the nail*, pagar a tocateja.
nail [neil] v. tr. Clavar, sujetar con clavos (*on, to*, en): *to nail a lid on a box*, clavar una tapa en una caja. || Clavetear (to decorate with nails). || FIG. Fijar (eyes, attention). | Averiguar, descubrir (to find out). || FIG. FAM. Coger, agarrar (to catch). || — FIG. *To nail a lie to the counter*, descubrir una mentira. || *To nail down*, clavar, sujetar con clavos (sth.), poner entre la espada y la pared (to corner a person), comprometer (to make s.o. give a promise). || *To nail up*, cerrar con clavos.
nailbrush [—brʌʃ] n. Cepillo (*m.*) para las uñas, cepillo (*m.*) de uñas.
nail claw [—klɔ:] n. Arrancaclavos, *m. inv.*, sacaclavos, *m. inv.*
nail clippers [—'klipəz] n. Cortaúñas, *m. inv.*
nailer [—ə*] n. Fabricante (*m.*) de clavos (nail maker). || FAM. As, *m.*, hacha, *m.* (person). | Cosa (*f.*) estupenda (thing).
nailery [—əri] n. Fábrica (*f.*) de clavos.
nail file [—fail] n. Lima (*f.*) de uñas.
nailing [—iŋ] n. Clavado, *m.* (of case). || Claveteado, *m.* (of boots). || Clavos *m. pl.* (nails).
nail polish [—'pɔliʃ] n. U. S. Esmalte (*m.*) de uñas *or* para las uñas.
nail puller [—pulə*] n. Arrancaclavos, *m. inv.*, sacaclavos, *m. inv.*
nail-scissors [—'sizəz] pl. n. Tijeras (*f.*) para las uñas.
nail varnish [—'vɑ:niʃ] n. Esmalte (*m.*) de uñas, esmalte (*m.*) para las uñas.
naïve or **naive** [nɑ:'i:v] adj. Ingenuo, nua; cándido, da.
naïveté or **naiveté** [nɑ:'i:vtei] n. Ingenuidad, *f.*, candidez, *f.*
naja ['neidʒə] n. Naja, *f.* (snake).
naked ['neikid] adj. Desnudo, da (body, part of body). || Descubierto, ta (head). || Descalzo, za (feet). || FIG. Pelado, da; desnudo, da (landscape). | Sin hojas, desnudo, da (tree). | Desnudo, da; sin adornos (wall). | Sin pantalla (light). | Sin protección (flame). | Desenvainado, da (a sword). || Indefenso, sa (helpless). || JUR. Unilateral. | Sin garantía (contract). || — *Invisible to the naked eye*, invisible a simple vista. || *The naked truth*, la verdad escueta, la verdad desnuda. || *To strip (o.s.) naked*, desnudarse.
nakedness [—nis] n. Desnudez, *f.* || FIG. Claridad, *f.*, evidencia, *f.*
namby-pamby ['næmbi'pæmbi] adj./n. Soso, sa; ñoño, ña.
name [neim] n. Nombre, *m.* (Christian name). || Apellido, *m.* (family name). || Nombre, *m.* (of places,

things, etc.). || Apodo, *m.* (nickname): *the last name they gave him was "lefty"*, el último apodo que le dieron era "zurdo". || Fama, *f.*, reputación, *f.* (reputation). || Título, *m.* (title). || Linaje, *m.* (lineage). || Personalidad, *f.*, celebridad, *f.* (celebrity). || — FIG. *Big name*, gran figura, *f.* || *By* o *under another name*, bajo otro nombre. || *By name*, por el nombre (to call people), de nombre (to know s.o.). || *By the name of*, llamado, da. || *Christian name*, nombre de pila, nombre. || *Family name*, apellido. || *First name*, nombre de pila, nombre. || *Full name*, nombre y apellidos. || *I'll do it or my name is not Brown*, lo haré, como me llamo Brown. || *In one's name*, en nombre de uno. || *In name* o *in name only*, sólo de nombre. || *In the name of*, en nombre de: *in the name of the law*, en nombre de la ley. || REL. *In the name of the Father*, en el nombre del Padre. || *Maiden name*, apellido de soltera. || *Married name*, apellido de casada. || *My name is Michael*, me llamo Miguel. || FIG. *Not to have a penny to one's name*, no tener un céntimo *or* un real. || *Pet name*, nombre cariñoso. || *Proper name*, nombre propio. || *Registered name*, nombre registrado. || *To answer to the name of*, responder al nombre de, tener por nombre, llamarse. || FIG. *To call s.o. names*, poner verde a alguien. || *To get o.s. a bad name*, hacerse una mala reputación. || *To go by the name of*, llamarse (real name), ser conocido por el nombre de (ficticious name). || *To know by name*, conocer de nombre. || *To make a name for o.s.*, darse a conocer, hacerse un nombre. || *To put one's name down*, inscribirse, apuntarse. || *What name shall I say?*, ¿de parte de quién? (on the phone), ¿a quién debo anunciar? (announcing arrival). || *What's your name?*, ¿cómo te llamas?

name [neim] v. tr. Llamar, poner: *what are you going to name your baby?*, ¿cómo vas a llamar al niño?, ¿cómo le vas a poner al niño? || Llamar, denominar, dar nombre a (a new product). || Nombrar (to appoint): *to name s.o. to an office*, nombrar a uno a un cargo. || Dar el nombre de: *the victim named his attacker*, la víctima dio el nombre del agresor. || Mencionar (to mention). || Elegir (to choose): *name your weapon*, elige el arma. || Dar, fijar (date, price). || Bautizar con el nombre de (a ship). || — *He is named Frederick Pelayo*, se llama Federico Pelayo. || *Name it*, pide lo que quieras. || *To be named in a list*, figurar en una lista. || *To name a child after his father*, poner a un niño el nombre de su padre.

name day [—dei] n. Santo, *m.*, día (*m.*) onomástico, onomástica, *f.*

name-dropping [—ˈdrɔpiŋ] n. FAM. Farol, *m.* (practice of mentioning important people to impress others).

nameless [—lis] adj. Anónimo, ma; sin nombre (without a name). || FIG. Sin nombre: *nameless atrocities were committed*, se cometieron atrocidades sin nombre. | Indecible (dread, grief). || *The accused who shall remain nameless*, el acusado, cuyo nombre debe permanecer en el anonimato.

namely [—li] adv. A saber (that is to say).

nameplate [—pleit] n. Placa (*f.*) *or* letrero (*m.*) con el nombre.

namesake [—seik] n. Tocayo, ya; homónimo, ma.

naming [—iŋ] n. Elección (*f.*) de un nombre (of a child). || Denominación, *f.* (of things). || Nombramiento, *m.* (appointment).

nandu [ˈnænˌdu] n. ZOOL. Ñandú, *m.*

nandubay [njɑ:ndəbai] n. Ñandubay, *m.*

nanduti [ˈnɑndʌti] n. Ñandutí, *m.*

nanism [ˈneiˌnizəm] n. MED. Enanismo, *m.*

nankeen [næŋˈki:n] n. Nanquín, *m.*, mahón, *m.* (cloth).

nanny or **nannie** [ˈnæni] n. Niñera, *f.* (child's nurse).

nanny goat [—gəut] n. ZOOL. FAM. Cabra, *f.* (female goat).

nanosecond [ˈneinəˈsekənd] n. Nanosegundo, *m.*

nap [næp] n. Siesta, *f.* (short sleep). || Lanilla, *f.*, pelusa, *f.* (of cloth). || BOT. Pelusa, *f.* || Informe (*m.*) seguro (in racing). || — *To go against the nap*, ir a contrapelo. || FIG. *To go nap*, jugárselo todo. || *To take* o *to have a nap*, dormir la siesta, descabezar un sueño.

nap [næp] v. tr. Levantar hacia atrás (the pile of a cloth). || Recomendar (a horse).

— V. intr. Dormitar (to sleep lightly). || Descabezar un sueño, dormir la siesta (to have a nap). || FIG. *To catch s.o. napping*, coger a uno desprevenido.

napalm [ˈneipɑ:m] n. Napalm, *m.*: *napalm bomb*, bomba de napalm.

nape [neip] n. ANAT. Cogote, *m.*, nuca, *f.*

napery [ˈneipəri] n. Mantelería, *f.* (table linen).

naphtha [ˈnæfθə] n. Nafta, *f.*

naphthalene [—li:n] n. CHEM. Naftalina, *f.*

naphthene [ˈnæfθi:n] n. Nafteno, *m.*

naphthol [ˈnæfθəl] n. CHEM. Naftol, *m.*

Napierian [nəˈpiəriən] adj. MATH. Neperiano, na.

napiform [ˈneipifɔ:m] adj. Nabiforme.

napkin [ˈnæpkin] n. Servilleta, *f.* (used at table). || Pañal, *m.* (for a baby). || U. S. Compresa (*f.*) higiénica *or* paño (*m.*) higiénico (sanitary towel).

napkin ring [—riŋ] n. Servilletero, *m.*

Naples [ˈneiplz] pr. n. GEOGR. Nápoles.

napoleon [nəˈpəuljən] n. Napoleón, *m.* (coin). || Milhojas, *m. inv.* (pastry).

Napoleon [nəˈpəuljən] pr. n. Napoleón, *m.*

Napoleonic [nəˌpəuliˈɔnik] adj. Napoleónico, ca.

nappy [ˈnæpi] n. Pañal, *m.* (napkin).

— Adj. Que tiene pelusa (cloth). || Fuerte (ale).

narcissism [nɑ:ˈsisizm] n. Narcisismo, *m.*

narcissist [nɑ:ˈsisist] n. Narcisista, *m.* & *f.*

narcissistic [ˌnɑ:siˈsistik] adj. Narcisista.

narcissus [nɑ:ˈsisəs] n. BOT. Narciso, *m.*

— OBSERV. El plural de *narcissus* es *narcissuses* o *narcissi*.

Narcissus [nɑ:ˈsisəs] pr. n. Narciso, *m.*

narcoanalysis [nɑ:kəuəˈnæləsis] n. MED. Narcoanálisis, *m.*

narcosis [nɑ:ˈkəusis] n. MED. Narcosis, *f.*

— OBSERV. El plural de la palabra inglesa es *narcoses*.

narcotic [nɑ:ˈkɔtik] adj. MED. Narcótico, ca; estupefaciente.

— N. MED. Narcótico, *m.*, estupefaciente, *m.*

narcotine [ˈnɑ:kəˌtin] n. CHEM. Narcotina, *f.*

narcotism [ˈnɑ:kətizəm] n. MED. Narcotismo, *m.*, narcosis, *f.*

narcotize [ˈnɑ:kətaiz] v. tr. MED. Narcotizar.

nard [nɑ:d] n. BOT. Nardo, *m.*

narghile [ˈnɑ:gili] n. Narguile, *m.* (pipe).

nark [nɑ:k] n. FAM. Soplón, *m.*

nark [nɑ:k] v. tr. FAM. Fastidiar (to annoy) || FAM. *To get narked*, ponerse furioso.

narratable [nəˈreitəbl] adj. Narrable.

narrate [nəˈreit] v. tr. Narrar, relatar, referir, contar.

narrater [—ə*] n. Narrador, ra.

narrating [—iŋ] n. Narración, *f.*, relato, *m.*

narration [nəˈreiʃən] n. Narración, *f.*, relato, *m.*

narrative [ˈnærətiv] adj. Narrativo, va.

— N. Narrativa, *f.*, narración, *f.* (art of relating stories). || Historia, *f.*, relato, *m.* (story).

narrator [nəˈreitə*] n. Narrador, ra. || MUS. Solista, *m.* & *f.*

narrow [ˈnærəu] adj. Estrecho, cha; angosto, ta (street, path, etc.): *a narrow bridge*, un puente estrecho. || Estrecho, cha (tight): *my trousers are narrow*, mi pantalón es estrecho. || FIG. De miras estrechas (person). | Estrecho, cha (views). | Escaso, sa; pequeño, ña; reducido, da (small): *a narrow majority*, una mayoría escasa. | Restringido, da; limitado, da: *a narrow interpretation*, una interpretación restringida. | Minucioso, sa (precise). || COMM. Poco activo, va (market). || — *In the narrowest sense of the word*, en el sentido más estricto de la palabra. || FAM. *The narrow bed*, la tumba. || *To grow narrow*, estrecharse, angostarse. || *To have a narrow escape* o *shave* o *squeak*, librarse por los pelos, escaparse por un pelo *or* por los pelos. || *To live in narrow circumstances*, vivir estrechamente, vivir con estrechez.

— N. Paso (*m.*) estrecho *or* angosto (narrow passage). || Estrecho, *m.* (strait).

narrow [ˈnærəu] v. tr. Estrechar, hacer más estrecho (to make less wide). || — *To narrow down*, limitar, reducir. || *To narrow sth. down to*, reducir algo a. || *To narrow the eyes*, entrecerrar los ojos.

— V. intr. Estrecharse, angostarse, hacerse más estrecho (a road, etc.). || Reducirse. || Entrecerrarse (eyes). || *To narrow down to*, reducirse a.

narrow-gauge [—geidʒ] adj. De vía estrecha (railway). || FIG. De miras estrechas.

narrowing [—iŋ] n. Estrechamiento, *m.* (of a road). || Menguado, *m.* (in knitting). || FIG. Limitación, *f.*

narrowly [—li] adv. Estrechamente. || De cerca, minuciosamente (closely). || *He narrowly missed being run over*, no le atropellaron por muy poco, faltó muy poco para que le atropellaran.

narrow-minded [—ˈmaindid] adj. De miras estrechas.

narrow-mindedness [—ˈmaindidnis] n. Estrechez (*f.*) de miras.

narrowness [—nis] n. Estrechez, *f.* || FIG. Lo reducido, lo limitado (of possibilities, etc.). | Minuciosidad, *f.* (of an inspection). | Estrechez, *f.* (of ideas).

narrows [—z] pl. n. Paso (*m.*) estrecho *or* angosto (narrow passage). || Estrecho, *m. sing.* (strait).

narthex [ˈnɑ:θeks] n. ARCH. Nártex, *m.*

narwal or **narwhal** or **narwhale** [ˈnɑ:wəl] n. ZOOL. Narval, *m.*

nasal [ˈneizəl] adj. Nasal: *nasal sounds*, sonidos nasales; *nasal fossae*, fosas nasales. || Gangoso, sa: *nasal voice*, voz gangosa.

— N. GRAMM. Nasal, *f.*

nasality [neiˈzæliti] n. Nasalidad, *f.*

nasalization [ˌneizəlaiˈzeiʃən] n. Nasalización, *f.*

nasalize [ˈneizəlaiz] v. tr. Nasalizar.

— V. intr. Ganguear, hablar con voz gangosa.

nasally [ˈneizəli] adv. Con voz gangosa.

nascent [ˈnæsnt] adj. Naciente.

naseberry [ˈneizbəri] n. BOT. Zapote, *m.* (fruit). | Zapotillo, *m.*, chicozapote, *m.* (tree).

nastily [ˈnɑ:stili] adv. De mala manera (in an unpleasant way). || Muy mal: *to behave nastily*, portarse muy mal. || Suciamente (dirtily). || Groseramente (rudely). || Peligrosamente (dangerously). || Gravemente (seriously).

nastiness [ˈnɑ:stinis] n. Sabor (*m.*) horrible (taste). || Peste, *f.* (odour). || Obscenidad, *f.* (obscenity). || Maldad, *f.* (wickedness). || Antipatía, *f.* (unfriendliness). || Suciedad, *f.* (dirtiness).

nasturtium [nəs'tə:ʃəm] n. BOT. Capuchina, *f.*
nasty ['nɑ:sti] adj. Sucio, cia; asqueroso, sa (dirty): *the bottom of the dustbin was really nasty*, el fondo del cubo de la basura estaba realmente asqueroso. || Repugnante; repulsivo, va (repugnant). || Horrible, espantoso, sa; asqueroso, sa (taste, smell, weather). || Desagradable (unpleasant): *nasty remark*, observación desagradable. || Antipático, ca (unfriendly): *she is a nasty girl*, es una chica antipática. || Malo, la; malévolo, la (wicked). || Vivo, va (temper). || Grosero, ra (rude). || Obsceno, na; asqueroso, sa (obscene). || Molesto, ta: *she has a very nasty cough*, tiene una tos muy molesta. || Feo, a (wound, cut). || Grave (accident). || Peligroso, sa (dangerous): *a nasty corner*, una esquina peligrosa. || Difícil (difficult). || — *Nasty business*, asunto malo *or* feo (affair), trabajo molesto (job). || *Nasty habit*, mala costumbre. || *Nasty trick*, mala jugada. || *To be nasty to s.o.*, portarse mal con uno, tratar mal a alguien. || *To have a nasty mind*, ser un mal pensado *or* una mal pensada. || FIG. *To leave a nasty taste in the mouth*, dejar mal sabor de boca. || *To smell nasty*, oler mal. || *To taste nasty*, saber mal, tener mal sabor. || *To turn nasty*, ponerse feo (an affair, the weather). || *To turn nasty on s.o.*, volverse antipático con alguien.
natal ['neitl] adj. Natal. || De nacimiento: *natal day*, día de nacimiento.
natality [nə'tæliti] n. Natalidad, *f.*: *natality rate*, índice de natalidad.
natation [nə'teiʃən] n. SP. Natación, *f.*
natatorial [,neitə'tɔ:riəl] or **natatory** [nə'teitəri] adj. Natatorio, ria.
natatorium [,neitə'tɔ:riəm] n. U. S. Piscina (*f.*) cubierta (swimming pool).

— OBSERV. El plural es *natatoriums* o *natatoria.*

nation ['neiʃən] n. Nación, *f.*: *the United Nations*, las Naciones Unidas.
national ['næʃənl] adj. Nacional: *national anthem*, himno nacional; *national income*, renta nacional. || — *Gross national product*, producto nacional bruto. || *National debt*, deuda pública. || *National park*, parque (*m.*) nacional.
— N. Nacional, *m.*, natural, *m.*
nationalism ['næʃnəlizəm] n. Nacionalismo, *m.*
nationalist ['næʃnəlist] adj./n. Nacionalista.
nationalistic [,næʃnə'listik] adj. Nacionalista.
nationality [,næʃə'næliti] n. Nacionalidad, *f.*: *dual nationality*, doble nacionalidad.
nationalization [,næʃnəlai'zeiʃən] n. Nacionalización, *f.* (of industry). || Naturalización, *f.* (of person).
nationalize ['næʃnəlaiz] v. tr. Nacionalizar (industry). || Naturalizar (person).
nationally ['næʃnəli] adv. Nacionalmente. || Desde el punto de vista nacional (from a national point of view). || A escala nacional: *to plan future constructions nationally rather than regionally*, planear construcciones futuras a escala nacional y no regional. || Por toda la nación, por todo el país (throughout a nation): *the company is divided nationally into fifteen branches*, la compañía está dividida por todo el país en quince sucursales.
National Socialism ['næʃənl'səuʃəlizəm] n. Nacionalsocialismo, *m.*
National Socialist ['næʃənl'səuʃəlist] adj./n. Nacionalsocialista.
National Syndicalism ['næʃənl'sindikəlizəm] n. Nacionalsindicalismo, *m.*
National Syndicalist ['næʃənl'sindikəlist] adj./n. Nacionalsindicalista.
nationhood ['neiʃənhud] n. Categoría (*f.*) de nación. || *To achieve nationhood*, alcanzar la independencia nacional.
nationwide ['neiʃənwaid] adj. A todo el país, a toda la nación (appeal, broadcast). || Por todo el país, por toda la nación (tour). || Nacional, a escala nacional: *nationwide scandal*, escándalo nacional.
native ['neitiv] adj. Nativo, va (inhabitant): *a native Spaniard*, un español nativo. || Natal (country, town). || Materno, na; nativo, va (language). || Del país (product). || Nacional (painter, writer). || Indígena, del país (labour). || Indígena (indigenous). || Innato, ta (innate). || Natural (simple). || MIN. Nativo, va: *native gold*, oro nativo. || Originario, ria: *customs native to England*, costumbres originarias de Inglaterra. || FAM. *To go native*, vivir como los indígenas.
— N. Natural, *m.* & *f.*, nativo, va: *I am a native of Scotland*, soy natural de Escocia. || Nativo, va; indígena, *m.* & *f.*, autóctono, na (original inhabitant of a country). || BOT. ZOOL. Originario, ria: *the elephant is a native of Asia*, el elefante es originario de Asia. || *You speak English like a native*, habla inglés como un inglés.
native-born [—bɔ:n] adj. De nacimiento: *a native-born Englishman*, un inglés de nacimiento.
nativism ['neitivizəm] n. PHIL. Nativismo, *m.* || Nacionalismo, *m.* (in politics).
nativist ['neitivist] adj./n. Nativista.
nativity [nə'tiviti] n. Nacimiento, *m.* (birth). || ASTR. Horóscopo, *m.*
Nativity [nə'tiviti] n. REL. Natividad, *f.* || Navidad, *f.*, Natividad, *f.* (Christmas). || ARTS. Natividad, *f.* (painting). | Nacimiento, *m.*, belén, *m.* (crib).

NATO ['neitəu] n. OTAN, *f.* (North Atlantic Treaty Organization).
natron ['neitrən] n. MIN. Natrón, *m.*
natter ['nætə*] n. FAM. Charla, *f.*
natter ['nætə*] v. intr. FAM. Charlar, charlotear (to chatter).
nattily ['nætili] adv. Elegantemente, con gusto.
nattiness ['nætinis] n. Elegancia, *f.*, buen gusto, *m.* (smartness). || Habilidad, *f.*, maña, *f.* (skill).
natty ['næti] adj. Elegante (smart). || Hábil, mañoso, sa (skilful). || Ingenioso, sa (clever).
natural ['nætʃrəl] adj. Natural: *natural resources*, recursos naturales; *natural gas*, gas natural. || Natural, sencillo, lla (simple). || Innato, ta; de nacimiento (innate). || Nato, ta: *he is a natural orator*, es un orador nato. || MATH. MUS. Natural. || — *Natural child*, hijo (*m.*) natural. || *Natural death*, muerte (*f.*) natural. || *Natural features*, geografía física. || *Natural historian*, naturalista, *m.* & *f.* || *Natural history*, historia (*f.*) natural. || *Natural law*, derecho (*m.*) natural, ley (*f.*) natural. || MATH. *Natural logarithm*, logaritmo (*m.*) natural. || *Natural person*, persona física. || *Natural sciences*, ciencias (*f.*) naturales. || *Natural to*, propio de. || *To be natural that*, ser natural *or* lógico que.
— N. FAM. Persona (*f.*) particularmente dotada (gifted person). | Cosa (*f.*) sensacional (good thing). || MUS. Nota (*f.*) natural (note). | Becuadro, *m.* (sign). || Tonto (*m.*) de nacimiento, tonta (*f.*) de nacimiento (half-wit). || — FAM. *He is a natural for the job*, es la persona más adecuada para este trabajo. || *The natural*, lo natural.
natural-born [—bɔ:n] adj. De nacimiento (native-born). || Nato, ta: *a natural-born pianist*, un pianista nato.
naturalism ['nætʃrəlizəm] n. Naturalismo, *m.*
naturalist ['nætʃrəlist] adj./n. Naturalista.
naturalistic [,nætʃrə'listik] adj. Naturalista.
naturalization [,nætʃrəlai'zeiʃən] n. Naturalización, *f.* (of an alien). || BOT. ZOOL. Aclimatación, *f.* || *Naturalization papers*, carta (*f. sing.*) de ciudadanía *or* de naturaleza.
naturalize ['nætʃrəlaiz] v. tr. Naturalizar (an alien). || BOT. ZOOL. Aclimatar. || *To become naturalized*, naturalizarse.
— V. intr. Naturalizarse (person). || Aclimatarse (plants, animals, etc.). || BOT. Herborizar.
naturally ['nætʃrəli] adv. Naturalmente, por supuesto, desde luego, claro (of course). || Por naturaleza: *he is naturally generous*, es generoso por naturaleza. || Con naturalidad, naturalmente: *people don't know how to behave naturally*, la gente no sabe comportarse con naturalidad.
naturalness ['nætʃrəlnis] n. Naturalidad, *f.*
nature ['neitʃə*] n. Naturaleza, *f.* (physical universe, essential characteristic or property): *nature is at its best in spring*, la naturaleza está en todo su esplendor en primavera; *human nature*, naturaleza humana; *the nature of the problem*, la naturaleza del problema. || Natural, *m.*, temperamento, *m.*, carácter, *m.*: *to be of a happy nature*, ser de natural alegre. || Índole, *f.*, género, *m.*, clase, *f.*, tipo, *m.*: *other things of that nature*, otras cosas de esta índole. || Esencia, *f.* (essence). || — *Against nature*, contra la naturaleza, contra natura. || *By nature*, por naturaleza. || *From nature*, del natural. || *Good nature*, amabilidad, *f.*; buen carácter. || *In a state of nature*, en estado natural. || *In the nature of things it's unlikely*, normalmente es improbable. || *It is not in his nature to shout*, no es propio de él gritar. || *It's the nature of things that*, es natural que. || *Learning languages is a second nature to him*, tiene mucha facilidad para los idiomas. || *Mother Nature*, la Madre Naturaleza. || *Nature lover*, amante (*m.* & *f.*) de la naturaleza. || *Nature study*, historia (*f.*) natural. || *Return to nature*, vuelta (*f.*) a la naturaleza. || *Something in the nature of*, una especie de. || *The laws of nature*, la leyes de la naturaleza. || *The nature of fish is to swim*, lo propio de los peces es nadar. || *To draw from nature*, dibujar del natural. || FIG. *To relieve nature*, hacer de *or* del cuerpo.
naturism ['neitʃərizəm] n. Naturismo, *m.* (nudism).
naturist ['neitʃərist] n. Naturista, *m.* & *f.* (nudist).
naturistic [neitʃə'ristik] adj. Naturista.
naught [nɔ:t] n. POET. Nada, *f.* || MATH. Cero, *m.* || — *All for naught*, en balde, para nada. || *To bring to naught*, frustrar (to ruin). || *To come to naught*, fracasar, reducirse a nada. || *To set at naught*, hacer caso omiso de, despreciar.
— Adj. Sin valor, inútil.
naughtily [—ili] adv. Mal: *to behave naughtily*, portarse mal.
naughtiness [—inis] n. Picardía, *f.*, travesuras, *f. pl.* (mischief). || Desobediencia, *f.* (disobedience). || Mala conducta, *f.* (bad behaviour). || Picardía, *f.*, lo verde (of a story).
naughty [—i] adj. Travieso, sa; pícaro, ra (mischievous). || Desobediente (disobedient). || Malo, la (bad): *he's been a very naughty boy*, ha sido muy malo. || Atrevido, da; verde, picante (slightly indecent): *a naughty joke*, un chiste atrevido.
nausea ['nɔ:siə] n. Náusea, *f.* (sickness). || FIG. Náuseas, *f. pl.*, asco, *m.* (strong disgust).
nauseate ['nɔ:sieit] v. tr. Dar náuseas a. || FIG. Dar asco a, repugnar a, dar náuseas a.

— V. intr. Tener náuseas (to be sick). || FIG. Asquear, dar náuseas (to disgust).
nauseating [—iŋ] adj. Nauseabundo, da; repugnante, asqueroso, sa.
nauseous [ˈnɔːsjəs] adj. Nauseabundo, da (causing nausea). || FIG. Nauseabundo, da; repugnante, asqueroso, sa (disgusting).
nauseousness [—nis] n. Náuseas, *f. pl.* (nausea). || FIG. Asco, *m.*, asquerosidad, *f.*
nautical [ˈnɔːtikəl] adj. MAR. Náutico, ca: *nautical chart*, carta náutica. | Marítimo, ma: *nautical term*, término marítimo. | Marino, na: *nautical mile*, milla marina.
nautilus [ˈnɔːtiləs] n. ZOOL. Nautilo, *m.* (small sea animal).
— OBSERV. El plural de *nautilus* es *nautiluses* o *nautili.*
naval [ˈneivəl] adj. MAR. Naval: *naval forces*, fuerzas navales; *naval engagement*, combate naval. || — *Naval attaché*, agregado (*m.*) naval. || *Naval base*, base (*f.*) naval. || *Naval college*, escuela (*f.*) naval [militar]. || *Naval hospital*, hospital (*m.*) de marina. || *Naval officer*, oficial (*m.*) de marina. || *Naval power*, potencia marítima. || *Naval station*, base (*f.*) naval.
Navarre [nəˈvɑː*] pr. n. GEOGR. Navarra, *f.*
Navarrese [nævəˈriːz] adj./n. Navarro, rra.
nave [neiv] n. ARCH. Nave, *f.* || Cubo, *m.* (of a wheel).
navel [ˈneivəl] n. ANAT. Ombligo, *m.* || FIG. Ombligo, *m.*, centro, *m.* || — *Navel orange*, naranja (*f.*) navel. || *Navel string*, cordón (*m.*) umbilical.
navelwort [—wəːt] n. BOT. Ombligo (*m.*) de Venus.
navicert [ˈnævisəːt] n. MAR. Navicert, *m.*, licencia (*f.*) de navegación (certificate).
navicula [nəˈvikjələ] n. REL. Naveta, *f.*
navigability [ˌnævigəˈbiliti] n. MAR. Navegabilidad, *f.*
navigable [ˈnævigəbl] adj. MAR. Navegable (river, etc.). || Gobernable, dirigible (steerable).
navigableness [—nis] n. Navegabilidad, *f.*
navigate [ˈnævigeit] v. tr. MAR. Navegar por (river, seas). | Gobernar (ship). || Pilotar (plane). || FIG. *To navigate a bill through Parliament*, llevar un proyecto de ley a buen término.
— V. intr. Navegar.
navigation [ˌnæviˈgeiʃən] n. Navegación, *f.* (art): *submarine, aerial navigation*, navegación submarina, aérea. || Náutica, *f.* (science). || — *Coastal navigation*, navegación costera *or* de cabotaje. || *Navigation chart*, carta náutica; carta aeronáutica. || *Navigation compass*, brújula (*f.*) de navegación. || *Navigation laws*, código marítimo. || *River navigation*, navegación fluvial.
navigator [ˈnævigeitə*] n. MAR. AVIAT. Navegante, *m.*,
navvy [ˈnævi] n. Peón (*m.*) caminero.
navy [ˈneivi] n. Marina, *f.* [de guerra] (organization and manpower). || Armada, *f.*, flota, *f.* (ships). || *Merchant navy*, marina mercante.
— Adj. De Marina: *Navy Department*, Ministerio de Marina. || Marino: *navy blue*, azul marino.
nay [nei] n. Voto (*m.*) en contra (in voting): *four ayes against three nays*, cuatro votos a favor y tres en contra. || Negativa, *f.* (refusal). || *To say s.o. nay*, decir que no a alguien.
— Adv. No (no). || Más aún, mejor dicho, más bien (or even): *I suspect, nay, I am certain, that he is wrong*, creo, mejor dicho, estoy seguro de que está equivocado.
Nazarene [ˌnæzəˈriːn] adj./n. Nazareno, na.
Nazareth [ˈnæzəriθ] pr. n. GEOGR. Nazaret.
naze [neiz] n. GEOGR. Cabo, *m.*
Nazi [ˈnɑːtsi] adj./n. Nazi.
Nazism [ˈnɑːtsizəm] n. Nazismo, *m.*
neap [niːp] n. MAR. Marea (*f.*) muerta.
— Adj. MAR. *Neap tide*, marea muerta.
Neapolitan [niəˈpɔlitən] adj./n. Napolitano, na.
near [niə*] adj. Cercano, na: *a near relative*, un pariente cercano. || Íntimo, ma (friend). || Estrecho, cha (friendship). || Cercano, na; próximo, ma (nearby): *the nearest inn*, la venta más cercana. || Próximo, ma; cercano, na (in time): *the near future*, el futuro próximo. || Grande (resemblance). || Bastante acertado, da (guess, estimate). || Directo, ta; corto, ta (road). || AUT. Izquierdo, da; de la izquierda (when driving on the left). | Derecho, cha; de la derecha (when driving on the right). || Literal: *near translation*, traducción literal. || Artificial: *near silk*, seda artificial. || Delicado, da; minucioso, sa (work). || Tacaño, ña (stingy). || SP. Reñido, da (race). || — *It was a near thing*, me he librado por los pelos. || *Near distance*, plano intermedio. || *Near one's end*, cercano a su fin. || *One's nearest and dearest*, los parientes y amigos íntimos. || *Or near offer*, precio a discutir (in advertisements). || *The near side*, el lado izquierdo (when driving on the left), el lado derecho (when driving on the right). || *To have a near escape*, librarse por los pelos. || *To take it to the nearest pound*, redondear la cifra hasta la libra más próxima.
— Adv. Cerca: *he lives near*, vive cerca; *you live near to my house*, vives cerca de mi casa. || FAM. Con parquedad, parcamente. || — *As near as I can remember*, que yo recuerde. || *Far and near*, en todas partes. || *He was very near asleep*, estaba casi dormido. || *I am nothing near so rich*, estoy muy lejos de ser tan rico. || *Near at hand*, a mano, muy cerca (object), a un paso, muy cerca (death, place, etc.), próximo, ma (time). || *Near by*, cerca. || *Near on*, casi. || *Near to Easter*, un poco antes de Pascua. || *Near upon*, cerca de. || *Quite near*, muy cerca. || FIG. *That's near enough*, está bien. || *To be as near as could be to doing sth.*, estar a punto de hacer algo. || *To bring near*, acercar. || *To come near*, see COME. || *To draw near*, acercarse. || *To keep as near as posible to the text*, ajustarse lo más posible al texto, acercarse lo más posible al texto.
— Prep. Cerca de: *near the door*, cerca de la puerta; *near death*, cerca de la muerte. || Casi: *we must have been near fifty*, debíamos de ser casi cincuenta. || — *Near here*, aquí cerca, cerca de aquí. || *Near the end of the month*, hacia fines de mes. || *Near the end of the text*, hacia el final del texto.
near [niə*] v. tr. Acercarse a, aproximarse a (a place). || Acercarse a (s.o.). || Acercarse a: *she is nearing sixty*, se acerca a los sesenta. || — *It was nearing midnight*, la medianoche se acercaba. || *Summer is nearing its end*, el fin del verano se acerca, el verano está a punto de terminarse. || *To be nearing ruin*, estar al borde de la ruina, estar muy cerca de la ruina.
nearby [—bai] adj. Cercano, na; próximo, ma.
— Adv. Cerca.
Near East [—iːst] pr. n. GEOGR. Cercano Oriente, *m.*
nearly [—li] adv. Casi: *it is nearly midnight*, son casi las doce de la noche; *he is nearly as old as her*, es casi tan viejo como ella; *we are nearly there*, casi hemos llegado. || De cerca (to affect s.o.): *the matter concerns me nearly*, el asunto me afecta de cerca. || Por poco, casi (in verbal constructions): *he nearly killed me*, por poco me mata, casi me mata. || — *Not nearly*, ni con mucho, ni mucho menos: *that will not be nearly enough for my journey*, no será ni mucho menos suficiente para el viaje. || *Or nearly so*, o casi. || *To be nearly acquainted with*, estar íntimamente relacionado con. || *Very nearly*, casi, casi.
near-miss [—ˈmis] n. Tiro (*m.*) cercano. || *To be a near-miss*, casi acertar, fallar por poco.
nearness [—nis] n. Proximidad, *f.*, cercanía, *f.* (of place). || Proximidad, *f.* (in time). || Intimidad, *f.* (of friends). || Fidelidad, *f.* (of translation). || FAM. Parquedad, *f.* || *Nearness of relationship*, parentesco cercano.
nearsighted [—ˈsaitid] adj. MED. Miope, corto de vista.
nearsightedness [—ˈsaitidnis] n. MED. Miopía, *f.*
neat [niːt] adj. Limpio, pia; pulcro, cra (person, clothes). || Limpio, pia (house, written work, worker). || Bien cuidado, da (garden). || Ordenado, da (orderly). || Esmerado, da; bien hecho, cha (job). || Elegante, pulcro, cra; pulido, da (style). || Claro, ra (handwriting). || Bien hecho, cha (speech). || Bien hecho, cha; bien proporcionado, da (shapely). || Fino, na (ankle). || Elegante (smart). || Ingenioso, sa (ingenious). || Hábil (skilful). || Solo, la (drinks): *a neat whisky*, un whisky solo. || — *As neat as a pin*, limpio como una patena. || U. S. FAM. *That's neat!*, ¡qué bien!
neat [niːt] n. Animal (*m.*) vacuno.
neatherd [—həːd] n. Vaquero, *m.*
neatly [—li] adv. Con cuidado, con esmero. || Pulcramente. || Con gusto, elegantemente: *neatly dressed*, vestido con gusto. || Hábilmente (skilfully).
neatness [—nis] n. Pulcritud, *f.*, limpieza, *f.* (of persons, clothes). || Limpieza, *f.* (of house, written work, worker). || Orden, *m.* (order). || Lo cuidado (of garden). || Esmero, *m.* (care). || Gusto, *m.*, elegancia, *f.* (of dress). || Elegancia, *f.*, pulcritud, *f.* (of style). || Claridad, *f.* (of handwriting). || Lo bien hecho (of speech, figure). || Ingenio, *m.* (ingenuity). || Destreza, *f.*, habilidad, *f.* (skill).
neb [neb] n. Pico, *m.* (beak). || Punta, *f.* (projecting tip).
Nebuchadnezzar [ˌnebjukədˈnezə*] pr. n. Nabucodonosor, *m.*
nebula [ˈnebjulə] n. ASTR. Nebulosa, *f.* || MED. Nube, *f.* (on eye).
— OBSERV. El plural de esta palabra es *nebulae.*
nebulize [ˈnebjuˌlaiz] v. tr. Atomizar.
nebulosity [ˌnebjuˈlɔsiti] n. Nebulosidad, *f.*
nebulous [ˈnebjuləs] adj. ASTR. Nebuloso, sa. || FIG. Vago, ga; nebuloso, sa; confuso, sa.
necessarily [ˈnesisərili] adv. Necesariamente.
necessary [ˈnesisəri] adj. Necesario, ria; indispensable, imprescindible. || — *If (it is) necessary*, si es necesario, si es preciso. || *It is necessary for you to do it o it is necessary that you do it*, es necesario *or* es preciso que lo hagas, tienes que hacerlo. || *To make it necessary for s.o. to do sth.*, obligar a alguien a que haga algo.
— N. Lo necesario, lo esencial, lo imprescindible. || Necesidad, *f.* (necessity). || — Pl. Lo necesario, *sing.* || — *The bare necessaries*, lo estrictamente necesario. || *The necessaries of life*, lo indispensable. || *To do the necessary*, hacer lo necesario.
necessitarian [niˌsesiˈtɛərjən] adj./n. PHIL. Determinista.
necessitarianism [niˌsesitɛəˈrijənizəm] n. PHIL. Determinismo, *m.*
necessitate [niˈsesiteit] v. tr. Necesitar, hacer necesario, exigir, requerir: *process that necessitates high pressures*, procedimiento que exige presiones elevadas.
necessitous [niˈsesitəs] adj. Necesitado, da; pobre, indigente (poor). || Urgente, apremiante (urgent).

necessity [ni'sesiti] n. Necesidad, *f.*: *necessity is the mother of invention*, la necesidad aguza el ingenio. || Requisito (*m.*) indispensable (requisite). || Necesidad, *f.*, indigencia, *f.* (poverty). || — Pl. Artículos (*m.*) de primera necesidad. || — *A car is a necessity nowadays*, el coche es una necesidad actualmente. || *A case of absolute* o *of sheer necessity*, un caso de fuerza mayor. || PHIL. *Doctrine of necessity*, determinismo, *m.* || *In case of necessity*, si fuese necesario, en caso de necesidad. || *Necessity knows no law*, la necesidad carece de ley. || *Of necessity* o *out of necessity*, por necesidad, por fuerza, forzosamente. || *The necessities of life*, lo indispensable. || *There is no necessity for him to do it*, no es necesario que lo haga. || *To be in necessity*, estar necesitado. || *To be under the necessity of*, verse obligado a. || *To make a virtue of necessity*, hacer de la necesidad virtud. || *To take the bare necessities*, tomar lo estrictamente necesario.

neck [nek] n. ANAT. Cuello, *m.* (of a man). || Pescuezo, *m.* (of an animal). || Cuello, *m.* (of garment). || Cuello, *m.*, gollete, *m.* (of bottle, etc.). || Mástil, *m.*, mango, *m.* (of violin, guitar, etc.). || Istmo, *m.* (isthmus). || Estrecho, *m.* (strait). || ARCH. Collarino, *m.* || ANAT. Cuello, *m.* (of tooth, of womb). || TECH. Estrangulamiento, *m.* (of pipe). | Garganta, *f.* (of axle). | Cuello, *m.* (of retort). || SP. Cabeza, *f.*: *to win by a neck*, ganar por una cabeza. || — *Low neck*, escote, *m.* || *Neck and neck*, parejos: *to be neck and neck*, ir parejos. || *Roll neck*, cuello vuelto. || MED. *Stiff neck*, tortícolis, *f.* || FIG. *To be in it up to the neck*, estar metido en ello hasta el cuello. | *To break one's neck*, romperse la crisma (after a fall), deslomarse (working), matarse (to obtain sth.). | *To break s.o.'s neck*, partir la cara a uno (to beat s.o. up). | *To fall on s.o.'s neck*, echar los brazos al cuello de alguien. || FIG. FAM. *To get it in the neck*, cargársela. | *To have a neck*, tener mucha cara. | *To risk one's neck*, jugarse el tipo. | *To save one's neck*, salvar el pellejo. | *To stick one's neck out*, arriesgarse (to take a risk), dar la cara (to face up to sth.). || *To throw* o *to fling one's arms around s.o.'s neck*, echarle a uno los brazos al cuello. || FIG. FAM. *To throw s.o. out neck and crop*, ponerle a uno de patitas en la calle. || *To wring s.o.'s neck*, retorcerle a uno el pescuezo. || *V neck*, cuello de pico.

neck [nek] v. intr. Besuquearse (to kiss). || Abrazarse (to hug). || Acariciarse (to caress).

— V. tr. Besuquear. || Abrazar. || Acariciar.

neckband [—bænd] n. Tirilla, *f.* (of a shirt).

neckerchief [—ətʃif] n. Pañuelo, *m.*

necking [—iŋ] n. ARCH. Collarino, *m.* || FAM. Besuqueo, *m.* (kissing). | Abrazos, *m. pl.* (hugging). | Caricias, *f. pl.* (caresses).

necklace [—lis] n. Collar, *m.*

necklet [—lit] n. Collar, *m.* (necklace). || Cuello, *m.* (of fur).

neckline [—lain] n. Escote, *m.* (of a dress).

necktie [—tai] n. Corbata, *f.*

necrological [nekrə'lɔdʒikəl] adj. Necrológico, ca.

necrologist [ne'krɔlədʒist] n. Necrólogo, *m.*

necrology [ne'krɔlədʒi] n. Necrología, *f.*

necromancer ['nekrəumænsə*] n. Nigromante, *m.* & *f.*, nigromántico, ca.

necromancy ['nekrəumænsi] n. Nigromancia, *f.*

necromantic [,nekrəu'mæntik] adj. Nigromante, nigromántico, ca.

necrophagous [ne'krɔfəgəs] adj. Necrófago, ga.

necrophilia [,nekrəu'filiə] n. Necrofilia, *f.*

necrophobia [,nekrəu'fəubiə] n. Necrofobia, *f.*

necropolis [ne'krɔpəlis] n. Necrópolis, *f.*

— OBSERV. El plural de la palabra inglesa es *necropolises* o *necropoles* o *necropoleis* o *necropoli*.

necropsy ['nekrɔpsi] n. Necropsia, *f.*

necrosis [ne'krəusis] n. MED. Necrosis, *f.*

— OBSERV. El plural de la palabra inglesa es *necroses*.

nectar ['nektə*] n. Néctar, *m.*

nectareous [nek'tɛəriəs] adj. Nectáreo, a.

nectarine ['nektərin] n. Nectarina, *f.* (variety of peach).

nectarous ['nektərəs] adj. Nectáreo, a.

née or **nee** [nei] adj. De soltera: *Mrs Mary Brown, née Watson*, la Sra. María Brown, de soltera Watson.

need [ni:d] n. Necesidad, *f.*: *the need for reinforcements*, la necesidad de refuerzos; *a little money is enough to satisfy my needs*, poco dinero me hace falta para satisfacer mis necesidades. || Requisito (*m.*) indispensable (requisite). || Necesidad, *f.*, indigencia, *f.* (poverty). || Carencia, *f.*, falta, *f.* (lack). || Necesidad, *f.*, apuro, *m.* (trouble): *in times of need*, en momentos de apuro. || — Pl. Necesidades, *f.* (wants): *to supply the needs of*, satisfacer las necesidades de. || FAM. Necesidades, *f.*: *bodily needs*, necesidades corporales. || — *If need be* o *in case of need*, en caso de necesidad, si fuera necesario, si hiciera falta. || *My needs are easily satisfied*, soy fácil de contentar. || *No need to hurry*, no es necesario *or* no hace falta darse prisa. || *No need to say that*, huelga decir que, no es necesario decir que. || *There is no need to*, no es necesario, no hace falta. || *To be badly in need of* o *in urgent need of*, necesitar urgentemente, tener gran necesidad de. || *To be in need*, estar necesitado (poor). || *To have need of* o *to stand in need of*, necesitar, tener necesidad de, hacerle falta a uno: *he has need of money*, necesita dinero, tiene necesidad de dinero, le hace falta dinero. || *To have need to do*, tener que hacer.

need [ni:d] v. tr. Necesitar, hacerle falta a uno: *I need to rest*, necesito descansar, me hace falta descansar; *I need twenty pounds*, necesito *or* me hacen falta veinte libras. || Requerir, exigir (to require): *a job which needs a lot of care*, un trabajo que requiere mucho cuidado. || Necesitar: *the soil needs rain*, la tierra necesita lluvia. || Carecer de, faltar (to lack). || Tener que, deber (to have to): *to need to do sth.*, tener que hacer algo. || Hacer falta: *these clothes need to be ironed*, hace falta planchar esta ropa. || — *That needs no saying*, ni que decir tiene. || *They need to be told everything*, hay que decírselo todo. || *Things needn't be that way*, las cosas no tienen por qué ser así.

— V. intr. Estar necesitado (to be needy).

— V. aux. Tener que, deber: *you needn't go if you don't want to*, no tienes que ir si no quieres; *need I do it?*, ¿tengo que hacerlo?, ¿debo hacerlo?

— V. impers. Hacer falta, ser necesario: *it needs much skill to do this work*, hace falta *or* es necesaria mucha habilidad para este trabajo.

— OBSERV. El verbo auxiliar es invariable en 3.ª persona del singular del presente de indicativo y en el pretérito. No tiene ni participio pasivo ni gerundio. Va siempre seguido por el infinitivo sin *to*.

needed [—id] adj. Necesario, ria. || *To be needed*, necesitarse, hacer falta, ser necesario.

needful [—ful] adj. Necesario, ria (necessary).

— N. Lo necesario: *do the needful*, haz lo necesario. || Dinero (*m.*) necesario (money).

needfulness [—fulnis] n. Necesidad, *f.*

neediness [—inis] n. Necesidad, *f.*, indigencia, *f.*

needle ['ni:dl] n. Aguja, *f.* (for knitting and sewing): *crochet needle*, aguja de ganchillo. || MED. BOT. Aguja. *f.* || Punta, *f.* (for engraving). || ARCH. Obelisco, *m.* || TECH. Aguja, *f.* || — *Darning needle*, aguja de zurcir. || *Knitting needle*, aguja de hacer punto *or* de hacer media. || *Larding needle*, aguja mechera. || *Magnetic needle*, aguja imantada *or* magnética. || BOT. *Shepherd's needle*, aguja de pastor *or* de Venus. || FIG. *To be as sharp as a needle*, ser un lince. | *To look for a needle in a haystack*, buscar una aguja en un pajar.

needle ['ni:dl] v. tr. Coser (to sew). || FAM. Hacer rabiar, pinchar, meterse con (to annoy): *stop needling him*, deja de pincharle. || U. S. Cargar (a drink).

needle case [—keis] n. Alfiletero, *m.*

needlecraft [—krɑ:ft] n. Costura, *f.*, labor (*f.*) de aguja.

needlefish [—fiʃ] n. ZOOL. Aguja, *f.*

needleful [—ful] n. Hebra, *f.* (of thread).

needlepoint [—pɔint] n. Encaje (*m.*) de aguja, puntas, *f. pl.* (lace). || Punta (*f.*) seca (of a compass). || FIG. Minuciosidad, *f.*

needless ['ni:dlis] adj. Innecesario, ria; inútil (unnecessary). || Inútil (useless). || *Needless to say*, ni que decir tiene que, huelga decir que, está de más decir que: *I was, needless to say, working*, huelga decir que yo estaba trabajando.

needlessness [—nis] n. Inutilidad, *f.* (of sth.). || Inoportunidad, *f.* (of a remark).

needle valve ['ni:dlvælv] n. Válvula (*f.*) de aguja.

needlewoman ['ni:dl'wumən] n. Costurera, *f.* || *To be a good needlewoman*, coser bien.

— OBSERV. El plural es *needlewomen*.

needlework ['ni:dlwə:k] n. Costura, *f.*, labor (*f.*) de aguja (sewing). || Bordado, *m.* (embroidery).

needn't ['ni:dnt] contraction of *need not*.

needs [ni:dz] adv. Necesariamente, forzosamente. || — *If needs must*, si hace falta. || *They must needs return*, no tienen más remedio que volver.

— OBSERV. *Needs* sólo se emplea antes o después de *must*.

needy ['ni:di] adj. Necesitado, da; indigente.

— N. *The needy*, los necesitados.

ne'er [nɛə*] adv. Nunca, jamás (never).

ne'er-do-well [—du,wel] adj./n. Inútil.

nefarious [ni'fɛəriəs] adj. Infame, inicuo, cua.

nefariousness [—nis] n. Infamia, *f.*, iniquidad, *f.*

negate [ni'geit] v. tr. Negar (to deny). || Anular, invalidar (to invalidate).

negation [ni'geiʃən] n. Negación, *f.*

negative ['negətiv] adj. Negativo, va: *a negative reply*, una contestación negativa; *negative personality, criticism*, personalidad, crítica negativa. || MATH. ELECTR. Negativo, va.

— N. Negativa, *f.*: *to reply in the negative*, contestar con una negativa. || MATH. Cantidad (*f.*) negativa, término (*m.*) negativo. || PHOT. Negativo, *m.* || ELECTR. Polo (*m.*) negativo. || GRAMM. Negación, *f.* || *Two negatives make an affirmative* o *a positive*, dos negaciones equivalen a una afirmación.

negative ['negətiv] v. tr. Rechazar, no aprobar (to reject). || Refutar (to refute). || Negar (to deny). || Contradecir (to contradict). || Neutralizar (to counteract).

negativism [—izəm] n. PHIL. Negativismo, *m.*

negaton ['negətɔn] or **negatron** ['negətrɔn] n. PHYS. Negatón, *m.*

neglect [ni'glekt] n. Negligencia, *f.*, descuido, *m.*, dejadez, *f.*, desidia, *f.*: *from* o *through* o *out of neglect*, por negligencia; *neglect for one's own cleanliness*,

negligencia en el aseo personal. || Inobservancia, *f.* (of a rule). || Incumplimiento, *m.* (of duties). || Abandono, *m.* (abandon): *in total neglect*, en el más completo abandono. || Dejadez, *f.* (self-neglect). || Desaliño, *m.*, dejadez, *f.* (in style). || Desatención, *f.* (*of*, con) [inattention]. || — *Neglect of one's duty*, negligencia en el cumplimiento del deber. || *To die in neglect*, morir abandonado.
neglect [niˈglekt] v. tr. Faltar a, no cumplir con, no cumplir (one's duty). || No observar (a rule). || Dejar de: *don't neglect to post the letter*, no dejes de echar la carta; *why did you neglect to go?*, ¿por qué dejaste de ir? || Descuidar, desatender: *she neglects her house, her child*, descuida la casa, al niño. || Descuidar (a garden). || No hacer caso de, despreciar, desdeñar (to disregard advice). || Abandonar (to abandon). || No aprovechar, desperdiciar (an opportunity). || Hacer poco caso de (one's friends). || Omitir, olvidar (to omit). || Ignorar (to ignore).
neglected [—id] adj. Descuidado, da; desaliñado, da (appearance, style). || Abandonado, da; dejado, da (person, garden).
neglectful [—ful] adj. Descuidado, da; negligente (careless). || Olvidadizo, za (forgetful). || *To be neglectful of*, descuidar, desatender.
neglectfulness [—fulnis] n. Negligencia, *f.*, descuido, *m.*, dejadez, *f.*, desidia, *f.*
néglígé or **negligee** [ˈnegli:ʒei] n. Salto (*m.*) de cama, bata, *f.*, "negligé", *m.*
negligence [ˈneglidʒəns] n. Negligencia, *f.*, descuido, *m.*: *through negligence*, por descuido. || *A piece of negligence*, un descuido.
negligent [ˈneglidʒənt] adj. See NEGLECTFUL.
negligible [ˈneglidʒəbl] adj. Insignificante (insignificant). || Despreciable, desdeñable: *the reward is by no means negligible*, la recompensa no es nada despreciable.
negotiability [ni,gəuʃjəˈbiliti] n. Negociabilidad, *f.*
negotiable [niˈgəuʃjəbl] adj. Negociable. || FAM. Transitable (road). | Salvable, franqueable (obstacle). || — COMM. *Negotiable paper*, efecto, *m.* || *Not negotiable*, que no se puede negociar.
negotiant [niˈgəuʃiənt] n. Negociador, ra.
negotiate [niˈgəuʃieit] v. intr. Negociar. || *To negotiate for*, negociar para obtener, entablar negociaciones para.
— V. tr. Negociar, gestionar: *to negotiate the sale of an estate*, gestionar la venta de una finca. || Negociar: *to negotiate a bill of exchange*, negociar una letra de cambio; *to negotiate a treaty*, negociar un tratado. || FIG. Salvar, franquear (obstacle). | Tomar (bends). | Subir (a hill).
negotiating [—iŋ] adj. Negociador, ra.
negotiation [ni,gəuʃiˈeiʃən] n. Negociación, *f.*, gestión, *f.*: *the negotiation of a contract*, la negociación de un contrato. || Negociación, *f.*: *to enter into* o *to open negotiations with*, entablar negociaciones con. || — *To be in negotiation with*, estar negociando con. || *Under negotiation*, en negociación.
negotiator [niˈgəuʃieitə*] n. Negociador, ra.
negotiatress [niˈgəuʃieitris] or **negotiatrix** [niˈgəuʃieitriks] n. Negociadora, *f.*
Negress [ˈni:gris] n. Negra, *f.*
Negrillo [neˈgriləu] n. Negrito, ta (from Africa).
— OBSERV. El plural de la palabra inglesa *Negrillo* es *Negrillos* o *Negrilloes*.
Negrito [neˈgri:təu] n. Negrito, ta (from Asia and Oceania).
— OBSERV. El plural de la palabra inglesa *Negrito* es *Negritos* o *Negritoes*.
negritude [ˈnigrə,tjud] n. Negritud, *f.*
Negro [ˈni:grəu] adj. Negro, gra.
— N. Negro, *m.*
— OBSERV. El plural de la palabra inglesa *Negro* es *Negroes*.
Negroid [ˈni:grɔid] adj. Negroide.
negus [ˈni:gəs] n. Bebida (*f.*) caliente de vino, agua y especias.
Negus [ˈni:gəs] n. Negus, *m.* (Ethiopian ruler).
neigh [nei] n. Relincho, *m.*
neigh [nei] v. intr. Relinchar.
neighbour (U. S. **neighbor**) [ˈneibə*] n. Vecino, na. || REL. Prójimo, *m.*: *love thy neighbour*, ama a tu prójimo. || — *Good Neighbour Policy*, política (*f.*) de buena vecindad. || *The new building dwarfs its neighbours*, el nuevo edificio empequeñece las casas colindantes.
neighbour (U. S. **neighbor**) [ˈneibə*] v. tr. Lindar con, estar contiguo a: *his land neighbours the river*, sus tierras lindan con el río *or* están contiguas al río.
— V. intr. *To neighbour on* o *upon*, lindar con, estar contiguo a (to be next to), rayar en: *his language neighboured on vulgarity*, sus palabras rayaban en la vulgaridad.
neighbourhood (U. S. **neighborhood**) [—hud] n. Barrio, *m.* (district). || Vecindad, *f.*: *my friend lives in the neighbourhood*, mi amigo vive en la vecindad. || Vecindad, *f.*, vecindario, *m.*, vecinos, *m. pl.*: *the whole neighbourhood came to the meeting*, todo el vecindario vino a la reunión. || Alrededores, *m. pl.*, cercanías, *f. pl.*: *Manchester and its neighbourhood*, Manchester y sus alrededores. || *In the neighbourhood of*, alrededor de, cerca de, aproximadamente (approximately), cerca de (near).
neighbouring (U. S. **neighboring**) [—riŋ] adj. Vecino, na: *neighbouring country*, país vecino. || Cercano, na (near).
neighbourliness (U. S. **neighborliness**) [—linis] n. Buenas relaciones (*f. pl.*) entre vecinos, relaciones (*f. pl.*) de buena vecindad.
neighbourly (U. S. **neighborly**) [—li] adj. De buena vecindad (relations). || Amable, amistoso, sa (action, person).
neither [ˈnaiðə*, U.S. ˈni:ðə*] adj. Ninguno de los dos, ninguna de las dos (not either of two): *neither concert pleased me*, no me gustó ninguno de los dos conciertos.
— Pron. Ninguno, na; ninguno de los dos, ninguna de las dos: *neither of the books is of any use to me*, ninguno de los dos libros me sirve para nada. || — *Neither of them*, ninguno de ellos, ninguno de los dos, ni el uno ni el otro. || *Neither of the parents*, ninguno de los padres.
— Adv. Ni tampoco, tampoco: *he didn't know the answer and neither did she*, él no conocía la respuesta ni ella tampoco. || Tampoco: *if you don't work neither shall I*, si tú no trabajas yo tampoco trabajaré. || — *Neither... nor*, ni... ni, no... ni... ni: *I want neither milk nor sugar*, no quiero ni leche ni azúcar; *neither wind nor rain will make me change my mind*, ni el viento ni la lluvia me harán cambiar de idea, no me harán cambiar de idea ni el viento ni la lluvia; *neither you nor I*, ni tú ni yo; *neither one nor the other*, ni uno ni otro. || FIG. *To be neither here nor there*, no tener nada que ver, no hacer al caso.
nemathelminths [,nemaˈθelminθz] pl. n. ZOOL. Nematelmintos, *m.*
nematodes [ˈnemətəudz] pl. n. ZOOL. Nematodos, *m.*
nemesis [ˈnemisis] n. Justo castigo, *m.* (punishment). || Vengador, *m.* (avenger).
— OBSERV. El plural de la palabra inglesa es *nemeses*.
nenuphar [ˈnenjufa:*] n. BOT. Nenúfar, *m.*
neo-Catholic [,ni:əuˈkæθəlik] adj./n. Neocatólico, ca.
neo-Catholicism [,ni:əukəˈθɔlisizəm] n. Neocatolicismo, *m.*
Neocene [ˈni:ə,si:n] n. GEOL. Neógeno, *m.*
neo-Christian [,ni:əuˈkristjən] adj./n. Neocristiano, na.
neo-Christianity [,ni:əu,kristiˈæniti] n. Neocristianismo, *m.*
neoclassic [,ni:əuˈklæsik] or **neoclassical** [—əl] adj. Neoclásico, ca.
neoclassicism [,ni:əuˈklæsisizəm] n. Neoclasicismo, *m.*
neoclassicist [,ni:əuˈklæsisist] n. Neoclásico, ca.
neocolonialism [,ni:əukəˈləunjəlizəm] n. Neocolonialismo, *m.*
neocolonialist [,ni:əukəˈləunjəlist] adj./n. Neocolonialista.
neofascism [,ni:əuˈfæʃizəm] n. Neofascismo, *m.*
neo-Gothic [,ni:əuˈgɔθik] adj. Neogótico, ca.
neo-Greek [,ni:əuˈgri:k] adj. Neogriego, ga.
neo-Impressionism [,ni:əuimˈpreʃnizəm] n. Neoimpresionismo, *m.*
neo-Latin [ˈni:əuˈlætin] adj. Neolatino, na; románico, ca.
Neolithic [,ni:əuˈliθik] adj. Neolítico, ca.
neologism [ni:ˈɔlədʒizəm] n. Neologismo, *m.*
neologist [ni:ˈɔlədʒist] n. Neólogo, ga.
neology [ni:ˈɔlədʒi] n. Neologismo, *m.*
neo-Malthusianism [,ni:əumælˈθju:ziənizəm] n. Neomaltusianismo, *m.*
neon [ˈni:ən] n. Neón, *m.*: *neon lighting*, alumbrado de neón.
neophyte [ˈni:əufait] n. Neófito, ta.
Neoplatonic [ˈni:əupləˈtɔnik] adj. Neoplatónico, ca
Neoplatonism [ˈni:əuˈpleitənizəm] n. PHIL. Neoplatonismo, *m.*
Neoplatonist [ˈni:əuˈpleitənist] n. Neoplatónico, ca.
neopositivism [,ni:əuˈpɔzitivizəm] n. PHIL. Neopositivismo, *m.*
neorealism [,ni:əuˈriəlizəm] n. Neorrealismo, *m.*
neorealist [,ni:əuˈriəlist] adj./n. Neorrealista.
neoromantic [,ni:əurəuˈmæntik] adj./n. Neorromántico, ca.
neoromanticism [,ni:əurəuˈmæntisizəm] n. Neorromanticismo, *m.*
neo-Scholastic [,ni:əuskəˈlæstik] adj. Neoescolástico, ca.
neo-Scholasticism [,ni:əuskəˈlæstisizəm] n. Neoescolástica, *f.*
neo-Thomism [ˈni:əuˈtəumizəm] n. Neotomismo, *m.*
Neozoic [,ni:əuˈzəuik] adj. GEOL. Neozoico, ca.
Nepal [niˈpɔ:l] pr. n. Nepal, *m.*
Nepalese [,nepɔ:ˈli:z] adj./n. Nepalés, esa. || *The Nepalese*, los nepaleses.
nephew [ˈnevju:] n. Sobrino, *m.*
nephralgia [neˈfrældʒiə] n. MED. Nefralgia, *f.*
nephritic [nəˈfritik] adj. MED. Nefrítico, ca.
nephritis [nəˈfraitis] n. MED. Nefritis, *f.*
nepotism [ˈnepətizəm] n. Nepotismo, *m.*
Neptune [ˈneptju:n] pr. n. MYTH. Neptuno, *m.*
Neptunian [nepˈtju:njən] adj. GEOL. Neptúnico, ca. || POET. Neptúneo, a.
neptunium [nepˈtju:njəm] n. CHEM. Neptunio, *m.*
Nereid [ˈniəriid] n. MYTH. Nereida, *f.*
Nero [ˈniərəu] pr. n. Nerón, *m.*
Neronian [niˈrəuniən] adj. Neroniano, na.

nervate [ˈnəːvit] adj. BOT. Nerviado, da.
nervation [nəːˈveiʃən] n. BOT. Nervadura, *f.*
nerve [nəːv] n. ANAT. Nervio, *m.*: *optic nerve*, nervio óptico. || BOT. Nervio, *m.* (of a leaf). || Nervadura, *f.* (of insects). || ARCH. Nervadura, *f.*, nervio, *m.* (rib). || FIG. Nervio, *m.*: *his nerves are on edge*, tiene los nervios de punta; *he has nerves of steel*, tiene nervios de acero. | Valor, *m.* (courage): *I have not the nerve to do it*, no tengo valor para llevarlo a cabo. || FAM. Cara, *f.*, caradura, *f.*, descaro, *m.* (cheek, insolence): *what a nerve!*, ¡qué descaro!; *he has got a nerve!*, ¡tiene una caradura! || — Pl. FAM. Nerviosismo, *m. sing.*, nerviosidad, *f. sing.*: *he couldn't control his nerves*, no podía dominar su nerviosismo; *to soothe s.o.'s nerves*, quitar a uno el nerviosismo. || — *A fit of nerves*, un ataque de nervios. || *Nerve specialist*, neurólogo, ga. || FIG. *To be a bundle of nerves*, estar hecho un manojo de nervios. | *To be in a state of nerves*, estar muy nervioso. | *To get on s.o.'s nerves*, crisparle los nervios a uno, ponerle nervioso a uno, ponerle a uno los nervios de punta. | *To have steady nerves*, tener los nervios bien templados. | *To lose one's nerve*, rajarse (to back down), ponerse nervioso (to get nervous). | *To set one's nerves on edge*, ponerle a uno los nervios de punta. | *To strain every nerve to*, hacer todo lo posible para. || *War of nerves*, guerra (*f.*) de nervios.
nerve [nəːv] v. tr. Animar, dar ánimos a. || *To nerve o.s. to*, animarse a.
nerve cell [—sel] n. ANAT. Neurona, *f.*, célula (*f.*) nerviosa.
nerve centre (U. S. **nerve center**) [—ˈsentə*] n. ANAT. Centro (*m.*) nervioso. || FIG. Punto (*m.*) neurálgico.
nerve impulse [—ˈimpʌls] n. Impulso (*m.*) nervioso.
nerveless [—lis] adj. Sin nervios (spiritless). || BOT. Sin nervadura. || MED. Sin nervios.
nerve-racking or **nerve-wracking** [—ˈrækiŋ] adj. Crispante (sound, etc.). || Desgarrador, ra (blood-curdling). || Horripilante (terrifying). || Exasperante (exasperating). || Muy agudo, da (pain).
nerviness [ˈnəːvinis] or **nervosity** [nəːˈvɔsiti] n. Nerviosidad, *f.*, nerviosismo, *m.*
nervous [ˈnəːvəs] adj. MED. Nervioso, sa (disease, system). || ARTS. Vigoroso, sa; enérgico, ca. || Tímido, da (timid). || Miedoso, sa (apprehensive). || Nervioso, sa: *nervous laugh*, risa nerviosa. || Nervioso, sa; irritable (irritable). || Inquieto, ta; preocupado, da (worried). || — *Don't be nervous*, no tengas miedo, no te asustes. || *Nervous breakdown*, depresión nerviosa. || *To be nervous of*, tener miedo a.
nervously [—li] adv. Tímidamente, con miedo. || Nerviosamente.
nervousness [—nis] n. Nerviosismo, *m.*, nerviosidad, *f.* (agitated mood). || Timidez, *f.* (shyness). || Miedo, *m.* (fear). || Vigor, *m.*, fuerza, *f.* (strength).
nervure [ˈnəːvjuə*] n. Nervadura, *f.* (of insects). || BOT. Nervio, *m.*, nervadura, *f.*
nervy [ˈnəːvi] adj. Nervioso, sa (nervous). || U. S. FAM. Descarado, da; fresco, ca (brazen).
nescience [ˈnesiəns] n. Ignorancia, *f.* || PHIL. Agnosticismo, *m.*
nescient [ˈnesiənt] adj. Ignorante.
— Adj./n. REL. Agnóstico, ca.
ness [nes] n. Promontorio, *m.*, cabo, *m.*
nest [nest] n. Nido, *m.* (of birds). || Nidal, *m.* (of hens). || Madriguera, *f.* (of mice, rabbits, etc.). || Nidada, *f.* (brood). || Hormiguero, *m.* (of ants). || Avispero, *m.* (of wasps). || FIG. Nido, *m.* (house). | Guarida, *f.*, cueva, *f.* (of criminals). || — *Nest box*, ponedero, *m.*, nidal, *m.* || *Nest of drawers*, archivador, *m.* (for office), costurero, *m.*, "chiffonnier", *m.* (for room). || *Nest of machine guns*, nido de ametralladoras. || *Nest of shelves*, casillero, *m.* || *Nest of tables*, mesas (*f. pl.*) de nido. || FIG. *To feather one's nest*, hacer su agosto.
nest [nest] v. tr. Encajar (to fit into). || Empalmar (to join).
— V. intr. Anidar (birds). || TECH. Empalmar (to join): *pipes that nest in each other*, tubos que empalman unos con otros. || Encajar (to fit into). || Buscar nidos (an egg collector).
nest egg [ˈnesteg] n. Nidal, *m.* (in a hen's nest). || FIG. Ahorrillos, *m. pl.*, ahorros, *m. inv.* (savings).
nestful [—ful] n. Nidada, *f.*
nestle [ˈnesl] v. intr. Arrellanarse: *he nestled in an armchair*, se arrellanó en un sillón. || Acurrucarse (in s.o.'s arms). || Recostar la cabeza: *she nestled against his shoulder*, recostó la cabeza sobre su hombro. || Anidar (to nest). || — *To nestle down*, acurrucarse, hacerse un ovillo. || *To nestle up to*, arrimarse a. || *Village nestling in a valley*, pueblo situado en el fondo de un valle.
— V. tr. Recostar (the head). || Poner con mimo: *she nestled the bird in her hand*, puso con mimo el pájaro en su mano.
nestling [—iŋ] n. Pajarito, *m.*, cría (*f.*) de pájaro.
Nestorian [nesˈtɔːriən] adj./n. Nestoriano, na.
Nestorianism [—izəm] n. Nestorianismo, *m.*
net [net] n. Red, *f.*: *net fishing*, pesca con red; *to cast the net*, echar la red. || Redecilla, *f.*: *hair net*, redecilla para el pelo. || Redecilla, *f.* (for shopping, luggage rack). || Malla, *f.* (mesh). || Tul, *m.* (fabric). || SP. Red, *f.*, malla, *f.* || Ganancia (*f.*) neta (benefit). || Peso (*m.*) neto (weight). || Cantidad (*f.*) neta (amount). || FIG. Red, *f.*, trampa, *f.*: *to fall into the net*, caer en la red. || *To sleep under a mosquito net*, dormir con mosquitero.
— Adj. Neto, ta: *a net profit*, un beneficio neto; *net weight*, peso neto.
net [net] v. tr. Coger [con red] (to catch with a net). || Pescar [con red] (to fish). || SP. Dar en la red con (the ball). || Tejer en forma de malla. || COMM. Ganar neto (to earn). | Producir neto (to yield).
netful [—ful] n. *A netful of fish*, una red llena de peces.
nether [ˈneðə*] adj. Inferior: *the nether lip*, el labio inferior. || *The nether regions* o *the nether world*, el infierno (hell), el otro mundo (the next world).
Netherlander [ˈneðələndə*] n. Holandés, esa; neerlandés, esa.
Netherlandish [ˈneðələndiʃ] adj./n. Holandés, esa.
Netherlands [ˈneðələndz] pl. n. GEOGR. Holanda, *f. sing.*, Países Bajos, *m.*

— OBSERV. *Netherlands* lleva siempre el artículo en inglés como *Países Bajos* en español, mientras que *Holanda* no lo lleva.

nethermost [ˈneðəməust] adj. Más profundo, más bajo.
nett [net] adj. See NET.
nett [net] v. tr. COMM. See NET.
netting [—iŋ] n. Fabricación (*f.*) *or* confección (*f.*) de redes. || Colocación (*f.*) de redes (for fishing or hunting). || Red, *f.* (net). || Redes, *f. pl.* (nets). || Tul, *m.* (fabric). || Malla, *f.* (mesh).
nettle [ˈnetl] n. BOT. Ortiga, *f.* || MED. *Nettle rash*, urticaria, *f.*
nettle [ˈnetl] v. tr. Picar con una ortiga (to sting). || FAM. Picar, hacer rabiar, irritar (to irritate).
network [ˈnetwəːk] n. Malla, *f.*, red, *f.* (net). || Red, *f.* (of railways, rivers, roads, telephones, etc.): *rail network*, red de ferrocarriles. || RAD. Canal, *m.*, cadena, *f.* (channel). || FIG. Tejido, *m.*, sarta, *f.*: *it is a network of lies*, es un tejido de mentiras. | Red, *f.*: *a network of drug pushers*, una red de vendedores de drogas.
neume [njuːm] n. MUS. Neuma, *m.*
neural [ˈnjuərəl] adj. De los nervios, nervioso, sa; neural.
neuralgia [njuəˈrældʒə] n. MED. Neuralgia, *f.*
neuralgic [njuəˈrældʒik] adj. MED. Neurálgico, ca.
neurasthenia [ˌnjuərəsˈθiːnjə] n. MED. Neurastenia, *f.*
neurasthenic [ˌnjuərəsˈθenik] adj./n. MED. Neurasténico, ca.
neuritic [njuəˈritik] adj. MED. Neurítico, ca.
neuritis [ˈnjuəˈraitis] n. MED. Neuritis, *f.*
neuroblast [ˈnjuərəˌblæst] n. BIOL. Neuroblasto, *m.*
neurological [ˌnjuərəˈlɔdʒəkəl] adj. MED. Neurológico, ca.
neurologist [njuəˈrɔlədʒist] n. MED. Neurólogo, *m.*
neurology [njuəˈrɔlədʒi] n. MED. Neurología, *f.*
neuroma [njuəˈrəumə] n. MED. Neuroma, *m.*

— OBSERV. El plural de la palabra inglesa *neuroma* es *neuromata* o *neuromas*.

neuron [ˈnjuərɔn] n. MED. Neurona, *f.* (cell).
neuropath [ˈnjuərəpæθ] n. MED. Neurópata, *m.*
neuropathology [ˌnjuərəpæˈθɔlədʒi] n. MED. Neuropatología, *f.*
neuropathy [njuəˈrɔpəθi] n. MED. Neuropatía, *f.*
neuroptera [njuəˈrɔptərə] pl. n. Neurópteros, *m.*
neuropteran [njuəˈrɔptərən] adj. Neuróptero (insect).
— N. Neuróptero, *m.* (insect).
neurosis [njuəˈrəusis] n. Neurosis, *f.*

— OBSERV. El plural de la palabra inglesa es *neuroses*.

neuroskeleton [ˌnjuərəˈskelitn] n. Neuroesqueleto, *m.*
neurosurgery [ˌnjuərəˈsəːdʒəri] n. Neurocirugía, *f.*
neurotic [njuəˈrɔtik] adj./n. Neurótico, ca.
neurotomy [njuəˈrɔtəmi] n. MED. Neurotomía, *f.*
neurovegetative [ˌnjuərəˈvedʒitətiv] adj. Neurovegetativo, va.
neuter [ˈnjuːtə*] adj. Neutro, tra. || GRAMM. Neutro, tra (gender). | Neutro, tra; intransitivo, va (verb).
— N. GRAMM. Neutro, *m.*: *in the neuter*, en neutro. || Obrera, *f.* (worker bee). || Animal (*m.*) castrado (castrated animal).
neuter [ˈnjuːtə*] v. tr. Castrar (to castrate).
neutral [ˈnjuːtrəl] adj. Neutro, tra. || JUR. MIL. Neutral: *to remain neutral*, permanecer neutral. || CHEM. ELECTR. Neutro, tra.
— N. Neutral, *m.* & *f.* || AUT. Punto (*m.*) muerto (of gearshift).
neutralism [—izəm] n. Neutralismo, *m.*
neutralist [—ist] adj./n. Neutralista, neutral.
neutrality [njuːˈtræliti] n. Neutralidad, *f.*
neutralization [ˌnjuːtrəlaiˈzeiʃən] n. Neutralización, *f.*
neutralize [ˈnjuːtrəlaiz] v. tr. Neutralizar.
neutralizer [—ə*] n. Neutralizador, *m.*, neutralizante, *m.*
neutralizing [—iŋ] adj. Neutralizador, ra.
neutrino [njuːˈtriːnəu] n. PHYS. Neutrino, *m.*
neutron [ˈnjuːtrɔn] n. PHYS. Neutrón, *m.*
never [ˈnevə*] adv. Nunca, jamás: *he never came*, nunca vino, no vino nunca; *never again* o *never more*, nunca más; *never yet*, jamás hasta ahora; *she said never a word about it*, nunca dijo una palabra sobre aquello. || — *I never expected it*, no me lo esperaba. || *I never heard anything like it*, no he oído nunca una

cosa parecida. || *Never!* o *you never did!*, ¡no me digas! || *Never a...*, ni: *never a care in the world*, ni una preocupación en el mundo. || *Never a one*, ni siquiera uno. || *Never fear*, no tema. || *Never in all my life*, jamás en la vida, en mi vida. || *Never mind*, no importa, da igual (it doesn't matter), no se preocupe (don't worry). || *Never never* o *never ever*, nunca jamás: *I shall never ever forget her*, no la olvidaré nunca jamás. || *Surely you never did it?*, ¿no me digas que lo has hecho? || *Well I never!*, ¡no me digas!

never-ceasing [—ˈsi:siŋ] adj. Incesante.

never-dying [—ˈdaiiŋ] adj. Imperecedero, ra.

never-ending [—ˈendiŋ] adj. Sin fin, interminable.

never-fading [—ˈfeidiŋ] adj. Imperecedero, ra.

never-failing [—ˈfeiliŋ] adj. Infalible.

nevermore [—ˈmɔ:*] adv. Nunca más: *nevermore shall I hear her voice*, nunca más oiré su voz; *nevermore to return*, para no volver nunca más.

never-never [—ˈnevə*] n. FAM. Compra (*f.*) a plazos. || — *Never-never land*, país (*m.*) de ensueños. || FAM. *To buy sth. on the never-never*, comprar algo a plazos.

nevertheless [—ðəˈles] adv. Sin embargo, no obstante.

nevus [ˈni:vəs] n. U. S. Nevo, *m.*

— OBSERV. El plural de *nevus* es *nevi*.

new [nju:] adj. Nuevo, va: *a new house*, una nueva casa, una casa nueva (see OBSERV.); *there is nothing new*, no hay nada nuevo; *new moon*, luna nueva; *new pupil*, alumno nuevo; *new suit*, traje nuevo. || Tierno (bread). || Fresco, ca (fish). || Nuevo, va: *new to one's job*, nuevo en el oficio. || GEOGR. Nuevo, va: *New Delhi*, Nueva Delhi; *New Mexico*, Nuevo México. || — *Are you new to this technique?*, ¿es nueva esta técnica para ti? || *It's as good as new*, está como nuevo, está nuevo. || *New Year*, Año Nuevo. || *New Year's Eve*, Nochevieja, *f.* || *There is nothing new under the sun*, no hay nada nuevo bajo el sol. || *To be new in o to a town*, acabar de llegar a una ciudad. || *To be new to the college*, ser nuevo en el colegio. || *What's new?*, ¿qué hay de nuevo?

— N. Lo nuevo: *to throw out the old and keep the new*, tirar lo viejo y quedarse con lo nuevo.

— Adv. Recién, recientemente: *new-made*, recién hecho.

— OBSERV. The translation *una nueva casa* would tend to suggest a recently acquired house, whereas *una casa nueva* would indicate a newly built house.

new arrival [—əˈraivəl] n. Recien llegado, da.

newborn [—bɔ:n] adj. Recién nacido, da.

New Caledonia [—ˌkæliˈdəunjə] pr. n. GEOGR. Nueva Caledonia, *f.*

newcomer [—ˈkʌmə*] n. Recién llegado, da; nuevo, va.

newel [—əl] n. ARCH. Nabo, *m.*, eje, *m.* (of stairs). | Pilastra, *f.* (at bottom of handrail).

New England [—ˈiŋglənd] pr. n. GEOGR. Nueva Inglaterra, *f.*

newfangled [—ˌfæŋgld] adj. Moderno, na; recién inventado, da.

newfound [—ˈfaund] adj. Nuevo, va.

Newfoundland [—fəndˈlænd] pr. n. GEOGR. Terranova, *f.* || *Newfoundland dog*, terranova, *m.*

New Guinea [—ˈgini] pr. n. GEOGR. Nueva Guinea, *f.*

new-laid [—leid] adj. Recién puesto, fresco (egg).

newly [—li] adv. Nuevamente (in a new way). || Recién, recientemente: *newly painted wall*, pared recién pintada. || *He is newly arrived*, acaba de llegar.

newlywed [—liˈwed] n. Recién casado, da.

newness [—nis] n. Novedad, *f.* (novelty). || FIG. Inexperiencia, *f.* (of s.o.).

New Orleans [—ˈɔ:liənz] pr. n. GEOGR. Nueva Orleáns, *f.*

news [nju:z] n. Noticia, *f.* (piece of news), noticias, *f. pl.*: *this is good news*, es una buena noticia; *to send news of o.s.*, dar noticias de uno. || Noticias, *f. pl.*, informaciones, *f. pl.*: *financial news*, informaciones financieras. || Crónica, *f.*: *musical news*, crónica musical. || Actualidad, *f.*: *to be in the news*, ser de actualidad. || Diario (*m.*) hablado, noticias, *f. pl.* (on the radio). || Noticias, *f. pl.*, telediario, *m.* (on television). || CINEM. Noticiario, *m.* (film). || — *A piece of news*, una noticia. || *Have I got news for you!*, ¡menuda noticia tengo que darte! || *Have you heard the news?*, ¿te has enterado de la última noticia? || *If the news breaks*, si la noticia llega a oídos del público. || *It was news to me*, me cogió de nuevas. || *Latest news*, últimas noticias. || *No news is good news*, las malas noticias llegan las primeras. || *That's no news*, eso no es ninguna novedad. || *To break the news to s.o.*, dar una noticia a alguien. || *What news?* o *what's the news?*, ¿qué hay de nuevo?

— OBSERV. *News* se construye siempre con el verbo en singular. Sin embargo es incorrecto decir *a news*. En su lugar debe emplearse *a piece of news* o *a news item*.

news agency [—ˈeidʒənsi] n. Agencia (*f.*) de información *or* de prensa.

newsagent [—ˌeidʒənt] n. Vendedor (*m.*) de periódicos.

newsboard [—bɔ:d] n. Tablero (*m.*) *or* tablón (*m.*) de anuncios.

newsboy [—bɔi] n. Muchacho (*m.*) vendedor de periódicos (seller). || Muchacho (*m.*) que reparte periódicos (deliverer).

news bulletin [—ˈbulitin] n. Boletín (*m.*) informativo, noticias, *f. pl.*, noticiario, *m.*

newscast [—kɑ:st] n. Noticiario, *m.*, noticias, *f. pl.*

newscaster [—ˈkɑ:stə*] n. Presentador, ra; locutor, ra [del telediario] (on television). || Locutor, ra [del boletín informativo] (on radio).

news conference [—ˈkɔnfərəns] n. Rueda (*f.*) de prensa, conferencia (*f.*) de prensa.

news correspondent [—ˌkɔrisˈpɔndənt] n. Corresponsal, *m.* & *f.* [de prensa, radio o televisión].

news dealer [—ˈdi:lə*] n. U. S. Vendedor (*m.*) de periódicos.

news flash [—flæʃ] n. Noticia (*f.*) de última hora, flash, *m.*

news item [—ˈaitəm] n. Noticia, *f.*

newsletter [—ˈletə*] n. Hoja (*f.*) informativa, boletín, *m.* (printed sheet).

newsman [—mən] n. Vendedor (*m.*) de periódicos (newsagent). || Periodista, *m.*, reportero, *m.* (reporter). || Locutor, *m.* [del boletín informativo] (newscaster on radio). || Presentador, *m.*, locutor, *m.* [del telediario] (newscaster on television).

— OBSERV. El plural de *newsman* es *newsmen*.

newsmonger [—ˈmʌŋgə*] n. Chismoso, sa.

newsmongering [—ˈmʌŋgəriŋ] n. Chismorreo, *m.*

newspaper [—ˈpeipə*] n. Periódico, *m.*, diario, *m.* (daily). || — *Newspaper correspondent*, corresponsal (*m.*) de periódico. || *Weekly newspaper*, semanario, *m.*

newspaperman [—ˈpeipəmən] n. Periodista, *m.*

— OBSERV. El plural de *newspaperman* es *newspapermen*.

newspaperwoman [—ˌpeipəˌwumən] n. Periodista, *f.*

— OBSERV. El plural es *newspaperwomen*.

newsprint [—print] n. Papel (*m.*) de periódico.

newsreel [—ri:l] n. Noticiario, *m.* (film).

— OBSERV. In Spain this word is usually translated by *No-Do* which stands for *noticiario documental*.

newsroom [—rum] n. Sala (*f.*) de lectura de los periódicos (in a library). || Sala (*f.*) de redacción (in a newspaper office, radio station, etc.).

newsstand [—stænd] n. Quiosco (*m.*) *or* puesto (*m.*) de periódicos.

newsworthy [—ˌwə:ði] adj. De interés periodístico.

newsy [—i] adj. U. S. Lleno de noticias.

newt [nju:t] n. ZOOL. Tritón, *m.*

newton [ˈnju:tn] n. Newton, *m.*, neutonio, *m.* (unit of force).

Newtonian [nju:ˈtəunjən] adj. Neutoniano, na; newtoniano, na.

New York [ˈnju:ˈjɔ:k] pr. n. GEOGR. Nueva York, *f.*

New Yorker [—ə*] n. Neoyorquino, na.

New Zealand [ˈnju:ˈzi:lənd] pr. n. GEOGR. Nueva Zelanda, *f.*, Nueva Zelandia, *f.*

New Zealander [—ə*] n. Neocelandés, esa; neozelandés, esa.

next [nekst] adj. Vecino, na; de al lado: *the next room*, la habitación de al lado. || Próximo, ma: *the next train to London*, el próximo tren para Londres; *(the) next time I sing*, la próxima vez que cante; *the next stop*, la próxima parada. || Siguiente: *the next chapter*, el capítulo siguiente; *the next day, morning*, el día, la mañana siguiente. || Que viene, próximo, ma: *next year*, el año que viene. || — *Next best*, el segundo [en calidad]. || *Next door*, [en] la casa de al lado. || *Next door but one to me*, dos casas más allá de la mía. || *Next please!*, ¡el siguiente por favor! || *On Sunday next*, el próximo domingo, el domingo que viene. || *On 23rd November next*, el 23 de noviembre próximo. || *The next but one*, el segundo después de éste. || *The next day but one*, dos días después. || *The next larger size*, una talla más grande, un número más grande. || *The next life*, la otra vida. || *The next of kin*, see KIN. || *This time next month, next year*, el mes, el año que viene por estas fechas. || *To be next after s.o.*, ser el primero después de alguien. || *To live next door to*, ser vecino de. || *What next?*, y ahora ¿qué? || *What next, please?*, ¿algo más? (in shop). || *Who is next?*, ¿a quién le toca?, ¿quién es el siguiente?, ¿de quién es el turno?

— Adv. Después, luego: *next came the bishop*, luego vino el obispo. || Ahora (now). || La próxima vez: *when we next see each other*, cuando nos veamos la próxima vez. || *Who comes next?*, ¿a quién le toca?, ¿quién es el siguiente?, ¿de quién es el turno?

— Prep. Cerca de, junto a, al lado de (s.o., sth.): *she was sitting next me*, estaba sentada junto a mí *or* a mi lado. || — *For next to nothing*, por casi nada. || *Next to*, cerca de, junto a, al lado de. || *Next to impossible*, casi imposible. || *Next to nobody*, casi nadie. || FAM. *The thing next my heart*, lo que más aprecio, lo más entrañable para mí. || *To come next to s.o.*, acercarse a uno. || *To wear wool next to one's skin*, llevar lana en contacto con la piel.

next-door [ˈneksˈdɔ:*] adj. De al lado.

nexus [ˈneksəs] n. Nexo, *m.*, vínculo, *m.*

— OBSERV. El plural de *nexus* es *nexus* o *nexuses*.

niacin [ˈnaiəsin] n. Ácido (*m.*) nicotínico.

Niagara [naiˈægərə] pr. n. GEOGR. Niágara, *m.*: *Niagara Falls*, Cataratas del Niágara.

nib [nib] n. Plumilla, *f.*, plumín, *m.* (of a pen). || Punta, *f.*, pico, *m.* (of tool). || Pico, *m.* (of bird).

nibble [ˈnibl] n. Mordisqueo, *m.*, mordedura, *f.* (act of nibbling). || Mordisco, *m.* (bite). || Roedura, *f.* (of mice). || Pizca, *f.*, pedacito, *m.* (bit). || Bocado, *m.* (bite to eat). || Mordida, *f.*, picada, *f.* (in fishing). || — *I never had a nibble all day*, no han picado en todo el día. || *To have a nibble*, picar un poco (at food).

nibble [ˈnibl] v. tr. Roer, mordisquear: *mice have been nibbling the cheese*, los ratones han mordisqueado el queso. || Picar (fish).

— V. intr. Mordisquear, mordiscar; *to nibble at a biscuit*, mordisquear una galleta. || Picar (fish at the bait). || FIG. Sentirse tentado: *to nibble at an offer*, sentirse tentado por una oferta. || *To nibble at one's food*, comisquear.

Nibelungen [ˈni:bəluŋən] pl. pr. n. Nibelungos, *m.*

nibs [nibz] n. FAM. *His nibs*, su señoría.

Nicaragua [ˌnikəˈrægjuə] pr. n. GEOGR. Nicaragua, *f.*

Nicaraguan [—n] adj./n. Nicaragüense.

nice [nais] adj. Simpático, ca (likeable): *she is very nice*, es muy simpática. || Amable [*Amer.*, gentil] (kind): *that is very nice of you*, es usted muy amable. || Bueno, na; agradable (agreeable): *nice dinner*, buena cena; *nice evening*, velada agradable. || Bonito, ta [*Amer.*, lindo, da]: *nice car*, bonito coche. || Mono, na; guapo, pa; bonito, ta [*Amer.*, lindo, da] (pretty): *you're looking very nice*, estás muy mona. || Ameno, na (pleasant): *a nice book*, un libro ameno. || Agradable: *to say nice things*, decir cosas agradables. || Bueno, na (weather). || Difícil, delicado, da (finicky). || Difícil, exigente, escrupuloso, sa; meticuloso, sa (punctilious). || Minucioso, sa; meticuloso, sa (enquiry). || Sutil (distinction). || Delicado, da; difícil (experiment, point). || Bueno, na: *to have a nice ear for music*, tener buen oído para la música. || Atinado, da; acertado, da: *a nice judgment*, un juicio atinado. || Preciso, sa (accurate). || Agudo, da (eye). || Delicado, da; fino, na (refined taste, manners). || Bien: *it smells, it tastes nice*, huele, sabe bien. || Decente: *it is not a nice joke*, no es un chiste decente. || FAM. Menudo, da (unsatisfactory): *a nice mess we are in now!*, ¡en menudo lío nos hemos metido!; *a nice friend you turned out to be!*, ¡menudo amigo me has salido! || — *A nice little sum*, una buena cantidad. || *As nice as nice can be*, de lo más agradable. || *How nice!*, ¡qué amable! (kind), ¡qué precioso!, ¡qué bonito! (pretty). || *How nice of you to come!*, ¡qué amable haber venido! || *It's nice and warm in here*, hace un calor agradable aquí dentro. || *It's nice here*, se está bien aquí. || *Nice and...*, bien, bastante (quite): *it is nice and easy*, es bien fácil; bien, muy (very): *nice and friendly*, bien simpático. || *Nice people*, buena gente. || *There's a nice thing to say!*, ¡qué agradable! (with irony). || *To be a nice fellow*, ser un buen chico. || *To have a nice time*, pasarlo bien, divertirse. || *What a nice gesture!*, ¡qué detalle más delicado!

nice-looking [—ˈlukiŋ] adj. Guapo, pa; mono, na; bien parecido, da [*Amer.*, lindo, da] (person). || Precioso, sa; bonito, ta [*Amer.*, lindo, da] (object).

nicely [—li] adv. Amablemente [*Amer.*, gentilmente] (kindly). || Agradablemente (pleasantly). || Cuidadosamente (carefully). || Bien: *very nicely, thank you*, muy bien, muchas gracias; *she speaks very nicely about you*, habla muy bien de ti; *we're very nicely situated*, estamos muy bien situados. || *That will do nicely*, así está muy bien.

niceness [—nis] n. Amabilidad, *f.*, simpatía, *f.* [*Amer.*, gentileza, *f.*] (kindness). || Lo agradable (pleasantness). || Meticulosidad, *f.* (punctiliousness). || Delicadeza, *f.* (refinement). || Sutileza, *f.*, sutilidad, *f.*, fineza, *f.*

nicety [—ti] n. Precisión, *f.*, exactitud, *f.* (exactness). || Sutileza, *f.* (subtlety). || Delicadeza, *f.* || — *Niceties*, sutilezas. || *To a nicety*, perfectamente.

niche [ni:ʃ] n. Hornacina, *f.*, nicho, *m.* (in a wall). || FIG. Hueco, *m.* (place): *he found his niche in administration*, encontró un hueco en la administración. | Buena colocación, *f.* (good job).

niche [ni:ʃ] v. tr. Poner en una hornacina.

nick [nik] n. Muesca, *f.* (notch). || Cran, *m.* (in printing). || Uña, *f.*, muesca, *f.* (for opening penknife). || Mella, *f.* (in edge of blade). || Hendidura, *f.* (in screw head). || Desportillado, *m.*, desportilladura, *f.* (of a dish). || Rasguño, *m.* (slight wound). || FAM. Chirona, *f.* (jail). || FIG. *In the nick of time*, en el momento preciso *or* oportuno, a punto (at the right moment), justo a tiempo (just in time).

nick [nik] v. tr. Hacer muescas en (to make nicks). || Cortar (to cut). || Hacer una hendidura en (a screw head). || Señalar, marcar (cards). || Desportillar (a dish). || Mellar (a blade). || Ganar (in dice games). || FAM. Acertar (to guess). | Coger, pillar, pescar, agarrar (to arrest). | Birlar (to steal).

— V. intr. *To nick at*, criticar. || *To nick in*, meterse en.

Nick [nik] pr. n. Nico, *m.*, Nicolás, *m.* (diminutive of Nicholas). || FAM. *Old Nick*, Patillas (the Devil).

nickel [ˈnikl] n. Níquel, *m.* (metal). || U. S. Moneda (*f.*) de cinco centavos. || — *Nickel bronze*, cuproníquel, *m.* || *Nickel silver*, plata alemana.

nickel [ˈnikl] v. tr. Niquelar.

nickelling [—iŋ] n. Niquelado, *m.*

nickel-plate [—ˈpleit] v. tr. Niquelar.

nickel-plating [—ˈpleitiŋ] n. Niquelado, *m.*

nickname [ˈnikneim] n. Apodo, *m.*, mote, *m.* (name). || Diminutivo, *m.* (diminutive).

nickname [ˈnikneim] v. tr. Apodar, poner de apodo *or* de mote: *they nicknamed him "toothy"*, le pusieron de mote "el dientes". || Llamar con un diminutivo.

nicotine [ˈnikəti:n] n. Nicotina, *f.*

nicotinic [ˌnikəˈti:nik] adj. Nicotínico, ca.

nicotinism [ˈnikəti:nizəm] n. Nicotinismo, *m.*, nicotismo, *m.*

nictation [nikˈteiʃən] n. Nictación, *f.*

nictitating [ˈniktiteitiŋ] adj. ZOOL. Nictitante.

nidation [niˈdeiʃən] n. Nidación, *f.*

nidification [ˌnidifiˈkeiʃən] n. Nidificación, *f.*

nidify [ˈnidifai] v. intr. Hacer el nido, anidar, nidificar.

nidus [ˈnaidəs] n. ZOOL. Nido, *m.* (of insects). || MED. Foco, *m.*, centro, *m.*

— OBSERV. El plural de *nidus* es *nidi* o *niduses*.

niece [ni:s] n. Sobrina, *f.*

niello [niˈeləu] n. TECH. Niel, *m.* (of metal). | Nielado, *m.* (process).

— OBSERV. El plural de *niello* es *nielli* o *niellos*.

niff [nif] n. FAM. Peste, *f.*, hedor, *m.*

niff [nif] v. intr. FAM. Apestar.

niffy [—i] adj. FAM. Apestoso, sa.

nifty [ˈnifti] adj. FAM. Formidable, estupendo, da (splendid).

nigella [naiˈdʒelə] n. Neguilla, *f.*

Niger [ˈnaidʒə*] n. pr. n. Níger, *m.*

Nigeria [naiˈdʒiəriə] pr. n. GEOGR. Nigeria, *f.*

Nigerian [—n] adj./n. Nigeriano, na.

niggard [ˈnigəd] adj./n. Tacaño, ña; avaro, ra (stingy).

niggardliness [—linis] n. Avaricia, *f.*, tacañería, *f.*

niggardly [—li] adj. Avaro, ra; tacaño, ña. || Miserable (portion, amount).

— Adv. Tacañamente, mezquinamente.

nigger [ˈnigə*] n. FAM. Negro, gra. || — FAM. *There is a nigger in the woodpile*, aquí hay gato encerrado. | *To work like a nigger*, trabajar como un negro.

— OBSERV. La palabra *nigger* es muy despectiva.

niggle [ˈnigl] v. intr. Reparar en minucias, pararse en pequeñeces.

niggling [—iŋ] adj. Insignificante, de poca monta (trifling). || Demasiado meticuloso, sa; demasiado cuidadoso, sa (punctilious). || Molesto, ta (annoying).

nigh [nai] adv. (Ant.). Cerca. || *Nigh on*, casi.

— Prep. (Ant.). Cerca de.

night [nait] n. Noche, *f.*: *in the silence of the night*, en el silencio de la noche. || FIG. Noche, *f.*, oscuridad, *f.*, tinieblas, *f. pl.*: *the night of ignorance*, las tinieblas de la ignorancia; *the dark nights of the soul*, las noches oscuras del alma. || THEATR. Representación, *f.*, función, *f.* || Velada, *f.* (musical evening). || — *All night* o *the whole night* o *all night long*, toda la noche. || *At night* o *by night*, por la noche, de noche. || *Dark night*, noche cerrada. || *Far into the night*, hasta altas horas de la noche, hasta muy entrada la noche. || *First night*, noche de estreno, primera representación (first performance). || *Good night!*, ¡buenas noches! || *I am used to late nights*, estoy acostumbrado a acostarme tarde. || *In the night*, por la noche, durante la noche. || *It is my night off* o *out*, es mi noche libre. || *It is night*, es de noche. || *It was 10 o'clock at night*, eran las 10 de la noche. || *Last night*, anoche, ayer por la noche (yesterday), último día, última función *or* representación (of a play), último día (of a film). || *Night is falling* o *is coming on*, está anocheciendo, se hace de noche, se está haciendo de noche. || *Night out*, noche de fiesta. || *Sleepless night*, noche en blanco, noche en claro, noche toledana. || *The Arabian Nights*, Las mil y una noches. || *The night before*, la noche anterior. || *The night before last*, antes de anoche, anteanoche. || *The night before the journey*, la víspera del viaje. || *Thursday is my chess night*, los jueves por la noche juego al ajedrez. || *To have a bad night*, pasar una mala noche, no poder dormir, dormir mal. || *To make a night of it*, pasarse la noche de juerga. || *Tomorrow night*, mañana por la noche. || *To pass the night*, pasar la noche. || *To say good night to s.o.*, dar las buenas noches a uno. || *To spend the night*, pasar la noche. || *To stay up all night*, pasar la noche en claro *or* en blanco. || *To turn day into night*, hacer de la noche día. || *To work day and night*, trabajar noche y día. || *To work nights*, trabajar de noche. || *Wedding night*, noche de bodas. || *When night fell*, al caer la noche.

— Adj. Nocturno, na; de noche: *night boat, train, flight*, barco, tren, vuelo nocturno.

night bird [—bə:d] n. Pájaro nocturno (in zoology). || Noctámbulo, *m.*, trasnochador, *m.*, pájaro nocturno (person).

night blindness [—ˈblaindnis] n. Ceguera (*f.*) nocturna.

nightcap [—kæp] n. Gorro (*m.*) de dormir (worn in bed). || Bebida (*f.*) tomada antes de acostarse (drink).

nightclothes [—kləuðz] pl. n. Ropa (*f. sing.*) de dormir.

nightclub [—klʌb] n. Club (*m.*) nocturno, sala (*f.*) de fiestas, "night club", *m.*

nightdress [—dres] n. Camisón, *m.*, camisa (*f.*) de dormir.

nightfall [—fɔ:l] n. Caída (*f.*) de la noche, anochecer, *m.*: *at nightfall*, al anochecer.

nightgown [—gaun] n. Camisón, *m.*, camisa (*f.*) de dormir.

nighthawk [—hɔ:k] n. ZOOL. Chotacabras, *m. inv.* (bird). || FAM. Pájaro (*m.*) nocturno, trasnochador, *m.*, noctámbulo, *m.* (person).
nightie [—i] n. FAM. Camisón, *m.*
nightingale [—iŋgeil] n. Ruiseñor, *m.* (bird).
nightjar [—dʒɑ:*] n. Chotacabras, *m. inv.* (bird).
night lamp [—læmp] n. Lamparita (*f.*) de noche.
night letter [—ˈletə*] n. Telegrama (*m.*) de noche.
night life [—laif] n. Vida (*f.*) nocturna.
night-light [—lait] n. Lamparilla, *f.*
nightlong [—lɔŋ] adj. Que dura toda la noche.
— Adv. Durante toda la noche.
nightly [—li] adj. Nocturno, na; de noche. || De cada noche.
— Adv. Por las noches (at night). || Todas las noches, cada noche (every night).
nightmare [—mɛə*] n. Pesadilla, *f.*
— Adj. De pesadilla: *a nightmare journey*, un viaje de pesadilla.
nightmarish [—mɛəriʃ] adj. De pesadilla.
night owl [—aul] n. See NIGHTHAWK.
night-robe [—rəub] n. Camisón, *m.*, camisa (*f.*) de dormir.
nights [—s] adv. FAM. Por la noche, de noche: *to work nights*, trabajar de noche.
night school [—sku:l] n. Escuela (*f.*) nocturna.
nightshade [—ʃeid] n. BOT. Hierba (*f.*) mora. || *Deadly nightshade*, belladona, *f.*
night shift [—ʃift] n. Turno (*m.*) de noche.
nightshirt [—ʃə:t] n. Camisón, *m.*, camisa (*f.*) de dormir (for men).
night soil [—sɔil] n. Estiércol, *m.* (fertilizer).
night spot [—spɔt] n. Sala (*f.*) de fiestas.
nightstick [—stik] n. U. S. Porra, *f.* (of a policeman).
night table [—ˈteibl] n. Mesilla (*f.*) de noche.
nighttime [—taim] n. Noche, *f.* || *At nighttime* o *in the nighttime*, por la noche, de noche.
night watch [—wɔtʃ] n. Guarda (*m.*) nocturno, vigilante (*m.*) nocturno [*Amer.*, nochero, *m.*] (person). || Sereno, *m.* (for houses in Spain). || Guardia (*f.*) de noche *or* nocturna (period of duty). || Ronda (*f.*) nocturna (of a guard, watchman).
night watchman [—ˈwɔtʃmən] n. Guarda (*m.*) nocturno [*Amer.*, nochero, *m.*]. || Sereno, *m.* (for houses in Spain).
— OBSERV. El plural de ***night watchman*** es ***night watchmen***.
nightwear [—wɛə*] n. Ropa (*f.*) de dormir.
nighty [—i] n. FAM. Camisón, *m.*
nigrescent [naiˈgresnt] adj. Negruzco, ca.
nigritude [ˈnigritju:d] n. Negrura, *f.*
nihilism [ˈnaiilizəm] n. Nihilismo, *m.*
nihilist [ˈnaiilist] adj./n. Nihilista.
nihilistic [naiiˈlistik] adj. Nihilista.
nihility [naiˈhiliti] n. Nada, *f.*
nil [nil] n. Nada, *f.* || Ninguno, na (on an official form). || SP. Cero, *m.*: *we beat them three nil*, les ganamos por tres a cero.
Nile [nail] pr. n. GEOGR. Nilo, *m.* (river): *Upper, Blue Nile*, Alto Nilo, Nilo Azul.
nimble [ˈnimbl] adj. Ágil (person, etc.): *nimble at doing sth.*, ágil para hacer algo. || Ágil, vivo, va; rápido, da (mind).
nimbleness [—lnis] n. Agilidad, *f.* || Vivacidad, *f.*, agilidad, *f.*, rapidez, *f.* (of mind).
nimbly [—li] adv. Ágilmente.
nimbostratus [ˈnimbəuˌstreitəs] n. Nimboestrato, *m.* (cloud).
nimbus [ˈnimbəs] n. Nimbo, *m.* (cloud). || Aureola, *f.*, nimbo, *m.* (halo).
— OBSERV. El plural de ***nimbus*** es ***nimbuses*** o ***nimbi***.
nincompoop [ˈninkəmpu:p] n. FAM. Lelo, la; memo, ma; mentecato, ta (idiot).
nine [nain] adj. Nueve. || *Nine times out of ten*, en el noventa por ciento de los casos.
— N. Nueve, *m.* (number, card). || — FAM. *Dressed up to the nines*, de punta en blanco. || *Nine o'clock*, las nueve. || *Ten past nine*, las nueve y diez. || MATH. *To cast out the nines*, hacer la prueba del nueve.
ninefold [—fəuld] adj. Multiplicado por nueve.
— Adv. Nueve veces.
nine hundred [—ˈhʌndrəd] adj./n. Novecientos, tas.
ninehundredth [—ˈhʌndrədθ] adj./n. Noningentésimo, ma.
ninepin [ˈnainpin] n. Bolo, *m.* (skittle). || — Pl. Juego (*m. sing.*) de bolos.
nineteen [ˈnainˈti:n] adj. Diecinueve, diez y nueve. || FIG. *To talk nineteen to the dozen*, hablar como una cotorra *or* por los codos.
— N. Diecinueve, *m.*, diez y nueve, *m.*
nineteenth [—θ] adj. Decimonoveno, na; decimonono, na (ordinal). || Diecinueveavo, va (partitive): *nineteenth part*, diecinueveava parte. || *The nineteenth century*, el siglo diecinueve.
— N. Decimonoveno, na; diez y nueve, *m.* & *f.*, diecinueve, *m.* & *f.* (in a series). || Diecinueveavo, *m.*, diecinueveava parte, *f.* (fraction). || Diecinueve, diez y nueve: *John XIX* (*the nineteenth*), Juan XIX [diez y nueve]. || Diecinueve, *m.*, día (*m.*) diecinueve (date): *the nineteenth of May*, el diecinueve de mayo.
ninetieth [ˈnaintiiθ] adj. Nonagésimo, ma; noventavo, va.
— N. Nonagésimo, ma; noventa, *m.* & *f.* (in a series). || Nonagésimo, *m.*, nonagésima parte, *f.* (fraction).
ninety [ˈnainti] adj. Noventa.
— N. Noventa, *m.*: *ninety-four*, noventa y cuatro. || — *The nineties*, los años noventa (period). || *To be in one's nineties*, tener unos noventa años.
ninetyfold [—fəuld] adj. Multiplicado por noventa.
— Adv. Noventa veces.
ninny [ˈnini] n. FAM. Memo, ma; mentecato, ta (idiot).
ninth [nainθ] adj. Noveno, na: *the ninth house*, la novena casa.
— N. Noveno, na: *I was the ninth in the queue*, era el noveno en la cola. || Novena parte, *f.* (fraction). || Nueve, *m.*, día (*m.*) nueve (day of the month): *the ninth of May*, el día nueve de mayo. || Nono: *Pious IX* (*the ninth*), Pío IX [nono]. || Noveno, na: *Alphonse IX* (*the ninth*), Alfonso IX [noveno]. || MUS. Novena, *f.*
ninthly [—li] adv. En noveno lugar.
niobium [naiˈəubiəm] n. CHEM. Niobio, *m.*
nip [nip] n. Pizca, *f.*, gota, *f.* (of liquid). || Trago, *m.* (drink). || Pellizco, *m.* (pinch). || Mordisco, *m.*, mordedura, *f.* (bite). || Estrechamiento, *m.* (narrowing). || Frío (*m.*) seco (in the air). || AGR. Helada, *f.* (freeze). || FIG. Palabras (*f. pl.*) mordaces, pulla, *f.* (cutting words). || MAR. Doblez, *f.*, vuelta, *f.* (in a cable). || GEOGR. Recorte, *m.* (of coastline). || — U. S. *The race was nip and tuck*, la carrera estuvo muy reñida. || *There was a nip in the air*, hacía algo de frío. || *To feel the nip of the wind*, sentir el viento penetrante.
nip [nip] v. tr. Pellizcar (to pinch). || Morder (to bite). || Coger, pillar: *to nip one's fingers in the door*, cogerse los dedos con la puerta. || Atenazar (with pincers). || Beber a traguitos (to drink). || AGR. Helar, quemar (a plant by the frost). || Cortar, recortar (to cut). || Cortar (cold). || FAM. Birlar (to steal). || FIG. *To nip in the bud*, cortar de raíz.
— V. intr. FAM. Correr (to run, to go fast): *we were nipping along at 100 m. p. h.*, corríamos a 100 millas por hora. || Beber a traguitos (to drink). || — *Nip across to the baker's for me*, pega un salto a la panadería, por favor. || *Nip along!*, ¡date prisa! || *To nip in*, entrar un momento. || *To nip off*, largarse. || *To nip on a bus*, coger al vuelo un autobús. || *To nip out for a moment*, salir un rato.
Nip [nip] n. U. S. FAM. Nipón, ona (Japanese).
— OBSERV. La palabra ***Nip*** es sumamente despectiva.
nipper [ˈnipə*] n. FAM. Chiquillo, *m.*, chaval, *m.* (young boy). || Boca, *f.*, pata, *f.* (of a crustacean). || Pala, *f.* (of a horse). || — Pl. Alicates, *m.* (pliers). || Tenazas, *f.* (pincers). || Pinzas, *f.* (forceps).
nipping [ˈnipiŋ] adj. Cortante (cold). || Mordiente, mordaz (remark).
nipple [ˈnipl] n. Pezón, *m.* (of female mammals). || Tetilla, *f.* (of male mammals). || Tetina, *f.*, tetilla, *f.*, boquilla, *f.* (of an infant's feeding bottle). || Protuberancia, *f.* (protuberance). || Cerro, *m.*, montecillo, *m.* (hill). || TECH. Pezón (*m.*) de engrase (for greasing). | Boquilla (*f.*) de unión (connexion). || AUT. Tuerca, *f.* (of a wheel). || Chimenea, *f.* (of a gun).
Nippon [ˈnipɔn] pr. n. Japón, *m.* (Japan).
Nipponese [ˌnipəˈni:z] adj./n. Nipón, ona: *they are Nipponese*, son japoneses.
nippy [ˈnipi] adj. FAM. Rápido, da (person). | Rápido, da; veloz (vehicle). | Que tiene buena aceleración (car). || Cortante, vivo, va (air). || Fresquito, ta (day). || *And be nippy about it*, y date prisa.
Nirvana [niəˈvɑ:nə] pr. n. REL. Nirvana, *m.*
nisei [ˈniˌsei] n. U. S. Nisei, ciudadano de los Estados Unidos de padres japoneses.
— OBSERV. El plural de ***nisei*** es ***nisei*** o ***niseis***.
nisi [ˈnaisai] adj. Bajo condición (decision). || Provisional (decree).
nit [nit] n. Liendre, *f.* (of a louse). || FAM. Papanatas, *m. inv.*, imbécil, *m.* & *f.* (idiot).
niter [ˈnaitə*] n. U. S. See NITRE.
nitrate [ˈnaitreit] n. CHEM. Nitrato, *m.*: *sodium nitrate*, nitrato sódico.
nitrate [ˈnaitreit] v. tr. CHEM. Nitratar.
nitrated [—id] adj. CHEM. Nitrado, da; nitratado, da.
nitration [naiˈtreiʃən] n. CHEM. Nitratación, *f.*, nitración, *f.*
nitre [ˈnaitə*] n. Nitro, *m.*, nitrato (*m.*) potásico, salitre, *m.*
nitre bed [—bed] n. Nitral, *m.*, nitrería, *f.*
nitric [ˈnaitrik] adj. CHEM. Nítrico, ca.
nitride [ˈnaitraid] n. CHEM. Nitruro, *m.*
nitriding [—iŋ] n. CHEM. Nitruración, *f.*
nitrification [ˌnaitrifiˈkeiʃən] n. CHEM. Nitrificación, *f.*
nitrify [ˈnaitrəfai] v. tr. CHEM. Nitrificar.
nitrifying [—iŋ] adj. CHEM. Nitrificador, ra.
nitrile [ˈnaitril] n. CHEM. Nitrilo, *m.*
nitrite [ˈnaitrait] n. CHEM. Nitrito, *m.*
nitrobenzene [ˈnaitrəuˌbenzi:n] n. CHEM. Nitrobenceno, *m.*
nitrocellulose [ˈnaitrəuˌseljuləus] n. CHEM. Nitrocelulosa, *f.*
nitrogen [ˈnaitrədʒən] n. CHEM. Nitrógeno, *m.*
nitrogenation [ˌnaitrədʒəˈneiʃən] n. Nitruración, *f.*
nitrogenization [naiˌtrɔdʒənaiˈzeiʃən] n. Nitrogenización, *f.*
nitrogenize [naiˈtrɔdʒənaiz] v. tr. Nitrogenar.
nitrogenous [naiˈtrɔdʒinəs] adj. Nitrogenado, da.

nitroglycerine or **nitroglycerin** [ˌnaitrəugliseˈri:n] n. CHEM. Nitroglicerina, *f.*

nitrotoluene [ˌnaitrəuˈtɔljuin] n. CHEM. Nitrotolueno, *m.*

nitrous [ˈnaitrəs] adj. CHEM. Nitroso, sa.

nitty [ˈniti] adj. Lleno de liendres.

nitwit [ˈnitwit] n. FAM. Burro, rra; mentecato, ta; cretino, na (idiot).

niveous [ˈniviəs] adj. Nevoso, sa; níveo, a.

nix [niks] n. FAM. Nada.
— Interj. ¡Ni hablar!

no [nəu] adj. Ninguno, na: *he's no genious*, no es ningún genio; *it's no trouble*, no es ninguna molestia. || — *He's no artist*, de artista no tiene nada, no es ningún artista. || *He's no friend of mine*, no es amigo mío. || *He's no great walker*, no es aficionado a andar. || *Make no mistake about it*, no lo dudes. || *No admittance*, prohibida la entrada. || *No fooling* o *no kidding*, en serio, sin broma. || *No man*, nadie, ninguno (nobody). || *No matter*, no importa. || *No... no...*, sin... no hay...: *no contestants, no championship*, sin competidores no hay campeonato. || *No nonsense!*, ¡sin tonterías! || *No one*, nadie, ninguno, na (nobody): *no one else*, nadie más. || *No one man can do it*, es demasiado para un hombre solo. || *No parking*, prohibido estacionar, prohibido aparcar. || *No smoking*, se prohibe fumar, prohibido fumar. || *No thoroughfare*, calle (*f.*) sin salida (no through road), calle interceptada (road blocked), prohibido el paso (no entry). || *No two men think alike*, no hay dos hombres que piensen igual. || *No use*, inútil. || *Of little or no interest*, de casi ningún interés. || *Orders or no orders, I'm staying*, no me importan las órdenes, me quedo. || *Say no more*, no digas más. || *She's no beauty*, no es nada guapa. || *There is no agreeing with him*, es imposible ponerse de acuerdo con él. || *To no purpose*, en vano (in vain), sin objetivo (aimlessly). || *We have no tea*, no tenemos té. || *With no*, sin: *with no money*, sin dinero.
— N. No, *m.*: *he wouldn't take no for an answer*, no estaba dispuesto a aceptar un no como respuesta. || Voto (*m.*) en contra (vote): *ayes and noes*, votos a favor y votos en contra. || *The noes have it*, hay mayoría de votos en contra.
— Adv. No: *no sir!*, ¡no señor!; *no better than before*, no mejor que antes; *whether he likes it or no*, le guste o no. || — FAM. *No can do*, imposible. || *No less than*, no menos de. || *No longer*, ya no, no... más. || *No more*, ya no. || *No more than*, no más de. || *No sooner*, apenas, no bien: *I had no sooner arrived than they called me*, apenas había llegado cuando me llamaron, no bien llegué me llamaron. || *No sooner said than done*, dicho y hecho. || *She is no nicer than you*, no es más mona que tú. || *To say no*, decir que no.

no-account [—əˈkaunt] adj. U. S. FAM. Insignificante, sin importancia.

Noah [ˈnəuə] pr. n. REL. Noé, *m.* || *Noah's ark*, el arca de Noé.

nob [nɔb] n. FAM. Pez (*m.*) gordo (important person). | Melón, *m.*, chola, *f.* (head).

no ball [ˈnəuˈbɔ:l] n. SP. Lanzamiento (*m.*) nulo (cricket). | Pelota (*f.*) mala *or* nula (tennis).

nobble [ˈnɔbl] v. tr. Drogar (a racehorse, greyhound). || Sobornar (a person). || FAM. Birlar (to steal). | Coger, pescar (to arrest).

nobelium [nəuˈbeliəm] n. CHEM. Nobelio, *m.*

nobiliary [nəuˈbiliəri] adj. Nobiliario, ria.

nobility [nəuˈbiliti] n. Nobleza, *f.*

noble [nəubl] adj. Noble: *of noble birth*, de noble cuna; *of noble descent*, de noble alcurnia *or* linaje; *noble sentiments*, sentimientos nobles; *noble metal*, metal noble. || Magnánimo, ma; generoso, sa: *noble gesture*, acción magnánima. || Grandioso, sa; magnífico, ca: *a noble mansion*, una mansión grandiosa. || *Noble gas*, gas (*m.*) inerte.
— N. Noble, *m.* & *f.* (peer or peeress).

nobleman [—mən] n. Noble, *m.*

— OBSERV. El plural de *nobleman* es *noblemen*.

nobleness [—nis] n. Nobleza, *f.* || Grandiosidad, *f.* (majesty).

noblewoman [—ˈwumən] n. Noble, *f.*

— OBSERV. El plural de *noblewoman* es *noblewomen*.

nobody [ˈnəubədi] pron. Nadie: *nobody came*, no vino nadie; *I spoke to nobody*, no hablé con nadie. || — *Nobody but*, nadie más que. || *Nobody else*, nadie más.
— N. FAM. Nadie, don nadie, *m.*

nock [nɔk] n. Muesca, *f.*

nock [nɔk] v. tr. Ajustar, empulgar (to place an arrow). || Hacer una muesca en (to notch).

noctambulant [nɔkˈtæmbjulənt] adj. Noctámbulo, la. || Sonámbulo, la; somnámbulo, la (sleepwalking).

noctambulism [nɔkˈtæmbjulizəm] n. Noctambulismo, *m.* || Sonambulismo, *m.*, somnambulismo, *m.* (sleepwalking).

noctambulist [nɔktˈæmbjulist] n. Noctámbulo, la. || Sonámbulo, la; somnámbulo, la (sleepwalker).

noctivagant [nɔkˈtivəgənt] adj./n. Noctámbulo, la.

noctivagation [ˌnɔktiviˈgeiʃən] n. Noctambulismo, *m.*

nocturnal [nɔkˈtə:nl] adj. Nocturno, na.

nocturne [ˈnɔktə:n] n. MUS. Nocturno, *m.* || ARTS. Escena (*f.*) nocturna.

nod [nɔd] n. Inclinación (*f.*) de cabeza. || Saludo (*m.*) con la cabeza. || Cabezada, *f.* (when falling asleep). || — FIG. *A nod is as good as a wink*, a buen entendedor con pocas palabras basta. | *A nod is as good as a wink to a blind horse*, es como si hablara a la pared. | *The land of Nod*, el mundo de los sueños. || *To give the nod*, asentir, aprobar.

nod [nɔd] v. intr. Asentir con la cabeza (as a sign of agreement). || Saludar con la cabeza (as a greeting). || Dar cabezadas (because of sleepiness). || Balancearse, mecerse: *the poppies nodded in the wind*, las amapolas se balanceaban con el viento. || *She nodded to him to begin*, inclinó la cabeza para que empezara, le hizo una señal con la cabeza para que empezase.
— V. tr. Inclinar, mover (the head). || — *To nod a greeting*, saludar con una inclinación de cabeza. || *To nod assent* o *to nod one's head*, asentir con la cabeza.

nodal [ˈnəudl] adj. ASTR. PHYS. Nodal. || *Nodal point*, punto nodal.

nodding [ˈnɔdiŋ] adj. Que se balancea.
— N. Inclinación (*f.*) de cabeza. || Cabezada, *f.* (when sleepy). || Balanceo, *m.* (swaying motion). || — *They are nodding acquaintances of mine*, sólo los conozco de vista. || *To have a nodding acquaintance with s.o.*, conocer a alguien de vista.

noddle [ˈnɔdl] n. FAM. Chola, *f.*, melón, *m.* (head). | Mollera, *f.* (brain).

node [nəud] n. BOT. Nudo, *m.* || ASTR. PHYS. ANAT. MED. Nodo, *m.* || Nudo, *m.* (of a story, play).

nodose [ˈnəudəus] adj. Nudoso, sa.

nodosity [nəuˈdɔsiti] n. Nudosidad, *f.*

nodular [ˈnɔdjulə*] adj. Nodular.

nodule [ˈnɔdju:l] n. Nódulo, *m.*

nodulose [ˈnɔdju:ləus] or **nodulous** [ˈnɔdju:ləs] adj. Nodular.

noël or **noel** [nəuˈel] n. Villancico, *m.* (Christmas carol).

Noël or **Noel** [nəuˈel] n. Navidad, *f.*

nog [nɔg] n. Tarugo (*m.*) de madera en la pared. || CULIN. Ponche (*m.*) de huevo (eggnog). | Cerveza (*f.*) muy fuerte (ale).

noggin [ˈnɔgin] n. Jarra (*f.*) pequeña (small mug). || Copita, *f.* (glass). || Cuarto (*m.*) de pinta (spirit measure).

no-good [ˈnəugud] adj. U. S. FAM. Malísimo, ma (very bad). | Inútil (useless).
— N. U. S. FAM. Inútil, *m.* & *f.* (person).

nohow [ˈnəuhau] adv. De ninguna manera.

noise [nɔiz] n. Ruido, *m.*: *the noise of traffic*, el ruido del tráfico; *to make a noise*, hacer ruido; *clanging noise*, ruido metálico. || Ruido (*m.*) parásito, interferencia, *f.* (in radio, acoustics, etc.). || Zumbido, *m.* (in the ears). || FIG. Sensación, *f.* || — FAM. *Big noise*, pez gordo. || FIG. *To make a lot of noise about*, hablar mucho de.

noise [nɔiz] v. tr. Divulgar, propalar. || — *To be noised*, rumorearse (to be rumoured), propagarse, divulgarse (to become known). || *To noise abroad*, divulgar.
— V. intr. Hacer ruido. || Hablar mucho.

noise abatement [—əˈbeitmənt] n. Defensa (*f.*) contra el ruido ambiental.

noiseless [—lis] adj. Silencioso, sa; sin ruido. || TECH. Insonorizado, da (soundproof).

noiselessness [—lisnis] n. Silencio, *m.*

noisemaker [—ˈmeikə*] n. Persona (*f.*) *or* cosa (*f.*) que hace ruido. || U. S. Matraca, *f.* (rattle).

noisemaking [—ˈmeikiŋ] adj. Que hace ruido.
— N. Ruido, *m.*

noiseproof [—pru:f] adj. Insonorizado, da.

noisiness [ˈnɔizinis] n. Ruido, *m.* (noise). || Lo ruidoso (being noisy).

noisome [ˈnɔisəm] adj. Fétido, da (stinking). || Dañino, na; nocivo, va (harmful, injurious). || Asqueroso, sa (repulsive).

noisomeness [—nis] n. Fetidez, *f.* (stench). || Nocividad, *f.* (harmfulness). || Asquerosidad, *f.* (repulsiveness).

noisy [ˈnɔizi] adj. Ruidoso, sa. || Bullicioso, sa: *a noisy crowd*, una muchedumbre bulliciosa. || FIG. Chillón, ona; llamativo, va (colours, clothes, etc.). | Clamoroso, sa; vivo, va (protest).

nomad [ˈnəuməd] adj./n. Nómada.

nomadic [nəuˈmædik] adj. Nómada.

nomadism [ˈnəumædizəm] n. Nomadismo, *m.*

no-man's-land [ˈnəumænzlænd] n. Tierra (*f.*) de nadie.

nom de plume [ˈnɔmdəˈplu:m] n. Seudónimo, *m.*

— OBSERV. El plural es *nom de plumes*.

nomenclature [nəuˈmenklətʃə*] n. Nomenclatura, *f.*

nominal [ˈnɔminl] adj. Nominal, sólo de nombre: *the nominal leader*, el jefe nominal. || COMM. Nominal: *nominal value*, valor nominal. | Nominativo, va (shares). || GRAMM. Nominal.

nominalism [—izəm] n. Nominalismo, *m.*

nominalist [—ist] adj./n. Nominalista.

nominalistic [nɔminəˈlistik] adj. Nominalista.

nominate [ˈnɔmineit] v. tr. Designar (to propose for appointment, to designate). || Nombrar (to appoint): *to nominate s.o. as secretary*, nombrar secretario a uno. || Proponer la candidatura de (to name as a candidate). || Nombrar (to name).

nomination [ˌnɔmiˈneiʃən] n. Designación, *f.* (designation). || Nombramiento, *m.* (appointment). || Propuesta, *f.* (as a candidate). || — *To accept nomination*, aceptar ser candidato. || *To put s.o.'s name in nomination for*, poner a alguien entre los candidatos para. || *To support a nomination*, apoyar una candidatura.
nominative [ˈnɔminətiv] n. GRAMM. Nominativo, *m.* || *Nominative absolute*, nominativo absoluto.
— Adj. GRAMM. Nominativo, va. || Nombrado, da (appointed). || Designado, da (designated). || Nominativo, va (shares).
nominator [ˈnɔmineitə*] n. Nominador, ra. || Persona (*f.*) que designa *or* que nombra *or* que propone.
nominee [ˌnɔmiˈni:] n. Candidato, *m.*
nonabsorbent [ˌnɔnəbˈsɔ:bənt] adj. Impermeable, que no absorbe.
nonacceptance [ˌnɔnəkˈseptəns] n. No aceptación, *f.*, falta (*f.*) de aceptación, rechazo, *m.*
nonage [ˈnəunidʒ] n. Minoría, *f.* (minority). || Juventud, *f.* (youth).
nonagenarian [ˌnəunədʒiˈnɛəriən] adj./n. Nonagenario, ria; noventón, ona.
nonaggression [ˌnɔnəˈgreʃən] n. No agresión, *f.*: *nonaggression pact*, pacto de no agresión.
nonalcoholic [ˈnɔnˌælkəˈhɔlik] adj. No alcohólico, ca.
nonaligned [ˌnɔnəˈlaind] adj. No alineado, da: *nonaligned country*, país no alineado.
nonalignment [ˌnɔnəˈlainmənt] n. No alineación, *f.*
nonappearance [ˌnɔnəˈpiərəns] n. JUR. Incomparecencia, *f.*
nonattendance [ˌnɔnəˈtendəns] n. Ausencia, *f.*, falta (*f.*) de asistencia.
nonbelligerency [ˌnɔnbiˈlidʒərənsi] n. No beligerancia, *f.*
nonbelligerent [ˌnɔnbiˈlidʒərənt] adj./n. No beligerante.
nonbreakable [nɔnˈbreikəbl] adj. Irrompible.
nonce [nɔns] n. *For the nonce*, por el momento. || *Nonce word*, palabra inventada para una circunstancia especial.
nonchalance [ˈnɔnʃələns] n. Tranquilidad, *f.*, sangre (*f.*) fría (casualness). || Indiferencia, *f.* (indifference). || Negligencia, *f.* || Inmutabilidad, *f.*, imperturbabilidad, *f.* (calmness). || Aplomo, *m.* (self-confidence).
nonchalant [ˈnɔnʃələnt] adj. Indiferente (unenthusiastic). || Imperturbable, inmutable (unperturbed). || Negligente (negligent). || Tranquilo, la (calm).
nonchalantly [—li] adv. Con indiferencia, indeferentemente (indifferently). || Con aplomo, con calma (calmly). || Negligentemente (negligently).
noncollapsible [ˌnɔnkəˈlæpsəbl] adj. Indesmontable.
noncollectible [ˌnɔnkəˈlektəbl] adj. Incobrable.
noncom [ˈnɔnkɔm] n. MIL. FAM. Suboficial, *m.*
noncombatant [ˌnɔnˈkɔmbətənt] adj./n. No combatiente.
noncombustible [nɔnkəmˈbʌstəbl] adj. Incombustible.
noncommissioned officer [ˌnɔnkəˈmiʃəndˈɔfisə*] n. MIL. Suboficial, *m.* || MIL. *Noncommissioned officers*, clases (*f.*) de tropa, suboficiales.
noncommittal [ˈnɔnkəˈmitl] adj. Evasivo, va (evasive). || Reservado, da (reserved). || Que no compromete a nada (answer, etc.). || *To answer in a noncommittal way*, contestar de forma poco comprometedora, contestar con evasivas.
noncompliance [ˈnɔnkəmˈplaiəns] n. Incumplimiento, *m.* (*with*, de) [failure to comply]. || Desobediencia, *f.* (disobedience).
nonconductor [ˈnɔnkənˌdʌktə*] n. Aislante, *m.*
nonconformist [ˈnɔnkənˈfɔ:mist] adj./n. REL. Disidente, no conformista.
nonconformity [ˈnɔnkənˈfɔ:miti] n. No conformismo, *m.*, no conformidad, *f.* || Disconformidad, *f.* (between two things). || REL. Disidencia, *f.*, no conformismo, *m.*
noncontagious [nɔnkənˈteidʒəs] adj. No contagioso, sa.
noncooperation [ˈnɔnkəuˌɔpəˈreiʃən] n. No cooperación, *f.*, falta (*f.*) de cooperación.
nondelivery [ˈnɔndiˈlivəri] n. Falta (*f.*) de entrega (of goods).
nondescript [ˈnɔndiskript] adj. Indescriptible. || Inclasificable (unclassifiable). || Anodino, na (mediocre).
none [nʌn] pron. Nadie, ninguno, na (nobody): *none but he can do it*, nadie sino él lo puede hacer; *none of them could do it*, ninguno de ellos lo pudo hacer. || Ninguno, na (not any, not one): *none of the books is mine*, ninguno de los libros es mío. || Nada (no part): *he understood none of the book*, no entendió nada del libro. || — *It is none of your business*, no es asunto suyo. || *None at all*, nada en absoluto: *is there any left? — No, none at all*, ¿queda algo? — No, nada en absoluto; ninguno: *are there any left? — No, none at all*, ¿queda alguno? — No, ninguno; nada: *a half is better than none at all*, la mitad es mejor que nada. || *None but*, solamente. || *None other than*, nada menos que: *he was none other than the King*, era nada menos que el rey. || *We'll have none of that here*, ¡nada de esto aquí!
— Adv. De ningún modo, de ninguna manera, no: *I am none the happier for the experience*, no estoy de ningún modo más contento con la experiencia; *I'm none the worse for it*, no estoy peor por ello. || — *None the less*, sin embargo, a pesar de todo. || *None too*, nada: *the pay is none too good*, el sueldo no es nada bueno. || *None too soon*, en buena hora. || *Reply gave he none*, respuesta no la dio. || *To be none the better off*, no haber avanzado nada.
noneffective [ˌnɔniˈfektiv] adj. Ineficaz (ineffective). || MIL. Inhabilitado (man). || JUR. No vigente.
nonego [ˈnɔˈni:gəu] n. PHIL. No yo, *m.*
nonentity [nɔˈnentiti] n. Cero (*m.*) a la izquierda, nulidad, *f.* (insignificant person). || Inexistencia, *f.*, no existencia, *f.*, nada, *f.* (nonexistence).
nones [nəunz] pl. n. HIST. Nonas, *f.* (day). || REL. Nona, *f. sing.* (hour).
nonessential [ˈnɔniˈsenʃəl] adj. No esencial.
nonesuch [ˈnʌnsʌtʃ] n. Persona (*f.*) *or* cosa (*f.*) sin igual *or* sin par.
nonetheless [ˈnʌnðəˈles] adv. U. S. Sin embargo, no obstante.
nonexecution [ˈnɔnˌeksiˈkju:ʃən] n. Incumplimiento, *m.* (of an order).
nonexigibility [ˈnɔnˌeksidʒiˈbiliti] n. Inexigibilidad, *f.*
nonexistence [ˈnɔnigˈzistəns] n. Inexistencia, *f.*, no existencia, *f.*
nonexistent [ˈnɔnigˈzistənt] adj. Inexistente, no existente.
nonfeasance [ˈnɔnˈfi:zəns] n. JUR. Omisión, *f.*, incumplimiento, *m.*
nonferrous [nɔnˈferəs] adj. No ferroso, sa.
nonfiction [nɔnˈfikʃən] n. Literatura (*f.*) no novelesca.
nonfulfilment (U. S. **nonfulfillment**) [ˈnɔnfulˈfilmənt] n. JUR. Incumplimiento, *m.*
noninflammable [ˈnɔninˈflæməbl] adj. Ininflamable.
nonintervention [ˈnɔnˌintə:ˈvenʃən] n. No intervención, *f.*
noniron [nɔnˈaiən] adj. Que no necesita plancha.
nonjuror [ˈnɔnˈdʒuərə*] n. HIST. Clérigo (*m.*) no juramentado.
nonmember [ˈnɔnˌmembə*] n. No miembro, *m.*
nonmetal [nɔnˈmetl] n. CHEM. Metaloide, *m.*
nonnegotiable [ˈnɔnniˈgəuʃjəbl] adj. COMM. No negociable.
nonobservance [ˈnɔnəbˈzə:vəns] n. Incumplimiento, *m.* (of a rule).
nonofficial [ˈnɔnəˈfiʃəl] adj. Oficioso, sa.
nonpareil [ˈnɔnpərəl] adj. Sin par, sin igual.
— N. Persona (*f.*) sin par *or* sin igual. || Cosa (*f.*) sin par *or* sin igual.
nonpartisan [ˈnɔnˌpɑ:tiˈzæn] adj. Independiente.
nonparty [nɔnˈpɑ:ti] adj. Independiente.
nonpayment [ˈnɔnˈpeimənt] n. Falta (*f.*) de pago.
nonperformance [ˈnɔnpəˈfɔ:məns] n. Incumplimiento, *m.* (of contract, etc.).
nonplus [ˈnɔnˈplʌs] v. tr. Asombrar, anonadar, dejar anonadado *or* perplejo.
nonproductive [ˈnɔnprəˈdʌktiv] adj. Improductivo, va.
nonproductiveness [—nis] n. Falta (*f.*) de productividad, improductividad, *f.*
nonprofessional [ˈnɔnprəˈfeʃənl] adj. No profesional.
nonprofit [ˈnɔnˈprɔfit] adj. No lucrativo, va.
nonprofitmaking [ˌnɔnˈprɔfitˌmeikiŋ] adj. No lucrativo, va.
nonrecurring [ˈnɔnriˈkə:riŋ] adj. COMM. Extraordinario, ria (expenditure).
nonrenewable [ˈnɔnriˈnju:əbl] adj. No renovable. || COMM. No prorrogable.
nonresident [ˈnɔnˈrezidənt] adj./n. No residente.
nonresistance [ˌnɔnriˈzistəns] n. Falta (*f.*) de resistencia, pasividad, *f.*
nonrestrictive [ˈnɔnriˈstriktiv] adj. Sin restricción.
nonreturnable [ˌnɔnriˈtə:nəbl] adj. Sin devolución.
nonreversible [ˌnɔnriˈvə:səbl] adj. Irreversible.
nonscheduled [ˈnɔnˈʃedju:ld] adj. No regular (airline, etc.).
nonsectarian [ˌnɔnsekˈtɛəriən] adj. No sectario, ria.
nonsense [ˈnɔnsəns] n. Tonterías, *f. pl.*, disparates, *m. pl.*: *to talk nonsense*, decir tonterías. || — *A nonsense* o *a piece of nonsense*, una tontería, un disparate. || *I want no more of your nonsense!*, ¡déjate de tonterías! || *That's nonsense*, esto es absurdo. || *To make nonsense*, no tener sentido.
— Interj. ¡Tonterías!, ¡bobadas!
nonsensical [nɔnˈsensikəl] adj. Disparatado, da; absurdo, da.
non sequitur [ˈnɔnˈsekwitə*] n. PHIL. Conclusión (*f.*) errónea.

— OBSERV. El plural de *non sequitur* es *non sequiturs.*

nonshrink [ˈnɔnʃriŋk] adj. Inencogible.
nonskid [ˈnɔnˈskid] adj. AUT. Antideslizante.
nonsmoker [ˈnɔnˈsməukə*] n. Persona (*f.*) que no fuma.
nonstop [ˈnɔnˈstɔp] adj. Directo, *m.* (train). || Sin escalas: *nonstop flight*, vuelo sin escalas. || Continuo, nua: *nonstop show*, sesión continua.
— Adv. Sin parar: *to drive nonstop to Rome*, conducir a Roma sin parar. || Directamente (by train). || Sin escalas (by plane).
nonsuch [ˈnʌnsʌtʃ] n. See NONESUCH.
nonsuit [ˈnɔnˈsju:t] n. JUR. Desestimación, *f.*, denegación, *f.*
nonsuit [ˈnɔnˈsju:t] v. tr. JUR. Desestimar, denegar.
nonsupport [ˌnɔnsəˈpɔ:t] n. JUR. Falta (*f.*) de pago de la pensión alimenticia.
nontaxable [ˌnɔnˈtæksəbl] adj. Exento de impuestos, no imponible.

nontransferable [ˌnɔntræns'fə:rəbl] adj. Intransferible.
nonunion [ˌnɔn'ju:njən] adj. No sindicado, da (not belonging to a union).
nonviolence [nɔn'vaiələns] n. No violencia, *f.*
nonviolent [nɔn'vaiələnt] adj. Pacífico, ca; no violento, ta.
noodle ['nu:dl] n. FAM. Melón, *m.*, chola, *f.* (head). | Lelo, la; memo, ma (idiot). || — Pl. CULIN. Fideos, *m.* (cylindrical). | Tallarines, *m.* (flat).
nook [nuk] n. Rincón, *m.* (recess, corner). || Refugio, *m.* (refuge). || Escondrijo, *m.* (hiding place).
noon [nu:n] n. Mediodía, *m.*: *at noon*, al mediodía. || FIG. Apogeo, *m.*
— Adj. De mediodía.
noonday [—dei] n. Mediodía, *m.* || — *The noonday meal*, el almuerzo. || *The noonday sun*, el sol de mediodía.
no one ['nəuwʌn] pron. Nadie: *no one heard me*, nadie me oyó; *I saw no one*, no vi a nadie; *I spoke to no one*, no hablé con nadie.
noose [nu:s] n. Nudo (*m.*) corredizo (knot). || Lazo, *m.* (for snaring animals, etc.). || Dogal, *m.*, soga, *f.* (of a hangman's rope). || FIG. Vínculo, *m.*, lazo, *m.* (link). | Trampa, *f.* (trap). || FIG. *To have one's head in the noose*, estar con la soga al cuello.
noose [nu:s] v. tr. Coger con un lazo (to catch in a noose). || Hacer un nudo corredizo en (to make a noose in). || Ahorcar (to hang).
nopal ['nəupəl] n. BOT. Nopal, *m.*, chumbera, *f.* [*Amer.*, tuna, *f.*]
nope [nəup] interj. U. S. FAM. ¡No!
nor [nɔ:*] conj. Ni: *he is neither big nor small*, no es ni grande ni pequeño; *neither you nor I*, ni tú ni yo. || Ni, ni tampoco: *they don't know him, nor do they want to*, no lo conocen, ni tampoco quieren conocerlo. || Tampoco: *nor had I forgotten the bread*, tampoco se me había olvidado el pan; *he had not gone there, nor had I*, él no había ido allí, yo tampoco.
Nordic ['nɔ:dik] adj./n. Nórdico, ca.
Norfolk jacket ['nɔ:fək'dʒækit] n. Cazadora, *f.*
noria ['nɔ:riə] n. Noria, *f.*
norm [nɔ:m] n. Norma, *f.* (standard). || *To deviate from the norm*, salir de lo normal.
normal [—əl] adj. Normal: *normal temperature*, temperatura normal; *a normal person*, una persona normal; *a normal reaction for a child of his age*, una reacción normal para un niño de su edad; *normal production figures*, cifras normales de producción. || MATH. Perpendicular, normal. || CHEM. Normal, neutro, tra (salt). | Normal (solution, chain of atoms). || *Normal school*, escuela (*f.*) normal.
— N. Lo normal: *above* (*the*) *normal*, por encima de lo normal, superior a lo normal. || Estado (*m.*) normal. || MATH. Normal, *f.*, perpendicular, *f.* || Normalidad, *f.*: *to return to normal*, volver a la normalidad.
normalcy ['nɔ:məlsi] n. Normalidad, *f.*
normality [nɔ:'mæliti] n. Normalidad, *f.*
normalization [ˌnɔ:məlai'zeiʃən] n. Normalización, *f.*
normalize ['nɔ:məlaiz] v. tr. Normalizar.
normally ['nɔ:məli] adv. Normalmente.
Norman ['nɔ:mən] adj./n. Normando, da.
Normandy ['nɔ:məndi] n. GEOGR. Normandía, *f.*
Norman-French ['nɔ:mən'frentʃ] n. Normando, *m.*
normative ['nɔ:mətiv] adj. Normativo, va.
Norse [nɔ:s] n. Nórdico, *m.* (language). || Noruego, ga (Norwegian). || Escandinavo, va; nórdico, ca (Scandinavian).
— Adj. Noruego, ga (of Norway). || Escandinavo, va; nórdico, ca (Scandinavian).
Norseman [—mən] n. Nórdico, *m.*, escandinavo, *m.*
— OBSERV. El plural de *Norseman* es *Norsemen*.
north [nɔ:θ] adj. Del norte, norteño, ña (belonging or situated towards the north). || Que da al norte (facing north). || [Que sopla] del norte (wind).
— Adv. Hacia el norte, al norte.
— N. Norte, *m.* || *The North*, el Norte, *m.*
North Africa [—'æfrikə] pr. n. GEOGR. África (*f.*) del Norte.
North African [—'æfrikən] adj./n. Norteafricano, na.
North America [—ə'merikə] n. GEOGR. América (*f.*) del Norte, Norteamérica, *f.*
North American [—ə'merikən] adj./n. Norteamericano, na.
northbound [—baund] adj. Que se dirige hacia el norte.
Northbound [—baund] adj. De dirección norte, que va hacia el norte.
north by east [—bai'i:st] n. MAR. Norte (*m.*) cuarta al nordeste.
north by west [—bai'west] n. MAR. Norte (*m.*) cuarta al noroeste.
northeast [—'i:st] adj. Del nordeste, nordeste.
— Adv. Hacia el nordeste.
— N. Nordeste, *m.*, noreste, *m.*
northeast by east [—'i:stbai'i:st] n. MAR. Nordeste (*m.*) cuarta al este.
northeast by north [—'i:stbai'nɔ:θ] n. MAR. Nordeste (*m.*) cuarta al norte.
northeaster [—'i:stə*] n. Nordeste, *m.* (wind).
northeasterly [—'i:stəli] adj. Nordeste, del nordeste.
— Adv. Hacia el nordeste.
— N. Nordeste, *m.* (wind).
northeastern [—'i:stən] adj. Del nordeste.
northeastward [—'i:stwəd] adj./adv. Hacia el nordeste.
northeastwards [—'i:stwədz] adv. Hacia el nordeste.
northerly ['nɔ:ðəli] adj. Norte, del norte. || [Que sopla] del norte (wind). || *The most northerly point*, el punto más septentrional.
— Adv. Hacia el norte.
— N. Norte, *m.*, viento (*m.*) del morte.
northern ['nɔ:ðən] adj. Del norte, septentrional (situated in the north). || Del Norte, norteño (of the North). || — *Northern hemisphere*, hemisferio norte *or* boreal. || *Northern lights*, aurora (*f. sing.*) boreal.
Northerner [—ə*] n. Norteño, ña (of a northern region). || Nórdico, ca (of a northern country).
Northern Ireland [—'aiələnd] pr. n. GEOGR. Irlanda (*f.*) del Norte.
northernmost [—məust] adj. Más septentrional: *the northernmost point*, el punto más septentrional.
northing ['nɔ:θiŋ] n. MAR. Rumbo (*m.*) norte.
northland ['nɔ:θlənd] n. Norte, *m.* (of a country).
Northman ['nɔ:θmən] n. Escandinavo, *m.*
— OBSERV. El plural de *Northman* es *Northmen*.
north-northeast ['nɔ:θnɔ:θ'i:st] adj. Nornordeste.
— N. Nornordeste, *m.*
north-northwest ['nɔ:θnɔ:θ'west] adj./adv. Nornoroeste, nornorueste.
— N. Nornoroeste, *m.*, nornorueste, *m.*
North Pole ['nɔ:θpəul] n. GEOGR. Polo (*m.*) Norte.
North Sea ['nɔ:θsi:] n. GEOGR. Mar (*m.*) del Norte.
North Star ['nɔ:θstɑ:*] n. ASTR. Estrella (*f.*) polar.
North Vietnam ['nɔ:θ'vjet'næm] pr. n. GEOGR. Vietnam (*m.*) del Norte.
North Vietnamese [—i:z] adj./n. Vietnamita del Norte, norvietnamita.
northward ['nɔ:θwəd] adj./adv. Hacia el norte.
— N. Dirección (*f.*) norte.
northwards [—z] adv. Hacia el norte.
northwest ['nɔ:θ'west] adj. Del noroeste, noroeste. || [Que sopla] del noroeste (wind).
— Adv. Hacia el noroeste. || [Que sopla] del noroeste (wind).
— N. Noroeste, *m.*
northwest by north [—bai'nɔ:θ] n. MAR. Noroeste (*m.*) cuarta al norte.
northwest by west [—bai'west] n. MAR. Noroeste (*m.*) cuarta al oeste.
northwester [—ə*] n. Noroeste, *m.* (wind).
northwesterly [—əli] adj. Noroeste, del noroeste.
— Adv. Hacia el noroeste.
— N. Noroeste, *m.* (wind).
northwestern [—ən] adj. Del noroeste.
northwestward [—wəd] adj./adv. Hacia el noroeste.
northwestwards [—wədz] adv. Hacia el noroeste.
Norway ['nɔ:wei] n. GEOGR. Noruega, *f.*
Norwegian [nɔ:'wi:dʒən] n. Noruego, ga (person). || Noruego, *m.* (language).
— Adj. Noruego, ga.
nose [nəuz] n. ANAT. Nariz, *f.* || ZOOL. Hocico, *m.* (of many animals). | Nariz, *f.* (of dog, etc.). || FIG. Olfato, *m.* (perspicacity): *to have a nose for business*, tener olfato para los negocios. | Olfato, *m.* (sense of smell). | Morro, *m.*, nariz, *f.* (front of an aircraft). | Nariz, *f.*, proa, *f.* (of a ship). | Morro, *m.* (of a car). | Boca, *f.*, aroma, *m.* (of a wine, drink). | Aroma, *m.* (of tobacco, herbs, etc.). || TECH. Boca, *f.* (of a tool). || — *Aquiline* o *Roman, turned-up, snub, flat, hooked nose*, nariz aguileña, respingona, chata, aplastada, de gancho. || FIG. *It is* (*right*) *under your nose*, está delante de tus narices. | *Not to be able to see further than the end of one's nose*, no ver más allá de sus narices. | *To be as plain as the nose on one's face*, estar más claro que el agua. || *To blow one's nose*, sonarse, sonarse la nariz. || FIG. *To cut off one's nose to spite one's face*, fastidiarse a sí mismo por querer fastidiar a los demás. | *To follow one's nose*, seguir recto (to go straight ahead), dejarse llevar por el instinto (to follow one's instinct). || *To hold one's nose*, taparse la nariz. || FIG. *To keep one's nose to the grindstone*, trabajar con ahínco (to work hard). | *To lead s.o. by the nose*, manejar a uno a su antojo, tener a uno agarrado por las narices. | *To look down one's nose at*, mirar por encima del hombro a. | *To make a long nose*, hacer un palmo de narices. | *To pay through the nose*, pagar un dineral. || *To pick one's nose*, hurgarse la nariz. || FIG. FAM. *To poke* o *to stick one's nose into other people's business*, meter la nariz *or* las narices en los asuntos de los demás. | *To put s.o.'s nose out of joint*, enfadar a alguien. || *To speak through the nose*, hablar con *or* por la nariz, hablar con voz gangosa. || FIG. *To thumb one's nose at s.o.*, hacer un palmo de narices a alguien. | *To turn up one's nose at*, despreciar, hacer una mueca de desprecio ante (sth.). || *Your nose is bleeding*, estás echando sangre *or* sangrando por la nariz *or* por las narices.
nose [nəuz] v. tr. Olfatear (to smell out). || — *To nose one's way through*, abrirse paso con cuidado entre. || *To nose out*, olfatear, husmear (an animal), conseguir descubrir (a secret).
— V. intr. *To nose about* o *around*, curiosear. || *To*

nose forward, avanzar con cuidado. || *To nose in* o *into*, meterse en, meter la nariz *or* las narices en.
nose bag [—bæg] n. Morral, *m.*
noseband [—bænd] n. Muserola, *f.*
nosebleed [—bli:d] n. Hemorragia (*f.*) nasal.
nose cone [—kəun] n. Morro, *m.* (of a rocket).
nose dive [—daiv] n. AVIAT. Picado, *m.*
nose-dive [—daiv] v. intr. AVIAT. Descender en picado.
nose flute [—flu:t] n. MUS. Flauta (*f.*) nasal.
nosegay [—gei] n. Ramillete (*m.*) de flores.
nosepiece [—pi:s] n. Puente, *m.* (of glasses). || Muserola, *f.* (noseband). || Lanza, *f.* (of a pipe).
nose ring [—riŋ] n. Nariguera, *f.* (ornament). || Aro, *m.* [que ponen en la nariz a los cerdos y a los toros].
nosey [—i] adj. FAM. Entrometido, da. || *Nosey parker*, entrometido, da; metomentodo, *m.* & *f.*
no-show [ˈnəuˈʃəu] n. Pasajero (*m.*) que no utiliza su reservación sin cancelarla.
nosing [—iŋ] n. ARCH. Borde (*m.*) saliente (edge of a step). | Saliente, *m.* (projection).
nostalgia [nɔstˈældʒiə] n. Nostalgia, *f.*
nostalgic [nɔstˈældʒik] adj. Nostálgico, ca.
nostril [ˈnɔstril] n. ANAT. Ventanilla (*f.*) *or* ventana (*f.*) de la nariz. || Ollar, *m.* (of a horse). || — Pl. Narices, *f.*
nostrum [ˈnɔstrəm] n. Panacea, *f.*
nosy [ˈnəuzi] adj. FAM. Entrometido, da (nosey).
not [nɔt] adv. No: *they did not come*, no vinieron; *not everybody*, no todos; *not a little*, no poco; *not a few*, no pocos; *I think not*, creo que no; *you like him, don't you?*, le gusta, ¿no?; *don't o do not do it*, no lo hagas; *I don't care whether he comes or not*, me da igual que venga o no; *we told you not to go*, te dijimos que no fueras. || ¿No?, ¿verdad?: *he is here, isn't he?*, está aquí, ¿verdad?; *it is this one, is it not?*, es éste, ¿verdad? || Ni: *not one of them knew it*, ni uno de ellos lo sabía. || Como no: *not wanting to disturb them, he kept quiet*, como no quería molestarles, se calló. || Sin: *not thinking that*, sin pensar que. || — *Absolutely not!*, ¡en absoluto! || *Certainly not!*, ¡de ninguna manera!, ¡por supuesto que no!, ¡ni hablar! || *Not a hope!* o *not a chance!*, ¡ni pensarlo! || *Not any*, ninguno, na. || *Not any more*, ya no. || *Not ... at all*, no ... nada, no ... en absoluto: *I do not like him at all*, no me gusta nada; *he is not handsome at all*, no es nada guapo. || *Not at all*, no hay de qué: *thank you — Not at all*, gracias. — No hay de qué; nada, en absoluto: *are you cross? — Not at all!*, ¿estás enfadado? — ¡En absoluto! || *Not even*, ni siquiera. || JUR. *Not guilty*, inocente. || *Not likely!*, ¡ni hablar! || *Not much!*, ¡ya lo creo!, ¡y cómo! (and how), ¡eso te lo crees tú! (I don't believe you). || *Not only ... but also*, no sólo ... sino también: *not only small but also bald*, no sólo bajo sino también calvo. || *Not she!*, ¡ella no! || *Not that*, no es que: *not that I don't want to go*, no es que no quiera ir. || || *Not to say*, por no decir. || *Not yet* o *still not*, todavía no, aún no. || *Of course not*, claro que no. || *Why not?*, ¿por qué no?, ¿cómo no?

— OBSERV. El adverbio *not* se suele contraer y combinar con los verbos que acompaña, particularmente en la lengua hablada : *don't* (do not), *won't* (will not), *isn't* (is not).

nota bene [ˈnəutəˈbi:ni] loc. lat. Nota bene.
notability [ˌneutəˈbiliti] n. Notabilidad, *f.* (quality, person).
notable [ˈnəutəbl] adj. Notable (admirable, noteworthy): *a notable success*, un éxito notable.
— N. Notabilidad, *f.*, notable, *m.* (person).
notarial [nəuˈtεəriəl] adj. Notarial: *notarial deeds*, actas notariales.
notarize [ˈnəutəraiz] v. tr. U. S. Hacer certificar por notario.
notary [ˈnəutəri] n. Notario, *m.* [*Amer.*, escribano, *m.*]
notary public [—ˈpʌblik] n. Notario, *m.*

— OBSERV. El plural de *notary public* es *notaries public*.

notation [nəuˈteiʃən] n. Anotación, *f.* (note). || MATH. MUS. Notación, *f.*
notch [nɔtʃ] n. Muesca, *f.*, corte, *m.* (a cut, indentation). || Grado, *m.*, punto, *m.* (a degree). || U. S. Desfiladero, *m.* (between mountains).
notch [nɔtʃ] v. tr. Hacer una muesca en, cortar (to make a cut in). || *To notch up*, apuntarse (to mark up): *the team notched up its third consecutive victory*, el equipo se apuntó la tercera victoria consecutiva.
note [nəut] n. Nota, *f.*: *he wrote me a note to say he wasn't coming*, me escribió una nota para decirme que no venía; *diplomatic note*, nota diplomática; *translator's note*, nota del traductor. || MUS. Nota, *f.* (sound, symbol). | Tecla, *f.* (key of piano, organ, etc.): *the black notes*, las teclas negras. || Sonido, *m.* (sound). || Canto, *m.* (of a bird). || Billete, *m.*: *a hundred peseta note*, un billete de cien pesetas. || Tono, *m.*, nota, *f.*: *a note of irony in his voice*, una nota de ironía en su voz. || Importancia, *f.*: *a person of note*, una persona de importancia. || Renombre, *m.*: *a restaurant of note*, un restaurante de renombre. || Marca, *f.*, señal, *f.* (mark, sign). || PRINT. Signo, *m.*: *note of exclamation*, signo de admiración. || — Pl. Apuntes, *m.*: *to take notes in a history lesson*, tomar apuntes en una clase de historia. || Notas, *f.*: *to make notes during a journey*, tomar notas durante un viaje. || — *Nothing of note*, nada especial. || *Promissory note*, pagaré, *m.* || FIG. *To change one's note*, cambiar de tono. | *To compare notes*, cambiar impresiones. || *To make a note of*, tomar nota de, apuntar. || *To speak from notes*, pronunciar un discurso utilizando notas or apuntes. || FIG. *To strike a false note*, desentonar. | *To strike the right note*, hacer *or* decir lo apropiado, acertar. || *To take note*, prestar atención. || *To take note of*, tomar nota de. || *Worthy of note*, digno de mención.
note [nəut] v. tr. Fijarse en, tomar nota de: *note carefully what I am about to say*, fíjense bien en lo que voy a decir. || Darse cuenta de, tener en cuenta: *but note that he is only ten years old*, pero date cuenta de que tiene sólo diez años. || Anotar, apuntar: *I noted the details in my exercise book*, anoté los detalles en mi cuaderno. || Tomar nota de: *we have noted your request*, hemos tomado nota de su solicitud. || Señalar: *the report noted a drop in sales*, el informe señaló un descenso en las ventas. || Notar, observar, advertir: *to note a difference between*, notar una diferencia entre; *I noted that he had holes in his shoes*, advertí que tenía agujeros en los zapatos. || *To note down*, apuntar, anotar.
notebook [—buk] n. Cuaderno, *m.*, libreta, *f.*
notecase [—keis] n. Billetero, *m.*, billetera, *f.* (wallet).
noted [—id] adj. Notable, eminente (eminent). || Famoso, sa; célebre (famous).
note of hand [—əvhænd] n. COMM. Pagaré, *m.*
notepaper [—ˌpeipə*] n. Papel (*m.*) de escribir, papel (*m.*) de cartas.
noteworthy [—ˌwə:ði] adj. Digno de mención, notable. || *It is noteworthy that ...*, es de notar que ...
nothing [ˈnʌθiŋ] n. No... nada: *to eat nothing*, no comer nada; *nothing happened*, no pasó nada. || Nada: *nothing new*, nada nuevo; *nothing else*, nada más; *nothing at all*, nada de nada. || Cero, *m.* (zero). || — *A mere nothing*, una fruslería, una bagatela. || *As though it were nothing at all*, como si nada. || *For nothing*, para nada (in vain), por nada, gratis (free), sin razón (for no reason). || *It's nothing to laugh about*, no tiene ninguna gracia. || *It's nothing to me*, me da igual (I don't care). || *Man risen from nothing*, hombre (*m.*) salido de la nada. || *Next to nothing*, casi nada. || *Nothing but*, sólo. || *Nothing but the truth*, nada más que la verdad. || *Nothing doing!*, ¡ni hablar! || *Nothing if not*, más que todo, antes que nada: *you are nothing if not selfish*, eres egoísta antes que nada. || *Nothing much*, poca cosa. || *Nothing on earth*, nada en el mundo. || FIG. *Nothing to write home about*, nada del otro mundo. || *Nothing ventured, nothing gained*, quien no se arriesga no pasa la mar. || *Sweet nothings*, ternezas, *f.* || *There's nothing for it but to*, no hay más remedio que. || *There's nothing in it*, no dice nada (not profound), es falso (untrue), no se puede sacar nada de ello (unprofitable), van muy iguales (in race). || *There is nothing like*, no hay nada mejor que, no hay nada como. || *There is nothing much to be said*, no hay mucho que decir. || *There is nothing stupid about her*, no es nada tonta. || *There is nothing to it*, es facilísimo, está tirado. || *Think nothing of it*, no hay de qué. || *To be nothing of a teacher*, ser muy mal profesor. || *To come to nothing*, reducirse a nada, quedar en nada, fracasar. || *To have nothing to do with*, no tener nada que ver con. || *To make nothing of*, no sacar nada en limpio de (to be unable to understand), no dar importancia a (to treat as unimportant), desaprovechar (to waste). || *To make nothing of doing sth.*, hacer algo como si nada. || *To mean nothing to*, no significar nada para, no querer decir nada para. || *To say nothing of*, por no hablar de. || *To think nothing of*, no suponer nada para uno: *he thinks nothing of working sixteen hours a day*, para él no supone nada trabajar dieciséis horas diarias; no encontrarle nada (not to like): *I'm afraid I think nothing of her*, lo siento, pero yo no le encuentro nada.
— Adv. De ninguna manera, de ningún modo. || — *It's nothing like as good as the first one*, no es ni mucho menos tan bueno como el primero. || *It looks nothing like you*, no se te parece nada. || *Nothing less than*, nada menos que.
nothingness [—nis] n. Nada, *f.*: *God created the world out of nothingness*, Dios creó el mundo de la nada. || Insignificancia, *f.*: *to realize one's own nothingness*, darse cuenta de su propia insignificancia.
notice [ˈnəutis] n. Atención, *f.* (attention): *to come into notice* o *to attract notice*, llamar la atención. || Anuncio, *m.* (announcement, advert). || Letrero, *m.* (sign): *the notice said "keep off the grass"*, el letrero decía "no pisar el césped". || Cartel, *m.* (poster). || Reseña, *f.* (review of a book). || Aviso, *m.*, notificación, *f.*: *subject to change without previous notice*, sujeto a cambio sin previo aviso *or* sin notificación previa. || Despido, *m.*, aviso (*m.*) de despido: *the firm gave him his notice*, la firma le comunicó su despido. || Dimisión, *f.*: *he handed in his notice*, presentó su dimisión. || Desahucio, *m.* (of a tenant). || Aviso, *m.*: *the landlady gave him notice to leave*, la dueña de la casa le dio el aviso de que se marchara. || Plazo, *m.*: *a week's notice*, una semana de plazo. || — *An event which attracted a lot of notice*, un acontecimiento que llamó mucho la atención. || *At a moment's notice*, en seguida, inmediatamente (at once). || *At short notice*, a corto plazo, con poco tiempo de antelación. || *At such short notice*, con tan poco plazo. || *On short notice*, en poco tiempo. || *Take notice that*, le advierto que. || *To bring to s.o.'s notice that*, hacer observar a uno que. || *To come to one's notice*, llegar al conocimiento

de uno. || *To escape one's notice*, pasarle desapercibido a uno, escapársele a uno. || *To give notice of*, avisar de. || *To give notice to*, despedir (an employee), despedirse (one's master), presentar la dimisión (one's employer). || *To give s.o. notice*, despedir a uno (to dismiss). || *To give two weeks notice*, avisar con dos semanas de anticipación. || *To serve notice on*, hacer saber, notificar, avisar. || FIG. *To sit up and take notice*, prestar atención. || *To take notice of s.o.*, hacer caso a alguien. || *To take notice of sth.*, observar (to observe), prestar atención a algo, hacer caso de algo (to pay attention). || *Under notice*, avisado, da; dimitido, da. || *Until further notice*, hasta nuevo aviso. || *Without notice*, sin previo aviso (without warning), desapercibido, da (unnoticed). || *Worthy of notice*, digno de atención.

notice [ˈnəutis] v. tr. Darse cuenta de, advertir (to realize, to see): *I noticed that it was getting dark*, me di cuenta de que estaba oscureciendo. || Fijarse, reparar en: *I had never noticed that picture before*, no me había fijado nunca en ese cuadro. || Observar, notar: *notice the harmony of colour*, observe la armonía de colores. || Ver, reconocer: *I noticed him in the crowd*, lo vi entre la multitud.||Prestar atención a (to pay attention). || Hacer la reseña de (to review). || Avisar (to notify).

noticeable [—əbl] adj. Notable, sensible: *a noticeable difference*, una diferencia notable; *a noticeable increase*, un aumento sensible. || Evidente, obvio, via (obvious). || — *Is the hole in my trousers very noticeable?*, ¿se ve mucho el agujero en mi pantalón? || *It is hardly noticeable*, casi no se nota.

notice board [— bɔ:d] n. Tablón (*m.*) de anuncios (for pinning notices). || Letrero, *m.* (for inscription). || AUT. Señal (*f.*) de tráfico.

notifiable [ˈnəutifaiəbl] adj. De declaración obligatoria, que hay que declarar a las autoridades (diseases).

notification [ˌnəutifiˈkeiʃən] n. Notificación, *f.*, aviso, *m.*

notify [ˈnəutifai] v. tr. Avisar, comunicar, notificar: *they notified me of your arrival*, me avisaron de su llegada, me comunicaron *or* me notificaron su llegada.

notion [ˈnəuʃən] n. Idea, *f.*, concepto, *m.*: *his notion of a good novel is different to mine*, su idea de una buena novela es diferente de la mía. || Concepto, *m.*, noción, *f.*: *the notion of law*, el concepto de ley. || Impresión, *f.*: *I have a notion he is right*, tengo la impresión de que tiene razón. || Teoría, *f.* (theory). || Idea, *f.*: *Anthony had no notion what was going on*, Antonio no tenía ni idea de lo que estaba pasando; *I haven't the slightest notion*, no tengo la más mínima idea. || Intención, *f.*: *to have a notion to do sth.*, tener intención de hacer algo. || FAM. Capricho, *m.*: *Victoria always acts as the notion takes her*, Victoria actúa siempre según su capricho. || — Pl. U. S. Artículos (*m.*) de mercería.

notional [ˈnəuʃənl] adj. Especulativo, va; teórico, ca (theoretical). || Imaginario, ria (imaginary). || U. S. Caprichoso, sa (capricious).

notoriety [ˌnəutəˈraiəti] n. Notoriedad, *f.* (fame). || Celebridad, *f.* (a celebrity). || Mala fama, *f.*, notoriedad, *f.* (ill repute).

notorious [nəuˈtɔ:riəs] adj. Célebre, famoso, sa; notorio, ria; muy conocido, da: *a notorious criminal*, un criminal notorio; *a place notorious for crime*, un sitio muy conocido por los crímenes que se cometen.

— OBSERV. *Notorious* casi siempre tiene un sentido despectivo en inglés.

notoriousness [—nis] n. Notoriedad, *f.*, mala fama, *f.*

no-trump [ˈnəuˈtrʌmp] adj. Sin triunfo.

notwithstanding [ˌnɔtwiθˈstændiŋ] prep. A pesar de.

— Adv. Sin embargo, no obstante.

— Conj. A pesar de que, por más que.

nougat [ˈnu:gɑ:] n. Turrón (*m.*) de almendras.

nought [nɔ:t] n. See NAUGHT.

noughts-and-crosses [ˈnɔ:tsəndˈkrɔsiz] n. Tres en raya, *m.* (game).

noumenon [ˈnu:məˌnɔn] n. PHIL. Nóumeno, *m.*

— OBSERV. El plural de la palabra inglesa es *noumena*.

noun [naun] n. GRAMM. Nombre, *m.*, sustantivo, *m.* || GRAMM. *Proper noun*, nombre propio.

— Adj. GRAMM. Sustantivo, va.

nourish [ˈnʌriʃ] v. tr. Alimentar, nutrir (with food). || FIG. Abrigar (hopes, etc.). | Fomentar (to encourage).

nourishing [—iŋ] adj. Nutritivo, va; alimenticio, cia.

nourishment [—mənt] n. Alimento, *m.* (food). || Alimentación, *f.*, nutrición, *f.* (feeding).

nous [naus] n. PHIL. Mente, *f.*, intelecto, *m.* || FAM. Sentido (*m.*) común.

nouveau riche [ˈnu:vəuˈri:ʃ] n. Nuevo rico, *m.*, nueva rica, *f.*

nova [ˈnəuvə] n. ASTR. Nova, *f.*

— OBSERV. El plural de la palabra inglesa *nova* es *novae* o *novas*.

Nova Scotia [ˈnəuvəˈskəuʃə] pr. n. GEOGR. Nueva Escocia, *f.*

novation [nəˈveiʃən] n. JUR. Novación, *f.*

novel [ˈnɔvəl] n. Novela, *f.*: *clock-and-dagger novel*, novela de capa y espada; *serialized novel*, novela por entregas.

— Adj. Nuevo, va (new). || Original, ingenioso, sa (new and ingenious).

novelette [ˌnɔvəˈlet] n. Novela (*f.*) corta (short novel). || Novela (*f.*) rosa (sentimental novel).

novelist [ˈnɔvəlist] n. Novelista, *m.* & *f.*

novelistic [nɔvəˈlistik] adj. Novelístico, ca.

novelize [ˈnɔvəlaiz] v. tr. Novelar, novelizar.

novelty [ˈnɔvəlti] n. Novedad, *f.* || COMM. Novedad, *f.*, fantasía, *f.*

November [nəuˈvembə*] n. Noviembre, *m.*: *on the fifth of November*, el cinco de noviembre.

novena [nəuˈvi:nə] n. REL. Novena, *f.*

— OBSERV. El plural de la palabra inglesa es *novenae*.

novice [ˈnɔvis] n. Principiante, *m.* & *f.*, novato, ta; novicio, cia (beginner). || REL. Novicio, cia. | Recién convertido, da (convert).

noviciate [nəuˈviʃiit] or **novitiate** [nəuˈviʃiit] n. REL. Noviciado, *m.* || Período (*m.*) de aprendizaje. || Novicio, cia; principiante (novice).

novocaine [ˈnəuvəˌkein] n. CHEM. Novocaína, *f.*

now [nau] adv. Ahora: *how do you feel now?*, ¿cómo te sientes ahora?; *I want to go now*, quiero irme ahora; *now or never*, ahora o nunca. || Ahora bien: *now, while this was happening...*, ahora bien, mientras esto ocurría ... || Entonces: *the general now changed his plan*, entonces el general cambió su plan. || Ya: *I have worked here a long time now*, hace ya mucho tiempo que trabajo aquí; *all was now ready*, todo estaba ya listo. || Ya, ahora: *it's six o'clock now*, ya son las seis, son las seis ahora; *you can go now*, ya te puedes marchar. || Inmediatamente (immediately). || Actualmente (at present). || — *He won't be long now*, ya no puede tardar. || *I can't help you just now*, no le puedo ayudar en este momento *or* ahora mismo. || *I saw him just now*, lo he visto ahora mismo, acabo de verlo. || *Not now*, ahora no. || *Now and again* o *now and then*, de vez en cuando, de cuando en cuando. || *Now... now...*, ya..., ya...; ora..., ora... || *Now, now!*, ¡vamos, vamos! || *Now then, where have you been?*, ahora bien, ¿dónde has estado? || *Right now*, ahora mismo.

— Conj. Ya que, ahora que: *now (that) you have come you may stay*, ahora que has venido te puedes quedar.

— N. *By now*, ya. || *For now*, por ahora. || *From now*, dentro de: *three days from now*, dentro de tres días. || *From now on*, de ahora en adelante, a partir de ahora. || *Long before now*, hace mucho tiempo ya. || *Till now*, hasta ahora. || *Up to now*, hasta ahora.

nowadays [—ədeiz] adv. Hoy, actualmente, ahora, hoy día, hoy en día.

noways [ˈnəuweiz] adv. U. S. De ninguna manera.

nowhere [ˈnəuwɛə*] adv. Por ninguna parte; *he was nowhere to be found*, no se le encontraba por ninguna parte. || A ninguna parte: *where are you going? — Nowhere*, ¿a dónde vas? — A ninguna parte. || En ninguna parte: *nowhere in the world*, en ninguna parte del mundo. || — *Nowhere else*, en ninguna otra parte. || *Nowhere near*, nada cerca: *it's nowhere near London*, no está nada cerca de Londres; ni mucho menos: *it was nowhere near as difficult as he expected*, no fue ni mucho menos tan difícil como pensaba. || *There's nowhere I can think of*, no se me ocurre ningún sitio. || *To be nowhere as good as*, distar mucho de ser tan bueno como. || FIG. *To come nowhere in a race*, quedarse muy atrás en una carrera. | *To get nowhere*, no conseguir nada.

— N. Nada, *f.*: *a man came out of nowhere and shot me*, un hombre salió de la nada y me disparó. || *At the back of nowhere*, en el quinto pino, en el quinto infierno.

nowise [ˈnəuwaíz] adv. De ninguna manera.

noxious [ˈnɔkʃəs] adj. Nocivo, va; perjudicial (harmful). || Nocivo, va; pernicioso, sa; dañino, na (corrupting).

noxiousness [—nis] n. Nocividad, *f.*

nozzle [ˈnɔzl] n. Boca, *f.*, boquilla, *f.* (serving as an outlet for a fluid, etc.). || TECH. Tobera, *f.*, inyector, *m.* || Cánula, *f.* (of a syringe). || FAM. Napias, *f. pl.* (nose).

nu [nju:] n. Ny, *f.* (Greek letter).

nuance [njuˈɑ̃:ns] n. Matiz, *m.*

nub [nʌb] n. Trocito, *m.* (small lump or piece). || Nudo, *m.* (crucial part of problem, etc.). || — *That's the nub of it*, ahí está el quid. || *To be worn to the nub*, estar molido (to be exhausted).

nubbin [ˈnʌbin] n. U. S. AGR. Mazorca (*f.*) defectuosa (stunted corn). | Verdura (*f.*) *or* fruta (*f.*) defectuosa (defective fruit).

nubecula [njuˈbi:kjulə] n. MED. Nefelión, *m.*

nubile [ˈnju:bail] adj. Núbil, casadera.

nubility [nju:ˈbiliti] n. Nubilidad, *f.*

nucha [ˈnju:kə] n. ANAT. Nuca, *f.*

nuchal [—l] adj. De la nuca.

nuclear [ˈnju:kliə*] adj. Nuclear: *nuclear energy*, *physics*, *warfare*, energía, física, guerra nuclear; *nuclear physicist*, *reactor*, *fission*, físico, reactor, fisión nuclear; *nuclear weapons*, armas nucleares.

nucleate [ˈnju:kliit] adj. Nucleado, da.

nucleate [ˈnju:klieit] v. intr. Formar núcleo.

nuclei [ˈnju:kliai] pl. n. See NUCLEUS.

nucleic [ˈnju:kliik] adj. Nucleico, ca: *nucleic acid*, ácido nucleico.

nuclein [ˈnju:kli:in] n. Nucleína, *f.*

nucleolar [ˈnju:kliəulə*] adj. Del nucléolo.

nucleolus [nju:ˈkli:ələs] n. Nucléolo, *m.*

NUCLEAR ENERGY — ENERGÍA (*f.*) NUCLEAR

A bomb, atomic bomb	bomba *f.*) atómica
absorption	absorción *f.*
accelerate (to)	acelerar
accelerating chamber	cámara (*f.*) de aceleración
accelerator	acelerador *m.*
alpha rays	rayos (*m.*) alfa
anion	anión *m.*
antimatter	antimateria *f.*
antiparticle	antipartícula *f.*
antiproton	antiprotón *m.*
atom	átomo *m.*
atomic boiler	caldera (*f.*) atómica
atomic number	número (*m.*) atómico
atomic power	energía (*f.*) atómica
atomic weight	peso (*m.*) atómico
attraction	atracción *f.*
barium	bario *m.*
berkelium	berkelio *m.*
beryllium	berilio *m.*
betatron	betatrón *m.*
bevatron	bevatrón *m.*
binding energy	energía (*f.*) de enlace *or* de unión
blast wave	onda (*f.*) de choque
bombardment	bombardeo *m.*
boron	boro *m.*
breeder reactor	reactor (*m.*) reproductor
bubble chamber	cámara (*f.*) de burbujas
burst	explosión *f.*
cadmium	cadmio *m.*
caesium, cesium	cesio *m.*
capture	captura *f.* (of neutrons)
cation	catión *m.*
chain reaction	reacción (*f.*) en cadena
charge	carga *f.*
cladding	revestimiento *m.*
clean bomb	bomba (*f.*) limpia
cobalt	cobalto *m.*
collide (to)	chocar
collision	choque *m.*, colisión *f.*
contamination	contaminación *f.*
coolant	refrigerante *m.*
cooling	refrigeración *f.*
cooling fluid	fluido (*m.*) refrigerante
cooling pond	piscina (*f.*) de desactivación
core	núcleo *m.*
cosmic rays	rayos (*m.*) cósmicos
counter	contador *m.*
critical mass	masa (*f.*) crítica
curie	curie *m.* (unit)
curium	curio *m.* (element)
cyclotron	ciclotrón *m.*
decay (to)	desintegrarse
decontamination	descontaminación *f.*
deflagration	deflagración *f.*
detector	detector *m.*
deuterium	deuterio *m.*
deuteron	deuterón *m.*
diffusion	difusión *f.*
disintegration	desintegración *f.*
dispersion	dispersión *f.*
electrode	electrodo *m.*
electron	electrón *m.*
electron beam	haz (*m.*) de electrones
electron cloud	nube (*f.*) de electrones
electron gun	cañón (*m.*) electrónico
electronic shell	capa (*f.*) electrónica
electron volt	electronvoltio *m.*
element	elemento *m.*
emission	emisión *f.*
enriched uranium	uranio (*m.*) enriquecido
enrichment	enriquecimiento *m.*
explosion	explosión *f.*
fertile element	elemento (*m.*) fértil
fission	fisión *f.*
fissionable material	materia (*f.*) fisible
free electron	electrón (*m.*) libre
fusion	fusión *f.*
gamma rays	rayos (*m.*) gama
gram atom	átomo-gramo *m.*
graphite	grafito *m.*
half-life	período *m.*
H-bomb, hydrogen bomb	bomba (*f.*) H, bomba (*f.*) de hidrógeno
heat exchanger	intercambiador (*m.*) de calor
heavy water	agua (*f.*) pesada
helium	helio *m.*
heterogeneous reactor	reactor (*m.*) heterogéneo
homogeneous reactor	reactor (*m.*) homogéneo
instability	inestabilidad *f.*
ion	ión *m.*
ionization	ionización *f.*
irradiation	irradiación *f.*
isomer	isómero *m.*
isotope	isótopo *m.*
kiloton	kilotón *m.*
krypton	kriptón *m.*
labelled *o* tagged molecule	molécula (*f.*) marcada
leakage	fuga *f.* (of neutrons)
lifetime	vida *f.*
lithium	litio *m.*
mass	masa *f.*
megaton	megatón *m.*
meson	mesón *m.*
moderator	moderator *m.*
molecule	molécula *f.*
mushroom cloud	hongo (*m.*) atómico
neptunium	neptunio *m.*
neutron	neutrón *m.*
neutron flux	flujo (*m.*) de neutrones
nuclear physics	física (*f.*) nuclear
nuclear power plant *o* station	central (*f.*) nuclear
nuclear reactor	reactor (*m.*) nuclear
nuclear tests	pruebas (*f.*) nucleares
nucleon	nucleón *m.*
nucleus	núcleo, *m.*
orbital *o* planetary electron	electrón (*m.*) planetario
particle	partícula *f.*
photon	fotón *m.*
pile	pila *f.*
plutonium	plutonio *m.*
positron	positrón *m.*, positón *m.*
power reactor	reactor (*m.*) generador de potencia
projectile	proyectil *m.*
proton	protón *m.*
quantum number	número (*m.*) cuántico
radiant energy	energía (*f.*) radiante
radiation	radiación *f.*
radioactive cloud	nube (*f.*) radiactiva
radioactive elements	radioelementos *m.*, elementos (*m.*) radiactivos
radioactive fallout	lluvia (*f.*) radiactiva
radioactive wastes	residuos (*m.*) *or* desechos (*m.*) radiactivos
radioactivity	radiactividad *f.*, radioactividad *f.*
radioisotope	radioisótopo *m.*
radiology	radiología *f.*
radiotherapy	radioterapia *f.*
radium	radio *m.*
radon	radón *m.*
rod	barra *f.*
roentgen	roentgen *m.*
scattering	dispersión *f.*
separation	separación *f.*
shield	protección *f.*, blindaje *m.*
shock wave	onda (*f.*) de choque
spectrometer	espectrómetro *m.*
spin	espín *m.*
split (to)	escindirse
stability	estabilidad *f.*
strontium	estroncio *m.*
synchrocyclotron	sincrociclotrón *m.*
synchrotron	sincrotrón *m.*
target	blanco *m.*
thermal neutron	neutrón (*m.*) térmico
thermal reactor	reactor (*m.*) térmico
thermionic	termoiónico, ca
thermonuclear	termonuclear
thorium	torio *m.*
tracer element	radioelemento (*m.*) trazador
trajectory	trayectoria *f.*
trinitrotoluene	trinitrotolueno *m.*
underwater test	prueba (*f.*) submarina
uranium	uranio *m.*
warhead	cabeza (*f.*) atómica
xenon	xenón *m.*

— OBSERV. El plural de *nucleolus* es *nucleoli.*

nucleon [ˈnju:kliɔn] n. PHYS. Nucleón, *m.*

nucleonic [nju:kliˈɔnik] adj. Nucleónico, ca.

nucleonics [—s] n. PHYS. Nucleónica, *f.*

nucleoplasm [ˈnju:kli:əplæzəm] n. Nucleoplasma, *m.*

nucleoprotein [ˈnju:kliəuˈprəuti:n] n. Nucleoproteína, *f.*

nucleus [ˈnju:kliəs] n. Núcleo, *m.*: *atomic nucleus,* núcleo atómico. || FIG. Núcleo, *m.*: *the nucleus of guerrillas grew into an army,* el núcleo de guerrilleros se transformó en un ejército.

— OBSERV. El plural de *nucleus* es *nuclei* o *nucleuses.*

nude [nju:d] adj. Desnudo, da (naked). || De color carne (stockings).

— N. Desnudo, *m.* || *In the nude,* desnudo, da.

nudge [nʌdʒ] n. Codazo, *m.*

nudge [nʌdʒ] v. tr. Dar un codazo a.

nudism [ˈnju:dizəm] n. Nudismo, *m.*, desnudismo, *m.*

nudist [ˈnju:dist] adj./n. Nudista.

nudity [ˈnju:diti] n. Desnudez, *f.* || Desnudo, *m.* (arts).

nugatory [ˈnju:gətəri] adj. Insignificante (of no importance). || Ineficaz (ineffective).

nugget [ˈnʌgit] n. MIN. Pepita, *f.*: *gold nugget,* pepita de oro.

nuisance [ˈnju:sns] n. Fastidio, *m.*, molestia, *f.*, pesadez, *f.*, lata, *f.* (thing): *these flies are a nuisance,* estas moscas son una pesadez. || Pesado, da; latoso, sa; persona (*f.*) molesta (person): *what a nuisance he is!,* ¡qué pesado es! || JUR. Perjuicio, *m.*, daño, *m.* || — *To make a nuisance of o.s.,* dar la lata, ponerse pesado. || *What a nuisance!,* ¡qué pesadez!

null [nʌl] adj. Nulo, la. || Inútil (useless). || JUR. *Null and void,* nulo y sin valor.

— N. Cero, *m.*

nullification [ˌnʌlifiˈkeiʃən] n. Anulación, *f.*

nullify [ˈnʌlifai] v. tr. Anular.

nullipara [nʌ lipərə] n. MED. Nulípara, *f.*

— OBSERV. El plural de la palabra inglesa es *nulliparae.*

nulliparous [—s] adj. MED. Nulípara.

nullity [ˈnʌliti] n. JUR. Nulidad, *f.*

Numantian [njuˈmænʃiən] adj./n. Numantino, na.

numb [nʌm] adj. Entumecido, da: *my feet were numb with cold,* tenía los pies entumecidos de frío. || FIG. Petrificado, da; paralizado, da: *numb with fear,*

petrificado de miedo. || *My foot has gone numb*, se me ha dormido el pie.
numb [nʌm] v. tr. Entumecer: *the cold numbed my feet*, el frío me entumeció los pies. || FIG. Dejar helado, paralizar: *the sad news numbed me completely*, la triste noticia me dejó completamente helado.
number [ˈnʌmbə*] n. Número, *m.*: *one is a number*, uno es un número; *the May number of a magazine*, el número de mayo de una revista; *reference number*, número de referencia; *the next number on the programme*, el próximo número del programa. || Grupo, *m.*: *she was not among their number*, no estaba en el grupo. || Total, *m.*, número, *m.* (total). || GRAMM. Número, *m.* || MIL. Número, *m.* || SP. Dorsal, *m.*, número, *m.* (worn by footballers, athletes). || — Pl. Números, *m.*: *he is no good at numbers*, no se le dan bien los números. || Cantidades, *f.*: *they attacked in great numbers*, atacaron en grandes cantidades. || Versos, *m.* (in poetry). || REL. Números, *m.* (Bible). || — FIG. FAM. *A nice little number*, una niña muy mona. || *A number of things to do*, varias cosas que hacer. || *Any number of times*, muchísimas veces. || *Atomic number*, número atómico. || *Beyond number*, innumerable. || REL. *Book of Numbers*, Libro (*m.*) de los Números. || *By the numbers*, mecánicamente; de uno en uno (file). || *Cardinal number*, número cardinal. || GRAMM. *Dual number*, número dual. || *Golden number*, número áureo. || *In round numbers*, en números redondos. || *Law of large numbers*, ley (*f*) de los grandes números. || *Number one*, número uno (best), primero, ra (first), mi menda, este cura (o.s.). || *Odd number*, número impar. || *On a number of occasions*, en varias *or* diversas ocasiones. || FIG. *Opposite number*, colega, *m.* & *f.* || *Ordinal number*, número ordinal. || *Prime number*, número primo. || *Registration number*, número de matrícula (of a car). || U. S. *The numbers*, la lotería clandestina. || *There is strength in numbers*, la unión hace la fuerza. || *They were four in number*, eran cuatro. || *They were not of our number*, no eran de los nuestros. || *To be few in number*, ser pocos. || U. S. FIG. *To have s.o.'s number*, tener a uno calado, conocer a alguien a fondo. || *To make up the number*, hacer número, rellenar. || *To swell the numbers*, hacer bulto. || *To take care of* o *to look after number one*, cuidarse a sí mismo. || *To the number of ten*, hasta el número diez. || *Whole number*, número entero. || *Winning number*, número premiado. || *Without number*, sin número, innumerable. || FIG. *Your number is up*, te llegó la hora, te llegó tu turno (you are going to die).
number [ˈnʌmbə*] v. tr. Numerar, poner número a: *he numbered the pages, the seats*, numeró las páginas, las sillas. || Contar (to count): *my days are numbered*, mis días están contados; *he numbered them among his friends*, los contaba entre sus amigos. || Ascender a, sumar (to amount to): *the population numbered ten thousand*, la población ascendía a diez mil.
— V. intr. *To number off*, numerarse.
numbering [ˈnʌmbəriŋ] n. Enumeración, *f.*, recuento, *m.* (counting). || Numeración, *f.* (of pages, etc.). || TECH. *Numbering machine*, numerador, *m.*
numberless [ˈnʌmbəlis] adj. Innumerable.
number plate [ˈnʌmbə*pleit] n. Matrícula, *f.* (of car).
numbers pool [ˈnʌmbəzpu:l] n. U. S. Lotería (*f.*) clandestina.
numbles [ˈnʌmblz] pl. n. Asaduras, *f.* (of deer).
numbness [ˈnʌmnis] n. Entumecimiento, *m.* (from cold, etc.). || FIG. Parálisis, *f.*
numbskull [ˈnʌmskʌl] n. Lelo, la; tonto, ta.
numen [ˈnju:mən] n. MYTH. Numen, *m.*

— OBSERV. El plural de la palabra inglesa es *numina*.

numerable [ˈnju:mərəbl] adj. Numerable.
numeral [ˈnju:mərəl] adj. Numeral.
— N. Número, *m.*, cifra, *f.*: *Roman, Arabic numerals*, números romanos, arábigos.
numerary [ˈnjumərəri] adj. Numerario, ria.
numeration [ˌnju:məˈreiʃən] n. Numeración, *f.*
numerator [ˈnju:məreitə*] n. Numerador, *m.*
numerical [nju:ˈmerikəl] adj. Numérico, ca.
numerosity [nju:məˈrɔsiti] n. Numerosidad, *f.*
numerous [ˈnju:mərəs] adj. Numeroso, sa: *a numerous family*, una familia numerosa; *on numerous occasions*, en numerosas ocasiones.
numismatic [ˌnju:mizˈmætik] adj. Numismático, ca.
numismatics [—s] n. Numismática, *f.*
numismatist [nju:ˈmizmətist] n. Numismático, ca.
nummulite [ˈnʌmjulait] n. Numulita, *f.* (fossil).
numskull [ˈnʌmskʌl] n. Lelo, la; tonto, ta.
nun [nʌn] n. Monja, *f.*, religiosa, *f.*: *to become a nun*, meterse a monja.
nunciature [ˈnʌnsiətʃə*] n. REL. Nunciatura, *f.*
nuncio [ˈnʌnʃiəu] n. REL. Nuncio, *m.*: *papal nuncio*, nuncio apostólico.
nunnery [ˈnʌnəri] n. Convento (*m.*) de monjas.
nuptial [ˈnʌpʃəl] adj. Nupcial.
— Pl. n. Nupcias, *f.*
nurse [nə:s] n. MED. Enfermera, *f.* || Niñera, *f.* (nanny). || Ama (*f.*) seca (dry nurse). || Nodriza, *f.*, ama (*f.*) de cría (wet nurse). || ZOOL. Obrera, *f.* (bee). || MED. *Male nurse*, enfermero.
nurse [nə:s] v. tr. Cuidar, atender, asistir (sick people, etc.). || Criar, amamantar (to suckle an infant). || Mecer (to cadle a child). || Cuidar (plants). || Curar (to try to cure). || FIG. Guardar, reservar (one's strength). | Abrigar (hopes). | Acariciar (plans). | Cultivar (one's popularity). | Fomentar (a business). || Juntar (billiard balls). || *To nurse a grudge against s.o.*, guardar rencor a uno.
— V. intr. Ser enfermera (to be a nurse). || Ser niñera (to be a nursemaid). || Dar de mamar (to suckle). || Mamar (to feed at the breast).
nurse-child [ˈnə:sˌtʃaild] n. Niño (*m.*) de pecho.
nurseling [ˈnə:sliŋ] n. Lactante, *m.*, niño (*m.*) de pecho.
nursemaid [—meid] n. Niñera, *f.*
nursery [ˈnə:səri] n. Habitación (*f.*) de los niños (in a house). || Guardería (*f.*) infantil (day nursery). || Escuela (*f.*) de párvulos (school). || AGR. Vivero, *m* (for young plants). || Vivero, *m.* (for young animals). || FIG. Vivero, *m.*, cantera, *f.*, semillero, *m.* (of politicians, etc.).
nurseryman [—mən] n. Encargado (*m.*) de un vivero, arbolista, *m.*

— OBSERV. El plural de *nurseryman* es *nurserymen*.

nursery rhyme [ˈnə:sriˌraim] n. Poesía (*f.*) infantil.
nursery school [ˈnə:srisku:l] n. Escuela (*f.*) de párvulos.
nursing [ˈnə:siŋ] adj. Lactante (mother). || *Nursing staff*, enfermeras, *f. pl.*
— N. Profesión (*f.*) *or* trabajo (*m.*) de enfermera (profession). || Cuidado, *m.*, asistencia, *f.* (of patient). || Lactancia, *f.* (suckling).
nursing bottle [—ˈbɔtl] n. Biberón, *m.*
nursing home [—həum] n. MED. Clínica, *f.*
nursling [ˈnə:sliŋ] n. Lactante, *m.*, niño (*m.*) de pecho.
nurture [ˈnə:tʃə*] n. Nutrición, *f.*, alimentación, *f.* (nourishment). || Alimento, *m.* (food). || Educación, *f.*, crianza, *f.* (upbringing).
nurture [ˈnə:tʃə*] v. tr. Nutrir, alimentar (to nourish). || Educar, criar (to educate). || FIG. Alimentar.
nut [nʌt] n. Nuez, *f.* (dry fruit). || TECH. Tuerca, *f.* || MUS. Ceja, *f.* (of stringed instruments). | Nuez, *f.* (of violin bow). || MAR. Cepo, *m.* (of an anchor). || Carbón (*m.*) de bola (coal). || FAM. Melón, *m.*, chola, *f.* (head). || FAM. Chiflado, da; chalado, da (crazy person). || — Pl. FAM. Huevos, *m.* (testicles). || — FIG. FAM. *A hard nut to crack*, un hueso duro de roer. | *Nuts!*, ¡naranjas de la China! | *To be off one's nut*, estar como una cabra. | *To do one's nut* echar el resto.
nut-brown [ˈnʌtbraun] adj. De color avellana (colour). || Castaño claro (hair).
nutcracker [ˈnʌtˌkrækə*] n. Cascanueces, *m. inv.* || ZOOL. Cascanueces, *m. inv.* (bird).
nutgall [ˈnʌtgɔ:l] n. BOT. Agalla, *f.*
nuthatch [ˈnʌthætʃ] n. Trepatroncos, *m. inv.* (bird).
nutmeg [ˈnʌtmeg] n. BOT. Nuez (*f.*) moscada.
nutria [ˈnju:triə] n. ZOOL. Nutria, *f.*
nutrient [ˈnju:triənt] adj. Nutritivo, va.
— N. Alimento (*m.*) nutritivo.
nutriment [ˈnju:trimənt] n. Alimento (*m.*) nutritivo.
nutrition [nju:ˈtriʃən] n. Nutrición, *f.*, alimentación, *f.*
nutritional [—əl] adj. Nutritivo, va; alimenticio, cia.
nutritious [nju:ˈtriʃəs] adj. Nutritivo, va; alimenticio, cia; nutricio, cia.
nutritiousness [—nis] n. Valor (*m.*) nutritivo.
nutritive [ˈnju:tritiv] adj. Nutritivo, va; alimenticio, cia.
nuts [nʌts] adj. FAM. Chiflado, da; chalado, da (crazy): *he is nuts about music*, está chiflado por la música. || — FAM. *To drive s.o. nuts*, volver loco a alguien. | *To go nuts*, volverse loco.
nutshell [ˈnʌtʃel] n. Cáscara (*f.*) de nuez. || FIG. *To put it in a nutshell*, decirlo en pocas palabras.
nutty [ˈnʌti] adj. Que sabe a nuez (taste). || Que da nueces (tree). || Con nueces (cake). || FAM. Tonto, ta; chiflado, da; chalado, da; loco, ca: *to be nutty about*, estar loco por; *to be as nutty as a fruitcake*, estar más loco que una cabra.
nux vomica [ˈnʌksˈvɔmikə] n. BOT. Nuez (*f.*) vómica.
nuzzle [ˈnʌzl] v. tr. Hocicar, hozar (a dog).
— V. intr. Hocicar. || Arrimarse cómodamente. || Acurrucarse (to nestle).
nyctalopia [ˈniktəˌləupiə] n. MED. Nictalopía, *f.*
nylon [ˈnailən] n. Nylon, *m.*, nilón, *m.*, nailon, *m.* (material). || — Pl. Medias (*f.*) de nilón.
— Adj. De nilón.
nymph [nimf] n. MYTH. ZOOL. Ninfa, *f.*
nympha [ˈnimfə] n. ZOOL. Ninfa, *f.*
nymphaea [ˈnimfi] n. BOT. Ninfea, *f.*, nenúfar, *m.*
nymphomania [ˌnimfəˈmeiniə] n. MED. Ninfomanía, *f.*
nymphomaniac [ˌnimfəuˈmeinjæk] n. MED. Ninfómana, *f.*, ninfomaníaca, *f.*

O

o [əu] n. O, *f.* (letter). || Cero, *m.* (zero).
— Interj. ¡Oh!
oaf [əuf] n. FAM. Zoquete, *m.*, ceporro, *m.*, bruto, *m.*
— OBSERV. El plural de *oaf* es *oafs* u *oaves*.
oafish [—iʃ] adj. FAM. Lerdo, da; tonto, ta; bruto, ta.
oafishness [—iʃnis] n. FAM. Necedad, *f.*, tontería, *f.* (foolishness). | Torpeza, *f.* (clumsiness).
oak [əuk] n. BOT. Roble, *m.* (tree). || — BOT. *Holm oak*, encina, *f.* | *Oak grove*, robledal, *m.*, robleda, *f.*, robledo, *m.* || FIG. *To sport one's oak*, cerrar la puerta.
— Adj. De roble.
oak apple [—ˌæpl] n. BOT. Agalla, *f.*
oaken [—ən] adj. De roble.
oak gall [—gɔ:l] n. BOT. Agalla, *f.*
oakum [—əm] n. Estopa, *f.*
oakwood [—wud] n. Roble, *m.* (wood). || Robledo, *m.*, robledal, *m.*, robleda, *f.* (grove of oaks).
oar [ɔ:*] n. MAR. Remo, *m.* (wooden shaft). | Remero, *m.* (oarsman). || — FIG. FAM. *To put* o *to shove* o *to stick one's oar in*, meter baza, entrometerse. || *To rest on one's oars*, dormirse en los laureles (to rest on one's laurels), dejar de remar (to stop rowing).
oar [ɔ:*] v. intr. MAR. Remar.
— V. tr. MAR. Hacer avanzar con el remo.
oared [ɔ:*d] adj. Provisto de remos.
oarlock [ɔ:*lɔk] n. MAR. Escálamo, *m.*, tolete, *m.*
oarsman [ˈɔ:zmən] n. MAR. Remero, *m.*
— OBSERV. El plural de *oarsman* es *oarsmen*.
oarsmanship [—ʃip] n. Arte (*m.*) de remar.
oarswoman [ˈɔ:zˌwumən] n. MAR. Remera, *f.*
— OBSERV. El plural de *oarswoman* es *oarswomen*.
oasis [əuˈeisis] n. Oasis, *m. inv.* || FIG. Remanso, *m.*, oasis, *m.*: *an oasis of peace*, un remanso de paz.
— OBSERV. El plural de la palabra inglesa *oasis* es *oases*.
oast [əust] n. Secadero (*m.*) para el lúpulo, el tabaco o la malta (kiln).
oasthouse [—haus] n. Secadero (*m.*) para el lúpulo, el tabaco o la malta (building).
oat [əut] n. BOT. Avena, *f.* || — Pl. BOT. Avena, *f. sing.* || — CULIN. *Rolled oats*, copos (*m.*) de avena. || FIG. *To be off one's oats*, estar indispuesto, no estar en forma. | *To feel one's oats*, sentirse en plena forma (to feel frisky), estar muy ancho (to feel important). | *To sow one's wild oats*, andar de picos pardos, correrla. || BOT. *Wild oats*, avena loca.
oatcake [—ˈkeik] n. Torta (*f.*) hecha con harina de avena.
oaten [ˈəutn] adj. De avena.
oatfield [ˈəutfi:ld] n. Avenal, *m.*, campo (*m.*) de avena.
oat grass [ˈəutgrɑ:s] n. BOT. Avena (*f.*) loca.
oath [əuθ] n. Juramento, *m.*: *to administer the oath to*, tomar juramento a. || Reniego, *m.*, voto, *m.*, blasfemia, *f.*, juramento, *m.* (blasphemy). || — *On* o *upon* o *under oath*, bajo juramento. || *Taking of an oath*, jura, *f.* || *To break one's oath*, romper un juramento. || *To make* o *to swear* o *to take an oath*, prestar juramento, jurar. || *To put s.o. on oath*, tomar juramento a alguien, hacer prestar juramento a alguien. || *To take one's oath of allegiance*, jurar bandera (in the army). || *Upon my oath*, palabra de honor (honestly), ¡por Dios!, ¡voto a tal! (expression of surprise). || *Witness on oath*, testigo juramentado.
oatmeal [ˈəutmi:l] n. Harina (*f.*) de avena.
oats [əuts] pl. n. See OAT.
obduracy [ˈɔbdjurəsi] n. Obstinación, *f.*, terquedad, *f.* (stubbornness). || Inflexibilidad, *f.*, inexorabilidad, *f.* (hardness). || REL. Impenitencia, *f.*
obdurate [ˈɔbdjurit] adj. Obstinado, da; terco, ca (stubborn). || Inflexible, inexorable (unyielding). || Duro, ra (hardhearted). || Endurecido, da (hardened). || REL. Impenitente.
obeah [ˈəubiə] n. Fetichismo, *m.*, hechicería, *f.* (witchcraft). || Fetiche, *m.* (fetish).
obedience [əˈbi:djəns] n. Obediencia, *f.*: *blind obedience*, obediencia ciega. || REL. Obediencia, *f.* || — *In obedience to*, conforme a, en *or* de conformidad con. | *To compel obedience from*, exigir obediencia de.
obedient [əˈbi:djənt] adj. Obediente. || Dócil (docile). || *To be obedient to*, obedecer a.
obediently [—li] adv. Con obediencia, obedientemente. || Dócilmente. || COMM. *Yours obediently*, queda siempre a su disposición *or* a sus órdenes.
obeisance [əuˈbeisəns] n. Reverencia, *f.* (curtsy). || Homenaje, *m.* (homage). || *To do* o *to make* o *to pay obeisance to*, rendir homenaje a.
obelisk [ˈɔbilisk] n. Obelisco, *m.* (stone shaft). || PRINT. Obelisco, *m.* (dagger).
obese [əuˈbi:s] adj. Obeso, sa.
obesity [—iti] n. Obesidad, *f.*
obey [əˈbei] v. tr. Obedecer: *to obey s.o.*, obedecer a alguien. || Cumplir (an order). || Acatar, respetar (the law). || Observar (the rules). || Obedecer a: *to obey the helm*, obedecer al timón.
— V. intr. Obedecer.
obeyer [—ə*] n. *Obeyer of the laws*, persona que acata la ley.
obfuscate [ˈɔbfʌskeit] v. tr. Ofuscar.
obfuscation [ˌɔbfʌsˈkeiʃən] n. Ofuscación, *f.*
obi [ˈəubi] n. Faja (*f.*) de seda japonesa (sash). || Fetichismo, *m.*, hechicería, *f.* (witchcraft). || Fetiche, *m.* (fetish).
obit [ˈɔbit] n. U. S. Necrología, *f.*, obituario, *m.*
obituarist [əˈbitjuərist] n. Necrólogo, *m.*
obituary [əˈbitjuəri] adj. Necrológico, ca. || — *Obituary column*, necrología, *f.* || *Obituary notice*, nota necrológica; esquela (*f.*) de defunción.
— N. Necrología, *f.*, obituario, *m.*
object [ˈɔbdʒikt] n. Objeto, *m.*: *a bag containing a round object*, una bolsa que contiene un objeto redondo. || Objeto, *m.*, cosa, *f.* (thing). || FIG. Objetivo, *m.*, meta, *f.*, objeto, *m.* (aim): *to accomplish one's object*, alcanzar su objetivo. | Propósito, *m.*, fin, *m.*, objeto, *m.*: *this law has several objects*, esta ley tiene varios propósitos. | Objeto, *m.*: *why is he the object of such strong dislike?*, ¿por qué es objeto de una antipatía tan grande? || PHIL. Objeto, *m.* || GRAMM. Complemento, *m.*: *direct object*, complemento directo. || — *To become an object of ridicule*, ponerse en ridículo. || FIG. *There is no object in doing that*, no sirve para nada hacer eso. | *To be no object*, no importar: *money is no object*, el dinero no importa. || *To make s.o. the object of*, hacerle a alguien objeto de. || *With this object*, con este fin, con este objeto.
object [əbˈdʒekt] v. intr. Oponerse: *no one objected to the decision*, nadie se opuso a la decisión; *he objected to my going out*, se opuso a que saliese. || Poner reparos, hacer objeciones (to raise objections). || Molestar: *do you object to my smoking?*, ¿le molesta que fume? || *I object* (*to that remark*)*!*, ¡protesto!
— V. tr. Objetar: *I objected that it was impossible*, objeté que era imposible.
object ball [ˈɔbdʒiktbɔ:l] n. Mingo, *m.* (in billiards).
object glass [ˈɔbdʒiktglɑ:s] n. PHYS. Objetivo, *m.*
objectification [əbˌdʒektifiˈkeiʃən] n. Objetivación, *f.*
objectify [ɔbˈdʒektifai] v. tr. Objetivar.
objecting [əbˈdʒektiŋ] adj. Objetante.
objection [əbˈdʒekʃən] n. Objeción, *f.*: *to raise an objection*, hacer una objeción. || Reparo, *m.*, objeción, *f.*: *he raises objections to everything*, pone reparos a todo, hace objeciones a todo. || Inconveniente, *m.*, dificultad, *f.* (difficulty): *can you see any objection?*, ¿ves algún inconveniente? || — *Have you any objection to my smoking?*, ¿le molesta que fume? || *If you have no objection*, si no tiene nada que objetar. || *We have no objection to your staying*, no tenemos inconveniente en que se quede.
objectionable [əbˈdʒekʃnəbl] adj. Censurable (criticizable): *objectionable conduct*, comportamiento censurable. || Desagradable, molesto, ta (unpleasant). || Grosero, ra: *objectionable language*, palabras groseras. || *I found the idea most objectionable*, la idea me pareció inaceptable.
objective [əbˈdʒektiv] adj. Objetivo, va. || GRAMM. Objetivo, va (case).
— N. Objetivo, *m.*
objectiveness [—nis] n. Objetividad, *f.*
objectivism [əbˈdʒektivizəm] n. Objetivismo, *m.*
objectivity [ˌɔbdʒekˈtiviti] n. Objetividad, *f.*
object lesson [ˈɔbdʒiktˌlesn] n. Lección (*f.*) práctica. || FIG. Ejemplo, *m.*
objector [əbˈdʒektə*] n. Objetante, *m.* || *Conscientious objector*, objetor (*m.*) de conciencia.
objurgate [ˈɔbdʒə:geit] v. tr. Reprender, amonestar.
objurgation [ˌɔbdʒə:ˈgeiʃən] n. Reprensión, *f.*, amonestación, *f.*, censura, *f.*
oblate [ˈɔbleit] adj. Achatado por los polos (spheroid).
— Adj./n. REL. Oblato, ta.
oblation [əuˈbleiʃən] n. REL. Oblación, *f.* (offering). | Oblata, *f.* (Eucharist).
obligate [ˈɔbligeit] v. tr. Obligar.
obligation [ˌɔbliˈgeiʃən] n. Obligación, *f.*: *to fulfil one's obligations*, cumplir con sus obligaciones; *marital obligations*, obligaciones matrimoniales. || COMM. Compromiso, *m.*: *without obligation*, sin compromiso; *to meet one's obligations*, cumplir sus compromisos. || — *I don't want him to put me under an obligation*, no quiero tener que agradecerle algo. || REL. *Of obligation*, de precepto, de guardar. || *To be under an obligation to do sth.*, tener la obligación de hacer algo, estar obligado a hacer algo. || *To be under an obligation to s.o.*, estarle muy agradecido a uno. || *To put s.o. under an obligation to do sth.*, obligarle a uno a hacer algo.

obligatoriness [ɔˈbligətərinis] n. Obligatoriedad, *f.*
obligatory [ɔˈbligətəri] adj. Obligatorio, ria. || *To make it obligatory upon s.o. to do sth.*, obligarle a uno a que haga algo.
oblige [əˈblaidʒ] v. tr. Obligar (to compel): *he obliged me to resign*, me obligó a dimitir. || Hacer un favor (to assist): *oblige me by thinking no more about it*, hágame el favor de no pensar más en eso; *can you oblige me with a light?*, ¿me haría el favor de darme lumbre? || Complacer (to please): *I'll do it in order to oblige you*, lo haré para complacerte. || — *I'm not obliged to do it*, nada me obliga a hacerlo. || *Much obliged!*, ¡muy agradecido!, ¡muchas gracias! || *To be obliged to do sth.*, verse *or* estar obligado a hacer algo. || *To be much obliged to s.o.*, estarle muy agradecido a uno. || *To be much obliged to s.o. for his help*, agradecerle mucho a uno su ayuda.
obligee [ˌɔbliˈdʒi:] n. Jur. Acreedor, ra.
obliger [əˈblaidʒə*] n. Persona (*f.*) a quien uno tiene que estar agradecido.
obliging [əˈblaidʒiŋ] adj. Complaciente, servicial (helpful). || Atento, ta; amable (kind).
obligingness [—nis] n. Complacencia, *f.* || Amabilidad, *f.* (kindness).
obligor [ˌɔbliˈgɔ:*] n. Jur. Deudor, ra.
oblique [əˈbli:k] adj. Oblicuo, cua: *oblique angle*, ángulo oblicuo. || Fig. Indirecto, ta (ways, means): *oblique criticism*, crítica indirecta.
— N. Anat. Oblicuo, *m.* (muscle). || Math. Oblicua, *f.* (line).
oblique [əˈbli:k] v. intr. Oblicuar (*to*, hacia).
oblique-angled [—æŋgld] adj. Oblicuángulo, la.
obliqueness [əˈbli:knis] or **obliquity** [əˈblikwiti] n. Oblicuidad, *f.*, inclinación, *f.* || Fig. Falta (*f.*) de rectitud (lack of rectitude). | Rodeos, *m. pl.* (obscure statement).
obliterate [əˈblitəreit] v. tr. Borrar (to blot out, to erase). || Quitar (to remove). || Tachar (to cross out). || Eliminar (to wipe out). || Arrasar, destruir (a town). || Med. Obliterar. || Matar, poner el matasellos sobre (a stamp).
obliterating [—iŋ] adj. Med. Obliterador, ra.
obliteration [əˌblitəˈreiʃən] n. Borradura, *f.* (erasure). || Tachadura, *f.* (crossing out). || Eliminación, *f.* (elimination). || Destrucción, *f.*, arrasamiento, *m.* (destruction). || Med. Obliteración, *f.* || Matado, *m.* (of a stamp).
obliterator [əˈblitəreitə*] n. Matasellos, *m. inv.*
oblivion [əˈbliviən] n. Olvido, *m.*: *to fall into oblivion*, caer en el olvido. || Inconsciencia, *f.* (unconsciousness). || Jur. Amnistía, *f.* || — *To cast into oblivion*, echar al olvido. || *To rescue from oblivion*, sacar del olvido.
oblivious [əˈbliviəs] adj. Olvidadizo, za (forgetful). || Inconsciente: *oblivious of* o *to danger*, inconsciente del peligro. || *Oblivious of my presence he started singing*, olvidando mi presencia empezó a cantar.
obliviousness [—nis] n. Olvido, *m.*
oblong [ˈɔblɔŋ] adj. Oblongo, ga.
— N. Rectángulo, *m.*
obloquy [ˈɔbləkwi] n. Calumnia, *f.* (abusive condemnation). || Deshonra, *f.*, oprobio, *m.* (shame).
obnoxious [əbˈnɔkʃəs] adj. Odioso, sa (odious). || Odiado, da (*to*, por) [hated]. || Desagradable, molesto, ta (unpleasant). || Repugnante: *obnoxious smell*, olor repugnante. || *I find him* o *it exceedingly obnoxious*, me repugna.
obnoxiousness [—nis] n. Lo odioso.
obnubilation [əbnjubiˈleiʃən] n. Obnubilación, *f.*, obcecación, *f.*
oboe [ˈəubəu] n. Mus. Oboe, *m.* (instrument). | Juego (*m.*) de lengüetas (of an organ).
oboe player [—ˈpleiə*] or **oboist** [ˈəubəuist] n. Oboe, *m.*, oboísta, *m.* & *f.*
obol [ˈɔbɔl] or **obolus** [—əs] n. Óbolo, *m.*
obscene [əbˈsi:n] adj. Obsceno, na; indecente (indecent). || Grosero, ra (coarse).
obscenity [əbˈsi:niti] n. Obscenidad, *f.* || Grosería, *f.*, obscenidad, *f.* (coarse language): *to utter obscenities*, decir obscenidades.
obscurant [əbˈskjuərənt] n. Oscurantista, obscurantista.
obscurantism [ˌɔbskjuəˈræntizəm] n. Oscurantismo, *m.*, obscurantismo, *m.*
obscurantist [ˌɔbskjuəˈræntist] adj./n. Oscurantista, obscurantista.
obscuration [ˌɔbskjuəˈreiʃən] n. Oscurecimiento, *m.* || Astr. Ocultación, *f.*
obscure [əbˈskjuə] adj. Oscuro, ra (dim): *obscure corner*, rincón oscuro. || Fig. Oscuro, ra (undistinguishable, abstruse). | Recóndito, ta; aislado, da; retirado, da (hidden): *to live in an obscure place in the country*, vivir en un lugar recóndito del campo. | Oscuro, ra; desconocido, da (not famous).
obscure [əbˈskjuə*] v. tr. Oscurecer (to darken). || Fig. Ocultar, disimular (the truth). | Esconder, ocultar (to hide): *a lake obscured by trees*, un lago escondido entre árboles. | Ocultar: *to obscure sth. from s.o.'s view*, ocultar algo a la vista de alguien. | Ofuscar (the understanding). | Eclipsar (to overshadow). || Fig. *To obscure the issue*, complicar las cosas.
obscureness [—nis] n. Falta (*f.*) de claridad (of style, etc.).
obscurity [əbˈskjuəriti] n. Oscuridad, *f.*: *the obscurity of the sky*, la oscuridad del cielo; *to live in obscurity*, vivir en la oscuridad.
obsequies [ˈɔbsikwiz] pl. n. Exequias, *f.*
obsequious [əbˈsi:kwiəs] adj. Obsequioso, sa.
obsequiousness [—nis] n. Obsequiosidad, *f.*
observable [əbˈzə:vəbl] adj. Observable. || — *As is observable*, como se puede comprobar *or* observar. || *No observable reaction*, ninguna reacción perceptible.
observance [əbˈzə:vəns] n. Observancia, *f.*, cumplimiento, *m.* (of a command). || Acatamiento, *m.*, observancia, *f.* (of the law). || Observancia, *f.* (of a religious order). || — Pl. Prácticas, *f.*: *religious observances*, prácticas religiosas. || *Strict observance*, observancia regular, estricta observancia.
observant [əbˈzə:vənt] adj. Observador, ra (quick to observe). || Atento, ta (attentive). || Cumplidor, ra (of one's duty). || Acatador, ra (of the law). || Observante (strict in observance). || *He is very observant*, se fija en todo, no se le escapa nada.
— N. Rel. Observante, *m.*
observantly [—li] n. Con cuidado.
observation [ˌɔbzə:ˈveiʃən] n. Observación, *f.* (remark, note, care, watching). || Observancia, *f.* (of rules, etc.). || — *Patient under observation*, enfermo (*m.*) en observación. || *To escape observation*, pasar inadvertido. || *To keep under observation*, vigilar.
observation car [—kɑ:*] n. U. S. Coche (*m.*) panorámico, coche (*m.*) con techo transparente (railway coach).
observatory [əbˈzə:vətri] Astr. Observatorio, *m.* || Mirador, *m.* (lookout).
observe [əbˈzə:v] v. tr. Observar (to look at with attention). || Cumplir, observar (rules). || Acatar, respetar (the law). || Guardar (silence). || Observar: *to observe an eclipse*, observar un eclipse. || Guardar (religious feasts). || Observar, notar (to notice). || Ver (to see): *I observed him stopping*, le vi pararse. || Decir (to say). || — *He observed to me that*, me advirtió que, me hizo observar que. || *To observe care in*, tener cuidado en.
— V. intr. Observar. || Hacer una observación *or* observaciones (*on* o *upon*, sobre) [to comment]. || Decir (to say).
observer [—ə*] n. Observador, ra.
observing [—iŋ] adj. Observador, ra (quick to observe). || Observante (strict in observance).
obsess [əbˈses] v. tr. Obsesionar (*with*, *by*, por): *it obsesses him*, le obsesiona.
obsession [əbˈseʃən] n. Obsesión, *f.* || *To have an obsession about*, estar obsesionado por.
obsessional [—əl] or **obsessive** [əbˈsesiv] adj. Obsesivo, va.
obsidian [əbˈsidiən] n. Min. Obsidiana, *f.* (dark volcanic rock).
obsolescence [ˌɔbsəuˈlesns] n. Caída (*f.*) en desuso. || Biol. Atrofia, *f.*
obsolescent [ˌɔbsəuˈlesnt] adj. Que cae en desuso. || Biol. Atrofiado, da.
obsolete [ˈɔbsəli:t] adj. Caído en desuso, anticuado, da [*Amer.*, obsoleto] (out of usage): *obsolete word*, palabra caída en desuso. || Pasado de moda (out of fashion). || Que ha caducado (expired). || Med. Atrofiado, da. || Tech. Aviat. Mil. Anticuado, da; fuera de uso.
obsoleteness [—nis] n. Desuso, *m.*
obstacle [ˈɔbstəkl] n. Obstáculo, *m.*: *to overcome an obstacle*, superar *or* vencer un obstáculo; *to put obstacles in the way of*, poner obstáculos a. || *Obstacle race*, carrera (*f.*) de obstáculos.
obstetric [ɔbˈstetrik] or **obstetrical** [—əl] adj. Med. Obstétrico, ca.
obstetrician [ˌɔbsteˈtriʃən] n. Med. Tocólogo, *m.*
obstetrics [ɔbˈstetriks] n. Med. Obstetricia, *f.*, tocología, *f.*
obstinacy [ɔˈbstinəsi] n. Obstinación, *f.*, terquedad, *f.* (stubbornness). || Med. Persistencia, *f.* (of a disease).
obstinate [ˈɔbstinit] adj. Obstinado, da (not yielding to reason). || Terco, ca; obstinado, da (stubborn). || Fig. Rebelde (stubbornly resisting). || Med. Rebelde: *an obstinate disease*, una enfermedad rebelde. || — *As obstinate as a mule*, terco *or* testarudo como una mula. || *To be obstinate in one's refusal to help*, negarse rotundamente a ayudar.
obstreperous [əbˈstrepərəs] adj. Ruidoso, sa (noisy). || Revoltoso, sa (unruly). || Protestón, ona (defying commands).
obstreperousness [—nis] n. Ruido, *m.*, alboroto, *m.* (noise). || Protestas, *f. pl.*
obstruct [əbˈstrʌkt] v. tr. Obstruir (a road, etc.). || Atorar, atascar, obstruir (pipes). || Estorbar (to hinder): *to obstruct the traffic*, estorbar el tráfico; *to obstruct s.o. in the execution of his duty*, estorbarle a uno en el desempeño de sus funciones. || Dificultar (to make it difficult). || Tapar (the view). || Med. Obstruir.
obstruction [əbˈstrʌkʃən] n. Obstrucción, *f.* (obstructing). || Atoramiento, *m.*, atasco, *m.*, obstrucción, *f.* (of pipes). || Obstáculo, *m.* (obstacle). || Estorbo, *m.* (hindrance). || Obstrucción, *f.* (in Parliament). || Med. Obstrucción, *f.*, oclusión, *f.*
obstructionism [—izəm] n. Obstruccionismo, *m.*

obstructionist [—ist] adj./n. Obstruccionista.
obstructive [əbˈstrʌktiv] adj. Que obstruye. || MED. Obstructor, ra. || De obstrucción: *obstructive tactics*, tácticas de obstrucción. || Obstruccionista (member of Parliament).
obstructor [əbˈstrʌktə*] n. Obstructor, ta.
obstruent [ˈɔbstruənt] adj. MED. Obstructor, ra.
obtain [əbˈtein] v. tr. Obtener, conseguir, lograr (to get): *to obtain good results*, conseguir buenos resultados. || Adquirir (to acquire). || Sacar: *to obtain sugar from beet*, sacar azúcar de la remolacha. || Valer: *his merits obtained him the post*, sus méritos le valieron el puesto.
— V. intr. Prevalecer (to prevail). || Existir (to exist).
obtainable [—əbl] adj. Que se puede conseguir. || *Obtainable in your local supermarket*, de venta en el supermercado de su barrio.
obtaining [—iŋ] n. Obtención, *f.*, consecución, *f.*
obtainment [—mənt] n. Obtención, *f.*, consecución, *f.*
obtrude [əbˈtru:d] v. tr. Imponer: *he is always obtruding his opinions upon others*, siempre impone sus opiniones a los demás. || Sacar (to thrust out). || — *To obtrude o.s. into*, entrometerse en. || *To obtrude o.s. on s.o.*, imponerse a alguien.
— V. intr. Manifestarse.
obtrusion [əbˈtru:ʒən] n. Intrusión, *f.* || Entrometimiento, *m.*
obtrusive [əbˈtru:siv] adj. Importuno, na; molesto, ta (annoying). || Entrometido, da (meddlesome). || Presumido, da (conceited). || Llamativo, va (too eye-catching). || Penetrante (smell).
obtrusiveness [—nis] n. Importunidad, *f.*
obturate [ˈɔbtjuəreit] v. tr. Obturar.
obturating [—iŋ] adj. Obturador, ra.
obturation [ˌɔbtjuəˈreiʃən] n. Obturación, *f.*
obturator [ˈɔbtjuəreitə*] n. Obturador, *m.*
obtuse [əbˈtju:s] adj. MATH. Obtuso, sa. || Obtuso, sa; romo, ma (blunt). || FIG. Tardo en comprender, torpe, obtuso, sa (dim-witted): *how can you be so obtuse?*, ¿cómo puedes ser tan obtuso? | Sordo (pain).
obtuse-angled [—æŋgld] adj. MATH. Obtusángulo: *obtuse-angled triangle*, triángulo obtusángulo.
obtuseness [—nis] n. Embotadura, *f.*, embotamiento, *m.* (bluntness). || FIG. Torpeza, *f.*, estupidez, *f.* (stupidity).
obverse [ˈɔbvə:s] adj. Del anverso.
— N. Anverso, *m.* (of a medal).
obvert [ɔbˈvə:t] v. tr. Invertir.
obviate [ˈɔbvieit] v. tr. Obviar: *to obviate a difficulty*, obviar una dificultad. || Evitar (a danger). || Adelantarse a (an objection).
obvious [ˈɔbviəs] adj. Obvio, via; evidente, patente (evident). || Vistoso, sa; llamativo, va (showy). || — *An obvious remark*, una perogrullada. || *It was the obvious thing to do*, era lo que había que hacer. || *To be glaringly obvious*, saltar a la vista.
obviously [—li] adv. Evidentemente, naturalmente, con toda evidencia. || Claro, por supuesto, naturalmente (in answers): *do you think she is right? — Obviously*, ¿crees que tiene razón? — Por supuesto. || — *He was obviously impressed*, se veía que estaba impresionado. || *They were not obviously convinced*, no parecían estar muy convencidos.
obviousness [—nis] n. Evidencia, *f.*
ocarina [ˌɔkəˈri:nə] n. MUS. Ocarina, *f.*
occasion [əˈkeiʒən] n. Ocasión, *f.*, oportunidad, *f.* (opportunity): *he took occasion to speak*, aprovechó la oportunidad para hablar; *the banquet was a good occasion for talking*, el banquete fue una buena ocasión para hablar. || Motivo, *m.* (cause): *you have no occasion to be alarmed*, no tiene ningún motivo para preocuparse. || Lugar, *m.*: *to give occasion to a rebellion*, dar lugar a una rebelión. || Caso, *m.*: *should the occasion arise, please mention it*, si viene al caso menciónelo. || Ocasión, *f.*, acontecimiento, *m.* (ceremony): *on great occasions*, en grandes ocasiones. || Momento, *m.*, ocasión, *f.*: *should the occasion arise, you know what to do*, si llega el momento *or* si se presenta la ocasión ya sabes lo que tienes que hacer. || Circunstancia, *f.*, ocasión, *f.*: *a speech prepared for the occasion*, un discurso preparado para la circunstancia. || — *As occasion requires*, eventualmente. || *On a certain occasion*, en cierta ocasión. || *On another occasion*, en otra oportunidad, otro día. || *On occasion*, de vez en cuando. || *On several occasions*, en varias ocasiones, varias veces. || *On the occasion of*, con motivo de, con ocasión de. || *On the present occasion*, actualmente (at present), en esta oportunidad, esta vez (this time). || *To be equal to the occasion*, estar a la altura de las circunstancias. || *To make it an occasion*, celebrarlo. || *To rise to the occasion*, ponerse a la altura de las circunstancias. || *Upon occasion*, de vez en cuando.
occasion [əˈkeiʒən] v. tr. Ocasionar, causar, provocar (to cause). || Incitar: *to occasion s.o. to do sth.*, incitar a alguien a que haga algo.
occasional [—əl] adj. Ocasional (fortuitous). || Que ocurre de vez en cuando (ocurring from time to time). || Para el caso: *an occasional poem*, un poema para el caso. || Alguno que otro: *despite our being so isolated we do get the occasional visitor*, a pesar de estar tan aislados tenemos alguna que otra visita. || Para casos de necesidad: *an occasional chair*, una silla para casos de necesidad. || *We give the occasional party*, damos una fiesta de vez en cuando.
occasionalism [əˈkeiʒnəlizəm] n. Ocasionalismo, *m.*
occasionalist [əˈkeiʒnəlist] n. Ocasionalista, *m.* & *f.*
occasionalistic [əˌkeiʒnəˈlistik] adj. Ocasionalista.
occasionally [əˈkeiʒənəli] adv. De vez en cuando, alguna que otra vez, ocasionalmente.
Occident [ˈɔksidənt] n. Occidente, *m.*
Occidental [ˌɔksiˈdentl] adj. Occidental.
Occidentalism [ˌɔksiˈdentəlizəm] n. Occidentalismo, *m.*
Occidentalist [ˌɔksiˈdentəlist] adj./n. Occidentalista.
Occidentalization [ˌɔksidentəlaiˈzeiʃən] n. Occidentalización, *f.*
Occidentalize [ˌɔksiˈdentəlaiz] v. tr. Occidentalizar.
occipital [ɔkˈsipitl] adj. ANAT. Occipital (bone).
— N. ANAT. Occipital, *m.*
occiput [ˈɔksipʌt] n. ANAT. Occipucio, *m.* (back part of the skull).

— OBSERV. El plural de la palabra *occiput* es *occipita*.

occlude [ɔˈklu:d] v. tr. Obstruir (a passage). || MED. CHEM. Ocluir. || *Occluded front*, oclusión, *f.* (in meteorology).
— V. intr. Encajarse, ocluirse (in dentistry).
occlusion [ɔˈklu:ʒən] n. Obstrucción, *f.* || MED. CHEM. Oclusión, *f.* || Oclusión, *f.* [de las muelas] (in dentistry).
occlusive [ɔˈklu:siv] adj. Oclusivo, va.
— N. Oclusiva, *f.* (consonant).
occult [ɔˈkʌlt] adj. Oculto, ta. || *Occult sciences* o *arts*, ciencias ocultas.
— N. Ciencias (*f. pl.*) ocultas.
occult [ɔˈkʌlt] v. tr. ASTR. Ocultar.
— V. intr. ASTR. Ocultarse.
occultation [ˌɔkəlˈteiʃən] n. ASTR. Ocultación, *f.*
occultism [ˈɔkəltizəm] n. Ocultismo, *m.*
occultist [ˈɔkəltist] adj./n. Ocultista.
occupancy [ˈɔkjupənsi] n. Ocupación, *f.* || Posesión, *f.* (of a post).
occupant [ˈɔkjupənt] n. Ocupante, *m.* & *f.* (of house, etc.). || Posesor, ra; titular (of a post).
occupation [ˌɔkjuˈpeiʃən] n. Ocupación, *f.* (of a house, a country): *the Roman occupation*, la ocupación romana. || Profesión, *f.*, ocupación, *f.* (employment): *what is your occupation?*, ¿cuál es su profesión? || Trabajo, *m.* (work). || Pasatiempo, *m.* (pastime).
occupational [—l] adj. Profesional: *occupational disease*, enfermedad profesional. || — *Occupational hazards* o *risks*, gajes (*m. pl.*) del oficio. || *Occupational therapy*, reeducación basada en un trabajo manual o intelectual.
occupier [ˈɔkjupaiə*] n. Ocupante, *m.* & *f.* || Inquilino, na (tenant).
occupy [ˈɔkjupai] v. tr. Ocupar, vivir en (to reside in): *my friends don't occupy the whole house*, mis amigos no ocupan toda la casa. || Ocupar (by military force). || Ocupar (a space, post, period of time): *his work occupies all his time*, el trabajo le ocupa todo el tiempo; *is that seat occupied?*, ¿está ocupado este sitio? || Emplear, ocupar: *to occupy one's time in doing sth.*, emplear su tiempo en hacer algo. || Ocupar (one's mind). || Emplear, dar trabajo, ocupar (to keep employed). || — *She is occupied in translating*, está traduciendo. || *To occupy o.s. in doing sth.*, ocuparse de algo *or* en hacer algo.
occur [əˈkə:*] v. intr. Ocurrir, suceder, acontecer (to happen): *the accident occurred in the afternoon*, el accidente ocurrió por la tarde. || Tener lugar (to take place): *festival that occurs every five years*, festival que tiene lugar cada cinco años. || Producirse: *a complete change has occurred*, se ha producido un cambio completo. || Presentarse (opportunity). || Encontrarse: *these plants rarely occur in this country*, estas plantas se encuentran muy poco en este país. || Ocurrirse: *it occurred to me that*, se me ocurrió que. || *I hope it won't occur again*, espero que no vuelva a suceder.
occurrence [əˈkʌrəns] n. Acontecimiento, *m.*, suceso, *m.* (event): *an unusual occurrence*, un suceso extraño. || Caso, *m.* (case). || Existencia, *f.*, presencia, *f.* (of minerals, plants, etc.). || REL. Coincidencia, *f.* || — *To be a common occurrence*, suceder *or* ocurrir frecuentemente. || *To be of frequent occurrence*, ocurrir frecuentemente *or* a menudo.
ocean [ˈəuʃən] n. Océano, *m.*: *the Atlantic Ocean*, el Océano Atlántico. || FIG. Mar, *m.*, océano, *m.*: *an ocean of sand*, un mar de arena. || — Pl. FAM. *Oceans of*, la mar de, un montón de.
— Adj. Oceánico, ca: *ocean currents*, corrientes oceánicas.
oceangoing [—ˈgəuiŋ] adj. MAR. Transatlántico, ca (liner). | De alta mar (capable of sailing across oceans). || *An oceangoing liner*, un transatlántico.
Oceania [əuʃiˈeinjə] pr. n. GEOGR. Oceanía, *f.*
Oceanian [—n] adj./n. Oceánico, ca (of Oceania).
oceanic [ˌəuʃiˈænik] adj. Oceánico, ca (of the ocean).
Oceanic [ˌəuʃiˈænik] adj. Oceánico, ca (Oceanian).
Oceanid [əuˈsi:ənid] n. Oceánida, *f.* (nymph).
oceanographer [ˌəuʃjəˈnɔgrəfə*] n. Oceanógrafo, fa.
oceanographic [ˌəuʃjənəuˈgræfik] or **oceanographical** [—əl] adj. Oceanográfico, ca.
oceanography [ˌəuʃjəˈnɔgrəfi] n. Oceanografía, *f.*
ocellus [əuˈseləs] n. Ocelo, *m.* (eye, mark).

— OBSERV. El plural de *ocellus* es *ocelli*.

ocelot [ˈəusilɔt] n. Ocelote, *m.* (wildcat).

ocher [ˊəukə*] n. U. S. Ocre, *m.*
ocherous [ˊəukərəs] adj. U. S. Ocre.
ochre [ˊəukə*] n. Ocre, *m.*: *red ochre*, ocre rojo.
ochreous [ˊəukriəs] or **ochrous** [ˊəukrəs] adj. Ocre.
o'clock [əˊklɔk] adv. *At three o'clock*, a las tres. || *It is one o'clock*, es la una. || *It is six o'clock*, son las seis.
octagon [ˊɔktəgən] n. MATH. Octógono, *m.*, octágono, *m.*
octagonal [ɔkˊtægənl] adj. Octagonal, octogonal, octágono, na; octógono, na.
octahedral [ˊɔktəˊhedrəl] adj. Octaédrico, ca.
octahedron [ˊɔktəˊhedrən] n. MATH. Octaedro, *m.*
— OBSERV. El plural de *octahedron* es *octahedrons* u *octahedra*.
octane [ˊɔktein] n. Octano, *m.*: *octane number*, índice de octano. || *High-octane fuel*, supercarburante, *m.*
octave [ˊɔktiv] n. MUS. POET. Octava, *f.*
octave [ˊɔkteiv] n. REL. Octava, *f.*
Octavian [ɔkˊteivjən] pr. n. Octavio, *m.*
— Adj. Octaviano, na: *Octavian peace*, paz octaviana.
octavo [ɔkˊteivəu] adj. En octavo (book).
— N. Libro (*m.*) en octavo.
octennial [ɔkˊtenjəl] adj. Que ocurre cada ocho años (occurring). || Que dura ocho años (lasting).
octet or **octette** [ɔkˊtet] n. MUS. Octeto, *m.*
October [ɔkˊtəubə*] n. Octubre, *m.*: *on the 12th of October 1492*, el 12 de octubre de 1492.
octogenarian [ˏɔktəudʒiˊnɛəriən] adj./n. Octogenario, ria.
octopod [ˊɔktəpɔd] n. ZOOL. Octópodo, *m.* | Pulpo, *m.* (octopus).
— Adj. ZOOL. Octópodo, da.
octopoda [ɔkˊtɔpədə] pl. n. ZOOL. Octópodos, *m.*
octopodan [—ən] adj. ZOOL. Octópodo, da.
— N. ZOOL. Octópodo, *m.*
octopus [ˊɔktəpəs] n. Pulpo, *m.* (mollusc).
— OBSERV. El plural de *octopus* es *octopuses* u *octopodes*.
octosyllabic [ˊɔktəusiˊlæbik] adj. Octosilábico, ca; octosílabo, ba.
— N. Octosílabo, *m.* (verse).
octosyllable [ˊɔktəuˏsiləbl] adj. See OCTOSYLLABIC.
— N. Octosílabo, *m.* (verse).
octuple [ˊɔktju:pl] v. tr. Multiplicar por ocho.
ocular [ˊɔkjulə*] adj. Ocular.
— N. Ocular, *m.* (of an optical instrument).
oculist [ˊɔkjulist] n. Oculista, *m.* & *f.*
odalisque or **odalisk** [ˊəudəlisk] n. Odalisca, *f.*
odd [ɔd] adj. Impar: *odd day*, día impar. || Impar, non (number). || Unos, unas; y pico: *a hundred-odd pounds*, cien libras y pico, unas cien libras. || Pequeño, na (amount). || Sobrante, de más (left over). || Suelto, ta (isolated). || Descabalado, da; deshermanado, da; desparejado, da: *an odd shoe*, un zapato desparejado. || Alguno, na; alguno que otro, alguna que otra: *on odd occasions*, en algunas ocasiones; *to receive the odd client*, recibir a algún que otro cliente. || Suelto, ta (money): *a few odd coins*, algunas monedas sueltas. || Cualquier, cualquiera: *in an odd corner*, en cualquier rincón. || Apartado, da (out-of-the-way). || Poco corriente: *an odd size*, una talla poco corriente. || Extraño, ña; raro, ra (strange): *an odd person*, una persona rara; *how very odd!*, ¡qué raro!; *the odd thing is that*, lo raro es que. || — *Odd job man*, factótum, *m.* (who does all kinds of work), hombre mañoso (skilful man). || *Odd jobs*, pequeños arreglos *or* reparaciones: *to do odd jobs around the house*, hacer pequeños arreglos en toda la casa; trabajitos, *m. pl.* [que uno hace de vez en cuando]: *he lives by odd jobs he picks up*, vive de los trabajitos que hace de vez en cuando. || *Odd man out*, excepción, *f.* (unlike the others), persona (*f.*) sobrante (person left over). || *Odd moments*, momentos (*m.*) de ocio, ratos perdidos. || *To eat the odd meal*, comer de vez en cuando. || *To play at odds or evens*, jugar a pares o nones.
oddball [ˊɔdbɔ:l] adj. Raro, ra; excéntrico, ca.
— N. Persona (*f.*) rara *or* excéntrica.
oddity [ˊɔditi] n. Rareza, *f.*, singularidad, *f.* (quality). || Curiosidad, *f.*, cosa (*f.*) rara (thing). || Excéntrico, ca; original, *m.* & *f.* (person). || *She has her oddities*, tiene sus cosas raras.
oddly [ˊɔdli] adv. Extrañamente. || — *Oddly enough*, por extraño que parezca. || *To behave oddly*, comportarse extrañamente *or* de una manera rara.
oddments [ˊɔdmənts] pl. n. COMM. Saldos, *m.* | Retales, *m.* (of fabric). || Cosillas, *f.* (odds and ends).
oddness [ˊɔdnis] n. Carácter (*m.*) impar (of day, number). || FIG. Excentricidad, *f.*, extravagancia, *f.*, rareza, *f.* (of a person). | Singularidad, *f.* (of a thing).
odds [ɔdz] pl. n. Desigualdad, *f. sing.*, disparidad, *f. sing.* (inequality): *overwhelming odds in his favour*, desigualdad enorme a su favor. || Fuerzas (*f.*) superiores: *to fight against odds*, luchar contra fuerzas superiores. || Posibilidades, *f.*, probabilidades, *f.* (chances). || Diferencia, *f. sing.* (difference). || SP. Ventaja, *f. sing.* | Apuesta, *f. sing.*: *the odds are four to one*, las apuestas están a cuatro contra uno. || — *By all odds*, indiscutiblemente, sin duda alguna. || *It makes no odds*, da lo mismo, no importa. || *Odds and ends*, pedazos, *m.*, trozos, *m.* (bits), cosillas, *f.*: *I've just a few odds and ends left to pack*, sólo me quedan algunas cosillas por poner en la maleta; fruslerías, *f.* (curios), restos, *m.* (food). || *The odds are in his favour*, tiene muchas probabilidades de ganar. || *The odds are that*, es probable que. || *To be at odds with s.o.*, estar peleado con uno, estar de punta con uno. || *To give odds*, dar ventaja. || *To put o to set two people at odds*, enemistar a dos personas, sembrar la discordia entre dos personas. || FAM. *What's the odds?*, ¿qué más da?, ¿qué importa?
odds-on [ˊɔdzɔn] adj. Seguro, ra. || — *He has an odds-on chance of winning*, tiene mucha probabilidad de ganar. || *Odds-on favourite*, caballo favorito (horse), favorito, ta (person).
ode [əud] n. Oda, *f.* (poetry).
odeon [əudjən] or **odeum** [ˊəudjəm] n. Odeón, *m.*
— OBSERV. El plural de *odeum* es *odeums* u *odea*.
odious [ˊəudjəs] adj. Odioso, sa.
odiousness [—nis] n. Odiosidad, *f.*, lo odioso.
odium [ˊəudjəm] n. Odio, *m.* (hatred). || Oprobio, *m.*, (ignominy). || Reprobación, *f.* (condemnation). || *To lose one's odium*, dejar de ser odiado.
odometer [ɔˊdɔmitə*] n. Odómetro, *m.*
odontologist [ˏɔdɔnˊtɔlədʒist] n. Odontólogo, *m.*
odontology [ˏɔdɔnˊtɔlədʒi] n. Odontología, *f.*
odor [ˊəudə*] n. U. S. See ODOUR.
odoriferous [ˏəudəˊrifərəs] adj. Odorífero, ra.
odorless [ˊəudəlis] adj. Inodoro, ra.
odorous [ˊəudərəs] adj. Odorante, oloroso, sa. || Perfumado, da: fragante.
odorousness [ˊəudərəsnis] n. Olor, *m.*, fragancia, *f.*
odour [ˊəudə*] n. Olor, *m.* (smell). || Perfume, *m.* (fragrance). || — *In the odour of sanctity*, en olor de santidad. || FAM. *To be in bad odour with*, estar mal visto por, no ser santo de la devoción de. | *To be in good odour with*, ser muy bien visto por.
odourless [—lis] adj. Inodoro, ra.
Odyssey [ˊɔdisi] pr. n. Odisea, *f.*
oecological [i:kəˊlɔdʒikəl] adj. Ecológico, ca.
oecology [i:ˊkɔlədʒi] n. Ecología, *f.*
oecumene [ˊi:kju:mi:n] n. REL. Ecumene, *m.*
oecumenical [ˏi:kjuˊmenikəl] adj. REL. Ecuménico, ca.
oecumenicalism [—izəm] or **oecumenism** [ˊi:kjumənizəm] n. REL. Ecumenismo, *m.*
oedema [iˊdi:mə] n. MED. Edema, *m.*
oedematous [iˊdemətəs] n. MED. Edematoso, sa.
Oedipus [ˊi:dipəs] pr. n. Edipo, *m.* || *Oedipus complex*, complejo (*m.*) de Edipo.
oenological [inəˊlɔdʒikəl] adj. Enológico, ca.
oenologist [i:ˊnɔlədʒist] n. Enólogo, ga.
oenology [i:ˊnɔlədʒi] n. Enología, *f.*
o'er [ˊəuə*] prep./adv. POET. See OVER.
oersted [ˊə:sted] n. Oersted, *m.*, oerstedio, *m.*
oesophagus [i:ˊsɔfəgəs] n. ANAT. Esófago, *m.*
— OBSERV. El plural de *oesophagus* es *oesophagi*.
oestrogen [ˊi:strədʒin] n. MED. Estrógeno, *m.*
oestrus [ˊi:strəs] n. Estro, *m.* (rut, insect).
of [ɔv, əv] prep. De (in most senses): *the events of last year*, los acontecimientos del año pasado; *she is proud of her daughter*, está orgullosa de su hija; *of good family*, de buena familia; *citizens of London*, ciudadanos de Londres; *the novels of Faulkner*, las novelas de Faulkner; *cured of his illness*, curado de su enfermedad; *a group of women*, un grupo de mujeres; *a basket of apples*, un cesto de manzanas; *one of his brothers*, uno de sus hermanos; *three of us went to university*, tres de nosotros fueron a la universidad; *made of gold*, [hecho] de oro. || Que tiene, de: *a man of resources*, un hombre de recursos; *a person of distinction*, una persona que tiene distinción. || En: *doctor of medicine*, doctor en medicina. || De parte de: *it is very kind of you*, es muy amable de su parte. || Por: *it can move of itself*, puede moverse por sí solo. || De: *of a child he was very naughty*, de niño era muy malo. || Por: *of an evening*, por la noche. || U. S. Menos, para (of time): *it is five of one*, es la una menos cinco, faltan cinco minutos para la una. || — *A beauty of beauties*, la belleza por excelencia. || *A child of seven*, un niño de siete años. || *A fine figure of a man*, un hombre bien hecho *or* bien proporcionado. || *A friend of mine, yours, etc.*, un amigo mío, tuyo, etc. || *A friend of my father's*, un amigo de mi padre. || *All of them*, todos ellos. || *A love of animals, of nature*, un amor a los animales, a la naturaleza. || *A smell of paint*, un olor a pintura. || *A terror of a child*, un monstruo de niño, un niño terrible. || *Dresses of her own making*, vestidos hechos por ella misma. || *Fleet of foot*, veloz, rápido, da. || *Hard of hearing*, duro de oído. || *Hard of heart*, duro de corazón, de corazón duro. || *Heart of gold*, corazón de oro. || *It was cruel of her*, fue una crueldad de su parte. || *King of kings*, rey de reyes. || *Of age*, mayor de edad. || *Of a Sunday*, los domingos (on Sundays), un domingo (one Sunday). || *Of late*, últimamente, recientemente. || *Of o.s.*, de motu propio. || *She is a marvel of marvels*, es de lo más maravilloso que hay. || *She is the queen of queens*, es la reina de las reinas. || *South of, north of*, al sur de, al norte de. || *The best of friends*, los mejores amigos del mundo, muy buenos amigos: *we are the best of friends*, somos muy buenos amigos. || *The fool of my brother*, el tonto de mi hermano. || *The love of God*, el amor de Dios. || *There were lots of us*, éramos muchos. || *Today of all days*, hoy precisamente. || *What of it?*, ¿y qué? (so what?), ¿qué te parece? (how about it?) || *You are no friend of mine*, no eres

amigo mío. || *You, of all men* o *of all people, should have more sense*, tú, más que nadie, tendrías que ser más sensato.

— OBSERV. Esta preposición se traduce de varias maneras cuando acompaña ciertos verbos como *to think, to smell, to taste*, etc. Consúltense los artículos dedicados a estos verbos para encontrar la traducción adecuada.

off [ɔf] adv. A (away): *the dam is twenty miles off*, la presa está a veinte millas; *some way off*, a cierta distancia. || A distancia: *to keep s.o. off*, mantener a alguien a distancia. || MAR. Viento en popa (with the wind). | Mar adentro, hacia alta mar, en alta mar (out to sea). || THEATR. Fuera de escena, entre bastidores (off stage). || En off: *voice off*, voz en off. || — *A long way off*, muy lejos (time, distance), muy equivocado (a guess, etc.): *to be a long way off in one's calculations*, estar muy equivocado en sus cálculos. || *Be off with you!*, ¡fuera de aquí! || *Further off*, más lejos, más allá. || *Off and on* o *on and off*, de vez en cuando. || *Off in the distance*, allá lejos. || *Off we go!*, ¡vámonos! || *Off with him* o *with you!*, ¡fuera!, ¡fuera de aquí! || *Off with his head!*, ¡que le corten la cabeza! || *Off with your boots!*, ¡quítate las botas! || *Right off* o *straight off*, see RIGHT & STRAIGHT. || FAM. *That's a bit off!*, ¡no hay derecho! || *The party is four days off*, la fiesta tendrá lugar dentro de cuatro días, faltan cuatro días para la fiesta. || *There are two shillings off*, hay un descuento de dos chelines. || POP. *To be having it off with*, hacer el amor con. || *To be off*, irse: *I'm off*, me voy; *I think it's time we were off*, creo que ya es hora de que nos vayamos *or* de irnos; *I'm off to Madrid this weekend*, me voy a Madrid este fin de semana; despegar (an aircraft), acabar de tomar la salida (in sports): *they're off!*, ¡acaban de tomar la salida!; estar fuera (absent). || *To give s.o. ten per cent off*, hacerle a uno un descuento del diez por ciento. || *To take a day off*, tomar un día de descanso. || *Why is the lid of the pan off?*, ¿por qué está destapada la cacerola?

— Prep. Fuera de: *our house is off the main road*, nuestra casa está fuera de la carretera principal. || De: *it fell off the table*, cayó de la mesa; *take that off the table*, quita eso de la mesa; *not far off each other*, no lejos uno de otro. || A ... de: *three yards off me*, a tres metros de mí. || Desde, de: *he jumped off the cliff*, saltó desde el acantilado. || Que arranca de, que sale de: *street off the main road*, calle que arranca de la carretera principal. || En: *to eat off gold plate*, comer en vajilla de oro. || De, con: *to feed off vegetables*, alimentarse de verduras. || A: *to borrow money off s.o.*, pedirle dinero prestado a uno. || MAR. A la altura de: *sailing off Gibraltar*, navegando a la altura de Gibraltar. || — *Height off the ground*, altura del suelo. || *He is off tobacco for life*, ha dejado definitivamente de fumar. || *I've gone right off the cinema*, ya no me gusta el cine. || MAR. *Off the wind*, viento en popa. || *Ten per cent off all our prices*, descuento del diez por ciento sobre todos nuestros precios. || *That's a load off my mind!*, ¡qué peso me he quitado de encima! || *To be off a job*, haber dejado un trabajo. || *To be off centre*, estar descentrado (crooked), no dar en el blanco (a shot). || *To be off form*, no estar en forma. || *To be off one's food*, no tener apetito. || *To be off work*, no trabajar. || FAM. *To be right off it*, estar completamente equivocado (wrong). || *To catch s.o. off guard*, cogerle a uno desprevenido. || *To dine off*, cenar. || *To live off s.o.*, vivir a costa de alguien. || *To take a fortnight off work*, tomarse quince días de vacaciones. || *You have a button off your coat*, te falta un botón del abrigo.

— Adj. Malo, la; pasado, da (meat, fish, fruit, vegetables). || Cortada (milk). || Agriado, da (wine). || Rancio, cia (butter). || Malo, la (not up to standard): *an off day*, un día malo. || Suspendido, da; cancelado, da: *the match, the trip is off*, el partido, el viaje ha sido suspendido. || Apagado, da (electrical appliances): *the lights were off*, las luces estaban apagadas. || Cerrado, da (tap). || Cortado, da (water). || Suelto, ta; quitado, da (brake). || Libre (free): *are you off on Thursday?*, ¿estás libre el jueves? || Lateral: *an off street*, una calle lateral. || Equivocado, da; erróneo, a (wrong): *his answer was slightly off*, su contestación fue ligeramente errónea. || Remoto, ta; lejano, na (remote): *an off chance*, una lejana posibilidad. || Secundario, ria: *an off issue*, una cuestión secundaria. || Derecho, cha (part of an animal). || SP. Derecho, cha (in cricket). || MAR. Mar adentro. || — *Chicken is off*, no hay pollo, no queda pollo (on a menu). || *For off consumption*, para llevar (goods). || *His shirt was off*, se había quitado la camisa. || *In the off position*, [en posición de] cerrado (a switch), en posición de paro (lever). || *In the off season*, fuera de temporada. || *Off season prices*, precios de fuera de temporada (in hotels), precios de temporada baja (of airlines). || AUT. *Off side*, lado izquierdo (when driving on the right), lado derecho (when driving on the left). || *To be badly off*, andar mal de dinero. || *To be badly off for*, andar mal de: *I am badly off for money*, ando mal de dinero. || *To be better off*, andar mejor de dinero (moneywise), estar mejor (of conditions). || *To be well off*, estar muy bien: *she is well off in her new job*, está muy bien en su nuevo trabajo; estar acomodado *or* desahogado (to enjoy financial comfort). || *To be with* o *to have one's coat off*, estar sin abrigo, haberse quitado el abrigo. || *To be worse off for*, estar *or* andar peor de. || *To have sth. off*, quitarse (to take off), estar sin (to be without). || *To walk with one's shoes off*, ir descalzo. || *We are only thirty pounds off*, sólo nos faltan treinta libras. || *We came on the off chance of finding you*, vinimos pensando que a lo mejor le encontraríamos, vinimos a ver si le encontrábamos. || *We'll go on the off chance*, iremos por si acaso, iremos a ver. || *Your aim was off*, apuntaste mal.

— N. SP. Salida, *f.* (start). | Campo (*m.*) derecho (in cricket).

— OBSERV. Como la palabra *off* modifica frecuentemente el sentido de los verbos que acompaña, es preciso consultar los artículos dedicados a estos verbos para encontrar la traducción adecuada.

off [ɔf] v. intr. MAR. Hacerse mar adentro. || Irse (to go away).

offal [—əl] n. Menudos, *m. pl.*, despojos, *m. pl.*, asaduras, *f. pl.* (of cattle). || Menudillos, *m. pl.* (of poultry). || Desechos, *m. pl.*, residuos, *m. pl.* (waste product). || Basuras, *f. pl.* (refuse).

offbeat [—bi:t] adj. U. S. Original, excéntrico, ca.

off-colour (U. S. **off-color**) [—ˈkʌlə*] adj. Pálido, da (pale). || Indispuesto, ta; malo, la (not in normal health): *he was feeling off-colour*, se encontraba indispuesto. || Desteñido, da (material). || Defectuoso, sa; que no es del color debido: *an off-colour diamond*, un diamante defectuoso. || Subido de color: *an off-colour joke*, un chiste subido de color.

offcut [—kʌt] n. Recorte, *m.*

offence [əˈfens] n. Ofensa, *f.* (act of offending s.o.). || Escándalo, *m.* (scandal). || JUR. Delito, *m.* || REL. Ofensa, *f.*, pecado, *m.*, falta, *f.* (sin). || MIL. Ataque, *m.*, ofensiva, *f.* || SP. Falta, *f.* (foul). || — JUR. *Capital offence*, crimen (*m.*) que merece la pena capital. | *Minor offence*, contravención, *f.*, infracción, *f.* || *No offence* o *no offence meant*, sin intención de ofenderle. || *No offence was intended*, no tenía la intención de ofender. || JUR. *Second offence*, reincidencia, *f.* || FIG. *To be an offence to the ear*, herir *or* lastimar el oído. || *To cause offence to s.o.*, ofender a alguien (to create resentment), escandalizar a alguien (to shock). || *To give offence*, ofender. || *To take offence at*, ofenderse por, sentirse ofendido por (to get resentful), escandalizarse por (to be shocked at). || *Without offence to you*, sin intención de ofenderle.

offenceless [—lis] adj. Inofensivo, va. || Inocente.

offend [əˈfend] v. tr. Ofender: *the remark offended him*, la observación le ofendió; *to offend s.o.'s dignity*, ofender la dignidad de uno. || Escandalizar (to shock). || FIG. Lastimar, herir (the eyes, the ears). || — *To be easily offended*, picarse *or* enfadarse fácilmente. || *To be offended at*, ofenderse por, estar enfadado por, tomar a mal. || *To be offended with s.o.*, estar enfadado con alguien.

— V. intr. *To offend against*, infringir, violar (the law, a regulation, etc.), pecar contra (to sin).

offender [—ə*] n. Ofensor, ra; ofendedor, ra. || REL. Pecador, ra (sinner). || JUR. Delincuente, *m. & f.* | Infractor, ra. || — JUR. *A first offender*, un delincuente sin antecedentes penales. | *Old offender*, reincidente, *m. & f.*

offending [—iŋ] adj. Ofendedor, ra; ofensor, ra.

offense [əˈfens] n. U. S. See OFFENCE.

offenseless [—lis] adj. U. S. Inofensivo, va. || Inocente.

offensive [—iv] adj. Ofensivo, va; insultante (insulting). || Repugnante (revolting): *an offensive smell*, un olor repugnante. || Chocante (shocking). || MIL. Ofensivo, va: *offensive weapons*, armas ofensivas. || — *Morally offensive*, que ofende la moral (book). || *Word offensive to the ear*, palabra malsonante *or* grosera.

— N. MIL. Ofensiva, *f.*: *to take the offensive*, tomar la ofensiva.

offensiveness [—ivnis] n. Lo ofensivo (of insulting words, etc.). || Lo chocante. || Repugnancia, *f.* || Grosería, *f.* (rudeness).

offer [ˈɔfə*] n. Oferta, *f.*: *a firm offer*, una oferta en firme; *to decline an offer*, rechazar una oferta. || Propuesta, *f.* (proposal). || — *Offer of marriage*, petición (*f.*) de mano. || *On offer*, en venta (on sale), en rebaja (cheap). || *That's my last offer*, es mi última oferta *or* mi última palabra, no puedo ofrecer más.

offer [ˈɔfə*] v. tr. Ofrecer, regalar (a gift). || Ofrecer: *can I offer you a cigarette?*, ¿le puedo ofrecer un cigarrillo? || Ofrecer (a post). || Proponer, ofrecer: *he offered his services*, propuso sus servicios. || Ofrecerse: *to offer to do a job*, ofrecerse para hacer un trabajo. || Proponer (to present for consideration): *to offer a plan*, proponer un proyecto. || Ofrecer: *to offer little resistance*, ofrecer poca resistencia. || Hacer (a remark). || Manifestar, expresar (an opinion). || Presentar (difficulties). || Presentar, ofrecer: *to offer few possibilities of success*, ofrecer pocas posibilidades de éxito; *to offer certain advantages*, ofrecer ciertas ventajas. || Ofrecer (to bid): *to offer a good price for sth.*, ofrecer un buen precio por algo. || Hacer como si, hacer el paripé de (to pretend to). || REL. Ofrecer (a sacrifice). | Ofrendar, ofrecer: *to offer one's soul to God*, ofrendar su alma a Dios. || — *To offer an apology*, pedir disculpas. || COMM. *To offer goods (for sale)*, vender mercancías. || *To offer one's arm*,

ofrecer su brazo. || *To offer one's help*, ofrecer su ayuda. || *To offer o.s.*, ofrecerse; presentarse: *to offer o.s. to a post*, presentarse a un puesto.
— V. intr. Presentarse (occasion). || REL. Hacer una ofrenda.
offerer [—rə*] n. Oferente, *m. & f.*
offering [—riŋ] n. Oferta, *f.* (action). || Regalo, *m.* (gift, present). || REL. Ofrenda, *f.* (sacrifice). | Don, *m.*, ofrenda, *f.* (donation). || — REL. *Burnt offering*, holocausto, *m.* || *To send a girl flowers as a peace offering*, mandar *or* regalar flores a una chica para hacer las paces. || REL. *Votive offering*, exvoto, *m.*
offertory [ˈɔfətəri] n. REL. Ofertorio, *m.* (part of the Mass). | Colecta, *f.* (collection of money).
offhand [ˈɔfˈhænd] adj. Improvisado, da (without preparation): *offhand speech*, discurso improvisado. || Desenvuelto, ta (casual). || Brusco, ca (brusque).
— Adv. Sin pensarlo, a primera vista (at once). || Improvisadamente, sin preparación (without preparation). || De una manera desenvuelta, con desenvoltura (casually). || Bruscamente (abruptly). || — *I can't remember offhand*, no me acuerdo en este momento *or* ahora mismo. || *I couldn't tell you offhand*, no se lo puedo decir así como así.
offhanded [—id] adj. See OFFHAND.
offhandedly [—idli] adv. See OFFHAND.
office [ˈɔfis] n. Oficina, *f.* (premises): *business office*, oficina comercial; *head office*, oficina central. || Oficina, *f.*, despacho, *m.* (room): *manager's office*, despacho del director. || Bufete, *m.* (of a lawyer). || Oficio, *m.* (service): *through s.o.'s good offices*, gracias a los buenos oficios de uno. || Favor, *m.* (favour): *to do s.o. a good office*, hacer a uno un gran favor. || Funciones, *f. pl.* (function): *to take office*, entrar en funciones. || Cargo, *m.*: *public office*, cargo público; *to hold office*, ocupar un cargo. || Ministerio, *m.* (ministry): *Foreign Office*, Ministerio de Asuntos Exteriores [*Amer.*, Ministerio de Relaciones Exteriores]; *Home Office*, Ministerio de Gobernación (in Spain), Ministerio del Interior (in other countries); *War office*, Ministerio del Ejército (in Spain), Ministerio de la Guerra (in other countries). || Cartera (*f.*) de ministro (portfolio): *to be called to office*, recibir una cartera de ministro. || Poder, *m.* (power): *the government in office*, el gobierno que está en el poder. || Oficina, *f.*: *Tourist Office*, oficina de turismo; *lost property office* [U. S., *lost and found office*], oficina de objetos perdidos. || Negociado, *m.* (administrative division). || REL. Oficio, *m.*: *office for the dead*, oficio de difuntos. || U. S. Consulta, *f.*, consultorio, *m.* (of a doctor). || — Pl. Dependencias, *f.* (of a house). || — *Holy Office*, Santo Oficio. || *International Labour Office*, Oficina Internacional del Trabajo. || *Last offices*, oficio de difuntos. || *Office hours*, horas (*f.*) de oficina. || *To leave office*, dimitir.
office boy [—bɔi] n. Recadero, *m.*
office clerk [—klɑ:k] n. Oficinista, *m. & f.*
officeholder [—ˌhəuldə*] n. U. S. Funcionario, ria.
officer [ˈɔfisə*] n. Funcionario, ria (who holds a public appointment). || Policía, *m.*, agente (*m.*) de policía (policeman). || Director, *m.* (of a company). || MIL. Oficial, *m.*: *naval, army officer*, oficial de marina, del ejército. || Dignatario, *m.* (of an order). || — *Customs officer*, aduanero, *m.* || MAR. *Executive officer*, segundo comandante. || MIL. *Field officer*, jefe, *m.* | *Officer of the day, of the watch*, oficial de servicio, de guardia. | *Reserve officer*, oficial retirado, de reserva. || *Sanitary officer*, oficial de sanidad.
officer [ˈɔfisə*] v. tr. MIL. Proveer de mandos. || Mandar (to command). || *To be well officered*, tener buenos mandos.
office seeker [—ˈsi:kə*] n. Político (*m.*) que intenta conseguir una cartera.
office work [—wə:k] n. Trabajo (*m.*) de oficina.
office worker [wə:kə*] n. Oficinista, *m. & f.*
official [əˈfiʃəl] adj. Oficial: *an official report*, un informe oficial; *the queen's official birthday*, el cumpleaños oficial de la reina; *official news*, noticias oficiales. || Titular (holding an office). || MED. Oficinal. || *In one's official capacity*, oficialmente.
— N. Funcionario, ria: *high officials*, altos funcionarios. || REL. Provisor, *m.*, oficial, *m.* (of an ecclesiastical court).
officialdom [—dəm] n. Burocracia, *f.* (bureaucracy). || Funcionarios, *m. pl.* (officials).
officialese [əˌfiʃəˈli:z] n. Lenguaje (*m.*) administrativo.
officialism [əˈfiʃəlizəm] n. Burocracia, *f.*
officiality [əˌfiʃiˈæliti] n. Oficialidad, *f.*
officialization [əˌfiʃəlaiˈzeiʃən] n. Oficialización, *f.*
officially [əˈfiʃəli] adv. Oficialmente.
officiant [əˈfiʃiənt] n. Celebrante, *m.*, oficiante, *m.* (priest, minister).
officiary [əˈfiʃiəri] adj. Por el cargo ocupado (title).
— N. Autoridades, *f. pl.*
officiate [əˈfiʃieit] v. tr./intr. Oficiar, celebrar (a religious service). || FAM. Ejercer las funciones (*as*, de).
officinal [ˌɔfiˈsainl] adj. MED. Oficinal.
officious [əˈfiʃəs] adj. Oficioso, sa (unofficial): *officious talks*, conversaciones oficiosas. || Entrometido, da; oficioso, sa (meddlesome).
officiousness [—nis] n. Oficiosidad, *f.*, carácter (*m.*) oficioso.
offing [ˈɔfiŋ] n. MAR. Alta mar, *f.*, lontananza, *f.* || FIG. *In the offing*, en perspectiva.
offish [ˈɔfiʃ] adj. Distante, altivo, va.
off-licence [ˈɔfˈlaisəns] n. Bodega, *f.* (shop). || Taberna, *f.*, tasca, *f.* (public house). || Permiso (*m.*) que concede el derecho de vender bebidas alcohólicas para consumo externo (licence).
off-peak [ˈɔfpi:k] adj. De menor consumo (electricity). || De menos tráfico, de menos afluencia (transport). || *Off-peak season*, temporada baja.
offprint [ˈɔfprint] n. Separata, *f.*
offscourings [ˈɔfˈskauəriŋz] pl. n. Heces, *f.*, hez, *f. sing.*: *the offscourings of humanity*, la hez de la humanidad.
offset [ˈɔfset] n. BOT. Renuevo, *m.*, vástago, *m.* || AGR. Acodo, *m.* (layer). || Rama, *f.* (of a family). || ARCH. Resalto, *m.* || GEOL. Estribación, *f.*, contrafuerte, *m.* (mountains). || Offset, *m.* (in printing). || TECH. Codo, *m.* (bend in a pipe). | Desviación, *f.* (deviation). || ELECTR. Ramal, *m.* || Ordenada, *f.*, perpendicular, *f.* (in surveying). || FIG. Compensación, *f.*: *to be an offset to losses*, ser una compensación a las pérdidas. | Contraste, *m.* (contrast).
offset [ˈɔfset] v. tr. Compensar (to balance): *his winnings offset my losses*, sus ganancias compensan mis pérdidas. || Desviar (to deviate). || Hacer un doble codo en, acodar (a pipe). || PRINT. Imprimir por el procedimiento offset (to print).
— V. intr. BOT. Echar renuevos *or* vástagos. || PRINT. Emplear el procedimiento offset.
offshoot [ˈɔfʃu:t] n. Vástago, *m.*, retoño, *m.*, renuevo, *m.* (from a main stem). || FIG. Ramificación, *f.* (subsidiary activity). | Vástago, *m.* (of a family).
offshore [ˈɔfʃɔ:*] adj. De la costa, de tierra: *an offshore wind*, un viento de la costa. || De altura (away from the shore). || — *Offshore derrick*, torre (*f.*) de perforación en el mar. || *Offshore islands*, islas cercanas a la costa.
— Adv. Mar adentro.
off side [ˈɔfˈsaid] adj. SP. Fuera de juego.
offside [ˈɔfˈsaid] n. SP. Fuera de juego, *m.* || AUT. Lado (*m.*) derecho (when driving on the left), lado (*m.*) izquierdo (when driving on the right).
offspring [ˈɔfspriŋ] n. Progenitura, *f.*, progenie, *f.*, descendencia, *f.* (children). || Hijo, ja (child). || FIG. Fruto, *m.*, resultado, *m.* (result).
offstage [ˈɔfsteidʒ] adj./adv. Entre bastidores, fuera del escenario. || FIG. Entre bastidores.
offtake [ˈɔfteik] n. Salida, *f.* (of goods).
off-the-peg [ˈɔfθəˈpeg] adj. De confección (clothes).
off-the-record [ˈɔfðəˈrekɔ:d] adj. Oficioso, sa (unofficial). || Confidencial.
off-white [ˈɔfwait] adj. Blancuzco, ca; de color hueso.
oft [ɔft] adv. POET. See OFTEN.
often [ˈɔfn] adv. A menudo, frecuentemente: *I often get angry with Michael*, me enfado a menudo con Miguel. || Muchas veces (many times). || — *As often as*, cada vez que, siempre que (each time that), con tanta frecuencia como. || *As often as not*, la mitad de las veces. || FAM. *Every so often*, alguna que otra vez. || *How often*, cuántas veces (how many times), cada cuánto (at what intervals). || *It's not often that one sees such generosity*, no es corriente ver a una persona tan generosa. || *More often than not*, la mayoría de las veces. || *Not very often*, pocas veces. || *Too often*, con demasiada frecuencia.
ofttimes [ˈɔftaimz] adv. (Ant.). A menudo.
ogee [ˈəudʒi:] n. ARCH. Cimacio, *m.*, talón, *m.*, gola, *f.*
ogee arch [—ɑ:tʃ] n. ARCH. Arco (*m.*) conopial.
ogival [əuˈdʒaivəl] adj. ARCH. Ojival, en ojiva.
ogive [ˈəudʒaiv] n. ARCH. Ojiva, *f.*
— Adj. Ojival, en ojiva.
ogle [ˈəugl] n. Mirada (*f.*) ávida.
ogle [ˈəugl] v. tr. Comerse con los ojos.
— V. intr. Guiñar el ojo (to make eyes at).
ogre [ˈəugə*] n. Ogro, *m.* (monster).
ogreish [—riʃ] or **ogrish** [—riʃ] adj. Monstruoso, sa.
ogress [ˈəugris] n. Ogresa, *f.* (monster).
oh [əu] interj. ¡Oh!
ohm [əum] n. ELECTR. Ohmio, *m.*, ohm, *m.*
ohmic [—ik] adj. ELECTR. Óhmico, ca.
oidium [əuˈidiəm] n. BOT. Oídio, *m.*
— OBSERV. El plural de *oidium* es *oidia*.
oil [ɔil] n. Aceite, *m.* (greasy substance). || CULIN. Aceite, *m.* (cooking oil): *olive, groundnut oil*, aceite de oliva, de cacahuete. || ARTS. Óleo, *m.* (painting). || MIN. Petróleo, *m.* || TECH. Aceite, *m.* (lubricant). | Fuel, *m.*, fuel-oil, *m.*, mazut, *m.* || REL. Óleo, *m.* || U. S. FAM. Coba, *f.* (flattery). || — *Castor oil*, aceite de ricino. || *Cod-liver oil*, aceite de hígado de bacalao. || *Heavy oil*, aceite pesado. || *Linseed oil*, aceite de linaza. || *Oil bottle*, aceitera, *f.* || *Oil of vitriol*, aceite de vitriolo. || *Paraffin oil*, petróleo lampante, queroseno, *m.* || *Siccative oil*, aceite secante. || *The Holy Oil*, los Santos Óleos. || *Thick oil*, aceitón, *m.* || FIG. *To burn the midnight oil*, quemarse las pestañas. || *To check the oil*, mirar el nivel del aceite (in a car). || FIG. *To know one's oil*, ser baquiano. || *To paint in oils*, pintar al óleo. || FIG. *To pour oil on the flames*, echar aceite *or* leña al fuego. | *To pour oil on troubled waters*, calmar la tempestad. | *To spread like oil*, extenderse como mancha de aceite. || *To strike oil*, encontrar petróleo (to find oil), encontrar una mina de

oro (to make a lot of money). || *Vegetable oil*, aceite vegetal.
— Adj. Aceitero, ra; de aceite: *oil production*, producción aceitera. || Petrolero, ra (industry, etc.). || De petróleo: *oil refinery*, refinería de petróleo.
oil [ɔil] v. tr. Aceitar, lubricar (to lubricate). || Echar aceite a (in cooking). || — FIG. FAM. *To be well oiled*, estar como una cuba. | *To oil one's tongue*, hablar con un tono meloso. | *To oil s.o.'s hand* o *s.o.'s palm*, untar la mano a alguien.
oil-bearing [—bεəriŋ] adj. Petrolífero, ra.
oil cake [—keik] n. Torta (*f.*) de aceite (fodder).
oilcan [—kæn] n. Aceitera, *f.*, alcuza, *f.* (for lubricating machinery, etc.). || Bidón (*m.*) de aceite (large can).
oilcloth [—klɔθ] n. Hule, *m.*
oil colour (U. S. **oil color**) [—ˌkʌlə*] n. Óleo, *m.*
oil cruet [—ˈkru:it] n. Aceitera, *f.*
oil engine [—ˈendʒin] n. Motor (*m.*) de petróleo.
oiler [—ə*] n. Engrasador, *m.* (person). || Aceitera, *f.*, alcuza, *f.* (oilcan). || MAR. Petrolero, *m.* || — Pl. U. S. FAM. Impermeable (*m. sing.*) de hule.
oil field [—fi:ld] n. Yacimiento (*m.*) petrolífero.
oil-fired [—ˌfaiəd] adj. Alimentado con mazut *or* fuel-oil. || *Oil-fired central heating*, calefacción (*f.*) central de mazut *or* de fuel-oil.
oil gun [—gʌn] n. Bomba (*f.*) de engrase, engrasador, *m.*
oiliness [—inis] n. Lo aceitoso. || FIG. Zalamerías, *f. pl.*
oiling [—iŋ] n. Aceitado, *m.*, engrase, *m.*, lubricación, *f.* (lubrication).
oil lamp [—læmp] n. Quinqué, *m.*, lámpara (*f.*) de aceite.
oilman [—mən] n. Petrolero, *m.* || Engrasador, *m.* (greaser).
— OBSERV. El plural de *oilman* es *oilmen*.
oil mill [—mil] n. Molino (*m.*) de aceite, almazara, *f.*
oil paint [—peint] n. Pintura (*f.*) al óleo.
oil painting [—peintiŋ] n. Pintura (*f.*) al óleo.
oil palm [ˈɔilpɑ:m] n. BOT. Palmera (*f.*) de aceite.
oilseed [—si:d] n. BOT. Semilla (*f.*) oleaginosa.
oil seller [—selə*] n. Aceitero, *m.*
oil shale [—ʃeil] n. Pizarra (*f.*) bituminosa.
oilskin [—skin] n. Hule, *m.* || — Pl. Traje (*m. sing.*) de hule (suit). | Impermeable (*m. sing.*) de hule (raincoat).
oil slick [—slik] n. Capa (*f.*) de aceite en la superficie del mar.
oilstone [—stəun] n. Afiladera, *f.*, piedra (*f.*) de afilar.
oilstove [—stəuv] n. Estufa (*f.*) de mazut *or* de fuel-oil.
oil tanker [—ˈtæŋkə*] n. MAR. Petrolero, *m.*
oil well [—wel] n. Pozo (*m.*) de petróleo.
oily [ˈɔili] adj. Aceitoso, sa (food). || Grasiento, ta (machines, etc.). || Graso, sa: *oily skin*, cutis graso. || FIG. FAM. Zalamero, ra.
ointment [ˈɔintmənt] n. Ungüento, *m.*, pomada, *f.*
OK or **okay** [ˈəuˈkei] adj. Bien, muy bien: *it is OK*, está bien. || — *Is it OK with you if I stay the night?*, ¿te importa *or* te molesta que pase la noche aquí? || *It's OK with me*, estoy de acuerdo.
— Adv. Muy bien.
— N. Visto (*m.*) bueno, aprobación, *f.* (approval).
— Interj. ¡De acuerdo!, ¡muy bien!, ¡vale!
OK or **okay** [ˈəuˈkei] v. tr. Dar el visto bueno a, aprobar (to approve).
okapi [əuˈkɑ:pi] n. Okapí, *m.* (African animal).
okoume or **okume** [əukəˈmei] n. Okumé, *m.* (tree and wood).
old [əuld] adj. Viejo, ja (aged): *his father is very old*, su padre es muy viejo. || Mayor (adult). || Viejo, ja; antiguo, gua (ancient): *old silver*, plata vieja. || Antiguo, gua (former): *our old school*, nuestro antiguo colegio; *an old pupil*, un antiguo alumno. || Viejo, ja; usado, da (clothes). || Pasado, da (food). || Sentado, da; duro, ra (bread). || Añejo (wine, cologne). || Viejo, ja (colour): *old rose*, rosa viejo. || Conocido, da; familiar: *the same old faces*, las mismas caras conocidas. || Viejo, ja: *he is an old friend of mine*, es un viejo amigo mío. || Antiguo, gua: *Old English*, inglés antiguo. || — *A little old lady*, una viejecita, una ancianita. || *An old family*, una familia antigua. || FIG. *An old hand*, un perro viejo, un veterano. | *An old head on young shoulders*, una persona joven con mentalidad de viejo. || *An old maid*, una solterona. || FIG. *An old salt*, un lobo de mar (sailor). || *An old woman*, una anciana, una vieja. || *Any old how*, de cualquier forma, de cualquier manera: *she dresses any old how*, se viste de cualquier forma. || *Any old thing*, cualquier cosa. || *As old as the hills*, más viejo que Matusalén *or* que andar a pie. || *At ten years old*, a los diez años [de edad]. || *A woman is as old as she feels*, una mujer no tiene más edad que la que representa. || *Come any old time*, ven cuando quieras. || *He is old enough to know better*, tiene bastante edad para ser más sensato. || *He is older than I am*, es mayor que yo. || *He is three years older than I*, tiene tres años más que yo. || *He is twelve years old today*, hoy cumple doce años. || *How old are you?*, ¿qué edad tienes?, ¿cuántos años tienes? || *I am the oldest*, soy el mayor. || *In days of old*, antaño, en tiempos antiguos. || *In the good old days*, en los buenos tiempos, en la buena época. || *In the old days*, antaño, en tiempos antiguos. || FAM. *My dear old fellow*, mi querido amigo. || *Never too old to learn*, nunca se es demasiado viejo para aprender. || *Of old*, antiguamente, antaño (formerly), de antaño: *knights of old*, los caballeros de antaño; de antiguo, desde hace mucho tiempo: *to know s.o. of old*, conocer a alguien de antiguo; por experiencia: *I know it of old*, lo sé por experiencia. || *Old age*, vejez, *f.* || *Old bachelor*, solterón, *m.* || *Older and wiser*, el tiempo no pasa en balde. || *Old gold*, oro viejo. || FAM. *Old John*, el tío Juan. | *Old man*, pariente, *m.*, media naranja, *f.*, marido, *m.* (husband), viejo, *m.*, padre, *m.* (father), jefe, *m.* (boss), viejo, *m.*: *a poor old man*, un pobre viejo; hombre, *m.*: *hello, old man!*, ¡hola, hombre! || *Old Testament*, Antiguo Testamento. || *The old*, los ancianos, los viejos. || *The old country*, la madre patria. || FAM. *The old lady* o *the old woman*, la parienta, la media naranja (the wife). || *The old world*, el viejo mundo. || *To be five years old*, tener cinco años (person, building), existir desde hace cinco años (firm, organization). || *To be old enough to do sth.*, tener edad suficiente para hacer algo. || *To be old in sin*, ser un pecador impenitente. || *To grow old*, envejecer. || *To live to a ripe old age*, vivir hasta una edad muy avanzada. || *To live to be ninety years old*, vivir hasta los noventa años. || *To make old*, envejecer. || *To throw out all the old things*, tirar todo lo viejo. || FIG. *You can't teach an old dog new tricks*, loro viejo no aprende a hablar, es un perro viejo.
Old Bailey [—ˈbeili] n. JUR. Tribunal (*m.*) de lo criminal en Londres.
old boy [—bɔi] n. Antiguo alumno, *m.*, ex alumno, *m.* (former pupil). || FAM. Viejo, *m.* (old man). | Hombre, *m.*: *hello, old boy!*, ¡hola, hombre! | Pariente, *m.* (husband).
Old Castile [—kæsˈti:l] pr. n. GEOGR. Castilla la Vieja.
old chap [—tʃæp] n. Hombre, *m.*
old-clothes [ˈəuldˈkləuðz] adj. *Old-clothes shop*, ropavejería, *f.*
old-clothesman [—ˌmæn] n. Ropavejero, *m.*
— OBSERV. El plural es *old-clothesmen*.
olden [ˈəuldən] adj. Antiguo, gua. || *In olden days* o *times*, antaño, en tiempos antiguos.
old-established [ˈəuldisˈtæbliʃt] adj. Antiguo, gua (brand, firm, etc.).
old-fashioned [ˈəuldˈfæʃənd] adj. Antiguo, gua (ancient). || Chapado a la antigua, anticuado, da (out-of-date): *old-fashioned opinions*, opiniones chapadas a la antigua. || Anticuado, da; pasado de moda (out-of-fashion).
old fogy or **old fogey** [ˈəuldˈfəugi] n. FAM. See FOGY.
old-fogyish or **old-fogeyish** [—iʃ] adj. Chapado a la antigua.
old girl [ˈəuldgə:l] n. Antigua alumna, *f.*, ex alumna, *f.* (former pupil). || FAM. Vieja, *f.* (old woman). | Parienta, *f.* (wife). | Mujer, *f.*: *come here, old girl!*, ¡ven aquí, mujer!
Old Glory [ˈəuldˈglɔ:ri] n. U. S. FAM. Bandera (*f.*) de los Estados Unidos.
Old Harry [ˈəuldˈhæri] n. U. S. FAM. Pedro Botero (the Devil).
oldish [ˈəuldiʃ] adj. Algo viejo, ja.
Old Latin [ˈəuldˈlætin] n. Latín (*m.*) clásico.
old-line [ˈəuldlain] adj. Antiguo, gua (old). || Chapado a la antigua, conservador, ra (conservative).
old-maidish [ˈəuldˈmeidiʃ] adj. Remilgado, da.
old master [ˈəuldˈmɑ:stə*] n. ARTS. Gran maestro, *m.* (painter of the 16th and 17th cc.).
Old Nick [ˈəuldnik] n. FAM. Pedro Botero (the Devil).
old school [ˈəuld-sku:l] n. Vieja escuela, *f.*: *the old school attitudes*, las ideas de la vieja escuela.
old school tie [ˈəuldsku:ltai] n. Corbata (*f.*) de antiguo alumno de un colegio británico (tie). || Conservadurismo, *m.* (attitude).
oldster [ˈəuldstə*] n. U. S. Viejo, ja.
old-style [ˈəuldˌstail] adj. Antiguo, gua.
old-time [ˈəuldtaim] adj. Antiguo, gua; de antaño.
old-timer [—ə*] n. Veterano, na (veteran). || Anciano, na; viejo, ja (old person). || Persona (*f.*) chapada a la antigua (old-fashioned person).
old wives' tale [ˈəuldwaivzteil] n. Cuento (*m.*) de viejas.
old-world [ˈəuldwə:ld] adj. GEOGR. Del viejo mundo. || Clásico, ca; chapado a la antigua (old-fashioned). || Antiguo, gua: *an old-world town*, un pueblo antiguo. || De los tiempos antiguos: *old-world charm*, encanto de los tiempos antiguos. || *The old-world charm of central Madrid*, el encanto del Madrid viejo.
oleaceae [ˌəuliˈeisii:] pl. n. BOT. Oleáceas, *f.*
oleaginous [ˌəuliˈædʒinəs] adj. Oleaginoso, sa.
oleaginousness [—nis] n. Oleaginosidad, *f.*
oleander [ˌəuliˈændə*] n. Adelfa, *f.* (shrub).
oleaster [ˌəuliˈæstə*] n. Acebuche, *m.* (shrub).
olecranon [ˌəuliˈkreinən] n. ANAT. Olécranon, *m.*, olecráneo, *m.*
oleiferous [əuliˈifərəs] adj. Oleífero, ra.
olein [ˈəuli:in] n. CHEM. Oleína, *f.*
oleo [ˈəuli:əu] n. U. S. FAM. Margarina, *f.*
oleograph [ˈəuliəugrɑ:f] or **oleography** [ˌəuliˈɔgrəFi] n. Oleografía, *f.*
oleometer [əuliˈɔmitə*] n. PHYS. Oleómetro, *m.*
oleum [ˈəuliəm] n. CHEM. Óleum, *m.*
olfaction [ɔlˈfækʃən] n. Olfato, *m.*
olibanum [ɔˈlibənəm] n. Olíbano, *m.*, incienso, *m.*

oligarch [ˈɔligɑ:k] n. Oligarca, *m.*
oligarchic [ˌɔliˈgɑ:kik] or **oligarchical** [—əl] adj. Oligárquico, ca.
oligarchy [ˈɔligɑ:ki] n. Oligarquía, *f.*
oligist [ˈɔlidʒist] n. MIN. Oligisto, *m.*
Oligocene [ɔˈligəusi:n] adj. GEOL. Oligoceno, na.
— N. GEOL. Oligoceno, *m.*
oligophrenia [ˌɔligəuˈfriniə] n. MED. Oligofrenia, *f.*
olivaceous [ˌɔliˈveiʃəs] adj. Oliváceo, a.
olive [ˈɔliv] n. Aceituna, *f.*, oliva, *f.* (fruit): *stuffed olive*, aceituna rellena. || BOT. Olivo, *m.* (tree). || Olivo, *m.* (wood). || Verde (*m.*) oliva (colour). || — *Crescent olive*, aceituna picudilla. || *Garden of Olives*, Huerto (*m.*) de los Olivos. || *Mount of Olives*, Monte (*m.*) de los Olivos. || *Queen olive*, aceituna gordal.
— Adj. Olivarero, ra; oleícola (olive-growing). || Verde oliva (colour). || Aceitunado, da (complexion).
olive branch [—brɑ:ntʃ] n. Ramo (*m.*) de olivo.
olive drab [—dræb] n. U.S. Verde (*m.*) oliva pardusco.
olive green [—gri:n] n. Verde (*m.*) oliva.
olive grove [—grəuv] n. Olivar, *m.*
olive grower [—grəuə*] n. Oleicultor, *m.*
olive growing [—grəuiŋ] n. Oleicultura, *f.*
olive-growing [—grəuiŋ] adj. Olivarero, ra; oleícola.
olive oil [—ɔil] n. Aceite (*m.*) de oliva.
oliviferous [ˌɔliˈvifərəs] adj. Olivífero, ra.
olivine [ˌɔliˈvi:n] n. MIN. Olivina, *f.*, olivino, *m.*
olla podrida [ˈɔləpɔˈdri:də] n. CULIN. Olla (*f.*) podrida.
Olympia [əuˈlimpiə] pr. n. GEOGR. Olimpia.
Olympiad [əuˈlimpiæd] n. Olimpiada, *f.*, olimpíada, *f.*
Olympian [əuˈlimpiən] adj. Olímpico, ca.
— N. MYTH. Dios (*m.*) olímpico. || SP. Participante (*m.* & *f.*) en los juegos olímpicos.
Olympic [əuˈlimpik] adj. Olímpico, ca: *Olympic games*, juegos olímpicos; *Olympic village*, ciudad olímpica.
— Pl. n. Juegos (*m.*) olímpicos.
Olympus [əuˈlimpəs] n. MYTH. GEOGR. Olimpo, *m.*
omasum [əuˈmeisəm] n. Omaso, *m.*, libro, *m.* (of ruminants).

— OBSERV. El plural de *omasum* es *omasa*.

ombre [ˈɔmbə*] n. Tresillo, *m.* (card game).
ombu [ɔmˈbu:] n. Ombú, *m.* (tree).
ombudsman [ˈɔmbudzmən] n. Mediador, *m.*
omega [ˈəumigə] n. Omega, *f.*
omelet or **omelette** [ˈɔmlit] n. CULIN. Tortilla, *f.*
omen [ˈəumen] n. Presagio, *m.*, augurio, *m.*, agüero, *m.* || — *Bird of ill omen*, pájaro de mal agüero. || *It's a good omen*, es un buen presagio.
omen [ˈəumen] v. tr. Augurar, presagiar.
omentum [əuˈmentəm] n. ANAT. Omento, *m.*

— OBSERV. El plural de *omentum* es *omenta*.

omicron [əuˈmaikrən] n. Ómicron, *f.* (Greek letter).
ominous [ˈɔminəs] adj. Siniestro, tra; inquietante, de mal agüero, ominoso, sa. || *That sounds ominous*, eso no augura nada bueno.
ominously [—li] adv. De manera amenazadora (menacingly). || De manera inquietante: *the building shook ominously*, el edificio tembló de una manera inquietante. || *The room was ominously quiet*, había un silencio impresionante en la sala, en la sala reinaba un silencio que no auguraba nada bueno.
omissible [əuˈmisibl] adj. Que se puede omitir.
omission [əˈmiʃən] n. Omisión, *f.*: *omission of accents*, omisión de acentos. || Olvido, *m.*, descuido, *m.* (slip): *it was an omission on your part*, fue un descuido tuyo.
omit [əˈmit] v. tr. Omitir: *I shall omit all mention of the matter*, omitiré toda referencia al asunto; *when I made the list I accidentally omitted two names*, al hacer la lista omití sin querer dos nombres. || Suprimir: *this chapter may be omitted*, se puede suprimir este capítulo. || Olvidar: *don't omit any name on the list*, no olvides ningún nombre en la lista. || *To omit to*, dejar de (deliberately), dejar de, olvidarse de (accidentally): *I omitted to mention it*, dejé de mencionarlo, se me olvidó mencionarlo.
Ommiads [ɔˈmæiædz] n. HIST. Omeyas, *m.*
omnibus [ˈɔmnibəs] n. Antología, *f.* (book). || Ómnibus, *m.*, autobús, *m.* (bus): *omnibus route*, línea de autobús. || *Omnibus train*, ómnibus.
— Adj. Que abarca varias cosas. || — *Omnibus bill*, proyecto (*m.*) de ley que abarca varias medidas. || *Omnibus edition*, antología, *f.*
omnidirectional [ˌɔmnidiˈrekʃənl] adj. Omnidireccional.
omnifarious [ˌɔmniˈfɛəriəs] adj. Muy variado, da; de todas clases.
omnipotence [ɔmˈnipətəns] n. Omnipotencia, *f.*
omnipotent [ɔmˈnipətənt] adj. Omnipotente.
— N. *The Omnipotent*, El Todopoderoso (God).
omnipresence [ɔmniˈprezəns] n. Omnipresencia, *f.*
omnipresent [ˈɔmniˈprezənt] adj. Omnipresente.
omniscience [ɔmˈnisiəns] n. Omnisciencia, *f.*
omniscient [ɔmˈnisiənt] adj. Omnisciente.
omnium-gatherum [ˈɔmniəmˈgæðərəm] n. Mezcolanza, *f.* (hotchpotch). || Reunión (*f.*) a la cual se invita a toda clase de personas.
omnivore [ˈɔmnivɔ*] n. Omnívoro, *m.*
omnivorous [ɔmˈnivərəs] adj. Omnívoro, ra. || FIG. *Omnivorous reader*, persona (*f.*) que lee todo lo que se publica.

on [ɔn, ən] prep. En: *to sit on a chair*, sentarse en una silla; *to strike on the face*, golpear en la cara; *a house on Madison Avenue*, una casa en Madison Avenue; *on page four*, en la página cuatro; *there is a good programme on channel one*, hay un buen programa en el primer canal; *there is a mirror on the wall*, hay un espejo en la pared; *on the Continent*, en el Continente; *I had a meal on the plane*, me dieron de comer en el avión; *on the high seas*, en alta mar. || En, sobre, encima de (on top of): *the book is on the table*, el libro está en la mesa; *it fell on my foot*, me cayó en el pie. || En, sobre: *he carved his name on a tree*, grabó su nombre en un árbol. || Sobre: *stone on stone*, piedra sobre piedra. || Tras: *he sent me letter on letter*, me mandó carta tras carta. || En, por: *he was walking on the road*, iba andando por la carretera. || De: *to live on one's income*, vivir de sus ingresos; *the stain on the ceiling*, la mancha del techo; *the mirror on the wall is broken*, el espejo de la pared está roto; *on a journey*, de viaje. || Sobre: *he has a great influence on me*, tiene una gran influencia sobre mí. || En, sobre (about): *we don't agree on that*, no estamos de acuerdo sobre eso; *a tax on luxury goods*, un impuesto en los productos de lujo. || Sobre, acerca de (concerning): *we could speak for a long time on that subject*, podríamos hablar mucho tiempo sobre ese tema. || Según (according to): *both houses are built on the same model*, las dos casas están construidas según el mismo modelo. || Por: *to swear on one's honour*, jurar por su honor; *on the orders of*, por mandato de; *on the afternoon of the 5th March*, el 5 de marzo por la tarde. || El (day): *he came on Sunday*, vino el domingo; *I usually go to the cinema on Thursdays*, generalmente voy al cine los jueves; *on the twenty-second of February*, el veintidós de febrero. || A: *on his request*, a petición suya. || Bajo: *on the recommendation of*, bajo la recomendación de. || Mediante: *on presentation of your ticket*, mediante presentación de su billete. || Contra (against): *an onslaught on the régime*, un ataque violento contra el régimen. || Con: *on whose authority?*, ¿con permiso de quién?; *I live on twenty pounds a week*, vivo con veinte libras a la semana. || A: *on his arrival*, a su llegada. || Al (with gerund): *on entering the room*, al entrar en la habitación. || A costa de, a expensas de: *he lives on his brother*, vive a costa de su hermano. || — *A curse on it!*, ¡maldito sea! || *Bent on learning English*, decidido a aprender inglés. || *Fate smiles on him*, la suerte le sonríe. || *Have a drink on me*, le invito a una copa. || *Have pity on me*, tenga piedad de mí. || *He has money on him*, lleva dinero encima *or* consigo. || *He is on drugs*, se droga. || *He is on pills*, toma píldoras. || *He was on T.V. last night*, anoche salió en la televisión. || *It is a new one on me*, es nuevo para mí. || *Madrid is on the Manzanares*, Madrid está a orillas del Manzanares, el Manzanares pasa por Madrid. || JUR. *On a charge of*, acusado de. || *On a fine day*, un buen día. || *On all sides*, por todas partes (everywhere), por todos los lados (on each side). || *On an equal footing*, en un pie de igualdad. || *On appearance*, por las apariencias. || *On average*, por término medio. || *On certain conditions*, bajo ciertas condiciones. || *On foot*, andando, a pie. || *On his arrival*, a su llegada. || *On holiday*, de vacaciones. || *On or after the 27th*, el día 27 o después. || *On our way to*, en el camino de, camino de, yendo a. || *On pain of death*, so pena de muerte. || *On principle*, por principio. || *On sale*, en venta. || *On strike*, en huelga. || *On that occasion*, en aquella ocasión. || *On that side, on this side*, del otro lado, de este lado. || *On the first day*, el primer día. || *On the next day*, al día siguiente. || *On the quiet* o *the sly*, a escondidas. || *On the right*, a la derecha: *it is on the right*, está a la derecha; por la derecha: *to drive on the right*, conducir por la derecha. || *On the spot*, see SPOT. || *On time*, a tiempo. || *The drinks are on me*, las bebidas corren de mi cuenta. || *The enemy was nearly on them*, el enemigo estaba a punto de caer sobre ellos. || *To be based on*, estar basado en, basarse en. || *To be on a diet*, estar a régimen. || *To be on a grapefruit diet*, seguir un régimen a base de pomelos. || *To be on an errand*, estar haciendo un recado. || *To be on the committee*, formar parte del comité, ser miembro del comité. || *To be on the staff*, estar en plantilla. || *To bet on a horse*, apostar a *or* por un caballo. || *To depend on*, depender de. || *To hang on the wall*, estar colgado de la pared. || *To have sth. on s.o.*, tener algún informe sobre alguien (information), tener algo sobre alguien: *do you have sth. on Freud?*, ¿tienes algo sobre Freud? || *To live on bread and water*, vivir de pan y agua, comer pan y agua. || *To march on London*, marchar sobre Londres. || *To play sth. on the piano*, tocar algo al piano. || *To send s.o. on an errand*, mandar a alguien a hacer un recado. || *To swear on the Bible*, jurar sobre la Biblia. || *What is on T.V. tonight?*, ¿qué ponen en la televisión esta noche?
— Adv. Más: *further on*, más lejos; *later on*, más tarde. || Más lejos, adelante (further) [See OBSERV.]. || — *And so on*, y así sucesivamente, etcétera. || *From now on*, a partir de ahora, de ahora en adelante. || *From that year on*, a partir de ese *or* de aquel año. || *Have you anything on tonight?*, ¿tienes algún plan para esta noche?, ¿tienes algo proyectado *or* previsto para esta noche? || *He danced on and on*, bailó sin parar. || *He is on in five minutes*, va a actuar dentro de cinco minutos. || *He is on one Sunday in two*, trabaja un

domingo sí y otro no. || FAM. *It's not on*, eso no se hace (it's not done). || *On and off*, de vez en cuando. || *On and on*, sin cesar, sin parar. || *On to*, hacia (towards). || *On with the show*, que empiece *or* que siga el espectáculo. || *On with your coat*, ponte el abrigo. || *Sing on!*, ¡siga cantando! || *The police are on to him*, la policía le sigue la pista. || *They talked on into the early hours of the morning*, siguieron hablando hasta la madrugada. || *To be on*, poner (film): *what film is on?*, ¿qué película ponen?; dar: *the show is now on in Madrid*, ahora dan el espectáculo en Madrid; estar en escena (actor). || *To be on to s.o.*, meterse con uno (to criticize), estar detrás de uno: *she is always on to me to clean the windows*, está siempre detrás de mí para que limpie los cristales. || *To be on to sth.*, enterarse de algo, comprender algo, caer en la cuenta de algo: *he was on to it at once*, se enteró en seguida. || *To be on to sth. good*, haber encontrado algo bueno. || *To have on*, see HAVE. || *To walk on*, seguir andando. || *Well on in the night*, muy entrada la noche. || *"What's on in London"*, "cartelera de espectáculos londinenses".
— Adj. Encendido, da; puesto ta (electrical appliances): *the television is always on*, la televisión está siempre encendida. || Puesto, ta: *the coffee is on*, el café está puesto; *the brake is on*, el freno está puesto. || Abierto, ta (tap). || Empezado, da: *the programme is already on*, ya ha empezado el programa. || En marcha (machine). || En el sitio (consumption). || FAM. Bueno, na (day).

— OBSERV. Cuando *on* acompaña ciertos verbos, como *to get, to go, to come*, etc., no se puede traducir literalmente. Por consiguiente es imprescindible consultar el artículo referente al verbo de que se trata.

onager [ˈɔnəgə*] n. ZOOL. Onagro, *m.*

— OBSERV. El plural de la palabra inglesa es *onagri* u *onagers*.

onanism [ˈəunənizəm] n. Onanismo, *m.*

onanist [ˈəunənist] adj. Onanista.

once [wʌns] adv. Una vez: *she saw him once*, le vio una vez; *once a day*, una vez al día. || Antes: *once he was young*, antes era joven. || Hace tiempo: *I knew her once*, le conocí hace tiempo. || Alguna vez: *if once the news got out*, si alguna vez saliese la noticia. || — *All at once*, de repente (suddenly), de una vez (at one go), todos al mismo tiempo (all together). || *At once*, en seguida (immediately), al mismo tiempo (at the same time), de una vez (at one go). || *For once*, por una vez. || *Just this once*, esta vez nada más. || *More than once*, más de una vez. || *Not once*, jamás, ni una [sola] vez. || *Once and for all*, de una vez para siempre. || *Once in a while*, de vez en cuando. || *Once more*, una vez más, otra vez. || *Once or twice*, un par de veces, una o dos veces. || *Once upon a time*, hace siglos (a long time ago). || *Once upon a time there was*, érase una vez, érase que se era (in stories).
— Conj. Una vez que: *once he starts he goes well*, una vez que empieza va bien. || Si alguna vez: *once he found out he would be furious*, si alguna vez se enterase se pondría furioso. || En cuanto: *once they arrive we can begin*, en cuanto lleguen podemos empezar.

once-over [—ˌəuvə*] n. FAM. Mirada, *f.*, ojeada, *f.*, vistazo, *m.*: *to give sth. the once-over*, echar una mirada a algo.

oncoming [ˈɔnˌkʌmiŋ] adj. Que viene, que se aproxima. || Venidero, ra: *the oncoming century*, el siglo venidero.
— N. Llegada, *f.*: *the oncoming of winter*, la llegada del invierno.

one [wʌn] adj. Uno, una: *one house*, una casa; *one man*, un hombre; *one day an old man came to see me*, un día un anciano vino a verme. || Primero, ra: *item one on the agenda*, primer punto del orden del día. || Único, ca; solo, la: *this is the one thing we can feel certain about*, es la única cosa de la cual podemos estar seguros; *the one person I know*, la única persona que conozco. || Mismo, ma: *we go all in one direction*, vamos todos en la misma dirección. || Un tal: *one Mr. X.*, un tal Sr. X. || — *For one thing*, primero. || FIG. *His one and only*, su Dulcinea. || *It's all one*, viene a ser lo mismo. || *It's all one to me*, me da igual. || *No one man*, ningún hombre, nadie. || *One and the same*, el mismo, la misma. || *One or two mistakes*, unas pocas faltas. || *That's the one thing I needed*, es exactamente lo que necesitaba. || *The last but one*, el penúltimo, la penúltima. || *The one and only*, el único, la única: *the one and only house in the street*, la única casa de la calle. || *To become one*, casarse. || *To be one with s.o.*, estar de acuerdo con alguien. || *To be one with sth.*, formar un conjunto con algo. || *With one voice*, a una voz.
— Indef. pron. Uno, una: *one of them*, uno de ellos; *have you one?*, ¿tienes uno? || Una persona, alguien: *he is one whom everybody admires*, es una persona a quien todos admiran. || Uno, una: *one cannot always be right*, uno no puede tener siempre razón. || Uno, una, se: *one cannot be working all day without stopping*, uno no puede estar trabajando todo el día sin parar, no se puede trabajar todo el día sin parar. || Se: *one does not smoke in high society*, no se fuma en la alta sociedad. || — *All in one*, a la vez. || *Any one of us*, cualquiera de nosotros. || *For one*, por lo menos: *I, for one, do not believe it*, yo, por lo menos, no me lo creo. || *He is not one to complain*, no es el tipo de persona que se queja. || FAM. *He's a one!*, ¡es único!, ¡es un caso! | *He's a real one for football*, le gusta muchísimo el fútbol. || *Many a one*, muchos, muchas. || *One after the other*, uno tras otro. || *One and all*, todo el mundo, absolutamente todos. || *One another*, se: *they love one another*, se quieren. || *One by one*, uno tras otro, uno por uno. || *One of my friends*, uno de mis amigos, un amigo mío. || *One's*, su: *to give one's opinion*, dar su opinión; *to visit one's friends*, ir a ver a sus amigos; el, la: *to cut one's hand*, cortarse la mano. || *The one and the other*, el uno y el otro. || *The one ... the other*, uno ... el otro. || *To be one of the family*, ser de la familia.
— Dem. pron. *That one*, ése *or* aquél, ésa *or* aquélla. || FAM. *That's a good one!*, ¡ésa sí que es buena! || *That's the one*, ése es. || *The big one*, el grande, la grande. || *The Evil One*, el demonio. || *The green one*, el verde, la verde. || *The little ones*, los pequeños. || *The one on the table*, el que está en la mesa. || *The ones who*, los que, las que. || *The one who*, el que, la que. || *The one whom*, al que, a la que. || *This one*, éste, ésta. || *Which one do you prefer?*, ¿cuál prefieres?
— N. Uno, *m.* (the number). || COMM. Unidad, *f.* || Uno, una: *two volumes in one*, dos volúmenes en uno. || La una (one o'clock): *he'll arrive between one and two*, llegará entre la una y las dos. || Un chelín: *one and three (pence)*, un chelín con tres peniques. || Punto, *m.* (point). || — *All in one*, de una sola pieza. || FAM. *A quick one*, un trago. || *One of two things*, una de dos. || FAM. *She gave him one with her handbag*, le dio un golpe con el bolso. || *They are at one*, están de acuerdo. || FAM. *To have one for the road*, tomar la espuela *or* la última copa [antes de marcharse].

— OBSERV. La palabra inglesa *one* no se emplea como artículo indefinido sino solamente para distinguir entre una cosa y varias. El artículo indefinido inglés es *a*.

one-act [—ækt] adj. De un [solo] acto.

one-armed [—ˈɑːmd] adj. Manco, ca. || FIG. *One-armed bandit*, máquina (*f.*) tragaperras.

one-cylinder [—ˈsilində*] adj. Monocilíndrico, ca.

one-eyed [—ˈaid] adj. Tuerto, ta.

one-handed [—ˈhændid] adj. Manco, ca.
— Adv. Con una sola mano.

one-horse [—ˈhɔːs] adj. De un caballo: *a one-horse carriage*, un carro de un caballo. || De segunda categoría, de poca monta: *a one-horse show*, un espectáculo de segunda categoría. || *A one-horse town*, un poblacho.

oneiric [əuˈnairik] adj. Onírico, ca.

one-legged [ˈwʌnˈlegd] adj. Con una sola pierna (person).

one-man [ˈwʌnˈmæn] adj. Que consiste en una sola persona (committee, staff). || Para una sola persona (job, play). || Individual: *one-man boat*, barco individual.

oneness [ˈwʌnnis] n. Unidad, *f.* || Identidad, *f.* (of opinions).

one-piece [ˈwʌnpiːs] adj. De una pieza.

onerous [ˈɔnərəs] adj. Oneroso, sa. || Pesado da (responsibility).

oneself [wʌnˈself] pron. Se (reflexive): *to wash oneself*, lavarse. || Sí, sí mismo, sí misma: *to speak of oneself*, hablar de sí mismo. || Uno mismo, una misma (emphatic). || — *By oneself*, solo, la: *it is impossible to do it by oneself*, es imposible hacerlo solo; *it is sad to be by oneself*, es triste estar solo. || *To be oneself*, ser natural, comportarse con naturalidad. || *To come to oneself*, volver en sí. || *To say sth. to oneself*, decir algo para su capote *or* para sus adentros *or* para sí. || *To take sth. upon oneself*, encargarse de algo. || *With oneself*, consigo mismo.

one-sided [ˈwʌnˈsaidid] adj. Unilateral: *a one-sided decision*, una decisión unilateral. || Parcial (biased). || Desigual (unequal). || Que sólo tiene un lado (having only one side). || Asimétrico, ca.

one-sidedness [—nis] n. Parcialidad, *f.*

onetime [ˈwʌntaim] adj. Antiguo, gua (former): *a onetime teacher*, un antiguo profesor.

one-to-one [ˈwʌntəˈwʌn] adj. Exacto, ta: *one-to-one correspondence*, correspondencia exacta.

one-track [ˈwʌnˈtræk] adj. De una sola vía, de un solo carril (road). || FIG. *To have a one-track mind*, no poder pensar más que en una cosa.

one-upmanship [wʌnˈʌpmənʃip] n. Arte (*m.*) que consiste en aventajar a los demás.

one-way [ˈwʌnˈwei] adj. De dirección única: *one-way street*, calle de dirección única. || De ida: *one-way ticket*, billete de ida. || *"One way traffic"*, "dirección única" (road sign).

ongoing [ˈɔnˌgəuiŋ] adj. En curso, actual (in process). || Progresivo, va (making progress).

onion [ˈʌnjən] n. BOT. Cebolla, *f.* || FAM. Chola, *f.* (head). || — FAM. *To know one's onions*, conocer muy bien la materia. || BOT. *Welsh onion*, cebollino, *m.*

onion bed [—bed] n. AGR. Cebollar, *m.*

onionskin [—skin] n. Binza, *f.*, tela (*f.*) de cebolla. || PRINT. Papel (*m.*) cebolla.

on-licence [ˈɔnˌlaisəns] n. Licencia (*f.*) para vender bebidas alcohólicas que se tienen que consumir en el mismo establecimiento.

onlooker [ˈɔnˌlukə*] n. Espectador, ra. || Mirón, ona: *there were many onlookers around the building site*, había muchos mirones alrededor del solar.

only [ˈəunli] adj. Solo, la; único, ca: *this is the only example I can give you,* es el único ejemplo que puedo darle. || Único, ca (child, son). || — *The only thing is that,* lo único es que. || *You were not the only one who noticed it,* no fue el único en darse cuenta de ello.
— Adv. Sólo, solamente: *I can tell you only what I know,* sólo le puedo decir lo que sé. || — *I am only the charlady,* no soy más que la asistenta. || *If only I had an orange!,* ¡ojalá tuviera una naranja! || *I only just caught the train,* por poco pierdo el tren. || *I saw him only last week,* no hace más de una semana que le he visto. || *Not only ... but,* no sólo... sino [también]. || *Only too pleased to,* encantado de. || *Only to think of it,* con sólo pensarlo. || *Take him if only for the company,* llévale por lo menos para estar acompañado. || *They have only just left,* acaban de marcharse ahora mismo. || *You have only to take it,* no tiene más que cogerlo.
— Conj. Pero, sólo que: *I wanted to do it only I could not,* quería hacerlo pero no pude.
only-begotten [—biˈgɔtn] adj. Unigénito, ta.
onomastic [ˌɔnəuˈmæstik] adj. Onomástico, ca.
onomastics [ˌɔnəuˈmæstiks] n. Onomástica, *f.*
onomatopoeia [ˌɔnəumætəuˈpiːə] n. Onomatopeya, *f.*
onomatopoeic [ˌɔnəumætəuˈpiːik] or **onomatopoetic** [ˌɔnəumætəuˈpiːtik] adj. Onomatopéyico, ca.
onrush [ˈɔnrʌʃ] n. Riada, *f.*, avalancha, *f.*, oleada, *f.*: *onrush of tourists,* avalancha de turistas. || Arremetida, *f.*, ataque, *m.* (of an army). || Embestida, *f.* (of a bull). || Fuerza, *f.*, ímpetu, *m.* (of water).
onset [ˈɔnset] n. Principio, *m.*, comienzo, *m.* (beginning). || MED. Ataque, *m.*, acceso, *m.* || MIL. Ataque, *m.*, arremetida, *f.* || — *At the onset,* al principio. || *From the onset,* desde el principio.
onshore [ˈɔnʃɔː*] adj. Que sopla hacia la tierra (wind).
— Adv. Hacia la tierra.
on side [ˈɔnsaid] adj./adv. SP. En posición correcta.
onslaught [ˈɔnˈslɔːt] n. MED. MIL. Ataque (*m.*) violento. || FIG. Crítica (*f.*) violenta, ataque (*m.*) violento.
onto [ˈɔntu] prep. See ON, adv. (*on to*).
ontological [ˌɔntəuˈlɔdʒikəl] adj. PHIL. Ontológico, ca.
ontologist [ɔnˈtɔlədʒist] n. PHIL. Ontólogo, *m.*
ontology [ɔnˈtɔlədʒi] n. PHIL. Ontología, *f.*
onus [ˈəunəs] n. Responsabilidad, *f.* || *The onus lies upon the government to,* le incumbe al gobierno.
onward [ˈɔnwəd] adj. Hacia adelante: *the onward march,* la marcha hacia adelante.
— Adv. See ONWARDS.
onwards [—z] adv. Hacia adelante. || — *From that time onwards,* desde entonces. || *From the 19th century onwards,* del siglo XIX en adelante, a partir del siglo XIX.
onyx [ˈɔniks] n. Ónice, *m. & f.*, ónix, *m.*
oocyte [ˈəuəsait] n. BIOL. Ovocito, *m.*
oodles [ˈuːdlz] pl. n. FAM. Montones, *m.*, cantidad, *f. sing.* (lots): *oodles of people,* cantidad de gente.
oolong [ˈuːlɔŋ] n. Té (*m.*) negro (black tea).
oomph [umf] n. FAM. Atractivo, *m.*, "sex-appeal", *m.* (personal charm). | Magnetismo, *m.* | Ánimo, *m.* (energy).
oosphere [ˈəuəsfiə*] n. Oosfera, *f.*
oospore [ˈəuəspɔː*] n. BOT. Oospora, *f.*
ooze [uːz] n. Cieno, *m.* (mud). || Agua (*f.*) de casca (for tanning leather).
ooze [uːz] v. intr. Rezumarse, rezumar (to flow). || Exudar (to sweat). || — FIG. *To ooze away,* faltar, acabarse: *he felt his courage oozing away,* sentía que le faltaba el valor, sentía que se le acababa el valor. | *To ooze with pride,* rebosar de orgullo.
— V. tr. Rezumar. || Sudar (to sweat). || FIG. Rebosar de.
oozy [—i] adj. Legamoso, sa; cenagoso, sa (muddy). || Húmedo, da (exuding liquid).
opacity [əuˈpæsiti] n. Opacidad, *f.* || FIG. Torpeza, *f.* (mental obtuseness). | Oscuridad, *f.* (of meaning).
opah [ˈəupə] n. ZOOL. Pez (*m.*) luna.
opal [ˈəupəl] n. MIN. Ópalo, *m.*
opalescence [ˌəupəˈlesns] n. Opalescencia, *f.*
opalescent [ˌəupəˈlesnt] adj. Opalescente.
opaline [ˈəupəliːn] adj. Opalino, na.
— N. Opalina, *f.*
opaque [əuˈpeik] adj. Opaco, ca (not transparent). || FIG. Obtuso, sa (obtuse). | Oscuro, ra (obscure).
— N. PHOT. Pintura (*f.*) opaca.
open [ˈəupən] adj. Abierto, ta: *an open window,* una ventana abierta; *an open book,* un libro abierto; *open shop,* tienda abierta; *open to the public,* abierto al público; *he is open to suggestions,* está abierto a las sugerencias. || Poco tupido, da (material). || Descubierto, ta: *open car,* coche descubierto. || Destapado, da (bottle). || Destapado, da; descubierto, ta: *open pot,* puchero destapado. || Despejado, da: *open view,* vista despejada. || Expuesto, ta: *open to attacks,* expuesto a los ataques. || Desplegado, da; extendido, da (unfolded): *the plan was open on the desk,* el plano estaba desplegado sobre el escritorio. || Abierto, ta: *an open rose,* una rosa abierta. || Franco, ca; abierto, ta: *he was very open with me,* fue muy franco conmigo. || Manifiesto, ta (patent). || Abierto a todos: *open tournament,* competición abierta a todos. || Público, ca: *open trial,* juicio público. || Sin resolver, pendiente (unsolved). || MIL. Abierto, ta: *open ranks,* filas abiertas. || Vacante (post): *the job is still open,* el puesto queda vacante. || Libre: *he keeps Saturday open,* tiene el sábado libre. || MED. Dilatado, da (pores). | Abierto, ta: *an open wound,* una herida abierta. || MAR. Alto, ta: *open sea,* alta mar. | Claro, ra (not foggy). || GRAMM. Abierto, ta: *open vowel,* vocal abierta. || COMM. Libre (market). | Abierto, ta (account, credit). || MUS. No pisado, da: *open string,* cuerda no pisada. || PRINT. Espaciado, da. || — *Half open,* entreabierto, ta; entornado, da. || *In the open country,* en descampado. || *It is open to you to do so,* Ud. puede perfectamente hacerlo. || *Membership is only open to retired officers,* sólo los oficiales retirados pueden hacerse socios. || *My invitation is still open,* mi invitación vale todavía. || *On the open road,* por la carretera. || *Open air,* aire libre: *in the open air,* al aire libre. || *Open arrest,* arresto (*m.*) simple. || CHEM. *Open chain,* cadena abierta. || *Open cheque,* cheque abierto. || ELECTR. *Open circuit,* circuito abierto. || MIL. *Open city,* ciudad abierta. || *Open date,* fecha (*f.*) que queda por fijar. || FIG. *Open door,* libre acceso, *m.* || *Open enemy,* enemigo declarado. || *Open letter,* carta abierta. || *Open mine,* mina (*f.*) a cielo abierto. || *Open order,* orden abierta (commercial meaning), orden abierto (military meaning). || *Open revolt,* franca rebeldía. || *Open secret,* secreto (*m.*) a voces. || *Open shop,* fábrica (*f.*) que emplea obreros que son miembros o no de un sindicato. || MIL. *Open sight,* alza (*f.*) de ranura (of gun). || *Open to doubt,* dudoso, sa. || *Open to improvement,* susceptible de mejora. || *Open verdict,* veredicto (*m.*) que no especifica ni el autor ni las circunstancias de un crimen. || MIL. *Open warfare,* guerra declarada. || *Our way lay open,* ya no quedaba ningún obstáculo en el camino. || *The meeting is open,* se abre la sesión. || *The road is open,* la vía está libre. || *The season is open,* se ha levantado la veda. || *To be open to misinterpretation,* poder interpretarse mal. || *To be unable to keep one's eyes open,* cerrársele a uno los ojos de sueño, tener sueño. || *To give with an open hand,* dar a manos llenas. || *To have an open hand,* ser generoso. || *To keep open house,* tener mesa franca *or* casa abierta. || *To lay a wound open,* descubrir una herida. || *To lay open,* abrir (to open), exponer (to expose). || *To lay o.s. open to criticism,* exponerse a las críticas, dar pie *or* dar pábulo a la crítica. || *To leave sth. open to s.o.,* dar a elegir algo a alguien, dejar algo a la elección de alguien: *he left it open to me,* me lo dio a elegir. || *To leave the matter open,* dejar el asunto *or* la cuestión pendiente. || *To throw open,* abrir de par en par. || *Two courses are open to you,* le quedan dos posibilidades. || *Wide open,* abierto de par en par. || *You have only one course open to you,* sólo le queda una posibilidad.
— N. *In the open,* al aire libre (in the open air), en el campo (in the country), en campo abierto: *to attack the enemy in the open,* atacar al enemigo en campo abierto. || *To bring into the open,* revelar, sacar a luz. || *To come into the open,* salir a luz (to appear), decir lo que piensa uno (to say what one thinks).
open [ˈəupən] v. tr. Abrir: *to open a door,* abrir una puerta; *to open a parcel,* abrir un paquete; *to open a road, a tunnel,* abrir una carretera, un túnel; *to open a hole,* abrir un agujero; *to open a bank account,* abrir una cuenta en el banco; *to open a testament,* abrir un testamento; *to open ranks,* abrir filas; *to open a wound,* abrir una herida; *to open one's eyes,* abrir los ojos; *that opens new prospects for him,* esto le abre nuevas perspectivas. || Desplegar (to unfold). || Abrir, poner (a shop). || Inaugurar (an exhibition). || AGR. Roturar. || Despejar (to clear). || Entablar, iniciar, empezar (negotiations, conversation). || Abrir (session, debate, ball). || Emprender (business). || Empezar: *my name opens the list,* mi nombre empieza la lista. || ELECTR. Abrir (a circuit). || JUR. Exponer (a case). || Iniciar (an institution). || Abrir (in cards). || Revelar (one's intentions). || — *To open fire,* romper el fuego. || FIG. *To open one's heart to s.o.,* abrir su pecho a alguien (to confide one's feelings). | *To open the door to,* abrir la puerta a.
— V. intr. Abrirse (shop, book, window, door, floor, etc.). || Empezar, comenzar (to begin): *the book opens with a long dialogue,* el libro empieza con un largo diálogo. || THEATR. Estrenarse. || Abrir (in cards). || *The shops open at eight in the morning,* las tiendas [se] abren a las ocho de la mañana.
— **To open into,** dar a, comunicar con: *this door opens into the bedroom,* esta puerta comunica con el dormitorio. || **To open on to,** dar a: *this room opens on to the street,* este cuarto da a la calle. || **To open out,** desplegar (to unfold). | Ensanchar (a hole). | Extenderse: *the moor opened out before us,* el páramo se extendía ante nosotros. | Abrirse: *the flowers will open out in spring,* las flores se abrirán en primavera. | Desplegarse: *this map opens out,* este mapa se despliega. || Desarrollarse (to develop). | Acelerar a fondo (to accelerate). | — *To open out to s.o.,* confiarse a alguien, abrirse con alguien. || **To open up,** abrir (mine, road, shop). | Abrir: *open up!,* ¡abran! | Abrir, conquistar: *to open up new outlets,* abrir nuevos mercados. | Abrir, crear (possibilities). | Explorar (to explore). | Desarrollar (to develop). | Inaugurar: *to open up a new house,* inaugurar una casa. | Iniciarse: *trade opened up between the two countries,* las relaciones comerciales

se iniciaron entre los dos países. | Empezar, comenzar (to begin). | Revelar (to disclose). | Abrirse (to speak freely). | Romper el fuego (to start shooting).

open-air [—'εə*] adj. Al aire libre.

open-and-shut ['əupən'ʃʌt] adj. U. S. FAM. Claro, ra; evidente, obvio, via.

opencast ['əupənkɑ:st] adj. MIN. A cielo abierto.

opencut ['əupənkʌt] adj. U. S. MIN. A cielo abierto.

open-door ['əupən'dɔ:*] adj. De puertas abiertas.

open-ended ['əupən'endid] adj. Abierto, ta.

opener ['əupənə*] n. Abrelatas, *m. inv.* (for tins). || SP. Primer partido, *m.* (first game). || — Pl. Cartas (*f.*) que por su valor permiten al jugador abrir (in cards).

open-eyed ['əupn'aid] adj. Con los ojos abiertos. || FIG. Boquiabierto, ta (with surprise).

open-faced ['əupn'feist] adj. Sincero, ra (frank).

openhanded ['əupn'hændid] adj. Generoso, sa.

openhandedness [—nis] n. Generosidad, *f.*

open-heart ['əupən'hɑ:t] adj. MED. A corazón abierto.

openhearted [—id] adj. Sincero, ra; franco, ca (frank). || Cordial (kindly). || Generoso, sa.

openheartedness [—idnis] n. Sinceridad, *f.*, franqueza, *f.* (sincerity). || Generosidad, *f.*

open-hearth ['əupən'hɑ:θ] adj. TECH. *Open-hearth furnace*, horno (*m.*) de hogar abierto.

opening ['əupniŋ] n. Abertura, *f.* (aperture). || Grieta, *f.*, abertura, *f.* (in a wall). || Apertura, *f.* (act of opening): *the opening of the conference*, la apertura de la conferencia. || Oportunidad, *f.* (opportunity): *it's a fine opening for you*, es una buena oportunidad para ti. || Vacante, *f.* (vacancy). || Principio, *m.*, comienzo, *m.* (beginning). || Brecha, *f.* (breach). || Claro, *m.* (in forest, clouds). || Estreno, *m.* (première of a play, etc.). || Inauguración, *f.* (of an exhibition). || Apertura, *f.* (in chess).

— Adj. Inaugural, de apertura (inaugural). || — *Opening night*, noche (*f.*) de estreno. || *Opening price*, cotización (*f.*) inicial (in the stock exchange).

openly ['əupənli] adv. Francamente (frankly). || Abiertamente (undisguisedly). || Públicamente (publicly).

open-minded ['əupn'maindid] adj. Liberal. || Imparcial (impartial).

open-mindedness [—nis] n. Liberalidad, *f.* || Imparcialidad, *f.*

openmouthed ['əupn'mauðd] n. Boquiabierto, ta.

openness ['əupənnis] n. Franqueza, *f.*

open-plan ['əupn'plæn] adj. ARCH. *Open-plan house*, casa (*f.*) cuya disposición se deja al arbitrio del dueño.

openwork ['əupnwə:k] n. Calado, *m.* || MIN. Explotación (*f.*) a cielo abierto.

opera ['ɔpərə] n. MUS. Ópera, *f.* (musical play). | Ópera, *f.* (theatre). | Compañía (*f.*) de ópera (company). || — *Comic opera*, ópera bufa. || *Grand opera*, ópera. || *Light opera*, opereta, *f.*

opera ['ɔpərə] pl. n. See OPUS.

operable ['ɔpərəbl] adj. MED. Operable. || Factible (practicable).

opéra bouffe ['ɔpərə'bu:f] n. MUS. Ópera (*f.*) bufa.

opéra comique ['ɔpeiræ'kɔmi:k] n. MUS. Ópera (*f.*) cómica, zarzuela, *f.*

opera glasses ['ɔpərə'glɑ:siz] pl. n. Prismáticos, *m.*, gemelos, *m.*

opera hat ['ɔpərəhæt] n. Clac, *m.*, sombrero (*m.*) de muelles.

opera house ['ɔpərə'haus] n. MUS. Ópera, *f.* [teatro].

operate ['ɔpəreit] v. tr. Manejar, hacer funcionar: *to operate a machine*, manejar una máquina. || Dirigir (to direct). || Efectuar, realizar, llevar a cabo: *to operate a plan*, realizar un proyecto. || Llevar: *to operate an affair*, llevar un asunto. || Producir (to bring about). || Accionar (a lever). || Hacer funcionar: *the switch operates the light*, el interruptor hace funcionar la luz. || Impulsar (to propel). || — *The machine is operated by electricity*, la máquina funciona con electricidad. || FAM. *To operate a switch*, efectuar un cambio (to make a change).

— V. intr. Funcionar: *the lift is not operating*, el ascensor no funciona. || Surtir efecto, operar: *is the aspirin operating yet?*, ¿ha surtido efecto ya la aspirina? || Obrar, actuar: *to operate freely*, obrar con libertad. || Trabajar: *the company operates on an international scale*, la compañía trabaja a escala internacional. || Cometer un delito (criminal, etc.): *the thief operated by night*, el ladrón cometió su delito por la noche. || MED. Operar, efectuar una operación. || COMM. Especular. || — MED. *To operate on s.o. for sth.*, operar a alguien de algo. | *To operate on s.o.'s heart*, operar a alguien del corazón.

operatic [,ɔpə'rætik] adj. MUS. Operístico, ca; de ópera.

operating ['ɔpəreitiŋ] adj. MED. Que opera (surgeon). || COMM. De explotación: *operating expenses*, gastos de explotación.

— N. Funcionamiento, *m.* || Acción, *f.* (of a medicine). || MED. Operación, *f.* || COMM. Explotación, *f.*

operating room ['ɔpəreitiŋru:m] n. MED. Quirófano, *m.*, sala (*f.*) de operaciones.

operating table ['ɔpəreitiŋteibl] n. MED. Mesa (*f.*) de operaciones.

operating theatre (U. S. **operating theater**) ['ɔpəreitiŋ'θiətə*] n. MED. Quirófano, *m.*, sala (*f.*) de operaciones.

operation [,ɔpə'reiʃən] n. MATH. MED. COMM. Operación, *f.* || Manejo, *m.*: *the operation of a crane*, el manejo de una grúa. || Funcionamiento, *m.*: *the operation of the valves is bad*, el funcionamiento de las válvulas es malo. || MIL. Operación, *f.* || Maniobra, *f.* (manoeuvre). || Aplicación, *f.* (of a law, a rule). || Actividad, *f.* (activity). || — Pl. Obras, *f.* (work): *operations begin tomorrow*, las obras empiezan mañana. || — *Shady operations*, maniobras turbias. || *To be in operation*, estar en vigor, ser vigente (law, rule), estar funcionando (to be working), estar en funcionamiento: *not all our machines are in operation yet*, todavía no están en funcionamiento todas nuestras máquinas. || *To bring* o *to put into operation*, poner en funcionamiento (a machine), poner en vigor, empezar a aplicar (a law). || *To come into operation*, entrar en vigor (a law). || MED. *To perform an operation on s.o. for cataract*, operar a alguien de catarata. | *To undergo an operation*, ser operado, sufrir una operación (*for*, de).

operational [,ɔpə'reiʃənl] adj. MIL. Operacional. | De operaciones. || En buen estado, capaz de funcionar (in working order). || — MIL. *Operational flight*, vuelo (*m.*) de servicio. || *We're not fully operational yet*, todavía no estamos en pleno funcionamiento.

operative ['ɔpərətiv] adj. Operativo, va; operante. || En vigor: *this law will be operative as from today*, esta ley entra en vigor hoy. || Eficaz (efficient). || MED. Operatorio, ria. || *Operative part*, parte resolutiva, parte dispositiva (of a resolution).

— N. Operario, ria; obrero, ra (workman). || U. S. Detective (*m.*) privado (private detective).

operator ['ɔpəreitə*] n. Operario, ria; maquinista, *m. & f.* (of machine). || Telefonista, *m. & f.* (of telephone). || Operador, *m.* (in the cinema). || MATH. MED. Operador, *m.* || U. S. Especulador, ra (speculator). | Explotador, *m.* (of mine, airline, etc.). | Empresario, *m.* (an industrial). | Negociante, *m.* (dealer). | Conductor, ra (driver). | FAM. Estafador, ra (swindler). | Ladrón, *m.* (thief). || — *Tour operator*, agente (*m.*) de viajes. || MIL. MAR. *Wireless operator*, radio, *m.*, radiotelegrafista, *m.*

operculum [ə'pə:kjuləm] n. Opérculo, *m.*

— OBSERV. El plural de *operculum* es *opercula* o *operculums*.

operetta [,ɔpə'retə] n. MUS. Opereta, *f.* | Zarzuela, *f.* (in Spain).

Ophelia [ɔ'fi:ljə] pr. n. Ofelia, *f.*

ophidian [ɔ'fidiən] n. ZOOL. Ofidio, *m.*

— Adj. ZOOL. Ofidio, dia.

ophthalmia [ɔf'θælmiə] n. MED. Oftalmía, *f.*

ophthalmic [ɔf'θælmik] adj. MED. Oftálmico, ca.

ophthalmologic [,ɔfθæl'mɔlədʒik] or **ophthalmological** [,ɔfθælmə'lɔdʒikəl] adj. MED. Oftalmológico, ca.

ophthalmologist [,ɔfθæl'mɔlədʒist] n. MED. Oftalmólogo, *m.*

ophthalmology [,ɔfθæl'mɔlədʒi] n. MED. Oftalmología, *f.*

ophthalmoscope [ɔf'θælməskəup] n. MED. Oftalmoscopio, *m.*

ophthalmoscopy [ɔfθæl'mɔskəpi] n. MED. Oftalmoscopia, *f.*

opiate ['əupieit] n. Narcótico, *m.*

opiate ['əupieit] v. tr. Dormir con opio (to put to sleep). || Mezclar con opio (to mix with opium).

opine [əu'pain] v. tr./intr. Opinar.

opiner [—ə*] n. Opinante, *m. & f.*

opinion [ə'pinjən] n. Opinión, *f.* || — *Advisory opinion*, dictamen, *m.* || *I am of your opinion*, estoy de acuerdo con Ud., comparto su opinión, soy de la misma opinión que Ud. || *I didn't ask your opinion*, no te he pedido tu opinión *or* tu parecer. || *In my opinion it is possible*, a mi parecer *or* a mi juicio *or* en mi opinión es posible. || *In the opinion of*, según opinión *or* la opinión de. || *Opinion of the experts*, dictamen (*m.*) pericial. || *Public opinion poll*, sondeo (*m.*) de la opinión pública. || *That is a matter of opinion*, es cuestión de opinión. || *To be of the opinion that*, ser de opinión que, ser del parecer que. || *To form an opinion*, formarse una opinión. || *To have a high opinion of o.s.*, ser muy creído. || *To have a high, a low opinion of s.o.*, tener buen, mal concepto de alguien. || *To share the opinion of*, compartir la opinión de. || FIG. *To stick to one's opinion*, casarse con su opinión, aferrarse a una opinión. || *What was your opinion of it?*, ¿qué le pareció?

opinionated [—eitid] or **opinionative** [—eitiv] adj. Testarudo, da; obstinado, da.

opinionativeness [—ətivnis] n. Testarudez, *f.*, obstinación, *f.*

opium ['əupjəm] n. Opio, *m.*

opium addict [—'ædikt] n. Opiómano, na.

opium addiction [—ə'dikʃən] n. Opiomanía, *f.*

opium den [—den] n. Fumadero (*m.*) de opio.

opiumism [—izəm] n. Opiomanía, *f.*

opium poppy [—'pɔpi] n. BOT. Adormidera, *f.*

opium smoker [—'sməukə*] n. Fumador (*m.*) de opio.

Oporto [əu'pɔ:təu] pr. n. GEOGR. Oporto.

opossum [ə'pɔsəm] n. ZOOL. Oposum, *m.*, zarigüeya, *f.*
opponent [ə'pəunənt] n. Adversario, ria; contrario, ria; oponente, *m. & f.*, contrincante, *m. & f.* (adversary). || Competidor, ra (competitor).
— Adj. Opuesto, ta; contrario, ria. || ANAT. Oponente (muscle).
opportune ['ɔpətju:n] adj. Oportuno, na: *he has come at an opportune moment*, llega en un momento oportuno.
opportuneness [—nis] n. Oportunidad, *f.*
opportunism ['ɔpətju:nizəm] n. Oportunismo, *m.*
opportunist ['ɔpətju:nist] adj./n. Oportunista.
opportunistic [ɔpətju:'nistik] adj. Oportunista.
opportunity [,ɔpə'tju:niti] n. Oportunidad, *f.*, ocasión, *f.*: *if I get the opportunity*, si la ocasión se presenta. || Oportunidad, *f.*: *equality of opportunity*, igualdad de oportunidades; *to have the opportunity to*, tener la oportunidad de. || — *Opportunity makes the thief*, la ocasión hace al ladrón. || *To seize, to miss an opportunity*, approvechar, perder una oportunidad. || *We should like to take this opportunity to*, quisiéramos aprovechar esta ocasión *or* esta oportunidad para.
opposable [ə'pəuzəbl] adj. Oponible.
oppose [ə'pəuz] v. tr. Oponerse a: *to oppose a motion, a plan*, oponerse a una moción, a un proyecto. || Oponer: *to oppose two teams*, oponer dos equipos.
— V. intr. Oponerse.
opposed [—d] adj. Opuesto, ta. || — *As opposed to*, en comparación con. || *To be opposed to*, oponerse a, estar en contra de (not to agree), ir en contra de: *what you say is opposed to all reason*, lo que Ud. dice va en contra del sentido común.
opposer [—ə*] n. Oponente, *m. & f.*, adversario, ria.
opposing [—iŋ] adj. Adversario, ria; contrario, ria; opuesto, ta: *opposing team*, equipo adversario.
opposite ['ɔpəzit] adj. Opuesto, ta; contrario, ria: *in the opposite direction*, en dirección contraria. || De enfrente: *he ran to the opposite house*, corrió a la casa de enfrente. || Contrario, ria: *a member of the opposite faction*, un miembro de la facción contraria. || Opuesto, ta: *his tastes were completely opposite to mine*, sus gustos eran completamente opuestos a los míos; *the opposite page*, la página opuesta; *the opposite bank*, la ribera opuesta. || PHYS. MATH. Opuesto, ta: *opposite angles*, ángulos opuestos. || BOT. Opuesto, ta. || — *Opposite number*, colega, *m. & f.* || *The opposite sex*, el otro sexo. || *To hold an opposite view to*, no estar de acuerdo con. || *To hold opposite views*, no estar de acuerdo. || *To take the opposite view*, defender la opinión contraria. || *Your house is opposite to mine*, su casa está frente a la mía *or* enfrente de la mía.
— N. Lo opuesto, lo contrario: *she says one thing but means the opposite*, dice una cosa pero piensa lo contrario: *"big" is the opposite of "small"*, "grande" es lo contrario de "pequeño". || *The opposite is true of women*, es todo lo contrario para las mujeres.
— Adv. Enfrente: *the post office is opposite*, Correos está enfrente.
— Prep. Enfrente de, frente a: *the hotel is opposite the church*, el hotel está frente a la iglesia.
opposition [,ɔpə'ziʃən] n. Oposición, *f.*, desacuerdo, *m.*: *I am in opposition to the policies of the country*, estoy en oposición *or* en desacuerdo con la política del país. || Oposición, *f.*, partido (*m.*) de la oposición (party not in power). || Oposición, *f.* (group opposed to plan, policy, etc.). || Resistencia, *f.*: *they met with little opposition*, encontraron poca resistencia. || ASTR. Oposición, *f.* || COMM. Competencia, *f.* (competition). || — *The opposition party* o *the party in opposition*, el partido de la oposición. || *To be in opposition*, estar en la oposición (a party).
oppositional [—əl] adj. De oposición.
oppositionist [ɔpə'ziʃənist] n. Oposicionista, *m. & f.*
oppress [ə'prəs] v. tr. Oprimir: *the tyrant oppressed the poor*, el tirano oprimía a los pobres. || Oprimir, agobiar (mentally).
oppressed [—t] adj. Oprimido, da.
— Pl. n. Oprimidos, *m.*
oppressing [—iŋ] adj. Opresor, ra.
oppression [ə'preʃən] n. Opresión, *f.*
oppressive [ə'presiv] adj. Opresor, ra; opresivo, va; tiránico, ca: *an oppressive government*, un gobierno opresivo. || Sofocante, bochornoso, sa: *the oppressive heat*, el calor sofocante. || Agobiante (mental burden).
oppressiveness [—nis] n. Opresión, *f.* (of government, etc.). || Bochorno, *m.* (of the atmosphere).
oppressor [ə'presə*] n. Opresor, ra.
opprobrious [ə'prəubriəs] adj. Oprobioso, sa.
opprobrium [ə'prəubriəm] n. Oprobio, *m.*
oppugn [ɔ'pju:n] v. tr. Opugnar, atacar.
oppugnation [ɔpju'neiʃən] n. Opugnación, *f.*, ataque, *m.* (attack).
oppugner [ɔ'pju:nə*] n. Opugnador, *m.*
opt [ɔpt] v. intr. *To opt for*, optar por, escoger (to choose). || *To opt to*, optar por.
optative ['ɔptətiv] adj. GRAMM. Optativo, va.
— N. GRAMM. Optativo, *m.*
optic ['ɔptik] adj. Óptico, ca: *optic nerve, angle*, nervio, ángulo óptico.
— N. FAM. Ojo, *m.* (eye).
optical [—əl] adj. Óptico, ca: *optical instruments*, instrumentos ópticos. || — *Optical illusion*, ilusión óptica. || *Optical telegraph*, telégrafo óptico.
optician [ɔp'tiʃən] n. MED. Óptico, *m.*
optics ['ɔptiks] n. PHYS. Óptica, *f.*
optimism ['ɔptimizəm] n. Optimismo, *m.*
optimist ['ɔptimist] n. Optimista, *m. & f.*
optimistic [,ɔpti'mistik] adj. Optimista.
optimistically [—əli] adv. Con optimismo.
optimize ['ɔptimaiz] v. tr. Mejorar *or* perfeccionar lo más posible.
optimum ['ɔptiməm] adj. Óptimo, ma: *optimum conditions*, condiciones óptimas.
— N. Lo óptimo.

— OBSERV. El plural de *optimum* es *optimums* u *optima*.

option ['ɔpʃən] n. Opción, *f.*: *to rent a house with the option of purchase*, alquilar una casa con opción a compra; *to take out an option on*, tomar una opción sobre. || Posibilidad, *f.* || Elección, *f.* (choice). || — *I had no option but to go*, no tuve más remedio que ir. || *To make one's option between*, escoger entre.
optional ['ɔpʃənl] adj. Facultativo, va (not compulsory). || — *Dress optional*, traje de etiqueta o de calle. || *It is optional with you whether you go or stay*, puede irse o quedarse:
opulence ['ɔpjuləns] n. Opulencia, *f.*
opulent ['ɔpjulənt] adj. Opulento, ta (rich, full). || Abundante.
opus ['əupəs] n. MUS. Obra, *f.*, opus, *m.*

— OBSERV. El plural de la palabra inglesa *opus* es *opuses* u *opera*.

opuscule [ɔ'pʌsk'ju:l] n. Opúsculo, *m.*
opusculum [ɔ'pʌskjələm] n. Opúsculo, *m.*

— OBSERV. El plural de la palabra inglesa es *opuscula*.

or [ɔ:*] n. HERALD. Oro, *m.*
or [ɔ:*] conj. O: *clean or dirty*, limpio o sucio; *the sea can be blue or green*, el mar puede ser azul o verde; *his accent is good, or at least not bad*, su acento es bueno o por lo menos no es malo. || Ni (with negation): *with no house or money*, sin casa ni dinero; *he cannot walk or run*, no puede andar ni correr. || — *A dozen or so*, una docena poco más o menos. || *Or else*, si no. || *Or not*, o no.

— OBSERV. In Spanish *o* changes to *u* before a word beginning with *o* or *ho* (*shame or pride*, vergüenza u orgullo; *woman or man*, mujer u hombre).

oracle ['ɔrəkl] n. Oráculo, *m.*
oracular [ɔ'rækjulə*] adj. Del oráculo. || Oscuro, ra (mysterious). || Sentencioso, sa. || Profético, ca.
oral ['ɔ:rəl] adj. Oral: *oral medicine*, medicina oral; *to pass the oral exams*, aprobar los exámenes orales.
— N. Examen (*m.*) oral, oral, *m.* (examination).
orally [—i] adv. Oralmente, de palabra.
orange ['ɔrindʒ] n. BOT. Naranjo, *m.* (tree). | Naranja, *f.* (fruit). || Naranja, *m.* (colour). || *Orange tree*, naranjo.
— Adj. Naranja, *inv.*, de color naranja.
Orange ['ɔrindʒ] pr. n. HIST. Orange.
orangeade ['ɔrindʒ'eid] n. Naranjada, *f.*
orange blossom ['ɔrindʒ,blɔsəm] n. BOT. Azahar, *m.*
orange-flower water ['ɔrindʒ'flauə*'wɔ:tə*] n. Agua (*f.*) de azahar.
orange grove ['ɔrindʒ'grəuv] n. BOT. Naranjal, *m.*
orange grower ['ɔrindʒ,grəuə*] n. Naranjero, ra.
orange juice ['ɔrindʒdʒu:s] n. Zumo (*m.*) de naranja, jugo (*m.*) de naranja.
orangery ['ɔrindʒəri] n. Invernadero (*m.*) de naranjos.
orange seller ['ɔrindʒ'selə*] n. Naranjero, ra.
orange stick ['ɔrindʒstik] n. Palito (*m.*) de naranjo (in manicuring).
orangewood ['ɔrindʒwud] n. Naranjo, *m.*, madera (*f.*) de naranjo.
orangoutang ['ɔ:rəŋ'u:tæŋ] or **orangutan** ['ɔ:rəŋ-'u:tæn] n. ZOOL. Orangután, *m.*
orant ['ɔrənt] n. Estatua (*f.*) orante.
orate [ɔ:'reit] v. intr. Perorar.
oration [ɔ:'reiʃən] n. Oración, *f.*, discurso, *m.* || *Funeral oration*, oración fúnebre.
orator ['ɔrətə*] n. Orador, ra.
Oratorian [ɔrə'tɔ:riən] n. REL. Oratoriano, *m.*
oratorical [,ɔrə'tɔrikəl] adj. Oratorio, ria: *oratorical style*, estilo oratorio.
oratorio [,ɔrə'tɔ:riəu] n. MUS. Oratorio, *m.*
oratory ['ɔrətəri] n. REL. Oratorio, *m.* (chapel). || Oratoria, *f.* (art of speech).
orb [ɔ:b] n. Orbe, *m.*
orbit ['ɔ:bit] n. ASTR. Órbita, *f.* || ANAT. Órbita, *f.* || FIG. Esfera, *f.*, órbita, *f.* || — *In orbit*, en órbita. || *Putting into orbit*, puesta (*f.*) en órbita. || *To put into orbit*, poner en órbita.
orbit ['ɔ:bit] v. intr. Estar en órbita (satellite). || Dar vueltas, girar (to revolve): *the moon orbits around the earth*, la luna da vueltas alrededor de la tierra.
— V. tr. Estar en órbita alrededor de (to be in orbit). || Poner en órbita (to put into orbit). || Dar vueltas a, girar alrededor de (a planet).
orbital [—l] adj. Orbital: *orbital flight*, vuelo orbital. || Orbitario, ria: *orbital index*, índice orbitario.
orc [ɔ:k] n. ZOOL. Orca, *f.* (grampus).
orchard ['ɔ:tʃəd] n. Huerto, *m.* (in general). || — *Apple orchard*, manzanal, *m.* || *Pear orchard*, peral, *m.*
orchestra ['ɔ:kistrə] n. MUS. Orquesta, *f.* || Foso (*m.*) de orquesta (pit). || Patio (*m.*) de butacas (in theatre, cinema). || — *Orchestra pit*, foso de orquesta. || *Orchestra seat*, butaca (*f.*) de patio.
orchestral [ɔ:'kestrəl] adj. Orquestal.

orchestrate [ˈɔ:kistreit] v. tr. Mus. Orquestar.
orchestration [ˌɔ:kesˈtreiʃən] n. Mus. Orquestación, *f.*
orchid [ˈɔ:kid] n. Bot. Orquídea, *f.*
orchidaceae [ˌɔ:kiˈdeisii:] pl. n. Bot. Orquidáceas, *f.*
orchidaceous [ˌɔ:kiˈdeiʃəs] adj. Orquídeo, a.
ordain [ɔ:ˈdein] v. tr. Rel. Ordenar: *to ordain s.o. deacon*, ordenar a uno de diácono. || Decretar, ordenar (to decree). || Fig. Destinar (to destine). || *To be ordained*, ser ordenado, ordenarse.
ordainer [—ə*] n. Rel. Ordenador, *m.*
ordaining [—iŋ] adj. Rel. Ordenador, ra.
ordeal [ɔ:ˈdi:l] n. Prueba (*f.*) muy dura, sufrimiento, *m.*: *twenty four hours of walking is an ordeal*, veinticuatro horas de marcha es una prueba muy dura. || — Pl. Hist. Ordalías, *f.* || *After such an ordeal*, después de tanto sufrir.
order [ˈɔ:də*] n. Orden, *m.*: *in alphabetical, in chronological order*, en *or* por orden alfabético, en *or* por orden cronológico; *to put one's affairs in order*, poner sus asuntos en orden; *in order of seniority*, por orden de antigüedad; *order of priority*, orden de prioridad. || Orden, *m.*: *law and order*, el orden público; *the police kept order*, la policía mantuvo el orden; *to call to order*, llamar al orden; *to keep order in a class*, mantener el orden en una clase. || Regla, *f.*: *your licence is in order*, su permiso está en regla; *it's all in order*, todo está en regla. || Orden, *f.* (title): *the Order of the British Empire, of the Garter*, la Orden del Imperio Británico, de la Jarretera; *order of knighthood, Order of the Golden Fleece*, orden de caballería, Orden del Toisón de Oro. || Condecoración, *f.* (medal). || Mil. Orden, *f.*: *to give orders*, dar órdenes; *to obey orders*, cumplir las órdenes. | Orden, *m.*: *in battle order*, en orden de combate; *close, open order*, orden cerrado, abierto. || Rel. Orden, *m.* (of the angels). | Orden, *f.*: *monastic order*, orden monástica; *the Dominican Order*, la orden dominicana; *Holy Orders*, órdenes sagradas. || Jur. Fallo, *m.*, sentencia, *f.* (of the court). | Mandato, *m.*, mandamiento, *m.*, orden, *f.* (of the judge). || Comm. Pedido, *m.*: *to place an order with*, hacer un pedido a; *order form*, orden de pedido; *rush order*, pedido urgente. | Giro, *m.*: *postal, banker's order*, giro postal, bancario. || Arch. Bot. Orden, *m.*: *Gothic, Ionic order*, orden gótico, jónico. || Math. Grado, *m.*: *equation of the first order*, ecuación de primer grado. || Fig. Calidad, *f.*, orden, *m.*, categoría, *f.*: *of the first order*, de primera calidad. | Tipo, *m.*, índole, *f.* (kind): *problems of a different order*, problemas de distinto tipo. || Zool. Orden, *m.*: *of the orthopteran order*, del orden de los ortópteros. || — Pl. Clase, *f. sing.* (class): *the lower orders*, la clase baja. || — *Am I in order?*, ¿me autoriza el reglamento? || *At the order of*, por orden de. || Mil. *At your orders!*, ¡a la orden! || Comm. *Bill to order*, pagaré, *m.*, billete (*m.*) a la orden. || *By order of*, por orden de. || Comm. *Cheque to order*, cheque nominativo. | *Delivery order*, orden (*f.*) de expedición. || Jur. *Departmental order*, orden (*f.*) ministerial. || *He gave me orders to do it*, me mandó hacerlo, me mandó que lo hiciera. || Mil. *In gala order*, en uniforme de gala. || *In order*, en orden (in the correct disposition), bien: *a piece of toast would be in order*, una tostada me vendría bien; que funciona (working): *is the machine in order again?*, ¿funciona ahora la máquina?; pertinente: *your question is in order, sir*, su pregunta es pertinente, señor; aceptable, admisible (motions, amendment), en regla: *your papers are in order*, sus papeles están en regla. || *In order of appearance*, por orden de aparición. || *In order that*, para que: *I did it in order that he should come out*, lo hice para que saliese. || *In order to*, para: *in order to be able to go*, para poder ir; para, a: *I went to London in order to see the Queen*, me fui a Londres para ver a la reina. || U. S. *In short order*, en seguida (at once). || *In working order*, que funciona: *everything is in working order*, todo funciona. || *Is it in order for me to suggest sth.?*, ¿puedo proponer algo?, ¿me permiten que proponga algo? || *Made to order*, hecho a la medida. || Rel. *Major, minor, mendicant orders*, órdenes (*f.*) mayores, menores, mendicantes. || *No-one gives me orders!*, ¡a mí nadie me da órdenes!, ¡a mí nadie me manda! || *Of the order of*, del mismo estilo que, parecido a (similar): *my village is of the order of yours*, mi pueblo es del mismo estilo que el tuyo; del orden de: *sth. of the order of five pounds*, una cantidad del orden de cinco libras. || *On order*, pedido, da: *we have twenty thousand books on order*, tenemos pedidos *or* hemos pedido veinte mil libros. || *Order of arrest*, orden (*f.*) de detención *or* de arresto. || *Order of Council*, Real Orden, *f.* || Mil. *Order of the day*, orden (*f.*) del día. || Comm. *Pay to the order of*, páguese a la orden de. || *Point of order*, cuestión (*f.*) de orden. || *Sailing orders*, últimas instrucciones [dadas al capitán de un barco]. || Comm. *Standing order*, pedido regular. || *Standing orders*, reglamento (*m.*) general (of committee, etc.). || *That's an order!*, ¡es una orden¡ || Fig. *That's a tall o a large order*, eso es mucho pedir. || *The meeting is called to order*, se abre la sesión. || *The new, the old order*, el nuevo, el antiguo régimen. || *Till further orders*, hasta nueva orden. || Rel. *To be in holy orders*, ser sacerdote. || *To be out of order*, no funcionar (a machine): *the lift is out of order*, el ascensor no funciona; estar en desorden (not in the correct sequence): *these pages are out of order*, estas páginas están en desorden; hablar cuando no se debe (in meetings, etc.), no ser pertinente (a question), estar descompuesto: *my tummy is out of order*, tengo el vientre descompuesto; estar fuera de lugar (out of place). || Fig. *To be the order of the day*, estar de moda. || Sp. *To be under starter's orders*, estar esperando la orden de salida. || *To be under the orders of*, estar bajo las órdenes *or* el mando de. || Mil. *To come to order*, descansar armas. || *To declare a candidature out of order*, rechazar una candidatura. || Fig. *To get one's marching orders*, ser despedido. || *To get out of order*, estropearse. || Fig. *To give s.o. his marching orders*, despedir a uno. || *To put in order*, poner en orden, ordenar (to arrange), poner en orden, arreglar (a matter). || *To put sth. on order*, pedir algo. || *To restore order*, restablecer el orden. || *To rule a question out of order*, rechazar una pregunta. || Rel. *To take holy orders*, tomar las órdenes sagradas, ordenarse. || Comm. *Unfilled orders*, pedidos pendientes.
order [ˈɔ:də*] v. tr. Ordenar, poner en orden: *to order one's affairs*, poner en orden sus asuntos. || Clasificar (to classify). || Organizar (one's life). || Ordenar, mandar: *I order you to do it*, le ordeno que lo haga. || Mandar: *to order s.o. in, out, back*, mandar a uno entrar, salir, volver. || Comm. Pedir, encargar, hacer un pedido de (goods). || Encargar: *yesterday I ordered a coat*, ayer encargué un abrigo. || Pedir, encargar (in restaurant, etc.). || Med. Mandar: *the doctor ordered him to stay in bed*, el médico le mandó que se quedara en la cama. | Recetar (to prescribe). || Mil. Mandar (to send, to command). || — *Order, arms!*, ¡descansen!, ¡ar! || *To order s.o. about*, mandar a uno de acá para allá, estar siempre dándole órdenes a uno. || *To order s.o. off*, mandar a uno que se vaya (to send away), expulsar (a player in sports).
order blank [—blæŋk] n. Orden (*f.*) de pedido.
order book [—buk] n. Libro (*m.*) de pedidos.
ordered [ˈɔ:dəd] adj. Ordenado, da.
ordering [ˈɔ:dəriŋ] n. Ordenamiento, *m.*
orderliness [ˈɔ:dəlinis] n. Orden, *m.* || Método, *m.* || Disciplina, *f.*
orderly [ˈɔ:dəli] adj. Ordenado, da; en orden (tidy). || Ordenado, da; metódico, ca (careful). || Pacífico, ca; disciplinado, da; tranquilo, la: *an orderly crowd*, una multitud disciplinada.
— N. Mil. Ordenanza, *m.* || U. S. Med. Enfermero, *m.* (nurse). || — *Orderly officer*, oficial (*m.*) de servicio. || *Orderly room*, oficina (*f.*) de la compañía.
ordinal [ˈɔ:dinl] adj. Ordinal.
— N. Número (*m.*) ordinal, ordinal, *m.* || Rel. Ordinal, *m.*
ordinance [ˈɔ:dinəns] n. Jur. Ordenanza, *f.* || Rel. Rito, *m.* (rite). | Eucaristía, *f.*
ordinarily [ˈɔ:dnrili] adv. Generalmente, en general, ordinariamente.
ordinariness [ˈɔ:dnrinis] n. Mediocridad, *f.*
ordinary [ˈɔ:dnri] adj. Corriente, habitual, usual: *in the ordinary way*, de la manera corriente. || Corriente, ordinario, ria: *the ordinary model*, el modelo corriente. || Corriente, cualquiera: *it cannot be done with an ordinary pencil*, no se puede hacer con un lápiz cualquiera. || Simple: *he was just an ordinary tourist*, no era más que un simple turista. || Medio, dia: *the ordinary reader*, el lector medio; *the ordinary Spaniard*, el español medio. || Regular, ordinario, ria; mediocre (mediocre): *a very ordinary piece of work*, un trabajo muy ordinario. || — *In ordinary use*, empleado normalmente *or* habitualmente. || Mar. *Ordinary seaman*, marinero, *m.* || *Ordinary shares*, acciones ordinarias.
— N. Lo corriente, lo ordinario (the usual). || Rel. Ordinario, *m.* (bishop). | Ordinario (*m.*) de la Misa (order of service). || Jur. Ordinario, *m.* (judge). || — *Above the ordinary*, fuera de lo común. || *In ordinary*, habitual: *purveyor in ordinary to*, proveedor habitual de. || *Out of the ordinary*, extraordinario, ria; fuera de lo común, excepcional: *the film was nothing out of the ordinary*, la película no era nada excepcional.
ordinate [ˈɔ:dnit] n. Math. Ordenada, *f.*
ordination [ˌɔ:diˈneiʃən] n. Rel. Ordenación, *f.* (of a priest). || Disposición, *f.*, ordenación, *f.* (arrangement).
ordnance [ˈɔ:dnəns] n. Mil. Artillería, *f.* (artillery): *ordnance officer*, oficial de artillería. | Material (*m.*) de guerra (material). | Servicio (*m.*) de material de guerra (department). || — *Ordnance Survey*, servicio (*m.*) oficial de topografía y cartografía. || *Ordnance survey map*, mapa (*m.*) de estado mayor.
ordure [ˈɔ:djuə*] n. Basura, *f.* (rubbish). || Porquería, *f.* (filth). || Excremento, *m.* (excrement). || Estiércol, *m.* (manure).
ore [ɔ:*] n. Min. Mineral, *m.*, mena, *f.*: *iron ore*, mineral de hierro.
oread [ˈɔ:riæd] n. Myth. Oréada, *f.*, oréade, *f.*
oregano [ɔˈregənəu] n. Orégano, *m.*
organ [ˈɔ:gən] n. Mus. Órgano, *m.* || Zool. Anat. Bot. Órgano, *m.*: *the organs of digestion*, los órganos de la digestión. || Fig. Órgano, *m.*: *the organ of the democratic party*, el órgano del partido democrático. || Mus. *Barrel organ*, organillo, *m.*, órgano de manubrio.
organdie (U. S. **organdy**) [ˈɔ:gəndi] n. Organdí, *m.*
organ-grinder [ˈɔ:gənˌgraində*] n. Organillero, ra.

organic [ɔ:ˈgænik] adj. Orgánico, ca: *organic chemistry*, química orgánica.
organism [ˈɔ:gənizəm] n. Organismo, *m.*
organist [ˈɔ:gənist] n. Mus. Organista, *m.* & *f.*
organizable [ˈɔ:gənaizəbl] adj. Organizable.
organization [ˌɔ:gənaiˈzeiʃən] n. Organización, *f.*
organize [ˈɔ:gənaiz] v. tr. Organizar: *to organize a party*, organizar una fiesta; *he organizes the trade union*, organiza el sindicato. || *To get organized*, organizarse.
— V. intr. Organizarse.
organized [—d] adj. Organizado, da. || *Organized labour*, obreros sindicados.
organizer [—ə*] n. Organizador, ra. || Biol. Organizador, *m.*
organizing [—iŋ] adj. Organizador, ra.
— N. Organización, *f.* (action).
organ stop [ˈɔ:gənˌstɔp] n. Mus. Registro (*m.*) de órgano.
organum [ˈɔ:gənəm] n. Mus. Organum, *m.*
organzine [ˈɔ:gənzi:n] n. Torzal, *m.*
orgasm [ˈɔ:gæzəm] n. Orgasmo, *m.*
orgeat [ˈɔ:ʒə] n. Horchata, *f.*
orgiastic [ˌɔ:dʒiˈæstik] adj. Orgiástico, ca.
orgy [ˈɔ:dʒi] n. Orgía, *f.* (debauchery). || Fig. Orgía, *f.*: *an orgy of colour*, una orgía de colores.
oriel [ˈɔ:riəl] n. Mirador, *m.*
orient [ˈɔ:riənt] n. Oriente, *m.* (lustre). || Perla (*f.*) fina (pearl). || Oriente, *m.* (east). || *The Orient*, el Oriente.
— Adj. Brillante. || Oriental.
orient [ˈɔ:riənt] v. tr. Orientar. || *To orient o.s.*, orientarse.
Oriental [ˌɔ:riˈentl] adj./n. Oriental.
Orientalism [ˌɔ:riˈentəlizəm] n. Orientalismo, *m.*
Orientalist [ˌɔ:riˈentəlist] adj./n. Orientalista.
orientalize [ˌɔ:riˈentəlaiz] v. tr. Orientalizar.
— V. intr. Orientalizarse.
orientate [ˈɔ:rienteit] v. tr. Orientar. || *To orientate o.s.*, orientarse.
orientation [ˌɔ:rienˈteiʃən] n. Orientación, *f.*
orifice [ˈɔrifis] n. Orificio, *m.*
oriflamme [ˈɔriflæm] n. Oriflama, *f.*
origan [ˈɔrigən] n. Bot. Orégano, *m.*
origin [ˈɔridʒin] n. Origen, *m.* || Origen, *m.*, procedencia, *f.*: *country of origin*, país de origen. || — Pl. Origen, *m. sing.*: *of humble origins*, de origen humilde.
original [əˈridʒənl] adj. Original: *original work, sin*, obra, pecado original. || Primero, ra: *one of the original members*, uno de los primeros miembros. || Original, primero, ra: *original sense of a word*, primer sentido de una palabra. || Original (not common): *original taste*, gusto original.
— N. Original, *m.* (work): *the original of this copy is in Paris*, el original de esta copia está en París. || Persona (*f.*) original (an eccentric).
originality [əˌridʒiˈnæliti] n. Originalidad, *f.*
originally [əˈridʒnəli] adv. En un principio, al principio, originariamente (initially). || Con originalidad (in an original manner).
originate [əˈridʒineit] v. tr. Originar, causar, provocar: *the spring thaw originates floods*, el deshielo primaveral origina inundaciones. || Crear, inventar (to create).
— V. intr. Comenzar, empezar (to begin): *how did your friendship originate?*, ¿cómo empezó vuestra amistad? || Ser originario de: *the custom originated in Wales*, la costumbre es originaria de Gales. || — *The plan originated with him*, es el autor del proyecto. || *To originate from*, ser descendiente de. || *To originate from* o *in*, tener su origen en.
origination [əˌridʒiˈneiʃən] n. Origen, *m.* (source). || Creación, *f.*, invención, *f.* (creation). || Principio, *m.* (beginning).
originative [əˈridzineitiv] adj. Inventivo, va; creador, ra.
originator [əˈridzineitə*] n. Autor, ra; creador, ra.
Orinoco [ˌɔriˈnəukəu] pr. n. Geogr. Orinoco, *m.*
oriole [ˈɔ:riəul] n. Oropéndola, *f.* (bird).
Orion [əˈraiən] pr. n. Astr. Orión, *m.*
orison [ˈɔrizən] n. Plegaria, *f.*, oración, *f.*
Orkney Islands [ˈɔ:kniˈailəndz] pl. pr. n. Geogr. Orcadas, *f.*
Orkneys [ˈɔ:kniz] pl. pr. n. Geogr. Orcadas, *f.*
orle [ɔ:l] n. Herald. Orla, *f.*
orlon [ˈɔ:lɔn] n. Orlón, *m.* (fabric).
orlop [ˈɔ:lɔp] n. Mar. Sollado, *m.*
ormer [ˈɔ:mə*] n. Zool. Oreja (*f.*) de mar (shell).
ormolu [ˈɔ:məulu:] n. Oro (*m.*) molido.
ornament [ˈɔ:nəmənt] n. Ornamento, *m.*, adorno, *m.* (embellishment). || Honra, *f.* (person). || Rel. Ornamento, *m.* || Aut. Embellecedor, *m.* || — Pl. Mus. Floreos, *m.*, adornos, *m.*
ornament [ˈɔ:nəmənt] v. tr. Adornar, ornamentar, ornar.
ornamental [ˌɔ:nəˈmentl] adj. Ornamental, decorativo, va; de adorno.
ornamentation [ˌɔ:nəmenˈteiʃən] n. Ornamentación, *f.*, decoración, *f.* || Adornos, *m. pl.*, decoración, *f.* (ornaments).
ornamenter [ˈɔ:nəməntə*] n. Decorador, ra.
ornate [ɔ:ˈneit] adj. Adornado, da; ornado, da (adorned). || Recargado, da (overadorned). || Fig. Florido, da (style).
ornateness [—nis] n. Adornos (*m. pl.*) excesivos. || Fig. Estilo (*m.*) florido.
ornery [ˈɔnəri] adj. U. S. Fam. Terco, ca; tozudo, da.
ornithological [ˌɔ:niθəˈlɔdʒikl] adj. Ornitológico, ca.
ornithologist [ˌɔ:niˈθɔlədʒist] n. Ornitólogo, *m.*
ornithology [ˌɔ:niˈθɔlədʒi] n. Ornitología, *f.*
ornithorhynchus [ˌɔ:niθəˈriŋkəs] n. Zool. Ornitorrinco, *m.*
orogenesis [ˌɔrəuˈdʒenisis] n. Geol. Orogénesis, *f.*
orogenic [ɔrəˈdʒenik] adj. Geol. Orogénico, ca.
orogeny [ɔˈrɔdʒəni] n. Geol. Orogenia, *f.*
orographic [ˌɔrəuˈgræfik] or **orographical** [—əl] adj. Orográfico, ca.
orography [ɔˈrɔgrəfi] n. Orografía, *f.*
orometry [ɔˈrɔmetri] n. Orometría, *f.*
orotund [ˈɔrəutʌnd] adj. Sonoro, ra (voice). || Pomposo, sa; rimbombante (bombastic).
orphan [ˈɔ:fən] adj./n. Huérfano, na.
orphan [ˈɔ:fən] v. tr. Dejar huérfano.
orphanage [ˈɔ:fənidʒ] n. Orfanato, *m.*, asilo (*m.*) de huérfanos (institution). || Orfandad, *f.* (condition).
orphaned [ˈɔ:fənd] adj. Huérfano, na.
orphanhood [ˈɔ:fənhud] n. Orfandad, *f.*
orphanize [ˈɔ:fənaiz] v. tr. Dejar huérfano.
Orphean [ɔ:ˈfiən] adj. Órfico, ca.
Orpheus [ˈɔ:fju:s] pr. n. Orfeo, *m.*
Orphic [ˈɔ:fik] adj. Órfico, ca. || Fig. Esotérico, ca. || Embelesador, ra (entrancing).
orrery [ˈɔrəri] n. Planetario, *m.*
orthocentre (U. S. **orthocenter**) [ɔ:θəˈsentə*] n. Math. Ortocentro, *m.*
orthochromatic [ˈɔ:θəukrəuˈmætik] adj. Ortocromático, ca.
orthodox [ˈɔ:θədɔks] adj. Ortodoxo, xa.
orthodoxy [ˈɔ:θədɔksi] n. Ortodoxia, *f.*
orthoepy [ˈɔ:θəuepi] n. Ortología, *f.*
orthogenesis [ɔ:θəˈdʒenesis] n. Ortogénesis, *f.*
orthogenetic [ɔ:θədʒiˈnetik] adj. Ortogenético, ca.
orthognathism [ɔ:ˈθɔgnəθizəm] n. Ortognatismo, *m.*
orthogonal [ɔ:ˈθɔgənl] adj. Math. Ortogonal.
orthographic [ˌɔ:θəuˈgræfik] or **orthographical** [—əl] adj. Ortográfico, ca. || Math. Ortogonal.
orthography [ɔ:ˈθɔgrəfi] n. Gramm. Ortografía, *f.* || Math. Proyección (*f.*) ortogonal.
orthopaedic (U. S. **orthopedic**) [ˌɔ:θəuˈpi:dik] adj. Ortopédico, ca.
orthopaedics (U. S. **orthopedics**) [—s] n. Med. Ortopedia, *f.*
orthopaedist (U. S. **orthopedist**) [ˌɔ:θəuˈpi:dist] n. Ortopedista, *m.* & *f.*, ortopédico, ca.
orthopteran [ɔ:ˈθɔptərən] adj. Ortóptero, ra.
— N. Zool. Ortóptero, *m.*
orthopteron [ɔ:ˈθɔptərən] n. Zool. Ortóptero, *m.*
— Observ. El plural de la palabra inglesa es *orthoptera*.
orthopterous [ɔ:ˈθɔptərəs] adj. Zool. Ortóptero, ra.
orthotropic [ˌɔ:θəuˈtrɔpik] adj. Bot. Ortótropo, pa.
orthotropous [ɔ:ˈθɔtrəpəs] adj. Bot. Ortótropo, pa.
ortolan [ˈɔ:tələn] n. Zool. Hortelano, *m.* (European bunting).
Oscar [ˈɔskə*] n. Oscar, *m.* (reward).
oscillate [ˈɔsileit] v. tr. Hacer oscilar.
— V. intr. Oscilar (to swing). || Fig. Oscilar, fluctuar, variar (to fluctuate): *the prices oscillate*, los precios oscilan. | Vacilar (to be indecisive).
oscillating [—iŋ] adj. Oscilante.
oscillation [ˌɔsiˈleiʃən] n. Oscilación, *f.* || Fig. Fluctuación, *f.*, variación, *f.* (fluctuation). | Vacilación, *f.*, oscilación, *f.* (hesitation).
oscillator [ˈɔsileitə*] n. Oscilador, *m.*
oscillatory [ˈɔsilətəri] adj. Oscilatorio, ria; oscilante. || Vibratorio, ria.
oscillogram [ɔˈsiləugræm] n. Phys. Oscilograma, *m.*
oscillograph [ɔˈsiləugræf] n. Phys. Oscilógrafo, *m.*
oscilloscope [ɔˈsiləskəup] n. Phys. Osciloscopio, *m.*
osculate [ˈɔskjuleit] v. tr. Besar (to kiss).
— V. intr. Besarse.
osculation [ˌɔskjuˈleiʃən] n. Ósculo, *m.*, beso, *m.* (kiss).
osculum [ˈɔskjuləm] n. Ósculo, *m.* (in sponges).
— Observ. El plural de *osculum* es *oscula*.
osier [ˈəuʒə*] n. Bot. Mimbrera, *f.*, mimbre, *m.* (tree). || Mimbre, *m.* (rod).
— Adj. De mimbre. || *Osier bed*, mimbrera, *f.*, mimbreral, *m.*, mimbral, *m.*
osiery [—ri] n. Mimbreral, *m.*, mimbral, *m.*, mimbrera, *f.* (osier bed). || Cestería, *f.* (basketwork).
Osiris [əuˈsaiəris] pr. n. Myth. Osiris, *m.*
Oslo [ˈɔzləu] pr. n. Geogr. Oslo.
osmanli [ɔzˈmænli] adj./n. Osmanlí, otomano, na.
osmic [ˈɔzmik] adj. Chem. Ósmico, ca.
osmium [ˈɔzmiəm] n. Chem. Osmio, *m.*
osmometer [ɔzˈmɔmitə*] n. Phys. Osmómetro, *m.*
osmosis [ɔzˈməusis] n. Ósmosis, *f.*
osmotic [ɔzˈmɔtik] adj. Osmótico, ca.
osmous [ˈɔzməs] adj. Ósmico, ca.
osprey [ˈɔspri] n. Quebrantahuesos, *m. inv.*, pigargo, *m.* (bird). || Airón, *m.* (trimming).
ossein [ˈɔsiin] n. Oseína, *f.*
osseous [ˈɔsiəs] adj. Óseo, a.
ossification [ˌɔsifiˈkeiʃən] n. Osificación, *f.*
ossifrage [ˈɔsifridʒ] n. Zool. See OSPREY.
ossify [ˈɔsifai] v. tr. Osificar.
— V. intr. Osificarse.
ossuary [ˈɔsjuəri] n. Osario, *m.*

osteal ['ɔstiəl] adj. Óseo, a.
ostein ['ɔstiin] n. CHEM. Osteína, *f.*
osteitis [ɔsti'aitis] n. MED. Osteítis, *f.*
ostensible [ɔs'tensəbl] adj. Aparente.
ostensibly [ɔs'tensəbli] adv. Aparentemente.
ostensive [ɔs'tensiv] adj. Aparente. || Ostensible, manifiesto, ta (obvious).
ostensory [ɔs'tensəri] n. REL. Custodia, *f.*
ostentation [,ɔsten'teiʃən] n. Ostentación, *f.*
ostentatious [,ɔsten'teiʃəs] asj. Ostentoso, sa.
ostentatiousness [—nis] n. Ostentación, *f.*
osteoarthritis [ɔstiəuɑ:r'θraitis] n. MED. Osteoartritis, *f.*
osteoblast ['ɔstiəblæst] n. Osteoblasto, *m.*
osteologic [,ɔstiə'lɔdʒik] or **osteological** [—əl] adj. Osteológico, ca.
osteologist [,ɔsti'ɔlədʒist] n. Osteólogo, ga.
osteology [ɔsti'ɔlədʒi] n. Osteología, *f.*
osteoma [ɔsti'əumə] n. MED. Osteoma, *m.*

— OBSERV. El plural de la palabra inglesa es *osteomas* u *osteomata.*

osteomyelitis [ɔstiəmaiə'laitis] n. MED. Osteomielitis, *f.*
osteopath ['ɔstiəpæθ] n. MED. Osteópata, *m. & f.*
osteopathic [,ɔstiə'pæθik] adj. MED Osteopático, ca.
osteopathist [,ɔsti'ɔpəθist] n. Osteópata, *m. & f.*
osteopathy [,ɔsti'ɔpəθi] n. MED. Osteopatía, *f.*
osteoplasty [ɔstiə'plæsti] n. MED. Osteoplastia, *f.*
osteotomy [ɔsti'ɔtəmi] n. MED. Osteotomía, *f.*
ostiary ['ɔstiəri] n. Ostiario, *m.*
ostler ['ɔstlə*] n. Mozo (*m.*) de cuadra, palafrenero, *m.*
ostmark ['ɔstmɑ:k] n. Marco, *m.* [de Alemania Oriental].
ostracism ['ɔstrəsizəm] n. Ostracismo, *m.*
ostracize ['ɔstrəsaiz] v. tr. Condenar al ostracismo.
ostreiculture ['ɔstriikʌltʃə*] n. Ostricultura, *f.*
ostrich ['ɔstritʃ] n. Avestruz, *m.* (bird).
Ostrogoth ['ɔstrəugɔθ] n. HIST. Ostrogodo, da.
Ostrogothic [—ik] adj. Ostrogodo, da.
otalgia [ə'tældʒiə] n. MED. Otalgia, *f.*
otalgic [ə'tældʒik] adj. Otálgico, ca.
otary ['əutəri] n. ZOOL. Otaria, *f.*
Othello [əu'θeləu] pr. n. Otelo, *m.*
other ['ʌðə*] adj. Otro, tra: *your other hand,* tu otra mano; *no other place to go,* ningún otro sitio a donde ir; *some other examples,* algunos otros ejemplos; *the youth of other days,* la juventud de otros tiempos; *the other day,* el otro día; *the other world,* el otro mundo. || Diferente, distinto, ta: *his tastes are quite other than mine,* sus gustos son bastante diferentes a *or* de los míos. || — *Among* o *amongst other things,* entre otras cosas. || *Every other day,* cada dos días, un día sí y otro no. || *On the other hand,* por otra parte, por otro lado. || *Other people,* otros. || *Other people's property,* los bienes ajenos. || *Some day or other,* un día u otro. || *The other one,* el otro, la otra.

— N./pron. Otro, tra: *show me the others,* enséñeme los otros; *open the other,* abra el otro. || — *A few others,* otros pocos. || *Among others,* entre otros. || *Each other,* uno a otro, el uno al otro. || *Many others,* otros muchos. || *No other,* ningún otro. || *No other than,* nadie más que (person). || *One after the other,* uno después del otro, uno tras otro. || *One or other of you,* uno de vosotros. || *Someone or other,* uno u otro. || *Some other,* otra persona, otro. || *The others,* los otros, los demás.

— Adv. *Other than,* de otra manera que.

otherwise [—waiz] adj. Distinto, ta; diferente, otro, tra: *if circumstances were otherwise,* si las circunstancias fuesen distintas.

— Adv. De otra manera, de otro modo (in a different way). || Si no, de lo contrario: *do it now, otherwise you will forget,* hazlo ahora, si no lo olvidarás. || Aparte de eso, por lo demás (in other respects): *he broke a leg but was otherwise unhurt,* se rompió una pierna, pero aparte de eso no le pasó nada.

otherworldiness [—'wə:ldlinis] n. Alejamiento (*m.*) *or* desapego (*m.*) del mundo.
otherworldly [—'wə:ldli] adj. Alejado del mundo, desapegado del mundo.
otiose ['əuʃiəus] adj. Ocioso, sa (idle). || Ocioso, sa; inútil (useless).
otiosity [əuʃi'ɔsiti] n. Ociosidad, *f.* (idleness). || Inutilidad, *f.* (uselessness).
otitis [əu'taitis] n. MED. Otitis, *f.*
otolaryngology [,əutəulærin'gɔlədʒi] n. MED. Otolaringología, *f.*
otologist [əu'tɔlədʒist] n. MED. Otólogo, *m.*
otology [əu'tɔlədʒi] n. MED. Otología, *f.*
otorhinolaryngologist [,ətaurainəulæriŋ'gɔlədʒist] n. MED. Otorrinolaringólogo, *m.*
otorhinolaryngology [,ətaurainəulæriŋ'gɔlədʒi] n. MED. Otorrinolaringología, *f.*
otoscope ['əutəskəup] n. Otoscopio, *m.*
otter ['ɔtə*] n. Nutria, *f.* (animal, fur).
Ottoman [—mən] adj./n. Otomano, na: *Ottoman Empire,* Imperio Otomano.
ottoman [—mən] n. Otomana, *f.* (divan).
oubliette [,u:bli'et] n. Mazmorra, *f.* (dungeon).
ouch [autʃ] interj. ¡Ay!
ought [ɔ:t] v. aux. Deber: *we ought to tell them,* deberíamos decírselo; *to sleep more than one ought,* dormir más de lo que se debe. || Tener que: *you ought to have been with us yesterday,* tenías que haber estado con nosotros ayer.

— OBSERV. El verbo *ought* va seguido por el infinitivo con *to.*

ought [ɔ:t] n. See AUGHT.
oughtn't [ɔ:tnt] contraction of *ought not.*
ouija ['wi:dʒɑ:] n. Tabla (*f.*) con signos.
ounce [auns] n. Onza, *f.* (weight of 28.35 gms). || FAM. Pizca, *f.*: *not an ounce of sympathy,* ni una pizca de simpatía. || ZOOL. Onza, *f.*
our ['auə*] poss. adj. Nuestro, nuestra; nuestros, nuestras: *our sisters,* nuestras hermanas.
ours [—z] poss. pron. Nuestro, nuestra, el nuestro, la nuestra, nuestros, nuestras, los nuestros, las nuestras: *this book is ours,* este libro es nuestro, este libro es el nuestro; *these are ours,* éstos son nuestros, éstos son los nuestros. || El nuestro, la nuestra, los nuestros, las nuestras: *your house is larger than ours,* su casa es más grande que la nuestra. || Nuestro, nuestra, nuestros, nuestras: *the fault is ours,* la culpa es nuestra. || — *It is not ours to blame him,* no somos quienes para criticarle. || *Of ours,* nuestro, nuestra: *a friend of ours,* un amigo nuestro; *it is no business of ours,* no es asunto nuestro. || FAM. *That gardener of ours!,* ¡ese maldito jardinero!
ourself [—'self] pron. (Ant.). Nos (myself). || — Pl. Nos (reflexive): *we can wash ourselves,* podemos lavarnos. || Nosotros, nosotras, nosotros mismos, nosotras mismas: *we always speak of ourselves,* siempre hablamos de nosotros. || Nosotros mismos, nosotras mismas (emphatic).

— OBSERV. El plural de *ourself* es *ourselves.*

oust [aust] v. tr. Expulsar, echar (to eject). || Desahuciar, desalojar (a tenant). || Desalojar, expulsar (the enemy). || Derribar (government). || Desbancar (s.o. from a post). || Destituir (to remove from office). || JUR. Desposeer (to dispossess). || FIG. Desbancar, sustituir, suplantar.
ouster [—ə*] n. JUR. Desposeimiento, *m.*
out [aut] adv. Fuera: *to lock s.o. out,* dejar a alguien fuera. || En huelga (on strike): *the workers are all out,* todos los trabajadores están en huelga. || MED. Dislocado, da (joint). || MIL. Preparado, da (troops). || Largado, da; soltado, da (rope). || Desplegado, da (sail). || — *All out,* a toda velocidad. || *Day out,* día (*m.*) libre. || *Inside out,* al revés. || *It's my day out,* es el día en que salgo. || *Out and away,* con mucho. || *Out and out,* completamente. || *Out at sea,* en alta mar, mar adentro. || *Out here,* por aquí (in these parts), aquí fuera (here outside). || *Out loud,* en voz alta. || *Out there,* por allí (in those parts), allí fuera (outside). || FAM. *Out with it!,* ¡desembucha! | *Out with you!,* ¡fuera de aquí! || *Right* o *straight out,* sin rodeos. || *The tide is out,* es marea baja. || *The voyage out,* el viaje de ida. || *To be far* o *a long way out,* estar muy equivocado (to make a mistake), estar muy lejos: *the house is far out,* la casa está lejos. || *To be out,* estar fuera, haber salido, no estar en casa: *Mrs Smith is out,* la Señora Smith ha salido; estar de viaje (traveling), pasar fuera: *to be out a lot,* pasar mucho tiempo fuera; salir: *I was out with some friends yesterday,* salí ayer con unos amigos; estar fuera, estar libre (prisoner), haber salido, haberse publicado: *the book is out,* ha salido el libro; haber salido (sun), estar abierto (flower), haber salido del cascarón (bird), estar sin conocimiento: *he was out for seven seconds,* estuvo sin conocimiento durante siete segundos; haberse apagado: *my cigarette is out,* se ha apagado mi cigarrillo; estar apagado: *the fire is out,* el fuego está apagado; acabarse, terminarse: *before the month is out,* antes de que se acabe el mes; haberse agotado: *my patience is out,* se me ha agotado la paciencia; haber pasado de moda, no estar ya de moda: *the miniskirt is out,* ya no está de moda la minifalda; haberse descubierto: *the secret is out,* el secreto se ha descubierto; estar fuera del poder: *now that my party is out,* ahora que mi partido está fuera del poder; quedar descartado (possibility), estar eliminado (player), estar fuera de juego (ball), estar fuera de combate (boxer), estar desenvainado (sword), estar equivocado (to be mistaken): *you are out in your accounts,* está equivocado en sus cuentas; faltar (to have too little): *I am five pounds out,* me faltan cinco libras; adelantar (to be fast): *his watch is ten minutes out,* su reloj adelanta diez minutos; atrasar (to be slow): *his watch is two minutes out,* su reloj atrasa dos minutos; haber vencido (lease), haber sido presentada en sociedad (young girl). || *To be out and about again,* estar de nuevo en pie (after an illness). || *To be out cold,* haber perdido completamente el sentido *or* el conocimiento. || *To be out for,* buscar: *to be out for revenge,* buscar venganza. || *To be out to do sth.,* estar decidido a *or* tener la intención de hacer algo. || *To be the best out,* ser el mejor que ha habido: *she is the best singer out,* es la mejor cantante que ha habido. || *To go all out to win,* hacer todo lo posible para ganar. || *To go out,* see GO. || *To go out to sea,* hacerse a la mar. || *To have a day out on the beach,* pasar un día en la playa. || *To have fallen out with,* haber reñido con. || *To have one's cry out,* llorar hasta más no poder. || *To hear out,* escuchar hasta el final. || *To put out,* see PUT. || *To run out,* salir corriendo.

— Prep. U. S. Por. || — *Out of,* fuera de: *out of the house,* fuera de la casa; *out of danger,* fuera de peligro; *out of place,* fuera de lugar; *out of season,* fuera de temporada; *out of wedlock,* fuera del matrimonio; por:

to jump out of the window, saltar por la ventana; *out of necessity*, por necesidad; *out of curiosity*, por curiosidad; entre: *one criticism out of many*, una crítica entre otras muchas; de cada: *ten out of fifteen*, diez de cada quince; de: *a paragraph out of a chapter*, un párrafo de un artículo; *built out of stone*, hecho de piedra; en: *he took a cigarette out of my case*, tomó un cigarrillo en mi petaca; sin: *out of breath*, sin aliento. || "*Out of order*", "no funciona". || COMM. *Out of print*, agotado, da. || *Out of reach*, fuera del alcance. || *Out of sight, out of mind*, ojos que no ven, corazón que no siente. || *Out of the corner of one's eye*, con el rabillo del ojo. || *Out of work*, sin trabajo, parado, da. || *To be out of*, habérsele agotado [a uno], no tener: *I am out of patience*, se me ha agotado la paciencia; habérsele acabado [a uno], no tener: *I am out of money*, se me ha acabado el dinero. || *To be out of it*, no estar metido en un asunto, quedar excluido (to be left out), no estar en el ajo (to be unaware). || *To be out of sight*, no poder verse. || *To drink out of*, beber en (a glass), beber de (a bottle). || *To feel out of a group*, sentirse fuera de un grupo. || *To feel out of it*, sentirse aislado. || FAM. *We're well out of it!*, ¡de buena nos hemos librado!

— Adj. Exterior, externo, na (part). || Muy grande (size).

— Interj. ¡Fuera!

— N. PRINT. Bordón, *m*. || U. S. FAM. Salida, *f*. (way out). || — Pl. U. S. Partido (*m. sing*) que está fuera del poder. || *The ins and outs*, see IN.

— OBSERV. Cuando *out* acompaña un verbo, en general no puede traducirse literalmente. Es imprescindible, por consiguiente, consultar el artículo referente al verbo de que se trata.

out [aut] v. intr. Descubrirse: *the truth will out*, la verdad se descubrirá.

— V. tr. Expulsar, echar.

outage [ˈautidʒ] n. Interrupción, *f*.

out-and-out [autndˈaut] adj. Empedernido, da; redomado, da; cien por cien (thorough): *an out-and-out drunkard*, un borracho empedernido; *an out-and-out liar*, un mentiroso empedernido. || Cien por cien: *an out-and-out nationalist*, un nacionalista cien por cien. || Acérrimo, ma (supporter).

out-and-outer [—ə*] n. Extremista, *m. & f*.

outback [ˈautbæk] n. Interior, *m*.

outbalance [autˈbæləns] v. tr. Exceder en peso, pesar más que (to weigh more). || Superar (to be more important).

outbid* [autˈbid] v. tr. Pujar más alto que, sobrepujar.

— OBSERV. Pret. & p. p. ***outbid***.

outbidder [autˈbidə*] n. Pujador, ra.

outboard [ˈautbɔ:d] adj. Fuera borda, fuera bordo: *two outboard motors*, dos motores fuera borda. || Exterior.

— Adv. Fuera de la embarcación.

— N. Motor (*m*.) fuera borda *or* fuera bordo (engine). || Fuera borda, *m. inv*., fuera bordo, *m. inv*. (boat).

outbound [ˈautbaund] adj. Que sale (ship, etc.).

outbrave [ˈautˈbreiv] v. tr. Arrostrar: *to outbrave the danger*, arrostrar el peligro. || Ser más valiente que (to exceed in courage).

outbreak [ˈautbreik] n. Comienzo, *m.*: *the outbreak of war*, el comienzo de la guerra. || Erupción, *f*. (of pimples). || Brote, *m*. (of an epidemic). || Epidemia, *f*. (of a disease): *an outbreak of influenza*, una epidemia de gripe. || Motín, *m*., insurrección, *f*., sublevación, *f*. (insurrection). || Ola, *f.*: *an outbreak of violence*, una ola de violencia; *a crime outbreak*, una ola de crímenes. || Arrebato, *m.*: *outbreak of temper*, arrebato de cólera. || — *At the outbreak of w*· ‑, cuando estalló la guerra. || *New outbreak*, recrudescencia, *f*.

outbred [ˈautbred] pret. & p. p. See OUTBREED.

outbreed* [ˈautbri:d] v. tr. Criar por cruce de razas.

— OBSERV. Pret. & p. p. ***outbred***.

outbreeding [ˈautˈbri:diŋ] n. Cría (*f*.) por cruce de razas. || U. S. Matrimonio (*m*.) entre razas o grupos sociales distintos.

outbuilding [ˈautˈbildiŋ] n. Dependencia, *f*.

outburst [ˈautbə:st] n. Explosión, *f*. || Arrebato, *m.*: *outburst of rage, of enthusiasm*, arrebato de ira, de entusiasmo. || Arranque, *m.*: *outburst of generosity*, arranque de generosidad. || Ataque, *m*. (of laughter). || — *Outburst of applause*, salva (*f*.) de aplausos. || *Outburst of temper*, arrebato de cólera, momento (*m*.) de mal humor.

outcast [ˈautkɑ:st] adj. Proscrito, ta.

— N. Paria, *m. & f*., proscrito, ta. || *To be a social outcast*, vivir rechazado por la sociedad.

outcaste [ˈautkɑ:st] n. Paria, *m. & f*.

outclass [autˈklɑ:s] v. tr. Aventajar con mucho, ser muy superior a, superar.

outcome [ˈautkʌm] n. Resultado, *m.*: *what was the outcome of the match?*, ¿cuál fue el resultado del partido? || Consecuencias, *f. pl*.

outcrop [ˈautkrɔp] n. GEOL. Afloramiento, *m*.

outcrop [ˈautkrɔp] v. intr. GEOL. Aflorar.

outcry [ˈautkrai] n. Protesta, *f*. || Alboroto, *m*. (din). || *To raise an outcry*, protestar ruidosamente, poner el grito en el cielo (to protest), provocar fuertes protestas (to provoke protest).

outdated [autˈdeitid] adj. Anticuado, da; pasado de moda.

outdid [autdid] pret. See OUTDO.

outdistance [autˈdistəns] v. tr. Dejar atrás.

outdo* [—ˈdu:] v. tr. Superar, aventajar: *to outdo s.o. in sth*., aventajar a uno en algo. || Vencer, derrotar (to defeat). || — *Not to be outdone*, para no ser menos, para no quedarse atrás. || *To outdo o.s*., superarse: *this time you have outdone yourself in generosity*, esta vez se ha superado en generosidad.

— OBSERV. Pret. ***outdid;*** p. p. ***outdone***.

outdone [autˈdʌn] p. p. See OUTDO.

outdoor [ˈautdɔ:*] adj. Al aire libre: *an outdoor restaurant, sport*, un restaurante, un deporte al aire libre. || De calle (clothes). || Externo, na (hospital activities, etc.). || JUR. A domicilio (relief). || — CINEM. *Outdoor scenes*, exteriores, *m*. || *To lead an outdoor life*, vivir al aire libre.

outdoors [autˈdɔ:z] adv. Fuera : *clean your boots outdoors*, límpiate las botas fuera. || Al aire libre (in the open air): *to eat outdoors*, comer al aire libre.

— N. Aire (*m*.) libre.

outer [ˈautə*] adj. Exterior, externo, na (side). || — *Outer ear*, oído externo. || *Outer space*, espacio (*m*.) exterior, espacio interplanetario.

— N. Círculo (*m*.) exterior del blanco (ring of target).

outermost [ˈautə:məust] adj. Más exterior. || Más alejado, da; extremo, ma (part of a city). || *To travel to the outermost parts of the globe*, recorrer las regiones más remotas de la Tierra.

outface [autˈfeis] v. tr. Hacer bajar los ojos (to stare down). || Desafiar (to defy).

outfall [ˈautfɔ:l] n. Desembocadura, *f*. (of a river). || Desagüe, *m*., desaguadero, *m*. (of a drain).

outfield [ˈautfi:ld] n. SP. Parte (*f*.) del campo más lejana del bateador (field).

outfit [ˈautfit] n. Equipo, *m*. (gear): *camping outfit*, equipo de camping. || Juego (*m*.) de herramientas (tools). || Piezas, *f. pl*. (components). || Ropa, *f*. (clothes): *summer outfit*, ropa de verano. || Traje, *m*. (suit). || Conjunto, *m*. (lady's costume): *to wear a new outfit for the first time*, estrenar un nuevo conjunto. || Uniforme, *m*. (uniform). || MIL. Unidad, *f*. || FAM. Grupo, *m*. (group): *the whole outfit was against him*, todo el grupo estaba en contra suya. | Equipo, *m*., cuadrilla, *f*. (of workers).

outfit [ˈautfit] v. tr. Equipar.

outfitter [ˈautˈfitə*] n. Vendedor (*m*.) de ropa confeccionada para caballero, camisero, *m*. || *Outfitter's*, camisería, *f*.

outflank [autˈflæŋk] v. tr. MIL. Desbordar, rebasar. || FIG. Burlar (to outwit).

outflow [ˈautfləu] n. Salida, *f*. (flowing out). || Corriente, *f*. (of lava). || Desagüe, *m*., salida, *f*. (of a sewer).

outgeneral [autˈdʒenərəl] v. tr. Superar en estrategia *or* en táctica.

outgo [ˈautˌgəu] n. U. S. Salida, *f*. (outflow). | Gastos, *m. pl*. (expense).

outgo* [autˈgəu] v. tr. Superar (to outdo).

— OBSERV. Pret. ***outwent;*** p. p. ***outgone***.

outgoer [—ˌgəuə*] n. El *or* la que se va. || *The outgoer must vacate the flat before 1st January*, el que ocupa actualmente el piso tiene que desalojarlo antes del primero de enero.

outgoing [ˈautˌgəuiŋ] adj. Saliente: *the outgoing president*, el presidente saliente. || Que sale: *the outgoing ship*, el barco que sale. || Saliente: *the outgoing tide*, la marea saliente. || U. S. Sociable.

— N. Salida, *f*. || — Pl. Gastos, *m*. (expenditure).

outgone [autˈgɔn] p. p. See OUTGO.

outgrew [autˈgru:] pret. See OUTGROW.

outgrow* [autˈgrəu] v. tr. Crecer más que: *he has outgrown his elder brother*, ha crecido más que su hermano mayor. || Perder con la edad: *you will outgrow your shyness*, perderás tu timidez con la edad. || — *To outgrow one's clothes*, quedarle la ropa pequeña a uno. || *To outgrow one's youthful habits*, perder las costumbres que se tenían de joven.

— OBSERV. Pret. ***outgrew;*** p. p. ***outgrown***.

outgrown [autˈgrəun] p. p. See OUTGROW.

outgrowth [ˈautgrəuθ] n. Excrecencia, *f*. (sth. which grows). || Consecuencia, *f*., resultado, *m*. (result).

outhaul [ˈauthɔ:l] n. MAR. Driza, *f*.

out-Herod [autˈherəd] v. tr. FAM. *To out-Herod Herod*, ser peor que Herodes.

outhouse [ˈauthaus] n. Dependencia, *f*. [de un edificio]. || U. S. Retrete, *m*. (outside lavatory).

outing [ˈautiŋ] n. Excursión, *f.*: *to go on a car outing*, ir de excursión en coche. || Paseo, *m*., vuelta, *f*. (walk).

outlander [ˈautˌlændə*] n. Extranjero, ra.

outlandish [autˈlændiʃ] adj. Extraño, ña; raro, ra (bizarre). || Extravagante (behaviour). || Apartado, da; alejado, da: *an outlandish place*, un lugar alejado. || Tosco, ca (uncouth). || (Ant.). Extranjero, ra (foreign).

outlandishness [autˈlændiʃnis] n. Aspecto (*m*.) extraño, lo extraño. || Extravagancia, *f*. (of behaviour).

outlast [autˈlɑ:st] v. tr. Durar más [tiempo] que: *the tyres have outlasted the car*, los neumáticos han durado más tiempo que el coche. || Sobrevivir a (person).

outlaw [ˈautlɔ:] n. Proscrito, ta; persona (*f*.) fuera de la ley.

outlaw [ˈautlɔ:] v. tr. Proscribir, declarar fuera de la ley: *the rebels have been outlawed*, los rebeldes han sido proscritos. || Prohibir, declarar ilegal: *the use of several medicines has been outlawed*, el uso de varias medicinas ha sido prohibido.

outlawry [ˈautˏlɔ:ri] n. Proscripción, *f.* || Bandolerismo, *m.*, bandidaje, *m.* (banditry).

outlay [ˈautlei] n. Gastos, *m. pl.*, desembolso, *m.*

outlet [ˈaulet] n. Salida, *f.* (way out). || Desagüe, *m.*, desaguadero, *m.* (of a drain). || Desagüe, *m.* (of a lake). || COMM. Mercado, *m.*, salida, *f.*: *the product has no outlet*, el producto no tiene mercado. | Distribuidor, *m.*, sucursal, *f.* (agency). || ELECTR. Toma, *f.* || — FIG. *An outlet for one's energies*, la posibilidad de emplear su energía. || COMM. *Retail outlet*, tienda, *f.*

outlier [ˈautˏlaiə*] n. GEOL. Afloramiento, *m.* [separado del macizo principal]. || Persona (*f.*) que vive lejos de donde trabaja.

outline [ˈautlain] n. Contorno, *m.* (line showing the boundary of an object). || Perfil, *m.*: *the outline of a mountain, of a building*, el perfil de una montaña, de un edificio. || Silueta, *f.* (indistinct): *a shadowy outline*, una silueta vaga. || Bosquejo, *m.*, esbozo, *m.* (draft): *a short outline of a plan*, un pequeño bosquejo de un proyecto. || ARTS. Bosquejo, *m.*, boceto, *m.*, esbozo, *m.* (sketch): *to draw a quick outline*, hacer un bosquejo rápido. || Trazado, *m.* (of a map). || Resumen, *m.* (summary): *here is an outline of his speech*, aquí tiene un resumen de su discurso. || Esquema, *m.*: *I will give you an outline of the organization*, le haré un esquema de la organización. || Signo (*m.*) taquigráfico (symbol). || Introducción, *f.*, reseña, *f.*: *outline of Spanish history*, introducción a *or* reseña de la historia de España. || — Pl. Líneas (*f.*) generales. || *In broad outline*, en líneas generales.

outline [ˈautlain] v. tr. Perfilar (to draw the outline of). || Bosquejar, esbozar (to sketch). || Trazar las líneas generales de (to give the main points of). || Resumir (to summarize). || *The tower was outlined against the sky*, la torre se perfilaba en el cielo.

outlive [autˈliv] v. tr. Durar más que (to last longer than). || Sobrevivir a (s.o., a disgrace).

outlook [ˈautluk] n. Vista, *f.* (view). || Panorama, *m.*, perspectiva, *f.*, perspectivas, *f. pl.*: *there is a bad outlook for trade*, las perspectivas relativas al comercio no son buenas. || Punto (*m.*) de vista: *he has an optimistic outlook*, tiene un punto de vista optimista. || Concepto, *m.*: *outlook upon life*, concepto de la vida.

outlying [autˏlaiiŋ] adj. Exterior, alejado del centro (lying away from the centre). || Remoto, ta; alejado, da; aislado, da: *outlying villages*, pueblos remotos.

outmanoeuvre (U. S. **outmaneuver**) [autməˈnu:və*] v. tr. Superar en estrategia. || Superar a (to put o.s. in a stronger position than).

outmarch [autˈmɑ:tʃ] v. tr. Dejar atrás.

outmatch [autˈmætʃ] v. tr. Aventajar, superar.

outmoded [autˈməudid] adj. Anticuado, da; pasado de moda.

outmost [ˈautməust] adj. Más exterior. || Más alejado, da; extremo, ma. || *At the outmost*, como máximo.

outnumber [autˏnʌmbə*] v. tr. Exceder en número, ser más numeroso que. || *They were outnumbered twenty to one*, éramos veinte veces más que ellos.

out-of-date [autəvˈdeit] adj. Pasado de moda, anticuado, da (old-fashioned). || Anticuado, da (not current, obsolete).

out-of-door [autəvˈdɔ:] adj. See OUTDOOR.

out-of-doors [ˈautəvˈdɔ:z] adv./n. See OUTDOORS.

out-of-pocket [ˈautəvˈpɔkit] adj. Efectivo, en efectivo. || *Out-of-pocket expenses*, gastos, *m.*, desembolsos, *m.*

out-of-school [autəvˈsku:l] adj. Extraescolar.

out-of-the-way [autəvðəˈwei] adj. Apartado, da; aislado, da; remoto, ta (distant): *a little out-of-the-way village*, un pueblecito aislado. || Poco corriente (unusual): *an out-of-the-way expression*, una expresión poco corriente. || Inaccesible, inasequible (price).

outpace [autˈpeis] v. tr. Dejar atrás.

outpatient [ˈautˏpeiʃənt] n. MED. Paciente (*m.*) no internado, enfermo (*m.*) no hospitalizado.

outplay [autˈplei] v. tr. Jugar mejor que. || *We were completely outplayed right from the beginning*, nos dominaron completamente desde el primer momento.

outpoint [autˈpoint] v. tr. Puntuar más alto que, sacar más puntos que (an opponent).

outport [ˈautpɔ:t] n. MAR. Antepuerto, *m.* (outer part of a port). | Puerto marítimo (of a city).

outpost [ˈautpəust] n. MIL. Avanzada, *f.* (detachment). | Puesto (*m.*) avanzado (post). | Puesto (*m.*) fronterizo (on a frontier).

outpouring [ˈautˈpɔ:riŋ] n. Efusión, *f.* (of heart). || Profusión, *f.* (of abuses).

output [ˈautput] n. Producción, *f.* || TECH. Rendimiento, *m.* (of a machine). | Potencia, *f.*, energía, *f.* (power). || ELECTR. Salida, *f.* (of a computer).

outrage [ˈautreidʒ] n. Ultraje, *m.*, atropello, *m.*, agravio, *m.* (on people's rights, feelings or property). || Desafuero, *m.* (against order or principles). || Ataque, *m.*, atentado, *m.*: *a wave of outrages and assassinations*, una ola de ataques y asesinatos. || Atrocidad, *f.* (atrocity). || — *Bomb outrage*, atentado con bomba. || *It's an outrage!*, ¡no hay derecho!, ¡es escandaloso! || *To commit an outrage against s.o.*, ultrajar a alguien, agraviar a alguien.

outrage [ˈautreidʒ] v. tr. Ultrajar, agraviar (to subject to an outrage). || Violentar (to do violence to). || Violar (to rape). || Atentar contra, ofender (public opinion). || Atropellar (the law). || Ir en contra de (common sense).

outrageous [autˈreidʒəs] adj. Ultrajante (constituting an outrage). || Extravagante (extravagant). || Escandaloso, sa (provoking disapproval): *his outrageous behaviour lost him many friends*, perdió muchos amigos por su conducta escandalosa. || Infame (accusation). || Flagrante (injustice). || Exorbitante, escandaloso, sa (price). || FAM. Horrible. || — *How outrageous!*, ¡qué vergüenza!, ¡qué barbaridad!, ¡es escandaloso! || *It is outrageous that he be allowed to do it*, es indignante que se le permita hacerlo.

outrageously [autˈreidʒəsli] adv. De una manera escandalosa.

outrageousness [autˈreidʒəsnis] n. Carácter (*m.*) ultrajante *or* escandaloso.

outran [autˈræn] pret. See OUTRUN.

outrange [autˈreindʒ] v. tr. Tener un alcance mayor que. || FIG. Superar.

outrank [autræŋk] v. tr. Ser superior a.

outré [ˈu:trei] adj. Exagerado, da; extravagante (exaggerated). || Chocante (shocking).

outreach [autˈri:tʃ] v. tr. Tener un alcance mayor que. || Superar (to exceed).

outridden [autˈridn] p. p. See OUTRIDE.

outride* [autˈraid] v. tr. Cabalgar mejor *or* más rápido que, adelantar (to surpass in riding). || MAR. Capear (a storm).

— OBSERV. Pret. ***outrode;*** p. p. ***outridden.***

outrider [ˈautˏraidə*] n. Persona (*f.*) que escolta a caballo (on horseback). || Motorista (*m.*) de escolta (on motorcycle).

outrigger [ˈautˏrigə*] n. MAR. Batanga, *f.*, balancín, *m.* (float). | Bote (*m.*) con batanga (boat equipped with a float). | Escálamo, *m.* (rowlock). | "Outrigger", *m.* (racing boat with projecting rowlocks). | Tangón, *m.*, botalón, *m.* (extending spar). || AVIAT. Larguero (*m.*) de soporte del plano fijo.

outright [ˈautrait] adj. Completo, ta; absoluto, ta; total: *outright dishonesty*, una falta completa de honradez. || Rotundo, da; categórico, ca: *outright denial*, negación rotunda. || Absoluto, ta; incondicional (unconditional). || Franco, ca (forthright).

outright [autˈrait] adv. Francamente (openly): *I told him outright he was mistaken*, le dije francamente que estaba equivocado. || En el acto (at once): *to be killed outright*, ser matado en el acto. || Al contado: *to pay outright*, pagar al contado. || En su totalidad (entirely). || Rotundamente, categóricamente (to refuse). || Abiertamente (to laugh).

outrightness [—nis] n. Franqueza, *f.* (forthrightness).

outrival [autˈraivəl] v. tr. Superar, aventajar.

outrode [autˈrəud] pret. See OUTRIDE.

outrun* [autˈrʌn] v. tr. Correr más de prisa que, dejar atrás (to run faster than). || FIG. Rebasar, sobrepasar: *his ambition outruns his talents*, su ambición sobrepasa su talento.

— OBSERV. Pret. ***outran;*** p. p. ***outrun.***

outsail [autˈseil] v. tr. MAR. Adelantar, dejar atrás.

outscore [autˈskɔ:*] v. tr. Puntuar más alto que.

outsell* [autˈsel] v. tr. Vender más que (to sell more than). || Venderse mejor que (a product).

— OBSERV. Pret. & p. p. ***outsold.***

outset [ˈautset] n. Principio, *m.*, comienzo, *m.*: *at the outset*, al principio; *from the outset*, desde el principio.

outshine* [autˈʃain] v. tr. Brillar más que (to shine brighter than). || FIG. Eclipsar: *she outshone all rivals*, eclipsó a todas sus rivales.

— OBSERV. El pretérito y el participio pasivo de ***outshine*** son ***outshone,*** aunque en Estados Unidos se emplea también ***outshined.***

outshoot [autˈʃu:t] v. tr. Disparar mejor que.
— V. intr. Sobresalir (to protrude).

outside [ˈautˈsaid] n. Exterior, *m.*: *the outside of the house*, el exterior de la casa. || Superficie, *f.* (surface). || Piso (*m.*) superior (of a bus). || Apariencia, *f.* (appearance). || SP. Extremo, *m.*: *outside left*, extremo izquierda. || — *At the outside*, como mucho, como máximo. || *From the outside*, desde fuera. || *On the outside*, por fuera.

— Adj. Exterior, externo, na: *the outside wheel*, la rueda exterior; *outside interests*, intereses exteriores. || Al aire libre (done outdoors). || Ajeno, na: *outside opinion*, opinión ajena. || Remoto, ta: *outside chance of living*, remota posibilidad de vivir. || Más elevado, da (highest): *they have exceeded the outside estimate*, han rebasado las previsiones más elevadas. || Máximo, ma; más elevado, da (price). || Del piso superior (of a bus). || Exterior, que trabaja fuera de la empresa (worker). || Independiente (independent). || RAD. Exterior. || — *Outside market*, bolsín, *m.* || *The outside world*, el mundo exterior.

— Adv. Fuera, afuera: *he is outside*, está fuera; *he went outside*, salió fuera. || En la calle (in the street), a la calle (into the street). || Fuera de la empresa: *work done outside*, trabajo realizado fuera de la empresa. || En el piso superior (on bus).

— Prep. Fuera de: *waiting outside the office*, esperando

fuera de la oficina; *outside the family*, fuera de la familia. || Más allá de, fuera de (beyond): *outside the city boundary*, más allá de los límites de la ciudad. || — *Interests outside work*, intereses ajenos al trabajo. || *Outside of*, fuera de.
outsider [—ə*] n. Intruso, sa (stranger to a group of people). || FIG. Forastero, ra (stranger to a place). || SP. Caballo (*m.*) no favorito (horse). || Candidato (*m.*) poco conocido (in an election). || Persona (*f.*) independiente (not included in a party).
outsize [ˈautsaiz] adj. De talla muy grande.
— N. Talla (*f.*) muy grande.
outskirts [ˈautskə:ts] pl. n. Afueras, *f.*, cercanías, *f.*
outsmart [autˈsmɑ:t] v. tr. U. S. Burlar, ser más listo que.
outsold [autˈsəuld] pret. & p. p. See OUTSELL.
outspoken [autˈspəukən] adj. Franco, ca; abierto, ta. || *To be outspoken*, no tener pelos en la lengua.
outspokenness [—nis] n. Franqueza, *f.*
outspread [ˈautˈspred] adj. Extendido, da. || Desplegado, da (sails).
— N. Extensión, *f.* || Despliegue, *m.*
outstanding [autˈstændiŋ] adj. Destacado, da; notable: *an outstanding event*, un acontecimiento notable. || Sobresaliente: *outstanding features*, características sobresalientes. || Eminente, notable, destacado, da (person). || Excepcional, fuera de lo común: *an outstanding success*, un éxito excepcional. || Sin pagar, pendiente (unpaid): *outstanding debts*, deudas sin pagar. || Sin resolver, pendiente (unsolved). || Por hacer, pendiente (still to be done).
outstare [autˈstɛə*] v. tr. Hacer bajar los ojos.
outstay [autˈstei] v. tr. Quedarse más tiempo que (to remain longer than). || Aguantar más que (to resist more than). || *To outstay one's welcome*, quedarse más tiempo de lo conveniente.
outstretched [autˈstretʃt] adj. Extendido, da.
outstrip [autˈstrip] v. tr. Dejar atrás (to leave behind, to surpass).
outturn [ˈaut,tə:n] n. Producción, *f.* || Rendimiento, *m.* (yield).
outvalue [autˈvælju:] v. tr. Sobrepasar en valor a, valer más que.
outvie [autˈvai] v. tr. Superar.
outvote [autˈvəut] v. tr. Vencer en una elección *or* en una votación. || *To be outvoted*, perder en una elección *or* en una votación.
outwalk [autˈwɔ:k] v. tr. Andar más rápidamente que, dejar atrás (to walk faster). || Andar más que (to walk longer).
outward [ˈautwəd] adj. De ida: *outward journey*, viaje de ida. || Exterior, externo, na (exterior). || MED. Externo, na (application).
— Adv. Hacia fuera. || Exteriormente.
— N. Exterior, *m.*
outward bound o **outward-bound** [—baund] adj. Que sale. || — *To be outward bound for Bilbao*, salir *or* ir rumbo a Bilbao. || *To be outward bound from Southampton*, haber salido de Southampton.
outwardly [—li] adj. Exteriormente, por fuera (externally). || Aparentemente (apparently).
outwardness [—nis] n. Objetividad, *f.* (of a judgment). || Exterioridad, *f.*
outwards [—z] adv. Hacia fuera. || Exteriormente.
outwear* [autˈwɛə*] v. tr. Durar más que (to last longer than): *this skirt will outwear the other one*, esta falda durará más que la otra. || Gastar, desgastar (to wear out). || Deshacerse de (to get rid of): *to outwear a habit*, deshacerse de una costumbre.
— OBSERV. Pret. **outwore;** p. p. **outworn.**
outweigh [autˈwei] v. tr. Pesar más que: *the advantages outweigh the disadvantages*, las ventajas pesan más que los inconvenientes. || Valer más que (to be more valuable).
outwent [autˈwent] pret. See OUTGO.
outwit [autˈwit] v. tr. Burlar, ser más listo que: *the thief outwitted the police and escaped*, el ladrón burló a la policía y se escapó.
outwore [autˈwɔ:*] pret. See OUTWEAR.
outwork [ˈautwə:k] n. MIL. Defensa (*f.*) exterior, obra (*f.*) accesoria. || Trabajo (*m.*) hecho fuera de la empresa (outside work).
outwork [autˈwə:k] v. tr. Trabajar mejor *or* más rápido que.
outworn [autˈwɔ:n] p. p. See OUTWEAR.
— Adj. Gastado, da; desgastado, da (worn-out). || Trillado, da (excessively used): *outworn phrase*, expresión trillada. || Anticuado, da; caduco, ca: *outworn ideas*, ideas caducas.
ouzel [ˈu:zl] n. Mirlo, *m.* (bird).
ova [ˈəuvə] pl. n. See OVUM.
oval [ˈəuvəl] adj. Oval, ovalado, da.
— N. Óvalo, *m.*
ovalization [əuvəlaiˈzeiʃən] n. Ovalización, *f.*
ovalize [ˈəuvəlaiz] v. tr. Ovalizar.
ovarian [əuˈvɛəriən] adj. Ovárico, ca.
ovariectomy [əu,vɛəriˈektəmi] n. MED. Ovariotomía, *f.*, ovariectomía, *f.* (removal of one or both ovaries).
ovariotomy [əu,vɛəriˈɔtəmi] n. MED. Ovariotomía, *f.*, ovariectomía, *f.* (ovariectomy). | Incisión (*f.*) de un ovario (incision).
ovary [ˈəuvəri] n. ANAT. BOT. Ovario, *m.*
ovate [ˈəuveit] adj. Ovado, da; aovado, da.
ovation [əuˈveiʃən] n. Ovación, *f.* || — *To give s.o. an ovation*, ovacionar a alguien. || *To receive an ovation*, ser ovacionado.
oven [ˈʌvn] n. Horno, *m.*: *baker's oven*, horno de panadero. || FIG. Estufa, *f.*, horno, *m.* (hot place).
ovenbird [—bə:d] n. ZOOL. Hornero, *m.* (passerine bird).
ovenproof [—pru:f] adj. De horno (dish).
over [ˈəuvə*] prep. Sobre: *the umbrella over his head*, el paraguas sobre su cabeza; *he increased his lead over the others*, aumentó su ventaja sobre los demás; *he has a great influence over me*, tiene una gran influencia sobre mí. || Sobre, por encima de: *the plane flew over the house*, el avión voló por encima de la casa. || Sobre, encima de: *books spread over the table*, libros esparcidos sobre la mesa. || Por encima de: *to throw a ball over a wall*, lanzar una pelota por encima de un muro; *he jumped over the fence*, saltó por encima de la valla; *he was over his ankles in water*, tenía agua por encima de los tobillos. || Encima de: *the clouds are over our heads*, las nubes están encima de nuestras cabezas. || Más de: *over a million*, más de un millón; *he is over fourty*, tiene más de cuarenta años; *to sleep for over three hours*, dormir más de tres horas. || Superior: *numbers over fifteen win a prize*, los números superiores a quince ganan un premio. || Junto a: *sitting over the fire*, sentado junto al fuego. || Al otro *or* del otro lado de: *Charles lives over the hill*, Carlos vive al otro lado de la colina. || Del otro lado de: *I live over the street*, vivo del otro lado de la calle. || Por: *we got this information over the phone*, recibimos esta información por teléfono; *to drive over a new road*, conducir por una nueva carretera; *to throw o.s. over a precipice*, despeñarse por un precipicio; *to fight over a woman*, pelearse por una mujer. || Durante: *over several days*, durante varios días; *can you stay over the weekend?*, ¿puede quedarse durante el fin de semana? || Hasta: *stay over Peter's birthday*, quédate hasta el cumpleaños de Pedro. || En, con: *how long will you be over it?*, ¿cuánto tiempo vas a estar con eso *or* vas a tardar en ello? || Con: *to stumble over a mat*, tropezar con un felpudo. || — *All over the house*, por toda la casa. || *All over the world*, en el mundo entero, en todo el mundo. || *Let's talk over a glass of beer*, hablemos mientras tomamos un vaso de cerveza. || *Over and above*, además de (in addition to), superior a (besides). || *Over the river*, que cruza el río (bridge), en la otra orilla del río (house, etc.). || *Over the road*, de enfrente: *the house over the road*, la casa de enfrente. || *Over the seas*, allende los mares. || *To be all over s.o.*, tener muchas atenciones con alguien. || *To have an advantage over s.o.*, llevar ventaja a uno. || *To help s.o. over the road*, ayudar a alguien a cruzar la calle. || *What's come over you?*, ¿qué le pasa? || *With his hat over his eyes*, con el sombrero calado hasta los ojos.
— Adv. Encima, por encima: *this one goes over*, éste pasa por encima. || Más: *it weighs tree tons and a bit over*, pesa tres toneladas y algo más. || Todo, da: *to search Paris over*, registrar todo París. || Hasta el final: *to read over*, leer hasta el final. || — *All over*, por todas partes (everywhere), completamente (completely). || *All the world over*, en el mundo entero, en todo el mundo. || *Children of fifteen and over*, mayores de quince años, chicos de quince años para arriba. || *He is over from Spain*, viene de España. || *He is his father all over*, es su padre cien por cien. || *He is Scottish all over*, es escocés cien por cien *or* hasta la médula. || *I ache all over*, me duele todo el cuerpo. || *I am over for the weekend*, he venido a pasar el fin de semana. || *It's all over!*, ¡se acabó! || *It's all over with me*, estoy perdido. || *Over again*, otra vez. || *Over against*, en frente de, frente a. || *Over and over (again)*, repetidas veces, una y otra vez. || *Over here*, aquí, acá. || *Over in China they eat rice*, allá en China se come arroz. || *Over there*, allí, allá. || *Sixteen divided by five equals three and one over*, dieciséis dividido por cinco da tres de cociente y queda uno de resto. || *That's over and done with!*, ¡se acabó! || *That's you all over*, eso es muy suyo. || *To ask s.o. over*, pedir a alguien que venga. || *To be all over dust*, estar cubierto de polvo. || *To bend over*, doblar (sth.), inclinarse. || *To be over*, haberse terminado *or* acabado: *the film is over*, la película se ha acabado; quedar: *is there any soup over?*, ¿queda algo de sopa? || *To boil over*, salirse (milk). || *To cross over*, atravesar, cruzar. || *Twice over*, dos veces [seguidas]. || *We have a pound over*, tenemos una libra de más, nos sobra una libra. || *What is left over*, lo que sobra.
— N. MIL. Tiro (*m.*) largo. || SP. Serie (*f.*) de seis saques (cricket). || COMM. Excedente, *m.*, superávit, *m.* (surplus).
— OBSERV. Cuando el adverbio *over* acompaña ciertos verbos no se puede traducir literalmente. Es preciso, por lo tanto, consultar el artículo referente al verbo de que se trata. En algunos casos este adverbio implica una idea de repetición que se puede expresar en español por "volver a" u "otra vez" (*to sing over*, volver a cantar: *to do over*, hacer otra vez).
overabundance [—əˈbʌndəns] n. Superabundancia, *f.*, sobreabundancia, *f.*
overabundant [—əˈbʌndənt] adj. Superabundante, sobreabundante.
overact [—ˈækt] v. tr. THEATR. Exagerar (a part).
— V. intr. THEATR. Exagerar el papel.

overacting [—ˈæktiŋ] n. THEATR. Exageración, *f.*
overactive [—ˈæktiv] adj. Demasiado activo, va.
overactivity [—ækˈtiviti] n. Superactividad, *f.*
overage [—idʒ] n. U. S. COMM. Excedente (*m.*) de mercancías.
overage [ˌəuvərˈeidʒ] adj. U. S. Con más edad de la requerida, demasiado viejo, ja.
overall [ˈəuvərˌɔːl] adj. Global, de conjunto (including everything). || Total: *the overall cost*, el coste total. || — *Overall dimensions*, dimensiones exteriores. || MAR. *Overall length*, eslora (*f.*) total, longitud máxima.
overall [ˌəuvərˈɔːl] adv. En conjunto (generally). || Por todas partes (everywhere).
overalls [ˈəuvərɔːlz] n. Guardapolvo, *m. sing.* (child's). || Bata, *f. sing.* (woman's). || Mono, *m.* (worker's).
overambitious [ˈəuvəræmˈbiʃəs] adj. Demasiado ambicioso, sa.
overanxious [ˈəuvərˈæŋkʃəs] adj. Demasiado preocupado, da (worried). || Excesivamente deseoso, sa (eagerly wishing). || *I am not overanxious to do it*, no tengo muchas ganas de hacerlo.
overate [ˌəuvərˈet] pret. See OVEREAT.
overawe [ˌəuvərˈɔː] v. tr. Intimidar, imponer respeto a, impresionar.
overbalance [ˌəuvəˈbæləns] n. Exceso, *m.* (of weight, value).
overbalance [ˌəuvəˈbæləns] v. tr. Hacer perder el equilibrio (to throw off balance). || Pesar más que (to weigh more than).
— V. intr. Perder el equilibrio (to lose one's balance). || Volcar (to overturn).
overbear* [ˌəuvəˈbeə*] v. tr. Oprimir (to press). || FIG. Intimidar (s.o.). | Hacer caso omiso de, no hacer caso de, no tener en cuenta (s.o.'s wishes). || Dominar (to domineer over).
— V. intr. Dar demasiados frutos.

— OBSERV. Pret. **overbore;** p. p. **overborne.**

overbearing [—riŋ] adj. Imperioso, sa; autoritario, ria (domineering).
overbid [ˈəuvəˌbid] n. Sobrepuja, *f.* (at auction). || Declaración (*f.*) más alta (in bridge).
overbid* [ˌəuvəˈbid] v. tr. Pujar más que, sobrepujar, hacer una mejor oferta que (to bid more than). || Ofrecer más del valor de (to bid more than the value of). || Declarar más que (in bridge).
— V. intr. Ofrecer más que otro. || Hacer una declaración más alta [que lo que permite su mano] (in bridge).

— OBSERV. Pret. & p. p. **overbid.**

overbidding [—iŋ] n. Sobrepuja, *f.*
overblown [ˈəuvəbləun] adj. Demasiado abierto, ta (flowers). || Pomposo, sa; rimbombante, ampuloso, sa (style).
overboard [ˈəuvəbɔːd] adv. Por la borda. || — *Man overboard!*, ¡hombre al agua! || U. S. FIG. *To go overboard*, pasarse de la raya. || *To throw overboard*, tirar por la borda.
overbold [ˌəuvəˈbəuld] adj. Temerario, ria; muy osado, da; muy atrevido, da.
overbore [ˌəuvəˈbɔː] pret. See OVERBEAR.
overborne [—n] p. p. See OVERBEAR.
overbought [ˈəuvəˈbɔːt] pret. & p. p. See OVERBUY.
overbuild* [ˈəuvəˈbild] v. tr. Construir demasiado en (an area).

— OBSERV. Pret. & p. p. **overbuilt.**

overburden [ˌəuvəˈbəːdn] n. Sobrecarga, *f.* (excess of burden). || FIG. Agobio, *m.*
overburden [ˌəuvəˈbəːdn] v. tr. Sobrecargar. || FIG. Agobiar, abrumar: *not overburdened with scruples*, poco agobiado por los escrúpulos.
overbuy* [ˈəuvəbai] v. tr./intr. Comprar demasiado.

— OBSERV. Pret. & p. p. **overbought.**

overcall [ˌəuvəˈkɔːl] n./v. tr./intr. See OVERBID.
overcame [ˌəuvəˈkeim] pret. See OVERCOME.
overcapitalization [ˈəuvəˌkæpitəlaiˈzeiʃən] n. Supercapitalización, *f.*
overcapitalize [ˌəuvəˈkæpitəlaiz] v. tr. Supercapitalizar.
overcast [ˈəuvəkɑːst] adj. Nublado, da; encapotado, da; cubierto, ta (the sky).
— N. Sobrehilado, *m.* (in sewing). || Revestimiento, *m.* (coating).
overcast* [ˈəuvəkɑːst] v. tr. Sobrehilar (in sewing). || Encapotar, cubrir (sky). || Oscurecer (to darken).

— OBSERV. Pret. & p. p. **overcast.**

overcautious [ˈəuvəˈkɔːʃəs] adj. Demasiado *or* excesivamente cauteloso, sa.
overcharge [ˈəuvəˈtʃɑːdʒ] n. Carga (*f.*) excesiva, sobrecarga, *f.* (weight). || Precio (*m.*) excesivo (very high price). || Recargo, *m.*, sobreprecio, *m.* (extra charge).
overcharge [ˈəuvəˈtʃɑːdʒ] v. tr. Cobrar más de lo debido a (to charge too high a price). || Recargar (price). || Cobrar de más (a certain amount). || Sobrecargar (to overload).
— V. intr. Sobrecargar. || Cobrar demasiado.
overcloud [ˌəuvəˈklaud] v. tr. Nublar, cubrir, encapotar (to cover over with clouds). || FIG. Oscurecer, entristecer: *fear of madness overclouded her last years*, el miedo a la locura oscureció sus últimos años.
— V. intr. Encapotarse, nublarse, cubrirse (sky).

overcoat [ˈəuvəkəut] n. Abrigo, *m.*
overcome* [ˌəuvəˈkʌm] v. tr. Vencer: *to overcome one's enemies*, vencer al enemigo. || Salvar, vencer, superar (difficulty, obstacle). || *She was overcome by fear*, estaba muerta de miedo.
— V. intr. Vencer, triunfar, salir victorioso.

— OBSERV. Pret. **overcame;** p. p. **overcome.**

overconfidence [ˈəuvəˈkɔnfidəns] n. Exceso (*m.*) de confianza, confianza (*f.*) excesiva. || Presunción, *f.*, suficiencia, *f.* (self-conceit).
overconfident [ˈəuvəˈkɔnfidənt] adj. Demasiado confiado, da. || Presumido, da; suficiente (conceited).
overconsumption [ˈəuvəkənˈsʌmpʃən] n. Consumo (*m.*) excesivo.
overcook [ˈəuvəˈkuk] v. tr. Cocer demasiado, recocer. || Requemar (to burn).
overcrop [ˈəuvəˈkrɔp] v. tr. Esquilmar, agotar (land).
overcrossing [ˈəuvəˈkrɔsiŋ] n. Paso (*m.*) superior (railway).
overcrowd [ˌəuvəˈkraud] v. tr. Atestar (*with*, de). || Superpoblar (a town).
overcrowded [—id] adj. Atestado, da [de gente]: *the bus is overcrowded*, el autobús está atestado de gente. || Superpoblado, da (a town, a country).
overcrowding [—iŋ] n. Atestamiento, *m.* [de gente]. || Superpoblación, *f.* (in a town, country).
overdevelop [—diˈveləp] v. tr. Desarrollar demasiado.
overdeveloped [—t] adj. Demasiado desarrollado, da; superdesarrollado, da.
overdevelopment [—mənt] n. Desarrollo (*m.*) excesivo, superdesarrollo, *m.*
overdid [ˌəuvədid] pret. See OVERDO.
overdo* [ˈəuvəˈduː] v. tr. Exagerar (to exaggerate). || Agotar (to exhaust). || CULIN. Cocer demasiado. || *To overdo it*, exagerar (to go too far), excederse: *I think I'm overdoing it at work*, creo que me estoy excediendo en el trabajo; recargar las tintas.

— OBSERV. Pret. **overdid;** p. p. **overdone.**

overdone [ˌəuvəˈdʌn] p. p. See OVERDO.
— Adj. Exagerado, da. || CULIN. Muy hecho, cha (meat). | Pasado, da (rice, etc.).
overdose [ˈəuvədəus] n. Dosis (*f.*) excesiva.
overdraft [ˈəuvədrɑːft] n. COMM. Giro (*m.*) en descubierto (sum overdrawn). | Saldo (*m.*) deudor, descubierto, *m.* (on account). || Corriente (*f.*) de aire [en un horno].
overdrank [ˈəuvəˈdræŋk] pret. See OVERDRINK.
overdraw* [ˈəuvəˈdrɔː] v. tr. COMM. Girar en descubierto. || Exagerar (to exaggerate). || *To be overdrawn*, tener un saldo deudor *or* un descubierto en su cuenta.
— V. intr. COMM. Girar en descubierto.

— OBSERV. Pret. **overdrew;** p. p. **overdrawn.**

overdrawn [ˈəuvəˈdrɔːn] p. p. See OVERDRAW.
overdress [ˈəuvəˈdres] v. tr. Vestir con exageración.
— V. intr. Ponerse de tiros largos (too elegantly). || Vestirse con exageración (too showily).
overdrew [ˈəuvəˈdruː] pret. See OVERDRAW.
overdrink* [ˈəuvəˈdriŋk] v. intr. Beber demasiado.
— OBSERV. Pret. **overdrank;** p. p. **overdrunk.**
overdrive [ˈəuvəˈdraiv] n. AUT. Superdirecta, *f.* (gear).
overdrive* [ˈəuvəˈdraiv] v. tr. Hacer trabajar con exceso (to give too much work). || Agotar (to exhaust).

— OBSERV. Pret. **overdrove;** p. p. **overdriven.**

overdriven [ˈəuvəˈdrivn] p. p. See OVERDRIVE.
overdrove [ˈəuvəˈdrəuv] pret. See OVERDRIVE.
overdrunk [ˈəuvəˈdrʌŋk] p. p. See OVERDRINK.
overdue [ˈəuvəˈdjuː] adj. Atrasado, da (train, rent, etc.). || COMM. Vencido y sin pagar. || FIG. Requerido *or* esperado desde hace tiempo (reform, etc.). || *The train is twenty minutes overdue*, el tren tiene veinte minutos de retraso.
overeat* [ˈəuvərˈiːt] v. intr. Comer excesivamente *or* demasiado.
— OBSERV. Pret. **overate;** p. p. **overeaten.**

overeaten [—n] p. p. See OVEREAT.
overeating [—iŋ] n. Comida (*f.*) excesiva.
overelaborate [ˈəuvəriˈlæbərit] adj. Demasiado complicado, da. || Con muchos detalles (with many details). || Muy rebuscado, da (affected).
overestimate [—ˈestimit] n. Sobrestimación, *f.*, estimación (*f.*) excesiva.
overestimate [ˈəuvərˈestimeit] v. tr. Sobrestimar.
overexcite [ˈəuvərikˈsait] v. tr. Sobreexcitar, sobrexcitar.
overexcitement [—mənt] n. Sobreexcitación, *f.*, sobrexcitación, *f.*
overexert [ˈəuvərigˈzəːt] v. tr. Agotar. || *To overexert o.s.*, hacer un esfuerzo excesivo.
— V. intr. Hacer un esfuerzo excesivo.
overexertion [ˈəuvərigˈzəːʃən] n. Esfuerzo (*m.*) excesivo. || Agotamiento, *m.* (exhaustion).
overexpose [ˈəuvəriksˈpəuz] v. tr. PHOT. Sobreexponer, exponer demasiado.
overexposure [ˈəuvəriksˈpəuʒə*] n. PHOT. Exposición (*f.*) excesiva, sobreexposición, *f.*
overfall [ˈəuvəfɔːl] n. Vertedero, *m.*
overfamiliar [ˈəuvəfəˈmiljə*] adj. Demasiado familiar, que se toma demasiada confianza [con los demás].
overfatigue [ˈəuvəfəˈtiːg] n. Cansancio (*m.*) excesivo, agotamiento, *m.*

overfatigue [ˈəuvəfəˈti:g] v. tr. Agotar, cansar demasiado.
overfed [ˈəuvəˈfed] pret. & p. p. See OVERFEED.
overfeed* [ˈəuvəˈfi:d] v. tr. Sobrealimentar.
— V. intr. Comer demasiado.

— OBSERV. Pret. & p. p. ***overfed***.

overfeeding [—iŋ] n. Sobrealimentación, *f.*
overfill [ˈəuvəˈfil] v. tr. Sobrellenar.
overflew [ˈəuvəflu:] pret. See OVERFLY.
overflow [ˈəuvəfləu] n. Desbordamiento, *m.* (of river, etc.). || Derrame, *m.* (from small containers). || Cañería (*f.*) de desagüe (pipe). || Inundación, *f.* (flooding). || FIG. Exceso, *m.*
overflow [ˈəuvəˈfləu] v. tr. Inundar (to flood). || Derramarse de (to flow over). || *The river overflowed its banks* el río se desbordó *or* se salió de madre.
— V. intr. Desbordarse (river, dam, etc.). || Derramarse, rebosar: *your cup is overflowing,* tu taza se está derramando. || FIG. Rebosar: *to overflow with joy,* rebosar de alegría.
overflown [ˈəuvəˈfləun] p. p. See OVERFLY.
overfly* [ˈəuvəˈflai] v. tr. Sobrevolar, volar por encima de.

— OBSERV. Pret. ***overflew;*** p. p. ***overflown***.

overfull [ˈəuvəˈful] adj. Rebosante (*of, with,* de).
overgarment [ˈəuvəˌgɑ:mənt] n. Abrigo, *m.* (overcoat). || Guardapolvo, *m.* (protective clothing).
overgild [ˌəuvəˈgild] v. tr. Sobredorar.
overglaze [ˈəuvəˌgleiz] n. Vidriado, *m.*
overglaze [ˈəuvəˌgleiz] v. tr. Vidriar.
overgrew [ˈəuvəˈgru:] pret. See OVERGROW.
overgrow* [ˈəuvəˈgrəu] v. tr. Cubrir (plants).

— OBSERV. Pret. ***overgrew;*** p. p. ***overgrown***.

overgrown [—n] p. p. See OVERGROW.
— Adj. Cubierto de hierba: *an overgrown garden,* un jardín cubierto de hierba. || Cubierto, ta: *a field overgrown with mushrooms,* un campo cubierto de hongos. || Demasiado crecido para su edad (too big for one's age).
overgrowth [ˈəuvəˈgrəuθ] n. Crecimiento (*m.*) excesivo (excessive growth). || Vegetación (*f.*) frondosa, frondosidad, *f.*
overhand [ˈəuvəˈhænd] adj. De arriba abajo. || SP. Por alto (stroke).
— Adv. Por alto.
overhang [əuvəˈhæŋ] n. Saliente, *m.* (projection). || ARCH. Alero, *m.*
overhang* [ˈəuvəhæŋ] v. tr. Sobresalir por encima de. || Adornar [con colgaduras] (a balcony). || FIG. Amenazar (to threaten).
— V. intr. Sobresalir.

— OBSERV. Pret. & p. p. ***overhung***.

overhanging [—iŋ] adj. Saliente, sobresaliente.
overhaul [ˈəuvəhɔ:l] n. Revisión, *f.*, examen (*m.*) detenido. || TECH. Revisión, *f.* | Reparación, *f.*, arreglo, *m.*
overhaul [ˌəuvəˈhɔ:l] v. tr. Revisar (to examine). || Examinar detenidamente (to look into). || TECH. Arreglar (to repair). || Alcanzar (to catch up). || Adelantar (to pass).
overhauling [—iŋ] n. See OVERHAUL.
overhead [ˈəuvəhed] adj. De arriba. || COMM. General (expenses). || A tanto alzado (price). || — *Overhead cable* o *wire,* cable aéreo. || *Overhead railway,* ferrocarril aéreo.
— Pl. n. COMM. Gastos (*m.*) generales.
overhead [ˈəuvəˈhed] adv. Por encima de la cabeza, arriba.
overhear* [ˌəuvəˈhiə*] v. tr. Oír por casualidad] (to hear). || Sorprender (a conversation).

— OBSERV. Pret. & p. p. ***overheard***.

overheard [ˌəuvəˈhə:d] pret. & p. p. See OVERHEAR.
overheat [ˈəuvəˈhi:t] v. tr. Recalentar, calentar demasiado. || FIG. Acalorar.
— V. intr. Recalentarse, calentar demasiado.
overheating [—iŋ] n. Recalentamiento, *m.* || FIG. Acaloramiento, *m.*
overhung [ˈəuvəˈhʌŋ] pret. & p. p. See OVERHANG.
overindulge [ˈəuvərinˈdʌldʒ] v. tr. Mimar demasiado a, ser demasiado indulgente con (s.o.). || Dar rienda suelta a (a passion).
— V. intr. *To overindulge in,* abusar de: *he overindulges in drinking,* abusa de la bebida.
overindulgence [—əns] n. Indulgencia (*f.*) excesiva. || Abuso, *m.*, exceso, *m.* [*in,* de].
overindulgent [—ənt] adj. Demasiado indulgente.
overissue [ˌəuvərˈiʃu:] n. COMM. Emisión (*f.*) excesiva.
overissue [ˌəuvərˈiʃu:] v. tr. COMM. Emitir en exceso.
overjoy [ˌəuvəˈdʒɔi] v. tr. Llenar de alegría. || *To be overjoyed at sth.,* no caber en sí de contento por algo.
overkill [ˈəuvəkil] n. Capacidad (*f.*) de destrucción superior al de las fuerzas enemigas.
overlaid [ˌəuveˈleid] pret. & p. p. See OVERLAY.
overlain [ˌəuvəˈlein] p. p. See OVERLIE.
overland [ˈəuvəlænd] adv. Por tierra, por vía terrestre.
— Adj. Terrestre (road). || Que viaja por tierra.
overlap [ˈəuvəlæp] or **overlapping** [ˌəuvəˈlæpiŋ] n. Imbricación, *f.*, superposición, *f.*, traslapo, *m.* || *Overlapping with other meetings,* coincidencia (*f.*) con otras reuniones.

overlap [ˌəuvəˈlæp] v. tr. Traslapar, superponerse a (to cover partially). || FIG. Coincidir parcialmente con.
— V. intr. Traslaparse, solaparse. || Sobresalir (to jut out). || FIG. Coincidir parcialmente.
overlay [ˈəuvəlei] n. Cubierta, *f.* (cover). || Chapa, *f.* (of wood, metal, etc.). || Capa, *f.* (coat). || Revestimiento, *m.* (new surface). || Colcha, *f.* (of a bed). || Colchón, *m.* (mattress). || PRINT. Alza, *f.*
overlay* [ˌəuvəˈlei] v. tr. Revestir, cubrir (to cover). || Asfixiar, ahogar (to overlie). || Oprimir (to oppress).

— OBSERV. Pret. & p. p. ***overlaid***.

overlay [ˌəuvəˈlei] pret. See OVERLIE.
overlaying [—ˈleiiŋ] n. Revestimiento, *m.*, capa, *f.*
overleaf [—ˈli:f] adv. A la vuelta. || *See overleaf,* véase al dorso.
overleap* [ˈəuvəˈli:p] v. tr. Saltar, salvar (to leap over). || Saltar más lejos que || FIG. Pasar por alto, omitir.

— OBSERV. Pret. & p.p. ***overleaped, overleapt***.

overlie* [ˌəuvəˈlai] v. tr. Cubrir (to cover). || Asfixiar, ahogar [a un niño echándose sobre él].

— OBSERV. Pret. ***overlay;*** p. p. ***overlain***.

overlive [ˌəuvəˈliv] v. tr. See OUTLIVE.
overload [ˈəuvələud] n. Sobrecarga, *f.*
overload [ˈəuvəˈləud] v. tr. Sobrecargar.
overlook [ˌəuvəˈluk] v. tr. Dar a, tener vista a (to command a view): *my window overlooks the sea,* mi ventana da al mar. || Dominar: *the Eiffel Tower overlooks all Paris,* la Torre Eiffel domina todo París. || Mirar desde lo alto (to look at from above). || Pasar por alto (to pretend not to notice). || No hacer caso de (to ignore). || Dejar pasar (to excuse): *to overlook an error,* dejar pasar un error. || Vigilar (to look after). || Inspeccionar, supervisar (to supervise).
overlooker [—ə*] n. Vigilante, *m.* (watchman). || Supervisor, ra; inspector, ra.
overlord [ˈəuvəlɔ:d] n. Señor (*m.*) feudal. || Jefe (*m*). supremo (supreme ruler).
overlordship [—ʃip] n. Soberanía (*f.*) *or* señorío (*m.*) feudal. || Jefatura (*f.*) suprema, mando (*m.*) supremo.
overly [ˈəuvəli] adv. Excesivamente, demasiado.
overman [ˈəuvəmæn] n. Capataz, *m.*

— OBSERV. El plural de *overman* es *overmen.*

overman [ˈəuvəˈmæn] v. tr. Emplear a más personal de lo necesario en.
overmaster [ˌəuvəˈmɑ:stə*] v. tr. Dominar.
overmastering [ˌəuvəˈmɑ:stəriŋ] adj. Dominante, dominador, ra. || FIG. Irresistible.
overmatch [ˌəuvəˈmætʃ] v. tr. Dominar, superar, patentizar una superioridad manifiesta sobre. || *To be overmatched,* ser dominado en todos los terrenos.
overmuch [ˈəuvəˈmʌtʃ] adj. Demasiado, da.
— Adv. Demasiado, excesivamente.
overnice [ˈəuvəˈnais] adj. Empalagoso, sa (too kind).
overnight [ˈəuvəˈnait] adj. De noche (journey). || Por una noche: *to have overnight guests,* tener invitados por una noche. || De la noche anterior. || — *Overnight bag,* neceser, *m.* || *To be an overnight success,* tener éxito de la noche a la mañana.
— Adv. Por la noche (during the night). || De la noche a la mañana: *he changed his mind overnight,* cambió de parecer de la noche a la mañana. || — *The milk won't keep overnight,* la leche no se conservará fresca hasta mañana. || *To stay overnight,* pernoctar, pasar la noche.
overornate [ˈəuvərɔ:ˈneit] adj. Recargado, da.
overpaid [ˈəuvəˈpeid] pret. & p. p. See OVERPAY.
— Adj. Pagado con exceso, demasiado pagado, da.
overparticular [ˈəuvəpəˈtikjulə*] adj. Melindroso, sa. || — *He is not overparticular about money,* no le importa mucho el dinero. || *He is not overparticular in how he gets his money,* tiene pocos escrúpulos para conseguir dinero.
overpass [ˈəuvəˌpɑ:s] n. Paso (*m.*) superior.
overpass [ˌəuvəˈpɑ:s] v. tr. Atravesar (a country). || Salvar, superar (an obstacle). || Sobrepasar (the limits). || Superar (s.o.).
overpay* [ˈəuvəˈpei] v. tr. Pagar con exceso a, pagar demasiado a (s.o.). || Pagar demasiado por (sth.)

— OBSERV. Pret. & p. p. ***overpaid***.

overpayment [—mənt] n. Pago (*m.*) excesivo.
overpersuade [ˈəuvepəˈsweid] v. tr. Persuadir.
overplacement [ˈəuvəˈpleismənt] n. Superposición, *f.*
overplay [ˈəuvəˌplei] v. tr. Exagerar (a part). || SP. Lanzar la pelota más allá de (the green).
overplus [ˈəuvəplʌs] n. Excedente, *m.*
overpopulated [ˈəuvəˈpɔpjuleitid] adj. Superpoblado, da.
overpopulation [ˈəuvəˌpɔpjuˈleiʃən] n. Exceso (*m.*) de población, superpoblación, *f.*
overpower [ˌəuvəˈpauə*] v. tr. Vencer, dominar (to beat). || Abrumar, agobiar, *the heat overpowered him,* el calor le abrumaba. || Dar demasiada potencia a.
overpowering [—riŋ] adj. Abrumador, ra. || Irresistible (desire).
overpraise [ˈəuvəˈpreiz] v. tr. Alabar con exceso.
overpressure [ˈəuvəˈpreʃə*] n. TECH. Superpresión, *f.* || FIG. Agotamiento, *m.*
overprint [ˈəuvəprint] n. Sobrecarga, *f.* (postmark). || Sello (*m.*) con sobrecarga (stamp). || PRINT. PHOT. Sobreimpresión, *f.*

overprint [ˈəuvəˈprint] v. tr. PRINT. PHOT. Sobreimprimir. || Imprimir demasiados ejemplares de (to print too many copies of). || Poner sobrecarga a (stamp).
overprize [ˌəuvəˈpraiz] v. tr. Supervalorar, sobrestimar.
overproduce [ˈəuvəprəˈdju:s] v. tr. Producir con exceso.
overproduction [ˈəuvəprəˈdʌkʃən] n. Superproducción, *f.*
overproof [ˈəuvəpru:f] adj. Con una proporción de alcohol superior al cincuenta por ciento.
overran [ˌəuvəˈræn] pret. See OVERRUN.
overrate [ˈəuvəˈreit] v. tr. Supervalorar, sobrestimar.
overreach [ˌəuvəˈri:tʃ] v. tr. Llegar más allá de, rebasar (to extend beyond). || Engañar (to cheat). || *To overreach o.s.*, extralimitarse.
— V. intr. Alcanzarse (horses).
overrefine [ˈəuvəriˈfain] v. tr. Refinar con exceso (a metal). || Alambicar (style).
overrefinement [—mənt] n. Afectación, *f.* || Preciosidad, *f.* (of style).
override* [ˌəuvəˈraid] v. tr. Pasar por encima de (to ride over). || Pisotear (to trample down). || No hacer caso de, hacer caso omiso de, no tener en cuenta (to disregard): *to override orders*, hacer caso omiso de las órdenes. || Anular (to invalidate). || Dejar a un lado (to set aside). || Dominar (to dominate). || Extralimitarse en, sobrepasar (to exceed). || Agotar, reventar (a horse).
— OBSERV. Pret. ***overrode;*** p. p. ***overridden.***
overridden [ˌəuvəˈridn] p. p. See OVERRIDE.
overriding [ˌəuvəˈraidiŋ] adj. Principal, primordial, esencial (principal). || — *Overriding clause*, cláusula derogatoria. || *Overriding principle*, principio absoluto.
overripe [ˈəuvəˈraip] adj. Demasiado maduro, ra; pasado, da (fruit). || Pasado, da; demasiado hecho (cheese).
overrode [ˌəuvəˈrəud] pret. See OVERRIDE.
overrule [ˌəuvəˈru:l] v. tr. Denegar (to refuse). || No aceptar (an objection). || Rechazar [una protesta]. || Anular (to rescind). || Dominar (to prevail over).
overrun [ˈəuvərʌn] n. PRINT. Recorrido, *m.* || Zona (*m.*) libre de obstáculos en un aeropuerto dispuesta para un aterrizaje forzoso.
overrun* [ˌəuvəˈrʌn] v. tr. Invadir (to invade). || Inundar (to flood). || Rebasar (to exceed). || ELECTR. Aumentar el voltaje de. || PRINT. Recorrer. || Pasar (a traffic signal). || *To overrun o.s.*, correr hasta el agotamiento.
— V. intr. Rebosar (liquid). || Desbordarse (river). || AUT. Correr más rápido que el motor.
— OBSERV. Pret. ***overran;*** p. p. ***overrun.***
overrunning [—iŋ] n. Invasión, *f.* (by people). || Inundación, *f.* (flood). || ELECTR. Aumento (*m.*) de voltaje, sobrevoltaje, *m.*, sobretensión, *f.*
oversaw [ˈəuvəˈsɔ:] pret. See OVERSEE.
overscrupulous [ˈəuvəˈskru:pjuləs] adj. See OVERPARTICULAR.
oversea [ˈəuvəˈsi:] or **overseas** [—z] adv. En *or* a ultramar (beyond the sea). || Por el extranjero, en el extranjero, al extranjero (abroad).
— Adj. Ultramarino, na; de ultramar. || Exterior (debt, trade). || Extranjero, ra (foreign).
oversee* [ˈəuvəˈsi:] v. tr. Supervisar (to supervise). || Vigilar (to watch).
— OBSERV. Pret. ***oversaw;*** p. p. ***overseen.***
overseen [—n] p. p. See OVERSEE.
overseer [ˈəuvəsiə*] n. Supervisor, ra. || Vigilante, *m.* (watchman). || Capataz, *m.* (foreman). || Regente, *m.* (in printing).
oversell* [ˈəuvəˈsel] v. tr. COMM. Vender con exceso. | Hacer una propaganda excesiva de.
— OBSERV. Pret. & p. p. ***oversold.***
oversensitive [ˈəuvəˈsensitiv] adj. Hipersensible, demasiado sensible.
overset* [ˈəuvəˈset] v. tr. See UPSET.
— OBSERV. Pret. & p. p. ***overset.***
oversew* [ˈəuvəˈsəu] v. tr. Sobrehilar (to overcast).
— OBSERV. Pret. ***oversewed;*** p. p. ***oversewn, oversewed.***
oversewn [—n] p. p. See OVERSEW.
overshade [ˌəuvəˈʃeid] v. tr. Sombrear.
overshadow [ˌəuvəˈʃædəu] v. tr. Oscurecer, sombrear (to cast a shadow over). || FIG. Eclipsar: *he is overshadowed by his brother*, es eclipsado por su hermano.
overshoe [ˈəuvəʃu:] n. Bota (*f.*) de goma, chanclo, *m.*
overshoot* [ˈəuvəˈʃu:t] v. tr. Ir *or* llegar más allá de (to go beyond). || Llegar más allá de [la pista] (an aeroplane). || FIG. FAM. *To overshoot the mark*, pasarse de la raya, rebasar los límites.
— OBSERV. Pret. & p. p. ***overshot.***
overshot [ˈəuvəˈʃɔt] pret. & p. p. See OVERSHOOT.
— Adj. ZOOL. Con la mandíbula superior saliente. || *Overshot wheel*, rueda (*f.*) de cangilones.
oversight [ˈəuvəsait] n. Descuido, *m.* (neglect): *by o through oversight*, por descuido. || Supervisión, *f.* (supervision). || Vigilancia, *f.*
oversimplification [ˈəuvəˌsimplifiˈkeiʃən] n. Simplificación (*f.*) excesiva.
oversimplify [ˈəuvəˈsimplifai] v. tr. Simplificar excesivamente *or* demasiado.
oversize [ˈəuvəsaiz] adj. Demasiado grande (too large). || De tamaño descomunal (unusually large).
— N. Tamaño (*m.*) descomunal.
overskirt [ˈəuvəskə:t] n. Sobrefalda, *f.*
oversleep* [ˈəuvəˈsli:p] v. intr. Dormir más de lo previsto, dormir demasiado, quedarse dormido más de la cuenta, no despertarse a la hora deseada. || *I overslept this morning*, se me pegaron las sábanas esta mañana (fam.).
— OBSERV. Pret. & p. p. ***overslept.***
overslept [ˈəuvəˈslept] pret. & p. p. See OVERSLEEP.
oversold [ˈəuvəˈsəuld] pret. & p. p. See OVERSELL.
overspend* [ˈəuvəˈspend] v. tr./intr. Gastar excesivamente *or* demasiado. || Gastar más que.
— OBSERV. Pret. & p. p. ***overspent.***
overspent [ˈəuvəˈspent] pret. & p. p. See OVERSPEND.
overspread* [ˌəuvəˈspred] v. tr. Extender sobre.
— OBSERV. Pret. & p. p. ***overspread.***
overstate [ˈəuvəˈsteit] v. tr. Exagerar.
overstatement [—mənt] n. Exageración, *f.*
overstay [ˈəuvəˈstei] v. tr. *To overstay one's leave* o *one's welcome*, quedarse más tiempo de lo conveniente.
overstep [ˈəuvəˈstep] v. tr. Sobrepasar, pasar de. || FIG. *To overstep the mark*, pasarse de la raya.
overstitch [ˈəuvəˈstitʃ] n. Punto (*m.*) por encima.
overstock [ˈəuvəˈstɔk] v. tr. *To be overstocked with*, poser existencias excesivas de.
overstocking [—iŋ] n. Existencias (*f. pl.*) excesivas.
overstrain [ˈəuvəˈstrein] n. Cansancio (*m.*) excesivo, agotamiento, *m.* (exhaustion). || Hipertensión, *f.* (nervous).
overstrain [ˈəuvəˈstrein] v. tr. Cansar excesivamente, agotar (to exhaust). || Producir hipertensión en (nervously). || — *Overstrained relations*, relaciones muy tensas. || *To overstrain o.s.*, agotarse.
— V. intr. Agotarse.
overstress [ˈəuvəˈstres] n. Sobrecarga, *f.*
overstress [ˈəuvəˈstres] v. tr. Sobrecargar. || FIG. Insistir demasiado en.
overstrung [ˈəuvəˈstrʌŋ] adj. Hipertenso, sa; sobreexcitado, da (very nervous). || Muy sensible (sensitive).
oversubscribe [ˈəuvəsəbˈskraib] v. tr. COMM. Suscribir en exceso de la emisión (shares, etc.).
oversupply [ˈəuvəsəˈplai] n. Exceso (*m.*) de provisión.
oversupply [ˈəuvəsəˈplai] v. tr. Proveer en exceso.
overt [ˈəuvə:t] adj. Abierto, ta; público, ca. || Evidente, manifiesto, ta (patent).
overtake* [ˌəuvəˈteik] v. tr. Adelantar, pasar [*Amer.*, rebasar] (to pass): *I overtook his car*, adelanté su coche. || Alcanzar (to catch up). || Sorprender: *a storm overtook them two hours later*, una tormenta les sorprendió dos horas después. || Abatirse: *misfortune overtook his family*, la desgracia se abatió sobre su familia. || Apoderarse : *panic overtook the crowd*, el pánico se apoderó de la muchedumbre.
— V. intr. Adelantar, pasar.
— OBSERV. Pret. ***overtook;*** p. p. ***overtaken.***
overtaken [—ən] p. p. See OVERTAKE.
overtaking [—iŋ] n. Adelantamiento, *m.* || *No overtaking*, prohibido adelantar.
overtask [ˈəuvəˈtɑ:sk] v. tr. Agobiar de trabajo.
overtax [ˈəuvəˈtæks] v. tr. Exigir demasiado a (to strain).
over-the-counter [ˈəuvəðəˈkauntə*] adj. Negociado fuera de la Bolsa (stocks).
overthrew [ˌəuvəˈθru:] pret. See OVERTHROW.
overthrow [ˌəuvəθrəu] n. Derrocamiento, *m.* (of a government). || Derrumbamiento, *m.* (of an empire). || Derrota, *f.* (of an army). || Desbaratamiento, *m.* (of plans).
overthrow* [ˌəuvəˈθrəu] v. tr. Derrocar, derribar: *to overthrow a government*, derrocar un gobierno. || Derrumbar (an empire). || Derrotar (an army). || Volcar (to overturn). || Echar abajo, desbaratar (plans).
— OBSERV. Pret. ***overthrew;*** p. p. ***overthrown.***
overthrown [—n] p. p. See OVERTHROW.
overtime [ˈəuvətaim] adv. Fuera de hora (beyond the usual hours). || U. S. SP. Fuera del tiempo reglamentario. || *To work overtime*, hacer horas extraordinarias.
— N. Horas (*f. pl.*) extraordinarias (work). || U. S. SP. Prórroga, *f.* || *An hour's overtime*, una hora extraordinaria.
overtime [ˈəuvəˈtaim] v. tr. PHOT. Sobreexponer.
overtire [ˈəuvəˈtaiə*] v. tr. Cansar demasiado, agotar.
overtone [ˈəuvətəun] n. MUS. Armónico, *m.* || FIG. Insinuación, *f.*, alusión, *f.*: *a reply full of overtones*, una contestación llena de insinuaciones.
overtook [ˈəuvəˈtuk] pret. See OVERTAKE.
overtop [ˈəuvətɔp] v. tr. Descollar entre, sobresalir entre.
overtrain [ˈəuvətrein] v. tr. Entrenar con exceso, sobreentrenar.
— V. intr. Entrenarse con exceso, sobreentrenarse.
overtraining [—iŋ] n. Exceso (*m.*) de entrenamiento, sobreentrenamiento, *m.*
overtrick [ˈəuvətrik] n. Baza (*f.*) de más (in card games).

overtrump [ˈəuvəˈtrʌmp] v. tr./intr. Contrafallar (in card games).

overture [ˈəuvətjuə*] n. Propuesta, *f.*, proposición, *f.*, oferta, *f.* (proposal): *we have made overtures of peace*, hemos hecho propuestas de paz. || MUS. Obertura, *f.*

overturn [ˈəuvəˈtə:n] n. See OVERTURNING.

overturn [ˌəuvəˈtə:n] v. tr. Volcar (to turn upside down). || MAR. Hacer zozobrar (a ship). || Derrocar, derribar (a government, etc.). || Trastornar (to disarrange).
— V. intr. Volcar (car, airplane, etc.). || MAR. Zozobrar (a ship).

overturning [ˌəuvəˈtə:niŋ] n. Vuelco, *m.* (of a car). || Vuelco, *m.*, zozobra, *f.* (of a ship). || Derrocamiento, *m.* (of a government, etc.).

overuse [ˈəuvəˈju:s] n. Empleo (*m.*) excesivo, uso (*m.*) excesivo.

overuse [ˈəuvəˈju:z] v. tr. Emplear *or* usar excesivamente.

overvaluation [ˈəuvəˌvæljuˈeiʃən] n. Sobrestimación, *f.*, supervaloración, *f.*

overvalue [ˈəuvəˈvælju:] v. tr. Supervalorar, sobrestimar.

overweening [ˌəuvəˈwi:niŋ] adj. Presuntuoso, sa; vanidoso, sa; arrogante.

overweight [ˈəuvəˈweit] adj. De peso excesivo, demasiado pesado, da. || — *To be overweight*, pesar demasiado, ser demasiado pesado. || *To be two pounds overweight*, pesar dos libras de más.
— N. Sobrepeso, *m.*, exceso (*m.*) de peso. || Exceso, *m.* (of luggage).

overweight [ˈəuvəˈweit] v. tr. Dar demasiada importancia a (to emphasize to excess). || Sobrecargar (to overload).

overwhelm [ˌəuvəˈwelm] v. tr. Inundar, sumergir (to inundate). || Aplastar, arrollar (in a discussion, an opponent). || Abrumar: *they were overwhelmed at the news*, la noticia les abrumó. || Agobiar, confundir: *overwhelmed by s.o.'s kindness*, confundido por la amabilidad de alguien. || Agobiar, abrumar: *overwhelmed with work*, agobiado de trabajo. || Colmar: *to overwhelm with honours*, colmar de honores. || *To be overwhelmed with joy*, rebosar de alegría.

overwhelming [—iŋ] adj. Abrumador, ra; aplastante, arrollador, ra (defeat). || Agobiante, abrumador, ra (work). || Irresistible (desire).

overwind* [ˈəuvəˈwaind] v. tr. Tensar demasiado la cuerda de (a watch).
— OBSERV. Pret. & p. p. **overwound.**

overwork [ˈəuvəˈwə:k] n. Exceso (*m.*) de trabajo, trabajo (*m.*) excesivo.

overwork [ˈəuvəˈwə:k] v. tr. Hacer trabajar demasiado (to make work excessively). || Usar demasiado, abusar de: *to overwork an expression*, usar demasiado una expresión. || *An overworked expression*, una expresión trillada.
— V. intr. Trabajar demasiado (to work excessively). || Trabajar horas extraordinarias (to work overtime).

overwound [ˈəuvəˌwaund] pret. & p. p. See OVERWIND.

overwrought [ˈəuvəˈrɔ:t] adj. Sobreexcitado, da: *an overwrought child*, un niño sobreexcitado. || Agotado por el trabajo excesivo, con los nervios destrozados (exhausted). || Recargado, da: *an overwrought style*, un estilo recargado.

Ovid [ˈɔvid] pr. n. Ovidio, *m.*

ovidae [ˈəuvidi:] pl. n. ZOOL. Óvidos, *m.*

oviduct [ˈəuvidʌkt] n. Oviducto, *m.*

oviform [ˈəuvifɔ:m] adj. Oviforme.

ovine [ˈəuvain] adj. ZOOL. Ovino, na; lanar.

oviparity [əuviˈpæriti] n. ZOOL. Oviparidad, *f.*

oviparous [əuˈvipərəs] adj. ZOOL. Ovíparo, ra.

oviposit [əuviˈpɔzit] v. intr. ZOOL. Poner huevos.

ovipositor [—ə*] n. ZOOL. Oviscapto, *m.*

ovoid [ˈəuvɔid] adj. Ovoide.
— N. Ovoide, *m.*

ovolo [ˈəuvələu] n. ARCH. Óvolo, *m.*
— OBSERV. El plural de la palabra inglesa es *ovoli.*

ovoviviparous [əuvəviˈvipərəs] adj. ZOOL. Ovovivíparo, ra.

ovular [ˈəuvjulə*] adj. Ovular.

ovulate [ˈəuvjuleit] v. intr. Ovular.

ovulation [əuvjuˈleiʃən] n. Ovulación, *f.*

ovule [ˈəuvju:l] n. Óvulo, *m.*

ovum [ˈəuvəm] n. ARCH. Ovo, *m.* || BIOL. Óvulo, *m.*
— OBSERV. El plural de *ovum* es *ova.*

owe [əu] v. tr. Deber: *to owe s.o. money*, deber dinero a alguien. || Deber: *to owe respect to s.o.*, deber respeto a alguien; *to owe allegiance to one's country*, deber lealtad al propio país *or* a la patria; *she owes her life to the doctors*, debe su vida a los médicos. || *I owe him my thanks*, le tengo que estar agradecido.
— V. intr. Tener deudas.

owing [ˈəuiŋ] adj. Que se debe: *a small quantity of money is owing*, se debe una pequeña cantidad de dinero. || *Owing to*, debido a, a causa de, por razones de.

owl [aul] n. ZOOL. Lechuza (*f.*) común (barn). | Mochuelo, *m.* (little). | Búho, *m.* (long-eared). | Cárabo, *m.*, autillo, *m.* (tawny). || — *Eagle owl*, búho real. || *Horned owl*, búho, *m.* || FIG. FAM. *Night owl*, ave nocturna. || U. S. FAM. *Owl train*, tren (*m.*) de noche.

owlet [ˈaulit] n. ZOOL. Mochuelo, *m.*

owlish [ˈauliʃ] adj. De búho. || FIG. FAM. Serio, ria.

own [əun] adj. Propio, pia: *her own money*, su propio dinero; *I saw it with my own eyes*, lo he visto con mis propios ojos. || — *Of one's own accord*, de motu propio. || *She makes her own dresses*, hace ella misma sus vestidos.
— N. Lo mío, lo tuyo, lo suyo, etc.: *to look after one's own*, ocuparse de lo suyo. || Los míos, los tuyos, los suyos (relatives). || — *For my own*, para mí solo. || *My, your, his own*, mío, mía, tuyo, tuya, suyo, suya: *the house is my own*, la casa es mía. || *Of my, your, his*, etc. *own*, mío, mía, tuyo, tuya, suyo, suya, etc.: *she has money of her own*, tiene dinero suyo; *he has nothing of his own*, no tiene nada suyo; propio, pia: *for reasons of his own*, por motivos propios; muy mío, muy mía, muy tuyo, muy tuya, muy suyo, muy suya, etc.: *she has a style of her own*, tiene un estilo muy suyo. || *On one's own*, solo, sola: *he did it on his own*, lo hizo solo; de motu propio (on one's own initiative), por su cuenta: *to work on one's own*, trabajar por su cuenta. || *To come into one's own*, tomar posesión de lo suyo; conseguir lo que uno se merece. || *To get one's own back*, desquitarse. || *To hold one's own*, mantenerse firme (not to give way), poder competir *or* rivalizar: *I can hold my own with you*, puedo competir con usted; defenderse: *I hold my own in English*, me defiendo en inglés. || *To make sth. one's own*, apoderarse de algo.

own [əun] v. tr. Poseer, tener (to possess): *I own a boat*, tengo un barco. || Reconocer (a child, a king, an authority). || Reconocer, admitir, confesar: *I own I was wrong*, reconozco que estaba equivocado. || *Who owns this land?*, ¿a quién pertenece este terreno?
— V. intr. *To own to*, reconocer, confesar. || *To own up*, confesar. || *To own up to*, confesar.

owner [—ə*] n. Dueño, ña; propietario, ria (of house, land, etc.). || Poseedor, ra (possessor). || — *Joint owner*, copropietario, ria. || JUR. *Rightful owner*, propietario legítimo, derecho habiente, *m.*

ownerless [—əlis] adj. Sin dueño.

ownership [—əʃip] n. Propiedad, *f.*: *bare ownership*, nuda propiedad. || Posesión, *f.* || — *Common ownership*, copropiedad, *f.* || *"Under new ownership"*, "cambio de propietario".

ox [ɔks] n. Buey, *m.* (animal).
— OBSERV. El plural de *ox* es *oxen.*

oxalic [ɔkˈsælik] adj. CHEM. Oxálico, ca (acid).

oxalidaceae [ɔksæliˈdeisi:i] pl. n. BOT. Oxalidáceas, *f.*

oxbow [ˈɔksbəu] n. Collera (*f.*) de yugo. || U. S. Recodo (*m.*) de un río (of a river).

oxcart [ˈɔkskɑ:t] n. Carreta (*f.*) de bueyes.

oxeye daisy [ˈɔksaiˈdeizi] n. BOT. Margarita, *f.*

Oxford [ˈɔksfəd] pr. n. GEOGR. Oxford.

Oxfordian [ˈɔksˈfɔdjən] adj./n. Oxoniense.

oxhide [ˈɔkshaid] n. Cuero (*m.*) de buey.

oxidable [ˈɔksidəbl] adj. Oxidable.

oxidant [ˈɔksidənt] n. Oxidante, *m.*

oxidation [ˌɔksiˈdeiʃən] n. Oxidación, *f.*

oxide [ˈɔksaid] n. CHEM. Óxido, *m.*: *copper oxide*, óxido de cobre.

oxidizable [ˈɔksidaizəbl] adj. Oxidable.

oxidize [ˈɔksidaiz] v. tr. Oxidar.
— V. intr. Oxidarse.

oxidizer [—ə*] n. Oxidante, *m.*

oxidizing [—iŋ] adj. Oxidante.
— N. Oxidación, *f.*

oxlip [ˈɔkslip] n. BOT. Prímula, *f.*

Oxonian [ɔkˈsəunjən] adj./n. Oxoniense.

oxtail [ˈɔksteil] n. Rabo (*m.*) de buey.

oxtongue [ˈɔkstʌŋ] n. BOT. Lengua (*f.*) de buey.

oxyacetylene [ˈɔksiəˈsetili:n] adj. CHEM. Oxiacetilénico, ca. || — *Oxyacetylene torch*, soplete oxiacetilénico, soplete de soldadura autógena. || *Oxyacetylene welding*, soldadura autógena *or* oxiacetilénica.

oxyacid [ˈɔksiˈæsid] n. CHEM. Oxácido, *m.*

oxygen [ˈɔksidʒən] n. CHEM. Oxígeno, *m.* || — *Oxygen acid*, oxácido, *m.* || *Oxygen cylinder*, balón (*m.*) de oxígeno. || *Oxygen mask*, máscara (*f.*) de oxígeno. || *Oxygen tent*, cámara (*f.*) de oxígeno. || *Oxygen treatment*, oxigenoterapia, *f.*

oxygenate [ɔkˈsidʒineit] v. tr. CHEM. Oxigenar.

oxygenation [ˌɔksidʒiˈneiʃən] n. CHEM. Oxigenación, *f.*

oxygen-hydrogen welding [ˈɔksidʒənˈhaidridʒən ˈweldiŋ] n. Soldadura (*f.*) oxhídrica.

oxygenize [ˈɔksidʒənaiz] v. tr. Oxigenar.

oxyhaemoglobin or **oxyhemoglobin** [ˈɔksihi:məˈgləubin] n. BIOL. Oxihemoglobina, *f.*

oxyhydrogen [ˈɔksiˈhaidridʒən] adj. Oxhídrico, ca: *oxyhydrogen torch*, soplete oxhídrico.

oxytone [ˈɔksitəun] adj. GRAMM. Oxítono, na.
— N. GRAMM. Oxítono, *m.*

oxyuris [ɔksiˈjuəris] n. Oxiuro, *m.*

oyer and terminer [ˈɔiə*ændˈtə:minə*] n. JUR. Audiencia (*f.*) de lo criminal.

oyes or **oyez** [əuˈjes] interj. ¡Atención!, ¡oíd!

oyster [ˈɔistə*] n. ZOOL. Ostra, *f.* || — *Oyster bed* o *farm*, criadero (*m.*) de ostras, ostral, *m.*, ostrero, *m.* || *Oyster catcher*, ostrero, *m.* (bird). || *Oyster culture* o *farming*, ostricultura, *f.* || *Oyster culturist* o *farmer*, ostricultor, *m.* || *Oyster seller*, ostrero, ra. || *The oyster industry*, la industria ostrícola.

oysterroot [—ru:t] n. BOT. Salsifí, *m.*
ozonation [əuzəuˈneiʃən] n. CHEM. Ozonización, *f.*
ozonator [əuzəuˈneitə*] n. CHEM. Ozonador, *m.*, ozonizador, *m.*
ozone [ˈəuzəun] n. CHEM. Ozono, *m.*
ozonic [əuˈzɔnik] adj. CHEM. Ozonizado, da.
ozonization [əuzəunaiˈzeiʃən] n. CHEM. Ozonización, *f.*
ozonize [ˈəuzəunaiz] v. tr. CHEM. Ozonizar, ozonar, ozonificar.
ozonizer [—ə*] n. CHEM. Ozonizador, *m.*, ozonador, *m.* (apparatus).
ozonometer [əuzəuˈnɔmitə*] n. Ozonómetro, *m.*
ozonosphere [əuˈzəunə,sfiə*] n. Ozonosfera, *f.*

P

p [pi:] n. P, *f.*: *capital p, small p:* p mayúscula, p minúscula. || FIG. *To mind one's P's and Q's*, darle siete vueltas a la lengua antes de hablar, tener cuidado de no meter la pata.
pa [pɑ:] n. FAM. Papá, *m.*
pabulum [ˈpæbjuləm] n. Alimento, *m.*, pábulo, *m.* (nourishment). || FIG. *Mental pabulum*, alimento del espíritu.
paca [ˈpækə] n. ZOOL. Paca, *f.* (rodent).
pacay [pəˈkai] n. *Amer.* Pacay, *m.* (tree).
pace [peis] n. Paso, *m.* (step): *ten paces off* o *away*, a diez pasos. || Paso, *m.* (speed): *to walk at a brisk pace*, andar con paso rápido; *to slacken one's pace*, aminorar el paso. || Ritmo, *m.*: *the present building pace*, el ritmo actual de la construcción. || — *At a good pace*, a buen paso. || *At a slow pace*, a paso lento. || *At a walking pace*, al paso. || FIG. *To go at a snail's pace*, andar a paso de tortuga *or* de buey *or* de carreta. || *To keep pace with s.o.*, andar al mismo paso que alguien. || FIG. *To keep pace with sth.*, correr parejas con algo, seguir el mismo ritmo que algo (to develop at the same speed), mantenerse al tanto de (to keep up to date with). || *To put through his* o *its paces*, poner a prueba (to test), entrenar (to train). || *To quicken one's pace*, apretar *or* alargar *or* acelerar *or* aligerar el paso. || FIG. *To set the pace*, dar la pauta.
pace [peis] v. intr. Ir al paso, andar al paso. || Amblar (a horse). || *To pace up and down the room*, ir y venir por la habitación.
— V. tr. Medir a pasos (to measure): *to pace a room*, medir una habitación a pasos. || DEP. Marcar el paso para (a runner, etc.). || Ir y venir por (a room). || *To pace off* o *out fifteen metres*, medir quince metros a pasos.
pacemaker [—,meikə*] n. Persona (*f.*) que da la pauta (s.o. who takes the lead). || SP. El que marca el paso (in a race). || MED. Marcapasos, *m. inv.*, regulador (*m.*) cardiaco, marcador (*m.*) de paso.
pacer [ˈpeisə*] n. SP. El que marca el paso.
pachyderm [ˈpækidə:m] n. ZOOL. Paquidermo, *m.*
pachydermatous [,pækiˈdə:mətəs] adj. ZOOL. Paquidermo, ma. || FIG. Insensible.
pacific [pəˈsifik] adj. Pacífico, ca.
Pacific [pəˈsifik] adj. Pacífico: *Pacific Ocean*, Océano Pacífico.
pacifically [pəˈsifikəli] adv. Pacíficamente.
pacification [,pæsifiˈkeiʃən] n. Pacificación, *f.*
pacifier [ˈpæsifaiə*] n. Pacificador, ra. || U. S. Chupete, *m.* (for babies).
pacifism [ˈpæsifizəm] n. Pacifismo, *m.*
pacifist [ˈpæsifist] adj./n. Pacifista.
pacify [ˈpæsifai] v. tr. Apaciguar, calmar, tranquilizar (s.o.). || Pacificar (a country).
pack [pæk] n. Bulto, *m.*, fardo, *m.* (bundle). || Paquete, *m.* (packet). || Manada, *f.* (of wolves). || Jauría, *f.* (of hounds). || Baraja, *f.* (of cards). || MIL. Mochila, *f.* || MED. Paño, *m.* [caliente]. | Compresa, *f.* || Emplasto, *m.* (cosmetic treatment). || Partida, *f.*, pandilla, *f.*, panda, *f.* (gang of people). || Serie, *f.*, montón, *m.* (of troubles). || Montón, *m.*, tejido, *m.*, sarta, *f.*: *a pack of lies*, una sarta de mentiras. || SP. "Pack", *m.*, delanteros, *m. pl.* (in rugby). || Banquisa, *f.*, banco (*m.*) de hielo (of ice). || Albarda, *f.* (carried by an animal). || Envase, *m.* (wrapping). || U. S. Cajetilla, *f.* (of cigarettes).
pack [pæk] v. tr. Llenar (to fill a container with sth.). || Embalar (to put sth. in a container): *a vacuum cleaner packed in a box*, una aspiradora embalada en una caja. || Envasar: *to pack flour in sacks*, envasar harina en sacos; *to pack milk in cartons*, envasar leche en cartones. || Envolver (to wrap). || Enlatar (to put in a tin). || Embotellar (to put in a bottle). || Empaquetar (to put in a packet or in a parcel). || Poner en cajas (to put in boxes). || Empacar (wool). || Embarrilar (to put into barrels). || Poner en la maleta: *I have to pack my things*, tengo que poner mis cosas en la maleta. || Hacer: *to pack a suitcase*, hacer la maleta. || Albardar (a horse). || Llenar hasta los topes, atestar (to fill tightly): *a train packed with people*, un tren atestado de gente. || TECH. Guarnecer (a piston). || Llenar de partidarios (a committee, a jury). || U. S. Llevar, cargar (a parcel, etc.). | Llevar [un arma] (to carry a gun). || — *The film is packing them in*, la película atrae a mucha gente. || *The town is packed with tourists*, la ciudad está llena de turistas. || *To pack down*, apretar (to press), pisotear (with the feet). || *To pack in*, apiñar (people), llenar de bote en bote, atestar (a place). || FAM. *To pack it in*, dejarlo. | *To pack one's bags*, liar el petate (to leave). | *To pack s.o. off*, mandar a alguien a paseo, echar *or* despedir a alguien con cajas destempladas (to tell s.o. to leave), mandar, despachar (to send). || *To pack up a tent*, recoger una tienda. || *To pack up one's bits and pieces*, preparar sus bártulos. || FAM. *To send s.o. packing*, echar *or* despedir a alguien con cajas destempladas.
— V. intr. Hacer la maleta *or* las maletas (to put one's things into a suitcase). || Volverse compacto, endurecerse (to become compact). || Apiñarse (to crowd together): *the crowd packed round the minister*, la muchedumbre se apiñó en torno al ministro. || Caber en la maleta: *small things pack easily*, las cosas pequeñas caben fácilmente en la maleta. || — *To pack badly*, arrugarse en la maleta. || FAM. *To pack off* o *away*, largarse (to leave). || *To pack together*, apretarse. || *To pack up*, hacer la maleta *or* las maletas (for a trip, etc.), amontonarse (to pile up), averiarse, estropearse (to break down), liar el petate (to die, to depart). || *To pack well*, no arrugarse en la maleta.
package [ˈpækidʒ] n. Paquete, *m.* (parcel). || Bulto, *m.* (bundle). || Embalaje, *m.* (packing). || Envase, *m.* (of liquids, etc.). || FIG. Conjunto (*m.*) de medidas (series of measures taken at one time). | Acuerdo (*m.*) global que supone concesiones mutuas (deal). || — FIG. *Package deal*, acuerdo global que supone concesiones mutuas (agreement), venta (*f.*) global de varios artículos (sale). | *Package holiday* o *tour*, viaje (*m.*) todo comprendido. || U. S. *Package store*, bodega, *f.*
package [ˈpækidʒ] v. tr. Embalar (to pack). || Envasar (liquids, grain, etc.).
packaging [—iŋ] n. Embalaje, *m.* (packing). || Envase, *m.* (of liquids, etc.).
pack animal [ˈpæk,æniməl] n. Animal (*m.*) de carga, acémila, *f.*
packed [pækt] adj. Lleno, na.
packer [ˈpækə*] n. Embalador, ra; empaquetador, ra. || Envasador, ra (of liquids, etc.).
packet [ˈpækit] n. Paquete, *m.* (small package). || Cajetilla, *f.* (of cigarettes). || Sobre, *m.* (of tea, etc.). || Paquebote, *m.* (packet boat). || FAM. Dineral, *m.* (money).
packet [ˈpækit] v. tr. Empaquetar, embalar. || Envasar.
packet boat [—bəut] n. Paquebote, *m.*
packhorse [ˈpækhɔ:s] n. Caballo (*m.*) de carga.
pack ice [ˈpækais] n. Banquisa, *f.*, banco (*m.*) de hielo.
packing [ˈpækiŋ] n. Embalaje, *m.* (in boxes): *the packing of goods*, el embalaje de mercancías. || Empaquetado, *m.* || Envase, *m.*, envasado, *m.* (of liquids, powders). || Embalaje, *m.* (material used): *to throw away the packing*, tirar el embalaje. || Envase, *m.* (recipient for liquids, flour, etc.). || Relleno, *m.* (filling). || MED. Paño (*m.*) caliente. || TECH. Guarnición, *f.* (of a piston). || *To do one's packing*, hacer las maletas.
packing case [—,keis] n. Cajón, *m.*, caja, (*f.*) de embalaje.
packing ring [—riŋ] n. TECH. Arandela, *f.*
packman [ˈpækmən] n. (Ant.). Vendedor (*m.*) ambulante, buhonero, *m.*

— OBSERV. El plural de *packman* es *packmen*.

packsaddle [ˈpæk,sædl] n. Albarda, *f.*

packthread [ˈpækθred] n. Bramante, *m.*, guita, *f.*
packtrain [ˈpæktrein] n. Reata (*f.*) de animales de carga.
pact [pækt] n. Pacto, *m.*: *nonaggresion pact*, pacto de no agresión.
pad [pæd] n. Almohadilla, *f.*, cojín, *m.* (cushion). || Rodete, *m.* (to carry loads). || Almohadilla, *f.*, tampón, *m.* (for inking). || Carpeta, *f.* (for blotting). || Bloc, *m.*, taco, *m.* (of paper). || Taco, *m.* (of a calendar). || Relleno, *m.*, almohadilla, *f.* (soft material to fill). || Hombrera, *f.*, almohadilla, *f.* (for shoulders). || SP. Espinillera, *f.* (for cricket, hockey, etc.). | Peto, *m.* (for fencing). || ZOOL. Almohadilla, *f.* (sole of the paw). | Pata, *f.* (paw). || MED. Cataplasma, *f.* || TECH. Portaherramientas, *m. inv.* (for several tools). || Pisada (*f.*) silenciosa (muffled step). || FAM. Camino, *m.* (road). | Casa, *f.* (house, flat). || Pista (*f.*) de despegue *or* de aterrizaje (for helicopters). || Plataforma (*f.*) de lanzamiento (for launching a rocket). || Hoja (*f.*) grande (of water plants). || — FAM. *Gentleman of the pad*, salteador (*m.*) de caminos, bandolero, *m.* | *To be on the pad*, vagabundear.
pad [pæd] v. tr. Acolchar, acolchonar, enguatar (door, material, etc.). || Rellenar (a cushion). || Poner hombreras (shoulders). || FIG. Rellenar, meter paja en: *to pad a book, a speech*, meter paja en un libro, en un discurso. || — *Padded cell*, loquera, *f.* || FAM. *To pad it* o *to pad the hoof*, ir en el coche de San Fernando. || FIG. *To pad out*, meter paja en, rellenar.
— V. intr. Andar, caminar (to walk). || Andar a pasos quedos *or* silenciosos (with muffled steps). || FAM. Vagabundear (unhurriedly).
padding [—iŋ] n. Acolchado, *m.*, acolchonado, *m.*, enguatado, *m.* (operation). || Relleno, *m.* (material). || FIG. Relleno, *m.*, paja, *f.*: *two chapters of pure padding*, dos capítulos de pura paja.
paddle [ˈpædl] n. Pagaya, *f.*, zagual, *m.*, canalete, *m.* (oar). || Paseo (*m.*) en canoa (voyage). || Álabe, *m.*, paleta, *f.* (of waterwheel). || ZOOL. Aleta, *f.* (flipper). || Paleta, *f.* (for mixing, for beating clothes). || FAM. *To go for a paddle*, ir a mojarse los pies.
paddle [ˈpædl] v. tr. MAR. Hacer avanzar con pagaya. || Mover con una paleta (a liquid). || U. S. FAM. Azotar (to spank).
— V. intr. Remar con pagaya (to row). || Mojarse los pies, chapotear (in the sea, etc.).
paddle boat [—bəut] n. MAR. Vapor (*m.*) de ruedas. | Hidropedal, *m.* (pedal boat).
paddle box [—bɔks] n. MAR. Tambor (*m.*) de ruedas (of a boat).
paddler [—ə*] n. Remero, ra; persona (*f.*) que rema con pagaya.
paddle steamer [—sti:mə*] n. MAR. Vapor (*m.*) de ruedas.
paddle wheel [—wi:l] n. Rueda (*f.*) de paletas *or* de álabes.
paddling pool [—iŋpu:l] n. Estanque (*m.*) para niños.
paddock [ˈpædək] n. Potrero, *m.*, "paddock", *m.* (grassy enclosed area). || "Paddock", *m.* (racecourse enclosure).
paddy [ˈpædi] n. Arroz (*m.*) con cáscara (rice). || Arrozal, *m.* (rice field). || FAM. Rabieta, *f.*, berrinche, *m.*: *to get into a paddy*, coger una rabieta.
paddy wagon [—ˈwægən] n. FAM. Coche (*m.*) celular.
padlock [ˈpædlɔk] n. Candado, *m.*
padlock [ˈpædlɔk] v. tr. Cerrar con candado.
padre [ˈpɑ:dri] n. MIL. MAR. Capellán, *m.*
paean [ˈpi:ən] n. Peán, *m.*, himno (*m.*) de alegría, himno (*m.*) triunfal.
paederast [ˈpedəræst] n. Pederasta, *m.*
paederasty [—i] n. Pederastia, *f.*
paediatrician [ˌpi:diəˈtriʃən] or **paediatrist** [ˌpidiˈætrist] n. MED. Pediatra, *m.*, pedíatra, *m.*
paediatrics [ˌpi:diˈætriks] n. MED. Pediatría, *f.*
pagan [ˈpeigən] adj./n. Pagano, na.
paganism [ˈpeigənizəm] n. Paganismo, *m.*
paganize [ˈpeigənaiz] v. tr. Paganizar.
page [peidʒ] n. Página, *f.* (of a book, etc.): *on page 2*, en la página 2. || PRINT. Plana, *f.* || FIG. Página, *f.* || Paje, *m.* (at court, at a wedding). || Botones, *m. inv.* (in a hotel). || Acomodador, *m.* (in a theatre). || — *Full page*, a toda plana. || *On the front page*, en primera plana.
page [peidʒ] v. tr. Paginar, foliar (to number the pages). || PRINT. Compaginar. || Mandar llamar por el botones (in a hotel). || Servir como paje (at court).
pageant [ˈpædʒənt] n. Cabalgata (*f.*) *or* desfile (*m.*) histórico (historical procession). || Espectáculo (*m.*) histórico (historical spectacle). || Pompa, *f.*, aparato, *m.*, boato, *m.* (pageantry). || *Air pageant*, fiesta (*f.*) aeronáutica.
pageantry [—ri] n. Pompa, *f.*, aparato, *m.*, boato, *m.* (display). || Espectáculo, *m.* (spectacle).
page boy [peidʒbɔi] n. Paje, *m.* (at court, at a wedding). || Botones, *m. inv.* (in a hotel).
page proof [peidʒpru:f] n. PRINT. Prueba (*f.*) de imprenta.
paginate [ˈpædʒineit] v. tr. Paginar.
pagination [ˌpædʒiˈneiʃən] n. Paginación, *f.*
pagoda [pəˈgəudə] n. Pagoda, *f.*
paid [peid] adj. Pagado, da; a sueldo (receiving wages). || Pagado, da: *paid holidays*, vacaciones pagadas. || See PAY. || — *Paid assassin*, asesino pagado *or* a sueldo. || *To put paid to*, acabar con, poner término a.
paid-up [—ˈʌp] adj. COMM. Liberado, da (share, capital). || *To be a paid-up member*, haber pagado su cotización (of a union, etc.).
pail [peil] n. Cubo, *m.* (bucket). || MAR. Balde, *m.*, cubo, *m.*
pailful [—ful] n. Cubo, *m.*
paillasse [ˈpæliæs] n. Jergón, *m.*, colchón (*m.*) de paja (palliasse).
paillette [pælˈjet] n. Lentejuela, *f.*
pain [pein] n. Dolor, *m.* (physical): *to cry out with pain*, gritar de dolor. || Pena, *f.*, dolor, *m.* (mental). || Sufrimiento, *m.* (suffering). || — Pl. MED. Dolores (*m.*) del parto. || Esfuerzos, *m.*, trabajo, *m. sing.*: *to take pains to do sth.*, hacer grandes esfuerzos *o* darse mucho trabajo para hacer algo. || — *On* o *upon* o *under pain of*, so pena de, bajo pena de. || FIG. FAM. *To be a pain in the neck*, ser un pesado (s.o.), ser una lata (sth.). || *To be in pain*, estar sufriendo, tener dolores. || *To be out of pain*, haber dejado de sufrir. || FIG. FAM. *To give s.o. a pain in the neck*, fastidiarle *or* darle la lata *or* chincharle a alguien. || *To have a pain in one's arm*, dolerle a uno el brazo. || *To spare no pains to get sth.*, no escatimar esfuerzos para lograr algo. || *To take pains over*, esmerarse en.
pain [pein] v. tr. Doler (physically): *my foot pains me*, me duele el pie. || Afligir, apenar, dar lástima, dar pena, doler (mentally): *it pains me to see him like that*, me duele verle así. || *It pains me to say so*, me cuesta decirlo, me duele decirlo.
pained [—d] adj. Dolorido, da; apenado, da (voice). || Afligido, da (expression).
painful [—ful] adj. Doloroso, sa: *a painful wound*, una llaga dolorosa; *a painful blow*, un golpe doloroso. || Dolorido, da (as a result of a blow). || Penoso, sa; difícil (task). || Afligente, lastimoso, sa; penoso, sa (spectacle). || Difícil, angustioso, sa (decision). || Doloroso, sa; desagradable: *it is painful to me to have to say so*, me es desagradable tener que decir estas cosas. || — *A painful performance*, una actuación deplorable *or* lamentable. || *It was painful to see her*, daba pena verla. || *My back is painful*, me duele la espalda.
painfully [—fuli] adv. Penosamente, con dificultad. || FIG. Muy, terriblemente. || FIG. *It is painfully obvious*, está clarísimo.
painfulness [—fulnis] n. Dolor, *m.*, lo doloroso.
pain killer [—kilə*] n. MED. Calmante, *m.*, analgésico, *m.*
painless [—lis] adj. Sin dolor, indoloro, ra (physically). || Sin dificultad, fácil (task, etc.). || *Painless childbirth*, parto (*m.*) sin dolor.
painstaking [ˈpeinzˌteikiŋ] adj. Cuidadoso, sa; esmerado, da: *a painstaking schoolboy*, un alumno cuidadoso. || Cuidadoso, sa (requiring great care). || Hecho con cuidado, esmerado, da (piece of work).
— N. Cuidado, *m.*, esmero, *m.*
paint [peint] n. Pintura, *f.*: *a box of paints*, una caja de pinturas; *a coat of paint*, una mano de pintura. || FAM. Pintura, *f.* (cosmetics). || "*Wet paint*", "cuidado con la pintura".
paint [peint] v. tr. Pintar: *to paint a landscape*, pintar un paisaje; *to paint the ceiling white*, pintar el techo de blanco. || Pintarse (with cosmetics): *to paint one's face*, pintarse la cara. || MED. Dar unos toques a, untar (a throat, etc.). || FIG. Describir, pintar. || — *To paint al fresco, in oils*, pintar al fresco, al óleo. || *To paint out*, tapar con una mano de pintura. || FIG. FAM. *To paint the town red*, irse de juerga, irse de parranda.
— V. intr. Pintar. || Ser pintor.
paintbox [—bɔks] n. Caja (*f.*) de pinturas.
paintbrush [—brʌʃ] n. Pincel, *m.* (for an artist). || Brocha, *f.* (for house painters).
painter [—ə*] n. Pintor, ra (artist). || Pintor (*m.*) de brocha gorda (who paints walls, etc.). || MAR. Amarra, *f.*, boza, *f.* || FIG. *To cut the painters*, soltar las amarras.
painting [—iŋ] n. Pintura, *f.*: *to study painting*, estudiar pintura; *painting in oils*, pintura al óleo. || Cuadro, *m.* (picture). || FIG. Descripción, *f.*, pintura, *f.* || MED. Pincelada, *f.*, toque, *m.* || — *Cave painting*, pintura rupestre. || *Spray painting*, pintura con pistola.
paint roller [—rəulə*] n. Rodillo, *m.*
paint spray [—sprei] n. Pistola, *f.* [para pintar].
paintwork [—wə:k] n. Pintura, *f.*
pair [pεə*] n. Par, *m.*: *a pair of shoes, of stockings*, un par de zapatos, de medias; *a pair of scissors*, un par de tijeras. || Pareja, *f.* (of people, animals). || Tronco, *m.* (of horses). || Yunta, *f.* (of oxen). || Pareja, *f.* (in cards). || TECH. Par, *m.*: *a pair of gears*, un par de engranajes. || — *Carriage and pair*, carruaje tirado por dos caballos. || *Pair of pants*, calzoncillos, *m. pl.* || *Pair of pyjamas*, pijama, *m.* || *Pair of scales*, balanza, *f.* || *Pair of spectacles*, gafas, *f. pl.* || *Pair of suspenders*, tirantes, *m. pl.* || *Pair of trousers*, pantalón, *m.*, pantalones, *m. pl.* || *The happy pair*, la feliz pareja, los novios. || *These two candlesticks are a pair*, estos dos candeleros hacen juego.
pair [pεə*] v. tr. Emparejar: *to pair gloves*, emparejar guantes. || Emparejar, juntar (people). || BIOL. Aparear.
— V. intr. Emparejarse (to form a pair). || Emparejar,

hacer pareja: *this glove pairs with the other*, este guante empareja con el otro. || BIOL. Aparearse (animals). || Formar parejas (people).

— OBSERV. La proposición *off* acompaña a veces este verbo sin cambiar por ello su significado.

pairing [—iŋ] n. Apareamiento, *m.* (of animals). || Emparejamiento, *m.*
paisley [ˈpeizli] n. Cachemira, *f.* (material, design).
pajamas [pəˈdʒɑːməz] pl. n. U. S. Pijama, *m. sing.* [*Amer.*, piyama, *m. sing.*].
Pakistan [ˌpɑːkisˈtɑːn] pr. n. GEOGR. Paquistán, *m.*, Pakistán, *m.*
Pakistani [ˌpɑːkisˈtɑːni] adj./n. Paquistaní, pakistaní.
pal [pæl] n. U. S. FAM. Amigote, *m.*, camarada, *m.* & *f.*, amigo, ga (close friend).
pal [pæl] v. intr. U. S. FAM. *To pal up*, hacerse amigos. | *To pal up with*, hacerse amigo de.
palace [ˈpæləs] n. Palacio, *m.*: *Royal Palace*, Palacio Real; *bishop's palace*, palacio episcopal.
paladin [ˈpælədin] n. Paladín, *m.*
palaeogeography [ˌpæliəudʒiˈɔgrəfi] n. Paleogeografía, *f.* (paleogeography).
palaeographer [ˌpæliˈɔgrəfə*] n. Paleógrafo, *m.*
palaeographic [ˌpæliəuˈgræfik] adj. Paleográfico, ca.
palaeography [ˌpæliˈɔgrəfi] n. Paleografía, *f.*
Palaeolithic [ˌpæliəuˈliθik] adj. Paleolítico, ca.
palaeologist [pæliˈɔlədʒist] n. Paleólogo, *m.*
Palaeologus [pæliˈɔləgəs] pr. n. Paleólogo.
palaeontologic [ˌpæliɔntəˈlɔdʒik] adj. Paleontológico, ca (paleontologic).
palaeontologist [ˌpæliɔnˈtɔlədʒist] n. Paleontólogo, *m.*
palaeontology [ˌpæliɔnˈtɔlədʒi] n. Paleontología, *f.*
Palaeozoic [pælia'zəuik] adj. Paleozoico, ca.
— N. Paleozoico, *m.*
palafitte [ˈpæləfit] n. Palafito, *m.* (lake dwelling).
palatability [pælətəˈbiliti] n. Lo sabroso, sabor (*m.*) agradable.
palatable [ˈpælətəbl] adj. Sabroso, sa (pleasant to taste). || Comestible, que se puede comer (eatable). || FIG. Agradable, aceptable.
palatal [ˈpælətl] adj. GRAMM. Palatal.
— N. GRAMM. Palatal, *f.*
palatalization [ˈpælətəlaiˈzeiʃən] n. GRAMM. Palatalización, *f.*
palatalize [ˈpælətəlaiz] v. tr. GRAMM. Palatalizar.
palate [ˈpælit] n. ANAT. FIG. Paladar, *m.*: *to have a refined palate*, tener el paladar delicado. || — ANAT. *Soft palate*, velo (*m.*) del paladar. || *The pleasures of the palate*, los placeres de la mesa.
palatial [ˌpəˈleiʃəl] adj. Magnífico, ca; espléndido, da; suntuoso, sa (splendid). || Palaciego, ga (of palace).
Palatinate [pəˈlætinit] pr. n. GEOGR. Palatinado, *m.*
palatine [ˈpælətain] adj./n. Palatino, na.
palaver [pəˈlɑːvə*] n. Conferencia, *f.*, discusión, *f.* (discussion): *a lengthy palaver between the union and the management*, una larga discusión entre el sindicato y la dirección. || Lío, *m.*, follón, *m.* (fuss): *what a palaver just to get a passport!*, ¡qué lío sólo para conseguir un pasaporte! || Palabrería, *f.* (worthless talk). || Charlatanería, *f.* (misleading talk). || Engatusamiento, *m.* (cajolery). || Asunto, *m.* (affair): *that's his palaver*, es asunto suyo. || *There's no need for all that palaver!*, ¡no es para tanto!
palaver [pəˈlɑːvə*] v. intr. Palabrear (to talk profusely). || Discutir (to converse).
— V. tr. FAM. Engatusar (to cajole): *he palavered me into signing*, me engatusó de tal manera que firmé.
pale [peil] adj. Pálido, da: *her face was pale*, su cara estaba pálida; *two pale blue ties*, dos corbatas de color azul pálido. || — *Pale as death* o *deadly pale*, blanco como el papel, más pálido que un muerto. || *To go* o *to turn pale*, ponerse pálido.
— N. Estaca, *f.* (of a fence). || HERALD. Palo, *m.* || FIG. Límites, *m. pl.* || — FIG. *Beyond the pale*, al margen de la sociedad. | *Within the pale of*, en el seno de.
pale [peil] v. intr. Palidecer.
— V. tr. Poner pálido, hacer palidecer.
paleface [—feis] n. Rostro (*m.*) pálido.
paleness [—nis] n. Palidez, *f.*
paleogeography [ˌpæliəudʒiˈɔgrəfi] n. Paleogeografía, *f.*
paleographer [ˌpæliˈɔgrəfə*] n. Paleógrafo, *m.*
paleographic [ˌpæliəuˈgræfik] adj. Paleográfico, ca.
paleography [ˌpæliˈɔgrəfi] n. Paleografía, *f.*
paleolithic [ˌpæliəuˈliθik] adj. GEOL. Paleolítico, ca.
paleologist [ˌpæliˈɔlədʒist] n. Paleólogo, *m.*
Paleologus [pæliˈɔləgəs] pr. n. Paleólogo.
paleontologic [ˌpæliɔnˈtɔlədʒik] adj. Paleontológico, ca.
paleontologist [ˌpæliɔnˈtɔlədʒist] n. Paleontólogo, *m.*
paleontology [ˌpæliɔnˈtɔlədʒi] n. Paleontología, *f.*
Paleozoic [pæliəˈzəuik] adj. GEOL. Paleozoico, ca.
— N. GEOL. Paleozoico, *m.*
Palestine [ˈpælistain] pr. n. GEOGR. Palestina, *f.*
Palestinian [ˌpælesˈtiniən] adj./n. Palestino, na.
palette [ˈpælit] n. ARTS. Paleta, *f.*
palette knife [—naif] n. ARTS. Espátula, *f.*
palfrey [ˈpɔːlfri] n. Palafrén, *m.*
palimpsest [ˈpælimpsest] n. Palimpsesto, *m.*
palindrome [ˈpælindrəum] n. Palíndromo, *m.*
palindromic [—ik] adj. Palíndromo, ma.
paling [ˈpeiliŋ] n. Estacada, *f.* (fence). || Estaca, *f.* (stake).
palingenesis [ˌpælinˈdʒenisis] n. Palingenesia, *f.*
palinode [ˈpælinəud] n. Palinodia, *f.*
palisade [ˌpæliˈseid] n. Empalizada, *f.*, estacada, *f.*, vallado, *m.*
palisade [ˌpæliˈseid] v. tr. Empalizar, vallar, cercar.
palish [ˈpeiliʃ] adj. Paliducho, cha.
pall [pɔːl] n. Paño (*m.*) mortuorio (over a coffin). || Féretro, *m.* (coffin). || REL. Palio, *m.* (pallium). || HERALD. Palio, *m.* || FIG. Cortina, *f.*, velo, *m.* (of smoke). | Manto, *m.*, capa, *f.* (of snow, etc.).
pall [pɔːl] v. intr. Perder su sabor [*on*, para] (to become insipid). || Cansar, dejar de gustar [*on*, a] (to become unattractive). || Cansarse: *to pall of too much music*, cansarse de un exceso de música.
— V. tr. Saciar, hartar (appetite).
palladium [pəˈleidjəm] n. CHEM. Paladio, *m.* (metal). || Paladión, *m.* (statue). || FIG. Paladión, *m.* (safeguard).
Pallas [ˈpælæs] pr. n. MYTH. Palas, *f.*
pallbearer [ˈpɔːlˌbɛərə*] n. Portador (*m.*) del féretro.
pallet [ˈpælit] n. Jergón, *m.* (hard bed, mattress). || Paleta, *f.*, espátula, *f.* (wooden tool, of painters). || TECH. Trinquete, *m.* (of a ratchet). | Paleta, *f.* (of a clock). | Paleta, *f.* (portable platform). || MUS. Válvula, *f.* (of an organ pipe).
pallet truck [—trʌk] n. Carretilla (*f.*) elevadora.
palliasse [ˈpæliæs] n. Jergón, *m.*, colchón (*m.*) de paja.
palliate [ˈpælieit] v. tr. Paliar, mitigar, atenuar: *to palliate a pain*, mitigar un dolor. || Reducir, disminuir (boredom).
palliation [ˌpæliˈeiʃən] n. Paliación, *f.*, disminución, *f.*
palliative [ˈpæliətiv] adj. Paliativo, va.
— N. Paliativo, *m.*
pallid [ˈpælid] adj. Pálido, da.
pallidity [—iti] or **pallidness** [—nis] n. Palidez, *f.*
pallium [ˈpæliəm] n. REL. Palio, *m.* || Manto, *m.* (of mollusks, birds).

— OBSERV. El plural de *pallium* es *pallia* o *palliums*.

pallor [ˈpælə*] n. Palidez, *f.*
pally [ˈpæli] adj. FAM. Amistoso, sa. || *To be pally with s.o.*, ser amigote de alguien.
palm [ˈpɑːlm] n. Palma, *f.* (of the hand, of a glove). || Pala, *f.* (of an implement): *the palm of a paddle*, la pala de una pagaya. || Palmo, *m.* (measure). || BOT. Palma, *f.*, palmera, *f.* (tree). | Palma, *f.* (leaf). || FIG. Palma, *f.* (success): *to carry off the palm*, llevarse la palma. || MAR. Uña, *f.* (of the anchor). || Pala, *f.* (of an antler). || — *Coconut palm*, cocotero, *m.* || *Date palm*, palma datilera. || *Palm cake*, palmera, *f.* || *Royal palm*, palmiche, *m.*, palma (*f.*) real. || FIG. FAM. *To grease s.o.'s palm*, untarle la mano a alguien. | *To have an itching palm*, ser codicioso. | *To hold* o *to have s.o. in the palm of one's hand*, tener a alguien en el bolsillo *or* en la palma de la mano *or* en el bote. | *To know like the palm of one's hand*, conocer como la palma de la mano. | *To yield the palm to*, conceder la victoria a.
palm [pɑːm] v. tr. Escamotear, escamotar. || FIG. *To palm sth. off on s.o.*, colar *or* encajar algo a alguien.
palmar [ˈpælmə*] adj. ANAT. De la palma, palmar: *palmar muscle*, músculo palmar.
palmary [—ri] adj. Sobresaliente.
palmate [ˈpælmit] adj. Palmeado, da.
palmer [ˈpɑːmə*] n. Palmero, *m.* (pilgrim).
palmetto [pælˈmetəu] n. BOT. Palmito, *m.*

— OBSERV. El plural de la palabra inglesa es *palmettos* o *palmettoes*.

palm grove [ˈpɑːmˈgrəuv] n. Palmar, *m.*, palmeral, *m.*
palm heart [pɑːmhɑːt] n. CULIN. Palmito, *m.*
palmiped [ˈpælmiped] adj. ZOOL. Palmípedo, da.
— N. ZOOL. Palmípeda, *f.*
palmist [ˈpɑːmist] n. Quiromántico, ca [*Amer.*, palmista, *f.*]
palmistry [—ri] n. Quiromancia, *f.*
palm leaf [ˈpɑːmliːf] n. Palma, *f.*
palm oil [ˈpɑːmɔil] n. Aceite (*m.*) de palma.
Palm Sunday [ˈpɑːmˈsʌndi] pr. n. REL. Domingo (*m.*) de Ramos.
palm tree [ˈpɑːmtriː] n. BOT. Palma, *f.*, palmera, *f.*
palm wine [ˈpɑːmˈwain] n. Vino (*m.*) de palma.
palmy [ˈpɑːmi] adj. FIG. Próspero, ra: *palmy days*, días prósperos.
palp [pælp] n. ZOOL. Palpo, *m.*
palpability [ˌpælpəˈbiliti] n. Palpabilidad, *f.* || FIG. Evidencia, *f.*
palpable [ˈpælpəbl] adj. Palpable. || FIG. Palpable, patente, evidente: *palpable falsehood*, falsedad patente.
palpableness [—nis] n. Palpabilidad, *f.* || FIG. Evidencia, *f.*
palpably [ˈpælpəbli] adv. Palpablemente, evidentemente.
palpate [ˈpælpeit] v. tr. Palpar.
palpation [pælˈpeiʃən] n. Palpación, *f.*, palpadura, *f.*, palpamiento, *m.*
palpitate [ˈpælpiteit] v. intr. Palpitar.
palpitating [—iŋ] adj. Palpitante (throbbing).
palpitation [ˌpælpiˈteiʃən] n. Palpitación, *f.*: *to suffer from palpitations*, tener palpitaciones.
palsied [ˈpɔːlzid] adj. MED. Paralizado, da.

palsy [ˈpɔ:lzi] n. Parálisis, *f.*
palter [ˈpɔ:ltə*] v. intr. Tergiversar (to talk insincerely). || Regatear (to bargain). || No tomar en serio: *to palter with a question*, no tomar una cuestión en serio.
paltriness [ˈpɔ:ltrinis] n. Mezquindad, *f.*
paltry [ˈpɔ:ltri] adj. Ínfimo, ma; miserable; insignificante: *a paltry sum*, una cantidad ínfima. || Mezquino, na (mean).
paludal [pæˈlju:dl] adj. Palúdico, ca.
paludism [ˈpæljəˌdizəm] n. MED. Paludismo, *m.*
pampas [ˈpæmpəs] pl. n. Pampa, *f. sing.*
pampean [ˈpæmpiən] adj./n. Pampero, ra.
pamper [ˈpæmpə*] v. tr. Mimar, consentir. || *He lead a pampered childhood*, se crió entre algodones.
pamphlet [ˈpæmflit] n. Folleto, *m.*, opúsculo, *m.* (booklet). || Octavilla, *f.* (one sheet handout). || Panfleto, *m.*, libelo, *m.* (lampoon).
pamphleteer [ˌpæmfliˈtiə*] n. Folletista, *m.* || Panfletista, *m.* (lampoonist).
pamphleteer [ˌpæmfliˈtiə*] v. intr. Escribir panfletos *or* folletos.
pan [pæn] n. Cacerola, *f.*, cazo, *m.* (metal container). || Cazuela, *f.* (of earthenware). || Sartén, *f.* (for frying). || Batea, *f.* (for washing gold). || Mortero, *m.* (for crushing). || Platillo, *m.* (of a balance). || Taza, *f.* (of lavatory). || MIL. Cazoleta, *f.* (of a musket). || BOT. Betel, *m.* || U. S. FAM. Jeta, *f.*, cara, *f.* (face). || *Pots and pans*, batería (*f.*) de cocina.
pan [pæn] v. tr. Lavar con batea (gold). || CINEM. Tomar una vista panorámica de *or* con. || FAM. Poner por los suelos, poner de vuelta y media (to criticize).
— V. intr. Extraer oro. || FIG. *To pan out*, salir: *things did not pan out as I wanted*, las cosas no salieron como quería; salir bien, ser un éxito (to turn out well).
Pan [pæn] pr. n. MYTH. Pan, *m.*
panacea [ˌpænəˈsiə] n. Panacea, *f.*
Pan-African [ˈpænˈæfrikən] adj. Panafricano, na.
Pan-Africanism [ˈpænˈæfriˈkənizəm] n. Panafricanismo, *m.*
panama [ˌpænəˈmɑ:] n. Jipijapa, *m.*, panamá, *m.* (hat).
Panama [ˌpænəˈmɑ:] pr. n. GEOGR. Panamá, *m.* (country). || *Panama Canal*, canal (*m.*) de Panamá.
Panama City [—ˈsiti] pr. n. GEOGR. Panamá (capital).
Panamanian [ˌpænəˈmeinjən] adj./n. Panameño, ña.
Pan-American [ˈpænəˈmerikən] adj. Panamericano, na. || *Pan-American Highway*, carretera panamericana.
Pan-Americanism [ˈpænəˈmerikənizəm] n. Panamericanismo, *m.*
Pan-Americanist [ˈpænəˈmerikənist] adj./n. Panamericanista.
Pan-Arabism [ˈpænəˈræbizəm] n. Panarabismo, *m.*
pancake [ˈpænkeik] n. Tortita, *f.*, "pancake", *m.* [*Amer.*, panqueque, *m*]. || AVIAT. Desplome, *m.* || FAM. *Flat as a pancake*, see FLAT.
pancake [ˈpænkeik] v. intr. AVIAT. Desplomarse.
Pancake Day [—dei] n. Martes (*m.*) de carnaval.
pancake landing [—ˈlændiŋ] n. AVIAT. Aterrizaje (*m.*) en desplome.
panchromatic [ˈpænkrəuˈmætik] adj. Pancromático, ca.
pancreas [ˈpæŋkriəs] n. ANAT. Páncreas, *m.*
pancreatic [ˌpæŋkriˈætik] adj. ANAT. Pancreático, ca: *pancreatic juice*, jugo pancreático.
panda [ˈpændə] n. ZOOL. Panda, *m.*
Pandects [ˈpændekts] pl. n. JUR. Pandectas, *f.*
pandemia [pænˈdimiə] n. Pandemia, *f.*
pandemic [pænˈdemik] adj. MED. Pandémico, ca.
— N. MED. Pandemia, *f.*
pandemonium [ˌpændiˈməunjəm] n. Pandemonio, *m.*, pandemónium, *m.* || FIG. Jaleo, *m.*: *it was absolute pandemonium*, había un jaleo tremendo.
pander [ˈpændə*] n. Alcahuete, *m.*, proxeneta, *m.*
pander [ˈpændə*] v. intr. Alcahuetear (to act as a pander). || *To pander to*, complacer: *he is always pandering to the director*, siempre está complaciendo al director; consentir (a child), agradar, contentar: *television programmes which pander to the lowest taste*, programas de televisión que agradan el gusto más vulgar.
pandit [ˈpændit] n. Pandit, *m.*
Pandora [pænˈdɔ:rə] pr. n. MYTH. Pandora, *f.*: *Pandora's box*, la caja de Pandora.
pane [pein] n. Cristal, *m.*, vidrio, *m.* (sheet of glass). || Cara, *f.*, lado, *m.* (flat side of an object).
panegyric [ˌpæniˈdʒirik] n. Panegírico, *m.*
panegyrical [—əl] adj. Panegírico, ca.
panegyrist [ˌpæniˈdʒirist] n. Panegirista, *m.* & *f.*
panegyrize [ˈpænidʒiraiz] v. tr. Panegirizar.
panel [ˈpænl] n. ARCH. Lienzo, *m.* (of a wall). | Panel, *m.*, cuarterón, *m.*, entrepaño, *m.* (of a door). | Artesón, *m.* (of a ceiling). || Panel, *m.*, tablero, *m.* (of plywood). || Paño, *m.* (of a dress). || Tablero, *m.* (of controls or instruments). || ARTS. Tabla, *f.* || Grupo, *m.*: *a panel of experts*, un grupo de expertos. || Jurado, *m.* (jury in a competition). || MED. Lista (*f.*) de médicos del seguro social.
panel [ˈpænl] v. tr. Revestir con paneles de madera (walls). || Artesonar (ceilings). || Dividir en paños (a dress). || JUR. Elegir jurado.
panel board [—bɔ:d] n. Tablero (*m.*) de mandos.
panel doctor [—ˈdɔktə*] n. Médico (*m.*) que presta sus servicios en el seguro social.
panel heating [—ˈhi:tiŋ] n. Calefacción (*f.*) por radiación.
panelist [ˈpænəlist] n. Miembro (*m.*) del jurado.
panelling (U. S. **paneling**) [ˈpænliŋ] n. Revestimiento (*m.*) de madera (of walls). || Artesonado, *m.* (of a ceiling).
Pan-European [ˈpænˌjuərəˌpi:ən] adj./n. Paneuropeo, a.
pang [pæŋ] n. Punzada, *f.* (of pain). || FIG. Remordimiento, *m.*: *pangs of conscience*, remordimientos de conciencia. | Punzada, *f.* (of hunger). | Herida, *f.* (of love). | Angustia, *f.*, tormento, *m.* (of jealousy). || — *The pangs of childbirth*, los dolores del parto. || *The pangs of death*, las ansias de la muerte.
Pan-Germanism [ˈpænˈdʒə:mənizəm] n. Pangermanismo, *m.*
Pan-Germanist [ˈpænˈdʒə:mənist] adj./n. Pangermanista.
pangolin [pænˈgəulin] n. Pangolín, *m.* (mammal).
panhandle [ˈpænˈhændl] n. U. S. Faja (*f.*) estrecha de un territorio que entra en otro.
panhandle [ˈpænˈhændl] v. intr. U. S. Pordiosear, mendigar, pedir limosna.
panhandler [—ə*] n. U. S. Pordiosero, *m.*, mendigo, *m.*
Panhellenism [ˈpænˈhelənizəm] n. Panhelenismo, *m.*
panic [ˈpænik] adj. Pánico, ca. || *Panic fear* o *terror*, miedo cerval *or* pánico, pavor, *m.*
— N. Pánico, *m.*: *he got into a panic*, le entró un pánico. || *To throw into a panic*, meter el miedo en el cuerpo a (a person), sembrar el pánico entre (a group of people).
panic [ˈpænik] v. intr. Asustarse, entrarle a uno pánico.
— V. tr. Sembrar el pánico entre.
— OBSERV. Pret. & p. p. ***panicked***.
panic grass [—grɑ:s] n. BOT. Panizo, *m.*
panicky [—i] adj. Lleno de pánico (person). || Alarmista (report). || *To get panicky*, entrarle a uno pánico, asustarse.
panic-stricken [—ˌstrikən] or **panic-struck** [—ˌstrʌk] adj. Preso de pánico.
Pan-Islamism [ˈpænˈizləmizəm] n. Panislamismo, *m.*
panjandrum [pənˈdʒændrəm] n. FAM. Archipámpano, *m.* (person of great self-importance).
panne [pæn] n. Pana, *f.* (soft fabric).
pannier [ˈpæniə*] n. Cesto, *m.* (basket). || Serón, *m.* (on a mule). || Cartera, *f.* (on a bicycle). || Miriñaque, *m.* (of a dress).
pannier bag [—bæg] n. Cartera, *f.* (on a bicycle). || Serón, *m.* (on a mule).
pannikin [ˈpænikin] n. Cubilete, *m.* (metal cup).
panoplied [ˈpænəplid] adj. De punta en blanco (elaborately dressed).
panoply [ˈpænəpli] n. Panoplia, *f.* || FIG. Boato, *m.*, pompa, *f.* (pomp).
panorama [ˌpænəˈrɑ:mə] n. Panorama, *m.* || CINEM. Panorámica, *f.*
panoramic [ˌpænəˈræmik] adj. Panomárico, ca: *panoramic windows*, ventanas panorámicas; *panoramic view*, vista panorámica.
panpipe [ˈpænpaip] n. MUS. Zampoña, *f.*
Pan-Slavism [ˈpænˈslɑ:vizəm] n. Paneslavismo, *m.*
Pan-Slavist [ˈpænˈslɑ:vist] adj./n. Paneslavista.
pansy [ˈpænzi] n. BOT. Pensamiento, *m.*, trinitaria, *f.* || FIG. FAM. Marica, *m.*
pant [pænt] n. Jadeo, *m.* (laboured breathing). || Latido, *m.*, palpitación, *f.* (of the heart). || Resoplido, *m.* (of an engine).
pant [pænt] v. intr. Jadear (to breathe quickly). || Palpitar, latir (to throb rapidly). || — *To pant for* o *after*, suspirar por. || *To pant for breath*, estar sin aliento, jadear.
— V. tr. *To pant out*, decir con palabras entrecortadas.
pantagruelian [pæntəgruˈeliən] adj. Pantagruélico, ca.
pantagruelism [pæntəˈgruelizəm] n. Pantagruelismo, *m.*
pantagruelist [pæntəˈgruelist] n. Pantagruelista, *m.* & *f.*
pantaloons [ˌpæntəˈlu:nz] pl. n. Pantalones, *m.*
pantechnicon [pænˈteknikən] n. Camión (*m.*) de mudanzas (furniture van).
pantheism [ˈpænθi:izəm] n. Panteísmo, *m.*
pantheist [ˈpænθi:ist] n. Panteísta, *m.* & *f.*
pantheistic [ˌpænθi:ˈistik] adj. Panteísta, panteístico, ca.
pantheon [ˈpænθiən] n. Panteón, *m.*
panther [ˈpænθə*] n. ZOOL. Pantera, *f.* || U. S. ZOOL. Puma, *m.* | Jaguar, *m.* || U. S. FIG. *Black Panthers*, panteras negras.
panties [ˈpæntiz] pl. n. Bragas, *f.*, braga, *f. sing.*
pantile [ˈpæntail] n. Teja (*f.*) flamenca.
panting [ˈpæntiŋ] n. Jadeo, *m.*
— Adj. Jadeante.
pantograph [ˈpæntəugrɑ:f] n. Pantógrafo, *m.*
pantomime [ˈpæntəmaim] n. THEATR. Pantomima, *f.* (dumb show). | Mimo, *m.* (actor). | Representación (*f.*) musical basada en cuentos de hadas que se da sobre todo por Navidades. || FAM. *It's a pantomime* o *what a pantomime!*, ¡es una farsa!, ¡qué farsa!
pantry [ˈpæntri] n. Despensa, *f.* (food store). || Oficio, *m.* (for preparing food).
pants [pænts] pl. n. Calzoncillos, *m.* (underpants). || Pantalones, *m.*, pantalón, *m. sing.* (trousers).
panty [ˈpænti] n. Bragas, *f. pl.* (panties). || *Panty girdle*, faja (*f.*) pantalón.
pantywaist [ˈpæntiweist] n. U. S. FAM. Afeminado, *m.*

Panzer [ˈpæntsə*] adj. MIL. Blindado, da: *Panzer division*, división blindada.
pap [pæp] n. Papilla, *f.* (for babies, etc.). || (Ant.). Teta, *f.*, pezón, *m.* (of breast). | Pico, *m.* (of a mountain). || U. S. FIG. Enchufe, *m.* (political patronage). | Tonterías, *f. pl.* (insubstantial reading matter, talk, etc.).
papa [pəˈpɑ:] n. Papá, *m.*
papable [ˈpeipəbl] adj. Papable.
papacy [ˈpeipəsi] n. Papado, *m.*, pontificado, *m.*
papain [pəˈpeiin] n. CHEM. Papaína, *f.*
papal [ˈpeipəl] adj. Papal: *papal decrees*, decretos papales. || — *Papal Chancery*, Cancillería Apostólica. || *Papal nuncio*, nuncio apostólico. || *Papal States*, Estados Pontificios.
papaveraceae [pəpeivəˈreisii] pl. n. BOT. Papaveráceas, *f.*
papaverine [pəˈpeivərin] n. CHEM. Papaverina, *f.*
papaw [pəˈpɔ:] or **papaya** [pəˈpaiə] n. BOT. Papaya, *f.* (fruit). | Papayo, *m.* (tree).
paper [ˈpeipə*] n. Papel, *m.* (for writing, wrapping, covering the walls, etc.): *ordinary paper*, papel corriente; *corrugated paper*, papel ondulado. || Documento, *m.*: *working papers*, documentos de trabajo. || Periódico, *m.*, diario, *m.* (newspaper): *morning paper*, periódico de la mañana; *evening paper*, diario de la tarde *or* vespertino. || Prueba, *f.* (examination): *to set a history paper*, poner una prueba de historia. || Comunicación, *f.*, ponencia, *f.*, informe, *m.* (learned composition to be read aloud): *to read a paper*, leer una comunicación. || Artículo, *m.* (written article). || Pases (*m.*) de favor (in theatre). || COMM. Efecto, *m.* || Paquete, *m.* (of pins, etc.). || — Pl. Documentación, *f. sing.*, documentos, *m.*, papeles, *m.* (to prove s.o.'s identity). || Papeles, *m.* (private documents). || — *Autographic paper*, papel autográfico. || *Ballot paper*, papeleta, *f.* || *Bible paper*, papel biblia. || *Blotting paper*, papel secante. || *Brown paper*, papel de estraza. || MIL. *Call-up papers*, llamamiento (*m.*) a filas. || *Carbon paper*, papel carbón. || *Cigarette paper*, papel de fumar. || *Coated paper*, papel cuché. || *Drawing paper*, papel de dibujo. || *Emery paper*, papel esmerilado *or* de lija, lija, *f.* || *Examination paper*, see EXAMINATION. || *Fashion paper*, revista (*f.*) de modas. || *Filter paper*, papel filtro. || *Glossy paper*, papel glaseado. || *Greaseproof paper*, papel vegetal. || *India paper*, papel de China. || *Laid paper*, papel vergé *or* verjurado. || *Litmus paper*, papel de tornasol. || *Music paper*, papel de música *or* pautado. || *On paper*, por escrito: *to put down on paper*, poner por escrito; sobre el papel, en teoría: *the project is a good one on paper*, el proyecto es bueno en teoría. || *Pelure paper*, papel cebolla. || *Rice paper*, papel de arroz. || MAR. *Ship's papers* o *boarding papers*, papeles de a bordo. || *Silver paper*, papel de plata. || *Sports paper*, periódico deportivo. || *Squared paper*, papel cuadriculado. || *Stamp* o *stamped paper*, papel sellado. || *Sticky* o *gummed paper*, papel de pegar *or* engomado. || *Tissue paper*, papel de seda. || *To commit to paper*, apuntar. || *Toilet paper*, papel higiénico *or* sánico. || *To put pen to paper*, comenzar a escribir. || FIG. *To send in one's papers*, presentar la dimisión. || *Tracing paper*, papel de calcar. || *Trade paper*, revista (*f.*) comercial. || *Untrimmed paper*, papel de barba. || *Vellum paper*, papel vitela. || *Waste paper*, papeles, *pl.* || *Waste paper basket*, cesto (*m.*) de los papeles, papelera, *f.* || *Weekly paper*, semanario, *m.* || *Wrapping paper*, papel de envolver *or* de embalar. || *Writing paper*, papel de escribir *or* de cartas.
— Adj. De papel: *a paper bag, handkerchief*, una bolsa, un pañuelo de papel. || Papelero, ra: *paper industry*, industria papelera. || FIG. Poco seguro, ra (hypothetical). || *A project still in the paper stage*, un proyecto todavía poco seguro.
paper [ˈpeipə*] v. tr. Envolver (to wrap). || Empapelar (walls).
paperback [—bæk] n. Libro (*m.*) en rústica. || *Paperback edition*, edición (*f.*) en rústica.
paperbacked [—bækt] adj. En rústica.
paper basket [—ˈbɑ:skit] n. Cesto (*m.*) de los papeles, papelera, *f.*
paperboard [—bɔ:d] n. Cartón, *m.*
paperbound [—baund] adj. En rústica.
paper boy [—bɔi] n. Repartidor (*m.*) de periódicos.
paper chase [—tʃeis] n. Juego (*m.*) que consiste en alcanzar a dos personas que han salido antes que los demás y que van sembrando papeles para señalar el camino que siguen.
paper clip [—klip] n. Sujetapapeles, *m. inv.*, clip, *m.*
paper cutter [ˈpeipəkʌtə] n. Guillotina, *f.*
paper fastener [—ˈfɑ:snə*] n. Grapa, *f.*
paper folder [—fəuldə*] n. Plegadera, *f.*
paperhanger [—ˌhæŋə*] n. Empapelador, *m.*
paperhanging [—ˌhæŋiŋ] n. Empapelado, *m.*
papering [—riŋ] n. Empapelado, *m.*
paper knife [—naif] n. Cortapapeles, *m. inv.*, plegadera, *f.*
paper mill [—mil] n. Fábrica (*m.*) de papel, papelera, *f.*
paper money [—mʌni] n. Papel (*m.*) moneda. || Billete (*m.*) de banco.
paperweight [—weit] n. Pisapapeles, *m. inv.*
paper work [—wə:k] n. Papeleo, *m.*
papery [ˈpeipəri] adj. Parecido al papel.
papier mâché [ˈpæpjeiˈmɑ:ʃei] adj. De cartón piedra
— N. Cartón (*m.*) piedra.
papilionaceae [pəpiliəˈneisii:] pl. n. BOT. Papilionáceas, *f.*
papilionaceous [pəpiliəˈneiʃəs] adj. BOT. Papilionáceo, a.
papilla [pəˈpilə] n. ANAT. Papila, *f.*
— OBSERV. El plural de *papilla* es *papillae*.
papillary [pəˈpiləri] adj. ANAT. Papilar.
papilloma [pæpiˈləumə] n. MED. Papiloma, *m.* (tumour).
— OBSERV. El plural de *papilloma* es *papillomata* o *papillomas*.
papillote [ˈpæpiˌləut] n. Papillote, *m.*
papism [ˈpeipizəm] n. REL. Papismo, *m.*
papist [ˈpeipist] adj./n. Papista.
papistic [pəˈpistik] or **papistical** [—əl] adj. Papista.
papistry [ˈpeipistri] n. Papismo, *m.*
pappy [ˈpæpi] adj. Pastoso, sa; pulposo, sa. || FIG. Blando, da (character).
— N. FAM. Papá, *m.*, papi, *m.*
paprika [ˈpæprikə] n. Paprika, *f.*, pimiento (*m.*) picante molido.
Papua [ˈpæpjuə] pr. n. GEOGR. Papuasia, *f.*
Papuan [—n] adj./n. Papú.
papyrus [pəˈpairəs] n. Papiro, *m.*
— OBSERV. El plural de la palabra inglesa *papyrus* es *papyri* o *papyruses*.
par [pɑ:] n. Igualdad, *f.* (equality). || COMM. Par, *f.*, paridad, *f.*: *at par*, a la par; *to be under, over par*, estar por debajo de, por encima de la par. || Valor (*m.*) nominal. || Promedio, *m.* (average). || SP. Par, *m.*, recorrido (*m.*) normal (in golf). || FAM. Párrafo, *m.* (paragraph). || Salmoncillo, *m.* (parr). || — *To be on a par with*, estar en un pie de igualdad con, correr parejas con. || FIG. *To feel below par*, no sentirse bien, no estar en forma. || SP. *To get round the course in four under par*, hacer el recorrido con cuatro por debajo del par. || *To put sth. on a par with*, equiparar algo con, poner algo en un pie de igualdad con.
— Adj. Normal. || COMM. A la par.
parable [ˈpærəbl] n. REL. Parábola, *f.*: *the parable of the prodigal son*, la parábola del hijo pródigo.
parabola [pəˈræbələ] n. MATH. Parábola, *f.*
parabolic [ˌpærəˈbɔlik] adj. Parabólico, ca.
parabolize [pəˈræbəlaiz] v. tr. Parabolizar.
parachute [ˈpærəʃu:t] n. Paracaídas, *m. inv.* || — *Parachute drop*, lanzamiento (*m.*) en paracaídas. || *Parachute flare*, bengala (*f.*) con paracaídas. || *Parachute jump*, salto (*m.*) en paracaídas. || *Parachute troops*, tropas (*f.*) paracaidistas.
parachute [ˈpærəʃu:t] v. intr. Saltar con paracaídas.
— V. tr. Lanzar en paracaídas.
parachuting [—iŋ] n. Lanzamiento (*m.*) en paracaídas (of arms, etc.). || Paracaidismo, *m.*: *to go in for parachuting*, practicar el paracaidismo.
parachutist [—ist] n. Paracaidista, *m.* & *f.*
parade [pəˈreid] n. Alarde, *m.*, ostentación, *f.*, gala, *f.*: *to make a parade of learning*, hacer alarde de erudición. || Paseo (*m.*) público (a promenade). || MIL. Desfile, *m.*: *parade of troops*, desfile de tropas. | Revista, *f.* (for inspection). || Desfile, *m.* (nonmilitary procession): *parade of floats*, desfile de carrozas. || Desfile, *m.*, presentación, *f.*: *fashion parade*, presentación de modelos. || SP. Quite, *m.*, parada, *f.* (fencing). || *Shopping parade*, zona (*f.*) comercial.
parade [pəˈreid] v. tr. Hacer alarde de, hacer ostentación de, hacer gala de, alardear de: *to parade one's talent*, hacer alarde de su talento. || Pasear (a banner, placard). || MIL. Pasar revista a (for inspection). | Formar (a regiment). | Hacer desfilar a (troops).
— V. intr. Pavonearse (to attract attention). || Desfilar (strikers, a model). || MIL. Desfilar (troops). || *To parade up and down*, pasearse [por]: *in the evening many Madrilenians parade up and down the Gran Via*, por la tarde muchos madrileños se pasean por la Gran Vía.
parade ground [—graund] n. MIL. Plaza (*f.*) de armas.
paradigm [ˈpærədaim] n. GRAMM. Paradigma, *m.* (example).
paradigmatic [ˌpærədigˈmætik] adj. Paradigmático, ca.
paradisaic [pærədiˈseiik] or **paradisaical** [—əl] adj. Paradisiaco, ca; paradisíaco, ca.
paradisal [ˌpærəˈdaisəl] adj. Paradisiaco, ca; paradisíaco, ca.
paradise [ˈpærədais] n. Paraíso, *m.*, Gloria, *f.*, Cielo, *m.* (heaven): *to go to paradise*, ir al Cielo. || FIG. Paraíso, *m.* (wonderful place): *a tourists' paradise*, el paraíso de los turistas. || — *Bird of paradise*, ave (*f.*) del paraíso. || *Earthly paradise*, edén, *m.*
paradisiac [ˌpærəˈdisiæk] or **paradisiacal** [ˌpærədiˈsaiəkəl] adj. Paradisiaco, ca; paradisíaco, ca.
paradox [ˈpærədɔks] n. Paradoja, *f.*
paradoxical [ˌpærəˈdɔksikəl] adj. Paradójico, ca.
paraffin [ˈpærəfin] n. Parafina, *f.* (solid). || Petróleo, *m.*, queroseno, *m.* (fuel): *paraffin lamp, stove*, lámpara, estufa de petróleo. || — *Liquid paraffin*, aceite (*m.*) de parafina, vaselina, *f.* || *Paraffin oil*, petróleo lampante, queroseno. || *Paraffin wax*, parafina, *f.*
paraffin [ˈpærəfin] v. tr. Parafinar.
paraffining [—iŋ] n. Parafinado, *m.*
paragoge [ˌpærəˈgəudʒi] n. Paragoge, *f.*

paragogic [ˌpærəˈgɔdʒik] adj. Paragógico, ca.
paragon [ˈpærəgən] n. Dechado, *m.*, modelo, *m.*: *a paragon of virtue*, un modelo de virtud. || Diamante (*m.*) sin defecto.
paragraph [ˈpærəgrɑːf] n. Párrafo, *m.* [*Amer.*, acápite, *m.*]: *a short paragraph*, un párrafo corto. || Suelto, *m.* (short article in a newspaper): *the accident got a paragraph in the Times*, hubo un suelto en el Times sobre el accidente. || Apartado, *m.* (subdivision): *the last paragraph of article three*, el último apartado del artículo tres. || *New paragraph*, punto y aparte.
paragraph [ˈpærəgrɑːf] v. tr. Dividir en párrafos.
— V. intr. Escribir sueltos *or* artículos cortos (in a newspaper).
paragrapher [—ə*] or **paragraphist** [—ist] n. Gacetillero, ra.
Paraguay [ˈpærəgwai] pr. n. GEOGR. Paraguay, *m.*
Paraguayan [ˌpærəˈgwaiən] adj./n. Paraguayo, ya.
parakeet [ˈpærəkiːt] n. Perico, *m.*, periquito, *m.* (bird).
parallax [ˈpærəlæks] n. PHYS. Paralaje, *f.*
parallel [ˈpærələl] adj. MATH. Paralelo, la: *to draw line AB parallel to CD*, trazar la línea AB paralela a CD. || FIG. Paralelo, la; similar, semejante, análogo, ga (similar): *parallel situations*, situaciones similares. | Correspondiente: *the progress of medicine and the parallel drop in the death rate*, el progreso de la medicina y la disminución correspondiente de la mortalidad. || — ELECTR. *In parallel*, en paralelo. || SP. *Parallel bars*, barras paralelas. || *To run parallel to*, correr paralelo a.
— N. MATH. Paralela, *f.* || GEOGR. Paralelo, *m.*: *the 38th parallel*, el paralelo 38. || ELECTR. Circuito (*m.*) paralelo. || FIG. Paralelo, *m.*: *one can draw a parallel between industrialization and pollution*, se puede hacer un paralelo entre la industrialización y la contaminación. || — Pl. PRINT. Barras, *f.* || FIG. *His behaviour is without parallel*, su conducta es única *or* no tiene paralelo.
parallel [ˈpærələl] v. tr. Comparar con, parangonar con (to compare): *to parallel the English parliamentary system with the French*, comparar el sistema parlamentario inglés con el francés. || Igualar a, ser comparable con, correr parejas con (to be comparable to): *his generosity parallels his amiability*, su generosidad es comparable con su amabilidad.
parallelepiped [ˌpærəleˈlepiped] n. MATH. Paralelepípedo, *m.*
parallelism [ˈpærəlelizəm] n. Paralelismo, *m.*
parallelogram [ˌpærəˈleləugræm] n. MATH. Paralelogramo, *m.*
paralogism [pəˈrælədʒizəm] n. Paralogismo, *m.*
paralyse [ˈpærəlaiz] v. tr. Paralizar: *paralysed in one leg*, paralizado de una pierna. || FIG. Paralizar: *the strike paralysed the country*, la huelga paralizó el país.
paralyser [—ə*] n. Paralizador, ra; paralizante, *m.* & *f.*
paralysing [—iŋ] adj. Paralizador, ra; paralizante.
paralysis [pəˈrælisis] n. MED. Parálisis, *f.*: *creeping paralysis*, parálisis progresiva. || FIG. Parálisis, *f.*, paralización, *f.*

— OBSERV. El plural de la palabra inglesa es *paralyses*.

paralytic [ˌpærəˈlitik] adj. Paralítico, ca. || FAM. Como una cuba (drunk).
— N. Paralítico, ca.
paralyzation [ˈpærəliˈzeiʃən] n. Paralización, *f.*
paralyze [ˈpærəlaiz] v. tr. See PARALYSE.
paramagnetic [pærəmægˈnetik] adj. Paramagnético, ca.
paramagnetism [pærəˈmægnətizəm] n. Paramagnetismo, *m.*
paramedical [ˈpærəˈmedikəl] adj. Paramédico, ca.
parament [ˈpærəmənt] n. Paramento, *m.*
parameter [pəˈræmitə*] n. MATH. Parámetro, *m.*
parametric [pærəˈmetrik] adj. Paramétrico, ca.
paramilitary [pærəˈmilitəri] adj. Paramilitar.
paramnesia [ˈpærəmˈniːzjə] n. MED. Paramnesia, *f.*
paramo [ˈpærəməu] n. Páramo, *m.*
paramount [ˈpærəmaunt] adj. Supremo, ma; extremo, ma; sumo, ma: *of paramount importance*, de extrema importancia. || Soberano, na (lord). || *Work is paramount with him*, el trabajo para él es lo más importante de todo.
paramour [ˈpærəmuə*] n. Amante, *m.* & *f.* (lover).
parang [ˈpɑːræŋ] n. Machete (*m.*) malayo.
paranoia [pærəˈnɔiə] n. MED. Paranoia, *f.*
paranoiac [—k] adj./n. MED. Paranoico, ca.
paranoid [ˈpærənɔid] adj./n. MED. Paranoico, ca.
parapet [ˈpærəpit] n. ARCH. Pretil, *m.*, antepecho, *m.* (of a bridge, balcony, etc.). || MIL. Parapeto, *m.* (of a trench). || *Parapet walk*, camino (*m.*) de ronda.
paraph [ˈpæræf] n. Rúbrica, *f.* (of a signature).
paraph [ˈpæræf] v. tr. Rubricar.
paraphernal [pærəˈfəːnl] adj. JUR. Parafernal.
paraphernalia [pærəfəːˈneiljə] n. Trastos, *m. pl.*, chismes, *m. pl.*, avíos, *m. pl.* (belongings). || Jaleo, *m.* (fuss). || JUR. Bienes (*m. pl.*) parafernales.
paraphrase [ˈpærəfreiz] n. Paráfrasis, *f. inv.*
paraphrase [ˈpærəfreiz] v. tr. Parafrasear, hacer una paráfrasis de.
paraphraser [—ə*] n. Parafraseador, ra.
paraphrastic [pærəˈfræstik] adj. Parafrástico, ca.
paraplegia [ˌpærəˈpliːdʒə] n. MED. Paraplejía, *f.*
paraplegic [—ik] adj./n. MED. Parapléjico, ca.
parapsychology [ˈpærəsaiˈkɔlədʒi] n. Parasicología, *f.*
paraselene [pærəsəˈliːni] n. Paraselene, *f.* (on the lunar halo).

— OBSERV. El plural de la palabra inglesa es *paraselenae*.

parasite [ˈpærəsait] n. Parásito, *m.* || FIG. Parásito, *m.*
parasitic [ˌpærəˈsitik] or **parasitical** [—əl] adj. Parásito, ta; parasitario, ria.
parasiticide [pærəˈsitisaid] n. Parasiticida, *m.*
— Adj. Parasiticida.
parasitism [ˈpærəsaitizəm] n. Parasitismo, *m.*
parasol [ˈpærəsɔl] n. Parasol, *m.*, sombrilla, *f.*, quitasol, *m.* (umbrella).
parasympathetic [ˈpærəsimpəˈθetik] adj. ANAT. Parasimpático, ca.
— N. Nervio (*m.*) parasimpático.
parathyroid [pærəˈθairɔid] adj. Paratiroides.
— N. Paratiroides, *f.*
paratroop [ˈpærətruːp] adj. Paracaidista.
paratrooper [—ə*] n. Soldado (*m.*) paracaidista, *m.*
paratroops [—s] n. Tropas (*f. pl.*) paracaidistas.
paratuberculosis [ˈpærətjuːˌbəːkjuˈləusis] n. MED. Paratuberculosis, *f.*
paratuberculous [ˈpærətjuːˈbəːkjuləs] adj. MED. Paratuberculoso, sa.
paratyphoid [ˈpærəˈtaifɔid] adj. MED. Paratifoideo, a.
— N. MED. Paratifoidea, *f.*
paravane [ˈpærəvein] n. MAR. Dispositivo (*m.*) contra las minas.
parboil [ˈpɑːbɔil] v. tr. CULIN. Cocer a medias, sancochar.
parbuckle [ˈpɑːbʌkl] n. MAR. Tiravira, *f.* (rope).
parbuckle [ˈpɑːbʌkl] v. tr. MAR. Arriar con la tiravira.
Parcae [ˈpɑːsiː] pl. pr. n. MYTH. Parcas, *f.* (fates).
parcel [ˈpɑːsl] n. Paquete, *m.*: *to make, to wrap a parcel*, hacer, envolver un paquete. || Parcela, *f.* (of land). || Grupo, *m.* (collection of things). || Partida, *f.* (of goods): *he bought the house and its contents in a single parcel*, compró la casa y su contenido en una sola partida. || Paquete, *m.* (of shares). || FAM. Sarta, *f.*, montón, *m.*, retahíla, *f.* (of lies). || — *Parcel delivery*, reparto (*m.*) de paquetes. || *Parcel post*, servicio (*m.*) de paquetes postales en Correos. || *Parcels office*, despacho (*m.*) de paquetes (in a railway station). || *Postal parcel*, paquete postal [*Amer.*, encomienda, *f.*]. || *To do up into parcels*, empaquetar.
parcel [ˈpɑːsl] v. tr. Empaquetar (to make into a parcel). || Envolver (to wrap). || — *To parcel out*, repartir (to share), parcelar (land). || *To parcel up*, empaquetar, embalar.
parcelling (U. S. **parceling**) [—iŋ] n. Empaquetado, *m.* (making into a parcel). || MAR. Precinta, *f.* (a strip of canvas). || Parcelación, *f.* (of land). || Reparto, *m.*, distribución, *f.* (sharing out).
parcenary [ˈpɑːsənəri] n. JUR. Herencia (*f.*) pro indiviso, copropiedad, *f.*
parcener [ˈpɑːsənə*] n. JUR. Heredero (*m.*) pro indiviso, coheredero, *m.*
parch [pɑːtʃ] v. tr. Tostar (to roast). || Secar (to dry beans, grain, etc.). || Abrasar (fever). || Resecar, agostar (sun). || *To be parched with thirst*, abrasarse de sed.
— V. intr. Resecarse.
parcheesi [pəˈtʃisi] n. Parchís, *m.*, parchesi, *m.* (game).
parchment [ˈpɑːtʃmənt] n. Pergamino, *m.* || *Parchment paper*, papel (*m.*) pergamino, pergamino vegetal.
parchment-like [—laik] adj. Apergaminado, da.
pardon [ˈpɑːdn] n. Perdón, *m.*: *to beg s.o.'s pardon*, pedir perdón a alguien. || JUR. Indulto, *m.* (release from a penalty). || REL. Indulgencia, *f.* || — JUR. *General pardon*, amnistía, *f.* || *I beg your pardon*, dispénseme, usted perdone, discúlpeme (excuse me). || *I beg your pardon?* o *pardon?*, ¿cómo? [*Amer.* ¿mande?] (what did you say?).
pardon [ˈpɑːdn] v. tr. Perdonar: *to pardon s.o. sth.*, perdonar algo a alguien. || Disculpar, dispensar, excusar (to excuse). || JUR. Indultar (to grant a pardon to). || — *Pardon me*, dispénseme, discúlpeme, perdóneme. || *Pardon my saying so*, perdone que se lo diga.
pardonable [—əbl] adj. Perdonable, excusable, disculpable.
pardonably [—əbli] adv. Con toda la razón: *he was pardonably furious*, estaba furioso y con toda la razón.
pardoner [—ə*] n. REL. Vendedor (*m.*) de indulgencias.
pare [pɛə*] v. tr. Pelar, mondar (fruit). || Cortar (nails). || Refilar (in bookbinding). || *To pare down*, disminuir, reducir (to reduce).
parenchyma [pəˈreŋkimə] n. Parénquima, *m.*
parent [ˈpɛərənt] n. Padre, *m.*, madre, *f.* (father, mother). || FIG. Madre, *f.*, causa, *f.*, origen, *m.* (source): *wealth is the parent of idleness*, la riqueza es madre de la ociosidad. || — Pl. Padres, *m.*: *our first parents*, nuestros primeros padres. || — *Parent branch*, rama (*f.*) principal (of a tree). || *Parent company, establishment*, casa central, casa matriz. || *Parent ship*, barco (*m.*) nodriza. || *Parent state*, madre (*f.*) patria.
parentage [—idʒ] n. Extracción, *f.*, linaje, *m.*, familia, *f.* || *Born of humble parentage*, de humilde cuna.

parental [pə'rentl] adj. De los padres, paternal, maternal.

parenthesis [pə'renθisis] n. Paréntesis, *m. inv.*: *in parentheses*, entre paréntesis.

— OBSERV. El plural de esta palabra es *parentheses*.

parenthesize [pə'renθesaiz] v. tr. Poner entre paréntesis.

parenthetic [pærən'θetik] or **parenthetical** [—əl] adj. Entre paréntesis.

parenthood ['pεərənthud] n. Paternidad, *f.*, maternidad, *f.* || *The joys of parenthood*, la alegría de tener hijos.

par excellence [pɑ:r'eksəlɑ̃:ns] adv. Por excelencia.

parget ['pɑ:dʒit] n. Enlucido, *m.*

parget ['pɑ:dʒit] v. tr. Enlucir.

parhelion [pɑ:'hi:ljən] n. ASTR. Parhelio, *m.*, parhelia, *f.*

— OBSERV. El plural de la palabra inglesa es *parhelia*.

pariah ['pæriə] n. Paria, *m.* & *f.*

parietal [pə'raiitl] adj. ANAT. Parietal. || *Parietal bone*, parietal, *m.*

pari-mutuel ['pæri'mju:tjuəl] n. Apuestas (*f. pl.*) mutuas (betting system). || Totalizador, *m.* (machine).

paring ['pεəriŋ] n. Mondadura, *f.*, peladura, *f.* (of a fruit). || Corte, *m.* (of nails). || Refilado, *m.* (of books).

pari passu ['pæri'pæsu:] adv. Al mismo ritmo.

Paris ['pæris] pr. n. Paris, *m.* (son of Priam).

Paris ['pæris] pr. n. GEOGR. París (capital of France).

parish ['pæriʃ] n. REL. Parroquia, *f.* (of a church). || Municipio, *m.* (division of local government). || — *Parish church*, parroquia, iglesia (*f.*) parroquial. || *Parish clerk*, sacristán, *m.* || *Parish council*, concejo (*m.*) municipal. || *Parish priest*, párroco, *m.* || *Parish register*, registro (*m.*) parroquial. || *To go on the parish*, correr a cargo del municipio.

parishioner [pə'riʃənə*] n. REL. Feligrés, esa.

parish-pump ['pæriʃ'pʌmp] adj. FAM. Pueblerino, na; localista: *parish-pump politics*, política pueblerina.

Parisian [pə'rizjən] adj./n. Parisiense, parisino, na.

parisyllabic ['pærisi'læbik] adj. Parisílabo, ba; parisilábico, ca.

parity ['pæriti] n. Igualdad, *f.*, paridad, *f.* (equality). || COMM. Paridad, *f.*: *the parity of the dollar*, la paridad del dólar; *exchange parities*, paridades de cambio.

park [pɑ:k] n. Parque, *m.*: *public park*, parque público. || U. S. Terreno, *m.* (baseball). || — *Car park*, aparcamiento (*m.*) de coches, parking, *m.* || MIL. *Gun park*, parque de artillería. || *Oyster park*, criadero (*m.*) de ostras, ostral, *m.*, ostrero, *m.*

park [pɑ:k] v. tr. Estacionar, aparcar [*Amer.*, parquear] (a vehicle). || AGR. Meter en el aprisco (sheep). || MIL. Poner en un parque de artillería. || FAM. Dejar (to deposit). || FAM. *To park o.s.*, instalarse.

— V. intr. Estacionarse, aparcar [*Amer.*, parquear].

parkerization [pɑ:kərai'zeiʃən] n. TECH. Parkerización, *f.*

parkin ['pɑ:kin] n. Bizcocho (*m.*) de avena y melaza.

parking ['pɑ:kiŋ] n. Aparcamiento, *m.*, estacionamiento, *m.* (of cars). || — *No parking*, prohibido aparcar. || *Parking attendant*, guardacoches, *m. inv.* || *Parking lights*, luces (*f. pl.*) de estacionamiento. || *Parking lot*, aparcamiento [*Amer.*, playa (*f.*) de estacionamiento]. || *Parking meter*, parcómetro, *m.*, parquímetro, *m.*, contador (*m.*) de aparcamiento. || *Parking space*, aparcamiento, sitio (*m.*) para aparcar.

parkway ['pɑ:kwei] n. Avenida, *f.*

parky ['pɑ:ki] adj. FAM. Frío, a; fresquito, ta.

parlance ['pɑ:ləns] n. Habla, *f.*, lenguaje, *m.* || *In common parlance*, en la lengua hablada, en el habla corriente.

parley ['pɑ:li] n. Conversación, *f.*, negociaciones, *f. pl.*, parlamento, *m.* || *To hold a parley with*, parlamentar con.

parley ['pɑ:li] v. intr. Parlamentar.

parliament ['pɑ:ləmənt] n. Parlamento, *m.* || Cortes, *f. pl.* (in Spain). || — *Houses of Parliament*, Parlamento, *m.* || *Member of Parliament*, miembro (*m.*) del Parlamento, diputado, *m.*

parliamentarian [ˌpɑ:ləmen'tεəriən] adj./n. Parlamentario, ria.

parliamentarianism [ˌpɑ:ləmen'tεəriənizm] n. Parlamentarismo, *m.*

parliamentary [ˌpɑ:ləmen'təri] adj. Parlamentario, ria. || *Parliamentary elections*, elecciones legislativas.

parlour (U. S. **parlor**) ['pɑ:lə*] n. Salón, *m.*, sala (*f.*) de recibir (in a house). || Locutorio, *m.* (of convent). || — *Bar parlour*, reservado, *m.* (in an inn). || *Beauty parlour*, salón (*m.*) de belleza, instituto (*m.*) de belleza. || *Funeral parlour*, funeraria, *f.* || *Hairdressing parlour*, peluquería, *f.* || *Ice-cream parlour*, heladería, *f.* || U. S. *Parlor car*, coche (*m.*) salón. || *Parlour game*, juego (*m.*) de sociedad.

parlourmaid (U. S. **parlormaid**) [—meid] n. Doncella, *f.*, criada (*f.*) de cuerpo de casa [*Amer.*, mucama, *f.*]

parlous ['pɑ:ləs] adj. Alarmante, peligroso, sa.

Parmesan [ˌpɑ:mi'zæn] adj./n. Parmesano, na. || *Parmesan cheese*, queso parmesano.

Parnassian [pɑ:'næsiən] adj./n. Parnasiano, na.

Parnassus [pɑ:'næsəs] pr. n. GEOGR. Parnaso, *m.*

parochial [pə'rəukjəl] adj. REL. Parroquial, de la parroquia (of a parish). || Municipal (of a civil parish). || FIG. Localista, pueblerino, na: *to have a parochial outlook*, tener una mentalidad pueblerina.

parochialism [—izəm] n. Mentalidad (*f.*) pueblerina, mentalidad (*f.*) localista (narrowness of opinions).

parodic ['pərɔdik] or **parodical** [—əl] adj. Paródico, ca.

parodist ['pærədist] n. Parodista, *m.*

parody ['pærədi] n. Parodia, *f.*

parody ['pærədi] v. tr. Parodiar, hacer una parodia de.

parole [pə'rəul] n. Palabra (*f.*) de honor (promise). || Libertad (*f.*) bajo palabra (of a prisoner). || U. S. Libertad (*f.*) condicional. || MIL. Santo (*m.*) y seña. || — *To break parole* o *one's parole*, faltar a su palabra. || *To put* o *to release on parole*, liberar bajo palabra.

parole [pə'rəul] v. tr. Liberar bajo palabra. || U. S. Poner en libertad condicional.

parolee [ˌpərəu'li] n. U. S. Persona (*f.*) en libertad condicional.

paronomasia [pərɔnə'meiziə] n. Paronomasia, *f.*

paronym ['pærənim] n. GRAMM. Parónimo, *m.*

paronymy [pə'rɔnimi] n. Paronimia, *f.*

paronymous [pə'rɔniməs] adj. GRAMM. Paronímico, ca; parónimo, ma.

parotid [pə'rɔtid] n. ANAT. Parótida, *f.*

parotitis [pærə'taitəs] n. MED. Parotiditis, *f.*

paroxysm ['pærəksizəm] n. Paroxismo, *m.* || FIG. Paroxismo, *m.* (extreme stage). | Crisis, *f.*, ataque, *m.* (of laughter, rage, etc.).

paroxytone [pə'rɔksitəun] adj. GRAMM. Paroxítono, na.

— N. GRAMM. Paroxítono, *m.*

parpen ['pɑ:pen] n. ARCH. Perpiaño, *m.*

parquet ['pɑ:kei] n. Entarimado, *m.*, parqué, *m.* (floor). || U. S. Patio (*m.*) de butacas (theatre).

parquet ['pɑ:kei] v. tr. Entarimar, poner parqué a.

parquet flooring [—'flɔ:riŋ] n. Entarimado, *m.*

parquetry ['pɑ:kətri] n. Entarimado, *m.*

parr [pɑ:*] n. Salmoncillo, *m.*, cría (*f.*) de salmón (fish).

parrakeet [pærə'ki:t] n. Perico, *m.*, periquito, *m.* (bird).

parricidal [ˌpæri'saidl] adj. Parricida.

parricide ['pærisaid] n. Parricida, *m.* & *f.* (person). || Parricidio, *m.* (crime).

parrot ['pærət] n. Loro, *m.*, papagayo, *m.* (bird). || FIG. Loro, *m.*, cotorra, *f.*, papagayo, *m.* (who repeats mechanically). || — MED. *Parrot disease* o *fever*, psitacosis, *f. inv.* || FIG. *Parrot fashion*, como un loro, mecánicamente.

parrot ['pærət] v. tr. Repetir como un loro.

parry ['pæri] n. Quite, *m.*, parada, *f.*

parry ['pæri] v. tr. Parar (a blow). || Parar, quitar (in fencing). || Rechazar (an attack). || FIG. Evitar, sortear (a difficulty). | Eludir (a question).

parse [pɑ:z] v. tr. GRAMM. Analizar gramaticalmente.

parsec [pɑ:'sek] n. ASTR. Parsec, *m.*

parsimonious [pɑ:si'məunjəs] adj. Parsimonioso, sa; parco, ca (sparing). || Frugal, escaso, sa: *parsimonious meal*, comida frugal. || Parsimonioso, sa; avaro, ra (mean).

parsimony ['pɑ:siməni] n. Parsimonia, *f.*, parquedad, *f.*, escasez, *f.* (frugality). || Parsimonia, *f.* avaricia, *f.* (meanness).

parsley ['pɑ:sli] n. BOT. Perejil, *m.*

parsnip ['pɑ:snip] n. BOT. Pastinaca, *f.*, chirivía, *f.*

parson ['pɑ:sn] n. REL. Sacerdote, *m.*, cura, *m.* (priest). || Pastor, *m.* (protestant). || FAM. *Parson's nose*, curcusilla, *f.*, rabadilla, *f.* (of a chicken).

parsonage [—idʒ] n. Casa (*f.*) del cura *or* parroquial, rectoral, *f.*

part [pɑ:t] n. Parte, *f.*: *part of the book is damaged*, una parte del libro está estropeada; *fifteen minutes is a fourth part of an hour*, quince minutos son la cuarta parte de una hora; *the greater part*, la mayor parte; *to be part of*, formar parte de. || Parte, *f.*: *on my part*, de mi parte; *on the part of*, de parte de; *on the one part..., on the other part ...*, por una parte ..., por otra... || Partido, *m.* (side): *to take s.o.'s part*, tomar el partido de alguien. || Deber, *m.* (duty): *to do one's part*, cumplir con su deber. || TECH. Pieza, *f.* (of a machine): *spare parts*, piezas de recambio *or* de repuesto. || Fascículo, *m.*, entrega, *f.* (of a serial publication). || THEATR. Papel, *m.*: *to play a part*, desempeñar un papel; *how did he play his part?*, ¿cómo representó su papel? || MUS. Parte, *f.*: *to sing the baritone part*, cantar la parte de barítono. || GRAMM. Parte, *f.*: *parts of speech*, partes de la oración. | Tiempo, *m.* (of a verb). || JUR. Parte, *f.* (in a transaction, dispute): *the other part*, la parte adversaria. || U. S. Raya (*f.*) del pelo (in hair). || — Pl. Regiones, *f.*, parajes, *m.*: *in tropical parts*, en regiones tropicales. || FIG. Talento, *m. sing.* (abilities): *a man of parts*, un hombre de talento. || ANAT. Partes, *f.* (genitals). || — *Aliquot part*, parte alícuota. || THEATR. *Bit part*, papel secundario. || *For my part*, en cuanto a mí, por lo que a mí se refiere, por mi parte. || *For the most part*, en la mayor parte. || *In foreign parts*, en el extranjero. || *In parts*, en parte: *the film is good in parts*, la película es buena en parte. || *In the early part of the week*, al principio de la semana. || *In these parts*, en estos parajes, por aquí. || FIG. *Part and parcel*, parte integrante *or* esencial.

|| ANAT. *Private parts*, partes pudendas *or* vergonzosas. || *The best part was when he...*, lo mejor fue cuando... || *The difficult part*, la parte difícil, lo difícil. || *The funny part about it is that*, lo gracioso del caso es que. || FIG. *To be just playing a part*, hacer teatro. || *To be three parts gone*, haberse gastado *or* consumido las tres cuartas partes. || *To have a part in*, tener algo que ver en. || *To have no part in*, no tener nada que ver en. || *To look the part*, encajar muy bien en el papel. || FIG. *To play a part in*, desempeñar un papel en. || *To sing in parts*, cantar a varias voces. || *To take in good, in bad part*, tomar en buena, en mala parte. || *To take part in*, participar en, tomar parte en. || *X parts of whisky to Y of water*, X partes de whisky e Y de agua.
— Adj. Parcial.
— Adv. En parte: *it is part finished*, está en parte terminado; *it is part wool, part nylon*, es en parte lana y en parte nylon.

part [pɑ:t] v. tr. Dividir [en dos] (to divide). || Separar: *he parted the fighting dogs*, separó a los perros que se peleaban. || Abrirse paso entre (the crowd). || Repartir (to share). || MAR. Romper (a cable). || — *To part company with*, separarse de. || *To part one's hair*, hacerse la raya.
— V. intr. Separarse (to separate): *he parted from her on bad terms*, se separó de ella en malos términos. || Despedirse, separarse (to say goodbye): *we parted at 10 o'clock*, nos separamos a las diez. || Abrirse (to draw apart): *the curtains parted*, las cortinas se abrieron. || Apartarse: *the crowd parted*, se apartó la multitud. || Romperse: *the rope parted in the middle*, la cuerda se rompió por en medio. || Bifurcarse (a road). || *To part with*, tener que separarse de: *I hate parting with my piano*, no me gusta tener que separarme del piano; deshacerse de (to get rid of), gastar (money), pagar, gastar (a certain sum): *I had to part with ten pounds*, tuve que gastar diez libras.

partake* [pɑ:ˈteik] v. intr. Participar, tomar parte (*in*, en) [to take part]. || — *To partake of*, compartir (to share): *to partake of s.o.'s meal*, compartir la comida con alguien; comer (to eat): *he partook of his dinner alone*, comió la cena solo; beber, tomar (to drink): *to partake of a glass of wine*, beber una copa de vino; tener algo de, participar de (to have some of the qualities of). || REL. *To partake of the Sacrament*, acercarse a la Sagrada Comunión, confesarse y comulgar.
— OBSERV. Pret. ***partook;*** p. p. ***partaken.***

partaken [—ən] p. p. See PARTAKE.
partaker [—ə*] n. Participante, *m.* & *f.*
parterre [pɑ:ˈtɛə*] n. Cuadro, *m.*, arriate, *m.* (of a garden). || Patio (*m.*) de butacas (theatre).
part exchange [pɑ:tiksˈtʃeindʒ] n. COMM. Cambio (*m.*) de un objeto por otro mejor pagando la diferencia. || COMM. *To offer, to take a car in part exchange*, ofrecer, tomar un coche como pago parcial de otro.
part-exchange [pɑ:tiksˈtʃeindʒ] v. tr. COMM. Cambiar [algún objeto] por otro mejor pagando la diferencia.
parthenogenesis [ˈpɑ:θinəuˈdʒenisis] n. Partenogénesis, *f.*
Parthenon [ˈpɑ:θinən] pr. n. Partenón, *m.*
Parthian [ˈpɑ:θjən] adj./n. HIST. Parto, ta: *Parthian shot*, flecha del parto.
partial [ˈpɑ:ʃəl] adj. Parcial: *a partial explanation*, una explicación parcial; *partial eclipse*, eclipse parcial. || Parcial (biased): *a partial judgment*, un juicio parcial. || FAM. Aficionado, da (fond of): *David is very partial to claret*, David es muy aficionado al clarete.
partiality [ˌpɑ:ʃiˈæliti] n. Parcialidad, *f.* (bias). || FAM. Predilección, *f.*, afición, *f.*, inclinación, *f.* (fondness): *a partiality for sweets*, una afición a los dulces.
partible [ˈpɑ:təbl] adj. Divisible, que se puede dividir.
participant [pɑ:ˈtisipənt] adj./n. Participante, partícipe.
participate [pɑ:ˈtisipeit] v. intr. Participar, tomar parte (to take part): *to participate in a game*, participar en un juego. || FAM. Tener algo (*of*, de) [to have some of the qualities of].
participating [—iŋ] adj. Participante. || *Participating stock*, acciones (*f. pl.*) preferenciales.
participation [pɑ:ˌtisiˈpeiʃən] n. Participación, *f.*
participator [pɑ:ˈtisipeitə*] n. Participante, *m.* & *f.*, partícipe, *m.* & *f.*
participle [ˈpɑ:tisipl] n. GRAMM. Participio, *m.*: *present participle*, participio de presente *or* activo; *past participle*, participio pasivo *or* de pretérito.
particle [ˈpɑ:tikl] n. Partícula, *f.* || Grano, *m.* (of dust). || FIG. Pizca, *f.*, átomo, *m.* (of common sense, truth). || GRAMM. Partícula, *f.* || PHYS. Partícula, *f.*: *particle accelerator*, acelerador (*m.*) de partículas.
parti-coloured (U. S. **parti-colored**) [ˈpɑ:tiˌkʌləd] adj. Abigarrado, da; con colores entremezclados, multicolor.
particular [pəˈtikjulə*] adj. Particular: *I have nothing particular to do*, no tengo nada particular que hacer. || Concreto, ta: *each particular case*, cada caso concreto. || Cierto, ta; determinado, da: *a particular object*, cierto objeto, un objeto determinado. || Especial: *take particular care not to offend him*, ten especial cuidado en no ofenderle; *she left me for no particular reason*, me dejó sin ninguna razón especial. || Detallado, da; minucioso, sa (with details): *a particular account of what occurred*, un relato detallado de lo que ocurrió. || Exigente (demanding): *he is very particular about punctuality*, es muy exigente con la puntualidad. || Exigente, delicado, da (about food): *she is very particular about what she eats*, es muy delicada con lo que come. || Personal: *my own particular sentiments*, mis propios sentimientos personales. || Íntimo, ma: *he is a particular friend of mine*, es un íntimo amigo mío. || — *I'm not particular about it*, me da igual, me da lo mismo, le doy poca importancia. || *In particular*, particularmente, especialmente, principalmente. || *That particular person*, aquella persona en particular.
— N. Detalle, *m.*, pormenor, *m.* (detail): *he gave me full particulars*, me dio todos los detalles. || *For further particulars apply to*, si desea más información diríjase a. || *In every particular*, en todos los detalles. || *Please give full particulars*, se ruega dar una información completa. || *To go into particulars*, entrar en pormenores.

particularism [—rizəm] n. Particularismo, *m.*
particularist [—rist] adj./n. Particularista.
particularistic [—ˈristik] adj. Particularista.
particularity [pəˌtikjuˈlæriti] n. Particularidad, *f.* || Minuciosidad, *f.*, lo detallado (of a description).
particularization [pətikjuləˈraiˈzeiʃən] n. Particularización, *f.*
particularize [pəˈtikjuləraiz] v. tr. Particularizar.
— V. intr. Especificar, concretar, entrar en detalles.
particularly [pəˈtikjuləli] adv. Particularmente, especialmente (especially): *it is particularly well done*, está especialmente bien hecho. || En particular, sobre todo, particularmente (in particular). || *I am not particularly rich*, no soy muy rico.
parting [ˈpɑ:tiŋ] n. Separación, *f.* || Despedida, *f.* (departure). || Ruptura, *f.* (of a cable). || Raya, *f.* (in the hair). || FIG. *To be at the parting of the ways*, estar en la encrucijada *or* en el momento crucial (critical point), haber llegado al momento de separarse (point of separation).
— Adj. De despedida (farewell): *parting visit*, visita de despedida. || Último, ma (words).
partisan [ˌpɑ:tiˈzæn] adj. Partidista (of a party): *partisan spirit*, espíritu partidista. || Partidario, ria (of a supporter). || MIL. De guerrilleros (of guerrillas).
— N. Partidario, ria (adept). || Seguidor, ra; partidario, ria (of a doctrine). || MIL. Guerrillero, *m.* (in guerrilla warfare). || *Partisan warfare*, guerrilla, *f.*
partisanship [—ʃip] n. Partidismo, *m.*
partition [pɑ:ˈtiʃən] n. División, *f.* || Parte, *f.* (section). || Tabique, *m.* (thin wall): *wooden partition*, tabique de madera.
partition [pɑ:ˈtiʃən] v. tr. Dividir. || Repartir (to share). || Poner un tabique a, tabicar (a room). || *To partition off*, separar con un tabique.
partitive [ˈpɑ:titiv] adj. Partitivo, va.
— N. GRAMM. Partitivo, *m.*
partizan [ˌpɑ:tiˈzæn] n. See PARTISAN.
partner [ˈpɑ:tnə*] n. Asociado, da; socio, cia (in business): *senior partner*, socio más antiguo. || Asociado, da; miembro asociado (of an organization): *our Common Market partners*, los demás asociados del Mercado Común. || Firmante, *m.* & *f.*; partícipe, *m.* & *f.* (of a treaty). || Interlocutor, ra (in a conversation). || Pareja, *f.* (in dancing): *take your partners, please*, elijan su pareja por favor. || Compañero, ra; pareja, *f.* (in cards, etc.). || SP. Pareja, *f.* || Cónyuge, *m.* & *f.*, consorte, *m.* & *f.* (husband, wife). || — Pl. TECH. Fogonadura, *f. sing.* || — *Partner in crime*, codelincuente, *m.* & *f.* || COMM. *Sleeping partner*, socio comanditario.
partner [ˈpɑ:tnə*] v. tr. Estar asociado con, asociarse con. || Acompañar, ser pareja de (in a dance).
partnership [—ʃip] n. Asociación, *f.* || Sociedad, *f.* (firm): *limited partnership*, sociedad en comandita. || Vida (*f.*) conyugal (married life). || — *To go into partnership with*, asociarse con. || *To take into partnership*, tomar como socio.
partook [pɑ:ˈtuk] pret. See PARTAKE.
part owner [ˈpɑ:tˈəunə*] n. Copropietario, ria.
partridge [ˈpɑ:tridʒ] n. Perdiz, *f.* (bird). || *Young partridge*, perdigón, *m.*
partridge-hunting [—ˈhʌntiŋ] adj. Perdiguero, ra: *partridge-hunting dog*, perro perdiguero.
part-song [ˈpɑ:tsɔŋ] n. MUS. Canción (*f.*) a varias voces.
part time [ˈpɑ:tˈtaim] adv. [A] media jornada: *to work part time*, trabajar media jornada.
— N. *To be on part time*, trabajar media jornada.
part-time [ˈpɑ:tˈtaim] adj. De media jornada: *a part-time job*, un trabajo de media jornada. || Que trabaja a media jornada: *a part-time typist*, un mecanógrafo que trabaja a media jornada.
parturient [pɑ:ˈtjuəriənt] adj. Parturienta
parturition [ˌpɑ:tjuəˈriʃən] n. Parto, *m.* (childbirth).
partway [ˈpɑ:tˈwei] adv. En parte, parcialmente.
party [ˈpɑ:ti] n. Partido, *m.*: *political parties*, partidos políticos; *Labour, Liberal, Conservative party*, partido laborista, liberal, conservador. || Partida, *f.*: *a shooting party*, una partida de caza. || Grupo, *m.*: *will you join our party?*, ¿quiere unirse a nuestro grupo?; *a*

party of tourists, un grupo de turistas. || JUR. Parte, *f.* (in a dispute, agreement, etc.): *contracting parties*, partes contratantes. || Reunión, *f.* (gathering). || Fiesta, *f.* (reception): *to give a birthday party*, dar una fiesta de cumpleaños. || Guateque, *m.*, fiesta, *f.* (young people's gathering). || Equipo, *m.*: *rescue party*, equipo de salvamento. || Cuadrilla, *f.* (of workers, bandits). || MIL. Destacamento, *m.* || Cómplice, *m.* & *f.*: *to be party to a crime*, ser cómplice en un crimen. || FAM. Individuo, *m.* (person): *a party of the name of Brown*, un individuo llamado Brown. || — *Dancing party*, baile, *m.* || *Dinner party*, cena, *f.* || MIL. *Firing party*, pelotón (*m.*) de ejecución, piquete (*m.*) de ejecución. || *Party dress*, traje (*m.*) de vestir. || *Party games*, juegos (*m.*) de sociedad. || *Party line*, línea política del partido (of a political group), línea telefónica compartida entre varios abonados (telephone), linde, *f.*, lindero, *m.* (between two properties). || *Party politics*, política (*f.*) de partidos (system), politiqueo, *m.* (political jobbery). || *Party spirit*, partidismo, *m.* || *Party ticket*, billete (*m.*) de grupo. || *Party wall*, pared medianera. || *Tea party*, té, *m.* || JUR. *Third party*, tercero, *m.* || *Third party insurance*, seguro (*m.*) contra tercera persona. || *To be a party to*, participar en, tener algo que ver con (to participate), estar interesado en (financially). || *To be a party to an agreement*, firmar un acuerdo. || *To be one of the party*, ser miembro del grupo.

parvenu [ˈpɑːvənjuː] n. Nuevo rico, nueva rica; advenedizo, za; arribista, *m.* & *f.*

parvis [ˈpɑːvis] n. ARCH. Atrio, *m.*

pas [pɑː] inv. n. Paso, *m.*

pascal [ˈpæskæl] n. Pascal, *m.* (pressure unit).

paschal [ˈpɑːskəl] adj. Pascual: *paschal lamb*, cordero pascual; *paschal candle*, cirio pascual.

pasha [ˈpɑːʃə] n. Bajá, *m.*, pachá, *m.*

pasquinade [pæskwiˈneid] n. Pasquín, *m.* (lampoon).

pass [pɑːs] n. GEOGR. Puerto, *m.*, desfiladero, *m.* || MAR. Paso, *m.*, pasaje, *m.* || Aprobado, *m.* (in an examination). || Pase, *m.* (document): *you need a pass to get into the research laboratories*, hace falta un pase para entrar en los laboratorios de investigación. || MIL. Permiso, *m.*: *to be on pass*, estar con permiso. || SP. Pase, *m.* (in football, etc.): *forward pass*, pase adelantado. | Pase, *m.* (in bullfighting, in fencing). || Pasa, *f.* (in cards). || Pase, *m.* (of a conjurer). || Pase (*m.*) de favor (in a theatre). || Billete (*m.*) de favor (on the railway). || FIG. Paso, *m.*, situación, *f.* (situation): *things have come to a pretty pass*, las cosas están en un mal paso. || TECH. Pasada, *f.* || — *It came to pass that*, ocurrió que. || *To bring to pass*, llevar a cabo. || *To get a pass in*, aprobar en (an exam). || FIG. *To make a pass at*, intentar conquistar. | *To sell the pass*, traicionar al país *or* al partido.

pass [pɑːs] v. intr. Pasar (to move along): *to pass before one's eyes*, pasar ante los ojos de uno; *will you pass into the dining room please?*, ¿quieren ustedes pasar al comedor, por favor? || Pasar, transcurrir (time): *a fortnight passed*, pasaron quince días. || Pasar, ocurrir (to happen): *I know what has passed*, sé lo que ha pasado. || Desaparecer (to disappear): *to pass into darkness*, desaparecer en la oscuridad. || Aprobar (in an examination): *to pass in maths*, aprobar en matemáticas. || Ser aprobado *or* adoptado (bill). || Ser aceptado (theory). || Tener curso legal (coin). || Aceptarse, admitirse: *what passes in Sweden*, lo que se admite en Suecia. || SP. Pasar, hacer un pase. || Pasar (in cards). || — *Be it said in passing*, dicho sea de paso. || *He passes for a liberal*, pasa por liberal. || *To let sth. pass*, dejar pasar algo, tolerar algo (a fault), dejar pasar (an opportunity). || *To pass into oblivion*, ser olvidado, caer en el olvido. || *To pass out of sight*, perderse de vista.

— V. tr. Pasar, cruzar, atravesar (to cross over): *to pass a river*, pasar un río; *to pass the frontier*, cruzar la frontera. || Pasar por delante de: *I passed your house yesterday*, pasé por delante de su casa ayer. || Cruzarse con: *I passed her on the street*, me crucé con ella en la calle. || Pasar: *to pass the thread through the eye of the needle*, pasar el hilo por el ojo de la aguja; *pass the sponge over the table*, pasa la esponja por la mesa. || Pasar (time): *they passed ten days in San Sebastian*, pasaron diez días en San Sebastián. || Aprobar (an examination, a candidate). || Aprobar, adoptar (a bill, a motion). || COMM. Aprobar (an invoice). || Aprobar, dar el visto bueno a: *the censor has passed the play*, la censura ha dado el visto bueno a la obra. || Ser aprobado *or* ser adoptado por: *bill that has passed the House of Commons*, ley que ha sido aprobada por la Cámara de los Comunes. || Tener el visto bueno de, ser aprobado por: *to pass the censor*, tener el visto bueno de la censura. || Superar, sobrepasar (to supass). || Pasar: *please, pass me that book, the salt*, por favor pásame ese libro, la sal. || Pasar (counterfeit money). || Escamotear (conjurer). || AUT. Pasar, adelantar (to overtake): *he passed me at a hundred miles an hour*, me adelantó a cien millas por hora. || Expresar (an opinion). || Hacer (a comment). || JUR. Pronunciar, dictar (a judgment). || SP. Pasar (ball). | Adelantar, dejar atrás (to overtake). || CULIN. Pasar, colar (through a sieve). || MED. Evacuar (faeces). || — *To pass each other*, cruzarse. || *To pass in review*, pasar revista a. || *To pass s.o. fit*, dar a alguien de alta (after illness), declarar a alguien apto (for military service).

— ***To pass across***, cruzar (street). | Pasar (a ball). || ***To pass along***, pasar por (street). | Pasar: *the procession passed along in perfect order*, el desfile pasó en un orden perfecto. | Pasar: *pass along the tray*, pasa la bandeja. | — *Pass along!*, ¡pasen para adelante! || ***To pass away***, pasar, desaparecer (to disappear). | Pasar a mejor vida (to die). | Pasar (time). || ***To pass by***, pasar (to go past). | Pasar por (to call in at): *I'll pass by your house tomorrow*, pasaré por su casa mañana. | Pasar de largo (to go straight past). | Pasar por alto, dejar de lado (to ignore). | Hacer caso omiso de (not to take into account). | Dejar pasar (a fault). || ***To pass down***, pasar para adelante. || ***To pass in***, entrar. || ***To pass off***, pasar. | Pasar (counterfeit money). | Hacer pasar (*as*, por) [to make sth. out to be]. | — *To pass off with*, disimular con. | *To pass o.s. off as*, hacerse pasar por. || ***To pass on***, pasar: *to pass on to a new subject*, pasar a un nuevo tema. | Pasar a mejor vida (to die). | Seguir para adelante. | Pasar, transmitir (news). | Dar: *to pass a message on to s.o.*, dar un mensaje a alguien. | Pasar: *read this and pass it on to the others*, lee esto y pásalo a los demás. || ***To pass out***, salir (to go out). | Desmayarse (to faint). | Pasar a mejor vida (to die). | Repartir, distribuir (to give out). | Graduarse (from school, academy). || ***To pass over***, cruzar (to cross over). | Hacer caso omiso de, pasar por alto, dejar de lado (to ignore). | Pasarse: *the soldier passed over to the enemy*, el soldado se pasó al enemigo. | Dar, transmitir (to give). | Decir (to say). | Alejarse (a storm). | Disiparse (clouds). | — FIG. *To pass s.o. over*, postergar a uno. || ***To pass round***, dar la vuelta a (an obstacle, a village). | Pasar de mano en mano: *the book passed round*, el libro pasó de mano en mano. | Pasar: *pass round the pastries*, pasa los pasteles. || ***To pass through***, pasar por: *to pass through Madrid*, pasar por Madrid. | Cruzar, atravesar (to cross): *we passed through Germany in two days*, cruzamos Alemania en dos días. | FIG. Pasar por: *the economy is passing through a crisis*, la economía está pasando por una crisis. || ***To pass up***, rechazar (to decline): *to pass up an offer*, rechazar una oferta. | Dejar pasar (an opportunity). | Renunciar a (hopes).

passable [—əbl] adj. Pasable, tolerable, admisible, aceptable, pasadero, ra (good enough). || Atravesable (river). || Transitable (road). || Promulgable (law).

passably [—i] adv. Bastante: *passably good*, bastante bueno.

passacaglia [ˌpæsəˈkɑːljə] n. MUS. Pasacalle, *m.*

passade [pəˈseid] n. Pasada, *f.* (of a horse).

passage [ˈpæsidʒ] n. Pasaje, *m.*, paso, *m.* (way): *underground passage*, pasaje subterráneo. || Callejón, *m.* (alley). || Corredor, *m.*, pasillo, *m.*, pasadizo, *m.* (in a house). || Paso, *m.*: *the passage of time*, el paso del tiempo. || Trozo, *m.*, pasaje, *m.* (of a book): *selected passages*, trozos escogidos. || Aprobación, *f.*: *the passage of a bill through Parliament*, la aprobación de un proyecto de ley por el Parlamento. || Paso, *m.* (passing). || MAR. Travesía, *f.* (crossing). | Pasaje, *m.* (ticket). || ANAT. Tubo, *m.* || Paso, *m.*: *birds of passage*, aves de paso. || MUS. Pasaje, *m.* || Paso (*m.*) de costado (of a horse). || — *Free passage* o *access*, paso franco *or* libre. || *Passage of arms*, combate, *m.*

passage money [—ˈmʌni] n. MAR. Pasaje, *m.*

passageway [—wei] n. Callejón, *m.* (alley). || Corredor, *m.*, pasillo, *m.* (in a house).

passant [ˈpæsənt] adj. HERALD. Pasante.

passbook [ˈpɑːsbuk] n. Libreta (*f.*) de depósitos.

pass degree [ˈpɑːsdiˈgriː] n. Aprobado, *m.*

passé [ˈpɑːsei] adj. Pasado de moda.

passementerie [pæsˈmɑːntri] n. Pasamanería, *f.*

passenger [ˈpæsindʒə*] n. Pasajero, ra; viajero, ra (traveller). || FIG. Persona (*f.*) inútil. || — *Passenger loading bridge*, pasarela (*f.*) de acceso. || *Passenger train, ship*, tren, buque de pasajeros.

passe-partout [ˈpæspɑːtuː] n. Orla, *f.*, "passe-partout", *m.* (frame of binding). || Llave (*f.*) maestra (key).

passe-partout [ˈpæspɑːtuː] v. tr. Orlar, poner una orla.

passer-by or **passerby** [ˈpɑːsəˈbai] n. Transeúnte, *m.* & *f.*

— OBSERV. El plural es *passers-by* y *passersby*.

passibility [ˌpæsiˈbiliti] n. Sensibilidad, *f.*

passible [ˈpæsibl] adj. Sensible.

passing [ˈpɑːsiŋ] adj. De paso, que pasa: *passing traveller*, viajero de paso. || Pasajero, ra; efímero, ra: *passing desire*, deseo pasajero. || Hecho de paso, de pasada: *passing remark*, observación hecha de paso. || — *A passing glance*, un vistazo rápido. || *Passing bell*, toque (*m.*) de difuntos. || U. S. *Passing mark*, aprobado, *m.*

— N. Paso, *m.* (of a train, of birds, etc.). || Adelantamiento, *m.* (overtaking). || Desaparición, *f.* (disappearance). || Paso, *m.*, transcurso, *m.* (of time). || Fallecimiento, *m.*, muerte, *f.* (death). || Adopción, *f.*, aprobación, *f.* (of a bill). || — *In passing*, de paso. || *With the passing of time*, andando el tiempo.

— Adv. (Ant.). Sumamente, extremadamente: *passing fair*, sumamente bello.

passion [ˈpæʃən] n. Pasión, *f.*: *to master one's passions*, dominar sus pasiones; *the debate aroused strong* *passions*, el debate despertó fuertes pasiones. || Cólera, *f.*, ira, *f.* (anger): *fit of passion*, ataque de cólera. || Pasión, *f.*, amor, *m.* (love): *to conceive a passion for*, tener una pasión por. || REL. Pasión, *f.* || — *I have a passion for strawberries*, me encantan las fresas, adoro las fresas. || *Passion Week*, Semana Santa, Semana de la Pasión. || *To be in a passion*, estar furioso. || *To fly into a passion*, encolerizarse, ponerse furioso. || *To put s.o. into a passion*, encolerizar *or* poner furioso a alguien.

passional [—əl] n. REL. Martirologio, *m.* (book).
— Adj. Pasional.

passionate [—it] adj. Apasionado, da (emotional): *a passionate speech*, un discurso apasionado. || Fervoroso, sa; ardiente, vehemente: *a passionate supporter*, un ardiente partidario. || Enfadado, da; furioso, sa (angry). || Irascible, colérico, ca (quick-tempered). || Ardiente (desire).

passionflower [—ˌflauə*] n. BOT. Pasionaria, *f.*, pasiflora, *f.*

passionless [—lis] adj. Desapasionado, da.

Passion play [—plei] n. Auto (*m.*) sacramental, misterio, *m.*

passive [ˈpæsiv] adj. Pasivo, va: *passive resistance*, resistencia pasiva. || GRAMM. Pasivo, va. || AVIAT. Sin motor.
— N. GRAMM. Voz (*f.*) pasiva.

passively [—li] adv. Pasivamente. || GRAMM. En voz pasiva.

passiveness [—nis] or **passivity** [pæˈsiviti] n. Pasividad, *f.*

passkey [ˈpɑ:ski:] n. Llave (*f.*) maestra.

Passover [ˈpɑ:sˌəuvə*] n. REL. Pascua, *f.* [de los Judíos].

passport [ˈpɑ:spɔ:t] n. Pasaporte, *m.*: *to issue a passport*, expedir un pasaporte. || FIG. *Passport to fame*, pasaporte a la fama.

password [ˈpɑ:swə:d] n. Contraseña, *f.*, santo y seña, *m.*

past [pɑ:st] adj. Pasado, da: *his past life*, su vida pasada; *in times past*, en tiempos pasados; *the past week*, la semana pasada. || Anterior, último, ma (former): *the past president*, el presidente anterior. || GRAMM. Pasado, da. || — *For some time past*, desde hace cierto tiempo. || *Past participle*, participio pasivo *or* de pretérito. || *Past perfect*, pluscuamperfecto, *m.* || *Past tense*, pretérito, *m.* || *The past few years*, estos últimos años. || *To be past*, haber pasado.
— N. Pasado, *m.*, lo pasado: *let us forget the past*, olvidemos el pasado; *to relive the past*, resucitar el pasado. || Antecedentes, *m. pl.* (record): *a man with a doubtful past*, un hombre con unos antecedentes dudosos. || FAM. Historia, *f.*: *a woman with a past*, una mujer con historia. || GRAMM. Pretérito, *m.*: *past absolute* o *historic*, *anterior*, pretérito indefinido, anterior. || — *In the past*, antes, anteriormente. || *It's a thing of the past*, pertenece al pasado. || *That's all in the past*, son cosas pasadas. || *Toledo is a town with a past*, Toledo es una ciudad llena de historia.
— Prep. Por delante de: *to walk past the house*, pasar por delante de la casa. || Más allá de: *it's just past the church*, está un poco más allá de la iglesia. || Más de: *he is past fifty*, tiene más de cincuenta años. || — *Bullets whistled past our ears*, las balas silbaban en nuestros oídos. || *He is past dancing*, ya no tiene edad para bailar. || *He pushed past me*, me empujó para pasar. || *I am past caring*, ya me trae sin cuidado. || *I am past worrying*, ya no me preocupa. || *It's half past*, es la media. || *It's past belief*, es increíble. || *It's past endurance*, es insoportable. || *It's past ten o'clock*, son las diez dadas, son más de las diez, son las diez y pico. || *It's past tolerance*, es intolerable. || *I wouldn't put it past you*, no me extrañaría de tu parte. || *My trousers are past mending*, mis pantalones están tan viejos que ya no se pueden arreglar. || *Ten past eight*, las ocho y diez.
— Adv. *To drive past*, pasar en coche. || *To fly past*, pasar volando. || *To go* o *to walk past*, pasar. || *To march past*, desfilar. || *To run past*, pasar corriendo.

pasta [ˈpæstə] n. Pastas, *f. pl.*

paste [peist] n. Masa, *f.* (for pastry crust). || Pasta, *f.*: *anchovy paste*, pasta de anchoas. || Pasta, *f.*: *paste for teeth*, pasta dentífrica. || Estrás, *m.* (for jewelry). || Barro, *m.* (clay). || Engrudo, *m.* (adhesive). || FAM. Puñetazo, *m.* (blow).

paste [peist] v. tr. Pegar (to stick). || Engrudar (to cover with paste). || FAM. Pegar (to hit). || SP. FAM. Dar una paliza a (to beat). || FAM. *To paste up*, pegar (to stick).

pasteboard [—bɔ:d] n. Cartón, *m.* (for boxes). || Cartulina, *f.* (for visiting cards). || Tarjeta (*f.*) de visita (visiting card). || Carta, *f.*, naipe, *m.* (playing card). || Billete, *m.* [*Amer.*, boleto, *m.*] (ticket).
— Adj. De cartón (box). || De cartulina (visiting card).

pastel [pæsˈtel] n. Pastel, *m.* (painting, colour). || — *Pastel blue*, azul (*m.*) pastel. || *Pastel drawing*, dibujo (*m.*) al pastel.

pastellist [pæsˈtəlist] or **pastelist** [ˈpæstəlist] n. Pastelista, *m.* & *f.*

pastern [ˈpæstə:n] n. Cuartilla, *f.* (of a horse).

paste-up [ˈpeistˈʌp] n. PRINT. Maqueta, *f.*

pasteurization [ˌpæstəraiˈzeiʃən] n. Pasterización, *f.*, pasteurización, *f.*

pasteurize [ˈpæstəraiz] v. tr. Pasterizar, pasteurizar.

pasticcio [pæsˈtitʃəu] or **pastiche** [pæsˈti:ʃ] n. Pastiche, *m.* (imitation).

pastil [ˈpæstəl] or **pastille** [pæsˈti:l] n. Pastilla, *f.*

pastime [ˈpɑ:staim] n. Pasatiempo, *m.*

pastiness [ˈpeistinis] n. Pastosidad, *f.*

pasting [ˈpeistiŋ] n. FAM. Paliza, *f.* (beating, criticism): *what a pasting I got!*, ¡menuda paliza me dieron!; *they gave him a pasting*, le dieron una paliza.

past master [ˈpɑ:stˈmɑ:stə*] n. FAM. *To be a past master in* o *at*, ser maestro en, ser perito en.

pastor [ˈpɑ:stə*] n. REL. Pastor, *m.*

pastoral [ˈpɑ:stərəl] adj. Pastoral, pastoril (relating to country life). || Pastoral, pastoril (literature). || REL. Pastoral: *pastoral ring*, anillo pastoral.
— N. Pastoral, *f.* (poem). || REL. Pastoral, *f.* (letter).

pastorale [ˌpæstəˈrɑ:li] n. MUS. Pastoral, *f.*

pastose [pæsˈtəus] adj. Pastoso, sa (paint).

pastosity [pæsˈtɔsiti] n. Pastosidad, *f.*

pastourelle [ˌpæstəˈrel] n. Pastorela, *f.*

pastry [ˈpeistri] n. Pasta, *f.* (dough). || Pasteles, *m. pl.* (cakes).

pastrycook [—kuk] n. Pastelero, ra; repostero, ra.

pastry shop [—ʃɔp] n. Pastelería, *f.*, repostería, *f.*

pasturable [ˈpɑ:stjurəbl] adj. Pacedero, ra.

pasturage [ˈpɑ:stjuridʒ] n. Pasto, *m.*, dehesa, *f.* (field). || Pasto, *m.* (grass). || Pasto, *m.*, pastoreo, *m.* (feeding). || *Common pasturage*, pasto comunal.

pasture [ˈpɑ:stʃə*] n. Pasto, *m.*

pasture [ˈpɑ:stʃə*] v. tr. Apacentar, pastorear (cattle). || Pacer (grass).
— V. intr. Pastar, pacer.

pasty [ˈpæsti] n. Pastel, *m.*, empanada, *f.*

pasty [ˈpeisti] adj. Pastoso, sa (like paste). || Pálido, da (complexion).

pat [pæt] adj. Adecuado, da; oportuno, na: *pat answer*, contestación adecuada. || *He always has an excuse pat*, siempre tiene una excusa preparada.
— Adv. Oportunamente, en el momento oportuno: *the reply came pat*, la contestación llegó en el momento oportuno. || — *To answer pat*, responder inmediatamente. || *To know sth. off pat*, saber algo al dedillo. || *To stand pat*, mantenerse en sus trece (to stand firm).
— N. Palmadita, *f.*, golpecito, *m.* (gentle stroke). || Caricia, *f.* (caress). || Porción, *f.* (small lump). || Ruido (*m.*) ligero (noise). || *To give s.o. a pat on the back*, dar a alguien palmaditas en la espalda (to tap lightly), felicitar a alguien (to congratulate).

pat [pæt] v. tr. Dar palmaditas: *to pat s.o. on the back*, dar palmaditas a alguien en la espalda. || Acariciar (a dog). || Dividir en porciones (butter, etc.). || — FIG. *To pat o.s. on the back*, congratularse. | *To pat s.o. on the back*, felicitar a alguien.

Patagonia [ˌpætəˈgəunjə] pr. n. GEOGR. Patagonia, *f.*

Patagonian [—n] adj. Patagón, ona; patagónico, ca.
— N. Patagón, ona.

patch [pætʃ] n. Pieza, *f.*, remiendo, *m.* (mend): *to put a patch on a coat*, echar *or* poner un remiendo a un abrigo. || Parche, *m.* (to cover a scratch, wound, puncture, etc.). || Bancal, *m.*: *potato patch*, bancal de patatas. || Parcela, *f.* (of land). || Parte, *f.*, trozo, *m.* (of a book, etc.). || Mancha, *f.* (of oil, colour). || Charco, *m.* (of water). || Lunar, *m.* (beauty spot). || — *A bad patch of road*, un tramo malo de carretera. || *Bald patch*, calva, *f.* || *Eye patch*, parche, *m.* || FIG. *Not to be a patch on*, no tener ni punto de comparación con. || *Patch of blue sky*, claro, *m.*, trozo (*m.*) de cielo azul. || *Patch pocket*, bolsillo (*m.*) de parche. || FIG. *To strike a bad patch*, tener mala suerte, pasar por un mal momento, tener una mala racha.

patch [pætʃ] v. tr. Remendar, poner un remiendo a: *to patch a hole*, remendar un roto. || Poner un parche a (a tyre). || *To patch up*, arreglar: *to patch up an old bicycle*, arreglar una vieja bicicleta; remendar (clothing), arreglar (differences).

patchouli [ˈpætʃuli] n. Pachulí, *m.*

patch test [ˈpætʃˈtest] n. MED. Prueba (*f.*) para descubrir una alergia.

patchwork [ˈpætʃwə:k] n. Labor (*f.*) hecha con trozos de varios colores. || — *A patchwork of fields*, un mosaico de campos. || *Patchwork quilt*, centón, *m.*, manta (*f.*) hecha con trozos de varios colores.

patchy [ˈpætʃi] adj. Desigual (unequal).

pate [peit] n. FAM. Coronilla, *f.* (top of the head). | Sesos, *m. pl.* (brains). || *Bald pate*, calva, *f.*

pâté [ˈpɑ:tei] n. CULIN. Pastel (*m.*) de carne. || *Pâté de foie gras*, pasta (*f.*) de hígado de ganso, "foie gras", *m.*

patella [pəˈtelə] n. ANAT. Rótula, *f.*
— OBSERV. El plural de *patella* es *patellae* o *patellas.*

patellar [pəˈtelə*] adj. ANAT. Rotular.

paten [ˈpætən] n. REL. Patena, *f.*

patency [ˈpeitənsi] n. Evidencia, *f.*

patent [ˈpeitənt] adj. Patente, evidente, manifiesto, ta (obvious): *you can't deny patent facts*, no puede negar hechos evidentes. || COMM. Patentado, da (an invention): *patent goods*, artículos patentados. | De patente (right). | De patentes (office). || Particular: *a patent way of pickling onions*, una manera particular de conservar cebollas. || MED. Abierto, ta (unobstructed). || — *Patent leather*, charol, *m.* || *Patent medicine*, específico, *m.*
— N. Patente, *f.*: *to take out a patent*, obtener una

patente. || *Infringement of patent*, imitación fraudulenta.

patent [ˈpeitənt] v. tr. Patentar.

patentee [ˌpeitənˈti:] n. Poseedor (*m.*) de una patente.

pater [ˈpeitə*] n. Fam. Padre, *m.* (father).

paterfamilias [ˈpeitəfəˈmiliæs] n. Paterfamilias, *m. inv.* (in ancient Rome). || Jefe (*m.*) de la familia.

— Observ. El plural es *patresfamilias*.

paternal [pəˈtə:nl] adj. Paternal (of or like a father). || Paterno, na: *paternal grandmother*, abuela paterna.

paternalism [pəˈtə:nəlizəm] n. Paternalismo, *m.*

paternalistic [pəˌtə:nəˈlistik] adj. Paternalista.

paternity [pəˈtə:niti] n. Paternidad, *f.* (fatherhood). || Fig. Paternidad, *f.*

paternoster [ˈpætəˈnɔstə*] n. Rel. Paternóster, *m.*, padrenuestro, *m.*

path [pɑ:θ] n. Camino, *m.*, sendero, *m.*, senda, *f.* (way): *he took the path that runs along the river*, cogió el camino que va a lo largo del río. || Calle, *f.* (of a garden). || Camino, *m.*: *the police cleared a path through the crowd for him*, la policía le abrió camino entre la multitud. || Pista, *f.* (track). || Órbita, *f.* (of a planet). || Curso, *m.* (of a star). || Curso, *m.*, recorrido, *m.* (of sun). || Trayectoria, *f.* (of bullet). || Fig. Paso, *m.*: *his path through life was hard*, su paso por la vida fue difícil. | Camino, *m.*: *path to glory*, camino hacia la gloria. || Fig. *The straight and narrow path*, el buen camino.

pathetic [pəˈθetik] or **pathetical** [—əl] adj. Patético, ca; lastimoso, sa (arousing pity). || Fam. Malísimo, ma: *the bullfighter was pathetic*, el torero fue malísimo. | Pobre: *she is a pathetic creature*, es una pobre mujer.

pathfinder [ˈpɑ:θˌfaində*] n. Explorador, ra (explorer). || Pionero, *m.*, adelantado, *m.* (pioneer).

pathless [ˈpɑ:θlis] adj. Sin senderos *or* caminos (without paths). || Inexplorado, da (unexplored).

pathogen [ˈpæθədʒən] or **pathogene** [pæθəˈdʒi:n] n. Agente (*m.*) patógeno.

pathogenesis [pæθəˈdʒenesis] n. Med. Patogenesia, *f.*, patogenia, *f.*

pathogenetic [pæθədʒəˈnetik] adj. Patógeno, na.

pathogenic [pæθəˈdʒenik] adj. Patógeno, na.

pathogeny [pəˈθɔdʒəni] n. Med. Patogenia, *f.*

pathologic [ˌpæθəˈlɔdʒik] or **pathological** [—əl] adj. Patológico, ca.

pathologist [pəˈθɔlədʒist] n. Med. Patólogo, ga.

pathology [pəˈθɔlədʒi] n. Patología, *f.*

pathos [ˈpeiθɔs] n. Patetismo, *m.*

pathway [ˈpɑ:θwei] n. Camino, *m.*, senda, *f.*, sendero, *m.* (path). || Acera, *f.* [*Amer.*, vereda, *f.*] (pavement).

patience [ˈpeiʃəns] n. Paciencia, *f.*: *to have patience*, tener paciencia; *to lose one's patience*, perder la paciencia; *my patience is exhausted*, se me ha agotado la paciencia. || Solitario, *m.* (card game): *to play patience*, hacer solitarios. || — *To be out of patience*, habérsele agotado a uno la paciencia. || *To have no patience with* o *for*, no aguantar: *I have no patience with that singer*, no aguanto a ese cantante. || *To possess one's soul in patience*, armarse de paciencia. || *To tax* o *to try s.o.'s patience*, probarle a alguien la paciencia.

patient [ˈpeiʃənt] adj. Paciente.

— N. Paciente, *m.* & *f.*, enfermo, ma.

patiently [—li] adv. Con paciencia, pacientemente.

patina [ˈpætinə] n. Pátina, *f.*: *to coat with a patina*, dar pátina a.

patinate [ˈpætineit] v. tr. Patinar.

patio [ˈpætiəu] n. Patio, *m.*

patois [ˈpætwɑ:] n. Dialecto, *m.*

patriarch [ˈpeitriɑ:k] n. Patriarca, *m.*

patriarchal [ˌpeitriˈɑ:kəl] adj. Patriarcal.

patriarchate [ˈpeitriɑ:kit] or **patriarchy** [ˈpeitriɑ:ki] n. Patriarcado, *m.*

patrician [pəˈtriʃən] adj./n. Patricio, cia.

patriciate [pəˈtriʃiit] n. Patriciado, *m.*

patricidal [ˈpætrisaidəl] adj. Parricida.

patricide [ˈpætrisaid] n. Parricidio, *m.* (crime). || Parricida, *m.* & *f.* (criminal).

Patrick [ˈpætrik] pr. n. Patricio, *m.*

patrilineal [pætrəˈliniəl] adj. Por línea paterna.

patrimonial [ˌpætriˈməunjəl] adj. Patrimonial.

patrimony [ˈpætriməni] n. Patrimonio, *m.*

patriot [ˈpeitriət] n. Patriota, *m.* & *f.*

patriotic [ˌpætriˈɔtik] adj. Patriótico, ca; patriota.

patriotism [ˈpætriətizəm] n. Patriotismo, *m.*

patristic [pəˈtristik] or **patristical** [—əl] adj. Rel. Patrístico, ca.

patristics [pəˈtristiks] n. Rel. Patrística, *f.*

patrol [pəˈtrəul] n. Patrulla, *f.* || U. S. Ronda, *f.* (of a policeman). || *To be on patrol*, estar de patrulla.

patrol [pəˈtrəul] v. tr. Hacer una ronda por: *he patrolled the area*, hizo una ronda por la región. || Hacer la ronda en, vigilar: *that watchman patrols this street*, aquel sereno hace la ronda en esta calle *or* vigila esta calle. || Patrullar por, estar de patrulla por: *police patrol the streets*, la policía patrulla por la calle. || Estar de patrulla: *soldiers patrol the border*, unos soldados están de patrulla en la frontera. || Fig. Rondar.

— V. intr. Patrullar.

patrol boat [—bəut] n. Patrullero, *m.*

patrol car [—kɑ:*] n. Coche (*m.*) patrulla.

patrol leader [—ˈli:də*] n. Jefe (*m.*) de patrulla.

patrolman [—mən] n. U. S. Policía, *m.*, guardia, *m.*

— Observ. El plural de *patrolman* es *patrolmen*.

patrol wagon [—ˈwægən] n. U. S. Coche (*m.*) celular.

patron [ˈpeitrən] n. Patrocinador, ra (person who gives practical support to a cause). || Patrón, *m.*, patrono, *m.*, patrona, *f.*: *St. Christopher is the patron of travellers*, San Cristóbal es el patrón de los viajeros. || Mecenas, *m.* (of arts). || Patrono, *m.* (of a charity). || Cliente, *m.* & *f.* (customer). || Rel. *Patron saint*, santo patrón, santa patrona.

patronage [ˈpætrənidʒ] n. Patrocinio, *m.* (sponsorship): *under the patronage of*, bajo el patrocinio de. || Patronato, *m.*: *royal patronage*, patronato real. || Mecenazgo, *m.* (of arts). || Clientela, *f.* (customers).

patronal [pəˈtrəunl] adj. Rel. Patronal.

patroness [ˈpeitrənis] n. Rel. Patrona, *f.* || Patrocinadora, *f.* (of a cause).

patronize [ˈpætrənaiz] v. tr. Patrocinar: *to patronize a firm*, patrocinar una empresa; *campaign patronized by*, campaña patrocinada por. || Favorecer, proteger (an artist). || Fomentar (arts). || Tratar con condescendencia *or* con aire protector (to be condescending towards). || Ser cliente de (to be customer at). || *This cinema is well patronized*, este cine tiene mucha clientela *or* atrae a mucha gente.

patronizing [—iŋ] adj. Protector, ra.

patronymic [ˌpætrəˈnimik] adj. Patronímico, ca.

— N. Patronímico, *m.*

patten [ˈpætn] n. Zueco, *m.*, chanclo, *m.*

patter [ˈpætə*] n. Jerga, *f.* (jargon). || Charloteo, *m.* (chat). || Charlatanería, *f.* (of a salesman). || Golpecitos, *m. pl.*, golpeteo, *m.* (noise). || Tamborileo, *m.*, repiqueteo, *m.* (of rain). || — *A patter of feet*, unos pasos ligeros y apresurados. || *To have a good patter*, tener mucha labia.

patter [ˈpætə*] v. tr. Chapurrear (a language). || Farfullar (to mumble). || Repetir mecánicamente (prayers, etc.).

— V. intr. Charlar (to chatter). || Tamborilear, repiquetear (rain). || Andar con paso ligero (walking). || *To patter about*, corretear.

pattern [ˈpætən] n. Dibujo, *m.* (design). || Estampado, *m.*, dibujo, *m.* (on cloth). || Dibujo, *m.*, diseño, *m.* (on china). || Muestra, *f.* (sample). || Forma, *f.* (form). || Tech. Patrón, *m.* (in dressmaking). | Escantillón, *m.*, plantilla, *f.* (for making moulds). || Dispersión, *f.* (of shots on a target). || Fig. Modelo, *m.*, ejemplo, *m.*: *to take s.o. as a pattern*, coger a alguien como modelo. | Pauta, *f.*: *to follow a fixed pattern*, seguir una pauta fija.

pattern [ˈpætən] v. tr. Adornar con dibujos (to decorate with a pattern). || Estampar (cloth). || — *To pattern o.s. on s.o.*, seguir el ejemplo de alguien, imitar a alguien. || *To pattern sth. after* o *on* o *upon*, hacer algo según el modelo de.

pattern book [—buk] n. Libro (*m.*) de muestras.

patternmaker [—meikə*] n. Modelista, *m.* & *f.*

patty [ˈpæti] n. Empanada, *f.* (fried meat pie). || Fritura, *f.*

paucity [ˈpɔ:siti] n. Escasez, *f.* (shortness, lack). || Falta, *f.* (of money).

Paul [pɔ:l] pr. n. Pablo, *m.* || *Paul VI* (*the sixth*), Paulo VI [sexto], Pablo VI [sexto].

Pauline [ˈpɔ:lain] adj. De San Pablo: *the Pauline Epistles*, las Epístolas de San Pablo.

Paulist [ˈpɔ:list] n. Rel. Paulista, *m.*

paunch [pɔ:ntʃ] n. Barriga, *f.*, panza, *f.* (belly).

paunch [pɔ:ntʃ] v. tr. Destripar.

paunchy [—i] adj. Panzudo, da; barrigón, ona.

pauper [ˈpɔ:pə*] n. Pobre, *m.* & *f.* || *Pauper's grave*, fosa (*f.*) común.

pauperism [—rizəm] n. Pauperismo, *m.*

pauperization [ˌpɔ:pəraiˈzeiʃən] n. Empobrecimiento, *m.*, pauperización, *f.*

pauperize [ˈpɔ:pəraiz] v. tr. Empobrecer, depauperar.

pause [pɔ:z] n. Pausa, *f.* || Descanso, *m.*: *after a brief pause I continued my work*, después de un breve descanso seguí trabajando. || Silencio, *m.*: *there was a pause in the conversation*, hubo un silencio en la conversación. || Mus. Poet. Pausa, *f.* || *To give pause to s.o.* o *to give s.o. pause*, hacer vacilar a alguien.

pause [pɔ:z] v. intr. Hacer una pausa (to make a pause). || Detenerse, pararse: *I paused at every shopwindow*, me paré delante de todos los escaparates. || Descansar (in working). || Vacilar (to hesitate): *to make s.o. pause*, hacer vacilar a alguien. || *To pause on a word*, recalcar una palabra.

pavan [ˈpævən] or **pavane** [ˈpævæn] n. Pavana, *f.*

pave [peiv] v. tr. Pavimentar (with asphalt). || Adoquinar (with cobbles). || Enlosar (with flagstones). || Enladrillar (with bricks). || Empedrar (with stones). || — Fig. *The road to hell is paved with good intentions*, el camino del infierno está empedrado de buenas intenciones. | *To pave the way for*, preparar el terreno para.

pavement [ˈpeivmənt] n. Acera, *f.* [*Amer.*, vereda, *f.*] (for pedestrians). || Pavimento, *m.* (paved surface). || U. S. Calzada, *f.* (roadway). || — *Brick pavement*, enladrillado, *m.* || *Cobblestone pavement*, adoquinado, *m.* || *Flagstone pavement*, enlosado, *m.* || *Stone pavement*, empedrado, *m.*

pavement artist [—ˈɑ:tist] n. Pintor (*m.*) callejero.

Pavia [pə'vi:ə] pr. n. GEOGR. Pavía.

pavilion [pə'viljən] n. Pabellón, *m.: the Spanish pavilion*, el pabellón español. || Vestuario, *m.* (changing room). || Quiosco, *m.* (bandstand). || ANAT. Pabellón, *m.* (outer ear). || Pabellón, *m.* (of a precious stone, in heraldry).

paving ['peiviŋ] n. Pavimento, *m.* || — *Brick paving*, enladrillado, *m.* || *Cobblestone paving*, adoquinado, *m.* || *Flagstone paving*, enlosado, *m.* || *Paving roller*, apisonadora, *f.* || *Paving stone*, adoquín, *m.* (brick), losa, *f.* (flagstone). || *Stone paving*, empedrado, *m.*

paw [pɔ:] n. Pata, *f.* (of animals). || Garra, *f.* (of cats). || Zarpa, *f.* (of lions). || FAM. Manaza, *f.* (hand). || FAM. *Keep your paws off!*, ¡las manos quietas!

paw [pɔ:] v. tr. Dar zarpazos a (a clawed animal). || Tocar con la pata (any animal). || FAM. Toquetear, manosear, sobar (to touch). || — FAM. *Stop pawing me!*, ¡las manos quietas! || *To paw the ground*, piafar (a horse).

— V. intr. Piafar (horse). || FAM. Manosear, toquetear, sobar (to touch).

pawkiness [—kinis] n. Astucia, *f.*

pawky [—ki] adj. Astuto, ta; ladino, na.

pawl [pɔ:l] n. TECH. Trinquete, *m.*

pawn [pɔ:n] n. Peón, *m.* (in chess). || FIG. Instrumento, *m.*, juguete, *m.* (person used by others). || Prenda, *f.* (object left as a deposit): *in pawn*, en prenda. || — *Pawn ticket*, papeleta (*f.*) del monte de piedad. || *To be in pawn*, estar empeñado, da. || FIG. *To be in pawn to*, estar en manos de. || *To put in pawn*, empeñar, dejar en prenda.

pawn [pɔ:n] v. tr. Empeñar.

pawnage ['pɔ:nidʒ] n. Empeño, *m.*

pawnbroker [—,brəukə*] n. Prestamista, *m.* & *f.* || *Pawnbroker's shop*, casa (*f.*) de empeños, monte (*m.*) de piedad.

pawnshop [—ʃɔp] n. Casa (*f.*) de empeños, monte (*m.*) de piedad.

pawpaw [pə'pɔ:] n. See PAPAW.

pax [pæks] n. REL. Paz, *f.*

— Interj. ¡Me rindo!

pay [pei] n. Paga, *f.*: *extra pay*, paga extraordinaria. || Sueldo, *m.* (of employee). || Salario, *m.* (of workman). || Jornal, *m.* (of day worker). || Emolumentos, *m. pl.* (of member of Parliament). || MIL. Paga, *f.* || — *Equal pay*, igualdad (*f.*) de salarios. || *Holidays with pay*, vacaciones retribuidas *or* pagadas. || *In the pay of*, pagado por, a sueldo de. || *Retirement pay*, pensión, *f.*, jubilación, *f.*, retiro, *m.* || FIG. *To be in the pay of*, estar al servicio de. || *To draw one's pay*, cobrar. || *To stop sth. out of s.o.'s pay*, descontar *or* deducir algo del sueldo de alguien.

pay* [pei] v. tr. Pagar (to hand over in payment): *to pay five pounds*, pagar cinco libras; *to pay one's debts*, pagar las deudas; *to pay s.o. five pounds*, pagar a alguien cinco libras; *to pay s.o. to do sth.*, pagar a alguien para que haga algo. || Producir, dar: *our investment paid five per cent*, nuestra inversión produjo el cinco por ciento. || Hacer (visit, compliment). || Rendir (homage). || Presentar (respects). || Prestar: *to pay attention*, prestar atención. || FIG. Compensar: *it will pay you to take that trip*, te compensará hacer ese viaje. | Ser rentable *or* ser provechoso para (to be profitable). | Pagar: *she paid his kindness with insults*, le pagó su amabilidad con insultos; *to pay the consequences*, pagar las consecuencias; *to pay sth. with one's life*, pagar algo con la vida. || MAR. Calafatear (to make waterproof). || — *To be paid every week*, cobrar todas las semanas. || FIG. FAM. *To pay a visit*, ir al excusado. || *To pay cash* o *on the nail*, pagar al contado *or* a tocateja. || FIG. *To pay court to*, cortejar a. || *To pay expenses*, cubrir gastos. || *To pay in cash*, pagar en metálico *or* en efectivo. || *To pay in instalments*, pagar a plazos. || *To pay in kind*, pagar en especie. || *To pay money into an account*, ingresar dinero en una cuenta. || *To pay on account*, pagar a cuenta. || *To pay one's way*, pagar su parte (to pay one's share), ser solvente (to be solvent).

— V. intr. Pagar: *have you paid yet?*, ¿has pagado ya? || FIG. Compensar: *crime does not pay*, el crimen no compensa. | Ser rentable *or* provechoso (to be profitable). || — FIG. *It pays*, vale *or* merece la pena: *it pays not to eat too much*, merece la pena no comer demasiado; es rentable (to be profitable). || *To pay in advance*, pagar por adelantado. || *To pay in full*, pagarlo todo.

— ***To pay away***, soltar (a rope). | Pagar. || ***To pay back***, reembolsar, devolver (money). | Pagar (s.o.). | Devolver (an insult, etc.). | — FIG. *To pay s.o. back in his own coin*, pagar a alguien con la misma moneda. || ***To pay down***, pagar al contado (cash). | Dejar una señal de, hacer un desembolso inicial de (as a first payment). || ***To pay for***, pagar: *he paid for the cigarettes*, pagó los cigarrillos. | Pagar por, pagar: *I paid five pounds for my watch*, pagué cinco libras por mi reloj, pagué mi reloj cinco libras. | FIG. Pagar por, pagar: *he paid for his crimes*, pagó por sus crímenes. | — *To pay for the sins of others*, pagar las culpas ajenas. | *You shall pay for it!*, ¡ya me las pagarás! || ***To pay in***, ingresar. || ***To pay off***, saldar, liquidar: *to pay off one's debts*, saldar las deudas. | Reembolsar (creditor). | Redimir (mortgage). | Despedir (employee, servant). | Licenciar (troops). | MAR. Despedir (crew), arriar (rope). | Merecer la pena: *it was a risk but it paid off*, fue un riesgo pero mereció la pena. | Dar resultado. || ***To pay out***, pagar (s.o.). | Desembolsar (money). | Distribuir (to distribute). | Arriar, soltar (rope). | — FIG. *I'll pay you out for that!*, ¡ya me las pagarás! | *To pay s.o. out*, pagar a alguien con la misma moneda. || ***To pay over***, pagar. || ***To pay up***, pagar.

— OBSERV. Pret. & p.p. ***paid***. — Cuando este verbo signfica "calafatear" se emplea también el pretérito y el participio pasivo *payed*.

payable [—əbl] adj. Pagadero, ra: *payable at sight, in instalments, to bearer*, pagadero a la vista, a plazos, al portador. || *To make a cheque payable to s.o.*, extender un cheque a favor de alguien.

pay-as-you-earn [peiæzjuə:n] n. Deducción (*f.*) del sueldo para los impuestos.

pay bill [—bil] n. Vale, *m.*

payday [—dei] n. Día (*m.*) de paga.

paydesk [—desk] n. Caja, *f.*

pay dirt [—də:t] n. U. S. Suelo (*m.*) rico en minerales (soil). | Información (*f.*) interesante (useful information). | Filón, *m.* (remunerative discovery).

payee [pei'i:] n. Beneficiario, ria (of a cheque, of a postal order). || Tenedor, ra (of a bill).

payer ['peiə*] n. Pagador, ra. || *Slow payer*, moroso, sa.

paying ['peiiŋ] adj. Que paga (who pays). || Rentable, provechoso, sa (profitable).

— N. Reembolso, *m.* (of a creditor). || Liquidación, *f.*, pago, *m.* (of debt). || Pago, *m.* (of money).

payload ['peiləud] n. Carga (*f.*) útil. || MIL. Carga (*f.*) explosiva.

paymaster ['pei,mɑ:stə*] n. Pagador, *m.* || MIL. Pagador, *m.*, habilitado, *m.*

payment ['peimənt] n. Pago, *m.*: *to make a payment*, efectuar *or* hacer un pago; *payment in (hard) cash*, pago en metálico. || FIG. Recompensa, *f.*, pago, *m.* (reward). || — *Advance payment* o *payment in advance*, pago adelantado *or* anticipado, anticipo, *m.* || *As* o *in payment for*, en pago de. || *Cash payment*, pago al contado. || *Deferred payment*, pago a plazos. || *Down payment*, desembolso (*m.*) inicial. || *Monthly payment*, mensualidad, *f.* || *Net payment*, líquido, *m.* || *On payment of two pounds*, mediante el pago de dos libras, pagando dos libras. || *Payment by instalments*, pago a plazos. || *Payment in full*, pago íntegro, liquidación, *f.* || *Payment in kind*, pago en especie. || *Payment on account*, pago a cuenta. || *To present a cheque for payment*, presentar un cheque al cobro, cobrar un cheque. || *To stop payments*, suspender los pagos. || *Without payment*, sin pagar, gratuitamente: *to get sth. without payment*, conseguir algo sin pagar; sin cobrar, gratuitamente: *I'll do it without payment*, lo haré gratuitamente.

payoff ['peiɔf] n. U. S. FAM. Pago, *m.* (payment). | Día (*m.*) de paga (payday). | Rentabilidad, *f.* (income). | Pago, *m.*, recompensa, *f.* (reward). | Resultado (*m.*) final (result). | Momento (*m.*) *or* factor (*m.*) decisivo. | Desenlace, *m.* (of a story).

pay office ['pei'ɔfis] n. Caja, *f.*, pagaduría, *f.*

pay rise ['pei 'raiz] n. Aumento (*m.*) de sueldo.

payroll ['peirəul] or **paysheet** ['pei ʃi:t] n. Nómina, *f.*: *he has 20 people on his payroll*, tiene una nómina de veinte personas.

pay slip ['pei ,slip] n. Hoja (*f.*) de paga.

pay station ['pei'steiʃən] or **pay telephone** ['pei'telifəun] n. U. S. Teléfono (*m.*) público.

pea [pi:] n. BOT. Guisante, *m.* [*Amer.*, arveja, *f.*, chícharo, *m.*]. || — BOT. *Green peas*, guisantes. | *Sugar pea*, guisante mollar. | *Sweet pea*, guisante de olor. || FIG. *To be as like as two peas* o *like two peas in a pod*, parecerse como dos gotas de agua.

peace [pi:s] n. Paz, *f.* (between countries). || Orden (*m.*) público (in a country): *to break the peace*, alterar el orden público. || Armonía, *f.* (between people). || Paz, *f.*, tranquilidad, *f.* (tranquillity). || — *At peace*, en paz (countries), en armonía (people). || *Go in peace!*, ¡vaya en paz! || *My conscience is at peace*, tengo la conciencia tranquila. || *Octavian peace*, paz octaviana. || *Peace be with you*, la paz sea con vosotros. || *Peace of mind*, tranquilidad de espíritu. || *Peace pipe*, pipa (*f.*) de la paz. || *Peace to his ashes!*, ¡paz a sus cenizas! || *Peace treaty*, tratado (*m.*) de paz. || *The King's peace* o *the Queen's peace*, el orden público. || *To give s.o. no peace*, no dejar a uno en paz. || *To hold* o *to keep one's peace*, guardar silencio, callarse. || *To keep the peace*, poner paz (between two people), mantener la paz (internationally), mantener el orden (in a country). || *To leave s.o. in peace*, dejar a alguien en paz. || *To live in peace*, vivir en paz. || *To make one's peace with*, hacer las paces con. || *To make peace*, hacer las paces (individuals), firmar la paz (after war), poner paz (to stop a fight). || *To rest in peace*, descansar en paz: *may he rest in peace*, que en paz descanse.

peaceable [—əbl] adj. Pacífico, ca.

peaceably [—əbli] adv. Pacíficamente, de modo pacífico: *to behave peaceably*, comportarse de modo pacífico. || En paz: *to live peaceably*, vivir en paz.

peaceful [—ful] adj. Pacífico, ca: *peaceful coexistence*, coexistencia *or* convivencia pacífica; *peaceful tribes*, tribus pacíficas. || Tranquilo, la (quiet).

peacefulness [—fulnis] n. Tranquilidad, *f.*, sosiego, *m.*, calma, *f.* (tranquillity). || Carácter (*m.*) pacífico.
peace-keeping [—ˌki:piŋ] adj. De pacificación.
— N. Mantenimiento (*m.*) de la paz.
peace-loving [—ˌlʌviŋ] adj. Amante de la paz.
peacemaker [—ˌmeikə*] n. Pacificador, ra. || Conciliador, ra.
peacemaking [—ˌmeikiŋ] n. Pacificación, *f.*
peace offering [—ˌɔfəriŋ] n. Rel. Ofrenda (*f.*) propiciatoria. || Fig. Regalo (*m.*) hecho para hacer las paces con una persona. || Oferta (*f.*) de paz (to make peace).
peacetime [—taim] n. Tiempo (*m.*) de paz.
peach [pi:tʃ] n. Bot. Melocotonero, *m.* [*Amer.*, duraznero, *m.*] (tree). | Melocotón, *m.* [*Amer.*, durazno, *m.*] (fruit). || Color (*m.*) melocotón (colour). || — Bot. *Peach tree*, melocotonero, *m.* [*Amer.*, duraznero, *m.*]. || Fam. *She is a peach*, es un bombón, es una monada.
— Adj. De color melocotón.
peach [pi:tʃ] v. intr. Fam. Chivarse (*on*, de), delatar (*on*, a).
— V. tr. Fam. Soplar, delatar.
peachy [—i] adj. Fig. Aterciopelado, da.
peacock [ˈpi:kɔk] n. Zool. Pavo (*m.*) real, pavón, *m.* || Fig. *To be as proud as a peacock*, see proud.
peacock [ˈpi:kɔk] v. intr. Pavonearse.
peacock blue [—blu:] n. Azul (*m.*) eléctrico (colour).
peacock butterfly [—ˈbʌtəflai] n. Zool. Pavón, *m.*
peafowl [ˈpi:faul] n. Zool. Pavo (*m.*) real, pava (*f.*) real.
pea green [ˈpi:ˈgri:n] n. Verde (*m.*) claro.
pea-green [ˈpi:ˈgri:n] adj. Verde claro.
peahead [ˈpi:hed] n. Fam. Mentecato, *m.*
peahen [ˈpi:ˈhen] n. Zool. Pava (*f.*) real.
pea jacket [ˈpi:ˌdʒækit] n. Chaquetón (*m.*) de marinero.
peak [pi:k] n. Pico, *m.* (mountain). || Cumbre, *f.*, cima, *f.* (summit). || Visera, *f.* (of a cap). || Punta, *f.* (point). || Mar. Puño (*m.*) de boca (of a sail). | Penol, *m.* (of lateen yard). | Uña, *f.* (of anchor). || Electr. Carga (*m.*) máxima. || Fig. Apogeo, *m.*, auge, *m.* (in a course of development). | Cumbre, *f.* (of glory). | Punto (*m.*) máximo *or* más alto: *the peak of production*, el punto máximo de la producción. || — *Peak hours*, horas (*f.*) punta *or* de mayor afluencia (transport), horas de mayor consumo (gas, etc.). || *Peak load*, carga máxima. || *Peak season*, temporada alta.
peak [pi:k] v. tr. Mar. Embicar. || Fig. Encumbrar.
— V. intr. Alcanzar el máximo.
peaked [—t] adj. Con visera (cap). || Puntiagudo, da (sharp-pointed). || *Peaked features*, cara cansada.
peaky [—i] adj. Fam. Paliducho, cha.
peal [pi:l] n. Repique, *m.*, repiqueteo, *m.* (of bells). || Sonido, *m.* (of organ). || Estruendo, *m.* (loud noise). || — *Peals of laughter*, carcajadas, *f.* || *Peals of thunder*, truenos, *m.*
peal [pi:l] v. tr. Repicar (bells).
— V. intr. Repicar, repiquetear (bells). || Retumbar (thunder). || Resonar (laugh).
peanut [ˈpi:nʌt] n. Bot. Cacahuete, *m.* [*Amer.*, cacahuate, *m.*, maní, *m.*]. || Fig. fam. Insignificancia, *f.* || — Pl. Fig. fam. Miseria, *f.*: *to work for peanuts*, trabajar por una miseria. | Nada (something small). || — *Peanut butter*, manteca (*f.*) de cacahuete. || U. S. Theatr. *Peanut gallery*, gallinero, *m.* || *Peanut oil*, aceite (*m.*) de cacahuete.
pear [pɛə*] n. Bot. Pera, *f.* (fruit). | Peral, *m.* (tree). || Bot. *Pear tree*, peral, *m.*
pearl [pə:l] n. Perla, *f.*: *cultured pearl*, perla cultivada; *real pearl*, perla fina. || Madreperla, *f.*, nácar, *m.* (mother-of-pearl). || Fig. Joya, *f.*, perla, *f.*, alhaja, *f.* (person). || Print. Perla, *f.* (four-point type). || Gris (*m.*) perla (colour). || Fig. *To cast pearls before swine*, echar margaritas a los cerdos *or* a los puercos.
— Adj. De perlas (necklace). || De perlas: *pearl diver o fisher*, pescador de perlas; *pearl fishing*, pesca de perlas. || De color perla (colour). || Perlero, ra (industry).
pearl [pə:l] v. intr. Pescar perlas (to fish for pearls). || Gotear (moisture, etc.).
pearl barley [—ˈbɑ:li] n. Bot. Cebada (*f.*) perlada.
pearl grey [—grei] n. Gris (*m.*) perla.
pearl oyster [—ˈɔistə*] n. Zool. Madreperla, *f.*, ostra (*f.*) perlífera.
pearl-shaped [—ʃeipt] adj. Perlado, da; en forma de perla.
pearl shell [—ʃel] n. Concha (*f.*) de perla.
pearly [ˈpə:li] adj. Nacarado, da; color de perla (colour). || De perla (made of pearl).
pearly nautilus [—ˈnɔ:tiləs] n. Zool. Nautilo, *m.*
pear-shaped [ˈpɛəʃeipt] adj. En forma de pera. || Fig. Suave (mellow).
peasant [ˈpezənt] adj./n. Campesino, na. || Fig. Paleto, ta; cateto, ta; palurdo, da.
peasantry [—ri] n. Campesinos, *m. pl.*
pease [pi:z] n. Guisantes, *m. pl.* (peas).
peashooter [ˈpi:ˌʃu:tə*] n. Cerbatana, *f.*
pea soup [ˈpi: su:p] n. Puré (*m.*) de guisantes (soup). || U. S. Fam. Niebla (*f.*) espesa de color amarillento (fog).
pea-souper [—ə*] n. Niebla (*f.*) espesa de color amarillento (fog).
peat [pi:t] n. Turba, *f.* || *Peat bog*, turbera, *f.*
peaty [—i] adj. Turboso, sa.
pebble [ˈpebl] n. Guijarro, *m.* (stone). || Fam. *You aren't the only pebble on the beach*, no eres el único en el mundo.
pebble [ˈpebl] v. tr. Enguijarrar, empedrar con guijarros.
pebbly [—i] adj. Guijarroso, sa.
pecan [piˈkæn] n. Bot. Pacana, *f.* (tree, nut).
peccadillo [ˌpekəˈdiləu] n. Pecadillo, *m.*, falta (*f.*) leve, peccata minuta, *f.*

— Observ. El plural de la palabra inglesa es *peccadilloes* o *peccadillos.*

peccancy [ˈpekənsi] n. Vicio, *m.*
peccant [ˈpekənt] adj. Culpable, pecador, ra.
peccary [ˈpekəri] n. Zool. Pecarí, *m.*, pécari, *m.* [*Amer.*, saíno, *m.*]
peck [pek] n. Medida (*f.*) de áridos parecida al celemín (measure). || Picotín, *m.* (of oats). || Picotazo, *m.* (of a bird, mark). || Picadura, *f.* (of an insect). || Fam. Beso, *m.* (kiss). || Fig. Montón, *m.*: *a peck of trouble*, un montón de problemas.
peck [pek] v. tr. Picotear (bird). || Fam. Besar (to kiss).
— V. intr. *To peck at*, picotear (bird), picar (to nibble at food). || *To peck out*, sacar a picotazos (the eyes).
pecker [—ə*] n. Fam. *To keep one's pecker up*, no dejarse desanimar.
peckerwood [ˈpekəwud] n. Pájaro (*m.*) carpintero (woodpecker).
pecking [ˈpekiŋ] n. Picoteo, *m.*
pecking order [—ˈɔ:də*] n. Fig. La ley del más fuerte.
peckish [ˈpekiʃ] adj. Fam. Hambriento, ta (hungry). || U. S. Fam. Irritable (irritable). || Fam. *To feel peckish*, tener gazuza.
pectineal [pekˈtiniəl] adj. Anat. Pectíneo, a (muscle).
pectoral [ˈpektərəl] adj. Anat. Pectoral. || Rel. *Pectoral cross*, pectoral, *m.*
— N. Anat. Músculo (*m.*) pectoral. || Med. Rel. Pectoral, *m.* || Pectoral, *m.* (ornament).
peculate [ˈpekjuleit] v. tr./intr. Jur. Desfalcar, malversar.
peculation [ˌpekjuˈleiʃən] n. Jur. Malversación, *f.*, desfalco, *m.*, peculado, *m.* (embezzlement).
peculator [ˈpekjuleitə*] n. Malversador, ra; desfalcador, ra; concusionario, ria.
peculiar [piˈkju:ljə*] adj. Raro, ra; extraño, ña (odd): *a peculiar girl*, una chica extraña. || Característico, ca; típico, ca; propio, pia; peculiar: *custom peculiar to a country*, costumbre típica de un país. || Propio, pia: *this gait is peculiar to him*, esta manera de andar es propia de él. || Especial, particular (special). || — *The condor is peculiar to the Andes*, el cóndor es un animal de los Andes. || *He is a bit peculiar*, está algo chalado (slightly mad).
peculiarity [piˌkju:liˈæriti] n. Particularidad, *f.*, peculiaridad, *f.* (particularity). || Rareza, *f.* (oddity). || Característica, *f.*, rasgo (*m.*) característico (special characteristic). || — *Everyone has his peculiarities*, todo el mundo tiene sus manías. || *Special peculiarities*, señas (*f.*) particulares (on passport).
peculiarly [piˈkju:ljəli] adv. Particularmente: *peculiarly difficult*, particularmente difícil. || De una manera extraña (strangely): *she dresses peculiarly*, se viste de una manera extraña.
peculium [piˈkju:ljəm] n. Peculio, *m.*

— Observ. El plural de *peculium* es *peculia.*

pecuniarily [piˈkju:njərili] adv. Pecuniariamente.
pecuniary [piˈkju:njəri] adj. Pecuniario, ria. || *Pecuniary troubles*, apuros de dinero *or* monetarios.
pedagog [ˈpedəgɔg] n. U. S. Pedagogo, *m.*
pedagogic [ˌpedəˈgɔdʒik] or **pedagogical** [—əl] adj. Pedagógico, ca.
pedagogics [—s] n. Pedagogía, *f.*
pedagogue [ˈpedəgɔg] n. Pedagogo, *m.*
pedagogy [ˈpedəgɔdzi] n. Pedagogía, *f.*
pedal [ˈpedl] n. Pedal, *m.*: *the pedals of a bicycle*, los pedales de una bicicleta; *clutch, brake pedal*, pedal de embrague, de freno. || — Mus. *Loud pedal*, pedal fuerte. | *Soft pedal*, sordina, *f.*
pedal [ˈpedl] v. tr. Dar a los pedales de (to move the pedals of): *to pedal a bicycle hard*, darle fuerte a los pedales de una bicicleta.
— V. intr. Pedalear.
pedal boat [—bəut] n. Hidropedal, *m.*
pedal brake [—breik] n. Freno (*m.*) de pie.
pedalling or **pedaling** [—iŋ] n. Pedaleo, *m.*
pedant [ˈpedənt] n. Pedante, *m.* & *f.*
pedantic [piˈdæntik] or **pedantical** [—əl] adj. Pedante (person). || Pedantesco, ca; pedante (manner).
pedantically [—əli] adv. Con pedantería, de una manera pedante, pedantescamente.
pedanticism [peˈdəntisizəm] or **pedantism** [ˈpedəntizəm] n. Pedantismo, *m.*, pedantería, *f.*
pedantry [ˈpedəntri] n. Pedantería, *f.*
peddle [ˈpedl] v. tr. Vender de puerta en puerta. || Fig. Divulgar, difundir.
— V. intr. Vender de puerta en puerta.
peddler [—ə*] n. Vendedor (*m.*) ambulante, buhonero, *m.*
peddling [—iŋ] n. Venta (*f.*) ambulante, buhonería, *f.*
pederast [ˈpedəræst] n. U. S. Pederasta, *m.*

pederasty [—i] n. U. S. Pederastia, *f.*
pedestal [ˈpedistl] n. Pedestal, *m.* || *To put* o *to set s.o. on a pedestal*, poner a alguien en un pedestal *or* por las nubes.
pedestal lamp [—læmp] n. Lámpara (*f.*) de pie.
pedestal table [—ˈteibl] n. Velador, *m.*
pedestrian [piˈdestriən] adj. Pedestre (relating to people on foot). || FIG. Vulgar, pedestre (commonplace). | Prosaico, ca (style).
— N. Peatón, *m.*
pedestrian crossing [—ˈkrɔsiŋ] n. Paso (*m.*) de peatones.
pedestrian traffic [—ˈtræfik] n. Peatones, *m. pl.*: *the town center is reserved for pedestrian traffic*, el centro de la ciudad está reservado a los peatones.
pediatric [ˌpi:diˈætrik] adj. MED. Pediátrico, ca.
pediatrician [ˌpi:diəˈtriʃən] or **pediatrist** [ˌpi:diˈætrist] n. U. S. MED. Pediatra, *m.*, pedíatra, *m.*
pediatrics [ˌpi:diˈætriks] n. U. S. MED. Pediatría, *f.*
pedicular [peˈdikjulə*] adj. Pedicular.
pedicure [ˈpedikjuə*] n. Pedicuro, ra; callista, *m.* & *f.* (chiropodist). || Pedicura, *f.*, quiropodia, *f.* (chiropody).
pedicurist [—rist] n. Pedicuro, ra; callista, *m.* & *f.*
pedigree [ˈpedigri:] n. Árbol (*m.*) genealógico (family tree). || Genealogía, *f.*, "pedigree", *m.*, pedigrí, *m.*, carta (*f.*) de origen (of animals). || Linaje, *m.* (ancestry). || — *Man of pedigree*, hombre (*m.*) de alta alcurnia. || *Pedigree animal*, animal (*m.*) de raza.
pediment [ˈpedimənt] n. ARCH. Frontón, *m.*
pedlar [ˈpedlə*] n. Vendedor (*m.*) ambulante, buhonero, *m.*
pedology [peˈdɔlədʒi] n. Pedología, *f.*, edafología, *f.* (soil science). || Pedología, *f.* (study of the development of children).
pedometer [piˈdɔmitə*] n. MED. Podómetro, *m.*
peduncle [piˈdʌŋkl] n. BOT. ANAT. Pedúnculo, *m.*
peduncular [peˈdʌŋkjulə*] adj. Peduncular.
pedunculate [peˈdʌŋkjulət] or **pedunculated** [peˈdʌŋkjuˌleitid] adj. Pedunculado, da.
pee [pi:] n. FAM. Pis, *m.*: *to have a pee*, hacer pis.
pee [pi:] v. intr. FAM. Hacer pis.
peek [pi:k] n. Ojeada, *f.*, mirada, *f.*: *to take a peek at*, echar una ojeada a.
peek [pi:k] v. intr. Mirar a hurtadillas (to look furtively). || Echar una ojeada (to glance).
peekaboo [ˈpi:kəˈbu:] n. Cucú, *m.* (game).
peel [pi:l] n. Piel, *f.* (skin). || Pala, *f.* (shovel). || Monda, *f.*, mondadura, *f.*, cáscara, *f.*, peladura, *f.* (removed skin of oranges, potatoes). || Pellejo, *m.* (of grapes). || — *Candied peel*, piel (*f.*) almibarada *or* confitada. || *Slice of peel*, cáscara, *f.* (in cocktails).
peel [pi:l] v. tr. Pelar, mondar (to take the skin off): *to peel an orange*, *potatoes*, pelar una naranja, patatas. || Descortezar (bark). || Descascarillar (nuts). || — *To peel off*, quitar, despegar (wallpaper, etc.), quitarse (clothes). || FIG. *To keep one's eyes peeled*, estar ojo avizor.
— V. intr. Pelarse: *apples that peel easily*, manzanas que se pelan fácilmente. || *To peel off*, desconcharse (paint), caerse a tiras, despegarse (wallpaper, etc.), despellejarse (skin), desnudarse (to undress), descortezarse (bark), descascarillarse (nails).
peeler [—ə*] n. (Ant.). Policía, *m.* (policeman). || FAM. Mujer (*f.*) que hace strip-tease. || *Potato peeler* pelapatatas, *m. inv.*
peeling [—iŋ] n. Peladura, *f.* (of fruit, etc.). || — Pl. Peladuras, *f.*, mondaduras, *f.*
peen [pin] n. Boca, *f.* (of a hammer).
peep [pi:p] n. Mirada (*f.*) furtiva, ojeada, *f.* (look): *to have* o *to take a peep at*, echar una ojeada a. || Pío pío, *m.*, pío, *m.* (of birds). || Grito (*m.*) agudo (of a mouse). || — *At peep of day* o *of dawn*, al amanecer. || *To get a peep at sth.*, conseguir ver algo un poco. || FAM. *We have not had a peep out of him all day*, no ha dicho ni pío en todo el día.
peep [pi:p] v. intr. Mirar furtivamente, echar una ojeada *or* una mirada furtiva (*at*, a) [to look]. || Piar (a bird). || — *To peep out*, asomar: *his head peeped out from behind the wall*, su cabeza asomó detrás del muro; aparecer, salir: *the moon peeped out from behind the clouds*, la luna salió detrás de las nubes. || *To peep through the curtains*, atisbar detrás de los visillos. || *To peep through the keyhole*, mirar por el ojo de la cerradura.
— V. tr. Asomar: *he peeped his head out of the window*, asomó la cabeza por la ventana.
peeper [—ə*] n. FAM. Ojo, *m.* (eye). | Mirón, ona (person). || Pollito, *m.* (bird).
peephole [—həul] n. Mirilla, *f.* (in the door).
peeping Tom [—iŋtɔm] n. Mirón, *m.*, curioso, *m.*
peep show [ˈpi:pʃəu] n. Mundonuevo, *m.* (box). || FAM. Espectáculo (*m.*) sicalíptico.
peep sight [—sait] n. Alza, *f.* (of a gun).
peer [piə*] n. Par, *m.* (nobleman). || Igual, *m.*, semejante, *m.* (equal). || — *Peer of the realm*, par del reino. || *You will not find his peer*, no encontrará otro igual.
peer [piə*] v. intr. Mirar (to look). || Mirar con atención *or* con ojos de miope, entornar los ojos (to look closely). || Aparecer, asomar (to peep out). || — *To peer at s.o.*, mirar a alguien de hito en hito. || *To peer into*, mirar dentro de.
— V. tr. Elevar a la dignidad de par.
peerage [—ridʒ] n. Pares, *m. pl.* (the peers of a country). || Dignidad (*f.*) de par (rank of a peer). || Libro (*m.*) nobiliario (book). || Nobleza, *f.* (nobility). || *To get a peerage*, recibir un título de nobleza.
peeress [—ris] n. Paresa, *f.*
peerless [—lis] adj. Sin par, sin igual.
peeve [pi:v] n. FAM. Malhumor, *m.*: *he got up in a peeve*, se levantó de malhumor. || *A pet peeve*, un motivo de enfado.
peeve [pi:v] v. tr. FAM. Irritar, poner de malhumor *or* furioso. || — FAM. *To be peeved*, estar furioso *or* de malhumor. | *To get peeved*, ponerse furioso *or* de malhumor.
— V. intr. Irritarse, ponerse de malhumor *or* furioso.
peevish [—iʃ] adj. Picajoso, sa (irritable). || Quejica (complaining). || Malhumorado, da; de malhumor (bad-tempered). || Terco, ca; testarudo, da (stubborn).
peevishly [—iʃli] adv. Con malhumor, malhumoradamente. || Quejándose.
peevishness [—iʃnis] n. Malhumor, *m.* (bad temper). || Terquedad, *f.* (stubbornness).
peewit [ˈpi:wit] n. Avefría, *f.* (bird).
peg [peg] n. Pinza, *f.* (for clothes). || Percha, *f.* (for hats, coats, etc.). || Gancho, *m.* (hook). || Estaca, *f.* (for tent). || TECH. Clavija, *f.* || MUS. Clavija, *f.* || Trago, *m.* (of spirits). || FIG. Escalón, *m.*, grado, *m.*: *to move up a peg in an organization*, ascender un escalón en una organización. | Nivel, *m.* (of prices). | Pretexto, *m.* (pretext): *he looked for a peg*, buscó un pretexto. || Estaca, *f.* (croquet). || Punto (*m.*) de apoyo (of an argument). || FAM. Pata, *f.* (leg). || — *Off the peg*, de confección (clothes). || FIG. *To be a square peg in a round hole*, estar como pez fuera del agua. | *To come down a peg* (*or two*), bajársele a uno los humos. | *To take s.o. down a peg* (*or two*), bajar los humos a alguien.
peg [peg] v. tr. Fijar con clavijas, enclavijar. || Estabilizar (stock exchange, prices). || SP. Marcar (the score). || — *To peg down*, sujetar con estacas, estacar. || *To peg out*, jalonar, señalar con estacas (to mark with pegs), tender (clothes).
— V. intr. *To peg away*, trabajar con ahínco. || *To peg away at*, afanarse por. || *To peg out*, acabar la partida (in croquet), estirar la pata (to die).
pegasus [ˈpegəsəs] n. Pegaso, *m.* (fish).
Pegasus [ˈpegəsəs] pr. n. MYTH. Pegaso, *m.*
pegbox [ˈpegˌbɔks] n. MUS. Clavijero, *m.*
pegleg [ˈpegleg] n. Pata (*f.*) de palo.
peg top [ˈpegtɔp] n. Peonza, *f.*
peignoir [ˈpeinwɑ:*] n. Bata, *f.*, salto (*m.*) de cama.
pejorative [ˈpi:dʒərətiv] adj. Peyorativo, va; despectivo, va.
— N. Palabra (*f.*) peyorativa *or* despectiva.
peke [pi:k] n. Pequinés, *m.*, pekinés, *m.* (dog).
Pekinese [pi:kiˈni:z] adj./n. See PEKINGESE.
Peking [pi:ˈkiŋ] pr. n. GEOGR. Pekín, Pequín.
Pekingese [ˌpi:kiŋˈi:z] adj. Pekinés, esa; pequinés, esa.
— N. Pekinés, esa; pequinés, esa (person). || Pequinés, *m.* (dog).
pelage [ˈpelidʒ] n. Pelaje, *m.*, pelo, *m.* (fur).
pelagian [pəˈleidʒiən] adj./n. REL. Pelagiano, na.
pelagianism [—izəm] n. REL. Pelagianismo, *m.*
pelagic [pəˈlædʒik] adj. Pelágico, ca: *pelagic fauna*, fauna pelágica.
Pelagius [pəˈleidʒiəs] pr. n. Pelagio, *m.*
Pelasgian [pəˈlæzgiən] adj./n. HIST. Pelasgo, ga.
Pelasgic [pəˈlæzgik] adj. Pelasgo, ga; pelásgico, ca.
pelerine [ˈpeləri:n] n. Esclavina, *f.* (woman's cape).
pelf [pelf] n. FAM. Vil metal, *m.* (money).
pelican [ˈpelikən] n. Pelicano, *m.*, pelícano, *m.* (bird).
pelisse [peˈli:s] n. Pelliza, *f.*
pellagra [peˈlægrə] n. MED. Pelagra, *f.*
pellet [ˈpelit] n. Bola, *f.*, bolita, *f.* (little ball). || Perdigón, *m.* (of a gun). || MED. Píldora, *f.* (pill).
pellicle [ˈpelikl] n. Película, *f.*
pellicular [peˈlikjulə*] adj. Pelicular.
pellitory [ˈpelitəri] n. BOT. Parietaria, *f.* || BOT. *Pellitory of Spain*, pelitre, *m.*
pellmell or **pell-mell** [ˈpelˈmel] adv. Atropelladamente. || Confusamente, desordenadamente.
— Adj. En desorden, confuso, sa.
pellucid [peˈlju:sid] adj. Translúcido, da; transparente. || FIG. Lúcido, da; claro, ra (mind). | Claro, ra (explanation).
pellucidity [peljuˈsiditi] n. Transparencia, *f.*, translucidez, *f.* || FIG. Lucidez, *f.*, claridad, *f.* (of mind). | Claridad, *f.* (of explanation).
Peloponnese [ˈpeləpəni:s] pr. n. GEOGR. Peloponeso, *m.*
Peloponnesian [ˌpeləpəˈni:ʃən] adj./n. Peloponense.
Peloponnesus [ˌpeləpəˈni:səs] n. GEOGR. Peloponeso, *m.*
pelota [peˈləutə] n. SP. Pelota (*f.*) vasca. || *Pelota player*, pelotari, *m.* & *f.*
pelt [pelt] n. Lluvia, *f.* (of stones). || Pellejo, *m.*, piel, *f.* (skin of an animal). || Golpe, *m.* (blow). || FAM. Piel, *f.*, pellejo, *m.* (skin). || — *At full pelt*, a toda mecha, a toda velocidad, a todo meter. || *Pelt of rain*, lluvia persistente *or* recia.
pelt [pelt] v. tr. Tirar, lanzar, arrojar: *they pelted us with snowballs*, nos tiraron bolas de nieve. || Apedrear (to stone). || Acribillar (with questions). || Colmar (with abuse).
— V. intr. Llover a cántaros (to rain). || FAM. Correr

a todo meter (to run). || — *He pelted away*, se fue corriendo. || *It's pelting down*, está lloviendo a cántaros. || *Pelting rain*, lluvia recia. || *To pelt at*, golpear fuertemente, aporrear.

peltry [ˈpeltri] n. Peletería, *f.*

pelure paper [pəˈljuə*ˈpeipə*] n. Papel (*m.*) cebolla.

pelvic [ˈpelvik] adj. ANAT. Pélvico, ca; pelviano, na.

pelvis [ˈpelvis] n. ANAT. Pelvis, *f.*

— OBSERV. El plural de la palabra inglesa *pelvis* es *pelves*.

pen [pen] n. Gallinero, *m.* (enclosure for hens). || Aprisco, *m.*, redil, *m.* (for sheep). || Pocilga *f.* (for pigs). || Corral, *m.* (for farm animals). || Toril, *m.* (at a bullring). || Hembra (*f.*) del cisne (female swan). || Pluma, *f.* (writing instrument, bird's feather). || Pluma, *f.*, plumilla, *f.* (nib). || Parque, *m.*, jaula, *f.* (child's play area). || FIG. Pluma, *f.*: *a journalist lives by his pen*, el periodista vive de su pluma. || FAM. Chirona, *f.* (jail). || — *Ball-point pen*, bolígrafo, *m.* || *Felt-tipped pen*, rotulador, *m.* || *Fountain pen*, pluma estilográfica. || *To have a ready pen*, tener facilidad para escribir. || *To let one's pen run on*, escribir al correr de la pluma *or* a vuela pluma. || *To put pen to paper*, tomar la pluma.

pen [pen] v. tr. Escribir. || *To pen in* o *up*, encerrar, acorralar.

penal [ˈpi:nl] adj. Penal: *penal code*, código penal. || Castigable (legally punishable). || — *Penal colony*, penal, *m.* || *Penal servitude*, trabajos forzados. || *Penal servitude for life*, cadena perpetua.

penalization [pi:nəlaiˈzeiʃən] n. Castigo, *m.*, penalización, *f.*

penalize [ˈpi:nəlaiz] v. tr. Penar, castigar, penalizar (to inflict punishment on). || Perjudicar: *the tobacco tax penalizes the smoker*, los impuestos sobre el tabaco perjudican al fumador. || SP. Castigar, penalizar.

penalty [ˈpenlti] n. Pena, *f.* (punishment for breaking a law, etc.): *death penalty*, pena de muerte. || Multa, *f.* (fine). || FIG. Castigo, *m.*: *his hangover was a penalty for drinking too much*, la resaca fue su castigo por haber bebido demasiado. | Precio, *m.*, contrapartida, *f.*: *penalty of fame*, precio de la gloria. | Consecuencias, *f. pl.*: *to pay the penalty of*, pagar las consecuencias de. || SP. Penalty, *m.*, castigo (*m.*) máximo (in football, hockey). | Penalización, *f.* (in golf). | Tiro (*m.*) de castigo *or* de penalidad (rugby). || Multa, *f.* (in bridge). || — *On* o *upon* o *under penalty of*, bajo pena de. || SP. *Penalty area*, área (*f.*) de castigo. || *Penalty clause*, cláusula (*f.*) penal. || SP. *Penalty kick*, penalty. | *Penalty spot*, punto (*m.*) de penalty.

penance [ˈpenəns] n. REL. Penitencia, *f.* || — *As penance*, como penitencia. || *To do one's penance*, cumplir la penitencia. || *To do penance*, hacer penitencia. || *To give s.o. a penance*, imponer una penitencia a uno.

pen-and-ink [ˈpenəndˈiŋk] adj. A pluma (drawing).

penates [peˈnɑ:teis] pl. n. Penates, *m.*

pence [pens] pl. n. See PENNY.

penchant [ˈpɑ̃:ŋʃɑ̃:ŋ] n. Inclinación, *f.*: *to have a penchant for music*, tener inclinación por la música.

pencil [ˈpensl] n. Lápiz, *m.*, lapicero, *m.*: *coloured pencil*, lápiz de color; *eyebrow pencil*, lápiz de ojos. || PHYS. Haz, *m.* (narrow beam of light). || — *In pencil*, a *or* con lápiz. || *Pencil drawing*, dibujo (*m.*) a lápiz. || *Propelling pencil*, lapicero, portaminas, *m. inv.*

pencil [ˈpensl] v. tr. Escribir con lápiz (to write). || Dibujar a lápiz (to draw). || Pintarse con lápiz (one's eyebrows).

pencil box [—bɔks] or **pencil case** [—keis] n. Estuche (*m.*) para lápices, plumero, *m.*

pencil holder [—ˌhəuldə*] n. Portalápiz, *m.*

pencil sharpener [—ˈʃɑ:pnə*] n. Sacapuntas, *m. inv.*, afilalápices, *m. inv.*

pendant [ˈpendənt] n. Colgante, *m.*, dije, *m.* (of necklace, chain, etc.). || Pendiente, *m.* (earring). || Colgante, *m.* (of a chandelier). || Colgante, *m.*, lámpara (*f.*) colgante (electrical fixture). || MAR. Grímpola, *f.*, gallardete, *m.*, banderín, *m.* (pennant). || Pareja, *f.* (companion piece of a picture, etc.).

— Adj. See PENDENT.

pendent [ˈpendənt] adj. Pendiente, colgante (hanging). || Que sobresale, sobresaliente (overhanging). || Pendiente (pending).

pendentive [pen dentiv] n. ARCH. Pechina, *f.*

pending [ˈpendiŋ] adj. Pendiente: *the case is still pending*, el caso está todavía pendiente; *pending orders*, pedidos pendientes.

— Prep. Hasta: *a temporary arrangement pending a final settlement*, un arreglo temporal hasta una solución definitiva. || Durante: *pending the discussions there are to be no troop movements*, durante las conversaciones, no debe haber movimiento de tropas.

pendular [ˈpendjulə*] adj. Pendular.

pendulous [ˈpendjuləs] adj. Colgante (hanging or bending down). || Oscilante (swinging to and fro).

pendulum [pendjuləm] n. Péndulo, *m.*

peneplain or **peneplane** [ˈpi:niplein] n. GEOL. Penillanura, *f.*

penetrability [ˌpenitrəˈbiliti] n. Penetrabilidad, *f.*

penetrable [ˈpenitrəbl] adj. Penetrable.

penetrate [ˈpenitreit] v. tr. Penetrar en (to go into by piercing): *the shell penetrated the hull*, el proyectil penetró en el casco. || Extenderse por: *the smell penetrated the whole house*, el olor se extendió por toda la casa. || FIG. Penetrar, descubrir (to discern, to see through): *to penetrate a secret*, penetrar un secreto.

— V. intr. Penetrar: *the bullet penetrated to the lung*, la bala penetró hasta el pulmón; *to penetrate into the jungle*, penetrar en la selva. || Entrar, penetrar: *water is penetrating everywhere*, el agua está entrando por todas partes. || *To penetrate through sth.*, atravesar algo.

penetrating [—iŋ] adj. Penetrante: *a penetrating gaze, wind*, una mirada, un viento penetrante. || Agudo, da (cry). || Perspicaz: *a penetrating mind*, una mente perspicaz. || *To have a penetrating eye*, tener la vista aguda *or* penetrante.

penetration [ˌpeniˈtreiʃən] n. Penetración, *f.*

penetrative [ˈpenitrətiv] adj. Penetrante.

penfriend [ˈpenfrend] n. Persona (*f.*) con quien uno se cartea.

penguin [ˈpeŋgwin] n. ZOOL. Pingüino, *m.*

penholder [ˈpenˌhəuldə*] n. Portaplumas, *m. inv.*, mango (*m.*) de la pluma.

penicillin [ˌpeniˈsilin] n. MED. Penicilina, *f.*

penicillium [peniˈsiliəm] n. BOT. Penicillium, *m.*

— OBSERV. El plural de la palabra inglesa es *penicillia*.

peninsula [piˈninsjulə] n. Península, *f.*: *the Iberian Peninsula*, la Península Ibérica.

peninsular [—*] adj. Peninsular. || HIST. *The Peninsular War*, la Guerra de Independencia (in Spain).

penis [ˈpi:nis] n. ANAT. Pene, *m.*

— OBSERV. El plural de *penis* es *penes* o *penises*.

penitence [ˈpenitəns] n. Penitencia, *f.* || Arrepentimiento, *m.*

penitent [ˈpenitənt] adj./n. Penitente. || Arrepentido, da: *a penitent thief*, un ladrón arrepentido.

penitential [ˌpeniˈtenʃəl] adj. Penitencial.

penitentiary [ˌpeniˈtenʃəri] n. Penitenciaría, *f.*, penal, *m.* (prison). || Reformatorio, *m.*, correccional, *m.* (institution to reform offenders). || REL. Penitenciaría, *f.* (office). | Penitenciario, *m.* (officer).

— Adj. Penitenciario, ria: *penitentiary system*, régimen penitenciario. || U. S. *Penitentiary offence*, delito castigado con el encarcelamiento en un penal.

penknife [ˈpennaif] n. Navaja, *f.*, cortaplumas, *m. inv.*

— OBSERV. El plural de esta palabra es *penknives*.

penman [ˈpenmən] n. Calígrafo, *m.* || Escritor, *m.* (writer).

— OBSERV. El plural de *penman* es *penmen*.

penmanship [—ʃip] n. Caligrafía, *f.* || Pluma, *f.* (style).

penna [ˈpenə] n. Pena, *f.* (feather).

— OBSERV. El plural de *penna* es *pennae*.

pen name [ˈpenneim] n. Seudónimo, *m.*

pennant [ˈpenənt] n. MAR. Gallardete, *m.*, grímpola, *f.* || Banderín, *m.* (small flag).

pennate [ˈpenet] adj. BOT. Pinado, da. || ZOOL. Alado, da.

pen nib [ˈpe nib] n. Plumilla, *f.* (of fountain pen). || Punta, *f.*

penniless [ˈpenilis] adj. Sin dinero. || *To be penniless*, estar sin un céntimo *or* sin un real.

Pennine Chain [ˈpenain tʃein] pr. n. GEOGR. Montes (*m. pl.*) Peninos.

Pennines [ˈpenainz] pl. pr. n. GEOGR. Peninos, *m.*, Montes (*m.*) Peninos.

pennon [ˈpenən] n. HIST. Pendón, *m.* (of a knight). || MAR. Gallardete, *m.*, grímpola, *f.* || Banderín, *m.* (small flag).

Pennsylvania [ˌpensilˈveinjə] pr. n. GEOGR. Pensivalnia, *f.*

Pennsylvanian [—n] adj./n. Pensilvano, na.

penny [ˈpeni] n. Penique, *m.*: *a new penny*, un nuevo penique; *sevenpence*, siete peniques. || U. S. Centavo, *m.* || FIG. Céntimo, *m.* || — *A penny for your thoughts*, ¿en qué estás pensando? || FIG. *Bad pennies always turn up*, bicho malo nunca muere. | *He is a bad penny*, es un gamberro. | *I am not a penny the wiser*, no me he enterado todavía. || *Not to have a penny to one's name* o *to bless o.s. with*, no tener un céntimo *or* un real. || FIG. *Take care of the pennies and the pounds will take care of themselves*, poco a poco la vieja hila el copo. | *The penny just dropped*, ahora caigo [en la cuenta], acabo de caer en la cuenta. | *To cost a pretty penny*, costar un dineral. | *To look twice at every penny*, reparar en gastos, ser tacaño. | *To make a pretty penny out of it*, sacar buen provecho de ello. || FIG. FAM. *To spend a penny*, llamar por teléfono (to go to the toilet). || *To turn an honest penny*, ganarse honradamente la vida.

— OBSERV. La palabra penny tiene dos plurales: *pence* (forma más empleada hoy) y *pennies*.

— La libra, hasta el año 1971, se dividía en 240 peniques y desde entonces se divide en 100, o sea que en la actualidad el penique es la centésima parte de la libra.

penny-a-liner [ˈpeniəˈlainə*] n. Escritorzuelo, *m.* (bad writer).

penny dreadful [ˈpeniˈdredful] n. Novela (*f.*) de muy poca categoría *or* barata, revista (*f.*) de muy poca categoría *or* barata.

penny-in-the-slot machine [ˈpeniinðəˈslɔtməˌʃi:n] n. Máquina (*f.*) tragaperras.
penny-pinching [ˈpenipintʃiŋ] adj. U. S. FAM. Tacaño, ña.
pennyweight [ˈpeniweit] n. Peso (*m.*) que equivale aproximadamente a un gramo y medio.
penny-wise [ˈpeniwaiz] adj. Que escatima en cosas pequeñas. || *To be penny-wise and pound-foolish,* hacer economías de chicha y nabo.
pennyworth [ˈpenəθ,US.ˈpeniwerθ] n. Valor (*m.*) de un penique: *to buy a pennyworth of,* comprar por el valor de un penique. || FIG. Pizca, *f.* || FIG. *There is not a pennyworth of food in the house,* no hay absolutamente nada de comer en la casa.
penologist [pi:ˈnɔlədʒist] n. JUR. Penalista, *m.* & *f.*, criminalista, *m.* & *f.*
penology [pi:ˈnɔlədʒi] n. JUR. Criminología, *f.*
penpusher [ˈpen,puʃə*] n. Chupatintas, *m. inv.*
pension [ˈpenʃən] n. Jubilación, *f.* (given to workers). || MIL. Retiro, *m.* || Pensión, *f.* (allowance). || Subvención, *f.* (given to artists). || — *Old-age pension* o *retirement pension,* jubilación, *f.* (of workers), retiro, *m.* (of soldiers), subsidio (*m.*) de vejez, pensión, *f.* (State aid). || *To retire on a pension,* jubilarse (a worker), retirarse (a soldier).
pension [ˈpɑ̃:ŋsiɔ̃:ŋ] n. Pensión, *f.* (board, lodging). || Internado, *m.* (school).
pension [ˈpenʃən] v. tr. Pensionar, dar una pensión a. || *To pension off,* jubilar (a worker), retirar (a soldier).
pensionable [—əbl] adj. Con derecho a la jubilación (a worker). || Con derecho al retiro (soldier). || *Pensionable age,* edad (*f.*) de la jubilación (of a worker), edad (*f.*) del retiro (of a soldier).
pensionary [—əri] n. Pensionado, da (who receives a pension). || Jubilado, da (worker). || Retirado, da (soldier). || Mercenario, *m.* (hireling).
pensioner [—ə*] n. Pensionista, *m.* & *f.*, pensionado, da. || Inválido, *m.* (in institution). || Pensionista, *m.* & *f.* (student).
pensive [ˈpensiv] adj. Pensativo, va; meditabundo, da.
pensiveness [—nis] n. Aire (*m.*) meditabundo. || Meditaciones, *f. pl.*
penstock [ˈpenstɔk] n. Compuerta, *f.* (sluice gate). || Caz, *m.* (millrace).
pent [pent] adj. See PENT-UP.
pentagon [ˈpentəgən] n. Pentágono, *m.* || *The Pentagon,* el Pentágono.
pentagonal [penˈtægənl] adj. MATH. Pentagonal, pentágono, na.
pentahedron [pentəˈhi:drən] n. MATH. Pentaedro.
pentarchy [ˈpentɑ:rki] n. Pentarquía, *f.*
pentasyllabic [pentəsiˈlæbik] adj. Pentasílabo, ba.
pentasyllable [pentəˈsiləbl] n. Pentasílabo, *m.*
Pentateuch [ˈpentətju:k] n. REL. Pentateuco, *m.*
pentathlon [penˈtæθlən] n. SP. Pentatlón, *m.*
Pentecost [ˈpentikɔst] n. REL. Pentecostés, *m.*
Pentecostal [,pentiˈkɔstl] adj. De Pentecostés.
penthouse [ˈpenthaus] n. Cobertizo, *m.* (shed). || Ático, *m.* (flat). || Alero, *m.* (over door or window).
pentode [ˈpentəud] n. PHYS. Pentodo, *m.*
pentothal [ˈpentəθɔl] n. MED. Pentotal, *m.*
pent-up [ˈpentʌp] adj. Encerrado, da (confined). || Reprimido, da; contenido, da (emotion).
penult [piˈnʌlt] n. Penúltima sílaba, *f.*
penultimate [piˈnʌltimit] adj. Penúltimo, ma.
— N. Penúltimo, ma. || Penúltima sílaba, *f.*
penumbra [piˈnʌmbrə] n. Penumbra, *f.*

— OBSERV. El plural de la palabra inglesa *penumbra* es *penumbrae* o *penumbras.*

penurious [piˈnjuəriəs] adj. Parsimonioso, sa; avaro, ra (stingy). || Mezquino, na (mean). || Pobre: *penurious family,* familia pobre. || Poco fértil (barren).
penury [ˈpenjuri] n. Penuria, *f.*, escasez, *f.* (lack). || Pobreza, *f.*, miseria, *f.* (extreme poverty): *to live in penury,* vivir en la miseria. || Pobreza, *f.* (of ideas, language, etc.).
peon [pju:n,US.ˈpi:ən] n. Peón, *m.*, bracero, *m.* (labourer). || Criado, *m.* (servant).
peonage [ˈpiənidʒ] n. Condición (*f.*) de peón. || FIG. Esclavitud, *f.* (servitude).
peony [ˈpiəni] n. BOT. Peonía, *f.*, saltaojos, *m. inv.*
people [ˈpi:pl] n. Personas, *f. pl.*: *five hundred people,* quinientas personas. || Gente, *f.*: *what will people say?,* ¿qué dirá la gente?; *many people,* mucha gente; *the country people,* la gente del campo; *business people,* gente de negocios; *all sorts of people,* toda clase de gente; *people say,* la gente dice. || Pueblo, *m.*, nación, *f.*: *the Spanish people,* el pueblo español; *to call on the people,* hacer un llamamiento al pueblo. || Súbditos, *m. pl.* (of a king). || Nacionales, *m. pl.* (of a country). || Pueblo, *m.*: *government by the people,* gobierno por el pueblo. || Habitantes, *m. pl.* (of a town). || Familia, *f.*: *to write to one's people,* escribir a la familia. || Amigos, *m. pl.* (friends). || Antepasados, *m. pl.* (ancestors). || — *Coloured people,* gente de color. || *I am going to write to my people,* voy a escribir a los míos *or* a mi familia. || *Lower class people,* pueblo bajo. || *Man of the people,* hombre (*m.*) del pueblo. || *Most people,* la mayoría de la gente. || *Ordinary people,* gente de la calle. || *People's court,* tribunal (*m.*) del pueblo. || *People's front,* frente (*m.*) popular. || *People's republic,* república (*f.*) popular. || *The common people,* el pueblo, la plebe. || *The people at large,* la gente en general. || *What do you people think?,* ¿qué piensan ustedes? || *Young people,* gente joven, jóvenes, *m. pl.*

— OBSERV. Cuando tiene un sentido colectivo *people* permanece invariable, pero se construye con el plural; en los demás casos la forma plural es *peoples.*

people [ˈpi:pl] v. tr. Poblar: *densely peopled country,* país muy poblado; *thinly peopled,* poco poblado.
pep [pep] n. FAM. Energía, *f.*: *full of pep,* lleno de energía.
pep [pep] v. tr. *To pep up,* animar (conversation, dance, person).
peplum [pepləm] n. Peplo, *m.*

— OBSERV. El plural de *peplum* es *peplums* o *pepla.*

pepper [ˈpepə*] n. Pimienta, *f.*: *black pepper,* pimienta negra. || BOT. Pimentero, *m.* (plant). | Pimiento, *m.*: *red pepper,* pimiento rojo; *sweet pepper,* pimiento morrón. || FAM. Tocino, *m.* (in skipping).
pepper [ˈpepə*] v. tr. Sazonar con pimienta (to season with pepper). || Acribillar: *they peppered him with shot,* le acribillaron a balazos. || FIG. Salpicar: *to pepper a speech with anecdotes,* salpicar un discurso con anécdotas.
pepper-and-salt [—ənˈsɔ:lt] adj. De mezclilla (cloth). || Entrecano, na (hair).
pepperbox [—bɔks] n. Pimentero, *m.*
peppercorn [—kɔ:n] n. Grano (*m.*) de pimienta. || FIG. *Peppercorn rent,* alquiler (*m.*) nominal.
pepper mill [—mil] n. Molinillo (*m.*) de pimienta.
peppermint [—mint] n. BOT. Hierbabuena, *f.*, yerbabuena, *f.*, menta, *f.* || Menta, *f.* (flavour). || Pipermín, *m.* (liqueur). || Pastilla (*f.*) de menta (sweet).
pepper patch [—pætʃ] n. Pimental, *m.*
pepper pot [—pɔt] n. Pimentero, *m.* (pepperbox). || CULIN. Guiso (*m.*) indio compuesto de carne *or* pescado y pimientos rojos. | Estofado (*m.*) muy picante (highly seasoned stew).
pepper shaker [—,ʃeikə*] n. U. S. Pimentero, *m.*
peppery [—ri] adj. Picante (tasting of pepper). || Irascible, enojadizo, za (quick-tempered). || Mordaz, picante (language).
pep pill [ˈpepˈpil] n. MED. Estimulante, *m.*
peppy [ˈpepi] adj. Lleno de vida.
pepsin [ˈpepsin] n. CHEM. Pepsina, *f.*
peptalk [ˈteptɔ:k] n. FAM. Discurso (*m.*) *or* palabras (*f. pl.*) destinadas a levantar los ánimos.
per [pə:*] prep. Por: *three shillings per person,* tres chelines por persona; *three per cent,* tres por ciento; *an increase of ten per cent,* un aumento del diez por ciento; *to decrease by five per cent,* bajar en un cinco por ciento. || Por, por medio de (by means of). || A, por: *per annum,* al año. || — *As per invoice,* según factura. || *As per usual,* como de costumbre. || *Per capita,* per cápita, por cabeza. || *Per hour,* por hora: *one hundred miles per hour,* cien millas por hora; por horas: *to work per hour,* trabajar por horas. || *Thirty pence per pound,* treinta peniques la libra.
peradventure [pərədˈventʃə*] adv. (Ant.). Quizás, tal vez (perhaps). | Por casualidad (by chance).
— N. (Ant.). *Beyond* o *without peradventure,* sin duda alguna.
perambulate [pəˈræmbjuleit] v. tr. Recorrer: *to perambulate the countryside,* recorrer el campo.
— V. intr. Andar, pasear.
perambulation [pə,ræmbjuˈleiʃən] n. Paseo, *m.* (stroll). || Viaje, *m.* (trip). || Inspección, *f.*
perambulator [ˈpræmbjuleitə*] n. Cochecito (*m.*) de niño (pram). || Paseante, *m.* & *f.* (person walking).
perborate [pə:ˈbɔ:reit] n. CHEM. Perborato, *m.*
percale [pə:ˈkeil] n. Percal, *m.*
percaline [pəkəˈlin] n. Percalina, *f.*
perceivable [pəˈsi:vəbl] adj. Perceptible.
perceive [pəˈsi:v] v. tr. Percibir (to hear): *he perceived a faint sound,* percibió un leve ruido. || Divisar (to see): *I perceived a boat in the distance,* divisé un barco a lo lejos. || Notar, darse cuenta (to notice): *he perceived that he was being watched,* se dio cuenta de que le estaban observando. || Comprender (to understand).
percent [pəˈsent] adj. Del... por ciento: *nine percent interest,* interés del nueve por ciento.
— N. Tanto (*m.*) por ciento, porcentaje, *m.* || Por ciento: *a commission of ten percent,* una comisión del diez por ciento. || *To agree a hundred per cent,* estar completamente de acuerdo, estar cien por cien de acuerdo.
percentage [—idʒ] n. Porcentaje, *m.*, tanto por ciento, *m.*: *to allow a percentage on all transactions,* conceder un tanto por ciento en todas las transacciones. || Porcentaje, *m.*, parte, *f.*: *only a small percentage of pupils were successful,* sólo una pequeña parte de los alumnos aprobó. || Proporción, *f.* (of acid, alcohol, etc.). || FIG. Provecho, *m.* (profit).
— Adj. Porcentual.
per centum [pəˈsentəm] n. See PERCENT.
percept [pə:sept] n. Percepción, *f.*
perceptibility [pə,septəˈbiliti] n. Perceptibilidad, *f.*
perceptible [pəˈseptəbl] adj. Perceptible. || Sensible: *perceptible difference,* diferencia sensible. || — *Perceptible to the ear,* audible, oíble. || *Perceptible to the eye,* visible.
perception [pəˈsepʃən] n. Percepción, *f.* (the act of perceiving). || Sensibilidad, *f.* || Comprensión, *f.*

perceptionism [—izəm] n. Percepcionismo, *m.*
perceptive [pəˈseptiv] adj. Perceptivo, va: *perceptive faculties*, facultades perceptivas. || Perspicaz (perspicacious).
perceptivity [—iti] n. Facultad (*f.*) perceptiva.
perch [pəːtʃ] n. Perca, *f.* (fish). || Percha, *f.*, vara, *f.* (for birds). || FIG. Posición. *f.*: *he had a good view from his perch on the rooftop*, tenía muy buena vista desde su posición en el tejado. || Medida (*f.*) de longitud de unos 5 metros. || FAM. *To knock s.o. off his perch*, derribar *or* desbancar a alguien.
perch [pəːtʃ] v. tr. Encaramar: *a castle perched on a rock*, un castillo encaramado en una roca. || Colocar [en un sitio elevado].
— V. intr. Posarse (bird). || Encaramarse: *the child perched on a stool*, el niño se encaramó en un taburete. || Subirse (to climb up).
perchance [pəˈtʃɑːns] adv. (Ant.). Tal vez, quizás (perhaps). | Por casualidad (by chance).
percheron [ˈpəːʃərən] n. Percherón, *m.* (horse).
perchlorate [pəːˈklɔːret] n. CHEM. Perclorato, *m.*
perchloride [pəːˈklɔraid] n. CHEM. Percloruro, *m.*
percipient [pəːˈsipiənt] adj./n. Perceptor, ra
percolate [ˈpəːkəleit] v. tr. Colar, filtrar (to filter). || Filtrar (coffee).
— V. intr. Filtrarse, colarse (liquid). || Filtrarse (coffee). || FIG. Infiltrarse.
percolation [ˌpəːkəˈleiʃən] n. Filtración, *f.*, filtrado, *m.* || FIG. Infiltración, *f.*
percolator [ˈpəːkəleitə*] n. Cafetera (*f.*) de filtro, percolador, *m.*
percuss [pəːˈkʌs] v. tr. MED. Percutir.
percussion [pəˈkʌʃən] n. Percusión, *f.*: *percussion instruments*, instrumentos de percusión; *percussion gun*, arma de percusión. || — *Percussion cap*, cápsula, *f.*, pistón, *m.* (of firearm). || *Percussion hammer*, percusor, *m.*
per diem [pəːˈdaiem] adv. Diariamente.
— Adj. Diario, ria.
— N. U. S. Dietas, *f. pl.* (allowance).
perdition [pəːˈdiʃən] n. Perdición, *f.*
perdurability [pəːˌdjuərəˈbiliti] n. Perdurabilidad, *f.*
perdurable [pəːˈdjuərəbl] adj. Perdurable.
peregrinate [ˈperigrineit] v. intr. Peregrinar.
peregrination [ˌperigriˈneiʃən] n. Peregrinación, *f.*
peregrine [ˈperigrin] n. ZOOL. Halcón (*m.*) peregrino.
peremptorily [pəˈremptərili] adv. Perentoriamente.
peremptoriness [pəˈremptərinis] n. Perentoriedad, *f.*
peremptory [pəˈremptəri] adj. Perentorio, ria: *in a peremptory tone*, con tono perentorio. || Autoritario, ria (person). || JUR. *Peremptory plea*, excepción perentoria.
perennial [pəˈrenjəl] adj. Perenne. || *Perennial youth*, juventud eterna.
— N. Planta (*f.*) perenne.
perfect [ˈpəːfikt] adj. Perfecto, ta: *a perfect example*, un ejemplo perfecto; *perfect knowledge*, conocimiento perfecto. || Perfecto, ta; verdadero, ra: *a perfect gentleman*, un verdadero caballero. || Perfecto, ta; consumado, da; completo, ta: *a perfect idiot*, un idiota completo. || Absoluto, ta: *perfect silence*, silencio absoluto. || BOT. Completo, ta: *perfect flower*, flor completa. || MATH. MUS. GRAMM. Perfecto, ta: *a perfect square*, un cuadrado perfecto; *perfect cadence*, cadencia perfecta; *perfect tense*, tiempo perfecto. || — GRAMM. *Future perfect*, futuro perfecto. | *Present perfect*, pretérito perfecto. || *She is a perfect stranger to me*, no la conozco absolutamente nada.
— N. GRAMM. Pretérito (*m.*) perfecto.
perfect [pəˈfekt] v. tr. Perfeccionar.
perfectibility [pəˌfektiˈbiliti] n. Perfectibilidad, *f.*
perfectible [pəˈfektəbl] adj. Perfectible.
perfection [pəˈfekʃən] n. Perfección, *f.* || Perfeccionamiento, *m.* || — *To be the perfection of kindness*, ser la bondad misma. || *To bring sth. to perfection*, rematar algo. || *To do sth. to perfection*, hacer algo a la perfección *or* a las mil maravillas.
perfectioning [—iŋ] n. Perfeccionamiento, *m.*
perfectionist [—ist] n. Perfeccionista, *m.* & *f.*
perfectly [ˈpəːfiktli] adv. Perfectamente. || — *It's perfectly silly*, es completamente tonto. || *To be perfectly happy*, ser muy feliz.
perfectness [ˈpəːfiktnis] n. Perfección, *f.*
perfervid [pəːˈfəːvid] adj. Ardiente, férvido, da.
perfidious [pəːˈfidiəs] adj. Pérfido, da.
perfidy [ˈpəːfidi] n. Perfidia, *f.*
perfoliate [pəːˈfəuliət] adj. BOT. Perfoliado, da.
perforate [ˈpəːfəreit] v. tr. Perforar. || *Perforated stamp*, sello dentado.
— V. intr. Perforarse. || Penetrar (*into*, en).
perforating [—iŋ] adj. Perforador, ra; perforante. || MED. *Perforating ulcer*, úlcera (*f.*) perforante.
— N. Perforado, *m.* (punching).
perforation [ˌpəːfəˈreiʃən] n. Perforación, *f.*, perforado, *m.* || Agujero, *m.* (hole). || MED. Perforación, *f.* || Trepado, *m.*, dentado, *m.* (of stamps).
perforator [ˈpəːfəreitə*] n. Perforador, ra (person). || Perforadora, *f.* (machine).
perforce [pəˈfɔːs] adv. (Ant.). Forzosamente, por fuerza.
perform [pəˈfɔːm] v. tr. Hacer, llevar a cabo, ejecutar, realizar (to carry out): *the work being performed*, el trabajo que se está realizando. || Cumplir (duty, promise). || Desempeñar (functions). || THEATR. Representar (a play). | Desempeñar, interpretar (a part). | Ejecutar, interpretar, tocar (piece of music). || Celebrar (a ceremony, rite). || *To perform wonders*, hacer maravillas.
— V. intr. Actuar, trabajar (actors): *who performs in that play?*, ¿quién trabaja en esa obra? || Tocar (musicians): *to perform on the flute*, tocar la flauta. || Cantar (singers). || Hacer un número, hacer trucos (animals). || TECH. Funcionar: *the engine performs well*, el motor funciona bien. | Portarse: *how does this car perform on slippery roads?*, ¿cómo se porta este coche en las carreteras resbaladizas?
performable [—əbl] adj. Hacedero, ra; realizable (task). || Representable (play). || Ejecutable (piece of music).
performance [—əns] n. Ejecución, *f.*, cumplimiento, *m.*, realización, *f.* (of a task). || Desempeño, *m.* (of functions). || Representación, *f.* (of a play). || Actuación, *f.*, interpretación, *f.* (of an actor, musician). || Interpretación, *f.* (of a piece of music, of a part). || Sesión, *f.* (in cinema): *the evening performance*, la sesión de la tarde. || Función, *f.* (in theatre). || Hazaña, *f.* (deed). || Celebración, *f.* (of ceremony, rite). || SP. Actuación, *f.* (of a team, athlete, horse, etc.). | Marca, *f.*, resultado, *m.*: *best performance*, mejor marca. || TECH. Funcionamiento, *m.* (of a machine). | Rendimiento, *m.* (of a motor, aircraft, etc.): *best performance*, rendimiento máximo. | Cualidades (*f. pl.*) técnicas (of a car). || — *Continuous performance*, sesión continua. || *First performance*, primera representación, estreno, *m.* || *No performance tonight*, no hay función esta noche. || FAM. *What a performance!*, ¡qué jaleo!
performer [—ə*] n. THEATR. Actor, *m.*, actriz, *f.*, artista, *m.* & *f.* || MUS. Músico, *m.*, intérprete, *m.* & *f.*, ejecutante, *m.* & *f.*
performing [—iŋ] adj. Amaestrado, da: *performing seals*, focas amaestradas.
perfume [ˈpəːfjuːm] n. Perfume, *m.* || — *Perfume atomizer*, atomizador, *m.*, vaporizador, *m.*, pulverizador, *m.* || *Perfume burner* o *pan*, pebetero, *m.*
perfume [pəˈfjuːm] v. tr./intr. Perfumar.
perfumery [—əri] n. Perfumería, *f.*
perfunctorily [pəˈfʌŋktərili] adv. A la ligera: *to perform a piece of work perfunctorily*, hacer un trabajo a la ligera. || Superficialmente. || Mecánicamente.
perfunctoriness [pəˈfʌŋktərinis] n. Negligencia, *f.*, descuido, *m.* (carelessness). || Superficialidad, *f.* || Indiferencia, *f.* (lack of interest).
perfunctory [pəˈfʌŋktəri] adj. Negligente, descuidado, da (careless). || Superficial, somero, ra (superficial): *a perfunctory inspection*, una inspección somera. || Hecho a la ligera: *perfunctory work*, trabajo hecho a la ligera. || Mecánico, ca (done as a duty or routine).
perfuse [pəːˈfjuːz] v. tr. Inundar (to cover with liquid). || Introducir, hacer penetrar (to force a liquid through).
perfusion [pəːˈfjuːʒən] n. Aspersión, *f.* || MED. Perfusión, *f.*
pergola [ˈpəːgələ] n. Pérgola, *f.*
perhaps [pəˈhæps] adv. Quizá, quizás, tal vez. || *Perhaps so*, puede ser, quizás.
perianth [ˈperiænθ] n. BOT. Periantio, *m.*
periapt [ˈperiæpt] n. Amuleto, *m.*, talismán, *m.*
pericardium [ˌperiˈkɑːdjəm] n. ANAT. Pericardio, *m.*

— OBSERV. El plural de *pericardium* es *pericardia*.

pericarp [ˈperikɑːp] n. BOT. Pericarpio, *m.*
pericranium [periˈkreiniəm] n. ANAT. Pericráneo, *m.*

— OBSERV. El plural de *pericranium* es *pericrania*.

peridot [ˈperidɔt] n. MIN. Peridoto, *m.*
perigee [ˈperidʒiː] n. ASTR. Perigeo, *m.*
peril [ˈperil] n. Peligro, *m.* (danger). || Riesgo, *m.* (risk). || — *At* o *to one's own peril*, por su cuenta y riesgo. || *In peril of*, en peligro de. || *In peril of one's life*, en peligro de muerte. || *To face the peril*, arrostrar el peligro.
perilous [—əs] adj. Peligroso, sa; arriesgado, da.
perimeter [pəˈrimitə*] n. Perímetro, *m.*
perimetric [periˈmetrik] adj. Perimétrico, ca.
perineum [periˈniːəm] n. ANAT. Perineo, *m.*

— OBSERV. El plural de la palabra inglesa es *perinea*.

period [ˈpiəriəd] n. Período, *m.*, periodo, *m.*, época, *f.*: *the Elizabethan period*, el período isabelino. || Período, *m.*: *a period of two months*, un período de dos meses. || Época, *f.*: *period costume*, traje de época. || Clase, *f.*: *the school day is divided into seven periods*, el día escolar está dividido en siete clases. || Plazo, *m.*: *within a period of two months*, en un plazo de dos meses. || PHYS. MATH. MUS. Período, *m.* || GRAMM. Período, *m.* | Punto, *m.* (orthography). || Pausa, *f.* (natural pause in speaking). || SP. Tiempo, *m.* (division of play). || MED. Período, *m.* (a single menstruation, stage of a disease). || GEOL. ASTR. Período, *m.*: *lunar period*, período lunar. || — *Bright period*, clara, *f.* (weather). || *Probationary period* o *period of instruction*, período de prácticas. || *To put a period to*, poner punto final a.
— Adj. Del período. || De época (costume, furniture).
periodic [ˌpiəriˈɔdik] adj. Periódico, ca: *the periodic motion of the planets*, el movimiento periódico de los planetas.
periodical [—əl] adj. Periódico, ca.
— N. Periódico, *m.*, revista, *f.*, publicación (*f.*) periódica.

periodicity [ˌpiəriəˈdisiti] n. Periodicidad, *f.* ‖ Frecuencia, *f.*
periosteum [periˈɔstiəm] n. ANAT. Periostio, *m.*
— OBSERV. El plural de la palabra inglesa es *periostea.*
peripatetic [ˌperipəˈtetik] adj. Ambulante. ‖ PHIL. Peripatético, ca.
— N. PHIL. Peripatético, ca.
peripateticism [peripəˈtetisizəm] n. Peripatetismo, *m.*
peripeteia [peripəˈtiə] or **peripetia** [peripəˈtaiə] n. Peripecia, *f.*
peripheral [pəˈrifərəl] or **peripheric** [periˈferik] adj. Periférico, ca.
periphery [pəˈrifəri] n. Periferia, *f.*
periphrase [ˈperifreiz] v. intr. Perifrasear.
periphrasis [pəˈrifrəsis] n. Perífrasis, *f.*
— OBSERV. El plural de la palabra inglesa es *periphrases.*
periphrastic [ˌperiˈfræstik] adj. Perifrástico, ca.
periplus [ˈperiplʌs] n. Periplo, *m.*
— OBSERV. El plural de *periplus* es *peripli.*
periscope [ˈperiskəup] n. Periscopio, *m.*
periscopic [periˈskɔpik] adj. Periscópico, ca.
perish [ˈperiʃ] v. intr. Perecer, fallecer, morir (person). ‖ Echarse a perder, estropearse (substance). ‖ — *Perish the thought!*, ¡Dios nos libre! ‖ FAM. *To perish with cold*, morirse de frío.
— V. tr. Estropear, echar a perder.
perishable [—əbl] adj. Perecedero, ra: *perishable goods*, productos perecederos. ‖ Efímero, ra; de corta duración: *perishable glory*, gloria efímera.
— Pl. n. Productos (*m.*) perecederos.
perisher [—ə*] n. FAM. Individuo, *m.* ‖ FAM. *You little perisher!*, ¡sinvergüenza!
perishing [—iŋ] adj. FAM. *It's perishing*, hace un frío de perros, hace un frío que pela.
peristaltic [ˌperiˈstæltik] adj. ANAT. Peristáltico, ca.
peristyle [ˈperistail] n. ARCH. Peristilo, *m.*
perisystole [ˈperisistəl] n. BIOL. Perisístole, *f.*
peritoneum or **peritonaeum** [ˌperitəuˈni:əm] n. ANAT. Peritoneo, *m.*
— OBSERV. El plural de las palabras inglesas es *peritonea* y *peritonaea.*
peritonitis [ˌperitəuˈnaitis] n. MED. Peritonitis, *f.*
periwig [ˈperiwig] n. Peluca, *f.* (wig).
periwinkle [ˈperiˌwiŋkl] n. Vincapervinca, *f.* (plant). ‖ Bígaro, *m.*, bigarro, *m.*, caracol (*m.*) de mar (mollusc).
perjure [ˈpə:dʒə*] v. tr. Perjurar. ‖ *To perjure o.s.*, perjurar, perjurarse.
perjured [pə:dʒəd] adj. Perjuro, ra.
perjurer [pə:dʒərə*] n. Perjuro, ra.
perjury [ˈpə:dʒəri] n. Perjurio, *m.* ‖ JUR. *To commit perjury*, jurar en falso (to swear), prestar falso testimonio (to testify).
perk [pə:k] v. tr. *To perk up*, entonar, animar (to make cheerful), levantar (one's head), levantar (the tail). ‖ *To perk up its ears*, aguzar las orejas (dog).
— V. intr. *To perk up*, entonarse, animarse (after depression), reponerse (after an illness).
perkily [—ili] adv. Con desenvoltura. ‖ Con descaro (saucily).
perkiness [—inis] n. Desenvoltura, *f.* (assurance). ‖ Descaro, *m.*, frescura, *f.* (sauciness). ‖ Alegría, *f.* (gaiety).
perks [—s] pl. n. See PERQUISITE.
perky [—i] adj. Despabilado, da; despierto, ta (alert). ‖ Desenvuelto, ta (assured). ‖ Descarado, da; fresco, ca (saucy). ‖ Alegre, de buen humor (gay).
perm [pə:m] n. FAM. Permanente, *f.* (hairdressing): *to have a perm*, hacerse la permanente.
perm [pə:m] v. tr. FAM. *To have one's hair permed*, hacerse una permanente.
permanence [ˈpə:mənəns] n. Permanencia, *f.* ‖ Estabilidad, *f.* (of law). ‖ Duración, *f.* (of conquest).
permanency [—i] n. Permanencia, *f.* (permanence). ‖ Algo definitivo (permanent thing). ‖ Puesto (*m.*) fijo (job, post).
permanent [ˈpə:mənənt] adj. Permanente. ‖ Definitivo, va. ‖ Estable (stable). ‖ Duradero, ra (lasting). ‖ — *Permanent address*, domicilio, *m.* ‖ *Permanent post*, puesto fijo. ‖ *Permanent president*, presidente vitalicio. ‖ *Permanent wave*, permanente, *f.* (hairdressing). ‖ *Permanent way*, vía férrea.
— N. Permanente, *f.* (hairdressing).
permanganate [pə:ˈmæŋgənit] n. CHEM. Permanganato, *m.*
permeability [ˌpə:mjəˈbiliti] n. Permeabilidad, *f.*
permeable [ˈpə:mjəbl] adj. Permeable.
permeate [ˈpə:mieit] v. tr. Penetrar (to penetrate). ‖ Empapar, impregnar (to soak): *the soil was permeated with water*, el suelo estaba empapado de agua.
— V. intr. Penetrar.
permeation [ˌpə:miˈeiʃən] n. Penetración, *f.* ‖ Empapamiento, *m.*, impregnación, *f.* (soaking).
Permian [ˈpə:miən] adj. GEOL. Pérmico, ca; permiano, na.
— N. GEOL. Pérmico, *m.*
permillage [pəˈmilidʒ] n. Tanto por mil, *m.*
permissible [pəˈmisəbl] adj. Permisible, lícito, ta. ‖ *Would it be permissible to say that...?*, ¿podemos decir que...?
permission [pəˈmiʃən] n. Permiso, *m.*: *to ask, to give, to have permission*, pedir, dar, tener permiso; *with your permission*, con su permiso.
permissive [pəˈmisiv] adj. Permisivo, va. ‖ Tolerante: *permissive society*, sociedad tolerante. ‖ Facultativo, va (optional).
permit [ˈpə:mit] n. Permiso, *m.* (permission). ‖ Permiso, *m.*, licencia, *f.*: *export, import permit*, licencia de exportación, de importación. ‖ Pase, *m.* (allowing free movement).
permit [pəˈmit] v. tr. Permitir: *he permitted them to come*, les permitió que viniesen; *smoking is not permitted in this theatre*, no está permitido fumar en este teatro.
— V. intr. Permitir. ‖ Dejar lugar: *your conduct permits of no other explanation*, su conducta no deja lugar a otra explicación. ‖ *Weather permitting*, si el tiempo no lo impide.
permutability [pə:mjutəˈbiliti] n. Permutabilidad, *f.*
permutable [pəˈmju:təbl] adj. Permutable.
permutation [ˌpə:mjuˈteiʃən] n. Permutación, *f.* (change).
permute [pəˈmju:t] v. tr. Permutar.
pernicious [pə:ˈniʃəs] adj. Pernicioso, sa (harmful). ‖ Funesto, ta (evil): *pernicious habits*, costumbres funestas. ‖ Peligroso, sa (dangerous): *pernicious doctrine*, doctrina peligrosa. ‖ MED. *Pernicious anaemia*, anemia perniciosa.
pernickety [pəˈnikiti] adj. Quisquilloso, sa; puntilloso, sa (person). ‖ Delicado, da; minucioso, sa (work). ‖ *To be pernickety about one's food*, ser muy exigente para la comida.
peroneal [perəuˈni:əl] adj. Peroneo, a; del peroné (of the fibula).
perorate [ˈperəreit] v. intr. Perorar.
peroration [ˌperəˈreiʃən] n. Peroración, *f.*, perorata, *f.*
peroxid or **peroxide** [pəˈrɔksaid] n. CHEM. Peróxido, *m.* ‖ — *Hydrogen peroxide*, agua oxigenada. ‖ FAM. *Peroxide blonde*, rubia oxigenada.
peroxided [—id] adj. Oxigenado, da (hair).
perpend [pəˈpend] n. U. S. ARCH. Perpiaño, *m.*
perpend [pəˈpend] v. tr. Considerar, meditar (to ponder sth.). ‖ Pesar, medir, sopesar (words).
— V. intr. Reflexionar, meditar.
perpendicular [ˌpə:pənˈdikjulə*] adj. Perpendicular: *line perpendicular to another*, línea perpendicular a *or* con otra. ‖ Vertical (cliff). ‖ ARCH. Flamígero, ra (English Gothic style).
— N. MATH. Perpendicular, *f.* ‖ Plomada, *f.* (plumb line). ‖ *To be out of (the) perpendicular*, no estar a plomo.
perpendicularity [ˈpə:pənˌdikjuˈlæriti] n. Perpendicularidad, *f.*
perpetrate [ˈpə:pitreit] v. tr. JUR. Perpetrar, cometer: *to perpetrate a crime*, perpetrar un crimen. ‖ Hacer: *to perpetrate a pun*, hacer un juego de palabras.
perpetration [ˌpə:piˈtreiʃən] n. Perpetración, *f.*
perpetrator [ˈpə:pitreitə*] n. Autor, ra: *the perpetrator of the joke*, el autor de la broma. ‖ JUR. Perpetrador, ra.
perpetual [pəˈpetʃuəl] adj. Perpetuo, tua: *perpetual calendar*, calendario perpetuo. ‖ Continuo, nua; incesante: *perpetual chatter*, charla continua. ‖ Eterno, na: *perpetual damnation*, condena eterna. ‖ *Perpetual motion*, movimiento continuo *or* perpetuo.
perpetuate [pəˈpetʃueit] v. tr. Perpetuar: *the pyramids perpetuate the memory of the pharaohs*, las pirámides perpetúan el recuerdo de los faraones.
perpetuation [pəˌpetʃuˈeiʃən] n. Perpetuación *f.*
perpetuity [ˌpə:piˈtju:iti] n. Perpetuidad, *f.* ‖ JUR. Renta (*f.*) perpetua (perpetual annuity). ‖ *In* o *to perpetuity*, a perpetuidad, para siempre (for ever).
perplex [pəˈpleks] v. tr. Dejar perplejo (to astonish). ‖ Complicar, enredar, embrollar (a situation, etc.).
perplexed [—t] adj. Perplejo, ja (astonished). ‖ Embrollado, da; enredado, da (entangled).
perplexedly [—idli] adv. Con perplejidad.
perplexing [—iŋ] adj. Que causa perplejidad. ‖ Confuso, sa; poco claro, ra: *a perplexing author*, un autor poco claro. ‖ Complicado, da (complex).
perplexity [pəˈpleksiti] n. Perplejidad, *f.* ‖ Confusión, *f.* ‖ *To be in perplexity*, estar perplejo.
perquisite [ˈpə:kwizit] n. Gratificación, *f.*, propina, *f.* (tip). ‖ Ganancia (*f.*) extra (extra profit).
perron [ˈperən] n. ARCH. Escalinata, *f.* (stairs).
perry [ˈperi] n. Sidra (*f.*) de pera.
persecute [ˈpə:sikju:t] v. tr. Perseguir (for religious or political reasons). ‖ Acosar, agobiar, atormentar (to harass): *to persecute a man with questions*, acosar a un hombre con preguntas. ‖ Molestar (to worry).
persecution [ˌpə:siˈkju:ʃən] n. Persecución, *f.* ‖ *Persecution mania*, manía persecutoria.
persecutor [ˈpə:sikju:tə*] n. Perseguidor, ra.
persecutory [—ri] adj. Persecutorio, ria.
perseverance [ˌpə:siˈviərəns] n. Perseverancia, *f.*
persevere [ˌpə:siˈviə*] v. intr. Perseverar (*with, in*, en): *to persevere in one's work*, perseverar en su trabajo. ‖ Persistir (*in*, en): *he perseveres in doing it*, persiste en hacerlo.
persevering [—riŋ] adj. Perseverante.
Persia [ˈpə:ʃə] pr. n. Persia, *f.*
Persian [—n] adj./n. Persa (of Persia). ‖ — *Persian blinds*, persianas, *f.* ‖ *Persian cat*, gato (*m.*) persa. ‖ *Persian lamb*, caracul, *m.*

Persian Gulf [—gʌlf] pr. n. GEOGR. Golfo (*m.*) Pérsico.

persiflage [ˌpɛəsiˈflɑ:ʒ] n. Zumba, *f.*, guasa, *f.*, burla, *f.*

persimmon [pə:ˈsimən] n. Caqui, *m.* (tree, fruit).

persist [pəˈsist] v. intr. Persistir. || Empeñarse (to continue insistently): *he persists in asking me the same question*, se empeña en hacerme la misma pregunta. || *To persist in one's opinion*, aferrarse a su opinión.

persistence [pəˈsistəns] or **persistency** [—i] n. Persistencia, *f.*: *persistence in error*, persistencia en el error. || Empeño, *m.* (insistence). || Perseverancia, *f.* (tenacity).

persistent [pəˈsistənt] adj. Persistente. || Continuo, nua; constante: *persistent attacks*, ataques continuos. || Perseverante (persevering). || Firme: *persistent in his intention to*, firme en su intención de.

persnickety [pəˈsnikəti] adj. U. S. See PERNICKETY.

person [ˈpə:sn] n. Persona, *f.* (human being): *he is a very important person*, es una persona muy importante. || GRAMM. Persona, *f.*: *in the first person*, en primera persona. || — JUR. *Artificial person*, persona jurídica *or* social *or* civil. || *In the person of*, en la persona de. || JUR. *Natural person*, persona natural. || *No person*, nadie. || *Private person*, particular, *m.* || *Some person said*, alguien dijo. || *To be delivered to the addressee in person*, a entregar en propia mano. || *To come in person*, venir en persona. || *Without respect of persons*, sin acepción de personas.

persona [pə:ˈsəunə] n. Persona, *f.*: *persona non grata*, persona no grata, persona non grata.

— OBSERV. El plural de la palabra inglesa es *personae*.

personable [ˈpə:snəbl] adj. De buen ver, bien parecido, da (good-looking).

personage [ˈpə:snidʒ] n. Personaje, *m.*

personal [ˈpə:snl] adj. Personal: *a personal opinion*, una opinión personal; *personal needs*, necesidades personales; *personal effects*, efectos personales; *personal business*, asunto personal. || Íntimo, ma: *personal friend*, amigo íntimo. || Privado, da; particular, personal (private). || Individual: *personal liberty*, libertad individual. || GRAMM. Personal (pronoun). || — *Personal column*, mensajes (*m. pl.*) personales (in newspapers). || *Personal equation*, factor (*m.*) personal (personal reason), opinión (*f.*) personal (opinion). || *Personal estate* o *property*, bienes (*m. pl.*) muebles. || *Personal file*, expediente (*m.*) personal. || *Personal injury*, daños (*m. pl.*) corporales. || *To be personal*, hacer alusiones personales, personalizar: *don't be personal*, no hagas alusiones personales. || *To make a personal appearance*, presentarse personalmente, personarse.

— Pl. Mensajes (*m.*) personales. || Ecos (*m.*) de sociedad (society column).

personalism [—izəm] n. Personalismo, *m.*

personalist [—ist] adj./n. Personalista.

personalistic [pə:snəˈlistik] adj. Personalista.

personality [ˌpə:səˈnæliti] n. Personalidad, *f.*: *to lack personality*, carecer de personalidad. || Personalidad, *f.*, personaje, *m.*, figura, *f.* (famous person). || — Pl. Alusiones (*f.*) personales. || *Personality cult*, culto a la personalidad.

personalization [pə:sənəlaiˈzeiʃən] n. Personalización, *f.*, personificación, *f.*

personalize [ˈpə:snəlaiz] v. tr. Personalizar, personificar.

personally [ˈpə:snəli] adv. Personalmente: *personally, I see no objection*, personalmente no veo ninguna objeción. || *Don't take that remark personally*, no se dé por aludido, no se lo tome como si fuera una alusión personal.

personalty [ˈpə:snlti] n. JUR. Bienes (*m. pl.*) muebles.

personate [ˈpə:səneit] v. tr. Hacerse pasar por, usurpar la personalidad de (s.o.). || THEATR. Hacer el papel de.

personation [ˌpə:səˈneiʃən] n. Usurpación (*f.*) de personalidad. || THEATR. Representación, *f.* || Personificación, *f.* (of a quality).

personator [ˈpə:səneitə*] n. THEATR. Intérprete, *m.* & *f.* || Impostor, ra (fake).

personification [pə:ˌsɔnifiˈkeiʃən] n. Personificación, *f.* || *He is the personification of selfishness*, es el egoísmo personificado, es la encarnación del egoísmo.

personify [pə:ˈsɔnifai] v. tr. Personificar: *the poets personify the sun and moon*, los poetas personifican el Sol y la Luna; *he is avarice personified*, es la avaricia personificada.

personnel [ˌpə:səˈnel] n. Personal, *m.*

perspective [pəˈspektiv] n. Perspectiva, *f.* || Vista *f.*, perspectiva, *f.* (view). || — *In perspective*, en perspectiva. || FIG. *To see a matter in its true perspective*, ver un asunto como es, apreciar un asunto en su justo valor.

— Adj. Perspectivo, va; en perspectiva.

perspectively [pəˈspektivli] adv. En perspectiva.

Perspex [ˈpə:speks] n. Plexiglás, *m.*

perspicacious [ˌpə:spiˈkeiʃəs] adj. Perspicaz.

perspicacity [ˌpə:spiˈkæsiti] n. Perspicacia, *f.*

perspicuity [ˌpə:spiˈkju:iti] n. Claridad, *f.*

perspicuous [pəˈspikjuəs] adj. Claro, ra; perspicuo, cua: *a perspicuous explanation*, una explicación clara.

perspiration [ˌpə:spəˈreiʃən] n. Transpiración, *f.*, sudor, *m.*: *to be dripping with perspiration*, estar bañado en sudor.

perspiratory [pə:ˈspaiərətəri] adj. Sudorífero, ra; sudoríparo, ra (glands, etc.). || MED. Sudorífico, ca.

perspire [pəsˈpaiə*] v. intr. Transpirar, sudar.

persuadable [pəˈsweidəbl] adj. Fácil de convencer.

persuade [pəˈsweid] v. tr. Persuadir: *they persuaded me to do it*, me persuadieron a que lo hiciese. || Convencer: *I am almost persuaded of his honesty*, estoy casi convencido de su honradez. || *To persuade s.o. not to do sth.*, disuadir a alguien de hacer algo.

persuasible [pəˈsweizəbl] adj. Fácil de convencer.

persuasion [pəˈsweiʒən] n. Persuasión, *f.*: *he spoke with great persuasion*, habló con gran persuasión. | Convicción, *f.*, creencia, *f.* (conviction). || Opinión, *f.*: *they are both of the same persuasion*, los dos son de la misma opinión. || REL. Creencia (*f.*) religiosa (belief). | Secta, *f.* (religious sect). || *It is my persuasion that*, estoy convencido de que.

persuasive [pəˈsweisiv] adj. Persuasivo, va; convincente.

persuasively [—li] adv. De modo convincente.

persuasiveness [—nis] n. Persuasión, *f.*, persuasiva, *f.*

persulphate (U. S. **persulfate**) [pə:ˈsʌlfeit] n. CHEM. Persulfato, *m.*

pert [pə:t] adj. Impertinente, insolente: *a pert answer*, una respuesta impertinente. || Alegre (jaunty): *a pert little spring outfit*, un alegre trajecito de primavera. || Animado, da (in good spirits). || Muy vivaracho, cha: *she is a pert little thing*, es una chiquilla muy vivaracha.

pertain [pə:ˈtein] v. intr. Pertenecer (to belong). || Ser propio de (to be characteristic): *the enthusiasm pertaining to youth*, el entusiasmo que es propio de la juventud. || Relacionarse (*to*, con) [to relate to]. || — *Pertaining to*, relacionado con, referente a, relativo a: *subjects pertaining to religion*, temas relacionados con la religión. || *This does not pertain to my office*, esto no es de mi incumbencia.

pertinacious [ˌpə:tiˈneiʃəs] adj. Pertinaz.

pertinaciously [—li] adv. Con pertinacia, pertinazmente.

pertinaciousness [—nis] or **pertinacity** [ˌpə:tiˈnæsiti] n. Pertinacia, *f.*

pertinence [ˈpə:tinəns] or **pertinency** [—i] n. Pertinencia, *f.* (of a reason). || Oportunidad, *f.*, pertinencia, *f.* (of a remark, etc.).

pertinent [ˈpə:tinənt] adj. Pertinente, oportuno, na: *a pertinent remark*, una observación pertinente. || Pertinente (reason). || *Pertinent to*, relacionado con, referente a, relativo a.

pertly [ˈpə:tli] adv. Impertinentemente, insolentemente. || Alegremente. || Animadamente.

pertness [ˈpə:tnis] n. Impertinencia, *f.*, insolencia, *f.* || Alegría, *f.* (jauntiness). || Animación, *f.* (liveliness).

perturb [pəˈtə:b] v. tr. Perturbar, turbar (to disturb). || Preocupar, inquietar (to worry).

perturbation [ˌpə:təˈbeiʃən] n. Perturbación, *f.* || Preocupación, *f.*, inquietud, *f.* (worry).

perturbing [pəˈtə:biŋ] adj. Perturbador, ra. || Inquietante (worrying).

Peru [pəˈru:] pr. n. GEOGR. Perú, *m.*

peruke [pəˈru:k] n. Peluca, *f.* (wig).

perusal [pəˈru:zəl] n. Examen, *m.* (examination). || Lectura (*f.*) atenta (reading).

peruse [pəˈru:z] v. tr. Examinar (to examine). || Leer atentamente (to read).

Peruvian [pəˈru:vjən] adj./n. Peruano, na. || *Peruvian bark*, chinchona, *f.*, quina, *f.*

Peruvianism [—izəm] n. Peruanismo, *m.*

pervade [pə:ˈveid] v. tr. Extenderse por, difundirse por (to spread). || Impregnar, empapar (to soak).

pervasion [pə:ˈveiʒən] n. Difusión, *f.* || Impregnación, *f.*, empapamiento, *m.* (soaking).

pervasive [pə:ˈveisiv] adj. Penetrante. || Que lo impregna todo.

perverse [pəˈvə:s] adj. Perverso, sa (wicked). || Obstinado, da; terco, ca; contumaz (obstinate). || Adverso, sa; contrario, ria: *perverse circumstances*, circunstancias adversas.

perverseness [—nis] n. Perversidad, *f.* (wickedness). || Obstinación, *f.*, terquedad, *f.* (stubbornness).

perversion [pəˈvə:ʃən] n. Perversión, *f.* || Desnaturalización, *f.* (of facts).

perversity [pəˈvə:siti] n. Perversidad, *f.* (wickedness). || Obstinación, *f.*, terquedad, *f.* (stubbornness).

perversive [pəˈvə:siv] adj. Pervertidor, ra.

pervert [ˈpə:və:t] n. Pervertido, da: *sexual pervert*, pervertido sexual.

pervert [pəˈvə:t] v. tr. Pervertir (a person). || Desvirtuar, desnaturalizar (words, facts). || Estragar, pervertir (taste). || Prostituir (talent).

perverter [—ə*] n. Pervertidor, ra.

pervious [ˈpə:vjəs] adj. Permeable.

perviousness [ˈpə:vjəsnis] n. Permeabilidad, *f.*

peseta [pəˈsetə] n. Peseta, *f.* (Spanish monetary unit).

pesky [ˈpeski] adj. U. S. FAM. Maldito, ta: *what pesky weather!*, ¡maldito tiempo!

peso [ˈpeisəu] n. Peso, *m.* (monetary unit).

pessary [ˈpesəri] n. MED. Pesario, *m.*

pessimism [ˈpesimizəm] n. Pesimismo, *m.*

pessimist [ˈpesimist] n. Pesimista, *m.* & *f.*

pessimistic [ˌpesiˈmistik] adj. Pesimista.

pessimistically [—əli] adj. Con pesimismo.

pest [pest] n. Insecto (*m.*) *or* animal (*m.*) nocivo *or* dañino, parásito, *m.* || FIG. Lata, *f.*, tostón, *m.*

(tiresome person). | Lata, *f.* (boring thing). | Peste, *f.*: *what pests these children are!*, ¡estos niños son la peste!

pester [—ə*] v. tr. Molestar, importunar, fastidiar (to annoy). || Acosar: *to pester s.o. with questions*, acosar a alguien con preguntas. || *To pester s.o. for sth.*, pedir algo a alguien con insistencia.

pesticide [ˈpestisaid] n. Pesticida, *m.*

pestiferous [pesˈtifərəs] adv. Nocivo, va; dañino, na (insects). || Pestífero, ra; pestilente (air). || FIG. Pernicioso, sa (harmful). | Pesado, da; molesto, ta; fastidioso, sa; latoso, sa (annoying).

pestilence [ˈpestiləns] n. MED. Pestilencia, *f.*, peste, *f.*

pestilent [ˈpestilənt] adj. Pestífero, ra; pestilente. || FIG. Pernicioso, sa; nocivo, va (harmful). | Pesado, da; latoso, sa (annoying).

pestilential [ˌpestiˈlenʃəl] adj. Pestífero, ra; pestilencial, pestilente. || Pestilente (smell). || FIG. Pesado, da; latoso, sa (annoying). | Pernicioso, sa; nocivo, va (harmful).

pestle [ˈpesl] n. Mano, *m.*, maja, *f.* (of a mortar).

pestle [ˈpesl] v. tr. Majar (in a mortar).

pet [pet] n. Animal (*m.*) favorito. || Ojo (*m.*) derecho, favorito, ta; preferido, da (favourite person). || — *He is a real pet*, es un cielo, es un encanto. || *My pet!*, ¡mi cielo! || *To be in a pet*, estar de mal humor. || *To make a pet of*, mimar a. || *To take pet*, ofenderse.

— Adj. Mimado, da. || — *Her pet cat*, su gato. || *Pet aversion*, pesadilla, *f.* || *Pet name*, nombre cariñoso. || *Pet panther*, pantera domesticada. || *Pet subject*, tema preferido, manía, *f.*

pet [pet] v. tr. Mimar (to pamper). || Acariciar (to caress).

— V. intr. Acariciarse (to caress). || Estar enfadado (to be angry).

petal [ˈpetl] n. Pétalo, *m.* (of a flower).

petaled or **petalled** [—d] adj. Con pétalos.

petard [peˈtɑ:d] n. Petardo, *m.* || FIG. *Hoist with one's own petard*, cogido en sus propias redes.

petcock [ˈpetkɔk] n. TECH. Llave (*f.*) de purga.

Pete [pi:t] pr. n. FAM. Perico, *m.*

— OBSERV. Esta palabra es el diminutivo de *Peter*.

peter [—ə*] v. intr. *To peter out*, agotarse (a mine, a stream), desaparecer (to disappear), quedarse en agua de borrajas (a plan), pararse (an engine).

Peter [—ə*] pr. n. Pedro, *m.* || — MAR. *Blue Peter*, bandera (*f.*) de salida. || *Peter's pence*, dinero (*m.*) de San Pedro. || FIG. *To rob Peter to pay Paul*, desnudar a un santo para vestir a otro.

petersham [ˈpi:təʃəm] n. Abrigo (*m.*) de ratina (coat). || Ratina, *f.* (material).

petiole [ˈpetiəul] n. BOT. Peciolo, *m.*, pecíolo, *m.*

petite [pəˈtit] adj. Chiquita (woman).

petition [piˈtiʃən] n. Petición, *f.*, solicitud, *f.*, instancia, *f.* (request). || Ruego, *m.*, súplica, *f.* (to God). || JUR. Demanda, *f.*, petición, *f.*, recurso, *m.* || *Petition for divorce*, demanda de divorcio.

petition [piˈtiʃən] v. tr. Solicitar a, presentar una solicitud a, dirigir una petición a. || JUR. Presentar demanda a. || Rogar: *to petition s.o. to do sth.* rogar a alguien que haga algo. || *To petition for sth.*, pedir *or* solicitar algo.

— V. intr. Presentar una petición, hacer una solicitud (to make a petition).

petitionary [piˈtiʃənəri] adj. Petitorio, ria.

petitioner [—ə*] n. Solicitador, ra; solicitante, *m.* & *f.* || JUR. Demandante, *m.* & *f.*

Petrarch [ˈpetrɑ:k] pr. n. Petrarca.

Petrarchan [—ən] adj. Petrarquista.

Petrarchism [—izəm] n. Petrarquismo, *m.*

Petrarchist [—ist] n. Petrarquista, *m.* & *f.*

petrel [ˈpetrəl] n. Petrel, *m.* (bird).

petrifaction [ˌpetriˈfækʃən] or **petrification** [ˌpetrifiˈkeiʃən] n. Petrificación, *f.*

petrify [ˈpetrifai] v. tr. Petrificar. || FIG. Petrificar, paralizar. || FIG. *We were petrified*, nos quedamos de piedra.

— V. intr. Petrificarse.

petrifying [—iŋ] adj. Petrificante.

petrochemical [petrəuˈkemikəl] adj. Petroquímico, ca.

— N. Producto (*m.*) petroquímico.

petrochemistry [petrəuˈkemistri] n. Petroquímica, *f.*

petrography [peˈtrɔgrəfi] n. Petrografía, *f.*

petrol [ˈpetrəl] n. Gasolina, *f.* [*Amer.*, nafta, *f.*]: *petrol pump*, surtidor de gasolina. || *High-grade petrol*, supercarburante, *m.*, súper, *f.*, gasolina (*f.*) plomo.

petrol can [—kæn] n. Bidón (*m.*) de gasolina.

petroleum [piˈtrauljəm] n. Petróleo, *m.* (mineral oil). || — *Petroleum-bearing*, petrolífero, ra [*Amer.*, petrolero, ra]. || *Petroleum-producing*, petrolífero, ra [*Amer.*, petrolero, ra].

petrol gauge [ˈpetrəlgeidʒ] n. Indicador (*m.*) del nivel de gasolina.

petroliferous [petrəˈlifərəs] adj. Petrolífero, ra [*Amer.*, petrolero, ra].

petrology [peˈtrɔlədʒi] n. Petrología, *f.*

petrol pump [ˈpetrəlpʌmp] n. Bomba (*f.*) de gasolina (in engine). || Surtidor (*m.*) de gasolina (in a garage).

petrol station [ˈpetrəl steiʃən] n. Gasolinera, *f.*, surtidor (*m.*) de gasolina.

petrol tank [ˈpetrəltæŋk] n. Depósito (*m.*) de gasolina.

petrous [ˈpetrəs] adj. Pétreo, a.

petticoat [ˈpetikəut] n. Enaguas, *f. pl.*, enagua, *f.* (underskirt). || FAM. Mujer, *f.* || — FAM. *Petticoat chaser*, mujeriego, *m.* | *Petticoat government*, dominación (*f.*) de la mujer.

pettifogger [ˈpetifɔgə*] n. Picapleitos, *m. inv.*, leguleyo, *m.*, abogadillo, *m.*

pettifoggery [ˌpetiˈfɔgəri] n. Argucia (*f.*) *or* trapacería (*f.*) de abogados.

pettifogging [ˈpetifɔgiŋ] adj. Pleitista (lawyer). || Quisquilloso, sa (person). || Insignificante (detail).

pettiness [ˈpetinis] n. Pequeñez, *f.* || Mezquindad, *f.*

petting [ˈpetiŋ] n. FAM. Caricias, *f. pl.*

pettish [ˈpetiʃ] adj. De mal humor, malhumorado, da (sulky).

pettitoes [ˈpetitəuz] pl. n. CULIN. Manos (*f.*) de cerdo.

petty [ˈpeti] adj. Pequeño, ña; insignificante, sin importancia (minor, trivial): *petty reforms*, reformas insignificantes. || Quisquilloso, sa (hairsplitting). || Mezquino, na (narrow-minded). || — *Petty cash*, dinero (*m.*) *or* fondo (*m.*) para gastos menores. || *Petty larceny*, hurto, *m.*, ratería, *f.* || *Petty monarch*, reyezuelo, *m.* || MAR. *Petty officer*, contramaestre, *m.* || *Petty thief*, ladronzuelo, *m.*, ratero, *m.*

petty-minded [—ˌmaindid] adj. Mezquino, na.

petulance [ˈpetjuləns] n. Irritabilidad, *f.*, susceptibilidad, *f.* (irritability). || Malhumor, *m.* (ill humour).

— OBSERV. *Petulancia* in Spanish means "arrogance".

petulant [ˈpetjulənt] adj. Irritable, susceptible, enojadizo, za (irritable). || Malhumorado, da; de mal humor (bad-tempered).

— OBSERV. *Petulante* in Spanish means "arrogant".

petunia [piˈtju:njə] n. Petunia, *f.* (flower).

pew [pju:] n. Banco (*m.*) de iglesia. || FAM. *Take a pew*, tome asiento.

pewee [ˈpiwi] n. Papamoscas (*m. inv.*) norteamericano (bird).

pewit [ˈpi:wit] n. Avefría, *f.* (lapwing). || Papamoscas (*m. inv.*) norteamericano (pewee).

pewter [ˈpju:tə*] n. Estaño, *m.*, peltre, *m.* (metal).

peyotl [peiˈɔtl] or **peyote** [peiˈəuti] n. Peyote, *m.*

phaeton [ˈfeitn] n. Faetón, *m.* (carriage).

phagocyte [ˈfægəusait] n. Fagocito, *m.*

phagocytic [fægəˈsitik] adj. Fagocitario, ria; fagocítico, ca.

phagocytosis [fægəsaiˈtəusis] n. Fagocitosis, *f.*

phalaena [fəˈli:nə] n. Falena, *f.* (moth).

phalange [ˈfælændʒ] n. Falange, *f.*

phalanger [—ə*] n. Falangero, *m.* (animal).

phalanges [—iz] pl. n. See PHALANX.

phalansterian [fælænˈsti:əriən] adj./n. Falansteriano, na.

phalanstery [ˈfælənstəri] n. Falansterio, *m.*

phalanx [ˈfælæŋks] n. ANAT. HIST. Falange, *f.*

— OBSERV. El plural es *phalanxes* o *phalanges* cuando se refiere al sentido histórico y *phalanges* en el otro caso.

phallic [ˈfælik] adj. Fálico, ca.

phallus [ˈfæləs] n. Falo, *m.*

— OBSERV. El plural es *phalli* o *phalluses*.

phanerogam [ˈfænərəugæm] n. BOT. Fanerógama, *f.*

phanerogamic [ˌfænərəuˈgæmik] or **phanerogamous** [ˌfænəˈrɔgəməs] adj. BOT. Fanerógamo, ma.

phantasm [ˈfæntæzəm] n. Fantasma, *m.* (spectre). || Ilusión, *f.*

phantasmagoria [ˌfæntæzməˈgɔriə] n. Fantasmagoría, *f.*

phantasmagoric [ˌfæntæzməˈgɔrik] adj. Fantasmagórico, ca.

phantasmal [fænˈtæzməl] adj. Fantasmal.

phantasy [ˈfæntəsi:] n. See FANTASY.

phantom [ˈfæntəm] adj. Fantasma: *the phantom ship*, el buque fantasma. || FIG. Ilusorio, ria; inexistente.

— N. Fantasma, *m.*

Pharaoh [ˈfɛərəu] n. Faraón, *m.* (Egyptian king).

Pharaonic [fɛəˈrɔnik] adj. Faraónico, ca.

Pharisaic [ˌfæriˈseiik] or **Pharisaical** [—əl] adj. Farisaico, ca.

Pharisaism [ˈfæriseiizəm] or **Phariseeism** [ˈfæriseiizəm] n. Farisaísmo, *m.*, fariseísmo, *m.*

Pharisee [ˈfærisi:] n. Fariseo, *m.*

pharmaceutic [ˌfɑ:məˈsju:tik] or **pharmaceutical** [—əl] adj. Farmacéutico, ca.

pharmaceutics [—s] n. Farmacia, *f.*

pharmaceutist [ˌfɑ:məˈsju:tist] n. Farmacéutico, ca.

pharmacist [ˈfɑ:məsist] n. Farmacéutico, ca.

pharmacological [fɑ:məkəˈlɔdʒikəl] adj. Farmacológico, ca.

pharmacologist [ˌfɑ:məˈkɔlədʒist] n. Farmacólogo, ga.

pharmacology [ˌfɑ:məˈkɔlədʒi] n. Farmacología, *f.*

pharmacopoeia [ˌfɑ:məkəˈpi:ə] n. Farmacopea, *f.*

pharmacy [ˈfɑ:məsi] n. Farmacia, *f.*

pharyngal [fəˈriŋgəl] or **pharyngeal** [ˌfærinˈdʒi:əl] adj. Faríngeo, a.

pharynges [færindʒiz] pl. n. See PHARYNX.

pharyngitis [ˌfærinˈdʒaitis] n. MED. Faringitis, *f.*

pharynx [ˈfæriŋks] n. ANAT. Faringe, *f.*

— OBSERV. El plural es *pharynges* o *pharynxes*.

phase [feiz] n. Fase, *f.*: *the phases of an illness*, las fases de una enfermedad; *the Moon's phases*, las

fases de la Luna. || ELECTR. Fase, *f.* || *Out of phase*, desfasado, da.
phase [feiz] v. tr. ELECTR. Poner en fase. || Escalonar (to plan in stages). || *To phase out*, reducir *or* hacer desaparecer progresivamente.
phasing [—iŋ] n. ELECTR. Ajuste (*m.*) de fase.
pheasant [ˈfeznt] n. Faisán, *m.* (bird). || — *Hen pheasant*, faisán hembra, faisana, *f.* || *Young pheasant*, pollo (*m.*) de faisán.
Phenicia [fiˈniʃiə] pr. n. GEOGR. Fenicia, *f.* (Phoenicia).
Phenician [fiˈniʃiən] adj./n. Fenicio, cia.
phenix [ˈfi:niks] n. Fénix, *m.* (phoenix).
phenol [ˈfi:nɔl] n. CHEM. Fenol, *m.*
phenomena [fiˈnɔminə] pl. n. See PHENOMENON.
phenomenal [—l] adj. Fenomenal.
phenomenalism [—lizəm] n. Fenomenismo, *m.*, fenomenalismo, *m.*
phenomenologist [fi,nɔmiˈnɔlədʒist] n. Fenomenólogo, *m.*
phenomenology [fi,nɔmiˈnɔlədʒi] n. Fenomenología, *f.*
phenomenon [fiˈnɔminən] n. Fenómeno, *m.*: *the phenomena of nature*, los fenómenos de la naturaleza.

— OBSERV. El plural es *phenomena* o *phenomenons*.

phenyl [ˈfi:nil] n. Fenilo, *m.*
phew [fju:] interj. ¡Uy!
phi [fai] n. Fi, *f.* (Greek letter).
phial [ˈfaiəl] n. Frasco, *m.* (small bottle). || Ampolla, *f.* (ampoule).
Philadelphia [,filəˈdelfjə] pr. n. GEOGR. Filadelfia.
philander [fiˈlændə*] v. intr. Flirtear (to flirt). || Mariposear (to have many love affairs).
philanderer [—rə*] n. Galanteador *m.* (who flirts). || Mariposón, *m.* (who has many love affairs).
philandering [—riŋ] adj. Mariposón.
— N. Flirteo, *m.*
philanthropic [,filənˈθrɔpik] or **philanthropical** [—əl] adj. Filantrópico, ca.
philanthropist [fiˈlænθrəpist] n. Filántropo, pa.
philanthropy [fiˈlænθrəpi] n. Filantropía, *f.*
philatelic [,filəˈtelik] adj. Filatélico, ca.
philatelist [fiˈlætəlist] n. Filatelista, *m.* & *f.*
philately [fiˈlætəli] n. Filatelia, *f.*
philharmonic [,filɑ:ˈmɔnik] adj. MUS. Filarmónico, ca.
philhellene [ˈfil,heli:n] n. Filheleno, na.
philhellenic [filheˈli:nik] adj. Filhelénico, ca; filheleno, na; helenófilo, la.
philhellenism [filˈhelinizəm] n. Filhelenismo, *m.*, helenismo, *m.*
philhellenist [filˈhelenist] n. Filheleno, na.
Philip [ˈfilip] pr. n. Felipe, *m.* (actual name). || Filipo, *m.* (king of Macedon).
Philippe [fiˈli:p] pr. n. Felipe, *m.* (king of France).
Philippians [fiˈlipiənz] pl. pr. n. Filipenses, *m.*: *Epistle to the Philippians*, Epístola a los Filipenses.
philippic [fiˈlipik] n. Filípica, *f.* (angry tirade).
Philippine [ˈfilipi:n] adj./n. Filipino, na. || GEOGR. *Philippine Islands*, Islas Filipinas.
Philippines [—z] pl. pr. n. GEOGR. Filipinas, *f.*
Philistine [ˈfilistain] adj./n. HIST. Filisteo, a. || — N. FIG. Filisteo, *m.*
philodendron [,filəˈdendrən] n. BOT. Filodendro, *m.*
philologic [,filəˈlɔdʒik] or **philological** [—əl] adj. Filológico, ca.
philologist [fiˈlɔlədʒist] n. Filólogo, ga.
philology [fiˈlɔlədʒi] n. Filología, *f.*
philosophaster [fiˈlɔsəfæstə*] n. Filosofastro, *m.*
philosopher [fiˈlɔsəfə*] n. Filósofo, fa. || — *Moral philosopher*, moralista, *m.* || *Philosopher's* o *philosophers' stone*, piedra (*f.*) filosofal.
philosophic [,filəˈsɔfik] or **philosophical** [—əl] adj. Filosófico, ca.
philosophize [fiˈlɔsəfaiz] v. intr. Filosofar.
philosophizer [fiˈlɔsəfaizə*] n. Filosofador, ra.
philosophy [fiˈlɔsəfi] n. Filosofía, *f.* || *Moral philosophy*, moral, *f.*
philtre (U. S. **philter**) [ˈfiltə*] n. Filtro, *m.*, bebedizo, *m.*, poción, *f.* (magic potion).
phimosis [faiˈməusis] n. MED. Fimosis, *f.*
phiz [fiz] n. FAM. Jeta, *f.*, cara, *f.* (face).
phlebitis [fliˈbaitis] n. MED. Flebitis, *f.*
phlebotomize [fliˈbɔtəmaiz] v. intr. MED. Hacer una sangría.
— V. tr. MED. Sangrar.
phlebotomy [fliˈbɔtəmi] n. MED. Flebotomía, *f.*, sangría, *f.*
phlegm [flem] n. MED. Flema, *f.* || FIG. Flema, *f.*
phlegmatic [flegˈmætik] or **phlegmatical** [—əl] adj. Flemático, ca.
phlegmon [ˈflegmɔn] n. MED. Flemón, *m.*
phloem [ˈfləuem] n. BOT. Líber, *m.*
phlogiston [flɔˈdʒistən] n. Flogisto, *m.*
phobia [ˈfəubiə] n. Fobia, *f.*
Phocian [ˈfəuʃjən] adj./n. Focense.
Phoebus [ˈfi:bəs] pr. n. Febo, *m.* (the sun).
Phoenicia [fiˈniʃiə] pr. n. Fenicia, *f.*
Phoenician [—n] adj./n. Fenicio, cia.
phoenix [ˈfi:niks] n. Fénix, *m.* (bird).
phon [fɔn] n. Fono, *m.*, fon, *m.*, fonio, *m.* (unit of loudness).
phonate [fəuˈneit] v. intr. Pronunciar un sonido.
phonation [fəuˈneiʃən] n. Fonación, *f.*
phone [fəun] n. GRAMM. Fonema, *m.* || FAM. Teléfono, *m.* || — *Phone box*, cabina telefónica. || *To be on the phone*, estar hablando [por teléfono].
phone [fəun] v. tr./intr. Telefonear, llamar por teléfono.
phoneme [ˈfəuni:m] n. GRAMM. Fonema, *m.*
phonetic [fəuˈnetik] adj. Fonético, ca
phonetically [fəuˈnetikəli] adv. Fonéticamente.
phonetician [,fəuniˈtiʃən] n. Fonetista, *m.* & *f.*
phonetics [fəuˈnetiks] n. GRAMM. Fonética, *f.*
phonetist [ˈfəunitist] n. Fonetista, *m.* & *f.*
phoney [ˈfəuni] adj./n. See PHONY.
phoniatrician [fəuniˈætriʃən] n. MED. Foniatra, *m.*
phoniatrics [fəuniˈætriks] n. MED. Foniatría, *f.*
phonic [ˈfəunik] adj. Fónico, ca.
phonics [—s] n. Acústica, *f.* || Fonética, *f.*
phoniness [ˈfəuninis] n. FAM. Falsedad, *f.*
phonogram [ˈfəunəgræm] n. Fonograma, *m.*
phonograph [ˈfəunəgrɑ:f] n. Fonógrafo, *m.*
phonographic [,fəunəˈgræfik] adj. Fonográfico, ca.
phonologist [fəuˈnɔlədʒist] n. Fonólogo, ga.
phonology [fəuˈnɔlədʒi] n. Fonología, *f.*
phonometer [fəuˈnɔmitə*] n. Fonómetro, *m.*
phonometry [fəuˈnɔmətri] n. Fonometría, *f.*
phony [ˈfəuni] adj. FAM. Falso, sa (not genuine): *a phony diamond*, un diamante falso.
— N. FAM. Farsante, *m.* & *f.*, camelista, *m.* & *f.* (person). | Camelo, *m.* (thing).
phosgene [ˈfɔzdʒi:n] n. CHEM. Fosgeno, *m.*
phosphate [ˈfɔsfeit] n. CHEM. Fosfato, *m.*: *phosphate of lime* o *calcium phosphate*, fosfato de cal.
phosphatic [fɔsˈfætik] adj. CHEM. Fosfático, ca.
phosphatize [ˈfɔsfətaiz] v. tr. CHEM. Fosfatar.
phosphatizing [—iŋ] n. AGR. Fosfatado, *m.*
phosphene [ˈfɔsfi:n] n. Fosfeno, *m.*
phosphite [ˈfɔsfait] n. CHEM. Fosfito, *m.*
phosphor [ˈfɔsfə*] n. Fósforo, *m.*
phosphorate [—reit] v. tr. Fosforar.
phosphoresce [,fɔsfəˈres] v. intr. Fosforecer, fosforescer.
phosphorescence [—ns] n. Fosforescencia, *f.*
phosphorescent [—nt] adj. Fosforescente.
phosphoretted (U. S. **phosphoreted**) [—reitid] adj. Fosforado, da.
phosphoric [fɔsˈfɔrik] adj. CHEM. Fosfórico, ca.
phosphorism [ˈfɔsfərizəm] n. MED. Fosforismo, *m.*
phosphorous [ˈfɔsfərəs] adj. Fosforoso, sa.
phosphorus [ˈfɔsfərəs] n. CHEM. Fósforo, *m.*
phosphuretted (U. S. **phosphureted**) [ˈfɔsfjuretid] adj. CHEM. Fosforado, da.
phot [fɔt] n. Foto, *m.*, fot, *m.* (unit of illumination).
photo [ˈfəutəu] n. Foto, *f.*
photo [ˈfəutəu] v. tr./intr. See PHOTOGRAPH.
photocell [—sel] n. Célula (*f.*) fotoeléctrica.
photochemistry [—ˈkemistri] n. Fotoquímica, *f.*
photochrome [—krəum] n. Fotocromía, *f.* (colour photograph).
photochromy [—,krəumi] n. Fotocromía, *f.* (colour photography).
photocomposition [—,kɔmpəˈziʃən] n. Fotocomposición, *f.*
photoconductive [—kənˈdʌktiv] adj. Fotoconductor, ra.
photocopier [—,kɔpiə*] n. Fotocopiadora, *f.*
photocopy [—,kɔpi] n. Fotocopia, *f.*
photocopy [—,kɔpi] v. tr. Fotocopiar.
photocurrent [—,kʌrənt] n. Corriente (*f.*) fotoeléctrica.
photoelasticity [—,elæsˈtisiti] n. PHYS. Fotoelasticidad, *f.*
photoelectric [—iˈlektrik] or **photoelectrical** [—iˈlektrikəl] adj. PHYS. Fotoeléctrico, ca: *photoelectric cell*, célula fotoeléctrica.
photoelectricity [—ilekˈtrisiti] n. PHYS. Fotoelectricidad, *f.*
photoelectron [—iˈlektrɔn] n. PHYS. Fotoelectrón, *m.*
photoemission [—iˈmiʃən] adj. PHYS. Fotoemisión, *f.*
photoengrave [—inˈgreiv] v. tr. Fotograbar.
photoengraver [—inˈgreivə*] n. Fotograbador, *m.*
photoengraving [—inˈgreiviŋ] n. Fotograbado, *m.*
photo finish [—ˈfiniʃ] n. SP. Final (*m.*) de carrera muy reñido (close race finish). || FIG. Competición (*f.*) muy reñida (close contest).
photoflash [—flæʃ] n. PHOT. Flash, *m.*, luz (*f.*) relámpago.
photoflood [—flʌd] n. Lámpara (*f.*) incandescente de gran voltaje.
photogenic [,fəutəuˈdʒenik] adj. Fotogénico, ca.
photogram [ˈfəutəugræm] n. Fotograma, *m.*
photogrammetry [ˈfəutəˈgræmətri] n. Fotogrametría, *f.*
photograph [ˈfəutəgrɑ:f] n. Fotografía, *f.*: *to take a photograph*, sacar una fotografía; *to have one's photograph taken*, hacerse *or* sacarse una fotografía. || — *Aerial photograph*, fotografía aérea, aerofotografía, *f.* || *Photograph library*, fototeca, *f.*
photograph [ˈfəutəgrɑ:f] v. tr. Fotografiar, hacer una fotografía, sacar una foto de.
— V. intr. Salir en una fotografía: *she photographs well*, sale bien en las fotografías.
photographer [fəˈtɔgrəfə*] n. Fotógrafo, fa: *street photographer*, fotógrafo callejero.
photographic [,fəutəˈgræfik] adj. Fotográfico, ca.
photographically [fəutəˈgræfikəli] adv. Fotográficamente.

PHOTOGRAPHY — FOTOGRAFÍA, *f.*

I. General terms. — Términos (*m.*) generales.

photo, photograph	foto *f.*, fotografía *f.*
snapshot, snap	instantánea *f.*
photographer	fotógrafo *m.*
cameraman	operador *m.*
backlighting	contraluz *m.*
backlighting photography	fotografía (*f.*) a contraluz
luminosity	luminosidad *f.*
to load	cargar [la máquina]
focus	foco *m.*
to focus	enfocar
focusing	enfoque *m.*
focal length	distancia (*f.*) focal
depth of focus	produndidad (*f.*) de foco
exposure	exposición *f.*
time of exposure	tiempo (*m.*) de exposición
to frame	encuadrar
framing	encuadre *m.*
slide, transparency	diapositiva *f.*, transparencia *f.*
microfilm	microfilm *m.*
photocopy	fotocopia *f.*
photocopier	fotocopiadora *f.*
duplicate, copy	duplicado *m.*, copia *f.*
reproduction	reproducción *f.*
photogenic	fotogénico, ca
overexposure	sobrexposición *f.*
underexposure	subexposición *f.*
projector	proyector *m.*

II. Camera. — Cámara, *f.*

still camera	cámara (*f.*) fotográfica, máquina (*f.*) de retratar *or* de fotografiar
cinecamera [U.S., movie camera]	cámara (*f.*) cinematográfica
television camera	cámara (*f.*) de televisión
box camera	máquina (*f.*) de cajón
folding camera	cámara (*f.*) de fuelle *or* plegable
lens	objetivo *m.*
aperture	abertura *f.* [del objetivo]
wide-angle lens	[objetivo *m.*] gran angular
diaphragm	diafragma *m.*
telephoto lens	teleobjetivo *m.*
eyepiece	ocular *m.*
filter	filtro *m.*
shutter	obturador *m.*
shutter release	disparador *m.*
viewfinder	visor *m.*
telemeter, range finder	telémetro *m.*
photometer, exposure meter	exposímetro *m.*
photoelectric cell	célula (*f.*) fotoeléctrica
mask	ocultador *m.*
sunshade	parasol *m.*
tripod	trípode *m.*
flash, flashlight	luz (*f.*) relámpago, flash *m.*
magazine	carga *f.*
cartridge	cartucho *m.*
spool	carrete *m.*, rollo *m.*
film	película *f.*
plate	placa *f.*
plateholder	chasis *m. inv.*
spotlight, floodlight	reflector *m.*, proyector *m.*, foco *m.*

III. Development. — Revelado, *m.*

darkroom	cámara (*f*) oscura
to develop	revelar
developer	revelador *m.*
bath	baño *m.*
to fix	fijar
emulsion	emulsión *f.*
drying	secado *m.*
to enlarge	ampliar
enlargement	ampliación *f.*
enlarger	ampliadora *f.*
negative	negativo *m.*, cliché *m.*, clisé *m.*
positive	positivo *m.*
print	prueba *f.*, copia *f.*
format	formato *m.*
oblong photography	fotografía (*f.*) apaisada
image, picture	imagen *f.*
blurred image	imagen (*f.*) movida *or* borrosa
grain	grano *m.*
foreground	primer plano *m.*

See also CINEMATOGRAPHY

photography [fəˈtɔgrəfi] n. Fotografía, *f.* || *Aerial photography*, fotografía aérea, aereofotografía, *f.*
photogravure [ˌfəutəgrəˈvjuə*] n. Fotograbado, *m.*
photolith [ˈfəutəuliθ] or **photolitho** [ˈfəutəuˈlaiθəu] n. Fotolito, *m.*
photolithograph [ˈfəutəˈliθəgrɑːf] n. Fotolitografía, *f.*
photolithograph [ˈfəutəˈliθəgrɑːf] v. tr. Fotolitografiar.
photolithographic [ˈfəutəliθəˈgræfik] adj. Fotolitográfico, ca.
photolithography [ˈfəutəliˈθɔgrəfi] n. Fotolitografía, *f.*
photoluminescence [ˈfəutəuluːmiˈnesəns] n. PHYS. CHEM. Fotoluminescencia, *f.*
photolysis [fəuˈtɔlisis] n. Fotólisis, *f.*
photomap [ˈfəutəumæp] n. Mapa (*m.*) hecho con una fotografía aérea.
photomechanical [ˈfəutəuməˈkænikəl] adj. PRINT. Fotomecánico, ca.
photometer [fəuˈtɔmiːtə*] n. Fotómetro, *m.*
photometric [fəutəˈmetrik] or **photometrical** [—əl] adj. Fotométrico, ca.
photometry [fəˈtɔmetri] n. Fotometría, *f.*
photomicrograph [fəutəˈmaikrəgrɑːf] n. Fotomicrografía, *f.*
photomicrography [fəutəmaiˈkrɔgrəfi] n. Fotomicrografía, *f.*
photomontage [ˈfəutəumɔnˈtɑːʒ] n. Fotomontaje, *m.*, montaje (*m.*) fotográfico.
photon [ˈfəutɔn] n. PHYS. Fotón, *m.*
photophore [ˈfəutəfɔː*] n. Fotóforo, *m.*
photophoresis [ˈfəutəufəˈrisis] n. Fotoforesis, *f.*
— OBSERV. El plural de *photophoresis* es *photophoreses.*
photoprint [ˈfəutəuprint] n. Fotocalco, *m.*
photosensitive [fəutəuˈsensitiv] adj. Fotosensible.
photosphere [ˈfəutəusfiə*] n. Fotosfera, *f.*
photostat [ˈfəutəustæt] n. Fotostato, *m.*, copia (*f.*) fotostática.
photostat [ˈfəutəustæt] v. tr. Hacer una copia fotostática, fotocopiar.
photostatic [ˌfəutəuˈstætik] adj. Fotostático, ca.
photosynthesis [fəutəˈsinθəsis] n. BOT. Fotosíntesis, *f.*
phototherapy [fəutəˈθerəpi] n. MED. Fototerapia, *f.*
phototropism [fəˈtɔtrəpizəm] n. Fototropismo, *m.*
phototype [ˈfəutətaip] n. PRINT. Fototipo, *m.*
phototypesetting [—ˈsetiŋ] n. PRINT. Fotocomposición, *f.*
phototypography [fəutətaiˈpɔgrəfi] n. PRINT. Fototipografía, *f.*
phototypy [ˈfəutətipi] n. PRINT. Fototipia, *f.*
phrase [freiz] n. Locución, *f.*, expresión, *f.*, frase, *f.* || GRAMM. Locución, *f.*: *adverbial phrase*, locución adverbial. || MUS. Frase, *f.* || — *Proverbial phrase*, frase proverbial. || *Set* o *stock phrase*, frase hecha *or* acuñada *or* estereotipada.
phrase [freiz] v. tr. Expresar (a thought). || Redactar (to write): *well-phrased letter*, carta bien redactada. || Frasear (to express in phrases). || MUS. Frasear.
— V. intr. Frasear.
phrase book [ˈfreizbuk] n. Repertorio (*m.*) de expresiones.
phraseology [ˌfreiziˈɔlədʒi] n. Fraseología, *f.*
phrasing [ˈfreiziŋ] n. Expresión, *f.* (of thought). || Redacción, *f.* (of a letter). || Estilo, *m.* (style). || Fraseología, *f.* (phraseology). || MUS. Fraseo, *m.*
phratry [ˈfreitri] n. Fratría, *f.* (in Athens).
phreatic [friˈætik] adj. Freático, ca.
phrenetic [friˈnetik] adj. Frenético, ca.
phrenic [ˈfrenik] adj. ANAT. Frénico, ca.
phrenologist [friˈnɔlədʒist] n. Frenólogo, *m.*
phrenology [friˈnɔlədʒi] n. Frenología, *f.*
Phrygia [ˈfridʒiə] pr. n. GEOGR. Frigia, *f.* (ancient country in Asia Minor).
Phrygian [—n] adj./n. Frigio, gia: *Phrygian cap*, gorro frigio.
phthalein [ˈfθæliin] n. CHEM. Ftaleína, *f.*
phthisic [ˈθaisik] or **phthisical** [—əl] adj. MED. Tísico, ca.
phthisis [ˈθaisis] n. MED. Tisis, *f.*
— OBSERV. El plural de *phtisis* es *phtises.*
phut [fʌt] adv. *To go phut*, estropearse (an engine), hundirse (a business), fracasar, fallar (a project).
phycomycete [faikəuˈmaisiːt] n. BOT. Ficomiceto, *m.*
phylactery [fiˈlæktəri] n. Filacteria, *f.*
phylloxera [ˌfilɔkˈsiərə] n. Filoxera, *f.*
phylum [ˈfailəm] n. BIOL. Filo, *m.*
— OBSERV. El plural de esta palabra es *phyla.*
physic [ˈfizik] n. MED. Medicamento, *m.*, medicina, *f.*, remedio, *m.*
physical [—əl] adj. Físico, ca (culture, force). || Físico, ca: *a physical change in a substance*, un cambio físico en una sustancia. || FIG. Físico, ca; material: *physical impossibility*, imposibilidad física. || — *Physical chemistry*, fisicoquímica, *f.* || *Physical education*, educación física. || *Physical examination*, reconocimiento médico. || *Physical fitness*, buena salud. || *Physical geography*, geografía física. || *Physical therapy*, fisioterapia, *f.*
— N. Reconocimiento (*m.*) médico.
physically [—əli] adv. Físicamente.
physician [fiˈziʃən] n. Médico, *m.* (doctor).
physicist [ˈfizisist] n. Físico, ca (specialist in physics).
physicochemical [ˈfisikəˈkemikəl] adj. Fisicoquímico, ca.
physics [ˈfiziks] n. Física, *f.*: *nuclear physics*, física nuclear.
physiocracy [fiziˈɔkrəsi] n. Fisiocracia, *f.*
physiocrat [ˈfiziəkræt] n. Fisiócrata, *m.* & *f.*
physiognomic [ˌfiziəˈnɔmik] or **physiognomical** [—əl] adj. Fisonómico, ca.

physiognomist [ˌfiziˈɔnəmist] n. Fisonomista, *m.* & *f.*, fisónomo, ma.
physiognomy [ˌfiziˈɔnəmi] n. Fisonomía, *f.*
physiographer [fiziˈɔgrəfə*] n. Fisiógrafo, *m.*
physiography [ˌfiziˈɔgrəfi] n. Fisiografía, *f.* || Geografía (*f.*) física.
physiologic [ˌfiziəˈlɔdʒik] or **physiological** [—əl] adj. Fisiológico, ca.
physiologist [ˌfiziˈɔlədʒist] n. Fisiólogo, ga.
physiology [ˌfiziˈɔlədʒi] n. Fisiología, *f.*
physiotherapist [fiziəuˈθerəpist] n. Fisioterapeuta, *m.* & *f.*
physiotherapy [fiziəˈθerəpi] n. Fisioterapia, *f.*
physique [fiˈzi:k] n. Constitución, *f.* (of a person's body). || Físico, *m.* (of a person).
physostome [ˈfaisəstəum] or **physostomous** [faisəsˈtəuməs] adj. Fisóstomo, ma (fish).
phytography [faiˈtɔgrəfi] n. Fitografía, *f.*
phytology [faiˈtɔlədʒi] n. Fitología, *f.* (botany).
phytophagous [faiˈtɔfəgəs] adj. Fitófago, ga (plant-eating).
phytozoon [faitəˈzəuɔn] n. BIOL. Fitozoario, *m.*, zoófito, *m.*
— OBSERV. El plural de esta palabra es *phytozoa.*
pi [pai] n. Pi, *f.* (Greek letter). || MATH. Pi, *f.* || PRINT. Pastel, *m.*
piacular [paiˈækjulə*] adj. Expiatorio, ria. || Pecaminoso, sa (requiring atonement).
pia mater [ˈpaiəˈmeitə*] n. ANAT. Piamadre, *f.*, piamáter, *f.*
pianissimo [pjæˈnisiməu] adj./adv. MUS. Pianísimo.
pianist [ˈpiənist] n. MUS. Pianista, *m.* & *f.*
pianistic [piəˈnistik] adj. Pianístico, ca.
piano [piˈænəu] n. MUS. Piano, *m.*: *grand, upright piano*, piano de cola, vertical *or* recto; *baby grand piano*, piano de media cola.
piano [ˈpjɑ:nəu] adv. MUS. Piano (softly).
pianoforte [ˌpjænəuˈfɔ:ti] n. MUS. Piano, *m.*, pianoforte, *m.*
pianola [piəˈnəulə] n. MUS. Pianola, *f.*
piano tuner [piˈænəuˌtju:nə*] n. Afinador (*m.*) de pianos.
piastre or **piaster** [piˈæstə*] n. Piastra, *f.*
piazza [piˈætsə] n. Plaza, *f.* (square). || Soportales, *m. pl.*, pórtico, *m.* (portico). || U. S. Galería, *f.*, porche, *m.* (veranda).
pibroch [ˈpi:brɔk] n. MUS. Pieza (*f.*) de música tocada con la gaita.
pica [ˈpaikə] n. Cícero, *m.* (printing). || MED. Pica, *f.*
picador [ˈpikədɔ:*] n. Picador, *m.* (bullfighting).
picaresque [ˌpikəˈresk] adj. Picaresco, ca.
picaroon [ˌpikəˈru:n] n. Pícaro, ra; bribón, ona (rogue). || Pirata, *m.*, corsario, *m.* (pirate).
picayune [piki:ˈju:n] adj. U. S. De poco valor, de poca monta, insignificante (of little value). | Baladí (trivial).
— N. U. S. Fruslería, *f.*, nadería, *f.*, nonada, *f.* || FAM. *It's not worth a picayune*, no vale un pepino.
piccalilli [ˈpikəlili] n. CULIN. Macedonia (*f.*) de verduras con salsa picante.
piccaninny [ˈpikənini] n. Negrito, ta.
piccolo [ˈpikələu] n. MUS. Flautín, *m.*
pick [pik] n. Elección, *f.*, selección, *f.* (choice). || Piqueta, *f.*, pico, *m.* (tool). || Ganzúa, *f.* (picklock). || MUS. Plectro, *m.* || Cosecha, *f.*, recolección, *f.* (of fruit). || — *Take your pick*, escoja el que quiera. || FIG. *The pick of the bunch*, lo más escogido, la flor y nata, lo más selecto, lo mejor de lo mejor. || *To have the pick of*, poder escoger entre. || *To take one's pick*, elegir a su gusto.
pick [pik] v. tr. Escoger (to choose): *to pick the best cake*, escoger el mejor pastel. || Seleccionar (to select carefully): *to pick a team*, seleccionar un equipo. || Coger (flowers). || Recoger (fruit). || Cavar (in the earth). || Escarbar (with the nails). || Abrir: *to pick a hole*, abrir un agujero *or* un boquete. || Mondarse, escarbarse (the teeth). || Hurgarse (one's nose). || Rascarse (a pimple, a wound). || Desplumar (to pluck poultry). || Picotear, picar (to peck, of a bird). || Roer (a bone). || Clasificar, seleccionar (minerals). || Forzar, abrir con ganzúa (a lock). || Picar (rocks). || Puntear, pulsar (a guitar, etc.). || Buscar (to seek): *to pick a quarrel with*, buscar camorra con. || Sacar (threads). || Deshilachar (a material). || — FIG. *To have a bone to pick with*, tener que ajustarle las cuentas a. || *To pick acquaintance with*, conocer a, trabar amistad con. || FIG. *To pick holes in*, encontrar defectos en (sth. done), criticar, desbaratar (an argument), criticar, poner verde (a person). || *To pick one's steps* o *way*, andar con tiento *or* con mucho cuidado (to go carefully), abrirse camino (*through*, entre) [through a crowd, etc.]. || *To pick one's words*, elegir las palabras. || *To pick pockets*, robar carteras. || FIG. *To pick s.o.'s brains*, explotar los conocimientos de alguien. || *To pick s.o.'s pocket*, robar algo del bolsillo de alguien. || *To pick to pieces*, see PIECE.
— V. intr. Picar (with a pick). || Picar, picotear (to eat): *to pick at one's food*, picar la comida. || Picotear (a bird). || Cogerse, recogerse (fruit, flowers, etc.). || Criticar (to criticize). || *To pick and choose*, ser muy exigente, escoger con sumo cuidado.
— ***To pick off***, quitar (to remove). | Eliminar *or* matar uno a uno (to kill). || ***To pick on***, escoger, elegir (to choose). | Criticar (to criticize). | Meterse con: *stop picking on your little brother*, deja de meterte con tu hermanito. || ***To pick out***, escoger, elegir (to select). | Ver, descubrir (to discover): *he hoped no one would pick him out in the crowd*, esperaba que nadie le descubriese en la muchedumbre. | Distinguir (to distinguish). | Discernir (to discern). | Hacer resaltar (to make sth. stand out). | Subrayar (to underline): *important words are picked out in red*, las palabras importantes están subrayadas en rojo. | Sacar, tocar de oído (a tune). || ***To pick over***, buscar en (to look for). || ***To pick up***, coger (to take): *pick the baby up*, coge al niño. | Levantar (to lift): *I can't pick it up, it's too heavy*, no lo puedo levantar, es demasiado pesado. | Recoger (to lift, to collect). | Descolgar, coger (telephone). | Recoger, reunir (information). | Sacar, lograr (a profit). | Recoger (to fetch): *I shall pick you up at your house*, le recogeré en su casa. | Adquirir (to acquire). | Comprar (to buy). | Tomar, coger (a train). | Encontrar (to meet, to find). | Coger: *to pick up speed*, coger velocidad. | Recobrar (strength, etc.). | Entonar (to tone up). | Recuperarse (to recover). | Mejorar (to get better). | Aprender (to learn). | Enterarse de, saber (a piece of news). | Captar (a message on the radio, signals, etc.). | Coger, detener (to arrest). | FAM. Ligar con (a girl). | Ganarse: *to pick up a living*, ganarse la vida. | — *To pick o.s. up*, levantarse. | *To pick up with*, conocer a, trabar amistad con.
pickaback [—əbæk] adv. A cuestas, en los hombros.
— N. Paseo (*m.*) a cuestas.
pickanniny [ˈpikənini] n. Negrito, ta.
pickaxe or **pickax** [—æks] n. Piocha, *f.*, piqueta, *f.* zapapico, *m.*
picked [—t] adj. Escogido, da; selecto, ta.
picker [—ə*] n. Recogedor, ra. || Desmotadora, *f.* (of cotton).
pickerel [—ərəl] n. Lucio, *m.* (fish).
picket [—it] n. Piquete, *m.*, pelotón, *m.* (of soldiers). || Piquete, *m.* (during a strike). || Huelguista, *m.* & *f.*, miembro (*m.*) de un piquete (person). || Manifestación, *f.* (riot, demonstration). || Manifestante, *m.* & *f.* (demonstrator). || Retén, *m.* (of firemen). || Estaca, *f.*, poste, *m.* (pointed stake). || Jalón, *m.*, mojón, *m.* (in surveying). || Poste, *m.* (for horses).
picket [—it] v. tr. Vallar *or* cercar con estacas (with a picket fence). || Atar al poste (an animal). || Vigilar las inmediaciones de (strikers, soldiers). || Poner de guardia a un piquete de huelguistas alrededor de (a factory). || Poner de guardia a unos soldados alrededor de (a military camp).
— V. intr. Vigilar, estar de guardia.
picketer [—itə*] n. Miembro (*m.*) de un piquete de huelguistas.
picking [ˈpikiŋ] n. Recolección, *f.*, cosecha, *f.* (of fruit). || Selección, *f.* (choice). || Forzamiento, *m.* (of a lock). || — Pl. Sobras, *f.*, restos, *m.* (leftovers). || Ganancias, *f.* (profits). || Botín, *m. sing.* (booty).
pickle [ˈpikl] n. Adobo, *m.*, salmuera, *f.* (for preserving meat). || Escabeche, *m.* (for fish). || Conserva (*f.*) en vinagre, encurtido, *m.* (preserve in vinegar). || TECH. Baño (*m.*) de ácido para desoxidar. || FAM. Lío, *m.*, aprieto, *m.*, apuro, *m.* (awkward situation). | Diablillo, *m.* (mischievous child). || — FIG. FAM. *To be in a nice* o *in a fine pickle*, estar metido en un lío. | *To get into a pickle*, meterse en un lío.
pickle [ˈpikl] v. tr. Conservar en vinagre, encurtir (to preserve in vinegar). || Adobar (meat). || Escabechar (fish). || TECH. Desoxidar.
pickled [—d] adj. Adobado, da; en adobo (meat). || Escabechado, da; en escabeche (fish). || En vinagre: *pickled onions*, cebollas en vinagre. || FIG. *To be pickled*, estar piripi (to be drunk).
picklock [ˈpiklɔk] n. Ganzúa, *f.* (device for picking locks). || Ladrón (*m.*) de ganzúa (burglar).
pick-me-up [ˈpikmiʌp] n. Tónico, *m.*, reconstituyente, *m.*, estimulante, *m.* (drink).
pickpocket [ˈpikˌpɔkit] n. Ratero, ra; carterista, *m.*
pickup [ˈpikʌp] n. Recogida (*f.*) de la pelota (cricket). || Recolección, *f.*, recogida, *f.* (harvest). || TECH. Fonocaptor, *m.* (of a gramophone). || Recepción, *f.*, toma, *f.*, captación, *f.* (of sound or light). || Receptor, *m.* (of a transmitter). || Recuperación, *f.*, restablecimiento, *m.* (of health). || Recuperación, *f.* (business recovery). || FAM. Ligue, *m.* (of a person). || Ganga, *f.* (bargain). || Camioneta (*f.*) de reparto, furgoneta (*f.*) de reparto (delivery truck). || Aceleración, *f.*, poder (*m.*) de aceleración (of a car). || Arresto, *m.*, detención, *f.* (arrest). || *Pickup truck*, camión (*m.*) de reparto.
picky [ˈpiki] adj. U. S. FAM. Difícil (finical).
picnic [ˈpiknik] n. Excursión (*f.*) al campo, merienda (*f.*) *or* comida (*f.*) campestre. || Merienda, *f.*, comida, *f.* (food). || FAM. Placer, *m.*: *life is not a picnic*, la vida no es ningún placer. | Cosa (*f.*) tirada (easy thing). || — *Picnic lunch*, bolsa (*f.*) de comida (given in a hotel, etc.), bocadillos, *m. pl.* (sandwiches). || *To go for a picnic*, ir a merendar al campo.
picnic [ˈpiknik] v. intr. Merendar *or* comer en el campo. || *We picnicked by the lake*, merendamos a orillas del lago.
— OBSERV. El pretérito y el participio pasivo de *picnic* son *picnicked* y el participio de presente es *picniking.*

picnicker [—ə*] n. Excursionista, *m.* & *f.*
picot [ˈpi:kəu] n. Puntilla, *f.* (of a ribbon).
picot [ˈpi:kəu] v. tr. Poner puntilla a (a ribbon).
picric [ˈpikrik] adj. Pícrico, ca.
Pict [pikt] adj./n. Picto, ta (people of Scotland).
Pictish [—iʃ] adj. Picto, ta.
pictograph [ˈpiktəugrɑ:f] n. Pictografía, *f.*
pictographic [piktˈəgræfik] adj. Pictográfico, ca.
pictography [pikˈtɔgrəfi] n. Pictografía, *f.*
pictorial [pikˈtɔ:riəl] adj. Pictórico, ca (of pictures): *pictorial art*, arte pictórica. || Gráfico, ca: *a very pictorial style of writing*, una manera de escribir muy gráfica. || Ilustrado, da (magazine).
— N. Revista (*f.*) ilustrada (magazine).
pictorially [—i] adv. Pictóricamente. || Gráficamente (graphically). || Con ilustraciones (through pictures).
picture [ˈpiktʃə*] n. Cuadro, *m.* (painting). || Dibujo, *m.* (drawing). || Grabado, *m.*, lámina, *f.* (engraving). || Ilustración, *f.* (in a magazine). || Película, *f.* (film). || Retrato, *m.* (portrait). || Fotografía, *f.*, foto, *f.* (photograph): *to have one's picture taken*, sacarse una fotografía. || FIG. Retrato, *m.*: *Alexander is the picture of his father*, Alejandro es el retrato de su padre. | Representación, *f.*, imagen, *f.*: *Mary is the picture of happiness*, María es la imagen de la felicidad. | Imagen, *f.* (mental image). | Pintura, *f.*, descripción, *f.*, cuadro, *m.*: *picture of the morals of the period*, descripción de las costumbres de la época. | Visión, *f.*: *these facts give you the general picture*, estos hechos le dan una visión general. | Situación, *f.* (panorama): *have you understood the picture?*, ¿has comprendido la situación? | Facha, *f.* (ridiculous sight): *what a picture you looked!*, ¡qué facha tenías!, ¡estabas hecho una facha! || — Pl. Cine, *m. sing.* (movies). || — FIG. *In the picture*, al corriente (well informed), de actualidad (of the moment). | *Out of the picture*, fuera de lugar. || *Silent pictures*, cine mudo. || *Talking pictures*, cine sonoro. || FIG. *The roses were a picture this year*, las rosas eran preciosas este año. | *To come into the picture*, entrar en escena. || *To give a good picture*, dar buena imagen (TV set). || *To go to the pictures*, ir al cine. || FIG. *To paint a very black picture of sth.*, pintar algo muy negro. | *To put s.o. in the picture*, poner a uno al corriente. | *To see the other side of the picture*, ver el reverso de la medalla. || *To take a picture*, sacar una fotografía. || FIG. *What a picture!*, ¡qué cuadro!, ¡había que verlo!
picture [ˈpiktʃə*] v. tr. Describir, pintar (to depict). || Pintar (to paint). || *To picture* (*to o.s.*), imaginarse, figurarse, representarse (to imagine): *can you picture the situation?*, ¿os imagináis la situación?
picture book [—buk] n. Libro (*m.*) ilustrado.
picture card [—kɑ:d] n. Figura, *f.*
picture frame [—freim] n. Marco, *m.*
picture gallery [—ˌgæləri] n. Museo (*m.*) de pintura, pinacoteca, *f.* (art museum). || Galería, *f.* (small exhibition room).
picturegoer [—ˌgəuə*] n. Aficionado (*m.*) al cine.
picture hat [—hæt] n. Pamela, *f.*
picture house [—haus] or **picture palace** [—ˈpælis] n. Cine, *m.*
picture postcard [—ˈpəustkɑ:d] n. Tarjeta (*f.*) postal.
picturesque [ˌpiktʃəˈresk] adj. Pintoresco, ca: *a picturesque village*, un pueblo pintoresco. || Gráfico, ca (style). || Típico, ca (typical).
picturesqueness [—nis] n. Lo pintoresco, pintoresquismo, *m.*
picture theatre [ˈpiktʃə*ˈθiətə*] n. Cine, *m.*
picture window [ˈpiktʃəˌwindəu] n. Ventanal, *m.*
picture writing [ˈpiktʃəˌraitiŋ] n. Pictografía, *f.*
piddle [pidl] v. intr. FAM. Hacer pipí. || U. S. Malgastar el tiempo.
piddock [ˈpidək] n. Dátil (*m.*) de mar (mollusc).
pidgin [ˈpidʒin] n. Lengua (*f.*) macarrónica. || — *Pidgin English*, "pidgin English", *m.*, inglés macarrónico. || FAM. *That's his pidgin, not yours*, eso es asunto suyo y no tuyo. || *To talk pidgin*, hablar como los indios.
pie [pai] n. ZOOL. Urraca, *f.* (bird). || CULIN. Pastel (*m.*) de carne, empanada, *f.* (with meat). | Pastel, *m.* (of fruit). || Pastel, *m.* (printing). || U. S. Tarta, *f.* (cake). || — FIG. *It's pie in the sky*, son ilusiones, son castillos en el aire, es como prometer la luna. || CULIN. *Shepherd's pie*, pastel (*m.*) de carne picada con puré de patatas. || FIG. *To be as easy as pie*, estar tirado, ser muy fácil. | *To eat humble pie*, reconocer su error. | *To have a finger in every pie*, estar metido en todo, meter las manos en todo. | *To have had a finger in the pie*, haber metido las manos *or* estar pringado en el asunto.
piebald [ˈpaibɔ:ld] adj. Pío, a; picazo, za (horse). || Con lunares de colores, moteado, da (with patches of different colours).
— N. Caballo (*m.*) pío, caballo *m.*) picazo.
piece [pi:s] n. Pedazo, *m.*, trozo, *m.*: *a piece of bread*, un pedazo de pan. || Parte, *f.* (part). || Pieza, *f.*: *a dinner service of 48 pieces*, una vajilla de 48 piezas. || Pieza, *f.* (of material). || Muestra, *f.* (sample). || Momento, *m.* (moment). || Moneda, *f.*, pieza, *f.* (of money): *a five pence piece*, una moneda de cinco peniques. || Pieza, *f.* (chess, draughts, etc.). || MUS. THEATR. Obra, *f.*, pieza, *f.* (musical composition, play). || Pasaje, *m.* (part of a work). || MIL. Pieza, *f.* (of artillery). || Parcela, *f.* (of land). || Poesía, *f.* (poem). || — *All of one piece* o *all in one piece*, de un solo bloque, de una sola pieza. || *A piece of advice*, un consejo. || *A piece of carelessness*, un descuido. || *A piece of folly*, una locura. || *A piece of insolence*, una insolencia. || *A piece of luck*, una suerte. || *A piece of luggage*, un bulto. || *A piece of news*, una noticia. || *A piece of rubbish*, una sandez. || FIG. *A pretty piece*, una preciosidad, una monería (girl, object). || *By the piece*, a destajo, por piezas. || *In pieces*, destrozado, da (destroyed), desmontado, da (machine), por piezas (piece by piece), hecho pedazos (in bits). || *It comes to pieces*, es desmontable, se puede desmontar *or* desarmar. || *Of a piece with*, parecido a. || *Piece by piece*, pieza por pieza, pieza a pieza. || *Piece of furniture*, mueble, *m.* || *Piece of ground* o *of land*, solar, *m.*, terreno, *m.*, parcela, *f.* || *Piece of water*, estanque, *m.* || *To arrive in one piece*, llegar sano y salvo, llegar indemne *or* ileso (a person), llegar en buen estado (a thing). || *To be of a piece with*, formar una sola pieza con (to be a whole), estar de acuerdo con, concordar con (to agree with). || *To be in pieces*, estar hecho pedazos (broken), estar desmontado *or* desarmado (taken apart). || *To break sth. in pieces* o *to pieces*, hacer algo trizas *or* pedazos. || *To come* o *to fall to pieces*, caerse a pedazos (house, person), hacerse pedazos (to break up, to fall apart), hundirse (business). || *To cut to pieces*, cortar en pedazos. || *To fly to pieces*, hacerse pedazos. || FIG. *To give s.o. a piece of one's mind*, decir a uno cuatro verdades. | *To go to pieces*, venirse abajo (to break up physically or morally), perder el dominio de sí mismo (to lose self-control). || *To pay by the piece*, pagar a destajo (a workman). || *To pick to pieces*, poner de vuelta y media, poner verde (to criticize), hacer polvo, no dejar un hueso sano (to beat up), desbaratar (an argument), hacer trizas (to break to pieces). || *To pull* o *to tear to pieces*, hacer pedazos (to break), echar abajo, echar por tierra (an argument), poner como un trapo, poner por los suelos (to criticize). || *To say one's piece*, decir su parecer. || *To take to pieces*, desmontar, desarmar (a machine), deshacer (a dress).
piece [pi:s] v. tr. Poner una pieza a (to add a piece). || — *To piece out*, completar. || FIG. *To piece things together*, atar cabos. || *To piece together*, juntar, juntar las partes de (to join), montar, armar (a machine), hacer (a jigsaw puzzle).
pièce de résistance [pjɛsdəreizistɑ̃:s] n. Atracción (*f.*) principal (main attraction). || CULIN. Plato (*m.*) fuerte *or* principal.
piecemeal [ˈpi:smi:l] adj. Hecho por partes *or* poco a poco. || Poco sistemático, ca (not methodical).
— Adv. Por partes, poco a poco.
piecework [ˈpi:swə:k] n. Trabajo (*m.*) a destajo. || — *Piecework price*, precio (*m.*) a destajo. || *To be on piecework* o *to do piecework*, trabajar a destajo.
pieceworker [—ə*] n. Destajista, *m.* & *f.*, trabajador (*m.*) a destajo.
piecrust [ˈpaikrʌst] n. CULIN. Pasta, *f.*
pied [paid] adj. De varios colores, moteado, da. || *Pied Piper*, el Flautista de Hamelín.
pied-à-terre [ˌpieitæˈtɛə*] n. Apeadero, *m.*
Piedmont [ˈpi:dmənt] pr. n. GEOGR. Piamonte, *m.*
Piedmontese [ˌpi:dmənˈti:z] adj./n. GEOGR. Piamontés, esa.
pier [piə*] n. Malecón, *m.*, rompeolas, *m. inv.*, espigón, *m.* (breakwater masonry). || Muelle, *m.*, embarcadero, *m.* (access to vessels). || ARCH. Pilar, *m.*, machón, *m.* (of an arch). | Entrepaño, *m.* (between two doors), entreventana, *f.* (between two windows). | Pila, *f.* (of a bridge).
pierce [piəs] v. tr. Perforar, taladrar (to bore, to punch a hole in). || Agujerear (to make a hole in). || Atravesar, traspasar (to go through): *the bullet pierced his heart*, la bala le atravesó el corazón. || Penetrar en (to penetrate). || Entrar en (to go into): *the arrow pierced his eye*, la flecha le entró en el ojo. || Abrirse paso por (to break through). || FIG. Traspasar (the heart). | Herir (with cries): *her cries pierced my ears*, sus gritos me hirieron los oídos. | Conmover, afectar (with emotions): *the news pierced him deeply*, la noticia le conmovió profundamente. | Penetrar, adivinar (a mystery, a secret). | Comprender (to understand). || — *A ray of light pierced the darkness*, un rayo de luz atravesó la oscuridad. || *A scream pierced the silent night*, un chillido rompió el silencio de la noche. || *The glass pierced the tyre*, el cristal pinchó la rueda. || *To pierce a hole in sth.*, hacer un agujero en algo. || *To pierce s.o. through*, atravesar a uno (with a spear, etc.), traspasarle el corazón a uno (with grief). || *To pierce the lid of a tin*, perforar una lata. || *When did you have your ears pierced?*, ¿cuándo le hicieron los agujeros en las orejas?
— V. intr. Salir (the teeth).
piercing [—iŋ] adj. Penetrante, agudo, da (cold, look, sound). || Punzante, agudo, da (pain). || Desgarrador, ra (cry). || Cortante (wind). || TECH. Perforador, ra: *piercing dies*, matrices perforadoras.
— N. Perforación, *f.*
pier glass [ˈpiəglɑ:s] n. Espejo (*m.*) de cuerpo entero.
pierrot [ˈpiərəu] n. Pierrot, *m.* (comic character).

pier table [ˈpiə*ˈteibl] n. Consola, *f.*
Pietà [ˌpiəˈtɑ:] pr. n. ARTS. Piedad, *f.*
pietism [ˈpaiətizəm] n. REL. Pietismo, *m.* (doctrine). ‖ Piedad, *f.* (piety). ‖ Beatería, *f.* (excessive piety).
pietist [ˈpaiətist] n. REL. Pietista, *m.* & *f.* ‖ Devoto, ta (pious). ‖ Beato, ta (excessively pious person).
pietistic [ˌpaiəˈtistik] adj. Devoto, ta (pious). ‖ Beato, ta (excessively pious).
piety [ˈpaiəti] n. Piedad, *f.* ‖ *Affected piety*, beatería, *f.*
piezoelectric [paiəzəiˈlektrik] adj. Piezoeléctrico, ca.
piezoelectricity [ˌpaiəzəilekˈtrisiti] n. Piezoelectricidad, *f.*
piezometer [paiəˈzɔmi:tə*] n. PHYS. Piezómetro, *m.*
piezometric [paiəzəˈmetrik] adj. Piezométrico, ca.
piezometry [paiəˈzɔmetri] n. Piezometría, *f.*
piffle [ˈpifl] n. FAM. Pamplina, *f.*, disparate, *m.*, tontería, *f.* (nonsense): *his argument was piffle*, su argumento era una pamplina. ‖ FAM. *A load of piffle*, pamplinas, disparates, tonterías.
piffle [ˈpifl] v. intr. FAM. Decir pamplinas, decir tonterías, soltar disparates, disparatar.
piffling [—iŋ] adj. Fútil, trivial (trivial). ‖ Disparatado, da (nonsensical). ‖ Insignificante, de poca importancia (insignificant).
pig [pig] n. Cerdo, *m.*, puerco, *m.* [*Amer.*, chancho, *m.*, guarro, *m.*] (animal). ‖ U. S. Cochinillo, *m.* (piglet). ‖ TECH. Lingote (*m.*) de arrabio (of iron). | Galápago, *m.* (of lead). | Lingotera, *f.* (mould in which metal is cast). ‖ FAM. Cerdo, da; cochino, na (dirty person): *what a pig!*, ¡qué cerdo! ‖ — FIG. *Greedy pig*, tragón, ona; comilón, ona. ‖ *Pig breeding*, cría (*f.*) de cerdos. ‖ *Roast pig*, cochinillo asado. ‖ *Sucking pig*, lechón, *m.*, cochinillo (*m.*) de leche. ‖ FIG. *To buy a pig in a poke*, comprar a ciegas. | *To make a pig of o.s.*, hincharse como un cerdo. | *To sell s.o. a pig in a poke*, dar a alguien gato por liebre. | *When pigs fly* o *have wings*, cuando las ranas críen pelos. ‖ *Wild pig*, jabalí, *m.* (wild boar). ‖ FAM. *You dirty pig!*, ¡qué cerdo eres!, ¡eres un guarro!, ¡qué guarro eres!
pig [pig] v. intr. Parir (the sow). ‖ FAM. Vivir como cerdos (to live like pigs).
pig bed [—bed] n. TECH. Era (*f.*) de colada.
pigeon [ˈpidʒin] n. ZOOL. Paloma, *f.*: *domestic, crested, carrier* o *homing, wild, wood, rock pigeon*, paloma casera, de moño, mensajera, silvestre, torcaz, zurita. ‖ SP. Pichón, *m.* (bird). | Plato, *m.* (clay pigeon). ‖ CULIN. Pichón, *m.* ‖ — SP. *Clay pigeon shooting*, tiro (*m.*) al plato. ‖ FAM. *That's his pigeon*, es asunto suyo.
pigeonhole [—həul] n. Casilla, *f.* ‖ (*Set of*)*pigeonholes*, casillas, *f. pl.*, casillero, *m. sing.*
pigeonhole [—həul] v. tr. Archivar (to store away). ‖ Encasillar, clasificar (to classify). ‖ Dar carpetazo a (to shelve).
pigeon house [—haus] or **pigeon loft** [—lɔft] n. Palomar, *m.*
pigeon shooting [—ʃu:tiŋ] n. Tiro (*m.*) de pichón.
pigeon-toed [—təud] adj. Con los pies torcidos hacia dentro.
piggery [ˈpigəri] n. Pocilga, *f.*, porqueriza, *f.* (pigsty). ‖ FIG. Pocilga, *f.* (a filthy place). | Porquería, *f.* (filthiness).
piggish [ˈpigiʃ] adj. Glotón, ona (greedy). ‖ Puerco, ca; cochino, na (dirty). ‖ Testarudo, da (stubborn).
piggy [ˈpigi] adj. Guarro, rra (dirty). ‖ Glotón, ona (greedy).
— N. Cochinillo, *m.*, lechón, *m.*, cerdito, *m.*
piggyback [—bæk] adv. A cuestas, en los hombros: *to carry s.o. piggyback*, llevar a alguien a cuestas. ‖ U. S. Sobre vagones plataformas.
— N. U. S. Sistema (*m.*) de transporte sobre vagones plataformas. ‖ Paseo (*m.*) a cuestas (pickaback ride).
piggy bank [—bæŋk] n. Hucha, *f.*, alcancía, *f.* (money box).
pigheaded [—ˈhedid] adj. Testarudo, da; terco, ca; cabezón, ona.
pigheadedness [—ˈhedidnis] n. Terquedad, *f.*, testarudez, *f.*, cabezonería, *f.*
pig iron [—ˌaiən] n. Arrabio, *m.*, hierro (*m.*) colado, hierro (*m.*) en lingotes.
pig Latin [—ˈlætin] n. Jerga, *f.*
piglet [—lit] n. Cochinillo, *m.*, lechón, *m.*
pigman [—mən] n. Porquero, *m.*, porquerizo, *m.*

— OBSERV. El plural de *pigman* es *pigmen*.

pigment [ˈpigmənt] n. Pigmento, *m.*
pigment [ˈpigmənt] v. tr. Pigmentar.
pigmentary [—məntəri] adj. Pigmentario, ria.
pigmentation [ˌpigmənˈteiʃən] n. Pigmentación, *f.*
pigmy [ˈpigmi] n. See PYGMY.
pignoraticious [ˌpignərəˈtiʃəs] or **pignorative** [ˈpignəˌreitiv] adj. Pignoraticio, cia.
pignus [ˈpignəs] n. Prenda, *f.*

— OBSERV. El plural de *pignus* es *pignora*.

pignut [ˈpignʌt] n. BOT. Pacana, *f.*
pigpen [ˈpigpen] n. U. S. Pocilga, *f.*, porqueriza, *f.*
pigskin [ˈpigskin] n. Piel (*f.*) de cerdo (skin). ‖ FAM. Silla (*f.*) de montar (saddle). | Balón, *m.*, pelota, *f.* (ball).
pigsty [ˈpigstai] n. Pocilga, *f.*, porqueriza, *f.* ‖ FIG. Pocilga, *f.* (dirty place).
pigswill [ˈpigswil] n. Bazofia, *f.*
pigtail [ˈpigteil] n. Coleta, *f.* (of Chinese, of bullfighter). ‖ Coleta, *f.*, trenza, *f.* (of girl).

pike [paik] n. Punta, *f.* (sharp tip). ‖ Pica, *f.* (weapon). ‖ Lucio, *m.* (fish). ‖ U. S. Peaje, *m.* (toll). | Barrera, *f.* (toll bar). | Carretera (*f.*) de peaje (toll road).
pikeman [—mən] n. MIL. Piquero, *m.*

— OBSERV. El plural de *pikeman* es *pikemen*.

piker [—ə*] n. U. S. FAM. Tacaño, ña; roñoso, sa (skinflint).
pikestaff [—stɑ:f] n. Asta (*f.*) de la pica (weapon staff). ‖ Báculo (*m.*) de peregrino (walking stick). ‖ *As plain as a pikestaff*, clarísimo, ma.

— OBSERV. El plural es *pikestaffs* o *pikestaves*.

pilaf or **pilaff** [ˈpilæf] n. CULIN. Plato (*m.*) oriental a base de arroz.
pilaster [piˈlæstə*] n. ARCH. Pilastra, *f.*
Pilate [ˈpailət] pr. n. HIST. Pilato, *m.*
pilau [piˈlau] n. CULIN. Plato (*m.*) oriental a base de arroz.
pilchard [ˈpiltʃəd] n. Sardina, *f.* (fish).
pile [pail] n. ARCH. Pilote, *m.* (support): *built on piles*, construido sobre pilotes. ‖ Estaca, *f.* (stake): *to drive piles in the ground*, clavar estacas en la tierra. ‖ Montón, *m.*, pila, *f.*: *a pile of books*, un montón de libros. ‖ FAM. Pila, *f.*, montón, *m.*: *a pile of things to do*, una pila de cosas que hacer. | Fortuna, *f.* (fortune). ‖ Pira (*f.*) funeraria (funeral pyre). ‖ ELECTR. Pila, *f.*, batería, *f.* ‖ PHYS. Pila, *f.*: *atomic pile*, pila atómica. ‖ Mole, *f.* (building). ‖ Pelo, *m.* (of carpets): *to have a thick pile*, tener el pelo largo. ‖ MIL. Pabellón, *m.* (of arms). ‖ MED. Almorrana, *f.*
pile [pail] v. tr. ARCH. Sostener con pilotes (to support). ‖ Hincar pilotes en (to drive piles into). ‖ Amontonar, apilar (to place in a heap): *he piled the books one on top of the other*, amontonó los libros uno encima de otro. ‖ Abarrotar (to cram). ‖ — MIL. *To pile arms*, formar pabellones. ‖ *To pile a table with books*, llenar una mesa de libros, amontonar libros sobre una mesa.
— V. intr. Amontonarse, apiñarse (in a heap). ‖ Acumularse (to accumulate).
— *To pile in* o *into*, meterse, amontonarse: *they all piled into the car*, se amontonaron todos en el coche. | Entrar en tropel (to crowd in). | — *Pile in everyone!*, ¡todos adentro! ‖ *To pile on*, echar un montón de: *to pile wood on the fire*, echar un montón de leña al fuego. | Aumentar, intensificar (to intensify). | — FIG. *To pile it on*, exagerar. | *To pile on the agony*, cargar las tintas. ‖ *To pile out*, salir en tropel. ‖ *To pile up*, amontonar, apilar (to put in a heap). | Cargar (to load). | Acumular: *he piled up evidence*, acumuló pruebas. | Amontonarse, acumularse: *the books piled up*, se amontonaban los libros; *the debts piled up*, se acumulaban las deudas. | Chocar uno contra otro (several cars). | — *To pile up against* o *on*, estrellarse contra.
pile driver [—ˌdraivə*] n. TECH. Martinete, *m.*
pile dwelling [—ˌdweliŋ] n. Vivienda (*f.*) sostenida por pilotes, vivienda (*f.*) lacustre.
piles [—z] pl. n. MED. Almorranas, *f.*
pileup [—ʌp] n. Accidente (*m.*) múltiple.
pileus [ˈpailiəs] n. Sombrerillo, *m.* (of a mushroom).
pilewort [ˈpailwə:t] n. BOT. Celidonia (*f.*) menor.
pilfer [ˈpilfə*] v. tr./intr. Sisar, hurtar, robar.
pilferage [ˈpilfəridʒ] n. Hurto, *m.*, robo, *m.*, sisa, *f.*
pilferer [—rə*] n. Ladronzuelo, la.
pilfering [—riŋ] n. Sisa, *f.*, hurto, *m.*, robo, *m.*
pilgrim [ˈpilgrim] n. Peregrino, na.
Pilgrim [ˈpilgrim] n. HIST. Padre (*m.*) Peregrino (one of the Pilgrim Fathers).
pilgrimage [—idʒ] n. Peregrinación, *f.*: *to go on a pilgrimage*, ir en peregrinación.
Pilgrim Father [—ˈfɑ:ðə*] n. HIST. Padre (*m.*) Peregrino.
piliferous [paiˈlifərəs] adj. BOT. Pilífero, ra.
piliform [ˈpailifɔ:m] adj. Piliforme.
piling [—iŋ] n. Pilotaje, *m.*
pill [pil] n. Píldora, *f.* (medicine). ‖ FIG. FAM. Lata, *f.* (person). | Bala, *f.* (bullet). | Pelota, *f.* (ball). ‖ — FIG. *It was a bitter pill to swallow*, era una píldora difícil de tragar. | *To sugar* o *to gild the pill*, dorar la píldora. | *To swallow the bitter pill*, tragarse la píldora.
pillage [ˈpilidʒ] n. Pillaje, *m.*, saqueo, *m.*
pillage [ˈpilidʒ] v. tr./intr. Saquear, pillar.
pillar [ˈpilə*] n. ARCH. Pilar, *m.* | Columna, *f.* ‖ FIG. Pilar, *m.*, soporte, *m.*, puntal, *m.*: *the pillars of the Church*, los pilares de la Iglesia. | Columna, *f.*: *a pillar of smoke*, una columna de humo. ‖ — FIG. *He is a pillar of strength*, es firme como una roca. ‖ *Pillars of Hercules*, Columnas de Hércules. ‖ FIG. *To be driven from pillar to post*, tener que ir de la Ceca a la Meca.
pillar [ˈpilə*] v. tr. Sostener con pilares.
pillar box [—bɔks] n. Buzón, *m.* (for letters).
pillbox [ˈpilbɔks] n. Cajita (*f.*) para pastillas *or* píldoras (for tablets). ‖ Sombrero (*m.*) sin ala (hat). ‖ MIL. Fortín, *m.*
pillion [ˈpiljən] n. Asiento (*m.*) trasero (of a motorcycle). ‖ Silla (*f.*) ligera de montar (saddle). ‖ Grupera, *f.* (pad). ‖ *To ride pillion*, ir en el asiento trasero (on a motorcycle), montar a la grupa (on a horse).
pillory [ˈpiləri] n. Picota, *f.*

pillory [ˈpiləri] v. tr. Poner en la picota (to punish). || FIG. Poner en la picota, exponer a la vergüenza pública (to ridicule).

pillow [ˈpiləu] n. Almohada, *f.* (cushion for the head). || TECH. Cojinete *m.* || Mundillo, *m.*, almohadilla, *f.* (in lace making).

pillow [ˈpiləu] v. tr. Apoyar en una almohada (to lean on a pillow). || Servir de almohada para (to serve as a pillow). || *To pillow one's head on one's arms*, reposar la cabeza en los brazos.

pillow block [—blɔk] n. TECH. Cojinete, *m.*

pillowcase [—keis] n. Funda (*f.*) de almohada.

pillow lace [—leis] n. Encaje (*m.*) de bolillos.

pillowslip [—slip] n. Funda (*f.*) de almohada.

pilose [ˈpailəus] adj. Piloso, sa.

pilosity [paiˈlɔsiti] n. Pilosidad, *f.*

pilot [ˈpailət] n. MAR. Piloto, *m.*, práctico, *m.* (of the harbour). | Timonel, *m.*, piloto, *m.* (of a boat). || AVIAT. Piloto, *m.* || Piloto, *m.* (light). || FIG. Guía, *m.* & *f.* (guide). || U. S. Quitapiedras, *m. inv.* (of a locomotive). || TECH. Guía, *f.* || — *Airline pilot*, piloto de línea. || *Automatic pilot*, piloto automático. || *Coast pilot*, práctico, *m.* || *Test pilot*, piloto de pruebas.
— Adj. Modelo, piloto: *a pilot factory*, una fábrica modelo.

pilot [ˈpailət] v. tr. Pilotar (a plane, a ship, etc.). || Guiar, dirigir (to guide). || — *To pilot a bill through Parliament*, defender un proyecto de ley en el Parlamento. || *To pilot through*, llevar a buen término (talks, etc.), guiar (people, etc.).

pilotage [—idʒ] n. Pilotaje, *m.*

pilot balloon [—bəˈlu:n] n. Globo (*m.*) sonda.

pilot boat [—bəut] n. MAR. Barco (*m.*) del práctico.

pilot engine [ˌ—ˈendʒin] n. Locomotora (*f.*) exploradora.

pilot fish [—fiʃ] n. Pez (*m.*) piloto (fish).

pilothouse [—haus] n. U. S. MAR. Timonera, *f.*, cabina (*f.*) del piloto.

piloting [—iŋ] n. Pilotaje, *m.*

pilot lamp [—læmp] n. Piloto, *m.*, lámpara (*f.*) indicadora.

pilot light [—lait] n. Piloto, *m.*, lámpara (*f.*) indicadora.

pilous [ˈpailəs] adj. Piloso, sa.

pilular [ˈpiljulə*] adj. En forma de píldora.

pimento [piˈmentəu] n. BOT. Pimienta (*f.*) de Jamaica. || Pimiento (*m.*) morrón (pimiento).

— OBSERV. El plural de *pimento* es *pimento* o *pimentos*.

pimiento [piˈmentəu] n. Pimiento (*m.*) morrón.

pimp [pimp] n. Chulo, *m.*, rufián, *m.*, proxeneta, *m.*, alcahuete, *m.*

pimp [pimp] v. intr. Alcahuetear. || *To pimp for*, ser alcahuete de.

pimpernel [ˈpimpənel] n. BOT. Murajes, *m. pl.*, pimpinela, *f.* (creeping plant).

pimple [—l] n. Grano, *m.*: *I came out in pimples*, me salieron granos. || Espinilla, *f.*, grano, *m.* (on the face).

pimpled [—ld] or **pimply** [—li] adj. Espinilloso, sa; con espinillas (face). || Con granos (body).

pin [pin] n. Alfiler, *m.* (used in sewing, etc.). || Horquilla, *f.* (hairpin). || Imperdible, *m.* (safety pin). || Broche, *m.* (brooch). || Insignia, *f.* (emblem). || Pinza, *f.*, alfiler, *m.* (for washing). || Clavija, *f.* (peg). || MUS. Clavija, *f.* (string instruments). || Macho, *m.* (of a dovetail joint). || Rodillo, *m.* (rolling pin). || TECH. Pezonera, *f.* (linchpin). | Chaveta, *f.* (cotter). | Paletón, *m.* (of key). | Perno, *m.* (bolt). || FIG. FAM. Pimiento, *m.*: *it's not worth a pin*, no vale un pimiento. || SP. Banderín, *m.* (in golf). | Bolo, *m.* (skittle). || Barrilete, *m.* (cask). || — Pl. FAM. Zancas, *f.*, patas, *f.* (legs). || — FIG. *Alike as two pins*, como dos gotas de agua. | *As clean as a new pin*, limpio como los chorros del oro, limpio como un espejo *or* como una patena. || MAR. *Belaying pin*, cabilla, *f.* || *Drawing pin*, chincheta, *f.* || *Firing pin*, percutor, *m.* || FIG. *For two pins I'd hit him*, un poco más y le pego. || FIG. FAM. *He is shaky on his pins*, le flaquean las piernas. || *Rolling pin*, rodillo, *m.* || FIG. *Pins and needles*, hormigueo, *m.* | *You could have heard a pin drop*, se podía oír el vuelo de una mosca.

pin [pin] v. tr. Prender con alfileres: *to pin the hem of a dress*, prender el dobladillo de un vestido con alfileres. || Sujetar (to hold, to fix). || Prender *or* coger con un alfiler: *to pin banknotes together*, prender billetes de banco con un alfiler. || ARCH. Apuntalar (a wall). || TECH. Enclavijar (with pegs). | Enchavetar (with cotters). | Sujetar con perno (with a bolt).
— ***To pin down***, sujetar a la fuerza (to hold down). | Sujetar (to fix, to attach): *pin it down with a few nails*, sujétalo con unos clavos. | Hacer que alguien concrete (to make s.o. specify). | Encontrar, localizar (to find). | Precisar: *there's sth. wrong but I can't quite pin it down*, hay algo que no va, pero no puedo precisar lo que es. | Inmovilizar (the enemy, etc.). | — *To pin sth. down to*, atribuir algo especialmente a. || ***To pin on***, prender (a brooch, a medal): *to pin a brooch on one's lapel*, prender un broche en la solapa. | Prender con alfiler (with pins). | Poner, cifrar: *to pin one's hopes on sth.*, poner sus esperanzas en algo. | Acusar: *they tried to pin the robbery on him*, intentaron acusarle del robo. || ***To pin out***, extender con el rodillo (dough). || ***To pin up***, fijar, sujetar: *how can I pin this poster up?*, ¿cómo puedo sujetar este cartel? | Sujetar (con horquillas) [hair]. | Sujetar con chinchetas (with drawing pins). | ARCH. Apuntalar.

pinafore [—əfɔ:*] n. Delantal, *m.* (apron). || U. S. Babero, *m.* (for baby). || *Pinafore dress*, falda (*f.*) con peto.

pinaster [paiˈnæstə*] n. BOT. Pino (*m.*) rodeno.

pinball table [ˈpinbɔ:lˌteibl] n. Billar (*m.*) automático.

pince-nez [ˈpɛ̃:nsnei] inv. n. Quevedos, *m. pl.*

pincers [ˈpinsəz] pl. n. TECH. Tenazas, *f.*, tenaza, *f. sing.* || ZOOL. Pinzas, *f.* || MIL. *Pincers movement*, movimiento (*m.*) de tenazas.

pinch [pintʃ] n. Pellizco, *m.*: *she gave him a pinch*, le dio un pellizco. || Pizca, *f.*: *a pinch of salt*, una pizca de sal. || Pulgarada, *f.* (of tobacco). || FIG. Necesidad, *f.* (need). || FAM. Robo, *m.* (robbery). | Pesca, *f.*, captura, *f.* (arrest). || — FIG. *At a pinch*, en caso de necesidad. | *To feel the pinch*, empezar a pasar apuros. | *To feel the pinch of hunger*, empezar a sentir hambre. | *To take sth. with a pinch of salt*, admitir algo con reservas. | *When it comes to the pinch*, cuando llega el momento decisivo.

pinch [pintʃ] v. tr. Pellizcar: *to pinch s.o.'s arm*, pellizcar a alguien en el brazo. || Pillarse, cogerse: *he pinched his finger in the door*, se pilló el dedo con la puerta. || Apretar: *do the new shoes pinch you?*, ¿te aprietan los zapatos nuevos? || FIG. Herir (pride). | Poner en un apuro *or* en un aprieto (to put in a tight spot). | Atenazar (hunger). || FAM. Mangar, birlar (to steal): *he had his car pinched*, le mangaron el coche. | Robar (an idea). | Coger (to grab). | Quitar (to take away). | Agarrar, pescar (to arrest). || — *Pinched features*, cara cansada. || *Pinched with cold*, aterido, transido de frío. || *To be pinched for*, andar mal de, andar escaso de (to be short of). || *To pinch off*, quitar con los dedos. || *To pinch pennies*, escatimar gastos.
— V. intr. Apretar: *these shoes pinch*, estos zapatos aprietan. || Economizar (to economize). || Tacañear, escatimar (to overeconomize). || FIG. *He knows where the shoe pinches*, sabe donde le aprieta el zapato.

pinch bar [—bɑ:*] n. Pie (*m.*) de cabra, alzaprima, *f.*

pinchbeck [—bek] n. Imitación, *f.*
— Adj. De pacotilla, de imitación.

pinchcock [—kɔk] n. TECH. Abrazadera, *f.*

pinched [—t] adj. See PINCH.

pinchers [—əz] pl. n. TECH. Tenazas, *f.*, tenaza, *f. sing.*

pinch-hit [—hit] v. intr. U. S. SP. Batear en sustitución del titular (in baseball). || U. S. FAM. Sustituir a otro en un momento de apuro (to substitute in an emergency).

pinch hitter [—ˌhitə*] n. U. S. SP. Bateador (*m.*) suplente. || U. S. FAM. Sustituto (*m.*) en un momento de apuro.

pinchpenny [—ˈpeni] adj. Tacaño, na.

pincushion [ˈpinˌkuʃən] n. Acerico, *m.*

Pindar [ˈpində*] pr. n. Píndaro, *m.* (Greek author).

pine [pain] n. BOT. Pino, *m.* (tree, wood). || FAM. Piña, *f.* (pineapple). || — *Aleppo pine*, pino carrasco. || *Cluster pine*, pino marítimo *or* rodeno. || *Scotch pine*, pino albar *or* royo. || *Stone* o *umbrella pine*, pino piñonero *or* real.

pine [pain] v. intr. Desfallecer, languidecer. || — *To pine away*, consumirse, languidecer. || *To pine for*, anhelar, suspirar por.

pineal body [ˈpiniəlˈbɔdi] or **pineal gland** [ˈpiniəlglænd] n. ANAT. Glándula (*f.*) pineal.

pineapple [ˈpainˌæpl] n. Piña, *f.*, ananás, *m.*

pinecone [ˈpainkəun] n. BOT. Piña, *f.*

pine grove [ˈpaingrəuv] n. Pinar, *m.*

pine kernel [ˈpainˌkə:nl] n. Piñón, *m.*

pine marten [ˈpainˌmɑ:tin] n. ZOOL. Marta, *f.*

pine needle [ˈpainˌni:dl] n. BOT. Aguja (*f.*) de pino.

pinery [ˈpainəri] n. BOT. Plantación (*f.*) de piñas *or* ananás (pineapple plantation). | Pinar, *m.* (pine grove).

pine seed [ˈpainsi:d] n. Piñón, *m.*

pine tree [ˈpaintri:] n. Pino, *m.*

pinetum [paiˈni:təm] n. BOT. Pinar, *m.*

— OBSERV. El plural de *pinetum* es *pineta*.

pinewood [ˈpainwud] n. Pinar, *m.* (forest). || Pino, *m.*, madera (*f.*) de pino (wood).

pinfeather [ˈpinfeðə*] n. ZOOL. Cañón, *m.*

pinfold [ˈpinfəuld] n. Perrera, *f.* (for stray dogs). || Depósito, *m.* (for stray animals).

ping [piŋ] n. Sonido (*m.*) corto y metálico. || Silbido, *m.* (of a bullet).

ping [piŋ] v. intr. Producir un sonido corto y metálico. || Silbar, zumbar (a bullet). || See PINK.

ping-pong [ˈpiŋpɔŋ] n. SP. Ping-pong, *m.*, tenis (*m.*) de mesa.

pinguid [ˈpiŋgwid] adj. Pingüe. || Feraz (soil).

pinhead [ˈpinhed] n. Cabeza (*f.*) de alfiler. || FIG. Nimiedad, *f.*, insignificancia, *f.* || U. S. FAM. Tonto ta; mentecato, ta (idiot).

pinhole [ˈpinhəul] n. Agujero (*m.*) de alfiler.

pinion [ˈpinjən] n. Ala, *f.* (wing). || TECH. Piñón, *m.* || *Pinion drive*, transmisión (*f.*) por engranaje.

pinion [ˈpinjən] v. tr. Cortar las alas a (birds). || Maniatar (people).

pink [piŋk] n. Clavel, *m.* (flower, plant). || Rosa, *m.* (colour). || Levita (*f.*) roja (hunting coat). || FIG. Modelo, *m.*, dechado, *m.* (example). || FAM. Rojillo, lla (Leftist). || *In the pink of health*, rebosante de salud.
— Adj. Rosa (colour). || FAM. Rojillo, lla (left-wing). || — FIG. FAM. *Strike me pink!*, ¡caray! || FIG. *To tickle (s.o.) pink*, see TICKLE.
pink [piŋk] v. tr. Picar (to ornament with holes). || Festonear (to edge). || Herir levemente (to wound). || *To pink out*, embellecer.
— V. intr. AUT. Picar.
pinkeye [ˈpiŋkai] n. MED. Conjuntivitis (*f.*) aguda.
pinkie [ˈpiŋki] n. FAM. Dedo (*m.*) meñique.
pinking shears [ˈpiŋkiŋˌʃiəz] pl. n. Tijeras (*f.*) dentadas.
pinkish [piŋkiʃ] adj. Rosáceo, a.
pin money [ˈpinˌmʌni] n. Dinero (*m.*) para gastos menudos.
pinna [ˈpinə] n. BOT. Pina, *f.*, folíolo, *m.* || ZOOL. Ala, *f.* (of birds). | Aleta, *f.* (of fishes). || ANAT. Pabellón (*m.*) de la oreja.
pinnace [ˈpinis] n. MAR. Pinaza, *f.*
pinnacle [ˈpinəkl] n. Pináculo, *m.* (turret). || Pico, *m.*, cima, *f.* (peak). || FIG. Cumbre, *f.*, apogeo, *m.*, pináculo, *m.*: *on the pinnacle of one's glory*, en la cumbre de la gloria.
pinnacle [ˈpinəkl] v. tr. Coronar, rematar (to top, to crown). || FIG. Poner en un pedestal.
pinnate [ˈpinit] adj. BOT. Pinada (leaf).
pinniped [ˈpiniped] adj. ZOOL. Pinnípedo, da.
pinny [ˈpini] n. Delantal, *m.*
pinole [pəˈnəuli:] n. Pinole, *m.*
pinpoint [ˈpinpɔint] n. Punta (*f.*) de alfiler.
— Adj. Preciso, sa; exacto, ta (exact). || De precisión (shooting).
pinpoint [ˈpinpɔint] v. tr. Localizar con toda precisión (to locate). || Apuntar con precisión (to aim). || Señalar (to point out). || Determinar con precisión (to determine).
pinprick [ˈpinprik] n. Alfilerazo, *m.* (with a pin). || Pinchazo, *m.* (small puncture). || FIG. Puya, *f.*, pinchazo, *m.* (malicious remark).
pinstripe [ˈpinstraip] adj. Rayado, da; a rayas.
pint [paint] n. Pinta, *f.* [medida de líquido equivalente a 0,568 litros en Gran Bretaña y a 0,473 en Estados Unidos]. || FAM. Cerveza, *f.* (beer). | Caña, *f.* (pot of beer).
pinta [ˈpintə] n. MED. Pinta, *f.*
pintail [ˈpinteil] n. ZOOL. Ánade (*m.*) de cola larga.
pintle [ˈpintəl] n. TECH. Perno, *m.* (bolt). || MAR. Macho, *m.* (of rudder).
pinto [ˈpintəu] n. Caballo (*m.*) pinto (horse). || Judía (*f.*) pinta (bean).
pinto bean [—bi:n] n. Judía (*f.*) pinta.
pinup [ˈpinʌp] n. FAM. Fotografía (*f.*) de una modelo. | Mujer (*f.*) atractiva. || *She is his pinup*, para él es la mujer ideal.
pinup girl [—gə:l] n. FAM. Modelo (*f.*) fotográfica. | Mujer (*f.*) atractiva.
pinwheel [ˈpinwi:l] n. U. S. Rueda (*f.*) de fuegos artificiales, girándula, *f.* (fireworks). | Molinillo, (toy).
pinworm [ˈpinwə:m] n. Lombriz (*f.*) intestinal.
piolet [ˈpi:əlei] n. "Piolet", *m.*, bastón (*m.*) de montañero [*Amer.*, piqueta, *f.*]
pioneer [ˌpaiəˈniə*] n. Colonizador, *m.*, pionero, *m.* (early settler). || MIL. Zapador, *m.* || FIG. Pionero, *m.*, iniciador, *m.*, adelantado, *m.*: *a pioneer of flying*, un pionero de la aviación.
pioneer [ˌpaiəˈniə*] v. tr. Promover (to foster). || Sentar las bases de (to lay the foundations for). || Iniciar, ser el iniciador de (to initiate). || Colonizar (to colonize).
— V. intr. Abrir *or* enseñar el camino.
pious [ˈpaiəs] adj. Piadoso, sa (devout). || FAM. Beato, ta (excessively religious). || FIG. Digno de alabanza: *pious intention*, intención digna de alabanza.
piousness [ˈpaiəsnis] n. Piedad, *f.* || FAM. Beatería, *f.* (religious bigotry).
pip [pip] n. VET. Moquillo, *m.* (of birds). || Punto, *m.* (on dice, playing cards). || MIL. Estrella, *f.* (on uniform). || BOT. Flor, *f.* (flower). | Pipa, *f.*, pepita, *f.* (seed). || RAD. Señal, *f.* [para dar las horas] (time signal). || FAM. Alhaja, *f.*, perla, *f.* (highly prized person). || — FAM. *To give s.o. the pip*, ponerle a uno enfermo. | *To have the pip*, estar disgustado.
pip [pip] v. tr. Romper [el cascarón] (a bird hatching). || Vencer (to beat). || Fastidiar (to spoil). || Dar en (to hit). || Suspender (to fail s.o. in an examination). || Ser suspendido en (to fail an examination). || Hacer el vacío a (to ignore). || FIG. *To pip s.o. at the post*, ganarle a uno por la mano.
— V. intr. Romper el cascarón (a bird). || Perder (to lose). || Fracasar (to fail). || FAM. *To pip out*, estirar la pata (to die).
pipage [ˈpaipidʒ] n. Transporte (*m.*) por tuberías (transportation). || Precio (*m.*) del transporte por tuberías (cost). || Tuberías, *f. pl.* (pipes).
pipe [paip] n. Pipa, *f.* (cask). || Tubo, *m.*, tubería, *f.*, cañería, *f.*, conducto, *m.*: *gas pipe*, tubo de gas. || MUS. Caramillo, *m.*, flautín, *m.*, flauta, *f.* (small flute). | Tubo, *m.* (of bagpipes). | Tubo, *m.*, cañón, *m.* (of an organ). || MAR. Pito, *m.* (whistle). || Pipa, *f.* (smoking device). || — Pl. MUS. Gaita, *f. sing.* (bagpipes). || Tubería, *f. sing.*, cañería, *f. sing.*, tubos, *m.*: *the water pipes*, la tubería del agua. (See OBSERV.). || — *Pipe of peace*, pipa de la paz. || FAM. *Put that in your pipe and smoke it!*, ¡chúpate ésa!

— OBSERV. Technically speaking, the words *tubería* and *cañería* mean a "set of pipes". They are however commonly used to denote a single "pipe" and the plural form *tuberías* and *cañerías* to denote "pipes".

pipe [paip] v. tr. Conducir por tubería (water, etc.). || Transportar por oleoducto (oil). || Instalar tuberías en (to furnish with pipes). || MUS. Interpretar *or* tocar con el caramillo. || Adornar con ribete (to adorn cloth with piping). || — *To pipe one's eye*, llorar. || *To pipe the captain aboard*, pitar cuando sube el capitán a bordo.
— V. intr. MUS. Tocar la gaita (to play the pipes). | Tocar el caramillo (flute). || Chillar (to make a shrill sound). || MAR. Convocar a la tripulación (to summon the crew). || — FAM. *To pipe down*, callarse. | *To pipe up*, empezar a hablar.
pipe clay [ˈpaipklei] n. Espuma (*f.*) de mar (for making pipes). || Blanco (*m.*) de España (for cleaning).
pipe-clay [ˈpaipklei] v. tr. Limpiar con blanco de España.
pipe cleaner [—ˌkli:nə*] n. Limpiapipas, *m. inv.*
pipe dream [—dri:m] n. FIG. Castillos (*m. pl.*) en el aire, ilusiones, *f. pl.*
pipefish [—fiʃ] n. ZOOL. Aguja. *f.*
pipeful [—ful] n. Pipa, *f.* (of tobacco).
pipeline [—lain] n. Oleoducto, *m.* (for oil). || Gasoducto, *m.* (for gas). || Tubería, *f.* (for water). || FIG. Conducto, *m.* (of information). || *To be in the pipeline*, estar en trámite.
pipe organ [—ˌɔ:gən] n. MUS. Órgano, *m.*
piper [—ə*] n. MUS. Gaitero, *m.* | Flautista, *m.* || — FIG. *He who pays the piper calls the tune*, manda el que paga. | *To pay the piper*, pagar el pato *or* los vidrios rotos.
piperaceae [pipəˈreisii] pl. n. Piperáceas, *f.*
pipe tobacco [ˈpaiptəˌbækəu] n. Tabaco (*m.*) de pipa.
pipette (U. S. **pipet**) [piˈpet] n. CHEM. Pipeta, *f.*
piping [ˈpaipiŋ] n. Sonido (*m.*) de la gaita (music of pipes). || Sonido (*m.*) de la flauta (of a flute). || Gorjeo, *m.* (of birds). || Pitido, *m.* (whistle). || Tubería, *f.*, tuberías, *f. pl.* (system of pipes). || Ribete, *m.* (decoration on cloth). || Adorno (*m.*) hecho sobre un pastel (on cakes).
— Adj. Agudo, da; aflautado, da: *a piping voice*, una voz aguda.
— Adv. *To be piping hot*, estar hirviendo.
pipistrelle [ˌpipiˈstrel] n. Pipistrelo, *m.* (bat).
pipit [ˈpipit] n. Pitpit, *m.* (bird).
pipkin [ˈpipkin] n. Puchero (*m.*) de barro.
pippin [ˈpipin] n. Reineta, *f.* (apple).
pipsqueak [ˈpipskwi:k] n. FAM. Cero (*m.*) a la izquierda.
piquancy [ˈpi:kənsi] n. Picante, *m.*, lo picante.
piquant [ˈpi:kənt] adj. Picante.
piquantly [—li] adv. De modo picante.
pique [pi:k] n. Resentimiento, *m.*, pique, *m.* (resentment). || — *He did it out of pique*, lo hizo por resentimiento. || *To be in a pique*, estar resentido.
pique [pi:k] v. tr. FIG. Herir (to hurt): *to pique s.o. with a remark*, herir a alguien con una observación. || Picar (to annoy). || FIG. Picar: *to pique s.o.'s curiosity*, picarle a alguien la curiosidad.
piqué [ˈpi:kei] n. Piqué, *m.* (material).
piquet [piˈket] n. Juego (*m.*) de los cientos.
piracy [ˈpaiərəsi] n. Piratería, *f.* || Edición (*f.*) pirata (of books).
Piraeus [paiˈri:əs] pr. n. GEOGR. El Pireo, *m.*
piragua [piˈrægwə] n. Piragua, *f.* (boat).
piranha [piˈrænə] n. Piraña, *f.*, piraya, *f.* (fish).
pirate [ˈpaiərit] n. Pirata, *m.* || — FIG. *Pirate edition*, edición (*f.*) pirata. | *Pirate of the air*, pirata del aire. | *Pirate radio*, radio (*f.*) pirata.
pirate [ˈpaiərit] v. tr. Hacer una edición pirata de.
— V. intr. Piratear.
piratical [paiˈrætikəl] adj. Pirata, pirático, ca.
pirogue [piˈrəug] n. Piragua, *f.* (boat).
pirouette [ˌpiruˈet] n. Pirueta, *f.*, cabriola, *f.*
pirouette [ˌpiruˈet] v. intr. Hacer piruetas, hacer cabriolas.
Pisces [ˈpisi:z] pl. n. ASTR. Piscis, *m.*
piscicultural [ˌpisiˈkʌltʃərəl] adj. Piscícola.
pisciculture [ˈpisikʌltʃə*] n. Piscicultura, *f.*
pisciculturist [ˌpisˈikʌltʃərəst] n. Piscicultor, *m.*
pisciform [ˈpisifɔ:m] adj. Pisciforme.
piscina [piˈsi:nə] n. REL. Piscina, *f.* || Vivero (*m.*) de peces (for fishes).

— OBSERV. El plural de la palabra inglesa *piscina* es *piscinas* o *piscinae*.

piscine [ˈpisain] adj. Pisciforme (like a fish). || De peces (relating to fish).
piscivorous [piˈsivərəs] adj. ZOOL. Piscívoro, ra.
pisiform [ˈpisifɔ:m] adj. Pisiforme.
pismire [ˈpismaiə*] n. Hormiga, *f.* (ant).
piss [pis] n. POP. Meada, *f.*
piss [pis] v. intr. POP. Mear. || POP. *Piss off!*, ¡vete al cuerno!

pissed [—t] adj. POP. Trompa (drunk). || — POP. *He got pissed*, cogió una trompa, se puso trompa. || POP. *To be pissed off at*, estar furioso con.

pistache [pisˈtɑ:ʃ] or **pistachio** [pisˈtɑ:ʃiəu] n. Pistachero, *m.*, alfóncigo, *m.* (tree). || Pistacho, *m.*, alfóncigo, *m.* (fruit).

pistil [ˈpistil] n. BOT. Pistilo, *m.*

pistol [ˈpistl] n. Pistola, *f.* || *Pistol shot*, pistoletazo, *m.*, tiro (*m.*) de pistola.

piston [ˈpistən] n. TECH. Émbolo, *m.*, pistón, *m.* || MUS. Llave, *f.*, pistón, *m.*

piston ring [—riŋ] n. AUT. Aro (*m.*) del émbolo, segmento (*m.*) del émbolo.

piston rod [—rɔd] n. AUT. Vástago (*m.*) del émbolo.

piston stroke [—strəuk] n. AUT. Carrera (*f.*) del émbolo.

piston travel [—ˌtrævl] n. AUT. Recorrido (*m.*) del émbolo.

piston valve [—vælv] n. MUS. Llave, *f.*, pistón, *m.*

pit [pit] n. Pozo, *m.*, hoyo, *m.* (natural or manmade hole). || Trampa, *f.* (trap). || MIN. Mina, *f.* (of coal, etc.). || Cantera, *f.* (quarry). || Picadura, *f.*, señal, *f.* (of smallpox). || Pozo, *m.* (in a garage). || Reñidero, *m.* (for fighting cocks). || SP. Puesto, *m.* (in motor racing). | Foso, *m.* (of jumpers). || THEATR. Patio (*m.*) de butacas (seats). | Foso (*m.*) de la orquesta (orchestra space). || ANAT. Boca, *f.* (of the stomach). || FIG. Abismo, *m.* (abyss). | Infierno, *m.* (hell). || U. S. Mercado, *m.*, bolsa, *f.* (exchange). | Hueso, *m.* (of fruits). || FIG. *To dig a pit for*, tender una trampa a.

pit [pit] v. tr. Oponer: *to pit one thing against another*, oponer una cosa a otra. || Picar: *face pitted by smallpox*, cara picada de viruelas. || Llenar de hoyitos, hacer hoyos en (a surface): *the sand was pitted by the rain*, la arena estaba llena de hoyitos después de la lluvia. || Echar a pelear: *to pit two animals*, echar a pelear a dos animales. || Almacenar (to store). || U. S. Deshuesar (a fruit). || *To pit o.s. against s.o.*, medirse con alguien, luchar con alguien.
— V. intr. Estar picado de viruelas (with smallpox). || Llenarse de agujeros.

pita [ˈpi:tə] n. BOT. Pita, *f.*, agave, *m.* [*Amer.*, maguey, *m.*].

pit-a-pat [ˈpitəˈpæt] n. Latido, *m.*, palpitación, *f.* (beating). || Paso (*m.*) ligero (footstep).
— Adv. *Her heart went pit-a-pat*, su corazón latía rápidamente.

pit-a-pat [ˈpitəˈpæt] v. intr. Ir con paso ligero (to move). || Latir rápidamente (heart).

pitch [pitʃ] n. Pez, *f.*, brea, *f.* (black sticky substance). || Resina, *f.* (resin). || Puesto, *m.* (space in market, etc.): *a beggar in his usual pitch*, un mendigo en su puesto habitual. || Charlatanería, *f.* (sales patter). || SP. Campo, *m.*: *football pitch*, campo de fútbol. || Tiro, *m.*, lanzamiento, *m.* (a throw). || MUS. Tono, *m.* (tone of sound). || Grado (*m.*) de inclinación, inclinación, *f.* (of slope). || Grado, *m.*, nivel, *m.* (of joy, etc.). || MIN. GEOL. Buzamiento, *m.* (dip). || TECH. Paso, *m.* (of screw, gearwheel, propellor). || ARCH. Pendiente, *f* (of a roof). || MAR. Cabezada, *f.* (rolling of ship). | — *Feelings were raised to a high pitch*, el ambiente estaba tenso. || *He ran full pitch into the door*, se dio de narices con la puerta. || *To reach fever pitch*, llegar a su punto culminante (emotion, tension, etc.). || *To reach such a pitch that...*, llegar a tal extremo que...

pitch [pitʃ] v. tr. Armar, montar: *to pitch a tent*, armar una tienda. || Colocar (to place). || Echar, lanzar, tirar, arrojar (to throw): *to pitch hay*, echar heno. || SP. Tirar, lanzar (to deliver the ball). || MUS. Entonar. || Embrear (to tar). || Calafatear (to caulk). || Contar: *to pitch s.o. a story*, contar una historia a alguien. || — U. S. FIG. *To be in there pitching*, estar luchando, estar bregando (to strive). || *To be pitched off one's horse*, ser desarzonado, caerse del caballo. || MIL. *To pitch battle*, trabar combate. || *To pitch camp*, acampar. || FIG. *To pitch it strong*, exagerar. | *To pitch one's aims very high*, picar muy alto. || *To pitch s.o. out*, echar a alguien. || *To pitch sth. away*, tirar algo.
— V. intr. Acampar (to encamp). || Instalarse (to install o.s.). || MAR. Cabecear (a ship). || Caerse, caer (to fall): *he pitched sideways*, se cayó de costado; *he pitched off his horse*, se cayó del caballo. || Inclinarse (to dip). || Lanzar (in baseball, etc.). || — *To pitch in*, ponerse a trabajar (to start working), echar una mano (to lend a hand), contribuir (to contribute). || *To pitch into*, atacar (to attack), arremeter contra (to attack verbally), echar un rapapolvo a (to scold severely), echarse encima de (a meal), emprender con energía (a job). || *To pitch upon*, tropezar con (to bump into, to come across), decidirse por (to choose).

pitch and toss [ˈpitʃənˈtɔs] n. Rayuela, *f.*

pitch-black [ˈpitʃˈblæk] adj. Negro como el carbón (intensely black). || Oscuro como boca de lobo (extremely dark).

pitchblende [ˈpitʃblend] n. MIN. Pechblenda, *f.*, pecblenda, *f.*

pitch-dark [ˈpitʃˈdɑ:k] adj. Oscuro como boca de lobo.

pitched battle [ˈpitʃtˈbætl] n. Batalla (*f.*) campal.

pitcher [ˈpitʃə*] n. Cántaro, *m.*, cántara, *f.*, jarra, *f.*, jarro, *m.* (jug). || U. S. SP. Lanzador, *m.* (in baseball).

pitchfork [ˈpitʃfɔ:k] n. Horca, *f.*, bieldo, *m.*

pitchfork [ˈpitʃfɔ:k] v. tr. Echar con la horca (hay, etc.). || FIG. Catapultar (into a post).

pitching [ˈpitʃiŋ] n. Cabeceo, *m.* (of a boat). || Lanzamiento, *m.* (throwing).

pitch pine [ˈpitʃpain] n. BOT. Pino (*m.*) tea.

pitch pipe [ˈpitʃpaip] n. MUS. Diapasón, *m.*

pitchy [ˈpitʃi] adj. Negro, gra (black). || Oscuro, ra (dark). || Parecido a la pez (like pitch).

piteous [ˈpitiəs] adj. Patético, ca; lastimoso, sa.

pitfall [ˈpitfɔ:l] n. FIG. Escollo, *m.*, peligro, *m.* (danger). | Trampa, *f.* (trap). | Dificultad, *f.*, pega, *f.* (difficulty).

pith [piθ] n. Médula, *f.* (medulla). || FIG. Médula, *f.*, meollo, *m.*, esencia, *f.*: *the pith of a matter*, el meollo de una cuestión. | Vigor, *m.* (vigour).

pith [piθ] v. tr. Matar cortando la médula (to kill by breaking spinal cord). || Quitar la médula a (to remove pith from a plant).

pithead [ˈpithed] n. MIN. Bocamina, *f.*

pithecanthrope [ˌpiθikænˈθrəup] or **pithecanthropus** [ˌpiθikænˈθrəupəs] n. Pitecántropo, *m.*
— OBSERV. El plural de la palabra inglesa *pithecanthropus* es *pithecanthropi*.

pithiness [ˈpiθinis] n. Fuerza, *f.* (vigour). || Concisión, *f.* (conciseness).

pithy [ˈpiθi] adj. FIG. Conciso, sa (concise). | Sustancial. | Expresivo, va. || Meduloso, sa (like or containing pith).

pitiable [ˈpitiəbl] adj. Lastimoso, sa; lastimero, ra (arousing pity). || Lamentable (bad). || *It was a pitiable sight*, daba lástima *or* pena verlo.

pitiful [ˈpitiful] adj. Lastimoso, sa; lastimero, ra; digno de compasión (arousing pity). || Despreciable, lamentable (contemptible). || *It was pitiful*, daba lástima.

pitifully [—i] adv. Lastimosamente, lastimeramente (arousing pity). || Lamentablemente (lamentably). || *To cry pitifully*, llorar que da lástima.

pitiless [ˈpitilis] adj. Despiadado, da; cruel, implacable.

pitman [ˈpitmən] n. Minero, *m.* (miner). || Pocero, *m.* (well digger). || U. S. TECH. Barra (*f.*) de conexión.
— OBSERV. El plural de *pitman* es *pitmen*, cuando significa "minero" o "pocero", y *pitmans* cuando significa "barra de conexión".

piton [ˈpi:tɔn] n. Pitón, *m.*, clavija (*f.*) de escala (in mountaineering).

pitprop [ˈpitprɔp] n. Puntal, *m.*

pit saw [ˈpitsɔ:] n. TECH. Sierra (*f.*) abrazadera.

pittance [ˈpitəns] n. Miseria, *f.*: *his wage is a pittance*, tiene un sueldo de miseria.

pitted [pitid] adj. Picado de viruelas (pockmarked). || U. S. Deshuesado, da (fruit).

pitter-patter [ˈpitəˌpætə*] n. Golpeteo, *m.* (tapping). || Tamborileo, *m.* (of rain). || Pasos (*m. pl.*) ligeros (light steps).
— Adv. *To go pitter-patter*, golpetear (to tap), tamborilear, repiquetear (rain).

pitter-patter [ˈpitəˌpætə*] v. intr. Golpetear (to tap). || Tamborilear, repiquetear (rain).

pituita [piˈtju:itə] n. ANAT. Pituita, *f.*
— OBSERV. El plural de la palabra inglesa es *pituitae*.

pituitary [piˈtju:itəri] adj. Pituitario, ria: *pituitary gland* o *body*, glándula pituitaria.
— N. ANAT. Pituitaria, *f.*, glándula (*f.*) pituitaria.

pit viper [ˈpitˌvaipə*] n. Crótalo, *m.* (snake).

pity [ˈpiti] n. Compasión, *f.* (sympathy): *to move s.o. to pity*, mover a uno a compasión, inspirar compasión a uno. || Lástima, *f.*, pena, *f.*: *it's a pity that it's raining*, es una lástima que esté lloviendo. || — *For pity's sake*, ¡por amor de Dios!, ¡por piedad! || *Man without pity*, hombre sin piedad *or* despiadado. || *More's the pity*, tanto peor. || *Out of pity*, por piedad. || *To have o to take pity on o to feel pity for*, tener lástima de, compadecerse *or* apiadarse de. || *What a pity!*, ¡qué lástima!, ¡qué pena!

pity [ˈpiti] v. tr. Compadecerse de, apiadarse de. || — *I pity him*, me da lástima. || *You are to be pitied*, eres digno de compasión, mereces compasión.

pitying [—iŋ] adj. De lástima, compasivo, va.

Pius [ˈpaiəs] pr. n. Pío, *m.*: *Pius IX*, Pío Nono.

pivot [ˈpivət] n. TECH. Gorrón, *m.*, pivote, *m.* || SP. Pivote, *m.* (in basketball). || FIG. Eje, *m.*, base, *f.* (central element).
— Adj. Giratorio, ria; que gira (which pivots). || FIG. Esencial, fundamental.

pivot [ˈpivət] v. tr. Montar sobre un gorrón *or* un pivote (to mount on a pivot). || Hacer girar (to spin).
— V. intr. Girar sobre su eje, dar vueltas sobre su eje (to turn). || FIG. *To pivot on*, depender de, basarse en.

pivotal [—l] adj. Giratorio, ria; que gira (which pivots). | FIG. Esencial, fundamental (fundamental).

pixie [ˈpiksi] n. Duendecillo, *m.*

pixilated or **pixillated** [ˈpiksileitid] adj. U. S. FAM. Chiflado, da.

pixy [ˈpiksi] n. Duendecillo, *m.*

pizza [ˈpi:tsə] n. CULIN. "Pizza", *f.*

pizzeria [pitsəˈri:ə] n. "Pizzería", *f.*

pizzicato [ˌpitsiˈkɑ:təu] n. MUS. Pizzicato, *m.*
— Adj./adv. Pizzicato, punteado.
— OBSERV. El plural del sustantivo inglés *pizzicato* es *pizzicatos* o *pizzicati*.

pizzle [ˈpizəl] n. Vergajo, *m.*

placable [ˈplækəbl] adj. Aplacable, apacible.
placard [ˈplækɑ:d] n. Cartel *m.* (poster, bill). || Letrero, *m.* (notice).
placard [ˈplækɑ:d] v. tr. Colocar *or* pegar carteles en (to place placards). || Anunciar en carteles (to advertise).
placate [pləˈkeit] n. Apaciguar, aplacar.
placation [pləˈkeiʃən] n. Apaciguamiento, *m.*
placatory [ˈplækətəri] adj. Apaciguador, ra.
place [pleis] n. Lugar, *m.*, sitio, *m.* (spot, position): *a place for everything and everything in its place*, un sitio para cada cosa y cada cosa en su sitio; *this is a pleasant place*, es un lugar agradable; *a very elegant place*, un sitio muy elegante; *he lost his place in the queue*, perdió el sitio en la cola. || Puesto, *m.*, empleo, *m.*, colocación, *f.* (post). || Página, *f.*: *I lost my place in the book*, perdí la página en el libro. || Parte, *f.*, momento, *m.*: *she always cries at the sad places in the book*, siempre llora en las partes tristes del libro. || Local *m.* (premises). || Edificio, *m.* (building). || Plaza, *f.* (square). || Casa, *f.* (house): *let's all go to my place*, vayamos todos a mi casa; *his place in the country*, su casa de campo. || Sitio, *m.* (seat, etc.): *are there any places left?*, ¿queda sitio? || Cubierto, *m.* (at table): *to lay a place for*, poner un cubierto para. || Asiento, *m.*, localidad, *f.* (seat in theatre, etc.). || SP. Lugar, *m.*, posición, *f.*: *in first place*, en primer lugar. || — *All over the place*, por todas partes. || FIG. *Another place*, la otra Cámara (in Parliament). || *Any place*, en cualquier sitio (without motion), a cualquier sitio (motion towards). || *From place to place*, de un sitio para otro. || *If I were in your place I would not do that*, yo en tu lugar *or* yo que tú no haría eso. || *In another place*, en otra parte. || *In no place*, en ninguna parte. || *In place*, en su sitio. || *In place of*, en lugar de, en vez de. || *In the first place*, en primer lugar. || *In the next place*, luego. || *It is not your place to criticize*, no eres quien para criticar. || *Market place*, mercado, *m.* || *Out of place*, fuera de lugar. || *People in high places*, gente bien situada. || *Place of business*, despacho, *m.* (office), comercio, *m.* (shop), domicilio (*m.*) social (premises). || *Place of decimal*, decimal, *m.* || *Place of refuge*, refugio, *m.* || *Place of residence*, domicilio, *m.* || *Place of worship*, lugar de culto. || REL. *The Holy Places*, los Santos Lugares. || *There's no place for you here*, estás de más aquí, estás sobrando aquí. || *This is no place for children*, éste no es lugar para niños, este sitio no es para niños. || *To back a horse for a place*, apostar a un caballo colocado. || *To change places*, cambiar de sitio. || *To give place to*, ceder el paso a. || FAM. *To go places*, llegar lejos (to get ahead), viajar (to travel), hacer progresos (to make progress), tener éxito (to be successful). || *To hold sth. in place*, sujetar algo. || *To keep one in his place*, mantener a alguien en su lugar. || *To know one's place*, saber cuál es su sitio. || *To put o.s. in s.o.'s place*, ponerse en el lugar de alguien. || *To put s.o. in his place*, poner a alguien en su sitio. || *To put sth. back in its place*, devolver algo a su sitio. || *To take place*, suceder ocurrir, tener lugar (to happen), tener lugar, celebrarse (a meeting, etc.). || *To take the place of*, sustituir a.
place [pleis] v. tr. Colocar, poner (to put). || Situar: *I knew his face but I couldn't place him*, su cara me era familiar, pero no la pude situar; *your house is very well placed*, su casa está muy bien situada. || Reconocer (to recognize). || Hacer: *place your bets!*, ¡hagan juego! || Poner: *to place one's confidence in* o *on* o *upon s.o.*, poner su confianza en alguien; *to place a matter in s.o.'s hands*, poner un asunto en manos de alguien. || Entonar [la voz] (in speech). || Emplear, colocar (to employ). || Lograr que se publique, hacer publicar (one's book). || COMM. Invertir, colocar (money). | Colocar, hacer (an order). | Encontrar salida para, vender, colocar (to find a market for). || — *To be placed*, colocarse, llegar; *to be placed third*, colocarse en tercer lugar; clasificarse, quedar clasificado (to be in the first three). || *To be well placed*, estar en buena posición. || *To place before*, someter a (a project, etc.). || *To place one's trust in*, fiarse de, confiar en. || *We are better placed now*, hemos mejorado de posición.
— V. intr. SP. Clasificarse.
place-kick [ˈpleiskik] n. SP. Tiro (*m.*) libre (in rugby).
place-kick [ˈpleiskik] v. intr. SP. Sacar un tiro libre.
placeman [ˈpleismən] n. Arribista, *m.*

— OBSERV. El plural de *placeman* es *placemen*.

place mat [ˈpleismæt] n. Mantel (*m.*) individual.
placement [ˈpleismənt] n. Colocación, *f.*
place-name [ˈpleisneim] n. Topónimo, *m.* || — Pl. Toponimia, *f. sing.*
placenta [pləˈsentə] n. ANAT. BOT. Placenta, *f.*

— OBSERV. El plural de la palabra inglesa *placenta* es *placentas* o *placentae*.

placental [—l] adj. Placentario, ria.
placer [ˈpleisə*] n. GEOL. Placer, *m.* (of gold).
placer mining [—ˌmainiŋ] n. MIN. Explotación (*f.*) de placeres.
placet [ˈpleiset] n. Plácet, *m.*
placid [ˈplæsid] adj. Apacible, plácido, da.
placidity [plæˈsiditi] n. Placidez, *f.*
placing [ˈpleisiŋ] n. Colocación, *f.*
placket [ˈplækit] n. Abertura, *f.*
plagal [ˈpleigəl] adj. MUS. Plagal.
plagiarism [ˈpleidʒjərizəm] n. Plagio, *m.*
plagiarist [ˈpleidʒjərist] n. Plagiario, ria.
plagiaristic [ˈpleidʒjəˌristik] adj. Plagiario, ria.
plagiarize [ˈpleidʒjəraiz] v. tr./intr. Plagiar.
plagiary [ˈpleidʒjəri] n. Plagiario, ria (person). || Plagio, *m.* (plagiarism).
plagiostomi [ˌpleidʒiˈɔstəmai] pl. n. Plagióstomos, *m.*
plague [pleig] n. Peste, *f.* (disease). || Plaga, *f.* (social scourge): *a plague of vandalism*, una plaga de vandalismo. || FIG. Molestia, *f.*, fastidio, *m.* (annoyance). || — *Plague on it!*, ¡maldito sea! || *The ten plagues of Egypt*, las diez plagas de Egipto. || *To avoid s.o. like the plague*, huir de alguien como de la peste *or* del demonio. || *To hate s.o. like the plague*, aborrecer *or* odiar a uno. || *What a plague she is!*, ¡qué pesada es!
plague [pleig] v. tr. Plagar, infestar: *plagued by insects*, plagado de insectos. || FIG. Atormentar: *the memory plagued him*, le atormentaba el recuerdo. | Plagar: *plagued with debts*, plagado de deudas. || *To plague s.o. with questions*, asar a alguien con preguntas.
plaguy (U. S. **plaguey**) [—i] adj. FAM. Latoso, sa; molesto, ta; fastidioso, sa; pesado, da.
plaice [pleis] n. Platija, *f.* (fish).
plaid [plæd] n. Gabán (*m.*) escocés (cloak). || Tartán, *m.* (cloth).
— Adj. Escocés, esa; de cuadros: *a plaid skirt*, una falda escocesa.
plaided [—id] adj. De cuadros.
plain [plein] adj. Claro, ra; evidente (clear, obvious): *it is plain*, está claro, es evidente. || Simple, sencillo, lla (simple). || Completo, ta: *that is plain madness*, es una locura completa. || Sencillo, lla (food). || Puro, ra; natural (unmixed). || Franco, ca; abierto, ta (frank). || Honrado, da (dealings). || Natural (unsophisticated). || Sin atractivo (unattractive). || Simple, sin lujo (living). || — *A plain answer*, una respuesta clara (clear), una respuesta categórica (categorical). || *He made it plain that*, dijo claramente que (verbally), dio a entender que (by attitude). || *In plain language*, en lenguaje corriente. || *Is that plain?*, ¿está claro? || *It was plain to see that*, estaba muy claro que. || *Let me make this plain*, quiero que quede claro. || *Plain clothes*, traje (*m. sing.*) de paisano. || *Plain English*, palabras (*f. pl.*) claras. || *Plain speaking*, palabras claras, franqueza, *f.* || *She's very plain*, no vale nada, no es ninguna belleza. || *The plain truth*, la verdad llana y lisa, la pura verdad. || *To do some plain talking*, hablar claro. || *To make sth. plain* (*to s.o.*), poner algo de manifiesto [ante alguien]: *his question made it plain that he had not been listening*, su pregunta puso de manifiesto que no había escuchado. || *Under plain cover* o *in a plain envelope*, con la mayor discreción (in advertisements), en un sobre blanco.
— N. Llanura, *f.*, planicie, *f.*, llano, *m.*
— Adv. Claramente (clearly). || Lisa y llanamente, claramente (candidly). || Francamente (frankly).
plainchant [ˈpleintʃɑ:nt] n. MUS. REL. Canto (*m.*) llano.
plainclothesman [pleinˈkləuðzmən] n. Policía (*m.*) en traje de paisano (when on duty).

— OBSERV. El plural es *plainclothesmen*.

plainly [ˈpleinli] adj. Claramente, evidentemente (obviously). || Claramente, con claridad (with clarity). || Sencillamente, simplemente (with simplicity). || Francamente (frankly). || *To put it plainly*, para ser claro.
plainness [ˈpleinnis] n. Claridad, *f.*, evidencia, *f.* || Simpleza, *f.*, sencillez, *f.* || Franqueza, *f.* (frankness). || Fealdad, *f.*, falta (*f.*) de atractivo (unattractiveness).
plainsman [ˈpleinzmən] n. Llanero, *m.*, hombre (*m.*) de la llanura.

— OBSERV. El plural de *plainsman* es *plainsmen*.

plainsong [ˈpleinsɔŋ] n. MUS. REL. Canto (*m.*) llano.
plainspoken [ˈpleinˈspəukən] adj. Franco, ca.
plaint [pleint] n. JUR. Querella, *f.*, demanda, *f.*
plaintiff [—if] n. JUR. Demandante, *m.* & *f.*, querellante, *m.* & *f.*
plaintive [—iv] adj. Quejumbroso, sa; lastimero, ra: *a plaintive voice*, una voz quejumbrosa.
plaintively [—ivli] adj. Lastimeramente, quejumbrosamente.
plait [plæt] n. Trenza, *f.* (hair). || Pliegue, *m.*, frunce, *m.* (fold). || *In plaits*, trenzado (hair), fruncido, da; plisado, da (folded).
plait [plæt] v. tr. Trenzar (hair). || Fruncir, plisar (to fold).
plan [plæn] n. Plano, *m.* (design, map). || Plan, *m.*, proyecto, *m.* (scheme, schedule): *work plan*, plan de trabajo; *what are your plans now?*, ¿ahora qué proyectos tiene?; *to make plans*, hacer proyectos. || ARCH. Plano, *m.*: *to draw up a plan of*, trazar el plano de. || — *Development plan*, plan de desarrollo. || *Five-year plan*, plan quinquenal. || *Have you any plans for tomorrow?*, ¿tienes algún plan para mañana?, ¿tienes algún compromiso para mañana? || *If everything goes according to plan*, si todo sale como está previsto. || *It all went according to plan*, todo salió como estaba previsto. || MIL. *Plan of campaign*, plan de campaña.

|| *The best plan would be to wait,* lo mejor sería esperar. || *The Marshall Plan,* el Plan Marshall.

plan [plæn] v. tr. Hacer el plano de (to design). || Planificar (production, economy). || Planear: *to plan a coup, a journey, a reform,* planear un golpe de estado, un viaje, una reforma. || Hacer el plan de (a book, holidays, etc.). || Hacer planes para (the future). || *I plan to go out tonight,* pienso salir esta noche, tengo la intención de salir esta noche.
— V. intr. Hacer planes, hacer proyectos.

planch [plɑ:nʃ] n. Plancha, *f.*

planchet [ˈplɑ:nʃət] n. Cospel, *m.*

planchette [plɑ:nˈʃet] n. Tabla (*f.*) usada en sesiones de espiritismo.

plane [plein] n. TECH. Cepillo, *m.* (of a carpenter). || MATH. Plano, *m.* (surface). || FIG. Plano, *m.*, nivel, *m.* (level of thought, etc.): *to be on another plane,* estar en otro plano. || AVIAT. Avión, *m.* (aircraft): *to go by plane,* ir en avión (people), ir por avión (goods, post). | Plano, *m.* (stabilizer). || BOT. Plátano, *m.*
— Adj. Plano, na: *plane geometry,* geometría plana.

plane [plein] v. tr. Cepillar (a carpenter).
— V. intr. Cepillar (to work with a plane). || Planear (to glide). || Viajar en avión (to go by aircraft).

plane sailing [—ˌseiliŋ] n. MAR. See SAILING.

planet [ˈplænit] n. ASTR. Planeta, *m.* || TECH. *Planet gear,* piñón planetario.

planetarium [ˌplæniˈtɛəriəm] n. Planetario, *m.*
— OBSERV. El plural de la palabra inglesa es *planetariums* o *planetaria.*

planetary [ˈplænitəri] adj. Planetario, ria.

planetoid [ˈplænətɔid] n. ASTR. Planetoide, *m.*, asteroide, *m.*

planet wheel [ˈplænitwi:l] n. TECH. Rueda (*f.*) planetaria.

plangent [ˈplændʒənt] adj. Resonante. || Plañidero, ra (plaintive).

planimeter [plæˈnimitə*] n. Planímetro, *m.*

planimetry [plæˈnimətri] n. Planimetría, *f.*

planing [pleiniŋ] n. Cepillado, *m.*

planish [ˈplæniʃ] v. tr. Aplanar, alisar (metals).

planisphere [ˈplænisfiə] n. Planisferio, *m.*

plank [plæŋk] n. Tablón, *m.*, tabla, *f.* (wooden board). || FIG. Punto, *m.* (in a policy). || — *Deck planks,* tablazón (*f.*) de cubierta (of a ship). || *To walk the plank,* ser castigado a arrojarse al mar desde un tablón que sobresale de la nave.

plank [plæŋk] v. tr. Entablar, entarimar (to cover with boards). || CULIN. Hacer a la plancha. || *To plank down,* tirar con violencia (to throw down with force), desembolsar (to pay out).

planking [—iŋ] n. Entarimado, *m.*, entablado, *m.* || MAR. Tablazón (*f.*) de cubierta.

plankton [ˈplæŋktən] n. BIOL. Plancton, *m.*

planned [plænd] adj. Planificado, da: *planned economy,* economía planificada.

planner [plænə*] n. Planificador, ra.

planning [ˈplæniŋ] n. Planificación, *f.* || *Family planning,* planificación familiar.
— Adj. Planificador, ra.

plano-concave [ˈplænəukɔnˈkeiv] adj. Planocóncavo, va.

plano-convex [ˈplænəukɔnˈveks] adj. Planoconvexo, xa.

plant [plɑ:nt] n. BOT. Planta, *f.* || Planta, *f.*, fábrica, *f.* (factory). || Instalación, *f.* (installation). || Maquinaria, *f.* (machinery). || FAM. Trampa, *f.* (trap). | Estratagema, *f.* (stratagem). || — *In plant,* en crecimiento. || *Plant kingdom,* reino (*m.*) vegetal. || *Plant life,* las plantas, la vida vegetal.

plant [plɑ:nt] v. tr. Plantar (plants): *he planted roses in the garden,* plantó rosas en el jardín. || Sembrar (a field): *to plant a field with corn,* sembrar un campo de trigo. || Cultivar (the land). || Colocar (to place). || Instalar, establecer (to establish). || FIG. Inculcar (ideas). | Plantar: *he planted himself in front of the door,* se plantó delante de la puerta. || FAM. Colocar a escondidas: *they planted marked notes in the drawer,* colocaron a escondidas billetes marcados en el cajón. | Asestar, plantar: *he planted him a blow on the nose,* le asestó un puñetazo en la nariz. || — *To plant out,* trasplantar (to transplant). || *To plant sth. on s.o.,* comprometer a uno escondiendo un objeto robado en su ropa *or* habitación.

plantain [ˈplæntin] n. BOT. Llantén, *m.*, plantaina, *f.* | Plátano, *m.* (banana tree). || BOT. *Water plantain,* llantén de agua.

plantar [ˈplæntɑ:*] adj. ANAT. Plantar, de la planta del pie.

plantation [plænˈteiʃən] n. Plantación, *f.*, plantío, *m.* (of plants). || Hacienda, *f.* (large estate). || Plantel, *m.* (of young trees). || HIST. Colonia, *f.* (colony). || — *Banana plantation,* platanal, *m.*, platanar, *m.* || *Coffee plantation,* cafetal, *m.*

planter [ˈplɑ:ntə*] n. Plantador, ra (person). || Plantadora, *f.* (machine). || HIST. Colono, *m.* (colonist).

plantigrade [ˈplæntigreid] adj./n. ZOOL. Plantígrado, da.

plant louse [ˈplɑ:ntˌlaus] n. ZOOL. Pulgón, *m.*

plantpot [ˈplɑ:ntˌpɔt] n. Maceta, *f.*, tiesto, *m.*

plaque [plɑ:k] n. Placa, *f.*: *commemorative plaque,* placa conmemorativa.

plaquette [plæˈket] n. Plaqueta, *f.*

plash [plæʃ] n. Salpicadura, *f.* (splashing). || Chapoteo, *m.* (sound). || Charca (*f.*) cenagosa (pool).

plash [plæʃ] v. tr. Salpicar (to splash). || Chapotear en. || Entrelazar, entretejer (to interweave).
— V. intr. Chapotear.

plashy [—i] adj. Cenagoso, sa.

plasm [ˈplæzəm] or **plasma** [ˈplæzmə] n. Plasma, *m.*

plaster [ˈplɑ:stə*] n. Yeso, *m.* (for walls, ceilings, etc.). || MED. Emplasto, *m.*, parche, *m.* | Escayola, *f.* (for injured leg, etc.). | Esparadrapo, *m.* (sticking plaster). || — MED. *Mustard plaster,* sinapismo, *m.* | *To have one's arm in plaster,* tener el brazo escayolado.

plaster [ˈplɑ:stə*] v. tr. Enyesar, enlucir (walls, etc.). || Cubrir: *his hands were plastered with paint,* tenía las manos cubiertas de pintura. || Pegar, fijar (to stick). || MED. Aplicar un emplasto a. | Enyesar, escayolar (a broken leg, etc.). || FIG. Colmar, llenar (with praise, etc.). | Bombardear (to bomb). || — FAM. *To be plastered,* estar trompa (to be drunk). || *To plaster down one's hair,* ponerse fijador en el pelo. || *To plaster over a crack,* tapar una grieta con yeso, enyesar una grieta.

plasterboard [—bɔ:d] n. Cartón (*m.*) yeso.

plaster cast [—kɑ:st] n. ARTS. Vaciado (*m.*) en yeso. || MED. Enyesado, *m.* || *To have one's leg in a plaster cast,* tener la pierna escayolada.

plasterer [ˈplɑ:stərə*] n. Yesero, *m.*, enlucidor, *m.*

plastering [ˈplɑ:stəriŋ] n. Enlucido, *m.* (of a wall). || FAM. Paliza, *f.* (thrashing): *to give s.o. a plastering,* dar *or* pegar una paliza a alguien.

plaster of Paris [ˈplɑ:stərəvˈpæris] n. Yeso (*m.*) blanco.

plastic [ˈplæstik] adj. Plástico, ca: *plastic substance,* materia plástica; *plastic arts,* artes plásticas. || De plástico (made of plastic). || — *Plastic bomb,* bomba (*f.*) de plástico. || *Plastic explosive,* plástico, *m.*
— N. Plástico, *m.*, materia (*f.*) plástica.

plasticene or **plasticine** [ˈplæstisi:n] n. ARTS. Arcilla (*f.*) de moldear.

plasticity [plæsˈtisiti] n. Plasticidad, *f.*

plasticization [plæstisiˈzeiʃən] n. Plastificado, *m.*, plastificación, *f.*

plasticize [ˈplæstisaiz] v. tr. Plastificar.

plasticizer [—ə*] n. Plastificante, *m.*

plasticizing [—iŋ] adj. Plastificante.

plastics [ˈplæstiks] n. Plástica, *f.*

plastic surgery [ˈplæstikˈsə:dʒəri] n. MED. Cirugía (*f.*) plástica.

plastify [ˈplæstifai] v. tr. Plastificar.

plastifying [—iŋ] adj. Plastificante.

plastron [ˈplæstrən] adj. ZOOL. Peto, *m.*, plastrón, *m.* || Peto, *m.*, plastrón, *m.* (breastplate). || Pechera (*f.*) postiza (dicky). || Plastrón, *m.* (of fencer).

plat [plæt] n. U.S. Parcela, *f.* (piece of land). | Plano, *m.* (plan). | Mapa, *m.* (map).

plat [plæt] v. tr. U. S. Hacer un plano de (to make a map of).

plate [pleit] n. Plato, *m.* (dish). || Placa, *f.* (plaque). || Chapa, *f.*, lámina, *f.*, plancha, *f.* (of metal). || Vajilla, *f.* (tableware). || PHOT. Placa, *f.* || MED. Placa (*f.*) de la dentadura postiza. || FAM. Dentadura (*f.*) postiza (false teeth). || REL. Bandeja, *f.*, platillo, *m.* (for collection). || PRINT. Estereotipo, *m.*, plancha, *f.*, clisé, *m.* (stereotype). | Lámina, *f.*, grabado, *m.* (illustration). || ARCH. Viga (*f.*) horizontal (of a roof). || MIL. Plancha (*f.*) de blindaje, blindaje, *m.* || SP. Premio, *m.*, copa (*f.*) de oro *or* de plata (in horse racing). || U. S. SP. Base (*f.*) del bateador (in baseball). || ANAT. ZOOL. Lámina, *f.* || TECH. Revestimiento, *m.* (coating). || Plancha, *f.* (grill). || ELECTR. Placa, *f.*, ánodo, *m.* || AUT. Matrícula, *f.* (number plate). || — FIG. *It was given to him on a plate,* se lo dieron en una bandeja de plata. || *Number plate* o *licence plate,* matrícula, *f.*, placa (*f.*) de matrícula. || FIG. *To have a lot on one's plate,* tener tela de que cortar.

plate [pleit] v. tr. Blindar (to armour). || Chapar (with metal). || Niquelar (with nickel). || Dorar (with gold). || Platear (with silver). || PRINT. Hacer un clisé *or* un estereotipo de.

plate armour (U. S. **plate armor**) [—ˈɑ:mə*] n. MIL. Blindaje, *m.* (of tank, ship).

plateau [ˈplætəu] n. GEOGR. Meseta, *f.* [*Amer.*, altiplano, *m.*].
— OBSERV. El plural de *plateau* es *plateaus* o *plateaux.*

plated [ˈpleitid] adj. Chapado, da (metals). || Blindado, da (armoured).

plateful [ˈpleitful] n. Plato, *m.*: *a plateful of chips,* un plato de patatas fritas.

plate glass [ˈpleitˈglɑ:s] n. TECH. Vidrio (*m.*) cilindrado, luna, *f.*

platelayer [ˈpleitˌleiə*] n. Asentador (*m.*) de vías.

platelet [ˈpleitlət] n. BIOL. Plaqueta, *f.*

plate mark [ˈpleitˌmɑ:k] n. Contraste, *m.* (hallmark).

platen [ˈplætən] n. PRINT. Platina, *f.* (of a press). | Rodillo, *m.* (of typewriter).

plater [ˈpleitə*] n. Chapista, *m.* (with metal). || Plateador, *m.* (with silver). || Dorador, *m.* (with gold). || Niquelador, *m.* (with nickel). || SP. Caballo (*m.*) de segunda categoría (horse).

plate rack [ˈpleitræk] n. Escurreplatos, *m. inv.*

plateresque [ˌplætəˈresk] adj. ARCH. Plateresco, ca.

Plate River [ˈpleitˈrivə*] pr. n. GEOGR. Río (*m.*) de la Plata.

platform [ˈplætfɔ:m] n. Plataforma, *f.* (raised planking). || Andén, *m.* (of railway station): *people waiting on the platform*, gente esperando en el andén. || Vía, *f.*: *the train standing at platform three*, el tren que está en la vía tres. || Plataforma, *f.* (on a bus or tram, for artillery, raised piece of ground). || Estrado, *m.* (stage). || Tribuna, *f.*, plataforma, *f.* (at a meeting, etc.). || Tablado, *m.* (for dancing, etc.). || Andamio, *m.* (of builders). || Programa, *m.* [político] (of a party).
platform car [—kɑ:*] n. U. S. Batea, *f.*, vagón (*m.*) plataforma (flatcar).
platform ticket [—ˈtikit] n. Billete (*m.*) de andén.
plating [ˈpleitiŋ] n. Enchapado, *m.*, chapado, *m.* || Capa (*f.*) metálica (layer of metal). || Blindaje, *m.* (armour). || — *Gold plating*, dorado, *m.* || *Nickel plating*, niquelado, *m.* || *Silver plating*, plateado, *m.*
platinizing [ˈplætinaiziŋ] n. Platinado, *m.*
platinize [ˈplætinaiz] v. tr. Platinar.
platinous [ˈplætinəs] adj. Platinoso, sa.
platinum [ˈplætinəm] n. Platino, *m.*
platinum black [—ˈblæk] n. CHEM. Negro (*m.*) de platino.
platinum blonde [—ˈblɔnd] n. Mujer (*f.*) rubia platino.
— Adj. Rubio platino (hair). || Rubia platino (woman).
platitude [ˈplætitju:d] n. Tópico, *m.*, lugar (*m.*) común.
platitudinize [ˌplætiˈtju:dinaiz] v. intr. Decir tópicos.
platitudinous [ˌplætiˈtju:dinəs] adj. Tópico, ca; trivial.
Plato [ˈpleitəu] pr. n. Platón, *m.*
Platonic [pləˈtɔnik] adj. Platónico, ca: *platonic love*, amor platónico.
Platonism [ˈpleitəunizəm] n. PHIL. Platonismo, *m.*
Platonist [ˈpleitəunist] n. PHIL. Platónico, ca.
platoon [pləˈtu:n] n. MIL. Pelotón, *m.*
platten [ˈplætən] n. See PLATEN.
platter [ˈplætə*] n. (Ant.). Plato, *m.* (dish). || U. S. Fuente, *f.* (serving dish). | Disco, *m.* (record).
platyhelminth [ˌplætiˈhelminθ] n. ZOOL. Platelminto, *m.* (flatworm).
platypus [ˈplætipəs] n. ZOOL. Ornitorrinco, *m.*
platyrrhine [ˈplætirain] n. ZOOL. Platirrino, *m.*
plaudits [ˈplɔ:dits] pl. n. Aplausos, *m.*
plausibility [ˌplɔ:zəˈbiliti] n. Plausibilidad, *f.*
plausible [ˈplɔ:zəbl] adj. Plausible: *a plausible excuse*, una excusa plausible. || Convincente pero poco de fiar (person).
play [plei] n. Juego, *m.*, entretenimiento, *m.*, diversión, *f.* (amusement). || SP. Juego, *m.* (manner of playing): *fair, foul play*, juego limpio, sucio. | Jugada, *f.* (manoeuvre): *a good play*, una buena jugada. || THEATR. Obra (*f.*) de teatro: *Lorca's plays*, las obras de teatro de Lorca. | Teatro, *m.*: *to go to the play*, ir al teatro. || Juego, *m.* (gambling). || TECH. Juego, *m.*, holgura, *f.* (looseness). || FIG. Rienda (*f.*) suelta (free rein). || — *A smart bit of play* o *a smart piece of play*, una buena jugada. || *At play*, en juego. || FIG. *Child's play*, juego de niños. || *Influences in play*, influencias (*f.*) en juego. || *In play*, en broma, de broma (joking): *to do sth. in play*, hacer algo en broma; en juego (sports). || *It's your play*, te toca a ti. || *Out of play*, fuera de juego. || SP. *Play has started*, ha empezado el partido. || *Play of light*, juego de luces. || *Play on words*, juego de palabras. || *To bring, to come into play*, poner, entrar en juego. || FIG. *To give full play to*, dar rienda suelta a. || *To make play of*, burlarse de. || *To watch the children at play*, mirar cómo juegan los niños, ver jugar a los niños.
play [plei] v. tr. Jugar a: *to play rugby, tennis, cards*, jugar al rugby, al tenis, a las cartas. || MUS. Tocar (an instrument, a song). | Interpretar (a song, a composer): *to play sth. on the piano*, tocar algo al piano. || THEATR. Hacer de, desempeñar *or* hacer el papel de (a role). | Representar, poner, dar: *they played Macbeth*, representaron Macbeth. | Actuar en: *they played Madrid for two months*, actuaron en Madrid durante dos meses. || Acompañar (to accompany). || Gastar, dar: *to play a joke on*, gastar una broma a. || Enfocar, dirigir: *to play a hose on*, dirigir la manguera hacia. || Jugar (in cards): *to play an ace*, jugar un as. || Jugarse (to gamble away). || Apostar por (to bet on). || SP. Colocar, mandar: *he played the ball into the net*, colocó la pelota en la red. | Jugar contra: *Wales played France*, Gales jugó contra Francia. | Alinear, hacer jugar: *England is playing a good kicker for this match*, Inglaterra hace jugar a un buen chutador para este partido. | Jugar de: *Joseph plays right half*, José juega de medio derecho. || Mover, jugar (a chessman). || Jugar a: *to play pirates*, jugar a los piratas. || FIG. Dárselas de, echárselas de: *to play the big shot*, dárselas de hombre importante. || COMM. Jugar a: *to play the stock exchange*, jugar a la Bolsa. || Dejar que se canse: *to play a fish*, dejar que se canse un pez. || — *To play a dirty trick on s.o.*, hacerle una mala jugada *or* hacerle una jugarreta a alguien, jugarle una mala pasada a alguien. || *To play a game of bridge*, jugar *or* echar una partida de bridge. || MUS. *To play by ear*, tocar de oído. || *To play false*, traicionar (to betray). || FIG. *To play one's part well*, desempeñar bien su papel. | *To play s.o.'s game*, hacer el juego de alguien. | *To play the arbitrator*, desempeñar el papel de árbitro. | *To play the fool*, hacer el tonto.
— V. intr. Jugar: *the children are playing*, los niños están jugando; *stop playing with your food!*, ¡deja de jugar con la comida!; *he played badly in the last match*, jugó mal en el último partido. || Bailar: *the shadows played on the walls*, las sombras bailaban en las paredes. || Fingirse (to pretend to be): *to play ill*, fingirse enfermo. || Conducirse, portarse (to behave). || MUS. Tocar: *he plays rather well*, toca bastante bien. | Sonar: *this piano plays better now*, este piano suena mejor ahora. || THEATR. CINEM. Actuar, trabajar: *he played at the best theatre in town*, actuó en el mejor teatro de la ciudad. | Desempeñar (a role). || Estar funcionando (a fountain). || Ser: *this court plays very slow*, esta pista es muy lenta. || Retozar (to gambol). || Jugar (to gamble). || Bromear (to joke): *they are only playing*, están sólo bromeando. || TECH. Tener juego, tener holgura (a steering wheel, etc.). | Funcionar (to work). || — FIG. *Are you sure he's not just playing with you?*, ¿estás segura de que no está jugando contigo? || SP. *How much time is left to play?*, ¿cuándo tiempo queda de juego? || FIG. *I'm playing with the idea*, estoy dándole vueltas en la cabeza a la idea. || *Love is not a thing to be played with*, con el amor no se juega. || *Run away and play!*, ¡vete a jugar! || *They are not people to be played with*, con esa gente no se juega. || *To play dead*, hacerse *or* hacer el muerto. || *To play fair, dirty*, jugar limpio, sucio. || *To play for money*, jugar por dinero. || *To play for time*, hacer tiempo. || *To play foul*, jugar sucio. || FIG. *To play into s.o.'s hands*, hacerle el juego a alguien. | *To play to the gallery*, actuar para la galería. | *To play upon words*, hacer juegos de palabras, jugar del vocablo. | *To play with fire*, jugar con fuego. | *To play with one's health*, jugar con la salud. | *To play with the cards on the table*, jugar con las cartas boca arriba. || *What's playing at the theatre?*, ¿qué ponen en el teatro?
— ***To play around*** or ***about***, hacer el tonto (to play the fool). | Juguetear (to fiddle). | Jugar: *he's playing about with you*, está jugando contigo. || ***To play at***, jugar a: *to play at chess*, jugar al ajedrez; *children playing at being adults*, niños jugando a adultos. | — FAM. *What are you playing at?*, ¿qué haces? (what are you doing), ¿a qué jugáis? (game). || ***To play back***, poner, volver a poner [algo grabado]. | Oír, escuchar [una cinta]: *let's play it back*, vamos a escucharlo. | — *Play it back for me*, déjeme oírlo. || ***To play down***, quitar importancia a, intentar minimizar. || ***To play off***, oponer: *to play one person off against another*, oponer a dos personas. | SP. Jugar un partido de desempate. || ***To play on***, aprovecharse de, explotar (to make use of). | Seguir jugando *or* tocando. | Disparar (a gun). | — *To play on s.o.'s nerves*, hacerle la guerra de nervios a alguien (to wage a war of nerves on), atacarle los nervios a alguien (to irritate). || ***To play out***, acabar (to finish). | Agotar (to exhaust). Representar hasta el final. || ***To play up***, jugar con toda el alma, darse por entero (to play heartily). | Jugar con más ánimo, jugar mejor (to play better). | Fastidiar, dar guerra (to annoy). | Hinchar (news, incident). | Exagerar (to exaggerate). || — *To play up to*, adular.
playable [—əbl] adj. MUS. Interpretable, que se puede interpretar. || THEATR. Representable (a play).
playact [—ækt] v. intr. Hacer teatro (to pretend). || THEATR. Desempeñar un papel.
playacting [—ˌæktiŋ] n. Comedia, *f.*, teatro, *m.*
playactor [—ˌæktə*] n. Actor, *m.*
playactress [—ˌæktris] n. Actriz, *f.*
playback [—bæk] n. Reproducción, *f.* (of a tape). || — *Playback head*, cabeza auditiva. || *To listen to the playback*, escuchar una cinta.
playbill [—bil] n. Cartel, *m.* [anunciador de una obra de teatro] (poster). || U. S. Programa, *m.*
playboy [—bɔi] n. "Playboy", *m.*
play-by-play [—baiˈplei] adj. U. S. Punto por punto, detallado, da.
playday [—dai] n. Día (*m.*) de fiesta.
playdown [—daun] n. Desempate, *m.*, partido (*m.*) de desempate.
played out [ˈpleidaut] adj. Agotado, da (exhausted). || Acabado, da (worn-out).
player [pleiə*] n. Jugador, ra (in games, sport, etc.). || MUS. Intérprete, *m.* & *f.*, músico, ca; ejecutante, *m.* & *f.* || THEATR. Actor, *m.*, actriz, *f.* | (Ant.) Cómico, ca. || — *Guitar player*, guitarrista, *m.* & *f.* || *Piano player*, pianista, *m.* & *f.* || *Violin player*, violinista *m.* & *f.*
player piano [—piˈænəu] n. MUS. Pianola, *f.*
playfellow [ˈpleiˌfeləu] n. Compañero (*m.*) de juego, compañera (*f.*) de juego, amigo, ga.
playful [ˈpleiful] adj. Juguetón, ona; retozón, ona (who likes to play). || Travieso, sa (mischievous). || Alegre (happy). || Guasón, ona (joking). || Festivo, va (humorous).
playfully [ˈpleifuli] adv. Jugando. || Alegremente. || En broma (jokingly).
playfulness [—nis] n. Alegría, *f.* (happiness). || Tono (*m.*) guasón (in voice).
playgoer [ˈpleiˌgəuə*] n. Aficionado al teatro.
playground [ˈpleigraund] n. Patio, *m.* (of a school). || Campo (*m.*) de juegos (place for children to play). || FIG. Lugar (*m.*) de predilección: *a millionaires'*

playground, un lugar de predilección para los millonarios.

playhouse [ˈpleihaus] n. Teatro, *m.* (theatre). || U. S. Casa (*f.*) de muñecas (dolls' house).

playing card [ˈpleiiŋkɑ:d] n. Carta, *f.*, naipe, *m.*

playing field [ˈpleiiŋfi:ld] n. Campo (*m.*) de deportes.

playmate [ˈpleimeit] n. Compañero (*m.*) de juego, compañera (*f.*) de juego, amigo, ga.

play-off [ˈpleiˌɔf] n. SP. Partido (*m.*) de desempate (to decide a tie).

playpen [ˈpleiˌpen] n. Parque, *m.*, corral, *m.* (for children).

playroom [ˈpleiˌru:m] n. Cuarto (*m.*) de jugar.

plaything [ˈpleiθiŋ] n. Juguete, *m.*

playtime [ˈpleiˌtaim] n. Recreo, *m.* (at school).

playwright [ˈpleiˌrait] n. Autor (*m.*) de teatro.

plea [pli:] n. Súplica, *f.* (appeal): *to ignore s.o.'s pleas*, no escuchar las súplicas de alguien. || Petición, *f.* (request). || Excusa, *f.*, disculpa, *f.* (excuse). || Pretexto, *m.* (pretext): *with the plea of*, con el pretexto de. || JUR. Alegato, *m.* || — JUR. *His plea was not guilty*, se declaró inocente. || *To make a plea for mercy*, pedir clemencia, pedir gracia.

pleach [pli:tʃ] v. tr. Entretejer.

plead [pli:d] v. intr. Implorar: *now you plead for mercy*, ahora imploras clemencia. || Suplicar: *to plead and plead with s.o.*, suplicar mil veces a alguien. || JUR. Hacer un alegato, abogar (*for*, por). || Defender, abogar (*for*, por): *to plead for s.o.'s cause*, defender la causa de alguien. || Intervenir (to intervene): *he pleaded for me*, intervino en mi favor.

— V. tr. JUR. Alegar (to cite in defence): *to plead extenuating circumstances*, alegar circunstancias atenuantes. | Defender: *to plead a case*, defender un caso. || — JUR. *To plead guilty*, declararse culpable. || *To plead ignorance*, pretextar su ignorancia. || JUR. *To plead not guilty*, declararse inocente. | *To plead self-defence*, alegar legítima defensa.

pleader [—ə*] n. JUR. Abogado (*m.*) defensor. || Intercesor, *m.*

pleading [—iŋ] n. Súplicas, *f. pl.*: *to give way to s.o.'s pleading*, ceder ante las súplicas de alguien. || JUR. Alegato, *m.*, defensa, *f.*

pleasant [ˈpleznt] adj. Agradable: *a pleasant surprise, evening*, una sorpresa, una velada agradable. || Simpático, ca; agradable (person). || *To have a pleasant time*, pasarlo muy agradablemente.

pleasantly [—li] adv. Agradablemente. || *We were pleasantly surprised*, fue una sorpresa agradable.

pleasantness [—nis] n. Agrado, *m.*, lo agradable. || Simpatía, *f.* (of a person).

pleasantry [—ri] n. Chanza, *f.*, broma, *f.*, chiste, *m.* (joke). || Jocosidad, *f.* (jocularity).

please [pli:z] v. tr. Gustar, agradar: *do you think this tie will please him?*, ¿cree que le gustará esta corbata?; *it pleases him to take a walk*, le gusta dar un paseo; *your essay pleased me considerably*, su ensayo me ha gustado mucho. || Contentar, complacer, agradar: *he is easy to please*, es fácil de contentar. || Caer bien, gustar, agradar: *you really pleased my mother when you met*, caíste muy bien a mi madre cuando os conocisteis; *do you think I please him?*, ¿crees que le gusto? || Dar gusto, agradar, gustar: *it pleases me to think that*, me gusta pensar que. || Satisfacer, contentar (to satisfy): *there's no pleasing him*, no hay manera de satisfacerle. || Complacer: *it pleases me to announce that*, me complace comunicar que. || Ser un placer para, agradar: *to please the ear, the eye*, ser un placer para el oído, para la vista. || — *If it so please you*, si usted quiere, si le parece bien. || FIG. *It might please you to know*, le interesará saber (with irony). || *Please yourself!*, ¡haga lo que quiera! || *To be hard to please*, ser difícil de contentar, ser muy exigente. || *To be pleased to*, tener el agrado de. || *To be pleased with*, estar satisfecho con. || *Where shall I sit? — Please yourself*, ¿dónde me siento? — Donde quiera *or* donde le parezca.

— V. intr. Agradar, gustar: *it is sure to please*, agradará sin duda alguna. || Querer, parecer: *to do as one pleases*, hacer lo que quiera uno, hacer lo que le parezca a uno; *he will do just as he pleases*, hará exactamente lo que quiera; *as you please*, como quiera; *when you please*, cuando quiera. || — *If you please*, por favor, tenga la amabilidad de (please), haga el favor de: *stop that noise if you please*, haga el favor de callarse; con su permiso (with your permission), ¡fíjate!, ¡fíjese!, ¡imagínate!, ¡imagínese!: *he called me a pig if you please!*, ¡fíjate que me trató de cerdo!; por raro que parezca (strange as it may seem). || *May I come in? — Please do!*, ¿puedo entrar? — ¡Por supuesto! *or* ¡Por favor! || *Please*, por favor: *please come in*, pase por favor. || *Please be seated* o *please take a seat*, siéntese por favor, tenga a bien sentarse. || "*Please do not speak to the driver*", "se ruega no hablar con el conductor". || *Please stop that noise!*, ¡haga el favor de no hacer ese ruido!

pleased [—d] adj. Contento, ta (content): *he is pleased with his new job*, está contento con su nuevo trabajo. || Contento, ta; alegre (happy): *everyone looked very pleased*, todos parecían muy contentos. || De satisfacción (of satisfaction): *a pleased smile*, una sonrisa de satisfacción. || Satisfecho, cha (satisfied): *she was pleased with the result*, estaba satisfecha del resultado; *he is very pleased with himself*, está muy satisfecho de sí mismo; *to be pleased with s.o.*, estar satisfecho con alguien. || — *I am pleased to announce that*, tengo el placer de comunicarles que, me complace comunicarles que, me complazco en comunicarles que. || *I am pleased to hear it*, me alegra saberlo, me alegro. || *I was pleased at the news*, me alegré de la noticia. || *Pleased to meet you*, encantado de conocerle. || *To be all but pleased* o *to be far from pleased*, no estar nada contento. || *To be as pleased as Punch*, estar como unas Pascuas.

pleasing [—iŋ] adj. Agradable.

pleasurable (U. S. **pleasureable**) [ˈpleʒərəbl] adj. Grato, ta; agradable.

pleasurably [—i] adv. Agradablemente. || *We were pleasurably surprised*, fue una agradable sorpresa.

pleasure [ˈpleʒə*] n. Placer, *m.*, gusto, *m.*: *with pleasure*, con gusto; *I have the pleasure of welcoming you here*, tengo el placer de darles la bienvenida; *with great pleasure*, con mucho gusto; *it is a pleasure to know that*, es un placer saber que, da gusto saber que; *what pleasure do you find in fishing?*, ¿qué placer encuentras en la pesca? || Voluntad, *f.*: *at pleasure*, a voluntad. || — *All the pleasures of Paris*, todos los placeres de París. || *I do it because it gives me pleasure*, lo hago porque me gusta. || *It gives me a certain amount of pleasure*, me da cierto placer. || *It gives me pleasure to introduce to the audience*, tengo el placer de *or* me complace presentar al público. || *It's a pleasure to see you*, da gusto verte. || *May I have the pleasure?*, ¿quiere usted bailar? || *The pleasure is mine*, de nada, no hay de qué (returning thanks), el gusto es mío (returning a greeting). || *To allow o.s. the pleasure of*, darse el gusto de. || *To be a pleasure lover*, ser amante de los placeres. || *To be at s.o.'s pleasure*, estar a la merced de alguien (at s.o.'s mercy), estar a la disposición de alguien (at s.o.'s service). || *To be to one's pleasure*, ser del gusto de alguien. || *To find pleasure in cards*, disfrutar jugando a las cartas. || *To take pleasure in*, disfrutar (to delight): *to take great pleasure in reading*, disfrutar mucho leyendo; *to take pleasure in music*, disfrutar con la música; divertirse (to amuse o.s.). || *What is your pleasure?*, ¿en qué puedo servirle? || *With the greatest of pleasure*, con sumo gusto. || *You may go or stay at your pleasure*, puede irse o quedarse, según prefiera.

pleasure boat [—bəut] n. Barco (*m.*) de recreo.

pleasure ground [—graund] n. Parque (*m.*) de atracciones.

pleasure trip [—trip] n. Viaje (*m.*) de recreo.

pleat [pli:t] n. Pliegue, *m.*

pleat [pli:t] v. tr. Plisar, hacer pliegues en.

pleating [—iŋ] n. Plegado, *m.*, plisado, *m.*, tableado, *m.*

pleb [pleb] n. FAM. Plebeyo, *m.*, persona (*f.*) ordinaria. || — FAM. *Don't be such a pleb*, no seas tan ordinario. | *The plebs*, la plebe.

plebeian (U. S. **plebian**) [pliˈbiən] adj./n. Plebeyo, ya.

plebeianism (U. S. **plebianism**) [—izəm] n. Plebeyez, *f.* || FIG. Plebeyez, *f.*, ordinariez, *f.* (vulgarity).

plebiscite [ˈpleibisit] n. Plebiscito, *m.*

plectognath [ˈplektɔgnæθ] adj. Plectognato, ta.
— N. Plectognato, *m.*

plectron [ˈplektrɔn] n. U. S. MUS. Púa, *f.*, plectro, *m.*

plectrum [ˈplektrəm] n. MUS. Púa, *f.*, plectro, *m.*

— OBSERV. El plural de *plectrum* es *plectra* o *plectrums.*

pledge [pledʒ] n. Prenda, *f.*, garantía, *f.* (guarantee): *in pledge of my good faith*, en prenda de mi buena fe, como garantía de mi buena fe. || Promesa (*f.*) solemne (promise). || JUR. Pignoración, *f.*, empeño, *m.* (pawning). || Compromiso, *m.* (commitment): *the country will honour its pledges*, el país hará honor a sus compromisos. || (Ant.). Brindis, *m.* (a toast). || — *As a pledge of*, en señal de. || *To keep the pledge*, cumplir la promesa. || *To put in pledge*, empeñar (to pawn), dar en prenda (to offer as a token). || *To take out of pledge*, desempeñar. || *To take the pledge*, hacer la promesa solemne de dejar de beber.

pledge [pledʒ] v. tr. Empeñar, pignorar (to pawn). || Dar en prenda: *to pledge sth. as a sign of one's good intentions*, dar algo en prenda como señal de sus buenas intenciones. || Comprometer (to commit). || Prometer (to promise): *to pledge assistance to s.o.*, prometer su ayuda a alguien. || Jurar (to swear): *to pledge allegiance*, jurar lealtad; *to be pledged to secrecy*, haber jurado guardar el secreto. || (Ant.). Brindar por (to toast). || *To pledge one's word*, dar or empeñar su palabra. || *To pledge o.s. to do sth.*, comprometerse a hacer algo.

pleiad [ˈplaiəd] n. Pléyade, *f.*

Pleiades [ˈplaiədiz] pl. n. ASTR. MYTH. Pléyades, *f.*

Pleiocene [ˈplaiəusi:n] n. GEOL. Plioceno, *m.*

Pleistocene [ˈplaistəusi:n] n. GEOL. Pleistoceno, *m.*
— Adj. Pleistoceno, na.

plenary [ˈpli:nəri] adj. Plenario, ria: *plenary session*, sesión plenaria; *plenary indulgence*, indulgencia plenaria. || Completo, ta.

plenipotentiary [ˌplenipəuˈtenʃəri] adj. Plenipotenciario, ria.
— N. Plenipotenciario, *m.*

plenitude [ˈplenitju:d] n. Plenitud, *f.* (fullness). || Abundancia, *f.* (abundance).

plenteous [ˈplentjəs] adj. Abundante (abundant): *a plenteous harvest*, una cosecha abundante. || Bueno, na; abundante (supply). || Copioso, sa (food). || *Oranges are plenteous this year*, hay abundancia de naranjas *or* abundan las naranjas este año.
plentiful [ˈplentiful] adj. See PLENTEOUS.
plentifulness [—nis] n. Abundancia, *f.*
plenty [ˈplenti] n. Abundancia, *f.*: *years of plenty*, años de abundancia. || Cantidad (*f.*) suficiente (sufficiency). || — *In plenty*, en abundancia. || *Plenty of*, suficiente, bastante (enough): *I have plenty of money to pay for both of us*, tengo bastante dinero para pagar por los dos; mucho, cha (many, much): *he has plenty of friends*, tiene muchos amigos; de sobra (more than enough): *there is plenty of time*, hay tiempo de sobra.
— Adj. Abundante (abundant). || Suficiente (sufficient).
— Adv. Más que: *this is plenty large enough*, es más que suficiente. || U. S. *I like it plenty*, me gusta mucho.
plenum [ˈpli:nəm] n. PHYS. Espacio (*m.*) lleno. || Asamblea (*f.*) plenaria, pleno, *m.* (assembly).
— OBSERV. El plural de *plenum* es *plenums* o *plena*.
pleonasm [ˈpli:ənæzəm] n. GRAMM. Pleonasmo, *m.*
pleonastic [pliəˈnæstik] adj. GRAMM. Pleonástico, ca.
plesiosaur [ˈpli:siəˈsɔ:*] n. Plesiosauro, *m.* (fossil).
plethora [ˈpleθərə] n. MED. FIG. Plétora, *f.*
plethoric [pleˈθɔrik] adj. MED. Pletórico, ca. || FIG. Pletórico, ca. | Ampuloso, sa (sentences).
pleura [ˈpluərə] n. ANAT. ZOOL. Pleura, *f.*
— OBSERV. El plural de la palabra inglesa *pleura* es *pleurae* o *pleuras*.
pleurisy [ˈpluərisi] n. MED. Pleuresía, *f.*, pleuritis, *f.*
pleuritic [pluəˈritik] adj. MED. Pleurítico, ca.
pleuritis [pluəˈritəs] n. MED. Pleuritis, *f.*, pleuresía, *f.*
plexiglass or **plexiglas** [ˈpleksəglɑ:s] n. TECH. Plexiglás, *m.*
plexor [ˈpleksɔ:*] n. MED. Martillo (*m.*) para comprobar los reflejos.
plexus [ˈpleksəs] n. ANAT. Plexo, *m.*: *solar plexus*, plexo solar. || FIG. Entrelazamiento, *m.* (interwoven structure).
pliability [ˌplaiəˈbiliti] n. Flexibilidad, *f.* || FIG. Docilidad, *f.*, flexibilidad, *f.*
pliable [ˈplaiəbl] adj. Flexible. || FIG. Dócil, flexible.
pliancy [ˈplaiənsi] n. See PLIABILITY.
pliant [ˈplaiənt] adj. See PLIABLE.
plica [ˈplaikə] n. Plica, *f.*
— OBSERV. El plural de la palabra inglesa es *plicae*.
plicate [ˈplaikeit] or **plicated** [—id] adj. BOT. ZOOL. Plegado, da.
plication [plaiˈkeiʃən] n. Plegamiento, *m.*, plegadura, *f.* (folding). || Pliegue, *m.* (fold). || GEOL. Plegamiento, *m.* (fold in a stratum).
pliers [ˈplaiəz] pl. n. Alicates, *m.* (tool).
plight [plait] n. Apuro, *m.*, aprieto, *m.* (tight spot). || Situación, *f.* || Situación (*f.*) difícil, crisis, *f.*
plight [plait] v. tr. Dar, empeñar (one's word). || — *To plight one's troth*, dar palabra de matrimonio *or* de casamiento. || *To plight o.s. to*, celebrar esponsales con.
Plimsoll line [ˈplimsəllain] n. MAR. Línea (*f.*) de máxima carga.
Plimsoll mark [ˈplimsəlmɑ:k] n. MAR. Línea (*f.*) de máxima carga.
plimsolls [ˈplimsəlz] pl. n. Zapatos (*m.*) de lona *or* de tenis, playeras, *f.*
plinth [plinθ] n. ARCH. Plinto, *m.* (of a column). | Zócalo, *m.* (of a wall). | Peana, *f.* (of a statue).
Pliny [ˈplini] pr. n. Plinio, *m.*: *Pliny the Elder, the Younger*, Plinio el Viejo, el Joven.
Pliocene [ˈplaiəusi:n] n. GEOL. Plioceno, *m.*
plod [plɔd] n. Paso (*m.*) pesado. || — *It's a long plod to the town*, queda mucho camino *or* una gran caminata para llegar a la ciudad. || *To go at a steady plod*, andar despacio pero sin parar.
plod [plɔd] v. tr./intr. Andar con paso pesado *or* con dificultad (to walk). | Trabajar laboriosamente (to work slowly). || — *To plod away at a dull task*, seguir haciendo un trabajo pesado a pesar de las dificultades que presenta. || *To plod one's way*, andar con paso pesado *or* con dificultad.
plodder [—ə*] n. FAM. Empollón, ona (student). | Persona que trabaja mucho sin tener grandes aptitudes (worker).
plodding [—iŋ] adj. Laborioso, sa.
plonk [plɔŋk] n. FAM. Pirriaque, *m.*, morapio, *m.* (cheap wine). || See PLUNK.
plonk [plɔŋk] v. tr./intr. See PLUNK.
plop [plɔp] n. Plaf, *m.* || *To go plop*, hacer plaf.
plop [plɔp] v. intr. Hacer plaf (to make a sound). || Caerse haciendo plaf (to fall with a plop). || *To plop down into a chair*, desplomarse pesadamente en un sillón.
plosive [ˈpləusiv] adj. GRAMM. Explosivo, va.
— N. Explosiva, *f.*
plot [plɔt] n. Parcela, *f.*, terreno, *m.* (of ground). || Cuadro, *m.* (in a garden): *a little vegetable plot*, un pequeño cuadro de hortalizas. || Solar, *m.* (for building). || Conspiración, *f.*, complot, *m.* (conspiracy). || Intriga, *f.* (intrigue). || Argumento, *m.*, trama, *f.* (story of a book, etc.). || MATH. Gráfico, *m.* (graph). || U. S. Plano, *m.*
plot [plɔt] v. tr. Tramar, urdir, maquinar, fraguar (a scheme): *to plot s.o.'s downfall*, tramar la caída de alguien. || Hacer el plano de (to map). || Idear el argumento de [un libro] (of a book, etc.). || Hacer un gráfico de (to make a graph of). || Trazar (to trace): *to plot one's course*, trazar su itinerario. || Marcar, señalar (points). || FIG. Tramar, maquinar, urdir: *what are you two plotting now?*, ¿qué estáis tramando ahora vosotros dos?
— V. intr. Conspirar, intrigar. || *They are plotting to overthrow the government*, están urdiendo un complot para derribar el gobierno.
plotter [ˈplɔtə*] n. Conspirador, ra (conspirator). || Maquinador, ra (schemer).
plotting paper [ˈplɔtiŋˈpeipə*]n. Papel (*m.*) cuadriculado (graph paper).
plough [plau] n. AGR. Arado, *m.* (implement). | Tierra (*f.*) arada (ploughed land). || Guillotina, *f.* (in bookbinding). || Guimbarda, *f.* (grooving plane). || ASTR. *The Plough*, El Carro, la Osa Mayor.
plough [plau] v. tr. Arar. || Abrir: *to plough one's way through a crowd*, abrirse paso entre la multitud. || Surcar (ships through the water). || Acanalar (in carpentry). || Guillotinar (in bookbinding). || FAM. Cargar, suspender (to fail an exam): *I was ploughed in English*, me cargaron en inglés.
— V. intr. Arar (to work with a plough). || Ararse: *this field ploughs easily*, este campo se ara fácilmente. || Trabajar con una guillotina (in bookbinding). || Trabajar con una guimbarda (in carpentry).
— COMM. ***To plough back***, reinvertir (to reinvest). || ***To plough in***, enterrar arando (seeds). || ***To plough into***, atacar (to attack). | Precipitarse contra: *the lorry ploughed into the crowd*, el camión se precipitó contra la multitud. || ***To plough through***, abrirse camino por (to make a path through). | — *I managed to plough through it*, conseguí acabarlo (book, work, etc.). | *To plough through a book*, leer un libro con dificultad. || ***To plough under***, enterrar (to bury). || ***To plough up***, arar, roturar: *to plough up a piece of ground*, arar un terreno. | Destrozar, levantar: *the rugby match has ploughed up the pitch*, el partido de rugby ha destrozado el campo. | Arrancar con el arado (to dig up with a plough). | FIG. Descubrir (to find out).
ploughboy [—bɔi] n. Mozo (*m.*) de labranza.
ploughing [—iŋ] n. Arada, *f.*
ploughland [—lænd] n. AGR. Tierra (*f.*) de labranza.
ploughman [—mən] n. Arador, *m.*, labrador, *m.*
— OBSERV. El plural de *ploughman* es *ploughmen*.
ploughshare [—ʃɛə*] n. Reja (*f.*) del arado.
ploughtail [—teil] n. Esteva, *f.*
plover [ˈplʌvə*] n. Chorlito, *m.* (bird).
plow [plau] n./v. tr./intr. U. S. See PLOUGH.
plowboy, plowing, etc. See PLOUGHBOY, PLOUGHING, etc.
ploy [plɔi] n. Trabajo, *m.*, actividad, *f.* (activity). || Táctica, *f.* (tactic). || Truco, *m.*, estratagema, *f.* (trick). || Diversión, *f.* (amusement).
pluck [plʌk] n. Tirón, *m.* (a sharp pull). || Asadura, *f.* (heart, liver, etc. of an animal). || Valor, *m.*, arrojo, *m.* (courage). || Agallas, *f. pl.* (guts). || MUS. Plectro, *m.* || — *I didn't have the pluck to ask him*, no tuve el valor de preguntárselo. || *It takes a lot of pluck*, hace falta tener agallas, hace falta mucho valor.
pluck [plʌk] v. tr. Arrancar (to pull out sharply): *he plucked it out of my hand*, me lo arrancó de la mano. || Desplumar: *to pluck a fowl*, desplumar un ave. || MUS. Pulsar, puntear (a stringed instrument). || Coger (flowers, etc.). || FAM. Robar, estafar (to rob). | Suspender (in an exam). || *To pluck one's eyebrows*, depilarse las cejas.
— ***To pluck at***, tirar de, dar un tirón a: *he plucked at my sleeve*, me tiró ligeramente de la manga. || ***To pluck off***, arrancar. || ***To pluck up***, animarse: *I wish he'd pluck up a bit*, ojalá se anime un poco. | Reunir (strength): *to pluck up enough strength*, reunir bastantes fuerzas. | Arrancar, coger bruscamente (to pick up suddenly). | — *He'll never pluck up the courage*, nunca tendrá el valor. | *To pluck up the* o *enough courage to*, armarse de valor para.
pluckiness [—inis] n. Valor, *m.*, ánimo, *m.*
plucking [—iŋ] n. MUS. Punteado, *m.*, punteo, *m.*
plucky [—i] adj. Valiente, valeroso, sa.
plug [plʌg] n. Tapón, *m.* (in sink, bath, etc.). || Taco (*m.*) de madera (wood for filling holes, etc.). || ELECTR. Enchufe, *m.*: *a two, three pin plug*, un enchufe bipolar, de tres polos; *there is only one plug in this room*, sólo hay un enchufe en este cuarto. || Clavija, *f.* (of telephone exchange). || AUT. Bujía, *f.* (sparking plug). || Andullo, *m.* (of tobacco). || Boca (*f.*) de incendio (fireplug). || U. S. FAM. Penco, *m.* (old horse). || Tiro, *m.* (shot). || FAM. *To give sth. a plug on the radio*, dar publicidad a algo en la radio (to publicize), mencionar algo en la radio (to mention).
plug [plʌg] v. tr./intr. Taponar (a sink, etc.). || Tapar (a hole). || Empastar (a tooth). || Enchufar (radio, etc.). || Atascar (to block up). || FAM. Dar publicidad a (to publicize). | Repetir (to repeat). | Poner constantemente (a record). | Hacer hincapié en, insistir en

(to emphasize): *they plug the advantages and ignore the disadvantages*, insisten en las ventajas y dejan de lado los inconvenientes. | Pegar (to hit). | Pegar un tiro a (to shoot). || — FAM. *To plug away at*, perseverar en (to persevere), aporrear (to hit). || ELECTR. *To plug in*, enchufar. || *To plug up*, atascarse, atorarse: *the sink has plugged up*, el lavabo se ha atascado.

plugged [—d] adj. Atascado, da; atorado, da (blocked). || Falsificado, da (money).

plughole [—həul] n. Desagüe, *m.*, desaguadero, *m.*

plug-in [—in] adj. Con enchufe.

plum [plʌm] n. Ciruela, *f.* (fruit). || Ciruelo, *m.* (tree). || FAM. Chollo, *m.*, breva, *f.* (sth. advantageous). || *Plum duff* o *plum pudding*, pudín, *m.*, budín (*m.*) de pasas.

plumage [ˈplu:midʒ] n. Plumaje, *m.*

plumb [plʌm] n. Plomada, *f.*, plomo, *m.* (for indicating verticality). || MAR. Plomo, *m.*, plomada, *f.*, sonda, *f.* || — *Plumb bob*, plomo, *m.* || *Plumb line*, plomada, *f.*, cuerda (*f.*) de plomada (in construction), sonda, *f.* (for measuring the depth of water). || *To be in plumb*, estar a plomo. || *To be out of plumb*, no estar a plomo.

— Adj. Vertical, a plomo (vertical). || FAM. Completo, ta: *plumb nonsense*, disparate completo.

— Adv. A plomo, verticalmente. || U. S. FAM. Completamente: *plumb crazy*, completamente loco. | De lleno (full): *it landed plumb in his eye*, le dio de lleno en el ojo.

plumb [plʌm] v. tr. Aplomar (to test for verticality). || MAR. Sondar. || FIG. Sondear: *to plumb s.o.'s mind*, sondear el pensamiento de alguien.

plumbaginaceae [plʌmˌbædʒəˈneisii] pl. n. BOT. Plumbagináceas, *f.*

plumbago [—ˈbeigəu] n. MIN. Plombagina, *f.* || BOT. Plumbaginácea, *f.*

plumbeous [ˈplʌmbiəs] adj. Plúmbeo, a (of or like lead). || Plomizo, za (lead-coloured).

plumber [ˈplʌmə*] n. Fontanero, *m.*

plumbiferous [plʌmˈbifərəs] adj. Plomífero, ra.

plumbing [ˈplʌmiŋ] n. Fontanería, *f.* (the craft of a plumber). || Instalación (*f.*) de cañerías, instalación (*f.*) sanitaria (water-supply and drainage system).

plumbism [ˈplʌmˌbizəm] n. MED. Saturnismo, *m.* (lead poisoning).

plumbum [ˈplʌmbəm] n. Plomo, *m.*

plume [plu:m] n. Pluma, *f.* (feather). || Penacho, *m.* (on hat). || *Plume of smoke*, penacho de humo.

plume [plu:m] v. tr. Emplumar (to adorn with feathers). || — *To plume o.s.*, arreglarse las plumas (the birds). || FIG. *To plume o.s. on*, vanagloriarse de.

plumed [—d] adj. Plumado, da (feathered). || Con penacho, empenachado, da (helmet).

plummet [ˈplʌmit] n. Plomo, *m.* (of plumb line, fishing line etc.). || Pesa, *f.* (of a clock). || Plomada, *f.* (plumb line). || MAR. Sonda, *f.* || FIG. Lastre, *m.*, peso, *m.*

plummet [ˈplʌmit] v. intr. Caer en picado (a bird, a plane). || Caer a plomo (object, person). || Caer verticalmente (prices).

plummy [ˈplʌmi] adj. Pastoso, sa (voice).

plump [plʌmp] adj. Rellenito, ta; regordete, ta (persons). || Gordo, da (animals). || Categórico, ca; terminante (denial).

— N. Ruido (*m.*) sordo (sound). || *To fail with a plump*, caer pesadamente.

— Adv. Con un ruido sordo (with a dull sound). || Pesadamente (heavily). || Justo (straight down). || Categóricamente, terminantemente (categorically).

plump [plʌmp] v. tr. Soltar bruscamente, dejar caer pesadamente (to drop). || Engordar (to fatten).

— V. intr. Caer de golpe, dejarse caer pesadamente (to fall heavily). || Ponerse regordete (to put on weight). || — *To plump for*, votar por; decidirse por. || *To plump out* o *up*, hincharse (sails, etc.), engordar (people).

plumpness [—nis] n. Gordura, *f.*

plumule [ˈplu:mju:l] n. BOT. Plúmula, *f.* || Plumón, *m.* (small or downy feather).

plumy [ˈplu:mi] adj. Plumoso, sa.

plunder [ˈplʌndə*] n. Saqueo, *m.*, pillaje, *m.* (the act of plundering). || Botín, *m.* (the goods obtained).

plunder [ˈplʌndə*] v. tr. Saquear, cometer pillaje en, pillar (a town, etc.). || Robar (a safe, tomb, pantry).

— V. intr. Robar.

plunderage [—ridʒ] n. See PLUNDER.

plunderer [—rə*] n. Saqueador, *m.*

plundering [ˈplʌndəriŋ] n. Saqueo, *m.*

plunge [plʌndʒ] n. Zambullida, *f.*, chapuzón, *m.* (short dive into water). || Salto, *m.* (leap, high dive). || Inmersión, *f.* (swim under water). || Piscina, *f.* (pool). || SP. Estirada, *f.* (dive in rugby, etc.). | Caída, *f.* (fall). || Baño, *m.*, remojón, *m.* (dip): *I'm going for a plunge*, voy a darme un baño. || *To take the plunge*, aventurarse, dar un paso decisivo.

plunge [plʌndʒ] v. tr. Hundir, meter: *to plunge a knife into sth.*, hundir un cuchillo en algo; *to plunge one's hand into one's pocket*, meter la mano en el bolsillo. || Hundir, clavar (a dagger). || Sumergir (to submerge). || Hundir, sumir: *plunged into despair*, hundido en la desesperación. || Templar (steel). || *The room, the town was plunged into darkness*, el cuarto, la ciudad quedó a oscuras.

— V. intr. Arrojarse (to throw o.s.). || Tirarse [de cabeza], zambullirse (into water). || Saltar (to dive). || Caer (to fall). || Sumergirse: *the submarine plunged*, el submarino se sumergió. || Cabecear (a ship). || Corcovear (a horse). || Ser muy escotado (a dress). || Precipitarse (to move suddenly). || Hundirse, sumirse (into despair). || Lanzarse: *he plunged into his speech*, se lanzó a hablar; *I hesitated before plunging*, vacilé antes de lanzarme. || Actuar precipitadamente, precipitarse: *he always plunges into things*, siempre actúa precipitadamente. || Jugar fuerte (to bet). || Arriesgar mucho dinero (in the stock exchange).

plunger [—ə*] n. TECH. Émbolo, *m.* (piston). || Desatascador, *m.* (for clearing drains, pipes, etc.).

plunging [—iŋ] adj. Muy bajo (neckline).

plunk [plʌŋk] n. Ruido (*m.*) sordo (dull, short sound). || Rasgueo, *m.*, punteo, *m.* (noise of a banjo, guitar, etc.). || Golpe (*m.*) seco (forceful blow). || FAM. Dólar, *m.*

— Adv. Con un ruido sordo *or* seco.

plunk [plʌŋk] v. tr. Dejar caer pesadamente (to put down suddenly and heavily). || Rasguear, puntear (a banjo, guitar, etc.).

— V. intr. Dejarse caer pesadamente (into a chair).

pluperfect [ˈplu:ˈpə:fikt] n. GRAMM. Pluscuamperfecto, *m.*

plural [ˈpluərəl] adj. Plural: *plural noun*, sustantivo plural. || Plural, del plural (form, ending).

— N. Plural, *m.*

pluralism [—izəm] n. Pluralismo, *m.* || REL. Multiplicidad (*f.*) de cargos.

pluralist [—ist] n. Pluralista, *m.* & *f.*

pluralistic [—istik] adj. Pluralista.

plurality [pluəˈræliti] n. Pluralidad, *f.* || Mayoría, *f.*, pluralidad, *f.*: *by a plurality of votes*, por mayoría de votos.

pluralize [ˈpluərəlaiz] v. tr. Pluralizar.

pluricellular [ˌpluəriˈseljulə*] adj. Pluricelular.

plus [plʌs] prep. Más: *four plus two is six*, cuatro más dos son seis. || FAM. Más, además de: *he arrived with a trunk plus a large suitcase*, llegó con un baúl más una maleta grande.

— Adj. Positivo, va: *plus number*, número positivo. || De ingresos, de entradas: *the plus column of an account*, la columna de ingresos de una cuenta. || ELECTR. Positivo, va. || Más: *the plus sign*, el signo más. || — *Plus sign*, signo (*m.*) más. || *To be plus five pounds on a sale*, ganar cinco libras en una venta. || *Twenty pounds plus*, algo más de veinte libras.

— N. Cantidad (*f.*) positiva (a positive quantity). || Signo (*m.*) más (plus sign).

— OBSERV. El plural del sustantivo *plus* es *plusses* en Gran Bretaña y *pluses* en Estados Unidos.

plus fours [ˈplʌsˈfɔ:z] pl. n. Pantalones (*m.*) de golf, pantalones (*m.*) bombachos.

plush [plʌʃ] n. Felpa, *f.*

— Adj. Afelpado, da; de felpa. || FIG. Lujoso, sa (luxurius).

plushy [—i] adj. Afelpado, da; de felpa. || FIG. Lujoso, sa (luxurious).

Plutarch [ˈplu:tɑ:k] pr. n. Plutarco, *m.*

Pluto [ˈplu:təu] pr. n. MYTH. ASTR. Plutón, *m.*

plutocracy [plu:ˈtɔkrəsi] n. Plutocracia, *f.*

plutocrat [ˈplu:təukræt] n. Plutócrata, *m.* & *f.*

plutocratic [ˌplu:təuˈkrætik] adj. Plutocrático, ca.

plutonium [plu:ˈtəunjəm] n. Plutonio, *m.*

pluvial [plu:vjəl] adj. Pluvial.

— N. REL. Capa (*f.*) pluvial.

pluviograph [ˈplu:viəgrɑ:f] n. Pluviógrafo, *m.*

pluviometer [plu:viˈɔmitə*] n. Pluviómetro, *m.*

pluviometric [ˌplu:viəˈmetrik] or **pluviometrical** [—əl] adj. Pluviométrico, ca.

pluviometry [pluviˈɔmitri] n. Pluviometría, *f.*

pluviosity [plu:viˈɔsiti] n. Pluviosidad, *f.*

pluvious [ˈplu:vjəs] adj. Pluvioso, sa; lluvioso, sa.

ply [plai] n. Cabo, *m.*: *two-ply wool*, lana de dos cabos. || Chapa, *f.* (layer of plywood). || Capa, *f.* (of fabric).

ply [plai] v. tr. Manejar, emplear: *to ply an axe*, manejar el hacha. || Ejercer (a trade, etc.). || Aplicarse a (to dedicate o.s.). || MAR. Hacer el trayecto de, ir y venir por: *this boat plies the Channel*, este barco hace el trayecto del Canal de la Mancha. || *To ply with*, acosar con: *to ply s.o. with questions*, acosar a alguien con preguntas; ofrecer *or* dar constantemente (to supply persistently).

— V. intr. *To ply between*, hacer el servicio entre, ir y venir entre. || *To ply for hire*, estar a la espera de clientes.

plywood [—wud] n. Contrachapado, *m.*, madera (*f.*) contrachapada.

p.m. [ˈpi:ˈem] abbrev. of *post meridiem*.

pneumatic [nju:ˈmætik] adj. Neumático, ca. || *Pneumatic tyre*, neumático, *m.*

pneumatically [njuˈmætikəli] adv. Neumáticamente.

pneumatics [—s] n. PHYS. Neumática, *f.*

pneumococcus [ˌnju:məuˈkɔkəs] n. Neumococo, *m.*

— OBSERV. El plural de *pneumococcus* es *pneumococci*.

pneumogastric [ˌnju:məuˈgæstrik] adj. ANAT. Neumogástrico, ca.

— N. ANAT. Nervio (*m.*) neumogástrico, neumogástrico, *m.*

pneumonia [njuˈməunjə] n. MED. Pulmonía, *f.*, neumonía, *f.*

pneumonic [njuˈmɔnik] adj. MED. Neumónico, ca.

pneumothorax [ˌnju:məuˈθɔ:ræks] n. MED. Neumotórax, *m.*
poach [pəutʃ] v. tr. CULIN. Escalfar (eggs). | Hervir (fish). || Cazar furtivamente, cazar en vedado (to hunt illegally). || Pescar furtivamente, pescar en vedado (to fish illegally). || Pisotear (to trample ground). || FIG. Robar (to steal).
— V. intr. Cazar furtivamente, cazar en vedado (to hunt illegally). || Pescar furtivamente, pescar en vedado (to fish illegally). || Enfangarse (to become soggy). || FIG. *To poach on s.o.'s preserves*, meter la hoz en mies ajena.
poached [—t] adj. Escalfado, da (egg).
poacher [—ə*] n. Cazador (*m.*) furtivo (hunter). || Pescador (*m.*) furtivo (fisherman).
poaching [—iŋ] n. Caza (*f.*) furtiva (hunting). || Pesca (*f.*) furtiva (fishing).
pock [pɔk] n. MED. Picadura, *f.*, señal, *f.*
pocket [—it] n. Bolsillo, *m.* (on a garment): *flap pocket*, bolsillo con cartera. || Hueco, *m.*, cavidad, *f.* (small hollow). || MIN. Bolsa, *f.* (deposit of oil, gas, etc.). | Filón, *m.* (of metal, mineral, etc.). || AVIAT. Bache, *m.* (air pocket). || Tronera, *f.* (of a billiard table). || Bolsa, *f.* (under the eyes). || MIL. Foco, *m.*: *pocket of resistance*, foco de resistencia. || ZOOL. Bolsa, *f.* (external pouch). || — *Breast pocket*, bolsillo de pecho. || FIG. *Empty pockets*, persona (*f.*) sin dinero. || *Patch pocket*, bolsillo de parche. || *Pocket battleship*, acorazado (*m.*) de bolsillo. || U. S. *Pocket billiards*, billar (*m.*) americano. | U. S. *Pocket book*, libro (*m.*) de bolsillo. || HIST. *Pocket borough*, municipio (*m.*) en el que han sido comprados los votos. || *Pocket dictionary, edition*, diccionario (*m.*), edición (*f.*) de bolsillo. || *Pocket handkerchief*, pañuelo (*m.*) de bolsillo. || *Pocket money*, dinero (*m.*) para gastos menudos, dinero de bolsillo. || *To be ten pounds out of pocket, in pocket*, salir perdiendo, ganando diez libras. || *To dip in one's own pocket*, poner de su bolsillo. || FIG. *To have s.o. in one's pocket*, tener a alguien en el bolsillo. | *To have sth. in one's pocket*, tener algo en el bolsillo (to be sure of victory, success, etc.). | *To line one's pockets*, llenarse los bolsillos, forrarse. | *To live beyond one's pocket*, vivir por encima de sus posibilidades económicas. || *To pay s.o. out of one's own pocket*, pagar a alguien de su bolsillo. || FIG. *To put one's hand in one's pocket*, echar mano al bolsillo. | *To put one's pride in one's pocket*, tragarse el orgullo.
pocket [—it] v. tr. Meterse en el bolsillo: *he pocketed the keys*, se metió las llaves en el bolsillo. || FIG. Embolsarse: *he had pocketed fifty pounds of the company's money*, se había embolsado cincuenta libras del dinero de la compañía. || FIG. FAM. Birlar, mangar (to pinch): *someone must have pocketed my lighter*, alguien me debe haber mangado el mechero. || Meter en la tronera (a billiard ball). || SP. Cerrar el paso a (in a race). || FIG. Tragarse: *to pocket one's pride*, tragarse el orgullo.
pocketbook [—itbuk] n. Cartera, *f.*, monedero, *m.*, billetero, *m.*, billetera, *f.* (purse, wallet). || Bolso, *m.* [*Amer.*, cartera, *f.*] (handbag).
pocketful [—itful] n. Bolsillo, *m.* (content).
pocketknife [—itnaif] n. Navaja, *f.*
pocket-size [—itsaiz] adj. De bolsillo.
pocket veto [ˈpɔkitˈvi:təu] n. U. S. Veto (*m.*) indirecto.
pockmark [ˈpɔkmɑ:k] n. Picadura (*f.*) de viruela, señal (*f.*) de viruela.
pockmarked [—t] adj. Picado de viruelas.
pod [pɔd] n. BOT. Vaina, *f.* (of peas, beans, etc.). || Capullo, *m.* (cocoon, etc.). || ZOOL. Manada, *f.* (of seals or whales). || TECH. Ranura, *f.* (groove, channel). | Mandril, *m.* (of a drill).
pod [pɔd] v. tr. Desvainar, pelar (peas).
— V. intr. Hincharse (to swell). || Producir vainas (to produce pods).
podagra [pəuˈdægrə] n. MED. Podagra, *f.*
podgy [ˈpɔdʒi] adj. Gordinflón, ona; regordete, ta.
podium [ˈpəudjəm] n. Podio, *m.* || MUS. Estrado, *m.* (of the conductor).
— OBSERV. El plural de *podium* es *podia* o *podiums*.
podology [pəˈdɔlədʒi] n. MED. Podología, *f.*
podzol [ˈpɔdzɔl] n. Podzol, *m.*
poem [ˈpəuim] n. Poesía, *f.*, poema, *m.* (short poem): *the poems of Lorca*, las poesías de Lorca. || Poema, *m.* (long): *Homer's poems*, los poemas de Homero.
poesy [ˈpəuizi] n. Poesía, *f.*
poet [ˈpəuit] n. Poeta, *m.*
poetaster [ˌpəuiˈtæstə*] n. Poetastro, *m.*
poetess [ˈpəuitis] n. Poetisa, *f.*
poetic [pəuˈetik] or **poetical** [—əl] adj. Poético, ca: *poetic licence*, licencia poética. || FIG. *Poetic justice*, justicia divina.
poeticize [pəuˈetisaiz] v. tr. Poetizar.
poetics [pəuˈetiks] n. Poética, *f.*, arte (*f.*) poética.
poetize [ˈpəuitaiz] v. tr. Poetizar.
poet laureate [ˈpəuitˈlɔ:riit] n. Poeta (*m.*) laureado.
— OBSERV. El plural es *poet laureates* o *poets laureate*.
poetry [ˈpəuitri] n. Poesía, *f.*
pogo stick [ˈpəugəustik] n. Saltador, *m.* (toy).
pogrom [ˈpɔgrəm] n. Pogrom, *m.*, pogromo, *m.*
poignancy [ˈpɔinənsi] n. Patetismo, *m.* (sadness). || Intensidad, *f.* (intensity). || Mordacidad, *f.* (of a satire).
poignant [ˈpɔinənt] adj. Conmovedor, ra (moving). || Intenso, sa; agudo, da (grief, pain). || Profundo, da; enorme: *of poignant interest*, de un interés enorme. || Mordaz (satire).
point [pɔint] n. Punto, *m.*: *four main points*, cuatro puntos principales; *to agree on a point*, estar de acuerdo en un punto; *point of departure*, punto de partida; *point of interest*, punto de interés; *melting, boiling point*, punto de fusión, de ebullición. || Cuestión, *f.*, punto, *m.* (problem). || Punto, *m.*, lugar, *m.* (place). || Aspecto, *m.* (aspect). || Momento, *m.* (moment). || Significado, *m.*, sentido, *m.*: *the point of a story*, el significado de una historia. || Gracia, *f.*, chiste, *m.* (of a joke). || Cualidad, *f.*: *generosity is not one of her better points*, la generosidad no es una de sus mejores cualidades; *to have one's good points*, tener sus cualidades. || Motivo, *m.*, interés, *m.*, razón, *f.*: *I see no point in it*, no le veo el interés; *is there any point in going on?*, ¿hay algún motivo para continuar? || Punta, *f.* (sharp end): *to sharpen the point of a pencil*, sacar punta a un lápiz; *the point of the arrow*, la punta de la flecha. || Objeto (*m.*) puntiagudo (sharp object). || Punto, *m.* (full stop). || MATH. Punto, *m.* (in geometry). | Coma, *f.* (in decimals): *five point seven* (5.7), cinco coma siete [5,7]. || Grado, *m.* (of thermometer): *to rise two points*, subir dos grados. || COMM. Entero, *m.*: *the shares dropped three points*, las acciones bajaron de tres enteros. || PRINT. Punto, *m.* || GEOGR. Cabo, *m.*, punta, *f.*, promontorio, *m.* || SP. Ataque, *m.* (in fencing). | Posición (*f.*) de uno de los jugadores (cricket). | Tanto, *m.*, punto, *m.*: *to score a point*, marcar un tanto. || Muestra, *f.* (of gundogs). || Cuerna, *f.* (of a deer). || Característica (*f.*) principal, cualidad, *f.* (of an animal). || MAR. Punto, *m.* (compass). || MIL. Punta, *f.* || Punto, *m.* (in Braille). || ELECTR. Contacto, *m.* (contact). || — Pl. Extremidades, *f.* (of a horse). || Agujas, *f.* (of railway). || — *At the point of death*, a punto de morirse, in articulo mortis. || *At the point where*, allí donde, donde (there where), cuando (when). || *At this point*, al llegar a este punto. || *At this point in time*, en este momento. || *Beside the point*, fuera de propósito, que no viene al caso. || *Cardinal points*, puntos cardinales. || *Critical point*, punto crítico. || *Focal point*, punto focal. || *He was severe to the point of cruelty*, fue severo hasta la crueldad. || *High point*, punto álgido. || *In point*, que viene al caso (relevant), de que se trata, en cuestión (in question). || *In point of*, en cuanto a, por lo que se refiere a: *in point of numbers*, por lo que se refiere al número. || *In point of fact*, en realidad. || *Not to put too fine a point on it*, hablando sin rodeos. || *Off the point*, fuera de propósito, que no viene al caso. || *On a point of clarification*, para una aclaración. || *On that point*, en ese momento (at that moment), en cuanto a eso (regarding that). || *On the point of*, a punto de: *he was on the point of falling*, estaba a punto de caerse. || *Penalty point*, punto de penalty. || *Point by point*, punto por punto. || *Point duty*, dirección (*f.*) del tráfico, control (*m.*) de la circulación. || *Point of conscience*, caso (*m.*) de conciencia. || *Point of fact*, hecho, *m.* || *Point of honour*, punto de honor. || *Point of impact*, punto de impacto. || *Point of order*, cuestión de orden. || *Point of reference*, punto de referencia. || *Point of view*, punto de vista. || *Starting point*, punto de partida. || *Strong point*, punto fuerte. || *Supporting point*, punto de apoyo. || *Suspension points*, puntos suspensivos. || *That's just the point!*, ¡eso es!, ¡ahí está! || *That's not the point*, eso no tiene nada que ver, no es eso. || *The point at issue*, el punto en cuestión. || *The point is that*, el caso es que. || *This is the point*, esto es lo importante, esto es lo que cuenta. || *To a certain point*, hasta cierto punto. || *To be beside o off the point*, no venir al caso, no tener nada que ver. || *To be to the point*, venir al caso. || *To carry one's point*, conseguir lo que uno quiere. || *To catch the point*, comprender. || *To get back to the point*, volver al tema. || *To get o to wander off the point*, salirse del tema. || *To get the point*, comprender. || *To get o to come to the point*, ir al grano. || *To give a twenty point advantage*, dar veinte puntos de ventaja. || *To give point to an objection*, dar valor or importancia a una objeción. || *To keep o to stick to the point*, no salirse del tema, ceñirse al tema. || *To make a point*, hacer una observación, llamar la atención sobre un punto. || *To make a point of*, creerse en la obligación de. || *To make one's point*, lograr lo que uno quiere, salirse con la suya. || *To miss the point*, no comprender: *he has completely missed the point*, no ha comprendido absolutamente nada. || *To press the point that*, insistir en que, hacer hincapié en que. || *To reach all points in England*, llegar a todos los puntos de Inglaterra. || *To speak to the point*, ceñirse al tema. || *To stretch a point*, hacer una excepción. || *To such a point*, hasta tal punto. || *To taper to a point*, terminarse en punta. || *To the point*, pertinente. || SP. *To win on points*, ganar por puntos (boxing). || *Up to a point*, hasta cierto punto. || *Weak point*, punto débil *or* flaco. || *We have reached the point of no return*, no podemos volver atrás. || *What's the point of having a horse?*, ¿para qué sirve tener un caballo?
point [pɔint] v. tr. Afilar, sacar punta a: *to point a pencil*, sacar punta a un lápiz. || Apuntar: *to point*

a gun at s.o., apuntar a uno con un arma. || TECH. Mampostear. || Poner los puntos a (Jewish writing). || Señalar, indicar: *Carol pointed the way*, Carol indicó el camino.
— V. intr. Señalar: *the compass needle always points north*, la aguja de la brújula siempre señala el norte. || Mostrar la caza, pararse (hunting dog).
— ***To point at***, señalar: *to point a finger at*, señalar con el dedo. | Apuntar (to aim). || ***To point out***, señalar, hacer notar, hacer observar: *Carol pointed out my mistake*, Carol señaló mi error; *she pointed out that it was not David's fault*, hizo notar que no era culpa de David. | Advertir: *she pointed out to me that it was dangerous*, me advirtió que era peligroso. | Señalar, indicar: *I'd like to point out that*, me gustaría señalar que. || ***To point to***, señalar: *an arrow pointing to Raymond's house*, una flecha señalando la casa de Ramón. | Indicar: *everything points to his guilt*, todo indica que es culpable. | Marcar: *the hands pointed to nine o'clock*, las manecillas marcaban las nueve. || ***To point up***, poner de relieve.
point-blank [—ˈblæŋk] adv. A boca de jarro, a quema ropa: *she shot him point-blank*, le disparó a quema ropa. || Sin rodeos, directamente, a boca de jarro, a quema ropa: *he asked her point-blank*, se lo preguntó sin rodeos. || Categóricamente: *she refused point-blank*, se negó categóricamente.
— Adj. Disparado a quema ropa *or* a boca de jarro (shot). || Directo, ta; hecho a quema ropa *or* a boca de jarro: *a point-blank question*, una pregunta directa. || Categórico, ca: *a point-blank refusal*, una negativa categórica.
pointed [—id] adj. Puntiagudo, da (having a sharp point). || FIG. Mordaz (critical): *a pointed attack*, un ataque mordaz. | Intencionado, da (intended): *pointed rudeness*, descortesía intencionada. | Picante (lively, piquant). || ARCH. *Pointed arch*, arco ojival *or* apuntado.
pointedly [—idli] adv. Con mordacidad (cuttingly). || Intencionadamente (deliberately).
pointer [—ə*] n. Indicador, *m.* (needle). || Manecilla, *f.* (of a clock). || Fiel, *m.* (of scales). || FIG. Indicación, *f.* (indication, clue). | Consejo, *m.* (suggestion). || Perro (*m.*) de muestra (dog). || Puntero, *m.* (for blackboard).
pointillism [ˈpwæntilizəm] n. ARTS. Puntillismo, *m.*
pointillist [ˈpwæntilist] n. ARTS. Puntillista, *m.* & *f.*
pointless [ˈpɔintlis] adj. Sin punta (without a point). | FIG. Insustancial, sin sentido (meaningless): *a pointless conversation*, una conversación insustancial. | Inútil: *it's pointless continuing*, es inútil continuar. | Sin sentido, que carece de sentido (existence).
pointlessly [—lisli] adv. Inútilmente (uselessly).
pointlessness [—lisnis] n. Inutilidad, *f.* (uselessness). || Insensatez, *f.*, falta (*f.*) de sentido (senselessness).
poise [pɔiz] n. PHYS. Poise, *m.* (viscosity unit). || Equilibrio, *m.* (balance). || Porte, *m.* (bearing). || Elegancia, *f.* (elegance). || Aplomo, *m.*, serenidad, *f.* (mental stability).
poise [pɔiz] v. tr. Poner en equilibrio (to balance). || Preparar: *to poise o.s. for an ordeal*, prepararse para una prueba.
— V. intr. Estar en equilibrio. || Estar suspendido (to hang as if suspended). || Cernerse (to hover).
poison [—n] n. Veneno, *m.*, ponzoña, *f.*: *deadly poison*, veneno mortífero; *selfishness is the poison of mankind*, el egoísmo es el veneno de la humanidad. || — FIG. *To hate like poison*, odiar a muerte. || FAM. *What's your poison?*, ¿con qué te quieres envenenar?, ¿qué quieres tomar? (drink).
— Adj. Venenoso, sa; ponzoñoso, sa (snake, etc.). || Tóxico, ca (gas, drug, etc.). || — *A poison arrow*, una flecha envenenada. || *Poison hemlock*, cicuta, *f.*
poison [—n] v. tr. Envenenar. || FIG. Envenenar, emponzoñar.
poisoner [—nə*] n. Envenenador, ra.
poisoning [—niŋ] n. Envenenamiento, *m.* || *To die of poisoning*, morir envenenado.
poisonous [—nəs] adj. Venenoso, sa; ponzoñoso, sa (snake, etc.). || Tóxico, ca (drug, gas, etc.). || FIG. Odioso, sa (hateful). | Nefasto, ta; pernicioso, sa (harmful). | Malísimo, ma (very bad).
poison-pen [ˈpɔiznˈpen] adj. *Poison-pen letter*, carta (*f.*) ofensiva anónima.
poke [pəuk] n. Hurgonada, *f.* (with a poker). || Empujón (*m.*) con el dedo (with a finger). || Pinchazo, *m.* (with sth. sharp). || Codazo, *m.* (with the elbow): *he gave me a poke in the ribs*, me dio un codazo en las costillas. || Golpe, *m.* (blow). || Trangallo, *m.* (for animals). || Bolsa, *f.*, saco, *m.* (bag). || — FIG. *To buy a pig in a poke*, comprar a ciegas. || *To give the fire a poke*, atizar el fuego.
poke [pəuk] v. tr. Atizar, hurgar: *to poke the fire*, atizar el fuego. || Hurgarse (one's nose). || Dar con la punta del dedo (with the finger): *he poked me in the arm*, me dio con la punta del dedo en el brazo. || Dar un codazo (with the elbow). || Meter: *to poke one's finger into a hole*, meter el dedo en un agujero; *he poked his finger in my eye*, me metió el dedo en el ojo; *to poke one's hand through a letterbox*, meter la mano en un buzón. || Hacer: *he poked a hole in the wall*, hizo un agujero en la pared. || Empujar (to push). || Asomar: *Raymond poked his head round the door*, Ramón asomó la cabeza por la puerta. || FAM. Dar un golpe *or* un puñetazo a (to hit). || — *To poke fun at*, reírse de. || FIG. *To poke one's nose into*, meter la nariz en, meter las narices en.
— V. intr. Hurgar (to make digs): *to poke at sth. with a stick*, hurgar algo con un bastón. || Asomar: *his head poked through the window*, su cabeza asomó por la ventana.
— ***To poke about*** o ***around***, fisgonear, hurgar (to search): *to poke around in a drawer*, fisgonear en un cajón. | Entrometerse (to meddle). | Husmear (to sniff around). | Curiosear: *to poke around in the shops*, curiosear en las tiendas. || ***To poke out***, sacar: *he poked her eye out*, le sacó un ojo. | Asomar, sacar (one's head). | Salirse: *a car poked out from the row*, un coche se salió de la fila.
poker [—ə*] n. Hurgón, *m.*, atizador, *m.* (for a fire). || Póker, *m.*, póquer, *m.* (card game): *poker of aces*, póker de ases. || FIG. *As stiff as a poker*, más tieso que un palo.
poker face [—əfeis] n. FAM. Cara (*f.*) inmutable.
poky (U. S. **pokey**) [ˈpəuki] adj. Diminuto, ta (very small). || U. S. Lento, ta. || — *A poky little room*, un cuartucho. || *A poky old town*, un pueblucho.
Poland [ˈpəulənd] pr. n. GEOGR. Polonia, *f.*
polar [ˈpəulə*] adj. Polar: *polar circle*, círculo polar; *polar coordinates*, coordenadas polares. || FIG. Opuesto, ta: *polar views*, ideas opuestas. || — *Polar bear*, oso (*m.*) polar. || *Polar cap*, casquete (*m.*) polar. || *Polar climate*, clima (*m.*) polar. || *Polar lights*, aurora (*f.*) boreal.
polarimeter [ˌpəuləˈrimitə*] n. PHYS. Polarímetro, *m.*
Polaris [pəuˈlæris] pr. n. Estrella (*f.*) polar.
polariscope [pəuˈlæriskəup] n. PHYS. Polariscopio, *m.*
polarity [pəuˈlæriti] n. Polaridad, *f.*
polarization [ˌpəuləraiˈzeiʃən] n. Polarización, *f.*
polarize [ˈpəuləraiz] v. tr. Polarizar.
polarizer [—ə*] n. Polarizador, *m.*
polarizing [ˈpəuləraiziŋ] adj. Polarizador, ra.
polaroid [ˈpəulərɔid] n. Polaroid, *m.*
polder [ˈpɔldə*] n. Pólder, *m.*
pole [pəul] n. ELECTR. MATH. BIOL. Polo, *m.*: *negative pole*, polo negativo; *magnetic pole*, polo magnético. || Palo, *m.*, vara, *f.* (long piece of wood). || Barra, *f.* (of metal). || Poste, *m.*: *telegraph pole*, poste telegráfico. || Estaca, *f.*, poste, *m.* (of a tent). || Lanza, *f.* (of carriage). || MAR. Mástil, *m.* (mast). || Asta, *f.*: *flag pole*, asta de bandera. || Pértiga, *f.* (for propelling a punt). || Palo, *m.*, estaca, *f.* (for climbing plants). || SP. Pértiga, *f.* [*Amer.*, garrocha, *f.*] : *pole vault*, salto de pértiga. || Medida (*f.*) de longitud de 5,03 m. || — *Greasy pole*, palo ensebado. || *Pole horse*, caballo (*m.*) de tronco. || FIG. *To be poles apart*, ser polos opuestos. | *To be up the pole*, estar como una cabra (crazy), estar metido en líos (in trouble).
pole [pəul] v. tr. Empujar con una pértiga (to propel with a pole).
Pole [pəul] n. Polaco, ca (native of Poland). || Polo, *m.*: *North Pole*, Polo Norte.
poleaxe (U. S. **poleax**) [—æks] n. HIST. Alabarda, *f.* (long-handled axe). | Hacha (*f.*) de abordaje (for grappling an enemy vessel). | Hacha (*f.*) de armas (battle-axe).
poleaxe (U. S. **poleax**) [—æks] v. tr. Desnucar.
pole bean [—biːn] n. BOT. Judía (*f.*) trepadora [*Amer.*, fríjol (*m.*) trepador].
polecat [—kæt] n. ZOOL. Turón, *m.* || U. S. Mofeta, *f.* (skunk).
polemic [pɔˈlemik] adj. Polémico, ca.
— N. Polémica, *f.* (controversy). || Polemista, *m.* & *f.* (person involved in a controversy).
polemical [pɔˈlemikəl] adj. Polémico, ca.
polemicist [pɔˈlemisist] n. Polemista, *m.* & *f.*
polemicize [pɔˈleməsaiz] v. tr. Polemizar.
polemics [pɔˈlemiks] n. Polémica, *f.*
polemist [pɔˈlemist] n. Polemista, *m.* & *f.*
polenta [pəuˈlentə] n. CULIN. Polenta, *f.*
polestar [ˈpəulstɑː*] n. Estrella (*f.*) polar.
police [pəˈliːs] n. Policía, *f.*: *to join the police*, entrar en la policía. || U. S. Mantenimiento (*m.*) del orden (keeping in order). | Control, *m.* (control). || U. S. MIL. Limpieza, *f.* (cleaning). || — Pl. Policía, *f. sing.*: *a squad of mounted police*, una escuadra de la policía montada; *the police were called in*, llamaron a la policía.
police [pɔˈliːs] v. tr. Vigilar, mantener el orden en: *the match will be policed by a detachment of forty*, el partido será vigilado por un destacamento de cuarenta hombres; *twenty men policed the town*, veinte hombres mantuvieron el orden en la ciudad. || Vigilar: *to police the border*, vigilar la frontera. || Tener un servicio de policía en (to provide with police). || Supervisar, vigilar (to supervise). || U. S. MIL. Limpiar (to clean up).
police car [—kɑː*] n. Coche (*m.*) de policía.
police constable [—ˈkʌnstəbl] n. Policía, *m.*, guardia, *m.*
police dog [—dɔg] n. Perro (*m.*) policía.
police force [—fɔːs] n. Cuerpo (*m.*) de policía: *to join the police force*, entrar en el cuerpo de policía. || Fuerza (*f.*) pública: *the police force intervened*, intervino la fuerza pública. || Policía, *f.*: *this town has an efficient police force*, esta ciudad tiene una policía eficiente.

police headquarters [—'hed'kwɔ:təz] n. Jefatura (*f.*) de policía.
policeman [—mən] n. Policía, *m.*, guardia, *m.*

— OBSERV. El plural de *policeman* es *policemen.*

police power [—'pauə*] n. Fuerza (*f.*) pública.
police record [—'rekɔ:d] n. Antecedentes (*m. pl.*) penales.
police state [—'steit] n. Estado (*m.*) policiaco.
police station [—'steiʃən] n. Comisaría (*f.*) de policía.
policewoman [—,wumən] n. Mujer (*f.*) policía.

— OBSERV. El plural de *policewoman* es *policewomen.*

policlinic [pɔli'klinik] n. Policlínica, *f.* [*Amer.*, policlínico, *m.*]
policy ['pɔlisi] n. Política, *f.* (of a government): *foreign policy*, política exterior; *a revolutionary policy*, una política revolucionaria. ‖ Norma, *f.*, principio, *m.*, sistema, *m.* (principle): *our policy is to satisfy our customers*, tenemos por norma satisfacer a nuestros clientes; *it is always my policy to ask people's opinion*, tengo por principio pedir a la gente su opinión. ‖ Táctica, *f.*: *would it be good policy to accept the invitation*, ¿sería buena táctica aceptar la invitación? ‖ Póliza, *f.*: *insurance policy*, póliza de seguros. ‖ U. S. Lotería (*f.*) clandestina (lottery). ‖ — *Good-neighbour policy*, política de buena vecindad. ‖ *To change one's policy*, cambiar de política *or* de táctica.
policyholder [—,həuldə*] n. Asegurado, da.
polio ['pəuliəu] n. MED. Polio, *f.*
poliomyelitis ['pəuliəumaiə'laitis] n. MED. Poliomielitis, *f.*
Polish ['pəuliʃ] adj. Polaco, ca.
— N. Polaco, *m.* (language).
polish ['pɔliʃ] n. Pulimento, *m.* (act of polishing). ‖ Lustre, *m.*, brillo, *m.* (shine, lustre): *it loses its polish very easily*, pierde su brillo muy fácilmente. ‖ Esmalte (*m.*) para las uñas, laca (*f.*) para las uñas (for nails). ‖ Cera, *f.* (for furniture, floors, etc.). ‖ Betún, *m.* [*Amer.*, cera, *f.*, bola, *f.*] (for shoes). ‖ FIG. Refinamiento, *m.*, finura, *f.*, elegancia, *f.*: *a show which lacks polish*, un espectáculo que carece de refinamiento. ‖ — *A high polish*, mucho brillo. ‖ *To give sth. a polish*, pulir algo, dar brillo a algo. ‖ FIG. *To have polish*, ser fino (person, show), ser pulido (style). | *Your style lacks polish*, su estilo no es muy pulido, le hace falta perfeccionar el estilo.
polish ['pɔliʃ] v. tr. Encerar (the floor, furniture). ‖ Limpiar [*Amer.*, embolar] (shoes). ‖ Limpiar, dar brillo a (silverware). ‖ Pulir, bruñir (metals). ‖ FIG. Pulir, refinar: *this child needs a little polishing*, a este niño hace falta pulirle un poco. | Pulir, perfeccionar (to perfect). | Pulir (the style). ‖ TECH. Pulir. ‖ — FAM. *To polish off*, zampar, zamparse (to consume quickly): *he polished off three chickens*, se zampó tres pollos; despachar (work), despachar, liquidar, cepillarse (to kill). ‖ *To polish up*, dar brillo a (to shine up), perfeccionar, pulir (to revise and improve).
polished [—t] adj. Pulido, da (cleaned with polish). ‖ FIG. Refinado, da; fino, na (refined). | Pulido, da (style, etc.).
polisher [—ə*] n. Pulidor, ra (person). ‖ Pulidora, *f.* (machine). ‖ Enceradora, *f.* (floor-polishing machine).
polishing [—iŋ] adj. Pulidor, ra. ‖ — TECH. *Polishing machine*, pulidora, *f.* ‖ *Polishing wax*, cera, *f.*
— N. Pulido.
Politburo [pɔ'litbjuərəu] n. Politburó, *m.*
polite [pə'lait] adj. Cortés (tactful, correct): *a polite answer*, una respuesta cortés. ‖ Educado, da; fino, na (refined): *in polite society*, entre gente educada. ‖ Atento, ta (considerate). ‖ — *It is not polite to yawn*, es de mala educación bostezar. ‖ *She was very polite to me*, me trató con mucha cortesía *or* educación, estuvo muy atenta conmigo. ‖ *This word is not in polite usage*, esta palabra es incorrecta.
politeness [—nis] n. Cortesía, *f.*, educación, *f.*, urbanidad, *f.* (good manners, etc.). ‖ Atenciones, *f. pl.* (consideration).
politic ['pɔlitik] adj. Diplomático, ca; prudente (prudent). ‖ Astuto, ta; sagaz (astute). ‖ Ingenioso, sa (clever).
political [pə'litikəl] adj. Político, ca. ‖ — *Political economy*, economía política. ‖ *Political jobbery*, politiqueo, *m.* ‖ *Political sciences*, ciencias políticas.
politicaster [pə'liti,kɑ:stə*] n. Politicastro, *m.*
politician [,pɔli'tiʃən] n. Político, *m.* ‖ *Petty politician*, politicastro, *m.*
politicize [pə'litisaiz] v. tr. Politizar.
politics ['pɔlitiks] n. Política, *f.*: *to talk politics*, hablar de política. ‖ — Pl. Política, *f. sing.*: *the politics of the last government were heavily criticized*, la política del último gobierno fue muy criticada.
politization [,pɔliti'zeiʃən] n. Politización, *f.*
polity ['pɔliti] n. Gobierno, *m.* (organized government). ‖ Constitución, *f.* (constitution). ‖ Estado, *m.* (state).
polje ['pəuljə] n. GEOL. Polje, *m.* (depression).
polka ['pɔlkə] n. Polca, *f.* (dance).
polka dot [—dɔt] n. Lunar, *m.* ‖ Tela (*f.*) de lunares (material).
poll [pəul] n. Votación, *f.* (the casting of votes, the number of votes cast): *a heavy poll*, una votación masiva. ‖ Escrutinio, *m.* (scrutiny). ‖ Elecciones, *f. pl.* (elections). ‖ Sondeo, *m.*, encuesta, *f.*: *public opinion poll*, sondeo de la opinión pública. ‖ Capitación, *f.* (tax). ‖ TECH. Cotillo, *m.* (blunt end of a hammer). ‖ — Pl. Centro (*m. sing.*) electoral: *the polls shut at nine*, el centro electoral cierra a las nueve. ‖ — *There was a poll of 65 %*, ha votado el 65 % del electorado. ‖ *To go to the polls*, ir a las urnas, votar. ‖ *To hold a Gallup poll on rising prices*, hacer una encuesta *or* un sondeo de la opinión pública sobre el alza de los precios.
poll [pəul] v. tr. Obtener: *he polled two thousand votes*, obtuvo dos mil votos. ‖ Registrar los votos de (to record the votes of). ‖ Sondear: *to poll public opinion*, sondear la opinión pública. ‖ Descornar (to cut off the horns of). ‖ Esquilar (to cut off wool, etc.). ‖ Trasquilar (to cut off hair). ‖ Desmochar (a tree).
— V. intr. Votar (to vote).
pollard ['pɔləd] n. Árbol (*m.*) desmochado (tree). ‖ Animal (*m.*) mocho (animal).
pollee [,pəu'li] n. Entrevistado, da.
pollen ['pɔlin] n. BOT. Polen, *m.* ‖ *Pollen count*, índice (*m.*) de polen contenido en el aire.
pollinate [—eit] v. tr. BOT. Polinizar.
pollination [,pɔli'neiʃən] n. BOT. Polinización, *f.*
polling ['pəuliŋ] n. Votación, *f.*
polling booth [—bu:θ] n. Cabina (*f.*) electoral.
polling day [—dei] n. Día (*m.*) de elecciones.
polling place [—pleis] o **polling station** [—'steiʃən] n. Centro (*m.*) *or* colegio (*m.*) electoral.
polliniferous [pɔli'nifərəs] n. BOT. Polinífero, ra.
polliwog ['pɔliwɔg] n. Renacuajo, *m.* (tadpole).
pollster ['pəulstə*] n. Entrevistador, ra; encuestador, ra.
poll tax ['pəultæks] n. Capitación, *f.*
pollutant [pə'lu:tənt] n. Contaminante, *m.*, agente (*m.*) contaminador.
pollute [pə'lu:t] v. tr. Contaminar. ‖ REL. Profanar. ‖ FIG. Corromper (to corrupt).
polluting [—iŋ] adj. Contaminante.
polluting agent [—iŋ'eidʒənt] n. Contaminante, *m.*, agente (*m.*) contaminador.
pollution [pə'lu:ʃən] n. Contaminación, *f.*, polución, *f.* ‖ Contaminación (*f.*) del medio ambiente (of the environment). ‖ REL. Profanación, *f.* ‖ *Air, river pollution*, contaminación del aire, de los ríos.
Pollux ['pɔləks] pr. n. Pólux, *m.*
pollywog ['pɔliwɔg] n. Renacuajo, *m.* (tadpole).
polo ['pəuləu] n. SP. Polo, *m.* | Polo (*m.*) acuático (water polo).
poloist [—ist] n. Polista, *m.*, jugador (*m.*) de polo.
polonaise [,pɔlə'neiz] n. MUS. Polonesa, *f.*
poloneck ['pəuləunek] n. Cuello (*m.*) vuelto (collar). ‖ Jersey (*m.*) de cuello vuelto (sweater).
polonium [pɔ'ləunjəm] n. CHEM. Polonio, *m.*
polo shirt ['pəuləuʃə:t] n. Polo, *m.*
poltergeist ['pɔltəgaist] n. Duende, *m.*
poltroon [pɔl'tru:n] adj./n. Cobarde.
poltroonery [—əri] n. Cobardía, *f.*
polyandry ['pɔliændri] n. Poliandria, *f.*
polyanthus [,pɔli'ænθəs] n. BOT. Prímula, *f.*

— OBSERV. El plural es *polyanthuses* o *polyanthi.*

polycephalous [pɔlike'fæləs] adj. Policéfalo, la.
polychroism ['pɔli,krəuizəm] n. PHYS. Policroísmo, *m.*
polychromatic [,pɔlikrə'mætik] adj. Policromo, ma.
polychrome ['pɔlikrəum] adj. Policromado, da; policromo, ma.
polychromy [—i] n. Policromía, *f.*
polyclinic [,pɔli'klinik] n. U. S. Policlínica, *f.* [*Amer.*, policlínico, *m.*]
polydactyl [,pɔli'dæktil] adj./s. Polidáctilo, la.
polyester ['pɔliestə*] n. CHEM. Poliéster, *m.*
polyethylene [,pɔli'eθəli:n] n. CHEM. Polietileno, *m.*
polygamist [pɔ'ligəmist] n. Polígamo, ma.
polygamous [pɔ'ligəməs] adj. Polígamo, ma.
polygamy [pɔ'ligəmi] n. Poligamia, *f.*
polyglot ['pɔliglɔt] adj. Polígloto, ta.
— N. Polígloto, ta (person). ‖ Libro (*m.*) políglota (book). ‖ *The Polyglot Bible*, La Biblia Políglota.
polyglotism [—izəm] n. Poliglotía, *f.*
polygon ['pɔligən] n. Polígono, *m.*
polygonaceae [pɔligə'neisi:i] pl. n. Poligonáceas, *f.*
polygonaceous [pɔligə'neisiəs] adj. Poligonáceo, a.
polygonal [pɔ'ligənl] adj. Poligonal.
polygraph ['pɔligrɑ:f] n. Polígrafo, *m.*
polygraphy [pə'ligrəfi] n. Poligrafía, *f.*
polygyny [pə'lidʒini] n. Poliginia, *f.*
polyhedral ['pɔli'hedrəl] adj. MATH. Poliédrico, ca.
polyhedron ['pɔli'hedrən] n. MATH. Poliedro, *m.*

— OBSERV. El plural de *polyhedron* es *polyhedra* o *polyhedrons.*

polymer ['pɔlimə*] n. CHEM. Polímero, *m.*
polymeric [,pɔli'merik] adj. CHEM. Polimérico, ca; polímero, ra.
polymerism ['pɔlimerizəm] n. CHEM. Polimería, *f.*
polymerization [pə,limərі'zeiʃən] n. CHEM. Polimerización, *f.*
polymerize [pə'limәraiz] v. tr. Polimerizar.
polymorph ['pɔli,mɔ:f] n. BIOL. Organismo (*m.*) polimorfo. ‖ MIN. Sustancia (*f.*) polimorfa.
polymorphic [,pɔli'mɔ:fik] adj. Polimórfico, ca.
polymorphism [,pɔli'mɔ:fizəm] n. Polimorfismo, *m.*
polymorphous [,pɔli'mɔ:fəs] adj. Polimorfo, fa.
Polynesia [,pɔli'ni:zjə] pr. n. GEOGR. Polinesia, *f.*
Polynesian [—n] adj./n. GEOGR. Polinesio, sia.

POLITICS — POLÍTICA, f.

I. Types of government. — Formas (f.) de gobierno.

monarchy; empire	monarquía *f.*; imperio *m.*
regency	regencia *f.*
princedom	principado *m.*
republic	república *f.*
directory	directorio *m.*
dictatorship	dictadura *f.*
tyranny; despotism	tiranía *f.*; despotismo *m.*
totalitarianism	totalitarismo *m.*
autonomy, self-government	autonomía *f.*
autocracy	autocracia *f.*
oligarchy	oligarquía *f.*
democracy	democracia *f.*
liberalism	liberalismo *m.*
demagogy	demagogia *f.*
parliamentary government *o* system	régimen (*m.*) parlamentario
absolute government	gobierno (*m.*) absoluto
centralism	centralismo *m.*
federal government	gobierno (*m.*) federal
federalism	federalismo *m.*
confederation	confederación *f.*
presidential government	presidencialismo *m.*
conservatism	conservadurismo *m.*
labourism [U.S., laborism]	laborismo *m.*
militarism	militarismo *m.*
anarchy	anarquía *f.*
anarchism	anarquismo *m.*
nationalism	nacionalismo *m.*
authoritarianism	autoritarismo *m.*
Fascism	fascismo *m.*
Socialism	socialismo *m.*
Communism; Marxism	comunismo *m.*; marxismo *m.*
Maoism	maoísmo *m.*
syndicalism	sindicalismo *m.*
protectorate	protectorado *m.*

II. Rulers. — Gobernantes, m.

sovereign; monarch	soberano *m.*; monarca *m.*
emperor	emperador *m.*
czar, tsar	zar *m.*
king; queen	rey *m.*; reina *f.*
prince	príncipe *m.*
regent; co-regent	regente *m.*; corregente *m.*
viceroy	virrey *m.*
dictator; tyrant	dictador *m.*; tirano *m.*
sultan	sultán *m.*
chancellor	canciller *m.*
head of state	jefe (*m.*) de Estado
Prime Minister, premier	primer ministro *m.*
Lord (High) Chancellor	presidente (*m.*) de la Cámara de los Lores
Speaker	presidente (*m.*) de la Cámara de los Comunes [U.S., de la Cámara de Representantes]
leader	dirigente *m.* & *f.*
caudillo	caudillo *m.*
minister	ministro *m.*
minister without portfolio	ministro (*m.*) sin cartera
Home Secretary [U.S., Secretary of the Interior]	ministro (*m.*) de la Gobernación *or* del Interior
Foreign Secretary [U.S., Secretary of State]	ministro (*m.*) de Asuntos Exteriores *or* de Relaciones Exteriores
Chancellor of the Exchequer [U.S., Secretary of the Treasury]	ministro (*m.*) de Hacienda [*Amer.*, de Finanzas]
Defence Minister	ministro (*m.*) de la Defensa
Army Minister	ministro (*m.*) del Ejército
First Lord of the Admiralty [U.S., Secretary of the Navy]	ministro (*m.*) de Marina
Air Minister	ministro (*m.*) del Aire
Secretary of State for War	ministro (*m.*) de la Guerra
head of the Department of Justice [U.S., Attorney General]	ministro (*m.*) de [Gracia y] Justicia
Minister of Public Works	ministro (*m.*) de Obras Públicas
Secretary of State for Industry	ministro (*m.*) de Industria
President of the Board of Trade	ministro (*m.*) de Comercio
Minister of Education [U.S., Secretary of Education]	ministro (*m.*) de Educación Nacional *or* de Instrucción Pública
Minister of Labour [U.S., Secretary of Labor]	ministro (*m.*) de Trabajo
Secretary of State for Agriculture	ministro (*m.*) de Agricultura
director general	director (*m.*) general
undersecretary	subsecretario *m.*
military governor	gobernador (*m.*) militar
provincial governor	gobernador (*m.*) civil
mayor	alcalde *m.*
(town) councillor	concejal *m.*

III. Politicians. — Hombres (m.) políticos.

politician	político *m.*, hombre (*m.*) político.
statesman	estadista *m.*, hombre (*m.*) de Estado
member of parliament [U.S., congressman]	parlamentario *m.*, diputado *m.*
member of the Cortes	procurador (*m.*) en Cortes
representative	miembro (*m.*) de la Cámara de Representantes
senator; peer	senador *m.*; par *m.*
substitute	suplente *m.*

IV. Institutions and laws. — Instituciones (f.) y leyes, f.

State	Estado *m.*
executive	poder (*m.*) ejecutivo
cabinet	consejo (*m.*) de ministros, gabinete *m.*
ministry	ministerio *m.*
undersecretariat	subsecretaría *f.*
department	departamento *m.*; dirección (*f.*) general; ministerio *m.*
government	gobierno *m.*
judiciary	poder (*m.*) judicial
justice	justicia *f.*
legislature	poder (*m.*) legislativo
legislation	legislación *f.*
code; codification	código *m.*; codificación *f.*
constitution	constitución *f.*
constitutional rights	garantías (*f. pl.*) constitucionales
bill	proyecto (*m.*) de ley
law	ley *f.*
decree; decree-law	decreto *m.*; decreto (*m.*) ley
edict; rule	edicto *m.*; norma *f.*
provision	disposición *f.*
Cortes, Spanish parliament	Cortes *f. pl.*
Assembly; House	Asamblea *f.*; Cámara *f.*
House of Representatives	Cámara (*f.*) de Representantes
House of Lords	Cámara (*f.*) de los Lores
Upper House	Cámara (*f.*) alta
House of Commons	Cámara (*f.*) de los Comunes
Lower House	Cámara (*f.*) baja
Parliament; Senate	Parlamento *m.*; Senado *m.*
convention	convención *f.*
Congress	congreso *m.*
county council	ayuntamiento *m.*; municipio *m.*
front bench	banco (*m.*) azul
town *o* city council	ayuntamiento *m.*, alcaldía *f.*, casa (*f.*) consistorial, consistorio *m.*, concejo (*m.*) municipal.
municipal corporation	municipio *m.*

V. Parties and tendencies. — Partidos (m.) y tendencias, f.

rightist	derechista
imperialist	imperialista
fascist	fascista
totalitarian	totalitario, ria
absolutist	absolutista
monarchist	monárquico, ca
royalist	realista
Conservative; Tory (in Great Britain)	conservador, ra
reactionary	reaccionario, ria
centralist	centralista
Democratic	demócrata
Liberal	liberal
reformist	reformista
progressive	progresista
moderate	moderado, da
radical	radical
federal; federalist	federal; federalista
secessionist	secesionista
separatist	separatista
regionalist	regionalista
leftist	izquierdista
Republican	republicano, na
extremist	extremista
revolutionary	revolucionario, ria
socialist	socialista
Labour [U.S., Labor]	laborista
Marxist	marxista
Communist	comunista
Maoist	maoísta
anarchist	anarquista
terrorist	terrorista
syndicalistic	sindicalista
Labour party	partido (*m.*) laborista, laboristas *m. pl.*
supporter, follower	partidario *m.*, adicto *m.*
adept	adepto *m.*
affiliate; member	afiliado *m.*; miembro *m.*
militant	militante *m.* & *f.*
trade union [U.S., labor union]	sindicato *m.*
spokesman	portavoz *m.* [*Amer.*, vocero *m.*]
chief whip	secretario (*m.*) general de un partido

VI. Political life. — Vida (f.) política.

politics; policy	política *f.*
administration	administración *f.*
govern (to), rule (to)	gobernar; dirigir; regir
reason of state	razón (*f.*) de Estado
legislate (to)	legislar
lawgiver, legislator [U.S., lawmaker]	legislador *m.*
session of the legislature	legislatura *f.*
enact (to)	promulgar
abrogate (to)	abrogar
summon (to)	convocar [el Parlamento]
seat	escaño *m.*, banco *m.*
mandate; term of office	mandato *m.*
duties, functions	funciones *f.*
majority	mayoría *f.*
opposition	oposición *f.*
recess	vacaciones (*f. pl.*) parlamentarias
dissolution of Parliament	disolución (*f.*) del Parlamento
cabinet crisis	crisis (*f.*) ministerial
cabinet reshuffle	reorganización (*f.*)

	ministerial
dismiss (to); dismissal	destituir; destitución *f.*
resign (to); resignation	dimitir; dimisión *f.*
lobby	grupo (*m.*) de presión
referendum	referéndum *m.*
plebiscite	plebiscito *m.*
president-elect	presidente (*m.*) electo
Inauguration Day	investidura *f.*
impeachment	acusación *f.*
demonstration	manifestación *f.*
strike	huelga *f.*
subversion	subversión *f.*
sedition	sedición *f.*
rising, insurrection	levantamiento *m.*, insurrección *f.*
mutiny, riot	motín *m.*
rebellion, revolt	rebelión *f.*, revuelta *f.*
revolution	revolución *f.*
coup d'état	golpe (*m.*) de Estado

VII. Foreign Affairs — Asuntos (*m.*) exteriores.

embassy	embajada *f.*
ambassador	embajador *m.*
consulate; consul	consulado *m.*; cónsul *m.*
legation	legación *f.*
office of attaché	agregaduría *f.*
diplomatic attaché	agregado (*m.*) de embajada
cultural, commercial, military, naval attaché	agregado (*m.*) cultural, comercial, militar, naval
plenipotentiary	plenipotenciario *m.*
chancellory, chancellery	cancillería *f.*
passport	pasaporte *m.*
visa	visado *m.* [*Amer.*, visa *f.*]
credential letters, letter of credence, letters credential	cartas (*f.*) credenciales
extraterritoriality	extraterritorialidad *f.*
diplomat	diplomático *m.*
diplomatic bag *o* pouch	valija (*f.*) diplomática
negotiations	negociaciones *f.*
negotiator	negociador *m.*
mediator	mediador *m.*
convention	convenio *m.*
commitment	compromiso *m.*
bilateral agreement	acuerdo (*m.*) bilateral
treaty; covenant	tratado *m.*; pacto *m.*
protocol; chart	protocolo *m.*; carta *f.*
nonintervention treaty	tratado (*m.*) de no intervención
contracting parties	partes (*f.*) contratantes
neutrality	neutralidad *f.*
belligerence	beligerancia *f.*

VIII. Elections. — Elecciones, *f.*

franchise, right to vote	derecho (*m.*) de voto
suffrage	sufragio *m.*
suffragist; suffragette	sufragista *m.*; sufragista *f.*
vote	votación *f.*; voto *m.*
vote (to); poll	votar; votación *f.*
constituency	distrito (*m.*) electoral
polling place *o* station	centro (*m.*) electoral
electoral college	colegio (*m.*) electoral
candidate	candidato *m.*
candidacy, candidature	candidatura *f.*
elegible	elegible
nominate (to)	presentar la candidatura de
to run for the office of	presentar su candidatura a
register	lista (*f.*) electoral
platform	plataforma *f.* programa *m.*
electioneering, election campaign	campaña (*f.*) electoral
electoral meeting	reunión (*f.*) electoral
meeting, rally	mitin *m.*
opinion poll	sondeo (*m.*) de opinión
electorate, voters	electores *m. pl.*, votantes *m. pl.*
by-election	elección (*f.*) parcial
primary	elección (*f.*) primaria
voting by list	escrutinio (*m.*) de lista
vote by proxy	votación (*f.*) por poderes
vote by show of hands, by roll call	votación (*f.*) a mano alzada, nominal
first, second ballot	primera, segunda votación *f.*
secret ballot	votación (*f.*) secreta
casting vote	voto (*m.*) de calidad
quorum	quórum *m.*
absolute *o* simple, relative majority	mayoría (*f.*) absoluta, relativa
minority	minoría *f.*
vote of confidence	voto (*m.*) de confianza
vote of censure *o* of no confidence	voto (*m.*) de censura
ballot paper, voting slip *o* paper	papeleta (*f.*) de votación
blank, null and void *o* invalid ballot paper	voto (*m.*) en blanco, nulo
polling booth	cabina (*f.*) electoral
ballot box	urna *f.*
voting machine	máquina (*f.*) de votar
teller	escrutador *m.*
to count the votes	hacer el escrutinio *or* el recuento de votos
registered voters	inscritos *m.*
votes cast	votos (*m.*) *or* sufragios (*m.*) emitidos
no-voter	abstencionista *m.* y *f.*
abstention	abstención *f.*
tie, draw, equality of votes	empate *m.*, igualdad (*f.*) de votos
veto	veto *m.*
veto (to)	vetar

See also JURÍDICO and CONFERENCES

polynomial [ˌpɔliˈnəumjəl] adj. MATH. Polinómico, ca.
— N. MATH. Polinomio, *m.*

polyp [ˈpɔlip] n. ZOOL. MED. Pólipo, *m.*

polypary [ˈpɔlipəri] n. ZOOL. Polípero, *m.*

polypeptide [ˌpɔliˈpeptaid] n. CHEM. Polipéptido, *m.*

polypetalous [pɔliˈpetələs] adj. BOT. Polipétalo, la.

polyphase [ˈpɔlifeiz] adj. ELECTR. Polifásico, ca.

polyphonic [ˌpɔliˈfɔnik] adj. Polifónico, ca.

polyphony [pəˈlifəni] n. Polifonía, *f.*

polypus [ˈpɔlipəs] n. MED. Pólipo, *m.*

— OBSERV. El plural de *polypus* es *polypi* o *polypuses.*

polysaccharide [pɔliˈsækəraid] n. CHEM. Polisacárido, *m.*

polysemy [ˈpɔlisəmi] n. Polisemia, *f.*

polystyrene [ˌpɔliˈstairiːn] n. CHEM. Poliestireno, *m.*

polysyllabic [ˈpɔlisiˈlæbik] or **polysyllabical** [—əl] adj. Polisílabo, ba; polisilábico, ca.

polysyllable [ˈpɔliˌsiləbl] n. Polisílabo, *m.*

polytechnic [ˌpɔliˈteknik] adj. Politécnico, ca.
— N. Escuela (*f.*) politécnica.

polytechnical [—əl] adj. Politécnico, ca.

polytheism [ˈpɔliθiːizəm] n. Politeísmo, *m.*

polytheist [ˈpɔliˌθiəst] n. Politeísta, *m.* & *f.*

polytheistic [ˌpɔliθiːˈistik] or **polytheistical** [—əl] adj. Politeísta.

polythene [ˈpɔliθiːn] n. CHEM. Polietileno, *m.*

polyvalence [ˌpɔliˈveiləns] n. Polivalencia, *f.*

polyvalent [ˌpɔliˈveilənt] adj. Polivalente.

polyvinyl [ˌpɔliˈvainil] n. CHEM. Polivinilo, *m.*

pomace [ˈpʌmis] n. Pulpa (*f.*) de manzana (apple pulp). || Pulpa, *f.* (of seeds).

pomaceous [pəuˈmeiʃəs] adj. BOT. Pomáceo, a.

pomade [pəˈmɑːd] n. Pomada, *f.*

pomander [pəuˈmændə*] n. Almohadilla (*f.*) perfumada.

pomatum [pəuˈmeitəm] n. Pomada, *f.*

pomegranate [ˈpɔmˌgrænit] n. BOT. Granada, *f.* (fruit). | Granado, *m.* (tree).

pomelo [ˈpɔmiləu] n. BOT. Pomelo, *m.* (grapefruit).

pomfret [ˈpɔmfrət] n. Japuta, *f.* (fish).

pommel [ˈpʌml] n. Pomo, *m.* (knob on sword handle). || Perilla, *f.* (of a saddle).

pommel [ˈpʌml] v. tr. Aporrear.

pommy [ˈpɔmi] n. FAM. Inglés, esa [palabra despectiva empleada en Australia].

pomp [pɔmp] n. Pompa, *f.*

pompadour [ˈpɔmpəduə*] n. Copete, *m.* (hairstyle).

pompano [ˈpɔmpənəu] n. ZOOL. Pámpano, *m.* (fish).

— OBSERV. El plural de la palabra inglesa *pompano* es *pompano* o *pompanos.*

Pompeian [pɔmˈpiːən] adj./n. Pompeyano, na.

Pompeii [pɔmˈpiːai] pr. n. GEOGR. Pompeya, *f.*

Pompeius [pɔmˈpeiəs] pr. n. Pompeyo, *m.* (Sextus).

Pompey [ˈpɔmpi] pr. n. Pompeyo, *m.* (Magnus).

pom-pom [ˈpɔmpɔm] n. MIL. Cañón (*m.*) antiaéreo.

pompon [ˈpɔ̃ːmpɔ̃ːŋ] n. Borla, *f.* (on a hat). || BOT. Rosa (*f.*) de pitiminí. | Variedad (*f.*) de crisantemo.

pomposity [pɔmˈpɔsiti] n. Pomposidad, *f.* (splendour, grandiloquence). || Presunción, *f.*, ostentación, *f.* (pretentiousness).

pompous [ˈpɔmpəs] adj. Pomposo, sa (style, occasion, etc.). || Presumido, da; ostentoso, sa (pretentious).

ponce [pɔns] n. FAM. Chulo, *m.*

poncho [ˈpɔntʃəu] n. Poncho, *m.*

pond [pɔnd] n. Charca, *f.* (natural). || Estanque, *m.* (artificial). || Vivero, *m.* (for breeding fish).

ponder [—ə*] v. tr. Considerar, examinar, sopesar.
— V. intr. Meditar, reflexionar. || *To ponder on* o *over,* meditar *or* reflexionar sobre.

ponderable [—ərəbl] adj. Ponderable.

ponderous [—ərəs] adj. Laborioso, sa; pesado, da: *ponderous style, movement,* estilo, movimiento laborioso. || Pesado, da (heavy).

pone [pəun] n. U. S. Pan (*m.*) de maíz, borona, *f.* [*Amer.*, arepa, *f.*]

pong [pɔŋ] v. intr. FAM. Apestar, heder.

poniard [ˈpɔnjəd] n. Puñal, *m.*

poniard [ˈpɔnjəd] v. tr. Apuñalar.

pons [pɔnz] n. ANAT. Puente (*m.*) de Varolio. || FIG. *Pons asinorum,* puente (*m.*) de los asnos.

pontifex [ˈpɔntifeks] n. HIST. Pontífice, *m.*

— OBSERV. El plural de *pontifex* es *pontifices.*

pontiff [ˈpɔntif] n. REL. Pontífice, *m.* || *Sovereign Pontiff,* Sumo Pontífice.

pontifical [pɔnˈtifikəl] adj. REL. Pontifical, pontificio, cia: *pontifical mass,* misa pontifical. || FIG. Presuntuoso, sa (pretentious). | Dogmático, ca; sentencioso, sa (dogmatic).
— N. REL. Pontifical, *m.* (book). || — Pl. Pontifical, *m. sing.* (garments and insignia).

pontificate [pɔnˈtifikit] n. REL. Pontificado, *m.*

pontificate [pɔnˈtifikeit] v. intr. Pontificar.

pontifices [pɔnˈtifisiːz] pl. n. See PONTIFEX.

Pontius Pilate [ˈpɔntjəsˈpailət] pr. n. Poncio Pilato, *m.*

ponton [ˈpɔntən] n. U. S. MIL. Pontón, *m.*

pontoneer (U. S. **pontonier**) [ˌpɔntəˈniə*] n. MIL. Pontonero, *m.*

pontoon [pɔn'tu:n] n. Pontón, *m.* (bridge of boats). || AVIAT. Flotador, *m.* || Veintiuna, *f.* (card game). || *Pontoon bridge*, puente de pontones.

pony ['pəuni] n. Poney, *m.*, jaca, *f.* (horse). || FAM. Veinticinco libras, *f. pl.* || U. S. FAM. Chuleta, *f.* [para exámenes] (crib). | Copa (*f.*) de licor (liqueur glass). || U. S. *Pony express*, sistema (*m.*) postal que consistía en enviar el correo por el intermediario de hombres a caballo.

ponytail [—teil] n. Cola (*f.*) de caballo (hairstyle).

pooch [putʃ] n. U. S. FAM. Perro, *m.*

poodle ['pu:dl] n. Perro, (*m.*) de lanas, caniche, *m.*

pooh [pu:] interj. ¡Bah!

pooh-pooh [pu:'pu:] v. tr. Despreciar, desdeñar (to treat with contempt).

pool [pu:l] n. Estanque, *m.* (artificial pond). || Charca, *f.* (natural pond). || Pozo, *m.* (in stream or river). || Charco, *m.*: *a pool of blood, rainwater*, un charco de sangre, de agua de lluvia. || Piscina, *f.* [*Amer.*, pileta, *f.*] (swimming pool). || Pozo, *m.*, bote, *m.*, banca, *f.*, plato, *m.* (in card games). || Guerra, *f.* (game of billiards played for money). || Billar (*m.*) americano (pocket billiards). || COMM. Fondos (*m. pl.*) comunes, capital (*m.*) común (common fund). | Recursos (*m. pl.*) comunes (combination of resources). | Consorcio, *m.* (consortium). || FIG. Reserva, *f.* (reserve). | Fuente, *f.* (source). || — Pl. Quinielas, *f.* (football pools). || — *Pool table*, billar, *m.*, mesa (*f.*) de billar. || *Typing pool*, servicio (*m.*) de mecanografía.

pool [pu:l] v. tr. Aunar, unir (knowledge, strength). || Poner en un fondo común (money). || Reunir (resources).

poolroom [—ru:m] n. Billar, *m.*, sala (*f.*) de billar.

poop [pu:p] n. MAR. Popa, *f.* (stern). | Toldilla, *f.* (poop deck).

poop [pu:p] v. tr. MAR. Recibir [un golpe de mar] por la popa. || Romper sobre la popa de [un barco] (waves).

poop deck [—dek] n. MAR. Toldilla, *f.*

poor [puə*] adj. Pobre: *the poor countries of the world*, los países pobres del mundo; *the tragedy of being old and poor*, la tragedia de ser viejo y pobre. || Pobre, necesitado, da: *a poor family*, una familia pobre. || Malo, la: *poor quality*, mala calidad; *poor memory*, mala memoria; *to have a poor night*, pasar una mala noche; *to be a poor actor*, ser mal actor; *poor excuse*, mala excusa. || Escaso, sa; poco numeroso, sa: *poor attendance*, asistencia poco numerosa. || Pobre: *poor in vitamins*, pobre en vitaminas. || Escaso, sa; malo, la (scanty): *a poor harvest*, una cosecha escasa; *poor output*, producción escasa. || Pobre, poco fértil: *poor soil*, terreno pobre. || Mediocre (lacking excellence): *a poor speaker*, un orador mediocre; *a poor worker*, un trabajador mediocre. || Tontaina, necio, cia (stupid): *poor character*, persona tontaina. || Malo, la; delicado, da: *poor health*, salud delicada. || Humilde (humble). || Pobre: *I am but a poor tramp*, no soy sino un pobre vagabundo. || Desgraciado, da (unfortunate, wretched). || Poco favorable: *to have a poor opinion of*, tener una opinión poco favorable de. || FIG. Pobre, pobrecito, ta: *poor child!*, ¡pobrecito niño!; *poor me!*, ¡pobre de mí!; *poor John broke his neck*, el pobre [de] Juan se rompió la nuca. || — *I have but a poor chance of success*, tengo poca probabilidad de éxito. || *Poor thing!*, ¡pobrecito!, ¡pobrecita! || *To be a poor liar*, mentir mal, no saber mentir. || *To be as poor as a church mouse*, ser más pobre que las ratas. || *To be poor at*, ser flojo en, ser poco fuerte en: *I am poor at mathematics*, soy flojo en matemáticas. || *To be two hundred pounds the poorer*, salir perdiendo doscientas libras. || FIG. *To give a poor performance*, hacer un pobre papel.
— N. *The poor*, los pobres.

poor box [—bɔks] n. Cepillo (*m.*) de los pobres.

poorhouse [—haus] n. U. S. Asilo (*m.*) para los pobres.

poorly [—li] adv. Mal: *poorly fed*, mal alimentado. || Pobremente. || — *To be doing poorly*, ir mal. || *To think poorly of*, tener mala opinión de.
— Adj. *To be poorly*, estar malo. || *You are looking very poorly*, tienes muy mala cara.

poorness [—nis] n. Pobreza, *f.* (poverty). || Mala calidad, *f.* (bad quality).

poor-spirited [puə'spiritid] adj. Pusilánime, apocado, da.

pop [pɔp] n. Explosión, *f.*, detonación, *f.* (sound). || Taponazo, *m.* (of a bottle opening). || FAM. Bebida (*f.*) gaseosa (fizzy drink). | Gaseosa, *f.* (lemonade). || FAM. Papá, *m.* (father). || — FAM. *In pop*, empeñado (in pawn). || *To go pop*, explotar, hacer pum.
— Adj. Popular. || — *Pop concert, festival*, concierto (*m.*), festival (*m.*) de música popular. || *Pop music*, música "pop".
— Interj. ¡Pum!

pop [pɔp] v. tr. Pinchar, hacer reventar (to burst with sth. sharp). || Meter: *to pop sth. into one's mouth*, meterse algo en la boca. || Hacer saltar (a cork). || FAM. Empeñar (to pawn). || — *To pop one's head out*, asomar [de repente] la cabeza. || FIG. *To pop the question*, declararse.
— V. intr. Explotar, estallar; reventar: *the balloon popped*, el globo explotó. || Saltar (a cork). || Disparar (to shoot).
— ***To pop across*** o ***by*** o ***over*** o ***round***, acercarse, pasar: *pop by the baker's on your way back*, acércate a la panadería a la vuelta; *pop by and see me*, acércate a verme. || ***To pop in***, entrar un momento: *are you sure you won't pop in?*, ¿está seguro de que no quiere entrar un momento? | Asomarse: *he only popped in at the meeting*, no hizo más que asomarse a la reunión. | Acercarse, pasar: *John popped in this morning*, Juan pasó esta mañana; *pop in at the baker's for me*, pasa por la panadería por favor. | Venir (to come). || ***To pop off***, irse, marcharse (to go). | FAM. Palmar (to die). || ***To pop out***, saltar (a cork, etc.). | Salir: *he's just popped out for a moment*, ha salido un momento; *pop out and buy some milk*, sal un momento a comprar leche. | Salir de pronto: *to pop out from behind a tree*, salir de pronto de detrás de un árbol. || ***To pop up***, aparecer de pronto (to appear suddenly). | Surgir (to arise): *this question has popped up before*, esta cuestión ha surgido ya.

popcorn [—kɔ:n] n. Palomitas (*f. pl.*) de maíz, rosetas (*f. pl.*) de maíz.

pope [pəup] n. REL. Papa, *m.*: *Pope Pious IX*, el Papa Pío IX. || Pope, *m.* (Orthodox priest).

popedom [—dəm] n. Papado, *m.*

popery ['pəupəri] n. REL. Papismo, *m.*

popeyed ['pɔpaid] adj. De ojos saltones. || *He looked at her popeyed*, le miró con los ojos desorbitados.

popgun ['pɔpgʌn] n. Pistola (*f.*) de aire comprimido (toy).

popinjay ['pɔpindʒei] n. Petimetre, *m.*, pedante, *m.*

popish ['pəupiʃ] adj. Papista.

poplar ['pɔplə*] n. BOT. Álamo, *m.* || U. S. Tulipero, *m.*, tulipanero, *m.* || — *Black poplar*, álamo negro, chopo, *m.* || *White poplar*, álamo blanco.

poplin ['pɔplin] n. Popelín, *m.*, popelina, *f.*

popliteal [pɔ'plitiəl] adj. ANAT. Poplíteo, a.

poppet ['pɔpet] n. TECH. Cabezal, *m.* (lathe head). || MAR. Escálamo, *m.* || FAM. *My poppet*, hijo mío, hija mía.

poppethead [—hed] n. TECH. Cabezal, *m.* (of a lathe).

popping crease ['pɔpiŋkri:s] n. SP. Línea (*f.*) del bateador (in cricket).

popple ['pɔpl] n. Chapoteo, *m.* (of water).

popple ['pɔpl] v. intr. Chapotear.

poppy ['pɔpi] n. BOT. Amapola, *f.* (red flower). | Adormidera, *f.* (used in pharmacy).

poppycock [—kɔk] n. Tonterías, *f. pl.*, necedades, *f. pl.* (nonsense).

popsy ['pɔpsi] n. FAM. Chica, *f.*, niña, *f.*

populace ['pɔpjuləs] n. Pueblo, *m.*, vulgo, *m.* (common people). || Populacho, *m.* (rabble).

popular ['pɔpjulə*] adj. Popular: *a popular play*, una obra popular; *popular prices*, precios populares. || Democrático, ca: *a popular election*, una elección democrática. || Corriente, generalizado, da: *popular opinions*, opiniones corrientes. || Estimado, da: *officer popular amongst his friends*, oficial estimado por sus amigos. || Popular, de moda (fashionable). || — *Popular front*, frente popular. || *To be popular with the girls*, tener éxito con las chicas.

popularity [,pɔpju'læriti] n. Popularidad, *f.*

popularization ['pɔpjulərai'zeiʃən] n. Popularización, *f.*, vulgarización, *f.*

popularize ['pɔpjuləraiz] v. tr. Popularizar, vulgarizar.

populate ['pɔpjuleit] v. tr. Poblar.

population [,pɔpju'leiʃən] n. Población, *f.*: *working population*, población activa: *the population of Spain*, la población española; *an increase in population*, un aumento de la población. || BIOL. Población, *f.* || *The population explosion*, la explosión demográfica.

Populist ['pɔpjulist] n. Populista, *m.* & *f.*

populous ['pɔpjuləs] adj. Muy poblado, da; populoso, sa.

populousness [—nis] n. Densidad (*f.*) de población.

porcelain ['pɔ:səlin] n. Porcelana, *f.*
— Adj. De porcelana.

porcellaneous or **porcelaneous** [,pɔ:sə'leinjəs] adj. De porcelana (made of porcelain). || De la porcelana (relative to porcelain). || Frágil.

porch [pɔ:tʃ] n. Pórtico, *m.* (of a building). || U. S. Porche, *m.*, portal, *m.*

porcine ['pɔ:sain] adj. Porcino, na.

porcupine ['pɔ:kjupain] n. ZOOL. Puerco (*m.*) espín.

pore [pɔ:*] n. ANAT. BOT. Poro, *m.*

pore [pɔ:*] v. intr. *To pore over*, estudiar detenidamente (to study), reflexionar sobre (to think about).

porgy ['pɔ:dʒi] n. Pargo, *m.*, pagro, *m.* (fish).
— OBSERV. El plural de *porgy* es *porgies* o *porgy*.

pork [pɔ:k] n. CULIN. Cerdo, *m.*, carne (*f.*) de cerdo: *pork chop*, chuleta de cerdo. || CULIN. *Pork sausage*, salchicha, *f.*

pork barrel [—'bærəl] n. FAM. Fondos (*m. pl.*) públicos asignados a un proyecto local para fines electorales.

pork butcher [—'butʃə*] n. Chacinero, ra; salchichero, ra [*Amer.*, chanchero, ra]. || *Pork butcher's*, chacinería, *f.*, salchichería, *f.* [*Amer.*, chanchería, *f.*].

porker [—ə*] n. Cebón, *m.*

porkpie [—,pai] n. Empanada (*f.*) de carne de cerdo. || Sombrero (*m.*) de copa baja (hat).

porky [—i] adj. FAM. Gordo, da; gordinflón, ona.

pornographer [pɔ:'nɔgrəfə*] n. Pornógrafo, *m.*

pornographic [,pɔ:nə'græfik] adj. Pornográfico, ca.

pornography [pɔ:'nɔgrəfi] n. Pornografía, *f.*

porosity [pɔ:'rɔsiti] n. Porosidad, *f.*

porous [ˈpɔːrəs] adj. Poroso, sa.
porousness [—nis] n. Porosidad, *f.*
porphyritic [pɔːfiˈritik] adj. MIN. Porfídico, ca; porfírico, ca.
porphyry [ˈpɔːfiri] n. MIN. Pórfido, *m.*, pórfiro, *m.*
porpoise [ˈpɔːpəs] n. ZOOL. Marsopa, *f.*, marsopla, *f.* (cetacean).
porridge [ˈpɔridʒ] n. CULIN. Gachas (*f. pl.*) de avena.
porringer [ˈpɔrindʒə*] n. Plato (*m.*) hondo (small bowl).
port [pɔːt] n. MAR. Puerto, *m.* (harbour): *sea port*, puerto marítimo; *fishing port*, puerto pesquero; *port of entry*, puerto de entrada. | Babor, *m.* (left side). | Portilla, *f.* (porthole). | Porta, *f.* (gunhole). || TECH. Lumbrera, *f.* || Oporto, *m.* (wine). || — FIG. *Any port in a storm*, la necesidad carece de ley. || *Commercial* o *trading port*, puerto comercial. || *Free port*, puerto franco *or* libre. || *Outer port*, antepuerto, *m.* || MAR. *Port of call*, puerto de escala *or* de arribada. | *Port of registry* o *home port*, puerto de amarre *or* de matrícula. || *To come into port* o *to put into port*, tomar puerto, arribar. || *To get safely into port*, llegar a buen puerto.
— Adj. Portuario, ria: *port duties*, derechos portuarios; *port authority*, autoridad portuaria; *port facilities*, instalaciones portuarias.
port [pɔːt] v. tr. MAR. Poner a babor. || MIL. Presentar: *port arms!*, ¡presenten armas! || MAR. *To port the helm*, poner el timón a babor, virar a babor.
— V. intr. MAR. Virar a babor.
portable [—əbl] adj. Portátil: *portable typewriter*, máquina de escribir portátil.
— N. Objeto (*m.*) portátil. || Máquina (*f.*) de escribir portátil (typewriter).
portage [—idʒ] n. Porteo, *m.*, transporte, *m.*, porte, *m.* (transportation). || Porte, *m.* (cost).
portal [ˈpɔːtl] adj. ANAT. Porta: *portal vein*, vena porta.
— N. ARCH. Pórtico, *m.*, portal, *m.* || ANAT. Vena (*f.*) porta.
portal-to-portal pay [ˈpɔːtəltəˈpɔrtəlˈpei] n. U. S. Remuneración (*f.*) que tiene en cuenta el tiempo pasado entre la empresa y el sitio donde se efectúa realmente el trabajo.
portative [ˈpɔːtətiv] adj. Portátil (portable).
Port-au-Prince [pɔːtəuprɛ̃s] pr. n. GEOGR. Puerto Príncipe (Haití).
portcullis [pɔːtˈkʌlis] n. Rastrillo, *m.*
portend [pɔːˈtend] v. tr. Presagiar, augurar. || Anunciar: *dark clouds that portend a storm*, nubarrones que anuncian una tempestad.
portent [ˈpɔːtent] n. Presagio, *m.*, augurio, *m.* (omen). || Portento, *m.*, prodigio, *m.* (prodigy).
portentous [pɔːˈtentəs] adj. De mal agüero, siniestro, tra (ominous): *portentous news*, noticias de mal agüero. || Portentoso, sa; prodigioso, sa (prodigious).
porter [ˈpɔːtə*] n. Portero, ra (doorkeeper). || Conserje, *m.* (in government buildings). || Maletero, *m.*, mozo, *m.* (baggage carrier). || Mozo (*m.*) de cuerda (person who carries things). || Mozo, *m.* (attendant). || Cerveza (*f.*) negra (dark-brown beer).
porterage [—ridʒ] n. COMM. Porte, *m.*, transporte, *m.* (transport, cost).
porterhouse [—haus] n. Mesón, *m.* || CULIN. *Porterhouse steak*, bistec (*m.*) de solomillo.
porter's lodge [—zˌlɔdʒ] n. Portería, *f.*
portfolio [pɔːtˈfəuljəu] n. Cartera, *f.* (briefcase). || Carpeta, *f.* (folder). || Cartera, *f.*: *minister without portfolio*, ministro sin cartera. || COMM. Cartera, *f.*: *securities in portfolio*, valores en cartera.
porthole [ˈpɔːthəul] n. MAR. Portilla, *f.* (window). || MIL. Tronera, *f.*, cañonera, *f.* (for cannon, etc.).
portico [ˈpɔːtikəu] n. ARCH. Pórtico, *m.*
— OBSERV. El plural de la palabra inglesa es *porticos* o *porticoes*.
portion [ˈpɔːʃən] n. Porción, *f.*, parte, *f.* || Parte, *f.*: *he got the biggest portion of the profits*, obtuvo la mayor parte de los beneficios. || Ración, *f.* (of food): *a portion of cheese*, una ración de queso. || Trozo, *m.*, porción, *f.* (of cake). || JUR. Parte, *f.* (of inheritance). || Dote, *f.* (dowry). || Sino, *m.*, destino, *m.* (destiny).
portion [ˈpɔːʃən] v. tr. Dividir (to divide). || Repartir, distribuir (to distribute). || Dotar (to endow).
— OBSERV. Este verbo va seguido muchas veces por *out* sin que cambie su sentido.
portionless [—lis] adj. Sin dote.
portland cement [ˈpɔːtləndsiˈment] n. Portland, *m.*
portliness [ˈpɔːtlinis] n. Corpulencia, *f.*, gordura, *f.*
portly [ˈpɔːtli] adj. Corpulento, ta; gordo, da (stout).
portmanteau [pɔːtˈmæntəu] n. Maleta, *f.* (suitcase).
— OBSERV. El plural de la palabra inglesa es *portmanteaus* o *portmanteaux*.
portmanteau word [—wəːd] n. GRAMM. Palabra (*f.*) formada por la combinación de otras dos.
Porto Rican [ˌpɔːtəuˈriːkən] adj./n. Puertorriqueño, ña; portorriqueño, ña.
Porto Rico [ˌpɔːtəuˈriːkəu] pr. n. GEOGR. Puerto Rico.
portrait [ˈpɔːtrit] n. Retrato, *m.*: *half-length portrait*, retrato de medio cuerpo; *full-length portrait*, retrato de cuerpo entero. || — *To have one's portrait painted* o *to sit for one's portrait*, hacerse retratar. || *To take s.o.'s portrait*, retratar a alguien.
portraitist [—ist] n. Retratista, *m.* & .
portraiture [ˈpɔːtritʃə] n. Retrato, *m.* || FIG. Descripción, *f.*
portray [pɔːˈtrei] v. tr. Retratar, pintar (in painting). || Retratar (with a camera). || FIG. Pintar, describir (to describe). | Representar (to represent).
portrayal [pɔːˈtreiəl] n. Retrato, *m.* (portrait). || FIG. Descripción, *f.* | Representación, *f.*
portress [ˈpɔːtris] n. Portera, *f.* (doorkeeper).
Portugal [ˈpɔːtjugəl] pr. n. GEOGR. Portugal, *m.*
Portuguese [ˌpɔːtjuˈgiːz] adj. Portugués, esa.
— N. Portugués, esa (people). || Portugués, *m.* (language). || *The Portuguese*, los portugueses.
pose [pəuz] n. Postura, *f.*, actitud, *f.* (of the body). || FIG. Afectación, *f.*, pose, *f.* (pretence).
pose [pəuz] v. tr. Colocar, hacer tomar una postura (model). || Plantear (a problem). || Formular, hacer (question): *I don't like the way you pose the question*, no me gusta su manera de formular la pregunta. || Dejar perplejo (to puzzle).
— V. intr. Posar (model). || FIG. Darse tono, presumir (to be conceited). || FIG. *To pose as*, dárselas de: *he poses as an intellectual*, se las da de intelectual.
Poseidon [pɔˈsaidən] pr. n. MYTH. Poseidón, *m.*
poser [ˈpəuzə*] n. Pregunta (*f.*) difícil (question). || Cuestión (*f.*) *or* problema (*m.*) difícil (problem).
poseur [pəuˈzəː*] n. Presumido, da.
posh [pɔʃ] adj. FAM. Elegante, distinguido, da (elegant): *posh clothes*, ropa elegante; *I live in a posh district*, vivo en un barrio elegante. | De lujo (luxurious): *a posh hotel*, un hotel de lujo. | Afectado, da: *he speaks with a posh accent*, habla con un acento afectado. | Cursi (in bad taste).
— Adv. *To talk posh*, hablar con un tono afectado.
posh [pɔʃ] v. tr. *To posh o.s. up*, arreglarse. || *To posh up*, arreglar.
posit [ˈpɔzit] v. tr. Postular (to postulate). || Proponer (to propose). || Colocar, situar (to situate).
position [pəˈziʃən] n. Posición, *f.*, situación, *f.* (place). || Sitio, *m.*: *from this position you can see the whole field*, desde este sitio se puede ver todo el campo. || Posición, *f.*, postura, *f.* (of the body, etc.): *vertical position*, posición vertical. || Situación, *f.*: *what is the position in Europe?*, ¿cuál es la situación en Europa? || Punto (*m.*) de vista (point of view). || Opinión, *f.*: *to state one's position*, manifestar su opinión. || Posición, *f.*, postura, *f.*: *to take up a position on a problem*, adoptar una postura sobre un problema. || Posición, *f.* [social], categoría, *f.*, rango, *m.* (rank). || Condiciones, *f. pl.*: *in a position to marry*, en condiciones de casarse. || Puesto, *m.*: *he has a good position in a ministry*, tiene un buen puesto en un ministerio. || Cargo, *m.*, puesto, *m.*, empleo, *m.* (employment). || Puesto, *m.* (in a class). || Taquilla, *f.* (at the post office). || MIL. MAR. Posición, *f.* || — *In a position to*, en condición *or* en condiciones de. || *Out of position*, fuera de lugar. || *Put yourself in my position*, ponte en mi lugar. || *To be in a position of trust*, tener *or* ocupar un puesto de confianza. || FIG. *To know one's position*, saber cuál es su sitio. || *To place in position*, colocar.
position [pəˈziʃən] v. tr. Situar, colocar, disponer.
position light [—lait] n. MAR. AVIAT. Luz (*f.*) de situación.
positive [ˈpɔzətiv] adj. Seguro, ra (convinced): *I am positive about* o *of it*, estoy seguro de ello. || Formal (order). || Tajante, categórico, ca: *positive tone of voice*, tono categórico. || Verdadero, ra; auténtico, ca: *it's a positive robbery*, es un verdadero robo; *a positive miracle*, un milagro auténtico. || Evidente: *positive proof*, prueba evidente. || Afirmativo, va; categórico, ca (affirmative): *don't be so positive*, no sea tan categórico. || Enérgico, ca: *he is a very positive person*, es una persona muy enérgica. || Positivo, va (not negative): *we reached a positive conclusion*, llegamos a una conclusión positiva. || PHYS. BIOL. CHEM. Positivo, va: *positive ray*, rayo positivo; *positive electricity*, electricidad positiva. || PHIL. GRAMM. MATH. Positivo, va. || COMM. Firme, en firme: *positive offer*, oferta firme. || PHOT. *Positive print*, positiva, *f.*
— N. PHOT. Positiva, *f.* || GRAMM. Positivo, *m.* || ELECTR. Polo (*m.*) positivo. || Lo positivo.
positively [—li] adv. Afirmativamente, positivamente (affirmatively): *I answered him positively*, le contesté afirmativamente. || Categóricamente, rotundamente: *I positively refused to go*, me negué rotundamente a ir. || Verdaderamente, realmente: *he is positively stupid*, es realmente estúpido. || Totalmente (completely). || *I can't speak positively*, no puedo asegurar nada.
positiveness [—nis] n. Seguridad, *f.*
positivism [ˈpɔzitivizəm] n. PHIL. Positivismo, *m.*
positivist [ˈpɔzitivist] n. PHIL. Positivista, *m.* & *f.*
positron [ˈpɔzitrɔn] n. PHYS. Positrón, *m.*, positón, *m.*
posology [pəˈsɔlədʒi] n. MED. Posología, *f.*
posse [ˈpɔsi] n. Pelotón, *m.* (of police). || Grupo, *m.* (of people).
possess [pəˈzes] v. tr. Poseer, tener: *he possesses an aeroplane*, posee un avión; *to possess endless patience*, tener una paciencia inagotable. || Poseer: *he is possessed by the devil*, está poseído por el demonio. || Dominar (to command): *he possesses French*, domina el francés. || Poseer (a woman). || — *To be possessed of*, tener (a quality, a property). || *To possess o.s. in*

patience, armarse de paciencia. || *To possess o.s. of*, apoderarse de. || *What possessed him to kill her?*, ¿cómo se le ocurrió matarla?

possessed [pəˈzest] adj. Poseído, da; poseso, sa (controlled by a spirit). || Obsesionado, da: *possessed with an idea*, obsesionado por una idea. || Poseído, da (by fear, etc.). || *To scream like one possessed*, gritar como un endemoniado *or* como un poseído.

possession [pəˈzeʃən] n. Posesión, *f.* (act, object): *to take possession of*, tomar posesión de. || REL. Posesión, *f.* (by a devil). || Posesión, *f.* (colony). || JUR. Tenencia, *f.*: *illicit possession of arms*, tenencia ilícita de armas. || — Pl. Bienes, *m.* (estate). || — *House for sale with vacant possession*, casa que se vende desocupada. || *In full possession of one's faculties*, con pleno dominio de sus facultades. || *To be in possession of*, tener. || *To be in the possession of*, estar en manos de. || *To come into possession of*, adquirir. || *To come into the possession of*, llegar a las manos de. || *To have sth. in one's possession*, tener algo [en su poder].

possessive [pəˈzesiv] adj. Posesivo, va. || GRAMM. Posesivo, va.
— N. GRAMM. Posesivo, *m.*

possessor [pəˈzesə*] n. Poseedor, ra.

possessory [pəˈzesəri] adj. Posesorio, ria.

possibility [ˌpɔsəˈbiliti] n. Posibilidad, *f.*: *I admit the possibility of your being right*, admito la posibilidad de que tenga razón. || Posibilidad, *f.*, eventualidad, *f.* (event): *to foresee all the possibilities*, prever todas las posibilidades. || — *If by any possibility*, si por casualidad. || *There is no possibility of my going there*, es imposible que vaya allí. || *To have possibilities*, ser prometedor (artist, project, etc.). || *Within the bounds of possibility*, dentro de lo posible.

possible [ˈpɔsəbl] adj. Posible: *a possible success*, un posible éxito. || Aceptable (reasonably satisfactory). || — *As best as possible*, lo mejor posible. || *As far as possible*, en la medida de lo posible, en lo posible. || *As much as possible*, todo lo posible. || *As often as possible*, lo más frecuentemente posible. || *As soon as possible*, tan pronto como sea posible, lo antes posible, cuanto antes. || *If possible*, de ser posible, si es posible. || *It is possible that*, puede ser que, es posible que. || *To make* o *to render possible*, hacer posible, posibilitar.
— N. Máximo, *m.* (maximum score). || Candidato (*m.*) posible: *there are two possibles for the post*, hay dos candidatos posibles para el puesto.

possibly [—i] adv. Probablemente, posiblemente. || Quizás, tal vez (perhaps). || *I cannot possibly do it*, no puedo hacerlo.

possum [ˈpɔsəm] n. ZOOL. Zarigüeya, *f.* || FAM. *To play possum*, hacerse el muerto.

post [pəust] n. Poste, *m.* (pole). || Estaca, *f.*, palo, *m.* (stake). || SP. Línea (*f.*) de llegada, llegada, *f.*, meta, *f.* (finishing). | Línea (*f.*) de salida (starting). || Correos, *m. pl.*, casa (*f.*) de correos (post office): *to take a letter to the post*, llevar una carta a correos. || Recogida, *f.* (collection of letters): *at what time does the post go?*, ¿a qué hora es la recogida? || Correo, *m.*: *has the post come?*, ¿ha venido el correo?; *registered post*, correo certificado; *by post*, por correo. || Cartas, *f. pl.*: *did you have any post this morning?*, ¿tuviste cartas esta mañana? || Reparto, *m.* (delivery of mail): *first post*, primer reparto. || HIST. Posta, *f.* || MIL. Puesto, *m.* (position): *advanced post*, puesto avanzado; *to stay at one's post*, quedarse en su puesto. || Puesto, *m.*, empleo, *m.*: *he has been given a post in industry*, se le ha asignado un puesto en la industria. || Cargo, *m.*: *to take up one's post*, tomar posesión de su cargo. || Factoría, *f.* (a trading post). || — *By return of post*, a vuelta de correo. || MIL. *Last post*, toque (*m.*) de retreta. || FIG. *There has been a general post in the Cabinet*, ha habido una reorganización ministerial. || FAM. *To be as deaf as a post*, estar más sordo que una tapia. | *To be as straight as a post*, estar más tieso que un poste. || FIG. *To be left at the post*, quedarse en la estacada.

post [pəust] v. tr. Fijar, pegar: *post no bills*, prohibido fijar carteles. || Poner: *results will be posted on the notice board*, los resultados se pondrán en el tablón de anuncios. || Fijar en: *to post a wall with notices*, fijar carteles en una pared. || Declarar: *to post s.o. missing*, declarar a alguien desaparecido. || Anunciar (to advertise by poster). || Echar [al correo]: *to post a letter*, echar una carta. || Mandar, enviar: *post me the photos*, mándame las fotos. || COMM. Pasar (in bookkeeping). || Informar, poner al tanto *or* al corriente (to inform). || MIL. Destinar, enviar: *posted to Germany*, destinado a Alemania. | Apostar (a sentry). || Nombrar, designar: *to post s.o. as captain*, nombrar a alguien capitán; *to post s.o. to a command*, designar a alguien para un mando. || — *To keep s.o. posted about the situation*, tener a alguien al tanto *or* al corriente de la situación. || *To post up*, fijar, pegar (bills, advertisements), poner al día (in bookkeeping), poner al corriente (s.o.).
— V. intr. Viajar en posta.

postage [ˈpəustidʒ] n. Franqueo, *m.* || — Pl. Gastos (*m.*) de correo. || *Postage paid*, franco de porte, porte pagado.

postage stamp [—stæmp] n. Sello, *m.* [*Amer.*, estampilla, *f.*].

postal [ˈpəustəl] adj. Postal: *postal order*, giro postal. || — *Postal card*, postal, *f.*, tarjeta (*f.*) postal. || *Postal reply coupon*, respuesta pagada.
— N. U. S. FAM. Tarjeta (*f.*) postal, postal, *f.*

postbellum [ˈpəustˈbeləm] adj. De la posguerra.

postbox [ˈpəustbɔks] n. Buzón, *m.*

postboy [ˈpəustbɔi] n. (Ant.) Postillón, *m.*

postcard [ˈpəustkɑːd] n. Tarjeta (*f.*) postal, postal, *f.*

post chaise [ˈpəustʃeiz] n. HIST. Silla (*f.*) de posta.

postdate [ˈpəustˈdeit] n. Posfecha, *f.*

postdate [ˈpəustˈdeit] v. tr. Poner fecha posterior a la verdadera, posfechar (to assign a later date to).

postdiluvian [ˈpəustdaiˈluːvjən] adj. Postdiluviano, na.

posted [ˈpəustid] adj. Al corriente, al tanto (informed). || Con postes (with poles).

poster [ˈpəustə*] n. Cartel, *m.* (notice). || Cartelero, *m.* (person).

poster designer [—diˈzainə*] n. Cartelista, *m.* & *f.*

poste restante [ˈpəustˈrestɑ̃ːnt] n. Lista (*f.*) de correos [*Amer.*, poste restante, *f.*].

posterior [pɔsˈtiəriə*] adj. Posterior, trasero, ra (situated behind). || Posterior (following). || ANAT. Posterior.
— N. FAM. Trasero, *m.*

posteriority [pɔsˌtiəriˈɔriti] n. Posterioridad, *f.*

posterity [pɔsˈteriti] n. Posteridad, *f.*

postern [ˈpəustəːn] n. Postigo, *m.* || MIL. Poterna, *f.*

post exchange [ˈpəustiksˈtʃeindʒ] n. MIL. Cantina, *f.*

postfix [ˈpəustˈfiks] n. GRAMM. Sufijo, *m.*, postfijo, *m.*

postfix [ˈpəustˈfiks] v. tr. GRAMM. Añadir [un sufijo] a.

post-free [ˈpəustˈfriː] adj. Franco de porte, con porte pagado.

postglacial [ˈpəustˈgleisjəl] adj. GEOL. Postglacial.

postgraduate [ˈpəustˈgrædjuit] adj. Graduado, da; diplomado, da (person). || Para graduados *or* diplomados (course).
— N. Graduado, da; diplomado, da.

posthaste [ˈpəustˈheist] adv. A toda prisa.

post horse [ˈpəusthɔːs] n. Caballo (*m.*) de posta.

posthumous [ˈpɔstjuməs] adj. Póstumo, ma.

posthumously [—li] adv. Después de la muerte.

postilion or **postillion** [pəsˈtiljən] n. Postillón, *m.*

postimpressionism [ˈpəustimˈpreʃnizəm] n. Postimpresionismo, *m.*

postimpressionist [ˈpəustimˈpreʃnist] adj./n. Postimpresionista.

postman [ˈpəustmən] n. Cartero, *m.*

— OBSERV. El plural de *postman* es *postmen.*

postmark [ˈpəustmɑːk] n. Matasellos, *m. inv.*: *letter with a London postmark*, carta con el matasellos de Londres.

postmark [ˈpəustmɑːk] v. tr. Matasellar, matar. || *The letter was postmarked London*, la carta llevaba el matasellos de Londres.

postmaster [ˈpəustˌmɑːstə*] n. Administrador (*m.*) de Correos. || *Postmaster general*, director (*m.*) general de Correos.

— OBSERV. El plural de esta palabra es *postmasters general* o *postmaster generals.*

postmeridian [ˈpəustməˈridiən] adj. Postmeridiano, na; de la tarde.

post meridiem [ˈpəustməˈridiəm] adv. De la tarde (of the afternoon). || De la noche (of the night).

— OBSERV. La expresión *post meridiem* se usa normalmente en forma abreviada, p.m. (*seven p.m.*, las siete de la tarde; *nine p.m.*, las nueve de la noche).

postmistress [ˈpəustˌmistris] n. Administradora (*f.*) de Correos.

postmortem [ˈpəustˈmɔːtəm] adj. MED. Que sucede después de la muerte. || MED. *Postmortem examination*, autopsia, *f.*
— N. MED. Autopsia, *f.*

postnatal [ˈpəustˈneitl] adj. Postnatal.

post office [ˈpəustˌɔfis] n. Correos, *m. pl.*, oficina (*f.*) de correos, casa (*f.*) de correos (office): *I have to go to the post office*, tengo que ir a correos. || — *District post office*, estafeta (*f.*) de correos. || *General Post Office*, Administración (*f.*) de Correos. || *Post-office box*, apartado (*m.*) de correos [*Amer.*, casilla (*f.*) postal].

postoperative [ˈpəustˈɔpərətiv] adj. Postoperatorio, ria.

postpaid [ˈpəustˈpeid] adj. Con porte pagado, franco de porte (parcel). || Franqueo concertado (letter, newspaper).

postpalatal [pəustˈpælətəl] adj. Postpalatal.

postpone [pəustˈpəun] v. tr. Aplazar: *to postpone a matter for a week*, aplazar un asunto hasta la semana siguiente.
— V. intr. MED. Tardar.

postponement [—mənt] n. Aplazamiento, *m.*

postposition [ˈpəustpəˈziʃən] n. GRAMM. Posposición, *f.*

postprandial [ˈpəustˈprændjəl] adj. De sobremesa (speech, talk, etc.). || Que se da después de comer (walk).

postscript [ˈpəusskript] n. Posdata, *f.*, post scriptum, *m.* (in a letter). || Nota (*f.*) final de un libro, advertencia (*f.*) final (in a book). || Comentario, *m.* (commentary).

postsynchronization [ˈpəustˌsiŋkrənaiˈzeiʃən] n. CINEM. Postsincronización, *f.*

postsynchronize [pəust'siŋkrənaiz] v. tr. CINEM. Postsincronizar.

postulant ['pɔstjulənt] n. Postulante, ta.

postulate ['pɔstjulit] n. Postulado, *m.*

postulate ['pɔstjuleit] v. tr. Postular, pedir (to demand). || Considerar como un postulado. || Dar por sentado (to assume).
— V. intr. *To postulate for*, pedir, postular.

postulation [,pɔstju'leiʃən] n. Postulación, *f.* (petition). || Supuesto, *m.* (assumption). || Postulado, *m.* (postulate).

postulator ['pɔstjuleitə*] n. REL. Postulador, *m.*

posture ['pɔstʃə*] n. Postura, *f.*, actitud, *f.* (of the body). || Situación, *f.* (of affairs).

posture ['pɔstʃə*] v. intr. Adoptar una postura (to pose). || Fingir ser, dárselas de: *posturing as an intellectual*, fingiendo ser un intelectual. || Darse tono, presumir (to be conceited).
— V. tr. Poner en una postura.

postwar ['pəust'wɔ:*] adj. De la posguerra. || *The postwar period*, la posguerra.

posy ['pəuzi] n. Ramillete (*m.*) de flores (bouquet). || U. S. Flor, *f.* (flower). | Lema, *m.*, inscripción, *f.* (motto).

pot [pɔt] n. Olla, *f.*, marmita, *f.*, puchero, *m.* (for cooking). || Tarro, *m.* (for preserving). || Tiesto, *m.*, maceta, *f.* (for flowers). || Nasa, *f.* (for fishing). || Orinal, *m.* (chamberpot). || Platillo, *m.*, pozo, *m.*, puesta, *f.* (in card games). || SP. FAM. Copa, *f.* (cup). || Premio, *m.* (prize). || FAM. Sombrerete, *m.* (of chimney). | Marihuana, *f.*, marijuana, *f.*, mariguana, *f.* || — Pl. FAM. Montones, *m.*: *pots of money*, montones de dinero. || — FAM. *Big pot*, pez gordo. || *Pots and pans*, batería (*f.*) de cocina. || FAM. *To go to pot*, echarse a perder. | *To keep the pot boiling*, calentar el puchero, ganarse la vida *or* el cocido.

pot [pɔt] v. tr. Poner en tiesto *or* en maceta (plants). || Meter en la tronera (billiards). || Conservar en tarros (to preserve food). || Guisar en una olla (to cook). || Matar (to shoot animals).
— V. intr. Tirar, disparar. || *To pot at s.o.*, disparar a alguien.

potable ['pəutəbl] adj. Potable.

potash ['pɔtæʃ] n. CHEM. Potasa, *f.*

potassic [pə'tæsik] adj. CHEM. Potásico, ca.

potassium [pə'tæsjəm] n. CHEM. Potasio, *m.*

potations [pəu'teiʃənz] pl. n. Libaciones, *f.*

potato [pə'teitəu] n. BOT. Patata, *f.* [*Amer.*, papa, *f.*]: *early* o *new potato*, patata temprana; *boiled potatoes*, patatas al vapor. || — *Mashed potatoes*, puré (*m.*) de patatas. || *Potato straws*, patatas paja. || *Sweet potato*, batata, *f.*
— OBSERV. El plural de *potato* es *potatoes*.

potato beetle [— bi:tl] n. ZOOL. Dorífora, *f.*, escarabajo (*m.*) de la patata.

potato chipper [—'tʃipə*] n. Freidora (*f.*) de patatas.

potato chips [—tʃips] pl. n. Patatas (*f.*) fritas [*Amer.*, papas (*f.*) fritas]. || U. S. Patatas (*f.*) fritas a la inglesa [*Amer.*, papas (*f.*) fritas a la inglesa].

potato crisps [—krisps] pl. n. Patatas (*f.*) fritas a la inglesa [*Amer.*, papas (*f.*) fritas a la inglesa].

potato field [—fi:ld] n. Campo (*m.*) de patatas, patatar, *m.*, patatal, *m.*

potato masher [—'mæʃə*] n. Pasapurés, *m. inv.*

potato peeler [—pi:lə*] n. Pelapatatas, *m. inv.*

potbellied ['pɔt,belid] adj. Barrigudo, da; barrigón, ona.

potbelly ['pɔt,beli] n. Barriga, *f.*, tripa, *f.* (stomach). || Barrigudo, da (person). || U. S. Salamandra, *f.* (stove).

potboiler ['pɔt,bɔilə*] n. Obra (*f.*) sin ningún valor hecha para ganar dinero.

poteen [pɔ'ti:n] n. Whisky (*m.*) irlandés [destilado ilegalmente].

potency ['pəutənsi] n. Potencia, *f.*, fuerza, *f.* (power, strength). || Potencia, *f.*, potencialidad, *f.* (potentiality).

potent ['pəutənt] adj. Potente (person). || Poderoso, sa (argument, poison). || Fuerte (drink). || Eficaz (remedy). || HERALD. *Potent cross*, potenza, *f.*, cruz potenzada.

potentate ['pəutənteit] n. Potentado, *m.*

potential [pəu'tenʃəl] adj. Posible, potencial, en potencia. || GRAMM. Potencial. || PHYS. Potencial: *potential energy*, energía potencial.
— N. Potencial, *m.* || Posibilidad, *f.* || GRAMM. PHYS. MATH. Potencial, *m.* || ELECTR. Voltaje, *m.*

potentiality [pəu,tenʃi'æliti] n. Potencialidad, *f.*

potentially [pəu'tenʃəli] adv. Potencialmente, en potencia.

potentiometer [pə,tenʃi'ɔmitə*] n. ELECTR. Potenciómetro, *m.*

pother ['pɔðə*] n. Confusión, *f.*, lío, *m.* || *To make a pother about sth.*, armar un lío por algo.

potherb ['pɔthə:b] n. Hierba, *f.* (to flavour food).

pothole ['pɔthəul] n. GEOL. Marmita (*f.*) de gigante. | Cueva, *f.* (cave). || Bache, *m.* (in a road).

pothole ['pɔthəul] v. intr. Dedicarse a la espeleología.

potholer [—ə*] n. Espeleólogo, *m.*

potholing [—iŋ] n. Espeleología, *f.*

pothook ['pɔthuk] n. Gancho, *m.*, llares, *m. pl.* (for hanging a pot). || Garabato, *m.* (writing).

pothunter ['pɔt,hʌntə*] n. Cazador (*m.*) que mata cualquier animal (hunter). || Cazador (*m.*) de premios (contestant).

potion ['pəuʃən] n. MED. Dosis, *f.*, pócima, *f.*, poción, *f.* || *Love potion*, filtro (*m.*) de amor.

pot lead ['pɔtled] n. Grafito, *m.*

pot-lead ['pɔtled] v. tr. Cubrir con grafito.

potluck ['pɔt'lʌk] n. Lo que haya: *to take potluck*, tomar lo que haya.

potpie ['pɔtpai] n. U. S. CULIN. Pastel (*m.*) de carne.

potpourri [pəu'puri] n. MUS. Popurrí, *m.* || CULIN. Olla (*f.*) podrida. || FIG. Popurrí, *m.* || Pebete, *m.* (to scent a room).

pot roast ['pɔtrəust] n. CULIN. Carne (*f.*) asada.

potsherd ['pɔtʃə:d] n. Tiesto, *m.*, casco, *m.*

potshot ['pɔt'ʃɔt] n. Tiro (*m.*) al azar (at random). || *To take a potshot at*, disparar al azar contra.

pottage ['pɔtidʒ] n. Sopa, *f.*, potaje, *m.* || FIG. *To sell one's birthright for a mess of pottage*, vender su primogenitura por un plato de lentejas.

potted ['pɔtid] adj. En conserva (food). || En tiesto, en maceta (plant).

potter ['pɔtə*] n. Alfarero, *m.* || Ceramista, *m.* & *f.* (artistic). || *Potter's wheel*, torno (*f.*) de alfarero.

potter ['pɔtə*] v. intr. *To potter about* o *around*, ocuparse en trabajos de poca importancia, no hacer nada de particular.

potter's clay [—z,klei] n. Arcilla (*f.*) figulina.

pottery ['pɔtəri] n. Alfarería, *f.* (craft). || Alfarería, *f.* (workshop). || Cacharros (*m. pl.*) de barro (pots). || Cerámica, *f.* (artistic).

potty ['pɔti] adj. FAM. Insignificante (trivial). | Chiflado, da (crazy). || — FIG. *To be potty about*, estar chiflado por. | *To drive s.o. potty*, volver loco a uno.
— N. FAM. Orinal, *m.* (chamberpot).

pouch [pautʃ] n. Bolsa (*f.*) pequeña (small bag). || Petaca, *f.* (for tobacco). || Cartuchera, *f.* (for ammunition). || Morral, *m.* (of hunters). || ZOOL. Bolsa, *f.* (abdominal sack). | Abazón, *m.* (cheek sack). || Bolsa, *f.* (under the eyes). || Valija, *f.* (locked bag for mail, etc.).

pouch [pautʃ] v. tr. Embolsar (to put in a bag). || Poner en una valija (to put in a locked bag). || Tragar (to swallow). || Formar bolsas en (to cause to form bags).

pouffe or **pouf** [pu:f] n. Puf, *m.*, taburete (*m.*) bajo de asiento relleno (seat).

poult [pəult] n. Pollo, *m.* (chicken). || Pavipollo, *m.* (turkey).

poulterer [—ərə*] n. Vendedor (*m.*) de aves, pollero, ra. || *Poulterer's shop*, pollería, *f.*

poultice ['pəultis] n. MED. Cataplasma, *f.*

poultice ['pəultis] v. tr. Poner una cataplasma a.

poultry ['pəultri] n. Aves (*f. pl.*) de corral.

poultry dealer [—'di:lə*] n. Pollero ra; vendedor (*m.*) de aves.

poultry farm [—fɑ:m] n. Granja (*f.*) avícola.

poultry farming [—fɑ:miŋ] n. Avicultura, *f.*, cría (*f.*) de aves de corral.

poultry house [—haus] n. Gallinero, *m.*

poultry keeper [—'ki:pə*] n. Avicultor, *m.*

poultry keeping [—ki:piŋ] n. Avicultura, *f.*

poultryman [—mən] n. Avicultor, *m.*
— OBSERV. El plural de esta palabra es *poultrymen*.

poultry yard [—jɑ:d] n. Corral, *m.*

pounce [pauns] n. ZOOL. Garra, *f.* || Arenilla, *f.* (powder). || Cisquero, *m.* (charcoal). || Salto, *m.*, ataque, *m.*: *the lion's pounce*, el ataque del león. || Salto (*m.*) repentino (spring).

pounce [pauns] v. tr. Estampar en relieve, repujar (to emboss). || Polvorear con arenilla (to sprinkle with fine powder). || Estarcir (to transfer a design).
— V. intr. Saltar. || *To pounce on* o *upon* o *at*, saltar sobre: *the lion pounces on the sheep*, el león salta sobre la oveja; abalanzarse sobre (birds), precipitarse sobre: *they pounced on the evening newspaper*, se precipitaron sobre el periódico de la tarde; no perder (an opportunity).

pound [paund] n. Libra, *f.* (weight, money): *pound sterling*, libra esterlina; *to sell by the pound*, vender por libras; *half a pound*, media libra. || Aprisco, *m.*, redil, *m.* (for sheep). || Perrera, *f.* (for dogs). || Depósito, *m.* (for animals, cars). || Garlito, *m.*, nasa, *f.* (fish trap). || Ruido, *m.* (noise). || FIG. *A question of pounds, shillings and pence*, un asunto de dinero.

pound [paund] v. tr. Aporrear (to thump). || Martillear (with a hammer). || Moler (to grind). || Machacar (to crush). || Azotar, batir: *the waves pounded the ship*, las olas azotaban el barco. || FAM. Dar una paliza, aporrear (to beat). || MIL. Machacar, martillear a cañonazos *or* con bombas. || Aporrear (a piano, a table). || — *To pound sth. to pieces*, destrozar algo a martillazos. || U. S. FAM. *To pound the asphalt*, callejear.
— V. intr. Dar golpes, aporrear (to strike). || Palpitar, latir violentamente (heart). || Picar (machine). || Resonar: *we heard feet pounding up the stairs*, oímos pasos que resonaban en las escaleras.
— ***To pound along***, andar *or* ir con paso pesado. || ***To pound at***, dar golpes en, aporrear: *he was pounding at the door*, estaba aporreando la puerta. || ***To pound***

away, machacar. || *To pound on*, aporrear, dar golpes en.
poundage [—idʒ] n. Impuesto (*m.*) *or* comisión (*f.*) por cada libra.
pounder [—ə*] n. Mazo, *m.* (big hammer). || Maja, *f.* (kitchen utensil). || Pisón, *m.* (beetle). || — *A twenty-five pounder*, un cañón de veinticinco. || *Ten-pounder*, algo que pesa diez libras.
pound-foolish [—ˈfu:liʃ] adj. Gastador, ra; manirroto, ta; derrochador, ra.
pounding [—iŋ] n. Golpeteo, *m.* (noise). || Embate, *m.*, azote, *m.* (of the sea). || Trituración, *f.* (crushing). || Molienda, *f.* (grinding). || MIL. Bombardeo, *m.*, martilleo, *m.*, machaqueo, *m.*
pound net [—net] n. Nasa, *f.*, garlito, *m.* (fish trap).
pound sterling [—ˈstə:liŋ] n. Libra (*f.*) esterlina.
pound-weight [—weit] n. PHYS. Libra, *f.*
pour [pɔ:*] n. Derrame, *m.* || Diluvio, *m.* (rain).
pour [pɔ:*] v. tr. Derramar, verter: *he poured the wine all over the table*, derramó el vino por toda la mesa. || Echar: *pour me a glass of wine*, échame un vaso de vino. || Servir: *may I pour the coffee?*, ¿sirvo el café? || Colar (metal). || — *To pour away o off*, vaciar, verter. || FIG. *To pour cats and dogs*, llover a cántaros. || *To pour out*, servir, echar (tea, etc.), echar (smoke). || *To pour out abuse on s.o.*, llenar a uno de improperios. || *To pour out one's feelings*, expansionarse. || *To pour out one's heart*, abrir el corazón, desahogar su corazón. || *To pour out one's thanks*, dar las gracias efusivamente. || *To pour out one's troubles*, confiar sus penas. || *To pour out threats*, desatarse en amenazas.
— V. intr. Diluviar, llover a cántaros (to rain). || Correr, fluir (water). || Salir a borbotones (to come out with a rush). || Servir: *the tea is ready, you pour*, el té está preparado, sírvelo tú || — *It is pouring down*, está lloviendo a cántaros. || FIG. *It never rains but it pours*, llueve sobre mojado. || *The crowds poured out of the theatre*, la gente salía del teatro en tropel. || *The letters were pouring in*, las cartas llegaban en abundancia. || *To pour in*, entrar a raudales *or* en tropel. || *To pour out*, salir a raudales *or* en tropel.
pouring [—riŋ] adj. Torrencial: *pouring rain*, lluvia torrencial.
pout [paut] n. FAM. Mala cara, *f.* || ZOOL. Abadejo, *m.* (fish). || *To have the pouts*, poner mala cara, hacer pucheros.
pout [paut] v. tr. *To pout one's lips*, poner mala cara, hacer pucheros.
— V. intr. Poner mala cara, hacer pucheros.
pouter [—ə*] n. Paloma (*f.*) buchona (pigeon).
poverty [ˈpɔvəti] n. Pobreza, *f.*: *the poverty of the land*, la pobreza de la tierra; *to live in poverty*, vivir en la pobreza. || Carencia, *f.*, escasez, *f.*: *poverty of ideas*, carencia de ideas. || — *Extreme poverty*, miseria, *f.* || FIG. *Poverty is no crime*, pobreza no es vileza.
poverty-stricken [—ˌstrikn] adj. Menesteroso, sa; necesitado, da; indigente.
powder [ˈpaudə*] n. Polvo, *m.*: *he reduced it to powder*, lo redujo a polvo. || Pólvora, *f.* (gun powder). || Polvos, *m. pl.* (cosmetic). || Arenilla, *f.* (pounce). || — FIG. *To keep one's powder dry*, no gastar pólvora en salvas. || U. S. FIG. *To take a powder*, poner pies en polvorosa.
powder [ˈpaudə*] v. tr. Reducir a polvo, pulverizar (to pulverize). || Espolvorear (to sprinkle). || *To powder one's face*, ponerse polvos en la cara.
— V. intr. Reducirse a polvo. || Ponerse polvos en la cara (to use cosmetic powder).
powder blue [—blu:] n. Azul (*m.*) pálido.
powder box [—bɔks] n. Polvera, *f.*
powder compact [—ˈkɔmpækt] n. Polvera, *f.*
powdered [—d] adj. En polvo.
powder flask [—flɑ:sk] n. Frasco (*m.*) para la pólvora.
powder keg [—keg] n. FIG. Polvorín, *m.*
powder magazine [—mægəˌzi:n] n. Polvorín, *m.* || MAR. Santabárbara, *f.*
powder monkey [—ˈmʌŋki] n. MAR. Grumete (*m.*) encargado de la pólvora.
powder puff [—pʌf] n. Borla, *f.*
powder room [—ru:m] n. U. S. Aseos, *m.pl.*, servicios, *m. pl.*
powdery [—ri] adj. En polvo: *powdery snow*, nieve en polvo. || Pulverizado, da (pulverized). || Polvoriento, ta; empolvado, da (dusty). || Quebradizo, za (friable).
power [ˈpauə*] n. Poder, *m.* (authority, control): *to be in the power of*, estar en poder *or* bajo el poder de; *to hand over power*, entregar los poderes; *with full power* o *powers*, con plenos poderes. || Potencia, *f.* (country): *the Great Powers*, las grandes potencias; *atomic power*, potencia atómica; *world power*, potencia mundial. || Poderío, *m.* (supremacy). || Facultad, *f.*, capacidad, *f.*, posibilidad, *f.*, poder, *m.* (gift): *the power to fly*, la facultad de volar. || Facultad, *f.*: *mental powers*, facultades mentales *or* intelectuales; *my powers are failing*, mis facultades decaen. || Fuerza, *f.*, potencia, *f.* (strength). || Fuerza, *f.*, poder, *m.*: *attractive power*, poder de atracción. || Ascendiente, *m.*, influencia, *f.* (influence). || Autoridad, *f.*, poder, *m.*, capacidad, *f.*, facultad, *f.* (legal authority): *to have the power to dismiss an employee*, tener capacidad para despedir a un empleado. || PHYS. ELECTR. TECH. Potencia, *f.* (rate of work done). | Fuerza, *f.*: *motive power*, fuerza motriz. | Energía, *f.* (energy): *electric, water power*, energía eléctrica, hidráulica. | Potencia, *f.* (of a lense). || MATH. Potencia, *f.*: *to raise a number to the power of four* o *to the fourth power*, elevar un número a la cuarta potencia; *to the nth power*, a la enésima potencia. || — Pl. Potestades, *f.* (of angels). || — *Absolute, executive, judicial, legislative power*, poder absoluto, ejecutivo, judicial, legislativo. || FAM. *A power of people*, una multitud. || *As far as lies within my power*, en la medida de lo posible. || *Five to the power of three, of two*, cinco elevado al cubo, al cuadrado. || *It is not within my power to help you*, no puedo ayudarle, no entra dentro de mis posibilidades ayudarle. || FIG. *More power to your elbow!*, ¡que le acompañe el éxito! || *Nuclear power*, energía nuclear. || JUR. *Power of attorney*, poderes, poder, procuración, *f.* || *Purchasing power*, poder adquisitivo. || *The powers that be*, las autoridades. || *To be in power*, estar en el poder. || *To come to power*, subir al poder; tomar el mando. || *To do all in one's power to*, hacer todo lo posible para. || FAM. *To do a power of good*, sentar bien, hacer mucho bien (a remedy). || *To exceed one's powers*, excederse. || *To fall into s.o.'s power*, caer en poder de alguien. || *To have s.o. in one's power*, tener a uno en su poder. || FAM. *To make a power of money*, ganar un dineral.
power [ˈpauə*] v. tr. *To be powered by*, estar impulsado *or* accionado por.
power axle [—ˈæksl] n. Eje (*m.*) de transmisión.
power brakes [—breiks] pl. n. AUT. Frenos (*m.*) asistidos, servofrenos, *m.*
power cable [—ˈkeibl] n. Cable (*m.*) de energía eléctrica, cable (*m.*) de transmisión.
power cut [—kʌt] n. Corte (*m.*) de corriente, apagón, *m.*
power dive [—daiv] n. AVIAT. Picado (*m.*) con motor.
power drill [—dril] n. TECH. Taladradora (*f.*) mecánica *or* eléctrica.
power-driven [—ˈdrivn] adj. Con motor. || Mecánico, ca (tool).
powerful [—ful] adj. Poderoso, sa: *a powerful nation*, una nación poderosa. || Potente (machine, engine). || Fuerte (strong). || Enérgico, ca; eficaz (medicines, etc.). || FIG. Intenso, sa (feelings). | Convincente (argument).
powerfully [—fuli] adv. Poderosamente. || *To be powerfully built*, ser fuerte *or* fornido.
power hammer [—ˈhæmə*] n. Martillo (*m.*) pilón.
powerhouse [—haus] n. Central (*f.*) eléctrica. || U. S. FIG. Persona (*f.*) enérgica.
powerless [—lis] adj. Impotente (helpless). || Ineficaz (remedy, etc.). || Sin autoridad, sin poder (not empowered). || — *To be powerless in a matter*, no poder hacer nada en un asunto. || *To be powerless to help s.o.*, no poder *or* ser incapaz de ayudar a alguien.
powerlessness [—lisnis] n. Impotencia, *f.* || Ineficacia, *f.* (inefficacy).
power line [—lain] n. Línea (*f.*) de fuerza eléctrica, línea (*f.*) de conducción *or* de transmisión eléctrica.
power plant [—plɑ:nt] n. Central (*f.*) eléctrica. || Grupo (*m.*) electrógeno (of a factory). || *Nuclear power plant*, central nuclear.
power politics [—ˌpɔlitiks] n. Política (*f.*) de fuerza.
power saw [—sɔ:] n. TECH. Sierra (*f.*) mecánica.
power shovel [—ˌʃʌvl] n. Excavadora, *f.*, pala (*f.*) mecánica.
power station [—ˌsteiʃən] n. Central (*f.*) eléctrica. || Grupo (*m.*) electrógeno (of a factory). || *Nuclear power station*, central nuclear.
power steering [—ˌstiəriŋ] n. AUT. Dirección (*f.*) asistida.
power tool [—tu:l] n. Herramienta (*f.*) mecánica *or* eléctrica.
power unit [—ˈju:nit] n. Unidad (*f.*) de potencia (for measurement). || Motor, *m.* (motor). || ELECTR. Generador, *m.* | Grupo (*m.*) electrógeno.
powwow [ˈpauwau] n. Conferencia, *f.*
powwow [ˈpauwau] v. intr. Conferenciar.
pox [pɔks] n. FAM. Sífilis, *f.* (syphilis). || Viruela, *f.*, viruelas, *f. pl.* (smallpox). || Varicela, *f.* (chicken pox). || *A pox on her!*, ¡maldita sea!
pozzolana [pɔtsəˈlɑ:nə] or **pozzuolana** [pɔttswəˈlɑ:nə] n. MIN. Puzolana, *f.*
practicability [ˌpræktikəˈbiliti] n. Practicabilidad, *f.*, factibilidad, *f.*
practicable [ˈpræktikəbl] adj. Factible, practicable, hacedero, ra; posible, realizable (which can be done): *a practicable plan*, un proyecto factible. || Utilizable (capable of being used). || Transitable (route). || THEATR. Practicable.
practical [ˈpræktikəl] adj. Práctico, ca: *practical experience*, experiencia práctica; *practical idea*, idea práctica. || — *Practical exam*, examen práctico. || *Practical lessons*, clases prácticas. || *Practical training period*, período (*m.*) de prácticas. || *The first night was a practical disaster*, el estreno fue casi un fracaso.
practicality [ˌpræktiˈkæliti] n. Espíritu (*m.*) práctico, sentido (*m.*) práctico (of a person). || Factibilidad, *f.* (of a project).
practical joke [ˈpræktikəldʒəuk] n. Broma (*f.*) pesada.

practically [ˈpræktikəli] adv. De manera práctica, eficazmente. || Prácticamente, casi (virtually): *practically a year ago*, hace prácticamente un año.
practical nurse [ˈpræktikəlnə:s] n. U. S. Enfermera (*f.*) sin título [que ha adquirido sus conocimientos gracias a la práctica].
practice [ˈpræktis] n. Práctica, *f.* (not theory): *in theory it is easy but in practice impossible*, en teoría es fácil, pero en la práctica es imposible; *to put into practice*, poner en práctica. || Costumbre, *f.*: *to make a practice of dining early*, tener la costumbre de cenar temprano. || Práctica, *f.* (exercise): *to learn by practice*, aprender con la práctica. || Ejercicios, *m. pl.* (on the piano). || SP. Entrenamiento, *m.* (training): *practice match*, partido de entrenamiento. || Ejercicio, *m.* (of a profession): *to devote o.s. to the practice of medicine*, dedicarse al ejercicio de la medicina. || Clientela, *f.*: *a dentist with a large practice*, un odontólogo con una clientela numerosa; *to sell one's practice*, vender su clientela. || JUR. Procedimiento, *m.*, práctica, *f.* (procedure). | Bufete, *m.* (lawyer's business): *to set up in practice*, poner un bufete. || Estratagema *f.* (stratagem). || — *He is no longer in practice*, ya no ejerce (a profession). || *It is not my practice to do that*, no acostumbro hacer eso. || *Practice makes perfect*, machacando se aprende el oficio. || *Restrictive practices*, normas restrictivas. || *Sharp practices*, mañas, *f.* || SP. *To be in practice*, estar bien entrenado, estar en forma. | *To be out of practice*, no estar bien entrenado, no estar en forma. || *To make it a practice to do sth.*, acostumbrar hacer algo.
practice [ˈpræktis] v. tr./intr. U. S. See PRACTISE.
practiced [—t] adj. U. S. See PRACTISED.
practician [prækˈtiʃən] n. See PRACTITIONER.
practicing [ˈpræktisiŋ] adj./n. U. S. See PRACTISING.
practise [ˈpræktis] v. tr. Practicar: *to practise a policy of neutrality*, practicar una política de neutralidad; *to practise one's English*, practicar el inglés; *to practise a religion*, practicar una religión. || Tener: *to practise patience, good manners*, tener paciencia, buenos modales. || Ejercer (a profession): *to practise medicine*, ejercer la medicina. || Ejercitarse en (to exercise o.s. in). || MUS. Hacer ejercicios en (an instrument). || Mandar hacer ejercicios sobre: *to practise a class in irregular verbs*, mandar hacer ejercicios sobre los verbos irregulares a una clase. || SP. Practicar (a stroke, a shot, a punch, etc.). | Entrenarse en (a sport): *to practise rugby*, entrenarse en el rugby. || — *To practise punctuality*, ser puntal. || *To practise what one preaches*, predicar con el ejemplo.
— V. intr. Ejercer (*as*, de) [professionally]. || Ejercitarse (to exercise o.s.). || Hacer ejercicios: *to practise on the piano*, hacer ejercicios en el piano. || SP. Entrenarse.
practised [—t] adj. Experto, ta; experimentado, da (expert). || Muy entrenado, da (well-trained).
practising [—iŋ] adj. Que ejerce, en ejercicio: *practising doctor, lawyer*, médico, abogado en ejercicio. || REL. Practicante.
— N. Ejercicio, *m.* (of a profession). || REL. Práctica, *f.* (of a faith). || Ejercicios, *m. pl.* (exercises). || SP. Entrenamiento, *m.* (training).
practitioner [prækˈtiʃnə*] n. Persona (*f.*) que ejerce una profesión. || MED. Facultativo, *m.*, médico, *m.* || MED. *General practitioner*, internista, *m.*
praedial [ˈpri:diəl] adj. Predial.
praenomen [pri:ˈnəumen] n. Prenombre, *m.*

— OBSERV. El plural es *praenomens* o *praenomina*.

praesidium [priˈsidiəm] n. Presidium, *m.*

— OBSERV. El plural de la palabra *praesidium* es *praesidia* o *praesidiums*.

praetexta [priˈ:tekstə] n. Pretexta, *f.*
praetor [ˈpri:tə*] n. Pretor, *m.*
praetorial [priˈtɔ:riəl] adj. Pretorial.
praetorian [priˈtɔ:riən] adj. Pretorial, pretoriano, na. || HIST. *Praetorian Guard*, guardia pretoriana.
— N. Pretoriano, *m.*
praetorianism [pritɔˈriəˌnizəm] n. Pretorianismo, *m.*
praetorium [priˈtɔriəm] n. Pretorio, *m.*
praetorship [ˈpri:təʃip] n. Pretoría, *f.*
pragmatic [prægˈmætik] or **pragmatical** [—əl] adj. Pragmático, ca. || Dogmático, ca (dogmatic). || Práctico, ca (practical). || Entrometido, da (meddling).
pragmatics [prægˈmætiks] n. Pragmática, *f.*
pragmatism [ˈprægmətizəm] n. Pragmatismo, *m.*
pragmatist [ˈprægmətist] n. Pragmatista, *m.* & *f.*
Prague [prɑ:g] pr. n. GEOGR. Praga.
prairie [ˈpreəri] n. Pradera, *f.*, llanura, *f.* [*Amer.*, pampa, *f.*].
prairie schooner [—ˈsku:nə*] n. U. S. HIST. Carromato (*m.*) en el que viajaban los pioneros.
prairie wolf [—wulf] n. ZOOL. Coyote, *m.*
praise [preiz] n. Alabanza, *f.*, alabanzas, *f. pl.*, elogio, *m.* || — *Praise be to God!*, ¡alabado sea Dios! || *To heap praises on s.o.*, cubrir a alguien de alabanzas. || *To sing* o *to shout the praises of*, cantar las alabanzas de.
praise [preiz] v. tr. Alabar, elogiar, ensalzar. || Alabar (God). || FIG. *To praise to the skies*, poner por las nubes.
praiser [—ə*] n. Ensalzador, ra; elogiador, ra; alabador, ra.
praiseworthily [—ˌwə:ðili] adv. De modo digno de elogio, loablemente, laudablemente.
praiseworthy [—ˌwə:ði] adj. Laudable, loable, digno de elogio.
Prakrit [ˈprɑ:krit] n. Pracrito, *m.*, prácrito, *m.* (Indic language).
praline [ˈprɑ:li:n] n. Almendra (*f.*) garapiñada.
pram [præm] n. Cochecito (*m.*) de niño (perambulator).
prance [prɑ:ns] n. Cabriola, *f.*
prance [prɑ:ns] v. intr. Encabritarse (to rear up). || Hacer cabriolas (to move by leaps). || Pavonearse (to swagger). || — *To prance with glee*, dar saltos *or* brincos de alegría. || *To prance with rage*, patalear de rabia.
prandial [ˈprændiəl] adj. De la comida (of a meal). || De la cena (of dinner).
prang [præŋ] v. tr. FAM. Derribar (an aircraft). | Bombardear (a building). | Chocar contra (to bump into).
— V. intr. FAM. Estrellarse (an aircraft).
prank [præŋk] n. Travesura, *f.* (a piece of mischief). || Broma, *f.* (joke): *to play a prank on s.o.*, gastar una broma a alguien.
prank [præŋk] v. tr. Ataviar, engalanar (to adorn).
prankish [—iʃ] adj. Travieso, sa; pícaro, ra.
prankster [—stə*] n. Bromista, *m.* & *f.*
praseodymium [ˌpreizioˈdimiəm] n. CHEM. Praseodimio, *m.*
prate [preit] n. Charla, *f.*, parloteo, *m.*, cháchara, *f.*
prate [preit] v. intr. Parlotear, charlar.
prater [—ə*] n. Charlatán, ana.
prating [—iŋ] adj. Parlanchín, ina; charlatán, ana.
pratique [ˈpræti:k] n. MAR. Libre plática, *f.*
prattle [ˈprætl] n. Balbuceo, *m.* (of a child). || Cháchara, *f.*, parloteo, *m.* (chatter).
prattle [ˈprætl] v. intr. Charlar, parlotear (to chatter).
— V. tr. Balbucear.
prattler [—ə*] n. Charlatán, ana.
prawn [prɔ:n] n. ZOOL. Camarón, *m.* (small). | Gamba, *f.*, langostino, *m.* (large).
praxis [ˈpræksis] n. Práctica, *f.*

— OBSERV. El plural de *praxis* es *praxes*.

pray [prei] v. intr. Rezar, orar: *to pray for s.o.*, rezar por alguien. || Rogar (to beg): *to pray for rain*, rogar que llueva. || *He's past praying for*, ya no se puede salvar.
— V. tr. Rogar, suplicar (to beg): *to pray s.o. to do sth.*, rogar a alguien que haga algo. || — *Pray be seated*, siéntese por favor, haga el favor de sentarse. || *Pray tell me*, le ruego me diga. || *What, pray, is the meaning of this?*, ¿qué significa esto, por favor?
prayer [preə*] n. REL. Oración, *f.*, rezo, *m.* || Súplica, *f.*, ruego, *m.* (entreaty). || — REL. *Book of Common Prayer*, libro (*m.*) de oraciones de la Iglesia Anglicana. | *Evening prayers*, vísperas, *f.* | *Lord's Prayer*, padrenuestro, *m.* | *Morning prayers*, maitines, *m.* | *To say a prayer* o *prayers for*, rezar por. | *To say one's prayers*, rezar sus oraciones, rezar. | *To spend one's life in prayer*, pasarse la vida rezando.
prayer beads [—bi:dz] pl. n. REL. Rosario, *m. sing.*
prayer book [—buk] n. REL. Devocionario, *m.*
prayerful [—ful] adj. Devoto, ta; piadoso, sa (devout).
prayer meeting [—ˌmi:tiŋ] n. REL. Reunión (*f.*) de fieles para rezar.
prayer rug [—rʌg] n. REL. Alfombra (*f.*) de rezo.
prayer shawl [—ʃɔ:l] n. REL. Taled, *m.*
prayer stool [—stu:l] n. REL. Reclinatorio, *m.*
prayer wheel [—wi:l] n. Molinillo (*m.*) de oraciones.
praying mantis [ˈpreiŋ ˈmæntis] n. Predicador, *m.*, santateresa, *f.* (insect).
preach [pri:tʃ] v. intr. Predicar: *he preaches very well*, predica muy bien. || Dar un sermón: *to preach about tolerance*, dar un sermón sobre la tolerancia. || Sermonear: *he is always preaching at his children*, está siempre sermoneando a sus hijos.
— V. tr. Predicar (the Gospel). || Dar, pronunciar (a sermon). || FIG. Aconsejar: *to preach moderation*, aconsejar la moderación.
preacher [—ə*] n. Predicador, ra (s.o. who preaches). || Pastor, *m.* (minister).
preachify [—ifai] v. intr. FAM. Sermonear.
preaching [—iŋ] adj. Sermoneador, ra (tone).
— N. Predicación, *f.* || Sermón, *m.* || FAM. Sermoneo, *m.* (tiresome moral advice).
preachy [—i] adj. FAM. Sermoneador, ra.
preamble [pri:ˈæmbl] n. Preámbulo, *m.*
preamplifier [ˈpri:ˈæmplifaiə*] n. RAD. Preamplificador, *m.*
prearrange [ˈpri:əˈreindʒ] v. tr. Organizar de antemano (to organize in advance): *a prearranged visit*, una visita organizada de antemano. || Preparar de antemano: *to ask a prearranged question*, hacer una pregunta preparada de antemano.
prebend [ˈprebənd] n. Prebenda, *f.* (stipend). || Prebendado, *m.* (prebendary).
prebendary [—əri] n. Prebendado, *m.*
prebook [ˈpri:buk] v. tr. Reservar de antemano.
Precambrian [priˈkæmbriən] adj. GEOL. Precámbrico, ca; precambriano, na.
— N. Precámbrico, *m.*
precarious [priˈkeəriəs] adj. Precario, ria.

precariousness [—nis] n. Precariedad, *f.*, carácter (*m.*) precario.
precast [pri:ˈkɑ:st] adj. Vaciado de antemano (concrete). || Prefabricado, da (concrete block, house).
precatory [ˈprekətəri] adj. Suplicante.
precaution [priˈkɔ:ʃən] n. Precaución, *f*: *as a precaution*, por precaución; *to take the precaution of doing sth.*, tomar la precaución de hacer algo.
precautionary [—əri] adj. Preventivo, va; de precaución: *precautionary measures*, medidas preventivas.
precautious [priˈkɔ:ʃəs] adj. Precavido, da; cauteloso, sa; cauto, ta.
precede [priˈsi:d] v. tr. Preceder, anteceder (in time, position, importance): *the stillness that precedes a storm*, la quietud que precede la tormenta. || Empezar, comenzar: *to precede a ceremony with a speech of welcome*, comenzar una ceremonia con un discurso de bienvenida.
— V. intr. Preceder, anteceder.
precedence [priˈsi:dəns] n. Precedencia, *f.*: *an archbishop has precedence over a bishop*, un arzobispo tiene precedencia sobre un obispo. || Prioridad, *f.*, preferencia, *f.*, prelación, *f.*: *exports take precedence over home production*, las exportaciones tienen prioridad sobre la producción para el mercado nacional.
precedent [priˈsi:dənt] adj. Precedente.
precedent [ˈpresidənt] n. Precedente, *m.*: *to establish a precedent*, sentar un precedente; *without precedent*, sin precedente; *there is no precedent for it*, no tiene precedente.
preceding [priˈsi:diŋ] adj. Precedente, anterior.
precentor [priˈsentə*] n. Rel. Chantre, *m.*
precept [ˈpri:sept] n. Precepto, *m.* (rule). || Jur. Mandato (*m.*) judicial.
preceptist [—ist] n. Preceptista, *m.* & *f.*
preceptive [priˈseptiv] adj. Preceptivo, va.
preceptor [priˈseptə*] n. Preceptor, *m.*
preceptorial [ˌpri:sepˈtɔ:riəl] adj. Preceptoril.
precession [priˈseʃən] n. Astr. Precesión, *f.*
precinct [ˈpri:siŋkt] n. Recinto, *m.* (grounds): *the cathedral precinct*, el recinto de la catedral. || Zona, *f.*: *pedestrian precinct*, zona reservada para peatones; *shopping precinct*, zona comercial [reservada para peatones]. || Frontera, *f.*, límite, *m.* (boundary). || U. S. Distrito (*m.*) electoral. | Barrio, *m.* (neighbourhood). || — Pl. Contornos, *m.*, alrededores, *m.*
preciosity [ˌpreʃiˈɔsiti] n. Preciosismo, *m.*, amaneramiento, *m.* (of style).
precious [ˈpreʃəs] adj. Precioso, sa: *precious metals*, metales preciosos; *precious stone*, piedra preciosa. || Inapreciable (priceless): *a precious friendship*, una amistad inapreciable. || Preciosista (exhibiting preciosity): *a precious writer*, un escritor preciosista. || Rebuscado, da (style): *a precious turn of phrase*, una locución rebuscada. || Afectado, da (manners). || Precioso, sa (term of endearment): *hello, precious!*, ¡hola, preciosa! || Querido, da (beloved): *he will be furious if you damage his precious car*, se pondrá furioso si estropeas su querido coche. || *A precious fool*, un perfecto imbécil.
— Adv. Muy (very): *precious little*, muy poco; *precious few*, muy pocos.
preciousness [—nis] n. Preciosidad, *f.* || Valor (*m.*) inapreciable.
precipice [ˈpresipis] n. Precipicio, *m.*
precipitance [priˈsipitəns] or **precipitancy** [—i] n. Precipitación, *f.*
precipitant [priˈsipitənt] adj. Precipitado, da (hasty).
precipitate [priˈsipitit] adj. Precipitado, da (hasty).
— N. Chem. Precipitado, *m.*
precipitate [priˈsipiteit] v. tr. Arrojar, precipitar (to hurl downward). || Apresurar, precipitar: *the assassination precipitated the war*, el asesinato precipitó la guerra. || Causar, producir, provocar (to cause). || Chem. Precipitar. || Condensar (vapour). || *To precipitate o.s.*, precipitarse, arrojarse.
— V. intr. Chem. Precipitarse. || Condensarse (vapour).
precipitation [priˌsipiˈteiʃən] n. Precipitación, *f.* (haste): *his precipitation cost him his life*, su precipitación le costó la vida. || Chem. Precipitación, *f.* | Precipitado, *m.* (precipitate). || Precipitación, *f.* (rain, snow, etc.).
precipitous [priˈsipitəs] adj. Empinado, da; escarpado, da (steep). || Precipitado, da; precipitoso, sa (hasty).
précis [ˈpreisi:] n. Resumen, *m.*
precise [priˈsais] adj. Preciso, sa; exacto, ta (detailed, exact): *a precise account*, un relato preciso. || Preciso, sa; claro, ra (clear). || Preciso, sa; mismo, ma: *at that precise moment*, en aquel momento preciso. || Meticuloso, sa (finicky). || — *It is the precise word I was looking for*, es precisamente *or* exactamente la palabra que estaba buscando. || *To be precise*, para ser preciso.
precisely [—li] adv. Precisamente, justamente, exactamente: *it is precisely what I want*, es precisamente lo que quiero. || Con precisión: *to speak, to write precisely*, hablar, escribir con precisión. || Meticulosamente (meticulously). || En punto: *it is precisely one o'clock*, es la una en punto. || — *At precisely six o'clock*, a las seis en punto. || *Precisely!*, ¡eso es!, ¡exactamente!
preciseness [—nis] n. Precisión, *f.*, exactitud, *f.* (accuracy). || Precisión, *f.* (in speaking, writing).
precisian [priˈsiʒən] n. Rigorista, *m.* & *f.*
precision [priˈsiʒən] n. Precisión, *f.*, exactitud, *f.* || *Precision instrument*, instrumento de precisión.
précis writer [ˈpreisi:raitə*] n. Redactor (*m.*) *or* secretario (*m.*) de actas.
preclude [priˈklu:d] v. tr. Impedir (to prevent): *to preclude s.o. from doing sth.*, impedir a alguien que haga algo. || Imposibilitar, impedir: *the use of one system precludes the use of another*, el uso de un sistema imposibilita el uso de otro. || Evitar: *to preclude any misunderstanding*, para evitar todo malentendido. || Excluir: *it does not preclude the possibility of...*, no excluye la posibilidad de...
preclusion [priˈklu:ʒən] n. Prevención, *f.* (prevention). || Exclusión, *f.* (exclusion).
preclusive [priˈklu:siv] adj. Que impide, que evita: *preclusive of a misunderstanding*, que evita un malentendido.
precocious [priˈkəuʃəs] adj. Precoz: *a precocious child*, un niño precoz.
precociousness [—nis] or **precocity** [priˈkɔsiti] n. Precocidad, *f.*
precognition [pri:kɔgˈniʃən] n. Precognición, *f.* (foreknowledge).
pre-Columbian [ˌpri:kəˈlʌmbjən] adj. Precolombino, na.
precombustion [pri:kəmˈbʌstʃən] n. Precombustión, *f.*
precompression [ˌpri:kəmˈpreʃən] n. Precompresión, *f.*
preconceive [ˈpri:kənˈsi:v] v. tr. Preconcebir.
preconception [ˈpri:kənˈsepʃən] n. Preconcepción, *f.*, idea (*f.*) preconcebida (preconceived idea). || Prejuicio, *m.* (prejudice).
preconcert [ˈpri:kənˈsə:t] v. tr. Concertar de antemano.
precondition [prikənˈdiʃən] n. Condición (*f.*) previa.
preconization [prikənaiˈzeiʃən] n. Rel. Preconización, *f.*
preconize [ˈpri:kənaiz] v. tr. Preconizar (a bishop). || Preconizar, encomiar (to extol).
precursive [pri:ˈkə:siv] adj. Precursor, ra.
precursor [priˈkə:sə*] n. Precursor, ra.
precursory [—ri] adj. Precursor, ra (which precedes). || Preliminar (preliminary).
predaceous or **predacious** [priˈdeiʃəs] adj. De rapiña, rapaz (animal).
predacity [priˈdæsiti] n. Rapacidad, *f.*
predate [pri:ˈdeit] v. tr. Preceder (to come before).
predator [ˈpredətə*] n. Animal (*m.*) de rapiña. || Depredador, ra (person).
predatory [ˈpredətəri] adj. De rapiña, rapaz (animal). || Depredador, ra (person).
predecease [ˈpri:diˈsi:s] v. tr. Morir antes que.
predecessor [ˈpri:disesə*] n. Predecesor, ra; antecesor, ra. || Antepasado, da (forefather).
predestinate [priˈdestinit] adj. Predestinado, da.
predestinate [priˈdestineit] v. tr. Predestinar.
predestination [priˌdestiˈneiʃən] n. Predestinación, *f.*
predestine [priˈdestin] v. tr. Predestinar.
predeterminate [ˌpri:diˈtə:mineit] adj. Predeterminado, da.
predetermination [ˈpri:diˌtə:miˈneiʃən] n. Predeterminación, *f.*
predetermine [ˈpri:diˈtə:min] v. tr. Predeterminar: *my fate is already predetermined*, mi destino está ya predeterminado. || Determinar de antemano: *we must predetermine the consequences*, debemos determinar de antemano las consecuencias.
predetermining [—iŋ] adj. Predeterminante.
predial [ˈpri:diəl] adj. Predial.
predicable [ˈpredikəbl] adj. Predicable.
— N. Predicable, *m.*
predicament [priˈdikəmənt] n. Apuro, *m.*, situación (*f.*) difícil. || Phil. Predicamento, *m.* (category). || *What a predicament to be in!*, ¡menudo lío!
predicant [ˈpredikənt] adj. Predicante.
— N. Predicador, *m.*
predicate [ˈpredikit] n. Gramm. Phil. Predicado, *m.*
predicate [ˈpredikeit] v. tr. Afirmar (to affirm). || Implicar (to imply). || U. S. Basar (to base).
predication [ˌprediˈkeiʃən] n. Afirmación, *f.* (affirmation). || Phil. Predicación, *f.*
predicative [priˈdikətiv] adj. Gramm. Predicativo, va.
predict [priˈdikt] v. tr. Predecir, pronosticar: *to predict rain*, pronosticar lluvia.
predictable [—əbl] adj. Previsible: *a predictable move*, una maniobra previsible. || De reacciones previsibles (person).
predicted [—id] adj. Previsto, ta.
prediction [priˈdikʃən] n. Predicción, *f.*, pronóstico, *m.*
predictive [priˈdiktiv] adj. Profético, ca.
predigested [pri:didˈʒestid; pri:daidˈʒestid] adj. Predigerido, da.
predigestion [pridəˈdʒestʃən] n. Predigestión, *f.*
predilection [ˌpri:diˈlekʃən] n. Predilección, *f.*
predispose [ˈpri:disˈpəuz] v. tr. Predisponer.
predisposition [ˈpri:ˌdispəˈziʃən] n. Predisposicion, *f.*, propensión, *f.*
predominance [priˈdɔminəns] or **predominancy** [priˈdɔminənsi] n. Predominio, *m.*
predominant [priˈdɔminənt] adj. Predominante.
predominate [priˈdɔmineit] v. intr. Predominar, prevalecer.
predominating [—iŋ] adj. Predominante.
predomination [priˌdɔmiˈneiʃən] n. Predominio, *m.*

preeminence [pri'eminəns] n. Preeminencia, *f.*
preeminent [pri'eminənt] adj. Preeminente.
preempt [pri'empt] v. tr. Comprar con derecho preferente. || U. S. Adueñarse de [un terreno] para conseguir el derecho preferente de compra. || Apropiarse de (to acquire).
preemption [pri'empʃən] n. JUR. Derecho (*m.*) preferente de compra (right). | Adquisición (*f.*) *or* apropiación (*f.*) por derecho preferente de compra.
preemptive [pri'emptiv] adj. Con derecho preferente.
preemptor [pri'emptə*] n. Comprador (*m.*) con derecho preferente.
preen [pri:n] v. tr. Arreglarse (feathers). || FIG. *To preen o.s.*, pavonearse (to show vanity), atildarse (to dress up).
preestablish [,pri:es'tæbliʃ] v. tr. Preestablecer, establecer de antemano.
preexist ['pri:ig'zist] v. intr. Preexistir.
— V. tr. Existir antes que.
preexistence [—əns] n. Preexistencia, *f.*
preexistent [—ənt] adj. Preexistente.
preexisting [—iŋ] adj. Preexistente.
prefab ['pri:fæb] n. FAM. Casa (*f.*) prefabricada.
prefabricate ['pri:'fæbrikeit] v. tr. Prefabricar.
prefabricated [—id] adj. Prefabricado, da.
prefabrication ['pri:,fæbri'keiʃən] n. Prefabricación, *f.*
preface ['prefis] n. Prólogo, *m.*, prefacio, *m.* (of a book). || FIG. Prólogo, *m.* || REL. Prefacio, *m.*
preface ['prefis] v. tr. Prologar (a book, etc.). || Introducir (to begin).
prefatorial [,prefə'tɔ:riəl] or **prefatory** ['prefətəri] adj. Preliminar, a modo de prólogo.
prefect ['pri:fekt] n. Prefecto, *m.*
prefecture ['pri:fektjuə*] n. Prefectura, *f.*
prefer [pri'fə:*] v. tr. Preferir: *I prefer this house to that one*, prefiero esta casa a aquélla; *I prefer not to think about it*, prefiero no pensar en ello. || JUR. Presentar (a complaint, etc.). | Entablar (an action). | Formular (a request). | Dar prioridad a (a creditor). || Ascender (to promote). || JUR. *To prefer a charge against s.o.*, acusar a alguien.
preferable ['prefərəbl] adj. Preferible.
preferably [—i] adv. Preferentemente, preferiblemente.
preference ['prefərəns] n. Preferencia, *f.* || JUR. Preferencia, *f.*, prioridad, *f.* || *In preference to*, preferentemente a.
— Adj. Preferencial (tariff). || Preferente: *preference shares*, acciones preferentes.
preferential [,prefə'renʃəl] adj. Preferente, preferencial: *preferential treatment*, trato preferente. || Privilegiado, da (creditor, debt). || COMM. *Preferential tariff*, aranceles (*m. pl.*) preferenciales, tarifa (*f.*) preferencial.
preferentialism [—izəm] n. Concesión (*f.*) de aranceles preferenciales.
preferment [pri'fə:mənt] n. Ascenso, *m.* || *To get preferment*, ser ascendido.
preferred stock [pri'fə:dstɔk] n. U. S. Acciones (*f. pl.*) preferentes.
prefiguration [pri,figjə'reiʃən] n. Prefiguración, *f.*
prefigure [pri'figə*] v. tr. Prefigurar (to represent beforehand). || Figurarse de antemano (to imagine).
prefix ['pri:fiks] n. GRAMM. Prefijo, *m.* || JUR. Título, *m.*
prefix [pri:'fiks] v. tr. GRAMM. Poner un prefijo. || FIG. Anteponer (to place before). || Prefijar (to fix beforehand).
preform [pri:'fɔ:m] v. tr. Preformar.
preformation [,pri:fɔ:'meiʃən] n. Preformación, *f.*
preglacial [pri:'gleisjəl] adj. Preglaciar.
pregnable ['pregnəbl] adj. MIL. Conquistable, vulnerable, expugnable. || FIG. Controvertible, discutible.
pregnancy ['pregnənsi] n. Embarazo, *m.* (of a woman).
pregnant ['pregnənt] adj. Embarazada, encinta, en estado (a woman), preñada (a female animal): *to be three months pregnant*, estar embarazada de tres meses. || FIG. Muy significativo, va. | Preñado, da; lleno, na; cargado, da (*with*, de) [full]. | Fecundo, da (fruitful).
preheat ['pri:'hi:t] v. tr. Precalentar.
preheater [—ə*] n. TECH. Precalentador, *m.*
preheating [—iŋ] n. TECH. Precalentamiento, *m.*
prehensile [pri'hensail] adj. Prensil: *prehensile tail*, cola prensil.
prehension [pri'henʃən] n. ZOOL. Prensión, *f.* || Comprensión, *f.*, aprehensión, *f.* (mental).
prehistorian [pri:his'tɔriən] n. Prehistoriador, ra.
prehistoric ['pri:his'tɔrik] or **prehistorical** [—əl] adj. Prehistórico, ca.
prehistory ['pri:'histəri] n. Prehistoria, *f.*
Pre-Inca [pri:'iŋkə] adj. HIST. Preincaico, ca.
prejudge ['pri:'dʒʌdʒ] v. tr. Prejuzgar. || Juzgar de antemano (s.o.).
prejudgment or **prejudgement** [—mənt] n. Prejuicio, *m.* (prejudice).
prejudice ['predʒudis] n. Prejuicio, *m.*: *racial prejudice*, prejuicio racial. || Parcialidad, *f.* (bias). || — *In prejudice of*, en detrimento de, con menoscabo de, en perjuicio de. || *Without prejudice to*, sin perjuicio de.
prejudice ['predʒudis] v. tr. Predisponer, prevenir (to cause to have a prejudice). || Perjudicar (to harm).
prejudiced [—t] adj. Parcial (partial). || Predispuesto, ta: *to be prejudiced against, in favour of*, estar predispuesto contra, a favor de.
prejudicial [,predʒu'diʃəl] or **prejudicious** [predʒu-diʃəs] adj. Perjudicial.
prelacy ['preləsi] n. REL. Prelacía, *f.*, prelatura, *f.* (office, dignity). | Episcopado, *m.* (prelates).
prelate ['prelit] n. REL. Prelado, *m.*
prelature ['prelətjə*] n. REL. Prelatura, *f.*, prelacía, *f.*
prelect [pri'lekt] v. intr. Dar una conferencia.
prelection [pri'lekʃən] n. Conferencia, *f.*
prelector [pri'lektə*] n. Conferenciante, *m.*
prelibation [prilaibeiʃən] n. Anticipación, *f.* (foretaste).
preliminary [pri'liminəri] adj. Premilinar.
— N. Preliminar, *m.* || Examen (*m.*) premilinar (examination). || — Pl. Preliminares, *m.*, preparativos, *m.*
prelude ['prelju:d] n. Preludio, *m.*: *the discussions were a prelude to the treaty*, las discusiones fueron el preludio del tratado. || MUS. Preludio, *m.*
prelude ['prelju:d] v. tr./intr. Preludiar.
prelusive [pri'lju:siv] adj. Preliminar.
premarital [pri:'mæritl] adj. Premarital, prenupcial.
premature [,premə'tjuə] adj. Prematuro, ra: *a premature baby*, un niño prematuro; *a premature crop*, una cosecha prematura. || Precoz.
prematurity [primə'tjuriti] n. Precocidad, *f.*, carácter (*m.*) prematuro.
premaxilla [,pri:mæk'silə] n. ANAT. ZOOL. Premaxilar, *m.*
— OBSERV. El plural de la palabra *premaxilla* es *premaxillae*.
premeditate [pri'mediteit] v. tr. Premeditar.
premeditation [pri,medi'teiʃən] n. Premeditación, *f.*
premeditative [pri'meditətiv] adj. Premeditado, da.
premier ['premjə*] adj. Primero, ra.
— N. Primer ministro, *m.*, presidente (*m.*) del consejo (prime minister).
première or **premiere** ['premiɛə*] n. THEATR. Estreno, *m.* (first public performance). || U. S. THEATR. Primera estrella, *f.*, protagonista, *f.* (female star).
premiership ['premjə*ʃip] n. Cargo (*m.*) de primer ministro, presidencia (*f.*) del consejo.
premilitary [pri'militəri] adj. Premilitar.
premise ['premis] n. Premisa, *f.* (in logic). || — Pl. Parte (*f. sing.*) inicial (of a deed). || Local, *m. sing.* (site). || Edificio, *m. sing.* (building). || *On the premises*, en el local, en el sitio.
premise [pri'maiz] v. tr. Sentar como premisa (in logic). || FIG. Hacer preceder [*with*, de], empezar [*with*, por].
premiss ['premis] n. Premisa, *f.*
premium ['pri:mjəm] n. Premio, *m.* (award). || Prima, *f.* (extra salary). || Prima, *f.* (in commerce, insurance). || — *To be at a premium*, estar sobre la par (above normal value), ser muy solicitado, da (to be in demand). || *To put a premium on*, dar un gran valor a (to value highly).
premium bond [—bɔnd] n. Bono (*m.*) del Estado que participa en un sorteo nacional.
premolar [pri:'məulə*] adj. Premolar.
— N. Premolar, *m.*
premonish [pri'moniʃ] v. tr. Avisar, advertir, prevenir.
premonition [,pri:mə'niʃən] n. Premonición, *f.*, presentimiento, *m.* (presentiment). || Advertencia, *f.* (forewarning).
premonitory [pri'mɔnitəri] adj. Premonitorio, ria.
prenatal ['pri:'neitl] adj. Prenatal.
prenuptial [pri'nʌpʃəl] adj. Prenupcial.
preoccupancy [pri'ɔkjupənsi] n. Ocupación (*f.*) anterior.
preoccupation [pri,ɔkju'peiʃən] n. Preocupación, *f.*
preoccupied [pri'ɔkjupaid] adj. Preocupado, da (worried): *to be preoccupied about*, estar preocupado por. || Absorto, ta; ensimismado, da (lost in thought): *to be preoccupied with*, estar absorto en. || Ocupado anteriormente (occupied before).
preoccupy [pri'ɔkjupai] v. tr. Preocupar (to worry). || Absorber, ensimismar (to absorb). || Ocupar anteriormente (a house).
preordain ['pri:ɔ:'dein] v. tr. Predeterminar.
prep [prep] n. Deberes, *m. pl.* (homework). || Escuela (*f.*) preparatoria.
prepaid ['pri:'peid] adj. Pagado con antelación *or* con anticipación *or* por adelantado. || Franqueado, da (letter). || Pagado, da (carriage, etc.). || Franco de porte, con el porte pagado (carriage paid, postpaid).
preparation [,prepə'reiʃən] n. Preparación, *f.*: *the preparation of the meal takes two hours*, la preparación de la comida requiere dos horas. || Deberes, *m. pl.* (homework). || Preparación, *f.*, preparado, *m.* (chemical substance, medicine). || — Pl. Preparativos, *m.*: *have you made all the preparations for the trip?*, ¿ha hecho todos los preparativos para el viaje?
preparative [pri'pærətiv] adj. Preparativo, va; preparatorio, ria.
— N. Preparativo, *m.*
preparatory [—i] adj. Preparatorio, ria; preliminar (preliminary). || — *Preparatory school*, escuela preparatoria. || *Preparatory to*, antes de (before), con miras a (with a view to).
prepare [pri'pɛə*] v. tr. Preparar, disponer (to get ready). || CULIN. Preparar: *I am preparing dinner*, estoy preparando la cena. || Preparar (s.o., document). || FIG. *To prepare the way for*, preparar el terreno para.

— V. intr. Prepararse: *he is preparing for an examination*, se está preparando para un examen. || MIL. *To prepare for action*, entrar en batería.
prepared [—d] adj. Listo, ta; preparado, da; dispuesto, ta. || — *Be prepared*, estad siempre listos. || *To be prepared for anything*, estar preparado para cualquier cosa. || *To be prepared to*, estar dispuesto a. || *We were not prepared for this*, no contábamos con esto. || *We were prepared for it*, lo teníamos previsto.
preparedness [—dnis] n. Preparación, *f.*, estado (*m.*) de preparación.
preparer [—rə*] n. Preparador, ra.
prepay* [ˈpriːˈpei] v. tr. Pagar por adelantado *or* por anticipado. || Franquear (a letter).

— OBSERV. Pret. & p. p. ***prepaid***.

prepayment [—mənt] n. Pago (*m.*) por adelantado *or* por anticipado. || Franqueo, *m.* (of a letter).
prepense [priˈpens] adj. Premeditado, da. || *With malice prepense*, con premeditación.
preponderance [priˈpɔndərəns] n. Preponderancia, *f.*, predominio, *m.*
preponderant [priˈpɔndərənt] adj. Preponderante, predominante.
preponderate [priˈpɔndəreit] v. intr. Preponderar, prevalecer, predominar.
preposition [ˌprepəˈziʃən] n. GRAMM. Preposición, *f.*
prepositional [ˌprepəˈziʃənl] adj. GRAMM. Prepositivo, va: *prepositional phrase*, locución prepositiva.
prepositive [priˈpɔzitiv] adj. GRAMM. Prepositivo, va.
prepossess [ˌpriːpəˈzes] v. tr. Predisponer (*in favour of*, a favor de). || Obseder, obsesionar, preocupar (to preoccupy).
prepossessing [—iŋ] adj. Atractivo, va; agradable.
prepossession [ˌpriːpəˈzeʃən] n. Prejuicio, *m.*, predisposición, *f.*
preposterous [priˈpɔstərəs] adj. Absurdo, da; ridículo, la; extravagante.
preposterousness [—nis] n. Lo absurdo, lo ridículo, ridiculez, *f.*
prepotency [priˈpəutənsi] n. Predominio, *m.* || BIOL. Prepotencia, *f.*
prepotent [priˈpəutənt] adj. Predominante. || BIOL. Prepotente.
prepuce [ˈpriːpjuːs] n. ANAT. Prepucio, *m.*
Pre-Raphaelite [ˈpriːˈræfəlait] adj./n. Prerrafaelista.
Pre-Raphaelitism [priˈræfəlaitizəm] n. Prerrafaelismo, *m.*
prerecord [pririˈkɔːd] v. tr. Grabar antes, grabar de antemano.
prerequisite [ˈpriːˈrekwizit] adj. Previamente necesario.
— N. Requisito (*m.*) previo, condición (*f.*) previa (precondition).
prerogative [priˈrɔgətiv] adj. Privilegiado, da.
— N. Prerrogativa, *f.*
Preromanticism [priraˈmæntisizəm] n. Prerromanticismo, *m.*
presage [ˈpresidʒ] n. Presagio, *m.* (that which foretells). || Presentimiento, *m.* (presentiment).
presage [ˈpresidʒ] v. tr. Presagiar (to portend, to predict). || Presentir, tener el presentimiento de (to have a presentiment of).
presbyopia [ˌprezbiˈəupjə] n. MED. Presbicia, *f.*
presbyopic [prezbiˈɔpik] adj. Présbita.
presbyter [ˈprezbitə*] n. REL. Presbítero, *m.*
presbyteral [prezˈbitiːəriəl] adj. Presbiteral.
presbyterate [presˈbitərət] n. REL. Presbiterado, *m.*
presbyterial [ˌprezbiˈtiːəriəl] adj. REL. Presbiteral.
Presbyterian [ˌprezbiˈtiəriən] adj./n. Presbiteriano, na.
Presbyterianism [—izəm] n. REL. Presbiterianismo, *m.*
presbytery [ˈprezbitəri] n. ARCH. Presbiterio, *m.* (part of a church). || Casa (*f.*) del cura, casa (*f.*) parroquial (priest's house).
preschool [priːˈskuːl] adj. Preescolar.
prescience [ˈpresiəns] n. Presciencia, *f.*
prescient [ˈpresiənt] adj. Que tiene presciencia, presciente.
prescind [priˈsind] v. tr. Separar (to isolate).
— V. intr. *To prescind from*, prescindir de.
prescribe [prisˈkraib] v. tr. Prescribir (to order). || MED. Recetar (a medicine). | Mandar, ordenar: *the doctor prescribed complete rest*, el médico le mandó reposo absoluto. || JUR. Prescribir. || — *In the prescribed time*, dentro del plazo fijado por la ley. || *In the prescribed way*, de conformidad con lo prescrito.
— V. intr. Establecer una norma, fijar una norma (to lay down a rule). || MED. Hacer una receta. || JUR. Prescribir.
prescript [ˈpriːskript] n. Norma, *f.*, regla, *f.*, precepto, *m.* (rule).
prescriptible [priˈskriptibl] adj. Prescriptible.
prescription [prisˈkripʃən] n. Prescripción, *f.* (act of prescribing). || Norma, *f.*, regla, *f.*, precepto, *m.* (prescript). || MED. Receta, *f.*, prescripción, *f.* || JUR. Prescripción, *f.*
prescriptive [prisˈkriptiv] adj. Preceptivo, va. || Establecido, da (established by usage).
presealed [priːˈsiːld] adj. Precintado, da.
preselection [priːsiˈlekʃən] n. RAD. Preselección, *f.*
preselector [priːseˈlektə*] n. RAD. Preselector, *m.*
presence [ˈprezns] n. Presencia, *f.*: *nobody noticed his presence in the room*, nadie advirtió su presencia en la sala; *of good presence*, de buena presencia; *supernatural presence*, presencia sobrenatural. || Asistencia, *f.*, presencia, *f.* (attendance). || Personalidad, *f.* (personality). || — *In the presence of*, en presencia de. || *Presence of mind*, presencia de ánimo. || *To be admitted to the Presence*, ser recibido en audiencia por el rey. || *To make one's presence felt*, imponerse, hacerse notar. || *Your presence is requested*, se ruega su asistencia.
presence chamber [—ˈtʃeimbə*] n. Sala (*f.*) de audiencia.
present [ˈpreznt] adj. Presente (in a place): *everybody was present*, todos estaban presentes. || Presente: *in the present case*, en el caso presente. || Presente, actual (time). || GRAMM. Presente: *present tense*, tiempo presente. || — *All present*, todos los presentes. || *At the present time*, en el momento actual, en este momento. || *Present company excepted*, mejorando lo presente. || *The present letter*, la presente carta, la presente. || *The present writer*, el que esto suscribe. || *The present year*, el año en curso. || *Those present*, los presentes. || *To be present*, asistir (to attend), haber: *nobody else was present*, no había nadie más. || *To be present at*, asistir: *we were present at the banquet*, asistimos al banquete; ser testigo de, presenciar: *he was present at the ceremony*, presenció la ceremonia.
— N. Regalo, *m.*, presente, *m.* (gift): *did you give him a present for his birthday?*, ¿le hizo un regalo para su cumpleaños? || Presente, *m.*, actualidad, *f.* (time). || GRAMM. Presente, *m.* (tense). || — *At present*, en la actualidad, actualmente, ahora (at the present day), por ahora (for the moment). || JUR. *By these presents*, por la presente. || *For the present*, por ahora, por el momento. || *To make s.o. a present of sth.*, regalar algo a alguien. || *Up to the present*, hasta ahora.
— Interj. ¡Presente!
present [priˈzent] v. tr. Presentar: *to present a candidate*, presentar a un candidato; *may I present Mrs. Robinson?*, le presento a la señora Robinson; *to present a bill*, presentar un proyecto de ley; *to present a report*, presentar un informe. || Exponer, presentar (an argument, case, etc.). || Presentar: *matter that presents many difficulties*, asunto que presenta muchas dificultades. || Plantear: *the dog presents a problem*, el perro plantea un problema. || JUR. Presentar (a charge, etc.). || Ofrecer, presentar: *to present a dismal aspect*, ofrecer un aspecto lúgubre. || Regalar, obsequiar (to give as a gift): *to present s.o. with a gold watch*, regalar un reloj de oro a alguien, obsequiar a alguien con un reloj de oro. || Presentar (in theatre, cinema, etc.). || REL. Designar, proponer, presentar (to an ecclesiastical benefice). || — *Presenting X as Romeo*, con X en el papel de Romeo. || MIL. *To present arms*, presentar armas. || *To present one's compliments to s.o.*, presentar sus respetos a alguien. || *To present o.s.*, presentarse.
presentability [priˌzəntəˈbiliti] n. Buena presencia, *f.*
presentable [priˈzentəbl] adj. Presentable. || *She is quite presentable*, tiene buena presencia.
presentation [ˌprezenˈteiʃən] n. Presentación, *f.* || Entrega, *f.*, ceremonia (*f.*) de entrega (ceremony). || Obsequio, *m.*, regalo, *m.* (gift). || THEATR. Presentación, *f.* (manner of presenting). | Representación, *f.* (performance). || REL. Presentación, *f.* || MED. Presentación, *f.* (of a foetus). || — *A presentation copy*, un ejemplar de cortesía, un ejemplar con la dedicatoria del autor (of a book). || *On presentation of*, al presentar.
presentative [priˈzentətiv] adj. REL. Colativo, va. || PHIL. Perceptible. | Intuitivo, va.
present-day [ˈprezntdei] adj. Actual, de hoy en día.
presentee [ˌprezənˈtiː] n. Persona (*f.*) presentada. || REL. Presentado, *m.*
presenter [priˈzentə*] n. Presentador, ra.
presentient [priˈsenʃiənt] adj. *To be presentient of*, presentir, tener el presentimiento de.
presentiment [priˈzentimənt] n. Presentimiento, *m.*, corazonada, *f.* || *To have the presentiment that*, tener el presentimiento de que.
presently [ˈprezntli] adv. Dentro de poco, luego (in a little while): *I'll come along presently*, iré dentro de poco. || Pronto (soon). || U. S. Ahora, en el momento presente (at present).
presentment [priˈzentmənt] n. Presentación, *f.* || REL. Reclamación, *f.*, queja, *f.* (complaint). || THEATR. ARTS. Representación, *f.* || JUR. Declaración (*f.*) del jurado. || FIG. Descripción, *f.* (of a place, etc.).
present participle [ˈprezntˈpɑːtisipl] n. GRAMM. Gerundio, *m.*, participio (*m.*) de presente.
present perfect [ˈprezntˈpəːfikt] n. GRAMM. Pretérito (*m.*) perfecto.
preservable [priˈzəːvəbl] adj. Conservable.
preservation [ˌprezəˈveiʃən] n. Conservación, *f.*: *preservation of fruit*, conservación de frutas. || Preservación, *f.* (protection). || *In good preservation*, bien conservado, da.
preservative [priˈzəːvətiv] adj. Preservativo, va.
— N. Preservativo, *m.* || Producto (*m.*) para la conservación, producto (*m.*) de conservación (for food).

preserve [pri'zə:v] n. Coto, *m.*, vedado, *m.* (for game or fish). || Conserva, *f.* (of food). || Confitura, *f.*, compota, *f.* (jam). || Fig. Terreno, *m.*: *to trespass on s.o.'s preserve*, meterse en terreno ajeno.
preserve [pri'zə:v] v. tr. Conservar, poner en conserva (foodstuffs). || Preservar, proteger (to protect). || Proteger (game). || Conservar (memory, custom). || Conservar, guardar, mantener (one's dignity, peace, etc.). || Observar, guardar (silence).
preserved [—d] adj. En conserva. || *Preserved food*, conservas, *f. pl.*
preserving [—iŋ] n. Conservación, *f.*
preshrunk ['pri'ʃrʌŋk] adj. Encogido de antemano, inencogible.
preside [pri'zaid] v. intr. Presidir: *to preside at* o *over a meeting*, presidir una reunión.
presidency ['prezidənsi] n. Presidencia, *f.* || Dirección, *f.* (of a bank, etc.). || U. S. Rectoría, *f.* (of a university).
president ['prezidənt] n. Presidente, *m.*, presidenta, *f.* || Director, *m.* (of a bank, etc.). || U. S. Rector, *m.* (of a university).
presidential [,prezi'denʃəl] adj. Presidencial.
presidentship ['prezidəntʃip] n. Presidencia, *f.* || Dirección, *f.* (of a bank, etc.). || U. S. Rectorado, *m.* (of a university).
presidio [pri'sidiəu] n. Presidio, *m.*
presidium [pri'sidiəm] n. Presidium, *m.*
press [pres] n. Presión, *f.* (pressure). || Apretón, *m.* (of hand). || Muchedumbre, *f.*, multitud, *f.* (crowd). || Apiñamiento, *m.* (crush of people). || Prisa, *f.*, urgencia, *f.* (urgency). || Apresuramiento, *m.* (haste). || Prensa, *f.*: *hydraulic press*, prensa hidráulica. || Print. Imprenta, *f.* (printing office): *to send to press*, mandar a la imprenta. | Impresión, *f.* (printing): *the edition is ready to go to press*, la edición está lista para la impresión. | Personal (*m.*) de imprenta (staff). || Prensa, *f.* (journalists, newspapers collectively): *will the press be admitted to the conference?*, ¿se admitirá a la prensa en la conferencia? || Prensa, *f.*, crítica, *f.*: *the play received a good press*, la obra tuvo muy buena prensa. || Ropero, *m.* (cupboard). || Sp. Presa, *f.* (in wrestling). | Levantada, *f.* (in weight lifting). | Prensa, *f.* (for a tennis racket). || Leva (*f.*) forzosa de marineros y soldados. || — *Freedom of the press*, libertad (*f.*) de prensa. || *In the press*, en prensa. || *Off the press*, recién salido de la imprenta. || *Press campaign*, campaña (*f.*) de prensa. || *Printing press*, prensa (machine). || *Rotary press*, rotativa, *f.* || *To go to press*, entrar en prensa. || *To pass for press*, dar el tirese. || *To write for the press*, escribir en los periódicos. || Fig. *Yellow press*, prensa sensacionalista.
press [pres] v. tr. Prensar (in a mechanical press). || Apretar, presionar (to push). || Apretar: *they press me here*, me aprietan aquí. || Planchar (to iron clothes): *to press a skirt*, planchar una falda. || Pulsar, presionar, dar a (a button, lever, etc.): *press the button*, dale al botón. || Tocar (a bell). || Apretar (trigger, hand, etc.). || Exprimir (fruits to obtain juice). || Estrujar (to squeeze). || Secar (flowers). || Prensar (a record). || Fig. Instar, apremiar, urgir (to urge): *to press s.o. to do sth.*, instar a alguien a que haga algo. | Insistir en (to insist upon): *to press one's opinion*, insistir en su opinión. | Hacer hincapié en (to emphasize). | Acosar, acuciar, apremiar (to harass): *to press a debtor for payment*, acosar a un deudor para que pague. | Imponer: *to press one's opinions on others*, imponer sus opiniones a otros. | Hostigar, acosar (the enemy). | Seguir muy de cerca, ir pisándole los talones a (in pursuit). || Tech. Calandrar (a fabric). | Sobar, adobar (hides). | Pisar, prensar (grapes). | Prensar (apples, olives). | Estampar, embutir (metals). | Satinar (paper). || Levar por fuerza (soldiers, sailors). || — *He didn't need much pressing*, no hubo que repetírselo dos veces, no se hizo de rogar. || *To be pressed for time, for money*, andar escaso de tiempo, de dinero. || *To press a claim*, insistir en una petición. || *To press a gift on s.o.*, obligar a alguien a aceptar un regalo. || *To press a point home*, conseguir convencer a alguien de algo. || *To press for payment*, apremiar para el pago. || *To press one's face to the window*, pegar la cara contra el cristal. || Fig. *To press s.o. for an answer*, insistir en que alguien conteste. || *To press s.o. into service*, recurrir a alguien. || *To press s.o. to one's heart*, abrazar a alguien estrechamente. || *To press sth. into service*, utilizar algo.
— V. intr. Apretar; *to press hard*, apretar fuerte *or* mucho. || Apretujarse, apiñarse (crowds). || Abrirse paso (through a crowd). || Apremiar, urgir, ser urgente (to be urgent): *the matter does not press*, el asunto no urge. || Apremiar (time): *time is pressing*, el tiempo apremia. || Pesar: *great responsibilities press on him*, grandes responsabilidades pesan sobre él. || Ejercer presión (to put pressure on).
— ***To press back***, rechazar (the enemy). | Contener (tears, desire). || ***To press down***, apretar. | — *To press down on sth.*, apretar algo (to force down), apoyarse en algo (to rest on, to lean on). || ***To press for***, pedir con insistencia. || ***To press forward***, activar, apresurar (to hasten). | Apresurarse (to make haste). | Seguir adelante (to advance with resolution). || ***To press in***, clavar (a drawing pin). | Meter a presión. || ***To press on***, activar, apresurar (to hasten). | Seguir adelante (to advance with resolution). | Apresurarse (to make haste). | — *To press on with*, activar, apresurar. || ***To press out***, exprimir (a fruit). | Planchar (creases). | Expulsar a presión. || ***To press up***, apretujarse, apretarse: *to press up to*, apretujarse contra.
press agency [—,eidʒənsi] n. Agencia (*f.*) de prensa.
press agent [—,eidʒənt] n. Agente (*m.*) de publicidad, agente (*m.*) de prensa.
press baron [—'bærən] n. Magnate (*m.*) de la prensa.
press box [—bɔks] n. Tribuna (*f.*) de la prensa.
press button [—'bʌtn] n. Botón, *m.*
press clipping [—'klipiŋ] n. Recorte (*m.*) de periódico *or* de prensa.
press conference [—,kɔnfərəns] n. Rueda (*f.*) *or* conferencia (*f.*) de prensa.
press cutting [—,kʌtiŋ] n. Recorte (*m.*) de periódico *or* de prensa.
presser [—ə*] n. Prensador, ra (press operator).
presser foot [—ə*fut] n. Pie (*m.*) prensatelas, prensilla, *f.* (of sewing machine).
press gallery [—'gæləri] n. Tribuna (*f.*) de la prensa.
press-gang [—gæŋ] n. Mil. Mar. Patrulla (*f.*) de enganche.
press house [—haus] n. Lagar, *m.* (for olives, grapes and apples). || Prensa, *f.* (for fruits and grains).
pressing [—iŋ] adj. Urgente: *he had a pressing engagement elsewhere*, tenía un compromiso urgente en otra parte. || Apremiante, acuciante: *a pressing need*, una necesidad apremiante. || Insistente.
— N. Prensado, *m.* (of fruits, records). || Planchado, *m.* (ironing). || Calandrado, *m.* (of fabric). || Estampado, *m.*, embutido, *m.* (of metals). || Satinado, *m.* (of paper).
pressman [—mən] n. Prensador, *m.* (press operator). || Impresor, *m.* (of a printing press). || Periodista, *m.* (journalist).

— Observ. El plural de *pressman* es *pressmen*.

pressmark [—mɑ:k] n. Signatura, *f.* (on books).
press money [—'mʌni] n. Prima (*f.*) de enganche.
press of canvas [—əv'kænvəs] or **press of sail** [—əv'seil] n. Mar. Velamen (*m.*) máximo.
press photographer [—fə'tɔgrəfə*] n. Fotógrafo (*m.*) de prensa, reportero (*m.*) gráfico.
press proof [—pru:f] n. Print. Última prueba (*f.*) de imprenta.
press release [—ri'li:s] n. Comunicado (*m.*) de prensa.
press roll [—rəul] n. Rodillo (*m.*) de presión.
pressroom [—ru:m] n. Taller (*m.*) de imprenta.
press stud [—stʌd] n. Automático, *m.*
pressure ['preʃə*] n. Phys. Tech. Presión, *f.*: *atmospheric pressure*, presión atmosférica. || Peso, *m.* (weight). || Fuerza, *f.* (strength). || Electr. Tensión, *f.*, voltaje, *m.* || Med. Tensión, *f.*: *blood pressure*, tensión arterial; *low blood pressure*, tensión baja. || Fig. Presión, *f.*, apremio, *m.*: *under the pressure of circumstances*, bajo la presión de las circunstancias. | Influencia, *f.*, presión, *f.* (influence). || — *At full pressure*, a toda presión. || *To act under pressure*, obrar bajo presión. || *To bring pressure to bear on s.o.*, ejercer presión sobre alguien. || *To do sth. under pressure from s.o.*, hacer algo presionado por alguien. || *To exert pressure on*, ejercer presión sobre. || *Tyre pressure*, presión de los neumáticos. || *Under the pressure of*, apremiado por, bajo la presión de.
pressure ['preʃə*] v. tr. Ejercer presión sobre.
pressure cabin [—,kæbin] n. Cabina (*f.*) presurizada.
pressure cooker [—,kukə*] n. Olla (*f.*) de presión.
pressure feed [—fi:d] n. Alimentación (*f.*) a presión.
pressure gauge [—geidʒ] n. Manómetro, *m.*
pressure group [—gru:p] n. Grupo (*m.*) de presión (in politics).
pressurization [preʃərai'zeiʃən] n. Presurización, *f.*
pressurize ['preʃəraiz] v. tr. Presurizar, sobrecomprimir.
presswork ['preswə:k] n. Print. Impresión, *f.*, tirada, *f.*
Prester John ['prestə:'dʒɔn] pr. n. Preste Juan.
prestidigitation ['presti,didʒi'teiʃən] n. Prestidigitación, *f.*
prestidigitator [,presti'didʒiteitə*] n. Prestidigitador, *m.*
prestige [pres'ti:ʒ] n. Prestigio, *m.*
prestigious [pres'tidʒəs] adj. Prestigioso, sa.
presto ['prestəu] adj./adv. Mus. Presto.
prestress ['prestris] v. tr. Pretensar: *prestressed concrete*, hormigón pretensado.
presumable [pri'zju:məbl] adj. Probable, presumible.
presumably [pri'zju:məbli] adv. Probablemente: *presumably she will come*, probablemente vendrá.
presume [pri'zju:m] v. tr. Suponer, imaginarse, figurarse, presumir (to suppose): *I presume that he will come tomorrow*, supongo que vendrá mañana. || Tomarse la libertad de, permitirse, atreverse a (to dare).
— V. intr. Presumir (to be presumptuous). || Abusar: *to presume on s.o.'s hospitality*, abusar de la hospitalidad de alguien.
presumed [—d] adj. Presunto, ta; supuesto, ta.
presumedly [—ədli] adv. Por lo visto, probablemente.
presuming [—iŋ] adj. Osado, da; atrevido, da (daring). || Presuntuoso, sa; presumido, da (conceited).

presumption [priˈzʌmpʃən] n. Presunción, *f.*, suposición, *f.* (supposition). || Presunción, *f.*, presuntuosidad, *f.* (vanity, conceit). || Atrevimiento, *m.*, osadía, *f.* (daring). || JUR. Presunción, *f.*

presumptive [priˈzʌmptiv] adj. Presunto, ta; supuesto, ta. || JUR. Presuntivo, va: *presumptive evidence*, pruebas presuntivas. || *Heir presumptive*, heredero presunto.

presumptuous [priˈzʌmptjuəs] adj. Presuntuoso, sa; presumido, da (conceited). || Atrevido, da; osado, da (daring).

presumptuousness [—nis] n. Presuntuosidad, *f.*, presunción, *f.* (vanity). || Atrevimiento, *m.*, osadía, *f.* (daring).

presuppose [ˌpri:səˈpəuz] v. tr. Presuponer, suponer.

presupposition [ˌpri:sʌpəˈziʃən] n. Presuposición, *f.*, presupuesto, *m.*

pretence (U. S. **pretense**) [priˈtens] n. Pretensión, *f.* (claim, pretentiousness): *no pretence to originality*, ninguna pretensión de originalidad. || Pretexto, *m.* (pretext). || Apariencia, *f.* (appearance). || Simulación, *f.*, fingimiento, *m.* (false show). || Ostentación, *f.* (display): *devoid of all pretence*, sin ninguna ostentación. || JUR. Procedimiento (*m.*) fraudulento. || — *False pretences*, fraude, *m. sing.* || *His anger was only pretence*, su cólera era fingida. || *To make a pretence of*, simular que, hacer como si. || *To make no pretence to know*, no pretender saber. || *To obtain sth. under false pretences*, obtener algo por fraude *or* fraudulentamente. || *Under the pretence of*, so pretexto de, con el pretexto de.

pretend [priˈtend] n. FAM. Simulacro, *m.* || FAM. *His anger was all pretend*, su cólera era fingida.

pretend [priˈtend] v. tr. Fingir, aparentar, simular: *to pretend ignorance*, fingir ignorancia. || Pretender (to claim): *he didn't pretend to know it*, no pretendía saberlo. || Suponer, imaginarse (to imagine): *let's pretend that we are on an island*, vamos a suponer que estamos en una isla. || — *To pretend to be*, fingirse, fingir: *he pretends to be dead*, se finge muerto, finge estar muerto; dárselas de: *he pretended he was a doctor*, se las daba de médico.

— V. intr. Disimular, fingir (to hide feelings, etc.): *don't pretend with me*, no disimules conmigo. || — *Let's not pretend to each other*, no nos engañemos uno a otro. || *To pretend to cleverness*, dárselas de listo, pretender ser listo. || *To pretend to the throne*, pretender el trono.

pretended [—id] adj. Fingido, da; simulado, da (emotion). || Supuesto, ta (person).

pretender [—ə*] n. Pretendiente, *m.* & *f.*: *pretender to the throne*, pretendiente al trono. || Simulador, ra (s.o. who pretends).

pretense [priˈtens] n. U. S. See PRETENCE.

pretension [priˈtenʃən] n. Pretensión, *f.* (claim). || Presunción, *f.*, pretensión, *f.* (pretentiousness).

pretentious [priˈtenʃəs] adj. Pretencioso, sa; presuntuoso, sa; presumido, da (conceited, showy). || Cursi (showy and in bad taste).

pretentiousness [—nis] n. Presunción, *f.*, presuntuosidad, *f.*, pretensión, *f.* (conceit). || Cursilería, *f.* (snobbishness).

preterite or **preterit** [ˈpretərit] adj. GRAMM. Pretérito. || FIG. Pretérito, ta; pasado, da.

— N. GRAMM. Pretérito, *m.*

preterition [pri:təˈriʃən] n. Preterición, *f.* (omission). || JUR. Preterición, *f.*

pretermission [ˌpri:təˈmiʃən] n. Preterición, *f.*

pretermit [ˌpri:təˈmit] v. tr. Omitir, preterir (to omit).

pretext [ˈpri:tekst] n. Pretexto, *m.* || — *Under the pretext of*, so pretexto de, con el pretexto de. || *Under the pretext that*, con el pretexto de que.

pretext [ˈpri:tekst] v. tr. Pretextar, dar como pretexto.

pretexta [—ə] n. Pretexta, *f.*

pretor, pretorial, pretorian, etc. See PRAETOR, PRAETORIAL, PRAETORIAN, etc.

prettification [ˌpritifiˈkeiʃən] n. Embellecimiento, *m.*

prettify [ˈpritifai] v. tr. Embellecer.

prettily [ˈpritili] adv. Bonitamente, lindamente. || Bien: *to behave prettily*, portarse bien.

prettiness [ˈpritinis] n. Lo bonito, lo mono, lo lindo, lindeza, *f.*, belleza, *f.* (beauty). || Preciosidad, *f.* (in style).

pretty [ˈpriti] adj. Bonito, ta; mono, na; lindo, da (thing). || Mono, na; guapo, pa; lindo, da (person). || FAM. Menudo, da: *a pretty mess*, menudo lío. | Importante, considerable, bueno, na (sum etc.). || FIG. *To cost a pretty penny*, costar caro, costar mucho dinero, costar un dineral.

— Adv. Bastante: *pretty good*, bastante bueno; *I am pretty busy*, estoy bastante ocupado. || *Pretty much the same*, más o menos lo mismo.

— N. Cosa (*f.*) bonita *or* linda. || *My pretty*, mi vida, mi cielo, guapa.

pretzel [ˈpretsəl] n. Galleta (*f.*) tostada cubierta con sal.

prevail [priˈveil] v. intr. Prevalecer: *truth will prevail*, la verdad prevalecerá; *the tradition still prevails in the South*, la tradición prevalece todavía en el Sur. || Triunfar, vencer: *we prevailed over o against the enemy*, vencimos al enemigo, triunfamos sobre el enemigo. || Predominar: *a region where strong winds prevail*, una región donde predominan vientos fuertes. || Imperar, predominar, regir, reinar: *the conditions that then prevailed*, las condiciones que imperaban entonces. || — *To be prevailed upon to*, dejarse convencer *or* persuadir de. || *To prevail on* o *upon*, persuadir, convencer.

prevailing [—iŋ] adj. Reinante, imperante, predominante: *the prevailing wind*, el viento predominante; *the prevailing cold*, el frío imperante. || Común (opinion). || Actual (present): *under prevailing conditions*, en las condiciones actuales.

prevalence [ˈprevələns] n. Uso (*m.*) corriente, costumbre, *f.* (common practice). || Predominio, *m.*: *the prevalence of good over evil*, el predominio del bien sobre el mal. || Frecuencia, *f.* (frequency).

prevalent [ˈprevələnt] adj. Predominante, que prevalece, que reina, que impera: *disease that is prevalent in a country*, enfermedad que impera en un país. || Extendido, da (widespread). || Corriente (common). || Actual (present-day): *the prevalent fashion*, la moda actual. || Frecuente (frequent).

prevaricate [priˈværikeit] v. intr. Andar con rodeos, tergiversar (to avoid the issue). || Mentir (to lie). || JUR. Prevaricar.

prevarication [priˌværiˈkeiʃən] n. Tergiversación, *f.*, equívocos, *m. pl.*, evasivas, *f. pl.* || Mentira, *f.* (lie). || JUR. Prevaricación, *f.*

prevaricator [priˈværikeitə*] n. Tergiversador, ra. || Mentiroso, sa (liar). || JUR. Prevaricador, *m.*

prevenient [priˈvi:njənt] adj. Previo, via; anterior (previous). || MED. Preventivo, va.

prevent [priˈvent] v. tr. Impedir: *illness prevented him from coming* o *prevented his coming*, la enfermedad le impidió venir. || Evitar (to avoid): *to prevent a serious accident*, evitar un accidente grave.

preventable or **preventible** [priˈventəbl] adj. Evitable.

preventative [priˈventətiv] adj./n. See PREVENTIVE.

preventer [priˈventə*] n. Impedimento, *m.*, obstáculo, *m.* || — MAR. *Preventer stay*, contraestay, *m.* | *Preventer tack*, contraamura, *f.*

prevention [priˈvenʃən] n. Prevención, *f.* || Impedimento, *m.* (hindrance): *in case of prevention*, en caso de impedimento. || Protección, *f.* || — *For the prevention of accidents*, para evitar accidentes. || *Prevention is better than cure*, más vale prevenir que curar. || *Prevention of unemployment*, medidas preventivas contra el paro *or* desempleo. || *Society for the prevention of cruelty to*, sociedad protectora de.

preventive [priˈventiv] adj. Preventivo, va.

— N. Medida (*f.*) preventiva. || MED. Medicamento (*m.*) profiláctico.

preventorium [privenˈtɔ:riəm] n. MED. Preventorio, *m.* (for preventive care or treatment).

preview [ˈpri:ˈvju:] n. CINEM. THEATR. Presentación (*f.*) a los críticos. | Trailer, *m.*, avance, *m.* (film extract).

preview [ˈpri:ˈvju:] v. tr. Asistir a la presentación [de una película u obra de teatro] a los críticos. || Presentar a los críticos (to present). || Ver antes que los demás.

previous [ˈpri:vjəs] adj. Anterior, previo, via: *the previous meeting*, la reunión anterior; *without previous notice*, sin previo aviso. || FAM. Prematuro, ra (premature). | Apresurado, da (hasty). || JUR. *Previous question*, cuestión previa.

— Adv. *Previous to*, antes de: *to check one's work previous to handing it in*, revisar el trabajo antes de entregarlo.

previously [—li] adv. Antes, anteriormente, previamente: *he didn't know what had happened previously*, no sabía lo que había ocurrido antes. || *Previously to*, antes de.

previousness [—nis] n. Anterioridad, *f.* || U. S. Prisa, *f.* (haste).

previse [priˈva:iz] v. tr. Prever (to foresee). || Prevenir, advertir (to warn).

prevision [priˈviʒən] n. Previsión, *f.*

previsional [—əl] adj. Previsor, ra.

prevue [ˈpri:ˈvju:] n./v. tr. U. S. See PREVIEW.

prewar [ˈpri:ˈwɔ:*] adj. De antes de la guerra. || *The prewar period*, la preguerra.

prey [prei] n. Presa, *f.* (of an animal). || FIG. Víctima, *f.*: *he fell prey to robbers*, fue víctima de los ladrones. || ZOOL. *Bird of prey*, ave (*f.*) de rapiña *or* de presa.

prey [prei] v. intr. Atacar (to attack). || Pillar (to plunder). || Aprovecharse de (to exploit). || FIG. Reconcomer, carcomer: *doubts preyed on him*, las dudas lo reconcomían. | Remorder (one's conscience). || Alimentarse (*on*, de) [animals]. || *To prey on one's mind*, preocupar mucho.

price [prais] n. Precio, *m.*: *asking, cash, cost, list, net price*, precio ofrecido, al contado, de coste, de lista, neto; *price fixing*, fijación de precios; *price rise*, subida de precio *or* de precios. || COMM. Cotización, *f.*: *closing, opening price*, cotización de cierre, inicial. || FIG. Precio, *m.*, valor, *m.* (value). || — FIG. *At any price*, a toda costa, cueste lo que cueste. || *At cost price*, a precio de coste. || *Beyond price*, inapreciable, sin precio. || *Factory price*, precio de fábrica. || *Fixed price*, precio fijo. || *Full price*, precio fuerte. || *Low price*, precio barato *or* bajo. || *Manufacturer's price*, precio de fábrica. || *Market price*, precio de mercado, precio corriente. || FIG. *Not at any price*, por nada del mundo. || *Price ceiling* o *maximum price*, precio tope. || *Price control*, control (*m.*) de precios, intervención, *f.* || *Price free on board*, precio franco a bordo. || *Price list*, lista (*f.*) de precios, tarifa, *f.* || *Price of money*, tipo (*m.*) de descuento, interés, *m.* || *Price range*, gama (*f.*) de precios. || *Price support*, mantenimiento (*m.*) de los precios. || *Purchase price*, precio de compra. || *Reserve price*, precio mínimo. || *Rock-bottom* o *cheapest possible price*, precio mínimo. || *Sale price*, precio de venta. || *Top* o *ceiling price*, precio tope. || *To put a price on*, poner precio a. || FIG. *To put a price on s.o.'s head*, poner a precio la cabeza de uno. | *To set a high price on sth.*, dar mucha importancia a algo. || *Unit price*, precio por unidad. || *Whatever the price*, a cualquier precio. || *What price autonomy?*, y la autonomía, ¿qué? || *Wholesale price*, precio al por mayor.

price [prais] v. tr. COMM. Poner precio a, tasar, valorar (*at*, en) [to fix the price of]. || Preguntar el precio de (to ask the price of). || FIG. Estimar, evaluar, valorar, tasar (to estimate the value of). || — COMM. *All the commodities are priced*, todos los artículos llevan precio. | *To be priced at*, costar, tener un precio de. | *To be priced out of the market*, no poder competir en los mercados internacionales [a causa de su elevado precio], no ser competitivo.

priceless [—lis] adj. Inapreciable, inestimable, que no tiene precio (invaluable). || FAM. Divertidísimo, ma; graciosísimo, ma (highly amusing). || *To be priceless*, no tener precio; ser divertidísimo.

pricelessness [—lisnis] n. Valor (*m.*) inapreciable.

prick [prik] n. Pinchazo, *m.* (act, pain, perforation). || Picadura, *f.* (of an insect). || Alfilerazo, *m.* (with a pin). || Pinchazo, *m.* (of a needle). || Aguijonazo, *m.* (with a goad). || Espolazo, *m.*, espolada, *f.* (with a spur). || POP. Polla, *f.* (penis). || FIG. *Prick of conscience*, remordimiento (*m.*) de conciencia.

prick [prik] v. tr. Pinchar, picar, punzar: *to prick sth. with a pin*, pinchar algo con un alfiler. || Pinchar: *to prick a balloon*, pinchar un globo. || Pinchar (a part of the body): *he pricked his finger*, se pinchó el dedo. || Abrir, reventar (an abscess). || Agujerear (to mark with holes). || Aguijar, aguijonear (to goad). || Espolear (to spur a horse). || Levantar, erguir (an animal its ears). || Trasplantar (to transplant). || FIG. Remorder: *his conscience pricked him*, le remordía la conciencia. || — *To prick out*, trasplantar (flowers). || *To prick up one's ears*, aguzar el oído, prestar atención (a person), levantar *or* erguir las orejas (an animal).

— V. intr. Causar comezón (to hurt). || Pinchar (to be prickly). || Agriarse, echarse a perder (a beverage). || Espolear (on horseback). || MED. Hormiguear (limbs). || Erguirse (ears, etc.).

prick-eared [—iəd] adj. Con las orejas levantadas *or* erguidas (animal). || Que aguza el oído (person).

pricker [—ə*] n. Punzón, *m.* (sharp instrument). || Montero (*m.*) de caza (in hunting).

pricket [ˈprikət] n. ZOOL. Corzo, *m.* [de un año]. || Pincho (*m.*) en un candelabro que sirve para sujetar la vela.

pricking [—iŋ] adj. Que pincha. || Punzante (pain).

— N. Pinchazo, *m.* || Punzada, *f.* || MED. Punción, *f.* (of an abscess). | Hormigueo, *m.* (of a limb). || — Pl. Remordimientos, *m.* (of conscience).

prickle [ˈprikl] n. BOT. Espina, *f.*, pincho, *m.*, púa, *f.* (thorn). || ZOOL. Púa, *f.* || Picor, *m.*, picazón, *f.* (prickly sensation).

prickle [ˈprikl] v. tr. Picar (to cause a prickly sensation). || Pinchar (to prick).

— V. intr. Sentir picor *or* picazón. || Hormiguear (a limb).

prickling [—iŋ] n. Picazón, *f.*, picor, *m.* (on the skin). || Hormigueo, *m.* (of a limb).

prickly [—li] adj. Espinoso, sa; lleno de pinchos *or* púas. || FIG. Espinoso, sa; delicado, da. | Quisquilloso, sa; susceptible (touchy). || — MED. *Prickly heat*, sarpullido causado por exceso de calor. || BOT. *Prickly pear*, nopal, *m.*, chumbera, *f.* (plant), higo chumbo (fruit).

pride [praid] n. Orgullo, *m.*: *to wound s.o.'s pride*, herir el orgullo de uno; *he is the pride of his family*, es el orgullo de la familia. || Amor (*m.*) propio (self-esteem). || Dignidad, *f.* (dignity). || Soberbia, *f.*, arrogancia, *f.* (arrogance). || Grupo, *m.* (of lions). || Brío, *m.* (of horse). || FIG. Apogeo, *m.*, esplendor, *m.* || — *False pride*, vanidad, *f.* || *In the full pride of youth*, en la flor de la edad. || *It is a source of pride to us that*, es para nosotros un motivo de orgullo que. || *Peacock in his pride*, pavo (*m.*) real haciendo la rueda. || FIG. *Puffed* o *blown up with pride*, hinchado de orgullo. || *To be s.o.'s pride and joy*, ser el orgullo de alguien. || *To pocket one's pride*, tragarse el orgullo *or* el amor propio. || *To take pride in*, enorgullecerse *or* vanagloriarse de, estar orgulloso de (to be proud of), esmerarse en (one's work, appearance, etc.).

pride [praid] v. tr. *To pride o.s. on* o *upon*, enorgullecerse de, vanagloriarse de, estar orgulloso de.

prideful [—ful] adj. Orgulloso, sa. || Arrogante (conceited).

prie-dieu [ˈpriːdjəː] n. Reclinatorio, *m.*

— OBSERV. El plural es *prie-dieux* o *prie-dieus*.

prier [ˈpraiə*] n. FAM. Fisgón, ona.

priest [priːst] n. REL. Sacerdote, *m.* || — *High priest*, Sumo Sacerdote. || *Parish priest*, párroco, *m.*, cura (*m.*) párroco.

priestcraft [—krɑːft] n. Clericalismo, *m.*

priestess [—is] n. REL. Sacerdotisa, *f.*

priesthood [—hud] n. Sacerdocio, *m.* (office). || Clero, *m.* (clergy). || *To enter the priesthood*, hacerse sacerdote, ordenarse de sacerdote.

priestly [—li] adj. Sacerdotal.

priest-ridden [—ˌridn] adj. Dominado por el clero.

prig [prig] n. Mojigato, ta; gazmoño, ña (prude). || Presumido, da; pedante, *m.* & *f.* (pedant).

priggish [—iʃ] adj. Presumido, da; pedante (pedantic). || Mojigato, ta; gazmoño, ña (prudish).

priggishness [—iʃnis] n. Presunción, *f.*, pedantería, *f.* (pedantry). || Mojigatería, *f.*, gazmoñería, *f.* (prudery).

prim [prim] adj. Remilgado, da (fussy). || Forzado, da (smile). || Etiquetero, ra; estirado, da (formal). || Recatado, da (demure).

prim [prim] v. tr. *To prim o.s. up*, acicalarse, arreglarse. || *To prim up one's mouth*, poner boca de corazoncito.

prima ballerina [ˈpriːməˌbæləˈriːnə] n. Primera bailarina, *f.*

primacy [ˈpraiməsi] n. Primacía, *f.*

prima donna [ˈpriːməˈdɔnə] n. Diva, *f.*, prima donna, *f.*

prima facie [ˈpraiməˈfeiʃiiː] adv. A primera vista.

prima-facie evidence [—evidəns] n. JUR. Prueba (*f.*) suficiente a primera vista.

primage [ˈpraimidʒ] n. MAR. Prima (*f.*) de flete.

primal [ˈpraiməl] adj. Primitivo, va; original. || Principal, fundamental, primordial (most important).

primarily [ˈpraimərili] adv. Ante todo, en primer lugar, principalmente, esencialmente (mainly). || Primitivamente (originally).

primary [ˈpraiməri] adj. Primario, ria: *primary school*, escuela primaria; *primary instincts*, instintos primarios. || Básico, ca; esencial, fundamental, principal (fundamental). || Primero, ra (not derived): *primary meaning of a word*, primer sentido de una palabra. || ELECTR. GEOL. CHEM. ASTR. MED. Primario, ria. || — *Primary accent*, acento primario. || *Primary education*, primera enseñanza, enseñanza primaria.

— N. Lo principal (most important thing). || Pluma (*f.*) primaria (feather). || Color (*m.*) primario (colour). || ASTR. Planeta (*m.*) primario. || ELECTR. Primario, *m.* || U. S. Elección (*f.*) primaria *or* preliminar para nombrar candidatos.

primary cell [—sel] n. Pila, *f.*

primate [ˈpraimit] n. REL. Primado, *m.*

primate [ˈpraimeit] n. ZOOL. Primate, *m.* (ape).

prime [praim] adj. Primero, ra (first). || Principal, fundamental, primordial (fundamental). || Original, primitivo, va (primary). || De primera calidad *or* categoría, selecto, ta (top-quality). || MATH. Primo, ma (number). || — *In prime condition*, en perfecto estado, en estado excelente. || *Of prime importance*, primordial, sumamente importante. || COMM. *Prime cost*, coste (*m.*) de producción. || *Prime mediridian*, primer meridiano. || *Prime minister*, primer ministro. || *Prime mover*, fuerza motriz (of a machine), causa primera (in philosophy), promotor, ra; instigador, ra (person behind an action).

— N. Flor (*f.*) de la vida *or* de la edad: *to be cut off in one's prime*, morir en la flor de la vida; *to be in one's prime*, estar en la flor de la vida. || POET. Albor, *m.*, principio, *m.* (beginning): *the prime of the world*, el albor del mundo. | Flor y nata, *f.*, lo mejor, lo más escogido (the best). || MATH. Número (*m.*) primo. || REL. Prima, *f.* || PRINT. Virgulilla, *f.* (apostrophe). || Átomo (*m.*) simple (atom). || SP. Primera posición, *f.* (in fencing). || MUS. Sonido (*m.*) fundamental. || *To be past one's prime*, haber pasado lo mejor de la vida.

prime [praim] v. tr. Cebar (a gun, a pump, a motor). || Preparar (a surface, etc.). || ARTS. Imprimar, aprestar. || FIG. Preparar (a person for an interview). | Informar: *they had primed him as to what to do*, le habían informado de lo que tenía que hacer. | Emborrachar (to make drunk). || FIG. *To be well primed*, estar alegre (to be drunk), estar bien preparado (for an examination).

primeness [—nis] n. Calidad (*f.*) superior, excelencia, *f.*

primer [—ə*] n. Cartilla, *f.* (for learning to read). || Libro (*m.*) elemental (elementary text book). || Cebador, *m.* (of a pump). || Cartucho (*m.*) cebo (of a gun). || Fulminante, *m.* (for firing a bomb). || REL. Libro (*m.*) de horas. || *Primer coat*, primera mano.

primeval [praiˈmiːvəl] adj. Primitivo, va; prístino, na. || Virgen (forest).

priming [ˈpraimiŋ] adj. De cebar.

— N. ARTS. Imprimación, *f.*, apresto, *m.* | Primera mano, *f.* (first coat). || Cebado, *m.* (of pump etc.). || Cebo, *m.* (of a gun).

primipara [praiˈmipərə] n. Primeriza, *f.*, primípara, *f.*

— OBSERV. El plural es *primiparae* o *primiparas*.

primiparous [praiˈmipərəs] adj. Primeriza, primípara.

primitive [ˈprimitiv] adj. Primitivo, va: *a primitive tribe*, una tribu primitiva. || Sencillo, lla; primitivo, va; primario, ria; rudimentario, ria: *primitive weapons*, armas rudimentarias. || BIOL. GRAMM. ARTS. Primitivo, va. || GEOL. Primario, ria.

— N. Primitivo, *m.*, hombre (*m.*) primitivo. || ARTS. Primitivo, *m.*

primitiveness [—nis] n. Carácter (*m.*) primitivo.
primitivism [—izəm] n. Primitivismo, *m.*
primness [ˈprimnis] n. Lo estirado, lo etiquetero (formality). || Remilgo, *m.* (fussiness).
primogenitor [ˌpraiməuˈdʒenitə*] n. Primer antepasado, *m.* (earliest ancestor). || FAM. Antepasado, *m.*
primogeniture [ˌpraiməuˈdʒenitʃə*] n. Primogenitura, *f.*
primordial [praiˈmɔːdjəl] adj. Primordial.
primp [primp] v. tr. Acicalar, emperejilar.
— V. intr. Acicalarse, emperejilarse.
primrose [ˈprimrəuz] n. Primavera, *f.*, prímula, *f.* (flower). || Amarillo (*m.*) claro (colour). || FIG. *Primrose path*, camino (*m.*) de flores, camino (*m.*) de rosas.
— Adj. Amarillo claro.
primula [ˈprimjulə] n. BOT. Prímula, *f.* (flower).
primulaceae [ˌprimjuˈleisii:] pl. n. Primuláceas, *f.*
prince [prins] n. Príncipe, *m.*: *Prince of Wales*, Príncipe de Gales. || — *Crown prince*, príncipe heredero. || *Prince Charming*, el Príncipe Azul. || *Prince consort*, príncipe consorte. || *Prince of Darkness*, príncipe de las tinieblas. || *Prince royal*, príncipe real.
princedom [—dəm] n. Principado, *m.*
princekin [—kin] or **princeling** [—liŋ] n. Principito, *m.* (insignificant prince).
princely [—li] adj. Principesco, ca. || FIG. Regio, gia; magnífico, ca: *a princely reward*, una magnífica recompensa.
princess [prinˈses] n. Princesa, *f.* || *Princess royal*, princesa real.
principal [ˈprinsəpəl] adj. Principal. || GRAMM. *Principal parts*, formas (*f.*) principales (of a verb).
— M. Director, ra (of a school, factory, etc.). || Rector, *m.* (of a university). || Jefe, *m.* (of a firm). || Mandante, *m.*: *principal and agent*, mandante y mandatario. || JUR. Autor, *m.* (of a crime). || COMM. Capital, *m.*, principal, *m.* (sum of money). || THEATR. Primera figura, *f.* || MUS. Solista, *m.* & *f.* | Principal, *m.* (organ stop). | Tema (*m.*) principal (of a fugue).
principality [ˌprinsiˈpæliti] n. Principado, *m.* || — Pl. REL. Principados, *m.* (order of angels).
principally [ˈprinsəpli] adv. Principalmente.
principalship [ˈprinsəpəlʃip] n. Dirección, *f.* (of a school, factory). || Rectorado, *m.* (of a university).
principle [ˈprinsəpl] n. Principio, *m.*: *Archimedes' principle*, el principio de Arquímedes; *my principles won't allow me to do it*, mis principios no me permiten hacerlo. || — *A man of principle*, un hombre de principios. || *I make it a principle never to do that*, tengo por principio no hacer nunca eso, tengo por norma jamás hacer eso. || *In principle*, en principio. || *It is a matter of principle*, es una cuestión de principios. || *On principle*, por principio. || *To go back to first principles*, volver a los principios fundamentales. || *To have high principles*, tener elevados *or* nobles principios. || *To lay it down as a principle that...*, sentar el principio de que...
principled [—d] adj. De principios.
prink [priŋk] v. tr. Emperejilar, emperifollar. || *To prink o.s. up*, emperejilarse, emperifollarse.
print [print] n. Huella, *f.* (of finger). || Huella, *f.*, señal, *f.* (of foot). || Marca, *f.*, impresión, *f.* (impression). || Prueba, *f.*, positiva, *f.* (photography). || Copia, *f.* (of a photograph). || Impreso, *m.*, texto (*m.*) impreso (printed paper). || Tirada, *f.* (edition). || Impresión, *f.* (printing). || Imprenta, *f.* (printing office). || Letras (*f. pl.*) de imprenta *or* de molde (handwriting). || Caracteres, *m. pl.*, letra, *f.* (letters in a book). || Tipo, *m.* (type). || Molde, *m.* (mould). || Estampado, *m.* (cloth, dress): *cotton prints*, estampados de algodón. || Estampa, *f.*, grabado, *m.* (picture). || — Pl. Huellas (*f.*) dactilares *or* digitales (fingerprints). || — *In print*, impreso, sa (in printed form), en venta, disponible (available). || *Out of print*, agotado, da. || *To find o.s. in print*, ver sus obras publicadas. || *To get into print*, publicarse: *I don't want that to get into print*, no quiero que eso se publique. || *To rush into print*, publicar algo precipitadamente.
— Adj. Estampado, da (dress, material).
print [print] v. tr. Imprimir: *where was this book printed?*, ¿dónde imprimieron este libro? || Tirar, hacer una tirada de (an edition). || Publicar (to publish): *the letter was printed in yesterday's paper*, la carta se publicó en el periódico de ayer. || Imprimir, grabar (drawings, etc.). || Dejar [huellas], imprimir, estampar (marks, traces, e.g. in the snow). || Estampar (seal). || Estampar (cloth, textiles). || Sacar, tirar, positivar (copies of a negative). || Escribir con letras de imprenta *or* de molde (when writing): *print your name, please*, por favor escriba su nombre con letras de imprenta. || FIG. Grabar, imprimir (sth. on the mind).
— V. intr. Imprimirse (book). || Escribir con letras de imprenta *or* de molde. || PHOT. *To print well*, salir bien (a negative).
printable [—əbl] adj. Imprimible.
printed [—id] adj. Impreso, sa (newspapers, books). || Estampado, da (cloth, seal). || De imprenta, de molde (letter). || — *Printed circuit*, circuito impreso. || *Printed matter*, impresos, *m. pl.*
printer [—ə*] n. Impresor, *m.* (of books). || — *Printer's devil*, aprendiz (*m.*) de imprenta. || *Printer's error*, errata, *f.*, error (*m.*) de imprenta. || *Printer's ink*, tinta (*f.*) de imprenta. || *Printer's mark*, pie (*m.*) de imprenta. || *Printer's reader*, corrector (*m.*) de pruebas.
printery [—əri] n. U. S. Imprenta, *f.* (printing house). || Fábrica (*f.*) de estampados.
printing [—iŋ] n. Impresión, *f.* (action): *colour printing*, impresión en color. || Imprenta, *f.* (art, profession): *to know everything about printing*, conocer perfectamente la imprenta. || Impresión, *f.* (quality of print). || Tipografía, *f.* (layout, etc.). || Tirada, *f.* (quantity printed). || Letras (*f. pl.*) de imprenta *or* de molde (handwriting). || PHOT. Tiraje, *m.*, positivado, *m.* (of a negative).
printing frame [—iŋfreim] n. Prensa (*f.*) de copiar.
printing house [—iŋhaus] n. Imprenta, *f.*
printing machine [—iŋməˌʃi:n] n. Prensa, *f.*
printing office [—iŋˌɔfis] n. Imprenta, *f.*, talleres (*m. pl.*) gráficos.
printing press [—iŋˌpres] n. Prensa, *f.*
printless [—lis] adj. Sin señal, sin marca, sin huellas.
print room [—ru:m] n. Sección (*f.*) de estampas.
prior [ˈpraiə*] adj. Anterior (previous). || Más importante, preferente (more important).
— Adv. *Prior to*, antes de (before).
— N. REL. Prior, *m.*
priorate [ˈpraiəret] n. REL. Priorato, *m.*
prioress [ˈpraiəris] n. REL. Priora, *f.*
priority [praiˈɔriti] n. Prioridad, *f.* (in order, importance). || Anterioridad, *f.* (in time). || — *According to priority*, por orden de prelación, por orden de prioridad. || *Priority share*, acción privilegiada.
priorship [ˈpraiəʃip] n. REL. Priorato, *m.* (rank, office).
priory [ˈpraiəri] n. REL. Priorato, *m.*
prise [praiz] n. Apalancamiento, *m.* (leverage). || Palanca, *f.* (lever).
prise [praiz] v. tr. *To prise open, up*, abrir, levantar por fuerza *or* con una palanca.
prism [ˈprizəm] n. MATH. PHYS. Prisma, *m.*
prismatic [prizˈmætik] adj. Prismático, ca. || *Prismatic colours*, colores (*m.*) del prisma.
prison [ˈprizn] n. Cárcel, *f.*, prisión, *f.* (building, punishment). || MIL. Prisión, *f.* || — *Model prison*, cárcel modelo. || *Sent to prison*, encarcelado, da (civil person), prisionero, ra (military man). || *To go to prison for three years*, ser condenado a tres años de prisión *or* de cárcel *or* de encarcelamiento. || *To put s.o. in prison* o *to send s.o. to prison*, encarcelar a alguien, meter a alguien en la cárcel. || *To put s.o. in prison for three years* o *to send s.o. to prison for three years*, condenar a alguien a tres años de prisión *or* de cárcel *or* de encarcelamiento.
— Adj. Carcelario, ria. || — *Prison breaking*, evasión, *f.* || *Prison camp*, campamento (*m.*) para prisioneros. || *Prison house*, cárcel, *f.*, prisión, *f.* || *Prison life*, la vida en la cárcel. || *Prison population*, población reclusa. || *Prison sentence of 20 years*, condena (*f.*) a veinte años de cárcel *or* de prisión *or* de encarcelamiento. || *Prison system*, régimen penitenciario. || *Prison van*, coche (*m.*) celular. || *Prison yard*, patio (*m.*) de la cárcel.
prison [ˈprizn] v. tr. Encarcelar.
prisoner [—ə*] n. Preso, sa (in a prison). || Detenido, da (under arrest). || JUR. Acusado, da (in the courtroom). || MIL. Prisionero, ra: *to take s.o. prisoner*, hacerle prisionero a uno. || — *Prisoner of war*, prisionero de guerra. || FIG. *To be a prisoner of*, estar aprisionado por. || *To hold s.o. prisoner*, tener detenido a uno. || *To take s.o. prisoner*, hacer prisionero a uno.
prisoner's base [ˈpriznəzbeis] n. Marro, *m.* (children's game).
prissy [ˈprisi] adj. Remilgado, da (very prim).
pristine [ˈpristain] adj. Prístino, na; original, primitivo, va.
prithee [ˈpriði] interj. ¡Te lo ruego!, ¡por favor!
privacy [ˈprivəsi] n. Intimidad, *f.*: *in the privacy of one's own home*, en la intimidad del hogar; *to respect s.o.'s privacy*, respetar la intimidad de uno. || Vida (*f.*) privada: *he doesn't get any privacy*, no tiene ninguna vida privada. || Aislamiento, *m.*, soledad, *f.* (isolation): *desire for privacy*, deseo de soledad. || Secreto, *m.* (secrecy).
private [praivit] adj. Privado, da: *private property*, propiedad privada; *private life*, vida privada; *private law*, derecho privado; *private interview*, entrevista privada. || Personal (personal): *private motives*, motivos personales; *my private opinion*, mi opinión personal; *private use*, uso personal. || Privado, da; íntimo, ma (thoughts). || Secreto, ta (secret). || Reservado, da: *she is very private about her affairs*, es muy reservada en sus cosas. || Confidencial (confidential). || Particular (lessons, arrangement, car, house, etc.). || En la intimidad (wedding). || Privado, da; no público ca (party). || Aislado, da; íntimo, ma (place). || MIL. Raso: *private soldier*, soldado raso. || — *Private bill*, proyecto (*m.*) de ley de interés local. || *Private citizen*, particular, *m.* || *Private detective*, detective privado. || *Private enterprise*, empresa privada. || U. S. MIL. *Private first class*, soldado (*m.*) de primera. || *Private fishing*, coto vedado. || *Private income*, renta, *f.* || ANAT. *Private parts*, partes pudendas. || THEATR. *Private performance*, representación privada. || *Private school*,

colegio privado. || *Private secretary*, secretario (*m.*) particular, secretaria (*f.*) particular. || CINEM. *Private showing*, sesión privada. || *Private view*, inauguración privada (of an exhibition). || *The ceremony was private*, la ceremonia se celebró en la intimidad. || *To have private means*, tener una fortuna personal. || *To keep a matter private*, no divulgar un asunto, mantener secreto un asunto.
— N. MIL. Soldado (*m.*) raso. || — Pl. ANAT. Partes (*f.*) pudendas (private parts). || *In private*, en privado: *they discussed the matter in private*, discutieron el asunto en privado; en secreto, confidencialmente (confidentially), a puerta cerrada (a meeting), en la intimidad (a ceremony).
privateer [ˌpraivəˈtiə*] n. MAR. Corsario, *m.* (ship, sailor).
privateering [—iŋ] n. MAR. Corso, *m.*, expedición, *f.*
privateersman [—zmən] n. MAR. Corsario, *m.*

— OBSERV. El plural de esta palabra es *privateersmen*.

privately [ˈpraivitli] adv. En privado, privadamente (in private). || En secreto, confidencialmente (confidentially). || Personalmente: *I spoke privately to him*, le hablé personalmente. || A puerta cerrada: *the meeting was held privately*, la reunión se celebró a puerta cerrada. || En la intimidad: *privately married*, casado en la intimidad. || En el fondo: *privately I was quite worried*, en el fondo estaba muy preocupado. || *Privately printed book*, libro editado por cuenta del autor.
privation [praiˈveiʃən] n. Privación, *f.* || Estrechez, *f.*, miseria, *f.*: *to live in privation*, vivir en la estrechez. || Apuro, *m.*: *he suffered many privations*, pasó muchos apuros.
privative [ˈprivətiv] adj. Privativo, va. || FIG. Negativo, va (quality).
— N. GRAMM. Prefijo (*m.*) privativo, sufijo (*m.*) privativo.
privet [ˈprivit] n. BOT. Alheña, *f.*
privilege [ˈprivilidʒ] n. Privilegio, *m.*, prerrogativa, *f.* || Honor, *m.*: *it has been a privilege to meet you*, ha sido un honor conocerle. || *Parliamentary privilege*, inmunidad parlamentaria.
privilege [ˈprivilidʒ] v. tr. Privilegiar. || *To privilege s.o. to do sth.*, conceder a alguien el privilegio de hacer algo.
privileged [—d] adj. Privilegiado, da (favoured). || Que goza del privilegio [*to*, de]. || Que goza de la inmunidad parlamentaria. || — *To be privileged from sth.*, estar dispensado por privilegio de algo. || *To be privileged to do sth.*, gozar del privilegio de hacer algo, tener el privilegio de hacer algo.
privily [ˈprivili] adv. En privado, en secreto.
privity [ˈpriviti] n. JUR. Vínculo (*m.*) legal, relación, *f.* | Obligación, *f.*: *privity in law*, obligación legal. || Conocimiento, *m.* (knowledge).
privy [ˈprivi] adj. Privado, da (private). || Secreto, ta (secret). || — *Privy Council*, Consejo privado. || ANAT. *Privy parts*, partes pudendas. || *Privy purse*, gastos (*m.*) personales del monarca. || *Privy seal*, sello (*m.*) real. || *To be privy to*, estar al tanto de.
— N. JUR. Derechohabiente, *m.*, interesado, *m.* || Cómplice, *m.* & *f.* (abettor). || FAM. Retrete, *m.*, excusado, *m.* (toilet).
prize [praiz] n. Premio, *m.*: *to win first prize* o *to carry off the prize*, ganar *or* llevarse el primer premio. || FIG. Recompensa, *f.*, premio, *m.*, galardón, *m.*: *cash prize*, premio en metálico; *a prize worthy of all the effort*, una recompensa digna del esfuerzo; *to award a prize*, conceder un premio. || MAR. Presa, *f.* (captured vessel). || TECH. Palanca, *f.* (lever). | Apalancamiento, *m.* (leverage). || — *Consolation prize*, premio de consolación. || *First prize*, premio gordo, primer premio (in a lottery). || *To take the prize*, llevarse el premio.
— Adj. Premiado, da; galardonado, da (prize-winning). || Digno de premio (worthy of a prize). || De primera categoría (first-class). || FAM. *You are a prize idiot*, eres un tonto de remate.
prize [praiz] v. tr. Apreciar, estimar (to value). || MAR. Capturar (a ship). || See PRISE.
prize court [—kɔːt] n. JUR. Tribunal (*m.*) de presas marítimas.
prizefight [—ˌfait] n. Combate (*m.*) de boxeo profesional.
prizefighter [—ˌfaitə*] n. SP. Boxeador (*m.*) profesional.
prizefighting [—ˌfaitiŋ] n. Boxeo (*m.*) profesional.
prizegiving [—ˌgiviŋ] n. Reparto (*m.*) de premios.
prize money [—ˌmʌni] n. Premio (*m.*) en metálico. || SP. Bolsa, *f.* (in boxing). || MAR. Parte (*f.*) de presa.
prize ring [—riŋ] n. SP. Cuadrilátero, *m.*, ring, *m.* (boxing ring). | Boxeo (*m.*) profesional (prizefighting).
prizewinner [—ˌwinə*] n. Premiado, da; galardonado, da.
prizewinning [—ˈwiniŋ] adj. Premiado, da; galardonado, da.
pro [prəu] prep. En pro de, pro.
— Adv. A favor.
— Adj. Favorable. || SP. Profesional.
— N. SP. Profesional, *m.* & *f.* || *The pros and cons*, el pro y el contra (arguments for and against), los votos a favor y los votos en contra (votes).
probabilism [ˈprɔbəbilizəm] n. Probabilismo, *m.*
probabilist [ˈprɔbəbilist] adj./n. Probabilista.
probability [ˌprɔbəˈbiliti] n. Probabilidad, *f.*: *in all probability*, según toda probabilidad.
probable [ˈprɔbəbl] adj. Probable: *rain isn't very probable*, no es muy probable que llueva. || Verosímil (credible).
probably [—i] adv. Probablemente. || *Most probably*, seguramente.
probang [ˈprəubæŋ] n. MED. Sonda, *f.*
probate [ˈprəubit] n. JUR. Legalización (*f.*) de un testamento.
probate [ˈprəubeit] v. tr. U. S. JUR. Legalizar (a will).
probation [prəˈbeiʃən] n. Período (*m.*) de prueba (trial period). || JUR. Libertad (*f.*) vigilada *or* condicional. || — *On probation*, a prueba (on trial): *to put on probation*, poner a prueba; en *or* bajo libertad vigilada *or* condicional (a convicted offender). || JUR. *Probation officer*, encargado (*m.*) de la vigilancia de los que están en libertad condicional.
probationary [prəˈbeiʃnəri] adj. De prueba, probatorio, ria. || JUR. *Probationary period*, período (*m.*) de libertad vigilada *or* condicional.
probationer [prəˈbeiʃnə*] n. JUR. Persona (*f.*) que está en libertad vigilada. || Persona (*f.*) a prueba.
probative [ˈprəubətiv] adj. Probatorio, ria.
probatory [ˈprəubətəri] adj. Probatorio, ria.
probe [prəub] n. MED. Sonda, *f.* (instrument). || Sondeo, *m.* (act). || Investigación, *f.*, encuesta, *f.* (*into*, sobre) [an investigation]. || Exploración, *f.* (*into*, de). || *Space probe*, sonda espacial.
probe [prəub] v. tr. MED. Sondear, sondar (with a medical probe). || Sondear (ground, etc.). || Examinar (to examine). || Investigar (to investigate). || Explorar (to explore). || Tantear (to judge the possibilities, etc.). || Sondear (opinion).
— V. intr. *To probe into*, tantear (possibilities), examinar (to examine), investigar (to investigate), explorar (to explore).
probing [—iŋ] adj. Minucioso, sa; meticuloso, sa (thorough). || Penetrante (penetrating).
— N. Sondeo, *m.* || Investigación, *f.* (investigation). || Exploración, *f.* || Toma (*f.*) de muestras (in the ground).
probity [ˈprəubiti] n. Probidad, *f.*
problem [ˈprɔbləm] n. Problema, *m.*: *that presents no problem*, no plantea ningún problema; *the housing problem*, el problema de la vivienda; *he poses me a lot of problems*, me plantea innumerables problemas.
— Adj. Problemático, ca. || Difícil (difficult): *a problem child*, un niño difícil. || — *Problem page*, consultorio, *m.* || *Problem play*, obra (*f.*) de tesis (theatre).
problematic [ˌprɔbliˈmætik] or **problematical** [—əl] adj. Problemático, ca. || Dudoso, sa (doubtful).
proboscideans or **proboscidians** [prɔbɔˈsidiənz] pl. n. ZOOL. Proboscidios, *m.*
proboscis [prəuˈbɔsis] n. ANAT. Probóscide, *f.*, trompa, *f.* || FAM. Napia, *f.* (nose).

— OBSERV. El plural de *proboscis* es *proboscises* o *proboscides*.

procain [ˈprəukein] n. CHEM. Procaína, *f.*
procedural [prəˈsiːdʒərəl] adj. JUR. Procesal: *procedural law*, derecho procesal. || De procedimiento: *a procedural question*, una cuestión de procedimiento.
procedure [prəˈsiːdʒə*] n. Procedimiento, *m.*: *legal procedure*, procedimiento legal; *to open a debate on procedure*, abrir un debate sobre el procedimiento. || Trámites, *m. pl.* (things one has to do). || Procedimiento, *m.*, proceder, *m.* (course of action). || — *Rules of procedure*, reglamento interno. || *The correct procedure would be...*, lo mejor sería... || *The usual procedure is...*, lo que se suele hacer es...
proceed [prəˈsiːd] v. intr. Seguir, continuar (to continue): *they proceeded to Leeds*, siguieron hacia Leeds; *to proceed on one's way*, seguir su camino; *the letter proceeds thus*, la carta continúa así. || Ir (to go): *before we proceed any further*, antes de ir más lejos; *the car proceeded at thirty kilometres per hour*, el coche iba a treinta kilómetros por hora. || Pasar, irse: *let us proceed to the dining room*, pasemos al comedor. || Obrar, actuar, proceder: *how should we proceed?*, ¿cómo hemos de proceder?, ¿cómo debemos actuar?; *this is a delicate matter, so please proceed with caution*, esto es un asunto delicado, así que por favor obren con cuidado. || Avanzar: *crossing a mine field, you must proceed with caution*, al cruzar un campo de minas se debe avanzar con cuidado. || Ponerse a, proceder a: *to proceed to do sth.*, ponerse a hacer algo; *to proceed to a vote*, proceder a votar. || Pasar a: *let us proceed to the next item on the agenda*, pasemos al punto siguiente del orden del día. || Venir, provenir, proceder (*from*, de): *the confusion proceeded from a misunderstanding*, la confusión vino de un malentendido. || Desarrollarse, suceder: *things are proceeding as usual*, las cosas se están desarrollando normalmente. || JUR. Proceder (*against*, contra). || — *The negotiations now proceeding in our country*, las negociaciones en curso en nuestro país. || *To proceed to blows*, llegar a las manos. || *To proceed with*, seguir con, proseguir.
proceeding [—iŋ] n. Proceder, *m.* (way). || Acción, *f.* (action). || — Pl. Debates, *m.*: *to conduct the proceedings*, dirigir los debates. || Reunión, *f. sing.* (meeting). ||

Actas, *f.* (minutes): *according to the proceedings of the last meeting*, según las actas de la última reunión. || JUR. Proceso, *m. sing.*: *to take proceedings against s.o.*, entablar un proceso contra alguien.

proceeds [ˈprəusi:dz] pl. n. Ganancias, *f.*, beneficios, *m.*: *he is entitled to one half of the proceeds*, tiene derecho a la mitad de los beneficios. || Ingresos, *m.*, producto, *m. sing.* (of a sale).

process [ˈprəuses] n. Proceso, *m.*: *the historic process*, el proceso histórico; *process of the mind*, proceso mental. || Procedimiento, *m.*: *the manufacturing process*, el procedimiento de fabricación. || Procedimiento, *m.*, método, *m.*, sistema, *m.* (method). || JUR. ANAT. Proceso, *m.* || — *In process*, en curso. || *In process of*, en vías de, en curso de. || *In the process of time*, con el tiempo, andando el tiempo. || TECH. *Process engraving*, fotomecánica, *f.*

process [ˈprəuses] v. tr. Tratar: *to process milk*, tratar la leche. || Transformar (raw materials). || Elaborar (to elaborate). || Tratar (data). || JUR. Procesar. || PHOT. Revelar (a negative). || PRINT. Reproducir por procedimientos fotomecánicos (to reproduce).

process [prəˈses] v. intr. Ir en procesión, desfilar.

processing [ˈprəusesiŋ] n. Tratamiento, *m.* (of food, information, etc.). || Procedimiento, *m.* || Transformación, *f.*: *processing industry*, industria de transformación. || *Data processing*, informática, *f.* (science), tratamiento (*m.*) de la información, proceso (*m.*) *or* procesamiento (*m.*) de datos.

procession [prəˈseʃən] n. Procesión, *f.*, desfile, *m.* (of people, animals). || Cortejo, *m.*, comitiva, *f.* (royal, wedding, etc.). || REL. Procesión, *f.* || FIG. Serie, *f.* (string).

procession [prəˈseʃən] v. intr. Desfilar. || REL. Ir en procesión.

processional [—l] adj. Procesional.
— N. Himno (*m.*) procesional (hymn). || Procesionario, *m.* (book).

processionary [—əri] adj. Procesionaria.

proclaim [prəˈkleim] v. tr. Proclamar (to announce publicly). || Declarar (war). || Proclamar (a king). || Revelar (to reveal). || Prohibir (to prohibit). || *To proclaim the banns*, correr las amonestaciones.

proclaimer [—ə*] n. Proclamador, ra.

proclamation [ˌprɔkləˈmeiʃən] n. Proclamación, *f.* (act). || Proclama, *f.* (document). || Bando, *m.* (edict). || Declaración, *f.* || Publicación, *f.* (of banns).

proclitic [prəuˈklitik] adj. GRAMM. Proclítico, ca.
— N. GRAMM. Proclítico, *m.*

proclivity [prəˈkliviti] n. Propensión, *f.*, tendencia, *f.*, inclinación, *f.*

proconsul [prəuˈkɔnsəl] n. Procónsul, *m.*

proconsular [prəuˈkɔnsjulə*] adj. Proconsular.

proconsulate [prəuˈkɔnsjulit] n. Proconsulado, *m.*

proconsulship [prəuˈkɔnsəlʃip] n. Proconsulado, *m.*

procrastinate [prəuˈkræstineit] v. intr. Andar con dilaciones, no decidirse, aplazar *or* diferir una decisión.
— V. tr. Aplazar, diferir.

procrastination [prəuˌkræstiˈneiʃən] n. Dilación, *f.*

procrastinator [prəuˈkræstineitə*] n. Indeciso, sa; persona (*f.*) que anda con dilaciones.

procreant [ˈprəukriənt] adj. Procreador, ra.

procreate [ˈprəukrieit] v. tr./intr. Procrear.

procreation [ˌprəukriˈeiʃən] n. Procreación, *f.*

procreative [ˈprəukrieitiv] adj. Procreador, ra.

procreator [ˈprəukrieitə*] n. Procreador, ra.

proctor [ˈprɔktə*] n. Oficial (*m.*) encargado de la disciplina (in a university). || U. S. Vigilante, *m.* (in an examination). || JUR. Procurador, *m.*

procumbent [prəuˈkʌmbənt] adj. BOT. Procumbente, rastrero, ra. || Boca abajo (face down).

procurable [prəˈkjuərəbl] adj. Asequible, alcanzable.

procurance [prəuˈkjurəns] n. Adquisición, *f.*, obtención, *f.* (obtaining). || Consecución, *f.* (bringing about, achieving).

procuration [ˌprɔkjuəˈreiʃən] n. Adquisición, *f.*, obtención, *f.* (obtaining). || Consecución, *f.* (achieving, bringing about). || Procuración, *f.*, poder, *m.* (power of attorney). || Proxenetismo, *m.* (procuring).

procurator [ˈprɔkjuəreitə*] n. HIST. Procurador, *m.* || JUR. Apoderado, *m.*

procuratory [ˈprɔkjuərətəri] n. JUR. Procuración, *f.*, poder, *m.*

procure [prəˈkjuə*] v. tr. Proporcionar, obtener, conseguir, lograr: *I procured a flat for him*, le proporcioné un piso. || Llevar a la prostitución (a woman).
— V. intr. Dedicarse al proxenetismo.

procurement [—mənt] n. Adquisición, *f.*, obtención, *f.* (obtaining). || Consecución, *f.* (achievement).

procurer [—rə*] n. Proxeneta, *m.* (who procures prostitutes).

procuress [—ris] n. Alcahueta, *f.*, proxeneta, *f.*

procuring [—riŋ] n. Proxenetismo, *m.*

prod [prɔd] n. Golpe, *m.*, golpecito, *m.* [que se da con la punta de algo]. || Pincho, *m.*, instrumento (*m.*) puntiagudo (sharp instrument). || Aguijón, *m.* (goad). || Pinchazo, *m.* (prick). || FIG. Acicate, *m.*, aguijón, *m.*, estímulo, *m.* (incentive).

prod [prɔd] v. tr. Darle [a algo *or* a alguien] con la punta del dedo, de un bastón, etc. (with finger, stick, etc.). || Picar, pinchar (to prick). || FIG. Aguijonear, estimular (to urge).

prodigal [ˈprɔdigəl] adj. Pródigo, ga. || — *Prodigal of*, pródigo en. || *The Prodigal Son*, el Hijo Pródigo.

prodigality [ˌprɔdiˈgæliti] n. Prodigalidad, *f.* (lavishness). || Derroche, *m.* (extreme abundance).

prodigious [prəˈdidʒəs] adj. Prodigioso, sa; portentoso, sa (wonderful). || Enorme, ingente (huge).

prodigiousness [—nis] n. Prodigiosidad, *f.*, carácter (*m.*) prodigioso *or* portentoso. || Enormidad, *f.* (hugeness).

prodigy [ˈprɔdidʒi] n. Prodigio, *m.* || *A child prodigy*, un niño prodigio.

prodrome [ˈprɔdrəm] n. MED. Pródromo, *m.* (symptom).

produce [ˈprɔdju:s] n. Productos, *m. pl.*: *farm produce*, productos agrícolas. || Producción, *f.* (yield). || FIG. Fruto, *m.* (of efforts).

produce [prəˈdju:s] v. tr. Presentar, mostrar, enseñar (to show): *I had to produce my passport*, tuve que enseñar el pasaporte. || Sacar (to take out): *he produced a handkerchief from his pocket*, se sacó un pañuelo del bolsillo. || Producir: *this author hasn't produced much lately*, este autor no ha producido mucho últimamente; *the factory produces a thousand cars a week*, la fábrica produce mil coches por semana. || Fabricar, hacer (to manufacture). || Producir, dar: *to produce profit*, producir beneficios. || Dar, producir (fruit). || Producir, ocasionar, causar (to cause, to give rise to). || MATH. Prolongar (a line). || THEATR. Dirigir (the making of a play). | Presentar (to present). || CINEM. Producir. || Realizar (in television). || JUR. Presentar (a witness, proof).
— V. intr. Producir.

producer [—ə*] n. Productor, ra. || Fabricante, *m.* (manufacturer). || THEATR. Escenógrafo, *m.*, director (*m.*) de escena. || CINEM. Productor, ra. || Realizador, ra (in television). || Gasógeno, *m.* (for cars).

producer gas [—ə*gæs] n. Gas (*m.*) pobre.

producer goods [—ə*gudz] pl. n. Elementos (*m.*) de producción. || Materias (*f.*) primas (raw materials).

producible [prəˈdju:səbl] adj. Producible.

producing [prəˈdju:siŋ] adj. Productor, ra.

producive [prəˈdju:siv] adj. Productivo, va. || *To be producive of*, producir.

product [ˈprɔdʌkt] n. Producto, *m.*: *manufactured products*, productos manufacturados. || Producto, *m.*, resultado, *m.* (result). || Producción, *f.* (of literature). || MATH. Producto, *m.* || *Gross national product*, producto nacional bruto.

production [prəˈdʌkʃən] n. Producción, *f.* || Presentación, *f.* (showing). || Fabricación, *f.* (manufacture). || Rendimiento, *m.* (output). || Producto, *m.* (product). || Obra, *f.* (artistic work). || THEATR. Dirección (*f.*) escénica, escenografía, *f.* (of a play). | Representación, *f.* (performance). | Dirección, *f.* (of actors). || Producción, *f.* (of a film). || Realización, *f.* (in television).
— Adj. De serie: *production car*, coche de serie. || *Production line*, línea (*f.*) de montaje, cadena (*f.*) de montaje.

productive [prəˈdʌktiv] adj. Productivo, va. || AGR. Fértil. || FIG. Fecundo, da; fértil [*of*, en] (fruitful). || *To be productive of*, producir.

productivity [ˌprɔdʌkˈtiviti] or **productiveness** [prəˈdʌktivnis] n. Productividad, *f.*

proem [ˈprəuem] n. Proemio, *m.*

prof [prɔf] n. FAM. Profe, *m.* (professor).

profanation [ˌprɔfəˈneiʃən] n. Profanación, *f.*

profanatory [prəˈfænətəri] adj. Profanador, ra.

profane [prəˈfein] adj. Profano, na (worldly, irreverent, uninitiated). || Impío, a; sacrílego, ga (sacrilegious). || Blasfemo, ma (blasphemous). || Soez (language). || Malhablado, da (person). || *Profane word*, blasfemia, *f.*, palabrota, *f.*

profane [prəˈfein] v. tr. Profanar.

profaner [—ə*] n. Profanador, ra.

profanity [prəˈfæniti] n. Lo profano, carácter (*m.*) profano. || Impiedad, *f.*, sacrilegio, *m.* (irreverence). || Blasfemia, *f.* (blasphemy). || Palabrota, *f.*, taco, *m.* (swearword).

profess [prəˈfes] v. tr. Pretender (to claim): *he doesn't profess to be an expert*, no pretende ser experto. || Declarar, manifestar (to state). || Asegurar, afirmar (to affirm): *he professed to be sorry*, aseguraba sentirlo. || Profesar (a religion, an opinion, esteem). || Ejercer, profesar (a profession). || Enseñar (to teach).

professed [—t] adj. Declarado, da (avowed): *a professed atheist*, un ateo declarado. || Fingido, da; supuesto, ta (pretended). || Llamado, da (so-called). || REL. Profeso, sa (monk, nun).

professedly [—idli] adv. Declaradamente, abiertamente (avowedly). || Supuestamente (supposedly). || *He is professedly an authority on the subject*, pretende ser una autoridad en la materia.

profession [prəˈfeʃən] n. Profesión, *f.*: *medical profession*, profesión médica; *to make a profession of*, hacer profesión de. || Profesión, *f.*, oficio, *m.* (trade). || Profesión, *f.*, miembros (*m. pl.*) de la profesión: *an insult to the profession*, un insulto a la profesión. || Manifestación, *f.*, declaración, *f.* (declaration). || Profesión, *f.*, declaración, *f.*: *profession of loyalty*, declaración de lealtad. || REL. Profesión, *f.* (of faith, vows). || — *By profession*, de profesión: *by profession he is an architect*, es arquitecto de profesión. || *Teaching profession*, profesorado, *m.*

professional [—əl] adj. Profesional, de profesión: *professional player*, jugador profesional. || *Professional diplomat*, diplomático de carrera.
— N. Profesional, *m.* & *f.*
professionalism [prəˈfeʃnəlizəm] or **professionality** [prəfəʃəˈnæliti] n. Profesionalismo, *m.*
professionalize [prəˈfeʃənəlaiz] v. tr. Profesionalizar, hacer profesional (a sport). || Hacer un oficio de (an occupation).
professionally [prəˈfeʃənəli] adv. Profesionalmente.
professor [prəˈfesə*] n. Profesor, ra; catedrático, ca (at University). || *Assistant, full, visiting professor*, profesor auxiliar, titular, visitante.
professorate [prəˈfesərit] n. Profesorado, *m.* (function). || Profesorado, *m.*, cuerpo (*m.*) de profesores, cuerpo (*m.*) docente (professors).
professorial [ˌprɔfeˈsɔːriəl] adj. Profesoral.
professoriate [ˌprɔfeˈsɔːriit] n. Profesorado, *m.*,
professorship [prəˈfesəʃip] n. Cátedra, *f.*: *to be appointed to a professorship*, ser nombrado a una cátedra. || Profesorado, *m.* (function).
proffer [ˈprɔfə*] n. Oferta, *n.*, propuesta, *f.* (offer).
proffer [ˈprɔfə*] v. tr. Ofrecer, proponer.
proficiency [prəˈfiʃənsi] n. Pericia, *f.*, destreza, *f.*, habilidad, *f.* (skilfulness). || Capacidad, *f.*, competencia, *f.* (competence).
proficient [prəˈfiʃənt] adj. Capaz, competente (capable). || Experto, ta; perito, ta (expert). || Diestro, tra; hábil (skilful).
— N. Experto, ta; perito, ta.
profile [ˈprəufail] n. Perfil, *m.* (of the face). || Silueta, *f.* (of the body). || Contorno, *m.*, perfil, *m.* (outline). || Línea, *f.* (of a car). || Sección, *f.*, corte, *m.* (cross section). || FIG. Retrato, *m.*, reseña (*f.*) biográfica (concise biography). | Descripción, *f.* (written study). || GEOL. ARCH. Perfil, *m.* || TECH. Perfil, *m.* | Calibre, *m.* (gauge). || *In profile*, de perfil.
profile [ˈprəufail] v. tr. Perfilar.
profit [ˈprɔfit] n. Provecho, *m.* (advantage, good): *with profit*, con provecho; *to derive profit from*, sacar provecho de. || Ganancia, *f.*, lucro, *m.* (financial gain). || COMM. Beneficios, *m. pl.*, beneficio, *m.*, ganancia, *f.*, utilidades, *f. pl.*: *to make a profit on*, sacar beneficios de. || — *Gross profit*, beneficio bruto. || *Margin of profit*, margen (*m.*) de beneficio. || *Net profit* o *net profits*, beneficio neto. || *Profit and loss account*, cuenta (*f.*) de ganancias y pérdidas. || *To my profit*, en mi provecho, en provecho mío. || *To sell sth. at a profit*, vender algo con ganancia. || *To show a profit*, dar beneficios. || *To the profit of*, en provecho de. || *To turn sth. to profit*, sacar provecho de algo.
profit [ˈprɔfit] v. intr. Ganar: *we profited from that deal*, ganamos en aquel negocio. || Sacar provecho, beneficiarse [*by*, de] (to benefit).
— V. tr. Servir a, aprovechar a (to be of advantage to).
profitability [ˌprɔfitəˈbiliti] n. Rentabilidad, *f.*
profitable [ˈprɔfitəbl] adj. Provechoso, sa; beneficioso, sa (advantageous). || Útil (useful). || Rentable, productivo, va (economical). || Lucrativo, va (lucrative).
profitableness [—nis] n. Utilidad, *f.*, carácter (*m.*) provechoso (usefulness). || Rentabilidad, *f.* || Carácter (*m.*) lucrativo (financially).
profit balance [ˈprɔfitˌbæləns] n. Saldo (*m.*) positivo.
profit-earning [ˈprɔfitˌəːniŋ] adj. Rentable, productivo, va. || *Profit-earning capacity*, rentabilidad, *f.*
profiteer [ˌprɔfiˈtiə*] n. Aprovechado, da.
profiteer [ˌprɔfiˈtiə*] v. intr. Aprovecharse.
profiteering [—riŋ] n. Ganancias (*f. pl.*) excesivas (extortionate profits). || Mercantilismo, *m.*
profitless [ˈprɔfitlis] adj. Improductivo, va; no rentable, que no rinde (financially). || Inútil (useless).
profit margin [ˈprɔfitˌmɑːdʒin] n. Margen (*m.*) de beneficio.
profit-seeking [ˈprɔfitˌsiːkiŋ] adj. Interesado, da (person). || De fines lucrativos, lucrativo, va (society).
profit sharing [ˈprɔfitˌʃεəriŋ] n. Participación (*f.*) en los beneficios (by workers). || Reparto (*m.*) de los beneficios (by a company).
profit taking [ˈprɔfitˌteikiŋ] n. COMM. Realización (*f.*) de beneficios.
profit tax [ˈprɔfitˌtæks] n. Impuesto (*m.*) de utilidades.
profligacy [ˈprɔfligəsi] n. Libertinaje, *m.* (dissolution). || Prodigalidad, *f.* (lavishness). || FAM. Profusión, *f.*
profligate [ˈprɔfligit] adj./n. Libertino, na; disoluto, ta (dissolute). || Despilfarrador, ra; pródigo, ga; derrochador, ra (lavish).
pro forma invoice [prəuˈfɔːməˈinvɔis] n. Factura (*f.*) pro forma.
profound [prəˈfaund] adj. Profundo, da: *profound poverty*, miseria profunda.
— N. Profundidades, *f. pl.*
profoundness [—nis] or **profundity** [prəˈfʌnditi] n. Profundidad, *f.*
profuse [prəˈfjuːs] adj. Profuso, sa; abundante: *profuse praise*, alabanzas profusas. || Pródigo, ga (a person): *he is profuse in his praise*, es pródigo de *or* en alabanzas. || MED. Profuso, sa (sweat).
profuseness [—nis] n. Profusión, *f.*, abundancia *f.*
profusion [prəˈfjuːʒən] n. Profusión, *f.*, abundancia, *f.* (abundance). || Prodigalidad, *f.*, liberalidad, *f.* (lavishness).
progenitor [prəuˈdʒenitə*] n. Progenitor, *m.* || Antepasado, *m.* (forefather).
progeny [ˈprɔdʒini] n. Progenie, *f.* (offspring). || Descendientes, *m. pl.* (issue). || FIG. Resultado, *m.*, consecuencia, *f.*
progesterone [prəuˈdʒestərəun] n. Progesterona, *f.*
progestin [prəuˈdʒestin] n. Progestina, *f.*
prognathic [prɔgˈnæθik] adj. Prognato, ta.
prognathism [ˈprɔgnəθizəm] n. Prognatismo, *m.*
prognathous [prɔgˈneiθəs] adj. Prognato, ta.
prognosis [prɔgˈnəusis] n. MED. Pronóstico, *m.*

— OBSERV. El plural de *prognosis* es *prognoses*.

prognostic [prɔgˈnɔstik] n. Pronóstico, *m.* (forecast). || Augurio, *m.*, presagio, *m.* (omen).
prognosticate [prəgˈnɔstikeit] v. tr. Pronosticar.
prognostication [prəgˌnɔstiˈkeiʃən] n. Pronóstico, *m.* (forecast). || Augurio, *m.*, presagio, *m.* (omen). || Presentimiento, *m.* (foreboding).
prognosticative [prəgˈnɔstikətiv] adj. Profético, ca. || *Prognosticative of*, que anuncia.
prognosticator [prəgˈnɔstikeitə*] n. Pronosticador, ra.
programme (U. S. **program**) [ˈprəugræm] n. Programa, *m.*
programme (U. S. **program**) [ˈprəugræm] v. tr. Programar (a computer). || Planear, programar: *to programme one's day*, planear el día; *to programme a reform*, programar una reforma.
programmer (U. S. **programer**) [—ə*] n. Programador, ra.
programming (U. S. **programing**) [—iŋ] n. Programación, *f.*
— Adj. Programador, ra.
programme music (U. S. **program music**) [—ˈmjuːzik] n. Música (*f.*) descriptiva.
programme seller (U. S. **program seller**) [—ˈselə*] n. THEATR. Vendedor (*m.*) de programas.
progress [ˈprəugres] n. Progreso, *m.*, marcha, *f.*, avance, *m.* (forward movement). || Progreso, *m.*, curso, *m.* (of a disease). || Curso, *m.* (of events). || Progresos, *m. pl.*: *he has made good progress at school*, ha hecho grandes progresos en el colegio. || Progreso, *m.*, adelanto, *m.* (of mankind, science). || Viaje (*m.*) oficial (official journey). || Etapa, *f.*, fase, *f.* (of career, life). || — *In progress*, en curso: *the negotiations in progress*, las negociaciones en curso. || *Progress report*, informe (*m.*) sobre la marcha de los trabajos. || *We don't seem to be making any progress*, parece que no avanzamos mucho, parece que no avanzamos nada.
progress [prəuˈgres] v. intr. Progresar, avanzar (to advance). || Ir: *how is the boy progressing?*, ¿cómo va el niño? || Hacer progresos, hacer adelantos, progresar, avanzar: *he has progressed well*, ha hecho muchos progresos, ha avanzado mucho. || MED. Mejorar, progresar (patient). || Hacer un viaje (official).
progression [prəuˈgreʃən] n. Progresión, *f.* || MUS. MATH. Progresión, *f.*: *arithmetic, geometric, harmonic progression*, progresión aritmética, geométrica, armónica.
progressionism [—izəm] n. Progresismo, *m.*
progressionist [prəuˈgreʃnist] n. Progresista, *m.* & *f.*
progressist [prəuˈgresist] n. Progresista, *m.* & *f.*
progressive [prəuˈgresiv] adj. Progresivo, va: *progressive development*, desarrollo progresivo; *progressive taxes*, impuestos progresivos. || Progresista (political and social ideas): *progressive newspaper*, periódico progresista. || GRAMM. Progresivo, va (form).
— N. Progresista, *m.* & *f.*
progressiveness [—nis] n. Progresividad, *f.* || Progresismo, *m.* (in politics).
progressivism [—izəm] n. Progresismo, *m.*
prohibit [prəˈhibit] v. tr. Prohibir: *smoking is prohibited*, está prohibido *or* se prohibe fumar. || Impedir, imposibilitar (to prevent): *his broken leg prohibits him from playing rugby*, la pierna rota le impide jugar al rugby, la pierna rota le imposibilita para jugar al rugby.
prohibition [ˌprəuiˈbiʃən] n. Prohibición, *f.* || U. S. Prohibicionismo, *m.*, prohibición, *f.*
prohibitionism [ˌprəuiˈbiʃnizəm] n. Prohibicionismo, *m.* (of liquor).
prohibitionist [ˌprəuiˈbiʃnist] adj./n. Prohibicionista.
prohibitive [prəˈhibitiv] adj. Prohibitivo, va: *prohibitive prices*, precios prohibitivos.
prohibitory [prəˈhibitəri] adj. Prohibitorio, ria.
project [ˈprɔdʒekt] n. Proyecto, *m.* (plan): *to carry out a project*, llevar a cabo un proyecto; *it is just a project*, no es más que un proyecto.
project [prəˈdʒekt] v. tr. Proyectar (a missile, film, shadow, plans, etc.). || Proyectar, planear (a trip). || MATH. Proyectar (a line). || Hacer resaltar (to cause to stick out). || FIG. *To project o.s. into*, imaginarse en.
— V. intr. Sobresalir, destacar, resaltar (to protrude).
projectile [prəuˈdʒektail] adj. Arrojadizo, za: *projectile weapons*, armas arrojadizas.
— N. Proyectil, *m.*
projecting [prəˈdʒektiŋ] adj. Saliente, saledizo, za.
projection [prəˈdʒekʃən] n. Proyección, *f.* || Saliente, *m.*, resalto, *m.* (part which sticks out). || GEOGR. Planisferio, *m.* || MATH. Proyección, *f.* || FIG. Concepción, *f.* (of a plan). || *Projection room* o *booth*, cabina (*f.*) de proyección.
projectionist [—ist] n. Operador (*m.*) de cine.

projective [prəˈdʒektiv] adj. MATH. Descriptivo, va (geometry).
projector [prəˈdʒektə*] n. Proyector, *m.*, aparato (*m.*) de proyección (of films). || Proyectista, *m.* & *f.* (planner). || Promotor, ra.
prolapse [ˈprəulæps] n. MED. Prolapso, *m.*
prolapsus [prəuˈlæpsəs] n. MED. Prolapso, *m.*
prole [prəul] n. FAM. Proletario, ria.
prolegomenon [ˌprəuleˈgɔminən] n. Prolegómeno, *m.*

— OBSERV. El plural de *prolegomenon* es *prolegomena.*

prolepsis [prəuˈlepsis] n. Prolepsis, *f.*

— OBSERV. El plural de la palabra inglesa es *prolepses.*

proletarian [ˌprəuliˈtɛəriən] adj./n. Proletario, ria.
proletarianization [ˌprəuliˌtɛəriənaiˈzeiʃən] n. Proletarización, *f.*
proletarianize [prəuliˈtɛəriənaiz] v. tr. Proletarizar.
proletariat [ˌprəuliˈtɛəriət] n. Proletariado, *m.*
proliferate [prəuˈlifəreit] v. intr. Proliferar.
proliferation [prəuˌlifəˈreiʃən] n. Proliferación, *f.*, multiplicación, *f.*
proliferous [prəˈlifərəs] adj. Prolífero, ra.
prolific [prəuˈlifik] adj. Prolífico, ca (*of,* en). || Fecundo, da.
prolificness [—nis] n. Fecundidad, *f.*
prolix [ˈprəuliks] adj. Prolijo, ja.
prolixity [prəuˈliksiti] n. Prolijidad, *f.*
prolocutor [prəuˈlɔkjutə*] n. Portavoz, *m.* [*Amer.*, vocero, *m.*] (spokesman). || Presidente, *m.* (chairman).
prologize [ˈprəulәgaiz] v. intr. Escribir prólogos.
prologue [ˈprəulɔg] n. Prólogo, *m.* (*to,* de).
prologue [ˈprəulɔg] v. tr. Prologar.
prologuize [ˈprəuləgaiz] v. intr. Escribir prólogos.
prolong [prəuˈlɔŋ] v. tr. Prolongar.
prolongate [ˈprəulɔŋgeit] v. tr. Prolongar.
prolongation [ˌprəulɔŋˈgeiʃən] n. Prolongación, *f.*
prolonge [prəˈlɔndʒ] n. MIL. Prolonga, *f.*
prolonger [prəuˈlɔŋgə*] n. Prolongador, ra.
prom [prɔm] n. FAM. Concierto (*m.*) en el que una parte del público no tiene localidades sentadas (concert). | Paseo (*m.*) marítimo (on the seafront). || U. S. FAM. Baile (*m.*) de gala (dance).
promenade [ˌprɔmiˈnɑ:d] n. Paseo, *m.* (place, walk, part of dance). || Paseo (*m.*) marítimo (on the seafront). || Pasillo, *m.* [sitio donde los espectadores están de pie] (theatre). || — *Promenade concert,* concierto (*m.*) en el que una parte del público no tiene localidades sentadas. || MAR. *Promenade deck,* cubierta (*f.*) de paseo.
promenade [ˌprɔmiˈnɑ:d] v. intr. Pasearse.
— V. tr. Pasear (to take for a walk or ride). || Pasearse por (the streets). || FIG. Hacer alarde de (to show).
promenader [—ə*] n. Paseante, *m.* & *f.*
Prometheus [prəˈmi:θju:s] pr. n. MYTH. Prometeo, *m.*
promethium [prəˈmi:θiəm] n. CHEM. Prometeo, *m.*
prominence [ˈprɔminəns] n. Prominencia, *f.* (hill, elevation). || Protuberancia, *f.*: *solar prominence,* protuberancia solar. || FIG. Importancia, *f.* || — FIG. *To bring into prominence,* hacer resaltar. | *To come into prominence,* empezar a destacar.
prominent [ˈprɔminənt] adj. Prominente (jutting out). || Saliente (tooth, cheekbone). || Saltón, ona (eye). || FIG. Preeminente (eminent). | Destacado, da; notable (outstanding). | Que llama la atención (striking).
promiscuity [ˌprɔmisˈkjuiti] n. Promiscuidad, *f.*
promiscuous [prəˈmiskjuəs] adj. Promiscuo, cua (mixed). || Heterogéneo, a. || Libertino, na (person). || FAM. Al azar (casual).
promiscuousness [prəˈmiskjuəsnis] n. Promiscuidad, *f.* (promiscuity).
promise [ˈprɔmis] n. Promesa, *f.* (pledge): *to keep one's promise,* cumplir su *or* con su promesa; *to break a promise,* faltar a una promesa; *empty promises,* promesas vanas. || Esperanza, *f.*, promesa, *f.* (hope). || — *Full of promise* o *of great promise,* muy prometedor, ra. || *Promise of marriage,* promesa *or* palabra de matrimonio. || *To be of great promise,* prometer. || *To hold* o *to keep s.o. to his promise,* hacer que alguien cumpla lo prometido. || *To release s.o. from his promise,* liberar a alguien de su promesa. || *To show promise,* prometer, ser prometedor, ra. || *Under promise of,* bajo palabra de. || FIG. *Wild promise,* promesa de borracho.
promise [ˈprɔmis] v. tr. Prometer: *you promised to help me,* prometió que me ayudaría; *to promise s.o. a rise,* prometerle a uno un aumento de sueldo. || Presagiar, augurar (to augur). || — *The production promises to be good,* la producción se anuncia muy buena, la producción promete ser muy buena. || FIG. *To promise the moon,* prometer la luna *or* el oro y el moro. || *To promise o.s.,* prometerse.
— V. intr. Prometer (to make a promise). || *To promise well,* prometer mucho.
promised [—t] adj. Prometido, da. || *Promised Land,* Tierra de Promisión.
promisee [prɔmiˈsi:] n. Persona (*f.*) que tiene una promesa.
promiser [ˈprɔmisə*] n. Prometedor, ra.
promising [ˈprɔmisiŋ] adj. Prometedor, ra; que promete: *he is a promising tennis player,* es un tenista que promete.
promisingly [prɔmisiŋli] adv. De modo prometedor.
promisor [ˈprɔmisɔ:*] n. JUR. Prometedor, *m.*
promissory [ˈprɔmisəri] adj. Promisorio, ria: *promissory oath,* juramento promisorio. || COMM. *Promissory note,* pagaré, *m.*
promontory [ˈprɔməntri] n. GEOGR. Promontorio, *m.* || ANAT. Protuberancia, *f.*, promontorio, *m.*
promote [prəˈməut] v. tr. Ascender (to raise in rank): *to promote s.o. captain,* ascender a uno a capitán. || Promover, ascender: *he has been promoted to foreman,* lo han ascendido a capataz. || Promocionar (product). || Promover, fomentar (disorder). || Suscitar, provocar, fomentar (hatred). || Fomentar, estimular (to encourage). || Contribuir a (a result). || Financiar (to finance). || Fundar (a company). || Presentar (a bill in Parliament). || CHEM. Provocar (a reaction). || Cambiar [un peón] por una pieza anteriormente comida (in chess). || Pasar de año (at school).
promoter [—ə*] n. Promotor, ra (originator). || Promotor, ra; fundador ra (of a company). || COMM. Promotor, ra. || Promotor, *m.* (in sports).
promoting [—iŋ] n. See PROMOTION.
promotion [prəˈməuʃən] n. Ascenso, *m.* (rise in rank). || Promoción, *f.* (of an employee, a product). || Fundación, *f.* (of a company). || Fomento, *m.* (encouragement). || Presentación, *f.* (of a bill in Parliament). || U. S. Publicidad, *f.* || — *Promotion list,* escalafón, *m.* || *Promotion match,* partido (*m.*) de promoción.
promotive [prəˈməutiv] adj. Promotor, ra.
prompt [prɔmpt] adj. Pronto, ta; rápido, da (quick). || Inmediato, ta; rápido, da: *a prompt reply,* una respuesta inmediata. || Puntual: *be prompt,* sea puntual. || Rápido, da (service). || COMM. Disponible.
— Adv. En punto: *at five o'clock prompt,* a las cinco en punto.
— N. COMM. Plazo (*m.*) límite (time limit). | Aviso, *m.* (reminder). || THEATR. Réplica, *f.* || Sugerencia, *f.* (suggestion). || *To give an actor a prompt,* apuntar a un actor.
prompt [prɔmpt] v. tr. Incitar, mover, impulsar (to rouse to action): *his anger prompted him to leave,* su enfado le movió a marcharse. || Inspirar, sugerir (to inspire). || Sugerir (to suggest). || THEATR. Apuntar. || FIG. Apuntar, soplar.
prompt box [—bɔks] n. THEATR. Concha (*f.*) del apuntador.
prompter [—ə*] n. THEATR. Apuntador, ra. || Instigador, ra; promotor, ra (instigator).
prompter's box [—zbɔks] n. THEATR. Concha (*f.*) del apuntador.
prompting [—iŋ] n. Instigación, *f.* || Incitación, *f.* (incitement).
promptitude [ˈprɔmptitju:d] or **promptness** [ˈprɔmptnis] n. Prontitud, *f.*, presteza, *f.*
promulgate [ˈprɔməlgeit] v. tr. Promulgar (a law). || FIG. Difundir: *to promulgate culture,* difundir la cultura.
promulgating [—iŋ] adj. Promulgador, ra.
promulgation [ˌprɔməlˈgeiʃən] n. Promulgación, *f.* (of a law). || FIG. Difusión, *f.*
promulgator [ˈprɔməlgeitə*] n. Promulgador, ra.
pronaos [prəˈneiɔs] n. ARCH. Pronaos, *m.* (of Greek temple).
pronate [ˈprəuˌneit] v. tr. Poner en posición prona, poner boca abajo.
pronating [—iŋ] adj. ANAT. Pronador, ra.
pronation [prəuˈneiʃən] n. ANAT. Pronación, *f.*
pronator [prəuˈneitə*] n. ANAT. Pronador, *m.*
prone [prəun] adj. Prono, na (hand, etc.). || Boca abajo (person). || Propenso, sa (inclined): *Mary is prone to fits of laughter,* María es propensa a los ataques de risa.
proneness [—nis] n. Propensión, *f.*, predisposición, *f.* (propensity).
prong [prɔŋ] n. Diente, *m.*, púa, *f.* (of a fork). || Pitón, *m.* (of horns). || Uña, *f.*, diente, *m.* (in mechanics).
prong [prɔŋ] v. tr. AGR. Remover con la horca *or* el bieldo. || Pinchar (to prick, to prod).
pronghorn [—hɔ:n] n. ZOOL. Berrendo, *m.* (deer).
pronominal [prəuˈnɔminl] adj. GRAMM. Pronominal.
pronoun [ˈprəunaun] n. GRAMM. Pronombre, *m.*
pronounce [prəˈnauns] v. tr. Pronunciar (words): *to pronounce a word well,* pronunciar bien una palabra. || Declarar (to declare): *the doctor pronounced Peter out of danger,* el médico declaró que Pedro estaba fuera de peligro. || JUR. Pronunciar (to pass): *to pronounce sentence,* pronunciar un fallo. || — *To be pronounced,* pronunciarse. || *To pronounce o.s.,* pronunciarse.
— V. intr. Pronunciar: *to pronounce badly,* pronunciar mal. || Pronunciarse, dar su opinión (to give one's opinion): *to pronounce on a matter,* dar su opinión sobre una cuestión; *to pronounce in favour of,* pronunciarse a favor de. || JUR. Pronunciarse.
pronounceable [—əbl] adj. Pronunciable.
pronounced [—t] adj. Pronunciado, da; acusado, da; marcado, da; fuerte.
pronouncement [—mənt] n. Declaración, *f.* (statement): *to make a pronouncement,* hacer una declaración.
pronouncing [—iŋ] n. JUR. Pronunciamiento, *m.* (of sentence).
pronouncing dictionary [—iŋˈdikʃənri] n. Diccionario (*m.*) fonético.

pronto [ˈprɔntə] adv. U. S. FAM. Pronto, en seguida, inmediatamente.

pronunciamento [prəˌnʌnsiəˈmentəu] n. Pronunciamiento, *m.*, proclama, *f.*, manifiesto, *m.*

pronunciation [prəˌnʌnsiˈeiʃən] n. Pronunciación, *f.*

proof [pru:f] adj. Resistente (*against*, a) [resistent to]. || Al abrigo de, fuera de: *proof against danger*, al abrigo de todo peligro. || A prueba de: *proof against bullets*, a prueba de balas. || De graduación normal (alcohol). || FIG. Insensible (*against*, a).
— N. Prueba, *f.*, pruebas, *f. pl.*: *I want proof*, quiero una prueba, quiero pruebas; *a proof of one's guilt*, una prueba de culpabilidad. || Prueba, *f.* (test). || MATH. JUR. PHOT. PRINT. Prueba, *f.* || Graduación (*f.*) normal (of an alcohol). || — *By way of proof*, como prueba. || *In proof of*, en prueba de. || *Negative proof*, prueba negativa. || *Proof of death*, acta (*f.*) de defunción. || *Proof of identity*, documentos (*m. pl.*) de identidad. || *The proof of it is*, prueba de ello es que. || FIG. *The proof of the pudding is in the eating*, por la muestra se conoce el paño. || *To give proof of*, dar prueba de. || *To put sth. to the proof*, poner algo a prueba.
— OBSERV. Muy frecuentemente el adjetivo *proof* se combina con un sustantivo para formar una palabra compuesta (*bulletproof*, a prueba de balas; *waterproof*, estanco, ca; impermeable). El lector tiene, por consiguiente, que consultar los artículos correspondientes a estas palabras.

proof [pru:f] v. tr. Impermeabilizar (cloth). || Hacer hermético, ca (to make watertight). || Hacer resistente (against fire, etc.). || PRINT. Tirar una prueba de (to make a trial proof of). | Corregir (to correct).

proofread* [—ˌri:d] v. tr. PRINT. Corregir.
— V. intr. PRINT. Corregir pruebas.
— OBSERV. Pret. & p. p. *proofread*.

proofreader [—ˌri:də*] n. Corrector (*m.*) de pruebas *or* de galeradas.

proofreading [—ˌri:diŋ] n. Corrección (*f.*) de pruebas *or* de galeradas.

proof sheet [—ʃi:t] n. Prueba, *f.*, galerada, *f.*

prop [prɔp] n. Puntal, *m.* (rigid support). || MIN. Puntal, *m.*, entibo, *m.* || AGR. Rodrigón, *m.* || MAR. Escora, *f.* || FIG. Sostén, *m.*, apoyo, *m.*, pilar, *m.* || Hélice, *f.* (propeller). || — Pl. THEATR. Accesorios, *m.*

prop [prɔp] v. tr. Apuntalar (a wall). || MIN. Entibar. || Apoyar (to lean). || Mantener: *prop the door open*, mantén la puerta abierta. || MAR. Escorar. || AGR. Poner rodrigones a, rodrigar (plants). || FIG. Apuntalar, apoyar, sostener. || *To prop o.s. against*, apoyarse en *or* contra.

propaganda [ˌprɔpəˈgændə] n. Propaganda, *f.*

propagandist [ˌprɔpəˈgændist] adj./n. Propagandista.

propagandize [ˌprɔpəˈgændaiz] v. tr. Hacer propaganda de.
— V. intr. Hacer propaganda.

propagate [ˈprɔpəgeit] v. tr. Propagar.
— V. intr. Propagarse.

propagating [—iŋ] adj. Propagador, ra.

propagation [ˌprɔpəˈgeiʃən] n. Propagación, *f.* (spreading).

propagative [ˈprɔpəgeitiv] adj. Propagativo, va; propagador, ra.

propagator [ˈprɔpəgeitə*] n. Propagador, ra; propalador, ra: *propagator of incorrect news*, propagador de noticias falsas.

propane [ˈprəupein] n. CHEM. Propano, *m.*

proparoxytone [ˌprəupəˈrɔksitəun] adj. Proparoxítono, na; esdrújulo, la.
— N. Palabra (*f.*) esdrújula.

propel [prəˈpel] v. tr. Propulsar, impeler, impulsar. || *Propelled by turbines*, propulsado por turbinas.

propellant or **propellent** [—ənt] adj. Propulsor, ra.
— N. Propulsor, *m.* || Propergol, *m.* (for rockets).

propeller [—ə*] n. Propulsor, *m.* || Hélice, *f.* (of ship or aircraft).

propeller shaft [—əʃɑ:ft] n. AUT. Árbol (*m.*) de transmisión. || MAR. Eje (*m.*) portahélice.

propelling [—iŋ] adj. Propulsor, ra; impelente.

propelling pencil [—iŋˈpensl] n. Portaminas, *m. inv.*, lapicero, *m.*

propense [prəˈpens] adj. Propenso, sa; inclinado, da.

propensity [prəˈpensiti] n. Propensión, *f.*: *propensity for lying*, propensión a mentir.

proper [ˈprɔpə*] adj. Apropiado, da; adecuado, da (appropriate): *a hat proper to the occasion*, un sombrero apropiado para el caso. || Oportuno, na (opportune): *at the proper time*, en el momento oportuno; *to deem it proper to do sth.*, juzgar oportuno hacer algo. || Propio, pia: *in the proper sense of the word*, en el sentido propio de la palabra. || Propio, pia; característico, ca (characteristic): *attitude proper to young people*, actitud propia de los jóvenes. || Propio, pia; mismo, ma: *my office is not in the building proper*, mi oficina no está en el propio edificio or en el edificio mismo. || Exacto, ta (accurate): *the proper word*, la palabra exacta. || Correcto, ta: *the proper use of the indicative*, el empleo correcto del indicativo. || Propiamente dicho, cha (properly speaking): *Great Britain proper excludes Ireland*, Gran Bretaña propiamente dicha excluye Irlanda. || Decente, como Dios manda (decent): *she is a very proper girl*, es una chica muy decente. || De verdad, verdadero, ra (real): *a proper rifle not a toy one*, un fusil de verdad no de juguete. || FAM. Verdadero, ra: *a proper idiot*, un verdadero idiota. || Hecho y derecho, cabal: *a proper man*, un hombre hecho y derecho. || GRAMM. Propio, pia: *proper noun* o *proper name*, nombre propio. || HERALD. Natural. || — *As you think proper*, como a usted le parezca. || *In proper condition*, en buen estado. || *In the proper way*, de forma adecuada, de la mejor manera. || *I think it proper to do this*, creo que conviene hacer esto. || *It was the proper thing to say*, es exactamente lo que había que decir. || MATH. *Proper fraction*, fracción propia. || FAM. *To do the proper thing by s.o.*, cumplir con alguien. || *To do what is proper*, hacer lo que se debe.
— Adv. FAM. Muy. || FAM. *Good and proper*, completamente.
— N. REL. Propio, *m.*

properly [—li] adv. Bien: *I like to do things properly*, me gusta hacer las cosas bien. || Debidamente, como es debido: *to thank s.o. properly*, dar a alguien las gracias como es debido. || Apropiadamente, adecuadamente (fitly). || De verdad, verdaderamente (really). || Correctamente (correctly). || GRAMM. En el sentido propio (word). || FAM. Completamente (completely): *properly mad*, completamente loco. || *Properly speaking*, propiamente dicho: *properly speaking he is not a writer*, no es un escritor propiamente dicho.

propertied [ˈprɔpətid] adj. Hacendado, da (landed). || Adinerado, da; acaudalado, da; rico, ca (wealthy).

property [ˈprɔpəti] n. Propiedad, *f.*, posesión, *f.* (possession). || Característica, *f.*, propiedad, *f.* (characteristic). || Finca, *f.*, propiedad, *f.* (land). || Bienes, *m. pl.*: *he left his property to me*, me dejó sus bienes. || Dominio, *m.*, propiedad, *f.*: *public property*, dominio público. || CHEM. MED. BOT. Propiedad, *f.* || THEATR. Accesorio, *m.* || — *It became the property of his son*, pasó a ser propiedad de su hijo. || *Man of property*, hombre hacendado, hombre rico. || *Personal property*, bienes muebles. || *That's my property*, eso es mío, eso es de mi propiedad || *To be common property*, ser del dominio público. || *Whose property is this?*, ¿de quién es esto?

property man [—mæn] n. Accesorista, *m.*, attrezzista, *m.* (in theatre, cinema).

property owner [—ˌəunə*] n. Terrateniente, *m.* & *f.*

property room [—ru:m] n. Guardarropía, *f.*

property tax [—tæks] n. Contribución (*f.*) territorial.

prophase [ˈprəufeiz] n. BIOL. Profase, *f.*

prophecy [ˈprɔfisi] n. Profecía, *f.*

prophesier [ˈprɔfisaiə*] n. Profeta, *m.*, profetisa, *f.* || Profetizador, ra.

prophesy [ˈprɔfisai] v. tr. Profetizar (to foretell). || Predecir, vaticinar (to predict).
— V. intr. Profetizar.

prophesying [—iŋ] adj. Profetizador, ra.

prophet [ˈprɔfit] n. REL. Profeta, *m.* || Adivino, *m.*, profeta, *m.* (s.o. who foretells the future). || FIG. *An early prophet of socialism*, uno de los primeros profetas del socialismo.

prophetess [ˈprɔfitis] n. Profetisa, *f.*

prophetic [prəˈfetik] or **prophetical** [—əl] adj. Profético, ca.

prophylactic [ˌprɔfiˈlæktik] adj. MED. Profiláctico, ca.
— N. MED. Medicamento (*m.*) profiláctico.

prophilaxis [ˌprɔfiˈlæksis] n. MED. Profilaxis, *f.*, profilaxia, *f.*

propinquity [prəˈpiŋkwiti] n. Cercanía, *f.*, proximidad, *f.*, propincuidad, *f.* (p.us.) [nearness]. || Parentesco, *m.* (kinship). || FIG. Parentesco, *m.*, afinidad, *f.* (of ideas).

propitiate [prəˈpiʃieit] v. tr. Propiciar, hacer propicio. || Aplacar (to appease).

propitiation [prəˌpiʃiˈeiʃən] n. Propiciación, *f.* || Aplacamiento, *m.*

propitiative [prəˈpiʃiətiv] adj. Propiciatorio, ria; expiatorio, ria.

propitiator [prəˈpiʃieitə*] n. Propiciador, ra.

propitiatory [prəˈpiʃiətəri] adj. Propiciatorio, ria.

propitious [prəˈpiʃəs] adj. Propicio, cia; favorable.

propitiousness [—nis] n. Carácter (*m.*) propicio.

propolis [ˈprɔpəlis] n. Propóleos, *m.*

proponent [prəˈpəunənt] n. Autor, ra; proponente, *m.* & *f.*, proponedor, ra (who makes a proposal). || Defensor, ra (who supports a cause).

proportion [prəˈpɔ:ʃən] n. Proporción, *f.* || Parte, *f.* (of expenses, profits). || — Pl. Dimensiones, *f.* || — MATH. *Arithmetic proportion*, proporción aritmética. || *In proportion as*, a medida que. || *In proportion to*, en proporción con. || *Sense of proportion*, sentido de la medida. || *To be out of proportion with*, no guardar proporción con.

proportion [prəˈpɔ:ʃən] v. tr. Proporcionar, adecuar. || Determinar las dimensiones de. || MED. Dosificar.

proportionable [prəˈpɔ:ʃnəbl] adj. Proporcionado, da.

proportional [prəˈpɔ:ʃənl] adj. Proporcional. || Proporcional, en proporción: *proportional to*, proporcional a, en proporción con. || MATH. Proporcional. || *Proportional representation*, representación (*f.*) proporcional (system of election).
— N. MATH. Número (*m.*) proporcional.

proportionality [prəˌpɔ:ʃəˈnæliti] n. Proporcionalidad, *f.*

proportionally [prəˈpɔːʃnəli] adv. Proporcionalmente. || *Proportionally to*, proporcionalmente a, en proporción con.
proportionate [prəˈpɔːʃnit] adj. Proporcionado, da (*to*, a).
proportionate [prəˈpɔːʃneit] v. tr. Proporcionar, adecuar.
proportionately [prəˈpɔːʃnitli] adv. Proporcionalmente. || *Proportionately speaking*, guardando las proporciones, teniéndolo todo en cuenta.
proposal [prəˈpəuzəl] n. Proposición, *f.*, propuesta, *f.*: *to make a proposal*, hacer una propuesta. || Oferta, *f.* (offer). || Propuesta (*f.*) de matrimonio, petición (*f.*) de mano (for marriage). || Fig. Proyecto, *m.*
propose [prəˈpəuz] v. tr. Proponer: *to propose a plan*, proponer un proyecto; *to propose s.o. for a post*, proponer a alguien para un puesto. || Proponerse, tener intención de: *he proposes to arrive early*, tiene la intención de llegar temprano. || Brindar por, proponer un brindis por (to toast). || Plantear (to pose a problem). || *To propose the health of*, brindar por, beber a la salud de.
— V. intr. Proponerse, tener intención (to intend). || Pedir la mano, ofrecer matrimonio. || Fig. *Man proposes, God disposes*, el hombre propone y Dios dispone.
proposer [—ə*] n. Proponente, *m.* & *f.*, autor, ra.
proposition [ˌprɔpəˈziʃən] n. Proposición, *f.*, propuesta, *f.* (proposal). || Oferta, *f.* (offer). || Proyecto, *m.* (plan). || Gramm. Phil. Math. Proposición, *f.* || Empresa, *f.* (undertaking). || Tarea, *f.* (job). || Propósito, *m.* (objective). || Perspectiva, *f.* || U. S. Fam. Proposición (*f.*) deshonesta (illicit invitation). || Fam. Tipo, *m.* (person). | Problema, *m.* (problem). || — Fig. *It's a tough proposition*, es un asunto difícil de resolver. | *That is a different proposition altogether*, eso es harina de otro costal.
proposition [ˌprɔpəˈziʃən] v. tr. U. S. Hacer una proposición a. | Fam. Hacer proposiciones deshonestas a (to propose sexual intercourse to).
propositional [—əl] adj. Phil. De la proposición. || Por silogismos (theology).
propound [prəˈpaund] v. tr. Proponer, exponer, presentar (a plan, question, etc.). || Plantear (a problem).
propounder [—ə*] n. Proponente, *m.* & *f.*
propraetor (U. S. **propretor**) [prəuˈpriːtə*] n. Propretor, *m.*
propraetorship (U. S. **propretorship**) [—ʃip] n. Propretura, *f.*
proprietary [prəˈpraiətəri] adj. Propietario, ria. || De propiedad (rights). || Patentado, da (article). || Rel. Privado, da (chapel). || Med. *Proprietary medicines*, especialidades farmacéuticas, específicos, *m.*
— N. Propiedad, *f.*, derecho (*m.*) de propiedad (ownership). || Propietarios, *m. pl.* (proprietors).
proprietor [prəˈpraiətə*] n. Propietario, ria.
proprietorship [—ʃip] n. Propiedad, *f.*, posesión, *f.* || Propiedad, *f.*, derecho (*m.*) de propiedad.
proprietress [prəˈpraiətris] n. Propietaria, *f.*
propriety [prəˈpraiəti] n. Conveniencia, *f.* (suitability). || Oportunidad, *f.* (of an action). || Decoro, *m.*, decencia, *f.* (decent behaviour). || Corrección, *f.* (correctness). || Propiedad, *f.* (of a word). || — Pl. Convenciones, *f.*, cánones (*m.*) sociales. || *Breach of propriety*, incorrección, *f.*
propulsion [prəˈpʌlʃən] n. Propulsión, *f.*: *jet propulsion*, propulsión a chorro *or* por reacción.
propulsive [prəˈpʌlsiv] adj. Propulsivo, va; propulsor, ra; impelente.
propylaeum [ˌprɔpiˈliəm] n. Arch. Propileo, *m.*

— Observ. El plural de la palabra inglesa es *propylaea*.

pro rata [prəuˈrɑːtə] adv. A prorrata, a prorrateo, proporcionalmente.
prorate [prəuˈreit] n. U. S. Prorrata, *f.*
prorate [prəuˈreit] v. tr. U. S. Prorratear.
proration [prəuˈreiʃən] n. U. S. Prorrateo, *m.*
prorogation [ˌprəurəˈgeiʃən] n. Prórroga, *f.*, prorrogación, *f.*
prorogue [prəˈrəug] v. tr. Prorrogar.
— V. intr. Ser prorrogado, prorrogarse.
prosaic [prəuˈzeiik] adj. Prosaico, ca.
prosaicness [—nis] n. Prosaísmo, *m.*: *the prosaicness of everyday tasks*, el prosaísmo de las tareas cotidianas.
prosaism [ˈprəuzeiizəm] n. Prosaísmo, *m.*
prosaist [ˈprəuzeiist] n. Prosista, *m.* & *f.* (writer). || Fig. Persona (*f.*) prosaica.
proscenium [prəuˈsiːnjəm] n. Theatr. Proscenio, *m.* || — *Proscenium arch*, embocadura, *f.* || *Proscenium box*, palco (*m.*) de proscenio.
proscribe [prəusˈkraib] v. tr. Proscribir.
proscribed [—d] adj. Proscrito, ta.
proscriber [—ə*] n. Proscriptor, *m.*
proscription [prəusˈkripʃən] n. Proscripción, *f.*
proscriptive [prəusˈkriptiv] adj. Proscriptor, ra.
prose [prəuz] n. Prosa, *f.* (in literature). || Fig. Prosaísmo, *m.* (of life). || *Prose writer*, prosista, *m.* & *f.*
— Adj. En prosa: *prose poem*, poema en prosa.
prose [prəuz] v. intr. Fam. Gastar mucha prosa.
— V. tr. Poner en prosa.
prosecutable [ˈprɔsiˌkjutəbl] adj. Jur. Que se puede enjuiciar.
prosecute [ˈprɔsikjuːt] v. tr. Jur. Procesar, enjuiciar (s.o.). | Entablar (an action). || Proseguir, continuar (to carry on): *to prosecute a war*, proseguir una guerra. || Llevar a cabo (to carry out). || Ejercer (a profession). || Hacer (studies). || Efectuar, realizar (a voyage).
— V. intr. Jur. Entablar una acción judicial.
prosecuting attorney [—iŋəˈtəːni] n. U. S. Jur. Acusador (*m.*) público, fiscal, *m.*
prosecution [ˌprɔsiˈkjuːʃən] n. Jur. Procesamiento, *m.*, enjuiciamiento, *m.* (action of prosecuting). | Acción (*f.*) judicial: *to start a prosecution against s.o.*, entablar una acción judicial contra alguien. | Proceso, *m.*, juicio, *m.* (trial). | Parte (*f.*) acusadora (party). | Acusación, *f.*, ministerio (*m.*) público *or* fiscal (public prosecutor). || Ejercicio, *m.* (of a profession). || Cumplimiento, *m.* (of duty). || Continuación, *f.*, prosecución, *f.* (continuation). || — Jur. *Counsel for the prosecution*, fiscal, *m.* | *Witness for the prosecution*, testigo de cargo.
prosecutor [ˈprɔsikjuːtə*] n. Jur. Demandante, *m.*, querellante, *m.* (plaintiff). | Acusador, *m.* (lawyer). | Fiscal, *m.*, acusador (*m.*) público (public prosecutor).
prosecutrix [ˈprɔsiˌkjuːtriks] n. Jur. Demandante, *f.*, querellante, *f.*
proselyte [ˈprɔsilait] n. Prosélito, *m.*
proselyte [ˈprɔsilait] v. intr. Ganar prosélitos, hacer prosélitos.
— V. tr. Convertir.
proselytism [ˈprɔsilitizəm] n. Proselitismo, *m.*
proselytize [ˈprɔsilitaiz] v. tr. Convertir.
— V. intr. Ganar prosélitos, hacer prosélitos.
prosenchyma [prɔsˈenkimə] n. Bot. Prosénquima, *m.*
proser [ˈprəuzə*] n. Fam. Prosador, *m.*
prose writer [prəuzˈraitə*] n. Prosista, *m.* & *f.*
prosimii [prəuˈsimii] pl. n. Zool. Prosimios, *m.*
prosiness [ˈprəuzinis] n. Prosaísmo, *m.*
prosist [ˈprəusist] n. Prosista, *m.* & *f.* (prose writer).
proslavery [prəuˈsleivəri] adj. Esclavista.
prosodic [ˌprəˈsɔdik] adj. Prosódico, ca.
prosodist [ˈprɔsədist] n. Especialista (*m.* & *f.*) en prosodia *or* en métrica.
prosody [ˈprɔsədi] n. Prosodia, *f.* || Métrica, *f.*
prosopopoeia [prɔsəpəˈpiːiə] n. Prosopopeya, *f.*
prospect [ˈprɔspekt] n. Perspectiva, *f.* (outlook): *the prospect of arriving too late*, la perspectiva de llegar demasiado tarde; *a job with good prospects*, un puesto con buenas perspectivas. || Vista, *f.*, panorama, *m.* (view): *a place with a splendid prospect*, un lugar con una vista espléndida. || Esperanza, *f.*, esperanzas, *f. pl.* (hope): *to hold out a prospect of*, dar esperanzas de; *there is no prospect of their leaving*, hay pocas esperanzas de que se vayan. || Expectativa, *f.* (expectation). || Posibilidad, *f.*, probabilidad, *f.* (possibility): *there is no prospect of agreement*, no hay ninguna probabilidad de acuerdo. || Muestra, *f.* (of ore). || U.S. Cliente (*m.*) *or* comprador (*m.*) eventual (possible client). | Partido, *m.* (for possible marriage). || — *To have a job in prospect*, tener un trabajo en perspectiva. || *To have prospects*, tener porvenir.
prospect [prəsˈpekt] v. tr. Prospectar, hacer una prospección en [*Amer.*, catear].
— V. intr. Hacer una prospección. || — *To prospect for*, buscar. || *To prospect well*, ser prometedor, prometer (mine, etc.).
prospect glass [ˈprɔspektglɑːs] n. Telescopio, *m.*
prospecting [prəsˈpektiŋ] n. Prospección, *f.*
prospection [prəsˈpekʃən] n. Prospección, *f.* (subsoil). || Prospección, *f.* (market).
prospective [prəsˈpektiv] adj. Eventual, probable: *a prospective client*, un cliente eventual. || Futuro, ra (future): *prospective mother-in-law*, futura suegra.
prospector [prəsˈpektə*] n. Explorador, ra (explorer). || Buscador, *m.*, prospector, *m.* [*Amer.*, cateador, *m.*] (of gold). || Prospector, *m.* (of oil, of clients).
prospectus [prəsˈpektəs] n. Prospecto, *m.*, folleto (*m.*) informativo.
prosper [ˈprɔspə*] v. intr. Prosperar, medrar.
— V. tr. Favorecer, hacer prosperar.
prosperity [prɔsˈperiti] n. Prosperidad, *f.*
prosperous [ˈprɔspərəs] adj. Próspero, ra: *prosperous business*, comercio próspero. || Favorable, propicio, cia (favourable). || Favorable (wind). || *Happy and prosperous New Year*, feliz y próspero Año Nuevo.
prosperousness [—nis] n. Prosperidad, *f.*
prostate [ˈprɔsteit] adj. Med. Prostático, ca.
— N. Med. Próstata, *f.*
prostatic [prɔˈstætik] adj. Med. Prostático, ca.
prostatitis [prɔstəˈtaitis] n. Med. Prostatitis, *f.*
prosthesis [ˈprɔsθisis] n. Med. Prótesis, *f.* || Gramm. Prótesis, *f.*, próstesis, *f.*
prosthetic [prɔsˈθetik] adj. Med. Protésico, ca. || Gramm. Protético, ca; prostético, ca.
prostitute [ˈprɔstitjuːt] n. Prostituta, *f.*
prostitute [ˈprɔstitjuːt] v. tr. Prostituir. || Fig. Prostituir: *to prostitute one's talent*, prostituir su talento. || *To prostitute o.s.*, prostituirse.
prostitution [ˌprɔstiˈtjuːʃən] n. Prostitución, *f.*
prostrate [ˈprɔstreit] adj. Boca abajo (face downwards). || Postrado, da; abatido, da (exhausted, defeated, grief-stricken, etc.). || Prosternado, da (bowing). || Bot. Procumbente.

prostrate [prɔs'treit] v. tr. Postrar. || *To prostrate o.s.*, postrarse (to lie down), prosternarse (to bow).
prostration [prɔs'treiʃən] n. Postración, *f.* (lying down, exhaustion). || Prosternación, *f.* (bowing).
prostyle ['prəustail] n. ARCH. Próstilo, *m.*
prosy ['prəuzi] adj. Prosaico, ca (style). || Monótono, na (life). || Aburrido, da (boring).
protactinium [,prəut,æk'tiniəm] n. CHEM. Protactinio, *m.* (radioactive element).
protagonist [prəu'tægənist] n. Protagonista, *m.* & *f.*
protargol [prəu'tɑ:gɔl] n. CHEM. Protargol, *m.*
protean [prəu'ti:ən] adj. Proteico, ca.
protect [prə'tekt] v. tr. Proteger. || MAR. Acorazar (a cruiser). || COMM. Proteger (industry). | Respaldar (a bill of exchange). | Salvaguardar (interests). || — *To protect against*, proteger contra. || *To protect from*, proteger de. || *Protected state*, estado bajo protectorado.
protecting [—iŋ] adj. Protector, ra.
protection [prə'tekʃən] n. Protección, *f.* (defence). || COMM. Protección, *f.* || MAR. Blindaje, *m.* || Salvoconducto, *m.* (pass). || U. S. Dinero (*m.*) pagado a una organización de gángsteres.
protectionism [prə'tekʃənizəm] n. Proteccionismo, *m.*
protectionist [prə'tekʃənist] adj./n. Proteccionista.
protective [prə'tektiv] adj. Protector, ra; de protección. || Proteccionista: *protective tariff*, tarifa proteccionista. || — ZOOL. *Protective colouring*, color (*m.*) que protege a un animal confundiéndolo con el medio donde se encuentra. || JUR. *Protective custody*, detención preventiva.
protector [prə'tektə*] n. Protector, *m.*
protectorate [—rit] n. Protectorado, *m.*
protectress [prə'tektris] n. Protectora, *f.*
protégé ['prəuteʒei] n. Protegido, *m.*
protégée ['prəuteʒei] n. Protegida, *f.*
proteic [prəu'ti:ic] adj. Proteico, ca.
proteid ['prəuti:d] n. CHEM. Proteido, *m.*
protein ['prəuti:n] n. Proteína, *f.*
proteinaceous [prəuti:'neiʃəs] or **proteinic** [prəu'ti:nik] or **proteinous** [prəu'ti:nəs] adj. Proteínico, ca; proteico, ca.
proteles ['prɔtəli:z] n. ZOOL. Proteles, *m.*
pro tem [prəu'tem] or **pro tempore** ['prəu'tempəri] adv. Por el momento (for the time being). || Provisionalmente (temporarily).
— Adj. Provisional (temporary).
protest ['prəutest] n. Protesta, *f.*, queja, *f.* (complaint): *to raise a protest*, hacer una protesta. || Objeción, *f.*, reparo, *m.* (objection). || COMM. Protesto, *m.* (of a bill of exchange). || MAR. Declaración (*f.*) de averías. || Protesta, *f.* (diplomatic). || *To do sth. under protest*, hacer algo de mala gana *or* contra su voluntad.
protest [prə'test] v. tr. Protestar de: *to protest one's innocence*, protestar de su inocencia. || JUR. Protestar (a bill of exchange, etc.). || Poner reparos a (to object to). || U. S. Recusar (a witness).
— V. intr. Protestar (to complain).
protestant ['prɔtistənt] adj. Protestador, ra.
Protestant ['prɔtistənt] adj./n. Protestante.
Protestantism [—izəm] n. Protestantismo, *m.*
protestation [,prəutes'teiʃən] n. Protesta, *f.*
protester [prə'testə*] n. Protestador, ra.
protest march [prə'testmɑ:tʃ] n. Manifestación, *f.*
Proteus ['prəutju:s] pr. n. MYTH. Proteo, *m.*
prothalamium [prəuθə'leimiəm] n. Canto (*m.*) nupcial.
— OBSERV. El plural de la palabra inglesa es *prothalamia.*
prothesis ['prɔθisis] n. REL. Prótesis, *f.* || GRAMM. Prótesis, *f.*, próstesis, *f.*
prothonotary [prəu'θɔnətəri] n. REL. Protonotario, *m.* (protonotary).
prothorax [prəu'θɔ:ræks] n. ZOOL. Protórax, *m.*
prothrombin [prəu'θrɔmbin] n. CHEM. Protrombina, *f.*
protides ['prəutaidz] pl. n. CHEM. Prótidos, *m.*
protocol ['prəutəkɔl] n. Protocolo, *m.*
protocol ['prəutəkɔl] v. tr. Protocolar, protocolizar.
— V. intr. Hacer un protocolo.
protocolize [—aiz] v. tr. Protocolar, protocolizar.
protohistoric [,prəutəhis'tɔrik] adj. Protohistórico, ca.
protohistory [,prəutə'histəri] n. Protohistoria, *f.*
protomartyr [,prəutə,mɑ:tə*] n. Protomártir, *m.* (first martyr).
proton ['prəutɔn] n. PHYS. Protón, *m.*
protonic [—ik] adj. PHYS. Protónico, ca.
protonotary [,prəutə'nəutəri] n. REL. Protonotario, *m.*: *protonotary apostolic*, protonotario apostólico.
protoplasm ['prəutəuplæzəm] n. BIOL. Protoplasma, *m.* (colloidal substance).
protoplasmic [prəutə'plæzmik] adj. BIOL. Protoplásmico, ca; protoplasmático, ca.
protoplast ['prəutəplæst] n. BIOL. Protoplasto, *m.*
prototype ['prəutəutaip] n. Prototipo, *m.*
protoxide [prəu'tɔksaid] n. CHEM. Protóxido, *m.*
protozoan [,prəutəu'zəuən] n. ZOOL. Protozoario, *m.*, protozoo, *m.*
protozoon [,prəutəu'zəuən] n. ZOOL. Protozoo, *m.*, protozoario, *m.*
— OBSERV. El plural de la palabra inglesa es *protozoa.*
protract [prə'trækt] v. tr. Prolongar (to lengthen in duration). || TECH. Levantar un plano de (to plot). || ZOOL. Sacar.
protractile [prə'træktail] adj. Protráctil: *protractile tongue*, lengua protráctil.
protraction [prə'trækʃən] n. Prolongación, *f.* (prolongation). || TECH. Levantamiento (*m.*) *or* trazado (*m.*) de un plano.
protractor [prə'træktə*] n. MATH. Transportador, *m.* || ANAT. Músculo (*m.*) protractor.
protrude [prə'tru:d] v. tr. Sacar (to stick out).
— V. intr. Salir (to come out). || Sobresalir (to jut out).
protruding [—iŋ] adj. Saliente, sobresaliente. || Saltón, ona (eyes). || Hacia fuera, salido, da (teeth). || Saliente (jaw, forehead). || MED. Herniado, da (bowel).
protrusion [prə'tru:ʒən] n. Saliente, *m.*
protrusive [prə'tru:siv] adj. Sobresaliente, saliente (protruding).
protuberance [prə'tju:bərəns] n. Protuberancia, *f.*
protuberant [prə'tju:bərənt] adj. Protuberante. || Saltón, ona (eyes).
proud [praud] adj. Orgulloso, sa (self-esteeming, properly satisfied, etc.): *he is proud of his son's success*, está orgulloso del éxito de su hijo. || Soberbio, bia; altivo, va; altanero, ra (arrogant). || Soberbio, bia; grandioso, sa; espléndido, da; imponente: *a proud cathedral*, una soberbia catedral. || Glorioso, sa: *a proud moment*, un momento glorioso. || Brioso, sa (a horse). || TECH. Saliente (rivet). || — *I am proud to*, tengo el honor de. || FIG. *To be as proud as a peacock*, ser más orgulloso que un pavo real. | *To do o.s. proud*, no privarse de nada. | *To do s.o. proud*, poner a alguien por las nubes (to praise), tratar a alguien a cuerpo de rey (to treat very well).
proud flesh [—fleʃ] n. MED. Tejido (*m.*) granulado (exuberant growth).
proudhearted [—'hɑ:tid] adj. Orgulloso, sa.
provable ['pru:vəbl] adj. Demostrable.
prove [pru:v] v. tr. Demostrar, probar (to establish the authenticity with proof, etc.): *I can prove I didn't do it*, puedo probar que no lo hice; *to prove s.o.'s innocence*, demostrar la inocencia de alguien. || Probar (one's identity). || Probar, poner a prueba (to test): *to prove a method*, probar un método. || Confirmar (to confirm): *to prove an alibi*, confirmar una coartada. || MATH. Hacer la prueba a, comprobar (an operation). | Demostrar (a theorem). || Verificar, comprobar: *to prove a document*, verificar un documento. || PRINT. Hacer pruebas de. || JUR. Justificar (damages). | Homologar (a will). || — *He was proved innocent*, se demostró su inocencia. || *He was proved right*, se demostró que era exacto. || *The exception proves the rule*, la excepción confirma la regla. || *To prove o.s.*, dar prueba de sus aptitudes.
— V. intr. Resultar: *it proved to be false*, resultó ser falso; *the movie proved to be very bad*, la película resultó ser muy mala.
proven [pru:vən] adj. Probado, da: *it is a proven remedy*, es un remedio probado.
provenance ['prɔvinəns] n. Procedencia, *f.*, origen, *m.*
Provençal [,prɔvɑ̃:n'sɑ:l] adj. Provenzal.
— N. Provenzal, *m.*, lengua (*f.*) de oc (language). || Provenzal, *m.* & *f.* (person).
Provence [prɔ'vɑ̃:ns] pr. n. GEOGR. Provenza, *f.*
provender ['prɔvində*] n. Forraje, *m.* (fodder). || FAM. Comida, *f.* (food).
provenience [prəu'vi:niəns] n. U. S. Procedencia, *f.*, origen, *m.*
prover ['pru:və*] n. TECH. Cuentahílos, *m. inv.* (for textiles). || PRINT. Tirador (*m.*) de pruebas.
proverb ['prɔvə:b] n. Refrán, *m.*, proverbio, *m.*
proverbial [prə'və:bjəl] adj. Proverbial.
Proverbs ['prɔvə:bz] pl. n. REL. Proverbios, *m.*
provide [prə'vaid] v. tr. Suministrar: *the underdeveloped countries provide most raw materials*, los países subdesarrollados suministran la mayoría de las materias primas. || Proveer de, dar: *to provide one's son with money*, proveer de dinero a su hijo, dar dinero a su hijo. || Proporcionar, dar: *the tree provides shade*, el árbol proporciona sombra. || Prestar: *to provide support*, prestar apoyo. || JUR. Estipular, disponer (to stipulate): *the law provides that*, la ley estipula que. || — *Not to provide a decent living*, no dar lo suficiente para vivir. || *To provide a topic of conversation*, dar que hablar. || *To provide o.s. with*, proveerse de.
— V. intr. Proveer: *God will provide*, Dios proveerá. || Tomar precauciones, precaverse: *to provide against a storm*, tomar precauciones contra una tormenta. || Satisfacer, atender a (to s.o.'s needs). || — *As provided for in*, de acuerdo con lo estipulado en. || *To provide for*, mantener: *to provide for a family*, mantener a una familia; estipular: *the treaty provides for*, el tratado estipula; prever: *to provide for an eventuality*, prever una posibilidad.
provided [—id] conj. Con tal que, a condición de que, siempre que: *you may come provided it is early*, puedes venir con tal que sea temprano. || *Provided that*, con tal que, a condición de que, siempre que.
— Adj. Previsto, ta: *provided by the statutes*, previsto por los estatutos. || — *Provided with*, provisto de, dotado de. || *Unless otherwise provided*, salvo disposición contraria.

providence [ˈprɔvidəns] n. Providencia, *f.*: *Divine Providence*, la Providencia Divina, la Divina Providencia. || Previsión, *f.* (foresightedness).

provident [ˈprɔvidənt] adj. Providente. || Previsor, ra (farsighted).

providential [ˌprɔviˈdenʃəl] adj. Providencial.

providently [ˈprɔvidəntli] adv. Con previsión.

provider [prəˈvaidə*] n. Proveedor, ra; suministrador, ra; abastecedor, ra.

providing [prəˈvaidiŋ] or **providing that** [—ðæt] conj. Con tal que, a condición de que, siempre que.

province [ˈprɔvins] n. Provincia, *f.* || FIG. Esfera, *f.*, campo, *m.* (field). | Competencia, *f.*, incumbencia, *f.*: *it's not within his province*, no es de su competencia. || JUR. Jurisdicción, *f.* || *In the provinces*, en la provincia.

provincial [prəˈvinʃəl] adj. Provincial, provinciano, na. || FIG. Pueblerino, na: *provincial likes*, gustos pueblerinos.
— N. Provinciano, na (s.o. who lives in the provinces). || REL. Provincial, *m.*

provincialate [—it] n. Provincialato, *m.*

provincialism [prəˈvinʃəlizəm] n. Provincialismo, *m.* || FIG. Mentalidad (*f.*) pueblerina.

provinciality [prəˌvinʃiˈæliti] n. Provincialismo, *m.*

proving [ˈpru:viŋ] n. Prueba, *f.* || MIL. *Proving ground*, polígono (*m.*) de pruebas.

provision [prəˈviʒən] n. Provisión, *f.* (providing). || Suministro, *m.*, abastecimiento, *m.* (supply). || Disposición, *f.* (of treaty, law, etc.). || — Pl. Provisiones, *f.*, comestibles, *m.*, suministro, *m. sing.* (food supplies). || — *To come within the provisions of the law*, estar previsto por la ley *or* por la legislación. || *To make provision for*, prever. || *To make provision for one's family*, atender a las necesidades de su familia; asegurar el porvenir de su familia.

provision [prəˈviʒən] v. tr. Proveer, abastecer, suministrar.

provisional [—l] adj. Provisional: *provisional liberty*, libertad provisional.

provisioner [—ə*] n. Proveedor, ra; suministrador, ra; abastecedor, ra.

proviso [prəˈvaizəu] n. Condición, *f.*: *with the proviso that*, con la condición de que. || JUR. Salvedad, *f.*

— OBSERV. El plural de *proviso* es *provisoes* o *provisos*.

provisory [prəˈvaizəri] adj. Provisional, provisorio, ria (provisional). || Condicional (conditional).

provocation [ˌprɔvəˈkeiʃən] n. Provocación, *f.*

provocative [prəˈvɔkətiv] adj. Provocador, ra; provocativo, va.
— N. Estimulante, *m.* || Afrodisiaco, *m.*

provoke [prəˈvəuk] v. tr. Provocar: *to provoke laughter*, provocar la risa; *to provoke a riot*, provocar disturbios. || Incitar, mover (*to*, a) [to induce]. || Provocar, irritar (to annoy).

provoker [—ə*] n. Provocador, ra.

provoking [—iŋ] adj. Provocador, ra. || Molesto, ta; fastidioso, sa (annoying). || Irritante (irritating).

provost [ˈprɔvəst] n. Director, *m.* (of a college). || Alcalde, *m.* (Scottish mayor). || REL. Preboste, *m.* || U. S. MIL. Preboste, *m.* (of military police). || — *Provost court*, tribunal (*m.*) de policía militar. || *Provost marshal*, capitán (*m.*) preboste.

provostship [—ʃip] n. Prebostazgo, *m.* || Alcaldía, *f.*, cargo (*m.*) de alcalde (in Scotland). || Dirección, *f.* (in a college).

prow [prau] n. MAR. Proa, *f.* || AVIAT. Morro, *m.*

prowess [—is] n. Valor, *m.* (courage). || Habilidad, *f.* (skill). || *Deed of prowess*, acto (*m.*) de valor, hazaña, *f.*, proeza, *f.*

prowl [—l] n. Ronda, *f.* (of police, etc.). || Merodeo, *m.* (of a person). || Caza, *f.* (of animals). || — U. S. *Prowl car*, coche (*m.*) patrulla. || *To be on the prowl*, rondar, merodear.

prowl [—l] v. intr. Rondar (police, etc.). || Merodear, vagar, rondar (to roam). || Cazar (animals).
— V. tr. Merodear por, rondar: *to prowl the streets*, merodear por las calles, rondar las calles.

prowler [—lə*] n. Merodeador, ra.

proximate [ˈprɔksimit] adj. Próximo, ma. || Aproximado, da (approximate).

proximity [prɔkˈsimiti] n. Proximidad, *f.* || *Proximity fuse* (U. S., *proximity fuze*), espoleta (*f.*) de proximidad.

proximo [ˈprɔksiməu] adj. COMM. Del mes próximo, del próximo mes.

— OBSERV. La abreviatura *prox.* suele sustituir a la palabra inglesa *proximo*.

proxy [ˈprɔksi] n. Procuración, *f.*, poder, *m.*, poderes, *m. pl.* (authority, document). || Poderhabiente, *m.* & *f.*, mandatario, ria; representante, *m.* & *f.*, apoderado, *m.* (person). || — *By proxy*, por poderes: *to vote by proxy*, votar por poderes. || *To stand proxy for s.o.*, tener los poderes de alguien.

prude [pru:d] n. FAM. Mojigato, ta; gazmoño, ña.

prudence [—əns] n. Prudencia, *f.*

prudent [—ənt] adj. Prudente.

prudential [pruˈdənʃəl] adj. Prudencial. || Industrial (insurance). || U. S. Asesor, ra (committee).

prudery [ˈpru:dəri] n. Mojigatería, *f.*, gazmoñería, *f.*

prudish [ˈpru:diʃ] adj. Mojigato, ta; pudibundo, da; gazmoño, ña.

prudishness [—nis] n. Mojigatería, *f.*, gazmoñería, *f.*, pudibundez, *f.*

prune [pru:n] n. Ciruela (*f.*) pasa (fruit). || U. S. FAM. Mentecato, ta (silly person).

prune [pru:n] v. tr. Podar, escamondar (trees). || FIG. Reducir, disminuir, cercenar: *to prune expenses*, reducir los gastos. | Mutilar, cortar: *to prune a text*, mutilar un texto.

pruner [ˈpru:nə*] n. Podador, *m.*

pruning [ˈpru:niŋ] n. Poda, *f.* || — *Pruning hook* o *knife* o *shears*, podadera, *f.* || *Pruning season*, poda, *f.*

prurience [ˈpruəriəns] n. Lascivia, *f.* (lewdness). || (Ant.). Comezón, *f.* (itch).

prurient [ˈpruəriənt] adj. Lascivo, va (lewd).

prurigo [pru:raigəu] n. MED. Prurigo, *m.*

pruritus [pruˈraitəs] n. MED. Prurito, *m.*

Prussia [ˈprʌʃə] pr. n. GEOGR. Prusia, *f.*

Prussian [—n] adj./n. Prusiano, na. || CHEM. *Prussian blue*, azul (*m.*) de Prusia.

prussiate [ˈprʌʃiit] n. CHEM. Prusiato, *m.*

prussic [ˈprʌsik] adj. CHEM. Prúsico, ca: *prussic acid*, ácido prúsico.

pry [prai] n. U. S. Palanca, *f.* (lever).

pry [prai] v. intr. Fisgar, curiosear, fisgonear (to snoop). || *To pry into*, entrometerse en (to meddle).
— V. tr. U. S. Abrir con una palanca (to prise). || *To pry a secret from* o *out of s.o.*, sacarle a alguien un secreto.

prying [—iŋ] adj. Fisgón, ona (snooping). || Entrometido, da (interfering).
— N. Fisgoneo, *m.*, curioseo, *m.*

psalm [sɑ:m] n. REL. Salmo, *m.*

psalmbook [—buk] n. Salterio, *m.*

psalmist [—ist] n. REL. Salmista, *m.*

psalmodize [—ədaiz] v. intr. Salmodiar.

psalmody [ˈsælmədi] n. REL. Salmodia, *f.*

psalter [ˈsɔ:ltə*] n. REL. Salterio, *m.*

psalterium [sɔ:lˈti:riəm] n. ZOOL. Omaso, *m.*

— OBSERV. El plural de la palabra inglesa es *psalteria*.

psaltery [ˈsɔ:ltəri] n. MUS. Salterio, *m.*

pseudo [ˈpsju:dəu] adj. Seudo, supuesto, ta.

pseudonym [ˈpsju:dənim] n. Seudónimo, *m.*

pseudonymous [psju:ˈdɔniməs] adj. Seudónimo, ma.

pseudopod [ˈpsju:dəˈpɔd] or **pseudopodium** [ˌpsju:dəˈpəudiəm] n. Seudópodo, *m.*

— OBSERV. El plural de *pseudopodium* es *pseudopodia*.

pshaw! [pʃɔ:] interj. ¡Bah!

psi [psai] n. Psi, *f.* (Greek letter).

psittacidae [psiˈtæsidi:] pl. n. ZOOL. Psitácidos, *m.*

psittacosis [ˌpsitəˈkəusis] n. MED. Psitacosis, *f. inv.*, sitacosis, *f. inv.*

psoas [ˈpsəuəs] n. Psoas, *m.*

psoriasis [psɔˈraiəsis] n. MED. Psoriasis, *f.*

psychasthenia [ˌsaikæsˈθi:njə] n. MED. Psicastenia, *f.*, sicastenia, *f.*

psychasthenic [ˌsaikæsˈθi:nik] adj. MED. Psicasténico, ca; sicasténico, ca.

psyche [ˈsaiki] n. Psique, *f.*, psiquis, *f.* (soul).

Psyche [ˈsaiki] n. MYTH. Psique, *f.*, Psiquis, *f.*

psychedelic [ˌsaikiˈdelik] adj. Psicodélico, ca; sicodélico, ca.

psychiatric [ˌsaikiˈætrik] adj. Psiquiátrico, ca; siquiátrico, ca.

psychiatrist [saiˈkaiətrist] n. Psiquiatra, *m.* & *f.*, siquiatra, *m.* & *f.*

psychiatry [saiˈkaiətri] n. MED. Psiquiatría, *f.*, siquiatría, *f.*

psychic [ˈsaikik] or **psychical** [—əl] adj. Psíquico, ca; síquico, ca.
— N. Medium, *m.*

psychics [—s] n. Metapsíquica, *f.*

psychism [ˈsaikizəm] n. Psiquismo, *m.*, siquismo, *m.*

psycho [ˌsaikəv] n. FAM. Psicópata, *m.* & *f.*

psychoanalyse [ˌsaikəuˈænəlaiz] v. tr. Psicoanalizar, sicoanalizar.

psychoanalysis [ˌsaikəuəˈnæləsis] n. Psicoanálisis, *m.*, sicoanálisis, *m.*

psychoanalyst [ˌsaikəuˈænəlist] n. Psicoanalista, *m.* & *f.*, sicoanalista, *m.* & *f.*

psychoanalytic [ˌsaikəuænəˈlitik] or **psychoanalytical** [—əl] adj. Psicoanalítico, ca; sicoanalítico, ca.

psychoanalyze [ˌsaikəuˈænəlaiz] v. tr. Psicoanalizar, sicoanalizar.

psychodelic [saikəˈdelik] adj. Psicodélico, ca; sicodélico, ca.

psychodrama [ˈsaikəuˌdrɑ:mə] n. MED. Psicodrama, *m.*, sicodrama, *m.*

psychologic [ˌsaikəˈlɔdʒik] or **psychological** [—əl] adj. Psicológico, ca; sicológico, ca.

psychologism [saiˈkɔlədʒizəm] n. Psicologismo, *m.*, sicologismo, *m.*

psychologist [saiˈkɔlədʒist] n. Psicólogo, ga; sicólogo, ga.

psychology [saiˈkɔlədʒi] n. Psicología, *f.*, sicología, *f.*

psychometry [saiˈkɔmitri] n. Psicometría, *f.*, sicometría, *f.*

psychomotor [ˈsaikəuˈməutə*] adj. Psicomotor, ra; sicomotor, ra.

psychoneurosis [ˈsaikəunjuəˈrəusis] n. MED. Psiconeurosis, *f.*, siconeurosis, *f.*

— OBSERV. El plural de *psychoneurosis* es *psychoneuroses*.

psychopath [ˈsaikəupæθ] n. MED. Psicópata, *m.* & *f.*, sicópata, *m.* & *f.*
psychopathic [ˌsaikəuˈpæθik] adj. MED. Psicopático, ca; sicopático, ca.
psychopathology [ˈsaikəupəˈθɔlədʒi] n. MED. Psicopatología, *f.*, sicopatología, *f.*
psychopathy [saiˈkɔpəθi] n. MED. Psicopatía, *f.*, sicopatía, *f.*
psychosis [saiˈkəusis] n. MED. Psicosis, *f.*, sicosis, *f.*

— OBSERV. El plural de *psychosis* es *psychoses*.

psychosomatic [ˌsaikəusəuˈmætik] adj. Psicosomático, ca; sicosomático, ca.
psychotechnological [ˈsaikəuteknəˈlɔdʒikəl] adj. Psicotécnico, ca; sicotécnico, ca.
psychotherapeutics [ˈsaikəuθerəˈpju:tiks] n. MED. Psicoterapia, *f.*, sicoterapia, *f.*
psychotherapy [ˌsaikəuˈθerəpi] n. MED. Psicoterapia, *f.*, sicoterapia, *f.*
psychotic [saiˈkɔtik] adj. Psicopático, ca; sicopático, ca.
— N. Psicópata, *m.* & *f.*, sicópata, *m.* & *f.*
ptarmigan [ˈtɑ:migən] n. Lagópedo, *m.* (grouse).
PT boat [ˈpi:ti:ˈbəut] n. U. S. MAR. Lancha (*f.*) torpedera.
pteridophyte [ˈptəridəfait] n. BOT. Pteridofita, *f.*
pterodactyl [ˌpterəuˈdæktil] n. ZOOL. Pterodáctilo, *m.*
pteropod [ˈterəpɔd] n. ZOOL. Pterópodo, *m.*
pterosaur [ˈpterəusɔ:*] n. ZOOL. Pterosaurio, *m.*
Ptolemaic [ˌtɔliˈmeiik] adj. Ptolemaico, ca; tolemaico, ca.
Ptolemy [ˈtɔlimi] pr. n. Ptolomeo, *m.*, Tolomeo, *m.*
ptomaine [ˈtəumein] n. BOT. Ptomaína, *f.*, tomaína, *f.*
ptosis [ˈtəusis] n. MED. Ptosis, *f. inv.*
ptyalin [ˈtaiəlin] n. BIOL. Ptialina, *f.*, tialina, *f.*
ptyalism [ˈtaiəlizəm] n. MED. Ptialismo, *m.*, tialismo, *m.* (excessive flow of saliva).
pub [pʌb] n. FAM. Taberna, *f.* (popular drinking place), bar, *m.* (more refined). || — *Pub crawl*, chateo, *m.*, copeo, *m.*, chiquiteo, *m.* || *Pub crawler*, persona (*f.*) a quien le gusta mucho ir de copeo. || *To pub crawl*, copear, estar de copeo.
puberty [ˈpju:bəti] n. Pubertad, *f.*
pubes [ˈpju:bi:z] n. ANAT. Pubis, *m.*
pubescence [pjuˈbesns] n. BOT. Pubescencia, *f.* || MED. Pubertad, *f.*, pubescencia, *f.*
pubescent [pjuˈbesnt] adj. BOT. Pubescente. || MED. Púber, pubescente.
pubic [ˈpju:bik] adj. Pubiano, na; púbico, ca.
pubis [ˈpju:bis] n. ANAT. Pubis, *m.*

— OBSERV. El plural de la palabra inglesa *pubis* es *pubes*.

public [ˈpʌblik] adj. Público, ca: *public opinion*, opinión pública; *a public figure*, un personaje público; *public life*, vida pública; *public enemy*, enemigo público; *public law*, derecho público; *public relations*, relaciones públicas; *public thoroughfare*, vía pública, *public works*, obras públicas. || *To make public*, hacer público, publicar.
— N. Público, *m.*: *notice to the public*, aviso al público; *the public are requested to remain seated*, se ruega al público que permanezca sentado. || — *In public*, en público. || *The general public*, el público en general. || *The television reaches a large public*, la televisión alcanza a un gran auditorio.
public-address system [—əˈdres-ˈsistim] n. Instalación (*f.*) de altavoces, megafonía, *f.*
publican [ˈpʌblikən] n. Tabernero, ra (in a public house). || Publicano, na (tax collector in Rome).
publication [ˌpʌbliˈkeiʃən] n. Publicación, *f.* || *Larousse Publications*, Ediciones (*f.*) Larousse, Editorial (*f. sing.*) Larousse.
public holiday [ˈpʌblikˈhɔlədi] n. Fiesta (*f.*) legal.
public house [ˈpʌblikˈhaus] n. Taberna, *f.* (popular drinking place). || Bar, *m.* || Posada, *f.* (inn).
publicist [ˈpʌblisist] n. Publicista, *m.* & *f.*
publicity [pʌbˈlisiti] n. Publicidad, *f.* || *To give publicity to*, dar publicidad a.
— Adj. Publicitario, ria.
publicize [ˈpʌbləˌsaiz] v. tr. Publicar, hacer público, divulgar.
public prosecutor [ˈpʌblikˈprɔsikju:tə*] n. JUR. Fiscal, *m.*
public school [ˈpʌblikˈsku:l] n. Colegio (*m.*) privado de enseñanza media (in Great Britain). || Instituto, *m.* (in United States).
public servant [ˈpʌblikˈsə:vənt] n. Funcionario, ria.
public spirit [ˈpʌblikˈspirit] n. Civismo, *m.*
public-spirited [—id] adj. De espíritu cívico, cívico, ca.
public utility [ˈpʌblikjuˈtiliti] n. Empresa (*f.*) de servicios públicos, servicio (*m.*) público (business concern). || Valores (*m. pl.*) de una empresa de servicios públicos (bonds).
publish [ˈpʌbliʃ] v. tr. PRINT. Publicar, editar. || Revelar, divulgar, publicar (news). || Correr (banns). || — *Just published*, de publicación reciente. || *Now publishing*, en prensa. || *Published by*, editado por.
publishable [—əbl] adj. Publicable.
publisher [—ə*] n. Editor, ra. || U. S. *Newspaper publisher*, propietario (*m.*) de un periódico.
publishing [—iŋ] n. Publicación, *f.* || *Publishing house*, casa (*f.*) editorial, editorial, *f.*, casa editora.
puce [pju:s] adj. De color pardo rojizo.
— N. Pardo (*m.*) rojizo.
puck [pʌk] n. SP. Disco, *m.* [en hockey sobre hielo]. || Duende, *m.* (goblin).
pucker [—ə*] n. Frunce, *m.*, fruncido, *m.*, pliegue, *m.* (pleat). || Arruga, *f.* (wrinkle).
pucker [—ə*] v. tr. Fruncir (to pleat). || Arrugar (to wrinkle). || — *To pucker one's brows*, fruncir el ceño. || *To pucker up*, fruncir.
— V. intr. Arrugarse. || *To pucker up*, arrugarse.
puckish [—iʃ] adj. Juguetón, ona; travieso, sa (mischievous). || Malicioso, sa (cunning).
pudding [ˈpudiŋ] n. CULIN. Pudín, *m.*, budín, *m.*, pudding, *m.* (sweet, pastry, etc.). | FAM. Postre, *m.* (dessert). || MAR. Andullo, *m.* (fender). || — CULIN. *Black pudding*, morcilla, *f.* || FAM. *Pudding face*, cara mofletuda. | *Pudding head*, majareta, *m.* & *f.* || *Pudding stone*, pudinga, *f.*
puddle [ˈpʌdl] n. Charco, *m.* (small pool). || TECH. Mezcla (*f.*) de arcilla y grava, argamasa, *f.*
puddle [ˈpʌdl] v. tr. TECH. Pudelar (iron). | Mezclar (clay). || Enturbiar (water).
— V. intr. Chapotear en el barro. || FIG. Hacer chapucerías (with paints, clay, etc.).
puddling [—iŋ] n. TECH. Pudelado, *m.*
puddly [—i] adj. Lleno de charcos, encharcado, da: *a puddly road*, una carretera llena de charcos. || Embarrado, da; fangoso, sa (muddy).
pudency [ˈpju:dənsi] n. Pudicicia, *f.*
pudenda [pjuˈdendə] pl. n. ANAT. Partes (*f.*) pudendas.
pudge [pʌdʒ] n. FAM. Gordito, ta; rechoncho, cha; gordinflón, ona.
pudgy [ˈpʌdʒi] adj. FAM. Gordito, ta; rechoncho, cha; gordinflón, ona.
pudicity [pjuˈdisiti] n. Pudicicia, *f.*
puerile [ˈpjuərail] adj. Pueril (childish).
puerilism [pjuəˈrilizəm] n. Puerilismo, *m.*
puerility [pjuəˈriliti] n. Puerilidad, *f.*
puerperal [pjuˈə:pərəl] adj. MED. Puerperal: *puerperal fever*, fiebre puerperal.
puerperium [pju:ə:ˈpiriəm] n. Puerperio, *m.*
Puerto Rican [ˈpwə:təuˈri:kən] adj./n. Puertorriqueño, ña.
Puerto Rico [ˈpwə:təuˈri:kəu] pr. n. GEOGR. Puerto Rico, *m.*
puff [pʌf] n. Soplo, *m.* (of air). || Racha, *f.*, ráfaga, *f.* (of wind). || Bocanada, *f.* (of smoke, cigarette). || Chorro, *m.*, escape, *m.* (of steam). || Resoplido, *m.* (of breathing, of engine). || Borla, *f.* (for powder). || Moña, *f.* (of ribbon). || Edredón, *m.* (bed covering). || CULIN. Buñuelo, *m.* (pastry). || Hinchazón, *f.* (swelling). || FAM. Bombo, *m.* (publicity). || Bullón, *m.*, pliegue (*m.*) ahuecado (on a skirt). || CULIN. *Cream puff*, petisú, *m.*
puff [pʌf] v. tr. Soplar (to blow). || Echar bocanadas de (to emit whiffs): *the train puffs smoke*, el tren echa bocanadas de humo. || Dar chupadas a (cigarette, pipe, etc.).
— V. intr. Jadear (to pant). || Soplar (to emit air through the mouth). || Echar humo (to emit smoke). || Echar vapor (to emit steam). || *To puff and pant*, jadear.
— ***To puff at***, dar chupadas a: *to puff at a cigarette*, dar chupadas a un cigarro. || ***To puff out***, echar bocanadas de (to emit whiffs). | Apagar (a candle, etc.). | Cardar (hair). | Ahuecar (a skirt). | Decir [words] jadeando. | — *To be puffed out*, estar sin aliento *or* sin resuello (breathless). | *To puff out one's cheeks*, hinchar los carrillos. || ***To puff up***, hinchar. | — *To puff o.s. up*, darse bombo, estar henchido de orgullo.
puffball [—bɔ:l] n. BOT. Pedo (*m.*) de lobo.
puffed [—t] adj. Sin aliento (out of breath). || De jamón (sleeve). || Hinchado, da (swollen). || FIG. Henchido, da: *to be puffed up with pride*, estar henchido de orgullo. | Ampuloso, sa (style). || FIG. *He was puffed up by his success*, se le subió el éxito a la cabeza.
puffer [ˈpʌfə*] n. FAM. Fumador, *m.* (smoker). | Locomotora, *f.* (locomotive).
puffin [ˈpʌfin] n. Frailecillo, *m.* (sea bird).
puffiness [ˈpʌfinis] n. Hinchazón, *f.* (swelling). || FIG. Ampulosidad, *f.* (of style).
puff pastry [ˈpʌfˈpeistri] or **puff paste** [ˈpʌfˈpeist] n. CULIN. Hojaldre, *m.*
puffy [ˈpʌfi] adj. Hinchado, da (swollen). || Ahuecado, da (skirt). || Sin aliento (out of breath).
pug [pʌg] n. Arcilla, *f.* (clay). || Doguillo, *m.* (dog).
pug [pʌg] v. tr. Amasar (clay). || Rellenar con arcilla *or* con argamasa (a wall, floor, etc.).
pugilism [ˈpju:dʒilizəm] n. Pugilato, *m.*, pugilismo, *m.* (boxing).
pugilist [ˈpju:dʒilist] n. Púgil, *m.*, pugilista, *m.* (boxer).
pugilistic [ˌpju:dʒiˈlistik] adj. Pugilístico, ca.
pugnacious [pʌgˈneiʃəs] adj. Belicoso, sa; batallador, ra; pugnaz.
pugnaciousness [—nis] or **pugnacity** [pʌgˈnæsiti] n. Belicosidad, *f.*, espíritu (*m.*) batallador, pugnacidad, *f.*
pug-nosed [—d] adj. Chato, ta.
puisne [ˈpju:ni] adj. Posterior (*to*, a). || JUR. Asesor (judge).
— N. JUR. Juez (*m.*) asesor.
puke [pju:k] n. FAM. Vomitona, *f.*
puke [pju:k] v. intr. FAM. Vomitar, cambiar la peseta (to vomit).

puking [—iŋ] n. FAM. Vomitona, *f.*
pukka [ˈpʌkə] adj. FAM. Auténtico, ca; genuino, na; legítimo, ma.
pulchritude [ˈpʌlkritu:d] n. Belleza, *f.*
pule [pju:l] v. intr. Gimotear, lloriquear (to whine). || Piar (birds).
pull [pul] n. Tracción, *f.*: *the pull of the engine on the wagons*, la tracción de los vagones por la locomotora. || Tirón, *m.*: *he gave the elastic a pull*, dio un tirón al elástico. || Arrastre, *m.* (of the tide). || Tensión, *f.* (of a bow). || Tirador, *m.* (knob, handle). || Cuerda, *f.* (rope of a bell). || Cadena, *f.* (chain). || FIG. Trecho, *m.* (distance): *it is a long pull from London to Glasgow*, hay un buen trecho de Londres a Glasgow. | Esfuerzo, *m.*, trabajo, *m.*: *it was a hard pull up to the top of the mountain*, hubo que hacer un gran esfuerzo para subir hasta la cumbre de la montaña, nos costó mucho trabajo subir hasta la cumbre de la montaña. | Enchufe, *m.*, influencia, *f.* (influence): *you need a lot of pull to get a job*, hay que tener mucho enchufe para conseguir un trabajo. | Ventaja, *f.*, superioridad, *f.* (advantage). | Atracción, *f.* (attraction): *the pull of Paris*, la atracción de París. | Rendimiento, *m.* (efficiency). || FAM. Chupada, *f.*: *I took a pull at my cigarette*, le di una chupada al cigarrillo. | Trago, *m.* (drink). || PHYS. Atracción, *f.*, fuerza (*f.*) de atracción (of a magnet). || TECH. Tracción, *f.* (movement). | Gancho (*m.*) de tracción (between an engine and the wagons). | Tiro, *m.* (of a chimney). || PRINT. Galerada, *f.*, primera prueba, *f.* || SP. Devolución (*f.*) de la pelota (in cricket). | Golpe (*m.*) oblicuo dado a la pelota (in golf). | Palada, *f.*, golpe (*m.*) de remo (oarstroke). | Sofrenada, *f.* (of a horse). | Distancia (*f.*) recorrida *or* tiempo (*m.*) pasado remando (distance, period of time). || — *To give a pull at* o *on the bell*, tocar la campana. || *To give a pull on the trigger*, apretar el gatillo. || *To give sth. a pull*, tirar de algo: *to give the door a pull*, tirar de la puerta. || *To go for a pull*, ir a remar (rowing). || FIG. *To have the pull over s.o.*, aventajar a alguien. || FAM. *To take a pull at a bottle*, beber de la botella.
pull [pul] v. tr. Tirar de: *pull the door to open it*, tira de la puerta para abrirla; *she pulled his hair*, le tiró de los pelos. || Arrastrar, tirar de (to drag): *the child was pulling a toy car*, el niño arrastraba un coche de juguete. || Sacar, arrancar, extraer (a tooth). || Arrancar (to uproot): *they are pulling beetroots*, están arrancando remolachas. || Sacar: *to pull a knife, a gun*, sacar un cuchillo, una pistola. || Tirar: *to pull beer from a barrel*, tirar cerveza de un barril. || Apretar: *to pull the trigger*, apretar el gatillo. || Tensar (a bow). || MAR. Halar (a rope). | Hacer avanzar remando (a boat). | Mover (oars). || SP. Golpear oblicuamente (ball). | Sujetar, sofrenar (a horse). || PRINT. Tirar (a proof). || FAM. Detener (to arrest). || U. S. Hacer (to perform): *the police pulled a raid*, la policía hizo una incursión. || Atraer (to attract). || — MED. *To have a pulled muscle*, tener un tirón en un músculo. || FIG. *To pull a face*, hacer una mueca. | *To pull a fast one* o *a trick on s.o.*, hacerle una mala jugada a uno, jugarle una mala pasada a uno. || *To pull one's punches*, no pegar a fondo (a boxer), andarse con rodeos, hacer críticas moderadas (to criticize halfheartedly). || FIG. *To pull s.o.'s leg*, tomarle el pelo a uno. | *To pull to pieces*, see PIECE.
— V. intr. Tirar: *to pull at a rope*, tirar de una cuerda. || Dar chupadas a (at a pipe). || Tirar (a dress). || Repropiarse (a horse). || MAR. Remar. || AUT. Tirar, irse: *this car pulls to the right*, este coche tira hacia la derecha. || FIG. Recomendar: *to pull for a candidate*, recomendar a un candidato. || — *The car pulled to a stop*, el coche se paró. || FIG. *They are pulling different ways*, cada uno tira por su lado. || *To pull at a bottle*, beber de la botella. || FIG. *To pull with*, influenciar a.
— ***To pull about***, manosear (to finger). | FAM. Maltratar (to handle roughly). || ***To pull ahead***, destacarse (runner). || ***To pull along***, arrastrar. | — *To pull o.s. along*, arrastrarse. || ***To pull apart***, separar (to separate). | Romper, hacer pedazos (to break). | Separarse (to become separated). | Destrozar, echar abajo, echar por tierra (an argument). || ***To pull away***, separar, apartar (s.o.). | Sacar, arrancar (sth.). | — *To pull away from s.o.*, apartarse bruscamente de alguien (to move away), dejar a uno atrás (in racing). || ***To pull back***, echar para atrás: *pull the chair back*, echa la silla para atrás. | Retrasar: *his failing the exam pulled him back considerably*, el suspenso que sacó en el examen le retrasó enormemente. || ***To pull down***, bajar: *pull down the curtain*, baja la cortina. | Encasquetarse (a hat). | Tirar: *I pulled him down on the sofa*, lo tiré en el sofá. | Echar abajo, derribar (to demolish): *they are going to pull the building down*, van a derribar el edificio. | FIG. Derribar, derrocar: *to pull down a government*, derribar a un gobierno; rebajar (price), debilitar mucho: *the disease pulled him down*, la enfermedad le ha debilitado mucho; desanimar (to depress), perjudicar (to prejudice). || U. S. FAM. ***To pull for***, animar. || ***To pull in***, entrar (to enter). | Entrar en la estación (train). | Llegar [en tren]: *we pulled in at four o'clock*, llegamos a las cuatro. | Sujetar, tirar de las riendas (a horse). | Tirar de: *let's pull in the line*, tiremos de la cuerda. | Cobrar (a rope). | Pararse (to stop). | Detener (to arrest). | Atraer (to attract). | — *To pull o.s. in*, ceñirse la cintura, apretarse la cintura. || ***To pull off***, quitar (to take off). | Quitarse: *he pulled off his coat*, se quitó el abrigo. | Arrancar: *to pull off a flower's petals*, arrancar los pétalos de una flor. | FIG. Conseguir (to obtain), llevar a cabo (to carry out): *to pull off a job*, llevar a cabo un trabajo; ganarse, llevarse (a prize, a victory). || ***To pull on***, ponerse (a coat, etc.). | Tirar de (a rope). || ***To pull out***, sacar (to take out). | Arrancar, sacar (tooth). | Irse, marcharse (to go). | Salir de la estación (train). | Retirarse (troops). | Estirar (to stretch). | MAR. Remar hacia alta mar. | Salirse [de la fila] (car). || ***To pull over***, ceñirse a: *the car pulled over to the left*, el coche se ciñó a la izquierda. | Volcar (to upset). | Acercar (to bring near): *pull the table over*, acerca la mesa. || ***To pull round***, reanimar: *a glass of sherry will pull him round*, una copa de jerez le reanimará. || Hacer levantar cabeza a (a patient). | Volver en sí, recobrar el sentido (to recover consciousness). | Recuperarse, reponerse (to recover from an illness). || ***To pull through***, sacar de un apuro (to get out of a difficulty). | Salir de un apuro (to survive danger). | Salvar, sacar de una enfermedad (to save). | Salvarse (to survive illness). | Llevar a cabo, llevar a buen término (to carry out). || ***To pull together***, aunar sus esfuerzos, actuar de común acuerdo (to cooperate). | — *To pull o.s. together*, serenarse, tranquilizarse (to regain control) ||. ***To pull up***, levantar, subir (to lift): *pull up the blind*, levante la persiana. | Encabritar (an aircraft). | Arremangarse (one's sleeves). | Recogerse (one's skirt). | Subirse (one's socks). | Acercar (to bring near): *pull up a chair*, acerca una silla. | Acercarse (to approach). | AGR. Arrancar. | Parar, detener (to make stop). | Pararse, detenerse (to come to a halt). | Contenerse (to restrain o.s.). | FAM. Regañar (to scold). | SP. Acercarse (*with, to*, a), recuperar terreno. | FIG. Ayudar (to help).
pullback [—bæk] adj. De retorno: *pullback spring*, muelle de retorno.
— N. Obstáculo, *m.* (hindrance). || Retirada, *f.* (of troops).
puller [—ə*] n. Arrancador, ra. || SP. Remero, ra.
pullet [ˈpulit] n. ZOOL. Polla, *f.*, pollo, *m.*
pulley [ˈpuli] n. Polea, *f.* || MAR. Motón, *m.*
pulley block [—blɔk] n. Aparejo, *m.* || MAR. Cuadernal, *m.*
pull-in [ˈpulin] n. AUT. Apartadero, *m.* (lay-by). | Restaurante (*m.*) de carretera (restaurant).
pulling [ˈpuliŋ] n. Tracción, *f.* || PRINT. Tirada, *f.* || *Pulling race*, carrera (*f.*) de remo.
pulling down [—daun] n. Demolición, *f.*, derribo, *m.* (of a building). || FIG. Derrocamiento, *m.* (of a government).
pulling in [—in] n. Llegada (*f.*) a la estación (of a train).
pulling out [—aut] n. Extracción, *f.* (of a tooth). || Arranque, *m.* (of a train). || Retirada, *f.* (of troops).
Pullman [—mən] n. Pullman, *m.* (railway coach).
pullout [—aut] adj. Corredero, ra; deslizable (slide).
— N. Restablecimiento, *m.* (of an aircraft). || Retirada, *f.* (of troops).
pullover [—ˌəuvə*] n. Jersey, *m.* (sweater). || Nicky, *m.* (shirt).
pullulate [ˈpʌljuleit] v. intr. Pulular.
pullulation [ˌpʌljuˈleiʃən] n. Pululación, *f.*
pull-up [ˈpulʌp] n. SP. Tracción, *f.* || Parada, *f.* (stop). || Restaurante (*m.*) de carretera (restaurant).
pulmonary [ˈpʌlmənəri] adj. ANAT. MED. Pulmonar: *pulmonary vein, artery*, vena, arteria pulmonar.
pulmonate [ˈpʌlmənit] adj. ZOOL. Pulmonado, da.
— N. ZOOL. Pulmonado, *m.*
pulmonic [pʌlˈmɔnik] adj. Pulmonar.
pulmotor [ˈpʌlməutə*] n. U. S. MED. Pulmón (*m.*) de acero.
pulp [pʌlp] n. Pulpa, *f.*: *dental pulp*, pulpa dentaria, pulpa dental; *pulp of a fruit*, pulpa de un fruto. || Pasta, *f.*, pulpa, *f.* (of paper, wood). || U. S. FAM. Revista (*f.*) *or* novela (*f.*) de poca categoría. || — FIG. FAM. *Crushed to pulp*, hecho papilla. || *Paper pulp*, pulpa de madera, pasta de papel. || FIG. FAM. *To reduce to pulp*, hacer papilla.
pulp [pʌlp] v. tr. Reducir a pulpa. || Reducir a pasta (paper). || Descascarillar (to husk). || Destruir (books).
— V. intr. Volverse pulposo.
pulpit [ˈpulpit] n. REL. Púlpito, *m.* || FIG. Predicadores, *m. pl.* (preachers).
pulpitis [pʌlˈpitis] n. MED. Pulpitis, *f.*
— OBSERV. El plural de la palabra inglesa es *pulpitides*.
pulpwood [ˈpʌlpwud] n. Madera (*f.*) para pasta de papel.
pulpy [ˈpʌlpi] adj. Pulposo, sa.
pulsate [pʌlˈseit] v. intr. Latir, palpitar (to move rhythmically). || Vibrar (music). || Brillar de forma intermitente (lights). || FIG. Vibrar, palpitar: *the crowd was pulsating with enthusiasm*, la multitud vibraba de entusiasmo.
pulsatile [ˈpʌlsətail] adj. Pulsátil.
pulsation [pʌlˈseiʃən] n. Pulsación, *f.* (beat). || Vibración, *f.* (vibration).
pulsatory [ˈpʌlsətəri] adj. Pulsátil, pulsativo, va (throbbing).

pulse [pʌls] n. Pulso, *m.*: *to take* o *to feel s.o.'s pulse*, tomarle el pulso a alguien. || Pulsación, *f.*, latido, *m.* (one single beat of the heart). || Compás, *m.*, cadencia, *f.*, ritmo, *m.* (the beat in music). || Cadencia, *f.*, ritmo, *m.* (the beat of verse). || PHYS. Pulsación, *f.* || Vibración, *f.* || RAD. Impulso, *m.* || Plantas (*f. pl.*) leguminosas (leguminous plants). || Legumbres, *f. pl.* (seeds of these plants). || — MED. *Irregular pulse*, pulso arrítmico *or* irregular. || *Pulse of light*, luz (*f.*) intermitente. || *Regular pulse*, pulso normal *or* sentado. || FIG. *To test the pulse of*, tomar el pulso a.

pulse [pʌls] v. intr. Latir, pulsar (to beat). || Vibrar (to vibrate). || FIG. Latir.

pulse-jet engine [—dʒet'endʒin] n. Pulsorreactor, *m.*

pulsimeter [pʌl'simitə*] n. Pulsímetro, *m.*

pulsometer [pʌl'sɔmitə*] n. Pulsómetro, *m.*

pulverizable ['pʌlvəraizəbl] adj. Pulverizable.

pulverization [,pʌlvərai'zeiʃən] n. Pulverización, *f.*

pulverize ['pʌlvəraiz] v. tr. Pulverizar. || FIG. Pulverizar: *to pulverize one's opponent, a record*, pulverizar a su adversario, un récord. | Machacar, dar una paliza a: *the team pulverized the opposition*, el equipo machacó al equipo contrario. || TECH. Machacar, triturar, pulverizar.

— V. intr. Pulverizarse.

pulverizer [—ə*] n. Pulverizador, *m.* (for liquid). || TECH. Machacadora, *f.*, trituradora, *f.* (for solids).

pulverulence [pʌl'verjuləns] n. Pulverulencia, *f.*

pulverulent [pʌl'verjulənt] n. Polvoriento, ta; pulverulento, ta (covered with powder). || Pulverulento, ta (crumbling to powder).

puma ['pju:mə] n. ZOOL. Puma, *m.* (cougar).

— OBSERV. El plural de la palabra inglesa es *puma* o *pumas*.

pumice ['pʌmis] n. Piedra (*f.*) pómez.

pumice ['pʌmis] v. tr. Limpiar *or* pulir con piedra pómez.

pummel ['pʌml] v. tr. Aporrear.

pummelling [—iŋ] n. Paliza, *f.*

pump [pʌmp] n. Bomba, *f.*: *bicycle pump*, bomba de bicicleta; *air pump*, bomba de aire; *suction pump*, bomba aspirante; *force pump*, bomba impelente; *suction and force pump*, bomba aspirante impelente. || Surtidor, *m.* (in petrol station or car engine): *petrol pump*, surtidor de gasolina. || Zapato (*m.*) bajo de charol, escarpín, *m.* (evening dress shoe). || Zapato (*m.*) de lona, playera, *f.* (plimsoll). || MAR. Pompa, *f.*, bomba, *f.* || — *Injection pump*, bomba de inyección. || *Stomach pump*, bomba gástrica. || *To give sth. a pump*, inflar algo.

pump [pʌmp] v. tr. Sacar con una bomba, bombear: *to pump water from a boat*, sacar agua de un barco con una bomba. || Sacar [por medio de una bomba]: *Mary is pumping water*, María está sacando agua. || Impulsar: *the heart pumps blood*, el corazón impulsa la sangre. || Inyectar: *to pump air into a machine*, inyectar aire en una máquina. || Echar [con bomba]: *to pump water into a bucket*, echar agua en un cubo con una bomba. || FIG. Pegar: *the bandit pumped four shots into the detective*, el bandido pegó cuatro tiros al detective. | Sonsacar: *they pumped the secret out of him*, le sonsacaron el secreto. | Sacar: *they pumped a lot of money out of me*, me sacaron mucho dinero. | Mover de arriba abajo (to shake, to move up and down). | Invertir, meter: *to pump money into a new industry*, invertir dinero en una nueva industria. || — *To pump dry*, secar: *to pump a polder dry*, secar un pólder; vaciar: *to pump a swimming pool dry*, vaciar una piscina. || *To pump full of lead*, acribillar a tiros. || *To pump out*, achicar (a boat, a flooded mine, etc.), agotar (to exhaust). || *To pump up*, inflar: *to pump up a tyre*, inflar un neumático; insuflar aire en (an organ), elevar con una bomba (to raise by pumping).

— V. intr. Accionar una bomba, dar a la bomba (to operate a pump). || Impulsar la sangre (the heart). || Latir (to beat).

pumpernickel ['pumpənikl] n. Pan integral (*m.*) de centeno.

pump handle [pʌmp'hændl] n. Guimbalete, *m.*

pumping ['pʌmpiŋ] adj. De bombeo: *pumping station*, estación de bombeo.

— N. Bombeo, *m.* (of water, etc.). || FIG. Sonsacamiento, *m.*, sondeo, *m.*

pumpkin ['pʌmpkin] n. BOT. Calabaza, *f.*

pun [pʌn] n. Retruécano, *m.*, juego (*m.*) de palabras (play on words).

pun [pʌn] v. intr. Hacer retruécanos, hacer juegos de palabras, jugar del vocablo.

punch [pʌntʃ] n. Puñetazo, *m.* (blow with the fist). || Pegada, *f.*: *to have a strong punch*, tener una gran pegada. || FIG. Fuerza, *f.*, empuje, *m.*, vigor, *m.*: *this story lacks punch*, a esta historia le falta fuerza. | Nervio, *m.*, energía, *f.* || TECH. Sacabocados, *m. inv.*, punzón, *m.* (instrument for making holes). | Punzón (*m.*) de clavo, botador (*m.*) de punta (for driving nails). | Perforadora, *f.* (for cutting holes in paper). | Máquina (*f.*) de picar [billetes] (for punching holes in tickets). || Ponche, *m.* (drink). || — *Rabbit punch*, golpe (*m.*) en la nuca. || *To pack a punch*, tener una gran pegada (a boxer), ser muy potente, tener mucha potencia (an engine).

punch [pʌntʃ] v. tr. Dar un puñetazo a: *he punched him on the nose*, le dio un puñetazo en la nariz. || Golpear, tener pegada, pegar: *Henry punches better than Joseph*, Enrique tiene mejor pegada que José. || TECH. Taladrar, agujerear, troquelar (to make a hole in metals). | Perforar (in paper): *punched cards*, tarjetas perforadas. || Picar (tickets). || Hacer (holes). || U. S. Aguijonear (cattle).

— V. intr. *To punch in* o *out*, fichar (employees).

Punch [pʌntʃ] n. Polichinela, *m.*

Punch-and-Judy show [,pʌntʃən'dʒudiʃəu] n. Teatro (*m.*) de marionetas.

punchball [—bɔ:l] n. SP. Punching ball, *m.*, saco (*m.*) de arena.

punch bowl [—bəul] n. Ponchera, *f.*

punch card [—kɑ:d] n. Tarjeta (*f.*) perforada.

punch-drunk [—drʌnk] adj. SP. Groggy, aturdido por los golpes.

puncheon ['pʌntʃən] n. Puntal, *m.*, estribo, *m.* (strut). || Punzón, *m.*, cuño, *m.* (patterned die used by silversmiths). || Pipa, *f.*, barril, *m.* (a cask and its contents).

puncher ['pʌntʃə*] n. Empleado (*m.*) que pica los billetes. || Troquelador, *m.* (of metal). || Sacabocados, *m. inv.* (tool). || Perforadora, *f.*, máquina (*f.*) perforadora (machine). || Pegador, *m.* (boxer). || U. S. Vaquero, *m.* (cowboy).

Punchinello [,pʌntʃi'neləu] pr. n. Polichinela, *m.*

punching ['pʌntʃiŋ] n. TECH. Taladro, *m.* || Puñetazos, *m. pl.* (blows).

punching bag [—bæg] n. SP. Punching ball, *m.*, saco (*m.*) de arena.

punching machine [—mə'ʃi:n] n. TECH. Taladradora, *f.*, perforadora, *f.*

punch line ['pʌntʃ,lain] n. Gracia, *f.* (witty remark).

punch mark ['pʌntʃ,mɑ:k] n. Marca, *f.*, señal, *f.*

punch press [,pʌntʃ,pres] n. TECH. Prensa (*f.*) troqueladora.

punctilio [pʌŋk'tiliəu] n. Formalismo, *m.* || Puntillo, *m.* (point of detail).

punctilious [pʌŋk'tiliəs] adj. Puntilloso, sa; quisquilloso, sa (particular). || Formalista, etiquetero, ra (ceremonious).

punctiliousness [—nis] n. Meticulosidad *f.* || Formalismo, *m.*, protocolo, *m.*

punctual ['pʌŋktjuəl] adj. Puntual. || *The bus was punctual*, el autobús llegó a la hora.

punctuality [,pʌŋktju'æliti] n. Puntualidad, *f.*

punctuate ['pʌŋktjueit] v. tr. GRAMM. Puntuar (to mark divisions of sentences). || Recalcar (to emphasize). || Interrumpir (to interrupt): *his speech was punctuated with applause*, su discurso fue interrumpido varias veces por los aplausos. || *His speech was punctuated with quotations*, intercaló citas en su discurso.

punctuation [,pʌŋktju'eiʃən] n. GRAMM. Puntuación, *f.* || *Punctuation marks*, signos (*m.*) de puntuación.

puncture ['pʌŋktʃə*] n. Pinchazo, *m.* (in tyre, sth. inflated). || Perforación, *f.* (perforation). || MED. Punción, *f.* || *Puncture patch*, parche, *m.*

puncture ['pʌŋktʃə*] v. tr. Pinchar (a tyre). || Perforar (to perforate). || MED. Puncionar, hacer una punción a. | Reventar (an abscess). || *The cyclist punctured a tyre*, al ciclista se le pinchó una rueda.

— V. intr. AUT. Pinchar (driver, car). || Pincharse (tyre).

puncture-proof [—pru:f] adj. Que no se pincha.

pundit ['pʌndit] n. Pandit (in India). || FIG. FAM. Lumbrera, *f.*, autoridad, *f.*

pungency ['pʌndʒənsi] n. Acritud, *f.* (of smell). || Lo picante (of taste). || FIG. Mordacidad, *f.*, causticidad, *f.* (of words).

pungent ['pʌndʒənt] adj. Acre (smell). || Picante, fuerte (taste). || Punzante (pain). || FIG. Mordaz, cáustico, ca (words). | Desgarrador, ra (sorrow).

Punic ['pju:nik] adj. Púnico, ca: *the Punic Wars*, las Guerras Púnicas.

puniness ['pju:ninis] n. Debilidad, *f.* (weakness). || Pequeño tamaño, *m.* (small size).

punish ['pʌniʃ] v. tr. Castigar (to give a punishment to): *the crime was punished by death*, el crimen fue castigado con la pena de muerte. || FIG. Maltratar (to treat harshly). | Dar una paliza a (to give s.o. a beating). | Castigar (a boxer). | Zamparse (food, drink). | Aprovecharse hasta el máximo de (to take advantage of).

punishable [—əbl] adj. Castigable, que merece castigo, penable, punible. || JUR. Delictivo, va. || *Punishable by*, merecedor de (a fine, etc.).

punisher [—ə*] n. Castigador, ra. || SP. Pegador, *m.* (boxer).

punishment [—mənt] n. Castigo, *m.*: *corporal punishment*, castigo corporal. || FIG. FAM. Paliza, *f.* (heavy defeat). | Castigo, *m.* (in boxing). || JUR. *Capital punishment*, pena capital *or* de muerte.

punitive ['pju:nitiv] adj. Punitivo, va: *a punitive expedition*, una expedición punitiva.

Punjab [pʌn'dʒɑ:b] pr. n. GEOGR. Pendjab, *m.*, Penjab, *m.*, Punjab, *m.*

punk [pʌŋk] adj. U. S. Malo, la (of poor quality).

— N. U. S. Yesca, *f.* (tinder). || U. S. FAM. Mocoso, sa (young inferior person). | Novato, *m.* (beginner). | Pobre hombre, *m.* (inferior person).

punnet ['pʌnit] n. Cestito, *m.*, canastilla, *f.*

punster [ˈpʌnstə*] n. Aficionado (*m.*) a los juegos de palabras.
punt [pʌnt] n. Batea, *f.* (boat). || SP. Patada, *f.* (in rugby). || Apuesta, *f.* (bet in gambling).
punt [pʌnt] v. tr. Llevar en batea (to carry s.o. in a punt). || Hacer avanzar con el bichero (to propel). || SP. Dar una patada a, dar un puntapié a, patear (a ball).
— V. intr. Ir en batea (to travel in a punt). || SP. Dar un puntapié a la pelota, patear la pelota. || Apostar (to bet). || Jugar contra la banca (in gambling).
punter [—ə*] n. Jugador, *m.* (gambler).
punt pole [—pəul] n. Bichero, *m.*
punty [—i] n. TECH. Puntel, *m.* (in glass blowing).
puny [ˈpju:ni] adj. Endeble, débil, enclenque (weak). || Escuchimizado, da (undersized). || Insignificante (insignificant).
pup [pʌp] n. Cachorro, *m.*, cría (*f.*) de perro (of dog). || Cría (*f.*) de foca (of seal). || FAM. Mocoso, *m.* (conceited young man). || FAM. *To sell s.o. a pup*, darle a uno gato por liebre.
pup [pʌp] v. intr. Parir [la perra].
pupa [ˈpju:pə] n. ZOOL. Crisálida, *f.*
— OBSERV. El plural de *pupa* es *pupas* o *pupae*.
pupil [ˈpju:pl] n. Alumno, na (in school). || JUR. Pupilo, la. || ANAT. Pupila, *f.* (of the eye).
pupilage or **pupillage** [ˈpju:pilidʒ] n. JUR. Pupilaje, *m.*, tutela, *f.* (wardship). | Minoría, *f.* (nonage). || Escolaridad, *f.*
pupillary [ˈpju:piləri] adj. Pupilar.
puppet [ˈpʌpit] n. THEATR. Títere, *m.*, marioneta, *f.* || FIG. Títere, *m.*, muñeco, *m.*, pelele, *m.* || FIG. *Puppet government*, gobierno títere.
puppeteer [ˌpʌpiˈtiə*] n. THEATR. Titiritero, *m.*
puppetry [ˈpʌpətri] n. Títeres, *m. pl.*
puppet show [ˈpʌpitʃəu] n. Títeres, *m. pl.*, teatro (*m.*) de marionetas.
puppy [ˈpʌpi] n. Cachorro, *m.* (pup). || Perrito, ta (young dog). || FIG. Mocoso, *m.* (young man).
puppy love [—lʌv] n. Amor (*m.*) de jóvenes.
purblind [ˈpə:blaind] adj. MED. Medio ciego, ga (partly blind). || FIG. Ciego, ga (unable to understand).
purblindness [—nis] n. Ceguera (*f.*) casi total. || FIG Ceguera, *f.*, ofuscación, *f.*
purchasable [ˈpə:tʃəsəbl] adj. Adquirible, comprable.
purchase [ˈpə:tʃəs] n. Compra, *f.*, adquisición, *f.* (a buy). || TECH. Palanca, *f.* (lever). || Agarre, *m.*, asidero, *m.* (hold). || Apoyo, *m.*, punto (*m.*) de apoyo (support). || MAR. Aparejo, *m.*, polipasto, *m.*
purchase [ˈpə:tʃəs] v. tr. Comprar (to buy). || Adquirir (to acquire). || Conseguir (to obtain). || MAR. Levar (the anchor). || Apalancar (to lift with a lever).
purchaser [—ə*] n. Comprador, ra (who buys). || Adjudicatario, ria (at auction).
purchase tax [—tæks] n. Impuesto (*m.*) sobre la venta.
purchasing [—iŋ] adj. Comprador, ra. || *Purchasing power*, poder adquisitivo.
— N. Compra, *f.*
pure [pjuə*] adj. Puro, ra.
pureblood [—blʌd] adj. De pura sangre (horse). || De pura raza (other animals).
— N. Pura sangre, *m.*, caballo (*m.*) de pura sangre (horse). || Animal (*m.*) de pura raza (any other animal).
pure-blooded [—ˈblʌdid] adj. De pura sangre (horse). || De pura raza (other animals).
purebred [—bred] adj./n. See PUREBLOOD.
purée (U. S., **puree**) [ˈpjuərei] n. CULIN. Puré, *m.*
purely [ˈpjuəli] adv. Puramente. || *Purely by chance*, por pura casualidad.
pure-minded [ˈpjuəˌmaindid] adj. Sano, na.
pureness [ˈpjuənis] n. Pureza, *f.*
purgation [pə:ˈgeiʃən] n. MED. REL. Purgación, *f.*
purgative [ˈpə:gətiv] adj. Purgante, purgativo, va.
— N. Purgante, *m.*, purga, *f.* (a medicine).
purgatorial [ˌpə:gəˈtɔ:riəl] adj. Purificador, ra; expiatorio, ria (expiatory). || REL. Del purgatorio.
purgatory [ˈpə:gətəri] n. REL. Purgatorio, *m.* || FIG. Purgatorio, *m.*
purge [pə:dʒ] n. MED. Purga, *f.* (act). | Purgante, *m.*, purga, *f.* (remedy). || TECH. Purga, *f.* || FIG. Purga, *f.* (in politics).
purge [pə:dʒ] v. tr. MED. Purgar (the bowels). | Purificar (blood). || TECH. Purgar, limpiar. || Limpiar (to cleanse). || FIG. Hacer una purga en: *to purge a political party*, hacer una purga en un partido político. | Deshacerse de (to get rid of). | Purgar, expiar: *to purge a sin*, purgar un pecado. | Sanear (the finances). | Exonerar (to clear of a charge).
purgecock [—kɔ:k] n. TECH. Purgador, *m.*
purger [—ə*] n. TECH. Purgador, *m.* || Autor (*m.*) de la purga (in politics).
purging buckthorn [pə:dʒiŋˈbʌkθɔ:n] n. BOT. Espino (*m.*) cerval.
purification [ˌpjuərifiˈkeiʃən] n. REL. Purificación, *f.* || FIG. Purificación, *f.* | Saneamiento, *m.* (of finances). || TECH. Depuración, *f.*
purificator [ˈpjuərifikeitə*] n. REL. Purificador, *m.*
purificatory [ˈpjuərifikeitəri] adj. Purificador, ra; purificatorio, ria.
purifier [ˈpjuərifaiə*] n. Purificador, ra (person who purifies). || TECH. Depurador, *m.*
purify [ˈpjuərifai] v. tr. Purificar. || TECH. Purificar, depurar. || FIG. *To purify s.o. from his sins*, librar a alguien de culpa.
— V. intr. Purificarse. || TECH. Purificarse, depurarse.
purifying [—iŋ] adj. Purificador, ra. || TECH. Depurador, ra.
— N. Purificación, *f.* || TECH. Depuración, *f.*
purism [ˈpjuərizəm] n. Purismo, *m.*
purist [ˈpjuərist] n. Purista, *m.* & *f.*
puristic [pjuəˈristik] or **puristical** [—əl] adj. Purista.
Puritan [ˈpjuəritən] adj./n. Puritano, na.
puritanical [ˌpjuəriˈtænikəl] adj. Puritano, na.
Puritanism [ˈpjuəritənizəm] n. Puritanismo, *m.*
purity [ˈpjuəriti] n. Pureza, *f.*
purl [pə:l] n. Puntilla, *f.* (on lace, ribbon). || Ribete (*m.*) de hilo de oro *or* de plata (golden or silver edging). || Hilo (*m.*) de oro *or* de plata (thread). || FIG. Susurro, *m.*, murmullo, *m.* (of a stream). || *Purl stitch*, punto (*m.*) del revés, punto (*m.*) al revés.
purl [pə:l] v. tr. Ribetear (sewing). || Hacer al revés (stitches). || Hacer con puntos al revés (garment).
— V. intr. FIG. Susurrar, murmurar (a stream).
purler [—ə*] n. FAM. Porrazo, *m.*, batacazo, *m.*: *to come a purler*, pegarse un porrazo, darse un batacazo.
purlieu [ˈpə:lju:] n. Límites, *m. pl.* (bounds). || Lindero, *m.*, linde, *f.* (of a forest). || — Pl. Alrededores, *m.*, cercanías, *f.*, inmediaciones, *f.*
purlin [ˈpə:lin] n. ARCH. Correa, *f.*
purling [ˈpə:liŋ] adj. Susurrante, murmurador, ra.
purloin [pə:ˈlɔin] v. tr. Hurtar, robar (to steal).
purloiner [—ə*] n. Ladrón, ona.
purple [ˈpə:pl] adj. Morado, da; purpúreo, a (colour). || FIG. *Purple passage*, pasaje muy lucido *or* de mucho efecto.
— N. Púrpura, *f.* (crimson cloth, emblem). || Morado, *m.*, violeta, *m.* (colour). || MED. Púrpura, *f.* || AGR. Añublo, *m.* || ZOOL. Púrpura, *f.* (mollusc).
purple [ˈpə:pl] v. tr. Purpurar, enrojecer.
purplish [ˈpə:pliʃ] or **purply** [ˈpə:pli] adj. Violáceo, a; purpurino, na; morado, da.
purport [ˈpə:pət] n. Significado, *m.*, sentido, *m.* (meaning). || Intención, *f.* (purpose). || Tenor, *m.*, contenido, *m.* (of a document). || Objeto, *m.* (of a letter).
purport [ˈpə:pət] v. tr. Pretender (to claim): *this book purports to be an original work*, este libro pretende ser original. || Significar (to mean). || Dejar suponer, implicar, dar a entender (to suggest).
purportless [—lis] adj. Sin ningún interés, desprovisto de interés.
purpose [ˈpə:pəs] n. Propósito, *m.*, objetivo, *m.*, intención, *f.*, deseo, *m.*: *for the purpose of doing sth. useful*, con el propósito de hacer algo útil. || Destino, *m.*, fin, *m.* (destination). || Resolución, *f.*, determinación, *f.* (determination). || Uso, *m.*: *I have got jeans for everyday purposes*, tengo pantalones vaqueros para uso diario. || Necesidad, *f.* (need): *for future purposes*, para las necesidades futuras. || Utilidad, *f.*: *public purpose*, utilidad pública. || — *Fixed purpose*, intención precisa. || *For all purpose*, para todo. || *For my purpose*, para lo que quiero. || *For the above purposes*, con los objetivos anteriormente mencionados. || *For the purpose*, al efecto. || *For the purpose of*, con el objeto de, con miras a, para. || *For this* o *that purpose*, con este propósito, con este fin. || *Infirm of purpose*, irresoluto, ta; indeciso, sa. || *Not to the purpose*, que no viene al caso, fuera de lugar. || *Novel with a purpose*, novela (*f.*) de tesis. || *Of set purpose*, deliberadamente, intencionadamente, a propósito. || *On purpose*, a propósito, adrede, a posta: *I did it on purpose*, lo hice adrede. || *Strength of purpose*, firmeza, *f.*, resolución, *f.* || *To achieve one's purpose*, conseguir el fin deseado, alcanzar su objetivo. || *To come to the purpose*, ir al grano. || *To good purpose*, con provecho, fructuosamente, con buenos resultados. || *To little purpose*, para poco. || *To no purpose*, para nada, en balde, en vano, sin resultado. || *To serve* o *to answer the purpose*, servir para el caso. || *To serve* o *to answer various purposes*, servir para varias cosas. || *To some purpose*, para algo: *all studies serve to some purpose*, cualquier estudio sirve para algo. || *To speak to the purpose*, no salirse del tema, ceñirse al tema. || *To the purpose*, que viene al caso, a propósito.
purpose [ˈpə:pəs] v. tr. Proponerse, tener la intención de (to intend).
purposeful [—ful] adj. Decidido, da; determinado, da; resuelto, ta (person). || Útil (activity). || Lleno de significado (speech).
purposefulness [—fulnis] n. Decisión, *f.*, determinación, *f.*, resolución, *f.* (determination). || Utilidad, *f.* (usefulness). || Significado, *m.* (meaning).
purposeless [—lis] adj. Sin objetivo, sin objeto (aimless). || Inútil (useless). || Irresoluto, ta (character). || Indeciso, sa; irresoluto, ta (person).
purposely [—li] adj. A propósito, adrede, a posta, deliberadamente, intencionadamente.
purposive [ˈpə:pəsiv] adj. Deliberado, da; intencionado, da (act). || Decidido, da; determinado, da; resuelto, ta (person). || Útil (useful). || Que desempeña una función (organ).
purpura [ˈpə:pjurə] n. MED. Púrpura, *f.*

purpure [ˈpə:puə*] n. HERALD. Púrpura, *f.*
purpurin [ˈpə:pjurin] n. Purpurina, *f.* (red crystalline compound).
purr [pə:*] n. Ronroneo, *m.* (of a cat). || Zumbido, *m.* (of an engine).
purr [pə:*] v. intr. Ronronear (a cat). || Zumbar (an engine).
purse [pə:s] n. Monedero, *m.*, portamonedas, *m. inv.* (for money). || Bolsa, *f.* (a sum of money). || Bolsa, *f.* (of a boxer). || Premio, *m.* (prize). || Colecta, *f.* (collection). || ANAT. Bolsa, *f.* || U. S. Bolso, *m.* [*Amer.*, cartera, *f.*] (handbag). || — *Belt purse*, escarcela, *f.* || FIG. *Beyond s.o.'s purse*, fuera de las posibilidades de uno, fuera del alcance de alguien. || *Public purse*, erario público. || *Purse bearer*, tesorero, ra. || *Purse strings*, cordones (*m.*) de la bolsa. || FIG. *To have a common purse*, hacer fondo común. | *To have a well-lined purse*, tener la bolsa repleta. | *To hold the purse strings*, manejar los cuartos, administrar el dinero. | *To loosen the purse strings*, aflojar la bolsa. || FIG. FAM. *You cannot make a silk purse out of a sow's ear*, no se pueden pedir peras al olmo.
purse [pə:s] v. tr. Fruncir: *to purse one's brows*, fruncir el entrecejo, fruncir el ceño. || Apretar (one's lips).
purse-proud [—praud] adj. Orgulloso de su riqueza.
purser [—ə*] n. MAR. Contador, *m.*
purslane [ˈpə:slin] n. BOT. Verdolaga, *f.*
pursuable [pə:ˈsjuəbl] adj. Perseguible (punishable, which can be followed). || Proseguible (continuable).
pursuance [pəˈsjuəns] n. Prosecución, *f.* (continuation). || Ejecución, *f.*, cumplimiento, *m.* (carrying out). || *In pursuance of*, según, conforme a, de conformidad con.
pursuant [pəˈsjuənt] adv. *Pursuant to*, según, conforme a, de conformidad con.
pursue [pəˈsju:] v. tr. Perseguir: *to pursue a thief*, perseguir a un ladrón. || Seguir la pista de (an animal). || FIG. Aspirar a, buscar, perseguir (to strive for). | Seguir (a line of conduct, a plan). | Ejercer (a profession). | Proseguir, continuar (to continue). || JUR. Demandar, perseguir judicialmente.
pursuer [—ə*] n. Perseguidor, ra. || JUR. Demandante, *m.* & *f.*
pursuit [pəˈsju:t] n. Persecución, *f.*: *in pursuit of*, en persecución de. || Profesión, *f.* || Ocupación, *f.*, trabajo, *m.* (work). || Pasatiempo, *m.* (pastime). || AVIAT. Caza, *f.* || FIG. Búsqueda, *f.*, busca, *f.*, (of an aim).
pursuit plane [—plein] n. AVIAT. Caza, *m.*, avión (*m.*) de caza.
pursy [ˈpə:si] adj. Barrigón, ona; barrigudo, da (corpulent). || Asmático, ca; que se ahoga (short-winded). || Encogido, da; apretado, da (lips). || Ricachón, ona (rich).
purulence [ˈpjuərulәns] n. MED. Purulencia, *f.* (condition). | Pus, *m.* (pus).
purulent [ˈpjuərulənt] adj. Purulento, ta.
purvey [pə:ˈvei] v. tr./intr. Proveer, abastecer, suministrar. || *To purvey for a person*, ser el proveedor de una persona.
purveyance [—əns] n. Abastecimiento, *m.*, suministro, *m.* (supply).
purveying [—iŋ] adj. Proveedor, ra; abastecedor, ra.
purveyor [—ə*] n. Proveedor, ra; abastecedor, ra.
purview [ˈpə:vju:] n. Articulado, *m.*, texto, *m.* (of a statute). || Alcance, *m.* (extent). || Esfera, *f.* (field). || Competencia, *f.* (concern, province).
pus [pʌs] n. MED. Pus, *m.*
push [puʃ] n. Empujón, *m.*: *he gave me a push in the back*, me dio un empujón por la espalda. || Empuje, *m.*, impulso, *m.* (force which pushes). || FIG. Apuro, *m.*, aprieto, *m.* (difficult moment). || ARCH. Empuje, *m.* || MIL. Ofensiva, *f.* || FAM. Enchufe, *m.* (influence). | Empuje, *m.* (drive): *he hasn't enough push to succeed as a salesman*, no tiene bastante empuje para ser un buen vendedor. | Empujón, *m.*: *we have to make a push to finish our work*, tenemos que dar un empujón para acabar nuestro trabajo. | Banda, *f.* (of thieves). | Embestida, *f.* (of a bull). || — *At a push*, en caso de necesidad, en un momento de apuro. || FAM. *To get the push*, ser despedido, ser puesto de patitas en la calle. || *To give a push on the bell*, tocar el timbre. || *To give a push on the button*, pulsar el botón. || FAM. *To give s.o. a push*, enchufar a alguien. | *To give s.o. the push*, despedir a alguien, poner de patitas en la calle a alguien. || *To make a push shot*, retacar (in billiards). || FIG. *When it comes to the push*, cuando llega el momento decisivo.
push [puʃ] v. tr. Empujar: *he pushed the door*, empujó la puerta; *the gardener was pushing a wheelbarrow*, el jardinero empujaba una carretilla. || Pisar: *he pushed the accelerator*, pisó el acelerador. || Apretar, pulsar: *he pushed the button*, apretó el botón. || Promocionar (goods, sale): *to push a product*, promocionar un producto. || Fomentar, promover, promocionar (trade, etc.): *the government is pushing agriculture*, el gobierno está fomentando la agricultura. || Extender (to extend). || Obligar: *they pushed him into marrying that girl*, le obligaron a casarse con esa chica. || Empujar: *my parents pushed me to go to University*, mis padres me empujaron a ir a la Universidad. || Aprovechar, aprovecharse de (to take advantage of). || Recomendar, enchufar (to recommend). || Insistir en (a claim). || FIG. Apremiar: *to push s.o. for payment*, apremiar a alguien para que pague. || — FAM. *Don't push him too far!*, ¡no le saque de quicio! || *He pushed his finger in his eye*, le metió el dedo en el ojo. || *I am pushed for time*, tengo prisa, ando escaso de tiempo. || *To be pushed for money*, andar muy justo de dinero, andar escaso de dinero. || *To push one's luck*, forzar la suerte. || *To push o.s.*, darse a fondo (sportsmen). || *To push s.o. out of the way*, apartar a alguien empujándole *or* a empujones. || *To push sth. open*, abrir algo empujándolo. || *We are pushed for an answer*, nos piden una contestación rápida.
— V. intr. Empujar: *Raymond's car stopped and we all had to push*, el coche de Ramón se paró y todos tuvimos que empujar. || Presionar, ejercer presión: *the trade unions are pushing for better wages*, los sindicatos están presionando para que aumenten los salarios. || Seguir: *we pushed as far as Manchester*, seguimos hasta Manchester. || Adentrarse: *we pushed a good way into Provence*, nos adentramos bastante en Provenza. || *Push*, empujen (notice on doors).
— ***To push ahead***, seguir adelante. | — *To push ahead with a plan*, llevar adelante un proyecto. || ***To push aside***, apartar a empujones (people). | Apartar con la mano (things). || ***To push away***, apartar. || ***To push back***, empujar. | Hacer retroceder: *the police pushed back the crowd*, la policía hizo retroceder a la multitud. | Hacer retroceder, rechazar: *we pushed back the enemy*, hicimos retroceder al enemigo. | Echar hacia atrás (hair, etc.). | Empujar hacia atrás. | Retroceder (to move back). || ***To push down***, derribar, tirar abajo (a house). | Hacer caer (s.o.). | Apretar (to press down): *to push down a button*, apretar un botón. || ***To push forward***, empujar hacia adelante (s.o.). | Avanzar (an army). | — *To push forward to the attack*, pasar a la ofensiva. | *To push o.s. forward*, ponerse en evidencia. || ***To push in***, empujar. | Hincar (a pole, etc.). | Entrar a empujones (to get in). | Colarse (in a queue). | — FAM. *To push s.o.'s face in*, romperle a uno la crisma. || ***To push off***, desatracar (a boat). | Quitar (to take off). | FAM. Largarse, irse (to go). | — *To push off from*, apartarse de. | *To push s.o. off a place*, echar a alguien de un sitio a empujones. || ***To push on***, activar, apresurar (work). | Avanzar: *the enemy pushed on to the village*, el enemigo avanzó hasta el pueblo. | Seguir: *we pushed on to Blackpool*, seguimos hasta Blackpool. | Seguir adelante, continuar: *now that we have rested let's push on*, ahora que hemos descansado sigamos adelante. | Empujar: *to push s.o. on to do sth.*, empujar a alguien a hacer algo. | Hacer adelantar: *to push on a pupil*, hacer adelantar a un alumno. | Irse, ponerse en camino: *it's time to push on*, es hora de irnos. || ***To push out***, echar a empujones: *they pushed him out of the room*, le echaron a empujones de la habitación. | Expulsar, desahuciar (a tenant). | Eliminar: *to push competitors out of the market*, eliminar a los competidores del mercado. | Echar al agua (a boat). | Echar (blossoms, roots). | Sacar: *the cat pushed out its claws*, el gato sacó las uñas. | — *To push out into*, adentrarse en: *the headland pushes out into the sea*, el promontorio se adentra en el mar. || ***To push over***, hacer caer (s.o.). | Volcar (sth.): *to push a car over*, volcar un coche. || ***To push through***, pasar por, sacar por: *they pushed the table through the window*, sacaron la mesa por la ventana. | Llevar a cabo *or* a buen término (to carry out). | Hacer aceptar (a bill in Parliament). | Salir (plants). | Abrirse paso a empujones entre (the crowd). | — *To push one's way through the crowd*, abrirse paso a empujones entre la muchedumbre. || ***To push to***, empujar (the door). || ***To push up***, levantar. | Hacer subir: *to push up the prices*, hacer subir los precios. | Ayudar a subir [empujándolo] (s.o.). | FIG. Dar un empujón, ayudar.
push-bike [—baik] n. FAM. Bicicleta, *f.*, bici, *f.*
push button [—ˌbʌtn] n. Pulsador, *m.*, botón, *m.*
push-button control [—ˌbʌtnkənˈtrəul] n. Mando (*m.*) por pulsador.
pushcart [—kɑ:t] n. Carretilla (*f.*) de mano.
push chair [—tʃɛə*] n. Coche silla, *m.*
pusher [—ə*] n. Persona (*f.*) que empuja. || FAM. Persona (*f.*) ambiciosa, arribista, *m.* & *f.* (ambitious person). | Vendedor (*m.*) de estupefacientes (narcotic seller). || AVIAT. Avión (*m.*) de hélice propulsora.
pushful [—ful] adj. Ambicioso, sa (ambitious). || Emprendedor, ra; que tiene empuje (energetic).
pushfulness [—fulnis] n. Ambición, *f.*, arribismo, *m.* (ambition). || Empuje, *m.* (energy).
pushing [—iŋ] adj. Ambicioso, sa (ambitious). || Emprendedor, ra; que tiene empuje (energetic). || Molesto, ta; insistente.
pushover [—ˌəuvə*] n. FAM. Cosa (*f.*) muy fácil de hacer (easy thing). | Persona (*f.*) fácil de convencer (person easily persuaded). || FAM. *It's a pushover*, está tirado.
pushpin [—pin] n. Chincheta, *f.* (nail).
push-up [—ʌp] n. Tracción, *f.* (in gymnastics).
pushy [—i] adj. U. S. FAM. Molesto, ta; insistente.
pusillanimity [ˌpju:siləˈnimiti] n. Pusilanimidad, *f.*
pusillanimous [ˌpju:siˈlænimәs] adj. Pusilánime.
puss [pus] n. Minino, *m.* (cat). || Liebre, *f.* (hare). || FAM. Chica, *f.* (girl). || U. S. FAM. Jeta, *f.*, cara, *f.* (face). || — *Puss in Boots*, el gato con botas. || *To play puss in the corner*, jugar a las cuatro esquinas.

pussy [—i] n. Minino, *m.* (cat). || BOT. Amento, *m.* (catkin). || FAM. Chica, *f.* (girl).

pussyfoot [—ifut] v. intr. Andar con mucho sigilo (to move stealthily). || U. S. FAM. No comprometerse.

pustular [ˈpʌstjulə*] adj. MED. Pustuloso, sa.

pustulate [ˈpʌstjuleit] adj. Pustuloso, sa.

pustule [ˈpʌstju:l] n. Pústula, *f.*

pustulous [ˈpʌstjuləs] adj. Pustuloso, sa.

put [put] n. SP. Lanzamiento, *m.* (of the shot). || COMM. Opción (*f.*) de venta.

put* [put] v. tr. Poner: *put all that on the floor*, ponga todo eso en el suelo. || Poner, colocar: *put the books on the table*, pon los libros en la mesa. || Meter (to introduce): *to put the key in the keyhole*, meter la llave en la cerradura. || Echar: *have you put salt in your soup?*, ¿le has echado sal a la sopa? || Someter (to submit): *to put a proposal before a committee*, someter una propuesta a una comisión. || Exponer, someter: *to put one's case before the jury* o *to the jury*, exponerle su caso al jurado. || Someter, presentar (to propose): *to put a project to the Parliament*, presentar un proyecto al Parlamento. || Someter *or* poner a votación (to a vote): *to put a motion*, poner a votación una moción. || Someter: *to put s.o. to a test*, someter a alguien a una prueba. || Hacer: *he put a question to me*, me hizo una pregunta. || Plantear (a problem). || Poner: *put it in writing*, ponlo por escrito. || Gravar con: *to put heavy taxes on alcohol*, gravar el alcohol con impuestos elevados. || Invertir, poner, colocar (to invest): *to put money to a firm*, poner *or* invertir dinero en una empresa. || Poner, meter: *to put money in the savings bank*, poner dinero en la caja de ahorros. || Meter: *I do not want to put you to expense*, no quiero meterle en gastos. || Causar: *to put s.o. to trouble*, causar molestias a alguien. || Echar (to impute to): *they put the blame* o *the responsibility on me*, me echaron la culpa. || Poner (to fix a price): *he put the price at five pounds*, puso el precio a cinco libras. || Echar, calcular (to estimate): *at first glance I would put this at ten pounds*, a primera vista le echaría diez libras. || Calcular: *I put the population of Malaga at 400 000*, calculo la población de Málaga en 400 000 habitantes. || Dar (to attribute): *to put a high value on sth.*, dar un gran valor a algo; *to put the proper interpretation on the clause of a contract*, dar la interpretación apropiada a la cláusula de un contrato. || Poner, decir (to state): *if you put it that way*, si lo pone así; *let's put it that you were not there*, pongamos que no estaba allí. || Decir (to say): *as Winston Churchill put it in his speech*, como dijo Winston Churchill en su discurso; *put it to him nicely*, dígaselo con buenos modales. || Exponer: *to put the case clearly*, exponer claramente el caso. || Expresar: *to put one's thoughts into words*, expresar sus pensamientos con palabras. || Traducir (to translate): *how would you put this into Spanish?*, ¿cómo traduciría esto al español? || Mandar (to oblige): *they put the troops to digging trenches*, mandaron que las tropas abriesen trincheras. || Poner de, meter a: *he put his boy to* o *into shoemaking*, metió a su hijo a zapatero. || Inscribir: *he put his horse in a race*, inscribió su caballo en una carrera. || Jugarse, poner (to bet): *he put his last penny on that horse*, se jugó el último penique en ese caballo. || Orientar, dirigir (to direct towards). || SP. Lanzar (the shot). || Echar (for reproduction): *to put a cow to a bull*, echar una vaca a un toro. || — *If I may put it so*, por decirlo así. || FIG. *I put it to you that you are lying*, me parece que está usted mintiendo. | *I would not put it past him to do sth. silly at the last moment*, no me extrañaría que hiciese una tontería en el último momento. | *Put it there!*, ¡chócala! (in a deal). || *To be hard put to do sth.*, serle a uno difícil hacer algo: *I'll be hard put to it*, me va a ser difícil hacerlo. || *To put a bullet in s.o.'s back*, pegarle un tiro a alguien por la espalda. || *To put a bullet through s.o.*, atravesar a alguien de un balazo. || *To put a child into a sailor's suit*, poner a un niño un traje de marinero, vestir a un niño de marinero. || *To put a child to bed*, acostar a un niño. || *To put a field under potatoes*, sembrar un campo de patatas. || SP. *To put a horse to a fence*, hacer que un caballo salte una valla. || *To put a knife in s.o.'s back*, clavarle un cuchillo a alguien por la espalda (for killing), dar una puñalada trapera a alguien (to trick). || *To put a matter into s.o.'s hands*, poner un asunto en manos de alguien. || *To put an animal out of his misery*, acortarle la agonía a un animal, rematar a un animal. || *To put an article on the market*, poner un artículo en el mercado, lanzar un artículo al mercado. || *To put an end* o *a stop to sth.*, poner fin *or* término a una cosa. || *To put it bluntly*, hablando sin rodeos. || *To put in danger*, poner en peligro. || *To put in safekeeping*, poner a buen recaudo. || FIG. *To put one's heart into one's work*, poner los cinco sentidos en un trabajo. | *To put one's mind to a problem*, poner los cinco sentidos en la resolución de un problema. | *To put one's pen through a word*, tachar una palabra. || *To put one's savings into francs, pounds, etc.*, cambiar sus ahorros en francos, libras, etc. || *To put one's signature to sth.*, firmar algo. || *To put on one side*, poner a un lado. || *To put on the stage*, montar, poner en escena (a play). || *To put o.s. in s.o.'s place*, ponerse en el lugar de uno. || *To put right*, see RIGHT (adj.). || FIG. *To put s.o. at ease*, tranquilizar a alguien. || *To put s.o. in a bad mood*, poner de malhumor a alguien. || *To put s.o. in a position to*, poner a alguien en condiciones de. || FIG. *To put s.o. in mind of sth.*, recordarle algo a alguien. || *To put s.o. on the right road to somewhere*, indicar a alguien el buen camino para ir a algún sitio. || *To put s.o. out of patience*, hacerle perder la paciencia a alguien. || *To put s.o.'s mind at rest*, tranquilizar a alguien. || *To put s.o. to death*, matar a alguien. || FIG. *To put s.o. to sleep*, darle sueño a alguien (to bore). || *To put s.o. to the sword*, pasar a alguien a cuchillo. || *To put sth. before sth. else*, anteponer una cosa a otra. || *To put sth. in doubt*, poner algo en duda *or* en tela de juicio. || *To put sth. into practice*, poner algo en práctica. || *To put sth. to good use*, hacer buen uso de algo. || *To put sth. to a vote*, someter *or* poner algo a votación. || *To put sth. to one's ear*, acercarse algo al oído. || *To put straight*, see STRAIGHT (adj.). || FIG. *To put the cards on the table*, poner las cartas sobre la mesa *or* boca arriba. || *To put the enemy to flight*, poner en fuga al enemigo. || *To put the finishing touch to*, dar el último toque a. || *To put the matter right*, arreglar el asunto. || *To put to fire and sword*, poner a fuego y a sangre. || *To put to the test*, poner a prueba. || *To stay put*, permanecer en el mismo sitio, no moverse (to remain in the same position), seguir igual (in the same condition).

— V. intr. MAR. Poner rumbo a (to take a specified course). || — MAR. *To put into port*, hacer escala en un puerto. | *To put to sea*, zarpar, hacerse a la mar.

— **To put about,** hacer correr, difundir (a rumour). | Preocupar (to worry). | Molestar (to trouble). | MAR. Hacer virar (a boat), virar, cambiar de rumbo (of a boat). | — *He put it about that John was getting married*, hizo correr la voz *or* el rumor de que Juan iba a casarse. || **To put across,** pasar (goods). | Hacer aceptar (idea, product). | Conseguir, lograr: *the play was put across very well*, la obra estaba muy conseguida. | Cerrar (a deal). | Traducir: *the book puts across the seriousness of the problem*, el libro traduce la gravedad del problema. | Transmitir, hacer comprender, comunicar (to communicate). | — FIG. *To put it across s.o.*, engañar a alguien (to trick), pegar una paliza a alguien (to defeat). | *You can't put that one across me*, esto no cuela, esto no me lo creo. || **To put aside,** poner *or* dejar a un lado. | Ahorrar (money). | Dejar, renunciar a: *to put drinking aside*, dejar de beber, renunciar a la bebida. | Rechazar (to reject). | Desechar (fears). || **To put away,** poner en su sitio, guardar: *put away your clothes*, pon tu ropa en su sitio. | Poner en el garaje (car). | FIG. Ahorrar (money), desechar (fears), apartar, alejar (a thought). | Repudiar (wife). | FAM. Zamparse, echarse entre pecho y espalda (drink, food), enjaular, meter en chirona (to jail), meter en un manicomio (a lunatic), suprimir, liquidar (to kill a person), sacrificar (to kill an animal), empeñar (to pawn). || **To put back,** volver a poner en su sitio: *put this book back*, vuelva a poner este libro en su sitio. | Volver a poner: *put it back on the table*, vuelva a ponerlo en la mesa. | Atrasar, retrasar (clock, time). | Aplazar (to postpone). | MAR. Volver *or* regresar [al puerto]. || **To put by,** guardar (to keep). | Ahorrar (money). | FIG. Eludir, evitar (to avoid). || **To put down,** bajar: *put your hand down*, baja la mano. | Dejar: *put this pen down on the table*, deja esta pluma en la mesa. | Poner, dejar: *to put sth. down on the ground*, poner algo en el suelo. | Soltar: *put that rifle down*, suelta ese fusil. | Cerrar (an umbrella). | Apuntar, poner por escrito (in writing). | Poner (on a bill, account, etc.). | Dejar [bajar] (passengers). | Acabar con (to put an end to). | Sofocar, reprimir (a rebellion). | Reprimir (to repress). | Suprimir (an abuse). | Disminuir, bajar (prices). | FIG. Achacar, atribuir (to ascribe): *to put a remark down to bad humour*, achacar una observación al mal humor; rebajar (pride), sacrificar (to kill animals), callar, hacer callar (to silence). | Degradar (to demote). | MATH. Poner. | MAR. Fondear (a buoy). | COMM. Hacer un desembolso inicial de (to deposit), abonar, poner: *put it down to my account*, póngalo en mi cuenta. | — *To put down as*, echar: *I put him down as forty*, le echo cuarenta años. | *To put down for*, tener por, considerar como: *they put him down for a fool*, le tienen por tonto. | *To put one's name down*, apuntar su nombre (on a paper), inscribirse (to enrol). || **To put forth,** proponer (to propose). | Mostrar (to show). | Emplear (one's efforts). | Publicar (to issue). | Tender, alargar (hand). | Extender, alargar (arm). | BOT. Echar [brotes]. | MAR. Zarpar. || **To put forward,** proponer, someter (a proposal). | Proponer, presentar la candidatura de (to propose as a candidate). | Exponer, emitir (an idea). | Hacer (a suggestion). | Valerse de (to use): *to put forward an argument*, valerse de un argumento. | Adelantar (clock, date). | — FIG. *To put o.s. forward*, ponerse en evidencia. | *To put o.s. forward as*, dárselas de. || **To put in,** meter, introducir (to insert). | Dedicar, pasar: *to put in one's time reading*, pasarse el tiempo leyendo, dedicar su tiempo a la lectura. | JUR. Presentar: *to put in a claim*, presentar una demanda; presentarse, presentar su candidatura (for an election). | AGR. Sembrar (seeds), plantar (trees, etc.). | FAM. Decir (a word). | MAR.

Tocar *or* hacer escala (*at*, en): *the Queen Mary put in at Malaga*, el Queen Mary hizo escala en Málaga. | Elegir: *the country has put the Conservatives in*, el país ha elegido a los conservadores. | — Fig. *To put a word in*, decir una palabra, intervenir en la conversación. | *To put in a good word for*, hablar por *or* en favor de. | *To put in out of one's own pocket*, poner de su bolsillo (money). | *To put in some overtime*, hacer unas horas extraordinarias. || **To put off,** quitarse (one's clothes): *he put his coat off*, se quitó el abrigo. | Aplazar, diferir (to postpone): *to put off a date, a payment*, aplazar una cita, un pago. | Aplazar una cita con (s.o.). | Cansar,hartar, hastiar (to disgust): *I went to the cinema so often that it put me off*, he ido tantas veces al cine que ya estoy harto. | Dar asco, asquear (to revolt): *the smell of this fish puts me off*, el olor de este pescado me da asco. | Disuadir, quitar de la cabeza: *we put him off his plan*, le hemos quitado de la cabeza el proyecto que tenía. | Desconcertar (to disconcert). | Desanimar (to dispirit). | Intimidar (to intimidate). | Alejar, apartar (to divert). | Entretener (with promises). | Engañar, dar el pego (to humbug). | Sp. Hacer fallar: *they tried to put me off my shot*, intentaron hacerme fallar el tiro. | Deshacerse de (to get rid of). | Mar. Hacerse a la mar. | — *To put s.o. off his meal* o *off his food*, quitarle a uno las ganas de comer. | *To put s.o. off the scent*, despistar a alguien. | *We had to put the guests off*, tuvimos que dejar para más tarde la invitación que habíamos hecho. || **To put on,** ponerse (clothes): *put on your jacket*, ponte la chaqueta. | Encender, dar a (light, radio, etc.). | Poner (record player, etc.). | Hacer funcionar (a machine). | Poner: *in August the airline puts on many extra flights*, en agosto la compañía pone muchos vuelos suplementarios. | Poner a calentar: *I am going to put some water on*, voy a poner agua a calentar. | Servir, poner (a dish). | Echar (brake). | Cobrar (speed). | Representar, dar (a show). | Echar, dar (a film). | Montar, poner en escena: *to put a play on*, poner una obra en escena. | Aumentar (to increase). | Fingir, simular (to pretend): *his anger was put on*, su cólera era fingida. | Afectar: *that accent isn't real, it's put on*, ese acento no es natural, es afectado. | Engordar: *I put on two pounds in a week*, engordé dos libras en una semana. | Adelantar (a clock). | Añadir (to add). | Designar (to appoint): *to put s.o. on to a job*, designar a alguien para un trabajo. | Poner, jugarse (to bet). | — Fam. *To put it on*, darse tono (to be conceited), exagerar (to exaggerate). | *To put on airs*, darse tono. | *To put on one's Sunday best*, ponerse de tiros largos. | *To put on weight*, engordar. | *To put s.o. on*, pasar la comunicación a alguien. | *To put s.o. on to s.o. else*, hablar a una persona de otra, dar a una persona el nombre de otra (to speak to s.o. about s.o. else), poner a una persona con otra (on the telephone). | *Who put you on to it?*, ¿quién le dio la información? || **To put out,** apagar, extinguir (flames, fire). | Apagar (light, radio, record player, etc.). | Echar, expulsar (to dismiss, to eject). | Sacar [por la noche] (a cat). | Alargar, tender (one's hand). | Alargar, extender (one's arm). | Asomar, sacar (one's head). | Sacar (one's tongue). | Sacar (s.o.'s eyes). | Sacar: *the snail puts out its horns*, el caracol saca los cuernos. | Bot. Echar (leaves) | Sacar, enseñar (to show). | Sacar, publicar (to issue): *this publisher puts out some very good books*, esta editorial publica unos libros muy buenos. | Extender, hacer correr (a rumour). | Hacer (an announcement). | Sacar, producir (to produce industrially). | Tender, poner a secar (clothes to dry). | Dislocar (a joint). | Dar fuera (to give work out of the premises). | Molestar (to bother, to annoy). | Desconcertar (to disconcert). | Enfadar (to irritate). | Izar (flags). | Mar. Hacerse a la mar (to head seawards), botar, echar al mar (to launch). | Comm. Invertir, colocar (money). | Sp. Poner fuera de combate (in boxing), eliminar (in cricket, baseball). | — *To put o.s. out*, molestarse: *don't put yourself out on my account*, no se moleste usted por mí. | *To put the washing out to dry*, poner a secar la ropa. || **To put over,** hacer aceptar (idea, product). | Aplazar, diferir (to postpone). | Conseguir (to succeed). | Comunicar, hacer comprender (to communicate). | — Fig. *To put one over on s.o.*, engañar a alguien. | *To put o.s. over*, impresionar, causar impresión. || **To put through,** hacer pasar (suffering). | Hacer aceptar (a proposal). | Hacer aprobar (a bill). | Llevar a cabo (a business deal). | Poner: *to put through a telephone call to Madrid*, poner una conferencia a Madrid. | Poner con: *put me through to this number*, póngame con este número de teléfono. | — *To put s.o. through an examination*, hacer sufrir un examen a alguien. | Fam. *To put s.o. through it*, hacerle pasar un mal rato a uno. || **To put to,** enganchar (to harness, to couple). || **To put together,** unir, reunir, juntar (to join). | Comparar (facts). | Math. Sumar. | Confeccionar (a dress). | Tech. Ensamblar, acoplar (pieces). | Montar (a machine). | — Fig. *To put two and two together*, atar cabos. || **To put up,** levantar (the window of a wagon, one's hand). | Colgar, poner (to hang up): *to put up a curtain*, colgar una cortina. | Recogerse (one's hair). | Subirse (one's collar). | Izar (flag). | Oponer (resistance). | Librar (a fight). | Aumentar, subir (prices). | Alojar, hospedar (to provide lodgings): *I can't put you up*, no puedo alojarle. | Alojarse (to lodge): *I put up at a small hotel*, me alojo en un hotel pequeño. | Fijar, pegar (to post up): *to put up a poster*, fijar un cartel. | Colocar, poner (a ladder). | Empaquetar, embalar, envolver (to pack). | Apostar (to stake money). | Comm. Proporcionar, dar, poner (funds): *to put up the money for an undertaking*, poner el dinero para una empresa. | Colgar (the telephone receiver). | Abrir (umbrella). | Envainar (a sword). | Construir (to build): *this building was put up in ten months*, este edificio fue construido en diez meses. | Preparar (meal, etc.). | Levantar (partridge, etc.). | Informar, decir (to inform): *to put s.o. up to a thing*, informar a alguien de algo, decir algo a alguien. | Representar, dar (a play). | Dar, ofrecer (prize). | Incitar, impulsar (to incite): *they put me up to do it*, me incitaron a hacerlo. | Fam. Tramar, urdir, preparar (a dirty trick), inventar (a yarn). || Jur. Presentar la candidatura de, proponer (s.o. as a candidate), presentar su candidatura, presentarse (o.s.), presentar (a petition). | Aut. Aparcar (a car). | U. S. Poner en conserva, conservar (to preserve fruit, etc.). | — *Put them up!*, ¡manos arriba! | *To put up a prayer to*, rezar a. | *To put up banns*, correr las amonestaciones. | *To put up for auction*, subastar, sacar a subasta. | *To put up for sale*, poner en venta. | *To put up with*, aguantar, soportar (to stand, to bear), arreglárselas con, conformarse con, contentarse con (to content o.s. with). || **To put upon,** engañar (to deceive). | Molestar (to bother).

— Observ. Pret. & p. p. **put.**

putative [ˈpju:tətiv] adj. Putativo, va (relation). || Supuesto, ta (supposed).

put-off [ˈputˌɔf] n. Aplazamiento, *m.* (postponement).

put-on [ˈputˌɔn] n. Afectación, *f.*

put-out [ˈputaut] n. Sp. Eliminación, *f.* (in baseball).

putrefaction [ˌpju:triˈfækʃən] n. Putrefacción, *f.*

putrefiable [ˈpju:trifaiəbl] adj. Putrescible.

putrefied [ˈpju:trifaid] adj. Putrefacto, ta.

putrefy [ˈpju:trifai] v. tr. Pudrir, podrir.

— V. intr. Pudrirse, podrirse. || Med. Supurar. | Gangrenarse. || Fig. Corromperse, pudrirse.

putrescence [pju:ˈtresns] n. Putrefacción, *f.*

putrescent [pju:ˈtresnt] adj. Putrescente.

putrescible [pjuˈtresibl] adj. Putrescible.

putrid [ˈpju:trid] adj. En putrefacción, pútrido, da; podrido, da; putrefacto, ta (rotten). || Fig. Depravado, da (depraved). || Fam. Asqueroso, sa (dirty). | Malísimo, ma (very bad). || Med. Gangrenoso, sa.

putridity [pju:ˈtriditi] or **putridness** [ˈpju:tridnis] n. Putridez, *f.*, putrefacción, *f.*

putsch [putʃ] n. Golpe (*m.*) de Estado, alzamiento, *m.*, pronunciamiento, *m.*, "putsch", *m.*

putt [pʌt] n. Sp. Golpe (*m.*) corto, tiro (*m.*) al hoyo, "put", *m.* (in golf).

putt [pʌt] v. tr. Sp. Dar un golpe corto a, tirar al hoyo (the ball).

puttee [ˈpʌti] n. Polaina, *f.*

putter [ˈpʌtə*] n. Sp. Palo (*m.*) para los golpes cortos, "putter", *m.* (in golf).

putter [ˈpʌtə*] v. intr. U. S. See potter.

putting [ˈputiŋ] n. Colocación, *f.* || Comm. Concesión, *f.* (of shares). || Fig. Presentación, *f.* || Puesta, *f.*: *putting into cultivation, into orbit, into service*, puesta en cultivo, en órbita, en servicio. || — *Putting about*, puesta (*f.*) en circulación (of rumours). || *Putting away*, colocación, *f.*, ahorro, *m.* (of money), colocación (*f.*) en orden (of things), alejamiento, *m.* (removal). || *Putting back*, colocación (*f.*) en su sitio (of things), aplazamiento, *m.* (postponement), regreso (*m.*) al puerto (of a boat), retraso, *m.* (delay). || *Putting by*, ahorro, *m.* (of money). || *Putting down*, inscripción, *f.* (in writing), sofocación, *f.* (of rebellion), rebajamiento, *m.* (of pride), fondeo, *m.* (of a buoy). || *Putting forth*, publicación, *f.* (of a book), despliegue, *m.* (display). || *Putting forward*, adelanto, *m.* (of a clock), presentación, *f.*, propuesta, *f.* (of a theory), exposición, *f.* || *Putting in*, introducción, *f.* (introduction), candidatura, *f.* (application), presentación, *f.* (of a legal document), escala, *f.* (for a boat), ejecución, *f.* (of an embargo). || *Putting off*, aplazamiento, *m.* (postponement). || *Putting on*, aumento, *m.*, subida, *f.* (of prices), adelanto, *m.* (of a clock), encendido, *m.* (of light), puesta (*f.*) en marcha (of radio, record player, etc.), colocación, *f.* (of a dress), montaje, *m.* (of a play), puesta (*f.*) en servicio (of trains), frenado, *m.* (of brakes), afectación, *f.* || *Putting out*, expulsión, *f.* (ejection), colocación, *f.* (of money), extinción, *f.* (of fire), alargamiento, *m.* (of arm), luxación, *f.* (of shoulder). || Sp. *Putting the shot* o *the weight*, el lanzamiento del peso. || *Putting through*, conexión, *f.* (telephone), éxito, *m.* (success), realización, *f.* (of a deal). || *Putting to*, enganche, *m.* || *Putting together*, acoplamiento, *m.*, ensambladura, *f.* (of pieces), montaje, *m.* (of machine), comparación, *f.* (of facts). || Mar. *Putting to sea*, salida, *f.* || *Putting up*, colocación, *f.* (hanging up), alojamiento, *m.* (lodging), empaquetado, *m.*, embalaje, *m.* (packing), aumento, *m.*, subida, *f.* (of prices), colocación, *f.* (of posters), publicación, *f.* (of bills, banns), presentación, *f.* (of a candidate), construcción, *f.* (building), garaje, *m.* (of cars).

putting [ˈpʌtiŋ] n. Sp. Deporte (*m.*) parecido al golf. || *Putting green*, campo (*m.*) más pequeño que el utilizado para jugar al golf.
putty [ˈpʌti] n. Masilla, *f.* (glazier's). || *Putty knife*, espátula (*f.*) para enmasillar.
putty [ˈpʌti] v. tr. Poner masilla a, enmasillar.
put-up [ˈputˈʌp] adj. Fam. Preparado de antemano: *it's a put-up job*, es una cosa preparada de antemano. | Amañado, da (match, etc.).
put-upon [ˈputəˌpɔn] adj. Engañado, da.
puzzle [ˈpʌzl] n. Enigma, *m.*, misterio, *m.*, lío, *m.* (a problem). || Perplejidad, *f.* (bewiderment). || Rompecabezas, *m. inv.* (game): *Chinese puzzle*, rompecabezas chino. || Acertijo, *m.*, adivinanza, *f.* (riddle). || — *Crossword puzzle*, crucigrama, *m.* || *Jigsaw puzzle*, rompecabezas, *m. inv.* || *To be in a puzzle*, estar hecho un lío. || *Your mother is a real puzzle to me*, no acabo de entender a su madre.
puzzle [ˈpʌzl] v. tr. Desconcertar, dejar perplejo (to bewilder). || — *He was puzzled how to answer the letter*, no sabía cómo contestar la carta. || *To puzzle out*, descifrar (a letter), esclarecer, aclarar (a mystery), resolver, solucionar (a problem).
— V. intr. Romperse la cabeza, devanarse los sesos [para resolver]: *to puzzle over a problem*, romperse la cabeza con un problema.
puzzled [—d] adj. Perplejo, ja; desconcertado, da.
puzzlement [—mənt] n. Perplejidad, *f.*, desconcierto, *m.* (bewilderment).
puzzler [—lə*] n. Enigma, *m.*, misterio, *m.* || Fam. Pega, *f.*: *to ask s.o. puzzlers*, plantearle a uno pegas. || *That's a puzzler!*, ¡qué pregunta más difícil!, ¡qué difícil!
puzzling [—liŋ] adj. Misterioso, sa; enigmático, ca. || *It is puzzling that he didn't come*, es extraño que no haya venido.
pycnometer [pikˈnɔmitə*] n. Picnómetro, *m.*
pyelitis [paiəˈlaitis] n. Med. Pielitis, *f.*
pygmaean [pigˈmi:ən] adj. Pigmeo, a.
Pygmalion [pigˈmeiljən] pr. n. Pigmalión, *m.*
pygmean [pigˈmi:ən] adj. Pigmeo, a.
pygmy [ˈpigmi] adj./n. Enano, na (dwarf).
Pygmy [ˈpigmi] adj./n. Pigmeo, a.
pyjamas [pəˈdʒɑ:məz] pl. n. Pijama, *m. sing.*
pyknic [ˈpiknik] adj. Pícnico, ca.
pylon [ˈpailən] n. Pilón, *m.* (of an Egyptian temple). || Electr. Poste, *m.*, torre (*f.*) metálica (for cables, etc.).
pyloric [paiˈlɔrik] adj. Pilórico, ca.
pylorus [paiˈlɔ:rəs] n. Anat. Píloro, *m.*

— Observ. El plural de *pylorus* es *pylori*.

pyorrhoea (U. S. **pyorrhea**) [ˌpaiəˈriə] n. Med. Piorrea, *f.*
pyramid [pirəmid] n. Arch. Math. Pirámide, *f.*
pyramidal [piˈræmidl] adj. Piramidal.
pyramidion [piraˈmidiən] n. Arch. Piramidión, *m.*
pyre [ˈpaiə*] n. Pira, *f.*, hoguera, *f.* (for burning).
Pyrenean [ˌpirəˈni:ən] adj. Pirenaico, ca.
Pyrenees [ˌpirəˈni:z] pl. pr. n. Geogr. Pirineos, *m.*
pyrethrum [pəiˈri:θrəm] n. Bot. Pelitre, *m.*
pyretic [paiˈretik] adj. Pirético, ca.
Pyrex [ˈpaireks] n. Culin. Pirex, *m.*
pyrexia [paiˈreksiə] n. Med. Pirexia, *f.*
pyrheliometer [pə:hi:liˈɔmitə*] n. Pirheliómetro, *m.*
pyrite [ˈpairait] n. Min. Pirita *f.*
pyrites [paiˈraiti:z] n. Min. Pirita, *f.*
pyrography [paiˈrɔgrəfi] or **pyrogravure** [pairəgrəˈvjuə*] n. Pirograbado, *m.*
pyrolysis [paiˈrɔlisis] n. Chem. Pirolisis, *f.*
pyromancy [ˈpairəumænsi] n. Piromancia, *f.*
pyromania [ˌpairəuˈmeiniə] n. Piromanía, *f.*
pyromaniac [ˌpairəuˈmeiˈniæk] n. Pirómano, na.
pyromaniacal [ˌpairəuməˈnaiəkəl] adj. Pirómano, na.
pyrometer [paiˈrɔmitə*] n. Pirómetro, *m.*
pyrometry [paiˈrɔmitri] n. Pirometría, *f.*
pyrophosphate [ˌpairəuˈfɔsfeit] n. Chem. Pirofosfato, *m.* (salt, ester).
pyrophosphoric [ˌpairəufɔsˈfɔrik] adj. Chem. Pirofosfórico (acid).
pyrosis [paiˈrəusis] n. Med. Pirosis, *f.*
pyrosphere [ˈpairəsfi:ə*] n. Geol. Pirosfera, *f.*
pyrotechnic [ˌpairəuˈteknik] adj. Pirotécnico, ca. || *Pyrotechnic display*, fuegos (*m. pl.*) artificiales.
pyrotechnical [—əl] adj. Pirotécnico, ca.
pyrotechnics [—s] n. Pirotecnia, *f.*
pyrotechnist [ˌpairəuˈteknist] n. Pirotécnico, *m.*, artificiero, *m.*
pyrotechny [ˌpairəuˈtekni] n. Pirotecnia, *f.*
piroxene [paiˈrɔksi:n] n. Piroxeno, *m.*
pyroxylin or **pyroxyline** [paiˈrɔksilin] n. Piroxilina, *f.*, algodón (*m.*) pólvora.
pyrrhic [ˈpirik] adj. Pírrico, ca: *pyrrhic victory*, victoria pírrica.
— N. Pirriquio, *m.* (poetry).
Pyrrhus [ˈpirəs] pr. n. Pirro, *m.*
Pythagoras [paiˈθægəræs] pr. n. Pitágoras, *m.*
Pythagorean [paiˌθægəˈriən] adj./n. Pitagórico, ca. || *Pythagorean table*, tabla pitagórica *or* de Pitágoras.
Pythia [ˈpiθiə] n. Pitia, *f.*
Pythian [—n] adj. Pitio, tia (of the oracle). || Pítico, ca (of the games).
python [ˈpaiθən] n. Pitón, *m.* (snake).
pythoness [ˈpaiθənes] n. Pitonisa, *f.*
pyx [piks] n. Rel. Copón, *m.*, píxide, *f.* || *Pyx cloth*, paño (*m.*) de cáliz.

Q

q [kju:] n. Q, *f.* (letter).
qua [kwei] adv. Como.
quack [kwæk] adj. Falso, sa. || De curandero (remedy). || — *Quack doctor*, curandero, *m.* || *Quack powder*, polvos (*m. pl.*) de la madre Celestina.
— N. Graznido, *m.* (of a duck). || Curandero, *m.* (fraudulent doctor). || Matasanos, *m. inv.* (bad doctor). || Charlatán, *m.* (impostor).
quack [kwæk] v. intr. Graznar (the duck). || Fam. Cotorrear (to chatter). | Dárselas de listo (to show off).
— V. tr. Encomiar, ensalzar (a remedy, etc.).
quackery [kwækəri] n. Curandería, *f.*, curanderismo, *m.* (of a quack doctor). || Charlatanismo, *m.* (of an impostor).
quad [kwɔd] n. See QUADRANGLE & QUADRAT. || — Pl. Cuatrillizos, zas (quadruplets).
quadragenarian [ˌkwɔdrədʒəˈnεəriən] adj/n. Cuadragenario, ria.
Quadragesima [ˌkwɔdrəˈdʒesimə] n. Rel. Cuadragésima, *f.*: *Quadragesima Sunday*, domingo de la Cuadragésima.
quadrangle [ˈkwɔdræŋgl] n. Math. Cuadrilátero, *m.* (figure with four sides). | Cuadrángulo, *m.* (figure with four angles). || Patio, *m.* (of a college).
quadrangular [kwɔˈdræŋgjulə*] adj. Cuadrangular. || Cuadrilátero, ra.
quadrant [ˈkwɔdrənt] n. Cuadrante, *m.*
quadrat [ˈkwɔdrit] n. Print. Cuadratín, *m.*
quadrate [kwɔˈdreit] v. intr. Cuadrar (*with*, con).
— V. tr. Cuadrar. || Hacer cuadrar (*to*, *with*, con).
quadratic [kwəˈdrætik] adj. Math. Cuadrático, ca; de segundo grado.
— N. Math. Ecuación (*f.*) de segundo grado.
quadrature [ˈkwɔdrətʃə*] n. Cuadratura, *f.*
quadrennial [ˌkwɔˈdreniəl] adj. Cuadrienal.
quadrennium [kwɔˈdreni:əm] n. Cuadrienio, *m.*, cuatrienio, *m.*

— Observ. El plural de la palabra *quadrennium* es *quadrenniums* o *quadrennia*.

quadriceps [ˈkwɔdriseps] n. Anat. Cuadríceps, *m.*
quadriga [kwəˈdri:gə] n. Cuadriga, *f.*

— Observ. El plural de la palabra inglesa es *quadrigae*.

quadrigeminal [kwɔdriˈdʒeminəl] adj. Anat. Cuadrigémino.
quadrilateral [ˌkwɔdriˈlætərəl] adj. Cuadrilátero, ra.
— N. Cuadrilátero, *m.*
quadrille [kwəˈdril] n. Cuadrilla, *f.* (dance). || Cuatrillo, *m.* (card game).
quadrillion [kwɔˈdriljən] n. Cuatrillón, *m.*

— Observ. Esta cifra equivale a 10^{24} en Gran Bretaña y en España y a 10^{15} en Estados Unidos.

quadripartite [ˌkwɔdriˈpɑ:tait] adj. Cuadripartido, da; cuadripartito, ta: *quadripartite convention*, convenio cuadripartito.
quadrisyllabic [ˈkwɔdrisiˈlæbik] adj. Cuatrisílabo, ba.
quadrisyllable [ˌkwɔdriˈsiləbl] n. Cuatrisílabo, *m.*

quadrivalent [ˌkwɔdriˈveilənt] adj. CHEM. Tetravalente, cuadrivalente.
quadrivium [kwɔˈdriviəm] n. Cuadrivio, *m.* (in medieval universities).

— OBSERV. El plural de *quadrivium* es *quadrivia*.

quadroon [kwɔˈdru:n] n. Cuarterón, ona.
quadrumane [ˈkwɔdrumein] n. Cuadrumano, *m.*
quadrumanous [kwɔˈdru:mənəs] adj. Cuadrumano, na.
quadruped [ˈkwɔdruped] adj. Cuadrúpedo, da.
— N. Cuadrúpedo, *m.*
quadrupedal [kwɔdruˈpədl] adj. Cuadrupedal.
quadruple [ˈkwɔdrupl] adj. Cuádruple. || MUS. *Quadruple measure* o *time*, compás (*m.*) de dos por cuatro.
— N. Cuádruplo, *m.*
quadruple [ˈkwɔdrupl] v. tr./intr. Cuadruplicar, cuadriplicar.
quadruplets [ˈkwɔdruplits] pl. n. Cuatrillizos, zas.
quadruplicate [kwɔˈdru:plikit] adj. Cuadruplicado, da; cuadriplicado, da. || *In quadruplicate*, en cuatro ejemplares, por cuadruplicado.
quadruplicate [kwɔˈdru:plikeit] v. tr. Sacar cuatro copias de (to make four copies of). || Cuadruplicar, cuadriplicar (to quadruple).
quadruplication [kwɔdru:pliˈkeiʃən] n. Cuadruplicación, *f.*
quaestor [ˈkwi:stə*] n. Cuestor, *m.*
quaestorship [ˈkwi:stəʃip] n. Cuestura, *f.*
quaff [kwɑ:f] v. tr./intr. Beber [a grandes tragos].
quag [kwæg] n. See QUAGMIRE.
quaggy [—i] adj. Pantanoso, sa; cenagoso, sa.
quagmire [ˈkwægmaiə*] n. Tremedal, *m.*, ciénaga, *f.*, cenagal, *m.* (boggy ground). || FIG. Atolladero, *m.*
quail [kweil] n. Codorniz, *f.* (bird).
quail [kweil] v. intr. Acobardarse (*before*, ante).
quaint [kweint] adj. Pintoresco, ca (picturesque): *a quaint little village*, un pueblecito pintoresco. || Original, singular: *a quaint person*, una persona original. || Extraño, ña (odd): *a quaint tale*, una historia extraña.
quaintness [—nis] n. Lo pintoresco (of a place, custom, etc.). || Originalidad, *f.*, singularidad, *f.* (of a person). || Lo extraño, rareza, *f.* (oddity).
quake [kweik] n. Temblor, *m.*
quake [kweik] v. intr. Temblar (to shake violently): *he was quaking with fear, with cold*, temblaba de miedo, de frío; *the earth quaked*, tembló la tierra. || Estremecerse (to shake inwardly). || — *He is quaking at the knees*, le flaquean las piernas. || FAM. *To quake in one's shoes*, temblar como un azogado.
Quaker [ˈkweikə*] n. REL. Cuáquero, ra.
Quakerism [—rizəm] n. REL. Cuaquerismo, *m.*
quaking bog [kweikiŋˈbɔg] n. Tremedal, *m.*
quaky [ˈkweiki] adj. Tembloroso, sa.
qualification [ˌkwɔlifiˈkeiʃən] n. Reserva, *f.*, restricción, *f.*: *we can accept his statement without qualification*, podemos aceptar su declaración sin reserva. || Aptitud, *f.*, capacidad, *f.*, competencia, *f.*: *to have the necessary qualifications for a post*, tener las aptitudes requeridas *or* la competencia requerida para un puesto. || Requisito, *m.*: *the qualifications for membership of a club*, los requisitos para ser miembro de un club. || Título, *m.*: *applicants must bring their qualifications with them*, los candidatos tienen que traer sus títulos. || Calificación, *f.* (description). || JUR. Capacidad, *f.*
qualified [ˈkwɔlifaid] adj. Competente: *qualified persons*, personas competentes. || Capacitado, da: *he is not qualified to do that job*, no está capacitado para hacer ese trabajo. || Cualificado, da; calificado, da (skilled). || Que tiene título, titulado, da: *qualified expert*, experto que tiene título. || Con reservas: *they gave the scheme their qualified approval*, aprobaron el proyecto con reservas. || Limitado, da; restringido, da: *in a qualified sense*, en un sentido limitado. || JUR. Capacitado, da: *he is qualified to vote*, está capacitado para votar.
qualify [ˈkwɔlifai] v. tr. Capacitar (to entitle): *he is not qualified to teach English*, no está capacitado para enseñar inglés. || Capacitar, habilitar, dar derecho: *residence qualifies you for membership*, la residencia le capacita para hacerse socio. || Calificar: *would you qualify his behaviour as offensive?*, ¿calificaría su comportamiento de ofensivo? || Modificar (to modify). || Mitigar, atenuar (to mitigate). || Limitar, restringir (to limit). || GRAMM. Calificar: *adverbs qualify verbs*, los adverbios califican los verbos. || JUR. Habilitar, capacitar. || — *To qualify one's acceptance*, aceptar con reservas. || *To qualify o.s. for a job*, adquirir la competencia *or* sacar los títulos necesarios para un puesto.
— V. intr. Capacitarse. || Estudiar: *to qualify for medicine*, estudiar medicina. || Sacar el título de: *to qualify as a doctor*, sacar el título de médico. || Satisfacer los requisitos (for a post, a vote, etc.). || SP. Clasificarse.
qualifying [—iŋ] adj. Calificativo, va (adjective). || Eliminatorio, ria (round, exam).
qualitative [ˈkwɔlitətiv] adj. Cualitativo, va: *qualitative analysis*, análisis cualitativo.
quality [ˈkwɔliti] n. Calidad, *f.*: *of good, of poor quality*, de buena, de mala calidad; *we aim at quality rather than quantity*, preferimos la calidad a la cantidad. || Calidad, *f.*, clase, *f.*, categoría, *f.* (degree of excellence): *goods of the first quality*, géneros de primera calidad. || Calidad, *f.* (status): *person of quality*, persona de calidad; *in quality of*, en calidad de. || Cualidad, *f.* (attribute): *she has many good qualities*, tiene muchas buenas cualidades. || Don, *m.*: *he has the quality of inspiring confidence*, tiene el don de inspirar confianza. || MUS. Timbre, *m.* || — *Quality control*, control (*m.*) de la calidad. || *The quality*, la nobleza (nobility), la flor y nata (the best).
— Adj. De calidad: *quality goods*, productos de calidad.
qualm [kwɑ:m] n. MED. Náusea, *f.*, ansias, *f. pl.* (nausea). | Mareo, *m.* (at sea). || FIG. Escrúpulo, *m.*: *to have no qualms about doing sth.*, no tener ningún escrúpulo en hacer algo. | Remordimiento, *m.*: *qualms of conscience*, remordimientos de conciencia. | Aprensión, *f.*, inquietud, *f.* (worry). | Duda, *f.*, incertidumbre, *f.* (doubt).
qualmish [—iʃ] adj. MED. Que tiene náuseas *or* ansias. || FIG. Escrupuloso, sa. | Preocupado, da; lleno de aprensión (worried). | Dudoso, sa; incierto, ta (uncertain).
quandary [ˈkwɔndəri] n. Dilema, *m.*: *to be in a quandary*, estar en un dilema. || Apuro, *m.*, aprieto, *m.* (difficulty).
quanta [ˈkwɔntə] pl. n. See QUANTUM.
quantic [ˈkwɔntik] adj. Cuántico, ca.
quantification [kwɔntifiˈkeiʃən] n. Cuantificación, *f.*
quantify [ˈkwɔntifai] v. tr. Determinar la cantidad de, cuantificar (to determine the quantity of). || PHIL. Cuantificar.
quantitative [ˈkwɔntitətiv] adj. Cuantitativo, va: *quantitative analysis*, análisis cuantitativo.
quantity [ˈkwɔntiti] n. Cantidad, *f.*: *a small quantity of cement*, una pequeña cantidad de cemento; *to buy in large quantities*, comprar en grandes cantidades. || Gran cantidad, *f.*: *a quantity of jewellery*, una gran cantidad de joyas. || MATH. GRAMM. PHIL. Cantidad, *f.* || — *Quantity production*, producción (*f.*) en serie. || *Quantity surveyor*, aparejador, *m.* || MATH. *Unknown quantity*, incógnita, *f.*
quantum [ˈkwɔntəm] n. Parte, *f.* (share). || PHYS. Quantum, *m.*, cuanto, *m.* || — PHYS. *Quantum number*, número cuántico. || *Quantum theory*, teoría (*f.*) de los quanta *or* de los cuanta *or* cuántica.

— OBSERV. El plural de la palabra *quantum* es *quanta*.

quarantine [ˈkwɔrənti:n] n. Cuarentena, *f.* (period of isolation): *to put in quarantine*, poner en cuarentena. || *Quarantine service*, servicio (*m.*) de sanidad.
quarantine [ˈkwɔrənti:n] v. tr. Poner en cuarentena.
quarrel [ˈkwɔrəl] n. Riña, *f.*, disputa, *f.*, pelea, *f.*, camorra, *f.* (angry dispute). || — *I have no quarrel with him*, no tengo nada en contra suya. || *To espouse* o *to take up s.o.'s quarrel*, tomar el partido de alguien. || *To have a quarrel with*, pelearse con, reñir con. || *To make up a quarrel*, hacer las paces, reconciliarse. || *To pick a quarrel with*, tener una pelea con. || *To try to pick a quarrel with s.o.*, buscar camorra con alguien.
quarrel [ˈkwɔrəl] v. intr. Pelearse, pelear, reñir (to argue): *children sometimes quarrel*, a veces los niños se pelean. || Reñir (to fall out). || Regañar: *he quarrelled with me for having done the wrong thing*, me regañó por haber hecho lo que no debía. || Quejarse (*with*, de) [to complain].
quarreller (U. S. **quarreler**) [—ə*] n. Pendenciero, ra; peleón, ona.
quarrelling (U. S. **quarreling**) [—iŋ] n. Disputas, *f. pl.* (quarrels).
— Adj. Pendenciero, ra; peleón, ona.
quarrelsome [—səm] adj. Peleón, ona; pendenciero, ra (inclined to quarrel). || Enfadadizo, za (quick-tempered).
quarrelsomeness [—səmnis] n. Carácter (*m.*) pendenciero. || Humor (*m.*) belicoso.
quarry [ˈkwɔri] n. MIN. Cantera, *f.* || Presa, *f.* (in hunting). || FIG. Mina, *f.*, cantera, *f.* (source of information, etc.). | Presa, *f.* (prey). | Persona (*f.*) acorralada (pursued person). || (Ant.). Encarne, *m.*, encarna, *f.* (fleshing of the hounds). || FIG. *He became the quarry of the nation's police force*, fue acorralado por la policía de todo el país.
quarry [ˈkwɔri] v. tr. MIN. Extraer, sacar. || FIG. Sacar (information from books).
— V. intr. MIN. Explotar una cantera. || FIG. Buscar información.
quarryman [—mən] n. Cantero, *m.*, picapedrero, *m.*

— OBSERV. El plural de *quarryman* es *quarrymen*.

quart [kwɔ:t] n. Cuarto (*m.*) de galón (measure).
quart [kɑ:t] n. See QUARTE.
quartan [ˈkwɔ:tn] adj. MED. Cuartanal.
— N. MED. Cuartana, *f.*
quarte [kɑ:t] n. SP. Cuarta, *f.* (in fencing). || Cuarta, *f.* (in card games).
quarter [ˈkwɔ:tə*] n. Cuarto, *m.* (of hour, circle, century, etc.): *quarter of an hour*, cuarto de hora; *three quarters*, tres cuartos; *to strike the quarters*, dar los cuartos; *an hour and a quarter*, una hora y cuarto; *a quarter past nine*, las nueve y cuarto; *a quarter*

to seven, las siete menos cuarto. || Cuarto, *m.* (of a pound): *a pound and a quarter*, una libra y un cuarto. || Cuarta parte, *f.*, cuarto, *m.*: *a quarter of an apple*, la cuarta parte de una manzana; *a quarter of the film was boring*, una cuarta parte de la película era aburrida; *what's a quarter of 64?*, ¿qué es la cuarta parte de 64? || Trimestre, *m.*: *during the first quarter of this year*, durante el primer trimestre de este año. || Alquiler (*m.*) trimestral (rent). || ASTR. Cuarto, *m.* (moon): *first, last quarter*, cuarto creciente, menguante. || SP. Tiempo, *m.* (period of playing time). | Cuarto (*m.*) de milla, cuatrocientos metros, *m. pl.* (race). || Cuarto, *m.* (of beef, etc.). || Barrio, *m.* (district): *the old quarter of the town*, el barrio viejo de la ciudad. || MAR. Cuarta, *f.* (division of the compass). | Cuarto (*m.*) de braza (fourth part of a fathom). | Aleta, *f.* (of a ship). | Dirección, *f.* (of the wind). || FIG. Lado, *m.*: *don't look for help from that quarter*, no busques ayuda por aquel lado. | Parte, *f.*, región, *f.* (region). | Fuente, *f.*: *information from a reliable quarter*, información de fuente fidedigna. || Cuartel, *m.*: *to give no quarter to the enemy*, no dar cuartel al enemigo. || U. S. Cuarto (*m.*) de dólar, veinticinco centavos, *m. pl.* (value and coin). || HERALD. Cuartel, *m.* (division of a shield). || — Pl. Cuartos (*m.*) traseros (of an animal). || MAR. Puesto (*m. sing.*) de combate. || Alojamiento, *m. sing.* (lodgings). || Residencia, *f. sing.*, domicilio, *m. sing.*: *to shift one's quarters*, cambiar de domicilio. || MIL. Residencia, *f. sing.*: *officers' quarters*, residencia de oficiales. | Cuartel, *m. sing.* (for soldiers): *winter quarters*, cuartel de invierno. || FAM. Trasero, *m. sing.* (bottom). || — *At close quarters*, muy cerca: *to explode at close quarters*, explotar muy cerca; de cerca: *to see s.o. at close quarters*, ver a alguien de cerca; cuerpo a cuerpo (to fight). || FIG. *From all quarters* o *from every quarter*, de todas partes. || *From all quarters of the globe*, de todas las partes del mundo. || *In high quarters*, en las altas esferas. || *It is a quarter as large*, es cuatro veces menos ancho. || *Living quarters*, alojamiento, residencia. || *To ask for quarter* o *to cry quarter*, pedir tregua. || *To give quarter to*, dar cuartel a. || *To take up one's quarters at* o *in*, alojarse en. || *What quarter is the wind in?*, ¿de qué lado sopla el viento?

quarter [ˈkwɔ:tə*] v. tr. Dividir en cuartos, cuartear (to divide into four parts). || MIL. Acuartelar (to lodge troops). || Alojar (to lodge). || Descuartizar (meat). || HERALD. Cuartelar. || HIST. Descuartizar (the body of a criminal).
— V. intr. Acuartelarse (troops). || Alojarse (to lodge).

quarter binding [—ˈbaindiŋ] n. Media pasta, *f.*, encuadernación (*f.*) a la holandesa.

quarter-bound [—baund] adj. Encuadernado a la holandesa *or* con media pasta.

quarter day [—dei] n. Primer día (*m.*) del trimestre.

quarterdeck or **quarter-deck** [—dek] n. MAR. Alcázar, *m.*

quarterfinal [—ˈfainl] n. SP. Cuarto (*m.*) de final.

quartering [—riŋ] n. División (*f.*) en cuatro partes (partition). || Corte (*m.*) a escuadra (of a log). || Descuartizamiento, *m.* (of a criminal). || Alojamiento, *m.* (lodging). || MIL. Acuartelamiento, *m.* || HERALD. Cuartel, *m.*

quarterly [—li] adj. Trimestral.
— Adv. Trimestralmente, cada tres meses.
— N. Publicación (*f.*) trimestral.

quartermaster [—ˌmɑ:stə*] n. MAR. Cabo (*m.*) de la Marina. || MIL. Oficial (*m.*) de Intendencia.

Quartermaster Corps [—ˌmɑ:stə*kɔ:*] n. MIL. Servicio (*m.*) de Intendencia.

quartermaster general [—ˌmɑ:stə*ˈdʒenərəl] n. MIL. Intendente (*m.*) general.

quartermaster sergeant [—ˌmɑ:stə*ˈsɑ:dʒənt] n. MIL. Sargento (*m.*) mayor.

quartern [ˈkwɔ:tə:n] n. Barra (*f.*) de pan de cuatro libras (loaf). || Cuarta parte, *f.*, cuarto, *m.* (quarter).

quarter note [ˈkwɔ:təˌnəut] n. MUS. Negra, *f.*

quarter-phase [ˈkwɔ:təˌfeiz] adj. Bifásico, ca.

quarter right [ˈkwɔ:təˌrait] n. MIL. Media vuelta (*f.*) a la derecha.

quarter round [ˈkwɔ:təraund] n. ARCH. Cuarto bocel, *m.*, óvolo, *m.*

quarter sessions [ˈkwɔ:təˈseʃənz] pl. n. Audiencia (*f. sing.*) trimestral.

quarterstaff [ˈkwɔ:tə*stɑ:f] n. Barra, *f.* (stick).

— OBSERV. El plural de esta palabra es *quarterstaves*.

quarter tone [ˈkwɔ:tətəun] n. Cuarto (*m.*) de tono.

quartet or **quartette** [kwɔ:ˈtet] n. MUS. Cuarteto, *m.*

quartile [ˈkwɔ:tail] n. MATH. Cuartila, *f.*, cuartil, *m.*

quarto [ˈkwɔ:təu] n. En cuarto, *m.*, libro (*m.*) en cuarto.

quartz [kwɔ:ts] n. MIN. Cuarzo, *m.*

quartzite [ˈkwɔ:tˌsait] n. MIN. Cuarcita, *f.*

quartzose [ˈkwɔ:tsəus] or **quartzous** [ˈkwɔ:tsəs] adj. Cuarzoso, sa.

quash [kwɔʃ] v. tr. JUR. Anular. || Reprimir, sofocar, ahogar (a feeling, an uprising): *to quash a rebellion*, reprimir una rebelión.

quasi [ˈkwɑ:zi:] adv. Cuasi, casi. || — JUR. *Quasi contract*, cuasicontrato, *m.* || *Quasi delict*, cuasidelito, *m.*

Quasimodo Sunday [ˌkwɑ:ziˈməudəuˈsʌndi] n. Domingo (*m.*) de Cuasimodo.

quassia [ˈkwɔʃə] n. BOT. Cuasia, *f.*

quatercentenary [ˌkwætəsenˈti:nəri] n. Cuarto centenario, *m.*

quaternary [kwəˈtə:nəri] adj. Cuaternario, ria.
— N. GEOL. Cuaternario, *m.*

quaternion [kwəˈtə:njən] n. MATH. Cuaternio, *m.*, cuaternión, *m.*

quatrain [ˈkwɔtrein] n. Cuarteto, *m.* (poetry).

quatrefoil [ˈkætrəfɔil] n. ARCH. Cuatrifolio, *m.*

quaver [ˈkweivə*] n. MUS. Corchea, *f.* (note). | Trino, *m.* (trill). || Temblor, *m.* (of the voice). || *With a quaver in his voice*, con voz trémula.

quaver [ˈkweivə*] v. intr. Temblar (voice). || MUS. Hacer trinos, trinar.
— V. tr. Decir con voz trémula.

quavering [—riŋ] or **quavery** [—ri] adj. Tembloroso, sa; trémulo, la: *in a quavering voice*, con voz temblorosa.

quay [ki:] n. Muelle, *m.* (wharf).

quayage [—idʒ] n. Derechos (*m. pl.*) de muelle, muellaje, *m.* (fees). || Espacio (*m.*) disponible en un muelle (mooring space).

quayside [—said] n. Muelle, *m.* (wharf).

quean [kwi:n] n. Mujer (*f.*) perdida (woman). || FIG. Marica, *m.* (homosexual).

queasiness [ˈkwi:zinis] n. Náuseas, *f. pl.*, bascas, *f. pl.* (sick feeling). || FIG. Escrupulosidad, *f.*, escrúpulos, *m. pl.*

queasy [ˈkwi:zi] adj. Mareado, da; con náuseas (feeling sick). || Repugnante, que da náuseas (food). || Delicado, da (easily upset). || Inquieto, ta; desasosegado, da (uneasy). || FIG. Escrupuloso, sa (scrupulous). | Complicado, da; difícil (difficult).

quebracho [keˈbrɑ:tʃəu] n. BOT. Quebracho, *m.*

Quechua [ˈketʃuə] n. Quechua, *m.* & *f.*, quichua, *m.* & *f.* (people, language).

Quechuan [ˈketʃuən] adj. Quechua, quichua.

queen [kwi:n] n. Reina, *f.*: *Queen Elizabeth*, la reina Isabel; *Queen mother*, reina madre; *Queen consort*, reina consorte; *Queen regent*, reina regente; *Queen dowager*, reina viuda. || FIG. Reina, *f.*: *the queen of jazz*, la reina del jazz. || ZOOL. Abeja (*f.*) maestra *or* maesa, reina, *f.* (of bees). || Dama, *f.*, reina, *f.* (playing card). || Reina, *f.* (chess). || FAM. Marica, *m.* (homosexual). || — FAM. *Queen Anne is dead*, eso es archisabido. || *Queen of the meadows*, reina de los prados (flower). || ARCH. *Queen post*, péndola, *f.*

queen [kwi:n] v. tr. Coronar (in chess). || Coronar reina (a woman).
— V. intr. Coronarse. || FIG. *To queen it*, darse aires, presumir.

queen bee [ˈkwi:nˈbi:] n. ZOOL. Abeja (*f.*) maestra *or* maesa, reina, *f.*

queenliness [—linis] n. Majestad, *f.*, realeza, *f.*

queenly [—li] or **queenlike** [—ˈlaik] adj. Regio, gia; de reina, majestuoso, sa.

queer [kwiə*] adj. Raro, ra; extraño, ña (strange): *a queer fish*, un tipo raro. || Curioso, sa (peculiar). || Misterioso, sa; turbio, bia; sospechoso, sa (suscipious). || Indispuesto, ta; malo, la (unwell). || FAM. Maricón, marica (homosexual). || — FAM. *Queer in the head*, chiflado, da. || *To feel queer*, no encontrarse bien, estar indispuesto *or* pachucho.
— N. FAM. Maricón, *m.*, marica, *m.* (homosexual). || U. S. FAM. Moneda (*f.*) falsa.

queer [kwiə*] v. tr. Fastidiar, estropear: *to queer s.o.'s pitch*, estropear los proyectos de alguien.

queerish [—riʃ] adj. Raro, ra; extraño, ña (strange). || FAM. Pachucho, cha; malo, la (ill).

queerness [—nis] n. Rareza, *f.* || FAM. Indisposición, *f.*

quell [kwel] v. tr. Calmar, mitigar (to mitigate): *to quell one's pains*, calmar los dolores. || Dominar, controlar (fear). || Reprimir, sofocar (rebellion). || Suprimir (to suppress).

quench [kwentʃ] v. tr. Apagar (flames). || Aplacar, mitigar, apagar (thirst). || TECH. Templar (hot steel). || ELECTR. Suprimir (sparks). || FIG. Sofocar (desire). | Apagar, enfriar, aplacar (enthusiasm). | Reprimir (emotion). || FAM. Callar (to shut up).

quenchable [—əbl] adj. Apagable.

quencher [—ə*] n. Bebida (*f.*) refrescante.

quenchless [—lis] adj. Inextinguible, inapagable.

querist [ˈkwiərist] n. Interrogador, ra.

quern [kwə:n] n. Molinillo (*m.*) de mano.

querulous [ˈkwerulәs] adj. Quejumbroso, sa.

query [ˈkwiəri] n. Pregunta, *f.* (question). || Duda, *f.* (doubt). || Signo (*m.*) de interrogación (question mark). || FIG. Interrogante, *m.*

query [ˈkwiəri] v. tr. Poner en duda, dudar de (to put in doubt). || Preguntar (s.o.): *is it true?, he queried*, ¿es verdad?, preguntó. || U. S. Interrogar (to interrogate). || Poner el signo de interrogación.
— V. intr. Hacer preguntas, interrogar. || *To query whether*, preguntarse si.

quest [kwest] n. Búsqueda, *f.*, busca, *f.* (search). || *In quest of*, en busca de.

quest [kwest] v. tr./intr. Buscar.

question [ˈkwestʃən] n. Pregunta, *f.*: *to ask s.o. a question*, hacer una pregunta a alguien; *indiscreet question*, pregunta indiscreta; *to ply with questions*, acosar con preguntas; *to put a written question*, formular una pregunta por escrito; *questions and answers*, preguntas y respuestas. || Problema, *m.* (in mathematics). || Pregunta, *f.* (in an examination). || Cuestión, *f.*, asunto, *m.*: *the question of capital punishment*, la cuestión de la pena capital; *open question*, asunto pendiente; *it is only a question of money*, es sólo una cuestión de dinero; *debate on special questions*, debate sobre asuntos especiales; *to raise a previous question*, plantear una cuestión previa. || Problema, *m.* (problem): *that is the question*, he aquí el problema; *the gipsy question*, el problema gitano. || Interrogación, *f.* (interrogation). || Cuestión, *f.* (torture). || — *Ask a silly question and you will get a silly answer*, a pregunta necia oídos sordos *or* de mercader. || *Begging the question*, petición (*f.*) de principio. || *Beside the question*, que no viene al caso. || *Beyond all question, beyond question*, fuera de toda duda, fuera de duda. || *Burning question*, asunto candente. || *Committee on legal questions*, comisión jurídica. || *In question*, de que se trata, en cuestión. || *It is a question of a quarter of an hour*, es cuestión de un cuarto de hora. || *It is not out of the question that*, es posible que. || *Out of all question*, completamente imposible. || *Out of the question*, imposible (impossible), ni hablar [de eso]: *please may I go out this evening? — No, it is out of the question*, por favor ¿puedo salir esta noche? — No, ni hablar. || *That's not the question*, no se trata de eso. || *There is no question about it*, no ofrece la menor duda. || *There is no question of going back now*, ya no hay posibilidad de volverse atrás. || *There was some question of*, se habló de. || *To call* o *to bring in question*, poner en tela de juicio. || *To come in question*, merecer consideración. || *To come into question*, plantearse. || *To make no question of*, no dudar de. || *To pop the question*, declararse. || *To put a question to s.o.*, hacer una pregunta a alguien. || *To put the question to the vote*, poner *or* someter el problema a votación. || *What is the question?*, ¿de qué se trata? || *Without question*, sin duda.

question [ˈkwestʃən] v. tr. Preguntar: *to question a student*, preguntar a un alumno. || Interrogar (the police, etc.). || Poner en duda, dudar de (to query).

questionable [ˈkwestʃənəbl] adj. Dudoso, sa (doubtful). || Discutible, controvertible: *it is a questionable matter*, es una cosa discutible.

questionary [ˈkwestʃənəri] n. Cuestionario, *m.*

questioner [ˈkwestʃənə*] n. Preguntador, ra (p. us.), interrogador, ra.

questioning [ˈkwestʃəniŋ] adj. Interrogativo, va.
— N. Preguntas, *f. pl.* (questions). || Interrogatorio, *m.* (by the police).

questionless [ˈkwestʃənlis] adj. Indiscutible, indudable.

question mark [ˈkwestʃənmɑːk] n. Signo (*m.*) *or* punto de interrogación. || FIG. Interrogante, *m.*

questionnaire [ˌkwestiəˈnɛə*] n. Cuestionario, *m.*

question time [ˈkwestʃəntaim] n. Ruegos y preguntas, *m. pl.* (in parliament).

questor [ˈkwiːstə*] n. Cuestor, *m.*

questorship [ˈkwestəˌʃip] n. Cuestura, *f.*

quetzal [ketˈsɔːl] n. Quetzal, *m.*

queue [kjuː] n. Cola, *f.* (line): *they formed a queue at the ticket window*, se pusieron en cola delante de la taquilla; *I was standing in a queue*, estaba haciendo cola. || Coleta, *f.* (Chinaman's plait).

queue [kjuː] v. intr. Hacer cola. || *To queue up*, hacer cola.

quibble [ˈkwibl] n. Sutileza, *f.* (subtlety). || Subterfugio, *m.*, evasiva, *f.* (evasion). || Pega, *f.*, objeción, *f.*

quibble [ˈkwibl] v. intr. Sutilizar (to split hairs). || Utilizar subterfugios (to equivocate). || Ser quisquilloso (to find fault with).

quibbler [—ə*] n. Sofista, *m. & f.*, casuista, *m. & f.* (equivocator).

quibbling [—iŋ] n. Sutilezas, *f. pl.*, sofismas, *m. pl.*

quick [kwik] adj. Rápido, da (fast): *it is quicker to go through the garden*, es más rápido ir por el jardín. || Vivo, va (alive, lively). || Agudo, da (clever). || Ágil (agile). || Ligero, ra (of feet). || Vivo, va (not dead). || Pronto, ta (reply). || AGR. Vivo, va (hedge). || Acelerado, da (pulse). || MIL. Acelerado, da (step). || Movedizo, za (ground). || — FIG. *As quick as a flash*, como un relámpago. || *Quick temper*, genio vivo. || FIG. *Quick with child*, embarazada (woman). || *To be quick*, darse prisa, apresurarse. || *To be quick about sth.*, hacer algo rápidamente. || FAM. *To have a quick one*, tomar [rápidamente] una copa. || *We had a quick luncheon*, almorzamos rápidamente *or* de prisa.
— N. Carne (*f.*) viva. || — *The quick and the dead*, los vivos y los muertos. || FIG. *To the quick*, hasta la médula. | *To touch* o *to cut* o *to hurt s.o. to the quick*, herir a alguien en lo vivo.
— Adv. Rápidamente, rápido.

quick-acting [—ˈæktiŋ] adj. De acción rápida.

quick assets [—ˈæsets] pl. n. COMM. Activo (*m.*) disponible.

quick-change [—ˌtʃeindʒ] adj. De cambio rápido. || *Quick-change artist*, transformista, *m. & f.*

quick-eared [—ˌiəd] adj. Fino de oídos.

quicken [ˈkwikən] v. tr. Acelerar, apretar: *to quicken one's pace*, apretar el paso. || Resucitar: *to quicken the dead*, resucitar a los muertos. || Acelerar (the pulse). || Estimular: *to quicken s.o.'s interest*, estimular el interés de alguien.
— V. intr. Apresurarse, acelerarse (to go faster). || MED. Moverse (foetus). | Sentir los movimientos del feto (a pregnant woman). || FIG. Vivificarse (hope).

quick-eyed [—ˌaid] adj. De vista aguda.

quick-fire [—ˈfaiə*] or **quick-firing** [—riŋ] adj. De tiro rápido (gun). || FIG. Rápido, da; hecho a bocajarro (question).

quick-freeze* [—ˈfriːz] v. tr. Congelar [rápidamente].

— OBSERV. Pret. ***quick-froze;*** p. p. ***quick-frozen.***

quick-freezing [—ˈfriːziŋ] n. Congelación (*f.*) rápida.

quick hedge [—hedʒ] n. Seto (*m.*) vivo.

quickie [ˈkwiki] n. Cosa (*f.*) hecha rápidamente. || *Let's pop in for a quickie*, tomemos rápidamente una copa.

quicklime [ˈkwiklaim] n. Cal (*f.*) viva (lime).

quickly [kwikli] adv. Rápidamente.

quickness [ˈkwiknis] n. Rapidez, *f.*, velocidad, *f.* (speed). || Prontitud, *f.* (promptness). || Viveza, *f.* (liveliness). || Agilidad, *f.* (agility). || Agudeza, *f.* (of ear, eyes, wit). || Aceleración, *f.*, frecuencia, *f.* (of pulse).

quicksand [ˈkwiksænd] n. Arena (*f.*) movediza (unstable sand).

quickset [ˈkwikset] n. BOT. Seto (*m.*) vivo (hedge). | Plantón, *m.* (slip). | Espino (*m.*) blanco, majuelo, *m.* (hawthorn).
— Adj. Vivo, va (hedge).

quick-sighted [ˈkwikˈsaitid] adj. De vista aguda. || FIG. Perspicaz.

quicksilver [ˈkwikˌsilvə*] adj. Variable.
— N. Mercurio, *m.*, azogue, *m.* (mercury).

quicksilver [ˈkwikˌsilvə*] v. tr. Azogar.

quicksilvering [—riŋ] n. Azogado, *m.*

quickstep [ˈkwikstep] n. MIL. Paso (*m.*) ligero.

quick-tempered [ˈkwikˈtempəd] adj. De genio vivo, irascible.

quick-witted [ˈkwikˈwitid] adj. Agudo, da; perspicaz; listo, ta.

quid [kwid] n. Mascada (*f.*) de tabaco. || FAM. Libra, *f.* (a pound). || FAM. *Quids in*, forrado de dinero.

— OBSERV. La palabra inglesa *quid* tiene como plural *quids* cuando significa "mascada" y *quid* cuando significa "libra" (*it cost me two quid*, me costó dos libras).

quiddity [—iti] n. Esencia, *f.* (essence). || Sutileza, *f.* (subtlety).

quidnunc [ˈkwidnʌŋk] n. Chismoso, sa (newsmonger).

quid pro quo [ˈkwidprəuˈkwəu] n. Compensación, *f.*,

quiescence [kwaiˈesns] n. Quietud, *f.*, tranquilidad, *f.*, inactividad, *f.*, reposo, *m.*

quiescent [kwaiˈesnt] adj. Quieto, ta; inactivo, va; en reposo (at rest).

quiet [ˈkwaiət] adj. Silencioso, sa; callado, da (silent). || Silencioso, sa (a motor). || Ligero, ra (footstep). || Tranquilo, la (peaceful, calm). || Callado, da; reservado, da (reserved). || Tranquilo, la (unworried). || Descansado, da (soothing). || Escondido, da; disimulado, da (secret). || Sencillo, lla; discreto, ta (not pretentious). || Poco llamativo va; sobrio, bria (a dress). || Privado, da; íntimo, ma (private). || COMM. Poco activo, va (business). | Encalmado, da (stock exchange). || — *All quiet on the front*, sin novedad en el frente. || *Be* o *keep quiet!*, ¡cállate! (shut up!), ¡estate quieto! (keep still!). || *It is as quiet as the grave*, hay un silencio sepulcral. || *To be quiet*, callarse (to stop talking), no hacer ruido (to make no noise).
— N. Tranquilidad, *f.*, calma, *f.*, quietud, *f.*, sosiego, *m.* (stillness, calm). || Silencio, *m.* (silence). || Reposo, *m.*, descanso, *m.* (rest). || *On the quiet*, a escondidas, a hurtadillas.

quiet [ˈkwaiət] v. tr. Calmar, tranquilizar, sosegar (to calm). || Hacer callar (to silence).
— V. intr. Calmarse, tranquilizarse, sosegarse.

quieten [ˈkwaiətn] v. tr. Callar (to silence). || Tranquilizar, calmar (to calm).
— V. intr. Callarse (to become silent). || Tranquilizarse, calmarse (to calm down). || *To quieten down*, tranquilizarse (to calm down), callarse (to shut up).

quietism [ˈkwaiitizəm] n. REL. Quietismo, *m.*

quietist [ˈkwaiitist] n. REL. Quietista, *m. & f.*

quietly [kwaiətli] adv. Sin hacer ruido, silenciosamente (silently). || Tranquilamente, con calma (calmly). || Con sobriedad, discretamente (to be dressed). || En la intimidad (in private).

quietness [ˈkwaiətnis] n. See QUIET.

quietude [ˈkwaiitjuːd] n. Quietud, *f.*, sosiego, *m.*

quietus [kwaiˈitəs] n. Muerte, *f.* (death). || Golpe (*m.*) de gracia (finishing stroke). || COMM. Finiquito, *m.*, descargo, *m.*

quiff [kwif] n. Copete, *m.* (of hair). || U. S. POP. Suripanta, *f.*, furcia, *f.* (woman).

quill [kwil] n. Pluma, *f.* (feather). || Cañón, *m.* (stem of the feather). || Púa, *f.* (of porcupine). || Pluma, *f.*, cálamo, *m.* (pen). || Canilla, *f.* (bobbin). || Mondadientes, *m. inv.* (toothpick). || Púa, *f.* (plectrum).

quill [kwil] v. tr. Encanillar (to wind). || Encañonar (to goffer).

quillai [kiːˈlai] n. BOT. Quillay, *m.*, palo (*m.*) de jabón.

quilling [ˈkwiliŋ] n. Encañonado, *m.*

quilt [kwilt] n. Colcha, *f.* (coverlet). || U. S. Edredón, *m.* (eiderdown).
quilt [kwilt] v. tr. Acolchar.
quilting [—iŋ] n. Acolchado, *m.* || "Piqué", *m.* (material).
quinary [ˈkwainəri] adj. Quinario, ria.
quince [kwins] n. Membrillo, *m.* (fruit, tree). || *Quince jelly*, carne (*f.*) de membrillo.
quincentenary [ˌkwinsenˈti:nəri] n. Quinto centenario, *m.*
quincuncial [kwinˈkʌnʃəl] adj. Al tresbolillo.
quincunx [ˈkwinkʌŋks] n. AGR. Tresbolillo, *m.*
quinine [kwiˈni:n] n. CHEM. Quinina, *f.*
quinoa [ki:ˈnəuə] n. BOT. Quinoa, *f.*, quinua, *f.*
quinone [kwiˈnəun] n. CHEM. Quinona, *f.*
quinquagenarian [ˌkwiŋkwədʒiˈnεəriən] adj./n. Quincuagenario, ria.
Quinquagesima [ˌkwiŋkwəˈdʒesimə] n. Quincuagésima, *f.*
quinquennial [kwiŋˈkweniəl] adj. Quinquenal.
— N. Quinquenio, *m.*
quinquennium [kwiŋˈkweniəm] n. Quinquenio, *m.*

— OBSERV. El plural de la palabra *quinquennium* es *quinquenniums* o *quinquennia*.

quins [kwinz] pl. n. Quintillizos, zas.
quinsy [ˈkwinzi] n. MED. Angina, *f.*
quint [kwint] n. Quinta, *f.* (cards). || MUS. Quinta, *f.* || U. S. FAM. Quintillizo, za (quintuplet).
quintain [ˈkwintin] n. Estafermo, *m.*
quintal [ˈkwintl] n. Quintal, *m.*
quinte [kε̃t] n. SP. Quinta, *f.* (in fencing).
quintessence [kwinˈtesns] n. Quintaesencia, *f.*
quintet or **quintette** [kwinˈtet] n. MUS. Quinteto, *m.*
quintillion [kwinˈtiljən] n. MATH. Quintillón, *m.*, diez elevado a treinta (in England). | Trillón, *m.*, diez elevado a dieciocho (in United States).
quintuple [ˈkwintjupl] adj. Quíntuplo, pla.
— N. Quíntuplo, *m.*
quintuple [ˈkwintjupl] v. tr. Quintuplicar.
— V. intr. Quintuplicarse.
quintuplets [ˈkwintjuplits] pl. n. Quintillizos, zas.
quip [kwip] n. Pulla, *f.*, burla, *f.*, sarcasmo, *m.*, ocurrencia, *f.*
quip [kwip] v. intr. Tirar pullas.
— V. intr. Decir sarcásticamente.
quipu [ˈki:pu:] n. Quipu, *m.*, quipo, *m.*
quire [ˈkwaiə*] n. Mano (*f.*) de papel. || *In quires*, en cuadernillos (book).
quirk [kwə:k] n. Peculiaridad, *f.*, rareza, *f.* (oddity). || Rasgo, *m.*, floreo, *m.* (in writing). || Ocurrencia, *f.* (quip). || Escapatoria, *f.* (subterfuge). || Capricho, *m.* (sudden fit). || ARCH. Mediacaña, *f.*
quirt [kwə:t] n. U. S. Cuarta, *f.*, látigo (*m.*) corto.
quirt [kwə:t] v. tr. U. S. Azotar con cuarta.
quisling [ˈkwizliŋ] n. Traidor, ra; colaboracionista, *m.* & *f.*
quit [kwit] adj. Libre: *to be quit of an obligation*, estar libre de una obligación.
quit* [kwit] v. tr. Dejar, abandonar: *to quit one's job*, abandonar el empleo; *to quit the army*, dejar el ejército. || Desocupar, dejar, abandonar (a place). || Abandonar, dejar: *he quit his wife*, dejó a su mujer. || Irse de (to depart from). || FAM. Dejar de: *quit shouting!*, ¡deja de gritar!
— V. intr. Irse, marcharse (to go away). || Dimitir (to resign a job). || Dejar de hacer algo: *he was shouting but when s.o. told him to be quiet he quit*, estaba gritando pero, cuando alguien le dijo que se callase, dejó de hacerlo. || Abandonar (to give up).

— OBSERV. Pret. & p.p. ***quitted, quit.***

quitch [kwitʃ] n. BOT. Grama, *f.*
quitclaim [ˈkwitkleim] n. JUR. Renuncia, *f.*
quitclaim [ˈkwitkleim] v. tr. JUR. Renunciar.
quite [kwait] adv. Completamente, totalmente: *we are quite alone*, estamos completamente solos. || Bastante: *it is quite near*, está bastante cerca; *it is quite good*, es bastante bueno. || Absolutamente, perfectamente (positively): *he quite understood it*, lo comprendió perfectamente. || Verdaderamente, realmente (truly): *he was quite a hero*, fue realmente un héroe. || Exactamente (exactly): *I don't quite know*, no sé exactamente. || — *It is quite three days ago*, hace por lo menos tres días. || *Quite a few* o *a lot of* o *a bit of*, bastante: *there were quite a few cows in the meadow*, había bastantes vacas en la pradera. || *Quite a while*, un buen rato, bastante tiempo. || *Quite so!*, ¡así es!, ¡efectivamente!, ¡en efecto! || *Quite the thing*, muy de moda. || *Quite the worst*, con mucho el peor: *he is quite the worst singer I have ever heard*, él es con mucho el peor cantante que he oído. || *That's quite enough!*, ¡ya está bien! || *You are quite right*, tiene toda la razón.
quits [kwits] adj. En paz: *to be quits with s.o.*, estar en paz con alguien; *now we are quits*, ahora estamos en paz. || *To call it quits* o *to cry quits*, hacer las paces.
quittance [ˈkwitəns] n. Descargo, *m.* (discharge). || Recibo, *m.* (receipt). || Compensación, *f.*
quitter [ˈkwitə*] n. Persona (*f.*) que abandona fácilmente lo que ha iniciado. || Cobarde, *m.* & *f.* (coward).
quiver [ˈkwivə*] n. Aljaba, *f.*, carcaj, *m.* (for arrow). || Temblor, *m.* (tremble). || Estremecimiento, *m.* (shiver). || Temblor, *m.* (of voice). || Parpadeo, *m.* (of eyelids).
quiver [ˈkwivə*] v. intr. Temblar (to tremble). || Estremecerse (to shiver). || Parpadear (the eyelids). || *To quiver its wings*, aletear.
quivering [—riŋ] adj. Tembloroso, sa: *with a quivering voice*, con voz temblorosa. || Parpadeante (eyelids).
— N. See QUIVER.
qui vive [ki:ˈvi:v] n. *To be on the qui vive*, estar ojo alerta *or* ojo avizor.
Quixote [ˈkwiksət] pr. n. Quijote, *m.*
Quixotic [kwikˈsɔtik] adj. Quijotesco, ca.
Quixotism [kwiksɔˌtizəm] n. Quijotismo, *m.*
quiz [kwiz] n. Encuesta, *f.* (enquiry). || Acertijo, *m.* (riddle). || Examen, *m.* (examination). || Interrogatorio, *m.* (questioning). || Concurso (*m.*) radiofónico (on radio). || Consurso (*m.*) de televisión (on television). || Broma, *f.* (joke). || Bromista, *m.* & *f.* (joker).
quiz [kwiz] v. tr. Interrogar (to interrogate). || Mirar con aire burlón (to stare at). || Burlarse de (to gibe at).
quizzical [—ikəl] adj. Curioso, sa: *a quizzical glance*, una mirada curiosa. || Burlón, ona (bantering): *quizzical remarks*, observaciones burlonas. || Extraño, ña (odd).
quizzing [—iŋ] adj. Burlón, ona. || *Quizzing glass*, impertinentes, *m. pl.*
quod [kwɔd] n. FAM. Chirona, *f.* (prison).
quoin [kɔin] n. ARCH. Piedra (*f.*) angular (stone). | Esquina, *f.*, ángulo, *m.* (corner). | Dovela, *f.* (of an arch). || PRINT. Cuña, *f.* (wedge).
quoit [kɔit; kwɔit] n. Tejo, *m.* || — Pl. Chito, *m. sing.*, tejo, *m. sing.* (game).
quondam [ˈkwɔndæm] adj. Antiguo, gua: *my quondam friends*, mis antiguos amigos.
quorum [ˈkwɔ:rəm] n. Quórum, *m.*: *we have a quorum* o *the quorum is reached*, hay quórum.
quota [ˈkwəutə] n. Cupo, *m.*: *each has his quota of work for the day*, cada uno tiene su cupo de trabajo para el día. || COMM. Cupo, *m.*, contingente, *m.*, cuota, *f.* || Cuota, *f.* (share). || *Taxable quota*, parte (*f.*) imponible.
quotable [ˈkwəutəbl] adj. Que merece citarse, citable. || COMM. Cotizable.
quotation [kwəuˈteiʃən] n. Cita, *f.*: *a quotation from the Bible*, una cita de la Biblia. || COMM. Cotización, *f.* || *Quotation marks*, comillas, *f.*
quote [kwəut] n. Cita, *f.* (quotation). || — Pl. Comillas, *f.* (quotation marks). || — *End of quote*, fin (*m.*) de la cita. || *Quote*, comienza la cita.
quote [kwəut] v. tr. Citar (to make a quotation from). || Dar (an example). || Entrecomillar, poner entre comillas (to enclose with quotation marks). || COMM. Cotizar.
— V. intr. Hacer citas, citar (from an author, etc.). || *And I quote*, y cito sus palabras.
quoth [kwəuθ] v. tr. *Quoth he*, dijo.

— OBSERV. Este verbo se emplea únicamente en la primera y tercera personas del singular del pretérito.

quotidian [kwɔˈtidiən] adj. Diario, ria; cotidiano, na (daily).
— N. MED. Fiebre (*f.*) cotidiana.
quotient [ˈkwəuʃənt] n. Cociente, *m.*

R

r [ɑ:*] n. R, *f.* (letter of the alphabet). || *The three R's*, lectura, escritura y aritmética.
Ra [rɑ:] pr. n. MYTH. Ra (ancient Egyptian god).
rabbet [ˈræbit] n. Ranura, *f.* (groove). || Rebajo, *m.*, renvalso, *m.* (for doors and windows). || *Rabbet plane*, guillame, *m.*
rabbet [ˈræbit] v. tr. Hacer una ranura *or* un rebajo en, renvalsar (to make a rabbet). || Ensamblar (to join).
rabbi [ˈræbai] or **rabbin** [ˈræbin] n. REL. Rabino, *m.* | Rabí, *m.* (before name). || *Chief rabbi*, gran rabino.
rabbinism [ˈræbinizəm] n. Rabinismo, *m.*
rabbit [ˈræbit] n. ZOOL. Conejo, *m.*: *Angora rabbit*, conejo de Angora. || FAM. Mal jugador, *m.* || — CULIN. *Buck rabbit*, pan tostado con queso derretido y un huevo frito. || ZOOL. *Doe rabbit*, coneja, *f.* || *Rabbit hole*, madriguera, *f.* || *Rabbit hutch*, conejera, *f.* || SP. *Rabbit punch*, golpe (*m.*) en la nuca. || *Rabbit warren*, conejal, *m.*, conejar, *m.* || *Tame rabbit*, conejo casero. || CULIN. *Welsh rabbit*, pan tostado con queso derretido. || ZOOL. *Wild rabbit*, conejo de campo *or* de monte.
rabbit [ˈræbit] v. intr. Cazar conejos.
rabble [ˈræbl] n. Multitud (*f.*) ruidosa, gentío, *m.* (crowd). || TECH. Hurgón, *m.* || *The rabble*, el populacho, la chusma.
rabble [ˈræbl] v. tr. TECH. Agitar (molten metal).
rabble-rouser [—ˌrauzə*] n. Agitador, ra.
rabble-rousing [—ˌrauziŋ] n. Agitación, *f.*
rabid [ˈræbid] adj. Rabioso, sa: *rabid dog*, perro rabioso. || Rábico, ca (virus). || FIG. Feroz (hate, hunger). | Rabioso, sa (thirst). | Furioso, sa (opponent). | Fanático, ca (supporter).
rabidity [raˈbiditi] or **rabidness** [—nis] n. Rabia, *f.* (rabies). || FIG. Violencia, *f.* (of passions, opinions). | Fanatismo, *m.*
rabies [ˈreibi:z] n. MED. Rabia, *f.*
raccoon [rəˈku:n] n. ZOOL. Mapache, *m.*
race [reis] n. Raza, *f.*: *the human race*, la raza humana. || Familia, *f.*: *the race of David*, la familia de David. || Estirpe, *f.*: *of noble race*, de noble estirpe. || SP. Regata, *f.*: *yatch race*, regata de balandros. | Carrera, *f.*: *cycling, horse, long-distance race*, carrera ciclista, de caballos, de fondo; *walking race*, carrera pedestre; *to run a race*, participar *or* tomar parte en una carrera. || ASTR. Curso, *m.*, recorrido, *m.* (of a star). || Curso, *m.* (of time). || Corriente (*f.*) fuerte (current of water). || TECH. Saetín, *m.*, caz, *m.* (of a mill). | Anillo (*m.*) de rodadura (of ball bearing). | Carrera, *f.* (of a shuttle). || FIG. Carrera, *f.* (rush). | Carrera, *f.*: *arms race*, carrera de armamentos. || — Pl. SP. Carreras, *f.*: *to go to the races*, ir a las carreras. || — FIG. *His race is run*, ha llegado al final de su vida. || SP. *Hurdle race*, carrera de vallas. || *Race against the clock* o *against time*, carrera contra el reloj. || *Race problem*, problema (*m.*) racial. || *Sack race*, carrera de sacos. || *True to race*, de raza (horse, dog, etc.).
race [reis] v. tr. Competir con *or* contra (to compete against). || Hacer correr: *to race a horse*, hacer correr un caballo. || Acelerar (a motor). || — *I'll race you home*, te echo una carrera a casa. || FIG. *To race a bill through the House*, hacer aprobar un proyecto de ley a toda prisa. || *To race away a fortune*, perder un dineral en las carreras. || FIG. *To race s.o. off one's feet*, agotar a alguien.
— V. intr. Correr: *I race every Saturday*, corro todos los sábados. || Ir corriendo: *I raced home*, fui corriendo a casa. || Embalarse (an engine). || Latir a ritmo acelerado (pulse). || — FIG. *To race about*, ajetrearse. || *To race against time*, correr contra el reloj. || *To race along*, ir corriendo. || *To race down the street*, bajar la calle corriendo.
race card [—kɑ:d] n. Programa (*m.*) de carreras.
racecourse [—kɔ:s] n. Hipódromo, *m.* (for horses). || Autódromo, *m.* (for cars). || Pista (*f.*) de carreras (racetrack).
racegoer [—ˈgəuə*] n. Aficionado (*m.*) a las carreras de caballos.
race hatred [—ˈheitrid] n. Odio (*m.*) racial.
racehorse [—hɔ:s] n. Caballo (*m.*) de carreras.
raceme [rəˈsi:m] n. BOT. Racimo, *m.*
race meeting [ˈreisˌmi:tiŋ] n. Concurso (*m.*) hípico.
racer [ˈreisə*] n. Corredor, ra (person). || Caballo (*m.*) de carreras (horse). || Coche (*m.*) de carreras (car). || Bicicleta (*f.*) de carreras (bicycle). || Motocicleta (*f.*) de carreras (motorbike). || Balandro (*m.*) de carreras (boat).
race riot [ˈreisˈraiət] n. Disturbio (*m.*) racial.
racetrack [ˈreistræk] n. Pista, *f.* || U. S. Hipódromo, *m.* (racecourse).
Rachel [ˈreitʃəl] pr. n. Raquel, *f.*
rachialgia [ˌreikiˈældʒiə] n. MED. Raquialgia, *f.*
rachidian [rəˈkidiən] adj. Raquídeo, a: *rachidian bulb*, bulbo raquídeo.
rachis [ˈreikis] n. ANAT. BOT. Raquis, *m.*
— OBSERV. El plural de *rachis* es *rachises* o *rachides*.
rachitic [ræˈkitik] adj. Raquítico, ca.
rachitis [ræˈkaitis] n. MED. Raquitismo, *m.*
racial [ˈreiʃəl] adj. Racial: *racial problems*, problemas raciales.
racialism [ˈreiʃəlizəm] n. Racismo, *m.*
racialist [ˈreiʃəlist] n. Racista, *m.* & *f.*
racialistic [reiʃəˈlistik] adj. Racista.
raciness [ˈreisinis] n. Picante, *m.* (of style). || Aroma, *m.*, buqué, *m.* (of wine).
racing [ˈreisiŋ] adj. De carreras: *racing car*, coche de carreras. || Embalado, da (engine). || *Racing driver*, corredor, *m.*, piloto, *m.*
— N. Carreras, *f. pl.* (races): *horse racing*, carreras de caballos.
racism [ˈreisizəm] n. Racismo, *m.*
racist [ˈreisist] adj./n. Racista.
rack [ræk] n. Estante, *m.*, anaquel, *m.* (shelf). || Perchero, *m.*, percha, *f.* (for hats, coats, etc.). || Escurreplatos, *m. inv.* (for plates). || Soporte (*m.*) para bicicletas (for bicycles). || Redecilla, *f.*, rejilla, *f.* (in a train). || Adral, *m.* (on a cart). || Pesebre, *m.* (in a stable). || Armero, *m.* (for arms). || Percha, *f.* (for tools). || Taquera, *f.*, portatacos, *m. inv.* (for billiard cues). || Archivador, *m.* (filing system). || PRINT. Chibalete, *m.* || TECH. Cremallera, *f.* || Potro, *m.* (torture instrument). || Nubes, *f. pl.* (mass of clouds). || Pasitrote, *m.* (horse's gait). || — *Bomb rack*, dispositivo (*m.*) portabombas. || *Rack and pinion*, engranaje (*m.*) de cremallera y piñón. || *Roof rack*, baca, *f.* || || FIG. *To be on the rack*, estar atormentado *or* en ascuas. | *To go to rack and ruin*, venirse abajo. | *To put on the rack*, atormentar.
rack [ræk] v. tr. Atormentar: *to be racked by remorse*, estar atormentado por los remordimientos. || Hacer sufrir atrozmente (physical pain). || Sacudir: *the cough racked his whole body*, la tos le sacudió todo el cuerpo. || Pedir un alquiler exorbitante: *the landlord racked the tenants*, el dueño pedía un alquiler exorbitante a los inquilinos. || Poner a un precio exorbitante (rent). || Trasegar (wine). || Poner en el pesebre (fodder). || (Ant.). Torturar en el potro. || FIG. *To rack one's brains*, devanarse los sesos.
— V. intr. Andar a pasitrote (a horse). || Dispersarse (clouds).
racket [ˈrækit] n. Raqueta, *f.* (light bat). || — Pl. Juego (*m. sing.*) parecido al frontón.
racket [ˈrækit] n. Alboroto, *m.*, barullo, *m.*, jaleo, *m.* (noise): *to kick up a racket*, armar jaleo. || FAM. Timo, *m.*, estafa, *f.* (swindle). | Chantaje, *m.* (blackmail). | Extorsión, *f.* (extortion). | Tráfico, *m.*: *drug racket*, tráfico de estupefacientes. | Chanchullo, *m.*, negocio (*m.*) sucio (dishonest work). || — FIG. *To go on the racket*, irse de juerga. | *To stand the racket*, pagar los vidrios rotos.
racket [ˈrækit] v. intr. FAM. *To racket about*, armar jaleo (to make a row), irse de juerga, correrla (to go on a spree).
racketeer [ˌrækiˈtiə*] n. Chantajista, *m.* (blackmailer). || Timador, *m.*, estafador, *m.* (swindler).
racketeering [—riŋ] n. Chantaje, *m.* (blackmail). || Crimen (*m.*) organizado.
racket press [ˈrækitpres] n. Prensa (*f.*) de raquetas.
racking [ˈrækiŋ] adj. Muy fuerte, terrible: *a racking pain*, un dolor terrible. || Exorbitante (rent).
— N. Trasiego, *m.* (of wine). || Tortura, *f.* (torment).
rack railway [ˈrækˈreilwei] or **rack railroad** [ˈrækˈreilrəud] n. Ferrocarril (*m.*) de cremallera.
rack rent [ˈrækrent] n. Alquiler (*m.*) exorbitante.
rack wheel [ˈrækwi:l] n. Rueda (*f.*) dentada.
raconteur [ˌrækɔnˈtə:*] n. Anecdotista, *m.*, persona (*f.*) que cuenta bien anécdotas.
racoon [rəˈku:n] n. ZOOL. Mapache, *m.*
racquet [ˈrækit] n. See RACKET (1st entry).
racy [ˈreisi] adj. Salado, da (person). || Picante (joke). || De raza (animal).
radar [ˈreidə*] n. Radar, *m.* || — *Radar beacon*, faro (*m.*) radar. || *Radar operator*, radarista, *m.*, operador (*m.*) de radar. || *Radar scanner*, antena giratoria de radar. || *Radar screen*, pantalla (*f.*) de radar.
radarman [—mən] n. Operador (*m.*) de radar.
— OBSERV. El plural de *radarman* es *radarmen*.
raddle [rædl] n. Almagre, *m.*, ocre (*m.*) rojo.
raddle [rædl] v. tr. Almagrar. || Maquillar exageradamente (a woman).
radial [ˈreidjəl] adj. Radial: *radial tyres*, neumáticos radiales. || *Radial engine*, motor (*m.*) en estrella.
— N. ANAT. Nervio (*m.*) radial (nerve). | Músculo

(*m.*) radial (muscle). | Vena (*f.*) radial (vein). | Arteria (*f.*) radial (artery).

radian [ˈreidjən] n. MATH. Radián, *m.*

radiance [ˈreidjəns] or **radiancy** [—i] n. Resplandor, *m.* (brightness). || PHYS. Radiación, *f.*

radiant [ˈreidjənt] adj. Resplandeciente, radiante (bright): *radiant sun*, sol resplandeciente. || Radiante (smile, face): *he was radiant with joy*, estaba radiante de alegría. || Resplandeciente (beauty). || PHYS. Radiante. || *Radiant heating*, calefacción (*f.*) por radiación.

radiantly [—li] adv. Con resplandor (to shine). || — *He was radiantly happy*, rebosaba de felicidad, estaba radiante de felicidad. || *She smiled radiantly at him*, le miró con una sonrisa radiante.

radiate [ˈreidieit] adj. Radiado, da.

radiate [ˈreidieit] v. tr. Irradiar (heat). || Emitir (rays). || FIG. Difundir (to spread). || RAD. Radiar, transmitir. — V. intr. Irradiar, radiar (to emit rays). || PHYS. Irradiar, emitir radiaciones. || Salir: *eight roads radiate from the square*, ocho carreteras salen de la plaza. || FIG. *Happiness radiated from her eyes*, la felicidad brillaba en sus ojos.

radiating [—iŋ] adj. Radiante: *radiating surface*, superficie radiante.

radiation [ˌreidiˈeiʃən] n. Radiación, *f.* || MED. *Radiation sickness*, enfermedad (*f.*) provocada por la radiación.

radiator [ˈreidieitə*] n. Radiador, *m.*: *gas radiator*, radiador de gas. || AUT. *Radiator cap*, tapón (*m.*) del radiador.

radical [ˈrædikəl] adj. Radical, fundamental: *radical change*, cambio radical; *radical differences*, diferencias radicales. || Radical: *radical point of view*, punto de vista radical. || MATH. BOT. GRAMM. Radical. || — *Radical Socialism*, radicalsocialismo, *m.* || *Radical Socialist*, radicalsocialista, *m.* & *f.*
— N. GRAMM. MATH. CHEM. Radical, *m.*

radicalism [—izəm] n. Radicalismo, *m.*

radicate [ˈrædikeit] v. tr. Radicar.

radices [ˈreidisi:z] pl. n. See RADIX.

radicle [ˈrædikl] n. BOT. Radícula, *f.* || CHEM. Radical, *m.* (radical).

radio [ˈreidiəu] n. Radio, *f.* (science, broadcasting): *he is going to talk on the radio*, va a hablar por la radio; *by radio* o *on the radio*, por radio. || Radio, *m.*,

RADIO AND TELEVISION — RADIO (*f.*) Y TELEVISIÓN, *f.*

I. General terms. — Generalidades, *f.*

broadcast (to)	radiar, emitir (by radio), transmitir (by television)
broadcasting	radiodifusión *f.* (by radio), transmisión *f.*, difusión *f.* (by television)
broadcast	emisión *f.*
live broadcast	emisión (*f.*) en directo
rebroadcast	nueva transmisión
recorded broadcast *o* transmission	emisión (*f.*) diferida
broadcasting station, transmitter	emisora *f.*
aerial	antena *f.*
indoor aerial	antena (*f.*) interior
network	red *f.* (of stations), canal *m.*, cadena *f.* (channel)
wave length	longitud (*f.*) de onda
long, medium, short wave	onda (*f.*) larga, media, corta
kilocycle	kilociclo *m.*
recording studio	estudio (*m.*) de grabación
echo chamber	cámara (*f.*) de resonancia
sound recording	toma (*f.*) de sonido
sound technician *o* engineer	ingeniero (*m.*) de sonido
microphone	micrófono *m.*
earphones	auriculares *m.* [*Amer.*, audífonos *m.*]
loudspeaker	altavoz *m.* [*Amer.*, altoparlante *m.*]
tape recorder	magnetófono *m.* [*Amer.*, grabadora *f.*]
track	pista *f.*
recording, playback, erasing head	cabeza (*f.*) sonora, auditiva, supresora
turntable	plato *m.*
tone control	control (*m.*) de tonalidad
tuner, tuning knob	sintonizador *m.*, mando (*m.*) de sintonización
frequency modulation	frecuencia (*f.*) modulada, modulación (*f.*) de frecuencia
high fidelity, hi-fi	alta fidelidad *f.*
interference	parásitos *m. pl.*, interferencias *f. pl.*
valve [U.S., tube]	lámpara *f.*, válvula *f.*

II. Radio. — Radio, *f.*

radio station	emisora *f.*
radio engineering, radiotechnology	radiotécnica *f.*
radiotechnologic, radiotechnological	radiotécnico, ca
radio engineer	radiotécnico *m.*, ingeniero (*m.*) radiotécnico
radio receiver, radio *o* receiving set, wireless	radiorreceptor *m.*, aparato (*m.*) receptor, receptor *m.*
radio transmission	radiotransmisión *f.*
radio transmitter	radiotransmisor *m.*
radio frequency	radiofrecuencia *f.*
dial	esfera *f.*, dial *m.* (disk), botón (*m.*) selector (knob)
dial (to), tune in (to)	sintonizar
signature tune	sintonía *f.*
listener	radioyente *m.* & *f.*

III. Television. — Televisión, *f.*

televise (to)	televisar
telecast, television broadcasting	teledifusión *f.*
colour television	televisión (*f.*) en color
closed-circuit television	televisión (*f.*) en circuito cerrado
telecommunication satellite	satélite (*m.*) de telecomunicación
television set *o* receiver	receptor (*m.*) de televisión, televisor *m.*
screen	pantalla *f.*
the small screen	la pequeña pantalla
channel selector	selector (*m.*) de canal
definition	definición *f.*
cathode-ray tube	tubo (*m.*) de rayos catódicos
scan (to)	explorar
scanning	exploración *f.*
scanning beam	haz (*m.*) explorador
contrast	contraste *m.*
picture	imagen *f.*
test chart	carta (*f.*) de ajuste
framing	encuadre *m.*
televiewer, viewer	televidente *m.* & *f.*, telespectador, ra
television camera	cámara (*f.*) de televisión
cameraman	cámara *m.*, cameraman *m.*, operador (*m.*) de televisión
console	mesa (*f.*) de control
relay	repetidor *m.*, relé *m.*
relay station	estación (*f.*) repetidora
video	video *m.*
magnetoscope	magnetoscopio *m.*
kinescope	cinescopio *m.*

IV. Programme. — Programa, *m.*

programme (to) [U. S., program (to)]	programar
programming [U. S., programing]	programación *f.*
programmer [U. S., programer]	programador, ra
live programme [U. S., live program]	emisión (*f.*) en directo
production	realización *f.*
produce (to)	realizar
producer	realizador, ra
announcer	locutor, ra
news bulletin, newscast	noticias *f. pl.*, noticiario *m.*, diario (*m.*) hablado (radio), telediario *m.* (television)
news flash	noticias (*f. pl.*) de última hora
newsroom	sala (*f.*) de redacción
interview (to)	entrevistar
interview	entrevista *f.*
interviewer	entrevistador, ra
radio play	emisión (*f.*) dramática
telefilm	telefilm *m.*
script	guión *m.*
shooting	rodaje *m.*, toma (*f.*) de vistas
shoot (to)	rodar
shot	plano *m.*
close shot	primer plano *m.*
dolly	travelín *m.*, plataforma (*f.*) rodante, travelling *m.*
set	decorado *m.*
set designer	decorador *m.*
lighting engineering	luminotecnia *f.*
lighting engineer	luminotécnico *m.*, ingeniero (*m.*) de luces
lighting effects	efectos (*m.*) luminosos
spotlight, spot	foco *m.*, proyector *m.*
rehearsal	ensayo *m.*
makeup girl	maquilladora *f.*
sound effects	efectos (*m.*) sonoros
background music	música (*f.*) de fondo
special effects	efectos (*m.*) especiales, trucajes *m.*

See also CINEMATOGRAPHY

aparato (*m.*) de radio, receptor (*m.*) de radio (receiving set).
— Adj. De radio (programme, announcer). || Radiofónico, ca: *radio advertising*, publicidad radiofónica.
radio [ˈreidiəu] v. tr. Radiar, transmitir por radio.
— V. intr. Mandar un mensaje por radio (*to*, a).
radioactive [—ˈæktiv] adj. Radiactivo, va; radioactivo, va.
radioactivity [—ækˈtiviti] n. Radiactividad, *f.*, radioactividad, *f.*
radio altimeter [—ˈæltimi:tə*] n. Radioaltímetro, *m.*
radio amateur [—ˈæmətə:*] n. Radioaficionado, da.
radio astronomy [—əsˈtrɔnəmi] n. Radioastronomía, *f.* (branch of astronomy).
radio beacon [—ˈbi:kən] n. Radiofaro, *m.*
radiobiology [—baiˈɔlədʒi] n. Radiobiología, *f.*
radiochemistry [—ˈkemistri] n. Radioquímica, *f.*
radiocobalt [—kəuˈbɔ:lt] n. Radiocobalto, *m.*
radio compass [—ˈkʌmpəs] n. Radiocompás, *m.*
radioconductor [—kənˈdʌktə*] n. Radioconductor, *m.*
radio contact [—ˈkɔntækt] n. Radiocomunicación, *f.*
radio control [—kənˈtrəul] n. Dirección (*f.*) a distancia, teledirección, *f.*
radio control [—kənˈtrəul] v. tr. Teledirigir.
radio-controlled [—kənˈtrəuld] adj. Teledirigido, da.
radioelectrical [—iˈlektrikəl] adj. Radioeléctrico, ca.
radioelectricity [—ilekˈtrisiti] n. Radioelectricidad, *f.*
radioelement [—ˈelimənt] n. Radioelemento, *m.*
radio engineer [—ˌendʒiˈniə*] n. Radiotécnico, *m.*, ingeniero (*m.*) radiotécnico.
radio engineering [—ˌendʒiˈniəriŋ] n. Radiotécnica, *f.*
radio frequency [—ˈfri:kwənsi] n. Radiofrecuencia, *f.*
radiogoniometer [—gəuniˈɔmitə*] n. Radiogoniómetro, *m.*
radiogoniometric [—gəuniəˈmetrik] adj. Radiogoniométrico, ca.
radiogoniometry [—gəuniˈɔmitri] n. Radiogoniometría, *f.*
radiogram [—græm] n. Radiograma, *m.* (wireless telegram). || MED. Radiografía, *f.* (radiograph). || Radiogramola, *f.* (radiogramophone).
radiogramophone [—ˈgræməfəun] n. Radiogramola, *f.* (wireless receiver and record player).
radiograph [—grɑ:f] n. Radiografía, *f.*
radiograph [—grɑ:f] v. tr. Radiografiar.
radiographer [ˌreidiˈɔgrəfə*] n. Radiógrafo, *m.*
radiographic [ˌreidiəuˈgræfik] adj. Radiográfico, ca.
radiography [ˌreidiˈɔgrəfi] n. Radiografía, *f.*
radioisotope [ˈreidiəuˈaisətəup] n. Radioisótopo, *m.*
radiolaria [reidiəˈlɛəriə] pl. n. ZOOL. Radiolarios, *m.*
radiolocation [ˈreidiəuləuˈkeiʃən] n. Radiolocalización, *f.*
radiologist [ˌreidiˈɔlədʒist] n. MED. Radiólogo, *m.*
radiology [ˌreidiˈɔlədʒi] n. MED. Radiología, *f.*
radiometer [ˌreidiˈɔmitə*] n. Radiómetro, *m.*
radiometric [ˌreidiəuˈmetrik] adj. Radiométrico, ca.
radiometry [ˌreidiˈɔmətri] n. Radiometría, *f.*
radiomicrometer [ˌreidiəumaiˈkrɔmitə*] n. Radiomicrómetro, *m.*
radio navigation [ˈreidiəuˌnæviˈgeiʃən] n. Radionavegación, *f.*
radio network [ˈreidiəuˈnetwə:k] n. Red. (*f.*) de emisoras.
radio officer [ˈreidiəuˈɔfisə*] n. Radionavegante, *m.*
radio operator [ˈreidiəuˈɔpəreitə*] n. Radiotelegrafista, *m.* & *f.*, radiotelefonista, *m.* & *f.*
radiophone [ˈreidiəufəun] n. Radiófono, *m.*
radiophoto [ˌreidiəuˈfəutəu] or **radiophotograph** [ˌreidiəuˈfeutəgrɑ:f] n. Radiofotografía, *f.*
radio play [ˈreidiəuˌplei] n. Emisión (*f.*) dramática.
radio receiver [ˈreidiəuriˈsi:və*] n. Radiorreceptor, *m.*
radioscopic [ˌreidiəuˈskɔpik] adj. Radioscópico, ca.
radioscopy [reidiˈɔskəpi] n. Radioscopia, *f.*
radiosensitivity [ˈreidiəuˌsensiˈtiviti] n. Radiosensibilidad, *f.*
radio set [ˈreidiəuset] n. Aparato (*m.*) *or* receptor (*m.*) de radio.
radiosonde [ˈreidiəuˌsɔnd] n. Radiosonda, *f.*
radio station [ˈreidiəuˈsteiʃən] n. Emisora, *f.*
radiotechnologic [ˈreidiəuˌteknəˈlɔdʒik] or **radiotechnological** [—əl] adj. Radiotécnico, ca.
radiotechnology [ˈreidiəutekˈnɔlədʒi] n. Radiotécnica, *f.*
radiotelegram [ˈreidiəuˈteligræm] n. Radiotelegrama, *m.* (message transmitted by radiotelegraphy).
radiotelegraph [ˈreidiəuˈteligrɑ:f] n. Aparato (*m.*) de radiotelegrafía.
radiotelegraph [ˈreidiəuˈteligrɑ:f] v. tr. Radiotelegrafiar.
radiotelegraphy [ˈreidiəuteˈlegrəfi] n. Radiotelegrafía, *f.*
radiotelephone [ˈreidiəuˈtelifəun] n. Radioteléfono, *m.*
radiotelephonic [ˈreidiəuˌteliˈfɔnik] adj. Radiotelefónico, ca.
radiotelephony [ˈreidiəutiˈlefəni] n. Radiotelefonía, *f.*
radio telescope [ˈreidiəuˈteliskəup] n. Radiotelescopio, *m.*
radiotherapeutic [ˈreidiəuˌθerəˈpju:tik] adj. Radioterápico, ca.
radiotherapy [ˈreidiəuˈθerəpi] n. Radioterapia, *f.*
radiothorium [ˈreidiəuˈθɔ:riəm] n. Radiotorio, *m.*
radio transmission [ˈreidiəutrænzˈmiʃən] n. Radiotransmisión, *f.*
radio transmitter [ˈreidiəutrænzˈmitə*] n. Radiotransmisor, *m.*
radish [ˈrædiʃ] n. BOT. Rábano, *m.* || — *Radish bed*, rabanal, *m.* || *Radish seed*, rabaniza, *f.*
radium [ˈreidjəm] n. CHEM. Radio, *m.* || *Radium therapy*, radioterapia, *f.*
radius [ˈreidjəs] n. MATH. ANAT. FIG. Radio, *m.*: *radius of curvature*, radio de curvatura; *within a radius of a hundred kilometres*, en un radio de cien kilómetros. || AVIAT. *Operational radius*, autonomía, *f.*
— OBSERV. El plural de *radius* es *radii* o *radiuses*.
radix [ˈreidiks] n. MATH. Base, *f.* || ANAT. BOT. Raíz, *f.*
— OBSERV. El plural de esta palabra es *radices*.
radon [ˈreidɔn] n. CHEM. Radón, *m.*
raff [ræf] n. Gentuza, *f.*, plebe, *f.*
raffia [ˈræfiə] n. BOT. Rafia, *f.*
raffish [ˈræfiʃ] adj. Chulo, la (flashy). || Chabacano, na (vulgar). || Disoluto, ta (dissolute).
raffle [ˈræfl] n. Rifa, *f.*
raffle [ˈræfl] v. tr. Rifar, sortear.
— V. intr. Participar en una rifa.
raft [rɑ:ft] n. Balsa, *f.* (floating platform). || Armadía, *f.*, almadía, *f.* (in logging). || Masa (*f.*) flotante (of ice). || U. S. FIG. Gran número, *m.*
raft [rɑ:ft] v. tr. Transportar en balsa (to transport). || Cruzar en balsa (to cross a river). || Construir una balsa con (to make a raft of).
— V. intr. Ir en balsa.
rafter [—ə*] n. ARCH. Par, *m.* (of a roof).
raftsman [ˈrɑ:ftsmən] n. Ganchero, *m.*
— OBSERV. El plural de esta palabra es *raftsmen*.
rag [ræg] n. Harapo, *m.*, andrajo, *m.* (waste piece of cloth). || Trapo, *m.* (for cleaning). || FAM. Periodicucho, *m.* (newspaper). | Bandera, *f.* (flag). || FIG. Pizca, *f.* (bit). || FAM. Payasadas, *f. pl.* (horseplay). | Broma, *f.* (joke). | Broma (*f.*) pesada (practical joke). || Pizarra, *f.* (slate). || — Pl. Trapos (*m.*) viejos (for papermaking). || Harapos, *m.*, andrajos, *m.* (old clothes). || FAM. Trapos, *m.* (clothes). || — *In rags*, hecho jirones (clothes), andrajoso, sa; con la ropa hecha jirones (person). || *In rags and tatters*, desastrado, da. || U. S. FAM. *To chew the rag*, estar de palique (to chatter). || FAM. *To feel like a wet rag*, estar hecho polvo. | *To put one's glad rags on*, ponerse los trapitos de cristianar. || *To tear to rags*, hacer jirones *or* pedazos.
rag [ræg] v. tr. Tomar el pelo a (to tease). || Dar *or* gastar bromas a (to play practical jokes on). || Echar una bronca a (to scold).
— V. intr. Armar jaleo. || Hacer payasadas.
ragamuffin [ˈrægəˌmʌfin] n. Golfo, *m.*
rag-and-bone man [ˌrægənˈbəunmæn] n. Trapero, *m.*
— OBSERV. El plural es *rag-and-bone men*.
ragbag [ˈrægbæg] n. Bolsa (*f.*) donde se guardan los trapos. || FIG. Mezcolanza, *f.* (mixture). | Fregona, *f.* (untidy woman).
rag book [ˈrægbuk] n. Libro (*m.*) de trapo para niños.
rag doll [ˈrægdɔl] n. Muñeca (*f.*) de trapo.
rage [reidʒ] n. Furia, *f.*, rabia, *f.* || Furia, *f.* (of the sea, etc.). || Pasión, *f.*, fervor, *m.* (passion). || Afán, *m.* (desire): *the rage of conquest*, el afán de conquista. || — FIG. *To be all the rage*, hacer furor, estar en boga. || *To fly into a rage*, enfurecerse, montar en cólera.
rage [reidʒ] v. intr. Estar furioso, rabiar (to be furious). || Hacer estragos (disease, fire). || Estar enfurecido (sea). || Bramar (wind).
rag fair [ˈrægfɛə*] n. Mercado (*m.*) de ropa vieja *or* de cosas viejas, Rastro, *m.* (in Madrid).
ragged [ˈrægid] adj. Desigual (surface). || Recortado, da (cloud, rock). || Mellado, da (edge). || Harapiento, ta; andrajoso, sa (people). || Roto, ta; hecho jirones (clothes). || FIG. Desigual (performance, work, style). | Descuidado, da (sentence). | Discordante (note). | Áspero, ra (voice). | Desordenado, da (formation). || — U. S. *On the ragged edge*, en situación precaria. | *On the ragged edge of*, al borde de.
raggedly [—li] adv. Con la ropa hecha jirones (in rags). || De una manera discordante (to sing).
raggedness [—nis] n. Estado (*m.*) andrajoso (of clothing). || Aspecto (*m.*) harapiento (of people). || Desigualdad, *f.* (of ground). || FIG. Desigualdad, *f.* (of style, performance, work). | Falta (*f.*) de cohesión (of a team).
raging [reidziŋ] n. Furor, *m.*
— Adj. Furioso, sa (person). || Encrespado, da (sea). || Incontenible, violento, ta (passion, anger). || Muy fuerte (fever, headache). || Voraz, feroz (hunger). || Terrible (thirst). || Extraordinario, ria; colosal (success, beauty, etc.).
raglan [ˈræglən] adj. Raglán: *raglan sleeve*, manga raglán.
— N. Raglán, *m.* (overcoat).
ragman [ˈrægˌmæn] n. Trapero, *m.*
— OBSERV. El plural de esta palabra es *ragmen*.
ragout [ˈrægu:] n. CULIN. Ragú, *m.*, guiso, *m.*
ragpicker [ˈrægˌpikə*] n. U. S. Trapero, ra.
ragtag [ˈrægtæg] n. FAM. Chusma, *f.* || FAM. *Ragtag and bobtail*, gentuza, *f.*, chusma, *f.*
ragtime [ˈrægtaim] n. MUS. Música (*f.*) de jazz de ritmo sincopado.
ragweed [ˈrægwi:d] n. BOT. Ambrosía, *f.*
ragwort [ˈrægwə:t] n. BOT. Hierba (*f.*) cana, zuzón, *m.*

raid [reid] n. Correría, *f.*, incursión, *f.*, ataque (*m.*) repentino (military attack). || Ataque, *m.*, incursión, *f.* (aerial attack). || Asalto, *m.* (robbery). || Redada, *f.*, batida, *f.* (by the police). || Maniobra (*f.*) para hacer bajar los precios (stock exchange).

raid [reid] v. tr. MIL. Atacar por sorpresa. || Asaltar (to rob). || Hacer una redada en (the police).
— V. intr. Hacer una incursión.

raider [reidə*] n. Invasor, *m.* (invader). || MAR. Buque (*m.*) corsario. || AVIAT. Bombardero, *m.* || Ladrón, *m.* (thief).

rail [reil] n. Barandilla, *f.*, baranda, *f.* (of balcony). || Pretil, *m.*, antepecho, *m.* (of bridge). || Antepecho, *m.* (of window). || Barandilla, *f.*, baranda, *f.*, pasamanos, *m. inv.* (of stairs). || Barrote, *m.* (of chair). || Pretil, *m.* (on high building). || Barra, *f.* (bar). || Adral, *m.* (of a cart). || Codal, *m.*, entibo, *m.* (brace, strut). || MAR. Barandilla, *f.*, batayola, *f.* || Cerco, *m.*, valla, *f.* (fence). || Verja, *f.* (fence of iron). || Cerca, *f.*, barrera, *f.* (of a racecourse). || Baranda, *f.* (of billiard table). || Riel, *m.*, raíl, *m.*, carril, *m.* (for trains, trams, etc.). || Ferrocarril, *m.*, vía (*f.*) férrea (method of transport): *to send by rail*, mandar por ferrocarril. || Rascón, *m.* (bird). || — Pl. Ferrocarriles, *m.* (shares). || — FIG. *On the rails*, en marcha. || TECH. *Rail chair*, cojinete (*m.*) del carril. || *Rail network*, red ferroviaria. || *Rail strike*, huelga (*f.*) de ferroviarios. || *To run off the rails*, descarrilar.

rail [reil] v. tr. Poner barandilla a (balcony, staircase). || Poner un pretil a (a bridge). || Poner un antepecho a (window). || Cercar, vallar (to fence). || Mandar por ferrocarril (to send by railway). || Transportar por ferrocarril (to transport by railway). || Poner rieles en (a track). || — *To rail against* o *at*, denostar contra. || *To rail in* o *off* o *round*, cercar.

railcar [—kɑ:*] n. Automotor, *m.*, autovía, *f.*

railer [—ə*] n. Denigrante, *m.* & *f.* (detractor). || Quejica, *m.* & *f.* (grouser).

rail gauge [—geidʒ] n. Ancho (*m.*) de vías.

railhead [—hed] n. Cabeza (*f.*) de línea. || MIL. Cabeza (*f.*) de etapa ferroviaria.

railing [ˈreiliŋ] n. Valla, *f.*, cerco, *m.* (fence of wood). || Verja, *f.* (fence of iron). || Barandilla, *f.*, baranda, *f.* (of balcony). || Pretil, *m.*, antepecho, *m.* (of bridge). || Pasamanos, *m. inv.* (on stairs). || Rieles, *m. pl.*, raíles, *m. pl.* (for trains, trams etc.).

raillery [ˈreiləri] n. Burla, *f.*

railroad [ˈreil,rəud] n. U. S. Vía (*f.*) férrea (track). || Ferrocarril, *m.* || — *Railroad car*, coche (*m.*) de ferrocarril. || *Railroad crossing*, cruce (*m.*) de vías. || *Railroad junction*, empalme, *m.* || *Railroad siding* o *switch*, apartadero, *m.*

railroad [ˈreil,rəud] v. tr. U. S. Transportar por ferrocarril *or* por vía férrea. || U. S. FAM. Hacer votar apresuradamente (motion, etc.). | Encarcelar bajo acusación falsa (to cause to be sent to prison).

railway [ˈreil,wei] n. Vía (*f.*) férrea (track). || Ferrocarril, *m.* (organization). || Línea (*f.*) de ferrocarril (route). || U. S. Tranvía, *m.* (tramcar).
— Adj. Férreo, a (line). || Por ferrocarril, por vía férrea (transport). || Ferroviario, ria: *railway traffic, bridge*, tráfico, puente ferroviario.

railway car [ˈreilweikɑ:*] n. U. S. Vagón, *m.*, coche, *m.*

railway carriage [ˈreilweiˈkæridʒ] n. Vagón, *m.*, coche, *m.*

railway crossing [ˈreilweiˈkrɔsiŋ] n. Cruce (*m.*) *or* intersección (*f.*) de vías. || Paso (*m.*) a nivel (level crossing).

railway engine [ˈreilweiˈendʒin] n. Locomotora, *f.*

railway line [ˈreilweilain] n. Línea (*f.*) *or* vía (*f.*) férrea.

railwayman [ˈreilweimən] n. Ferroviario, *m.*

— OBSERV. El plural de esta palabra es *railwaymen*.

railway station [ˈreilweiˈsteiʃən] n. Estación, *f.* [de ferrocarril].

railway system [ˈreilweiˈsistim] n. Red (*f.*) ferroviaria.

raiment [ˈreimənt] n. Vestimenta, *f.*

rain [rein] n. Lluvia, *f.*: *in the rain*, bajo la lluvia. || FIG. Lluvia, *f.* (of bullets, questions, etc.). | Mar, *m.* (of tears). || — FIG. *Come rain or shine*, llueva o truene, pase lo que pase. || *Drizzling rain*, llovizna, *f.* || *It looks like rain*, parece que va a llover. || *The rains*, la época de las lluvias.

rain [rein] v. impers. Llover. || — FIG. *It never rains but it pours*, las desgracias nunca vienen solas, llueve sobre mojado. | *It rained presents that day*, llovieron los regalos aquel día. | *To rain cats and dogs, to rain buckets*, llover a cántaros, caer chuzos de punta.
— V. intr. Llover (blows, etc.). || Correr (tears).
— V. tr. *To rain blows on*, llover golpes sobre.

rain belt [ˈreinbelt] n. Zona (*f.*) de lluvias.

rainbow [ˈreinbəu] n. Arco (*m.*) iris.

rainbow-hued [ˈreinbəuˈhjud] adj. Irisado, da.

rainbow trout [ˈreinbəutraut] n. Trucha (*f.*) arco iris.

rain chart [ˈreintʃɑ:t] n. Mapa (*m.*) pluviométrico.

rain check [ˈreintʃek] n. U. S. Contraseña (*f.*) que se da a los espectadores, cuando se suspende un espectáculo a causa de la lluvia, para que puedan presenciarlo en el momento en que se celebre.

rain cloud [ˈreinklaud] n. Nubarrón, *m.*

raincoat [ˈreinkəut] n. Impermeable, *m.*

raindrop [ˈreindrɔp] n. Gota (*f.*) de lluvia.

rainfall [ˈreinfɔ:l] n. Precipitación, *f.* (falling of rain). || Aguacero, *m.*, chaparrón, *m.* (shower). || Pluviometría, *f.*, cantidad (*f.*) de lluvia caída durante un tiempo determinado.

rain gauge [ˈreingeidʒ] n. Pluviómetro, *m.*

raininess [ˈreininis] n. Pluviosidad, *f.*, lo lluvioso.

rainless [ˈreinlis] adj. Sin lluvia, seco, ca: *rainless region*, región seca.

rainproof [ˈreinpru:f] adj. Impermeable.

rainproof [ˈreinpru:f] v. tr. Impermeabilizar.

rainsquall [ˈreinskwɔ:l] n. Chubasco, *m.*

rainstorm [ˈreinstɔ:m] n. Tempestad (*f.*) de lluvia, temporal, *m.*

raintight [ˈreintait] adj. Impermeable.

rainwater [ˈrein,wɔ:tə*] n. Agua (*f.*) de lluvia, agua (*f.*) llovediza.

rainwear [ˈrein,wɛə*] n. Ropa (*f.*) impermeable, impermeables, *m. pl.*

rainy [ˈreini] adj. Lluvioso, sa (climate, region). || Lluvioso, sa; de lluvia: *a rainy afternoon*, una tarde lluviosa. || De las lluvias: *the rainy season*, la estación de las lluvias. || — *It is rainy*, parece que va a llover. || FIG. *Rainy day*, tiempos (*m.*) *or* momentos (*m.*) difíciles.

raise [reiz] n. Sobremarca, *f.* (at cards). || U. S. Aumento, *m.*, subida, *f.* (of prices, wages, etc.).

raise [reiz] v. tr. Levantar, alzar (to make stand up): *to raise a fallen statue*, levantar una estatua caída. || Levantar (an object, a weight): *to raise sth. from the floor*, levantar algo del suelo. || Levantar, subir: *would you raise the window, please?*, ¿puede subir la ventanilla, por favor? || Levantar (one's head, arm, eyes). || Levantar, erigir, alzar: *they raised a statue to the mayor*, levantaron una estatua al alcalde. || Levantar, construir (to build): *they have raised a very high building*, han construido un edificio muy alto. || Subir (to heighten): *to raise sth. two metres*, subir algo dos metros. || Dar mayor altura a (a building). || Levantar (a piece of ground). || Extraer (coal). || Aumentar, subir (to increase): *to raise the temperature, the price*, subir la temperatura, el precio; *he raised his offer to two hundred pounds*, subió la oferta a doscientas libras. || Aumentar (production). || Levantar (a cloud of dust). || Izar (a flag). || Erizar (feathers, hair). || Levantar: *to raise s.o.'s spirits*, levantar los ánimos a alguien. || Ascender, elevar (to a dignity). || Provocar, levantar, causar (to provoke): *the joke raised laughter*, el chiste provocó la risa; *the book raised considerable controversy*, el libro provocó una gran controversia. || Suscitar (hopes, doubts, etc.). || Dar: *he raised a cry*, dio un grito. || Formular, presentar, hacer (a claim, a complaint). || Hacer: *I'd like to raise a point*, quisiera hacer una observación; *he raised a very good question*, hizo una pregunta muy buena. || Plantear (a problem): *this reform will raise many problems*, esta reforma va a plantear muchos problemas. || Formular, hacer, poner (objection). || Alzar, levantar (one's tone, one's voice). || Levantar (to remove): *to raise an embargo, an injunction*, levantar un embargo, un entredicho. || Sublevar, alzar, levantar (to incite to rebellion): *to raise the people*, sublevar al pueblo. || Reunir (funds). || Conseguir (money). || Emitir (loan). || MIL. Reclutar: *to raise an army of ten thousand men*, reclutar un ejército de diez mil hombres. | Levantar: *to raise a blockade, a siege*, levantar un bloqueo, un sitio. || Ascender (an officer). || MAR. Levantar, levar (anchor). | Guindar, izar (a mast). | Poner a flote (a ship). || Educar, criar (children). || Mantener (a family). || Evocar, llamar: *to raise the spirits*, evocar los espíritus. || Envidar (in card games). || REL. Resucitar: *to raise the dead*, resucitar a los muertos. || JUR. Gravar con (a tax). || MED. Producir, levantar (blisters). || CULIN. Hacer subir (dough). || AGR. Criar (livestock). | Cultivar (vegetables). || ARTS. Subir (a colour). || MATH. Elevar. || TECH. Cardar. || — *To raise game*, levantar la caza. || *To raise money on*, conseguir un préstamo sobre. || *To raise one's glass to*, brindar por. || *To raise one's hat*, descubrirse. || *To raise one's hat to s.o.*, saludar a alguien. || *To raise one's voice in protest*, levantar la voz en son de protesta. || *To raise o.s. to a sitting position*, incorporarse. || MUS. *To raise the pitch of*, subir el tono de. || *To raise s.o. from the gutter*, sacar a alguien del arroyo. || *To raise up*, levantar (to lift up).

raisin [ˈreizn] n. Pasa, *f.*

raising [ˈreiziŋ] n. Aumento, *m.*, subida, *f.* (increase). || Levantamiento, *m.* (of a building, eyes, arm, weight, etc.). || Elevación, *f.* (of one's voice). || Evocación, *f.* (of ghosts). || Reclutamiento, *m.* (of soldiers). || Levantamiento, *m.*, suspensión, *f.* (of an embargo, injunction, etc.). || Izado, *m.* (of a flag). || Resurrección, *f.* (of dead). || Elevación, *f.* (of a wall, etc.). || AGR. Cría, *f.*, crianza, *f.* (of livestock). | Cultivo, *m.* (of vegetables). || Extracción, *f.* (of coal). || Aumento, *m.* (of production). || Erizamiento, *m.* (of hair). || Ascenso, *m.*, elevación, *f.* (to a dignity). || Formulación, *f.* (of a claim, a complaint, a point). || Sublevación, *f.*, alzamiento, *m.*, levantamiento, *m.* (riot). || Consecución, *f.* (of money). || Emisión, *f.* (of a loan). || Levantamiento, *m.* (of a siege). || Ascenso, *m.* (of an officer). || Educación, *f.* (of children). || Mantenimiento, *m.*

(of a family). || Imposición, *f.* (with taxes). || Envite, *m.* (in card games). || MATH. Elevación, *f.*
raison d'être [ˈreizɔ̃:nˈdeitr] n. Razón (*f.*) de ser.
raj [rɑ:dʒ] n. Soberanía, *f.* || Imperio, *m.*: *the British raj in India*, el imperio británico en India.
raja or **rajah** [ˈrɑ:dʒə] n. Rajá, *m.*
rake [reik] n. Rastrillo, *m.* (for gardening). || AGR. Rastro, *m.*, rastrillo, *m.* || Hurgón, *m.* (for the fire). || Rastrillo, *m.*, raqueta, *f.* (for gambling). || Inclinación, *f.* (slant). || Calavera, *m.* (dissolute man).
rake [reik] v. tr. Rastrillar: *to rake the garden, the soil*, rastrillar el jardín, la tierra. || Recoger con el rastrillo: *to rake leaves*, recoger hojas con el rastrillo. || Atizar, hurgar: *to rake the fire*, hurgar el fuego. || FIG. Rastrear: *the police raked the district for the criminals*, la policía rastreó el barrio en busca de los criminales. | Buscar en: *to rake history for examples*, buscar ejemplos en la historia. | Abarcar [con la mirada] (to scan). | Dominar: *window that rakes the valley*, ventana que domina el valle. || MIL. Ametrallar, barrer, batir en enfilada (to sweep with gun fire). || Inclinar (to incline). || MAR. Inclinar. || — *To rake away* o *off*, quitar con el rastrillo. || *To rake in*, recoger con el rastrillo (gambling chips), amasar (money). || *To rake one's hand through one's hair*, pasar la mano por el pelo. || *To rake out*, quitar las cenizas de (a stove). || FAM. *To rake over the coals*, echar un rapapolvo *or* una bronca a. || *To rake together* o *up*, reunir (facts, information). || *To rake up*, sacar a luz: *to rake up an old quarrel*, sacar a luz una vieja disputa. || *To rake up the past*, sacar a relucir el pasado.
— V. intr. Inclinarse (to slant).
rake-off [—ˌɔf] n. FAM. Comisión, *f.*
raker [ˈreikə*] n. Rastrillador, ra.
raking [—iŋ] n. AGR. Rastrillado, *m.*, rastrillaje, *m.* || FAM. *Raking over the coals*, bronca, *f.*, rapapolvo, *m.*
— Adj. MIL. De enfilada (fire).
rakish [ˈreikiʃ] adj. MAR. Aerodinámico, ca (having a trim appearance). || Desenvuelto, ta (jaunty). || Libertino, na (dissolute).
rakishness [—nis] n. Desenvoltura, *f.* (jauntiness). || Vida (*f.*) disoluta, libertinaje, *m.*
rale [rɑ:l] n. MED. Estertor, *m.*
rally [ˈræli] n. Reunión, *f.*, mitin, *m.*: *political rally*, mitin político. || Reunión, *f.*: *youth rally*, reunión de jóvenes. || SP. Peloteo, *m.* (in tennis). || MED. COMM. Recuperación, *f.* || AUT. Rallye, *m.*
rally [ˈræli] v. tr. Reunir (to gather): *to rally troops, supporters*, reunir tropas, partidarios. || Recobrar: *to rally one's spirits*, recobrar el ánimo. || Reanimar (to revive). || Reírse de (to mock).
— V. intr. Reunirse (to come together). || Reorganizarse (troops). || Recuperarse (to regain strength). || Reponerse, recuperarse (from an illness). || COMM. Recuperarse. || — *To rally round s.o.*, tomar el partido de alguien. || *To rally to*, adherirse a (a party, s.o.'s opinion).
rallying [—iŋ] n. Reunión, *f.*: *rallying point*, punto de reunión.
— Adj. Burlón, ona.
ram [ræm] n. ZOOL. Carnero, *m.*, morueco, *m.* || TECH. Maza, *f.*, pilón, *m.* (of steam hammer). | Émbolo, *m.* (of a pump). | Ariete, *m.* (hydraulic). | Pisón, *m.* (rammer). || MAR. Espolón, *m.* (on prow of ship). || MIL. Ariete, *m.* (battering ram). || MIN. Taco, *m.* || ASTR. Aries, *m.* || FAM. Conquistador, *m.* (seducer).
ram [ræm] v. tr. Apisonar (to pound earth, etc.). || Hincar (with a pile driver). || Dar con: *he rammed his head against the wall*, dio con la cabeza contra la pared. || Meter a la fuerza, apretar: *he rammed it all into the suitcase*, lo metió todo en la maleta a la fuerza. || Dar con, chocar con: *he rammed the car into the wall*, dio con el coche contra la pared. || MIL. Atacar (a charge into a gun). || FIG. Meter: *to ram ideas into s.o.'s head*, meter a alguien ideas en la cabeza. || Golpear con el ariete (with the battering ram). || Embestir con el espolón (ships). || — *To ram down*, apisonar (earth), hincar (to drive in). || *To ram in*, hincar. || FIG. *To ram sth. down s.o.'s throat*, hacer tragar algo a alguien. || *To ram up*, tapar (a hole).
Ramadan [ˌræməˈdɑ:n] n. REL. Ramadán, *m.*
ramble [ˈræmbl] n. Paseo, *m.*, vuelta, *f.* (walk): *to go for a ramble*, ir a dar un paseo. || FIG. Divagaciones, *f. pl.* (talk).
ramble [ˈræmbl] v. intr. Pasear (to go for a walk). || Callejear, vagar (to roam). || FIG. Divagar (to talk or write aimlessly). | Serpentear, dar vueltas (stream, road, path, etc.). | Trepar, extenderse (plant).
rambler [—ə*] n. Paseante, *m.* & *f.* (walker). || Excursionista, *m.* & *f.* (excursionist). || Divagador, ra (one who talks without aim). || BOT. Rosal (*m.*) trepador.
rambling [—iŋ] adj. De distribución irregular, laberíntico, ca: *a rambling house*, una casa de distribución irregular. || Tortuoso, sa (street). || Sin orden ni concierto (conversation). || Errante (existence). || Sin ilación, incoherente (speech, thoughts). || BOT. Trepador, ra. || *Rambling talk*, divagaciones, *f. pl.*
— N. Excursiones, *f. pl.*, paseos, *m. pl.* || FIG. Divagaciones, *f. pl.*
ramekin or **ramequin** [ˈræmkin] n. CULIN. Pastelillo (*m.*) de queso [*Amer.*, quesadilla, *f.*]. || Recipiente (*m.*) en el que se sirve el pastelillo de queso (dish).
ramification [ˌræmifiˈkeiʃən] n. Ramificación, *f.* || FIG. Ramificación, *f.*: *the ramifications of a plot*, las ramificaciones de una conspiración.
ramify [ˈræmifai] v. tr. Hacer ramificarse, ramificar.
— V. intr. Ramificarse.
ramjet [ˈræmdʒet] n. Estatorreactor, *m.*
rammer [ˈræmə*] n. Pisón, *m.* (paviour's). || Baqueta, *f.* (ramrod).
ramose [ræˈməus] adj. Ramoso, sa.
ramp [ræmp] n. Rampa, *f.* (slope). || Elevador, *m.*: *hydraulic ramp*, elevador hidráulico. || FAM. Subida (*f.*) injustificada de los precios (price increase). | Timo, *m.*, estafa, *f.* (swindle).
ramp [ræmp] v. intr. Inclinarse (to slope). || Levantarse sobre las patas traseras (a lion). || HERALD. Estar en posición rampante (lion). || FIG. Estar hecho una furia (to rush about in anger). || Trepar (plants).
rampage [ræmˈpeidʒ] n. *To be on a rampage*, andar destrozándolo todo a su paso, alborotar.
rampage [ræmˈpeidʒ] v. intr. Comportarse violentamente (to act wildly). || Estar hecho una furia (to rush about in anger). || Andar destrozándolo todo a su paso, alborotar (to play havoc).
rampageous [—əs] adj. Alborotador, ra.
rampancy [ˈræmpənsi] n. Abundancia, *f.*, exuberancia, *f.* (of vegetation, etc.). || Proliferación, *f.* (of crime, disease, etc.).
rampant [ˈræmpənt] adj. HERALD. Rampante (lion). || Violento, ta; agresivo, va (aggressive). || Exuberante, abundante (vegetation). || Desenfrenado, da: *rampant inflation*, inflación desenfrenada. || ARCH. Por tranquil (arch). || *To be rampant*, estar extendido *or* difundido (plague, vice).
rampart [ˈræmpɑ:t] n. Muralla, *f.*: *the ramparts of a castle*, las murallas de un castillo. || FIG. Defensa, *f.*, amparo, *m.*, escudo, *m.*
rampart [ˈræmpɑ:t] v. tr. Rodear con una muralla.
rampion [ˈræmpjən] n. BOT. Ruiponce, *m.*, rapónchigo, *m.*
ramrod [ˈræmrɔd] n. MIL. Baqueta, *f.* (of rifle). | Escobillón, *m.* (of gun). || FAM. *Straight as a ramrod*, más tieso que un huso.
ramshackle [ˈræmˌʃækl] adj. Desvencijado, da.
ran [ræn] pret. See RUN.
ranch [rɑ:ntʃ] n. Rancho, *m.* (in United States). || Hacienda, *f.*, estancia, *f.* (in Latin America).
ranch [rɑ:ntʃ] v. intr. Llevar un rancho (in United States). || Llevar una hacienda *or* una estancia (in Latin America).
rancher [—ə*] or **ranchman** [—mən] n. Ranchero, *m.*, ganadero, *m.*

— OBSERV. El plural de *ranchman* es *ranchmen*.

rancid [ˈrænsid] adj. Rancio, cia: *to get rancid*, ponerse rancio.
rancidity [rænˈsiditi] or **rancidness** [ˈrænsidnis] n. Rancidez, *f.*, ranciedad, *f.*
rancorous [ˈræŋkərəs] adj. Rencoroso, sa.
rancour (U. S. **rancor**) [ˈræŋkə*] n. Rencor, *m.*
randiness [—inis] n. FAM. Cachondez, *f.*
random [ˈrændəm] adj. Hecho al azar: *random bombing*, bombardeo hecho al azar; *a random selection of articles*, una selección de artículos hecha al azar. || Escogido al azar: *a random passage in a book*, un fragmento de un libro escogido al azar. || Fortuito, ta: *random remark*, observación fortuita. || Aleatorio, ria. || — *At a random guess*, a ojo de buen cubero. || *Random shot*, bala perdida (stray bullet), tiro pegado sin apuntar (chance shot).
— N. *At random*, al azar. || *To talk at random*, hablar sin orden ni concierto *or* sin ton ni son.
randy [ˈrændi] adj. FAM. Cachondo, da.
rang [ræŋ] pret. See RING.
range [ˈreindʒ] n. Fila, *f.*, hilera, *f.* (row): *a range of houses*, una hilera de casas. || Cadena, *f.* (of mountains). || Extensión, *f.*, zona, *f.* (area): *a wide range of meadows*, una gran extensión de praderas. || Alcance, *m.* (maximum attainable distance): *the range of a rocket, a gun, a telescope*, el alcance de un cohete, de un fusil, de un telescopio. || Distancia, *f.*: *the gun fired at a range of two hundred metres*, el cañón tiró a una distancia de doscientos metros. || Autonomía, *f.*, radio (*m.*) de acción (maximum attainable distance without refuelling): *the range of an aircraft*, la autonomía de un avión. || MIL. Campo (*m.*) de tiro (for rifles). | Polígono, *m.* (for artillery). || Barraca (*f.*) de tiro al blanco (in a fair). || MUS. Registro, *m.* (of voice, instrument). || FIG. Alcance, *m.* (scope): *within the range of*, al alcance de; *Kant is out of my range*, Kant no está a mi alcance. | Gama, *f.*, escala, *f.* (of frequencies, of colours, of prices). | Variedad, *f.*: *a wide range of subjects*, una gran variedad de temas. | Surtido, *m.*: *this shop has a large range of ties*, esta tienda tiene un gran surtido de corbatas. | Esfera, *f.*: *the upper ranges of society*, las altas esferas de la sociedad. | Campo, *m.*: *the range of science*, el campo de la ciencia. | Extensión, *f.* (of knowledge). || Cocina (*f.*) económica (cooking stove). || Habitación, *f.*, área (*f.*) que habita una especie animal *or* vegetal. || U. S. Dehesa, *f.* (grazing land for cattle). || — *At*

close range, de cerca. || *Out of range*, fuera de alcance. || *Range of action*, campo de actividad, esfera de acción *or* de actividad. || *Range of mountains*, cordillera, *f.*, sierra, *f.* || *Range of vision*, campo (*m.*) visual. || *To be in range*, estar al alcance *or* a tiro. || *To be in range with*, estar alineado con. || *To give free range to*, dar rienda suelta a (one's imagination). || MIL. *To rectify the range*, corregir el tiro.

range [ˈreindʒ] v. tr. Alinear (to set in a row): *the trees were ranged along the road*, los árboles estaban alineados a lo largo de la carretera. || Colocar (to place). || Clasificar (to classify). || Recorrer (to wander through): *to range the countryside*, recorrer el campo. || PRINT. Alinear (to set type in line). || MAR. Costear, bordear (the coast). || MIL. Apuntar: *to range a gun on an enemy ship*, apuntar un cañón hacia un barco enemigo. || Enfocar (a telescope). || U. S. Apacentar (to graze). || — FIG. *To range o.s. against s.o.*, ponerse en contra de alguien. | *To range o.s. with the opposition*, ponerse del lado de la oposición.

— V. intr. Alinearse (to be in line): *the peaks ranged as far as he could see*, las cimas se alineaban hasta donde alcanzaba la vista. || Extenderse: *the frontier ranges from north to south*, la frontera se extiende del norte al sur. || Oscilar, fluctuar, variar: *the temperature ranges between eighty and ninety degrees*, la temperatura oscila entre ochenta y noventa grados; *prices range between one and twenty pounds*, los precios oscilan entre una y veinte libras. || Tener un alcance: *this gun ranges over eight miles*, este cañón tiene un alcance de más de ocho millas. || — *Latitudes between which a plant ranges*, latitudes entre las cuales se encuentra una planta. || *To range along*, bordear. || *To range over*, recorrer: *to range over the country*, recorrer el país; *his eyes ranged over the audience*, recorrió al público con la mirada; abarcar: *the talk ranged over a number of topics*, el discurso abarcó muchos temas; vivir en: *this animal ranges over the southern regions*, este animal vive en las regiones del sur. || *To range with the great poets*, ser uno de los poetas más grandes.

range finder [ˈreindʒˌfaində*] n. Telémetro, *m.*

ranger [ˈreindʒə*] n. Guardabosques, *m. inv.* (park or forest keeper). || MIL. Soldado (*m.*) de un comando. || — Pl. U. S. Policía (*f. sing.*) montada.

rangy [ˈreindzi] adj. Ágil (agile). || Espacioso, sa (wide).

ranidae [ˈrænədi:] pl. n. ZOOL. Ránidos, *m.*

rank [ræŋk] n. MIL. Fila, *f.* (of soldiers). | Graduación, *f.*, grado, *m.*: *what rank are you?*, ¿qué graduación tiene usted? || Fila, *f.*, hilera, *f.* (row, line). || Categoría, *f.*, clase, *f.*: *dancer of the first rank*, bailarina de primera categoría; *people of all ranks*, gente de todas clases. || Rango, *m.*, categoría, *f.*: *to have the rank of ambassador*, tener rango de embajador. || Calidad, *f.*: *a man of rank*, un hombre de calidad. || AUT. Parada, *f.* (of taxis). || Fila, *f.* (chess). || — Pl. MIL. Tropa, *f. sing.*, soldados (*m.*) rasos. || — *Rank and file*, soldados rasos (soldiers), masa, *f.*, gente (*f.*) del montón (ordinary people), base, *f.* (of trade unions, etc.). || MIL. *To be in the ranks*, estar en filas. | *To break ranks*, romper filas. | *To close the ranks*, estrechar *or* cerrar las filas. | *To fall in rank*, ponerse en filas. | *To join the ranks*, alistarse (a soldier). || FIG. *To join the ranks of*, unirse a. || MIL. *To rise from the ranks*, ser ascendido a oficial, ser patatero (fam.) | *To serve in the ranks*, ser soldado raso.

— Adj. Exuberante (vegetation). || Tupido, da (thick): *rank grass*, hierba tupida. || Fértil, rico, ca (soil). || Completo, ta; absoluto, ta (deceit). || Manifiesto, ta; flagrante (injustice). || Rematado, da; completo, ta: *he is a rank idiot*, es un idiota completo. || Verdadero, ra; auténtico, ca (poison). || Grosero, ra; vulgar (coarse). || Rancio, cia (rancid). || Fétido, da; maloliente (foul-smelling). || — *Rank lie*, pura mentira. || *To smell rank*, oler muy mal.

rank [ræŋk] v. tr. MIL. Alinear, poner en fila (soldiers). || Situar, colocar, poner (to estimate): *I rank him amongst the greatest*, le sitúo entre los mejores. || U. S. Ser superior a (to outrank).

— V. intr. Figurar, estar, encontrarse: *he ranks amongst the best*, figura entre los mejores. || Considerarse: *it ranks as one of his best films*, se considera como una de sus mejores películas. || — *To rank above*, ser superior a. || *To rank below*, ser inferior a. || *To rank high*, sobresalir, distinguirse. || *To rank with*, estar al mismo nivel que.

ranker [—ə*] n. MIL. Oficial (*m.*) que antes fue soldado raso, patatero, *m.* (fam.) [officer].

ranking [—iŋ] adj. De mayor categoría.

rankle [ˈræŋkl] v. intr. Causar rencor. || *The insult rankled in her mind*, todavía le dolía el insulto.

rankly [—i] adv. Con exuberancia (to grow). || Con un olor fétido (to smell).

rankness [—nis] n. Exuberancia, *f.* (of vegetation). || Olor (*m.*) fétido (smell). || Rancidez, *f.*, ranciedad, *f.* (taste). || Enormidad, *f.* (of a lie).

ransack [ˈrænsæk] v. tr. Saquear (to rob). || Registrar (to search thoroughly): *to ransack a drawer for a document*, registrar un cajón para encontrar un documento.

ransom [ˈrænsəm] n. Rescate, *m.* (for a prisoner). || REL. Redención, *f.* || — FIG. *To be worth a king's ransom*, valer su peso en oro. || *To hold s.o. to ransom*, pedir *or* exigir rescate por uno (for a prisoner), hacer chantaje a alguien (to blackmail).

ransom [ˈrænsəm] v. tr. Rescatar (to pay ransom for): *he was ransomed for ten thousand pounds*, fue rescatado por diez mil libras. || Pedir *or* exigir rescate por (to demand ransom for). || REL. Redimir (of sins).

ransoming [—iŋ] n. Rescate, *m.*

rant [rænt] n. Discurso (*m.*) rimbombante.

rant [rænt] v. tr. Decir con rimbombancia.

— V. intr. Hablar con rimbombancia (to speak bombastically). || Divagar, desvariar (to rave). || Declamar con exageración (an actor). || Vociferar, echar pestes (to be noisily angry).

rantan [ˈrænˌtæn] n. FAM. *To go on the rantan*, ir de francachela, ir de parranda.

ranter [—ə*] n. Orador (*m.*) rimbombante. || Energúmeno, *m.*

ranting [—iŋ] adj. Rimbombante, ampuloso, sa.

— N. Discurso (*m.*) rimbombante *or* violento.

ranunculaceae [rænʌŋkjuˈleisii:] pl. n. BOT. Ranunculáceas, *f.*

ranunculus [ræˈnʌŋkjuləs] n. BOT. Ranúnculo, *m.*, botón (*m.*) de oro.

— OBSERV. El plural de *ranunculus* es *ranunculuses* o *ranunculi.*

rap [ræp] n. Golpecito, *m.*, golpe (*m.*) seco: *a rap at the door*, un golpecito en la puerta. || — FIG. *Not to be worth a rap*, no valer un comino. | *Not to care a rap*, importarle a uno un comino. | *To give s.o. a rap on the knuckles*, llamar a uno al orden, poner a uno en su sitio. | *To take the rap*, pagar el pato.

rap [ræp] v. tr. Golpear, dar un golpe en. || Arrebatar (to stir). || Regañar (to scold). || *To rap out*, espetar, soltar: *he rapped out a command*, espetó una orden; transmitir por golpes (a message).

— V. intr. *To rap at* o *on*, golpear, dar un golpe en.

rapacious [rəˈpeiʃəs] adj. De rapiña, rapaz (bird, animal). || FIG. Rapaz.

rapaciously [—li] adv. Con rapacidad.

rapaciousness [—nis] or **rapacity** [rəˈpæsiti] n. Rapacidad, *f.*

rape [ˈreip] n. JUR. Violación, *f.* (forcible sexual intercourse). || FIG. Asolamiento, *m.*, saqueo, *m.* (plundering). | Violación, *f.* (invasion). || BOT. Colza, *f.* || Orujo, *m.* (of grapes). || — *Rape cake*, torta (*f.*) de orujo, borujo, *m.* || *Rape oil*, aceite (*m.*) de colza. || *The Rape of the Sabine Women*, el Rapto de las Sabinas.

rape [ˈreip] v. tr. JUR. Violar. || FIG. Saquear, asolar (to plunder). | Violar (to invade).

rapeseed [—si:d] n. Semilla (*f.*) de colza.

Raphael [ˈræfeiəl] pr. n. Rafael, *m.*

Raphaelesque [ˌræfiəˈlesk] adj. Rafaelesco, ca.

rapid [ˈræpid] adj. Rápido, da: *rapid movement*, movimiento rápido; *to make rapid progress*, hacer progresos rápidos. || Muy empinado, da; muy pendiente (slope).

— N. Rápido, *m.* (in a river): *to shoot the rapids*, salvar los rápidos.

rapid-fire [—ˈfaiə*] or **rapid-firing** [—ˈfaiəriŋ] adj. De tiro rápido (gun).

rapidity [rəˈpiditi] n. Rapidez, *f.*

rapier [ˈreipjə*] n. Espadín, *m.*, estoque, *m.* || *Rapier thrust*, estocada, *f.*

rapine [ˈræpain] n. Rapiña, *f.*, saqueo, *m.*

rapist [ˈreipist] n. Violador, *m.* || Raptor, *m.*

rappee [ræˈpi:] n. Rapé, *m.* (snuff).

rapping [ˈræpiŋ] n. Golpecitos, *m. pl.*, golpes (*m. pl.*) secos.

rapport [ræˈpɔ:] n. Relación, *f.* (connection). || Compenetración, *f.*, armonía, *f.* (sympathy).

rapporteur [ˌræpɔ:ˈtə:*] n. Ponente, *m.* [*Amer.*, relator, *m.*]

rapprochement [ræˈprɔʃmɑ̃:ŋ] n. Acercamiento, *m.*, aproximación, *f.*

rapscallion [ræpˈskæljən] n. Golfo, *m.*, bribón, *m.*

rapt [ræpt] adj. Absorto, ta; ensimismado, da: *rapt in thought*, absorto en sus pensamientos. || Profundo, da: *rapt attention*, atención profunda. || Embelesado, da (enraptured).

raptorial [ræpˈtɔ:riəl] adj. ZOOL. De rapiña, de presa.

rapture [ˈræptʃə*] n. Éxtasis, *m.*, arrobamiento, *m.*, embeleso, *m.* (ecstasy). || — *To be in raptures*, estar extasiado. || *To go into raptures over*, extasiarse por.

rapture [ˈræptʃə*] v. tr. Arrobar, extasiar, embelesar.

rapturous [ˈræptʃərəs] adj. Entusiasta (applause, cries). || Desbordante (joy). || Embelesado, da; extasiado, da; en éxtasis (people).

rare [rɛə*] adj. Raro, ra; poco frecuente: *a rare event*, un acontecimiento poco frecuente. || Poco común (uncommon). || Excepcional, raro, ra (extraordinary). || CHEM. Raro, ra. || Enrarecido, da (atmosphere). || FAM. Enorme: *you gave me a rare fright*, me has dado un susto enorme. | Estupendo, da; excelente: *we had a rare meal last night*, tuvimos una comida estupenda anoche. || CULIN. Poco hecho (meat).

rarebit [ˈrɛəbit] n. *Welsh rarebit*, pan (*m.*) tostado con queso derretido.

rarefaction [ˌrɛəriˈfækʃən] n. Rarefacción, *f.*, enrarecimiento, *m.*

rarefactive [ˌrɛəriˈfæktiv] adj. Rarificativo, va; rarificante.

rarefied [ˈrɛərifaid] adj. Enrarecido, da (atmosphere).

rarefy [ˈrɛərifai] v. tr. Enrarecer, rarificar (gas). || FIG. Hacer más sutil (to make more subtle). | Refinar (to refine).
— V. intr. Enrarecerse, rarificarse (gases).
rarely [ˈrɛəli] adv. Raramente, raras veces, poco frecuentemente (not frequently). || FAM. Estupendamente, maravillosamente.
rareness [ˈrɛənis] n. Rareza, *f.* || Enrarecimiento, *m.*, rarefacción, *f.* (of atmosphere).
raring [ˈrɛəriŋ] adj. Deseoso, sa.
rarity [ˈrɛəriti] n. Rareza, *f.* (rareness, object): *this object is a rarity*, este objeto es una rareza. || *Rain is a rarity here*, es raro que llueva aquí, no llueve casi nunca aquí.
rascal [ˈrɑ:skəl] n. Tunante, *m.*, bribón, *m.*, pícaro, *m.*
rascality [rɑ:sˈkæliti] n. Bribonería, *f.*, picardía, *f.*
rascally [ˈrɑ:skəli] adj. Pícaro, ra; bribón, ona. || *My rascally son*, el pícaro de mi hijo.
rase [reiz] v. tr. Arrasar.
rash [ræʃ] adj. Precipitado, da; irreflexivo, va (action). || Temerario, ria; impetuoso, sa (person). || Imprudente (promise, words).
— N. MED. Sarpullido, *m.*, salpullido, *m.*, erupción (*f.*) cutánea.
rasher [—ə*] n. Loncha, *f.*, lonja, *f.* (bacon, ham).
rashly [—li] adj. Sin reflexionar (to act). || A la ligera (to speak).
rashness [—nis] n. Precipitación, *f.* || Temeridad, *f.*, impetuosidad, *f.* (impetuosity). || Irreflexión, *f.* || Imprudencia, *f.*
rasp [rɑ:sp] n. TECH. Escofina, *f.* (file). || Chirrido, *m.* (noise).
rasp [rɑ:sp] v. tr. Raspar, escofinar (to file). || CULIN. Rallar (bread). || FIG. Dañar, lastimar (ears). | Herir (s.o.'s feelings). | Crispar (to annoy). || — *To rasp away*, quitar con la escofina (with a file), rallar (bread). || *To rasp out*, decir con voz áspera (an oath, order).
— V. intr. Chirriar (sound). || Hablar con voz áspera.
raspberry [ˈrɑ:zbəri] n. BOT. Frambuesa, *f.* (fruit). | Frambueso, *m.* (plant). || Color (*m.*) frambuesa (colour). || — FAM. *To blow s.o. a raspberry*, hacer un gesto de desprecio a uno, hacer la higa a uno. | *To get a raspberry from*, recibir una bronca de. | *To give s.o. a raspberry*, abuchear a alguien (to boo).
raspberry bush [—buʃ] or **raspberry cane** [—kein] n. BOT. Frambueso, *m.*
rasping [rɑ:spiŋ] n. Raspado, *m.*, raspadura, *f.* (act). || Chirrido, *m.* (sound). || — Pl. CULIN. Pan (*m. sing.*) rallado.
— Adj. Áspero, ra (voice). || Chirriante (sound).
rat [ræt] n. ZOOL. Rata, *f.*: *brown rat*, rata de alcantarilla; *water rat*, rata de agua. || FAM. Esquirol, *m.* (blackleg). | Traidor, ra (betrayer). | Delator, ra (accuser). | Canalla, *m.* (contemptible person). | Desertor, *m.* (quitter). || U. S. FAM. Postizo, *m.* (hair). || — *Extermination of rats*, desratización, *f.* || FAM. *I smell a rat*, hay gato encerrado. | *Like a drowned rat*, calado hasta los huesos, hecho una sopa. | *Rats!*, ¡cáscaras! (expression of annoyance), ¡ni hablar! (out of the question!). | *To be caught like a rat in a trap*, caer en la ratonera. | *To smell a rat*, sospechar algo.
rat [ræt] v. intr. Cazar ratas (to hunt rats). || FAM. Ser esquirol (worker). | Desertar (to let one's side down). | Chaquetear, volver casaca (to turn coat). || FAM. *To rat on*, chivarse de, denunciar: *to rat on a pal*, denunciar a un amigote.
ratable [ˈreitəbl] adj. See RATEABLE.
ratafia [ˌrætəˈfiə] n. Ratafía, *f.*
ratal [ˈreitl] n. Valor (*m.*) imponible.
ratan [rəˈtæn] n. BOT. Rota, *f.*, junco (*m.*) de Indias. || Bastón (*m.*) de caña (walking stick).
ratcatcher [ˈrætˌkætʃə*] n. Cazador (*m.*) de ratas.
ratch [rætʃ] n. TECH. Trinquete, *m.*
ratchet [—it] n. TECH. Trinquete, *m.* (hinged catch). | Rueda (*f.*) de trinquete (ratchet wheel). | Uña, *f.* (of a ratch).
ratchet wheel [—itˌwi:l] n. TECH. Rueda (*f.*) de trinquete.
rate [reit] n. Proporción, *f.* (ratio). || Índice, *m.*, coeficiente, *m.*: *birth rate*, índice de natalidad; *rate of increase*, coeficiente de incremento; *rate of growth*, índice de crecimiento. || Velocidad, *f.* (speed): *he drives at a moderate rate*, conduce a una velocidad moderada. || Ritmo, *m.*: *the rate of production is very rapid*, el ritmo de la producción es muy rápido. || Precio, *m.*, tarifa, *f.* (price): *reduced rate*, tarifa reducida; *advertising rates*, precios de la publicidad; *buying rate*, precio de compra; *free market rate*, precio libre; *full rate*, precio sin descuento; *selling rate*, precio de venta. || Tanto (*m.*) por ciento, porcentaje, *m.* (percentage). || Tipo, *m.* (of discount, interest): *rate of interest*, tipo de interés; *bank rate*, tipo de descuento bancario. || Interés, *m.*: *rates for money on loan*, intereses de un préstamo. || Prima, *f.* (of insurance): *insurance rate*, prima de seguros. || Nivel, *m.* (of salaries, etc.). || COMM. Cotización, *f.* (in the stock exchange): *market rates*, cotizaciones en el mercado; *rate of gold*, cotización del oro. || MED. Frecuencia, *f.* (of the pulse). || — Pl. Contribución (*f. sing.*) municipal, impuesto (*m. sing.*) municipal. || — *Annual rate*, anualidad, *f.* || *A second-rate hotel*, un hotel de segunda categoría. || *At any rate*, de todos modos, de todas formas, en todo caso. || *At that rate*, de ese modo. || *At the rate of 500 litres per day*, a razón de 500 litros por día. || *At this rate*, si continuamos así. || *Basic salary rate* o *base rate*, sueldo (*m.*) base. || *Borough rates*, impuestos municipales. || *Commission rates*, comisión, *f.* || *Discount rate*, tipo de descuento. || *Effective rates*, cotización real. || *Exchange rates*, cambio, *m.* || *First rate*, de primera clase. || *Freight rate*, flete, *m.* || *Inclusive rate*, precio a tanto alzado. || *Inland rate*, precio nacional *or* interior. || *Letter rate*, franqueo, *m.* || *Postage rate*, tarifa. || *Rate of exchange*, cambio, *m.*, tipo de cambio. || *Rate of flow*, caudal medio (of water), régimen, *m.* (of electricity). || *Rate of living*, tren (*m.*) de vida.
rate [reit] v. tr. Tasar, valorar (*at*, en) [to assess the value of]. || Estimar (to estimate): *to rate s.o. highly*, estimar mucho a alguien. || Considerar: *they rate him as a public menace*, le consideran como una amenaza pública. || MAR. AUT. Clasificar. || Reñir, echar una bronca (to scold). || U. S. Merecer (to deserve). | Clasificar (a pupil). || — *I rate him among my friends*, le cuento entre mis amigos. || *What is the house rated at?*, ¿cuál es la contribución que hay que pagar por la casa?
— V. intr. Ser considerado (*as*, como): *he rates as a fine workman*, es considerado como un buen trabajador. || FAM. *To rate with s.o.*, gozar de la estima de alguien.
rateable [—əbl] adj. Valorable. || Imponible (value).
ratepayer [ˈreitˌpeiə*] n. Contribuyente, *m.* & *f.*
ratepaying [ˈreitˌpeiiŋ] adj. Contribuyente (taxpayer).
— N. Pago (*m.*) de impuestos.
rather [ˈrɑ:ðə*] adv. Más bien: *rather long than short*, más bien largo que corto. || Bastante: *this matter is rather important*, esta cuestión es bastante importante; *I rather like it*, me gusta bastante. || Algo, un poco (somewhat): *John is rather stupid*, Juan es algo estúpido; *rather better*, un poco mejor. || — *Anything rather than*, todo menos. || *I had rather not* o *I would rather not*, no me apetece. || *I rather like it*, no me disgusta. || *I would rather leave than stay here*, preferiría *or* prefiero irme que quedarme aquí. || *I would rather not go*, preferiría *or* prefiero no ir. || *Or rather*, mejor dicho.
— Interj. ¡Ya lo creo!, ¡por supuesto! [*Amer.*, ¡cómo no!]: *do you know him? — Rather!*, ¿le conoce? — ¡Ya lo creo! || *Rather not!*, ¡claro que no!
raticide [ˈrætisaid] n. Raticida, *m.*
ratification [ˌrætifiˈkeiʃən] n. Ratificación, *f.*
ratify [ˈrætifai] v. tr. Ratificar.
ratifying [—iŋ] adj. Ratificatorio, ria.
rating [ˈreitiŋ] n. Estimación, *f.*, tasación, *f.*, valoración, *f.* (estimate). || Rango, *m.* (rank). || MAR. Marinero, *m.* || Clasificación, *f.* (of engines, cars, ships). || SP. Clase, *f.*, categoría, *f.* || Crédito, *m.* (of a business concern). || Derrama, *f.* (of local taxes). || ELECTR. Condiciones (*f. pl.*) normales de funcionamiento. || FAM. Bronca, *f.* (scolding): *to give s.o. a rating*, echarle una bronca a alguien. || U. S. Clasificación, *f.* (of a pupil).
ratio [ˈreiʃiəu] n. Proporción, *f.*, relación, *f.*: *the ratio of men to women is two to three*, la proporción entre los hombres y las mujeres es de dos a tres; *in the ratio of*, en la proporción de. || MATH. Razón, *f.* || *In direct, indirect ratio to*, en razón directa, inversa con.
ratiocinate [ˌrætiˈɔsineit] v. intr. Raciocinar, razonar.
ratiocination [ˌrætiɔsiˈneiʃən] n. Raciocinio, *m.*, razonamiento, *m.*
ration [ˈræʃən] n. Ración, *f.* (food). || Porción, *f.* (time). || — Pl. Víveres, *m.*, suministro, *m. sing.*, aprovisionamiento, *m. sing.* || — *Emergency* o *iron ration*, reserva (*f.*) de víveres. || *To be off the ration*, no estar racionado. || *To be on the ration*, estar racionado. || FIG. *To put on short rations*, racionar, poner a media ración. || *To put on the ration*, racionar.
ration [ˈræʃən] v. tr. Racionar: *to ration bread*, racionar el pan. || *To ration out*, racionar.
rational [—l] adj. Racional: *man is a rational animal*, el hombre es un animal racional; *his criticism is very rational*, su crítica es muy racional. || Razonable, sensato, ta (reasonable). || Lógico, ca (logical). || Racionalista (tendencies). || MATH. Racional. || FAM. Práctico, ca.
rationale [ˌræʃəˈnɑ:l] n. Razón (*f.*) fundamental, base, *f.*, fundamento, *m.* (basis). || Análisis (*m.*) razonado, exposición (*f.*) razonada (explanation).
rationalism [ˈræʃnəlizəm] n. Racionalismo, *f.*
rationalist [ˈræʃnəlist] adj./n. Racionalista.
rationalistic [ˌræʃnəˈlistik] adj. Racionalista.
rationality [ˌræʃəˈnæliti] n. Racionalidad, *f.*
rationalization [ˌræʃnəlaiˈzeiʃən] n. Racionalización, *f.* (of industry, etc.).
rationalize [ˈræʃnəlaiz] v. tr. Racionalizar.
ration book [ˈræʃənbuk] or **ration card** [ˈræʃən kɑ:d] n. Cartilla (*f.*) de racionamiento.
rationing [ˈræʃniŋ] n. Racionamiento, *m.*
ratline [ˈrætlin] n. MAR. Flechaste, *m.*
rat poison [ˈrætˈpɔizn] n. Matarratas, *m. inv.*, raticida, *m.*
rat race [ˈrætreis] n. FIG. Competición, *f.*, competencia, *f.*, lucha (*f.*) incesante [para triunfar].

rattan [rəˈtæn] n. BOT. Rota, *f.*, junco (*m.*) de Indias. || Bastón (*m.*) de caña (walking stick).
rat-tat-tat [ˈrætəˈtæt] interj. ¡Pum! ¡pum!
ratteen [rəˈti:n] n. Ratina, *f.* (cloth).
ratter [ˈrætə*] n. Perro (*m.*) ratero. || FIG. FAM. Traidor, *m.* (betrayer). | Esquirol, *m.* (blackleg).
rattle [rætl] n. Sonajero, *m.* (baby's toy). || Carraca, *f.*, matraca, *f.* (of football fans). || Traqueteo, *m.* (noise of train, carriage). || Ruido (*m.*) de sonajero (of baby's toy). || Ruido (*m.*) metálico (of chains, bicycle). || Tamborileo, *m.*, repiqueteo, *m.* (of hail, rain). || Golpe, *m.* (of door, window, etc.). || Chasquido, *m.*, repiqueteo, *m.*, tableteo, *m.* (of machine gun). || Castañeteo, *m.* (of teeth). || ZOOL. Cascabel, *m.* (of a snake). || FAM. Alboroto, *m.*, jaleo, *m.* (shindy). || *Death rattle*, estertor (*m.*) de la muerte.
rattle [rætl] v. tr. Hacer sonar. || Agitar, sacudir (to shake). || FIG. Desconcertar (to disconcert): *the questions rattled the witness*, las preguntas desconcertaron al testigo. | Poner nervioso, crispar (to annoy): *that noise is beginning to rattle me*, ese ruido empieza a ponerme nervioso. || *To rattle off*, despachar (a piece of work, a speech). || MAR. *To rattle up*, levantar rápidamente (the anchor).
— V. intr. Hacer un ruido metálico (bicycle, chains). || Traquetear (train, carriage): *Raymond's car does not rattle*, el coche de Ramón no traquetea. || Chasquear, repiquetear, tabletear (machine gun). || Tamborilear, repiquetear (hail, rain). || Golpetear: *the window rattled in the wind*, la ventana golpeteaba con el viento. || Castañetear: *his teeth rattled with fear*, le castañeteaban los dientes de miedo. || MED. Tener un estertor. || — *To rattle along*, traquetear, ir traqueteando. || *To rattle at the door*, llamar a la puerta (to knock), sacudir la puerta (to shake). || *To rattle away*, irse con mucho ruido (coach), charlotear (to talk). || *To rattle down*, caer con gran estrépito. || *To rattle off*, irse con mucho ruido (coach). || *To rattle on*, seguir traqueteando (train), seguir hablando (to talk).
rattlebrain [—ˈbrein] or **rattlehead** [—hed] or **rattlepate** [—peit] n. FAM. Persona (*f.*) ligera de cascos, cabeza (*f.*) de chorlito.
rattlebrained [—breind] adj. FAM. Ligero de cascos, casquivano, na.
rattler [—ə*] n. FAM. Tío (*m.*) estupendo (person). | Cosa (*f.*) estupenda (thing). || U. S. ZOOL. Crótalo, *m.*, serpiente (*f.*) de cascabel. || U. S. FAM. Cacharro, *m.*, trasto, *m.* (car).
rattlesnake [—sneik] n. ZOOL. Crótalo, *m.*, serpiente (*f.*) de cascabel.
rattletrap [—træp] adj. Desvencijado, da.
— N. Cacharro, *m.*, trasto, *m.* (old car). || — Pl. Cachivaches, *m.* (baubles).
rattling [—iŋ] adj. Rápido, da (pace). || FAM. Muy bueno, estupendo, da (extraordinarily good).
— Adv. FAM. Muy.
rattrap [ˈrættræp] n. Ratonera, *f.*
ratty [ˈræti] adj. Infestado de ratas (place). || A rata (smell). || FAM. Furioso, sa.
raucous [ˈrɔ:kəs] adj. Ronco, ca (hoarse, harsh). || Estridente (shrill).
raucousness [—nis] n. Ronquedad, *f.*
ravage [ˈrævidʒ] n. Destrozo, *m.*, asolamiento, *m.* (devastation). || — Pl. Estragos, *m.* || FIG. *The ravages of time*, las injurias del tiempo, los estragos de los años.
ravage [ˈrævidʒ] v. tr. Destrozar, asolar: *the crops were ravaged by hail*, las cosechas fueron destrozadas por el granizo. || *Face ravaged by disease*, cara desfigurada por la enfermedad.
— V. intr. Causar estragos.
rave [reiv] n. FAM. Desvarío, *m.*, delirio, *m.* (nonsense). | Juerga, *f.* (good time): *the party was quite a rave*, la fiesta fue una verdadera juerga. || FAM. *Rave review*, relato (*m.*) entusiasta.
rave [reiv] v. intr. Delirar, desvariar: *he raved in his delirium*, desvarió en su delirio. || Estar desencadenado (wind). || — *To rave about* o *over*, deshacerse en alabanzas sobre, entusiasmarse por, estar loco por. || *To rave at* o *against s.o.*, tronar contra alguien, encolerizarse con alguien.
ravel [ˈrævəl] n. Enmarañamiento, *m.* (entanglement). || Hilacha, *f.*, hilacho, *m.* (ravelled thread). || Maraña, *f.*, embrollo, *m.* (sth. tangled).
ravel [ˈrævəl] v. tr. Enredar, enmarañar (to entangle). || *To ravel out*, deshilachar (material), desenredar, desenmarañar (threads), desenmarañar, desenredar, aclarar (a matter).
— V. intr. Enredarse, enmarañarse (to become tangled). || *To ravel out*, deshilacharse (to fray).
ravelin [ˈrævlin] n. Revellín, *m.* (of a fort).
ravelling (U. S. **raveling**) [ˈrævliŋ] n. Deshilachadura, *f.* || Hilacha, *f.*, hilacho, *m.* (ravelled thread).
raven [ˈreivn] adj. Negro como el azabache.
— N. Cuervo, *m.* (bird).
raven [ˈrævn] v. tr. Devorar.
— V. intr. Buscar una presa (animal). || Vivir de rapiña (person). || FIG. *To raven for*, tener sed de.
ravening [—iŋ] adj. Voraz.
— N. Voracidad, *f.*
ravenous [ˈrævənəs] adj. Hambriento, ta (very hungry). || Voraz (voracious). || *To be ravenous*, tener un hambre canina (to be hungry), estar ansioso, tener muchas ganas (*for*, de) [to long for].
ravenously [—li] adv. Vorazmente. || *To be ravenously hungry*, tener un hambre canina.
ravenousness [—nis] n. Voracidad, *f.* || Hambre (*f.*) canina.
ravine [rəˈvi:n] n. Barranco, *m.*
raving [ˈreiviŋ] adj. Delirante. || FIG. FAM. Extraordinario, ria. || *Raving mad*, loco de atar.
— N. Delirio, *m.*, desvarío, *m.* || — Pl. Divagaciones, *f.*, desvaríos, *m.*
ravioli [ˌrɑviˈəuli] pl. n. CULIN. Ravioles, *m.*, raviolis, *m.* (pasta).
ravish [ˈræviʃ] v. tr. Raptar (to kidnap). || Llevarse, arrebatar (sth.). || Violar (a woman). || FIG. Encantar, embelesar (to enrapture).
ravisher [—ə*] n. Raptor, ra (kidnapper). || Violador, *m.* (rapist).
ravishing [—iŋ] adj. Encantador, ra.
ravishment [—mənt] n. Rapto, *m.* (of s.o.). || Violación, *f.* (rape). || FIG. Encanto, *m.*, embeleso, *m.*
raw [rɔ:] adj. CULIN. Crudo, da (uncooked): *raw meat*, carne cruda. || Bruto, ta; sin refinar (oil). || En bruto, bruto, ta (metal). || Puro, ra: *raw spirit*, alcohol puro. || Sin cocer (brick). || Sin curtir, verde, en verde (hide, skins). || En rama (cotton). || ARTS. Crudo, da (colours). || No aguerrido, da (troops). || Vivo, va (flesh). || En carne viva (wound). || A flor de piel (nerves). || FIG. Frío, a (air). | Frío y húmedo (weather). | Novato, ta; inexperto, ta (inexperienced). | Basto, ta; tosco, ca (uncouth). || FAM. Verde (story). || — *Raw deal*, injusticia, *f.*, tratamiento injusto (injustice), jugarreta, *f.*, mala pasada (dirty trick). || *Raw material*, materia (*f.*) prima. || *Raw silk*, seda cruda. || *Raw umber*, ocre (*m.*) natural.
— N. U. S. FAM. *In the raw*, en cueros (naked), en su estado original (in the original state). || FIG. *To touch s.o. on the raw*, herir a uno en lo vivo.
rawboned [—bəund] adj. Esquelético, ca; huesudo, da (person). || Flaco, ca (horse).
rawhide [—haid] n. Cuero (*m.*) sin curtir *or* verde (untanned skin). || Látigo (*m.*) de cuero verde (whip).
rawness [—nis] n. Crudeza, *f.* || Frío (*m.*) húmedo (weather). || FIG. Falta (*f.*) de experiencia. | Tosquedad, *f.* (coarseness).
ray [rei] n. PHYS. Rayo, *m.*: *a ray of light*, un rayo de luz; *the sun's rays*, los rayos del sol; *cosmic rays*, rayos cósmicos; *cathode rays*, rayos catódicos. || MATH. Radio, *m.* (radius). || BOT. Radio, *m.*: *medullary ray*, radio medular. || ZOOL. Raya, *f.* (fish). || MUS. Re, *m.* (note). || FIG. Rayo, *m.*, resquicio, *m.* (of hope). || ZOOL. *Electric ray*, torpedo, *m.*
Raymond [ˈreimənd] pr. n. Raimundo, *m.*, Ramón, *m.* (Christian name).
rayon [ˈreiɔn] n. Rayón, *m.*, rayona, *f.*, seda (*f.*) artificial (cloth).
raze [reiz] v. tr. Arrasar (to demolish). || Tachar (to erase). || Borrar de la memoria (a memory). || Arañar (the skin). || *To raze to the ground*, arrasar, destruir por completo.
razor [ˈreizə*] n. Navaja (*f.*) de afeitar (with unprotected blade). || Maquinilla (*f.*) de afeitar (safety). || Máquina (*f.*) de afeitar eléctrica (electric).
razorback [—bæk] n. Rorcual, *m.* (whale).
razor-backed [—ˈbækt] adj. En escarpa (hill).
razorbill [—bil] n. Alca, *f.* (bird).
razor blade [—bleid] n. Hoja (*f.*) de afeitar, cuchilla (*f.*) de afeitar.
razor clam [—klæm] n. Navaja, *f.* (mollusc).
razor-edge [ˈreizərˈedʒ] n. Filo, *m.* || FIG. *To be on a razor-edge*, estar con el agua al cuello, estar en una situación difícil.
razor-sharp [ˈreizəˈʃɑ:p] adj. Afilado, da. || Muy agudo, da (wit).
razor shell [—ʃel] n. Navaja, *f.* (mollusc).
razor strop [—strɔp] n. Suavizador, *m.*
razz [ræz] v. tr. U. S. FAM. Tomar el pelo a (to tease, to rag).
razzia [ˈræziə] n. Razzia, *f.*
razzle [ˈræzl] or **razzle-dazzle** [—ˌdæzl] n. FAM. Juerga, *f.*: *to go on the razzle*, irse de juerga.
re [rei] n. MUS. Re, *m.*
re [ri:] prep. COMM. Respecto a, relativo a, con referencia a.
reabsorb [riəbˈsɔ:b] v. tr. Reabsorber.
reabsorption [riəbˈsɔ:pʃən] n. Reabsorción, *f.*
reach [ri:tʃ] n. Alcance, *m.*: *out of my reach*, fuera de mi alcance. || Tramo, *m.* (canal). || Tramo (*m.*) recto (river). || SP. Extensión (*f.*) del brazo (boxer). || MAR. Bordada, *f.* (tack). || Facultad, *f.* (of mind). || — *Beyond s.o.'s reach*, fuera del alcance de uno. || *Oxford is within easy reach of London*, Oxford está muy cerca de Londres. || *Planets within reach of small telescopes*, planetas visibles con telescopios pequeños. || *The upper reaches of the Amazon*, la cuenca alta del Amazonas. || *To make a reach for*, intentar alcanzar. || *Within reach of*, al alcance de.
reach [ri:tʃ] v. tr. Llegar a, alcanzar: *we reached Paris at ten o'clock*, llegamos a París a las diez; *the plant reaches the ceiling*, la planta alcanza el techo. || Cumplir, llegar a: *to reach fifty*, cumplir cincuenta años, llegar a los cincuenta años. || Llegar a (a conclusion, an agreement, a compromise, perfection). || Llegar a

las manos de (to come into the possession of): *the letter reached me yesterday*, la carta llegó a mis manos ayer. || Alcanzar, dar en (with a shot). || SP. Alcanzar: *he could not reach his opponent*, no pudo alcanzar a su adversario. || Pasar, acercar, dar, alargar: *reach me that dictionary*, acércame ese diccionario. || Comunicar con: *we tried to reach John by radio*, tratamos de comunicar con Juan por radio. || Llamar [por teléfono] (to telephone): *you can reach me at this number*, me puede llamar a este número. || FIG. Llegar al corazón *or* al alma, impresionar: *his words reached me*, sus palabras me llegaron al corazón. || — *To reach an amount*, ascender a *or* alcanzar una cantidad. || *To reach down*, bajar. || *To reach home*, llegar a casa. || *To reach into one's pocket*, meter la mano en el bolsillo. || *To reach out one's hand*, tender la mano (for money), alargar la mano (to get sth.), dar la mano (to shake hands).

— V. intr. Extenderse (to extend): *the woods reach as far as the river*, los bosques se extienden hasta el río. || Llegar: *I cannot reach*, no llego; *she reaches to my shoulder*, me llega al hombro. || Alargar la mano: *he reached over the table*, alargó la mano por encima de la mesa. || Alcanzar: *as far as the eye could reach*, hasta donde alcanzaba la vista. || Intentar alcanzar *or* coger: *he reached for the lighter*, intentó alcanzar el mechero. || MAR. Navegar de bolina. || — *The books reach up to the ceiling*, los libros llegan hasta el techo. || *The curtains reach down to the floor*, las cortinas llegan hasta el suelo. || FIG. *To reach for o after*, aspirar a.

reachable [—əbl] adj. Accesible. || — *Are you reachable by telephone?*, ¿tiene teléfono?, ¿le puedo llamar por teléfono? || *I am always reachable*, siempre puede ponerse en contacto conmigo.

reach-me-down [—mi‚daun] adj. De segunda mano (second-hand). || Heredado del hermano *or* de la hermana (handed down).

— N. Ropa (*f.*) de segunda mano (second-hand). || Ropa (*f.*) heredada (from one's brother or sister).

re-act [ˈri:ˈækt] v. tr. Volver a representar.

react [riˈækt] v. intr. Reaccionar: *how did they react to the news?*, ¿cómo reaccionaron ante la noticia? || PHYS. CHEM. Reaccionar. || *To react upon*, producir efecto en.

reactance [—əns] n. ELECTR. Reactancia, *f.*

reaction [riˈækʃən] n. Reacción, *f.*: *the decision produced a violent reaction*, la decisión provocó una reacción violenta. || CHEM. PHYS. Reacción, *f.*: *chain reaction*, reacción en cadena. || — *Reaction engine*, motor (*m.*) de reacción.

reactionary [—əri] adj./n. Reaccionario, ria.

reactivate [riˈæktiveit] v. tr. Reactivar.

reactivation [riækti'veiʃən] n. Reactivación, *f.*

reactive [riˈæktiv] adj. Reactivo, va.

reactor [riˈæktə*] n. PHYS. Reactor, *m.*: *nuclear reactor*, reactor nuclear. || CHEM. Reactivo, *m.*

read [red] adj. Leído, da. || Leído, da; instruido, da: *he is better read than most*, él es más leído que la mayoría de la gente; *to be well-read in history*, ser muy leído en historia.

read [ri:d] n. Lectura. || — *I had a good read in the plane*, estuve leyendo un buen rato en el avión. || *To have a quick read of the paper*, echar un vistazo al periódico.

read* [ri:d] v. tr. Leer: *to read a book, music, French*, leer un libro, música, en francés; *read me a story*, léeme un cuento; *to read fluently*, leer de corrido; *to read sth. aloud*, leer algo en voz alta. || Estudiar (at university): *to read history*, estudiar historia. || PRINT. Corregir, leer (proofs). || Consultar, mirar, leer (an instrument). || Marcar: *the thermometer reads thirty degrees*, el termómero marca treinta grados. || Interpretar: *it may be read several ways*, se puede interpretar de varias maneras. || Leer: *for "dead" read "lead"*, léase "lead" en lugar de "dead." || Leer, predecir (to predict). || Descifrar (signs, codes). || — MUS. *To read at sight*, leer a primera vista, repentizar. || FIG. *To read one a lesson*, leerle a uno la cartilla. || *To read out*, leer en voz alta (aloud), expulsar (from an association). || *To read s.o.'s palm*, leerle la mano a uno. || *To read s.o.'s thoughts*, adivinar *or* leer los pensamientos de alguien. || *To read s.o. to sleep*, adormecer a alguien leyendo. || *To read sth. in s.o.'s eyes*, leer algo en los ojos *or* en la mirada de alguien. || *To read sth. into a phrase*, leer en una frase algo que no hay. || *To read sth. over o through*, leer rápidamente algo, echar un vistazo a algo (to read quickly), volver a leer algo (to reread). || *To read sth. right through*, leer algo de cabo a rabo. || *To read sth. up*, estudiar algo.

— V. intr. Leer: *he is reading aloud*, está leyendo en voz alta. || Leerse: *a magazine which reads easily*, una revista que se lee con facilidad. || Estar escrito: *to read well, badly*, estar bien escrito, mal escrito. || Decir, rezar: *the constitution reads as follows*, la constitución dice lo siguiente. || Poder interpretarse, indicar: *his letter reads as if he isn't coming*, su carta parece indicar que *or* se puede interpretar en el sentido de que no va a venir. || — *To read about Churchill*, leer un libro sobre Churchill. || *To read about sth. in the newspaper*, leer un artículo sobre algo *or* ver algo en el periódico. || *To read between the lines*, leer entre líneas. || JUR. *To read for the bar*, prepararse para el foro. || *To read on*, seguir leyendo.

— OBSERV. Pret. & p. p. ***read*** [red].

readable [—əbl] adj. Legible (legible). || Que merece la pena leerse, entretenido, da (pleasant to read).

readapt [ˈri:əˈdæpt] v. tr. Readaptar.

readaptation [ri‚ædæpˈteiʃən] n. Readaptación, *f.*

readdress [ˈri:əˈdres] v. tr. Cambiar la dirección en.

reader [ˈri:də*] n. Lector, ra (person who reads). || Libro (*m.*) de lectura (book). || Antología, *f.* (anthology). || PRINT. Corrector, *m.* (proofreader). || Aficionado, da [a la lectura] (person fond of reading). || Lector (*m.*) de manuscritos (publisher's critic). || Profesor (*m.*) adjunto (of a university staff).

readership [—ʃip] n. Cargo (*m.*) de profesor adjunto (in a university). || Lectores, *m. pl.*: *a newspaper with a readership of fifty thousand*, un periódico con cincuenta mil lectores.

readily [ˈredili] adv. De buena gana (willingly): *I will lend you the money readily*, le dejaré el dinero de buena gana. || En seguida: *funds are readily available*, los fondos están disponibles en seguida. || Con soltura: *he writes readily*, escribe con soltura. || Pronto: *you must not criticize too readily*, no hay que criticar demasiado pronto. || Libremente: *she talks readily of her divorce*, habla libremente de su divorcio. || Fácilmente (easily): *readily understandable*, fácilmente comprensible.

readiness [ˈredinis] n. Buena disposición, *f.*: *readiness to help*, buena disposición para ayudar. || Disponibilidad, *f.* (of funds). || Rapidez, *f.* (of a reply). || Soltura, *f.*: *the readiness with which he writes*, la soltura con la cual escribe. || Agudeza, *f.* (of s.o.'s wit). || — *To be in readiness*, estar listo *or* preparado. || *To hold o.s. in readiness*, estar listo.

reading [ˈri:diŋ] n. Lectura, *f.*: *the reading of a book*, la lectura de un libro; *to be fond of reading*, ser aficionado a la lectura. || Recital, *m.* (aloud): *a poetry reading*, un recital de poesía. || Versión, *f.* (textual version). || PRINT. Corrección, *f.* (of proofs). || Indicación, *f.* (of instruments). || Interpretación, *f.*: *my reading of the situation differs somewhat*, mi interpretación de la situación difiere algo. || JUR. Lectura, *f.* (of a will, a bill in Parliament). || *A man of wide reading*, un hombre culto, un hombre que ha leído mucho.

— Adj. De lectura (of reading). || De los lectores (of readers). || Lector, ra; que lee (who reads). || — *Reading desk*, mesa (*f.*) de lectura (table), atril, *m.* (lectern). || *Reading lamp*, lámpara (*f.*) portátil. || *Reading matter*, lectura, *f.* || *Reading room*, sala (*f.*) de lectura.

readjust [ˈri:əˈdʒʌst] v. tr. Ajustar de nuevo, reajustar, readaptar.

readjustment [—mənt] n. Reajuste, *m.*

readmission [ˈri:ədˈmiʃən] n. Readmisión, *f.* || THEATR. *Readmission ticket*, contraseña, *f.*

readmit [ˈri:ədˈmit] v. tr. Readmitir, volver a admitir.

readmittance [—əns] n. Readmisión, *f.*

ready [ˈredi] adj. Listo, ta; preparado, da: *is supper ready?*, ¿está la cena preparada?; *ready for use*, listo para usar. || Dispuesto, ta: *she is ready to starve in order to slim*, está dispuesta a morirse de hambre para adelgazar. || Disponible: *a ready supply of money*, una cantidad disponible de dinero. || Rápido, da (reply). || Vivo, va; agudo, da (wit). || Pronto, ta; dispuesto, ta (prompt): *he is very ready with his criticism*, es muy pronto en criticar. || A punto de: *she looked ready to drop*, parecía a punto de caerse. || De buen grado: *he gave me his ready consent*, me dio su consentimiento de buen grado. || — *Now ready* o *just ready*, a punto de publicarse (book). || *Ready cash* o *money*, dinero (*m.*) contante *or* líquido. || *Ready reckoner*, tabla (*f.*) de cálculo. || *Ready!, set!, go!* o *ready!, steady!, go!*, ¡preparados!, ¡listos!, ¡ya! || *To be ready to hand*, estar a mano. || *To get ready*, prepararse (to prepare o.s.), arreglarse (before going out). || *To get* o *to make sth. ready*, preparar algo. || *To have a ready pen*, escribir con soltura. || *To have a ready tongue*, no tener pelillos en la lengua. || *To hold o.s. ready to do sth.*, estar listo para hacer algo.

— N. MIL. Posición (*f.*) de fuego *or* de apresto (firearms). || FAM. *The ready*, la pasta (money).

ready [ˈredi] v. tr. Preparar. || *To ready o.s.*, prepararse.

ready-made [—ˈmeid] adj. Confeccionado, da; hecho, cha: *ready-made clothing*, ropa hecha. || *Ready-made beliefs*, prejuicios, *m.*

ready-to-wear [—təˈwɛə*] adj. Confeccionado, da; hecho, cha (clothing).

reaffirm [ˈri:əˈfə:m] v. tr. Reafirmar.

reaffirmation [ri:‚æfəˈmeiʃən] n. Reafirmación, *f.*

reafforest [ˈri:əˈfɔrist] v. tr. Repoblar con árboles.

reafforestation [ˈri:‚əfɔrisˈteiʃən] n. Repoblación (*f.*) forestal.

reagent [riˈeidʒənt] n. CHEM. Reactivo, *m.*

real [riəl] adj. Real, verdadero, ra: *his pain is real, not imaginary*, su dolor es real, no imaginario. || Auténtico, ca; verdadero, ra: *this is real summer weather*, esto es un auténtico tiempo de verano; *a real surprise*, una verdadera sorpresa. || Legítimo, ma; auténtico, ca; genuino, na: *real sherry*, vino de Jerez legítimo; *a real pearl*, una perla legítima; *real gold*,

oro legítimo. || PHIL. JUR. MATH. Real. || — FAM. *For real*, de veras. || JUR. *Real estate* o *property*, bienes (*m. pl.*) raíces. | *Real estate agency*, agencia inmobiliaria. || PHYS. *Real image*, imagen real. || *Real time*, tiempo (*m.*) real. || FAM. *The real McCoy*, el auténtico, la auténtica. || *They are real men*, son hombres de verdad.
— Adv. U. S. FAM. Realmente, verdaderamente: *I am real pleased*, estoy verdaderamente contento.
— N. *The real*, lo real, la realidad.
real [reiˈɑ:l] n. Real, *m.* (former Spanish coin).
realgar [riˈælgə*] n. MIN. Rejalgar, *m.*
realise [ˈriəlaiz] v. tr. See REALIZE.
realism [ˈriəlizəm] n. Realismo, *m.*
realist [ˈriəlist] n. Realista, *m.* & *f.*
realistic [riəˈlistik] adj. Realista.
realistically [riəˈlistikəli] adv. De una manera realista.
reality [riˈæliti] n. Realidad, *f.* || Realismo, *m.* (of a description). || — *In reality*, en realidad, de hecho. || *To get back to realities*, volver a la realidad.
realizable [ˈriəlaizəbl] adj. Realizable, factible. || FIG. Imaginable.
realization [ˈriəlaiˈzeiʃən] n. Realización, *f.* (of a project, assets). || Comprensión, *f.*
realize [ˈriəlaiz] v. tr. Darse cuenta de: *he realized that she was in danger*, se dio cuenta de que ella estaba en peligro. || Realizarse, hacerse realidad: *her wish was realized at last*, su deseo al fin se hizo realidad. || Realizar (to convert into money): *to realize one's assets*, realizar sus bienes. || Sacar, lograr (profit). || — *I realize your position*, comprendo su posición. || *To realize a high price*, venderse caro.
really [ˈriəli] adv. Realmente, en realidad, de verdad (in reality): *it is not really a storm, just a shower*, no es una tormenta de verdad, sino sólo un chubasco. || Verdaderamente, realmente (truly): *really beautiful weather*, tiempo verdaderamente espléndido; *I really like it*, me gusta realmente. || — *Have we really finished?*, ¿será verdad que hemos terminado? || *Really!*, ¡hay que ver! || *Really?*, ¿de veras?, ¿de verdad?
realm [relm] n. Reino, *m.* (kingdom). || FIG. Esfera, *f.*, terreno, *m.* (domain). || FIG. *Within the realm of possibility*, dentro de lo posible.
realtor [riˈæltə*] n. U. S. Corredor (*m.*) de fincas.
realty [ˈriəlti] n. Bienes (*m. pl.*) raíces.
ream [ri:m] n. Resma, *f.* (of paper). || — Pl. FIG. Montones, *m.*, gran cantidad, *f. sing.* || FIG. *To write reams about a subject*, escribir mucho sobre un tema.
ream [ri:m] v. tr. TECH. Abocardar, ensanchar, escariar (to widen or shape with a reamer). || MIL. Avellanar (to widen the bore with a reamer). || U. S. Exprimir (fruit). | Extraer con exprimidor (fruit juice).
reamer [—ə*] n. TECH. Escariador, *m.* || MIL. Avellanador, *m.* || U. S. Exprimelimones, *m. inv.*, exprimidor, *m.*
reanimate [ri:ˈænimeit] v. tr. Reanimar.
reanimation [ri:æniˈmeiʃən] n. Reanimación, *f.*
reap [ri:p] v. tr. AGR. Segar (to cut). | Recoger, cosechar (to harvest). || FIG. Cosechar, recoger: *to reap the fruits of one's labours*, cosechar los frutos de su trabajo. || *To reap the benefits*, llevarse los beneficios.
— V. intr. Cosechar, hacer la cosecha.
reaper [—ə*] n. AGR. Segador, ra (s.o. who reaps). | Segadora, *f.* (machine). || — *Reaper and binder*, segadora agavilladora. || FIG. *The Reaper* o *the Grim Reaper*, la Parca.
reaping [—iŋ] n. Siega, *f.* || *Reaping hook*, hoz, *f.* || *Reaping machine*, segadora, *f.* || *Reaping time*, siega, *f.*
reappear [ˈri:əˈpi:ə*] v. intr. Reaparecer.
reappearance [ˈri:əˈpiə:rəns] n. Reaparición, *f.*
reappoint [ˈri:əˈpɔint] v. tr. Nombrar de nuevo.
reappointment [—mənt] n Nuevo nombramiento, *m.*
reappraisal [ˈri:əˈpreizəl] n Revaluación, *f.*
reapportion [riəˈpɔ:ʃən] v. tr. Repartir de nuevo.
rear [ˈri:ə*] adj. Posterior, de atrás, trasero, ra. || MIL. De retaguardia. || — *Rear admiral*, contraalmirante, *m.* || MIL. *Rear guard*, retaguardia, *f.* || *Rear seat, axle*, asiento, eje trasero. || *Rear window, drive*, ventanilla, tracción trasera.
— N. Parte (*f.*) posterior, parte (*f.*) de atrás (the back of sth.). || MIL. Retaguardia, *f.*: *five hundred yards to the rear*, quinientas yardas a retaguardia. | Cola, *f.* (of a column). || FAM. Letrina, *f.* (latrine). | Trasero, *m.* (buttocks). || — *At the rear of*, detrás de. || *In the rear*, atrás; por detrás (to attack). || *To bring up the rear*, cerrar la marcha; cubrir la retaguardia (soldiers).
rear [ˈri:ə*] v. tr. Levantar, erigir (to erect): *to rear a monument*, levantar un monumento. || Levantar, erguir: *to rear one's head*, levantar la cabeza. || Cultivar (to cultivate). || Criar: *to rear dogs*, criar perros; *to rear a family*, criar niños.
— V. intr. Encabritarse, empinarse (a horse). || Levantarse (to rise up).
rear-engined [—rˈendʒind] adj. Con motor trasero.
rear guard [—gɑ:d] n. MIL. Retaguardia, *f.*
rearing [—iŋ] n. Erección, *f.* (of a monument, etc.). || Erguimiento, *m.* (of the head). || Cultivo, *m.* (cultivation). || Cría, *f.* (of animals). || Crianza, *f.* (of children). || Encabritamiento, *m.* (of a horse).
rearm [ˈri:ˈɑ:m] v. tr. Rearmar.
— V. intr. Rearmarse.
rearmament [—əmənt] n. MIL. Rearme, *m.*
rearmost [ˈriəməust] adj. Último, ma.
rearrange [ˈri:əˈreindʒ] v. tr. Volver a arreglar (to arrange again). || Disponer de otro modo (to arrange in a different way). || Adaptar (to adapt).
rearrangement [—mənt] n. Nuevo arreglo, *m.*, nueva disposición, *f.* || Adaptación, *f.*
rearview [ˈriəvju:] adj. AUT. *Rearview mirror*, retrovisor, *m.*
rearward [ˈriəwə:d] adj. Posterior, último, ma.
— Adv. Hacia atrás.
— N. Retaguardia, *f.*
reason [ˈri:zn] n. Razón, *f.*: *his reason has shown him the right course*, su razón le ha enseñado el buen camino; *to lose one's reason*, perder la razón. || Razón, *f.*, causa, *f.*, motivo, *m.*: *she understands the reason for his behaviour*, ella entiende la razón de su comportamiento; *for this reason*, por esta razón. || PHIL. Razón, *f.* || — *All the more reason you should not go*, razón de más para que no vaya. || *By reason of*, en virtud de. || *In reason*, razonablemente (reasonably), dentro de lo razonable (within reasonable limits). || *It is contrary to reason*, no es razonable. || *Reason of State*, razón de Estado. || *The reason why*, el porqué, la razón por la cual. || *To bring to reason*, hacer entrar en razón. || *To have reason to believe that*, tener motivo para creer que. || *To listen to reason*, avenirse a razones. || *To stand to reason*, ser evidente. || *With good reason*, con razón.
reason [ˈri:zn] v. tr. Razonar (to analyse by reasoning). || Discutir (to discuss). || — *To reason out*, resolver (a problem), llegar a: *to reason out a settlement*, llegar a una solución; comprender: *I cannot reason it out*, no llego a comprenderlo; disuadir: *to reason s.o. out of doing sth.*, disuadir a alguien de hacer algo. || *To reason whether...*, intentar saber si...
— V. intr. Razonar, raciocinar (to think logically). || Discutir (with s.o.).
reasonable [ˈri:znəbl] adj. Razonable, sensato, ta (person). || Razonable: *a reasonable excuse*, una disculpa razonable; *the book had a reasonable success*, el libro tuvo un éxito razonable. || Módico, ca; razonable: *a reasonable rent*, un alquiler módico.
reasonableness [—nis] n. Moderación, *f.*, sensatez, *f.*, lo razonable.
reasoner [ˈri:znə*] n. Razonador, ra. || Discutidor, ra.
reasoning [ˈri:zniŋ] n. Razonamiento, *m.* || Cálculos, *m. pl.*: *according to my reasoning*, según mis cálculos.
— Adj. Dotado de raciocinio, racional.
reasonless [ˈri:znlis] adj. Sin razón.
reassemble [ˈri:əˈsembl] v. tr. Reunir, volver a juntar. || TECH. Volver a montar.
— V. intr. Reunirse, volverse a juntar.
reassert [ˈri:əˈsə:t] v. tr. Reafirmar.
reassess [ˈri:əˈses] v. tr. Valorar de nuevo (to revalue). || Fijar de nuevo (a tax). || Examinar de nuevo (to reconsider).
reassume [ˌri:əˈsju:m] v. tr. Reasumir, volver a asumir.
reassumption [ˌri:əˈsʌmpʃən] n. Reasunción, *f.*
reassurance [ˌri:əˈʃuərəns] n. Tranquilidad, *f.* || Noticia (*f.*) tranquilizadora (reassuring news). || Palabras (*f. pl.*) tranquilizadoras (words). || Promesa (*f.*) tranquilizadora (promise). || COMM. Reaseguro, *m.*
reassure [ˌri:əˈʃuə*] v. tr. Tranquilizar (to tranquillize). || COMM. Reasegurar.
reassuring [—riŋ] adj. Tranquilizador, ra.
reattach [ˈri:əˈtætʃ] v. tr. Reatar.
reawaken [ˈri:əˈweikən] v. tr. Volver a despertar.
— V. intr. Volver a despertarse.
reawakening [—iŋ] n. Despertar, *m.*
rebaptize [ri:bæpˈtaiz] v. tr. Rebautizar.
rebarbative [riˈbɑ:bətiv] adj. Repelente.
rebate [ˈri:beit] n. Rebaja, *f.*, descuento, *m.* (discount). || Reembolso, *m.* (repayment). || TECH. Rebajo, *m.* (in carpentry).
rebate [ˈri:beit] v. tr. U. S. Rebajar, descontar (to discount). || Reembolsar (to repay). || TECH. See RABBET.
rebec [ˈri:bek] n. MUS. Rabel, *m.*
Rebecca [riˈbekə] pr. n. Rebeca, *f.*
rebel [ˈrebl] adj./n. Rebelde.
rebel [riˈbel] v. intr. Rebelarse, sublevarse.
rebellion [riˈbeljən] n. Rebelión, *f.*, sublevación, *f.*
rebellious [riˈbeljəs] adj. Rebelde.
rebelliousness [—nis] n. Rebeldía, *f.*
rebind* [ˈri:ˈbaind] v. tr. Volver a atar (to fasten again). || Reencuadernar (a book).

— OBSERV. Pret. & p. p. **rebound.**

rebinding [—iŋ] n. Reencuadernación, *f.* (of a book).
rebirth [ˈri:ˈbə:θ] n. Renacimiento, *m.* (second birth).
rebore [ˈri:ˈbɔ:*] n. TECH. Rectificado, *m.*
rebore [ˈri:ˈbɔ:*] v. tr. TECH. Rectificar.
reborn [ˈri:ˈbɔ:n] p. p. *To be reborn*, renacer, volver a nacer.
rebound [riˈbaund] n. Rebote, *m.* || FIG. *On the rebound*, en pleno choque emocional.
rebound [ˈriˈbaund] v. intr. Rebotar.
rebound [ˈriˈbaund] pret. & p. p. See REBIND.
rebroadcast [ˈri:ˈbrɔ:dkɑ:st] n. Nueva transmisión, *f.*
rebroadcast [ˈri:ˈbrɔ:dkɑ:st] v. tr. Volver a transmitir.
rebuff [riˈbʌf] n. Negativa, *f.* (rejection). || Desaire, *m.* (snub).

rebuff [riˈbʌf] v. tr. Rechazar (to reject). ‖ Desairar (to snub).
rebuild* [ˈri:ˈbild] v. tr. Reconstruir.
— OBSERV. Pret. & p. p. ***rebuilt***.
rebuilding [—iŋ] n. Reconstrucción, *f.*
rebuke [riˈbju:k] n. Reproche, *m.*, reprimenda, *f.*
rebuke [riˈbju:k] v. tr. Reprender, regañar.
rebus [ˈri:bəs] n. Jeroglífico, *m.* ‖ Acertijo, *m.* (riddle).
rebut [riˈbʌt] v. tr. Rebatir, refutar, impugnar.
rebuttal [—l] n. Refutación, *f.*, impugnación, *f.*
rebutter [—ə*] n. JUR. Contrarréplica, *f.*
recalcification [ri,kælsifiˈkeiʃən] n. Recalcificación, *f.*
recalcitrance [riˈkælsitrəns] n. Terquedad, *f.*, obstinación *f.*
recalcitrant [riˈkælsitrənt] adj. Recalcitrante, refractario, ria; reacio, cia. ‖ MED. Que no responde al tratamiento.
recalcitrate [riˈkælsitreit] v. intr. Oponerse.
recalcitration [rikælsiˈtreiʃən] n. Oposición, *f.*
recalculate [riˈkæljuleit] v. tr. Calcular de nuevo.
recall [riˈkɔ:l] n. Llamada, *f.* (the act of recalling). ‖ Revocación, *f.*, anulación, *f.* ‖ Retirada, *f.* (of a diplomat). ‖ Recuerdo, *m.* (memory). ‖ MIL. Llamada, *f.*, toque (*m.*) de llamada. ‖ *Beyond recall* o *past recall*, irrevocable.
recall [riˈkɔ:l] v. tr. Llamar, hacer volver (to order to return). ‖ Retirar: *to recall an ambassador*, retirar a un embajador; *to recall an edition from the bookshops*, retirar una edición de las librerías. ‖ Revocar (a decision, a judgment). ‖ Retirar (one's word). ‖ MIL. Llamar a filas (a reservist). ‖ Recordar, acordarse de (to remember): *she recalled meeting him last year*, se acordó de haberle conocido el año pasado. ‖ Recordar, hacer pensar en (to remind): *that music recalls my stay in Spain*, esa música me recuerda mi estancia en España.
recant [riˈkænt] v. tr. Retractar.
— V. intr. Retractarse.
recantation [,ri:kænˈteiʃən] n. Retractación, *f.* (of a statement).
recap [ˈriˈkæp] n. FAM. Recapitulación, *f.* ‖ Recauchutado, *m.* (of a tyre).
recap [ˈriˈkæp] v. tr./intr. FAM. Recapitular. | Resumir (to summarize). ‖ Recauchutar (a tyre).
recapitalization [ˈri:,kæ,pitəlaiˈzeiʃən] n. Recapitalización, *f.*
recapitulate [,ri:kəˈpitjuleit] v. tr./intr. Recapitular. ‖ Resumir (to summarize).
recapitulation [ˈri:kə,pitjuˈleiʃən] n. Recapitulación, *f.*
recapitulative [,ri:kəˈpitjulətiv] adj. Recapitulativo, va.
recapture [ˈri:ˈkæptʃə*] n. Nueva detención, *f.* (recapturing). ‖ Reconquista, *f.* (of a town).
recapture [ˈri:ˈkæptʃə*] v. tr. Volver a capturar (a prisoner). ‖ Reconquistar (a town, area). ‖ FIG. Hacer revivir (to recreate): *to recapture the atmosphere of the twenties*, hacer revivir el ambiente de los años veinte. ‖ JUR. Recobrar.
recast* [ˈri:ˈkɑ:st] v. tr. Refundir (metal). ‖ Refundir (a book). ‖ THEATR. Cambiar el reparto de (a play). ‖ Rehacer (to remodel).
— OBSERV. Pret. & p. p. ***recast***.
recasting [—iŋ] n. Refundición, *f.*
recede [riˈsi:d] v. intr. Retroceder, retirarse: *the sea receded*, el mar retrocedió. ‖ Retroceder: *the shore gradually receded*, la playa retrocedía gradualmente. ‖ Descender (tide). ‖ MIL. Retirarse. ‖ Disminuir (to lessen). ‖ Volverse atrás (to withdraw from a position, promise, etc.). ‖ *Receding hairline*, entradas, *f. pl.*
receipt [riˈsi:t] n. Recepción, *f.*, recibo, *m.* (the act of receiving). ‖ Recibo, *m.* (document): *to ask for a receipt*, pedir un recibo. ‖ (Ant.). Receta, *f.* (recipe). ‖ — Pl. Ingresos, *m.*, recaudación, *f. sing.*, entradas, *f.* (amount collected). ‖ — *I am in receipt of your letter of the third*, he recibido *or* obra en mi poder su atenta carta del tres del corriente. ‖ *On receipt of*, al recibo de, al recibir. ‖ *To acknowledge receipt of*, acusar recibo de. ‖ *Upon receipt of the goods*, al recibir las mercancías.
receipt [riˈsi:t] v. tr. U. S. Acusar recibo de, dar un recibo por.
— V. intr. U. S. Dar un recibo.
receipt book [—buk] n. Talonario (*m.*) de recibos.
receivable [riˈsi:vəbl] adj. Admisible, procedente (that can be accepted or received). ‖ Válido, da (candidature). ‖ COMM. Por cobrar: *receivable bills*, cuentas por cobrar.
— Pl. n. COMM. Efectos (*m.*) *or* deudas(*f.*) por cobrar.
receive [riˈsi:v] v. tr. Recibir: *they received him with applause*, le recibieron con aplausos; *to receive good advice*, recibir buenos consejos; *to receive a refusal*, recibir una negativa; *to receive a letter*, recibir una carta; *the canal receives water from several rivers*, el canal recibe agua de varios ríos. ‖ Aceptar (to accept): *if she sends me a gift I shall refuse to receive it*, si me manda un regalo me negaré a aceptarlo. ‖ Acoger (to welcome into one's home): *to receive an orphan for Christmas*, acoger a un huérfano para pasar las Navidades. ‖ Admitir (to admit): *to be received into a society*, ser recibido en una sociedad. ‖ Cobrar: *to receive one's salary*, cobrar el sueldo. ‖ Tener: *to receive serious wounds*, tener lesiones graves. ‖ JUR. Ocultar, encubrir (stolen goods). ‖ SP. Recibir: *to receive a pass*, recibir un pase. ‖ Soportar, aguantar (to take the weight of). ‖ REL. Recibir (Communion). ‖ Contener: *large enough to receive two gallons*, suficientemente grande para contener dos galones. ‖ RAD. Captar (a broadcast). ‖ — JUR. *He received ten years*, le echaron diez años, recibió diez años. ‖ GRAMM. *Received pronunciation*, pronunciación generalmente admitida. ‖ COMM. *Received with thanks*, recibí. ‖ *To be well, badly received*, tener una buena, una mala acogida (a play, etc.). ‖ REL. *To receive into the Church*, recibir en el seno de la Iglesia, bautizar.
— V. intr. Recibir: *to receive on Thursdays*, recibir los jueves. ‖ REL. Recibir la comunión, comulgar (to take communion). ‖ JUR. Ser encubridor.
receiver [—ə*] n. Recibidor, ra; receptor, ra (s.o. who receives). ‖ Destinatario, ria (of a letter). ‖ Recaudador, ra (tax collector). ‖ JUR. Síndico, *m.* (syndic). | Ocultador, *m.*, encubridor, *m.* (of stolen goods). ‖ Auricular, *m.* (earpiece of a telephone). ‖ RAD. Receptor, *m.* (television or radio set). ‖ CHEM. Recipiente, *m.* (receptacle). ‖ *To lift the receiver*, descolgar el teléfono.
receiving [—iŋ] n. Recepción, *f.* (reception). ‖ JUR. Encubrimiento, *m.* (of stolen goods). ‖ — *Receiving room*, sala (*f.*) de recibo, recibidor, *m.* ‖ *Receiving set*, receptor, *m.* ‖ *Receiving station*, estación receptora.
recency [ˈri:snsi] n. Carácter (*m.*) reciente, novedad, *f.*
recension [riˈsenʃən] n. Recensión, *f.*
recent [ˈri:snt] adj. Reciente.
recently [—li] adv. Recientemente. ‖ *Until quite recently*, hasta hace poco.
recentness [—nis] n. Carácter (*m.*) reciente, novedad, *f.*
receptacle [riˈseptəkl] n. Receptáculo, *m.*, recipiente, *m.* (container). ‖ BOT. Receptáculo, *m.*
reception [riˈsepʃən] n. Recepción, *f.*, recibo, *m.*: *reception of goods*, recepción de mercancías. ‖ Admisión, *f.* (admission). ‖ Recibimiento, *m.*, acogida, *f.* (welcoming). ‖ Recepción, *f.* (social gathering). ‖ RAD. Recepción, *f.* (of radio or television signals). ‖ Recepción, *f.* (part of a hotel). ‖ — *Reception clerk*, encargado (*m.*) de la recepción, recepcionista, *m.* & *f.* ‖ *Reception desk*, recepción. ‖ *Reception room*, sala (*f.*) de espera (for receiving the patients of a doctor, dentist, etc.), sala (*f.*) de recibir (for receiving guests). ‖ *To get a cold, a warm reception*, tener una acogida fría, calurosa.
receptionist [riˈsepʃənist] n. Recepcionista, *m.* & *f.*
receptive [riˈseptiv] adj. Receptivo, va.
receptiveness [—nis] or **receptivity** [—iti] n. Receptividad, *f.*
receptor [riˈseptə*] n. Receptor, *m.*
recess [riˈses] n. ARCH. Hueco, *m.* (in a wall). | Nicho, *m.* (for a statue). | Alcoba, *f.* (for a bed). ‖ Escondrijo, *m.* (hiding place). ‖ Lugar (*m.*) apartado: *in the farthest recesses of Argentina*, en los lugares más apartados de Argentina. ‖ Parte (*f.*) recóndita: *the recesses of the mind*, las partes recónditas de la mente. ‖ Suspensión, *f.* (of activity). ‖ Descanso, *m.* (rest). ‖ Período (*m.*) de clausura, intermedio, *m.* (of parliament). ‖ Interrupción, *f.* (of a meeting). ‖ Retroceso, *m.* (of water). ‖ ANAT. Fosa, *f.* ‖ U. S. Recreo, *m.* (period between school classes). ‖ — *To be in recess*, estar clausurado (parliament). ‖ *To have a recess*, suspender la sesión.
recess [riˈses] v. tr. Hacer un hueco en (to construct a recess in). ‖ Poner en un hueco (to put into a recess).
— V. intr. Suspender la sesión.
recession [riˈseʃən] n. Retroceso, *m.*, retirada, *f.* (retreat). ‖ Hueco, *m.* (receding part). ‖ REL. Procesión (*f.*) del clero hacia la sacristía. ‖ GEOGR. Retroceso, *m.* ‖ COMM. Recesión, *f.* ‖ JUR. Retrocesión, *f.*
recessional [—əl] adj. REL. De la procesión del clero [una vez terminado el servicio]. ‖ Del período de clausura (parliament).
— N. Himno (*m.*) de fin de oficio.
recessive [riˈsesiv] adj. Que tiende a retroceder. ‖ BIOL. Recesivo, va.
recharge [ˈri:ˈtʃɑ:dʒ] v. tr. Recargar.
recherché [rəˈʃeəʃei] adj. Rebuscado, da.
rechristen [ˈriˈkrisn] v. tr. Rebautizar. ‖ FIG. Dar un nuevo nombre a.
recividism [riˈsidivizəm] n. Reincidencia, *f.*
recividist [riˈsidivist] adj./n. Reincidente.
recipe [ˈresipi] n. CULIN. MED. Receta, *f.* ‖ FIG. Receta, *f.*: *a sure recipe for success*, una receta segura para el éxito.
recipient [riˈsipiənt] adj./n. Receptor, ra (receiver). ‖ Destinatario, ria (of a letter, cheque, etc.).
reciprocal [riˈsiprəkəl] adj. Recíproco, ca; mutuo, tua: *reciprocal feelings of affection*, sentimientos mutuos de afecto. ‖ GRAMM. MATH. Recíproco, ca.
— N. MATH. Cantidad (*f.*) recíproca. ‖ Lo recíproco.
reciprocate [riˈsiprəkeit] v. tr. Corresponder a (to give in return): *to reciprocate s.o.'s love*, corresponder al amor de alguien. ‖ Cambiar, intercambiar (to give and receive mutually): *the two presidents reciprocated expressions of goodwill*, los dos presidentes intercambiaron palabras reveladoras de su buena voluntad. ‖ TECH. Producir un movimiento alternativo en.
— V. intr. Corresponder (to respond): *I tried to*

be nice but she didn't reciprocate, intenté ser amable pero no me correspondió. || TECH. Tener movimiento alternativo.

reciprocating [ri'siprəkeitiŋ] adj. TECH. Alternativo, va.

reciprocation [ri,siprə'keiʃən] n. Reciprocidad, *f.*

reciprocity [,resi'prɔsiti] n. Reciprocidad, *f.*

recital [ri'saitl] n. Relato, *m.*, relación, *f.* (a relating of facts, sth. which is related). || Recital, *m.* (of music, dancing): *organ recital*, recital de órgano. || Recitación, *f.*, recital, *m.* (of poetry).

recitation [,resi'teiʃən] n. Relato, *m.*, relación, *f.*: *a long recitation of what had happened*, una larga relación de lo que había pasado. || Enumeración, *f.* (listing). || Recitación, *f.* (of a poem). || Poesía, *f.* (piece of poetry).

recitative [,resitə'ti:v] adj. Recitativo, va.
— N. MUS. Recitativo, *m.*

recite [ri'sait] v. tr. Recitar (to repeat aloud): *to recite a poem*, recitar un poema. || Relatar, narrar (to give a detailed account of). || Enumerar (to list in detail). || JUR. Exponer (facts).
— V. intr. Recitar.

reciter [—ə*] n. Recitador, ra.

reck [rek] v. tr. (Ant.). Preocuparse por.

reckless [—lis] adj. Imprudente (careless): *a reckless driver*, un conductor imprudente. || Arrojado, da; temerario, ria (indifferent to danger). || Inconsiderado, da; imprudente (ill-considered): *a reckless thing to say*, una declaración inconsiderada. || *Reckless speed*, velocidad peligrosa.

recklessness [—lisnis] n. Imprudencia, *f.* (carelessness). || Temeridad, *f.* (temerity).

reckon ['rekən] v. tr. Calcular (to calculate): *reckon how much you have spent*, calcule cuánto ha gastado. || Contar (to count): *she reckons him among her best friends*, le cuenta entre sus mejores amigos. || Estimar, creer: *I reckon she is thirty*, creo que tiene treinta años. || Considerar: *he is reckoned as one of the best runners*, está considerado como uno de los mejores corredores. || — *Reckoning everything*, todo incluido, contándolo todo (all included), pensándolo bien, considerándolo todo (everything considered). || *To reckon in*, incluir. || *To reckon up*, calcular.
— V. intr. Calcular (to calculate). || Contar: *she reckoned on her fingers*, contaba con los dedos; *we are reckoning on a devaluation of the peseta*, contamos con una devaluación de la peseta. || Suponer, imaginar (to suppose). || Creer, pensar (to think). || — *Reckoning from yesterday*, a contar de ayer, a partir de ayer. || *To reckon without*, prescindir de. || *To reckon with s.o.*, ajustar cuentas con alguien (to settle accounts with), contar con (to contend with): *if you marry her you will have her mother to reckon with*, si se casa con ella tendrá que contar con su madre.

reckoner [—ə*] n. Calculador, ra. || MATH. Tabla, *f.*

reckoning [—iŋ] n. Cuenta, *f.*, cálculo, *m.*: *to be out in one's reckoning*, equivocarse en las cuentas. || Estimación, *f.*, apreciación, *f.*: *to the best of my reckoning*, según mi estimación. || COMM. Cuenta, *f.*, factura, *f.*, nota, *f.* (account). | Ajuste (*m.*) de cuentas (settling of accounts). || MAR. Estima, *f.* || *It's a lot of money by any reckoning*, se mire como se mire representa mucho dinero.

reclaim [ri'kleim] n. *Past* o *beyond reclaim*, perdido para siempre.

reclaim [ri'kleim] v. tr. Reformar (to reform). || Sacar (from vice). || AGR. Roturar, aprovechar. || Ganar: *land reclaimed from the sea*, tierra ganada al mar. || Sanear (marshland). || TECH. Recuperar, regenerar: *reclaimed rubber*, caucho regenerado. || *Reclaimed woman*, mujer arrepentida.

re-claim [ri'kleim] v. tr. Reclamar.

reclaimable [—əbl] adj. Enmendable, corregible (reformable). || Recuperable: *reclaimable deposit*, fianza recuperable. || AGR. Roturable (land). || Que puede ser ganado [al mar] (from the sea). || Que puede ser saneado (marshland). || TECH. Recuperable, regenerable.

reclaiming [—iŋ] n. See RECLAMATION.

reclamation [,reklə'meiʃən] n. Enmienda, *f.*, corrección, *f.* (moral salvation). || Reclamación, *f.* (claiming back). || AGR. Roturación, *f.*, aprovechamiento, *m.* (of land). || Saneamiento, *m.* (of marshland). || TECH. Recuperación, *f.*, regeneración, *f.*

recline [ri'klain] v. tr. Apoyar, reclinar (one's head).
— V. intr. Recostarse, reclinarse (*on*, en). || Apoyarse, descansar (head).

recluse [ri'klu:s] n. Recluso, sa; solitario, ria.

reclusion [ri'klu:ʒən] n. Reclusión, *f.*, aislamiento, *m.*

recognition [,rekəg'niʃən] n. Reconocimiento, *m.*: *recognition of a new state*, reconocimiento de un nuevo estado; *in recognition of*, en reconocimiento de. || *It has changed beyond recognition* o *out of all recognition*, ha llegado a ser irreconocible.

recognizable ['rekəgnaizəbl] adj. Reconocible.

recognizance [ri'kɔgnizəns] n. JUR. Fianza, *f.* (guarantee). | Compromiso, *m.* (obligation). || *To enter into recognizances to*, comprometerse a.

recognize ['rekəgnaiz] v. tr. Reconocer: *to recognize s.o. by the way he dresses*, reconocer a alguien por su modo de vestirse; *to recognize a new state*, reconocer un nuevo estado; *to recognize s.o. as leader*, reconocer a alguien como jefe. || Admitir, reconocer (a mistake). || Admitir: *this word is not recognized*, esta palabra no está admitida. || U. S. Dar la palabra a.

recoil [ri'kɔil] n. Culatazo, *m.* (of a gun). || Retroceso, *m.* (of a cannon). || Aflojamiento, *m.* (of a spring). || FIG. Asco, *m.*, repugnancia, *f.*, horror, *m.* (repugnance). || Retirada, *f.*, retroceso, *m.* (of soldiers). || *Recoil spring*, muelle (*m.*) de retroceso.

recoil [ri'kɔil] v. intr. Dar culatazo (a gun). || Retroceder (a cannon). || Aflojarse (a spring). || Retirarse, retroceder, replegarse (soldiers). || Echarse atrás (to draw back). || FIG. Rechazar, negarse a, rehusar (to refuse): *to recoil from doing sth.*, rechazar hacer algo. | Tener horror a *or* asco a, sentir repugnancia por (to feel disgust). | Recaer sobre (to have repercussions): *his dishonesty recoiled on him*, su falta de honradez recayó sobre él.

recoilless [—lis] adj. Sin retroceso (gun).

recoin [ri'kɔin] v. tr. Acuñar de nuevo.

recoinage [—idʒ] n. Reacuñación, *f.*, nueva acuñación, *f.*

recollect [,rekə'lekt] v. tr. Recordar, acordarse de (to remember): *as far as I recollect*, si mal no recuerdo. || *To recollect o.s.*, recogerse.

re-collect ['ri:kə'lekt] v. tr. Reunir (to gather). || Recuperar (to recover). || *To re-collect o.s.*, serenarse.

recollection [,rekə'lekʃən] n. Recuerdo, *m.* (thing remembered): *I have happy recollections of my stay there*, tengo buenos recuerdos de mi estancia allí. || Memoria, *f.* (power of recollecting). || Recogimiento, *m.* (spiritual contemplation). || *To the best of my recollection*, que yo recuerde.

recommence ['ri:kə'mens] v. tr./intr. Volver a empezar, empezar de nuevo *or* otra vez, recomenzar.

recommend [,rekə'mend] v. tr. Recomendar: *can you recommend a good restaurant?*, ¿puede recomendar un buen restaurante?; *I have been recommended to you*, me han recomendado a usted. || Aconsejar, recomendar (to advise): *I recommend you to accept*, le aconsejo que acepte. || Encomendar: *I recommend my soul to God*, encomiendo mi alma a Dios. || — *He has little to recommend him*, poca cosa tiene que hable en su favor. || *Not to be recommended*, que no es de aconsejar, que no es recomendable, poco aconsejable.

recommendable [—əbl] adj. Recomendable. || Aconsejable (advisable).

recommendation [,rekəmen'deiʃən] n. Recomendación, *f.*: *the recommendations of a committee*, las recomendaciones de un comité; *when I left he wrote me a good recommendation*, cuando me marché me hizo una buena recomendación. || Consejo, *m.*, recomendación, *f.* (advice). || — *In recommendation of*, recomendando. || *On the recommendation of*, por recomendación de. || *Recommendation to mercy*, petición (*f.*) de indulto.

recommendatory [,rekə'mendətəri] adj. De recomendación, recomendatorio, ria.

recompense ['rekəmpens] n. Recompensa, *f.* (reward). || Compensación, *f.*, indemnización, *f.*, resarcimiento, *m.* (for damage).

recompense ['rekəmpəns] v. tr. Recompensar (to reward). || Compensar, indemnizar, resarcir (in return for a loss or damage).

recompose ['ri:kəm'pəuz] v. tr. Calmar, tranquilizar, serenar (s.o.). || Recomponer (sth.).

recomposition [ri,kɔmə'ziʃən] n. Recomposición, *f.*

reconcilable ['rekənsailəbl] adj. Reconciliable (person). || Conciliable, compatible (statements).

reconcile ['rekənsail] v. tr. Reconciliar (persons). || Arreglar, poner fin a (a dispute). || Conciliar (different statements). || — *To become reconciled to* o *to reconcile o.s. to*, resignarse a, conformarse con (sth). || *To become reconciled with*, reconciliarse con (s.o.).

reconcilement [—mənt] or **reconciliation** [,rekənsili'eiʃən] n. Reconciliación, *f.* (of two persons). || Conciliación, *f.* (of theories). || Arreglo, *m.* (of a dispute).

reconciliatory [,rekən'siljətəri] adj. Reconciliador, ra.

recondite [ri'kɔndait] adj. Recóndito, ta; oculto, ta (obscure). || Abstruso, sa (difficult to understand).

recondition [,ri:kən'diʃən] v. tr. Arreglar, poner como nuevo (to restore). || *Reconditioned car, engine*, coche, motor revisado.

reconfirm ['ri:kən'fə:m] v. tr. Reconfirmar.

reconnaissance or **reconnoissance** [ri'kɔnisəns] adj. De reconocimiento: *reconnoissance plane, flight*, avión, vuelo de reconocimiento.
— N. Reconocimiento, *m.* || *To go on reconnoissance*, reconocer el terreno.

reconnoitre (U. S. **reconnoiter**) [,rekə'nɔitə*] v. tr. Reconocer.
— V. intr. Hacer un reconocimiento, reconocer el terreno.

reconnoitrer (U. S. **reconnoiterer**) [—rə*] n. MIL. Explorador, *m.*

reconquer ['ri:'kɔŋkə*] v. tr. Reconquistar.

reconquest ['ri:'kɔŋkwest] n. Reconquista, *f.*

reconsider ['ri:kən'sidə*] v. tr. Volver a considerar, examinar de nuevo, reconsiderar (to consider again). || Revisar (a judgment).

reconsideration ['ri:kən,sidə'reiʃən] n. Nuevo examen, *m.* || Revisión, *f.*

reconstituent [ˈri:kənsˈtitjuənt] adj. Reconstituyente.
— N. Reconstituyente, *m.*

reconstitute [ˈri:ˈkɔnstitju:t] v. tr. Reconstituir. || CULIN. Hidratar (dried food).

reconstitution [ˈri:ˌkɔnstiˈtju:ʃən] n. Reconstitución, *f.*

reconstruct [ˈri:kənsˈtrʌkt] v. tr. Reconstruir, reedificar (a building). || Reconstruir (a road). || JUR. Reconstituir (a crime).

reconstruction [ˈri:kənsˈtrʌkʃən] n. Reconstrucción, *f.*, reedificación, *f.* (of a building). || Reconstrucción, *f.* (of a road). || JUR. Reconstitución, *f.* (of a crime). || U. S. Reorganización, *f.*

reconstructive [ˈri:kənsˈtrʌktiv] adj. Reconstructivo, va.

reconvene [ˈrikənˈvi:n] v. tr. Convocar de nuevo (a meeting).
— V. intr. Reanudar la sesión, volverse a reunir.

reconvention [ˈrikənˈvenʃən] n. Reconvención, *f.*

reconversion [ˈri:kənˈvə:ʃən] n. Readaptación, *f.* || TECH. Reconversión, *f.*

reconvert [ˈri:kənˈvə:t] v. tr. Readaptar. || Reconvertir.

reconvey [ˈri:kənˈvei] v. tr. Devolver, restituir (to give back). || JUR. Hacer la retrocesión de, retroceder.

reconveyance [—əns] n. JUR. Retrocesión, *f.* || Devolución, *f.*, restitución, *f.*

recook [ˈri:kuk] v. tr. Volver a cocer, recocer.

record [ˈrekɔ:d] n. Anotación, *f.*, inscripción, *f.*, registro, *m.* (writing down). || Registro, *m.* (register). || Documento, *m.* (document). || Relación, *f.* (account): *a detailed record of what happened*, una relación detallada de lo que pasó. || Actas, *f. pl.*, acta, *f.* (minutes): *the record of a meeting*, las actas de una reunión; *court record*, actas de un tribunal. || Expediente, *m.* (file): *I'll go and get out your record*, voy a sacar su expediente. || Expediente (*m.*) académico (at university). || Historial (*m.*) médico (medical). || Historial, *m.*, hoja (*f.*) de servicios (of s.o.): *I have a good record*, tengo una buena hoja de servicios. || Mención, *f.*: *there is no record of it in history*, no se hace mención de ello en la historia. || Nota, *f.*: *to make a record of an observation*, tomar nota de una observación. || Boletín, *m.*: *official record of a society*, boletín oficial de una sociedad. || Calificación, *f.*, notas, *f. pl.*: *his son has a good record at school*, su hijo tiene buenas notas en el colegio. || SP. Récord, *m.*, marca, *f.*, plusmarca, *f.*: *to break, to hold, to set a record*, batir, tener, establecer un récord; *five records fell*, se batieron cinco récords. || Grabación, *f.* (of sounds). || Disco, *m.* (of gramophone): *long-playing record*, disco de larga duración. || Cinta, *f.* (of tape recorder). || Rollo, *m.* (of a pianola). || — Pl. Anales, *m.*, archivos, *m.* (archives). || — *Matter of record*, hecho establecido. || *Music on record*, música grabada. || *Off the record*, confidencialmente, oficiosamente. || *Off-the-record statement*, declaración oficiosa. || *Police record* o *criminal record*, registro de antecedentes penales. || *Service record*, hoja de servicios, historial. || *The Public Record Office*, los Archivos Nacionales. || *There is no record of it*, no hay constancia de ello. || *To be on record*, estar registrado (to be registered), constar (fact) || *To go on record*, declarar públicamente: *the Prime Minister went on record as saying*, el Primer Ministro declaró públicamente que; constar: *let it go on record that*, que conste que. || *To have a clean record*, no tener antecedentes penales. || *To place on record in the minutes*, hacer constar en las actas. || *To put a resolution on record*, consignar una resolución, hacer constar una resolución. || *Verbatim record*, actas taquigráficas *or* literales.
— Adj. Récord, nunca alcanzado, da: *at record speed*, a una velocidad nunca alcanzada.

record [riˈkɔ:d] v. tr. Tomar nota de, apuntar (to make a note of): *to record an appointment in one's diary*, tomar nota de una cita en su agenda. || Registrar (to register). || Hacer constar, consignar (in the minutes): *to record a resolution*, consignar una resolución. || Informar de, relatar (to relate). || Declarar: *to record a birth with the authorities*, declarar un nacimiento al registro civil. || Empadronar, hacer el censo de (population). || Grabar (sounds). || Marcar (a thermometer, etc.). || — *Recorded broadcast* o *transmission*, emisión diferida. || *To be recorded*, constar.

record breaker [ˈrekɔ:dˈbreikə*] n. Plusmarquista, *m.* & *f.*, "recordman", *m.*, "recordwoman", *f.*

record-breaker [ˈrekɔ:dˈbreikiŋ] adj. Récord, *inv.* (time, jump, production). || Que ha batido muchos records (team).

record cabinet [rekɔ:dˈkæbinit] n. Discoteca, *f.*, armario (*m.*) para discos.

record card [ˈrekɔ:dkɑ:d] n. Ficha, *f.*

record changer [ˈrekɔ:dˈtʃeindʒə*] n. Cambiadiscos, *m. inv.*

record dealer [ˈrekɔ:dˈdi:lə*] n. Vendedor (*m.*) de discos.

recorder [riˈkɔ:də*] n. JUR. Magistrado (*m.*) municipal. || Secretario (*m.*) del registro civil (registrar). || Archivero, ra; archivista, *m.* & *f.* (keeper of records). || MUS. Flauta, *f.* (flute). | Artista (*m.* & *f.*) que graba discos. || Grabadora, *f.* (sound recording device). || Contador, *m.*, indicador, *m.* (recording device): *speed recorder*, indicador de velocidad. || — AVIAT. *Flight recorder*, registrador (*m.*) de vuelo. || *Recorder of deeds*, registrador (*m.*) de la propiedad. || *Sound recorder*, grabadora, *f.* || *Tape recorder*, magnetófono, *m.*, magnetofón, *m.* [*Amer.*, grabadora, *f.*]

record holder [ˈrekɔ:dˈhəuldə*] n. SP. Plusmarquista, *m.* & *f.*, "recordman", *m.*, "recordwoman", *f.*

recording [riˈkɔ:diŋ] adj. JUR. Encargado del empadronamiento (official). || Que graba discos (artist). || De grabación (studio, van, session). || Magnetofónico, ca (tape). || *Recording head*, cabeza sonora.
— N. Consignación, *f.*: *the recording of a motion*, la consignación de una moción. || Narración, *f.*, relación, *f.* (narration). || Censo, *m.*, empadronamiento, *m.* (of the population). || Registro, *m.* (registration). || Grabación, *f.* (of sound).

record library [ˈrekɔ:dˈlaibrəri] n. Discoteca, *f.*

record player [ˈrekɔ:dˌpleiə*] n. Tocadiscos, *m. inv.*

recount [riˈkaunt] v. tr. Contar, relatar (a story).

re-count or **recount** [ˈri:ˈkaunt] n. Recuento, *m.*, segundo escrutinio, *m.*: *to have a recount*, hacer un recuento.

re-count or **recount** [ˈri:ˈkaunt] v. tr. Hacer el recuento de *or* un segundo escrutinio de, volver a contar (votes).

recountal [riˈkauntəl] n. Relato, *m.*

recoup [riˈku:p] v. tr. Indemnizar (*for*, por) [to compensate]. || Recuperar, resarcirse (to recover): *to recoup a loss*, resarcirse de una pérdida. || Recobrar (strength). || JUR. Deducir, descontar (to deduct).

recoupment [—mənt] n. Indemnización, *f.* (compensation). || Recuperación, *f.*, resarcimiento, *m.* (of losses). || JUR. Deducción, *f.*

recourse [riˈkɔ:s] n. Recurso, *m.* || *To have recourse to*, recurrir a.

recover [riˈkʌvə*] v. tr. Recuperar, recobrar (the appetite, voice, breath, senses, consciousness, strength, love, etc.). || Recuperar (lost time, a town, lost or stolen property). || Sacar del agua (sth. floating). || Rescatar (to rescue). || Sacar, recuperar: *to recover by-products from oil*, sacar subproductos del petróleo. || Obtener (to obtain): *to recover damages from s.o.*, obtener daños y perjuicios de alguien. || Resarcirse de (to make good a loss). || Hacer volver en sí (a fainting person). || Ganar (land from sea). || Cobrar (a debt). || *To recover one's legs*, ponerse de pie.
— V. intr. Reponerse, restablecerse, recuperarse (from an illness). || Volver en sí, recobrar el sentido (to regain consciousness). || Recuperarse: *to recover from civil war*, recuperarse de la guerra civil. || Reponerse, salir: *he recovered from his astonishment*, se repuso de su asombro. || Recuperarse: *the economy has recovered*, la economía se ha recuperado. || Volver a subir (prices). || JUR. Ganar el pleito.

re-cover [ˈri:ˈkʌvə*] v. tr. Volver a cubrir, cubrir de nuevo (to cover again). || Forrar de nuevo (a book, furniture, etc.).

recoverable [—ərəbl] adj. Recuperable. || MED. Curable.

recovery [riˈkʌvəri] n. Recuperación, *f.* (of sth. lost): *recovery of one's appetite, of lost time, of a stolen car*, recuperación del apetito, del tiempo perdido, de un coche robado. || MED. Restablecimiento, *m.*, recuperación, *f.* || Recuperación, *f.* (of the economy, business). || Rescate, *m.* (rescue). || Subida, *f.* (of prices). || Obtención, *f.* (of damages). || FIG. Restablecimiento, *m.* (after a setback). || Recuperación, *f.* (from waste products). || MED. *Past recovery*, en estado desesperado, desahuciado, da.

recreancy [ˈrekriənsi] n. Cobardía, *f.* (cowardice). || Deslealtad, *f.* (disloyalty).

recreant [ˈrekriənt] adj./n. Cobarde (coward). | Traidor, ra; desleal (betrayer).

recreate [ˈrekrieit] v. tr. Divertir, entretener.
— V. intr. Divertirse, entretenerse.

re-create [ˈri:kriˈeit] v. tr. Volver a crear, recrear.

recreation [ˌrekriˈeiʃən] n. Esparcimiento, *m.*, expansión, *f.*, descanso, *m.* (leisure-time activity): *a moment of recreation*, un momento de esparcimiento. || Diversión, *f.*, entretenimiento, *m.* (pastime): *my favourite recreation*, mi diversión preferida. || Recreo, *m.* (playtime in school).

re-creation [ˈri:kriˈeiʃən] n. Nueva creación, *f.*

recreational [ˌrekriˈeiʃənəl] adj. Recreativo, va: *recreational evening*, velada recreativa; *recreational facilities*, instalaciones recreativas.

recreative [ˈrekrieitiv] adj. Recreativo, va.

recrement [ˈrekrimənt] n. Recremento, *m.*

recriminate [riˈkrimineit] v. intr. Recriminar.

recrimination [riˌkrimiˈneiʃən] n. Recriminación, *f.*

recriminative [riˈkrimiˌneitiv] or **recriminatory** [rekrimiˈneitəri] adj. Recriminatorio, ria; recriminador, ra.

recross [ˈri:ˈkrɔs] v. tr./intr. Volver a cruzar.

recrudesce [ˌri:kru:ˈdes] v. intr. Recrudecer.

recrudescence [—ns] n. Recrudescencia, *f.*: *recrudescence of crime*, recrudescencia de la criminalidad. || Recrudecimiento, *m.*: *recrudescence of the cold weather*, recrudecimiento del frío.

recrudescent [ˌri:kru:ˈdesnt] adj. Recrudescente.

recruit [riˈkru:t] n. MIL. Recluta, *m.*, quinto, *m.* || Neófito, ta; nuevo adherente (new member).

recruit [riˈkru:t] v. tr. MIL. Reclutar, alistar (to enlist). || Contratar (employees). || Recuperar (one's health). || MIL. *To recruit supplies*, abastecerse.

— V. intr. MIL. Reclutar (to take on recruits). | Abastecerse (with supplies). || Restablecerse, reponerse, recuperarse (one's health).
recruiter [—ə*] n. Reclutador, *m.*
recruiting [—iŋ] or **recruitment** [—mənt] n. MIL. Reclutamiento, *m.* || Contratación, *f.* (of employees). || MED. Restablecimiento, *m.* (recovery). || MIL. *Recruiting board*, junta (*f.*) de clasificación.
rectal [ˈrektəl] adj. ANAT. Rectal, del recto.
rectangle [ˈrek,tæŋgl] n. MATH. Rectángulo, *m.*
rectangular [rekˈtæŋgjulə*] adj. MATH. Rectangular.
rectifiable [ˈrektifaiəbl] adj. Rectificable.
rectification [,rektifiˈkeiʃən] n. Rectificación, *f.*
rectifier [ˈrektifaiə*] n. TECH. Rectificador, *m.*
rectify [ˈrektifai] v. tr. Rectificar, corregir: *to rectify an error*, rectificar un error. || MATH. CHEM. ELECTR. Rectificar. || MIL. Corregir (a shot).
rectifying [—iŋ] adj. Rectificador, ra.
rectilineal [,rektiˈliniəl] or **rectilinear** [,rektiˈliniə*] adj. Rectilíneo, a.
rectitude [ˈrektitju:d] n. Rectitud, *f.*
recto [ˈrektəu] n. Recto, *m.* (of a page).
rector [ˈrektə*] n. Director, *m.* (of a school). || Rector, *m.* (of a university). || REL. Párroco, *m.* (parish priest). | Superior, *m.* (of a religious order).
rectorate [ˈrektərit] or **rectorship** [ˈrektəʃip] n. Rectorado, *m.*, rectoría, *f.*
rectorial [rekˈtɔ:riəl] adj. Rectoral.
rectory [ˈrektəri] n. REL. Rectoral, *f.*, rectoría, *f.*, casa (*f.*) del párroco.
rectum [ˈrektəm] n. ANAT. Recto, *m.*
— OBSERV. El plural de *rectum* es *rectums* o *recta*.
recumbency [riˈkʌmbənsi] n. Posición (*f.*) yacente *or* recostada.
recumbent [riˈkʌmbənt] adj. Recostado, da. || *Recumbent statue*, estatua (*f.*) yacente.
recuperable [riˈkju:pərəbl] adj. Recuperable.
recuperate [riˈkju:pəreit] v. tr. Recuperar: *to recuperate lost time*, recuperar el tiempo perdido. || Recobrar (one's health). || TECH. Recuperar (waste products).
— V. intr. Restablecerse, recuperarse, reponerse.
recuperation [ri,kju:pəˈreiʃən] n. Recuperación, *f.* || Restablecimiento, *m.*, recuperación, *f.* (of health).
recuperative [riˈkju:pərətiv] adj. Recuperativo, va.
recuperator [riˈkju:pəreitə*] n. Recuperador, *m.*
recur [riˈkə:*] v. intr. Volver: *this idea recurred to my mind*, esta idea volvió a mi mente; *to recur to a subject*, volver a un tema. || Volver a ocurrir, repetirse, reproducirse (to occur again): *the noise recurred several times*, el ruido se repitió varias veces. || Repetirse (a question). || Volver a plantearse (a problem). || MATH. Reproducirse (figures). || MED. Reproducirse.
recurrence [riˈkʌrəns] n. Vuelta, *f.* (return). || Reaparición, *f.*, repetición, *f.* (repetition): *the recurrence of a noise*, la reaparición de un ruido. || Periodicidad, *f.* (regular repetition). || MED. Reaparición, *f.*, reproducción, *f.* (of a disease).
recurrent [riˈkʌrənt] adj. Que vuelve, que se repite. || Periódico, ca (at regular intervals). || MED. ANAT. Recurrente. || *It was a recurrent idea in his speech*, la idea reapareció constantemente en su discurso.
— N. ANAT. Nervio (*m.*) recurrente. | Arteria (*f.*) recurrente.
recurring [riˈkə:riŋ] adj. Periódico, ca.
recusancy [ˈrekjuzənsi] n. Recusación, *f.*
recusant [ˈrekjuzənt] adj./n. Recusante.
recusation [,rekjəˈzeiʃən] n. JUR. Recusación, *f.*
recuse [riˈkjuz] v. tr. JUR. Recusar.
red [red] adj. Rojo, ja; encarnado, da; colorado, da (colour). || Rojo, ja (beard, hair). || Enrojecido, da; rojo, ja (eyes). || Rojo, ja: *red with anger*, rojo de ira. || Colorado, da (with embarrassment): *to go red*, ponerse colorado. || Rojo, ja (in politics). || Tinto (wine). || Rojo, ja (ink). || Ahumado, da (herring). || Poco hecha (meat). || FIG. Sanguinario, ria: *red vengeance*, venganza sanguinaria. || — FIG. *Red as a peony* o *as a beetroot* o *as a turkey-cock* o *as a lobster*, más rojo que un cangrejo (from the sun), más rojo que un tomate (with embarrassment). || ANAT. *Red blood cell*, glóbulo rojo. || U. S. FAM. *Red cent*, céntimo, *m.*, centavo, *m.* (a trifling sum of money). || *Red Cross*, Cruz Roja (international organization). || MAR. *Red duster* o *red ensign*, bandera (*f.*) de la marina mercante británica. || *Red hands*, manos teñidas de sangre. || *Red hat*, capelo cardenalicio. || *Red heat*, calor rojo. || *Red herring*, see HERRING. || *Red Indian*, piel (*m.*) roja. || *Red lead*, minio, *m.* || *Red light*, disco rojo (traffic), luz roja (to draw attention), señal (*f.*) de peligro (danger signal). || ZOOL. *Red mullet*, salmonete, *m.* (fish). || *Red ochre* [U. S., *red ocher*], ocre rojo, almagre, *m.* || *Red Riding Hood*, Caperucita Roja. || GEOGR. *Red Sea*, Mar (*m.*) Rojo. || FIG. *Red tape*, papeleo, *m.*, trámites, *m. pl.* || *To go* o *to turn red*, ruborizarse, sonrojarse, ponerse colorado (a person), enrojecer (the sky).
— N. Rojo, *m.*, encarnado, *m.*, colorado, *m.*: *dressed in red*, vestido de rojo. || Rojo, *m.* (in politics). || Mingo, *m.* (ball in billiards). || — *Cherry red*, rojo cereza. || FIG. *To be in the red*, deber dinero, tener deudas. | *To be in the red at the bank*, tener la cuenta bancaria en rojo. | *To make s.o. see red*, sacar a uno de quicio. | *To see red*, ponerse furioso, ponerse rojo de ira.
redact [riˈdækt] v. tr. Redactar.
redaction [riˈdækʃən] n. Redacción, *f.*
redactor [riˈdæktə*] n. Redactor, *m.*
redan [riˈdæn] n. Rediente, *m.* (fortification).
red-blooded [ˈredˈblʌdəd] adj. Fuerte, vigoroso, sa (vigorous). || Enérgico, ca; vigoroso, sa (in writing).
redbreast [ˈredbrest] n. Petirrojo, *m.* (bird).
redcap [ˈredkæp] n. Policía (*m.*) militar. || U. S. Mozo (*m.*) de equipajes (in a railway station).
red-carpet [ˈredˈkɑ:pit] adj. FAM. Suntuoso, sa.
redcoat [ˈredkəut] n. Soldado (*m.*) inglés en la guerra de Independencia de los Estados Unidos.
redden [ˈredn] v. intr. Enrojecer (sky). || Ruborizarse, ponerse colorado (a person).
reddish [ˈrediʃ] adj. Rojizo, za.
reddle [ˈredl] n. Almagre, *m.*
redeem [riˈdi:m] v. tr. Cancelar, redimir (a mortgage). || Recobrar, recuperar (one's rights). || REL. Redimir (mankind). || Liberar, desempeñar (sth. pawned). || Amortizar, liberarse de (a debt). || Pagar (a bill). || Redimir (a slave). || Rescatar (by ransom). || Cumplir (a promise). || Compensar, salvar (a failing). || Expiar (a fault). || Recuperar (lost time). || *To redeem o.s.*, desquitarse.
redeemable [—əbl] adj. Redimible. || Amortizable (a debt). || Liberable (from pawn).
redeemer [—ə*] n. Redentor, ra. || *The Redeemer*, el Redentor.
redeeming [riˈdi:miŋ] adj. Redentor, ra. || Compensatorio, ria; que compensa.
redemand [ˈri:diˈma:nd] v. tr. Pedir de nuevo.
redemption [riˈdempʃən] n. Cancelación, *f.*, extinción, *f.* (of a mortgage). || Desempeño, *m.*, liberación, *f.* (from pawn). || Amortización, *f.* (of a debt). || Reembolso, *m.* (of a loan). || Expiación, *f.* (of a fault). || REL. Redención, *f.* || Rescate, *m.* (of a slave). || — *Redemption fund*, caja (*f.*) de amortización. || *Past redemption*, sin redención, irremediable. || *Sale with power of redemption*, venta (*f.*) con pacto de retro, retroventa, *f.*
redemptive [riˈdemptiv] adj. Redentor, ra.
Redemptorist [riˈdemptərist] n. REL. Redentorista, *m.*
redeploy [ˈri:diˈplɔi] v. tr. Cambiar de frente (military forces).
red-eyed [ˈred,aid] adj. Con los ojos inyectados en sangre.
red-faced [ˈredˈfeist] adj. Coloradote, ta (with a reddish complexion). || Rojo de ira (angry). || Colorado, da; avergonzado, da (embarrassed).
red-handed [ˈredˈhændid] adj. En flagrante delito, con las manos en la masa: *to catch s.o. red-handed*, coger a uno con las manos en la masa.
redhead [ˈredˈhed] n. Pelirrojo, ja.
redheaded [—id] adj. Pelirrojo, ja.
redhibition [redhiˈbiʃən] n. JUR. Redhibición, *f.*
redhibitory [redˈhibitəri] adj. JUR. Redhibitorio, ria.
red-hot [ˈredˈhɔt] adj. Al rojo, candente: *to make sth. red-hot*, poner algo al rojo. || FIG. Acérrimo, ma (supporter). | Ardiente, vehemente (ardent). | De última hora (news, etc.). | Muy peligroso, sa (very dangerous). | Sensacional, formidable (story). | Muy cotizado, da; favorito, ta (favourite). | Animado, da (full of pep). || FIG. FAM. *Red-hot blonde*, rubia incendiaria *or* explosiva.
redid [ˈri:ˈdid] pret. See REDO.
redingote [ˈrediŋgəut] n. Redingote, *m.*, levita, *f.*
redintegrate [reˈdintigreit] v. tr. Reintegrar (s.o.). || Volver a dar, devolver (to give back).
redintegration [redinteˈgreiʃən] n. Reintegro, *m.* || Devolución, *f.* (restitution).
redirect [ˈri:diˈrekt] adj. U. S. JUR. *Redirect examination*, segundo interrogatorio de un testigo.
redirect [ˈri:daiˈrekt] v. tr. Remitir *or* reexpedir al destinatario, remitir a las nuevas señas del destinatario (a letter).
redirection [—ʃən] n. Reexpedición, *f.*
rediscount [ˈridisˈkaunt] n. Redescuento, *m.*
rediscover [ˈri:disˈkʌvə*] v. tr. Descubrir de nuevo, volver a descubrir, redescubrir.
rediscovery [ˈri:disˈkʌvəri] n. Nuevo descubrimiento, *m.*, redescubrimiento, *m.*
redistribute [ˈri:disˈtribju:t] v. tr. Distribuir de nuevo, redistribuir.
redistribution [ˈri:,distriˈbju:ʃən] n. Nueva distribución, *f.*, redistribución, *f.*
red-letter day [ˈredˈletə*dei] n. Día (*m.*) memorable *or* señalado.
red-light district [ˈredˈlaitˈdistrikt] n. Barrio (*m.*) de mala fama.
redness [ˈrednis] n. Color (*m.*) rojo.
redo* [ˈri:ˈdu:] v. tr. Volver a hacer, rehacer.
— OBSERV. Pret. ***redid***; p. p. ***redone***.
redolence [ˈredəuləns] n. Perfume, *m.*, fragancia, *f.* || FIG. Evocación, *f.*
redolent [ˈredəulənt] adj. Fragante, oloroso, sa. || FIG. Evocador, ra. || *Redolent with*, impregnado de.
redone [ˈri:ˈdʌn] p. p. See REDO.
redouble [riˈdʌbl] n. Redoble, *m.* (bridge).
redouble [riˈdʌbl] v. tr./intr. Redoblar (to intensify); *to redouble one's efforts*, redoblar sus esfuerzos. || Redoblar (bridge).

redoubling [—iŋ] n. Aumento, *m.*, incremento, *m.*, redoblamiento, *m.*, intensificación, *f.*
redoubt [riˈdaut] n. MIL. Reducto, *m.*
redoubtable [—əbl] adj. Temible.
redound [riˈdaund] v. intr. Contribuir (to contribute). || Recaer (*upon*, sobre) [to reflect]. || *To redound to*, redundar en beneficio de (to benefit).
redpoll [ˈredpəul] n. Pardillo, *m.* (bird).
redraft [ˈriːˈdrɑːft] n. Nueva redacción, *f.* || COMM. Resaca, *f.*
redraft [ˈriːˈdrɑːft] v. tr. Redactar de nuevo, escribir de nuevo.
redraw* [ˈriːˈdrɔː] v. tr./intr. Volver a dibujar *or* a trazar.
— OBSERV. Pret. **redrew**; p. p. **redrawn**.
redrawn [ˈriːˈdrɔːn] p. p. See REDRAW.
redress [riˈdres] n. Reparación, *f.*, desagravio, *m.* (of a wrong). || Enmienda, *f.*, corrección, *f.* (of an error). || — *Beyond redress*, irreparable. || *To seek redress at s.o.'s hands*, exigir un desagravio a alguien.
redress [riˈdres] v. tr. Restablecer (balance). || Corregir, enmendar (an error). || Reparar, deshacer, enderezar (a wrong). || Aliviar (to relieve).
redresser [—ə*] n. *Redresser of wrongs*, desfacedor (*m.*) de entuertos, deshacedor (*m.*) de agravios.
redrew [ˈriːˈdruː] pret. See REDRAW.
redskin [ˈredskin] n. Piel roja, *m.* & *f.*
redstart [ˈredstɑːt] n. ZOOL. Colirrojo, *m.* (bird).
reduce [riˈdjuːs] v. tr. Reducir: *to reduce expenses*, reducir los gastos; *to reduce by a quarter*, reducir en una cuarta parte; *to reduce to dust*, reducir a polvo; *to reduce s.o. to obedience, to silence*, reducir a alguien a la obediencia, al silencio. || Reducir: *he reduces everything to a simple principle*, lo reduce todo a un principio sencillo. || Consignar: *to reduce sth. to writing*, consignar algo por escrito. || Poner: *to reduce a theory to practice*, poner una teoría en práctica. || Sofocar, reducir (a revolt). || Rebajar (to a lower rank). || MIL. Degradar (an officer). || COMM. Rebajar, reducir (a price). || Acortar (in length). || Estrechar (in width). || Reducir, aminorar, disminuir (to lessen). || Hacer adelgazar (a fat person). || MATH. CHEM. MED. Reducir. || CULIN. Trabar (a sauce). || PHOT. Rebajar. || — *At reduced prices*, a precios reducidos, con rebaja. || FIG. *In reduced circumstances*, apurado, da (poor). | *They were reduced to begging*, no tuvieron más remedio que pedir limosna. | *To reduce s.o. to poverty*, llevar a alguien a la pobreza.
— V. intr. Adelgazar (to slim). || Reducirse, disminuir.
reducer [—ə*] n. Reductor, *m.* || PHOT. Rebajador, *m.*
reducibility [riˌdjuːsəˈbiliti] n. Reductibilidad, *f.*
reducible [riˈdjuːsəbl] adj. Reducible, reductible.
reducing [riˈdjuːsiŋ] adj. Reductor, ra. || — CHEM. *Reducing agent*, reductor, *m.* || TECH. *Reducing gear*, engranaje desmultiplicador.
reduction [riˈdʌkʃən] n. Reducción, *f.* (in general). || Acortamiento, *m.* (in length). || Estrechamiento, *m.* (in width). || Adelgazamiento, *m.* (in weight). || MIL. Degradación, *f.* (to a lower rank). || MED. Reducción, *f.* (of a fracture). || MATH. CHEM. Reducción, *f.* || COMM. Disminución, *f.* (of prices, of wages). || Rebaja, *f.*, descuento, *m.* (discount): *to get a good reduction on an article*, conseguir un buen descuento en un artículo. || Baja, *f.*, disminución, *f.* (in temperature). || ELECTR. Disminución, *f.* (of voltage). || TECH. Desmultiplicación, *f.* (gearing down). || PHOT. Rebajamiento, *m.* || TECH. *Reduction gear*, engranaje desmultiplicador.
redundance [riˈdʌndəns] or **redundancy** [—i] n. GRAMM. Redundancia, *f.* || Superabundancia, *f.* (excess). || Superfluidad, *f.* || Exceso (*m.*) de mano de obra (of labour). || Desempleo, *m.* (unemployment).
redundant [riˈdʌndənt] adj. Excesivo, va; superfluo, a. || GRAMM. Redundante, pleonástico, ca; tautológico, ca (word). || — *Redundant labour*, exceso (*m.*) de mano de obra. || *To become redundant*, perder su empleo (worker).
reduplicate [riˈdjuːplikit] adj. Repetido, da. || BOT. Reduplicado, da. || GRAMM. Repetido, da; reduplicado, da.
reduplicate [riˈdjuːplikeit] v. tr. Repetir. || BOT. Reduplicar. || GRAMM. Repetir, reduplicar.
reduplication [riˌdjuːpliˈkeiʃən] n. Repetición, *f.* || BOT. Reduplicación, *f.* || GRAMM. Repetición, *f.*, reduplicación, *f.*
reduplicative [riˈdjuːplikətiv] adj. Reduplicativo, va.
redwing [ˈredwiŋ] n. Malvís, *m.* (bird).
redwood [ˈredwud] n. Secoya, *f.* (tree).
redye [ˈriːˈdai] v. tr. Teñir de nuevo.
reecho [riˈekəu] v. intr. Resonar.
— V. tr. Repetir.
reed [riːd] n. BOT. Caña, *f.*, junco, *m.*, carrizo, *m.* || MUS. Caramillo, *m.* (instrument). | Lengüeta, *f.* (in mouthpiece): *reed instrument*, instrumento de lengüeta. || TECH. Peine, *m.* (of a loom). || Paja, *f.*, rastrojo, *m.* (of a roof). || Junquillo, *m.* (molding). || — Pl. MUS. Instrumentos (*m.*) de lengüeta.
reed [riːd] v. tr. Poner lengüeta a (an instrument). || Techar con paja (a roof).
reedbed [—bed] n. Cañaveral, *m.*, carrizal, *m.*, juncal, *m.*
reed mace [—meis] n. BOT. Anea, *f.*, espadaña, *f.*
reed organ [—ˈɔːgən] n. MUS. Armonio, *m.*
reed pipe [—paip] n. MUS. Cañón (*m.*) de lengüeta (of an organ). | Caramillo, *m.* (instrument).
reed stop [—stɔp] n. MUS. Cañones (*m. pl.*) de lengüeta (of an organ).
reeducate [ˈriːˈedjukeit] v. tr. Reeducar.
reeducation [ˈriːˌedjuˈkeiʃən] n. Reeducación, *f.*
reedy [ˈriːdi] adj. Lleno de juncos *or* cañas *or* carrizos. || FIG. Delgado, da (person). | Aflautado, da (voice). | Agudo, da (sound).
reef [riːf] n. MAR. Arrecife, *m.*, escollo, *m.*: *coral reef*, arrecife de coral. || MIN. Vena, *f.*, filón, *m.* || MAR. Rizo, *m.* (in a sail): *to take in a reef*, tomar rizos. || FIG. Escollo, *m.* (hazard). || — FIG. *To let out a reef*, aflojarse el cinturón. | *To take in a reef*, apretarse el cinturón. || *Reef knot*, nudo (*m.*) de rizo.
reef [riːf] v. tr. MAR. Arrizar.
reefer [—ə*] n. Chaquetón, *m.*, chubasquero, *m.* (jacket). || Guardiamarina, *m.* (midshipman). || U. S. FAM. Cigarrillo (*m.*) de marijuana, porro, *m.* (joint).
reek [riːk] n. Humo, *m.* (smoke). || Vaho, *m.*, vapor, *m.* (vapour). || Tufo, *m.*, mal olor, *m.*, hedor, *m.* (unpleasant smell).
reek [riːk] v. intr. Humear (sth. burning). || Apestar: *this room reeks of tobacco*, este cuarto apesta a tabaco. || FIG. Destilar, rebosar de, rezumar: *his speech reeks of hypocrisy*, su discurso destila hipocresía. || *To reek with blood*, estar bañado en sangre.
reel [riːl] n. Carrete, *m.*, bobina, *f.*: *reel of cotton*, bobina de algodón. || CINEM. Bobina, *f.*, cinta, *f.*: *to change reels*, cambiar de bobina. || PHOT. Carrete, *m.*, rollo, *m.* || SP. Carrete, *m.* (of fishing rod). || Baile (*m.*) escocés muy rápido (Scottish dance). || TECH. Devanadera, *f.* (spool). | Bobina, *f.* (of paper). || Titubeo, *m.* (staggering). || FIG. *Off the reel*, de un tirón, sin parar.
reel [riːl] v. intr. Hacer eses, vacilar, tambalearse (to stagger). || Dar vueltas: *my head is reeling*, la cabeza me da vueltas. || Tener vértigo (to feel giddy). || Tambalearse (to be shaken). || — FIG. *His mind reeled at the thought*, este pensamiento le daba vértigo. || *To reel down the street*, bajar la calle tambaleándose.
— V. tr. Devanar (thread, etc.). || — *To reel in* o *up*, cobrar (rope). || *To reel in a fish*, sacar un pez del agua enrollando el sedal. || *To reel off*, devanar (thread, etc.), recitar de un tirón, soltar (to recite without interruption).
reelect [ˈriːiˈlekt] v. tr. Reelegir.
reelected [—id] adj. Reelegido, da, || Reelecto, ta (not yet having taken office).
reelection [ˈriːiˈlekʃən] n. Reelección, *f.*
reeligibility [ˈriːˌelidʒəˈbiliti] n. Reelegibilidad, *f.*
reeligible [ˈriːˈelidʒəbl] adj. Reelegible.
reembark [ˈriːimˈbɑːk] v. tr. Reembarcar.
— V. intr. Reembarcarse.
reembarkation [ˌriːimbɑːˈkeiʃən] n. Reembarco, *m.*
reemerge [ˈriːiˈməːdʒ] v. intr. Resurgir.
reemploy [ˌriːimˈplɔi] v. tr. Volver a emplear.
reenact [ˈriːiˈnækt] v. tr. Volver a promulgar (law, etc.). || Volver a representar (a play). || Reconstituir (a crime).
reenforce [ˈriːinˈfɔːs] v. tr. See REINFORCE.
reenforcement [—mənt] n. See REINFORCEMENT.
reengage [ˈriːinˈgeidʒ] v. tr. Contratar de nuevo, volver a contratar (employees).
reengagement [—mənt] n. Nuevo contrato, *m.*
reenlist [ˈriːinˈlist] v. tr. MIL. Reenganchar.
— V. intr. MIL. Reengancharse.
reenlistment [—mənt] n. MIL. Reenganche, *m.*
reenter [ˈriːˈentə*] v. tr. Volver a entrar: *they never reentered that house*, no volvieron nunca a entrar en esa casa. || Reingresar en, volver a ingresar en: *to reenter an organization*, reingresar en una organización. || Volver a matricular (a child in a school). || Volver a apuntar (in a register, etc.).
— V. intr. Volver a entrar: *Raymond went out and reentered*, Ramón salió y volvió a entrar. || Volver a presentarse: *he reentered for his English exam*, se volvió a presentar al examen de inglés.
reentrance [ˈriːˈentrəns] n. Reingreso, *m.*
reentrant [ˈriːˈentrənt] adj. Entrante: *a reentrant angle*, un ángulo entrante.
— N. MIL. Entrante, *m.* (part of a defence).
reentry [riːˈentri] n. Nueva entrada, *f.*: *the reentry of a spacecraft into the atmosphere*, la nueva entrada de un vehículo espacial en la atmósfera. || Reingreso, *m.*: *his reentry into university*, su reingreso en la universidad.
reestablish [ˈriːisˈtæbliʃ] v. tr. Restablecer: *to reestablish order*, restablecer el orden. || Restaurar: *to reestablish the king on the throne*, restaurar al rey en el trono. || Reintegrar: *to reestablish s.o. in his possessions*, reintegrar a alguien sus bienes. || *To reestablish one's health*, restablecerse, recuperarse, reponerse.
reestablishment [—mənt] n. Restablecimiento, *m.* (act of reestablishing). || Restauración, *f.* (restoration). || Reintegración, *f.* (of fortune, property). || *Reestablishment of one's health*, restablecimiento, *m.*
reeve [riːv] n. Baile, *m.* (king's agent). || Presidente (*m.*) del concejo (in Canada).
reeve* [riːv] v. tr. MAR. Pasar por una polea *or* por un ojal (a rope).
— V. intr. MAR. Laborear.
— OBSERV. Pret. & p. p. **rove, reeved.**

reexamination [ˈriːigˌzæmiˈneiʃən] n. Nuevo examen, *m.* (second exam). || JUR. Nuevo interrogatorio, *m.* (of a witness). || Reexaminación, *f.*
reexamine [ˈriːigˈzæmin] v. tr. Examinar de nuevo, reexaminar (to examine again). || JUR. Volver a interrogar.
reexport [ˈriːˈekspɔːt] n. Reexportación, *f.*: *goods for reexport*, mercancías destinadas a la reexportación.
reexport [ˈriːˈekspɔːt] v. tr. Reexportar.
reexportation [ˈriːˌekspɔːˈteiʃən] n. Reexportación, *f.*
ref [ref] n. Árbitro, *m.* (referee).
reface [ˈriːˈfeis] v. tr. ARCH. Rehacer la fachada de. || TECH. Rectificar (a surface). || Arreglar (garment).
refashion [ˈriːˈfæʃən] v. tr. Rehacer.
refection [riˈfekʃən] n. Colación, *f.*, refrigerio, *m.*
refectory [riˈfektəri] n. Refectorio, *m.*
refer [riˈfəː*] v. tr. Remitir (a matter to s.o.). || Remitir: *he referred me to a Spanish dictionary*, me remitió a un diccionario español. || Enviar: *to refer a patient to a specialist*, enviar un paciente a un especialista. || Situar (an event to a date): *historians refer this event to the sixteenth century*, los historiadores sitúan este acontecimiento en el siglo dieciséis. || Atribuir (to attribute): *the discovery of gunpowder is usually referred to China*, generalmente el descubrimiento de la pólvora se atribuye a China. || Atribuir, achacar (an effect to its cause): *he refers his emotional problems to his childhood*, atribuye sus problemas emocionales a su infancia. || JUR. Remitir, enviar (an affair to a tribunal). || COMM. *To refer a cheque to drawer*, negarse a pagar un cheque [por falta de fondos].
— V. intr. Referirse, aludir, mencionar (to allude to); *in his speech he referred to football in Spain*, en su discurso se refirió al fútbol en España *or* mencionó el fútbol en España. || Referirse (to look at for information): *the speaker referred to his notes*, el orador se refirió a sus notas. || Calificar: *he referred to them as idealists*, los calificó de idealistas. || Remitirse: *this man is an idiot, I refer to the facts*, ese hombre es un idiota, me remito a los hechos. || Consultar: *for further information refer to the archives*, para mayor información consultar los archivos. || — COMM. *Referring to your letter of the twentieth*, con relación a su carta del día veinte. || *Refer to page 10*, véase la página 10.
referable [riˈfəːrəbl] adj. *Referable to*, atribuible a.
referee [ˌrefəˈriː] n. Árbitro, *m.* (in an argument, sports). || Garante, *m.* (for character reference).
referee [ˌrefəˈriː] v. tr./intr. Arbitrar.
reference [ˈrefrəns] n. Referencia, *f.* (act of referring). || Relación, *f.*: *all parts have reference to one another*, todas las partes tienen relación las unas con las otras. || Alusión, *f.*, mención, *f.*, referencia, *f.*: *to make a reference to a fact*, hacer alusión a un hecho. || Fiador, *m.*, garante, *m.* (person giving character reference). || Informe, *m.*, referencia, *f.* (testimonial). || Llamada, *f.* (mark indicating a footnote). || Referencia, *f.*, nota, *f.* (footnote). || Fuente, *f.* (source of information). || — *Point of reference*, punto (*m.*) de referencia. || *Reference book*, libro (*m.*) de consulta. || *Reference library*, biblioteca (*f.*) de consulta. || *Reference mark*, llamada. || *Reference number*, número (*m.*) de referencia. || *Terms of reference*, mandato, *m.* || *To make reference to*, referirse a, hacer referencia a. || *Without reference to*, sin consultar (without consulting), sin mencionar (without mentioning). || *With reference to*, en cuanto a (as regards), con referencia a, con relación a, respecto a (in a business letter).
reference [ˈrefrəns] v. tr. Poner notas a.
referendum [ˌrefəˈrendəm] n. Referéndum, *m.*: *to have a referendum on a matter*, hacer un referéndum sobre un asunto.
— OBSERV. El plural de *referendum* es *referendums* o *referenda*.
referential [ˌrefəˈrenʃəl] adj. De referencia.
refill [ˈriːfil] n. Recambio, *m.*: *ballpoint refill*, recambio de bolígrafo. || Carga, *f.*: *gas refill*, carga de gas.
refill [ˈriːˈfil] v. tr. Rellenar (to fill up). || Cargar: *to refill a pen, a lighter*, cargar una pluma, un encendedor.
refillable [—əbl] adj. Recargable, recambiable.
refinance [riˈfaiˌnæns] v. tr. Financiar de nuevo.
refine [riˈfain] v. tr. Refinar: *to refine oil, sugar*, refinar petróleo, azúcar. || Depurar, purificar (water). || Purificar, acrisolar (metal). || FIG. Refinar, pulir, hacer *or* volver más fino (a person, an accent). | Pulir (style). | Perfeccionar (a technique).
— V. intr. Refinarse. || Purificarse. || *To refine on* o *upon*, sutilizar.
refinement [—mənt] n. FIG. Refinamiento, *m.* (of a person). | Finura, *f.*, educación, *f.* (good manners). | Elegancia, *f.* (of style). | Perfección, *f.*, perfeccionamiento, *m.* (of a technique). || TECH. Refinado, *m.*, refinación, *f.* (of oil, sugar). | Purificación, *f.* (of metal). | Depuración, *f.* (of water). || — *Refinements of cruelty*, barbaridades, *f.* || *Refinements of meaning*, sutilezas, *f.*
refiner [—ə*] n. Refinador, *m.*
refinery [riˈfainəri] n. TECH. Refinería, *f.*
refining [riˈfainiŋ] n. TECH. Refinado, *m.*, refinación, *f.*: *oil refining*, refinado del petróleo. | Purificación, *f.* (of metal). | Depuración, *f.* (of water). || FIG. Refinamiento, *m.* (of a person). | Perfeccionamiento, *m.* (of a technique).
refit [ˈriːˈfit] n. Reparación, *f.*
refit [ˈriːˈfit] v. tr. Reparar. || Volver a equipar.
reflect [riˈflekt] v. tr. Reflejar: *mirrors reflect light*, los espejos reflejan la luz; *his behaviour reflects his upbringing*, su comportamiento refleja su educación. || *To reflect credit on*, hacer recaer el prestigio en, honrar.
— V. intr. Reflejarse (light, sound). || Reflexionar, meditar, pensar (to think): *give him time to reflect*, dale tiempo para reflexionar. || — *To reflect ill on s.o.*, desacreditar a alguien (an action). || *To reflect on* o *upon*, perjudicar: *such an act reflects on him*, una acción así le perjudica; meditar sobre: *to reflect on the past*, meditar sobre el pasado; pensar: *I shall reflect on it*, lo pensaré. || *To reflect well on s.o.*, honrar a alguien (an action).
reflectance [—əns] n. PHYS. Reflectancia, *f.*
reflected [—id] adj. Reflejado, da. || *Reflected ray*, rayo reflejado *or* reflejo.
reflecting [riˈflektiŋ] adj. Reflectante: *reflecting surface*, superficie reflectante.
reflecting telescope [—ˈteliskəup] n. PHYS. Telescopio (*m.*) reflector.
reflection [riˈflekʃən] n. Reflexión, *f.* (act). || Reflejo, *m.* (image produced). || ANAT. Repliegue, *m.* (of tissue). || Reflexión, *f.*, meditación, *f.* (meditation). || Reflexión, *f.*, comentario, *m.* (opinion). || Crítica, *f.* (criticism): *I don't mean this as any reflection on your work*, con eso no quiero hacer ninguna crítica de su trabajo. || — *A pale reflection of his former self*, una sombra de lo que era. || *On reflection*, después de pensarlo, pensándolo bien. || *To cast reflections on*, criticar a. || *To see s.o.'s reflection in the mirror*, ver la imagen de alguien reflejada en el espejo.
reflective [riˈflektiv] adj. Reflector, ra: *reflective surface*, superficie reflectora. || Reflexivo, va; pensativo, va (pensive). || GRAMM. Reflexivo, va.
reflector [riˈflektə*] n. PHYS. Reflector, *m.* || AUT. Catafaro, *m.*
reflex [ˈriːfleks] adj. Reflejo, ja: *a reflex action*, una acción refleja. || Reflejado, da: *reflex light*, luz reflejada.
— N. Reflejo, *m.* || Imagen (*f.*) reflejada (image). || — *Reflex arc*, arco reflejo. || PHOT. *Reflex camera*, cámara (*f.*) reflex.
reflexibility [riˌfleksiˈbiliti] n. Reflexibilidad, *f.*
reflexible [riˈfleksibl] adj. Reflexible.
reflexion [riˈflekʃən] n. See REFLECTION.
reflexive [riˈfleksiv] adj. GRAMM. Reflexivo, va. || Reflejo, ja (of a reflex).
— N. GRAMM. Reflexivo, *m.*, verbo (*m.*) reflexivo (verb). | Pronombre (*m.*) reflexivo (pronoun).
reflexivity [—iti] n. Poder (*m.*) de reflexión.
refloat [ˈriːˈfləut] v. tr. MAR. Desencallar, poner a flote. || FIG. Sacar a flote (a company).
refloating [—iŋ] n. MAR. Desencalladura, *f.*, desencallamiento, *m.* || FIG. Salida (*f.*) a flote (of a company).
reflourish [ˈriˈflʌriʃ] v. intr. Reflorecer.
refluence [ˈrefluəns] n. Reflujo, *m.*
refluent [ˈrefluənt] adj. Menguante (tide).
reflux [ˈriːflʌks] n. Reflujo, *m.* || Menguante, *m.*, reflujo, *m.* (of a tide).
reforest [riˈfɔrist] v. tr. U. S. Repoblar [con árboles].
reforestation [ˈriˌfɔrisˈteiʃən] n. U. S. Repoblación (*f.*) forestal.
reform [riˈfɔːm*] n. Reforma, *f.*: *agrarian* o *land reform*, reforma agraria. || *Reform school*, reformatorio, *m.* (reformatory).
reform [riˈfɔːm] v. tr. Reformar.
— V. intr. Reformarse.
re-form [ˈriːˈfɔːm] v. tr. Formar de nuevo, volver a formar.
— V. intr. Formarse de nuevo.
reformable [riˈfɔːməbl] adj. Reformable.
reformation [ˌrefəˈmeiʃən] n. Reforma, *f.* || REL. *Reformation*, la Reforma.
re-formation [ˌrifɔˈmeiʃən] n. Nueva formación, *f.*
reformational [ˌrefəˈmeiʃənəl] adj. REL. De la Reforma.
reformative [riˈfɔːmətiv] adj. Reformatorio, ria; reformativo, va.
reformatory [riˈfɔːmətəri] adj. Reformatorio, ria.
— N. Reformatorio, *m.*
reformed [riˈfɔːmd] adj. Reformado, da: *reformed Church*, Iglesia reformada.
reformer [riˈfɔːmə*] n. Reformista, *m.* & *f.*; reformador, ra.
reformism [riˈfɔːmizəm] n. Reformismo, *m.*
reformist [riˈfɔːmist] adj./n. Reformista.
refract [riˈfrækt] v. tr. Refractar.
refracting telescope [riˈfræktiŋˈteliskəup] n. Telescopio (*m.*) refractor.
refraction [riˈfrækʃən] n. PHYS. Refracción, *f.*
refractive [riˈfræktiv] adj. Refractivo, va; refringente. || PHYS. *Refractive index*, índice (*m.*) de refracción.
refractometer [rifrækˈtɔmitə*] n. PHYS. Refractómetro, *m.*
refractor [riˈfræktə*] n. Refractor, *m.*
refractory [—ri] adj. Refractario, ria.
— N. Material (*m.*) refractario.
refrain [riˈfrein] n. Estribillo, *m.*
refrain [riˈfrein] v. intr. Abstenerse: *please refrain from smoking*, por favor absténganse de fumar. || *I couldn't refrain from making a comment*, no pude contenerme e hice una observación.

refrangibility [ri,frændʒi'biliti] n. PHYS. Refrangibilidad, *f.*
refrangible [ri'frændʒibl] adj. PHYS. Refrangible.
refresh [ri'freʃ] v. tr. Refrescar: *to refresh one's face with a little water*, refrescarse la cara con un poco de agua. || — *They refreshed themselves in a roadside inn*, se restauraron en una posada. || *To refresh the memory*, refrescar la memoria.
— V. intr. Refrescarse.
refresher [—ə*] n. Refresco, *m.* (drink). || JUR. Honorarios (*m. pl.*) suplementarios. || *Refresher course*, cursillo (*m.*) de perfeccionamiento *or* de repaso.
refreshing [—iŋ] adj. Refrescante: *a refreshing drink*, una bebida refrescante. || Reparador, ra (sleep). || Reconfortante (comforting). || — *It makes a refreshing change to live in the country*, irse a vivir al campo representa un cambio muy agradable. || *It makes a refreshing change to meet an honest person*, da gusto encontrar a una persona honrada.
refreshment [—mənt] n. Refresco, *m.* (drink). || — Pl. Refrigerio, *m. sing.*: *refreshments will be served in the interval*, se servirá un refrigerio durante el descanso. || — *They offered us some refreshment*, nos ofrecieron algo de comer *or* de tomar. || *Would you like some refreshment?*, ¿quiere tomar algo?
refreshment room [—məntru:m] n. Fonda, *f.*
refried [ri'fraid] adj. Refrito, ta.
refrigerant [ri'fridʒərənt] n. Refrigerante, *m.*
refrigerate [ri'fridʒəreit] v. tr. Refrigerar.
refrigeration [ri,fridʒə'reiʃən] n. Refrigeración, *f.*
refrigerative [ri'fridʒərətiv] adj. Refrigerante.
refrigerator [ri'fridʒəreitə*] n. Refrigerador, *m.*, nevera, *f.*, frigorífico, *m.* || *Refrigerator car, lorry*, vagón, camión frigorífico.
refringence [ri'frindʒəns] n. Refringencia, *f.*
refringent [ri'frindʒənt] adj. Refringente.
refry [ri'frai] v. tr. Volver a freír, refreír.
refuel [ri'fjuəl] v. tr. Poner combustible *or* carburante a (a boiler, plane, ship). || Echar gasolina a (a car).
— V. intr. Repostar, repostarse: *they stopped to refuel in Paris*, hicieron escala en París para repostar.
refuge ['refju:dʒ] n. Refugio, *m.*: *to seek refuge*, buscar refugio. || — *To give refuge to*, dar refugio a. || *To take refuge in*, regugiarse en.
refugee [,refju'dʒi:] n. Refugiado, da.
refulgence [ri'fʌldʒəns] n. Refulgencia, *f.*, resplandor, *m.* (brightness).
refulgent [ri'fʌldʒənt] adj. Refulgente.
refund ['ri:fʌnd] n. Devolución, *f.*, reembolso, *m.* (of money). || Reembolso, *m.* (of expenses, of a debt). || *To demand a refund*, exigir la devolución *or* el reembolso de su dinero.
refund [ri:'fʌnd] v. tr. Reintegrar, devolver, reembolsar (money). || Reembolsar (person): *they refunded him*, le reembolsaron; *they refunded his expenses*, le reembolsaron los gastos. || Consolidar (a debt). || *To refund the cost of one's ticket*, devolver a uno el importe de la entrada *or* del billete.
refurbish ['ri:'fə:biʃ] v. tr. Restaurar (an old house, table, etc.).
refurnish ['ri:'fə:niʃ] v. tr. Amueblar de nuevo (with furniture).
refusable [ri'fju:zəbl] adj. Rechazable.
refusal [ri'fju:zəl] n. Negativa, *f.*: *a flat refusal*, una negativa rotunda. || COMM. Opción, *f.* || — *They met the offer with a flat refusal*, rechazaron la oferta rotundamente. || *Your refusal to cooperate caused a lot of difficulty*, el hecho de que se negara a cooperar nos causó muchas dificultades.
refuse ['refju:s] adj. Desechado, da.
— N. Basura, *f.* (rubbish). || Desperdicios, *m. pl.* (waste material). || — *Refuse bin*, cubo (*m.*) de la basura. || *Refuse dump*, vertedero, *m.* || *Refuse lorry*, camión (*m.*) de la basura.
refuse [ri'fju:z] v. tr. Rechazar (to reject): *he refused my offer*, rechazó mi oferta. || No aceptar, no querer aceptar (invitation, food, present, etc.). || Negar, denegar: *to refuse admittance to s.o.*, denegar a alguien la entrada. || Negarse a, rehusar: *he refused to shake hands*, se negó a darle la mano. || No servir en (in card games). || SP. Rehusar saltar (a fence). || *To refuse o.s.*, privarse de.
— V. intr. Negarse (to make a refusal). || SP. Pararse, plantarse (a horse).
refutable ['refjutəbl] adj. Refutable, rebatible.
refutal [ri'fju:təl] or **refutation** [,refju'teiʃən] n. Refutación, *f.*, rebatimiento, *m.*
refute [ri'fju:t] v. tr. Refutar, rebatir (an argument, etc.). || Contradecir (s.o.).
regain [ri'gein] v. tr. Recobrar, recuperar (sth. lost): *to regain one's breath*, recobrar el aliento. || Volver a (to go back to). || — *To regain consciousness*, recobrar *or* recuperar el conocimiento, volver en sí. || *To regain one's composure*, serenarse.
regal ['ri:gəl] adj. Real, regio, gia.
regale [ri'geil] v. tr. Agasajar (to entertain richly). || Entretener (to amuse).
— V. intr. Regalarse.
regalia [ri'geiljə] pl. n. Insignias, *f.* (insignia). || Atributos, *m.* (of an office).
regalism ['ri:gəlizəm] n. Regalismo, *m.*
regalist ['ri:gəlist] n. Regalista.
regality [ri'gæliti] n. Soberanía, *f.*
regally ['ri:gəli] adv. Regiamente.
regard [ri'gɑ:d] n. Estima, *f.* (esteem). || Consideración, *f.*, respeto, *m.* (consideration). || (Ant.) Mirada, *f.* (look). || — Pl. Recuerdos, *m.*: *give my regards to your mother*, dale recuerdos a tu madre. || — *Having regard to*, teniendo en cuenta. || *In* o *with regard to*, en cuanto a, con respecto a, con relación a. || *In this regard*, a este respecto, al respecto. || *To have no regard to*, no tener en cuenta (not to take into account), no tener que ver con (to have nothing to do with). || *To have the highest regard for s.o.*, tener a alguien en gran estima. || *To pay regard to*, hacer caso de. || *To show no regard to*, hacer caso de. || *To show no regard for other people*, no tener ninguna consideración con los demás. || *To stand high in s.o.'s regard*, gozar de la estima de uno. || *With kind regards*, con muchos recuerdos. *Without regard to the dangers*, indiferente a los peligros, sin hacer caso de *or* sin prestar atención a los peligros.
regard [ri'gɑ:d] v. tr. Considerar, juzgar (to consider): *I regard it as a crime*, lo considero un crimen. || Considerar (to treat): *regard this letter as confidential*, considere esta carta como confidencial. || Concernir, atañer (to concern): *this order does not regard me*, esta orden no me concierne. || Tener en cuenta (to take into account). || Tomar en consideración, hacer caso de (to have respect for). || (Ant.). Mirar (to look at). || *As regards your work*, con respecto a su trabajo, en cuanto a su trabajo.
regardant [—ənt] adj. HERALD. Contornado, da.
regardful [—ful] adj. Atento, ta (heedful): *regardful of my words*, atento a mis palabras. || Respetuoso, sa (of people).
regarding [—iŋ] prep. Con respecto a, en cuanto a, por lo que se refiere a. || Relativo, va; referente: *everything regarding sales*, todo lo relativo *or* todo lo referente a las ventas.
regardless [—lis] adj. Indiferente (*of*, a) [indifferent]. || Insensible (*of*, a) [insensitive]. || Sin tener en cuenta: *regardless of expense*, sin tener en cuenta los gastos. || *Regardless of the cost*, a toda costa, cueste lo que cueste: *he wanted to buy it, regardless of the cost*, lo quería comprar costase lo que costase.
— Adv. A pesar de todo (despite everything). || Pase lo que pase (whatever happens). || *I warned him, but he went on regardless*, le advertí pero siguió adelante sin hacerme caso.
regatta [ri'gætə] n. SP. Regata, *f.*
regency ['ri:dʒənsi] n. Regencia, *f.*
Regency ['ri:dʒənsi] adj. Regencia, de estilo regencia.
regeneracy [ri'dʒenərəsi] n. Regeneración, *f.*
regenerate [ri'dʒenərit] adj. Regenerado, da.
regenerate [ri'dʒenəreit] v. tr. Regenerar.
— V. intr. Regenerarse.
regeneration [ri,dʒenə'reiʃən] n. Regeneración, *f.*
regenerative [ri'dʒenərətiv] adj. Regenerador, ra.
regenerator [ri'dʒenəreitə*] n. TECH. Regenerador, *m.*
regent ['ri:dʒənt] adj. Regente: *the Prince regent*, el príncipe regente.
— N. Regente, *m.* & *f.*
regicidal [,redʒi'saidl] adj. Regicida.
regicide ['redʒisaid] n. Regicidio, *m.* (crime). || Regicida, *m.* & *f.* (person).
regild ['ri:'gild] v. tr. Volver a dorar, redorar.
régime or **regime** [rei'ʒi:m] n. Régimen, *m.*: *political régime*, régimen político.
regimen ['redʒimən] n. MED. Régimen, *m.*
regiment ['redʒimənt] n. MIL. Regimiento, *m.* || FIG Regimiento, *m.*, ejército, *m.*, multitud, *f.* (large number).
regiment ['redʒimənt] v. tr. MIL. Regimentar. || FIG. Reglamentar estrictamente, regimentar.
regimental [,redʒi'mentl] adj. MIL. De *or* del regimiento.
— Pl. n. Uniforme (*m. sing.*) del regimiento. || Uniforme (*m. sing.*) militar.
regimentation [,redʒimen'teiʃən] n. Reglamentación (*f.*) estricta.
region ['ri:dʒən] n. Región, *f.*: *barren region*, región árida. || Zona, *f.* (area). || ANAT. Región, *f.* || *In the region of a hundred pounds*, unas cien libras, alrededor de cien libras.
regional [—l] adj. Regional.
regionalism [—əlizəm] n. Regionalismo, *m.*
regionalist [—əlist] n. Regionalista, *m.* & *f.*
regionalistic [,ri:dʒənə'listik] adj. Regionalista.
regionalization [,ri:dʒənəlai'zeiʃən] n. Regionalización, *f.*
regionalize ['ri:dʒənəlaiz] v. tr. Regionalizar.
regisseur ['reiʒi'sə*] n. THEATR. Regidor (*m.*) de escena.
register ['redʒistə*] n. Registro, *m.*: *hotel register*, registro de hotel; *register of births, marriages and deaths*, registro civil. || Lista, *f.* (in school): *to call the register*, pasar lista. || MUS. TECH. Registro, *m.* (of voice, instrument, stove). || MAR. Matrícula, *f.* (list of men, of boats). || Registrador, *m.* (recording instrument). || PRINT. Registro, *m.* || Indicador, *m.* contador, *m.* (gauge). || — *Cash register*, caja registradora. || *Electoral register*, censo (*m.*) *or* registro electoral. || *Land register*, registro de la propiedad.
register ['redʒistə*] v. tr. Registrar (to note in a register). || Declarar (birth, deaths). || Presentar (a complaint). || Facturar (luggage). || Registrar (a

trademark, an invention). || FIG. Reflejar, denotar, expresar: *her face registered surprise*, su cara reflejaba sorpresa. || Experimentar: *to register an increase, an improvement*, experimentar una subida, una mejora. || Certificar (a letter): *registered letter*, carta certificada. || Marcar: *the gauge registered 300 revolutions*, el indicador marcaba 300 revoluciones. || Matricular (a car, a boat, students). || TECH. Hacer corresponder (parts).
— V. intr. Inscribirse (to sign on). || Registrarse (in a hotel, in the registrar's office). || Matricularse (at university). || Coincidir *or* corresponder exactamente (parts). || PRINT. Estar en registro. || *It weighed so little that it didn't register on the scale*, pesaba tan poco que no se movía el fiel de la balanza.

registered [—d] adj. Registrado, da: *registered trademark*, marca registrada. || Facturado, da (luggage). || Certificado, da (letter). || Matriculado, da (student).

registered nurse [—nə:s] n. Enfermera (*f.*) titulada.

register office [—ˈɔfis] n. U. S. Registro (*m.*) civil (for births, marriages, deaths). | Registro, *m.* (for other things).

register ton [—tʌn] n. MAR. Tonelada (*f.*) de arqueo.

registrar [ˌredʒisˈtrɑ:*] n. Registrador, *m.*, archivero, *m.* (keeper of a register). || Secretario (*m.*) general (of university). || Secretario (*m.*) del registro civil (of registry office). || Secretario, *m.* (secretary).

registrate [ˈredʒistreit] v. intr. MUS. Seleccionar el registro.

registration [ˌredʒisˈtreiʃən] n. Inscripción, *f.* (inscription). || Declaración, *f.* (of a birth, etc.). || Registro, *m.* (of a trademark). || Matrícula, *f.* (at university). || Certificación, *f.* (of letters). || Facturación, *f.* (of luggage). || AUT. MAR. Matrícula, *f.* (number, nationality). || U. S. MUS. Registros, *m. pl.* || — *Registration number*, número (*m.*) de matrícula. || *Registration plate*, placa (*f.*) de matrícula.

registry [ˈredʒistri] n. Registro, *m.* || — *Registry office*, registro (*m.*) civil (for births, marriages, deaths), registro, *m.* (for other things). || *To get married at a registry office*, casarse por lo civil.

regius [ˈri:dʒəs] adj. *Regius professor*, profesor (*m.*) nombrado por el rey.

reglet [ˈreglet] n. PRINT. Regleta, *f.* || ARCH. Filete, *m.*

regnal [ˈregnəl] adj. De un reinado. || *Regnal day*, aniversario (*m.*) de la coronación de un monarca.

regnant [ˈregnənt] adj. Reinante: *regnant queen*, soberana reinante.

regorge [ri:ˈgɔ:dʒ] v. tr. Arrojar, vomitar.
— V. intr. Brotar de nuevo.

regress [ˈri:gres] n. Retroceso, *m.*

regress [riˈgres] v. intr. Retroceder.

regression [riˈgreʃən] n. Retroceso, *m.*, regresión, *f.*

regressive [riˈgresiv] adj. Regresivo, va.

regret [riˈgret] n. Arrepentimiento, *m.* (remorse). || Pesar, *m.*, pena, *f.*: *the old man's death caused everybody deep regret*, la muerte del anciano dio mucha pena a todos. || — Pl. Excusas, *f.* (on refusing an invitation): *to send one's regrets*, enviar sus excusas. || — *Much to my regret*, con gran sentimiento mío, sintiéndolo mucho, con gran pesar mío. || *To express one's regret to s.o.*, disculparse con uno (to apologize), dar el pésame a alguien (for s.o.'s death). || *To have no regrets*, no arrepentirse de nada. || *With regret*, con pena, con pesar (with sorrow), a disgusto, contra su voluntad (against one's will).

regret [riˈgret] v. tr. Sentir, lamentar: *I regret to have to say that*, siento tener que decir que; *it is to be regretted that*, es de lamentar que. || Arrepentirse de: *to regret one's sins*, arrepentirse de los pecados; *to regret the past*, arrepentirse del pasado; *if you go you won't regret it*, si vas no te arrepentirás; *he bitterly regretted his action*, estaba profundamente arrepentido de lo que había hecho.

regretful [—ful] adj. Arrepentido, da (remorseful). || Pesaroso, sa (sorrowful). || — *To be regretful that*, lamentar que. || *We are not regretful of having done it*, no nos arrepentimos de haberlo hecho, no lamentamos haberlo hecho.

regretfully [—fuli] adv. Con pesar, con sentimiento, sentidamente (with sorrow). || Con disgusto (against one's will). || Desafortunadamente (unfortunately).

regrettable [—əbl] adj. Lamentable, deplorable.

regrettably [—əbli] adv. Lamentablemente, desgraciadamente.

regroup [ˈri:ˈgru:p] v. tr. Reagrupar.
— V. intr. Reagruparse.

regrouping [—iŋ] n. Reagrupamiento, *m.*, reagrupación, *f.*

regular [ˈregjulə*] adj. Regular: *regular pulse*, pulso regular. || Normal: *it's perfectly regular*, es completamente normal; *in the regular manner*, de manera normal. || Normal, acostumbrado, da: *his regular job, time*, su trabajo acostumbrado, su hora acostumbrada. || Uniforme: *a regular stroke*, una brazada uniforme. || Regular (features). || Corriente (usual). || Habitual, asiduo, dua: *a regular customer*, un cliente asiduo. || Permanente (permanent): *regular staff*, personal permanente. || MIL. REL. Regular: *regular army, clergy*, ejército, clero regular. || Regular, ordenado, da: *a regular life*, una vida regular. || BOT. MATH. GRAMM. Regular: *regular flower, triangle, verb*, flor, triángulo, verbo regular. || FAM. Verdadero, ra; auténtico, ca: *a regular idiot*, un auténtico idiota. | Estupendo, da: *a regular guy*, un tipo estupendo. || — *To be as regular as clockwork*, ocurrir con la regularidad de un cronómetro *or* con una regularidad cronométrica. || *To make a regular thing of arriving late*, tener la costumbre de llegar tarde, llegar siempre tarde. || *To make regular use of*, emplear con regularidad. || *Where is your regular assistant?*, ¿dónde está la persona que suele ayudarle?
— N. REL. MIL. Regular, *m.* || Asiduo, dua (of a bar, a club). || Cliente (*m.* & *f.*) habitual (of a shop).

regularity [ˌregjuˈlæriti] n. Regularidad, *f.* || *Regularity of attendance*, asiduidad, *f.*

regularization [ˌregjuləraiˈzeiʃən] n. Regularización, *f.*

regularize [ˈregjuləraiz] v. tr. Regularizar (document, situation, etc.).

regularly [ˈregjuləli] adv. Con regularidad, regularmente. || Normalmente.

regulate [ˈregjuleit] v. tr. Regular: *to regulate prices, the flow of water, a machine*, regular los precios, la salida del agua, una máquina. || Reglamentar (to make rules for). || *To regulate one's life by one's work*, vivir con arreglo a su trabajo.

regulating [—iŋ] adj. Regulador, ra.

regulation [ˌregjuˈleiʃən] n. Regulación, *f.* (action): *regulation of a watercourse*, regulación de un curso de agua. || Reglamentación, *f.* (setting rules for). || Regla, *f.* (a rule). || — Pl. Reglamento, *m. sing.*, reglas, *f.* (set of rules).
— Adj. Reglamentario, ria.

regulative [ˈregjulətiv] adj. Regulativo, va.
— N. Regulador, *m.*

regulator [ˈregjuleitə*] n. Regulador, *m.*

regulus [ˈregjuləs] n. CHEM. Régulo, *m.* || Reyezuelo, *m.* (bird).

— OBSERV. El plural de *regulus* es *reguluses* o *reguli*.

regurgitate [riˈgə:dʒiteit] v. tr. Vomitar [sin esfuerzo] (to bring up). || FIG. Reproducir *or* repetir maquinalmente (things learnt).
— V. intr. Regurgitar.

regurgitation [ˌrigə:dʒiˈteiʃən] n. Regurgitación, *f.* (by animals). || FIG. Reproducción (*f.*) maquinal.

rehabilitate [ˌri:əˈbiliteit] v. tr. Rehabilitar (to restore rank, privileges, reputation). || Restaurar (to restore to good condition). || MED. Rehabilitar, reeducar.

rehabilitation [ˈri:əˌbiliˈteiʃən] n. Rehabilitación, *f.* || Restauración, *f.* (restoration). || Reconstrucción, *f.*, reorganización, *f.* (of a country). || MED. Reeducación, *f.* (of a disabled person).

rehash [ˈri:hæʃ] n. Refrito, *m.*, refundición, *f.*: *his last book is just a rehash of his previous works*, su último libro es un refrito de sus obras anteriores. || Comida (*f.*) recalentada (meal). || U. S. Repetición, *f.*

rehash [ˈri:ˈhæʃ] v. tr. Volver a sacar, volver a repetir, machacar (arguments, ideas). || Recalentar (food).

rehearing [ˈˌriˈhiəriŋ] n. JUR. Revisión, *f.*

rehearsal [riˈhə:səl] n. Ensayo, *m.* (of a play, ceremony). || Enumeración, *f.* (enumeration). || — *Dress rehearsal*, ensayo general. || *There was a rehearsal of the fire drill*, se hizo un simulacro de incendio.

rehearse [riˈhə:s] v. tr. Ensayar (a play, ceremony). || Enumerar (to enumerate): *to rehearse a list of complaints*, enumerar una lista de quejas.
— V. intr. Ensayar.

reheat [riˈhi:t] v. tr. Recalentar.

reheater [—ə*] n. Recalentador, *m.*

reheating [—iŋ] n. Recalentamiento, *m.*

rehouse [ˈri:ˈhauz] v. tr. Proporcionar nueva vivienda a.

rehydrate [riˈhaiˌdreit] v. tr. Rehidratar, volver a hidratar.

reification [ˌriəfəˈkeiʃən] n. Materialización, *f.*

reify [ˈriəˌfai] v. tr. Materializar, concretar (an abstraction).

reign [rein] n. Reinado, *m.* (of a monarch): *under the reign of*, bajo el reinado de. || FIG. Dominio, *m.*, predominio, *m.* (dominion). | Régimen, *m.* (régime): *reign of terror*, régimen de terror.

reign [rein] v. intr. Reinar: *to reign over*, reinar sobre. || FIG. Reinar: *silence reigned in the assembly*, el silencio reinaba en la asamblea. | Predominar, imperar (to prevail).

reigning [—iŋ] adj. Reinante (monarch). || FIG. Dominante, predominante (tendency, etc.).

reimbursable [ˌri:imˈbə:səbl] adj. Reembolsable.

reimburse [ˌri:imˈbə:s] v. tr. Reembolsar: *to reimburse s.o.'s expenses*, reembolsarle los gastos a uno.

reimbursement [—mənt] n. Reembolso, *m.*

reimport [ˈri:imˈpɔ:t] n. Reimportación, *f.*: *reimports amounted to a million pounds*, las reimportaciones alcanzaron el valor de un millón de libras. || Artículo (*m.*) reimportado *or* de reimportación (goods).

reimport [ˈri:imˈpɔ:t] v. tr. Reimportar.

reimportation [ˈri:impɔ:ˈteiʃən] n. Reimportación, *f.*

reimpression [ˈri:imˈpreʃən] n. Reimpresión, *f.*

rein [rein] n. Rienda, *f.* (for animals). || — Pl. Riendas, *f.* (for animals). || Andadores, *m.* (for children). || FIG. Riendas, *f.*: *the reins of government*, las riendas del gobierno; *to hold the reins*, llevar las riendas. || — *To draw rein*, tirar de las riendas. || *To give rein to*, aflojar las riendas a (to loosen the reins), dar rienda suelta a (the imagination, etc.). || *To keep a tight rein on s.o.*, atar corto a uno. || *To take the reins*, tomar las riendas.

rein [rein] v. tr. Poner riendas a. || *To rein in o up*, refrenar.

— V. intr. *To rein in*, detenerse.

reincarnate [riːˈinkɑːneit] v. tr. Reencarnar.

reincarnation [ˈriːinkɑːˈneiʃən] n. Reencarnación, *f.*

reindeer [ˈreindiə*] n. Zool. Reno, *m.*

— Observ. El plural de la palabra *reindeer* es *reindeer* o *reindeers.*

reinforce [ˌriːinˈfɔːs] v. tr. Reforzar, fortalecer. || Armar (concrete).

reinforcement [—mənt] n. Refuerzo, *m.* (strengthening). || Armazón, *f.* (of concrete). || — Pl. Mil. Refuerzos, *m.*

reinsert [ˌriinˈsəːt] v. tr. Volver a insertar *or* introducir, reinsertar.

reinstall [ˈriːinˈstɔːl] v. tr. Volver a instalar, reinstalar.

reinstate [ˈriːinˈsteit] v. tr. Reintegrar, reinstalar, restituir: *to reinstate s.o. in a job*, reintegrar a uno en su puesto, restituir el puesto a alguien. || Volver a poner (to put back). || Rehabilitar (to rehabilitate). || Restablecer (a law, etc.).

reinstatement [—mənt] n. Restablecimiento, *m.* || Reintegración, *f.*, reinstalación, *f.* (in a job). || Rehabilitación, *f.*

reinsurance [ˈriːinˈʃuərəns] n. Reaseguro, *m.*

reinsure [ˈriːinˈʃuə*] v. tr. Reasegurar.

reintegrate [ˈriːˈintigreit] v. tr. Reintegrar.

reintegration [ˈriːˌintiˈgreiʃən] n. Reintegro, *m.*, reintegración, *f.*

reinter [ˈriːinˈtəː*] v. tr. Volver a enterrar.

reintroduce [ˈriːˌintrəˈdjuːs] v. tr. Volver a presentar (s.o.). || Volver a introducir (sth.).

reinvest [ˈriːinˈvest] v. tr. Comm. Volver a invertir, reinvertir.

reinvestment [—mənt] n. Comm. Nueva inversión, *f.*, reinversión, *f.*

reinvigorate [ˈriːinˈvigəreit] v. tr. Revigorizar.

reissue [ˈriːˈiʃuː] n. Reedición, *f.* (of books). || Nueva emisión, *f.* (of stamps, etc.).

reissue [ˈriːˈiʃuː] v. tr. Reeditar (books, etc.). || Volver a emitir (stamps, shares, etc.).

reiterate [riːˈitəreit] v. tr. Reiterar.

reiteration [riˌitəˈreiʃən] n. Reiteración, *f.*

reiterative [riːˈitərətiv] adj. Reiterativo, va.

reject [ˈriːdʒekt] n. Persona (*f.*) rechazada. || Cosa (*f.*) rechazada, desecho, *m.* (object).

reject [riˈdʒekt] v. tr. Rechazar: *to reject an attack, an offer, a request*, rechazar un ataque, una oferta, una petición. || Arrojar (from the stomach).

rejection [riˈdʒekʃən] n. Rechazamiento, *m.* (action). || Cosa (*f.*) rechazada, desecho, *m.* (reject). || *I've already had two rejections*, ya me han rechazado dos veces.

rejoice [riˈdʒɔis] v. intr. Alegrarse, regocijarse. || Disfrutar: *he rejoices in pulling her leg*, disfruta tomándole el pelo. || *To rejoice in the name of*, tener el honor de llamarse.

— V. tr. Alegrar, regocijar.

rejoicing [—iŋ] n. Alegría, *f.*, regocijo, *m.*, júbilo, *m.* (happiness). || Fiesta, *f.*: *rejoicing went on right through the night*, la fiesta continuó toda la noche.

— Adj. Alegre.

rejoin [ˈriːˈdʒɔin] v. tr. Volver a juntarse con, volver a unirse a (two objects). || Reincorporarse a (clubs, army, society). || Encontrar, reunirse con: *I'll rejoin you at the station*, os encontraré en la estación.

rejoin [riˈdʒɔin] v. tr. Replicar, responder (to reply).

— V. intr. Replicar, responder (to reply). || Jur. Contestar (to answer to a charge).

rejoinder [—də*] n. Réplica, *f.*, respuesta, *f.* (reply). || Jur. Contestación, *f.*, contrarréplica, *f.* (answer).

rejuvenate [riˈdʒuːvineit] v. tr. Rejuvenecer.

— V. intr. Rejuvenecerse.

rejuvenating [—iŋ] adj. Rejuvenecedor, ra.

rejuvenation [riidʒuːviˈneiʃən] or **rejuvenescence** [ˌridzuːviˈnesns] n. Rejuvenecimiento, *m.*

rejuvenescent [ˌridʒuːviˈnesnt] adj. Rejuvenecedor, ra.

rekindle [ˈriːˈkindl] v. tr. Volver a encender (a fire). || Fig. Reavivar, reanimar.

relapse [riˈlæps] n. Recaída, *f.*, recidiva, *f.* (into bad health): *to have a relapse*, tener una recaída. || Reincidencia, *f.* (into crime, etc.).

relapse [riˈlæps] v. intr. Recaer (into bad health). || Reincidir (into crime, etc.). || — Rel. *Relapsed heretic*, relapso, sa. || Jur. *Relapsed offender*, reincidente, *m.* & *f.* (recidivist).

relatable [riˈleitəbl] adj. Narrable, contable.

relate [riˈleit] v. tr. Contar, relatar: *to relate a story*, relatar una historia. || Relacionar: *to relate two facts*, relacionar dos hechos.

— V. intr. Relacionarse (*to*, con), tener que ver (*to*, con), estar relacionado (*to*, con), ser relativo (*to*, a), referirse (*to*, a): *everything relating to aircraft interests him*, todo lo que tiene que ver con los aviones le interesa.

related [—id] adj. Relacionado, da: *related subjects, objects*, temas, objetos relacionados. || Emparentado, da (through birth or by marriage). || — *His answer was in no way related to the question*, su respuesta no tenía nada que ver con la pregunta. || *She is related to me*, es parienta mía. || *They are closely related*, hay un estrecho parentesco entre ellos, son parientes cercanos (people). || *To be distantly related to*, ser pariente lejano de.

relater [—ə*] n. Relator, ra.

relation [riˈleiʃən] n. Relato, *m.*, narración, *f.*, relación, *f.* (account). || Pariente, ta (a relative). || Parentesco, *m.*: *what relation is he to you?*, ¿qué parentesco tiene contigo? || Relación, *f.*, conexión, *f.*: *the relation between two events*, la relación entre dos acontecimientos. || Jur. Relación, *f.* || — Pl. Relaciones, *f.*: *business relations*, relaciones comerciales *or* de negocios; *political relations*, relaciones políticas; *good relations*, buenas relaciones. || — *In* o *with relation to*, en relación con, con relación a, en lo que se refiere a. || *Public relations officer*, encargado de relaciones públicas. || *Sexual relations*, relaciones sexuales. || *To bear no relation to reality*, no tener ninguna relación *or* nada que ver con la realidad. || *To bear relation to*, guardar relación con. || *To break off relations with*, romper con (a friend), romper las relaciones diplomáticas con (a country).

relationship [—ʃip] n. Relación, *f.* (connection). || Relaciones, *f. pl.*: *theirs is a strange relationship*, tienen unas relaciones muy extrañas. || Relaciones, *f. pl.* (between countries). || Parentesco, *m.* (kinship): *relationship by marriage*, parentesco político; *what is your relationship to her?*, ¿qué parentesco tienes con ella? || *Theirs is a beautiful relationship*, se llevan perfectamente.

relative [ˈrelətiv] adj. Relativo, va: *questions relative to what I have been saying*, preguntas relativas a lo que he dicho; *the relative difference between two things*, la diferencia relativa entre dos cosas; *relative humidity*, humedad relativa. || Gramm. Relativo, va: *relative pronoun*, pronombre relativo. || *The mass of the earth relative to that of the sun*, la masa de la tierra en relación con la del sol.

— N. Pariente, ta (connected by birth or marriage). || Gramm. Relativo, *m.*

relativeness [—nis] n. Relatividad, *f.*

relativism [ˈrelətivizəm] n. Relativismo, *m.*

relativist [ˈrelətivist] adj./n. Relativista.

relativistic [ˌrelətivˈistik] adj. Relativista.

relativity [ˌreləˈtiviti] n. Relatividad, *f.*

relax [riˈlæks] v. tr. Aflojar (to loosen): *to relax one's grip*, aflojar la mano. || Relajar (muscles). || Relajar, aflojar (to make less strict): *to relax discipline*, relajar la disciplina. || Disminuir (to diminish): *to relax one's efforts*, disminuir los esfuerzos. || Mitigar (pain). || Med. Soltar: *to relax the bowels*, soltar el vientre.

— V. intr. Relajarse (nerves, muscles, social relations). || Descansar, relajarse (after work): *to relax on a golf course*, descansar jugando al golf. || Relajarse (to become less strict). || — *Relax!*, ¡tranquilo!, ¡cálmate! (take it easy!). || *To relax in one's efforts*, disminuir los esfuerzos, aflojar.

relaxant [riˈlæksənt] n. Relajante, *m.*

relaxation [ˌriːlækˈseiʃən] n. Relajación, *f.* (of muscles, nerves). || Relajación, *f.*, relajamiento, *m.* (of discipline). || Disminución, *f.* (of efforts). || Recreo, *m.* (recreation). || Descanso, *m.*, desahogo, *m.*, relajamiento, *m.*, relajación, *f.* (after work). || Distracción, *f.*: *my favourite relaxation*, mi distracción preferida.

relaxed [riˈlækst] adj. Tranquilo, la; sosegado, da (peaceful, calm). || Relajado, da (muscles, etc.).

relaxing [riˈlæksiŋ] adj. Relajante.

relay [riˈlei] n. Relevo, *m.* (fresh supply of people, animals, etc.). || Posta, *f.* (of horses). || Electr. Rad. Repetidor, *m.*, relé, *m.*, relevador, *m.*: *television relay*, repetidor de televisión. || Sp. Carrera (*f.*) de relevos (race). || — Sp. *Medley relay*, relevo estilos. | *Relay race*, carrera (*f.*) de relevos. || *Relay station*, estación repetidora. || Sp. *The 100 metres relay*, los 100 metros relevos.

relay [ˈriːˈlei] v. tr. Divulgar, difundir: *to relay the news*, divulgar la noticia. || Retransmitir (to transmit to another station). || Transmitir (a message to s.o.). || Electr. Regular con relevador.

re-lay [ˈriːˈlei] v. tr. Volver a poner, volver a colocar. | Volver a tender (rail).

release [riˈliːs] n. Liberación, *f.*, puesta (*f.*) en libertad (from prison). || Orden (*f.*) de puesta en libertad (document). || Exención, *f.*, descargo, *m.* (from duty or obligation). || Salida, *f.*, estreno, *m.* (of film, record, etc.). || Anuncio, *m.*, comunicación, *f.* (of information, the information itself). || Disminución, *f.* (reduction). || Aflojamiento, *m.* (loosening). || Liberación, *f.* (from difficulties). || Alivio, *m.* (from a pain). || Escape, *m.* (of steam, gas). || Disparo, *m.* (discharge). || Lanzamiento, *m.* (of a bomb). || Suelta, *f.* (of pigeons). || Autorización (*f.*) para publicar (permission to publish news). || Jur. Cesión, *f.* (surrender of a right to another). | Acta (*f.*) de cesión (document). || Tech. Disparador, *m.* || Comm. Puesta (*f.*) en venta. || Fig. Arrebato, *m.* (fit): *in a release of rage*, en un arrebato de furia. || — *Press release*, comunicado (*m.*) de prensa. || *Release spring*, muelle (*m.*) antagonista. || *Release valve*, válvula (*f.*) de seguridad.

release [riˈliːs] v. tr. Liberar, poner en libertad (from prison). || Liberar, librar, descargar (from a duty, obligation). || Dejar salir (an employee). || Jur. Ceder (to surrender). || Estrenar (a film, a record). || Publicar (a book). || Poner en venta (to put on sale). || Anunciar, comunicar (information). || Soltar (to let go): *he released the dog, her arm*, soltó el perro, le soltó el brazo. || Liberar (in a chemical reaction). || Echar, desprender, emitir (smoke). || Lanzar (a bomb). || Arrojar, tirar: *to release waste in the sea*, arrojar residuos al mar. || Phot. Disparar. || Soltar (a catch). ||

Disparar (a mechanism). || Jur. *To release on bail*, poner en libertad bajo fianza.

releaser [—ə*] n. Tech. Disparador, *m.*

relegate [ˈreligeit] v. tr. Relegar. || Someter, remitir: *to relegate a matter to s.o.*, someter un asunto a alguien. || Desterrar (to banish). || — *The officer was relegated to the ranks*, el oficial fue degradado. || *To be relegated*, bajar [a una división inferior] (a team).

relegation [ˌreliˈgeiʃən] n. Relegación, *f.* || Destierro, *m.* (banishment). || Sp. Descenso, *m.*

relent [riˈlent] v. intr. Ablandarse, aplacarse (to become less severe). || Ceder (to give way).

relentless [—lis] adj. Despiadado, da; implacable, cruel (without pity). || Incesante (unceasing).

relet [ˈriːˈlet] v. tr. Realquilar.

relevance [ˈrelivəns] or **relevancy** [—i] n. Pertinencia, *f.*

relevant [ˈrelivənt] adj. Pertinente: *a relevant remark*, una observación pertinente. || Relacionado, da; referente: *information relevant to the matter*, información relacionada con el asunto *or* referente al asunto.

reliability [riˌlaiəˈbiliti] n. Seriedad, *f.*, formalidad, *f.* (of a person). || Tech. Fiabilidad, *f.*, seguridad, *f.* (of a machine). || Exactitud, *f.* (of figures). || Veracidad, *f.* (of facts).

reliable [riˈlaiəbl] adj. De fiar, de confianza: *a reliable man*, un hombre de confianza. || Seguro, ra: *reliable information*, información segura; *a reliable car*, un coche seguro. || Serio, ria (firm, company): *a reliable lawyer*, un abogado serio. || Tech. Fiable, seguro, ra (machine). || — *Information from a reliable source*, información de fuente fidedigna. || *Reliable friend*, amigo de confianza, amigo seguro, amigo del que uno se puede fiar.

reliableness [—nis] n. See reliability.

reliably [—i] adv. *To be reliably informed*, estar bien informado. || *To be reliably informed that*, saber de fuente fidedigna que.

reliance [riˈlaiəns] n. Dependencia, *f.* (dependence): *their reliance on foreign aid*, su dependencia de la ayuda extranjera. || Confianza, *f.* (trust). || *To place reliance on*, fiarse de, tener confianza en.

reliant [riˈlaiənt] adj. Dependiente. || *To be reliant on*, depender de (to depend upon), tener confianza en, fiarse de (to trust).

relic [ˈrelik] n. Reliquia, *f.*, vestigio, *m.* (of sth. no longer existent). || Rel. Reliquia, *f.* || Fig. Vejestorio, *m.* (old person or thing). || — Pl. Fig. Restos (*m.*) mortales (of a dead person).

relict [ˈrelikt] n. Viuda, *f.* (widow).

relief [riˈliːf] n. Alivio, *m.*: *the medicine gave him relief*, la medicina le proporcionó alivio; *it is a relief to get outside*, es un alivio salir fuera; *to come as a great relief to everybody*, ser un gran alivio para todos. || Socorro, *m.*, auxilio, *m.*, ayuda, *f.*: *relief for refugees*, socorro para los refugiados; *to bring relief to a besieged town*, llevar auxilio a una ciudad sitiada. || Beneficencia, *f.*, auxilio (*m.*) social (for the poor). || Alivio, *m.*, descanso, *m.*: *a relief for the eyes*, un descanso para la vista. || Relevo, *m.* (person who carries on work for another). || Relieve, *m.*: *lettering in relief*, escritura en relieve. || Arts. Relieve, *m.*: *high, low relief*, alto, bajo relieve. || Geogr. Relieve, *m.*: *the relief of Spain*, el relieve de España; *relief map*, mapa en relieve. || Jur. Desagravio, *m.* || — *Relief train*, tren suplementario *or* adicional. || *Relief valve*, válvula (*f.*) de seguridad. || *Tax relief*, desgravación (*f.*) de impuestos. || *To go to s.o.'s relief*, acudir en ayuda de alguien. || *To heave a sigh of relief*, dar un suspiro de alivio. || *To stand out in relief against*, resaltar sobre. || *To throw into relief*, poner de relieve. || *What a relief!*, ¡qué alivio!, ¡qué descanso!

relieve [riˈliːv] v. tr. Aliviar, mitigar (to alleviate pain, distress, anxiety). || Liberar, sacar (to free): *to relieve s.o. of his worries*, liberar a alguien de sus preocupaciones; *to relieve s.o. from doubt*, sacar a alguien de dudas. || Coger, tomar: *to relieve s.o. of his coat*, cogerle el abrigo a alguien. || Liberar, librar: *to relieve s.o. of an obligation*, librar a alguien de una obligación. || Exonerar (to exonerate). || Destituir: *to relieve s.o. of his post*, destituirle a uno de su puesto. || Relevar, sustituir, reemplazar (to replace). || Socorrer, auxiliar (a besieged town, the poor, refugees, etc.). || Disipar: *to relieve the monotony*, disipar la monotonía. || Alegrar (to brighten up). || Mil. Relevar (sentries, etc.). || Poner de relieve, realzar (to bring out). || Jur. Desagraviar. || Fam. Limpiar (to steal): *to relieve s.o. of his purse*, limpiar a alguien la cartera. || — Arch. *Relieving arch*, arco (*m.*) de descarga. || *Their intervention relieved the situation momentarily*, su intervención remedió la situación momentáneamente. || *To relieve one's feelings*, desahogarse. || *To relieve o.s.*, hacer sus necesidades (to go to the toilet). || *To relieve o.s. of a problem*, quitarse un problema de encima, liberarse de un problema. || Fig. *To relieve nature*, hacer sus necesidades. || *To relieve s.o.'s anxiety*, tranquilizarle a uno.

relievo [riˈliːvəu] n. Arts. Relieve, *m.*

religion [riˈlidʒən] n. Religión, *f.* || Fig. Religión, *f.*: *football is his religion*, el fútbol es su religión. || *To take to religion*, darle a uno por la religión.

religiosity [riˌlidʒiˈɔsiti] n. Religiosidad, *f.*

religious [riˈlidʒəs] adj. Religioso, sa: *to fulfil one's religious duties*, cumplir con sus deberes religiosos. || Fig. Religioso, sa; exacto, ta; escrupuloso, sa. || *Religious wars*, guerras de religión.
— N. Religioso, sa.

religiousness [—nis] n. Religiosidad, *f.*

reline [ˈriːˈlain] v. tr. Cambiar el forro de (clothes, brakes).

relinquish [riˈliŋkwiʃ] v. tr. Renunciar a: *to relinquish a right*, renunciar a un derecho. || Soltar (to let go).

relinquishment [—mənt] n. Renuncia, *f.* (*of*, *a*).

reliquary [ˈrelikwəri] n. Relicario, *m.*

relish [ˈreliʃ] n. Gusto, *m.*, deleite, *m.*, fruición, *f.* (pleasure). || Entusiasmo, *m.* (enthusiasm). || Atracción, *f.*: *the relish of novelty*, la atracción de la novedad. || Culin. Condimento, *m.*, sazón, *f.* (seasoning). | Gusto, *m.*, sabor, *m.* (taste). | Pizca, *f.* (pinch). | Gustillo, *m.* (slight taste). || — *To do sth. with relish*, hacer algo con deleite *or* con entusiasmo. || *To have a relish for sth.*, encantarle algo a alguien, tener mucha afición a algo.

relish [ˈreliʃ] v. tr./intr. Culin. Condimentar, sazonar. || Saborear (to take pleasure in food). || Encantar: *I relish oysters*, me encantan las ostras. || Disfrutar con: *Peter relishes a good joke*, Pedro disfruta con un buen chiste. || — *I don't relish the idea of going*, no me gusta mucho *or* no me hace ninguna gracia la idea de ir. || *I relish a walk in the country*, disfruto dando un paseo por el campo, me encanta dar un paseo por el campo. || *To relish of*, saber a, tener sabor a.

relive [ˈriˈliv] v. tr. Volver a vivir (an experience).

reload [ˈriːˈləud] v. tr. Recargar.

relocate [ˈriːləuˈkeit] v. tr. Volver a situar, cambiar de sitio.

reluct [riˈlʌkt] v. intr. Sentir repulsión (*at*, *against*, por).

reluctance [riˈlʌktəns] n. Desgana, *f.*: *to do sth. with reluctance*, hacer algo con *or* a desgana. || Electr. Reluctancia, *f.* || *To affect reluctance*, hacerse de rogar.

reluctant [riˈlʌktənt] adj. Reacio, cia (reticent). || — *He gave his reluctant consent*, consintió de mala gana. || *To be reluctant to do sth.*, estar poco dispuesto a hacer algo, no querer hacer algo (not to want to), vacilar en hacer algo (to hesitate to). || *To go on a reluctant errand*, hacer un recado a disgusto.

reluctantly [—li] adv. De mala gana, contra su voluntad, a regañadientes, a disgusto.

rely [riˈlai] v. intr. Depender: *he relied on the money*, dependía del dinero. || Contar, confiar: *to rely on s.o. to do sth.*, contar con alguien para hacer algo, confiar en que alguien haga algo. || Fiarse: *you can't rely on the timetable*, uno no se puede fiar del horario.

remade [ˈriːˈmeid] pret. & p.p. See remake.

remain [riˈmein] v. intr. Quedarse, permanecer (to stay): *and they have remained there ever since*, y se han quedado allí desde entonces; *to remain silent*, permanecer silencioso. || Quedar, sobrar (to be left over). || Quedar: *the few joys that remained to him*, las pocas alegrías que le quedaban. || Quedar, faltar: *nothing remains to be done*, nada queda por hacer; *that remains to be seen*, eso queda por ver; *it only remains for us but to sign it*, ahora sólo nos queda firmarlo. || Seguir: *I remain certain that*, sigo convencido de que; *they remained faithful*, siguieron fieles; *the weather remains good*, el tiempo sigue bueno. || — *I remain yours faithfully*, reciba un atento saludo de, le saluda atentamente (in a letter). || *It remains, nevertheless, that*, sin embargo. || *Nothing remained but to go back*, no quedaba más remedio que volver. || *One thing remains sure*, una cosa es segura. || *There remains one solution*, queda una solución. || *To let it remain as it is*, dejarlo como es *or* como está. || *To remain behind*, quedarse (to stay). || *To remain in s.o.'s memory*, quedar grabado en la memoria de uno. || *To remain with*, quedar en manos de.

remainder [riˈmeində*] n. Resto, *m.*: *the remainder of the year, of the money*, el resto del año, del dinero. || Math. Resto, *m.* (in division, substraction). || — Pl. Saldo, *m. sing.*, restos (*m.*) de edición (books). || Comm. Saldo, *m. sing.* || Los demás, las demás, los otros, las otras: *some are good, the remainder are bad*, algunos son buenos, los demás son malos. || *Two into nine goes four, remainder one*, nueve dividido por dos son cuatro y queda uno.

remainder [riˈmeində*] v. tr. Saldar (books).

remaining [riˈmeiniŋ] adj. Otro, otra; que queda: *the remaining two were shot*, los dos que quedaban *or* los otros dos fueron fusilados. || Restante, sobrante.

remains [riˈmeinz] pl. n. Restos, *m.* (of a building). || Vestigios, *m.* (of a civilization, etc.). || Sobras, *f.*, restos, *m.* (of a meal). || Restos, *m.* (the dead human body): *mortal remains* restos mortales. || Fig. Vestigios, *m.* (of former beauty, etc.). || Obra (*f. sing.*) póstuma (of a writer).

remake [ˈriːˈmeik] n. Nueva versión, *f.* (of a film).

remake* [ˈriːˈmeik] v. tr. Rehacer, volver a hacer.

— Observ. Pret. & p. p. ***remade***.

reman [ˈriːˈmæn] v. tr. Mar. Proveer de nueva tripulación.

remand [riˈmaːnd] n. Jur. Detención, *f.* (keeping in custody). | Libertad (*f.*) condicional (release on bail). | Remisión, *f.* (of a case).

remand [riˈmaːnd] v. tr. Jur. Remitir: *to remand a case to another court*, remitir el caso a otro tribunal.

|| — JUR. *To remand in custody*, mantener bajo custodia. | *To remand on bail*, liberar bajo fianza.
remanence [ˈremənəns] n. PHYS. Remanencia, *f.*
remanent [ˈremənənt] adj. Remanente.
remark [riˈmɑːk] n. Observación, *f.*, comentario, *m.* (comment): *to let sth. by without remark*, dejar pasar algo sin hacer comentarios; *to make a remark*, hacer una observación. || — *His remark went home*, su observación tuvo efecto. || *Introductory remarks*, observaciones preliminares. || *To escape remark*, pasar desapercibido *or* inadvertido. || *To make the remark that*, observar que. || *To pass remarks on*, hacer comentarios sobre (to comment), criticar (to criticize). || *Worthy of remark*, notable.
remark [ˈriˈmɑːk] v. tr. Observar, advertir, notar (to say, to notice).
— V. intr. *To remark on* o *upon*, hacer una observación *or* hacer observaciones sobre, comentar.
remarkable [—əbl] adj. Notable: *remarkable for its size*, notable por su estatura. || Extraordinario, ria; excelente (excellent): *a remarkable singer*, un cantante extraordinario. || Admirable: *he did a remarkable piece of work*, ha hecho un trabajo admirable. || Singular (strange).
remarkableness [—əblnis] n. Notabilidad, *f.*
remarriage [ˈriːˈmæridʒ] n. Segundas nupcias, *f. pl.*, nuevo casamiento, *m.*
remarry [ˈriːˈmæri] v. intr. Volver a casarse.
rematch [ˈriˌmætʃ] n. Partido (*m.*) de vuelta.
remediable [riˈmiːdjəbl] adj. Remediable.
remedial [riˈmiːdjəl] adj. Remediador, ra; reparador, ra: *remedial effect*, efecto remediador. || MED. Reparador, ra (surgery). | Curativo, va (treatment). | Correctivo, va (exercises). || *Remedial education*, enseñanza (*f.*) de niños atrasados.
remediless [ˈremidilis] adj. Irremediable. || MED. Incurable.
remedy [ˈremidi] n. Remedio, *m.*: *there's no remedy for it*, no tiene remedio. || JUR. Recurso, *m.*: *remedy of appeal*, recurso de apelación. || Tolerancia, *f.* (coinage).
remedy [ˈremidi] v. tr. Remediar (to correct by removing a fault): *that should remedy the situation*, eso debería remediar la situación. || Curar (to heal).
remember [riˈmembə*] v. tr./intr. Acordarse de, recordar: *easily remembered*, fácil de recordar; *he could not remember your name*, no podía acordarse de *or* recordar tu nombre; *to remember a friend on his birthday*, acordarse de un amigo en el día de su cumpleaños; *I remember going*, recuerdo haber ido, me acuerdo de haber ido. || Dar recuerdos a: *remember me to your parents*, deles recuerdos a sus padres. || Acordarse de, dar propina a (to give a tip to): *remember the guide*, acuérdense del guía. || — *As far as I can remember*, si mal no recuerdo. || *Easy to remember*, fácil de recordar. || *He asked me to remember him to you all*, os manda recuerdos a todos. || *Here's sth. to remember me by*, te doy un recuerdo mío. || *Remember to turn to the left*, acuérdate de torcer a la izquierda, que no se te olvide torcer a la izquierda, recuerda que tienes que torcer a la izquierda. || *Remember where you are!*, ¡recuerde donde está usted! ¿usted dónde se cree?
remembrance [riˈmembrəns] n. Recuerdo, *m.*, rememoración, *f.* (recollection). || Recuerdo, *m.*, memoria, *f.* (memory). || Recuerdo, *m.* (souvenir). || Pl. Recuerdos, *m.* (greeting). || — *In remembrance of*, en conmemoración de, para conmemorar. || *Remembrance Day*, día (*m.*) de la conmemoración del armisticio de 1918. || *To have no remembrance of*, no recordar, no acordarse de.
remex [ˈriːmeks] n. Remera, *f.*, rémige, *f.* (of a bird's wing).

— OBSERV. El plural de *remex* es *remiges*.

remilitarization [ˈriːˌmilitəraiˈzeiʃən] n. Remilitarización, *f.*
remilitarize [ˈriːˈmilitəraiz] v. tr. Remilitarizar.
remind [riˈmaind] v. tr. Recordar: *to remind s.o. of sth.*, recordar algo a alguien; *he reminds me of your brother*, me recuerda a tu hermano; *remind me to write to her*, recuérdame que le escriba. || *That reminds me!*, ¡por cierto!, ¡a propósito!
reminder [—ə*] n. Recordatorio, *m.* (of a date). || Notificación, *f.* (of outstanding bill). || Advertencia, *f.* (warning). || Recuerdo, *m.* (souvenir).
reminisce [ˌremiˈnis] v. intr. Recordar el pasado.
reminiscence [ˌremiˈnisns] n. Recuerdo, *m.*, reminiscencia, *f.* (sth. which is remembered). || Recuerdo, *m.* (souvenir, memory). || — Pl. Memorias, *f.* (personal memories). || *To spend evenings in reminiscence*, pasar las tardes recordando el pasado.
reminiscent [ˌremiˈnisnt] adj. Evocador, ra; que evoca (evocative). || Lleno de recuerdos: *reminiscent photographs*, fotos llenas de recuerdos. || — *A room full of reminiscent old men*, una sala llena de ancianos que recuerdan el pasado. || *To be reminiscent of*, recordar, hacer pensar en: *it is reminiscent of his first book*, recuerda su primer libro.
remintage [riːˈmintidʒ] n. Reacuñación, *f.*
remise [riˈmaiz] v. tr. JUR. Ceder.
remiss [riˈmis] adj. Negligente, descuidado, da (neglectful). || Remiso, sa (slack).
remissibility [ˌrimisəˈbiləti] n. Remisibilidad, *f.*
remissible [—əbl] adj. Remisible.
remission [riˈmiʃən] n. Remisión, *f.*, perdón, *m.*: *the remission of sins*, el perdón de los pecados. || Disminución, *f.* (decrease in the magnitude of a force, etc.). || Exoneración, *f.* (of a debt, fine, etc.). || MED. Remisión, *f.* || JUR. Remisión, *f.* (of a case). || *To give s.o. six months remission for good conduct*, remitirle a uno seis meses de pena por buena conducta.
remissive [riˈmisiv] adj. Remisivo, va.
remissness [riˈmisnis] n. Negligencia, *f.*, descuido, *m.*
remit [riˈmit] v. tr. Remitir (to send). || Remitir, enviar (money). || Remitir (sth. for further consideration). || Devolver a un tribunal inferior (to return to a lower court). || Aplazar (to postpone). || Perdonar, remitir (to forgive). || Perdonar, remitir (a debt, fine, penalty, etc.).
— V. intr. Moderarse (to moderate). || Remitir (fever, storm). | Aliviarse (pain).
remittal [—əl] n. Remisión, *f.*, perdón, *m.* (forgiveness). || Exoneración, *f.* (of a debt, fine, etc.). || JUR Remisión, *f.*
remittance [—əns] n. Remesa, *f.*, giro, *m.* (sending of money). || *Remittance man*, hombre (*m.*) que vive en el extranjero gracias al dinero que le envían de su casa.
remittee [remiˈtiː] n. Destinatario, ria.
remittent [riˈmitənt] adj. Remitente: *remittent fever*, fiebre remitente.
remitter [riˈmitə*] n. Remitente, *m.* & *f.* (sender).
remnant [ˈremnənt] n. Resto, *m.*, remanente, *m.* (a remaining part). || Retal, *m.* (piece of fabric): *remnant sale*, venta de retales. || FIG. Vestigio, *m.* || — Pl. Saldos, *m.* (sales).
remodel [ˈriːˈmɔdl] v. tr. Modelar de nuevo (to give new shape to). || Transformar || Reorganizar.
remonetization [riˌmʌnitəˈzeiʃən] n. Restablecimiento (*m.*) del curso legal (of a metal).
remonetize [ˈriːˈmʌnitaiz] v. tr. Dar de nuevo curso legal a (a metal).
remonstrance [riˈmɔnstrəns] n. Amonestación, *f.*, reprimenda, *f.*, reconvención, *f.* (reprimand). || Protesta, *f.* (protest). || HIST. Protesta, *f.*
remonstrant [riˈmɔnstrənt] adj. Que protesta (person). || De protesta (tone, etc.).
remonstrate [ˈremənstreit] v. tr. Decir en señal de protesta.
— V. intr. Protestar (to protest). || Amonestar (to reprimand s.o.): *to remonstrate with s.o. upon sth.*, amonestar a alguien por algo.
remora [ˈremərə] n. Rémora, *f.* (fish).
remorse [riˈmɔːs] n. Remordimiento, *m.* || — *A twinge of remorse*, un remordimiento. || *To feel remorse*, tener remordimientos. || *Without remorse*, sin piedad.
remorseful [—ful] adj. Lleno de remordimiento, muy arrepentido, da.
remorsefully [—fuli] adv. Con remordimiento.
remorseless [—lis] adj. Sin remordimiento (without remorse). || Despiadado, da; implacable, inexorable (merciless).
remorselessly [—lisli] adv. Sin remordimiento (without remorse). || Despiadadamente, implacablemente, inexorablemente (mercilessly).
remorselessness [—lisnis] n. Implacabilidad, *f.*, inexorabilidad, *f.*
remote [riˈməut] adj. Remoto, ta (in space or time). || Lejano, na; distante (distant). || Retirado, da; apartado, da (out-of-the-way): *a remote little beach*, una playita retirada. || Lejano, na: *remote theories*, teorías lejanas. || Ligero, ra; remoto, ta (very slight): *a remote possibility*, una posibilidad remota, una ligera posibilidad; *I haven't the remotest idea*, no tengo la más remota idea. || Lejano, na: *a remote cousin*, un primo lejano. || Distante (standoffish). || — *Remote control*, mando (*m.*) a distancia, telemando, *m.* || FIG. *Remote from*, ajeno a.
remote-controlled [—kənˈtrəuld] adj. Teledirigido, da. (operated by remote control).
remoteness [—nis] n. Alejamiento, *m.*, lejanía, *f.* (in time or space). || Improbabilidad, *f.* (of a prospect).
remount [ˈriːmaunt] n. MIL. Remonta, *f.*
remount [riːˈmaunt] v. tr. Volverse a montar en (bicycle, horse, etc.). || Remontar (to supply with fresh mounts). || Volver a subir (a hill). || Volver a enmarcar (a photo, etc.).
— V. intr. Volverse a montar.
removability [riˌmuːvəˈbiliti] n. Amovilidad, *f.*
removable [riˈmuːvəbl] adj. Movible, móvil, trasladable (moveable). || Transportable (machine). || Amovible (part, civil servant). || De quita y pon (shirt collar). || Que se puede quitar (a stain).
removal [riˈmuːvəl] n. Traslado, *m.* (transfer). || Despido, *m.*, destitución, *f.* (discharge from office). || Mudanza, *f.* (moving house). || Eliminación, *f.* (elimination). || Supresión, *f.* (of an article, word, etc.). || MED. Extirpación, *f.* || Alivio, *m.* (of a suffering). || FAM. Liquidación, *f.* (murder). || *Removal van*, camión (*m.*) de mudanzas.
remove [riˈmuːv] n. Grado, *m.* (degree). || Grado (*m.*) de parentesco (of kinship). || Distancia, *f.* (distance). || Mudanza, *f.* (removal). || Paso (*m.*) a la clase superior. || Cambio (*m.*) de platos (eating). || — *Cousin at the first remove*, tío segundo (one's parent's first cousin),

sobrino segundo (one's first cousin's child). || FIG. *It is but one remove from*, raya en. || *Not to get one's remove*, repetir el curso. || *To be many removes from*, distar de ser.

remove [riˈmu:v] v. tr. Quitar (to take off or away): *s.o. has removed my radio*, alguien me ha quitado la radio. || Quitar de en medio (to get sth. out of the way). || Quitar (a stain). || Eliminar, borrar (traces). || Quitarse (to take off): *please remove your coat*, quítese el abrigo, por favor. || Destituir, despedir (to dismiss from office). || Trasladar (to transfer). || Mudar, trasladar (one's personal effects). || Quitar: *he removed the lid*, quitó la tapa. || Suprimir (tax, passage, word). || Tachar, borrar (from a list). || Disipar (doubt, fear). || Eliminar (difficulties, etc.). || Deshacerse de (to get rid of). || MED. Extirpar, quitar (tumour, etc.). || — *The accident removed him from racing*, el accidente le hizo abandonar *or* retirarse de las carreras. || *To remove o.s.*, irse, marcharse (to go away). || *To remove one's hat*, descubrirse, quitarse el sombrero. || *To remove sth. to another place*, cambiar algo de sitio, trasladar algo a otro sitio. || *To remove to hospital* o *to the hospital*, hospitalizar, llevar al hospital.

— V. intr. Mudarse, trasladarse.

removed [—d] adj. Distante. || *First cousin once removed*, tío segundo (one's parent's first cousin), sobrino segundo (one's first cousin's child).

remover [—ə*] n. Empresario (*m.*) de mudanzas (agent). || Mozo (*m.*) de cuerda *or* de mudanzas (workman). || — *Makeup remover*, desmaquillador, *m.* || *Nail polish remover*, quitaesmalte, *m.* || *Stain remover*, quitamanchas, *m. inv.*

remunerable [riˈmjunərəbl] adj. Remunerable.

remunerate [riˈmju:nəreit] v. tr. Remunerar, retribuir.

remunerating [—iŋ] adj. Remunerador, ra.

remuneration [ri,mju:nəˈreiʃən] n. Remuneración, *f.*

remunerative [riˈmju:nərətiv] adj. Remunerativo, va.

remunerator [riˈmju:nə,reitə*] n. Remunerador, ra.

remuneratory [riˈmju:nərətəri] adj. Remuneratorio, ria; remunerativo, va.

Remus [ˈri:məs] pr. n. Remo, *m.*

renaissance [rəˈneisəns] n. Renacimiento, *m.* || *The Renaissance*, el Renacimiento.

renal [ˈri:nəl] adj. Renal.

rename [ˈri:ˈneim] v. tr. Poner un nuevo nombre a.

renascence [riˈnæsns] n. Renacimiento, *m.* || *The Renascence*, el Renacimiento.

renascent [riˈnæsnt] adj. Renaciente.

rend* [rend] v. tr. Rasgar, rajar, hender (to split violently). || Rasgar, desgarrar (to tear). || Arrancar (to pull away or out). || Destrozar (to cause emotional pain to). || Dividir (to divide). || — FIG. *A cry rent the air*, un grito hendió el aire. | *To rend one's hair*, arrancarse los cabellos. | *To rend s.o.'s heart*, partirle el corazón a uno. || *To rend sth. asunder*, partir algo por medio.

— OBSERV. Pret. & p. p. *rent.*

render [—ə*] n. Primera capa (*f.*) de enlucido (building). || Contribución, *f.*

render [—ə*] v. tr. Dar: *to render thanks to God*, dar gracias a Dios. || Rendir (homage). || Rendir, dar: *to render an account of*, dar cuenta de. || Presentar (to present). || Hacer: *to render s.o. a service*, hacer un favor a alguien; *to render s.o. happy*, hacer feliz a alguien. || Dar, prestar (assistance). || Devolver (to give back). || Dejar: *the accident rendered him blind*, el accidente le dejó ciego. || Hacer (to do). || Entregar, rendir (to hand over, to surrender). || Representar (to represent): *the picture rendered the scene perfectly*, el cuadro representaba perfectamente la escena. || Reproducir (to reproduce). || Producir (a benefit). || Traducir (to translate). || Interpretar (to interpret artistically). || JUR. Administrar (justice). | Pronunciar (a sentence, a verdict). || CULIN. Derretir (to melt fat). || COMM. Mandar, presentar (a bill). || ARCH. Enlucir, dar una capa de enlucido a (building). || TECH. Extraer derritiendo (to extract fats). || — *For services rendered to the nation*, por los servicios prestados a la nación. || *The poor soil renders irrigation necessary*, la pobreza del suelo hace que sea necesario el regadío. || *To render sth. impossible*, imposibilitar algo, hacer que algo sea imposible.

rendering [—riŋ] n. Enlucido, *m.* (of a building). || Interpretación, *f.* (artistic interpretation). || Traducción, *f.* (translation).

rendezvous [ˈrɔndivu:] inv. n. Cita, *f.*: *to have a rendezvous with*, tener cita con. || Lugar (*m.*) de reunión (place). || MIL. Punto (*m.*) de reunión.

rendezvous [ˈrɔndivu:] v. tr. MIL. Reunir (to assemble).

— V. intr. Reunirse.

rendition [renˈdiʃən] n. Traducción, *f.* (translation). || Interpretación, *f.* (artistic interpretation). || Rendición, *f.* (surrender).

renegade [ˈrenigeid] adj./n. Renegado, da.

renegade [ˈrenigeid] v. intr. Renegar.

renege [riˈni:g] n. U. S. Renuncio, *m.* (cards).

renege [riˈni:g] v. intr. U. S. No cumplir una promesa (on a promise). | Dar marcha atrás, volverse atrás (on an agreement, etc.). || Renunciar (in cards).

renegotiate [,riniˈgəuʃi,eit] v. tr. Negociar de nuevo.

renew [riˈnju:] v. tr. Renovar: *to renew a passport, vows, a contract*, renovar un pasaporte, votos, un contrato. || Extender, prorrogar (to extend). || Reanudar: *to renew one's efforts*, reanudar sus esfuerzos; *to renew talks*, reanudar las conversaciones; *to renew one's acquaintance with*, reanudar una amistad con. || Reavivar (one's interest). || Renovar (to replace). || COMM. Renovar. || — *To renew the attack*, volver a atacar. || *With renewed strength*, con nuevas fuerzas.

— V. intr. Renovarse (strength). || Reanudarse (to resume). || COMM. Hacer una renovación.

renewable [—əbl] adj. Renovable.

renewal [riˈnju:əl] n. Renovación, *f.* (of passport, subscription, contract, etc.). || Prórroga, *f.*, extensión, *f.* (extension). || Reanudación, *f.* (continuation after a break). || COMM. Renovación, *f.*

rennet [ˈrenit] n. Cuajo, *m.* (curdled milk). || Cuajar, *m.* (abomasum). || *Rennet stomach*, cuajar.

renounce [riˈnauns] n. Renuncio, *m.* (in cards).

renounce [riˈnauns] v. tr. Repudiar (to repudiate). || Renunciar a (a claim, a right). || Denunciar (a treaty).

— V. intr. Renunciar (in cards).

renouncement [—mənt] n. Renuncia, *f.*

renovate [ˈrenəuveit] v. tr. Renovar (to brighten up). || Restaurar (to restore).

— V. intr. Renovarse.

renovation [,renəuˈveiʃən] n. Renovación, *f.* || Restauración, *f.* (restoration).

renovator [ˈrenəuveitə*] n. Renovador, ra. || Restaurador, ra (restorer).

renown [riˈnaun] n. Renombre, *m.*, fama, *f.*, reputación, *f.*

renowned [—d] adj. Renombrado, da; famoso, sa; célebre.

rent [rent] n. Alquiler, *m.* (for house, car, television, etc.). || Arrendamiento, *m.* (of agricultural land). || Raja, *f.*, hendidura, *f.* (split). || Rasgón, *m.*, rasgadura, *f.* (tear). || Escisión, *f.*, división, *f.* (schism). || — *Cars for rent*, coches (*m.*) de alquiler. || *For rent*, se alquila. || *I pay five pounds rent*, pago cinco libras de alquiler.

rent [rent] v. tr. Alquilar (house, property): *to rent s.o. a flat*, alquilar un piso a alguien; *to rent a house from s.o.*, alquilar una casa a alguien. || Arrendar (land).

— V. intr. Alquilarse: *the house rents at a high price*, se alquila la casa a un precio elevado. || Arrendarse (land).

rent [rent] pret. & p. p. See REND.

rentable [ˈrentəbl] adj. Que se alquila, alquilable (house). || Arrendable (land).

rental [—əl] n. Alquiler, *m.* (quantity paid): *monthly rental*, alquiler mensual. || Arriendo, *m.*, arrendamiento, *m.* (of agricultural land). || Renta, *f.* (income from rents). || Alquiler, *m.* (renting). || U. S. Propiedad (*f.*) alquilada.

— Adj. De alquiler.

renter [ˈrentə*] n. Inquilino, na (in a house, flat). || Arrendatario, ria (of land). || CINEM. Distribuidor, ra (distributor).

rent-free [ˈrentˈfri:] adv. Gratuitamente, sin pagar alquiler.

— Adj. Exento de alquiler, gratuito, ta (a house).

rentier [ˈrɔntiei] n. Rentista, *m.* & *f.*

rent-roll [ˈrentrəul] n. Registro (*m.*) de propiedades en alquiler (register). || Ingresos (*m. pl.*) de propiedades en alquiler.

renumber [ˈri:ˈnʌmbə*] v. tr. Volver a numerar.

renunciation [ri,nʌnsiˈeiʃən] n. Renuncia, *f.*, renunciación, *f.*

renunciative [riˈnʌnsiətiv] or **renunciatory** [ri,nʌnsiətəri] adj. Renunciante.

reoccupation [ˈri:,ɔkjuˈpeiʃən] n. Nueva ocupación, *f.*

reoccupy [ˈri:ˈɔkjupai] v. tr. Volver a ocupar.

reopen [ˈri:ˈəupən] v. tr. Volver a abrir, reabrir (a shop). || JUR. Volver a estudiar (a case).

— V. intr. Volver a abrirse, reabrirse (a shop). || Volverse a estudiar (a case).

reopening [—iŋ] n. Reapertura, *f.*

reorder [ri:ˈɔ:də*] n. Nuevo pedido, *m.*

reorder [ri:ˈɔ:də*] v. tr. Pedir de nuevo *or* hacer un nuevo pedido de (goods). || Volver a ordenar *or* a poner en orden (to put in order). || Reorganizar (to reorganize).

— V. intr. Hacer un nuevo pedido.

reorganization [ˈri:,ɔ:gənaiˈzeiʃən] n. Reorganización, *f.*

reorganize [ˈri:ˈɔ:gənaiz] v. tr. Reorganizar.

— V. intr. Reorganizarse.

reorganizer [—ə*] n. Reorganizador, ra.

reorient [ˈri:ˈɔ:rient] v. tr. Reorientar, dar nueva orientación a.

reorientation [ˈri:,ɔ:rienˈteiʃən] n. Nueva orientación, *f.*

rep [rep] n. Reps, *m.* (fabric).

rep [rep] n. FAM. Viajante, *m.*, representante, *m.* (salesman). | Reputación, *f.*, fama, *f.*

repack [ri:ˈpæk] v. tr. Volver a embalar (to wrap up again). || Volver a hacer (suitcase).

repackage [ri:ˈpækidʒ] v. tr. Volver a embalar.

repaid [ˈri:ˈpeid] pret. & p. p. See REPAY.

repaint [ri:ˈpeint] v. tr. Volver a pintar, repintar: *to repaint sth. red*, repintar algo de rojo.

repair [riˈpεə*] n. Reparación, *f.* (of car, house, etc.). || Remiendo, *m.* (of clothes). || — *Closed for repairs*, cerrado por reformas *or* obras. || *In bad repair*, en mal estado. || *It is out of repair*, no tiene arreglo, no se puede reparar. || *Repair kit*, caja (*f.*) de herramientas. || *Repair* *parts*, repuestos, *m.*, recambios, *m.* || *Repair shop*, taller (*m.*) de reparaciones. || *Repair squad*, equipo (*m.*) de reparación. || *To be (damaged) beyond repair*, no tener arreglo (object, situation). || *To be under repair*, estar en reparación (appliance, etc.), estar en obras (house). || *To keep in good repair* o *in repair*, mantener en buen estado.

repair [riˈpɛə*] v. tr. Reparar, arreglar, componer (to fix). || Remendar (shoes, clothes). || Remediar (a wrong). || Restablecer (health).
— V. intr. Acudir.

repairable [—rəbəl] adj. Reparable.

repairing [—riŋ] n. See REPAIR.

repairman [—mæn] n. Reparador, *m.*
— OBSERV. El plural de *repairman* es *repairmen*.

reparable [ˈrepərəbl] adj. Reparable: *reparable damage*, daño reparable.

reparation [ˌrepəˈreiʃən] n. Reparación, *f.* || Satisfacción, *f.* (satisfaction). || — Pl. COMM. Indemnización, *f. sing.* (compensation).

reparative [riˈpærətiv] adj. Reparador, ra.

repartee [ˌrepɑːˈtiː] n. Rápida sucesión (*f.*) de réplicas *or* salidas (exchange between speakers). || Réplica, *f.* (art).

repartition [ˈrepɑːˈtiʃən] n. Reparto, *m.*, distribución, *f.*

repass [ˈriːˈpɑːs] v. tr. Volver a pasar (to pass again).
— V. intr. Volver a pasar.

repast [riˈpɑːst] n. Comida, *f.*

repatriate [riːˈpætrieit] n. Repatriado, da.

repatriate [riːˈpætrieit] v. tr. Repatriar.
— V. intr. Repatriarse.

repatriation [ˈriːpætriˈeiʃən] n. Repatriación, *f.*

repay* [ˈriːˈpei] v. tr. Devolver, reembolsar (money). || Pagar, liquidar (a debt). || Compensar, pagar (s.o.). || Corresponder a, devolver (to return): *to repay an invitation*, corresponder a una invitación. || Recompensar (to recompense). || Hacer pagar, desquitarse de: *he repaid the trick by setting his dog on them*, les hizo pagar la broma echándoles el perro. || — *Book that repays reading*, libro que merece la pena ser leído. || *How can I ever repay you?*, ¿cómo puedo pagarle? || *I'll repay you for that!*, ¡ya me las pagarás! || *To repay s.o. in full*, reembolsar a alguien integralmente. || FIG. *To repay s.o. in kind*, pagar a uno con la misma moneda.
— V. intr. Hacer un pago, pagar.
— OBSERV. Pret. & p. p. ***repaid***.

repayable [—əbl] adj. Reembolsable, reintegrable.

repayment [—mənt] n. Devolución, *f.*, pago, *m.*, reintegro, *m.*, reembolso, *m.* (of money). || Recompensa, *f.* (reward).

repeal [riˈpiːl] n. Revocación, *f.* (revocation). || Abrogación, *f.* (abrogation). || Anulación, *f.* (annulment).

repeal [riˈpiːl] v. tr. Revocar. || Abrogar. || Anular.

repealing [—iŋ] adj. Derogatorio, ria.

repeat [riˈpiːt] n. Repetición, *f.* (a repeating or sth. repeated). || MUS. Repetición, *f.* || CINEM. Reestreno, *m.* (of a film). || THEATR. Reposición, *f.* (of play). || *This programme is a repeat*, es una segunda difusión de este programa.

repeat [riˈpiːt] v. tr. Repetir: *to repeat a sentence*, repetir una frase; *to repeat an experience*, repetir una experiencia. || Repetir, volver a hacer: *to repeat a visit*, volver a hacer una visita. || Recitar (to recite). || Contar, decir, repetir (sth. one has been told): *don't repeat this to anybody*, no se lo cuente a nadie. || Repetir (a course, term, etc.). || CINEM. Volver a poner (a film). || THEATR. Volver a representar (a play). || *To repeat o.s.*, repetirse.
— V. intr. Repetir (a taste, a gun, etc.). || U. S. Votar más de una vez [en unas elecciones]. || — *Garlic repeats on me*, el ajo se repite. || *Not to bear repeating*, no merecer la pena repetirse.

repeated [—id] adj. Repetido, da.

repeatedly [—idli] adv. Repetidas veces, reiteradamente, reiteradas veces.

repeater [—ə*] n. Reloj (*m.*) de repetición (watch or clock). || Arma (*f.*) de repetición (a repeating gun). || Repetidor *m.* (telegraphy). || U. S. Elector (*m.*) que vota más de una vez (elections). | Repetidor, ra (student).

repeating [—iŋ] adj. De repetición (rifle, clock). || MATH. *Repeating decimal*, fracción (*f.*) decimal periódica.

repel [riˈpel] v. tr. Repeler, rechazar: *to repel an attack*, rechazar un ataque. || Reprimir, contener: *to repel a desire*, contener un deseo. || Rechazar: *to repel an offer of friendship*, rechazar un ofrecimiento de amistad. || Repeler: *this paint repels water*, esta pintura repele el agua. || PHYS. Repeler. || FIG. Repeler, repugnar (to repulse).

repellent [—ənt] adj. Repelente. || FIG. Repugnante, repelente.
— N. Producto (*m.*) contra los insectos (for repelling insects). || Producto (*m.*) para impermeabilizar (to make sth. impermeable).

repent [ˈriˈpent] adj. BOT. Rastrero, ra. || ZOOL. Reptante, que se arrastra.

repent [riˈpent] v. tr. Arrepentirse de.
— V. intr. Arrepentirse.

repentance [—əns] n. Arrepentimiento, *m.*

repentant [—ənt] adj. Arrepentido, da.

repeople [ˈriːˈpiːpl] v. tr. Repoblar.

repercussion [ˌriːpəˈkʌʃən] n. Repercusión, *f.* || Reverberación, *f.*, eco, *m.* (reverberation). || Repercusión, *f.* (indirect reaction to some event): *to have grave repercussions*, tener graves repercusiones.

repertoire [ˈrepətwɑː*] or **repertory** [ˈrepətəri] n. Repertorio, *m.*: *to have a very varied repertory*, tener un repertorio muy variado. || *Repertory theatre*, teatro de repertorio.

repetend [repəˈtend] n. Estribillo, *m.*, cantinela, *f.*

repetition [ˌrepiˈtiʃən] n. Repetición. *f.* || Recitación, *f.* || Réplica, *f.* (copy).

repetitious [ˌrepəˈtiʃəs] adj. Lleno de repeticiones.

repetitive [riˈpetitiv] adj. Reiterativo, va (tending to repeat). || Lleno de repeticiones (repetitious).

rephrase [ˈriːˈfreiz] v. tr. Decir con otras palabras, decir de otra manera (when speaking). || Volver a redactar (sth. in writing).

repine [riˈpain] v. intr. Quejarse, afligirse: *to repine at*, quejarse de.

repining [—iŋ] n. Quejas, *f. pl.*

replace [riˈpleis] v. tr. Reponer, volver a poner en su lugar (to put back). || Sustituir, reemplazar: *Smith replaced Brown*, Smith sustituyó a Brown; *to replace one thing by another*, sustituir una cosa por otra; *he replaced Brown by Smith*, reemplazó a Brown por Smith. || Pagar (to pay for sth. broken). || *Please replace the receiver*, cuelgue por favor (phone).

replaceable [—əbl] adj. Reemplazable, sustituible.

replacement [—mənt] n. Reposición, *f.* (action of putting back). || Sustitución, *f.*, reemplazo, *m.* (action of substituting). || Sustituto, ta; suplente, *m.* & *f.* (s.o. who replaces). || Repuesto, *m.*, recambio, *m.* (spare part). || MIL. Reemplazo, *m.* || *I can't find a replacement for the vase I broke*, no consigo encontrar un jarrón para sustituir el que rompí.

replant [ˈriːˈplɑːnt] v. tr. Replantar, volver a plantar.

replanting [—iŋ] n. Replantación, *f.*

replay [ˈriːplei] n. SP. Repetición (*f.*) de un partido (match). || Repetición, *f.* (on television).

replay [ˈriːˈplei] v. tr. Volver a jugar. || MUS. Volver a tocar. || THEATR. Volver a representar.

repleadar [riˈpliːdə*] n. JUR. Segundo alegato, *m.*

replenish [riˈpleniʃ] v. tr. Rellenar, llenar de nuevo (to fill again). || Abastecer *or* aprovisionar de nuevo (*with*, de). || Reponer: *to replenish one's stocks*, reponer las existencias.

replenishment [—mənt] n. Relleno, *m.* || Reabastecimiento, *m.*

replete [riˈpliːt] adj. Repleto, ta; lleno, na.

repletion [riˈpliːʃən] n. Saciedad, *f.*, repleción, *f.* || *To eat to repletion*, comer hasta hartarse *or* saciarse.

replevin [riˈplevin] n. JUR. Desembargo, *m.*

replevin [riˈplevin] v. tr. U. S. JUR. Obtener un desembargo de.

replevy [riˈplevi] n. U. S. JUR. Desembargo, *m.*

replevy [riˈplevi] v. tr. JUR. Obtener un desembargo de.
— V. intr. JUR. Obtener un desembargo.

replica [ˈreplikə] n. Copia, *f.*, reproducción, *f.*, réplica, *f.*

replicate [ˈreplikət] adj. Replegado, da.

replicate [ˈreplikeit] v. tr. Repetir, duplicar.

replicated [—id] adj. Replegado, da.

replication [repliˈkeiʃən] n. Copia, *f.*, reproducción, *f.*, réplica, *f.* (copy). || Réplica, *f.* (answer). || JUR. Réplica, *f.* || Repercusión, *f.*

reply [riˈplai] n. Respuesta, *f.*, contestación, *f.* || — *In reply they said that...*, contestaron que... || COMM. *In reply to your letter of the 5th inst.*, en respuesta a su atenta del 5 del corriente. || *Reply coupon*, cupón, *m.* || *Reply paid*, respuesta pagada.

reply [riˈplai] v. tr. Responder, contestar: *he replied that he was tired*, contestó que estaba cansado.
— V. intr. Contestar, responder: *to reply to s.o.*, contestar a uno. || *To reply to a letter*, contestar una carta.

repolish [ˈriːˈpɔliʃ] v. tr. Repulir, pulir de nuevo.

repopulate [ˈriːˈpɔpjuleit] v. tr. Repoblar.

repopulation [ˈriːpɔpjuˈleiʃən] n. Repoblación, *f.*

report [riˈpɔːt] n. Informe, *m.* (official): *preliminary, provisional, final report*, informe preliminar, provisional, definitivo; *to bring a report up-to-date*, poner al día un informe; *to amend a report*, enmendar un informe. || Noticia, *f.* (piece of news). || Reportaje, *m.* (account in newspaper, on radio). || Relato, *m.*, relación, *f.* (spoken account). || Informe, *m.*, ponencia, *f.* (speech at a public meeting). || Reputación, *f.*, fama, *f.*: *of good report*, de buena reputación. || Boletín, *m.* (at school, etc.). || Rumor, *m.*, voz, *f.* (rumour): *there are reports that*, corre la voz de que. || Estampido, *m.*, detonación, *f.* (of gun, etc.). || Informe, *m.* (of a policeman). || MIL. Parte, *m.*: *to make one's report*, dar el parte. || — *Chairman's report*, informe del presidente. || *Expert report*, dictamen (*m.*) pericial, peritaje, *m.* || *Factual report*, exposición (*f.*) de hechos. || *I have heard reports that he is ill*, me han dicho que está enfermo. || *Information report*, nota informativa. || *Progress report*, informe sobre la marcha de los trabajos. || COMM. *Report on activities* o *on the management*, informe sobre la gestión. || JUR. *To draw up a report against s.o.*, levantar un atestado contra alguien. || *Weather report*, parte meteorológico.

report [riˈpɔːt] v. tr. Relatar (to recount). || Redactar las actas de (the secretary in a meeting). || Hacer la

crónica de (a trial, a meeting for a newspaper). || Presentar un informe sobre. || Repetir (a message). || Denunciar (to make an official complaint about s.o.): *to report a criminal*, denunciar a un criminal; *to report a theft to the police*, denunciar un robo a la policía. || Declarar, anunciar (to declare, to announce). || Comunicar: *to report the results of an investigation*, comunicar los resultados de una investigación. || MIL. Dar parte de. || *It is reported that*, se dice que.
— V. intr. Presentar un informe (to present a formal report). || Hacer un informe (*on*, sobre) [to draw up a report]. || Ser reportero, hacer reportajes (to work as reporter). || Presentarse: *to report for work*, presentarse para trabajar. || — *Report back to me when you finish*, vuelva a verme cuando acabe. || MIL. *To report sick*, darse de baja por enfermedad. | *To report to one's unit*, incorporarse a su unidad.
reportage [ˌrepɔ:ˈtɑ:ʒ] n. Reportaje, *m.*
report card [—kɑ:d] n. U. S. Boletín (*m.*) de notas.
reporter [riˈpɔ:tə*] n. Periodista, *m.* & *f.*, reportero, *m.* (of a newspaper). || Relator, *m.* (in court, official meetings, etc.). || Presentador, ra (on television).
reporting [riˈpɔ:tiŋ] n. Reporterismo, *m.*
reportorial [repəˈtɔriəl] adj. Reporteril.
repose [riˈpəuz] n. Reposo, *m.*, descanso, *m.* (rest). || Sueño, *m.* (sleep). || Calma, *f.*, sosiego, *m.* (calm).
repose [riˈpəuz] v. intr. Reposar, descansar. || — *To repose in state*, estar de cuerpo presente. || *To repose on*, basarse en: *his argument reposes on a new theory*, su argumento se basa en una nueva teoría.
— V. tr. Descansar, reposar (to rest). || FIG. Poner, depositar (confidence).
repository [riˈpɔzitəri] n. Depósito, *m.*, (place for keeping things). || Almacén, *m.* (warehouse). || Depositario, ria (person): *repository of one's secrets*, depositario de los secretos de uno. || Fuente, *f.* (source). || Panteón, *m.* (burial vault). || *Furniture repository*, guardamuebles, *m. inv.*
repossess [ˌripəˈzes] v. tr. Volver a tomar posesión de, recuperar (to take possession of). || Devolver (to give back). || *To repossess o.s. of*, recuperar, volver a tomar posesión de.
repossession [ˌripəˈzeʃən] n. Recuperación, *f.*
repoussé [rəˈpu:sei] adj. TECH. Repujado, da.
— N. TECH. Repujado, *m.*
repp [rep] n. Reps, *m.*
reprehend [ˌrepriˈhend] v. tr. Reprender: *he reprehended her for her bad behaviour*, le reprendió por su mala conducta.
reprehensible [ˌrepriˈhensəbl] adj. Reprensible, censurable.
reprehension [ˌrepriˈhenʃən] n. Reprensión, *f.*, reprobación, *f.*
represent [ˌrepriˈzent] v. tr. Representar: *to represent a minister at the inauguration of a monument*, representar a un ministro en la inauguración de un monumento; *the painting represents three Spaniards*, el cuadro representa a tres españoles; *this book represents twenty years' work*, este libro representa un trabajo de veinte años. || Equivaler: *that represents a slander*, eso equivale a una calumnia. || Describir (to describe): *you represented it to me quite differently*, me lo describió de forma muy diferente. || JUR. COMM. Representar. || THEATR. Representar.
re-present [ˈri:ˈprizent] v. tr. Presentar de nuevo, volver a presentar.
representation [ˌreprizenˈteiʃən] n. Representación, *f.*: *proportional representation*, representación proporcional; *a representation of the battle*, una representación de la batalla. || Descripción, *f.* (description). || Representantes, *m. pl.*, delegación, *f.* (representatives). || THEATR. Representación, *f.* || *To make a representation* o *representations to*, presentar una petición a (to petition), formular *or* elevar una protesta a (to protest).
representational [—əl] adj. ARTS. Figurativo, va.
representative [ˌrepriˈzentətiv] adj. Representativo, va: *representative government*, gobierno representativo. || *A song representative of South American music*, una canción representativa de la música sudamericana, una canción que representa la música sudamericana.
— N. Representante, *m.* & *f.*: *commercial representative*, representante comercial; *to send a representative to a conference*, mandar un representante a una conferencia. || U. S. Diputado, *m.*, representante, *m.*
representatively [—li] adv. De manera representativa.
repress [riˈpres] v. tr. Reprimir, contener: *to repress an uprising*, reprimir una insurrección; *to repress tears*, reprimir el llanto.
repression [riˈpreʃən] n. Represión, *f.*
repressive [riˈpresiv] adj. Represivo, va: *repressive measures*, medidas represivas.
repressiveness [—nis] n. Lo represivo.
reprieve [riˈpri:v] n. JUR. Indulto, *m.* (pardon). | Conmutación, *f.* (commutation). | Suspensión, *f.* (suspension). || FIG. Alivio, *m.*, respiro, *m.* (relief). || *The right of reprieve*, el derecho de gracia.
reprieve [riˈpri:v] v. tr. JUR. Indultar (to pardon). | Conmutar la pena de (to commute a sentence). | Suspender la pena de (to suspend sentence). || FIG. Aliviar (to relieve). | Aplazar (to postpone).
reprimand [ˈreprimɑ:nd] n. Reprimenda, *f.*, reprensión, *f.*
reprimand [ˈreprimɑ:nd] v. tr. Reprender, reconvenir.
reprint [ˈri:print] n. Reimpresión, *f.*, reedición, *f.* || Separata, *f.*, tirada (*f.*) aparte (offprint).
reprint [ˈri:ˈprint] v. tr. Reimprimir (to print again). || Tirar aparte (to extract).
reprisal [riˈpraizəl] n. Represalia, *f.*: *to take reprisals*, ejercer represalias.
reprise [riˈpraiz] n. MUS. Repetición, *f.* || JUR. *Revenue above reprises*, renta neta.
reproach [riˈprəutʃ] n. Reproche, *m.*, crítica, *f.*, censura, *f.* (reproof). || Deshonra, *f.*, oprobio, *m.* (shame, disgrace). || — *Above reproach*, sin tacha. || *To be a reproach to*, ser vergonzoso para. || *To be beyond reproach*, ser impecable (work, etc.), ser intachable (conduct, reputation, etc.). || *To bring reproach on*, ser un oprobio para.
reproach [riˈprəutʃ] v. tr. Reprochar, criticar, censurar: *to reproach s.o. with* o *for sth.*, reprocharle algo a alguien. || — *To reproach o.s. with sth.*, reprocharse algo. || *To reproach s.o. for doing sth.*, reprochar a alguien que haya hecho algo.
reproachable [—əbəl] adj. Reprochable, criticable, censurable.
Reproaches [—iz] pl. n. REL. Improperios, *m.*
reproachful [—ful] adj. Reprobador, ra; de reproche (look, etc.). || *To be reproachful of sth.*, reprochar algo.
reproachfully [—fuli] adv. Con reproche, de manera reprobatoria.
reprobate [ˈreprəubeit] adj./n. REL. Réprobo, ba. || Malvado, da (wicked).
reprobate [ˈreprəubeit] v. tr. Reprobar.
reprobation [ˌreprəuˈbeiʃən] n. Reprobación, *f.*
reprobative [ˈreprəˌbeitiv] or **reprobatory** [ˈreprəbəˌtəri] adj. Reprobatorio, ria.
reproduce [ˌri:prəˈdju:s] v. tr. Reproducir.
— V. intr. Reproducirse.
reproducer [—ə*] n. Reproductor, ra.
reproducibility [ˌri:prədju:siˈbiliti] n. Reproducibilidad, *f.*
reproducible [ˌri:prəˈdju:sibl] adj. Reproducible.
reproducing machine [ˌri:prəˈdju:siŋməˈʃi:n] n. Máquina (*f.*) reproductora.
reproduction [ˌri:prəˈdʌkʃən] n. Reproducción, *f.*
reproductive [ˌri:prəˈdʌktiv] adj. Reproductor, ra. || *Reproductive organs*, órganos reproductores.
reproductivity [ˌri:prədʌkˈtiviti] n. Reproductividad, *f.* (capacity of being reproductive).
reproof [riˈpru:f] n. Reprobación, *f.*, censura, *f.*, reprensión, *f.*
reprovable [riˈpruvəbəl] adj. Reprobable, censurable (reproachable).
reproval [riˈpru:vəl] n. Reprobación, *f.*, censura, *f.*, reprensión, *f.*
reprove [riˈpru:v] v. tr. Reprobar, condenar, censurar, criticar, reprender.
reproving [—iŋ] adj. Reprobatorio, ria; de reprobación.
reprovingly [riˈpru:viŋli] adv. Con reprobación.
reptant [ˈreptənt] adj. ZOOL. Reptante. || BOT. Rastrero, ra: *reptant roots*, raíces rastreras.
reptile [ˈreptail] adj. Reptil. || FIG. Rastrero, ra.
— N. Reptil, *m.*
reptilian [repˈtiliən] adj. Reptil.
— N. Reptil, *m.*
republic [riˈpʌblik] n. República, *f.* || *Republic of letters*, república de las letras.
republican [—ən] adj./n. Republicano, na. || *Republican Party*, Partido Republicano.
republicanism [—ənizəm] n. Republicanismo, *m.*
republicanize [riˈpʌblikənaiz] v. tr. Republicanizar.
republication [ˈri:ˌpʌblikeiʃən] n. Reedición, *f.*
republish [ˈri:ˈpʌbliʃ] v. tr. Reeditar.
repudiable [riˈpju:dieibl] adj. Repudiable.
repudiate [riˈpju:dieit] v. tr. Repudiar (a person). || Rechazar (to reject). || JUR. Negarse a cumplir (a contract). | Negarse a reconocer (debt, claim, etc.).
repudiation [ripju:ˈdieiʃən] n. Repudiación, *f.*, repudio, *m.* (of one's wife). || Rechazo, *m.* (rejection). || Desconocimiento, *m.* (of debts, etc.).
repugnance [riˈpʌgnəns] or **repugnancy** [—i] n. Repugnancia, *f.*, repulsión, *f.*
repugnant [riˈpʌgnənt] adj. Repugnante, repulsivo, va; repelente (repellent). || Incompatible: *repugnant to*, incompatible con. || *I find them repugnant*, me repugnan.
repulse [riˈpʌls] n. Repulsa, *f.*, rechazamiento, *m.* || *He suffered a repulse*, fue rechazado.
repulse [riˈpʌls] v. tr. Rechazar (to drive back). || Repeler, rechazar (to reject).
repulsion [riˈpʌlʃən] n. Repulsión, *f.*, repugnancia, *f.* (revulsion). || Rechazamiento, *m.*, repulsa, *f.*, repulsión, *f.* (rejection). || PHYS. Repulsión, *f.*
repulsive [riˈpʌlsiv] adj. Repulsivo, va; repelente.
repulsiveness [—nis] n. Carácter (*m.*) repulsivo. || PHYS. Fuerza (*f.*) repulsiva.
repurchase [ri:ˈpə:tʃəs] n. Nueva compra, *f.*, nueva adquisición, *f.*
repurchase [ri:ˈpə:tʃəs] v. tr. Volver a comprar, comprar de nuevo.
reputability [ˈrepjutəˈbiliti] n. Buena reputación, *f.*, honorabilidad, *f.*
reputable [ˈrepjutəbl] adj. Reputado, da (well known). || Acreditado, da (having a good reputation). ||

Honroso, sa; estimable (honourable). || De confianza, seguro, ra (reliable). || Puro, ra; castizo, za (word).
reputation [ˌrepju:'teiʃən] n. Reputación, *f.*, fama, *f.*: *to have a good reputation*, tener buena reputación; *to have the reputation of being stupid*, tener fama de estúpido. || *This region has a reputation for good wine*, esta región es famosa por la calidad de sus vinos.
repute [ri'pju:t] n. Reputación, *f.*, fama, *f.*: *a man of good repute*, un hombre de buena reputación; *a city of evil repute*, una ciudad de mala fama; *to know a person by repute*, conocer a una persona por su reputación. || *House of ill repute*, casa de mala fama. || *Of repute* o *of good repute*, famoso, sa. || *To hold s.o. in high repute*, tener a alguien en gran estima.
repute [ri'pju:t] v. tr. Considerar. || — *He is reputed to have married three times*, dicen que se casó tres veces. || *It is reputed that Caesar was murdered by Brutus*, se supone que César fue asesinado por Bruto. || *To be reputed to be rich*, tener fama de rico.
reputed [—id] adj. Reputado, da (well known): *highly reputed*, muy reputado. || Supuesto, ta (supposed): *the reputed journalist turned out to be a criminal*, el supuesto periodista resultó ser un criminal.
reputedly [—idli] adv. Según dicen, según se dice: *it is reputedly easy to play the piano*, según dicen, es fácil tocar el piano.
request [ri'kwest] n. Petición, *f.*, ruego, *m.*, solicitud, *f.*: *to make a request*, hacer una petición, dirigir una solicitud. || COMM. Demanda, *f.* || — *At the request of*, a petición de, a instancia de. || *By request*, a petición del público. || *In request*, solicitado: *the famous yodeller is very much in request*, el célebre cantante tirolés es muy solicitado por el público. || *On request*, a petición de los interesados, solicite: *a list of prices is available on request*, una lista de precios está disponible a petición de los interesados, solicite una lista de precios. || *On the request of*, a petición de. || *Request programme*, emisión (*f.*) de discos solicitados por los radioyentes. || *Request stop*, parada discrecional. || *To send a request for reinforcements*, pedir refuerzos.
request [ri'kwest] v. tr. Pedir, solicitar: *in his speech he requested better conditions for widows*, en su discurso pidió mejores condiciones para las viudas; *he requested me to attend the meeting*, me pidió que asistiese a la reunión; *I requested that he be shot*, pedí que lo fusilaran. || Rogar: *silence is requested*, se ruega silencio. || — *Mr. Andrews requests the pleasure of your company for dinner*, el señor Andrés tiene el placer de invitarle a cenar. || *Passengers are requested not to alight between stops*, se ruega no bajen entre las paradas. || *To request sth. of s.o.*, pedir algo a alguien.
requiem ['rekwiəm] n. REL. Réquiem, *m.*
require [ri'kwaiə*] v. tr. Disponer, exigir: *the law requires that all criminals be punished*, la ley dispone que todos los criminales sean castigados. || Requerir, necesitar (to need): *this illness requires a lot of care*, esta enfermedad requiere muchos cuidados. || Exigir, requerir (to demand): *the circumstances require that a decision be taken at once*, las circunstancias exigen que se tome una decisión en seguida. || Desear (to desire). || — *If required*, si es preciso, en caso de necesidad. || *It required all my strength to move it*, necesité *or* tuve que aplicar toda mi fuerza para moverlo. || *The radiator requires constant filling*, hay que rellenar el radiador constantemente. || *To be required*, necesitarse, requerirse: *a great deal of application is required to study medicine*, para estudiar medicina se necesita mucha aplicación. || *To require s.o. to do sth.*, pedir a alguien que haga algo (to ask), exigir que alguien haga algo (to demand). || *We have all we require*, tenemos todo lo que nos hace falta. || *What do you require of me?*, ¿qué desean que haga yo? (what do you want me to do), ¿qué exigen de mí? (what do you demand of me). || *What is required to make an omelette?*, ¿qué hace falta para hacer una tortilla? || *What qualifications are required?*, ¿qué títulos se exigen? || *When required*, en caso de necesidad. || *Your presence is required*, se requiere su asistencia. || *Your presence will not be required*, su asistencia no es necesaria.
required [—d] adj. Requerido, da: *a table of the required height*, una mesa de la altura requerida. || Necesario, ria: *the required papers*, los documentos necesarios. || Obligatorio, ria (compulsory). || Prescrito, ta (fixed): *within the required time*, dentro del plazo prescrito.
requirement [—mənt] n. Requisito, *m.*: *it fulfils all the requirements*, satisface todos los requisitos; *the requirements include two foreign languages*, entre los requisitos figura el conocimiento de dos idiomas. || Necesidad, *f.* (need): *his requirements are very humble*, sus necesidades son muy modestas.
requirer [ri'kwairə*] n. Requeridor, ra.
requisite ['rekwizit] adj. See REQUIRED.
— N. Requisito, *m.*
requisition [ˌrekwi'ziʃən] n. Petición, *f.*, solicitud, *f.* (formal request). || MIL. Requisición, *f.*, requisa, *f.* || JUR. Requisitoria, *f.* || *To call into* o *to put in requisition*, requisar.
requisition [ˌrekwi'ziʃən] v. tr. Requisar: *to requisition vehicles*, requisar vehículos. || Requerir: *the householders were requisitioned to open their houses to refugees*, se requirió a los dueños de casas que acogiesen a los refugiados.
requital [ri'kwaitl] n. Desquite, *m.* (retaliation). || Compensación, *f.*, satisfacción, *f.*
requite [ri'kwait] v. tr. Desquitar: *to requite s.o. for breakage caused*, desquitar a alguien por los estropicios producidos. || Devolver: *to requite good for evil*, devolver bien por mal. || Corresponder a: *to requite s.o.'s love*, corresponder al amor de alguien. || Pagar: *she requites me with ingratitude*, me paga con ingratitud. || Desquitarse de, vengarse de (a wrong).
reread ['ri:'ri:d] v. tr. Releer, volver a leer.
rereading [—iŋ] n. Relectura, *f.*
reredos ['riədɔs] n. ARCH. Retablo, *m.*
reroute [ri'rut] v. tr. Cambiar el itinerario de.
rerun ['ri:'rʌn] n. CINEM. Reestreno, *m.*
rerun* ['ri:'rʌn] v. tr. CINEM. Reestrenar (a film).

— OBSERV. Pret. ***rer[illegible]n***; p.p. ***rerun***.

resale [ri:'seil] n. Reventa, *f.*
rescind [ri'sind] v. tr. Rescindir.
rescindable [—əbl] or **rescissible** [ri'sisəbl] adj. Rescindible.
rescission [ri'siʒən] n. Rescisión, *f.*
rescissory [ri'sisəri] adj. Rescisorio, ria.
rescript ['ri:skript] n. Rescripto, *m.* || Nueva redacción, *f.* (rewriting). || Nueva versión, *f.*
rescue ['reskju:] n. Rescate, *m.*, salvamento, *m.*: *rescue party, operations*, equipo, operaciones de salvamento; *rescue boat*, bote de salvamento. || *To go to the rescue of*, ir *or* acudir en auxilio de.
rescue ['reskju:] v. tr. Rescatar, salvar (a captive, a town, s.o. in danger). || FIG. Rescatar, salvar: *to rescue from oblivion*, rescatar del olvido.
rescuer [—ə*] n. Rescatador, ra; salvador, ra.
research [ri'sə:tʃ] n. Investigación, *f.*, investigaciones, *f. pl.*: *scientific research*, investigación científica. || Búsqueda, *f.*, busca, *f.* (search). || — *Market research*, estudio (*m.*) *or* investigación (*f.*) de mercados. || *Research establishment* o *centre*, instituto (*m.*) de investigación, centro (*m.*) de investigación. || *Research worker*, investigador, ra. || *To do the background research for an article*, documentarse para escribir un artículo (a reporter). || *To go into research*, dedicarse a la investigación.
research [ri'sə:tʃ] v. intr. Investigar. || *To research into*, investigar, efectuar investigaciones sobre.
researcher [—ə*] n. Investigador, ra.
reseat ['ri:'si:t] v. tr. TECH. Rectificar (valves). || Poner nuevo asiento en (a chair). || Sentar en otro sitio (a person).
resect [ri:'sekt] v. tr. MED. Resecar.
resection [ri:'sekʃən] n. MED. Resección, *f.*
reseda ['residə] n. BOT. Reseda, *f.*
resedaceae [ˌresi'deisii] pl. n. BOT. Resedáceas, *f.*
reseed ['ri:'si:d] v. tr. Replantar.
resell* ['ri:'sel] v. tr. Revender.

— OBSERV. Pret. & p. p. ***resold***.

reseller [—ə*] n. Revendedor, ra.
resemblance [ri'zembləns] n. Parecido, *m.* (between people). || Semejanza, *f.* (between things). || — *There is hardly any resemblance between them*, no se parecen casi nada. || *To bear a strong resemblance to s.o.*, parecerse mucho a alguien.
resemble [ri'zembl] v. tr. Parecerse a: *John resembles his brother*, Juan se parece a su hermano; *John and his brother resemble each other a great deal*, Juan y su hermano se parecen mucho.
resent [ri'zent] v. tr. Resentirse de: *I resent what you said*, me resiento de lo que dijiste. || Tomar a mal (to take badly). || Ofenderse por (to be offended). || Guardar rencor por (to bear a grudge).
resentful [—ful] adj. Resentido, da; ofendido, da.
resentment [—mənt] n. Resentimiento, *m.*, rencor, *m.* || *To hold resentment against* o *for s.o.*, guardar rencor a alguien.
reservable [ri'zə:vəbl] adj. Reservable.
reservation [ˌrezə'veiʃən] n. Reserva, *f.* [*Amer.*, reservación, *f.*] (act of booking). || Reserva, *f.* (seat, room, etc. booked). || Reserva, *f.* (for Indians). || Reserva, *f.*: *without reservation*, sin reserva; *mental reservation*, reserva mental. || JUR. Reserva, *f.*, salvedad, *f.* (in a contract). || REL. Reserva, *f.* || — *To receive a piece of news with reservation*, acoger una noticia con reservas. || *We've made the reservation*, hemos reservado las plazas.
reserve [ri'zə:v] n. Reserva, *f.* (of character, attitude): *without reserve*, sin reserva. || MIL. Reservista, *m.* || COMM. Reserva, *f.* || SP. Reserva, *m.* & *f.*, suplente, *m.* & *f.* || — *Cash reserves*, reservas en metálico. || *Game reserve*, coto (*m.*) de caza. || *In reserve*, en reserva, de reserva: *troops in reserve*, tropas de reserva; *provisions in reserve*, provisiones en reserva. || *Reserve supplies*, provisiones (*f.*) en *or* de reserva. || *To keep in reserve*, guardar en reserva.
reserve [ri'zə:v] v. tr. Reservar: *to reserve seats*, reservar asientos; *to reserve one's strength*, reservar sus fuerzas. || *To reserve one's judgment on*, reservarse el juicio acerca de.
reserved [—d] adj. Reservado, da. || *All rights reserved*, reservados todos los derechos, es propiedad.
reservedly [—dli] adv. Con reserva, reservadamente.
reservedness [—dnis] n. Reserva, *f.*
reservist [—ist] n. MIL. Reservista, *m.*

reservoir [ˈrezəvwɑ:*] n. Represa, *f.*, embalse, *m.* (artificial lake). || Depósito, *m.*, tanque, *m.*: *petrol reservoir*, depósito de gasolina.
reset* [ˈri:ˈset] v. tr. Poner en su sitio (to put in place). || Poner en hora (a watch). || MED. Encajar, volver a encajar (a bone). || Volver a engastar (jewel). || PRINT. Recomponer. || TECH. Reajustar.
— OBSERV. Pret. & p. p. **reset.**
resettle [ˈri:ˈsetl] v. tr. Volver a establecer (a person). || Colonizar de nuevo, volver a colonizar, repoblar (land).
— V. intr. Volver a establecerse.
resettlement [—mənt] n. Nueva colonización, *f.*, repoblación, *f.* (colonization). || Restablecimiento, *m.*
resew* [ˈri:ˈsəu] v. tr. Recoser.
— OBSERV. Pret. **resewed;** p. p. **resewed, resewn.**
reshape [ˈri:ˈʃeip] v. tr. Reformar, rehacer. || Reorganizar.
reship [ˈri:ˈʃip] v. tr. MAR. Reembarcar. || Reenviar, reexpedir (to forward).
— V. intr. MAR. Reembarcarse.
reshipment [—mənt] n. Reembarque, *m.* || Reenvío, *m.*, reexpedición, *f.* (forwarding).
reshuffle [ˈri:ˈʃʌfl] n. Reorganización, *f.* (of a government). || Nueva mezcla, *f.* (of cards).
reshuffle [ˈri:ˈʃʌfl] v. tr. Reorganizar (a goverment). || Volver a barajar (cards).
reside [riˈzaid] v. intr. Vivir, residir: *to reside in Paris*, residir en París. || FIG. Residir, radicar: *there resides the problem*, ahí reside el problema; *legislative power resides in Parliament*, el poder legislativo reside en el Parlamento.
residence [ˈrezidəns] n. Residencia, *f.* (building, action, etc.). || Permanencia, *f.*, residencia, *f.* (stay). || — *Hall of residence*, residencia. || *In residence*, en residencia. || *Official residence*, residencia oficial. || *Place of residence*, domicilio, *m.* (on forms). || *Residence permit*, permiso (*m.*) de residencia. || *To take up one's residence*, instalarse (in a house), establecer su residencia (in a country). || *Town and country residences for sale*, se venden fincas rústicas y urbanas.
residency [—i] n. Residencia, *f.*
resident [ˈrezidənt] adj./n. Residente. || Permanente (servant). || Interno, na (doctor). || — *Minister resident*, ministro (*m.*) residente. || *Resident population*, población fija. || *Spaniards resident in France*, los españoles residentes en Francia. || *To be resident in a town*, residir en una ciudad.
residential [ˌreziˈdenʃəl] adj. Residencial: *residential area*, barrio residencial.
residentiary [reziˈdenʃəri] adj. REL. Residente: *a canon residentiary*, un canónigo residente.
residual [riˈzidjuəl] adj. Residual.
— N. Residuo, *m.*
residuary [riˈzidjuəri] adj. Residual. || JUR. *Residuary legatee*, heredero (*m.*) universal.
residue [ˈrezidju:] n. Residuo, *m.* || JUR. Bienes (*m. pl.*) residuales.
residuum [riˈzidjuəm] n. Residuo, *m.* || JUR. Bienes (*m. pl.*) residuales.
— OBSERV. El plural de *residuum* es *residua.*
resign [ˈrizain] v. tr. Dimitir, renunciar: *to resign one's charge*, dimitir el cargo. || Renunciar a (task, claim, etc.): *to resign one's rights*, renunciar a sus derechos. || Ceder (to hand over). || *To resign o.s. to*, resignarse a, conformarse con: *to resign o.s. to one's fate*, resignarse *or* conformarse con su suerte.
— V. intr. Dimitir, presentar la dimisión: *the prime minister has resigned*, el primer ministro ha dimitido. || Abandonar (in chess).
resignation [ˌrezigˈneiʃən] n. Dimisión, *f.* (from a post). || Resignación, *f.*, conformidad, *f.* (conformity with a situation): *he accepted with resignation*, aceptó con resignación. || Renuncia, *f.* (*of*, a) [giving up]. || *To submit* o *to tender* o *to send in* o *to hand in one's resignation*, presentar la dimisión, dimitir.
resigned [riˈzaind] adj. Resignado, da: *to be resigned to*, estar resignado a.
resignedly [riˈzainədli] adv. Con resignación.
resignee [riˈzaini:] n. Resignatario, *m.*
resilience [riˈziliəns] or **resiliency** [—i] n. Elasticidad, *f.*, resiliencia, *f.* (of a body or material). || Resistencia, *f.* (of human body). || FIG. Fuerza (*f.*) moral (of temperament).
resilient [riˈziliənt] adj. Elástico, ca. || Resistente (human body). || De carácter fuerte.
resin [ˈrezin] n. Resina, *f.*
resinate [ˈrezineit] v. tr. Untar con resina.
resiner [ˈrezinə*] n. Resinero, *m.*
resinous [ˈrezinəs] adj. Resinoso, sa.
resist [riˈzist] v. tr. Resistir a: *to resist the enemy*, resistir al enemigo. || Resistir (to endure): *I cannot resist the heat as well as I could when I was young*, no puedo resistir el calor como cuando era joven; *asbestos resists the heat very well*, el amianto resiste muy bien el calor. || — *I can't resist chocolate*, me encanta el chocolate. || *I couldn't resist asking her*, no pude resistir la tentación de preguntárselo. || *No man could resist her*, no había hombre que se le resistiera. || *To resist temptation*, resistir [a] la tentación.
— V. intr. Resistir: *Madrid resisted for three years*, Madrid resistió durante tres años.
resistance [—əns] n. Resistencia, *f.*: *passive resistance*, resistencia pasiva. || TECH. Resistencia, *f.* || — *French Resistance*, Resistencia francesa. || MIL. *Resistance fighter*, resistente, *m.* || *Resistance thermometer*, termómetro de resistencia. || *To offer* o *to put up resistance*, oponer resistencia, resistir. || *To take the line of least resistance*, seguir la ley del mínimo esfuerzo, optar por lo más fácil (to take the easy way).
resistant [—ənt] adj./n. Resistente.
resistible [—əbl] adj. Resistible.
resistive [—iv] adj. Resistente.
resistivity [riˌzisˈtiviti] n. ELECTR. Resistividad, *f.*
resistless [riˈzistlis] adj. Incontenible, irresistible (tears, laugh). || Ineluctable (unavoidable). || Sin defensa, indefenso, sa (defenceless): *a resistless old man*, un anciano sin defensa.
resistor [riˈzistə*] n. ELECTR. Reóstato, *m.*
resold [ˈri:ˈsəuld] pret. & p. p. See RESELL.
resole [ˈri:ˈsəul] v. tr. Poner medias suelas a (to put stick-on soles on). || Remontar (to remake the sole of).
resoluble [riˈzɔljubl] adj. Soluble, resoluble.
resolute [ˈrezəlu:t] adj. Resuelto, ta; determinado, da.
resoluteness [—nis] n. Resolución, *f.*, determinación, *f.*
resolution [ˌrezəˈlu:ʃən] n. Resolución, *f.* (resoluteness). || Resolución, *f.*, propósito, *m.*: *good resolutions*, buenos propósitos. || Resolución, *f.* (proposal): *draft joint resolution*, proyecto (*m.*) de resolución común. || — *To make a resolution*, tomar una resolución. || *To oppose a resolution*, oponerse a una resolución. || *To show resolution*, mostrarse resuelto.
resolutive [ˈrezəljutiv] or **resolutory** [ˈrezəljutəri] adj. JUR. Resolutorio, ria.
resolvable [riˈzɔlvəbl] adj. Soluble, resoluble.
resolve [riˈzɔlv] n. Resolución, *f.* || *To make a resolve to*, resolverse a, decidir.
resolve [riˈzɔlv] v. tr. Resolver, solucionar (a problem). || Resolver, disipar (a doubt). || Resolver, decidir: *to resolve to leave*, resolver marcharse. || MATH. CHEM. PHYS. MED. Resolver. || FIG. *To resolve into*, convertir en.
— V. intr. Resolverse. || MED. Resolverse. || Resolver, decidir, acordar (to decide). || *To resolve upon* o *on*, decidirse por (with noun), decidirse a (with verb): *they resolved on going*, se decidieron a ir.
resolved [riˈzɔlvd] adj. Resuelto, ta.
resolvent [riˈzɔlvənt] adj. MED. Resolutivo, va.
— N. MED. Resolutivo, *m.*
resonance [ˈreznəns] n. Resonancia, *f.*
resonant [ˈreznənt] adj. Resonante.
resonate [ˈrezɔneit] v. intr. Resonar.
resonator [—ə*] n. Resonador, *m.*
resorb [riˈsɔ:b] v. tr. Resorber.
resorption [riˈsɔ:pʃən] n. Resorción, *f.*
resort [riˈzɔ:t] n. Estación, *f.*: *seaside resort*, estación balnearia; *winter resort*, estación de invierno; *summer resort*, estación veraniega. || Centro, *m.*: *holiday resort* o *tourist resort*, centro de turismo. || Recurso, *m.*: *as a last resort*, como último recurso. || — *A resort for beggars and thieves*, un lugar frecuentado por mendigos y ladrones. || *To have resort to*, recurrir a. || *Without resort to violence*, sin recurrir a la violencia.
resort [riˈzɔ:t] v. intr. Recurrir: *to resort to torture*, recurrir a la tortura. || Acudir a, frecuentar: *the people resort to church*, la gente acude a la iglesia.
resound [riˈzaund] v. tr. Ensalzar, cantar: *to resound the glory of a nation*, cantar la gloria de una nación.
— V. intr. Resonar: *her shout resounded in the empty street*, su grito resonó en la calle desierta; *the streets resounded with joyful shouting*, gritos de alegría resonaban por las calles. || FIG. Tener resonancias: *a discovery which was to resound the world over*, un descubrimiento que tendría resonancia en el mundo entero.
resounding [—iŋ] adj. Resonante, clamoroso, sa: *a resounding victory*, un triunfo resonante. || Retumbante: *resounding thunder*, trueno retumbante. || Sonoro, ra: *a resounding voice*, una voz sonora. || Tremendo, da: *a resounding blow*, un golpe tremendo.
resource [riˈsɔ:s] n. Recurso, *m.*, medio, *m.* (expedient). || Habilidad, *f.*, recursos, *m. pl.*, inventiva, *f.*, ingenio, *m.* (skill, resourcefulness). || — Pl. Distracciones, *f.* (amusements). || Recursos, *m.*: *to be without resources*, estar sin recursos; *natural resources*, recursos naturales; *untapped resources*, recursos sin explotar. || Reserva, *f. sing.* (of energy). || *To be at the end of one's resources*, haber agotado todos los recursos.
resourceful [—ful] adj. Ingenioso, sa; despabilado, da; listo, ta.
resourcefulness [—fulnis] n. Recursos, *m. pl.*, inventiva, *f.*, habilidad, *f.*, ingenio, *m.*: *to show great resourcefulness in handling a matter*, demostrar gran habilidad en el manejo de un negocio.
respect [risˈpekt] n. Respeto, *m.*: *lack of respect*, falta de respeto; *to have great respect for s.o.*, tenerle mucho respeto a alguien. || Consideración, *f.* (consideration). || Respecto, *m.*: *with respect to what you were saying*, con respecto a lo que estaba diciendo; *in this respect*, a este respecto. || Aspecto, *m.*, punto (*m.*) de vista: *in every respect*, en todos los aspectos, desde todos los puntos de vista; *in no respect*, en ningún aspecto. || — Pl. Respetos, *m.*, recuerdos, *m.*: *give him my respects*, preséntale mis respetos. || —

I have the greatest respect for your opinion, but..., tengo el mayor respeto por su opinión, pero... || *In other respect*, por otro lado. || *In respect of*, respecto a *or* de. || *In that respect*, en cuanto a eso. || *Out of respect for*, en consideración a, por respeto a. || *To command respect*, infundir respeto. || *To hold in respect*, tener estima a, respetar. || *To pay one's respects to*, presentar sus respetos a. || *To pay respect to*, tomar en consideración. || *To show no respect for s.o.*, no tener ningún respeto a alguien. || *With all due respect*, con el respeto debido. || *Without respect of persons*, sin acepción de personas.

respect [ris'pekt] v. tr. Respetar. || — *As respects...*, por lo que respecta a... || *My respected colleague*, mi estimado colega. || *To make o.s. respected*, hacerse respetar.

respectability [ris,pektə'biliti] n. Respetabilidad, *f.*

respectable [ris'pektəbl] adj. Respetable: *a respectable person, place*, una persona, un sitio respetable; *a respectable sum of money*, una suma respetable de dinero. || Decente, respetable (decent). || Decente: *a respectable performance*, una representación decente. || *To keep at a respectable distance*, mantener a una distancia respetable *or* prudencial.

respectful [ris'pektful] adj. Respetuoso, sa.

respectfully [—i] adv. Respetuosamente. || *Yours respectfully*, le saluda respetuosamente.

respectfulness [—nis] n. Respetuosidad, *f.*

respecting [ris'pektiŋ] prep. Respecto a, con respecto a, en cuanto a.

respective [ris'pektiv] adj. Respectivo, va: *they went off with their respective girlfriends*, se fueron con sus novias respectivas.

respectively [—li] adv. Respectivamente.

respell* ['ri:'spel] v. tr. Volver a deletrear (to spell again). || Transcribir fonéticamente (in phonetics).

— OBSERV. El pretérito y el participio pasivo de *to respell* son irregulares ***(respelt)***. Además de éstos, en Estados Unidos se usa también la forma ***respelled***.

respelt [—t] pret. & p. p. See RESPELL.

respirable ['respirəbl] adj. Respirable.

respiration [,respə'reiʃən] n. Respiración, *f.*

respirator ['respəreitə*] n. MED. Respirador, *m.* || Careta, *f.*, mascarilla, *f.* (for filtering air). || Careta (*f.*) antigás (gas mask).

respiratory [ris'paiərətəri] adj. Respiratorio, ria.

respire [ris'paiə*] v. tr./intr. Respirar.

respite ['respait] n. Respiro, *m.*, tregua, *f.*: *to work without respite*, trabajar sin respiro; *the pain does not give him a moment's respite*, el dolor no le deja ni un momento de respiro. || Prórroga, *f.*, plazo, *m.* (postponement of an obligation). || Suspensión, *f.* (of a sentence).

respite ['respait] v. tr. Prorrogar, aplazar. || Suspender (a sentence).

resplendence [ris'plendəns] or **resplendency** [—i] n. Resplandor, *m.*

resplendent [ris'plendənt] adj. Resplandeciente. || *To be resplendent*, resplandecer, ser resplandeciente.

respond [ris'pɔnd] n. ARCH. Ménsula, *f.* || REL. Responsorio, *m.*

respond [ris'pɔnd] v. intr. Contestar, responder (to reply). || Responder: *the patient responded to treatment*, el enfermo respondió al tratamiento. || Reaccionar (to react). || Ser sensible a (to be sensitive to). || REL. Contestar (to make a response).

respondent [—ənt] n. JUR. Demandado, da (a defendant).

response [ris'pɔns] n. Contestación, *f.*, respuesta, *f.* (reply): *he made no response*, no dio contestación. || Acogida, *f.*: *the response to a charity campaign*, la acogida de una campaña de caridad. || Reacción, *f.*: *his response to the treatment is satisfactory*, su reacción al tratamiento es satisfactoria; *his question met with no response*, su pregunta no suscitó ninguna reacción. || REL. Contestación, *f.* (words said in answer to the priest). | Responsorio, *m.* (responsory). || — *In response to*, en *or* como respuesta a. || *The response to the appeal has been poor*, la llamada ha suscitado poco interés, la llamada no ha sido acogida con mucho entusiasmo.

responsibility [ris,pɔnsə'biliti] n. Responsabilidad, *f.*: *to take the responsibility of*, asumir la responsabilidad de; *on one's own responsibility*, bajo su propia responsabilidad. || Seriedad, *f.*, formalidad, *f.* (responsible behaviour). || — *That's not my responsibility*, eso no es cosa mía *or* asunto mío. || *The decision is your responsibility*, le incumbe a Ud. decidir, le corresponde a Ud. decidir.

responsible [ris'pɔnsəbl] adj. Responsable: *to be responsible for*, ser responsable de; *a responsible person*, una persona responsable; *those responsible*, los responsables; *to be responsible to s.o.*, ser responsable ante alguien. || De responsabilidad: *a responsible position*, un cargo de responsabilidad.

responsibly [—i] adv. Con seriedad, con formalidad.

responsive [ris'pɔnsiv] adj. Sensible: *responsive to sympathy*, sensible a la simpatía; *a responsive engine*, un motor sensible. || *They weren't very responsive*, no demostraron mucho interés.

responsiveness [—nis] n. Sensibilidad, *f.* (sensitivity). || Interés, *m.* (interest).

responsory [ris'pɔnsəri] n. REL. Responsorio, *m.*

rest [rest] n. Descanso, *m.*: *a five minute rest*, un descanso de cinco minutos; *day of rest*, día de descanso; *eternal rest*, descanso eterno. || Reposo, *m.*, descanso, *m.*: *to enjoy a well-earned rest*, gozar de un bien merecido descanso; *half an hour's rest after dinner*, media hora de reposo después de la cena. || MUS. Pausa, *f.*, silencio, *m.* (period of silence, symbol thereof). || Cesura, *f.* (in poetry). || Pausa, *f.* (in speech). || Taquera, *f.* (for billiard cue). || Apoyo, *m.*: *the tree made a rest for his back*, el árbol le sirvió de apoyo. || Tranquilidad, *f.*, sosiego, *m.*: *I shall have no rest until I find the solution*, no tendré un momento de tranquilidad hasta que encuentre la solución. || Resto, *m.*: *the rest of the day*, el resto del día. || Resto, *m.*, lo demás: *take some and leave the rest*, toma un poco y deja el resto; *I'll tell you the rest*, le contaré lo demás. || Los demás, las demás, los otros, las otras: *the rest of them didn't mind*, a los otros les daba igual; *the rest of the women*, las otras *or* las demás mujeres; *we went and the rest stayed*, nosotros fuimos y los demás se quedaron. || Ristre, *m.* (of lance). || COMM. Reserva, *f.* || TECH. Base, *f.* (base). | Soporte, *m.* (support). | Horquilla, *f.* (of telephone). || — *After a good night's rest*, después de haber pasado una buena noche. || *All he needs is a good night's rest*, lo que le hace falta es dormir bien una noche. || *Arm rest*, brazo, *m.* (of chair). || *As for the rest*, por lo demás. || *At rest*, parado da: *the train was at rest*, el tren estaba parado; quieto, ta (motionless), tranquilo, la (quiet), en reposo: *a body at rest*, un cuerpo en reposo; en paz: *he is at rest with his family*, descansa en paz con su familia. || *Back rest*, respaldo, *m.* || MED. *Complete rest*, reposo absoluto. || *Have a good night's rest!*, ¡que descanse! || *Rest cure*, cura (*f.*) de reposo. || *To come to rest*, pararse (to stop), venir a parar *or* a pararse (car, bird, arrow, etc.). || *To give a rest*, dejar descansar. || *To have a rest*, descansar. || *To lay to rest*, enterrar. || *To put* o *to set s.o.'s mind at rest*, tranquilizar a alguien. || *To take a rest*, descansar un rato. || *To try and get a little rest*, intentar descansar *or* dormir un poco.

rest [rest] v. intr. Pararse (to stop): *the ball rested at the edge of the hole*, la pelota se paró al borde del agujero. || Descansar: *to rest after a day's work*, descansar después de un día de trabajo; *to rest in peace*, descansar en paz. || Descansar, reposar: *you have to rest after meals*, tienes que reposar después de las comidas. || Descansar: *the vase rests on a marble column*, el florero descansa sobre una columna de mármol. || Depender de: *the decision rests on his testimony*, la decisión depende de su testimonio; *it rests with France*, depende de Francia. || Quedar: *there the matter rests*, allí queda el asunto. || Radicar, estribar, basarse: *his fame rests in his books*, su fama radica en sus libros; *in this rests the problem*, en esto radica el problema. || Pesar sobre: *a great responsibility rests on his shoulders*, una gran responsabilidad pesa sobre él. || Quedarse tranquilo, descansar: *I can't rest till I find the answer*, no me quedaré tranquilo *or* no descansaré mientras no encuentre la solución. || AGR. Descansar: *to leave ground to rest*, dejar descansar la tierra. || JUR. Terminar su alegato. || — FIG. *His eyes rested on the object*, fijó la mirada en el objeto, sus ojos se posaron en el objeto. | *Let it rest*, déjalo estar. | *Rest assured that*, tenga la seguridad de que. | *To rest easy*, dormir tranquilo. | *To rest on one's oars* o *on one's laurels*, dormirse en los laureles.

— V. tr. Apoyar: *to rest a ladder against a wall*, apoyar una escalera contra una pared. || Apoyar, descansar: *to rest one's head on s.o.'s shoulder*, descansar la cabeza en el hombro de alguien. || Descansar: *to rest one's feet*, descansar los pies; *these sunglasses rest my eyes*, estas gafas de sol me descansan la vista. || Dejar descansar: *to rest a player*, dejar descansar a un jugador. || Basar: *to rest one's case on the insanity of the accused*, basar la defensa en la enajenación mental del acusado. || Poner (hopes). || — *God rest his soul*, que Dios le tenga en su gloria. || JUR. *To rest one's case*, terminar su alegato. || *To rest one's eyes on*, fijar la mirada en.

restart ['ri:'stɑ:t] v. tr. Volver a poner en marcha (motor, etc.). || Volver a empezar (to begin again).

— V. intr. Volver a arrancar (motor). || Volver a empezar.

restate ['ri:'steit] v. tr. Volver a exponer (case, theory). || Volver a plantear (problem). || Repetir (to repeat).

restatement [—mənt] n. Nueva exposición, *f.* || Nuevo planteamiento, *m.* (of problem). || Repetición, *f.*

restaurant ['restərɔ̃:ŋ] n. Restaurante, *m.*, restaurant, *m.*, restorán, *m.* || *Restaurant car*, coche (*m.*) restaurante.

restaurateur [,restɔrə'tə:*] n. Dueño (*m.*) de un restaurante.

restful ['restful] adj. Descansado, da; tranquilo, la; reposado, da: *restful holidays*, vacaciones descansadas.

restharrow [rest,hærəu] n. BOT. Gatuña, *f.*

rest home ['resthəum] n. Casa (*f.*) de reposo (for rest cures). || Asilo (*m.*) de ancianos (old people's home).

resting-place ['restiŋpleis] n. Lugar (*m.*) de descanso. || Última morada, *f.* (of the dead).

restitute ['resti,tju:t] v. tr. Restituir.

restitution [ˌresti'tju:ʃən] n. Restitución, *f.* || Indemnización, *f.*
restive ['restiv] adj. Intranquilo, la; inquieto, ta (uneasy). || Repropio, pia (horse).
restiveness [—nis] n. Inquietud, *f.*, intranquilidad, *f.* (uneasiness). || Impaciencia, *f.* (impatience). || Agitación, *f.* (agitation).
restless ['restlis] adj. Agitado, da; inquieto, ta: *a restless sea*, un mar agitado. || Intranquilo, la; agitado, da; inquieto, ta; desasosegado, da: *a restless person*, una persona intranquila; *a restless night*, una noche agitada. || Descontento, ta (discontented). || — *The guests are getting restless*, los invitados se están impacientando. || *The students are restless*, los estudiantes se están agitando. || *To be restless to do sth.*, impacientarse por hacer algo. || *To be the restless kind*, no poder estarse quieto.
restlessly [—li] adv. Con impaciencia, nerviosamente (impatiently). || Con inquietud, nerviosamente (worriedly). || *To toss and turn restlessly in one's bed*, agitarse *or* dar vueltas en la cama.
restlessness [—nis] n. Impaciencia, *f.* (impatience). || Inquietud, *f.*, desasosiego, *m.* (worry). || Agitación, *f.* (agitation). || Descontento, *m.* (discontent). || Insomnio, *m.* (sleeplessness).
restock ['ri:'stɔk] v. tr. Repoblar (with animals, trees). || Reabastecer (shop with provisions).
— V. intr. Reponer las existencias.
restorable [ris'tɔ:rəbl] adj. Rehabilitable.
restoration [ˌrestə'reiʃən] n. Restauración, *f.* (reparation, reestablishment): *restoration of a painting, of the monarchy*, restauración de un cuadro, de la monarquía. || Restitución, *f.*, devolución, *f.* (giving back). || Reintegración, *f.*, restitución, *f.* (returning to original rank, role). || Restablecimiento, *m.*: *restoration of peace*, restablecimiento de la paz. || HIST. *The Restoration*, la Restauración.
restorative [ris'tɔrətiv] adj. Reconstituyente, fortificante.
— N. Reconstituyente, *m.*, fortificante, *m.*
restore [ris'tɔ:*] v. tr. Restituir, devolver: *to restore sth. to its owner*, restituir algo a su dueño. || Restaurar (painting, building, monarch). || Reconstituir (a text). || Reintegrar, restablecer (to bring back to a previous rank or position). || Devolver: *to restore s.o. to health*, devolver la salud a alguien; *to restore s.o. to liberty*, devolverle a alguien la libertad. || Restablecer: *to restore order*, restablecer el orden; *to restore old customs*, restablecer viejas costumbres. || Volver a poner (to put back into place).
restorer [—rə*] n. Restaurador, ra (one who restores). || Tónico, *m.*: *hair restorer*, tónico capilar. || Reconstituyente, *m.* (reconstituent).
restrain [ris'trein] v. tr. Impedir (to prevent). || Limitar, frenar, restringir (to limit). || Contener, reprimir, refrenar (to repress): *he restrained his anger*, reprimió su cólera. || Recluir, encerrar (to confine).
restrainable [—əbl] adj. Restringible.
restrainedly [—dli] adv. Comedidamente.
restraint [ris'treint] n. Restricción, *f.*: *restraint of trade*, restricción del comercio. || Limitación, *f.* (limitation). || Traba, *f.* (hindrance). || Represión, *f.* (of one's feelings). || Moderación, *f.*, reserva, *f.*, comedimiento, *m.*: *lack of restraint*, falta de moderación. || Dominio (*m.*) de sí mismo (self-control). || Internamiento, *m.*, reclusión, *f.* (confinement). || — *To put under restraint*, internar, recluir, encerrar. || *Without restraint*, libremente, sin restricción.
restrict [ris'trikt] v. tr. Restringir, limitar (to limit). || — *To restrict o.s. to the main points*, limitarse a los puntos principales. || *Use of the library is restricted to teachers*, sólo los profesores pueden utilizar la biblioteca, la biblioteca está reservada a los profesores.
restricted [—id] adj. Restringido, da; limitado, da (limited). || Estrecho, cha (mentality, outlook). || *Restricted area*, zona (*f.*) de velocidad limitada (speed limit), zona prohibida [a ciertas personas] (security zone).
restriction [ris'trikʃən] n. Restricción, *f.*, limitación, *f.*
restrictive [ris'triktiv] adj. Restrictivo, va.
rest room ['restru:m] n. Aseos, *m. pl.*, lavabos, *m. pl.*, tocador, *m.*
result [ri'zʌlt] n. Resultado, *m.*: *the result of the experiment*, el resultado del experimento; *the election results*, los resultados de las elecciones; *the exam results*, los resultados de los exámenes. || Resultado, *m.*, consecuencia, *f.*: *his action had grave results*, su acción tuvo consecuencias graves. || SP. MATH. Resultado, *m.* || — *As a result of*, a *or* como consecuencia de, a causa de. || *With the result that*, con el resultado de que.
result [ri'zʌlt] v. intr. Resultar: *it resulted badly*, resultó mal.
— ***To result from***, derivarse de: *the consequences resulting from an act*, las consecuencias que se derivan de un acto; resultar de: *the misery that results from warfare*, la miseria que resulta de la guerra; *it results from this that...*, de ello resulta que... | Ser causado *or* producido por (to be produced by): *his death resulted from a fall*, su muerte fue provocada por una caída. || ***To result in***, tener por *or* como resultado: *the election resulted in an opposition victory*, las elecciones tuvieron por resultado la victoria de la oposición. | Tener como resultado, conducir a: *the modernization resulted in increased productivity*, la modernización condujo a un aumento de la productividad. | Conducir *or* llevar a: *the negotiations resulted in an agreement*, las negociaciones condujeron a un acuerdo. | Dar resultado: *it resulted in nothing*, no dio ningún resultado. | Ser: *the expedition resulted in a failure*, la expedición fue un fracaso. | — *The illness resulted in his death*, murió a consecuencia de la enfermedad.
resultant [—ənt] adj. Resultante.
— N. Resultante, *f.*
resultful [—ful] adj. Fructuoso, sa.
resume [ri'zju:m] v. tr. Volver a tomar (to take again). || Reasumir (one's duties): *to resume command*, reasumir el mando. || Recuperar (a territory, etc.). || Reanudar (a journey, job, etc.): *to resume talks*, reanudar las conversaciones. || Continuar, seguir: *to resume one's speech*, seguir su discurso. || Resumir (to sum up): *to resume the main points of a debate*, resumir los puntos principales de un debate. || *To resume one's seat*, volver a sentarse.
— V. intr. Reanudar sus trabajos. || Proseguir (to take up an interrupted discourse).
résumé ['rezju:mei] n. Resumen, *m.* (summary). || U. S. Curriculum vitae, *m.*
resumption [ri'zʌmpʃən] n. Reanudación, *f.* (of talks, work, etc.). || Reasunción, *f.* (of office). || Continuación, *f.* || *Upon the resumption of talks*, al reanudarse las conversaciones.
resurface ['ri:'sə:fis] v. tr. Rehacer el firme de (road). || Revestir (floors, walls, etc.).
— V. intr. Volver a salir a la superficie (submarine).
resurgence [ri'sə:dʒəns] n. Resurgimiento, *m.*, resurrección, *f.*
resurgent [ri':sə:dʒənt] adj. Que resurge. || Renaciente.
resurrect [ˌrezə'rekt] v. tr. Resucitar (to bring back to life). || FIG. Resucitar (old stories, customs, etc.).
— V. intr. Resucitar.
resurrection [ˌrezə'rekʃən] n. Resurrección, *f.* || REL. *The Resurrection*, la Resurrección.
resuscitate [ri'sʌsiteit] v. tr./intr. Resucitar.
resuscitation [riˌsʌsi'teiʃən] n. MED. Resucitación, *f.*
ret [ret] v. tr. Enriar (flax).
retable [ri'teibl] n. REL. Retablo, *m.*
retail ['ri:teil] n. Venta (*f.*) al por menor, venta (*f.*) al detall.
— Adj./adv. Al por menor, al detall. || *Retail dealer*, detallista, *m.* & *f.*, minorista, *m.* & *f.*, comerciante (*m.* & *f.*) al por menor.
retail [ri:'teil] v. tr. Vender al por menor, vender al detall (to sell goods). || Repetir (gossip).
— V. intr. Venderse al por menor, venderse al detall: *these goods retail at five pounds each*, estos artículos se venden al por menor a cinco libras la unidad.
retailer [—ə*] n. Detallista, *m.* & *f.*, minorista, *m.* & *f.*, comerciante (*m.* & *f.*) al por menor.
retain [ri'tein] v. tr. Conservar: *he retained his British sense of humour to the end*, conservó el sentido del humor británico hasta el final. || Retener: *a dyke to retain water*, un dique para retener el agua. || Recordar, acordarse de, retener: *I have great difficulty in retaining names*, tengo mucha dificultad en recordar los nombres. || Contratar: *to retain s.o.'s services*, contratar los servicios de alguien. || Quedarse con (to keep).
retainer [—ə*] n. Dispositivo (*m.*) de retención (device for retaining). || Criado, da (servant). || Partidario, ria (follower). || JUR. Anticipo (*m.*) sobre los honorarios (of a barrister). || U. S. Contrato (*m.*) con un abogado.
retaining fee [—iŋfi:] n. Anticipo, *m.*
retaining wall [—iŋwɔ:l] n. Muro (*m.*) de contención.
retake ['ri:teik] n. CINEM. Repetición (*f.*) de la toma, nueva toma, *f.* [de una escena].
retake* ['ri:'teik] v. tr. Volver a tomar, recuperar: *the army retook the fortress*, el ejército volvió a tomar la fortaleza. || Capturar [de nuevo], [volver a] capturar: *the fugitive was retaken*, capturaron al fugitivo. || CINEM. Volver a rodar *or* a tomar (a scene in a film).
— OBSERV. Pret. ***retook;*** p. p. ***retaken.***
retaken [—ən] p. p. See RETAKE.
retaliate [ri'tælieit] v. tr. Devolver (blow, insult, etc.).
— V. intr. Vengarse, tomar represalias: *he is a person who won't retaliate*, es el tipo de persona que no toma represalias. || Desquitarse, vengarse: *he retaliated with a blow*, se desquitó con un golpe.
retaliation [riˌtæli'eiʃən] n. Venganza, *f.*, desquite, *m.* (revenge). || Represalias, *f. pl.* (retaliatory measures). || *In retaliation*, para vengarse, para desquitarse, como represalias.
retaliative [ri'tæliˌeitiv] adj. Vengativo, va.
retaliatory [ri'tæliətəri] adj. Vengativo, va. || — *A retaliatory bombardment*, un bombardeo de represalias. || *To take retaliatory measures*, tomar *or* ejercer represalias.
retard [ri'tɑ:d] v. tr. Retrasar, retardar: *the storm retarded his arrival by an hour*, la tormenta retrasó su llegada en una hora.
— V. intr. Retrasar, atrasar (sth.). || Tardar (s.o.).
retardation [ˌri:tɑ:'deiʃən] n. Retraso, *m.*, atraso, *m.* || MED. Atraso (*m.*) mental.

retardative [riˈtɑːdətiv] adj. Que retarda. || Retardatriz (force).
retarded [riˈtɑːdid] adj. Atrasado, da. || *Mentally retarded person*, atrasado (*m.*) mental.
retch [retʃ] n. Náusea, *f.*, basca, *f.*
retch [retʃ] v. intr. Tener náuseas.
retell* [ˈriːˈtel] v. tr. Volver a contar.
— OBSERV. Pret. & p. p. ***retold***.
retention [riˈtenʃən] n. Retención, *f.* || Retentiva, *f.*, memoria, *f.* (memory).
retentive [riˈtentiv] adj. Retentivo, va. || Bueno, na (memory). || *To be retentive of sth*, recordar algo, acordarse de algo.
retentiveness [—nis] n. Retentiva, *f.*
retesting [ˈriːˈtestiŋ] n. Reensayo, *m.* (machine).
rethink* [ˈriːˈθiŋk] v. tr. Volver a pensar.
— OBSERV. Pret. & p.p. ***rethought***.
reticence [ˈretisəns] n. Reserva, *f.*
reticent [ˈretisent] adj. Reservado, da. || *To be reticent about sth.*, no querer revelar nada sobre algo.
reticle [ˈretikl] n. Retícula, *f.*, retículo, *m.*
reticular [reˈtikjulə*] adj. Reticular.
reticulate [riˈtikjuleit] v. tr. Dar forma de red a (to give sth. the form of a net).
— V. intr. Esta dividido en forma de red.
reticulated [—id] adj. Reticulado, da.
reticule [ˈretikjuːl] n. Retícula, *f.*, retículo, *m.* (reticle). || Ridículo, *m.* (small handbag).
reticulum [reˈtikjuləm] n. ZOOL. Redecilla, *f.*, retículo, *m.* (in ruminants). || BIOL. Retículo, *m.* (network structure in cells).
— OBSERV. El plural de *reticulum* es *reticula*.
retile [ˈriːˈtail] v. tr. Retejar.
retin [ˈriːˈtin] v. tr. Restañar.
retina [ˈretinə] n. ANAT. Retina, *f.*
— OBSERV. El plural de la palabra inglesa es *retinas* o *retinae*.
retinal [—l] adj. Retiniano, na; retinal.
retinitis [ˌretiˈnaitis] n. MED. Retinitis, *f.*
retinning [riːtiniŋ] n. Restañadura, *f.*, restañamiento, *m.*
retinue [ˈretinjuː] n. Séquito, *m.*, comitiva, *f.*
retire [riˈtaiə*] v. intr. Jubilarse (from a job, occupation). || Retirarse (soldier, trader). || Retirarse (to draw back, to seek privacy, etc.). || Abandonar, retirarse (from a race). || Dimitir (to resign). || Recogerse (to go to bed). || MIL. Replegarse, retirarse (troops). || *To retire into o.s.*, recogerse en sí mismo.
— V. tr. COMM. Retirar (to withdraw). || Jubilar (a civilian). || Retirar (a soldier). || Retirer (bank notes from circulation). || *To apply to be retired on a pension*, pedir la jubilación (civilian), pedir el retiro (soldier).
retired [—d] adj. Retirado, da (soldier, trader): *retired officer*, oficial retirado. || Jubilado, da (civilian): *retired civil servant*, funcionario jubilado. || Retirado, da (life). || Retirado, da; apartado, da: *a retired corner of the garden*, un apartado rincón del jardín. || — *A retired person*, un jubilado (civilian), un retirado (soldier, trader). || *Retired list*, escalafón (*f.*) de retirados. || *Retired pay*, retiro, *m.* (of soldier), jubilación, *f.* (of civilian).
retiredness [—dnis] n. Vida (*f.*) retirada. || Amor (*m.*) a la soledad. || Reserva, *f.*
retirement [—mənt] n. Retiro, *m.* (of soldiers, traders): *to reach retirement age*, llegar a la edad del retiro. || Jubilación, *f.* (from a job). || MIL. Retirada, *f.*, repliegue, *m.* (of troops). || Abandono, *m.* (from a race). || Retirada, *f.* (of an actor). || FIG. Recogimiento, *m.* (of a person). || *To live in retirement*, vivir apartado del mundo.
retiring [—riŋ] n. Retraído, da; tímido, da; reservado, da (reserved). || Saliente: *the retiring president*, el presidente saliente. || De jubilación, de retiro (pension).
retold [ˈriːˈtəuld] pret. & p. p. See RETELL.
retook [ˈriːˈtuk] pret. See RETAKE.
retort [riˈtɔːt] n. CHEM. Retorta, *f.* || Réplica, *f.* (reply).
retort [riˈtɔːt] v. tr. Devolver (an insult). || Replicar: *why should I?, he retorted*, ¿por qué yo?, replicó. || CHEM. Destilar en retortas.
retortion [riˈtɔːʃən] n. Retorcimiento, *m.*, retorcedura, *f.* (bending back). || Retorsión, *f.*, represalia, *f.* (retaliation).
retouch [ˈriːˈtʌtʃ] n. Retoque, *m.* (a retouching). || Fotografía (*f.*) retocada (retouched photo).
retouch [ˈriːˈtʌtʃ] v. tr. Retocar.
retoucher [—ə*] n. PHOT. Retocador, ra.
retrace [riˈtreis] v. tr. Volver a trazar, repasar (to go over again). || Reconstruir, reconstituir: *to retrace s.o.'s past*, reconstituir el pasado de alguien. || Remontarse a: *to retrace one's childhood*, remontarse a la niñez. || *To retrace one's steps*, desandar lo andado, volver sobre sus pasos.
retract [riˈtrækt] v. tr. Retractar, retirar (a promise, statement). || ZOOL. Meter, encoger (the head, body or limbs). | Retraer (the claws). || TECH. Replegar (the undercarriage, wheels, etc.).
— V. intr. Retraerse, encogerse (to draw back). || Retractarse, desdecirse (to recant). || ZOOL. Meterse, encogerse (head, body or limbs). | Retraerse (claws). || TECH. Replegarse, meterse (wheels, etc.).
retractable [—əbl] adj. Retractable. || Replegable, retráctil (the undercarriage, wheels).
retractation [ˌriːtrækˈteiʃən] n. Retractación, *f.*
retractile [riˈtræktail] adj. Retráctil.
retractility [ˌritrækˈtiliti] n. Retractilidad, *f.*
retracting [riˈtræktiŋ] adj. Retráctil.
retraction [riˈtrækʃən] n. Retracción, *f.* (of claws, wheels, etc.). || Retractación, *f.* (of claim, promise, etc.).
retractive [riˈtræktiv] adj. Retractor, ra.
retractor [riˈtræktə*] n. Músculo (*m.*) retractor, retractor, *m.* || MED. Retractor, *m.* (instrument).
retrain [ˈriːˈtrein] v. tr. Reconvertir (workers).
retraining [—iŋ] n. Reconversión, *f.* (for another job). || Curso (*m.*) de perfeccionamiento (refresher course).
retral [ˈriːtrəl] adj. Posterior.
retransmission [ˌriˈtrɑːnsˈmiʃən] n. RAD. Retransmisión, *f.*
retread [ˈriːˈtred] n. Neumático (*m.*) recauchutado.
re-tread* [ˈriːˈtred] v. tr. Pisar de nuevo. || Seguir de nuevo (a path). || Volver a (a place).
— OBSERV. Pret. ***re-trod;*** p. p. ***re-trodden, re-trod.***
retread [ˈriːˈtred] v. tr. Recauchutar (a tyre).
— OBSERV. Este verbo, a diferencia de su homónimo anterior, es regular.
retreading [—iŋ] n. Recauchutado, *m.*
retreat [riˈtriːt] n. MIL. Retirada, *f.* (from battle, territory, etc.). | Retreta, *f.* (signal): *to sound the retreat*, tocar retreta. || Retirada, *f.*, retiro, *m.* (from life). || Refugio, *m.*: *the world of books is his retreat*, el mundo de los libros es su refugio; *a country retreat*, un refugio en el campo. || Guarida, *f.* (of thieves). || Retroceso, *m.*, retirada, *f.* (of the sea water). || REL. Retiro: *spiritual retreat*, retiro espiritual. || — MIL. *To beat a retreat*, batirse en retirada. | *To cut off the retreat*, cortar la retirada.
retreat [riˈtriːt] v. intr. Retirarse. || MIL. Retirarse, batirse en retirada. || Retirarse, aislarse (from life, for spiritual reasons). || Retroceder (to draw back). || Refugiarse: *to retreat into the mountains*, refugiarse en las montañas.
— V. tr. Mover hacia atrás (in chess).
retrench [riˈtrentʃ] v. tr. Reducir, disminuir (to reduce). || Restringir (to restrict). || Suprimir, quitar (a passage). || Cortar (a text). || MIL. Atrincherar.
— V. intr. Ahorrar.
retrenchment [—mənt] n. Reducción, *f.*, disminución, *f.* || Supresión, *f.* || Ahorro, *m.* (saving). || MIL. Trinchera, *f.* (trench). | Atrincheramiento, *m.* (entrenchment).
retrial [ˈriːˈtraiəl] n. Nuevo juicio, *m.* || Revisión, *f.* (of a case).
retribution [ˌretriˈbjuːʃən] n. Pena (*f.*) merecida, castigo (*m.*) justo (merited punishment). || Recompensa, *f.* (reward). || *The Day of Retribution*, el día del Juicio Final.
retributive [riˈtribjutiv] adj. Justiciero, ra: *retributive punishment*, castigo justiciero. || Retributivo, va (of reward).
retrievable [riˈtriːvəbl] adj. Recuperable. || FIG. Reparable (error).
retrieval [riˈtriːvəl] n. Recuperación, *f.* (of sth. lost). || Rehabilitación, *f.* (of reputation, etc.). || Reparación, *f.* (of an error). || Restablecimiento, *m.* (of one's position). || Resarcimiento, *m.* (of damages). || Cobranza, *f.* (in hunting). || *Beyond* o *past retrieval*, irreparable.
retrieve [riˈtriːv] n. SP. Devolución, *f.* || Reparación, *f.* (of an error). || *Beyond* o *past retrieve*, irreparable.
retrieve [riˈtriːv] v. tr. Cobrar (to bring back fallen game). || Recuperar, recobrar (sth. lost). || Resarcirse de (damages). || Rehabilitar (reputation, etc.). || Salvar (from ruin, etc.). || Enmendar, subsanar, reparar (a mistake). || Recoger (to pick up). || SP. Devolver (to return a difficult shot).
— V. intr. Cobrar (hunting dogs).
retriever [—ə*] n. Perro (*m.*) cobrador.
retroact [ˌretrəuˈækt] v. intr. Tener efecto retroactivo (a law, etc.). || Reaccionar (to react).
retroaction [ˌretrəuˈækʃən] n. Retroactividad, *f.* (of a law, etc.). || Reacción, *f.*
retroactive [ˌretrəuˈæktiv] adj. Retroactivo, va. || *Retroactive law*, ley con efecto retroactivo.
retroactivity [ˌretrəuækˈtiviti] n. Retroactividad, *f.*
retrocede [ˌretrəuˈsiːd] v. intr. Retroceder (to go backwards).
— V. tr. Devolver (to give back).
retrocession [ˌretrəuˈseʃən] n. Retroceso, *m.* (backwards movement). || JUR. Retrocesión, *f.*
retrochoir [ˈretrəˌkwaiə*] n. REL. Trascoro, *m.*
re-trod [ˈriːˈtrɔd] pret. & p. p. See RE-TREAD.
re-trodden [—ən] p. p. See RE-TREAD.
retroflex [ˈretrəufleks] adj. Vuelto hacia atrás.
retroflexion [ˌretrəuˈflekʃən] n. MED. Retroflexión, *f.*, retroversión, *f.*
retrogradation [ˌretrəugreiˈdeiʃən] n. Retroceso, *m.*, regresión, *f.* || ASTR. Retrogradación, *f.*
retrograde [ˈretrəugreid] adj. Retrógrado, da: *retrograde movement*, movimiento retrógrado. || Inverso, sa (order). || FIG. Retrógrado, da.
retrograde [ˈretrəugreid] v. intr. Retroceder (to move backwards). || ASTR. Retrogradar. || FIG. Degenerar.
retrogress [ˌretrəuˈgres] v. intr. Retroceder. || Degenerar.

retrogression [ˌretrəuˈgreʃən] n. Retroceso, *m.*, regresión, *f.* ‖ ASTR. Retrogradación, *f.* ‖ FIG. Degeneración, *f.*
retrogressive [ˌretrəuˈgresiv] adj. Retrógrado, da.
retrorocket [ˈretrəuˌrɔkit] n. Retrocohete, *m.*
retrorse [riˈtrɔːs] adj. Vuelto hacia atrás.
retrospect [ˈretrəuspekt] n. Retrospección, *f.*, examen (*m.*) retrospectivo. ‖ *In retrospect*, retrospectivamente.
retrospect [ˈretrəuspekt] v. intr. *To retrospect on* o *to*, recordar.
retrospection [ˌretrəuˈspekʃən] n. Retrospección, *f.*, examen (*m.*) retrospectivo.
retrospective [ˌretrəuˈspektiv] adj. Retrospectivo, va. ‖ JUR. Con efecto retroactivo.
retroussé [rəˈtruːsei] adj. Respingona (nose).
retroversión [ˌretrəuˈvəːʃən] n. MED. Retroversión, *f.*
retry [riˈtrai] v. tr. Volver a juzgar *or* procesar (s.o.). ‖ Revisar, volver a examinar (a case).
return [riˈtəːn] n. Vuelta, *f.*, regreso, *m.*, retorno, *m.* (coming back): *on his return*, a su vuelta. ‖ Retorno, *m.*, vuelta, *f.*: *the return of the spring*, la vuelta de la primavera. ‖ Reexpedición, *f.* (of a letter). ‖ Cambio, *m.*: *to give a pen in return for a pencil*, dar una pluma a cambio de un lápiz. ‖ Recompensa, *f.* (reward). ‖ Devolución, *f.*, restitución, *f.* (the giving back): *the return of a book to its owner*, la devolución de un libro a su dueño. ‖ Ganancias, *f. pl.* (profit): *to bring a return*, proporcionar ganancias. ‖ Rédito, *m.*, interés, *m.* (interest): *return on capital*, interés del capital. ‖ Producto, *m.*, rendimiento, *m.* (productivity): *the return for the year*, el rendimiento del año. ‖ Cambio, *m.*, vuelta, *f.* (change in a shop). ‖ Reembolso, *m.*, devolución, *f.* (of a sum): *return of a capital*, reembolso de un capital. ‖ Restablecimiento, *m.*: *return to public order*, restablecimiento del orden público. ‖ Reelección, *f.*, elección, *f.*: *the return of the same members is likely*, la reelección de los mismos miembros es probable. ‖ Estadística, *f.* (statistic): *the official returns*, las estadísticas oficiales. ‖ Estado, *m.*: *return of expenses*, estado de gastos. ‖ Informe (*m.*) oficial (report). ‖ Censo, *m.* (of the population). ‖ Lista, *f.*: *return of killed and wounded*, lista de muertos y heridos. ‖ Declaración, *f.* (of taxes): *to send in one's return of income*, enviar la declaración de impuestos. ‖ Repercusión, *f.* (of a sound). ‖ Retroceso, *m.* (in typewriter). ‖ Réplica, *f.* (in cards). ‖ Respuesta, *f.* (in fencing). ‖ Curva, *f.* (bend). ‖ ARCH. Ala, *f.* ‖ SP. Devolución, *f.* (of ball). | Resto, *m.* (in tennis). ‖ TECH. Rendimiento, *m.* (of a machine). ‖ — Pl. Remanente (*m. sing.*) de periódicos no vendidos (of unsold newspapers). ‖ Resultados, *m.* (of ballot): *have the election returns come in yet?*, han llegado ya los resultados de las elecciones? ‖ COMM. Ingresos, *m.*: *gross returns*, ingresos brutos. ‖ Respuestas, *f.*: *there were enormous returns to our advertisement*, ha habido muchas respuestas a nuestro anuncio. ‖ — *A return ticket*, un billete de ida y vuelta (in Great Britain), un billete de vuelta (in United States). ‖ *As a return for your kindness*, para corresponder a su amabilidad. ‖ *By return of post* o *by return mail*, a vuelta de correo. ‖ *In return*, en recompensa (as a reward), a cambio (in exchange). ‖ *Many happy returns* (*of the day*)*!*, ¡feliz cumpleaños! ‖ *On my return home*, a mi vuelta a casa. ‖ *On sale or return*, en depósito (goods). ‖ *Quick return*, venta rápida. ‖ *Return address*, remite, *m.*, remitente, *m.* ‖ *Return game* o *match*, partido (*m.*) de vuelta. ‖ *Return of an illness*, recaída, *f.* ‖ *Return spring*, muelle (*m.*) antagonista *or* de retorno. ‖ *Return stroke*, carrera (*f.*) de vuelta (of a piston). ‖ *Return to school*, reapertura (*f.*) del año escolar. ‖ *Return trip*, viaje de ida y vuelta (round trip), viaje de regreso (journey back). ‖ *To bring in a good return*, dar mucho beneficio.
return [riˈtəːn] v. tr. Devolver (to bring back, to give back): *to return a book to its owner*, devolver un libro a su dueño; *to return a bill to drawer*, devolver una letra de cambio al girador; *to return blow for blow*, devolver golpe por golpe; *to return a call*, devolver una visita; *to return good for evil*, devolver bien por mal. ‖ Repercutir, devolver: *to return a sound*, repercutir un sonido. ‖ Reflejar (a light). ‖ Reembolsar (to refund). ‖ Restituir (lost or stolen goods, etc.). ‖ Poner de nuevo, volver a colocar (to put back): *to return a book to its place*, volver a colocar un libro en su sitio. ‖ Contestar con, responder con (to reply): *to return a blasphemy*, contestar con una blasfemia. ‖ Corresponder (to s.o.'s love, kindness, etc.): *to return s.o.'s love*, corresponder al amor de alguien. ‖ COMM. Declarar (income): *to return one's income to the tax authorities*, declarar sus ingresos a Hacienda. | Evaluar, estimar, valorar (to estimate). | Dar, proporcionar, rendir: *investment that returns very good interest*, inversión que da muy buenos intereses. ‖ Elegir, reelegir (to elect). ‖ Replicar con, devolver (in cards). ‖ Responder (in fencing). ‖ SP. Devolver (the ball). | Restar (tennis). ‖ JUR. Dar, pronunciar, dictar (a verdict, sentence, etc.). | Declarar (guilty): *the prisoner was returned guilty*, declararon culpable al acusado. ‖ TECH. Rendir, producir (productivity). ‖ Presentar (to submit statistics, documents, etc.). ‖ Dar [las gracias] (thanks). ‖ Dar a conocer (results). ‖ Hacer retroceder (typewriter carriage). ‖ — *Return to sender*, devuélvase al remitente (letter). ‖ *To return like for like*, pagar en *or* con la misma moneda.
— V. intr. Volver, regresar, retornar (to come back, to go back): *to return home*, volver a casa; *to return to poverty*, retornar a la pobreza; *my thoughts return to my childhood*, mis pensamientos vuelven a mi niñez; *they are about to return*, están a punto de regresar. ‖ Volver (to a former owner or state). ‖ Reanudar: *to return to a task*, reanudar un trabajo. ‖ Volver (*to*, a) [a subject]. ‖ Reaparecer (to reappear). ‖ *To return from the dead*, resucitar de entre los muertos.
returnable [—əbl] adj. Que se puede devolver, restituible, reintegrable. ‖ JUR. Devolutivo, va. | Elegible (candidate). ‖ *Non returnable*, sin consigna (packing).
returned [—d] adj. De vuelta (person). ‖ Devuelto al remitente (letter, packet). ‖ Devuelto, ta: *returned article*, artículo devuelto; *returned empties*, envases devueltos vacíos.
returning officer [—iŋˌɔfisə*] n. Escrutador, *m.*
retype [ˈriːˈtaip] v. tr. Volver a escribir a máquina, volver a mecanografiar.
retyre [riːˈtaiə*] v. tr. Poner neumáticos nuevos a.
reunification [riːˈjuːnifiˈkeiʃən] n. Reunificación, *f.*
reunify [ˈriːˈjuːnifai] v. tr. Reunificar.
reunion [ˈriːˈjuːnjən] n. Reunión, *f.*
reunite [ˈriːjuːˈnait] v. tr. Reunir. ‖ Reconciliar (two friends).
— V. intr. Reunirse. ‖ Reconciliarse.
reuse [ˈriːˈjuːs] n. Nuevo empleo, *m.*
reuse [ˈriːˈjuːz] v. tr. Volver a emplear.
rev [ˈrev] n. FAM. Revolución, *f.* (of an engine). | Cura, *m.* (short for reverend). ‖ *Rev counter*, cuentarrevoluciones, *m. inv.*
rev [rev] v. tr. FAM. *To rev up*, acelerar (car).
— V. intr. FAM. *To rev up*, embalarse (car).
revaccinate [ˈriːˈvæksineit] v. tr. MED. Revacunar.
revaccination [ˈrivæksiˈneiʃən] n. MED. Revacunación, *f.*
revalorization [riːvæləraiˈzeiʃən] n. Revalorización, *f.*
revalorize [riːˈvæləraiz] v. tr. Revalorizar.
revaluation [riːvæljuˈeiʃən] n. Revaluación, *f.*, revalorización, *f.*
revalue [ˈriːˈvæljuː] v. tr. Revaluar, revalorizar.
revamp [ˈriːˈvæmp] v. tr. Remendar, arreglar (shoes). ‖ FIG. Renovar, modernizar.
revanche [rəˈvɑːnʃ] n. Venganza, *f.*, revancha, *f.*
reveal [riˈviːl] n. ARCH. Derrame, *m.* (of door, window).
reveal [riˈviːl] v. tr. Revelar, manifestar: *to reveal one's real intentions*, manifestar sus verdaderas intenciones. ‖ Revelar, descubrir (to uncover). ‖ Revelar, descubrir, divulgar (a secret).
revealer [riˈviːlə*] n. Revelador, ra.
revealing [riˈviːliŋ] adj. Revelador, ra: *revealing letter*, carta reveladora.
revealment [riˈviːlmənt] n. Revelación, *f.*
reveille [riˈvæli] n. MIL. Diana, *f.*: *to sound reveille*, tocar diana.
revel [ˈrevl] n. Diversión, *f.*, fiesta, *f.* (amusement). ‖ Juerga, *f.*, jarana, *f.* (spree).
revel [ˈrevl] v. intr. Deleitarse, gozar: *she revels in dancing*, goza bailando. ‖ Divertirse (to amuse o.s.). ‖ Juerguearse, ir *or* estar de juerga (to have a good time).
— V. tr. *To revel away*, gastar en placeres (money).
revelation [ˌreviˈleiʃən] n. Revelación, *f.* ‖ *Revelations*, el Apocalipsis (last book of the New Testament).
reveler or **reveller** [ˈrevlə*] n. Juerguista, *m.* & *f.*
revelry [ˈrevlri] n. Jolgorio, *m.*, jarana, *f.*, juerga, *f.*
revendication [riˌvendiˈkeiʃən] n. Reivindicación, *f.*
revenge [riˈvendʒ] n. Venganza, *f.* ‖ SP. Desquite, *m.*, revancha, *f.* ‖ — *In revenge for*, para vengarse de. ‖ *To be full of revenge*, arder en deseos de venganza. ‖ *To take revenge on s.o. for sth.*, vengarse de algo en uno.
revenge [riˈvendʒ] v. tr. Vengar, vengarse de. ‖ *To revenge o.s.* o *to be revenged on s.o.*, vengarse en alguien.
revengeful [—ful] adj. Vengativo, va (avenging). ‖ Vindicativo, va (vindictive).
revengefulness [—fulnis] n. Carácter (*m.*) vengativo.
revenger [—ə*] n. Vengador, ra.
revenue [ˈrevinjuː] n. Entrada, *f.*, ingreso, *m.*, renta, *f.* (income). ‖ Fuente (*f.*) de ingresos (source of income). ‖ Rentas (*f. pl.*) públicas (from taxes, etc.). ‖ Hacienda (*f.*) Pública (administration). ‖ — Pl. Ingresos, *m.*, entradas, *f.*, rentas, *f.* ‖ — *Inland Revenue*, contribuciones, *f. pl.* (government income), hacienda, *f.*, fisco, *m.* (government department). ‖ *Public Revenue*, Tesoro Público. ‖ *Revenue office*, oficina (*f.*) de recaudación. ‖ *Revenue officer*, agente (*m.*) de aduanas (of customs), delegado (*m.*) de Hacienda (of finance). ‖ *Revenue stamp*, timbre (*m.*) fiscal.
revenue cutter [—ˌkʌtə*] n. MAR. Guardacostas, *m. inv.* (boat).
reverberant [riˈvəːbərənt] adj. Reverberante.
reverberate [riˈvəːbəreit] v. tr. Reverberar, reflejar (heat and light). ‖ Reflejar, reverberar (sound).
— V. intr. Reverberarse, reflejarse (heat and light). ‖ Resonar, retumbar, reverberarse (sound).
reverberation [riˌvəːbəˈreiʃən] n. Reverberación, *f.* (of heat, light). ‖ Reverberación, *f.*, repercusión, *f.*, eco, *m.* (of sound).

reverberative [ri'və:bəreitiv] adj. Reverberante.
reverberator [ri'və:bəreitə*] n. Reflector, *m.*
reverberatory [ri'və:bərətəri] adj. De reverbero: *reverberatory furnace*, horno de reverbero.
— N. Horno (*m.*) de reverbero.
revere [ri'viə*] v. tr. Reverenciar, venerar.
reverence ['revərəns] n. Reverencia, *f.* (respect, bow). || — *Saving your reverence*, con perdón sea dicho. || *To hold in reverence*, reverenciar, venerar. || *To pay reverence to*, rendir homenaje a. || REL. *Your Reverence*, Su Reverencia.
reverence ['revərəns] v. tr. Reverenciar, venerar.
reverend ['revərənd] adj. REL. Reverendo, da. || *Most* o *right Reverend*, reverendísimo.
— N. REL. Pastor, *m.* (Anglican Church). | Cura, *m.*, padre, *m.* (Roman Catholic Church).
reverent ['revərənt] adj. Reverente.
reverential [,revə'renʃəl] adj. Reverencial.
reverie ['revəri] n. Ensueño, *m.* || *To be lost in reverie*, estar absorto, ta.
revers [ri'viə*] inv. n. Solapa, *f.*
reversal [ri'və:səl] n. Inversión, *f.* || JUR. Revocación, *f.* (of a judgment). || FIG. Cambio (*m.*) completo (of opinion).
reverse [ri'və:s] adj. Opuesto, ta; contrario, ria (opposite): *in the reverse direction*, en dirección contraria. || Inverso, sa (inverse): *in reverse order*, en orden inverso. || AUT. De marcha atrás. || *The reverse side*, el revés, la vuelta (of cloth), el dorso (of a sheet), el reverso (of a medal), el reverso, la cruz (of coin).
— N. Lo contrario: *what you say is the reverse of what I say*, lo que dice usted es lo contrario de lo que digo yo. || Revés, *m.*, vuelta, *f.* (of cloth). || Reverso, *m.* (of medal). || Cruz, *f.*, reverso, *m.* (of coin). || Dorso, *m.* (of printed form). || Revés, *m.* (of fortune). || Revés, *m.*, derrota, *f.* (defeat). || AUT. Marcha (*f.*) atrás (gear). || — *He is the reverse of polite*, no es nada cortés, es todo lo contrario de un hombre cortés. || *Quite the reverse*, todo lo contrario. || AUT. FIG. *To go into reverse*, dar marcha atrás. || AUT. *To put in* o *into reverse*, poner en marcha atrás.
reverse [ri'və:s] v. tr. Invertir: *a mirror reverses the image*, el espejo invierte la imagen. || Volver al revés (to turn the other way round). || MIL. Llevar a la funerala (arms). || Cambiar completamente (policy, situation). || JUR. Revocar, anular, cancelar (a decision). || TECH. Invertir la marcha de (engine). | Invertir (current, steam). || — *To reverse one's car*, dar marcha atrás. || *To reverse the (telephone) charges*, poner una conferencia a cobro revertido.
— V. intr. AUT. Dar marcha atrás (to put an engine in reverse). | Ir marcha atrás (to drive backwards). || Ir en sentido inverso (in dancing).
reverse-charge [—tʃɑ:dʒ] adj. *To make a reverse-charge call*, poner una conferencia a cobro revertido.
reverse current [—'kʌrənt] n. Contracorriente, *f.*
reverse gear [—giə*] n. AUT. Marcha (*f.*) atrás.
reversely [—li] adv. Al revés.
reverser [—ə*] n. ELECTR. Inversor, *m.*
reversibility [ri,və:sə'biliti] n. Reversibilidad, *f.*
reversible [ri'və:səbl] adj. Reversible. || JUR. Revocable (decision). || De dos caras, reversible (material).
reversion [ri'və:ʃən] n. Reversión, *f.* (return to a former condition). || BIOL. Salto (*m.*) atrás, reversión, *f.* || JUR. Reversión, *f.* || PHOT. Inversión, *f.*
reversionary [ri'və:ʃənəri] adj. De reversión.
reversive [ri'və:siv] adj. Reversivo, va.
revert [ri'və:t] v. intr. Volver a: *the tribe reverted to paganism*, la tribu volvió al paganismo; *reverting to your original statement*, volviendo a su declaración inicial. || JUR. Revertir: *property which reverts to the Crown*, bienes que revierten a la Corona. || BIOL. Saltar atrás.
revertibility [rivə:ti'biliti] n. JUR. Reversibilidad, *f.*
revertible [ri'və:təbl] adj. JUR. Reversible.
revet [ri'vet] v. tr. Revestir.
revetment [—mənt] n. Revestimiento, *m.*
revictual ['ri:'vitl] v. tr. Reabastecer.
— V. intr. Reabastecerse.
review [ri'vju:] n. Examen, *m.*, análisis, *m.*: *to make a review of the situation*, hacer un análisis de la situación. || MIL. Revista, *f.* || JUR. Revisión, *f.* || Crítica, *f.*, reseña, *f.* (critic). || Revista, *f.* (magazine). || THEATR. Revista, *f.* (revue). || U. S. Revisión, *f.* (revision). || — *Review copy*, ejemplar (*m.*) para la prensa. || *To come under review*, ser examinado.
review [ri'vju:] v. tr. Examinar, analizar (to consider). || Volver a examinar (to reconsider). || MIL. Pasar revista a: *to review a regiment*, pasar revista a un regimiento. || Hacer una crítica de, hacer una reseña de (a book). || JUR. Revisar. || U. S. Revisar (to revise).
— V. intr. Hacer críticas *or* reseñas (to write reviews).
reviewal [—əl] n. Crítica, *f.*, reseña, *f.* (of a book). || Revisión, *f.*
reviewer [—ə*] n. Crítico, ca.
revigorate [ri'vigəreit] v. tr. Revigorizar.
revile [ri'vail] v. tr. Insultar, injuriar: *he was reviling his father*, estaba insultando a su padre.
— V. intr. Proferir injurias (*against*, contra).
revilement [—mənt] n. Insulto, *m.*, injuria, *f.*
reviler [—ə*] n. Injuriador, ra.
reviling [—iŋ] adj. Injurioso, sa.

revindicate ['ri:'vindikeit] v. tr. Reivindicar.
revindicating [—iŋ] adj. Reivindicatorio, ria; reivindicativo, va.
revindication ['ri:vindi'keiʃən] n. Reivindicación, *f.*
revisable [ri'vaizəbl] adj. Que puede ser revisado, revisable.
revisal [ri'vaizəl] n. Revisión, *f.*
revise [ri'vaiz] n. PRINT. Segunda prueba, *f.* || *Second revise*, tercera prueba.
revise [ri'vaiz] v. tr. Revisar, volver a examinar (to reexamine). || Repasar (a lesson). || Corregir, revisar (to correct): *to revise a manuscript*, revisar un manuscrito. || Modificar (to modify). || Refundir (to make a new version): *to revise a dictionary*, refundir un diccionario. || PRINT. Corregir (proofs).
reviser [—ə*] n. Revisor, ra (who reexamines). || Revisor, ra; corrector, ra (who corrects a manuscript). || Refundidor, ra (of dictionary, etc.). || PRINT. Corrector, ra (of proofs).
revision [ri'viʒən] n. Revisión, *f.* || Repaso, *m.* (of a lesson). || Corrección, *f.*, revisión, *f.* (of a manuscript). || Modificación, *f.* (modification). || Refundición, *f.* (of a dictionary, etc.). || PRINT. Corrección, *f.* (of proofs).
revisionism [—izəm] n. Revisionismo, *m.*
revisionist [—ist] adj./n. Revisionista.
revisit ['ri:'vizit] v. tr. Volver a visitar.
revisor [ri'vaizə*] n. See REVISER.
revisory [ri'vaizəri] adj. Revisor, ra.
revitalization [ri,vaitəlai'zeiʃən] n. Revitalización, *f.*, revivificación, *f.*
revitalize ['ri:'vaitəlaiz] v. tr. Revitalizar, revivificar.
revivable [ri'vaivəbl] adj. Reanimable.
revival [ri'vaivəl] n. MED. Reanimación, *f.* (bringing back to life). | Resucitación, *f.* (of a dead person). | Restablecimiento, *m.* (recovery). || COMM. Reactivación, *f.*, nuevo desarrollo, *m.* (of business, economy). || REL. Despertar (*m.*) religioso (awakening of religious fervour). | Asamblea (*f.*) evangelística (meeting). || Renacimiento, *m.* (of interest, style of art, etc.). || Reaparición, *f.* (of fashion). || Restablecimiento, *m.* (of an old custom). || Resurgimiento, *m.* (of a country). || THEATR. Reposición, *f.*, reestreno, *m.* (of a play). || JUR. Restablecimiento, *m.*, nueva aplicación, *f.* (of a law, etc.). || ARTS. Renacimiento, *m.* || *The Revival of learning*, el Renacimiento.
revivalism [ri'vaivəlizəm] n. REL. Evangelismo, *m.*
revivalist [ri'vaivəlist] n. REL. Evangelista, *m.*
revive [ri'vaiv] v. tr. MED. Reanimar (to bring back to consciousness). | Resucitar (to bring back to life). || THEATR. Reponer, reestrenar (a play). || JUR. Restablecer, volver a aplicar (a law). || Volver a poner de moda, resucitar (fashion). || Reactivar, dar nueva vida *or* nuevo impulso a (trade). || Restablecer (an old custom). || Reanimar, animar (the conversation). || Resucitar (feelings, memories). || Despertar (wish, hopes). || Animar (to cheer up). || Renovar (interest). || Atizar, avivar (fire).
— V. intr. MED. Reanimarse, volver en sí, recobrar el sentido (to come back to consciousness). | Resucitar (to come back to life). | Restablecerse, reponerse, recuperarse (to recover strength). || Despertar (nature). || Renacer, volver a nacer (to be renewed): *our hopes revived*, nuestras esperanzas volvieron a nacer. || Resucitar (feelings, memories). || Renacer (interest). || COMM. Reactivarse, recuperarse. || *His spirits revived*, recobró el ánimo.
reviver [ri'vaivə*] n. Reanimador, ra; persona (*f.*) *or* cosa (*f.*) que reanima. || FAM. *To have an early morning reviver*, matar el gusanillo.
revivification [ri,vivəfə'keiʃən] n. Revivificación, *f.*
revivify [ri'vivifai] v. tr. Revivificar.
revocability [,revəkə'biliti] n. Revocabilidad, *f.*
revocable ['revəkəbl] adj. Revocable.
revocation [,revə'keiʃən] n. JUR. Revocación, *f.* (of a decree). | Suspensión, *f.* (of a licence).
revocative ['revəkətiv] adj. Revocativo, va.
revocatory ['revəkətəri] adj. Revocatorio, ria.
revokable ['revəkəbl] adj. Revocable.
revoke [ri'vəuk] n. Renuncio, *m.* (at cards).
revoke [ri'vəuk] v. tr. JUR. Revocar: *to revoke an order, a law, a decree*, revocar una orden, una ley, un decreto. | Suspender (a licence).
— V. intr. Renunciar (at cards).
revolt [ri'vəult] n. Rebelión, *f.*, sublevación, *f.*, revuelta, *f.* (rebellion). || Rebeldía, *f.* (state of mind). || — *In revolt*, en rebelión. || *To rise in revolt*, sublevarse, levantarse. || *To stir up to revolt*, sublevar, levantar.
revolt [ri'vəult] v. tr. Repugnar, dar asco, asquear (to fill with repugnance): *snails revolt me*, los caracoles me repugnan. || Escandalizar, indignar (to fill with horror): *the scene revolted him*, la escena le escandalizó. || Sublevar, incitar a la rebelión (to incite to rebellion).
— V. intr. Rebelarse, sublevarse: *to revolt against the government*, rebelarse contra el gobierno. || Sentir repugnancia *or* asco *or* repulsión (to feel disgust). || Escandalizarse, indignarse (to be filled with horror): *human nature revolts at such a crime*, la naturaleza humana se indigna ante semejante crimen.
revolting [—iŋ] adj. Repugnante, asqueroso, sa (repulsive). || Rebelde, sublevado, da (rebellious).
revolution [,revə'lu:ʃən] n. Revolución, *f.* (political, social, etc.): *industrial Revolution*, la Revolución

industrial. || TECH. Rotación, *f.*, giro, *m.* (round an axis). | Revolución, *f.* (of a wheel): *40 revolutions per minute*, cuarenta revoluciones por minuto. || ASTR. Revolución, *f.* (round an orbit). | Rotación, *f.* (of heavenly bodies round their axis). || *Revolution counter*, cuentarrevoluciones, *m. inv.*
revolutionary [ˌrevəˈlu:ʃnəri] adj./n. Revolucionario, ria.
revolutionist [ˌrevəˈlu:ʃnist] n. Revolucionario, ria.
revolutionize [ˌrevəˈlu:ʃnaiz] v. tr. Revolucionar (to change completely).
revolvable [riˈvɔlvəbəl] adj. Giratorio, ria.
revolve [riˈvɔlv] v. tr. Hacer girar (to make turn). || FIG. Dar vueltas en la cabeza a (problem, thought). | Meditar (scheme).
— V. intr. Girar (to move around an axis). || Volver, repetirse: *the seasons revolve each year*, las estaciones se repiten cada año. || — FIG. *The problem is revolving in his mind*, el problema le está dando vueltas en la cabeza. || *To revolve around*, girar alrededor de: *to revolve around an axis*, girar alrededor de un eje; girar alrededor de, girar en torno a: *all the conversation revolved around politics*, toda la conversación giró alrededor de la política.
revolver [—ə*] n. Revólver, *m.*
revolving [—iŋ] adj. Giratorio, ria: *revolving door*, puerta giratoria. || Que se repite (year, season). || ASTR. Rotatorio, ria. || *Revolving fund*, fondo (*m.*) de rotación.
revue [riˈvju:] n. THEATR. Revista, *f.*
revulsion [riˈvʌlʃən] n. MED. Revulsión, *f.* || FIG. Repulsión, *f.*, repugnancia, *f.* (repugnance). | Cambio (*m.*) brusco (sudden change). | Reacción, *f.* (reaction).
revulsive [riˈvʌlsiv] adj. MED. Revulsivo, va.
— N. MED. Revulsivo, *m.*
reward [riˈwɔ:d] n. Recompensa, *f.*: *as a reward for*, en recompensa de; *a ten pound reward*, diez libras de recompensa.
reward [riˈwɔ:d] v. tr. Recompensar, premiar.
rewarding [—iŋ] adj. Remunerador, ra. || Que merece la pena, que compensa (experience, film, etc.).
rewind* [ˈri:ˈwaind] v. tr. Rebobinar. || Dar cuerda a (clock, watch).

— OBSERV. Pret. & p. p. ***rewound.***

rewinding [—iŋ] n. Rebobinado, *m.*
rewire [ˈri:ˈwaiə*] v. tr. Poner nueva instalación eléctrica a (a house). || Cambiar el alambre de (electric circuit). || Telegrafiar de nuevo.
reword [ˈri:ˈwə:d] v. tr. Expresar con otras palabras. || Volver a redactar.
rewound [ˈri:ˈwaund] pret. & p. p. See REWIND.
rewrite* [ˈri:ˈrait] v. tr. Volver a escribir (to write again). || Volver a redactar, redactar con otras palabras (to alter the wording).

— OBSERV. Pret. ***rewrote;*** p. p. ***rewritten.***

Rhaetian [ˈri:ʃjən] adj./n. Rético, ca.
Rhaeto-Romanic [ˈri:təurəuˈmænik] n. Retorromano, *m.*, rético, *m.*
rhamnaceae [ræmˈneisii:] pl. n. BOT. Ramnáceas, *f.*
rhapsodic [ræpˈsɔdik] or **rhapsodical** [—əl] adj. Rapsódico, ca.
rhapsodist [ˈræpsədist] n. Rapsoda, *m.*
rhapsodize [ˈræpsədaiz] v. intr. Extasiarse (*over*, ante), estar entusiasmado (*over*, por). || Celebrar, poner por las nubes (to praise).
rhapsody [ˈræpsədi] n. Rapsodia, *f.* || FIG. *To go into rhapsodies over*, poner por la nubes, celebrar.
rhatany [ˈrætəni] n. BOT. Ratania, *f.*
rhea [riə] n. Ñandú, *m.* (bird).
Rhea [riə] pr. n. MYTH. Rea, *f.*
Rhenish [ˈri:niʃ] adj. Renano, na. || Del Rin (wine).
— N. Vino (*m.*) del Rin.
rhenium [ˈri:niəm] n. CHEM. Renio, *m.*
rheometer [riˈɔmitə*] n. Reómetro, *m.*
rheophore [ˈri:əfɔ:*] n. PHYS. Reóforo, *m.*
rheostat [ˈriəustæt] n. ELECTR. Reóstato, *m.*
rheostatic [riəuˈstætik] adj. Reostático, ca.
rhesus [ˈri:səs] n. Macaco (*m.*) de la India (monkey). || BIOL. *Rhesus factor*, factor (*m.*) Rhesus.
rhetor [ˈri:tə*] n. Retórico, *m.*
rhetoric [ˈretərik] n. Retórica, *f.*
rhetorical [riˈtɔrikəl] adj. Retórico, ca.
rhetorician [ˌretəˈriʃən] n. Retórico, *m.*
rheum [ru:m] n. MED. Legaña, *f.* (in the eyes). | Mucosidades, *f. pl.* (in the nose).
rheumatic [ruˈmætik] adj. MED. Reumático, ca: *rheumatic fever*, fiebre reumática.
— N. MED. Reumático, ca (person). || — Pl. FAM. Reumatismo, *m. sing.*, reúma, *m. sing.* (disease).
rheumatism [ˈru:mətizəm] n. MED. Reumatismo, *m.*, reúma, *m.*
rheumatoid [ˈru:mətɔid] adj. MED. Reumatoideo, a. || *Rheumatoid arthritis*, reúma (*m.*) articular.
rheumy [ˈru:mi] adj. MED. Legañoso, sa (eyes).
rhinal [ˈrainəl] adj. ANAT. Nasal.
Rhine [rain] pr. n. GEOGR. Rin, *m.*
Rhineland [—lænd] pr. n. GEOGR. Renania, *f*
Rhinelander [—ˌlændə*] n. Renano, na.
rhinestone [ˈrainstəun] n. Diamante (*m.*) falso.
rhinitis [raiˈnaitis] n. MED. Rinitis, *f. inv.*
rhino [ˈrainəu] n. FAM. Rinoceronte, *m.* (rhinoceros). || FAM. Parné, *m.*, pasta, *f.* (money).
rhinoceros [raiˈnɔsərəs] n. ZOOL. Rinoceronte, *m.*

— OBSERV. El plural es *rhinoceroses* o *rhinoceros*.

rhinologist [raiˈnɔlədʒist] n. Rinólogo, *m.*
rhinology [raiˈnɔlədʒi] n. MED. Rinología, *f.*
rhinopharyngitis [ˈrainəuˌfærinˈdʒaitis] n. MED. Rinofaringitis, *f. inv.*
rhinopharynx [ˌrainəuˈfæriŋks] n. Rinofaringe, *f.*
rhinoplasty [ˈrainəplæsti] n. MED. Rinoplastia, *f.*
rhizome [ˈraizəum] n. BOT. Rizoma, *m.*
rhizophagous [raiˈzɔfəgəs] adj. Rizófago, ga (animal).
rhizopod [ˈraizəpɔd] n. Rizópodo, *m.*
rhizopoda [raiˈzɔpədə] pl. n. Rizópodos, *m.*
rhizopodous [raiˈzɔpədəs] adj. Rizópodo.
Rhodes [rəudz] pr. n. GEOGR. Rodas.
Rhodesia [rəuˈdi:zjə] pr. n. GEOGR. Rodesia, *f.*
Rhodesian [—n] adj./n. Rodesiano, na.
rhodium [ˈrəudjəm] n. CHEM. Rodio, *m.*
rhododendron [ˌrəudəˈdendrən] n. Rododendro, *m.*
rhomb [rɔm] n. MATH. Rombo, *m.* (rhombus).
rhombic [ˈrɔmbik] adj. MATH. Rómbico, ca; rombal.
rhombohedral [ˌrɔmbəˈhi:drəl] adj. MATH. Romboédrico, ca.
rhombohedron [rɔmbəˈhi:drən] n. MATH. Romboedro, *m.*

— OBSERV. El plural de la palabra inglesa es *rhombohedrons* o *rhombohedra*.

rhomboid [ˈrɔmbɔid] adj. MATH. Romboidal, romboideo, a.
— N. Romboide, *m.*
rhomboidal [—əl] adj. MATH. Romboidal.
rhombus [ˈrɔmbəs] n. MATH. Rombo, *m.*

— OBSERV. El plural de la palabra *rhombus* es *rhombuses* o *rhombi*.

Rhône [rəun] pr. n. GEOGR. Ródano, *m.*
rhotacism [ˈrəutəsizəm] n. Rotacismo, *m.* (phonetics).
rhubarb [ˈru:bɑ:b] n. BOT. Ruibarbo, *m.*
rhumb [rʌm] n. MAR. Rumbo, *m.*
rhyme [raim] n. Rima, *f.* || Poesía, *f.*, versos, *m. pl.* (poetry). || — *Nursery rhyme*, poesía infantil. || *To put into rhyme*, poner en verso. || FIG. *Without rhyme or reason*, a tontas y a locas, sin ton ni son.
rhyme [raim] v. tr./intr. Rimar.
rhymer [—ə*] or **rhymester** [—stə*] n. Rimador, ra.
rhyming [ˈraimiŋ] adj. Rimador, ra (person). || Rimado, da (words).
— N. Versificación, *f.*
rhyming dictionary [—ˈdikʃənri] n. Diccionario (*m.*) de rimas.
rhythm [ˈriðəm] n. Ritmo, *m.*: *to put rhythm into*, dar ritmo a. || *Rhythm method*, método (*m.*) Ogino.
rhythmic [ˈriðmik] or **rhythmical** [—əl] adj. Rítmico, ca.
rhythmically [—əli] adv. Rítmicamente, de modo rítmico.
rhythmics [—s] n. Rítmica, *f.*
ria [ˈri:ə] n. GEOGR. Ría, *f.*
rib [rib] n. ANAT. Costilla, *f.*: *true, false, floating rib*, costilla verdadera, falsa, flotante. || ARCH. Nervio, *m.*, nervadura, *f.* (of an arch). | Arista, *f.* (of a vault). || ZOOL. BOT. Nervio, *m.* (of leaf, insect's wing). | Cañón, *m.* (of feather). || MAR. Cuaderna, *f.*, costilla, *f.* || Cordoncillo, *m.* (in knitting). || Nervio, *m.* (in bookbinding). || Varilla, *f.* (of umbrella, fan, etc.). || CULIN. Costilla, *f.* (of meat). || AVIAT. Costilla, *f.* || MUS. Armazón, *f.* || FAM. Costilla, *f.* (wife).
rib [rib] v. tr. MAR. Poner cuadernas a (a ship). || Poner nervios a (a book). || U. S. FAM. Tomar el pelo a (to tease). || *Ribbed socks*, calcetines acanalados.
ribald [ˈribəld] adj. Verde, obsceno, na; chusco, ca.
— N. Persona (*f.*) verde *or* chusca.
ribaldry [—ri] n. Chusquería, *f.*, obscenidad, *f.*
riband [ˈribənd] n. See RIBBON.
ribband [ˈribənd] n. MAR. Cinta, *f.* || See RIBBON.
ribbon [ˈribən] n. Cinta, *f.* (narrow strip of material). || Cordón, *m.* (of an order). || Galón, *m.* (of a decoration). || — Pl. Riendas, *f.* (reins). | FAM. Jirones, *m.*, trizas, *f.*: *the flag was in ribbons*, la bandera estaba hecha jirones. || — *Steel ribbon*, fleje, *m.* || FIG. *To handle* o *to take the ribbons*, tomar las riendas. || *Typewriter ribbon*, cinta de máquina de escribir.
ribbon development [—diˈveləpmənt] n. Urbanización (*f.*) realizada a lo largo de una carretera.
ribbon saw [—sɔ:] n. TECH. Sierra (*f.*) de cinta.
rib cage [ˈribkeidʒ] n. ANAT. Caja (*f.*) torácica.
ribonucleic [ˈraibəuˈnju:kliik] adj. Ribonucleico, ca (acid).
ribwort [ˈribˌwə:t] n. BOT. Llantén (*m.*) menor.
rice [rais] n. Arroz, *m.*: *husked rice*, arroz descascarillado. || — *Boiled rice*, arroz blanco. || *Broken rice*, arroz quebrantado *or* picón. || *Creamed rice*, arroz con leche.
rice [rais] v. tr. U. S. CULIN. Pasar (cooked potatoes).
rice field [—fi:ld] n. Arrozal, *m.*
rice grower [—ˌgrəuə*] n. Arrocero, ra.
rice mill [—mil] n. Molino (*m.*) arrocero.
rice paper [—ˌpeipə*] n. Papel (*m.*) de arroz.
rice pudding [—ˈpudiŋ] n. Arroz (*m.*) con leche.
ricer [—ə*] n. U. S. Pasapuré, *m.*
rich [ritʃ] adj. Rico, ca (wealthy): *a rich property owner*, un rico propietario. || Rico, ca: *person rich in virtues*, persona rica en virtudes. || Magnífico, ca;

espléndido, da (splendid): *rich gifts*, regalos magníficos. || Suntuoso, sa (sumptuous). || Precioso, sa (elaborate). || Rico, ca: *adorned with rich embroidery*, adornado con ricos bordados. || Abundante, rico, ca (abundant): *a rich harvest*, una cosecha abundante. || AGR. Fértil, rico, ca (soil). | Ubérrimo, ma (pasture). || CULIN. Rico, ca; sabroso, sa (food). | Con mucha materia grasa (pastries). | Generoso, sa (wine). || FIG. Pingüe (earnings, profits). | Vivo, va; subido, da (colours). | Sonoro, ra; potente (voice). | Muy fuerte (perfume). | Opíparo, ra (meal). | Rico, ca (language). || Rico, ca: *ore rich in silver*, mineral rico en plata. || FAM. Gracioso, sa; muy divertido, da (funny). | Absurdo, da. || — *A land rich in minerals*, un terreno rico en minerales. || *To become* o *to get* o *to grow rich*, hacerse rico, enriquecerse. || *To be rich in*, abundar en. || *To make s.o. rich*, enriquecer a uno.

— Pl. n. *The rich*, los ricos.

Richard [ˈritʃəd] pr. n. Ricardo, *m.*

riches [ˈritʃiz] pl. n. Riquezas, *f.*, riqueza, *f. sing.*: *to pile up riches*, amontonar riquezas.

richly [ˈritʃli] adv. Ricamente (in a rich way). || Magníficamente, espléndidamente (splendidly). || Suntuosamente (sumptuously). || Abundantemente (abundantly). || FAM. Bien: *he richly deserves it*, lo tiene bien merecido.

richness [ˈritʃnis] n. Riqueza, *f.* || Suntuosidad, *f.* (sumptuousness). || Preciosidad, *f.* (beauty). || Abundancia, *f.* (abundance). || Fertilidad, *f.* (of soil). || Lo sabroso (of food). || Sonoridad, *f.* (of voice).

rick [rik] n. Almiar, *m.* (of hay). || Esguince, *m.* (twist).

rick [rik] v. tr. Amontonar [en almiares] (hay).

rickets [ˈrikits] n. MED. Raquitismo, *m.*

rickety [ˈrikiti] adj. MED. Raquítico, ca. || FIG. Cojo, ja (shaky): *a rickety chair*, una silla coja. | Poco seguro, ra (unsteady). | Desvencijado, da: *a rickety old car*, un viejo coche desvencijado. | Canijo, ja: *a rickety old man*, un viejo canijo.

rickshaw [ˈrɪkʃɔ:] n. Cochecillo (*m.*) tirado por un hombre.

ricochet [ˈrikəʃei] n. Rebote, *m.*

ricochet [ˈrikəʃei] v. intr. Rebotar.

rictus [ˈriktəs] n. Rictus, *m.*, gesto, *m.*

rid* [rid] v. tr. Librar: *to rid a country of bandits*, librar de bandidos un país. || — *To be rid of*, estar libre de. || *To get rid of s.o., of sth.*, deshacerse de alguien, de algo. || *To rid o.s. of*, librarse de: *to rid o.s. of an obligation*, librarse de una obligación. || *To rid o.s. of an idea*, quitarse una idea de la cabeza.

— OBSERV. Pret. & p. p. ***rid, ridded.***

ridable [ˈraidəbəl] adj. See RIDEABLE.

riddance [ˈridəns] n. Liberación, *f.* || *Good riddance!*, ¡vete con viento fresco! (go to blazes!), ¡menudo alivio!, ¡qué bien! (what a relief!).

ridden [ˈridn] p. p. Acosado, da; agobiado, da. || Infestado, da (invaded). || See RIDE.

riddle [ˈridl] n. Acertijo, *m.*, adivinanza, *f.*: *to ask s.o. a riddle*, poner un acertijo a alguien. || FIG. Enigma, *m.* (puzzling person, situation). || Criba, *f.* (sieve). || *To speak in riddles*, hablar en clave.

riddle [ˈridl] v. tr. Cribar (to sieve). || Acribillar (with holes, bullets, etc.). || Criticar (an argument). || Infestar (to corrupt). || Resolver *or* adivinar [un acertijo] (to solve a riddle).

— V. intr. Hablar en clave.

ride [raid] n. Paseo (*m.*) a caballo (on a horse). || Paseo (*m.*) en coche (in a car). || Paseo (*m.*) en bicicleta (on a bicycle). || Viaje (*m.*) en tren (in a train). || Viaje (*m.*) en barco (on a ship). || Viaje en avión (in a plane). || Camino (*m.*) de herradura, vereda, *f.* (path). || Trayecto, *m.*, viaje, *m.* (journey). || Vuelta, *f.*, paseo, *m.*: *the children had a ride on a camel*, los niños dieron una vuelta en un camello. || Precio (*m.*) del viaje *or* del paseo (price). || — *He gave me a ride from London to Blackpool*, me llevó de Londres a Blackpool. || *It's a ten penny ride on the bus*, cuesta diez peniques en autobús. || *It's only a short ride by bus*, no se tarda mucho en autobús. || *To give a child a ride on one's back*, llevar a un niño a cuestas. || *To go for a ride*, dar un paseo [en coche, a caballo, etc.]. || FAM. *To take s.o. for a ride*, dar gato por liebre a uno (to deceive s.o.), dar el paseo a uno (to kill).

ride* [raid] v. tr. Montar, ir montado en: *he was riding a black horse*, montaba un caballo negro. || Montar a: *I can't ride a horse*, no sé montar a caballo. || Montar en (a bicycle, a donkey). || Ir en: *to ride a bus*, ir en autobús. || Conducir, guiar [*Amer.*, manejar] (to drive a bicycle, etc.). || Recorrer (to cover a distance). || Cruzar *or* atravesar a caballo (a country, a town): *to ride the deserts*, atravesar los desiertos a caballo. || Surcar, hender: *to ride the waves*, surcar las olas. || Llevar: *to ride a baby on one's back*, llevar a un niño a cuestas. || SP. Correr, participar en (a race). || Montar, acaballar (to mate). || FIG. Dominar, tiranizar (to dominate). | Acosar, agobiar : *ridden by doubts*, acosado por las dudas. || U. S. FAM. Meterse con (to tease). || — *I rode my horse down to the river*, llevé el caballo al río, fui a caballo al río. || *I rode my horse up the hill*, subí la colina a caballo. || *The motorcycle was ridden by*, la motocicleta iba conducida por. || *To ride to death*, agotar (a horse), repetir hasta la saciedad (an idea, a theory).

— V. intr. Montar, ir montado: *he was riding on a donkey*, iba montado en un burro. || Montar: *to ride sidesaddle*, montar a la amazona. || Ir [a caballo, en bicicleta, etc.]: *to ride to a place*, ir a un sitio; *to ride a good pace*, ir a buen paso; *I rode by bicycle to London*, fui a Londres en bicicleta. || Viajar (to travel). || Montar a caballo: *we rode* o *we went riding all morning*, montamos *or* estuvimos montando a caballo toda la mañana. || Cabalgar: *I rode hard all morning*, cabalgué toda la mañana sin parar. || Viajar en coche (in a car). || Viajar en tren (in a train). || Montar en bicicleta (on a bicycle). || Ser llevado a cuestas (on s.o.'s back). || Recorrer: *to ride fifty miles*, recorrer cincuenta millas. || Moverse: *to ride on an axis*, moverse en un eje. || MAR. Flotar. || Flotar (sun or moon). || FIG. Seguir su curso: *let the problem ride*, deja que el problema siga su curso. || — *I rode all the way*, hice todo el camino a caballo. || *The ground rides hard*, el terreno es muy duro para ir a caballo. || *The moon was riding high in the heavens*, la luna estaba alta en el cielo. || FIG. *To be riding high*, estar en plena forma. || *To ride astride*, montar a horcajadas. || MAR. *To ride at anchor*, estar fondeado *or* anclado. || FIG. *To ride for a fall*, ir a la ruina.

— ***To ride along,*** pasar. || ***To ride away,*** irse [a caballo, etc.]. || ***To ride back,*** volver [a caballo, etc.]. || ***To ride behind,*** montar a la grupa (on same horse). | Ir en el asiento trasero (in carriage). | Ir detrás (to follow). || ***To ride by,*** pasar [a caballo, etc.]. || ***To ride down,*** adelantar a caballo (to overtake on a horse). | Atropellar (to run over). || ***To ride in,*** entrar [a caballo, etc.]. | Ir en [un vehículo]. || ***To ride off,*** irse [a caballo, etc.]. || ***To ride on,*** seguir adelante [a caballo, etc.]. || ***To ride out,*** salir [a caballo, etc.]. | — *To ride out the storm*, capear el temporal. || ***To ride up,*** llegar [a caballo, etc.]. | Subirse: *this pullover always rides up*, este jersey siempre se sube.

— OBSERV. Pret. ***rode;*** p. p. ***ridden.***

rideable [—əbl] adj. Que se puede montar (horse). || Transitable (path).

rider [—ə*] n. Jinete, *m.*, caballista, *m.* (on horse). || Ciclista, *m.* & *f.* (on a bicycle). || Motociclista, *m.* (on a moped). || Motorista, *m.* & *f.* (on a motorbike). || Caballista, *m.* & *f.* (in a circus). || SP. Jockey, *m.* || JUR. Cláusula (*f.*) adicional. || MATH. Ejercicio (*m.*) de aplicación.

ridge [ridʒ] n. GEOGR. Cadena, *f.*, cordillera, *f.* (of hills). | Cumbre, *f.*, cresta, *f.* (crest). | Loma, *f.* (hillock). | Arista, *f.*, estría, *f.* (on a rock). | Ondulación, *f.* (on sand). | Escollo, *m.* (of reefs, etc.). || AGR. Caballón, *m.* (between furrows). || ANAT. Caballete, *m.* (of nose). || ARCH. Caballete, *m.* (of a roof). || Cordoncillo, *m.* (in cloth).

ridge [ridʒ] v. tr. Surcar. || ARCH. Cubrir con un caballete.

— V. intr. Rizarse (sea).

ridgepiece [—pi:s] n. ARCH. Caballete, *m.*, cumbrera, *f.*, parhilera, *f.* (of a roof).

ridgepole [—pəul] n. Caballete, *m.*, cumbrera, *f.*, parhilera, *f.* (of a roof).

ridge tile [—tail] n. Teja (*f.*) de caballete *or* de cumbrera.

ridgy [—i] adj. Surcado de estrías, estriado, da. || Con aristas. || ARCH. A dos aguas (roof).

ridicule [ˈridikju:l] n. Irrisión, *f.*, burla, *f.* (mockery). || — *To expose s.o. to ridicule*, poner a uno en ridículo. || *To hold s.o. up to ridicule*, ridiculizar a uno. || *To invite ridicule*, hacer reír, causar la risa. || *To lay o.s. open to ridicule*, exponerse al ridículo.

ridicule [ˈridikju:l] v. tr. Ridiculizar, poner en ridículo.

ridiculous [riˈdikjuləs] adj. Ridículo, la: *to say ridiculous things*, decir cosas ridículas. || *To make s.o. ridiculous*, poner en ridículo a alguien.

ridiculousness [—nis] n. Ridiculez, *f.*, lo ridículo.

riding [ˈraidiŋ] adj. De montar: *riding habit*, traje de montar; *riding breeches*, pantalones de montar. || De silla (horse). || — *Riding crop*, fusta, *f.* || *Riding light*, luz (*f.*) de posición (ship, planes). || *Riding master*, profesor (*m.*) de equitación. || *Riding school*, escuela (*f.*) de equitación, picadero, *m.* || *Riding whip*, fusta, *f.*

— N. Camino (*m.*) de herradura (path). || AUT. Suspensión, *f.* || MAR. Anclaje, *m.* || SP. Equitación, *f.* || TECH. Imbricación, *f.* || *Riding is easy*, es fácil montar a caballo.

Rif [rif] pr. n. GEOGR. Rif, *m.*

rife [raif] adj. Abundante (*with*, en). || *To be rife*, abundar, ser muy corriente.

riffle [ˈrifl] n. U. S. Ranura (*f.*) de una artesa (for catching gold particles). | Rápido, *m.*, rabión, *m.* (in a river). | Peinado, *m.* (of cards).

riffle [ˈrifl] v. tr. U. S. Hacer pasar por la ranura de una artesa (in gold mining). | Pasar rápidamente [las hojas de un libro]. | Hojear (book). | Peinar (cards).

riffraff [ˈrifræf] n. FAM. Canalla, *f.*, chusma, *f.*, gentuza, *f.* (disreputable persons).

rifle [ˈraifl] n. Rifle, *m.* (for hunting). || Fusil, *m.* (soldier's). || Raya, *f.*, estría, *f.* (groove). || — Pl. Fusileros, *m.* (soldiers).

rifle [ˈraifl] v. tr. Saquear, desvalijar (to steal everything of value from). || Saquear (to plunder). || Vaciar (the pockets). || Rayar (to cut grooves in). || Disparar a (to shoot).

rifleman [—mən] n. MIL. Fusilero, *m.*

— OBSERV. El plural de la palabra inglesa es *riflemen.*

rifle range [—reindʒ] n. Campo (*m.*) de tiro, polígono (*m.*) de tiro (for target practice). || Alcance (*m.*) del fusil *or* del rifle (distance). || Barraca (*f.*) de tiro al blanco (in fairground).

rifle shot [—ʃɔt] n. Disparo, *m.*, tiro, *m.* || *Within rifle shot,* a tiro de fusil.

rifling [—iŋ] n. Rayado, *m.*

rift [rift] n. Grieta, *f.*, fisura, *f.* (crack, fissure). || Claro, *m.* (opening in clouds, mist). || GEOL. Falla, *f.* (a fault). || FIG. Ruptura, *f.* (in friendship, etc.). | Escisión, *f.* (in a political party, etc.). || FIG. *A rift in the lute,* una desavenencia.

rift saw [—sɔ:] n. Sierra (*f.*) para cortar madera.

rig [rig] n. MAR. Aparejo, *m.* || Equipo, *m.* (equipment). || Instalación, *f.* || FAM. Traje, *m.*, vestimenta, *f.*, indumentaria, *f.*: *the rig of an Englishman,* la vestimenta de un inglés. || Broma, *f.* (joke). || Mala pasada, *f.* (trick). || Artimaña, *f.*, engañifa, *f.* (piece of trickery). || Especulación (*f.*) en la Bolsa.

rig [rig] v. tr. MAR. Aparejar (a ship). | Enjarciar (a mast). || Armar (a plane). || Montar, armar, instalar (machines). || Equipar (to provide with equipment). || Preparar: *the fire was rigged to throw blame on the caretaker,* el incendio fue preparado para que se le achacara la culpa al portero. || Arreglar (to arrange). || Amañar: *to rig an election,* amañar una elección. || Especular en (on the stock exchange). || Hacer trampas con (cards). || — *The fight was rigged,* hubo tongo en el combate. || *To rig out,* ataviar, vestir. || *To rig up,* improvisar.

rigadoon [rigəˈdu:n] n. Rigodón, *m.* (dance).

rigamarole [ˈrigəmə,rəul] n. See RIGMAROLE.

rigger [ˈrigə*] n. MAR. Aparejador, ra. || AVIAT. Montador, *m.* || ARCH. Andamio (*m.*) protector (in construction). || Especulador, ra (in the stock exchange).

rigging [ˈrigiŋ] n. MAR. Aparejo, *m.*, jarcia, *f.* || TECH. Montaje, *m.* (of a machine). || Equipo, *m.* (equipment).

right [rait] adj. Bueno, na (obeying moral law): *right conduct,* buena conducta. || Bien: *to know what is right and what is wrong,* saber lo que está bien y lo que está mal. || Justo, ta; equitativo, va (fair): *God is right,* Dios es justo. || Correcto, ta; exacto, ta (correct): *the right answer,* la respuesta correcta. || Exacto, ta: *the bill is not right,* la cuenta no es exacta; *have you got the right time?,* ¿tiene la hora exacta? || Exacto, ta; justo, ta: *the right conclusion,* la conclusión exacta; *I can't find the right word,* no puedo encontrar la palabra exacta. || Exacto, ta; verdadero, ra (true). || Fundado, da (justified): *our suspicions were right,* las sospechas eran fundadas. || Oportuno, na; bueno, na (opportune): *at the right moment,* en el momento oportuno. || Apropiado, da; conveniente (most appropriate): *I thought it right to tell you,* pensé que era conveniente decírselo. || Adecuado, da; conveniente (suitable): *the right word in this context,* la palabra adecuada en este contexto. || Que hace falta: *this painting is just right for the bedroom,* este cuadro es exactamente lo que hace falta para el dormitorio. || Decente: *it is not the right film for a young girl,* no es una película decente para una chica. || Respetable (respectable). || Bien (physically and mentally sound): *I don't feel right,* no me encuentro bien; *he is not right in the head,* no está bien de la cabeza. || Bueno, na: *we'll leave tomorrow if the weather is right,* nos iremos mañana si hace buen tiempo. || En orden, ordenado, da (in order). || FAM. Verdadero, ra (complete): *he is a right idiot,* es un verdadero idiota; *this is a right mess!,* ¡es un verdadero lío! || Derecho, cha: *the right leg,* la pierna derecha; *the right bank of a river,* la orilla derecha de un río. || SP. Derecha: *the right winger,* el extremo derecha. | De derecha: *a right hook,* un gancho de derecha. || De derecha, derechista (politics). || MATH. Recto, ta: *a right angle,* un ángulo recto; *right line,* línea recta. || — *All right,* bien (well): *I am all right,* estoy bien; bastante bien (well enough), de confianza (trustworthy). || *All right!,* ¡bueno!, ¡bien! (now then), ¡de acuerdo!, ¡muy bien!, ¡vale! (agreed), ¡está bien! (enough!). || *All right?,* ¿de acuerdo? || *Are you all right?,* ¿te encuentras bien? || *Everything will be all right,* todo saldrá bien. || *Is it all right for me to go?,* ¿puedo ir? || *Is that right?,* ¿de verdad? || *Is this the right house?,* ¿es ésta la casa que buscamos? || *Is this the right road for...?,* ¿es ésta la carretera de...?, ¿vamos bien para...? || *It is all right,* no importa, déjalo (it doesn't matter). || *It is all right for some,* los hay con suerte. || *It is all right for you,* Ud. no tiene problemas. || *It is right that,* es justo que. || *It's not right!,* ¡no hay derecho! || *My watch is right,* mi reloj va bien. || *Quite right!,* ¡perfectamente! || *Right?,* ¿vale? || *Right!* o *right you are!* o *right ho!,* ¡bueno!, ¡de acuerdo! || *Right side up,* en posición vertical. || FAO. *She's a bit of all right,* está muy bien, es para comérsela. || *That's right,* eso es. || *The right side of a fabric,* el derecho de una tela. || FAM. *To be as right as rain,* estar perfectamente bien. || *To be in one's right mind,* estar en su sano juicio *or* en sus cabales. || *To be right,* tener razón. || *To be right to,* hacer bien en. || FIG. *To be s.o.'s right hand,* ser el brazo derecho de alguien. || *To come out* o *to turn out right,* salir bien. || *To do the right thing,* hacer bien. || *To put* o *to set right,* poner en el buen camino (to put on the right road), desengañar (to show the truth), corregir (to correct), curar (to cure), ordenar, poner en orden, arreglar (to put in order), arreglar (to repair), poner bien (to put in the right position), poner en hora (watch). || *To say the right thing,* decir lo que se debe.

— N. Bien, *m.*: *right and wrong,* el bien y el mal. || Justicia, *f.*: *to fight for the right,* luchar por la justicia; *to do s.o. right,* hacerle justicia a alguien. || Equidad, *f.* (equity). || Derecho, *m.*: *divine right,* derecho divino; *the rights of man,* los derechos del hombre; *right to the throne,* derecho al trono; *what right have you to enter?,* ¿de qué derecho se vale para entrar? || Derecha, *f.* (the right hand side): *to turn to the right,* torcer a la derecha; *it's on your right,* está a su derecha. || SP. Derechazo, *m.* (a blow with the right hand). || Derecha, *f.* (the right hand). || Pie (*m.*) derecho (in dancing): *to lead with the right,* empezar con el pie derecho. || — Pl. Derechos, *m.*: *civil rights,* derechos civiles; *feudal rights,* derechos señoriales. || — *All rights reserved,* reservados todos los derechos, es propiedad. || *By right* o *by rights,* de derecho: *it is yours by right,* te corresponde de derecho. || MIL. *By the right,* ¡derecha! || *By what right do you arrest me?,* ¿con qué derecho me detiene usted? || *In one's own right,* por derecho propio. || *Keep to the right,* circulen por la derecha. || *Member as of right,* miembro (*m.*) por derecho propio. || *Might and right,* la fuerza y el derecho. || *On the right,* a la derecha. || *Right of pardon,* derecho de gracia. || *Right of way,* servidumbre (*m.*) de paso, derecho de paso (land), preferencia (*f.*) de paso, prioridad, *f.* (roads). || COMM. *Sole right,* exclusiva, *f.* || *The Right,* la derecha (politics). || *The rights and wrongs of,* lo bueno y lo malo de. || *To be in the right,* tener razón. || *To be within one's rights,* estar en su derecho. || *To have a right to,* tener derecho a (sth.), tener derecho de *or* a (to do sth.). || *To know the rights of a case,* conocer todos los pormenores de un asunto. || *To put* o *to set things to rights,* arreglar las cosas. || *To put to rights,* poner en orden, ordenar (to put in order), deshacer, enderezar (a wrong). || *To waive one's right to speak,* renunciar al uso de la palabra. || *With a right to vote,* con voz y voto. || *Without a right to vote,* con voz pero sin voto.

— Adv. Bien, como es debido (well): *I think you did right,* creo que obraste bien. || Correctamente, bien: *add the figures right,* suma bien las cifras. || A la derecha: *turn right,* tuerza a la derecha. || Exactamente, justo (exactly): *right where you are now,* exactamente donde estás tú ahora. || De lleno: *he ran right into the tree,* dio de lleno contra el árbol. || Inmediatamente, justo: *right after dinner,* justo después de la cena; *right by the church,* justo al lado de la iglesia. || Directamente, derecho: *go right home,* vete directamente a casa. || Muy (very): *I was right glad to see him,* estuve muy contento de verlo. || — MIL. *Eyes right!,* ¡vista a la derecha! || *Go right ahead,* siga, continúe. || *He owed money right and left,* debía dinero a diestro y siniestro. || *He's coming right enough,* va a venir por supuesto. || *He put his finger right into the cake,* metió todo el dedo en el pastel. || *If I remember right,* si mal no recuerdo. || *I knew he was coming all right,* sabía perfectamente que venía. || *It serves you right!,* ¡bien merecido lo tienes!, ¡te está bien empleado! || *Right against the wall,* muy pegado a la pared (sin que haya movimiento), de lleno contra la pared (dar, arrojar algo, etc.). || *Right and left,* a diestro y siniestro. || *Right at the top,* en todo lo alto. || *Right away,* en seguida, inmediatamente. || *Right here,* aquí mismo. || *Right in the middle,* en pleno centro. || *Right now,* en este momento, ahora mismo. || *Right off,* inmediatamente, en seguida (at once), de un tirón (in one go), seguidos, das (one after the other). || U. S. *Right on!,* ¡adelante! || *Right Reverend,* reverendísimo. || *Right to the end,* hasta el final. || MIL. *Right turn!,* ¡media vuelta a la derecha! || *To do right,* obrar bien. || *To do right by s.o.,* tratar bien a alguien. || *To get right away,* escaparse sin dejar rastro. || *To go right,* salir bien. || *To go right on,* seguir adelante. || *To speak right out,* hablar sin rodeos. || *We had to pass right through the town centre,* tuvimos que pasar por el centro mismo de la ciudad.

— OBSERV. A veces la palabra *right* en su uso adverbial tiene un carácter enfático y no se traduce (*he threw the ball right over the wall,* echó el balón por encima del muro).

right [rait] v. tr. Enderezar (to put in an upright position). || MAR. Enderezar, adrizar: *to right a boat,* enderezar un barco. || Enderezar (a wrong). || Hacer justicia a (a person). || Corregir, rectificar (to correct): *to right an error,* corregir un error.

— V. intr. Enderezarse.

right about or **right-about** [—ə,baut] adj. MIL. *Right-about turn,* media vuelta a la derecha.

— N. MIL. Media vuelta (*f.*) a la derecha.

— Adv. *To turn right about,* dar media vuelta.

right-about-face [—ə,bautˈfeis] n. U. S. MIL. Media vuelta (*f.*) a la derecha. || U. S. Cambio (*m.*) completo (of opinion).

right-about-face [—ə,bautˈfeis] v. intr. U. S. Dar media vuelta a la derecha. || Cambiar completamente.

right angle [—æŋgl] n. MATH. Ángulo (*m.*) recto. || *At right angles*, en ángulo recto.
right-angled [—ˈæŋgld] adj. MATH. Rectángulo, la (triangle). | Rectangular: *right-angled figure*, figura rectangular. || En ángulo recto (bend).
right ascension [—əˈsenʃən] n. ASTR. Ascensión (*f.*) recta.
right-down [—ˌdaun] adj. FAM. Completo, ta.
— Adv. FAM. Muy.
righteous [—ʃəs] adj. Recto, ta; honrado, da: *a righteous ruler*, un gobernante honrado. || Justo, ta: *righteous anger*, cólera justa. || Justificado, da (act).
righteousness [—ʃəsnis] n. Rectitud, *f.* (uprightness). || Justicia, *f.* (fairness).
righter [—ə*] n. Enderezador (*m.*) de entuertos.
right field [—fi:ld] n. U. S. SP. Parte (*f.*) derecha del campo (in baseball).
rightful [—ful] adj. Legítimo, ma: *rightful owner*, propietario legítimo. || Equitativo, va; justo, ta (fair).
right-hand [—hænd] adj. De la derecha: *right-hand door*, puerta de la derecha. || A la derecha: *a right-hand turn*, una vuelta a la derecha. || Por la derecha: *right-hand drive*, conducción por la derecha. || — FIG. *Right-hand man*, brazo derecho. || *Right-hand side*, derecha, *f.*, lado derecho.
right-handed [—ˈhændid] adj. Que usa la mano derecha (person). || Para la mano derecha (tools, etc.). || TECH. Dextrógiro, ra (dextrorotatory). || Torcido de izquierda a derecha (rope). || Con la mano derecha (boxing).
right hander [—hændə*] n. Persona (*f.*) que usa la mano derecha. || Derechazo, *m.* (in boxing).
rightism [—izəm] n. Derechismo, *m.*
rightist [—ist] adj. De derechas, derechista.
— N. Derechista, *m.* & *f.*
rightly [—li] adv. Como es debido, debidamente, correctamente (correctly). || Exactamente (exactly). || Justamente, con justicia (fairly, justly). || Con derecho, con razón (reasonably). || Prudentemente, cuerdamente (wisely). || — *And rightly so*, y con razón. || *Rightly or wrongly*, con razón o sin ella.
right-minded [—maindid] adj. Honrado, da; recto, ta.
rightness [—nis] n. Exactitud, *f.*, precisión, *f.* (accuracy). || Rectitud, *f.*, honradez, *f.* (honesty). || Justicia, *f.* (fairness). || JUR. Lo bien fundado, legitimidad, *f.*
right-thinking [—ˈθiŋkiŋ] adj. Honrado, da; recto, ta.
right wing [—ˈwiŋ] n. Derecha, *f.* (in politics). || SP. Extremo (*m.*) derecha, ala (*m.*) derecha.
right-wing [—ˈwiŋ] adj. De derecha, derechista.
right winger [—ˈwiŋə*] n. Derechista, *m.* & *f.* (in politics). || SP. Extremo (*m.*) derecha, ala (*m.*) derecha (in rugby).
rigid [ˈridʒid] adj. Rígido, da: *his arm went rigid with cold*, su brazo se puso rígido con el frío. || Fijo, ja: *a rigid stare*, una mirada fija. || Severo, ra; riguroso, sa; inflexible: *rigid discipline*, disciplina rigurosa. || Riguroso, sa; rígido, da: *a rigid regard for rules*, un concepto rígido del reglamento. || Preciso, sa; exacto, ta; riguroso, sa (precise). || AVIAT. Rígido, da.
rigidness [—nis] n. See RIGIDITY.
rigidity [riˈdʒiditi] n. Rigidez, *f.* || Fijeza, *f.* (of glance). || Rigor, *m.*, severidad, *f.*, inflexibilidad, *f.* (of discipline, etc.).
rigmarole [ˈrigmərəul] n. Galimatías, *m.*, sarta (*f.*) de disparates.
rigor [ˈrigə*] n. MED. Escalofríos, *m. pl.* (shivering fit). | Rigidez, *f.* (stiffness). || U. S. See RIGOUR. || MED. *Rigor mortis*, rigidez cadavérica.
rigorism [ˈrigərizəm] n. Rigorismo, *m.*
rigorist [ˈrigərist] n. Rigorista, *m.* & *f.*
rigorous [ˈrigərəs] adj. Riguroso, sa.
rigorousness [—nis] n. Rigurosidad, *f.*
rigour [ˈrigə*] n. Rigor, *m.*, severidad, *f.* (strictness): *the rigour of the law*, el rigor de la ley. || Rigor, *m.*, austeridad, *f.* (austerity). || MATH. PHIL. Exactitud, *f.* || Rigor, *m.* (of weather).
rile [rail] v. tr. FAM. Irritar, poner nervioso, sacar de quicio (to exasperate).
rill [ril] n. Riachuelo, *m.*
rillet [ˈrilet] n. Arroyuelo, *m.*
rim [rim] n. Llanta, *f.* (of a wheel). || Borde, *m.* (of cup, vase). || Canto, *m.* (of a coin). || Montura, *f.* (of spectacles). || ASTR. Cerco, *m.*
rim [rim] v. tr. Poner una llanta a (a wheel). || Bordear.
rime [raim] n. Escarcha, *f.* (frost). || See RHYME.
rime [raim] v. tr. Cubrir de escarcha.
rimer [raimə*] or **rimester** [ˈraimstə*] n. Rimador, ra.
rimmed [ˈrimd] adj. Bordeado de, con un borde de (cup, vase). || Con una montura de (spectacles).
rimose or **rimous** [ˈraiˈməus] adj. BOT. Agrietado, da.
rimy [ˈraimi] adj. Escarchado, da.
rind [raind] n. Cáscara, *f.* (of fruits). || Corteza, *f.* (of bacon). || Corteza, *f.*, costra, *f.* (of cheese).
rinderpest [ˈrindəpest] n. VET. Peste (*f.*) bovina.
ring [riŋ] n. Sonido, *m.* (sound). || Tañido, *m.*, repique, *m.*, campaneo, *m.* (of a large bell). || Toque, *m.* (act of sounding a bell). || Toque, *m.*, timbrazo, *m.*, toque (*m.*) de timbre (of an electric bell). || Campanilleo, *m.*, toque (*m.*) de la campanilla (of handbell). || Timbre, *m.* (of the alarm clock). || Llamada, *f.*, timbre, *m.* (of phone). || Sonido (*m.*) metálico (metallic sound). || Resonancia, *f.* (resonance). || Tintineo, *m.*, retintín, *m.* (tinkle). || Timbre, *m.* (of the voice). || Tono, *m.*, entonación, *f.* (tone). || Cascabeleo, *m.* (of laughter). || Círculo, *m.* (circle). || Anillo, *m.*, sortija, *f.* (on finger). || Aro, *m.* (rim, ornament). || Arete, *m.* (earring). || Aro, *m.*, servilletero, *m.* (for napkins). || Llavero, *m.* (for keys). || Anillo, *m.* (of smoke, tree, fire). || Anilla, *f.* (for birds, curtains). || Corte (*m.*) circular (on tree trunks). || Anilla, *f.* (in gymnastics). || Pista, *f.* (circus). || SP. Ring, *m.*, cuadrilátero, *m.* (in boxing). || Ruedo, *m.*, redondel, *m.* (in bullring). || Aro, *m.*, segmento, *m.* (of a piston). || Recinto, *m.*, cercado (*m.*) para apuestas (racecourse). || Corro, *m.* (of children): *sitting in a ring*, sentados en corro. || Círculo, *m.*, grupo, *m.* (of people). || Camarilla, *f.* (coterie). || Banda, *f.* (of thieves, etc.). || COMM. Cártel, *m.* || Red, *f.*, organización, *f.* (of spies). || ASTR. Anillo, *m.* (of a planet). | Halo, *m.* (of moon). | Cerco, *m.* (of sun). || BOT. Cerco, *m.* || MAR. Arganeo, *m.* (of the anchor). || CHEM. Cadena, *f.* || — *A ring of bells*, un juego de campanas. || *There is a ring at the door*, llaman a la puerta, tocan el timbre. || SP. *The ring*, los corredores de apuestas (bookmakers), el boxeo (boxing), los boxeadores (boxers). || *To give s.o. a ring*, llamar por teléfono a alguien, dar un telefonazo a alguien, telefonear a alguien. || *To have rings round the eyes*, tener ojeras, estar ojeroso. || FIG. *To make* o *to run rings round s.o.*, dar cien vueltas a alguien. | *To throw one's hat in the ring*, echarse al ruedo. || *Wedding ring*, alianza, *f.*, anillo (*m.*) de boda. || *With a ring of defiance*, en son de reto.
ring* [riŋ] v. tr. Tocar: *to ring a bell*, tocar una campana. || Hacer sonar (coins). || FIG. Cantar (s.o.'s praises). || Rodear, circundar: *trees ring the lake*, unos árboles rodean el lago. || Anillar (bird, animal). || Acorralar (to ride round). || AGR. Hacer un corte circular en la corteza de [un árbol]. | — *That rings a bell*, eso me suena. || FIG. *To ring the bell*, dar en el blanco.
— V. intr. Sonar (to sound). || Repicar, tañer, sonar: *the bell rang*, sonó la campana. || Llamar [con una campana *or* con un timbre]: *s.o. rang at the door*, alguien llamó a la puerta. || Tocar la campanilla (the altar boy). || Resonar: *the room rang with laughter*, la sala resonó con risas. || Tintinear (coins). || Zumbar, pitar: *the noise made my ears ring*, el ruido me hizo zumbar los oídos. || Llamar [por teléfono], telefonear: *I'll ring tomorrow*, llamaré mañana. || Llamar: *to ring for the lift*, llamar el ascensor. || Formar círculo *or* corro (to form a circle). || Moverse en círculo (to move in a circle). || Subir en espiral (smoke). || — *To ring false*, sonar a falso. || *To ring true*, parecer verdad. || *To set all the bells ringing*, echar las campanas a vuelo.
— ***To ring back***, volver a llamar (telephone). || ***To ring down***, bajar (the curtain). | — *To ring the curtain down on*, acabar con. || ***To ring in***, tocar las campanas por la llegada de, anunciar: *to ring in the New Year*, anunciar el Año Nuevo. || ***To ring off***, colgar. || ***To ring out***, oírse: *a shot rang out*, se oyó un tiro. | Tocar las campanas por la ida de. || ***To ring up***, llamar [por teléfono], telefonear (to telephone). | Subir (curtain).
— OBSERV. Este verbo es irregular en todos los sentidos referentes a sonido (pret. ***rang***; p. p. ***rung***) y regular en las demás acepciones.
ring-a-ring-a-roses [—əˈriŋəˈrəuziz] n. Corro, *m.*
ringbolt [—bəult] n. TECH. Cáncamo, *m.*, armella, *f.*
ringdove [—dʌv] n. ZOOL. Paloma (*f.*) torcaz.
ringed [—d] adj. Anillado, da (finger, birds). || En anillo (circular). || ASTR. Rodeado por un anillo (planet).
ringer [—ə*] n. Campanero, ra (person who rings a bell). || Timbre, *m.* (doorbell). || Badajo, *m.* (bell clapper). || SP. Aro (*m.*) que da en el blanco (quoits). || FIG. FAM. Intruso, sa (illegal entry in a race). || U. S. FIG. *He's a ringer for his brother*, es la viva imagen de su hermano.
ring fence [—fens] n. Cercado, *m.* || FIG. Barrera, *f.*
ring finger [—ˌfiŋgə*] n. Anular, *m.*
ringing [—iŋ] adj. Que suena (bell). || Resonante, sonoro, ra (cry). || Estruendoso, sa (laughter). || Clamoroso, sa (applause).
— N. Tañido, *m.* (of bells). || Toque (*m.*) de timbre (of an electric bell). || Sonido, *m.* (sound). || Zumbido, *m.*, pitido, *m.* (in one's ears).
ringleader [—ˌli:də*] n. Cabecilla, *m.*
ringlet [—lit] n. Arillo, *m.*, anillito, *m.* || Bucle, *m.*, rizo, *m.* (of hair).
ringmaster [—ˌmɑ:stə*] n. Maestro (*m.*) de ceremonias.
ring road [—rəud] n. Carretera (*f.*) de circunvalación.
ringside [—said] n. Cercanías (*f. pl.*) del cuadrilátero (boxing). || FIG. Primera fila, *f.*
— Adj. De primera fila.
ringworm [—wə:m] n. MED. Tiña, *f.*
rink [riŋk] n. SP. Pista (*f.*) de hielo (ice skating). | Pista (*f.*) de patinaje (roller skating). | Terreno, *m.* (bowling). | Equipo (*m.*) de cuatro (bowling or curling team).
rinse [rins] n. Enjuague, *m.* (of dishes). || Aclarado, *m.* (of clothes, hair). || Reflejo, *m.* (hair colouring).
rinse [rins] v. tr. Enjuagar (dishes). || Aclarar (clothes). || Dar reflejos a (to dye).

rinsing [—iŋ] n. See RINSE. || — Pl. Agua (*f. sing.*) de aclarado. || Heces, *f.* (dregs).

riot [ˈraiət] n. Disturbio, *m.*: *race riots*, disturbios raciales. || Motín, *m.* (uprising). || FIG. Derroche, *m.* (of colours). | Exuberancia, *f.* (of plants). || — FAM. *He's a riot*, es divertidísimo. || *Riot Act*, ley (*f.*) de orden público. || U. S. *Riot policeman*, guardia (*m.*) de asalto. || FIG. *To be a riot*, tener mucho éxito, tener un éxito clamoroso (a theatre play). || FAM. *To read the riot act to s.o.*, echar un rapapolvo a alguien, leerle la cartilla a alguien. || *To run riot*, desmandarse, desenfrenarse (people), proliferar, pulular (plants).

riot [ˈraiət] v. tr. *To riot away*, perder (time), derrochar, despilfarrar (money).
— V. intr. Alborotarse, amotinarse: *the people rioted in the streets*, la gente se amotinó en las calles. || Causar alboroto, armar jaleo (to make a row). || FIG. *To riot in*, entregarse a.

rioter [—ə*] n. Alborotador, ra; amotinado, da; revoltoso, sa. || Juerguista, *m.* & *f.* (reveller).

riotous [—əs] adj. Alborotado, da; sedicioso, sa; amotinado, da (engaging in riots). || Ruidoso, sa; bullicioso, sa (noisy). || Desenfrenado, da: *riotous living*, vida desenfrenada. || Juerguista, jaranero, ra (revelling). || FIG. *A riotous success*, un éxito clamoroso.

rip [rip] n. Rasgón, *m.*, desgarrón, *m.* (a tear). || Descosido, *m.* (split seam). || Aguas (*f. pl.*) revueltas (rough water). || FAM. Tunante, *m.*, bribón, *m.* (child). | Mal bicho, *m.*, mala persona, *f.* (rogue). | Calavera, *m.* (rotter). || Matalón, *m.*, rocín, *m.* (horse).

rip [rip] v. tr. Rasgar, desgarrar (to tear): *I ripped my trousers*, me rasgué el pantalón. || Descoser (to tear a seam): *rip the hem*, descosa el dobladillo. || Serrar al hilo (in carpentry). || Quitar las tejas de, destejar (a roof). || *To rip open*, abrir de un tirón *or* desgarrando.
— V. intr. Rasgarse, desgarrarse (to tear). || FAM. Volar (to move fast). || FAM. *Let her rip!*, ¡a todo gas!, ¡pisa el acelerador! (car).
— ***To rip along***, ir a todo gas, ir a toda mecha (quickly). || ***To rip away*** o ***off***, arrancar, quitar (to remove). || FAM. ***To rip into***, atacar. || ***To rip out***, arrancar (to tear out). | Soltar (to utter). || ***To rip up***, desgarrar (to tear to pieces). | Romper (to break). | Destrozar (to destroy). | Deshacer, descoser (a seam). | Abrir (to open up). | Rajar, partir, hender (wood). | Destripar, despanzurrar (s.o.). | Reavivar (old grievances).

riparian [raiˈpɛəriən] adj. Ribereño, ña.

rip cord [ˈripkɔːd] n. Cuerda (*f.*) de desgarre (of a balloon). || Cuerda (*f.*) de abertura (of a parachute).

ripe [raip] adj. Maduro, ra: *a ripe apple*, una manzana madura; *a ripe plan*, un proyecto maduro. || Hecho, cha: *a ripe cheese*, un queso hecho. || Listo, ta; preparado, da (ready). || Oportuno, na (suitable): *when the time is ripe*, cuando llegue el momento oportuno. || Sensato, ta; maduro, ra: *a ripe judgment*, un juicio sensato. || MED. Maduro, ra (abscess). || Encarnado, da; rojo, ja (lips). || — *The ripe old age of ninety*, la avanzada edad de noventa años. || *The time is ripe for action*, ha llegado el momento de hacer algo.

ripen [ˈraipən] v. tr./intr. Madurar.

ripeness [ˈraipnis] n. Madurez, *f.*

ripening [ˈraipniŋ] adj. Que madura.
— N. Madurez, *f.*, maduración, *f.*

rip-off [ˈripɔf] n. FAM. Timo, *m.* (swindle). || FAM. *This place is a real rip-off*, en este sitio le clavan a uno.

riposte or **ripost** [riˈpəust] n. SP. Respuesta, *f.* (in fencing). || Respuesta, *f.*, réplica, *f.* (a retort).

riposte or **ripost** [riˈpəust] v. intr. SP. Parar atacando (in fencing). || Replicar, responder (to retort).

ripper [ˈripə*] n. TECH. Sierra (*f.*) de cortar al hilo *or* de hender (ripsaw). || Destripador, *m.*: *Jack the Ripper*, Jack el Destripador. || FAM. Persona (*f.*) *or* cosa (*f.*) estupenda.

ripping [ˈripiŋ] adj. FAM. Formidable, estupendo, da.

ripple [ˈripl] n. Onda, *f.*, rizo, *m.* (on water). || Chapoteo, *m.* (sound of water, waves). || Murmullo, *m.* (of a river). || Ondulación, *f.* (of hair). || Murmullo, *m.* (of a conversation). || Ondulación (*f.*) dejada por la marea en la arena (ripple mark). || TECH. Desgranadora, *f.* (textiles). || *Ripple mark*, ondulación dejada por la marea en la arena.

ripple [ripl] v. tr. Ondular, rizar (water). || TECH. Desgranar (textiles).
— V. intr. Rizarse (to form waves). || Murmurar (a stream). || Ondular (corn, hair).

ripplet [ˈriplit] n. Onda (*f.*) *or* ola (*f.*) pequeña.

ripply [ˈripli] adj. Rizado, da; ondulado, da.

riprap [ˈripræp] n. U. S. Fondo (*m.*) de roca (foundation). | Escollera, *f.*, muro (*m.*) de rocas (wall).

riprap [ˈripræp] v. tr. U. S. Echar cimientos de roca a.

rip-roaring [ˈripˈrɔːriŋ] adj. FAM. Clamoroso, sa (success). | Muy animado, da (party).

ripsaw [ˈripsɔː] n. TECH. Sierra (*f.*) de cortar al hilo *or* de hender.

rise [raiz] n. Elevación, *f.*, altura, *f.* (hill). || Cuesta, *f.*, pendiente, *f.*, subida, *f.* (slope). || Subida, *f.*, ascensión, *f.* (of a hill, slope, etc.). || Subida, *f.* (in social status). || Ascenso, *m.* (in rank). || Subida, *f.*, ascensión, *f.* (to power). || Salida, *f.* (of sun, moon). || Desarrollo, *m.* (development): *the rise of industry*, el desarrollo de la industria. || Crecimiento, *m.* (of town). || Subida, *f.*, alza, *f.*, aumento, *m.* (price): *rise in prices*, aumento de los precios. || Aumento, *m.*, elevación, *f.* (in rate). || Aumento, *m.* (in value, salary, etc.). || Alza, *f.* (in the stock exchange). || PHYS. Aumento, *m.* (of pressure). || Aumento, *m.*, elevación, *f.*, subida, *f.* (of temperature). || Subida, *f.* (in a thermometer, etc.). || Crecida, *f.* (in water level). || Flujo, *m.* (of the tide). || Aparición, *f.* (of an empire). || Elevación, *f.* (in the voice). || THEATR. Subida, *f.* (of the curtain). || Manantial, *m.*, fuente, *f.* (source of a river). || FIG. Fuente, *f.*, origen, *m.* (source). || — FIG. *I haven't had a rise all day*, no han picado en todo el día (in fishing). || *Rise and fall*, grandeza (*f.*) y decadencia (of an empire), flujo y reflujo (of the sea). || *To ask for a rise*, pedir un aumento de sueldo. || *To be on the rise*, estar subiendo. || FIG. *To get* o *to take a rise out of s.o.*, tomarle el pelo a alguien. || *To give rise to*, provocar, causar, ocasionar, dar origen a. || *To shoot a bird on the rise*, disparar a un pájaro al levantar el vuelo.

rise* [raiz] v. tr. Espantar, hacer que levanten el vuelo (birds). || Atraer, hacer picar al anzuelo (fish).
— V. intr. Levantarse: *he rose from the chair*, se levantó de la silla; *I rise early in the morning*, me levanto por la mañana temprano; *to rise from one's bed*, levantarse de la cama; *a strong wind rose*, se levantó un viento fuerte. || Levantarse, ponerse de pie: *the men all rose as she came in*, todos los hombres se pusieron de pie cuando ella entró. || Levantarse, alzarse: *mountains rose in the distance*, los montes se levantaban a lo lejos. || Elevarse: *the balloon rose in the air*, el globo se elevó en el aire. || Subir, ascender (to slope up). || Subir (ground). || Levantar *or* alzar el vuelo (birds). || Picar, morder (fish). || Subir, aumentar: (temperature). || Mejorar de posición, subir, medrar: *to rise in society*, mejorar de posición en la sociedad. || Ascender (in rank): *he rose to an important post*, ascendió a un cargo importante. || Subir (to power). || Subir, aumentar (prices, salary): *prices rose by ten per cent*, los precios aumentaron en un diez por ciento. || Estar en alza (stock exchange). || Aumentar (the pressure). || Desarrollarse (to develop). || Alzarse, levantarse; *her voice rose in anger*, su voz se alzó con ira. || Crecer (river): *the Seine is rising fast*, el Sena está creciendo rápidamente. || Subir (tide). || Salir (sun, moon, stars). || THEATR. Subir (the curtain). || FIG. Crecer, aumentar (anger, hopes). | Surgir, aparecer, presentarse (to appear). | Surgir, armarse, haber (a quarrel). || Nacer: *the river rises in the mountains*, el río nace en las montañas. || Tener su origen, originarse (*from*, en) [to originate]. || Levantarse, sublevarse (to revolt). || Arreciar (to get stronger). || Levantarse (to adjourn a meeting). || Levantar la sesión (to end a meeting). || Erizarse: *fear made his hair rise*, el pelo se le erizó de miedo. || CULIN. Leudarse (bread, cakes). || Brotar (plants). || Hincharse (to swell). || MED. Salir (blister, bruise, etc.). || — *Tears rose to her eyes*, se le subieron las lágrimas a los ojos. || FIG. *To rise above*, sobreponerse a. || *To rise early*, madrugar, levantarse temprano. || *To rise from nothing*, haber empezado con nada, salir de la nada. || REL. *To rise from the dead*, resucitar de entre los muertos. || *To rise on a point of order*, plantear *or* formular una cuestión de orden (during a meeting). || FIG. *To rise to*, ser capaz de hacer, poder hacer. | *To rise to a challenge*, aceptar un reto. || *To rise to one's feet*, ponerse de pie, levantarse. || *To rise to the occasion*, ponerse a la altura de las circunstancias. || *To rise to the surface*, salir a la superficie. || *To rise up in arms*, alzarse en armas.

— OBSERV. Pret. ***rose;*** p. p. ***risen.***

risen [ˈrizn] p. p. See RISE.

riser [ˈraizə*] n. Contrahuella, *f.* (of stair). || Tubo (*m.*) de subida (pipe). || Columna (*f.*) ascendente (of gas, water, etc.). || — *Early riser*, madrugador, ra. || *Late riser*, dormilón, ona.

risibility [ˌriziˈbiliti] n. Risibilidad, *f.*

risible [ˈrizibl] adj. Risible (causing laughter). || Risueño, ña (inclined to laugh).

rising [ˈraiziŋ] adj. Naciente: *the rising sun*, el sol naciente. || Que se levanta (wind). || Ascendente (quantity). || Creciente (number, tide, anger, importance). || Que sube, que aumenta, creciente (price). || En cuesta, pendiente (sloping). || Nuevo, va; joven: *the rising generation*, la nueva generación. || Que tiene casi, que raya en: *rising forty five*, que raya en los cuarenta y cinco años. || Prometedor, ra (promising): *rising man*, hombre prometedor. || *Rising vote*, votación (*f.*) por levantados y sentados.
— N. Salida, *f.*: *the rising of the sun*, la salida del sol. || REL. Resurrección, *f.*: *the rising of Jesus from the dead*, la resurreción de Cristo de entre los muertos. || Levantamiento, *m.*, alzamiento, *m.* (rebellion). || JUR. Clausura, *f.* || Levantamiento, *m.* (of a meeting). || THEATR. Subida, *f.* (curtain). || Subida, *f.*, ascensión, *f.* (of a slope, etc.). || Elevación, *f.* (of ground). || Aumento, *m.*, subida, *f.* (of prices, salary). || Ascenso, *m.* (in rank). || Subida, *f.* (of fever, thermometer). || Crecida, *f.* (of river). || Nacimiento, *m.* (source of river). || *On the rising of the meeting*, al levantarse la sesión.

risk [risk] n. Riesgo, *m.*, peligro, *m.* || Riesgo, *m.* (in insurance). || — *At one's own risk*, bajo su propia responsabilidad, por su cuenta y riesgo. || *At the risk*

of, a *or* con riesgo de. || *At the risk of one's life*, con peligro de su vida. || *At your own risk*, por su cuenta y riesgo. || *To run the risk of*, correr el riesgo de. || *To take risks*, arriesgarse.
risk [risk] v. tr. Arriesgar: *to risk one's life*, arriesgar la vida. || Exponerse a: *to risk a defeat*, exponerse a una derrota. || Arriesgarse a, correr el riesgo de: *you can't risk doing it*, no puede arriesgarse a hacerlo; *he risked breaking his arm*, corrió el riesgo de romperse el brazo. || — FIG. *To risk everything on one throw*, jugarse el todo por el todo. || FAM. *To risk one's neck*, jugarse el tipo.
riskiness [—inis] n. Riesgo, *m.*, peligro, *m.*, lo arriesgado.
risky [—i] adj. Arriesgado, da; peligroso, sa; aventurado, da.
risorius [riˈsɔriəs] n. Risorio, *m.* (muscle).
— OBSERV. El plural de la palabra inglesa es *risorii*.
risqué [ˈriskei] adj. Escabroso, sa; de color subido, subido de color: *a risqué joke*, un chiste de color subido.
rissole [ˈrisəul] n. CULIN. Empanadilla (*f.*) rellena.
rite [rait] n. Rito, *m.* || — *The Rite of Spring*, la Consagración de la Primavera (work by Stravinsky). || REL. *The Roman Rite*, el rito romano.
ritornello [ritɔːˈneləu] n. MUS. Ritornelo, *m.*, retornelo, *m.*
— OBSERV. El plural de *ritornello* es *ritornelli*.
ritual [ˈritjuəl] adj. Ritual: *ritual dances*, danzas rituales.
— N. Ritual, *m.*, ceremonial, *m.* (rites). || Ritual, *m.* (book).
ritualism [—izəm] n. Ritualismo, *m.* || Ritualidad, *f.*
ritualist [ˈritjuəlist] n. Ritualista, *m.* & *f.*
ritualistic [ˌritjuəˈlistik] adj. Ritualista.
ritzy [ˈritsi] adj. U. S. Lujoso, sa.
rival [ˈraivəl] n. Rival, *m.* & *f.*, competidor, ra.
— Adj. Rival, competidor, ra.
rival [ˈraivəl] v. tr. Competir con, rivalizar con (to be in competition with): *her beauty rivalled that of the queen*, su belleza competía con la de la reina. || Poder rivalizar con (to equal).
— V. intr. Rivalizar, competir (*with*, con).
rivalize [ˈraivəlaiz] v. intr. Rivalizar.
rivalry [ˈraivəlri] n. Rivalidad, *f.*, competencia, *f.*
rive* [raiv] v. tr. Rajar, hender, partir. || *To rive sth. from s.o.*, arrancar algo a alguien.
— V. intr. Rajarse, henderse.
— OBSERV. Pret. ***rived;*** p. p. ***riven, rived.***
riven [ˈrivən] p. p. See RIVE.
river [ˈrivə*] n. Río, *m.* || FIG. Río, *m.* || — *Down the river*, río abajo. || FIG. *To be up the river*, estar en chirona, estar en la cárcel. | *To sell s.o. down the river*, traicionar a alguien. || *Up the river*, río arriba.
— Adj. De río, del río: *river fish*, pez de río; *river diversion*, desviación del río. || Fluvial: *river harbour*, puerto fluvial.
— OBSERV. La palabra *river* precede el nombre en Gran Bretaña *(the River Thames)* y lo sigue en los Estados Unidos *(the Hudson River)*.
riverain [ˈrivərein] adj./n. Ribereño, ña.
riverbank [ˈrivəˈbæŋk] n. Orilla, *f.*, ribera, *f.*
river basin [ˈrivəˌbeisn] n. Cuenca (*f.*) de río.
riverbed [ˈrivəˈbed] n. Lecho (*m.*) del río, cauce (*m.*) del río.
riverhead [ˈrivəˌhed] n. Fuente (*f.*) *or* nacimiento (*m.*) de un río.
river horse [ˈrivəˌhɔːs] n. Hipopótamo, *m.* (animal).
riverine [ˈrivərain] adj. Ribereño, ña (situated or living by a river). || Fluvial (relating to a river).
river lamprey [ˈrivəˈlæmpri] n. ZOOL. Lampreílla, *f.*, lamprehuela, *f.*
riverman [ˈrivəmən] n. Barquero, *m.*
— OBSERV. El plural de la palabra inglesa es *rivermen*.
River Plate [ˈrivəˌpleit] pr. n. GEOGR. Río (*m.*) de la Plata.
riverside [ˈrivəsaid] n. Ribera, *f.*, orilla, *f.*
— Adj. Ribereño, ña.
rivet [ˈrivit] n. TECH. Remache, *m.*, roblón, *m.*: *flathead rivet*, roblón de cabeza plana.
rivet [ˈrivit] v. tr. TECH. Remachar, roblonar. || FIG. Captar (the attention). | Sellar, cimentar (a friendship). | Fijar (one's eyes).
riveter [—ə*] n. Remachador, *m.* (person). || Remachadora, *f.* (machine).
riveting or **rivetting** [—iŋ] n. Remachado, *m.*, remache, *m.* (operation). || *Riveting hammer*, martillo (*m.*) de remachar, remachadora, *f.*
Riviera [ˌriviˈɛərə] n. Riviera, *f.* (in Italy). || Costa (*f.*) Azul (in France).
rivière [riviˈɛə*] n. Collar (*m.*) de brillantes.
rivulet [ˈrivjulit] n. Arroyo, *m.*
rix-dollar [ˈriksˈdɔlə*] n. Rixdal, *m.*
roach [rəutʃ] n. ZOOL. Cucaracha, *f.* (cockroach). | Gobio, *m.* (European freshwater fish). || MAR. Borde (*m.*) curvo de la parte inferior de la vela.
road [rəud] n. Carretera, *f.*: *the road to London*, la carretera de Londres. || Calle, *f.* (in a town). || Calzada, *f.* (roadway). || Camino, *m.* (way). || FIG. Camino, *m.*, vías, *f. pl.*: *the road to success*, el camino de la gloria; *he's well on the road to recovery*, está en vías de recuperación. || U. S. FAM. Vía (*f.*) férrea (track). | Ferrocarril, *m.* (railway). || — Pl. Rada, *f. sing.*, fondeadero, *m. sing.* (roadsted). || — *"A" road*, carretera nacional *or* general. || *Arterial* o *trunk road*, carretera nacional. || *"B" road*, carretera secundaria *or* comarcal. || *Country road*, camino vecinal. || *Main road*, carretera general (highway), calle mayor (high street). || THEATR. *On the road*, de gira. || *Road accidents*, accidentes (*m.*) de tráfico. || U. S. *Road agent*, bandolero, *m.*, salteador (*m.*) de caminos. || *Road narrows*, estrechamiento (*m.*) de carretera (traffic sign). || *Road network*, red (*f.*) de carreteras. || *Road safety*, seguridad (*f.*) en carretera. || *Road traffic*, tránsito rodado, circulación rodada. || *Road transport*, transporte (*m.*) por carretera. || *Road up*, obras, *f. pl.* || FIG. *To be on the right road*, ir por buen camino. | *To be on the road*, estar de gira (actors), estar de viaje (salesman). || FIG. FAM. *To hit the road*, largarse, irse. || AUT. *To hold the road*, agarrarse, tener buena adherencia *or* estabilidad.
roadbed [—bed] n. U. S. Infraestructura, *f.* (foundation of a road). | Firme, *m.* (surface of a road). | Terraplén, *m.* (of a railway).
roadblock [—blɔk] n. MIL. Barricada, *f.*
road hog [—hɔg] n. Conductor (*m.*) imprudente.
roadhouse [—haus] n. Parador, *m.*, albergue (*m.*) de carretera (inn). || U. S. Sala (*f.*) de fiestas en las afueras de una ciudad.
road labourer [—ˈleibərə*] n. Peón (*m.*) caminero.
road making [—ˌmeikiŋ] n. Construcción (*f.*) de carreteras.
roadman [—mən] or **roadmender** [—ˌmendə*] n. Peón (*m.*) caminero.
— OBSERV. El plural de *roadman* es *roadmen*.
road map [—mæp] n. Mapa (*m.*) de carreteras.
road metal [—ˌmetl] n. Grava, *f.*
road race [—reis] n. Carrera (*f.*) en carretera.
road roller [—ˈrəulə*] n. Apisonadora, *f.*
roadside [—said] n. Borde (*m.*) de la carretera.
— Adj. Situado al borde de la carretera. || *Roadside hotel*, albergue (*m.*) de carretera.
road sign [—sain] n. Señal (*f.*) de tráfico.
roadstead [—sted] n. Fondeadero, *m.*, rada, *f.*
roadster [—stə*] n. Dos plazas, *m. inv.* (car).
road sweeper [—ˌswiːpə*] n. Barrendero, *m.*
road trial [—ˌtraiəl] n. Prueba (*f.*) *or* carrera (*f.*) en carretera.
roadway [—wei] n. Calzada, *f.* (of a road). || Tablero, *m.* (of a bridge).
roam [rəum] n. Paseo, *m.* (ramble): *I went for a roam in the forest*, di un paseo por el bosque. || Vagabundeo, *m.* (wandering).
roam [rəum] v. tr. Rondar, vagar por. || *To roam the seas*, surcar los mares.
— V. intr. Vagar, errar.
roamer [—ə*] n. Azotacalles, *m. inv.* (loafer). || Vagabundo, *m.*
roaming [—iŋ] n. Vagabundeo, *m.*, || Paseos, *m. pl.*
roan [rəun] n. Caballo (*m.*) ruano (horse). || Marrón (*m.*) rojizo (colour). || Badana, *f.* (in bookbinding).
— Adj. Ruano, na (horse).
roar [rɔː*] n. Rugido, *m.* (of lion): *the lion let out a roar*, el león lanzó un rugido. || Mugido, *m.* (of cow). || Bramido, *m.* (of bull). || Estruendo, *m.* (noise). || Fragor, *m.* (of thunder). || Bramido, *m.* (of wind, sea). || Zumbido, *m.* (of an engine). || Rugido, *m.*, berrido, *m.*, vociferaciones, *f. pl.* (of a man). || Clamor, *m.* (of crowd). || *Roars of laughter*, carcajadas, *f.*
roar [rɔː*] v. tr. Vociferar (an order). || Berrear (a song). || *To roar s.o. down*, callar a alguien a gritos.
— V. intr. Rugir (lion). || Mugir (cow). || Bramar (bull). || Vociferar, berrear (to shout). || Bramar (sea, wind). || Zumbar (an engine). || Retumbar (to resound). || Respirar trabajosamente, padecer huélfago (horses). || — *The cars roared by*, los coches pasaban zumbando. || *To roar with anger*, rugir de cólera. || *To roar with laughter*, reírse a carcajadas. || *To roar with pain*, rugir de dolor.
roaring [—riŋ] adj. Rugiente (lion). || Bramante (bull). || Vociferante (people). || FAM. Clamoroso, sa: *roaring success*, éxito clamoroso. | Formidable, estupendo, da: *a roaring trade*, negocios formidables. || — FIG. *The roaring twenties*, los felices años veinte. | *We had a roaring night*, pasamos una noche estupenda.
— N. See ROAR.
roast [rəust] adj. Asado, da: *roast chicken*, pollo asado. || Tostado, da; torrefacto, ta (coffee). || FIG. Asado, da; achicharrado, da (very hot). || *Roast beef*, rosbif, *m.*, carne de vaca asada.
— N. Asado, *m.* || U. S. Barbacoa, *f.* (barbecue).
roast [rəust] v. tr. Asar (meat). || Tostar, torrefactar (coffee). || FIG. Achicharrar, asar: *the sun was roasting us*, el sol nos achicharraba. || TECH. Tostar, calcinar (minerals). || FAM. Meterse con, burlarse de (to banter). || U. S. FAM. Poner como los trapos a, desollar vivo a, vapulear a (to criticize). || — FIG. *To roast o.s.*, asarse, achicharrarse. | *To roast o.s. before a fire*, tostarse al fuego.
— V. intr. Asarse (meat). || Tostarse, torrefactarse (coffee). || FIG. Achicharrarse, asarse (to feel hot).
roasted [—id] adj. Tostado, da; torrefacto, ta (coffee).

roaster [—ə*] n. Animal (*m.*) para asar (animal). || Pollo (*m.*) para asar (chicken). || Asador, *m.* (oven). || TECH. Horno (*m.*) de calcinación (for minerals). || Torrefactor, *m.*, tostador (*m.*) de café (for coffee).
roasting [—iŋ] adj. Achicharrante, abrasador, ra (fire). — N. Asado, *m.* (of meat). || Torrefacción, *f.*, tostado, *m.* (of coffee). || TECH. Calcinación, *f.* (of minerals). || FAM. Burla, *f.*, tomadura (*f.*) de pelo (mockery). || U. S. FAM. Rapapolvo, *m.*, sermón, *m.* (ticking off): *he gave me a roasting*, me echó un rapapolvo. | Crítica, *f.*, vapuleo, *m.* (slander). || *Roasting jack* o *roasting spit*, asador, *m.*
rob [rɔb] v. tr. Robar (to steal): *to rob a thousand pesetas*, robar mil pesetas; *in this shop they rob you*, en esta tienda te roban; *he robbed me of my handbag*, me robó el bolso. || Asaltar, atracar: *to rob a bank*, asaltar un banco. || FIG. Quitar: *fear robbed him of speech*, el miedo le quitó el habla. || FIG. *To rob Peter to pay Paul*, desnudar un santo para vestir a otro.
— V. intr. Robar.
robalo [rəu'bɑ:ləu] n. Róbalo, *m.*, robalo, *m.* (fish).

— OBSERV. El plural de la palabra inglesa es *robalos* o *robalo*.

roband ['rəubənd] n. MAR. Envergue, *m.*
robber ['rɔbə*] n. Ladrón, ona (thief). || Atracador, ra (of a bank). || Salteador, *m.* (highwayman). || Bandido, *m.* (brigand). || *Robber baron*, señor (*m.*) feudal que vivía del robo (feudal noble), capitalista enriquecido por la explotación (capitalist).
robbery ['rɔbəri] n. Robo, *m.*: *to commit a robbery*, cometer un robo; *armed robbery*, robo a mano armada. || *Highway robbery*, atraco, *m.*, asalto, *m.*
robe [rəub] n. Toga, *f.*: *a judge's robe*, la toga de un juez. || Bata, *f.* (dressing gown). || Traje, *m.* (dress, costume). || Traje (*m.*) de noche (evening gown). || Hábito, *m.* (of a monk). || Sotana, *f.* (of a priest). || Albornoz, *m.* (after bathing). || Mantillas, *f. pl.* (in the baptism). || U. S. Manta (*f.*) de viaje (rug). || *Gentlemen of the robe*, togados, *m.*
robe [rəub] v. tr. Vestir.
— V. intr. Vestirse.
robin ['rɔbin] n. ZOOL. Petirrojo, *m.* (bird). || *Robin Hood*, Robín (*m.*) de los Bosques.
robinia [rə'biniə] n. BOT. Robinia, *f.*
robot ['rəubɔt] n. Robot, *m.*, autómata, *m.*
robust [rəu'bʌst] adj. Robusto, ta; vigoroso, sa; fuerte (person). || Duro, ra: *a robust job*, un trabajo duro. || Resistente (plants).
robustious [rə'bʌstjəs] adj. Ruidoso, sa (boisterous). || Robusto, ta (strong).
robustness [rəu'bʌstnis] n. Robustez, *f.*, fuerza, *f.*, vigor, *m.*
rochet ['rɔtʃit] n. REL. Roquete, *m.*
rock [rɔk] n. GEOL. Roca, *f.*: *igneous rock*, roca ígnea. || GEOGR. Roca, *f.*, peña, *f.* || MAR. Escollo, *m.* (reef). || FIG. Base, *f.* (foundation). | Escollo, *m.* (obstacle). || U. S. Piedra, *f.* (stone). || POP. Diamante, *m.* (diamond). || Pirulí, *m.* (sweet). || Balanceo, *m.* (swaying movement). || Cuneo, *m.*, mecedura, *f.* (of a cradle). || — FIG. FAM. *A business on the rocks*, un negocio que va a la ruina, un negocio en bancarrota. || *Bare rock*, roca viva. || FIG. *Built on rock*, sólido, da. || FAM. *On the rocks*, con cubitos de hielo. || REL. *Rock of Ages*, Jesucristo, *m.* || *The Rock of Gibraltar*, el Peñón de Gibraltar. || FAM. *To be on the rocks*, no tener un céntimo, estar sin blanca, no tener una perra (penniless), ir a la ruina (to go to ruin). || *To give the child a rock*, mecer *or* acunar al niño.
— Adj. Rupestre: *rock drawings*, pinturas rupestres. || Rocoso, sa: *rock face*, vertiente rocosa. || De roca: *rock water*, agua de roca. || De rocas: *rock garden*, jardín de rocas; *rock fall*, corrimiento de rocas.
rock [rɔk] v. tr. Mecer: *to rock a baby's cradle*, mecer la cuna de un niño. || Acunar, mecer: *to rock a baby to sleep*, acunar a un niño para que se duerma. || Balancear, mover (to move). || Zarandear (a ship). || Sacudir, hacer temblar (to shake). || Mover, dar a (a lever). || MIN. Lavar. || FIG. Mecer.
— V. intr. Mecerse, balancearse: *stop rocking in that chair*, deja de mecerte en la silla. || Temblar, vibrar (to vibrate): *the earthquake made the whole house rock*, el terremoto hizo que toda la casa vibrase. || Sacudirse (to shake violently). || FAM. *To rock with laughter*, partirse de risa, desternillarse de risa.
rock and roll [—ənd'rəul] n. MUS. "Rock and roll", *m.*
rock bottom [—'bɔtəm] n. Fondo (*m.*) rocoso (of the sea). || FIG. Fondo, *m.*
rock-bottom [—'bɔtəm] adj. Mínimo, ma; bajísimo, ma: *rock-bottom prices*, precios mínimos.
rockbound [—baund] adj. Rocoso, sa.
rock candy [—,kændi] n. Azúcar (*m.*) candi.
rock-climber [—,klaimə*] n. Escalador (*m.*) de rocas.
rock-climbing [—'klaimiŋ] n. Escalada, *f.*
rock crystal [—,kristl] n. MIN. Cristal (*m.*) de roca.
rock dove [—dʌv] n. Paloma (*f.*) zorita, paloma (*f.*) zurita (bird).
rock drill [—dril] n. Perforadora, *f.*
rocker ['rɔkə*] n. Arco, *m.* (leg of rocking chair or cradle). || Mecedora, *f.* (rocking chair). || MIN. Criba, *f.* || AUT. Balancín, *m.* || U. S. SP. Patín (*m.*) de cuchilla curva. || — FAM. *To go off one's rocker*, perder la chaveta. | *Michael is off his rocker*, Miguel está mal del coco *or* está chalado.
rocker arm [—rɑ:m] n. AUT. Balancín, *m.*
rockery [—ri] n. Jardín (*m.*) de rocas.
rocket ['rɔkit] n. Cohete, *m.* (projectile): *space rocket*, cohete espacial. || BOT. Jaramago, *m.*, oruga, *f.* (plant). || FAM. Bronca, *f.*, rapapolvo, *m.* (reprimand). || — *Rocket bomb*, proyectil teledirigido. || *Rocket launcher*, lanzacohetes, *m. inv.* || *Rocket ship*, nave (*f.*) espacial.
rocket ['rɔkit] v. intr. Subir vertiginosamente: *prices rocketed*, los precios subieron vertiginosamente. || Levantar el vuelo (birds). || — *He rocketed into the room*, entró como un cohete en la habitación. || *He rocketed to stardom*, tuvo una ascensión vertiginosa.
rocketry [—ri] n. Estudio (*m.*) y uso (*m.*) de los cohetes.
rockfish ['rɔkfiʃ] n. Rescaza, *f.*, escorpina, *f.* (fish).
Rockies ['rɔkiz] pl. n. GEOGR. Montañas Rocosas, *f.*
rocking ['rɔkiŋ] adj. Oscilante (oscillating). || Basculante (tilting, tipping). || — *Rocking chair*, mecedora, *f.* || *Rocking horse*, caballito (*m.*) de balancín. || *Rocking shaft*, eje (*m.*) de balancín.
rock'n'roll [—ən'rəul] n. MUS. "Rock and roll", *m.*
rock oil [—ɔil] n. Petróleo, *m.*
rock pigeon ['rɔk,pidʒin] n. Paloma (*f.*) zorita *or* zurita (bird).
rock-ribbed ['rɔk'ribd] adj. Rocoso, sa.
rockrose ['rɔk'rəuz] n. BOT. Jara, *f.*
rock salt ['rɔk'sɔ:lt] n. Sal (*f.*) gema.
rockshaft ['rɔk'ʃɑ:ft] n. Eje (*m.*) de balancín.
rock wool ['rɔk'wul] n. Lana (*f.*) mineral.
rocky ['rɔki] adj. Rocoso, sa (full of or made of rocks). || Duro como una piedra (hard as a rock). || FAM. Bamboleante (shaky). | Poco firme, débil (government).
Rocky Mountains [—'mauntinz] pl. n. GEOGR. Montañas (*f.*) Rocosas.
rococo [rəu'kəukəu] n. Rococó, *m.*
— Adj. Rococó.
rod [rɔd] n. Barra, *f.* (bar, pole). || Jalón, *m.* (topography). || Caña, *f.* (for fishing). || AUT. Biela, *f.* || Cetro, *m.* (of a king). || Vara, *f.*, bastón, (*m.*) de mando (symbol of authority). || Varilla, *f.* (of fasces). || Varilla, *f.*, barra, *f.* (for curtains). || Medida (*f.*) de longitud equivalente a 5,029 m (measure). || Vara (*f.*) de medir (measuring stick). || ANAT. BIOL. Bastoncillo, *m.* || U. S. FAM. Pistolón, *m.* (gun). || — FIG. *Spare the rod and spoil the child*, quien bien te quiere te hará llorar. || *The rod*, castigo (*m.*) corporal, varas, *f. pl.*, azotes, *m. pl.*, disciplinas, *f. pl.* || FAM. *To make a rod for one's own back*, hacer algo contraproducente. | *To rule s.o. with a rod of iron*, mandar a alguien a la baqueta.
rode [rəud] pret. See RIDE.
rodent ['rəudənt] n. ZOOL. Roedor, *m.*
— Adj. Roedor, ra.
rodeo [rəu'deiəu] n. U. S. Rodeo, *m.*
rodomontade [,rɔdəmɔn'teid] n. Fanfarronada, *f.*
— Adj. Fanfarrón, ona; jactancioso, sa (bragging).
rodomontade [,rɔdəmɔn'teid] v. intr. Fanfarronear, jactarse.
roe [rəu] n. ZOOL. Hueva, *f.* (fish eggs). | Freza, *f.* (eggs of shellfish). | Corzo, za (deer).
roebuck ['rəubʌk] n. ZOOL. Corzo, *m.*
roe deer ['rəudiə*] n. ZOOL. Corzo, za.
roentgen ['rɔntjən] n. PHYS. Roentgen, *m.* || *Roentgen rays*, rayos (*m.*) X.
roentgenogram ['rɔntjənəgræm] n. PHYS. Radiografía, *f.*
roentgenotherapy [,rɔntgənə'θerəpi] n. Roentgenoterapia, *f.*
rogation [rəu'geiʃən] n. REL. Rogativa, *f.*
rogatory ['rɔgətəri] adj. U. S. JUR. Rogatorio, ria: *rogatory commission*, comisión rogatoria.
Roger ['rɔdʒə*] pr. n. Rogelio, *m.*, Roger, *m.* || — RAD. *Roger!*, ¡recibido! || *The Jolly Roger*, el pabellón negro (of pirates).
rogue [rəug] n. Granuja, *m.*, pícaro, *m.* (crook). || Pillo, lla (mischievous person or child). || Animal (*m.*) solitario y bravo. || Elefante (*m.*) solitario (elephant). || *Rogues' gallery*, registro (*m.*) central de delincuentes.
roguery [—əri] n. Granujada, *f.*, picardía, *f.* (of a person). || Pillería, *f.*, travesura, *f.*, diablura, *f.* (of a child).
roguish [—iʃ] adj. De granuja, picaresco, ca (relating to a rogue). || Pillo, lla; travieso, sa (mischievous). || Picaruelo, la (glance, smile).
roguishness [—iʃnis] n. Tunantería, *f.*, picardía, *f.* || Travesura, *f.*
roil [rɔil] v. tr. See RILE.
roily [—i] adj. U. S. Turbio, bia.
roister ['rɔistə*] v. intr. Andar de jarana, estar de juerga.
roisterer [—rə*] n. Jaranero, ra; juerguista, *m.* & *f.*
role or **rôle** [rəul] n. THEATR. CINEM. Papel, *m.*: *leading role*, papel principal; *supporting role*, papel secundario. || FIG. Papel, *m.*, función, *f.*: *the role of concrete in modern building*, el papel del hormigón en la arquitectura moderna. || *To play* o *to take a role*, hacer un papel, desempeñar un papel.
roll [rəul] n. Rollo, *m.* (of paper). || Carrete, *m.*, rollo, *m.* (of camera film). || Rollo, *m.*, bobina, *f.* (of cinema film). || Bucle, *m.* (of hair). || Rosca, *f.*, michelín, *m.*

(of fat). || Panecillo, *m.*, bollo, *m.* (piece of baked dough). || Rollo (*m.*) de mantequilla (of butter). || Rollo, *m.* (of tobacco). || Pieza, *f.* (of cloth). || Rollo (*m.*) de pergamino (scroll). || Nómina, *f.* (list of names). || Lista, *f.* (list of things). || Registro, *m.*, estado, *m.* (register). || Relación, *f.* (record). || Censo, *m.*, lista, *f.*: *electoral roll*, censo electoral. || Catálogo, *m.* (catalogue). || PRINT. Rodillo, *m.* (tool). || ARCH. Junquillo, *m.* (curved moulding). | Voluta, *f.* (of an Ionic capital). || MAR. Oleaje, *m.* (of the sea). | Balanceo, *m.* (of a ship). | Rol, *m.* (list). || Balanceo, *m.* (a swaying movement). || Contoneo, *m.* (gait). || AVIAT. Balanceo, *m.* | Tonel, *m.* (aerobatics). || Redoble, *m.* (of a drum). || Fragor, *m.*, retumbo, *m.* (of thunder). || Gorjeo, *m.* (trill). || FIG. Ritmo, *m.*, cadencia, *f.* (of a sentence). || TECH. Rodillo, *m.* (of a steel mill). | Maza, *f.* (of a drop hammer). | Pisón, *m.* (for roads). || U. S. FAM. Fajo, *m.* (of paper money): *a big roll of bills*, un gran fajo de billetes. || — Pl. Escalafón (*m. sing.*) de abogados (solicitors). || Archivos, *m.* (archives). || TECH. Tren (*m. sing.*) laminador. || — MAR. AVIAT. *Angle of roll*, ángulo (*m.*) de balanceo. || CULIN. *French roll*, panecillo, *m.* || FIG. *On the rolls of fame*, en los anales de la gloria. | *On the rolls of saints*, entre los santos. || *Roll collar*, cuello vuelto. || *Roll shutter*, persiana (*f.*) enrollable. || CULIN. *Swiss roll*, brazo (*m.*) de gitano. || *The roll of honour*, la lista de los caídos por la patria. || *To call the roll*, pasar lista. || MIL. *To enter* o *to put a man on the rolls*, incluir a un hombre en las listas. || MIL. JUR. *To strike s.o. off the rolls*, excluir a alguien de la lista, tachar a uno de la lista.

roll [rəul] v. tr. Hacer rodar: *to roll a marble*, hacer rodar una canica. || Liar (cigarette): *I roll my own cigarettes*, yo lío mis cigarrillos. || Envolver, enrollar (to envelop). || Mover (to move). || Empujar (to push). || Balancear (one's body). || Arrastar: *the waves rolled the bathers towards the shore*, las olas arrastraban a los bañistas hacia la playa. || Allanar con un rodillo, pasar el rodillo por (to level with a roller). || Apisonar (with a steamroller). || CULIN. Pasar el rodillo por (dough). | Dar vueltas, girar (roast). || Laminar (metals). || Tocar redobles en (drums). || PRINT. Entintar con el rodillo. || U. S. FAM. Desplumar (to rob s.o.). || — CULIN. *To roll and fold*, hojaldrar. || *To roll one's eyes*, poner los ojos en blanco (to show the white of one's eyes), hacer juegos de ojos (to rotate the eyes). || *To roll one's r's*, pronunciar fuerte las erres.

— V. intr. Rodar: *the marble rolled across the floor*, la canica rodó por el suelo; *the car rolled down the slope*, el coche rodó cuesta abajo. || Revolcarse: *to roll in the mud*, revolcarse en el barro. || Ondular (to have an ondulating surface). || Retumbar (thunder). || Tronar (cannons). || Redoblar (the drum). || Trinar (to trill). || MAR. AVIAT. Balancearse (a ship, plane). || Andar bamboleándose *or* balanceándose *or* contoneándose (to walk). || Enrollarse (to curl up). || Desenvolverse normalmente (to proceed smoothly). || TECH. Laminarse (metals).

— ***To roll about***, vagar, ir de acá para allá (to wander). | Llevar de acá para allá (to make s.o. go to and fro). || ***To roll along***, rodar por. | Andar: *the car was rolling along nicely*, el coche andaba perfectamente. | Hacer rodar por: *they rolled the barrel along the corridor*, hicieron rodar el barril por el pasillo. || ***To roll away***, alejarse (to go away). | Apartar (to push sth. away). || ***To roll back***, hacer retroceder (to cause to retreat). | Poner en blanco (eyes). | U. S. Bajar, reducir (prices). || ***To roll by***, pasar: *as the months roll by*, a medida que pasan los meses. || ***To roll down***, caerse rodando por: *he rolled down the stairs*, se cayó rodando por las escaleras. | Bajar sin motor (a car). | Hacer rodar por: *they rolled the barrel down the stairs*, hicieron rodar el barril por las escaleras. | Correr por: *tears were rolling down his face*, las lágrimas le corrían por la cara. || ***To roll in***, llegar en abundancia *or* a raudales (to arrive in large quantity). | FAM. Acostarse (to go to bed). | FAM. *He is rolling in money* o *in plenty*, nada en dinero *or* en la abundancia, apalea oro. || ***To roll off***, caer rodando. | PRINT. Tirar, imprimir. || ***To roll on***, seguir rodando (to continue to roll). | Pasar (time). | Correr, seguir su curso (river). | Extender con el rodillo (to spread on). || ***To roll out***, extender con el rodillo (pastry). | Desenrollar (to unroll). || ***To roll over***, derribar (s.o.). || Dar una vuelta (to turn over). || ***To roll up***, enrollar: *to roll up a newspaper, a map*, enrollar un periódico, un mapa. | Envolver (to wrap). | Remangar, arremangar (sleeves). | MIL. Arrollar. | Elevarse formando espirales (smoke). | Enrollarse (blind, paper, etc.). | Encogerse, enroscarse (a dying insect). | FAM. Presentarse, aparecer (to arrive). | — *To roll o.s. up in*, envolverse en. | *To roll o.s. up into a ball*, acurrucarse, hacerse una bola *or* un ovillo.

rollaway bed [—əwei'bed] n. U. S. Cama (*f.*) plegable.

rollback [—bæk] n. U. S. Reducción (*f.*) de precios.

roll call [—kɔ:l] n. Lista, *f.*, el pasar lista. || *Vote by roll call*, votación (*f.*) nominal.

roller ['rəulə*] n. Rodillo, *m.* (cylinder). || Ruedecilla, *f.* (small wheel). || TECH. Rodillo, *m.* (for flattening metal). | Apisonadora, *f.* (for road). || Ola (*f.*) larga, ola (*f.*) grande (wave). || ZOOL. Pichón (*m.*) volteador (pigeon). || Rulo, *m.* (for the hair).

roller bearing [—,bɛəriŋ] n. TECH. Cojinete (*m.*) de rodillos.

roller blind [—blaind] n. Persiana (*f.*) enrollable.

roller coaster [—'kəustə*] n. U. S. Montaña (*f.*) rusa.

roller skate [—skeit] n. Patín (*m.*) de ruedas.

roller-skate [—skeit] v. intr. Patinar sobre ruedas.

roller skating [—,skeitiŋ] n. Patinaje (*m.*) sobre ruedas.

roller towel [—,tauəl] n. Toalla (*f.*) de rodillo.

rollick ['rɔlik] v. intr. Juguetear, retozar. || Divertirse.

rollicking [—iŋ] adj. Jovial, alegre (gay). || Ajetreado, da (life). | Animado, da (lively). | Divertido, da (funny). || *To have a rollicking time*, pasarlo bomba.

rolling ['rəuliŋ] adj. Que rueda, rodante (stone). || Ondulado, da (ground). || MAR. Agitado, da; encrespado, da (sea). | Que se balancea (ship). || Oscilante.

— N. Rodamiento, *m.* || MAR. Balanceo, *m.* (of ship). || Redoble, *m.* (of drum). || TECH. Apisonamiento, *m.* (of ground). | Laminado, *m.* (of metal).

rolling mill [—mil] n. TECH. Taller (*m.*) de laminación (workshop). | Tren (*m.*) de laminación, laminador, *m.*, laminadora, *f.* (machine).

rolling pin [—pin] n. Rodillo, *m.*

rolling stock [—stɔk] n. Material (*m.*) móvil *or* rodante (railway).

rolling stone [—'stəun] n. Canto (*m.*) rodado. || — FIG. *Rolling stone gathers no moss*, piedra movediza nunca moho la cobija, agua pasada no mueve molino. | *To be a rolling stone*, rodar por el mundo.

roll-on ['rəulɔn] n. Faja (*f.*) elástica.

rolltop ['rəultɔp] adj. De tapa corrediza (desk).

roly-poly ['rəuli'pəuli] adj. Rechoncho, cha; regordete, ta.

— N. Persona (*f.*) rechoncha (person). || CULIN. Brazo (*m.*) de gitano (pudding).

romaine lettuce [rəu'mein'letis] n. U. S. Lechuga (*f.*) romana.

Roman ['rəumən] adj. Romano, na (of Rome). || REL. Romano, na. || PRINT. Romano, na (type). || Aguileño, ña (nose).

— N. Romano, na (native of Rome). || REL. Católico, ca. || PRINT. Letra (*f.*) romana.

Roman arch [—'ɑ:tʃ] n. ARCH. Arco (*m.*) de medio punto.

Roman Catholic [—'kæθəlik] adj./n. REL. Católico romano, católica romana.

Roman Catholic Church [—'kæθəlik'tʃə:tʃ] n. REL. Iglesia (*f.*) Católica Romana.

Roman Catholicism [—kə'θɔlisizəm] n. REL. Catolicismo, *m.*

romance [rəu'mæns] n. Romance, *m.* (medieval literary form, language). || Novela (*f.*) romántica (love story). || Libro (*m.*) de aventuras *or* de caballería. || Amores, *m. pl.*, idilio, *m.*, amor, *m.*, aventura (*f.*) amorosa, amorío, *m.* (love affair): *she was the one romance in my life*, fue el único amor de mi vida. || Lo romántico (romantic character). || Lo poético, poesía, *f.* (poetic character). || Encanto, *m.* (charm). || Fantasía, *f.* (exaggeration, falsehood). || MUS. Romanza, *f.*

— Adj. Románico, ca; neolatino, na; romance (language).

romance [rəu'mæns] v. tr. Novelar: *a romanced biography*, una biografía novelada.

— V. intr. Exagerar, fantasear (to exaggerate).

romancer [—ə*] n. Fantaseador, ra.

Romanesque [,rəumə'nesk] n. ARCH. Románico, *m.*, arte (*m.*) románico.

— Adj. Románico, ca.

Romania [ru'meinjə] pr. n. GEOGR. Rumania, *f.*

Romanian [ru'meinjən] adj./n. Rumano, na.

Romanic [rəu'mænik] adj. Románico, ca; romance.

— N. Romance, *m.*

Romanism ['rəumənizəm] n. REL. Romanismo, *m.*

Romanist ['rəumənist] adj. REL. Romanista, católico, ca.

Romanize ['rəumənaiz] v. tr. Romanizar.

Roman numerals ['rəumən'nju:mərəlz] pl. n. Números (*m.*) romanos.

Romansh or **Romansch** [rəu'mænʃ] n. Retorromano, *m.*, rético, *m.*

romantic [rəu'mæntik] adj. Romántico, ca: *a romantic novel*, una novela romántica; *a romantic person*, una persona romántica.

— N. Romántico, ca.

romanticism [rəu'mæntisizəm] n. Romanticismo, *m.*

romanticist [rəu'mæntisist] n. Romántico, ca.

romanticize [rəu'mæntisaiz] v. tr. Hacer romántico.

— V. intr. Obrar de modo romántico. || Fantasear (to dream).

Romany ['rɔməni] n. Gitano, na (gipsy). || Lengua (*f.*) de los gitanos (gipsy language), caló, *m.* (in Spain).

— Adj. Gitano, na.

Rome [rəum] pr. n. GEOGR. Roma. || — FIG. *All roads lead to Rome*, por todas partes se va a Roma, todos los caminos llevan a Roma. | *Rome was not built in a day*, no se ganó Zamora en una hora. | *When in Rome do as the Romans do*, cuando a Roma fueres, haz lo que vieres.

Romeo ['rəumiəu] pr. n. Romeo, *m.*

Romish ['rəumiʃ] adj. Papista, católico, ca.

romp [rɔmp] n. Jugueteo, *m.*, retozo, *m.* (playing). || Niño (*m.*) travieso (child). || Marimacho, *m.* (tomboy).

romp [rɔmp] v. intr. Juguetear, retozar. || — FAM. *To romp home*, ganar con facilidad. | *To romp through sth.*, hacer algo con facilidad.

rompers [—əz] pl. n. Pelele, *m. sing.* (child's one-piece garment).

rompish [—iʃ] or **rompy** [—i] adj. Juguetón, ona; retozón, ona.

Romulus [ˈrɔmjuləs] pr. n. MYTH. Rómulo, *m.*

rondeau [ˈrɔndəu] n. Letrilla, *f.* (poem).

— OBSERV. El plural de la palabra inglesa es *rondeaux*.

rondel [ˈrɔndl] n. POET. Rondel, *m.*

rondo [ˈrɔndəu] n. MUS. Rondó, *m.*

Roneo [ˈrəuniəu] n. Multicopista, *f.*

Roneo [ˈrəuniəu] v. tr. Reproducir con multicopista.

röntgen [ˈrɔntjən] n. PHYS. See ROENTGEN.

rood [ru:d] n. REL. Crucifijo, *m.* (crucifix). || Cuarta parte (*f.*) de un acre (measure). || — *Rood loft*, galería (*f.*) encima de la reja de separación entre el coro y la nave. || *Rood screen*, reja (*f.*) que separa el coro de la nave.

roof [ru:f] n. ARCH. Tejado, *m.* (of a building). || Techo, *m.*: *the roof of a cave*, el techo de una cueva; *thatched roof*, techo de papa; *the roof of a car*, el techo de un coche. || Capota, *f.* (of a convertible car). || Cielo, *m.* (of mouth). || FIG. Techo, *m.*: *I have no roof to cover me*, no tengo un techo donde cobijarme; *to live under the same roof*, vivir bajo el mismo techo. || Bóveda (*f.*) celeste (sky). || AVIAT. Altura (*f.*) máxima, techo, *m.* || — *Flat roof*, azotea, *f.* || *Roof light*, luz (*f.*) cenital *or* del techo (in cars). || *Sliding* o *sun roof*, techo corredizo. || *Tiled roof*, tejado, *m.* || FAM. *To raise* o *to hit the roof*, poner el grito en el cielo (with anger), armar un alboroto (with enthusiasm).

roof [ru:f] v. tr. Techar. || FIG. Alojar, cobijar (s.o.). || *To be roofed with*, tener tejado *or* techo de.

roofer [—ə*] n. Techador, *m.*

roof garden [—ˌgɑ:dn] n. Jardín (*m.*) en una azotea. || U. S. Restaurante (*m.*) en la azotea de un edificio (terrace restaurant).

roofing [—iŋ] n. Material (*m.*) para techar. || Techumbre, *f.*, techado, *m.* (roof).

roofless [—lis] adj. Sin techo (house). || Sin hogar (people).

rooftop [ˈru:fˌtɔp] n. Tejado, *m.*

rooftree [—tri:] n. ARCH. Cumbrera, *f.*, parhilera, *f.*

rook [ruk] n. Grajo, *m.* (bird). || FAM. Timador, *m.*, estafador, *m.* (swindler). | Fullero, *m.* (in gambling). || Torre, *f.* (in chess).

rook [ruk] v. tr. FAM. Estafar, timar (to swindle).

— V. intr. Enrocar (in chess). || FAM. Hacer trampas (to cheat). | Fullear (in gambling).

rookery [—əri] n. Colonia (*f.*) de grajos (of rooks). || Colonia, *f.* [de animales gregarios] (of gregarious animals). || FAM. Tugurio, *m.*

rookie [—i] n. MIL. FAM. Quinto, *m.*, recluta, *m.* || FAM. Novato, *m.* (novice).

room [ru:m] n. Habitación, *f.*, cuarto, *m.*: *hotel room*, habitación de hotel; *single room*, habitación individual. || Sala, *f.* (public room): *committee room*, sala de comisiones; *conference room*, sala de conferencias. || Sitio, *m.*: *is there room for me in your car?*, ¿queda sitio para mí en su coche? || Espacio, *m.*: *leave room at the beginning of this page*, deja espacio al principio de esta página; *there was hardly any room to breathe*, casi no había espacio para respirar. || Sala, *f.* (people). || — Pl. Alojamiento, *m. sing.* (accommodation). || Piso, *m. sing.* (flat): *bachelor's rooms*, piso de soltero. || *Allocation of rooms*, distribución (*f.*) de las salas. || *Room and board*, cama y comida, pensión completa. || *There is no room for doubt*, no cabe duda. || *There is room for improvement*, podría mejorarse. || *To make room for*, hacer *or* dejar sitio *or* espacio.

room [ru:m] v. intr. Alojarse: *where is he rooming?*, ¿dónde se aloja? || Compartir la habitación (*with*, con).

— V. tr. Alojar.

roomer [—ə*] n. U. S. Inquilino, na (tenant). | Huésped, da (lodger).

roomful [—ful] n. Habitación (*f.*) llena, cuarto (*m.*) lleno (*of*, de).

roominess [—inis] n. Dimensiones (*f. pl.*) espaciosas, amplitud, *f.*

rooming house [—iŋˌhaus] n. U. S. Pensión, *f.*, casa (*f.*) de huéspedes.

roommate [—eit] n. Compañero (*m.*) de habitación, compañera (*f.*) de habitación.

room service [—ˈsə:vis] n. Servicio (*m.*) de habitaciones.

roomy [—i] adj. Espacioso, sa; amplio plia (place). || Holgado, da (garment).

roost [ru:st] n. Varilla, *f.*, percha, *f.*, palo, *m.* (in a cage). || Palo, *m.* (for domestic fowls). || Gallinero, *m.* || — FAM. *Chickens and curses come home to roost*, si escupes al cielo, en la cara te caerá. | *To come home to roost*, ser contraproducente, volverse en contra de uno. | *To go to roost*, irse a dormir. | *To rule the roost*, llevar la voz cantante, llevar la batuta, dirigir el cotarro.

roost [ru:st] v. intr. Posarse [para dormir] (birds). || FIG. Pasar la noche.

rooster [—ə*] n. ZOOL. Gallo, *m.* (cock).

root [ru:t] n. BOT. Raíz, *f.* (underground part of a plant). | Tubérculo, *m.* (tubercle). || ANAT. Raíz, *f.* (of hair, teeth). || FIG. Raíz, *f.*, origen, *m.* (origin, source). | Fundamento, *m.*, base, *f.* (base). || MATH. GRAMM. Raíz, *f.*: *square root*, raíz cuadrada. || — FIG. *To get to the root of*, ir a la raíz de. || *To pull up by the roots*, extirpar, arrancar, cortar *or* arrancar de raíz. || FIG. *To put down one's roots in a country*, radicarse *or* establecerse en un país. || *To strike* o *to take root*, echar raíces, arraigar, enraizar.

root [ru:t] v. tr. FIG. Arraigar (to fix firmly): *a rooted idea*, una idea arraigada. || — *To root out* o *to root up*, desarraigar, arrancar de raíz (a plant), extirpar, arrancar *or* cortar de raíz (to remove completely). || FAM. *To root s.o. to the spot*, paralizar *or* dejar inmovilizado a alguien.

— V. intr. Echar raíces (to grow roots). || FIG. Arraigar, echar raíces (to become firmly fixed). || Hurgar con el hocico, hozar (swine). || Hurgar (to search about). || U. S. FAM. *To root for*, animar, alentar: *to root for one's team*, animar a su equipo.

root beer [—ˈbiə*] n. Cerveza (*f.*) de raíces.

root cap [—kæp] n. BOT. Pilorriza, *f.*, cofia, *f.*

rooter [—ə*] n. U. S. FAM. Hincha, *m.*, partidario, ria.

root hair [—hɛə*] n. BOT. Pelos (*m. pl.*) absorbentes.

rootless [ˈru:tlis] adj. Desarraigado, da.

rootlet [ˈru:tlet] n. BOT. Radícula, *f.*, raicilla, *f.*

rootstalk [ˈru:tstɔ:k] n. BOT. Rizoma, *m.*

rootstock [ˈru:tstɔk] n. BOT. Rizoma, *m.*

rooty [ˈru:ti] adj. Lleno de raíces.

rope [rəup] n. Cuerda, *f.*: *I slid down the rope*, me deslicé por la cuerda. || Soga, *f.* (of hemp, flax). || Cable, *m.* (of wire). || Tirador, *m.* (of a handbell). || Sarta, *f.*, hilo, *m.* (of pearl). || Ristra, *f.* (of garlic, onions). || MAR. Maroma, *f.*, cabo, *m.* || Lazo, *m.* (a lasso). || SP. Cordada, *f.* (of mountaineers): *first on the rope* o *head of the rope*, primero *or* cabeza *or* jefe de cordada. || — Pl. Cuerdas, *f.* (in boxing). || — FIG. *At the end of one's rope*, en un aprieto (in a desperate situation). || *Hangman's rope*, dogal, *m.* || FIG. *To give s.o. enough rope to hang himself*, dar completa libertad a alguien con la esperanza de que vaya a enredarse. | *To give s.o. plenty of rope*, dar rienda suelta a alguien, dar completa libertad a alguien. | *To know the ropes*, estar al tanto. | *To learn the ropes*, ponerse al tanto.

rope [rəup] v. tr. Amarrar, atar (to fasten). || Coger con lazo (to lasso). || Encordar (climbers). || MAR. Relingar (sails). || Sujetar con las riendas (a horse). || — *To rope off*, acordonar. || FIG. *To rope s.o. in*, conseguir que alguien participe en algo.

— V. intr. Ahilarse (wine, beer). || *To rope up*, encordarse (mountaineers).

ropedancer [—ˌdɑn:sə*] n. Funámbulo, la.

ropedancing [—ˌdɑn:siŋ] n. Baile (*m.*) en la cuerda floja.

rope ladder [—ˈlædə*] n. Escala (*f.*) de cuerda.

ropemaker [—ˌmeikə*] n. Cordelero, *m.*

ropewalk [—wɔ:k] n. Cordelería, *f.*

ropewalker [—ˌwɔ:kə*] n. Funámbulo, la.

ropeway [—wei] n. Teleférico, *m.*

ropiness [—inis] n. Viscosidad, *f.* (of beer).

ropy [—i] adj. Viscoso, sa (viscous). || Fibroso, sa (stringy). || Ahilado, da (wine, beer). || FAM. Malo, la (unsatisfactory).

Roquefort [ˈrɔkfɔ:*] n. Queso (*m.*) de Roquefort (cheese).

rorqual [ˈrɔ:kwəl] n. Rorcual, *m.* (cetacean).

rosaceous [rəˈzeiʃəs] adj. BOT. Rosáceo, a.

rosarium [rəuˈzɛəriəm] n. Rosaleda, *f.*

rosary [ˈrəuzəri] n. Rosaleda, *f.* (rose garden). || REL. Rosario, *m.*: *to say the rosary*, rezar el rosario.

rose [rəuz] n. BOT. Rosal, *m.* (plant). | Rosa, *f.* (flower). || Rosa, *f.* (emblem). || Rosa, *m.*, color (*m.*) de rosa (colour). || Diamante (*m.*) rosa, rosa, *f.* (diamond). || Alcachofa, *f.* (sprinkler). || Rosa (*f.*) náutica, rosa (*f.*) de los vientos. || ARCH. Rosetón, *m.* (window). | Roseta, *f.* (decoration). || MED. Roseta, *f.* || — FIG. *Every rose has its thorn*, no hay rosa sin espinas. | *Life is not a bed of roses*, la vida no es un camino de rosas. || *Rose of Jericho*, rosa de Jericó. || *Tea rose*, rosa de té. || *The Wars of the Roses*, la guerra de las Dos Rosas. || FIG. *To be in a bed of roses*, estar en un lecho de rosas.

— Adj. De rosa: *rose petals*, pétalos de rosa; *rose perfume*, perfume de rosa. || Rosa, rosado, da; color de rosa (colour).

rose [rəuz] pret. See RISE.

rosé [rəuˈzei] n. Rosado, *m.*, clarete, *m.* (wine).

roseate [ˈrəuziit] adj. Róseo, a; rosado, da. || FIG. Optimista.

rosebay [ˈrəuzbei] n. BOT. Adelfa, *f.*

rose bed [ˈrəuzbed] n. Rosaleda, *f.*

rosebud [ˈrəuzbʌd] n. BOT. Capullo, *m.* || FIG. Pimpollo, *m.*

rosebush [ˈrəuzbuʃ] n. BOT. Rosal, *m.*

rose-coloured (U. S. **rose-colored**) [ˈrəuzˌkʌləd] adj. Rosa, rosado, da (pink). || FIG. Optimista (optimistic). || FIG. *To see everything through rose-coloured spectacles* o *rose-coloured glasses*, verlo todo color de rosa.

rose garden [ˈrəuzˌgɑ:dn] n. Rosaleda, *f.*

rose hip [ˈrəuzˈhip] n. Escaramujo, *m.*

rose honey [ˈrəuzˌhʌni] n. Rodomiel, *m.*

rose mallow [ˈrəuzˈmæləu] n. U. S. BOT. Malvarrosa, *f.*, malva (*f.*) loca *or* real *or* rósea.

rosemary [ˈrəuzməri] n. Bot. Romero, *m.*
roseola [rəuˈziːələ] n. Med. Roséola, *f.*
rose-red [ˈrəuzˈred] adj. [De] color de rosa.
rose tree [ˈrəuztriː] n. Rosal, *m.*
rosette [rəuˈzet] n. Escarapela, *f.* (of ribbons). ‖ Arch. Florón, *m.* (representation of the wild rose). | Rosetón, *m.* (rose window). ‖ Bot. Roseta, *f.*
rose water [ˈrəuzˌwɔːtə*] n. Agua (*f.*) de rosas.
rose window [ˈrəuzˈwindəu] n. Arch. Rosetón, *m.*
rosewood [ˈrəuzwud] n. Bot. Palisandro, *m.* | Palo (*m.*) de rosa.
rosily [ˈrəuzili] adv. De color de rosa (with rose colour). ‖ Fig. Alegremente (cheerfully).
rosin [ˈrɔzin] n. Colofonia, *f.*
rosin [ˈrɔzin] v. tr. Frotar con colofonia.
rosiness [ˈrəuzinis] n. Color (*m.*) de rosa (of flowers). ‖ Aspecto (*m.*) prometedor (of future).
roster [ˈrəustə*] n. Lista, *f.*, rol, *m.* ‖ *Promotion roster*, escalafón, *m.*
rostral [ˈrɔstrəl] adj. Rostrado, da; rostral.
rostrate [ˈrɔstreit] adj. Rostrado, da; rostral.
rostrum [ˈrɔstrəm] n. Tribuna, *f.* (platform): *to go up to the rostrum*, subir a la tribuna. ‖ Zool. Rostro, *m.*, pico, *m.* ‖ Mar. Espolón, *m.*, rostro, *m.*

— Observ. El plural de *rostrum* es *rostrums* o *rostra*.

rosy [ˈrəuzi] adj. Sonrosado, da (complexion). ‖ De color de rosa, rosado, da; rosa (rose-coloured). ‖ Fig. De color de rosa, prometedor, ra (future). | Optimista (view, outlook).
rot [rɔt] n. Putrefacción, *f.* (action of rotting). ‖ Podredumbre, *f.* (rotten substance). ‖ Vet. Comalia, *f.* ‖ Fam. Bobadas, *f. pl.*, tonterías, *f. pl.*, sandeces, *f. pl.*, majaderías, *f. pl.*: *don't talk rot!*, ¡no digas tonterías! ‖ Fig. Desmoralización, *f.* (of a team, army). | Decadencia, *f.* (decline).
— Interj. ¡Tonterías!, ¡sandeces!
rot [rɔt] v. tr. Pudrir, podrir: *rain rotted the wood*, la lluvia pudrió la madera. ‖ Descomponer (to decompose). ‖ Fam. Tomar el pelo a (to tease). ‖ Enriar (hemp, flax).
— V. intr. Pudrirse, podrirse, descomponerse (to decay). ‖ Degenerar (to degenerate). ‖ Fam. Bromear (to joke). | Pudrirse. ‖ *To rot away*, pudrirse, descomponerse.
rota [ˈrəutə] n. Lista, *f.*, rol, *m.* (list).
Rota [ˈrəutə] pr. n. Rel. Rota, *f.*
Rotarian [rəuˈtɛəriən] n. Rotario, ria.
rotary [ˈrəutəri] adj. Rotatorio, ria; giratorio, ria; rotativo, va.
— N. Rotativa, *f.* (press). ‖ U. S. Plaza (*f.*) circular, glorieta, *f.* (roundabout, intersection). ‖ *Rotary Club*, Club (*m.*) Rotario.
rotary press [—ˈpres] n. Print. Rotativa, *f.*
rotate [rəuˈteit] adj. Bot. Rotáceo, a.
rotate [rəuˈteit] v. tr. [Hacer] girar, dar vueltas a (to cause to revolve). ‖ Agr. Alternar (crops). ‖ Alternar (work).
— V. intr. Girar, dar vueltas (to revolve). ‖ Alternar: *the seasons rotate*, las estaciones alternan. ‖ Turnarse (in a job).
rotating [—iŋ] adj. Giratorio, ria. ‖ Agr. Alternativo, va (crops).
rotation [rəuˈteiʃən] n. Giro, *m.*, rotación, *f.* (turning). ‖ Revolución, *f.* (turn). ‖ Turno, *m.*: *by* o *in rotation*, por turno. ‖ Agr. *Rotation of crops*, rotación de cultivos.
rotational [—əl] adj. Giratorio, ria (rotating).
rotative [ˈrəutətiv] adj. Rotatorio, ria; giratorio, ria; rotativo, va (which revolves). ‖ Rotativo, va (of rotation).
rotator [rəuˈteitə*] n. Anat. Músculo (*m.*) rotatorio. ‖ Mar. Hélice, *f.* (of a ship's log).

— Observ. El plural de la palabra *rotator* en el sentido anatómico es *rotatores*.

rotatory [ˈrəutətəri] adj. Rotatorio, ria; giratorio, ria; rotativo, va (rotary). ‖ Alternativo, va (alternate).
rote [rəut] n. Rutina, *f.* ‖ *By rote*, de memoria (by heart), maquinalmente, por rutina.
rotgut [ˈrɔtgʌt] n. Fam. Matarratas, *m. inv.* (spirits).
rotifer [ˈrəutifə*] n. Zool. Rotífero, *m.*
rotogravure [ˌrəutəugrəˈvjuə*] n. Rotograbado, *m.*
rotor [ˈrəutə*] n. Tech. Rotor, *m.*
rotproof [ˈrɔtˈpruːf] adj. Imputrescible.
rotten [ˈrɔtn] adj. Podrido, da (decayed). ‖ Estropeado, da; echado a perder (fruit). ‖ Cariado, da; picado, da (tooth). ‖ Carcomido, da (worm-eaten). ‖ Vet. Infectado de comalia (sheep). ‖ Desmenuzable, friable (rocks). ‖ Fig. Corrompido, da (corrupt). ‖ Fam. Malísimo, ma; pésimo, ma; infame: *rotten weather*, tiempo infame. | Malo, la: *that was a rotten trick*, fue una mala jugada. ‖ Asqueroso, sa (dirty). ‖ — Fig. Fam. *I feel rotten today*, hoy me encuentro fatal. | *To be rotten with money*, estar podrido de dinero. ‖ *To smell rotten*, oler a podrido. ‖ Fam. *What rotten luck!*, ¡qué suerte más negra!, ¡qué mala pata!
rottenness [—nis] n. Podredumbre, *f.*, putrefacción, *f.* ‖ Fig. Corrupción, *f.*
rotter [ˈrɔtə*] n. Fam. Sinvergüenza, *m.* & *f.*
rotulian [rɔˈtjuːliən] adj. Anat. Rotuliano, na; rotular.
rotund [rəuˈtʌnd] adj. Corpulento, ta (person). ‖ Redondo, da (round). ‖ Fig. Rimbombante, ampuloso, sa; grandilocuente (bombastic).
rotunda [—ə] n. Arch. Rotonda, *f.*
rotundity [—iti] n. Grandilocuencia, *f.*, ampulosidad, *f.* (of bombastic speech). ‖ Rotundidad, *f.* (of language). ‖ Corpulencia, *f.* (corpulence). ‖ Redondez, *f.* (of a person's figure).
rouble [ˈruːbl] n. Rublo, *m.* (Russian currency).
roué [ˈruːei] n. Libertino, *m.*
rouge [ruːʒ] n. Colorete, *m.*, arrebol, *m.* (cosmetic in powder). ‖ Lápiz (*m.*) de labios (lipstick). ‖ Colcótar, *m.* (jewellers' rouge).
rouge [ruːʒ] v. tr. Poner colorete a, pintar. ‖ *To rouge o.s.*, ponerse colorete.
— V. intr. Ponerse colorete, pintarse.
rouge et noir [ˈruːʒeinˈwɑː*] n. Treinta y cuarenta, *m.* (card game).
rough [rʌf] adj. Áspero, ra (surface, skin, etc.). ‖ Calloso, sa (hands). ‖ Tosco, ca; chapucero, ra (hastily or badly made). ‖ Accidentado, da; fragoso, sa; desigual (ground). ‖ Pedregoso, sa (path). ‖ Accidentado, da; desigual (road). ‖ Basto, ta; burdo, da (cloth). ‖ Áspero, ra (sound, touch, taste). ‖ Bronco, ca (voice). ‖ Desgreñado, da (hair). ‖ Inculto, ta; tosco, ca (person). ‖ Tosco, ca; grosero, ra (character, manner). ‖ Rudo, da; ordinario, ria; grosero, ra (language). ‖ Tosco, ca (style). ‖ Difícil, duro, ra (work). ‖ Duro, ra; brutal: *he was very rough with me*, fue muy brutal conmigo. ‖ Severo, ra; duro, ra (severe): *rough punishment*, castigo severo. ‖ Duro, ra; malo, la (life, journey, etc.): *they had a rough time of it*, pasaron una temporada muy mala. ‖ Tempestuoso, sa; borrascoso, sa (weather). ‖ Encrespado, da; alborotado, da; agitado, da (sea). ‖ Movido, da; agitado, da (sea crossing). ‖ Violento, ta: *children play rough games*, los niños tienen juegos violentos. ‖ Alborotador, ra (rowdy). ‖ Violento, ta (wind). ‖ Aspirado, da (in phonetics). ‖ Sumario, ria (justice). ‖ Preliminar (not elaborated). ‖ Aproximado, da (approximate): *this will give you a rough idea*, esto le dará una idea aproximada. ‖ Sp. Duro, ra (play). ‖ Tech. Bruto, ta; en bruto (diamond). | Sin desbastar (timber). ‖ — *At a rough guess* o *estimate*, haciendo un cálculo aproximado, a ojo de buen cubero. ‖ *It's rough on him!*, ¡qué mala suerte tiene! ‖ *Rough draft*, borrador, *m.* ‖ *Rough notes* o *copy*, borrador, *m.* ‖ *Rough sketch*, esbozo, *m.*, boceto, *m.*, bosquejo, *m.* ‖ *Rough stuff*, violencia, *f.* ‖ *To be rough on s.o.*, tratar brutalmente a alguien (to treat harshly), ser una mala suerte para alguien (to be bad luck). ‖ *To give s.o. a rough time*, hacer pasar a alguien un mal rato.
— Adv. Duro: *to play rough*, jugar duro. ‖ Brutalmente. ‖ Ásperamente. ‖ Chapuceramente, toscamente (manual work). ‖ — Fam. *To cut up rough*, ponerse hecho una fiera. ‖ *To sleep rough*, domir en el suelo (inside), dormir al raso (outside).
— N. Terreno (*m.*) accidentado *or* desigual (uneven ground). ‖ Aspereza, *f.* (of a surface). ‖ Boceto, *m.* (sketch). ‖ Borrador, *m.* (first draft). ‖ Estado (*m.*) bruto. ‖ Estado (*m.*) basto *or* burdo. ‖ Ramplón, *m.* (of horseshoe). ‖ Fam. Matón, *m.*, duro, *m.* (tough). ‖ Fig. Lado (*m.*) malo de las cosas. ‖ Sp. Terreno (*m.*) apenas cuidado (in golf). ‖ — *In the rough*, en bruto (in the crude state), en líneas generales (project, etc.), en la hierba alta (in golf). ‖ Fig. *To take the rough with the smooth*, tomar la vida como es, estar a las duras y a las maduras.
rough [rʌf] v. tr. Poner ramplones a (a horseshoe). ‖ Desgreñar, despeluznar (the hair). ‖ Maltratar (to ill-treat). ‖ — *To rough down*, desbastar. ‖ *To rough in*, bosquejar. ‖ *To rough it*, vivir sin comodidades, pasar muchas dificultades. ‖ *To rough out*, bosquejar (a map, a statue), esbozar (a plan). ‖ *To rough up*, erizar, poner de punta (hair, fur, etc.), pegarle una paliza a (a person).
roughage [—idʒ] n. Agr. Forraje (*m.*) duro (fodder). ‖ Alimento (*m.*) poco digerible.
rough-and-ready [—ənˈredi] adj. Tosco, ca (not well finished): *a rough-and-ready piece of work*, un trabajo tosco. ‖ Improvisado, da (makeshift). ‖ Tosco pero eficaz (crude, but efficient).
rough-and-tumble [—ənˈtʌmbl] adj. Agitado, da; movido, da: *a rough-and-tumble life*, una vida agitada. ‖ Desordenado, da (fight).
— N. Pelea, *f.* (fight). ‖ Agitación, *f.* (of life).
rough breathing [—ˈbriːðiŋ] n. Gramm. Aspiración, *f.*
roughcast [—kɑːst] n. Mezcla (*f.*) gruesa, revoque, *m.* (for covering a wall). ‖ Modelo (*m.*) tosco (rough model). ‖ Boceto, *m.*, esbozo, *m.* (sketch).
roughcast [—kɑːst] v. tr. Revocar (wall). ‖ Esbozar, bosquejar (to sketch).
roughdry [—ˈdrai] v. tr. Secar sin planchar.
roughen [—ən] v. tr. Poner áspero *or* tosco.
— V. intr. Ponerse áspero *or* tosco. ‖ Volverse calloso (hands). ‖ Volverse accidentado (a road). ‖ Encresparse (the sea).
roughhew [—ˈhjuː] v. tr. Desbastar (to cut roughly into shape). ‖ Labrar toscamente (to make a rough model of).
roughhewn [—ˈhjuːn] adj. Desbastado, da (wood). ‖ Toscamente labrado (statue). ‖ Fig. Esbozado, da; bosquejado, da (sketched).
roughhouse [—haus] n. Jaleo, *m.*, trapatiesta, *f.*, trifulca, *f.* (row).

roughhouse [—haus] v. intr. Armar jaleo, armar una trapatiesta *or* una trifulca.
— V. tr. Zarandear.

roughly [—li] adv. Toscamente (manual work): *roughly made*, toscamente hecho. || Ásperamente. || Brutalmente (brutally). || Aproximadamente, más o menos (approximately). || *To treat s.o. roughly*, maltratar a alguien.

roughneck [—nek] n. U. S. FAM. Duro, *m.*, matón, *m.* (tough). | Palurdo, *m.*, rústico, *m.* (rustic).

roughness [—nis] n. Aspereza, *f.*, rugosidad, *f.* (of surface, skin). || Aspereza, *f.* (of taste, sound, touch). || Callosidad, *f.* (of hands). || Tosquedad, *f.* (crudeness). || Desigualdad, *f.* (of the land, a road). || Brusquedad, *f.* (of character, manner). || Brutalidad, *f.* (of treatment). || Severidad, *f.* (severity). || Ordinariez, *f.*, grosería, *f.* (of language). || Agitación, *f.*, encrespamiento, *m.* (of the sea). || Violencia, *f.* (of wind). || Inclemencia, *f.* (of weather). || Incultura, *f.* (lack of culture). || Falta (*f.*) de educación (impoliteness). || Chapucería, *f.* (of sth. badly made). || SP. Dureza, *f.* (of playing).

roughrider [—ˌraidə*] n. Domador (*m.*) de caballos.

roughshod [—ʃɔd] adj. Herrado con ramplones (horse).
— Adv. FIG. *To ride roughshod over*, pisotear (to ill-treat), hacer caso omiso de (to ignore).

rough-spoken [—ˈspəukən] adj. Malhablado, da.

roulade [ru:ˈlɑ:d] n. MUS. Trino, *m.*, gorgorito, *m.*

rouleau [ruˈləu] n. Cartucho, *m.*

roulette [ruˈlet] n. Ruleta, *f.* (game): *Russian roulette*, ruleta rusa. || Ruleta, *f.* (toothed wheel). || Perforación, *f.* (of a postage stamp).

roulette [ruˈlet] v. tr. Perforar con la ruleta.

Roumania [ruˈmeinjə] pr. n. GEOGR. Rumania, *f.*

Roumanian [—n] adj. Rumano, na.
— N. Rumano, na (person). || Rumano, *m.* (language).

round [raund] adj. Redondo, da: *a round table*, una mesa redonda; *round cheeks*, mejillas redondas; *a round hole*, un agujero redondo; *round handwriting*, letra redonda. || Arqueado, da (shoulders). || Sonoro, ra (voice, sound). || Redondo, da: *in round figures*, en números redondos. || Completo, ta; bueno, na: *a round dozen*, una docena completa. || Rotundo, da; categórico, ca; terminante (refusal). || Pronunciada con los labios redondeados (a vowel). || — *Round trip*, viaje (*m.*) de ida y vuelta (return), viaje (*m.*) circular (circular). || *To be round with s.o.*, ser franco *or* sincero con alguien. || *To go at a good round pace*, ir a buen paso.
— Adv. Por todas partes (everywhere): *leaves scattered round*, hojas esparcidas por todas partes. || De un lado para otro (to and fro): *people walking round*, la gente que anda de un lado para otro. || De perímetro, de circunferencia (in circumference): *a tower sixty feet round*, una torre de sesenta pies de perímetro. || A la redonda (in a circle): *the sound could be heard a mile round*, el ruido se podía oír a una milla a la redonda. || Alrededor (around): *the people standing round*, la gente que está de pie alrededor. || A *or* por casa [de alguien]: *come round when you like*, pasa por casa cuando quieras; *to invite s.o. round*, invitar a alguien a casa. || — *All round*, para todos (for everybody). || *All the year round*, durante todo el año. || *An orchard with a wall all round*, una huerta rodeada por un muro. || *Is there enough to go round?*, ¿hay para todos? || *It's a long way round*, hay que dar un gran rodeo. || *Round about*, en los alrededores. || *Round and round*, dando vueltas a la redonda (in circles): *birds flying round and round*, pájaros dando vueltas a la redonda. || *Taken all round*, en conjunto. || *To gather round*, apiñarse. || *To go the long way round*, ir por el camino más largo. || *To pass* o *to hand round*, pasar de mano en mano, hacer circular. || *To send s.o. round for*, mandar a alguien a buscar *or* a traer. || *To show s.o. round the town*, hacer visitar la ciudad a alguien. || *To spin round*, girar, dar vueltas. || *To whirl round*, girar, dar vueltas. || *To win s.o round*, convencer a uno.
— Prep. Alrededor de: *the wind blew round the house*, el viento soplaba alrededor de la casa; *round the world*, alrededor del mundo; *sitting round the table*, sentados alrededor de la mesa; *the earth turns round its axis*, la tierra gira alrededor de su eje; *round 1830*, alrededor de 1830. || Que rodea: *the wall round the garden*, la tapia que rodea el jardín. || A la vuelta de: *the bar round the corner*, el bar a la vuelta de la esquina. || En: *to wear a scarf round one's neck*, llevar una bufanda en el cuello. || Cerca de, por (near): *somewhere round the High Road*, cerca de la calle Mayor; *it's round here somewhere*, está por aquí cerca. || Por: *to walk round the town singing*, andar cantando por la ciudad. || A eso de: *round (about) five o'clock*, a eso de las cinco. || Acerca de: *to write a book round an incident*, escribir un libro acerca de un incidente. || De: *to measure twenty inches round the neck*, medir veinte pulgadas de cuello. || — *Just round the corner*, a la vuelta de la esquina. || *To go round an obstacle*, dar la vuelta a un obstáculo. || MAR. *To sail round*, doblar un cabo. || *To swim, to run round the island*, dar la vuelta a la isla a nado, corriendo. || FAM. *To talk round a subject*, andar con rodeos, andarse por las ramas.
— N. Círculo, *m.* (circle). || Curva, *f.* (curve). || Esfera, *f.* (sphere). || Rodaja, *f.* (slice). || Vuelta, *f.* (in knitting). || Escalón, *m.*, peldaño, *m.* (of a ladder). || Vuelta, *f.* (circular movement). || Revolución, *f.* (of earth). || Recorrido, *m.* (of a salesman). || Viaje (*m.*) de negocios (of a tradesman). || Visita, *f.* (of a doctor): *to go the rounds*, hacer visitas. || Serie, *f.*, sucesión, *f.*: *a round of parties*, una serie de fiestas. || Ronda, *f.* (of drinks): *to stand a round of drinks*, invitar a una ronda. || Ronda, *f.* (of negotiations). || Vuelta, *f.* (of elections). || Salva, *f.* (of applause). || Rutina, *f.*: *the daily round*, la rutina cotidiana. || MIL. Ronda, *f.* (patrol). | Visita (*f.*) de inspección. | Tiro, *m.* (shot). | Cartucho, *m.* (of ammunition). | Descarga, *f.*, salva, *f.* (salvo). || SP. Asalto, *m.*, "round", *m.* (in boxing). | Vuelta, *f.* (stage of a competition). | Circuito, *m.* (lap). | Partido, *m.*: *to play a round of golf*, jugar un partido de golf. || Partida, *f.* (game). || MUS. Canon, *m.* || — *In the round*, en alto relieve (a sculpture). || *To go the round* o *the rounds*, ir de boca en boca (a story, rumour). || *To go the round of the pubs looking for s.o.*, ir por todas las tabernas en busca de alguien.

round [raund] v. tr. Redondear (to make round). || Dar la vuelta a, doblar, torcer (a corner). || Doblar (a cape). || Costear (an island). || Dar la vuelta a (an obstacle). || Pulir (written work, style).
— V. intr. Redondearse (to become round).
— ***To round off*** redondear (a sharp end, a number, etc.). | Acabar, rematar (to end, to close). | Pulir (one's sentences). || ***To round on,*** denunciar (to betray). | Volverse en contra de (to turn on). | *To round on one's heels*, dar media vuelta. || ***To round out,*** acabar (to end). | Ponerse rellenito (to become plump). || MAR. ***To round to,*** ponerse al pairo. || ***To round up,*** acorralar, rodear (cattle, etc.). | Reunir (people).

roundabout [—əbaut] adj. Indirecto, ta (indirect). || Tortuoso, sa (tortuous). || — *Roundabout means*, rodeos, *m.* || *Roundabout phrase*, circunloquio, *m.*, rodeo, *m.*
— N. Tiovivo, *m.* (merry-go-round). || Plaza (*f.*) circular, glorieta, *f.* (at the intersection of crossroads). || Rodeo, *m.* (circumlocution). || Rodeo, *m.*, vuelta, *f.* (detour).

roundel [—l] n. Ventana (*f.*) circular (window). || Letrilla, *f.*, rondel, *m.* (poetry). || HERALD. Roel, *m.*

roundelay [—ilei] n. MUS. Rondó, *m.* | Baile (*m.*) en corro. | Canción (*f.*) cantada en corro.

rounder [—ə*] n. TECH. Herramienta (*f.*) para redondear. || U. S. FAM. Calavera, *m.* (gay dog).

rounders [—əz] n. SP. Juego (*m.*) parecido al béisbol.

round-eyed [—aid] adj. Con los ojos desorbitados: *to gaze round-eyed at*, mirar con los ojos desorbitados.

Roundhead [—hed] n. HIST. Cabeza (*f.*) redonda.

roundhouse [—haus] n. MAR. Toldilla, *f.*, chupeta, *f.* || Depósito (*m.*) de locomotoras (circular building for railway engines).

roundish [—iʃ] adj. Regordete, ta (plump). || Casi redondo, da.

roundly [—li] adv. Completamente (completely). || Abiertamente (openly). || Francamente (frankly). || FIG. Rotundamente, categóricamente, terminantemente.

roundness [—nis] n. Redondez, *f.*

round robin [—ˈrɔbin] n. Petición, *f.* [hecha de modo que ningún nombre encabece la lista]. || Torneo, *m.* (contest).

round-shouldered [—ˈʃəuldəd] adj. Cargado de espaldas.

roundsman [—zmən] n. Repartidor, *m.* (delivery man). || U. S. Cabo (*m.*) de policía.
— OBSERV. El plural de *roundsman* es *roundsmen.*

Round Table [—ˈteibl] n. Tabla (*f.*) Redonda (in the Arthurian legend).

round table conference [—ˈteiblˈkɔnfərəns] n. Mesa (*f.*) redonda.

round-the-clock [ˈraundðəˈklɔk] adj. Que dura veinticuatro horas.

roundtop [—tɔp] n. MAR. Gavia, *f.*, cofa, *f.*

roundup [—ʌp] n. Rodeo, *m.* (of cattle). || FIG. Redada, *f.* (of suspects). | Resumen, *m.* (summary).

roundworm [—wə:m] n. ZOOL. Ascáride, *f.*

roup [rup] n. VET. Moquillo, *m.*

rouse [rauz] v. tr. Despertar (to wake up). || Animar (to make active). || Despertar (a feeling, indignation). || Suscitar, provocar (admiration). || Sacudir (from indifference). || Irritar, enfadar (to make angry). || MAR. Halar (to haul). || Avivar (the fire). || Levantar (the game). || — *To rouse o.s.*, animarse. || *To rouse s.o. to action*, hacer que alguien haga algo.
— V. intr. Despertarse, despertar.

rouser [—ə*] n. Agitador, *m.* || Estimulante, *m.* (stimulus). || FAM. Bola, *f.*, mentira, *f.* (lie).

rousing [—iŋ] adj. Conmovedor, ra (moving). || Caluroso, sa (applause). || Vigorizante, estimulante (invigorating). || FAM. Descomunal, enorme: *rousing lie*, mentira enorme.

Roussillon [ˈru:sijɔ̃n] n. GEOGR. Rosellón, *m.*

roustabout [ˈraustəbaut] n. Estibador, *m.* (in a dock). || U. S. Peón, *m.* (labourer).

rout [raut] n. Derrota (*f.*) completa, desbandada, *f.* (defeat). || Fuga (*f.*) desordenada (flight). || Canalla, *f.*, chusma, *f.* (rabble). || Pandilla, *f.* (of revellers). || Alboroto, *m.*, tumulto, *m.* (uproar).

rout [raut] v. tr. Derrotar (to defeat). || Poner en fuga (to put to flight). || Hacer salir (to make s.o. come out). || Descubrir (to discover).
— V. intr. Hozar, hocicar (swine). || Hurgar (to search about).
route [ru:t] n. Ruta, *f.*, itinerario, *m.* (for a journey): *to map out a route*, trazar un itinerario. || Camino, *m.* (path). || Línea, *f.*, recorrido, *m.* (bus route). || MAR. Rumbo, *m.*, derrota, *f.* (of a ship): *to change route*, cambiar de rumbo. || Ruta (*f.*) aérea (airway). || MIL. Itinerario, *m.* || U. S. Recorrido, *m.* (round). || — *Route map*, mapa (*m.*) de carreteras. || MIL. *Route march*, marcha (*f.*) de entrenamiento. | *Route order*, orden (*m.*, de marcha. || *Sea route*, vía marítima.
route [ru:t] v. tr. Encaminar, mandar (to send).
router [ˈrautə*] n. TECH. Guimbarda, *f.* (plane). | Fresa, *f.*, fresadora, *f.* (milling machine).
routine [ru:ˈti:n] n. Rutina, *f.*: *the daily routine*, la rutina cotidiana; *as a matter of routine*, por rutina. || MIL. *Routine orders*, órdenes (*f.*) de servicio.
— Adj. Rutinario, ria: *a routine job*, un trabajo rutinario.
routinist [ruˈti:nist] n. Rutinario, ria.
rove [rəuv] n. Arandela, *f.* (washer). || Madeja, *f.* (of cotton, wool). || Torzal, *m.* (of silk). || FAM. *To be on the rove*, errar, vagar.
rove [rəuv] v. tr. Torcer (thread). || Recorrer (to travel round). || Errar por, vagar por (to roam).
— V. intr. Andar errante, vagar, errar. || *His eyes roved over the landscape*, recorría el paisaje con la mirada.
rove [rəuv] pret. & p. p. See REEVE.
rover [—ə*] n. Vagabundo, *m.* (vagabond). || Explorador, *m.* (senior boy scout). || Blanco, *m.* (target). || MAR. Pirata, *m.*, corsario, *m.* (pirate).
roving [—iŋ] adj. Errante (wandering). || Ambulante (salesman). || Itinerante (ambassador).
row [rəu] n. Fila, *f.*, hilera, *f.*: *a row of houses*, una hilera de casas. || Fila, *f.* (of seats, persons). || Vuelta, *f.* (of knitting). || Paseo (*m.*) en bote (trip in a rowboat). || — *In a row*, en fila (in a line), seguidos, das (one after the other). || *In rows*, en filas. || *To go for a row*, pasearse en bote.
row [rəu] v. tr. Hacer avanzar con el remo (a boat). || Remar en (a race). || Competir con (to compete against). || Llevar a remo (a person). || Ser movido por: *a boat which rows ten oars*, una barca que es movida por diez remos.
— V. intr. Remar. || *To row across the river*, cruzar el río a remo *or* remando.
row [rau] n. Alboroto, *m.*, estrépito, *m.*, jaleo, *m.*, escándalo, *m.* (noise, disturbance). || Jaleo, *m.*, escándalo, *m.* (fuss). || Bronca, *f.*, pelea, *f.* (quarrel). || Riña, *f.*, regañuza, *f.* (scolding). || — *Family rows*, peleas or riñas familiares. || FAM. *Hold your row!*, ¡cállate! || FIG. *If they catch you, you will get into a row*, si te cogen, cobrarás. || *To kick up* o *to make a row*, armar jaleo (to make a lot of noise), armar un escándalo (to protest strongly).
row [rau] v. intr. Reñir, pelearse.
— V. tr. FAM. Echar una regañuza a, reñir.
rowan [ˈrauən] n. BOT. Serbal, *m.* (tree). | Serba, *f.* (fruit).
rowboat [ˈrəubəut] n. Bote (*m.*) de remos.
rowdiness [ˈraudinis] n. Carácter (*m.*) pendenciero (quarrelsomeness). || Alboroto, *m.* (disturbance). || Ruido, *m.* (noise).
rowdy [ˈraudi] adj. Ruidoso, sa (noisy). || Camorrista, pendenciero, ra (loud and quarrelsome).
— N. Camorrista, *m.* & *f.*, pendenciero, ra.
rowdyism [—ˌizəm] n. Disturbios, *m. pl.*, pendencias, *f. pl.*, alboroto, *m.* (disturbance).
rowel [ˈrauəl] n. Rodaja, *f.* (of a spur).
rowel [ˈrauəl] v. tr. Espolear.
rower [rəuə*] n. Remador, ra; remero, ra.
rowing [ˈrəuiŋ] n. Remo, *m.*
rowing boat [—bəut] n. Bote (*m.*) de remos.
rowlock [ˈrɔlək] n. MAR. Escálamo, *m.*, tolete, *m.* || ARCH. Sardinel, *m.*
royal [ˈrɔiəl] adj. Real: *the royal family*, la familia real. || Principesco, ca (princely). || Grandioso, sa; magnífico, ca; espléndido, da; regio, gia (splendid): *they gave her a royal send-off*, le hicieron una despedida magnífica. || MAR. De sobrejuanete. || BOT. Real. || — *Royal flush*, escalera real (in card games). || *The Royal Academy of Music*, La Real Academia de Música. || FIG. *To have a royal time*, pasarlo en grande.
— N. ZOOL. Ciervo (*m.*) de doce cuernos. || MAR. Sobrejuanete, *m.* || Miembro (*m.*) de la familia real.
royalism [—izəm] n. Monarquismo, *m.*, realismo, *m.*
royalist [—ist] adj./n. Monárquico, ca; realista.
royally [—i] adv. FIG. Regiamente, magníficamente.
royal palm [—ˈpɑ:m] n. BOT. Palma (*f.*) real, palmiche, *m.* (ornamental palm).
royalty [—ti] n. Realeza, *f.* || Miembro (*m.*) de la familia real. || Familia (*f.*) real (royal family). || — Pl. Derechos (*m.*) de autor *or* de inventor, regalías, *f.*
rub [rʌb] n. Fricción, *f.*, frotamiento, *m.*, frote, *m.* (voluntary). || Roce, *m.* (accidental, unwanted). || Desigualdad (*f.*) del terreno (in bowls). || Dificultad, *f.*, obstáculo, *m.* (hindrance). || — FIG. *There's the rub*, allí está el busilis, ésa es la dificultad, ahí está el quid. || *To give one's shoes a rub*, sacar brillo a los zapatos. || *To give the silver a rub*, limpiar la plata.
rub [rʌb] v. tr. Friccionar: *to rub one's leg with ointment*, friccionar la pierna con una pomada. || Limpiar, dar brillo a: *to rub the silverware*, dar brillo a la plata. || Lustrar, encerar (floors). || Limpiar frotando (to clean). || Rozar: *my shoes rub my heels*, los zapatos me rozan los talones. || Rozar contra: *to rub the kerb with one's ankle*, rozar con el tobillo contra el borde de la acera. || Frotar, restregar: *to make fire by rubbing two pieces of wood together*, hacer fuego frotando dos trozos de madera. || Frotarse: *to rub one's hands together*, frotarse las manos. || Lijar (with sandpaper). || Estarcir (a drawing). || — FIG. *To rub elbows* o *shoulders with*, codearse con. | *To rub noses with*, ser amigo íntimo de. | FAM. *To rub* (*up*) *the wrong way*, coger a contrapelo.
— V. intr. Rozar: *the wheel rubs against the mudguard*, la rueda roza contra el guardabarros. || Friccionarse (a person). || Desviarse (a ball in bowls). || Desgastarse (to wear out).
— ***To rub along***, ir tirando, ganar justo lo suficiente para vivir (to get by). | Evitar fricciones (to avoid frictions). | — *To rub along in a language*, defenderse en una lengua. | *To rub along very well together*, llevarse bien. || ***To rub away***, quitar frotando (to remove by rubbing). | Desgastar (to wear out). | Hacer desaparecer (to make disappear). || ***To rub down***, almohazar (a horse). | Friccionar (s.o.). | Raspar (a surface). | Lijar (with sandpaper). || ***To rub in***, frotar [una parte del cuerpo] con (ointment). | — FIG. *Don't rub it in!*, ¡no insista! || ***To rub off***, quitar frotando (to remove). | Quitarse frotando (to be removable): *that stain will rub off*, esa mancha se quitará frotando. | Desaparecer (to disappear). | — FIG. *To rub off on s.o.*, pegársele a uno (bad habits), transmitírsele a uno (another's intelligence, etc.). || ***To rub out***, borrar (to erase). | Borrarse (to be erased). | FAM. Liquidar (to kill). || ***To rub through***, salir adelante. || ***To rub up***, limpiar, dar brillo a (to polish). | Refrescar (memory).
rub-a-dub [ˈrʌbəˈdʌb] or **rub-a-dub-dub** [— dʌb] n. Rataplán, *m.* (of drums).
rubber [ˈrʌbə*] n. BOT. Caucho, *m.* || Goma, *f.*, caucho, *m.* (synthetic substance). || Goma (*f.*) de borrar (eraser). || Masajista, *m.* & *f.* (person). || Chanclo, *m.* (overshoe). || FAM. Goma, *f.*, condón, *m.* (contraceptive sheath). || "Rubber", *m.* (bridge).
— Adj. De goma: *rubber ball*, pelota de goma. || Sin fondos (cheque). || — *Rubber band*, goma, *f.* || *Rubber industry*, industria (*f.*) del caucho.
rubberize [ˈrʌbəraiz] v. tr. Cauchutar.
rubberneck [ˈrʌbənek] n. U. S. FAM. Curioso, sa (inquisitive person). | Mirón, ona (sightseer). | Turista, *m.* & *f.* (tourist).
rubberneck [ˈrʌbənek] v. intr. U. S. FAM. Curiosear, meter las narices.
rubber plant [ˈrʌbəplɑ:nt] n. BOT. Árbol (*m.*) del caucho, gomero, *m.*
rubber ring [ˈrʌbəˈriŋ] n. Goma, *f.* (rubber band). || Flotador, *m.* (for swimming).
rubber stamp [ˈrʌbəˈstæmp] n. Tampón, *m.*, sello (*m.*) de goma. || FIG. Aprobación (*f.*) maquinal.
rubber-stamp [ˈrʌbəˈstæmp] v. tr. Marcar con un sello de goma (to put a stamp on). || FIG. Aprobar maquinalmente (go give one's approval).
rubber tree [ˈrʌbəˈtri:] n. Gomero, *m.*, árbol (*m.*) del caucho.
rubbery [ˈrʌbəri] adj. Parecido a la goma. || Elástico, ca (elastic).
rubbing [ˈrʌbiŋ] n. Frotamiento, *m.* (voluntary). || Roce, *m.* (undesirable): *the rubbing of one's shoes*, el roce de los zapatos. || MED. Fricción, *f.*
rubbish [ˈrʌbiʃ] n. Basura, *f.* (refuse). || Desperdicios, *m. pl.* (waste). || Escombros, *m. pl.* (from building). || FIG. FAM. Birria, *f.*, porquería, *f.*, asquerosidad, *f.*: *these photographs are rubbish*, estas fotos son una birria. | Tonterías, *f. pl.*, disparates, *m. pl.*, sandeces, *f. pl.*: *to talk rubbish*, decir tonterías.
rubbish bin [—bin] n. Cubo (*m.*) de la basura.
rubbish chute [—ʃu:t] n. Vertedero (*m.*) de basuras, colector (*m.*) de basuras.
rubbish dump [—dʌmp] or **rubbish heap** [—hi:p] n. Basurero, *m.*, muladar, *m.*, vertedero, *m.*
rubbishy [ˈrʌbiʃi] adj. Sin valor, de pacotilla. || Lleno de sandeces (book, speech, etc.).
rubble [ˈrʌbl] n. Escombros, *m. pl.* (loose bricks, debris, etc.). || Cascotes, *m. pl.*, ripios, *m. pl.* (for foundations, roadbuilding). || Morrillo, *m.* (masonry).
rubblework [—wə:k] n. Morrillo, *m.*
rubdown [—daun] n. Masaje, *m.* || Secado (*m.*) con una toalla. || *To give a horse a rubdown*, almohazar un caballo.
rube [ru:b] n. U. S. FAM. Paleto, *m.*, palurdo, *m.* (bumpkin).
rubefacient [ˌru:biˈfeiʃjənt] adj. MED. Rubefaciente.
— N. MED. Rubefaciente, *m.*
rubefaction [ˌru:biˈfækʃən] n. MED. Rubefacción, *f.*
rubefy [ˈru:bifai] v. tr. MED. Rubificar.
rubella [ru:ˈbelə] n. MED. Rubéola, *f.* (German measles).
rubeola [ru:ˈbi:ələ] n. MED. Sarampión, *m.* (measles). | Rubéola, *f.* (German measles).
rubescent [ru:ˈbesənt] adj. Rubescente.

rubiaceae [rubi'eisii] pl. n. BOT. Rubiáceas, *f.*
rubicelle ['ru:bisel] n. MIN. Rubicela, *f.*
Rubicon ['ru:bikən] pr. n. GEOGR. Rubicón, *m.*: *to cross the Rubicon*, pasar el Rubicón.
rubicund ['ru:bikənd] adj. Rubicundo, da.
rubicundity [,ru:bi'kʌnditi] n. Rubicundez, *f.*
rubidium [ru'bidiəm] n. Rubidio, *m.* (metal).
rubied ['ru:bid] adj. De color del rubí.
ruble ['ru:bl] n. Rublo, *m.* (Russian currency).
rubric ['ru:brik] n. Rúbrica, *f.*
ruby ['ru:bi] n. Rubí, *m.* (stone). || PRINT. Tipo (*m.*) de 5,5 puntos. || Color (*m.*) de rubí.
— Adj. De color de rubí.
ruche [ru:ʃ] n. Encañonado (*m.*) de encaje (lace frills).
ruck [rʌk] n. Vulgo, *m.* (ordinary people). || Pelotón, *m.* (in racing). || "Melée", *f.* (in rugby). || Arruga, *f.* (wrinkle).
ruck [rʌk] or **ruckle** [—l] v. tr. Arrugar.
— V. intr. Arrugarse.
rucksack [—sæk] n. Mochila, *f.*
ruckus [—əs] or **ruction** [—ʃən] n. FAM. Jaleo, *m.*, cisco, *m.*, jollín, *m.* (noisy disturbance). || FAM. *There will be ructions*, se va armar la de San Quintín *or* la gorda.
rudder ['rʌdə*] n. MAR. AVIAT. Timón, *m.* || *Rudder bar*, caña (*f.*) del timón, timón, *m.* (of a ship), palanca (*f.*) de mando del timón (of a plane).
rudderless [—lis] adj. Sin timón.
rudderpost [—,pəust] n. MAR. Codaste, *m.*
ruddiness [—inis] n. Color (*m.*) rubicundo *or* rojizo, rubicundez, *f.*
ruddle ['rʌdl] n. Almagre, *m.*
ruddy [—i] adj. Rubicundo, da; rojizo, za. || FAM. Maldito, ta; condenado, da (damned).
rude [ru:d] adj. Grosero, ra; ordinario, ria (coarse): *rude behaviour*, comportamiento grosero. || Descortés, mal educado, da; grosero, ra (impolite): *don't be rude*, no sea mal educado; *he was very rude to me*, estuvo muy descortés conmigo. || Tosco, ca: *a rude table*, una mesa tosca; *a rude plough*, un arado tosco. || Duro, ra: *a rude blow*, un golpe duro. || Penoso, sa; desagradable (painful): *a rude surprise*, una sorpresa penosa. || Escabroso, sa; verde, indecente, grosero, ra: *rude story*, historia indecente. || Inculto, ta (uneducated). || Crudo, da; riguroso, sa (weather). || Violento, ta (sea, wind). || Brusco, ca; repentino, na (sudden). || Aproximado, da (estimation). || Fuerte, robusto, ta (health). || — *It's rude*, es de mala educación, es descortés. || *To make rude remarks*, decir groserías.
rudeness [—nis] n. Grosería, *f.*, descortesía, *f.* (impoliteness, vulgarity). || Mala educación, *f.* (bad breeding). || Indecencia, *f.*, lo verde, escabrosidad, *f.*, grosería, *f.* (obscenity). || Tosquedad, *f.*, lo basto (roughness). || Dureza, *f.*, rudeza, *f.* (of a blow, a shock). || Incultura, *f.* (lack of education). || Rigor, *m.*, lo crudo (of weather). || Violencia, *f.* (of wind, sea).
rudiment ['ru:dimənt] n. BIOL. Rudimento, *m.* || — Pl. Rudimentos, *m.*: *the rudiments of grammar*, los rudimentos de la gramática.
rudimentary [,ru:di'mentəri] adj. Rudimentario, ria.
rue [ru:] n. Ruda, *f.* (plant). || Arrepentimiento, *m.* (regret).
rue [ru:] v. tr. Arrepentirse de, lamentar, sentir mucho. || *You'll live to rue the day you left him*, un día lamentarás haberle dejado.
rueful [—ful] adj. Pesaroso, sa; arrepentido, da (regretful). || Triste (sad): *the Knight of the Rueful Countenance*, el Caballero de la Triste Figura. || Lastimoso, sa; lamentable (deplorable).
ruefulness [—fulnis] n. Tristeza, *f.*, pesar, *m.*
rufescent [ru:'fesənt] adj. Rojizo, za.
ruff [rʌf] n. Collarín, *m.* (on animals and birds). || Gorguera, *f.*, gola, *f.* (starched collar). || Fallo, *m.* (in cards). || Paloma (*f.*) moñuda (bird).
ruff [rʌf] v. tr./intr. Fallar (in card games).
ruffian [—jən] n. Rufián, *m.*, canalla, *m.*
ruffianly [—jənli] adj. Canallesco, ca; rufianesco, ca.
ruffle ['rʌfl] n. Chorrera, *f.* (on the chest): *a blouse with a ruffle*, una blusa con chorrera. || Volante, *m.* (at the wrists, etc.). || Gorguera, *f.*, gola, *f.* (around the neck). || Collarín, *m.* (of a bird, etc.). || Rizo, *m.* (ripple of water). || Redoble, *m.* (of drums). || Agitación, *f.* (disturbance). || FIG. Enfado, *m.*, enojo, *m.*, disgusto, *m.* (anger).
ruffle ['rʌfl] v. tr. Agitar (to disturb). || Desgreñar (hair). || Agitar, rizar (water). || Erizar (bird's feathers). || Arrugar (to wrinkle). || Fruncir (to gather cloth). || FIG. Enojar, disgustar (to offend). | Perturbar (to perturb). || Barajar (cards).
— V. intr. Agitarse, rizarse (water, etc.). || Encresparse (with waves). || Erizarse (feathers). || Desgreñarse (hair).
rufous ['ru:fəs] adj. Rojizo, za.
rug [rʌg] n. Alfombra, *f.* (carpet). || Alfombrilla (*f.*) de cama (bedside rug). || Alfombrilla, *f.*, tapete, *m.* (small carpet). || Piel, *f.*: *a tiger skin rug*, una piel de tigre. || Manta (*f.*) de viaje (travelling rug).
rugby ['rʌgbi] n. SP. Rugby, *m.* || *Rugby League*, rugby a trece.
rugby football [—'futbɔ:l] n. SP. Rugby, *m.*
rugged ['rʌgid] adj. Accidentado, da; desigual (ground, road). || Escarpado, da (mountain, rock). || Rugoso, sa (bark). || Duro, ra (features). || Desabrido, da (character). || Desigual, tosco, ca (style). || Duro, ra (way of life). || Riguroso, sa (climate). || Basto, ta; tosco, ca (manners). || U. S. Robusto, ta; fuerte (strong).
ruggedness [—nis] n. Lo accidentado, desigualdad, *f.* (of the ground). || Lo escarpado (of mountains, rocks). || Dureza, *f.* (of face, features, way of life). || Desabrimiento, *m.* (of character). || Tosquedad, *f.* (of manners). || U. S. Robustez, *f.*
rugger ['rʌgə*] n. FAM. Rugby, *m.*
rugose ['ru:gəus] or **rugous** ['ru:gəus] adj. Rugoso, sa.
rugosity [ru'gɔsiti] n. Rugosidad, *f.*
ruin [ruin] n. Ruina, *f.*: *drink led to his ruin*, la bebida le llevó a la ruina; *the palace is now a ruin*, el palacio es ahora una ruina. || Ruina, *f.*, perdición, *f.*: *the flood will be the ruin of the crops*, la inundación será la ruina de las cosechas; *she will be the ruin of me*, será mi perdición. || Ruina, *f.* (financial disaster). || — Pl. Ruinas, *f. pl.*: *the ruins of a castle*, las ruinas de un castillo. || — FIG. *He is but the ruin of what he was*, no es ni sombra de lo que fue, está hecho una ruina. || FAM. *Mother's ruin*, matarratas, *m. inv.*, ginebra muy mala. || *To be in ruins*, estar en ruinas. || *To be on the road to ruin*, ir a la ruina. || *To bring to ruin*, arruinar. || FIG. *To go to rack and ruin*, venirse abajo. || *To go to ruin*, caer en ruinas (building), venirse abajo (project). || *To lie in ruin*, estar en ruinas.
ruin [ruin] v. tr. Arruinar (financially): *inflation ruined the firm*, la inflación arruinó la empresa. || Asolar (to destroy): *the earthquake ruined the city*, el terremoto asoló la ciudad. || Estropear (to spoil): *to ruin s.o.'s hairdo*, estropear el peinado de alguien. || Echar abajo: *bad weather ruined my plans*, el mal tiempo echó abajo mis planes. || Arruinar, echar a perder (health). || Arruinar, estropear (one's life). || Arruinar, echar por tierra (one's reputation). || Estragar (one's taste). || Desacreditar (to disparage). || Perder (to cause moral downfall, to seduce).
ruination [rui'neiʃən] n. Arruinamiento, *m.*, ruina, *f.*, perdición, *f.* (cause of ruin).
ruined [ruind] adj. Arruinado, da (financially). || En ruinas (in ruins).
ruinous ['ruinəs] adj. Ruinoso, sa: *ruinous expenses*, gastos ruinosos; *ruinous houses*, casas ruinosas.
rule [ru:l] n. Regla, *f.*, norma, *f.*: *rules of conduct*, normas de conducta. || Regla, *f.*: *rules of arithmetic*, reglas aritméticas; *rule of three*, regla de tres; *rule of an order*, regla de una orden; *an exception to the rule*, una excepción a la regla. || Dominio, *m.*, mando, *m.*: *country under British rule*, país bajo dominio británico. || Imperio, *m.*: *the rule of law*, el imperio de la ley. || Reinado, *m.*: *England under the rule of Elizabeth I*, Inglaterra bajo el reinado de Isabel I. || Regla (*f.*) graduada (ruler). || Metro, *m.* (metre). || PRINT. Filete, *m.* || JUR. Fallo, *m.*, decisión, *f.* || — Pl. Reglas, *f.*, normas, *f.* (in sports, etc.). || Reglamento, *m. sing.* (regulations): *to abide by the rules*, respetar el reglamento. || — MATH. *Alligation rule*, regla de aligación. || *As a rule*, generalmente, por regla general. || *By rule*, de acuerdo con las reglas. || *By rule of thumb*, de modo empírico. || *Folding rule*, metro plegable. || *Home rule*, autonomía, *f.* || *Rules and regulations*, reglamento. || *Rules of the game*, reglas del juego. || *Rules of the road*, reglamento del tráfico. || *Slide rule*, regla de cálculo. || *The exception proves the rule*, la excepción confirma la regla. || *To act according to the rules*, obrar según las reglas. || *To make it a rule to*, ser un deber para uno. || FIG. *To play by the rules*, obrar como es debido *or* como Dios manda. || *To work to rule*, ceñirse al reglamento, negarse a hacer horas extraordinarias.
rule [ru:l] v. tr. Mandar, gobernar (to govern): *he ruled the country for ten years*, gobernó el país durante diez años. || Dirigir (a firm). || Aconsejar, guiar (to advise). || Llevar (a household, one's life, etc.). || Decretar (to decree). || Decidir (to decide): *the chairman ruled that the question was out of order*, el presidente decidió que no se podía discutir la cuestión. || Dominar (one's passions, s.o.): *is it true that she rules her husband?*, ¿es verdad que domina a su marido? || Trazar, tirar (a line). || Rayar, reglar, pautar (paper). || JUR. Fallar. || — *To rule off*, trazar una línea debajo de (a paragraph, etc.), cerrar (an account). || *To rule out*, excluir (s.o.), excluir, descartar (sth.). || *To rule over*, dominar, regir. || *To rule the waves*, dominar los mares.
— V. intr. Gobernar (to govern). || Reinar (to reign). || Reinar, imperar: *silence ruled*, reinaba el silencio. || Regir (prices). || JUR. Fallar, decidir. || — *To rule high*, mantenerse a un nivel alto (prices). || *To rule over*, reinar en.
ruler [—ə*] n. Gobernante, *m.* & *f.* (person who governs). || Soberano, na (sovereign). || Regla, *f.* (for drawing lines). || — Pl. Gobernantes, *m.*, dirigentes, *m.*
rulership [—əʃip] n. Poder, *m.*, autoridad, *f.*
ruling [—iŋ] adj. Dirigente: *ruling classes*, clases dirigentes. || Que rige, actual (price). || Dominante (passion).
— N. JUR. Fallo, *m.*, decisión, *f.* || Gobierno, *m.* (action). || *To give a ruling on*, pronunciar un fallo sobre.
rum [rʌm] adj. FAM. Extraño, ña; raro, ra (strange). || FAM. *He is a rum customer*, es un tipo raro.
— N. Ron, *m.* (drink). || U. S. Bebida (*f.*) alcohólica.
Rumania [ru:'meinjə] pr. n. GEOGR. Rumania, *f.*

Rumanian [—n] adj./n. Rumano, na.
rumba [ˈrʌmbə] n. Rumba, *f.* (dance, music).
rumble [ˈrʌmbl] n. Ruido (*m.*) sordo, el retumbar (sound). || Rodar, *m.* (of a vehicle). || Estruendo, *m.*, fragor, *m.* (of thunder). || Borborigmo, *m.* (of the stomach). || AUT. Picado (*m.*) de la biela.
rumble [ˈrʌmbl] v. tr. Decir con voz cavernosa (to say in a deep voice). || FAM. Calar (s.o.). | Olerse (sth.). || *To rumble out a remark*, hacer una observación con voz cavernosa.
— V. intr. Rodar con gran estrépito (vehicle). || Retumbar (thunder). || Hacer ruidos (stomach).
rumble seat [—si:t] n. U. S. Asiento (*m.*) trasero descubierto.
rumbling [—iŋ] adj. Retumbante.
— N. Ruido (*m.*) sordo, estruendo, *m.*
rumbustious [rʌmˈbʌstʃəs] adj. Bullicioso, sa.
rumen [ˈru:men] n. Herbario, *m.* (of a ruminant).

— OBSERV. El plural de *rumen* es *rumina*.

ruminant [ˈru:minənt] adj. ZOOL. Rumiante.
— N. ZOOL. Rumiante, *m.*
ruminate [ˈru:mineit] v. tr./intr. Rumiar (animals). || FIG. Rumiar: *to ruminate a project*, rumiar un proyecto.
rumination [ˌru:miˈneiʃən] n. Rumia, *f.* || FIG. Meditación, *f.*, reflexión, *f.*
ruminative [ˈru:minətiv] adj. FIG. Meditabundo, da.
rummage [ˈrʌmidʒ] n. Búsqueda (*f.*) desordenada (search). || Objetos (*m. pl.*) diversos.
rummage [ˈrʌmidʒ] v. tr. Registrar: *to rummage a house from top to bottom*, registrar una casa de arriba abajo.
— V. intr. Buscar desordenadamente, revolver: *to rummage in a drawer*, revolver en un cajón.
rummage sale [—seil] n. Venta (*f.*) de artículos con fines benéficos (for a church, etc.). || Liquidación, *f.* (clearance sale).
rummy [ˈrʌmi] n. Rami, *m.* (card game).
— Adj. FAM. Extraño, ña; raro, ra.
rumour (U. S. **rumor**) [ˈru:mə*] n. Rumor, *m.*: *according to rumours*, según los rumores. || *Rumor has it that* o *there are rumours that*, se rumorea que, se dice que, corre el rumor de que.
rumour (U. S. **rumor**) [ˈru:mə*] v. tr. Rumorear. || *It is rumoured that*, se rumorea que, se dice que, corre el rumor de que.
rump [rʌmp] n. Ancas, *f.pl.*, grupa, *f.* (of a quadruped). || Rabadilla, *f.* (of birds). || CULIN. Cuarto (*m.*) trasero. || FAM. Trasero, *m.* (of person).
rumple [ˈrʌmpl] v. tr. Arrugar (to crease). || FAM. Enfadar, molestar (to annoy). || *To rumple s.o.'s hair*, despeinar a uno.
rumpus [ˈrʌmpəs] n. FAM. Jaleo, *m.* (shindy): *to kick up a rumpus*, armar jaleo. | Agarrada, *f.*: *to have a rumpus with s.o.*, tener una agarrada con alguien.
rumpus room [—ru:m] n. Cuarto (*m.*) de juegos.
rumrunner [ˈrʌmˌrʌnə*] n. U. S. Contrabandista (*m.*) de bebidas alcohólicas.
run [rʌn] n. Carrera, *f.* (race). || Serie, *f.*, racha, *f.*: *a run of mishaps*, una serie de contratiempos. || Período, *m.*: *a run of bad weather*, un período de mal tiempo. || Escalera, *f.* (in card games). || Gran demanda, *f.*: *there has been a run on sugar today*, ha habido gran demanda de azúcar hoy. || Libre uso, *m.*, libre disposición, *f.*: *to give s.o. the run of one's house*, dar a alguien libre uso de su casa, dejar a alguien la libre disposición de su casa. || Sendero, *m.* (habitual course of an animal). || Corral, *m.* (for farm animals). || Pasto, *m.* (pasture). || Migración, *f.* (of fish). || Vuelta, *f.*, paseo, *m.* (short journey): *to go for a run in the car*, dar una vuelta en coche; *to go for a run over to the coast*, darse una vuelta por la costa. || Recorrido, *m.*, trayecto, *m.* (of a train, railway, etc.): *the run from Los Angeles to San Francisco is not very long*, el trayecto de Los Ángeles a San Francisco no es muy largo. || Tendencia, *f.* (general tendency): *the run of the market*, la tendencia del mercado. || Dirección, *f.* (direction). || Disposición, *f.*: *the run of the streets is perpendicular to the river*, la disposición de las calles es perpendicular al río. || Curso, *m.* (of a liquid). || Corriente, *f.* (of the tide). || Arroyo, *m.* (stream). || Curso, *m.*: *the present run of events*, el curso actual de los acontecimientos. || Funcionamiento, *m.* (of a machine). || Pasada, *f.* (of a machine tool). || Colada, *f.* (of a blast furnace). || Producción, *f.* (production). || Prueba, *f.* (trial). || Ritmo, *m.*, cadencia, *f.* (of a phrase). || FIG. Hilo, *m.*: *to lose the run of the speech*, perder el hilo de la conversación. | Boga, *f.*, moda, *f.* (popularity). | Gran demanda, *f.* (demand). | Carrera, *f.*, carrerilla, *f.* (in stockings). || MUS. Carrerilla, *f.* || SP. Carrerilla, *f.*: *to take a long run*, coger mucha carrerilla. | Pista, *f.* (ski slope). | Punto, *m.* (point scored). | Carrera, *f.* (in baseball and cricket). || PRINT. Tirada, *f.*: *a run of 10 000 copies*, una tirada de diez mil ejemplares. || COMM. Categoría, *f.* (of goods). || MIL. Pasada, *f.* (of bombers). || MIN. Dirección, *f.* (of a vein). || GEOL. Desprendimiento, *m.* (of ground). || — *A run of bad luck*, una mala racha. || *A run of luck*, una buena racha. || *At a run*, corriendo: *he came up at a run*, llegó corriendo. || *Birmingham is two hour's run from London*, Birmingham está a dos horas [de tren *or* de coche] de Londres. || MAR. *Day's run*, singladura, *f.* || CINEM. *First run*, período (*m.*) de estreno (of a film). || *I have a ten-minute run before breakfast*, corro *or* echo una carrera de diez minutos antes del desayuno. || *In the long run*, a la larga. || *It's only half an hour's run*, está sólo a media hora de aquí. || *Landing run*, distancia recorrida al aterrizar. || *Out of the common run*, fuera de lo común. || *Prices came down with a run*, los precios experimentaron una caída vertical. || *The common run of men*, el común de los mortales. || FIG. *The play had a run of a year*, la obra estuvo en cartel durante un año. || *There was a run on the bank*, el banco sufrió el asedio de los cuentacorrentistas que querían retirar el dinero. || *To be always on the run*, estar siempre corriendo. || *To be on the run*, haberse fugado *or* escapado. || *To break into a run*, echar a correr. || FIG. *To give s.o. a run for his money*, hacer pasar un mal rato a alguien (to give a bad time), permitir a alguien que le saque jugo al dinero (to give good value). | *To have a good* o *a long run*, estar mucho tiempo en cartel (play, show), ser popular durante mucho tiempo (person), estar de moda durante mucho tiempo (fashion). | *To have a good run for one's money*, dar buena cuenta de sí (working for a long time), sacarle jugo al dinero (to have good value). || *To keep the enemy on the run*, hostigar al enemigo. || *To make a run for it*, escaparse. || *Trial run*, prueba, *f.*

run* [rʌn] v. intr. Correr (to move quickly): *he set off running*, echó a correr; *the lions ran loose in the street*, los leones corrían sueltos por la calle; *the rope runs in the pulley*, la cuerda corre por la polea. || Echar a correr: *he grabbed the money and ran*, cogió el dinero y echó a correr. || Ir corriendo: *to run for the doctor*, ir corriendo en busca del médico. || Correr (rumour). || Irse, huir: *to run from a place*, irse de un sitio. || Resbalar, deslizarse (to slide): *sledges run on snow*, los trineos se deslizan por la nieve. || Circular: *the traffic runs day and night*, los coches circulan día y noche. || Circular, hacer el servicio: *trains running between London and the coast*, trenes que circulan entre Londres y la costa. || Salir: *the train runs every two hours*, el tren sale cada dos horas. || MAR. Hacer, marchar a, navegar a: *the ship runs 12 knots*, el barco marcha a doce nudos. | Navegar: *to run before the wind*, navegar con el viento en popa. || MED. Supurar (abscess). | Llorar (eyes). | Moquear (nose). || SP. Correr, participar: *to run in a race*, participar en una carrera. | Llegar: *to run third in a race*, llegar el tercero en una carrera. | Disputarse (a cup). || THEATR. Estar en cartel (a play etc.). || TECH. Funcionar (machine): *the engine is still running*, el motor funciona todavía. | Girar (wheel, spindle). | Marchar: *this car runs very well*, este coche marcha muy bien. || Derretirse: *the ice cream is beginning to run*, el helado está empezando a derretirse. || Correrse: *the ink is running*, la tinta se corre. || Desteñirse, correrse (colours). || Salirse (to leak). || GEOGR. Tener un curso (*for*, de): *river that runs for 100 miles*, río que tiene un curso de cien millas. || Estar colocado: *the shelves run all round the room*, los estantes están colocados alrededor de la habitación. || Extenderse: *the mountains run across the country*, la cordillera se extiende a través del país. || Pasar: *the road runs quite close to the village*, la carretera pasa bastante cerca del pueblo. || Decir, rezar (to say): *the poem runs like this*, el poema dice así. || Girar (*on*, sobre), tratar (*on*, de): *the talk ran on this subject*, la conversación giró sobre este tema. || Gotear (to drip). || Correr (to flow). || Manar, correr (blood). || Hacerse una carrerilla (stockings). || JUR. Ser válido *or* estar vigente (decree). || COMM. Ser válido: *the contract has two years to run*, el contrato es válido para dos años. || BOT. Extenderse (roots). || Emigrar (to migrate). || — *A heavy sea is running*, el mar está encrespado. || *His funds were running low*, le quedaba poco dinero. || *I can't run to that*, no puedo comprar eso, no tengo bastante dinero para eso, no puedo permitirme eso. || *It runs in the family*, viene de familia. || *Money runs through his fingers like water*, tiene un boquete en la mano, es un manirroto. || *My pen runs*, a mi pluma se le sale la tinta. || *Prices run from a pound to ten pounds*, los precios oscilan entre una libra y diez libras. || *Run for your lives!*, ¡sálvese quien pueda! || *The floor was running with water*, el suelo estaba lleno de agua. || *The gutters were running with water*, el agua corría por los arroyos. || *The money will not run to a car*, no hay bastante dinero para comprar un coche. | *The play ran for 200 nights*, la obra estuvo en cartel doscientos días, la obra tuvo doscientas representaciones *or* se representó doscientas veces. || *The river ran blood*, el río estaba teñido de sangre. || *The song kept running through his head*, tenía esa canción metida en la cabeza. || *The tap is running*, el grifo está abierto. || *The thought keeps running through my head*, esta idea me está dando vueltas en la cabeza, no me puedo sacar esta idea de la cabeza. || *The tide is running strongly*, la marea sube [*or* baja] rápidamente. || *This defect runs through all his work*, esta falta se encuentra en todo su trabajo. || MAR. *To run aground* o *ashore*, encallar, varar, embarrancarse. || *To run cold*, helarse (the blood). || *To run dry*, secarse. || *To run high*, see HIGH. || *To run like the devil* o *a hare* o *hell*, correr como un descosido. || *To run low*, escasear. || ELECTR. *To run off the mains*, funcionar con electricidad. || *To run past s.o.*, pasar delante de alguien corriendo (to pass by), adelantar (to overtake). || *To run short of money*, andar escaso de dinero. || *To run smoothly*, transcurrir tranquilamente (life), marchar bien (engine), correr tranquilamente (river), ir bien (for s.o.): *things never run smoothly for me*, nunca me van bien las cosas. || *To run to*, ascender a, alcanzar: *production runs to a million tons*, la producción asciende a un millón de toneladas; durar: *our holidays ran to three weeks*, nuestras vacaciones duraron tres semanas; tener: *this paper runs to twenty pages*, este periódico tiene veinte páginas. || *To run to fat*, engordar. || *To run to help s.o.*, correr en ayuda de alguien. || *To run to meet s.o.*, correr al encuentro de alguien. || AGR. *To run to seed*, granar. || *To run upstairs*, subir las escaleras corriendo. || *To run with sweat*, chorrear sudor. || *We are running short of oranges*, nos quedan pocas naranjas. || *Your bath is running*, el baño se está llenando. || *Your nose is running* o *you are running at the nose*, tienes mocos (fam.).

— V. tr. Recorrer (a distance): *to run a mile*, recorrer una milla. || Andar por: *to run the streets*, andar por las calles. || Hincar (to drive in). || Empujar (to push). || Manejar, llevar (to operate): *to run a tractor*, manejar un tractor. || Manejar, atender al funcionamiento de, ocuparse de (a machine). || Dirigir, llevar: *to run a factory*, dirigir una fábrica; *to run s.o.'s affairs*, llevar los asuntos de alguien. || Llevar (a house). || Organizar, dirigir (a campaign). || Poner, meter: *he ran his car into the garage*, puso el coche en el garaje. || Pasar: *you'll have to run the pipe through this wall*, tendrá que pasar el tubo por esta pared. || Pasar de contrabando (to smuggle): *to run arms*, pasar armas de contrabando. || Forzar, burlar (a blockade). || Correr, exponerse a (risk). || Publicar (a story in a newspaper, etc.). || Exhibir, echar (a film). || Presentar como candidato: *the Conservatives are running their best representative*, los conservadores presentan a su mejor representante como candidato. || SP. Correr en, participar en: *to run a race*, correr en una carrera. | Correr: *he ran a bad race*, corrió muy mal; *to run a horse*, correr un caballo. || Hacer correr: *to run a rope through a pulley*, hacer correr una cuerda por una polea. || Deslizar, pasar: *to run one's fingers along a table*, deslizar los dedos sobre la mesa. || Pasar: *he ran his hand through his hair*, se pasó la mano por el pelo. || Tener (to possess): *it is very expensive to run a car these days*, es muy caro tener un coche actualmente. || Establecer un servicio de: *to run trains between two towns*, establecer un servicio de trenes entre dos ciudades. || Poner: *airlines run extra flights in August*, las compañías aéreas ponen vuelos extraordinarios en agosto. || Llevar: *could you run me to London in your car?*, ¿me podría llevar a Londres en coche? || Correr (in hunting): *to run a wild boar*, correr un jabalí. || AGR. Pacer (cattle). || COMM. Vender (goods). || TECH. Vaciar, colar: *to run molten metal into a mould*, vaciar un metal fundido en un molde. || — *Cheap to run*, económico, ca. || *He ran a needle into his finger*, se clavó una aguja en el dedo. || *Let the affair run its course*, deja que el asunto siga su curso. || *To be run*, estar en servicio (planes, trains, etc.). || *To run a chance of being*, tener posibilidad de ser. || *To run a line around sth.*, rodear algo con una línea, trazar una línea alrededor de algo. || *To run an errand* o *a message*, hacer un recado. || FIG. *To run a parallel too far*, llevar una comparación demasiado lejos. || *To run a temperature*, tener fiebre. || *To run its course*, seguir su curso. || *To run one's pen through a word*, tachar una palabra. || *To run s.o. close* o *hard*, seguir de cerca a uno, pisarle los talones a uno. || *To run s.o. off his legs*, hacer correr a alguien hasta agotarle. || *To run s.o. through with a sword* o *to run a sword through s.o.*, traspasar a uno con una espada. || *To run the length of sth.*, correr de un extremo a otro de algo.

— **To run about**, correr por todas partes. || **To run across**, cruzar corriendo: *he ran across the street*, cruzó la calle corriendo. | Tropezar con (s.o., sth.): *I ran across him yesterday*, tropecé con él ayer. || **To run after**, perseguir, ir detrás de (s.o., sth.). | Solicitar: *she is very much run after*, está muy solicitada. || **To run against**, chocar contra (to collide). | Ir en contra de: *this runs against my interests*, esto va en contra de mis intereses. || **To run along**, ir corriendo: *he was running along shouting*, iba corriendo y gritando. | Correr a lo largo de: *the landing strip runs along the beach*, la pista de aterrizaje corre a lo largo de la playa. | MAR. Costear. | FAM. *Run along!*, ¡vete! || **To run around with**, asociarse con. || **To run at**, abalanzarse sobre, arremeter contra. || **To run away**, escaparse, fugarse, evadirse: *the prisoner ran away from jail*, el preso se escapó de la cárcel. | Huir (from one's responsibilities). | Desbocarse (a horse). | — *Don't run away with the idea that*, no te vayas a creer que. | *His temper ran away with him*, perdió el control de sí mismo. | *That runs away with a lot of money*, esto hace gastar mucho dinero. | *To run away from home*, escaparse *or* huir de casa. | *To run away from the facts*, negarse a reconocer los hechos. | *To run away with*, llevarse: *the thief ran away with five hundred pounds*, el ladrón se llevó quinientas libras; ganar fácilmente (a race). || **To run back**, volver corriendo. || **To run by**, pasar corriendo: *he has just run by*, acaba de pasar corriendo. || Pasar corriendo delante de: *he ran by my house*, pasó corriendo delante de mi casa. | Ser conocido por (a name). || **To run down**, bajar corriendo: *he ran down the street*, bajo la calle corriendo. | Correr (water). | Pararse, quedarse sin cuerda (watch). | Atropellar, cillar (to knock over): *the car ran down a child*, el poche pilló a un niño. | Atropellar (to run over). | MAR. Hundir (a ship). | Acorralar (a stag). | Encontrar: *the police ran him down*, la policía le encontró. | FAM. Echar abajo (an argument), poner por los suelos (s.o.). || Agotar (to exhaust). | TECH. Descargar. | Dejar de funcionar (an engine). || **To run for**, presentar su candidatura a *or* para, presentarse a *or* para: *he ran for Parliament last year*, presentó su candidatura al Parlamento el año pasado. | — *To run for it*, darse a la fuga, fugarse. || **To run in**, detener (to arrest). | Entrar corriendo (to enter at a run). | Rodar, hacer funcionar (engine, car, etc.). | Entrar un momento (to pay a quick call). | — AUT. *To be running in*, estar en rodaje. || **To run into**, entrar corriendo en (to enter at a run). || Chocar contra (to collide with): *the car ran into a tree*, el coche chocó contra un árbol. | Tropezar con, encontrarse a (to meet by chance). | Tropezar con: *to run into difficulties*, tropezar con dificultades. | Enfrentarse con (danger). | Desembocar en (rivers, streets). | Llegar a: *the expenses run into hundreds of pounds*, los gastos llegan a cientos de libras. | — *To run into debt*, contraer deudas. | *To run s.o. into debt*, hacer que alguien contraiga deudas. | MAR. *To run into port*, entrar en el puerto. || **To run off**, salirse (a liquid). | Escaparse, fugarse (person). | Salirse: *to run off the subject*, salirse del tema. | SP. Correr (a race). | Dejar correr (water). | TECH. Colar, vaciar (metal). | PRINT. Tirar. | Redactar rápidamente (an article). | Recitar de un tirón (a poem). | — FAM. *To run off at the mouth*, irse de la boca, hablar más de la cuenta. | *To run off the rails*, descarrilarse. | *To run off with*, llevarse. || **To run on**, funcionar con: *this car runs on petrol*, este coche funciona con gasolina. | Seguir corriendo (to continue running). | Continuar, seguir (to continue). | Transcurrir, pasar (time). | PRINT. Enlazar. | FAM. Hablar sin parar (to talk without stopping). || **To run out**, salirse (liquid). | Desenrollarse (rope). | Salir corriendo (to exit at a run). | Acabarse, agotarse (to finish): *my patience is running out*, se me está acabando la paciencia. | Agotarse (stocks). | Expirar, vencer (contract, lease). | Bajar (tide). | FAM. Echar, expulsar (of a club, etc.). | SP. Poner fuera de juego. | — *To run out of*, quedarse sin: *we are running out of coal*, nos estamos quedando sin carbón. | *To run out on*, dejar, abandonar: *Anthony has run out on Mary*, Antonio ha abandonado a María. || **To run over**, pillar (to hit): *the car ran over a hedgehog*, el coche pilló un erizo. | Atropellar: *he was run over*, fue atropellado. | Echar un vistazo a (a text). | Volver a ensayar (to rehearse). | Rebosar (to overflow). | Derramarse: *the milk ran over*, la leche se derramó. | Desbordarse, salir de madre (a river). | — *The meeting ran over by five minutes*, la reunión duró cinco minutos más de lo previsto. | *To run over to*, pegar un salto a. || **To run through**, atravesar corriendo (a room, etc.). | Pasar por (a river). | Echar un vistazo a, leer por encima (a document). | Hojear (a book). | Despilfarrar (fortune). | Despachar (an affair). | Filtrar, colar (a liquid). | Atravesar, traspasar (to transpierce). | Tachar (to cross out). || **To run up**, izar (a flag). | Hacer rápidamente (to make quickly). | Construir (a house). | Dejar que se acumule (debt). | Hacer subir (prices). | Llegar corriendo (to arrive at a run). | Subir corriendo: *he ran up the stairs*, subió corriendo las escaleras. | Crecer rápidamente (plant). | — *To run up against*, tropezar con. | *To run up bills*, endeudarse, contraer deudas.

— OBSERV. Pret. **ran**; p. p. **run**.

runabout [—əbaut] n. Coche (*m.*) pequeño (car). | Lancha (*f.*) pequeña (boat). || U. S. Vagabundo, *m.* (tramp).

runaway [—əwei] adj. Fugitivo, va (fugitive). | Clandestino, na: *runaway marriage*, casamiento clandestino. || Fácilmente ganado, fácil (a race). | Abrumador, ra; holgado, da; amplio, plia (victory). || Desbocado, da (a horse). || Incontrolado, da: *the runaway lorry hurtled into the crowd*, el camión incontrolado se precipitó contra la muchedumbre. | Galopante: *runaway inflation*, inflación galopante. — N. Fugitivo, *m.* (fugitive). || MIL. Desertor, *m.* (deserter). || Huida, *f.* (flight). || Caballo (*m.*) desbocado (horse).

run-down [— daun] adj. Agotado, da (exhausted). || Parado, da; sin cuerda, que no tiene cuerda (clocks). || Descargado, da (accumulator). || Ruinoso, sa (houses, etc.).

rundown [—daun] n. Informe (*m.*) detallado.

rune [ru:n] n. Runa, *f.* (ancient Scandinavian character).

rung [rʌŋ] n. Escalón, *m.*, peldaño, *m.* (of a ladder). || Barrote, *m.* (of a chair).

rung [rʌŋ] p. p. See RING.

runic [ˈru:nik] adj. Rúnico, ca.

run-in [ˈrʌnin] n. PRINT. Palabras (*f. pl.*) insertadas. || U. S. FAM. Riña, *f.* (argument).

runlet [ˈrʌnlet] or **runnel** [ˈrʌnl] n. Arroyo, *m.*

runner [ˈrʌnə*] n. SP. Corredor, ra (athlete). | Caballo (*m.*) de carrera (horse). | Cuchilla, *f.* (of skate). | Patín, *m.* (of sledge). || Mensajero, *m.*, recadero, *m.* (messenger). || MIL. Enlace, *m.* || Contrabandista, *m.* & *f.* (smuggler). || BOT. Estolón, *m.* | Planta (*f.*) trepadora (climbing plant). || Tapete, *m.* (for a table). || Alfombra (*f.*) de un pasillo (long rug). || TECH. Carro, *m.* | Guía, *f.*, cursor, *m.* (of a drawer, etc.). | Polea, *f.* (pulley). | Anillo (*m.*) móvil (ring). | Rueda, *f.* (wheel). | Orificio (*m.*) de colada (in metallurgy). || AVIAT. Patín, *m.* || Rascón, *m.* (bird). || Malla (*f.*) suelta (in fabric). || Carrerilla, *f.* (in stockings). || U. S. Mecánico, *m.* (of a railway engine). | Cobrador, *m.* (of a bank). || *Runner bean*, judía (*f.*) escarlata.

runner-up [—ˈʌp] n. Subcampeón, ona; segundo, da.
— OBSERV. El plural es *runners-up*.

running [ˈrʌniŋ] adj. Que está corriendo (that is running). || De carrera (horse, etc.). || MIL. En retirada: *running fight*, combate en retirada. | Graneado, da: *running fire*, fuego graneado. || Corriente: *running water*, agua corriente. || Corredizo, za: *running knot*, nudo corredizo. || Movedizo, za (land). || En marcha: *running machine*, máquina en marcha. || MED. Supurante: *a running sore*, una llaga supurante. || COMM. Corriente (account, expenses). || TECH. Móvil: *running block*, polea móvil. || — *In running order*, en buen estado. || *Running cold*, constipado (*m.*) muy fuerte. || RAD. *Running commentary*, reportaje (*m.*) en directo. || *Running handwriting*, letra cursiva. || SP. *Running kick*, puntapié dado al correr. || *Running reading*, lectura corrida. || SP. *Running start*, salida lanzada. || *Three months running*, tres meses seguidos. || *Twice running*, dos veces seguidas.
— N. Carrera, *f.* (race). || Derrame, *m.* (of a liquid). || Chorro, *m.* (of water). || Circulación, *f.* (of trains, etc.). || Contrabando, *m.* (smuggling). || MED. Supuración, *f.* || COMM. Dirección, *f.* (of a firm). || TECH. Funcionamiento, *m.*, marcha, *f.* || — *To be in the running*, tener posibilidades de ganar. || *To be out of the running*, no tener ninguna posibilidad de ganar.

running aground [—ə graund] n. MAR. Varada, *f.*, encallamiento, *m.*

running board [—bɔːd] n. AUT. Estribo, *m.*

running head [—hed] or **running title** [—ˈtaitl] or **running headline** [—ˈhedlain] PRINT. Titulillo, *m.*

running in [—ˈin] n. Rodaje, *m.*

running light [—lait] n. Luz (*f.*) de situación.

running mate [—meit] n. U. S. Candidato (*m.*) a la vicepresidencia.

running track [—træk] n. SP. Pista, *f.*

runny [ˈrʌni] adj. Blando, da (soft). || Líquido, da (liquid). || Que moquea (nose).

runoff [ˈrʌnɔf] n. SP. Carrera (*f.*) de desempate *or* final.

run-of-the-mill [ˈrʌnəvðəˈmil] adj. Corriente y moliente.

runproof [ˈrʌnpruːf] adj. Indesmallable (stockings).

runt [rʌnt] n. Bóvido (*m.*) de raza pequeña (cattle). || Rocín, *m.* (horse). || FAM. Enano, na (small person).

run-through [ˈrʌnθruː] n. Ensayo (*m.*) rápido. || Lectura (*f.*) rápida.

runty [—i] adj. U. S. Chiquitejo, ja; enano, na.

runway [ˈrʌnwei] n. AVIAT. Pista, *f.* [de aterrizaje *or* de despegue]. || Cauce, *m.* (of a river). || — *Overhead runway*, transportador aéreo. || *Runway light*, baliza, *f.* (of an airport).

rupee [ruːˈpiː] n. Rupia, *f.*

rupestral [ruˈpestrəl] or **rupestrian** [ruˈpestriən] adj. Rupestre.

rupture [ˈrʌptʃə*] n. Ruptura, *f.* || MED. Hernia, *f.*

rupture [ˈrʌptʃə*] v. tr. Romper. || MED. Hacer una hernia en. || *To rupture o.s.*, herniarse, quebrarse, hacerse una hernia.
— V. intr. MED. Quebrarse, hacerse una hernia, herniarse.

rural [ˈruərəl] adj. Rural: *rural problems*, problemas rurales; *rural farm*, finca rural; *rural policeman*, guarda rural. || *Rural dwellers*, campesinos, *m.*

ruralism [ˈruərəlizəm] n. Rusticidad, *f.* || U. S. Regionalismo, *m.* (word).

ruse [ruːz] n. Astucia, *f.*, treta, *f.*, ardid, *m.*

rush [rʌʃ] adj. Urgente: *a rush job*, un trabajo urgente. || *Rush hour*, hora (*f.*) punta, hora (*f.*) de mayor afluencia.
— N. Ímpetu, *m.* (impetus). || Prisa, *f.*, precipitación, *f.* (haste): *what's your rush?*, ¿por qué tiene prisa? || Afluencia, *f.*, riada, *f.*, avalancha, *f.* (flow of people). || Aglomeración (*f.*) de gente (crowd). || Bullicio, *m.*, confusión, *f.* (crush). || Torrente, *m.*: *the rush of water*, un torrente de agua; *a rush of words*, un torrente de palabras. || Bullicio, *m.*, ajetreo, *m.*: *the rush of city life*, el bullicio de la vida de la ciudad. || Agobio, *m.*: *a rush of work*, un agobio de trabajo. || MED. Aflujo, *m.*, agolpamiento, *m.*: *a rush of blood to the head*, un agolpamiento de sangre en la cabeza. || Arrebato, *m.*: *a rush of tenderness*, un arrebato de ternura. || Bocanada, *f.* (of air). || Ráfaga, *f.* (of wind). || COMM. Gran demanda, *f.*: *there was a rush on oranges*, hubo una gran demanda de naranjas. || SP. Ataque, *m.* || MIL. Ataque, *m.*, acometida, *f.*, asalto, *m.* || ELECTR. Aumento (*m.*) brusco de la corriente, sobrevoltaje, *m.* || Primeras pruebas, *f. pl.* (first proofs of a film). || BOT. Junco, *m.*: *the swamp was full of rushes*, las marismas estaban llenas de juncos. || — *In a rush*, de prisa. || *There is no rush*, no corre prisa. || *There was a rush to the emergency exit*, la gente se precipitó hacia la salida de emergencia. || *To be always in a rush*, tener siempre prisa. || *To do sth. in a rush*, hacer algo precipitadamente. || *To make a rush at*, abalanzarse sobre, precipitarse sobre. || *With a rush*, de repente.

rush [rʌʃ] v. tr. Hacer precipitadamente *or* de prisa: *to rush a job*, hacer precipitadamente una tarea. || Ejecutar urgentemente (an order). || Dar *or* meter prisa: *don't rush me!*, ¡no me metas prisa! || Precipitarse, abalanzarse, lanzarse contra: *the crowd rushed the building*, la muchedumbre se precipitó hacia el edificio. || Llevar de prisa, transportar de prisa *or* con urgencia: *they rushed the child to the doctor*, llevaron de prisa al niño al médico. ||Empujar a, forzar a: *to rush s.o. into marriage*, forzar a alguien a casarse. || MIL. Tomar por asalto (a position). || FAM. Sacar: *he rushed me 5 pounds for it*, me sacó cinco libras para ello. | Ir tras de (to court assiduously). || — *I don't want to rush you*, hágalo con tranquilidad. || *To rush into print*, publicar precipitadamente.
— V. intr. Precipitarse, abalanzarse (to haste): *everyone rushed to the doors*, todos se precipitaron hacia las puertas. || Ir de prisa, correr (to go quickly). || Darse prisa, apresurarse: *they rushed to help her*, se apresuraron *or* se dieron prisa en ayudarle. || Irse corriendo, marcharse: *I simply must rush*, me tengo que ir corriendo. || — *Tears rushed to her eyes*, se le llenaron los ojos de lágrimas. || *The blood rushed to his face*, se puso colorado, se sonrojó. || *To rush to conclusions*, sacar conclusiones apresuradas.
— ***To rush about***, correr de un lado a otro. || ***To rush across***, atravesar rápidamente. || ***To rush at***, abalanzarse sobre. || ***To rush forward***, abalanzarse, precipitarse. || ***To rush in*** o ***into***, meterse en (an affair). | Surgir en, venir a (one's memory). | Hacer irrupción en, entrar precipitadamente en (a room). || ***To rush off***, irse a toda velocidad. || ***To rush out***, salir precipitadamente. || ***To rush through***, leer de prisa (a book). | Visitar precipitadamente (a museum). | Atravesar a toda velocidad (a town). | Despachar rápidamente (one's work). | Hacer de prisa (to do quickly). | — *To rush a bill through Parliament*, hacer aprobar rápidamente un proyecto de ley.

rushing [—iŋ] n. Precipitación, *f.*, apresuramiento, *m.*
— Adj. Impetuoso, sa (torrent).

rushlight [—lait] n. Vela (*f.*) de junco.

rushy [—i] adj. De junco. || Cubierto de juncos.

rusk [rʌsk] n. Galleta, *f.* (biscuit). || Bizcocho, *m.*

russet [ˈrʌsit] adj. Rojizo, za.
— N. Color (*m.*) rojizo.

Russia [ˈrʌʃə] pr. n. GEOGR. Rusia, *f.*

Russian [—n] adj. Ruso, sa.
— N. Ruso, sa (inhabitant of Russia). || Ruso, *m.* (language).

Russianization [ˌrʌʃənaiˈzeiʃən] or **Russification** [rʌsifiˈkeiʃən] n. Rusificación, *f.*

Russianize [ˈrʌʃənaiz] or **Russify** [ˈrʌsifai] v. tr. Rusificar.

Russophil [ˈrʌsəufil] or **Russophile** [ˈrʌsəufail] adj./n. Rusófilo, la.

Russophobe [ˈrʌsəufəub] adj./n. Rusófobo, ba.

rust [rʌst] n. Oxidación, *f.*, corrosión, *f.* (action). || Orín, *m.*, herrumbre, *f.*, moho, *m.* (on metal). || Color (*m.*) de orín (colour). || BOT. Roya, *f.*, añublo, *m.*, tizón, *m.*

rust [rʌst] v. tr. Oxidar, enmohecer, poner mohoso.
— V. intr. Oxidarse, enmohecerse, ponerse mohoso. || FIG. Entumecerse (a person).

rustic [—ik] adj. Campesino, na; campestre, rústico, ca (rural). || Paleto, ta; palurdo, da (boorish).
— N. Rústico, ca; campesino, na (peasant). || Palurdo, da; paleto, ta (bumpkin).

rusticate [—ikeit] v. intr. [Ir a] vivir en el campo.
— V. tr. Expulsar temporalmente (from a college).

rustication [ˌrʌstiˈkeiʃən] n. Vida (*f.*) en el campo. || Expulsión (*f.*) temporal (from a college).

rusticity [rʌsˈtisiti] n. Rusticidad, *f.*

rustiness [ˈrʌstinis] n. Herrumbre, *f.*, moho, *m.*, oxidación, *f.* (of metals). || FIG. Enmohecimiento, *m.*

rustle [ˈrʌsl] n. Susurro, *m.* (of leaves). || Crujido, *m.*, frufrú, *m.* (of a dress). || Crujido, *m.* (of paper).

rustle [ˈrʌsl] v. intr. Susurrar (leaves). || Crujir (paper, material). || U. S. Robar ganado (to steal cattle). | Moverse, agitarse (to move busily).
— V. tr. Hacer susurrar (sound). || Hacer crujir (paper, material). || U. S. Robar [ganado] (to steal cattle).

rustler [—ə*] n. U. S. Ladrón (*m.*) de ganado. | Hombre (*m.*) emprendedor.

rustless [ˈrʌstlis] adj. Inoxidable.

rustproof [ˈrʌstˌpruːf] adj. Inoxidable.

rusty [ˈrʌsti] adj. Oxidado, da; mohoso, sa; herrumbroso, sa (metal). || De color de orín, de color mohoso (colour). || Ronco, ca (voice). || FIG. Desentrenado, da; falto de práctica: *I am a little rusty in French*, estoy un poco falto de práctica en francés. || FIG. *My French is rusty*, me falta práctica en francés, tengo que practicar el francés.

rut [rʌt] n. Surco, *m.* (furrow). || Carril, *m.*, carrilada, *f.*, rodada, *f.* (of wheels). || Ranura, *f.* (groove). || Bache, *m.* (pothole): *a road full of ruts*, una carretera

llena de baches. || FIG. Rutina, *f.*, camino (*m.*) trillado (routine). || Celo, *m.* (of animals). || FIG. *To be in a rut*, ser esclavo de la rutina.
rut [rʌt] v. tr. Surcar.
— V. intr. Estar en celo (animals).
rutabaga [ˈruːtəˌbeigə] n. U. S. BOT. Colinabo, *m.*, nabo sueco, *m.*
rutaceae [ruˈteisiː] pl. n. BOT. Rutáceas, *f.*
ruth [ruːθ] n. Piedad, *f.*, compasión, *f.*
Ruth [ruːθ] pr. n. Rut, *f.*
ruthenium [ruːˈθiːniəm] n. CHEM. Rutenio, *m.*
ruthless [ˈruːθlis] adj. Despiadado, da; cruel. || Implacable.
ruthlessness [—nis] n. Crueldad, *f.*, falta (*f.*) de piedad. || Implacabilidad, *f.*
rutilant [ˈruːtilənt] adj. Rutilante.
rutile [ˈruːtil] n. MIN. Rutilo, *m.*
rutty [ˈrʌti] adj. Lleno de baches.
rye [rai] n. BOT. Centeno, *m.* || U. S. Whisky (*m.*) de centeno (drink).
ryegrass [—grɑːs] n. BOT. Ballico, *m.*
ryot [ˈraiət] n. Campesino (*m.*) indio.

S

s [es] n. S, *f.* (letter).
's [—iz] possessive ending. *The girl's handbag*, el bolso de la chica; *the girls' handbags*, los bolsos de las chicas.
Saar [sɑː*] pr. n. GEOGR. Sarre, *m.*
— OBSERV. Esta palabra siempre lleva el artículo en español, lo mismo que en inglés.
Saarland [ˈsɑːlænd] pr. n. GEOGR. Sarre, *m.*
— OBSERV. See SAAR.
Sabaean [səˈbiən] adj./n. Sabeo, a.
sabbath [ˈsæbəθ] n. REL. Domingo, *m.* (Sunday). | Sábado, *m.* (of the Jewish week). || Aquelarre, *m.* (witches').
sabbatical [səˈbætikəl] adj. Sabático, ca. || *Sabbatical year*, año (*m.*) de permiso (granted to teachers).
sabbatine [ˈsæbətain] adj. Sabatino, na: *sabbatine bull*, bula sabatina.
Sabean [səˈbiːən] adj./n. Sabeo, a.
saber [ˈseibə*] n. U. S. Sable, *m.*
saber [ˈseibə*] v. tr. U. S. Herir *or* matar a sablazos, acuchillar.
Sabine [ˈsæbain] adj./n. Sabino, na.
sable [ˈseibl] n. ZOOL. Marta (*f.*) cebellina, cebellina, *f.*, cibelina, *f.* || HERALD. Sable, *m.* || — Pl. Trajes (*m.*) de luto (black clothing).
— Adj. Negro, gra (black). || HERALD. Color de sable.
sabot [ˈsæbəu] n. Zueco, *m.* (clog). || MIL. Casquillo, *m.*
sabotage [ˈsæbətɑːʒ] n. Sabotaje, *m.*
sabotage [ˈsæbətɑːʒ] v. tr. Sabotear.
saboteur [ˌsæbəˈtəː*] n. Saboteador, ra.
sabre [ˈseibə*] n. Sable, *m.* || FIG. *Saber rattling*, amenazas, *f. pl.*
sabre [ˈseibə*] v. tr. Herir *or* matar a sablazos, acuchillar.
sabretache [ˈsæbətæʃ] n. (Ant.). MIL. Portapliegos, *m. inv.* (leather case).
sac [sæk] n. ANAT. Bolsa, *f.*, saco, *m.*
sacchariferous [ˈsækəˈrifərəs] adj. Sacarífero, ra.
saccharification [sæˌkərifiˈkeiʃən] n. CHEM. Sacarificación, *f.*
saccharify [sæˈkærifai] v. tr. CHEM. Sacarificar.
saccharimeter [ˌsækəˈrimitə*] n. Sacarímetro, *m.*
saccharin [ˈsækərin] n. CHEM. Sacarina, *f.*
saccharine [ˈsækərain] adj. CHEM. Sacarino, na. || FIG. Empalagoso, sa.
saccharoid [ˈsækərɔid] adj. GEOL. Sacaroideo, a (granular in structure).
saccharometer [sækəˈrɔmitə*] n. Sacarímetro, *m.*
saccharomyces [ˌsækərəˈmaisiːz] pl. n. Sacaromicetos, *m.* (yeasts).
saccharose [ˈsækərəus] n. CHEM. Sacarosa, *f.*
sacerdotal [ˌsæsəˈdəutl] adj. Sacerdotal.
sachem [ˈseitʃəm] n. Sachem, *m.* (Indian chief). || U. S. FIG. FAM. Pez (*m.*) gordo.
sachet [ˈsæʃei] n. Saquito, *m.*, bolsita, *f.* (small bag). || Almohadilla (*f.*) perfumada (perfumed).
sack [sæk] n. Saco, *m.* (for goods). || Costal, *m.* (for grains). || Vestido (*m.*) saco (dress). || FAM. Cama, *f.* (bed). || MIL. Saqueo, *m.*, saco, *m.* || — *Sack race*, carrera (*f.*) de sacos. || FIG. FAM. *To get the sack*, ser despedido. | *To give s.o. the sack*, poner a alguien de patitas en la calle, echar a alguien, despedir a alguien (to dismiss).
sack [sæk] v. tr. Ensacar (to put into sacks). || MIL. Saquear, entrar a saco en. || FIG. FAM. Poner de patitas en la calle, echar, despedir (to dismiss).
sackbut [—bʌt] n. MUS. Sacabuche, *m.*
sackcloth [—klɔθ] n. Tela (*f.*) de saco, arpillera, *f.* (coarse cloth). || Sayal, *m.* (penitential clothing). || FIG. *To wear sackcloth and ashes*, arrepentirse.
sacker [—ə*] n. Saqueador, ra.
sackful [—ful] n. Saco, *m.* (content): *a sackful of coal*, un saco de carbón.
sacking [—iŋ] n. Tela (*f.*) de saco, arpillera, *f.* (coarse cloth). || FAM. Despido, *m.* (dismissal).
sacral [ˈseikrəl] adj. ANAT. Sacro, cra. || REL. Sagrado, da.
sacrament [ˈsækrəmənt] n. REL. Sacramento, *m.*: *to administer the last sacraments*, administrar los últimos sacramentos; *the Holy Sacrament*, el Santísimo Sacramento. || (Ant.) Juramento, *m.* (solemn oath).
sacramental [ˌsækrəˈmentl] adj. Sacramental.
— N. Sacramental, *m.*
Sacramentarian [ˌsækrəmenˈteəriən] n. Sacramentario, *m.*
sacred [ˈseikrid] adj. Sacro, cra; sagrado, da: *sacred history*, historia sacra *or* sagrada. || Religioso, sa (song, picture, procession). || Consagrado, da; dedicado, da: *sacred to the memory of*, consagrado a la memoria de. || Mayor (religious order). || De música religiosa (concert). || FIG. Sagrado, da: *the siesta is sacred in Spain*, en España la siesta es sagrada. || — FIG. *Nothing is sacred any more*, ya no se respeta nada. || *Sacred College*, Sacro Colegio. || *Sacred cow*, vaca sagrada. || *Sacred fire*, fuego sacro. || *Sacred Heart*, Sagrado Corazón. || *Sacred music*, música sacra. || *The Sacred Way*, la Vía Sacra.
sacredness [—nis] n. Santidad, *f.* || FIG. Lo sagrado.
sacrifice [ˈsækrifais] n. Sacrificio, *m.*: *to make a sacrifice to the gods*, ofrecer un sacrificio a los dioses. || Ofrenda, *f.* (thing offered). || FIG. Sacrificio, *m.*: *to make sacrifices for one's children*, hacer sacrificios por sus hijos. || — COMM. *At a sacrifice*, con pérdida. || FIG. *At the sacrifice of*, en detrimento de, sacrificando.
sacrifice [ˈsækrifais] v. tr. Sacrificar. || COMM. Vender a un precio sacrificado, vender con pérdida. || FIG. Sacrificar (one's interests, etc.). || FIG. *To sacrifice o.s.*, sacrificarse.
— V. intr. Ofrecer un sacrificio.
sacrificeable [—əbl] adj. Sacrificable.
sacrificer [—ə*] n. Sacrificador, ra.
sacrificial [ˌsækriˈfiʃəl] adj. Sacrificatorio, ria. || — COMM. *Sacrificial price*, precio sacrificado. | *Sacrificial sale*, venta (*f.*) con pérdida.
sacrilege [ˈsækrilidʒ] n. Sacrilegio, *m.*
sacrilegious [ˌsækriˈlidʒəs] adj. Sacrílego, ga. || *Sacrilegious person*, sacrílego, ga.
sacring bell [ˈseikriŋˈbel] n. REL. Campanilla (*f.*) de la Elevación.
sacrist [ˈsækrist] or **sacristan** [ˈsækristən] n. REL. Sacristán, *m.*
sacristy [ˈsækristi] n. REL. Sacristía, *f.*
sacroiliac [seikrəˈiliæk] adj. ANAT. Sacroilíaco, ca.
sacrosanct [ˈsækrəusæŋkt] adj. Sacrosanto, ta.
sacrum [ˈseikrəm] n. ANAT. Sacro, *m.*
— OBSERV. El plural de *sacrum* es *sacra* o *sacrums.*
sad [sæd] adj. Triste: *he is sad because his cat has died*, está triste porque su gato ha muerto; *a sad place, book*, un sitio, un libro triste. || Doloroso, sa: *a sad loss*, una pérdida dolorosa. || Lamentable, deplorable, triste (deplorable): *a sad mistake*, un error deplorable; *a sad lack of manners*, una falta de educación lamentable. || Apagado, da; triste (colour). || FAM. Malísimo, ma (very bad). || — *A sadder and a wiser man*, un hombre que ha escarmentado. || *To be sad at heart*, tener el corazón oprimido. || *To make s.o. sad*, entristecer a alguien.
sadden [ˈsædn] v. tr. Entristecer.
— V. intr. Entristecerse, ponerse triste.
saddle [ˈsædl] n. Silla, *f.* (of a horse): *riding saddle*, silla de montar. || Sillín, *m.* (of a bicycle, a harness).

|| CULIN. Faldilla, *f.*, cuarto (*m.*) trasero (of mutton). | Rabadilla, *f.* (of hare). || GEOGR. Puerto, *m.*, paso, *m.* (between mountains). || TECH. Carro (*m.*) de bancada (of a lathe). || — *English* o *hunting saddle*, silla inglesa. || *Saddle horse*, caballo (*m.*) de silla. || ARCH. *Saddle roof*, tejado (*m.*) de dos aguas. || SP. *The favourite is the Flying Dutchman with John Smith in the saddle*, el favorito es el Flying Dutchman montado por John Smith. || FIG. *To be in the saddle*, llevar las riendas. || *To be thrown out of the saddle*, perder los estribos.

saddle [ˈsædl] v. tr. Ensillar. || — FIG. FAM. *To get saddled with* o *to saddle o.s. with a reponsibility*, cargar con una responsabilidad. || *To saddle s.o. with the blame*, echar la culpa a alguien.

saddleback [—bæk] n. ARCH. Tejado (*m.*) de dos aguas (roof). || Ensillada, *f.* (hill). || ZOOL. Animal (*m.*) albardado (with a different-coloured back).

saddle-backed [—bækt] adj. ARCH. De dos aguas (roof). || ZOOL. Ensillado, da (with a hollow back).

saddlebag [—bæg] n. Alforja, *f.* (on a horse). || Cartera, *f.* (on a bicycle).

saddlebow [—bəu] n. Arzón, *m.*

saddlecloth [—klɔθ] n. Manta (*f.*) sudadera, sudadero, *m.*

saddler [—ə*] n. Guarnicionero, *m.*, talabartero, *m.*

saddlery [—əri] n. Guarniciones, *f. pl.*, arreos, *m. pl.* (harness). || Guarnicionería, *f.*, talabartería, *f.* (saddler's trade).

saddletree [—tri:] n. Arzón, *m.* || U. S. BOT. Tulipanero, *m.*

Sadducean [ˌsædjuˈsi:ən] adj. Saduceo, a.

Sadducee [ˈsædjusi:] n. Saduceo, a.

sadiron [ˈsædaiən] n. Plancha, *f.* (for pressing).

sadism [ˈseidizəm] n. Sadismo, *m.*

sadist [ˈseidist] n. Sádico, ca.

sadistic [səˈdistik] adj. Sádico, ca.

sadness [ˈsædnis] n. Tristeza, *f.*

sad sack [ˈsædsæk] n. FAM. Desgraciado, da.

safari [səˈfɑ:ri] n. Safari, *m.*

safe [seif] adj. Sano y salvo, ileso, sa; indemne (uninjured): *the car crashed but they were safe*, el coche se estrelló pero salieron ilesos. || Intacto, ta; en buen estado (undamaged). || Seguro, ra; en seguridad, a salvo (secure): *if we hide here, we shall be safe*, si nos escondemos aquí, estaremos a salvo. || Seguro, ra: *a safe retreat*, un retiro seguro; *a safe bridge*, un puente seguro. || Prudente (cautious): *at a safe distance*, a una distancia prudente; *safe policy*, política prudente. || De fiar, digno de confianza (trustworthy): *you must not tell him anything because he is not safe*, no debe decirle nada porque no es de fiar. || Inofensivo, va (harmless). || Salvado, da: *your honour is safe*, su honor está salvado. || Seguro, ra (certain): *safe investment*, inversión segura. || — *As safe as houses*, completamente seguro. || *In order to be on the safe side*, para mayor seguridad. || *Is it safe to leave her alone?*, ¿no es peligroso dejarla sola? || *It is safe to say that...*, se puede decir con seguridad que... || *Safe and sound*, sano y salvo, ileso, sa. || *Safe from*, a salvo de. || *The safest course would be to go*, lo mas seguro sería marcharse. || *This toy is not safe*, este juguete es peligroso. || *To be on the safe side*, see SIDE. || *To get safe into port*, llegar a buen puerto.

— N. Caja (*f.*) de caudales, caja (*f.*) fuerte (strongbox). || Fresquera, *f.* (for storing foods).

safeblower [—ˌbləuə*] or **safebreaker** [ˈseifˌbreikə*] n. Ladrón (*m.*) de cajas de caudales.

safe-conduct [—ˈkɔndʌkt] n. Salvoconducto, *m.*

safecracker [—ˌkrækə*] n. Ladrón (*m.*) de cajas de caudales.

safecracking [—ˌkrækiŋ] n. Fractura (*f.*) de cajas de caudales.

safe deposit [—diˌpɔzit] n. Sala (*f.*) donde se guardan las cajas de seguridad en un banco.

safe-deposit box [—diˌpɔzitˌbɔks] n. Caja (*f.*) de seguridad.

safeguard [—gɑ:d] n. Salvaguardia, *f.*, salvaguarda, *f.*: *the law is the safeguard of freedom*, las leyes son la salvaguardia de la libertad. || Protección, *f.* (protection). || Garantía, *f.* (assurance): *I give you a safeguard that you will not suffer in any way*, le doy la garantía de que no sufrirá ningún perjuicio. || Salvoconducto, *m.* (safe-conduct). || Escolta, *f.* (convoy). || Dispositivo (*m.*) de seguridad (safety device). || — *As a safeguard against*, para evitar. || *To put money aside as a safeguard*, poner dinero a un lado como reserva *or* por si acaso.

safeguard [—gɑ:d] v. tr. Salvaguardar, proteger.

safekeeping [—ˈki:piŋ] n. Custodia, *f.* || *To put into safekeeping*, poner a buen recaudo *or* a salvo.

safely [—li] adv. A buen puerto, sin accidente: *we arrived safely*, llegamos a buen puerto. || Sin peligro: *now you can cross the bridge safely*, ahora puede cruzar el puente sin peligro. || Con toda seguridad, sin temor a equivocarse: *you can safely say that population is increasing*, puedes decir con toda seguridad que la población está aumentando. || Por lo menos, fácilmente: *she is eighteen safely*, tiene por lo menos diez y ocho años. || — *Put it away safely*, póngalo en un sitio seguro. || *Safely and soundly*, sano y salvo, ileso, sa. || *Safely invested money*, dinero bien invertido.

safeness [—nis] n. Seguridad, *f.*

safety [—ti] n. Seguridad, *f.*: *safety measures*, medidas de seguridad; *public safety*, seguridad pública. || — *At safety*, con el seguro puesto (a weapon). || *For safety's sake*, para mayor seguridad. || *In a place of safety*, en un sitio seguro. || *In safety*, seguro, en seguridad, a salvo. || *Safety belt*, cinturón (*f.*) de seguridad. || *Safety bolt*, cerrojo (*m.*) de seguridad. || *Safety catch*, seguro, *m.* (of firearms, of machinery), cadena (*f.*) de seguridad (of bracelets, brooches), retenedor, *m.*, cadena (*f.*) de seguridad (of doors). || *Safety chain*, cadena (*f.*) de seguridad. || *Safety curtain*, telón metálico. || *Safety device*, dispositivo (*m.*) de seguridad. || *Safety film*, película (*f.*) incombustible. || *Safety first!*, ¡seguridad ante todo! || *Safety first campaign*, campaña (*f.*) pro seguridad. || *Safety fuse*, mecha lenta *or* de seguridad, espoleta (*f.*) de seguridad (for detonators), fusible, *m.* (in an electric circuit). || *Safety glass*, vidrio (*m.*) inastillable *or* de seguridad. || *Safety island*, refugio, *m.* (in a street). || *Safety lamp*, lámpara (*f.*) de seguridad. || *Safety lock*, cerradura (*f.*) de seguridad (on a door), seguro, *m.* (on firearms). || *Safety match*, fósforo (*m.*) de seguridad. || *Safety net*, red, *f.* (in a circus). || *Safety pin*, imperdible, *m.* || *Safety razor*, maquinilla (*f.*) de afeitar. || *Safety valve*, válvula (*f.*) de seguridad. || U. S. *Safety zone*, zona (*f.*) de seguridad. || *To be able to do sth. with safety*, poder hacer algo sin peligro. || *To reach safety*, llegar a buen puerto (s.o. who was travelling), llegar a un sitio seguro (s.o. who is hiding), ponerse a salvo (to avoid danger).

saffron [ˈsæfrən] n. BOT. CULIN. Azafrán, *m.*

— Adj. Azafranado, da; de color de azafrán.

sag [sæg] n. Hundimiento, *m.* (sinking). || Pandeo, *m.* (of a beam, a wall). || Comba, *f.*, pandeo, *m.* (of a plank). || Caída, *f.* (of prices). || MAR. Deriva, *f.* || Flexión, *f.* (in a rope).

sag [sæg] v. intr. Hundirse (to sink). || Pandear (beam, wall). || Combarse, pandear (plank). || Aflojarse (rope, cable, etc.). || Colgar (flesh, clothes). || Caer, bajar (prices). || MAR. Ir a la deriva. || FIG. Perder interés: *the programme began to sag towards the end*, el programa empezó a perder interés hacia el final. | Decaer (one's spirits). || *His shoulders sagged*, tenía los hombros caídos.

— V. tr. Hundir.

saga [ˈsɑ:gə] n. Saga, *f.* || FIG. Epopeya, *f.* (epic). | Novela (*f.*) que relata la vida de una familia.

sagacious [səˈgeiʃəs] adj. Sagaz.

sagacity [səˈgæsiti] n. Sagacidad, *f.*

sagamore [ˈsægəmɔ:*] n. U. S. Sachem, *m.* (Indian chief).

sage [seidʒ] adj. Sabio, bia (wise). || Sensato, ta; cuerdo, da (sensible).

— N. Sabio, *m.* (wise man). || BOT. Salvia, *f.*

sagebrush [—brʌʃ] n. BOT. Artemisa, *f.*

sageness [—nis] n. Sabiduría, *f.* (wiseness). || Sensatez, *f.*, cordura, *f.* (sensibleness).

saggar (U. S. **sagger**) [ˈsægə*] n. TECH. Gaceta (*f.*) refractaria (container). | Arcilla (*f.*) refractaria (fireclay).

sagging [ˈsægiŋ] adj. Hundido, da (sunken): *a sagging floor*, un piso hundido. || Decreciente (prices). || Flojo, ja (market). || Decaído, da (one's spirits).

— N. Hundimiento, *m.* (of a roof, etc.). || Baja, *f.* (of prices).

Sagittarius [ˌsædʒiˈtɛəriəs] n. ASTR. Sagitario, *m.*

saguntine [sæˈgʌntain] adj./n. Saguntino, na.

Sagunto [sæˈgʌntəu] pr. n. GEOGR. Sagunto.

Sahara [səˈhɑ:rə] pr. n. GEOGR. Sáhara, *m.*, Sahara, *m.*

Saharan [—ən] or **Saharian** [—iən] adj. Sahariano, na; sahárico, ca (place). || Saharaui (people).

— N. Saharaui *m.* & *f.* (people).

said [sed] pret. & p. p. See SAY.

sail [seil] n. MAR. Vela, *f.* | Velamen, *m.*, velas, *f. pl.* (collectively). | Velero, *m.*, barco (*m.*) de vela: *not a sail in sight*, ni un velero a la vista. | Viaje, *m.* [en barco]: *it is a five-day sail away*, está a cinco días de viaje. | Travesía, *f.* (crossing). | Paseo, *m.* [en barco]: *to go for a sail on the lake*, ir de paseo por el lago. | Manga (*f.*) de ventilación, manga (*f.*) veleta (windsail). || Brazo, *m.*, aspa, *f.* (of a windmill). || ZOOL. Aleta, *f.* (fin). || — *(At) full sail*, a toda vela, a todo trapo. || *Sail ho!*, ¡barco a la vista! || *To get under sail* o *to set sail*, hacerse a la vela (sailing ship), hacerse a la mar, zarpar (any boat). || *To strike sail*, arriar las velas. || *To take in sail*, arriar las velas (to haul down), apocar las velas (to reduce the number of sails), recoger velas (to curb one's ambitions). || FIG. FAM. *To take the wind out of s.o.'s sails*, bajarle los humos a alguien. || *Under full sail*, a toda vela. || *Under sail*, con las velas alzadas (sailing ship), en camino (any boat).

sail [seil] v. tr. Cruzar, atravesar [en barco]: *to sail the Atlantic*, cruzar el Atlántico. || Gobernar (to manage a boat). || Botar: *I sail my boat every Saturday*, boto mi barco cada sábado. || Jugar con (toy boats). || *To sail the seas*, surcar los mares.

— V. intr. Navegar: *a boat sailing to New York*, un barco que navega rumbo a Nueva York. || Marchar, navegar: *to sail at 10 knots*, marchar a diez nudos. || Ir en barco: *I sailed to America*, fui a América en barco. || Zarpar, salir: *the ship sails tomorrow*, el barco zarpa mañana. || Volar (to move through the air): *the book sailed through the air*, el libro voló por los aires. || Cernerse (birds). || Planear (a glider). || Andar majestuosamente (to walk in a stately manner). || — FIG. *I sailed through customs in two minutes*, pasé por la aduana en dos minutos. | *I sailed through the exam*, hice el examen muy fácilmente, el examen no me planteó ningún problema. || *To sail against the wind*, hurtar el viento (a ship), actuar contra viento y marea (person).

— ***To sail away***, irse. || ***To sail in***, entrar (a boat). | Entrar majestuosamente (a person). || ***To sail into***, emprender, acometer (a task). | Atacar (to eat greedily). | Atacar, arremeter contra (to attack). | Entrar majestuosamente en (a room). | Tropezar con, topar con (to bump into). || ***To sail out***, salir. || ***To sail round***, doblar (a headland). | Dar la vuelta a (the world).

sail arm [—ɑ:m] n. Brazo, *m.* (of windmill).

sailboat [—bəut] n. U. S. Velero, *m.*, barco (*m.*) de vela.

sailcloth [—klɔθ] n. Lona, *f.* (canvas cloth for sails, tents, etc.).

sailer [—ə*] n. Velero, *m.* (sailing boat).

sailfish [—fiʃ] n. ZOOL. Pez (*m.*) vela (kind of swordfish).

sailing [—iŋ] n. MAR. Navegación, *f.* | Salida, *f.* (departure): *sailings every half hour*, salidas cada media hora. | Travesía, *f.* (voyage). || — MAR. *Plane sailing*, navegación loxodrómica. | *Sailing boat*, velero, *m.*, barco (*m.*) de vela. | *Sailing orders*, últimas instrucciones. | *Sailing ship*, velero, *m.*, barco (*m.*) de vela. || FIG. *To be plain sailing*, ser coser y cantar, ser pan comido.

sailmaker [—,meikə*] n. Velero, *m.*

sailor [ˈseilə*] n. Marinero, *m.*, marino, *m.* || — *To be a bad sailor*, marearse fácilmente. || *To be a good sailor*, no marearse. || *Sailor hat*, sombrero (*m.*) de paja. || *Sailor suit*, traje (*m.*) de marinero.

sailoring [—iŋ] n. Marinería, *f.*

sailplane [ˈseilplein] n. Planeador, *m.* (glider).

sainfoin [ˈsænfɔin] n. BOT. Pipirigallo, *m.*

saint [seint] n. Santo, ta. || FIG. Santo, ta (good person). || — *All Saints' Day*, Fiesta (*f.*) de Todos los Santos. || *Saint John the Baptist*, San Juan Bautista. || FIG. *To be with the Saints*, estar con Dios.

— OBSERV. The word *Santo* apocopates to *San* before all masculine names (*Saint Paul*, San Pablo), except in the cases of *Domingo, Tomás, Tomé* and *Toribio* (*Saint Thomas*, Santo Tomás).

saint [seint] v. tr. Canonizar.

Saint Bernard [sntˈbə:nəd] n. Perro (*m.*) de San Bernardo.

SAILING — NAVEGACIÓN, *f.*

aboard	a bordo
adrift (to be)	[ir] a la deriva
anchor (to)	anclar, echar anclas, fondear
anchorage	anclaje *m.*, fondeo *m.* (action), fondeadero *m.*, ancladero *m.* (place)
bail (to), bale (to)	achicar
beacon	baliza *f.*
binnacle	bitácora *f.*
bound for	con rumbo a
breakwater	rompeolas *m. inv.*, escollera *f.*
buoy	boya *f.*
cabotage	cabotaje *m.*
calk (to), caulk (to)	calafatear
call at a port (to)	hacer escala en un puerto
capsize (to)	hacer zozobrar (transitive), zozobrar (intransitive)
careen (to)	carenar
careen	carena *f.*
cargo	carga *f.*, cargamento *m.*
cast anchor (to)	echar anclas, fondear
charter (to)	fletar
coast (to)	costear (to follow the coast), hacer cabotaje (from port to port)
costal traffic *o* trading	cabotaje *m.*
compass	compás *m.*, brújula *f.*
crew	tripulación *f.*
cruise	crucero *m.*
day's run	singladura *f.*
dead calm	calma (*f.*) chicha, bonanza *f.*
derelict	derrelicto *m.*, pecio *m.*
dike	dique *m.*
disembark (to)	desembarcar (people)
dismast (to)	desarbolar
distress signal	señal (*f.*) de socorro
dock	dársena *f.*
dockyard	astillero *m.* (shipbuilder's yard), arsenal *m.* (naval yard)
draught	calado *m.*
dredge (to)	dragar
dredge, dredger	draga *f.*
drop anchor (to)	echar anclas, anclar
dry dock	dique (*m.*) seco
embark (to)	embarcar (people)
fathom line	sonda *f.*
fleet	flota *f.*
floating dock	dique (*m.*) flotante
flotsam	pecios *m. pl.*
freight, freightage	flete *m.*
freight (to)	fletar
furl (to)	aferrar (the sails)
gale	vendaval *m.*
ground (to)	encallar, varar
harbour [U. S., harbor]	puerto *m.*
harbour entrance	boca (*f.*) del puerto
head wind	viento (*m.*) en contra
heave to (to)	ponerse al pairo, pairar
helmsman	timonel *m.*
hurricane	huracán *m.*
in full sail	a toda vela
jetsam	echazón *f.*, carga (*f.*) arrojada al mar
jettison	echazón *f.*
jetty	malecón *m.*, escollera *f.*, muelle *m.*
knot	nudo *m.*
land (to)	atracar, arribar
landing stage	desembarcadero *m.*
launch (to)	botar
launch, launching	botadura *f.*
lead	sonda *f.*, escandallo *m.*
leak	vía (*f.*) de agua
leeward	sotavento *m.*
lie at anchor (to)	estar anclado
lie to (to)	estar al pairo, pairar
life saving	salvamento *m.*
lighthouse	faro *m.*
list	escora *f.*
list (to)	escorar
loading dock	embarcadero *m.*
log, logbook, ship's log	cuaderno (*m.*) de bitácora, diario (*m.*) de a bordo
log line	cordel (*m.*) de la corredera

luff	orza *f.*
luff (to)	orzar
mate	piloto *m.*
mile	milla *f.*
mole	malecón *m.*
moor (to)	amarrar
moorage	amarre *m.*, amarradura *f.*
moorings	amarras *f.*
navigable	navegable
navigate (to)	navegar
navy	marina *f.*
oar	remo *m.*
outer port, outport	antepuerto *m.*
pier	malecón *m.*, rompeolas *m. inv.*, espigón *m.*
pilot	práctico *m.*, piloto *m.* (of the harbour), timonel *m.*, piloto *m.* (of a boat)
pitch (to)	cabecear
pitching, pitch	cabeceo *m.*
port	puerto *m.* (harbour), babor *m.* (direction)
port of call	puerto (*m.*) de escala
port of registry	puerto (*m.*) de matrícula
put in (to), put into port (to)	hacer escala
put off (to)	hacerse a la mar
quay	muelle *m.*
radar	radar *m.*
radio beacon	radiofaro *m.*
ride at anchor (to)	estar anclado *or* fondeado
riding lights	luces (*f.*) de posición
roadstead	rada *f.*
roll (to)	balancearse
rolling	balanceo *m.*
row (to)	remar
run aground (to)	encallar, embarrancarse
sail (to)	navegar
sailer	marinero *m.*, marino *m.*
set afloat (to)	poner a flote
set sail (to)	hacerse a la mar, zarpar (any boat), hacerse a la vela (sailing boat)
ship (to)	embarcar (to load), transportar (to transport)
shipbreaker	desguazador *m.*
ship broker	agente (*m.*) marítimo, consignatario (*m.*) de buques
shipowner	naviero *m.*, armador *m.*
shipway	grada *f.*
shipwreck	naufragio *m.*
shipyard	astillero *m.*
signal flare	bengala (*f.*) de señales
sink (to)	hundir, echar a pique (transitive), hundirse, irse a pique (intransitive)
slip, slipway	grada *f.*
sound (to)	sondear
sounding line	sonda *f.*
squall	borrasca *f.*
starboard	estribor *m.*
steer (to)	llevar el timón
storm	tempestad *f.*, temporal *m.*
stow (to)	estibar, arrumar
stowage	estiba *f.*, arrumaje *m.*
tack (to)	virar de bordo
take the helm (to)	tomar el timón
tonnage	tonelaje *m.*
tow (to), tug (to)	remolcar
towage	remolque *m.*
transship (to)	transbordar
unfurl (to)	desplegar (the sails)
unship (to)	desembarcar (goods)
veer (to)	virar
wake	estela *f.*
watch	guardia *f.*
weather (to)	doblar (a cape), capear (a storm)
weigh anchor (to)	levar anclas
wharf	muelle *m.*
wharfage	muellaje *m.*
windward	barlovento *m.*
wreck	naufragio *m.* (shipwreck), barco (*m.*) naufragado (wrecked ship)
wreckage	barco (*m.*) naufragado

See also BOATS

sainted [ˈseintid] adj. Santo, ta; canonizado, da (canonized). || Santo, ta; sagrado, da (holy). || Piadoso, sa (pious, saintly). || FIG. FAM. *My sainted aunt!*, ¡Dios mío!
Saint Elmo's fire [sntˈelməuzˈfaiə*] n. Fuego (*m.*) de San Telmo.
sainthood [ˈseintˌhud] n. Santidad, *f.* || Santos, *m. pl.* (saints).
Saint-John's-wort [sntˈdʒɔnzˌwəːt] n. BOT. Corazoncillo, *m.*, hipérico, *m.*, hierba (*f.*) de San Juan.
saintliness [ˈseintlinis] n. Santidad, *f.*
saintly [ˈseintli] adj. Santo, ta; piadoso, sa (holy, pious). || Santo, ta (pertaining to a saint).
saint's day [ˈseintsˈdei] n. Fiesta (*f.*) *or* día (*m.*) del santo patrón (of a place). || Santo, *m.*, día (*m.*) onomástico (of a person): *today is my saint's day*, hoy es mi santo.
Saint Simonian [sntsiˈməunjən] adj./n. Sansimoniano, na.
Saint-Simonianism [—izəm] n. Sansimonismo, *m.*
Saint Valentine's day [sntˈvæləntains dei] n. Día (*m.*) de San Valentín, día (*m.*) de los enamorados.
Saint Vitus's dance [sntˈvaitəsizˈdɑːns] n. MED. Baile (*m.*) de San Vito.
saith [seθ] archaic 3rd. pers. sing. pres. ind. See SAY.
saké (U. S. **sake**) [ˈsɑːki] n. Saki, *m.*
sake [seik] n. *For brevity's sake*, para ser breve. || *For God's* o *for goodness' sake*, por el amor de Dios. || *For old times' sake*, para recordar el pasado. || *For pity's sake!*, ¡por [el] amor de Dios! || *For the sake of, for...'s sake*, por: *he did it for the sake of his children* o *for his children's sake*, lo hizo por sus hijos; *for my sake*, por mí; *he fought for the sake of his country* o *for his country's sake*, luchó por su patria; *art for art's sake*, el arte por el arte; *to argue for the sake of it*, discutir por discutir; *to talk for talking's sake*, hablar por hablar. || *For your own sake*, por tu propio bien.
saki [ˈsɑːki] n. ZOOL. Sakí, *m.* (monkey). || Saki, *m.* (drink).
sal [sæl] n. CHEM. Sal, *f.* || — *Sal ammoniac*, sal amoniaca, sal amoniaco. || *Sal volatile*, sal volátil.
salaam [səˈlɑːm] n. Zalema, *f.*
salaam [səˈlɑːm] v. tr. Hacer zalemas a.
— V. intr. Hacer zalemas.
salability [ˌseiləˈbiliti] n. Facilidad (*f.*) de venta, posibilidad (*f.*) de venta.
salable [ˈseiləbl] adj. Vendible, de fácil venta.
salacious [səˈleiʃəs] adj. Salaz.
salaciousness [—nis] or **salacity** [səˈlæsiti] n. Salacidad, *f.*
salad [ˈsæləd] n. CULIN. Ensalada, *f.*: *tomato salad*, ensalada de tomates; *lobster salad*, ensalada de langosta. || Lechuga, *f.* (lettuce). || — *Fruit salad*, macedonia (*f.*) *or* ensalada de frutas. || *Salad bowl*, ensaladera, *f.* || *Salad cream*, salsa parecida a la mayonesa. || *Salad days*, días (*m.*) de juventud. || *Salad dressing*, vinagreta, *f.*, aderezo, *m.*, aliño, *m.* || *Salad oil*, aceite, *m.* [para ensalada]. || *Vegetable salad*, ensaladilla, *f.*
Salamanca [ˌsæləˈmæŋkə] pr. n. GEOGR. Salamanca.
salamander [ˈsæləˌmændə*] n. ZOOL. Salamandra, *f.* || *Salamander stove*, salamandra, *f.* (heater).
salami [səˈlɑːmi] n. CULIN. Especie (*f.*) de salchichón [*Amer.* salame, *m.*].
salaried [ˈsælərid] adj. Asalariado, da: *salaried employee, staff*, empleado, personal asalariado. || Retribuido, da (position). || A sueldo (work). || *High-salaried officials*, funcionarios bien pagados.
salary [ˈsæləri] n. Sueldo, *m.*, salario, *m.* || — *Salary earner*, persona (*f.*) que cobra un sueldo. || *To be on a salary*, estar a sueldo.
salary [ˈsæləri] v. tr. Pagar un sueldo a.
sale [seil] n. Venta, *f.*: *wine sales are rising*, están aumentando las ventas de vino. || Saldo, *m.*, liquidación, *f.*, rebajas, *f. pl.* (of old unwanted stock): *to hold a sale*, hacer una liquidación; *to buy sth. at the sales*, comprar algo en las rebajas. || Mercado, *m.*, salida, *f.* (market): *an object that has a good sale*, un objeto que tiene un buen mercado. || Subasta, *f.* (by auction). || — Pl. Venta, *f. sing.*: *sales department*, servicio de venta. || — "*Car for sale*", "se vende coche". || *Closing-down sale*, liquidación. || *Credit sale*, venta a crédito. || *For* o *on sale*, en venta. || *It is not for sale*, no se vende, no está en venta. || *Sale price*, precio (*m.*) de venta (selling price), precio (*m.*) de saldo (reduced price). || U. S. *Sales check*, factura, *f.* || *Sales goods*, saldos, *m.* || *Sales talk*, cameleo, *m.* || *Sales tax*, impuesto (*m.*) sobre las ventas. || *Sale value*, valor (*m.*) comercial. || *To put a piece of land up for sale*, poner un terreno en venta. || *To put a product on sale*, poner un producto en venta. || *White sale*, quincena blanca.
saleability [seiləˈbiliti] n. Facilidad (*f.*) de venta, posibilidad (*f.*) de venta.
saleable [ˈseiləbl] adj. Vendible, de fácil venta.
saleratus [ˌsæləˈreitəs] n. U. S. CHEM. Bicarbonato (*m.*) de sosa.
saleroom [ˈseilrum] n. Sala (*f.*) de subasta.
salesclerk [ˈseilzˌklɑːk] n. Dependiente, *m.*
salesgirl [ˈseilzgəːl] n. Dependienta, *f.*
Salesian [səˈliːʒən] adj./n. REL. Salesiano, na.
saleslady [ˈseilzˌleidi] n. Dependienta, *f.*
salesman [ˈseilzmən] n. Dependiente, *m.* (in a shop). || Vendedor, *m.* (seller). || Representante, *m.* (representative). || *Travelling salesman*, viajante (*m.*) de comercio (commercial traveller).
— OBSERV. El plural de la palabra inglesa es *salesmen*.
salesmanship [—ʃip] n. Arte (*m.*) de vender. || *His salesmanship is good*, es un buen vendedor.
salesroom [ˈseilzrum] n. Sala (*f.*) de subasta (saleroom). || U. S. Sala (*f.*) de exposición (showroom).
saleswoman [ˈseilzˈwumən] n. Dependienta, *f.* (in a shop). || Vendedora, *f.* (seller).
— OBSERV. El plural de la palabra inglesa es *saleswomen*.
Salian [ˈseiljən] adj./n. HIST. Salio, lia.
Salic [ˈsælik] adj. HIST. Sálico, ca: *Salic law*, ley sálica.
salicylate [sæˈlisileit] n. CHEM. Salicilato, *m.*
salicylic [ˌsæliˈsilik] adj. Salicílico, ca.
salience [ˈseiliəns] or **saliency** [—i] n. Prominencia, *f.* (protruding part). || FIG. Rasgo (*m.*) sobresaliente (striking feature). || *To give saliency to a fact*, subrayar *or* destacar un hecho.
salient [ˈseiljənt] adj. Saliente (projecting): *salient angle*, ángulo saliente. || FIG. Sobresaliente, destacado, da: *the salient points of a speech*, los puntos sobresalientes de un discurso.
— N. Saliente, *m.*
salientian [ˌseiliˈentʃən] n. ZOOL. Anuro, *m.*
— Adj. ZOOL. Anuro, ra.
saliferous [sæˈlifərəs] adj. GEOL. Salífero, ra.
salification [ˌsælifiˈkeiʃən] n. CHEM. Salificación, *f.*
salify [ˈsælifai] v. tr. CHEM. Salificar.
— V. intr. CHEM. Salificarse.
salina [səˈlainə] n. Salina, *f.* (salt marsh).
saline [ˈseilain] adj. Salino, na (containing salt). || Salado, da (tasting of salt). || MED. Salino, na.
— N. Salina, *f.* (salina, deposit of salt). || Solución (*f.*) salina (solution). || Sal (*f.*) metálica (metallic salt).
salinity [səˈliniti] n. Salinidad, *f.*
saliva [səˈlaivə] n. Saliva, *f.*
salivary [ˈsælivəri] adj. Salival: *salivary glands*, glándulas salivales.
salivate [ˈsæliveit] v. tr. Hacer salivar.
— V. intr. Salivar.
salivation [ˌsæliˈveiʃən] n. Salivación, *f.*
salivous [səˈlivəs] adj. Salivoso, sa.
sallet [ˈsælit] n. Celada, *f.* (helmet).
sallow [ˈsæləu] adj. Cetrino, na: *sallow complexion*, tez cetrina.
— N. BOT. Sauce, *m.* (willow). || BOT. *Goat sallow*, sauce cabruno.
sallow [ˈsæləu] v. tr. Poner cetrino.
sallowness [—nis] n. Color (*m.*) cetrino, palidez, *f.*
Sallust [ˈsæləst] pr. n. Salustio.
sally [ˈsæli] n. Agudeza, *f.*, ocurrencia, *f.*, salida, *f.* (of wit). || Arranque, *m.* (outburst): *sally of activity*, arranque de energía. || Acceso, *m.* (of anger). || MIL. Salida, *f.*: *to make a sally*, hacer una salida. || Paseo, *m.*, vuelta, *f.* (trip): *we made a sally into the woods*, dimos un paseo por los bosques.
sally [ˈsæli] v. intr. MIL. Hacer una salida. || *To sally forth* o *out*, salir, ponerse en marcha.
Sally Lunn [—ˈlʌn] n. Bollo (*m.*) que se come caliente con mantequilla.
sally port [—pɔːt] n. MIL. Poterna, *f.*
salmagundi [ˌsælməˈgʌndi] n. CULIN. Salpicón, *m.* || FIG. Revoltijo, *m.*
salmi (U. S. **salmis**) [ˈsælmi] n. CULIN. Guiso (*m.*) de caza menor.
salmon [ˈsæmən] n. ZOOL. Salmón, *m.*
— Adj. Color salmón.
salmon trout [—traut] n. ZOOL. Trucha (*f.*) asalmonada.
salon [ˈsælɔ̃ːŋ] n. Salón, *m.* (drawing room). || Tertulia, *f.*, salón, *m.* (group of writers, etc.). || Exposición, *f.*, salón, *m.* (exhibition). || *Beauty salon*, instituto (*m.*) de belleza.
saloon [səˈluːn] n. Salón, *m.*, sala, *f.* (hall): *billiard saloon*, salón de billar. || Salón, *m.* (salon). || Coche, *m.*, vagón, *m.* (on a train): *dining saloon*, coche restaurante. || AUT. Sedán, *m.* || Salón (*m.*) interior (of a public house). || U. S. Taberna, *f.*, bar, *m.* || *Hairdressing saloon*, peluquería, *f.*, salón de peluquería. || *Ice-cream saloon*, heladería, *f.*
saloon bar [—bɑː*] n. Salón (*m.*) interior (of a public house).
saloon car [—kɑː*] n. Coche (*m.*) salón (in a train).
saloon deck [—dek] n. MAR. Cubierta (*f.*) de primera clase.
saloonkeeper [—kiːpə*] n. U. S. Tabernero, *m.*
salsify [ˈsælsifi] n. BOT. Salsifí, *m.*
sal soda [sælˈsəudə] n. U. S. CHEM. Sal (*f.*) de sosa (crystallized sodium carbonate).
salt [sɔːlt] n. Sal, *f.*: *table salt*, sal de mesa; *cooking* o *kitchen salt*, sal de cocina; *sea salt*, sal marina; *rock salt*, sal gema. || CHEM. Sal, *f.* || FIG. Salero, *m.*, sal, *f.* (piquancy, interest). || — Pl. Sales, *f.*: *bath salts*, sales de baño. || — *Fruit salts*, sal de frutas. || *Liver* o *Epsom salts*, sal de la Higuera. || MIN. *Mineral salts*, sales minerales. || FIG. *Not to be worth one's salt*, no valer gran cosa, no merecerse lo que se gana. | *Old salt*, lobo (*m.*) de mar (sailor). || *Smelling salts*, sales aromáticas. || FIG. *The salt of the earth*, la sal de la tierra. | *To take sth. with a grain* o *a pinch of salt*, admitir algo con reservas.
— Adj. Salado, da: *salt water*, agua salada. || Salinero,

ra: *salt industry*, industria salinera. || Para la sal: *salt spoon*, cucharilla para la sal; *salt mill*, molinillo para la sal. || De sal: *salt mine*, mina de sal.
salt [sɔ:lt] v. tr. Salar (to treat with salt): *to salt beef*, salar carne de vaca. || Echar sal a (to give flavour). || FIG. Salpicar (to sprinkle): *to salt a speech with jokes*, salpicar un discurso con chistes. | Colocar mineral en [una mina] para darle valor (a mine). || — *To salt away* o *down*, conservar en sal (to preserve in salt), ahorrar (money, etc.). || *To salt out*, precipitar [una sustancia] añadiendo sal.
saltation [sæl'teiʃən] n. Salto, *m.* (jump). || Mutación, *f.* (evolution).
saltatory ['sæltətəri] adj. ZOOL. Saltador, ra. || FIG. Intermitente.
saltcellar ['sɔ:lt,selə*] n. Salero, *m.*
salter ['sɔ:ltə*] n. Salinero, *m.* (person who makes or sells salt). || Salador, *m.* (person who salts meat, fish, etc.).
saltern ['sɔ:ltə:n] n. Salina, *f.*
saltiness ['sɔ:ltinis] n. Salinidad, *f.* (of the sea). || Salobridad, *f.* (brackishness). || Lo salado (of food). || FIG. Ingenio, *m.*, sal, *f.*, picante, *m.*
salting ['sɔltiŋ] n. Salazón, *f.*, saladura, *f.* || — Pl. Saladar, *m. sing.*
salt lick ['sɔ:ltlik] n. Salegar, *m.*
salt marsh ['sɔ:ltmɑ:ʃ] n. Salina, *f.*
salt pan ['sɔ:ltpæn] n. Salina, *f.* (depression). || Recipiente (*m.*) utilizado para obtener sal, previa evaporación del agua (vessel).
saltpetre (U. S. **saltpeter**) ['sɔ:lt,pi:tə*] n. Salitre, *m.*, nitro, *m.* (potassium nitrate). || Nitro (*m.*) de Chile, caliche, *m.* (sodium nitrate). || *Salpetre works*, salitrería, *f.*, salitral, *m.*
saltpetrous ['sɔ:lt,pi:trəs] adj. Salitrado, da; salitroso, sa.
salt pit ['sɔ:ltpit] n. Salina, *f.*
salt shaker ['sɔ:lt,ʃeikə*] n. U. S. Salero, *m.*
saltwater ['sɔ:lt,wɔtə*] adj. De agua salada.
saltworks ['sɔ:ltwə:ks] n. Salinas, *f. pl.* || Refinería (*f.*) de sal.
saltwort ['sɔ:ltwə:t] n. BOT. Salicor, *m.*, barrilla, *f.*
salty ['sɔ:lti] adj. Salado, da (containing salt): *the soup is too salty*, la sopa está demasiado salada. || Que huele a mar (smelling of the sea). || FIG. Picante: *salty joke*, chiste picante.
salubrious [sə'lu:briəs] adj. Sano, na; salubre, saludable (good for the health): *a salubrious climate*, un clima sano. || Sano, na (morally wholesome).
salubrity [sə'lu:briti] n. Salubridad, *f.*, sanidad, *f.* (of a climate, region, etc.). || Lo sano (moral wholesomeness).
salutariness ['sæljutərinis] n. Salubridad, *f.*, sanidad, *f.* (of a climate). || Lo saludable (of an example, a punishment, etc.).
salutary ['sæljutəri] adj. Saludable: *a salutary climate*, un clima saludable. || Benéfico, ca (beneficial).
salutation [,sælju'teiʃən] n. Saludo, *m.* (greeting or military salute). || Encabezamiento, *m.* (of a letter). || REL. *The Angelic Salutation*, la Salutación angélica.
salutatorian [,sælju:tə'tɔ:riən] n. U. S. Estudiante (*m.*) que pronuncia el discurso de apertura en la ceremonia de fin de curso.
salutatory [sə'lju:tətəri] adj. De saludo (of salutation). || U. S. De bienvenida.
— N. Discurso (*m.*) de apertura.
salute [sə'lu:t] n. Saludo, *m.* (greeting). || MIL. Saludo, *m.* | Salva, *f.*: *to fire a salute of ten guns*, disparar una salva de diez cañonazos.
salute [sə'lu:t] v. tr. Saludar.
— V. intr. Hacer un saludo.
salvable ['sælvəbl] adj. Salvable.
Salvadoran [,sælvə'dɔ:rən] or **Salvadorian** [,sælvə'dɔ:riən] adj./n. Salvadoreño, ña.
salvage ['sælvidʒ] n. Objetos (*m. pl.*) salvados (things salvaged). || Salvamento, *m.* (act of salvaging). || JUR. Derecho (*m.*) de salvamento.
salvage ['sælvidʒ] v. tr. Salvar.
salvager [—ə*] n. MAR. Salvador, ra.
salvation [sæl'veiʃən] n. Salvación, *f.*
Salvation Army [—'ɑ:mi] n. Ejército (*m.*) de Salvación.
Salvationist [sæl'veiʃnist] n. Salutista, *m.* & *f.*
salve [sɑ:v] n. MED. Ungüento, *m.*, pomada, *f.*, bálsamo, *m.* (ointment). || FIG. Bálsamo, *m.* (sth. that soothes). | Halago, *m.* (flattery).
salve [sɑ:v] v. tr. MED. Poner pomada en. || FIG. Tranquilizar, sosegar (to soothe).
salve [sælv] v. tr. Salvar (to rescue).
salver ['sælvə*] n. Salvilla, *f.*, bandeja, *f.*: *silver salver*, bandeja de plata.
salvia ['sælviə] n. BOT. Salvia, *f.*
salvo ['sælvəu] n. Salva, *f.*: *salvo of shots, of applause*, salva de cañonazos, de aplausos. || Reserva, *f.*, salvedad, *f.* (reservation).
salvor ['sælvə*] n. MAR. Salvador, ra.
Samaritan [sə'mæritn] adj./n. Samaritano, na.
samarium [sə'mærjəm] n. Samario, *m.* (metallic element).
samba ['sæmbə] n. Samba, *f.* (dance).
Sam Browne belt ['sæm'braun'belt] n. MIL. Correaje (*m.*) de oficial.
same [seim] adj. Mismo, ma: *I read the same newspaper every day*, leo el mismo periódico todos los días; *several women had on the same dress at the party*, varias mujeres llevaban el mismo traje en la fiesta; *it was hotter at the same time last year*, hizo más calor el año pasado en la misma época; *you cannot write and eat at the same time*, no se puede escribir y comer al mismo tiempo; *he is of the same age as you*, tiene la misma edad que tú. || Igual, idéntico, ca: *the two buildings are the same*, los dos edificios son iguales. || — *In the same way*, del mismo modo. || *It amounts* o *it comes to the same thing*, viene a ser lo mismo. || *The same old story*, la historia de siempre. || *Very same*, mismísimo, ma: *at the very same moment*, en ese mismísimo momento.
— Adv. De la misma forma, igual: *they both felt the same about it*, los dos pensaban igual respecto a aquello. || — *All the same*, sin embargo. || *If it's all the same to you*, si no le importa, si le da lo mismo, si le da igual. || *It's all the same to me*, me da igual, me da lo lo mismo. || *Just the same*, sin embargo (nevertheless), exactamente igual (exactly the same, in the same way). || *Things go on much the same as ever*, todo sigue más o menos como siempre.
— Pron. El mismo, la misma: *"Mr Smith?"*... — *"The same"*, "Sr. Smith?"... — « El mismo »; *I am the same as I have always been*, soy el mismo de siempre. || Lo mismo: *the same applies to you*, lo mismo vale por Ud. || — *I'd do the same again*, volvería a hacer lo mismo. || *Same here*, yo también. || *The prime minister and foreign minister are one and the same*, el primer ministro y el ministro de Asuntos Exteriores son la misma persona. || *The same to you!*, ¡igualmente!
sameness ['seimnis] n. Igualdad, *f.*, identidad, *f.* (identity). || Similaridad, *f.* (similarity). || Monotonía, *f.*, uniformidad, *f.* (lack of variety).
samiel [səm'jel] n. Simún, *m.* (wind).
samisen ['sæmisen] n. MUS. Guitarra (*f.*) japonesa.
samite ['sæmait] n. HIST. Brocado (*m.*) de seda.
samlet ['sæmlet] n. ZOOL. Salmoncillo, *m.*
Samnite ['sæmnait] adj./n. HIST. Samnita.
Samothrace ['sæməuθreis] n. GEOGR. Samotracia.
samovar [,sæməu'vɑ:*] n. Samovar, *m.*
samp [sæmp] n. U. S. Sémola (*f.*) gruesa de maíz (maize). | Gachas (*f. pl.*) de sémola gruesa de maíz (porridge).
sampan ['sæmpæn] n. MAR. Sampán, *m.*
samphire ['sæmfaiə*] n. BOT. Hinojo (*m.*) marino.
sample ['sɑ:mpl] n. Muestra, *f.*: *free sample*, muestra gratuita; *a sample of the population*, una muestra de la población.
sample ['sɑ:mpl] v. tr. Probar: *to sample a dish*, probar un plato. || Catar (drinks). || Tomar una muestra *or* muestras de (to take samples).
sample book [—buk] n. Muestrario, *m.*
sampler [—ə*] n. Dechado, *m.* (in sewing). || Catador, *m.* (of drinks).
sampling [—iŋ] n. Catadura, *f.* (of food and drink). || Toma (*f.*) de muestras, muestreo, *m.* (sample taking). || Muestra, *f.* (sample).
Samson ['sæmsn] pr. n. Sansón, *m.*
samurai ['sæmurai] inv. n. HIST. Samurai, *m.*
sanatarium [,sænə'teriəm] n. U. S. Sanatorio, *m.*
— OBSERV. El plural de la palabra americana es *sanatariums* o *sanataria*.
sanatorium [,sænə'tɔ:riəm] n. Sanatorio, *m.* (for patients undergoing treatment). || Enfermería, *f.* (in a school, etc.).
— OBSERV. El plural de la palabra inglesa es *sanatoriums* o *sanatoria*.
sanatory ['sænətəri] adj. Sanador, ra; curativo, va.
sanbenito [,sænbə'ni:təu] n. HIST. Sambenito, *m.* (robe).
sanctification [,sæŋktifi'keiʃən] n. Santificación, *f.*
sanctifier ['sæŋktifaiə*] n. Santificador, ra.
sanctify ['sæŋktifai] v. tr. Santificar (to make holy) || Venerar (to revere). || Consagrar (to give authority to).
sanctifying [—iŋ] adj. Santificador, ra; santificante.
sanctimonious [,sæŋkti'məunjəs] adj. Beato, ta; mojigato, ta.
sanctimoniousness [—nis] or **sanctimony** ['sæŋktiməni] n. Beatería, *f.*, mojigatería, *f.*
sanction ['sæŋkʃən] n. Sanción, *f.* (punishment). || Sanción, *f.*, aprobación, *f.* (approval). || Autorización, *f.* (authorization). || Consagración, *f.* (by usage). || Decreto, *m.* (decree).
sanction ['sæŋkʃən] v. tr. Sancionar.
sanctity ['sæŋktiti] n. Santidad, *f.* (holiness). || Inviolabilidad, *f.* (inviolability). || Lo sagrado (of an oath, a promise).
sanctuary ['sæŋktjuəri] n. REL. Santuario, *m.* (a sacred place). | Sagrario, *m.* (part of church). || Refugio, *m.* (of birds). || JUR. Derecho (*m.*) de asilo, inmunidad (*f.*) de los lugares sagrados (immunity). | Asilo, *m.* (place). || — *To seek sanctuary in* o *with*, acogerse a. || *To take sanctuary*, acogerse a sagrado.
sanctum ['sæŋktəm] n. Santuario, *m.* (a sacred place). || FIG. Sanctasanctórum, *m.* (place of retreat).
— OBSERV. El plural de *sanctum* es *sanctums* o *sancta*.
sanctum sanctorum [—sæŋk'tɔ:rəm] n. Sanctasanctórum, *m.*

sand [sænd] n. Arena, *f.* || MED. Arenilla, *f.* || — Pl. Playa, *f. sing.* (beach). || Banco (*m. sing.*) de arena (sandbank). || — FIG. *To build on sand*, edificar sobre arena. || U. S. FAM. *To have plenty of sand*, tener agallas.
sand [sænd] v. tr. Lijar (to abrade). || Enarenar (to cover with sand). || Secar con arena (to dry with sand). || Mezclar con arena (to falsify the weight).
sandal [—l] n. Sandalia, *f.* (shoe): *beach sandals*, sandalias de playa. || BOT. Sándalo, *m.* (sandalwood).
sandalled (U. S. **sandaled**) [—ld] adj. Que lleva sandalias, con sandalias.
sandalwood [—lwud] n. BOT. Sándalo, *m.*
sandarac [—əræk] n. BOT. Alerce (*m.*) africano (tree). || Sandáraca, *f.* (resin). || MIN. Sandáraca, *f.*, rejalgar, *m.* (realgar).
sandbag [—bæg] n. Saco (*m.*) terrero. || Porra, *f.* (used as a weapon).
sandbag [—bæg] v. tr. Proteger con sacos terreros (to protect with sandbags). || Golpear con una porra (to stun). || U. S. FAM. Forzar, obligar (to coerce).
sandbank [—bæŋk] n. Banco (*m.*) de arena.
sandbar [—bɑ:*] n. Banco (*m.*) de arena.
sandblast [—ˌblɑ:st] n. TECH. Chorro (*m.*) de arena (jet of sand). | Limpiadora (*f.*) de chorro de arena (machine).
sandblast [—blɑ:st] v. tr. TECH. Pulir *or* limpiar con chorro de arena.
sandbox [—bɔks] n. Arenero, *m.* (in a locomotive). || Salvadera, *f.* (to dry ink). || U. S. Cajón (*m.*) de arena para juegos infantiles (sandpit).
sand-cast [—kɑ:st] v. tr. Vaciar en molde de arena (metal).
sandcastle [—ˈkɑ:sl] n. Castillo (*m.*) de arena.
sand dollar [—ˈdɔlə*] n. ZOOL. Erizo (*m.*) de mar poco grueso.
sand dune [—ˈdju:n] n. Duna, *f.*
sand flea [—ˈfli:] n. ZOOL. Pulga (*f.*) de mar (beach flea). | Nigua, *f.* (chigoe).
sand fly [—ˈflai] n. Jején, *m.*, mosquito, *m.*
sandglass [—ˌglɑ:s] n. Reloj (*m.*) de arena.
sandgrouse [—graus] n. Ortega, *f.* (bird).
sandhog [—hɔg] n. U. S. Trabajador (*m.*) que efectúa obras subterráneas en una campana.
sandlot [—lɔt] n. U. S. Solar, *m.*
sandman [—ˌmæn] n. Ser (*m.*) imaginario que adormece a los niños.
sandpaper [—ˌpeipə*] n. Papel (*m.*) de lija.
sandpaper [—ˌpeipə*] v. tr. Lijar.
sand pie [—pai] n. Flan (*m.*) de arena (for children).
sandpiper [—ˌpaipə*] n. ZOOL. Lavandera, *f.* (bird).
sandpit [—ˌpit] n. Cajón (*m.*) de arena para juegos infantiles (for children). || Mina (*f.*) de arena (for extracting sand).
sandshoe [—ʃu:] n. Playera, *f.*
sandstone [—stəun] n. MIN. Arenisca, *f.*
sandstorm [—stɔ:m] n. Tempestad (*f.*) de arena.
sandwich [ˈsænwidʒ] n. Bocadillo, *m.* (made with a roll). || Sandwich, *m.*, emparedado, *m.* (made with square sliced bread).
sandwich [ˈsænwidʒ] v. tr. Intercalar (to place between). || *To be sandwished between*, estar entre.
sandwich board [—bɔ:d] n. Carteles (*m. pl.*) que lleva el hombre anuncio.
sandwich man [—mæn] n. Hombre anuncio, *m.*

— OBSERV. El plural es *sandwich men.*

sandy [ˈsændi] adj. Cubierto de arena (full of sand). || Arenoso, sa (covered with or like sand). || Rubio rojizo (hair).
sane [sein] adj. Cuerdo, da; sensato, ta (sensible). || Sano, na (mind). || *He is sane*, está en sus cabales *or* en su sano juicio.
sanforized [ˈsænfəraizd] adj. Sanforizado, da (cotton, etc.).
sang [sæŋ] pret. See SING.
sangaree [ˈsæŋgəˈri:] n. Sangría, *f.*
sangfroid [ˈsɑ̃:ŋˈfrwɑ:] n. Sangre (*f.*) fría.
Sangrail [sæŋˈgreil] n. REL. Santo Grial, *m.*
sanguinary [ˈsæŋgwinəri] adj. Sangriento, ta (accompanied by much bloodshed). || Sanguinario, ria (murderous): *a sanguinary tyrant*, un tirano sanguinario.
sanguine [ˈsæŋgwin] adj. Sanguíneo, a (complexion). || Optimista (optimistic). || Sanguinario, ria (sanguinary).
— N. Sanguina, *f.* (drawing, pencil).
sanguineness [—nis] n. Optimismo, *m.*, confianza, *f.*
sanguineous [sæŋˈgwiniəs] adj. Sanguíneo, a (pertaining to blood). || Sanguíneo, a; de color rojo sangre (bloodred). || Sanguíneo, a (complexion). || Sanguinario, ria (bloodthirsty).
sanguinolent [ˈsæŋgwinələnt] adj. Sanguinolento, ta.
Sanhedrim [ˈsænidrim] or **Sanhedrin** [ˈsænidrin] n. HIST. Sanedrín, *m.*
sanies [ˈseini:z] n. MED. Sanies, *f.*, sanie, *f.*

— OBSERV. La palabra inglesa es invariable.

sanitarian [ˌsæniˈtɛəriən] adj. Sanitario, ria.
sanitarium [ˌsæniˈtɛəriəm] n. U. S. Sanatorio, *m.*

— OBSERV. El plural de la palabra americana es *sanitariums* o *sanitaria.*

sanitary [ˈsænitəri] adj. Sanitario, ria; higiénico, ca. || MIL. Sanitario, ria. || — *Sanitary inspector*, inspector (*m.*) de sanidad. || *Sanitary napkin o towel*, compresa, *f.*, paño higiénico.
sanitate [ˈsæniteit] v. tr. Sanear (to make sanitary).
sanitation [ˌsæniˈteiʃən] n. Saneamiento, *m.* || Higiene, *f.*
sanity [ˈsæniti] n. Cordura, *f.*, juicio, *m.* (soundness of mind). || Sensatez, *f.* (sensibleness). || — *To be restored to sanity*, recobrar el juicio. || *To lose one's sanity*, perder el juicio, perder la razón. || *To regain one's sanity*, recobrar el juicio.
sank [sæŋk] pret. See SINK.
sansei [sænˈsei] n. U. S. Ciudadano (*m.*) americano descendiente de japoneses.

— OBSERV. El plural de esta palabra es *sansei* o *sanseis.*

Sanskrit [ˈsænskrit] adj. Sánscrito, ta.
— N. Sánscrito, *m.*
sans serif [sænˈserif] n. PRINT. Tipo (*m.*) basto.
Santa Claus [ˈsæntəˈklɔ:z] n. San Nicolás, *m.*, Papá Noel, *m.*
sap [sæp] n. BOT. Savia, *f.* || FIG. Savia, *f.* || MIL. Zapa, *f.* (trench or tunnel). || FAM. Bobo, ba; memo, ma (fool).
sap [sæp] v. tr. MIL. Zapar, socavar (to dig). | Minar (to undermine). || FIG. Agotar (to weaken): *the heat saps your strength*, el calor agota las fuerzas. | Socavar.
sapajou [ˈsæpədʒu:] n. Sapajú, *m.* (monkey).
sapanwood [ˈsæpənwud] n. BOT. Sibucao, *m.*, sapan, *m.* (sappanwood).
saphead [ˈsæphed] n. FAM. Bobo, ba; memo, ma.
saphena [sæˈfi:nə] n. ANAT. Safena, *f.*
saphenous [sæˈfi:nəs] adj. Safena (vein).
sapid [ˈsæpid] adj. Sabroso, sa; sápido, da.
sapidity [sæˈpiditi] n. Sapidez, *f.*, sabor, *m.*
sapience [ˈseipiəns] n. Sapiencia, *f.*
sapient [ˈseipjənt] adj. Sapiente.
sapiential [ˌseipiˈenʃəl] adj. Sapiencial. || REL. *Sapiential books*, libros sapienciales.
sapless [ˈsæplis] adj. BOT. Sin savia (plant). || Estéril (soil). || FIG. Débil (character). | Insípido, da; trivial (idea).
sapling [ˈsæpliŋ] n. BOT. Árbol (*m.*) joven. || ZOOL. Galgo (*m.*) joven. || FIG. FAM. Pimpollo, *m.*, jovenzuelo, *m.* (youth).
sapodilla [sæpəˈdilə] n. BOT. Zapote, *m.*
saponaceous [ˌsæpəuˈneiʃəs] adj. Saponáceo, a. || FIG. Meloso, sa.
saponification [səˌpɔnifiˈkeiʃən] n. CHEM. Saponificación, *f.*
saponify [səˈpɔnifai] v. tr. CHEM. Saponificar.
— V. intr. CHEM. Saponificarse.
saponite [ˈsæpənait] n. MIN. Saponita, *f.*
sapor [ˈseipə*] n. Sabor, *m.*
saporous [ˈseipərəs] adj. Sabroso, sa.
sappanwood [ˈsæpənwud] n. BOT. Sibucao, *m.*, sapan, *m.*
sapper [ˈsæpə*] n. MIL. Zapador, *m.*
Sapphic [ˈsæfik] adj. Sáfico, ca. || Lesbiano, na.
— N. POET. Sáfico, *m.*, verso (*m.*) sáfico (metre). || — Pl. POET. Poesía (*f. sing.*) sáfica.
sapphire [ˈsæfaiə*] n. Zafiro, *m.*
— Adj. De color zafiro.
sapphirine [ˈsæfirain] adj. Zafirino, na.
— N. MIN. Zafirina, *f.*
sapphism [ˈsæfˌizəm] n. Safismo, *m.*
Sappho [ˈsæfəu] pr. n. Safo, *f.*
sappiness [ˈsæpinis] n. Jugosidad, *f.* || FIG. FAM. Sensiblería, *f.* (mawkishness). | Tontería, *f.* (silliness).
sappy [ˈsæpi] adj. BOT. Jugoso, sa; lleno de savia. || FIG. FAM. Sensiblero, ra (mawkish). | Tontuelo, la (silly).
saprophyte [ˈsæprəfait] n. BIOL. Saprófito, *m.*
saprophytic [sæprəˈfitik] adj. BIOL. Saprófito, ta.
sapsucker [ˈsæpˌsʌkə*] n. ZOOL. Pájaro (*m.*) carpintero americano.
sapwood [ˈsæpwud] n. Albura, *f.*
saraband or **sarabande** [ˈsærəbænd] n. MUS. Zarabanda, *f.*
Saracen [ˈsærəsn] adj./n. HIST. Sarraceno, na.
Saragossa [ˌsærəˈgɔsə] pr. n. GEOGR. Zaragoza.
Sarah [ˈsɛərə] pr. n. Sara, *f.*
Saratoga trunk [ˌsærəˈtəugəˌtrʌŋk] n. Baúl (*m.*) mundo.
sarcasm [ˈsɑ:kæzəm] n. Sarcasmo, *m.*
sarcastic [sɑ:ˈkæstik] adj. Sarcástico, ca.
sarcastically [—əli] adv. Con sarcasmo, sarcásticamente.
sarcoma [sɑ:ˈkəumə] n. MED. Sarcoma, *m.*

— OBSERV. El plural de la palabra inglesa es *sarcomas* o *sarcomata.*

sarcomatous [—təs] adj. MED. Sarcomatoso, sa.
sarcophagus [sɑ:ˈkɔfəgəs] n. Sarcófago, *m.*

— OBSERV. El plural de *sarcophagus* es *sarcophagi* o *sarcophaguses.*

sardana [sɑ:ˈdɑ:nə] n. Sardana, *f.* (Catalan dance).
Sardanapalian [ˈsɑ:dənəˈpeiliən] adj. Sardanapalesco, ca.
Sardanapalus [ˌsɑ:dəˈnæpələs] pr. n. Sardanápalo, *m.*
sardine [sɑ:ˈdi:n] n. ZOOL. Sardina, *f.* || FIG. *To be packed like sardines*, estar como sardinas en banasta *or* en lata.
Sardinia [sɑ:ˈdinjə] pr. n. GEOGR. Cerdeña, *f.*

Sardinian [—n] n. Sardo, da (person). || Sardo, *m.* (language).
— Adj. Sardo, da.
sardonic [sɑːˈdɔnik] adj. Sardónico, ca.
sardonically [—əli] adv. Sardónicamente.
sargasso [sɑːˈgæsəu] n. BOT. Sargazo, *m.*
Sargasso Sea [—siː] pr. n. GEOGR. Mar (*m.*) de los Sargazos.
sarge [sɑːdʒ] n. FAM. Sargento, *m.*
sargo [ˈsɑːgəu] n. ZOOL. Sargo, *m.* (fish).
sari [ˈsɑːri] n. Sari, *m.*
sarmentose [sɑːˈmen,təus] adj. BOT. Sarmentoso, sa.
sarsaparilla [,sɑːsəpəˈrilə] n. BOT. Zarzaparrilla, *f.*
sartorial [sɑːˈtɔːriəl] adj. De sastre, de sastrería. || *Sartorial elegance*, elegancia (*f.*) en el vestir.
sartorius [sɑːˈtɔːriəs] n. ANAT. Sartorio, *m.*, músculo (*m.*) sartorio.
sash [sæʃ] n. Marco, *m.* (frame). || Hoja (*f.*) móvil de la ventana de guillotina (of a sash window). || Banda, *f.* (broad ribbon worn across the chest). || Fajín, *m.* (worn around the waist by officers, officials, etc.). || Faja, *f.* (in local costume).
sashay [—ˈei] v. intr. U. S. FAM. Andar pavoneándose (to swagger). | Zigzaguear (to zigzag).
sash cord [—kɔːd] n. Cuerda (*f.*) de ventana.
sash window [—ˈwindəu] n. Ventana (*f.*) de guillotina.
sasin [ˈseisin] n. ZOOL. Antílope (*m.*) indio.
sass [sæs] n. U. S. FAM. Descaro, *m.*, insolencia, *f.* (impudent talk).
sass [sæs] v. tr. U. S. FAM. Hablar con descaro a, insolentarse con.
sassafras [ˈsæsəfræs] n. BOT. Sasafrás, *m.*
Sassanian [sæˈseinjən] or **Sassanid** [ˈsæsənid] adj./n. HIST. Sasánida.
Sassenach [ˈsæsənæk] n. Inglés, esa.
sassy [ˈsæsi] adj. U. S. FAM. Descarado, da.
sat [sæt] pret. & p. p. See SIT.
Satan [ˈseitən] n. REL. Satán, *m.*, Satanás, *m.*
satanic [səˈtænik] adj. Satánico, ca.
Satanism [səˈtænizəm] n. Satanismo, *m.*
satchel [ˈsætʃəl] n. Cartera, *f.*, cartapacio, *m.* (for schoolchildren). || Morral, *m.* (for hunters). || Cartera, *f.* (for bicycles).
sate [seit] v. tr. Saciar (one's appetite). || Hartar (to surfeit).
sateen [sæˈtiːn] n. Satén, *m.*
satellite [ˈsætəlait] n. ASTR. Satélite, *m.*: *artificial satellite*, satélite artificial. || FIG. Acólito, *m.*, satélite, *m.* (servile follower). || *Satellite country, town*, país, ciudad satélite.
satiable [ˈseiʃəbl] adj. Saciable.
satiate [ˈseiʃicit] v. tr. Saciar (to satisfy). || Hartar (to surfeit).
satiate [ˈseiʃieit] adj. Saciado, da; harto, ta.
satiation [,seiʃiˈeiʃən] or **satiety** [səˈtaiəti] n. Saciedad, *f.* (sufficiency). || Hartura, *f.*, hartazgo, *m.* (excess).
satin [ˈsætin] n. Raso, *m.*, satén, *m.*
— Adj. De raso: *a satin dress*, un vestido de raso. || Satinado, da: *satin paper*, papel satinado. || *Satin stitch*, plumetís, *m.*
satin [ˈsætin] v. tr. Satinar.
satinet or **satinette** [,sætiˈnet] n. Rasete, *m.*
satinwood [ˈsætinwud] n. BOT. Satín, *m.*
satiny [ˈsætini] adj. Satinado, da.
satire [ˈsætaiə*] n. Sátira, *f.*
satiric [səˈtirik] or **satirical** [—əl] adj. Satírico, ca.
satirist [ˈsætərist] n. Satírico, *m.*, autor (*m.*) de sátiras.
satirize [ˈsætəraiz] v. tr./intr. Satirizar.
satisfaction [,sætisˈfækʃən] n. Satisfacción, *f.*: *to give complete satisfaction*, dar entera satisfacción; *the satisfaction of one's appetite, of an ambition*, la satisfacción del apetito, de una ambición. || Aplacamiento, *m.* (of one's thirst). || Liquidación, *f.* (of a debt). || Reembolso, *m.* (of a creditor). || Compensación, *f.* (compensation). || Cumplimiento, *m.* (of requirements, promise). || FIG. Satisfacción, *f.*, reparación, *f.*: *to demand satisfaction for an offence*, pedir satisfacción de una ofensa. || — *To express one's satisfaction*, declararse satisfecho, expresar su satisfacción. || *To prove sth. to s.o.'s satisfaction*, convencer a alguien de algo. || *To the satisfaction of*, a satisfacción de.
satisfactorily [,sætisˈfæktərili] adv. Satisfactoriamente.
satisfactoriness [,sætisˈfæktərinis] n. Carácter (*m.*) satisfactorio, lo satisfactorio.
satisfactory [,sætisˈfæktəri] adj. Satisfactorio, ria: *satisfactory answer*, contestación satisfactoria.
satisfied [ˈsætisfaid] adj. Satisfecho, cha.
satisfy [ˈsætisfai] v. tr. Satisfacer: *to satisfy s.o.'s desires*, satisfacer los deseos de alguien: *to satisfy one's appetite*, satisfacer el apetito. || Aplacar (one's thirst). || Cumplir con, satisfacer: *he satisfied the requirements*, cumplió con los requisitos. || Cumplir con, cumplir (a promise). || Pagar, liquidar (a debt). || Pagar una deuda a, reembolsar (a creditor). || Indemnizar (to compensate). || Responder satisfactoriamente a (to counter): *to satisfy s.o.'s objections*, responder satisfactoriamente a las objeciones de uno. || Convencer (to convince): *I am not absolutely satisfied that it is true*, no estoy completamente convencido de que sea verdad. || — *I am afraid you will have to be satisfied with that*, lo siento, pero usted tendrá que contentarse con eso. || *I have satisfied myself that he is telling the truth*, estoy convencido de que dice la verdad.
— V. intr. Satisfacer.
satisfying [—iŋ] adj. Satisfactorio, ria: *a satisfying piece of news*, una noticia satisfactoria. || Agradable: *driving a sports car is a satisfying experience*, es una experiencia agradable conducir un coche deportivo. || Sustancioso, sa (food). || Convincente (argument).
satrap [ˈsætrəp] n. Sátrapa, *m.*
satrapy [—i] n. Satrapía, *f.*
saturability [,sætjurəˈbiliti] n. CHEM. Saturabilidad, *f.*
saturable [ˈsætjurəbl] adj. Saturable.
saturate [ˈsætʃərit] adj. Saturado, da.
saturate [ˈsætʃəreit] v. tr. Saturar: *to saturate a market with a product*, saturar un mercado con un producto. || Empapar (to soak): *the tablecloth is saturated with wine*, el mantel está empapado en vino. || PHYS. CHEM. Saturar.
saturated [—id] adj. PHYS. CHEM. Saturado, da. || FAM. Empapado, da (wet). || FIG. *Saturated with conceit*, convencido de su propia importancia.
saturater or **saturator** [—ə*] n. Saturador, *m.*
saturation [,sætʃəˈreiʃən] n. Saturación, *f.* || *Saturation point*, punto (*m.*) de saturación.
Saturday [ˈsætədi] n. Sábado, *m.*: *on Saturday*, el sábado; *on Saturdays*, los sábados. || *Easter Saturday*, Sábado Santo *or* de Gloria.
Saturn [ˈsætən] pr. n. MYTH. ASTR. Saturno, *m.*
Saturnalia [,sætəːˈneiljə] n. HIST. Saturnales, *f. pl.* || FIG. Bacanales, *f. pl.* (orgy).
— OBSERV. El plural de la palabra inglesa es *Saturnalias* o *Saturnalia* cuando tiene un sentido figurado.
Saturnalian [—n] adj. HIST. De las saturnales. || FIG. Orgiástico, ca.
Saturnian [sæˈtəːnjən] adj. Saturnal, saturnio, nia. || FIG. *The Saturnian age*, la edad de oro.
saturnic [ˈsætəːnik] adj. MED. Saturnino, na.
saturnine [ˈsætənain] adj. Saturnino, na.
saturnism [ˈsætənizəm] n. MED. Saturnismo, *m.*
satyr [ˈsætə*] n. MYTH. FIG. Sátiro, *m.* || ZOOL. Sátiro, *m.* (butterfly).
satyric [səˈtirik] or **satyrical** [—əl] adj. Satírico, ca.
sauce [sɔːs] n. CULIN. Salsa, *f.*: *white sauce*, salsa blanca; *tartare sauce*, salsa tártara. | Compota, *f.* (stewed fruit). || FIG. Salsa, *f.* (appetizer): *hunger is the best sauce*, no hay mejor salsa que el apetito. | Sal, *f.* (wit). || FAM. See SAUCINESS. || — *Tomato sauce*, salsa de tomate. || *To thicken a sauce*, trabar una salsa. || *White cream sauce*, salsa bechamel or besamel.
sauce [sɔːs] v. tr. Añadir salsa a, sazonar (to put sauce on). || FAM. Insolentarse con.
sauceboat [—bəut] n. Salsera, *f.*
saucebox [—bɔks] n. FAM. Fresco, ca (cheeky person).
saucepan [—pən] n. Cazo, *m.*, cacerola, *f.*
saucer [—ə*] n. Platillo, *m.* || *Flying saucer*, platillo volante.
sauciness [—inis] n. FAM. Descaro, *m.*, frescura, *f.*, insolencia, *f.* (impudence). || *That's enough of your sauciness!*, ¡déjate de frescuras!, ¡no seas tan descarado!
saucy [—i] adj. FAM. Descarado, da; insolente, fresco, ca (impudent). | Pícaro, ra: *a saucy look*, una mirada pícara. || *A saucy little hat*, un sombrerito coquetón.
Saudi Arabia [ˈsɔːdiəˈreibjə] pr. n. GEOGR. Arabia (*f.*) Saudita *or* Saudí.
sauerkraut [ˈsauəkraut] n. CULIN. Sauerkraut, *m.* (fermented cabbage).
sauna [ˈsaunə] n. Sauna, *f.*
saunter [ˈsɔːntə*] n. Paseo, *m.* (walk): *to go for a saunter*, ir de paseo. || Paso (*m.*) lento (gait).
saunter [ˈsɔːntə*] v. intr. Deambular, pasearse (to stroll). || *To saunter up to s.o.*, acercarse lentamente a alguien.
saunterer [—rə*] n. Paseante, *m.* & *f.*
saurel [sɔˈrel] n. Jurel, *m.* (fish).
saurian [ˈsɔːriən] adj. ZOOL. Saurio, ria.
— N. ZOOL. Saurio, *m.*
sausage [ˈsɔsidʒ] n. CULIN. Embutido, *m.*, salchicha, *f.* (for cooking): *pork sausage*, salchicha de carne de cerdo. || Salchichón, *m.* (cured).
sausage meat [—miːt] n. CULIN. Carne (*f.*) de salchicha.
sausage roll [—rəul] n. CULIN. Empanadilla (*f.*) de salchicha.
sauté [ˈsəutei] adj. CULIN. Salteado, da.
sauté [ˈsəutei] v. tr. CULIN. Saltear.
savable [seivəbl] adj. Salvable.
savage [ˈsævidʒ] adj. Salvaje (primitive, wild): *savage tribe, land*, tribu, tierra salvaje. || Feroz (ferocious): *savage animal*, animal feroz. || Cruel (cruel). || Violento, ta (attack). || Violento, ta; acerbo, ba (criticism, etc.). || FAM. Rabioso, sa (angry).
— N. Salvaje, *m.* & *f.*
savage [ˈsævidʒ] v. tr. Embestir (to attack). || Lacerar (to lacerate).
savageness [—nis] or **savagery** [—əri] n. Salvajismo, *m.*: *still in a state of complete savagery*, todavía en un estado de completo salvajismo. || Salvajada, *f.* (savage act). || Ferocidad, *f.* (of an animal). || Crueldad, *f.* (of a tyrant). || Violencia, *f.* (of an attack, criticism, etc.).
savanna or **savannah** [səˈvænə] n. Sabana, *f.*

savant [ˈsævənt] n. Sabio, *m.*, erudito, *m.*
save [seiv] n. SP. Parada, *f.* (in football).
— Prep. Salvo, excepto: *all his children save one are married*, todos sus hijos, salvo uno, están casados. || *Save for*, fuera de: *he is penniless save for a few shares*, no tiene dinero fuera de unas cuantas acciones; si no fuese por: *he would do it save for his position*, lo haría si no fuese por su posición.
— Conj. A no ser que. || *Save that*, excepto que: *I know nothing about him save that he is a foreigner*, no sé nada de él excepto que es extranjero.
save [seiv] v. tr. Salvar: *to save s.o. from danger*, salvar a alguien del peligro; *to save s.o. from drowning*, salvar a alguien que se está ahogando. || Evitar (to avoid): *we shall save a lot of trouble if we catch the bus*, evitaremos muchas molestias si cogemos el autobús. || Ganar, ahorrarse (time, distance): *you can save ten minutes if you catch the underground*, se puede ahorrar diez minutos si coge el metro. || Ahorrar (money, electricity, gas, etc.): *put out the fire to save coal*, apaga el fuego para ahorrar carbón. || Proteger (to protect): *these covers will save the chairs*, estas fundas protegerán los sillones. || Guardar (to keep for later): *to save the best till the end*, guardar lo mejor para lo último; *I'll save you a seat*, te guardaré un asiento. || Coleccionar (to collect). || SP. Parar (a goalkeeper). || — FIG. *A stitch in time saves nine*, no dejes para mañana lo que puedes hacer hoy. || *God save the Queen!*, ¡Dios guarde a la Reina! || FAM. *Save it!*, ¡déjalo! || *To save appearances* o *face*, salvar las apariencias. || *To save one's soul*, salvar el alma. || *To save one's strength* o *to save o.s.*, escatimar sus fuerzas, reservarse. || *To save the day* o *the situation*, salvar la situación. || *You might as well save your breath, she isn't listening*, no gastes saliva en balde ya que no está escuchando.
— V. intr. Ahorrar. || *To save up*, ahorrar: *I am saving up for a house*, estoy ahorrando para comprar una casa.
saveable [—əbl] adj. Salvable.
save-all [—ɔ:l] n. Apuracabos, *m. inv.*
saver [ˈseivə*] n. Salvador, ra. || Ahorrador, ra (of money).
saving [ˈseiviŋ] adj. Atenuante: *saving circumstances*, circunstancias atenuantes. || Económico, ca; ahorrador, ra; ahorrativo, va (not wasteful). || *Saving clause*, cláusula (*f.*) de salvaguardia.
— Prep. Salvo, excepto.
— N. Salvamento, *m.* (rescue). || Ahorro, *m.*, economía, *f.*: *saving of time*, ahorro de tiempo. || REL. Salvación, *f.* || JUR. Salvedad, *f.* || — Pl. Ahorros, *m.* (money saved).
savings account [ˈseiviŋzəˈkaunt] n. U. S. Cuenta (*f.*) de ahorros.
savings bank [ˈseiviŋzˈbæŋk] n. Caja (*f.*) de ahorros.
saviour (U. S. **savior**) [ˈseivjə*] n. Salvador, ra. || REL. *The Saviour*, El Salvador.
savoir faire [ˈsævwɑ:ˈfɛə*] n. Tacto, *m.*, habilidad, *f.* (tact). || Habilidad, *f.* (know-how). || Don (*m.*) de gente, mundo, *m.* (easy assurance).
savoir vivre [ˈsævwɑ:ˈvi:vr] n. Mundología, *f.*
savor [ˈseivə*] n. U. S. See SAVOUR.
savoriness [—rinis] n. U. S. See SAVOURINESS.
savorless [—lis] adj. U. S. See SAVOURLESS.
savory [ˈseivəri] n. BOT. Ajedrea, *f.* || — Pl. U. S. Tapas, *f.*
— Adj. U. S. See SAVOURY.
savour (U. S. **savor**) [ˈseivə*] n. Sabor, *m.*, gusto, *m.* (flavour, tastiness). || Aroma, *m.* (smell). || FIG. Sabor, *m.* (*of*, a): *it has a savour all of its own*, tiene un sabor muy propio.
savour (U. S. **savor**) [ˈseivə*] v. tr. Dar sabor a (to give taste to). || Saborear (to enjoy the taste of). || FIG. Saborear (to enjoy): *to savour a moment's rest*, saborear un momento de descanso. || FIG. *I don't savour the idea of going alone*, no me apetece la idea de ir solo.
— V. intr. Saber (*of*, a) [to taste]. || Oler (*of*, a) [to smell]. || FIG. Oler (to smack): *this savours of subterfuge*, esto huele a subterfugio.
savouriness (U. S. **savoriness**) [—rinis] n. Sabor (*m.*) agradable (pleasant taste). || Olor (*m.*) agradable (pleasant smell).
savourless (U. S. **savorless**) [—lis] adj. Soso, sa; insípido, da.
savoury (U. S. **savory**) [—ri] adj. Sabroso, sa (tasty). || Salado, da (salted): *I prefer savoury things*, me gustan más las cosas saladas. || FIG. *Not very savoury*, poco edificante (affair, film), malsano, na (district), sospechoso, sa (hotel).
— N. pl. Tapas, *f.* (food eaten with an apéritif, etc.).
savoy [səˈvɔi] n. BOT. Col (*f.*) rizada, col (*f.*) de Milán.
Savoy [səˈvɔi] pr. n. GEOGR. Saboya, *f.*
Savoyard [səˈvɔiɑ:d] adj./n. Saboyano, na.
savvy [ˈsævi] n. FAM. Entendederas, *f. pl.*
savvy [ˈsævi] v. tr. FAM. Chanelar, comprender.
saw [sɔ:] n. Sierra, *f.* (cutting instrument): *band* o *belt* o *ribbon saw*, sierra de cinta; *bow saw*, sierra de arco; *circular saw*, sierra circular; *compass saw*, sierra de contornar; *pit saw*, sierra abrazadera. || Serrucho, *m.* (handsaw). || ZOOL. Sierra, *f.* || Máxima, *f.* (maxim). || Refrán, *m.* (proverb). || Dicho, *m.* (saying).
saw* [sɔ:] v. tr. Serrar, aserrar (to cut). || FIG. Hender: *to saw the air*, hender el aire. || FAM. Rascar (a violin). | Tocar rascando el violín (a tune). || Dentar (in bookbinding).
— V. intr. Serrar, aserrar (to work with a saw). || Cortarse (to be sawn): *this wood saws easily*, esta madera se corta fácilmente. || FAM. *To saw on the fiddle*, rascar el violín.

— OBSERV. Pret. ***sawed;*** p. p. ***sawn, sawed.***

saw [sɔ:] pret. See SEE.
sawbones [—bəunz] n. FAM. Matasanos, *m. inv.*, cirujano, *m.*
sawbuck [—bʌk] n. U. S. Burro, *m.* (sawhorse). | Billete (*m.*) de diez dólares (bill).
sawdust [—dʌst] n. Serrín, *m.*, aserrín, *m.*
sawed-off [—dˈɔf] adj. U. S. *Sawed-off shotgun*, escopeta (*f.*) con los cañones cortados.
sawfish [—fiʃ] n. ZOOL. Pez (*m.*) sierra.
sawhorse [—hɔ:s] n. TECH. Burro, *m.*
sawlike [—laik] adj. En forma de sierra.
sawlog [—lɔg] n. Tronco (*m.*) serradizo.
sawmill [—mil] n. Aserradero *m.*, serrería, *f.*
sawn [sɔ:n] p. p. See SAW.
sawn-off [—ɔf] adj. See SAWED-OFF.
saw set [ˈsɔ:set] n. TECH. Triscador, *m.*
sawtooth [ˈsɔ:tu:θ] n. TECH. Diente (*m.*) de sierra.

— OBSERV. El plural de esta palabra es *sawteeth.*

sawtooth [ˈsɔ:tu:θ] or **saw-toothed** [—t] adj. Serrado, da.
sawyer [ˈsɔ:jə*] n. Aserrador, *m.*
sax [sæks] n. Hacha, *f.* (axe). || MUS. FAM. Saxófono, *m.*
Saxe [sæks] pr. n. Sajonia, *f.*
saxhorn [—hɔ:n] n. MUS. Bombardino, *m.*
saxifrage [ˈsæksifridʒ] n. BOT. Saxífraga, *f.*
Saxon [ˈsæksn] adj./n. Sajón, ona.
Saxony [—i] pr. n. GEOGR. Sajonia, *f.*
saxophone [ˈsæksəfəun] n. MUS. Saxofón, *m.*, saxófono, *m.*
saxophonist [sækˈsɔfənist] n. MUS. Saxofón, *m.*, saxófono, *m.* (person).
say [sei] n. *I had no say in it*, no me pidieron mi opinión. || *Let him have his say*, déjele hablar. || *She is the one with the say*, ella lleva la voz cantante. || *We have no say in the matter*, en este asunto no tenemos ni voz ni voto.
say* [sei] v. tr. Decir: *what did he say?*, ¿qué dijo?; *he said she was coming*, dijo que ella iba a venir; *do what he says*, haz lo que él dice; *let us say X is the unknown quantity*, digamos que X es la incógnita. || Expresar (to express). || Afirmar, declarar, decir (to affirm): *he said that he would not do as I asked*, declaró que no haría lo que yo le pedía. || Decir, rezar (a text, a proverb, a notice, etc.): *what does the sign say?*, ¿cómo reza el rótulo? || Decir (mass). | Rezar (a prayer). || Dar (a lesson). || Marcar (a clock, an instrument): *the clock says half past six*, el reloj marca las seis y media; *the thermometer says a hundred degrees*, el termómetro marca cien grados. || Opinar, pensar (to think): *what do you say to this idea?*, ¿qué piensa de esta idea? || Poner, decir (as an example or an estimate): *let us say about ten metres*, digamos unos diez metros; *half the population, say, will not vote*, pongamos que la mitad de la población no votará. || Suponer (to imagine): *say the king were to die*, supongamos que muriese el rey. || — *As they say*, como dicen. || *Enough said!*, ¡basta! || *He doesn't have much to say for himself*, es muy reservado. || *I say!*, ¡oiga!, ¡oye! (to draw attention), ¡ya lo creo! || *It goes without saying*, por supuesto, ni que decir tiene, huelga decir (needless to say), eso cae de su peso (it is obvious). || *It is said that...*, dicen que..., se dice que ... || *It's easier said than done*, es más fácil decirlo que hacerlo. || *No sooner said than done*, dicho y hecho. || *Not to say*, por no decir: *it is difficult, not to say impossible*, es difícil, por no decir imposible. || U. S. *Say*, oiga, oye: *say, what do you think of this?*, oye, ¿qué piensas de esto? || U. S. *Say!*, ¡vaya! (surprise). || *Say no more!*, ¡no me diga más! || *So to say*, por decirlo así. || *That is to say*, es decir, o sea. || *That film is said to be worth seeing*, dicen que merece la pena ver esa película. || *There is a lot to be said for not overeating*, existen múltiples argumentos en contra del exceso de comida. || *There is sth. to be said for his argument*, su argumento tiene cierto valor. || *There's no saying*, es imposible decir. || *They say that...*, dicen que..., se dice que ... || *To say good-bye to s.o.*, despedirse de alguien. || *To say good morning to s.o.*, dar los buenos días a alguien. || *To say grace*, bendecir la mesa. || *To say no*, decir que no. || *To say nothing of*, sin mencionar, sin hablar de, por no hablar de. || *To say no to*, rechazar (an offer, etc.). || *To say the word*, dar la orden. || *To say to o.s.*, decir para sí. || U. S. FAM. *To say uncle*, rendirse. || *To say yes to*, aceptar (an offer, etc.). || *What say you?*, ¿qué te parece? || *What would you say if we accepted?*, ¿qué te parece si aceptamos? || *When all is said and done*, al fin y al cabo. || *You can say that again!*, ¡dímelo a mí! || *You don't say!*, ¡no me diga! || *You may well say so*, tiene toda la razón. || *You said it!*, ¡dímelo a mí! || *Their conduct says a lot about them*, su conducta revela gran parte de su personalidad.

— OBSERV. Pret. & p. p. ***said.***

saying [—iŋ] n. Decir, *m.* (act of speaking): *saying and doing are two different things*, una cosa es decir y otra es hacer. || Decir, *m.*, refrán, *m.*, dicho, *m.* (a maxim): *it's an old saying*, es un viejo refrán. || Rumor, *m.* (rumour). || *As the saying goes...*, como dice or reza el refrán...

say-so [—səu] n. Fam. Afirmación, *f.* (assertion). || Opinión, *f.* (judgment). || Autoridad, *f.* (authority). || Aprobación, *f.*, visto (*m.*) bueno: *you need his say-so before you can go ahead*, necesita su visto bueno para seguir adelante.

scab [skæb] n. Med. Costra, *f.*, postilla, *f.* || Bot. Vet. Roña, *f.* (disease). || Fam. Esquirol, *m.* (blackleg). | Canalla, *m.* (scoundrel).

scab [skæb] v. intr. Med. Formar costra. || Fam. Sustituir a un huelguista.

scabbard [—əd] n. Vaina, *f.* (of a weapon).

scabbiness [—inis] n. Med. Estado (*m.*) costroso. || Fam. Mezquindad, *f.*

scabble [—l] v. tr. Desbastar.

scabby [—i] adj. Med. Costroso, sa. || Vet. Roñoso, sa. || Fam. Despreciable (contemptible). | Mezquino, na.

scabies [ˈskeibii:z] inv. n. Med. Sarna, *f.*

scabious [ˈskeibjəs] adj. Med. Sarnoso, sa.
— N. Bot. Escabiosa, *f.*

scabrous [ˈskeibrəs] adj. Escabroso, sa.

scads [skædz] pl. n. U. S. Fam. Montón, *m. sing.*, montones, *m.*: *scads of money*, un montón de dinero.

scaffold [ˈskæfəld] n. Andamio, *m.* (round a building, etc.). || Cadalso, *m.*, patíbulo, *m.* (for executing criminals). || Tarima, *f.* (platform). || Tribuna, *f.*

scaffold [ˈskæfəld] v. tr. Poner un andamio a.

scaffolding [—iŋ] n. Andamio, *m.*, andamiaje, *m.*

scagliola [skæˈljəulə] n. Escayola, *f.*

scalage [ˈskeilidʒ] n. U. S. Clasificación, *f.*

scalar [ˈskeilə*] adj. Math. Phys. Escalar.

scalawag [ˈskæləwæg] n. Fam. Canalla, *m.* (rogue). | Pícaro, ra (child).

scald [skɔ:ld] n. Escaldadura, *f.* (burn).

scald [skɔ:ld] v. tr. Escaldar (to burn): *to scald one's hand*, escaldarse la mano. || Culin. Escaldar. | Calentar (milk).

scalding [—iŋ] adj. Hirviendo, hirviente.
— N. Escaldado, *m.*

scale [skeil] n. Escala, *f.*: *measuring scale*, escala graduada; *centigrade scale*, escala centígrada; *sliding wage scale*, escala móvil salarial; *a large-scale map*, un mapa a gran escala. || Amplitud, *f.* (of a project, etc.). || Extensión, *f.* (of a disaster, damage, etc.). || Escala, *f.*, nivel, *m.*: *financial operations on an international scale*, operaciones financieras a escala internacional. || Platillo, *m.* (of a balance). || Mus. Escala, *f.*, gama, *f.*: *the scale of F sharp*, la escala de fa sostenido; *he is practising* o *running over his scales*, está haciendo gamas. || Escalafón, *m.* (hierarchy of employees). || Zool. Escama, *f.* (of fish). || Med. Escama, *f.* (on skin). | Sarro, *m.* (on teeth). || Incrustaciones, *f. pl.* (on a ship's hull, in a boiler, etc.). || Chem. Óxido, *m.* || — Pl. Balanza, *f. sing.* (balance). | Báscula, *f. sing.* (weighing machine). || Astr. Libra, *f. sing.* || — *On a large scale*, a gran escala. || *Out of scale*, desproporcionado, da. || *Scale drawing*, dibujo hecho a escala. || *Social scale*, jerarquía (*f.*) social. || *To draw sth. to scale*, dibujar algo a escala. || *To tip the scales at*, pesar más de: *it tips the scales at fifty kilogrammes*, pesa más de cincuenta kilos. || Fig. *To turn* o *to tip the scales*, inclinar el fiel de la balanza, decidir: *his past record turned the scales in his favour*, su historial decidió en su favor.

scale [skeil] v. tr. Escalar (to climb): *to scale a peak*, escalar un pico. || Subir (the stairs). || Trepar a (a tree). || Pesar (to weigh): *the fish scaled ten pounds*, el pescado pesaba diez libras. || Quitar las escamas a, escamar (fish). || Quitar el sarro a (teeth). || Depositar incrustaciones en (to cover with scales a boiler, etc.). || Tech. Desincrustar (to remove the scales from a boiler, etc.). | Decapar, desoxidar (a metal). || Clasificar (to classify). || Adaptar, ajustar (to adapt). || Dibujar a escala (a map). || — *To scale a stone on water*, lanzar una piedra para hacerla rebotar sobre el agua. || *To scale down*, reducir proporcionalmente (to reduce proportionally), reducir a escala (a map). || *To scale up*, aumentar proporcionalmente (to increase proportionally), aumentar a escala (a map).
— V. intr. Desconcharse (to form or to shed scales): *the wall is beginning to scale*, la pared esta empezando a desconcharse. || Zool. Descamarse, perder la escamas (fish). || Descamarse (skin). || Cubrirse de sarro (teeth). || Pesar (to weigh). || — *To scale off*, desconcharse (paint), descamarse (skin). || *To scale up*, cubrirse de incrustaciones (the hull of a ship, etc.).

scaleboard [—bɔ:d] n. Tabla (*f.*) delgada [de madera].

scaled [—d] adj. Escamoso, sa.

scalene [ˈskeili:n] adj. Math. Escaleno, na.

scaler [ˈskeilə*] n. Tech. Contador (*m.*) de impulsos. || Escalador, ra (climber). || Escamador, ra (person who scales fish).

scaling [ˈskeiliŋ] n. Escalada, *f.* (climbing). || Tech. Desincrustación, *f.* (of a boiler, etc.). | Decapado, *m.*, desoxidación, *f.* (of metals). || Ajuste, *m.* (adjustment).

scallawag [ˈskæləwæg] n. Canalla, *m.* (rogue). || Pícaro, ra (child).

scallion [ˈskæljən] n. Bot. Chalote, *m.*, escalonia, *f.* (shallot). | Cebollino, *m.* (young onion).

scallop [ˈskɔləp] n. Zool. Venera, *f.*, vieira, *f.* || Herald. Venera, *f.* || Festón, *m.* (as a decoration). || Culin. Escalope, *m.*

scallop [ˈskɔləp] v. tr. Culin. Guisar al gratén. || Festonear (to cut an edge into scallops).

scallywag [ˈskæliwæg] n. Canalla, *m.* (rogue). | Pícaro, ra (child).

scalp [skælp] n. Anat. Cuero (*m.*) cabelludo. || Escalpe, *m.*, escalpo, *m.* (Indian trophy). || Fig. *To clamour for s.o.'s scalp*, pedir la cabeza de alguien.

scalp [skælp] v. tr. Escalpar, quitar el cuero cabelludo a (Indians). || Fam. Pelar (barber). | Dar un palo a (to defeat). || U. S. Comm. Especular en (shares, etc.). | Dedicarse a la reventa de (theatre tickets, etc.).

scalpel [ˈskælpəl] n. Med. Escalpelo, *m.*

scalper [ˈskælpə*] n. U. S. Comm. Especulador, *m.* (on the stock market). || Revendedor (*m.*) de billetes de teatro.

scaly [ˈskeili] adj. Escamoso, sa (skin, fish). || Sarroso, sa (teeth). || Tech. Con incrustaciones (boiler, ship's hull, etc.). || Fam. Vil, mezquino, na (mean).

scaly anteater [—ˈæntˌi:tə*] n. Zool. Pangolín, *m.*

scamp [skæmp] n. Pícaro, ra.

scamp [skæmp] v. tr. Chapucear (a piece of work).

scamper [—ə*] n. Correteo, *m.*

scamper [—ə*] v. intr. Corretear. || Precipitarse, correr (to make a dash): *to scamper for shelter*, precipitarse hacia un refugio. || *To scamper away* o *off*, irse corriendo.

scan [skæn] v. tr. Escrutar, escudriñar (to scrutinize). || Recorrer con la mirada (to look round). || Echar un vistazo a (to glance at). || Hojear (a book). || Tech. Explorar (television, radar). || Escandir (in poetry). || *To scan the horizon*, otear el horizonte.
— V. intr. Estar bien medido: *this line does not scan*, este verso no está bien medido. || Tech. Explorar una superficie.

scandal [ˈskændl] n. Escándalo, *m.*: *political, financial scandal*, escándalo político, financiero; *to create a scandal*, formar un escándalo. || Chismorreo, *m.*, habladurías, *f. pl.* (gossiping). || Chismes, *m. pl.* (pieces of gossip): *they do nothing but talk scandal all day*, se pasan el día contando chismes. || Jur. Difamación, *f.* || *It's a scandal!*, qué escándalo!, ¡qué vergüenza!

scandalize [—aiz] v. tr. Escandalizar: *his behaviour scandalized the local population*, su conducta escandalizó a la gente del barrio. || *To be scandalized*, escandalizarse.

scandalmonger [—ˌmʌŋgə*] n. Chismoso, sa.

scandalous [ˈskændələs] adj. Escandaloso, sa; vergonzoso, sa (conduct, happening). || Jur. Difamatorio, ria.

Scandinavia [ˌskændiˈneivjə] pr. n. Escandinavia, *f.*

Scandinavian [—n] adj./n. Escandinavo, va.

scandium [ˈskændiəm] n. Chem. Escandio, *m.*

scanner [ˈskænə*] n. Escudriñador, ra (s.o. who scans). || Tech. Dispositivo (*m.*) explorador (television). | Antena (*f.*) giratoria (radar). | Med. Scanner, *m.*, tomógrafo, *m.*

scanning [—iŋ] n. Exploración, *f.*
— Adj. Explorador, ra: *scanning beam*, haz explorador.

scant [skænt] adj. Escaso, sa (measure, etc.). || Muy ligero (clothes). || Muy corto (dress). || — *To be scant of*, tener poco. || *To meet with scant success*, tener poco éxito.

scant [skænt] v. tr. Escatimar.

scantily [—ili] adv. Escasamente. || Muy ligeramente: *scantily dressed*, muy ligeramente vestido.

scantiness [—inis] n. Escasez, *f.*

scantlings [—liŋz] pl. n. Escantillones, *m.*

scanty [—i] adj. Escaso, sa: *a scanty knowledge of Latin*, unos conocimientos escasos de latín. || Escaso, sa; muy ligero, ra: *scanty clothes*, ropa escasa. || Muy corto, ta: *she was wearing a scanty skirt*, llevaba una falda muy corta. || *Scanty meal*, comida parca.

scape [skeip] n. Bot. Bohordo, *m.* (stem). || Zool. Cañón, *m.* (of a feather). || Arch. Fuste, *m.*

scapegoat [—gəut] n. Fig. Cabeza (*f.*) de turco, víctima (*f.*) propiciatoria. || Rel. Chivo (*m.*) expiatorio.

scapegrace [—greis] n. Granuja, *m.*, canalla, *m.* (unprincipled person). || Pícaro, ra; granujilla, *m.* & *f.* (child).

scape wheel [—wi:l] n. Rueda (*f.*) dentada (of a clock).

scaphoid [ˈskæfɔid] adj. Anat. Escafoides.
— N. Anat. Escafoides, *m.*

scapula [ˈskæpjulə] n. Anat. Omóplato, *m.*, escápula, *f.* (shoulder blade). || Zool. Escápula, *f.*
— Observ. El plural de la palabra inglesa es *scapulae* o *scapulas*.

scapular [ˈskæpjulə*] n. Anat. Zool. Escápula, *f.* (scapula). | Pluma (*f.*) escapular (feather). || Rel. Escapulario, *m.*
— Adj. Anat. Zool. Escapular: *scapular feather*, pluma escapular.

scapulary [—ri] n. Rel. Escapulario, *m.*

scar [skα:*] n. Cicatriz, *f.*: *a scar on one's leg*, una cicatriz en la pierna. || Cicatriz, *f.*, señal, *f.*, chirlo, *m.*, costurón, *m.* (on the face). || Fig. Cicatriz, *f.* || Geogr. Farallón, *m.*, roca (*f.*) escarpada.

scar [skα:*] v. tr. Marcar con una cicatriz (to leave a scar on). || Marcar con un chirlo, señalar (the face). || Fig. Marcar: *the experience scarred him for life*,

aquella experiencia le marcó para toda la vida. || *The doors are scarred with bullet marks*, en las puertas se ven señales de balas.
— V. intr. Cicatrizar, cicatrizarse.
scarab [ˈskærəb] n. ZOOL. Escarabajo, *m.*
scarabaeus [ˌskærəˈbi:əs] n. ZOOL. Escarabajo, *m.*
— OBSERV. El plural de la palabra inglesa es *scarabeuses* o *scarabei*.
scarce [skɛəs] adj. Escaso, sa (in short supply, barely sufficient): *medicines were scarce after the war*, después de la guerra las medicinas eran escasas. || Raro, ra; poco común (rare): *a scarce species of plant*, una especie de planta poco común. || — *Blacksmiths are now scarce*, los herreros escasean ahora, los herreros ya se ven muy poco. || *To become scarce*, escasear. || FIG. *To make o.s. scarce*, esfumarse (to go away), no aparecer [por un sitio] (to stay away).
— Adv. Apenas (scarcely).
scarcely [—li] adv. Apenas: *he is scarcely twenty-one*, apenas tiene veintiún años; *I had scarcely arrived when they served me with a meal*, apenas había llegado cuando me sirvieron una comida. || Seguramente no (certainly not). || — *He can scarcely have finished already*, es muy difícil que haya terminado ya. || *He will scarcely come at this hour*, es poco probable que venga a estas horas. || *I scarcely believe it*, no lo creo. || *Scarcely anybody*, casi nadie. || *Scarcely ever*, casi nunca.
scarcement [—mənt] n. Saliente, *m.*
scarceness [—nis] or **scarcity** [—iti] n. Escasez, *f.*, falta, *f.*: *scarcity of money*, escasez de dinero; *scarcity of labour*, falta de mano de obra. || Rareza, *f.*, poca frecuencia, *f.* (uncommonness).
scare [skɛə*] n. Pánico, *m.*: *to create a scare*, sembrar el pánico. || Susto, *m.*: *what a scare you gave me!*, ¡qué susto me has dado! || Alarma, *f.*: *the epidemic created a great scare*, la epidemia produjo gran alarma. || *The radioactive fallout scare produced by the explosion*, el miedo a las lluvias radiactivas producido por la explosión.
scare [skɛə*] v. tr. Asustar, espantar: *the sudden noise scared her*, el ruido repentino le asustó. || Dar miedo: *old houses scare me*, las casas viejas me dan miedo; *aircraft scare me to death* o *out of my wits*, los aviones me dan un miedo espantoso. || — FAM. *To be scared stiff*, estar muerto de miedo, tener un miedo espantoso. || *To scare away* o *off*, ahuyentar, espantar. || *To scare s.o. into doing sth.*, intimidar a alguien para que haga algo. || U. S. FAM. *To scare up*, juntar, reunir.
— V. intr. Asustarse.
scarecrow [—krəu] n. Espantapájaros, *m. inv.*, espantajo, *m.* || FIG. Esperpento, *m.*, espantajo, *m.* (ugly person).
scarehead [—hed] n. U. S. FAM. Titulares (*m. pl.*) sensacionalistas.
scaremonger [—ˌmʌŋgə*] n. Alarmista, *m.* & *f.*
scarf [skɑ:f] n. Bufanda, *f.* (woollen). || Pañuelo, *m.* (light neckerchief or headwear). || Fular, *m.* (of silk). || Corte, *m.*, canal, *f.* (of a whale). || TECH. Empalme, *m.* || U. S. Tapete, *m.* (table cover). || U. S. MIL. Banda, *f.* (sash).
— OBSERV. El plural de *scarf*, cuando significa "bufanda," "pañuelo", "fular", "tapete" o "banda", es *scarves* o *scarfs*. En los demás casos es *scarfs* solamente.
scarf [skɑ:f] v. tr. TECH. Empalmar, ensamblar. || Descuartizar (a whale).
scarfing [—iŋ] n. TECH. Ensambladura, *f.*
scarfskin [—ˌskin] n. Epidermis, *f. inv.*
scarification [ˌskɛərifiˈkeiʃən] n. Escarificación, *f.*
scarificator [ˈskɛərifikeitə*] n. Escarificador, *m.*
scarifier [ˈskɛərifaiə*] n. Escarificador, *m.*
scarify [ˈskɛərifai] v. tr. MED. AGR. Escarificar. || FIG. Desollar (by criticism).
scarlatina [ˌskɑ:ləˈti:nə] n. MED. Escarlatina, *f.*
scarlet [ˈskɑ:lit] adj. Escarlata: *scarlet dress*, vestido escarlata. || Colorado, da: *his face turned scarlet*, su cara se puso colorada. || — MED. *Scarlet fever*, escarlatina, *f.* || *Scarlet woman*, prostituta, *f.* || BOT. *Scarlet pimpernel*, murajes, *m. pl.* | *Scarlet runner*, judía (*f.*) escarlata.
— N. Escarlata, *f.* (colour, cloth). || REL. Púrpura, *f.*
scarp [skɑ:p] n. GEOL. MIL. Escarpa, *f.*
scarp [skɑ:p] v. tr. Escarpar.
scarves [skɑ:vz] pl. n. See SCARF.
scary [ˈskɛəri] adj. FAM. Asustadizo, za (easily frightened). | Espantoso, sa; pavoroso, sa (frightening). || De miedo (film).
scat [skæt] v. intr. Largarse (to go away).
scathe [skeið] v. tr. Fustigar, vituperar (to criticize severely). || Perjudicar (to harm).
scatheless [—lis] adj. Ileso, sa.
scathing [—iŋ] adj. Mordaz, cáustico, ca.
scatological [ˌskætəˈlɔdʒikəl] adj. Escatológico, ca.
scatology [skəˈtɔlədʒi] n. Escatología, *f.*
scatter [ˈskætə*] n. PHYS. Dispersión, *f.* || *There was no more than a scatter of people there*, había solamente unas pocas personas.
scatter [skætə*] v. tr. Esparcir, desparramar: *wreckage was scattered all over the field*, los restos estaban esparcidos por todo el campo; *she slipped and scattered her shopping over the floor*, resbaló y desparramó sus compras por el suelo. || Salpicar: *she scatters her novels with Spanish words*, salpica sus novelas con palabras españolas. || Dispersar: *the dog scattered the sheep*, el perro dispersó las ovejas. || Disipar (to dispel). || Sembrar al voleo (seed). || PHYS. Dispersar.
— V. intr. Dispersarse: *the crowd scattered when the police charged*, la multitud se dispersó cuando la policía atacó. || Desparramarse: *the family has scattered over the whole world*, la familia se ha desparramado por el mundo entero.
scatterbrain [—brein] n. Cabeza (*f.*) de chorlito.
scatterbrained [—breind] adj. Ligero de cascos, atolondrado, da.
scattered [ˈskætəd] adj. Disperso, sa; desparramado, da: *scattered villages*, pueblos dispersos. || Intermitente: *scattered showers*, chubascos intermitentes. || Diseminado, da: *scattered army*, ejército diseminado. || — *A meadow scattered with flowers*, una pradera salpicada de flores. || *The floor is scattered with toys*, hay juguetes esparcidos por el suelo.
scattering [ˈskætəriŋ] n. Dispersión, *f.*, esparcimiento, *m.* || *A scattering of*, un pequeño número de, unos pocos, unos cuantos (a few).
scavenge [ˈskævindʒ] v. tr. Recoger (rubbish). || Barrer (streets). || Buscar entre (to search amongst). || Revolver: *the tramp scavenged the dustbin for food*, el vagabundo revolvió el cubo de la basura buscando comida. || TECH. Expulsar (gases). | Limpiar (metal).
— V. intr. Recoger la basura (to remove waste). || Buscar comida (to search for food).
scavenger [—ə*] n. Basurero, *m.* (refuse collector). || Barrendero, *m.* (road sweeper). || ZOOL. Animal (*m.*) or insecto (*m.*) que se alimenta de carroña.
scavenger beetle [—əˌbi:tl] n. ZOOL. Necróforo, *m.*
scavengery [—ri] or **scavenging** [—iŋ] n. Recogida (*f.*) de la basura (rubbish collection). || Barrido, *m.* (of streets). || Búsqueda (*f.*) de comida (searching for food). || Búsqueda (*f.*) de objetos útiles (amongst rubbish). || TECH. Expulsión, *f.* (of gases).
scenario [siˈnɑ:riəu] n. THEATR. Argumento, *m.* || CINEM. Guión, *m.*
scenarist [ˈsi:nərist] n. CINEM. Guionista, *m.* & *f.*
scene [si:n] n. CINEM. THEATR. Escena, *f.* (division of a play, film): *Act 1, Scene 2*, primer acto, segunda escena; *the big scene*, la escena principal; *a love scene*, una escena de amor. | Escena, *f.* (place where the action is set): *the scene is Venise*, la escena representa Venecia; *the scene changes*, cambia la escena. | Decorado, *m.* (scenery). || THEATR. Escenario, *m.* (stage). || Panorama, *m.*, vista, *f.*, perspectiva, *f.* (view): *the scene from the window is magnificent*, la vista desde la ventana es espléndida. || Paisaje, *m.* (landscape): *wooded scene*, paisaje arbolado. || FIG. Escenario, *m.*, lugar, *m.* (place where sth. takes place): *the scene of the disaster*, el lugar del desastre; *the scene of the crime*, el escenario del crimen. | Teatro, *m.*: *the scene of the war*, el teatro de la guerra; *the scene of operations*, el teatro de operaciones. | Panorama, *m.* (situation): *the present political scene*, el panorama político actual. || Escándalo, *m.*, escena, *f.* (fuss): *he made an awful scene in the restaurant*, armó un escándalo espantoso en el restaurante. || Riña, *f.*, pelea, *f.*, escena, *f.* (argument): *he had a scene with his wife in front of everybody*, tuvo una riña con su mujer delante de todo el mundo. || — FIG. *Behind the scenes*, entre bastidores. | *The scene was set for a tragedy*, todo estaba preparado para la tragedia. | *To come on the scene*, aparecer. | *To disappear from the scene*, desaparecer. | *To paint a scene of gloom*, crear un mundo de tristeza (a writer). || RAD. *To set the scene*, describir el escenario (before an event). || FIG. *You need a change of scene*, necesita cambiar de aire.
scenery [—əri] n. Paisaje, *m.* (landscape): *a town set in mountain scenery*, un pueblo situado en un paisaje montañoso. || Paisajes, *m. pl.* (landscapes): *there is a lot of beautiful scenery in Spain*, en España hay muchos paisajes hermosos. || THEATR. Decorado, *m.* (painted background).
sceneshifter [—ˌʃiftə*] n. THEATR. Tramoyista, *m.* (stagehand).
scenic [ˈsi:nik] or **scenical** [—əl] adj. Escénico, ca (of stage scenery). || Dramático, ca (dramatic). || Del paisaje (of the countryside): *scenic beauty*, belleza del paisaje. || Pintoresco, ca (picturesque). || FIG. Espectacular.
scenic railway [— reilwei] n. Montaña (*f.*) rusa (big dipper). || Tren (*m.*) de recreo (miniature railway).
scenographer [si:ˈnɔgrəfə*] n. Escenógrafo, fa.
scenographic [ˌsi:nəˈgræfik] or **scenographical** [ˌsi:nəˈgræfikəl] adj. Escenográfico, ca.
scenography [si:ˈnɔgrəfi] n. Escenografía, *f.*
scent [sent] n. Olor, *m.* (smell). || Perfume, *m.*, fragancia, *f.* (pleasing smell): *the scent of violets*, el perfume de las violetas. || Aroma, *m.* (of food). || Perfume, *m.* (perfume): *a bottle of scent*, un frasco de perfume. || Rastro, *m.* (in hunting). || FIG. Pista, *f.* (in crime detection). || Olfato, *m.* (sense of smell): *to have no scent*, carecer de olfato, no tener olfato. || — FIG. *To lose the scent*, perder la pista. | *To pick up the scent*, encontrar la pista. | *To throw off the scent*, despistar.
scent [sent] v. tr. Olfatear, oler: *the dog scented the rabbit*, el perro olfateó el conejo. || FIG. Oler, presentir: *to scent danger*, presentir el peligro. || Perfumar:

to scent soap, perfumar el jabón; *the roses scented the air*, las rosas perfumaban el aire.

— V. intr. Olfatear.

scented [—id] adj. Fragante: *a scented garden, flower*, un jardín, una flor fragante. || Perfumado, da: *she is always heavily scented*, siempre va muy perfumada. || — *A keen-scented dog*, un perro con buen olfato. || *The room was scented with lavender*, el cuarto olía a lavanda.

scepsis [ˈskepsis] n. PHIL. Escepticismo, *m.*

scepter [ˈseptə*] n. U. S. Cetro, *m.*

sceptic [ˈskeptik] n. Escéptico, ca.

sceptical [—əl] adj. Escéptico, ca: *to be sceptical about sth.*, ser escéptico acerca de algo.

scepticism [ˈskeptisizəm] n. Escepticismo, *m.*

sceptre [ˈseptə*] n. Cetro, *m.*

schedule [ˈʃedju:l; U. S. ˈskedju:l] n. Lista, *f.*, inventario, *m.* (list). || Apéndice, *m.* (appendix). || Programa, *m.*: *my schedule for today*, mi programa para hoy. || Calendario, *m.* (of meetings). || Horario, *m.* (timetable): *train schedule*, horario de trenes. || — *The train arrived on schedule*, el tren llegó a la hora. || *The train is behind schedule*, el tren tiene *or* lleva retraso. || *The work is behind schedule*, el trabajo está atrasado. || *The work is up to schedule* or *is going according to schedule*, el trabajo no tiene retraso, el trabajo se desarrolla como está previsto. || *Work schedule*, plan (*m.*) de trabajo.

schedule [ˈʃedju:l; U. S. ˈskedju:l] v. tr. Catalogar (to make a list of). || Registrar (to put on a register): *this building is scheduled as being of historic interest*, este edificio está registrado como monumento histórico. || Programar (to plan). || Fijar el horario de (trains, aeroplanes, etc.). || Fijar: *their departure was scheduled for five o'clock*, se fijó su salida para las cinco. || *The concert is scheduled for eight o'clock* o *is scheduled to start at eight o'clock*, el concierto está previsto para las ocho.

Scheldt [skelt] pr. n. GEOGR. Escalda, *m.*

schema [ˈski:mə] n. Esquema, *m.* (outline, diagram). || Proyecto, *m.*, plan, *m.* (plan). || PHIL. Esquema, *m.*

— OBSERV. El plural de esta palabra es *schemata*.

schematic [skiˈmætik] adj. Esquemático, ca.

schematism [ˈskimətizəm] n. Esquematismo, *m.*

schematize [ˈskiməˌtaiz] v. tr. Esquematizar.

scheme [ski:m] n. Combinación, *f.*: *colour scheme*, combinación de colores. || Esquema, *m.* (schema). || Programa, *m.* (program). || Proyecto, *m.* (plan): *the airport scheme*, el proyecto de aeropuerto. || Idea, *f.*: *I've just thought of a marvellous scheme*, acabo de tener una idea genial. || Intriga, *f.* (plot). || Ardid, *m.*, estratagema, *f.* (ruse): *it is a scheme to get him here*, es una estratagema para que venga. || Sistema, *m.*: *a marking scheme*, un sistema de notas; *a firm's pension scheme*, el sistema de pensión de una empresa.

scheme [ski:m] v. tr. Proyectar (to plan). || Tramar (to plot).

— V. intr. Hacer planes *or* proyectos (to make plans). || Intrigar, conspirar (to plot).

schemer [—ə*] n. Intrigante, *m.* & *f.*, maquinador, ra (plotter).

scheming [—iŋ] adj. Intrigante.

scherzo [ˈskɛətsəu] n. MUS. Scherzo, *m.*

schilling [ˈʃiliŋ] n. Schilling, *m.* (Austrian coin).

schism [ˈsizəm] n. Cisma, *m.*

schismatic [sizˈmætik] adj./n. Cismático, ca.

schismatical [—əl] adj. Cismático, ca.

schist [ʃist] n. MIN. Esquisto, *m.*

schistose [ˈʃistəus] or **schistous** [ˈʃistəs] adj. MIN. Esquistoso, sa.

schizo [ˈskitsəu] adj./n. FAM. Esquizofrénico, ca.

schizophrene [ˌskitsəuˈfri:n] n. MED. Esquizofrénico, ca.

schizophrenia [ˌskitsəuˈfri:njə] n. MED. Esquizofrenia, *f.*

schizophrenic [ˌskitsəuˈfrenik] adj./n. MED. Esquizofrénico, ca.

schmaltz [ʃmɔlts] n. FAM. Música (*f.*) sentimental (music). | Sentimentalismo (*m.*) excesivo, sensiblería, *f.* (extreme sentimentality).

schmaltzy [—i] adj. FAM. Sentimentaloide.

schnapps [ʃnæps] n. Aguardiente, *m.*

schnorkel [ˈʃnɔ:kəl] n. MAR. Esnórquel, *m.* (of a submarine). || Tubo (*m.*) de respiración (swimmer's).

scholar [ˈskɔlə*] n. Erudito, ta; sabio, bia (learned person). || Becario, ria (scholarship holder). || Alumno, na (pupil). || — *Classical scholar*, humanista, *m.* & *f.* || *Greek scholar*, helenista, *m.* & *f.* || *Latin scholar*, latinista, *m.* & *f.*

scholarly [—li] adj. Erudito, ta.

scholarship [—ʃip] n. Saber, *m.*, erudición, *f.* (learning). || Beca, *f.* (grant): *to be on a scholarship*, tener una beca; *to win a scholarship*, conseguir una beca. || *Scholarship holder*, becario, ria.

scholastic [skəˈlæstik] adj. PHIL. Escolástico, ca (relative to scholasticism). || Escolar: *scholastic year*, año escolar. || Docente (profession). || FIG. Pedante.

— N. PHIL. Escolástico, *m.*

scholasticism [skəˈlæstisizəm] n. PHIL. Escolástica, *f.*, escolasticismo, *m.* || FIG. Escolasticismo, *m.*

scholium [ˈskəuljəm] n. Escolio, *m.*

— OBSERV. El plural de la palabra inglesa es *scholia*.

school [sku:l] n. Escuela, *f.* (in general). || Escuela, *f.* (state primary). || Colegio, *m.* (private primary or secondary). || Instituto, *m.* (state secondary). || Academia, *f.*, escuela, *f.* (specialized): *language school*, academia de idiomas; *drama school*, academia de arte dramático. || Clase, *f.*: *to miss school*, faltar a clase; *to go to school*, ir a clase; *there will be no school today*, hoy no hay clase. || Alumnado, *m.*, alumnos, *m. pl.*: *the school will have a holiday next week*, los alumnos estarán de vacaciones la semana que viene. || U. S. Universidad, *f.*: *to be in school*, ir a la universidad. || Facultad, *f.* (of a university): *School of Medicine*, facultad de medicina. || Escuela, *f.* (group): *the Impressionist school*, la escuela impresionista; *school of Aristotle*, escuela aristotélica. || Educación, *f.*: *he was brought up in a hard school*, recibió una educación severa. || Instrucción, *f.*, educación, *f.*, formación, *f.* (formal education): *he had only three years of school*, tuvo una formación que sólo duró tres años. || MUS. Método, *m.*, manual, *m.* || Banco, *m.* (of fish). || — *Comprehensive school*, instituto de segunda enseñanza. || *Driving school*, autoescuela, *f.* || *Grammar school*, instituto de segunda enseñanza (in Great Britain), escuela primaria (in U. S.). || U. S. *High school*, instituto de segunda enseñanza. || *Infant school*, colegio *or* escuela de párvulos. || U. S. *Junior high school*, instituto de bachillerato elemental. || *Lower school*, primero y segundo de bachillerato. || *Middle school*, tercero y cuarto de bachillerato. || *Military school*, academia militar. || *Night school*, escuela nocturna. || *Of the old school*, de la vieja escuela. || *Prep* o *preparatory school*, escuela preparatoria. || *Primary school*, escuela primaria *or* de primera enseñanza. || *Public school*, colegio privado de segunda enseñanza (in Great Britain), instituto (in the U.S.A.). || *School leaving age*, edad (*f.*) en que se acaba la escolaridad obligatoria. || *School of thought*, escuela filosófica (in philosophy), opinión, *f.*, idea, *f.*: *there are several schools of thought as to how to make tea*, existen varias opiniones sobre la manera de hacer el té. || *Secondary modern school*, instituto de segunda enseñanza [centrado en estudios prácticos]. || *Summer school*, cursos (*m. pl.*) de verano. || *Sunday school*, catequesis, *f.* || *Technical school*, instituto laboral. || U. S. *To teach school*, ser profesor, dar clases.

— Adj. Escolar: *school age*, edad escolar; *school curriculum*, programa escolar; *school year*, año escolar.

school [sku:l] v. tr. Instruir, educar, formar (to educate s.o.). || Enseñar: *to school s.o. to do sth.*, enseñar a alguien a hacer algo. || Ejercitar (to train). || Amaestrar (animal). || Disciplinar (one's temper). || Dominar (one's feelings). || *To school o.s. to patience*, aprender a ser paciente.

— V. intr. Nadar en bancos.

schoolbook [—buk] n. Libro (*m.*) escolar, libro (*m.*) de texto.

schoolboy [—bɔi] n. Alumno, *m.*, colegial, *m.*

schoolchild [—ˌtʃaild] n. Alumno, *m.*, alumna, *f.*

— OBSERV. El plural es *schoolchildren*.

schooldays [—deiz] pl. n. Años (*m.*) *or* tiempos (*m.*) de colegio: *in my schooldays*, en mis tiempos de colegio.

schoolfellow [—ˌfeləu] n. Compañero, ra [de clase].

schoolgirl [—gə:l] n. Alumna, *f.*, colegiala, *f.* || *Schoolgirl complexion*, tez (*f.*) de colegiala.

schoolhouse [—haus] n. Colegio, *m.*, escuela, *f.*

schooling [—iŋ] n. Instrucción, *f.*, educación, *f.*, enseñanza, *f.* (formal education). || Estudios, *m. pl.*: *she paid for her brother's schooling*, pagó los estudios de su hermano. || *Compulsory schooling*, escolaridad obligatoria.

schoolma'am [—ˈmæəm] or **schoolmarm** [—mɑ:m] n. U. S. Profesora, *f.* (in a secondary school). | Maestra, *f.* (in a primary school).

schoolman [—mən] n. PHIL. Escolástico, *m.*

— OBSERV. El plural de esta palabra es *schoolmen*.

schoolmaster [—ˌmɑ:stə*] n. Profesor, *m.* (in a secondary school). || Maestro, *m.* (in a primary school).

schoolmate [—meit] n. Compañero, ra [de clase].

schoolmistress [—ˌmistris] n. Profesora, *f.* (in a secondary school). || Maestra, *f.* (in a primary school).

schoolroom [—rum] n. Clase, *f.*, aula, *f.*, sala (*f.*) de clase.

school ship [—ʃip] n. Buque (*m.*) escuela.

schoolteacher [—ˌti:tʃə*] n. Profesor, ra (in a secondary school). || Maestro, tra (in a primary school).

schoolyard [—jɑ:d] n. Patio (*m.*) de recreo.

schooner [ˈsku:nə*] n. MAR. Goleta, *f.* || U. S. Jarra, *f.* (of beer).

schooner-rigged [—ˌrigd] adj. MAR. De velas cangrejas.

schorl [ʃɔ:l] n. MIN. Turmalina (*f.*) negra.

schottische [ʃɔˈti:ʃ] n. Chotis, *m.*

schuss [ʃus] n. SP. Recta, *f.*

schuss [ʃus] v. intr. SP. Esquiar rápidamente en línea recta.

sciatic [saiˈætik] adj. Ciático, ca.

sciatica [—ə] n. MED. Ciática, *f.*

science [ˈsaiəns] n. Ciencia, *f.*: *the advances of science*, los adelantos de la ciencia; *the physical sciences*, las ciencias físicas. || Arte, *f.*: *the science of fencing*, el arte de la esgrima. || — REL. *Christian science*, ciencia

cristiana. || *Social science*, sociología, *f.* || *To blind s.o. with science*, deslumbrar a uno con sus conocimientos.
science fiction [—ˊfikʃən] n. Ciencia (*f.*) ficción.
scientific [ˌsaiənˊtifik] adj. Científico, ca: *scientific principles*, principios científicos; *scientific management*, organización científica del trabajo. || FIG. Estudiado, da (cruelty). || SP. Que tiene mucha técnica.
scientifically [—əli] adv. Científicamente.
scientist [ˊsaiəntist] n. Científico, ca.
scilicet [ˊsailiset] adv. A saber, es decir.
scilla [ˊsilə] n. BOT. Cebolla (*f.*) albarrana.
Scilly Isles [ˊsiliailz] pl. pr. n. GEOGR. Islas (*f.*) Sorlingas.
scimitar [ˊsimitə*] n. Cimitarra, *f.*
scintilla [sinˊtilə] n. Centella, *f.* (light trace). || Chispa, *f.*, centella, *f.* (spark).
scintillant [ˊsintilənt] adj. See SCINTILLATING.
scintillate [ˊsintileit] v. intr. Centellear (to twinkle). || Titilar (stars). || Destellar, chispear (to sparkle). || FIG. Brillar.
scintillating [—iŋ] adj. Titilante (star). || Centelleante, relumbrante (dazzling). || FIG. Chispeante (wit). | Brillante (style, conversation, etc.).
scintillation [ˌsintiˊleiʃən] n. Centelleo, *m.* (twinkling). || Titilación, *f.* (of stars). || FIG. Viveza, *f.* (wit). || PHYS. Centelleo, *m.*: *scintillation counter*, contador de centelleo.
sciolism [ˊsaiəulizəm] n. Falsa erudición, *f.*
sciolist [ˊsaiəulist] n. Erudito (*m.*) a la violeta, falso erudito, *m.*, falsa erudita, *f.*
sciolistic [ˊsaiəˊlistik] adj. Falsamente erudito, ta.
scion [ˊsaiən] n. AGR. Retoño, *m.*, renuevo, *m.* (bud). | Púa, *f.*, injerto, *m.*, esqueje, *m.* (shoot used for grafting). || FIG. Vástago, *m.*, descendiente, *m.* (descendant).
Scipio [ˊskipiəu] pr. n. HIST. Escipión, *m.*: *Scipio Africanus*, Escipión el Africano.
scissile [ˊsisil] adj. Hendible, escindible.
scission [ˊsiʒən] n. Escisión, *f.*, corte, *m.* (cut, cutting). || Escisión, *f.*, división, *f.* (division).
scissor [ˊsizə] v. tr. Cortar con tijeras.
scissors [ˊsizəz] pl. n. Tijeras, *f.* (tool). || SP. Salto (*m.*) de tijera (in gymnastics). | Tijera, *f.*, tijereta, *f.* (in wrestling). || *A pair of scissors*, unas tijeras.
scissors jump [—dʒʌmp] n. SP. Salto (*m.*) de tijera.
scissors kick [—kik] n. SP. Tijereta, *f.*
sclera [ˊskliːərə] n. ANAT. Esclerótica, *f.*
sclerosed [skliːəˊrəust] adj. MED. Escleroso, sa.
sclerosis [skliəˊrəusis] n. MED. Esclerosis, *f.*

— OBSERV. El plural de *sclerosis* es *scleroses*.

sclerotic [skliəˊrɔtik] adj. MED. Escleroso, sa.
— N. ANAT. Esclerótica, *f.* (sclera).
sclerous [ˊskliːərəs] adj. Escleroso, sa.
scoff [skɔf] n. Mofa, *f.*, burla, *f.*: *he said it with a scoff*, lo dijo con mofa. || Hazmerreír, *m.* (laughing-stock). || FAM. Comida, *f.* (meal). || FAM. *To have a good scoff*, pegarse una comilona.
scoff [skɔf] v. tr. FAM. Tragarse, zamparse (food).
— V. intr. Mofarse, burlarse: *to scoff at superstition*, mofarse de la superstición. || *That's not to be scoffed at*, no es para tomarlo a broma.
scoffer [—ə*] n. Mofador, ra; burlón, ona.
scoffing [—iŋ] n. Mofa, *f.*, burla, *f.*, escarnio, *m.* || FAM. Comer, *m.*, jamancia, *f.* (eating).
scold [skəuld] n. Regañona, *f.*, gruñona, *f.* (woman). || Reprensión, *f.*, regaño, *m.*, reprimenda, *f.* (scolding).
scold [skəuld] v. tr. Regañar, reñir: *to scold one's children*, regañar a los niños.
— V. intr. Chillar, gritar.
scolding [—iŋ] n. Reprimenda, *f.*, regaño, *m.*, reprensión, *f.* || *To give s.o. a severe scolding*, regañar severamente a alguien.
scoliosis [ˌskɔliˊəusis] n. MED. Escoliosis, *f.*
scollop [ˊskɔləp] n. See SCALLOP.
scollop [ˊskɔləp] v. tr. See SCALLOP.
scolopendra [ˌskɔləˊpendrə] n. ZOOL. Escolopendra, *f.*
sconce [skɔns] n. Candelabro (*m.*) de pared (wall candle holder). || Palmatoria, *f.* (handled candle stick). || MIL. Fortín, *m.*
scone [skɔn] n. Torta, *f.*
scoop [skuːp] n. Pala, *f.* (hollow utensil for serving flour, etc.). || Cuchara, *f.* (spoon). || Platillo, *m.* (of a balance). || Pinzas, *f. pl.* (for ice cream). || Recogedor, *m.* (for dust, rubbish). || Cubo (*m.*) para el carbón (for coal). || Palada, *f.* (content of a scoop). || MAR. Achicador, *m.* (for bailing out). || TECH. Cuchara, *f.* (of an excavator). | Gubia, *f.* (carpenter's tool). | Cangilón, *m.* (of a dredge). || MED. Legra, *f.* (surgical instrument). || GEOL. Depresión, *f.* || FAM. Ganancia (*f.*) grande (profit). || Noticia (*f.*) sensacional que se tiene en exclusiva (in journalism).
scoop [skuːp] v. tr. Sacar (profit). || — *To scoop in*, sacar (money). || *To scoop out*, sacar [con pala] (flour, etc.), achicar (water from a boat), cavar (to excavate), escotar (a neckline). || *To scoop the other newspapers*, adelantarse a los otros periódicos en la publicación de una noticia. || *To scoop up*, sacar [con pala] (flour, etc.), achicar (water from a boat), sacar [del agua] (sth. from the water), recoger (dust, rubbish), coger: *to scoop s.o. up in one's arms*, coger a uno en brazos.
scooper [—ə*] n. Gubia, *f.* (tool). || Avoceta, *f.* (bird).
scoop net [—net] n. Red (*f.*) barredera.
scoot [skuːt] v. intr. FAM. Correr rápidamente (to go quickly). | Largarse (to go away).
scooter [—ə*] n. Patineta, *f.* (child's toy). || Scooter, *m.* (motor vehicle).
scope [skəup] n. Ámbito, *m.*: *such subjects are not within the scope of this book*, temas de esa índole no están dentro del ámbito de este libro. || Esfera (*f.*) *or* campo (*m.*) de acción (person's field of action): *it does not come within my scope*, no cae dentro de mi esfera de acción. || Incumbencia, *f.*, competencia, *f.* (person's responsibilities): *outside my scope*, fuera de mi incumbencia. || Competencia, *f.* (ability): *his scope is fairly limited*, su competencia es bastante limitada. || Alcance, *m.* (reach): *beyond the scope of his imagination*, fuera del alcance de su imaginación; *a new car is quite beyond my scope*, comprar un coche nuevo está completamente fuera de mi alcance. || Amplitud, *f.* (of a project). || Campo (*m.*) de aplicación (of a law). || — *He needs more scope to develop his talents*, necesita más libertad para desarrollar sus capacidades. || *To give s.o. full scope*, dar carta blanca a alguien.
scops owl [ˊskɔpsəul] n. ZOOL. Buharro, *m.*
scorbutic [skɔːˊbjuːtik] adj. MED. Escorbútico, ca.
scorch [skɔːtʃ] n. Quemadura, *f.*
scorch [skɔːtʃ] v. tr. Quemar: *fields scorched by the summer sun*, campos quemados por el sol de verano; *the iron scorched the sheet*, la plancha quemó la sábana; *the cook has scorched the food*, la cocinera ha quemado la comida. || Chamuscar (to singe). || FIG. Herir. || MIL. Arrasar (to devastate).
— V. intr. Quemarse (to become burnt): *the grass scorched in the sun*, con el sol se quemó la hierba. || Chamuscarse (to become singed). || FAM. Ir volando *or* a gran velocidad (to go very fast). || FAM. *They scorched past at a hundred*, pasaron [volando] a cien millas por hora.
scorched-earth policy [skɔːtʃtəːθˊpɔlisi] n. MIL. Táctica (*f.*) que consiste en arrasar todo lo que puede facilitar el avance del enemigo.
scorcher [ˊskɔːtʃə*] n. FAM. Día (*m.*) abrasador (hot day). | Crítica (*f.*) severa (criticism). | Loco (*m.*) del volante (driver). | Ciclista (*m.*) suicida (cyclist). | Persona (*f.*) *or* cosa estupenda.
scorching [ˊskɔːtʃiŋ] adj. Abrasador, ra (very hot). || FIG. Mordaz (comment, criticism).
score [skɔː*] n. Muesca, *f.*, incisión, *f.* (notch). || Raya, *f.* (line). || Arañazo, *m.* (on leather, cardboard, etc.). || Estría, *f.* (on rock). || TECH. Raya, *f.* (on a cylinder, bearing). || Señal, *f.* (on a tree). || SP. Tanteo, *m.* (number of points, goals, etc.): *the score at half time was two to one*, al terminar el primer tiempo el tanteo era de dos a uno. | Resultado, *m.* (result): *what was the score?*, ¿cuál fue el resultado? | Tanto, *m.* (a point scored in a game). | Puntuación, *f.* (in golf, shooting, cards, etc.). || Calificación, *f.*, nota, *f.* (in a test, exam): *to get a score of nine out of ten*, sacar una nota de nueve sobre diez. || FAM. Cuenta, *f.* (debt). | Observación (*f.*) mordaz (well-directed remark). || Veintena, *f.* (twenty): *a score of people*, una veintena de personas. || MUS. Partitura, *f.*: *full score*, partitura de orquesta. || — Pl. Montones, *m.*: *scores of people*, montones de gente. || — *On that score*, por lo que se refiere a eso, a ese respecto. || *On the score of*, con motivo de, por causa de. || SP. *There was no score in the second half*, no marcaron en el segundo tiempo. || *Three score years and ten*, setenta años. || SP. *To keep the score*, tantear. || FIG. *To know the score*, conocer el percal (to know about sth.), ser muy despabilado (not to be easily deceived). | *To pay off old scores* o *to settle an old score with s.o.*, ajustar cuentas con alguien.
score [skɔː*] v. tr. Hacer una muesca en (to notch). || Rayar (to scratch a line on). || Subrayar (to underline). || Estriar (rock). || TECH. Rayar (a bearing, piston, etc.). || Apuntar [por medio de rayas *or* muescas] (to keep account of). || SP. Marcar (point, goal, etc.). | Conseguir (a victory). || Valer: *ace scores ten*, el as vale diez. || MUS. Orquestar (a composition). || Sacar *or* obtener [una nota de] (in a test): *to score five*, sacar un cinco. || U. S. Calificar (to grade). | Reprender, regañar (to scold). || *To score out*, tachar (to cross out).
— V. intr. SP. Tantear (to keep a score). | Marcar un tanto (to win a point). | Marcar un gol (in football). || Aventajar: *to score over a rival*, aventajar a un rival. || FAM. Tener éxito (to have a success). || — FIG. *That's where you score*, es en eso donde llevas ventaja. || *To score off s.o.*, marcar un tanto a costa de alguien (to win at s.o.'s expense), reírse de uno (to make a joke about s.o.).
scoreboard [—bɔːd] n. Marcador, *m.*, tanteador, *m.*
scorecard [—kɑːd] n. SP. Tanteador, *m.*
scorekeeper [—kiːpə*] n. Tanteador, *m.*
scorer [—ə*] n. SP. Goleador, *m.* (in football). || Tanteador, *m.* (scorekeeper). || *The team's top scorer*, el jugador que más goles ha marcado.
scoresheet [—ʃiːt] n. SP. Tanteador, *m.*
scoria [ˊskɔriə] n. Escoria, *f.*

— OBSERV. El plural de la palabra inglesa es *scoriae*.

scorification [ˌskɔrifiˊkeiʃən] n. Escorificación, *f.*
scorify [ˊskɔriˌfai] v. tr. Escorificar.
scoring [ˊskɔːriŋ] n. SP. Tanteo, *m.* || Rayado, *m.* (scratching). || Incisión, *f.* (cutting). || Estriación, *f.*

(of rock). || TECH. Rayado, *m.* (of bearing, piston, etc.). || MUS. Orquestación, *f.* || U. S. Reprimenda, *f.*, reprensión, *f.* (reprimand).

scorn [skɔ:n] n. Desprecio, *m.*, desdén, *m.*, menosprecio, *m.* || — *She is the scorn of her friends*, sus amigas la desprecian. || *To laugh to scorn*, ridiculizar.

scorn [skɔ:n] v. tr. Despreciar, desdeñar, menospreciar. || *To scorn to do sth.*, no dignarse a hacer algo, negarse a hacer algo.

scornful [—ful] adj. Despreciativo, va; desdeñoso, sa.

Scorpio [ˈskɔ:piəu] n. ASTR. Escorpión, *m.*

scorpion [ˈskɔ:pjən] n. ZOOL. Escorpión, *m.*, alacrán, *m.* || ASTR. Escorpión, *m.* || *Scorpion fish*, rascacio, *m.*, rescaza, *f.*

scorzonera [ˌskɔ:zəˈni:ərə] n. BOT. Escorzonera, *f.*

scot [skɔt] n. Parte, *f.*, escote, *m.* (share in joint expenses): *to pay one's scot*, pagar su parte. || HIST. Contribución, *f.* (money levied as a tax).

Scot [skɔt] n. Escocés, esa.

scotch [skɔtʃ] n. Calza, *f.* (for wheel). || Muesca, *f.* (notch). || Herida, *f.* (wound). || Whisky (*m.*) escocés.

scotch [skɔtʃ] v. tr. Calzar (to prevent from rolling). || Frustrar (to thwart): *to scotch s.o.'s plans*, frustrar los proyectos de alguien. || Herir (to wound without killing). || Suprimir (to suppress). || *To scotch a conspiracy*, hacer fracasar una conspiración.

Scotch [skɔtʃ] adj. Escocés, esa: *Scotch terrier*, terrier escocés: *Scotch whisky*, whisky escocés; *Scotch broth*, sopa escocesa. || *Scotch tape*, cinta adhesiva.

— N. Escocés, *m.* (language). || *The Scotch*, los escoceses.

Scotchman [—mən] n. Escocés, *m.*

— OBSERV. El plural de esta palabra es *Scotchmen.*

Scotchwoman [—ˌwumən] n. Escocesa, *f.*

— OBSERV. El plural de esta palabra es *Scotchwomen.*

scot-free [ˈskɔtˈfri:] adj. Sin castigo, impune (without punishment). || Ileso, sa (unhurt). || Sin pagar (without paying).

Scotland [ˈskɔtlənd] pr. n. GEOGR. Escocia, *f.* || *Scotland Yard*, sede (*f.*) de la policía londinense.

Scots [skɔts] adj. Escocés, esa: *Scots Guards*, Guardia escocesa.

— N. Escocés, *m.* (language).

Scotsman [—mən] n. Escocés, *m.*

— OBSERV. El plural de esta palabra es *Scotsmen.*

Scotswoman [—ˌwumən] n. Escocesa, *f.*

— OBSERV. El plural de esta palabra es *Scotswomen.*

Scotticism [ˈskɔtisizəm] n. GRAMM. Giro (*m.*) escocés.

scottie [ˈskɔti] n. FAM. Terrier (*m.*) escocés (dog).

Scottie [ˈskɔti] n. FAM. Escocés, esa.

Scottish [ˈskɔtiʃ] adj. Escocés, esa: *Scottish terrier*, terrier escocés.

— N. Escocés, *m.* (language). || *The Scottish*, los escoceses.

scoundrel [ˈskaundrəl] n. Sinvergüenza, *m.*, canalla, *m.*

scoundrelly [—i] adj. Canallesco, ca.

scour [ˈskauə*] n. Restregón, *m.*, fregado, *m.* (act of scouring). || Detergente, *m.* (cleansing agent). || Lugar (*m.*) derrubiado (eroded place). || — Pl. VET. Diarrea, *f. sing.*

scour [ˈskauə*] v. tr. Restregar, fregar (to clean by rubbing hard): *to scour a pan*, restregar una cacerola. || Revocar (with high-pressure water). || Limpiar (wool). || MED. Purgar (to purge). || Derrubiar, erosionar (to erode). || FIG. Batir, registrar, recorrer: *police are scouring the district searching for the girl*, la policía está batiendo el barrio en busca de la niña; *to scour the town*, recorrer la ciudad.

— V. intr. Correr: *to scour after*, correr en busca de.

scourer [—rə*] n. Estropajo, *m.* (abrasive pad).

scourge [skə:dʒ] n. Látigo, *m.* (whip). || FIG. Azote, *m.*, plaga, *f.* (cause of misery). | Castigo, *m.* (divine punishment). || FIG. *Attila, the Scourge of God*, Atila, el Azote de Dios.

scourge [skə:dʒ] v. tr. Azotar, flagelar (to whip). || FIG. Azotar: *a country scourged by disease and famine*, un país azotado por la enfermedad y el hambre. | Atormentar (to torment).

scouring [ˈskauəriŋ] n. Restregadura, *f.*, fregado, *m.* (of a cooking utensil, etc.). || Revoque, *m.* (of a building's exterior). || Limpieza, *f.* (of wool). || Derrubio, *m.* (erosion). || — Pl. Basura, *f. sing.* (refuse). || Hez, *f. sing.* (of society). || *Scouring pad*, estropajo, *m.* (scourer).

scout [skaut] n. MIL Explorador, *m.* (soldier sent ahead). | Escucha, *m.* (sent out to listen). | Reconocimiento, *m.*, exploración, *f.* (scouting). || Explorador, *m.* (boy scout). || Criado, *m.* (at Oxford). || U. S. Observador, *m.* (person who observes rival sport team). | Descubridor (*m.*) de personas de talento (talent scout). | Tipo, *m.* (fellow). || — MIL. *Scout plane*, avión (*m.*) de reconocimiento. || *To be on the scout for*, estar buscando.

scout [skaut] v. tr. MIL. Explorar, batir, reconocer (to reconnoitre). || Rechazar (to reject).

— V. intr. Hacer un reconocimiento (to reconnoitre). || Hacer una batida (to search). || *To scout for*, buscar.

scouting [—iŋ] n. MIL. Exploración, *f.*, reconocimiento, *m.* || Actividades (*f. pl.*) de los exploradores (boy scouts).

scoutmaster [—ˌmɑ:stə*] n. Jefe (*m.*) de exploradores.

scow [skau] n. MAR. Chalana, *f.* (boat).

scowl [skaul] n. Ceño, *m.* || "*No*", *he answered with a scowl*, "no", contestó frunciendo el entrecejo.

scowl [skaul] v. intr. Fruncir el entrecejo. || FIG. Tener un aspecto amenazador.

— V. tr. *To scowl an answer*, contestar frunciendo el entrecejo. || *To scowl one's dissatisfaction*, manifestar su descontento frunciendo el entrecejo.

scowling [—iŋ] adj. Ceñudo, da.

scrabble [ˈskræbl] v. intr. Escarbar (to make scratching movements). || Garabatear, garrapatear (to scrawl). || Subir gateando (to climb). || — *She scrabbled in her bag for her matches*, revolvió todo lo que tenía en el bolso para encontrar sus cerillas. || *To scrabble on the floor for sth.*, buscar algo en el suelo a gatas.

— V. tr. Garabatear (to write illegibly).

scrag [skræg] n. Persona (*f.*) esquelética, animal (*m.*) esquelético (scrawny person or animal). || CULIN. Pescuezo, *m.* (of mutton or veal). || Pescuezo, *m.* (of a person).

scrag [skræg] v. tr. FAM. Ahorcar (to kill by hanging). | Torcer el pescuezo a (to kill by twisting the neck). | Agarrar por el pescuezo, torcer el pescuezo a (to grab by the neck): *scrag him!*, ¡tuércele el pescuezo!

scragginess [—inis] n. Flacura, *f.*, delgadez, *f.* (of the body). || Aspereza, *f.* (of rocks).

scraggly [—li] adj. U. S. Desaseado, da (unkempt). | Ralo, la (of sparse growth).

scraggy [—i] adj. Flaco, ca; delgado, da (scrawny). || Escabroso, sa; áspero, ra (rocks, etc.).

scram [skræm] v. intr. FAM. Largarse.

scramble [—bl] n. Camino (*m.*) difícil: *it is a scramble to get down the hillside*, es un camino difícil para bajar la colina. || Lucha, *f.*, arrebatiña, *f.*, pelea, *f.*: *a scramble to get tickets*, una lucha para conseguir entradas. || SP. Carrera (*f.*) de motocross.

scramble [—bl] v. tr. Revolver (to jumble). || Mezclar (to mix). || RAD. Perturbar. || CULIN. Revolver: *scrambled eggs*, huevos revueltos.

— V. intr. Trepar, gatear (to climb with struggling movements). || Pelearse: *they scrambled for the best seats*, se pelearon para conseguir los mejores sitios. || — *To scramble into one's clothes*, vestirse rápidamente. || *To scramble out*, salir a gatas.

scrambler [—blə*] n. RAD. Aparato (*m.*) para perturbar las emisiones radiofónicas *or* telefónicas. || SP. Motocicleta (*f.*) de motocross.

scrambling [—bliŋ] n. Pelea, *f.*, arrebatiña, *f.*, lucha, *f.*: *I don't like all this scrambling for seats*, no me gusta toda esta pelea para obtener asientos. || Trepa, *f.* (struggling uphill). || SP. Motocross, *m.*

scrap [skræp] n. Trozo, *m.*, pedazo, *m.* (of paper, food, etc.). || Recorte, *m.* (piece of material, printed excerpt of book, speech, etc., newspaper cutting). || Chatarra, *f.* (old metal): *scrap value*, valor como chatarra; *to sell sth. for scrap*, vender algo como chatarra. || Ápice, *m.*: *there is not a scrap of truth in it*, no tiene un ápice de verdad. || Pizca, *f.* (very small piece): *not a scrap of food*, ni una pizca de comida. || FAM. Pelea, *f.* (fight). || — Pl. Restos, *m.*, sobras, *f.* (leftovers): *table scraps*, las sobras de la mesa. || Residuos, *m.*, desechos, *m.* (waste). || CULIN. Chicharrones, *m.* || — *A few scraps of knowledge*, algunos conocimientos. || *To catch scraps of conversation*, poder oír algunas palabras de una conversación. || FAM. *To have a scrap with s.o.*, pelearse con alguien.

scrap [skræp] v. tr. Desechar (to discard). || Desguazar (to break up). || Desechar, descartar (idea).

— V. intr. FAM. Pelearse (to fight).

scrapbook [—buk] n. Álbum (*m.*) de recortes.

scrape [skreip] n. Raspado, *m.* (act of scraping). || Chirrido, *m.* (noise of scraping). || Arañazo, *m.* (scraped mark on paintwork, leather, etc.). || Rasguño, *m.* (graze on skin). || FAM. Lío, *m.*, apuro, *m.* (awkward situation). | Reverencia (*f.*) obsequiosa (bow).

scrape [skreip] v. tr. Raspar: *to scrape a ship's hull*, raspar el casco de un barco; *to scrape the paint off a door*, raspar la pintura de una puerta. || Decapar, desoxidar (a metal). || Limpiar (to clean). || Arañar (to graze the skin, scratch paintwork, leather, etc.). || CULIN. Rallar. || Arrastrar (to drag): *to scrape furniture across the floor*, arrastrar un mueble por el suelo; *to scrape one's feet along the ground*, arrastrar los pies por el suelo. || Rozar: *to scrape the seabed*, rozar el fondo del mar. || Rasgar (a violin). || Hacer chirriar: *he scraped the chalk on the blackboard*, hizo chirriar la tiza en la pizarra. || MED. Legrar, raspar. || — FIG. *To scrape a living*, vivir muy apretadamente. || *To scrape off* o *away*, quitar [raspando]. || FIG. FAM. *To scrape one's plate*, dejar el plato limpio. || *To scrape out a tune on the violin*, tocar una melodía rascando el violín. || *To scrape together* o *up*, reunir.

— V. intr. Rozar: *to scrape along the wall*, pasar rozando la pared. || Chirriar: *the chalk scraped on the blackboard*, la tiza chirrió en la pizarra. || Economizar (to live economically). || — FIG. *To bow and scrape*, hacer zalemas. || FIG. FAM. *To scrape along* o *by*, ir tirando. || *To scrape through*, pasar muy justo por (a gap), aprobar por los pelos (an exam).

scraper [ˈskreipə*] n. Raspador, *m.*, rascador, *m.* (tool). || MAR. Rasqueta, *f.* || MED. Legra, *f.* || Limpiabarros, *m. inv.* (for scraping mud off one's shoes). || FAM. Rascatripas, *m. inv.* (violinist).

scrap heap [ˈskræphi:p] n. Montón (*m.*) de chatarra (pile of scrap). || Cementerio (*m.*) de coches (for old cars). || Montón (*m.*) de desechos (rubbish heap).

scraping [ˈskreipiŋ] n. Raspado, *m.* (act). || Chirrido, *m.* (noise). || MED. Raspado, *m.*, legrado, *m.*

scrap iron [skræpˈaiən] n. Chatarra, *f.*

scrap merchant [skræpˈmə:tʃənt] n. Chatarrero, *m.*

scrapper [ˈskræpə*] n. FAM. Pendenciero, *m.*, peleón, *m.*, camorrista, *m.*

scrappy [ˈskræpi] adj. Pobre, hecho con sobras *or* restos (meal). || Incompleto, ta (information, collection, education). || Deshilvanado, da (style, speech). || FAM. Peleón, ona; pendenciero, ra. || *Scrappy knowledge*, unos conocimientos fragmentarios.

scrapyard [ˈskræpjɑ:d] n. Cementerio (*m.*) de coches.

scratch [skrætʃ] n. Arañazo, *m.*, rasguño, *m.* (on the skin): *to escape without a scratch*, escapar sin un rasguño. || Arañazo, *m.* (on paintwork, wood, etc.). || Raya, *f.* (on a record, photograph). || Chirrido, *m.* (sound of scratching). || Rascadura, *f.* (to relieve itching). || Garabato, *m.* (meaningless mark made by pen, etc.). || SP. Línea (*f.*) de salida (in athletics). | Chiripa, *f.* (in billiards). || — *To be* o *to come up to scratch*, satisfacer los requisitos (to fulfil the requirements), ser tan bueno como siempre (to be as good as ever): *her performance was up to scratch*, su actuación fue tan buena como siempre; estar a la altura de las circunstancias (to be good enough). || *To feel up to scratch*, sentirse en forma (fit). || *To start from scratch*, empezar sin nada (with nothing), empezar desde el principio (from the beginning).

— Adj. Improvisado, da: *a scratch team*, un equipo improvisado; *a scratch meal*, una comida improvisada. || Sin homogeneidad. || SP. Sin ventaja (who has no handicap).

scratch [skrætʃ] v. tr. Rayar: *to scratch the paintwork*, rayar la pintura. || Grabar: *I scratched my name on the tree*, grabé mi nombre en el árbol. || Rascar: *to scratch one's head*, rascarse la cabeza. || Arañar, rasguñar: *the dog scratched me*, el perro me arañó; *I have scratched my hand*, me he rasguñado la mano. || Frotar (a match). || Escarbar: *hens scratch the ground*, las gallinas escarban la tierra. || Tachar, borrar (to cross out): *scratch his name from the list*, tacha su nombre de la lista. || Garabatear (to scrawl). || SP. Cancelar (a match, race, etc.). | Retirar (a horse, competitor, etc.). || — *To scratch a hole in sth.*, rascar algo hasta hacer un agujero. || *To scratch s.o.'s eyes out*, sacar los ojos a alguien. || FIG. *To scratch the surface*, no profundizar. || FIG. FAM. *To scratch together* o *up*, reunir. | *You scratch my back and I'll scratch yours*, un favor con favor se paga.

— V. intr. Arañar: *a cat that scratches*, un gato que araña. || Rascarse (to relieve itching). || Escarbar (a hen). || Raspear (a pen). || SP. Retirarse (to withdraw). || FAM. *To scratch along* o *by*, ir tirando.

scratcher [—ə*] n. Raspador, *m.* (tool). || Raspador, ra (person).

scratch pad [—pæd] n. Bloc, *m.* [para apuntes].

scratch paper [—ˈpeipə*] n. Papel (*m.*) de borrador.

scratch test [—test] n. Cutirreacción, *f.* [para casos alérgicos].

scratchy [—i] adj. Arañado, da; rayado, da (covered with scratches). || Que pica (causing irritation or itching). || Que chirria, chirriante (making a harsh sound). || Que raspea (pen). || Garabatoso, sa (writing).

scrawl [skrɔ:l] n. Garabato, *m.*: *his signature is just a scrawl*, su firma no es más que un garabato. || Garabatos, *m. pl.* (scrawling writing): *I can't read this scrawl*, no consigo leer estos garabatos.

scrawl [skrɔ:l] v. tr./intr. Garabatear: *to scrawl a note*, garabatear unas palabras. || *To scrawl over*, cubrir de garabatos.

scrawny [ˈskrɔ:ni] adj. Flaco, ca; flacucho, cha.

screak [skrik] n. Chirrido, *m.*

screak [skrik] v. intr. Chirriar.

scream [skri:m] n. Grito, *m.*, chillido, *m.* (of pain, fear). || FAM. Persona (*f.*) *or* cosa (*f.*) divertidísima. || — Pl. Carcajadas, *f.* (of laughter). || — FAM. *He's an absolute scream*, es divertidísimo, es mondante. | *It was a scream*, fue la monda. || *To give a scream of horror*, dar un grito de horror.

scream [skri:m] v. tr. Vociferar: *to scream insults*, vociferar insultos. || Gritar: *yes!, he screamed*, ¡sí!, gritó. || Berrear: *the baby screamed itself to sleep*, el niño berreó hasta dormirse.

— V. intr. Gritar, chillar (in fear, pain, anger, hysteria): *to scream with pain*, gritar de dolor. || Chillar, chirriar (bird). || FIG. Ser muy llamativo: *posters screamed outside the theatre*, los carteles del teatro eran muy llamativos. || FAM. *To scream with laughter*, partirse *or* mondarse de risa, reír a carcajadas.

screamer [—ə*] n. Chillón, ona; gritón, ona (person who screams). || Ave (*f.*) chillona (bird). || FAM. Chiste (*m.*) graciosísimo (joke). | Obra (*f.*) divertidísima (play). | Tipo (*m.*) muy chistoso (person). | Titulares (*m. pl.*) sensacionalistas (headlines). | Punto (*m.*) de exclamación (exclamation mark).

screaming [—iŋ] adj. FIG. Mondante, graciosísimo, ma; divertidísimo, ma (funny). || Estridente (noise). || Llamativo, va; chillón, ona (colour): *painted in screaming red*, pintado de rojo chillón. || FIG. *Screaming headlines*, titulares (*m.*) sensacionalistas.

screamingly [—iŋli] adv. *Screamingly funny*, mondante, de morirse de risa.

scree [skri:] n. GEOL. Piedra, *f.* (stone). | Guijarro, *m.* (pebble). | Acumulación (*f.*) de piedras y rocas.

screech [skri:tʃ] n. Chillido, *m.*

screech [skri:tʃ] v. intr. Chillar (to give a shrill scream). || Chirriar: *the brakes screeched*, los frenos chirriaron.

— V. tr. Decir a gritos, gritar (to scream shrilly).

screech owl [—aul] n. ZOOL. Lechuza, *f.*

screed [skri:d] n. Discurso (*m.*) largo y aburrido, perorata, *f.*, rollo, *m.* (fam.) [speech]. || Escrito (*m.*) largo y aburrido (piece of writing). || Sarta, *f.*, lista (*f.*) larga (long list). || TECH. Maestra, *f.* (used in plastering). | Reglón, *m.* (in paving).

screen [skri:n] n. Biombo, *m.* (movable partitition made of wood, metal, etc.): *folding screen*, biombo plegable. || ARCH. Tabique, *m.* (partition wall). || Reja, *f.* (of a window). || AUT. Parabrisas, *m. inv.* (windscreen). || FIG. Cortina, *f.*: *a smoke screen*, una cortina de humo. || MIL. Cobertura, *f.* (of men). || MAR. Protección, *f.* (of vessels). || Tablón (*m.*) de anuncios (notice board). || PHYS. CINEM. Pantalla, *f.*: *cinema screen, television screen*, pantalla de cine, de televisión; *the small screen*, la pequeña pantalla. || Cine, *m.*: *screen star*, estrella de cine; *screen music*, música de cine. || PRINT. Trama, *f.* || Criba, *f.* (sieve). || SP. Pantalla, *f.* (cricket). || — *Fire screen*, pantalla. || *Safety screen*, pantalla de seguridad. || *Screen door*, puerta (*f.*) de tela metálica. || *Screen of trees*, pantalla de árboles.

screen [skri:n] v. tr. Proteger, resguardar (to shelter): *to screen one's eyes from the light*, protegerse los ojos de la luz. || Tapar, ocultar (to conceal): *sun screened by clouds*, sol tapado por las nubes; *to screen (off) part of a room*, tapar una parte de una habitación. || MIL. MAR. Cubrir, proteger. || Cribar, tamizar (to sift). || Adaptar para el cine (to make into a film). || Proyectar (a film): *the film will be screened after the meal*, proyectarán la película después de la comida. || FIG. Pasar por el tamiz *or* por la criba: *to screen candidates for a job*, pasar por el tamiz los candidatos a un puesto. || FIG. *To screen out*, seleccionar (to select), eliminar (to eliminate).

— V. intr. Adaptarse para el cine: *this book will screen well*, este libro se adaptará bien para el cine.

screener [—ə*] n. Cribador, ra.

screening [—iŋ] n. Protección, *f.* (protection). || Ocultación, *f.* (hiding). || Cribado, *m.* (sifting). || Proyección, *f.* (of a film). || — Pl. Cribaduras, *f.*, cerniduras, *f.* (refuse). || FIG. *To submit s.o. to a security screening*, hacer una investigación sobre los antecedentes de alguien.

screenplay [—plei] n. Guión, *m.*

screen test [—test] n. Prueba (*f.*) cinematográfica.

screenwriter [—ˌraitə*] n. Guionista, *m.* & *f.*

screw [skru:] n. Tornillo, *m.*: *endless screw*, tornillo sin fin. || Tuerca, *f.* (female screw). || Vuelta, *f.* (one turn of a screw): *to give another screw*, dar otra vuelta. || AVIAT. MAR. Hélice, *f.* (propeller). || SP. Efecto, *m.* (of a ball). || FAM. Tacaño, ña (miser). | Sueldo, *m.* (salary): *to be on a good screw*, ganar un buen sueldo. | Penco, *m.* (horse). | Carcelero, *m.* (prison warder). || POP. Polvo, *m.* (sexual intercourse). || — Pl. Empulgueras, *f.* (torture). || — FIG. FAM. *To have a screw loose*, tener flojos los tornillos, faltarle un tornillo a uno. | *To put the screws on s.o.*, apretar las clavijas *or* los tornillos a uno.

screw [skru:] v. tr. Atornillar (to turn). || Apretar (to tighten). || Fijar con tornillos: *to screw sth. (on) to the wall*, fijar algo en la pared con tornillos. || Retorcer (to twist). || FAM. Sacar: *to screw a dollar out of s.o.*, sacarle un dólar a alguien. || POP. Joder (to make love to, to ruin things for). || — *He screwed the letter into a ball*, hizo una bola con la carta. || *To screw off*, destornillar. || *To screw on*, enroscar. || *To screw up*, arrugar (paper), torcer (one's face), apretar (one's lips), fastidiar (to spoil): *to screw up the whole deal*, fastidiar todo el negocio; armarse de: *to screw up one's courage*, armarse de valor.

— V. intr. Enroscarse (to be joined or to turn like a screw): *the top screws on to the jar*, la tapa se enrosca en el tarro. || Estar atornillado, estar fijado con tornillos: *the shelf screws on to the wall*, el estante está atornillado en la pared. || Apretarse (to tighten).

screwball [—bɔ:l] adj. U. S. FAM. Chiflado, da; chalado, da; excéntrico, ca.

— N. U. S. SP. Pelota (*f.*) lanzada con efecto (in baseball). || U. S. FAM. Excéntrico, ca.

screw bolt [—bəult] n. TECH. Perno (*m.*) roscado.

screw cap [—kæp] n. Tapón (*m.*) de rosca *or* de tuerca.

screw coupling [—ˈkʌpliŋ] n. TECH. Manguito (*m.*) roscado.

screwdriver [—ˌdraivə*] n. TECH. Destornillador, *m.* || Cóctel (*m.*) de vodka con naranja (drink).

screwed [—d] adj. TECH. Roscado, da (bolt, etc.). || Torcido, da; retorcido, da (twisted). || FAM. Achispado, da (drunk). || U. S. FAM. Fastidiado, da.

screwed-up [—dʌp] adj. FAM. Fastidiado, da.

screw eye [—ai] n. Armella, *f.*, cáncamo, *m.*

screwhead [—ˌhed] n. Cabeza (*f.*) de tornillo.

screw propeller [—prəˈpelə*] n. Hélice, *f.*

screw tap [—tæp] n. TECH. Macho (*m.*) de aterrajar *or* de roscar.
screw thread [—θred] n. Rosca (*f.*) de tornillo.
screw wrench [—rentʃ] n. Llave (*f.*) inglesa.
screwy [—i] adj. FAM. Chiflado, da; chalado, da (crazy). | Absurdo, da (absurd).
scribble [ˈskribl] n. Garabato, *m.* (scrawl).
scribble [ˈskribl] v. tr./intr. Garabatear (to scrawl). || Escribir de prisa y sin cuidado (to write hastily).
scribbler [—ə*] n. Emborronador (*m.*) de cuartillas (s.o. who writes illegibly). || Emborronador (*m.*) de cuartillas, escritorzuelo, la (bad writer).
scribe [skraib] n. HIST. Escriba, *m.* (of Jewish law). || Amanuense, *m.*, escribiente, *m.* (copyist). || FAM. Emborronador (*m.*) de cuartillas. || TECH. Punta (*f.*) de trazar (scriber).
scribe [skraib] v. tr. Trazar.
— V. intr. Desempeñar el trabajo de escribiente (to act as a copyist). || HIST. Actuar de escriba (of Jewish law).
scriber [—ə*] n. TECH. Punta (*f.*) de trazar.
scrimmage [—idʒ] n. Escaramuza, *f.* (skirmish). || SP. Melée (*f.*) abierta (open scrum in American football). | Entrenamiento, *m.* (practice).
scrimmage [—idʒ] v. intr. Pelearse, tener una escaramuza.
scrimp [skrimp] v. tr. Escatimar: *to scrimp the servants' food*, escatimar la comida a los criados.
— V. intr. Ahorrar, hacer economías. || *To scrimp and save*, apretarse el cinturón.
scrimpy [—i] adj. Escaso, sa; parco, ca: *a scrimpy meal*, una comida escasa. || Mezquino, na; avaro, ra; cicatero, ra (person).
scrimshaw [ˈskrimʃɔ:] n. Talla (*f.*) en marfil *or* en concha *or* en barba de ballena.
scrimshaw [ˈskrimʃɔ:] v. tr. Tallar (whalebone, ivory, shells, etc.).
— V. intr. Hacer tallas en marfil *or* en concha *or* en barba de ballena.
scrip [skrip] n. Trozo (*m.*) de papel (piece of paper). || Vale, *m.* (certificate of indebtedness). || Título (*m.*) provisional de propiedad (of ownership of stock, property, etc.). || U. S. HIST. Papel (*m.*) moneda [que valía menos de un dólar].
script [skript] n. Escritura, *f.*, letra, *f.* (handwriting). || Escritura: *phonetic script*, escritura fonética. || PRINT. Letra (*f.*) cursiva. || Manuscrito, *m.* (manuscript). || THEATR. Argumento, *m.* || CINEM. Guión, *m.* || Ejercicio (*m.*) escrito (of an examination). || JUR. Original, *m.*
script girl [—gə:l] n. Secretaria (*f.*) de rodaje, script-girl, *f.*
scriptorium [skripˈtɔ:riəm] n. Escritorio, *m.* (in a monastery).

— OBSERV. El plural de *scriptorium* es *scriptoria*.

scriptural [ˈskriptʃərəl] adj. Bíblico, ca.
Scripture [ˈskriptʃə*] n. REL. Sagrada Escritura, *f.*, Biblia, *f.* (the Bible). | Pasaje (*m.*) de la Sagrada Escritura (passage). | Religión, *f.* (as a school subject). | Libros (*m. pl.*) sagrados (of any religion). || — Pl. REL. Sagradas Escrituras, *f.*
scriptwriter [ˈskriptˌraitə*] n. Guionista, *m.* & *f.*
scrivener [ˈskrivnə*] n. HIST. Amanuense, *m.* (copyist). | Notario, *m.* (notary).
scrod [skrɔd] n. U. S. Bacalao, *m.* (cod).
scrofula [ˈskrɔfjulə] n. MED. Escrófula, *f.*
scrofulous [ˈskrɔfjuləs] adj. MED. Escrofuloso, sa.
scroll [skrəul] n. Rollo (*m.*) de papel *or* de pergamino. || ARTS. Voluta, *f.* || Rúbrica, *f.* (of a signature). || *Dead Sea Scrolls*, manuscritos (*m.*) del Mar Muerto.
scroll [skrəul] v. tr. Enrollar (to form into a scroll). || Decorar con volutas (to decorate with scrolls).
— V. intr. Enrollarse.
scroll saw [—sɔ:] n. Sierra (*f.*) de marquetería.
scrollwork [—wə:k] n. ARTS. Volutas, *f. pl.*
Scrooge [skru:dʒ] n. Avariento, ta; tacaño, ña (miser): *to be a real Scrooge*, ser muy tacaño.

— OBSERV. *Scrooge* es un personaje de Dickens que simboliza la avaricia.

scrotum [ˈskrəutəm] n. ANAT. Escroto, *m.*

— OBSERV. El plural de *scrotum* es *scrota* o *scrotums*.

scrounge [skraundʒ] v. tr. FAM. Conseguir gorroneando, sacar de gorra (to get by cadging). | Birlar, robar (to pilfer).
— V. intr. FAM. Gorronear (to eat, etc. at s.o.'s expenses) | Dar sablazos (to borrow money). | — FAM. *To scrounge around for*, buscar. | *To scrounge on s.o.*, vivir a costa de alguien.
scrounger [—ə*] n. FAM. Gorrón, ona; sablista, *m.* & *f.* (cadger).
scrounging [—iŋ] n. Gorronería, *f.*
scrub [skrʌb] n. Maleza, *f.*, monte (*m.*) bajo (undergrowth). || Matorral, *m.* (land covered with scrubby undergrowth). || Árbol (*m.*) achaparrado (stunted tree). || Arbusto (*m.*) achaparrado (shrub). || FAM. Aborto, *m.* (very small person). | Don nadie, *m.* (insignificant person). || Cepillo (*m.*) de cerdas cortas (brush). || Barba (*f.*) corta (beard). || Pequeño bigote, *m.* (moustache). || Fregado, *m.* (act of scrubbing). || U. S. SP. Jugador (*m.*) suplente, reserva, *m.* (player). | Equipo (*m.*) de reservas (team). || *To give sth. a good scrub*, fregar algo vigorosamente.
— Adj. Achaparrado, da (tree, shrub). || FAM. Achaparrado, da; canijo, ja (small). | Inferior.
scrub [skrʌb] v. tr. Fregar (the floor, the dishes). || Restregar (clothes). || TECH. Depurar (gases). || FIG. FAM. Cancelar, anular: *to scrub a plan*, cancelar un proyecto.
— V. intr. Fregar.
scrubber [—ə*] n. Fregón, ona (person who scrubs). || Cepillo (*m.*) de fregar (brush). || TECH. Depurador, *m.* (of gases).
scrubbing [—iŋ] n. Fregado, *m.* (of floor, dishes). || TECH. Depuración, *f.* (of gases).
scrubbing brush [—brʌʃ] n. Cepillo (*m.*) de fregar.
scrubby [—i] adj. Achaparrado, da (stunted). || Cubierto de maleza (covered with scrub).
scrubwoman [—ˌwumən] n. U. S. Fregona, *f.*

— OBSERV. El plural de esta palabra es *scrubwomen*.

scruff [skrʌf] n. Cogote, *m.*, nuca, *f.* (of neck). || *To seize s.o. by the scruff of the neck*, coger a alguien por el cogote.
scruffy [ˈskrʌfi] adj. FAM. Desaliñado, da (neglected-looking): *a scruffy person, house*, una persona, una casa desaliñada.
scrum [skrʌm] n. SP. Melée, *f.* (rugby). || — SP. *Scrum half*, medio (*m.*) de melée. | *Open scrum*, melée abierta.
scrummage [—idʒ] n. SP. Melée, *f.* (rugby).
scrummage [—idʒ] v. intr. SP. Hacer una melée.
scrumptious [ˈskrʌmpʃəs] adj. FAM. De chuparse los dedos (food). || FAM. *A scrumptious girl*, un bombón.
scrunch [skrʌntʃ] n. Crujido, *m.*
scrunch [skrʌntʃ] v. tr./intr. See CRUNCH.
scruple [ˈskru:pl] n. Escrúpulo, *m.* (weight). || Escrúpulo, *m.*: *he has no scruples about thieving*, no tiene ningún escrúpulo en robar.
scruple [ˈskru:pl] v. intr. Tener escrúpulos. || *He does not scruple to betray his friends*, no tiene escrúpulos *or* no vacila en traicionar a sus amigos.
scrupulosity [ˌskru:pjuˈlɔsiti] n. Escrupulosidad, *f.*
scrupulous [ˈskru:pjuləs] adj. Escrupuloso, sa.
scrupulously [—li] adv. Escrupulosamente. || *Scrupulously careful*, sumamente cuidadoso.
scrupulousness [—nis] n. Escrupulosidad, *f.* (uprightness, care). || Escrúpulos, *m. pl.* (scruples).
scrutator [skru:ˈteitə*] or **scrutineer** [ˌskru:tiˈniə*] n. Escudriñador, ra. || Escrutador, ra (of votes).
scrutinize [ˈskru:tinaiz] v. tr. Hacer el recuento de, efectuar el escrutinio de (votes). || Examinar a fondo, escudriñar (to examine): *to scrutinize a document*, examinar un documento a fondo.
scrutinizer [—ə*] n. Escudriñador, ra. || Escrutador, ra (of votes).
scrutinizing [—iŋ] n. Examen (*m.*) profundo (examination). || Recuento, *m.* (of votes).
scrutiny [ˈskru:tini] n. Escrutinio, *m.*, recuento, *m.* (of votes). || Examen, *m.* [profundo] (of a document, etc.): *this plan does not stand up to scrutiny*, este proyecto no resiste al examen.
scuba [ˈskjubə] n. Escafandra (*f.*) autónoma.
scud [skʌd] n. Carrera, *f.* (rush). || Nubes (*f. pl.*) ligeras empujadas por el viento (clouds driven by the wind). || Ráfaga, *f.* (gust of wind). || Chaparrón, *m.* (brief shower of rain). || Espuma, *f.* (ocean spray).
scud [skʌd] v. intr. Correr (to run). || — *To scud across the sky*, pasar rápidamente por el cielo (clouds). || *To scud before the wind*, ir viento en popa (a sailing ship).
scuff [skʌf] n. Arrastre (*m.*) de los pies (dragging of the feet). || Chancleta, *f.* (slipper). || Parte (*f.*) desgastada (worn spot).
scuff [skʌf] v. tr. Arrastrar (to drag): *to scuff one's feet*, arrastrar los pies. || Estropear (to damage): *to scuff one's shoes*, estropear los zapatos. || Rozar (to touch lightly). || Rasguñar, arañar (to scratch).
— V. intr. Andar arrastrando los pies (to walk scraping the feet). || Estropearse (to become worn).
scuffle [—l] n. Riña, *f.*, pelea, *f.* (struggle).
scuffle [—l] v. intr. Reñir, pelearse (to struggle). || Arrastar los pies (to scuff one's feet).
scull [skʌl] n. Remo, *m.* (oar). || Espadilla, *f.* (used at the stern in propelling a boat). || U. S. Barco (*m.*) de remo (boat).
scull [skʌl] v. tr. Impulsar con el remo *or* la espadilla.
— V. intr. Remar.
sculler [—ə*] n. Remero, *m.* (person who sculls). || Barco (*m.*) de remo (boat).
scullery [—əri] n. Oficio, *m.*, office, *m.*, trascocina, *f.*
scullery maid [ˈskʌləriˈmeid] n. Fregona, *f.*
scullion [ˈskʌljən] n. Pinche, *m.*, marmitón, *m.*
sculpt [skʌlpt] v. tr. Esculpir.
— V. intr. Hacer esculturas, esculpir.
sculptor [—ə*] n. Escultor, *m.*
sculptress [—tris] n. Escultora, *f.*
sculptural [ˈskʌlptʃərəl] adj. Escultórico, ca; escultural.
sculpture [ˈskʌlptʃə*] n. Escultura, *f.*
sculpture [ˈskʌlptʃə*] v. tr. Esculpir: *to sculpture a statue in stone*, esculpir una estatua en piedra.
— V. intr. Hacer esculturas, esculpir.
sculpturesque [ˌskʌlptʃəˈresk] adj. Escultórico, ca.

scum [skʌm] n. Espuma, *f.* (froth, bubbles). || Telilla, *f.* (skinlike mass). || Nata, *f.* (on milk). || Verdín, *m.* (on a pond). || TECH. Escoria, *f.* (of molten metals). || FIG. Hez, *f.*, escoria, *f.* (despicable people): *the scum of society*, la escoria de la sociedad.
scum [skʌm] v. tr. Espumar (to skim). || Desnatar (milk). || Quitar la escoria de (molten metals).
— V. intr. Cubrirse de espuma.
scumble [—bl] v. tr. ARTS. Esfumar (to soften).
scumble [—bl] n. ARTS. Esfumado, *m.*, difuminado, *m.* (effect produced by scumbling). | Difumino, *m.*, esfumino, *m.* (used for scumbling).
scummy [—i] adj. Espumoso, sa (a liquid). || Cubierto de escoria (metals). || FIG. Canallesco, ca.
scupper [ˈskʌpə*] n. MAR. Imbornal, *m.*
scupper [ˈskʌpə*] v. tr. MAR. Hundir. || FAM. Frustrar, fastidiar (a plan, etc.).
scurf [skə:f] n. Caspa, *f.* (dandruff). || TECH. Incrustación, *f.* (in a boiler).
scurfy [—i] adj. Casposo, sa (full of dandruff). || TECH. Cubierto de incrustaciones.
scurrility [skʌˈriliti] n. Lo difamatorio, carácter (*m.*) injurioso (of an accusation, etc.). || Grosería, *f.* (coarseness).
scurrilous [ˈskʌriləs] adj. Injurioso, sa; calumnioso, sa; difamatorio, ria (insulting). || Grosero, ra (coarse).
scurry [ˈskʌri] n. Carrera, *f.* (run). || Huida, *f.* (flight).
scurry [ˈskʌri] v. intr. Correr (to run). || — *To scurry away* o *off*, escabullirse. || *To scurry by* o *past*, pasar corriendo.
scurviness [ˈskə:vinis] n. Vileza, *f.*
scurvy [ˈskə:vi] adj. Vil, ruin.
— N. MED. Escorbuto, *m.*
scut [skʌt] n. Rabo, *m.*, rabito, *m.* (short tail).
scutch [skʌtʃ] n. Agramadera, *f.*, agramador, *m.*
scutch [skʌtʃ] v. tr. Agramar (flax, etc.).
scutcheon [—ən] n. See ESCUTCHEON.
scutcher [—ə*] n. Agramadera, *f.*, agramador, *m.* (tool). || Agramador, ra (person).
scute [skju:t] n. ZOOL. Escudo, *m.* (of a reptile).
scutter [ˈskʌtə*] n. Carrera, *f.* (scurry).
scutter [ˈskʌtə*] v. intr. Correr (to scurry).
scuttle [skʌtl] n. Huida, *f.*, carrera, *f.* (scurry). || Cubo (*m.*) del carbón (small container holding coal). || Cesta, *f.* (basket). || MAR. Escotilla, *f.* || Trampa, *f.* (trapdoor). || U. S. Trampilla, *f.* (in the roof or floor of a building).
scuttle [skʌtl] v. tr. MAR. Barrenar, dar barreno a. || FIG. Barrenar, desbaratar (plans, etc.).
— V. intr. See SCURRY.
scuttlebutt [—ˌbʌt] n. MAR. Barril (*m.*) de agua fresca. || FAM. Rumor, *m.* (rumour). | Habladuría, *f.*, chisme, *m.* (gossip).
scutum [ˈskju:təm] n. ZOOL. Escudo, *m.* || Escudo, *m.* (shield). || ANAT. Rótula, *f.*

— OBSERV. El plural de *scutum* es *scuta*.

Scylla [ˈsilə] pr. n. GEOGR. Escila. || FIG. *To be between Scylla and Charybdis*, estar entre Escila y Caribdis.
scyphus [ˈsaifəs] n. HIST. Copa (*f.*) con dos asas (drinking cup).
scythe [saið] n. AGR. Guadaña, *f.*
scythe [saið] v. tr. AGR. Guadañar, segar.
Scythia [ˈsiðiə] pr. n. GEOGR. Escitia, *f.*
sea [si:] n. Mar, *m.* or *f.*: *rough sea*, mar agitado; *angry* o *raging* o *stormy sea*, mar enfurecido; *choppy sea*, mar picado; *at sea*, en el mar; *by the sea*, a orillas del mar; *out at sea*, en alta mar; *to travel by sea*, viajar por mar; *to put to sea*, hacerse a la mar. || Mar, *m.*, vía (*f.*) marítima: *to send by sea*, enviar por vía marítima. || Mar, *m.*: *Mediterranean Sea*, Mar Mediterráneo; *Caspian Sea*, Mar Caspio; *Black Sea*, Mar Negro; *Dead Sea*, Mar Muerto. || Lago, *m.*: *Sea of Galilee* o *of Tiberias*, Lago de Tiberíades. || Oleada, *f.*, ola, *f.* (wave). || FIG. Mar, *m.*: *to be swamped in a sea of doubt*, estar sumido en un mar de dudas; *a sea of tears*, un mar de lágrimas. || — *Beyond the sea* o *the seas*, allende los mares. || *Heavy sea*, marejada, *f.*, mar gruesa. || *Inland sea*, mar (*m.*) interior. || *On the high seas* o *on the open sea*, en alta mar. || *Strong sea*, marejada, *f.* || FIG. *To be all at sea*, estar en un mar de confusiones. | *To be half seas over*, estar achispado. || *To follow the sea*, ser marinero. || *To go to sea*, hacerse marinero. || *To ship a sea*, ser cubierto por una ola grande. || *To stand out to sea*, irse *or* hacerse mar adentro.
— Adj. Del mar, marino, na: *sea air*, aire marino. || Marítimo, ma: *sea transport*, transporte marítimo. || — *Sea battle*, batalla (*f.*) naval. || *Sea chart*, carta (*f.*) de marear. || *Sea current*, corriente marina. || *Sea voyage*, viaje por mar *or* en barco, viaje marítimo.

— OBSERV. *Mar* is generally masculine in everyday usage, but feminine when used by fishermen and seamen. It is also feminine in certain expressions (see MAR).

sea anchor [—ˈæŋkə*] n. Ancla (*f.*) flotante.
sea anemone [—əˈneməni] n. ZOOL. Anémona (*f.*) de mar.
seabag [—bæg] n. Saco (*m.*) de marinero.
seabed [—ˌbed] n. Fondo (*m.*) del mar.
sea bird [—bə:d] n. Ave (*f.*) marina.
sea biscuit [—ˈbiskit] n. Galleta, *f.*
seaboard [—bɔ:d] n. Costa, *f.*, litoral, *m.*
— Adj. Costero, ra.
seaborne [—bɔ:n] adj. Transportado por mar (goods). || Marítimo, ma (trade).
sea bream [—ˈbri:m] n. ZOOL. Besugo, *m.*
sea breeze [—ˈbri:z] n. Brisa (*f.*) marina.
sea calf [—kɑ:f] n. ZOOL. Foca, *f.*, becerro (*m.*) marino (seal).
seacoast [—ˈkəust] n. Litoral, *m.*, costa, *f.*
sea cow [—ˈkau] n. ZOOL. Manatí, *m.*, vaca (*f.*) marina (manatee). | Morsa, *f.* (walrus). | Hipopótamo, *m.* (hippopotamus).
sea cucumber [—ˈki:ju:kʌmbə*] n. ZOOL. Cohombro (*m.*) de mar, holoturia, *f.*
sea devil [—ˈdevil] n. Raya, *f.* (devilfish).
sea dog [—dɔg] n. Lobo (*m.*) de mar (experienced sailor). || Pirata, *m.* (pirate). || ZOOL. Foca, *f.*, becerro (*m.*) marino (sea calf). | Cazón, *m.* (dogfish).
sea eagle [—ˈi:gl] n. ZOOL. Águila (*f.*) marina, águila (*f.*) pescadora. | Quebrantahuesos, *m. inv.* (osprey).
sea-ear [—ˈiə*] n. ZOOL. Oreja (*f.*) de mar.
sea elephant [—ˈelifənt] n. ZOOL. Elefante (*m.*) marino.
sea fan [—fæn] n. ZOOL. Abanico (*m.*) de mar (coral).
seafarer [—ˌfɛərə*] n. Marinero, *m.*, marino, *m.* (sailor). || Navegante, *m.* & *f.* (s.o. who travels by sea).
seafaring [—ˌfɛəriŋ] n. Oficio (*m.*) de marinero, marinería, *f.* (occupation of a sailor). || Viajes (*m. pl.*) por mar (sea travel).
— Adj. Marinero, ra: *a seafaring people*, un pueblo marinero. || Que viaja por mar (travelling by sea). || — *In my seafaring days*, en mi época de marinero. || *Seafaring yarn*, historia (*f.*) de marinero.
seaflower [—ˈflauə*] n. Anémona (*f.*) de mar.
sea foam [—fəum] n. Espuma (*f.*) de mar (froth, meerschaum).
seafood [—fu:d] n. Mariscos, *m. pl.* (shellfish). || Pescado, *m.* (fish). || *Seafood restaurant*, marisquería, *f.*
seafowl [—faul] n. Ave (*f.*) marina.
seafront [—frʌnt] n. Paseo (*m.*) marítimo.
seagirt [—ˌgə:t] adj. Rodeado por el mar.
seagoing [—ˌgəuiŋ] adj. MAR. De alta mar (vessel). | Marinero, ra (people). | Marítimo, ma (trade).
sea green [—ˈgri:n] n. Verdemar, *m.* (colour).
sea-green [—ˈgri:n] adj. Verdemar.
sea gull [—gʌl] n. Gaviota, *f.* (bird).
sea hare [—hɛə*] n. Liebre (*f.*) de mar.
sea hog [—hɔg] n. Marsopa, *f.*, marsopla, *f.* (porpoise).
sea horse [—hɔ:s] n. ZOOL. Caballo (*m.*) de mar, hipocampo, *m.* | Morsa, *f.* (walrus). || MYTH. Criatura (*f.*) mitad caballo mitad pez.
sea kale [—keil] n. BOT. Col (*f.*) marina.
seal [si:l] n. Foca, *f.* (sea mammal). || Piel (*f.*) de foca (hide). || Sello, *m.* (piece of wax, lead, etc. stamped with a design): *wax seal*, sello de lacre; *great seal*, sello real. || Precinto, *m.* (paper sticker): *do not buy the bottle if the seal is broken*, no compre la botella si el precinto está roto. || Junta, *f.*: *a watertight seal between the glass and the frame*, una junta estanca entre el cristal y el marco. || FIG. Sello, *m.* (hallmark): *his work bears the seal of genius*, sus obras llevan el sello del genio. | Garantía, *f.*: *the seal of approval*, la garantía de una aprobación. || — Pl. Sellos, *m.*: *breaking of seals*, quebrantamiento *or* violación de sellos. || — *To set one's seal to*, aprobar. || *Under the seal of secrecy*, bajo secreto.
seal [si:l] v. tr. Sellar, marcar con un sello (a document, etc.): *signed and sealed*, firmado y sellado. || Lacrar, sellar con lacre (with wax). || Emplomar (with lead). || Precintar (with a paper sticker): *the boxes of cigars are sealed before leaving the factory*, las cajas de puros son precintadas antes de salir de la fábrica. || Cerrar (to close): *a sealed envelope*, un sobre cerrado. || JUR. Precintar. || Tapar (a crack). || Cerrar herméticamente (two pipes, etc.). || Impermeabilizar (to make waterproof). || FIG. Sellar (a friendship, agreement, etc.). | Decidir, determinar: *that sealed his fate*, aquello decidió su destino. || — *My lips are sealed*, he prometido no decir nada, no puedo decir nada. || TECH. *Sealed circuit*, circuito sellado. || *To seal off*, cerrar (to close), acordonar: *the police sealed off the area*, la policía acordonó el barrio.
— V. intr. Cazar focas.
sea-lane [ˈsi:ˈlein] n. Ruta (*f.*) *or* vía (*f.*) marítima.
sea lavender [ˈsi:ˈlævində*] n. BOT. Acelga (*f.*) silvestre.
sea lawyer [ˈsi:ˈlɔ:jə*] n. FAM. Marinero (*m.*) protestón.
sea legs [ˈsi:ˈlegz] pl. n. Equilibrio, *m. sing* [para andar en un barco]. || *To get one's sea legs*, acostumbrarse a andar en un barco.
sealer [ˈsi:lə*] n. Cazador (*m.*) de focas (hunter). || Barco (*m.*) para cazar focas (boat). || U. S. Verificador (*m.*) de pesas y medidas.
sea level [ˈsi:ˈlevl] n. Nivel (*m.*) del mar: *the town is a thousand feet above sea level*, la ciudad está a mil pies de altura sobre el nivel del mar.
sea lily [ˈsi:ˈlili] n. ZOOL. Crinoideo, *m.*
sealing wax [ˈsi:liŋwæks] n. Lacre, *m.*
sea lion [ˈsi:ˌlaiən] n. ZOOL. León (*m.*) marino, otaria, *f.* (large seal).
sea loch [ˈsi:ˌlɔk] n. Ría, *f.*
seal ring [ˈsi:lriŋ] n. Sello, *m.* (signet ring).
sealskin [ˈsi:lskin] n. Piel (*f.*) de foca.

seam [si:m] n. Costura, *f.* (in sewing). || TECH. Juntura, *f.*, junta, *f.* (joint in a surface). || Grieta, *f.* (in rock). || MIN. Veta, *f.*: *a coal seam*, una veta de carbón. || ANAT. Sutura, *f.* || Arruga, *f.* (wrinkle). || Cicatriz, *f.* (scar). || *To burst at the seams*, estallar por las costuras (a garment), rebosar de gente (to overflow): *the hall was bursting at the seams*, la sala rebosaba de gente.
seam [si:m] v. tr. Unir con una costura, coser (in needlework). || TECH. Juntar (to join). || Arrugar (to wrinkle). || Marcar: *scars seamed his face*, tenía la cara marcada de cicatrices. || Agrietar (a rock).
sea-maid [ˈsi:ˌmeid] n. Sirena, *f.* (mermaid).
seaman [ˈsi:mən] n. MAR. Marinero, *m.*, marino, *m.*

— OBSERV. El plural de *seaman* es *seamen*.

seamanlike [—laik] adj. MAR. Propio de un buen marinero.
seamanship [—ʃip] n. MAR. Náutica, *f.*
seamark [ˈsi:mɑ:k] n. MAR. Marca, *f.*, baliza, *f.* (object on land which guides navigators). | Línea que indica el límite de la altura de las mareas (high tide line).
sea mew [ˈsi:mju:] n. ZOOL. Gaviota, *f.* (sea gull).
sea mile [ˈsi:mail] n. Milla (*f.*) marina.
seamless [ˈsi:mlis] adj. Sin costura.
seamstress [ˈsi:mstris] n. Costurera, *f.*
seamy [ˈsi:mi] adj. Que tiene costuras (in sewing). || Arrugado, da (wrinkled). || Que tiene cicatrices (covered with scars). || Sórdido, da: *the seamy side of life*, el lado sórdido de la vida. || *The seamy side of a garment*, el revés de un traje.
séance [ˈseiɑ̃:ns] n. Sesión, *f.* (session). || Sesión (*f.*) de espiritismo (spiritualist meeting).
sea needle [ˈsi:ˈni:dl] n. Aguja, *f.* (fish).
sea onion [ˈsi:ˈʌnjən] n. BOT. Cebolla (*f.*) albarrana.
sea otter [ˈsi:ˈɔtə*] n. ZOOL. Nutria (*f.*) de mar.
sea pass [ˈsi:pa:s] n. MAR. Pasavante, *m.*
seaplane [ˈsi:plein] n. Hidroavión, *m.*
seaport [ˈsi:pɔ:t] n. Puerto (*m.*) de mar, puerto marítimo.
sea power [ˈsi:ˌpauə*] n. Potencia (*f.*) naval (country). || Fuerza (*f.*) naval (naval strength).
seaquake [ˈsi:ˌkweik] n. Maremoto, *m.*
sear [siə*] n. Quemadura, *f.*
— Adj. Marchito, ta.
sear [siə*] v. tr. Marchitar (to wither). || Abrasar, quemar (to scorch). || CULIN. Soasar. || MED. Cauterizar (to cauterize). || FIG. Endurecer (the conscience). | Endurecer, volver insensible (the heart).
— V. intr. Marchitarse (to wither).
search [sə:tʃ] n. Búsqueda, *f.* (in order to find sth.). || Registro, *m.* (of a house, car, etc.): *to carry out a search*, efectuar un registro. || Cacheo, *m.* (of a person). || Investigación, *f.* (in order to gain information). || MAR. Visita, *f.* (by customs). || — *In search of*, en busca de. || MAR. *Right of search*, derecho (*m.*) de visita.
search [sə:tʃ] v. tr. Buscar en (in order to find sth., gain information, etc.): *to search the woods for a missing child*, buscar en el bosque a un niño que se ha perdido; *to search the files*, buscar en los archivos. || Registrar (police, customs, etc.): *to search a car for weapons*, registrar un coche para ver si lleva armas. || Cachear (a person). || Examinar (one's conscience). || MED. Sondar (a wound). || — *Search me!*, ¡yo qué sé!, ¡a mí que me registren! || *To search one's memory for sth.*, intentar recordar algo. || *To search out*, descubrir.
— V. intr. Buscar (in order to find sth.). || Indagar, investigar (in order to gain information). || Hacer un registro (to find sth. concealed). || *To search after* o *for*, buscar.
searcher [—ə*] n. Buscador, ra. || Vista, *m.* (customs officer). || Investigador, ra (of information). || JUR. Indagador, ra; pesquisidor, ra. || MED. Sonda, *f.*
searching [—iŋ] adj. Minucioso, sa (thorough). || FIG. Penetrante (penetrating): *a searching look*, una mirada penetrante.
— N. Búsqueda, *f.* || Registro, *m.* (of luggage). || Cacheo, *m.* (of people). || Pesquisa, *f.* (of premises).
searchlight [—lait] n. Reflector, *m.*, proyector, *m.*
search party [—ˌpɑ:ti] n. Equipo (*m.*) de salvamento.
search warrant [—ˌwɔrənt] n. Mandamiento (*m.*) de registro.
sea risk [ˈsi:risk] n. Peligro (*m.*) de mar.
sea room [ˈsi:ru:m] n. Espacio (*m.*) de maniobra.
sea rover [ˈsi:ˌrəuvə] n. Pirata, *m.* (pirate). || Barco (*m.*) pirata (ship).
seascape [ˈsi:skeip] n. ARTS. Marina, *f.* || Vista (*f.*) marina (view of the sea).
seascapist [—əst] n. ARTS. Marinista, *m.* & *f.*
sea serpent [ˈsi:ˌsə:pənt] n. ZOOL. Serpiente (*f.*) de mar, serpiente (*f.*) marina (sea snake). || Serpiente (*f.*) de mar (mythological sea monster).
sea shanty [ˈsi:ˌʃænti] n. MAR. Saloma, *f.* (song).
seashell [ˈsi:ʃel] n. Concha (*f.*) marina.
seashore [ˈsi:ʃɔ:*] n. Playa, *f.*, orilla (*f.*) del mar (beach). || Costa, *f.*, litoral, *m.* (seacoast).
seasick [ˈsi:sik] adj. Mareado, da. || *To get seasick*, marearse.
seasickness [—nis] n. Mareo, *m.*
seaside [ˈsi:ˈsaid] n. Playa, *f.*: *to spend a day at* o *by the seaside*, pasar un día en la playa. || Costa, *f.*, litoral, *m.* (coast). || *To spend one's summer holiday at* o *by the seaside*, veranear a orillas del mar *or* en el mar.
— Adj. Costero, ra. || *Seaside resort*, estación balnearia.
sea snail [ˈsi:ˈsneil] n. ZOOL. Caracola, *f.*
sea snake [ˈsi:ˈsneik] n. ZOOL. Serpiente (*f.*) de mar, serpiente (*f.*) marina. || Serpiente (*f.*) de mar (mythological sea monster).
season [ˈsi:zn] n. Estación, *f.*: *the four seasons of the year*, las cuatro estaciones del año. || Época, *f.*: *the mating season*, la época del celo. || Temporada, *f.*: *football season*, temporada de fútbol; *bullfighting season*, temporada de toros; *tourist season*, temporada turística; *strawberry season*, temporada de las fresas; *concert season*, temporada de conciertos. || — *At the height of the season*, en plena temporada. || *In due season*, a su debido tiempo. || *In season*, en sazón (fruit), en celo (on heat), oportuno (remark). || FIG. *In season and out of season*, a tiempo y a destiempo. || *Out of season*, fuera de temporada *or* de sazón (fruit, etc.), inoportuno (remark). || *Slack season*, temporada baja *or* de poca venta *or* de venta reducida. || *The close season*, la veda (hunting and fishing). || *The off season*, la temporada baja. || *The open season*, la temporada de caza *or* de pesca. || *The summer season*, el verano. || *To last for a season*, estar en cartel por una temporada (a play). || *With the compliments of the season*, deseándole felices Pascuas.
season [ˈsi:zn] v. tr. Sazonar, condimentar (food). || Madurar (wine). || Secar (wood). || Curar (pipe). || Acostumbrar: *one gets seasoned to cold weather*, uno se acostumbra al frío. || Madurar: *a man seasoned by many misfortunes*, un hombre madurado por muchas desgracias. || Acostumbrar al mar (sailors). || Aguerrir (troops). || Moderar: *a judgment seasoned by goodwill*, un fallo moderado por la benevolencia. || Sazonar, amenizar: *a letter seasoned with verse*, una carta sazonada con versos. || *A seasoned sailor*, un marinero experimentado.
— V. intr. Secarse (wood). || Madurar (wine). || Acostumbrase (to become accustomed). || Acostumbrarse al mar (sailors). || Aguerrirse (troops).
seasonable [—əbl] adj. Propio de la estación: *seasonable weather*, tiempo propio de la estación. || Oportuno, na: *seasonable piece of advice*, consejo oportuno.
seasonableness [—əblnis] n. Oportunidad, *f.*
seasonably [—əbli] adv. Oportunamente, a propósito.
seasonal [ˈsi:zənl] adj. Estacional (characteristic of the season). || Apropiado para la estación (suited to the season): *seasonal dress*, ropa apropiada para la estación. || Temporal: *seasonal work*, trabajo temporal. || Estacional (worker).
seasoner [ˈsi:zənə*] n. Persona (*f.*) que sazona. || Condimento, *m.*
seasoning [ˈsi:zniŋ] n. Condimento, *m.*, aderezo, *m.* || TECH. Secado, *m.* (of wood). || Maduramiento, *m.* (of wine). || Endurecimiento, *m.* (hardening). || Acostumbramiento, *m.*
season ticket [ˈsi:znˌtikit] n. Abono, *m.* (for football, theatre, trains, etc.).
seat [si:t] n. Asiento, *m.*: *front*, *rear seat*, asiento delantero, trasero. || Silla, *f.* (chair). || Asiento, *m.* (of a chair). || Plaza, *f.* (when considering the number): *a car with four seats*, un coche de cuatro plazas. || CINEM. THEATR. Localidad, *f.*, entrada, *f.*: *to book seats*, reservar localidades. || Centro, *m.*: *a seat of learning*, un centro de estudios. || Sede *f.*: *seat of government*, sede del gobierno. || Fondo, *m.*: *the seat of the problem*, el fondo del problema. || Escaño, *m.*, puesto, *m.* [*Amer.*, banco, *m.*] (in Parliament): *to lose one's seat*, perder su escaño. || Sillín, *m.* (of a bicycle). || Tabla, *f.* (of toilet). || Trasero, *m.*, posaderas, *f. pl.* (buttocks). || Fondillos, *m. pl.* (of trousers). || TECH. Asiento, *m.* || MED. Foco, *m.* (of an illness). || MIL. Teatro, *m.* (of operations). || — *To have a good seat*, montar bien a caballo (in riding). || *To keep one's seat*, permanecer sentado. || *To take a seat*, sentarse. || *To take one's seat*, colocarse. || *To take one's seat in Parliament*, tomar posesión de su cargo en el Parlamento.
seat [si:t] v. tr. Sentar: *he seated the child on the chair*, sentó al niño en la silla. || Tener cabida para: *the theatre seats a hundred people*, el teatro tiene cabida para cien personas. || Tener sitio para: *the table seats six easily*, la mesa tiene sitio de sobra para seis personas. || Colocar (to allot a seat to s.o.): *the younger members were seated at the back of the room*, los socios más jóvenes fueron colocados al fondo de la sala; *to seat the audience round the stage*, colocar al público alrededor del escenario. || Poner asiento a (a chair). || TECH. Ajustar (an axle, a valve). | Colocar (a machine). || ARCH. Asentar. || — *To be seated*, sentarse: *please be seated*, siéntese, por favor; estar sentado (to be sitting), estar localizado (*in*, en) [a disease] || *To remain seated*, quedarse sentado. || TECH. *To seat on*, descansar en. || *To seat o.s.*, sentarse.
seat belt [—belt] n. Cinturón (*m.*) de seguridad.
seater [—ə*] n. *A fifty-seater coach*, un autocar de cincuenta plazas. || *A three-seater settee*, un sofá de tres plazas. || *A two seater*, un dos plazas (car, plane)
seating [—iŋ] n. Asientos, *m. pl.* (seats): *the seating is rather poor*, los asientos son bastante malos. || Distribución (*f.*) de los asientos (arrangement of seats): *the man in charge of seating*, el encargado de la distribución de los asientos. || Colocación, *f.*: *the*

seating of the guests, la colocación de los invitados. || Tapicería, *f.* (material for covering seats). || TECH. Asiento, *m.* || *Seating capacity*, número (*m.*) de plazas.
sea trout [ˈsiːtraut] n. ZOOL. Trucha (*f.*) de mar.
sea urchin [ˈsiːˈəːtʃin] n. ZOOL. Erizo (*m.*) de mar.
sea wall [ˈsiːˈwɔːl] n. Dique, *m.*, rompeolas, *m. inv.*
seaward [ˈsiːwəd] n. Lado (*m.*) del mar.
— Adj. Que da al mar, del lado del mar.
seaward [ˈsiːwəd] or **seawards** [—z] adv. Hacia el mar, mar adentro.
seaware [ˈsiːwɛə*] n. Algas, *f. pl.*
seawater [ˈsiːˌwɔːtə*] n. Agua (*f.*) de mar.
seaway [ˈsiːwei] n. Ruta (*f.*) *or* vía (*f.*) marítima (route). || Canal (*m.*) marítimo (ship canal). || MAR. Avance, *m.* (ship's progress). | Estela, *f.* (trace). | Mar (*f.*) gruesa (heavy sea).
seaweed [ˈsiːwiːd] n. BOT. Alga, *f.*
sea wolf [—ˌwulf] n. Lubina, *f.*, robalo, *m.* (fish). || Pirata, *m.* (pirate).
seaworthiness [ˈsiːˌwəːðinis] n. Navegabilidad, *f.*
seaworthy [ˈsiːˌwəːði] adj. En buen estado para navegar, marinero, ra.
sea wrack [ˈsiːræk] n. Algas, *f. pl.* (mass of seaweed).
sebaceous [siˈbeiʃəs] adj. Sebáceo, a: *sebaceous glands*, glándulas sebáceas.
seborrhea or **seborrhoea** [ˌsebəˈriːə] n. MED. Seborrea, *f.*
sebum [ˈsiːbəm] n. BIOL. Sebo, *m.*
secant [ˈsiːkənt] adj. MATH. Secante.
— N. MATH. Secante, *f.*
secateurs [ˌsekəˈtəːz] pl. n. Podadera, *f. sing.*
secede [siˈsiːd] v. intr. Separarse: *to secede from a federation*, separarse de una federación.
seceder [—ə*] n. Separatista, *m.* & *f.*, secesionista, *m.* & *f.*
secession [siˈseʃən] n. Secesión, *f.*, separación, *f.* || U. S. *War of Secession*, Guerra (*f.*) de Secesión.
secessionism [siˈseʃnizəm] n. Separatismo, *m.*
secessionist [siˈseʃnist] n. Secesionista, *m.* & *f.*, separatista, *m.* & *f.*
seclude [siˈkluːd] v. tr. Recluir (to keep apart). || Aislar (to isolate). || *To seclude o.s. from*, apartarse de, retirarse de.
secluded [—id] adj. Aislado, da (isolated). || Retirado, da (withdrawn).
seclusion [siˈkluːʒən] n. Reclusión, *f.* (forceable keeping apart). || Aislamiento, *m.*, retiro, *m.* (withdrawn existence). || *To live in seclusion*, vivir aislado.
seclusive [siˈkluːsiv] adj. Que tiene tendencia a aislarse, solitario, ria.
second [ˈsekənd] adj. Segundo, da: *he married for the second time*, se casó en segundas nupcias; *he came in the second place*, llegó en segundo lugar. || Otro, otra: *you will need a second pair of shoes*, le hará falta otro par de zapatos; *he seems to think he's a second Napoleon!*, ¡parece que se cree otro Napoleón! || — *Every second*, uno de cada dos. || *Every second day*, un día sí y otro no, cada dos días. || *On second thoughts*, pensándolo bien. || REL. *Second Advent*, segundo advenimiento. | *Second Adventist*, adventista, *m.* & *f.* || SP. *Second base*, segunda base (in baseball). || *Second chamber*, cámara alta. || *Second childhood*, segunda infancia. || *Second class*, segunda clase, segunda (in a train). || *Second cousin*, primo segundo, prima segunda. || *Second cousin once removed*, sobrino tercero, sobrina tercera. || *Second floor*, segundo piso (in Great Britain and other countries), primer piso (in United States). || MIL. *Second lieutenant*, alférez, *m.*, subteniente, *m.* || MAR. *Second mate*, segundo (*m.*) de a bordo. || *Second mortgage*, segunda hipoteca. || *Second nature*, segunda naturaleza. || *Second offence*, reincidencia, *f.* || *Second offender*, reincidente, *m.* & *f.* || GRAMM. *Second person*, segunda persona. || *Second self*, alter ego, *m.* || *Second sight*, clarividencia, *f.* || *Second teeth*, segunda dentición. || *Second wind*, segundo aliento. || *The second day of March*, el dos de marzo. || *The second largest city*, la segunda ciudad en importancia. || *To be second to none*, no ser inferior a nadie, no ir a la zaga a nadie. || *To have a second helping*, repetir de una cosa. || *To play second fiddle*, desempeñar un papel secundario.
— N. Segundo, *m.* (time). || Segundo, da (in rank, in a series): *she came in second*, llegó segunda. || SP. Segundo, *m.*, cuidador, *m.* (in boxing). || Padrino, *m.* (in a duel). || Notable, *m.* (university degree): *to obtain a second*, sacar un notable. || Segundo premio, *m.* (prize). || AUT. Segunda, *f.* (gear). || Día (*m.*) dos, dos, *m.* (of a month): *the second of May*, el dos de mayo. || MUS. Segunda, *f.* (interval). | Segunda parte, *f.* (of a composition). || MATH. Segundo, *m.* || — Pl. Artículos (*m.*) de segunda clase (goods). || — *Just a second!*, ¡un momento! || *In a split second*, en un dos por tres. || *Philip II* (*the Second*), Felipe II [segundo].
— Adv. En segundo lugar (in the second place). || En segunda, en segunda clase: *to travel second*, viajar en segunda.
second [ˈsekənd] v. tr. Apoyar, secundar (to assist). || Apoyar (a proposal, a speaker): *a few delegates seconded the motion*, unos delegados apoyaron la moción.
second [siˈkɔnd] v. tr. MIL. Destinar, destacar.
secondary [ˈsekəndəri] adj. Secundario, ria. || JUR. Indirecto, ta (evidence). || GRAMM. Derivado, da (meaning). || — ELECTR. *Secondary cell*, acumulador, *m.* || *Secondary colour*, color secundario. || *Secondary education*, enseñanza media, segunda enseñanza. || PHYS. *Secondary emission*, emisión secundaria. || ASTR. *Secondary planet*, planeta secundario, satélite, *m.* || *Secondary school*, instituto (*m.*) de enseñanza media.
— N. Subalterno, *m.* (secondary person). || GEOL. Secundario, *m.*
second best [ˈsekəndbest] n. Segundo, da (in quality). || — FIG. *It's a second best*, es una manera de salir del paso. || *To come off second best*, ser vencido, perder, llevar la peor parte.
second-best [ˈsekəndbest] adj. Mejor después del primero, segundo, da.
second born [ˈsekəndˈbɔːn] adj./n. Segundogénito, ta.
second-class [ˈsekəndˈklɑːs] adj. De segunda clase, de segunda (trains, etc.). || De segunda categoría, de segunda clase (hotels, goods, etc.).
— Adv. En segunda, en segunda clase: *to travel second-class*, viajar en segunda.
seconde [səˈkɔnd] n. Segunda, *f.* (in fencing).
seconder [ˈsekəndə*] n. Persona (*f.*) que apoya [una moción, etc.].
second hand [ˈsekəndhænd] n. Segundero, *m.* (of a watch). || *At second hand*, de segunda mano.
secondhand [ˈsekəndˈhænd] adj. De segunda mano, de ocasión: *secondhand books*, libros de segunda mano. || Usado, da; viejo, ja: *secondhand clothes*, ropa vieja. || — *Secondhand bookseller*, librero (*m.*) de lance. || *Secondhand bookshop*, librería (*f.*) de lance. || *Secondhand dealer*, chamarilero, ra. || *Secondhand information*, información conseguida indirectamente, información de segunda mano.
second-in-command [ˌsekəndinkəˈmend] n. MIL. Segundo jefe, *m.*
secondly [ˈsekəndli] adv. En segundo lugar.
second-rate [ˈsekəndˈreit] adj. De segunda categoría.
secrecy [ˈsiːkrisi] n. Secreto, *m.*: *done in secrecy*, hecho en secreto; *professional secrecy*, secreto profesional. || Discreción, *f.*: *you can rely on Peter's secrecy*, se puede confiar en la discreción de Pedro. || *Under pledge of secrecy*, bajo secreto.
secret [ˈsiːkrit] adj. Secreto, ta: *a secret agreement*, un acuerdo secreto; *there was a secret passage behind the fireplace*, había un pasillo secreto detrás de la chimenea; *secret society*, sociedad secreta; *secret agent, service*, agente, servicio secreto. || Reservado, da; callado, da (secretive). || Escondido, da; recóndito, ta (place). || — *Secret partner*, socio comanditario. || FIG. ANAT. *Secret parts*, partes pudendas. || *To keep sth. secret*, mantener algo secreto.
— N. Secreto, *m.*: *trade secret*, secreto de fabricación. || REL. Secreta, *f.* || — Pl. Misterios, *m.* (of nature). || FIG. ANAT. Partes (*f.*) pudendas. || — *An open secret*, un secreto a voces. || *As a secret*, secretamente, de modo confidencial. || *In secret*, en secreto. || *To be in on the secret*, estar en el secreto. || *To keep a secret*, guardar un secreto. || *To let s.o. into a secret*, revelar un secreto a alguien. || *To make no secret of sth.*, no ocultar algo. || *State secret*, secreto de Estado.
secretaire [sekriˈtɛə*] n. Secreter, *m.*
secretarial [ˌsekrəˈtɛəriəl] adj. De secretario, de secretaria.
secretariat or **secretariate** [ˌsekrəˈtɛəriət] n. Secretaría, *f.*, secretariado, *m.*
secretary [ˈsekrətri] n. Secretario, ria (person): *general secretary*, secretario general; *private secretary*, secretario particular. || Secreter, *m.*, escritorio, *m.* (desk). || U. S. Ministro, *m.* (minister): *Secretary of the Treasury*, ministro de Hacienda. || — ZOOL. *Secretary bird*, secretario, *m.*, serpentario, *m.* || *Secretary of State*, ministro con cartera (in Britain), secretario de Estado, ministro de Asuntos Exteriores [*Amer.*, ministro de Relaciones Exteriores] (in United States).
secretary-general [—ˈdʒenərəl] n. Secretario (*m.*) general.

— OBSERV. El plural es *secretaries-general.*

secretaryship [—ʃip] n. Secretaría, *f.*, secretariado, *m.* || U. S. Ministerio, *m.*
secrete [siˈkriːt] v. tr. Secretar, segregar (to emit a substance). || Ocultar (to hide). || JUR. Encubrir, ocultar.
secretin [siˈkriːtin] n. Secretina, *f.* (hormone).
secretion [siˈkriːʃən] n. Secreción, *f.*: *the secretion of saliva*, la secreción de la saliva. || Ocultación, *f.* (hiding). || JUR. Encubrimiento, *m.*, ocultación, *f.*
secretive [siˈkriːtiv] adj. Sigiloso, sa (disposed to secrecy). || Reservado, da; callado, da (silent).
secretiveness [—nis] n. Sigilo, *m.*, discreción, *f.* (discretion). || Reserva, *f.*
secretory [siˈkriːtəri] adj. Secretor, ra; secretorio, ria.
— N. ANAT. Órgano (*m.*) secretorio.
sect [sekt] n. Secta, *f.*
sectarian [sekˈtɛəriən] adj./n. Sectario, ria.
sectarianism [—izəm] n. Sectarismo, *m.*
sectary [ˈsektəri] n. Sectario, ria (sectarian). || Cismático, ca.
section [ˈsekʃən] n. Sección, *f.*: *that section of the house over there belongs to the servants*, aquella sección de la casa pertenece al servicio; *the string section of the orchestra*, la sección de cuerdas de la

orquesta. || Parte, *f.* (part). || Parte, *f.*, distrito, *m.* (of a town). || Parte, *f.*, región, *f.* (of a country). || Sector, *m.* (of population). || JUR. Artículo, *m.* (of a law). || Párrafo, *m.* (of book, document). || Página, *f.*, sección, *f.* (in a newspaper). || Trozo, *m.* (of cheese, cake). || Gajo, *m.* (of orange). || Casilla, *f.* (of a drawer). || MIL. Sección, *f.* || AVIAT. Patrulla, *f.* || TECH. Tramo, *m.* (of a tube). | Perfil, *m.* (of metal). | Tramo, *m.*, ramal, *m.* (of railway track). || Departamento, *m.*, compartimiento, *m.* (of a sleeper). || MATH. Sección, *f.* || ARTS. ARCH. Corte, *m.*, sección, *f.* || Pliego, *m.* (in bookbinding). || *Cross section*, sección transversal.

section [ˈsekʃən] v. tr. Seccionar, cortar (to cut). || Dividir en secciones (to divide).

sectional [—l] adj. Particular, local, regional: *sectional interests*, intereses particulares. || En corte (plans, designs). || Cuadriculado, da (paper). || En compartimentos (bookcase). || TECH. En perfil (metal). | Desmontable (dismountable).

sectionalism [ˈsekʃənəlizəm] n. Localismo, *m.*, regionalismo, *m.*

sectionalize [ˈsekʃənəˌlaiz] v. tr. Dividir en regiones.

sectioning [ˈsekʃəniŋ] n. Seccionamiento, *m.*

sector [ˈsektə*] n. MATH. Sector, *m.* (area). | Compás (*m.*) de proporciones (instrument). || MIL. COMM. Sector, *m.*: *public, private sector*, sector público, privado. || Zona, *f.* (of a town).

sectorial [sekˈtɔːriəl] adj. Sectorial (of a sector).

secular [ˈsekjulə*] adj. Profano, na: *secular music*, música profana. || REL. Secular, seglar (clergy). | Seglar: *the secular apostolate*, el apostolado seglar. || Laico, ca: *secular school*, escuela laica. || Mundano, na: *a very secular life*, una vida muy mundana. || Secular (occurring once a century). || JUR. Secular (justice). || FIG. Secular (very ancient). | Duradero, ra (renown).
— N. REL. Seglar, *m.*, secular, *m.*

secularism [ˈsekjulərizəm] n. Laicismo, *m.* (in education). || PHIL. Materialismo, *m.*

secularist [ˈsekjulərist] n. Partidario (*m.*) del laicismo. || PHIL. Materialista, *m.* & *f.*, libre pensador, ra.

secularization [ˈsekjuləraiˈzeiʃən] n. Secularización, *f.*

secularize [ˈsekjuləraiz] v. tr. Secularizar.

secure [siˈkjuə*] adj. Seguro, ra (certain, free from anxiety, safe): *our victory is secure*, nuestra victoria es segura; *do you feel secure about your future?*, ¿se siente seguro en cuanto a su porvenir? || Seguro, ra; firme, sólido, da: *is this ladder secure?*, ¿está segura esta escalera? || COMM. Seguro, ra (investment). || — *Secure from attack*, protegido contra los ataques. || *To make secure*, fijar, sujetar, afianzar, asegurar (door, beam, etc.).

secure [siˈkjuə*] v. tr. Asegurar, afianzar (to make firm). || Poner a buen recaudo (to put in a safe place). || Cerrar firmemente (a door, a window). || Garantizar (a loan, a creditor): *secured by mortgage*, garantizado por una hipoteca. || Conseguir, obtener (to obtain). || Reservar: *to secure seats at the theatre*, reservar entradas en el teatro. || Asegurar (to procure): *to secure employment*, asegurar el empleo. || Proteger (to protect). || Consolidar, reforzar, asegurar: *to secure one's positions*, consolidar sus posiciones. || TECH. Bloquear (a screw). || JUR. Detener, encarcelar (to take into custody). || MAR. Amarrar (a boat). || AGR. Recoger (crop). || *To secure o.s. against*, protegerse contra.

security [siˈkjuəriti] n. Seguridad, *f.*: *the security of the home*, la seguridad del hogar; *national security*, la seguridad nacional; *security measures to protect a secret weapon*, medidas de seguridad para proteger un arma secreta. || Fianza, *f.*, garantía, *f.* (guarantee): *on security*, bajo fianza; *in security for*, en garantía de; *to lodge a security*, dejar una fianza. || Fiador, ra (guarantor). || FIG. Salvaguardia, *f.*, defensa, *f.*: *the family is the security of society*, la familia es la salvaguardia de la sociedad. || — Pl. COMM. Valores, *m.*, títulos, *m.*: *public securities*, valores públicos; *gilt-edged securities*, valores de máxima garantía; *securities in hand*, valores en cartera. || — COMM. *Government securities*, fondos (*m. pl.*) del Estado. || *Security Council*, Consejo (*m.*) de Seguridad (of U. N.). || COMM. *Security market*, la Bolsa. || *Social Security*, seguridad social. || *To stand security for*, salir *or* ser fiador de, garantizar a.

sedan [siˈdæn] n. AUT. Sedán, *m.*, automóvil (*m.*) de carrocería cerrada. || Silla (*f.*) de manos (portable chair). || *Sedan chair*, silla (*f.*) de manos.

sedate [siˈdeit] adj. Sosegado, da; tranquilo, la (conduct, person). || Sentado, da; serio ria; formal (temperament).

sedateness [—nis] n. Tranquilidad, *f.*, sosiego, *m.* (calmness). || Seriedad, *f.*, formalidad, *f.* (seriousness).

sedation [siˈdeiʃən] n. MED. Sedación, *f.*

sedative [ˈsedətiv] adj. Sedativo, va; sedante, calmante.
— N. MED. Sedante, *m.*, sedativo, *m.*, calmante, *m.*

sedentariness [ˈsedntərinis] n. Sedentarismo, *m.*, vida (*f.*) sedentaria.

sedentary [ˈsedntəri] adj. Sedentario, ria: *a sedentary occupation*, un trabajo sedentario. || ZOOL. Sedentario, ria. || ARTS. Sedente.

sedge [sedʒ] n. BOT. Juncia, *f.*

sedge warbler [—ˌwɔːblə*] n. Curruca, *f.* (bird).

sediment [ˈsedimənt] n. Sedimento, *m.* || Poso, *m.* (of a liquid). || Borra, *f.* (of ink). || Poso, *m.*, heces, *f. pl.* (of wine). || GEOL. Sedimento, *m.*

sedimentary [ˌsediˈmentəri] adj. Sedimentario, ria: *sedimentary rock*, roca sedimentaria.

sedimentation [ˈsedimenˈteiʃən] n. Sedimentación, *f.*

sedition [siˈdiʃən] n. Sedición, *f.*

seditious [siˈdiʃəs] adj. Sedicioso, sa.

seduce [siˈdjuːs] v. tr. Seducir. || *To seduce a man from his duty*, apartar a un hombre de su deber.

seducer [—ə*] n. Seductor, ra.

seduction [siˈdʌkʃən] n. Seducción, *f.* || FIG. Atractivo, *m.* (attractiveness): *the seductions of wealth*, los atractivos de la riqueza.

seductive [siˈdʌktiv] adj. Seductor, ra; seductivo, va. || Seductor, ra; atractivo, va; tentador, ra (offer). || Provocativo, va (smile).

seductiveness [—nis] n. Seducción, *f.*, atractivo, *m.* (of a woman). || Atractivo, *m.* (of an offer).

sedulity [siˈdjuːliti] n. Diligencia, *f.*

sedulous [ˈsedjuləs] adj. Diligente.

sedulousness [—nis] n. Diligencia, *f.*

see [siː] n. REL. Sede, *f.*: *the Holy See*, la Santa Sede. | Arzobispado, *m.* (of an archbishop). | Obispado, *m.* (of a bishop).

see* [siː] v. tr. Ver: *I see you*, te veo; *I'm going to see a bullfight*, voy a ver una corrida; *I'd like to see more of you*, me gustaría verle más a menudo; *let me see your papers*, déjame ver tus papeles; *I saw him running*, le he visto correr; *I saw it done*, lo vi hacer; *monument that can be seen from afar*, monumento que se ve desde lejos. || Visitar: *to see the town*, visitar la ciudad. || Mirar: *see if this coat suits you*, mire si le sienta bien este abrigo. || Ver (friends): *when shall I see you again?*, ¿cuándo le volveré a ver?; *can I see her for a minute?*, ¿puedo verla un momento? || Comprender, entender, ver: *I don't see what you mean*, no comprendo lo que quiere decir. || Comprender, entender: *I don't see that joke*, no entiendo ese chiste. || Ver: *I can't see the advantage of*, no veo el interés de; *I see that you have changed your mind*, veo que ha cambiado de parecer. || Imaginarse, figurarse, ver: *I just can't see them married*, no me los imagino casados. || Ver: *go and see what he wants*, vaya a ver lo que quiere. || Tener una entrevista con, entrevistarse con, ver (to have an interview): *I'll see the Prime Minister tomorrow*, tendré una entrevista mañana con el Primer Ministro. || Recibir (visitors): *the doctor will see you in a moment*, el doctor le recibirá dentro de un momento. || Ir a ver, consultar: *Mary, you must see the dentist*, María, tienes que ir a ver al dentista. || Asegurarse de: *see that you take all your papers with you*, asegúrese de que se lleva todos los papeles. || Procurar: *see that we are housed*, procure encontrarnos alojamiento. || Tener cuidado de: *see that you don't fall down the stairs*, ten cuidado de no caerte por las escaleras. || Acompañar: *to see s.o. home*, acompañar a alguien a casa; *I'll see you to the door*, le acompaño hasta la puerta. || Llevar (to carry): *to see s.o. to bed*, llevar a alguien a la cama. || Conocer (changes, life, etc.): *we have seen better days*, hemos conocido tiempos mejores. || Aceptar (a bet, a challenge). || — *As I see it*, por lo que veo, por lo visto. || *He has seen a good deal of the world*, ha corrido mucho mundo. || FIG. *He will never see fifty again*, tiene cincuenta años cumplidos, tiene más de cincuenta años. | *I don't know what you see in him*, no sé lo que usted encuentra en él. | *I don't see it*, no creo que sea posible. || *I fail to see how he did it*, no consigo ver cómo pudo hacerlo. || FIG. FAM. *I have to see a man about a dog*, tengo que ir a llamar por teléfono (to go to the toilet). || FAM. *I'll see him damned first!*, ¡que le parta un rayo! || *I saw it with my own eyes*, lo vi con mis propios ojos. || *I shall be seing you for lunch*, ya nos veremos en el almuerzo. || *It's not fit to be seen*, no se puede ver. || *It's worth seing*, merece la pena verlo. || *I wanted to see you on business*, quería verle para hablar de negocios. || *Let's see*, vamos a ver, a ver: *let's see what film they're showing*, vamos a ver qué película echan. || FIG. *Nothing could be seen of him*, no se le veía nada, no se le veía en ninguna parte. || *Seeing is believing*, ver para creer. || *See page 20*, véase página veinte. || *See you!*, ¡hasta luego! || *See you later!*, *see you soon!*, ¡hasta luego!, ¡hasta pronto! || *See you on Thursday!*, ¡hasta el jueves! || *That remains to be seen*, eso está por ver. || *There's nothing to see*, no hay nada que merezca la pena verse. || *This is how I see it*, esta es mi manera de verlo *or* de enfocarlo. || *To go and see s.o.* o *to call and see s.o.* o *to call to see s.o.*, ir a ver a alguien. || *To make s.o. see sth.*, hacer ver algo a alguien. || *To see no one*, no ver a nadie. || *To see o.s. in one's children*, verse [retratado] en sus hijos. || *To see one's way clear*, ver claramente la manera de hacer las cosas. || FIG. FAM. *To see red*, ponerse furioso. || FAM. *To see stars*, ver las estrellas. || FIG. *To see the light* o *the light of day*, nacer, ver la luz (to be born), salir a luz (work). || *We can't see to read*, no vemos lo suficiente para leer. || *You have to see it to believe it*, hay que verlo para creerlo. || FIG. *You're seeing things!*, ¡está usted viendo visiones! || *You see...*, es que: *you see I haven't got any money*, es que no tengo dinero.

— V. intr. Ver: *I can see very well*, veo muy bien; *to see poorly*, ver mal; *let me see*, vamos a ver. || Comprender, entender, ver (to understand). || — *As far as I can see*, por lo visto, por lo que veo. || *As far as the eye can see*, hasta donde alcanza la vista. || *Do as you see fit*, haz como te parezca. || *I see!*, ¡ya veo! || *Let's see*, a ver, veamos, vamos a ver. || FAM. *Not to see further than the end of one's nose*, no ver más allá de sus narices. || *See for yourself*, vea usted mismo. || FAM. *See here!*, ¡oiga!, ¡mire! || *You see?*, ¿me entiendes?, ¿comprendes?

— ***To see about***, encargarse de, ocuparse de (to attend to): *don't worry, I'll see about it*, no se preocupe, me encargaré de ello. | Pensar: *you'd better see about it*, sería mejor que usted lo pensara. || ***To see after*** o ***to see to***, ocuparse de: *to see to the children*, ocuparse de los niños. | Encargarse de: *I'll see to the tickets*, me encargaré de las entradas. | — *To see to it that*, procurar que: *see to it that all is ready*, procure que todo esté listo. || ***To see in***, celebrar (the New Year). || ***To see into***, investigar, examinar (to investigate): *we must see into this matter*, tenemos que examinar este asunto. | Penetrar (secret, etc.). | Ver (the future). || ***To see off***, ir a despedir (to say good-bye). | — *To see s.o. off the premises*, acompañar a alguien hasta la puerta. || ***To see out***, acompañar hasta la puerta (to say good-bye). | Quedarse hasta el final de (to stay till the end): *I saw the film out*, me quedé hasta el final de la película. | Llevar a cabo (to carry out). | — FIG. *He will see us all out!*, ¡nos enterrará a todos! || ***To see over***, visitar. || ***To see through***, ver a través de: *I saw him through the curtains*, le vi a través de los visillos. | Calar, ver claramente las intenciones de (not to be deceived by). | Penetrar (a mystery). | Ayudar a salir de un apuro (to help). | Llevar a cabo (to carry out): *to see a business through*, llevar a cabo una empresa.

— OBSERV. Pret. ***saw***; p. p. ***seen***.

seeable [ˈsiəbəl] adj. Visible.

seed [si:d] n. BOT. Semilla, *f.* (in general). | Pepita, *f.* (of fruit). || AGR. Simiente, *f.*, semilla, *f.* (for sowing). || ANAT. Semen, *m.* (sperm). || FIG. Semilla, *f.*, germen, *m.*, origen, *m.*: *the seeds of revolution*, las semillas de la revolución. | Descendencia, *f.* (descendants). || Freza, *f.* (of an oyster). || — FIG. *To broadcast seed*, sembrar a los cuatro vientos. || *To go o to run to seed*, granar, dar grana (a plant), ajarse (a person), echarse a perder (to deteriorate). || FIG. *To sow the seeds of discord*, sembrar la discordia.

seed [si:d] v. tr. Despepitar (to take the seed out). || AGR. Sembrar (to sow): *when did you seed the lawn?*, ¿cuándo sembró usted el césped? || Fumigar (clouds). || SP. Preseleccionar (players).

— V. intr. AGR. Granar, dar grana (to go to seed). || Desgranarse (to shed seed). || Sembrar (to sow).

seedbed [—bed] n. AGR. Semillero, *m.* || FIG. Semillero, *m.*, foco, *m.*: *a seedbed of subversion*, un foco de subversión.

seedcake [—keik] n. CULIN. Torta (*f.*) de alcaravea.

seedcase [—keis] n. BOT. Vaina, *f.* (pod).

seed corn [—kɔ:n] n. BOT. Trigo (*m.*) de siembra. || U. S. Maíz (*m.*) de siembra.

seed drill [—dril] n. AGR. Sembradora, *f.*, sembradera, *f.*

seeder [—ə*] n. AGR. Sembradora, *f.*, sembradera, *f.* (sowing machine). | Máquina (*f.*) de despepitar (seed removing machine).

seediness [—inis] n. Aspecto (*m.*) raído (of a garment). || Lo desastrado (of appearance, dress). || FAM. Indisposición, *f.*, malestar, *m.*

seed leaf [—ˌli:f] n. BOT. Cotiledón, *m.*

seedless [—lis] adj. BOT. Sin semillas | Sin pepitas (fruit).

seedling [—liŋ] n. BOT. Planta (*f.*) de semillero. | Plantón, *m.* (young plant).

seed pearl [—ˈpə:l] n. Aljófar, *m.*

seedsman [—zmən] n. Vendedor (*m.*) de semillas.

— OBSERV. El plural de esta palabra es *seedsmen*.

seed sowing [—ˌsəuiŋ] n. Siembra, *f.*

seedtime [—taim] n. Siembra, *f.*

seed vessel [—vesl] n. BOT. Pericarpio, *m.*

seedy [—i] adj. BOT. Granado, da. || FAM. Raído, da (clothing). | Desastrado, da (appearance, person). | Sórdido, da (place). | Pachucho, cha (in poor health).

seeing [ˈsi:iŋ] adj. Vidente.

— N. Vista, *f.* (sense of sight). || Visión, *f.* (act of perceiving). || *Seeing is believing*, ver para creer.

— Conj. *Seeing that*, en vista de que, visto que: *seeing that it is so late you can stay*, en vista de que es tan tarde te puedes quedar.

seek* [si:k] v. tr. Buscar: *he sought shelter*, buscaba abrigo; *to go and seek s.o.*, ir a buscar a alguien; *he is seeking employment*, está buscando trabajo. || Tratar, procurar: *he seeks to persuade everybody*, trata de convencer a todo el mundo. || Pedir: *to seek advice*, pedir consejo. || Solicitar (a post). || *To seek s.o.'s life*, atentar contra la vida de alguien.

— V. intr. Buscar. || — *To be much sought after*, ser muy solicitado (person), ser muy cotizado (thing). || *To seek after* o *for*, buscar: *to seek for information*, buscar información.

— OBSERV. Pret. & p. p. ***sought***.

seeker [—ə*] n. Buscador, ra.

seem [si:m] v. intr. Parecer: *it seems to me that*, me parece que; *it seems interesting*, parece interesante; *he seems to be working*, parece que está trabajando. || — *I seem to remember that*, me parece recordar que. || *It seems not*, parece que no. || *So it seems*, así parece, eso parece. || *What seems to be the trouble?*, ¿qué pasa?

seeming [—iŋ] adj. Aparente, supuesto, ta.

— N. Apariencia, *f.*

seemingly [—iŋli] adv. Al parecer, por lo visto, aparentemente. || *He was seemingly content*, parecía satisfecho.

seemliness [—linis] n. Decoro, *m.*, decencia, *f.* (correctness). || Atractivo, *m.* (attractiveness).

seemly [—li] adj. Decente, decoroso, sa; correcto, ta (correct). || Atractivo, va (attractive).

seen [si:n] p. p. See SEE.

seep [si:p] v. intr. Rezumarse.

seepage [—idʒ] n. Filtración, *f.*

seer [siə*] n. Vidente, *m.* & *f.*, adivino, na.

seesaw [ˈsi:sɔ:] n. Subibaja, *m.*, columpio, *m.* (for children). || FIG. Vaivén, *m.*: *the seesaw of prices*, el vaivén de los precios.

— Adj. De vaivén: *seesaw motion*, movimiento de vaivén.

seesaw [ˈsi:sɔ:] v. intr. Columpiarse. || TECH. Oscilar. || FIG. Vacilar, oscilar: *to seesaw between two opinions*, vacilar entre dos opiniones.

seethe [si:ð] v. intr. Borbotar, hervir (liquid). || FIG. Hervir: *the streets were seething with people*, las calles hervían de gente. || FIG. *To be seething with anger*, estar bufando de cólera.

seething [—iŋ] adj. Hirviente. || Agitado, da (waters). || FIG. Hormigueante (mass). | Agitado, da (country).

see-through [ˈsi:θru:] adj. Transparente.

segment [ˈsegmənt] n. MATH. ZOOL. Segmento, *m.* || Gajo, *m.* (of orange).

segment [segˈment] v. tr. Dividir en segmentos, segmentar.

— V. intr. Segmentarse, dividirse en segmentos.

segmental [—əl] adj. Segmentario, ria. || ARCH. Rebajado, da (arch). || Parcial, fragmentario, ria (part).

segmentary [—əri] adj. Segmentario, ria.

segmentation [ˌsegmənˈteiʃən] n. Segmentación, *f.*, división (*f.*) en segmentos.

segmented [segˈmentid] adj. Segmentario, ria. || *Segmented mirror*, espejo (*m.*) de varios cuerpos.

Segovian [seˈgəuviən] adj./n. Segoviano, na.

segregate [ˈsegrigit] adj. Aislado, da; separado, da.

segregate [ˈsegrigeit] v. tr. Segregar, separar, aislar.

— V. intr. Dividirse, separarse.

segregation [ˌsegriˈgeiʃən] n. Segregación, *f.*: *racial segregation*, segregación racial.

segregationist [ˌsegriˈgeiʃnist] n. Segregacionista, *m.* & *f.*

segregative [ˈsegrigeitiv] adj. Segregativo, va.

seguidilla [segiˈdi:ljə] n. MUS. Seguidilla, *f.*

seignior [ˈseinjə*] n. Señor (*m.*) feudal.

seigniory [—ri] n. Señorío, *m.*

seine [sein] n. Jábega, *f.* (fishing net).

seine [sein] v. tr./intr. Pescar con jábega.

Seine [sein] pr. n. GEOGR. Sena, *m.*

seism [ˈsaizəm] n. Seísmo, *m.* [*Amer.*, sismo, *m.*].

seismic [ˈsaizmik] adj. Sísmico, ca.

seismism [ˈsaizmizəm] n. Fenómenos (*m. pl.*) sísmicos.

seismogram [ˈsaizməgræm] n. Sismograma, *m.*

seismograph [ˈsaizməgrɑ:f] n. Sismógrafo, *m.*

seismologic [ˌsaizməˈlɔdʒik] or **seismological** [—əl] adj. Sismológico, ca.

seismology [saizˈmɔlədʒi] n. Sismología, *f.*

seismometer [saizˈmɔmitə*] n. Sismómetro, *m.*

seizable [ˈsi:zəbl] adj. Asible. || JUR. Embargable.

seize [si:z] v. tr. Agarrar, asir, coger (to grab firmly): *to seize s.o. by the collar*, agarrar a alguien por el cuello. || Tomar (to take hold of). || JUR. Embargar, incautarse de (property). | Incautarse de: *the police seized fifty kilograms of drugs on the border*, la policía se incautó de cincuenta kilos de drogas en la frontera. | Secuestrar, retirar de la circulación (newspapers). | | Detener, arrestar (a person). || MIL. Apoderarse de, tomar (fortress, etc.). || FIG. Apoderarse de: *panic seized him*, el pánico se apoderó de él. | Captar, comprender (to understand): *to seize the meaning of sth.*, comprender el sentido de algo. | No dejar escapar, aprovechar (an opportunity). || MAR. Amarrar. || *To be seized with*, estar sobrecogido por: *to be seized with fear*, estar sobrecogido por el miedo; darle [a uno]: *he was seized with apoplexy*, le dio un ataque de apoplejía; entrarle [a uno]: *to be seized with a desire to do sth.*, entrarle a uno el deseo de hacer algo.

— V. intr. *To seize on* o *upon*, valerse de (a pretext), echar mano de (to take hold of). || TECH. *To seize up*, agarrotarse (an engine), atorarse, atascarse (to become clogged).

seizin [ˈsi:zin] n. JUR. Toma (*f.*) de posesión.

seizure [ˈsi:ʒə*] n. Asimiento, *m.* || JUR. Detención, *f.* (of a person). | Incautación, *f.*, embargo, *m.* (of property). | Secuestro, *m.* (of newspapers). || MIL. Toma, *f.* (of fortress, ship). || MED. Ataque, *m.* || TECH. Agarrotamiento, *m.* (of an engine). | Atoramiento, *m.*, atascamiento, *m.* (clogging).

sejant or **sejeant** ['si:dʒənt] adj. HERALD. Sentado, da.
selachian [si'lækiən] n. ZOOL. Selacio, *m.*
seldom ['seldəm] adv. Raramente, rara vez, muy pocas veces: *to be seldom seen,* verse raramente.
select [si'lekt] adj. Selecto, ta; escogido, da: *select society,* sociedad selecta. || Selecto, ta; exclusivo, va (club, etc.). || Escogido, da: *select passages from,* trozos escogidos de. || COMM. De primera calidad.
select [si'lekt] v. tr. Escoger, elegir. || SP. Seleccionar. || COMM. Clasificar.
selected [—id] adj. SP. Seleccionado, da. || Selecto, ta; escogido, da: *selected poems,* poesías selectas.
selection [si'lekʃən] n. Selección, *f.*: *natural selection,* selección natural; *a selection of books,* una selección de libros. || Elección, *f.* (choice). || Surtido, *m.*: *a large selection of wines,* un gran surtido de vinos. || — Pl. Trozos (*m.*) escogidos (of a writer, a musician). || SP. Pronósticos, *m.* (in horse racing).
selective [si'lektiv] adj. Selectivo, va.
selectivity [silek'tiviti] n. Selectividad, *f.*
selectman [si'lektmən] n. U. S. Concejal, *m.*

— OBSERV. El plural de esta palabra es *selectmen.*

selector [si'lektə*] n. SP. Seleccionador, ra. || TECH. Selector, *m.*
selenite ['seli:nait] n. MIN. Selenita, *f.*
selenium [si'li:njəm] n. CHEM. Selenio, *m.*
selenographer [selə'nɔgrəfə*] n. ASTR. Selenógrafo, *m.*
selenographic [sə,li:nə'græfik] adj. ASTR. Selenográfico, ca.
selenography [,selə'nɔgrəfi] n. ASTR. Selenografía, *f.*
Seleucid [si'lju:sid] n. HIST. Seleúcida, *m.* & *f.*
self [self] n. Personalidad, *f.*: *he showed his true self,* mostró su verdadera personalidad. || Sí mismo, sí misma: *to think of others before self,* pensar en los demás antes que en sí mismo. || Egoísmo, *m.*, interés (*m.*) personal (selfishness). || COMM. Al portador (en cheques). || PHIL. Yo, *m.*: *my other self,* mi otro yo. || BOT. Flor (*f.*) unicolor. || — *All by one's very self,* completamente solo. || *He is his old self again,* se ha recuperado completamente, vuelve a ser el mismo de siempre. || *He is only a shadow of his former self,* es sólo una sombra de lo que fue. || *His better self,* su lado bueno. || *My humble self,* ese servidor. || *My second self,* mi alter ego. || *Our noble selves,* nosotros. || *Your good selves,* ustedes.
— Adj. BOT. Unicolor. || Idéntico, ca; igual (of same kind, material, etc.). || Puro, ra (whisky).

— OBSERV. El plural de *self* es *selves.*

self-abandonment [—ə'bændənmənt] n. Olvido (*m.* de sí mismo. || Falta (*f.*) de moderación.
self-abasement [—ə'beismənt] n. Autodegradación, *f.*, rebajamiento (*m.*) de sí mismo.
self-absorption [—əb'sɔ:pʃən] n. Ensimismamiento, *m.*
self-abuse [—ə'bju:s] n. Masturbación, *f.*, onanismo, *m.* (masturbation). || Autocrítica, *f.* (reproach of o.s.).
self-accusation [—,ækju'zeiʃən] n. Autoacusación, *f.*
self-acting [—'æktiŋ] adj. Automático, ca.
self-addressed [—ə'drest] adj. Con su propia dirección, con la dirección de uno mismo: *a self-addressed envelope,* un sobre con su propia dirección. || Dirigido a sí mismo.
self-adhesive [—əd'hi:siv] adj. Autoadhesivo, va.
self-advertisement [əd'və:tismənt] n. Autobombo, *m.*
self-analysis [—ə'næləsis] n. Autoanálisis, *m. inv.*
self-apparent [—ə'pærənt] adj. Evidente.
self-appointed [—ə'pɔintid] adj. Nombrado por sí mismo.
self-approving [—ə'pru:viŋ] adj. Suficiente.
self-assertion [—ə'sə:ʃən] n. Presunción, *f.* (presumption). || Agresividad, *f.*
self-assertive [—ə'sə:tiv] adj. Presumido, da (conceited). || Agresivo, va.
self-assurance [—ə'ʃuərəns] n. Seguridad (*f.*) *or* confianza (*f.*) en sí mismo.
self-assured [—ə'ʃuəd] adj. Seguro de sí mismo.
self-binder [—'baində*] adj. AGR. Segadora (*f.*) agavilladora.
self-centred (U. S. **self-centered**) [—'sentəd] adj. Egocéntrico, ca.
self-closing [—'kləuziŋ] adj. De cierre automático.
self-coloured (U. S. **self-colored**) [—'kʌləd] adj. De color natural (having the natural colour). || Unicolor (having one colour). || Liso, sa; de un solo color (a fabric).
self-command [—kə'mɑ:nd] n. Dominio (*m.*) de sí mismo.
self-communion [—kə'mju:njən] n. Recogimiento, *m.*
self-complacency [—kəm'pleisnsi] n. Suficiencia, *f.*, engreimiento, *m.*
self-complacent [—kəm'pleisnt] adj. Suficiente, pagado *or* creído de sí mismo, engreído, da.
self-composed [—kəm'pəuzd] adj. Dueño de sí mismo.
self-conceit [—kən'si:t] n. Suficiencia, *f.*, vanidad, *f.*, engreimiento, *m.*
self-conceited [—kən'si:tid] adj. Suficiente, vanidoso, sa; engreído, da.
self-confidence [—'kɔnfidəns] n. Seguridad (*f.*) *or* confianza (*f.*) en sí mismo.
self-confident [—'kɔnfidənt] adj. Seguro de sí mismo.
self-conscious [—'kɔnʃəs] adj. Cohibido, da; tímido, da. || *To make s.o. self-conscious,* cohibir a alguien.
self-consciousness [—'kɔnʃəsnis] n. Timidez, *f.*
self-contained [—kən'teind] adj. Autónomo, ma (complete). || Independiente, con entrada particular (a flat, house). || Autosuficiente, independiente (independant). || Reservado, da (reserved).
self-contempt [—kən'tempt] n. Desprecio (*m.*) de sí mismo.
self-contradiction [—,kɔntrə'dikʃən] n. Contradicción, *f.*
self-contradictory [—,kɔntrə'diktəri] adj. Contradictorio, ria; que lleva implícita una contradicción.
self-control [—kən'trəul] n. Dominio (*m.*) de sí mismo, sangre (*f.*) fría.
self-cooker [—'kukə*] n. Olla (*f.*) de presión.
self-criticism [—'kritisizəm] n. Autocrítica, *f.*
self-deception [—di'sepʃən] n. Engaño (*m.*) de sí mismo, ilusión, *f.*
self-defeating [—di'fi:tiŋ] adj. Contraproducente.
self-defence (U.S. **self-defense**) [—di'fens] n. Autodefensa, *f.* (physical). || JUR. Legítima defensa, *f.*, defensa (*f.*) propia.
self-delusion [—di'lu:ʒən] n. Engaño (*m.*) de sí mismo, ilusión, *f.*
self-denial [—di'naiəl] n. Abnegación, *f.*
self-denying [—di'naiiŋ] adj. Abnegado, da.
self-dependent [—di'pendənt] adj. Independiente.
self-destruction [—dis'trʌkʃən] n. Suicidio, *m.*, autodestrucción, *f.*
self-determination [—di,tə:mi'neiʃən] n. Autodeterminación, *f.*
self-determining [—di'tə:miniŋ] adj. Autodeterminado, da.
self-discipline [—'disiplin] n. Autodisciplina, *f.*
self-distrust [—dis'trʌst] n. Inseguridad, *f.*, falta (*f.*) de seguridad en sí mismo.
self-driven [—'drivn] adj. Automotor, ra; automóvil.
self-educated [—'edjukeitid] adj. Autodidacto, ta.

— OBSERV. Although the form *autodidacto, audidacta* is the only one the Real Academia de la Lengua accepts as correct, the form *autodidacta* is most generally used for both the masculine and feminine.

self-effacement [—i'feismənt] n. Modestia, *f.*, humildad, *f.*
self-effacing [—i'feisiŋ] adj. Modesto, ta; humilde.
self-employed [—im'plɔid] adj. Que trabaja por cuenta propia.
self-esteem [—is'ti:m] n. Amor (*m.*) propio.
self-evident [—'evidənt] adj. Evidente, patente, manifiesto, ta.
self-examination [—ig,zæmi'neiʃən] n. Examen (*m.*) de conciencia.
self-excitation [—,eksi'teiʃən] n. ELECTR. Autoexcitación, *f.*
self-explanatory [—iks'plænətəri] adj. Que se explica por sí mismo.
self-expression [—iks'preʃən] n. Expresión (*f.*) de la propia personalidad.
self-feeding [—'fi:diŋ] adj. TECH. De alimentación automática.
self-fertilization [—,fə:tilai'zeiʃən] n. BIOL. Autofecundación, *f.* || BOT. Polinización (*f.*) directa.
self-fulfilment (U.S. **self-fulfillment**) [—ful'filmənt] n. Realización (*f.*) de las ambiciones de uno.
self-governed [—'gʌvənd] or **self-governing** [—'gʌvəniŋ] adj. Autónomo, ma.
self-government [—'gʌvnmənt] n. Gobierno (*m.*) autónomo, autonomía, *f.* (of a country). || Dominio (*m.*) de sí mismo (self-control).
self-help [—'help] n. Esfuerzo (*m.*) personal.
selfhood [—,hud] n. Individualidad, *f.*, personalidad, *f.* || Egoísmo, *m.* (selfishness).
self-ignition [—ig'niʃən] n. Autoencendido, *m.*
self-importance [—im'pɔ:təns] n. Presunción, *f.*, vanidad, *f.*
self-important [—im'pɔ:tənt] adj. Presumido, da; vanidoso, sa.
self-imposed [—im'pəuzd] adj. Que uno se impone a sí mismo (penalty).
self-induction [—in'dʌkʃən] n. ELECTR. Autoinducción, *f.*, selfinducción, *f.* || *Self-induction coil,* self, *f.*
self-indulgence [—in'dʌldʒəns] n. Satisfacción (*f.*) inmoderada de sus deseos.
self-indulgent [—in'dʌldʒənt] adj. Inmoderado, da; que satisface todos sus deseos.
self-inflicted [—in'fliktid] adj. Que uno se inflige a sí mismo (penance). || Voluntario, ria (wound).
self-interest [—'intrist] n. Interés (*m.*) propio (one's own interest). || Egoísmo, *m.* (selfishness).
selfish [—iʃ] adj. Egoísta. || Interesado, da (having an ulterior motive).
selfishness [—iʃnis] n. Egoísmo, *m.*
self-knowledge [—'nɔlidʒ] n. Conocimiento (*m.*) de sí mismo.
selfless [—lis] adj. Desinteresado, da.
self-locking [—'lɔkiŋ] adj. De cierre automático.
self-love [—'lʌv] n. Egoísmo, *m.* (selfishness). || Egolatría, *f.* (self-worship). || PHIL. Narcisismo, *m.*
self-made man [—'meidmən] n. Hombre (*m.*) que ha triunfado por su propio esfuerzo.
self-moving [—'mu:viŋ] adj. Automotor, ra.
self-opinionated [—ə'pinjəneitid] adj. Obstinado, da; testarudo, da; terco, ca.

self-pity [—ˈpiti] n. Lástima (*f.*) de sí mismo.
self-pollinated [—ˈpɔlineitid] adj. Fecundado por polinización directa.
self-pollution [—pəˈlu:ʃən] n. Masturbación, *f.*
self-portrait [—ˈpɔ:trit] n. Autorretrato, *m.*
self-possessed [—pəˈzest] adj. Sereno, na; dueño de sí mismo.
self-possession [—pəˈzeʃən] n. Dominio (*m.*) de sí mismo, serenidad, *f.*, sangre (*f.*) fría.
self-praise [—ˈpreiz] n. Autobombo, *m.*
self-preservation [—ˌprezəˈveiʃən] n. Instinto (*m.*) de conservación.
self-propelled [—prəˈpeld] adj. Autopropulsado, da: *self-propelled rocket*, cohete autopropulsado.
self-propelling [—prəˈpeliŋ] adj. Autopropulsor, ra.
self-propulsion [—prəˈpʌlʃən] n. Autopropulsión, *f.*
self-recording [—riˈkɔ:diŋ] adj. Registrador, ra.
self-regard [—riˈgɑ:d] n. Dignidad, *f.*, amor (*m.*) propio.
self-regulating [—ˈregjuleitiŋ] adj. TECH. Autorregulador, ra.
self-regulation [—ˌregjuˈleiʃən] n. TECH. Autorregulación, *f.*
self-reliance [—riˈlaiəns] n. Confianza (*f.*) *or* seguridad (*f.*) en sí mismo. || Independencia, *f.*
self-reliant [—riˈlaiənt] adj. Seguro de sí mismo. || Independiente.
self-renunciation [—riˌnʌnsiˈeiʃən] n. Abnegación, *f.*
self-reproach [—riˈprəutʃ] n. Remordimiento, *m.*
self-respect [—risˈpekt] n. Dignidad, *f.*, amor (*m.*) propio.
self-respecting [—risˈpektiŋ] adj. Que se precie, que tiene amor propio: *as every self-respecting man should know*, como debería de saber todo hombre que se precie.
self-restraint [—risˈtreint] n. Dominio (*m.*) de sí mismo.
self-rewarding [—riˈwɔ:diŋ] adj. Que compensa.
self-righteous [—ˈraitʃəs] adj. Farisaico, ca.
self-righteousness [—ˈraitʃəsnis] n. Fariseísmo, *m.*, farisaísmo, *m.*
self-rule [—ˈrul] n. Autonomía, *f.*
self-sacrifice [—ˈsækrifais] n. Sacrificio (*m.*) de sí mismo, abnegación, *f.*
self-sacrificing [—ˈsækrifaisiŋ] adj. Sacrificado, da; abnegado, da.
selfsame [—seim] adj. Mismísimo, ma: *at that selfsame moment*, en ese mismísimo momento.
self-satisfaction [—ˌsætisˈfækʃən] n. Suficiencia, *f.*, satisfacción (*f.*) de sí mismo.
self-satisfied [—ˈsætisfaid] adj. Suficiente, satisfecho de sí mismo.
self-sealing [—ˈsi:liŋ] adj. Que se cierra automáticamente. || Autoadhesivo, va (envelopes, etc.).
self-seeker [—ˈsi:kə*] n. Egoísta, *m.* & *f.*
self-seeking [—ˈsi:kiŋ] adj. Egoísta.
— N. Egoísmo, *m.*
self-service [—ˈsə:vis] adj. De autoservicio.
— N. Autoservicio, *m.*
self-starter [—ˈstɑ:tə*] n. TECH. Arranque (*m.*) automático.
self-starting [—ˈstɑ:tiŋ] adj. TECH. De arranque automático (motor).
self-styled [—ˈstaild] adj. Supuesto, ta.
self-sufficiency [—səˈfiʃənsi] n. Independencia, *f.*, autosuficiencia, *f.* (independence). || Seguridad (*f.*) *or* confianza (*f.*) en sí mismo.
self-sufficient [—səˈfiʃənt] adj. Independiente, autosuficiente. || Seguro de sí mismo (self-conceited).
self-suggestion [—səˈdʒestʃən] n. Autosugestión, *f.*
self-support [—səˈpɔ:t] n. Independencia (*f.*) económica.
self-supporting [—səˈpɔ:tiŋ] adj. Económicamente independiente, que vive con sus propios recursos. || *He is self-supporting*, se mantiene a sí mismo, vive con sus propios recursos.
self-surrender [—səˈrendə*] n. Abandono (*m.*) de sí mismo.
self-taught [—ˈtɔ:t] adj. Autodidacto, ta. || *Self-taught person*, autodidacto, ta.

— OBSERV. Although the form *autodidacto, ta* is the only one the Real Academia de la Lengua accepts as correct, the form *autodidacta* is most generally used for both the masculine and feminine.

self-will [—ˈwil] n. Obstinación, *f.*, terquedad, *f.* (obstinacy).
self-willed [—ˈwild] adj. Obstinado, da; terco, ca (obstinate).
self-winding [—ˈwaindiŋ] adj. De cuerda automática (watch).
self-worship [—ˈwə:ʃip] n. Egolatría, *f.*
self-worshipper [—ˈwə:ʃipə*] n. Persona (*f.*) ególatra.
self-worshipping [—ˈwə:ʃipiŋ] adj. Ególatra.
sell [sel] n. FAM. Engaño, *m.*, camelo, *m.* (trick). || Decepción, *f.* (disappointment). || Venta, *f.* (selling). || — *Hard sell*, publicidad agresiva. || *Soft sell*, publicidad discreta.
sell* [sel] v. tr. Vender: *he sold his car*, vendió su coche; *to sell a painting for ten thousand pesetas*, vender un cuadro en *or* por diez mil pesetas; *to sell wholesale*, vender al por mayor; *to sell on credit*, vender a plazos [*Amer.*, vender a cuota]. || Hacer vender: *television sells many products*, la televisión hace vender muchos productos. || FIG. Vender: *to sell one's soul*, vender su alma; *he sold his friend to the police*, vendió su amigo a la policía. | Hacer aceptar, convencer (scheme, idea). || — FIG. *To be sold on*, estar entusiasmado por (to be enthusiastic about), convencerle a uno: *I am sold on this idea*, esta idea me convence. || *To sell at a loss*, vender con pérdida. || FIG. FAM. *To sell down the river*, traicionar. | *To sell for a song*, vender en cuatro cuartos. || *To sell for cash*, vender al contado. || *To sell off*, liquidar. || FIG. *To sell one's life dearly*, vender cara su vida. | *To sell o.s.*, venderse. || *To sell out*, liquidar (to get rid of), realizar (shares), agotarse, estar agotado: *the edition sold out overnight*, la edición se agotó en una noche; traicionar, vender (to betray). || *To sell short* o *to sell a bear*, vender al descubierto (Stock Exchange). || JUR. *To sell up*, hacer embargar. || *We are sold out of this article*, se nos ha agotado este artículo. || FIG. FAM. *You've been sold!*, ¡le han dado gato por liebre!
— V. intr. Venderse: *these books sell well*, estos libros se venden bien; *eggs are selling at* o *for twenty pesetas a dozen*, los huevos se venden a veinte pesetas la docena. || FIG. Ser aceptado (scheme, idea). || — FIG. *To sell like hot cakes*, venderse como rosquillas. || *To sell out*, liquidar todas las existencias; traicionar (to betray).

— OBSERV. Pret. & p. p. ***sold***.

seller [—ə*] n. Vendedor, ra (person who sells). || Comerciante, *m.* (dealer). || — *Quick seller*, artículo que se vende fácilmente. || *Seller's market*, mercado (*m.*) favorable al vendedor (in the Stock Exchange).
selling [—iŋ] adj. De venta: *selling price*, precio de venta. || De fácil venta (product).
sell-off [—ˈɔf] n. Baja (*f.*) de valores (in the Stock Exchange).
sellout [—aut] n. Traición, *f.* (betrayal). || Lleno, *m.*, función (*f.*) para la que se han vendido todas las localidades, éxito (*m.*) de taquilla (in a theatre, stadium, etc.). || COMM. Agotamiento (*m.*) de todas las existencias.
Seltzer [ˈseltsə*] or **Seltzer water** [—ˈwɔ:tə*] n. Agua (*f.*) de Seltz.
selvage or **selvedge** [ˈselvidʒ] n. Orillo, *m.* (edge of cloth).
selves [selvz] pl. n. See SELF.
semantic [siˈmæntik] or **semantical** [—əl] adj. Semántico, ca.
semantics [—s] n. GRAMM. Semántica, *f.*
semaphore [ˈseməfɔ:*] n. MAR. Semáforo, *m.*
semaphore [ˈseməfɔ:*] v. tr. Transmitir por semáforo.
— V. intr. Hacer señales con semáforo.
semasiology [siˌmeisiˈɔlədʒi] n. GRAMM. Semasiología, *f.*
semblance [ˈsembləns] n. Apariencia, *f.*: *under a semblance of friendship*, bajo una apariencia de amistad; *in semblance*, en apariencia. || *To put on a semblance of gaiety*, fingir alegría.
semeiologic [ˌsi:maiˈɔlədʒik] adj. Semiológico, ca.
semeiologist [ˌsi:maiˈɔlədʒist] n. Semiólogo, *m.*
semeiology [ˌsi:maiˈɔlədʒi] n. Semiología, *f.*
semeiotic [si:maiˈɔtik] adj. Semiótico, ca.
semeiotics [—s] n. Semiótica, *f.*
semen [ˈsi:mən] n. Semen, *m.*

— OBSERV. El plural de la palabra inglesa es *semina* o *semens*.

semester [simestə*] n. U. S. Semestre, *m.* (academic half year).
semi [ˈsemi] n. FAM. Casa (*f.*) unida a otra por una pared medianera.
semiannual [—ˈænjuəl] adj. Semestral.
semiarid [—ˈærid] adj. Semiárido, da.
semiautomatic [—ˌɔ:təˈmætik] adj. Semiautomático, ca.
semiaxis [—ˈæksis] n. Semieje, *m.*
semibreve [—bri:v] n. MUS. Semibreve, *f.*
semichromatic [—krəuˈmætik] adj. MUS. Semicromático, ca.
semicircle [—ˌsə:kl] n. MATH. Semicírculo, *m.*
semicircular [—ˈsə:kjulə*] adj. Semicircular. || ARCH. De medio punto (arch).
semicircumference [—səˈkʌmfərəns] n. MATH. Semicircunferencia, *f.*
semicolon [—ˈkəulən] n. GRAMM. Punto y coma, *m.*
semiconductor [—kənˈdʌktə*] n. ELECTR. Semiconductor, *m.*
semiconscious [—ˈkɔnʃəs] adj. Semiconsciente.
semiconsonant [—ˈkɔnsənənt] n. GRAMM. Semiconsonante, *f.*
semiconsonantal [—ˌkɔnsəˈnæntl] adj. GRAMM. Semiconsonante.
semidarkness [—ˈdɑ:knis] n. Media luz, *f.*, penumbra, *f.*
semidetached [—diˈtætʃt] adj. *Semidetached houses*, casas separadas por una pared medianera.
semidiameter [—daiˈæmitə*] n. MATH. Semidiámetro, *m.*
semidirect [—diˈrekt] adj. Semidirecto, ta.
semidouble [—ˈdʌbl] adj. BOT. Semidoble.
semifinal [—ˈfainl] n. SP. Semifinal, *f.*
— Adj. SP. Semifinalista: *the two semifinal teams*, los dos equipos semifinalistas.

semifinalist [—ˈfainəlist] n. Semifinalista, *m.* & *f.*
semifine [—fain] adj. Semifino, na.
semilunar [—ˈlu:nə*] adj. Semilunar.
semi-manufactured [—ˌmænjuˈfæktʃəd] adj. Semimanufacturado, da.
seminal [ˈsi:minl] adj. Seminal: *seminal fluid*, líquido seminal.
seminar [ˈseminɑ:*] n. Seminario, *m.* (of students, experts).
seminarian [semiˈnεəriən] or **seminarist** [ˈseminərist] n. Estudiante (*m.* & *f.*) *or* experto (*m.*) que asiste a un seminario. || REL. Seminarista, *m.*
seminary [ˈseminəri] n. REL. Seminario, *m.*
seminiferous [ˌsemiˈnifərəs] adj. Seminífero, ra.
seminomad [ˈsemiˈnəuməd] n. Seminómada, *m.* & *f.*
seminomadic [ˈseminəuˈmædik] adj. Seminómada.
semiofficial [ˈsemiəˈfiʃəl] adj. Semioficial.
semiologic [ˌsemiˈələdʒik] adj. U. S. MED. Semiológico, ca.
semiologist [ˌsemiˈələdʒist] n. U. S. Semiólogo, *m.*
semiology [ˌsemiˈələdʒi] n. U. S. MED. Semiología, *f.*
semiotic [ˌsemiˈətik] adj. U. S. Semiótico, ca.
semiotics [—s] n. U. S. Semiótica, *f.*
semiprecious [ˈsemiˌpreʃəs] adj. Fino, na; semiprecioso, sa: *semiprecious stone*, piedra fina.
semiquaver [ˈsemiˌkweivə*] n. MUS. Semicorchea, *f.*: *semiquaver rest*, silencio de semicorchea.
semi-refined [ˈsemiriˈfaind] adj. Semirrefinado, da.
semirigid [ˈsemiˈridʒid] adj. Semirrígido, da.
semiskilled [ˈsemiˈskild] adj. Semicualificado, da.
semisolid [ˈsemiˈsɔlid] adj. Semisólido, da.
— N. Semisólido, *m.*
Semite [ˈsi:mait] n. Semita, *m.* & *f.*
Semitic [siˈmitik] adj. Semítico, ca; semita.
Semitism [ˈsemitizəm] n. Semitismo, *m.*
Semitist [ˈsemitist] n. Semitista, *m.* & *f.*
semitone [ˈsemitəun] n. MUS. Semitono, *m.*
semitrailer [ˈsemiˈtreilə*] n. Semirremolque, *m.*
semitransparent [ˈsemitrænsˈpεərənt] adj. Semitransparente.
semitropic [ˈsemiˈtrɔpik] or **semitropical** [—əl] adj. Subtropical.
semivocalic [ˈsemivəuˈkælik] adj. GRAMM. Semivocal.
semivowel [ˈsemiˌvauəl] n. GRAMM. Semivocal, *f.*
semiweekly [ˈsemiˈwi:kli] adj. Bisemanal.
— N. Publicación (*f.*) bisemanal.
semolina [ˌseməˈli:nə] n. CULIN. Sémola, *f.*
sempiternal [ˌsempiˈtə:nl] adj. Sempiterno, na (everlasting).
sempstress [ˈsempstris] n. Costurera, *f.*
senate [ˈsenit] n. Senado, *m.* || Consejo, *m.* (in a university).
senator [ˈsenətə*] n. Senador, *m.*
senatorial [ˌsenəˈtɔ:riəl] adj. Senatorial.
senatorship [ˈsenətəʃip] n. Senaduría, *f.*
send* [send] v. tr. Mandar: *she sent him to his grandmother's*, lo mandó a casa de su abuela; *I shall send him for her*, le mandaré buscarla; *did he send any message?*, ¿mandó algún recado? || Mandar, enviar: *to send a postcard*, mandar una postal. || Poner, mandar (telegram): *I have a telegram to send*, tengo que poner un telegrama. || Echar: *she wrote the letter but she forgot to send it*, escribió la carta pero se le olvidó echarla. || Adjuntar, mandar adjunto, enviar adjunto (to enclose): *with this letter I'm sending you a price list*, en esta carta le adjunto una lista de precios. || Enviar: *the prophets were sent from God*, los profetas fueron enviados por Dios. || Lanzar (to throw). || Volver: *the noise sent him crazy*, el ruido le volvió loco. || RAD. Transmitir. || FAM. Chiflar: *this record sends me*, este disco me chifla. || — *God send him victorious*, Dios le dé la victoria. || *He sent the book flying at me*, me tiró el libro a la cabeza. || *It sent a shiver down my spine*, me dio escalofríos. || *To be sent into the world*, venir al mundo. || *To send one's love to s.o.*, mandar *or* enviar cariñosos saludos a alguien. || *To send s.o. sprawling*, hacer que uno se caiga. || FIG. *To send s.o. to Coventry*, hacer el vacío a alguien.
— V. intr. Mandar a alguien: *she sent to inquire after you*, mandó a alguien a preguntar por ti; *I shall send for it*, mandaré a alguien a buscarlo. || Mandar un recado: *send to me in the morning*, mándeme un recado por la mañana. || RAD. Emitir, transmitir. || *To send for the doctor*, llamar al médico, enviar a alguien a buscar al médico.
— ***To send along***, mandar: *send him along!*, ¡mándemelo! || ***To send away***, echar, despedir (an employee). | Escribir pidiendo: *I have sent away for the latest catalogue*, he escrito pidiendo el último catálogo. | Enviar, mandar, expedir (a package). || ***To send back***, devolver: *he sent the ball back with a magnificent backhand stroke*, devolvió la pelota con un magnífico revés; *I have sent back the umbrella*, devolví el paraguas. | Hacer volver, enviar *or* mandar de nuevo (to make s.o. return). || ***To send down***, hacer bajar: *to send down prices*, hacer bajar los precios. | Expulsar (a student). | Encarcelar (a thief). | MAR. Desaparejar. || ***To send forth***, echar (odour, leaves, etc.). || ***To send in***, devolver (to return): *you have to send the form in after you have filled it in*, tiene que devolver el formulario después de haberlo rellenado. | Mandar: *send in your suggestions on a postcard*, mándenos sus sugerencias en una postal; *he has sent in his bill*, ha mandado su factura. | Presentar (a calling card, a resignation). | Hacer entrar, hacer pasar (s.o.). | — *Send her in!*, ¡que pase! | *To send in one's name*, dar su nombre para ser recibido. || ***To send off***, mandar, echar al correo (a letter). | Escribir pidiendo: *I have sent off for the latest catalogue*, he escrito pidiendo el último catálogo. | Mandar, enviar: *they sent soldiers off on an important mission*, mandaron soldados con una importante misión. | Despedir (to see s.o. off). | SP. Expulsar: *the player was sent off in the sixth minute*, el jugador fue expulsado en el minuto seis *or* a los seis minutos. || ***To send on***, mandar, reexpedir: *if you write to me at home, mummy will send the letter on to me*, si me escribe a casa, mamá me mandará la carta. | Transmitir (orders). || ***To send out***, echar (s.o.). | Echar, despedir (an odour). | Echar (smoke, leaves). | Mandar (a circular letter). | Emitir (to emit). | Dar (a shout). || ***To send round***, hacer circular: *word was sent round that*, se hizo circular la noticia de que. | Mandar: *I sent him round to the butcher's*, le mandé a la carnicería. || ***To send up***, satirizar (to caricature). | Hacer subir (to make s.o. come up). | Mandar arriba (to make s.o. go up). | Hacer subir (prices, temperature). | Lanzar (balloon, ball). | Presentar (a calling card). | Meter en la cárcel (to put in jail).
— OBSERV. Pret. & p. p. **sent**.
sendal [ˈsendəl] n. Cendal, *m.* (fabric).
sender [—ə*] n. Remitente, *m.* & *f.* (of a letter, etc.). || RAD. Transmisor, *m.*
send-off [—ˈɔf] n. Despedida, *f.* (farewell). || *The press has given the play a good send-off*, la prensa ha acogido muy favorablemente la obra.
Seneca [ˈsenikə] pr. n. Séneca, *m.*
Senegal [ˌseniˈgɔ:l] pr. n. GEOGR. Senegal, *m.*
Senegalese [ˈsenigəˈli:z] adj./n. Senegalés, esa. || *The Senegalese*, los senegaleses.
senescence [seˈnesəns] n. Senectud, *f.*
senescent [seˈnesənt] adj. Senescente.
seneschal [ˈseniʃəl] n. Senescal, *m.*
senile [ˈsi:nail] adj. Senil.
senility [siˈniliti] n. Senilidad, *f.*
senior [ˈsi:njə*] adj. Padre: *John Brown senior*, John Brown padre. || Mayor (in age). || Superior (in rank, grade). || Más antiguo, gua (of prior enrolment): *senior members*, los socios más antiguos. || SP. Senior. || — U. S. *Senior citizen*, jubilado, da. | *Senior college*, colegio universitario para los dos últimos años. || *The senior partner*, el socio mayoritario. || *The senior Service*, la marina. || *To be senior to s.o.*, ser mayor que alguien. || *To be three years senior to s.o.*, tener tres años más que alguien, llevarle tres años a alguien.
— N. Mayor, *m.* & *f.* (in age). || Mayor, *m.* & *f.* (at school). || Miembro (*m.*) más antiguo (member). || Socio (*m.*) principal *or* mayoritario (partner). || U. S. Estudiante (*m.* & *f.*) de último año. || — *She is his senior*, es mayor que él. || *She is his senior by three years*, le lleva tres años, tiene tres años más que él.
seniority [ˌsi:niˈɔriti] n. Antigüedad, *f.*
sensation [senˈseiʃən] n. Sensación, *f.*: *I have a slight sensation of dizziness*, tengo una ligera sensación de mareo; *this act was the sensation of the evening*, este número fue la sensación de la noche. || — *She was a great sensation as Cleopatra*, estuvo sensacional en el papel de Cleopatra. || *To create* o *to make* o *to cause a sensation*, causar sensación.
sensational [senˈseiʃənl] adj. Sensacional (excellent). || Sensacionalista (writer, novel). || Sensacional (event).
sensationalism [senˈseiʃnəlizəm] n. Sensacionalismo, *m.* (in journalism, philosophy).
sensationalist [senˈseiʃnəlist] n. Sensacionalista, *m.* & *f.* (in journalism, philosophy).
sensationalistic [senˌseiʃnəˈlistik] adj. Sensacionalista.
sense [sens] n. Sentido, *m.*: *the five senses*, los cinco sentidos; *the sense of sight*, *of smell*, el sentido de la vista, del olfato; *sense of direction*, *honour*, *humour*, sentido de la orientación, del honor, del humor. || Sentido, *m.*, significado, *m.* (meaning): *the sense of a word*, el sentido de una palabra; *figurative sense*, sentido figurado; *in the literal sense*, en sentido propio. || Sentido (*m.*) común, juicio, *m.* (intelligence). || Sensación, *f.* (sensation): *sense of pain*, sensación de dolor; *sense of insecurity*, sensación de inseguridad. || Sentimiento, *m.* (of injustice, etc.). || Sentir (*m.*) general, parecer, *m.*, opinión, *f.* (consensus): *the sense of the assembly*, la opinión de la asamblea. || — Pl. MED. Juicio, *m. sing.* (reason): *to be out of one's senses*, haber perdido el juicio. | Sentido, *m. sing.* (consciousness): *to regain one's senses*, recobrar el sentido. || — *Against common sense* o *in defiance of common sense*, en contra del sentido común. || *Common sense*, sentido común. || *Good sense*, buen sentido, juicio, *m.*, sentido común, sensatez, *f.* || *I can't make any sense of it*, no le encuentro sentido alguno. || *In a sense*, en cierto sentido. || *In every sense*, en todos los sentidos. || *In no sense*, de ninguna forma. || *In the best sense of the word*, en el buen sentido de la palabra. || *In the broad sense* o *in all senses of the word*, en el sentido amplio de la palabra, en toda la extensión de la palabra. || *Person of sense*, persona sensata. || *There is no sense in that*, eso no tiene sentido. || *This doesn't*

make sense, esto no tiene sentido. || *To be in one's senses*, estar en su sano juicio. || *To bring s.o. to his senses*, hacer sentar la cabeza a alguien, hacer entrar en razón a alguien (to bring s.o. to reason), hacer volver a alguien en sí (s.o. who is unconscious). || *To come to one's senses*, recobrar el juicio, sentar la cabeza (to become sensible), volver en sí (after unconsciousness). || *To have the sense to*, tener la inteligencia *or* la cordura de. || FIG. *To lose one's senses*, perder el sentido, volverse loco. || *To make sense*, tener sentido. || *To make sense of sth.*, comprender el sentido de algo, entender algo. || FIG. *To make s.o. lose his senses*, hacerle perder el sentido a uno, volverle loco a uno. | *To take leave of one's senses*, perder el juicio, volverse loco. || *To take the sense of the meeting*, consultar a la asamblea, pedir el parecer de la asamblea. || *To talk sense*, hablar razonablemente *or* con sentido común. || *To talk sense into*, meter en razón. || *What is the sense of talking like that?* ¿de qué sirve hablar así?

sense [sens] v. tr. Sentir. || PHIL. Percibir.

senseless [—lis] adj. Inconsciente, sin conocimiento, sin sentido (unconscious): *the blow knocked him senseless*, el golpe le dejó sin sentido. || Insensato, ta (foolish): *a senseless act*, una acción insensata; *senseless person*, persona insensata.

senselessness [—lisnis] n. Insensatez, *f.* (foolishness).

sense organ [—'ɔ:gən] n. ANAT. Órgano (*m.*) sensorio.

sensibility [ˌsensi'biliti] n. Sensibilidad, *f.* || — Pl. Susceptibilidad, *f. sing.*

sensible ['sensəbl] adj. Sensato, ta (showing good sense): *sensible decision*, decisión sensata. || Sensato, ta; cuerdo, da; razonable: *sensible person*, persona razonable. || Acertado, da (choice). || Cómodo, da; práctico, ca (clothing). || Sensible (perceivable). || Sensible, apreciable, notable: *sensible difference*, diferencia notable. || *To be sensible of*, darse cuenta de.

sensibleness [—nis] n. Sensatez, *f.*, juicio, *m.*, cordura, *f.* || Inteligencia, *f.* || *The sensibleness of a choice*, lo acertado de una elección.

sensitive ['sensitiv] adj. Sensible: *sensitive to light*, sensible a la luz; *sensitive scales*, balanza sensible; *the scar is still very sensitive*, la cicatriz está todavía muy sensible. || PHOT. Sensible (film). || Susceptible (easily offended): *he is very sensitive on questions of honour*, es muy susceptible para las cuestiones de honor. || COMM. Inestable: *a sensitive market*, un mercado inestable. || — *To be sensitive to cold*, ser friolero. || *To have a sensitive ear*, ser fino de oídos, tener un oído fino.

sensitiveness ['sensitivnis] or **sensitivity** [sensi'tiviti] n. Susceptibilidad, *f.* (susceptibility). || Sensibilidad, *f.* (responsiveness).

sensitive plant ['sensitiv'plɑ:nt] n. BOT. Sensitiva, *f.*

sensitization [sensitai'zeiʃən] n. Sensibilización, *f.*

sensitize ['sensitaiz] v. tr. Sensibilizar.

sensorial [sen'sɔ:riəl] or **sensory** ['sensəri] adj. Sensorio, ria.

sensual ['sensjuəl] adj. Sensual: *sensual pleasures*, placeres sensuales; *a sensual woman*, una mujer sensual; *a sensual mouth*, una boca sensual.

sensualism [—izəm] n. Sensualismo, *m.*

sensualist [—ist] n. Sensualista, *m.* & *f.*

sensualistic [ˌsensjuə'listik] adj. Sensualista.

sensuality [ˌsensju'æliti] n. Sensualidad, *f.*

sensualize ['sensjuəlaiz] v. tr. Volver sensual.

sensuous ['sensjuəs] adj. Sensual.

sensuousness [—nis] n. Sensualidad, *f.*

sent [sent] pret. & p. p. See SEND.

sentence ['sentəns] n. GRAMM. Oración, *f.* (grammatical term), frase, *f.* (common term). || JUR. Sentencia, *f.* || — *Death sentence*, pena (*f.*) de muerte. || *Life sentence*, condena perpetua. || *To be under sentence of death*, estar condenado a muerte. || *To pass sentence on*, sentenciar, condenar. || *To serve one's sentence*, cumplir la sentencia.

sentence ['sentəns] v. tr. JUR. Sentenciar, condenar: *to sentence s.o. to five years' imprisonment*, sentenciar a alguien a cinco años de prisión.

sententious [sen'tenʃəs] adj. Sentencioso, sa.

sententiousness [—nis] n. Tono (*m.*) sentencioso.

sentient ['senʃənt] adj. Sensible.

sentiment ['sentimənt] n. Sentimiento, *m.*: *to have noble sentiments*, tener sentimientos nobles. || Sentimiento, *m.*, sensibilidad, *f.*: *to play a tune with sentiment*, tocar una melodía con sentimiento. || Sentimentalismo, *m.*, sensiblería, *f.* (sentimentality). || Parecer, *m.*, opinión, *f.* (opinion). || *Those are my sentiments*, es mi opinión.

sentimental [ˌsenti'mentl] adj. Sentimental. || Sentimental, sensiblero, ra (mawkish). || Sentimental, romántico, ca (romantic).

sentimentalism [—izəm] n. Sentimentalismo, *m.*

sentimentalist [—ist] n. Sentimental, *m.* & *f.*

sentimentality [ˌsentimen'tæliti] n. Sentimentalismo, *m.* || Sentimentalismo, *m.*, sensiblería, *f.* (mawkishness).

sentimentalize [ˌsenti'mentəlaiz] v. tr. Hablar con sentimentalismo de.

— V. intr. Ponerse sentimental.

sentinel ['sentinl] n. MIL. Centinela, *m.* || *To stand sentinel*, hacer guardia.

sentry ['sentri] n. MIL. Centinela, *m.* || *To be on sentry* o *to stand sentry*, estar de guardia, hacer guardia.

sentry box [—bɔks] n. Garita, *f.* [de centinela].

sentry go [—gəu] n. Guardia, *f.*: *to be on sentry go*, estar de guardia.

sepal ['sepəl] n. BOT. Sépalo, *m.*

separability [ˌsepərə'biliti] n. Posibilidad (*f.*) de separación.

separable ['sepərəbl] adj. Separable.

separate ['seprit] adj. Separado, da. || Particular (entrance, room). || Distinto, ta: *cut it into three separate parts*, córtelo en tres partes distintas. || Suelto, ta: *there are several separate sheets of instructions*, hay varias hojas sueltas de instrucciones. || Otro, otra: *please give details of former employment on a separate sheet*, se ruega den informes sobre su empleo anterior en otra hoja. || Aislado, da (existence). || Independiente (interests). || *Under separate cover*, por separado.

— N. PRINT. Separata, *f.*

separate ['sepəreit] v. tr. Separar: *to separate two boxers*, separar a dos boxeadores; *the border separates France and Spain*, la frontera separa Francia y España; *different cultures separate these countries*, distintas culturas separan estos dos países. || Dividir: *to separate sth. into several parts*, dividir algo en varias partes. || Distinguir entre: *I find it hard to separate good from evil*, me es difícil distinguir entre el bien y el mal. || Clasificar (to sort out): *to separate mail*, clasificar el correo. || CULIN. Desnatar (milk).

— V. intr. Separarse: *they separated when they reached the crossroads*, se separaron al llegar a la encrucijada; *my husband and I have decided to separate*, mi marido y yo hemos decidido separarnos.

separately ['sepritli] adv. Separadamente, por separado.

separation [ˌsepə'reiʃən] n. Separación, *f.* || Clasificación, *f.* || CULIN. Desnatado, *m.* (of milk). || JUR. *Legal separation*, separación matrimonial.

separatism ['sepərətizəm] n. Separatismo, *m.*

separatist ['sepərətist] adj./n. Separatista.

separative ['sepərətiv] adj. Separador, ra.

separator ['sepəreitə*] n. TECH. Separador, *m.*

Sephardi [se'fɑ:di] n. Sefardí, *m.* & *f.*, sefardita, *m.* & *f.*

— OBSERV. El plural de la palabra inglesa es *Sephardim.*

Sephardic [—k] adj. Sefardí, sefardita.

sepia ['si:pjə] n. Sepia, *f.*

sepoy ['si:pɔi] n. Cipayo, *m.*

seps [seps] n. ZOOL. Sepedón, *m.*, seps, *m.*

sepsis [—is] n. MED. Septicemia, *f.*

septangular [sep'tæŋgjulə*] adj. Heptagonal.

September [sep'tembə*] n. Septiembre, *m.*, setiembre, *m.*: *I went on the 29th of September*, fui el 29 de septiembre.

— OBSERV. See SEPTIEMBRE in the other part.

septemvir [sep'temvə*] n. Septenviro, *m.*

septennate [sep'tenət] n. Septenado, *m.*, septenato, *m.*, septenio, *m.*

septennial [sep'tenjəl] adj. Septenal.

septennium [sep'teniəm] n. Septenio, *m.*

— OBSERV. El plural de *septennium* es *septenniums* o *septennia.*

septet or **septette** [sep'tet] n. MUS. Septeto, *m.*

septic ['septik] adj. MED. Séptico, ca: *septic tank*, fosa séptica.

septicaemia (U. S. **septicemia**) [septi'si:miə] n. MED. Septicemia, *f.*

septicaemic (U. S. **septicemic**) [septi'si:mik] adj. MED. Septicémico, ca.

septicity [sep'tisiti] n. Septicidad, *f.*

septime ['septi:m] n. Séptima, *f.* (in fencing).

septimole ['septiməul] n. MUS. Septillo, *m.*

septuagenarian [ˌseptjuədʒi'nɛəriən] adj./n. Septuagenario, ria.

Septuagesima [ˌseptjuə'dʒesimə] n. REL. Septuagésima, *f.*

septuple ['septjupl] adj. Séptuplo, pla.

— N. Séptuplo, *m.*

septuple ['septjupl] v. tr. Septuplicar.

sepulcher ['sepəlkə*] n./v. tr. U. S. See SEPULCHRE.

sepulchral [si'pʌlkrəl] adj. Sepulcral: *sepulchral stone*, lápida sepulcral; *sepuchral voice*, voz sepulcral. || *Sepuchral vault*, panteón, *m.*

sepulchre ['sepəlkə*] n. Sepulcro, *m.*: *the Holy Sepulchre*, el Santo Sepulcro. || *Whited sepulchre*, sepulcro blanqueado.

sepulchre ['sepəlkə*] v. tr. Sepultar.

sepulture ['sepəltʃə*] n. Sepultura, *f.*

sequacious [se'kweiʃəs] adj. Coherente (argument). || Servil (imitator).

sequel ['si:kwəl] n. Continuación, *f.* (of speech, narrative). || Consecuencia, *f.*, resultado, *m.* (consequence).

sequela [si'kwi:lə] n. Secuela, *f.*

— OBSERV. El plural de *sequela* es *sequelae.*

sequence ['si:kwəns] n. Sucesión, *f.*: *the sequence of events that led to his downfall*, la sucesión de acontecimientos que lo llevaron a la caída. || Serie, *f.*: *a sequence of sonnets*, una serie de sonetos. || Orden, *m.* (historical). || Resultado, *m.*, consecuencia, *f.* (result).

|| Escalera, *f.* (of cards). || CINEM. Secuencia, *f.* || REL. Secuencia, *f.* | GRAMM. Concordancia, *f.* (of tenses).
sequent [si'kwent] or **sequential** [si'kwenʃəl] adj. Sucesivo, va (successive). || Consecutivo, va (consecutive). || Consecuente, subsecuente (consequent).
sequester [si'kwestə*] v. tr. JUR. Embargar, confiscar, secuestrar (property). | Secuestrar (a person). || Apoderarse de (to seize). || Aislar (to isolate). || *To sequester o.s.*, retirarse, confinarse.
sequestered [—əd] adj. Retirado, da; aislado, da (isolated). || JUR. Embargado, da; confiscado, da; secuestrado, da.
sequestrate ['sikwestreit] v. tr. JUR. Embargar, confiscar, secuestrar (to sequester).
sequestration [,si:kwes'treiʃən] n. JUR. Embargo, *m.*, confiscación, *f.*, secuestro, *m.* (of a property). | Secuestro, *m.*, secuestración, *f.* (of a person). || Aislamiento, *m.*, retiro, *m.* (isolation).
sequestrator [si'kwestreitə*] n. JUR. Embargador, ra; secuestrador, ra.
sequestrum [se'kwestrəm] n. MED. Secuestro, *m.*

— OBSERV. El plural de *sequestrum* es *sequestra* o *sequestrums*.

sequin ['si:kwin] n. Lentejuela, *f.* (spangle). || Cequí, *m.* (old coin).
sequoia [si'kwɔiə] n. Secoya, *f.* (tree).
sera ['siərə] pl. n. See SERUM.
serac ['seræk] n. GEOL. Sérac, *m.*
seraglio [se'rɑ:liəu] n. Serrallo, *m.*, harén, *m.*

— OBSERV. El plural de *seraglio* es *seraglios* o *seragli*.

serai [se'rai] n. Caravanserallo, *m.* (caravansary).
serape [se'rɑ:pei] n. Sarape, *m.*
seraph ['serəf] n. REL. Serafín, *m.*

— OBSERV. El plural de *seraph* es *seraphs* o *seraphim*.

seraphic [se'ræfik] or **seraphical** [—əl] adj. Seráfico, ca. || *Seraphic Doctor*, Doctor Seráfico [San Buenaventura].
seraphim ['serəfim] pl. n. Serafines, *m.*
Serb [sə:b] adj./n. See SERBIAN.
Serbia [—jə] pr. n. GEOGR. Serbia, *f.*, Servia, *f.*
Serbian [—jən] adj. Serbio, bia; servio, via.
— N. Serbio, bia; servio, via (inhabitant of Serbia). || Serbio, *m.*, servio, *m.* (language).
Serbo-Croat ['sə:bəu'krəuæt] n. Serbocroata, *m.*, servocroata, *m.*
Serbo-Croatian [,sə:bəukrəu'eiʃən] adj. Serbocroata, servocroata.
— N. Serbocroata, *m.*, servocroata, *m.* (language).
sere [siə*] adj. Marchito, ta (withered).
serenade [,seri'neid] n. MUS. Serenata, *f.*
serenade [,seri'neid] v. tr. MUS. Dar una serenata a.
— V. intr. MUS. Dar una serenata.
serene [si'ri:n] adj. Sereno, na (person, sea, sky). || *His Serene Highness*, Su Alteza Serenísima.
— N. Mar (*m.*) en bonanza (sea). || Cielo (*m.*) sereno (sky).
serenely [—li] adv. Tranquilamente, con tranquilidad, serenamente.
serenity [si'reniti] n. Serenidad, *f.* || *Your Serenity*, Su Serenidad.
serf [sə:f] n. Siervo, va.
serfage [—idʒ] or **serfdom** [—dəm] or **serfhood** [—hud] n. Servidumbre, *f.*
serge [sə:dʒ] n. Sarga, *f.* (textile).
sergeancy ['sɑ:dʒənsi] n. Grado (*m.*) de sargento.
sergeant ['sɑ:dʒənt] n. MIL. Sargento, *m.* || Cabo, *m.* (of police). || Ujier, *m.* (sergeant at arms).
sergeant at arms [—ət'ɑ:mz] n. Ujier, *m.*
sergeant-at-law [—ət'lɔ:] n. JUR. Abogado, *m.*
sergeant major [—'meidʒə*] n. MIL. Sargento (*m.*) mayor.
sergeantship [—ʃip] n. Grado (*m.*) de sargento.
serial ['siəriəl] adj. Consecutivo, va (consecutive). || De serie: *serial number*, número de serie. || Seriado, da (radio, television programme, etc.). || Por entregas (novel). || De publicación por entregas: *serial rights*, derechos de publicación por entregas.
— N. Serial, *m.*, novela (*f.*) por entregas, folletín, *m.* (in a magazine). || Serial, *m.* (on television, radio).
serialization [,siəriəlai'zeiʃən] n. Publicación (*f.*) por entregas.
serialize ['si:əriəlaiz] v. tr. Publicar por fascículos *or* por entregas *or* como serial (a novel). || TECH. Fabricar en serie.
serially ['si:əriəli] adv. En serie. || Por entregas, por fascículos (novel).
seriate ['siəriət] adj. En serie.
seriate ['si:ərieit] v. tr. Seriar.
seriatim [,siəri'eitim] adv. Sucesivamente, por separado.
sericeous [si'riʃəs] adj. Sedoso, sa.
sericultural [,seri'kʌltʃurəl] adj. Sericícola.
sericulture [,seri'kʌltʃə*] n. Sericultura, *f.*, sericicultura, *f.*
sericulturist [—rist] n. Sericultor, *m.*, sericicultor, *m.* (who raises silkworms).
series ['siəri:z] n. Serie, *f.* || ELECTR. *In series*, en serie.

— OBSERV. El plural de la palabra inglesa es *series*.

series-wound [—waund] adj. Arrollado en serie.
serigraphy [sə'rigrəfi] n. Serigrafía, *f.*
serin ['serin] n. Canario, *m.* (bird).
seringa [si'riŋgə] n. Siringa, *f.* (rubber tree).
seriocomic ['siəriəu'kɔmik] adj. Tragicómico, ca; jocoserio, ria.
serious ['siəriəs] adj. Serio, ria: *a serious decision*, una decisión seria; *a serious book*, un libro serio; *a serious promise*, una promesa seria. || Serio, ria; formal (earnest). || Grave, serio, ria: *serious illness*, enfermedad grave; *a serious situation*, una situación grave; *a serious mistake*, un grave error. || Grave, de gravedad (wound). || Serio, ria; importante (damage, loss, etc.). || — *I am serious*, estoy hablando en serio. || *To make a serious attempt to*, esforzarse realmente por.
seriously [—li] adv. Seriamente. || Seriamente, gravemente, de gravedad (ill, wounded). || En serio: *don't take things so seriously*, no tome las cosas tan en serio.
serious-minded [—'maindid] adj. Serio, ria.
seriousness [—nis] n. Seriedad, *f.* || Gravedad, *f.*, seriedad, *f.* (of illness, situation, etc.). || *In all seriousness*, en serio, con toda seriedad.
serjeant ['sɑ:dʒənt] n. See SERGEANT.
serjeant at arms [—ət'ɑ:mz] n. Ujier, *m.*
serjeant-at-law [—ət'lɔ:] n. JUR. Abogado, *m.*
sermon ['sə:mən] n. REL. FIG. Sermón, *m.* || *The Sermon on the Mount*, el Sermón de la Montaña.
sermonize ['sə:mənaiz] v. tr./intr. Sermonear.
sermonizer [—ə*] n. Sermoneador, ra.
serology [siə'rɔlədʒi] n. Serología, *f.*
serosity [si'rɔsiti] n. Serosidad, *f.*
serotherapy [siərə'θerəpi] n. MED. Sueroterapia, *f.*, seroterapia, *f.*
serous ['siərəs] adj. Seroso, sa. || ANAT. *Serous membrane*, membrana serosa.
Serpens ['sə:penz] pr. n. ASTR. Serpentario, *m.*
serpent ['sə:pənt] n. ZOOL. Serpiente, *f.* || FIG. Víbora, *f.*, serpiente, *f.* (person). || Buscapiés, *m. inv.* (firework).
Serpentarium [,sə:pən'teəriəm] pr. n. ASTR. Serpentario, *m.*

— OBSERV. El plural de *serpentarium* es *serpentariums* o *serpentaria*.

serpent charmer ['sə:pənt'tʃɑ:mə*] n. Encantador (*m.*) de serpientes.
serpentine ['sə:pəntain] adj. Serpentino, na. || FIG. Sinuoso, sa (road). | Viperino, na; pérfido, da (person).
— N. MIN. Serpentina, *f.*
serrate ['serit] adj. BOT. Dentado, da; serrado, da. || TECH. Dentado, da.
serrated [se'reitid] adj. BOT. Dentado, da; serrado, da. || Serrato (muscle). || — *Serrated edge*, dientes, *m. pl.* || *Serrated suture*, juntura (*f.*) serrátil.
serration [se'reiʃən] n. Borde (*m.*) dentado.
serratus [sə'rætəs] n. ANAT. Serrato, *m.* (muscle).

— OBSERV. El plural de *serratus* es *serrati*.

serried ['serid] adj. Apretado, da.
serum ['siərəm] n. MED. Suero, *m.* || — *Protective serum*, suero inmunizador. || *Serum therapy*, sueroterapia, *f.*, seroterapia, *f.* || *Serum vaccination*, vacuna (*f.*) con suero.

— OBSERV. El plural de *serum* es *serums* o *sera*.

serval ['sə:vəl] n. ZOOL. Gato (*m.*) cerval.
servant ['sə:vənt] n. Criado, da; sirviente, ta (domestic help, valet, maid, etc.). || Empleado, da (in industry). || Funcionario, ria (of a government): *public servant*, funcionario público. || Servidor, ra (epistolary form): *your humble servant*, su seguro servidor. || — Pl. Servicio, *m. sing.*, servidumbre, *f. sing.* || — *Civil servant*, funcionario, ria. || *Servant of the Lord*, siervo de Dios. || *Your servant, Sir!*, ¡un servidor!
serve [sə:v] n. SP. Saque, *m.*, servicio, *m.* (in tennis): *to break the serve*, romper el saque.
serve [sə:v] v. tr. Servir: *to serve God, one's country*, servir a Dios, a la patria; *to serve lunch*, servir la comida; *to serve s.o. with soup*, servir sopa a alguien; *fish served with tomato sauce*, pescado servido con salsa de tomate. || Servir, estar al servicio de: *I served Lord Fotheringale for twenty years*, serví a lord Fotheringale durante veinte años. || Ser útil, servir: *his old car served him very well*, su antiguo coche le fue muy útil. || Despachar (in a shop): *to serve s.o. with a pound of butter*, despachar a alguien una libra de mantequilla. || Atender: *are you being served?*, ¿le atienden? || Ejercer, desempeñar (a function): *he served an office*, desempeñó un cargo. || Cumplir (an assignment). || Ser suficiente, bastar: *this amount serves him for two months*, esta cantidad le basta para dos meses. || JUR. Entregar (a writ, a summons). | Entregar a (to a person). | Cumplir (a term of punishment): *to serve one's sentence*, cumplir la sentencia. || REL. Ayudar a (Mass). || Abastecer (to supply). || Tratar: *fate served her badly*, el destino le trató mal. || ZOOL. Cubrir, montar (to mount the female). || MIL. Servir (a gun). || MAR. Forrar (a rope). || TECH. Ocuparse de, manejar (a machine). || — *If my memory serves me right*, si la memoria no me falla, si mal no recuerdo. || FAM. *I'll serve him out!*, ¡me las pagará! || *It serves you right!*, ¡te está bien empleado!, ¡bien merecido lo tienes! || *It will serve you nothing to*, no le servirá para nada. || *Localities served by a railway line*, localidades por donde pasa una vía ferrea *or* donde hay una vía férrea. || *Lunch is served, madam*, la señora está servida. || *To serve one's apprenticeship*, hacer el aprendizaje. || *To serve out*, repartir (to distribute), servir (food). || SP. *To serve the ball*,

hacer el saque, sacar, servir (in tennis). || *To serve the purpose*, servir para el caso: *this example will serve the purpose*, este ejemplo servirá para el caso. || *To serve the purpose of*, utilizarse como. || *To serve up*, servir.

— V. intr. Servir: *I served in the residence of Lord Fotheringale as a butler*, serví en la casa de lord Fotheringale de mayordomo; *to serve in the army*, servir en el ejército; *this cushion will serve*, este cojín servirá; *this box will serve as a table*, esta caja servirá de mesa; *to serve at the table*, servir la mesa. || SP. Sacar, hacer *or* tener el saque, servir (in tennis). || REL. Ayudar (at Mass). || Despachar (in a shop). || — *As occasion serves*, cuando se presente la ocasión. || *That serves to show that he is honest*, eso demuestra que es honrado. || *To serve as a waiter in a restaurant*, ser camarero *or* servir de camarero en un restaurante. || *To serve for*, servir para. || *To serve on the jury*, ser miembro del jurado.

server [—ə*] n. Monaguillo, *m.*, acólito, *m.* (at Mass). || SP. Saque, *m.* (in tennis). || Cubierto, *m.* (utensil for salad, etc.). || Pala, *f.* (for fish). || Bandeja, *f.* (tray). || Criado, *m.* (servant). || Camarero, *m.* [*Amer.*, mozo, *m.*] (waiter).

service [ˈsə:vis] n. Servicio, *m.*: *I was in the service of Lord Fotheringale*, estuve al servicio de lord Fotheringale; *military service*, servicio militar; *the service in this restaurant is bad*, el servicio en este restaurante es malo; *after-sales service*, servicio postventa; *bus service*, servicio de autobuses; *public service*, servicio público; *social service*, servicio social; *repair service*, servicio de reparaciones. || MIL. Servicio (*m.*) militar: *compulsory service*, servicio militar obligatorio. | Servicio, *m.*: *he saw service on several fronts*, prestó servicio en varios frentes; *active service*, servicio activo. || Favor, *m.*, servicio, *m*: *you have rendered me a great service*, me has hecho un gran favor, me has prestado un gran servicio. || Utilidad, *f.*: *to be of great service*, ser de gran utilidad. || Uso, *m.* (use). || REL. Oficio, *m.*, servicio, *m.* || JUR. Entrega, *f.* (of a writ, a summons, etc.). || SP. Saque, *m.*, servicio, *m.* (in tennis): *to break the service*, romper el saque. || Juego, *m.*, servicio, *m.*: *tea service*, juego de té. || Vajilla, *f.* (crockery). || ZOOL. Cubrición, *f.*, monta, *f.* (mating). || BOT. Serbal, *m.* (tree). || MAR. Funda, *f.*, forro, *m.* (of gear). || Revisión, *f.* (of a car, etc.). || — Pl. Servicios, *m.*: *to dispense with s.o.'s services*, prescindir de los servicios de alguien. | Servicios, *m.* (third sector of the economy). || — *At your service*, a su disposición, a sus órdenes. || *At your service, sir*, para servirle, señor. || *Civil service*, administración pública. || *Diplomatic service*, cuerpo diplomático, diplomacia, *f.*, carrera diplomática. || *How can I be of service to you?*, ¿en qué puedo ayudarle? || *In service*, en funcionamiento. || *Intelligence service*, servicio de información. || *National Health Service*, Seguridad (*f.*) Social. || *Secret service*, servicio secreto. || MIL. *The senior Service*, la marina. || *The three services*, el ejército, la marina y la aviación, las fuerzas armadas. || *To be in the civil service*, ser funcionario. || *To be of service* o *to do service*, ser útil, servir. || MIL. *To be on active service*, estar en [servicio] activo. || *To be out of service*, no funcionar. || *To bring into service*, poner en servicio. || *To come into service*, empezar a utilizarse (machine), aplicarse (timetable). || MIL. *To go into service*, entrar a servir. || FAM. *To have seen long service*, haberse utilizado mucho tiempo. || *What good service this pen has done me!*, ¡lo que me ha servido esta pluma!

— Adj. De servicio: *service staircase*, escalera de servicio. || MIL. Militar (military). | De diario (uniform). || — REL. *Service book*, misal, *m.* || *Service brake*, freno (*m.*) de pedal. || *Service charge*, servicio, *m.*: *service charge included*, servicio incluido. || *Service families*, familias (*f.*) de militares. || SP. *Service line*, línea (*f.*) de saque (in tennis). || MIL. *Service record*, hoja (*f.*) de servicios. || *Service road*, vía (*f.*) de acceso. || *Service station*, estación (*f.*) de servicio. || MIL. *Service stripe*, galón (*m.*) de servicio. || BOT. *Service tree*, serbal, *m.* || *Service workshop*, taller (*m.*) de reparaciones.

service [ˈsə:vis] v. tr. Mantener (to maintain). || Revisar (to check): *to service a car*, revisar un coche. || Atender a (to treat). || Cubrir (a mare).

serviceability [ˈsə:visəˈbiləti] n. Utilidad, *f.*

serviceable [ˈsə:visəbl] adj. Utilizable, servible (that can be used). || Práctico, ca; útil (practical). || Resistente, duradero, ra (lasting). || Servicial (obliging).

serviceableness [ˈsə:visəblnis] n. Utilidad, *f.* (usefulness). || Solidez, *f.*, resistencia, *f.* (of clothing). || Solicitud, *f.* (of a person).

serviceman [ˈsə:vismən] n. MIL. Militar, *m.* || TECH. Reparador, *m.*

— OBSERV. El plural de esta palabra es *servicemen*.

serviette [ˌsə:viˈet] n. Servilleta, *f.*

servile [ˈsə:vail] adj. Servil.

servility [sə:ˈviliti] n. Servilismo, *m.*

serving [ˈsə:viŋ] n. Servicio, *m.* (of a master). || CULIN. Porción, *f.* (helping). | Servicio, *m.* (of a meal). || SP. Saque, *m.*, servicio, *m.* || JUR. Entrega, *f.* || MAR. Funda, *f.*, forro, *m.* || ZOOL. Cubrición, *f.*, monta, *f.* (mating).

— Adj. De servir.

Servite [ˈsə:vait] n. REL. Servita, *m.*

servitor [ˈsə:vitə*] n. Criado, *m.* (servant).

servitude [ˈsə:vitju:d] n. Servidumbre, *f.* || JUR. *Penal servitude*, trabajos forzados.

servo brake [ˈsə:vəuˈbreik] n. TECH. Servofreno, *m.*

servo control [ˈsə:vəukənˈtrəul] n. Servomando, *m.*

servomechanism [ˈsə:vəuˌmekənizəm] n. TECH. Servomecanismo, *m.*

servomotor [ˈsə:vəuˌməutə*] n. Servomotor, *m.*

sesame [ˈsesəmi] n. BOT. Sésamo, *m.*, ajonjolí, *m.*, alegría, *f.* || *Open sesame!*, ¡ábrete, sésamo!

sesamoid [ˈsesəmɔid] adj. ANAT. Sesamoideo, a (bone, cartilage).

— N. ANAT. Hueso (*m.*) sesamoideo (bone). | Cartílago (*m.*) sesamoideo (cartilage).

sesquicentennial [ˈseskwisenˌtenjəl] adj. Sesquicentenario, ria.

— N. Sesquicentenario, *m.*

sesquioxide [ˈseskwiˌɔksaid] n. CHEM. Sesquióxido, *m.*

sesquipedalian [ˈseskwipiˈdeiljən] adj. FIG. Larguísimo, ma; que no acaba nunca (word). | Pesado, da (style).

session [ˈseʃən] n. Sesión, *f.* (meeting): *opening, plenary, closed session*, sesión de apertura, plenaria, a puerta cerrada; *closing* o *final session*, sesión de clausura. || Período (*m.*) de sesiones, reunión, *f.* (series of meetings). || JUR. Audiencia, *f.* || CINEM. Sesión, *f.* || Curso (*m.*) académico (academic period).

sessional [—l] adj. De una sesión (in parliament, court, cinema). || De fin de curso (exam).

sesterce [ˈsestə:s] n. HIST. Sestercio, *m.* (ancient Roman coin).

sestet [sesˈtet] n. POET. Dos últimos tercetos (*m. pl.*) de un soneto. || MUS. Sexteto, *m.*

sestina [sesˈti:nə] n. POET. Sextina, *f.*

set [set] adj. Fijado, da; señalado, da (date, time). || Establecido, da (form, manner): *a set practice*, una práctica establecida. || Determinado, da: *a set intention*, una intención determinada. || Inmóvil (immovable). || Rígido, da (stiff). || Firme (opinion). || Fijo, ja: *set gaze*, mirada fija; *set price*, precio fijo. || Estable (weather). || Cuajado, da (jelly, blancmange, etc.). || Fraguado, da (cement). || Montado, da; armado, do (a machine). || Engastado, da (a jewel). || Arraigado, da (habits). || Preparado, da (prepared): *a set speech*, un discurso preparado. || Estereotipado, da (stereotyped): *set smile*, sonrisa estereotipada. || Dispuesto, ta: *set for trouble*, dispuesto a la lucha. || Listo, ta: *set to go*, listo para salir. || Campal (battle). || Apretado, da (teeth). || — *Everyone has his own set task*, cada uno tiene un trabajo determinado. || *Set phrase*, frase hecha *or* estereotipada. || *The set books*, los libros que hay que estudiar durante el curso. || *To be all set*, estar completamente listo. || *To be dead set against*, estar resueltamente opuesto a. || *To be set in one's ways*, tener costumbres arraigadas. || *To be set on*, estar empeñado en: *she was set on being an actress*, estaba empeñada en ser actriz. || *To be set on an idea*, aferrarse a una idea.

— N. Conjunto, *m.*: *a set of laws*, un conjunto de leyes. || Serie, *f.*: *a set of measures*, una serie de medidas. || Juego, *m.*: *tea set*, juego de té. || Batería, *f.* (of kitchen implements). || Tiro, *m.*, tronco, *m.* (of horses). || Juego, *m.*, aderezo, *m.* (of jewelry). || Colección, *f.* (of volumes, etc.): *a set of poems*, una colección de poemas. || Juego, *m.*, surtido, *m.* (of buttons). || Grupo, *m.* (group). || Clase, *f.*: *ask any set of people*, pregunte a cualquier clase de personas. || Pandilla, *f.* (of friends): *he is a member of Antonio's set*, es un miembro de la pandilla de Antonio. || Banda, *f.* (of thieves). || Círculo, *m.*: *we don't move in the same set*, no pertececemos al mismo círculo. || Camarilla, *f.* (political). || Categoría, *f.* (of thinkers, writers). || Caída, *f.* (of clothes, drapery). || Marcado, *m.* (of hair). || Forma, *f.*, porte, *m.*: *I recognized him by the set of his head*, lo reconocí por su porte de cabeza. || Tendencia, *f.* (of opinion). || Aparato, *m.* (radio, television). || TECH. Tren, *m.* (of wheels). | Grupo, *m.*, equipo, *m.* (of turbines, etc.): *generating set*, grupo electrógeno. | Dispositivo, *m.* (device). | Estuche, *m.* (of tools). | Entibado, *m.* (of a mine). | Bastidor, *m.* (of timber). || SP. Set, *m.* (in tennis). || BOT. Esqueje, *m.* || MAR. Dirección, *f.* (of wind, current). | Juego, *m.* (of oars). || ARCH. Asiento, *m.* (of a beam). | Alabeo, *m.* (under pressure). || Puesta, *f.* (of sun). || PRINT. Ojo, *m.*, anchura, *f.* (of type). || Puesta, *f.* (of eggs). || Muestra, *f.* (of hunting dog). || CINEM. Plató, *m.* || THEATR. Decorado, *m.* || — *Dinner set*, servicio (*m.*) de mesa, vajilla, *f.* || *On the set*, en el escenario. || *Set of false teeth*, dentadura postiza. || *Set of features*, fisonomía, *f.* || *Set of furniture*, muebles, *m. pl.*, mobiliario, *m.* || *Set of mind*, manera (*f.*) de ser, mentalidad, *f.* || *Set of points*, agujas, *f. pl.*, cambio (*m.*) de agujas. || *Set of teeth*, dentadura, *f.* || *The smart set*, la gente elegante. || FIG. *To make a dead set at*, meterse con (to attack vigorously), intentar conquistar a (a woman).

set* [set] v. tr. Colocar, poner (to put). || Poner: *to set sentries at the gate*, poner centinelas en la entrada; *to set s.o. to work*, poner a alguien a trabajar; *to set the table*, poner la mesa; *to set an examination*, poner un examen; *I set my alarm clock for 8 o'clock*, puse el despertador para las ocho; *to set s.o. amongst the great writers*, poner a alguien entre los grandes escritores. || Poner en hora (watch, clock): *I want to set my clock*, quiero poner mi reloj en hora. || Fijar, señalar (date): *the time and date of the meeting have not yet been set*, no se ha fijado todavía ni la hora ni la fecha de la reunión. || Fijar, señalar (colour, price, etc.). || Dar, citar: *to set an example*, dar un ejemplo. || Sentar (a precedent). || Establecer (a record, a standard). || Dar (to assign work): *he set me seven pages to do*, me dio siete páginas para que las hiciese. || Señalar: *to set books for an exam*, señalar libros para un examen. || Hacer (a question). || Plantear (a problem). || Imponer (a fashion). || Cuajar (jelly, milk, etc.). || Coagular (blood). || Fraguar (cement). || Marcar (hair). || Situar: *to set a novel in Spain*, situar una novela en España; *town set in the mountains*, pueblo situado en las montañas. || Dirigir (to direct). || Armar, preparar (a trap). || Hacer: *the smoke set him coughing*, el humo le hizo toser. || MUS. Afinar (to tune). | Poner: *Peter set words to the music I had composed*, Pedro le puso la letra a la música que yo había compuesto; *Michael set the words to music*, Miguel le puso música a la letra. || Afilar (a blade): *to set a razor*, afilar una cuchilla de afeitar. || MED. Reducir, encajar (a bone). | Reducir (a fracture). || Desarrollar: *too much exercise sets a boy's muscles prematurely*, demasiado ejercicio desarrolla prematuramente los músculos de los chicos. || THEATR. CINEM. Montar (scenery). || MAR. Desplegar (the sails). || CULIN. Dejar reposar (dough). || TECH. Ajustar (to adjust). | Triscar (a saw). | Engastar, montar (gem). || PRINT. Componer. || Poner a empollar (hen, eggs). || — FIG. *He is setting his career on this interview*, de esta entrevista depende su carrera. || *Set your mind at ease*, tranquilícese. || *To set a glass to one's lips*, llevarse un vaso a la boca. || *To set a match to* o *to set fire to*, prenderle fuego a. || *To set an engine going*, poner un motor en marcha. || *To set a price on s.o.'s head*, poner a precio la cabeza de alguien. || FIG. *To set a trap*, tender un lazo, poner una trampa. || *To set a watch*, poner un reloj en hora (time), poner guardia *or* centinela (a guard). || *To set eyes on*, see EYE. || *To set foot on*, pisar. || *To set free*, see FREE. || *To set great store by*, valorar en mucho. || *To set limits to*, poner límites a. || *To set one's hand to*, firmar. || *To set one's jaw* o *one's teeth*, apretar los dientes. || *To set on fire*, prender fuego. || *To set right*, see RIGHT. || *To set sail*, hacerse a la vela. || *To set s.o. a problem*, poner a alguien un problema. || *To set s.o.'s teeth on edge*, darle dentera a uno. || *To set straight*, see STRAIGHT. || *To set the fashion*, dictar la moda. || *To set thinking*, dar que pensar a.

— V. intr. Cuajarse (jelly). || Coagularse (blood). || Fraguarse (cement). || Fijarse (colours). || Ponerse fijo (eyes). || Seguir con la misma expresión (face). || Ponerse rígido (corpse). || Empollar (fowl). || Ponerse (moon, sun). || Dirigirse (to go in a specified direction). || Soplar (wind). || MED. Encajarse (a bone). || Caer (clothes): *the jacket sets badly*, la chaqueta cae mal. || BOT. Formarse. || Mermar, declinar (reputation). || Formarse (character). || Estar completamente desarrollado (body). || Parar (a hunting dog).

— **To set about**, ponerse a (to begin): *I must set about my packing*, tengo que ponerme a hacer las maletas. | Emprender (to undertake). | Difundir, propagar, propalar (to spread): *to set a rumour about*, propagar un rumor. | Atacar (to attack). | — *They set about each other at once*, en seguida llegaron a las manos. || **To set above** o **before**, anteponer: *he sets honour before glory*, antepone el honor a la gloria. || **To set after**, seguir la pista de, perseguir (to pursue). | Echar tras: *to set a dog after s.o.*, echar un perro tras alguien. || **To set against**, enemistar con (to turn against): *he is trying to set you against me*, está ir tentando enemistarte conmigo. | Comparar con: *to set advantages against disadvantages*, comparar las ventajas con los inconvenientes. | Oponerse a: *public opinion is setting against the proposal*, la opinión pública se opone a la propuesta. || **To set apart**, poner aparte, apartar: *to set the women apart from the men*, apartar a las mujeres de los hombres. | Reservar (money, time). || **To set aside**, apartar, poner aparte: *set the best apples aside*, aparta las mejores manzanas. | Dejar de lado (to pay no attention to): *to set aside one's own feelings*, dejar de lado sus sentimientos. | Desechar, rechazar (to reject): *he set all their offers aside*, rechazó todas sus ofertas. | JUR. Anular (to annul), casar, anular (a judgment), rechazar (a claim). || **To set at**, lanzar contra. | — *To set at liberty*, poner en libertad. || **To set back**, detener, frenar (to halt progress). | Retrasar (to delay): *this accident set me back three weeks*, este accidente me ha retrasado tres semanas. | Atrasar (a watch, clock). | FAM. Costar, salir por (to cost): *my car set me back six thousand dollars*, mi coche me ha costado seis mil dólares. | — *House set back from the road*, casa que no está al borde de la carretera. | *House set back from the street*, casa que no está alineada con las demás en una calle. || **To set by**, ahorrar (money). || **To set down**, poner por escrito (to write down): *set down the main arguments*, ponga por escrito los principales argumentos. | Apuntar: *set me down for ten pounds*, apúnteme para diez libras. | Dejar *or* poner en el suelo (to lay down): *he set the parcel down*, dejó el paquete en el suelo. | Dejar: *I'll set you down at your door*, le dejaré en su casa. | Dejar bajar, dejar apearse: *the train stopped at the station to set down three passengers*, el tren se detuvo en la estación para dejar bajar a tres viajeros. | Hacer aterrizar (a plane). | Considerar, tomar por (to consider). | Fijar, prever: *the meeting is set down for Tuesday*, la reunión está prevista para el martes. | Establecer, fijar (to prescribe): *rules have been set down and must be obeyed*, las reglas han sido establecidas para ser respetadas. | — *To set down to*, atribuir a: *to set one's success down to hard work*, atribuir su éxito a un trabajo intenso. || **To set forth**, enunciar. | Desarrollar (an argument). | Exponer: *to set forth one's views*, exponer sus opiniones. | Salir, ponerse en camino (to begin a journey). || **To set forward**, adelantar. | Exponer (a theory). | Salir (to start). || **To set in**, engastar (a stone). | Encajar (to insert). | Empezar, llegar: *the rainy season has set in*, la época de las lluvias ha empezado. | Cerrar (night). | Levantarse (wind). | Subir (tide). | Montar (in dressmaking). | — *It is setting in for a wet day*, parece que va a llover. | *This fashion is setting in*, esto se está poniendo de moda. || **To set off**, ponerse en camino, salir (to begin a journey). | Hacer resaltar, realzar, poner de relieve: *the red scarf sets off the dark jacket*, el pañuelo rojo hace resaltar la chaqueta oscura. | Adornar, embellecer (to adorn). | Hacer explotar, hacer estallar (a bomb). | Volar (a mine). | Hacer: *the joke set him off laughing*, el chiste lo hizo reír. | Compensar (a debt, a loss). | — *To set off running*, salir corriendo. | *To set s.o. off*, hacer hablar a alguien. || **To set on**, atacar (to attack). | Instigar contra (to provoke). | Azuzar contra: *he set the dog on me*, azuzó el perro contra mí. | Seguir adelante (to go on). || **To set out**, ponerse en camino, salir (to begin a journey). | Declarar (to state). | Exponer, explicar: *he set out his reasons for his behaviour*, expuso las razones por las cuales había actuado así. | Proponerse: *he set out to prove that Shakespeare was a woman*, se propuso demostrar que Shakespeare era una mujer. | Disponer (to arrange). | Exponer (to display): *to set out goods*, exponer mercancías. | Adornar (to adorn). | Presentar (one's work). | MAR. Bajar (tide). | PRINT. Espaciar. | — *To set out the table*, poner la mesa. || *To set out to do*, empezar a hacer. || **To set over**, poner por encima de. || **To set to**, ponerse a trabajar. | Empezar a, ponerse a: *to set to work*, empezar a trabajar. | FAM. Pelearse. || **To set up**, establecerse: *to set up as a butcher*, establecerse de carnicero. | Abrir, poner (a business). | Levantar (a statue). | Construir, edificar (a house). | Instalar (an exhibition). | Fundar, crear: *this school was set up in 1927*, esta escuela fue creada en 1927. | Crear, constituir: *to set up a committee*, crear una comisión. | Colocar (a person). | TECH. Montar, armar (a piece of machinery). | Establecer (a record). | Instaurar, establecer (a government): *to set up a monarchy*, instaurar una monarquía. | Planear, proyectar (to plan). | Exponer (theory). | Lanzar, dar, soltar, pegar (a yell). | Convidar, invitar (to invite). | Abastecer, proveer (to supply with). | Provocar, causar (to be the cause of). | Restablecer, reponer: *a fortnight in the country will set him up*, unos quince días en el campo le restablecerán. | PRINT. Componer. | — *To be set up for life*, tener el porvenir asegurado. | *To set up as a model*, dar como ejemplo. | *To set up for* o *to set o.s. up as*, dárselas de, presumir de (to pretend to be): *although he's such an ignorant fellow he sets up for an expert*, aunque sea tan ignorante se las da de experto. || **To set upon**, atacar: *to set upon the enemy*, atacar al enemigo. | Emprender (a task). | Instigar contra (to provoke).

— OBSERV. Pret. & p. p. **set**.

setaceous [si'teiʃəs] adj. Cerdoso, sa.
setback ['setbæk] n. Revés, *m.* (misfortune): *he met with many setbacks*, sufrió muchos reveses. || Contratiempo, *m.* (sth. which stops progress). || Baja, *f.*, caída, *f.* (of prices). || Regresión, *f.* (of trade). || MED. Recaída, *f.*
setdown ['setdaun] n. Repulsa, *f.*
set-in ['setin] adj. Empotrado, da.
setoff ['set'ɔf] n. Contrapeso, *m.* (sth. that counterbalances). || Compensación, *f.* (of a debt). || Contrapartida, *f.* (counterpart). || Realce, *m.*, relieve, *m.* (bringing out). || ARCH. Saliente, *m.*
seton ['si:tn] n. MED. Sedal, *m.*
setout [set'aut] n. Principio, *m.* (beginning). || Salida, *f.* (departure). || Preparativos, *m. pl.* (preparations). || Exposición, *f.*, presentación, *f.* (display).
setscrew ['set'skru:] n. TECH. Tornillo (*m.*) de fijación.
set square ['setskwɛə*] n. Cartabón, *m.*, escuadra, *f.*
settee [se'ti:] n. Sofá, *m.*
settee-bed [—bed] n. Sofá cama, *m.*
setter ['setə*] n. Setter, *m.*, perro (*m.*) de muestra (dog). || Engastador, ra (of gems).
setting ['setiŋ] n. Colocación, *f.* || Engaste, *m.*, montura, *f.* (of a gem). || Puesta, *f.* (of sun). || FIG. Marco, *m.* (background). | Escenario, *m.*, teatro, *m.*: *the setting of the battle*, el escenario de la batalla. | Declinación, *f.*, disminución, *f.* (of fame). || Escenario, *m.*, escena, *f.* (of a play, of a film). || MUS. Música, *f.*: *I prefer Handel's setting of the twenty third psalm to Haydn's*,

prefiero la música que Haendel ha puesto al salmo veintitrés a la de Haydn. | Arreglo, *m.* (arrangement). || Puesta, *f.* (of eggs). || TECH. Ajuste, *m.* (of a machine). | Afilado, *m.* (of a tool). | Fraguado, *m.* (of cement). || PRINT. Composición, *f.* || MED. Reducción, *f.* (of bone, fracture).

— Adj. Poniente (sun).

setting lotion [—ˈləuʃən] n. Fijador, *m.* [para el pelo].

setting-up [—ʌp] n. Instalación, *f.* || Establecimiento, *m.*: *setting-up of a new order*, establecimiento de un nuevo régimen. || Creación, *f.*, fundación, *f.* (of an organization, institution, etc.). || Construcción, *f.* (of a house). || PRINT. Composición, *f.*

settle [ˈsetl] n. Banco, *m.* (wooden seat).

settle [ˈsetl] v. tr. Establecer, instalar (people). || Colonizar, poblar (land, country). || Estabilizar (to stabilize): *a good thunderstorm would settle the weather*, una buena tempestad estabilizaría el tiempo. || Colocar (to put). || Asentar (to put firmly). || Colocar, establecer (one's children). || Clarificar, dejar asentarse (a liquid). || Hacer caer: *the rain settled the dust*, la lluvia hizo caer el polvo. || Disipar (a doubt). || Calmar (nerves). || Arreglar (stomach). || Fijar (date). || Acordar, decidir (to agree on): *to settle to do sth.*, acordar hacer algo. || Resolver, solucionar (problem): *to settle a question once and for all*, resolver definitivamente una cuestión. || Resolver, arreglar, dirimir (a dispute). || Arreglar: *to settle a matter amicably*, arreglar una cuestión amistosamente. || Arbitrar (an arbitrator). || Satisfacer (a claim). || Terminar *or* acabar con (to put an end to). || Saldar, liquidar (an account). || Pagar (a debt). || JUR. Asignar (an annuity, an inheritance). || Poner en orden, ordenar, arreglar (to put in order). || — FAM. *I'll settle accounts with him!*, ¡voy a ajustarle las cuentas! | *It's as good as settled*, está prácticamente resuelto, está prácticamente en el bote (fam.). || *Questions not yet settled*, cuestiones pendientes. || *That settles it!*, ¡eso resuelve el problema! (that solves the problem), ¡no hay más que hablar! (let's say no more about it). || *To settle an affair out of court*, llegar a un arreglo amistoso sobre un asunto. || *To settle o.s.*, instalarse.

— V. intr. Posarse: *the bird settled on a branch*, el pájaro se posó en una rama. || Domiciliarse, instalarse, establecerse: *to settle in London*, domiciliarse en Londres. || Fijar la residencia, afincarse (to take up residence). || Arrellanarse (in an armchair). || Estabilizarse, serenarse (weather). || Localizarse (a disease): *the inflammation settled on his lungs*, la inflamación se localizó en los pulmones. || Depositarse, asentarse (sediment): *the dregs settled and the wine was clear*, se depositaron las heces y el vino quedó claro. || Asentarse, clarificarse (liquid). || Depositarse, caer: *the dust settled on everything*, el polvo se depositó por todas partes. || Asentarse (building). || Calmarse (excitement). || Arreglarse, resolverse (business matters). || Espesarse (fog). || Caer, venir (the night). || Cuajar (snow). || Volver a la normalidad, normalizarse: *the situation has settled*, la situación ha vuelto a la normalidad. || Pagar: *please settle as quickly as possible*, haga el favor de pagar cuanto antes. || MAR. Hundirse poco a poco (ship). || — *He can't settle down anywhere*, no puede estarse quieto. || *He can't settle to anything*, no consigue decidirse por nada. || *The wind is settling in the north*, el viento sopla del norte. || *To settle down*, domiciliarse, establecerse, instalarse (to take up permanent residence), calmarse (to calm), sentar cabeza (to lead a more serious life), casarse (to get married), normalizarse, volver a la normalidad: *since the war things have settled down*, desde la guerra las cosas se han normalizado; acostumbrarse: *he is settling down to his new job*, se está acostumbrando a su nuevo trabajo. || *To settle down to work*, ponerse seriamente a trabajar. || *To settle for*, contentarse con. || *To settle in*, instalarse. || *To settle on* o *upon*, decidirse por, escoger (to choose), ponerse de acuerdo sobre: *they settled on the terms of the treaty*, se pusieron de acuerdo sobre los términos del tratado. || *To settle o.s. down in an armchair*, arrellanarse en un sillón. || *To settle to work*, ponerse seriamente a trabajar. || *To settle up*, ajustar cuentas, saldar cuentas (to adjust accounts).

settlement [—mənt] n. Establecimiento, *m.* (of people). || Colonización, *f.*, población, *f.* (of land, country). || Colonia, *f.* (colony). || Poblado, *m.*, pueblo, *m.* (little village). || Acuerdo, *m.* (agreement): *the terms of the settlement are quite just*, los términos del acuerdo son completamente justos. || Arreglo, *m.* (of an argument): *a friendly settlement*, un arreglo amistoso. || Solución, *f.* (of a problem). || Liquidación, *f.* (of an account). || Pago, *m.* (of a debt). || Asentamiento, *m.*, hundimiento, *m.* (of a building). || JUR. Pensión, *f.*, renta, *f.* (pension). | Dote, *f.* (dowry). | Asignación, *f.* (of an annuity, an endowment). | Domicilio, *m.* (residence). || — *Act of settlement*, ley (*f.*) de sucesión al trono (in England). || *Marriage settlement*, capitulaciones, *f. pl.* || *Penal settlement*, penal, *m.*

settler [—ə*] n. Colonizador, ra; colono, *m.*, poblador, ra.

settling [—iŋ] n. See SETTLEMENT.

set-to [ˈsetˈtu:] n. FAM. Lucha, *f.*, refriega, *f.* (fight). | Agarrada, *f.* (verbal). || SP. Asalto, *m.* (in fencing).

setup [ˈsetʌp] n. Porte, *m.* (of the body). || Organización, *f.* || Disposición, *f.* (of the parts of a machine). || Plan, *m.*, proyecto, *m.* (plan). || Situación, *f.* || FAM. Combate (*m.*) amañado.

seven [ˈsevn] adj. Siete. || — *The seven deadly sins*, los siete pecados capitales. || *The seven wise men*, los siete sabios de Grecia.

— N. Siete, *m.* (number, card). || *It's seven o'clock*, son las siete.

sevenfold [—fəuld] adj. Séptuplo, pla.

— Adv. Siete veces.

seven hundred [—ˈhʌndrəd] n. Setecientos, *m.*

seven hundredth [—ˈhʌndrədθ] adj./n. Septingentésimo, ma.

seventeen [—ti:n] adj. Diecisiete, diez y siete.

— N. Diecisiete, *m.*, diez y siete, *m.*

seventeenth [—ti:nθ] adj. Decimoséptimo, ma. || *The seventeenth century*, el siglo diecisiete.

— N. Decimoséptimo, ma; diecisiete, *m.* & *f.*, diez y siete, *m.* & *f.* (in a series). || Diecisieteava parte, *f.*, decimoséptima parte, *f.*, diecisieteavo, *m.* (fraction). || Día (*m.*) diecisiete, diecisiete, *m.* (day of month). || Diecisiete, diez y siete: *John XVII* (*the seventeenth*), Juan XVII [diecisiete].

seventh [—θ] adj. Séptimo, ma. || En séptima posición: *he came seventh*, llegó en séptima posición. || — *Seventh century*, siglo (*m.*) siete. || FIG. *Seventh heaven*, séptimo cielo.

— N. Séptimo, ma (person or thing in seventh position). || Séptima parte, *f.* (fraction). || MUS. Séptima, *f.* (interval). || Día (*m.*) siete, siete, *m.* (day of month). || *Charles VII* (*the Seventh*), Carlos VII [Séptimo].

seventhly [—θli] adv. En séptimo lugar.

seventieth [—iəθ] adj. Septuagésimo, ma.

— N. Septuagésimo, ma; setenta, *m.* & *f.* (in seventieth position). || Setentavo, *m.*, septuagésima parte, *f.* (one of seventy parts).

seventy [—ti] adj. Setenta.

— N. Setenta, *m.* (number). || *The seventies*, los años setenta (years), los setenta grados (temperature), los setenta (age).

seventy-one [—tiˈwʌn] adj. Setenta y uno.

— N. Setenta y uno, *m.* (number).

seventy-two [—tiˈtu:] adj. Setenta y dos.

— N. Setenta y dos, *m.* (number).

sever [ˈsevə*] v. tr. Cortar: *to sever a rope with a knife*, cortar una cuerda con un cuchillo. || Separar (*from*, de). || FIG. Romper (connections, etc.): *to sever a friendship*, romper una amistad.

— V. intr. Romperse (things). || Separarse (persons).

several [ˈsevrəl] adj. Varios, rias: *I have seen him several times*, lo he visto varias veces; *he and several others*, él y varios más. || Distinto, ta: *the several members of the committee*, los distintos miembros de la comisión. || Respectivo, va: *our several rights*, nuestros derechos respectivos. || JUR. Individual. || — JUR. *Joint and several bond*, obligación solidaria. || *They went their several ways*, cada uno se fue por su lado.

— Pron. Varios, rias: *several were in the garden*, varios estaban en el jardín; *several of the team were absent*, faltaban varios del equipo.

severally [—i] adj. Separadamente, individualmente, por separado (one by one). || Respectivamente.

severalty [—ti] n. JUR. Propiedad (*f.*) individual. || *In severalty*, en propiedad exclusiva.

severance [ˈsevərəns] n. División, *f.* (division in two parts). || Separación, *f.* (breaking away from main body). || Interrupción, *f.* (of communications). || FIG. Ruptura, *f.* (of relations). || *Severance pay*, indemnización (*f.*) por despido.

severe [siˈviə*] adj. Severo, ta: *a severe critic*, un crítico severo; *a severe punishment*, un castigo severo; *he is very severe with his children*, es muy severo con sus hijos. || Duro, ra; fuerte (blow). || Riguroso, sa: *to take severe measures*, tomar medidas rigurosas. || Fuerte, severo, ra (reprimand). || Grave, serio, ria; grande (loss). || Violento, ta (fight). || Intenso, sa (bombardment). || Duro, ra: *a severe trial*, una dura prueba. || Austero, ra; severo, ra: *severe architecture*, arquitectura austera. || Duro, ra; riguroso, sa (climate). || Intenso, sa (heat). || MED. Grave, serio, ria (illness). | Agudo, da (pain). || Minucioso, sa; serio, ria: *my car will have to undergo a severe test*, habrá que someter mi coche a una revisión minuciosa. || *To be severe on*, tratar con severidad, tratar severamente.

severely [—li] adv. Severamente, con severidad. || MED. De gravedad (ill, wounded). || Austeramente (built). || — *He has suffered severely*, ha sufrido mucho. || *Severely plain*, muy austero, de lo más austero. || *To leave severely alone*, dejar completamente de lado.

severity [siˈveriti] n. Severidad, *f.* (of character, punishment). || Rigor, *m.* (of climate). || Dificultad, *f.* (of an ordeal). || Gravedad, *f.*, importancia, *f.* (of a loss). || Austeridad, *f.*, severidad, *f.* (of style). || MED. Gravedad, *f.*, seriedad, *f.* (of an illness). | Agudeza, *f.* (of a pain).

Seville [səˈvil] pr. n. GEOGR. Sevilla.

Sevillian [—jən] adj./n. Sevillano, na.

sew* [səu] v. tr./intr. Coser: *I make my living by sewing*, me gano la vida cosiendo. || MED. Coser. ||

Encuadernar, coser (in bookbinding). || — *To sew on*, coser: *to sew a button on*, coser un botón. || *To sew up*, coser, remendar (a tear), cerrar con una costura (tear, wound, etc.), monopolizar (to monopolize), arreglar (to settle).

— OBSERV. Pret. **sewed;** p. p. **sewn, sewed.**

sewage ['sju:idʒ] n. Aguas (*f. pl.*) residuales. || — *Sewage disposal*, depuración (*f.*) de las aguas residuales. || *Sewage farm*, huerta abonada con aguas residuales. || *Sewage system*, alcantarillado, *m.*
sewer ['sjuə*] n. Alcantarilla, *f.*, cloaca, *f.*, albañal, *m.* || FIG. Cloaca, *f.* || — *Main sewer*, colector, *m.* || *Sewer gas*, gas mefítico. || *Sewer man*, alcantarillero, *m.* || *Sewer rat*, rata (*f.*) de alcantarilla.
sewerage ['sjuəridʒ] n. Alcantarillado, *m.* (system). || Aguas (*f. pl.*) residuales (sewage).
sewing ['səuiŋ] n. Costura, *f.* || Encuadernación, *f.* (in bookbinding).
— Adj. De coser: *sewing machine*, máquina de coser. || *Sewing basket*, cesto (*m.*) de la costura.
sewn [səun] p. p. See SEW.
sex [seks] n. Sexo, *m.* || — *Fair sex*, bello sexo. || *Gentle* o *weaker sex*, sexo débil. || *Stronger sex*, sexo fuerte.
— Adj. Sexual: *sex education*, educación sexual; *sex life*, vida sexual; *sex organs*, órganos sexuales.
sex [seks] v. tr. Determinar el sexo de.
sexagenarian [,seksədʒi'nεəriən] adj./n. Sexagenario, ria.
sexagenary [,seks'ædʒinəri] adj. Sexagesimal. || Sexagenario, ria (sexagenarian).
Sexagesima [,seksə'dʒesimə] n. REL. Sexagésima, *f.*
sexagesimal [—l] adj. Sexagesimal.
sex appeal ['seksə,pi:l] n. Atractivo (*m.*) sexual, "sex appeal", *m.*
sexed [sekst] adj. Sexuado, da. || FAM. *To be highly sexed*, tener mucho temperamento.
sexennial [seks'enjəl] adj. Que ocurre cada seis años. || Que dura seis años.
— N. Sexenio, *m.*
sexiness ['seksinis] n. FAM. Atractivo (*m.*) sexual.
sexless ['sekslis] adj. Asexuado, da; asexual. || FAM. Sin atractivo.
sex-linked ['seks'liŋkt] adj. Ligado al sexo.
sexologist [seks'ɔlədʒist] n. Sexólogo, *m.*
sexology [seks'ɔlədʒi] n. Sexología, *f.*
sext [sekst] n. REL. Sexta, *f.*
sextant ['sekstənt] n. MAR. Sextante, *m.*
sextet or **sextette** [seks tet] n. MUS. Sexteto, *m.* (musical composition, group).
sextodecimo ['sekstəu'desiməu] adj. PRINT. En dieciseisavo.
— N. PRINT. Libro (*m.*) en dieciseisavo, tamaño (*m.*) en dieciseisavo.
sexton ['sekstən] n. REL. Sacristán, *m.* || FAM. Sepulturero, *m.* (gravedigger).
sextuple ['sekstjupl] adj. Séxtuplo, pla.
— N. Séxtuplo, *m.*
sextuple ['sekstjupl] v. tr. Sextuplicar.
— V. intr. Sextuplicarse.
sextuplet [—et] n. MUS. Seisillo, *m.*, sextillo, *m.*
sexual ['seksjuəl] adj. Sexual. || — *Sexual intercourse*, relaciones (*f. pl.*) sexuales. || *Sexual organs*, órganos (*m.*) genitales *or* sexuales.
sexuality [,seksju'æliti] n. Sexualidad, *f.* || Vida (*f.*) sexual.
sexy ['seksi] adj. Atractivo, va (woman). || Erótico, ca; verde (film, book, etc.). || Provocativo, va (dress).
sh [ʃ] interj. ¡Chitón!
shabbiness ['ʃæbinis] n. Aspecto (*m.*) andrajoso *or* desharrapado (of a person). || Lo raído (of clothing). || Pobreza, *f.*, aspecto (*m.*) lastimoso (of furniture, house, district). || Mezquindad, *f.* (of behaviour).
shabby ['ʃæbi] adj. Andrajoso, sa; desharrapado, da (poorly dressed). || Raído, da (clothing). || Lamentable, de aspecto lastimoso, pobre (furniture, house, district). || Mezquino, na (behaviour). || *To play a shabby trick*, hacer una mala jugada.
shabby-looking [—'lukiŋ] adj. De aspecto lastimoso.
shack [ʃæk] n. Choza, *f.*
schack [ʃæk] v. intr. U.S. FAM. *To shack up with*, vivir con, juntarse con.
shackle [—l] n. Argolla, *f.* (of a chain). || — Pl. Grilletes, *m.*, grillos, *m.* (for prisoners). || Trabas, *f.* (for animals). || FIG. Trabas, *f.* (hindrance).
shackle [—l] v. tr. Poner grilletes a (a prisoner). || Poner trabas a (animals). || FIG. Atar, poner trabas a (to restrict the freedom of).
shad [ʃæd] n. Sábalo, *m.* (fish).
shaddock ['ʃædək] n. Pomelo, *m.* (fruit).
shade [ʃeid] n. Sombra, *f.*: *he was sitting in the shade*, estaba sentado a la sombra; *light and shade*, luz y sombra; *temperature in the shade*, temperatura a la sombra; *to give shade*, dar sombra. || Visera, *f.* (eyeshade). || Pantalla, *f.* (lampshade). || Persiana, *f.* (window blind). || Fanal (*m.*) de cristal (for clocks). || Tono, *m.*, matiz, *m.*: *a different shade of pink*, un tono diferente de rosa, || Tono, *m.*: *I don't like the shade of this dress*, no me gusta el tono de este traje. || Matiz, *m.* (of a meaning, an opinion). || Tendencia, *f.*: *newspapers of every shade*, periódicos de todas las tendencias. || FIG. Poquito, *m.*, pizca, *f.*: *he is a shade better*, está un poquito mejor. | Fantasma, *m.*, sombra, *f.* (ghost). || — Pl. Sombras, *f.*: *the shades of the evening*, las sombras del crepúsculo. || Tinieblas, *f.* (of night). || MYTH. Averno, *m. sing.* || — ARTS. *Light and shade*, claroscuro, *m.* (of a painting). || FAM. *Of every shade and hue*, de toda calaña, de todas clases. || FIG. *Shades of Wagner!*, ¿qué diría Wagner si lo oyera? | *To put s.o.* o *sth. in the shade*, hacer sombra a alguien *or* a algo, eclipsar a alguien *or* algo.
shade [ʃeid] v. tr. Dar sombra a: *trees that shade the house*, árboles que dan sombra a la casa. || Proteger contra el sol, resguardar: *a hat that shades one's eyes*, un sombrero que protege los ojos contra el sol. || Tamizar (light). || Poner una pantalla a (lamp). || ARTS. Sombrear. || COMM. Reducir progresivamente (prices). || FIG. Matizar (a meaning). | Entristecer (face). || *To shade off*, degradar.
— V. intr. Oscurecerse. || *To shade into* o *to shade off into*, fundirse en.
shadeless [—lis] adj. Sin sombra.
shadiness ['ʃeidinis] n. Sombra, *f.* || FAM. Lo turbio, aspecto (*m.*) turbio (of a deal). | Honradez (*f.*) dudosa (of a person).
shading ['ʃeidiŋ] n. Protección (*f.*) contra la luz *or* contra el sol. || Sombra, *f.* (shadow). || ARTS. Degradación *f.* (of colours). | Sombreado, *m.* (of a drawing).
shadow ['ʃædəu] n. Sombra, *f.*: *I could see your shadow on the wall*, veía su sombra en la pared; *he was sitting in the shadow*, estaba sentado a la sombra; *he is only a shadow of his former self*, es sólo una sombra de lo que fue; *not a shadow of doubt*, ni sombra de duda; *that friend is your shadow*, ese amigo es tu sombra. | Oscuridad, *f.* (darkness). || FIG. Policía, *m.* (policeman). || Sombra, *f.*, fantasma, *m.* (ghost). || Sombreado, *m.*, sombra, *f.* (of a drawing). || Sombreador, *m.* (for eyelids). || Sombra, *f.* (in television). || Poquito, *m.*, pizca, *f.* (a little). || — Pl. Oscuridad, *f.* || — MATH. *Cast shadow*, sombra proyectada. || FIG. *Not to even trust one's own shadow*, desconfiar hasta de su sombra, no fiarse ni de su sombra. || *Shadow play* o *theatre*, sombras chinescas. || FIG. *To be afraid even of one's own shadow*, tener miedo hasta de su sombra. | *To be under the shadow of misfortune*, tener muchas desgracias. || *To cast a shadow*, hacer sombra. || FIG. *To cast a shadow over the festivities*, aguar la fiesta. || *To have shadows under the eyes*, tener ojeras. || FIG. *To run after a shadow*, soñar con quimeras. | *To wear o.s. to a shadow*, agotarse.
shadow ['ʃædəu] v. tr. Sombrear (to throw into shadow). || Oscurecer (to darken). || FIG. Seguir [la pista a] (to follow in secret): *the spy was shadowed by detectives*, el espía era seguido por detectives. || *To shadow forth*, anunciar.
shadowbox [—bɔks] v. intr. SP. Entrenarse con un adversario imaginario (in boxing).
shadow cabinet [—'kæbinit] n. Gabinete (*m.*) fantasma.
shadowy ['ʃædəui] adj. Oscuro, ra (dark). || Sombrío, a (a place). || Sombreado, da (shaded). || FIG. Quimérico, ca (dream). | Vago, ga; indistinto, ta (outline). | Vago, ga (plan). | Oscuro, ra (mysterious).
shady ['ʃeidi] adj. Sombreado, da: *a shady place*, un sitio sombreado. || Que da sombra (tree). || FAM. Turbio, bia (dealings): *there is sth. shady in the business*, hay algo turbio en el asunto. | Dudoso, sa; sospechoso, sa (person): *shady character*, persona dudosa. || FIG. *To be on the shady side of fifty*, tener más de cincuenta años.
shaft [ʃɑ:ft] n. Mango, *m.* (handle). || Flecha, *f.* (arrow). || Astil, *m.* (of an arrow). || Asta, *f.* (of a lance). || TECH. Árbol, *m.*, eje, *m.* (for transmitting motion): *driving shaft*, árbol motor. | Varal, *m.* (of carriage). || ARCH. Hueco, *m.*, caja, *f.* (of a lift). | Fuste, *m.*, caña, *f.* (of a column). | Aguja, *f.* (of a tower). || Pozo, *m.* (of mines, wells, etc.): *ventilation shaft*, pozo de ventilación. || Conducto, *m.* (duct). || ANAT. Caña, *f.* (of bone). || ZOOL. Cañón, *m.* (of feather). || BOT. Tallo, *m.* (of plants). || Rayo, *m.* (of light, of lightning). || FIG. Pullazo, *m.*, pulla, *f.* (remark). || FIG. *Cupid's shafts*, flechas de Cupido.
shag [ʃæg] n. Cormorán (*m.*) moñudo (bird). || Picadura, *f.* (tobacco). || Greñas, *f. pl.* (hair). || Pelusa, *f.* (of textiles). || Borra, *f.* (of wool).
shagginess ['ʃæginis] n. Aspecto (*m.*) desgreñado (of hair). || *The shagginess of his beard*, su barba enmarañada.
shaggy ['ʃægi] adj. Peludo, da (with long hair). || Desgreñado, da (hair). || Enmarañado, da (beard, eyebrows). || Lanudo, da (with long wool). || Con pelusa (textiles). || BOT. Cubierto de maleza (field). | Tupido, da (hedge). | Velludo, da; velloso, sa (leaf). || FAM. *Shaggy dog story*, chiste largo y pesado.
shagreen [ʃæ'gri:n] n. Zapa, *f.*
shah [ʃɑ:] n. Sha, *m.*, chah, *m.*, cha, *m.*
shake [ʃeik] n. Sacudida, *f.* (a shaking or being shaken). || Temblor, *m.*, estremecimiento, *m.* (tremble). || Movimiento, *m.*, meneo, *m.* (of the head). || Apretón (*m.*) de manos (of hands). || Grieta, *f.* (crack). || FAM. Batido, *m.* (milkshake). || MUS. Trino, *m.* (trill). || — FAM. *In two shakes*, en un momento, en un periquete, en un dos por tres. || *Shake of hands*, apretón (*m.*) de manos. || *To be all of a shake*, estar todo tembloroso, estar temblequeando. || FIG. *To be no*

great shakes, no valer gran cosa. || *To give sth. a good shake*, sacudir bien algo. || FIG. *To have the shakes*, temblar como un azogado (of fear), tener escalofríos (of fever). || *With a shake in his voice*, con la voz temblorosa.

shake* [ʃeik] v. tr. Sacudir (to agitate): *to shake a carpet*, sacudir una alfombra. || Agitar (bottle). || Hacer temblar (a table, etc.). || Esgrimir (to brandish). || Mover, menear (head). || Zarandear, sacudir (s.o.). || Mover (dice). || FIG. Hacer vacilar (s.o.'s faith, courage, etc.). | Librarse de (a habit). | Conmocionar, trastornar (to upset). | Desconcertar (to disconcert). | Mermar, hacer mella en (s.o.'s reputation). | Quebrantar (health). | Estremecer: *new ideas which shake the foundations of society*, nuevas ideas que estremecen los cimientos de la sociedad. || — FAM. *To shake a leg*, see LEG. || *To shake hands*, darse la mano, estrecharse la mano. || *To shake hands with*, dar la mano a, estrechar la mano a. || *To shake one's finger at*, decir que no con el dedo a. || *To shake one's fist at*, amenazar con el puño. || *To shake one's head*, negar con la cabeza (in dissent), dar muestras de desaprobación (disapproval).

— V. intr. Temblar (to tremble, to quiver): *the earth was shaking*, la tierra estaba temblando; *he was shaking with cold*, estaba temblando de frío. || Vibrar (to vibrate). || Agitarse, moverse, menearse (to move rapidly). || MUS. Trinar. || — U. S. FAM. *Shake!*, ¡enhorabuena! (congratulations), ¡chócala! (to seal bargain). || FIG. *To shake like a leaf*, temblar como un azogado. || *To shake with*, temblar de, estremecerse de (fear), tiritar de, temblar de (cold). || *To shake with laughter*, desternillarse de risa.

— **To shake down**, hacer caer sacudiendo: *to shake fruit down from a tree*, hacer caer las frutas sacudiendo un árbol. | Esparcir (straw). | Echar en el suelo (blanket). | Acostarse (to lie down). | Acostumbrarse (to become accustomed). | Instalarse (to settle down). | U. S. FAM. Sacar dinero a. || **To shake off**, deshacerse de, quitarse de encima, librarse de: *to shake off a bad habit*, librarse de una mala costumbre. | — FIG. *To shake off the yoke*, sacudir el yugo. || **To shake out**, sacudir. | Desplegar (flag, sail). || **To shake up**, agitar, mover: *to shake up a bottle*, agitar una botella. | Sacudir (a pillow, etc.). | Conmocionar, trastornar (to shock). | Estimular (to stimulate). | Reorganizar (to reorganize).

— OBSERV. Pret. **shook;** p. p. **shaken.**

shakedown [—'daun] n. FAM. Cama (*f.*) improvisada (bed). || U. S. FAM. Exacción (*f.*) de dinero (by a racketeer).

shaken [—ən] p. p. See SHAKE.

shaker [—ə*] n. Criba (*f.*) vibradora (sieve). || — *Cocktail shaker*, coctelera, *f.* || REL. *The Shakers*, los cuáqueros, *m.*, los tembladores, *m.*

Shakespearean or **Shakespearian** [ʃeiks'piəriən] adj. Shakesperiano, na.

shake-up ['ʃeik'ʌp] n. Reorganización, *f.* (reorganization): *government shake-up*, reorganización ministerial. || Sacudida, *f.* (shake).

shakily ['ʃeikili] adv. Con voz temblorosa (speaking). || Con paso inseguro (walking). || Con mano temblorosa (writing). || De modo poco estable (built).

shakiness ['ʃeikinis] n. Inestabilidad, *f.* (unsteadiness). || Temblor, *m.* (of the hand). || Debilidad, *f.* (of health).

shaking ['ʃeikiŋ] adj. Tembloroso, sa: *shaking voice*, voz temblorosa. || Desconcertante (disconcerting). || Que conmociona (upsetting).

— N. Sacudida, *f.*

shako ['ʃækəu] n. MIL. Chacó, *m.*

shaky ['ʃeiki] adj. Inestable (situation, etc.): *a shaky table*, una mesa inestable. || Tembloroso, sa (hand, voice). || Temblón, ona (handwriting). || Vacilante, inseguro, ra (step). || Delicado, da (health). || Cortado, da (style). || Sin ilación (speech). || Tambaleante (building). || Poco sólido, da: *a shaky argument*, un argumento poco sólido. || — *He got off to a shaky start*, tuvo un comienzo incierto. || *His English is shaky*, no domina el inglés, no tiene conocimientos muy seguros en inglés. || *To be shaky on one's legs*, tener las piernas poco firmes.

shale [ʃeil] n. GEOL. Esquisto, *m.* || *Shale oil*, aceite (*m.*) de esquisto bituminoso.

shall [ʃæl] v. aux. Se usa para expresar el futuro de indicativo [primera persona del sing. y del pl.]: *I shall go tomorrow*, iré mañana; *shall we be back in time?*, ¿estaremos de vuelta a tiempo?; *he said I was not to go but I certainly shall*, dijo que yo no iba a ir pero seguramente iré. || Se utiliza para expresar una promesa, una amenaza, una intención o una obligación [segundas y terceras personas]: *they shall be set free*, serán liberados; *he should not have gone if I could have stopped him*, no se hubiera ido si hubiese podido impedírselo; *you say you will not do it, but I say you shall (do it)*, usted dice que no lo hará pero yo digo que usted lo va a hacer. || Expresa el deber, un mandato o una obligación [todas las personas]: *shall I close the door?*, ¿cierro la puerta?; *you should have been more careful*, tenía que haber sido más prudente. || Equivale al subjuntivo [todas las personas]: *I'm anxious that it shall be done at once*, deseo que se haga en seguida; *it is surprising that he should be so foolish*, es extraño que sea tan estúpido. || *Let's go, shall we?*, vamos, ¿os parece?

— OBSERV. El verbo auxiliar *shall* puede contraerse cuando le antecede un pronombre personal (*I'll, you'll, he'll, we'll, they'll*). Si va seguido por la negación *not* puede formar con ella la palabra *shan't* (*you shan't do it*, no lo hará; *shan't I go?*, ¿no puedo ir?).
— El pretérito de *shall* es *should*. *Should* se emplea también para expresar la probabilidad (*they should be there by now*, ya deben de estar allí).

shallop [—əp] n. MAR. Chalupa, *f.*

shallot [ʃə'lɔt] n. BOT. Chalote, *m.*

shallow ['ʃæləu] adj. Poco profundo, da: *shallow water*, agua poco profunda. || Llano, na: *a shallow plate*, un plato llano. || AGR. Superficial (soil). || MAR. Poco, ca (ship's draught). || FIG. Superficial (person, knowledge, etc.).

— Pl. n. MAR. Bajío, *m. sing.*, bajos, *m.*

shallow ['ʃæləu] v. tr. Hacer menos profundo.

— V. intr. Hacerse menos profundo.

shallow-minded [—'maindid] adj. Superficial.

shallowness ['ʃæləunis] n. Poca profundidad, *f.* (of water). || FIG. Superficialidad, *f.* (of knowledge, etc.).

shalt [ʃælt] 2nd pers. sing. of shall. (Ant.) *Thou shalt not steal*, no robarás.

shaly ['ʃeili] adj. Esquistoso, sa.

sham [ʃæm] adj. Fingido, da; simulado, da: *a sham illness*, una enfermedad fingida. || De imitación, de bisutería (jewelry). || Falso, sa (title, knowledge). || COMM. Ficticio, cia (dividend). || Adulterado, da (food). || MIL. *A sham battle*, un simulacro de combate.

— N. Impostor, ra (person). || Impostura, *f.*, engaño, *m.*, farsa, *f.* (thing, act). || Joya (*f.*) de imitación, bisutería, *f.* (jewelry).

sham [ʃæm] v. tr. Fingir, simular: *he shams illness*, simula que está enfermo.

— V. intr. Fingir, fingirse, simular: *to sham dead*, fingirse muerto; *he is not ill, he is only shamming*, no está enfermo, sólo está simulando.

shamble ['ʃæmbl] v. intr. Andar arrastrando los pies.

shambles [—z] n. Matadero, *m.* (slaughterhouse). || FIG. Ruinas, *f. pl.* (great destruction). | Carnicería, *f.*, matanza, *f.* (carnage). | Follón, *m.* (extreme disorder). | Confusión, *f.*

shame [ʃeim] n. Vergüenza, *f.*: *the shame of having to admit defeat*, la vergüenza de tener que admitir la derrota; *to flush with shame*, ruborizarse de vergüenza; *you are a shame to your country*, eres una vergüenza para tu país; *red with shame*, colorado de vergüenza. || Deshonra, *f.* (dishonour). || FAM. Pena, *f.*, lástima, *f.*: *it's a shame the rain spoiled our holidays*, es una pena que la lluvia nos haya estropeado las vacaciones; *what a shame!*, ¡qué lástima! || — *For shame!*, ¡qué vergüenza! || *Shame on you!*, ¡qué vergüenza! || *To be without shame* o *to be lost to all sense of shame*, no tener vergüenza alguna. || *To bring shame upon s.o.*, deshonrar a alguien. || *To cry shame*, poner el grito en el cielo. || *To feel shame at having done sth.*, avergonzarse de haber hecho algo. || *To my shame*, con gran vergüenza mía. || *To put to shame*, avergonzar.

shame [ʃeim] v. tr. Avergonzar (to cause to feel shame). || Deshonrar (to bring shame upon). || *To shame s.o. into doing sth.*, avergonzar a alguien de tal manera que se sienta obligado a hacer algo.

shamefaced [—feist] adj. Avergonzado, da (showing shame). || Vergonzoso, sa; tímido da (shy).

shamefacedly [—feistli] adv. Con vergüenza.

shamefacedness [—feistnis] n. Vergüenza, *f.* (shame). || Vergüenza, *f.*, timidez, *f.* (shyness).

shameful [—ful] adj. Vergonzoso, sa: *shameful behaviour*, comportamiento vergonzoso. || *How shameful!*, ¡qué vergüenza!, ¡es vergonzoso!

shamefully [—fuli] adv. Vergonzosamente.

shamefulness [—fulnis] n. Vergüenza, *f.*

shameless [—lis] adj. Desvergonzado, da; descarado, da (behaviour). || Sinvergüenza, descarado, da; desvergonzado, da (person). || Vergonzoso, sa (action).

shamelessness [—lisnis] n. Desvergüenza, *f.*, falta (*f.*) de vergüenza, descaro, *m.*

shammer ['ʃæmə*] n. Impostor, ra; simulador, ra.

shammy ['ʃæmi] n. Gamuza, *f.* (chamois).

shampoo [ʃæm'pu:] n. Champú, *m.* || *To give s.o. a shampoo*, lavar la cabeza a alguien, dar un champú a alguien.

shampoo [ʃæm'pu:] v. tr. Dar un champú a, lavar la cabeza a (person). || Lavar (hair).

shamrock ['ʃæmrɔk] n. BOT. Trébol, *m.*

shandy ['ʃændi] or **shandygaff** [—gæf] n. Cerveza (*f.*) con gaseosa.

shanghai [ʃæŋ'hai] v. tr. Emborrachar *or* drogar [a alguien] para llevarlo como marinero.

Shangri-la ['ʃæŋgri'lɑ:] n. Jauja, *f.*, tierra (*f.*) de Jauja.

shank [ʃæŋk] n. ANAT. Pierna, *f.* (leg). | Espinilla, *f.* (part of the leg). || Caña, *f.* (of a horse). || CULIN. Pierna, *f.* || TECH. Mango, *m.* (of a tool). | Pierna, *f.* (of scissors, pliers). | Tija, *f.* (of a key, of a pin). || MAR. Caña, *f.* (of an anchor). || BOT. Peciolo, *m.* (of a leaf). | Rabillo, *m.* (of flowers). | Tallo, *m.* (of a plant). || ARCH. Fuste, *m.*, caña, *f.* || PRINT. Cuerpo, *m.* || FIG. FAM. *To ride on Shanks' mare* o *on Shanks' pony*, ir en el coche de San Fernando.

shank [ʃæŋk] v. intr. Bot. *To shank off*, caerse (fruit), pudrirse por el tallo (plant).

shan't [ʃɑ:nt] contraction of *shall not*.

shantung [ʃænˈtʌŋ] n. Shantung, *m*.

shanty [ˈʃænti] n. Mus. Saloma, *f*. (sailor's song). || Chabola, *f*. (poor dwelling).

shantytown [—taun] n. Barrio (*m*.) de las latas [*Amer*., villa (*f*.) miseria].

shape [ʃeip] n. Forma, *f*.: *what shape is his hat?*, ¿de qué forma es su sombrero? || Figura *f*. (figure). || Aspecto, *m*., apariencia, *f*. (aspect). || Tipo, *m*.: *what shape was the man you saw?*, ¿qué tipo tenía el hombre que viste? || Silueta, *f*., bulto, *m*.: *two shapes came up to me in the darkness*, dos siluetas vinieron hacia mí en la oscuridad. || Aparición, *f*. (ghost). || Condición, *f*., estado, *m*.: *my business is in bad shape*, mis negocios están en mal estado. || Sp. Forma, *f*.: *this athlete is in bad shape*, este atleta está en baja forma; *he kept in shape*, se mantuvo en forma. || Culin. Molde, *m*. || Horma, *f*. (for hats). || Hechura, *f*., corte, *m*. (of a garment). || Tech. Perfil, *m*. (of iron). || — Fig. *An enemy in the shape of a friend*, un enemigo que se las da de amigo *or* que finge ser amigo. || *In shape*, en orden, arreglado, da. || *In the shape of*, en forma de. || *Out of shape*, deformado, da. || *Something in the shape of*, una especie de. || *To get into shape*, ordenar, poner en orden. || *To lick into shape*, pulir, poner a punto (an article), formar: *travel licks a young man into shape*, los viajes forman a los jóvenes; pulir, desbastar (an uncouth person). || *To put an idea into shape*, dar forma a una idea. || *To put into shape*, arreglar, preparar, poner a punto. || *To put out of shape*, deformar. || *To take shape*, tomar forma, concretarse: *our plans are taking shape*, nuestros proyectos se están concretando. || *You are in no shape to go on*, no estás en condiciones de continuar.

shape [ʃeip] v. tr. Dar forma a: *to shape the rock into a statue*, dar a la piedra la forma de una estatua. || Labrar, tallar: *to shape a statue out of stone*, labrar una estatua en piedra. || Tallar (wood). || Modelar (clay). || Cortar: *to shape a coat*, cortar un abrigo. || Formar: *to shape s.o.'s character*, formar el carácter de alguien. || Determinar: *to shape the destiny of men*, determinar el destino de los hombres. || Amoldar, conformar, ajustar: *to shape one's life to certain principles*, ajustar su vida a ciertos principios. || Concebir (an idea, plan). || Formular (an idea). || Construir (an essay). || — *To shape one's course towards*, dirigirse hacia. || Mar. *To shape the course*, determinar el rumbo.

— V. intr. Tomar forma, formarse (to acquire a particular shape). || Formarse: *clouds shaping on the horizon*, nubes formándose en el horizonte. || Suceder, ocurrir (to arrive). || Desarrollarse (to develop). || — *As things are shaping*, tal y como van las cosas. || *He is shaping well at Latin*, se le da bien el latín, hace progresos en latín. || *Shaped like*, en forma de. || *To shape up to s.o.*, prepararse a luchar contra alguien. || *To shape well*, tomar buen cariz, prometer, ser prometedor.

shaped [—t] adj. En forma de: *pear-shaped*, en forma de pera.

shapeless [—lis] adj. Informe (formless). || Deforme (not shapely).

shapelessness [—lisnis] n. Falta (*f*.) de forma. || Deformidad, *f*.

shapeliness [—linis] n. Formas (*f. pl*.) bien proporcionadas.

shapely [—li] adj. Bien proporcionado, da.

shaper [—ə*] n. Tech. Moldeador, *m*. (workman). | Embutidora, *f*. (machine). || Fig. Autor, ra.

shard [ʃɑ:d] n. Casco, *m*. (of broken earthenware). || Élitro, *m*. (of a beetle).

share [ʃɛə*] n. Parte, *f*.: *to get one's share of the booty*, recibir su parte del botín; *he did his share of the work*, hizo su parte del trabajo; *what share had he in their success?*, ¿qué parte tuvo en su éxito? || Contribución, *f*. (contribution). || Comm. Acción, *f*. (of stock): *bearer, registered share*, acción al portador, nominal. | Aportación, *f*. (of capital). | Participación, *f*.: *share in profits*, participación en los beneficios. | Cupo, *m*. (quota). | Cuota, *f*. (part). || Agr. Reja, *f*. (of a plough). || — *Everyone will pay his own share*, pagaremos a escote. || *I have had my share of worries*, ya tuve mi parte de preocupaciones. || *Share and share alike*, por partes iguales. || Fig. *The lion's share*, la parte del león, la mejor parte, la mejor tajada. || *To come in for one's full share of*, recibir la parte que le corresponde a uno de. || *To do one's share*, hacer de su parte. || *To fall to s.o.'s share*, tocar a uno, corresponder a uno. || *To go half shares with s.o.*, ir a medias con alguien. || *To go shares in*, compartir. || *To have a share in*, participar en. || *To pay share and share alike*, pagar a escote, compartir los gastos. || *You had a share in this*, ha tenido algo que ver en esto.

share [ʃɛə*] v. tr. Compartir: *he will share the prize with you*, compartirá el premio con usted; *I share your opinion*, comparto su opinión; *two children who share a bedroom*, dos niños que comparten un dormitorio. || Partir, dividir (to divide): *he shared the cake among us*, dividió el pastel entre nosotros. || *To share out*, repartir, distribuir.

— V. intr. *To share and share alike*, participar por igual, participar por partes iguales. || *To share in*, participar en, tener parte en.

share certificate [—səˈtifikeit] n. Acción, *f*.

sharecrop [—krɔp] v. tr./intr. U. S. Agr. Trabajar como aparcero.

sharecropper [—ˈkrɔpə*] n. U. S. Agr. Aparcero, *m*.

shareholder [—ˈhəuldə*] n. Comm. Accionista, *m*. & *f*.

share-out [—aut] n. Reparto, *m*.

sharer [—ə*] n. Partícipe, *m*. & *f*.

sharif [ˈʃerif] n. Jerife, *m*.

shark [ʃɑ:k] n. Tiburón, *m*. (fish). || Fig. Estafador, *m*. (swindler). || U. S. Fam. As, *m*. (expert).

sharkskin [—skin] n. Zapa, *f*. (skin of a shark).

sharp [ʃɑ:p] adj. Afilado, da; aguzado, da (able to cut or pierce): *sharp knife*, cuchillo afilado. || Puntiagudo, da (sharp-pointed). || Cerrado, da (bend): *a sharp bend in the road*, una curva cerrada en la carretera. || Agudo, da (angle). || Anguloso, sa (feature). || Puntiagudo, da (roof). || Definido, da (outline). || Nítido, da (photograph). || Marcado, da (contrast, opposition). || Empinado, da (slope). || Fuerte (incline). || Brusco, ca; repentino, na (change). || Agudo, da (pain, eyesight, cry). || Seco, ca (noise). || Chillón, ona (voice). || Acre (taste). || Ácido, da (fruit). || Penetrante (cold, wind). || Frío, a (air). || Fuerte (frost). || Mordaz (criticism). || Violento, ta (argument). || Arisco, ca (temper). || Acerbo, ba; áspero, ra (tone). || Severo, ra (reproof). || Áspero, ra (answer). || Encarnizado, da; feroz (struggle). || Aplastante (defeat). || Profundo, da; intenso, sa (feeling, regret, remorse). || Intenso, sa (attention). || Fino, na (hearing, sense of smell). || Rápido, da (pace). || Perspicaz, penetrante, agudo, da (mind). || Listo, ta; inteligente (clever): *a sharp child*, un chico inteligente. || Astuto, ta; vivo, va; despabilado, da (quick-witted). || Deshonesto, ta; poco honrado (practice, procedure). || Mus. Sostenido, da. || — *Sharp edge*, filo, *m*. || *Sharp words*, palabras (*f*.) mayores. || Fig. *That was sharp work*, lo has hecho muy rápido *or* en un dos por tres. | *To be as sharp as a needle*, ser un lince. || *To be sharp at arithmetic*, ser muy bueno en matemáticas. || *To have a sharp appetite*, tener un apetito feroz. || *To have a sharp tongue*, tener una lengua viperina. || *We must be sharp if we are to catch the train*, tenemos que darnos prisa si queremos coger el tren.

— N. Mus. Sostenido, *m*. || Aguja (*f*.) afilada (needle). || Fam. Estafador, ra (swindler). | Fullero, ra (cardsharper). || U. S. Fam. Experto, *m*.

— Adv. En punto: *at ten o'clock sharp*, a las diez en punto. || De pronto, repentinamente: *he turned sharp right*, torció repentinamente a la derecha. || En seco: *he stopped sharp*, se paró en seco. || Mus. Demasiado alto, desafinadamente. || *Look sharp!*, ¡pronto!, ¡rápido!

sharp [ʃɑ:p] v. tr. Mus. Marcar con un sostenido. || Fam. Estafar (to cheat).

— V. intr. Hacer fullerías en el juego (in cards). || Mus. Dar un agudo.

sharp-edged [—ˈedʒd] adj. Afilado, da; aguzado, da.

sharpen [—ən] v. tr. Afilar (blade). || Sacar punta a (pencil). || Fig. Aguzar, abrir (appetite). | Aguzar (intelligence). | Avivar, acentuar, agudizar (desire, enmity). | Despabilar (s.o.). | Hacer más severo (a law). | Hacer más encarnizado (a struggle). | Hacer más agudo (a pain).

— V. intr. Volverse más agudo (noise). || Afilarse (features). || Fig. Agudizarse (faculties).

sharpener [—nə*] n. Sacapuntas, *m. inv*., afilalápices, *m. inv*. (for pencil). || Tech. Afiladora, *f*. (machine).

sharpening [—niŋ] n. Afilado, *m*. (of tools, etc.). || Fig. Agudizamiento, *m*. (of faculties).

sharper [—ə*] n. Fam. Fullero, ra (cardsharper). | Estafador, ra (swindler).

sharp-eyed [—aid] adj. De vista aguda, de mirada penetrante, que tiene ojos de lince (having good sight). || Perspicaz (perspicacious). || Observador, ra (observant).

sharply [—li] adv. Bruscamente, repentinamente: *he turned sharply*, torció repentinamente. || Con aspereza, abruptamente: *she answered him sharply*, le contestó con aspereza. || De modo incisivo (remark). || Claramente: *sharply divided*, dividido claramente. || Severamente, con severidad: *he spoke sharply to her*, le habló severamente. || Rápidamente: *he walked sharply*, andaba rápidamente. || Pronunciadamente (sloping). || Fuerte (freezing, hitting). || Atentamente (listening). || Con un ruido seco (sounding). || Mucho (suffering). || — *Sharply edged*, afilado, da. || *Sharply pointed*, puntiagudo, da.

sharpness [—nis] n. Lo afilado (of edge). || Agudeza, *f*. (of noise, senses, pain). || Lo cerrado (of a bend). || Nitidez, *f*. (clarity). || Lo empinado (of a slope). || Brusquedad, *f*. (of a change, gesture). || Acritud, *f*. (of taste). || Violencia, *f*. (of an argument). || Acritud, *f*., lo arisco (of temper). || Aspereza, *f*. (of tone). || Mordacidad, *f*. (of criticism). || Severidad, *f*. (of a reprimand). || Rigor, *m*. (of the weather). || Agudeza, *f*., perspicacia, *f*. (of mind). || Inteligencia, *f*. (intelligence). || Lo profundo, intensidad, *f*. (of feeling, remorse). || Culin. Acidez, *f*. (of a fruit). | Lo picante (of a sauce).

sharp-pointed [—ˈpɔintid] adj. Puntiagudo, da.

sharpshooter [—ˌʃu:tə*] n. Mil. Tirador (*m*.) de primera.

sharpshooting [—,ʃu:tiŋ] n. Puntería (*f.*) certera.
sharp-sighted [—ˈsaitid] adj. See SHARP-EYED.
sharp-sightedness [—ˈsaitidnis] n. Vista (*f.*) aguda (keen eyesight). || Perspicacia, *f.*, sagacidad, *f.*
sharp-tongued [—ˈtʌŋd] adj. De lengua viperina.
sharp-witted [—ˈwitid] adj. Listo, ta (clever). || Agudo, da; ingenioso, sa (witty). || Perspicaz (shrewd).
shatter [ˈʃætə*] v. tr. Hacer añicos, hacer pedazos, romper, destrozar: *he shattered the window*, rompió la ventana; *the explosion shattered the house*, la explosión destrozó la casa. || FIG. Echar por tierra: *this objection shatters your theory*, esta objeción echa por tierra su teoría. | Destruir, echar por tierra, frustar: *to shatter s.o.'s hopes*, destruir las esperanzas de alguien. | Dejar pasmado (to stun). || MED. Quebrantar (health). | Destrozar (nerves).
— V. intr. Hacerse pedazos, hacerse añicos, romperse.
shatterproof [—pru:f] adj. Inastillable (glass).
shave [ʃeiv] n. Afeitado, *m.* (act of shaving). || Roce, *m.* (act of passing very near). || TECH. Cepillo, *m.* (plane). | Viruta, *f.* (slice of wood). || — *To get a shave*, afeitarse. || *To give s.o. a shave*, afeitar a alguien. || FIG. *To have a close shave*, librarse por los pelos. || *To have a shave*, afeitarse.
shave [ʃeiv] v. tr. Afeitar. || Rapar: *to shave s.o.'s head*, rapar la cabeza a alguien. || TECH. Cepillar (wood). || FIG. Cercenar (to reduce): *to shave the budget estimates*, cercenar las previsiones presupuestarias. | Pasar rozando (to pass very close): *the car shaved a wall*, el coche pasó rozando un muro. || — *To shave off one's moustache*, afeitarse el bigote. | *To shave one's legs*, afeitarse las piernas.
— V. intr. Afeitarse.
shaveling [—liŋ] n. U. S. Chaval, *m.*
shaven [ˈʃeivn] adj. Afeitado, da (face). || Rapado, da (head). || Tonsurado, da (monk). || TECH. Cepillado, da (wood).
shaver [ˈʃeivə*] n. Maquinilla (*f.*) de afeitar eléctrica, afeitadora, *f.* (electric razor). || Barbero, *m.* (barber). || FAM. *Little* o *young shaver*, chaval, *m.* (young boy).
shaving [ˈʃeiviŋ] n. Afeitado, *m.* || TECH. Cepillado, *m.* (act of shaving wood). | Viruta, *f.* (slice of wood or metal). || — *Shaving bowl*, bacía, *f.* || *Shaving brush*, brocha (*f.*) de afeitar. || *Shaving cream*, crema (*f.*) de afeitar. || *Shaving horse*, banco (*m.*) de carpintero. || *Shaving is obligatory in the army*, es obligatorio afeitarse en el ejército. || *Shaving soap* o *shaving stick*, jabón (*m.*) de afeitar.
shawl [ʃɔ:l] n. Chal, *m.*
shawm [ʃɔ:m] n. MUS. Caramillo, *m.* (instrument).
she [ʃi:] n. ZOOL. Hembra, *f.*: *is it a he or a she?*, ¿es macho o hembra?
— Pron. Ella: *she didn't speak*, ella no habló; *it is she*, es ella. || — *If I were she*, si fuera ella, si estuviera en su lugar. || MAR. *Isn't she a beautiful boat?*, es un barco precioso ¿verdad? || *She who*, la que, aquella que, quien.
— Adj. *She-ass*, burra, *f.* || *She-bear*, osa, *f.* || *She-cat*, gata, *f.* || *She-devil*, diabla, *f.*, diablesa, *f.* || *She-elephant*, elefante (*m.*) hembra. || *She-monkey*, mona, *f.*
sheaf [ʃi:f] n. AGR. Gavilla, *f.* || Haz, *m.* (of arrows). || Fajo, *m.* (of papers, tickets).
— OBSERV. El plural de esta palabra es *sheaves*.
sheaf [ʃi:f] v. tr. AGR. Agavillar.
shear* [ʃiə*] v. tr. Esquilar (sheep). || Cortar (a branch). || Rapar (hair). || FIG. Privar, despojar: *shorn of his power*, privado de su poder. || FIG. FAM. Pelar, desplumar (of money). || TECH. Cizallar (metal). || Tundir (cloth). || — *Shorn of*, sin. || *To shear off* o *through*, cortar.
— V. intr. Esquilar ovejas (to clip sheep). || TECH. Romperse por cizallamiento. || FIG. Abrirse camino.
— OBSERV. Pret. ***sheared;*** p. p. ***shorn, sheared.***
shearer [—rə*] n. Esquilador, ra.
shearing [—riŋ] n. Esquileo, *m.* (of sheep). || TECH. Cizallamiento, *m.* (of metals). || — Pl. Lana (*f. sing.*) esquilada.
shearing machine [—iŋməˈʃi:n] n. Esquiladora, *f.*
shear legs [—legz] n. TECH. Cabria, *f.* (for hoisting).
shearling [—liŋ] n. Añal, *m.*, cordero (*m.*) esquilado una vez.
shears [—z] pl. n. Tijeras, *f.* (for hedging). || TECH. Cizalla, *f. sing.* (for cutting metal). | Cabria, *f. sing.* (for hoisting).
sheatfish [ˈʃi:tfiʃ] n. Siluro, *m.* (catfish).
sheath [ʃi:θ] n. Funda, *f.* (for knife, scissors, umbrella). || Vaina, *f.* (of sword). || BOT. Vaina, *f.* || Vaina, *f.* (of an organ, an artery). || MED. Preservativo, *m.* (contraceptive).
sheath dress [—dres] n. Vestido (*m.*) tubo *or* tubular.
sheathe [ʃi:ð] v. tr. Envainar (a sword). || Enfundar (a knife). || Cubrir (a boat, a roof, etc.). || Retraer (claws). || TECH. Forrar (a cable). || Hundir en la carne (a dagger, fang, etc.).
sheathing [—iŋ] n. Enfundadura, *f.* (of a knife). || Acción (*f.*) de envainar (of a sword). || Revestimiento, *m.* (covering). || TECH. Forro, *m.* (of a cable, metal).
sheath knife [—naif] n. Cuchillo (*m.*) de monte.
sheave [ʃi:v] n. Roldana, *f.* (of a pulley). || Escudo, *m.* (of a keyhole).
sheave [ʃi:v] v. tr. AGR. Agavillar.
sheaves [—z] pl. n. See SHEAF.
Sheba [ˈʃi:bə] pr. n. GEOGR. Saba: *the Queen of Sheba*, la reina de Saba.
shebang [ʃiˈbæŋ] n. U. S. FAM. *The whole shebang*, todo el asunto (affair), todos los bártulos (things).
shed [ʃed] n. Cobertizo, *m.* (lean-to). || Hangar, *m.* (for engines). || Nave, *f.* (workshop). || Barraca, *f.* (for workmen). || Almacén, *m.* (warehouse). || AGR. Establo, *m.* (for cattle).
shed* [ʃed] v. tr. Quitarse, despojarse de (clothes). || Deshacerse de (to get rid of). || ZOOL. Mudar (skin). || BOT. Despojarse de (leaves). || Derramar (tears). || Verter, derramar (blood). || Despedir (a smell). || Dar (light). || Verter (water). || FIG. Traer: *to shed happiness*, traer la felicidad. | Perder (weight). || FIG. *To shed light on a subject*, aclarar un asunto.
— V. intr. ZOOL. Pelechar, mudar.
— OBSERV. Pret. & p. p. ***shed.***
she'd [ʃi:d] contraction of *she had, she would*.
shedder [—ə*] n. Animal (*m.*) que pelecha.
shedding [—iŋ] n. Muda, *f.* (of skin, plumage). || Derramamiento, *m.* (of blood, tears).
sheen [ʃi:n] n. Brillo, *m.* (brightness). || Viso, *m.* (of silk). || Brillo, *m.*, espejeo, *m.* (of water).
sheeny [—i] adj. Brillante.
sheep [ʃi:p] inv. n. ZOOL. Oveja, *f.* || FIG. Corderito, ta; cordero, ra (easily led person). || REL. Grey, *f.* || AGR. Ganado (*m.*) lanar, ovinos, *m. pl.* || — FIG. *A wolf in sheep's clothing*, un lobo con piel de oveja. | *The black sheep of the family*, la oveja negra de la familia. | *To cast sheep's eyes at s.o.*, mirar a alguien con ternura. | *To feel like a lost sheep*, sentirse perdido. | *To separate the sheep from the goats*, separar la cizaña del buen grano.
sheep bot [—bɔt] n. Rezno, *m.*
sheepdip [—dip] n. Desinfectante, *m.* (liquid). || Baño (*m.*) desinfectante (bath).
sheep dog [—dɔg] n. Perro (*m.*) pastor (dog).
sheep farming [—ˈfɑ:miŋ] n. AGR. Cría (*f.*) de las ovejas para la lana.
sheepfold [—,fəuld] n. Aprisco, *m.*, majada, *f.*, redil, *m.*
sheepherder [—,hɔ:də*] n. U. S. Pastor, *m.*
sheepherding [—,hə:diŋ] adj. Pastoril.
— N. Pastoreo, *m.*
sheephook [—huk] n. Cayado, *m.*
sheepish [—iʃ] adj. Tímido, da; vergonzoso, sa (bashful).
sheepishness [—iʃnis] n. Timidez, *f.*, vergüenza, *f.*
sheepman [—mən] n. Propietario (*m.*) de ganado lanar, ganadero, *m.*
— OBSERV. El plural de esta palabra es *sheepmen*.
sheep run [—rʌn] n. Redil, *m.*, aprisco, *m.*
sheepshearer [—,ʃiərə*] n. Esquilador, ra (person). || Esquiladora, *f.* (machine).
sheepshearing [—,ʃiəriŋ] n. Esquileo, *m.*
sheepskin [—skin] n. Piel (*f.*) de carnero *or* de oveja, zamarra, *f.* (hide). || Badana, *f.* (leather). || Pergamino, *m.* (parchment). || U. S. FAM. Diploma, *m.*, pergamino, *m.* (diploma). || *Sheepskin jacket* o *coat*, zamarra, *f.*, pelliza, *f.*
sheepwalk [—wɔ:k] n. Pasto, *m.*, dehesa, *f.*
sheer [ʃiə*] adj. Completo, ta; total, absoluto, ta (impossibility). || Total: *a sheer waste of time*, una pérdida total de tiempo. || Puro, ra [*Amer.*, mero, ra] (kindness, etc.): *out of sheer malice*, por pura maldad; *it is sheer nonsense*, es pura necedad. || Verdadero, ra: *it is sheer robbery*, es un verdadero robo. || Escarpado, da; cortado a pico (cliff). || Acantilado, da (coast). || Vertical (drop, fall). || Fino, na; transparente (cloth). || — *By sheer force*, a viva fuerza. || *In sheer desperation*, en último extremo.
— Adv. Perpendicularmente, a pico (perpendicularly). || Completamente: *the tree was torn sheer out by the roots*, el árbol fue completamente desarraigado.
— N. MAR. Arrufadura, *f.*, arrufo, *m.* (curve of ship). | Desviación, *f.* (deviation from a course). | Guiñada, *f.* (yaw).
sheer [ʃiə*] v. intr. MAR. Guiñar, desviarse. || Caer a pico (rock, etc.). || *To sheer off*, desviarse (ship), desviarse (from a subject), largarse (to go away).
sheerlegs [—legz] n. MAR. Cabria, *f.* (hoist).
sheet [ʃi:t] n. Sábana, *f.* (of bed): *bottom, top sheet*, sábana bajera, encimera. || Hoja, *f.* (of paper, tin). || Lámina, *f.* (of glass). || Chapa, *f.*, lámina, *f.* (of metal, etc.). || Capa, *f.* (of water, snow, ice). || Cortina, *f.* (of fog, smoke, rain). || COMM. Hoja, *f.* (for orders). || MAR. Escota, *f.* (rope). || FAM. Periodicucho, *m.* (newspaper). || — FIG. *As white as a sheet*, blanco como el papel. || *Balance sheet*, balance, *m.* || *In sheets*, en pliegos, sin encuadernar (book). || *Loose sheet*, hoja suelta. || PRINT. *Proof sheet*, prueba, *f.* || *Sheet anchor*, ancla (*f.*) de la esperanza (of a ship), tabla (*f.*) de salvación (last resort). || *Sheet brass*, chapa de latón. || *Sheet glass*, vidrio plano, vidrio laminado. || *Sheet iron*, chapa. || *Sheet lightning*, fucilazo, *m.* || *Sheet metal*, chapa de metal, metal (*m.*) en chapa. || *Sheet pile*, tablestaca, *f.* || *Sheet shop*, hojalatería, *f.* || *Sheet steel*, chapa de acero, acero (*m.*) en chapa. || FAM. *To be three sheets in the wind*, estar como una cuba. | *To get between the sheets*, meterse entre sábanas *or* en la cama. || *Winding sheet*, mortaja, *f.* (shroud).

sheet [ʃi:t] v. tr. Cubrir con una sábana (to cover with a sheet). || Cubrir con una capa (of tar, mist, etc.). || Cubrir: *river sheeted with ice*, río cubierto de hielo. || Amortajar (in a winding sheet).
sheeting [—iŋ] n. Tela (*f.*) de sábana (fabric). || Chapas, *f. pl.* (sheets of metal).
sheik or **sheikh** [ʃeik] n. Jeque, *m.* (Arab chief). || FAM. Seductor, *m.*, conquistador, *m.*
shekel [ˈʃekl] n. Siclo, *m.* (Hebrew coin). || — Pl. FAM. Pasta, *f. sing.* [*Amer.*, plata, *f. sing.*] (money).
shelf [ʃelf] n. Anaquel, *m.*, estante, *m.* (in a library). || Estante, *m.*, repisa, *f.* (in a room, kitchen, etc.). || Tabla, *f.*, anaquel, *m.* (in a cupboard, closet). || Parrilla, *f.* (in oven, fridge). || GEOL. Saliente, *m.* (projecting rock). | Graderío, *m.*, escalón, *m.*, rellano, *m.* (of a cliff). || MAR. Banco, *m.* (of sand). | Arrecife, *m.* (of rock, coral). || — Pl. Estantería, *f. sing.* || — *Continental shelf*, plataforma (*f.*) continental. || *Shelf ice*, plataforma (*f.*) de hielo. || FAM. *To be left on the shelf*, quedarse para vestir santos.
— OBSERV. El plural de esta palabra es *shelves*.
shell [ʃel] n. Concha, *f.* (of molluscs): *I have a lovely collection of shells*, tengo una colección de conchas preciosa. || Caparazón, *m.* (of crustacean). || Concha, *f.*, caparazón, *m.* (of tortoise). || Concha, *f.*, carey, *m.* (for making combs, etc.). || Cáscara, *f.*, cascarón, *m.* (of eggs). || Cáscara, *f.* (of nuts). || Vaina, *f.* (of peas). || Armazón, *f.*, esqueleto, *m.* (of a building). || Caja, *f.* (of a car). || MIL. Proyectil, *m.*, granada, *f.* (cannon projectile). | Casquillo, *m.* (of a bullet). || Taza, *f.* (of a sword). || MAR. Casco, *m.* (hull). | Yola, *f.* (boat). || TECH. Revestimiento, *m.* (of a furnace, etc.). | Soporte, *m.* (of pulley). || Capa, *f.* (of an atom). || FIG. Líneas (*f. pl.*) generales (plan). | Apariencia, *f.* (outward appearance). || — *Sea shell*, concha. || FIG. *To come out of one's shell*, salir de su concha. | *To retire into one's shell*, meterse en su concha.
shell [ʃel] v. tr. Pelar, desvainar (peas). || Quitar la cáscara de (eggs). || Descascarar (nuts). || Sacar de la concha *or* del caparazón (molluscs, crustaceans). || Abrir, desbullar (oysters). || Pelar (shrimps). || MIL. Bombardear. || FAM. *To shell out*, soltar, aflojar (money).
— V. intr. *To shell off*, desconcharse (paint). || FAM. *To shell out*, cascar, aflojar (money).
she'll [ʃil] contraction of *she will, she shall.*
shellac (U. S. **shellack**) [ʃəˈlæk] n. Laca, *f.*, goma (*f.*) laca.
shellac (U. S. **shellack**) [ʃəˈlæk] v. tr. Dar laca, laquear. || U. S. FAM. Dar una paliza (to beat).
shellacking [—iŋ] n. U. S. FAM. Paliza, *f.* (beating).
shellfire [—ˈfaiə*] n. MIL. Bombardeo, *m.*, cañoneo, *m.*
shellfish [—fiʃ] n. ZOOL. Marisco, *m.* (cockles, mussels, etc.). | Crustáceo, *m.* (crabs, lobsters, etc.). || CULIN. Mariscos, *m. pl.*
shelling [—iŋ] n. Pelado, *m.* (of peas). || Descascarillado, *m.* (of nuts). || Desbulla, *f.* (of oysters). || Pelado, *m.* (of shrimps). || MIL. Bombardeo, *m.*
shellproof [—pru:f] adj. MIL. A prueba de bombas.
shell shock [—ʃɔk] n. MED. Trauma (*m.*) causado por la guerra, conmoción (*f.*) debida a los bombardeos.
shelter [ˈʃeltə*] n. Refugio, *m.*, abrigo, *m.* (place of safety). || Asilo, *m.* (for the old, the homeless): *night shelter*, asilo nocturno. || Cobertizo, *m.* (against the rain). || Albergue, *m.* (for mountaineers). || FIG. Amparo, *m.* (protection). | Albergue, *m.*, refugio, *m.*: *to find shelter with a friend*, encontrar albergue en casa de un amigo. || MIL. Garita, *f.* (for a sentry). || — *Fallout shelter*, refugio atómico. || *Shelter tent*, tienda (*f.*) de campaña. || *To take shelter*, ponerse a cubierto, refugiarse. || FIG. *To take s.o. under one's shelter*, amparar a alguien. || *Under shelter*, al abrigo, a cubierto. || *Under the shelter of*, al abrigo de.
shelter [ˈʃeltə*] v. tr. Abrigar, proteger: *to shelter sth. from the rain*, abrigar algo de la lluvia. || Proteger, resguardar: *the trenches sheltered the soldiers from the enemy's fire*, las trincheras protegían a los soldados del fuego enemigo. || Dar hospitalidad, recoger, acoger, dar asilo (poor people, etc.). || FIG. Amparar, proteger. || *To shelter o.s.*, refugiarse.
— V. intr. Resguardarse: *to shelter from the wind*, resguardarse del viento. || Ponerse a cubierto, refugiarse: *to shelter under a tree*, ponerse a cubierto debajo de un árbol.
sheltered [—d] adj. Protegido, da.
shelterless [—lis] adj. Sin hogar, desamparado, da.
shelve [ʃelv] v. tr. Poner en un estante (to put on a shelf): *to shelve some books*, poner unos libros en un estante. || Poner estantes en (to fit with shelves). || FAM. Dar carpetazo a (a matter). | Dejar de lado (a discussion). | Arrinconar (s.o., sth.).
— V. intr. Estar en declive.
shelves [—z] pl. n. See SHELF.
shelving [—iŋ] n. Estantería, *f.* (shelves). || Disposición (*f.*) en los estantes (of books). || FIG. Aplazamiento (*m.*) indefinido (of a matter). | Arrinconamiento, *m.* (of s.o.).
shenanigans [ʃiˈnænigəns] pl. n. U. S. FAM. Engaños, *m.*, trampas, *f.* (trickery).
shepherd [ˈʃepəd] n. Pastor, *m.* || — *Shepherd boy*, zagal, *m.* || *Shepherd's pie*, pastel (*m.*) de carne y patatas. || REL. *The Good Shepherd*, el Buen Pastor.
shepherd [ˈʃepəd] v. tr. Cuidar de (animals).
shepherdess [—is] n. Pastora, *f.*
sherbet [ˈʃə:bət] n. Sorbete, *m.*
sherd [ʃə:d] n. Casco, *m.* (of broken earthenware). | ZOOL. Élitro, *m.*
shereef or **sherif** [ˈʃerif] n. Jerife, *m.*
sheriff [ˈʃerif] n. JUR. Gobernador (*m.*) civil (in England). | Primer presidente (*m.*) del tribunal de un condado (in Scotland). || U. S. "Sheriff", *m.* (law officer).
sherry [ˈʃeri] n. Jerez, *m.* (wine).
she's [ʃiz] contraction of *she is, she has.*
shibboleth [ˈʃibəleθ] n. Contraseña, *f.*, santo y seña, *m.* (password).
shield [ʃi:ld] n. MIL. ZOOL. HERALD. Escudo, *m.* || TECH. Capa (*f.*) protectora (coating). | Blindaje, *m.* (of an atomic reactor, etc.). | Pantalla (*f.*) protectora (on a machine, for welding, etc.). | Careta (for workers). || BOT. Escudete, *m.*, escudo, *m.* || FIG. Escudo, *m.*, protección, *f.* || Sobaquera, *f.* (for a garment). || U. S. Placa, *f.* (of policeman).
shield [ʃi:ld] v. tr. Proteger (to protect). || Tapar (to mask). || TECH. Blindar. || FIG. Proteger, escudar.
shield bearer [—ˈbεərə*] n. Escudero, *m.*
shield budding [—ˈbʌdiŋ] or **shield grafting** [—ˈgrα:ftiŋ] n. AGR. Injerto (*m.*) de escudete.
shieldless [—lis] adj. Sin escudo. || FIG. Sin defensa.
shift [ʃift] n. Cambio, *m.*: *a shift in position*, un cambio de posición. || Salto, *m.* (of wind). || Movimiento, *m.* (moving). || Cambio, *m.*: *a shift in public opinion*, un cambio en la opinión pública. || Turno, *m.*, tanda, *f.*: *to work in shifts*, trabajar por turnos; *the night shift was going to work*, el turno de la noche iba a trabajar. || Expediente, *m.*, recurso, *m.* (expedient). || Subterfugio, *m.*, artificio, *m.* (trick). || Escapatoria, *f.* (evasion). || Traje (*m.*) recto (frock). || GEOL. Falla, *f.* || MUS. Cambio (*m.*) de posición (in violin playing). || GRAMM. Cambio, *m.* || Variación, *f.* (in the Stock Exchange). || SP. Desplazamiento (*m.*) lateral. || — AGR. *Shift of crops*, rotación (*f.*) de cultivos. || *To make a shift*, cambiar de sitio. || *To make shift to*, arreglárselas para. || *To make shift with*, arreglárselas con. || *To make shift without*, prescindir de.
— Adj. Por turno (work). || — *Shift key*, tecla (*f.*) de mayúsculas. || *Shift pedal*, pedal (*m.*) de sordina (on a piano).
shift [ʃift] v. tr. Cambiar: *the river shifts its course*, el río cambia su curso; *to shift the scenery*, cambiar los decorados. || Cambiar de sitio, trasladar, desplazar: *he shifted his chair*, cambió su silla de sitio. || Mover: *I can't shift it*, no lo puedo mover. || Pasar: *to shift a burden from one shoulder to the other*, pasar una carga de un hombro al otro. || Cambiar de, mudar de: *to shift one's opinion*, cambiar de opinión. || Retrasar (to put back a train schedule). || Adelantar (to put forward a train schedule). || FIG. Echar: *to shift the blame upon s.o.*, echar la culpa a alguien. | Quitarse de encima (to get rid of). || — U. S. *To shift gears*, cambiar de velocidad. || FIG. *To shift one's ground*, cambiar de táctica.
— V. intr. Cambiar de sitio (to change place). || Moverse (to move). || MAR. Desplazarse (cargo). || Cambiar (wind, scenery, opinion). || FAM. Tergiversar. || U. S. AUT. Cambiar de velocidad (gears). || — *To shift about*, cambiar constantemente de sitio. || FIG. *To shift for o.s.*, arreglárselas solo, valerse por sí mismo.
shiftiness [—inis] n. Falsedad, *f.* (falsehood). || Astucia, *f.* (cunning).
shifting [—iŋ] adj. Movedizo, za (sand).
shiftless [—lis] adj. Vago, ga; perezoso, sa (lazy). || Indolente (indolent). || Torpe, inútil (incapable).
shiftlessness [—lisnis] n. Pereza, *f.* (laziness). || Inutilidad, *f.*, incapacidad, *f.* (incapacity).
shifty [—i] adj. Falso, sa (untrustworthy). || Astuto, ta; taimado, da (wily). || Sospechoso, sa (behaviour). || *To have shifty eyes*, no mirar nunca a los ojos *or* a la cara.
shifty-eyed [ˈʃiftiaid] adj. *To be shifty-eyed*, no mirar nunca a los ojos *or* a la cara.
Shiite [ˈʃi:ait] n. REL. Chiita, *m.* & *f.*
shill [ʃil] n. U. S. FAM. Cómplice, *m.* (of a gambler).
shillalah [ʃiˈleilə] or **shillelagh** [ʃiˈleilə] n. Porra, *f.* (cudgel).
shilling [ˈʃiliŋ] n. Chelín, *m.* (coin). || — FIG. *To cut s.o. off with a shilling*, desheredar a alguien. | *To take the King's shilling*, alistarse en el ejército.
shilly-shally [ˈʃili,ʃæli] n. Titubeo, *m.*, vacilación, *f.*, indecisión, *f.*, irresolución, *f.*
— Adj. Titubeante, vacilante, indeciso, sa.
shilly-shally [ˈʃili,ʃæli] v. intr. Titubear, vacilar, no decidirse.
shim [ʃim] n. TECH. Calce, *m.*
shim [ʃim] v. tr. TECH. Calzar, poner un calce.
shimmer [—ə*] n. Luz (*f.*) trémula, resplandor (*m.*) tenue (wavering shine). || Brillo, *m.* (of pearls, jewelry). || *The shimmer of the moon in the sea*, el reflejo de la luna en el mar, la luna que riela en el mar.
shimmer [ˈʃimə*] v. intr. Rielar, relucir, brillar.
shimmering [—riŋ] or **shimmery** [—ri] adj. Trémulo, la (light). || Reluciente (glittering). || Tornasolado, da (tints).

shimmy [′ʃimi] n. "Shimmy", *m.* (dance). || AUT. "Shimmy", *m.*, abaniqueo, *m.*, trepidación (*f.*) oscilante (of wheels). || U. S. Camisa, *f.* (chemise).

shimmy [′ʃimi] v. intr. Bailar el shimmy (to dance). || AUT. Abaniquear, oscilar (the wheels).

shin [ʃin] n. ANAT. Espinilla, *f.* (of the leg). || Caña, *f.* (of a horse). || CULIN. Jarrete, *m.*, corva, *f.*, corvejón, *m.* (of beef, etc.). || TECH. Eclisa, *f.*, mordaza, *f.*

shin [ʃin] v. intr. *To shin down*, bajar como por una cuerda. || *To shin up*, trepar: *to shin up a tree*, trepar a un árbol.
— V. tr. Dar una patada *or* patadas en las espinillas a (s.o.).

shinbone [—bəun] n. ANAT. Tibia, *f.* (bone).

shindig [′ʃindig] or **shindy** [′ʃindi] n. FAM. Jaleo, *m.* (noise): *to kick up a shindy*, armar un jaleo. | Pelea, *f.* (row): *to have a shindy with s.o.*, tener una pelea con alguien. || U. S. FAM. Fiesta, *f.* (party).

shine [ʃain] n. Brillo, *m.*, lustre, *m.* || Buen tiempo, *m.* (good weather). || — *Give my shoes a shine*, límpieme los zapatos, sáqueme brillo a los zapatos [*Amer.*, lústreme los zapatos]. || *Rain or shine*, llueva o truene, aunque llueva, independientemente del tiempo que haga. || FAM. *To take a shine to*, coger cariño a, aficionarse a. || *To take the shine off sth.*, quitarle el brillo a algo, deslustrar algo (a surface), quitar a algo su encanto (sth. attractive). || FIG. *To take the shine out of*, eclipsar.

shine* [ʃain] v. tr. Sacar brillo a (by polishing). || Hacer brillar. || Dirigir (a light). || Limpiar [*Amer.*, lustrar] (shoes).
— V. intr. Brillar, relucir: *the sun shines*, el sol brilla. || Brillar, relucir (polished article). || FIG. Rebosar de (with health). | Resplandecer de, rebosar de: *his face shone with happiness*, su cara resplandecía de felicidad. | Brillar, sobresalir, lucirse (to excel at). || — *The moon is shining*, hay un claro de luna. || *To shine on*, iluminar. || FAM. *To shine up to*, intentar caer en gracia a.

— OBSERV. El pretérito y el participio pasivo de *to shine* son irregulares ***(shone)***. En Estados Unidos se usa también la forma ***shined*** en el participio pasivo.

shiner [—ə*] n. Limpiabotas, *m. inv.* [*Amer.*, lustrabotas, *m. inv.*] (of shoes). || Moneda (*f.*) de oro (gold coin). || U. S. FAM. Ojo (*m.*) a la funerala (black eye). || — Pl. FAM. Pasta, *f. sing.* [*Amer.*, plata, *f. sing.*] (money).

shingle [′ʃiŋgl] n. Tablilla, *f.* (in roofing). || Corte (*m.*) a lo "garçon" (hairstyle). || Guijarros, *m. pl.* (mass of pebbles). || Playa (*f.*) de guijarros (beach). || U. S. FAM. Placa, *f.* (signboard). || — Pl. MED. Zona, *f. sing.* || U. S. FAM. *To hang out one's shingle*, abrir consulta (doctor), abrir un bufete (lawyer).

shingle [′ʃiŋgl] v. tr. Cortar a lo "garçon" (hair). || Cubrir con tablillas (roof).

shingly [—i] adj. De guijarros, guijarroso, sa (covered with pebbles).

shin guard [′ʃingɑ:d] n. Espinillera, *f.*

shininess [′ʃaininis] n. Brillo, *m.*

shining [′ʃainiŋ] adj. Brillante, reluciente (things). || Radiante (face). || Excelente (remarkable).

shinny [′ʃini] v. tr. U. S. FAM. *To shinny up*, trepar a.

shin pad [′ʃinpæd] n. Espinillera, *f.*

Shinto [′ʃintəu] or **Shintoism** [—izəm] n. REL. Sintoísmo, *m.*

Shintoist [′—ist] n. REL. Sintoísta, *m.* & *f.*

shiny [′ʃaini] adj. Brillante (bright). || Radiante (face). || Con brillo (through wear).

ship [ʃip] n. MAR. Barco, *m.*, buque, *m.*, navío, *m.* (vessel). | Tripulación, *f.* (crew). || U. S. FAM. Avión, *m.* (aircraft). | Dirigible, *m.* || — MAR. *Capital ship*, acorazado, *m.* || *Her o His Majesty's Ship* (*H M.S.*), buque de la marina británica. | *Hospital ship*, buque hospital. | *Merchant ship*, buque mercante. | *Mother ship*, buque nodriza. | *On board ship*, a bordo. | *Passenger ship*, buque de pasajeros. | *Ship biscuit*, galleta, *f.* | *Ship of the line*, buque de línea. | *Ship's boat*, lancha, *f.* [que permite bajar a tierra], bote (*m.*) salvavidas. | *Ship's company*, tripulación. | *Ship's papers*, documentación (*f.*) del barco. || FIG. *The ship of the desert*, el camello. || *To take ship*, embarcarse. || FIG. *When one's ship comes home*, cuando lleguen las vacas gordas.

ship [ʃip] v. tr. MAR. Embarcar (a cargo, passengers, water). | Armar (a mast). | Montar (a rudder). | Desarmar (oars). | Enrolar (crew). || Transportar (to transport). || Enviar, mandar, expedir (to send): *I'll ship my car to New York*, mandaré mi coche a Nueva York. || FAM. *To ship off*, echar, despedir.
— V. intr. MAR. Embarcarse (to go on board ship). || Soportar el transporte: *fruit ships badly*, la fruta soporta mal el transporte. || Enrolarse (sailors).

shipboard [—,bɔ:d] n. MAR. *On shipboard*, a bordo.

shipboy [—,bɔi] n. Grumete, *m.*

shipbreaker [—,breikə*] n. MAR. Desguazador, *m.*

ship broker [—′brəukə*] n. Agente (*m.*) marítimo, consignatario (*m.*) de buques.

shipbuilder [—,bildə*] n. MAR. Constructor (*m.*) de buques.

shipbuilding [—,bildiŋ] n. MAR. Construcción (*f.*) naval.

ship canal [—kə′næl] n. Canal (*m.*) navegable.

ship chandler [—′tʃɑ:ndlə*] n. Abastecedor (*m.*) de buques.

shipload [—ləud] n. MAR. Cargamento, *m.*, carga, *f.*

shipmaster [—,mɑ:stə*] n. MAR. Capitán (*m.*) de un buque mercante (captain). | Patrón, *m.* (owner).

shipmate [—meit] n. MAR. Compañero (*m.*) de a bordo *or* de tripulación.

shipment [—mənt] n. MAR. Embarque, *m.* (loading). | Enrolamiento, *m.* (of a crew). | Transporte, *m.* (transporting). | Envío, *m.* (goods to be delivered): *this shipment is for Spain*, este envío es para España. | Carga, *f.*, cargamento, *m.* (goods shipped): *a boat with a shipment of bananas*, un barco con una carga de plátanos.

shipowner [—,əunə*] n. Naviero, *m.*, armador, *m.*

shipper [—ə*] n. MAR. Expedidor, *m.*, cargador, *m.* || AVIAT. Transportista, *m.*

shipping [—iŋ] n. MAR. Embarque, *m.* (loading on board ship): *shipping port*, puerto de embarque. | Transporte, *m.* (transporting). | Envío, *m.*, expedición, *f.* (sending): *shipping expenses*, gastos de envío. | Barcos, *m. pl.*, buques, *m. pl.* (ships of a port). | Flota, *f.* (of a country). | Navegación, *f.*: *dangerous for shipping*, peligroso para la navegación. | Montaje, *m.* (of rudder, etc.).

shipping agent [—iŋ′eidʒənt] n. Agente (*m.*) marítimo, consignatario (*m.*) de buques (ship broker). || Expedidor, *m.* (shipper).

shipping bill [—iŋbil] n. MAR. Conocimiento, *m.*

shipping clerk [—iŋ′klɑ:k] n. COMM. Expedidor, *m.*

shipping company [—iŋ′kʌmpəni] n. Compañía (*f.*) naviera.

shipping line [—iŋlain] n. MAR. Compañía (*f.*) naviera.

shipping master [—iŋ′mɑ:stə*] n. MAR. Persona (*f.*) encargada de enrolar a la tripulación.

shipping office [—iŋ′ɔfis] n. MAR. Oficina (*f.*) de enrolamiento de marineros. | Agencia (*f.*) marítima.

shipping room [—iŋru:m] n. U. S. COMM. Despacho (*m.*) de envíos.

shipshape [—ʃeip] adj. En orden, ordenado, da.

shipside [—said] n. Dársena, *f.*

ship's log [lɔg] n. Diario (*m.*) de a bordo, cuaderno (*m.*) de bitácora.

shipway [—wei] n. MAR. Grada, *f.* (support for launching). | Canal (*m.*) navegable (ship canal).

shipwreck [—rek] n. MAR. Naufragio, *m.* || FIG. Catástrofe, *f.*, ruina, *f.*

shipwreck [—rek] v. tr. MAR. Hacer naufragar. || *To be shipwrecked*, naufragar.

shipwright [—rait] n. MAR. Carpintero (*m.*) de barcos (carpenter).

shipyard [—jɑ:d] n. MAR. Astillero, *m.*

shire [′ʃaiə*] n. Condado, *m.* || *The Shires*, los condados de Leicestershire, Northamptonshire y Rutland.

shire town [—taun] n. Capital (*f.*) de condado.

shirk [ʃə:k] v. tr. Eludir (a question). || Esquivar, eludir, zafarse de (a duty). || Rehuir (a task). || Esquivar, evitar (danger, difficulties). || FAM. Fumarse (school).
— V. intr. Esquivarse (to practise evasion). || No cumplir con el deber (to neglect one's duty). || MIL. Escurrir el bulto. || Hacer el vago, gandulear (to idle).

shirker [—ə*] n. Gandul, la.

shirr [ʃə:*] n. Frunce, *m.* (sewing).

shirr [ʃə:*] v. tr. Fruncir (in dressmaking). || U. S. CULIN. Cocer en el horno (eggs).

shirt [ʃə:t] n. Camisa, *f.* (for men): *stiff shirt*, camisa almidonada. || Blusa, *f.* (for women). || (Ant.) Cota, *f.* (of mail). || — *In shirt sleeves*, en mangas de camisa. || FIG. *Keep your shirt on!*, ¡no te sulfures! | *Stiff shirt*, persona envarada *or* estirada. | *To lose one's shirt*, perder hasta la camisa. | *To put one's shirt on a horse*, apostar todo lo que se tiene a un caballo.

shirtband [—bænd] n. Tirilla (*f.*) de la camisa.

shirtfront [—frʌnt] n. Pechera, *f.*

shirting [—iŋ] n. Tela (*f.*) de camisa.

shirtless [—lis] adj. Sin camisa, descamisado, da.

shirtmaker [—′meikə*] n. Camisero, ra.

shirt-sleeve [—sli:v] or **shirt-sleeves** [—,sli:vz] or **shirt-sleeved** [—sli:vd] adj. En mangas de camisa. || U. S. Sencillo, lla (informal). | Casero, ra (homespun). | Elemental.

shirttail [—teil] n. Faldón, *m.*

shirtwaist [—weist] n. U. S. Blusa, *f.* (of women). || *Shirtwaist dress*, vestido camisero.

shirty [—i] adj. FAM. Furioso, sa; enfadado, da (angry).

shit [ʃit] n. POP. Mierda, *f.*

shit [ʃit] v. tr./intr. POP. Cagar. || POP. *To shit bricks*, cagarse de miedo.

shiver [′ʃivə*] n. Escalofrío, *m.* (with cold). || Temblor, *m.*, escalofrío, *m.*, estremecimiento, *m.* (with fear). || Astilla, *f.* (of wood). || Fragmento, *m.*, pedazo, *m.* (fragment). || Piedra (*f.*) esquistosa (stone). || — *A shiver went down his back*, le dio un escalofrío. || *It gives me the shivers to think of it*, cuando lo pienso me echo a temblar. || *To have the shivers*, estar temblando.

shiver [′ʃivə*] v. tr. Hacer añicos *or* astillas (to break). || MAR. Hacer flamear (sails).
— V. intr. Tiritar (with cold). || Temblar, estremecerse (with fear). || Hacerse añicos *or* astillas (to break).

shivery [—ri] adj. Estremecido, da (shivering). || Estremecedor, ra (causing shivers). || Friolero, ra (sensitive to the cold). || Destemplado, da (feverish).

shoal [ʃəul] n. Banco (*m.*) de arena, bajío, *m.* (sandbank). || Banco, *m.*, cardumen, *m.* (of fish). || Fig. Multitud, *f.* (of people): *a shoal of tourists*, una multitud de turistas. | Montón, *m.* (of things). | Peligro (*m.*) oculto (hidden danger). || Fig. *In shoals*, a montones.
— Adj. Poco profundo (water).

shoal [ʃəul] v. intr. Disminuir en profundidad, hacerse menos profundo (to become shallow). || Desplazarse *or* ir en bancos (fish). || Fig. Agruparse (people).

shoat [ʃəut] n. U. S. Zool. Cochinillo, *m.*, lechón, *m.*

shock [ʃɔk] n. Sacudida, *f.* (violent shaking). || Seísmo, *m.*, sacudida, *f.* (of an earthquake). || Choque, *m.* (of a collision, an explosion, etc.): *when the cars collided there was a terrible shock*, al entrar en colisión los coches se produjo un choque terrible. || Med. "Shock", *m.*, choque, *m.*, conmoción, *f.* || Fig. Conmoción, *f.* (commotion). | Sobresalto, *m.*, susto, *m.* (start, scare): *he died of the shock*, se murió del susto. | Golpe, *m.*: *his marriage was a great shock to her*, su casamiento fue un golpe muy duro para ella. || Mil. Choque, *m.*, refriega, *f.* || Agr. Tresnal, *m.* || Greñas, *f. pl.*, melena, *f.* (mass of hair). || *Electric shock*, descarga *or* sacudida eléctrica: *to get an electric shock*, sentir una sacudida eléctrica; electrochoque, *m.* (treatment).

shock [ʃɔk] v. tr. Producir una conmoción a, conmocionar a (to cause an emotional or physical shock). || Escandalizar, chocar (to give offence): *book that is shocking everybody*, libro que escandaliza a todos. || Indignar, dar un disgusto (to anger). || Sobresaltar, dar un susto (to startle). || Lastimar (the ear). || Agr. Hacinar. || *To be shocked at*, escandalizarse por.
— V. intr. Chocar.

shock absorber [—əbˌzɔːbə*] n. Amortiguador, *m.*

shocker [—ə*] n. Fam. Sinvergüenza, *m.* & *f.*, horror, *m.* (person). | Cosa (*f.*) horrible, horror, *m.* (thing). | Novela (*f.*) escandalosa (novel). | Obra (*f.*) de teatro escandalosa (play). || Sorpresa (*f.*) desagradable.

shock-head [—hed] n. Cabeza (*f.*) desgreñada.

shock-headed [—ˈhedid] adj. Desgreñado, da.

shocking [—iŋ] adj. Escandaloso, sa; vergonzoso, sa; chocante (morally incorrect): *shocking behaviour*, comportamiento escandaloso. || Espantoso, sa; horroroso, sa; horrible (causing horror): *shocking spectacle*, espectáculo horrible. || Aterrador, ra: *the shocking news of his death*, la noticia aterradora de su muerte. || Fam. Espantoso, sa; horrible, horroroso, sa; malísimo, ma (very bad): *shocking weather*, tiempo espantoso.
— Adv. See SHOCKINGLY.

shockingly [—iŋli] adv. De manera chocante *or* escandalosa (incorrectly). || Muy mal, horrorosamente, espantosamente: *he writes shockingly*, escribe muy mal. || Muy, sumamente, espantosamente: *shockingly dear, difficult*, sumamente caro, difícil.

shockproof [—pruːf] adj. A prueba de choques. || Fig. Inquebrantable.

shock tactics [—ˈtæktiks] pl. n. Mil. Táctica (*f. sing.*) de choque.

shock therapy [—ˈθerəpi] or **shock treatment** [—ˈtriːtmənt] n. Med. Tratamiento (*m.*) por electrochoques.

shock troops [—truːps] pl. n. Mil. Tropas (*f.*) de choque *or* de asalto.

shock wave [—weiv] n. Phys. Onda (*f.*) de choque *or* expansiva.

shod [ʃɔd] pret. & p. p. See SHOE.

shoddy [—i] n. Lana (*f.*) regenerada (cloth). || Fig. Mercancía (*f.*) de mala calidad (goods). | Pacotilla, *f.* (anything of poor quality).
— Adj. Regenerado, da (cloth). || Fig. De mala calidad, de pacotilla (goods, etc.). | Mal hecho (work).

shoe [ʃuː] n. Zapato, *m.*: *to put on one's shoes*, ponerse los zapatos; *to take off one's shoes*, quitarse los zapatos; *brown shoes*, zapatos marrones. || Herradura, *f.* (for a horse): *to cast a shoe*, perder una herradura. || Aut. Zapata, *f.* (of brake). | Cubierta, *f.* (of tyre). || Regatón, *m.* (metal end). || Tech. Patín, *m.* (of sledge, etc.). | Calzo, *m.* (chock). || Electr. Frotador, *m.* || Mar. Zapata, *f.* (of anchor). || Carrito, *m.* (in baccarat). || — Fig. fam. *As hard as shoe leather*, como suela de zapato (very hard). || Fig. *I should not like to be in his shoes*, no me gustaría estar en su pellejo *or* en su lugar. || *Shoe industry*, industria (*f.*) del calzado. || Fig. *To be waiting for dead men's shoes*, esperar que se muera alguien para ocupar su puesto. | *To know where the shoe pinches*, saber dónde le aprieta el zapato. | *To put the shoe on the right foot*, echar la culpa al que la tiene. | *To step into s.o.'s shoes*, ocupar el puesto de alguien.

shoe* [ʃuː] v. tr. Calzar (a person): *to be well shod*, ir bien calzado. || Herrar (a horse). || Poner un regatón a (a stick, etc.). || Poner una cubierta a (a wheel). || Tech. Poner un patín *or* un calzo a.

— Observ. Pret. & p. p. ***shod.***

shoeblack [—blæk] n. Limpiabotas, *m. inv.* [*Amer.*, lustrabotas, *m. inv.*].

shoeblacking [—ˈblækiŋ] n. U. S. Betún, *m.* [*Amer.*, bola, *f.*, lustre, *m.*].

shoe brush [—brʌʃ] n. Cepillo (*m.*) para los zapatos.

shoe cream [—kriːm] n. Betún, *m.*, crema (*f.*) para el calzado [*Amer.*, bola, *f.*, lustre, *m.*].

shoehorn [—hɔːn] n. Calzador, *m.*

shoelace [—leis] n. Cordón, *m.*

shoe leather [—ˌleðə*] n. Cuero (*m.*) para zapatos. || Fig. Zapatos, *m. pl.* (shoes).

shoemaker [—ˌmeikə*] n. Zapatero, *m.* || *Shoemaker's*, zapatería, *f.*

shoemaking [—ˌmeikiŋ] n. Zapatería, *f.*

shoe mender [—ˌmendə*] n. Zapatero (*m.*) remendón.

shoe polish [—ˈpɔliʃ] n. Betún, *m.*, crema (*f.*) para el calzado [*Amer.*, bola, *f.*, lustre, *m.*].

shoer [—ə*] n. Herrador, *m.*

shoe repairer [—riˈpɛərə*] n. Zapatero (*m.*) remendón, zapatero (*m.*) de viejo.

shoe repair shop [—riˈpɛə*ʃɔp] n. Zapatería (*f.*) de viejo.

shoeshine [—ʃain] n. U. S. Betún, *m.*, crema (*f.*) para el calzado [*Amer.*, bola, *f.*, lustre, *m.*] (polish). || Limpieza (*f.*) de los zapatos [*Amer.*, lustrada, *f.*] (polishing). || *Shoeshine boy*, limpiabotas, *m. inv.* [*Amer.*, lustrabotas, *m. inv.*] (shoeblack).

shoe shop (U. S. **shoe store**) [—ʃɔp] n. Zapatería, *f.*, tienda (*f.*) de zapatos, tienda (*f.*) de calzado.

shoestring [—striŋ] n. Cordón, *m.* (shoelace). || — Fam. *On a shoestring*, con muy poco dinero. || U. S. Culin. *Shoestring potatoes*, patatas (*f.*) paja.

shoe tree [—triː] n. Horma, *f.*

shone [ʃɔn] pret. & p. p. See SHINE.

shoo [ʃuː] interj. ¡Fuera! (to children). || ¡Zape! (to animals).

shoo [ʃuː] v. tr. Espantar, ahuyentar (animals). || Fig. Mandar a otra parte (children).

shook [ʃuk] pret. See SHAKE.

shoot [ʃuːt] n. Bot. Brote, *m.*, retoño, *m.*, renuevo, *m.* || Rápido, *m.* (river). || Plano (*m.*) inclinado (a slope down). || Tobogán, *m.* (in swimming pool). || Vertedero, *m.* (for rubbish). || Aliviadero, *m.*, vertedero, *m.* (for overflow). || Punzada, *f.* (of pain). || Carrera (*f.*) rápida [de algo lanzado]. || Rebote (*m.*) hacia adelante (of a ball). || Coto (*m.*) de caza (land for hunting). || Cacería, *f.* (hunting party). || Caza, *f.* (the game shot). || Mil. Ejercicio (*m.*) de tiro, tiro, *m.* || Concurso (*m.*) de tiro al blanco (shooting contest). || Lanzamiento, *m.* (of a rocket). || Fam. *The whole shoot*, todos los bártulos, toda la pesca.

shoot* [ʃuːt] v. tr. Lanzar, tirar (a projectile). || Arrojar (by violent motion). || Disparar (arrow, bullet, gun). || Herir (to wound): *he shot him in the leg*, le hirió en la pierna. || Matar (to kill): *to shoot a rabbit*, matar un conejo. || Pegar un tiro (to fire on): *he shot his father*, le pegó un tiro a su padre. || Fusilar (to execute). || Cazar: *he is in Africa shooting lions*, está cazando leones en África. || Echar, tender (fishing net). || Salvar: *to shoot a rapid*, salvar un rápido. || Pasar rápidamente por debajo de (a bridge). || Soltar, espetar (question). || Echar (glance). || Verter (coal, rubbish). || Echar (beams, rays). || Sp. Marcar (a goal). | Tirar (the ball). || Lanzar, tirar (a marble). || Cinem. Rodar, filmar. || Fotografiar, tomar, sacar (photograph). || Mar. Tomar la altura de (the sun). || Echar (dice). || Correr (a bolt). || Bot. Echar. || Med. Fam. Poner una inyección. || — *He was shot through the arm*, una bala le atravesó el brazo. || Fig. *I'll be shot if...!*, ¡que me ahorquen si ...! || *To shoot a match*, participar en un concurso de tiro. || *To shoot craps*, jugar a los dados. || Fig. *To shoot one's bolt*, quemar su último cartucho. || *To shoot s.o. dead*, matar a alguien de un tiro *or* a tiros. || Fam. *To shoot the bull*, see BULL. || *To shoot to death*, matar a tiros.
— V. intr. Precipitarse, lanzarse (to move swiftly). || Cazar (to hunt): *he is out shooting*, se ha ido a cazar. || Disparar (with a bow, a gun): *he shot at me*, disparó contra mí. || Tirar: *to shoot at a target*, tirar al blanco. || Tirar a, tener un alcance de (to reach). || Cinem. Rodar, filmar. || Fotografiar (photograph). || Sobresalir, proyectarse (to project). || Sp. Chutar (in football). | Tirar (to attempt to score): *to shoot at goal*, tirar a gol. || Correrse, echarse, cerrarse (a bolt). || Pasar rápidamente *or* fugazmente (a star). || Dar punzadas (a pain). || Bot. Brotar (bud). | Crecer (plant). | Echar brotes (tree). || — Fam. *Shoot!*, ¡suéltalo!, ¡habla! || *To shoot past* o *by*, pasar como un rayo. || *To shoot through*, cruzar rápidamente.
— ***To shoot ahead,*** tomar rápidamente la delantera (in a race). || ***To shoot away,*** arrancar de un tiro. | Quemar (all one's ammunition). | Disparar sin parar (to shoot incessantly). || ***To shoot down,*** derribar (an aeroplane). | Matar de un tiro (s.o.). | Echar abajo (an argument). || ***To shoot forth,*** echar (buds). || ***To shoot in,*** entrar como un torbellino. || ***To shoot off,*** salir disparado (to rush out). | Arrancar de un tiro. | — *She had a foot shot off*, una bala le arrancó el pie. || ***To shoot out,*** salir disparado (to rush out). | Brotar (water). | Salir (flames). | Sobresalir, proyectarse (to project). | Sacar (to stick out): *the snake shot out its tongue*, la serpiente sacó la lengua. | Echar (sparks, buds, etc.). | — *To shoot it out*, resolverlo a tiros. || ***To shoot up,*** subir rápidamente (aeroplane, ball, etc.). | Subir vertiginosamente (prices). || Bot. Crecer. | Fig. Crecer, espigar (children). | Salir (flames): *flames shot up from the house*, las llamas salían de la casa. || U. S. Aterrorizar, atemorizar [pegando tiros] (village, district).

— Observ. Pret. & p. p. ***shot.***

shooter [—ə*] n. Tirador, ra. || Cazador, ra (hunter). || SP. Goleador, *m.* || FIG. Estrella (*f.*) fugaz. || U. S. Arma (*f.*) de fuego (firearm). || *Six-shooter rifle*, rifle (*m.*) de seis tiros.

shooting [—iŋ] n. Disparo, *m.*, tiro, *m.* (of an arrow, a bullet, a gun). || Herida (*f.*) mortal (wound). || Asesinato, *m.* (murder). || Fusilamiento, *m.* (execution). || Tiros, *m. pl.*, disparos, *m. pl.* (shots). || Tiroteo, *m.* (exchange of shots). || MIL. Cañoneo, *m.*, bombardeo, *m.* (bombing). || Tiro (*m.*) al blanco: *shooting competition*, concurso de tiro al blanco. || Caza, *f.* (of animals). || Paso, *m.* (of rapids). || BOT. Brote, *m.* (of buds). | Salida, *f.* (of branches). || Punzadas, *f. pl.* (of pain). || CINEM. Toma (*f.*) de vistas, rodaje, *m.*, filmación, *f.* || Foto, *f.* (photograph).
— Adj. Punzante, lancinante (pain).

shooting box [—iŋbɔks] n. Pabellón (*m.*) de caza.

shooting brake [—iŋbreik] n. AUT. Furgoneta, *f.*, rubia, *f.* (fam.).

shooting gallery [—iŋ,gæləri] n. Barraca (*f.*) de tiro al blanco (at the fair). || MIL. Galería (*f.*) de tiro.

shooting jacket [—iŋ,dʒækit] n. Chaquetón, *m.*

shooting licence [—iŋ,laisəns] n. Licencia (*f.*) de caza.

shooting lodge [—iŋ,lɔdʒ] n. Pabellón (*m.*) de caza.

shooting match [—iŋ,mætʃ] n. Concurso (*m.*) de tiro al blanco.

shooting party [—iŋ,pɑ:ti] n. Cacería, *f.*

shooting range [—iŋ,reindʒ] n. MIL. Campo (*m.*) de tiro (for rifles). | Polígono (*m.*) de tiro (for artillery). || CINEM. Distancia (*f.*) de toma de vistas. || *Within shooting range*, a tiro.

shooting script [—iŋ,skript] n. CINEM. Guión, *m.*

shooting star [—iŋ,stɑ:*] n. Estrella (*f.*) fugaz.

shooting stick [—iŋ,stik] n. Bastón (*m.*) que sirve de asiento.

shop [ʃɔp] n. Tienda, *f.*: *grocer's shop*, tienda de ultramarinos. || Almacén, *m.* (large store). || Departamento, *m.*, sección, *f.* (of a department store). || Despacho, *m.* (for wine). || Expendeduría, *f.* (for tobacco). || FAM. Negocios, *m. pl.* (business). | Oficina, *f.* (office). || U. S. Taller, *m.* (workshop). || — *Baker's shop*, panadería, *f.* || *Shop!*, ¿quién despacha? (when entering a shop). || FAM. *To be all over the shop*, estar en desorden, estar patas arriba. || *To keep a shop*, tener una tienda. || *To set up shop*, abrir *or* poner una tienda (to open a shop), poner un negocio (to open a business). || *To shut up shop*, cerrar una tienda (to close a shop), dejar los negocios, dejar su trabajo (to go out of business). || *To talk shop*, hablar de negocios, hablar de asuntos profesionales.

shop [ʃɔp] v. intr. Hacer compras: *I spent the whole afternoon shopping*, pasé toda la tarde haciendo compras. || — *To go shopping*, ir de compras. || *To shop for*, ir a buscar, ir a comprar.
— V. tr. FAM. Denunciar, delatar.

shop assistant [—ə,sistənt] n. Dependiente, ta.

shop boy [—bɔi] n. Recadero, *m.*, chico (*m.*) de los recados.

shop front [—frʌnt] n. Escaparate, *m.* [*Amer.*, vidriera, *f.*, vitrina, *f.*].

shopgirl [—gə:l] n. Dependienta, *f.*

shop hours [—,auəz] pl. n. Horas (*f.*) de apertura y cierre [durante las cuales están abiertas las tiendas].

shopkeeper [—,ki:pə*] n. Tendero, ra; comerciante, *m.* & *f.*

shoplifter [—,liftə*] n. Ladrón (*m.*) que roba en las tiendas, mechero, ra; ratero, ra.

shoplifting [—,liftiŋ] n. Ratería, *f.*, hurto, *m.*

shopman [—mən] n. Dependiente, *m.* (employee). || Tendero, *m.* (shopkeeper).

— OBSERV. El plural de esta palabra es *shopmen.*

shopper [—ə*] n. Comprador, ra.

shopping [—iŋ] n. Compras, *f. pl.*: *she is doing her shopping*, está de compras.

shopping bag [—iŋ,bæg] n. Bolsa (*f.*) de la compra.

shopping basket [—iŋ,bɑ:skit] n. Cesta (*f.*) de la compra.

shopping cart [—iŋ,kɑ:t] n. Carrito, *m.*

shopping centre (U. S. **shopping center**) [—iŋ,sentə*] n. Centro (*m.*) comercial.

shop-soiled [—sɔild] adj. Estropeado, da.

shop steward [—stjuəd] n. Enlace (*m.*) sindical.

shoptalk [—tɔ:k] n. Argot, *m.* (specialized vocabulary). || Conversación (*f.*) sobre asuntos profesionales (conversation).

shopwalker [—'wɔ:kə*] n. Jefe (*m.*) de sección *or* de departamento (person who supervises clerks).

shopwindow [—'windəu] n. Escaparate, *m.* [*Amer.*, vidriera, *f.*, vitrina, *f.*].

shopworn [—wɔ:n] adj. Estropeado, da (damaged). || FIG. Trasnochado, da: *shopworn ideas*, ideas trasnochadas.

shore [ʃɔ:*] n. Orilla, *f.* (sea or river edge): *how far is it to the other shore?*, ¿qué distancia hay a la otra orilla? || Playa, *f.* (beach). || Costa, *f.* (coast). || Tierra, *f.* (land): *on shore*, en tierra. || ARCH. Puntal, *m.* || MAR. Escora, *f.*, puntal, *m.* || — *In shore*, cerca de la costa. || *Off shore*, see OFFSHORE.

shore [ʃɔ:*] v. tr. Desembarcar (a cargo). || Escorar (to prop a ship). || ARCH. Apuntalar. || *To shore up*, apuntalar.

shore battery [—'bætəri] n. Batería (*f.*) costera.

shore leave [—li:v] n. MAR. Permiso (*m.*) para bajar a tierra.

shoreless [—lis] adj. Sin límites.

shore patrol [—pə'trəul] n. U. S. MAR. Patrulla (*f.*) guardacostas.

shoreward [—wəd] or **shorewards** [—wədz] adv. Hacia la costa.

shoring [—iŋ] n. Puntales, *m. pl.* (shores).

shorn [ʃɔ:n] p. p. See SHEAR.

short [ʃɔ:t] adj. Corto, ta (of little length): *a short skirt*, una falda corta; *to go by the shortest road*, ir por el camino más corto; *the rope is too short*, la cuerda es demasiado corta. || Bajo, ja (not tall): *person of short stature*, persona de baja estatura. || Pequeño, ña; corto, ta: *short distance*, distancia pequeña; *a short stick*, un bastón corto; *short steps*, pasos pequeños. || Escaso, sa (insufficient): *short crops*, cosechas escasas; *I was short of money*, andaba escaso de dinero. || Corto, ta; breve (not long in time). || Poco, ca: *of short duration*, de poca duración. || Conciso, sa (style). || Seco, ca (brusque). || Tajante (tone, answer). || Vivo, va: *very short temper*, carácter muy vivo. || CULIN. Curruscante, crujiente (pastry). || GRAMM. Breve. || COMM. A corto plazo (bill, payment, loan). | Al descubierto: *short sale*, venta al descubierto. || Rápido, da (pulse). || Cerrado, da (turn). || RAD. Corto, ta (wave). || TECH. Quebradizo, za (iron). || — *A short distance from*, a poca distancia de. || *A short eight kilometres*, unos ocho kilómetros escasos. || *A short time ago*, hace poco tiempo. || *A short way off*, a poca distancia, cerca. || *A short while ago*, hace un momento. || *Dick is short for Richard*, Dick es el diminutivo de Richard. || *For a short time*, durante *or* por poco tiempo. || *For short*, para abreviar. || *I am twenty pounds short*, me faltan veinte libras. || *In a short time*, dentro de poco. || *In short order*, en seguida. || *In short supply*, escaso, sa. || *It is one pound short*, falta una libra. || *Not far short of*, no lejos de, casi: *he is not far short of forty*, no está lejos de tener cuarenta años; *not far short of a masterpiece*, casi una obra maestra. || *Nothing short of*, nada menos que, nada fuera de, nada excepto, sólo: *nothing short of an operation can save you*, sólo una operación le salvará. || *On short notice*, en poco tiempo. || *Pram is short for perambulator*, "pram" es la abreviatura de "perambulator." || FIG. *Short and sweet*, corto y bueno. || *Short drink*, bebida corta, bebida alcohólica servida sin agua. || CINEM. *Short film*, cortometraje, *m.* || SP. *Short head*, media cabeza (in horse racing). || *Short list*, lista (*f.*) de seleccionados. || *Short sight*, vista corta, miopía, *f.* || *Short story*, novela corta. || *Short time*, jornada reducida. || *Short ton*, tonelada corta. || FAM. *Something short*, una copita. || *To be short in one's payments*, quedarse corto en el pago. || *To be short in the arms*, tener los brazos cortos (person), tener las mangas demasiado cortas (garment). || *To be short of*, andar escaso de, tener poco: *to be short of money*, tener poco dinero. || *To be short on*, tener poco. || *To be short with s.o.*, hablar a alguien con tono tajante. || *To get the short end of the stick*, llevarse la peor parte. || *To give short measure*, dar de menos. || *To give short weight*, dar menos que el peso exacto. || *To go short of*, privarse de. || *To grow short*, menguar (days). || *To make short work of*, despachar rápidamente. || *To run short*, agotarse: *our supplies run short*, nuestras provisiones se agotan. || *To run short of*, acabársele [a uno], agotársele [a uno]: *we ran short of oil*, se nos acabó el aceite. || *To take shorter steps*, aminorar el paso. || *We are still a mile short of our destination*, nos falta todavía una milla para llegar a nuestro destino.
— Adv. En seco: *to stop short*, pararse en seco. || Bruscamente (in a brusque manner). || Cerca (near). || COMM. A corto plazo (borrowing). | Al descubierto: *to sell short*, vender al descubierto. || — *Short of*, excepto, menos: *he would do anything short of murder*, haría cualquier cosa excepto matar. || *To be taken up short*, cogerle a uno desprevenido. || *To come o to fall short of*, no cumplir (one's duty), no alcanzar (one's mark), no corresponder a (one's expectations), no satisfacer (requisites), estar muy por debajo de (a model). || *To cut s.o. short*, see CUT.
— N. Abreviatura, *f.* (abbreviation). || Diminutivo, *m.* (of a name). || Apodo, *m.*, mote, *m.* (nickname). || CINEM. Cortometraje, *m.* || COMM. Vendedor (*m.*) al descubierto (person). | Venta (*f.*) al descubierto (sale). | Déficit, *m.* || GRAMM. Sílaba (*f.*) breve (syllable). | Vocal (*f.*) breve (vowel). || ELECTR. Cortocircuito, *m.* || FAM. Bebida (*f.*) corta, bebida (*f.*) alcohólica servida sin agua. || — Pl. "Shorts", *m.*, pantalones (*m.*) cortos. || U. S. Calzoncillos, *m.* (underpants). || *In short*, en resumen.

short [ʃɔ:t] v. tr. ELECTR. Poner en cortocircuito.
— V. intr. ELECTR. Ponerse en cortocircuito.

shortage [—idʒ] n. Falta, *f.*, escasez, *f.*, insuficiencia, *f.*: *labour shortage*, falta de mano de obra. || Crisis, *f.*: *housing shortage*, crisis de la vivienda. || COMM. Déficit, *m.*: *to make up the shortage*, enjugar el déficit.

shortbread [—bed] n. Especie (*f.*) de mantecada.

shortcake [—keik] n. CULIN. Especie (*f.*) de mantecada (shortbread). || U. S. CULIN. Torta (*f.*) de frutas.

shortchange [—tʃeindʒ] v. tr. FAM. Dar de menos en la vuelta, devolver menos de lo debido en el cambio. || FIG. Estafar (to cheat).
short circuit [—'sə:kit] n. ELECTR. Cortocircuito, *m.*
short-circuit [—'sə:kit] v. tr. ELECTR. Poner en cortocircuito. || FIG. Saltarse, hacer caso omiso de.
— V. intr. ELECTR. Ponerse en cortocircuito.
shortcoming [—'kʌmiŋ] n. Defecto, *m.*, punto (*m.*) flaco (defect). || Falta, *f.* (shortage).
shortcut [—,kʌt] n. Atajo, *m.*
shorten [—n] v. tr. Acortar (to make shorter): *I'm going to shorten my skirt*, voy a acortar mi falda; *I had to shorten my holiday*, tuve que acortar mis vacaciones. || Compendiar, resumir (a text). || Reducir (a task). || Disminuir, reducir (rations). || Abreviar (to abbreviate).
— V. intr. Acortarse (to become shorter). || Menguar (days). || Disminuir, reducirse (to diminish). || Abreviarse: *Member of Parliament shortens to M.P.*, "Member of Parliament" se abrevia en M.P.
shortening [—niŋ] n. Acortamiento, *m.* (of garment, holiday, etc.). || Compendio, *m.*, resumen, *m.* (of a text). || Reducción, *f.*, disminución, *f.* (decrease). || Abreviación, *f.* (abbreviation). || CULIN. Materia (*f.*) grasa.
shortfall [—fɔ:l] n. COMM. Déficit, *m.*
shorthand [—hænd] n. Taquigrafía, *f.* || — *Shorthand typewriter*, estenotipo, *m.*, máquina (*f.*) de taquigrafía. || *Shorthand typist*, taquimecanógrafo, fa. || *Shorthand writer*, taquígrafo, fa; estenógrafo, fa. || *To take down in shorthand*, tomar taquigráficamente.
— Adj. Taquigráfico, ca (system, symbol). || Tomado en taquigrafía (report, etc.).
shorthanded [—'hændid] adj. Falto de mano de obra.
shorthead [—hed] n. Braquicéfalo, la.
shortish [—iʃ] adj. Bastante corto. || Bajito, ta (person).
short-lived [—'livd] adj. Efímero, ra.
shortly [—li] adv. En pocas palabras (in a few words). || Dentro de poco (soon). || Secamente (discourteously). || — *Shortly after*, poco después. || *Shortly before four o'clock*, poco antes de las cuatro.
shortness [—nis] n. Brevedad, *f.* (duration). || Pequeñez, *f.* (length, size). || Falta, *f.*, escasez, *f.* (of money, provisions). || Sequedad, *f.* (of manner). || Falta, *f.* (of breath, memory). || *Shortness of sight*, miopía, *f.*
short-range [—'reindʒ] adj. MIL. De corto alcance. || AVIAT. De autonomía limitada.
shortsighted [—'saitid] adj. Miope, corto de vista (myopic). || FIG. Corto de vista, miope (without foresight).
shortsightedness [— saitidnis] n. Miopía, *f.* || FIG. Cortedad (*f.*) de vista, miopía, *f.*, falta (*f.*) de perspicacia, imprevisión, *f.*
short-spoken [—'spəukən] adj. Tajante, seco, ca.
short-tempered [—'tempəd] adj. De mal genio.
short-term [—tə:m] adj. A corto plazo: *short-term loan*, préstamo a corto plazo.
shortwave [—weiv] n. Onda (*f.*) corta.
— Adj. De onda corta.
short-winded [— windid] adj. De respiración corta, corto de resuello.
shorty [—i] n. FAM. Retaco, *m.*, tapón (*m.*) de alberca (small person).
shot [ʃɔt] n. Bala, *f.* (of a gun). || Bala (*f.*) de cañón (of a cannon). || Perdigones, *m. pl.* (for hunting). || Tiro, *m.*, disparo, *m.* (act of shooting, detonation, wound): *at a shot*, de un tiro. || Cañonazo, *m.* (of cannon). || Alcance, *m.* (range of shoot): *out of shot*, fuera de alcance. || Tirador, ra (person who shoots): *he is a good shot*, es un buen tirador. || FIG. Indirecta, *f.* (hinting criticism): *that was a shot at you*, eso fue una indirecta dirigida a ti. | Oportunidad, *f.* (chance). | Conjetura, *f.* (guess). | Tentativa, *f.* (intent). || CINEM. Toma, *f.* | Plano, *m.*: *close shot*, primer plano; *long shot*, plano largo. || PHOT. Foto, *f.*, instantánea, *f.* (photograph). || SP. Peso, *m.* [*Amer.*, pesa, *f.*, bala, *f.*] (weight): *to put the shot*, lanzar el peso. | Tiro, *m.* (at goal). | Chut, *m.* (at goal in football). || Golpe, *m.*, jugada, *f.* (in billiards). || Redada, *f.* (in fishing). || FAM. Trago, *m.* (of drinks). || MED. Inyección, *f.* (injection). | Dosis, *f.* (dose). || — FIG. *At the first shot*, a la primera. || FAM. *Big shot*, pez gordo. || *Exchange of shots*, tiroteo, *m.* || CINEM. *Exterior shots*, exteriores, *m. pl.* || FIG. *Good shot!*, ¡muy bien! || *It's your shot*, te toca a ti. || FIG. *Like a shot*, como movido por un resorte: *he was out of the chair like a shot*, saltó del sillón como movido por un resorte. || *Moon shot*, lanzamiento (*m.*) de un cohete hacia la Luna. || FIG. *Not by a long shot*, ni mucho menos. || CINEM. *Three-quarter shot*, plano americano. || FIG. *To be off like a shot*, salir disparado (to rush out). | *To do sth. like a shot*, hacer algo sin vacilar. || *To have a flying shot at*, tirar al vuelo. || FIG. *To have a shot at sth.*, probar suerte con algo, intentar hacer algo. | *To have sth. within shot*, tener algo a tiro. | *To make a shot at an answer*, contestar a la buena de Dios *or* al azar. | *To pay one's shot*, pagar su parte. || *Without firing a shot*, sin pegar un tiro.
— Adj. Tornasolado, da (fabric). || FAM. Gastado, da (worn-out). | Agotado, da (completely exhausted). | Destrozado, da (ruined): *his nerves are shot*, tiene los nervios destrozados. || FAM. *To get shot of*, quitarse de encima (to get rid of).
shot [ʃɔt] pret. & p. p. See SHOOT.
shote [ʃəut] n. U. S. ZOOL. Cochinillo, *m.*, lechón, *m.*
shotgun ['ʃɔtgʌn] n. Escopeta, *f.*: *double-barrelled shotgun*, escopeta de dos cañones. || FAM. *It was a shotgun marriage*, se casaron de prisa y corriendo.
shot put ['ʃɔtput] n. U. S. SP. Lanzamiento (*m.*) de peso.
shot-putter [—ə*] n. Lanzador (*m.*) de peso.
should [ʃud] v. aux. Se emplea para formar el potencial [primera persona del sing. y del pl.]: *I should have arrived earlier if the train had not been late*, hubiera llegado más temprano si el tren no hubiese tenido retraso. || Deber, tener que (suggestion): *you should walk faster if you want to arrive in time*, deberías andar más de prisa si quieres llegar a tiempo. || Tener que (obligation): *all doors should be locked by ten*, todas las puertas tienen que estar cerradas a las diez. || Deber de (probability): *they should be there by now*, ya deben de estar allí. || — *How should I know?*, ¿cómo iba yo a saber? || *I should if I were you*, lo haría si estuviese en tu lugar, yo que tú lo haría. || *I should think so*, supongo que sí. || *It should rain tonight if the wind drops*, lloverá probablemente esta noche si amaina el viento.
— OBSERV. *Should* es el pretérito de *shall* (See SHALL). El verbo auxiliar *should* puede contraerse cuando le antecede un pronombre personal (*I'd, we'd*). Si va seguido por la negación *not* puede formar con ella la palabra *shouldn't* (*I shouldn't do it, shouldn't we go?*) — En la primera persona del potencial *would* sustituye frecuentemente a *should* (*I would have arrived earlier if...*). — Cuando *should* se encuentra en una oración que expresa una condición o una finalidad, el verbo que acompaña tiene que ir en subjuntivo en español (*should he come, he would be welcome*, si viniera sería el bienvenido: *he gave me an umbrella so that I should not get wet*, me dio un paraguas para que no me mojara). Lo mismo ocurre en los casos en que se halla en una oración subordinada precedida por la expresión de un sentimiento (*I am astonished that he should say that*, me extraña que diga eso).
shoulder ['ʃəuldə*] n. ANAT. Hombro, *m.* || Espaldilla, *f.*, codillo, *m.*, paletilla, *f.* (of meat). || Hombro, *m.* (of a garment). || Desnivel, *m.* (of ground). || Rellano, *m.* (of hill). || Estribación, *f.* (of mountain). || Andén, *m.* (of road). || — Pl. Hombros, *m.*, espalda, *f. sing.* || — *On the shoulders*, a *or* en hombros. || *Shoulder to shoulder*, hombro a hombro, hombro con hombro. || FIG. *Straight from the shoulder*, francamente, con toda sinceridad, sin rodeos. | *To give s.o. the cold shoulder*, tratar a alguien con frialdad, volver la espalda a alguien. | *To have one's head squarely on one's shoulders*, tener la cabeza en su sitio. || *To have round shoulders*, ser cargado de espaldas. || FIG. *To put one's shoulder to the wheel*, arrimar el hombro. | *To put the blame on s.o.'s shoulders*, echarle la culpa a alguien. | *To rub shoulders with s.o.*, codearse con alguien. || *To shrug one's shoulders*, encogerse de hombros. || *To sling sth. over one's shoulder*, echarse algo al hombro. || *To stand head and shoulders above s.o.*, llevarle la cabeza a uno, sacarle la cabeza a uno. || *To take a responsibility on one's shoulders*, cargar con una responsabilidad.
shoulder ['ʃəuldə*] v. tr. Empujar con el hombro (to push). || Echarse al hombro (to put on one's shoulder). || Llevar en hombros (to carry on the shoulders). || Cargar con (task, responsibility). || — MIL. *Shoulder arms!*, ¡arma al hombro! || *To shoulder one's way through a crowd*, abrirse paso a codazos entre la muchedumbre. || *To shoulder s.o. out of the way*, apartar a alguien con el hombro.
shoulder bag [—bæg] n. Bolso (*m.*) de bandolera.
shoulder belt [—belt] n. Tahalí, *m.* (baldric). || Bandolera, *f.* (bandoleer).
shoulder blade [—bleid] n. ANAT. Omóplato, *m.*, omoplato, *m.* || Paletilla, *f.* (of an animal).
shoulder braid [—breid] n. MIL. Forrajera, *f.*
shoulder-high [—'hai] adv. A hombros: *to carry shoulder-high*, llevar *or* sacar a hombros.
shoulder knot [—nɔt] n. Cordones, *m. pl.*, charretera, *f.* (insignia, decoration).
shoulder pad [—pæd] n. Hombrera, *f.*
shoulder plate [—pleit] n. Hombrera, *f.* (of armour).
shoulder strap [—stræp] n. Bandolera, *f.*, correa, *f.* (of bag, knapsack). || Tirante, *m.* (on underwear). || MIL. Dragona, *f.*
shouldn't ['ʃudənt] contraction of *should not.*
shout [ʃaut] n. Grito, *m.* (cry, call). || — *Shout of laughter*, carcajada, *f.* || *Shouts of applause*, aclamaciones, *f.*
shout [ʃaut] v. tr. Gritar: *he shouted to me that it was not safe*, me gritó que era peligroso. || Vociferar, soltar a voz en grito (an insult). || Expresar en alta voz *or* a voz en grito (an opinion). || — *To shout o.s. hoarse*, volverse ronco a fuerza de gritar, desgañitarse gritando. || *To shout out*, gritar. || *To shout s.o. down*, callar a alguien a gritos. || *To shout sth. down*, abuchear algo.
— V. intr. Gritar: *to shout at the top of one's voice*, gritar a voz en cuello; *to shout for joy*, gritar de alegría. || — *To shout at s.o.*, gritarle a uno. || *To shout for s.o.*, llamar a alguien a gritos. || *To shout like mad*, gritar como un desaforado. || *To shout with laughter*, reírse a carcajadas.

shouting [—iŋ] n. Gritos, *m. pl.* || *Within shouting distance*, al alcance de la voz.
— Adj. Que grita.
shove [ʃʌv] n. Empujón, *m.* || *To give a shove*, empujar, dar un empujón.
shove [ʃʌv] v. tr. Empujar (by pushing). || Meter, meterse (to put): *shove it in your pocket*, métaselo en el bolsillo. || FIG. *To shove the responsibility on to s.o.*, cargar a uno la responsabilidad de.
— V. intr. Empujar. || — FAM. *To shove along* o *off*, largarse. || *To shove by* o *past s.o.*, empujar *or* dar un empujón a alguien al pasar. || MAR. *To shove off*, desatracar (a boat). || *To shove through*, abrirse paso a codazos entre (a crowd).
shovel [ˈʃʌvl] n. Pala, *f.*: *coal shovel*, pala para el carbón. || TECH. Pala (*f.*) mecánica *or* cargadora, excavadora, *f.*
shovel [ˈʃʌvl] v. tr. Mover con la pala (to move with a shovel). || Echar con la pala (to put with a shovel). || Sacar con pala (to clear with a shovel). || FIG. FAM. Echar una gran cantidad de: *he shoveled sugar into his coffee*, echó una gran cantidad de azúcar en el café. || — *To shovel a path through the snow*, despejar un camino quitando la nieve con la pala. || FAM. *To shovel food into one's mouth*, zamparse la comida.
shovelboard [—bɔ:d] n. Juego (*m.*) de tejo.
shoveler [—ə*] n. See SHOVELLER.
shovelful [—ful] n. Pala, *f.*, paletada, *f.*
shovel hat [—hæt] n. REL. Sombrero (*m.*) de teja.
shoveller [—ə*] n. Paleador, *m.* (worker). || Espátula (*f.*) común (bird).
show [ʃəu] n. Demostración, *f.* (showing): *a show of strength*, una demostración de fuerza. || Exposición, *f.* (exhibition): *flower show*, exposición de horticultura. || Apariencia, *f.* (appearance). || Feria, *f.*: *agricultural show*, feria del campo. || Concurso, *m.*: *horse show*, concurso hípico. || Salón, *m.*: *motor show*, salón del automóvil. || Función, *f.* (performance). || Espectáculo, *m.* (entertainment): *to go to a show*, ir a ver un espectáculo. || RAD. Programa, *m.* || Sombra, *f.*, traza, *f.*, vestigio, *m.* (trace). || Indicación, *f.*, señal, *f.* (sign). || Vista, *f.* (view). || Oportunidad, *f.* (chance). || Alarde, *m.* (pretence): *to make a show of wealth*, hacer alarde de riqueza. || Ostentación, *f.* (display). || Aparato, *m.* (pomp). || Actuación, *f.*, papel, *m.*: *he put up a good show*, tuvo una buena actuación, hizo un buen papel. || FAM. Negocio, *m.* (undertaking): *he wrecked the whole show*, estropeó todo el negocio. || U. S. FAM. Tercer lugar, *m.* (in horse racing). || — FAM. *Bad show!*, ¡malo! || *By show of hands*, a mano alzada (vote). || *Dumb show*, pantomima, *f.* || *Fashion show*, desfile (*m.*) de modelos. || *For show*, para impresionar a los demás. || FAM. *Good show!*, muy bien! || *Lord Mayor's show*, desfile organizado en honor del alcalde de Londres. || *One-man show*, recital, *m.* || COMM. *On show*, expuesto, ta. || *Show of hands*, votación (*f.*) a mano alzada. || *To deceive s.o. under a show of friendship*, engañar a alguien fingiendo amistad. || FAM. *To give the show away*, descubrir el pastel. | *To make a show of*, hacer gala de, alardear de. | *To make a show of o.s.*, hacer el ridículo. || *To put up a show of resistance*, hacer el paripé de resistir, fingir resistencia. || FAM. *To run* o *to boss the show*, llevar la voz cantante, ser el que manda, tener la sartén por el mango. | *To steal the show*, llevarse todos los aplausos.
show* [ʃəu] v. tr. Enseñar, mostrar: *he showed his books to me*, me enseñó sus libros; *show me your hands*, enséñame las manos. || Dejar ver: *this dress shows your slip*, este traje deja ver tu combinación. || Llevar, conducir: *she showed me to my seat*, me condujo a mi asiento. || Explicar: *this letter shows why she could not come*, esta carta explica por qué no pudo venir. || Exponer: *to show one's reasons*, exponer sus razones. || Demostrar, mostrar, probar (to demonstrate): *the evidence shows that he was right*, las pruebas demuestran que tenía razón. || Manifestar, mostrar (to manifest): *she showed her displeasure*, manifestó su descontento. || Demostrar, mostrar: *his attempt shows courage*, su intento demuestra valor. || Tener: *they showed no reaction*, no tuvieron reacción alguna. || Conceder, hacer (to grant): *he showed me a favour*, me hizo un favor. || Tener (mercy). || Registrar, arrojar: *the firm showed a profit*, la empresa registró un beneficio. || Experimentar: *exports showed an important increase last year*, las exportaciones experimentaron un gran aumento el año pasado. || Indicar, señalar, mostrar, enseñar (the way). || Indicar, señalar, mostrar (time, a place, etc.): *the traffic lights show that we must stop*, los semáforos indican que tenemos que pararnos || Marcar, indicar (temperature). || Indicar, revelar (to reveal). || Indicar: *place shown in a map*, sitio indicado en un mapa. || Presentar: *the account shows him as a rascal*, el relato lo presenta como un bribón. || ARTS. Representar. || COMM. Presentar (to present): *the firm showed its new designs*, la empresa presentó sus nuevos diseños. | Exponer, presentar, exhibir (in a display window). || Representar, dar (a play). || Poner, echar, proyectar, exhibir (film). || Proyectar, enseñar (slides). || Exponer (in an exhibition): *he won prizes for all the roses he showed*, ganó premios por todas las rosas que expuso. || JUR. Alegar, hacer constar (one's right). || — *As shown in the illustration*, como se ve en el grabado. || FIG. *He has been working all day and has nothing to show for it*, ha estado trabajando todo el día para nada. || *He is beginning to show his age*, ya empieza a notarse la edad que tiene. || FAM. *He will never show his face here again*, nunca más aparecerá *or* se dejará ver por aquí. | *I'll show you!*, ¡te vas a enterar!, ¡ya me las pagarás! || FIG. *To have nothing to show for it*, no sacar ningún provecho. | *To show one's hand*, poner las cartas boca arriba, descubrir su juego. || *To show o.s.*, dejarse ver. || *To show o.s. a coward*, mostrarse cobarde, demostrar ser un cobarde. || *To show s.o. a light*, iluminar a alguien. || *To show s.o. how to read*, enseñar a alguien a leer. || *To show s.o. into a room*, hacer pasar *or* entrar a alguien en una habitación. || *To show s.o. round the town*, hacer visitar la ciudad a alguien. || FAM. *To show s.o. the door*, echar a alguien con cajas destempladas. || *What can I show you, Madam?*, ¿qué desea la señora?
— V. intr. Verse, notarse (to be noticeable): *the parts that do not show*, las partes que no se ven; *does the mark of the wound still show?*, ¿se ve todavía la marca de la herida?; *your petticoat is showing*, se te ven las enaguas; *it doesn't show that you are tired*, no se nota que estás cansado. || Aparecer, salir: *the buds are beginning to show*, los retoños empiezan a salir. || THEATR. Dar una función. || CINEM. Exhibirse, proyectarse (a film). || U. S. FAM. Llegar en tercer lugar (in horse racing). || — *It just goes to show!*, ¡hay que ver! || *To show to advantage*, apreciarse mejor: *his talent shows to advantage when he plays a Stradivarius*, su talento se aprecia mejor cuando toca con un Stradivarius. || *What is showing at the cinema?*, ¿qué ponen en el cine?, ¿qué echan en el cine?, ¿qué dan en el cine?
— ***To show in***, hacer pasar (a visitor). || ***To show off***, hacer alarde de: *he likes to show off his strength*, le gusta hacer alarde de su fuerza. | Realzar, hacer resaltar: *setting that shows off a stone*, engaste que hace resaltar una piedra. | Presumir, darse pisto (to boast). || ***To show out***, acompañar a la puerta. || ***To show through***, transparentarse. || ***To show up***, hacer subir (a guest). | Poner en evidencia, sacar a luz (a thing): *to show up s.o.'s faults*, poner en evidencia los defectos de alguien. | Poner de manifiesto: *when he plays on a Stradivarius his talent is shown up*, cuando toca con un Stradivarius su talento se pone de manifiesto. | Revelar, descubrir: *to show up a fraud*, revelar un fraude. | Desenmascarar (an impostor). | Hacer resaltar, realzar: *this dress shows up her figure*, este traje hace resaltar su figura. | Entregar (one's work). | Destacarse, sobresalir, resaltar (against a background). | Perfilarse (on the horizon). | FAM. Venir, aparecer (to be present at): *he didn't show up at the meeting*, no vino a la reunión.
— OBSERV. Pret. ***showed***; p. p. ***shown, showed.***
show bill [—bil] n. Cartel, *m.* (poster).
show biz [—biz] n. FAM. Mundo (*m.*) del espectáculo, espectáculos, *m. pl.*
showboat [—bəut] n. U. S. Barco (*m.*) donde se dan representaciones teatrales.
show business [—ˈbiznis] n. Mundo (*m.*) del espectáculo, espectáculos, *m. pl.*
show card [—kɑ:d] n. Rótulo, *m.*, letrero, *m.* (in a shopwindow). || Muestrario, *m.*, colección (*f.*) de muestras (samples).
showcase [—keis] n. Vitrina, *f.* (in a museum). || Escaparate, *m.* [*Amer.*, vidriera, *f.*, vitrina, *f.*] (in a shop).
showdown [—daun] n. Momento (*m.*) decisivo, hora (*f.*) de la verdad (decisive moment). || Confrontación, *f.* (of two persons).
shower [ˈʃauə*] n. Chubasco, *m.*, aguacero, *m.*, chaparrón, *m.* (of rain). || Granizada, *f.* (of hail). || Nevada, *f.* (of snow). || FIG. Lluvia, *f.* (of blows, stones). | Avalancha, *f.* (of insults). | Diluvio, *m.*, lluvia, *f.* (of letters). | Haz, *m.* (of sparks). || Ducha, *f.* (bath). || FAM. Panda (*f.*) de imbéciles (stupid people). || U. S. Fiesta (*f.*) en que todos traen un regalo (gathering). || — *Showers of*, montones de. || *To take a shower*, ducharse, tomar una ducha, darse una ducha.
shower [ˈʃəuə*] n. Expositor, ra (exhibitor).
shower [ˈʃauə*] v. tr. Derramar (to pour). || FIG. Colmar: *to shower attentions on s.o.*, colmar a alguien de atenciones. | Inundar: *my friends showered me with presents*, mis amigos me inundaron de regalos. || — FIG. *I was showered with invitations*, me llegaron las invitaciones de todas partes. | *Questions were showered on him*, le acosaron con preguntas.
— V. intr. Llover (to rain). || Ducharse (to take a shower). || FIG. *Congratulations showered on her*, todos la felicitaban.
shower bath [—bɑ:θ] n. Ducha, *f.*
showerproof [—pru:f] adj. Impermeable.
showery [—ri] adj. Lluvioso, sa (weather).
show flat [ˈʃəuflæt] n. Piso (*m.*) de muestra, piso (*m.*) piloto.
show girl [ˈʃəugə:l] n. THEATR. Corista, *f.*
showily [ˈʃəuili] adv. Con ostentación (displayed). || Vistosamente, de una manera llamativa (dressed). || Lujosamente pero con mal gusto (furnished).
showiness [ˈʃəuinis] n. Ostentación, *f.* (ostentation): *dressed without showiness*, vestido sin ostentación. ||

Lo aparatoso (of a ceremony). || Lo llamativo, lo vistoso (of a dress). || Lujo (*m.*) que revela mal gusto (of furniture).

showing [ˈʃəuiŋ] n. Exposición, *f.* (exhibition). || Actuación, *f.* (performance). || Proyección, *f.* (of film). || Manifestación, *f.* (of one's feelings). || Demostración, *f.* (of evidence). || Presentación, *f.* (of facts). || Resultados, *m. pl.* (results). || — *On this showing*, mirando así las cosas. || *On your own showing*, según lo que usted mismo dice, según sus propias palabras. || *To make a good showing*, hacer un buen papel, quedar bien.

show jumping [ˈʃəuˈdʒʌmpiŋ] n. SP. Concurso (*m.*) hípico.

showman [ˈʃəumən] n. Organizador (*m.*) *or* empresario (*m.*) de espectáculos. || Feriante, *m.* (in a fair). || Director (*m.*) de circo (of a circus). || FIG. Exhibicionista, *m.* | Comediante, *m.*

— OBSERV. El plural de esta palabra es *showmen*.

showmanship [—ʃip] n. Talento (*m.*) para organizar espectáculos. || FIG. Exhibicionismo, *m.* | Teatralidad, *f.* (theatricality).

shown [ʃəun] p. p. See SHOW.

show-off [ˈʃəuˈɔf] n. FAM. Presumido, da (conceited person). | Alarde, *m.*, ostentación, *f.* (ostentation).

showpiece [ˈʃəupi:s] n. Obra (*f.*) maestra. || FIG. Modelo, *m.*

showplace [ˈʃəupleis] n. Sitio (*m.*) de interés turístico.

showroom [ˈʃəurum] n. Sala (*f.*) de muestras. || ARTS. Sala (*f.*) de exposición.

show window [ˈʃəuˈwindəu] n. Escaparate, *m.* [*Amer.*, vidriera, *f.*, vitrina, *f.*].

showy [ˈʃəui] adj. Ostentoso, sa (people). || Aparatoso, sa (ceremony). || Llamativo, va; vistoso, sa: *a showy dress*, un traje llamativo.

shrank [ʃræŋk] pret. See SHRINK.

shrapnel [ˈʃræpnl] n. MIL. "Shrapnel", *m.* (projectile). | Metralla, *f.* (shell fragment).

shred [ʃred] n. Fragmento, *m.*, trozo, *m.* (fragment). || Jirón, *m.* (of cloth): *in shreds*, hecho jirones. || Tira, *f.* (strip): *to cut sth. into shreds*, cortar algo en tiras. || FIG. Chispa, *f.*, pizca, *f.*, átomo, *m.*: *there is not a shred of truth in what he says*, no hay ni chispa de verdad en lo que dice. || — *There isn't a shred of evidence*, no hay la menor prueba de ello. || *To tear to shreds*, hacer trizas, destrozar (sth.), echar abajo *or* por tierra (an argument).

shred [ʃred] v. tr. Hacer trizas, destrozar. || CULIN. Despedazar (meat). | Cortar en tiras (vegetables). || TECH. Desfibrar (paper, rags).

shredder [—ə*] n. TECH. Desfibradora, *f.*

shredding [—iŋ] n. TECH. Desfibrado, *m.*, desfibración, *f.*

shrew [ʃru:] n. ZOOL. Musaraña, *f.* || FIG. Arpía, *f.* (brawling woman). || *The Taming of the Shrew*, la fierecilla domada, la doma de la bravía (Shakespeare's play).

shrewd [—d] adj. Perspicaz (perspicacious). || Sagaz, listo, ta (clever). || Astuto, ta (astute). || Juicioso, sa; atinado, da (reasoning). || Hábil (answer). || Fino, na (wit). || (Ant.) Duro, ra (blow). | Penetrante (cold). || — *I can make a shrewd guess as to who is the author*, me es muy fácil adivinar quién es el autor. || *I have a shrewd idea that*, me parece que.

shrewdly [—dli] adv. Con perspicacia.

shrewdness [—dnis] n. Perspicacia, *f.* (perspicacity). || Sagacidad, *f.*, inteligencia, *f.* (cleverness). || Astucia, *f.* (astuteness).

shrewish [—iʃ] adj. De mal genio, regañón, ona (ill-tempered).

shrewishness [—iʃnis] n. Mal genio, *m.*

shrewmouse [—maus] n. ZOOL. Musaraña, *f.*

shriek [ʃri:k] n. Chillido, *m.* (piercing cry). || Grito, *m.* (scream). || *Shrieks of laughter*, carcajadas, *f.*

shriek [ʃri:k] v. intr. Chillar (to utter a piercing cry). || Gritar (to scream). || FIG. FAM. Darse patadas (two colours). || — *To shriek at the top of one's voice*, gritar a voz en cuello. || *To shriek with laughter*, reírse a carcajadas.

— V. tr. Gritar. || *To shriek out a cry for help*, pedir socorro a voz en grito.

shrieking [—iŋ] adj. Chillón, ona (colour).

— N. Chillidos, *m. pl.*, gritos, *m. pl.*

shrift [ʃrift] n. (Ant.) Confesión, *f.* (confession). | Absolución, *f.* (remission). || FIG. *To give s.o. short shrift*, despachar a alguien.

shrike [ʃraik] n. Alcaudón, *m.* (bird).

shrill [ʃril] adj. Chillón, ona; agudo, da (voice, tone). || Agudo, da; estridente (cry, sound). || Estridente (whistle).

shrill [ʃril] v. intr. Tener un sonido agudo *or* estridente.

— V. tr. Chillar. || *To shrill out*, gritar (insults), cantar con voz aguda (a song).

shrillness [—nis] n. Lo chillón, lo agudo (of a voice, tone). || Lo estridente, lo agudo, estridencia, *f.* (of a sound).

shrilly [—i] adv. Con tono agudo. || Con un sonido estridente.

shrimp [ʃrimp] n. ZOOL. Camarón, *m.* || FAM. Renacuajo, *m.* (small person).

shrimp [ʃrimp] v. intr. Pescar camarones.

shrine [ʃrain] n. REL. Relicario, *m.* (reliquary). | Capilla, *f.* (chapel). | Altar, *m.* (altar). | Mausoleo, *m.*, sepulcro, *m.* (tomb). | Lugar (*m.*) santo (place). | Santuario, *m.* (sanctuary). || FIG. Santuario, *m.*

shrink* [ʃriŋk] v. tr. Encoger (clothes, etc.): *this soap won't shrink woolen goods*, este jabón no encogerá los artículos de lana. || TECH. Contraer (metal). | Montar en caliente. || Reducir (heads, value): *shrunken head*, cabeza reducida.

— V. intr. Encoger (to become smaller): *woolen clothes often shrink when they are washed*, la ropa de lana encoge a menudo cuando se lava. || Disminuir (value). || TECH. Contraerse (metal). || FIG. Encogerse. || — FIG. *To shrink away* o *back*, echarse atrás (to draw back). | *To shrink from doing sth.*, horrorizarle a uno hacer algo. | *To shrink into o.s.*, recogerse en sí mismo, meterse en el caparazón.

— OBSERV. Pret. ***shrank;*** p. p. ***shrunk***. En Estados Unidos también existe el pretérito ***shrunk***. El participio pasivo ***shrunken*** sólo se usa como adjetivo.

shrink [ʃriŋk] n. Encogimiento, *m.* || FAM. Psiquiatra, *m.* (psychiatrist).

shrinkable [—əbl] adj. Que puede encoger.

shrinkage [—idʒ] n. Encogimiento, *m.* (of cloth). || Contracción, *f.* (of metal): *shrinkage factor*, coeficiente de contracción. || FIG. Disminución, *f.*, reducción, *f.*

shrive* [ʃraiv] v. tr. (Ant.) REL. Confesar.

— V. intr. (Ant.) REL. Confesarse.

— OBSERV. Pret. ***shrove;*** p. p. ***shriven***.

shrivel [ˈʃrivl] v. tr. Encoger (to shrink). || Apergaminar, arrugar (to wrinkle). || Marchitar, secar (plants), || Quemar (to burn). || Consumir (to waste away).

— V. intr. *To shrivel up*, encogerse (to shrink), apergaminarse, arrugarse, consumirse (people), marchitarse, consumirse, secarse (plants), quemarse (to burn up).

shriven [ˈʃrivn] p. p. See SHRIVE.

shroud [ʃraud] n. Sudario, *m.*, mortaja, *f.* (for corpses). || FIG. Velo, *m.*: *a shroud of mystery*, un velo de misterio. | Manto, *m.*: *the shroud of night*, el manto de la noche. || MAR. Obenque, *m.* || REL. *The Holy Shroud*, el Santo Sudario.

shroud [ʃraud] v. tr. Amortajar (a corpse). || FIG. Ocultar, tapar (to hide). | Envolver (to surround): *shrouded in mist*, envuelto en la niebla. || FIG. *Shrouded in mystery*, misterioso, sa; envuelto en el misterio.

shroud-laid [—leid] adj. MAR. De cuatro cabos (rope).

shrove [ʃrəuv] pret. See SHRIVE.

Shrovetide [—taid] n. Carnestolendas, *f. pl.*

Shrove Tuesday [—ˈtju:zdi] n. Martes (*m.*) de carnaval.

shrub [ʃrʌb] n. Arbusto, *m.* (small tree). || Matorral, *m.* (bush). || Zumo (*m.*) de frutas con ron *or* con coñac.

shrubbery [—əri] n. Arbustos, *m. pl.*, matorrales, *m. pl.* (shrubs).

shrubby [—i] adj. Lleno de arbustos (full of shrubs). || Parecido a un arbusto (like a shrub). || Arbustivo, va (plantation).

shrug [ʃrʌg] n. Encogimiento (*m.*) de hombros. || *He answered with a shrug*, contestó encogiéndose de hombros *or* con un encogimiento de hombros.

shrug [ʃrʌg] v. tr. Encoger, encogerse de: *to shrug one's shoulders*, encogerse de hombros. || FIG. *To shrug off the difficulties*, no dejarse impresionar por las dificultades, minimizar las dificultades.

— V. intr. Encogerse de hombros.

shrunk [ʃrʌŋk] pret. & p. p. See SHRINK.

shrunken [—ən] adj. Encogido, da (material). || Reducido, da (head). || Apergaminado, da; arrugado, da (skin).

shuck [ʃʌk] n. U. S. Cáscara, *f.* (of nuts). | Vaina, *f.* (of peas). | Espata, *f.* (of corn). | Concha, *f.* (of oysters, etc.). || U. S. FAM. *Not worth shucks*, que no vale un pimiento *or* un comino.

shuck [ʃʌk] v. tr. U. S. Desvainar (peas). | Descascarillar (cereals). | Pelar (fruits, nuts). | Desbullar (oysters). || U. S. FAM. *To shuck off*, desechar, arrumbar.

shucks! [—s] interj. ¡Cáscaras!

shudder [ˈʃʌdə*] n. Repeluzno, *m.*, escalofrío, *m.*, estremecimiento, *m.* (of fear, etc.). || Vibración, *f.* (of machines, motor, etc.).

shudder [ˈʃʌdə*] v. intr. Estremecerse: *he shuddered at the news*, se estremeció ante la noticia. || Sentir un escalofrío, darle a uno un escalofrío, estremecerse: *we shuddered with fear*, nos dió un escalofrío de miedo.

shuffle [ˈʃʌfl] n. Arrastramiento (*m.*) de los pies (of feet). || Barajada, *f.* (of cards). || FIG. Evasiva, *f.* (evasion). || *Whose shuffle is it?*, ¿a quién le toca barajar?

shuffle [ˈʃʌfl] v. tr. Revolver, mezclar (to stir). || Barajar (cards). || Arrastrar (feet). || — *To shuffle off*, quitarse, despojarse de (clothes), quitarse de encima (responsibilities). || *To shuffle on*, ponerse rápidamente (clothes).

— V. intr. Andar arrastrando los pies (to walk). || Bailar arrastrando los pies (to dance). || Moverse de un lado para otro (to move nervously). || Barajar (in cards). || FIG. Andar con rodeos. || — *He came shuffling towards me*, se acercó a mí arrastrando los pies. || *To shuffle in* o *into*, entrar arrastrando los pies en. || FIG. *To shuffle into a job*, conseguir un trabajo por medios poco recomendables. || *To shuffle off*, irse arrastrando los pies. || FIG. *To shuffle out of a tricky situation*, conseguir salir de una situación difícil. || *To shuffle through*, hacer sin cuidado, hacer con los pies (a task).

shuffleboard [—bɔ:d] n. Juego (*m.*) de tejo (game).

shuffler [—ə*] n. Persona (*f.*) que baraja (in cards). || U. S. Pato (*m.*) marino (duck).

shuffling [—iŋ] adj. Lento, ta (gait). || Que arrastra los pies (person). || FIG. Evasivo, va.
— N. Arrastramiento (*m.*) de los pies.

shun [ʃʌn] v. tr. Rehuir, huir de, evitar (people, responsibilities, etc.).

shunt [ʃʌnt] n. Maniobras, *f. pl.* (of trains). || Agujas, *f. pl.* (railway points). || ELECTR. Derivación, *f.*, shunt, *m.* || ELECTR. *Shunt circuit*, circuito derivado.

shunt [ʃʌnt] v. tr. Desviar. || Cambiar de vía (train). || ELECTR. Derivar. || FIG. Desviar (conversation). || — *To shunt s.o. aside*, apartar a alguien. || *To shunt s.o. backwards and forwards*, mandar a uno de acá para allá. || *To shunt s.o. off* o *out of the way*, dejar de lado a uno (lo leave aside).
— V. intr. Cambiar de vía (trains). || ELECTR. Derivarse.

shunter [—ə*] n. Guardagujas, *m. inv.*

shunting [—iŋ] n. Maniobras, *f. pl.* || *Shunting engine*, locomotora (*f.*) de maniobras.

shunt-wound [—waund] adj. ELECTR. Devanado en derivación.

shush [ʃʌʃ] interj. ¡Chitón!

shush [ʃʌʃ] v. tr. Hacer callar.

shut [ʃʌt] adj. Cerrado, da: *the door is shut*, la puerta está cerrada. || FAM. *To get shut of sth.*, deshacerse de algo, quitarse algo de encima.

shut* [ʃʌt] v. tr. Cerrar (door, shop, eyes, mouth, etc.). || Encerrar: *to shut a dog in the kitchen*, encerrar un perro en la cocina. || — *To shut one's ears to sth.*, hacer oídos sordos a algo. || *To shut one's eyes to sth.*, cerrar los ojos ante algo. || *To shut one's finger in the door*, pillarse el dedo en la puerta. || *To shut the door in s.o.'s face*, dar a alguien con la puerta en las narices.
— V. intr. Cerrarse.
— **To shut away**, guardar bajo llave (to keep under lock and key). | Encerrar (to imprison). || **To shut down**, cerrar (curtain, etc.). | Cerrar (factory, etc.). | Cerrarse (to close). || **To shut in**, encerrar (to imprison). | Rodear, cercar (to surround). || **To shut off**, cortar (gas, electricity, water). | Desconectar (machine). | Aislar (to isolate). | Apartar: *to shut o.s. off from society*, apartarse de la sociedad. | — *To be shut off from*, estar apartado *or* aislado de. || **To shut out**, no admitir (not to admit). | Dejar fuera (to leave outside): *they shut me out of the house*, me dejaron fuera de la casa. | Excluir (to exclude). | Evitar: *to shut out all risk of fire*, evitar todo peligro de incendio. | Tapar (the light, a view). | — *To be shut out*, quedarse fuera. || **To shut up**, guardar bajo llave (to keep under lock and key). | Encerrar (to imprison, to enclose). | Cerrar: *to shut up a shop*, cerrar una tienda; *the shop is shutting up*, la tienda está cerrando. | Obstruir (to block). | Callar, hacer callar (to cause to be quiet). | Callarse: *shut up!*, ¡cállate! | — *He spends the whole day shut up in his workshop*, se pasa el día entero encerrado en su taller. | FIG. *To shut up shop*, liquidar el negocio.
— OBSERV. Pret. & p.p. **shut.**

shutdown [—daun] n. Cierre, *m.*

shut-eye [—ai] n. FAM. *To get some shut-eye*, echar un sueño.

shut-in [—in] n. U. S. Enfermo (*m.*) que tiene que guardar cama *or* quedarse en su casa.
— Adj. U. S. Encerrado, da. || Introvertido, da.

shutoff [—ɔf] n. Válvula, *f.* (valve). || Interrupción, *f.*, cierre, *m.*

shutout [—aut] n. U. S. Cierre (*m.*) patronal (lockout). || U. S. SP. Victoria (*f.*) ganada sin que el adversario marque un tanto.

shutter [—ə*] n. Postigo, *m.*, contraventana, *f.* (on window). || PHOT. Obturador, *m.* || — PHOT. *Shutter speed*, tiempo (*m.*) de exposición. || FIG. *To put up the shutters*, cerrar definitivamente (to close down), desistir (to give up).

shutter [—ə*] v. tr. Poner postigos a (to provide with shutters). || Cerrar los postigos de (to close).

shuttle [ʃʌtl] n. Lanzadera, *f.* (in sewing and weaving). || U. S. Vehículo (*m.*) que hace trayectos cortos y regulares entre dos puntos (vehicle). || Trayecto (*m.*) corto y regular entre dos puntos (journey). || SP. Volante, *m.* (shuttlecock). || *Space shuttle*, transbordador (*m.*) espacial.

shuttle [ʃʌtl] v. tr. Transportar [en trayectos cortos y regulares] (to transport in a shuttle service). || *To shuttle s.o. about*, mandar a alguien de acá para allá.
— V. intr. Hacer trayectos cortos y regulares (a shuttle service). || FIG. Ir y venir, ir de acá para allá (to go back and forth).

shuttlecock [—kɔk] n. SP. Volante, *m.*

shuttle service [—'sə:vis] n. Servicio (*m.*) regular de ida y vuelta entre dos puntos.

shy [ʃai] adj. Tímido, da: *a shy person, smile*, una persona, una sonrisa tímida. || Vergonzoso, sa (bashful). || Asustadizo, za (animals). || Cauteloso, sa (cautious). || U. S. Escaso, sa: *shy of money*, escaso de dinero. || — *Come on, don't be shy!*, ¡venga, no tengas vergüenza! || *I can't, I'm shy*, no puedo, me da vergüenza. || FIG. *I'm ten pounds shy*, me faltan *or* he perdido diez libras. | *To be shy of*, desconfiar de (to distrust). | *To be shy of doing sth.*, no atreverse a hacer algo. | *To fight shy of*, evitar.
— N. Tiro, *m.*, lanzamiento, *m.* (a throw). || Respingo, *m.*, espantada, *f.* (of a horse). || FIG. Tentativa, *f.*, intento, *m.* (try). || FIG. *To have a shy at doing sth.*, intentar hacer algo.

shy [ʃai] v. tr. Tirar, lanzar (to throw).
— V. intr. Asustarse, sobresaltarse: *I shied at the noise*, me sobresalté al oír el ruido. || Negarse a saltar: *to shy at a fence*, negarse a saltar una valla. || — *To shy away*, espantarse (to be frightened). || *To shy away from*, huir: *he shies away from reporters*, huye de los periodistas; negarse a, rehusar: *to shy away from doing sth.*, negarse a hacer algo.

Shylock [—lɔk] n. FIG. Usurero, *m.*

shyly [—li] adv. Tímidamente, con vergüenza.

shyness [—nis] n. Timidez, *f.* (bashfulness). || Cautela, *f.* (caution).

shyster ['ʃaistə*] n. U. S. FAM. Picapleitos, *m. inv.*

si [si:] n. MUS. Si, *m.*

sial ['saiəl] n. GEOGR. Sial, *m.*

Siam ['saiæm] pr. n. GEOGR. Siam, *m.*

Siamese [,saiə'mi:z] adj. Siamés, esa: *Siamese twins*, hermanos siameses. || *Siamese cat*, gato siamés.
— N. Siamés, esa (inhabitant of Thailand). || Siamés, *m.* (language). || *The Siamese*, los siameses.

sib [sib] n. Hermano, na (sibling). || Pariente, *m.* (relative). || Parientes, *m. pl.* (kinfolk).

Siberia [sai'biəriə] pr. n. GEOGR. Siberia, *f.*

Siberian [—n] adj./n. Siberiano, na.

sibilance ['sibiləns] or **sibilancy** [—i] n. Carácter (*m.*) sibilante.

sibilant ['sibilənt] adj. Sibilante. || MED. Silbante.
— N. GRAMM. Sibilante, *f.*

sibilate ['sibileit] v. tr. Pronunciar con sibilante.
— V. intr. Silbar (to hiss).

sibilation [,sibi'leiʃən] n. Pronunciación (*f.*) sibilante.

sibling ['sibliŋ] n. Hermano, na (brother, sister). || Medio hermano, media hermana (half brother, half sister).

sibyl ['sibil] n. Sibila, *f.*

sibylline [si'bilain] adj. Sibilino, na. || *Sibylline Books*, libros sibilinos.

sic [sik] adv. Sic.

sic [sik] v. tr. See SICK.

siccative ['sikətiv] adj. Secante.
— N. Secante, *m.*, aceite (*m.*) secante.

Sicilian [si'siljən] adj. Siciliano, na.
— N. Siciliano, na (native of Sicily). || Siciliano, *m.* (Italian dialect).

Sicily ['sisili] pr. n. GEOGR. Sicilia, *f.*

sick [sik] adj. Enfermo, ma (ill, unhealthy): *how long has he been sick?*, ¿desde cuándo está enfermo? || Enfermizo, za (sickly). || FIG. Enfermo, ma: *he was sick with envy*, se puso enfermo de envidia. || FIG. FAM. Enfermo, ma; malo, la: *his bad manners make me sick*, su mala educación me pone enfermo; *you make me sick!*, ¡me pones malo! | Morboso, sa; negro, gra: *sick humour*, humor negro. | Morboso, sa (joke). || (Ant.) Ansioso, sa; anhelante (longing). || — *I feel sick when you go this fast*, me mareo cuando vas tan de prisa. || FIG. *I get sick of it*, me cansa. | *It makes me sick to think that*, me pone malo pensar que. | *My car looks pretty sick next to yours*, mi coche es muy poca cosa al lado del suyo. | *Our economy is sick at present*, actualmente nuestra economía va mal. || *Sick person*, enfermo, ma. || *To be off sick*, estar ausente por enfermedad. || *To be sick*, estar enfermo (to be ill), vomitar (to vomit). || FIG. *To be sick for*, anhelar. | *To be sick of*, estar harto de. || *To be sick with flu*, estar con gripe. || *To fall* o *to go* o *to take sick*, caer *or* ponerse enfermo. || *To feel sick*, tener náuseas, estar mareado. || FIG. *To feel sick at heart*, estar desesperado. | *To feel* o *to be sick and tired of*, estar harto de, estar hasta las narices de. || *To get sick*, marearse (seasick, airsick, etc.), caer *or* ponerse enfermo (to take sick). || *To report sick*, darse de baja por enfermedad.
— N. *The sick*, los enfermos.

sick [sik] v. tr. Atacar, coger (to attack). || Echar (*on*, a) [a dog on s.o.]. || — *Sick!*, ¡a por él! || FAM. *To sick up*, vomitar.

sick bay [—bei] n. Enfermería, *f.*

sickbed [—bed] n. Lecho (*m.*) de enfermo.

sick benefit [—'benifit] n. Subsidio (*m.*) de enfermedad.

sicken ['sikn] v. tr. Poner enfermo (to make ill). || Empalagar: *sweet things sicken me*, las cosas dulces me empalagan. || Dar náuseas, marear (to cause nausea). || FIG. Hartar (to bore). || FIG. *It sickens me that there is so much violence*, me pone enfermo que haya tanta violencia.
— V. intr. Enfermar, ponerse *or* caer enfermo (to get ill). || Marearse (to become nauseated). || — *To sicken for*, echar de menos (to miss), anhelar (to yearn for), incubar (an illness). || FIG. *To sicken of*, hartarse de.

sickening [—iŋ] adj. Nauseabundo, da; repugnante (revolting). || Deprimente (distressing).

sickeningly [—iŋli] adv. Repugnantemente. || *Sickeningly dirty*, tan sucio que da asco.

sick headache [—'hedeik] n. U. S. MED. Jaqueca, *f.*: *to have a sick headache*, tener jaqueca.

sickish [ˈsikiʃ] adj. Enfermizo, za (person). || Empalagoso, sa (taste, smell).
sickle [ˈsikl] n. Hoz, *f.*
sick leave [ˈsikli:v] n. Baja (*f.*) por enfermedad.
sickliness [ˈsiklinis] n. Mala salud, *f.*, salud (*f.*) delicada (of a person). || Palidez, *f.* (of complexion). || Lo empalagoso (of cakes, etc.).
sickly [ˈsikli] adj. Enfermo, ma (ill). || Enfermizo, za (prone to sickness, weak). || Pálido, da (pale). || Forzado, da: *a sickly smile*, una sonrisa forzada. || Nauseabundo, da (nauseating). || Empalagoso, sa (taste). || Macilento, ta (light). || Malsano, na (climate). || *Sickly sweet*, empalagoso, sa; dulzón, ona.
sickness [ˈsiknis] n. Enfermedad, *f.* (illness): *absence through sickness*, ausencia por enfermedad; *sleeping sickness*, enfermedad del sueño. || Ganas (*f. pl.*) de vomitar, náuseas, *f. pl.* (desire to vomit). || Mareo, *m.* (seasickness, airsickness).
sick pay [ˈsikpei] n. Subsidio (*m.*) de enfermedad.
sickroom [ˈsikrum] n. Cuarto (*m.*) de un enfermo.
side [said] n. Lado, *m.*: *the right, the left side*, el lado derecho, izquierdo. || Lado, *m.*, costado, *m.* (of the body). || Ijar, *m.*, ijada, *f.* (of an animal). || Lonja, *f.*: *a side of bacon*, una lonja de tocino. || Ladera, *f.*, falda, *f.* (of a hill, mountain). || Cara, *f.*, lado, *m.* (of a paper, a record). || Lado, *m.* (of a tape). || Borde, *m.* (edge). || Orilla, *f.* (shore). || Banda, *f.*, costado, *m.* (of a boat). || Lado, *m.*, parte, *f.*: *whose side are you on?*, ¿de qué lado estás?, ¿de parte de quién estás?; *I'm on your side*, estoy de tu lado; *on the side of*, del lado de. || Lado, *m.*, parte, *f.*, línea, *f.*: *an uncle on my mother's side*, un tío por parte de mi madre *or* por el lado materno. || Aspecto, *m.*, lado, *m.*: *a new side to the matter*, un nuevo aspecto del asunto; *the many sides of his character*, los múltiples aspectos de su carácter; *to consider a problem from all sides*, examinar todos los aspectos de un problema. || MIL. Flanco, *m.*, lado, *m.* (flank). || MATH. Lado, *m.*: *a triangle has three sides*, un triángulo tiene tres lados. | Cara, *f.* (face). || SP. Equipo, *m.* (team): *to field a good side*, sacar un buen equipo. | Efecto, *m.* (spin on a ball). || JUR. Parte, *f.*: *the other side*, la parte adversa. || RAD. Canal, *m.* (on television): *what's on the other side?*, ¿qué hay en el otro canal? || — *At* o *by the side of*, al lado de. || COMM. *Credit side*, haber, *m.* | *Debit side*, debe, *m.* || *From all sides*, de todos lados, de todas partes. || *From side to side*, de un lado para otro (with movement), de ancho: *the room measures four metres side to side*, el cuarto mide cuatro metros de ancho. || *God is on our side*, Dios está de nuestro lado. || *It's best to be on the safe side*, más vale estar seguro. || *It's on the other side of the forest*, está del otro lado del bosque. || *It's on this side of the forest*, está antes del bosque *or* de este lado del bosque. || *On all sides*, por todos lados, por todas partes. || *On both sides*, por ambas partes, por ambos lados. || *On either side*, de cada lado. || *On one's blind side*, fuera de la vista de uno. || *On one side..., on the other...*, por una parte... por otra... || *On the French side of the border*, en el lado francés de la frontera. || *On the large, the cold, the sweet side*, bastante grande, frío, dulce. || *On the left-hand side*, a la izquierda. || *On the right-hand side*, a la derecha. || U. S. *On the side*, por añadidura. || *On this side*, por este lado. || *Side by side*, juntos, uno al lado del otro, lado a lado. || FIG. *The other side of the picture*, el reverso de la medalla. || *There are two sides to the problem*, el problema se divide en dos partes *or* presenta dos aspectos. || *The right side*, el derecho (of cloth), el lado derecho, la derecha (right-hand side), el lado bueno (the correct side). || *The under, the upper side*, la parte inferior, superior. || *To be on the safe side*, para mayor seguridad, para estar tranquilo (for safety's sake), ir sobre seguro, obrar sin riesgos. || FIG. *To be on the wrong side of forty*, tener cuarenta años bien cumplidos, tener más de cuarenta años. || *To be sitting side by side*, estar sentados uno al lado del otro. || FIG. *To change sides*, cambiar de partido. | *To get on the right side of s.o.*, congraciarse con alguien, granjearse la simpatía de alguien. | *To get on the wrong side of s.o.*, tomar a alguien a contrapelo. || *To go side by side*, ir juntos, ir lado a lado. || FIG. *To keep on the good* o *on the right side of s.o.*, tratar de llevarse bien con alguien. | *To keep on the right side of the law*, mantenerse dentro de la ley. | *To let the side down*, dejar mal a los suyos [a su equipo, a su regimiento, etc.]. | *To look on the bright side*, ver el lado bueno de las cosas. || FAM. *To make a bit on the side*, ganar algún dinero fuera de su trabajo normal. || *To move to one side*, apartarse, hacerse a un lado. || FIG. *To put on side*, tener muchos humos. || *To put* o *to leave on* o *to one side*, poner a un lado, poner aparte. || *To sleep on one's side*, dormir de costado. || FIG. *To split one's sides laughing*, partirse *or* desternillarse de risa. || *To take sides*, tomar partido. || *To take sides with s.o.*, ponerse del lado *or* de parte de alguien. || *To turn over on one's side*, ponerse de costado (a person), volcar (a car, etc.). || *Wrong side out*, al revés, del revés.
— Adj. Lateral: *a side wall*, un muro lateral; *a side street*, una calle lateral. || Secundario, ria (secondary): *side issue*, cuestión secundaria; *side effects*, efectos secundarios; *side road*, carretera secundaria. || Adicional (supplementary). || Indirecto, ta: *a side comment*, un comentario indirecto. || — *Side door*, puerta (*f.*) lateral (secondary), entrada (*f.*) de servicio (tradesmen's entrance). || *Side view*, vista (*f.*) de perfil.
side [said] v. tr. Poner lados a.
— V. intr. *To side with*, ponerse del lado *or* de parte de. || *To side with nobody*, no tomar partido.
side arms [—ɑ:mz] pl. n. MIL. Armas (*f.*) de mano, armas (*f.*) blancas.
sideboard [—bɔ:d] n. Aparador, *m.* (furniture). || — Pl. Patillas, *f.* (of hair).
sideburns [—bə:nz] pl. n. Patillas, *f.* (of hair).
sidecar [—kɑ:*] n. Sidecar, *m.* (of motorcycle). || Cóctel (*m.*) de coñac, licor de naranja y zumo de limón (drink).
side dish [—diʃ] n. Plato (*m.*) que acompaña el principal.
side drum [—drʌm] n. MUS. Tambor, *m.*
side face [—feis] n. Perfil, *m.*
— Adj./adv. De perfil.
side-glance [—glɑ:ns] n. Mirada (*f.*) de reojo *or* de soslayo.
sidehead [—hed] n. Título (*m.*) al margen.
sidekick [—kik] n. U. S. FAM. Compañero, *m.*, amigo, *m.* (friend). | Socio, *m.* (partner).
sidelight [—lait] n. Luz (*f.*) lateral. || Piloto, *m.*, luz (*f.*) de posición (of a car). || MAR. Luz (*f.*) de situación (of ship). || FIG. Aclaración, *f.* (enlightening comment).
sideline [—lain] n. Negocio (*m.*) suplementario (supplementary trade). || Empleo (*m.*) suplementario, actividad (*f.*) suplementaria (second job). || Vía (*f.*) secundaria (of railway). || SP. Línea (*f.*) de banda. || — Pl. SP. Banquillo, *m. sing.*: *to sit on the sidelines*, quedarse en el banquillo. || FIG. *From the sidelines*, desde la barrera, desde fuera.
sidelong [—lɔŋ] adj. De reojo, de soslayo: *a sidelong glance*, una mirada de reojo. || Lateral (lateral). || Oblicuo, cua (oblique). || De costado, lateral (fall, dive, etc.).
— Adv. De reojo, de soslayo: *to glance sidelong*, mirar de reojo. || Lateralmente. || Oblicuamente. || De costado (to dive, etc.).
sidenote [—nəut] n. Nota (*f.*) al margen.
sidepiece [—pi:s] n. Pieza (*f.*) lateral.
sidereal [saiˈdiəriəl] adj. Sideral, sidéreo, a. || — *Sidereal day*, día (*m.*) sideral. || *Sidereal year*, año sideral.
siderite [ˈsaidərait] n. MIN. Siderita, *f.*, siderosa, *f.*
siderosis [sidəˈrəusis] n. MED. Siderosis, *f.*
siderurgy [ˈsidəˌrə:dʒi] n. Siderurgia, *f.*
sidesaddle [ˈsaidˌsædl] n. Silla (*f.*) de amazona. || *To ride sidesaddle*, montar a mujeriegas, montar a la amazona.
sideshow [ˈsaidʃəu] n. Atracción (*f.*) secundaria (supporting act). || Caseta, *f.* (stall). || FIG. Acontecimiento (*m.*) secundario (event). || MIL. Diversión, *f.*
sideslip [ˈsaidslip] n. Deslizamiento (*m.*) lateral (slip to the side). | Patinazo, *m.*, resbalón, *m.* (of a car). | AVIAT. Resbalamiento, *m.*
sideslip [ˈsaidslip] v. intr. Deslizarse lateralmente (to slip sideways). | Patinar, resbalar (a car). || AVIAT. Resbalar.
sidesman [saidzmən] n. Mayordomo, *m.* (of Anglican church).

— OBSERV. El plural de esta palabra es *sidesmen*.

sidesplitting [ˈsaidˈsplitiŋ] n. FAM. Divertidísimo, ma; mondante, de partirse de risa (funny).
side step [ˈsaidstep] n. Paso (*m.*) lateral. || SP. Quiebro, *m.* | MIL. Paso (*m.*) de lado *or* lateral.
side-step [ˈsaidstep] v. tr. Esquivar, evitar (to avoid, to dodge). || Evitar (a problem, an issue).
— V. intr. Dar un paso lateral. || SP. Dar un quiebro.
sidestroke [ˈsaidstrəuk] n. *To swim sidestroke*, nadar de costado.
sideswipe [ˈsaidswaip] n. Golpe (*m.*) de refilón (blow). | FIG. Indirecta, *f.* (remark).
sideswipe [ˈsaidswaip] v. tr. Chocar de refilón contra.
sidetrack [ˈsaidtræk] n. Apartadero, *m.*, vía (*f.*) muerta (siding). || FIG. Cuestión (*f.*) de interés secundario.
sidetrack [ˈsaidtræk] v. tr. Poner en vía muerta, apartar (a train). || FIG. Despistar (a person). | Dejar de lado (an issue). | Desviar (from a course).
sidewalk [ˈsaidwɔ:k] n. U. S. Acera, *f.* || U. S. *Sidewalk artist*, artista callejero.
sideward [ˈsaidwə:d] or **sidewards** [—z] adj. Lateral, de lado, a un lado (to one side): *a sideward step, movement*, un paso, un movimiento lateral. || De reojo, de soslayo: *a sideward glance*, una mirada de soslayo. || De costado, de lado: *a sideward dive*, un salto de costado. || Oblicuo, cua (oblique).
— Adv. De lado, lateralmente, de costado: *it goes in sidewards*, entra de lado; *to walk sidewards*, andar de lado. || De lado, de costado (to dive, to fall). || || A un lado, hacia un lado: *to step sidewards*, dar un paso hacia un lado. || Oblicuamente (obliquely). || De reojo, de soslayo (to look, to glance).
sideways [ˈsaidweiz] (U. S. **sideway**) [ˈsaidwei] adj./adv. See SIDEWARD.
side-wheeler [ˈsaidˌwilə*] n. Vapor (*m.*) de ruedas (paddle steamer).
side-whiskers [ˈsaidˈwiskəz] pl. n. Patillas, *f.*
sidewise [ˈsaidwaiz] adj./adv. See SIDEWARD.

siding [ˈsaidiŋ] n. Apartadero, *m.*, vía (*f.*) muerta.

sidle [ˈsaidl] n. Movimiento (*m.*) furtivo (furtive movement). || Movimiento (*m.*) lateral (sideways movement).

sidle [ˈsaidl] v. intr. Avanzar *or* moverse furtivamente (to move furtively). || FAM. *To sidle up to s.o.*, acercarse furtivamente a alguien.

siege [si:dʒ] n. MIL. Sitio, *m.*, cerco, *m.* || FIG. Acoso, *m.* (insistence). || U. S. Calvario, *m.* (exhausting period). || — *To lay* o *to stand siege to*, sitiar, poner sitio a, asediar, cercar. || *To raise the siege*, levantar el sitio.

sienna [siˈenə] n. Tierra (*f.*) de siena, siena, *f.*

sierra [ˈsiərə] n. GEOGR. Sierra, *f.*

siesta [siˈestə] n. Siesta, *f.*: *to have a siesta*, dormir *or* echar una siesta.

sieve [siv] n. Cedazo, *m.*, cernedor, *m.*, tamiz, *m.*, criba, *f.* || FIG. Indiscreto, ta. || FIG. *To have a memory like a sieve*, tener una memoria como un colador.

sieve [siv] v. tr. Cerner, tamizar, cribar.

sift [sift] v. tr. Tamizar, cerner, cribar (to sieve). || Espolvorear (to sprinkle). || FIG. Examinar cuidadosamente (to examine). || — FIG. *To sift out*, encontrar (to find), seleccionar (to choose), separar (to separate). | *To sift through*, examinar cuidadosamente.
— V. intr. Filtrarse: *light sifted through the curtains*, la luz se filtraba a través de las cortinas.

sifter [—ə*] n. Cedazo, *m.*, cernedor, *m.*, tamiz, *m.*

sifting [—iŋ] n. Cernido, *m.* || — Pl. Cerniduras, *f.* (residue).

sigh [sai] n. Suspiro, *m.*: *to heave* o *to breathe a sigh of relief*, dar un suspiro de alivio. || FIG. Susurro, *m.*, gemido, *m.* (of the wind).

sigh [sai] v. tr. Decir suspirando.
— V. intr. Suspirar (to emit a sigh). || FIG. Susurrar, gemir: *the wind sighs in the trees*, el viento susurra entre los árboles. || FIG. *To sigh for*, suspirar por.

sight [sait] n. Vista, *f.*: *the gift of sight*, el don de la vista; *within sight*, a la vista. || Visión, *f.* (vision). || Examen, *m.* (examination). || Mira, *f.* (of a gun). || — Pl. Cosas (*f.*) dignas de verse (things worth seeing). || Monumentos, *m.* (monuments). || — *A sight more*, mucho más. || *At* o *on first sight*, a primera vista. || *Guilty in the sight of the law*, culpable a los ojos de la ley. || *I hate the sight of him*, no le puedo ver [ni en pintura]. || *It was a sight to see!*, ¡era una cosa digna de verse! || *It was love at first sight*, fue un flechazo. || *Not to let s.o. out of one's sight*, no perder de vista a alguien. || *Not to lose sight of*, no perder de vista (a person, an object), tener presente (a fact, etc.). || *On sight*, a primera vista, nada más verlo: *I recognized them on sight*, los reconocí nada más verlos. || *Out of sight, out of mind*, ojos que no ven, corazón que no siente. || COMM. *Payable on* o *at sight*, pagadero a la vista. || *People on the streets after curfew will be shot on sight*, se disparará inmediatamente contra toda persona que circule por la calle después del toque de queda. || *Short sight*, miopía, *f.* || *Sight translation*, traducción (*f.*) a libro abierto *or* a la vista. || *Sight unseen*, sin haberlo visto. || *The accident was not a pretty sight*, el accidente fue un espectáculo bastante desagradable. || *The end is in sight*, el final está a la vista *or* está cerca. || *The oasis was a sight for sore eyes*, la vista del oasis era un verdadero alivio. || *The sight of blood makes me faint*, me desmayo cuando veo sangre. || *To be a sight* o *a long sight* o *a darned sight bigger*, ser muchísimo más grande. || *To be in sight of land*, divisar tierra. || *To be out of sight*, estar fuera de la vista, no poder verse. || *To catch sight of*, divisar. || *To come into sight*, aparecer. || *To drop out of sight*, desaparecer. || *To find favour in the sight of s.o.*, ser acogido favorablemente por alguien (an idea, etc.), caerle en gracia a alguien (a person). || *To get a sight of*, conseguir *or* lograr ver (to get a look at). || MAR. *To heave into sight*, aparecer. || *To keep out of sight*, no dejarse ver. || *To keep sth. in sight*, no perder de vista (an object, a person), tener presente (a fact, etc.). || *To know by sight*, conocer de vista. || *To lose one's sight*, perder la vista, quedar ciego. || *To lose sight of*, perder de vista. || *To make a sight of o.s.*, ir hecho una facha, estar hecho un adefesio. || *To play music at sight*, repentizar. || *To regain one's sight*, recobrar la vista. || *To see the sights (of the city)*, visitar la ciudad. || *To set one's sights on sth.*, echar el ojo a algo. || *To set one's sights very high*, apuntar muy alto. || *To take sight*, apuntar (to aim). || *Victory was in sight*, la victoria estaba cerca. || *What a sight he looked!*, ¡había que verlo!, ¡menuda pinta tenía! || *You look a real sight in that cap!*, ¡menuda pinta tienes con esa gorra! || *You're a sight for sore eyes!*, ¡qué gusto verte!, ¡cuánto me alegro de verte!, ¡felices los ojos que te ven!

sight [sait] v. tr. Divisar, avistar, ver: *to sight land*, divisar tierra. || Observar (to observe): *to sight a star*, observar una estrella. || Descubrir (to discover). || Apuntar, apuntar con [un arma] (to aim): *to sight a gun at s.o.*, apuntar a alguien con un fusil. || Poner una mira a [un arma] (to provide with a sight).
— V. intr. Apuntar (to take aim). || Mirar detenidamente (to look carefully).

sight draft [—dra:ft] n. U. S. Letra (*f.*) a la vista.

sighted [—id] adj. Que ve, de vista normal.

sighthole [—həul] n. Mirilla, *f.* (peephole).

sighting [—iŋ] n. Observación, *f.*

sightless [—lis] adj. Ciego, ga (blind). || Invisible.

sightlessness [—lisnis] n. Ceguera, *f.*

sightliness [—linis] n. Hermosura, *f.*

sightly [—li] adj. Agradable a la vista, hermoso, sa.

sight-read [—ri:d] v. tr. Leer a primera vista. || MUS. Repentizar.

sight reading [—ˌri:diŋ] n. MUS. Acción (*f.*) de repentizar, ejecución (*f.*) a primera vista.

sight-seeing [—ˌsi:iŋ] n. Turismo, *m.*: *I don't like sight-seeing*, no me gusta hacer turismo. || *To go sight-seeing*, visitar la ciudad, hacer turismo.

sightseer [—ˌsi:ə*] n. Turista, *m.* & *f.*

sigillography [sidʒiˈlɔgrəfi] n. Sigilografía, *f.*

Sigismund [ˈsigismənd] pr. n. Segismundo, *m.*

sigma [ˈsigmə] n. Sigma, *f.* (Greek letter).

sigmate [ˈsigmeit] adj. En forma de S.

sigmoid [ˈsigmɔid] adj. Sigmoideo, a; sigmoides. || ANAT. *Sigmoid flexure*, flexura sigmoidea.

sign [sain] n. MATH. MUS. ASTR. Signo, *m.*: *the sign of the Bull*, el signo del Tauro. || Símbolo, *m.* (symbol). || Seña, *f.*: *to converse in signs*, conversar por señas. || Señal, *f.*: *to make a sign with one's hand*, hacer una señal con la mano. || Gesto, *m.*, ademán, *m.* (gesture). || Muestra, *f.*: *he is showing signs of weakness*, da muestras de debilidad. || Rastro, *m.*, huella, *f.* (trace): *they left no sign of their passage*, no dejaron ningún rastro de su paso. || Señal, *f.*: *good, bad sign*, buena, mala señal. || Presagio, *m.* (omen): *a sign of doom*, un presagio de catástrofe. || Señal, *f.*, indicio, *m.* (of rain, etc.). || Anuncio, *m.* (notice): *put a sign in the window*, pon un anuncio en la ventana. || Cartel, *m.* (poster). || Letrero, *m.* (board): *the sign says it is forbidden to walk on the grass*, el letrero dice que está prohibido pisar la hierba. || Letrero, *m.*, rótulo, *m.* (over shop, doorway, etc.). || MED. Síntoma, *m.* (symptom). || Huella, *f.*, rastro, *m.* (track of animal). || — *As a sign of good faith*, como prueba de buena fe. || *At the slightest sign of*, al menor signo de. || *He made a sign for me to come*, me hizo una señal para que viniese. || "*No parking*" *sign*, señal de prohibición de estacionamiento. || *Not to show any signs of life*, no dar señales de vida. || *Road sign*, señal de tráfico. || *Sign of the times*, signo del tiempo en que vivimos. || *There was no sign of them anywhere*, no se les veía por ninguna parte. || *The sign of the Cross*, la señal de la Cruz.

sign [sain] v. tr. Firmar (name, document, treaty). || Hacer la señal de la cruz sobre, santiguar (to bless). || Indicar (to express). || — *To sign and seal*, firmar y sellar. || REL. *To sign o.s.*, persignarse.
— V. intr. Firmar. || Hacer señas (to make signs).
— ***To sign away*** o ***over***, ceder (a property). || ***To sign off***, acabar el programa (on the radio). | Terminar (to finish). || ***To sign on*** o ***up***, alistarse(to join the army, navy, etc.). | MAR. Enrolar (to take on). | MAR. Enrolarse (to enrol). | SP. Fichar (a player): *to sign on a player*, fichar a un jugador. | COMM. Contratar (to take on). | Firmar un contrato (to engage o.s.). | — *To sign up for*, matricularse en (a class).

signal [ˈsignəl] n. Señal, *f.* (agreed sign): *to give the signal for*, dar la señal de *or* para. || RAD. Sintonía, *f.* || Señal, *f.* (traffic, railway, etc.). || — *Alarm signal*, señal de alarma. || U. S. *Busy signal*, señal de ocupado (telephone). || *Distress signals*, señales de socorro.
— Adj. Señalado, da; notable.

signal [ˈsignəl] v. tr. Dar la señal de *or* para (to order by signal): *he signalled them to stop*, les dio la señal de pararse. || Indicar (to convey by signals). || — *He signalled that he was turning left*, indicó *or* avisó que iba a torcer a la izquierda. || *He signalled them on*, les indicó que avanzaran. || *To signal before overtaking*, indicar que se va a adelantar.
— V. intr. Hacer señales, avisar.

signal book [—buk] n. Código (*m.*) de señales.

signal box [—bɔks] n. Cabina (*f.*) del cambio de agujas.

signal code [—kəud] n. Código (*m.*) de señales.

Signal Corps [—kɔ:] n. MIL. Servicio (*m.*) de Transmisiones.

signal flag [—flæg] n. Bandera (*f.*) de señales.

signal flare [—flεə*] n. Bengala (*f.*) de señales.

signaling [—iŋ] n. U. S. Señalización, *f.*

signalize [ˈsignəlaiz] v. tr. Señalar, distinguir (to distinguish). || Señalar (to point out).

signalling [ˈsignəliŋ] n. Señalización, *f.*

signalman [ˈsignəlmən] n. Guardavía, *m.* (on a railway).
— OBSERV. El plural de esta palabra es *signalmen*.

signalment [ˈsignəlmənt] n. Descripción, *f.*, filiación, *f.* (of a person).

signal tower [ˈsignəlˈtauə*] n. U. S. Cabina (*f.*) del cambio de agujas.

signatory [ˈsignətəri] adj./n. Signatario, ria; firmante: *the signatory countries*, los países firmantes; *the signatories to an agreement*, los firmantes de un acuerdo.

signature [ˈsignitʃə*] n. Firma, *f.* (of name, document, treaty): *blank signature*, firma en blanco. || RAD. Sintonía, *f.* || MUS. Armadura, *f.* (of key). || Signatura, *f.* (in bookbinding). || U. S. MED. Parte (*f.*) de una receta en que se indica la posología.

signature tune [—tju:n] n. Sintonía, *f.* (on radio, etc.).

signboard [ˈsainbɔ:d] n. Letrero, *m.* (sign). || Cartel, *m.* (poster). || Tablón (*m.*) de anuncios (notice board).

signer [ˈsainə*] n. Firmante, *m.* & *f.*, signatario, ria.

signet [ˈsignit] n. Sello, *m.*

signet ring [—riŋ] n. Sortija (*f.*) de sello, sello, *m.*

significance [sigˈnifikəns] or **significancy** [—i] n. Significado, *m.* (meaning). || Significación, *f.*, importancia, *f.* (importance).

significant [sigˈnifikənt] adj. Significativo, va (meaningful). || Importante: *a significant increase*, un aumento importante. || Mucho, cha (a lot of): *to place significant emphasis on*, dar mucho énfasis a. || MATH. *Significant figures*, cifras significativas.

significantly [—li] adv. De modo significativo. || *To smile significantly*, dirigir una sonrisa de entendimiento.

signification [ˌsignifiˈkeiʃən] n. Significado, *m.* (meaning). || Significación, *f.* (act of signifying).

significative [sigˈnifikətiv] adj. Significativo, va.

signify [ˈsignifai] v. tr. Indicar (to indicate). || Significar (to mean). || Dar a conocer (an opinion).

— V. intr. Tener importancia (to be significant). || *Please signify*, le ruego tenga a bien dar su opinión.

signing [ˈsainiŋ] n. Firma, *f.*

sign language [ˈsainˈlæŋgwidʒ] n. Lenguaje (*m.*) por señas. || *To speak to each other in sign language*, hablarse por señas.

sign manual [ˈsainˈmænjuəl] n. Firma, *f.*

signpost [ˈsainpəust] n. Señal (*f.*) de tráfico, poste (*m.*) indicador (traffic sign). || Letrero, *m.* (notice).

signpost [ˈsainpəust] v. tr. Señalizar. || *The way is well signposted*, el camino está bien indicado.

signposting [—iŋ] n. Señalización, *f.*

signwriter [ˈsainˈraitə*] n. Rotulista, *m.* & *f.*

silage [ˈsailidʒ] n. Ensilaje, *m.*

silage [ˈsailidʒ] v. tr. Ensilar.

silence [ˈsailəns] n. Silencio, *m.*: *deadly silence*, silencio sepulcral; *to suffer in silence*, sufrir en silencio. || — *Silence!*, ¡silencio! || FIG. *Silence gives consent*, quien calla otorga. | *Silence is golden*, el silencio es oro. || *To break the silence*, romper el silencio. || *To call for silence*, pedir *or* imponer silencio. || *To pass over sth. in silence*, silenciar algo, callar algo, pasar algo por alto.

silence [ˈsailəns] v. tr. Hacer callar (to cause to be quiet). || Silenciar, callar (to quieten). || Amortiguar (a sound). || TECH. Silenciar (a motor). || FIG. Reducir al silencio (guns, s.o. who knows too much).

silencer [—ə*] n. Silenciador, *m.* (of gun, engine).

silent [ˈsailənt] adj. Silencioso, sa (making no sound): *a silent audience*, *motor*, un público, un motor silencioso. || Callado, da; silencioso, sa (person). || Mudo, da: *a silent letter*, *film*, una letra, una película muda. || — *Be silent!*, ¡cállate!, ¡cállese! || COMM. *Silent partner*, socio comanditario. || *The house was deathly silent*, en la casa había un silencio sepulcral. || *The silent majority*, la mayoría silenciosa. || *To keep silent about sth.*, guardar silencio respecto a algo.

silently [—li] adv. Silenciosamente, en silencio.

silex [ˈsaileks] n. Sílex, *m.*, pedernal, *m.*

silhouette [ˌsiluˈet] n. Silueta, *f.*

silhouette [ˌsiluˈet] v. tr. Siluetear (to represent as an outline). || *The firemen were silhouetted against the burning building*, la silueta de los bomberos se perfilaba *or* se destacaba en el edificio en llamas.

silica [ˈsilikə] n. CHEM. Sílice, *f.*

silicate [ˈsilikit] n. CHEM. Silicato, *m.*

siliceous [siˈliʃəs] adj. CHEM. Silíceo, a.

silicic [siˈlisik] adj. CHEM. Silícico, ca (acid).

silicify [siˈlisifai] v. tr. CHEM. Impregnar de sílice (to impregnate). | Convertir en sílice (to turn into silica).

— V. intr. CHEM. Impregnarse de sílice (to become impregnated). | Convertirse en sílice (to turn into silica).

silicon [ˈsilikən] n. MIN. Silicio, *m.*

silicone [ˈsilikəun] n. CHEM. Silicona, *f.*

silicosis [ˌsiliˈkəusis] n. MED. Silicosis, *f.*

silk [silk] n. Seda, *f.* (fabric, fibre). || FAM. Toga, *f.* (of lawyer). || BOT. Estigma (*m.*) del maíz (of maize). || — Pl. U. S. Gorra (*f. sing.*) y chaquetilla (*f. sing.*) del jockey. || — *As smooth as silk*, suave como la seda. || *To take silk*, tomar la toga, hacerse abogado.

— Adj. De seda: *a silk dress*, un vestido de seda; *silk paper*, papel de seda. || Sedero, ra; *silk industry*, industria sedera.

silk [silk] v. intr. U. S. Madurar (maize).

silk cotton [—ˈkɔtn] n. Seda (*f.*) vegetal.

silk culture [—ˈkʌltʃə*] n. Sericultura, *f.*, sericicultura, *f.* (sericulture).

silken [ˈsilkən] adj. Sedoso, sa (lustrous). || Suave, sedoso, sa (smooth). || Suave (suave). || De seda (made of silk).

silk hat [hæt] n. Sombrero (*m.*) de copa, chistera, *f.*

silkiness [ˈsilkinis] n. Suavidad, *f.* || Aspecto (*m.*) sedoso (of fabric).

silk-screen [ˈsilkskri:n] adj. PRINT. *Silk-screen process o print*, serigrafía, *f.*

silk-screen [ˈsilkskri:n] v. tr. Estampar por serigrafía.

silk stocking [ˈsilkˈstɔkiŋ] n. U. S. FIG. Aristócrata, *m.* & *f.*

silk-stocking [ˈsilkˈstɔkiŋ] adj. U. S. FIG. Elegante. | Aristocrático, ca.

silkworm [ˈsilkwə:m] n. ZOOL. Gusano (*m.*) de seda.

silky [ˈsilki] adj. Sedoso, sa (fabric, etc.). || Suave (voice).

sill [sil] n. Alféizar, *m.* (of window). || Umbral, *m.* (of a door). || ARCH. Solera, *f.* || GEOL. Capa, *f.*

sillabub [ˈsiləbʌb] n. Batido (*m.*) de leche, azúcar y licores.

silliness [ˈsilinis] n. Necedad, *f.*, estupidez, *f.* (quality of being silly). || Tontería, *f.* (silly act). || *Such silliness does not become your age*, esas tonterías no son propias de tu edad.

silly [ˈsili] adj. Tonto, ta; bobo, ba: *don't be silly!*, ¡no seas tonto! || Ridículo, la (ridiculous). || Absurdo, da (absurd). || — *That was a silly thing to do*, eso fue una tontería, hiciste una tontería. || FAM. *To knock s.o. silly*, pegar una paliza a alguien (to beat s.o. up), dejar atontado a alguien (to leave s.o. senseless). || *To make s.o. look silly*, poner a alguien en ridículo.

— N. Tonto, ta; bobo, ba.

silo [ˈsailəu] n. Silo, *m.*

silo [ˈsailəu] v. tr. Ensilar.

silt [silt] n. Cieno, *m.*, limo, *m.*, légamo, *m.* (mud).

silt [silt] v. tr. *To silt up*, encenagar (canal), enarenar (port).

— V. intr. *To silt up*, cegarse (canal), enarenarse (port).

Silurian [saiˈljuəriən] adj./n. Siluriano, na; silúrico, ca.

silvan [ˈsilvən] n. adj./n. See SYLVAN.

silver [ˈsilvə*] n. MIN. Plata, *f.* (metal): *silver foil*, hoja de plata. || Color (*m.*) plateado (colour). || FIG. Monedas (*f. pl.*) de plata (silver coins). | Suelto, *m.* (change). || Plata, *f.* (silverware). || *German silver*, plata alemana.

— Adj. De plata (made of silver): *a silver tray*, una bandeja de plata; *silver coin*, moneda de plata. || Plateado, da (like silver). || Argentino, na (voice). || Argentífero, ra (mineral). || — *Silver gilt*, plata dorada || *Silver nitrate*, nitrato (*m.*) de plata.

silver [ˈsilvə*] v. tr. Platear (to silver-plate). || Azogar (a mirror). || Volver cano (hair).

silver age [—reidʒ] n. Edad (*f.*) de plata.

silver anniversary [—ˌræniˈvə:səri] n. Bodas (*f. pl.*) de plata.

silver fir [—ˈfə:*] n. BOT. Abeto (*m.*) blanco, pinabete, *m.*

silverfish [—fiʃ] n. ZOOL. Lepisma, *f.* (insect). | Pez (*m.*) plateado (fish).

silver fox [—fɔks] n. ZOOL. Zorro (*m.*) plateado.

silvering [—riŋ] n. Plateado, *m.*

silver lining [—ˈlainiŋ] n. FIG. Resquicio (*m.*) de esperanza, perspectiva (*f.*) esperanzadora. || *Every cloud has a silver lining*, see CLOUD.

silver paper [ˈpeipə*] n. Papel (*m.*) de plata *or* de estaño.

silver plate [—ˈpleit] n. Baño (*m.*) de plata, plateado, *m.* (thin coating of silver). || Plata, *f.*, vajilla (*f.*) de plata (silverware).

silver-plate [—ˈpleit] v. tr. Platear, dar un baño de plata a.

silver plater [—pleitə*] n. Plateador, *m.*

silver-plating [—ˈpleitiŋ] n. Plateado, *m.*

silversmith [—ˌsmiθ] n. Platero, *m.* || *Silversmith's*, platería, *f.*

silversmithing [—iŋ] n. Platería, *f.*, orfebrería, *f.*

silver-tongued [—ˈtʌŋd] adj. Elocuente, con pico de oro.

silverware [—wɛə*] n. Plata, *f.*, vajilla (*f.*) de plata.

silver wedding [—ˈwediŋ] n. Bodas (*f. pl.*) de plata.

silvery [ˈsilvəri] adj. Plateado, da (of or like silver). || Argentino, na (tone, voice).

silviculture [ˈsilvikʌltʃə*] n. Silvicultura, *f.*

silviculturist [ˌsilviˈkʌltʃərist] n. Silvicultor, *m.*

simian [ˈsimiən] adj. ZOOL. Símico, ca; simiesco, ca.

— N. ZOOL. Simio, *m.*

similar [ˈsimilə*] adj. Similar, parecido, da; semejante. || MATH. Semejante. || — *It is very similar to the one you have*, se parece mucho al que tiene Ud. || *They are quite similar*, se parecen bastante.

similarity [ˌsimiˈlæriti] n. Similitud, *f.*, semejanza, *f.*, parecido, *m.*

similarly [—li] adv. Del mismo modo.

simile [ˈsimili] n. Símil, *m.*

similitude [siˈmilitju:d] n. Similitud, *f.*, parecido, *m.*, semejanza, *f.* (similarity). || Imagen, *f.* (image). || Forma, *f.* (form).

simmer [ˈsimə*] n. *To be o to keep on the simmer*, hervir a fuego lento.

simmer [ˈsimə*] v. tr. Hervir a fuego lento.

— V. intr. Hervir a fuego lento (to be boiling gently). || Estar a punto de hervir (to be almost boiling). || FIG. Fermentar, estar a punto de estallar (revolt, etc.). || — FIG. *He was simmering with rage*, estaba a punto de estallar. | *To simmer down*, calmarse.

simnel cake [ˈsimnlkeik] n. Torta (*f.*) de frutas que se prepara para Pascuas.

simoniac [saiˈməuniæk] adj./n. Simoniaco, ca; simoniático, ca.

simonist [ˈsaimənist] n. Simoniaco, ca; simoniático, ca.

simon-pure [ˈsaimənˈpjuə*] adj. Auténtico, ca.

simony [ˈsaiməni] n. Simonía, *f.*

simoom or **simoon** [siˈmu:m] n. Simún, *m.* (wind).

simp [simp] n. U. S. FAM. Tonto, ta; bobo, ba.

simper [ˈsimpə*] n. Sonrisa (*f.*) afectada (affected smile). || Sonrisa (*f.*) boba *or* tonta (silly smile).

simper [ˈsimpə*] v. tr. Decir con una sonrisa afectada *or* tonta.
— V. intr. Sonreír con afectación *or* tontamente.
simple [ˈsimpl] adj. Sencillo, lla; simple: *a simple dress*, un vestido sencillo; *he is a simple man*, es un hombre sencillo; *the simple life*, la vida sencilla. || Natural: *simple beauty*, belleza natural. || Fácil, sencillo, lla; simple (easy). || Inocente, ingenuo, nua (guileless): *he is simple enough to believe anything*, es tan inocente que se lo cree todo. || Simple (half-witted). || Simple (mere): *he is a simple herdsman*, es un simple pastor. || JUR. CHEM. MED. Simple. || — *A simple soul*, un alma de Dios. || ZOOL. *Simple eye*, ojo (*m.*) simple. || MATH. *Simple equation*, ecuación (*f.*) del primer grado. | *Simple fraction*, fracción ordinaria. || COMM. *Simple interest*, interés (*m.*) simple. || BOT. *Simple leaf*, hoja (*f.*) simple. || GRAMM. *Simple sentence*, oración (*f.*) simple.
— N. Simple, *m.* & *f.* (silly person). || Simple, *m.* (plant).
simplehearted [—ˈhɑ:tid] adj. Sencillo, lla (unsophisticated). || Inocente, ingenuo, nua (artless).
simpleminded [—ˈmaindid] adj. Sencillo, lla (unsophisticated). || Ingenuo, nua (guileless). || Simple (of subnormal intelligence). || Tonto, ta (silly).
simplemindedness [—ˈmaindidnis] n. Simpleza, *f.* (silliness). || Ingenuidad, *f.* (ingenuousness).
simpleness [—nis] n. See SIMPLICITY.
Simple Simon [—ˈsaimən] n. Bobo, *m.*, simplón, *m.*
simpleton [ˈsimpltən] n. Simplón, ona; tontuelo, la; bobalicón, ona.
simplicity [simˈplisiti] n. Sencillez, *f.* (lack of affectation or complexity). || Naturalidad, *f.* (naturalness). || Ingenuidad, *f.* (guilelessness). || Simpleza, *f.* (silliness).
simplifiable [ˈsimplifaiəbl] adj. Simplificable.
simplification [ˌsimplifiˈkeiʃən] n. Simplificación, *f.*
simplifier [ˈsimplifaiə*] n. Simplificador, ra.
simplify [ˈsimplifai] v. tr. Simplificar.
simplifying [—iŋ] adj. Simplificador, ra.
simplism [ˈsimˌplizəm] n. Simplismo, *m.*
simplistic [simˈplistik] adj. Simplista.
simply [ˈsimpli] adv. Simplemente, sencillamente, con sencillez (in a simple way): *I simply left*, me fui sencillamente; *simply dressed*, vestido sencillamente. || Meramente, simplemente, solamente (merely). || Realmente, francamente: *the play was simply awful*, la obra era francamente horrible. || *You simply must see it*, tienes que verlo, no puedes dejar de verlo.
simulacrum [ˌsimjuˈleikrəm] n. Simulacro, *m.*

— OBSERV. El plural de la palabra *simulacrum* es *simulacra* o *simulacrums*.

simulate [ˈsimjuleit] v. tr. Simular, fingir. || — *A simulated attack*, un simulacro de ataque. || AVIAT. *Simulated flight*, vuelo simulado.
simulation [ˌsimjuˈleiʃən] n. Simulación, *f.*, fingimiento, *m.* (pretence). || Simulacro, *m.* (simulacrum).
simulator [ˈsimjuleitə*] n. TECH. Simulador, *m.*
simulcast [ˈsimʌlˌkɑ:st] n. Transmisión (*f.*) simultánea por radio y televisión (of programme, event, etc.).
simulcast [ˈsimʌlˌkɑ:st] v. tr. Transmitir simultáneamente por radio y televisión.
simultaneity [ˌsiməltəˈniəti] n. Simultaneidad, *f.*
simultaneous [ˌsiməlˈteinjəs] adj. Simultáneo, a: *simultaneous translation*, traducción simultánea. || MATH. *Simultaneous equations*, sistema (*m. sing.*) de ecuaciones.
simultaneousness [—nis] n. Simultaneidad, *f.*
sin [sin] n. Pecado, *m.*: *mortal, venial, original sin*, pecado mortal, venial, original; *the seven deadly sins*, los siete pecados capitales. || — FIG. FAM. *As ugly as sin*, más feo que un pecado. || *Every sin carries its own punishment*, en el pecado va la penitencia. || *For my sins*, por mis pecados. || FIG. *It would be a sin to miss this chance*, sería un pecado no aprovechar esta oportunidad. || *There is forgiveness for every sin*, todo pecado merece perdón. || *To be in sin*, estar en pecado. || FIG. *To live in sin*, vivir en el pecado.
sin [sin] v. intr. Pecar.
Sinai [ˈsainiai] pr. n. GEOGR. Sinaí, *m.*
sinapism [ˈsinəpizəm] n. MED. Sinapismo, *m.*
since [sins] adv. Desde entonces: *he moved away three years ago but she has seen him since*, hace tres años que se marchó pero ella le ha visto desde entonces. || — *A short time since*, hace poco. || *Ever since*, desde entonces. || *He has married long since*, hace tiempo *or* hace mucho tiempo que se ha casado, se ha casado desde hace tiempo *or* desde hace mucho tiempo. || *How long since?*, ¿cuánto tiempo hace?, ¿desde cuándo? || *Not long since*, hace poco.
— Prep. Desde: *since childhood*, desde la niñez. || *Since that time*, desde entonces, a partir de entonces.
— Conj. Desde que: *much has happened since they last met*, muchas cosas han pasado desde que se vieron por última vez. || Ya que: *since you have come you can do the washing up*, ya que has venido puedes fregar los platos. || — *How long is it since he left?*, ¿cuánto tiempo hace que se fue? || *How long is it since you've seen him?*, ¿cuánto tiempo hace que no le ves? || *It's just a month since he left*, sólo hace un mes que se fue. || *Since he was a child*, desde niño.
sincere [sinˈsiə*] adj. Sincero, ra.
sincerely [—li] adv. Sinceramente. || *Yours sincerely*, le saluda atentamente (in a letter).
sincerity [sinˈseriti] n. Sinceridad, *f.*: *in all sincerity*, con toda sinceridad.
sine [sain] n. MATH. Seno, *m.* || *Sine curve*, sinusoide, *f.*
sine die [ˈsainiˈdaii:] adv. phr. Sine die.
sinecure [ˈsainikjuə*] n. Sinecura, *f.*, canonjía, *f.*
sinew [ˈsinju:] n. ANAT. Tendón, *m.* || Nervio, *m.* (in meat). || FIG. Nervio, *m.*, vigor, *m.* (strength). || — Pl Recursos, *m.* (means). || *The sinews of war*, el nervio de la guerra.
sinewy [—i] adj. Nervudo, da (hands, body). || Estropajoso, sa (meat). || FIG. Vigoroso, sa; enérgico, ca (vigorous).
sinfonia [ˌsinfəˈni:ə] n. MUS. Sinfonía, *f.*

— OBSERV. El plural de la palabra inglesa *sinfonia* es *sinfonie*.

sinful [ˈsinful] adj. Pecaminoso, sa (deed, thought). || Pecador, ra (person). || De perdición (place). || FIG. Escandaloso, sa (scandalous).
sinfulness [—nis] n. Maldad, *f.* (wickedness). || Culpabilidad, *f.* (guilt). || Pecado, *m.* (sin).
sing [siŋ] n. Silbido, *m.*, zumbido, *m.* (shrill sound): *the sing of a bullet*, el silbido de una bala. || Canto, *m.* (singing).
sing* [siŋ] v. tr. Cantar. || — *To sing a baby to sleep*, arrullar a un niño. || FIG. *To sing a different tune*, cambiar de tono. || *To sing out*, gritar (to shout), celebrar cantando (the old year). || FIG. *To sing the praises of*, cantar las alabanzas de.
— V. intr. Cantar (music, poetry, birds). || Silbar, zumbar (bullets, etc.). || Zumbar (insects, ears). || Silbar (kettle). || FIG. FAM. Cantar (to confess). || — *To sing out*, gritar. || *To sing out of tune*, desafinar. || FIG. *To sing small*, achantarse. || *To sing up*, cantar más fuerte (louder).

— OBSERV. Pret. ***sang***; p. p. ***sung***.

singable [ˈsiŋəbl] adj. Cantable.
Singapore [ˌsingəˈpɔ:*] pr. n. GEOGR. Singapur.
singe [sindʒ] n. Chamusquina, *f.*
singe [sindʒ] v. tr. Chamuscar, socarrar. || Quemar las puntas de (hair).
singer [siŋə*] n. Cantante, *m.* & *f.*, cantor, ra (s.o. who sings). || Cantor, ra (in a choir). || Cantante, *m.* & *f.*, cantor, *m.*, cantatriz, *f.* (of opera). || Cantante, *m.* & *f.* (pop singer, folk singer, etc.). || Ave (*f.*) canora (a bird that sings). || *Flamenco singer*, cantaor (*m.*) de flamenco.
Singhalese [ˌsiŋhəˈli:z] adj./n. Cingalés, esa.
singing [ˈsiŋiŋ] n. MUS. Canto, *m.* (operatic, etc.). || Canción, *f.* (pop singing). || Zumbido, *m.*, silbido, *m.* (buzz). || Silbido, *m.* (whistle). || — *I can hear singing*, oigo a alguien que canta. || *I enjoyed their singing*, me gustó mucho como cantaron.
single [ˈsiŋgl] adj. Solo, la: *a single spectator remained*, un solo espectador se quedó; *there wasn't a single seat left*, no quedaba ni un solo asiento. || Único, ca (sole, only). || Suelto: *a single copy of a magazine*, un número suelto de una revista. || Individual (for one person): *a single room, bed*, una habitación, una cama individual. || Soltero, ra (unmarried): *to stay single*, quedarse soltero. || De soltero: *single life is very difficult*, la vida de soltero es muy difícil. || Simple (not compound). || BOT. Simple. || De ida: *one single ticket*, un billete de ida. || — *Every single person*, todos [y cada uno]. || *Not a single*, ninguno, na. || *Not a single one*, ni uno, ni una. || *Not a single person*, ninguno, na; nadie. || *Not a single thing*, nada. || *Single file*, fila india. || SP. *Single game*, partido (*m.*) individual *or* simple.
— N. Individuo, *m.*, persona, *f.* (person). || Objeto, *m.*, cosa, *f.* (thing). || Billete (*m.*) de ida (ticket). || SP. Golpe (*m.*) que marca un tanto (in cricket). | Primera base, *f.* (in baseball). || — Pl. SP. Individual, *m. sing.*, simple, *m. sing.* (in tennis, golf): *men's singles*, individual caballeros.
single [siŋgl] v. tr. *To single out*, separar (to isolate), escoger, seleccionar, elegir (to choose), distinguir, singularizar (to distinguish).
— V. intr. U. S. SP. Pasar a la primera base (baseball).
single-acting [—ˈæktiŋ] adj. De efecto simple.
single-barrelled (U. S. **single-barreled**) [—ˈbærəld] adj. De un cañón (rifle).
single-breasted [—ˈbrestid] adj. Recto, ta; sin cruzar: *a single-breasted jacket*, una chaqueta recta.
single-cell [—sel] adj. Unicelular.
single combat [—ˈkɔmbət] n. Combate (*m.*) singular. || *To engage the enemy in single combat*, luchar cuerpo a cuerpo con el enemigo.
single-cylinder [—ˈsilində*] adj. Monocilíndrico, ca.
single-engined [—ˈendʒind] adj. Monomotor.
single entry [—ˈentri] n. COMM. Partida (*f.*) simple.
single-foot [—fut] n. U. S. Ambladura, *f.*
single-foot [—fut] v. intr. U. S. Amblar.
single-handed [—ˈhændid] adj. Sin ayuda (done without assistance). || Manco, ca (having only one hand). || Que se emplea con una sola mano (used with one hand).
— Adv. Sin ayuda, solo, la.
single-hearted [—ˈhɑ:tid] adj. Leal (loyal).
single-minded [—ˈmaindid] adj. Que tiene un solo objetivo, resuelto, ta (with one purpose). || Leal (single-hearted).

single-mindedness [—ˈmaindidnis] n. Perseverancia, *f.* || Franqueza, *f.* (frankness).
singleness [—nis] n. Lealtad, *f.*, honradez, *f.* (sincerity). || Unidad, *f.* (unity). || Soltería, *f.* (unmarried state). || *With singleness of purpose*, con un solo objetivo, con determinación.
single-phase [—feiz] adj. ELECTR. Monofásico, ca.
single-pole [—ˈpəul] adj. Unipolar.
single-seater [—ˈsi:tə*] n. Monoplaza, *m.* (plane).
single-stage [—steidʒ] adj. De un solo cuerpo (rocket).
singlestick [—stik] n. Bastón, *m.* (in fencing).
singlet [ˈsiŋglit] n. Camiseta, *f.*
singleton [ˈsiŋgltən] n. Semifallo, *m.* (in cards).
single-track [—træk] adj. De vía única (railway). || FIG. Limitado, da; de pocos alcances (mind).
singletree [ˈsiŋgltri:] n. U. S. Balancín, *m.*
singly [ˈsiŋgli] adv. Individualmente, por separado, separadamente (separately). || Uno a uno (one by one). || Sin ayuda, solo, la (singlehanded).
singsong [ˈsiŋsɔŋ] n. Tono (*m.*) monótono, sonsonete, *m.*, canto (*m.*) monótono (tone of voice). || *We had a little singsong after the meal*, cantamos un poco después de la comida.
— Adj. Monótono, na.
singular [ˈsiŋgjulə*] adj. GRAMM. Singular. || Singular, excepcional: *singular beauty*, belleza singular. || Singular, raro, ra; extraño, ña (strange). || Individual. || Solo, la; único, ca (single).
— N. GRAMM. Singular, *m.*: *in the singular*, en singular.
singularity [ˌsiŋgjuˈlæriti] n. Singularidad, *f.* (strangeness, distinctiveness). || Peculiaridad, *f.* (peculiarity).
singularize [ˈsiŋgjuləraiz] v. tr. Singularizar.
sinister [ˈsinistə*] adj. Siniestro, tra (evil). || HERALD. Siniestrado, da (left).
sink [siŋk] n. Lavabo, *m.* (in bedroom, bathroom). || Fregadero, *m.*, pila, *f.* (in kitchen). || Sumidero, *m.* (drain). || Pozo (*m.*) negro (cesspool). || Depresión, *f.* (depressed land). || FIG. Cloaca, *f.* (place of vice).
sink* [siŋk] v. tr. Hundir, sumergir: *to sink one's hand in boiling water*, sumergir la mano en agua hirviendo. || Echar al fondo del mar *or* de un río: *to sink a hundred tons of explosives*, echar cien toneladas de explosivos al fondo del mar. || Hundir, echar a pique: *the torpedo sank the ship*, el torpedo echó el barco a pique. || Hincar: *to sink a post in the ground*, hincar un poste en el suelo; *to sink one's teeth into an apple*, hincar los dientes en una manzana. || Meter: *I sank my hand in my pocket*, metí la mano en el bolsillo. || Clavar, hundir: *to sink a knife into the ground*, clavar un cuchillo en el suelo. || Cavar, excavar (a well, mine, etc.). || TECH. Avellanar (to countersink). | Grabar en hueco (in engraving). || Bajar (to reduce in intensity, volume): *to sink one's voice*, bajar la voz. || COMM. Invertir (to invest). | Enterrar, gastar (one's fortune). || Meter [la bola] en el agujero (billiards). || Meter [la pelota en el hoyo] (in golf). || FIG. Acabar con: *to sink s.o.'s hopes*, acabar con las esperanzas de uno. | Echar abajo: *to sink s.o.'s plans*, echar abajo los planes de uno; *to sink a theory*, echar abajo una teoría. | Hundir (person). | Bajar (one's head, eyes). | Beberse (a drink). | Echar tierra sobre, olvidar (to cover up, to hush up). || — FIG. FAM. *Now we're sunk!*, ¡estamos perdidos! || FIG. *To be sunk in*, estar sumido en (thought, despair, melancholy, etc.).
— V. intr. Hundirse: *the cart sunk into the mud*, el carro se hundió en el barro; *sinking into the cushions*, hundiéndose en los cojines; *land that is sinking*, tierra que se está hundiendo. || Hundirse, irse a pique (boat, drowning man). || Ponerse, bajar, ocultarse (heavenly body): *the sun was sinking behind the hills*, el sol estaba bajando detrás de las colinas. || Desaparecer: *to sink into the distance*, desaparecer en la lejanía. || Arrellanarse: *he sank back into the chair*, se arrellanó en la silla. || Dejarse caer (to drop): *he sank heavily into the chair*, se dejó caer pesadamente en la silla. || Descender, bajar, estar en declive: *hills that sink to the sea*, colinas que bajan hacia el mar. || Disminuir, bajar: *over the years sales figures have sunk*, a través de los años las ventas han bajado. || Bajar (opinion, etc.): *he has sunk in my esteem*, ha bajado en mi estima. || Amainar (the wind). || Hundirse (the cheeks). || Bajar (voice). || FIG. Caer: *night sank upon the town*, la noche cayó sobre la ciudad. | Venirse abajo: *his hopes sunk*, sus esperanzas se vinieron abajo. | Doblarse: *to sink under a heavy load*, doblarse bajo una carga pesada. | Debilitarse, consumirse (a sick person): *he is sinking fast*, se está debilitando rápidamente. || COMM. Bajar (value, shares). || — FIG. *His heart sank*, se le cayó el alma a los pies. | *His legs sank under him*, le flaquearon las piernas. | *To leave s.o. to sink or swim*, abandonar a alguien a su suerte. || *To sink in* o *into*, hundirse en: *the knife sank into his flesh*, el cuchillo se le hundió en la carne; penetrar: *the rain sank into the dry ground*, la lluvia penetró en la tierra seca; fijarse (dye), caer en: *to sink into oblivion*, caer en el olvido; *to sink into decay*, caer en la decadencia; grabarse en: *to sink into the memory*, grabarse en la memoria; causar impresión (words). || *To sink into a deep sleep*, caer *or* sumirse en un profundo sueño. || *To sink to one's knees*, hincarse de rodillas. || FIG. *When the importance of the news finally sank in*, cuando por fin nos dimos cuenta de la importancia de la noticia.
— OBSERV. Pret. *sank*; p. p. *sunk*.
sinkage [—idʒ] n. Hundimiento, *m.*
sinker [—ə*] n. Plomo, *m.* (to sink a fishing line, net, etc.). || Pocero, *m.* (well digger). || Excavador, *m.* (shaft sinker). || U. S. FAM. Buñuelo, *m.* (doughnut).
sinkhole [—həul] n. Sumidero, *m.* (drain). || Pozo (*m.*) negro (cesspool).
sinking [—iŋ] n. Hundimiento, *m.* (of boat, road, building, etc.). || Excavación, *f.* (excavation). || Amortización, *f.* (of debt). || Debilitación, *f.*, disminución, *f.* (of debt). || Debilitación, *f.*, disminución, *f.* (of strength). || Bajada, *f.* (of voice). || FIG. *To have that sinking feeling*, tener el sentimiento de que todo se acaba.
sinking fund [—iŋfʌnd] n. Fondo (*m.*) de amortización.
sinless [ˈsinlis] adj. Inmaculado, da; puro, ra; sin pecado.
sinlessness [—nis] n. Pureza, *f.*
sinner [ˈsinə*] n. Pecador, ra.
Sino-Japanese [ˈsainəudʒæpəˈni:z] adj. Sinojaponés, esa.
Sinologist [saiˈnɔlədʒist] or **Sinologue** [ˈsainəlɔg] n. Sinólogo, ga.
Sinology [siˈnɔlədʒi] n. Sinología, *f.*
sinter [ˈsintə*] n. GEOL. Toba (*f.*) caliza. || TECH. Frita, *f.* (product of sintering).
sinter [ˈsintə*] v. tr. TECH. Sinterizar.
sintering [—riŋ] n. TECH. Sinterización, *f.*
sinuate [ˈsinjuet] adj. BOT. Ondeado, da; sinuoso, sa.
sinuosity [ˌsinjuˈɔsiti] n. Sinuosidad, *f.*
sinuous [ˈsinjuəs] adj. Sinuoso, sa (winding, having many curves). || BOT. Ondeado, da; sinuoso, sa.
sinus [ˈsainəs] n. ANAT. MED. BOT. Seno, *m.*
sinusitis [ˌsainəˈsaitis] n. MED. Sinusitis, *f.*
sinusoid [ˈsainəsɔid] n. Sinusoide, *f.*
sinusoidal [sainəsˈɔidəl] adj. Sinusoidal.
Sioux [su:] adj./n. Siux.
— OBSERV. El plural de la palabra *Sioux* es *Sioux* [su:z].
sip [sip] n. Sorbo, *m.*: *let me have a sip from your glass*, déjame tomar un sorbo de tu vaso.
sip [sip] v. tr./intr. Sorber, beber a sorbos (to drink). || Probar (to taste).
siphon [ˈsaifən] n. Sifón, *m.* || *Siphon bottle*, sifón, *m.*
siphon [ˈsaifən] v. tr. Trasegar con sifón. || *To siphon off* o *out*, sacar con un sifón.
— V. intr. Pasar por un sifón.
sippet [ˈsipit] n. Picatoste, *m.* (for soaking in soup, for garnishing). || FIG. Trozo, *m.*, fragmento, *m.* (morsel).
sir [sə:*] n. Señor, *m.*, caballero, *m.*: *excuse me, Sir*, perdone usted, señor. || Sir, *m.* (title). || — *Dear Sir*, Muy Señor mío. || *My dear sir!*, ¡amigo mío! || MIL. *Yes, Sir!*, ¡Sí, mi General [mi Capitán, etc.]!, ¡a sus órdenes, mi General [mi Capitán, etc.]!
— OBSERV. En plural se emplean las formas *Sirs* o *Gentlemen*. El título *Sir* va siempre seguido del nombre de pila de la persona considerada.
sir [sə:*] v. tr. Dar el tratamiento de señor.
sire [ˈsaiə*] n. (Ant.) Mi Señor, *m.*, Majestad, *f.* (form of address to a king). || ZOOL. Padre, *m.* (of a quadruped). | Semental, *m.* (stud animal).
sire [ˈsaiə*] v. tr. Ser el padre de, engendrar. || — *He sired eleven children*, fue el padre de once hijos. || *This horse was sired by...*, el padre de este caballo es *or* fue...
siren [ˈsaiərən] n. MYTH. MAR. TECH. Sirena, *f.* || FIG. Mujer (*f.*) fatal, sirena, *f.*
sirenian [saiˈri:niən] n. ZOOL. Sirenio, *m.*
sirloin [ˈsə:lɔin] n. CULIN. Solomillo, *m.*
sirocco [siˈrɔkəu] n. Siroco, *m.* (wind).
sirup [ˈsirəp] n. See SYRUP.
sisal [ˈsaisəl] n. Sisal, *m.*, pita, *f.*, henequén, *m.*
siskin [ˈsiskin] n. Chamariz, *m.* (bird).
sissy [ˈsisi] n. FAM. Blandengue, *m.* (softy). | Gallina, *m.* (coward). | Afeminado, *m.*, mariquita, *m.* (effeminate man).
sister [ˈsistə*] n. Hermana, *f.* || Enfermera (*f.*) jefe (in hospital). || REL. Hermana, *f.*, monja, *f.* (nun). || FIG. Mujer, *f.* (woman). || — *Sister Mary*, Sor María. || *Sister nations*, naciones hermanas. || *Sister ships*, barcos gemelos.
sister-german [—ˈdʒə:mən] n. Hermana (*f.*) carnal.
— OBSERV. El plural de *sister-german* es *sisters-german*.
sisterhood [—hud] n. Hermandad, *f.* || REL. Comunidad (*f.*) religiosa.
sister-in-law [—rinlɔ:] n. Cuñada, *f.*, hermana (*f.*) política.
— OBSERV. El plural de *sister-in-law* es *sisters-in-law*.
sisterly [—li] adj. Fraternal, de hermana.
Sistine [ˈsistain] adj. Sixtino, na: *the Sistine Chapel*, la Capilla Sixtina.
sit* [sit] v. tr. Sentar: *sit him on her left*, siéntale a su izquierda. || Montar (a horse). || Presentarse a: *to sit an exam*, presentarse a un examen. || Tener cabida para (to accommodate): *it sits fifty people*, tiene cabida para cincuenta personas. || — *To sit o.s.*, sentarse. || *To sit out*, no bailar: *do you mind if we sit this one*

out?, ¿te importa que no bailemos esta vez?; quedarse hasta el final de, aguantar hasta el final de (a meeting, film, etc.). || *To sit s.o. up*, incorporar a alguien.
— V. intr. Sentarse: *sit on my left*, siéntese a mi izquierda; *tables are not meant for sitting on*, las mesas no están hechas para que uno se siente encima. || Estar sentado: *when everyone was sitting*, cuando todos estuvieron sentados; *they were sitting round the fire*, estaban sentados alrededor del fuego. || Posarse (bird, insect). || Empollar: *the hen sits on the eggs*, la gallina empolla los huevos. || Posar (to pose): *to sit for a portrait*, posar para un retrato. || Sentar (clothes): *to sit very well on one*, sentarle bien a uno. || Yacer, estar situado (to lie, to be situated). || Quedarse, estar, permanecer: *the car sits there all day long*, el coche se queda allí todo el día. || Ser miembro: *to sit on a committee*, ser miembro de una comisión. || Ocupar un escaño: *to sit in Parliament*, ocupar un escaño en el parlamento. || Reunirse, celebrar sesión (an assembly, court, etc.): *the committee is sitting*, la comisión está reunida. || Actuar: *the assembly will sit as a general committee*, la asamblea actuará como comité. || Cuidar niños (to look after children). || FIG. Corresponder: *conduct that sits badly on a young lady*, conducta que no corresponde a una señorita. | Pesar (to weigh): *the responsibility sits heavily on him*, la responsabilidad le pesa mucho. || Soplar (wind). || — FIG. *Now we just have to sit back and wait*, ahora sólo tenemos que esperar. || *They sat looking at each other*, estaban sentados mirándose el uno al otro. || *To be sitting at breakfast, at dinner*, estar desayunando, cenando. || *To be sitting at table*, estar sentado a la mesa. || FIG. *To make s.o. sit up*, sorprender a alguien (to surprise), despertarle el interés a alguien (to arouse s.o.'s interest). || *To shoot a pheasant sitting*, disparar un faisán en tierra. || *To sit at home doing nothing*, quedarse en casa sin hacer nada. || *To sit back in one's chair*, recostarse en la silla. || *To sit down*, sentarse: *please sit down*, siéntese por favor; *they sat down to a meal of chicken*, se sentaron para comer un pollo; *to sit down to a game of cards*, sentarse a jugar a las cartas. || FIG. *To sit down on*, suprimir (to suppress), reprimir (to repress), oponerse firmemente a (to oppose). | *To sit down under*, aguantar (to accept). || *To sit for a constituency*, representar un distrito electoral. || *To sit for an examination*, presentarse a un examen. || FIG. *To sit in for s.o.*, sustituir a alguien. | *To sit on o over a matter*, discutir un asunto, examinar un asunto. | *To sit on s.o.*, poner a alguien en su sitio, bajarle los humos a alguien. | *To sit over a book*, estar leyendo un libro. | *To sit over a glass of brandy*, estar sentado con una copa de coñac. || *To sit still*, no moverse. || *To sit up*, incorporarse (from a lying position): *to sit up in bed*, incorporarse en la cama; ponerse derecho (to straighten one's back), quedarse levantado, no acostarse: *I sat up all night*, no me acosté en toda la noche; quedar asombrado: *everybody sat up at the news*, todos quedaron asombrados con la noticia. || *To sit up and take notice*, aguzar el oído, prestar atención. || *To sit up for s.o.*, quedarse esperando a alguien. || *To sit up with s.o.*, hacer compañía a alguien (to keep s.o. company), cuidar a alguien (to look after). || FIG. *We can't just sit back and let them get away*, no podemos cruzarnos de brazos y dejar que se escapen.

— OBSERV. Pret. & p. p. **sat**.

sit-down strike [—daun'straik] n. Huelga (*f.*) de brazos caídos *or* de brazos cruzados, sentada, *f.*
site [sait] n. Situación, *f.*, emplazamiento, *m.*: *the site of ancient Carthage*, la situación de la antigua Cartago. || Solar, *m.*: *the site for the new factory*, el solar para la nueva fábrica. || Lugar, *m.*, escenario, *m.*, sitio, *m.*: *the exact site of the battle*, el lugar exacto de la batalla. || — *Building site*, obra, *f.* (under construction): *I work on that building site*, trabajo en esa obra; solar, *m.* (for sale, etc.). || *On site*, en el sitio.
site [sait] v. tr. Situar: *where will it be sited?*, ¿dónde estará situado?
sit-in ['sitin] n. Ocupación, *f.* || *To stage a sit-in in a building*, ocupar un edificio.
siting ['saitiŋ] n. Emplazamiento, *m.*, localización, *f.*, situación, *f.*
sitter ['sitə*] n. Modelo, *m.* & *f.* (painter's model). || Persona (*f.*) que cuida a los niños (baby-sitter). || FAM. Gol (*m.*) facilísimo (easy goal). | Blanco (*f.*) facilísimo (easy target): *to miss a sitter*, errar un blanco facilísimo. || Gallina (*f.*) clueca (broody hen).
sitting ['sitiŋ] n. Sentada, *f.*, tirón, *m.*: *she read the novel at one sitting*, leyó la novela de un tirón. || Sesión, *f.*: *a portrait painted in two sittings*, un retrato pintado en dos sesiones. || Sesión, *f.* (of an assembly): *the sitting is open o is called to order*, queda abierta la sesión; *to hold a sitting*, celebrar [una] sesión. || Servicio, *m.* (in a restaurant). || Asiento (*m.*) reservado (in a church). || Incubación, *f.* (brooding of a hen). || Nidada, *f.* (of eggs). || — *Final sitting*, sesión de clausura. || *Opening sitting*, sesión de apertura. || *To resume a sitting*, reanudar la sesión.
— Adj. Sentado, da. || — FIG. FAM. *Sitting duck*, blanco facilísimo. || *Sitting hen*, gallina clueca.
sitting room [—rum] n. Cuarto (*m.*) de estar, sala (*f.*) de estar.
situate ['sitjueit] v. tr. Situar [*Amer.*, ubicar].
situated [—id] adj. Situado, da: *to be well situated*, estar bien situado.
situation [ˌsitju'eiʃən] n. Situación, *f.* [*Amer.*, ubicación, *f.*] (location). || Situación, *f.*: *an embarrassing situation*, una situación embarazosa. || Colocación, *f.* (paid occupation). || — *Situations vacant*, ofertas (*f.*) de trabajo. || *Situations wanted*, solicitudes (*f.*) de trabajo. || *To save the situation*, salvar la situación.
sitz bath ['sitsbɑːθ] n. Baño (*m.*) de asiento.
six [siks] adj. Seis. || — *Six hundred*, seiscientos, tas. || *Six hundredth*, sexcentésimo, ma.
— N. Seis, *m.* (number, card, figure). || SP. Equipo (*m.*) de seis (team). || — *Half past six*, las seis y media. || *He is six*, tiene seis años. || *He is six today*, cumple seis años hoy. || FIG. *It's six of one and half a dozen of the other*, olivo y aceituno todo es uno. || *Six o'clock*, las seis. || *To be at sixes and sevens*, estar en desorden (to be in disorder), estar reñidos (at loggerheads).
sixfold [—fəuld] adj. Séxtuplo, pla.
— Adv. Seis veces.
sixpence [—pəns] n. Seis peniques, *m. pl.* (value). || Moneda (*f.*) de seis peniques (coin).
sixpenny [—pəni] adj. De seis peniques. || FIG. De tres al cuarto (cheap).
six-shooter [—'ʃuːtə*] n. Revólver (*m.*) de seis tiros.
sixteen ['siks'tiːn] adj. Dieciséis, diez y seis.
— N. Dieciséis, *m.*, diez y seis, *m.*
sixteenmo [siks'tiːnməu] n. Libro (*m.*) en dieciseisavo (book).
sixteenth ['sikst'tiːnθ] adj. Decimosexto, ta (in a series). || Dieciseisavo, va (one of sixteen parts).
— N. Decimosexto, ta. || Dieciséis, diez y seis: *John XVI* (*the sixteenth*), Juan XVI [dieciséis]. || Dieciseisavo, *m.* (one of sixteen equal parts). || — *On the sixteenth of May*, el día dieciséis de mayo. || U. S. MUS. *Sixteenth note*, semicorchea, *f.*
sixth [siksθ] adj. Sexto, ta.
— N. Sexto, ta (of a series): *John VI* (*the sixth*), Juan VI [sexto]. || MUS. Sexta, *f.* || Seis, *m.* (in dates). || *On the sixth of July*, el [día] seis de julio.
sixthly [—li] adv. En sexto lugar.
sixtieth ['sikstiiθ] adj. Sexagésimo, ma (in a series). || Sexagésimo, ma; sesentavo, va (being one of sixty equal parts).
— N. Sexagésima parte, *f.*, sesentavo, *m.* (one of sixty equal parts). || Sexagésimo, ma (of a series).
Sixtus ['sikstəs] pr. n. Sixto, *m.*
sixty ['siksti] adj. Sesenta.
— N. Sesenta, *m.* || *The sixties*, los años sesenta.
sixty-fourth note [—fɔːθnəut] n. U. S. MUS. Semifusa, *f.*
sizable ['saizəbl] adj. Grande: *a sizable majority*, una gran mayoría. || Considerable, importante (quantity).
sizar ['saizə*] n. Becario, ria.
size [saiz] n. Tamaño, *m.*: *it is about the size of a football*, tiene aproximadamente el tamaño de un balón de fútbol; *medium size*, tamaño mediano; *life size*, tamaño natural. || Talla, *f.*, estatura, *f.* (of a person). || Número, *m.* (of shoes, gloves). || Talla, *f.* (of garments): *what is your size?*, ¿cuál es su talla? || Formato, *m.*, tamaño, *m.* (of a book). || FIG. Talla, *f.* (capacity): *it is not a job for a man of his size*, no es un trabajo para un hombre de su talla. | Magnitud, *f.* (magnitude). | Alcance, *m.* (scope). || Apresto, *m.*, cola, *f.* (for paper, textile, etc.). || Calibre, *m.* (of a cartridge). || — *A bump the size of an egg*, un bulto del tamaño de un huevo. || *Of a size*, igual, del mismo tamaño. || FAM. *That's about the size of it*, es más o menos eso. || *This is a size too small*, esta talla me está un poco pequeña. || FIG. *To be quite a size*, ser muy grande. | *To cut s.o. down to size*, bajarle los humos a alguien, ponerle en su sitio a alguien. || *To cut sth. to size*, cortar algo del tamaño que se necesita. || *To take the size of*, medir. || *What size collar do you take?*, ¿qué cuello tiene? || *What size shoes do you take?*, ¿qué número calza usted?
size [saiz] v. tr. Clasificar según el tamaño (to arrange according to size). || Calibrar (to gauge). || Aprestar (paper, textiles, etc.). || *To size up*, evaluar (to estimate), medir con la vista, evaluar el tamaño de (to estimate the size of), juzgar (the character or qualities of): *it's difficult to size him up*, es difícil juzgarle; comparar (to compare).
sizeable [—əbl] adj. See SIZABLE.
sizing [—iŋ] n. Apresto, *m.*
sizzle ['sizl] n. Chisporroteo, *m.* (sound).
sizzle ['sizl] v. intr. Chisporrotear.
sizzling [—iŋ] adj. Muy caliente (very hot). || Candente (issue).
— N. Chisporroteo, *m.* (sizzle).
skate [skeit] n. Patín, *m.* (ice or roller skate). || Raya, *f.* (fish). || FAM. Matalón, *m.*, rocín, *m.* (old horse). | Desgraciado, *m.* (despicable person).
skate [skeit] v. intr. Patinar. || FIG. *To skate on thin ice*, pisar un terreno peligroso.
skater [—ə*] n. Patinador, ra.
skating [—iŋ] n. Patinaje, *m.*: *ice skating*, patinaje sobre hielo; *roller skating*, patinaje sobre ruedas.
skating rink [—iŋriŋk] n. Pista (*f.*) de patinaje.
skedaddle [ski'dædl] n. FAM. Huida, *f.*

skedaddle [skiˈdædl] v. intr. FAM. Salir pitando.
skeet [ski:t] n. U. S. Tiro (*m.*) al plato.
skein [skein] n. Madeja, *f.*, ovillo, *m.* (of thread, wool, silk, etc.). || Bandada, *f.* (of birds). || FIG. Enredo, *m.*, maraña, *f.*
skeletal [ˈskelətəl] adj. Esquelético, ca.
skeleton [ˈskelitn] n. ANAT. Esqueleto, *m.* || TECH. Armazón, *f.*, armadura, *f.* (of a building). || FIG. Estructura, *f.*: *the skeleton of the organization*, la estructura de la organización. | Mínimo, *m.*: *to reduce sth. to a skeleton*, reducir algo al mínimo. | Esqueleto, *m.* (thin person). | Esquema, *m.*, bosquejo, *m.* (outline). || — FIG. *Skeleton at the feast*, aguafiestas, *m. inv.* | *Skeleton in the cupboard* o *in the closet*, vergüenza (*f.*) de la familia, secreto (*m.*) de familia. || *Skeleton key*, llave (*f.*) maestra (master key), ganzúa, *f.* (for picking locks). || FIG. *To work with a skeleton team*, trabajar con un equipo muy reducido.
skeletonize [skelitnaiz] v. tr. Reducir al mínimo (to reduce greatly). || Esbozar, bosquejar (to outline).
skene [ski:n] n. Puñal, *m.*, daga, *f.*
skep [skep] n. Cesta, *f.* (basket, basketful). || Colmena (*f.*) de paja (straw beehive).
skeptic [—tik] adj./n. U. S. Escéptico, ca.
skeptical [—tikəl] adj. U. S. Escéptico, ca.
skepticism [ˈskeptisizəm] n. U. S. Escepticismo, *m.*
sketch [sketʃ] n. Croquis, *m.*, apunte, *m.* (quick drawing). || Bosquejo, *m.*, esbozo, *m.* (preliminary drawing). || Dibujo, *m.* (drawing). || Descripción, *f.*: *character sketch*, descripción de un personaje. || Esquema, *m.* (outline). || THEATR. Sketch, *m.*, obra (*f.*) corta. || MUS. Pieza (*f.*) corta.
sketch [sketʃ] v. tr. Hacer un croquis de (rough drawing). || Bosquejar, esbozar (preliminary drawing): *to sketch in pencil*, esbozar a lápiz. || Dibujar (to draw). || FIG. *To sketch in the details for s.o.*, resumirle los detalles a alguien.
— V. intr. Dibujar.
sketchbook [—buk] n. Bloc (*m.*) de dibujo (of drawings). || Colección (*f.*) de obras cortas (of literary sketches).
sketcher [—ə*] n. Dibujante, *m.* & *f.*
sketchiness [—inis] n. Superficialidad, *f.*, falta (*f.*) de detalles, imprecisión, *f.*
sketchy [—i] adj. Incompleto, ta (incomplete). || Sin detalles, impreciso, sa; superficial (not detailed). || Vago, ga; impreciso, sa (idea).
skew [skju:] adj. Oblicuo, cua; sesgado, da (not straight). || Asimétrico, ca (lacking symmetry). || ARCH. Esviado, da (wall, arch, etc.).
— N. Oblicuidad, *f.*, sesgo, *m.* || Sesgo, *m.* (in cloth). || Esviaje, *m.* (of wall, arch, etc.).
skew [skju:] v. tr. Sesgar (to cut or set slantingly). || Tergiversar, desvirtuar (to distort).
— V. intr. Torcerse.
skewback [—bæk] n. ARCH. Salmer, *m.*
skewbald [—bɔ:ld] adj. Pío, a (horse).
skewer [—ə*] n. Pincho, *m.*, broqueta, *f.*, brocheta, *f.* (for meat, cooked food, etc.). || Espetón, *m.* (for sardines). || FAM. Espada, *f.* (sword).
skewer [—ə*] v. tr. Ensartar, espetar.
skew-eyed [—aid] adj. Bizco, ca.
skewness [—nis] n. Oblicuidad, *f.* (obliquity). || Falta (*f.*) de simetría (lack of symmetry).
skewwhiff [—ˈwif] adj./adv. FAM. See ASKEW.
ski [ski:] n. Esquí, *m.* || — *Ski boots*, botas (*f.*) de esquiar. || *Ski jump*, salto (*m.*) con esquís (action), pista (*f.*) de salto (course). || *Ski lift*, telesquí, *m.* || *Ski run* o *slope*, pista (*f.*) de esquí. || *Ski stick* o *ski pole*, bastón, *m.* || *Ski tow*, telesquí, *m.*

— OBSERV. El plural de la palabra inglesa es *ski* o *skis*.

ski [ski:] v. intr. Esquiar.
skid [skid] n. Patinazo, *m.* (of a wheel, car). || Calzo, *m.* (block of wood, metal). || Rampa (*f.*) de descarga (for unloading). || AVIAT. Patín, *m.* || MAR. Varadera, *f.* (for protection). || — FIG. *To be on the skids*, estar *or* andar de capa caída. | *To put the skids under s.o.*, poner chinas en el camino de uno.
skid [skid] v. tr. Hacer deslizar [sobre maderos, etc.] (to slide down a ramp). || Poner un calzo a, calzar (to block). || Hacer patinar (a car). || MAR. Poner varaderas a.
— V. intr. Patinar (car, wheel, etc.).
skiddoo [skiˈdu:] v. intr. U. S. FAM. Largarse.
skid row [ˈskidˈrəu] n. U. S. Barrio (*m.*) bajo.
skier [ˈski:ə*] n. Esquiador, ra.
skiff [skif] n. Esquife, *m.*
skiing [ˈski:iŋ] n. Esquí, *m.* || *To go skiing*, ir a esquiar.
skilful [ˈskilful] adj. Hábil, diestro, tra.
skilfulness [—nis] n. Habilidad, *f.*, destreza, *f.*
skill [skil] n. Habilidad, *f.*, destreza, *f.* (ability to do sth. well). || Técnica, *f.*, arte, *f.* (particular technique): *a difficult skill to acquire*, una técnica difícil de adquirir. || Oficio, *m.* (trade): *one learns several skills in the army*, se aprenden varios oficios en el ejército. || Experiencia, *f.* (experience).
skilled [—d] adj. Hábil, habilidoso, sa; diestro, tra (having skill). || Cualificado, da; especializado, da: *skilled workman*, obrero cualificado. || Especializado, da: *skilled work*, trabajo especializado. || Experto, ta: *to be skilled in a craft*, ser experto en un arte.
skillet [ˈskilət] n. Cacerola, *f.* [con patas y mango largo]. || U. S. Sartén, *f.* (frying pan).
skillful [ˈskilful] adj. U. S. See SKILFUL.
skillfulness [—nis] n. U. S. See SKILFULNESS.
skim [skim] n. Espumado, *m.* (act of skimming). || Leche (*f.*) desnatada (milk). || Capa (*f.*) fina (thin covering). || *Skim milk*, leche desnatada.
skim [skim] v. tr. Espumar (a liquid). || Desnatar (milk). || Hacer cabrillas con (a stone). || Rozar (a surface): *to skim the ground*, rozar el suelo. || FIG. Echar una ojeada a: *to skim the headlines*, echar una ojeada a los títulos. | Tocar, tratar superficialmente (a subject).
— V. intr. Pasar rozando (to go smoothly over): *to skim along at treetop height*, pasar rozando los árboles. || U. S. Cubrirse con una capa fina (to become coated). || — AVIAT. *To skim along the ground, the water*, volar a ras de tierra, a ras del agua, volar rozando el suelo, el agua. || *To skim over*, pasar rozando (a surface), volar rozando, volar a ras de (an aeroplane), tocar, tratar superficialmente (a subject). || *To skim through*, hojear (to flick through), echar una ojeada a (to read quickly).
skimmer [—ə*] n. Espumadera, *f.* (for skimming liquids). || Desnatadora, *f.* (for milk).
skimp [skimp] v. tr. Escatimar: *to skimp material in making a curtain*, escatimar tela para hacer una cortina; *to skimp s.o. in money*, escatimarle dinero a alguien. || Chapucear: *to skimp a piece of work*, chapucear un trabajo.
— V. intr. Escatimar los gastos, vivir con estrechez.
skimpily [—ili] adv. Insuficientemente, escasamente. || — *To be skimpily dressed*, ir ligero de ropa. || *To feed s.o. skimpily*, darle poco de comer a alguien.
skimpiness [—inis] n. Insuficiencia, *f.* (insufficiency). || Tacañería, *f.* (stinginess).
skimpy [—i] adj. Escaso, sa (scarce, scanty, poor). || Pequeño, ña (too small). || Mezquino, na (mean). || Tacaño, ña (stingy). || Corto, ta (dress).
skin [skin] n. Piel, *f.* (membrane of body, animal hide). || Cutis, *m.* (of face). || Tez, *f.* (complexion). || Pellejo, *m.*, odre, *m.* (container). || Pellejo, *m.* (of sausage). || Piel, *f.* (of drum). || Piel, *f.* (of fruit). || Cáscara, *f.*, piel, *f.* (of orange, banana). || Nata, *f.* (of boiled milk, custard, etc.). || MAR. AVIAT. Forro, *m.* || — Pl. FAM. Batería, *f. sing.*, tambores, *m.* (drums). || — FIG. *He has a thick skin*, es poco sensible. | *He has a thin skin*, es muy susceptible. | *He is nothing but skin and bone*, está en los huesos, está hecho un esqueleto. | *It's no skin off my back*, esto no me va ni me viene. || *Soaked to the skin*, calado hasta los huesos. || FIG. *To escape by the skin of one's teeth*, escapar *or* librarse por los pelos. || FIG. FAM. *To get under one's skin*, irritarle a uno. | *To have s.o. under one's skin*, tener a alguien en la masa de la sangre. | *To jump out of one's skin*, llevarse un susto tremendo. | *To play the skins*, tocar la batería. | *To save one's skin*, salvar el pellejo. || *To strip to the skin*, desnudarse completamente.
skin [skin] v. tr. Despellejar, desollar: *to skin a rabbit*, despellejar un conejo. || Pelar (fruit, vegetables). || Desollar, arañar (to graze, to scrape): *I skinned my knuckles*, me desollé los nudillos. || Quitarse (clothes). || FIG. FAM. Despojar (to take from): *he skinned me of all I had*, me despojó de todo lo que tenía. || MAR. AVIAT. Proveer de forro. || — *Dark skinned*, de piel morena. || *To skin s.o. alive*, desollar vivo a alguien.
— V. intr. Cubrirse de nata (custard, etc.). || MED. *To skin over*, cicatrizarse.
skin-deep [—ˈdi:p] adj. Superficial: *skin-deep wound*, herida superficial; *skin-deep feelings*, sentimientos superficiales.
skin disease [—diˈzi:z] n. MED. Dermatosis, *f.*, enfermedad (*f.*) de la piel.
skin diving [—ˈdaiviŋ] n. SP. Natación (*f.*) submarina (swimming). | Pesca (*f.*) submarina (fishing).
skin effect [—iˈfekt] n. ELECTR. Efecto (*m.*) superficial.
skinflint [—flint] n. Tacaño, ña; roñoso, sa.
skinful [—ful] n. Odre, *m.*, pellejo, *m.* || FAM. *He's got a good skinful*, está como una cuba.
skin game [—geim] n. FAM. Estafa, *f.*, timo, *m.*
skin grafting [—ˈgrɑ:ftiŋ] n. Injerto (*m.*) de piel.
skink [skiŋk] n. Escinco, *m.* (lizard).
skinner [ˈskinə*] n. Desollador, ra (s.o. who strips skin). || FAM. Estafador, ra (swindler). || Peletero, *m.* (furrier).
skinniness [ˈskininis] n. Delgadez, *f.*, flacura, *f.*
skinny [ˈskini] adj. Flaco, ca; enjuto, ta (person). || Trasijado, da; flaco, ca (horse).
skin test [ˈskintest] n. MED. Cutirreacción, *f.*, dermorreacción, *f.*
skintight [ˈskintait] adj. Muy ajustado, da; muy ceñido, da.
skip [skip] n. Salto, *m.*, brinco, *m.* (jump). || Rebote, *m.* (rebound). || FIG. Salto, *m.*, omisión, *f.* || Capitán, ana (in games). || MIN. Montacargas, *m. inv.* (lift).
skip [skip] v. tr. Saltarse: *to skip a year at school*, saltarse un curso en el colegio. || Saltarse, saltar, omitir: *to skip a passage in a book*, saltarse un párrafo en un libro. || Hacer rebotar (to skim a stone, etc.). || FAM. Fumarse: *to skip a lecture*, fumarse una clase. || *Skip it!*, ¡déjalo!
— V. intr. Ir dando saltos: *to skip along the street*, ir

dando saltos por la calle. || Saltar, brincar (to jump). || Saltar (over a skipping rope, fence, etc.). || Saltar a la comba: *the girls were in the garden skipping*, las niñas estaban saltando a la comba en el jardín. || Saltar, pasar: *to skip to another subject*, saltar a otro tema. || Rebotar (to rebound). || U. S. FAM. Largarse (to leave hurriedly). || FIG. *To skip over*, saltar, saltarse.

skip-bomb [ˈskip,bɔm] v. tr. MIL. Bombardear de rebote.

skipper [—ə*] n. Saltador, ra. || Capitán, *m.*, patrón, *m.* (of a small vessel). || AVIAT. Capitán, *m.* || SP. FAM. Capitán, ana.

skipper [—ə*] v. tr. Capitanear (games).

skipping rope [—iŋrəup] n. Comba, *f.*, saltador, *m.*

skirl [skə:l] n. Sonido (*m.*) agudo. || *The skirl of the pipes*, el sonido de las gaitas.

skirl [skə:l] v. intr. Tener un sonido agudo. || Sonar: *the bagpipes skirl*, suenan las gaitas.

skirmish [ˈskə:miʃ] n. MIL. Escaramuza, *f.* || Pelea, *f.* (fight). || Agarrada, *f.* (slight conflict).

skirmish [ˈskə:miʃ] v. intr. MIL. Escaramuzar, escaramucear, tener una escaramuza *or* escaramuzas. || Pelear (to fight).

skirmisher [—ə*] n. MIL. Tirador, *m.*

skirr [skə:] n. Aleteo, *m.*

skirr [skə:] v. intr. Aletear.

skirt [skə:t] n. Falda, *f.*: *bell, straight skirt*, falda acampanada, estrecha. || Faldones, *m. pl.* (of a coat). || FAM. Gachí, *f.* (girl, woman). || — Pl. Afueras, *f.* (of a city). || *Divided* o *split skirt*, falda pantalón.

skirt [skə:t] v. tr./intr. Rodear (to surround). || Rodear, dar la vuelta a (a hill, a mountain, etc.). || Bordear (a lake, a coast).

skirting [—iŋ] n. Borde, *m.* (edge). || Zócalo, *m.*, cenefa, *f.* (of a wall).

skirting board [—iŋbɔ:d] n. Zócalo, *m.*, cenefa, *f.*

skit [skit] n. Relato (*m.*) corto y satírico (story). || THEATR. Sketch (*m.*) satírico. || Escarnio, *m.*, burla, *f.* (gibe).

skitter [—ə*] v. intr. Pasar rozando el agua (to skim the surface of water).

skittish [—iʃ] adj. Frívolo, la (fickle). || Caprichoso, sa (whimsical). || Asustadizo, za (horse).

skittishness [—iʃnis] n. Frivolidad, *f.* (fickleness). || Inconstancia, *f.*

skittle [—l] n. Bolo, *m.* (pin, in bowling). || — Pl. Juego (*m. sing.*) de bolos, bolos, *m.* (game): *to play skittles*, jugar a los bolos. || — FIG. *It's not all beer and skittles*, see BEER. || *Skittle alley*, bolera, *f.*

skive [skaiv] v. tr. Chiflar (to pare leather). || Cortar en capas finas (rubber). || Pulir (a diamond). || FAM. Fumarse: *to skive a lecture*, fumarse una clase. | Remolonear (to slack).

skiver [—ə*] n. Chifla, *f.* (knife for cutting leather). || Cuero (*m.*) fino y blando [para encuadernar, etc.] (leather).

skivvy [ˈskivi] n. Criada, *f.* (maid). || — Pl. FAM. Ropa (*f. sing.*) interior (underwear).

skulduggery [skʌlˈdʌgəri] n. Trampas, *f. pl.*, engaños, *m. pl.* (trickery).

skulk [skʌlk] n. FAM. Remolón, ona.

skulk [skʌlk] v. intr. Esconderse (to hide). || FAM. Escurrir el bulto, zafarse.

skull [skʌl] n. Calavera, *f.* (lay term). || ANAT. Cráneo, *m.* (scientific term): *to break one's skull*, romperse el cráneo. || FAM. Caletre, *m.* (mind). || *Skull and crossbones*, calavera (danger sign, pirate flag).

skullcap [—kæp] n. Solideo, *m.* (of a priest). || Gorro, *m.* (of Jews).

skunk [skʌŋk] n. Mofeta, *f.* (mammal). || FAM. Canalla, *m.*

skunk [skʌŋk] v. tr. FAM. Dar una paliza a (to defeat).

sky [skai] n. Cielo, *m.* || Clima, *m.* (weather). || — Pl. Cielo, *m. sing.*: *a week of blue skies*, una semana con cielo azul. || — *Sky blue*, azul (*m.*) celeste. || FIG. *Out of a clear blue sky*, de repente. | *To praise to the skies*, poner por las nubes. | *Under the open sky*, al aire libre.

sky [skai] v. tr. FAM. Bombear (a ball). || Colgar muy alto (to hang up high).

sky-blue [—ˈblu:] adj. Azul celeste, celeste.

sky-high [—ˈhai] adj. Muy alto, ta. || — *Prices are sky-high*, los precios están por las nubes. || *Sky-high prices*, precios astronómicos.

— Adv. Hasta las nubes, por las nubes (very high). || — *To blow sky-high*, destruir completamente (to blow up), echar por tierra (arguments). || *To praise s.o. sky-high*, poner a alguien por las nubes.

skyjack [—,dʒæk] v. tr. Secuestrar en vuelo (an aircraft).

skylark [—lɑ:k] n. Alondra, *f.* (bird).

skylark [—lɑ:k] v. intr. Hacer travesuras (to be mischievous). || Divertirse, estar de juerga (to have fun). || — *Stop skylarking about!*, ¡déjate de tonterías! || *To skylark about*, hacer el tonto.

skylight [—lait] n. Claraboya, *f.*, tragaluz, *m.* (window in a roof). || Luz (*f.*) cenital.

skyline [—lain] n. Horizonte, *m.* (horizon). || Perfil, *m.*, silueta, *f.* (of a building). || Contorno, *m.*, perfil, *m.* (of a city).

sky pilot [—ˈpailət] n. FAM. Sacerdote, *m.* (priest). | Capellán, *m.* (chaplain).

skyrocket [—,rɔkit] n. Cohete, *m.* (fireworks).

skyrocket [—,rɔkit] v. intr. Subir como un cohete (to shoot up). || Subir vertiginosamente (prices).

skyscraper [—,skreipə*] n. Rascacielos, *m. inv.*

skyward [—wəd] adj./adv. Hacia el cielo.

skywards [—wədz] adv. Hacia el cielo.

sky wave [—weiv] n. Onda (*f.*) ionosférica.

skyway [—,wei] n. Ruta (*f.*) aérea.

skywriting [—,raitiŋ] n. Publicidad (*f.*) aérea [formando palabras en el cielo con humo].

slab [slæb] n. Trozo, *m.* (piece). || Porción, *f.* (of cake, etc.). || Losa, *f.* (of stone, marble). || Plancha, *f.*, lámina, *f.* (of metal). || Tableta, *f.* (of chocolate). || Rodaja, *f.* (of fish). || Tajada, *f.* (of meat). || Costero, *m.* (of a log). || Bloque, *m.* (block): *a slab of ice*, un bloque de hielo.

slab [slæb] v. tr. Cortar los costeros de (to cut slabs from wood). || Aplicar una capa espesa de: *to slab paint on canvas*, aplicar una capa espesa de pintura al lienzo. || Enlosar (to pave with slabs).

slabber [—ə*] n. See SLOBBER.

slabber [—ə*] v. tr./intr. See SLOBBER.

slack [slæk] adj. Flojo, ja: *a slack rope*, una cuerda floja; *a slack screw*, un tornillo flojo. || Descuidado, da; negligente (careless): *a slack workman*, un trabajador negligente. || Tranquilo, la; descansado, da: *a slack job*, un trabajo tranquilo. || Vago, ga; perezoso, sa (lazy). || Bajo, ja: *the slack season*, la temporada baja. || De poco trabajo, de poca actividad: *to go through a slack period*, atravesar un período de poca actividad. || Quieto, ta; tranquilo, la: *slack sea*, mar quieta. || — *Business is slack*, hay poco trabajo. || *Slack demand*, poca demanda. || *Slack hours*, horas (*f. pl.*) de poca actividad. || *Slack lime*, cal muerta. || *Slack water*, aguas muertas. || *The market is slack*, el mercado está flojo, hay poca actividad en el mercado. || *They are very slack about whom they let in*, son muy tolerantes con respecto a quienes dejan entrar.

— N. Período (*m.*) de poca actividad (dull period). || Baja temporada, *f.* (season). || Aguas (*f. pl.*) muertas (slack water). || Cisco, *m.* (coal particles). || Parte (*f.*) floja (of a rope). || — Pl. Pantalones, *m.* (trousers). || — *There is a lot of slack in the rope*, la cuerda está muy floja. || *To take up the slack in a rope*, tensar una cuerda.

slack [slæk] v. tr. Aflojar (rope, screw). || Aminorar (pace). || Disminuir (activity). || Apagar (lime). || *To slack off*, disminuir.

— V. intr. Aflojarse (rope, etc.). || Apagarse (lime). || Aflojar: *he has slacked in his work*, ha aflojado en su trabajo. || FAM. Gandulear, holgazanear (to be lazy). || — *To slack off*, disminuir. || *To slack up*, ir más despacio, reducir la velocidad.

slacken [—ən] v. tr. Disminuir, reducir (to lessen): *the driver slackened his speed*, el conductor disminuyó la velocidad; *to slacken the rhythm*, disminuir el ritmo. || Aminorar (one's pace). || Aflojar (rope, effort, etc.). || FIG. *To slacken the reins*, soltar las riendas.

— V. intr. Aflojarse (rope, etc.). || Disminuir (rhythm, speed). || Aflojar (to reduce one's efforts). || Amainar (wind). || *Business is slackening*, los negocios están aflojando.

slacker [—ə*] n. FAM. Gandul, la; holgazán, ana (lazybones). || MIL. Prófugo, *m.*

slackness [—nis] n. Flojedad, *f.* (looseness). || Estancamiento, *m.* (of business). || Inactividad, *f.* (inactivity). || Relajamiento, *m.*, relajación, *f.* (of discipline). || Pereza, *f.*, gandulería, *f.* (laziness). || Descuido, *m.*, negligencia, *f.* (carelessness).

slag [slæg] n. Escoria, *f.* (from metals and mines). || Escoria, *f.*, lava, *f.* (from a volcano). || *Slag heap*, escorial, *m.*

slag [slæg] v. intr. Escorificar.

slagging [—iŋ] n. Escorificación, *f.*

slain [slein] p. p. See SLAY.

slake [sleik] v. tr. Apagar, aplacar (thirst). || Satisfacer, saciar (passions). || Apagar (lime). || *Slaked lime*, cal apagada *or* muerta.

slakeless [—lis] adj. FIG. Insaciable.

slalom [ˈsleiləm] n. SP. Slalom, *m.*, prueba (*f.*) de habilidad (in skiing).

slam [slæm] n. Portazo, *m.* (of a door). || Golpe, *m.* (blow). || FAM. Vapuleo, *m.* (harsh criticism). || Slam, *m.* (in card games): *grand slam*, gran slam.

slam [slæm] v. tr. Cerrar de un golpe (to shut noisily). || Hacer golpear: *the wind slammed the shutters against the window*, el viento hacía golpear las persianas contra la ventana. || FAM. Disparar: *to slam a ball*, disparar una pelota. | Vapulear (to criticize harshly): *the critics slammed the play*, los críticos vapulearon la obra. || — SP. *To slam in a goal*, marcar un gol. || *To slam sth. down on a table*, poner algo violentamente en la mesa. || *To slam sth. down on the ground*, tirar algo al suelo. || *To slam the brakes on*, dar un frenazo. || *To slam the door*, dar un portazo. || *To slam the door in s.o.'s face*, dar con la puerta en las narices de alguien. || FIG. *To slam the door on*, cerrar la puerta a. || SP. FAM. *To slam the opposing team*, darle una paliza al equipo contrario. || U. S. *To slam through*, hacer aprobar (a proposal).

— V. intr. Cerrarse de golpe (to shut violently). || — *I was kept awake all night by slamming doors*, no dormí en toda la noche a causa de los portazos que se oían.

|| *She slammed down the corridor*, se fue corriendo por el pasillo.

slander [ˈslɑ:ndə*] n. Calumnia, *f.* (false statement). || JUR. Difamación, *f.* [oral]: *to sue s.o. for slander*, demandar a alguien por difamación.

slander [ˈslɑ:ndə*] v. tr. Calumniar. || JUR. Difamar.

slanderer [—rə*] n. Calumniador, ra. || JUR. Difamador, ra.

slanderous [—rəs] adj. Calumnioso, sa. || JUR. Difamatorio, ria.

slang [slæŋ] n. Germanía, *f.*, argot, *m.* (of criminals, etc.). || Jerga, *f.* (jargon): *student's slang*, jerga estudiantil. || Argot, *m.* (colloquial language).
— Adj. De germanía. || De jerga. | De argot.

slang [slæŋ] v. tr. FAM. Poner verde, insultar.

slanginess [—inis] n. Vulgaridad, *f.* (of language).

slangy [—i] adj. Vulgar.

slant [slɑ:nt] n. Inclinación, *f.*: *a slant of ten degrees*, una inclinación de diez grados. || Pendiente, *f.*, declive, *m.* (slope). || FIG. Giro, *m.*: *the affair took on a new slant*, el asunto tomó un nuevo giro. | Punto (*m.*) de vista, parecer, *m.* (opinion). || — *To be on a slant* o *on the slant*, estar inclinado: *the ground is on a slant*, el terreno está inclinado; estar sesgado, estar al bies (a picture, etc.).
— Adj. Inclinado, da (inclined). || *Slant eyes*, ojos achinados.

slant [slɑ:nt] v. intr. Estar inclinado: *the table slants*, la mesa está inclinada.
— V. tr. Inclinar (to incline). || Poner al sesgo *or* al bies, sesgar (to put out of line). || FIG. Enfocar de modo parcial (a problem, etc.).

slanting [—iŋ] adj. Inclinado, da (roof, handwriting, etc.). || Que cae en sentido oblicuo (rain, snow). || Al sesgo, sesgado, da (not straight). || Oblicuo, cua (oblique). || *Slanting eyes*, ojos achinados.

slantingly [—iŋli] or **slantways** [—weiz] or **slantwise** [—waiz] adv. Oblicuamente.

slap [slæp] n. Bofetada, *f.* (blow on the face). || Palmada, *f.* (on thigh, back, etc.). || Azote, *m.* (on child's bottom). || — FIG. *A slap in the face*, un bofetón, una bofetada, un feo, una afrenta, un desaire (affront). | *To give s.o. a slap on the back*, dar una palmada en la espalda a alguien (in greeting, etc.), dar a alguien la enhorabuena (to congratulate s.o.). || FAM. *To have a slap at*, intentar [hacer] (to try sth.), dar un bofetón a (to attack in criticism).
— Adv. De lleno: *he ran slap into the lamppost*, dio de lleno contra el farol. || Justo: *slap in the middle of the pond*, justo en medio de la charca.

slap [slæp] v. tr. Abofetear (to hit). || Dar una palmada: *to slap s.o. on the back*, dar a alguien una palmada en la espalda. || Poner violentamente, tirar: *he slapped the book on the table*, tiró el libro en la mesa. || — *To slap a new wing on a building*, ponerle un anexo a un edificio. || *To slap paint on a wall*, pintar una pared a brochazos. || *To slap s.o.'s face* o *to slap s.o. on the face*, darle una bofetada *or* un tortazo a alguien.
— V. intr. Romper: *the waves slapped against the boat*, las olas rompían contra el barco.

slap-bang [—ˈbæŋ] adv. De sopetón, de golpe y porrazo (with suddenness). || Violentamente (violently).

slapdash [—dæʃ] adj. Descuidado, da; chapucero, ra.
— Adv. Descuidadamente.

slap-happy [—ˈhæpi] adj. Aturdido, da (dazed). || Inconsciente (carefree).

slapjack [—dʒæk] n. U. S. Torta, *f.* (flapjack).

slapstick [—stik] n. Payasada, *f.*, bufonada, *f.* (farcical comedy).
— Adj. Bufonesco, ca.

slap-up [—ʌp] adj. FAM. Elegante (elegant). | Excelente, de primera categoría (first-rate). || FAM. *Slap-up meal*, comilona, *f.*, banquete, *m.*

slash [slæʃ] n. Cuchillada, *f.*, tajo, *m.* (with a knife). || Cuchillada, *f.* (slit in clothing). || Latigazo, *m.* (with a whip). || Reducción, *f.* (of costs, prices, etc.). || Tala, *f.* (in a forest). || U. S. Pantano, *m.* (bog).

slash [slæʃ] v. tr. Acuchillar (with a knife). || Azotar (with a whip). || Dar un tajo a (with the edge of a sword). || Acuchillar (to put a slit in clothes). || FIG. Poner por los suelos, vapulear (to criticize). | Sacrificar (prices). | Reducir (wages, etc.). | Cortar (a speech). || Talar (trees).
— V. intr. Tirar tajos y estocadas.

slashing [—iŋ] adj. Mordaz, áspero, ra (criticism). || Extraordinario, ria (success).
— N. See SLASH.

slat [slæt] n. Tablilla, *f.* (short, thin piece of wood). || Listón, *m.* (long, thin piece of wood).

slat [slæt] v. tr. Hacer con listones (to lath). || Poner listones a (to furnish with laths). || Tirar (to throw). || Pegar (to beat).
— V. intr. MAR. Gualdrapear (sails).

slate [sleit] n. Pizarra, *f.* (rock, roofing, writing surface). || Color (*m.*) pizarra (colour). || U. S. Lista (*f.*) de candidatos. || — *Slate pencil*, pizarrín, *m.* || *Slate quarry*, pizarral, *m.* || FIG. *To clean the slate* o *to wipe the slate clean*, hacer borrón y cuenta nueva. | *To start with a clean slate*, empezar una nueva vida.
— Adj. De color pizarra (colour). || De pizarra (made of slate).

slate [sleit] v. tr. Empizarrar (to cover with slates). || FIG. Vapulear (to criticize). | Echar una bronca a (to scold). | Castigar (to punish). || U. S. Inscribir (on a list). | Designar (to appoint).

slater [—ə*] n. Pizarrero, *m.*

slating [—iŋ] n. FIG. Vapuleo, *m.* (criticism). | Bronca, *f.* (scolding). | Reprimenda, *f.* (reprimand). || Empizarrado, *m.* (work, material).

slattern [ˈslætə:n] n. Mujer (*f.*) desaseada.

slatternliness [—linis] n. Desaseo, *m.*, dejadez, *f.*

slatternly [—li] adj. Desaseado, da; dejado, da.
— Adv. Desaseadamente.

slaty [ˈsleiti] adj. Pizarroso, sa (like slate). || De color pizarra (slate-coloured).

slaughter [ˈslɔ:tə*] n. Matanza, *f.*, sacrificio, *m.* (of animals). || Matanza, *f.*, degollina, *f.* (massacre). || *The Slaughter of the Innocents*, la Degollación de los Inocentes.

slaughter [ˈslɔ:tə*] v. tr. Matar, sacrificar (animals for food). || Matar brutalmente (to kill brutally). || Exterminar (to kill in large numbers). || FIG. Dar una paliza a (an opponent).

slaughterer [—rə*] n. Jifero, *m.*, matarife, *m.* (of animals). || Asesino, na (of people).

slaughterhouse [—haus] n. Matadero, *m.*

slaughterous [—rəs] adj. Asesino, na; sanguinario, ria.

Slav [slɑ:v] adj./n. Eslavo, va.

slave [sleiv] n. Esclavo, va. || FIG. Esclavo, va: *a slave to work*, un esclavo del trabajo. || *To make a slave of*, esclavizar.

slave [sleiv] v. intr. Trabajar como un negro (*at*, en).

slave driver [—ˌdraivə*] n. Negrero, *m.*

slaveholder [—ˌhəuldə*] n. Negrero, *m.*

slaveholding [—ˌhəuldiŋ] adj. Que posee esclavos.
— N. Posesión (*f.*) de esclavos.

slave labour (U. S. **slave labor**) [—ˌleibə*] n. Trabajo (*m.*) de negros (job). || Esclavos, *m. pl.* (people).

slaver [—ə*] n. Negrero, *m.* (person). || Barco (*m.*) negrero (ship). || *White slaver*, tratante (*m.*) de blancas.

slaver [ˈslævə*] n. Baba, *f.* (dribble). || U. S. Tonterías, *f. pl.* (nonsense).

slaver [—ə*] v. tr. Babosear (to cover with spittle).
— V. intr. Babear.

slavery [—əri] n. Esclavitud, *f.*: *to live in slavery*, vivir en la esclavitud; *slavery is forbidden in most countries*, la esclavitud está prohibida en la mayoría de los paises; *this job is pure slavery*, este trabajo es una esclavitud. || — *To sell s.o. into slavery*, vender a alguien como esclavo. || *White slavery*, trata (*f.*) de blancas.

slave ship [—ʃip] n. Barco (*m.*) negrero.

slave trade [—treid] n. Trata (*f.*) de esclavos. || *White slave trade*, trata de blancas.

slave trader [—ˌtreidə*] n. Negrero, *m.*

slavey [ˈslævi] n. FAM. Criada, *f.* (servant).

Slavic [—k] adj. Eslavo, va.
— N. Eslavo, *m.* (language).

slavish [ˈsleiviʃ] adj. De esclavo (life, etc.). || Servil: *slavish person*, persona servil; *slavish imitation*, imitación servil.

slavishness [—nis] n. Servilismo, *m.*

Slavonic [sləˈvɔnik] adj. Eslavo, va.
— N. Eslavo, *m.* (language).

slaw [slɔ:] n. Ensalada (*f.*) de col.

slay* [slei] v. tr. Matar, asesinar (to kill). || U. S. FAM. Encantar, chiflar (to be immensely pleasing): *he slays me*, me chifla. | Hacer mucha gracia (to be funny).

— OBSERV. Pret. **slew**; p. p. **slain**.

slayer [—ə*] n. Asesino, *m.*

sleaziness [ˈsli:zinis] n. Mala calidad, *f.* (poor quality). || Sordidez, *f.* (shabbiness).

sleazy [ˈsli:zi] adj. De mala calidad (of poor quality). || Sórdido, da (shabby): *a sleazy joint*, un lugar sórdido.

sled [sled] n. Trineo, *m.*

sled [sled] v. tr. Transportar *or* llevar en trineo.
— V. intr. Ir en trineo.

sledding [—iŋ] n. Transporte (*m.*) por trineo. || FIG. *It was hard sledding*, fue muy difícil.

sledge [sledʒ] n. Trineo, *m.* (sled). || TECH. Almádana, *f.*, almádena, *f.* (sledgehammer).

sledge [sledʒ] v. tr. Transportar *or* llevar en trineo.
— V. intr. Ir en trineo (to sled). || U. S. Golpear con la almádena (to use a sledgehammer).

sledgehammer [—ˌhæmə*] n. Almádana, *f.*, almádena, *f.* (heavy hammer).

sledgehammer [—ˌhæmə*] v. tr./intr. Golpear con la almádena.

sleek [sli:k] adj. Liso y brillante, lustroso, sa (smooth and shiny). || Impecable: *a sleek appearance*, un aspecto impecable. || Elegante (elegant). || FAM. Meloso, sa; empalagoso, sa (manners).

sleek [sli:k] v. tr. Alisar.

sleekness [—nis] n. Lustre, *m.*, brillo, *m.* || Elegancia, *f.* || FAM. Melosidad, *f.* (of manners).

sleep [sli:p] n. Sueño, *m.*: *deep sleep*, sueño profundo; *lack of sleep*, falta de sueño. || — FIG. *Eternal sleep*, sueño eterno. || *Hypnotic sleep*, sueño hipnótico. || FIG. *Last sleep*, ultimo sueño (death). || *Not to have a wink of sleep all night*, no pegar ojo en toda la noche. || FIG. *To abandon o.s. to sleep*, entregarse al sueño. || *To cry o.s. to sleep*, llorar hasta dormirse. || *To drop off to sleep*, quedarse dormido. || *To fall into a deep sleep*, caer en un sueño profundo. || *To get some sleep*, dormir un poco. || *To get to sleep*, conciliar el sueño. ||

To go for an after-dinner sleep, ir a dormir la siesta. || *To go to sleep*, dormirse: *he went to sleep*, se durmió; *my leg has gone to sleep*, la pierna se me ha dormido. || *To have a sleep*, echar un sueñecito. || *To lose sleep*, perder el sueño. || FIG. *To put an animal to sleep*, sacrificar un animal. || *To put* o *to send somebody to sleep*, dormir a alguien. || FIG. *To sleep the sleep of the just*, dormir el sueño de los justos. || *To walk in one's sleep*, ser sonámbulo. || FIG. *To ward off sleep*, espantar el sueño.

sleep* [—sli:p] v. tr. Dormir: *he slept five hours before leaving*, durmió cinco horas antes de marcharse. || Tener cabida para, poder alojar: *this hotel sleeps fifty guests*, este hotel tiene cabida para cincuenta personas. || — *To sleep away*, pasar durmiendo: *he sleeps the hours away*, pasa las horas durmiendo. || FAM. *To sleep it off*, dormir la mona. || *To sleep off*, dormir para que desaparezca (fatigue, headache, etc.).
— V. intr. Dormir: *to sleep like a log*, dormir como un tronco; *he was sleeping soundly* o *deeply*, dormía profundamente. || Pasar la noche, dormir: *we slept at a very good hotel*, pasamos la noche en un hotel muy bueno. || — FAM. *To sleep around*, acostarse con todos. || *To sleep in*, dormir en casa (a domestic servant). || *To sleep on* o *over sth.*, consultar algo con la almohada. || *To sleep out*, dormir fuera. || *To sleep with*, acostarse con.

— OBSERV. Pret. & p. p. **slept**.

sleeper [—ə*] n. Persona (*f.*) que duerme (s.o. who sleeps). || Traviesa, *f.*, durmiente, *m.* (on railway lines). || Coche (*m.*) cama (sleeping car). || U. S. Pelele, *m.* (child's sleeping garment). | Éxito (*m.*) inesperado (success). || *To be a heavy, a light sleeper*, tener el sueño pesado, ligero.

sleepily [—ili] adv. Soñolientamente: *he walked sleepily up the stairs*, subió soñolientamente la escalera. || *She replied sleepily*, contestó soñolienta *or* entre sueños.

sleepiness [—inis] n. Somnolencia, *f.* || *To try to hide one's sleepiness*, intentar disimular el sueño.

sleeping [—iŋ] adj. Durmiente, dormido, da.
— N. Sueño, *m.*

sleeping bag [—iŋbæg] n. Saco (*m.*) de dormir.

Sleeping Beauty [—iŋ'bju:ti] n. Bella (*f.*) durmiente del bosque.

sleeping car [—iŋkɑ:*] n. Coche (*m.*) cama.

sleeping partner [—iŋ'pɑ:tnə*] n. COMM. Socio (*m.*) comanditario.

sleeping pill [—iŋpil] n. Somnífero, *m.*

sleeping sickness [—iŋ,siknis] n. MED. Enfermedad (*f.*) del sueño, tripanosomiasis, *f.* (transmitted by the tsetse fly). | Encefalitis (*f.*) letárgica (inflammation of the brain).

sleepless [—lis] adj. En blanco (with no sleep): *a sleepless night*, una noche en blanco. || Insomne, desvelado, da (insomnious). || Incansable (unceasingly active).

sleeplessness [—lisnis] n. Insomnio, *m.*

sleepwalker [—,wɔ:kə*] n. Sonámbulo, la; somnámbulo, la.

sleepwalking [—,wɔ:kiŋ] n. Sonambulismo, *m.*, somnambulismo, *m.*

sleepy [—i] adj. Soñoliento, ta (tired): *sleepy eyes*, ojos soñolientos. || FIG. Dormido, da: *a sleepy village*, un pueblo dormido. | Soporífero, ra: *a sleepy atmosphere*, un ambiente soporífero. | Letárgico, ca (lethargic). | Pasado, da (fruit). || — *Sleepy face*, cara dormida. || *To be awfully sleepy*, caerse de sueño. || *To be sleepy*, tener sueño. || *To make sleepy*, dar sueño.

sleepyhead [—ihed] n. Dormilón, ona.

sleepy sickness [—i,siknis] n. MED. Encefalitis (*f.*) letárgica.

sleet [sli:t] n. Aguanieve, *f.* (snow mixed with rain).

sleet [sli:t] v. intr. Cellisquear, caer aguanieve (to rain snow and water).

sleety [—i] adj. Con aguanieve. || Cubierto de aguanieve *or* de hielo (roads, etc.).

sleeve [sli:v] n. Manga, *f.* (of a garment). || Funda, *f.* (of record). || TECH. Manguito, *m.* (of shaft, etc.). | Camisa, *f.* (of cylinder). || — FIG. *To have sth. up one's sleeve*, tener algo en reserva, traer algo en la manga. | *To laugh up one's sleeve*, reírse para su capote. || *To roll up one's sleeves*, arremangarse.

sleeved [—d] adj. Con mangas. || — *Long-sleeved*, de manga larga. || *Short-sleeved*, de manga corta.

sleeveless [—lis] adj. Sin mangas.

sleigh [slei] n. Trineo, *m.* (sledge).

sleigh [slei] v. intr. Ir en trineo.

sleight [slait] n. Habilidad, *f.*, destreza, *f.* (skill). || FIG. Artimañas, *f. pl.* (trickery).

sleight of hand ['slaitəv'hænd] n. Prestidigitación, *f.*, juego (*m.*) de manos (of conjurers).

slender ['slendə*] adj. Delgado, da; fino na (thin). || Esbelto, ta (thin and graceful). || FIG. Ligero, ra: *slender hopes*, ligeras esperanzas; *slender chance*, ligera posibilidad. | Bajo, ja: *slender income*, sueldo bajo. | Escaso, sa (resources). | Malo, la; pobre (excuse).

slenderize ['slendəraiz] v. tr. Adelgazar.

slenderness ['slendənis] n. Delgadez, *f.* (thinness). || Esbeltez, *f.* (gracefulness). || FIG. Ligereza, *f.* (slightness). | Escasez, *f.* (scarcity).

slept [slept] pret. & p. p. See SLEEP.

sleuth [slu:θ] n. Detective, *m.* (detective).

sleuth [slu:θ] v. intr. Hacer una investigación, investigar. || Hacer de detective.

sleuthhound [—'haund] n. Sabueso, *m.* (dog, man).

slew [slu:] n. Giro, *m.* (turn). || U. S. FAM. Gran cantidad, *f.* (a lot). || U. S. Lodazal, *m.*, cenagal, *m.* (slough).

slew [slu:] pret. See SLAY.

slew [slu:] v. tr. Hacer girar a (to turn round).
— V. intr. Girar (to turn). || MAR. Virar.

slice [slais] n. Rebanada, *f.* (of bread). || Lonja, *f.*, loncha, *f.* (of ham). || Tajada, *f.* (of meat). || Rodaja, *f.*, raja, *f.* (of salami). || Raja, *f.* (of fish, of cheese). || Raja, *f.*, tajada, *f.* (of melon). || Pala, *f.*, paleta, *f.* (for serving fish). || FIG. Parte, *f.* (part): *a large slice of my income*, una gran parte de mis ingresos. || FAM. Tajada, *f.* (benefit). || SP. Golpe (*m.*) que da efecto a la pelota *or* al balón.

slice [slais] v. tr. Partir en rodajas [*or* rajas, rebanadas, lonjas, etc.] (to cut into slices). || Cortar (to cut). || SP. Dar efecto a (a ball). | Cortar (a ball in tennis). || *To slice off*, cortar.
— V. intr. Dar efecto a la pelota.

slicer [—ə*] n. Máquina (*f.*) de cortar.

slick [slik] adj. Diestro, tra; hábil (skilful). || Astuto, ta (astute). || Liso, sa (hair). || Elegante (elegant). || U. S. Resbaladizo, za (slippery).
— Adv. Hábilmente (skilfully). || Rápidamente (quickly).
— N. U. S. Superficie (*f.*) resbaladiza (smooth surface). | Capa (*f.*) de aceite (oil slick). | Herramienta (*f.*) para alisar (tool for smoothing).

slick [slik] v. tr. Alisar: *to slick one's hair*, alisarse el pelo. || Acicalar (to spruce up). || *To slick o.s. up*, acicalarse.

slicker [—ə*] n. U. S. FAM. Estafador, ra (swindler). | Impermeable, *m.* (raincoat).

slid [slid] pret. & p. p. See SLIDE.

slide [slaid] n. Deslizamiento, *m.*, desliz, *m.* (the act of sliding). || Superficie (*f.*) resbaladiza (smooth surface). || Tobogán, *m.* (for children, parcels, etc.). || Resbaladero, *m.* (for logs). || Tapa (*f.*) corrediza (lid). || Cursor, *m.* (of mathematical instrument). || PHOT. Diapositiva, *f.*, transparencia, *f.*: *colour slide*, diapositiva en color. || Portaobjeto, *m.* (of a microscope). || Desprendimiento, *m.* (of rock, earth, etc.). || Pasador, *m.* (for hair). || FIG. Baja, *f.* (drop). || MUS. Vara (*f.*) corredera (of an instrument).

slide* [slaid] v. tr. Hacer resbalar. || Deslizar: *to slide a letter under the door, into s.o.'s hand*, deslizar una carta por debajo de la puerta, en la mano de alguien. || Correr: *slide your chair nearer*, corre la silla más cerca. || Arrastrar (to drag). || Añadir: *he slid a clause into the contract*, añadió una cláusula al contrato. || — *Slide it down* o *over to me*, échamelo. || *To slide a box across to s.o.*, mandar una caja a alguien de un empujón. || *To slide a glance at s.o.*, mirar a alguien de reojo. || *To slide a ring on s.o.'s finger*, ponerle a alguien un anillo en el dedo.
— V. intr. Resbalar (to slip): *he slid over and broke an arm*, resbaló y se rompió un brazo. || Deslizarse: *children sliding in the snow*, niños deslizándose por la nieve. || — *The rain slid down the windows*, la lluvia corría por las ventanas. || FIG. *To let things slide*, desatenderse de lo que pasa, dejar que ruede la bola. | *To slide by* o *away*, pasar (time, procession). || *To slide down*, bajar deslizándose [por]. || *To slide into*, introducirse en (a place), caer imperceptiblemente en (a habit). || FIG. *To slide over*, pasar por alto (a subject). | *To slide up to s.o.*, acercarse furtivamente a alguien.

— OBSERV. Pret. & p. p. **slid**.

slide fastener [—'fɑ:snə*] n. U. S. Cremallera, *f.* (zip fastener).

slider [—ə*] n. Guía, *f.*, cursor, *m.*, corredera, *f.*

slide rule [—ru:l] n. Regla (*f.*) de cálculo.

slide projector [—prə'dʒektə*] n. Proyector (*m.*) de diapositivas *or* de transparencias.

slide trombone [—trɔm'bəun] n. MUS. Trombón (*m.*) de varas.

slide valve [—vælv] n. TECH. Corredera, *f.*

sliding [—iŋ] adj. Corredizo, za (roof). || Corredera, de corredera (door). || Móvil (scale).
— N. Deslizamiento (*m.*) por una corredera.

slight [slait] adj. Ligero, ra; pequeño, ña: *a slight difference, improvement*, una ligera diferencia, mejora; *slight error, pause*, pequeño error, pequeña pausa. || Menudo, da (small): *a slight person*, una persona menuda. || Delgado, da (slim). || Esbelto, ta (slender). || Leve (not serious). || Insignificante. || — *A slight amount of difficulty*, cierta dificultad. || *A slight wound*, una pequeña herida, una herida superficial. || *I have a slight headache*, me duele un poco la cabeza, tengo un ligero dolor de cabeza. || *I haven't the slightest idea*, no tengo la más remota *or* la más mínima *or* la menor idea. || *Not in the slightest*, en absoluto. || *Of slight intelligence*, de corta inteligencia, corto de inteligencia. || *There is not the slighest hope*, no queda ninguna esperanza, no queda ni la más remota esperanza.
— N. Desaire, *m.*, feo, *m.* (affront): *a slight on the family*, un desaire a la familia.

slight [slait] v. tr. Despreciar, menospreciar: *he slighted my efforts*, despreció mis esfuerzos. || Desairar (to treat with rudeness). || Ofender, insultar (to offend, to insult). || U. S. Desatender, descuidar: *to slight one's work*, descuidar el trabajo.
slighting [—iŋ] adj. Despreciativo, va; menospreciativo (scornful). || Ofensivo, va (offensive).
slightly [—li] adv. Ligeramente. || Un poco: *the patient is slightly better today*, hoy el enfermo está un poco mejor. || *Slightly built*, menudo, da (small), esbelto, ta (slender), delgado, da (slim).
slightness [—nis] n. Pequeñez, *f.* (smallness). || Delgadez, *f.* (slimness). || Insignificancia, *f.* (insignificance). || Superficialidad, *f.*, levedad, *f.*, poca gravedad, *f.* (of wound, etc.).
slim [slim] adj. Delgado, da (thin): *a slim person*, una persona delgada. || Esbelto, ta (slender). || Delgado, da; fino, na (thing). || FIG. Pequeño, na; ligero, ra: *a slim chance*, una ligera posibilidad. | Escaso, sa; poco, ca (public). | Escaso, sa (resources). || *To get slim* o *slimmer*, adelgazar (a person), disminuir (hopes, etc.).
slim [slim] v. tr./intr. Adelgazar.
slime [slaim] n. Limo, *m.*, cieno, *m.*, fango, *m.*, lodo, *m.* (mud). || Baba, *f.*, babaza, *f.* (of slugs, snails, etc.).
slime [slaim] v. tr. Enfangar, cubrir de limo *or* de cieno (with mud).
sliminess [—inis] n. Fangosidad, *f.* (of mud). || Lo baboso (of snails). || Viscosidad, *f.* (viscosity). || FIG. Obsequiosidad, *f.*
slimming [ˈslimiŋ] adj. Que no engordan (foods). || Que adelgaza (dress). || *To be on a slimming diet*, seguir un régimen para adelgazar.
slimness [ˈslimnis] n. Delgadez, *f.* (of s.o.). || FIG. Escasez, *f.* (of chances, etc.).
slimy [ˈslaimi] adj. Fangoso, sa (covered with mud). || Baboso, sa: *the snail left a slimy trail*, el caracol dejó un rastro baboso. || Viscoso, sa (sticky). || FIG. Rastrero, ra; adulón, ona (obsequious). || U. S. Asqueroso, sa (filthy). || FIG. *A slimy trick*, una mala jugada.
sling [sliŋ] n. Honda, *f.* (for throwing stones). || Tirador, *m.* (toy). || Portafusil, *m.* (for rifle). || MAR. Eslinga, *f.* (rope). || MED. Cabestrillo, *m.* (for injured arm). || U. S. Cóctel, *m.* [hecho con ginebra, agua, azúcar y limón].
sling* [sliŋ] v. tr. Colgar (to hang). || Tirar con honda: *he slung a stone at it*, le tiró una piedra con honda. || Tirar, arrojar (to throw). || MED. Poner en cabestrillo (an arm). || FIG. FAM. *To sling one's hook*, irse con la música a otra parte.
— OBSERV. Pret. & p. p. ***slung.***
slinger [—ə*] n. Hondero, *m.* || Lanzador, ra (thrower).
slingshot [—ʃɔt] n. Tirador, *m.* (catapult). || Honda, *f.* (sling).
slink* [sliŋk] v. intr. *To slink in*, entrar furtivamente. || *To slink off* o *away*, escabullirse.
— V. tr. Malparir (an animal).
— OBSERV. Pret. & p. p. ***slunk.***
slinky [—i] adj. Sigiloso, sa (stealthy). || Ceñido, da (women's clothes). || Esbelto, ta (woman's figure). || Provocativo, va (provocative).
slip [slip] n. Resbalón, *m.* (a slipping). || Traspiés, *m.*, paso (*m.*) en falso (trip): *one slip and he'll fall to his death*, un traspiés y se mata. || Equivocación, *f.*, error, *m.* (mistake in writing, calculating, etc.). || Desliz, *m.*, descuido, *m.* (mistake in one's actions, words, etc.). || Funda, *f.*: *pillow slip*, funda de la almohada. || Combinación, *f.* (long petticoat). || Combinación (*f.*) de medio cuerpo (short petticoat). || Correa, *f.* (dog's leash). || Esqueje, *m.* (plant cutting). || Tira, *f.* (strip). || Trozo, *m.*: *a slip of paper*, un trozo de papel. || Papel, *m.* (with a note). || Ficha, *f.* (filing card). || Desprendimiento, *m.* (of land, stones, etc.). || ARTS. Barbotina, *f.* (liquid clay). || PRINT. Galerada, *f.*, galera, *f.* (galley proof). || MAR. Grada, *f.* (shipway). || — Pl. THEATR. Bastidores, *m.* || — FAM. *A slip of a girl*, una chiquilla. || *Gym slip*, traje (*m.*) de gimnasia. || *Slip of the pen*, lapsus (*m.*) cálami. || *Slip of the tongue*, lapsus (*m.*) linguae. || *There's many a slip' twixt the cup and the lip*, de la mano a la boca se pierde la sopa. || *To give s.o. the slip*, dar esquinazo a alguien.
slip [slip] v. tr. Pasar: *to slip a rope round s.o.'s neck*, pasarle una cuerda por el cuello a alguien; *he slipped his hand round her waist*, le pasó la mano por la cintura. || Poner, meter (to put): *he slipped his biro back into his pocket*, volvió a meter el bolígrafo en el bolsillo. || Poner disimuladamente (to put furtively). || Escaparse de, librarse de: *she slipped her pursuers*, se escapó de sus perseguidores. || Soltar (to let loose). || Descorrer (to slide open): *to slip the catch*, descorrer el cerrojo. || Correr (to slide shut). || Dejar [un punto] sin hacer (in knitting). || Mudar (snakes, etc.). || Parir antes de tiempo (animals). || MAR. Soltar, largar (a cable, an anchor). || MED. Dislocar (to dislocate). || — *The dog slipped its leash*, el perro se soltó de la correa. || *To slip in*, introducir. || *To slip off*, quitarse [rápidamente] (clothes). || *To slip on*, ponerse [rápidamente] (clothes). || FIG. FAM. *To slip one over on s.o.*, engañar a alguien. || FIG. *To slip one's memory* o *one's mind*, írsele de la memoria *or* de la cabeza, olvidársele. | *To slip s.o.'s notice*, pasarle desapercibido a uno. || FAM. *To slip s.o. a pound*, deslizar *or* poner en la mano *or* darle una libra a alguien (de propina, etc.). || *Try to slip in a good word for me*, a ver si me recomiendas, a ver si hablas bien de mí.
— V. intr. Resbalar: *he slipped on the ice*, resbaló en el hielo. || Escurrirse, escabullirse: *he slipped out of the room*, se escabulló de la habitación. || Ir un momento (to go): *slip round to the baker's, please*, ve un momento a la panadería, por favor. || Equivocarse (to be wrong). || Dislocarse (bone). || Desprenderse (rocks). || Desatarse, soltarse (a knot). || FIG. Ir para atrás, empeorar (to drop from previous standards). || AUT. Patinar (clutch). || AVIAT. Resbalar. || — *My foot slipped*, se me fue el pie. || *To let an opportunity slip*, perder *or* dejar pasar una oportunidad. || FIG. *To let sth. slip* (*out*), escapársele algo a uno, decir algo sin querer (to disclose inadvertently).
— ***To slip away,*** correr (time). | Escabullirse (to go stealthily). | Desaparecer (to disappear). || ***To slip back,*** volver sigilosamente. || ***To slip by,*** correr (time). | Pasar inadvertido (to pass unnoticed). || ***To slip down,*** dejarse caer. || ***To slip in,*** meterse, introducirse. || ***To slip into,*** ponerse rápidamente (clothes). | Introducirse. | — *To slip into bad habits*, coger malas costumbres. || ***To slip off,*** escabullirse (to go stealthily). | Caerse (to fall off). || ***To slip out,*** salir. | Escapársele a uno (a secret). || ***To slip through,*** escabullirse por. | — *To slip through one's fingers*, escapársele de las manos. || FAM. ***To slip up,*** meter la pata (to make a mistake). | Salir mal (a plan, etc.).
slipcase [—keis] or **slipcover** [—ˈkʌvə*] n. Funda, *f.* (for records). || Estuche, *m.* (for books).
slipknot [—nɔt] n. Nudo (*m.*) corredizo.
slip-on [—ɔn] adj. Sin cordones (shoes). || De quitaipón (garment).
slipper [—ə*] n. Zapatilla, *f.*, babucha, *f.* (shoe). || TECH. Zapata, *f.*, patín, *m.* (of a brake).
slipperiness [—ərinis] n. Lo resbaladizo. || *The accident was caused by the slipperiness of the road*, el accidente tuvo lugar porque la carretera estaba resbaladiza.
slippery [—əri] adj. Resbaladizo, za; escurridizo, za *a slippery ball, surface*, un balón escurridizo, una superficie resbaladiza. || FIG. Evasivo, va; escurridizo, za (evasive): *a slippery customer*, un tipo escurridizo. | Delicado, da: *a slippery problem*, un problema delicado. | Que no es de fiar (untrustworthy).
slippy [—i] adj. FAM. Escurridizo, za; resbaladizo, za (slippery). || FAM. *To be* o *to look slippy*, darse prisa: *look slippy!*, ¡date prisa!
slipshod [—ʃɔd] adj. Descuidado, da; negligente (careless). || Gastado, da (shoe heel). || Con zapatos gastados (person).
slipslop [—slɔp] n. Aguachirle, *f.* (watery food). || FIG. Disparate, *m.*
slipstream [—striːm] n. Estela, *f.*
slipup [—ʌp] n. FAM. Metedura (*f.*) de pata, error, *m.* (mistake). | Desliz, *m.*, descuido, *m.* (neglect, carelessness).
slipway [—wei] n. MAR. Grada, *f.*
slit [slit] n. Raja, *f.*, abertura, *f.* (in a long dress). || Corte, *m.* (cut). || Abertura, *f.*, rendija, *f.*, hendidura, *f.* (long, thin opening).
— Adj. Con una abertura, con una raja (skirt, etc.). || Achinado, da; rasgado, da (eyes).
slit* [slit] v. tr. Partir *or* cortar a lo largo (to cut lengthwise). || Rasgar, cortar en tiras (to tear into strips). || Hacer una abertura *or* abrir una rendija en (to make a long opening in). || Hender (to split). || Cortar (to cut). || *To slit s.o.'s throat*, cortarle el cuello a alguien.
— OBSERV. Pret. & p. p. ***slit.***
slither [ˈsliðə*] n. Deslizamiento, *m.*
slither [ˈsliðə*] v. tr. Hacer resbalar (to cause to slide).
— V. intr. Resbalar (to slide). || Arrastrarse (to crawl). || Deslizarse: *to slither down from a tree*, bajar deslizándose por un árbol.
slit trench [slit trentʃ] n. Trinchera, *f.*
sliver [ˈslivə*] n. Astilla, *f.* (of wood). || Pequeña lonja, *f.* (of ham). || Pequeña tajada, *f.* (of meat). || Pequeña rodaja, *f.* (of salami). || Pedacito, *m.*, trocito, *m.* (bit). || Cebo, *m.* (bait). || Torzal, *m.* (of cotton, etc.).
sliver [ˈslivə*] v. tr. Astillar (wood). || Cortar en tiras (to cut into very thin pieces).
— V. intr. Astillarse (wood).
slob [slɔb] n. U. S. FAM. Palurdo, *m.*, patán, *m.* (boor).
slobber [—ə*] n. Baba, *f.*, baboseo, *m.* (dribbling saliva). || FAM. Sensiblería, *f.* (sentimentality).
slobber [—ə*] v. tr. Babosear.
— V. intr. Babear (to dribble). || Decir sensiblerías (to gush sentimentality).
sloe [sləu] n. BOT. Endrino, *m.* (shrub). | Endrina, *f.* (fruit).
sloe-eyed [—aid] adj. De ojos endrinos (dark-blue eyed). || De ojos achinados (slant eyed).
sloe gin [—dʒin] n. Ginebra (*f.*) de endrinas.
slog [slɔg] n. Golpetazo, *m.* (hard blow). || FAM. Pesadez, *f.* (drag). || FIG. FAM. *It was a hard slog, but we made it*, nos costó trabajo, pero lo conseguimos.
slog [slɔg] v. tr. Golpear (a ball).
— V. intr. Avanzar *or* caminar con dificultad (to

walk). || FAM. *To slog away*, sudar tinta, trabajar como un negro.

slogan ['sləugən] n. "Slogan", *m.*, lema (*m.*) publicitario (in sales promotion). || Lema, *m.* (in politics).

slogger ['slɔgə*] n. SP. Pegador, *m.* (boxer). || FAM. Trabajador, ra.

sloop [slu:p] n. MAR. Balandro, *m.* || MAR. *Sloop of war*, corbeta, *f.*

slop [slɔp] n. Aguachirle, *f.* (watery food). || Bazofia, *f.* (leftover food, bad food, pigswill). || Fango, *m.*, barro, *m.* (mud). || FIG. Sensiblería, *f.* (sentimental rubbish). || — Pl. Lavazas, *f.*, agua (*f. sing.*) sucia (dirty water). || Posos (*m.*) de té (of tea). || Ropa (*f. sing.*) barata (cheap clothes).

slop [slɔp] v. tr. Derramar, verter (to pour). || Salpicar (to splash). || Servir con brusquedad (to serve clumsily). || Comer con torpeza (to eat).

— V. intr. Derramarse, verterse (a liquid). || Chapotear, avanzar chapoteando (to plod through mud, etc.). || Chapotear (to make a slapping sound). || *To slop over*, derramarse.

slop basin [—,beisn] n. Recipiente (*m.*) para echar los posos de té.

slope [sləup] n. Cuesta, *f.*, pendiente, *f.*, declive, *m.* (incline): *a steep slope*, una cuesta empinada. || || Vertiente, *f.* (of roof). || Vertiente, *f.*, ladera, *f.*, falda, *f.* (of mountain): *we camped on the western slope*, acampamos en la vertiente oeste. || — *Degree of slope*, inclinación, *f.* || *The ground is on a slope*, la tierra está en declive.

slope [sləup] v. tr. Inclinar. || *Slope arms!*, ¡armas al hombro!

— V. intr. Inclinarse: *the roof slopes*, el tejado se inclina. || FAM. Andar (to walk). || — *To slope down*, descender, bajar. || FIG. FAM. *To slope off*, largarse. || *To slope up*, ascender, subir.

sloping [—iŋ] adj. Inclinado, da; en pendiente: *sloping roof, ground*, tejado inclinado, tierra en pendiente. || Al bies, al sesgo, oblicuo, cua (slanted, crooked). || Inclinado, da (handwriting).

slop pail ['slɔppeil] n. Cubo (*m.*) para el agua sucia.

sloppiness ['slɔpinis] n. Estado (*m.*) fangoso (of the ground). || Estado (*m.*) líquido (of food). || Descuido, *m.*, mala presentación, *f.* (of work): *the sloppiness of his work*, su descuido en el trabajo, la mala presentación de su trabajo. || Desaseo, *m.* (slovenliness). || Suciedad, *f.* (dirtiness). || Sensiblería, *f.* (sentimental rubbish). || Blandura, *f.* (of character). || Descuido, *m.* (of style).

sloppy ['slɔpi] adj. Mojado, da (wet). || Aguado, da (food). || Fangoso, sa; cenagoso, sa (ground). || Encharcado, da (with puddles). || Sensiblero, ra; empalagoso, sa (sentimental). || Desaliñado, da (slovenly). || Muy ancho, cha (garment). || Chapucero, ra (careless). || Sucio, cia (dirty). || Flojo, ja; poco enérgico, ca (unenergetic).

slops [slɔps] pl. n. See SLOP.

slop shop ['slɔp,ʃɔp] n. U. S. FAM. Tienda (*f.*) de ropa barata.

slopwork ['slɔpwə:k] n. Confección (*f.*) de ropa barata. || FAM. Chapucería, *f.* (bad work).

slopworker [—ə*] n. FAM. Chapucero, ra.

slosh [slɔʃ] n. See SLUSH.

slosh [slɔʃ] v. tr. Aplicar a brochazos (paint). || Salpicar (to splash). || FAM. Pegar (to beat). || FAM. *To get sloshed*, coger una tajada (to get drunk).

— V. intr. Andar chapoteando (to walk splashing): *to slosh along a wet path*, andar chapoteando por un camino mojado. || Chapotear (water in a bucket, etc.). || *To slosh about in the bath*, chapotear en el baño.

slot [slɔt] n. Ranura, *f.*, muesca, *f.* (groove). || Abertura, *f.*, rendija, *f.* (narrow opening). || Ranura, *f.* (for coins). || Rastro, *m.*, huella, *f.* (of an animal).

slot [slɔt] v. tr. Hacer una ranura *or* muesca en (to cut a groove in). || Encajar (one part into another).

— V. intr. Encajarse.

sloth [sləuθ] n. Pereza, *f.*, indolencia, *f.* (laziness). || Apatía, *f.* (spiritual apathy). || ZOOL. Perezoso, *m.* || ZOOL. *Sloth bear*, oso (*m.*) bezudo.

slothful [—ful] adj. Perezoso, sa; indolente (lazy). || Apático, ca (spiritually apathetic).

slot machine ['slɔtmə,ʃi:n] n. Distribuidor (*m.*) automático (vending machine). || Máquina (*f.*) tragaperras (for games of chance).

slouch [slautʃ] n. Andar (*m.*) desgarbado (bad posture). || U. S. Holgazán, ana; perezoso, sa (lazy person). || *To walk with a slouch*, andar con los hombros caídos y arrastrando los pies.

slouch [slautʃ] v. tr. Bajar (shoulders). || Echar hacia adelante (a hat).

— V. intr. Andar con los hombros caídos y arrastrando los pies (walking). || Bajar (the brim of a hat). || — *To slouch about*, holgazanear, gandulear (to loaf). || *To slouch in a chair*, estar repantigado en un sillón. | *To slouch on a table*, apoyarse con dejadez en una mesa.

slouch hat [—hæt] n. Flexible, *m.*, sombrero (*m.*) flexible.

slouchy [—i] adj. Desgarbado, da.

slough [slʌf] n. Camisa, *f.*, piel, *f.* (of snake, etc.). || MED. Costra, *f.*, postilla, *f.*, escara, *f.*

slough [slau] n. Ciénaga, *f.*, lodazal, *m.*, fangal, *m.*, cenagal, *m.* (swamp). || U. S. Estero, *m.* || FIG. Abismo, *m.* (abyss). || *In the slough of despair*, en la desesperación más profunda.

slough [slʌf] v. tr. Mudar (to shed). || Descartar (cards). || — FIG. *To slough off*, deshacerse de. | *To slough over*, quitar importancia a.

— V. intr. Caerse (the skin).

sloughy ['slaui] adj. Cenagoso, sa; pantanoso, sa.

sloven ['slʌvn] n. Persona (*f.*) desaseada (untidy). || Vago, ga (idle person).

slovenliness ['slʌvnlinis] n. Lo desaseado, desaliño, *m.* (of appearance). || Dejadez, *f.* (of habits). || Suciedad, *f.* (dirtiness). || Descuido, *m.* (*of*, en) [work].

slovenly ['slʌvnli] adj. Desaseado, da; desaliñado, da (in appearance). || Dejado, da (in character). || Descuidado, da; chapucero, ra (work). || Sucio, cia (dirty).

slow [sləu] adj. Lento, ta: *slow response*, respuesta lenta; *slow worker*, trabajador lento; *slow recovery*, recuperación lenta; *a rather slow boy*, un chico bastante lento; *in a slow oven*, a fuego lento; *slow to grasp an opportunity*, lento en aprovechar una oportunidad. || Frío, a: *a slow audience*, un público frío. || Atrasado, da: *my watch is slow*, mi reloj está atrasado. || Difícil: *slow to take offence*, difícil de ofender. || Aburrido, da (boring): *slow conversation*, conversación aburrida. || MED. Perezoso, sa (liver, etc.). || SP. Pesado, da (pitch, field, track, etc.). || — *Business is slow*, hay poca actividad *or* poco trabajo. || *Life was too slow for me there*, allí la vida era muy aburrida *or* lenta para mi gusto. || *My watch is always slow*, mi reloj atrasa siempre. || *My watch is ten minutes slow*, mi reloj tiene diez minutos de retraso *or* está diez minutos atrasado. || *Slow fire*, fuego lento. || *Slow match*, mecha (*f.*) de combustión lenta. || *Slow train*, tren (*m.*) ómnibus. || *To be slow to*, tardar en: *he was slow to answer*, tardó en contestar.

— Adv. Lentamente, despacio. || FIG. *To go slow*, trabajar a ritmo lento [con fines reivindicativos].

slow [sləu] v. tr. *To slow down* o *up*, aminorar la velocidad de, reducir la marcha de (machine, car etc.), retrasar (to hold up).

— V. intr. *To slow down* o *up*, aminorar la velocidad, reducir la marcha (in a car, etc.), aminorar el paso (walking), ir más despacio (to go slower), disminuir (to decrease). || *Slow down!*, ¡más despacio!

slow coach [—kəutʃ] n. FIG. FAM. Tortuga, *f.* (slow person). | Torpe, *m.* & *f.* (stupid person).

slowdown [—daun] n. Retraso, *m.* || U. S. See GO-SLOW.

slowish [—iʃ] adj. Algo lento, ta.

slowly [—li] adv. Lentamente, despacio. || — *Slowly but surely*, lenta pero seguramente. || *Slowly does it!*, ¡despacito!

slow motion [—'məuʃən] n. Cámara (*f.*) lenta: *in slow motion*, a cámara lenta.

slow-motion [—'məuʃən] adj. A cámara lenta: *a slow-motion picture*, una película a cámara lenta.

slowness [—nis] n. Lentitud, *f.* || Torpeza, *f.* (stupidity). || FIG. Pesadez, *f.*, aburrimiento, *m.* (boredom). || Retraso, *m.* (of watch).

slowpoke [—pəuk] n. U. S. Tortuga, *f.* (slow person). | Torpe, *m.* & *f.* (stupid person).

slow-witted [—'witid] adj. Lento, ta (person).

slowworm [—wə:m] n. Lución, *m.*

slub [slʌb] v. tr. Torcer [el hilo].

sludge [slʌdʒ] n. Fango, *m.*, cieno, *m.*, lodo, *m.* (mud). || Lodo, *m.* (in drilling). || Sedimento, *m.*, residuos, *m. pl.* (sediment). || Fango (*m.*) de alcantarillado (sewage). || Capa (*f.*) de hielo flotante (of sea ice).

sludgy [—i] adj. Fangoso, sa; cenagoso, sa; lodoso, sa.

slue [slu:] n. See SLEW.

slue [slu:] v. tr./intr. See SLEW.

slug [slʌg] n. Posta, *f.* (bullet). || Trozo (*m.*) de metal (roughly shaped piece of metal). || PRINT. Lingote, *m.* (for spacing type). | Línea (*f.*) de linotipia. || ZOOL. Babosa, *f.* || Porrazo, *m.* (heavy blow). || U. S. Ficha, *f.* (for telephone, slot machine, etc.). | Moneda (*f.*) falsa (coin used in machines).

slug [slʌg] v. tr. FAM. Pegar un porrazo a (to hit): *he slugged him*, le pegó un porrazo.

sluggard [—əd] n. Holgazán, ana; vago, ga (loafer).

sluggish [—iʃ] adj. Lento, ta (slow). || COMM. Flojo, ja; inactivo, va; encalmado, da (trade). || Perezoso, sa; holgazán, ana (lazy). || MED. Perezoso, sa (liver, etc.). || *The market is sluggish*, hay poca actividad en el mercado.

sluggishness [—nəs] n. Lentitud, *f.* || Pereza, *f.* (of s.o., of liver). || COMM. Inactividad, *f.*

sluice [slu:s] n. Canal, *m.* (artificial waterway). || Compuerta, *f.*, esclusa, *f.* (gate to control water level). || Canal (*m.*) de desagüe (drainage channel). || Saetín, *m.* (of a water mill). || — *To give sth. a sluice down*, lavar algo con mucha agua. || FAM. *To have a quick sluice*, lavarse rápidamente.

sluice [slu:s] v. tr. Regar: *to sluice the floor*, regar el suelo. || Transportar por un canal (logs). || Lavar [en lavadero] (ores). || *To sluice sth. down*, regar algo con agua.

sluice gate [—'geit] n. Compuerta, *f.*

sluiceway [—wei] n. Canal, *m.* (artificial channel). || Aliviadero, *m.* (of reservoir).

slum [slʌm] n. Barrio (*m.*) bajo, tugurios, *m. pl.* (area). || Tugurio, *m.* (house). || — Pl. Barrio (*m. sing.*) bajo, tugurios, *m.* (slum area). || *Slum clearance*, demolición (*f.*) y reconstrucción de los barrios bajos.

slum [slʌm] v. intr. Visitar los barrios bajos.
slumber [ˈslʌmbə*] n. Sopor, *m.*, sueño (*m.*) ligero (light sleep). || Sueño, *m.* (sleep).
slumber [ˈslʌmbə*] v. tr. *To slumber away*, pasar durmiendo: *to slumber away the afternoon*, pasar la tarde durmiendo.
— V. intr. Dormir (to sleep). || Dormitar (to sleep lightly). || FIG. Estar inactivo (to lie inactive).
slumberous or **slumbrous** [—rəs] adj. Dormido, da (asleep). || Soñoliento, ta (sleepy). || FIG. Inactivo, va (inactive). | Adormecedor, ra (soporific).
slummy [ˈslʌmi] adj. Sórdido, sa (sordid). || De tugurios (area).
slump [slʌmp] n. COMM. Caída (*f.*) vertical, baja (*f.*) repentina (*in*, de) [prices]. | Depresión (*f.*) económica, crisis (*f.*) económica (economic depression). | Disminución (*f.*) brusca (of production, etc.). || FIG. *A slump in morale*, una depresión.
slump [slʌmp] v. intr. Hundirse (to fall into water, through ice, etc.). || Desplomarse: *he slumped to the floor*, se desplomó en el suelo. || Desplomarse, dejarse caer pesadamente (into a chair, etc.). || COMM. Caer verticalmente, bajar de pronto (prices). | Disminuir bruscamente (production, demand). || *The country's economy slumped*, hubo una depresión económica en el país.
slung [slʌŋ] pret. & p. p. See SLING.
slunk [slʌŋk] pret. & p. p. See SLINK.
slur [slə:*] n. Calumnia, *f.*, difamación, *f.* (slanderous remark, etc.). || FIG. Mancha, *f.*, borrón, *m.* (stain). | Afrenta, *f.*, ofensa, *f.*, insulto, *m.* (affront). || Pronunciación (*f.*) incomprensible (indistinct pronunciation). || MUS. Ligado, *m.* || PRINT. Maculatura, *f.* || *To cast a slur on s.o.'s reputation*, manchar la reputación de alguien.
slur [slə:*] v. tr. Calumniar, difamar (to slander). || Pronunciar mal (words). || MUS. Ligar. || FIG. Manchar, mancillar (one's reputation). || PRINT. Macular (to mackle).
— V. intr. Articular mal (to speak indistinctly). || Borrarse (to blur, to fade). || *To slur over*, pasar por alto (not to mention), ocultar (to hide).
slurry [—ri] n. Lechada, *f.*
slush [slʌʃ] n. Nieve (*f.*) medio derretida, aguanieve, *f.* (melting snow). || Lodo, *m.*, fango, *m.*, cieno, *m.* (mud). || Grasa, *f.* (for lubricating). || FAM. Sentimentalismo (*m.*) exagerado, sensiblería, *f.* || U. S. *Slush fund*, dinero utilizado con fines deshonestos.
slush [slʌʃ] v.tr./intr. See SLOSH.
slushy [—i] adj. Medio derretida (snow). || Lodoso, sa; fangoso, sa (muddy). || FAM. Sensiblero, ra; sentimentaloide.
slut [slʌt] n. Marrana, *f.*, puerca, *f.* (slovenly woman). || Mujerzuela, *f.* (loose woman).
sluttish [—iʃ] adj. Puerco, ca; marrano, na (dirty). || De mujerzuela (of a loose woman).
sly [slai] adj. Astuto, ta (artful). || Furtivo, va; sigiloso, sa (furtive). || Malicioso, sa (showing underhandedness). || — *He's a sly old devil* o *fox*, es muy zorro. || *To do sth. on the sly*, hacer algo a hurtadillas *or* a escondidas.
slyness [—nis] n. Astucia, *f.* (artfulness). || Disimulo, *m.* (feigning). || Malicia, *f.* (wickedness).
smack [smæk] n. Tortazo, *m.*, bofetada, *f.* (slap on the face). || Palmada, *f.* (soft blow). || Chasquido, *m.* (of a whip). || Azote, *m.* (to punish a child). || Golpe, *m.* (blow, stroke). || Sabor, *m.*, gusto, *m.* (flavour). || Poco, *m.* (small quantity). || FAM. Beso (*m.*) sonoro (loud kiss). || MAR. Barco (*m.*) de pesca con velas áuricas. || FIG. FAM. *To have a smack at*, probar (to have a try at).
— Adv. De lleno: *the ball hit him smack in the face*, la pelota le dio de lleno en la cara. || *Smack in the middle*, justo en medio.
smack [smæk] v. tr. Dar una bofetada *or* un tortazo, abofetear (to slap): *she smacked him on the face*, le dio una bofetada. || Dar una palmada: *he smacked him on the back*, le dio una palmada en la espalda. || Dar un azote: *she smacked his bottom*, le dio un azote en el trasero. || Chasquear: *to smack a whip*, chasquear un látigo. || Hacer un chasquido con: *to smack one's tongue*, hacer un chasquido con la lengua. || Pegar (to hit). || FAM. Besar sonoramente (to kiss).
— V. intr. Saber (to taste): *it smacks of almonds*, sabe a almendras. || FIG. Oler a: *his stories smack of the sea*, sus historias huelen a mar. || Chasquear, restallar (whip). || Resonar (a kiss).
smacker [—ə*] n. FAM. Beso (*m.*) sonoro (loud kiss). | Bofetón, *m.* (heavy blow). | Dólar, *m.* (dollar). | Maravilla, *f.* (wonder).
small [smɔ:l] adj. Pequeño, ña: *a small garden*, un jardín pequeño. || Pequeño, ña; bajo, ja (person). || Sin importancia, pequeño, ña; insignificante (unimportant): *a small matter*, un asunto sin importancia. || Escaso, sa: *a small spoonful of sugar*, una cucharilla escasa de azúcar. || Humilde, modesto, ta (modest): *small people*, gente modesta; *to live in a small way*, vivir de manera modesta. || Pequeño, ña; exiguo, gua; bajo, ja: *a small salary*, un sueldo pequeño. || Mezquino, na (petty): *it's small of her*, es mezquino de su parte. || Débil (voice). || Flojo, ja (liqueur). || Ligero, ra (meal). || — *A small time*, un tiempo corto, poco tiempo. || *Four times smaller*, cuatro veces más pequeño. || *He is smaller than you*, es más pequeño *or* más bajo que tú. || *How much smaller is it?*, ¿cómo es de pequeño? || *In small numbers*, poco numerosos, pocos. || *It was small recompense for all his efforts*, era poca recompensa para todos los esfuerzos que había hecho. || *My smaller brother*, mi hermano menor. || *Small arms*, armas (*f.*) portátiles. || *Small beer*, cerveza floja (weak bear), persona (*f.*) *or* cosa (*f.*) sin importancia (s.o. or sth.). || *Small calorie*, pequeña caloría. || PRINT. *Small capital*, versalita, *f.* || *Small change*, cambio, *m.*, dinero suelto. || *Small craft*, pequeña embarcación. || *Small fry*, see FRY. || *Small game*, caza (*f.*) menor. || *Small holding*, pequeña propiedad, minifundio, *m.* || ANAT. *Small intestine*, intestino delgado. || *Small letters*, minúsculas, *f.* || FIG. *Small potatoes*, don nadie, *m.* (person), cosa (*f.*) sin importancia (thing). || *Small print*, letra pequeña. || *Small shopkeeper*, pequeño comerciante. || *Small shot*, perdigones, *m. pl.* (ammunition). || *Small talk*, charla, *f.*, charloteo, *m.* || FIG. *To feel small*, sentirse pequeño, sentirse poca cosa. | *To make o. s. small*, achicarse. | *To make s.o. look* o *feel small*, achicar a alguien. || *When I was small*, cuando era pequeño.
— N. Parte (*f.*) pequeña (small part of sth.). || — Pl. Paños (*m.*) menores, ropa (*f. sing.*) interior (underclothes). || Examen (*m. sing.*) preliminar de ingreso (in Oxford). || *Small of the back*, región (*f.*) lumbar.
— Adv. En trozos pequeños (to cut). || Finamente (to grind). || FIG. Desdeñosamente (to look, to treat).
— OBSERV. In everyday spoken Spanish the diminutive is sometimes used to convey the idea of smallness (*a small house*, una casita).
smallholder [—ˈhəuldə*] n. Propietario (*m.*) de un minifundio.
smallish [—iʃ] adj. Más bien pequeño, más bien pequeña, bastante pequeño, ña.
small-minded [—ˈmaindid] adj. Mezquino, na (petty). || De miras estrechas (narrow-minded).
small-mindedness [—ˈmaindidnis] n. Mezquindad, *f.* (pettiness). || Estrechez (*f.*) de miras (narrow-mindedness).
smaliness [—nis] n. Pequeñez, *f.* (in size). || Escasez, *f.* (scantiness). || Exigüidad, *f.* (of salary). || Mezquindad, *f.* (meanness). || Insignificancia, *f.* (insignificance).
smallpox [—pɔks] n. MED. Viruela, *f.*
small-scale [—skeil] adj. En pequeña escala.
smallsword [—sɔ:d] n. Espada (*f.*) de esgrima corta.
small-time [—taim] adj. U. S. FAM. De poca categoría, de poca monta.
small-town [—taun] adj. U. S. Provinciano, na; pueblerino, na.
smalt [smɔ:lt] n. Esmalte, *m.* (colour).
smarm [smα:m] v. tr. *To smarm one's hair down*, alisarse el pelo.
smarmy [—i] adj. Zalamero, ra; cobista.
smart [smα:t] adj. Elegante: *a smart hat*, un sombrero elegante; *she looks very smart*, está muy elegante. || De moda (fashionable). || Ligero, ra; rápido, da: *smart pace*, paso ligero. || Rápido, da: *his smart action prevented a disaster*, su acción rápida evitó un desastre. || Inteligente, listo, ta (intelligent). || Espabilado, da (alert). || Vivo, va (lively). || Sagaz: *a smart politician*, un político sagaz. || Ingenioso, sa (ingenious). || Punzante, agudo, da (pain). || Que escuece *or* pica (itching). || FAM. Listo, ta (in the bad sense): *don't get smart with me*, no te hagas el listo conmigo. || — FIG. *He was too smart for me*, era demasiado listo para mí. || *Look smart about it!*, ¡date prisa! || FIG. *The smart set of Madrid*, la gente más selecta *or* distinguida de Madrid.
— N. Punzada, *f.* (sharp pain). || Escozor, *m.* (sting). || FIG. Resquemor, *m.* (mental pain).
smart [smα:t] v. intr. Escocer, picar (to sting): *my eyes are smarting*, me pican *or* me escuecen los ojos. || Dar punzadas (to cause a sharp pain). || — FIG. *To smart under*, sufrir con. || *You shall smart for this!*, ¡lo vas a pagar!, ¡te va a escocer!
smart aleck or **smart alec** [—ˈælik] n. Sabihondo, *m.*, sabelotodo, *m.*
smarten [—n] v. tr. Arreglar, acicalar (a person). || Arreglar (a house). || FAM. Espabilar (to wake up).
— V. intr. Arreglarse (a person).

— OBSERV. Este verbo va generalmente seguido por *up* sin que cambie el sentido.

smarting [—iŋ] adj. Punzante (pain). || Que pica, que escuece (itching).
— N. Punzada, *f.* (sharp pain). || Escozor, *m.* (sting).
smartly [—li] adv. Elegantemente, con elegancia (elegantly). || A la moda (fashionably). || Inteligentemente. || Astutamente (cunningly). || Ingeniosamente (wittily). || De repente (suddenly). || Secamente, bruscamente (to answer, etc.). || Rápidamente (quickly). || Violentamente (violently).
smartness [—nis] n. Elegancia, *f.* (elegance). || Inteligencia, *f.* (intelligence). || Astucia, *f.* (cunning). || Ingeniosidad, *f.*, ingenio, *m.* (wit). || Sequedad, *f.*, brusquedad, *f.* (sharpness). || Rapidez, *f.* (speed). || Violencia, *f.* (of a slap, etc.).
smarty [—i] n. FAM. Sabelotodo, *m.* & *f.*, sabihondo, da. (know-all).
smash [smæʃ] n. Rotura, *f.* (the act of breaking). || Estrépito, *m.* (loud crash). || Puñetazo, *m.* (heavy

blow). || Choque, *m.* (collision). || Accidente, *m.* (accident): *a rail smash*, un accidente ferroviario. || COMM. Crisis (*f.*) económica (crisis). | Quiebra, *f.* (bankruptcy). | Ruina, *f.* (ruin). || SP. Mate, *m.*, "smash", *m.* (tennis).
— Adj. Descomunal, enorme. || *Smash hit*, exitazo, *m.*, gran éxito, *m.*
— Adv. Violentamente: *to go smash into a tree*, chocar violentamente contra un árbol. || Con gran estrépito (noisily).
smash [smæʃ] v. tr. Romper (to break): *to smash a window*, romper un cristal. || Destrozar, hacer pedazos (to shatter). || Aplastar (to crush). || Estrellar: *he smashed the car into a tree*, estrelló el coche contra un árbol; *she smashed the glass against the wall*, estrelló el vaso contra la pared; *to smash a boat against the rocks*, estrellar un barco contra las rocas. || FIG. Arruinar (to ruin). || Destruir (to destroy): *to smash s.o.'s hopes*, destruir las esperanzas de alguien; *the police smashed the spy ring*, la policía destruyó la red de espías. | Aplastar (to defeat resoundingly). || — FAM. *His face was badly smashed up*, tenía la cara destrozada. || *To smash a place up*, destrozar un local. || *To smash s.o.'s face in*, romper la cara a uno. || *To smash sth. through a window*, arrojar algo por una ventana. || SP. *To smash the ball*, dar un mate (tennis).
— V. intr. Chocar (to come into collision). || Estrellarse: *he smashed into the door*, se estrelló contra la puerta; *the car smashed into the tree*, el coche se estrelló contra el árbol. || Hacerse pedazos (to shatter). || Romperse (to break). || Quebrar, arruinarse (to go bankrupt). || Abrirse paso: *to smash through the forest*, abrirse paso a través del bosque. || SP. Dar un mate (tennis).
smasher [—ə*] n. FAM. Maravilla, *f.* (wonder). | Golpe (*m.*) demoledor (blow). | Destructor, ra (destructive person).
smashing [—iŋ] adj. Aplastante: *smashing victory*, victoria aplastante. || Demoledor, ra: *smashing blow*, golpe demoledor. || FAM. Estupendo, da; extraordinario, ria (marvellous). || FAM. *I had a smashing time*, me lo pasé en grande, lo pasé estupendamente.
smashup [—ʌp] n. Choque (*m.*) violento (violent collision). || Accidente, *m.* (accident). || Quiebra, *f.*, ruina, *f.* (bankruptcy). || MED. Colapso, *m.*
smattering [ˈsmætəriŋ] n. Ligero conocimiento, *m.*, nociones, *f. pl.*: *to have a smattering of French*, tener un ligero conocimiento del francés.
smear [smiə*] n. Mancha, *f.* (stain, mark). || FIG. Calumnia, *f.*, mancha, *f.* (slur). || MED. Frotis, *m.* (for microscopic examination). || *To cast a smear on s.o.*, manchar la reputación de alguien.
smear [smiə*] v. tr. Untar: *to smear butter on bread*, untar mantequilla en el pan; *to smear bread with butter*, untar pan con mantequilla. || Estropear (a freshly painted surface). || Manchar (to soil or stain sth.): *the baby's face was smeared with chocolate*, la cara del niño estaba manchada de chocolate. || FIG. Manchar (s.o.'s reputation). | Calumniar (to defame). || MED. Preparar un frotis de (for microscopic examination). || U. S. FAM. Aplastar (to defeat overwhelmingly).
smeary [—ri] adj. Manchado, da. || Grasiento, ta (greasy).
smell [smel] n. Olor, *m.*: *a strong smell of gas*, un olor fuerte a gas; *the smell of freshly cut grass*, el olor de la hierba recién cortada. || Olor, *m.*, perfume *m.*: *a wonderful smell of roses*, un perfume agradable de rosas. || Olfato, *m.* (sense): *to have a keen sense of smell*, tener buen olfato. || — *Have a smell*, huélelo. || FIG. *There is a smell of treason in all this*, todo esto huele a traición. || *This room has a funny smell in it*, esta habitación huele raro *or* tiene un olor extraño.
smell* [smel] v. tr. Oler. || Olfatear (animals). || FIG. Olfatear, olerse, husmear (to detect): *he smelt danger*, olfateó el peligro. || — FIG. *I smell a rat*, hay gato encerrado. || *To smell out*, olfatear, husmear (a dog), descubrir (to discover).
— V. intr. Oler: *the cake smells good*, el pastel huele bien; *the old man smelt of whisky*, el anciano olía a whisky; *it smells musty*, huele a cerrado. || Tener olfato (to have a sense of smell). || Apestar (to stink). || — *It doesn't smell of anything*, no huele a nada, no tiene olor. || FIG. *It smells fishy to me*, me huele a chamusquina.
— OBSERV. Pret. & p. p. **smelt, smelled.**
smeller [—ə*] n. Husmeador, ra. || FAM. Napias, *f. pl.*, nariz *f.* (nose).
smelling salts [—iŋsɔ:lts] pl. n. Sales (*f.*) aromáticas.
smelly [—i] adj. Maloliente, apestoso, sa.
smelt [smelt] pret. & p. p. See SMELL.
smelt [smelt] n. Eperlano, *m.* (fish).
— OBSERV. El plural de *smelt* es *smelts* o *smelt.*
smelt [smelt] v. tr. Fundir (ores).
smelter [—ə*] n. Fundidor, *m.* (person). || Fundición, *f.* (smelting works).
smeltery [—əri] n. Fundición, *f.*
smelting [—iŋ] n. Fundición, *f.* || — *Smelting furnace*, horno (*m.*) de fundición. || *Smelting works*, fundición.
smew [smju:] n. Mergo, *m.* (duck).
smilax [ˈsmailæks] n. BOT. Zarzaparrilla, *f.*
smile [smail] n. Sonrisa, *f.* || — *Bitter smile*, sonrisa amarga. || *Broad smile*, sonrisa abierta. || *Forced smile*, sonrisa forzada. || *Stereotyped smile*, sonrisa estereotipada. || *To give s.o. a smile*, sonreír a alguien, dirigir una sonrisa a alguien. || FIG. *To knock* o *to take* o *to wipe the smile off s.o.'s face*, quitarle a uno las ganas de sonreír *or* de reír.
smile [smail] v. intr. Sonreír, sonreírse. || FIG. Sonreír, favorecer: *if fortune smiles on me*, si la fortuna me sonríe. || FIG. *To smile at*, reírse de (to regard with amusement, contempt, etc.).
— V. tr. Dirigir una sonrisa de: *to smile a welcome*, dirigir una sonrisa de bienvenida. || — *To smile a sad smile*, sonreír tristemente. || *To smile one's thanks, one's encouragement*, dar las gracias, animar con una sonrisa.
smiling [—iŋ] adj. Sonriente, risueño, ña. || *A smiling landscape*, un paisaje risueño.
smilingly [—iŋli] adv. Sonriendo, con una sonrisa.
smirch [smə:tʃ] n. Mancha, *f.* (stain). || FIG. Mancha, *f.*, mancilla, *f.*, tacha, *f.*
smirch [smə:tʃ] v. tr. Manchar (to stain). || FIG. Manchar, mancillar.
smirk [smə:k] n. Sonrisa (*f.*) afectada.
smirk [smə:k] v. intr. Sonreír afectadamente.
smite* [smait] v. tr. Golpear con violencia (to hit). || Aplastar (to inflict a crushing defeat on). || Castigar (to punish). || FIG. Remorder (conscience). | Ocurrírsele [a uno] (an idea). || — *To be smitten with*, estar aquejado de (an illness), estar lleno de (fear), estar encaprichado por (a girl, an idea). || *To be smitten with remorse*, remorderle a uno la conciencia.
— OBSERV. Pret. **smote;** p. p. **smitten.**
smith [smiθ] n. Herrero, *m.* (blacksmith).
smithereens [ˈsmiθəˈri:nz] or **smithers** [ˈsmiðəz] pl. n. FAM. Añicos, *m.*: *to break sth. to smithereens*, hacer algo añicos.
smithery [ˈsmiθəri] n. Herrería, *f.*
smithy [ˈsmiði] n. Herrería, *f.*
smitten [ˈsmitn] p. p. See SMITE.
smock [smɔk] n. Bata (*f.*) corta (woman's garment). || Babero, *m.* (for very small children). || Delantal, *m.* (for children). || Guardapolvo, *m.* (of artist, etc.).
smock [smɔk] v. tr. Adornar con pliegues fruncidos y bordados, adornar con punto de nido de abeja.
smocking [—iŋ] n. Nido (*m.*) de abeja (stitch).
smockmill [—mil] n. Molino (*m.*) de viento holandés.
smog [smɔg] n. Niebla (*f.*) espesa con humo [*Amer.*, "smog", *m.*]
smokable [ˈsməukəbəl] adj. Fumable.
smoke [sməuk] n. Humo, *m.* || FAM. Cigarrillo, *m.*, pitillo, *m.* (cigarette). || — *Smoke bomb*, bomba (*f.*) de humo, bomba fumígena. || *Smoke screen*, cortina (*f.*) de humo. || FIG. *There's no smoke without fire*, cuando el río suena, agua lleva. || *To go up in smoke*, ser destruido por un incendio (house, etc.), esfumarse, evaporarse, irse en humo (money), quedar en agua de borrajas, irse en humo (plans). || FAM. *To have a smoke*, fumar un cigarrillo, echar un pitillo, fumar (cigarette), fumarse una pipa (pipe).
smoke [sməuk] v. tr. Ahumar: *to smoke glass, meat*, ahumar cristal, carne. || Fumar: *I never smoke cigars*, no fumo nunca puros. || Fumar, fumarse: *I must smoke a cigarette*, tengo que fumar un cigarrillo; *she smokes twenty cigarettes a day*, se fuma veinte cigarrillos diarios. || Fumigar (to fumigate). || — *To smoke a pipe*, fumar en pipa. || *To smoke out*, desalojar con bombas fumígenas (people, animals), ahuyentar con humo (insects), llenar de humo (a room).
— V. intr. Fumar: *he smokes too much*, fuma demasiado. || Echar humo (chimney, fire, etc.). || — *Do you mind if I smoke?*, ¿le molesta que fume? || FAM. *To smoke like a chimney*, fumar como una chimenea.
smokebox [—bɔks] n. Caja (*f.*) de humos (in a steam boiler).
smoked [—t] adj. Ahumado, da (food, glass, etc.): *smoked salmon*, salmón ahumado.
smoke-dried [—ˈdraid] adj. Ahumado, da.
smokehouse [—haus] n. Lugar (*m.*) donde se ahuma [carne, pescado, pieles, etc.].
smokeless [—lis] adj. Sin humo.
smoker [—ə*] n. Fumador, ra (of cigarettes, etc.). || Compartimiento (*m.*) de fumadores (train compartment). || U. S. Tertulia (*f.*) de hombres (meeting for men only). || *To be a heavy smoker*, fumar mucho, ser un fumador empedernido.
smokeroom [—rum] n. Salón (*m.*) de fumar.
smokestack [—stæk] n. Chimenea, *f.* || Conducto (*m.*) de humos (flue).
smoking [—iŋ] adj. Que echa humo, humeante. || — *Smoking car*, coche (*m.*) de fumadores. || *Smoking jacket*, batín, *m.* || *Smoking room*, salón (*m.*) de fumar.
— N. El fumar. || Fumigación, *f.* (against insects). || CULIN. Ahumado, *m.* || *No smoking*, se prohíbe fumar, prohibido fumar.
smoking-room [—rum] adj. FIG. Atrevido, da.
smoky [—i] adj. Humeante (giving off smoke). || Que huele a humo (smelling of smoke). || Ahumado, da (colour). || Ennegrecido por el humo (sooty). || Ahumado, da (tasting of smoke). || Lleno de humo (filled with smoke). || *Smoky quartz*, cuarzo ahumado.
smolder [ˈsməuldə*] n./v. intr. U. S. See SMOULDER.
smolt [sməult] n. Esguín, *m.*, murgón, *m.* (fish).

smooch [ˈsmuːtʃ] n. Mancha, *f.* (stain). || FAM. Beso, *m.* (kiss).
smooch [ˈsmuːtʃ] v. intr. FAM. Besuquearse (to kiss). | Acariciarse, abrazarse (to hug).
— V. tr. Manchar.
smooth [smuːð] adj. Liso, sa (having an even surface). || Llano, na (flat). || Sin grumos: *smooth paste*, masa sin grumos. || Suave: *smooth wine*, vino suave; *smooth voice*, voz suave. || Liso, sa (hair). || Terso, sa; suave (skin). || Sin arrugas (brow). || Pulido, da (glass). || Imberbe, lampiño, ña (beardless). || Tranquilo, la (day, journey). || Sin novedad (uneventful). || En calma, tranquilo, la (the sea). || Gastado, da (worn): *a smooth tyre*, un neumático gastado. || Grato, ta; agradable (pleasant). || Afable (affable). || Suelto, ta; fluido, da (style). || Fácil (easy). || FAM. Refinado, da (refined). | Zalamero, ra; meloso, sa (ingratiating). || GRAMM. Suave (not aspirated). || — FIG. *As smooth as silk*, suave como la seda. || *Smooth talk*, zalamerías, *f. pl.*
— N. Alisado, *m.* (act of smoothing). || Parte (*f.*) lisa (smooth side). || Llano, *m.* (ground). || Zona (*f.*) de calma (smooth patch of sea).
smooth [smuːð] v. tr. Alisar (hair). || Igualar, alisar (a surface). || Cepillar (wood). || Pulir (metals). || Esmerilar (glass). || Suavizar (an angle). || Desarrugar, hacer desfruncir (one's brow). || Hacer desaparecer (wrinkles). || FIG. Calmar (to soothe): *to smooth s.o. down*, calmar a alguien. | Aliviar, hacer llevadero (grief). | Refinar, pulir (to polish, to refine). || — FIG. *To smooth the way for*, allanar el camino para, preparar el terreno para. | *To smooth things over*, limar asperezas (to settle differences, etc.).
smoothbore [—bɔː*] adj. De ánima lisa (firearm).
— N. Ánima (*f.*) lisa.
smooth-chinned [—ˈtʃind] adj. Barbilampiño, ña; imberbe (young). || Bien afeitado (clean-shaven).
smooth-faced [—feist] adj. Barbilampiño, ña; imberbe (young). || Bien afeitado, da (clean-shaven). || Zalamero, ra; meloso, sa (flattering). || Liso, sa (surface).
smoothie [—i] n. U. S. FAM. Zalamero, ra.
smoothing [ˈsmuːðiŋ] adj. Suavizador, ra. || Allanador, ra.
— N. Allanamiento, *m.*, igualación, *f.* (of a surface). || Cepillado, *m.* (of wood). || Pulido, *m.* (of metals). || Esmerilado, *m.* (of glass). || Desaparición, *f.* (of wrinkles).
smoothing iron [—ˈaiən] n. Plancha, *f.*
smoothing plane [—plein] n. TECH. Cepillo, *m.*
smoothness [ˈsmuːðnis] n. Suavidad, *f.* (softness). || Uniformidad, *f.* (of surface). || Tranquilidad, *f.* (peacefulness). || Fluidez, *f.* (of style). || Afabilidad, *f.* (affability). || Zalamería, *f.* (flattery).
smooth-running [ˈsmuːðˈrʌniŋ] adj. Que funciona normalmente.
smooth-shaven [ˈsmuːðˈʃeivn] adj. Bien afeitado.
smooth-spoken [ˈsmuːðˈspəukən] adj. Afable. || Zalamero, ra (flattering).
smooth-tongued [ˈsmuːðtʌŋd] adj. Zalamero, ra (flattering).
smorgasbord [ˈsmɔːgəsbɔːd] n. Buffet (*m.*) sueco.
smote [sməut] pret. See SMITE.
smother [ˈsmʌðə*] n. Humareda, *f.* (thick cloud of smoke). || Polvareda, *f.* (thick cloud of dust). || Asfixia, *f.* (asphyxia).
smother [ˈsmʌðə*] v. tr. Sofocar (to stifle, to suffocate). || Asfixiar (to asphyxiate, to kill). || Sofocar, apagar (a fire). || Contener (yawn, anger, laughter). || Cubrir: *to smother s.o. with a blanket*, cubrir a alguien con una manta; *to smother s.o. with kisses*, cubrir a alguien de besos. || Colmar, abrumar: *to smother with attentions*, colmar de atenciones. | Echar tierra a, enterrar (a scandal).
— V. intr. Asfixiarse (to die of suffocation). || Sofocarse (to be unable to breathe).
smoulder [ˈsməuldə*] n. Fuego (*m.*) lento.
smoulder [ˈsməuldə*] v. intr. Arder sin llama. || FIG. Arder: *eyes smouldering with indignation*, ojos que arden de indignación. | Latir: *smouldering hatred*, odio latente.
smudge [smʌdʒ] n. Mancha, *f.* (stain). || Borrón, *m.* (of ink). || Humo (*m.*) para fumigar (used to repel insects).
smudge [smʌdʒ] v. tr. Correr (ink, paint, etc.). || Emborronar (a piece of writing). || Manchar (by touching with sth. dirty): *to smudge paint on one's shirt*, mancharse la camisa de pintura. || U. S. Fumigar (an orchard). || FIG. Manchar, mancillar (a reputation).
— V. intr. Correrse (ink, paint, etc.). || Emborronarse (a piece of writing). || Mancharse (to stain).
smudginess [—inis] n. Suciedad, *f.* (dirtiness).
smudgy [—i] adj. Emborronado, da (a piece of writing). || Manchado, da (stained).
smug [smʌg] adj. Pagado de sí mismo.
smuggle [ˈsmʌgl] v. tr. Pasar de contrabando (goods liable to customs duty): *to smuggle sth. through customs*, pasar algo de contrabando por la aduana. || Pasar clandestinamente (to pass secretly). || — *To smuggle sth. into the country*, pasar algo de contrabando al país, meter algo de contrabando en el país. || *To smuggle sth. out*, sacar algo de contrabando (through customs), sacar algo clandestinamente (secretly).
— V. intr. Hacer contrabando, contrabandear.
smuggled [—d] adj. De contrabando.
smuggler [—ə*] n. Contrabandista, *m.* & *f.*
smuggling [—iŋ] n. Contrabando, *m.*
smugly [—i] adv. Con aire satisfecho, con suficiencia.
smugness [ˈsmʌgnis] n. Presunción, *f.*, suficiencia, *f.*
smut [smʌt] n. Carbonilla, *f.*, hollín, *m.* (in the air). || Mancha (*f.*) de tizne (mark). || AGR. Tizón, *m.*, añublo, *m.* (fungus and disease). || FIG. FAM. Verdulerías, *f. pl.* (indecent talk, picture, etc.).
smut [smʌt] v. tr. Tiznar (to mark with smuts). || Manchar, ensuciar (to dirty). || AGR. Atizonar, añublar: *smutted corn*, maíz atizonado.
— V. intr. Tiznarse (to stain). || AGR. Atizonarse, añublarse (plants).
smuttiness [—inis] n. Suciedad, *f.*, negrura, *f.* (dirtiness). || FIG. Obscenidad, *f.*, escabrosidad, *f.*
smutty [—i] adj. Tiznado, da; manchado, da (soiled with smut). || AGR. Atizonado, da. || FIG. FAM. Verde, obsceno, na (indecent). || Negruzco, ca (colour).
Smyrna [ˈsməːnə] pr. n. GEOGR. Esmirna.
snack [snæk] n. Bocado, *m.*, piscolabis, *m.*, tentempié, *m.*: *to have a snack*, tomarse un tentempié. || *Snack bar*, cafetería, *f.*, bar, *m.*
snack [snæk] v. intr. Tomarse un bocado.
snaffle [ˈsnæfl] n. Filete, *m.*, bridón, *m.* (of horse's harness).
snaffle [ˈsnæfl] v. tr. Poner filete a (a horse). || Sujetar con filete (to control with a snaffle). || FIG. Controlar. || FAM. Mangar, birlar (to filch).
snafu [snæˈfuː] adj. U. S. FAM. Liado, da; embrollado, da (mixed up).
— N. U. S. FAM. Lío, *m.*, embrollo, *m.* (mess). | Confusión, *f.*
— OBSERV. Esta palabra es la abreviatura de *Situation Normal, All Fouled Up*.
snag [snæg] n. Gancho, *m.* (of a branch). || Tocón, *m.* (of a tree). || Raigón, *m.* (of a tooth). || Tronco (*m.*) sumergido (wood in a river). || FIG. Pega, *f.*, obstáculo, *m.* (difficulty): *there's just one snag*, hay una pega; *the only snag is that*, la única pega es que. || Protuberancia, *f.* (protuberance). || — FIG. *That's the snag*, ahí está la pega. | *To come across* o *to run into* o *to strike* o *to hit a snag*, encontrarse con una pega *or* un obstáculo.
snag [snæg] v. tr. Enganchar (a jumper, material). || Encallar (a boat on a snag). || FIG. Estorbar, obstaculizar.
snaggletooth [ˈsnægltuːθ] n. U. S. Raigón, *m.* (broken stump of tooth). | Diente (*m.*) salido.
snaggy [ˈsnægi] adj. FIG. Sembrado de obstáculos.
snail [sneil] n. ZOOL. Caracol, *m.* || FIG. Tortuga, *f.* (slow person). || FIG. *To walk at a snail's pace*, andar a paso de tortuga.
snake [sneik] n. ZOOL. Serpiente, *f.* (in general). | Culebra, *f.* (harmless). || FIG. Víbora, *f.*, bicho, *m.* (malevolent person). || — FIG. *Snakes and ladders*, juego (*m.*) de la oca. | *There is a snake in the grass*, hay gato encerrado (sth.), hay un traidor (s.o.). | *To cherish a snake in one's bosom*, criar cuervos.
snake [sneik] v. intr. Serpentear: *the river snaked across the valley*, el río serpenteaba a través del valle. || *To snake out*, extenderse (a tentacle).
— V. tr. Hacer serpentear. || U. S. Arrastrar (to haul logs). | Hacer deslizar (to skid logs).
snakebite [—bait] n. Mordedura (*f.*) de serpiente.
snake charmer [—ˌtʃɑːmə*] n. Encantador (*m.*) de serpientes.
snakelike [—laik] adj. Serpentino, na; en forma de serpiente.
snaky [—i] adj. Sinuoso, sa; serpentino, na (winding). || Lleno de serpientes (snake infested). || Traidor, ra (treacherous).
snap [snæp] adj. Instantáneo, a; rápido, da: *a snap decision*, una decisión instantánea. || Rápido, da: *a snap vote*, una votación rápida. || U. S. FAM. Tirado, da (simple, easy).
— N. Chasquido, *m.* (of wood breaking, whip, etc.). || Crujido, *m.*, ruido (*m.*) seco (of the teeth, mouth, joints). || Mordisco, *m.*, dentellada, *f.* (bite): *to make a snap at*, dar un mordisco en. || Castañeteo, *m.* (of the fingers). || PHOT. Instantánea, *f.*, foto, *f.* (snapshot). || Ola, *f.* (of bad weather): *a cold snap*, una ola de frío. || Galleta, *f.* (thin hard biscuit). || FAM. Energía, *f.*, vigor, *m.* (vigour). | Réplica (*f.*) mordaz (answer). || U. S. Automático, *m.* (snap fastener). | Cosa (*f.*) tirada *or* fácil (easy task). || — *He shut the book with a snap*, cerró el libro de golpe. || FAM. *Put some snap into it!*, ¡venga!
— Adv. Con un chasquido, con un crujido. || *To go snap*, romperse con un chasquido (to break), crujir (joints).
snap [snæp] v. tr. Partir: *to snap a branch in two*, partir una rama en dos. || Romper (bones). || Hacer crujir (joints). || Intentar morder (to try to bite). || Agarrar (to seize). || Castañetear: *to snap one's fingers*, castañetear los dedos. || Chasquear: *to snap a whip*, chasquear un látigo. || Tomar una instantánea de, sacar una foto a (to take a snapshot of). || — FIG. *To snap one's fingers at*, burlarse de. || *To snap open*, abrir de golpe. || *To snap out*, soltar, decir con brusquedad (words), espetar (order). || *To snap shut*, cerrar de golpe. || FIG. FAM. *To snap s.o.'s head off*, poner verde

a alguien, echar un rapapolvo a alguien. || FIG. *To snap up*, agarrar: *to snap up an offer*, agarrar una oportunidad; llevarse: *to snap up the last tickets*, llevarse las últimas entradas.
— V. intr. Partirse, romperse: *the rope snapped*, la cuerda se rompió. || Regañar: *don't snap at the boy*, no regañes al niño. || Intentar morder (to make as if to bite). || Morder: *to snap at the bait*, morder el anzuelo. || Crujir: *a twig snapped*, una rama crujió. || Chasquear (a whip). || Castañetear, crujir (fingers). || Dar un estampido (gun). || Ponerse: *to snap into action*, ponerse en acción. || — FIG. *Snap out of it!*, ¡anímate! | *To snap at*, agarrarse a: *he snapped at the chance to go*, se agarró a la oportunidad de marcharse; intentar morder (a dog), hablar con brusquedad a (to speak harshly to). || *To snap off*, desprenderse, caerse. || *To snap open*, abrirse de golpe. || FIG. FAM. *To snap out of it*, recuperarse (to recover), olvidarlo (to forget it). || *To snap shut*, cerrarse de golpe.
snap bean [—bi:n] n. Judía (*f.*) verde.
snapdragon [—ˌdrægən] n. Dragón, *m.* (flower).
snap fastener [—ˈfɑ:snə*] n. Automático, *m.*
snappish [—iʃ] adj. Irritable (irritable). || Mordedor, ra (dog).
snappy [—i] adj. Irritable, irascible (short-tempered). || Mordedor, ra (dog). || Animado, da (lively). || Rápido, da (fast). || FAM. Elegante (stylish). || *Be snappy about it!* o *make it snappy!*, ¡date prisa!
snapshot [—ʃɔt] n. PHOT. Instantánea, *f.*, foto, *f.*
snare [snεə*] n. Trampa, *f.*, cepo, *m.*, lazo, *m.* (for catching animals). || FIG. Trampa, *f.*, lazo, *m.*, celada, *f.* (trap, trick). || MUS. Cuerda, *f.* (of a drum). || *Snare drum*, tambor, *m.*
snare [snεə*] v. tr. Cazar con trampa, coger con lazo. || FIG. Hacer caer en la trampa (to trick).
snarl [snɑ:l] n. Gruñido, *m.* (of a dog, person, etc.). || Maraña, *f.*, enredo, *m.*: *a snarl of hair*, una maraña de pelo. || — *To say sth. with a snarl*, decir algo gruñendo. || U. S. FAM. *Traffic snarl*, embotellamiento, *m.*, atasco, *m.* (traffic jam).
snarl [snɑ:l] v. tr. Enredar, enmarañar (to entangle).
— V. intr. Enredarse, enmarañarse (to become entangled). || Gruñir (to growl).
snarler [—ə*] n. Gruñón, ona.
snatch [snætʃ] n. Arrebatamiento, *m.* (snatching). || Fragmento, *m.* (portion of talk, song, etc.). || FAM. Robo, *m.* (robbery). | Secuestro, *m.* (kidnapping). || Rato, *m.*: *in snatches*, a ratos: *to work in snatches*, trabajar a ratos. || SP. Arrancada, *f.* (weight lifting). || *To make a snatch at sth.*, intentar arrebatar algo (to take it from s.o.), intentar agarrar algo (to grab at).
snatch [snætʃ] v. tr. Arrebatar (to seize from s.o.): *he snatched it from my hands*, me lo arrebató de las manos. || Agarrar, coger (to pick up). || Sacar tiempo para: *to snatch a meal, a sleep*, sacar tiempo para comer, para dormir. || Sacar: *they snatched the drowning man from the river*, sacaron al ahogado del río. || FAM. Robar (to steal). | Secuestrar (to kidnap). || — FIG. *To snatch an opportunity*, agarrar una oportunidad al vuelo. || *To snatch up*, agarrar rápidamente.
— V. intr. Agarrar. || — *Don't snatch!*, ¡no me lo quites así de las manos! || *To snatch at an opportunity*, agarrar una oportunidad al vuelo. || *To snatch at sth.*, intentar agarrar algo.
snatch block [—blɔk] n. MAR. Pasteca, *f.*
snatchy [—i] adj. Irregular.
snazzy [ˈsnæzi] adj. FAM. Bonito, ta (pretty). | Llamativo, va (flashy).
sneak [sni:k] n. FAM. Chivato, ta; soplón, ona (s.o. who betrays one). || Ladronzuelo, la (thief). || Salida (*f.*) disimulada (exit). || — Pl. Zapatos (*m.*) de lona (sneakers).
sneak [sni:k] v. tr. Hacer furtivamente (to do stealthily). || Meter a escondidas: *he sneaked the papers into his desk*, metió los papeles a escondidas en su escritorio. || FAM. Mangar, birlar (to steal). || *To sneak a look at*, mirar furtivamente.
— V. intr. *To sneak away* o *off*, escabullirse. || *To sneak in, out*, entrar, salir furtivamente *or* a hurtadillas. || *To sneak off with sth.*, llevarse algo furtivamente. || *To sneak on s.o.*, traicionar *or* acusar a alguien.
sneakers [—əz] pl. n. U. S. Zapatos (*m.*) de lona.
sneaking [—iŋ] adj. Furtivo, va (furtive). || Ligero, ra (slight). || Secreto, ta (secret).
sneak preview [—ˈpri:ˈvju:] n. U. S. Proyección (*f.*) anterior al estreno para conocer la opinión del público (of a film).
sneak thief [—θi:f] n. Ratero, *m.*
sneaky [—i] adj. Vil, bajo, ja; rastrero, ra (low, despicable). || Secreto, ta (secret). || Furtivo, va (furtive): *to have a sneaky look at*, echar un vistazo furtivo a. || Solapado, da (sly).
sneer [sniə*] n. Desprecio, *m.* (scorn). || Burla, *f.*, chifla, *f.*, escarnio, *m.* (mockery). || Sonrisa (*f.*) de desprecio (scornful smile). || Sonrisa (*f.*) burlona (mocking smile). || Sarcasmo, *m.* (sarcasm).
sneer [sniə*] v. tr. Decir con desprecio.
— V. intr. Reír burlonamente *or* sarcásticamente. || *To sneer at*, despreciar (an offer), mofarse *or* burlarse de (to mock).
sneerer [—rə*] n. Burlón, ona; socarrón, ona.
sneering [—riŋ] adj. Burlón, ona; socarrón, ona.
sneeze [sni:z] n. Estornudo, *m.*
sneeze [sni:z] v. intr. Estornudar. || FIG. *It is not to be sneezed at*, no es de despreciar.
sneezewort [—wə:t] n. BOT. Milenrama, *f.*
snell [snel] n. Hilo (*m.*) para atar el anzuelo.
snick [snik] n. Muesca, *f.* (small cut in wood, etc.). || Tijeretada, *f.* (in paper, cloth). || SP. Golpe (*m.*) con el borde del bate (in cricket).
snick [snik] v. tr. Hacer una muesca en (wood). || Cortar un poco (to cut slightly). || SP. Golpear con el borde del bate (in cricket).
snicker [—ə*] n./v. intr. See SNIGGER.
snide [snaid] adj. FAM. Bajo, ja; vil (mean, cheap). | Sarcástico, ca: *to make snide remarks*, hacer comentarios sarcásticos. || FAM. *What a snide thing to do!*, ¡qué cochinada!
sniff [snif] n. Aspiración, *f.* (of air). || Olfateo, *m.* (of dogs). || Inhalación, *f.*: *one sniff is enough to kill*, una inhalación basta para matar. || — FIG. FAM. *I didn't even get a sniff of the champagne*, ni siquiera olí el champán. || *To open the window and take a sniff of fresh air*, abrir la ventana y aspirar el aire fresco. || *To take a sniff at*, oler. || *With a scornful sniff*, con un gesto de desprecio.
sniff [snif] v. tr. Oler (to smell): *to sniff a rose*, oler una rosa. || Olfatear, husmear (a dog): *to sniff the ground*, olfatear la tierra. || Aspirar (smelling salts, etc.). || FIG. Oler, olfatear: *to sniff danger*, oler el peligro. || — FIG. *To sniff out*, oler, olfatear. || *To sniff up*, sorber (liquids), aspirar (snuff, smelling salts, powder, etc.).
— V. intr. Aspirar por la nariz, sorber. || — FIG. *It's not to be sniffed at*, no es de despreciar. || *To sniff at*, oler (to smell), olfatear, husmear (a dog), despreciar (to scorn).
sniffle [—l] n. Sorbo, *m.* || *To have the sniffles*, estar resfriado.
sniffle [—l] v. intr. Sorberse los mocos (because of catarrh). || Sorberse las lágrimas (when weeping).
sniffy [—i] adj. FAM. Desdeñoso, sa; despreciativo, va (scornful). | Maloliente (bad-smelling). || *To be sniffy about sth.*, tratar algo con desdén *or* desprecio.
snifter [ˈsniftə*] n. U. S. FAM. Copa, *f.*, trago, *m.* (drink): *to have a snifter*, echarse un trago.
snigger [ˈsnigə*] n. Risa (*f.*) disimulada, risita, *f.*
snigger [ˈsnigə*] v. intr. Reír disimuladamente.
snip [snip] n. Tijereteo, *m.* (action and noise): *the snip of the barber's scissors*, el tijereteo del peluquero. || Tijeretazo, *m.*, tijeretada, *f.* (cut made with scissors). || Recorte, *m.* (piece snipped off). || FAM. Ganga, *f.* (bargain). | Ganga, *f.*, cosa (*f.*) fácil (easy task). | Sastre, *m.* (tailor). || U. S. FAM. Joven (*m.*) impertinente.
snip [snip] v. tr. Tijeretear. || *To snip off*, cortar con tijeras.
snipe [snaip] n. Agachadiza, *f.* (bird).
snipe [snaip] v. intr. Cazar agachadizas (to shoot snipe). || MIL. Tirar desde una posición emboscada (to fire shots from a hiding place).
sniper [—ə*] n. MIL. Tirador (*m.*) emboscado, francotirador, *m.*
snippet [ˈsnipit] n. Recorte, *m.* (fragment cut off). || FIG. Retazo, *m.*, fragmento, *m.*, trozo, *m.* (fragment). || FIG. *Snippets of news*, noticias sueltas.
snitch [snitʃ] v. tr. FAM. Birlar (to steal).
— V. intr. FAM. Chivarse (to inform).
snivel [ˈsnivl] n. Lloriqueo, *m.*, gimoteo, *m.* (whimpering). || Moco, *m.* (in the nose).
snivel [ˈsnivl] v. intr. Caérsele a uno los mocos (to have a runny nose). || Lloriquear, gimotear (to whine).
sniveller (U. S. **sniveler**) [—ə*] n. Llorón, ona (whiner).
snivelling (U. S. **sniveling**) [—iŋ] adj. Llorón, ona (whining).
— N. Lloriqueo, *m.*, gimoteo, *m.*
snob [snɔb] n. Snob, *m.*, esnob, *m.*
snobbery [—əri] n. Snobismo, *m.*, esnobismo, *m.*
snobbish [—iʃ] adj. Snob, esnob.
snobbishness [—iʃnis] n. Snobismo, *m.*, esnobismo, *m.*
snobby [—i] adj. Snob, esnob.
snood [snu:d] n. Redecilla, *f.* (hair net). || Cintillo, *m.* (ribbon). || Hilo (*m.*) para atar el anzuelo (in fishing).
snook [snu:k] n. Robalo, *m.*, róbalo, *m.* (fish). || FIG. *To cock a snook at*, hacer un palmo de narices a, hacer burla con la mano a (to thumb one's nose at), mofarse de, burlarse de, reírse de (to laugh at).
snooker [—ə*] n. Billar (*m.*) ruso.
snooker [—ə*] v. tr. Imposibilitar el tiro directo a (the opponent in snooker). || FIG. Fastidiar (to hinder s.o.).
snoop [snu:p] or **snooper** [—ə*] n. Entrometido, da; fisgón, ona (nosey person). || FAM. Detective, *m.* (detective). || *I had a snoop around, but found nothing*, estuve husmeando *or* fisgando, pero no encontré nada.
snoop [snu:p] v. intr. Entrometerse (to pry). || *To snoop around*, husmear, fisgonear, curiosear.
snoopy [ˈsnu:pi] adj. U. S. FAM. Entrometido, da; curioso, sa.
snootily [ˈsnu:tili] adv. FAM. Con esnobismo, con presunción.
snootiness [ˈsnu:tinis] n. FAM. Snobismo, *m.*, esnobismo, *m.*, presunción, *f.*
snooty [ˈsnu:ti] adj. FAM. Snob, esnob, presumido, da.

snooze [snu:z] n. Cabezada, *f.* (short light sleep): *to have a snooze*, dar una cabezada.
snooze [snu:z] v. intr. Dar una cabezada, dormitar.
snore [snɔ:*] n. Ronquido, *m.*
snore [snɔ:*] v. intr. Roncar.
snoring [—riŋ] n. Ronquidos, *m. pl.*
snorkel [ˈsnɔ:kəl] n. Tubo (*m.*) de respiración (swimmer's). || Esnórquel, *m.* (of a submarine).
snort [snɔ:t] n. Resoplido, *m.*: *the snorts of the horses*, los resoplidos de los caballos. || FIG. Zumbido, *m.*, ronquido, *m.* (of an engine). | Resoplido, *m.*, bufido, *m.* (of a person): *a snort of rage*, un bufido de rabia. || U. S. FAM. Trago, *m.* (drink).
snort [snɔ:t] v. tr. Decir con un bufido.
— V. intr. Bufar, resoplar. || Zumbar (an engine). || *To be snorting with rage*, estar bufando de rabia.
snorter [—ə*] n. Ventarrón, *m.* (violent gale). || FAM. Cosa (*f.*) impresionante. || — FAM. *A snorter of a letter*, una carta impresionante. | *His new car is a snorter*, su nuevo coche es impresionante.
snot [snɔt] n. Moco, *m.* (in the nose). || FAM. Mocoso, sa (person). || POP. *Snot rag*, pañuelo, *m.*
snotty [—i] adj. Mocoso, sa (dirty with snot). || FAM. Despreciable (contemptible). | Snob, esnob, presumido, da (snooty). | De mal humor (angry).
— N. FAM. Guardiamarina, *m.*
snout [snaut] n. Hocico, *m.* (of a pig, bull, boar, dog, etc.). || FAM. Napias, *f. pl.* (nose). | Hocico, *m.*, jeta, *f.* (face). | Pitillo, *m.* (cigarette). || FIG. Morro, *m.* (of a plane). | Pitorro, *m.* (of a teapot, hosepipe).
snow [snəu] n. Nieve, *f.* || Nevada, *f.* (a fall of snow). || FAM. Mandanga, *f.* (cocaine). || — *A heavy fall of snow*, una fuerte nevada. || *As white as snow*, blanco como la nieve.
snow [snəu] v. tr. Hacer caer como copos (like flakes). || Bloquear: *to be snowed in* o *up*, estar bloqueado por la nieve. || FIG. *To be snowed under with work, with debts*, estar abrumado *or* agobiado de trabajo, de deudas.
— V. intr. Nevar.
snowball [—bɔ:l] n. Bola (*f.*) de nieve (snow pressed into a ball). || BOT. Mundillo, *m.*, bola (*f.*) de nieve.
snowball [—bɔ:l] v. tr. Tirar bolas de nieve a.
— V. intr. Aumentar rápidamente (to grow rapidly). || Acumularse (to accumulate). || Tirar bolas de nieve (to throw snowballs).
snowbird [—bə:d] n. Pinzón (*m.*) de las nieves.
snow-blind [—ˈblaind] adj. Cegado por el reflejo de la nieve.
snow-blindness [—ˈblaindnis] n. Ceguera (*f.*) producida por el reflejo de la nieve.
snowbound [—baund] adj. Bloqueado por la nieve.
snow-capped [—kæpt] or **snow-covered** [—ˈkʌvəd] adj. Cubierto de nieve, nevado, da.
snowdrift [—drift] n. Acumulación (*f.*) de nieve, ventisquero, *m.* [producida por el viento].
snowfall [—fɔ:l] n. Nevada, *f.*
snowfield [—fi:ld] n. Campo (*m.*) de nieve.
snowflake [—fleik] n. Copo (*m.*) de nieve.
snow leopard [—ˈlepəd] n. ZOOL. Onza, *f.*
snow line [—lain] n. Límite (*m.*) de las nieves perpetuas.
snowman [—mæn] n. Muñeco (*m.*) de nieve. || *The abominable snowman*, el abominable hombre de las nieves.

— OBSERV. El plural de *snowman* es *snowmen*.

snowplough (U. S. **snowplow**) [—plau] n. Quitanieves, *m. inv.* (device for cleaning snow). || Cuña, *f.* (in skiing).
snowshoe [—ʃu:] n. Raqueta, *f.*
snowslide [—slaid] n. Alud (*m.*) de nieve (avalanche).
snowstorm [—stɔ:m] n. Tormenta (*f.*) de nieve.
snow-white [—ˈwait] adj. Blanco como la nieve.
Snow White [—ˈwait] n. *Snow White and the Seven Dwarfs*, Blancanieves y los siete enanitos.
snowy [—i] adj. Nevado, da (snow-covered). || Blanco como la nieve (white). || De las nieves (season). || De mucha nieve, nevoso, sa (region, climate). || *It was very snowy last week*, la semana pasada nevó mucho, hubo mucha nieve la semana pasada.
snub [snʌb] n. Desaire, *m.* (of a person). || Rechazo, *m.* (of an offer).
snub [snʌb] v. tr. Desairar, despreciar (to slight or to ignore s.o.). || Despreciar (an offer). || Parar con brusquedad (to stop abruptly). || *To snub out*, apagar (a cigarette).
snubber [—ə*] n. U. S. TECH. Amortiguador, *m.* (shock absorber). | Tambor (*m.*) del freno (of the brake).
snub nose [—nəuz] n. Nariz (*f.*) chata y respingona.
snub-nosed [—ˈnəuzd] adj. De nariz chata y respingona.
snuff [snʌf] n. Inhalación, *f.* (act of snuffing). || Rapé, *m.* (powdered tobacco): *pinch of snuff*, toma de rapé. || Pabilo, *m.* (of a candle). || — FIG. *To be up to snuff*, ser muy despabilado. || *To take snuff*, tomar rapé.
snuff [snʌf] v. tr. Inhalar, aspirar (to inhale). || Oler, olfatear (to sniff). || Despabilar (to cut the wick off). || — FIG. FAM. *To snuff it*, estirar la pata. || *To snuff out*, apagar (a candle), terminar con (conspiracy, etc.).
— V. intr. Tomar rapé.
snuffbox [—bɔks] n. Caja (*f.*) de rapé, tabaquera, *f.*
snuffer [—ə*] n. Apagavelas, *m. inv.* || Tomador (*m.*) de rapé. || — Pl. Despabiladeras, *f.* (scissors).
snuffle [—l] n. Resuello, *m.* (sniff). || Obstrucción (*f.*) nasal, respiración (*f.*) ruidosa (noisy breathing). || Tono (*m.*) gangoso. || — Pl. Romadizo, *m. sing.* (cold). || *To have the snuffles*, estar resfriado *or* constipado *or* acatarrado.
snuffle [—l] v. intr. Respirar ruidosamente. || Ganguear (to speak with a twang).
snug [snʌg] adj. Cómodo, da; confortable: *a snug room*, una habitación confortable. || Calentito, ta (nice and warm). || Ajustado, da; ceñido, da (tight-fitting): *a snug jacket*, una chaqueta ajustada. || MAR. Bien aparejado (ship). || Abrigado, da (sheltered). || FIG. Bueno, na: *a snug income*, un buen sueldo. | Agradable (job). || FIG. *To be as snug as a bug in a rug*, estar muy cómodo.
snug [snʌg] v. tr. MAR. *To snug down*, preparar [para hacer frente a la tempestad]. || Abrigar (to shelter). || Ajustar, ceñir (a garment).
snuggery [—əri] n. Habitación (*f.*) cómoda.
snuggle [—l] v. tr. Acurrucar, apretar.
— V. intr. Arrimarse: *she snuggled up to him*, se arrimó a él. || Acurrucarse (to curl up): *he snuggled up in the hay, in bed*, se acurrucó en el heno, en la cama; *the cat snuggled up on her lap*, el gato se acurrucó en sus rodillas. || *To snuggle up with a book*, ponerse cómodo para leer un libro.
snugly [—li] adv. Cómodamente (comfortably). || Al abrigo (under shelter). || *To fit snugly*, ajustar perfectamente (clothes), caber perfectamente (one object inside another).
snugness [—nis] n. Comodidad, *f.* (comfort). || Ajuste, *m.*, ajustamiento, *m.* (of a garment).
so [səu] adv. Así, de esta manera: *it must be done so*, debe hacerse así; *she wrapped up well and so was warm*, se arropó bien y así consiguió tener calor. || Tan: *he was so ill that we thought he would die*, estaba tan enfermo que creíamos que se iba a morir; *it's not so difficult*, no es tan difícil; *it won't be so bad as you think*, no será tan malo como crees; *so happy*, tan feliz; *he is so kind*, es tan amable. || También: *he wants to go and so do I*, él quiere ir y yo también; *so did she*, ella también. || Tanto: *she misses him so*, le echa tanto de menos; *why do you protest so?*, ¿por qué protesta usted tanto? || — *And in doing so*, y al hacer eso. || *And so forth*, y así sucesivamente, etcétera. || *And so it was that*, y ocurrió que (and it happened that), y así fue como (and that was how). || *And so on*, y así sucesivamente, etcétera. || *And so to bed*, y después a la cama. || *Be so kind as to*, tenga la bondad de. || *Ever so*, muy, infinitamente (grateful). || *Ever so little*, muy pequeño, pequeñísimo: *he is ever so little*, es muy pequeño; muy poco: *give me ever so little*, dame muy poco. || *How so?*, ¿cómo es eso? || *If so*, en ese caso, si es así (in that case). || *I hope so*, eso espero, espero que sí. || *In so far as*, en la medida en que. || *In so many words*, see WORD. || *Is that so?*, ¿es verdad?, ¿de verdad? || *I think so*, creo que sí. || *I told you so*, ya te lo dije. || *It so happens that*, resulta que, da la casualidad de que. || *Just so* o *quite so*, ni más ni menos, así es. || *Not so*, no es así. || *Not so much as*, ni siquiera. || *Not so much... as*, no... sino más bien. || *Only more so*, pero más aún. || *Or so*, o poco más o menos. || *So as to*, para: *so as not to be heard*, para no ser oído. || *So ... as*, tan ... como: *he is not so kind as his wife*, no es tan amable como su mujer. || *So ... as to*, tan ... como para, tantos ... que: *cars so numerous as to block the traffic*, coches tan numerosos como para bloquear el tráfico, tantos coches que bloquearon el tráfico. || *So be it*, así sea. || *So far*, hasta aquí *or* allí: *you can go so far in the car, but eventually you'll have to get out and walk*, se puede ir hasta allí en coche, pero luego hay que bajar e ir andando; hasta ahora (until now). || *So far as*, hasta. || *So far as I am concerned*, por lo que a mi respecta *or* se refiere. || *So far as I can make out*, por lo que veo. || *So far as I know*, que yo sepa. || *So far so good*, hasta ahora todo va bien. || *So forth and so on*, y así sucesivamente. || *So he says*, eso dice él, según dice él. || *So it is!*, ¡es verdad!, ¡así es! || *So it seems*, eso parece. || *So long*, tanto tiempo: *they did not stay so long*, no se quedaron tanto tiempo; hasta luego, hasta pronto (good-bye). || *So long as*, mientras que. || *So many*, tanto, ta: *so many people*, tanta gente: *so many guests*, tantos invitados. || *So much*, tanto, ta: *so much money*, tanto dinero; tanto: *so much has been said that*, tanto se ha dicho que. || *So much for that*, ¿qué le vamos hacer? || *So much so that*, tanto que. || *So much the better*, tanto mejor. || *So so*, así, así. || *So that*, para que, de manera que (in order that): *I helped him so that he might finish earlier*, le ayudé para que terminase antes; de modo que, de manera que (with the result that). || *So that's that*, así son las cosas. || *So then*, así pues. || *So to speak*, por decirlo así. || *So what?*, ¿y qué? || *They are just so many thieves*, no son más que unos ladrones. || *They did not so much as answer*, ni siquiera contestaron. || *They get so much per day*, ganan tanto por día. || *Very much so*, mucho. || *What he said was so much nonsense*, lo que dijo no fueron más que tonterías. || *Why so?*, ¿por qué? || *Without so much as a by*

your leave, sin decir nada a nadie, sin pedirle siquiera permiso a nadie.
— Conj. Así que, por lo tanto: *you are not listening so I'll shut up*, no me estás escuchando, así que me callaré. || Así que, conque, entonces, de modo que: *so you are not coming*, ¿así que no vienes?; *so it was you who did it*, conque fuiste tú el que lo hiciste. || U. S. Para que: *I'll show you so you can see how it is done*, te lo voy a enseñar para que veas como se hace; *I only said it so you'd stay*, sólo lo dije para que te quedases. || De manera que, de modo que (with the result that).
soak [səuk] n. Remojo, *m.* (washing, food). || Empapamiento, *m.* (of soil, etc.). || Remojón, *m.*, empapamiento, *m.* (of a person). || FAM. Borrachín, ina (drunkard). | Borrachera, *f.* (spree).
soak [səuk] v. tr. Remojar, poner en remojo (washing, food): *to soak a shirt before washing it*, poner una camisa en remojo antes de lavarla. || Empapar, calar: *we got absolutely soaked*, nos empapamos *or* nos calamos completamente. || Empapar, mojar (to wet): *soak the cotton wool in antiseptic*, empapa el algodón en un antiséptico. || — *Soaked to the skin*, calado hasta los huesos. || *To soak in* o *up*, absorber (a liquid). || *To soak o.s.*, calarse hasta los huesos (to get soaked). || FIG. *To soak o.s. in*, empaparse de. || *To soak out*, quitar *or* sacar remojando: *to soak the stains out of sth.*, quitar las manchas de algo remojándolo. || FIG. FAM. *To soak s.o. for twenty pounds*, clavarle veinte libras a alguien.
— V. intr. Estar en remojo, remojarse (clothes, food). || FIG. FAM. Pimplar, soplar (to drink a lot). || — *To leave sth. to soak*, dejar algo en remojo. || *To soak in*, penetrar. || *To soak through*, penetrar (to penetrate), calar: *the rain has soaked through his overcoat*, la lluvia le ha calado el abrigo.
soakage [—idʒ] n. Empapamiento, *m.*
soaking [—iŋ] n. Remojón, *m.* (accidental). || — *To get a soaking*, empaparse. || *To give sth. a soaking*, poner algo en remojo.
— Adj. *Soaking* (*wet*), empapado, da; calado hasta los huesos.
so-and-so [ˈsəuənsəu] n. Fulano, na. || — FAM. *He's a useless so-and-so*, es un inútil. || *Mr. So-and-so*, don Fulano de Tal.
soap [səup] n. Jabón, *m.* || — *Soap bubble*, pompa (*f.*) de jabón. || *Soap dish*, jabonera, *f.* || U. S. FAM. *Soap opera*, serial, *m.*
soap [səup] v. tr. Jabonar, enjabonar.
soapbark [—bɑːk] n. BOT. Quillay, *m.*
soapberry [—ˈberi] n. BOT. Jaboncillo, *m.*
soapbox [—bɔks] n. Tribuna (*f.*) improvisada (of open-air speaker).
— Adj. *Soapbox orators*, oradores (*m.*) callejeros.
soap flakes [—fleiks] pl. n. Jabón (*m. sing.*) en escamas.
soap plant [—plɑːnt] n. BOT. Jabonera, *f.*
soap powder [—ˈpaudə*] n. Jabón (*m.*) en polvo.
soapstone [—stəun] n. MIN. Esteatita, *f.* || Jaboncillo, *m.* (in dressmaking).
soapsuds [—sʌdz] pl. n. Espuma, *f. sing.*, jabonaduras, *f.* (lather).
soapwort [—wəːt] n. BOT. Jabonera, *f.*
soapy [—i] adj. Jabonoso, sa: *soapy water, hands*, agua jabonosa, manos jabonosas. || FIG. Meloso, sa.
soar [sɔː*] n. Vuelo, *m.* (flight). || Subida (*f.*) vertiginosa (of prices).
soar [sɔː*] v. intr. Elevarse, remontarse (up into the air): *the plane soared to ten thousand metres*, el avión se elevó a diez mil metros. || Volar, planear: *the birds were soaring high above us*, los pájaros volaban muy alto por encima de nosotros. || FIG. Elevarse: *the tower soared above the town*, la torre se elevaba por encima de la ciudad. | Subir vertiginosamente (prices). || FIG. *Our hopes soared*, cobramos nuevas esperanzas.
soaring [—riŋ] n. Vuelo, *m.* (flight). || Subida (*f.*) vertiginosa (of prices).
— Adj. Que planea en las alturas (bird, plane, etc.). || Altísimo, ma (very high). || *To check soaring prices*, controlar la subida excesiva de los precios.
sob [sɔb] n. Sollozo, *m.*
sob [sɔb] v. tr. Decir sollozando *or* con sollozos. || — *She sobbed herself to sleep*, se durmió sollozando. || *To sob one's heart out*, llorar a lágrima viva.
— V. intr. Sollozar.
sobbing [—iŋ] n. Sollozos, *m. pl.*
sober [ˈsəubə*] adj. Sobrio, bria (not drunk). || Moderado, da; sobrio, bria (temperate): *sober habits*, costumbres moderadas. || Sensato, ta: *a sober opinion*, una opinión sensata. || Equilibrado, da (showing discretion). || Grave, serio, ria (serious, grave): *his expression was very sober*, tenía una expresión muy seria. || Sobrio, bria (not ornamented): *a sober style, dress*, un estilo, un vestido sobrio. || Discreto, ta: *sober colours*, colores discretos. || Puro, ra: *the sober truth*, la pura verdad. || — *As sober as a judge* o *stone-cold sober*, completamente sobrio. || *In sober fact*, en realidad. || *We'll have to wait until he's sober*, tendremos que esperar hasta que se le pasen los efectos de la bebida.
sober [ˈsəubə*] v. tr. Desembriagar (a drunken person). || FIG. Calmar (to calm).
— V. intr. *To sober down*, calmarse (to calm down). || *To sober up*, pasársele a uno la embriaguez.
sober-minded [—ˈmaindid] adj. Sensato, ta.
soberness [—nis] n. See SOBRIETY.
sobersides [—saidz] n. Persona (*f.*) muy seria.
sobriety [səuˈbraiəti] n. Sobriedad, *f.* || Moderación, *f.* (moderation). || Serenidad, *f.* (sedateness). || Seriedad, *f.* (seriousness). || Sensatez, *f.* (good sense). || Discreción, *f.* (discretion).
sobriquet [ˈsəubrikei] n. Apodo, *m.*, mote, *m.* (nickname).
sob sister [ˈsɔbˌsistə*] n. U. S. FAM. Periodista (*f.*) que escribe artículos sentimentales.
sob story [ˈsɔbˌstɔːri] n. FAM. Historia (*f.*) sentimental.
socage or **soccage** [ˈsɔkidʒ] n. HIST. Arriendo, *m.*
so-called [ˈsəuˈkɔːld] adj. Llamado, da; supuesto, ta: *a so-called liberal*, un llamado liberal.
soccer [ˈsɔkə*] n. SP. Fútbol, *m.*
sociability [ˌsəuʃəˈbiliti] n. Sociabilidad, *f.*, carácter (*m.*) sociable.
sociable [ˈsəuʃəbl] adj. Sociable: *he is a very sociable person*, es una persona muy sociable. || Amistoso, sa; afable (friendly).
sociableness [—nis] n. Sociabilidad, *f.*, carácter (*m.*) sociable.
social [ˈsəuʃəl] adj. Social: *social legislation*, legislación social; *social rank*, rango *or* posición social; *social life*, vida social; *social events*, acontecimientos sociales. || Amistoso, sa (friendly). || Sociable (sociable): *man is a social being*, el hombre es un ser sociable. || — *Social climber*, arribista, *m.* & *f.*, advenedizo, za. || *Social column*, ecos (*m. pl.*) de sociedad (in a newspaper). || *Social Democracy*, democracia (*f.*) social, socialdemocracia, *f.* || *Social Democrat*, socialdemócrata, *m.* & *f.* || *Social disease*, enfermedad causada por condiciones precarias de vida (disease related to social conditions), enfermedad venérea (venereal disease). || *Social insurance*, seguro (*m.*) social. || *Social reformer*, reformador (*m.*) de la sociedad. || *Social science*, sociología, *f.* || *Social scientist*, sociólogo, ga. || *Social security*, seguridad (*f.*) social. || *Social service*, servicio (*m.*) social. || *Social settlement*, centro (*m.*) de asistencia social. || *Social welfare*, asistencia (*f.*) social. || *Social work*, asistencia (*f.*) social. || *Social worker*, asistente (*m.*) social, asistenta (*f.*) social. || *To be a social outcast*, vivir rechazado por la sociedad.
— N. Reunión, *f.*, tertulia, *f.*
socialism [—izəm] n. Socialismo, *m.*
socialist [—ist] adj./n. Socialista.
socialistic [ˌsəuʃəˈlistik] adj. Socialista.
socialite [ˈsəuʃəlait] n. FAM. Mundano, na.
sociality [səuˈʃæliti] n. Sociabilidad, *f.*
socialization [ˌsəuʃəlaiˈzeiʃən] n. Socialización, *f.*
socialize [ˈsəuʃəlaiz] v. tr. Socializar.
socialized medicine [—dˈmedsin] n. Medicina (*f.*) estatal.
socially [ˈsəuʃəli] adv. Socialmente. || Para la sociedad: *socially unacceptable*, inaceptable para la sociedad. || Por la sociedad (accepted, etc.). || — *I never meet my colleagues socially*, nunca me reúno con mis colegas fuera del trabajo. || *Socially inferior*, de condición social inferior.
society [səˈsaiəti] n. Sociedad, *f.*: *feudal society*, sociedad feudal; *American society*, la sociedad americana; *high society*, alta sociedad. || Alta sociedad, *f.* (upper class). || Asociación, *f.* (organized group). || Compañía, *f.* (company). || ZOOL. Sociedad, *f.* || — *Cooperative society*, sociedad cooperativa. || *Friendly* o *provident society*, sociedad de socorro mutuo, mutualidad, *f.* || *Society column* o *news*, ecos (*m. pl.*) de sociedad. || *Society woman*, mujer mundana. || *To go into society*, ponerse de largo, ser presentada en sociedad.
Society of Friends [—əvˌfrendz] n. REL. Sociedad (*f.*) de los amigos.
Society of Jesus [—əvˌdʒiːzəs] n. REL. Compañía (*f.*) de Jesús.
socioeconomic [ˈsəusjəuˌiːkəˈnɔmik] adj. Socioeconómico, ca.
sociologic [ˌsəusjəˈlɔdʒik] or **sociological** [—əl] adj. Sociológico, ca.
sociologist [ˌsəusiˈɔlədʒist] n. Sociólogo, ga.
sociology [ˌsəusiˈɔlədʒi] n. Sociología, *f.*
sociopolitical [ˈsəusjəupəˈlitikəl] adj. Sociopolítico, ca.
sock [sɔk] n. Calcetín, *m.* (foot garment). || Plantilla, *f.* (inner sole of a shoe). || Manga, *f.* (showing wind direction). || (Ant.) Coturno, *m.* (for actors). || FAM. Puñetazo, *m.* (blow). || — FAM. *Put a sock in it!*, ¡cierra la boca!, ¡cállate! || FIG. *To pull up one's socks*, hacer un esfuerzo.
sock [sɔk] v. tr. Pegar.
socket [ˈsɔkit] n. Hueco, *m.*, cubo, *m.* (for holding sth.). || ELECTR. Enchufe, *m.*, enchufe (*m.*) hembra (electrical connection). | Casquillo, *m.* (of a bulb). || Arandela, *f.* (of a candlestick). || ANAT. Cuenca, *f.* (of the eye). | Alveolo, *m.* (of teeth). | Glena, *f.* (of bones).
socket wrench [—rentʃ] n. U. S. TECH. Llave (*f.*) de tubo.
sockeye [ˈsɔkai] n. Salmón (*m.*) rojo.
socle [ˈsɔkəl] n. ARCH. Zócalo, *m.* (for a wall). | Pedestal, *m.*, peana, *f.* (for a statue).
Socrates [ˈsɔkrətiːz] pr. n. Sócrates, *m.*
Socratic [sɔˈkrætik] adj./n. Socrático, ca.

sod [sɔd] n. Césped, *m.* (surface soil with grass growing). || Tepe, *m.* (piece of turf). || POP. Cabrón, *m.* (term of abuse). || FAM. *Under the sod,* debajo de tierra.
sod [sɔd] v. tr. Cubrir de césped.
soda [ˈsəudə] n. CHEM. Sosa, *f.*: *caustic soda,* sosa cáustica. || Soda, *f.*, sifón, *m.*, agua (*f.*) de Seltz (soda water): *a whisky and soda,* un whisky con soda. || — *Soda ash,* carbonato sódico. || *Soda biscuit* (U. S. *soda cracker*), galleta ligeramente salada. || U. S. *Soda fountain,* bar (*m.*) donde sólo se venden bebidas sin alcohol (bar), sifón (siphon). || U. S. FAM. *Soda jerk,* camarero, *m.* || *Soda water,* agua de Seltz, soda, sifón.
sodality [səuˈdæliti] n. Asociación, *f.* (organized society). || REL. Cofradía, *f.*, hermandad, *f.*
sodden [ˈsɔdn] adj. Empapado, da (saturated). || Mal cocido, da (bread). || Embrutecido por el alcohol (from frequent drunkenness).
sodium [ˈsəudjəm] n. CHEM. Sodio, *m.* || — *Sodium bicarbonate,* bicarbonato sódico *or* de sosa. || *Sodium carbonate,* carbonato sódico. || *Sodium chloride,* cloruro sódico *or* de sodio. || *Sodium hydroxide* hidróxido sódico. || *Sodium nitrate,* nitrato sódico *or* de sodio.
sodium-vapour-lamp [—ˈveipə,læmp] n. Lámpara (*f.*) de vapor de sodio.
Sodom [ˈsɔdəm] pr. n. HIST. Sodoma.
sodomite [ˈsɔdəmait] n. Sodomita, *m.*
sodomitical [,sɔdəˈmitikəl] adj. Sodomítico, ca.
sodomy [ˈsɔdəmi] n. Sodomía, *f.*
sofa [ˈsəufə] n. Sofá, *m.*
sofa bed [—bed] n. U. S. Sofá (*m.*) cama.
soffit [ˈsɔfit] n. ARCH. Sofito, *m.*
Sofia [ˈsəufjə] pr. n. GEOGR. Sofía.
soft [sɔft] adj. Blando, da: *soft bed,* cama blanda. || Suave: *soft hair,* pelo suave; *soft skin,* cutis suave; *soft colours,* colores suaves. || Confuso, sa; borroso, sa (outline). || Silencioso, sa (silent). || Bajo, ja (low): *in a soft voice,* en voz baja. || Dulce (sweet): *soft words,* palabras dulces. || Débil (weak). || Benigno, na; templado, da; suave (climate). || No alcohólico, ca (drinks). || Blando, da; suave (diet). || Blando, da (water). || Flexible (hat). || FAM. Fácil (easy). | Blando, da; tolerante (tolerant). | Tonto, ta; lelo, la (silly). || PHOT. Borroso, sa; desenfocado, da. || PHYS. Blando, da; poco penetrante (rays). || GRAMM. Suave (consonant). || — FAM. *A soft job,* un chollo. || *As soft as silk,* suave como la seda. || *Soft answer,* respuesta suave. || *Soft coal,* hulla grasa, carbón bituminoso. || *Soft currency,* moneda *or* divisa débil *or* blanda. || FIG. FAM. *Soft in the head,* bobo, ba; lelo, la; tonto, ta. || *Soft iron,* hierro (*m.*) dulce. || *Soft palate,* velo (*m.*) del paladar. || *Soft sell,* publicidad discreta. || *Soft solder,* soldadura (*f.*) de estaño. || *Soft spot,* debilidad, *f.* (weakness): *to have a soft spot for s.o.* o *for sth.,* tener una debilidad por alguien *or* por algo. || *Soft to the touch,* blando *or* suave al tacto. || FAM. *To be soft on s.o.,* ser poco severo con alguien (to be too lenient), estar encaprichado por *or* enamoriscado de alguien (to be fond of). || *To go soft,* ponerse blando (butter, etc.), perder la cabeza (to go mad). || FAM. *To go soft in the head,* perder la cabeza.
— N. Parte (*f.*) blanda *or* suave.
softball [—bɔ:l] n. SP. Variedad (*f.*) de béisbol que se juega con pelota blanda.
soft-boiled [—bɔild] adj. Pasado por agua (egg).
soften [ˈsɔfn] v. tr. Ablandar: *to soften the heart,* ablandar el corazón; *to soften leather,* ablandar el cuero. || Amortiguar (to deaden): *to soften a blow,* amortiguar un golpe. || Atenuar: *to soften the light,* atenuar la luz. || Suavizar (contours, the skin, etc.). || Bajar, templar (the voice). || MED. Reblandecer (the brain). || Destemplar, adulzar (steel). || Templar (the temperature). || *To soften up,* debilitar (to weaken), ablandar (leather, etc.).
— V. intr. Ablandarse: *he softened,* se ablandó; *the leather softens with time,* el cuero se ablanda con el tiempo. || Templarse (weather). || Debilitarse (to weaken). || MED. Reblandecerse (the brain). || — *To soften up on s.o.,* ablandarse con alguien. || *To soften up on the rules,* aplicar las reglas con más flexibilidad.
softener [—ə*] n. Suavizador, *m.*
softening [—iŋ] n. Ablandamiento, *m.* (of leather, etc.). || Amortiguamiento, *m.* (deadening). || Debilitación, *f.* (weakening). || Reblandecimiento, *m.* (of the brain). || Adulzado, *m.* (of steel). || Suavización, *f.* (of design, skin, character).
soft-footed [ˈsɔft,futid] adj. Que anda sin hacer ruido.
softhead [ˈsɔft,hed] n. Bobo, ba; tonto, ta.
softheaded [—id] adj. Bobo, ba; tonto, ta.
softhearted [ˈsɔftˈhɑ:tid] adj. Bondadoso, sa.
softness [ˈsɔftnis] n. Blandura, *f.* (of bed). || Suavidad, *f.* (of hair, colours). || Dulzura, *f.* (sweetness). || Tolerancia, *f.*, indulgencia, *f.* (tolerance). || Debilidad, *f.*, falta (*f.*) de energía (weakness). || Estupidez, *f.*
soft pedal [sɔftˈpedl] n. Sordina, *f.* (of a piano).
soft-pedal [ˈsɔftˈpedl] v. tr. Tocar con sordina (piano). || FIG. Suavizar, moderar.
soft soap [ˈsɔftsəup] n. Jabón (*m.*) líquido. || FAM. Jabón, *m.*, pelotilla, *f.*, coba, *f.* (flattery).
soft-soap [ˈsɔftsəup] v. tr. FAM. Dar jabón a, hacer la pelotilla a, dar coba a (to flatter).
soft-spoken [ˈsɔft,spəukən] adj. De voz baja *or* dulce.
software [ˈsɔftwɛə*] n. "Software", *m.*, logicial, *m.* [programación almacenada en una computadora].
softwood [ˈsɔftwud] n. Madera (*f.*) blanda.
softy [ˈsɔfti] n. FAM. Blando, da (indulgent person). | Sensiblero, ra (sentimental). | Bobo, ba (idiot).
soggy [ˈsɔgi] adj. Empapado, da (soaked). || Pesado, da (atmosphere). || Pastoso, sa (bread).
soh [səu] n. MUS. Sol, *m.*
soi-disant [swɑ:dízɑ̃ŋ] adj. Supuesto, ta.
soigné [ˈswænjei] adj. Elegante (carefully dressed). || Cuidadoso, sa (attentive to detail).
soil [sɔil] n. Suelo, *m.*, tierra, *f.*: *he came home covered in soil,* vino a casa cubierto de tierra; *when Colombus first stepped on American soil,* cuando Colón pisó tierra americana por primera vez. || Mancha, *f.* (dirty mark). || Estiércol, *m.* (excrement). || Basura, *f.* (refuse). || *One's native soil,* su tierra natal, su país.
soil [sɔil] v. tr. Ensuciar, manchar: *to soil a dress,* manchar un traje. || FIG. Manchar, mancillar: *to soil s.o.'s reputation,* manchar la reputación de alguien. || Alimentar con forraje verde (cattle).
— V. intr. Ensuciarse, mancharse.
soil pipe [—paip] n. Tubo (*m.*) de desagüe sanitario.
soirée [ˈswɑ:rei] n. Sarao, *m.*, velada, *f.*
soja bean [ˈsɔiəbi:n] n. BOT. Soja, *f.*
sojourn [ˈsɔdʒə:n] n. Residencia, *f.*, estancia, *f.*, permanencia, *f.* [*Amer.*, estada, *f.*] (stay).
sojourn [ˈsɔdʒə:n] v. intr. Residir, permanecer.
sojourner [—ə*] n. Residente (*m.*) temporal.
soke [səuk] n. HIST. Derecho (*m.*) de jurisdicción.
sol [sɔl] n. MUS. CHEM. Sol, *m.* || Sol, *m.* (monetary unit).
solace [ˈsɔləs] n. Consuelo, *m.*, alivio, *m.*
solace [ˈsɔləs] v. tr. Consolar, aliviar.
solanaceae [sɔləˈneisii:] pl. n. BOT. Solanáceas, *f.*
solan goose [ˈsəulənguːs] n. ZOOL. Alcatraz, *m.*
solanum [səuˈleinəm] n. BOT. Solanácea, *f.*
solar [ˈsəulə*] adj. Solar. || — *Solar battery, flare, month, plexus, prominence, system, year,* batería, erupción, mes, plexo, protuberancia, sistema, año solar.
solarium [səuˈlɛəriəm] n. Solario, *m.*
— OBSERV. El plural de *solarium* es *solaria* o *solariums.*
sold [səuld] pret. & p. p. See SELL.
solder [—ə*] n. Soldadura, *f.*
solder [—ə*] v. tr. Soldar.
— V. intr. Soldarse.
soldering [—riŋ] n. Soldadura, *f.* || *Soldering iron,* soldador, *m.*
soldier [ˈsəuldʒə*] n. MIL. Soldado, *m.* (non officer): *raw soldier,* soldado bisoño; *discharged soldier,* soldado licenciado; *volunteer soldier,* soldado voluntario. | Militar, *m.* (a man serving in an army). || — *Old soldier,* veterano, *m.* || *Private soldier,* soldado raso. || *Soldier ant,* hormiga (*f.*) soldado. || *Tin* o *toy soldier,* soldadito (*m.*) de plomo. || *To become a soldier,* hacerse soldado.
soldier [ˈsəuldʒə*] v. intr. Servir como soldado. || FIG. *To soldier on,* seguir adelante a pesar de todo.
soldierly [—li] adj. Militar, marcial.
soldier of fortune [—əvˈfɔ:tʃən] n. MIL. Mercenario, *m.* || FIG. Aventurero, *m.*
soldiery [—ri] n. MIL. Tropa, *f.*, soldadesca, *f.* || Arte (*f.*) militar (military science).
sole [səul] adj. Único, ca: *the sole survivor,* el único superviviente. || Exclusivo, va: *sole agent, right,* agente, derecho exclusivo. || JUR. *Sole legatee,* legatario (*m.*) universal.
— N. Planta, *f.* (of a foot). || Suela, *f.* (of a shoe): *half soles,* medias suelas. || Base, *f.* (lower part of sth.). || AGR. Cama, *f.* (of ploughshare). || Lenguado, *m.* (fish).
sole [səul] v. tr. Poner suela a (to provide with a sole).
solecism [ˈsɔlisizəm] n. GRAMM. Solecismo, *m.* || FIG. Incorrección, *f.* (bad social manners).
solely [ˈsəulli] adv. Únicamente, solamente.
solemn [ˈsɔləm] adj. Solemne: *solemn ceremony,* ceremonia solemne; *a solemn mass,* una misa solemne. || Serio, ria: *don't look so solemn!,* ¡no te pongas tan serio! || Estirado, da (pompous).
solemnity [səˈlemniti] or **solemness** [ˈsɔləmnis] n. Solemnidad, *f.*, seriedad, *f.* (of behaviour). || Solemnidad, *f.*, ceremonia (*f.*) solemne (solemn rite). || JUR. Requisito, *m.* (formality).
solemnization [ˈsɔləmnaiˈzeiʃən] n. Solemnización, *f.* || Celebración, *f.*
solemnize [ˈsɔləmnaiz] v. tr. Solemnizar (to perform with ceremony). || Celebrar (a marriage).
solenoid [ˈsəulinɔid] n. PHYS. Solenoide, *m.*
soleus [səˈli:əs] n. ANAT. Sóleo, *m.* (muscle).
sol-fa [sɔlˈfɑ:] n. MUS. Solfeo, *m.*
sol-fa [sɔlˈfɑ:] v. tr. MUS. Solfear.
solfatara [sɔlfəˈtɑ:rə] n. GEOL. Solfatara, *f.*
solfège [sɔlˈfeʒ] n. Solfeo, *m.*
solfeggio [sɔlˈfedʒiəu] n. MUS. Solfeo, *m.*
— OBSERV. El plural de *solfeggio* es *solfeggi* o *solfeggios.*
solicit [səˈlisit] v. tr. Solicitar (to request): *to solicit s.o. for sth.,* solicitar algo a alguien. || Importunar (to importune). || Abordar (a prostitute). || FIG. Requerir (to require). | Incitar (to incite). | Inducir (to induce).
— V. intr. Hacer de buscona (a prostitute).
solicitation [sə,lisiˈteiʃən] n. Solicitación, *f.* (request). || Provocación, *f.* (of a prostitute).

solicitor [sə'lisitə*] n. JUR. Procurador, *m.* (lawyer who prepares a case). | Notario, *m.* (for will, deeds, etc.). | Abogado, *m.* (in lower courts). || U. S. Agente, *m.*, representante, *m.* (agent).

— OBSERV. El *solicitor* acumula las funciones de procurador, notario, asesor y, en algunos casos, de abogado defensor.

solicitor general [—'dʒenərəl] n. Procurador (*m.*) de la Corona. || U. S. Subsecretario (*m.*) de Justicia.
solicitous [sə'lisitəs] adj. Solícito, ta; atento, ta (attentive). || Preocupado, da; ansioso, sa (*to*, de) [eager].
solicitude [sə'lisitju:d] n. Solicitud, *f.*, cuidado, *m.* (care, attention). || Preocupación, *f.*, afán, *m.*, ansiedad, *f.* (eagerness).
solid ['sɔlid] adj. Sólido, da: *solid body, state*, cuerpo, estado sólido; *solid foods*, alimentos sólidos. || Firme: *solid conviction*, convicción firme. || Continuo, nua: *a solid line*, una línea continua. || Denso, sa (fog, smoke). || Espeso, sa (jungle). || Entero, ra: *a solid day's work*, un día entero de trabajo. || Consistente, sólido, da; sustancial (arguments). || Bien fundado, da; poderoso, sa: *solid reasons*, razones poderosas. || Serio, ria (serious). || Fuerte, resistente (building, structure). || Sin interlíneas (typography). || Compacto, ta: *a solid mass*, una masa compacta. || Macizo, za (gold, silver, ebony, tyre): *a solid gold watch*, un reloj de oro macizo. || Sustancioso, sa (meal). || Duro, ra: *solid snow*, nieve dura. || Uniforme, unido, da (colour). || Cúbico, ca: *solid yard*, yarda cúbica. || Unánime (unanimous): *solid vote, support*, votación, apoyo unánime. || Incondicional (friends). || Atestado, da (full): *the room was solid with people*, el cuarto estaba atestado de gente. || — *As solid as a rock*, tan firme como una roca. || *Person of solid build*, persona (*f.*) fuerte. || MATH. *Solid angle*, ángulo sólido. | *Solid geometry*, geometría (*f.*) del espacio. || *Solid measure*, medida (*f.*) de volumen. || *To become solid*, solidificarse. || *To be* o *to go solid for*, estar unánimemente en favor de. || *To rain for three solid weeks* o *for three weeks solid*, llover durante tres semanas enteras, llover sin parar durante tres semanas.
— N. Sólido, *m.*
solidarity [,sɔli'dæriti] n. Solidaridad, *f.*: *out of* o *in solidarity with*, por solidaridad con.
solidary ['sɔlidəri] adj. Solidario, ria.
solidification [sə,lidifi'keiʃən] n. Solidificación, *f.*
solidify [sə'lidifai] v. tr. Solidificar.
— V. intr. Solidificarse.
solidity [sə'liditi] n. Solidez, *f.*
solidly ['sɔlidli] adv. Unánimemente, por unanimidad (unanimously). || Sin parar (non-stop). || *Solidly built*, sólidamente construido, de construcción sólida.
solidness ['sɔlidnis] n. Solidez, *f.* || Unanimidad, *f.* (of a vote).
solidungulate [sɔlid'ʌŋgjulət] adj./n. See SOLIPED.
soliloquist [sə'liləkwist] n. Persona (*f.*) que habla a solas.
soliloquize [sə'liləkwaiz] v. intr. Soliloquiar, hablar a solas, monologar.
soliloquy [sə'liləkwi] n. Soliloquio, *m.*, monólogo, *m.*
soliped ['sɔliped] adj. ZOOL. Solípedo, da.
— N. ZOOL. Solípedo, *m.*
solipsism ['səulipsizəm] n. Solipsismo, *m.*
solitaire [,sɔli'tεə*] n. Solitario, *m.* (card game, diamond).
solitariness ['sɔlitərinis] n. Soledad, *f.*
solitary ['sɔlitəri] adj. Solitario, ria (alone, lonely). || Único, ca; solo, la (only). || — *I didn't see a solitary soul*, no había ni un alma. || *Solitary confinement*, incomunicación, *f.* || *To be in solitary confinement*, estar incomunicado.
— N. Solitario, ria (person who lives alone). || U. S. FAM. Incomunicación, *f.* || U. S. FAM. *To put s.o. in solitary*, dejar a alguien incomunicado.
solitude ['sɔlitju:d] n. Soledad, *f.* (loneliness). || Aislamiento, *m.* (isolation). || Lugar (*m.*) solitario (lonely place).
solleret [sɔlə'ret] n. HIST. Escarpe, *m.*
solmization [sɔlmi'zeiʃən] n. MUS. Solfeo, *m.*
solo ['səuləu] n. MUS. Solo, *m.*: *a drum solo*, un solo de tambor; *a soprano solo*, un solo para soprano. || Solo, *m.* (in cards).
— Adj. MUS. Solo, la. || *My first solo flight*, la primera vez que vuelo solo.
— Adv. A solas. || *To fly solo*, volar solo.
soloist ['səuləuist] n. Solista, *m.* & *f.*
Solomon ['sɔləmən] pr. n. Salomón, *m.*
Solomonic [,sɔlə'mɔnik] adj. Salomónico, ca.
solstice ['sɔlstis] n. Solsticio, *m.*: *winter, summer solstice*, solsticio de invierno, de verano.
solubility [,sɔlju'biliti] n. Solubilidad, *f.*
soluble ['sɔljubl] adj. Soluble.
solution [sə'lu:ʃən] n. Solución, *f.*: *to find the solution to a problem*, encontrar la solución de un problema. || Resolución, *f.* (act of solving). || CHEM. Solución, *f.* || MED. *Physiological salt solution* o *physiological saline solution*, suero fisiológico.
solvability [,sɔlvə'biliti] n. Solubilidad, *f.*
solvable ['sɔlvəbl] adj. Soluble.
solve [sɔlv] v. tr. Resolver, solucionar.
solvency ['sɔlvənsi] n. Solvencia, *f.*
solvent ['sɔlvənt] adj. Solvente (able to pay debts). || Soluble (able to dissolve).
— N. Disolvente, *m.*, solvente, *m.* (chemical which dissolves).
soma ['səumə] n. BIOL. Soma, *m.*

— OBSERV. El plural de la palabra inglesa *soma* es *somata* o *somas.*

Somali [səu'mɑ:li] adj./n. Somalí.
Somalia [—ə] pr. n. GEOGR. Somalia, *f.*
Somaliland [—lænd] pr. n. GEOGR. Somalia, *f.*
somatic [sə'mætik] adj. Somático, ca.
somatology [səumə'tɔlədʒi] n. BIOL. Somatología, *f.*
sombre (U. S. **somber**) ['sɔmbə*] adj. Sombrío, a (dark and shadowy). || Melancólico, ca (melancholic). || Pesimista (pessimistic).
sombreness (U. S. **somberness**) [—nis] n. Aspecto (*m.*) sombrío. || Melancolía, *f.* || Pesimismo, *m.*
sombrero [sɔm'brεərəu] n. Sombrero (*m.*) de ala ancha.
some [sʌm] adj. Algunos, nas: *some people can't take decisions*, algunas personas no pueden tomar decisiones; *leave us some oranges*, déjanos algunas naranjas. || Alguno, na: *some fool left the light on*, algún idiota ha dejado la luz encendida. || Unos, unas; varios, rias: *some weeks ago*, hace unas semanas; *there are some men waiting for you*, hay unos hombres que te esperan. || Unos, unas, algo como: *some ten hours*, unas diez horas. || Cierto, ta: *some distance away*, a cierta distancia; *that might take some time*, podría tardar cierto tiempo. || FAM. Menudo, da; valiente (with irony): *some friend you are*, menudo amigo eres; *some help you were*, menuda ayuda me diste. | Extraordinario, ria (very good): *it was some game*, fue un partido extraordinario. || — *Do you want some tea?*, ¿quieres té?, ¿quieres un poco de té? || *For some reason or other*, por alguna razón, por una razón o por otra. || *I gave him some money*, le di un poco de *or* algo de dinero. || *I have some money*, tengo dinero, tengo un poco *or* algo de dinero. || *I'll give it some thought*, lo pensaré. || *In some regulation or other*, en algún reglamento, en algún que otro reglamento. || *Some day*, algún día, algún día de éstos, un día de éstos. || *Some hopes!*, ¡espérate sentado! || *Some luck!*, ¡vaya suerte! || *Some meal!*, ¡vaya comida! || *Some people I could mention*, algunos a quienes podría nombrar. || *Some other time* o *day*, otro día. || *Some way or other*, de una manera o de otra, de cualquier manera. || *That was some party!*, ¡eso sí que fue una buena fiesta!, ¡menuda fiesta! || *They must have found some other way*, han debido encontrar algún otro medio. || *They only finished some of the food*, sólo terminaron una parte de la comida. || *Try to get some sleep*, intenta dormir un poco.
— Pron. Algunos, nas; unos, unas: *some left and some stayed*, algunos se fueron y otros se quedaron. || Un poco: *some of that paper*, un poco de ese papel; *this cake is nice, do you want some?*, este pastel está muy rico, ¿quieres un poco? || Algunos, nas: *some of my friends*, algunos de mis amigos. || Parte, *f.*: *some of the time*, parte del tiempo; *I liked some of the film*, me gustó parte de la película, la película me gustó en parte; *some of what he said*, parte de lo que dijo. || — *And then some*, y algunos más. || *I already have some, thank you*, ya tengo, gracias. || *I've no money.* — *I have some*, no tengo dinero. — Yo sí tengo. || *Please take some*, tome un poco (a little), tome unos cuantos (a few). || *There are some who would disagree*, los hay *or* hay algunos que no estarían de acuerdo, hay quienes no estarían de acuerdo.
— Adv. Unos, unas: *some six months*, unos seis meses; *some 500 people*, unas quinientas personas; *some few*, unos pocos, unos cuantos. || U. S. FAM. Un poco, algo (a little): *we chatted some*, charlamos un poco. | Bastante (quite a lot).
somebody [—bədi] pron. Alguien: *somebody is calling you*, alguien te está llamando. || Alguien, alguno, na: *somebody probably picked it up*, lo habrá cogido alguno *or* alguien. || — *Somebody was asking for you*, alguien estaba preguntando por ti, han estado preguntando por ti. || *Somebody else*, otro, otra; algún otro, alguna otra.
— N. Personaje, *m.*, alguien: *he must be somebody to receive a welcome like that*, debe ser alguien *or* un personaje para que le hagan tal recibimiento; *he thinks he is somebody*, se cree alguien.
someday [—dei] adv. Algún día.
somehow [—hau] adv. De algún modo, de una forma o de otra: *we shall manage somehow*, nos las arreglaremos de algún modo. || Por alguna razón (for some unknown reason). || *This doesn't seem right to me somehow*, no sé por qué, pero no me parece bien.
someone [—wʌn] pron./n. See SOMEBODY.
someplace [—pleis] adv. U. S. See SOMEWHERE.
somersault ['sʌməsɔ:lt] n. Salto (*m.*) mortal: *back somersault*, salto mortal hacia atrás; *to turn a somersault*, dar un salto mortal. || Vuelta (*f.*) de campana (of a car, etc.): *to turn a somersault*, dar una vuelta de campana. || FIG. Cambio (*m.*) total.
somersault ['sʌməsɔ:lt] v. intr. Dar un salto mortal (a person). || Dar una vuelta de campana, volcar (a car, etc.).
something ['sʌmθiŋ] pron./n. Algo: *there must be something we can do*, debe de haber algo que podamos

hacer; *something to eat*, algo de comer; *I need something to eat*, necesito comer algo; *something of a problem*, algo problemático. || — *A hundred and something*, ciento y pico. || *Her name is Mary something*, se llama Mary algo *or* Mary y no sé qué más. || *Her name is Mary Trotter or something*, se llama Mary Trotter o algo así *or* algo por el estilo, se llama algo así como Mary Trotter. || *His new book is quite something*, su nuevo libro es algo extraordinario. || *Is something the matter?*, ¿le pasa algo?, ¿pasa algo? || *It's quite something to be able to speak six languages*, no es cualquier cosa hablar seis idiomas. || *She has a certain something*, tiene un no sé qué. || *Something else*, otra cosa: *and there's something else*, y hay otra cosa; algo extraordinario: *that film was something else!*, ¡esa película fue algo extraordinario! || *Something like*, algo como. || *Something of a coward*, algo cobarde. || *Something of the kind*, algo por el estilo. || *Something or other*, una cosa u otra, alguna cosa. || *That certain something was missing*, faltaba un no sé qué. || *The figure represents something of an increase*, la cifra demuestra cierto aumento. || *There's something in his theory*, su teoría tiene cierto valor. || *To be something of an artist*, tener algo de artista. || *To see something of s.o.*, ver a alguien de vez en cuando. || *Well, that's something*, ya es algo.

— Adv. Algo: *something over fifty*, algo más de cincuenta; *something like fifty pounds*, algo así como cincuenta libras; *something like yours*, algo parecido al tuyo. || — FAM. *It hurts something shocking*, duele una barbaridad. | *Now that's something like it!*, ¡eso sí que es!

sometime [ˈsʌmtaim] adv. Algún día, alguna vez. || — *Sometime before Saturday*, antes del sábado. || *Sometime last week*, [un día de] la semana pasada. || *Sometime next week*, [un día de] la semana que viene. || *Sometime or other*, tarde o temprano (sooner or later). || *Sometime soon*, pronto, algún día de éstos.

— Adj. Ex, antiguo, gua: *the sometime chairman*, el ex presidente.

sometimes [—z] adv. De vez en cuando, a veces, unas veces. || *Sometimes ... sometimes...*, unas veces ... y otras ...; ya ... ya ...: *sometimes sad sometimes gay*, ya triste, ya alegre.

someway [ˈsʌmwei] or **someways** [—z] adv. De alguna manera.

somewhat [ˈsʌmwɔt] adv. Algo, un poco: *to be somewhat suprised*, estar algo sorprendido.

— N. Algo, *m.*: *he was somewhat of a coward, of an athlete*, tenía algo de cobarde, de atleta. || *This is somewhat of a relief*, en cierto modo es un alivio.

somewhere [ˈsʌmwεə*] adv. En alguna parte: *somewhere in the world*, en alguna parte del mundo. || A alguna parte (with motion). || — *Somewhere between*, entre: *somewhere between two and three o'clock*, entre las dos y las tres; de: *somewhere between two and three weeks*, de dos a tres semanas. || *Somewhere else*, en otra parte (without motion), a otra parte (with motion). || *Somewhere in the region of twenty pounds*, unas veinte libras poco más o menos. || *Somewhere near here*, cerca de aquí, por aquí.

— N. Sitio, *m.*, lugar, *m.*

somnambulant [sɔmˈnæmbjulənt] adj. Sonámbulo, la; somnámbulo, la.

somnambulate [sɔmˈnæmbjuleit] v. intr. Andar dormido.

somnambulism [sɔm næmbjulizəm] n. Sonambulismo, *m.*, somnambulismo, *m.*

somnambulist [sɔmˈnæmbjulist] n. Sonámbulo, la; somnámbulo, la.

somnambulistic [sɔmnæmbjuˈlistik] adj. Sonámbulo, la; somnámbulo, la.

somniferous [sɔmˈnifərəs] adj. Somnífero, ra.

somniloquist [sɔmˈniləkwist] n. Persona que habla dormida, somnílocuo, cua.

somnolence [ˈsɔmnələns] or **somnolency** [—i] n. Somnolencia, *f.*

somnolent [ˈsɔmnələnt] adj. Soñoliento, ta; somnoliento, ta; somnolento, ta.

son [sʌn] n. Hijo, *m.*: *eldest, youngest son*, hijo mayor, menor. || FIG. Hijo, *m.*: *the sons of Spain*, los hijos de España. || — FAM. *Every mother's son*, todo quisque, todo hijo de vecino. || *Prodigal son*, hijo pródigo. || *Second son*, segundogénito, *m.*, segundón, *m.* || POP. *Son of a bitch!*, ¡hijo de puta! || REL. *The Son*, el Hijo (second person of the Trinity).

sonance [ˈsəunəns] n. Sonoridad, *f.*

sonant [ˈsəunənt] adj. Sonoro, ra.

— N. GRAMM. Sonora, *f.* (consonant).

sonar [ˈsəunɑ:*] n. TECH. Sonar, *m.*

sonata [səˈnɑ:tə] n. MUS. Sonata, *f.*

sonatina [ˌsɔnəˈti:nə] n. MUS. Sonatina, *f.*

sonde [sɔnd] n. Sonda, *f.*

son et lumière [ˌsɔ̃elu:ˈmjε:r] n. Espectáculo (*m.* de luz y sonido.

song [sɔŋ] n. Canto, *m.* (art of singing). || Canción, *f.* (musical composition): *to sing a romantic song*, cantar una canción romántica. || Canto, *m.* (of birds). || FIG. Rumor, *m.* (of waves). | Poesía, *f.*, canto, *m.* (poetry). || REL. Cántico, *m.* || — *Drinking song*, canción báquica. || *Hit song*, éxito, *m.* || *Song festival*, festival (*m.*) de la canción. || FIG. FAM. *There's no need to make such a song and dance about it*, no es para tanto. || REL. *The Song of Songs*, el Cantar de los Cantares. || *To burst into song*, empezar a cantar. || FIG. FAM. *To buy sth. for a song*, comprar algo por una bicoca *or* por cuatro cuartos. || U. S. FAM. *To give s.o. a song and dance*, contarle toda una historia a alguien, colocarle un rollo a alguien. || FIG. *To make a song and dance*, armar un follón. | *To sing the same old song*, volver a la misma cantilena.

songbird [—bə:d] n. Ave (*f.*) canora, pájaro (*m.*) cantor.

songbook [—buk] n. Cancionero, *m.*

songster [—stə*] n. Ave (*f.*) canora, pájaro (*m.*) cantor (bird). || MUS. Cantor, *m.*, cantante, *m.*

songstress [—stris] n. Cantante, *f.*, cantora, *f.*

songwriter [—ˈraitə*] n. Compositor, ra (who composes the music). || Autor (*m.*) de la letra (lyrics writer). || Autor (*m.*) de canciones (who composes the lyrics and music).

sonic [ˈsɔnik] adj. Acústico, ca: *sonic depth finder*, sonda acústica. || Sónico, ca (of the speed of sound). || — *Sonic bang* o *boom*, estampido supersónico. || *Sonic barrier*, barrera (*f.*) del sonido.

son-in-law [ˈsʌninlɔ:] n. Yerno, *m.*, hijo (*m.*) político.

— OBESRV. El plural de *son-in-law* es *sons-in-law*.

sonnet [ˈsɔnit] n. POET. Soneto, *m.*

sonneteer [ˌsɔniˈtiə*] n. Sonetista, *m.*

sonny [ˈsʌni] n. FAM. Hijito, *m.*, hijo, *m.*

sonometer [səuˈnɔmitə*] n. Sonómetro, *m.*

sonority [səˈnɔriti] n. Sonoridad, *f.*

sonorous [səˈnɔ:rəs] adj. Sonoro, ra.

sonorousness [—nis] n. Sonoridad, *f.*

soon [su:n] adv. Pronto, dentro de poco (within a short time): *it will soon be dinner time*, pronto será la hora de cenar. || Pronto: *write to me soon*, escríbeme pronto. || Rápidamente, en seguida (quickly): *he will soon solve the problem*, en seguida resolverá el problema. || Pronto, temprano (early): *you needn't go so soon*, no necesitas marcharte tan pronto; *to arrive too soon*, llegar demasiado temprano. || — *As soon as* o *so soon as*, en cuanto, nada más: *as soon as she saw him she remembered him*, en cuanto lo vio se acordó de él. || *As soon as possible*, en cuanto pueda, cuanto antes, lo más pronto posible: *he came as soon as possible*, vino en cuanto pudo; *we will come as soon as possible*, vendremos en cuanto podamos. || *How soon can you send it?*, ¿cuándo me lo puede mandar? || *How soon will it be ready?*, ¿para cuándo estará listo? || *It's still too soon to ask him*, todavía es muy pronto *or* es demasiado pronto todavía para preguntárselo. || *I would as soon o I had sooner do it by myself*, me gustaría más *or* preferiría hacerlo yo solo. || *My holidays ended all too soon*, mis vacaciones acabaron demasiado pronto. || *No sooner ... than*, en cuanto, nada más: *no sooner had he arrived than he began to complain*, en cuanto llegó *or* nada más llegar empezó a quejarse; *no sooner had he arrived than they interrupted the concert*, nada más llegar él *or* en cuanto llegó interrumpieron el concierto. || *No sooner said than done*, dicho y hecho. || *Soon after*, poco después: *soon after twelve*, poco después de las doce. || *Sooner or later*, tarde o temprano. || *Sooner than*, antes que. || *The reinforcements arrived none too soon*, los refuerzos llegaron justo en el momento oportuno. || *The sooner ... the better*, cuanto más pronto ... mejor: *the sooner you do it, the better it will be for you*, cuanto más pronto lo hagas, mejor será para ti. || *The sooner the better*, cuanto antes mejor.

soot [sut] n. Hollín, *m.*

soot [sut] v. tr. Cubrir de hollín.

sooth [su:θ] n. Realidad, *f.*: *in sooth*, en realidad.

soothe [su:ð] v. tr. Apaciguar, calmar, tranquilizar, sosegar (to calm). || Aplacar (temper, anger, etc.). || Aliviar, calmar (pain).

soothing [—iŋ] adj. MED. Calmante, sedante. || Tranquilizador, ra (calming). || Dulce (sweet).

soothsayer [ˈsu:θˌseiə*] n. Adivino, na.

soothsaying [ˈsu:θˌseiiŋ] n. Adivinación, *f.*

sootiness [ˈsutinis] n. Fuliginosidad, *f.* (resemblance to soot). || Suciedad, *f.* (dirtiness).

sooty [ˈsuti] adj. Fuliginoso, sa (like soot). || Cubierto de hollín (soot covered). || Negro como el hollín (as black as soot).

sop [sɔp] n. Sopa, *f.* (bread soaked in liquid). || Soborno, *m.*, regalo, *m.* (bribe). || Compensación, *f.* (compensation).

sop [sɔp] v. tr. Remojar. || *To sop up*, absorber.

sophism [ˈsɔfizəm] n. Sofisma, *m.*

sophist [ˈsɔfist] n. Sofista, *m.*

sophistic [səˈfistik] or **sophistical** [—əl] adj. Sofístico, ca; sofista.

sophisticate [səˈfistikeit] v. tr. Sofisticar (to make complex or affected). || Falsificar (a text). || Adulterar (wine). || Perfeccionar (system, method, mechanism, etc.).

sophisticated [—id] adj. Sofisticado, da; complejo, ja; complicado, da (made complex). || Falsificado, da (text). || Adulterado, da (wine). || Perfeccionado, da (system, method, etc.). || Sofisticado, da; carente de naturalidad (person).

sophistication [səˌfistiˈkeiʃən] n. Sofisticación, *f.*, complejidad, *f.* (complexity). || Perfección, *f.* (perfection). || Sofisticación, *f.*, falta (*f.*) de naturalidad (affectation).

sophistry [ˈsɔfistri] n. Sofistería, *f.* (the use of sophisms). || Sofisma, *m.* (sophism).
Sophocles [ˈsɔfəkli:z] pr. n. Sófocles, *m.*
sophomore [ˈsɔfəmɔ:*] n. U. S. Estudiante (*m.* & *f.*) de segundo año.
sophomoric [sɔfəˈmɔ:rik] adj. U. S. De estudiante de segundo año. || FIG. Carente de madurez (immature).
soporiferous [sɔpəˈrifərəs] adj. Soporífero, ra.
soporific [sɔpəˈrifik] adj. Soporífico, ca; soporífero, ra.
— N. Somnífero, *m.* (sleep pill).
sopping [ˈsɔpiŋ] adj. Empapado, da. || *Sopping wet*, calado hasta los huesos (person), empapado, da (thing).
soppy [ˈsɔpi] adj. Empapado, da (soaked). || FAM. Bobo, ba; tonto, ta (silly). | Sensiblero, ra (foolishly sentimental).
soprano [səˈprɑ:nəu] n. MUS. Soprano, *m.* & *f.*
— Adj. De soprano.
sorb [sɔ:b] n. BOT. Serbal, *m.* (tree). | Serba, *f.* (fruit). || *Sorb apple*, serba, *f.*
sorbet [ˈsɔ:bət] n. Sorbete, *m.*
sorcerer [ˈsɔ:sərə*] n. Brujo, *m.*, hechicero, *m.*
sorceress [ˈsɔ:səris] n. Bruja, *f.*, hechicera, *f.*
sorcery [ˈsɔ:səri] n. Brujería, *f.*, hechicería, *f.*
sordid [ˈsɔ:did] adj. Sórdido, da: *sordid dwellings*, viviendas sórdidas. || Sucio, cia: *a sordid affair*, un asunto sucio; *a sordid story*, una historia sucia. | Sórdido, da (mean, contemptible).
sordidness [—nis] n. Sordidez, *f.* || Suciedad, *f.*
sordino [sɔ:ˈdi:nəu] n. MUS. Sordina, *f.*
— OBSERV. El plural de *sordino* es *sordini*.

sore [sɔ:*] adj. Malo, la (bad): *a sore foot*, un pie malo. || Dolorido, da; que duele; doloroso, sa (which hurts). || FIG. Doloroso, sa: *a sore memory*, un recuerdo doloroso. | Grande: *a sore disappointment*, una gran decepción; *sore need*, gran necesidad. | Penoso, sa (work, etc.). || U. S. FAM. Molesto, ta; resentido, da: *to feel sore about not being promoted*, sentirse molesto *or* estar resentido por no haber sido ascendido. || — FIG. *A sore point* o *subject*, un tema delicado, un asunto espinoso. || *His wound is still very sore*, todavía le duele mucho la herida. || *My eyes are sore*, me pican *or* me duelen los ojos. || *My nose is sore*, me duele la nariz. || FIG. *To be sore at heart*, tener el corazón dolorido. || U. S. FAM. *To be sore at s.o.*, estar enfadado con alguien. | *To get sore*, ofenderse (to take offence), enfadarse (*at*, con) [to get angry]. || *To have a sore throat*, dolerle a uno la garganta, tener dolor de garganta.
— N. Llaga, *f.*, úlcera, *f.* (on people). || FIG. Dolor, *m.*, pena, *f.* || FIG. *To reopen an old sore*, renovar la herida.
— Adv. See SORELY.
sorehead [—hed] n. U. S. FAM. Cascarrabias, *m.* & *f.* *inv.*, resentido, da.
sorely [—li] adv. Muy (very). || Mucho (a lot). || Profundamente (deeply): *sorely offended*, profundamente ofendido. || Gravemente (seriously). || — *To be sorely afraid*, tener mucho miedo. || *To be sorely tempted to*, sentir una gran tentación de. || *When the sorely needed supplies arrived*, cuando llegaron las provisiones que tanta falta hacían.
soreness [—nis] n. Dolor, *m.* (pain). || U. S. Resentimiento, *m.* (resentment).
sorghum [ˈsɔ:gəm] n. BOT. Zahína, *f.*, sorgo, *m.*
sorites [səˈraiti:z] inv. n. PHIL. Sorites, *m.*
sororicide [səˈrɔrəsaid] n. Fratricidio, *m.* (crime). || Fratricida, *m.* & *f.* (criminal).
sorority [səˈrɔriti] n. U. S. Club (*m.*) femenino de estudiantes.
sorption [ˈsɔ:pʃən] n. Absorción, *f.*, adsorción, *f.*
sorrel [ˈsɔrəl] adj. Alazán, ana.
— N. Alazán, *m.* (colour). || Alazán, *m.* (horse). || BOT. Acedera, *f.*
sorriness [ˈsɔrinis] n. Pesar, *m.*, tristeza, *f.* (sadness). || Compasión, *f.* (pity).
sorrow [ˈsɔrəu] n. Tristeza, *f.*, pesar, *m.*, dolor, *m.*, pena, *f.* (sadness). || — *More in sorrow than in anger*, con más pesar que enojo. || *Much to my sorrow*, con gran pesar mío. || FIG. *To drown one's sorrows*, ahogar sus penas.
sorrow [ˈsɔrəu] v. intr. Entristecerse (to become sad). || Sentir pesar *or* pena, sentirse afligido (to feel sorrow): *to sorrow over sth.*, sentir pesar *or* pena por algo. || *To sorrow for*, añorar.
sorrowful [—ful] adj. Afligido, da; triste, pesaroso, sa (air, person). || Entristecedor, ra; triste, lastimoso, sa; doloroso, sa (news, sight, etc.).
sorrow-stricken [—ˈstrikən] adj. Muy afligido, da.
sorry [ˈsɔri] adj. Triste: *a sorry sight*, un triste espectáculo; *the sorry truth*, la triste verdad *or* realidad. || — *A sorry fellow*, un infeliz, un desgraciado. || *I can't say I'm sorry to hear it*, no puedo decir que lo sienta. || *I don't want you to feel sorry for me*, no quiero que me tengas lástima *or* que tengas pena por mí. || *I'm not at all sorry for what I did*, no me arrepiento en absoluto de *or* no me pesa nada lo que hice. || *I'm sorry about the other night*, siento lo que ocurrió la otra nocha, me disculpo por lo de la otra noche. || *To be in a sorry plight*, estar en una situación lamentable. || *To be in a sorry state*, estar en un estado lamentable *or* lastimoso. || *To be sorry*, sentir: *I'm very sorry*, lo siento mucho; *to be sorry about not having done sth.*, sentir no haber hecho algo; *I was sorry not to be there*, sentí mucho no estar allí; *I am sorry to have to tell you*, siento tener que decirle; arrepentirse, sentir: *you'll be sorry!*, ¡te arrepentirás! || *To feel sorry for*, compadecer: *I feel sorry for him*, le compadezco; sentir (to regret). || *To feel sorry for o.s.*, sentirse desgraciado.
— Interj. ¡Perdone!, ¡perdóneme!, ¡disculpe!, ¡perdón!, ¡lo siento!
sort [sɔ:t] n. Clase, *f.*, tipo, *m.*: *all sorts of flowers*, toda clase de flores; *and all that sort of thing*, y todo ese tipo de cosas. || Especie, *f.*: *it formed a sort of arch*, formaba una especie de arco. || Modo, *m.*, forma, *f.*, manera, *f.* (manner). || Tipo, *m.* (type of person): *to be a strange sort*, ser un tipo extraño. || Persona, *f.* (person): *to be a good sort*, ser buena persona. || — *After a sort*, en cierta manera. || *An unusual sort of film*, una película extraña. || *A sort of big black ball*, una especie de bola grande y negra. || *Did you tell him? — Sort of*, ¿se lo has dicho? — En cierto modo. || *He has bought some sort of sports car*, ha comprado no sé qué clase de coche deportivo. || *He sort of smiled*, esbozó una especie de sonrisa. || *He's some sort of officer*, es oficial, pero no sé qué graduación tiene. || *He's the sort that will take advantage*, es de los que se aprovechan. || *I know his sort*, sé la clase de persona que es. || *I'm sort of lost*, estoy como perdido. || *Is this the sort of thing you had in mind?*, ¿es eso *or* es algo así lo que busca usted? || *It's sort of big*, es más bien grande. || *It's sort of presentable*, está más o menos presentable. || *It takes all sorts to make a world*, de todo hay en el mundo *or* en la viña del Señor. || *Nothing of the sort!*, ¡nada de eso!, ¡ni hablar! || *Of a sort* o *of sorts*, una especie de: *there is a cupboard of sorts*, hay una especie de aparador. || *Out of sorts*, pachucho, cha (unwell), de mal humor, enfadado, da (cross). || *She's not that sort of woman*, no es de ésas. || *Something of the sort*, algo por el estilo. || *To have a sort of idea that*, tener una ligera idea de que.
sort [sɔ:t] v. tr. Seleccionar (to select). || Clasificar (to classify). || Ordenar, arreglar (to put in order). || — *To sort goods into lots*, distribuir mercancías en lotes. || *To sort out*, separar: *to sort out the good from the bad*, separar lo bueno de lo malo; apartar: *to sort out the bad ones*, apartar los malos; resolver (problems, difficulties), ordenar, arreglar (to put in order), seleccionar (to select), clasificar (to classify). || FAM. *To sort s.o. out*, ajustarle a uno las cuentas.
sorter [—ə*] n. Clasificador, ra (person). || Clasificadora, *f.* (machine).
sortie [ˈsɔ:ti] n. MIL. Salida, *f.*
sortilege [ˈsɔ:tilidʒ] n. Sortilegio, *m.*
sorting [ˈsɔ:tiŋ] n. Clasificación, *f.* || *Sorting office*, sala (*f.*) de batalla (in post office).
SOS [esəuˈes] n. S.O.S., *m.*: *to pick up an SOS*, recibir un S.O.S.
so-so [ˈsəusəu] adj./adv. Regular.
sot [sɔt] n. Borracho, cha.
sottish [ˈsɔtiʃ] adj. Borracho, cha; embrutecido por la bebida.
sotto voce [ˈsɔtəuˈvəutʃi] adv. En voz baja.
sou [su:] n. (Ant.). Moneda (*f.*) francesa de cinco *or* diez céntimos. || FAM. Gorda, *f.*, perra, *f.*, céntimo, *m.* [*Amer.*, centavo, *m.*]: *they haven't a sou*, no tienen una gorda.
soubrette [su:ˈbret] n. THEATR. Confidenta, *f.*
soubriquet [ˈsu:brikei] n. Apodo, *m.*, mote, *m.* (nickname).
Soudan [suˈdɑ:n] pr. n. GEOGR. Sudán, *m.*
Soudanese [ˌsu:dəˈni:z] adj./n. Sudanés, esa.
souffle [su:fl] n. MED. Soplo, *m.*
soufflé [ˈsu:flei] n. CULIN. "Soufflé", *m.*
sough [sau] n. Murmullo, *m.*, susurro, *m.*
sough [sau] v. intr. Murmurar, susurrar.
sought [sɔ:t] pret. & p. p. See SEEK.
sought-after [—ˈɑ:ftə*] adj. Solicitado, da (job, person, etc.). || Deseado, da (desired). || Codiciado, da (coveted).
soul [səul] n. Alma, *f.*: *to commend one's soul to God*, encomendar su alma a Dios; *with all one's soul*, con toda el alma. || FIG. Imagen, *f.*, personificación, *f.*, mismo, ma: *to be the soul of honour*, ser la personificación del honor, ser el honor mismo. || FAM. Garra, *f.*: *his performance lacks soul*, su actuación carece de garra. || — *A good* o *a simple soul*, un alma de Dios. || REL. *All Souls' Day*, Día (*m.*) de Difuntos. || *Bless my soul!*, ¡Dios mío! || *Every living soul*, todo ser viviente. || *God rest his soul*, que Dios le tenga en su gloria. || *Like a lost soul*, como un alma en pena. || *Not a soul was in sight*, no se veía ni un alma. || *Poor little soul*, pobre criatura, *f.* || *Poor soul*, pobre, *m.* & *f.*, pobrecito, ta. || *Put some soul into it!*, ¡venga, un poco de ánimo! || *The ship went down with all souls*, el barco se hundió con todos los que iban a bordo. || FIG. *To be the life and soul of the party*, ser el alma de la fiesta. | *To be the soul of discretion*, ser la discreción personificada. | *To throw o.s. life and soul* o *body and soul into sth.*, darse de lleno a algo, entregarse cuerpo y alma a algo. | *Unable to call one's soul one's own*, completamente esclavizado. || *Upon my soul!*, ¡por mi vida!, ¡vaya por Dios!

soul-destroying [—disˈtrɔiiŋ] adj. Embrutecedor, ra.
soul-felt [—felt] adj. Sincero, ra; sentido, da (sincere).
soulful [—ful] adj. Lleno de sentimiento (showing feeling). || Expresivo, va (expressive). || Sentimental. || Conmovedor, ra (moving).
soulless [—lis] adj. Sin alma (having no soul). || Inexpresivo, va (unexpressive). || Monótono, na; sin interés (dull, boring).
soul mate [—meit] n. Amigo (*m.*) del alma, amiga (*f.*) del alma.
soul-stirring [—stə:riŋ] adj. Emocionante (exciting). || Conmovedor, ra (moving).
sound [saund] adj. Sano, na (healthy). || Bueno, na: *sound character*, buen carácter; *sound health*, buena salud; *sound investment*, buena inversión; *sound piece of advice, argument*, buen consejo, argumento. || Profundo, da (sleep). || Válido, da (valid). || Bien fundado, da (well-founded). || Razonado, da; lógico, ca (reasoned). || Acertado, da (propitious): *a sound policy considering the situation*, una política acertada dada la situación. || Competente (competent). || Sólido, da (strong). || Seguro, ra (trustworthy). || Ortodoxo, xa (orthodox). || COMM. Solvente (solvent). | Seguro, ra (business). || MAR. En buen estado, en buenas condiciones (goods, ship). || — *Safe and sound*, sano y salvo. || FIG. *To be sound as a bell*, ser muy seguro (to be very solid), estar más sano que una manzana (to be healthy). || *To be sound in body and mind*, ser sano de cuerpo y alma. || *To be sound in wind and limb*, estar más sano que una manzana. || *To be sound of mind* o *of sound mind*, estar en su sano juicio.
— N. Sonido, *m.*: *the sound of her voice*, el sonido de su voz. || Ruido, *m.* (noise): *the sound of wheels*, el ruido de las ruedas. || MAR. Estrecho, *m.* (channel connecting two seas). | Brazo (*m.*) de mar (ocean inlet). || MED. Sonda, *f.* || ZOOL. Vejiga (*f.*) natatoria. || — FIG. FAM. *I don't like the sound of it*, no me huele bien. || *Light and sound*, luz y sonido. || *The speed of sound*, la velocidad del sonido. || *To live within the sound of the sea*, vivir a orillas del mar *or* donde todavía se oye el romper de las olas. || *To the sound of*, al son de. || *We camped within the sound of the battle*, desde donde acampamos se oían los cañonazos. || *Within, out of sound*, al alcance, fuera del oído.
— Adv. *To sleep sound*, dormir profundamente.
sound [saund] v. tr. Tocar: *to sound the trumpets*, tocar las trompetas; *to sound the bells*, tocar las campanas; *to sound the retreat*, tocar retreta. || Pronunciar: *sound your consonants clearly*, pronuncia bien las consonantes. || MED. Auscultar (with a stethoscope). | Sondar (with a sound). || MAR. Sondar, sondear, escandallar (to measure the depth of). | Estudiar, examinar (the ocean floor, seabed, etc.). || FIG. Sondear, tantear (s.o.'s opinion). || — FIG. *To sound s.o. out*, tantear *or* sondear a alguien. || *To sound the horn*, tocar el claxon.
— V. intr. Sonar: *the alarm, a gun, a bell sounded*, sonó la alarma, un tiro, una campana; *piano note that is not sounding*, una nota de piano que no suena; *it sounds like an aircraft*, suena como un avión; *it sounds hollow, full*, suena a hueco, a lleno. || FIG. Sonar: *it sounds wrong, funny*, suena mal, raro. | Parecer: *it sounds marvellous, silly*, parece estupendo, tonto. | Sonar: *it sounds like a lie to me*, me suena a mentira. || Sumergirse (a whale). || MAR. Hacer sondeos, sondear (to measure the depth of water). || U. S. FAM. *To sound off about sth.*, protestar a voz en grito sobre algo.
sound absorber [—əbˈsɔ:bə*] n. Amortiguador (*m.*) del sonido.
sound barrier [—ˌbæriə*] n. Barrera (*f.*) del sonido.
soundboard [—bɔ:d] n. MUS. Tabla (*f.*) de armonía (of piano). | Secreto, *m.* (of organ). || Tornavoz, *m.* (to reflect the voice).
sound box [—bɔks] n. Captador (*m.*) acústico (of gramophone). || Caja (*f.*) de resonancia (of musical instrument).
sound effects [—iˌfekts] pl. n. Efectos (*m.*) sonoros.
sound film [—film] n. Película (*f.*) sonora.
sound head [—hed] n. Cabeza (*f.*) sonora.
sound hole [—həul] n. Ese, *f.* (of a violin).
sounding [—iŋ] adj. Resonante, sonoro, ra (resonant). || Sonoro, ra (making a sound). || Altisonante (high-sounding). || — *Sounding balloon*, globo (*m.*) sonda. || *Sounding board*, tabla (*f.*) de armonía (of a piano), secreto, *m.* (of an organ), tornavoz, *m.* (to reflect the voice), portavoz, *m.*: *the government uses the press as a sounding board*, el gobierno emplea la prensa como portavoz. || *Sounding line* o *lead*, sonda, *f.*, escandallo, *m.*, sondaleza, *f.*
— N. MAR. GEOL. Sondeo, *m.* || FIG. Sondeo, *m.* (of opinion).
soundless [—lis] adj. Mudo, da (silent). || Silencioso, sa; sin ruido (noiseless). || Insondable, sin fondo (bottomless).
soundlessly [—lisli] adv. Sin sonido, silenciosamente, sin ruido (silently).
soundly [—li] adv. Sólidamente (firmly). || Sensatamente: *he advised them soundly*, les aconsejó sensatamente. || Profundamente: *he slept soundly all through the journey*, durmió profundamente durante todo el viaje. || *To thrash s.o. soundly*, dar una buena paliza a alguien (to punish, to defeat).
soundness [—nis] n. Validez, *f.* (validity). || Seguridad, *f.* (of an investment). || Firmeza, *f.*, solidez, *f.* (firmness). || Acierto, *m.*, sensatez, *f.* (good sense). || Solvencia, *f.* (solvency). || *Soundness of health*, buena salud.
sound post [—pəust] n. Alma, *f.* (of a violin).
soundproof [—pru:f] adj. A prueba de sonido, insonoro, ra.
soundproof [—pru:f] v. tr. Insonorizar.
soundproofing [—ˈpru:fiŋ] n. Aislante (*m.*) acústico (material). || Insonorización, *f.* (action).
sound track [—træk] n. Banda (*f.*) sonora, pista (*f.*) sonora.
sound wave [—weiv] n. Onda (*f.*) sonora *or* acústica.
soup [su:p] n. Sopa, *f.*: *tomato soup*, sopa de tomate; *vegetable soup*, sopa de verduras *or* de legumbres. || FAM. Niebla (*f.*) espesa (fog). || — U. S. FAM. *From soup to nuts*, de cabo a rabo. || FIG. FAM. *To be in the soup*, estar en un apuro *or* en un aprieto.
— Adj. Sopero, ra: *soup dish*, plato sopero. || — *Soup kitchen*, comedor (*m.*) de beneficencia. || *Soup ladle*, cucharón, *m.* || *Soup tureen*, sopera, *f.*
soup [su:p] v. tr. FAM. *To soup up*, aumentar la potencia de (a car).
soupçon [ˈsu:psɔ̃:ŋ] n. Pizca, *f.*, algo, *m.*: *a soupçon of irony*, una pizca de ironía.
soup spoon [ˈsu:pspu:n] n. Cuchara (*f.*) sopera.
soupy [ˈsu:pi] adj. Espeso, sa.
sour [ˈsauə*] adj. Ácido, da; agrio, gria; amargo, ga: *sour taste*, sabor agrio. || Acre (smell). || Cortado, da: *sour milk*, leche cortada. || Rancio, cia (bread). || FIG. Amargo, ga: *a sour smile*, una sonrisa amarga. | Acre, desabrido, da (character). | Agrio, gria; amargado, da: *a sour person*, una persona agria. || — FIG. *Sour grapes*, see GRAPE. || *To turn sour*, cortarse (milk), agriarse (wine, etc.), agriarse (character, situation, etc.).
sour [sauə*] v. tr. Agriar. || Cortar (milk). || Poner rancio (bread). || FIG. Amargar: *her death soured his character*, su muerte le amargó el carácter.
— V. intr. Agriarse. || Cortarse (milk). || Ponerse rancio (bread). || FIG. Amargarse (to turn bitter).
source [sɔ:s] n. Nacimiento, *m.*, manantial, *m.* (of a river). || FIG. Fuente, *f.*, origen, *m.*: *the source of the trouble*, el origen del problema. | Fuente, *f.* (of supply, information): *well-informed sources*, fuentes bien informadas. || MED. Foco, *m.* (of infection). || — *Reliable source*, fuente fidedigna. || *Source book*, libro (*m.*) de consulta.
sourdine [suəˈdi:n] n. MUS. Sordina, *f.*
sour-faced [ˈsauəfeist] adj. Arisco, ca.
sourly [ˈsauəli] adv. Agriamente.
sourness [ˈsauənis] n. Amargura, *f.*, acidez, *f.* (of taste). || FIG. Acritud, *f.*, desabrimiento, *m.* (of character).
sourpuss [ˈsauəpus] n. FAM. Persona (*f.*) desabrida.
soursop [ˈsauəsɔp] n. BOT. Guanábano, *m.* (tree). | Guanábana, *f.* (fruit).
sousaphone [ˈsu:zəfəun] n. U. S. MUS. Instrumento (*m.*) de cobre parecido a la tuba.
souse [saus] n. Conserva (*f.*) en vinagre (pickled food). || Adobo, *m.* (preparation for pickling meat). || Escabeche, *m.* (for pickling fish). || Remojón, *m.* (soaking). || FAM. Borracho, cha (drunkard).
souse [saus] v. tr. Adobar (meat). || Escabechar (fish). || Empapar (to soak). || Sumergir (to plunge). || — FAM. *To be soused*, estar trompa (drunk). | *To get soused*, empaparse, calarse (to get soaked), entromparse, coger una trompa (to get drunk).
soutache [ˈsutæʃ] n. Trencilla, *f.*
soutane [ˈsu:tæn] n. Sotana, *f.*
south [sauθ] n. Sur, *m.* (direction). || Sur, *m.*, mediodía, *m.* (region).
— Adj. Del sur: *south wind*, viento del sur. || — *South Pole*, Polo (*m.*) Sur. || *South Seas*, Mares (*m.*) del Sur.
— Adv. Hacia el sur: *to travel south*, viajar hacia el sur. || Al sur: *my house lies south of London*, mi casa está al sur de Londres; *my window looks south*, mi ventana da al sur.
south [sauθ] v. intr. MAR. Ir rumbo al sur.
South Africa [—ˈæfrikə] pr. n. GEOGR. África (*f.*) del Sur (the South of Africa). | República (*f.*) Sudafricana, África (*f.*) del Sur (South African Republic).
South African [—ˈæfrikən] adj./n. Sudafricano, na.
South America [—əˈmerikə] pr. n. GEOGR. Sudamérica, *f.*, Suramérica, *f.*, América (*f.*) del Sur.
South American [—əˈmerikən] adj./n. Sudamericano, na; suramericano, na.
southbound [—baund] adj. Con rumbo al sur.
south by east [—baiˈi:st] n. Sur (*m.*) cuarta al sudeste.
south by west [—baiˈwest] n. Sur (*m.*) cuarta al suroeste.
southeast [—ˈi:st] n. Sudeste, *m.*
— Adj. Del sudeste (of the southeast). || Sudeste (direction, part).
— Adv. Hacia el sudeste.
southeast by east [—i:stbaiˈi:st] n. Sudeste (*m.*) cuarta al este.
southeast by south [—i:stbaiˈsauθ] n. Sudeste (*m.*) cuarta al sur.
southeaster [—ˈi:stə*] n. Viento (*m.*) del sudeste.
southeasterly [—ˈi:stəli] adj. Sudeste (direction). || Del sudeste (wind).
— Adv. Hacia el sudeste.

southeastern [—'i:stən] adj. Del sudeste (of the southeast). || Sudeste (direction, part).
southeastward [—'i:stwəd] or **southeastwards** [—'i:stwədz] adv. Hacia el sudeste. || MAR. Rumbo al sudeste.
southerly ['sʌðəli] adj. En el sur (in the south). || Del sur (wind). || Sur (part, direction). || *The most southerly part*, la parte más meridional.
— Adv. Hacia el sur.
southern ['sʌðən] adj. Sur, meridional: *the southern part of the country*, la parte sur del país. || Del sur: *the southern region*, la región del sur. || Hacia el sur, sur: *in a southern direction*, en dirección sur *or* hacia el sur. || HIST. Sudista. || — *Southern Asia*, el sur de Asia. || *Southern Cross*, Cruz (*f.*) del Sur. || *Southern hemisphere*, hemisferio (*m.*) sur *or* austral.
southerner [—ə*] n. Habitante (*m.*) del sur, meridional, *m.* & *f.* (person). || HIST. Sudista, *m.* & *f.* || — *He's a southerner*, es del sur. || *The southerners are friendlier*, la gente del sur es más abierta, los del sur *or* los meridionales son más abiertos.
southern lights [—laits] pl. n. Aurora (*f. sing.*) austral.
southernmost [—məust] adj. Del extremo sur.
southernwood [—,wud] n. BOT. Abrótano, *m.*
South Korea ['sauθkə'riə] pr. n. GEOGR. Corea (*f.*) del Sur.
South Korean [—n] adj./s. Surcoreano, na.
southpaw ['sauθpɔ:] adj./s. U. S. FAM. Zurdo, da.
south-southeast ['sauθsauθ i:st] n. Sudsudeste, *m.*
— Adj. Sudsudeste. || Del sudsudeste (winds).
— Adv. Hacia el sudsudeste.
south-southwest ['sauθsauθ'west] n. Sudsudoeste, *m.*
— Adj. Sudsudoeste. || Del sudsudoeste (winds).
— Adv. Hacia el sudsudoeste.
South Vietnam ['sauθ'vjet'næm] pr. n. Vietnam (*m.*) del Sur.
South Vietnamese ['sauθ-vjetnə'mi:z] adj./n. Survietnamita.
southward ['sauθwəd] adj. Sur (direction).
— Adv. Hacia el sur.
— N. Sur, *m.*: *to the southward*, hacia el sur.
southwards [—z] adv. Hacia el sur.
southwest ['sauθ'west] n. Sudoeste, *m.*, suroeste, *m.*
— Adj. Del sudoeste (wind). || Sudoeste (direction, part).
— Adv. Hacia el sudoeste.
southwest by south [—bai'sauθ] n. Sudoeste (*m.*) cuarta al sur.
southwest by west [—bai'west] n. Sudoeste (*m.*) cuarta al oeste.
southwester [—'westə*] n. Viento (*m.*) del sudoeste (wind). || Sueste, *m.* (sailor's waterproof hat).
southwesterly [—'westəli] adj. Del sudoeste (wind). || Sudoeste (direction).
southwestern [—'westən] adj. Del sudoeste.
southwestward [—'westwəd] adj. Sudoeste.
— Adv. Hacia el sudoeste.
southwestwards [—'westwədz] adv. Hacia el sudoeste.
souvenir ['su:vəniə*] n. Recuerdo, *m.*
sou'wester [sau'westə*] n. Sueste, *m.* (sailor's waterproof hat).
sovereign ['sɔvrin] adj. Soberano, na: *sovereign power, state*, poder, estado soberano. || Eficaz (effective). || FIG. Soberano, na (absolute, supreme, unmitigated): *sovereign contempt*, soberano desprecio.
— N. Soberano, na (king, etc.). || Soberano, *m.* (coin).
sovereignty ['sɔvrənti] n. Soberanía, *f.* || Estado (*m.*) soberano (state).
soviet ['səuviət] n. Soviet, *m.*
— Adj. Soviético, ca: *Soviet Russia*, la Rusia Soviética; *the Soviet Union*, la Unión Soviética.
sovietization [,səuviəti'zeiʃən] n. Sovietización, *f.*
sovietize ['səuviətaiz] v. tr. Sovietizar.
sow [sau] n. Cerda, *f.* (female pig). || Tejón (*m.*) hembra (female badger). || Hembra, *f.* (female animal). || TECH. Reguera, *f.* (ditch). | Galápago, *m.*, lingote, *m.* (ingot).
sow* [səu] v. tr. Sembrar: *to sow wheat*, sembrar trigo; *to sow a field with wheat*, sembrar un campo de trigo; *to sow discontent, panic*, sembrar el descontento, el pánico. || FIG. Colocar, sembrar (mines). || Introducir [ostras, anchoas, etc.] en un criadero (oysters, etc.). || — FIG. *To sow on stony ground*, sembrar en el desierto. | *To sow the seeds of discord*, sembrar la discordia.
— V. intr. Sembrar.

— OBSERV. Pret. ***sowed***; p. p. ***sowed, sown***.

sowbread ['sau,bred] n. BOT. Pamporcino, *m.*
sow bug ['saubʌg] n. Cochinilla, *f.* (wood louse).
sower ['səuə*] n. Sembrador, ra.
sowing ['səuiŋ] n. Siembra, *f.* (action). || — *Sowing machine*, sembradora, *f.* || *Sowing time*, sementera, *f.*, siembra, *f.*
sown [səun] p. p. See SOW.
sow thistle ['sau,θisl] n. BOT. Cerraja, *f.*
soy [sɔi] n. CULIN. Salsa (*f.*) picante de soja (sauce). || Soja, *f.* (soya bean).
soya bean ['sɔiəbi:n] n. Soja, *f.*
soybean ['sɔibi:n] n. U. S. Soja, *f.*
sozzled [sɔzld] adj. FAM. Trompa (drunk): *he is sozzled*, está trompa. || FAM. *To get sozzled*, coger una trompa.
spa [spɑ:] n. Balneario, *m.* (resort). || Manantial (*m.*) de agua mineral (spring).
space [speis] n. Espacio, *m.*: *a space of six metres*, un espacio de seis metros; *in the space of half an hour*, en el espacio de media hora; *a journey into space*, un viaje al espacio; *write your name in the blank space*, ponga su nombre en el espacio en blanco. || Sitio, *m.*, espacio, *m.* (room): *to take up a lot of space*, ocupar mucho sitio. || MUS. PRINT. Espacio, *m.*: *double space*, doble espacio. || — *Space age*, era (*f.*) espacial. || PRINT. *Space band*, espaciador, *m.* | *Space bar*, espaciador, *m.* (of typewriter). || *Space capsule*, cápsula (*f.*) espacial. || PHYS. *Space charge*, carga (*f.*) espacial. || *Space flight*, vuelo (*m.*) espacial. || PHYS. *Space lattice*, red (*f.*) cristalina. || PRINT. *Space line*, interlínea, *f.* || *Space programme* o *program*, programa (*m.*) de vuelos espaciales. || *Space shot*, lanzamiento (*m.*) de un cohete espacial. || *Space station*, estación (*f.*) espacial. || *Space suit*, traje (*m.*) espacial. || *Space travel*, viaje (*m.*) espacial, viajes (*m. pl.*) espaciales. || *Space vehicle*, vehículo (*m.*) espacial. || *Space writer*, escritor pagado por líneas. || *To stare into space*, tener la mirada perdida.
space [speis] v. tr. Espaciar, separar: *to space (out) posts at ten metre intervals*, espaciar los postes a intervalos de diez metros. || Espaciar: *to space payments*, espaciar los pagos; *to space lines of type*, espaciar los renglones. || Distanciar (to move apart). || Distribuir (to distribute). || MIL. Escalonar (to stagger). || *Well spaced out*, bastante separados *or* distanciados.
spacecraft [—krɑ:ft] n. Nave (*f.*) espacial, astronave, *f.*, vehículo (*m.*) espacial.
spaceless [—lis] adj. Sin límites, ilimitado, da.
spaceman [—mən] n. Astronauta, *m.*, cosmonauta, *m.*

— OBSERV. El plural de *spaceman* es *spacemen*.

spacer [—ə*] n. Espaciador, *m.* (of a typewriter).
spaceship [—ʃip] n. Nave (*f.*) espacial, astronave, *f.*
space-time [—taim] n. Espacio tiempo, *m.*
spaceward [—wəd] adv. En dirección al espacio, hacia el espacio.
spacial ['speiʃəl] adj. Espacial, del espacio.
spacing ['speisiŋ] n. Espaciamiento, *m.* (arrangement of spaces). || Espacio, *m.* (space, room). || PRINT. Espacio, *m.*: *double spacing*, doble espacio.
spacious ['speiʃəs] adj. Espacioso, sa; amplio, plia (roomy). || Amplio, plia (wide). || *To live a spacious life*, vivir holgadamente.
spaciousness [—nis] n. Espaciosidad, *f.*, amplitud, *f.*
spade [speid] n. Pala, *f.* (for digging). || Laya, *f.* (for cutting turf). || MIL. Arado, *m.* (of a gun carriage). || Pico, *m.* (card or mark). || — Pl. Picos, *m.* (in international cards). || Espadas, *f.* (in Spanish cards). || — *The ace of spades*, el as de picos. || FIG. *To call a spade a spade*, llamar al pan pan y al vino vino.
spade [speid] v. tr. Remover con laya *or* pala.
spadeful [—ful] n. Pala, *f.*, paletada, *f.*
spader [—ə*] n. Pala (*f.*) mecánica.
spadework [—wə:k] n. FIG. Trabajo (*m.*) preparatorio.
spaghetti [spə'geti] n. CULIN. Espaguetis, *m. pl.*
Spain [spein] pr. n. GEOGR. España, *f.*
spake [speik] pret. (Ant.). See SPEAK.
spall [spɔ:l] n. Astilla, *f.* (of wood). || Laja, *f.* (of stone).
spall [spɔ:l] v. tr. Descantillar (to chip). || Astillar (wood). || Labrar (stone). || Machacar (ore).
— V. intr. Descantillarse (to get chipped). || Astillarse (wood). || Desprenderse (rock).
span [spæn] n. Envergadura, *f.* (of wings). || Lapso, *m.*, espacio, *m.* (of time): *over a span of ten years*, en un lapso de diez años. || Duración, *f.*: *life span*, duración de la vida. || Período, *m.* (period). || Distancia, *f.* (of space). || Pareja, *f.* (of horses). || Yunta, *f.* (of oxen). || Palmo, *m.*, cuarta, *f.* (measurement). || FIG. Esfera, *f.* (sphere). || ARCH. Tramo, *m.* (part of a bridge): *a bridge consisting of two fifty metre spans*, un puente con dos tramos de cincuenta metros. | Luz, *f.*, ojo, *m.* (distance between supports): *an arch with a fifty metre span*, un arco con una luz de cincuenta metros. || MAR. Envergadura, *f.* (of sails). || AVIAT. Envergadura, *f.* (of wings).
span [spæn] v. tr. MAR. Amarrar (to fasten with ropes). || Atravesar: *the bridge spans the river*, el puente atraviesa el río. || Tender sobre: *to span a river with a bridge*, tender un puente sobre un río. || Salvar, atravesar, pasar por encima de (to jump over). || Durar: *his life spanned fifty years*, su vida duró cincuenta años. || Medir en palmos (to measure). || Abarcar, comprender (to include): *this theme spans many subjects*, este tema abarca muchas materias.
span [spæn] pret. See SPIN.
spandrel ['spændrəl] n. ARCH. Tímpano, *m.*, enjuta, *f.*
spangle ['spæŋgl] n. Lentejuela, *f.*
spangle ['spæŋgl] v. tr. Adornar con lentejuelas (clothes): *a spangled dress*, un vestido adornado con lentejuelas. || FIG. Salpicar: *the sky was spangled with stars*, el cielo estaba salpicado de estrellas.
— V. intr. Brillar.
Spaniard ['spænjəd] n. Español, la.

spaniel [ˈspænjəl] n. Perro (*m.*) de aguas (dog).

Spanish [ˈspæniʃ] adj. Español, la.
— N. Español, *m.*, castellano, *m.* (language). || *The Spanish*, los españoles.

Spanish America [—əˈmerikə] pr. n. GEOGR. Hispanoamérica, *f.*

Spanish American [—əˈmerikən] n. Hispanoamericano, na.

Spanish-American [—əˈmerikən] adj. Hispanoamericano, na.

— OBSERV. See LATIN-AMERICAN (*Observ.*).

Spanish Armada [—ɑːˈmɑːdə] n. HIST. Armada (*f.*) Invencible.

Spanish bayonet [—ˈbeiənit] n. BOT. Yuca, *f.*

Spanish fir [—fəː*] n. BOT. Pinsapo, *m.*

Spanish fly [—flai] n. Cantárida, *f.* (insect).

Spanish leather [—ˈleðə*] n. Cordobán, *m.*

Spanish Main [—mein] n. MAR. Caribe, *m.* || Tierra (*f.*) firme (terra firma).

Spanish moss [—mɔs] n. BOT. Liquen, *m.*

Spanishness [—nis] n. Españolismo, *m.*, carácter (*m.*) español.

Spanish-speaking [—ˌspiːkiŋ] adj. De habla española *or* castellana, hispanohablante, hispanoparlante.

Spanish white [—wait] n. Blanco (*m.*) de España, albayalde, *m.*

spank [spæŋk] n. Azote, *m.* (single smack). || Zurra, *f.*, azotaina, *f.* (beating).

spank [spæŋk] v. tr. Dar un azote a, dar una zurra a.
— V. intr. Ir volando, ir a toda mecha: *they were spanking along*, iban a toda mecha.

spanker [—ə*] n. Caballo (*m.*) veloz (fast horse). || Azotador, ra (person). || MAR. Cangreja, *f.* || — MAR. *Spanker boom*, botavara, *f.* || FIG. FAM. *To be a spanker*, ser fenomenal (a flat, a car, etc.).

spanking [—iŋ] adj. Rápido, da; veloz: *spanking pace*, paso veloz. || Estupendo, da; fenomenal (impressive). || Fuerte (breeze).
— N. Zurra, *f.*, azotaina, *f.* (beating).

spanner [ˈspænə*] n. TECH. Llave, *f.* || — TECH. *Adjustable spanner*, llave inglesa. | *Box spanner*, llave de tubo. | *Double-ended spanner*, llave plana de doble boca. || FAM. *To throw a spanner in the works*, poner chinitas en el camino.

span-new [ˈspænˈnju] adj. Flamante.

span roof [spænruːf] n. Cubierta (*f.*) de dos aguas.

spanworm [ˈspænwəːm] n. ZOOL. Oruga, *f.*

spar [spɑː*] n. MAR. Palo, *m.* || AVIAT. Larguero, *m.* || MIN. Espato, *m.*: *Iceland spar*, espato de Islandia. || SP. Combate (*m.*) de entrenamiento, entrenamiento, *m.* (in boxing). | Amago, *m.*, finta, *f.* (feint). | Pelea (*f.*) con espolones (in cockfight).

spar [spɑː*] v. tr. MAR. Poner palos a. || AVIAT. Poner largueros a.
— V. intr. SP. Entrenarse (in boxing). | Hacer fintas, fintar (to feint). | Pelear con espolones (cocks). || FIG. Discutir (to argue).

sparable [ˈspærəbl] n. Puntilla, *f.* (nail).

spare [spɛə*] adj. Disponible (available): *I'm afraid we have no men spare*, lo siento, pero no tenemos a nadie disponible. || Sobrante, que sobra (left over, remaining): *are there any spare apples?*, ¿hay manzanas sobrantes? || Delgado, da (thin). || Frugal (frugal): *a spare meal*, una comida frugal. || Mezquino, na (mean). || De repuesto, de recambio (part): *a spare wheel*, una rueda de repuesto. || Libre: *if you have a spare moment*, si tiene un momento libre; *in my spare time*, en mis ratos libres. || — *Have you any spare glasses you could lend me?*, ¿tienes algún vaso de sobra que me podrías prestar? || *Spare of speech*, parco en palabras. || *Spare room*, cuarto (*m.*) de los invitados. || *There was some cheese spare*, sobraba un poco de queso. || *This one seems to be going spare*, parece que sobra éste.
— N. Pieza (*f.*) de recambio, repuesto, *m.* (spare part). || *You can have it, it is a spare*, cógelo, está de sobra.

spare [spɛə*] v. tr. Reservar (to conserve): *to spare one's strength*, reservar las fuerzas. || Perdonar la vida a: *they only spared the women and children*, sólo perdonaron la vida a las mujeres y a los niños. || Salvar [de la destrucción]: *Paris has been spared*, París ha sido salvado. || No herir, tener en consideración: *to spare s.o.'s feelings*, no herir los sentimientos de alguien. || Escatimar: *no effort was spared to save him*, ningún esfuerzo fue escatimado para salvarle; *to spare no expense*, no escatimar gastos; *don't spare the wine*, no escatimes el vino. || Ahorrar (to save): *spare me the details*, ahórrate los detalles; *you can spare yourself the trouble*, te puedes ahorrar el esfuerzo. || Prescindir de (to do without): *I can't spare him right now*, no puedo prescindir de él en este momento. || Dar, dejar: *can you spare me five hundred dollars?*, ¿puedes darme quinientos dólares? || Dispensar: *he was spared answering*, fue dispensado de responder. || Disponer de, tener: *can you spare two minutes?*, ¿puedes disponer de *or* tienes dos minutos? || Conceder, dedicar: *I can only spare you two minutes*, le puedo conceder dos minutos solamente. || — *Are you sure you can spare it?*, ¿está seguro de que no le hace falta? || *Have you any to spare?*, ¿le sobra alguno *or* algo? || *He spares neither himself nor his employees*, es muy exigente *or* duro tanto consigo mismo como con sus empleados. || *It fits in the box with room to spare*, cabe holgadamente en la caja. || *Nothing was spared for his comfort*, se hizo todo lo posible para su comodidad. || *Spare me*, tenga piedad de mí. || *The flood spared nothing*, la inundación no respetó *or* no perdonó nada. || *There is room and to spare*, hay sitio de sobra. || *To be spared a horrible fate*, librarse de un terrible destino. || *Very few lives were spared by the flood*, la inundación dejó a muy pocas personas con vida. || *We arrived with time to spare*, llegamos con tiempo de sobra. || *We have no time to spare*, no tenemos tiempo que perder.
— V. intr. Ser frugal. || Tener piedad (to have mercy).

spareable [—rəbl] adj. Disponible. || De sobra.

spareness [—nis] n. Escasez, *f.* || Frugalidad, *f.*

spare part [—pɑːt] n. Recambio, *m.*, pieza (*f.*) de recambio *or* de repuesto, repuesto, *m.*

spareribs [—ribs] pl. n. CULIN. Costillas (*f.*) de cerdo.

sparing [—riŋ] adj. Frugal (frugal). || Escaso, sa (scarce, sparse). || Limitado, da (limited). || Económico, ca (economical). || Parco, ca: *to be sparing of words*, ser parco en el hablar *or* en palabras; *sparing of compliments*, parco en cumplidos. || — *He is sparing in his use of adjectives*, emplea los adjetivos con parquedad. || *His sparing use of adjectives*, su parquedad en el empleo de los adjetivos.

sparingly [—riŋli] adv. Con moderación (with moderation). || Poco (little). || Frugalmente (frugally). || En pequeñas cantidades (in small amounts).

spark [spɑːk] n. Chispa, *f.*: *to give off sparks*, echar chispas. || ELECTR. Chispa, *f.* || AUT. Encendido, *m.* || FIG. Destello, *m.*, chispa, *f.*: *not a spark of life*, ni un destello de vida. || FIG. FAM. Galán, *m.* (dandy). || — FIG. FAM. *Bright spark*, listillo, *m.* (person). | *Sparks*, radiotelegrafista, *m.* || FIG. FAM. *Sparks are going to fly when he finds out*, echará chispas cuando se entere. | *Sparks flew*, se armó la gorda.

spark [spɑːk] v. intr. Chispear, echar chispas.
— V. tr. Encender. || FIG. *To spark off*, provocar, causar.

spark arrester [—əˈrestə*] n. Parachispas, *m. inv.*

spark coil [—kɔil] n. ELECTR. Bobina (*f.*) de inducción.

spark gap [—gæp] n. ELECTR. Distancia (*f.*) explosiva, entrehierro, *m.*

sparking plug [ˈspɑːkiŋplʌg] n. AUT. Bujía, *f.*

sparkle [ˈspɑːkl] n. Destello, *m.*, centelleo, *m.*: *sparkle of the diamond*, centelleo del diamante. || FIG. Viveza, *f.*, vivacidad, *f.* (liveliness).

sparkle [ˈspɑːkl] v. intr. Centellear, destellar: *a diamond sparkles in the sun*, un diamante centellea al sol. || Echar chispas, chispear (to spark). || FIG. Ser muy animado (to be vivacious). || Brillar, chispear: *eyes that sparkle with happiness*, ojos que brillan de alegría. || Burbujear, ser espumoso (wine). || FIG. FAM. Lucirse, brillar (to perform brilliantly). || FIG. *To sparkle with wit*, tener un ingenio chispeante.

sparkler [—ə*] n. Fuego (*m.*) de artificio [que desprende chispas blancas] (firework). || U. S. FAM. Diamante, *m.* (diamond).

sparkling [—iŋ] adj. Centelleante, brillante (stars, jewels, etc.). || FIG. Chispeante, brillante (wit, eyes). | Vivaz (vivacious). | Espumoso, sa (liquid): *sparkling wine*, vino espumoso. || U. S. *Sparkling water*, soda, *f.* (soda water).

spark plug [ˈspɑːkplʌg] n. U. S. AUT. Bujía, *f.*

sparling [ˈspaliŋ] n. ZOOL. Eperlano, *m.* (fish).

sparring partner [ˈspɑːriŋˌpɑːtnə*] n. SP. "Sparring-partner", *m.*, boxeador (*m.*) que entrena a otro antes de un combate.

sparrow [ˈspærəu] n. Gorrión, *m.* (bird).

sparrow hawk [—hɔːk] n. Gavilán, *m.* (bird).

sparry [ˈspɑːri] adj. MIN. Espático, ca.

sparse [spɑːs] adj. Escaso, sa; disperso, sa: *sparse vegetation*, vegetación escasa. || Poco denso, sa (not dense). || Ralo, la (hair).

sparsely [—li] adv. Escasamente: *sparsely forested*, escasamente poblado de árboles; *sparsely populated*, escasamente poblado. || *Sparsely scattered*, esparcidos.

Sparta [ˈspɑːtə] pr. n. GEOGR. Esparta, *f.*

Spartan [ˈspɑːtən] adj./n. Espartano, na.

spasm [ˈspæzəm] n. MED. Espasmo, *m.* (contraction). | Acceso, *m.*, ataque, *m.* (of fever, coughing, etc.). || FIG. Arrebato, *m.* (surge of anger, of enthusiasm). | Arranque, *m.* (of humour, of gaiety). || *To work in spasms*, trabajar irregularmente.

spasmodic [spæzˈmɔdik] adj. MED. Espasmódico, ca. | Involuntario, ria (movement). || FIG. Irregular, intermitente (not continuous).

spastic [ˈspæstik] adj. MED. Espástico, ca.
— N. MED. Espástico, ca.

spat [spæt] pret. & p. p. See SPIT.

spat [spæt] n. Polaina, *f.* (gaiter). || ZOOL. Freza, *f.*, hueva, *f.* (spawn). | Ostra (*f.*) joven (young oyster). || U. S. FAM. Riña, *f.*

— OBSERV. En el sentido zoológico el plural de *spat* es *spat* o *spats*.

spat [spæt] v. intr. U. S. FAM. Reñir (to quarrel). || ZOOL. Frezar (to spawn).

spate [speit] n. Avenida, *f.*, crecida, *f.* (of a river). || FIG. Torrente, *m.*: *a spate of words*, un torrente de palabras. || *In spate*, crecido, da (a river).

spathe [speiːð] n. BOT. Espata, *f.*
spathic [ˈspæθik] or **spathose** [spæˈθəus] adj. MIN. Espático, ca.
spatial [ˈspeiʃəl] adj. Espacial, del espacio.
spatter [ˈspætə*] n. Salpicón, *m.*, salpicadura, *f.* (splash). || — *Spatter of applause*, unos cuantos aplausos. || *Spatter of rain*, un poco de lluvia.
spatter [ˈspætə*] v. tr. Salpicar, rociar: *to spatter with mud*, salpicar de barro. || FIG. Mancillar, manchar.
— V. intr. Salpicar.
spatterdash [—dæʃ] n. Polaina, *f.* (gaiter).
spatula [ˈspætjulə] n. Espátula, *f.*
spatulate [ˈspætjulit] adj. Espatulado, da.
spavin [ˈspævin] n. VET. Esparaván, *m.*
spawn [spɔːn] n. Freza, *f.*, hueva, *f.* (of fish). | Huevos, *m. pl.* (of a frog). || BOT. Micelio, *m.* (of mushrooms). || FIG. Resultado, *m.*: *the spawn of my research*, el resultado de mi investigación. | Semilla, *f.*, germen, *m.* (origin). | Engendro, *m.* (offspring).
spawn [spɔːn] v. tr. Depositar (eggs). || Producir, engendrar (to produce).
— V. intr. Frezar, desovar (fishes). || Multiplicarse, reproducirse (to reproduce).
spawning [—iŋ] n. Desove, *m.*, freza, *f.*
spay [spei] v. tr. Quitar los ovarios.
speak* [spiːk] v. tr. Decir: *to speak the truth*, decir la verdad; *to speak nonsense*, decir tonterías. || Hablar: *do you speak Spanish?*, ¿habla usted español?; *English spoken*, se habla inglés. || FIG. Expresar: *her eyes spoke a warm welcome*, sus ojos expresaban una cordial bienvenida. | Cantar, hablar de: *his deeds speak his bravery*, sus hazañas cantan su valor. | Indicar (indicate). || MAR. Comunicar con. || — *He didn't speak a word*, no dijo ni una palabra, no habló. || *To speak one's mind* o *to speak straight from the shoulder*, decir lo que uno piensa, hablar sin rodeos. || *To speak pidgin English*, hablar un inglés macarrónico, hablar como los indios. || *To speak volumes*, see VOLUME.
— V. intr. Hablar: *he speaks clearly*, habla claramente; *he was too sad to speak*, estaba demasiado triste para hablar; *he is going to speak at the meeting*, va a hablar en la reunión; *to speak about sth.*, hablar de algo; *to speak to s.o.*, hablar con alguien; *you must speak to John about the noise he makes*, tienes que hablar con Juan del ruido que hace. || Hablarse (to each other): *they aren't speaking*, no se hablan. || Tomar la palabra (to take the floor). || Pronunciar un discurso (to give a speech). || FIG. Sonar: *the organ spoke*, el órgano sonó. || — *Did s.o. speak?*, ¿ha hablado alguien?, ¿alguien ha dicho algo? || *Generally speaking*, hablando en general. || *I don't know him to speak to*, no he hablado nunca con él. || *I'll never speak to you again*, no te volveré a dirigir la palabra. || FIG. *It almost speaks*, sólo le falta hablar (portrait, animal). || *Roughly speaking*, aproximadamente. || *So to speak*, por así decirlo, como quien dice. || *Speaking*, al aparato (on the telephone). || *This is Elena speaking*, soy Elena (on the telephone). || *To speak behind s.o.'s back*, hablar a espaldas de alguien. || *To speak cryptically*, hablar a medias palabras. || *To speak like a book*, hablar como un libro. || *To speak like a fishwife*, hablar como una verdulera. || *To speak through one's nose*, hablar con *or* por la nariz, hablar con voz gangosa.
— **To speak for**, recomendar (to recommend). | Hablar en nombre de (on behalf of). | Hablar en favor de (a motion). | FAM. Coger, comprometer: *I am spoken for*, estoy cogido (engaged, married, etc.), coger, reservar: *this table is spoken for*, esta mesa está cogida. | — *It speaks for itself*, es evidente, habla por sí mismo. | *Speaking for myself*, personalmente. | *The evidence speaks for itself*, las pruebas hablan por sí solas. | FIG. *To speak well for s.o.*, decir mucho en favor de uno. || **To speak of**, hablar de (to talk about). | Revelar (to indicate). | — *Speaking of marriage...*, hablando de matrimonio... | *To be nothing to speak of*, no ser nada especial. | *To speak ill of*, hablar mal de. | *To speak well of*, hablar bien de. || **To speak out**, hablar claro. | Hablar más fuerte. || **To speak to**, garantizar, confirmar. | — *To speak to the point*, ceñirse al tema, ir al grano. || **To speak up**, hablar más fuerte: *speak up, he's deaf*, habla más fuerte, que es sordo. | — *To speak up for*, intervenir en favor de.

— OBSERV. Pret. **spoke;** p. p. **spoken**.

speakeasy [—iːzi] n. U. S. FAM. Despacho (*m.*) de bebidas clandestino.
speaker [—ə*] n. Orador, ra: *a good speaker*, un buen orador; *to interrupt the speaker*, interrumpir al orador. || Persona (*f.*) que habla (person speaking). || Presidente, *m.* (in Parliament). || Portavoz, *m.* [*Amer.*, vocero, *m.*] (spokesman). || ELECTR. Altavoz, *m.* [*Amer.*, altoparlante, *m.*] (loudspeaker). || *Speakers of English*, los que hablan inglés.
speakership [—əʃip] n. Presidencia, *f.* (of Parliament).
speaking [—iŋ] adj. Hablante, parlante (who is speaking). || De habla: *English-speaking people*, personas de habla inglesa. || Manifiesto, ta: *a speaking resemblance*, un parecido manifiesto. || Fiel (likeness). || Elocuente: *a speaking glance*, una mirada elocuente. || Expresivo, va (face). || Elocuente (proof). || Cuando habla: *his speaking voice is better than his singing voice*, su voz cuando habla es mejor que cuando canta. || Hablado, da: *he has a speaking part in the play*, tiene una parte hablada en la obra de teatro. || — *To be on speaking terms*, hablarse: *I am not on speaking terms with him*, no me hablo con él; *they are not on speaking terms*, no se hablan. || *Within speaking distance*, al alcance de la voz.
— N. Habla, *f.* (speech, use of voice). || — *Public speaking*, arte (*m.*) de la oratoria. || *Speaking acquaintance*, conocido, da. || *Speaking trumpet*, megáfono, *m.*, bocina, *f.*
spear [spiə*] n. Lanza, *f.* (weapon). || Arpón, *m.* (harpoon). || SP. Jabalina, *f.* (javelin). || *With a thrust of his spear*, de una lanzada.
spear [spiə*] v. tr. Traspasar, atravesar [con una lanza]: *to spear s.o. through the heart*, traspasarle el corazón a alguien. || Arponear (to harpoon).
spearhead [—hed] n. Punta (*f.*) de lanza. || FIG. Vanguardia, *f.*: *the cavalry was the spearhead of the attack*, la caballería constituyó la vanguardia del ataque.
spearhead [—hed] v. tr. Encabezar.
spearman [—mən] n. Lancero, *m.*

— OBSERV. El plural de *spearman* es *spearmen*.

spearmint [—mint] n. BOT. Menta (*f.*) verde.
spec [spek] n. COMM. Especulación, *f.* || FIG. *On spec*, por si acaso.
special [ˈspeʃəl] adj. Especial, particular: *each spice imparts a special flavour*, cada especia da un sabor particular; *it requires special knowledge*, requiere un conocimiento especial. || Superior: *special brand*, marca superior. || Íntimo, ma: *special friends*, amigos íntimos. || Especial: *special licence*, autorización especial. || Extraordinario, ria (edition). || — *Nothing special*, nada especial, nada extraordinario. || *Special constable*, guardia (*m.*) auxiliar. || *Special delivery*, carta (*f.*) *or* correo (*m.*) urgente (letter), entrega inmediata (delivery). || *This week's special offer*, la oferta especial de esta semana. || *What's so special about it?*, ¿qué tiene de particular?
— N. Tren (*m.*) especial (train). || Guardia (*m.*) auxiliar (policeman). || Número (*m.*) extraordinario (edition).
specialism [—izəm] n. Especialización, *f.*
specialist [—ist] n. Especialista, *m.* & *f.*
speciality [ˌspeʃiˈæliti] n. Especialidad, *f.* || *Speciality of the house* o *our speciality*, especialidad de la casa.
specialization [ˌspeʃəlaiˈzeiʃən] n. Especialización, *f.*
specialize [ˈspeʃəlaiz] v. intr. Especializarse: *to specialize in French*, especializarse en francés. || BIOL. Diferenciarse.
— V. tr. Especializar: *to specialize one's studies*, especializar los estudios. || BIOL. Adaptar.
specially [ˈspeʃəli] adv. Especialmente.
specialty [ˈspeʃəlti] n. Especialidad, *f.* (speciality). || JUR. Contrato (*m.*) formal.
speciation [spiʃiˈeiʃən] n. Evolución (*f.*) de las especies.
specie [ˈspiːʃiː] n. Metálico, *m.*, efectivo, *m.* || *In specie*, en metálico.
species [ˈspiːʃiːz] n. Especie, *f.*, clase, *f.*: *a species of cherry*, una clase de cereza. || BIOL. Especie, *f.*: *the human species*, la especie humana. || REL. Especies (*f. pl.*) sacramentales.

— OBSERV. El plural de *species* es *species*.

specific [spiˈsifik] adj. Específico, ca. || *He wasn't very specific*, no especificó, no concretó, no fue muy explícito.
— N. MED. Específico, *m.* || — Pl. Datos (*m.*) específicos.
specification [ˌspesifiˈkeiʃən] n. Especificación, *f.* || Estipulación, *f.* (of a contract, etc.). || Requisito, *m.* (requirement). || — Pl. Descripción (*f. sing.*) detallada (detailed description). || Pliego (*m.*) de condiciones (list of requirements).
specific gravity [—ˈgræviti] n. PHYS. Peso (*m.*) específico.
specific heat [—hiːt] n. PHYS. Calor (*m.*) específico.
specify [ˈspesifai] v. tr. Especificar, precisar, concretar. || *Unless otherwise specified*, salvo indicación contraria.
specimen [ˈspesimin] n. Modelo, *m.* (model). || Muestra, *f.* (sample). || Ejemplar, *m.* (example). || BIOL. Espécimen, *m.* || FAM. Individuo, *m.*, tipo, *m.*: *he is a queer specimen*, es un tipo extraño. || — MED. *Blood specimen*, muestra de sangre. || PRINT. *Specimen page* o *copy*, espécimen.
speciosity [ˌspiːʃiˈɔsiti] n. Especiosidad, *f.*
specious [ˈspiːʃəs] adj. Especioso, sa.
speciousness [—nis] n. Especiosidad, *f.*
speck [spek] n. Partícula, *f.*, mota, *f.* (small particle). || Mota, *f.* (small defect). || FIG. Punto, *m.*: *he was a speck on the horizon*, era un punto en el horizonte. | Pizca, *f.*: *there's not a speck of kindness in him*, no tiene ni pizca de generosidad.
speck [spek] v. tr. Motear, salpicar de manchas.
speckle [ˈspekl] n. Mancha, *f.*, mota, *f.* (small spot). || Peca, *f.* (freckle).
speckle [spekl] v. tr. Motear, salpicar de manchas.
specs [speks] pl. n. FAM. Gafas, *f.* [*Amer.*, lentes, *m.*, anteojos, *m.*]
spectacle [ˈspektəkl] n. Espectáculo, *m.* (display). || — Pl. Gafas, *f.* [*Amer.*, lentes, *m.*, anteojos, *m.*]

(glasses): *spectacle case*, estuche de las gafas. || — FAM. *To make a spectacle of o.s.*, dar el espectáculo, ponerse en ridículo. || FIG. *To see life through rose-coloured spectacles*, ver la vida color de rosa.
spectacled [—d] adj. Que lleva gafas, con gafas. || ZOOL. *Spectacled snake*, serpiente (*f.*) de anteojos.
spectacular [spekˈtækjulə*] adj. Espectacular.
— N. Espectáculo (*m.*) grandioso.
spectator [spekˈteitə*] n. Espectador, ra.
specter [ˈspektə*] n. U. S. Espectro, *m.*
spectra [ˈspektrə] pl. n. See SPECTRUM.
spectral [ˈspektrəl] adj. Espectral.
spectre [ˈspektə*] n. Espectro, *m.*
spectrogram [ˈspektrəugræm] n. Espectrograma, *m.*
spectrograph [ˈspektrəugrɑ:f] n. Espectrógrafo, *m.*
spectrography [spekˈtrɔgrəfi] n. Espectrografía, *f.*
spectrometer [spekˈtrɔmitə*] n. Espectrómetro, *m.*
spectroscope [ˈspektrəskəup] n. Espectroscopio, *m.*
spectroscopic [ˌspektrəsˈkɔpik] adj. Espectroscópico, ca.
spectroscopy [spekˈtrɔskəpi] n. Espectroscopia, *f.*
spectrum [ˈspektrəm] n. Espectro, *m.*

— OBSERV. El plural de la palabra inglesa *spectrum* es *spectra* o *spectrums*.

specula [ˈspekjulə] pl. n. See SPECULUM.
speculate [ˈspekjuleit] v. intr. Especular: *to speculate on the Stock Exchange, in cereals*, especular en la Bolsa, en cereales; *to speculate about what might have happened*, especular sobre lo que hubiera podido acontecer.
speculation [ˌspekjuˈleiʃən] n. Especulación, *f.*
speculative [ˈspekjulətiv] adj. Especulativo, va.
speculator [ˈspekjuleitə*] n. Especulador, ra.
speculum [ˈspekjuləm] n. MED. Espéculo, *m.* || ZOOL. Espéculo, *m.*, espejo, *m.*

— OBSERV. El plural de la palabra *speculum* es *specula* o *speculums*.

sped [sped] pret. & p. p. See SPEED.
speech [spi:tʃ] n. Habla, *f.* (capacity to speak): *he lost his speech*, perdió el habla. || Conferencia, *f.* (lecture): *he gave a speech on Spanish gypsies*, dio una conferencia sobre los gitanos españoles. || Discurso, *m.*: *to deliver a speech in Parliament*, pronunciar un discurso en el parlamento. || Conversación, *f.* (talk). || Palabras, *f. pl.* (words). || Pronunciación, *f.*: *speech defect* o *impediment*, defecto de pronunciación. || Diálogo, *m.* (dialogue in play, film). || Habla, *f.*: *the speech of the Incas*, el habla de los Incas. || MUS. Sonoridad, *f.* (of an instrument). || GRAMM. Oración, *f.*: *direct, indirect speech*, oración directa, indirecta; *part of speech*, parte de la oración. || — *Figure of speech*, see FIGURE. || *Free speech*, libertad (*f.*) de expresión. || *Opening, closing speech*, discurso inaugural *or* de apertura, de clausura.
speech area [—ˈɛəriə] n. Área (*f.*) lingüística.
speech community [—kəˈmju:niti] n. U. S. Comunidad (*f.*) lingüística.
speech day [—dei*] n. Día (*m.*) del reparto de premios.
speechify [—ifai] v. intr. Perorar.
speechless [—lis] adj. Sin habla, mudo, da (dumb): *I was speechless*, me quedé mudo.
speed [spi:d] n. Velocidad, *f.*: *the speed of a car*, la velocidad de un coche. || PHYS. Velocidad, *f.* || Rapidez, *f.*, velocidad, *f.*: *the speed at which one works*, la rapidez con la que se trabaja. || PHOT. Velocidad, *f.* || U. S. TECH. Velocidad, *f.* (gear). || FAM. Droga (*f.*) estimulante. || — *At full* o *top speed*, a toda velocidad. || MAR. *Full speed ahead!*, ¡adelante a toda máquina! || *Its top* o *maximun speed is*, su velocidad máxima es de. || *They were doing quite a speed*, llevaban mucha velocidad. || *To make good speed*, llevar buena velocidad. || *To pick up* o *to gain speed*, coger velocidad. || *To put on speed*, acelerar.
speed* [spi:d] v. intr. Ir corriendo, correr, ir de prisa (a person). || Ir a toda velocidad (a car, etc.). || Apresurarse (to hurry). || JUR. Conducir con exceso de velocidad (to break the speed limit). || — *He sped round the corner*, dio la vuelta a la esquina a toda velocidad. || *To speed up*, acelerar.
— V. tr. Despedir (to say good-bye to). || Disparar (an arrow). || Acelerar (en engine). || — *God speed you!*, ¡que Dios le ampare! || *To speed up*, acelerar (car, process, matters), dar prisa a (a person).

— OBSERV. Pret. & p. p. ***sped, speeded***.

speedboat [—bəut] n. Lancha (*f.*) motora.
speeder [—ə*] n. Regulador (*m.*) de velocidad.
speedily [—ili] adv. Rápidamente.
speed indicator [—ˌindikeitə*] n. Indicador (*m.*) de velocidad, velocímetro, *m.*
speediness [—inis] n. Rapidez, *f.*, velocidad, *f.*
speeding [—iŋ] n. Exceso (*m.*) de velocidad.
speed limit [—ˌlimit] n. Límite (*m.*) de velocidad (restriction). || Velocidad (*f.*) máxima (on road signs).
speedometer [spiˈdɔmitə*] n. Velocímetro, *m.*, indicador (*m.*) de velocidad.
speedup [ˈspi:dʌp] n. U. S. Aceleración, *f.* | Aumento (*m.*) de productividad (increase in productivity).
speedway [ˈspi:dwei] n. Pista (*f.*) de carreras (for racing). || U. S. Autopista, *f.* (motorway).
speedwell [ˈspi:dwel] n. BOT. Verónica, *f.*
speedy [ˈspi:di] adj. Veloz, rápido, da. || FAM. Drogado, da.
speleological [ˌspi:liəˈlɔdʒikəl] adj. Espeleológico, ca.
speleologist [ˌspi:liˈɔlədʒist] n. Espeleólogo, *m.*
speleology or **spelaeology** [ˌspi:liˈɔlədʒi] n. Espeleología, *f.*
spell [spel] n. Turno, *m.* (shift): *a spell on watch*, un turno de vigilancia. || Temporada, *f.*: *I am going to the country for a spell*, me voy al campo por una temporada. || Rato, *m.*: *we chatted for a spell*, charlamos un rato. || Descanso, *m.* (a rest). || Racha, *f.*: *he is going through a good, a bad spell*, está atravesando una buena, una mala racha. || Acceso, *m.* (of bad temper). || Ataque, *m.* (of disease). || Sortilegio, *m.*, maleficio, *m.* (evil spell). || Encanto, *m.*: *the spell of Ireland*, el encanto de Irlanda; *the light broke the spell*, la luz rompió el encanto. || — *Cold, warm spell*, racha *or* ola (*f.*) de frío, de calor. || *To be under a spell*, estar hechizado. || *To cast* o *to put a spell on s.o.*, hechizar a alguien.
spell* [spel] v. tr. Escribir: *he spells my name wrong*, escribe mal mi nombre. || Deletrear (letter by letter). || FIG. Significar, representar, equivaler a: *the flood spelled disaster for many people*, la inundación significó un desastre para mucha gente. || Encantar, hechizar (to bewitch). || U. S. Remplazar, reemplazar, relevar (to take over from). || — *C-a-t spells cat*, g-a-t-o significa gato. || *How do you spell his name?*, ¿cómo se escribe su nombre? || *To spell backward*, escribir *or* deletrear al revés. || *To spell out*, deletrear (to read letter by letter), explicar (to explain), captar (to understand), entrever (to see).
— V. intr. Escribir. || U. S. Tomarse un descanso (to rest). | Tomar su turno (to shift). || *He spells well*, su ortografía es buena, tiene buena ortografía.

— OBSERV. Pret. & p. p. ***spelled, spelt***.

spellbind* [—baind] v. tr. Hechizar, encantar.

— OBSERV. Pret. & p.p. ***spellbound***.

spellbinder [—ˌbaində*] n. Orador (*m.*) arrebatador.
spellbound [—baund] adj. Hechizado, da; embrujado, da (bewitched). || FIG. Fascinado, da: hechizado, da: *he held his audience spellbound*, tenía fascinado al auditorio.
speller [—ə*] n. Abecedario, *m.* (spelling book). || *To be a bad, a good speller*, tener mala, buena ortografía.
spelling [—iŋ] n. Ortografía, *f.* || Deletreo, *m.* (letter by letter).
spelling bee [—iŋbi:] n. Concurso (*m.*) de ortografía.
spelling book [—iŋbuk] n. Abecedario, *m.*
spelt [spelt] pret. & p. p. See SPELL.
spelter [—ə*] n. CHEM. Cinc, *m.*
spelunker [spiˈlʌŋkə*] n. U. S. FAM. Espeleólogo, *m.*
spelunking [spiˈlʌŋkiŋ] n. U. S. FAM. Espeleología, *f.*
spencer [ˈspensə*] n. MAR. Vela (*f.*) cangreja. || Chaqueta (*f.*) corta (jacket).
spend* [spend] v. tr. Gastar, gastarse (money): *he spent a lot on cigarettes*, gastó mucho en cigarrillos. || Pasar: *to spend a week in bed*, pasar una semana en la cama; *to spend one's holidays abroad*, pasar las vacaciones en el extranjero. || Emplear, usar (to use). || Dedicar: *you must spend more time on your homework*, tiene que dedicar más tiempo a los deberes. || Agotar (to exhaust).
— V. intr. Gastar dinero.

— OBSERV. Pret. & p. p. ***spent***.

spender [—ə*] n. Gastador, ra; derrochador, ra.
spending [—iŋ] n. Gasto, *m.* || — *Spending money*, dinero para gastos menudos. || *Spending power*, poder adquisitivo.
spendthrift [—θrift] adj./n. Manirroto, ta; gastador, ra; derrochador, ra; despilfarrador, ra.
spent [spent] pret. & p. p. See SPEND.
— Adj. Agotado, da (exhausted). || Gastado, da; acabado, da (worn-out). || — *Spent bullet*, bala muerta. || *The storm was spent*, la tormenta se había calmado.
sperm [spə:m] n. Esperma, *f.*, esperma, *m.*
spermaceti [ˌspə:məˈseti] n. Espermaceti, *m.*, esperma (*f.*) de ballena.
spermatic [spə:ˈmætik] adj. Espermático, ca.
spermatocyte [ˌspə:ˈmətəsait] n. Espermatocito, *m.*
spermatogenesis [ˌspə:mætəˈdʒenəsis] n. Espermatogénesis, *f.*
spermatogenetic [ˌspə:mætədʒiˈnetik] adj. Espermatógeno, na.
spermatophyte [ˈspə:mətəfait] n. BOT. Espermatofita, *f.*
spermatozoid [ˌspə:mətəˈzəuid] n. Espermatozoide, *m.* (of a plant).
spermatozoon [ˌspə:mətəuˈzəuən] n. Espermatozoo, *m.*, espermatozoide, *m.*

— OBSERV. El plural de *spermatozoon* es *spermatozoa*.

sperm oil [ˈspə:mɔil] n. Aceite (*m.*) de ballena.
sperm whale [ˈspə:mweil] n. ZOOL. Cachalote, *m.*
spew [spju:] n. Vómito, *m.*
spew [spju:] v. tr. Vomitar, devolver, arrojar (to vomit). || FIG. Vomitar, arrojar (smoke, flames, etc.).
— V. intr. Vomitar, devolver, arrojar.
Speyer [ˈʃpaiə*] pr. n. GEOGR. Espira.

sphenoid [ˈsfi:nɔid] adj. ANAT. Esfenoideo, a; esfenoidal, esfenoides.
— N. ANAT. Esfenoides, *m.*
sphenoidal [—əl] adj. ANAT. Esfenoidal.
sphere [sfiə*] n. MATH. Esfera, *f.* || FIG. Esfera, *f.*: *sphere of activity*, esfera de actividad; *sphere of influence*, esfera de influencia. | Competencia, *f.* (province).
spheric [ˈsferik] or **spherical** [—əl] adj. Esférico, ca. || *Spherical trigonometry*, trigonometría esférica.
sphericity [sfeˈrisiti] n. MATH. Esfericidad, *f.*
spherics [ˈsferiks] n. MATH. Trigonometría (*f.*) esférica.
spheroid [ˈsfiərɔid] n. MATH. Esferoide, *m.*
spheroidal [sfiəˈrɔidl] adj. MATH. Esferoidal.
spherometer [sfiəˈrɔmitə*] n. Esferómetro, *m.*
sphincter [ˈsfiŋktə*] n. ANAT. Esfínter, *m.*
sphinx [sfiŋks] n. MYTH. Esfinge, *f.* || FIG. Esfinge, *f.* || ZOOL. Esfinge, *f.* (hawkmoth).
spice [spais] n. Especia, *f.* || FIG. Picante, *m.*, sabor, *m.*, sal, *f. to give spice to a book*, dar sabor a un libro. || — *Spice of life*, lo sabroso de la vida, sal de la vida. | *Variety is the spice of life*, en la variedad está el gusto.
spice [spais] v. tr. Condimentar, sazonar. || FIG. Sazonar, salpimentar.
spice box [—bɔks] n. Especiero, *m.*, caja (*f.*) de especias.
spicery [—əri] n. Especias, *f. pl.*
spiciness [—inis] n. Picante, *m.*, sabor *m.* || FIG. Picante, *m.*
spick-and-span [ˈspikəndˈspæn] adj. Flamante, impecable (cleaned up). || Nuevo, va (new). || Impecable (person).
spicule [ˈspaikju:l] n. Espícula, *f.*
spicy [ˈspaisi] adj. Picante, sazonado con especias (food). || FIG. Picante.
spider [ˈspaidə*] n. ZOOL. TECH. Araña, *f.* || U. S. Trébedes, *f. pl.* (frying pan). || — ZOOL. *Spider crab, sea spider*, centollo, *m.*, centolla, *f.*, araña (*f.*) de mar. || *Spider's web*, telaraña, *f.*, tela (*f.*) de araña.
spidery [ˈspaidəri] adj. De alambre: *John has spidery legs*, Juan tiene patas de alambre. || Que tiene forma de telaraña (like spider's web). || Lleno de arañas (full of spiders). || *Spidery handwriting*, patas (*f. pl.*) de mosca, garabatos, *m. pl.*
spiegeleisen [ˈspi:gəlaizən] n. Arrabio, *m.* (pig iron).
spiel [spi:l] n. U. S. FAM. Perorata, *f.* (speech). | Charlatanería, *f.* (sales patter). | Camelo, *m.*, cuento, *m.* (story). | Publicidad, *f.* (publicity).
spiel [spi:l] v. tr. U. S. FAM. *To spiel off*, soltar (a speech, a list, etc.).
— V. intr. U. S. FAM. Perorar.
spiffing [ˈspifiŋ] or **spiffy** [ˈspifi] adj. FAM. Estupendo, da.
spigot [ˈspigət] n. Espita, *f.*, bitoque, *m.* (of a barrel). || Macho, *m.*, enchufe, *m.* (of a tube). || Macho, *m.*, espiga, *f.* (tenon). || U. S. Grifo, *m.*, espita, *f.* (tap).
spike [spaik] n. Punta, *f.*, púa, *f.*, pincho, *m.* (sharp-pointed object). || Estaca, *f.* (pointed rod or bar). || Barrote, *m.* (on a railing). || Bastón (*m.*) con pincho (for picking up litter). || Pincho, *m.*, clavo, *m.* (for filing bills). || Clavo, *m.* (of running shoes). || ZOOL. Pitón, *m.* (a single antler). || BOT. Espiga, *f.* || — Pl. Zapatillas (*f.*) con clavos (running shoes).
spike [spaik] v. tr. Clavar (to fix with a spike). || Empalar, atravesar (to impale). || FIG. Frustrar (s.o.'s plans). | Acabar con, poner fin a (a rumour). || MIL. Clavar (a cannon). || U. S. Añadir alcohol a (a drink).
— V. intr. Formar espigas.
spiked [—t] adj. Claveteado, da (shoes).
spikelet [ˈspaiklət] n. BOT. Espiguilla, *f.*
spikenard [ˈspaiknɑ:d] n. BOT. Nardo, *m.*
spiky [ˈspaiki] adj. Erizado, da (with many sharp points). || Puntiagudo, da (sharp-pointed).
spile [spail] n. Tarugo, *m.* (wedge). || Espita, *f.* (plug). || Estaca, *f.*, pilote, *m.* (stake, pile). || U. S. Gotera (*f.*) para sangrar un árbol.
spile [spail] v. tr. Poner una espita a (to put a spile on). || Asegurar con pilotes (to pile). || U. S. Sangrar con gotera (trees).
spill [spil] n. Espita, *f.* (spile). || Clavija, *f.* (peg). || Tarugo, *m.* (wedge). || Astilla, *f.* (splinter). || Pajuela, *f.* (for lighting fire). || Derramamiento, *m.*, derrame, *m.* (of a liquid). || Caída, *f.* (from a horse). || *To take a spill*, caerse (to fall).
spill* [spil] v. tr. Derramar: *he spilled the water on the table*, derramó el agua sobre la mesa. || Volcar (to knock over). || Verter (to pour). || Hacer caer: *the horse spilled the rider to the ground*, el caballo hizo que el jinete cayese al suelo. || FIG. Derramar: *a lot of blood has been spilt*, ha sido derramada mucha sangre. || FAM. Soltar (to divulge). || FIG. FAM. *To spill the beans*, descubrir el pastel.
— V. intr. Derramarse, verterse (a liquid): *mind your coffee doesn't spill*, cuidado que no se derrame el café. || Salirse: *as he walked petrol spilled from the can*, al andar se le salía la gasolina de la lata. || Romper (waves). || Caer: *the wine spilt over her dress*, el vino le cayó en el vestido. || — *To spill out*, salir: *as the crowd spilled out of the football ground*, mientras los espectadores salían del campo de fútbol; desparramarse (objects). || *To spill over*, salirse: *the bathwater was spilling over*, el agua del baño se salía; rebosar, estar rebosante (to be full to overflowing).
— OBSERV. Pret. & p. p. ***spilled, spilt.***
spillikin [ˈspilikin] n. Palillo, *m.* || — Pl. Juego (*m. sing.*) de los palillos.
spillway [ˈspilwei] n. Aliviadero, *m.*, derramadero, *m.*
spilt [spilt] pret. & p. p. See SPILL.
spin [spin] n. Giro, *m.*, vuelta, *f.* (act of revolving). || Efecto, *m.*: *to put spin on a ball*, dar efecto a una pelota. || Vuelta, *f.*, paseo, *m.*: *to go for a spin on a motorbike*, dar un paseo en moto. || Aturdimiento, *m.*, confusión, *f.* (confusion). || AVIAT. Barrena, *f.*: *to go into a spin*, entrar en barrena. || PHYS. Espín, *m.*, "spin", *m.*, giro, *m.* (of electrons). || — FIG. *My head is in a spin*, estoy aturdido. || *To give sth. a spin*, hacer girar algo. || *To risk a fortune on the spin of a coin*, jugarse una fortuna a cara o cruz.
spin* [spin] v. tr. Hacer girar, dar vueltas a: *to spin a wheel, a top*, hacer girar una rueda, una peonza. || Hilar: *to spin cotton*, hilar algodón. || Tejer: *the spider spins his web*, la araña teje su tela. || Fabricar, hacer (a cocoon). || Hacer girar (a dancing partner). || Contar: *to spin a tale*, contar un cuento. || Suspender: *to spin a candidate*, suspender a un candidato. || SP. Dar efecto a (a ball). || TECH. Tornear (metal on a lathe). || — *To spin a coin for sth.*, echar algo a cara o cruz. || *To spin out*, estirar, hacer dar de sí (time, money), alargar (holiday), prolongar (trial), alargar, prolongar (speech). || FIG. *To spin s.o. a yarn*, contarle a uno una historia.
— V. intr. Girar, dar vueltas: *the top was spinning*, la peonza estaba dando vueltas. || Perturbarse, volverse loco (a compass). || Hilar (cotton, silk, etc.). || Tejer la tela (spiders). || FIG. Dar vueltas (ideas, thoughts). || AUT. Patinar (wheels). || AVIAT. Entrar or descender en barrena (a plane). || — *My head was spinning*, me daba vueltas la cabeza, estaba mareado. || *The blow sent him spinning*, el golpe le hizo rodar. || *To send sth. spinning*, echar algo a rodar. || *To spin along*, ir volando (to speed along). || *To spin round*, dar una vuelta, girar en redondo (to turn round), girar, dar vueltas (a top, a wheel, etc.).

— OBSERV. Pret. & p. p. ***spun.***

spinach [ˈspinidʒ] n. BOT. Espinaca, *f.* || CULIN. Espinacas, *f. pl.*
spinal [ˈspainl] adj. ANAT. Espinal, vertebral. || — ANAT. *Spinal column*, columna (*f.*) vertebral, espina (*f.*) dorsal. | *Spinal cord*, médula (*f.*) espinal. || MED. *Spinal curvature*, desviación (*f.*) de la columna vertebral, escoliosis, *f.*
spindle [ˈspindl] n. TECH. Eje, *m.* (axle, shaft). | Mandril, *m.* (of a lathe). | Vástago, *m.* (of a valve). | Huso, *m.* (of a spinning wheel or spinning machine). | Espiga, *f.* (of gramophone). || MAR. Mecha, *f.* (of a capstan). || AUT. Mangueta, *f.* || U. S. Pincho, *m.*, clavo, *m.* (filing device). || BOT. *Spindle tree*, bonetero, *m.* (shrub).
spindle [spindl] v. intr. Crecer alto y delgado, espigar.
spindleshanks [—ʃæŋks] n. FAM. Zanquilargo, ga (person). || — Pl. FIG. FAM. Palillos, *m.* (long legs).
spindly [ˈspindli] adj. FAM. Largirucho, cha.
spindrift [ˈsprindrift] n. Rocío (*m.*) del mar, salpicaduras (*f. pl.*) de las olas.
spin dryer [ˈspinˈdraiə*] n. Secador (*m.*) centrífugo.
spine [spain] n. ANAT. Espina (*f.*) dorsal, columna (*f.*) vertebral (backbone). || ZOOL. Púa, *f.* || BOT. Espina, *f.* || GEOL. Cresta, *f.* || PRINT. Lomo, *m.* (back of a book). || FIG. Temple, *m.*
spineless [—lis] adj. Invertebrado, da (invertebrate). || Sin espinas (having no spines or thorns). || Sin púas (a hedgehog). || FIG. Sin carácter, blando, da; débil (characterless).
spinet [spiˈnet] n. MUS. Espineta, *f.*
spinnaker [ˈspinəkə*] n. MAR. "Spinnaker", *m.*, vela (*f.*) balón, velón, *m.* (sail).
spinner [ˈspinə*] n. Máquina (*f.*) de hilar (spinning machine). || Rueca, *f.* (spinning wheel). || Hilandero, ra; hilador, ra (person who spins). || SP. Cebo (*m.*) artificial de cuchara (in fishing). | Pelota (*f.*) con efecto (in cricket). || AVIAT. Cono, *m.*, ojiva, *f.* (of a propeller).
spinneret [ˈspinəret] n. Hilera, *f.*
spinney [ˈspini] n. Soto, *m.*
spinning [ˈspiniŋ] n. Hilado, *m.* (production of thread). || Rotación, *f.* (circular motion). || MAR. Perturbación (*f.*) de la brújula. || AUT. Patinazo, *m.* (of wheels). || AVIAT. Barrena, *f.* || — *Spinning factory* o *mill*, hilandería, *f.*, fábrica (*f.*) de hilados. || *Spinning frame* o *machine*, máquina (*f.*) de hilar. || *Spinning jenny*, "jenny", *f.*, máquina (*f.*) de hilar algodón. || *Spinning top*, peonza, *f.*, trompo, *m.* || *Spinning wheel*, rueca, *f.*
spinose [ˈspainəus] or **spinous** [ˈspainəs] adj. Espinoso, sa.
spinster [ˈspinstə*] n. Soltera, *f.* (unmarried woman). || Solterona, *f.* (old maid).
spinsterhood [—hud] n. Soltería, *f.*
spiny [ˈspaini] adj. Espinoso, sa. || FIG. Peliagudo, da; espinoso, sa (problem, etc.). || *Spiny lobster*, langosta, *f.*
spiral [ˈspaiərəl] adj. Espiral: *spiral curve*, curva espiral. || De caracol, en espiral: *spiral staircase*, escalera de caracol. || Helicoidal (helical). || — *Spiral*

ascent, ascenso (*m.*) en espiral. || *Spiral descent*, descenso (*m.*) en espiral.
— N. MATH. Espiral, *f.* || FIG. Espiral, *f.*: *spiral of smoke*, espiral de humo. || COMM. Espiral, *f.* (of prices). || AVIAT. Espiral, *f.* || U. S. SP. Pase (*m.*) de la pelota con efecto (in American football).

spiral [ˈspaiərəl] v. tr. Aumentar, hacer subir (prices).
— V. intr. Moverse en espiral, dar vueltas. || — *To spiral down*, descender en espiral. || *To spiral up*, ascender en espiral (to rise upwards), subir vertiginosamente (prices).

spirally [—i] adv. En espiral.

spirant [ˈspaiərənt] n. Espirante, *f.*, fricativa, *f.* (consonant).

spire [spaiə*] n. ARCH. Aguja, *f.* || BOT. Brizna, *f.* || MATH. Espiral, *f.* (spiral). || Vuelta, *f.*, rosca, *f.* (single turn).

spire [spaiə*] v. intr. Rematar en punta.

spirit [ˈspirit] n. Espíritu, *m.*, alma, *f.* (soul): *the spirit leaves the body at the moment of death*, el espíritu *or* el alma se separa del cuerpo en el momento de la muerte. || Espíritu, *m.* (ghost, etc.): *to summon the spirits*, llamar a los espíritus; *evil spirit*, espíritu maligno; *to believe in spirits*, creer en los espíritus. || Ser, *m.*, alma, *f.* (person). || Persona, *f.*, ser, *m.*: *she was one of the weaker spirits among us*, era una de las personas más débiles entre nosotros. || Carácter, *m.* (strong character): *a man of spirit*, un hombre de carácter; *he lacks spirit*, no tiene carácter. || Ánimo, *m.*, energía, *f.* (liveliness): *to be full of spirit*, estar lleno de ánimo. || Vigor, *m.* (vigour). || Vitalidad, *f.* (vitality). || Valor, *m.* (courage). || Espíritu, *m.*: *the spirit of the law*, el espíritu de la ley. || Temple, *m.*, humor, *m.* (mood): *in good spirit*, de buen humor. || Espíritu, *m.*: *team, fighting spirit*, espíritu de equipo, de lucha. || Alcohol, *m.* || — Pl. Humor, *m. sing.* (mood). || Ánimos, *m.*, ánimo, *m. sing.* (liveliness): *to dampen s.o.'s spirits*, rebajarle los ánimos a alguien. || Alcohol, *m. sing.* (drink): *I never touch spirits*, no bebo nunca alcohol. || CHEM. Espíritu, *m. sing.*: *spirits of salt, of wine*, espíritu de sal, de vino. | Alcohol, *m. sing.*: *methylated spirits*, alcohol metílico *or* de quemar. || — *Community* o *public spirit*, civismo, *m.* || *Familiar spirit*, demonio (*m.*) familiar. || *I'll do it when the spirit moves me*, lo haré cuando me dé la gana. || *In a friendly spirit*, de manera amistosa. || *In spirit*, para sus adentros, en su fuero interno. || *Leading* o *moving spirit*, alma. || *Poor in spirit*, pobre de espíritu. || *Spirit lamp*, lámpara (*f.*) de alcohol. || *Spirit level*, nivel (*m.*) de burbuja. || *Spirit of turpentine*, esencia (*f.*) de trementina. || *Spirit rapping*, comunicación (*f.*) con los espíritus.|| *That's the spirit!*, ¡así me gusta! || REL. *The Holy Spirit*, el Espíritu Santo. || *The spirit world*, el mundo de los espíritus. || *To be full of spirits*, estar muy animado *or* muy alegre. || *To be in high spirits*, estar muy animado *or* alegre. || *To be in low spirits*, estar desanimado. || *To come in the spirit of peace*, venir en son de paz. || *To do sth. in a spirit of mischief*, hacer algo para gastar una broma. || *To enter into the spirit of sth.*, meterse *or* entrar en el espíritu de algo, entrar *or* meterse en el ambiente de algo. || *To keep up one's spirits*, no desanimarse. || *To raise s.o.'s spirits*, animarle *or* levantarle el ánimo a alguien. || *To take sth. in good spirit* o *in the right spirit*, tomar algo a bien, tomar algo como es debido.

spirit [ˈspirit] v. tr. Alentar, animar (to cheer up). || *To spirit away* o *off*, hacer desaparecer.

spirited [—id] adj. Animado, da: *a spirited argument*, una discusión animada. || Vigoroso, sa; enérgico, ca (vigorous, energetic). || Fogoso, sa (horse). || Alegre (music).

spiritism [—izəm] n. Espiritismo, *m.*

spiritist [—ist] n. Espiritista, *m.* & *f.*

spiritless [—lis] adj. Desanimado, da (downhearted). || Sin vigor *or* energía (flabby). || Irresoluto, ta; indeciso, sa (irresolute).

spiritual [ˈspiritjuəl] adj. Espiritual: *spiritual life*, vida espiritual. || REL. Eclesiástico, ca: *spiritual court*, tribunal eclesiástico. || *Spiritual adviser, director, father, home*, consejero (*m.*), director (*m.*), padre (*m.*), patria (*f.*) espiritual.
— N. "Negro spiritual", *m.* (song).

spiritualism [ˈspiritjuəlizəm] n. PHIL. Espiritualismo, *m.* || Espiritismo, *m.*

spiritualist [ˈspiritjuəlist] adj./n. PHIL. Espiritualista. || Espiritista: *spiritualist séance*, sesión espiritista.

spiritualistic [ˌspiritjuəˈlistik] adj. PHIL. Espiritualista. || Espiritista.

spirituality [ˌspiritjuˈæliti] n. Espiritualidad, *f.* || — Pl. REL. Bienes (*m.*) eclesiásticos.

spiritualization [spiritjuəlaiˈzeiʃən] n. Espiritualización, *f.*

spiritualize [ˈspiritjuəlaiz] v. tr. Espiritualizar.

spiritually [ˈspiritjuəli] adv. Espiritualmente.

spirituous [ˈspiritjuəs] adj. Espirituoso, sa (drink).

spirochaete (U. S. **spirochete**) [spairəˈkiːtiː] n. BIOL. Espiroqueta, *f.*

spiroid [ˈspairɔid] adj. Espiroidal.

spirometer [ˌspaiəˈrɔmitə*] n. MED. Espirómetro, *m.*

spirt [spəːt] n./v.tr./intr. See SPURT.

spit [spit] n. Escupitajo, *m.*, gargajo, *m.*, salivazo, *m.* (saliva expelled from the mouth). || Saliva, *f.* (in the mouth). || MED. Esputo, *m.*: *a spit of blood*, un esputo de sangre. || Bufido, *m.* (of a cat). || Espuma, *f.* (of insects). || Rocío, *m.* (of rain). || CULIN. Asador, *m.*, espetón, *m.* || GEOL. Banco, *m.* (of sand). | Punta, *f.* (of land). || Paletada, *f.* (spadeful). || — FIG. *He is the spit and image* o *the very spit of his father*, es el vivo retrato de su padre. || *Spit and polish*, limpieza, *f.* (clean, cleanliness), preocupación exagerada por la limpieza (exaggerated cleanliness), material (*m.*) de limpieza (tools).

spit* [spit] v. tr. Escupir: *I spat in his face*, le escupí en la cara; *to spit blood*, escupir sangre. || FIG. Echar, escupir, arrojar: *the guns spat fire*, los cañones escupían fuego. | Soltar, proferir: *to spit insults*, proferir insultos. || Encender (a fuse, match). || Espetar, atravesar, ensartar (to pierce). || — FAM. *Spit it out!*, ¡suéltalo!, ¡desembucha! || *To spit sth. out*, escupir algo.
— V. intr. Escupir (to emit saliva): *it is rude to spit*, escupir es de mala educación. || FIG. Chisporrotear: *the fire, the frying pan was spitting*, el fuego, la sartén chisporroteaba. || Dar un bufido (cat). || Gotear, chispear (to rain lightly). || FIG. *To spit at* o *on* o *upon*, despreciar (to scorn).

— OBSERV. Pret. & p. p. ***spat, spit.***

spitball [—bɔːl] n. Pelotilla (*f.*) de papel mascado.

spite [spait] n. Rencor, *m.*, ojeriza, *f.* (animosity): *to have a spite against s.o.*, tener ojeriza a alguien. || — *In spite of*, a pesar de, pese a: *in spite of everyone, of everything*, a pesar de todos, de todo. || *To do sth. out of spite*, hacer algo por despecho.

spite [spait] v. tr. Molestar, fastidiar (to annoy). || *To cut off one's nose to spite one's face*, fastidiarse a sí mismo por querer fastidiar a los demás.

spiteful [—ful] adj. Rencoroso, sa (person). || Viperino, na (tongue). || Malévolo, la (remark, etc.).

spitefulness [—fulnis] n. Rencor, *m.* || Malevolencia, *f.*

spitfire [ˈspitfaiə*] n. Colérico, ca.

spitting [ˈspitiŋ] n. MED. Expectoración, *f.*

spitting image [—ˈimidʒ] n. Vivo retrato, *m.*

spittle [ˈspitl] n. Escupitajo, *m.*, salivazo, *m.*, gargajo, *m.* (spit). || Espuma, *f.* (of insects). || MED. Esputo, *m.*

spittoon [spiˈtuːn] n. Escupidera, *f.*

spitz [spits] n. Lulú, *m.*, perro (*m.*) de Pomerania (dog).

spiv [spiv] n. FAM. Gandul, *m.* (layabout). | Caballero (*m.*) de industria (well-dressed trickster). | Estraperlista, *m.* (blackmarketeer).

splash [splæʃ] n. Salpicadura, *f.*: *splashes of paint*, salpicaduras de pintura. || Chapoteo, *m.* (lapping, slopping sound). || Mancha, *f.* (of colour). || Chorro, *m.*: *a whisky with a splash of soda, please!*, un whisky con un chorro de soda, por favor. || FIG. Grandes titulares, *m. pl.* (of news). || — *The splash of the waves against the rocks*, el golpe de las olas contra las rocas, las olas que rompen contra las rocas. || FIG. *To make a splash*, causar sensación. || *To fall into the water with a splash*, caer ruidosamente al agua.

splash [splæʃ] v. tr. Salpicar: *a car splashed him with mud*, un coche le salpicó de barro; *I splashed ink on the wall*, salpiqué la pared de tinta. || Chapotear, agitar: *to splash one's feet in the water*, chapotear los pies en el agua. || Rociar (to spray). || FIG. Derrochar: *to splash one's money about*, derrochar el dinero. | Salpicar (the sky with stars). | Poner en primera plana: *to splash a piece of news*, poner una noticia en primera plana.
— V. intr. Chapotear: *we splashed about in the water*, chapoteamos en el agua. || Salpicar: *the water splashed all around*, el agua lo salpicó todo. || Ir chapoteando: *we splashed through the waves*, fuimos chapoteando entre las olas. || — *To splash down*, amerizar (spaceship). || FIG. *To splash out*, derrochar *or* tirar el dinero (to spend a lot). || *To splash over*, saltar por encima: *the waves splashed over the breakwater*, las olas saltaban por encima del rompeolas.

splashboard [—bɔːd] n. AUT. Guardabarros, *m. inv.* [*Amer.*, guardafango, *m.*] (mudguard). || U. S. Alza, *f.* (of a dam).

splashdown [—daun] n. Amerizaje, *m.*

splasher [—ə*] n. Guardabarros, *m. inv.* [*Amer.*, guardafango, *m.*] (car's splashboard).

splash guard [—gɑːd] n. Guardabarros, *m. inv.* [*Amer.*, guardafango, *m.*].

splashing [—iŋ] n. Salpicadura, *f.*

splashy [—i] adj. Fangoso, sa (muddy). || Salpicado, da (of water, etc.). || ARTS. Pintarrajeado, da. || FAM. Llamativo, va (people, clothes).

splat [splæt] n. Listón (*m.*) del espaldar (of a chair).

splatter [—ə*] n. Salpicadura, *f.*

splatter [—ə*] v. tr. Salpicar: *the car splattered him with mud*, el coche le salpicó de barro. || Aplastar: *he splattered an egg against the wall*, aplastó un huevo contra la pared.

splay [splei] n. ARCH. Derrame, *m.*, alféizar, *m.* (of a window). | Chaflán, *m.* (bevelled edge). || Extensión, *f.* (a spreading).

splay [splei] v. tr. Extender. || ARCH. Hacer un derrame en (a window). | Abocinar (an arch). | Achaflanar (to bevel).
— V. intr. Ensancharse, extenderse.

splayfoot [—fut] n. Pie (*m.*) plano y torcido.

splayfooted [—ˈfutid] adj. De pies planos.

spleen [spli:n] n. ANAT. Bazo, *m.* || Esplín, *m.* (depression). || Melancolía, *f.*, (melancholy). || Mal humor, *m.* (ill-temper). || Capricho, *m.* (whim).
spleenful [—ful] adj. Irritable.
spleeny [—i] adj. Irritable.
splendent [ˈsplendənt] adj. Brillante.
splendid [ˈsplendid] adj. Espléndido, da; magnífico, ca: *splendid palaces*, palacios magníficos. || Espléndido, da; estupendo, da: *a splendid performance*, una actuación espléndida.
splendiferous [splenˈdifərəs] adj. FAM. Espléndido, da.
splendour (U. S. **splendor**) [ˈsplendə*] n. Esplendor, *m.*, esplendidez, *f.*: *the splendour of the Golden Age*, el esplendor del Siglo de Oro. || Brillantez, *f.*, resplandor, *m.* (brilliance). || Magnificencia, *f.*, esplendor, *m.* (magnificence).
splenetic [spliˈnetik] adj. MED. Esplénico, ca. || FIG. Malhumorado, da.
— N. Persona (*f.*) malhumorada.
splenic [ˈsplenik] adj. MED. Esplénico, ca.
splenius [ˈspli:niəs] n. ANAT. Esplenio, *m.* (muscle).
splice [splais] n. Empalme, *m.* || FIG. FAM. Casorio, *m.*
splice [splais] v. tr. Empalmar (ropes, wood). || FIG. FAM. Unir, casar. || Encolar, pegar (a film). || FIG. FAM. *To get spliced*, pasar por la vicaría (to get married).
splicer [—ə*] n. Encoladora, *f.*
splicing [—iŋ] n. Empalme, *m.* (of wood, ropes). || Encolado, *m.* (of films).
spline [splain] n. Tira, *f.* (thin strip of wood, plastic, etc.). || TECH. Lengüeta, *f.* | Ranura, *f.* (slot).
spline [splain] v. tr. Acanalar (to cut a groove in).
splint [splint] n. MED. Tablilla, *f.* || VET. Sobrecaña, *f.* || — MED. *In a splint*, entablillado, da. | *To put in splints*, entablillar (an arm, etc.).
splint [splint] v. tr. MED. Entablillar.
splinter [ˈsplintə*] n. Astilla, *f.* (of wood). || Fragmento, *m.*, pedazo, *m.* (small piece). || MED. Esquirla, *f.* (of bone). || Casco, *m.*, metralla, *f.* (of a bomb).
— Adj. Disidente: *splinter group*, grupo disidente.
splinter [ˈsplintə*] v. tr. Astillar, rajar, hender.
— V. intr. Astillarse, rajarse.
splinter bone [—bəun] n. ANAT. Peroné, *m.*
splintering [—riŋ] n. MED. Entablillado, *m.*
splinterless [—lis] adj. Inastillable.
splinterproof [—pruf] adj. Inastillable (glass).
splintery [—ri] adj. Astilloso, sa.
split [split] adj. Partido, da; hendido, da (wood). || Agrietado, da (a rock, etc.). || Desgarrado, da (clothes). || Reventado, da (burst): *the sack is split*, el saco se ha reventado. || Dividido, da: *the party is split on this issue*, el partido está dividido sobre este asunto; *I am split between love and hate*, mis sentimientos están divididos entre el amor y el odio. || — *Split pea*, guisante seco. || MED. *Split personality*, desdoblamiento (*m.*) de la personalidad. || *Split pin*, pasador, *m.* || *Split second*, fracción (*f.*) de segundo.
— N. Raja, *f.*, desgarrón, *m.*: *I had a split in my shirt*, tenía un desgarrón en la camisa. || Grieta, *f.*, hendidura, *f.* (fissure): *a split in the table, in the rock*, una grieta en la mesa, en la roca. || Escisión, *f.*, división, *f.*, ruptura, *f.* (of a group). || CULIN. Helado, *m.*: *banana split*, helado de plátano. || Media botella, *f.* (half bottle). || Diente, *m.* (of a comb). || Claro, *m.* (space between teeth). || Tira (*f.*) de piel (of leather). || SP. Disposición (*f.*) separada de los bolos (in bowling). || MED. Grieta, *f.* (in the skin). || — Pl. "Ecart", *m.*, despatarrada, *f. sing.* (in ballet).
split* [split] v. tr. Agrietar, hender: *the pressure split the rock*, la presión agrietó la roca. || Partir (into two parts): *the lightning split the tree*, el rayo partió el árbol. || Desgarrar, rajar: *I split my dress*, me desgarré el vestido. || Resquebrajar, cuartear, agrietar: *the earthquake split all the walls of the house*, el terremoto resquebrajó todas las paredes de la casa. || Repartir, dividir: *they split the prize between the two winners*, repartieron el premio entre los dos vencedores. || Dividir: *the abdication split the country*, la abdicación dividió al país. || MED. Agrietar (the skin). || GRAMM. Separar (an infinitive). || CHEM. Descomponer (a compound). || PHYS. Descomponer (a molecule). | Desintegrar (the atom). || — FIG. *To split hairs*, hilar muy fino. || *To split off*, separar. || FIG. *To split one's sides laughing*, partirse de risa. || *To split one's vote*, dividir el voto. || *To split the difference*, partir la diferencia. || *To split up*, dividir (to divide), dispersar (a meeting), compartir (to share), descomponer (a fraction, a compound), desintegrar (the atom), separar (friends, lovers).
— V. intr. Partirse: *the piece of wood split*, la madera se partió. || Agrietarse, henderse (rock). || Desgarrarse, rajarse (cloth). || Reventarse (shoes). || Cuartearse, resquebrajarse: *the wall split with the earthquake*, la pared se resquebrajó con el terremoto. || Estrellarse, hacerse pedazos: *the boat split on a reef*, el barco se estrelló contra un arrecife. || Separarse, dividirse, fraccionarse (groups): *the party split into several factions*, el partido se dividió en diversas facciones. || Doler atrozmente: *my head is splitting*, me duele atrozmente la cabeza. || MED. Agrietarse (skin). || FAM. Delatar vender: *he split on us to the police*, nos vendió a la policía. || — FAM. *Let's split*, vayámonos, larguémonos. || *To split off*, separarse. || *To split open*, abrirse. || *To split up*, dividirse (to go different ways), separarse (a married couple).
— OBSERV. Pret. & p. p. ***split***.
split-level [—ˈlevl] adj. De pisos construidos a desnivel (house).
splitter [—ə*] n. *Atom splitter*, ciclotrón, *m.*
splitting [—iŋ] adj. Hendedor, ra (which splits). || Atroz, insoportable, horrible (headache). || Para partirse *or* desternillarse de risa (very funny).
— N. Hendimiento, *m.* || Cuarteo, *m* (of a wall). || PHYS. Desintegración, *f.*, fisión, *f.*, escisión, *f.* (of the atom). || FIG. División, *f.*
splodge [splɔdʒ] n. Manchón, *m.*, mancha, *f.*
splodge [splɔdʒ] v. tr. See SPLOTCH.
splodgy [—i] adj. Manchado, da.
splotch [splɔtʃ] n. Mancha, *f.*, manchón, *m.*
splotch [splɔtʃ] v. tr. Manchar (to stain). || *To splotch paint on a canvas*, pintar a brochazos un lienzo.
splotchy [—i] adj. Manchado, da.
splurge [ˈsplə:dʒ] n. FAM. Faroleo, *m.*, fachenda, *f.*
splurge [ˈsplə:dʒ] v. intr. FAM. Farolear, fachendear (to show off).
— V. tr. FAM. Derrochar, gastar: *to splurge five hundred pounds on a fur coat*, derrochar quinientas libras en un abrigo de piel.
splutter [ˈsplʌtə*] n. Farfulla, *f.* || Chisporroteo, *m.*
splutter [ˈsplʌtə*] v. tr. Balbucear, farfullar.
— V. intr. Farfullar (a person). || Chisporrotear (candle). || ELECTR. Chisporrotear (a collector).
splutterer [—rə*] n. Farfullador, ra.
spoil [spɔil] n. MIN. Escombros, *m. pl.* (waste). || — Pl. Botín, *m. sing.*: *the burglar's spoils*, el botín del ladrón; *the spoils of war*, el botín de la guerra. || Ventajas, *f.* (political privilege): *the spoils of office*, las ventajas del oficio. || U. S. FAM. Prebenda, *f. sing.*, sinecura, *f. sing.*, canonjía, *f. sing.* (sinecure). || — *Spoil heap*, escorial, *m.* || *To have one's share of the spoils*, sacar tajada, sacar su parte.
spoil* [spɔil] v. tr. Estropear, aguar: *the quarrel spoilt the party*, la discusión estropeó la fiesta. || Echar a perder, estropear (to damage): *the rain spoiled the crop*, la lluvia estropeó la cosecha; *heat spoils food*, el calor estropea los alimentos. || MED. Estropear: *reading in poor light spoils the eyes*, leer con poca luz estropea la vista. || Cortar (appetite). || Afear, estropear: *her hat spoiled her outfit*, su sombrero afeaba su vestimenta; *the landscape has been spoiled by the new building*, el paisaje ha sido afeado por el nuevo edificio. || Consentir, mimar (a child). || Saquear (a town). || Despojar (to deprive). || FAM. Despachar, liquidar (to kill). || *To spoil s.o.'s fun*, aguarle la fiesta a uno.
— V. intr. Estropearse, echarse a perder: *the fruit spoiled with the heat*, la fruta se estropeó con el calor. || FAM. *To be spoiling for a fight*, tener ganas de pelearse.
— OBSERV. Pret. & p. p. ***spoilt, spoiled***.
spoilage [—idʒ] n. Desperdicios, *m. pl.*, desechos, *m. pl.* (waste). || Putrefacción, *f.* (process of decay).
spoiler [—ə*] n. Expoliador, ra (pillager). || Aguafiestas, *m. & f. inv.* (killjoy).
spoilsman [—zmən] n. U. S. FAM. Aprovechón, *m.*, oportunista, *m.* (opportunist).
— OBSERV. El plural de *spoilsman* es *spoilsmen*.
spoilsport [—spɔ:t] n. Aguafiestas, *m.* & *f.* inv. (killjoy).
spoils system [—zˈsistim] n. Acaparamiento (*m.*) de los cargos públicos por el partido victorioso.
spoilt [spɔilt] pret. & p. p. See SPOIL.
— Adj. Estropeado, da. || Mimado, da; consentido, da (child). || COMM. Deteriorado, da; estropeado, da (merchandise).
spoke [spəuk] n. Radio, *m.* (of a wheel). || Escalón, *m.*, peldaño, *m.* (of a ladder). || FAM. *To put a spoke in s.o.'s wheel*, poner trabas a alguien.
spoke [spəuk] v. tr. Enrayar.
spoke [spəuk] pret. See SPEAK.
spoken [—ən] p. p. See SPEAK.
— Adj. Hablado, da: *spoken English*, inglés hablado. || "*English spoken*", "se habla inglés".
spokeshave [—ʃeiv] n. TECH. Raedera, *f.*
spokesman [—smən] n. Portavoz, *m.* [*Amer.*, vocero, *m.*]. || *To be spokesman for a group of people*, ser portavoz de un grupo de personas, hablar en nombre de un grupo de personas.
— OBSERV. El plural de *spokesman* es *spokesmen*.
spoliate [ˈspəulieit] v. tr. Expoliar, despojar de.
spoliation [ˌspəuliˈeiʃən] n. Expoliación, *f.*, despojo, *m.* (pillage). || JUR. Alteración (*f.*) de documentos.
spoliator [ˈspəulieitə*] n. Expoliador, ra.
spondaic [spɔnˈdeiik] adj. POET. Espondaico, ca.
spondee [ˈspɔndi:] n. POET. Espondeo, *m.*
spondulicks [spɔnˈdju:liks] n. FAM. Pasta, *f.* (money).
spondyl [ˈspɔndil] or **spondyle** [ˈspɔndail] n. ANAT. Espóndilo, *m.*, vértebra, *f.*
sponge [spʌndʒ] n. ZOOL. Esponja, *f.* || Esponja, *f.* (for domestic use). || CULIN. Bizcocho (*m.*) esponjoso (cake). || MIL. Escobillón, *m.* (for cleaning a cannon). || FIG. FAM. Gorrón, ona (sponger). || — FIG. FAM. *To drink like a sponge*, beber como una esponja. ||

FIG. *To pass the sponge over*, pasar la esponja por. | *To throw in the sponge*, tirar la esponja (in boxing, etc.).

sponge [spʌndʒ] v. tr. Limpiar con esponja (to clean). || Pasar una esponja por (to wipe). || Limpiar con un escobillón. || FAM. Sacar de gorra, gorronear: *to sponge a meal*, sacar una comida de gorra. | Dar un sablazo: *to sponge five pounds off s.o.*, dar un sablazo de cinco libras a alguien. || — *To sponge off* o *out*, quitar con una esponja. || *To sponge up*, absorber.
— V. intr. Pescar esponjas. || FAM. Sablear, dar sablazos (to borrow money). | Vivir de gorra, gorrear, gorronear (to eat, etc. at s.o.'s expense). || — *The stain will sponge off easily*, la mancha se quitará fácilmente con un trapo mojado. || FAM. *To sponge on s.o.*, vivir a costa de alguien.

sponge bath [—bɑ:θ] n. Lavado (*m.*) con esponja.

sponge cake [—'keik] n. CULIN. Bizcocho (*m.*) esponjoso.

sponger [—ə*] n. Pescador (*m.*) de esponjas (who harvests sponges). || FAM. Gorrón, ona (person who lives parasitically). | Sablista, *m.* & *f.* (who borrows money).

sponge rubber [—'rʌbə*] n. Goma (*f.*) esponjosa.

spongiae ['spʌndʒii:] pl. n. Espongiarios, *m.*

sponginess ['spʌndʒinis] n. Esponjosidad, *f.*

sponging ['spʌndʒiŋ] n. Limpieza (*f.*) con esponja (cleaning). || FAM. Gorronería, *f.* (cadging).
— Adj. FAM. Gorrón, ona (cadging).

spongy ['spʌndʒi] adj. Esponjoso, sa.

sponsion ['spɔnʃən] n. JUR. Garantía, *f.*

sponson ['spɔnsn] n. Saliente (*m.*) en un buque de guerra para colocar el cañón. || AVIAT. Flotador, *m.* (of a hydroplane). || MAR. Cámara (*f.*) de aire (of a canoe).

sponsor ['spɔnsə*] n. Patrocinador, ra (who gives financial support). || Garante, *m.*, fiador, ra (warrantor). || Padrino, *m.*, madrina, *f.* (of a child, club member). || RAD. Patrocinador, ra (of a program).

sponsor ['spɔnsə*] v. tr. Patrocinar (to support, to finance). || Fiar, garantizar (to accept responsibility for). || Apadrinar (to act as godparent to, to introduce to a society). || RAD. *To sponsor a television programme*, presentar or patrocinar un programa de televisión.

sponsorial [spɔn'sɔ:riəl] adj. Del padrino. || Patrocinador, ra. || Garantizador, ra.

sponsorship ['spɔnsəʃip] n. Patrocinio, *m.* || *Under the sponsorship of*, bajo el patrocinio de, patrocinado por.

spontaneity [,spɔntə'ni:iti] n. Espontaneidad, *f.*

spontaneous [spɔn'teinjəs] adj. Espontáneo, a.

spontaneousness [—nis] n. Espontaneidad, *f.*

spoof [spu:f] n. FAM. Engaño, *m.* (hoax). | Broma, *f.* (parody).

spoof [spu:f] v. tr. Engañar.
— V. intr. Bromear, burlarse.

spook [spu:k] n. FAM. Espectro, *m.*, aparición, *f.*

spooky [—i] adj. FAM. Fantasmal (like a ghost). | Tétrico, ca (scary). | Encantado, da; visitado por duendes (haunted).

spool [spu:l] n. Carrete, *m.*, bobina, *f.* (of sewing thread). || Canilla, *f.* (of a sewing machine). || TECH. Devanadera, *f.* (in spinning). | Enjulio, *m.* (in weaving). || Carrete, *m.* (of a typewriter, fishing rod, still camera). || Bobina, *f.* (of magnetic tape, cine film).

spool [spu:l] v. tr. Enrollar, encanillar (thread, etc.). || TECH. Devanar.

spoon [spu:n] n. Cuchara, *f.* || Cucharada, *f.* (spoonful): *two spoons of flour*, dos cucharadas de harina. || SP. "Spoon", *m.*, cuchara, *f.* (golf club). | Cuchara, *f.* (in fishing). || — *Basting spoon*, cucharón, *m.* || *Coffee spoon*, cuchara or cucharilla (*f.*) de café. || *Dessert spoon*, cuchara de postre. || *Serving spoon*, cuchara de servir. || *Soup spoon*, cuchara sopera. || FIG. *To be born with a silver spoon in one's mouth*, criarse en buenos pañales.

spoon [spu:n] v. tr. Sacar con cuchara. || Dar forma de cuchara. || SP. Elevar [la pelota] de un golpe. || *To spoon out the soup*, servir la sopa con cuchara.
— V. intr. Pescar con cuchara (in fishing). || FAM. Hacerse carantoñas.

spoon bait [—beit] n. Cuchara, *f.* (in fishing).

spoonbill [—bil] n. Espátula, *f.* (bird).

spoonerism [—arizəm] n. Lapsus (*m.*) burlesco de trastrocamiento de letras.

spoon-fed [—fed] adj. FIG. Mimado, da (spoilt). | Subvencionado, da (enterprise). || Que come con cuchara.
— Pret. & p. p. See SPOON-FEED.

spoon-feed* [—fi:d] v. tr. Dar de comer con cuchara (to feed with a spoon). || FIG. Mimar (to spoil). | Subvencionar (an enterprise).

— OBSERV. Pret. & p. p. *spoon-fed*.

spoonful [—ful] n. Cucharada, *f.*: *heaped spoonful of flour*, cucharada colmada de harina. || *Small spoonful*, cucharadita, *f.*

— OBSERV. El plural es *spoonfuls* o *spoonsful*.

spoony [—i] adj. FAM. Acaramelado, da; enamorado, da (in love).

spoor [spuə*] n. Rastro, *m.*, pista, *f.*

spoor [spuə*] v. tr. Rastrear, seguir el rastro de, seguir la pista de.
— V. intr. Seguir el rastro or la pista de un animal.

sporadic [spə'rædik] adj. Esporádico, ca.

sporadicalness [—əlnis] n. Esporadicidad, *f.*

sporangium [spə'rændʒiəm] n. BOT. Esporangio, *m.*

spore [spɔ:*] n. Espora, *f.* || *Spore case*, esporangio, *m.*

sporidium [spə'ridiəm] n. BOT. Esporidio, *m.*

sporozoan [,spɔrə'zəuən] n. BIOL. Esporozoo, *m.*, esporozoario, *m.*

sporran ['spɔrən] n. Bolsa (*f.*) que llevan los escoceses sobre la falda.

sport [spɔ:t] n. Deporte, *m.*: *winter sports*, deportes de invierno; *to go in for sport*, practicar deportes. || Caza, *f.* (hunting): *to have a good day's sport*, pasar un buen día de caza. || Presa, *f.* (prey): *such people are easy sport for pickpockets*, tales personas son presa fácil para los rateros. || Víctima, *f.* (victim): *the sport of fortune*, *of other people's jokes*, la víctima del destino, de las bromas de los demás. || Juguete, *m.* (plaything). || Burla, *f.*, diversión, *f.* (amusement): *a moment's sport*, un momento de diversión. || Buen perdedor, *m.* (good loser). || BIOL. Mutación, *f.* || — Pl. Competiciones, *f.*, campeonatos, *m.* (organized meetings for athletes). || — *Athletic sports*, atletismo, *m.* || *Be a sport!*, ¡sé bueno!, ¡sé amable! || *In sport*, en broma. || *To be a good sport*, portarse como un caballero (to be a gentleman), ser buen chico (likeable). || *To make sport of*, burlarse or mofarse de.
— Adj. U. S. Deportivo, va; de sport (sports).

sport [spɔ:t] v. intr. Jugar, divertirse (to play). || Bromear (to joke). || Juguetear (to frolic).
— V. tr. Lucir: *to sport a new dress*, lucir un traje nuevo.

sporting [—iŋ] adj. Deportivo, ca: *sporting event*, encuentro deportivo; *sporting spirit*, espíritu deportivo. || Aficionado a los deportes (fond of sport): *sporting man*, hombre aficionado a los deportes. || Que juega (gambling). || — *Sporting chance*, buena posibilidad de éxito. || *Sporting offer*, oferta interesante.

sportive [—iv] adj. Juguetón, ona.

sports [—s] adj. Deportivo, va; de sport. || — *Sports car*, coche deportivo. || *Sports day*, día dedicado a los deportes. || *Sports ground*, campo deportivo. || *Sports jacket*, chaqueta (*f.*) de sport.

sportscast [—kɑ:st] n. Retransmisión (*f.*) deportiva.

sportsman [—smən] n. Deportista, *m.* (who practices a sport). || Hombre (*m.*) de espíritu deportivo, caballero, *m.* (gentleman). || Buen perdedor, *m.* (good loser).

— OBSERV. El plural de *sportsman* es *sportsmen*.

sportsmanlike [—smənlaik] adj. De espíritu deportivo (person). || Caballeroso, sa (attitude).

sportsmanship [—smənʃip] n. Deportividad, *f.* || Caballerosidad, *f.*

sportswear [—wɛə*] n. Ropa (*f.*) de deporte (clothes for sport). || Ropa (*f.*) de sport (casual wear).

sportswoman [—s'wumən] n. Deportista, *f.* (who practices a sport). || Señora, *f.* (real lady).

— OBSERV. El plural de *sportswoman* es *sportswomen*.

sportswriter [—s,raitə*] n. Cronista (*m.*) deportivo.

sporty [—i] adj. De espíritu deportivo (sportsmanlike). || Aficionado a los deportes (fond of sport). || Deportivo, va (suitable for sport): *a sporty little boat*, un pequeño bote deportivo. || De sport (clothes). || Alegre (gay). || U. S. FAM. Ostentoso, sa (flashy).

sporulation [spɔrju'leiʃən] n. Esporulación, *f.*

spot [spɔt] n. Mancha, *f.* (of dirt, on a leopard skin, on fruit, leaves, etc., on the sun, planets): *dog with a brown spot*, perro con una mancha de color marrón. || Lunar, *m.* (pattern on material): *shirt with blue spots*, camisa con lunares azules. || MED. Grano, *m.* (on the body): *to come out in spots*, salirle granos a uno. | Espinilla, *f.* (on the face). || Sitio, *m.*, lugar, *m.* (place): *a quiet spot*, un sitio tranquilo; *the spot where the accident occurred*, el sitio donde ocurrió el accidente. || Puesto, *m.*, sitio, *m.* (job). || Parte, *f.*: *a wet spot on a painting*, una parte mojada en un cuadro. || Punto, *m.* (on billiard table, ball). || Marca, *f.* (distinguishing mark). || RAD. Espacio, *m.*: *advertising spot*, espacio publicitario. || FIG. Mancha, *f.*, baldón, *m.*: *a spot on one's reputation*, una mancha en la reputación de uno. || Gota, *f.* (of liquid): *a few spots of rain*, unas gotas de lluvia. || Gota, *f.*, gotita, *f.* (of drink): *just a spot, please*, sólo una gotita, por favor. || FAM. Poco, *m.*, poquito, *m.*: *a spot of work*, un poco de trabajo; *a spot to eat*, un poquito de comida. | Foco, *m.*, proyector, *m.* (spotlight). || — Pl. COMM. Mercancías (*f.*) disponibles. || — *Accident black spot*, lugar en que ocurren muchos accidentes. || FAM. *A spot of bother*, cierta dificultad. || *Beauty spot*, lunar, *m.* || *Black spot*, mancha, *f.* (on one's record). || *Night spot*, sala (*f.*) de fiestas. || *On the spot*, en el lugar: *police were on the spot within five minutes*, la policía se personó en el lugar en cinco minutos; en el momento: *he dealt with it on the spot*, se ocupó de ello en el momento; en el acto: *killed on the spot*, matado en el acto. || *Our man on the spot*, nuestro representante (representative), nuestro corresponsal (correspondent). || FIG. *Sore spot*, punto sensible. | *Tender spot*, punto sensible. | *To be in a tight spot*, estar en un apuro, estar en un aprieto. | *To have a soft spot for s.o.*, *for sth.*, tener una debilidad por alguien, por algo. | *To hit the spot*, venirle muy bien a uno, ser lo mejor. | *To knock spots off*, dar una paliza a (to triumph over), dejar muy atrás (to be better than). | *To put s.o. on the spot*, poner a uno en un aprieto (in a difficult position). | *Weak spot*, punto flaco.

— Adj. COMM. Contante: *spot cash*, dinero contante. | En existencia, disponible (goods). | Con pago al contado (sell). || [Hecho] al azar (at random): *spot check*, inspección hecha al azar. || RAD. Local (from a local station). | Realizado entre programas (announcement, etc.).

spot [spɔt] v. tr. Cubrir con manchas (to mark with spots). || Salpicar, motear (to speckle): *the passing car spotted me with mud*, el coche me salpicó de barro al pasar. || Manchar (to dirty). || Pronosticar, adivinar: *to spot the winner*, pronosticar el ganador. || Escoger (to select). || Reconocer (to recognize). || Divisar: *she spotted him in the crowd*, le divisó en medio de la multitud. || Notar, ver: *did you spot the errors?*, ¿notaste los errores? || MIL. Localizar (to find the position of). | Concentrar (artillery fire). | Emplazar (to position). || U. S. FAM. Dar como ventaja (to allow as a handicap).

— V. intr. Mancharse (to become stained). || Manchar (to stain). || MIL. Observar el tiro. || *To spot with rain*, gotear.

spotless [—lis] adj. Sin tacha (character). || Intachable (reputation). | Inmaculado, da (clean).

spotlessly [—lisli] adv. *Spotlessly clean*, limpísimo, ma; inmaculado, da.

spotlessness [—lisnis] n. Limpieza (*f.*) perfecta.

spotlight [—lait] n. THEATR. Proyector, *m.*, foco, *m.* || Foco, *m.* (beam of light). || Lámpara, *f.*, linterna, *f.* (torch). || AUT. Faro (*m.*) auxiliar. || FIG. *To be in the spotlight*, ser objeto de la atención pública, ser el blanco de las miradas.

spotlight [—lait] v. tr. Iluminar con un proyector (to light up). || FIG. Poner de relieve: *his speech spotlighted the difference between the two parties*, en su discurso puso de relieve la diferencia que existe entre los dos partidos.

spot news [—nju:z] n. Noticias (*f. sing.*) de última hora.

spot-remover [—ri'mu:və*] n. Quitamanchas, *m. inv.*

spotted [—id] adj. Moteado, da (speckled). || De lunares: *spotted tie*, corbata de lunares. || Con manchas: *spotted dog*, perro con manchas. || Sucio, cia (dirty). || MED. *Spotted fever*, tifus *or* tifo exantemático (typhus), meningitis (*f.*) cerebroespinal.

spotter [—ə*] n. Coleccionista, *m.* & *f.* (collector). || AVIAT. Avión (*m.*) de observación. || MIL. Observador (*m.*) de tiro.

spotting [—iŋ] n. MIL. Observación (*f.*) del tiro.

spotty [—i] adj. Lleno de manchas (covered in spots). || MED. Con granos (skin). | Espinilloso, sa (face). || FIG. Irregular, desigual (uneven in quality).

spot-weld [—,weld] v. tr. Soldar por puntos.

spot-welding [—,weldiŋ] n. Soldadura (*f.*) por puntos.

spousals ['spauzəls] pl. n. Desposorios, *m.*

spouse [spauz] n. Esposo, sa; cónyuge, *m.* & *f.*

spout [spaut] n. Pico, *m.* (of a jug). || Pitorro, *m.* (of a teapot). || ARCH. Canalón, *m.* (of roof). || Caño, *m.*, conducto, *m.* (pipe for rainwater, etc.). || Chorro, *m.* (jet). || Alcachofa, *f.* (of watering can). || Tromba, *f.* (waterspout). || FAM. *Up the spout*, empeñado, da (in pawn), perdido, da (beyond remedy).

spout [spaut] v. tr. Echar, arrojar: *the well started to spout oil*, el pozo empezó a echar petróleo. || FAM. Soltar: *to spout nonsense*, soltar tonterías.

— V. intr. Salir a chorro, chorrear (a fluid). || FAM. Declamar, perorar (to talk excessively).

sprag [spræg] n. Calce, *m.*, cuña, *f.*

sprag [spræg] v. tr. Calzar.

sprain [sprein] n. MED. Torcedura, *f.*, esguince, *m.*

sprain [sprein] v. tr. MED. Torcer: *to sprain one's ankle*, torcerse el tobillo.

sprang [spræŋ] pret. See SPRING.

sprat [spræt] n. Espadín, *m.*, "sprat", *m.* (fish).

sprawl [sprɔ:l] n. Postura (*f.*) desgarbada. || *Urban sprawl*, urbanización (*f.*) irregular.

sprawl [sprɔ:l] v. tr. Extender.

— V. intr. Dejarse caer, tumbarse: *he sprawled on the sofa*, se dejó caer en el sofá. || Extenderse: *London sprawls over a wide area*, Londres se extiende sobre una gran zona. || — *He went sprawling*, cayó cuan largo era. || *To send s.o. sprawling*, tumbar *or* derribar a uno.

spray [sprei] n. Rociada, *f.* (water). || MAR. Espuma, *f.* || Pulverizador, *m.*, vaporizador, *m.* (device for spraying). || Ramo, *m.*, ramillete, *m.* (of flowers). || Barra, *f.* (of diamonds).

spray [sprei] v. tr. Pulverizar (to project a liquid): *to spray a plant with insecticide*, pulverizar una planta con insecticida. || Rociar (to sprinkle). || AGR. Fumigar (crops). || *To spray paint on*, pintar con pistola.

— V. intr. Vaporizarse.

sprayer [—ə*] n. Pulverizador, *m.*, vaporizador, *m.* (atomizer). || Pistola, *f.* (for painting). || Quemador, *m.* (for fuel oil).

spray gun [—gʌn] n. Pistola, *f.*

spraying [—iŋ] n. Pulverización, *f.* (of a liquid). || AGR. *Crop spraying*, fumigación (*f.*) de los cultivos.

spread [spred] n. Propagación, *f.*, difusión, *f.*: *spread of a disease*, *of ideas*, propagación de una enfermedad, de ideas. || Extensión, *f.* (of an area): *the spread of the city*, la extensión de la ciudad; *the spread of one's arms*, la extensión de los brazos; *the spread of a country*, *of a speech*, la extensión de un país, de un discurso. || Envergadura, *f.* (of wings, sails). || Expansión, *f.*, desarrollo, *m.* (of an enterprise). || Gama, *f.* (range): *a wide spread of prices*, *of books*, una ancha gama de precios, de libros. || CULIN. Pasta, *f.* (paste): *anchovy spread*, pasta de anchoa. || Colcha, *f.* [*Amer.*, cubrecama, *m.*] (bedspread). || Tapete, *m.* (for a table). || FAM. Comilona, *f.* (meal). || ARCH. Anchura, *f.* (of a vault). || PRINT. Anuncio (*m.*) a doble página. || — CULIN. *Cheese spread*, queso (*m.*) de untar. || FAM. *Middle-age spread*, la curva de la felicidad *or* del cincuentón.

— Pret & p. p. See SPREAD.

spread* [spred] v. tr. Extender: *to spread clothes to dry*, extender ropa para secar; *to spread a newspaper on the ground*, extender un periódico en el suelo; *to spread one's arms*, extender los brazos; *to spread a privilege to more than one person*, extender un privilegio a más de una persona; *to spread one's influence*, extender su influencia. || Exponer: *the potter spread his wares*, el alfarero expuso la mercancía. || Untar: *to spread marmalade on bread*, untar mermelada en el pan; *to spread bread with marmalade*, untar el pan con mermelada. || Cubrir: *to spread the floor with newspapers*, cubrir el suelo con periódicos. || Poner (to set): *to spread the table*, poner la mesa. || Llenar: *to spread the table with exquisite morsels*, llenar la mesa con exquisitos manjares. || PRINT. Imprimir a doble página. | Espaciar (lines). || Propagar: *coughs and sneezes spread diseases*, toses y estornudos propagan las enfermedades. || Difundir: *to spread ideas*, difundir ideas. || Propagar, hacer correr, difundir: *to spread a rumour*, hacer correr un rumor. || Sembrar (panic, terror). || COMM. Espaciar (payment). || Tender (a net). || Aflojar (to distend). || Desplegar (wings, sails, flags). || — *To spread its tail*, hacer la rueda (peacock). || *To spread o.s.*, ponerse a sus anchas (to have plenty of room), dedicarse a muchas actividades (to have many interests), superarse (in performing a task), darse aires, presumir (to give o.s. airs), extenderse, hablar extensamente (on a subject). || *To spread out*, esparcir (to scatter), extender: *to spread out a newspaper*, extender un periódico; exponer (goods), espaciar (to space out).

— V. intr. Esparcirse: *dust spread over the books*, el polvo se esparció sobre los libros. || Extenderse: *the woods spread as far as the valley*, el bosque se extendía hasta el valle; *the ink spread over the paper*, la tinta se extendió sobre el papel; *the damp spread into the next room*, la humedad se extendió hasta la habitación siguiente. || Ensancharse (a river). || Untarse: *butter spreads more easily if warmed slightly*, la mantequilla se unta más fácilmente si se calienta un poco. || Correr: *the rumour has spread*, ha corrido el rumor. || Propagarse: *the disease quickly spread*, la enfermedad se propagó rápidamente. || Difundirse, propagarse, diseminarse (news, ideas). || Propagarse (fire). || Desplegarse (flags, wings, sails). || Separarse (to move apart). || FAM. Engordar (to grow stout). || *To spread out*, esparcirse, desparramarse (to scatter), separarse (to separate), extenderse (to stretch), desarrollarse (to develop), ensancharse: *here the river spreads out*, aquí se ensancha el río.

— OBSERV. Pret. & p. p. ***spread***.

spread-eagle [—'i:gl] adj. Con los miembros extendidos. || U. S. Patriotero, ra (chauvinistic). | Fanfarrón, ona (boasting).

spread-eagle [—'i:gl] v. tr. Extender los miembros de (as a punishment).

spreader [—ə*] n. Propagador, ra.

spree [spri:] n. Juerga, *f.*, jarana, *f.* [*Amer.*, parranda, *f.*]: *to go on a spree*, ir de juerga, andar de parranda. || *To go on a shopping o a spending spree*, hacer muchas compras.

sprig [sprig] n. Ramito, *m.*: *a sprig of holly*, un ramito de acebo. || TECH. Puntilla, *f.*, tachuela, *f.* (nail).

sprig [sprig] v. tr. Adornar con ramitos (to decorate). || TECH. Clavar con puntillas *or* con tachuelas.

sprightliness ['spraitlinis] n. Vivacidad, *f.* (liveliness). || Energía, *f.* (energy). | Agilidad, *f.* (in an old person).

sprightly ['spraitli] adj. Vivo, va (lively): *a sprightly style*, un estilo vivo. || Enérgico, ca (energetic). || Ágil: *he is very sprightly for his age*, es muy ágil para la edad que tiene.

spring [spriŋ] n. Salto, *m.* (jump): *to take a spring*, dar un salto. || Primavera, *f.* (season): *in spring*, en la primavera; *spring is in the air*, huele a primavera. || Manantial, *m.*, fuente, *f.* (of water): *hot spring*, manantial de agua caliente. || Muelle, *m.*, resorte, *m.* (of watch, mattress, etc.): *coil spring*, muelle helicoidal. || AUT. Ballesta, *f.* || FIG. Fuente, *f.*: *spring of life*, fuente de vida. || ARCH. Arranque, *m.* (of an arch, a vault). || Elasticidad, *f.* (elasticity). || Grieta, *f.* (crack). || FIG. *To walk with a spring in one's step*, andar con paso ligero.

— Adj. Primaveral: *spring morning*, mañana primaveral; *spring flowers*, flores primaverales. || Resistente (resilient). || De muelles (a watch, mattress, etc.). || Montado sobre ballestas (carriage). || De manantial (water).

spring* [spriŋ] v. tr. Saltar: *the dog sprang the river*, el perro saltó el río. || Hacer surgir *or* brotar (water, etc.). || Soltar (to release). || Poner muelles a (to put springs on). || Hacer funcionar (a trap). || FAM. Soltar de repente: *he sprang a question on me*, de repente me soltó una pregunta. || Volar, hacer explotar (to cause to explode). || Torcer, combar (to warp). || Hender (to split). || Levantar [caza] (game). || FAM. Poner en libertad, soltar (prisoners). || — *To spring a leak*, empezar a hacer agua. || *To spring an ambush*, tender una emboscada. || *To spring a surprise on s.o.*, coger de sorpresa a alguien.
— V. intr. Saltar (to jump): *to spring over a fence*, saltar una valla. || Levantarse de un salto (to get up suddenly): *he sprang from his bed*, de un salto se levantó de la cama. || Descender: *he springs from aristocratic stock*, desciende de una familia aristocrática. || Surgir, derivarse: *the quarrel sprang from a misunderstanding*, la riña surgió de un malentendido. || Brotar: *the point where the water springs from the rock*, el lugar donde el agua brota de la roca; *the corn is springing*, brota el maíz. || Salir a chorros: *the wine was springing from the hole in the barrel*, el vino salía a chorros por el agujero en el tonel. || Torcerse, alabearse (to warp). || Henderse (to split). || Explotar (a mine). || ARCH. Arrancar: *several arches spring from the column*, varios arcos arrancan de la columna. || — *Hope springs eternal*, la esperanza es lo último que se pierde. || *Tears sprang to his eyes*, se le llenaron los ojos de lágrimas. || *To spring at s.o.*, abalanzarse sobre alguien. || *To spring back*, volver a su posición original: *the branch sprang back*, la rama volvió a su posición original; saltar para atrás, dar un salto para atrás (a person). || *To spring forth*, brotar. || *To spring forward*, dar un salto hacia adelante. || *To spring open*, abrirse de un golpe. || *To spring to one's feet*, levantarse de un salto. || *To spring to s.o.'s rescue*, acudir rápidamente en ayuda de alguien. || *To spring up*, brotar, surgir, manar (a liquid), elevarse, levantarse (a building), levantarse de un salto (to get up quickly), levantarse (the wind), crecer rápidamente (to grow quickly), espigarse (a child), surgir (a problem), nacer (a friendship). || *Where did you spring from?*, ¿de dónde salió usted?
— OBSERV. Pret. ***sprang, sprung;*** p. p. ***sprung.***

spring balance [—ˈbæləns] n. Peso (*m.*) de muelle.
spring bed [—ˈbed] n. Colchón (*m.*) de muelles.
springboard [—bɔ:d] n. Trampolín, *m.*
spring bolt [—bəlt] n. Pestillo (*m.*) de golpe.
spring-clean [—kli:n] v. tr. Hacer una limpieza general de, limpiar completamente.
— V. intr. Hacer una limpieza general.
spring-cleaning [—ˌkli:niŋ] n. Limpieza (*f.*) general. || *To do the spring-cleaning*, hacer una limpieza general, limpiar toda la casa.
springe [sprindʒ] n. Lazo, *m.*
springe [sprindʒ] v. tr. Atrapar con lazo.
springer [spriŋə*] n. Tipo de podenco, *m.* (dog). || Sotabanco, *m.* (of an arch).
spring fever [ˈspriŋfi:və*] n. Desasosiego, *m.* [debido a la llegada de la primavera].
springhead [ˈspriŋhed] n. Manantial, *m.*, fuente, *f.*
springiness [ˈspriŋinis] n. Elasticidad, *f.*
springing [ˈspriŋiŋ] n. Muelles, *m. pl.* (springs). || ARCH. Arranque, *m.*
spring leaf [ˈspriŋli:f] n. Hoja (*f.*) de ballesta.
springlet [ˈspriŋlet] n. Manantial (*m.*) pequeño.
springlike [ˈspriŋlaik] adj. Elástico, ca (like a spring). || Primaveral: *springlike weather*, tiempo primaveral.
spring lock [ˈspriŋlɔk] n. Cerradura (*f.*) de golpe.
spring mattress [ˈspriŋˌmætris] n. Colchón (*m.*) de muelles.
spring tide [ˈspriŋtaid] n. MAR. Marea (*f.*) viva, aguas (*f. pl.*) vivas.
springtide [ˈspriŋtaid] or **springtime** [ˈspriŋtaim] n. Primavera, *f.*
springwater [ˈspriŋˌwɔ:tə*] n. Agua (*f.*) de manantial.
springiness [ˈspriŋinis] n. Elasticidad, *f.*
springy [ˈspriŋi] adj. Elástico, ca (resilient). || FIG. Ligero, ra: *springy step*, paso ligero.
sprinkle [ˈspriŋkl] n. Rociada, *f.*, salpicadura, *f.* || — *A sprinkle of grated cheese*, un poquito de queso rallado. || *A sprinkle of rain*, unas gotas de lluvia.
sprinkle [ˈspriŋkl] v. tr. Rociar: *to sprinkle with water*, rociar de agua. || Asperjar (with holy water). || Salpicar: *to sprinkle with sugar*, salpicar con azúcar; *a speech sprinkled with long words*, un discurso salpicado de palabras largas. || Diseminar, desparramar: *he has relatives sprinkled all over the country*, tiene parientes diseminados por todo el país. || TECH. Jaspear (book).
— V. intr. Chispear, lloviznar (to drizzle). || Rociar (to spray).
sprinkler [—ə*] n. AGR. Regadera, *f.* || REL. Hisopo, *m.*, aspersorio, *m.* || Extintor, *m.* (to extinguish fire). || *Sprinkler system*, sistema (*m.*) de regadío (in agriculture), sistema (*m.*) de aspersión automática (fire precaution).
sprinkling [—iŋ] n. Aspersión, *f.* (of a liquid). || REL. Aspersión, *f.* (of holy water). || FIG. Un poco, algo de: *a sprinkling of sugar*, un poco de azúcar. || — *A sprinkling of Latinisms in a letter*, una carta salpicada de latinajos. || *A sprinkling of rain*, unas gotas de lluvia. || *There was a sprinkling of peers at the reception*, en la fiesta había unos cuantos aristócratas.
sprint [sprint] n. SP. "Sprint", *m.*, esprint, *m.* || FIG. *It was quite a sprint for us to get the work finished on time*, tuvimos que apresurarnos mucho para terminar a tiempo el trabajo.
sprint [sprint] v. tr. SP. Sprintar en, esprintar en: *to sprint the last hundred metres*, esprintar en los últimos cien metros.
— V. intr. SP. Sprintar, esprintar. || Correr a toda velocidad (to run at full speed).
sprinter [—ə*] n. SP. Sprinter, *m.* & *f.*, esprinter, *m.* & *f.*, corredor (*m.*) de velocidad.
sprit [sprit] n. MAR. Verga, *f.* (spar). | Bauprés, *m.* (bowsprit).
sprite [sprait] n. Duende, *m.*, trasgo, *m.* (elf). || Hada, *f.* (fairy).
spritsail [ˈspritseil] n. MAR. Vela (*f.*) de abanico, vela (*f.*) tarquina, cebadera, *f.*
sprocket [ˈsprɔkit] n. TECH. Diente, *m.* (of a chain, pinion). | Rueda (*f.*) dentada, rueda (*f.*) catalina (wheel).
sprocket wheel [—wi:l] n. TECH. Rueda (*f.*) dentada, rueda (*f.*) catalina.
sprout [spraut] n. Brote, *m.*, retoño, *m.* (shoot).
— Pl. *Brussels sprouts*, coles (*f.*) de Bruselas.
sprout [spraut] v. tr. BOT. Echar: *the tree has sprouted leaves*, el árbol ha echado hojas. || Echar, salirle [a un animal] (horns). || Dejarse: *to sprout a moustache*, dejarse bigote.
— V. intr. BOT. Brotar: *after the rain the flowers sprouted*, después de la lluvia brotaron las flores. | Echar brotes (branch). || FIG. Crecer rápidamente.
spruce [spru:s] adj. Cuidado, da (tidy). || Pulcro, cra (neat). || Elegante (smart). || Acicalado, da (trim).
— N. BOT. Picea, *f.* (tree).
spruce [spru:s] v. tr. *To spruce o.s. up*, acicalarse, ataviarse. || *To spruce up*, arreglar (sth.), acicalar, ataviar (s.o.).
spruceness [—nis] n. Pulcritud, *f.* (neatness). || Elegancia, *f.* (smartness).
sprue [spru:] n. TECH. Piquera, *f.*, orificio (*m.*) de colada (hole). | Mazarota, *f.* (waste metal).
sprung [sprʌŋ] pret. & p. p. See SPRING.
— Adj. De muelles (mattress, etc.).
spry [ˈsprai] adj. Vivo, va (lively). || Activo, va (active).
spud [spʌd] n. AGR. Escarda, *f.*, escardillo, *m.* (tool). || FAM. Patata, *f.* [*Amer.*, papa, *f.*] (potato).
spud [spʌd] v. tr. Escardar.
spue [spju:] n./v. tr./intr. See SPEW.
spume [spju:m] n. Espuma, *f.*
spume [spju:m] v. intr. Espumar, hacer espuma.
spumous [—əs] or **spumy** [—i] adj. Espumoso, sa.
spun [spʌn] pret. & p. p. See SPIN.
— Adj. Hilado, da: *spun silk*, seda hilada. || — *Spun glass*, lana (*f.*) de vidrio. || MAR. *Spun yarn*, meollar, *m.* (rope).
spunk [spʌŋk] n. FAM. Valor, *m.*, arrojo, *m.*, agallas, *f. pl.* (courage). || Yesca, *f.* (tinder).
spunky [—i] adj. FAM. Valiente, arrojado, da; que tiene agallas.
spur [spə:*] n. Espuela, *f.* (for horsemen). || ZOOL. Espolón, *m.* || BOT. Cornezuelo, *m.* || Espolón, *m.* (of a gamecock). || Trepador, *m.* (for climbing). || Vía (*f.*) muerta, apartadero, *m.* (in railways). || Estribación, *f.* (of mountain). || ARCH. Riostra, *f.*, puntal, *m.* (strut). | Contrafuerte, *m.* (buttress). || FIG. Estímulo, *m.*, espuela, *f.*, aguijón, *m.*, acicate, *m.* || MAR. Espolón, *m.*, tajamar, *m.* || — FIG. *On the spur of the moment*, sin pensarlo. || *To dig one's spurs into one's horse*, espolear un caballo, picar un caballo con las espuelas. || FIG. *To give a spur to s.o.'s efforts*, estimular los esfuerzos de alguien. | *To win one's spurs*, dar pruebas de sus aptitudes.
spur [spə:*] v. tr. Espolear, picar con las espuelas (a horse). || Poner espuelas en (a horseman). || Poner espolones a (a gamecock). || FIG. *To spur on*, estimular, incitar: *to spur s.o. on to do sth.*, incitar a alguien a que haga algo; espolear, aguijonear: *spurred on by desire*, aguijoneado por el deseo.
— V. intr. *To spur on* o *forward*, hincar las espuelas (to spur a horse), apresurarse (to hurry).
spur gear [—giə*] n. TECH. Engranaje (*m.*) cilíndrico.
spurious [ˈspjuəriəs] adj. Falso, sa (money, sentiments). || Apócrifo, fa (document). || Espúreo, a (child).
spuriousness [—nis] n. Falsedad, *f.* || Carácter (*m.*) espúreo, ilegitimidad, *f.* (of a child).
spurn [spə:n] n. Desprecio, *m.*, desdén, *m.*
spurn [spə:n] v. tr. Despreciar, desdeñar (to disdain). || Dar una patada a (to kick).
spurt [spə:t] n. Gran esfuerzo, *m.*, momento (*m.*) de energía (sudden effort). || Arrebato, *m.*, acceso, *m.* (sudden outburst): *a spurt of anger*, un arrebato de cólera. || Chorro, *m.* (sudden gush). || — SP. *Final spurt*, esfuerzo final. || FAM. *To put on a spurt*, acelerar.
spurt [spə:t] v. intr. Hacer un gran esfuerzo (to make a big effort). || SP. Acelerar. || Chorrear, salir a chorros (to gush forth).
— V. tr. Echar (a liquid).
spur track [ˈspə:træk] n. Apartadero, *m.*, vía (*f.*) muerta.

spur wheel [ˈspəːwiːl] n. TECH. Engranaje (*m.*) cilíndrico.
sputnik [ˈsputnik] n. "Sputnik", *m.* (satellite).
sputter [ˈspʌtə*] n./v. tr./intr. See SPLUTTER.
sputum [ˈspjuːtəm] n. MED. Esputo, *m.*

— OBSERV. El plural de esta palabra es *sputa*.

spy [spai] n. Espía, *m.* & *f.* || — FAM. *Police spy*, confidente, *m.*, soplón, *m.*, chivato, *m.* || *Spy story*, novela (*f.*) de espionaje.
spy [spai] v. tr. Divisar (to catch sight of). || Ver (to see). || Conseguir ver (by careful observation). || Espiar (to watch). || *To spy out*, reconocer (the land), descubrir valiéndose de artimañas (a secret).
— V. intr. Ser espía. || — *To spy into*, mirar de cerca (to examine), intentar descubrir (a secret). || *To spy on* o *upon s.o.*, espiar a alguien.
spyglass [—glɑːs] n. Catalejo, *m.*
spyhole [—həul] n. Mirilla, *f.* (in a door). || Registro, *m.* (in machinery).
spying [—iŋ] n. Espionaje, *m.*
squab [skwɔb] adj. Rechoncho, cha; regordete, ta (plump). || ZOOL. Sin plumas.
— N. Pichón, *m.* (young pigeon). || Pollito, *m.* (young bird). || Cojín, *m.*, almohadón, *m.* (cushion). || Sofá, *m.* (couch). || FAM. Tapón (*m.*) de alberca, persona (*f.*) rechoncha *or* regordeta.
squabble [—l] n. Riña, *f.*, disputa, *f.*, pelea, *f.*
squabble [—l] v. tr. PRINT. Empastelar.
— V. intr. Reñir, pelearse, disputar.
squabbler [—lə*] n. Pendenciero, ra.
squabbling [—liŋ] n. Peleas, *f. pl.*, riñas, *f. pl.*
squabby [—i] adj. FAM. Rechoncho, cha; regordete, ta.
squad [skwɔd] n. MIL. Pelotón, *m.*: *firing squad*, pelotón de ejecución. || Brigada, *f.* (of police): *drug squad*, brigada de estupefacientes. || U. S. Equipo, *m.* (team).
squad car [—kɑː*] n. U. S. Coche (*m.*) patrulla.
squadron [ˈskwɔdrən] n. MIL. Escuadrón, *m.* || AVIAT. Escuadrilla, *f.* || MAR. Escuadra, *f.*
squadron leader [—ˌliːdə*] n. Comandante, *m.*
squalid [ˈskwɔlid] adj. Mugriento, ta; asqueroso, sa; escuálido, da (very dirty). || Sórdido, da (sordid). || Miserable (poor).
squalidity [skwɔˈliditi] or **squalidness** [ˈskwɔlidnis] n. Asquerosidad, *f.*, escualidez, *f.* (dirtiness). || Miseria, *f.* (poverty).
squall [skwɔːl] n. Ráfaga, *f.*, racha, *f.* (sudden wind). || MAR. Turbonada, *f.* (sudden storm). || FAM. Tormenta, *f.*, borrasca, *f.* || Chillido, *m.*, berrido, *m.* (harsh cry).
squall [skwɔːl] v. intr. Chillar, berrear (to scream).
squaller [—ə*] n. Chillón, ona.
squalling [—iŋ] n. Chillidos, *m. pl.*, berridos, *m. pl.*
squally [—i] adj. Tempestuoso, sa; borrascoso, sa.
squalor [—ə*] n. Mugre, *f.*, asquerosidad, *f.* (dirtiness). || Miseria, *f.* (poverty).
squama [ˈskweimə] n. Escama, *f.*

— OBSERV. El plural de esta palabra es *squamae*.

squamate [ˈskweimət] or **squamosal** [ˈskweiˈməusəl] or **squamose** [ˈskweiˌməus] or **squamous** [ˈskweiməs] adj. Escamoso, sa.
squander [ˈskwɔndə*] v. tr. Malgastar, derrochar, despilfarrar (money). || Desperdiciar (time).
squanderer [—rə*] n. Despilfarrador, ra; derrochador, ra (spendthrift).
squandering [—riŋ] n. Despilfarro, *m.* derroche, *m.* (of money). || Desperdicio, *m.* (of time).
square [skwεə*] adj. Cuadrado, da (having four equal sides): *a square table*, una mesa cuadrada. || Rectangular. || En ángulo recto, a escuadra (sides of a box). || MATH. Cuadrado, da: *square mile*, milla cuadrada; *square root*, raíz cuadrada. | De superficie (measure). || Cuadrado, da (chin, shoulders). || FIG. Justo, ta; equitativo, va (fair): *square deal*, trato justo. | Honrado, da (honest). | Rotundo, da; categórico, ca; terminante: *square statement*, afirmación categórica; *a square refusal*, una negación rotunda. || En orden (orderly): *to get things square*, poner las cosas en orden. || FAM. Satisfactorio, ria (meal). | Anticuado, da; chapado a la antigua (old-fashioned). || SP. Empatado, da (tied). || — FIG. *All square*, en paz: *now we are all square*, ahora estamos en paz; iguales, empatado, da (in sport). | *Of square frame*, fornido, da; cuadrado, da (person). || *Square bracket*, corchete, *m.* || *Square dance*, baile (*m.*) de figuras. || *Square knot*, nudo (*m.*) de envergue *or* de rizo. || MAR. *Square sail*, vela cangreja. || FIG. *To get square with s.o.*, ajustarle las cuentas a uno.
— Adv. A escuadra, en ángulo recto (*to*, *with*, con) (at right angles). || En forma cuadrada (in square shape). || FIG. Directamente (directly). | Justo, exactamente: *the library is square in the middle of the town*, la biblioteca está justo en medio de la ciudad. | Honradamente (honestly). | Equitativamente, con justicia (fairly). | Cara a cara (face to face).
— N. Cuadrado, *m.* (shape). || Cuadro, *m.*: *decorated with black squares*, decorado con cuadros negros. || Escuadra, *f.* (instrument). || MATH. Cuadrado, *m.* (figure, multiple): *nine is the square of three*, nueve es el cuadrado de tres. || Casilla, *f.* (of a chessboard). || Cristal, *m.* (of a window). || ARCH. Plaza, *f.* (in a town). | Plaza (*f.*) ajardinada, plazoleta, *f.* (with garden). || MIL. Cuadro, *m.* (of soldiers). || Pañuelo, *m.* (handkerchief). || FAM. Anticuado, da; persona (*f.*) chapada a la antigua (old-fashioned person). || U. S. Manzana, *f.* [*Amer.*, cuadra, *f.*] (block of houses). || — *On the square*, en ángulo recto. || FIG. *To be on the square*, ser honrado.
square [skwεə*] v. tr. Cuadrar (to make square). || TECH. Escuadrar, labrar a escuadra (stone). | Escuadrar (timber). || Cuadricular (paper, etc.). || MATH. Cuadrar, elevar al cuadrado *or* a la segunda potencia (a number). || FAM. Sobornar, untar la mano a (to bribe). || FIG. Adaptar (to adapt). | Ajustar (accounts). | Arreglar (to settle): *to square matters*, arreglar las cosas. || SP. Igualar, empatar (a score). || — FIG. *To square accounts with*, ajustarle las cuentas a. || *To square one's shoulders*, sacar el pecho. || FIG. *To square with*, conformar con, ajustar a.
— V. intr. Cuadrar, estar de acuerdo: *his ideas do not square with mine*, sus ideas no cuadran con las mías. || *To square up*, ponerse en guardia, disponerse a luchar [*to*, contra] (to be ready to fight), saldar cuentas [*with*, con] (to settle accounts), enfrentarse con (to face up to).
square-built [—bilt] adj. De forma cuadrada (building). || Fornido, da; cuadrado, da (person).
squared [ˈskwεəd] adj. Cuadriculado, da (paper). || Escuadrado, da (stone, timber). || MATH. Elevado al cuadrado, elevado a la segunda potencia.
squarely [ˈskwεəli] adv. En ángulo recto, a escuadra (forming a right angle). || Con ángulos rectos (with right angles). || FIG. Honradamente (honestly). | Justo, exactamente (exactly). | Justo enfrente (directly opposite). | Cara a cara, de frente (face to face). | Firmemente (firmly).
square-necked [ˈskwεəˈnekt] adj. Con escote cuadrado (dress).
squareness [ˈskwεənis] n. Forma (*f.*) cuadrada. || FIG. Honradez, *f.*
square-shouldered [ˈskwεəˈʃəuldəd] adj. Ancho de espaldas, con las espaldas cuadradas.
square-toed [ˈskwεəˈtəud] adj. Con la punta cuadrada (shoe). || FAM. Anticuado, da; chapado a la antigua (old-fashioned).
squaring [ˈskwεəriŋ] n. Corte (*m.*) a escuadra (of a stone). || Cuadriculado, *m.* || MATH. Cuadratura, *f.*: *squaring the circle*, cuadratura del círculo.
squarish [ˈskwεəriʃ] adj. Casi cuadrado, aproximadamente cuadrado.
squash [skwɔʃ] n. Zumo, *m.* (juice). || Aplastamiento, *m.* (crushing). || Tropel, *m.*, gentío, *m.* (closely packed crowd). || BOT. Calabaza, *f.* [*Amer.*, cidra, *f.*, chayote, *m.*] || Chapoteo, *m.* (walking). || SP. Juego (*m.*) parecido a la pelota vasca que se juega con raquetas y contra una pared. || — *Lemon squash*, limón (*m.*) natural, zumo de limón. || *Squash hat*, sombrero (*m.*) flexible.
squash [skwɔʃ] v. tr. Aplastar (to crush): *I'm afraid I squashed the cake*, temo haber aplastado el pastel. || Apretar (to squeeze). || Meter (to put). || FAM. Aplastar, sofocar (to suppress): *to squash a rebellion*, sofocar una rebelión. | Echar por tierra (an objection). | Apabullar, callar (to silence a conceited person).
— V. intr. Aplastarse (to crush). || Apretarse, apretujarse (to crowd together). || — *To squash into*, conseguir meterse en, conseguir entrar en: *I squashed into the lift*, conseguí meterme en el ascensor. || *To squash through*, entrar atropelladamente por.
squash rackets or **squash racquets** [—ˌrækits] n. SP. Juego (*m.*) parecido a la pelota vasca que se juega con raquetas y contra una pared.
squashy [—i] adj. Blando, da (easily crushed). || Cenagoso, sa (earth). || De pulpa blanda (fruit).
squat [skwɔt] adj. En cuclillas (crouching). || Agazapado, da (animals). || Rechoncho, cha; achaparrado, da (person).
— N. Posición (*f.*) en cuclillas.
squat [skwɔt] v. intr. Ponerse en cuclillas, agacharse (to crouch). || Agazaparse (animals). || FAM. Sentarse (to sit). || JUR. Ocupar ilegalmente un sitio (to occupy property illegally).
squatter [—ə*] n. JUR. Persona (*f.*) que occupa ilegalmente un sitio.
squaw [skwɔː] n. India (*f.*) norteamericana.
squawk [skwɔːk] n. Graznido, *m.*, chillido, *m.*
squawk [skwɔːk] v. intr. Graznar, chillar.
squeak [skwiːk] n. Chillido, *m.* (of mice, rats, rabbits). || Chirrido, *m.*, rechinamiento, *m.* (of a hinge). || Chirrido, *m.* (of certains birds). || Crujido, *m.* (of shoes). || — FAM. *I don't want to hear a squeak out of you*, no quiero oírte, no quiero que rechistes. | *To have a narrow squeak*, librarse por los pelos.
squeak [skwiːk] v. tr. Decir con voz aguda.
— V. intr. Chillar (mice, rats, rabbits). || Chirriar, rechinar (hinge). || Rechinar (spring). || Chirriar (certain birds). || Crujir (shoes). || Raspear (pen). || U. S. FAM. Cantar, confesar (a secret). || — FIG. *To squeak by*, arreglárselas. | *To squeak through*, pasar dificultosamente.
squeaker [—ə*] n. Pichón, *m.* (pigeon). || Pollito, *m.* (young bird). || FAM. Soplón, *m.*, chivato, *m.* (informer).

squeaky [—i] adj. Chirriador, ra; chirriante (birds). || Que cruje (shoe). || Chillón, ona (voice). || Que rechina, chirriante (hinge).
squeal [skwi:l] n. Chillido, *m.* || FAM. Protesta, *f.*, queja, *f.* (complaint). | Denuncia, *f.* (denunciation).
squeal [skwi:l] v. intr. Chillar (to make a shrill cry). || FAM. Protestar, quejarse (to complain). | Cantar, confesar (to inform). || FAM. *To squeal on*, chivarse de (one's accomplices).
— V. tr. *To squeal out sth.*, decir algo chillando.
squeamish [ˈskwi:miʃ] adj. Remilgado, da (oversensitive). || Delicado, da (excessively fastidious). || Demasiado escrupuloso (excessively scrupulous). || Pudibundo, da (prudish). || — *To be squeamish about*, tener horror a. || MED. *To feel squeamish*, estar mareado, sentir náuseas.
squeamishness [—nis] n. Remilgos, *m. pl.* || Delicadeza, *f.*
squeegee [ˈskwi:ˈdʒi:] n. Enjugador, *m.*, rodillo (*m.*) de goma.
squeeze [skwi:z] n. Apretón, *m.* (of the hand). || Abrazo, *m.* (hug). || Presión, *f.* (compression). || Reducción, *f.*, disminución, *f.* || Gentío, *m.*, bullicio, *m.* (crowd). || Unas gotas: *a squeeze of lemon*, unas gotas de limón. || FIG. Aprieto, *m.* (difficulty): *if you are ever in a squeeze, come and see me*, si alguna vez se encuentra en un aprieto, venga a verme. || ARTS. Molde, *m.* || FAM. Exacción, *f.* || — *It was a tight squeeze*, estábamos muy apretados. || *To give s.o. a squeeze*, abrazar a alguien. || FIG. *To put the squeeze on s.o.*, apretarle las clavijas a uno.
squeeze [skwi:z] v. tr. Apretar, estrechar (to press): *to squeeze somebody's hand*, apretar la mano a alguien. || Estrujar (to press very hard). || Exprimir: *to squeeze an orange to extract the juice*, exprimir una naranja para extraer el zumo; *to squeeze the juice out of an orange*, exprimir el zumo de una naranja. || FIG. Ejercer presión (to put pressure upon). || Moldear (to mould). || Abrazar (to hug). || FAM. Sacar, sonsacar: *to squeeze money from*, sacar dinero a. || — *The doctor managed to squeeze him in before lunch*, el médico consiguió darle hora antes del almuerzo [aunque tenía muchos clientes]. || *To squeeze in one's waist*, ceñirse la cintura. || *To squeeze into*, meter (by force). || *To squeeze one's finger*, pillarse *or* cogerse el dedo. || *To squeeze o.s. into*, meterse [con dificultad] en. || *To squeeze o.s. through*, abrirse paso [con dificultad] entre, conseguir pasar entre. || *To squeeze out*, sacar (water, money, a confession), derramar (a tear). || *To squeeze through*, hacer pasar por.
— V. intr. *To squeeze into*, meterse [con dificultad] en. || *To squeeze out*, salir [con dificultad] de. || *To squeeze through*, abrirse paso [con dificultad], conseguir pasar entre (to force one's way). || *To squeeze together* o *up*, apretarse, apretujarse, apiñarse.
squeezer [—ə*] n. Exprimidor, *m.*, exprimelimones, *m. inv.* (for juice).
squelch [skweltʃ] n. Chapoteo, *m.* || FAM. Réplica, *f.* (retort).
squelch [skweltʃ] v. tr. Despachurrar, aplastar (to squash). || FIG. Aplastar, sofocar (a revolt). | Callar, apabullar (s.o.)
— V. intr. Chapotear, ir chapoteando.
squib [skwib] n. Buscapiés, *m. inv.* (firework). || Detonador, *m.* (detonator). || FIG. Pasquín, *m.* (lampoon). || FIG. *A damp squib*, un fallo.
squid [skwid] n. Calamar, *m.* (fish).
squiffy [ˈskwifi] adj. FAM. Achispado, da.
squill [skwil] n. Esquila, *f.*, cebolla (*f.*) albarrana (onion). || Esquila, *f.*, camarón, *m.* (prawn).
squilla [—ə] n. Esquila, *f.*, camarón, *m.* (prawn).

— OBSERV. El plural de esta palabra es *squillas* o *squillae*.

squint [skwint] n. Estrabismo, *m.*, bizquera, *f.* (strabismus). || Mirada (*f.*) bizca (cross-eyed look). || FAM. Ojeada, *f.*, vistazo, *m.* (quick look): *I had a squint at his paper*, eché un vistazo a su periódico. || Mirada (*f.*) de reojo (sidelong glance). || FIG. Inclinación, *f.* (tendency). || *To have a squint*, ser bizco.
— Adj. Bizco, ca (eyes). || Que mira de reojo.
squint [skwint] v. tr. Cerrar casi, entrecerrar (eyes).
— V. intr. Bizquear, ser bizco (to be cross-eyed). || Mirar de reojo (to look from the corner of the eye). || Cerrar casi *or* entrecerrar los ojos (to keep the eyes partly closed). || *To squint at*, echar un vistazo *or* una ojeada a (to have a look at), mirar de reojo (to look from the corner of the eye), mirar con los ojos entrecerrados.
squint-eyed [—aid] adj. Bizco, ca (s.o.). || FIG. De reojo (look). || FIG. Avieso, sa (malicious).
squire [ˈskwaiə*] n. HIST. Escudero, *m.* || Propietario, *m.*, terrateniente, *m.* [*Amer.*, hacendado, *m.*, estanciero, *m.*] (landowner). || Señor, *m.* (term of address). || FIG. Galán, *m.* (lady's escort). || *The squire*, el señor (in a village).
squire [ˈskwaiə*] v. tr. Acompañar (a lady).
squirearchy [—rɑ:ki] n. Aristocracia (*f.*) rural, terratenientes, *m. pl.*
squirm [skwə:m] n. Retorcimiento, *m.*
squirm [skwə:m] v. intr. Retorcerse (to wriggle). || FIG. Estar violento (to be embarrassed).
squirrel [ˈskwirəl] n. ZOOL. Ardilla, *f.*
squirt [skwə:t] n. Chorro, *m.* (of liquid). || Jeringa, *f.* (syringe). || Atomizador, *m.* (atomizer). || FAM. Mequetrefe, *m.* (whippersnapper).
squirt [skwə:t] v. tr. Dejar salir a chorros: *the cracked pipe was squirting water*, el tubo roto dejaba salir el agua a chorros. || Echar agua: *to squirt s.o. with a water pistol*, echar agua a alguien con una pistola de agua. || Inyectar (with a syringe).
— V. intr. Salir a chorros: *beer squirted from the barrel*, la cerveza salía a chorros del tonel.
squirter [—ə*] n. FAM. Atomizador, *m.*
squirt gun [—gʌn] n. Pistola (*f.*) de agua (toy).
squirting [—iŋ] n. Salida (*f.*) a chorros (of liquid). || Inyección, *f.* (with a syringe).
stab [stæb] n. Puñalada, *f.* (with a dagger). || Navajazo, *m.* (with a knife). || Herida, *f.* (wound). || FAM. Tentativa, *f.*, intento, *m.* (attempt). || FIG. Punzada, *f.* (of pain). || — FIG. *Stab in the back*, puñalada trapera. || FAM. *Taking a stab in the dark, I would say that*, a ojo de buen cubero diría que. || *To die of stab wounds*, morir apuñalado. || FAM. *To have a stab at sth.*, intentar [hacer] algo.
stab [stæb] v. tr. Apuñalar, dar una puñalada a (to pierce with a dagger). || Dar una navajazo (with a knife). || FIG. Partir (s.o.'s heart). || — *To be stabbed to death*, morir apuñalado. || FIG. *To stab s.o. in the back*, darle a uno una puñalada por la espalda *or* una puñalada trapera. || *To stab s.o. to death*, matar a alguien a puñaladas.
— V. intr. Dar una puñalada. || *To stab at*, intentar apuñalar a (to try to wound), mancillar (s.o.'s reputation), señalar (sth. with one's finger).
stabber [—ə*] n. Apuñalador, ra; asesino, na.
stabbing [—iŋ] adj. Punzante (pain).
— N. Puñaladas, *f. pl.* (stabs). || Asesinato (*m.*) a puñaladas (murder).
stability [stəˈbiliti] n. Estabilidad, *f.* || Firmeza, *f.*, entereza, *f.* (firmness of character).
stabilization [ˌsteibilaiˈzeiʃən] n. Estabilización, *f.*
stabilize [ˈsteibilaiz] v. tr. Estabilizar.
— V. intr. Estabilizarse.
stabilizer [—ə*] n. Estabilizador, *m.*
stabilizing [—iŋ] adj. Estabilizador, ra.
stable [ˈsteibl] adj. Estable: *a stable building, situation*, un edificio, una situación estable. || Estable, fijo, ja (job). || Firme (conviction). || Estable (person). || *To become stable*, estabilizarse.
— N. Cuadra, *f.*, caballeriza, *f.*, establo, *m.* (stall of horses). || Cuadra, *f.* (group of race horses). || Equipo, *m.* (of persons). || AUT. Escudería, *f.* (of race cars). || MYTH. *Augean stables*, establos (*m.*) de Augias.
stable [ˈsteibl] v. tr. Poner en una cuadra.
— V. intr. Estar en la cuadra.
stableboy [—bɔi] or **stableman** [—mən] n. Mozo (*m.*) de cuadra.

— OBSERV. El plural de *stableman* es *stablemen*.

stableness [—nis] n. Estabilidad, *f.*
staccato [stəˈkɑ:təu] adj. Staccato. || FIG. Entrecortado, da (style, voice).
— N. MUS. Staccato, *m.* || FIG. Repiqueteo, *m.*: *a staccato of machine gun fire*, el repiqueteo de una ametralladora.
stack [stæk] n. AGR. Almiar, *m.*, hacina, *f.* || Montón, *m.* (pile): *a stack of dishes*, un montón de platos. || MIL. Pabellón, *m.* (of rifles). || Cañón, *m.* (of chimney). || Chimenea, *f.* (of train, ship). || FAM. Montón, *m.* (large number). || U. S. AUT. Tubo (*m.*) de escape. || — Pl. Biblioteca, *f. sing.*, estantería, *f. sing.*, estantes, *m.* (bookcase). || FAM. Montón, *m. sing.*: *I have stacks of things to do*, tengo un montón de cosas que hacer.
stack [stæk] v. tr. Amontonar, apilar (to pile). || AGR. Hacinar. || Llenar, atiborrar (to load): *the room is stacked with books*, el cuarto está lleno de libros. || — FIG. *The cards are stacked against me*, las circunstancias están en contra mía. || MIL. *To stack arms*, armar pabellones. || U. S. *To stack the cards*, hacer fullerías con las cartas (in card games), hacer trampas (to prearrange circumstances). || *To stack up*, amontonar, apilar.
stadia [ˈsteidjə] n. Estadía, *f.* || *Stadia rod*, estadía.
stadium [ˈsteidjəm] n. Estadio, *m.*: *olympic stadium*, estadio olímpico. || FIG. Estadio, *m.*, fase, *f.*, etapa, *f.* (phase). || Estadio, *m.* (ancient measure).

— OBSERV. El plural de esta palabra es *stadiums* en los dos primeros sentidos y *stadia* en el tercero.

staff [stɑ:f] n. Personal, *m.*, empleados, *m. pl.* (personnel). || Palo, *m.* (stick). || Bastón, *m.* (walking stick). || REL. Báculo, *m.* (of a bishop). || Bordón, *m.* (of pilgrims). || Cayado, *m.* (of shepherd). || Bastón (*m.*) de mando (rod). || Asta, *f.* (flagpole). || Mira, *f.* (measure). || Estaf, *m.* (in construction). || MIL. Estado (*m.*) Mayor. || Servidumbre, *f.* (of a house). || MUS. Pentagrama, *m.* || FIG. Sostén, *m.*: *the staff of life*, el sostén de la vida. || — *Editorial staff*, redactores, *m. pl.*, redacción, *f.* || *Teaching staff*, cuerpo (*m.*) docente, profesorado, *m.* || *To be on the staff*, estar en plantilla. || FIG. *To be the staff of s.o.'s old age*, ser el báculo de la vejez de alguien. || *To leave the staff*, dimitir.
— Adj. Del personal: *staff entrance*, entrada del personal. || MIL. Del Estado Mayor.

— OBSERV. El plural de esta palabra es *staffs* cuando significa "personal, Estado Mayor, profesorado" y "estaf", y *staffs* o *staves* en los demás casos.

staff [stɑ:f] v. tr. Proveer de personal.

staff officer [—ˈɔfisə*] n. Oficial (*m.*) de Estado Mayor.

stag [stæg] adj. FAM. Para hombres. || *Stag party*, reunión (*f.*) de hombres, despedida (*f.*) de soltero.

— N. ZOOL. Venado, *m.*, ciervo, *m.* (deer). | Macho, *m.* (of certain animals). | Animal (*m.*) castrado (castrated animal). || COMM. Especulador, *m.* || FAM. Soltero, *m.* (bachelor). || *Stag beetle*, ciervo (*m.*) volante.

stage [steidʒ] n. THEATR. Escenario, *m.*, escena, *f.*, tablas, *f. pl.* (raised platform): *I can't see the stage from this seat*, no puedo ver el escenario desde este asiento. | Teatro, *m.*, tablas, *f. pl.* (art, profession): *my sister is trying to get on the stage*, mi hermana está intentando dedicarse al teatro *or* subir a las tablas. || Estrado, *m.*, tribuna, *f.*, plataforma, *f.* (platform). || Andamio, *m.* (scaffold). || FIG. Escena, *f.*, escenario, *m.*: *England was the stage for one of the most important historical events of the century*, Inglaterra fue escena de uno de los acontecimientos más importantes del siglo. | Campo, *m.* (area). || Etapa, *f.* (step): *the first stage of the journey is the longest*, la primera etapa del viaje es la más larga; *by easy stages*, en pequeñas etapas; *it is necessary to learn Basque in several stages*, es necesario aprender el vasco en varias etapas. || Etapa, *f.*, fase, *f.* (of development, evolution): *this project is in the first stage of its development*, este proyecto está en la primera etapa de su desarrollo. || Fase, *f.*, periodo, *m.* (phase): *the early stages of existence*, el primer período de la existencia; *to reach a critical stage*, llegar a una fase crítica. || MAR. Desembarcadero, *m.* (landing stage). || Portaobjeto, *m.*, platina, *f.* (of a microscope). || GEOL. Piso, *m.* || Cuerpo, *m.* (of a rocket). || Diligencia, *f.* (stagecoach). || Relevo, *m.*: *horses were changed at every stage*, se cambiaban los caballos en cada relevo. || — *By stages*, progresivamente. || *Fare stage*, sección, *f.* (in a bus). || *Front of the stage*, proscenio, *m.* || *In stages*, por etapas. || *To come on the stage*, salir a escena. || *To go on the stage*, hacerse actor, subir a las tablas. || *To put a novel on the stage*, llevar a la escena una novela. || *To write for the stage*, escribir para el teatro.

stage [steidʒ] v. tr. Representar, poner en escena (a play): *the play was poorly staged*, la obra estuvo mal representada. || Llevar a la escena (a novel). || Efectuar: *to stage a counteroffensive*, efectuar una contraofensiva. || Organizar (to arrange).

— V. intr. Representarse: *this play stages easily*, esta obra se representa fácilmente.

stage box [—bɔks] n. Palco (*m.*) de proscenio.

stagecoach [—kəutʃ] n. Diligencia, *f.*

stagecraft [—krɑ:ft] n. Arte (*m.*) escénico.

stage direction [—diˈrekʃən] n. THEATR. Acotación, *f.*

stage door [—dɔ:*] n. THEATR. Entrada (*f.*) de artistas.

stage effect [—iˈfekt] n. Efecto (*m.*) teatral *or* escénico.

stage fright [—frait] n. Miedo (*m.*) al público, nerviosismo, *m.*

stagehand [—hænd] n. Tramoyista, *m.*, maquinista, *m.*

stage-manage [—ˈmænidʒ] v. tr. Dirigir la tramoya de (a play). || FIG. Manipular (to rig).

stage manager [—ˈmænidʒə*] n. THEATR. Regidor (*m.*) de escena. || CINEM. Director (*m.*) de producción, regidor, *m.*

stage name [—neim] n. Nombre (*m.*) de artista.

stage play [—plei] n. Obra (*f.*) de teatro.

stage player [—ˈpleiə*] n. Actor, *m.*, actriz, *f.*

stage properties [—ˈprɔpətiz] pl. n. THEATR. Accesorios, *m.*

stager [—ə] n. FAM. *Old stager*, perro viejo, hombre de gran experiencia.

stagestruck [—strʌk] adj. Apasionado por el teatro.

stage whisper [—ˈwispə*] n. THEATR. Aparte, *m.*

stagey [ˈsteidʒi] adj. Teatral.

stagflation [stægˈfleiʃən] n. Inflación (*f.*) acompañada por el estancamiento de la economía.

stagger [ˈstægə*] n. Tambaleo, *m.* (staggering movement).

stagger [ˈstægə*] v. tr. Hacer tambalearse, hacer titubear: *the blow staggered him*, el golpe le hizo tambalearse. || Asombrar (to astonish). || Escalonar: *to stagger the hours of the factories*, escalonar las horas de las fábricas; *staggered holidays*, vacaciones escalonadas. || Alternar (to alternate). || TECH. Colocar al tresbolillo.

— V. intr. Tambalearse, titubear. || Vacilar, titubear (to hesitate).

staggerer [—rə*] n. FAM. Argumento (*m.*) desconcertante (argument). | Noticia (*f.*) asombrosa (piece of news).

staggering [—riŋ] adj. FIG. Asombroso, sa (amazing). || Tambaleante (reeling).

— N. Escalonamiento, *m.*: *staggering of holidays*, escalonamiento de las vacaciones.

staggers [—z] n. VET. Modorra, *f.*

staghound [—haund] n. Sabueso, *m.* (dog).

staging [steidʒiŋ] n. Puesta (*f.*) en escena, escenificación, *f.* (in theatre). || Andamio, *m.* (scaffold). || MIL. Estacionamiento, *m.*

stagnancy [ˈstægnənsi] n. Estancamiento, *m.*

stagnant [ˈstægnənt] adj. Estancado, da (water). || FIG. Estancado, da; paralizado, da (paralysed). || COMM. Inactivo, va (market).

stagnate [stægˈneit] v. intr. Estancarse.

stagnation [stægˈneiʃən] n. Estancamiento, *m.* (of water). || FIG. Estancamiento, *m.*, paralización, *f.*

stagy [ˈsteidʒi] adj. Teatral.

staid [steid] adj. Serio, ria; formal.

staidness [—nis] n. Seriedad, *f.*, formalidad, *f.*

stain [stein] n. Mancha, *f.*: *coffee stain*, mancha de café; *to remove* o *to take out a stain*, sacar *or* quitar una mancha. || Tinte, *m.*, tintura, *f.* (dye). || Colorante, *m.* (for microscopic study). || FIG. Mancha, *f.*: *a stain on one's reputation*, una mancha en la reputación de uno. || *Stain remover*, quitamanchas, *m. inv.*

stain [stein] v. tr. Manchar, ensuciar: *the coffee stained her dress*, el café le manchó el vestido; *to stain with ink*, manchar con *or* de tinta. || Teñir (to dye). || Colorar (to colour). || FIG. Manchar, mancillar: *to stain s.o.'s reputation*, manchar la reputación de alguien.

— V. intr. Manchar, ensuciar: *be careful with the coffee, it stains*, ten cuidado con el café, mancha. || Mancharse, ensuciarse (to become stained).

stainable [—əbl] adj. Que puede colorarse *or* teñirse.

stained glass [—dˈglɑ:s] n. Vidrio (*m.*) de color.

stained-glass window [—dˈglɑ:sˈwindəu] n. Vidriera, *f.* (in churches, etc.).

stainer [—ə*] n. Tintorero, ra (person). || Tinte, *m.* (substance).

stainless [—lis] adj. Que no se mancha (that cannot be stained). || Inmaculado, da; sin mancha (immaculate). || *Stainless steel*, acero (*m.*) inoxidable.

stair [stɛə*] n. Escalón, *m.*, peldaño, *m.* (single step). || — Pl. Escaleras, *f.*, escalera, *f. sing.*: *to go up, to go down the stairs*, subir, bajar la escalera. || — FIG. *Below stairs*, sitio (*m.*) donde se encuentra la servidumbre. || *Flight of stairs*, tramo (*m.*) de escalera.

staircase [—keis] n. Escalera, *f.*: *spiral staircase*, escalera de caracol. || *Moving staircase*, escalera mecánica.

stairhead [—hed] n. Rellano, *m.*, descansillo, *m.*

stair rod [—rɔd] n. Varilla (*f.*) para sujetar la alfombra de la escalera.

stairway [—wei] n. See STAIRCASE.

stairwell [—wel] n. Caja (*f.*) de la escalera.

stake [steik] n. Estaca, *f.* (stick). || Poste, *m.* (post). || AGR. Rodrigón, *m.*, tutor, *m.* || Jalón, *m.* (in surveying). || Hoguera, *f.*: *Joan of Arc was condemned to the stake*, Juana de Arco fue condenada a la hoguera. || Intereses, *m. pl.*: *I have a stake in the company*, tengo intereses en la compañía. || Puesta, *f.*, apuesta, *f.* (bet). || Tas, *m.* (small anvil). || — Pl. Premio, *m. sing.* || — *At stake*, en juego: *your honour is at stake*, su honor está en juego; en peligro (in danger). || *Put down your stakes!*, ¡hagan juego! || *The issue at stake*, el asunto de que se trata. || U. S. FAM. *To pull up stakes*, irse.

stake [steik] v. tr. Estacar, sujetar con estacas (to secure with stakes). || Delimitar con estacas (to mark). || Amarrar a un poste (to tether). || AGR. Rodrigar. || Apostar (to bet). || Arriesgar, jugarse: *he has staked his life on this interview*, se juega la vida en esta entrevista. || Presentar (a claim). || — *To stake off* o *out*, jalonar (in surveying). || *To stake one's all*, jugarse el todo por el todo.

stakeholder [—ˈhəuldə*] n. Tenedor (*m.*) de apuestas.

stakhanovism [stəˈkænəvizəm] n. Stajanovismo, *m.*

stakhanovite [stəˈkænəvait] n. Stajanovista, *m.* & *f.*

stalactite [ˈstæləktait] n. GEOL. Estalactita, *f.*

stalagmite [ˈstæləgmait] n. GEOL. Estalagmita, *f.*

stale [steil] adj. Rancio, cia; pasado, da (food). || Picado, da; echado a perder (wine, beer). || Poco fresco (egg). || Duro, ra (bread). || Viciado, da (air). || A cerrado (smell). || Averiado, da; echado a perder (goods). || Viejo, ja (news). || Trillado, da (joke). || Decaido, da (run-down). || Caducado, da (expired). || Vencido, da (cheque). || Desanimado, da (market). || SP. Entrenado con exceso, sobreentrenado, da.

stale [steil] v. intr. Echarse a perder (food). || Perder novedad *or* interés (news, joke). || ZOOL. Orinar.

— V. tr. Echar a perder (food). || Quitar novedad a, quitar interés a (news, joke).

stalemate [ˈsteilˈmeit] n. Ahogado, *m.* (in chess). || FIG. Paralización, *f.*, punto (*m.*) muerto, estancamiento, *m.* (halt in progress). || FIG. *To reach a stalemate*, llegar a un punto muerto, estancarse.

stalemate [ˈsteilˈmeit] v. tr. Ahogar (in chess). || FIG. Paralizar, llevar a un punto muerto, estancar (to halt the progress of).

staleness [—nis] n. Ranciedad, *f.* (of food). || Lo poco fresco (of egg). || Dureza, *f.* (of bread). || Olor (*m.*) a cerrado (of a room). || Lo viciado (of the air). || Deterioro, *m.* (of goods). || Vencimiento, *m.* (of a cheque). || Caducidad, *f.* (of legal document). || SP. Sobreentrenamiento, *m.* || Falta (*f.*) de novedad (of news, joke).

Stalinism [ˈstɑ:linizəm] n. Stalinismo, *m.*

Stalinist [ˈstɑ:linist] adj./n. Staliniano, na; stalinista.

stalk [stɔ:k] n. BOT. Tallo, *m.* (stem). | Pedúnculo, *m.* (of flower). | Peciolo, *m.* (of leaf). | Caña, *f.* (of bamboo). | Troncho, *m.* (of cabbages). || Pie, *m.* (of a glass). || Paso (*m.*) *or* andar (*m.*) majestuoso (majestic gait). || Caza (*f.*) al acecho (in hunting).

stalk [stɔ:k] v. tr. Cazar al acecho *or* en puestos (to hunt). || Acechar (animals). || Seguir los pasos a, acechar a (s.o.). || Cundir: *terror stalked the city*, el terror cundía por la ciudad.
— V. intr. Andar con paso majestuoso. || — *He stalked out of the room in anger*, salió con paso airado de la habitación. || *The plague stalked through the country*, la peste se extendía por el país.

stalker [—ə*] n. Cazador (*m.*) en puestos.

stalking-horse [—iŋhɔ:s] n. FIG. Tapadera, *f.*, pantalla, *f.* (screen). || Candidato (*m.*) presentado para engañar a la oposición (in politics).

stalky [—i] n. Talludo, da.

stall [stɔ:l] n. Pesebre, *m.* (manger). || Establo, *m.* (stable). || Departamento (*m.*) para un caballo en las cuadras (compartment in a stable). || Jaula, *f.*, departamento (*m.*) en un garaje (for cars). || COMM. Puesto, *m.* (in a market). || Caseta, *f.* (in a fair, exhibition). || Silla (*f.*) de coro, sitial, *m.* (in church). || Butaca, *f.* (in theatre, cinema). || Dedil, *m.* (for fingers). || AVIAT. Pérdida (*f.*) de velocidad. || FIG. Pretexto, *m.* || *Newspaper stall*, quiosco (*m.*) de periódicos.

stall [stɔ:l] v. tr. Poner en el establo (horses). || Atascar (cart). || Parar (a car, an engine). || AVIAT. Hacer perder velocidad. || FIG. *To stall s.o. off*, quitarse a uno de encima con pretextos (to get rid of), evitar a alguien (to avoid).
— V. intr. Calarse, pararse (a car, an engine). || Atascarse (a cart). || AVIAT. Entrar en pérdida de velocidad, perder velocidad. || FIG. Andar con rodeos.

stall-feed [—fi:d] v. tr. Engordar en un establo.

stallion [ˈstæljən] n. Semental, *m.*

stalwart [ˈstɔ:lwət] adj. Robusto, ta; vigoroso, sa; fornido, da (sturdy). || Leal (loyal). || Firme, decidido, da; resuelto, ta (resolute). || Incondicional (unconditional).
— N. Partidario (*m.*) incondicional (supporter). || Persona (*f.*) fornida (sturdy person).

stalwartness [—nis] n. Robustez, *f.* || Firmeza, *f.*, resolución, *f.*

stamen [ˈsteimen] n. BOT. Estambre, *m.*

stamina [ˈstæminə] n. Vigor, *m.*, energía, *f.*, nervio, *m.* (energy). || Aguante, *m.*, resistencia, *f.* (endurance).

staminate [ˈstæmineit] adj. BOT. Estaminífero, ra.

staminiferous [stæmiˈnifərəs] adj. BOT. Estaminífero, ra.

stammer [ˈstæmə*] n. Tartamudez, *f.*, tartamudeo, *m.* (stuttering).

stammer [ˈstæmə*] v. tr. Decir tartamudeando.
— V. intr. Tartamudear (to stutter).

stammerer [—rə*] n. Tartamudo, da.

stammering [—riŋ] adj. Tartamudo, da.
— N. Tartamudez, *f.*

stammeringly [—riŋli] adv. Tartamudeando.

stamp [stæmp] n. Sello, *m.* [*Amer.*, estampilla, *f.*] (postage stamp). || Timbre, *m.* (fiscal). || Cupón, *m.* (of shares). || Sello, *m.*, tampón, *m.* (mark left by rubber stamp, seal). || Marca, *f.*, huella, *f.*, señal, *f.* (mark). || Taconazo, *m.*, zapatazo, *m.* (with foot). || TECH. Estampa, *f.* (for forging). | Cuño, *m.* (for metals). | Troquel, *m.* (for coins). | Punzón, *m.* (graver). | Prensa (*f.*) de estampar (for printing). | Triturador, *m.*, machacadora, *f.* (for crushing ore). || FIG. Cuño, *m.*, marchamo, *m.*, sello, *m.*: *bearing the stamp of genius*, marcado con el sello del genio. | Estampa, *f.*: *he has the stamp of a soldier*, tiene la estampa de un soldado. | Clase, *f.*, calaña, *f.*, indole, *f.*: *of the same stamp*, de la misma calaña. || *Rubber stamp*, tampón, *m.*, sello, *m.*

stamp [stæmp] v. tr. Estampar, imprimir: *to stamp one's foot in the sand*, estampar el pie en la arena. || Sellar, poner el sello a [*Amer.*, estampillar] (letter, document). || Timbrar (with fiscal stamp). || FIG. Señalar, catalogar: *his attitude stamped him as a revolutionary*, su actitud le catalogaba como revolucionario. | Marcar, impresionar, afectar: *stamped by his experiences as a prisoner*, marcado por sus experiencias de prisionero. | Estampar, grabar (to engrave): *he stamped it on his memory*, lo grabó en su memoria. || TECH. Poner el contraste a (gold). | Acuñar (coins). | Estampar, forjar (a metal). | Triturar, machacar (ore). || — *Paper stamped with one's name*, papel con membrete. || *To stamp one's feet*, patear (in anger), patalear (a child), golpear el suelo con los pies (to warm o.s., etc.), zapatear (in dancing). || *To stamp one's foot*, golpear el suelo con el pie. || *To stamp out*, extirpar (to eliminate), acabar con, sofocar: *to stamp out a rebellion*, acabar con una rebelión; apagar con el pie: *to stamp out a cigarette*, apagar un cigarrillo con el pie; estampar (to punch out): *to stamp out washers*, estampar arandelas.
— V. intr. Dar zapatazos, golpear con los pies (with feet). || Patear (angrily). || Piafar (a horse). || *To stamp on*, pisar: *to stamp on s.o.'s foot*, pisarle el pie a uno; pisotear (principles).

stamp album [—ˌælbəm] n. Álbum (*m.*) de sellos.

stamp collecting [—kəˌlektiŋ] n. Colección (*f.*) de sellos [*Amer.*, colección (*f.*) de estampillas], filatelia, *f.*

stamp collector [—kəˌlektə*] n. Coleccionista (*m.* & *f.*) de sellos [*Amer.*, coleccionista (*m.* & *f.*) de estampillas], filatelista, *m.* & *f.*

stamp duty [—ˌdju:ti] n. Póliza, *f.*, timbre, *m.*, impuesto (*m.*) del timbre.

stampede [stæmˈpi:d] n. Espantada, *f.*, desbandada, *f.*, fuga, *f.* (flight). || Desbocamiento, *m.* (of horses).

stampede [stæmˈpi:d] v. tr. Provocar la espantada *or* la desbandada de: *the shot stampeded the elephants*, el disparo provocó la desbandada de los elefantes. || Infundir terror a (to frighten).
— V. intr. Dar una espantada, salir en desbandada. || Abalanzarse, precipitarse (to rush).

stamper [ˈstæmpə*] n. Máquina (*f.*) de estampar (machine). || Troquel, *m.* (for coins). || Triturador, *m.* (for ore). || Estampador, *m.* (person).

stamping [ˈstæmpiŋ] n. Estampación, *f.*, estampado, *m.* (of design, metal). || Timbrado, *m.* (with fiscal stamp). || Trituración, *f.* (of ore).

stamping ground [—graund] n. U. S. FAM. Lugar (*m.*) predilecto *or* de elección: *this town was formerly the democrats' stamping ground*, esta ciudad era antiguamente el lugar predilecto de los demócratas.

stamp machine [ˈstæmpməˌʃi:n] n. Máquina (*f.*) automática que distribuye sellos de correos.

stamp mill [ˈstæmpmil] n. Trapiche, *m.* (for pulverizing ore).

stance [stæns] n. Postura, *f.*: *he took up a stance*, adoptó una postura.

stanch [stɑ:ntʃ] v. tr. Restañar (to staunch blood).

stanchion [ˈstɑ:nʃən] n. Puntal, *m.* (prop). || Montante, *m.* (upright bar). || MAR. Candelero, *m.* || U. S. Yugo, *m.* (yoke).

stanchion [ˈstɑ:nʃən] v. tr. Sujetar con puntal, apuntalar.

stand [stænd] n. Parada, *f.* (stop). || Posición, *f.*, situación, *f.*, sitio, *m.* (position). || Posición, *f.*, postura, *f.* (stance). || Plataforma, *f.* (platform). || Tribuna, *f.* (in stadium). || MUS. Quiosco (*m.*) de música (bandstand). | Atril, *m.* (lectern). || Puesto, *m.* (at market): *he has a vegetable stand*, tiene un puesto de verduras. || Quiosco, *m.* (of newspapers). || Caseta, *f.*, "stand", *m.* (at an exhibition, etc.). || Caseta, *f.*, barraca, *f.* (at fair). || Parada, *f.* (of buses, taxis, etc.). || Pie, *m.*, pedestal, *m.* (of lamp). || Velador, *m.* (table). || Percha, *f.*, perchero, *m.* (for coats, hats). || Paragüero, *m.* (umbrella rest). || AGR. Cosecha (*f.*) en pie. || THEATR. Representación, *f.*, función, *f.* (performance): *one-night stand*, representación única. || FIG. Postura, *f.*, posición, *f.*: *the Government has taken a stand in favour of emigration*, el Gobierno ha tomado una postura en favor de la emigración. || TECH. Soporte, *m.* || U. S. Bosque, *m.*: *a stand of pines*, un bosque de pinos. || U. S. JUR. Estrado, *m.*, tribuna, *f.* (witness box). || — *To come to a stand*, pararse, detenerse. || *Liqueur stand*, licorera, *f.* || FIG. *To maintain one's stand*, mantenerse firme en su postura. | *To make a stand against*, oponerse a, resistir a (s.o.), alzarse contra (an abuse). || MIL. *To make a stand against the enemy*, resistir al enemigo. || *To take a firm stand*, plantarse (standing), adoptar una actitud firme (decision). || *To take one's stand behind a tree*, apostarse detrás de un árbol. || *To take one's stand on a principle*, basarse *or* fundarse en un principio. || U. S. JUR. *To take the stand*, subir al estrado, comparecer ante un tribunal. || *To take up one's stand by the entrance*, ponerse cerca de la entrada.

stand* [stænd] v. tr. Poner, colocar (to place): *to stand sth. upright* o *on end*, poner algo de pie; *stand it over there*, ponlo ahí. || Poner de pie (to set upright). || Resistir: *it will stand heat up to 200 degrees*, resistirá el calor hasta 200 grados; *this book won't stand criticism*, este libro no resistirá a la crítica. || Someterse a: *to stand trial*, someterse a juicio. || Soportar, aguantar (to endure): *I can't stand work*, no puedo soportar el trabajo; *I can't stand him*, no puedo aguantarle. || FAM. Sufragar, pagar (to pay for): *to stand a round of drinks*, pagar una ronda; *to stand the cost*, sufragar los gastos. | Invitar, convidar: *to stand s.o. a drink, a dinner*, invitar a alguien a tomar una copa, a cenar. || — *I can't stand it any longer*, ya no lo puedo aguantar, ya estoy harto. || *To stand a chance*, tener una posibilidad. || MIL. *To stand fire*, aguantar el fuego del enemigo. || *To stand one's ground*, see GROUND. || MIL. *To stand siege to*, see SIEGE.
— V. intr. Estar de pie: *he is standing near John*, está de pie junto a Juan. || Estar de pie, quedarse de pie: *to stand waiting*, estar de pie esperando. || Levantarse, ponerse de pie (to an upright position): *all stand!*, ¡levántense todos! || Ponerse, colocarse: *I'll stand under the clock and wait for you*, me pondré debajo del reloj para esperarle. || Mantenerse en pie: *the house still stood after the earthquake*, la casa se mantuvo en pie después del terremoto. || Andar: *how do you stand for money?*, ¿cómo andas de dinero? || Estar: *how do they stand in the matter of clothes?*, ¿cómo están de ropa? || Tener, medir: *he stands five feet tall*, tiene cinco pies de altura. || Cotizarse (securities, commodities). || Marcar (thermometer). || Reposar: *let the dough stand an hour*, deja la masa reposar una hora. || Mantenerse (a position, point of view). || Pararse (to stop): *the retreating army stood and fought*, el ejército, que se batía en retirada, se paró y luchó. || Quedarse: *stand where you are!*, ¡quédese donde está!; *I stood in the rain*, me quedé bajo la lluvia; *I stood and looked at him*, me quedé

mirándole. || Quedarse: *this page must stand as it is*, esta página tiene que quedarse tal cual. || Ponerse (hunting dog). || Estancarse (water). || Estar: *his house stands on the hill*, su casa está en la colina; *she stood in the doorway*, estaba en la puerta; *I stand opposed to that*, estoy opuesto a esto. || Estar, encontrarse: *to stand in the front rank*, encontrarse en primera fila. || Figurar: *this page must stand in the dictionary*, esta página debe figurar en el diccionario. || Ser: *to stand first*, ser el primero; *that's how it stands*, así es. || Estar en condiciones de: *he stands to win all*, está en condiciones de ganarlo todo. || Presentarse: *he stood as a candidate for the election*, se presentó como candidato a la elección. || Permanecer (to remain unchanged). || Seguir siendo válido: *my offer still stands*, mi oferta sigue siendo válida. || Durar (to last): *the house will stand another century*, la casa durará todavía un siglo. || Regir, tener validez: *these rules still stand*, estas reglas tienen validez todavía. || MAR. Ir rumbo (*to*, a). || — *As it stands* o *as things stand*, tal y como están las cosas. || *How does my account stand?*, ¿qué tengo en la cuenta? || *I don't know where I stand*, no sé cuál es mi situación. || *I found the door standing open*, encontré la puerta abierta. || *It stands to reason*, es lógico, es evidente. || *It stands to reason that*, ni que decir tiene que, es evidente que. || *Nothing stands between you and me*, nada nos separa. || *Nothing stands between you and success*, nada se opone a su éxito. || *Stand and deliver!*, ¡la bolsa o la vida! || MIL. *Stand at ease*, en su lugar ¡descanso! || *Stand out of the way!*, ¡quítese de en medio! || *This is how I stand*, ésta es mi posición. || *To let stand*, dejar: *don't let the car stand in the middle of the street*, no dejes el coche en medio de la calle. || *To stand alone*, estar solo. || MIL. *To stand at attention*, cuadrarse. | *To stand fast*, mantenerse firme (on one's opinion), resistir (to resist). || *To stand for nothing*, no contar para nada. || *To stand in need of*, necesitar. || *To stand in s.o.'s name*, estar a nombre de alguien. || *To stand in the way*, see WAY. || *To stand on end*, erizarse (hair). || FIG. *To stand on one's own two feet*, see FOOT. || U. S. *To stand pat*, mantenerse en sus trece. || *To stand ready to*, estar dispuesto a. || *To stand sentry*, montar guardia, estar de guardia. || *To stand still*, no moverse, estarse quieto. || *To stand together*, mantenerse unidos. || *To stand to it that*, sostener que. || *To stand to lose*, tener las de perder. || *To stand to lose a lot*, tener mucho que perder. || *To stand to lose nothing*, no tener nada que perder. || *To stand well with s.o.*, llevarse bien con alguien, tener buenas relaciones con alguien. || *Your account stands at 100 pounds in your credit*, tiene cien libras en su haber.

— **To stand about**, esperar de pie (to wait). | — *We stood about watching the football match*, miramos el partido de fútbol de pie. || **To stand against**, resistir a, oponerse a. || **To stand aside**, apartarse, echarse a un lado: *to stand aside to let s.o. pass*, apartarse para dejar pasar a alguien. | Retirarse: *to stand aside in favour of s.o.*, retirarse en favor de alguien. || **To stand away**, apartarse. || **To stand back**, retroceder: *to make the crowd stand back*, hacer retroceder a la muchedumbre. | — *House standing back from the road*, casa que no está al borde de la carretera. || **To stand by**, estar preparado (to be ready to act). | MIL. Estar dispuesto para el combate. | Estar dispuesto a prestar ayuda *or* a socorrer: *to stand by a sinking ship*, estar dispuesto a socorrer un barco en perdición. | Estar cerca (to be near). | Estar al lado de: *I'll always stand by you in case of trouble*, estaré siempre a su lado en caso de dificultad. | Estar atento: *stand by for the latest news*, esté usted atento a las noticias de última hora. | Apoyar, sostener (to support). | Atenerse a (a decision): *I stand by what I said*, me atengo a lo que dije. | Cumplir (a promise, one's word). | Quedarse sin hacer nada (to stand near as an onlooker): *please help instead of merely standing by*, por favor ayude en vez de quedarse sin hacer nada. || — MAR. *Stand by!*, ¡listo! || **To stand down**, retirarse. || **To stand for**, significar (to mean). | Representar (to represent): *in this code each number stands for a letter*, en este código cada número representa una letra. | Ser las siglas de: *U. N. stands for United Nations*, U. N. son las siglas de las Naciones Unidas. | Abogar por, ser partidario de: *to stand for free trade*, abogar por el libre comercio. | Presentarse como candidato a (a post). | Presentarse como candidato en, presentar su candidatura en: *I'm standing for Orpington*, presento mi candidatura en Orpington. | FAM. Aguantar, tolerar: *I won't stand for such behaviour*, no toleraré semejante conducta. | MAR. Ir rumbo a. | — *To stand for Parliament*, presentarse como candidato a las elecciones parlamentarias. || **To stand in**, unirse, asociarse (*with*, a). | Compartir los gastos: *let me stand in with you if it's too expensive*, déjeme compartir los gastos con usted si es demasiado caro. | Estar en buenos términos (*with*, con) [to be friendly]. | MAR. Hacer rumbo (*for*, a). | CINEM. Sustituir (*for*, a). | Costar. || **To stand off**, apartarse. | Mantenerse apartado (to keep at a distance). | MAR. Apartarse de la costa. | Dejar sin trabajo (workers). | FIG. Evitar (to evade), rechazar (an assailant), aplazar (to put off). || **To stand on**, mantener el rumbo (ship). | FIG. Dar mucha importancia a. | Insistir en (to insist upon). | Valerse de: *I'm going to stand on my rights*, me valdré de mis derechos. || **To stand out**, sobresalir: *his house stands out from the others*, su casa sobresale de las demás. | Destacarse: *mountains that stand out on the horizon*, montañas que se destacan en el horizonte. | FIG. Descollar, destacarse, sobresalir: *the qualities that stand out in his work*, las cualidades que sobresalen en su obra. | — *To stand out against*, oponerse a, resistir a. | FAM. *To stand out a mile*, verse a la legua. | *To stand out for*, insistir en. | MAR. *To stand out to sea*, hacerse a la mar. || **To stand over**, vigilar: *if I don't stand over him he does nothing*, si no le vigilo no hace nada. | Quedar pendiente (to be postponed). | — *To let sth. stand over*, dejar algo pendiente. || **To stand to**, estar alerta. | — MIL. *Stand to your arms!*, ¡a las armas! || **To stand up**, levantarse, ponerse de pie (to rise). | Resistir. | U. S. FAM. Dejar plantado: *he stood me up at the last minute*, me dejó plantado en el último momento. | — *This soup is so thick you could stand a spoon up in it*, esta sopa es tan espesa que una cuchara podría quedarse de pie. | *To stand up for*, defender, salir en defensa de, dar la cara por: *if we don't stand up for him nobody will*, si no damos la cara por él nadie lo hará. | *To stand up to*, resistir a. | *To stand up to a test*, salir bien de una prueba. || **To stand upon**, insistir en.

— OBSERV. Pret. & p. p. **stood**.

standard [—əd] adj. Normal, corriente: *of standard size*, de tamaño normal. || Standard, tipo (model). || Clásico, ca (author, book). || De ley (gold). || Oficial, legal (time). || Legal (weight). || COMM. Standard, estándar, estandard, corriente: *standard model of a washing machine*, modelo standard de una lavadora. || AUT. De serie, standard, estándar, estandard. || CHEM. Reactivo, va (paper). || BOT. De tronco (tree). || FIG. Clásico, ca (joke). || — *A Standard Spanish Dictionary*, un diccionario general de la lengua española. || *Standard English*, el inglés correcto. || *Standard measure*, medida (*f.*) tipo. || *The standard Spanish dictionary for schools is*, el diccionario español que se utiliza generalmente en las escuelas es.

— N. Patrón, *m.* (money): *gold standard*, patrón oro. || Patrón, *m.* (of weight and length): *the metre is the standard of length*, el metro es el patrón de longitud. || Nivel, *m.*: *standard of living*, nivel de vida; *the standard of wages*, el nivel de los salarios; *standard of knowledge*, nivel de conocimientos. || Clase, *f.* (of products). || Modelo, *m.*, tipo, *m.* (model). || Regla, *f.*, norma, *f.* (norm): *standards of behaviour*, normas de conducta. || Criterio, *m.* (criterion): *judged by that standard*, juzgado según ese criterio. || Valor (*m.*) moral (moral value). || MIL. Estandarte, *m.*, bandera, *f.* (flag). || MAR. Bandera, *f.*, pabellón, *m.* || CHEM. Ley, *f.* (of a metal). | Dosificación, *f.* (of a solution). || Pie, *m.* (of a lamp). || Poste, *m.* (of a streetlamp). || TECH. Bancada, *f.* (of a machine). || BOT. Árbol (*m.*) de tronco (tree). || Clase, *f.*, grado, *m.* (in a primary school). || — U. S. *Bureau of standards*, Oficina (*f.*) de pesas y medidas. || *Not to come up to the standard*, no satisfacer los requisitos. || *Of low standard*, de baja calidad. || FIG. *To raise the standard of*, ser el abanderado de.

standard-bearer [—əd·bɛərə*] n. MIL. Abanderado, *m.*, portaestandarte, *m.* || FIG. Jefe, *m.*, adalid, *m.*, abanderado, *m.* (of a movement, etc.).

standard gauge [—əd·geidʒ] n. Vía (*f.*) normal.

standard-gauge [—əd·geidʒ] adj. De vía normal.

standardization [·stændədaiˈzeiʃən] n. COMM. Estandardización, *f.*, standardización, *f.*, producción (*f.*) en serie. || TECH. Normalización, *f.*, tipificación, *f.* || Uniformación, *f.* (of methods).

standardize [ˈstændədaiz] v. tr. COMM. Standardizar, estandardizar, producir en serie. || TECH. Normalizar, tipificar. || Uniformar (methods).

standby [ˈstændbai] n. Recurso, *m.* (thing): *that story is an old standby of his*, esa historia es un viejo recurso suyo. || Persona (*f.*) segura, persona (*f.*) con quien siempre se puede contar (person). || Sustituto, ta (substitute). || AVIAT. Persona (*f.*) que está en la lista de espera. || *To be on standby*, estar preparado para salir.

— Adj. De reserva (machine). || *A stand-by passenger*, un pasajero que está en la lista de espera.

standee [ˈstændi:] n. U. S. Espectador (*m.*) que asiste de pie [a un espectáculo].

stander [ˈstændə*] n. Viajero (*m.*) que hace el trayecto de pie.

stand-in [ˈstændˈin] n. CINEM. Doble, *m.* & *f.* || THEATR. Suplente, *m.* & *f.* || Sustituto, ta (substitute). || SP. Suplente, *m.* & *f.*

standing [ˈstændiŋ] adj. De pie (upright). || Vertical (position). || Clásico, ca: *standing joke*, broma clásica. || Fijo, ja: *standing rule*, regla fija. || Arraigado, da (custom). || Permanente: *standing body*, *committee*, órgano, comisión permanente. || MIL. Permanente (army, camp). || AGR. En pie (crops). || Parado, da (not in use). || Estancado, da (water). || SP. A pie juntillas (jump). | Parado, da: *standing start*, salida parada. || AUT. Estacionado, da. || — *Standing expenses*, gastos (*m.*) generales. || *Standing order*, see ORDER. || *Standing wave*, onda estacionaria. || FIG.

To leave s.o. standing, dejar atrás a alguien.
— N. Posición (*f.*) vertical (upright position). || Parada, *f.* (of a car). || Posición, *f.*, situación, *f.* (position): *social standing*, posición social. || Situación, *f.*: *financial standing of a firm*, situación financiera de una empresa. || Importancia, *f.*: *standing of a firm*, importancia de una empresa. || Reputación, *f.*: *firm of international standing*, empresa de reputación internacional. || Categoría, *f.*: *a man of high standing*, un hombre que tiene mucha categoría. || Duración, *f.* (duration). || — *Agreement of ten months' standing*, acuerdo (*m.*) vigente desde hace diez meses. || *Employee of ten months' standing*, empleado (*m.*) que lleva diez meses en la empresa. || *Friend of long standing*, viejo amigo, amigo de toda la vida. || *Habit of long standing*, vieja costumbre.
standing rigging [—ˊrigiŋ] n. MAR. Jarcia (*f.*) muerta.
standing room [—ru:m] n. Sitio (*m.*) donde la gente está de pie (in a bus, etc.). || Pasillo, *m.* (in a theatre). || *Standing room only*, no quedan asientos.
standoff [ˊstændˊɔf] n. Reserva, *f.*, distancia, *f.* || Empate, *m.* (in game or contest).
standoffish [ˊstændˊɔfiʃ] adj. Distante, reservado, da.
standout [ˊstændaut] n. U. S. FAM. Original, *m.*
standpat [ˊstændpæt] adj. U. S. FAM. Inmovilista, conservador, ra.
standpatter [—ə*] n. U. S. FAM. Inmovilista, *m.* & *f.*, conservador, ra.
standpipe [ˊstændpaip] n. Tubo (*m.*) vertical. || Columna (*f.*) de alimentación.
standpoint [ˊstændpɔint] n. Punto (*m.*) de vista.
standstill [ˊstændstil] n. Parada, *f.* (stop). || COMM. Estancamiento, *m.*, marasmo, *m.* (of economy). || — *To be at a standstill*, estar parado, estar estancado (economy). || *To bring to a standstill*, parar (a car), producir el estancamiento de (trade, etc.). || *To come to a standstill*, pararse (people, cars), estancarse (economy, etc.).
stand-up [ˊstændʌp] adj. Tomado de pie (lunch). || Vertical. || Campal (battle). || Duro, ra (collar).
stank [stæŋk] pret. See STINK.
stannary [ˊstænəri] n. MIN. Mina (*f.*) de estaño (tin mine).
stannate [ˊstæneit] n. CHEM. Estannato, *m.*
stannic [ˊstænik] adj. CHEM. Estánnico, ca.
stanniferous [stæˊnifərəs] adj. CHEM. Estannífero, ra (tin-bearing).
stannous [ˊstænəs] adj. CHEM. Estañoso, sa.
stanza [ˊstænzə] n. POET. Estancia, *f.*, estrofa, *f.*
stapedes [stəˊpi:di:z] pl. n. See STAPES.
stapes [ˊsteipi:z] n. ANAT. Estribo, *m.*

— OBSERV. El plural de *stapes* es *stapes* o *stapedes*.

staphylococcus [stæfiləˊkɔkəs] n. Estafilococo, *m.*

— OBSERV. El plural de *staphylococcus* es *staphylococci*.

staple [ˊsteipl] adj. Básico, ca: *staple food*, alimento básico. || Principal, básico, ca: *staple industry*, industria básica. || FIG. Clásico, ca; principal: *staple topic of conversation*, tema clásico de conversación. || *Staple commodity*, artículo (*m.*) de primera necesidad.
— N. Producto (*m.*) principal: *coffee is the staple of Brasil*, el café es el producto principal del Brasil. || Elemento (*m.*) básico: *rice is the staple of their diet*, el arroz es el elemento básico de su alimentación. || Materia (*f.*) prima (raw material). || TECH. Grapa, *f.* (for fastening papers, etc.). | Armella, *f.* (to hold a hook, etc.). || Fibra, *f.* (of wool, cotton). || Calidad, *f.* (fineness). || FIG. Tema (*m.*) principal.
staple [ˊsteipl] v. tr. Sujetar *or* coser con una grapa *or* grapas (to fasten with staples). || Clasificar según la longitud de las fibras (textiles).
stapler [—ə*] or **stapling machine** [—iŋməˊʃi:n] n. Grapadora, *f.*, máquina (*f.*) de coser papeles con grapas.
star [stɑ:*] n. Estrella, *f.* (luminous heavenly body): *the sky is full of stars tonight*, el cielo está lleno de estrellas esta noche. || Astro, *m.* (heavenly body). || Lucero, *m.*, estrella, *f.* (of a horse). || Estrella, *f.*: *movie star*, estrella de cine. || THEATR. Primer actor, *m.*, primera actriz, *f.* (of a play). || Figura, *f.* (in sports). || MIL. Estrella, *f.* || Asterisco, *m.* (asterisk). || FIG. Estrella, *f.*: *he was born under a lucky star*, nació con buena estrella. || — Pl. Astros, *m.* (in astrology). || — *Evening star*, estrella vespertina. || *Morning star*, estrella matutina, lucero del alba. || *Pole star*, estrella polar. || *Shooting star*, estrella fugaz. || *Star aniseed*, anís estrellado. || REL. *Star of David*, estrella de David. || U. S. HIST. *Stars and Bars*, primera bandera de los Estados Unidos. || *Stars and Stripes*, bandera estrellada (of the United States). || FIG. *To see stars*, ver las estrellas. | *To sleep under the stars*, dormir al raso *or* bajo las estrellas. | *To thank one's lucky stars*, dar las gracias a Dios.
— Adj. Principal. || Más destacado, más brillante (outstanding). || Estelar: *star bout*, combate estelar.
star [stɑ:*] v. tr. Estrellar, sembrar de estrellas (to cover with stars). || Señalar con un asterisco, poner un asterisco a (to put an asterisk on). || Presentar como protagonista (to present in a leading role).
— V. intr. Ser protagonista, protagonizar: *Jimmy Neville stars in the film*, Jimmy Neville es el protagonista de la película. || Destacarse, descollar (to be outstanding).
starboard [—bəd] n. MAR. Estribor, *m.*: *land to starboard!*, ¡tierra a estribor!
— Adj. MAR. De estribor, a estribor.
starboard [—bəd] v. tr. MAR. Poner a estribor.
— V. intr. MAR. Ponerse a estribor.
starch [stɑ:tʃ] n. CHEM. Almidón, *m.* || Fécula, *f.* (in food). || FIG. Rigidez, *f.* (unbending manners). | Tiesura, *f.*, estiramiento, *m.* (stiffness).
starch [stɑ:tʃ] v. tr. Almidonar.
Star Chamber [ˊstɑ:ˊtʃeimbə*] n. Antiguo tribunal (*m.*) británico de inquisición.
starchiness [ˊstɑ:tʃinis] n. FIG. Rigidez, *f.* | Tiesura, *f.*, estiramiento, *m.* (stiffness).
starching [ˊstɑ:tʃiŋ] n. Almidonado, *m.*
starchy [ˊstɑ:tʃi] n. Almidonado, da (of or like starch). || Amiláceo, a (containing starch). || Feculento, ta (food). || FIG. Rígido, da (unbending). | Tieso, sa; estirado, da (stiff).
star-crossed [ˊstɑ:ˊkrɔst] adj. Desgraciado, da; malhadado, da.
stardom [ˊstɑ:dəm] n. FAM. Estrellato, *m.*
stardust [ˊstɑ:dʌst] n. ASTR. Polvo (*m.*) de estrellas, enjambre, *m.* || FIG. Encanto, *m.*
stare [stεə*] n. Mirada (*f.*) fija (steady look). || Mirada (*f.*) de extrañeza (with astonishment). || Mirada (*f.*) despavorida (with fear).
stare [stεə*] v. tr. Mirar fijamente, fijar la mirada en. || — *To stare s.o. down*, hacer bajar los ojos a alguien mirándole fijamente. || FIG. *To stare s.o. in the face*, saltar a la vista: *it's staring you in the face*, salta a la vista. || *To stare s.o. up and down*, mirar a alguien de arriba abajo.
— V. intr. Mirar fijamente: *to stare in amazement*, mirar fijamente con asombro; *he stared at me*, me miró fijamente. || Abrir desmesuradamente los ojos, abrir los ojos de par en par, tener los ojos desorbitados (to gaze in wonder). || Saltar a la vista (to be glaringly obvious). || FIG. *To stare into space*, mirar a las musarañas.
starfish [ˊstɑ:fiʃ] n. ZOOL. Estrella (*f.*) de mar, estrellamar, *f.*
stargaze [ˊstɑ:ˊgeiz] v. intr. Mirar las estrellas (to watch the stars). || FIG. Mirar a las musarañas (to indulge in dreamy thoughts).
stargazer [—ə*] n. Astrónomo, *m.* || FIG. Soñador, ra.
stargazing [—iŋ] n. Astronomía, *f.* || FIG. Distracción, *f.* (absentmindedness).
staring [ˊstεəriŋ] adj. Que mira fijamente. || Llamativo, va; chillón, ona (colour). || *Staring eyes*, mirada fija (stare), ojos desorbitados (wide eyes).
stark [stɑ:k] adj. Rígido, da; tieso, sa (stiff). || Resuelto, ta; decidido, da (determined). || Desolado, da; desierto, ta (bleak). || Desnudo, da (unadorned). || Puro, ra; absoluto, ta; completo, ta (utter).
— Adv. Completamente. || *Stark mad*, loco de atar.
stark-naked [—ˊneikid] adj. En cueros.
starless [ˊstɑ:lis] adj. Sin estrellas.
starlet [ˊstɑ:lət] n. Actriz (*f.*) principiante (young actress). || Pequeña estrella, *f.* (small star).
starlight [ˊstɑ:lait] n. Luz (*f.*) de las estrellas: *by starlight*, a la luz de las estrellas.
starlike [ˊstɑ:laik] adj. Estrellado, da (star-shaped). || Brillante, radiante (brilliant).
starling [ˊstɑ:liŋ] n. Estornino, *m.* (bird). || Espolón, *m.*, tajamar, *m.* (of bridges).
starlit [ˊstɑ:lit] adj. Iluminado por las estrellas.
starred [stɑ:d] adj. Estrellado, da (full of stars). || Presentado como protagonista (actor). || Marcado con un asterisco.
starry [ˊstɑ:ri] adj. Estrellado, da; sembrado de estrellas (night, sky). || Estelar (of the stars). || Brillante, resplandeciente (shining).
starry-eyed [—aid] adj. Idealista (idealistic). || Soñador, ra (daydreaming).
star shell [ˊstɑ:ʃel] n. MIL. Cohete (*m.*) luminoso, bengala, *f.*
star shower [ˊstɑ:ʃauə*] n. Lluvia (*f.*) de estrellas.
star-spangled [ˊstɑ:ˊspæŋgld] adj. Estrellado, da; salpicado *or* tachonado de estrellas. || *Star-Spangled Banner*, bandera estrellada (flag of the U.S.A.), himno (*m.*) nacional de los Estados Unidos (anthem).
start [stɑ:t] n. Principio, *m.*, comienzo, *m.* (of action, journey, course of events): *it was a failure from start to finish*, fue un fracaso desde el principio hasta el final; *to get a good start in life*, tener un buen principio en la vida. || Salida, *f.* (of a race): *false start*, salida nula; *flying start*, salida lanzada. || Ventaja, *f.*: *I'll give you ten metres start*, te daré diez metros de ventaja. || Sobresalto, *m.* (nervous jump). || Respingo, *m.* (of a horse). || Susto, *m.*: *what a start you gave me!*, ¡qué susto me has dado! || — *At the start*, al principio: *at the very start*, muy al principio. || *By fits and starts*, a trompicones, a rachas. || *For a start*, para empezar. || *Odd* o *rum start*, aventura peregrina, hecho extraño. || FIG. *The sales of his book got off to a good start*, al principio su libro tenía buena venta. | *To get off to a flying* o *a good start*, empezar muy bien, empezar con buen pie. || *To get one's start*, empezar. || *To give a sudden start*, sobresaltarse. || *To give s.o. a start in life*, ayudar a uno en sus comienzos. || *To make a fresh start*, volver

a empezar. || *To make a start*, empezar, comenzar. || *To wake up with a start*, despertarse sobresaltado.

start [stɑ:t] v. tr. Empezar, comenzar, iniciar: *they started the meeting with questions*, comenzaron la reunión con preguntas; *they started negotiations, a discussion*, iniciaron las negociaciones, la discusión. || Entablar (conversation). || Plantear (a question). || Emitir (a doubt). || Empezar a, comenzar a: *it's starting to rain*, está empezando a llover; *she started feeling ill just after the dessert*, empezó a sentirse enfermo inmediatamente después del postre; *she started singing*, empezó a cantar. || Poner en marcha, arrancar: *to start a car*, poner un coche en marcha. || Poner en marcha, hacer funcionar (a clock). || Cebar (a dynamo). || Hacer salir, dar la salida a (a train). || Dar la señal de salida a (a race). || Fundar, crear (to establish). || Emprender (a business). || FIG. Ayudar a emprender: *to start s.o. in a career*, ayudar a alguien a emprender una carrera. || Levantar (an animal from its lair). || Aflojar, soltar (mechanical parts). || FIG. Lanzar, hacer nacer (rumour): *who started the rumour?*, ¿quién lanzó este rumor? | Provocar, causar: *to start a fire*, provocar un incendio. | Provocar, armar: *to start a row*, provocar una riña. | Hacer: *he started everyone laughing*, hizo reír a todo el mundo. || Verter (a liquid). || *To start s.o. learning Latin*, iniciar a alguien en el aprendizaje del latín.

— V. intr. Empezar, comenzar (to begin): *to start by doing sth.*, empezar por hacer algo; *to start in life*, empezar en la vida; *don't start again!*, ¡no empieces de nuevo! || Salir (a train). || Arrancar (car, etc.). || Ponerse en marcha (a machine): *the engine started*, la máquina se puso en marcha. || Salir, irse (to set off): *to start on a journey for*, salir de viaje para. || Salir (in a race). || Aflojarse, soltarse (a screw). || Abrirse (seams). || Salirse (eyes). || Sobresaltarse (to jump). || — *Starting from*, a partir de: *starting from last month*, a partir del mes pasado. || *To start afresh*, volver a empezar. || *To start at the beginning*, empezar desde el principio.

— **To start after**, ir *or* salir en busca de. || **To start aside**, echarse a un lado. | **To start back**, iniciar la vuelta (to return). | Dar un salto atrás, retroceder. || **To start in**, empezar. || **To start off**, empezar, comenzar (to begin). | Salir, ponerse en camino (on a journey). | Salir (a train). | Arrancar (a car). || **To start on**, empezar. || **To start out**, salir, ponerse en camino (on a journey). | Empezar (to begin). | — *To start out to*, ponerse a. || **To start up**, empezar (to begin). | Arrancar (engine). | Levantarse de un golpe (to rise up). || **To start with**, empezar con. | — *To start with*, para empezar (used as an adverbial phrase).

starter [—ə*] n. SP. Juez (*m.*) de salida (signal giver). | Participante, *m.* & *f.*, competidor, ra (competitor). || AUT. Arranque, *m.* || FIG. Promotor, ra (of a discussion). | Autor, ra (of an objection). | Iniciador, ra (of a project). || — *He is a fast runner but a slow starter*, es un corredor rápido pero lento al salir. || *To give as a starter*, dar para empezar.

starting [—iŋ] n. AUT. Arranque, *m.* || TECH. Puesta (*f.*) en marcha (of a machine). || Salida, *f.* (start). || Comienzo, *m.*, principio, *m.* (beginning). || Sobresalto, *m.*, susto, *m.* (fear).

starting gate [—iŋgeit] n. SP. Barrera (*f.*) en la línea de salida.

starting handle [—iŋ'hændl] n. AUT. Manivela, *f.* [de arranque].

starting line [—iŋ'lain] n. SP. Línea (*f.*) de salida.

starting motor [—iŋ'məutə*] n. Motor (*m.*) de arranque.

starting point [—iŋpoint] n. Punto (*m.*) de partida.

starting post [—iŋpəust] n. SP. Línea (*f.*) de salida.

starting price [—iŋprais] n. Precio (*m.*) inicial (in stock exchange). || SP. Última cotización antes de iniciarse una carrera de caballos.

starting switch [—iŋswitʃ] n. AUT. Arranque, *m.*, botón (*m.*) de arranque.

startle ['stɑ:tl] v. tr. Asustar, sobresaltar.

— V. intr. Asustarse, sobresaltarse.

startling [—iŋ] adj. Sorprendente, asombroso, sa (amazing). || Sobrecogedor, ra (frightening). || Alarmante (alarming). || Llamativo, va (colour, dress).

star turn ['stɑ:tə:n] n. Atracción (*f.*) principal (featured number).

starvation [stɑ:'veiʃən] n. Hambre, *f.* || MED. Inanición, *f.*: *he died of starvation*, murió de inanición. || *Starvation wages*, sueldos (*m.*) de hambre.

starve [stɑ:v] v. tr. Hacer morir de hambre, matar de hambre (to cause to die of hunger). || Privar de comida *or* de alimentos, hacer pasar hambre: *they starved him*, le hicieron pasar hambre. || FIG. Privar: *to starve s.o. of love*, privar a alguien de amor. || *To starve into surrender* o *to starve out*, hacer rendirse por hambre.

— V. intr. Morir de hambre (to die of hunger). || Pasar hambre (to suffer from hunger). || FAM. Morirse de hambre, estar muerto de hambre (to be hungry). | Morirse de frío, estar helado (to be cold). || — FIG. *To starve for*, carecer de (to be in great need of), anhelar (to have a strong desire for). || *To starve to death*, morir de hambre.

starveling [—liŋ] adj./n. Muerto de hambre, muerta de hambre, hambriento, ta. || *Starveling wages*, sueldos (*m.*) de hambre.

starving [—iŋ] adj. Hambriento, ta; muerto de hambre.
— N. See STARVATION.

stash [stæʃ] v. tr. U. S. FAM. Esconder, guardar.

stasis ['steisis] n. MED. Estasis, *f.*

— OBSERV. El plural de la palabra inglesa es *stases*.

state [steit] n. Estado, *m.* (in general): *in a bad state*, en mal estado. || Estado, *m.*: *the United States*, los Estados Unidos; *Church and State*, la Iglesia y el Estado. || Condición, *f.*: *he lived in a style befitting his state*, vivía de la forma que correspondía a su condición. || Lujo, *m.*: *to live in state*, vivir en el lujo. || Gran pompa, *f.*, gran ceremonia, *f.* (pomp, display): *to escort s.o. in state*, escoltar a alguien con gran pompa. || PHYS. CHEM. Estado, *m.*: *the solid state*, el estado sólido. || — *He is not in a fit state to travel*, no está en condiciones de viajar. || *Married state*, estado matrimonial, matrimonio, *m.* || *Reason of State*, razón (*f.*) de Estado. || *Single state*, celibato, *m.*, soltería, *f.* || *State of emergency*, estado de emergencia (disaster), estado de excepción (political measure). || *State of grace*, estado de gracia. || *State of mind*, estado de ánimo. || REL. *State of nature*, estado de naturaleza. || *State of siege*, estado de sitio. || *State of things*, estado de cosas. || *State of war*, estado de guerra. || *States General*, Estados Generales. || *The States*, los Estados Unidos. || FAM. *To be in a great state*, estar fuera de sí. | *To get into a state*, ponerse nervioso. || *To lie in state*, estar de cuerpo presente.

— Adj. Estatal, del Estado. || Público, ca: *state education*, enseñanza pública. || Oficial. || Solemne: *a state occasion*, una ocasión solemne. || De gala (apartment, etc.). || *State secret*, secreto (*m.*) de Estado.

state [steit] v. tr. Declarar, afirmar (to declare): *I state that I heard it*, afirmo haberlo oído. || Decir: *he did not state why*, no dijo por qué. || Dar, expresar, manifestar: *I have stated my opinion*, he dado mi opinión. || Escribir (to write down). || Consignar: *as stated in the rules*, como está consignado en el reglamento. || JUR. Exponer, formular (a claim). || Fijar, determinar (condition, date, time). || Dar a conocer: *you must state full particulars*, debe dar a conocer todos los detalles. || Plantear (a problem). || — *As stated below*, como se indica a continuación. || *To state one's name*, dar su nombre. || JUR. *To state the case*, exponer los hechos.

state bank [—bæŋk] n. Banco (*m.*) nacional (national), banco (*m.*) del Estado (State's).

state capitalism [—'kæpitəlizəm] n. Capitalismo (*m.*) de Estado.

statecraft [—krɑ:ft] n. Habilidad (*f.*) política, diplomacia, *f.*, arte (*m.*) de gobernar.

stated [—id] adj. Dicho, cha; indicado, da.

State Department [—di'pɑ:tmənt] n. U. S. Ministerio (*m.*) de Asuntos Exteriores [*Amer.*, Ministerio (*m.*) de Relaciones Exteriores].

statehouse [—haus] n. U. S. Cámara (*f.*) legislativa de un estado de los Estados Unidos.

stateless [—lis] adj. Apátrida.

stateliness [—linis] n. Majestad, *f.*, majestuosidad, *f.*

stately [—li] adj. Majestuoso, sa (majestic). || Impresionante (imposing).

statement [—mənt] n. Declaración, *f.*: *a statement to the police*, una declaración a la policía. || Informe, *m.*, relación, *f.* (report): *to draw up a statement*, redactar un informe. || Afirmación, *f.*: *to contradict a statement*, contradecir una afirmación. || Exposición, *f.*: *bare statement of the facts*, simple exposición de los hechos. || Comunicado, *m.*: *an official statement to the press*, un comunicado oficial a la prensa. || Planteamiento, *m.* (of a problem). || COMM. Extracto (*m.*) de cuentas, estado (*m.*) de cuenta. || MUS. Exposición, *f.* || COMM. *Monthly statement*, balance (*m.*) mensual.

stateroom [—ru:m] n. Camarote, *m.* (ship). || Compartimento (*m.*) privado (train).

State's attorney [—sə'tə:ni] n. U. S. Fiscal, *m.*

stateside [—said] adj. FAM. Estadounidense.

statesman [—smən] n. Estadista, *m.*, hombre (*m.*) de Estado.

— OBSERV. El plural de *statesman* es *statesmen.*

statesmanlike [—smənlaik] adj. Propio de estadista.

statesmansly [—smənli] adj. Propio de estadista.

statesmanship [—smənʃip] n. Habilidad (*f.*) política, arte (*m.*) de gobernar.

static ['stætik] adj. Estático, ca.
— N. RAD. Parásitos, *m. pl.*, interferencias, *f. pl.*

statical [—əl] adj. Estático, ca.

statics [—s] n. Estática, *f.*

station ['steiʃən] n. Puesto, *m.*, lugar, *m.*: *the policeman took up his station near the door*, el guardia ocupó su puesto junto a la puerta. || Sitio, *m.* (place). || Estación, *f.*: *weather station*, estación meteorológica; *tracking station*, estación de seguimiento. || Estación, *f.* (train, etc.): *goods station*, estación de mercancías: *railroad station*, estación de ferrocarril. || Granja (*f.*) de ganado lanar (sheep farm). || MIL. Puesto, *m.*: *action station*, puesto de combate. || Posición (*f.*) social, condición, *f.* (social standing). || RAD. Estación, *f.*: *radio, relay station*, estación de radio, repetidora. || REL. Estación, *f.* (of the Cross). || — *Bus station*, término, *m.*, final (*m.*) de línea. || *First-aid station*, casa (*f.*) de socorro. || MIL. *Military station*, guarnición, *f.* || *Naval station*, puerto (*m.*) militar. || *Petrol station*, surtidor (*m.*) de gasolina, gasolinera, *f.* || *Police station*, comisaría, *f.* || AUT. *Service station*, estación de servicio. || *To marry below one's station*, malcasarse, casarse con una persona de posición social inferior.

station [ˈsteiʃən] v. tr. Apostar: *to station sentries*, apostar centinelas. || Estacionar: *to station troops abroad*, estacionar tropas en el extranjero. || Colocar, situar (to place).

stationary [ˈsteiʃnəri] adj. Fijo, ja; estacionario, ria (unchanging). || Inmóvil (not moving). || PHYS. *Stationary wave*, onda estacionaria.

stationer [ˈsteiʃnə*] n. Librero, ra; papelero, ra. || *Stationer's*, librería, *f.*, papelería, *f.*

stationery [ˈsteiʃnəri] n. Objetos (*m. pl.*) de escritorio (writing materials). || Papel (*m.*) de escribir y sobres.

station house [ˈsteiʃənhaus] n. Comisaría, *f.* (of police). || Cuartel (*m.*) de bomberos (of firemen). || U. S. Estación (*f.*) de ferrocarril.

stationmaster [ˈsteiʃənˌmɑːstə*] n. Jefe (*m.*) de estación.

station wagon [ˈsteiʃənˌwægən] n. Break, *m.*

statism [ˈsteitizəm] n. Estatismo, *m.*

statist [ˈsteitist] n. Partidario (*m.*) del estatismo.

statistic [stəˈtistik] n. Estadística, *f.*

— Adj. Estadístico, ca.

statistical [—əl] adj. Estadístico, ca.

statistically [—əli] adv. Según las estadísticas, estadísticamente.

statistician [ˌstætisˈtiʃən] n. Estadístico, ca.

statistics [stəˈtistiks] n. Estadística, *f.* (science). || — Pl. Estadísticas, *f.* (data).

stator [ˈsteitə*] n. TECH. Estator, *m.*

statoscope [ˈsteitəˌskəup] n. PHYS. Estatoscopio, *m.* (aneroid barometer).

statuary [ˈstætjuəri] adj. Estatuario, ria: *statuary marble, art*, mármol, arte estatuario.

— N. Estatuaria, *f.* (art of making statues). || Estatuas, *f. pl.* (statues collectively). || Estatuario, *m.* (artist).

statue [ˈstætjuː] n. Estatua, *f.*: *equestrian statue*, estatua ecuestre; *recumbent statue*, estatua yacente.

statuesque [ˌstætjuˈesk] adj. Escultural.

statuette [ˌstætjuˈet] n. Figurina, *f.*, estatuilla, *f.*

stature [ˈstætʃə*] n. Estatura, *f.*, talla, *f.* (height). || FIG. Talla, *f.*, categoría, *f.*

status [ˈsteitəs] n. Condición, *f.*, estado, *m.* (state). || Posición (*f.*) social (position). || Categoría, *f.* (standing). || JUR. Estado, *m.*: *marital* o *civil status*, estado civil.

status quo [—ˈkwəu] n. Statu quo, *m.*

statutable [ˈstætjuːtəbl] adj. See STATUTORY.

statute [ˈstætjuːt] n. JUR. Estatuto, *m.*, decreto, *m.* (formally recorded law). || — Pl. Estatutos, *m.* (of a chartered body): *in accordance with the statutes*, según los estatutos. || *Statute book*, código, *m.* || *Statute law*, derecho escrito. || *Statute mile*, milla (*f.*) terrestre.

statutory [ˈstætjutəri] adj. Establecido por la ley *or* los estatutos, estatutario, ria (established by a statute). || Reglamentario, ria; estatutario, ria (conforming to a statute). || Establecido por la ley (offence).

staunch [stɔːntʃ] adj. Fiel; seguro, ra: *a staunch friend*, un amigo fiel. || Inquebrantable (courage). || MAR. Estanco, ca; hermético, ca (watertight).

staunch [stɔːntʃ] v. tr. Restañar (blood). || Restañar la sangre de (a wound).

staunchness [—nis] n. Lealtad, *f.*, seguridad, *f.* (of friendship). || Firmeza, *f.* (of courage). || Estanquidad, *f.*, hermeticidad, *f.* (watertightness).

stave [steiv] n. Duela, *f.* (of barrel). || Peldaño, *m.* (of a ladder). || Barrote, *m.* (of a chair). || Bastón, *m.* (stick). || MUS. Pentagrama, *m.* || Estrofa, *f.* (of a poem).

stave* [steiv] v. tr. Poner duelas a (a barrel). || — *To stave in*, desfondar (a cask, a ship), romper (to break). || *To stave off*, rechazar (an attack), apartar, (to put aside), evitar: *to stave off a disaster*, evitar un desastre; diferir, aplazar (to delay).

— V. intr. Desfondarse.

— OBSERV. Pret. & p. p. **stove, staved.**

staves [—z] pl. n. See STAFF.

stay [stei] n. Estancia, *f.*, permanencia, *f.* [*Amer.*, estadía, *f.*]: *a stay of one week*, una estancia de una semana; *during my stay in Cordoba*, durante mi estancia en Córdoba. || JUR. Aplazamiento, *m.* (postponement). | Sobreseimiento, *m.* (of proceedings). || ARCH. Sostén, *m.*, soporte, *m.*, puntal, *m.* (prop). || Apoyo *m.*, sostén, *m.* (support). || Ballena, *f.* (stiffener). || MAR. Estay, *m.* || — Pl. Corsé, *m. sing.*

stay [stei] v. tr. JUR. Aplazar, diferir (to postpone). || Quedarse, permanecer: *he stayed a month*, se quedó un mes. || Resistir, aguantar (to endure): *to stay a race*, resistir una carrera. || Detener, parar (to stop). || Frenar (to check). || Soportar, apoyar, sostener, apuntalar (to prop up, to secure). || FIG. Sostener, mantener (to support). || — *To stay one's hand*, contenerse. || *To stay one's hunger*, engañar el hambre. || *To stay out*, quedarse hasta el final de: *he stayed the month, the film out*, se quedó hasta el final del mes, de la película; terminar (a race).

— V. intr. Quedarse, permanecer: *to stay indoors*, quedarse dentro. || Estar, vivir, alojarse, hospedarse: *I stayed in a very good hotel*, estuve en un hotel muy bueno; *to stay with one's grandparents*, estar en casa de sus abuelos. || Pararse, detenerse (to stop). || Esperar, quedarse (to wait): *stay a little*, espera un poco. || Resistir, aguantar: *the winner stayed well*, el ganador resistió bien. || MAR. Virar (to tack). || — *It has come to stay*, se ha implantado. || *To stay away*, ausentarse (to absent o.s.), no venir (not to come). | — *To stay away from*, no acercarse a. || *To stay in*, quedarse en casa, no salir (not to go out), estar castigado sin salir (at school). || *To stay on*, quedarse. || *To stay out*, quedarse fuera. || *To stay over*, pasar la noche. || *To stay put*, see PUT. || *To stay to dinner*, quedarse a cenar. || *To stay up*, no acostarse. || *To stay up late*, acostarse tarde.

stay-at-home [—əthəum] adj. Casero, ra; hogareño, ña.

— N. Persona (*f.*) casera *or* hogareña.

stayer [—ə*] n. Caballo (*m.*) para carreras de fondo (horse). || Corredor (*m.*) de fondo (racer). || FIG. Persona (*f.*) que tiene mucha resistencia.

staying power [—iŋˌpauə*] n. Resistencia, *f.*, aguante, *m.*

stay-in strike [—inˌstraik] n. Huelga (*f.*) de brazos caídos *or* de brazos cruzados.

staysail [—seil] n. MAR. Vela (*f.*) de estay.

stead [sted] n. Utilidad, *f.* || — *In s.o.'s* o *sth's stead*, en lugar de alguien, de algo. || *To stand s.o. in good stead*, ser muy útil a alguien, ser de gran utilidad para alguien: *this will stand you in good stead*, esto le será muy útil.

steadfast [—fəst] adj. Constante, firme (constant). || Inquebrantable (not wavering). || Estable (not changing). || Fijo, ja (gaze). || *Steadfast in danger*, impertérrito, ta.

steadfastness [—fəstnis] n. Constancia, *f.*, firmeza, *f.*, tenacidad, *f.* || Estabilidad, *f.*

steadily [—dili] adv. Firmemente. || Fijamente: *he looked at her steadily*, la miró fijamente. || A velocidad constante: *to drive steadily at 100*, conducir a una velocidad constante de 100. || Normalmente: *to walk steadily*, andar normalmente. || Sin parar, continuamente (continuously): *he works steadily*, trabaja sin parar. || Constantemente: *prices rise steadily*, los precios aumentan constantemente. || En equilibrio: *a table that stands steadily*, una mesa que se mantiene en equilibrio. || Prudentemente, sensatamente (sensibly).

steadiness [—inis] n. Estabilidad, *f.*, equilibrio, *m.* (of person or object). || Firmeza, *f.*, seguridad, *f.* (of hand, mind). || Regularidad, *f.* (in action). || Constancia, *f.* (of demand, faith, etc.). || Estabilidad, *f.* (of prices). || Continuidad, *f.* (continuity). || Sensatez, *f.*, juicio, *m.* (good sense). || Formalidad, *f.* (seriousness). || Perseverancia, *f.* (perseverance). || Fijeza, *f.*: *steadiness of gaze*, fijeza en la mirada.

steady [—i] adj. Constante (constant). || Firme, seguro, ra: *steady rest*, sostén firme; *with a steady hand*, con mano segura. || En equilibrio: *to make a table steady*, poner una mesa en equilibrio. || Tranquilo, la; manso, sa (horse). || Regular: *to play a steady game*, tener un juego regular; *steady pace*, paso regular. || Ininterrumpido, da; continuo, nua: *steady progress*, progresos continuos. || Estable: *steady weather*, tiempo estable. || Continuo, nua; persistente: *steady downpour*, lluvia continua. || Tenaz, firme (faith). || Fiel, leal: *to be steady in one's principles*, ser fiel a sus principios. || Sensato, ta; formal, equilibrado, da (sensible): *steady young man*, joven sensato. || Asiduo, dua; aplicado, da (worker, student). || Fijo, ja; seguro, ra: *he got a steady job*, consiguió un empleo fijo. || Fijo, ja: *a steady gaze*, una mirada fija. || Uniforme, regular: *steady heartbeat*, pulso regular. || Estacionario, ria: *steady barometer*, barómetro estacionario. || Sostenido, da (in the Stock Exchange). || COMM. Constante, continuo, nua; *steady demand for*, pedido constante de. | Estable: *steady prices*, precios estables. || — *Ship steady in a sea*, barco (*m.*) que navega bien. || *Steady!*, ¡quieto! (remain calm!), ¡despacio! (take it easy!), mantenga el rumbo (command to the helmsman). || *To go steady (with)*, tener relaciones [con], salir [con]. || *To keep steady*, no moverse, quedarse quieto.

— N. Novio, via (sweetheart).

steady [—i] v. tr. Estabilizar (to stabilize). || Hacer sentar cabeza (to make serious). || Uniformar, regularizar (to make uniform). || Calmar (nerves). || Mantener firme, sostener (to hold). || — *To steady o.s.*, recuperar el equilibrio. || *To steady o.s. against sth.*, apoyarse en algo.

— V. intr. Estabilizarse (to become stable). || Sentar cabeza (a wild person). || Uniformarse, regularizarse (to become uniform). || Calmarse (to quieten down).

steak [steik] n. Filete, *m.* (slice of meat or fish). || Bistec, *m.*, filete, *m.* (beefsteak).

steak house [—haus] n. Restaurante (*m.*) especializado en bistecs.

steal [stiːl] n. Robo, *m.* (robbery). || Plagio, *m.* (plagiarism). || U. S. FAM. Ganga, *f.* (real bargain).

steal* [stiːl] v. tr. Robar, hurtar (to rob): *I didn't steal anything*, no robé nada. || FIG. Robar: *to steal a kiss*, robar un beso. || SP. Robar (in baseball). || — *To steal a glance at*, echar una mirada furtiva a. || *To*

steal a march on, adelantarse a, anticiparse a. || *To steal the show*, llevarse todos los aplausos.
— V. intr. Robar, hurtar. || — *To steal away*, escabullirse, marcharse sigilosamente. || *To steal in, out*, entrar, salir furtivamente *or* a hurtadillas.

— OBSERV. Pret. **stole**; p. p. **stolen**.

stealer [—ə*] n. Ladrón, ona.
stealing [—iŋ] n. Robo, *m.*
stealth [stelθ] n. Cautela, *f.*, sigilo, *m.* || *By stealth*, a hurtadillas, furtivamente: *he did it by stealth*, lo hizo a hurtadillas.
stealthily [—ili] adv. A hurtadillas, furtivamente.
stealthiness [—inis] n. Cautela, *f.*, sigilo, *m.* (caution). || Lo furtivo (of an action).
stealthy [—i] adj. Cauteloso, sa; sigiloso, sa (person). || Furtivo, va (action). || *With stealthy step*, con mucho sigilo.
steam [sti:m] n. Vapor, *m.* (from boiling water): *does it run on steam or electricity?*, ¿funciona a vapor o con electricidad? || Vaho, *m.* (from wet grass, the mouth, etc.). || — *At full steam*, a todo vapor. || *To get up steam*, dar presión (boiler), hacer acopio de energía (person). || FIG. *To let off steam*, desfogarse. | *Under one's own steam*, por sus propios medios, por sí mismo.
— Adj. De vapor: *steam launch*, lancha de vapor; *steam locomotive*, locomotora de vapor; *steam bath*, baño de vapor.
steam [sti:m] v. tr. CULIN. Cocer al vapor. || Limpiar con vapor (to clean). || Tratar al vapor (to treat with steam). || Arrojar, despedir (to emit). || Empañar (window). || — *To steam open*, abrir por medio de vapor. || *To steam up*, empañar.
— V. intr. Humear (to emit steam or vapour). || Echar vapor: *the train steamed into the station*, el tren entró en la estación echando vapor. || Evaporarse, salir en forma de vapor (to evaporate). || Empañarse (windows, etc.). || Funcionar con vapor (to work). || Navegar, hacer, marchar a: *to steam at twelve knots*, hacer doce nudos. || — *To steam ahead*, avanzar. || MAR. *To steam out*, zarpar (a ship). || *To steam up*, empañarse.
steamboat [—bəut] n. Vapor, *m.*, buque (*m.*) de vapor.
steam boiler [—ˌbɔilə*] n. Caldera (*f.*) de vapor.
steam box [—bɔks] or **steam chest** [—tʃest] n. Cámara (*f.*) de vapor.
steam-driven [—ˌdrivn] adj. A vapor, de vapor.
steam engine [—ˌendʒin] n. Máquina (*f.*) de vapor.
steamer [—ə*] n. Vapor, *m.*, buque (*m.*) de vapor (steamship). || Máquina (*f.*) de vapor (steam engine). || CULIN. Olla (*f.*) de estofar.
steam fitter [—ˌfitə*] n. Montador (*m.*) de calderas *or* de tuberías de vapor.
steam gauge (U. S. **steam gage**) [—geidʒ] n. Manómetro, *m.*
steam hammer [—ˌhæmə*] n. Martillo (*m.*) pilón.
steaminess [—inis] n. Humedad, *f.*
steam iron [—ˈaiən] n. Plancha (*f.*) de vapor.
steamroller [—ˌrəulə*] n. TECH. Apisonadora, *f.* || FAM. Fuerza (*f.*) arrolladora (overwhelming power).
steamroller [—ˌrəulə*] v. tr. Apisonar, allanar (to flatten with a steamroller). || FAM. Aplastar, arrollar: *to steamroller any opposition*, aplastar toda oposición. | Imponer (idea, policy).
steamship [—ʃip] n. Vapor, *m.*, buque (*m.*) de vapor. || *Steamship company*, compañía naviera.
steam shovel [—ˌʃʌvl] n. Excavadora, *f.*, pala (*f.*) mecánica.
steamy [—i] adj. Húmedo, da (atmosphere). || Empañado, da (glass). || Humeante (giving off steam). || Vaporoso, sa (of or like steam).
stearate [ˈstiəreit] n. CHEM. Estearato, *m.*
stearic [stiˈærik] adj. Esteárico, ca: *stearic acid*, ácido esteárico.
stearin [ˈstiərin] or **stearine** [ˈstiəri:n] n. CHEM. Estearina, *f.*
steatite [ˈstiətait] n. MIN. Esteatita, *f.*
stedfast [ˈstedfəst] adj. See STEADFAST.
steed [sti:d] n. Corcel, *m.* (horse).
steel [sti:l] n. Acero, *m.* (metal): *stainless steel*, acero inoxidable; *cast steel*, acero colado; *steel casting*, fundición del acero. || Eslabón, *m.*, chaira, *f.* (for sharpening knives). || Eslabón, *m.* (for making sparks). || Acero, *m.* (sword). || Ballena, *f.* (stiffener). || FIG. Resolución, *f.*, firmeza, *f.* (determination). | Acero, *m.* (strength). || — *Cold steel*, arma blanca. || FIG. *To be made of steel*, ser de hierro. || *To turn into steel*, acerar: *to turn iron into steel*, acerar el hierro.
— Adj. De acero.
steel [sti:l] v. tr. Acerar (to cover with steel). || FIG. Endurecer (one's heart). | Fortalecer (to strengthen). || — FIG. *To steel one's heart*, endurecerse, volverse insensible. | *To steel o.s.*, fortalecerse (to strengthen), endurecerse, volverse insensible (to harden). | *To steel o.s. against*, acorazarse contra.
steel-clad [—klæd] adj. Acorazado, da; cubierto de acero.
steel engraving [—inˈgreiviŋ] n. Grabado (*m.*) en acero.
steel grey (U. S. **steel gray**) [—ˈgrei] n. Gris (*m.*) metálico.
steel industry [—ˈindəstri] n. Industria (*f.*) siderúrgica.
steeliness [—inis] n. Dureza, *f.*, inflexibilidad, *f.*
steel mill [—mil] n. Acería, *f.*, fábrica (*f.*) de acero.
steel wool [—ˈwul] n. Estropajo, *m.*
steelwork [—wə:k] n. Estructura (*f.*) de acero. || — Pl. Acería, *f. sing.*, fundición (*f. sing.*) de acero.
— OBSERV. *Steelworks* se construye con el singular o con el plural.
steely [—i] adj. Acerado, da (of or like steel). || FIG. Duro, ra (hard). | Inflexible.
steelyard [—jɑ:d] n. Romana, *f.* (balance).
steep [sti:p] adj. Empinado, da; escarpado, da; abrupto, ta (slope): *steep hillside*, ladera escarpada. || Cortado a pico (cliff). || FAM. Excesivo, va; exorbitante (price). | Increíble, exagerado, da (story).
— N. Pendiente, *f.*, cuesta (*f.*) empinada (steep slope). || Remojo, *m.* (soaking).
steep [sti:p] v. tr. Remojar (to soak). || Enriar (hemp). || FIG. Empapar, impregnar (to saturate): *to be steeped in*, estar empapado de.
— V. intr. Estar en remojo. || Estar en infusión (tea).
steepen [—ən] v. tr. Volver más empinado (slope). || Aumentar (prices).
— V. intr. Empinarse (slope). || Aumentar (prices).
steeple [—l] n. Aguja, *f.* (spire). || Campanario, *m.*, torre, *f.* (tower and spire).
steeplechase [—ltʃeis] n. SP. Carrera (*f.*) de obstáculos (horse racing, athletics).
steeplechaser [—lˌtʃeisə*] n. SP. Jockey (*m.*) *or* caballo (*m.*) *or* corredor (*m.*) de obstáculos.
steeplechasing [—lˌtʃeisiŋ] n. Carrera (*f.*) de obstáculos.
steeplejack [—ldʒæk] n. Reparador (*m.*) de chimeneas *or* de campanarios.
steeply [—li] adv. En pendiente. || — *Prices rose steeply*, los precios subieron vertiginosamente. || *Steeply inclined road*, carretera muy empinada.
steepness [—nis] n. Pendiente, *f.*, inclinación, *f.*
steer [stiə*] n. Novillo, *m.* (young bull). || U. S. FAM. Consejo, *m.* (friendly suggestion).
steer [stiə*] v. tr. Dirigir, encaminar (one's steps). || Dirigir, guiar (vehicle). || Gobernar (a boat). || Llevar (a bicycle). || Conducir [*Amer.*, manejar] (a car). || Seguir: *to steer a course*, seguir un rumbo. || FIG. Conducir, llevar, guiar (to lead). | Orientar (to guide).
— V. intr. Llevar el timón (in a boat). || Obedecer al timón (boat). || Llevar el volante, conducir [*Amer.*, manejar] (in a car). || Conducirse [*Amer.*, manejarse]: *a car that steers easily*, un coche que se conduce fácilmente. || — *To steer clear of*, evitar. || *To steer for*, dirigirse a.
steerage [—ridʒ] n. MAR. Entrepuente, *m.*, tercera clase, *f.* (cheapest quarters on a ship). | Gobierno, *m.* (ship's reaction to the helm).
steerageway [—ridʒˌwei] n. MAR. Velocidad (*f.*) mínima para gobernar.
steerer [—rə*] n. Timonero, *m.*, timonel, *m.*
steering [—riŋ] n. MAR. Gobierno, *m.* || AUT. Conducción, *f.* [*Amer.*, manejo, *m.*] (of a car).
steering column [—riŋˌkɔləm] n. Columna (*f.*) de dirección.
steering committee [—riŋkəˈmiti] n. Comité (*m.*) de dirección *or* directivo.
steering gear [—riŋgiə*] n. Mecanismo (*m.*) de dirección.
steering wheel [—riŋwi:l] n. Volante, *m.* (of a car). || Rueda (*f.*) del timón (of a ship).
steersman [—zmən] n. MAR. Timonero, *m.*, timonel, *m.* (helmsman).

— OBSERV. El plural de la palabra inglesa es *steersmen*.

steeve [sti:v] n. MAR. Inclinación, *f.* (of bowsprit). | Esteba, *f.* (for steeving cargo).
steeve [sti:v] v. tr. MAR. Estibar (to stow). | Inclinar (to angle a bowsprit).
— V. intr. MAR. Inclinarse (bowsprit).
stein [stain] n. U. S. Jarra, *f.* (beer mug).
steinbock [—bɔk] n. ZOOL. Íbice, *m.* (ibex).
steinbok [—bɔk] n. ZOOL. Antílope (*m.*) africano.
stele [ˈsti:li:] n. Estela, *f.* (monument). || BOT. Estela, *f.*
stellar [ˈstelə*] adj. Estelar (relating to the stars). || Estrellado, da (stellate). || U. S. Principal, estelar: *a stellar role*, un papel principal.
stellate [ˈsteleit] or **stellated** [ˈsteleitid] adj. Estrellado, da (shaped like a star). || Radiado, da (leaves, cells, etc.).
stellionate [ˈsteliəneit] n. JUR. Estelionato, *m.*
stellular [ˈsteljulə*] adj. See STELLATE.
stem [stem] n. Tallo, *m.* (of a flower). || Tronco, *m.* (of a tree). || Rabo, *m.*, pedúnculo, *m.* (of leaf). || Rabo, *m.* (of fruit). || Racimo, *m.* (of bananas). || Pie, *m.* (of a glass). || Tubo, *m.*, cañón, *m.* (of a pipe). || Cañón, *m.* (of feathers). || TECH. Vástago, *m.* (rod). || Tija, *f.* (of a key). || MUS. Rabo, *m.* (of a note). || Grueso, *m.* (of a letter). || GRAMM. Radical, *m.* || Tronco, *m.*, origen, *m.*, estirpe, *f.* (line of descent). || MAR. Tajamar, *m.*, roda, *f.* (vertical piece of bow). | Proa, *f.* (bow). || SP. Cuña, *f.* (in skiing). || *From stem to stern*, de proa a popa.
stem [stem] v. tr. Despalillar (to remove the stem from). || MAR. Hacer frente a, mantenerse contra (to make headway). || Restañar (blood). || Estancar,

represar (to dam up). || Detener, contener: *to stem an attack*, detener un ataque. || Frenar (to stop).
— V. intr. Pararse en cuña (skiing). || *To stem from*, derivarse de, ser el resultado de (to result).
stemless [—lis] adj. Sin tallo.
stench [stentʃ] n. Peste, *f.*, hedor, *m.* (foul smell).
stencil [ˈstensl] n. Plantilla, *f.* (for reproducing letters, designs, etc.). || Cliché (*m.*) de multicopista (for duplicator, typewriter, etc.). || Estarcido, *m.* (patterns or letters produced).
stencil [ˈstensl] v. tr. Estarcir. || Sacar con multicopista (documents).
stenocardia [ˌstenəˈkɑːdiə] n. Med. Estenocardia, *f.*
stenograph [ˈstenəgrɑːf] n. Taquigrafía, *f.* (symbols). || Máquina (*f.*) de taquigrafía (machine).
stenograph [ˈstenəgrɑːf] v. tr. Taquigrafiar, estenografiar.
stenographer [steˈnɔgrəfə*] n. Taquígrafo, fa; estenógrafo, fa.
stenographic [steˈnɔgrəfik] or **stenographical** [—əl] adj. Taquigráfico, ca; estenográfico, ca.
stenography [steˈnɔgrəfi] n. Taquigrafía, *f.*, estenografía, *f.*
stenotype [ˈstenətaip] n. Estenotipo, *m.*
stenotypist [ˈstenətaipist] n. Estenotipista, *m.* & *f.*
stenotypy [ˈstenətaipi] n. Estenotipia, *f.*
stentor [ˈstentɔ*] n. Esténtor, *m.*
stentorian [stenˈtɔːriən] adj. Estentóreo, a.
step [step] n. Paso, *m.*: *to take three steps*, dar tres pasos; *three steps away*, a tres pasos; *to walk with a heavy step*, andar con paso pesado; *to take a step backwards*, dar un paso hacia atrás. || Paso, *m.*, huella, *f.* (footprint): *to follow in s.o.'s steps*, seguir los pasos de alguien. || Paso, *m.*, pisada, *f.* (sound made by the foot): *steps were heard*, se oían pasos. || Paso, *m.* (movement or sequence in dancing). || Paso, *m.* (pace): *at a fast step*, a paso rápido. || Peldaño, *m.*, escalón, *m.* (of stairs, ladder): *I sat down on the top step*, me senté en el último escalón. || Estribo, *m.* (of a vehicle). || Umbral, *m.* (of doorway). || Fig. Escalón, *m.* (a degree in scale): *to go up a step in one's job*, subir un escalón en su empleo. | Paso, *m.*, etapa, *f.* (stage in a process, activity): *the first step towards liberty*, el primer paso hacia la libertad; *a process that is done in three steps*, un proceso que se hace en tres etapas. | Medida, *f.* (measure): *to take steps to cut down inflation*, tomar medidas para reducir la inflación. | Paso, *m.*, gestión, *f.*: *to take the necessary steps to get a passport*, hacer las gestiones necesarias *or* dar los pasos necesarios para conseguir un pasaporte. || Mus. Nota, *f.* (degree on a scale). | Intervalo, *m.* (interval). || Mar. Carlinga, *f.* (socket). || Min. Tajo (*m.*) escalonado (shelf). || Graderío, *m.* (in a stadium). || — Pl. Escalinata, *f. sing.* (flight of outdoor stairs). || Escaleras, *f.*, escalera, *f. sing.* (staircase). || Escalera (*f. sing.*) de tijera (stepladder). || Escalerilla, *f. sing.* (of a plane). || — *A few steps forward*, a dos pasos. || *A great step forward*, un gran paso adelante. || Fig. *At every step*, a cada paso. || *First steps*, primeros pasos (of children). || *Flight of steps*, tramo, *m.* (of a staircase), escalinata, *f.* (of an entrance). || *Goose step*, paso de la oca. || *Mind your step!*, ¡tenga cuidado! || *Pair of steps*, escalera (*f.*) de tijera. || *Step by step*, paso a paso, poco a poco. || *Sure step*, paso firme. || *To be a step away*, estar a dos pasos. || *To be in step*, llevar el paso. || *To be out of step*, no llevar el paso. || *To break step*, romper el paso. || *To get* o *to fall into step*, coger el paso. || *To keep in step*, llevar el compás (dancing), llevar el paso, ir con paso acompasado (marching). || *To retrace one's steps*, desandar lo andado, volverse atrás. || Fig. *To take a false step*, dar un mal paso, dar un paso en falso. || *To take a great step*, dar un buen paso. || Fig. *To take the first steps*, dar los primeros pasos. || *To turn one's steps towards*, encaminarse hacia, dirigirse hacia. || Fig. *To watch one's step*, ir con cuidado. | *With measured steps*, a pasos contados.
step [step] v. tr. Dar: *to step three paces to the left*, dar tres pasos a la izquierda. || Poner (the foot). || Bailar (a dance). || Mar. Plantar (the mast into its socket). || Escalonar (to construct in steps). || Medir a pasos (a distance).
— V. intr. Dar un paso, dar pasos: *to step forward*, dar un paso adelante. || Ir (to go). || — *Step this way please*, pase por aquí, por favor. || *To step ashore*, tomar tierra. || Fam. *To step round to the tobacconist's*, darse una vuelta *or* pasarse por el estanco. || *To step short*, andar a paso corto.
— ***To step aside***, apartarse, hacerse a un lado. | Fig. Hacer una digresión. || ***To step back***, retroceder, echarse atrás. || ***To step down***, bajar: *to step down from the bus*, bajar del autobús. | Renunciar a (from office). | Electr. Reducir (current). || ***To step in***, entrar. | Fig. Intervenir. | — *Step in!*, ¡adelante! || ***To step into***, poner el pie en: *to step into the road*, poner el pie en la calzada. | Fig. Heredar (a fortune). | Ocupar (position). || ***To step off***, medir [a pasos] (to measure). | Bajar de: *to step off the pavement*, bajar de la acera. || ***To step on***, pisar: *to step on s.o.'s foot*, pisar el pie a alguien; *to step on the brake*, pisar el freno; *to step on the grass*, pisar la hierba. | — *To step on board*, subir a bordo. | Fam. *To step on it*, darse prisa (to hurry), acelerar (to accelerate). || ***To step out***, apretar el paso (to walk fast). | Salir (to go out): *to step out for a while*, salir un rato. | Apartarse (of one's way). | U. S. Irse de juerga (to have a good time). || ***To step over***, pasar por encima de (an obstacle). | Darse una vuelta por, pasarse por (to go). || ***To step up***, subir: *to step up into the bus*, subir al autobús. | Ascender (to promote). | Aumentar: *to step up production*, aumentar la producción. | Electr. Aumentar (current). | Acercarse (to approach).
stepbrother [—ˌbrʌðə*] n. Hermanastro, *m.*, medio hermano, *m.*
step-by-step [—baiˌstep] adj. Progresivo, va; gradual: *a step-by-step method of learning English*, un método progresivo para aprender inglés.
stepchild [—tʃaild] n. Hijastro, tra.

— Observ. El plural es *stepchildren*.

stepdaughter [—ˌdɔːtə*] n. Hijastra, *f.*
step-down [—daun] n. Reducción, *f.*
— Adj. Reductor, ra.
stepfather [—ˌfɑːðə*] n. Padrastro, *m.*
stepladder [ˈstepˌlædə*] n. Escalera (*f.*) de tijera.
stepmother [ˈstepˌmʌðə*] n. Madrastra, *f.*
stepparent [ˈstepˌpɛərənt] n. Padrastro, *m.*, madrastra, *f.*
steppe [step] n. Estepa, *f.*
stepped [—t] adj. Con escalones. || Escalonado, da. || Fig. Gradual, progresivo, va.
stepped-up [—tʌp] adj. Aumentado, da. || Ascendido, da (promoted).
stepping-stone [—iŋˌstəun] n. Pasadera, *f.*, cada una de las piedras usadas para cruzar un río. || Fig. Trampolín, *m.* (a means of advancement).
stepsister [ˈstepˌsistə*] n. Hermanastra, *f.*, media hermana, *f.*
stepson [ˈstepsʌn] n. Hijastro, *m.*
step-up [ˈstepʌp] adj. Electr. Elevador, ra.
stere [ˈstiːə*] n. Estéreo, *m.* (cubic metre).
stereo [ˈstiəriəu] adj. Estereoscópico, ca. || Estereofónico, ca; estéreo, a: *a stereo record*, un disco estéreo. || Print. Estereotipado, da.
— N. Print. Estereotipo, *m.* || Estereoscopia, *f.* (stereoscopy). || Estereofonía, *f.* (stereophony). || Equipo (*m.*) estereofónico (equipment).
stereobate [ˈstiəriəubeit] n. Arch. Estereóbato, *m.*
stereochemistry [stiəriəuˈkemistri] n. Estereoquímica, *f.*
stereogram [ˈstiəriəgræm] n. Estereograma, *m.*
stereograph [ˈstiəriəugrɑːf] n. Estereograma, *m.*, estereografía, *f.*
stereography [stiəriˈɔgrəfi] n. Estereografía, *f.*
stereometer [ˌstiəriˈɔmitə*] n. Estereómetro, *m.*
stereometry [stiəriˈɔmətri] n. Estereometría, *f.*
stereophonic [stiəriəˈfɔnik] adj. Estereofónico, ca.
stereophony [steriˈɔfəni] n. Estereofonía, *f.*
stereoscope [ˈstiəriəskəup] n. Estereoscopio, *m.*
stereoscopic [stiəriəˈskɔpik] or **stereoscopical** [—əl] adj. Estereoscópico, ca.
stereoscopy [stiəriˈɔskəpi] n. Estereoscopia, *f.*
stereotomy [stiəriˈɔtəmi] n. Estereotomía, *f.*
stereotype [ˈstiəriətaip] n. Print. Estereotipo, *m.* (plate). | Estereotipia, *f.* (machine). || Fig. Estereotipo, *m.* (conventional idea, character, etc.).
stereotype [ˈstiəriətaip] v. tr. Estereotipar. || Fig. Estereotipar: *stereotyped smile, attitude, phrase*, sonrisa, actitud, expresión estereotipada.
stereotyping [—iŋ] n. Estereotipado, *m.*
stereotypy [stiəriəˈtaipi] n. Estereotipia, *f.*
sterile [ˈsterail] adj. Estéril.
sterility [steˈriliti] n. Esterilidad, *f.*
sterilization [ˌsterilaiˈzeiʃən] n. Esterilización, *f.*
sterilize [ˈsterilaiz] v. tr. Esterilizar.
sterilizer [—ə*] n. Esterilizador, *m.*
sterilizing [—iŋ] adj. Esterilizador, ra.
sterling [ˈstəːliŋ] adj. Esterlina: *the pound sterling*, la libra esterlina. || De la libra esterlina: *sterling area*, zona de la libra esterlina. || Fig. Excelente, de buena ley, de buena calidad: *sterling fellow*, persona excelente. | Verdadero, ra; auténtico, ca (genuine). || *Sterling silver*, plata (*f.*) de ley.
— N. Libra (*f.*) esterlina (money). || Plata (*f.*) de ley (sterling silver).
stern [stəːn] adj. Severo, ra; austero, ra: *stern discipline*, disciplina severa. || Sombrío, a (air). || Severo, ra: *stern judge*, juez severo; *stern look*, mirada severa. || Severo, ra; riguroso, sa (punishment). || Austero, ra: *stern landscape*, paisaje austero. || Triste (reality). || Firme: *stern resolve*, firme resolución.
— N. Mar. Popa, *f.* || Fam. Parte (*f.*) trasera, trasero, *m.* (of a person). || Cuarto (*m.*) trasero (of an animal).
sternforemost [—ˈfɔːməust] adv. Mar. Con la popa hacia adelante.
sternmost [—məust] adj. Mar. Más a popa.
sternness [—nis] n. Austeridad, *f.*, severidad, *f.* | Severidad, *f.* (of judge, look, punishment). || Austeridad, *f.* (of a landscape). || Lo sombrío (of air). || Tristeza, *f.* (sadness). || Firmeza, *f.* (of resolve).
sternpost [—pəust] n. Mar. Codaste, *m.*
sternum [ˈstəːnəm] n. Anat. Esternón, *m.*

— Observ. El plural de *sternum* es *sternums* o *sterna*.

sternutation [ˌstəːnjuˈteiʃən] n. Estornudo, *m.*
sternway [ˈstəːnwei] n. Mar. Marcha (*f.*) atrás, retroceso, *m.*
sterol [ˈstərɔl] n. Chem. Esterol, *m.*

stertor [ˈstəːtəː*] n. MED. Estertor, *m.*
stertorous [ˈstəːtərəs] adj. MED. Estertoroso, sa.
stet [stet] n. Vale [lo tachado].
stet [stet] v. tr. Marcar como válido [lo tachado].
stethoscope [ˈsteθəskəup] n. MED. Estetoscopio, *m.*
stethoscopy [steˈθɔskəpi] n. MED. Estetoscopia, *f.*
stevedore [ˈstiːvidɔː*] n. MAR. Estibador, *m.*
stevedore [ˈstiːvidɔː*] v. tr. MAR. Estibar.
stew [stjuː] n. CULIN. Estofado, *m.*, guisado, *m.* (of mutton, etc.). | Encebollado, *m.* (of hare). | Compota, *f.* (of fruit). || Vivero, *m.*, criadero, *m.* (for fish, oysters). || Lupanar, *m.* (brothel). || FIG. FAM. Preocupación, *f.*, agitación, *f.* (worry). || FAM. *To be in a stew*, estar hecho un lío.
stew [stjuː] v. tr. CULIN. Estofar, guisar, cocer a fuego lento (meat). || Hacer una compota de, cocer (fruit). — V. intr. Cocer a fuego lento. || Pasarse (tea). || FIG. FAM. Cocerse, ahogarse (to stifle). | Empollar (to study hard). | Estar en ascuas (to worry). || FIG. FAM. *To stew in one's own juice*, cocerse en su propia salsa.
steward [stjuəd] n. Mayoral, *m.* (of a farm). || Administrador, *m.* (of an estate). || AVIAT. Auxiliar (*m.*) de vuelo. || Camarero, *m.* (on a passenger ship). || Mayordomo, *m.* (butler). || Despensero, *m.*, administrador (*m.*) de la cocina (in charge of serving and preparing meals on a boat). || Organizador, *m.* (of public meetings). || *Shop steward*, enlace (*m.*) sindical.
stewardess [—is] n. Camarera, *f.* (on a passenger ship). || AVIAT. Azafata, *f.* [*Amer.*, aeromoza, *f.*].
stewardship [—ʃip] n. Mayordomía, *f.* (catering). || Administración, *f.*
stewed [stjuːd] adj. FAM. Bebido, da; como una cuba (drunk).
stewpan [ˈstjuːpæn] or **stewpot** [ˈstjuːpɔt] n. Cazuela, *f.*, olla, *f.*
sthene [ˈsθiːn] n. Estenio, *m.* (unit of force).
stibium [ˈstibiəm] n. CHEM. Antimonio, *m.*
stick [stik] n. Madero, *m.*, trozo (*m.*) de madera (piece of wood). || Estaca, *f.* (stake). || Garrote, *m.*, porra, *f.* (club, weapon). || Vara, *f.*, palo, *m.* (for hitting with): *I hit him with a stick*, le golpeé con un palo. || Bastón, *m.* (for walking): *I knocked on the door with my stick*, llamé a la puerta con el bastón. || Rodrigón, *m.* (for plants). || Palo, *m.*, mango, *m.* (of a broom). || Palillo, *m.* (drumstick, cocktail stick). || MUS. Batuta, *f.* (of conductor). || MIL. Baqueta, *f.* (of guns). || Barra, *f.* (of toffee, wax, chewing gum). || Palo, *m.* (for lollipop). || SP. Palo, *m.*, "stick", *m.* (hockey). || Tallo, *m.* (of rhubarb). || Rama, *f.* (of celery). || MAR. Mástil, *m.*, verga, *f.*, palo, *m.* (mast). || AVIAT. Palanca, *f.* [de mando] (control lever). || Cartucho, *m.* (of dynamite). || Ráfaga, *f.* (of machine gun). || Haz, *m.* (of bombs). || PRINT. Componedor, *m*, (composing stick). || Pinchazo, *m.*: *a stick in the ribs*, un pinchazo en el costado. || Adhesión, *f.* (power of adhering). || — Pl. Leña, *f. sing.*, astillas *f.* (to make a fire). || — FIG. *Big stick policy*, política (*f.*) del gran garrote. | *Poor stick*, desgraciado, *m.* | *Odd* o *rum stick*, tipo extraño. || *Stick of furniture*, mueble, *m.* || FIG. *To be in a cleft stick*, estar entre la espada y la pared. || *To give s.o. the stick*, dar a alguien una paliza.
stick* [stik] v. tr. Clavar (to thrust): *to stick a pin into sth.*, clavar un alfiler en algo. || Prender: *stuck with pins*, prendido con alfileres. || Pinchar (to penetrate): *that pin is sticking me*, este alfiler me está pinchando; *to stick a cushion with a pin*, pinchar un cojín con un alfiler. || Fijar, sujetar (with tacks). || Clavar, hincar (a knife, bayonet). || Poner: *she stuck a flower in her hair*, se puso una flor en la cabeza. || Picar (with a stick). || Pegar: *to stick a postage stamp on a letter*, pegar un sello de correos en una carta. || FAM. Colocar, poner: *he stuck knicknacks all over the room*, colocó cositas por toda la habitación. | Colocar, poner, clavar (on a spike). | Meter: *he stuck the letter in his pocket*, metió la carta en el bolsillo. | Timar, estafar: *to stick s.o. (for) five pounds*, timar a alguien cinco libras. | Soportar, aguantar: *I can't stick him*, no le puedo aguantar. | Meter: *don't stick your nose into other people's business*, no meta la nariz en asuntos ajenos. | Cargar: *they have stuck me with all the cooking*, me han cargado toda la cocina. | Desconcertar (a problem). || Degollar (a pig). || Apuñalar (a person).|| — FAM. *I got stuck in geography*, me cogieron en geografía. | *To stick one's hat on one's head*, calarse el sombrero. | *You can stick it!*, ¡aguántate!, ¡te aguantas! (telling s.o. to put up with sth.), ¡te lo puedes quedar! (keep it!).
— V. intr. Clavarse: *the pin stuck in the cushion*, el alfiler se clavó en el cojín. || Estar prendido (pins). || Clavarse, hincarse (a knife, a bayonet). || Pegar: *this glue doesn't stick*, esta goma no pega. || Pegarse (to adhere): *the paper sticks to my fingers*, el papel se me pega a los dedos. || Atascarse, quedarse atascado (to become bogged down): *the car stuck in the mud*, el coche se atascó en el barro. || Atascarse, atrancarse, bloquearse (a machine). || Quedarse parado, pararse, detenerse (to come to a stop): *the car stuck on the hill*, el coche se quedó parado en la colina. || Quedarse, permanecer (to stay). || Pegarse (cooking). || FAM. Pegarse: *he sticks like a leech*, se pega como una sanguijuela *or* como una lapa.
— ***To stick around***, quedarse. || ***To stick at***, tropezar con (a difficulty). | Seguir [con]: *he is sticking at the work he started*, sigue el trabajo que empezó. | Vacilar en (to hesitate at). | — FIG. *He sticks at nothing*, no se para en barras. || ***To stick by***, ser fiel a (a friend). || ***To stick down***, poner (to put down). | Apuntar (to write down). | Pegar (to fasten with paste). || ***To stick on***, pegar (stamp). | Pegarse (a person). | — FAM. *To be stuck on*, estar chalado por. | FIG. *To stick it on*, exagerar. || ***To stick out***, sacar: *to stick out one's tongue*, sacar la lengua. | Asomar (one's head). | Sobresalir: *the eaves are the part of the roof which sticks out*, el alero es la parte del tejado que sobresale. | Aguantar (to endure). | FAM. Obstinarse (to be obstinate). | — *His tongue was sticking out*, estaba con la lengua fuera, tenía la lengua fuera. | FIG. *It sticks out a mile*, se ve a la legua. | *To stick it out*, aguantar hasta el final. | *To stick out for*, obstinarse en pedir. || ***To stick to***, ser fiel a (a friend). | Atenerse a, mantener: *I am sticking to what I said*, me atengo a lo que he dicho, mantengo lo dicho. | Cumplir con (one's duty). | Cumplir (a promise). | Seguir (to continue, to follow). | Ceñirse: *to stick to the truth, to the text*, ceñirse a la verdad, al texto. | — *Stick to it!*, ¡sigue! | *To stick to one's guns*, mantenerse en sus trece. || ***To stick together***, no separarse (persons). | Pegar (to fasten). || ***To stick up***, fijar (posters). | Aguzar (one's ears). | Erizarse (hair, etc.). | Salir, sobresalir (to project). | U. S. FAM. Atracar (to rob). | — *Stick'em up!*, ¡arriba las manos! | *To stick up for*, defender, dar *or* sacar la cara por: *I would have been expelled if my friend had not stuck up for me*, me habrían expulsado si mi amigo no me hubiera defendido. | *To stick up to*, resistir a.
— OBSERV. Pret. & p. p. ***stuck***.
sticker [—ə*] n. Letrero (*m.*) engomado, cartel, *m.*, pegatina, *f.* (poster). || Etiqueta (*f.*) adhesiva (label). || Fijasellos, *m. inv.* (for stamps). || Matarife, *m.*, jifero, *m.* (in a slaughterhouse). || Espina, *f.* (thorn). || FAM. Persona (*f.*) tenaz (tenacious person). | Lapa, *f.*, pelma, *m.* & *f.* (tiresome person). | Pega, *f.* (puzzling question).
stickiness [—inis] n. Pegajosidad, *f.* (viscosity). || Humedad, *f.* (of climate). || Pegajosidad, *f.* (of heat). || Adherencia, *f.*, adhesividad, *f.* (power of adhering). || Dificultad, *f.* (of a problem).
sticking [—iŋ] adj. Engomado, da. || *Sticking plaster*, esparadrapo, *m.*
— N. Adherencia, *f.*, adhesividad, *f.* (stickiness). || TECH. Agarrotamiento, *m.* (of pistons, etc.).
stick-in-the-mud [—inðəmʌd] n. Persona (*f.*) chapada a la antigua.
stickle [—l] v. intr. Ser rigorista.
stickleback [—lbæk] n. Picón, *m.* (fish).
stickler [—lə*] n. Rigorista, *m.* & *f.* || FAM. Rompecabezas, *m. inv.*, problema (*m.*) peliagudo (puzzle). || — FIG. *To be a stickler for*, dar mucha importancia a. | *To be a stickler for etiquette*, ser muy etiquetero.
stickpin [—pin] n. U. S. Alfiler (*m.*) de corbata.
stickup [—ʌp] n. U. S. Robo (*m.*) a mano armada, atraco, *m.*
sticky [—i] adj. Pegajoso, sa (viscous): *my fingers are sticky*, tengo los dedos pegajosos. || Engomado, da (label, envelope, etc.). || Resbaladizo, za (slippery). || Húmedo, da (climate). || Pegajoso, sa; bochornoso, sa (heat): *what a sticky day!*, ¡qué día más pegajoso! || FAM. Quisquilloso, sa (touchy). | Difícil, peliagudo, da (difficult). || *To come to a sticky end*, acabar mal.
stiff [stif] adj. Rígido, da (rigid). || Duro, ra: *stiff cardboard*, cartón duro. || Tieso, sa (corpse). || Almidonado, da; duro, ra (collar, cuffs, etc.). || Empinado, da (slope, stairs). || Espeso, sa (substance, paste, etc.). || MED. Anquilosado, da (joint). | Tieso, sa (leg). | Entumecido, da; embotado, da (numb). | Con agujetas (after exercise). || AGR. Arcilloso, sa (soil). || Duro, ra (hard to move). || TECH. Agarrotado, da (pistons, etc.). || FIG. Estirado, da; envarado, da (not natural). | Ceremonioso, sa; etiquetero, ra; protocolario, ria (excessively formal). | Inflexible (unyielding). | Difícil, duro, ra (difficult): *stiff piece of work*, trabajo difícil. | Reñido, da: *stiff battle*, batalla reñida. | Fuerte (wind). || FAM. Fuerte, cargado, da (drink). | Alto, ta; subido, da (prices). | Firme (market). | Severo, ra (punishment). | Como una cuba, borracho, cha (drunk). || *Stiff with cold*, aterido *or* yerto de frío.
— Adv. *To be scared stiff*, estar muerto de miedo.
— N. FAM. Fiambre, *m.* (corpse). | Vagabundo, *m.* (tramp). || FAM. *Big stiff*, tonto (*m.*) de capirote.
stiffen [—n] v. tr. Poner tieso *or* rígido, atiesar. || Endurecer (to harden). || Espesar, hacer más espeso (substance, sauce, paste). || Poner ballenas a (a bodice). || Almidonar (a collar, cuffs, etc.). || MED. Anquilosar (a joint). | Entumecer, embotar (limbs). | Agarrotar (muscles). || FAM. Cargar (a drink).
— V. intr. Ponerse tieso *or* rígido. || Endurecerse (to harden). || Hacerse más espeso (to become thicker). || MED. Anquilosarse (a joint). | Entumecerse, embotarse (limbs). | Agarrotarse (muscles). || FIG. Volverse más duro. | Ponerse más fuerte (wind).
stiffener [—nə*] n. Contrafuerte, *m.*, refuerzo, *m.* (of boots).
stiffening [—niŋ] n. Almidonado, *m.* (of fabrics). || Almidón, *m.* (starch). || Endurecimiento, *m.* (hardening). || Refuerzo, *m.*: *stiffening plate*, chapa de refuerzo. || Rigidez, *f.* (stiffness).

stiff neck [—'nek] n. Tortícolis, *f.*
stiff-necked [—'nekt] adj. Terco, ca; testarudo, da (stubborn). || FAM. Estirado, da; envarado, da (not natural). | Ceremonioso, sa; etiquetero, ra; protocolario, ria (excessively formal).
stiffness [—nis] n. Rigidez, *f.* || Dureza, *f.* || Espesura, *f.* (of a sauce). || Consistencia, *f.* || MED. Anquilosamiento, *m.* (of a joint). | Embotamiento, *m.* (of limbs). | Agarrotamiento, *m.* (of muscles). || FAM. Fuerza, *f.* (of a drink). || FIG. Dificultad, *f.*, lo difícil (difficulty). | Obstinación, *f.*, testarudez, *f.* (stubbornness). | Envaramiento, *m.* (formality). | Firmeza, *f.* (of market). || *Stiffness of the legs*, agujetas (*f. pl.*) en las piernas (after exercise).
stifle ['staifl] n. ZOOL. Babilla, *f.* (of quadrupeds).
stifle ['staifl] v. tr. Ahogar, sofocar (to prevent from breathing). || Contener (cough, yawn). || Sofocar, reprimir (a revolt). || Amortiguar, sofocar (sound).
— V. intr. Ahogarse, sofocarse.
stifling [—iŋ] adj. Sofocante. || Bochornoso, sa (atmosphere).
stigma ['stigmə] n. Estigma, *m.*
— OBSERV. El plural de *stigma* es *stigmata* o *stigmas*.
stigmata [—tə] pl. n. REL. Estigmas, *m.*
stigmatism ['stigmətizəm] n. PHYS. Estigmatismo, *m.*
stigmatization [ˌstigmətai'zeiʃən] n. Estigmatización, *f.*
stigmatize ['stigmətaiz] v. tr. Estigmatizar.
stile [stail] n. Escalera (*f.*) para pasar por encima de una cerca (to cross a fence). || Montante, *m.* (of a door).
stiletto [sti'letəu] n. Estilete, *m.* (dagger). || Punzón, *m.* (tool). || *Stiletto heels*, tacones (*m.*) de aguja.
— OBSERV. El plural es *stilettos* o *stilettoes*.
still [stil] adj. Tranquilo, la (quiet, calm). || Apacible, sosegado, da (peaceful). || Suave, sordo, da (noise). || Silencioso, sa (silent). || Durmiente, estancado, da (water). || No espumoso (wine). || No gaseoso, sa (other drinks). || Inmóvil (not moving). || — *Keep still!*, ¡estate quieto! || *Keep still about this*, no diga nada de esto. || *The air is still*, no corre aire. || *To stand still*, estarse quieto, no moverse (to stop fidgetting), no moverse (not to move), pararse (to stop).
— Adv. Todavía, aún: *I am still in Paris*, estoy todavía en París; *the green one is still bigger*, el verde es todavía más grande. || — *He is still here*, está todavía aquí, aún está aquí, sigue aquí. || *In spite of his faults she loved him still*, a pesar de sus defectos le seguía queriendo. || *Still more*, más aún.
— Conj. Sin embargo, no obstante, con todo [y con eso] (nervertheless): *still, you did the right thing*, no obstante hizo lo que había que hacer.
— N. Calma, *f.*, quietud, *f.*, tranquilidad, *f.* (calm). || Sosiego, *m.*, tranquilidad, *f.* (peacefulness). || Silencio, *m.* (silence). || Estancamiento, *m.* (of water). || Alambique, *m.* (for distilling). || Destilería, *f.* (distillery). || PHOT. Vista (*f.*) fija, fotografía, *f.*
still [stil] v. tr. Tranquilizar, calmar (to quieten). || Calmar (fears). || Callar, hacer callar (to make silent). || Amortiguar (a noise). || Aplacar (to allay). || CHEM. Destilar.
— V. intr. Calmarse, aplacarse.
stillbirth [—bə:θ] n. Alumbramiento (*m.*) de un mortinato, nacimiento (*m.*) de un niño muerto.
stillborn [—bɔ:n] adj. Mortinato, ta; nacido muerto. || FIG. Malogrado, da.
still life [—laif] n. Bodegón, *m.*, naturaleza (*f.*) muerta.
— OBSERV. El plural de *still life* es *still lives* o *still lifes*.
stillness [—nis] n. Calma, *f.*, quietud, *f.*, tranquilidad, *f.* (peacefulness). || Silencio, *m.*, quietud, *f.* (silence).
stillson wrench [—sənrentʃ] n. U. S. Llave (*f.*) de tubos.
stilly [—i] adj. Tranquilo, la; silencioso, sa; quieto, ta.
— Adv. Tranquilamente.
stilt [stilt] n. Zanco, *m.* (for walking). || Zampa, *f.*, pilote, *m.* (for buildings). || AGR. Esteva, *f.* (plough handle). || *Stilt walker*, zancuda, *f.* (bird).
stilted [—id] adj. Construido sobre pilotes (building). || Peraltado, da (arch, road). || FIG. Envarado, da (person). | Pomposo, sa; afectado, da (style).
stimulant ['stimjulənt] n. MED. Estimulante, *m.* || FIG. Bebida (*f.*) alcohólica.
stimulate ['stimjuleit] v. tr. MED. Estimular. || FIG. Estimular, animar, incitar.
— V. intr. Actuar como estimulante. || FIG. Servir de estímulo.
stimulating [—iŋ] adj. Estimulante. || Interesante (interesting). || Alentador, ra (encouraging).
stimulation [ˌstimju'leiʃən] n. Estímulo, *m.*
stimulative ['stimjulətiv] adj. Estimulante.
— N. Estimulante, *m.*
stimulus ['stimjuləs] n. Estímulo, *m.*, incentivo, *m.*: *his words were a stimulus for me*, sus palabras fueron un estímulo para mí. || Estímulo, *m.* (to activate the functioning of an organ, etc.).
— OBSERV. El plural de *stimulus* es *stimuli*.
stimy ['staimi] v. tr. Obstruir [el hoyo] con una bola (in golf). || FIG. Obstaculizar (to hinder). || FAM. *To be stimied*, estar fastidiado.
sting [stiŋ] n. ZOOL. Aguijón, *m.* (of bee, wasp, etc.). | Colmillo, *m.* (of a snake). || Picadura, *f.* (wound). || Escozor, *m.* (pain). || BOT. Pelo (*m.*) urticante. || FIG. Punzada, *f.*: *the sting of remorse*, la punzada del remordimiento. | Mordacidad, *f.* (of an attack, a remark). | Herida, *f.*: *the sting of an insult*, la herida provocada por un insulto. | Veneno, *m.*: *the sting of his words*, el veneno de sus palabras. || FIG. *To give a sting to*, hacer mordaz.
sting* [stiŋ] v. tr. Picar: *the wasp stung me*, me picó la avispa. || Escocer, picar (a blow, etc.). || FIG. Herir, picar en lo vivo: *stung by an insult*, herido por un insulto. || FAM. Clavar (to overcharge). || — FIG. *His conscience will sting him*, le remorderá la conciencia. | *To sting s.o. to do sth.*, incitar a alguien a que haga algo.
— V. intr. Picar (bees, wasps, etc.). || Escocer, picar: *my wound stings*, me escuece la herida.
— OBSERV. Pret. & p. p. **stung**.
stinger [—ə*] n. U. S. Aguijón, *m.* (of bees, wasps). || U. S. FAM. Pulla, *f.* (painful remark). | Cóctel (*m.*) de coñac y licor. | Bofetada, *f.* (blow).
stingfish [—fiʃ] n. Peje (*m.*) araña.
stingily ['stindʒili] adv. Tacañamente, mezquinamente.
stinginess ['stindʒinis] n. Tacañería, *f.*, mezquindad, *f.*, roñosería, *f.* (avarice).
stinging hair ['stiŋiŋhεə*] n. Pelo (*m.*) urticante.
stingless ['stiŋlis] adj. Sin aguijón.
stingray ['stiŋrei] n. Pastinaca, *f.* (fish).
stingy ['stindʒi] adj. FAM. Tacaño, ña; mezquino, na; roñoso, sa (avaricious). | Escaso, sa; parco, ca (meagre).
stink [stiŋk] n. Peste, *f.*, hedor, *m.* (unpleasant smell). || FAM. *To cause* o *to kick up* o *to raise a stink*, armar un escándalo, organizar un follón.
stink* [stiŋk] v. intr. Apestar, oler mal, heder. || FIG. Oler: *it stinks of corruption*, huele a corrupción. || FAM. Estar fatal: *his performance stank*, su actuación estuvo fatal. || FAM. *He stinks of money*, tiene tanto dinero que da asco.
— V. tr. *To stink out*, hacer salir *or* ahuyentar por el mal olor. || U. S. *To stink up*, dar mal olor a.
— OBSERV. Pret. **stank**, **stunk**; p. p. **stunk**.
stink bomb [—bɔm] n. Bomba (*f.*) fétida.
stinkbug [—bʌg] n. U. S. ZOOL. Chinche (*f.*) hedionda.
stinker [—ə*] n. FAM. Mala persona, *f.*, mal bicho, *m.* (person). | Problema (*m.*) peliagudo (problem). | Examen (*m.*) difícil (examination). || Cosa (*f.*) *or* persona (*f.*) maloliente.
stinking [—iŋ] adj. Hediondo, da; apestoso, sa; fétido, da; pestilente (smelly). || FAM. Asqueroso, sa (disgusting). || BOT. *Stinking iris*, lirio hediondo.
— Adv. FAM. Muy, enormemente, terriblemente. || FAM. *He is stinking rich*, tiene tanto dinero que da asco.
stint [stint] n. Limitación, *f.*, restricción, *f.*, límite, *m.* (limit). || Tarea, *f.*, trabajo, *m.* (work).
stint [stint] v. tr. Escatimar (expenses, efforts, etc.). || Limitar, restringir (to limit). || Privar: *to stint s.o. of sth.*, privar a uno de algo. || *To stint o.s.*, privarse.
stipe [staip] n. Estípite, *m.*
stipend ['staipənd] n. Estipendio, *m.*, remuneración, *f.* salario, *m.*
stipendiary [stai'pendjəri] adj. Remunerado, da; asalariado, da.
— N. Asalariado, da.
stipple ['stipl] n. Punteado, *m.*
stipple ['stipl] v. tr. Puntear.
stipulate ['stipjuleit] v. tr. Estipular.
— V. intr. *To stipulate for*, estipular.
stipulation [ˌstipju'leiʃən] n. Estipulación, *f.*, condición, *f.* || JUR. Cláusula, *f.*, estipulación, *f.*
stir [stə:*] n. Movimiento, *m.*: *he gave a stir*, hizo un movimiento. || FIG. Agitación, *f.* (disturbance). | Murmullo, *m.*: *there was a stir among the audience*, hubo un murmullo entre el público. | Emoción, *f.*, conmoción, *f.* (commotion). | Sensación, *f.*, gran impresión, *f.* | Escándalo, *m.*, revuelo, *m.*: *he raised quite a stir with his new novel*, provocó un escándalo con su nueva novela. || FAM. Chirona, *f.*, cárcel, *f.* (jail). || *Give the tea a stir*, mueve *or* remueve el té.
stir [stə:*] v. tr. Mover, remover, revolver: *to stir tea*, mover el té. || Mezclar: *to stir water into paint*, mezclar agua con pintura. || Mover, agitar: *the wind stirred the leaves*, el viento movía las hojas. || Agitar: *stir before using*, agítese antes de usarse. || FIG. Incitar, animar: *he stirred me into doing my chores*, me incitó a hacer mis quehaceres. | Conmover (to touch). | Provocar (s.o.'s anger). | Excitar: *to stir the imagination*, excitar la imaginación. || Atizar, avivar (the fire). || — FIG. *To stir o.s.*, hacer un esfuerzo. || *To stir s.o. to pity*, dar lástima a alguien. || *To stir up*, mover (a liquid), provocar, armar: *to stir up trouble*, provocar un escándalo; excitar (passions), fomentar (discord, revolt), despertar (curiosity), levantar (courage), atizar, avivar (hatred), aguijonear, espolear (s.o.), remover (the past), atizar, avivar (the fire).
— V. intr. Moverse: *nobody stirred*, nadie se movía; *to stir in one's sleep*, moverse durmiendo. || Levantarse (to get up).
stirabout [—ə'baut] n. Gachas, *f. pl.* (of oatmeal). || FAM. Revuelo, *m.*

stirless [—lis] adj. Inmóvil.
stirps [—ps] n. JUR. Estirpe, *f* || Raza, *f.* (of animals).

— OBSERV. El plural de *stirps* es *stirpes*.

stirrer [—ə*] n. CHEM. Agitador, *m.* || FIG. Fomentador, ra; promotor, ra (of trouble).
stirring [—iŋ] adj. Bullicioso, sa; revoltoso, sa (child). || FIG. Agitado, da; movido, da (life). | Sensacional (event). | Conmovedor, ra (speech, etc.). | Que anima, animado, da (music).
stirrup [ˈstirʌp] n. Estribo, *m.* || TECH. Trepador, *m.* || — *Stirrup bone*, estribo, *m.* (in the ear). || FAM. *Stirrup cup*, espuela, *f.* (drink). || *Stirrup leather*, ación, *m.* || *Stirrup pump*, bomba (*f.*) de mano (for water).
stitch [stitʃ] n. Puntada, *f.* (in sewing). || Punto, *m.* (in knitting). || Punto, *m.* (style in sewing, embroidering, etc.): *chain stitch*, punto de cadeneta. || MED. Punto (*m.*) de sutura. || Dolor (*m.*) de costado, punzada (*f.*) en el costado (pain in the side). || — FAM. *He has not done a stitch of work all day*, no ha dado puntada en todo el día. | *Not to have a dry stitch on*, estar empapado. | *Not to have a stitch on*, estar en cueros. | *To be in stitches*, desternillarse de risa.
stitch [stitʃ] v. tr. Coser. || MED. Suturar. || Encuadernar en rústica (books). || *To stitch up*, volver a coser, remendar.
— V. intr. Coser.
stiver [ˈstaivə*] n. FAM. Ochavo, *m.*
stoa [ˈstəuə] n. ARCH. Pórtico, *m.*

— OBSERV. El plural de *stoa* es *stoae* o *stoas*.

stoat [stəut] n. Armiño, *m.* (animal).
stock [stɔk] n. COMM. Existencias, *f. pl.*, reservas, *f. pl.*, "stock", *m.* (of tradesmen and manufacturers). | Surtido, *m.*: *have you a good stock of men's wear?*, ¿tiene un buen surtido de ropa de caballero? | Reserva, *f.*, depósito, *m.* (of money). | Capital (*m.*) social (of a company). | Acciones, *f. pl.*, títulos, *m. pl.*, valores, *m. pl.* (in stock exchange): *I advise you not to buy those stocks*, le aconsejo que no adquiera esas acciones. || Caudal, *m.* (of knowledge). || Linaje, *m.*, familia, *f.*, estirpe, *f.*, cepa, *f.*: *he is of very ancient stock*, es de una familia muy antigua. || Familia, *f.* (family of animals, plants etc.). || Raza, *f.* (race): *are these animals of healthy stock?*, ¿son estos animales de buena raza? || AGR. Ganado, *m.* (livestock). | Alhelí, *m.* (flower). | Tronco, *m.* (trunk). | Cepa, *f.*, tocón, *m.* (tree stump). | Cepa, *f.* (of vine). | Patrón, *m.* (in grafting). || TECH. Materia (*f.*) prima (raw material). | Cepo, *m.* (of an anvil, an anchor). | Cabezal, *m.* (of a lathe). | Caja, *f.* (of smoothing plane). | Mango, *m.* (of a tool, whip). | Esteva, *f.*, mancera, *f.* (of plough). | Caja, *f.*, culata, *f.* (of gun). | Material (*m.*) rodante *or* móvil (railways). || CULIN. Extracto, *m.* (of meat, etc.). | Caldo, *m.* (of vegetables). || Pechera (*f.*) negra (worn over the chest by clergymen). || THEATR. Repertorio, *m.* (of plays). || — Pl. Picota, *f. sing.*, cepo, *m. sing.* (punishment). || MAR. Grada (*f. sing.*) de construcción, astillero, *m. sing.* || — *Government stock*, papel (*m.*) del Estado. || *In stock*, en existencia, en almacén, en reserva, en depósito. || *Joint stock*, capital (*m.*) social. || *Joint-stock company*, sociedad anónima. || MAR. *Off the stocks*, botado. || *On the stocks*, en los astilleros, en construcción (a boat), en el telar, en preparación: *he has two novels on the stocks*, tiene dos novelas en el telar. || *Out of stock*, agotado, da. || *Stock in hand*, existencias disponibles. || *Surplus stock*, excedentes, *m. pl.* || *To have sth. in stock*, tener existencias de algo. || *To lay in a stock of*, abastecerse de. || FIG. *To put* o *to take stock in*, hacer poco caso de. || *To take stock*, hacer el inventario. || FIG. *To take stock of*, examinar (to consider), evaluar (to appraise).
— Adj. En existencia: *stock goods*, mercancías en existencia. || De las existencias: *stock clerk*, encargado de las existencias. || Corriente, normal, de serie (size). || Clásico, ca: *stock argument*, argumento clásico. || Acuñado, da; estereotipado, da: *stock phrase*, expresión acuñada. || THEATR. Del repertorio. || AGR. Reproductor, ra (animal). | Ganadero, ra (farm).
stock [stɔk] v. tr. Surtir, abastecer (to provide): *he stocked his shop with tinned foods*, abasteció su tienda con conservas. || Tener existencias de, tener en el almacén (to have in stock). || Almacenar (to store). || Tener (to have): *he does not stock that kind of food*, no tiene esa clase de alimentos. || Poblar (with fishes, trees). || AGR. Ensilar, entrojar (a crop). || MAR. Encepar (an anchor). || Poner mango a (a whip). || Poner culata a (a gun). || FIG. Enriquecer (one's memory).
— V. intr. Brotar (plants). || *To stock up with* o *on*, abastecerse de.
stockade [stɔˈkeid] n. Estacada, *f.*, empalizada, *f.*, vallado, *m.*
stockade [stɔˈkeid] v. tr. Empalizar, poner una estacada, vallar.
stock book [ˈstɔkbuk] n. Libro (*m.*) de almacén.
stockbreeder [ˈstɔk,bri:də*] n. Ganadero, ra.
stockbreeding [ˈstɔk,bri:diŋ] n. Ganadería, *f.*, cría (*f.*) del ganado.
stockbroker [ˈstɔk,brəukə*] n. Corredor (*m.*) de Bolsa, agente (*m.*) de Bolsa.
stockbrokerage [—ridʒ] or **stockbroking** [ˈstɔk,brəukiŋ] n. Correduría (*f.*) de Bolsa, corretaje (*m.*) de Bolsa.
stockcar [ˈstɔkkɑ:*] n. U. S. Vagón (*m.*) para el ganado.
stock car [ˈstɔkkɑ:*] n. "Stock-car", *m.*, automóvil (*m.*) que participa en carreras donde se permiten choques y obstrucciones.
stock company [ˈstɔk,kʌmpəni] n. COMM. Sociedad (*f.*) anónima. || THEATR. Compañía (*f.*) de repertorio.
stock exchange [ˈstɔkiks,tʃeindʒ] n. COMM. Bolsa, *f.*
stock farm [ˈstɔkfɑ:m] n. Ganadería, *f.*
stock farmer [—ə*] n. Ganadero, *m.*
stock farming [—iŋ] n. Ganadería, *f.*
stockfish [ˈstɔkfiʃ] n. Estocafís, *m. inv.*, pejepalo, *m.*
stockholder [ˈstɔk,həuldə*] n. Accionista, *m.* & *f.*
Stockholm [ˈstɔkhəum] pr. n. GEOGR. Estocolmo.
stockiness [ˈstɔkinis] n. Robustez, *f.*
stockinet or **stockinette** [,stɔkiˈnet] n. Tejido (*m.*) elástico de punto.
stocking [ˈstɔkiŋ] n. Media, *f.* (for ladies). || Calcetín, *m.* (sock). || — *Horse with white stockings*, caballo calzado de blanco. || *In one's stocking feet*, con medias *or* calcetines pero sin zapatos, descalzo, za.
stock-in-trade [ˈstɔkinˈtreid] n. Existencias, *f. pl.* || TECH. Herramientas, *f. pl.*, instrumentos, *m. pl.*, útiles, *m. pl.* || FIG. Repertorio, *m.*
stockist [ˈstɔkist] n. Distribuidor, *m.*, depositario, *m.*
stockjobber [ˈstɔk,dʒɔbə*] n. Agiotista, *m.*
stockjobbing [ˈstɔk,dʒɔbiŋ] n. Agiotaje, *m.*
stock list [ˈstɔklist] n. Cotizaciones (*f. pl.*) de la Bolsa.
stockman [ˈstɔkmən] n. Ganadero, *m.* (of a stock farm). || Almacenero, *m.* (of a stockroom).

— OBSERV. El plural de *stockman* es *stockmen*.

stock market [ˈstɔk,mɑ:kit] n. COMM. Bolsa (*f.*) *or* mercado (*m.*) de valores.
stockpile [ˈstɔkpail] n. Reservas, *f. pl.*
stockpile [ˈstɔkpail] v. tr. Almacenar, acumular.
— V. intr. Almacenarse ,acumularse.
stockpot [ˈstɔkpɔt] n. Olla, *f.*, marmita, *f.*
stock raiser [ˈstɔk,reizə*] n. Ganadero, ra.
stock raising [ˈstɔk,reiziŋ] n. Ganadería, *f.*, cría (*f.*) del ganado.
stockroom [ˈstɔkrum] n. Almacén, *m.*, depósito, *m.*
stock-still [ˈstɔkˈstil] adj. Completamente inmóvil.
stocktaking [ˈstɔk,teikiŋ] n. Inventario, *m.*, balance, *m.* || *Stocktaking sale*, venta (*f.*) postbalance.
stocky [ˈstɔki] adj. Rechoncho, cha; achaparrado, da (chubby). || Robusto, ta (heavily built). || BOT. Achaparrado, da.
stockyard [ˈstɔkjɑ:d] n. Corral (*m.*) de ganado.
stodge [stɔdʒ] n. FAM. Comida (*f.*) indigesta.
stodge [stɔdʒ] v. tr. FAM. Atiborrar (with food). | Abarrotar (with facts). || FAM. *To stodge o.s.*, atiborrarse, hartarse.
stodgy [—i] adj. FAM. Indigesto, ta; pesado, da (food). | Abarrotado, da (crammed full). | Pesado, da (dull). | Rechoncho, cha (stocky).
stogie or **stogy** [ˈstəugi] n. U. S. Puro (*m.*) largo y barato.
stoic [ˈstəuik] adj./n. Estoico, ca: *the Stoic doctrine*, la doctrina estoica; *stoic in the face of misfortune*, estoico ante la desgracia.
stoical [—əl] adj. Estoico, ca.
stoicalness [—əlnis] n. Estoicismo, *m.*
stoicism [ˈstəuisizəm] n. PHIL. Estoicismo, *m.* || FIG. Estoicismo, *m.*
stoke [stəuk] v. tr. Alimentar (fire, boiler).
— V. intr. FAM. *To stoke up*, atiborrarse (to eat).
stokehold [—həuld] n. MAR. Sala (*f.*) de máquinas, sala (*f.*) de fogoneros, cuarto (*m.*) de calderas.
stokehole [—həul] n. Boca (*f.*) del horno (mouth of furnace). || MAR. Sala (*f.*) de máquinas, sala (*f.*) de fogoneros, cuarto (*m.*) de calderas.
stoker [—ə*] n. Fogonero, *m.* (person). || TECH. Cargador (*m.*) mecánico (machine).
stole [stəul] n. Estola, *f.*
stole [stəul] pret. See STEAL.
stolen [—ən] p. p. See STEAL.
stolid [ˈstɔlid] adj. Impasible, imperturbable.
stolidity [stɔˈliditi] or **stolidness** [ˈstɔlidnis] n. Impasibilidad, *f.*, imperturbabilidad, *f.*
stolon [ˈstəulən] n. Estolón, *m.*, latiguillo, *m.*
stoma [ˈstəumə] n. BOT. ANAT. Estoma, *m.*

— OBSERV. El plural de *stoma* es *stomata* o *stomas*.

stomach [ˈstʌmək] n. ANAT. Estómago, *m.* || FAM. Vientre, *m.*, barriga, *f.* (belly). || FIG. Afición, *f.* (inclination): *I have no stomach for politics*, no tengo ninguna afición a la política. | Ganas, *f. pl.*, deseo, *m.* (desire). | Valor, *m.*, estómago, *m.* (courage). || — *On an empty stomach*, con el estómago vacío. || *Pit of the stomach*, boca (*f.*) del estómago. || || FIG. *That turns my stomach*, eso me revuelve el estómago. | *To have a cast-iron stomach*, tener un estómago de piedra. || *To have an empty stomach*, tener el estómago vacío. || FIG. *To put some stomach into s.o.*, infundir ánimo a alguien.
stomach [ˈstʌmək] v. tr. FIG. Soportar, aguantar, tragar (to bear).
stomachache [—eik] n. Dolor (*m.*) de estómago.
stomacher [ˈstʌməkə*] n. Peto, *m.* (ornamental garment).

stomachic [stə'mækik] adj. Estomacal.
— N. MED. Estomacal, *m.*, digestivo, *m.*
stomach pump ['stʌmək·pʌmp] n. MED. Bomba (*f.*) gástrica.
stomach tooth ['stʌmək·tu:θ] n. FAM. Colmillo, *m.*, canino, *m.*
stomach upset ['stʌməkʌp'set] n. Trastorno (*m.*) gástrico.
stomata ['stəumətə] pl. n. See STOMA.
stomatitis [stɔmə'taitis] n. MED. Estomatitis, *f.*
stomatologist [stɔmə'tɔlədʒist] n. MED. Estomatólogo, ga.
stomatology [stɔmə'tɔlədʒi] n. MED. Estomatología, *f.*
stone [stəun] n. Piedra, *f.* (rock, piece of rock): *to throw a stone*, tirar una piedra; *precious stone*, piedra preciosa. || Lápida, *f.* (on graves). || MED. Cálculo, *m.*, piedra, *f.* (disease). || Piedra, *f.*, muela, *f.* (of a mill). || Granizo, *m.* (hailstone). || BOT. Hueso, *m.* (of fruit). || PRINT. ARTS. Piedra, *f.* || Peso (*m.*) que equivale a 6 kilos 350 gramos (weight). || — *Meteoric stone*, piedra meteórica. || FIG. *Not to leave a stone standing*, no dejar piedra sobre piedra. || *Philosopher's stone*, piedra filosofal. || *Pumice stone*, piedra pómez. || *Semiprecious stone*, piedra fina. || FIG. *To cast the first stone*, tirar la primera piedra. || *To lay the foundation stone*, poner la primera piedra. || FIG. *To leave no stone unturned*, no dejar piedra por mover, revolver Roma con Santiago. | *To melt a heart of stone*, ablandar las piedras. | *To throw stones at s.o.*, tirar piedras contra uno. | *Within a stone's throw*, muy cerca, a tiro de piedra.
— Adj. De piedra.
— OBSERV. Cuando tiene el sentido de peso, la palabra *stone* es invariable.
stone [stəun] v. tr. Apedrear, lapidar (to throw stones at). || Quitar el hueso, deshuesar (a fruit). || Empedrar, pavimentar (to face with stone). || FAM. Emborrachar (to make drunk). | Drogar (to drug). || — FAM. *To get stoned*, coger una trompa. || *To stone s.o. to death*, matar a alguien a pedradas.
Stone Age [—eidʒ] n. Edad (*f.*) de Piedra.
stone-blind [—'blaind] adj. Completamente ciego.
stone-broke [—'brəuk] adj. FAM. Sin blanca, sin un centavo (without money).
stone coal [—kəul] n. Carbón (*m.*) de piedra, antracita, *f.*
stone-cold [—'kəuld] adj. FAM. Helado, da: *the soup is stone-cold*, la sopa está helada; *I am stone-cold*, estoy helado.
stonecrop [—krɔp] n. BOT. Uva (*f.*) de gato.
stone crusher [—·krʌʃə*] n. Trituradora, *f.*, machacadora, *f.*
stone curlew [—'kə:lju:] n. ZOOL. Alcaraván, *m.* (bird).
stonecutter [—·kʌtə*] n. Cantero, *m.*, picapedrero, *m.*
stone-dead [—'ded] adj. FAM. Tieso, sa.
stone-deaf [—'def] adj. FAM. Sordo como una tapia.
stone fruit [—fru:t] n. BOT. Drupa, *f.*, fruta (*m.*) con hueso.
stone marten [—·mɑ:tin] n. ZOOL. Garduña, *f.*
stonemason [—·meisn] n. Albañil, *m.* (bricklayer). || Cantero, *m.*, picapedrero, *m.* (in quarry).
stone pit [—pit] or **stone quarry** [—·kwɔri] n. Cantera (*f.*) de piedras.
stoner [—ə*] n. Apedreador, ra (stone thrower). || Deshuesadora, *f.* (for fruit).
stonewall [—'wɔ:l] v. intr. SP. Jugar a la defensiva. || FIG. Practicar el obstruccionismo (in Parliament).
stoneware [—wɛə*] n. Gres, *m.*: *stoneware pot*, vasija de gres. || Objetos (*m. pl.*) de barro.
stonework [—wə:k] n. ARCH. Construcción (*f.*) de piedra (stone construction). | Cantería, *f.*, sillería, *f.* (masonry).
stonily [—ili] n. FIG. Glacialmente, fríamente.
stoniness [—inis] n. FIG. Frialdad, *f.*
stony [—i] adj. Pedregoso, sa (with many stones). || Pétreo, a (like stone). || FIG. De piedra, pétreo, a: *a stony heart*, un corazón de piedra. | Frío, a; glacial: *a stony look*, una mirada fría. | Sepulcral: *a stony silence*, un silencio sepulcral.
stony-broke ['stəuni'brəuk] adj. FAM. Sin blanca, sin un centavo (without money).
stonyhearted ['stəuni'hɑ:tid] adj. Con el corazón de piedra, insensible.
stood [stud] pret. & p. p. See STAND.
stooge [stu:dʒ] n. THEATR. Comparsa, *m.* || Secuaz, *m.* (underling). || Soplón, ona; chivato, ta (informer).
stook [stuk] n. Hacina, *f.*, fajina, *f.*
stook [stuk] v. tr. Hacinar.
stool [stu:l] n. Taburete, *m.*, banquillo, *m.* (seat without back or arms). || Silla (*f.*) de tijera (folding). || Escabel, *m.* (footstool). || BOT. Planta (*f.*) madre. || Alféizar, *m.* (of window). || Reclamo, *m.* (decoy bird). || Chivato, ta; soplón, ona (informer). || Deposiciones, *f. pl.*, deyecciones, *f. pl.* (faeces). || *Folding stool*, silla (*f.*) de tijera.
stool [stu:l] v. intr. Echar retoños (plants). || Defecar.
stool pigeon [—·pidʒin] n. Reclamo, *m.* (decoy bird). || FAM. Chivato, ta; soplón, ona (informer).
stoop [stu:p] n. Inclinación (*f.*) de hombros, espaldas (*f. pl.*) encorvadas (posture). || U. S. Pórtico, *m.* (porch). || See STOUP. || — *To have a stoop*, ser cargado de espaldas. || *To walk with a stoop*, andar encorvado.
stoop [stu:p] v. tr. Inclinar, agachar (one's head). || Encorvar (one's back).
— V. intr. Encorvarse, agacharse, inclinarse (to bend forwards). || Ser cargado de espaldas (habitually). || FIG. Rebajarse: *to stoop to cheating*, rebajarse a hacer trampas.
stooping [—iŋ] adj. Encorvado, da; cargado de espaldas. || Inclinado, da.
stop [stɔp] n. Parada, *f.* (act, halt): *it made a stop*, hizo una parada; *five-minute stop*, parada de cinco minutos. || Parada, *f.* (place where buses, etc. stop): *request stop*, parada discrecional. || Escala, *f.* (of a ship, plane). || Estancia, *f.* (stay). || Pausa, *f.* (pause). || Detención, *f.* (holdup). || Interrupción, *f.* (interruption). || Cesación, *f.* (cessation). || Suspensión, *f.* (suspension). || Tapón, *m.* (stopper of bottle, etc.). || TECH. Tope, *m.* (of a mechanism). || Marginador, *m.* (of typewriter). || PHOT. Diafragma, *m.* || MAR. Boza, *f.* || MUS. Llave, *f.* (of clarinet, saxophone). | Agujero, *m.* (of flute, wind instruments). | Traste, *m.* (of guitar). | Registro, *m.* (of organ). || FAM. Fin, *m.*, término, *m.* (end): *to put a stop to sth.*, poner fin a algo. || Punto, *m.*, "stop", *m.* (in telegrams). || "Stop", *m.*, señal (*f.*) de parada (on road). || GRAMM. Punto, *m.* (full stop). | Oclusión, *f.* (in phonetics). || — *Full stop*, punto, *m.* || *To be at a stop*, estar parado. || *To come to a stop*, pararse. || *To come to a sudden stop*, pararse en seco. || FIG. FAM. *To pull out all the stops*, tocar todos los registros. || MUS. *To pull out a stop*, sacar un registro.
stop [stɔp] v. tr. Parar, detener: *he stopped his car near the house*, paró su coche junto a la casa; *stop the bus*, pare el autobús. || Interrumpir: *she stopped him in the middle of the speech*, le interrumpió en medio del discurso; *the rain stopped the match*, la lluvia interrumpió el partido. || Dejar de: *to stop crying*, dejar de llorar. || Impedir: *he will not stop me from going*, no me impedirá ir. || Evitar, parar (a danger). || Tapar, taponar (a hole). || Rellenar (a gap). || Obturar, obstruir (a pipe). || Empastar (a tooth). || Restañar, detener (the flow of blood). || Interceptar, cortar, cerrar (a road). || Tapar: *to stop s.o.'s ears*, tapar los oídos a alguien; *I stopped my ears*, me tapé los oídos. || Cortar, interrumpir: *to stop supplies*, cortar el suministro. || Cortar (electricity, gas, water). || Parar, paralizar (production). || Suprimir (s.o.'s holidays). || Suspender: *they stopped my pay*, me suspendieron el sueldo. || Deducir de, descontar de, retener de (to deduct). || Anular, cancelar (a cheque). || Oponerse a (payment of a cheque). || FAM. Parar: *to stop a blow*, parar un golpe. || Rechazar, contener (an attack). || Poner fin *or* término a, acabar con: *I am going to stop his nonsense*, voy a poner fin a sus tonterías. || GRAMM. Puntuar. || MUS. Tapar los agujeros de (a flute). | Pisar (a string). || — FAM. *He stopped a bullet*, recibió un balazo. || *Stop it!*, ¡basta!, ¡ya está bien! || *Stop thief!*, ¡al ladrón!, ¡ladrones! || *What's stopping you?*, ¿qué te impide continuar?, ¿qué te detiene?
— V. intr. Pararse, detenerse (to come to a halt, to cease to operate): *we stopped at the end of the road*, nos paramos al final de la calle; *my watch has stopped*, se ha parado mi reloj. || Parar, pararse (to cease to do sth.): *he was crying and then he stopped*, estaba llorando y entonces se paró; *the rain has stopped*, ha parado la lluvia. || Parar, pararse (buses, trains, etc.): *the bus stops near my house*, el autobús para cerca de mi casa. || Cesar: *the noise stopped*, el ruido cesó. || Terminarse, acabarse (to finish). || Cortarse (electricity, gas, water). || Suspenderse (to be suspended). || Alojarse, vivir, parar: *I stop at my parents' place*, vivo en casa de mis padres. || Quedarse (to stay). || — *To stop at nothing*, no pararse en barras. || *To stop dead* o *short*, pararse en seco. || *To stop to think*, pararse a pensar, reflexionar. || *Without stopping*, sin parar, sin cesar, sin interrupción.
— ***To stop away***, no venir (not to come). | Ausentarse (to go away). || ***To stop behind***, rezagarse, quedarse atrás (to lag behind). | Quedarse (to stay). || ***To stop by***, pasar, hacer una visita corta (to visit). | Pasar por. || ***To stop down***, diafragmar (a lens). || ***To stop in***, quedarse en casa, no salir (to stay at home). | Quedarse en el colegio, no salir (after school). || ***To stop off***, pararse (during a journey). | Detenerse un rato: *let's stop off at the bar*, detengámonos un rato en el bar. || ***To stop out***, tapar una parte de (a surface to be printed). | Quedarse fuera (to stay out). || ***To stop over***, pasar la noche (to spend the night). | Quedarse: *stop over at my place for a few days*, quédese unos días en casa. || ***To stop up***, taponar, obturar, obstruir (a leak). | Tapar (a hole). | Velar, no acostarse (to stay awake). || ***To stop with***, vivir *or* alojarse *or* quedarse en casa de.
stopcock [—kɔk] n. Llave (*f.*) de paso.
stope [stəup] n. MIN. Bancada, *f.*
stopgap ['stɔpgæp] n. Sustituto, ta (person). || Recurso, *m.* (thing).
stoplight ['stɔplait] n. AUT. Luz (*f.*) de frenado. || U. S. Disco (*m.*) rojo, semáforo (*m.*) rojo (of traffic lights).
stopover ['stɔp·əuvə*] n. Parada, *f.* [temporal] (during a journey). || Escala, *f.* (of plane, ship).
stoppage ['stɔpidʒ] n. Parada, *f.* (stop). || Paro, *m.* (industrial). || Huelga, *f.* (strike). || MED. Oclusión, *f.*

|| Suspensión, *f.* (of payments). || Detención, *f.*: *stoppage of play*, detención de juego. || Cesación, *f.* (ceasing). || Interrupción, *f.* || Deducción, *f.*, retención *f.* (of wages). || Obstrucción, *f.*, taponamiento, *m.* (blockage).

stopper [ˈstɔpə*] n. Tapón, *m.* (of bottle, etc.). || TECH. Tope, *m.* (in mechanics). | Obturador, *m.* (of pipe). || MAR. Boza, *f.* || FAM. Coto, *m.*, término, *m.*, tope, *m.*: *to put a stopper on*, poner tope a.

stopper [ˈstɔpə*] v. tr. Taponar, tapar.

stopping [ˈstɔpiŋ] n. See STOP.

stop press [ˈstɔpˈpres] n. Noticias (*f. pl.*) de última hora.

stop-press [ˈstɔpˈpres] adj. De última hora: *stop-press news*, noticias de última hora.

stop sign [ˈstɔpsain] or **stop signal** [ˈstɔpˌsignl] n. Stop, *m.*

stop valve [ˈstɔpvælv] n. TECH. Válvula (*f.*) de retención.

stopwatch [ˈstɔpwɔtʃ] n. Cronómetro, *m.*

storage [ˈstɔ:ridʒ] n. Almacenamiento, *m.*, almacenaje, *m.* (action). || Almacenaje, *m.* (cost). || Almacén, *m.*, depósito, *m.* (place). || Guardamuebles, *m. inv.* (for furniture). || ELECTR. Acumulación, *f.*

storage battery [—ˌbætəri] n. ELECTR. Acumulador, *m.*, batería, *f.*

storage cell [—sel] n. ELECTR. Acumulador, *m.*

storax [ˈstɔ:ræks] n. BOT. Estoraque, *m.*

store [stɔ:*] n. Provisión, *f.* (supply). || Almacén, *m.*, depósito, *m.* (warehouse). || Almacén, *m.* (large shop). || Tienda, *f.* (any shop). || FIG. Reserva, *f.*: *I had sth. in store*, tenía algo en reserva. || — Pl. Provisiones, *f.* (supplies, provisions). || Pertrechos, *m.* (equipment). || — *Department store*, gran almacén. || FIG. *He has a large store of knowledge about history*, tiene grandes conocimientos de historia. || *In store*, en almacén, en depósito. || *Store guide*, indicador, *m.* || FIG. *There was a surprise in store for him*, le esperaba una gran sorpresa. | *To hold in store for*, reservar *or* guardar para. | *To set great store by*, valorar en mucho, estimar enormemente. | *To set little store by*, valorar *or* estimar en poco.

— Adj. De confección (clothes). || Que viene de los grandes almacenes (furniture).

store [stɔ:*] v. tr. Almacenar (to put into storage). || Guardar (to keep). || Abastecer, suministrar (to supply). || AGR. Ensilar (crop). || Archivar (documents). || — *To store away*, guardar, tener en reserva. || *To store up*, almacenar, acumular.

— V. intr. Conservarse: *eggs do not store well*, los huevos no se conservan bien.

storehouse [—haus] n. Almacén, *m.*, depósito, *m.* || FIG. Mina, *f.* (of information).

storekeeper [—ˌki:pə*] n. Almacenero, *m.* (of a warehouse). || U. S. Tendero, *m.* (shopkeeper). || MAR. Pañolero, *m.*

storeroom [—rum] n. Despensa, *f.* || MAR. Pañol, *m.* || AVIAT. Bodega, *f.*

storey [ˈstɔ:ri] n. See STORY (2nd art.).

storeyed [ˈstɔ:rid] or **storied** [ˈstɔrid] adj. *A five-storied building*, un edificio de cinco pisos.

storied [ˈstɔ:rid] adj. Celebrado por la historia. || Historiado, da (decorated).

stork [stɔ:k] n. Cigüeña, *f.* (bird).

storm [stɔ:m] n. Tormenta, *f.* (thunderstorm). || Tempestad, *f.*, temporal, *m.* (at sea). || Borrasca, *f.* (of wind). || Vendaval, *m.* (gale). || FIG. Bombardeo, *m.*, lluvia, *f.* (of missiles). | Arrebato, *m.* (of rage, jealousy, etc.). | Frenesí, *m.* (frenzy). | Tormenta, *f.* (noisy argument). | Torrente, *m.*, lluvia, *f.* (of protests, etc.). | Salva, *f.* (of applause). || MIL. Asalto, *m.*: *to take by storm*, tomar por asalto. || — FIG. *A storm in a teacup*, una tempestad en un vaso de agua, mucho ruido y pocas nueces. | *To raise a storm of laughter*, provocar carcajadas. || *To ride out o to weather the storm*, capear el temporal.

storm [stɔ:m] v. tr. MIL. Asaltar, tomar por asalto.

— V. intr. Haber tormenta: *it is storming*, hay tormenta. || Ser tempestuoso (wind). || FIG. Echar pestes, vociferar (*at*, contra) [with anger].

stormbound [—baund] adj. Detenido por la tormenta.

storm cellar [—ˌselə*] n. U. S. Refugio (*m.*) contra los ciclones.

storm centre (U. S. **storm center**) [—ˌsentə*] n. Centro (*m.*) de la tormenta *or* del ciclón. || FIG. Centro (*m.*) *or* foco (*m.*) de disturbios.

storm cloud [—klaud] n. Nubarrón, *m.*

storm door [—dɔ:*] n. Contrapuerta, *f.*

storminess [—inis] n. Estado (*m.*) tempestuoso (of the weather). || FIG. Lo borrascoso (of a meeting).

storm-tossed [—tɔst] adj. Zarandeado por la tempestad.

storm troops [—tru:ps] pl. n. Tropas (*f.*) de asalto.

storm window [—ˌwindəu] n. Contraventana, *f.*

stormy [—i] adj. Tempestuoso, sa (weather). || FIG. Borrascoso, sa; agitado, da; acalorado, da (meeting, etc.): *stormy discussion*, discusión acalorada. | Agitado, da (life).

stormy petrel [ˈstɔ:miˌpetrəl] n. Petrel, *m.* (bird). || FIG. Promotor (*m.*) de disturbios (who brings trouble).

story [ˈstɔ:ri] n. Historia, *f.* (history): *the story of my life*, la historia de mi vida; *true story*, historia verídica. || Cuento, *m.*, relato, *m.* (tale): *he told me a story*, me contó un cuento; *adventure story*, cuento de aventuras. || Relato, *m.*, relación, *f.*, narración, *f.* (account). || Argumento, *m.*, trama, *f.* (plot of book, play, film). || Artículo, *m.* (in a newspaper). || Chiste, *m.* (joke): *dirty story*, chiste verde. || Rumor, *m.* (rumour). || Mentira, *f.*, cuento, *m.*, embuste, *m.*, historia, *f.* (lie). || — *As the story goes*, según lo que se cuenta. || *Funny story*, chiste. || *It's a long story*, es muy largo de contar. || FIG. *It's always the same old story*, es siempre la misma canción, es la historia de siempre. || *Short story*, novela corta. || *Tall story*, historia increíble. || FAM. *That's another story*, eso es otro cantar. || *That's not the whole story*, no se lo ha dicho todo. || *The full story has still to be told*, no se ha contado todavía todo. || *To cut a long story short*, en pocas palabras, en resumidas cuentas. || *Your story is that...*, según lo que Ud. dice...

story [ˈstɔ:ri] n. Piso, *m.* || FAM. *To be weak in the upper story*, estar majareta, estar mal de la azotea *or* del tejado, faltarle a uno un tornillo.

storybook [—buk] n. Libro (*m.*) de cuentos.

storyteller [—ˌtelə*] n. Cuentista, *m.* & *f.*, autor (*m.*) de cuentos (author). || Narrador, ra (narrator). || FAM. Cuentista, *m.* & *f.*, mentiroso, sa; embustero, ra (liar, fibber).

storytelling [—ˌteliŋ] n. Narración, *f.* || FAM. Cuentos, *m. pl.* (lies). || *He is good at storytelling*, sabe muy bien contar las historias.

stoup [stu:p] n. REL. Pila (*f.*) para el agua bendita. || Jarra, *f.* (drinking mug).

stout [staut] adj. Robusto, ta; corpulento, ta (corpulent). || Fuerte (strong). || Fuerte, resistente, sólido, da: *stout beams*, vigas sólidas. || Valiente (brave). || Firme, resuelto, ta; decidido, da (undaunted): *stout resistance*, resistencia firme.

— N. Cerveza (*f.*) de malta, cerveza (*f.*) negra y fuerte (beer).

stouthearted [—ˈhɑ:tid] adj. Valiente (courageous).

stoutheartedness [—ˈhɑ:tidnis] n. Valor, *m.*

stoutness [—nis] n. Corpulencia, *f.*, robustez, *f.* (of body). || Vigor, *m.*, fuerza, *f.* (vigour). || Solidez, *f.*, resistencia, *f.* (strength). || Valor, *m.* (courage). || Firmeza, *f.*, resolución, *f.*, decisión, *f.* (resoluteness).

stove [stəuv] n. Estufa, *f.* (for heating). || Cocina, *f.* (cooker). || Hornillo, *m.* (cooking ring). || Horno, *m.* (oven).

stove [stəuv] pret. & p. p. See STAVE.

stovepipe [—paip] n. Tubo (*m.*) de cocina (of cooker). || Tubo (*m.*) de estufa (of heater). || FAM. Chistera, *f.* (hat).

stow [stəu] v. tr. Guardar (to put away): *to stow the books in a cupboard*, guardar los libros en un armario. || Almacenar (to stock). || Poder contener (to hold). || MAR. Estibar, arrumar (a cargo). | Aferrar (sails). || — FAM. *Stow it!*, ¡cierra el pico! || *To stow away*, guardar (to put away), zamparse (food).

— V. intr. *To stow away*, viajar de polizón (to travel clandestinely).

stowage [—idʒ] n. MAR. Estiba, *f.*, arrumaje, *m.* || Depósito, *m.* (storage place). || Almacenaje, *m.* (storage).

stowaway [—əwei] n. Polizón, *m.* (on board a ship).

stower [—ə*] n. Estibador, *m.*

stowing [—iŋ] n. MAR. Estiba, *f.*, arrumaje, *m.*

strabismal [strəˈbizməl] or **strabismic** [strəˈbizmik] or **strabismical** [strəˈbizmikəl] adj. Estrábico, ca.

strabismus [strəˈbizməs] n. MED. Estrabismo, *m.*

straddle [ˈstrædl] n. Posición (*f.*) a horcajadas (position). || MIL. Encuadramiento, *m.* (of target). || COMM. Operación (*f.*) de Bolsa con opción de compra y venta. || U. S. FAM. Posición (*f.*) ambigua.

straddle [ˈstrædl] v. tr. Estar con una pierna a cada lado de (to stand over). || Sentarse *or* montar a horcajadas sobre (to sit). || Abrir [las piernas] (to spread the legs). || Pasar por encima de, cruzar (a bridge). || Encuadrar [el blanco] (target). || U. S. FAM. No tomar ningún partido en, no comprometerse acerca de (an issue).

— V. intr. Esparrancarse (to spread the legs). || Sentarse a horcajadas (to sit astride sth.). || U. S. FAM. Nadar entre dos aguas.

Stradivarius [ˌstrædiˈvɑ:riəs] n. Estradivario, *m.* (violin).

strafe [strɑ:f] n. MIL. Bombardeo, *m.*, castigo, *m.*

strafe [strɑ:f] v. tr. MIL. Bombardear, castigar.

straggle [ˈstrægl] v. intr. Rezagarse (to lag behind). || Extraviarse (to get lost). || Dispersarse (to disperse). || Desparramarse (to spread).

straggler [—ə*] n. Rezagado, da.

straggling [—iŋ] or **straggly** [—i] adj. Disperso, sa; diseminado, da (dispersed). || Rezagado, da (left behind). || Desordenado, da; en desorden (in disorder).

straight [streit] adj. Recto, ta; derecho, cha (not bent): *stand up straight*, póngase derecho. || Recto, ta: *in a straight line*, en línea recta. || Lacio, cia; liso, sa (hair). || Erguido, da (erect). || Seguido, da (continuous): *I work ten hours straight*, trabajo diez horas seguidas. || Certero, ra (aim). || Honrado, da (honest): *are you straight?*, ¿eres honrado? || Justo, ta; equitativo, va (fair). || Serio, ria (serious). || Sincero, ra; franco, ca (sincere). || Claro, ra; preciso, sa (unqualified): *straight answer*, contestación clara. || Auténtico, ca: *straight democrat*, demócrata auténtico. || Seguro, ra;

fidedigno, na (information). || Incondicional (follower). || En orden (in order): *everything is straight now*, todo está en orden ahora. || Arreglado, da (tidy). || Bien puesto, ta: *is the picture straight?*, ¿está bien puesto el cuadro? || En posición correcta (cricket bat). || Correcto, ta (correct). || Solo, la; sin mezcla, puro, ra (drinks). || Fijo, ja (price). || TECH. Con los cilindros en línea recta (engine). || — *As straight as an arrow*, derecho como una vela. || *Let's get the facts straight*, pongamos las cosas claras. || *Straight face*, cara seria *or* impávida. || *Straight fight*, campaña (*f.*) electoral de dos candidatos. || *Straight flush*, escalera (*f.*) de color (in cards). || *Straight run*, candidatura segura. || FIG. *To have a straight eye*, tener buena vista. || *To keep a straight face*, mantenerse impávido. || *To put o to set straight*, poner en el buen camino (to put on the right road), desengañar (to show the truth), corregir (to correct), curar (to cure), ordenar, poner en orden, arreglar (to put in order), arreglar (to repair), poner bien (to put in the right position), poner en hora (watch).

— Adv. En línea recta (in a straight line): *to fly straight*, volar en línea recta. || Derecho, cha: *the book is standing up straight*, el libro está derecho; *the house stands up straight*, la casa está derecha. || Honradamente (honestly). || Sinceramente, francamente, sin rodeos (sincerely): *to speak straight out*, hablar sinceramente. || Derecho, directamente: *we will go straight to Salford*, iremos directamente a Salford. || Correctamente: *to think straight*, pensar correctamente. || Certeramente: *to shoot straight*, tirar certeramente. || — *He walked straight in*, entró directamente. || *I shall come straight back*, vuelvo en seguida. || *It is straight across the road*, está justo en frente. || *Straight ahead*, todo recto, todo seguido (further on), en frente (in front). || *Straight off*, inmediatamente (at once), de un tirón, sin interrupción (in one go). || *Straight on*, todo recto, todo seguido. || *Straight out*, sin rodeos, francamente, sinceramente. || FIG. *To go straight*, enmendarse (a former criminal). || *To look s.o. straight in the face*, mirar a alguien en los ojos. || *To read a book straight through*, leer un libro desde el principio hasta el final. || FIG. *To talk to s.o. straight from the shoulder*, hablar francamente con alguien. | *To tell s.o. sth. straight*, decir algo a alguien francamente. | *To tell s.o. straight* o *to let s.o. have it straight*, decirle cuatro verdades a alguien.

— N. Línea (*f.*) recta (straight line). || Recta, *f.* (the straight part of sth.): *the last straight*, la última recta. || Escalera, *f.* (in cards). || — FIG. *To keep to the straight and narrow*, ir por buen camino. | *To stray from the straight and narrow*, apartarse del buen camino.

straight angle [—ˌæŋgl] n. MATH. Ángulo (*m.*) plano.

straightaway [—əˌwei] adv. En seguida, inmediatamente.

— Adj. Recto, ta; derecho, cha.

— N. Recta, *f.*

straightedge [—edʒ] n. Regla, *f.*

straighten [—n] v. tr. Enderezar, poner derecho (sth.). || Estirar (hair). || Ordenar, arreglar (a room). || Poner bien (one's tie). || — FIG. *To straighten out*, arreglar (one's affairs), resolver (a problem). || *To straighten up*, enderezar.

— V. intr. Enderezarse, ponerse derecho. || FIG. Arreglarse.

straightening [—niŋ] n. Estirado, *m.* (of hair). || Enderezamiento, *m.*

straight-faced [—ˈfeist] adj. Imperturbable, impávido, da (showing no emotion). || Serio, ria (showing no amusement).

straightforward [—ˌfɔːwəd] adj. Sincero, ra; franco, ca (sincere). || Honrado, da (honest). || Abierto, ta (open). || Claro, ra (clear): *a straightforward answer*, una contestación clara. || Sencilo, lla (easy).

straightforwardness [—ˈfɔːwədnis] n. Sinceridad, *f.*, franqueza, *f.* (sincerity). || Sencillez, *f.* (easiness). || Honradez, *f.* (honesty).

straightforwards [—ˈfɔːwədz] adv. Sinceramente, francamente (sincerely). || Abiertamente (openly). || Honradamente (honestly).

straight-haired [—hɛəd] adj. Con el pelo lacio *or* liso.

straightjacket [—ˌdʒækit] n. Camisa (*f.*) de fuerza.

straight-laced [—leist] adj. Mojigato, ta; gazmoño, ña.

straight-line [—lain] adj. Lineal, rectilíneo, a.

straight-lined [—laind] adj. Rectilíneo, a.

straight man [—mən] n. U. S. THEATR. Actor (*m.*) que da pie a un cómico.

straightness [—nis] n. Rectitud, *f.*

straight-out [—aut] adj. Franco, ca; sincero, ra (sincere). || Abierto, ta (open). || Completo, ta.

straight razor [—ˌreizə*] n. Navaja, *f.*

straightway [—wei] adv. En seguida, inmediatamente (straightaway).

strain [strein] n. Tendencia, *f.* (tendency). || Vena, *f.*: *a strain of madness*, una vena de loco. || Tono, *m.*: *to speak in a cheerful strain*, hablar con un tono alegre. || Tenor, *m.*, sentido, *m.*: *he said much more in the same strain*, dijo muchas cosas del mismo tenor. || Tensión, *f.* (on an elastic body). || Presión, *f.* (pressure). || TECH. Deformación, *f.* || FIG. Tensión, *f.*, tirantez, *f.* (of atmosphere). | Esfuerzo, *m.*: *he put a great strain on him*, le sometió a un gran esfuerzo; *it is a great strain to read by candlelight*, requiere mucho esfuerzo leer a la luz de una vela. | Tensión, *f.* (nervous, mental). | Agotamiento, *m.* (exhaustion). || MED. Torcedura, *f.* || Torsión, *f.* (twisting). || Raza, *f.* (race). || Cepa, *f.* (descent). || — Pl. Sonidos (*m.*) lejanos (sounds). || MUS. Son, *m. sing.*, compases, *m.*, acordes, *m.*: *to the strains of the national anthem*, a los acordes del himno nacional. || Acentos, *m.* (in poetry). || *To bear the strain of sth.*, llevar el peso de algo.

strain [strein] v. tr. Estirar, poner tirante, tensar (to stretch). || Torcer (to twist). || Encorvar (to bend). || Estrechar (s.o.): *to strain s.o. to one's bosom*, estrechar a alguien contra el pecho. || Agotar, cansar (to exhaust). || Agotar los nervios (nervously). || Forzar (one's voice). || Cansar (the heart). || Cansar: *to strain one's eyes*, cansar la vista. || Aguzar: *to strain one's ears*, aguzar el oído. || MED. Torcer (a limb): *he strained his ankle*, se torció el tobillo. | Dislocar: *I strained my shoulder*, me disloqué el hombro. | Sufrir un tirón en (muscle). || FIG. Abusar de: *to strain s.o.'s generosity*, abusar de la generosidad de alguien. | Sobrepasar, extralimitarse en (one's powers). | Poner tirante, crear una tirantez en (a relationship). | Forzar: *to strain a point*, forzar las cosas. | Desnaturalizar (a meaning). || Filtrar (to filter). || Tamizar (to sieve). || Colar (vegetables, etc.): *strain the tea*, cuele el té. || TECH. Deformar (to deform). || JUR. Violar (the law). || FIG. Sacar (money). || — *To strain one's back*, derrengarse. || *To strain o.s.*, agotarse (to be exhausted), hacer un mal movimiento.

— V. intr. Esforzarse, hacer un gran esfuerzo (to make a great effort). || Estar tirante (a rope). || Filtrar, filtrarse (to filter). || TECH. Deformarse (to deform). || — *To strain after sth.*, esforzarse por *or* hacer un gran esfuerzo para conseguir algo. || *To strain at*, tirar de (to pull hard). || *To strain under a burden*, soportar un peso con gran dificultad.

strained [—d] adj. Muy tirante *or* tenso (rope). || Dislocado, da (joint). || Torcido, da (ankle). || Cansado, da (heart, eyes). || Tenso, sa (nerves). || FIG. Tirante, tenso, sa (relations). | Forzado, da (voice, laugh). || Colado, da (liquid).

strainer [—ə*] n. Colador, *m.* (kitchen utensil). || Filtro, *m.* (filter). || Tamiz, *m.* (sieve). || Depurador, *m.* (of water, etc.).

strait [streit] n. GEOGR. Estrecho, *m.* || FIG. Aprieto, *m.*, apuro, *m.*: *to be in desperate straits*, estar en un gran aprieto, estar en grandes aprietos, estar en el mayor apuro. || *The Strait of Gibraltar*, el estrecho de Gibraltar.

— OBSERV. La palabra inglesa se emplea sobre todo en plural.

straiten [—n] v. tr. Estrechar. || FIG. *To be in straitened circumstances*, estar en un apuro, estar apurado de dinero.

straitjacket [—ˌdʒækit] n. Camisa (*f.*) de fuerza.

straitlaced [—ˈleist] adj. Mojigato, ta; gazmoño, ña.

strait waistcoat [—ˈweiskəut] n. Camisa (*f.*) de fuerza.

strake [streik] n. MAR. Traca, *f.*

stramonium [strəˈməuniəm] n. BOT. Estramonio, *m.* [*Amer.*, chamico, *m.*].

strand [strænd] n. Playa, *f.* (beach). || Costa, *f.* (coast). || Mechón, *m.* (tuft). || Trenza, *f.* (plait). || Pelo, *m.* (hair). || Ramal, *m.* (of rope). || Cable *m.* (cable). || Hebra, *f.*, hilo, *m.* (of thread). || Sarta, *f.* (of beads, etc.). || BOT. ZOOL. Fibra, *f.* || FIG. *To tie up the loose strands*, atar cabos.

strand [strænd] v. tr. Varar, hacer encallar (a ship). || FIG. Dejar desamparado, dejar en la estacada (to leave helpless). || Trenzar (to twist strands).

— V. intr. MAR. Varar, encallar.

strange [streindʒ] adj. Desconocido, da (unknown): *the town was strange to him*, la ciudad le era desconocida. || Inesperado, da: *a strange result*, un resultado inesperado. || Extraño, ña; raro, ra (odd, bizarre, arousing wonder): *it is strange he has not come*, es extraño que no haya venido. || Nuevo, va; recién llegado, da: *I am strange here*, aquí soy nuevo. || — *Strangest of all...*, lo más curioso del caso es que... || *Strange to say*, aunque parezca extraño. || *To feel strange*, sentirse extraño.

strangely [—li] adv. Extrañamente, de una manera extraña. || *Strangely enough*, aunque parezca extraño.

strangeness [—nis] n. Lo extraño, lo raro, lo curioso. || Novedad, *f.*

stranger [—ə*] n. Desconocido, da (unknown person): *he is a stranger to me*, es un desconocido para mí. || Extranjero, ra (foreigner). || Forastero, ra (outsider): *he is a stranger in this town*, es un forastero en esta ciudad. || — *He is no stranger here*, es muy conocido aquí. || *He is no stranger to fear*, sabe perfectamente lo que es el miedo. || *He is no stranger to London*, conoce bien Londres. || *Hello, stranger!*, ¡cuánto tiempo sin verte! || *I am stranger to the subject*, soy profano en la materia, no conozco el tema. || *To make a stranger of*, tratar con frialdad a. || *You are quite a stranger!*, ¡hace siglos que no te vemos!

strangle [ˈstræŋgl] v. tr. Estrangular. || FIG. Ahogar (voice). | Sofocar (rebellion). | Amordazar (press).
— V. intr. Estrangularse. || FIG. Ahogarse.
stranglehold [—həuld] n. SP. Collar (*m.*) de fuerza (in wrestling, etc.). || FIG. Dominio (*m.*) completo (complete control). || FIG. *To have a stranglehold on s.o.*, dominar por completo a alguien.
strangler [—ə*] n. Estrangulador, ra.
strangling [—iŋ] n. Estrangulación, *f.*, estrangulamiento, *m.*
— Adj. Estrangulador, ra.
strangulate [ˈstræŋgjuleit] v. tr. MED. Estrangular (hernia, vein, etc.).
— V. intr. Estar estrangulado (hernia, vein, etc.).
strangulation [ˌstræŋgjuˈleiʃən] n. Estrangulación, *f.* || MED. Estrangulación, *f.*, estrangulamiento, *m.* (of hernia, vein, blood circulation).
strangury [ˈstræŋgjəri] n. MED. Angurria, *f.*
strap [stræp] n. Correa, *f.*, tira, *f.* (strip of leather). || Tirante, *m.* (of a dress). || Tira, *f.*, banda, *f.* (of material). || Correa, *f.* (watch strap). || Tirante, *m.* (on boots). || Tira, *f.* (on shoes). || Trabilla, *f.* (on trousers). || TECH. Collar, *m.*, abrazadera, *f.* (for pipes). | Correa, *f.* (belt). || Suavizador, *m.* (razor strop).
strap [stræp] v. tr. Atar con correa (to tie up). || Azotar (to beat). || Suavizar (a razor). || MED. Vendar.
straphang [—hæŋ] v. intr. Viajar de pie sujetándose a la correa.
straphanger [—ˌhæŋə*] n. FAM. Pasajero de pie que se agarra a la correa (standing passenger).
strap iron [—ˌaiən] n. Fleje, *m.*
strapless [—lis] adj. Sin tirantes (dress).
strappado [strəˈpeidəu] n. Estrapada, *f.*
strapper [ˈstræpə*] n. FAM. Buen mozo, *m.*
strapping [ˈstræpiŋ] adj. FAM. Fornido, da; robusto, ta (very big and strong).
— N. Atadura (*f.*) con correas. || Correas, *f. pl.* (belts). || MED. Esparadrapo, *m.* || FAM. Azote, *m.*, paliza, *f.* (beating).
strass [stræs] n. Estrás, *m.* (glass).
strata [ˈstrɑːtɑː] pl. n. See STRATUM.
stratagem [ˈstrætidʒəm] n. Estratagema, *f.*
strategic [strəˈtiːdʒik] or **strategical** [—əl] adj. Estratégico, ca.
strategist [ˈstrætidʒist] n. Estratega, *m.* || FAM. *Armchair strategist*, estratega de café.
strategy [ˈstrætidʒi] n. Estrategia, *f.*
strath [stræθ] n. Valle, *m.*
strathspey [—ˈspei] n. Danza (*f.*) escocesa.
stratification [ˌstrætifiˈkeiʃən] n. Estratificación, *f.*
stratify [ˈstrætifai] v. tr. Estratificar.
— V. intr. Estratificarse.
stratocumulus [ˌstreitəuˈkjuːmjuləs] n. Estratocúmulo, *m.* (cloud formation).
stratosphere [ˈstrætəusfiə*] n. Estratosfera, *f.* || *Stratosphere balloon*, globo estratosférico.
stratospheric [ˌstrætəuˈsferik] adj. Estratosférico, ca.
stratum [ˈstrɑːtəm] n. BIOL. Capa, *f.*, estrato, *m.* (layer of tissue). || Capa, *f.* (in meteorology). || GEOL. Estrato, *m.* || FIG. Estrato, *m.*, capa, *f.*: *social stratum*, estrato social.
— OBSERV. El plural de *stratum* es *strata* o *stratums*.
stratus [ˈstreitəs] n. Estrato, *m.* (cloud formation).
— OBSERV. El plural de *stratus* es *strati*.
straw [strɔː] n. Paja, *f.* [*Amer.*, popote, *m.*] (of cereals and for drinking). || FIG. FAM. Ardite, *m.*, comino, *m.*: *she doesn't care a straw*, [no] le importa un comino. || — FIG. *A straw in the wind*, un indicio. | *It's the last straw that breaks the camel's back*, es la última gota que hace rebasar la copa. | *Man of straw*, testaferro, *m.*, hombre (*m.*) de paja. | *That is the last straw*, esto es el colmo. | *To cling o to clutch at a straw*, agarrarse a un clavo ardiendo. || *To draw straws*, echar pajas.
— Adj. De paja: *straw hat*, sombrero de paja; *straw hut*, choza de paja. || Pajizo, za (colour). || — *Straw bed* o *straw mat*, jergón (*m.*) de paja. || *Straw loft*, pajar, *m.* || *Straw rick*, almiar, *m.*
strawberry [—bəri] n. BOT. Fresa, *f.* [*Amer.*, frutilla, *f.*] (wild), fresón, *m.* (cultivated and larger). || Color (*m.*) fresa (colour). || — *Strawberry bed*, fresal, *m.* || *Strawberry blonde*, pelirroja, *f.* || *Strawberry jam*, mermelada (*f.*) de fresa. || *Strawberry mark*, antojo, *m.* || *Strawberry patch*, fresal, *m.* || *Strawberry tomato*, alquequenje, *m.* || *Strawberry tree*, madroño, *m.*
strawboard [—bɔːd] n. Cartón, *m.* (coarse cardboard).
straw-coloured (U. S. **straw-colored**) [—ˌkʌləd] adj. Pajizo, za; de color de paja.
straw man [—mæn] n. Testaferro, *m.*, hombre (*m.*) de paja (man of straw). || Don nadie, *m.*, pelele, *m.* (nonentity).
straw vote [—vəut] n. U. S. Votación (*f.*) de prueba.
straw wine [—wain] n. Vino (*m.*) de paja.
strawy [—i] adj. De paja. || Pajizo, za; de color de paja (colour).
stray [strei] adj. Perdido, da; extraviado, da (animal). || Aislado, da; disperso, sa (houses). || Perdido, da (bullet). || Descarriado, da (morally). || — *Stray child*, niño abandonado. || *Stray dog*, perro callejero.
— N. Animal (*m.*) perdido *or* extraviado. || Perro (*m.*) callejero (dog). || Gato (*m.*) callejero (cat). || Niño (*m.*) abandonado (child). || ELECTR. Dispersión, *f.* || — Pl. RAD. Parásitos, *m.*, interferencias, *f.*
stray [strei] v. intr. Desviarse, apartarse: *they strayed from the path and got lost*, se desviaron del camino y se perdieron. || Extraviarse, perderse (to lose o.s.). || Descarriarse (morally). || Errar (to roam).
streak [ˈstriːk] n. Raya, *f.*, lista, *f.*, línea, *f.* (stripe). || Señal, *f.*: *the tears have left streaks on her face*, tiene señales de haber llorado. || Fondo, *m.*, lado, *m.*: *he has a serious streak you'd never suspect*, tiene un fondo serio en el que nunca se pensaría. || Racha, *f.* (of luck, good weather, etc.). || Vena, *f.* (of madness, genious). || Haz, *m.*, rayo, *m.* (of light). || MIN. Veta, *f.* (in minerals). || — *A streak of irony*, cierta ironía. | *Streak of lightning*, rayo, *m.*
streak [ˈstriːk] v. tr. Rayar (to stripe). || Vetear: *white marble streaked with red*, mármol blanco veteado de rojo.
— V. intr. FIG. Pasar como un rayo.
streakiness [—inis] n. Rayado, *m.*, rayadura, *f.*, aspecto (*m.*) rayado.
streaky [—i] adj. Rayado, da (streaked). || Entreverado, da (bacon). || Veteado, da (veined).
stream [striːm] n. Corriente, *f.* (current). || Río, *m.* (river). || Arroyo, *m.*, riachuelo, *m.* (small river). || Torrente, *m.* (of lava). || Chorro, *m.* (of water, blood). || Raudal, *m.* (of light). || Serie, *f.*, sucesión, *f.* (of events). || Torrente, *m.* (of tears). || Sarta, *f.*: *a stream of oaths*, una sarta de improperios. || Torrente, *m.*, flujo, *m.*: *a stream of words*, un torrente de palabras. || Oleada, *f.*, riada, *f.*, flujo, *m.*: *stream of immigrants*, oleada de inmigrantes. || Desfile (*m.*) continuo: *a stream of cars*, un desfile continuo de coches. || Grupo, *m.* (of pupils). || — *Against the stream*, a contracorriente. || FIG. *To go with the stream*, ir con la corriente, seguir la corriente.
stream [striːm] v. tr. Hacer correr, derramar (liquid). || Hacer ondear: *the wind streamed the flag*, el viento hacía ondear la bandera. || MAR. Echar, fondear (the anchor). || MIN. Lavar (minerals). || Clasificar, poner en grupos (pupils in a school). || *Her eyes streamed tears*, estaba hecha un mar de lágrimas.
— V. intr. Correr, fluir (liquid). || Manar, correr, chorrear (blood). || Ondear, flotar (to wave in the wind): *the flags were streaming in the wind*, flotaban las banderas en el viento. || — *His eyes were streaming with tears*, tenía la cara bañada en lágrimas. || *To stream in*, entrar a raudales (sunlight, people). || *To stream out*, brotar (a liquid), salir en tropel: *people streamed out*, la gente salía en tropel.
streamer [—ə*] n. Serpentina, *f.* (of paper). || MAR. Gallardete, *m.* || U. S. Titulares, *m. pl.* (of newspaper). || — Pl. Aurora (*f. sing.*) boreal.
streamlet [—lit] n. Riachuelo, *m.*, arroyuelo, *m.*
streamline [—lain] n. Corriente (*f.*) natural (of liquid, gas). || Línea (*f.*) *or* forma (*f.*) aerodinámica (of car, plane).
streamline [—lain] v. tr. Carenar, dar línea aerodinámica a (cars, etc.). || FIG. Modernizar, simplificar, racionalizar (measure, system).
streamlined [—laind] adj. De línea aerodinámica, aerodinámico, ca; carenado, da (cars, planes). || FIG. Moderno, na (modernized).
street [striːt] n. Calle, *f.*: *he walked down the street*, bajaba la calle; *main* o *high street*, calle mayor; *down the street*, calle abajo; *up the street*, calle arriba; *the whole street knew about it*, toda la calle lo sabía. || — FIG. *He's streets above you*, está muy por encima de ti. | *Not to be in the same street as s.o.*, no estar a la altura de alguien, no llegarle a alguien a la suela del zapato. || *One-way street*, calle de dirección única. || *Street accident*, accidente (*m.*) de tráfico *or* de circulación. || FIG. *That's right up my street*, eso es lo mío. | *The man in the street*, el hombre de la calle. | *To be on easy street*, llevar una vida acomodada. || *To go out into the street*, echarse a la calle. || *To line the streets*, hacer calle (soldiers). || *To roam the streets*, callejear, azotar las calles. || FAM. *To turn s.o. out into the streets*, poner a alguien de patitas en la calle. || *To walk the streets*, correr las calles, callejear (anyone), hacer la carrera (prostitute).
street arab [—ˌærəb] n. Golfillo, *m.*, niño (*m.*) de la calle, pilluelo, *m.*
streetcar [—kɑː*] n. U. S. Tranvía, *m.*
street cleaner [—ˌkliːnə*] n. Barrendero, *m.*
street cry [—krai] n. Pregón, *m.*, grito (*m.*) de los vendedores ambulantes.
street door [—dɔ*] n. Puerta (*f.*) principal, puerta (*f.*) de la calle.
street floor [—flɔː*] n. U. S. Planta (*f.*) baja.
street guide [—gaid] n. Callejero, *m.*, guía (*f.*) de la ciudad.
streetlamp [—læmp] or **streetlight** [—lait] n. Farol, *m.* (gas). || Poste (*m.*) de alumbrado (electric).
street lighting [—ˌlaitiŋ] n. Alumbrado (*m.*) público.
street musician [—mjuːˈziʃən] n. Músico (*m.*) callejero.
street sweeper [—ˌswiːpə*] n. Barrendero, *m.* (person). || Barredora, *f.* (lorry).
street urchin [—ˌəːtʃin] n. Golfillo, *m.*, niño (*m.*) de la calle.
streetwalker [—ˌwɔːkə*] n. Carrerista, *f.*, buscona, *f.* (prostitute).

strength [streŋθ] n. Fuerza, *f.*: *a man of great strength*, un hombre de gran fuerza. || Resistencia, *f.*, solidez, *f.*: *the strength of a wall*, la resistencia de una muralla. || Intensidad, *f.*, fuerza, *f.* (of a colour). || Fuerza, *f.* (of drugs, drinks). || Número, *m.*: *they came in full strength*, vinieron en gran número. || Validez, *f.*, fuerza, *f.* (of an argument). || Poder, *m.*, potencia, *f.*, fuerza, *f.* (power). || MIL. Efectivos, *m. pl.*, fuerzas, *f. pl.* || ELECTR. Intensidad, *f.* (of a current). || TECH. Resistencia, *f.*: *the strength of a metal under pressure*, la resistencia de un metal a la presión. || CHEM. Proporción, *f.*, cantidad, *f.*, graduación, *f.*: *alcoholic strength*, graduación de alcohol. || COMM. Firmeza, *f.* || — *By sheer strength*, a viva fuerza. || || *On the strength of*, teniendo como base, fundándose en. || *Strength of character*, entereza, *f.*, firmeza, *f.* || *Strength of mind*, fortaleza, *f.* || *Strength of will*, fuerza de voluntad, resolución, *f.* || *To be present in great strength*, estar en gran número. || *To bring a battalion up to strength*, completar un batallón. || *To recover one's strength*, recuperar *or* recobrar las fuerzas. || *To reserve* o *to save one's strength*, reservarse.

strengthen [—ən] v. tr. Fortalecer, consolidar: *to strengthen a house*, consolidar una casa. || Reforzar: *to strengthen a wall*, reforzar un muro. || Dar mayor intensidad a (colour, sound). || FIG. Intensificar (relations). | Estrechar (links). | Afianzar, consolidar (s.o.'s authority, etc.). | Fortalecer, reforzar, consolidar (friendship). || MED. Fortificar, fortalecer. || MIL. Reforzar.

— V. intr. FIG. Reforzarse, fortalecerse, consolidarse: *their friendship strengthened*, su amistad se consolidó. | Intensificarse (relations). | Estrecharse (links). | Afianzarse, consolidarse (s.o.'s authority, etc.).

strengthening [—əniŋ] n. Fortalecimiento, *m.* || Refuerzo, *m.* || Consolidación, *f.*

— Adj. MED. Fortificante, tonificante.

strengthless [—lis] adj. Débil, sin fuerzas.

strenuous [ˈstrenjuəs] adj. Activo, va; vigoroso, sa; enérgico, ca: *a strenuous person*, una persona activa. || Intenso, sa; activo, va: *a strenuous life*, una vida intensa. || Fatigoso, sa; cansado, da; arduo, dua: *a strenuous occupation*, un trabajo cansado. || Intenso, sa (effort). || Tenaz, porfiado, da; firme (opposition). || Encarnizado, da (fight). || — *Through much strenuous work*, a fuerza de mucho trabajo. || *To offer strenuous opposition to*, oponerse firmemente a.

strenuousness [—nis] n. Energía, *f.*

streptococcosis [ˌstreptəukɔˈkəusais] n. MED. Estreptococia, *f.*

streptococcus [ˌstreptəuˈkɔkəs] n. MED. Estreptococo, *m.*

— OBSERV. El plural de la palabra inglesa es *streptococci*.

streptomycin [ˌstreptəuˈmaisin] n. MED. Estreptomicina, *f.*

stress [stres] n. MED. Tensión (*f.*) *or* fatiga (*f.*) nerviosa: *I am under stress*, sufro una tensión nerviosa. || Hincapié, *m.*: *he put the stress on the salary increase*, hizo hincapié en el aumento de salarios. || Presión, *f.*, coacción, *f.*, fuerza, *f.* (compulsion). || GRAMM. Acento (*m.*) tónico. || TECH. PHYS. Esfuerzo, *m.* || — *By stress of weather*, a causa del temporal. || *The laws of stress in Spanish*, las reglas de la acentuación en español. || *To lay stress on*, insistir en, hacer hincapié en, subrayar (to emphasize), acentuar, poner el acento en (in linguistics). || *Stress system*, acentuación, *f.* || *Times of stress*, períodos (*m. pl.*) difíciles. || *Under the stress of a violent emotion*, preso de una intensa emoción.

stress [stres] v. tr. Insistir en, recalcar, hacer hincapié en, subrayar (to emphasize): *he stressed the importance of the reform*, recalcó la importancia de la reforma. || GRAMM. Acentuar. || TECH. Someter a un esfuerzo.

stressless [—lis] adj. Sin acento.

stretch [stretʃ] n. Alargamiento, *m.* (extension). || Elasticidad, *f.* (of elastic fabric). || Trozo, *m.*: *a stretch of rope*, un trozo de cuerda. || Trecho, *m.*, tramo, *m.*: *this stretch of the road is dangerous*, este tramo de carretera es peligroso. || Recta, *f.* (in a race track). || Extensión, *f.*: *a stretch of land*, una extensión de terreno. || Envergadura, *f.* (of wings). || Extensión, *f.* (of arms). || Intervalo, *m.*, tiempo, *m.*, período, *m.* (time). || Vuelta, *f.* (short walk). || Esfuerzo, *m.* (of imagination). || GRAMM. Extensión, *f.* (of meaning). || — FIG. *At a stretch*, de un tirón (in one go), seguido, da: *I can work for ten hours at a stretch*, puedo trabajar durante diez horas seguidas. | *At full stretch*, a todo gas, a toda mecha. | *Home stretch*, última etapa. || FAM. *To do a stretch*, estar en chirona. || *To give a stretch as one wakes up*, estirarse al despertar.

— Adj. Elástico, ca.

stretch [stretʃ] v. tr. Estirar, alargar: *he stretched the elastic*, estiró la goma. || Tender: *they stretched the wires across the valley*, tendieron los cables sobre el valle. || Alargar, extender: *he stretched his arm to reach the book*, extendió el brazo para coger el libro. || Tender, alargar (the hand). || Desentumecer, estirar: *to stretch one's legs*, estirar las piernas. || Desplegar, extender, abrir (the wings). || Distender (a tendon). || Ensanchar: *he stretched his shoes*, ensanchó sus zapatos. || Extender: *they stretched him on the operating table*, le extendieron sobre la mesa de operaciones. || FIG. Estirar: *they stretched their food over three days*, estiraron la comida para tres días. | Forzar (meaning). | Sobrepasar los límites de (law). | Violar (one's principles). || MUS. TECH. Tensar. || FAM. Derribar (to knock down). || — FIG. *To stretch a point*, hacer una excepción. | *To stretch it*, exagerar. || *To stretch o.s.*, estirarse. || *To stretch out*, alargar, extender (one's arm), estirar (one's leg), estirar (a speech, etc.).

— V. intr. Estirarse, alargarse (elastic). || Estirarse: *he got up and stretched*, se levantó y se estiró. || Extenderse: *the road stretched into the distance*, la carretera se extendía a lo lejos. || Ensancharse, dar de sí (shoes). || FIG. Dar de sí (money). || *To stretch out*, estirarse, desperezarse (one's limbs), tumbarse, echarse (to lie down), separarse (a line of runners, etc.), extenderse (a country), alargar la mano (to reach sth.), aligerar el paso (walking).

stretchable [—əbl] adj. Estirable.

stretcher [—ə*] n. Camilla, *f.*, parihuelas, *f. pl.* (small portable bed). || Horma, *f.* (for shoes). || Ensanchador, *m.* (for gloves). || TECH. Tensor, *m.* || ARCH. Soga, *f.* || ARTS. Bastidor, *m.* (for canvas). || Travesaño, *m.* (of a tent). || Apoyo, *m.* (in a rowing boat). || FIG. Mentira, *f.*, exageración, *f.*

stretcher-bearer [—əˌbεərə*] n. Camillero, *m.*

stretching [—iŋ] n. Estiramiento, *m.*

stretchy [—i] adj. Elástico, ca. || Que ensancha, que da de sí (shoes, etc.).

strew* [struː] v. tr. Regar, esparcir, derramar: *to strew sand*, regar arena. || Salpicar, desparramar (to scatter). || Cubrir, llenar: *a table strewn with books*, una mesa cubierta de libros.

— OBSERV. Pret. **strewed;** p. p. **strewed, strewn.**

stria [ˈstraiə] n. GEOL. Estría, *f.* || ARCH. Estría, *f.*, ranura, *f.*, acanaladura, *f.*

— OBSERV. El plural de *stria* es *striae*.

striate [ˈstraiit] adj. Estriado, da.

striate [ˈstraiit] v. tr. Estriar.

striated [straiˈeitid] adj. Estriado, da. || ANAT. *Striated muscle*, músculo estriado.

striation [straiˈeiʃən] n. Estriación, *f.*, estriado, *m.* (striated appearance). || GEOL. Estría, *f.* || ARCH. Estría, *f.*, ranura, *f.*, acanaladura, *f.*

stricken [ˈstrikən] adj. Afectado, da: *the stricken village*, el pueblo afectado. || Destrozado, da (damaged). || Afligido, da; *the stricken families*, las familias afligidas; *he was stricken with*, estaba afligido por. || Afectado, da; aquejado, da; atacado, da: *stricken with tuberculosis*, aquejado de *or* atacado por la tuberculosis. || Herido, da (wounded).

— P. p. See STRIKE.

strickle [strikl] n. Rasero, *m.* (for removing surplus grain). || Piedra (*f.*) de afilar (sharpening stone). || Plantilla, *f.*, terraja, *f.* (template).

strickle [strikl] v. tr. Dar forma con la plantilla *or* la terraja.

strict [strikt] adj. Estricto, ta; preciso, sa; exacto, ta: *in the strict sense of the word*, en el sentido estricto de la palabra. || Estricto, ta; severo, ra; riguroso, sa: *a strict headmaster*, un director estricto; *strict discipline*, disciplina severa. || Estricto, ta; riguroso, sa: *a strict Catholic*, un católico estricto. || Terminante, estricto, ta (order). || Absoluto, ta; completo, ta: *in strict seclusion*, en un aislamiento absoluto.

strictly [—li] adv. Terminantemente: *smoking strictly forbidden*, terminantemente prohibido fumar, se prohibe terminantemente fumar. || Exactamente: *it is not strictly true*, no es exactamente cierto. || Con precisión: *to define a word strictly*, definir una palabra con precisión. || Severamente, estrictamente: *I was brought up very strictly*, fui educado muy severamente. || *Strictly speaking*, hablando con propiedad (in the strict sense), en realidad: *strictly speaking it is not true*, en realidad no es verdad.

strictness [—nis] n. Exactitud, *f.* (exactness). || Severidad, *f.* (severity). || Lo terminante (of an order).

stricture [ˈstriktʃə*] n. Crítica, *f.* (criticism). || MED. Estrechamiento, *m.*

stridden [ˈstridn] p. p. See STRIDE.

stride [straid] n. Zancada, *f.* (long step): *with big strides*, a grandes zancadas. || Paso, *m.* (step). || FIG. Progreso, *m.*, adelanto, *m.*: *making great strides in English*, haciendo grandes progresos en inglés. || — *To get into one's stride*, coger el ritmo. || *To take sth. in one's stride*, tomarse las cosas con calma, hacer las cosas con tranquilidad. || SP. *To take the hurdles in one's stride*, saltar las vallas sin perder el ritmo.

stride* [straid] v. tr. Pasar *or* saltar *or* salvar *or* franquear de una zancada (to cross over). || Sentarse a horcajadas en (a branch, etc.). || Montar a horcajadas (a horse).

— V. intr. Andar a zancadas *or* a grandes pasos. || — *To stride away*, alejarse a grandes zancadas. || *To stride up to s.o.*, acercarse a alguien a grandes zancadas.

— OBSERV. Pret. **strode;** p. p. **stridden.**

stridence [—əns] or **stridency** [—i] n. Estridencia, *f.*

strident [—ənt] adj. Estridente.

stridor [ˈstraidɔː*] n. MED. Estridor, *m.* (harsh vibrating sound).

stridulate [ˈstridjuleit] v. intr. Chirriar, estridular (p.us.) [cicadas, grasshoppers, etc.].

stridulation [stridjuˈleiʃən] n. Chirrido, *m.*, estridor, *m.*, estridulación, *f.*

strife [straif] n. Disensión, *f.*, disputa, *f.* (enmity). ‖ Contienda, *f.*, lucha, *f.*, conflicto, *m.* (struggle). ‖ Disensiones, *f. pl.*, discordias, *f. pl.*: *internal strife*, disensiones internas. ‖ Querellas, *f. pl.*, peleas, *f. pl.*: *domestic strife*, querellas domésticas.

strike [straik] n. Golpe, *m.* (blow). ‖ Huelga, *f.* (ceasing to work): *to go on strike*, declararse en huelga; *to be on strike*, estar en huelga. ‖ Acuñación, *f.* (of coins). ‖ Descubrimiento, *m.* (of ore, oil, etc.). ‖ Rasero, *m.* (for removing surplus grain). ‖ Piedra (*f.*) de afilar (sharpening stone). ‖ Patrón, *m.*, plantilla, *f.* (template). ‖ GEOL. Dirección (*f.*) horizontal (of a stratum). ‖ MIL. Ataque, *m.* ‖ U. S. SP. Golpe, *m.* (in baseball). ‖ "Strike", *m.* (in bowling). ‖ Mordida, *f.*, picada, *f.* (in fishing). ‖ FAM. Suerte, *f.*, chamba, *f.*, potra, *f.* (good luck). ‖ — *Hunger strike*, huelga del hambre. ‖ *Sit-down strike*, sentada, *f.*, huelga de brazos caídos *or* de brazos cruzados. ‖ *Staggered strike*, huelga escalonada *or* alternativa *or* por turno. ‖ *Strike pay*, subsidio (*m.*) de huelga. ‖ *Sympathetic* o *sympathy strike*, huelga por solidaridad.

strike* [straik] v. tr. Pegar, golpear: *he struck her on the face*, le pegó en la cara. ‖ Dar, asestar, pegar (a blow): *I struck a blow at him*, le di un golpe. ‖ Golpear, dar un golpe en: *he struck the table with his fist*, golpeó la mesa con el puño. ‖ Golpear (a ball). ‖ Herir (to wound). ‖ Alcanzar, dar (with a bullet). ‖ Tocar (the keys of an instrument). ‖ Dar, tocar: *the clock struck two*, el reloj dio las dos. ‖ Encender: *strike a match*, encienda un fósforo. ‖ Chocar contra, dar contra, dar un golpe contra (to collide with): *his head struck the wall*, su cabeza chocó contra la pared. ‖ Chocar con (a car). ‖ Atropellar: *he was struck by a car*, fue atropellado por un coche. ‖ Clavar, hundir, meter: *he struck the knife into her heart*, le clavó el cuchillo en el corazón. ‖ Llegar: *the news struck him to the heart*, la noticia le llegó al alma; *the cold struck him to the bone*, el frío le llegó hasta los huesos. ‖ Acuñar, (coins, medals). ‖ Batir (iron). ‖ Atravesar (fog): *the rays strike through the mist*, los rayos atraviesan la neblina. ‖ Hacer saltar (sparks). ‖ Caer en (lightning). ‖ Dar en: *the light strikes the wall*, la luz da en la pared; *to strike the target*, dar en el blanco. ‖ Herir, lastimar: *a sound strikes my ear*, un ruido me hiere el oído. ‖ Impresionar: *we were struck by his intelligence*, nos impresionó su inteligencia. ‖ Hacer impresión: *how did it strike me?*, ¿qué impresión me hizo? ‖ Sorprender (to astonish): *what struck me was*, lo que me sorprendió fue. ‖ Ocurrírsele a uno: *the thought struck me that*, se me ocurrió la idea de que. ‖ Parecer: *it strikes me as impossible*, me parece imposible; *it struck me that*, me pareció que. ‖ Atraer (the eyes). ‖ Llamar (attention). ‖ Infundir (terror). ‖ Sobrecoger: *he was struck with panic*, estaba sobrecogido por el pánico. ‖ Aquejar: *struck with deafness*, aquejado de sordera. ‖ Abatirse sobre (disaster). ‖ Adoptar, tomar (a pose). ‖ Constituir, formar (a jury, a committee). ‖ Concertar (an agreement). ‖ Cerrar (a bargain). ‖ Liquidar, cerrar (an account). ‖ Hacer (a balance). ‖ Rasar (to level off). ‖ MAR. Amainar, recoger (sails). | Arriar (flags). ‖ Coger, enganchar con el anzuelo (to hook a fish). ‖ Arponear, arponar (a whale). ‖ Morder (a snake). ‖ Descubrir (oil, track): *they struck oil*, descubrieron petróleo. ‖ Dar con: *they struck the main road*, dieron con la carretera principal. ‖ Encontrar, dar con, topar con (difficulties, obstacles). ‖ BOT. Echar (roots). ‖ MIL. Levantar (camp). |Desmontar (tents). | Concertar (a truce). | Atacar (to attack). ‖ THEATR. Desmontar (scenery). ‖ MATH. Hacer, calcular (an average). | Trazar (a circle, a line). ‖ — FIG. *Strike me dead if...!*, ¡que me muera si...! | *Strike when the iron is hot*, al hierro caliente batir de repente. ‖ *The house was struck by lightning*, cayó un rayo en la casa. ‖ *To be struck all of a heap*, quedarse pasmado. ‖ *To be struck by a stone*, recibir una pedrada. ‖ *To strike it lucky*, tener suerte. ‖ *To strike it rich*, hacerse rico. ‖ FIG. *To strike oil*, encontrar una mina de oro. ‖ *To strike s.o. dead*, matar a uno. ‖ *To strike s.o. deaf*, dejarle sordo a uno, ensordecer a uno. ‖ *To strike s.o. dumb*, dejarle a uno mudo *or* sin habla. ‖ MAR. *To strike the bottom*, dar con el fondo. | *To strike the rocks*, chocar contra las rocas. ‖ *To strike work*, declararse en huelga.

— V. intr. Golpear, dar un golpe *or* golpes (to hit): *he struck at me*, me dio un golpe. ‖ Atacar: *the enemy struck at dawn*, el enemigo atacó al amanecer. ‖ Dirigirse hacia: *he struck south*, se dirigió hacia el sur. ‖ Sonar (a bell). ‖ Dar: *one o'clock struck*, dio la una. ‖ Dar la hora: *the clock struck*, el reloj dio la hora. ‖ Dar [*on*, *upon*, en] (light). ‖ Penetrar (cold). ‖ Atravesar (sun). ‖ Dar, chocar (*against*, *on*, contra) [to collide]. ‖ Caer, tropezar (*on*, *upon*, en, con) [a difficulty]. ‖ Encenderse (match). ‖ Ocurrir (disaster). ‖ Declararse en huelga (to stop working). ‖ Morder (snake). ‖ MAR. Encallar (to run aground). | Arriar bandera (flag). ‖ Rendirse (town). ‖ BOT. Echar raíces (to take root). | Agarrar (cutting). ‖ — FIG. *His hour has struck*, ha llegado su hora. ‖ *To strike home*, dar en el blanco.

— **To strike aside**, apartar de un golpe. ‖ **To strike back**, devolver un golpe *or* golpe por golpe *or* los golpes. ‖ **To strike down**, derribar (to knock down). | Hacer soltar de un golpe (firearm, etc.). | Fulminar (disease). ‖ **To strike in**, clavar (a nail). | Intervenir (to interrupt). ‖ **To strike into**, echarse a, empezar a: *he struck into song*, empezó a cantar. ‖ **To strike off**, cortar (to cut). | Quitar de golpe (to remove). | Borrar (to rub out). | Tachar (to cross out). | Deducir, rebajar (to deduct). | PRINT. Tirar. ‖ **To strike on** o **upon**, ocurrírsele [a uno]: *he struck on a good idea*, se le ocurrió una buena idea. ‖ **To strike out**, borrar (to rub out). | Tachar (to cross out). | Idear (a plan). | Pegar, dar un golpe *or* golpes (to hit). | — *To strike out for*, ponerse en camino hacia (walking, etc.), ponerse a remar hacia (rowing), ponerse a nadar hacia (swimming). | *To strike out for o.s.*, volar con sus propias alas. ‖ **To strike through**, tachar. ‖ **To strike to**, torcer hacia *or* a: *the road strikes to the left*, la carretera tuerce hacia la izquierda. ‖ **To strike up**, empezar (to begin). | Entablar, iniciar (conversation). | Trabar, entablar (friendship). | Entonar (a song). | Atacar (a piece of music). | Empezar a cantar (to start singing). | Empezar a tocar (to start playing).

— OBSERV. Pret. ***struck;*** p. p. ***struck, stricken.***

strikebound [—baund] adj. Paralizado por la huelga (industry, economy, etc.).

strikebreaker [—ˌbreikə*] n. Esquirol, *m.*, rompehuelgas, *m. inv.*

strikebreaking [—ˌbreikiŋ] n. Medidas (*f.pl.*) encaminadas a hacer fallar una huelga.

striker [—ə*] n. Huelguista, *m.* & *f.* (person). ‖ Badajo, *m.* (of a bell). ‖ TECH. Percutor, *m.* ‖ Percusor, *m.* (of firearm). ‖ U. S. MIL. Ordenanza, *m.*

striking [—iŋ] adj. Notable, grande, sorprendente: *striking difference*, notable diferencia. ‖ Llamativo, va: *a striking colour*, un color llamativo. ‖ Impresionante: *a striking spectacle*, un espectáculo impresionante. ‖ [Que está] en huelga (on strike). ‖ Que da las horas (clock). ‖ *Within striking distance*, al alcance.

— N. Golpeteo, *m.*, golpes, *m. pl.* ‖ Acuñación, *f.* (of coins). ‖ Campanada, *f.* (of clock).

string [striŋ] n. Cuerda, *f.*, bramante, *m.*, cordel, *m.* (for tying up). ‖ Cordón, *m.* (lace). ‖ Hilo, *m.* (of a puppet). ‖ Hebra, *f.* (of beans, meat). ‖ Ristra, *f.* (of garlic, onions, sausages). ‖ Cuerda, *f.* (of tennis racket). ‖ Fila, *f.*, hilera, *f.* (of cars, animals). ‖ Fila, *f.* (of barges). ‖ Reata, *f.* (of horses). ‖ Cadena, *f.*, sucesión, *f.* (of events). ‖ Cadena, *f.* (of hotels, etc.). ‖ Serie, *f.* (of questions, etc.). ‖ Sarta, *f.* (of lies). ‖ Retahila, *f.* (of curses). ‖ MUS. Cuerda, *f.*: *string instrument*, instrumento de cuerda. ‖ ARCH. Zanca, *f.* (of a staircase). | Hilada (*f.*) volada (stringcourse). ‖ GEOL. Veta, *f.* ‖ SP. Cuadra, *f.* (in horse racing). | Serie, *f.*: *first string athlete*, atleta de primera serie. | Línea (*f.*) de arranque (in billiards). ‖ FIG. Condición, *f.*: *a loan with strings attached*, un préstamo con ciertas condiciones. ‖ — Pl. MUS. Instrumentos (*m.*) de cuerda. ‖ — *String of beads*, rosario, *m.* (rosary), collar, *m.* (necklace). ‖ *String orchestra*, orquesta (*f.*) de cuerdas. ‖ FIG. *To have s.o. on a string*, tener a uno en un puño. | *To have two strings to one's bow*, ser persona de recursos. | *To pull all the strings one can*, tocar todos los resortes. | *To pull the strings*, mover los hilos. | *To touch a string*, tocar el punto sensible.

string* [striŋ] v. tr. Poner una cuerda a (to provide with a string). ‖ Atar con una cuerda (to fasten). ‖ Armar (a bow). ‖ MUS. Poner cuerdas a, encordar (to put strings on). | Templar (to tune). ‖ Ensartar, enhebrar (pearls). ‖ Enristrar (garlic, onions). ‖ Quitar las hebras de (beans). ‖ Estirar (to stretch). ‖ Tender: *to string a wire down the corridor*, tender un cable a lo largo del pasillo. ‖ FIG. Ensartar (ideas). ‖ — FIG. *Highly strung*, see HIGHLY. ‖ FIG. FAM. *To string s.o. along*, tomarle el pelo a alguien. | *To string up*, ahorcar (to hang).

— V. intr. Ahilarse, formar hilos (to form stringy fibres). ‖ Extenderse (to stretch out). ‖ *To string along with s.o.*, acompañar a alguien.

— OBSERV. Pret. & p. p. ***strung.***

string bean [—bi:n] n. U. S. Judía (*f.*) verde.

stringboard [—bɔ:d] n. ARCH. Zanca, *f.*, limón, *m.*

stringcourse [—kɔ:s] n. ARCH. Hilada (*f.*) volada.

stringed [—d] adj. MUS. De cuerda.

stringency [ˈstrindʒənsi] n. Rigor, *m.*, severidad, *f.* (of rules, conditions). ‖ Fuerza, *f.* (of an argument). ‖ COMM. Escasez, *f.* ‖ *Financial stringency*, situación económica apurada.

stringent [ˈstrindʒənt] adj. Estricto, ta; riguroso, sa; severo, ra: *stringent rules*, reglas severas. ‖ Convincente, fuerte (argument). ‖ COMM. Escaso, sa (credit). | Apurado, da (financial situation).

stringer [ˈstriŋə*] n. ARCH. Travesaño, *m.*, larguero, *m.* ‖ AVIAT. Larguero, *m.* (of fuselage or wings). ‖ U. S. Durmiente, *m.* (railway sleeper). ‖ Corresponsal (*m.*) pagado por líneas (news correspondent).

stringiness [ˈstriŋinis] n. Lo fibroso (of vegetables, etc.). ‖ Viscosidad, *f.* (viscosity).

stringpiece [ˈstriŋpi:s] n. ARCH. Riostra, *f.*

string tie [ˈstriŋtai] n. Lazo, *m.* (necktie).
stringy [ˈstriŋi] adj. Fibroso, sa; filamentoso, sa (like a string). || Lleno de hebras, fibroso, sa (vegetables). || Correoso, sa; lleno de hebras (meat). || Viscoso, sa (liquid). || Enjuto, ta; flacucho, cha (person).
strip [strip] n. Banda, *f.*, faja, *f.* || Franja, *f.*: *a strip of land*, una franja de terreno. || Tira, *f.*, historieta, *f.* (comic strip). || Pista, *f.* [de aterrizaje] (airstrip). || Cinta, *f.* (of film). || Tira, *f.* (of paper, material). || Listón, *m.* (of wood). || Tira, *f.* (of leather). || Fleje, *m.* (of metal). || FIG. *To tear a strip off s.o.*, echar una reprimenda *or* una bronca a alguien.
strip [strip] v. tr. Quitar (clothing). || Desnudar (to undress). || Quitar, sacar (to deprive sth. of its covering). || Deshacer, quitar la ropa de (a bed). || Desamueblar, quitar los muebles de (a room). || Deshojar (to remove leaves from). || Despalillar (tobacco leaves). || Descortezar (a tree). || Pelar (fruit). || Descarnar (a bone). || Quitar el pelo a (a dog). || TECH. Desmontar, desarmar (to dismantle). | Estropear (a screw thread, the cogs of a gear). | Quitar el forro a (a wire, a cable). || MAR. Desencapillar (a mast). | Desaparejar (a ship). || FAM. Aligerar (to lighten a car for speed). || — *To strip down*, raspar (to remove paint), desmontar (a motor). || *To strip of*, despojar de (possessions, honours etc.). || *To strip off*, quitar.
— V. intr. Desnudarse, desvestirse (to undress): *strip to the waist*, desnúdese hasta la cintura. || Hacer "strip-tease" (to perform striptease). || Pasarse de rosca (a screw). || Desconcharse, desprenderse (paint). || Despegarse (paper, wood, etc.). || Deshojarse (tree). || Descortezarse (the trunk of a tree). || — *To strip off*, desnudarse. || *To strip to the skin*, desnudarse completamente.
strip cartoon [—kɑ:ˈtu:n] n. Tira (*f.*) de periódico ilustrado, historieta, *f.*
strip cropping [—ˈkrɔpiŋ] n. AGR. Cultivo (*m.*) en fajas *or* en franjas.
stripe [straip] n. Azote, *m.*, latigazo, *m.* (stroke of the whip). || Latigazo, *m.* (mark made by this). || Raya, *f.*, lista, *f.* (band of colour, material). || Raya, *f.* (on trousers). || Tira, *f.* (of leather). || MIL. Galón, *m.* || U. S. Índole, *f.*, clase, *f.*, tipo, *m.* (kind).
stripe [straip] v. tr. Hacer rayas en, rayar.
striped [—t] adj. A rayas, rayado, da.
strip lighting [—ˈlaitiŋ] n. Alumbrado (*m.*) con lámparas fluorescentes.
stripling [ˈstripliŋ] n. Mozalbete, *m.*, joven, *m.*
strip mining [ˈstripˈmainiŋ] n. Explotación (*f.*) de una mina a cielo abierto.
stripper [ˈstripə*] n. Mujer (*f.*) que hace "striptease".
striptease [ˈstripti:z] n. "Strip-tease", *m.*
stripteaser [—ə*] n. Mujer (*f.*) que hace "striptease".
stripy [ˈstraipi] adj. Rayado, da.
strive* [straiv] v. intr. Esforzarse, procurar: *to strive to win the victory*, esforzarse por conseguir la victoria, procurar conseguir la victoria || Luchar (to fight). || Rivalizar, competir (to rivalize). || *To strive for* o *after sth.* esforzarse por conseguir algo, procurar conseguir algo.

— OBSERV. Pret. ***strove;*** p. p. ***striven.***

striven [ˈstrivn] p. p. See STRIVE.
stroboscope [ˈstrəubəskəup] n. Estroboscopio, *m.*
strode [strəud] pret. See STRIDE.
stroke [strəuk] n. Golpe, *m.* (blow, attempt to strike a ball). || Campanada, *f.* (of bell, clock). || Latido, *m.* (heartbeat). || MED. Ataque, *m.* [fulminante], apoplejía, *f.* (attack of apoplexy). || Rayo, *m.* (lightning). || Caricia, *f.* (caress). || Pincelada, *f.* (with a brush). || Trazo, *m.* (with pencil, pen). || PRINT. Raya, *f.* (oblique line). || SP. Tacada, *f.* (in billiards). | Brazada, *f.* (single movement when swimming). | Estilo, *m.* (swimming style). | Primer remero, *m.* (oarsman). | Palada, *f.*, golpe (*m.*) de remo (with an oar, style of rowing). | Golpe, *m.*, jugada, *f.* (in tennis, golf, cricket, etc.). || TECH. Recorrido, *m.*, carrera, *f.* (of a piston). || — *At a* o *with one stroke of the pen*, de un plumazo. || *At one fell stroke*, de un golpe. || SP. *Butterfly stroke*, estilo mariposa. || FIG. *By a stroke of luck*, por suerte. | *Finishing stroke*, golpe de gracia. || *Four-stroke engine*, motor de cuatro tiempos. || FAM. *Not to do a stroke of work*, no dar golpe. || *On the stroke of ten*, al dar las diez. || FIG. *Stroke of genius*, rasgo (*m.*) de ingenio, idea (*f.*) genial. || *To keep stroke*, llevar el compás. || FIG. *To put the finishing strokes to*, dar la última mano *or* el último toque a. || *Witty stroke*, agudeza, *f.*
stroke [strəuk] v. tr. Acariciar (with the hand): *he stroked the dog*, acarició el perro. || Ser el primer remero en (to be stroke for a boat). || — FAM. *To stroke s.o. down*, ablandar a alguien. | *To stroke s.o. the wrong way*, tomar a alguien a contrapelo.
stroll [strəul] n. Paseo, *m.*, vuelta, *f.*: *to go for a stroll*, [ir a] dar una vuelta.
stroll [strəul] v. tr. Dar un paseo por, dar una vuelta por, pasearse por. || *Strolling players*, cómicos (*m.*) de la legua.
— V. intr. Pasearse, vagar.
stroller [—ə*] n. Paseante, *m.* & *f.* || Cómico (*m.*) de la legua (actor). || U. S. Cochecito (*m.*) de niño (pram).
strong [strɔŋ] adj. Fuerte (cheese, drink, wind, current, light, smell, acid, tobacco). || Fuerte, robusto, ta (person): *a strong man*, un hombre fuerte. || Fuerte: *a very strong fabric*, una tela muy fuerte. || Fuerte, sólido, da (object). || Resistente: *is this ladder strong enough to hold me?*, ¿es esta escalera de manos bastante resistente para aguantarme? || Fuerte, potente (voice). || Poderoso, sa (lenses). || Fuerte (performed with physical strength): *a strong kick*, una patada fuerte. || Fuerte (morally powerful): *a strong will*, una voluntad fuerte. || Poderoso, sa; fuerte: *a strong nation*, una nación poderosa. || Fuerte, enérgico, ca; decidido, da (resolute): *a strong character*, un carácter enérgico. || Convincente (argument, evidence). || Fuerte (proficient): *to be strong in Latin*, estar fuerte en latín. || Acusado, da; fuerte (characteristic). || Fuerte, marcado, da (accent). || Bueno, na (sight). || Drástico, ca; severo, ra; enérgico, ca: *strong measures*, medidas drásticas. || Firme, profundo, da (conviction, devotion, faith). || Fervoroso, sa (believer). || Fuerte, profundo, da (impression). || Fuerte, intenso, sa (emotion). || Acérrimo, ma (supporter). || Arraigado, da (habit). || Fuerte: *strong currency*, moneda fuerte. || Fuerte, intenso, sa; vivo, va (colours). || Fuerte, marcado, da; notable (resemblance). || Subido de tono, subido de color (language). || Fuerte, violento, ta (terms). || Rancio, cia (butter, bacon, etc.). || ELECTR. Intenso, sa (current). || GRAMM. Fuerte (verbs). || COMM. Firme. || — *An army 2000 strong*, un ejército de dos mil hombres. || *As strong as an ox*, fuerte como un toro *or* un roble. || *Strong man*, hércules, *m.* (in circus). || *Strong point*, fuerte, *m.*: *politeness is not his strong point*, la corrección no es su fuerte. || *Strong nerves*, nervios bien templados. || *Strong reason*, causa (*f.*) mayor. || FIG. *That's too strong*, eso es demasiado. || *The strong and the weak*, el fuerte y el débil. || *To be strong in numbers*, ser numerosos. || *To be stronger*, estar mejor (in health). || *To have a strong character*, tener mucho carácter. || *To have a strong head*, aguantar mucho [alcohol]. || *To have a strong stomach*, tener un buen estómago. || *To have strong feelings about sth.*, tener ideas muy precisas *or* muy firmes sobre algo. || *To use the strong arm*, utilizar la fuerza.
— Adv. Muy bien: *at 80 he is still going strong*, tiene ochenta años y todavía se conserva muy bien; *the work is going strong*, el trabajo marcha muy bien. || Fuertemente.
strong-arm [—ɑ:m] adj. Severo, ra; de mano dura (policy, method, etc.). || — *Strong-arm man*, guardaespaldas, *m. inv.* || *Strong-arm tactics*, fuerza, *f.*
strong-arm [—ɑ:m] v. tr. Pegar (to beat). || Intimidar (to intimidate).
strongbox [—bɔks] n. Caja (*f.*) fuerte *or* de caudales.
stronghold [—həuld] n. MIL. Fortaleza, *f.*, plaza (*f.*) fuerte (fortress). || FIG. Baluarte, *m.*: *conservative stronghold*, baluarte del partido conservador.
strong-minded [—ˈmaindid] adj. Resuelto, ta; decidido, da (resolute).
strong-mindedness [—ˈmaindidnis] n. Resolución, *f.*, decisión, *f.*, carácter, *m.* (determination).
strongpoint [—pɔint] n. Plaza (*f.*) fuerte, fuerte, *m.*
strongroom [—rum] n. Cámara (*f.*) acorazada (for storing money or valuables).
strong-willed [ˈstrɔŋˈwild] adj. Resuelto, ta; decidido, da (resolute). || Obstinado, da (obstinate).
strontian [ˈstrɔnʃiən] n. Estroncio, *m.*
strontium [ˈstrɔntiəm] n. Estroncio, *m.*
strop [strɔp] n. Suavizador, *m.* (of razors).
strop [strɔp] v. tr. Suavizar (a razor).
strophe [ˈstrəufi] n. Estrofa, *f.*
strove [strəuv] pret. See STRIVE.
struck [strʌk] pret. & p. p. See STRIKE.
struck jury [—ˈdʒuəri] n. U. S. JUR. Jurado (*m.*) compuesto por 12 miembros escogidos entre 48 candidatos.
structural [ˈstrʌktʃərəl] adj. Estructural. || — *Structural engineering*, ingeniería (*f.*) de construcción de pantanos, puentes y otras grandes obras. || *Structural steel*, acero (*m.*) para la construcción.
structuralism [ˈstrʌktʃərəlizəm] n. Estructuralismo, *m.*
structure [ˈstrʌktʃə*] n. Estructura, *f.* || Construcción, *f.* (building). || FIG. Base, *f.* (of arguments). | Estructura, *f.* (of a play, etc.): *social structure*, estructura social.
structure [ˈstrʌktʃə*] v. tr. Estructurar. || Construir (to build).
structuring [—riŋ] n. Estructuración, *f.*
struggle [strʌgl] n. Lucha, *f.*, combate, *m.*, contienda, *f.* (a contending): *desperate struggle*, combate desesperado; *hand-to-hand struggle*, lucha cuerpo a cuerpo. || Esfuerzo, *m.* (a great effort). || Lucha, *f.*: *class struggle*, lucha de clases; *struggle for survival*, lucha por la vida. || *Without a struggle*, sin resistencia, sin luchar: *he gave in without a struggle*, se rindió sin resistencia.
struggle [ˈstrʌgl] v. intr. Luchar: *to struggle to survive*, luchar por la vida; *I am struggling with adversity*, lucho contra la adversidad. || Forcejear: *he struggled to free himself*, forcejeó para liberarse. || Esforzarse, luchar: *to struggle to succeed*, esforzarse por triunfar. || — *To struggle against* o *with*, pelear contra, luchar contra. || *To struggle along*, avanzar penosamente. ||

To struggle for, luchar por conseguir. || *To struggle to one's feet*, levantarse con dificultad.
struggler [—ə*] n. Luchador, ra.
struggling [—iŋ] adj. Combativo, va.
— N. Lucha, *f.*
strum [strʌm] n. Rasgueo, *m.* (on the guitar).
strum [strʌm] v. tr./intr. Rasguear (the guitar). || Rascar, tocar mal (an instrument).
struma [strumə] n. MED. Escrófula, *f.* (scrofula). | Bocio, *m.* (goitre).
— OBSERV. El plural de *struma* es *strumae*.
strumming [strʌmiŋ] n. Rasgueo, *m.*, rasgueado, *m.*
strumose [ˈstruməus] or **strumous** [ˈstruməs] adj. MED. Escrofuloso, sa. | Que tiene bocio.
strumpet [ˈstrʌmpit] n. FAM. Fulana, *f.*, furcia, *f.* (prostitute).
strung [strʌŋ] pret. & p. p. See STRING.
strut [strʌt] n. Pavoneo, *m.* (way of walking). || ARCH. Puntal, *m.*, riostra, *f.* || AVIAT. Montante, *m.*
strut [strʌt] v. tr. Apuntalar (to fit struts to).
— V. intr. Pavonearse (to walk).
strychnia [ˈstrikniə] or **strychnine** [ˈstrikni:n] n. CHEM. Estricnina, *f.*
Stuart [ˈstjuət] pr. n. Estuardo.
stub [stʌb] n. Tocón, *m.*, cepa, *f.* (of tree). || Raigón, *m.* (of tooth). || Cabo, *m.* (of pencil, crayon, candle, etc.). || Colilla, *f.* (of cigarette). || Talón, *m.*, matriz, *f.* (of a cheque). || Resguardo, *m.* (of a ticket, receipt).
stub [stʌb] v. tr. Arrancar (to pull up by the roots). || Rozar (to clear land). || — *To stub one's foot* o *one's toe against*, tropezar con. || *To stub out*, apagar (a cigarette). || *To stub up*, arrancar.
stubble [—l] n. Rastrojo, *m.* (stalks). || Barba (*f.*) incipiente (beard). || *Stubble field*, campo (*m.*) de rastrojos.
stubbly [—li] adj. Cubierto de rastrojo (with stalks). || Con una barba incipiente (chin). || Al cepillo (hair). || *Stubbly beard*, barba incipiente.
stubborn [—ən] adj. Obstinado, da; terco, ca; testarudo, da (obstinate): *a stubborn child*, un niño testarudo. || Porfiado, da; tenaz; tesonero, ra (effort). || Rebelde: *a stubborn illness*, una enfermedad rebelde. || Terco, ca; testarudo, da (animals). || Duro, ra; difícil de labrar (wood, stone). || Ingrato, ta; poco fructífero, ra (soil). || Difícil (problems, etc.). || Rotundo, da (refusal).
stubbornness [—ənnis] n. Obstinación, *f.*, terquedad, *f.*, testarudez, *f.*
stubby [—i] adj. Rechoncho, cha (person). || Lleno de cepas *or* de tocones (land).
stucco [ˈstʌkəu] n. Estuco, *m.*
— Adj. De estuco. || *Stucco plasterer* o *stucco worker*, estucador, *m.*, estuquista, *m.*
— OBSERV. El plural de *stucco* es *stuccoes* o *stuccos*.
stucco [ˈstʌkəu] v. tr. Estucar.
stuccowork [—wə:k] n. Estucado, *m.*
stuck [stʌk] pret. & p. p. See STICK.
stuck-up [—ʌp] adj. FAM. Presumido, da; engreído, da; pagado de sí mismo.
stud [stʌd] n. Cuadra, *f.* (collection of horses). || Cuadra, *f.*, caballeriza, *f.* (place). || Semental, *m.*, caballo (*m.*) semental (studhorse). || Tachón, *m.* (ornamental nail or rivet). || Clavo, *m.* (of pedestrian crossing). || Taco, *m.* (on football boots). || Botón (*m.*) de camisa (for shirt collar). || Gemelo, *m.* (for shirt cuffs). || ELECTR. Contacto, *m.* || Travesaño, *m.* (of chain). || Espiga, *f.*, husillo, *m.* (spindle, pin). || ARCH. Montante, *m.* || *Stud mare*, yegua (*f.*) de cría.
stud [stʌd] v. tr. Tachonar, adornar con clavos (to furnish with studs). || Poner tacos a (boots). || FIG. Llenar de: *the piano was studded with ornaments*, el piano estaba lleno de adornos. | Sembrar, cubrir, salpicar, tachonar (to scatter).
studbook [—buk] n. Registro (*m.*) genealógico de caballos.
student [ˈstju:dənt] n. Estudiante, *m.* & *f.* (who attends university, college, etc.). || Alumno, na (pupil): *that's one of my best students*, es uno de mis mejores alumnos. || Investigador, ra (researcher). || — *Law student*, estudiante de derecho. || *Student demonstrations*, manifestaciones estudiantiles. || *They are serious students of the subject*, estudian el tema a fondo.
student body [—ˈbɔdi] n. Estudiantes, *m. pl.*, estudiantado, *m.*
studentship [—ʃip] n. Beca, *f.* (grant). || Estudios, *m. pl.* (time).
stud farm [ˈstʌdfɑ:m] n. Acaballadero, *m.*
studhorse [ˈstʌdhɔ:s] n. Caballo (*m.*) semental, semental, *m.*
studied [ˈstʌdid] adj. Premeditado, da; calculado, da (premeditated). || Pensado, da; estudiado, da: *a well-studied plot*, un argumento bien pensado. || Estudiado, da; afectado, da: *a studied gesture*, un gesto estudiado.
studio [ˈstju:diəu] n. Estudio, *m.*, taller, *m.* (of an artist). || Estudio, *m.*: *photographer's studio*, estudio fotográfico; *television studio*, estudio de televisión. || CINEM. Estudios, *m. pl.*, estudio, *m.* || *Studio couch*, sofá (*m.*) cama.
studious [ˈstju:djəs] adj. Estudioso, sa; aplicado, da (devoted to study). || Solícito, ta; atento, ta (thoughtful). || See STUDIED.
studiousness [—nis] n. Aplicación, *f.*
study [ˈstʌdi] n. Estudio, *m.*: *a life devoted to study*, una vida dedicada al estudio. || Estudio, *m.*, investigación, *f.*: *studies of animal behaviour*, estudios de *or* investigaciones sobre el comportamiento de los animales. || Estudio, *m.*, examen, *m.* (consideration). || Asignatura, *f.*: *my favorite study*, mi asignatura preferida. || Estudio, *m.*: *he has published several studies in that field*, ha publicado varios estudios sobre este tema. || ARTS. MUS. Estudio, *m.* || Estudio, *m.*: *Macbeth is a study of evil*, Macbeth es un estudio de la maldad. || Despacho, *m.*, estudio, *m.*, escritorio, *m.* (room). || Sala (*f.*) de estudios (at school). || Preocupación, *f.* (earnest effort). || — Pl. Estudios, *m.*: *to stop one's studies*, dejar los estudios. || — FIG. *His face was a study!*, ¡la cara que puso! || THEATR. *To be a good, a slow study*, aprender rápidamente, lentamente su papel (an actor). || FIG. *To be in a brown study*, estar en las nubes, estar meditando profundamente.
study [ˈstʌdi] v. tr. Estudiar: *to study Spanish*, estudiar español. || Estudiar, examinar (to consider): *to study the possibilities*, examinar las posibilidades. || Estudiar, observar: *to study the stars*, observar las estrellas. || Estudiar, investigar, hacer un estudio sobre: *to study animal behaviour*, hacer un estudio sobre el comportamiento de los animales. || Estudiar, meditar, pensar: *to study one's answer*, meditar su respuesta. || Aprender [de memoria] (a part in a play). || *To study out*, reflexionar *or* meditar en (a question), resolver (a problem).
— V. intr. Hacer estudios, estudiar (to be a student). || Aplicarse, estudiar: *to study hard*, estudiar mucho. || — *To study for an exam*, preparar un examen. || *To study to be*, estudiar para: *he is studying to be a doctor*, estudia para médico. || *To study under*, ser alumno de, estudiar con.
study hall [—hɔ:l] n. Sala (*f.*) de estudios.
stuff [stʌf] n. Material, *m.*, materia, *f.*: *what stuff is it made of?*, ¿de qué materia está hecho? || Tejido, *m.*, tela, *f.*, paño, *m.*, género, *m.* (cloth). || Cosas, *f. pl.*: *the plumber went to collect his stuff*, el fontanero fue a recoger sus cosas; *leave your stuff in the hall*, deja tus cosas en la entrada; *they have produced a lot of new stuff*, han producido muchas cosas nuevas; *there's good stuff in her*, tiene cosas buenas; *there's some good stuff in your dictionary*, hay cosas buenas en tu diccionario. || Eso: *does she call this stuff tobacco?*, ¿llama a eso tabaco? || FIG. Tonterías, *f. pl.* (worthless ideas, opinions). | Madera, *f.*: *he has the stuff of a general, of an artist*, tiene madera de general, de artista. || FAM. Pasta, *f.*, moni, *m.* (money). || MAR. Galipote, *m.* || — FAM. *A nice bit of stuff*, un bombón, una monería. | *Did you bring the stuff?*, ¿lo trajiste? | *Give me the stuff*, dámelo. || *Green stuff*, verduras, *f. pl.* (vegetables). || FAM. *Horrible stuff*, porquería, *f.*, mejunje, *m.*, pócima, *f.* (bad tasting potion). || *Stuff and nonsense!*, ¡tonterías! || FIG. *That's the stuff!*, ¡eso es! | *The same old stuff*, las tonterías de siempre. | *To be good stuff*, ser muy bueno. || FAM. *To be hot stuff*, ser fenomenal *or* extraordinario *or* estupendo (to be fantastic), ser un as *or* un hacha (to be a champion, a wizard, etc.), ser sensacional (news), ser muy picante (spicy food), ser caliente (a woman). | *To do one's stuff*, hacer lo que uno debe (to do one's duty), mostrar lo que uno sabe (to show one's worth). | *To know one's stuff*, saber lo que uno se hace, conocer el percal.
stuff [stʌf] v. tr. Llenar, rellenar: *to stuff a jar with olives*, llenar de aceitunas un tarro; *to stuff a cushion with feathers*, rellenar un cojín con plumas. || Llenar completamente de: *to stuff olives into a jar*, llenar completamente de aceitunas un tarro. || Meter: *I stuffed my things in a suitcase*, metí mis cosas en una maleta. || Disecar (animals in taxidermy). || Rellenar (toys, dolls). || CULIN. Rellenar. || FAM. Atiborrar, llenar: *they stuffed us with food*, nos atiborraron de comida. | Meter [en la cabeza], llenar [la cabeza] de (to cram into the mind). || Impregnar con aceite (leather). || U. S. Poner votos falsos en (a ballot box). || — FAM. *Get stuffed!*, ¡vete a paseo! || *To stuff o.s.*, atiborrarse, hartarse, llenarse. || *To stuff up*, tapar, taponar (to block). || FIG. *To stuff with*, meter en la cabeza, llenar la cabeza de (ideas).
— V. intr. Atiborrarse, hartarse, llenarse.
stuffed [—t] adj. CULIN. Relleno, na: *stuffed olives*, aceitunas rellenas. || FAM. *Stuffed shirt*, persona envarada *or* estirada.
stuffer [—ə*] n. Disecador, ra.
stuffiness [—inis] n. Falta (*f.*) de ventilación, mala ventilación, *f.* (poor ventilation). || Congestión, *f.* (in the nose). || FIG. Envaramiento, *m.* (pomposity). | Pesadez, *f.* (dullness). | Mal humor, *m.* (sulkiness).
stuffing [—iŋ] n. Relleno, *m.* (for food, cushions, animals, etc.). || Disecación, *f.* (of animals). || FIG. Paja, *f.* (padding). || FIG. *To knock the stuffing out of s.o.*, quitarle los humos a uno (to deflate), pegarle una paliza a uno (to beat).
stuffing box [—iŋbɔks] n. Prensaestopas, *m. inv.*
stuffy [—i] adj. Mal ventilado, da (poorly ventilated). || Cargado, da (air). || Congestionado, da; taponado, da: *a stuffy nose*, la nariz taponada. || FAM. Estirado, da; envarado, da; pomposo, sa (pompous). | Pesado,

da (dull). | Chapado a la antigua (old-fashioned). | Malhumorado, da (sulky).

stultification [ˌstʌltifiˈkeiʃən] n. Ridiculización, *f.* (a ridiculing). || Anulación, *f.*, aniquilamiento, *m.* (a making worthless). || JUR. Incapacitación, *f.*

stultify [ˈstʌltifai] v. tr. Poner en ridículo, ridiculizar (to make ridiculous). || Anular, aniquilar (to make worthless). || JUR. Alegar incapacidad mental.

stum [stʌm] n. Mosto, *m.* (unfermented grape juice).

stumble [—bl] n. Tropezón, *m.*, traspié, *m.* (trip). || Lapsus (*m.*) lingüe (in speech). || Desliz, *m.* (error, sin).

stumble [—bl] v. intr. Tropezar (against an obstacle). || Dar traspiés: *he stumbled along the road*, iba por la calle dando traspiés. || Tropezar, topar [*over*, con] (a difficulty). || Cometer un desliz (to do wrong). || Vacilar (to hesitate). || Balbucear, decir torpemente: *to stumble through one's speech*, decir torpemente un discurso. || *To stumble across* o *on* o *upon*, tropezar con, encontrar.

stumbling block [—bliŋblɔk] n. FIG. Escollo, *m.*, tropiezo, *m.*

stumblingly [—bliŋli] adv. A tropezones, dando traspiés.

stump [stʌmp] n. Tocón, *m.*, cepa, *f.* (of a tree). || Troncho, *m.* (stalk of a cabbage). || Raigón, *m.* (of tooth). || Muñón, *m.* (of arm or leg). || Cabo, *m.* (of pencil, candle, etc.). || Colilla, *f.* (of cigarette). || Matriz, *f.*, talón, *m.* (of cheque, ticket, etc.). || Paso (*m.*) pesado (heavy step). || Pisada, *f.* (sound of footstep). || Difumino, *m.* (in drawing). || SP. Estaca, *f.* (in cricket). || U. S. Tribuna (*f.*) política (political rostrum). || FAM. Pata (*f.*) de palo (wooden leg). || — Pl. FAM. Zancas, *f.*, patas, *f.* (legs). || — *To go on the stump*, hacer una campaña electoral. || FAM. *To stir one's stumps*, menearse, moverse.

stump [stʌmp] v. tr. Arrancar los tocones de (land). || SP. Expulsar [a un bateador] derribando la puerta antes de que llegue a ella (in cricket). || U. S. Recorrer haciendo propaganda electoral (to canvass an area). || FAM. Dejar perplejo *or* confuso (to baffle). | Suspender (a candidate). || Difuminar (to blur). || — *To be stumped*, quedarse mudo. || FAM. *To stump up*, apoquinar, cascar, aflojar: *to stump up twenty pounds*, apoquinar veinte libras.
— V. intr. Renquear (to walk heavily). || U. S. Pronunciar discursos en una campaña electoral. || FAM. *To stump up*, aflojar la mosca *or* los cuartos.

stumping [—iŋ] n. Difuminación, *f.*

stump orator [—ˌɔrətə*] or **stump speaker** [—ˌspi:kə*] n. Orador (*m.*) callejero.

stumpy [—i] adj. Rechoncho, cha; achaparrado, da (people). || Corto, ta (things). || Lleno de tocones (land).

stun [stʌn] n. Aturdimiento, *m.*, atontamiento, *m.* || Perplejidad, *f.* || Choque, *m.* (shock).

stun [stʌn] v. tr. Aturdir, atontar (to make unconscious). || Pasmar, dejar estupefacto *or* pasmado (to stupefy). || *Stunned with surprise*, pasmado, da.

stung [stʌŋ] pret. & p. p. See STING.

stunk [stʌŋk] pret. & p. p. See STINK.

stunner [ˈstʌnə*] n. FAM. Persona (*f.*) estupenda, maravilla, *f.* (person). | Cosa (*f.*) estupenda, maravilla, *f.* (thing).

stunning [ˈstʌniŋ] adj. Imponente, bárbaro, ra; fenomenal (very attractive). || Que aturde, aturdidor, ra: *a stunning blow*, un golpe aturdidor. || Sorprendente; pasmoso, sa (astonishing).

stunt [stʌnt] n. Proeza, *f.*, hazaña, *f.* (exhibition of skill). || Acrobacia, *f.* (acrobatics). || Noticia (*f.*) sensacional (in newspapers). || Truco (*m.*) publicitario (publicity). || Recurso (*m.*) *or* maniobra (*f.*) sensacional (to attract attention). || Engendro, *m.* (malformed animal or plant). || Atrofia, *f.* (atrophy).

stunt [stʌnt] v. tr. Atrofiar, impedir el crecimiento *or* el desarrollo de (to stop the growth of).
— V. intr. Hacer acrobacias (in a plane).

stunted [—id] adj. Canijo, ja; encanijado, da. || *To become stunted*, encanijarse, ponerse canijo.

stunt flying [—ˌflaiiŋ] n. Vuelo (*m.*) acrobático.

stunt man [—mæn] n. Doble (*m.*) especial (in film).

stupa [ˈstju:pə] n. REL. Stupa, *f.*

stupe [stju:p] n. Compresa, *f.*

stupefacient [ˌstju:piˈfeiʃənt] adj. Estupefaciente.
— N. Estupefaciente, *m.*

stupefaction [ˌstju:piˈfækʃən] n. Estupefacción, *f.*

stupefactive [ˈstju:pifæktiv] adj. Estupefaciente.

stupefy [ˈstju:pifai] v. tr. Dejar estupefacto, dejar pasmado (to amaze): *the news stupefied him*, la noticia le dejó estupefacto. || Atontar (to make lethargic or dull).

stupefying [—iŋ] adj. Pasmoso, sa; asombroso, sa.

stupendous [stjuˈpendəs] adj. Estupendo, da: *she is a stupendous girl*, es una chica estupenda. || Prodigioso, sa; formidable: *a stupendous effort*, un esfuerzo formidable.

stupid [ˈstju:pid] adj. Estúpido, da; tonto, ta (slow-witted). || Atontado, da (in a state of stupor). || — FIG. *As stupid as a donkey*, más tonto que una mata de habas. || *That was stupid of me*, fue una estupidez mía, fue una tontería de mi parte. || *To drink o.s. stupid*, atontarse bebiendo.
— N. Estúpido, da; tonto, ta.

stupidity [stjuˈpiditi] or **stupidness** [ˈstju:pidnis] n. Estupidez, *f.*, tontería, *f.* (silliness). || Atontamiento, *m.* (daze).

stupor [ˈstju:pə*] n. Estupor, *m.* || *In a drunken stupor*, atontado por la bebida.

stuporous [ˈstju:pərəs] adj. Letárgico, ca.

sturdiness [ˈstə:dinis] n. Robustez, *f.*, fuerza, *f.* (robustness). || Energía, *f.* (energy). || Firmeza, *f.*, determinación, *f.* (resolution).

sturdy [ˈstə:di] adj. Robusto, ta; fuerte (strong or healthy). || Firme, resuelto, ta; decidido, da (resolute). || Enérgico, ca (energetic).
— N. VET. Modorra, *f.* (in sheep).

sturgeon [ˈstə:dʒən] n. Esturión, *m.* (fish).

stutter [ˈstʌtə*] n. Tartamudeo, *m.*

stutter [ˈstʌtə*] v. tr. Tartamudear, farfullar.
— V. intr. Tartamudear.

stutterer [—rə*] n. Tartamudo, da.

stuttering [—riŋ] adj. Tartamudo, da.
— N. Tartamudeo, *m.*

sty [stai] n. Pocilga, *f.* (for pigs). || FAM. Tugurio, *m.*, pocilga, *f.* (filthy place).

sty [stai] v. tr. Tener en la pocilga.
— V. intr. Vivir en una pocilga.

sty or **stye** [stai] n. MED. Orzuelo, *m.* (in the eye).

Stygian [ˈstidʒiən] adj. Estigio, gia. || FIG. Tenebroso, sa (night). | Inviolable (oath).

style [stail] n. Estilo, *m.* (distinctive type, way of expression): *the Byzantine style*, el estilo bizantino. || Manera, *f.*, estilo, *m.* (manner): *his style of playing the piano*, su manera de tocar el piano. || Tipo, *m.* (kind): *an American-style comedy*, una comedia de tipo americano. || Modelo, *m.*, tipo, *m.* (of manufactures). || Moda, *f.* (fashion): *it's the latest style*, es la última moda. || Hechura, *f.* (cut of clothes). || Peinado, *m.* (of hair). || Estilo, *m.*, elegancia, *f.*, clase, *f.*, distinción, *f.*: *that girl has style*, esa chica tiene estilo. || Título, *m.*, tratamiento, *m.* (mode of address). || Título, *m.* (title). || BOT. Estilo, *m.* || TECH. Buril, *m.* || Estilete, *m.* (for writing on wax). || Estilo, *m.*, gnomón, *m.* (of a dial). || Aguja, *f.* (of gramophone). || COMM. Razón (*f.*) social (name of a company). || — *A general in the old style*, un general de la vieja escuela. || *In the style of*, al estilo de. || *That's the style!*, ¡muy bien! || *To do sth. in style*, hacer algo como es debido. || *To live in style*, vivir con gran lujo. || *To travel in style*, viajar con la mayor comodidad. || *To win in fine style*, ganar limpiamente.

style [stail] v. tr. Llamar, dar el nombre de, titular (to give a name to). || Hacer a la moda (clothes). || Peinar a la moda (hair). || Diseñar (to design).

stylet [—it] n. MED. Estilete, *m.* || Estilete, *m.* (stiletto). || ZOOL. Púa, *f.*, pincho, *m.*

styling [ˈstailiŋ] n. Estilización, *f.*

stylish [ˈstailiʃ] adj. Elegante (elegant). || A la moda (fashionable). || Con estilo, que tiene estilo (behaviour).

stylishness [—nis] n. Elegancia, *f.*, estilo, *m.*

stylism [ˈstailizəm] n. Estilismo, *m.*

stylist [ˈstailist] n. Estilista, *m.* & *f.* (writer or fashion consultant). || Diseñador, ra (of cars, etc.). || Peluquero, ra (hairdresser).

stylistic [staiˈlistik] or **stylistical** [—əl] adj. Estilístico, ca.

stylistics [—s] n. Estilística, *f.*

stylization [ˌstailaiˈzeiʃən] n. Estilización, *f.*

stylize [ˈstailaiz] v. tr. Estilizar.

stylograph [ˈstailəgrɑ:f] n. Estilográfica, *f.*

stylographic [ˌstailəˈgræfik] adj. Estilográfico, ca.

stylus [ˈstailəs] n. Estilete, *m.* (for writing on wax). || Punzón, *m.* (for writing Braille). || Aguja, *f.* (of a record player).

— OBSERV. El plural de *stylus* es *styluses* o *styli*.

stymie [ˈstaimi] v. tr. See STIMY.

styptic [ˈstiptik] adj. Estíptico, ca; astringente.
— N. MED. Estíptico, *m.*, astringente, *m.*

styrax [ˈstaiəræks] n. BOT. Estoraque, *m.*

styrene [ˈstairi:n] n. CHEM. Estireno, *m.*, estiroleno, *m.*

Styx [stiks] n. MYTH. Laguna (*f.*) Estigia.

suable [ˈsju:əbl] adj. Que puede ser citado ante la justicia, demandable.

suasion [ˈsweiʒən] n. Persuasión, *f.*

suave [swɑ:v] adj. Suave. || Afable, amable (kind). || Zalamero, ra (ingratiating).

suavity [ˈswɑ:viti] n. Suavidad, *f.* || Afabilidad, *f.*, amabilidad, *f.* (kindness). || Zalamería, *f.* (excessive politeness).

sub [sʌb] n. FAM. Subalterno, *m.*, subordinado, *m.* (subordinate). | Submarino, *m.* (submarine). | Subteniente, *m.* (sublieutenant). | Sustituto, ta (substitute). | Suscripción, *f.* (subscription). | Anticipo, *m.*, adelanto, *m.* (an advance).

sub [sʌb] v. intr. *To sub for*, sustituir a.

subacid [ˈsʌbˈæsid] adj. Agridulce, ligeramente agrio (taste). || FIG. Agridulce (remarks).

subaltern [ˈsʌbltən] adj. Subordinado, da; subalterno, na.
— N. Subalterno, *m.*, subordinado, *m.* || MIL. Alférez, *m.* (subaltern officer). | Subalterno, *m.*

subaquatic [ˌsʌbəˈkwætik] adj. Subacuático, ca.

subaqueous [ˈsʌbˈeikwiəs] adj. Subacuático, ca.

subarctic [sʌbˈɑ:ktik] adj. Subártico, ca.

subastral [sʌbˈæstrəl] adj. Sublunar, terrestre.

subbasement [ˈsʌbˌbeismənt] n. Segundo (*m.*) sótano.
subcelestial [ˈsʌbsiˈlestjəl] adj. Terrenal.
subclass [ˈsʌbklɑːs] n. Subclase, *f.*
subclavian [ˌsʌbˈkleiviən] adj. Subclavio, via: *subclavian vein*, vena subclavia.
subcommittee [ˈsʌbkəˌmiti] n. Subcomisión, *f.*, subcomité, *m.*
subconscious [ˈsʌbˈkɔnʃəs] adj. Subconsciente.
— N. Subconsciente, *m.*
subconsciousness [ˈsʌbˈkɔnʃəsnis] n. Subconsciencia, *f.*
subcontinent [ˈsʌbˈkɔntinənt] n. Subcontinente, *m.*
subcontract [sʌbˈkɔntrækt] n. Subcontrato, *m.*
subcontract [ˌsʌbkənˈtrækt] v. tr. Ceder *or* tomar en subcontrato, subcontratar.
subcontractor [—ə*] n. Subcontratista, *m.*, segundo contratista, *m.*
subcutaneous [ˈsʌbkjuˈteinjəs] adj. Subcutáneo, a.
subdeacon [ˈsʌbˈdiːkən] n. REL. Subdiácono, *m.*
subdeaconry [—ri] n. REL. Subdiaconado, *m.*, subdiaconato, *m.*
subdelegate [ˈsʌbˈdeligit] n. Subdelegado, da.
subdelegate [ˈsʌbˈdeligeit] v. tr. Subdelegar.
subdelegation [ˈsʌbdeliˈgeiʃən] n. Subdelegación, *f.*
subdiaconate [ˈsʌbdaiˈækənit] n. REL. Subdiaconado, *m.*, subdiaconato, *m.*
subdivide [ˈsʌbdiˈvaid] v. tr. Subdividir.
— V. intr. Subdividirse.
subdivision [ˈsʌbdiˌviʒən] n. Subdivisión, *f.*
subdominant [ˈsʌbˈdɔminənt] n. MUS. Subdominante, *f.* (tone).
subdue [səbˈdjuː] v. tr. Sojuzgar, someter, dominar (a country, etc.). || Atenuar, suavizar (sound, colour, light, etc.). || Bajar (voice). || Calmar, aliviar (pain). || Reprimir, contener, sojuzgar, dominar (passion). || Deprimir, abatir (s.o.'s spirits). || Poner en cultivo (land).
subdued [—d] adj. Sojuzgado, da; sometido, da; dominado, da (a country, etc.). || Sumiso, sa (docile). || Suave, suavizado, da (colour, sound, light, etc.). || Bajo, ja (voice). || Aliviado, da (pain). || Reprimido, da; contenido, da; sojuzgado, da; dominado, da (one's passion). || Deprimido, da; abatido, da (depressed).
subedit [ˈsʌbˈedit] v. tr. Corregir (an article).
subeditor [—ə*] n. Redactor, *m.* (of a newspaper).
suberose [ˈsjuːbərəus] o **suberous** [ˈsjuːbərəs] adj. Suberoso, sa.
subfamily [ˈsʌbˌfæmili] n. Subfamilia, *f.*
subfluvial [ˈsʌbˈfluːvjəl] adj. Subfluvial, subálveo, a.
subfusc [ˈsʌbfʌsk] adj. Oscuro, ra.
subgenus [ˈsʌbˌdʒiːnəs] n. Subgénero, *m.*
subgroup [ˈsʌbgruːp] n. Subgrupo, *m.*
subhead [ˈsʌbhed] o **subheading** [—iŋ] n. Subtítulo, *m.* (subtitle). || Subdirector, *m.* (of a school).
subhuman [ˈsʌbˈhjuːmən] adj. Infrahumano, na.
subindex [ˌsʌbˈindeks] n. MATH. Subíndice, *m.*

— OBSERV. El plural de la palabra inglesa es *subindices*.

subjacent [sʌbˈdʒeisənt] adj. Subyacente.
subject [ˈsʌbdʒikt] adj. Sometido, da; dominado, da (people, race). || — *Subject to*, sujeto a (charge, fee, etc.): *we are subject to the laws of the country*, estamos sujetos a las leyes del país. || *Subject to correction*, que puede ser corregido. || *Subject to earthquakes*, propenso a terremotos. || *Subject to government approval*, previa aprobación del gobierno.
— N. Súbdito, ta (of a country): *British subject*, súbdito británico. || Tema, *m.* (of conference, conversation, book): *let's change the subject*, cambiemos de tema. || Sujeto, *m.* (of an experiment). || Motivo, *m.* (of a painting). || Objeto, *m.* (of meditation, gossip). || Motivo, *m.* (reason). || GRAMM. PHIL. Sujeto, *m.* || MED. Paciente, *m.* & *f.* || Asignatura, *f.* (in school). || MUS. Tema, *m.* || — *Enough on that subject*, dejemos de hablar de esto. || *On the subject of*, a propósito de, referente al tema de. || *To come to one's subject*, entrar en materia. || *To keep off a subject*, no tocar un tema. || *While we are on the subject*, mientras hablamos del tema.
subject [səbˈdʒekt] v. tr. Sojuzgar, dominar (to conquer). || Supeditar (to subordinate). || Someter (to an examination). || — *To subject o.s. to*, sujetarse a, someterse a. || *To subject to*, someter a: *the thief was subjected to severe punishment*, el ladrón fue sometido a un castigo severo; exponer a: *such behaviour will subject you to criticism*, tal comportamiento le expondrá a críticas.
subjection [səbˈdʒekʃən] n. Sojuzgamiento, *m.*, avasallamiento, *m.*, dominación, *f.* (domineering). || Sujeción, *f.*, supeditación, *f.* (subordination). || Sometimiento, *m.* (submission). || *To bring into subjection*, sojuzgar, avasallar.
subjective [səbˈdʒektiv] adj. Subjetivo, va. || GRAMM. Nominativo, va.
subjectivism [səbˈdʒektivizəm] n. Subjetivismo, *m.*
subjectivity [ˌsʌbdʒekˈtiviti] n. Subjetividad, *f.*
subject matter [ˈsʌbdʒiktˌmætə*] n. Tema, *m.*, materia, *f.* (theme, matter). || Contenido, *m.* (contents).
subjoin [ˈsʌbˈdʒɔin] v. tr. Adjuntar.
sub judice [sʌbˈdʒuːdisi] adj. JUR. Pendiente, por resolver, sub judice.
subjugate [ˈsʌbdʒugeit] v. tr. Sojuzgar.
subjugating [—iŋ] adj. Sojuzgador, ra.
subjugation [ˌsʌbdʒuˈgeiʃən] n. Dominación, *f.*, sometimiento, *m.*, sojuzgamiento, *m.*
subjugator [ˈsʌbdʒugeitə*] n. Sojuzgador, ra.
subjunctive [səbˈdʒʌŋktiv] adj. GRAMM. Subjuntivo, va: *subjunctive mood*, modo subjuntivo.
— N. Subjuntivo, *m.*
subkingdom [ˈsʌbˌkiŋdəm] n. BIOL. Subreino, *m.*
sublease [ˈsʌbˈliːs] n. Subarriendo, *m.*, subarrendamiento, *m.*
sublease [ˈsʌbˈliːs] v. tr. Subarrendar.
sublessee [ˈsʌbleˈsiː] n. Subarrendatario, ria.
sublessor [ˈsʌbleˈsɔː*] n. Subarrendador, ra.
sublet [ˈsʌbˈlet] v. tr. Subarrendar.
sublieutenant [ˈsʌbleˈtenənt] n. MAR. Alférez (*m.*) de navío. || MIL. Alférez, *m.*, subteniente, *m.*
sublimate [ˈsʌblimit] n. CHEM. Sublimado, *m.*
sublimate [ˈsʌblimeit] v. tr. Sublimar.
sublimation [ˌsʌbliˈmeiʃən] n. CHEM. Sublimación, *f.* (process). | Sublimado, *m.* (product). || FIG. Sublimación, *f.*
sublime [səˈblaim] adj. Sublime (exalted, inspiring admiration). || Supremo, ma (supreme, outstanding): *sublime indifference*, indiferencia suprema. || Majestuoso, sa; sublime (scenery). || MED. Epidérmico, ca.
— N. *The sublime*, lo sublime. || *To go from the sublime to the ridiculous*, volverse cada vez más ridículo.
sublime [səˈblaim] v. tr. Sublimar.
— V. intr. Sublimarse.
sublimeness [—nis] n. Sublimidad, *f.*
subliminal [sʌbˈliminl] adj. Subconsciente.
— N. Subconsciente, *m.*
sublimity [səˈblimiti] n. Sublimidad, *f.* || Cosa (*f.*) sublime.
sublunar [sʌbˈluːnə*] or **sublunary** [—ri] adj. Sublunar. || FIG. Terrenal (earthly).
submachine gun [ˈsʌbməˈʃiːngʌn] n. MIL. Pistola (*f.*) ametralladora, metralleta, *f.*
submarine [ˌsʌbməˈriːn] adj. Submarino, na.
— N. Submarino, *m.* || *Submarine chaser*, cazasubmarinos, *m. inv.*
submariner [sʌbˈmærinə*] n. Submarinista, *m.*
submaxilla [ˌsʌbmækˈsilə] n. ANAT. Mandíbula (*f.*) inferior.

— OBSERV. El plural de *submaxilla* es *submaxillae*.

submaxillary [ˌsʌbmækˈsiləri] adj. Submaxilar: *submaxillary gland*, glándula submaxilar.
submediant [sʌbˈmiːdiənt] n. MUS. Superdominante, *f.*
submerge [səbˈməːdʒ] v. tr. Sumergir. || Inundar (land).
— V. intr. Sumergirse.
submergence [—əns] n. Sumersión, *f.*
submergible [—əbl] adj. Sumergible.
submerse [sʌbˈməːs] v. tr. Sumergir.
submersed [—t] adj. Sumergido, da.
submersible [səbˈməːsəbl] adj. Sumergible.
— N. Submarino, *m.*, sumergible, *m.*
submersion [səbˈməːʃən] n. Sumersión, *f.*
submission [səbˈmiʃən] n. Sumisión, *f.* (act of submitting). || Resignación, *f.*, conformidad, *f.* (resignation). || JUR. Sumisión (*f.*) a la jurisdicción de un juez *or* tribunal. | Sumisión, *f.* (to arbitration). || Sometimiento, *m.* (to an examination). || Presentación, *f.* (of documents).
submissive [sʌbˈmisiv] adj. Sumiso, sa (willing to submit). || Obediente (obedient).
submissiveness [—nis] n. Sumisión, *f.*
submit [səbˈmit] v. tr. Someter: *to submit s.o. to torture*, someter a alguien a la tortura. || Presentar (a proposal). || Proponer, exponer (a theory). || Sugerir, proponer (to suggest). || Señalar, indicar: *I submit that there is another point of view*, señalo que existe otro punto de vista. || Someter (to refer for consideration): *to submit sth. for s.o.'s approval*, someter algo a la aprobación de alguien.
— V. intr. Rendirse, someterse (to cease to resist). || Someterse (to defer to s.o.'s wishes). || Conformarse (to resign o.s.).
submittal [səbˈmitəl] n. Sumisión, *f.*
submultiple [ˈsʌbˈmʌltipl] n. MATH. Submúltiplo, *m.*
subnormal [ˈsʌbˈnɔːməl] adj. MED. Subnormal.
— N. MED. Subnormal, *m.* & *f.* || MATH. Subnormal, *f.*
suborbital [sʌbˈɔːbitəl] adj. ANAT. Suborbitario, ria.
suborder [ˈsʌbˌɔːdə*] n. Suborden, *m.*
subordinate [səˈbɔːdnit] adj. Subordinado, da; subalterno, na. || GRAMM. Subordinado, da: *subordinate clause*, oración subordinada.
— N. Subordinado, da; subalterno, na.
subordinate [səˈbɔːdineit] v. tr. Subordinar.
subordination [səˌbɔːdiˈneiʃən] n. Subordinación, *f.*
suborn [sʌˈbɔːn] v. tr. Sobornar, cohechar.
subornation [ˌsʌbɔːˈneiʃən] n. Soborno, *m.*, corrupción, *f.*, cohecho, *m.* (bribery).
suborner [sʌˈbɔːnə*] n. Sobornador, ra; cohechador, ra (briber).
subplot [ˈsʌbplɔt] n. Argumento (*m.*) secundario (of novel, film, play, etc.).
subpoena [səbˈpiːnə] n. JUR. Citación, *f.*
subpoena [səbˈpiːnə] v. tr. JUR. Citar, mandar comparecer.
sub-post office [ˌsəbˈpəustˌɔfis] n. Estafeta (*f.*) de Correos.

subprefect [ˈsʌbˈpriːfekt] n. Subprefecto, *m.*
subprefecture [ˈsʌbpriːˈfektjə*] n. Subprefectura, *f.*
subprincipal [ˈsʌbˈprinsəpl] n. Subdirector, *m.* (of a school).
subrent [ˈsʌbˈrent] v. tr. Subarrendar.
subreption [səbˈrepʃən] n. Subrepción, *f.*
subreptitious [ˌsʌbrepˈtiʃəs] adj. Subrepticio, cia.
subrogate [ˈsʌbrəgeit] v. tr. JUR. Subrogar.
subrogation [ˌsʌbrəˈgeiʃən] n. JUR. Subrogación, *f.*
sub rosa [ˈsʌbˈrəuzə] adv. En secreto, confidencialmente.
subscribe [səbˈskraib] v. tr. Poner (one's name on a document). || Firmar, suscribir (a document). || Suscribir, aprobar, estar de acuerdo con (to support). || Pagar (to pay). || Suscribirse por (to promise to pay).
— V. intr. Suscribirse, abonarse (to make a subscription). || *To subscribe to*, aprobar, estar de acuerdo con, suscribir (to agree with), abonarse a, suscribirse a (a newspaper, magazine, etc.), suscribir, firmar (a document, etc.).
— OBSERV. The verb *suscribir* may also be spelt *subscribir*.
subscribed [—d] adj. Suscrito, ta.
subscriber [—ə*] n. Suscriptor, ra; el que suscribe. || Suscriptor, ra; abonado, da (to a newspaper).
subscript [ˈsʌbskript] adj. GRAMM. Escrito debajo de una letra.
— N. Signo (*m.*) escrito debajo de una letra. || MATH. Subíndice, *m.*
subscription [səbˈskripʃən] n. Suscripción, *f.* (act of subscribing). || Firma, *f.* (on a document). || Adhesión, *f.* (to a doctrine). || Abono, *m.*, suscripción, *f.* (to a newspaper, magazine). || Cuota (*f.*) *or* cantidad (*f.*) suscrita (sum subscribed). || Cuota, *f.* (membership fees).
— OBSERV. The word *suscripción* may also be spelt *subscripción*.
subsection [ˈsʌbˌsekʃən] n. Subdivisión, *f.* || Apartado, *m.* (of a law).
subsequence [ˈsʌbsikwəns] n. Consecuencia, *f.* (happening). || Posterioridad, *f.* (posteriority).
subsequent [ˈsʌbsikwənt] adj. Subsiguiente, consecutivo, va. || Posterior: *subsequent to*, posterior a.
subsequently [—li] adv. Posteriormente, más tarde.
subserve [səbˈsəːv] v. tr. Favorecer, ayudar.
subservience [səbˈsəːvjəns] or **subserviency** [—i] n. Utilidad, *f.* (usefulness). || Servilismo, *m.* (servility). || Subordinación, *f.* (subordination). || Sumisión, *f.* (submissiveness).
subservient [səbˈsəːvjənt] adj. Servil (servile). || Subordinado, da (subordinate). || Sumiso, sa (submissive).
subside [səbˈsaid] v. intr. Hundirse (ground, building). || Bajar, descender (flood water, fever). || Depositarse, asentarse (sediment). || Calmarse, apaciguarse (the sea, anger, excitement). || Amainar (storm, wind, etc.). || Desplomarse, dejarse caer: *to subside into a chair*, dejarse caer en una silla.
subsidence [—əns] n. Hundimiento, *m.* (of ground, building). || Bajada, *f.*, descenso, *m.* (of flood water, fever). || Depósito, *m.*, asentamiento, *m.* (of sediment). || Apaciguamiento, *m.* (of sea, anger, etc.). || Amaine, *m.* (of storm, wind).
subsidiary [səbˈsidjəri] adj. Subsidiario, ria. || Secundario, ria. || Auxiliar. || *Subsidiary company*, sucursal, *f.*, filial, *f.*
— N. Auxiliar, *m.* & *f.*, ayudante, *m.* & *f.* (assistant). || Sucursal, *f.*, filial, *f.* (company).
subsidize [ˈsʌbsidaiz] v. tr. Subvencionar (an enterprise). || Dar subsidios a (a family).
subsidy [ˈsʌbsidi] n. Subvención, *f.* (to an enterprise, a country). || Subsidio, *m.* (to a family, a person).
subsist [səbˈsist] v. intr. Subsistir, perdurar (to continue to exist). || Subsistir (to continue to live). || *To subsist on*, mantenerse con, sustentarse con.
— V. tr. Mantener.
subsistence [—əns] n. Subsistencia, *f.*, existencia, *f.* || Mantenimiento, *m.*, subsistencia, *f.*, sustento, *m.* (livelihood). || PHIL. Subsistencia, *f.* || *Subsistence allowance*, dietas, *f. pl.* [*Amer.*, viático, *m.*].
subsistent [—ənt] adj. Subsistente.
subsoil [ˈsʌbsɔil] n. Subsuelo, *m.*
subsonic [ˈsʌbˈsɔnik] adj. Subsónico, ca.
subspecies [ˈsʌbˌspiːʃiːz] n. BOT. BIOL. Subespecie, *f.*
— OBSERV. El plural de *subspecies* es *subspecies*.
substance [ˈsʌbstəns] n. Sustancia, *f.*, substancia, *f.* (material). || Esencia, *f.*: *the substance of an argument*, la esencia de un argumento. || Sustancia, *f.*, substancia, *f.*: *his arguments have little substance*, sus argumentos tienen poca sustancia. || Fondo, *m.*: *form and substance*, forma y fondo. || FIG. Caudal, *m.*, fortuna, *f.*, bienes, *m. pl.* (wealth): *a man of substance*, un hombre con fortuna. || PHIL. Sustancia, *f.*, substancia, *f.* || Consistencia, *f.*, cuerpo, *m.* (of a material, cloth). || Solidez, *f.* (solidity). || *In substance*, en esencia, en sustancia.
substandard [ˈsʌbˈstændəd] adj. Inferior [al nivel medio].
substantial [səbˈstænʃəl] adj. Real, verdadero, ra (real). || Sustancial, substancial: *a substantial argument*, un argumento sustancial. || Considerable, sustancial, substancial: *substantial income*, ingresos considerables. || Importante. || Abundante: *substantial meal*, comida abundante. || Sustancioso, sa; substancioso, sa; nutritivo, va (food, drink). || Consistente, fuerte, sólido, da (made to last). || FIG. Con fortuna, rico, ca; acaudalado, da; adinerado, da (wealthy).
substantialism [—izəm] n. PHIL. Sustancialismo, *m.*, substancialismo, *m.*
substantiality [səbˌstænʃiˈæliti] n. Realidad, *f.* (reality). || Solidez, *f.* (solidity).
substantially [—i] adv. Sustancialmente, substancialmente (in a substantial manner). || Considerablemente (considerably).
substantiate [səbˈstænʃieit] v. tr. Establecer (a charge). || Justificar (a claim). || *Non-substantiated*, sin pruebas que lo justifiquen.
substantiation [səbˌstænʃiˈeiʃən] n. Justificación, *f.*
substantival [ˌsʌbstənˈtaivəl] adj. GRAMM. Sustantivo, va; substantivo, va.
substantivate [səbˈstæntiveit] v. tr. Sustantivar, substantivar.
substantive [ˈsʌbstəntiv] adj. GRAMM. Sustantivo, va; substantivo, va. || Considerable (substantial). || Real (actual). || Esencial (essential). || Autónomo, ma; independiente (not dependent). || JUR. Positivo, va: *substantive law*, derecho positivo.
— N. GRAMM. Sustantivo, *m.*, substantivo, *m.*
substantiveness [—nis] n. Sustantividad, *f.*, substantividad, *f.*
substantivize [sʌbˈstæntivaiz] or **substantize** [ˈsʌbstəntaiz] v. tr. Sustantivar, substantivar.
substation [ˈsʌbˌsteiʃən] n. ELECTR. Subestación, *f.*
substitutable [ˈsʌbstitjuːəbl] adj. Sustituible, substituible.
substitute [ˈsʌbstitjuːt] n. Sustituto, ta; substituto, ta; suplente, *m.* & *f.* (person). || Sucedáneo, *m.* (goods). || Imitación, *f.* || SP. Suplente, *m.*, reserva, *m.*
substitute [ˈsʌbstitjuːt] v. tr. Sustituir, substituir: *to substitute nylon for cotton* o *to substitute cotton by nylon*, sustituir el algodón por el nylon
— V. intr. Sustituir, substituir, suplir, reemplazar: *he is substituting for his brother*, está sustituyendo a su hermano.
substitution [ˌsʌbstiˈtjuːʃən] n. Sustitución, *f.*, substitución, *f.*
substitutional [—l] or **substitutive** [ˈsʌbstitjuːtiv] adj. Sustituidor, ra; substituidor, ra; sustitutivo, va; substitutivo, va.
substrata [ˈsʌbˈstrɑːtə] pl. n. See SUBSTRATUM.
substratum [ˈsʌbˈstrɑːtəm] n. Sustrato, *m.*, substrato, *m.* || FIG. Fondo, *m.*: *a substratum of truth*, un fondo de verdad. || AGR. GEOL. Subsuelo, *m.*
— OBSERV. El plural de *substratum* es *substrata*.
substructure [ˈsʌbˌstrʌktʃə*] n. Infraestructura, *f.* || FIG. Base, *f.*
subsume [səbˈsjuːm] v. tr. PHIL. Incluir [en una categoría, clase, etc.].
subsurface [ˈsʌbˈsəːfis] adj. Subterráneo, a.
subtangent [ˈsʌbˈtændʒənt] n. Subtangente, *f.*
subtenancy [ˈsʌbˈtenənsi] n. Subarriendo, *m.*
subtenant [ˈsʌbˈtenənt] n. Subarrendatario, ria.
subtend [səbˈtend] v. tr. MATH. Subtender.
subterfuge [ˈsʌbtəfjuːdʒ] n. Subterfugio, *m.*
subterranean [ˌsʌbtəˈreinjən] or **subterraneous** [sʌbtəˈreinjəs] adj. Subterráneo, a.
subtility [sʌbˈtiləti] n. See SUBTLETY.
subtilization [sʌtilaiˈzeiʃən] n. Sutilización, *f.*
subtilize [ˈsʌtilaiz] v. tr./intr. Sutilizar.
subtitle [ˈsʌbˈtaitl] n. Subtítulo, *m.*
subtitle [ˈsʌbˌtaitl] v. tr. Subtitular, poner subtítulos a.
subtle [ˈsʌtl] adj. Sutil (thin, not dense). || Sutil: *a subtle difference*, una diferencia sutil. || Agudo, da; sutil, perspicaz (keen): *a subtle mind*, una mente aguda. || Ingenioso, sa; astuto, ta (clever): *a subtle argument*, un argumento ingenioso. || Insidioso, sa (insidious). || Misterioso, sa (charm). || Delicado, da (perfume). || Fino, na (irony, etc.).
subtleness [—nis] n. See SUBTLETY.
subtlety [—ti] n. Sutilidad, *f.*, sutileza, *f.* (of distinctions, ideas, etc.). || Astucia, *f.*, sutileza, *f.* (cunning).
subtly [ˈsʌtli] adv. Sutilmente.
subtonic [ˈsʌbˈtɔnik] n. MUS. Nota (*f.*) sensible.
subtract [səbˈtrækt] v. tr. Restar, sustraer, substraer: *to subtract 13 from 20*, restar 13 a 20. || FIG. Sustraer, quitar.
subtraction [səbˈtrækʃən] n. MATH. Resta, *f.*, sustracción, *f.*, substracción, *f.* || FIG. Sustracción, *f.*
subtractive [səbˈtræktiv] adj. Que se tiene que sustraer.
subtrahend [ˈsʌbtrəhend] n. MATH. Sustraendo, *m.*, substraendo, *m.*
subtropic [ˈsʌbˈtrɔpik] or **subtropical** [—əl] adj. Subtropical: *subtropical climate*, clima subtropical.
subtropics [—s] pl. n. Regiones (*f.*) subtropicales.
subtype [ˈsʌbtaip] n. BIOL. Subtipo, *m.*
suburb [ˈsʌbəːb] n. Suburbio, *m.*, arrabal, *m.*
suburban [səˈbəːbən] adj. Suburbano, na. || *Suburban train*, tren (*m.*) de cercanías.
suburbanite [sʌˈbəːbənait] adj. De las afueras, suburbano, na.
— N. Persona (*f.*) que vive en las afueras.
suburbia [sʌˈbəːbiə] pl. n. Suburbios, *m.*, afueras, *f.*

subvention [səb'venʃən] n. Subvención, *f.*, ayuda, *f.*, subsidio, *m.*
subversion [səb'və:ʃən] n. Subversión, *f.*
subversive [səb'və:siv] adj. Subversivo, va.
— N. Persona (*f.*) subversiva.
subvert [sʌb'və:t] v. tr. Derribar, derrocar (a government, etc.). || Derribar (sth. established). || Corromper, pervertir (a person).
subway ['sʌbwei] n. Paso (*m.*) subterráneo (under street, etc.). || Conducto (*m.*) subterráneo (underground conduit). || U. S. Metro, *m.* [*Amer.*, subte, *m.*] (underground).
succedaneous [sʌksi'deiniəs] adj. Sucedáneo, a.
succedaneum [sʌksi'deiniəm] n. Sucedáneo, *m.*, sustituto, *m.*
— Observ. El plural de *succedaneum* es *succedanea.*
succeed [sək'si:d] v. intr. Tener éxito (to be successful). || Salir bien: *the plan succeeded*, el proyecto salió bien. || Triunfar: *he succeeded in life*, triunfó en la vida. || Seguir, suceder: *a long peace succeeded*, siguió un largo período de paz. || — *To succeed in doing sth.*, conseguir *or* lograr hacer algo: *did you succeed in getting him on the phone?*, ¿logró hablar con él por teléfono? || *To succeed to a fortune*, heredar una fortuna. || *To succeed to the throne*, heredar el trono.
— V. tr. Suceder a: *he succeeded his father in the business*, sucedió a su padre en el negocio. || Seguir (to follow).
succeeding [—iŋ] adj. Siguiente (following). || Sucesivo, va (successive).
succentor [sək'sentə*] n. Rel. Sochantre, *m.*
success [sək'ses] n. Éxito, *m.*, triunfo, *m.*: *he was a great success*, tuvo un gran éxito; *to make a success of*, tener éxito en. || — *Box-office success*, éxito de taquilla *or* taquillero. || *The portrait is a success*, el retrato ha salido muy bien.
successful [—ful] adj. Que tiene éxito, de éxito [*Amer.*, exitoso, sa]: *a successful record*, un disco de éxito. || Afortunado, da (person). || Próspero, ra; venturoso, sa: *successful business*, negocio próspero. || Logrado, da; conseguido, da: *successful attempt*, intento logrado. || Elegido, da; afortunado, da (candidate). || Acertado, da; atinado, da: *successful union*, unión acertada.
successfully [—fuli] adv. Con éxito.
succession [sʌk'seʃən] n. Sucesión, *f.*, serie, *f.*: *a succession of defeats*, una serie de derrotas. || Sucesión, *f.* (right to succeed to a position, to inherit): *succession duties*, derechos de sucesión. || Descendencia, *f.*, descendientes, *m. pl.* (heirs). || Geol. Biol. Serie, *f.* || — *In close succession*, a cortos intervalos. || *In succession*, seguido, da; uno tras otro: *six shots in succession*, seis tiros uno tras otro; consecutivo, va; seguido, da: *for three years in succession*, durante tres años consecutivos. || *In succession to*, como sucesor *or* heredero de. || *Universal succession*, sucesión universal.
successional [—əl] adj. Sucesorio, ria.
successive [sʌk'sesiv] adj. Sucesivo, va; consecutivo, va: *six successive months*, seis meses seguidos.
successor [sʌk'sesə*] n. Sucesor, ra.
successory [—ri] adj. Sucesorio, ria.
succinct [sək'siŋkt] adj. Sucinto, ta (concise).
succinctness [—nis] n. Concisión, *f.*
succinic ['sʌk'sinik] adj. Chem. Succínico, ca (acid).
succor ['sʌkə*] n./v.tr. U. S. See succour.
succory [—ri] n. Bot. Achicoria, *f.*
succour ['sʌkə*] n. Socorro, *m.*, auxilio, *m.*
succour ['sʌkə*] v. tr. Socorrer, auxiliar.
succulence ['sʌkjuləns] or **succulency** [—i] n. Suculencia, *f.*
succulent ['sʌkjulənt] adj. Suculento, ta. || Bot. Carnoso, sa (plant).
— N. Bot. Planta (*f.*) carnosa.
succumb [sə'kʌm] v. intr. Sucumbir: *to succumb to temptation*, sucumbir a la tentación. || Ceder, rendirse (to give up resistance). || Sucumbir (to die).
succursal [sʌ'kə:səl] adj. Filial, sucursal.
— N. Filial, *f.*, sucursal, *f.*
such [sʌtʃ] adj. Tal: *it gave me such a fright!*, ¡me dio tal susto!; *the noise was such that I couldn't sleep*, el ruido era tal que no podía dormir. || Tal, semejante: *I had never seen such luxury*, nunca había visto semejante lujo; *such luxury is a sin*, semejante lujo es un pecado; *I can't afford such a price*, no puedo pagar semejante precio; *such men as he and I*, hombres tales como él y yo. || Semejante, parecido, da: *is there such a book in English?*, ¿hay un libro parecido en inglés? || Tan, tan grande: *he is such a liar!*, ¡es tan mentiroso!, ¡es un mentiroso tan grande! || De esta índole, de semejante índole, de este tipo: *any such reason*, cualquier razón de esta índole. || En tales condiciones: *the road is such that it can be travelled only on foot*, la carretera está en tales condiciones que sólo se puede recorrer a pie. || Tanto, ta: *don't be in such a hurry*, no tengas tanta prisa. || — *In such a way that*, de tal forma *or* de tal manera que. || *No such thing!*, ¡no hay tal!, ¡nada de eso! || *On just such a day*, un día exactamente igual. || *Such a lot*, tanto. || *Such a lot of things*, tantas cosas. || *Such and such*, tal, tal o cual, tal y cual: *on such and such a day*, en tal o cual día; *at such and such a time*, a tal hora. || *Such as*, como: *a friend such as Peter*, un amigo como Pedro; *books such as these*, libros como éstos. || *Such as it is*, tal y como es, tal cual. || *Such is life*, así es la vida. || *Until such time as*, hasta que.
— Pron. Los que, las que: *such as laugh today*, los que se ríen hoy; *such as heard the news came*, los que se enteraron de la noticia vinieron. || Todo lo que: *I will give you such as I have*, te daré todo lo que tenga. || Lo que: *the castle, such of it as remained, was beautiful*, lo que quedaba del castillo era muy bonito. || Esto, éste, ésta: *such is my opinion*, ésta es mi opinión. || [Cosas, gente, etc.] de este tipo *or* clase, cosas similares, gente similar: *he plays football, hockey and such*, juega al fútbol, hockey y deportes similares; *he knows bishops, priests and such*, conoce obispos, curas y gente de este tipo. || *As such*, en sí, de por sí, como tal: *the book as such was not bad*, el libro de por sí no era malo; como tal: *he was a foreigner and they treated him as such*, era un extranjero y le trataron como tal.
— Adv. Tan: *such a pretty girl!*, ¡una chica tan guapa!; *not such a happy person as I imagined*, una persona no tan feliz como pensaba. || *Such a long time ago*, hace tanto tiempo.
suchlike [—laik] adj. De este tipo, de esta clase, de esta índole, semejante, similar: *he plays football, rugby and suchlike games*, juega al fútbol, al rugby y a deportes de ese tipo.
— N. Cosas (*f. pl.*) *or* gente (*f.*) de este tipo *or* de esta clase *or* de esta índole, cosas (*f. pl.*) similares, gente (*f.*) similar: *tramps, beggars and suchlike*, vagabundos, mendigos y gente de esta clase; *peas, beans and suchlike*, guisantes, judías y cosas similares.
suck [sʌk] n. Succión, *f.* || Chupada, *f.*, sorbo, *m.* (action or noise). || Mamada, *f.* (of babies).
suck [sʌk] v. tr. Sorber (a liquid). || Aspirar (air, dust). || Absorber, chupar: *roots suck water from the earth*, las raíces absorben el agua de la tierra. || Chupar (an orange, thumb, sweet, pipe, blood, etc.). || Chupar, mamar (babies). || Aspirar, sacar (with a pump). || Zool. Libar (butterflies, bees, etc.). || — *To suck one's fingers*, chuparse los dedos. || Fam. *To suck s.o. dry*, chuparle a uno la sangre.
— V. intr. Chupar: *to suck at a sweet*, chupar un caramelo. || Dar chupadas. || Mamar (babies). || Aspirar (pump, vacuum cleaner).
— ***To suck down,*** tragar (whirlpool, sand). || ***To suck in,*** tragar (whirlpool, sand). | Aspirar (air). | Fig. Absorber. || ***To suck out,*** chupar: *to suck out poison from a wound*, chupar el veneno de una herida. || ***To suck up,*** absorber. | — Fam. *To suck up to*, hacer la pelotilla a, dar coba a.
sucker [—ə*] n. Chupador, ra; chupón, ona (person that sucks). || Zool. Ventosa, *f.* (of leech, octopus). | Trompa, *f.* (of insects). | Lechón, *m.* (sucking pig). || Bot. Chupón, *m.*, mamón, *m.* (of plant roots). | Retoño, *m.*, vástago, *m.* (shoot). || Tech. Émbolo, *m.* (piston). | Tubo (*m.*) de aspiración (pipe). || Fam. Primo, *m.* (simpleton). | Novato, *m.*, primerizo, *m.* (beginner). || U. S. Pirulí, *m.*, chupón, *m.* (lollipop).
suckfish [—fiʃ] n. Zool. Rémora, *f.*
sucking [—iŋ] adj. De leche (animals). || Lechal (lamb). || De pecho (child). || *Sucking pig*, lechón, *m.*, cochinillo (*m.*) de leche.
suckle ['sʌkl] v. tr. Amamantar a, dar de mamar a, dar el pecho a, criar a.
suckling ['sʌkliŋ] n. Cría, *f.* (animal). || Lactante, *m.* (child). || Lactancia, *f.*, crianza, *f.* (act).
sucre ['su:krə] n. Sucre, *m.* (money of Ecuador).
sucrose ['sju:krəus] n. Sucrosa, *f.*, sacarosa, *f.*
suction ['sʌkʃən] n. Succión, *f.*, aspiración, *f.* (of liquid). || Aspiración, *f.* (of air). || Succión, *f.* (sucking force).
— Adj. De succión, aspirante, de aspiración.
suction pump [—pʌmp] n. Bomba (*f.*) aspirante.
suction valve [—vælv] n. Válvula (*f.*) de aspiración.
Sudan [su'dɑ:n] pr. n. Geogr. Sudán, *m.*
Sudanese [ˌsu:də'ni:z] adj./n. Sudanés, esa. || *The Sudanese*, los sudaneses.
Sudanic [su'dænik] adj./n. Sudanés, esa.
sudarium [sju:'dɛəriəm] n. Rel. Sudario, *m.*
— Observ. El plural de *sudarium* es *sudaria.*
sudation [sju:'deiʃən] n. Sudación, *f.*
sudatorium [ˌsju:də'tɔ:riəm] n. Sudadero, *m.*
— Observ. El plural de *sudatorium* es *sudatoria.*
sudatory ['sju:dətəri] adj. Sudorífico, ca.
— N. Sudadero, *m.*
sudden ['sʌdn] adj. Repentino, na; súbito, ta. || Inesperado, da; imprevisto, ta (unexpected): *a sudden bend in the road*, una curva inesperada en la carretera. || Brusco, ca. || — *All of a sudden*, de repente, de pronto: *all of a sudden he remembered*, de repente se acordó. || *To die a sudden death*, morir de repente, fallecer de muerte repentina.
suddenly [—li] adv. Repentinamente, súbitamente, de repente, de pronto.
suddenness [—nis] n. Lo repentino, lo súbito. || Lo imprevisto. || Brusquedad, *f.*
Sudetes [su'ditˌiz] or **Sudeten Mountains** [su:'deitn'mauntinz] pl. n. Geogr. Sudetes, *m.*, Montes (*m.*) de los Sudetes.
sudoriferous [ˌsju:də'rifərəs] adj. Sudorífero, ra.

sudorific [ˌsju:dəˈrifik] adj. Sudorífico, ca.
— N. Sudorífico, *m.*
sudoriparous [ˌsju:dəˈripərəs] adj. Sudoríparo, ra.
suds [sʌdz] pl. n. Espuma (*f. sing.*) de jabón, jabonaduras, *f.* (soapy water). || FAM. Cerveza, *f. sing.* (beer).
sudsy [—i] adj. Espumoso, sa; jabonoso, sa.
sue [sju:] v. tr. JUR. Demandar, poner pleito a (to bring legal action against): *to sue s.o. for damages,* demandar a alguien por daños y perjuicios. | Presentar una demanda a [un tribunal] (to petition a court for justice). || Cortejar (a young lady).
— V. intr. JUR. Entablar acción judicial. || Hacer la corte (to woo). || — *To sue for,* pedir: *to sue for peace,* pedir la paz; suplicar: *to sue for mercy,* suplicar misericordia. || *To sue for divorce,* solicitar el divorcio, presentar demanda de divorcio. || *To sue to s.o. for sth.,* pedir algo a alguien.
suède (U. S. **suede**) [sweid] n. Ante, *m.* (for shoes, coats, etc.). || Cabritilla, *f.* (for gloves).
suet [sjuit] n. Sebo, *m.*
suety [—i] adj. Grasiento, ta; seboso, sa.
Suez [ˈsuiz] pr. n. GEOGR. Suez. || *Suez canal,* canal (*m.*) de Suez.
suffer [ˈsʌfə*] v. tr. Sufrir: *to suffer punishment, injury,* sufrir un castigo, una herida; *to suffer a loss, a defeat,* sufrir una pérdida, una derrota. || Sentir, padecer: *are you suffering any pain?,* ¿siente algún dolor? || Tolerar, permitir: *he will suffer no insult,* no tolera ningún insulto. || Soportar, aguantar: *I had to suffer her insults,* tuve que soportar sus insultos. || Permitir, dejar: *suffer the little children to come unto me,* dejad que los niños se acerquen a mí.
— V. intr. Sufrir: *to suffer acutely,* sufrir mucho. || Ser dañado, da (to be damaged). || *To suffer from,* padecer de, padecer: *to suffer from neuralgia,* padecer de neuralgia; adolecer de: *Madrid suffers from overcrowding,* Madrid adolece de superpoblación. || *You'll suffer for it!,* ¡pagarás las consecuencias!
sufferable [—rəbl] adj. Soportable, tolerable.
sufferance [—rəns] n. Consentimiento (*m.*) tácito. || Tolerancia, *f.*: *on sufferance,* por tolerancia. || *Beyond sufferance,* intolerable.
sufferer [—rə*] n. Víctima, *f.* (victim). || MED. Paciente, *m.* & *f.*, enfermo, ma (patient).
suffering [—riŋ] n. Sufrimiento, *m.*, padecimiento, *m.* || Dolor, *m.* (pain).
— Adj. Que sufre, que padece. || MED. Doliente, enfermo, ma.
suffice [səˈfais] v. tr. Ser suficiente [a alguien], bastar [a alguien]: *a meal a day suffices him,* una comida al día le basta. || Satisfacer: *to suffice s.o.'s needs,* satisfacer las necesidades de uno.
— V. intr. Ser suficiente, bastar. || *Suffice it to say,* basta con decir.
sufficiency [səˈfiʃənsi] n. Cantidad (*f.*) suficiente: *a sufficiency of bread,* la cantidad suficiente de pan. || Lo suficiente: *to eat a sufficiency,* comer lo suficiente. || Eficacia, *f.*: *the sufficiency of the law,* la eficacia de la ley. || Desahogo, *m.*, holgura, *f.*, buena posición (*f.*) económica (wealth).
sufficient [səˈfiʃənt] adj. Suficiente, bastante.
suffix [ˈsʌfiks] n. GRAMM. Sufijo, *m.* || MATH. Subíndice, *m.* (subindex).
suffix [ˈsʌfiks] v. tr. GRAMM. Añadir como sufijo.
suffixal [—əl] adj. GRAMM. Sufijo, ja.
suffocate [ˈsʌfəkeit] v. tr. Asfixiar, ahogar (to kill). || Sofocar, asfixiar, ahogar (to hinder the respiration of). || FIG. Ahogar (to oppress).
— V. intr. Asfixiarse, ahogarse. || *The heat was suffocating,* el calor era sofocante.
suffocation [ˌsʌfəˈkeiʃən] n. Asfixia, *f.*, ahogo, *m.*
suffragan [ˈsʌfrəgən] n. REL. Obispo (*m.*) sufragáneo.
— Adj. Sufragáneo, a.
suffrage [ˈsʌfridʒ] n. Sufragio, *m.* (vote): *election by universal suffrage,* elección por sufragio universal. || Derecho (*m.*) al voto (right to vote). || Aprobación, *f.*, asentimiento, *m.* (vote of assent).
suffragette [ˌsʌfrəˈdʒet] n. Sufragista, *f.*
suffragist [ˈsʌfrədʒist] n. Sufragista, *m.* & *f.*
suffuse [səˈfju:z] v. tr. Cubrir (to cover): *a blush suffused her cheeks,* el rubor cubría sus mejillas. || Bañar: *the room was suffused with light,* la habitación estaba bañada de luz; *suffused with tears,* bañado en lágrimas. || Difundirse por, extenderse por (to spread over).
suffusion [səˈfju:ʒən] n. Difusión, *f.* || Rubor, *m.* (blush).
sugar [ˈʃugə*] n. Azúcar, *m.* or *f.*: *brown sugar,* azúcar morena; *to put sugar in,* echar azúcar a; *a lump of sugar,* un terrón de azúcar. || Terrón, *m.* (lump). || — *Cane sugar,* azúcar de caña. || *Castor sugar,* azúcar extrafina. || *Icing sugar,* azúcar en polvo. || *Loaf sugar,* azúcar de pilón. || *Lump sugar,* azúcar de cortadillo *or* en terrones. || *Refined sugar,* azúcar refinada. || FIG. FAM. *To be all sugar,* ser meloso.
— Adj. Azucarero, ra; del azúcar: *sugar industry,* industria azucarera.
sugar [ˈʃugə*] v. tr. Azucarar, poner *or* echar azúcar a *or* en (to sweeten with sugar). || Echar azúcar a (to sprinkle with sugar). || FIG. Endulzar, suavizar (to make more agreeable). || FIG. *To sugar the pill,* dorar la píldora.
— V. intr. Granularse (to become granular).
sugar almond [—ˈɑ:mənd] n. Peladilla, *f.*
sugar basin [—ˈbeisn] n. Azucarero, *m.*
sugar beet [—bi:t] n. Remolacha (*f.*) azucarera.
sugar bowl [—bəul] n. Azucarero, *m.*
sugar candy [—ˈkændi] n. Azúcar (*m.*) candi, azúcar (*m.*) cande.
sugarcane [—kein] n. Caña (*f.*) de azúcar.
sugarcoat [—kəut] v. tr. Garapiñar (nuts). || Cubrir con una capa de azúcar (food, sweets, etc.). || U. S. FIG. Endulzar, suavizar (to make more agreeable). | Dorar (the pill).
sugarcoated [—ˌkəutid] adj. Garapiñado, da (nuts). || Cubierto con una capa de azúcar (food, sweets).
sugarcoating [—ˌkəutiŋ] n. Capa (*f.*) de azúcar.
sugar crop [—krɔp] n. Zafra, *f.*
sugar daddy [—ˌdædi] n. FAM. Amigo, *m.* [viejo].
sugarhouse [—haus] n. U. S. Azucarera, *f.*, fábrica (*f.*) de azúcar.
sugariness [—rinis] n. Dulzura, *f.* (sweetness). || FIG. Melosidad, *f.*
sugarloaf [—ləuf] n. Pilón, *m.*, pan (*m.*) de azúcar.
sugar maple [—ˌmeipl] n. Arce (*m.*) azucarero.
sugar mill [—mil] n. Trapiche, *m.*, ingenio (*m.*) de azúcar.
sugarplum [—plʌm] n. Confite, *m.*
sugar refinery [—riˌfainəri] n. Refinería (*f.*) de azúcar.
sugar tongs [—tɔŋz] pl. n. Tenacillas (*f.*) para el azúcar.
sugary [—ri] adj. Azucarado, da (like or containing sugar). || Dulce (sweet). || Granular (granular). || FIG. Meloso, sa (excessively sweet in manners).
suggest [səˈdʒest] v. tr. Sugerir, proponer: *to suggest a different plan,* sugerir un proyecto distinto; *I suggest that you go now,* sugiero que vayas ahora. || Proponer: *to suggest s.o. for a post,* proponer a alguien para un puesto. || Sugerir, hacer pensar en, evocar: *the symphony suggests a sunrise,* la sinfonía evoca una salida del sol. || Dar: *that suggested to me the idea of travelling,* esto me dio la idea de viajar. || Inspirar: *my success suggested me further efforts,* mi éxito me inspiró la continuación de mis esfuerzos. || Aconsejar (to advise). || Indicar: *from Malaga as his accent suggests,* malagueño como su acento indica. || Insinuar (to hint): *are you suggesting that I'm lying?,* ¿estás insinuando que miento? || *A solution suggested itself to me,* se me ocurrió una solución.
suggestibility [sʌdʒestiˈbiliti] n. Sugestibilidad, *f.*
suggestible [sʌˈdʒestibl] adj. Sugestionable: *a suggestible person,* una persona sugestionable. || Que puede proponerse (thing).
suggestion [səˈdʒestʃən] n. Sugerencia, *f.*: *to make a suggestion,* hacer una sugerencia. || Sugestión, *f.* (a suggesting). || Indicación, *f.*, indicaciones, *f. pl.*: *you will follow my suggestion,* seguirá mis indicaciones; *at the suggestion of you,* por indicación suya. || Insinuación, *f.* (hint). || Idea, *f.* (idea). || FIG. Tinte, *m.*, matiz, *m.* (nuance). | Sombra, *f.*, traza, *f.* (trace). | Poquitín, *m.*, pizca, *f.* (bit). || Sugestión, *f.* (in psychology): *hypnotic suggestion,* sugestión hipnótica. || *Your suggestion was that,* usted proponía que.
suggestive [səˈdʒestiv] adj. Sugestivo, va (stimulating ideas). || Evocador, ra: *suggestive of a sunrise,* evocador de una salida del sol. || Sugestivo, va; insinuante (insinuating). || *To be suggestive of sth.,* evocar algo, hacer pensar en algo.
suggestiveness [—nis] n. Lo sugestivo, lo insinuante.
suicidal [sjuiˈsaidl] adj. Suicida: *suicidal tendencies,* tendencias suicidas. || FAM. *It's suicidal to,* es un suicidio.
suicide [ˈsjuisaid] n. Suicida, *m.* & *f.* (person). || Suicidio, *m.* (act). || — *To attempt suicide,* atentar contra su vida. || *To commit suicide,* suicidarse.
suint [swint] n. Churre, *m.*, grasa (*f.*) de la lana.
suit [sju:t] n. Traje, *m.* (clothes, uniform, etc.): *ready-made suit,* traje de confección. || Traje (*m.*) sastre (woman's). || Conjunto, *m.*, juego, *m.* (set, series). || Palo, *m.* (in cards). || JUR. Pleito, *m.*: *to bring a suit,* entablar un pleito. || Petición, *f.* (petition, request): *at the suit of,* a petición de. || Galanteo, *m.*, cortejo, *m.* (courtship). || MAR. Velamen, *m.* (sails). || — *Bathing suit,* bañador, *m.*, traje de baño. || *Suit of armour,* armadura, *f.* [completa]. || *Suit of clothes,* traje. || *To follow suit,* servir, jugar del mismo palo (in cards), seguir el ejemplo (to follow the example set). || *Two-piece suit,* conjunto.
suit [sju:t] v. tr. Convenir, venir bien a: *would it suit you to come tomorrow?,* ¿te convendría venir mañana?; *that suits me best,* eso me viene mejor. || Adaptarse a, ajustarse a, acomodarse a: *that suits my plans,* esto se ajusta a mis planes. || Ir bien a, sentar bien a: *green suits you,* el verde le sienta bien. || Satisfacer, agradar (to please): *does the program suit you?,* ¿le agrada el programa? || Adaptar al gusto: *try to suit the play to the audience,* intente adaptar la comedia al gusto del público. || — *He can be very cruel if it suits him,* puede ser muy cruel cuando quiere. || *He is not suited for engineering,* no ha nacido para ingeniero. || *He is suited for this job,* es la persona adecuada para este trabajo. || FIG. *It suits me to a T,* me viene de perlas. || *To be suited with,* haber encontrado (a servant, situation). || *To suit o.s.,* hacer lo que uno quiere. || *With a hat to suit,* con un sombrero haciendo juego.

— V. intr. Convenir, ir bien.
suitability [ˌsju:təˈbiliti] n. Conveniencia, *f.*, oportunidad, *f.*: *the suitability of a certain date*, la conveniencia de cierta fecha. || Oportunidad, *f.* (of a remark, answer, etc.). || Compatibilidad, *f.* (of two people). || Aptitud, *f.*: *the suitability of a political candidate*, la aptitud de un candidato político.
suitable [ˈsju:təbl] adj. Conveniente, oportuno, na; idóneo, a (convenient). || Oportuno, na; adecuado, da; apropiado, da (appropriate). || Compatible (two people). || Apto, ta (apt). || Satisfactorio, ria (satisfactory).
suitableness [—nis] n. See SUITABILITY.
suitcase [ˈsju:tkeis] n. Maleta, *f.*
suite [swi:t] n. Juego, *m.*: *a bedroom suite*, un juego de dormitorio. || "Suite", *f.*, apartamento, *m.* (in a hotel). || Séquito, *m.*, cortejo, *m.* (of a king). || Comitiva, *f.*, acompañantes, *m. pl.* (of a minister, etc.). || Serie, *f.*, sucesión, *f.* (series). || MUS. "Suite", *f.*
suiting [ˈsju:tiŋ] n. Tela, *f.* [para trajes] (material).
suitor [ˈsju:tə*] n. JUR. Demandante, *m.* & *f.* || Galán, *m.*, pretendiente, *m.* (pretender, lover).
sulcate [ˈsʌlkeit] or **sulcated** [—id] adj. ANAT. Surcado, da.
sulcus [ˈsʌlkəs] n. ANAT. Surco, *m.*

— OBSERV. El plural de *sulcus* es *sulci*.

sulfa drug [ˈsʌlfəˌdrʌg] n. U. S. MED. Sulfamida, *f.*
sulfate [ˈsʌlfeit] n. U. S. CHEM. Sulfato, *m.*
sulfate [ˈsʌlfeit] v. tr. U. S. Sulfatar.
sulfating [—iŋ] n. U. S. See SULPHATING.
sulfide [ˈsʌlfaid] n. U. S. CHEM. Sulfuro, *m.*
sulfite [ˈsʌlfait] n. U. S. CHEM. Sulfito, *m.*
sulfonamide [sʌlˈfɔnəmaid] n. U. S. MED. Sulfamida, *f.*
sulfur [ˈsʌlfə*] n./v. tr. U. S. See SULPHUR.
sulfurate [ˈsʌlfjurit] adj. U. S. CHEM. Sulfurado, da.
sulfurate [ˈsʌlfjureit] v. tr. U. S. See SULPHURATE.
sulfuration [sʌlfjuˈreiʃən] n. U. S. See SULPHURATION.
sulfurator [ˈsʌlfjureitə*] n. U. S. AGR. Sulfatador, *m.*
sulfureous [sʌlˈfjuəriəs] adj. U. S. Sulfuroso, sa.
sulfuretted [ˈsʌlfjuretid] adj. U. S. CHEM. Sulfurado, da.
sulfuric [sʌlˈfjuərik] adj. U. S. Sulfúrico, ca.
sulfurize [ˈsʌlfjəraiz] v. tr. U. S. See SULPHUR.
sulfurous [ˈsʌlfərəs] adj. U. S. See SULPHUROUS.
sulfury [ˈsʌlfəri] adj. U. S. Azufrado, da.
sulk [sʌlk] n. Enfado, *m.*, enfurruñamiento, *m.*, mal humor, *m.* || *To be in the sulks* o *to have the sulks*, estar enfadado *or* enfurruñado, poner mala cara, poner cara larga.
sulk [sʌlk] v. intr. Estar malhumorado, enfurruñarse, poner mala cara, poner cara larga.
sulkily [—ili] adv. Con mal humor.
sulkiness [—inis] n. Mal humor, *m.*
sulky [—i] adj. Malhumorado, da (cross). || Resentido, da (resentful). || Triste (gloomy). || *To be sulky with*, poner mala cara a, poner cara larga a (s.o.).
sullage [ˈsʌlidʒ] n. Barro, *m.*, cieno, *m.* (mud). || Escoria, *f.* (of molten metal). || Aguas (*f. pl.*) residuales (sewage).
sullen [ˈsʌlən] adj. Hosco, ca; ceñudo, da; malhumorado, da (unsociable). || Triste, taciturno, na (sad). || Resentido, da (resentful). || Triste, tétrico, ca; lúgubre, sombrío, a (place). || Plomizo, za (sky). || Amenazador, ra (cloud). || Repropio, pia (horse). || Lento, ta (slow): *sullen pace*, paso lento.
sullenness [—nis] n. Malhumor, *m.* || Tristeza, *f.* || Taciturnidad, *f.* || Resentimiento, *m.*
sully [ˈsʌli] v. tr. Manchar, mancillar.
sulpha drug [ˈsʌlfəˌdrʌg] n. MED. Sulfamida, *f.*
sulphate [ˈsʌlfeit] n. CHEM. Sulfato, *m.*
sulphate [ˈsʌlfeit] v. tr. Sulfatar.
sulphating [—iŋ] n. CHEM. Sulfatación, *f.*, sulfatado, *m.* || *Sulphating machine*, sulfatadora, *f.*
sulphide [ˈsʌlfaid] n. CHEM. Sulfuro, *m.*
sulphite [ˈsʌlfait] n. CHEM. Sulfito, *m.*
sulphonamide [sʌlˈfɔnəmaid] n. MED. Sulfamida, *f.*
sulphur [ˈsʌlfə*] n. Azufre, *m.* || *Sulphur water*, agua sulfurosa.
sulphur [ˈsʌlfə*] or **sulphurate** [ˈsʌlfjureit] v. tr. Azufrar. || CHEM. Sulfurar.
sulphurate [ˈsʌlfjurit] adj. CHEM. Sulfurado, da.
sulphuration [sʌlfjuˈreiʃən] n. Azufrado, *m.*, azuframiento, *m.* || CHEM. Sulfuración, *f.* || AGR. Sulfatado, *m.*, sulfurado, *m.*
sulphurator [ˈsʌlfjureitə*] n. AGR. Sulfatador, *m.*
sulphureous [sʌlˈfjuəriəs] adj. Sulfuroso, sa.
sulphuretted [ˈsʌlfjuretid] adj. CHEM. Sulfurado, da.
sulphuric [sʌlˈfjuərik] adj. Sulfúrico, ca.
sulphurize [ˈsʌlfjəraiz] v. tr. See SULPHUR.
sulphurous [ˈsʌlfərəs] adj. Sulfuroso, sa. || FIG. Acalorado, da.
sulphury [ˈsʌlfəri] adj. Azufrado, da.
sultan [ˈsʌltən] n. Sultán, *m.*
sultana [sʌlˈtɑ:nə] n. Sultana, *f.* (wife of a sultan). || Pasa (*f.*) de Esmirna (raisin).
sultanate [ˈsʌltənit] n. Sultanato, *m.*, sultanía, *f.*
sultriness [ˈsʌltrinis] n. Bochorno, *m.*, calor (*m.*) sofocante (of weather). || FIG. Sensualidad, *f.*
sultry [ˈsʌltri] adj. Bochornoso, sa; de bochorno, sofocante (weather). || FIG. Sensual.
sum [sʌm] n. Suma, *f.*, cantidad, *f.*: *a sum of money*, una cantidad de dinero. || Total, *m.*, suma, *f.* (the whole amount, entirety). || MATH. Suma, *f.*, adición, *f.* (addition). | Cálculo, *m.*: *a quick mental sum*, un cálculo mental rápido. || — Pl. Aritmética, *f. sing.* (arithmetic). || — *In sum*, en suma, en resumen, en resumidas cuentas. || *The sum and substance of the matter*, el fondo de la cuestión.
sum [sʌm] v. tr. Sumar. || *To sum up*, sumar (to add up), resumir, recapitular (to summarize), evaluar (to evaluate). || *To sum up I would say that*, para resumir *or* en resumen yo diría que.
— V. intr. *To sum to*, sumar, ascender a (to total).
sumach or **sumac** [ˈsu:mæk] n. BOT. Zumaque, *m.* (shrub).
Sumerian [sjuˈmiəriən] adj./n. Sumerio, ria.
summarily [ˈsʌmərili] adv. Sumariamente.
summarization [ˌsʌməraiˈzeiʃən] n. Resumen, *m.*
summarize [ˈsʌməraiz] v. tr. Resumir.
summary [ˈsʌməri] adj. Sumario, ria. || U. S. *Summary court-martial*, consejo de guerra sumarísimo.
— N. Resumen, *m.*
summation [sʌˈmeiʃən] n. Adición, *f.*, suma, *f.* || Total, *m.*, suma (*f.*) total. || Resumen, *m.* (summary). || Recapitulación, *f.*
summer [ˈsʌmə*] n. Verano, *m.*, estío, *m.* || ARCH. Viga (*m.*) maestra. || — FIG. *A girl of twenty summers*, una chica de veinte abriles. || *Indian Summer*, veranillo (*m.*) de San Martín. || *In summer*, en verano, durante el verano.
— Adj. Veraniego, ga; estival.
summer [ˈsʌmə*] v. tr. Pastar durante el verano (cattle).
— V. intr. Veranear, pasar el verano.
summer holidays [—ˈhɔlidiz] pl. n. Vacaciones (*f.*) de verano, veraneo, *m. sing.*
summerhouse [—haus] n. Cenador, *m.*, glorieta, *f.*
summer house [—haus] n. Casa (*f.*) de verano.
summer lightning [—ˌlaitniŋ] n. Fucilazo, *m.*
summer resort [—riˌzɔ:t] n. Lugar (*m.*) de veraneo.
summersault [—sɔ:lt] n./v. intr. See SOMERSAULT.
summer solstice [—ˌsɔlstis] n. Solsticio (*m.*) de verano.
summer stock [—stɔk] n. U. S. THEATR. Repertorio (*m.*) de obras representadas en verano.
summer time [—taim] n. Hora (*f.*) de verano.
summertime [—taim] n. Verano, *m.*, estío, *m.*
summery [—ri] adj. Veraniego, ga; estival.
summing-up [ˈsʌmiŋˈʌp] n. Resumen, *m.*

— OBSERV. El plural de *summing-up* es *summings-up*.

summit [ˈsʌmit] n. Cima, *f.*, cumbre, *f.* (of a hill, mountain). || FIG. Cima, *f.*, apogeo, *m.*, cumbre, *f.*: *to reach the summit of honours*, alcanzar la cima de los honores. || Conferencia (*f.*) de alto nivel *or* en la cumbre (conference). || *Summit conference*, conferencia de alto nivel *or* en la cumbre.
summon [ˈsʌmən] v. tr. Convocar (a meeting): *to summon parliament*, convocar el parlamento. || Pedir (aid). || JUR. Citar, emplazar. || FIG. Evocar: *a picture that summons up many happy memories*, un cuadro que evoca muchos recuerdos felices. | Reunir: *to summon one's strength*, reunir sus fuerzas. || Llamar (to call a servant, s.o.). || MIL. Intimar (a town to surrender). || *To summon up one's courage*, armarse de valor.
summons [ˈsʌmənz] n. JUR. Citación (*f.*) judicial, requerimiento (*m.*) judicial, emplazamiento, *m.*, auto (*m.*) de comparecencia. || Llamada, *f.*, llamamiento, *m.* (call). || Convocatoria, *f.* (convocation). || *To take out a summons against s.o.*, citar a uno ante la justicia.

— OBSERV. El plural de *summons* es *summonses*.

summons [ˈsʌmənz] v. tr. JUR. Citar ante la justicia.
sump [sʌmp] n. AUT. Cárter, *m.* || MIN. Sumidero, *m.* (of mine). || Letrina, *f.*, pozo (*m.*) negro (cesspool). || FIG. FAM. Vertedero, *m.*, muladar, *m.*, estercolero, *m.*
sumpter [—tə*] n. Bestia (*f.*) de carga, acémila, *f.*
sumptuary [—tjuəri] adj. Suntuario, ria: *sumptuary law*, ley suntuaria.
sumptuous [—tjuəs] adj. Suntuoso, sa.
sumptuousness [—tjuəsnis] n. Suntuosidad, *f.*
sum total [ˈsʌmˈtəutl] n. Suma (*f.*) total, total, *m.* || FIG. *And that is the sum total of his experience*, y ésa es toda su experiencia.
sun [sʌn] n. Sol, *m.*: *setting, midnight sun*, sol poniente, de medianoche; *in summertime the sun rises early and sets late*, en verano el sol sale temprano y se pone tarde. || — *From sun to sun*, de sol a sol. || FIG. *There is everything under the sun*, hay de todo como en botica. | *There is nothing new under the sun*, no hay nada nuevo bajo el Sol. || *The rising sun*, el sol naciente. || *The sun is shining today*, hoy hace sol. || *The Sun King*, el Rey Sol. || *To bask in the sun*, tomar el sol. || FIG. *To have a place in the sun*, tener una buena situación. || *To sit in the sun*, estar sentado al sol. || *Touch of the sun*, quemadura (*f.*) de sol. || FIG. *Under the sun*, en el mundo. || MAR. *With the sun*, en el sentido de las agujas de un reloj.
— Adj. Del sol, solar.
sun [sʌn] v. tr. Exponer al sol. || *To sun o.s.*, tomar el sol.
sunbaked [—beikt] adj. Curtido por el sol (person). || Quemado por el sol (place). || Secado al sol (brick).
sunbath [—bɑ:θ] n. Baño (*m.*) de sol.
sunbathe [—beið] v. intr. Tomar el sol.

sunbather [—ˌbeiðə*] n. Persona (*f.*) que toma el sol.
sunbathing [—ˌbeiðiŋ] n. Baños (*m. pl.*) de sol.
sunbeam [—bi:m] n. Rayo (*m.*) de sol.
sunblind [—blaind] n. Toldo, *m.* (awning). || Persiana, *f.* (Venetian blind).
sunbonnet [—ˌbɔnit] n. Sombrero (*m.*) para protegerse del sol.
sunburn [—bə:n] n. Quemadura (*f.*) de sol (burn). || Bronceado, *m.* (tan).
sunburn [—bə:n] v. tr. Quemar al sol (to burn). || Broncear (to tan).
— V. intr. Sufrir quemaduras de sol (to burn). || Broncearse (to tan).
sunburnt [—bə:nt] adj. Bronceado, da; tostado por el sol (tanned). || Quemado por el sol (burnt).
sundae [ˈsʌndei] n. Helado (*m.*) con frutas y nueces.
Sunda Islands [ˈsʌndəˈailəndz] pl. n. GEOGR. Islas (*f.*) de la Sonda.
Sunday [ˈsʌndi] n. Domingo, *m.*: *Easter Sunday*, Domingo de Resurrección; *Palm Sunday*, Domingo de Ramos; *Shrove Sunday*, Domingo de Carnaval; *Low Sunday*, Domingo de Cuasimodo. || — FIG. *Never in a month of Sundays*, nunca. || *On Sunday*, el domingo: *I shall come on Sunday*, vendré el domingo.
— Adj. Del domingo, dominical (rest, mass). || Dominguero, ra (clothes, etc.).
Sunday best [—best] n. Traje (*m.*) de los domingos, trapitos (*m. pl.*) de cristianar.
Sunday-go-to-meeting [—ˌgəutəˈmi:tiŋ] adj. U. S. Dominguero, ra; del domingo.
Sunday school [—sku:l] n. REL. Catequesis, *f.*
sun deck [ˈsʌndek] n. MAR. Cubierta (*f.*) superior. || Terraza (*f.*) donde se toma el sol (terrace).
sunder [ˈsʌndə*] v. tr. Partir (to tear apart). || Separar (to separate).
— V. intr. Partirse.
sundial [ˈsʌndaiəl] n. Reloj (*m.*) de sol.
sun dog [ˈsʌndɔg] n. Parhelio, *m.*
sundown [ˈsʌndaun] n. Puesta (*f.*) del sol, ocaso, *m.* || Anochecer, *m.*: *at sundown*, al anochecer.
sundress [ˈsʌndres] n. Traje (*m.*) de playa.
sun-dried [ˈsʌndraid] adj. Secado al sol.
sundries [ˈsʌndriz] pl. n. Miscelánea, *f. sing.*, artículos (*m.*) diversos. || Gastos (*m.*) diversos (expenses).
sundry [ˈsʌndri] adj. Diversos, sas; varios, rias: *sundry objects*, diversos objetos. || *All and sundry*, todos sin excepción.
sunfast [ˈsʌnfɑ:st] adj. Resistente al sol.
sunfish [ˈsʌnfiʃ] n. ZOOL. Pez (*m.*) luna.
sunflower [ˈsʌnˌflauə*] n. BOT. Girasol, *m.*
sung [sʌŋ] p. p. See SING.
sunglasses [ˈsʌnˌglɑ:siz] pl. n. Gafas (*f.*) de sol [*Amer.*, anteojos (*m.*) de sol].
sunglow [ˈsʌngləu] n. Arrebol, *m.*
sun-god [ˈsʌngɔd] n. Dios (*m.*) del sol.
sun helmet [ˈsʌnˌhelmit] n. Salacot, *m.*
sunk [sʌŋk] p. p. See SINK.
sunken [—ən] adj. Hundido, da (ships, ground, eyes, cheeks, etc.).
sunlamp [ˈsʌnlæmp] n. Lámpara (*f.*) solar, lámpara (*f.*) de rayos ultravioletas. || CINEM. Foco, *m.*
sunless [ˈsʌnlis] adj. Sin sol.
sunlight [ˈsʌnlait] n. Luz (*f.*) del sol, sol, *m.*: *in the sunlight*, al sol, a la luz del sol.
sunlit [ˈsʌnlit] adj. Iluminado por el sol.
Sunna or **Sunnah** [ˈsunə] n. REL. Sunna, *f.*
Sunni [ˈsuni] or **Sunnite** [ˈsunait] n. REL. Sunnita, *m.*
sunny [ˈsʌni] adj. De sol: *a sunny day*, un día de sol. || Soleado, da: *a sunny place*, un lugar soleado. || Iluminado por el sol (sunlit). || Expuesto al sol. || FIG. Risueño, ña; sonriente: *a sunny future*, un porvenir risueño. || — FIG. *A sunny smile*, una sonrisa alegre. || *It is sunny today*, hoy hace sol. || FIG. *To see the sunny side of things*, ver siempre el lado bueno de las cosas.
sun parlour (U. S. **sun parlor**) [ˈsʌnˌpɑ:lə*] n. Solario, *m.*, solana, *f.*
sunproof [ˈsʌnpru:f] adj. Inalterable a los rayos de sol, resistente al sol.
sunray [ˈsʌnrei] n. Rayo (*m.*) de sol.
— Adj. *Sunray lamp*, lámpara (*f.*) solar, lámpara (*f.*) de rayos ultravioletas. || *Sunray treatment*, helioterapia, *f.*
sunrise [ˈsʌnraiz] n. Salida (*f.*) del sol. || *I work from sunrise to sunset*, trabajo de sol a sol.
sun room [ˈsʌnrum] n. Solario, *m.*, solana, *f.*
sunset [ˈsʌnset] n. Puesta (*f.*) del sol, ocaso, *m.* || FIG. Ocaso, *m.* (of life).
sunshade [ˈsʌnʃeid] n. Sombrilla, *f.*, quitasol, *m.* (parasol). || Toldo, *m.* (awning). || PHOT. Parasol, *m.*
sunshine [ˈsʌnʃain] n. Sol, *m.*: *it is rather pleasant to be here in the sunshine*, es muy agradable estar aquí al sol; *in the bright sunshine*, en pleno sol. || FIG. Alegría, *f.*: *bring a little sunshine into the life of an old man*, da un poco de alegría a la vida de un anciano. || *Hours of sunshine*, horas (*f.*) de sol.
sunshiny [—i] adj. Soleado, da. || FIG. Alegre.
sunspot [ˈsʌnspɔt] n. Mancha (*f.*) solar.
sunstroke [ˈsʌnstrəuk] n. Insolación, *f.* [*Amer.*, asoleada, *f.*].
sunstruck [ˈsʌnstrʌk] adj. Con insolación.
sunsuit [ˈsʌnsju:t] n. Traje (*m.*) de playa.
suntan [ˈsʌntæn] n. Bronceado, *m.* || *To have a suntan*, estar bronceado, estar moreno.
suntan [ˈsʌntæn] v. intr. Broncearse, ponerse moreno.
suntrap [ˈsʌntræp] n. Sitio (*m.*) muy soleado.
sunup [ˈsʌnʌp] n. Salida (*f.*) del sol.
sunwise [ˈsʌnwaiz] adj./adv. En el sentido de las agujas de un reloj.
sup [sʌp] n. Sorbo, *m.* (sip).
sup [sʌp] v. tr. Sorber (to sip). || Dar de cenar a, hacer cenar (to provide with supper).
— V. intr. Cenar (to have supper).
super [ˈsju:pə*] adj. FAM. Estupendo, da; formidable, de primera categoría.
— N. FAM. Tamaño (*m.*) muy grande (size). | Calidad (*f.*) extrafina (quality). | Súper, *f.*, supercarburante, *m.*, plomo, *m.*, gasolina (*f.*) súper (petrol). || Parte (*f.*) superior de una colmena (of beehive). || THEATR. Comparsa, *m.* & *f.*, figurante, *m.* & *f.* || CINEM. Extra, *m.* || Superintendente, *m.* (superintendent). || Segundo jefe, *m.*, subjefe, *m.* (of police).
superable [—rəbl] adj. Superable.
superabound [ˌsupərəˈbaund] v. intr. Superabundar, sobreabundar.
superabundance [ˌsju:pərəˈbʌndəns] n. Superabundancia, *f.*, sobreabundancia, *f.*
superabundant [ˌsju:pərəˈbʌndənt] adj. Superabundante, sobreabundante.
superadd [ˌsju:pərˈæd] v. tr. Sobreañadir.
superannuate [ˌsju:pəˈrænjueit] v. tr. Jubilar (s.o.). || Arrinconar, arrumbar (sth.).
superannuated [—id] adj. Jubilado, da (retired). || Anticuado, da (out-of-date).
superannuation [ˌsju:pəˌrænjuˈeiʃən] n. Jubilación, *f.* (retirement). || Jubilación, *f.*, pensión, *f.* (pension).
superb [sjuˈpə:b] adj. Magnífico, ca; excelente, soberbio, bia.
supercargo [ˈsju:pəˌkɑ:gəu] n. MAR. Sobrecargo, *m.*

— OBSERV. El plural de *supercargo* es *supercargoes* o *supercargos*.

supercharge [ˈsju:pətʃɑ:dʒ] v. tr. TECH. Supercomprimir. | Sobrealimentar (motor).
supercharger [—ə*] n. Compresor, *m.*
supercharging [—iŋ] n. TECH. Supercompresión, *f.* | Sobrealimentación, *f.* (of a motor).
superciliary [ˌsju:pəˈsiliəri] adj. Superciliar: *superciliary arch* o *ridge*, arco superciliar.
supercilious [ˌsju:pəˈsiliəs] adj. Arrogante, desdeñoso, sa; altanero, ra.
superciliousness [—nis] n. Desdén, *m.*, arrogancia, *f.*, altanería, *f.*
supercool [ˈsju:pəku:l] v. tr. CHEM. Someter a la sobrefusión.
supercooling [—iŋ] n. CHEM. Sobrefusión, *f.*
superdominant [ˌsju:pəˈdɔminənt] n. MUS. Superdominante, *f.*
supereminence [ˌsju:pərˈeminəns] n. Supereminencia, *f.* (distinguished eminence).
supereminent [ˌsju:pərˈeminənt] adj. Supereminente.
supererogation [ˌsju:pərˌerəˈgeiʃən] n. Supererogación, *f.*
superexcellent [ˌsju:pərˈeksələnt] adj. Excelentísimo, ma.
superfetation [ˌsju:pəfi:ˈteiʃən] n. Superfetación, *f.*
superficial [ˌsju:pəˈfiʃəl] adj. Superficial: *superficial injury*, herida superficial.
superficiality [ˌsju:pəˌfiʃiˈæliti] n. Superficialidad, *f.*
superficially [ˌsju:pəˈfiʃəli] adv. Superficialmente.
superficies [ˌsju:pəˈfiʃi:z] inv. n. Superficie, *f.*
superfine [ˈsju:pəˈfain] adj. Superfino, na; extrafino, na. || FIG. Refinado, da.
superfluity [ˌsju:pəˈfluiti] n. Superfluidad, *f.* || Exceso, *m.*, superabundancia, *f.* (excess).
superfluous [sjuˈpə:fluəs] adj. Superfluo, flua.
superfluousness [—nis] n. Superfluidad, *f.*
superfortress [ˈsju:pəˌfɔ:tris] n. AVIAT. Superfortaleza, *f.*
superheat [ˈsju:pəhi:t] n. Sobrecalentamiento, *m.*, recalentamiento, *m.*
superheat [ˈsju:pəˈhi:t] v. tr. Sobrecalentar, recalentar.
superheater [—ə*] n. Sobrecalentador, *m.*, recalentador, *m.*
superheterodyne [ˈsju:pəˈhetərədain] n. RAD. Superheterodino, *m.*
superhighway [ˌsju:pəˈhaiwei] n. U. S. Autopista, *f.*
superhuman [ˌsju:pəˈhju:mən] adj. Sobrehumano, na.
superhumeral [ˌsjupəˈjhumərəl] n. REL. Superhumeral, *m.*
superimpose [ˈsju:pərimˈpəuz] v. tr. Sobreponer, superponer.
superimposed [ˈsju:pərimˈpəuzd] adj. Superpuesto, ta.
superimposition [ˈsju:pərˌimpəˈziʃən] n. Superposición, *f.*
superimpression [ˌsju:pərimˈpreʃən] n. PHOT. CINEM. Sobreimpresión, *f.*
superincumbent [sju:pərinˈkʌmbənt] adj. Superpuesto, ta; sobrepuesto, ta.
superintend [ˌsju:pərinˈtend] v. tr. Supervisar (to supervise). || Vigilar (to watch over).
superintendence [—əns] or **superintendency** [—i] n. Supervisión, *f.*, dirección, *f.* || Superintendencia, *f.*
superintendent [—ənt] n. Superintendente, *m.* || Supervisor, *m.*, director, *m.* || Vigilante, *m.* (custodian). || Inspector, *m.*

superior [sju'piəriə*] adj. Superior: *he is superior to everybody*, es superior a todos. || Superior, arrogante, altanero, ra (proud). || — GEOGR. *Lake Superior*, Lago (*m.*) Superior. || *To be superior to flattery*, estar muy por encima de la adulación.
— N. Superior, *m.* || REL. Superior, *m.*, superiora, *f.* || *Mother Superior*, superiora, *f.*, madre (*f.*) superiora.
superiority [sju,piəri'ɔriti] n. Superioridad, *f.*: *superiority complex*, complejo de superioridad.
superlative [sju'pə:lətiv] adj. Superlativo, va; supremo, ma. || GRAMM. Superlativo, va. || *To a superlative degree*, en grado superlativo.
— N. GRAMM. Superlativo, *m.* || *To speak in superlatives*, deshacerse en elogios.
superlunary [,sju:pə'lu:nəri] adj. Situado más allá de la luna. || FIG. Celestial.
superman ['sju:pəmæn] n. Superhombre, *m.*

— OBSERV. El plural de esta palabra es *supermen*.

supermarket ['sju:pə,mα:kit] n. Supermercado, *m.*
supernal [sju:'pə:nl] adj. Celestial. || Excelso, sa.
supernatant [,sju:pə'neitənt] adj. Sobrenadando, flotante.
supernatural [,sju:pə'nætʃrəl] adj. Sobrenatural: *supernatural force*, fuerza sobrenatural. || *The supernatural*, lo sobrenatural.
supernaturalism [—izəm] n. Sobrenaturalismo, *m.*
supernaturalness [—nis] n. Lo sobrenatural, carácter (*m.*) sobrenatural.
supernumerary [,sju:pə'nju:mərəri] adj. Supernumerario, ria. || Superfluo, flua.
— N. Supernumerario, ria. || THEATR. Figurante, *m.*, comparsa, *m.* & *f.* || CINEM. Extra, *m.*
superphosphate [,sju:pə'fɔsfeit] n. CHEM. Superfosfato, *m.*
superpose ['sju:pə'pəuz] v. tr. Superponer, sobreponer.
superposition ['sju:pəpə'ziʃən] n. Superposición, *f.*
superpower ['sju:pə,pauə*] n. Superpotencia, *f.*
supersaturate [,sju:pə'sætjureit] v. tr. Supersaturar, sobresaturar.
supersaturation ['sju:pə,sætju'reiʃən] n. Supersaturación, *f.*, sobresaturación, *f.*
superscribe ['sju:pə'skraib] v. tr. Poner una indicación en (a parcel). || Poner la dirección en (a letter).
superscription [,sju:pə'skripʃən] n. Inscripción, *f.*, indicación, *f.* || Dirección, *f.* (on letter). || Membrete, *m.* (on document).
supersede [,sju:pə'si:d] v. tr. Desbancar, suplantar: *buses have superseded trams*, los autobuses han desbancado los tranvías. || Reemplazar, sustituir: *the written exam has been superseded by an oral exam*, el examen escrito ha sido sustituido por un examen oral; *John has superseded Joseph as director*, Juan ha sustituido a José como director.
supersensible [,sju:pə'sensibl] adj. Suprasensible.
supersensitive [,sju:pə'sensitiv] adj. Hipersensible (person). || PHOT. Muy sensible.
supersensory [,sju:pə'sensəri] or **supersensual** [,sju:pə'sensjuəl] adj. Suprasensible.
supersession [,sju:pə'seʃən] n. Reemplazo, *m.*, sustitución, *f.* (replacement, substitution). || Desbancamiento, *m.*, suplantación, *f.* (of a colleague, etc.).
supersonic ['sju:pə'sɔnik] adj. Supersónico, ca: *supersonic aircraft*, avión supersónico.
supersonics [—s] n. Ciencia (*f.*) que estudia los fenómenos supersónicos.
supersound ['sju:pə,saund] n. Ultrasonido, *m.*
superstition [,sju:pə'stiʃən] n. Superstición, *f.*
superstitious [,sju:pə'stiʃəs] adj. Supersticioso, sa.
superstratum [,sju:pə'strα:təm] n. GEOL. Capa (*f.*) superior.

— OBSERV. El plural de esta palabra es *superstrata* o *superstratums*.

superstructure ['sju:pə,strʌktʃə*] n. ARCH. MAR. Superestructura, *f.*
supertanker ['sjupə,tænkə*] n. Petrolero (*m.*) gigante.
supertax ['sju:pətæks] n. Sobretasa, *f.*, impuesto (*m.*) adicional.
supervene [,sju:pə'vi:n] v. intr. Sobrevenir, ocurrir.
supervise ['sju:pəvaiz] v. tr. Supervisar.
supervision [,sju:pə'viʒən] n. Supervisión, *f.*
supervisor ['sju:pəvaizə*] n. Supervisor, ra.
supervisory ['sju:pəvaizəri] adj. De supervisión.
supervoltage [,sju:pə'vəultidʒ] n. ELECTR. Sobretensión, *f.*, supervoltaje, *m.*
supinate ['sju:pineit] v. tr. Enseñar la palma de (one's hand).
supinating [—iŋ] adj. ANAT. Supinador.
supination [,sju:pi'neiʃən] n. Supinación, *f.*
supinator ['sju:pineitə*] n. ANAT. Supinador, *m.*
supine [sju:pain] adj. Supino, na (face up). || FIG. Indolente, flojo, ja.
— N. GRAMM. Supino, *m.* (in Latin).
supinely [—li] adv. Boca arriba, en posición supina. || FIG. Indolentemente.
supineness [—nis] n. Indolencia, *f.*
supper ['sʌpə*] n. Cena, *f.* || — REL. *The Last Supper*, la Última Cena. | *The Lord's Supper*, el pan eucarístico. || *To have supper*, cenar. || *To have sth. for supper*, cenar algo. || *To stay to supper*, quedarse a cenar.
suppertime [—taim] n. Hora (*f.*) de cenar.
supplant [sə'plα:nt] v. tr. Suplantar (by cunning). || Reemplazar, sustituir (to take the place of).
supplantation [səplα:n'teiʃən] n. Suplantación, *f.* || Reemplazo, *m.*, sustitución, *f.*
supplanter [sə'plα:ntə*] n. Suplantador, ra. || Sustituto, ta.
supple ['sʌpl] adj. Flexible: *supple stick*, palo flexible. || FIG. Flexible, adaptable. | Influenciable (easily influenced). | Complaciente, obsequioso, sa (obsequious).
supple ['sʌpl] v. tr. Volver flexible. || Domar (horse).
— V. intr. Volverse flexible.
supplement ['sʌplimənt] n. Suplemento, *m.*, complemento, *m.* || MATH. PRINT. Suplemento, *m.*
supplement ['sʌplimənt] v. tr. Suplir, completar (to add what lacks). || Aumentar: *he has taken a second job to supplement his wages*, ha tomado un segundo empleo para aumentar su sueldo.
supplemental [,sʌpli'mentl] adj. See SUPPLEMENTARY.
supplementary [,sʌpli'mentəri] adj. Suplementario, ria; supletorio, ria; adicional. || MAT. *Supplementary angles*, ángulos suplementarios.
suppleness ['sʌplnis] n. Flexibilidad, *f.* || FIG. Flexibilidad, *f.* | Obsequiosidad, *f.*, complacencia, *f.*
suppletory ['sʌplitəri] adj. Suplementario, ria; supletorio, ria.
suppliant ['sʌpliənt] adj./n. Suplicante.
supplicant ['sʌplikənt] adj./n. Suplicante.
supplicate ['sʌplikeit] v. tr./intr. Suplicar, rogar.
supplicating ['sʌpli,keitiŋ] adj. Suplicante.
supplication [,sʌpli'keiʃən] n. Súplica, *f.*
supplicatory ['sʌplikətəri] adj. Suplicante.
supplier [sə'plaiə*] n. Suministrador, ra: *the supplier of arms*, el suministrador de armas. || COMM. Proveedor, ra; abastecedor, ra.
supply [sə'plai] n. Oferta, *f.*: *the law of supply and demand*, la ley de la oferta y la demanda. || Abastecimiento, *m.*, suministro, *m.* (act of supplying). || Provisión, *f.*: *I need a supply of coal*, necesito una provisión de carbón. || Suministro, *m.*: *electricity supply*, suministro de electricidad. || Surtido, *m.* (stock): *we have a large supply of bathing costumes*, tenemos un gran surtido de trajes de baño. || — Pl. Suministros, *m.* || Provisiones, *f.*, víveres, *m.* (stores, provisions). || MIL. Pertrechos, *m.*, municiones, *f.* (munitions). || Material, *m. sing.*, artículos, *m.* (for office, etc.). || Créditos, *m.* (credits). || — *Committee of Supplies*, Comisión (*f.*) del Presupuesto. || MIL. *Supply department*, intendencia, *f.* || *Supply teacher*, profesor (*m.*) suplente. || *To be in short supply*, escasear. || *To lay in a supply of*, hacer provisión de.
supply [sə'plai] v. tr. Proveer (to provide): *to supply s.o. with clothes*, proveer a alguien de ropa. || Abastecer (*with*, con), suministrar, aprovisionar (*with*, con): *to supply a town with electricity*, suministrar electricidad a una ciudad. || COMM. Surtir. || MIL. Avituallar, aprovisionar. || Alimentar (a machine). || Dar, presentar: *to supply proof, an explanation*, dar pruebas, una explicación. || Facilitar, proporcionar: *to supply a bus service*, proporcionar un servicio de autobuses. || Proporcionarse (to procure): *when you go to university you must supply your own books*, cuando uno va a la universidad tiene que proporcionarse sus propios libros. || Traer (to bring): *you will have to supply your own wine*, tendrás que traer tu propio vino. || Poner: *I will supply the butter if you supply the cheese*, yo pondré la mantequilla si tú pones el queso. || Satisfacer (a need). || Reparar (an omission). || Enjugar (a deficit). || Corregir, remediar: *to supply a defect in manufacture*, corregir un defecto de fabricación. || Cubrir (a vacancy). || Suplir, sustituir (to supplement, to replace): *to supply a teacher who is ill*, suplir a un profesor que está enfermo.
— V. intr. Sustituir (*for*, a).
support [sə'pɔ:t] n. Apoyo, *m.*: *to give s.o. support*, prestar apoyo a alguien. || Apoyo, *m.*, ayuda, *f.*: *he solicited my support*, me pidió ayuda, pidió mi apoyo. || Apoyo, *m.* (base, sth. that supports, act of supporting): *a column which acts as a support*, una columna que sirve de apoyo. || TECH. Soporte, *m.* || ARCH. Soporte, *m.*, pilar, *m.* || FIG. Sostén, *m.* (of one's family). | Mantenimiento, *m.*, sustento, *m.*: *several relatives depend on him for their support*, varios parientes dependen de él para su mantenimiento. || — *In support of*, en apoyo de (an allegation, etc.), a favor de, en defensa de: *he spoke in support of my idea*, habló a favor de mi idea; a beneficio de. || *To lean on s.o. for support*, apoyarse en uno.
support [sə'pɔ:t] v. tr. Sostener (to carry the weight of): *the beams support the roof*, la vigas sostienen el tejado. || Apoyar (to lean). || Apoyar (to back up): *I'll support your claims*, apoyaré sus peticiones; *to support a motion, a candidature*, apoyar una moción, una candidatura; *Mary does not agree with me, but John supports me*, María no está de acuerdo conmigo, pero Juan me apoya. || Sustentar, respaldar: *this supports your theory*, esto respalda su teoría. || Confirmar, corroborar (suspicions). || Mantener (a family). || Soportar, aguantar: *that bridge is not strong enough to support so much weight*, este puente no es bastante fuerte para aguantar tanto peso. || Soportar: *Eskimoes can support intense cold*, los esquimales pueden soportar un frío intenso. || Dar la entrada a (a leading actor). || — *Supporting film*, película secundaria. || MIL. *Supporting fire*, fuego (*m.*) de apoyo. || *Supporting role*, papel secundario. || *To*

support o.s., ganarse la vida, mantenerse (to earn one's living), apoyarse (to lean).
supportable [—əbl] adj. Sostenible. || Soportable.
supporter [—ə*] n. Partidario, ria: *a supporter of democracy*, un partidario de la democracia. || Seguidor, ra; hincha, *m.* (of a team). || Aficionado, da (of a sport): *football supporter*, aficionado al fútbol. || Soporte, *m.*, apoyo, *m.* (support). || HERALD. Tenante, *m.* || *Supporters' club*, peña deportiva.
supposable [səˈpəuzəbl] adj. *It is supposable that*, es de suponer que.
suppose [səˈpəuz] v. tr. Suponer: *let us suppose that what he says is true*, supongamos que es verdad lo que dice; *he is not supposed to know it*, se supone que no lo sabe. || Suponer, presuponer (to presuppose). || Imaginarse (to imagine): *as you may suppose*, como te puedes imaginar. || Creer (to think). || — *I suppose so*, supongo que sí. || *I suppose you are right*, tendrás razón, debes de tener razón. || *Suppose* o *supposing she came back*, y ¿si volviese? || *They are supposed to be at midday*, tienen que estar aquí a las doce. || *This tower is supposed to be the highest in the world*, se considera que esta torre es la más alta del mundo. || *We are not supposed to do it*, no nos corresponde *or* no nos toca hacerlo (we have not to), no podemos *or* no debemos hacerlo (we are not allowed to). || *We are not supposed to tell you that*, nos dijeron que no te lo contásemos. || *You are supposed to be in London!*, ¡creíamos que estabas en Londres!
supposed [—d] adj. Supuesto, ta; presunto, ta.
supposedly [səˈpəuzidli] adv. Según cabe suponer, probablemente.
supposition [ˌsʌpəˈziʃən] n. Suposición, *f.* || *On the supposition that*, en la hipótesis de que, en el supuesto de que.
suppositional [—l] adj. Hipotético, ca.
supposititious [səˌpɔziˈtiʃəs] adj. Hipotético, ca (suppositional). || Falso, sa (counterfeit). || JUR. Supuesto, ta.
suppository [səˈpɔzitəri] n. MED. Supositorio, *m.*
suppress [səˈpres] v. tr. Suprimir. || Contener, reprimir (laughter, feeling, yawn, cough, etc.). || Dominar (passions). || Disimular (a fact). || Callar, no revelar, ocultar (secret, name, news, etc.). || Prohibir (a publication). || Sofocar, reprimir (a revolt). || Echar tierra a (a scandal). || Contener (blood, etc.).
suppression [səˈpreʃən] n. Supresión, *f.* || Represión, *f.* (of anger, revolt, etc.). || Dominio, *m.* (of passions). || Ocultación, *f.* (of facts, truth, etc.). || Prohibición, *f.* (of publications).
suppressive [səˈpresiv] adj. Represivo, va.
suppressor [səˈpresə*] n. ELECTR. Supresor, *m.* || TECH. Silencioso, *m.* (muffler). || RAD. Antiparásito, *m.*
suppurate [ˈsʌpjuəreit] v. intr. MED. Supurar.
suppurating [—iŋ] adj. MED. Supurante.
suppuration [ˌsʌpjuəˈreiʃən] n. MED. Supuración, *f.*
suppurative [ˈsʌpjəˌreitiv] adj. Supurativo, va; supurante.
supranational [ˌsju:prəˈnæʃənl] adj. Supranacional.
suprarenal [ˈsju:prəˈri:nl] adj. ANAT. Suprarrenal: *suprarenal gland*, glándula suprarrenal.
— N. Glándula (*f.*) suprarrenal.
supremacy [sjuˈpreməsi] n. Supremacía, *f.*
supreme [sjuˈpri:m] adj. Supremo, ma (highest). || Supremo, ma; sumo, ma (greatest). || — *Supreme Being*, Ser Supremo. || *Supreme commander*, generalísimo, *m.*, jefe supremo. || *Supreme court*, tribunal supremo.
sura [ˈsuərə] n. REL. Sura, *f.*, surata, *f.*
surah [ˈsjuərə] n. Surá, *m.* (material).
surbase [ˈsə:beis] v. tr. ARCH. Rebajar.
surcharge [ˈsə:tʃɑ:dʒ] n. Sobrecarga, *f.* (load). || Sobretasa, *f.* (surtax). || Recargo, *m.* (of taxes). || Sobrecarga, *f.* (on postage stamps).
surcharge [sə:ˈtʃɑ:dʒ] v. tr. Sobrecargar, recargar (to overcharge, to overload). || Sobrellenar (to overfill). || Poner sobretasa a (a letter). || Sobrecargar, poner sobrecarga a (a postage stamp). || Gravar con impuestos suplementarios *or* tasas suplementarias.
surcingle [ˈsə:siŋgl] n. Sobrecincha, *f.* (harness). || Faja, *f.* (of a cassock).
surcoat [ˈsə:kəut] n. Sobretodo, *m.*
surd [sə:d] adj. GRAMM. Sordo, da. || MATH. Irracional, sordo, da.
— N. MATH. Número (*m.*) sordo, número (*m.*) irracional. || GRAMM. Sonido (*m.*) sordo.
sure [ʃuə*] adj. Seguro, ra: *a sure friend*, un amigo seguro; *I'm sure he will come*, estoy seguro de que vendrá; *it is by no means sure that*, no es nada seguro que. || Seguro, ra; cierto, ta: *it's a sure sign of rain*, es una señal segura de lluvia. || Seguro, ra; firme (hand). || Certero, ra (shot). || — *Be sure and wear* o *be sure to wear your overcoat*, no deje de ponerse el abrigo. || *Be sure not to lose it*, tenga cuidado en no perderlo. || *Be sure to come*, venga sin falta, no deje de venir. || *Don't be too sure*, no tenga tanta seguridad, no esté tan seguro. || *He is sure to succeed*, seguramente tendrá exito. || *I am sure he may go out if he wants to*, por supuesto puede salir si así lo desea. || *I'm sure I can't tell you*, te aseguro que no puedo decírtelo. || *Sure thing!*, ¡claro!, ¡seguro!, ¡por supuesto! || *To be sure!*, ¡claro!, ¡por supuesto! || *To be sure of o.s.*, estar seguro de sí mismo. || *To be sure that*, estar seguro de que, tener la seguridad de que. || *To make s.o. sure of sth.*, asegurar a uno algo. || *To make sure*, asegurarse: *I just want to make sure of the time*, sólo quiero asegurarme de la hora.
— Adv. Seguramente. || Realmente. || Claro, por supuesto: *sure, I'll do it*, claro que lo haré. || FAM. Sí que, vaya si: *he is very ugly but he sure sings well*, es muy feo pero vaya si canta bien. || — *For sure*, seguramente (certainly), con seguridad: *do you know that for sure?*, ¿lo sabe con seguridad? || *Sure enough*, efectivamente: *I said he would come, and sure enough he came*, dije que vendría y efectivamente vino.
surefire [—ˌfaiə*] adj. U. S. De éxito seguro, seguro, ra.
surefooted [—ˌfutid] adj. De pie firme.
surely [—li] adv. Sin duda, seguramente (without a doubt). || Seguramente (in a sure manner). || *Surely!*, ¡por supuesto!
sureness [—nis] n. Seguridad, *f.*, certeza, *f.* || Firmeza, *f.* (of hand).
surety [—ti] n. Seguridad, *f.*, certeza, *f.* || Fiador, *m.*, garante, *m.* & *f.* (guarantor). || Fianza, *f.*, garantía, *f.* (guarantee). || — *Surety bond*, fianza. || *To go* o *to stand surety for*, salir fiador *or* garante de.
suretyship [—tiʃip] n. Fianza, *f.*, garantía, *f.*
surf [sə:f] n. Rompientes, *m. pl.*, resaca, *f.* (breaking waves). || Espuma, *f.* (foam).
surface [ˈsə:fis] n. Superficie, *f.*: *the surface of the water*, la superficie del agua; *friction surface*, superficie de rozamiento; *land surface*, superficie terrestre. || Firme, *m.* (of road). || FIG. Aspecto (*m.*) superficial, apariencia, *f.* || FIG. *On the surface*, superficialmente, en apariencia.
— Adj. De la superficie, superficial. || De superficie: *surface transportation*, transporte de superficie. || A cielo abierto (mine). || PHYS. Superficial (tension). || *By surface mail*, por vía terrestre *or* marítima.
surface [ˈsə:fis] v. tr. Pulir, alisar (to polish). || Allanar (to flatten). || Revestir (a road). || Sacar a la superficie (a submarine).
— V. intr. Salir a la superficie (to come to the surface). || MIN. Trabajar a cielo abierto.
surface-to-air [—tuˈɛə*] adj. *Surface-to-air missile*, proyectil tierra-aire.
surfboard [ˈsə:fbɔ:d] n. Tabla (*f.*) hawaiana.
surfeit [ˈsə:fit] n. Exceso, *m.*: *there is a surfeit of apples*, hay un exceso de manzanas. || Empacho, *m.* (indigestion). || Saciedad, *f.*, hartura, *f.* (satiety).
surfeit [ˈsə:fit] v. tr. Colmar, saciar (to oversupply). || Hartar, empachar (to overfeed). || Saciar, hartar (to satiate).
surfing [ˈsə:fiŋ] n. SP. "Surf", *m.*
surge [sə:dʒ] n. Oleada, *f.*, oleaje, *m.* (of waves). || Mar (*m.*) de fondo (enormous billow). || FIG. Oleada, *f.*, ola, *f.* (of indignation, etc.). | Arranque, *m.*: *a surge of pity, anger*, un arranque de compasión, de ira. || ELECTR. Sobretensión, *f.*
surge [sə:dʒ] v. tr. MAR. Largar (a cable).
— V. intr. Encresparse, levantarse (the sea). || — FIG. *People surged into the cinema*, la gente entró a manadas en el cine. || *Rage surged up within him*, la rabia se apoderó de él. || *The blood surged to my cheeks*, se me subió la sangre a la cara. || ELECTR. *The current surges*, hay una sobretensión de corriente.
surgeon [ˈsə:dʒən] n. MED. Cirujano, *m.* || — *Dental surgeon*, odontólogo, *m.*, dentista, *m.* || *Veterinary surgeon*, veterinario, *m.*
surgery [ˈsə:dʒəri] n. MED. Cirugía, *f.* (work of a surgeon). | Consultorio, *m.* (consulting room). | Clínica, *f.* (clinic). | Dispensario, *m.* (dispensary). || U. S. MED. Sala (*f.*) de operaciones, quirófano, *m.* (operating theatre). || — *Plastic surgery*, cirugía estética *or* plástica. || *Surgery hours*, horas (*f.*) de consulta.
surgical [ˈsə:dʒikəl] adj. MED. Quirúrgico, ca.
surging [ˈsə:dʒiŋ] adj. Agitado, da; encrespado, da.
surliness [ˈsə:linis] n. Malhumor, *m.*, mal genio, *m.* (bad temper). || Hosquedad, *f.*, desabrimiento, *m.* (sullenness).
surly [ˈsə:li] adj. Malhumorado, da (bad-tempered). || Hosco, ca; desabrido, da; arisco, ca (unfriendly).
surmise [ˈsə:maiz] n. Conjetura, *f.*, suposición, *f.*
surmise [sə:ˈmaiz] v. tr. Conjeturar, suponer.
surmount [sə:ˈmaunt] v. tr. Superar: *to surmount a difficult situation*, superar una situación difícil. || Coronar (to crown, to lie at the top of).
surmountable [—əbl] adj. Superable.
surmullet [sə:ˈmʌlet] n. Salmonete, *m.* (fish).
surname [ˈsə:neim] n. Apellido, *m.* (family name). || Apodo, *m.* (nickname).
surname [ˈsə:neim] v. tr. Apellidar. || Apodar.
surpass [sə:ˈpɑ:s] v. tr. Sobrepasar, superar, aventajar: *to surpass s.o. in intelligence*, superar a alguien en inteligencia. || Rebasar, superar: *to surpass all expectations*, rebasar todas las esperanzas.
surpassable [—əbl] adj. Superable.
surpassing [—iŋ] adj. Sobresaliente, incomparable, sin igual, sin par.
surplice [ˈsə:pləs] n. REL. Sobrepelliz, *f.*
surplus [ˈsə:pləs] n. Excedente, *m.* || COMM. Superávit, *m.* (of budget). | Excedente, *m.* (of goods).
— Adj. Excedente, sobrante. || *Sale of surplus stock*, liquidación (*f.*) de saldos.

surplusage [—idʒ] n. Excedente, *m.* (surplus). || JUR. Redundancia, *f.* (of words).
surprise [səˈpraiz] n. Sorpresa, *f.*, asombro, *m.*: *much to my surprise*, con gran asombro mío. || Sorpresa, *f.*: *he gave me a surprise*, me dio una sorpresa. || — FAM. *Surprise, surprise!*, ¡vaya, vaya! || *To spring a surprise on s.o.*, dar una sorpresa a alguien. || *To take by surprise*, coger desprevenido. || *What a surprise!*, ¡vaya sorpresa!
— Adj. Inesperado, da: *a surprise visit*, una visita inesperada. || — *Surprise attack*, ataque (*m.*) por sorpresa. || *Surprise party*, asalto, *m.*, guateque, *m.*
surprise [səˈpraiz] v. tr. Sorprender asombrar (to astonish): *his behaviour surprised me*, me asombró su conducta. || Sorprender (a secret, a robber). || MIL. Coger por sorpresa. || *To be surprised at*, sorprenderle a uno: *I was surprised at his indifference*, me sorprendió su indiferencia.
surprising [—iŋ] adj. Sorprendente, asombroso, sa.
surprisingly [—iŋli] adv. Terriblemente, asombrosamente. || De modo sorprendente.
surrealism [səˈriəlizəm] n. Surrealismo, *m.*
surrealist [səˈriəlist] adj./n. Surrealista.
surrealistic [səriəˈlistik] adj. Surrealista.
surrender [səˈrendə*] n. Rendición, *f.*: *their surrender meant the end of the war*, su rendición significó el fin de la guerra. || Entrega, *f.* (handing over). || Abandono, *m.* (abandoning). || JUR. Renuncia, *f.*, cesión, *f.* || Rescate, *m.* (of insurance policy). || *In surrender*, en señal de rendición.
surrender [səˈrendə*] v. tr. Rendir, entregar (to hand over): *to surrender the town*, entregar la ciudad. || Ceder (to give up): *to surrender one's place to a lady*, ceder el sitio a una señora. || Abandonar (hope). || JUR. Ceder, renunciar a. || — *To surrender o.s.*, rendirse. || FIG. *To surrender o.s. to vice*, entregarse al vicio.
— V. intr. Rendirse: *I surrender!*, ¡me rindo! || Entregarse: *to surrender to justice*, entregarse a la justicia; *to surrender to vice*, entregarse al vicio.
surreptitious [ˌsʌrəpˈtiʃəs] adj. Subrepticio, cia.
surrey [ˈsʌri] n. U. S. Coche (*m.*) de punto, simón, *m.*
surrogate [ˈsʌrəgit] n. Sustituto, *m.* || REL. Vicario, *m.*
surround [səˈraund] v. tr. Cercar, rodear: *the sea surrounds the island*, el mar rodea la isla; *surrounded by people*, rodeado de gente. || FIG. Rodear: *I am surrounded by friends*, estoy rodeado de amigos. || MIL. Sitiar, rodear, cercar.
surrounding [—iŋ] adj. Circundante.
— Pl. n. Alrededores, *m.* (environs). || Medio, *m. sing.*, ambiente, *m. sing.*, medio (*m.*) ambiente (environment).
surtax [ˈsə:tæks] n. Sobretasa, *f.*, recargo, *m.*
surtax [ˈsə:tæks] v. tr. Poner un recargo a.
surveillance [sə:ˈveiləns] n. Vigilancia, *f.*
surveillant [sə:ˈveilənt] n. Vigilante, *m.* (watchman). || Guardián, *m.* (of prison).
survey [ˈsə:vei] n. Inspección, *f.* (inspection). || Reconocimiento, *m.* (reconnaissance). || Examen, *m.*, estudio, *m.* (of a question). || Encuesta, *f.* (inquiry). || Informe, *m.* (report). || Panorama, *m.*, vista (*f.*) de conjunto: *a survey of the economic situation*, una vista de conjunto de la situación económica. || Idea (*f.*) de conjunto. || Medición, *f.* (in topography). || Alzado, *m.*, levantamiento, *m.* (of a map). || Mapa (*m.*) topográfico (map). || *Market survey*, estudio del mercado.
survey [sə:ˈvei] v. tr. Inspeccionar (to inspect). || Reconocer (ground). || Examinar (to examine). || Estudiar (to study). || Hacer una encuesta de (to make an inquiry into). || Contemplar (to look at). || Medir (to measure land). || Levantar un plano de (to make a map). || Hacer el catastro de (a parish).
surveying [—iŋ] n. Topografía, *f.*, agrimensura, *f.* (topography). || Levantamiento (*m.*) de planos (of maps). || Inspección, *f.* (inspection). || *Naval surveying*, hidrografía, *f.*
surveyor [—ə*] n. Agrimensor, *m.*, topógrafo, *m.* (of land). || Inspector, *m.* || U. S. Vista, *m.*, inspector (*m.*) de aduanas (in the customs). || — *Surveyor's chain*, cadena (*f.*) de agrimensor. || *Surveyor's cross*, escuadra (*f.*) de agrimensor.
surveyorship [—əʃip] n. Topografía, *f.*, agrimensura, *f.*
survival [səˈvaivəl] n. Supervivencia, *f.* || *Survival of the fittest*, selección (*f.*) natural.
survive [səˈvaiv] v. tr. Sobrevivir a: *he survived his wife*, sobrevivió a su mujer.
— V. intr. Sobrevivir (to continue to live). || Subsistir: *we are trying to survive on 4 pounds a week*, estamos intentando subsistir con cuatro libras a la semana. || Quedar, sobrevivir, subsistir: *only four houses have survived*, no han quedado más que cuatro casas.
surviving [—iŋ] adj. Superviviente, sobreviviente.
survivor [—ə*] n. Superviviente, *m.* & *f.*, sobreviviente, *m.* & *f.*
survivorship [—əʃip] n. JUR. Supervivencia, *f.*
susceptibility [səˌseptəˈbiliti] n. Susceptibilidad, *f.* || Sensibilidad, *f.* (sensitivity). || ELECTR. Susceptibilidad, *f.* || MED. Predisposición, *f.*, propensión, *f.*
susceptible [səˈseptəbl] adj. Susceptible. || Sensible (sensitive): *susceptible to beauty*, sensible a la belleza. || ELECTR. Susceptible. || Vulnerable, expuesto, ta (vulnerable). || MED. Predispuesto, ta; propenso, sa. || — *To be susceptible of*, estar expuesto a. || *To be susceptible of proof*, poder demostrarse. || *To be susceptible to*, ser propenso *or* predispuesto a: *to be susceptible to disease*, ser propenso a enfermedades.
susceptive [səˈseptiv] adj. Susceptible. || Sensible (sensitive).
suspect [ˈsʌspekt] adj./n. Sospechoso, sa.
suspect [səsˈpekt] v. tr. Sospechar: *I would never had suspected him*, nunca le hubiera sospechado. || Recelar de (to distrust). || Sospechar, tener la impresión de: *we suspect he is a genius*, tenemos la impresión de que es un genio. || Sospechar, tener la sospecha de: *I suspect him of being a thief*, sospecho que es un ladrón.
— V. intr. Sospechar, tener sospechas. || Imaginarse, figurarse (to believe): *I suspected as much*, ya me lo imaginaba.
suspend [səsˈpend] v. tr. Suspender, colgar (to hang). || Suspender, interrumpir (to interrupt). || Suspender, privar temporalmente de sus funciones (to debar). || Suspender (payment, newspaper). || Reservar (one's judgment). || JUR. Suspender (proceedings). || *Suspended animation*, suspensión momentánea de las funciones vitales.
suspender [—ə*] n. Liga, *f.* (for socks or stockings). || — Pl. U. S. Tirantes, *m.* (for trousers). || *Suspender belt*, liguero, *m.*
suspense [səsˈpens] n. Ansiedad, *f.* (anxiety). || Incertidumbre, *f.*, duda, *f.* (uncertainty): *to keep in suspense*, mantener en la incertidumbre. || Tensión, *f.* || CINEM. "Suspense", *m.* || JUR. Suspensión, *f.* (of proceedings). || *To remain in suspense*, quedar pendiente.
suspension [səsˈpenʃən] n. Suspensión, *f.* || — *Points of suspension* o *suspension points*, puntos suspensivos. || *Suspension bridge*, puente (*m.*) colgante.
suspensive [səsˈpensiv] adj. Suspensivo, va.
suspensory [—ri] adj. Suspensorio, ria.
— N. MED. Suspensorio, *m.*
suspicion [səsˈpiʃən] n. Sospecha, *f.*: *the police has suspicions about him*, la policía tiene sospechas de él. || Recelo, *m.*, desconfianza, *f.* (mistrust): *to cast suspicion on s.o.'s good faith*, tener recelo de la buena fe de alguien; *with suspicion*, con desconfianza. || Ligera idea, *f.*: *he hadn't a suspicion of the truth*, no tenía la más ligera idea de la verdad. || Pizca, *f.*, poco, *m.*: *a suspicion of garlic*, una pizca de ajo. || — *Above suspicion*, por encima *or* fuera de toda sospecha. || *Detention on suspicion*, detención preventiva. || *On suspicion*, como sospechoso. || *Suspicion fell on me*, se empezó a sospechar de mí, las sospechas recayeron sobre mí. || *To arouse suspicion*, despertar sospechas. || *To hold s.o. in suspicion*, sospechar de alguien. || *To lay o.s. open to suspicion*, hacerse sospechoso. || *Under suspicion*, bajo sospecha. || *Without a shadow of a suspicion*, sin la menor sospecha.
suspicion [səsˈpiʃən] v. tr. U. S. Sospechar.
suspicious [səsˈpiʃəs] adj. Sospechoso, sa (suspected). || Suspicaz, receloso, sa; desconfiado, da (suspecting).
suspiciousness [—nis] n. Suspicacia, *f.*, recelo, *m.*, desconfianza, *f.* (mistrust). || Carácter (*m.*) sospechoso.
suspiration [ˌsʌspiˈreiʃən] n. Suspiro, *m.* (sigh).
suspire [sʌsˈpaiə*] v. intr. Suspirar: *to suspire for*, suspirar por.
sustain [səsˈtein] v. tr. Mantener: *to sustain a conversation*, mantener una conversación. || Sostener, mantener, sustentar (a family). || Sostener (weight, burden). || Mantener, continuar, sostener (effort). || Soportar, aguantar (to endure). || Apoyar (an assertion, a theory). || MUS. Sostener (a note). || Sufrir: *to sustain injuries, losses*, sufrir heridas, pérdidas. || Sostener (an attack). || Desempeñar (a rôle). || Admitir: *to sustain an objection*, admitir una objeción.
sustainable [—əbl] adj. Sostenible.
sustained [—d] adj. Ininterrumpido, da; sostenido, da; continuo, nua. || MUS. Sostenido, da (note).
sustenance [ˈsʌstinəns] n. Sustento, *m.*, alimento, *m.* (food). || Subsistencia, *f.*: *means of sustenance*, medios de subsistencia.
sustentation [ˌsʌstenˈteiʃən] n. Mantenimiento, *m.* || Sustentación, *f.* (of the body).
sutler [ˈsʌtlə*] n. MIL. Cantinero, *m.*
sutra [ˈsu:trə] n. REL. Sutra, *m.*
suttee [ˈsʌti] n. REL. Inmolación (*f.*) voluntaria de una viuda hindú.
sutural [ˈsju:turəl] adj. MED. Sutural, de sutura.
suture [ˈsju:tʃə*] n. MED. Sutura, *f.*
suture [ˈsju:tʃə*] v. tr. MED. Suturar, coser.
suzerain [ˈsu:zərein] n. HIST. Señor (*m.*) feudal. || JUR. Estado (*m.*) protector.
suzerainty [—ti] n. HIST. Soberanía (*f.*) feudal, señorío (*m.*) feudal. || JUR. Soberanía, *f.*
svelte [svelt] adj. Esbelto, ta.
swab [swɔb] n. Estropajo, *m.* (mop). || MAR. Lampazo, *m.* || MIL. Escobillón, *m.* (of gun). || MED. Tapón, *m.* || FAM. Patán, *m.* (loutish person).
swab [swɔb] v. tr. Fregar con estropajo (to mop). || MAR. Lampacear. || MED. Limpiar con tapón.
Swabian [ˈsweibjən] adj./n. Suabo, ba.
swaddle [ˈswɔdl] v. tr. Poner los pañales a (a baby). || Envolver (to wrap). || — *Swaddling clothes*, pañales, *m.*, pañal, *m. sing.* || FIG. *To be still in swaddling clothes*, estar en pañales, estar en mantillas.

swag [swæg] n. FAM. Botín, *m.* (booty). || Festón, *m.* (festoon). || Bulto, *m.* (bundle, in Australia).
swag [swæg] v. intr. Vagar, vagabundear.
swage [sweidʒ] n. Tas (*m.*) de estampar.
swage [sweidʒ] v. tr. Forjar, embutir, estampar.
swagger [ˈswægə*] n. Contoneo, *m.*, pavoneo, *m.* (walking). || Fanfarronada, *f.* (boast).
— Adj. FAM. Pera, elegante.
swagger [ˈswægə*] v. intr. Contonearse, pavonearse, andar pavoneándose (to walk). || Fanfarronear, vanagloriarse (to boast).
swagger cane [—kein] n. Junco, *m.* (stick).
swaggerer [—rə*] n. Fanfarrón, ona.
swaggering [—riŋ] adj. Jactancioso, sa.
swagger stick [—stik] n. Junco, *m.* (stick).
swain [swein] n. Pretendiente, *m.*, galán, *m.* (suitor). || Zagal, *m.* (boy, shepherd).
swallow [ˈswɔləu] n. Golondrina, *f.* (bird). || Deglución, *f.* (swallowing). || Gaznate, *m.* (throat). || Trago, *m.* (of drink, etc.): *at* o *with one swallow*, de un trago. || Bocado, *m.* (of food). || TECH. Garganta (*f.*) de polea. || FIG. *One swallow doesn't make a summer*, una golondrina no hace verano.
swallow [ˈswɔləu] v. tr. Tragar (to take down food, etc.). || MED. Tomar (a pill). || FIG. Tragar, creer, tragarse (to believe): *he swallows everything he's told*, se traga cuanto le dicen. | Tragar, tragarse, soportar: *he swallows all the insults*, se traga todos los insultos. | Desdecirse de, retractarse de: *to swallow one's words*, desdecirse de sus palabras. | Tragarse: *to swallow one's laughter*, tragarse la risa. | Comerse, tragarse: *to swallow one's pride*, tragarse el orgullo. | Comerse: *the Andalusians swallow many of their letters*, los andaluces comen muchas de las letras. | Tragarse: *the sea swallowed the boat*, el mar se tragó el barco. || *To swallow up*, tragarse (to engulf), consumir: *to swallow up one's savings*, consumir los ahorros.
— V. intr. Tragar.
swallow dive [—daiv] n. Salto (*m.*) del ángel.
swallow fish [—fiʃ] n. ZOOL. Golondrina (*f.*) de mar.
swallowtail [—teil] n. Cola (*f.*) de golondrina. || Macaón, *m.* (butterfly). || TECH. Cola (*f.*) de milano.
swallow-tailed coat [—teildˈkəut] n. Frac, *m.*
swallowwort [—wəːt] n. BOT. Vencetósigo, *m.*
swam [swæm] pret. See SWIM.
swamp [ˈswɔmp] n. Pantano, *m.*, terreno (*m.*) pantanoso, ciénaga, *f.*
swamp [ˈswɔmp] v. tr. Hundir (a boat). || Encenagar, empantanar (in marsh, mud). || Inundar, anegar, sumergir (with water). || FIG. Inundar (to inundate): *swamped with orders*, inundado de pedidos. | Agobiar, abrumar (with work).
— V. intr. Hundirse (to sink). || Inundarse (to become flooded). || Empantanarse, encenagarse.
swamp fever [—ˈfiːvə*] n. MED. Fiebre (*f.*) de los pantanos, malaria, *f.*, paludismo, *m.*
swampy [—i] adj. Pantanoso, sa.
swan [swɔn] n. Cisne, *m.* (bird).
swan dive [—daiv] n. U. S. Salto (*m.*) del ángel.
swank [swæŋk] n. Ostentación, *f.* || Fanfarronada, *f.*
swank [swæŋk] v. intr. Fanfarronear.
swanker [—ə*] n. Fanfarrón, ona.
swanky [—i] adj. Ostentoso, sa. || Fanfarrón, ona.
swannery [ˈswɔnəri] n. Criadero (*m.*) de cisnes.
swansdown [ˈswɔnzdaun] n. Muletón, *m.* (cotton flannel). || Plumón (*m.*) de cisne.
swan song [ˈswɔnsɔŋ] n. Canto (*m.*) del cisne.
swap [swɔp] n. Cambio, *m.*, canje, *m.*
swap [swɔp] v. tr. Cambiar, canjear.
— V. intr. Hacer un intercambio.
sward [swɔːd] n. Césped, *m.*
swarf [swɔːf] n. Limalla, *f.*, limaduras, *f. pl.*
swarm [swɔːm] n. Enjambre, *m.* (of bees). || FIG. Enjambre, *m.*, multitud, *f.* (of people, etc.).
swarm [swɔːm] v. intr. Salir en enjambre, enjambrar (bees). || FIG. Hormiguear, pulular: *the tourists swarmed all over the park*, los turistas hormigueaban por todo el parque. | Rebosar, ser un hervidero, hervir: *the place was swarming with tourists*, el lugar era un hervidero de turistas, el lugar rebosaba *or* hervía de turistas. || Escaparse [los zoosporas del zoosporangio]. || *To swarm up*, trepar.
— V. tr. FIG. Invadir, inundar.
swart [swɔːt] adj. Moreno, na.
swarthiness [ˈswɔːðinis] n. Tez (*f.*) morena, piel (*f.*) atezada.
swarthy [ˈswɔːði] adj. Moreno, na; atezado, da.
swash [swɔʃ] n. Chapoteo, *m.*
swash [swɔʃ] v. tr. Echar, arrojar (to splash).
— V. intr. Chapotear (water). || U. S. FAM. Fanfarronear (to boast).
swashbuckler [—ˌbʌklə*] n. Espadachín, *m.*, bravucón, *m.*, matón, *m.*
swashbuckling [—ˌbʌkliŋ] n. Bravuconería, *f.*
— Adj. Bravucón, ona.
swastika [ˈswɔstikə] n. Esvástica, *f.*, cruz (*f.*) gamada.
swat [swɔt] n. Golpe (*m.*) repentino (blow).
swat [swɔt] v. tr. Aplastar (flies, etc.).
swath [swɔːθ] n. AGR. Andana, *f.*, ringlera, *f.* (line of grass or grain).
swathe [sweið] n. Venda, *f.* (bandage). || Banda, *f.* (of mummies).

swathe [sweið] v. tr. Envolver: *woman swathed in a shawl*, mujer envuelta en un chal. || Vendar (with bandage).
swatter [ˈswɔtə*] n. Matamoscas, *m. inv.*
sway [swei] n. Vaivén, *m.*, balanceo, *m.*, oscilación, *f.* (oscillation). || Movimiento, *m.*: *the sway of the train makes me sick*, el movimiento del tren me marea. || FIG. Dominio, *m.* (power, influence). || — FIG. *To be under the sway of*, estar dominado por. | *To have* o *to hold sway over*, dominar.
sway [swei] v. tr. Hacer oscilar (to move from side to side). || Agitar, mover (trees, etc.). || Inclinar (to cause to lean). || Blandir, esgrimir (a cudgel, a sword). || Llevar (a sceptre). || FIG. Gobernar, dirigir, dominar (to rule). | Ejercer influencia en, influir en: *considerations that sway our opinions*, consideraciones que influyen en nuestras opiniones. | Convencer, persuadir (to convince): *his advice swayed the whole assembly*, su consejo convenció a toda la asamblea. || — *To sway s.o. from*, apartar *or* desviar a alguien de. || MAR. *To sway up*, izar.
— V. intr. Oscilar, balancearse (to swing). || Inclinarse (to lean). || Tambalearse (to move unsteadily): *the drunken man was swaying along*, el borracho iba tambaleándose. || FIG. Vacilar (to hesitate). | Gobernar, dirigir (to rule).
swaying [—iŋ] adj. Oscilante. || *To walk with a swaying gait*, andar tambaleándose.
swear [swɛə*] n. Blasfemia, *f.*, juramento, *m.*, voto, *m.*, reniego, *m.* (blasphemous word). || Tacos, *m. pl.*, palabrotas, *f. pl.* (obscene words). || *To have a good swear*, soltar una sarta de palabrotas.
swear* [swɛə*] v. tr. Jurar: *I swear that it is true*, juro que es verdad; *to swear sth. on the Bible*, jurar algo sobre la Biblia. || JUR. Tomar juramento a (to put on oath). | Declarar bajo juramento. || Jurar, prometer: *to swear to do sth.*, prometer hacer algo. || — *To be sworn in*, prestar juramento, jurar. || *To swear an oath*, prestar juramento, jurar. || *To swear away s.o.'s life*, levantar un falso testimonio que hace condenar a alguien a muerte. || *To swear in*, tomar juramento a. || *To swear s.o. to secrecy*, hacer que uno jure guardar un secreto.
— V. intr. Jurar, prestar juramento (to make an oath). || Jurar, blasfemar (to blaspheme). || Soltar tacos, decir palabrotas, jurar (to use obscene language). || — FIG. *He swears by castor oil*, para él no hay nada como el aceite de ricino. | *I would have sworn to him*, hubiera jurado que era él. || *To swear at*, echar pestes de. || *To swear by*, jurar por: *to swear by all that one holds sacred*, jurar por lo más sagrado; fiarse enteramente de, tener entera fe *or* confianza en (to have great confidence in). || *To swear off*, prometer *or* jurar renunciar a. || *To swear to*, jurar: *I wouldn't swear to it*, no lo juraría; declarar bajo juramento (a witness).
— OBSERV. Pret. ***swore;*** p. p. ***sworn.***
swearer [—ə*] n. El que presta juramento. || Blasfemador, ra.
swearword [—wəːd] n. Palabrota, *f.*, taco, *m.*
sweat [swet] n. Sudor, *m.* (perspiration): *to be in a sweat*, estar bañado en sudor. || Sudor, *m.*, sudación, *f.* (act of perspiring). || Rezumamiento, *m.* (on a wall). || FIG. Trabajo (*m.*) pesado (hard work). || — FIG. *By the sweat of one's brow*, con el sudor de su frente. || *Cold sweat*, sudor frío. || REL. *In the sweat of thy face shalt thou eat bread*, ganarás el pan con el sudor de tu frente. || FAM. *Old sweat*, veterano, *m.* || *Running with sweat*, sudando a chorros *or* a mares. || FIG. FAM. *To be dripping with sweat*, sudar la gota gorda, sudar tinta. | *To cause s.o. a lot of sweat*, costarle a uno muchos sudores.
sweat* [swet] v. tr. Hacer sudar (to cause to perspire): *the doctor sweated his patient*, el médico hizo sudar al enfermo. || Empapar de sudor (to make wet). || FIG. Explotar (workers). || Estregar, cepillar (a horse). || Hacer fermentar (tobacco). || TECH. Calentar (to heat). | Soldar (to solder). || Secar en la estufa (hides). || U. S. FAM. Hacer cantar a (to get information from). || — FAM. *To make s.o. sweat his guts out*, hacer sudar a alguien la gota gorda. | *To sweat blood*, sudar sangre *or* tinta, sudar la gota gorda. | *To sweat it out*, pasar un mal rato, pasar muchos sudores. || *To sweat out a cold*, curar un resfriado sudando.
— V. intr. Sudar (people, plants). || Fermentar (tobacco). || Rezumar, sudar (wall). || FIG. Sudar (worker, etc.). || FAM. Tener sudores fríos.
— OBSERV. Pret. & p. p. ***sweat, sweated.***
sweatband [—bænd] n. Badana (*f.*) de un sombrero.
sweat cloth [—klɔθ] n. Sudadero, *m.*
sweated [—id] adj. FIG. Explotado, da; mal pagado, da (labour).
sweater [—ə*] n. Suéter, *m.*, jersey, *m.* (pullover). || MED. Sudorífico, *m.* || FIG. Explotador, *m.* (employer).
sweat gland [—glænd] n. ANAT. Glándula (*f.*) sudorípara.
sweatiness [—inis] n. Sudor, *m.* (of body). || Humedad, *f.* (of clothes).
sweating [—iŋ] n. Sudación, *f.* || FIG. Explotación, *f.*
— Adj. Sudoroso, sa.

sweating room [—iŋrum] n. Sudadero, *m.* || TECH. Estufa, *f.*
sweating system [—iŋˈsistim] n. Explotación (*f.*) de los obreros.
sweat shirt [—ʃə:t] n. Chandal, *m.* (for athletes).
sweatshop [—ʃɔp] n. Fábrica (*f.*) donde se explota al obrero.
sweaty [—i] adj. Sudoroso, sa; sudoso, sa (body, hand). || A sudor (odour). || Empapado de sudor (clothes). || Que hace sudar (causing sweat). || FIG. Agotador, ra; que hace sudar (work).
swede [swi:d] n. BOT. Colinabo, *m.*, nabo (*m.*) sueco.
Swede [swi:d] n. Sueco, ca.
Sweden [—n] pr. n. GEOGR. Suecia, *f.*
Swedish [—iʃ] adj. Sueco, ca.
— N. Sueco, *m.* (language). || *The Swedish*, los suecos.
sweep [swi:p] n. Barrido, *m.*: *to give the room a sweep*, dar un barrido a la habitación. || Deshollinador, *m.* (chimney cleaner). || Curva, *f.* (of a river, road). || Extensión, *f.* (of a plain). || Movimiento (*m.*) amplio (of the arm). || Envergadura, *f.* (of wings). || Lo aerodinámico (of motor car's lines). || MIL. Alcance, *m.* (of weapons): *within the sweep of the guns*, al alcance de los cañones. || Giro, *m.* (of telescope, radar). || Aspa, *f.* (of a mill). || FIG. Redada, *f.*: *the police made a sweep*, la policía hizo una redada. | Alcance, *m.* (of an argument). || MAR. Remo, *m.* (oar). || Draga, *f.* (for dredging sea beds). || Cigoñal, *m.* (of a well). || ARCH. Curvatura, *f.* || SP. "Sweepstake", *m.* || — FIG. *At one sweep*, de una vez. | *To make a clean sweep*, llevárselo todo (in gaming). | *To make a clean sweep of*, hacer tabla rasa de (to get rid of), acaparar, llevarse todo (to get hold of): *the Russian team made a clean sweep of the awards*, el equipo ruso se llevó todos los premios.
sweep* [swi:p] v. tr. Barrer (the dust, ground, room): *they haven't swept the streets*, no han barrido las calles. || Deshollinar (a chimney). || Dragar (a river bed). || Arrasar, asolar: *the earthquake swept the town*, el terremoto arrasó la ciudad. || Arrastrarse por: *her dress swept the floor*, su vestido se arrastraba por el suelo. || Barrer: *the bullets swept the beach*, las balas barrieron la playa. || Arrastrar, llevarse: *a wave swept her overboard*, una ola se la llevó por la borda. || Recorrer: *he swept the valley with his binoculars*, recorrió el valle con los prismáticos; *he swept the map with his finger*, recorrió el mapa con el dedo. || Explorar, barrer (the horizon): *the searchlight swept the sky*, los proyectores barrían el cielo. || Pasar ligeramente por: *she swept her fingers over the strings of the harp*, pasó ligeramente los dedos por las cuerdas del arpa. || Tocar, rozar: *she swept the strings of the guitar with her fingers*, rozó las cuerdas de la guitarra con los dedos. || Pasar: *she swept her hand through her hair*, pasó la mano por el pelo. || Explorar (radar, television). || Rastrear (mines). || FIG. Limpiar, librar: *to sweep the seas of one's enemies*, limpiar los mares de enemigos. | Llevarse, ganar de una manera aplastante (to win overwhelmingly). || — *To sweep a path through the snow*, abrir un camino limpiando *or* quitando la nieve. || *To sweep s.o. off his feet*, entusiasmar a alguien, volverle loco a uno: *she swept him off his feet*, le volvió loco; arrastrar: *the waves swept him off his feet*, las olas le arrastraron; llevarse (a crowd). || *To sweep the board*, see BOARD. || *To sweep the room with a glance*, recorrer la habitación con la mirada. || *To sweep the seas*, ser dueño de los mares.
— V. intr. Extenderse, difundirse: *the news of his death swept over the country*, la noticia de su muerte se extendió por todo el país; *a feeling of horror swept through the crowd*, un sentimiento de horror se extendió por la multitud. || Extenderse: *the shore sweeps to the south*, la costa se extiende hacia el sur. || Arrastrarse: *her dress swept along the floor*, su vestido se arrastraba por el suelo. || Barrer: *you wash the window and I'll sweep*, tú lavas las ventanas y yo barro. || — *She swept into the room*, entró en la sala con paso majestuoso. || *The car swept past the house*, el coche pasó rápidamente delante de la casa. || *The car swept round the corner*, el coche dobló rápidamente la esquina. || *The crowd swept over the pitch*, la multitud invadió el campo. || *The road sweeps round the lake*, la carretera rodea el lago.
— ***To sweep across***, barrer. || ***To sweep along***, arrastrar, llevarse: *the current swept him along*, la corriente le arrastró. | Entusiasmar, arrebatar (to fill with enthusiasm). | Andar con paso majestuoso (to move with dignity). | Andar rápidamente (to go quickly). || ***To sweep aside***, apartar: *to sweep the curtains aside*, apartar las cortinas. | Descartar (a suggestion). || ***To sweep away***, barrer. | Limpiar (snow). | Llevar, arrastrar: *the current swept away the bridge*, la corriente se llevó el puente. | Suprimir (to remove). || ***To sweep by***, pasar rápidamente (quickly). | Pasar majestuosamente (majestically). || ***To sweep down***, arrastrar, llevarse (to carry). | Caer sobre, echarse encima: *the storm swept down on us*, la tormenta se nos echó encima. | Bajar suavemente (to descend): *hills sweeping down to the sea*, colinas que bajan suavemente hacia el mar. | Bajar rápidamente (to go down quickly). | Bajar majestuosamente: *she swept down the stairs*, bajó la escalera majestuosamente. || ***To sweep in***, estrecharse: *the hull sweeps in at the prow*, el casco se estrecha en la proa. | Entrar rápidamente (quickly). | Entrar majestuosamente (majestically). || ***To sweep off***, llevarse. || ***To sweep on***, seguir avanzando. || ***To sweep out***, barrer (a room). | Limpiar, quitar (dust). || ***To sweep up***, barrer (a room). | Recoger (dust, etc.): *to sweep up dead leaves*, recoger las hojas muertas. | Llegar rápidamente (quickly). | Llegar majestuosamente (majestically). | Describir una curva (to curve). | Emprender *or* alzar el vuelo (bird).
— OBSERV. Pret. & p. p. ***swept***.
sweeper [—ə*] n. Barrendero, ra (person). || Barredora, *f.*, barredera, *f.* (machine). || Deshollinador, *m.* (chimney sweep).
sweeping [—iŋ] adj. Aplastante; arrollador, ra: *sweeping victory*, victoria aplastante. || Amplio, plia (gesture). || Radical: *sweeping changes*, cambios radicales. || Demasiado general: *a sweeping statement*, una declaración demasiado general. || Profundo, da (bow). || COMM. Increíble, insuperable (reduction). || Fuerte, violento, ta (blow). || Aerodinámico, ca (car). || — *Sweeping machine*, barredora, *f.*, barredera, *f.* || *To give a sweeping glance*, recorrer con la vista.
— N. Barrido, *m.*, barredura, *f.* (act of clearing away). || — Pl. Barreduras, *f.*, basuras, *f.* (rubbish). || FIG. Heces, *f.* (of society, etc.).
sweep net [—net] n. MAR. Jábega, *f.*
sweep seine [—sein] n. MAR. Jábega, *f.*
sweepstake [—steik] or **sweepstakes** [—steiks] n. "Sweepstake", *m.*
sweet [swi:t] adj. Dulce (taste): *sweet oranges*, naranjas dulces. || Azucarado, da; dulce (containing sugar): *this tea is very sweet*, este té está muy azucarado. || Fresco, ca (milk, meat, fish, breath, air). || Dulce (wine). || Fértil (land). || Suave (engine). || Melodioso, sa; suave (music): *she has a very sweet voice*, tiene una voz muy suave. || Fragante, bueno, na (smell). || Potable (water). || Mono, na; bonito, ta [*Amer.*, lindo, da] (facial features, dress, etc.). || Amable, encantador, ra (friendly): *sweet old lady*, viejecita encantadora. || Querido, da (dear). || Amable: *that was very sweet of you*, fue muy amable de su parte. || Afable, bondadoso, sa (kind): *he has a very sweet disposition*, tiene un carácter muy afable. || Agradable: *it was sweet to be able to do it*, fue agradable poder hacerlo. || — *As sweet as honey*, dulce como la miel. || *At one's own sweet will*, a su antojo. || *Isn't she sweet!*, ¡es un encanto!, ¡es una monería! || *Revenge is sweet*, la venganza es placer de dioses. || BOT. *Sweet basil*, albahaca, *f.* || *Sweet cider*, sidra (*f.*) dulce. || BOT. *Sweet corn*, maíz tierno. || *Sweet oil*, aceite (*m.*) de oliva. || BOT. *Sweet pea*, guisante (*m.*) de olor. | *Sweet pepper*, pimiento (*m.*) morrón. | *Sweet potato*, batata, *f.*, boniato, *m.* [*Amer.*, camote, *m.*]. || *Sweet sixteen*, quince abriles. || *Sweet stuff*, golosinas, *f. pl.*, dulces, *m. pl.* || *To be sweet on s.o.*, estar enamorado de alguien. || *To have a sweet tooth*, ser goloso, gustarle a uno los dulces *or* las golosinas. || *To smell sweet*, oler bien. || *To taste sweet*, estar dulce. || *What a sweet little cat!*, ¡qué gatito más mono!
— N. Caramelo, *m.* (toffee). || Dulce, *m.* (candy). || Postre, *m.* (dessert). || Amor, *m.*, amor mío, *m.*, cielo, *m.*, cariño, *m.* (a beloved person). || — Pl. Deleites, *m.*, delicias, *f.*, dulzura, *f. sing.*: *the sweets of victory*, los deleites de la victoria. || U. S. Dulces, *m.*, golosinas, *f.* (sweet edible things).
sweet-and-sour [—ənˈsauə*] adj. Agridulce.
sweetbread [—bred] n. Mollejas, *f. pl.*, lechecillas, *f. pl.*
sweeten [ˈswi:tn] v. tr. Azucarar, endulzar (by adding sugar). || Suavizar (a sound). || Aplacar, calmar (a person). || Purificar (air). || Depurar (seawater). || Sanear (soil). || FIG. Endulzar, dulcificar (to make more enjoyable). || CHEM. Neutralizar (an acid). || FIG. *To sweeten the pill*, dorar la píldora.
— V. intr. Endulzarse.
sweetener [—ə*] n. Dulcificante, *m.*
sweetening [—iŋ] n. Endulzamiento, *m.*, dulcificación, *f.* || Dulcificante, *m.* (sweetener). || FIG. Suavizamiento, *m.*
sweetheart [—hɑ:t] n. Amor, *m.*, novio, via (loved one). || *My sweetheart*, mi cielo, mi cariño, amor mío, mi amor.
sweetie [—i] n. Caramelo, *m.* (candy). || FIG. Amor, *m.* || *Isn't she a sweetie?*, ¡es un encanto!
sweetish [—iʃ] adj. Dulzón, ona.
sweetmeat [—mi:t] n. Caramelo, *m.* (candy). || — Pl. Dulces, *m.* (a piece of confectionery).
sweetness [—nis] n. Dulzor, *m.*, lo dulce (of sugar). || Suavidad, *f.* (to the touch). || Dulzura, *f.*, suavidad, *f.* (of character). || Buen olor, *m.* (smelling). || Amabilidad, *f.* (kindness).
sweet-scented [—ˈsentid] adj. Perfumado, da; fragante.
sweetshop [—ʃɔp] n. Confitería, *f.*
sweet-smelling [—ˈsmeliŋ] adj. Perfumado, da; fragante.
sweet-tempered [—ˈtempəd] adj. Afable, amable, bondadoso, sa.
sweet-toothed [—tu:θt] adj. Goloso, sa.
swell [swel] adj. Elegantísimo, ma. || U. S. FAM. Fenomenal, bárbaro, ra (fabulous).

— N. Inflamiento, *m.*, inflado, *m.* (action). || Hinchazón, *f.*: *the swell of her belly*, la hinchazón de su vientre. || Curvatura, *f.*, redondez, *f.*: *the swell of a pot*, la redondez de un puchero. || Abultamiento, *m.*: *the swell of a column*, el abultamiento de una columna. || Alabeo, *m.* (through distortion). || GEOL. Ondulación, *f.* (of ground). || MAR. Elevación, *f.* (of seabed). | Marejada, *f.*, oleaje, *m.* (of waves). || FAM. Ricachón, ona (wealthy person). | Guapo, pa (handsome person). | Pez (*m.*) gordo, personaje, *m.* (important person). || *The swells*, la gente bien.

swell* [swel] v. tr. Hinchar. || Hacer crecer (a river). || Hacer aumentar, engrosar: *immigration swelled the population*, la inmigración hizo aumentar la población. || — *Eyes swollen with tears*, ojos hinchados de lágrimas. || FIG. *To get a swollen head*, engreírse, envanecerse. || *To swell the ranks*, engrosar las filas del ejército.

— V. intr. Hincharse, inflamarse: *the boil began to swell*, el divieso empezó a hincharse. || Inflarse, hincharse (to inflate). || Subir, crecer: *the river swelled*, el río creció. || Levantarse (the sea). || Abombarse: *the barrel is swollen in the middle*, el barril está abombado en el centro. || Hincharse: *chickpeas swell when cooked*, los garbanzos se hinchan al cocer. || CULIN. Subir (pastry). || MUS. Aumentar, subir (sound). || FIG. Crecer, aumentar (to increase). | Hincharse, ensoberbecerse, engreírse: *to swell with pride*, hincharse de orgullo. || — *To swell out*, hincharse, inflarse. || *To swell up*, hincharse (part of the body), crecer, aumentar (to increase).

— OBSERV. Pret. **swelled;** p. p. **swollen, swelled.**

swellhead [—hed] n. Vanidoso, sa; engreído, da.
swellheaded [—'hedid] adj. Vanidoso, sa; engreído, da.
swelling [—iŋ] n. Inflamiento, *m.*, inflado, *m.* (increase in size). || Crecida, *f.* (of a river). || Levantamiento, *m.* (of waves). || Inflamiento, *m.* (of sails). || Abultamiento, *m.* (of a column). || MED. Hinchazón, *f.*, tumefacción, *f.*: *the swelling of the belly*, la hinchazón del vientre. | Ganglio, *m.* (ganglion). | Chichón, *m.*, bulto, *m.* (bruise).

— Adj. Inflado, da (in size). || Crecido, da (a river). || Levantado, da; encrespado, da (waves). || MED. Hinchado, da. || FIG. Ampuloso, sa (speech). | Exaltado, da (emotion).

swelter ['sweltə*] n. Calor (*m.*) sofocante, bochorno, *m.* (oppressive heat).
swelter ['sweltə*] v. intr. Chorrear sudor, sudar a mares, sofocarse de calor.
sweltering [—riŋ] or **sweltry** [—ri] adj. Abrasador, ra; sofocante (day, office). || Sudando a mares, chorreando sudor (person).
swept [swept] pret. & p. p. See SWEEP.
swept-back [—bæk] adj. En flecha (wing).
swerve [swə:v] n. Viraje, *m.*: *the car did a violent swerve*, el coche dio un viraje brusco. || Desviación, *f.* (deviation). || SP. Regate, *m.* (of a player). | Efecto, *m.* (of a ball).
swerve [swə:v] v. tr. Desviar: *to swerve s.o. from his duty*, desviar a uno de su deber. || Dar efecto a, cortar (a ball). || *He swerved the car to the left*, torció a la izquierda.

— V. intr. Dar un viraje: *the car swerved*, el coche dio un viraje. || Desviarse, apartarse: *I had to swerve to avoid him*, tuve que apartarme para evitar chocar contra él; *he never swerves from his duty*, nunca se desvía de su deber. || SP. Hacer un regate, dar un regate (a player). | Tener efecto (a ball).

swift [swift] adj. Veloz, rápido, da: *a swift horse*, un caballo veloz. || Ligero, ra; rápido, da: *swift step*, paso ligero. || Pronto, ta; rápido da: *he was very swift to act*, fue muy pronto en obrar. || Rápido, da: *a swift answer*, una respuesta rápida.

— N. Vencejo, *m.* (bird). || Lagartija, *f.* (lizard). || Carrete, *m.* (reel). || Tambor, *m.* (cylinder in a carding machine).

swifter [—ə*] n. MAR. Andarivel (*m.*) del cabrestante (of a capstan).
swift-footed [—'futid] adj. De pies ligeros.
swift-handed [—'hændid] adj. Hábil.
swiftness [—nis] n. Rapidez, *f.*, velocidad, *f.* (speed). || Prontitud, *f.* (promptness).
swig [swig] FAM. Trago, *m.*
swig [swig] v. tr. FAM. Beber a tragos.
swill [swil] n. Desperdicios, *m. pl.*, bazofia, *f.* (pig's food). || Basura, *f.* (rubbish). || FAM. Bazofia, *f.*, basura, *f.*: *I can't eat that swill*, no puedo comer esa bazofia. | Trago, *m.* (a swig). || *Give the bucket a swill*, limpia el cubo con mucha agua.
swill [swil] v. tr. Enjuagar, lavar con mucha agua: *to swill the bucket*, lavar el cubo con mucha agua. || Beber a tragos (to drink).

— V. intr. Beber a tragos (to drink). || Emborracharse (to get drunk).

swim [swim] n. Baño, *m.*: *I am going for a swim*, me voy a dar un baño. || Natación, *f.* (swimming). || Parte (*f.*) de un río en la que abundan los peces (part of river). || MED. FAM. Vértigo, *m.*, mareo, *m.* || — *In the swim*, al tanto (informed), al día (up to date). || *My head is in a swim*, la cabeza me da vueltas. || *To go for a swim*, ir a nadar, ir a bañarse, ir a darse un baño.

swim* [swim] v. tr. Cruzar *or* atravesar a nado: *to swim a river*, cruzar a nado un río. || Hacer nadar (an animal). || Nadar: *to swim the hundred metres*, nadar los cien metros; *to swim the butterfly*, nadar la braza mariposa.

— V. intr. Nadar: *he swims very well*, nada muy bien. || Flotar (to be afloat). || Dar vueltas: *my head is swimming*, la cabeza me da vueltas. || Dar vueltas, bailar: *the room is swimming before my eyes*, la habitación está bailando ante mis ojos. || Estar cubierto de, estar lleno de, estar inundado: *the floor is swimming with blood*, el suelo está cubierto de sangre; *the yard is swimming with water*, el patio está inundado de agua. || — *To go swimming*, ir a bañarse, ir a nadar. || *To swim against the tide*, nadar contra la corriente. || *To swim backstroke* o *on one's back*, nadar de espalda. || *To swim for it*, salvarse a nado. || *To swim like a brick*, nadar como un plomo. || *To swim like a fish*, nadar como un pez. || *To swim out to sea*, alejarse a nado de la playa. || *To swim under water*, bucear, nadar debajo del agua. || FIG. *To swim with the tide*, seguir la corriente.

— OBSERV. Pret. **swam;** p. p. **swum.**

swim bladder [—'blædə*] n. ZOOL. Vejiga (*f.*) natatoria.
swim fin [—fin] n. Aleta, *f.* (of swimmer).
swimmer [—ə*] n. Nadador, ra.
swimming [—iŋ] n. Natación, *f.*: *swimming is my favourite sport*, la natación es mi deporte favorito. || Mareo, *m.*, vértigo, *m.* (of the head).

— Adj. Inundado, da (eyes). || Que nada, nadador, ra. || Que da vueltas (head).

swimming bath [—iŋbɑ:θ] n. Piscina, *f.* [*Amer.*, pileta, *f.*] (swimming pool).
swimming belt [—iŋbelt] n. Flotador, *m.*
swimming cap [—iŋkæp] n. Gorro (*m.*) de baño.
swimming costume [—iŋ'kɔstju:m] n. Traje (*m.*) de baño, bañador, *m.*
swimmingly [—iŋli] adv. A las mil maravillas.
swimming pool [—iŋpu:l] n. Piscina, *f.* [*Amer.*, pileta, *f.*]: *indoor, outdoor swimming pool*, piscina cubierta, al aire libre.
swimming suit [—iŋ'sju:t] or **swimsuit** [—sju:t] n. Traje (*m.*) de baño, bañador, *m.* (bathing suit).
swindle ['swindl] n. Estafa, *f.*, timo, *m.*
swindle ['swindl] v. tr. Estafar, timar (to cheat): *to swindle s.o. out of money*, estafar dinero a alguien.

— V. intr. Estafar, timar.

swindler [—ə*] n. Estafador, ra; timador, ra.
swindling [—iŋ] n. Estafa, *f.*, timo, *m.*
swine [swain] n. Cerdo, *m.*, cochino, *m.*, puerco, *m.* [*Amer.*, chancho, *m.*]. || — *To eat like a swine*, comer como un cerdo. || FAM. *You swine!*, ¡canalla!, ¡cerdo!

— OBSERV. El plural de *swine* es *swine*.

swineherd [—hə:d] n. Porquero, *m.*, porquerizo, *m.*
swinery [—əri] n. Pocilga, *f.*
swing [swiŋ] n. Balanceo, *m.*, vaivén, *m.*, oscilación, *f.* (oscillation). || Columpio, *m.*, balancín, *m.* (plaything): *the child is sitting on the swing*, el niño está sentado en el columpio. || Oscilación, *f.* (of pendulum). || Recorrido, *m.* (distance). || Impulso, *m.*, ímpetu, *m.* (force). || Paso (*m.*) rítmico (walk). || Golpe, *m.* (blow). || FIG. Cambio (*m.*) brusco, viraje, *m.*: *there has been a swing to the left in public opinion*, ha habido un cambio brusco hacia la izquierda en la opinión pública. || COMM. Movimiento, *m.*, fluctuación, *f.* (in share prices). || MUS. Ritmo, *m.* (of music). | "Swing", *m.* (jazz style). || SP. "Swing", *m.* (in boxing, golf). || — FIG. *At full swing*, con toda rapidez, a toda velocidad. || FIG. *The party is in full swing*, la fiesta está en pleno apogeo. | *The plant is in full swing*, la fábrica está en plena actividad. | *To get into the swing of*, ponerse al corriente de, coger el truco a. || *To give a swing*, columpiar (a child), empujar (a hammock), girar (a starting handle). || FIG. *To give full swing to*, dar libre curso a. | *To go with a swing*, ir sobre ruedas.

— Adj. Giratorio, ria (bridge, etc.).

swing* [swiŋ] v. tr. Dar vueltas a, hacer girar: *to swing the cane*, dar vueltas al bastón. || Hacer oscilar, balancear (sth. suspended). || Mecer (in the arms). || Columpiar, balancear (on a swing). || Balancear, menear: *to swing one's hips*, menear las caderas; *swinging his legs*, balanceando las piernas. || Colgar (to hang up): *to swing a hammock*, colgar una hamaca. || Blandir (sword, etc.). || Hacer girar: *to swing the wheels of a car*, hacer girar las ruedas de un coche. || MUS. Tocar con ritmo. || — SP. *To swing a blow*, pegar un golpe. || *To swing a car round*, dar un viraje brusco. || *To swing a jury*, poner de su parte al jurado, ganar al jurado. || *To swing an election*, ganar una elección. || AVIAT. *To swing a propeller*, hacer girar una hélice. || FAM. *To swing it*, fingirse enfermo. | *To swing it on s.o.*, engañar a uno. || *To swing the cargo ashore*, descargar las mercancías. || *To swing the bells*, echar las campanas a vuelo. || *To swing s.o. round and round*, dar vueltas en volandas a uno. || *To swing sth. right round*, dar una vuelta completa a algo. || *To swing up a load with a crane*, levantar un peso con una grúa.

— V. intr. Oscilar: *the pendulum swung*, el péndulo

osciló. || Girar: *the door swung on its hinges*, la puerta giró sobre sus goznes. || Columpiarse, balancearse: *she was swinging in the hammock*, se estaba balanceando en la hamaca. || Colgar (to hang). || FIG. Dar un giro, volverse, virar: *public opinion swung in his favour*, la opinión pública dio un giro en su favor. || Contonearse: *she was swinging down the road*, iba contoneándose por la calle. || Bailar (to dance). || Intentar golpear, intentar dar un golpe: *he swung at me but missed*, intentó golpearme pero falló. || Montar de un salto: *to swing aboard a bus*, montar de un salto en el autobús. || — FAM. *He swung for murder*, le colgaron por homicidio. || *The troops swung in through the gates*, las tropas atravesaron la puerta a paso rápido. || *To swing clear*, dar un viraje para evitar un choque. || *To swing open*, abrirse de par en par (a door). || *To swing round*, dar media vuelta (person), girar (car). || *To swing to*, cerrarse (door). || *To swing to and fro*, balancearse; oscilar (pendulum).
— OBSERV. Pret. & p. p. ***swung***.

swing bridge [—ˈbridʒ] n. Puente (*m.*) giratorio.
swing door [—dɔ:*] n. Puerta (*f.*) de batiente.
swingeing [ˈswindʒiŋ] adj. Inmenso, sa.
swinging [ˈswiŋiŋ] adj. Oscilante. || MUS. Rítmico, ca. || FAM. De vida alegre. | Muy moderno, na. || *Swinging door*, puerta (*f.*) de batiente.
— N. Oscilación, *f.* || Balanceo, *m.* || MUS. Ritmo, *m.*
swingletree [—tri:] n. Balancín, *m.*
swing shift [ˈswiŋʃift] n. U. S. Turno (*m.*) de la tarde.
swinish [ˈswainiʃ] adj. Cochino, na. || *A swinish eater*, una persona glotona *or* tragona.
swinishness [—nis] n. Cochinada, *f.* || Glotonería, *f.*
swipe [swaip] n. Golpetazo, *m.* (blow). || Tortazo, *m.* (slap). || — Pl. Cerveza (*f. sing.*) floja.
swipe [swaip] v. tr. FAM. Afanar, limpiar, birlar (to steal). || Golpear con fuerza (to hit). || Dar un tortazo a (to slap).
swirl [swə:l] n. Remolino, *m.*, torbellino, *m.* (of water, dust, air).
swirl [swə:l] v. tr. Formar remolinos con, formar torbellinos con.
— V. intr. Arremolinarse, hacer remolinos *or* torbellinos (water). || Dar vueltas (ideas, one's head).
swirling [—iŋ] adj. Turbulento, ta; revuelto, ta.
swish [swiʃ] adj. Elegante.
— N. Crujido, *m.*, silbido, *m.* (hissing sound). || Chasquido, *m.* (of a whip). || Susurro, *m.* (of receding waves). || Frufrú, *m.*, crujido, *m.* (of silk). || Latigazo, *m.* (lash).
swish [swiʃ] v. tr. Blandir (sword). || Hacer chasquear (a cane, a whip). || Sacudir, menear: *the bull swished its tail*, el toro sacudió el rabo. || Azotar (the air, s.o.).
— V. intr. Susurrar (water). || Dar un chasquido (a whip). || Hender el aire (a sword). || Crujir (silk).
Swiss [swis] adj./n. Suizo, za. || — *The Swiss*, los suizos. || *The Swiss Guard*, la Guardia Suiza.
switch [switʃ] n. ELECTR. Interruptor, *m.*, conmutador, *m.* || Agujas, *f. pl.* (railway points). || Desviación, *f.* (change of line). || Cambio, *m.*, paso, *m.*: *the switch from steam trains to electric trains*, el paso de los trenes de vapor a los trenes eléctricos. || Cambio, *m.*: *a switch in public opinion*, un cambio de la opinión pública. || Látigo, *m.* (whip). || Fusta, *f.* (riding whip). || Palmeta, *f.* (carpet beater). || Varilla, *f.* (for punishing). || Golpe (*m.*) de fusta *or* de palmeta *or* de varilla (blow). || Trenza (*f.*) postiza (tress of hair). || Mechón, *m.*, punta (*f.*) de la cola (end of animal's tail).
switch [switʃ] v. tr. Desviar, cambiar de vía (a train). || Cambiar (places). || Cambiar de (policy). || Menear, agitar, sacudir: *the horse switched its tail*, el caballo meneó el rabo. || Blandir (the whip). || Azotar, golpear, dar golpes (to beat). || FIG. Encaminar, orientar, encauzar (to guide).
— V. intr. Cambiar, pasar: *to switch from one to the other*, pasar de uno a otro. || Desviarse.
— ***To switch off***, desconectar. | Apagar (a light, radio, TV). | Cortar (the current). | Parar (car, engine). || ***To switch on***, encender (light). | Encender, poner (radio, TV). | Poner en marcha, arrancar (car, engine). || ***To switch round***, cambiar de sitio *or* de idea.
switchback [—bæk] Carretera (*f.*) en zigzag (road). || Vía (*f.*) de tren en zigzag (railway). || Montaña (*f.*) rusa (scenic railway).
switchblade knife [—ˌbleidnaif] n. U. S. Navaja (*f.*) de muelle.
switchboard [—bɔ:d] n. ELECTR. Cuadro (*m.*) *or* tablero (*m.*) de distribución. || Centralita (*f.*) de teléfonos (of phone). || *Switchboard operator*, telefonista, *m.* & *f.*
switchgear [—giə*] n. Dispositivos (*m. pl.*) de distribución.
switch knife [—naif] n. Navaja (*f.*) de muelle.
switchman [—mən] n. Guardagujas, *m. inv.*
— OBSERV. El plural de *switchman* es *switchmen*.

switchyard [ˈswitʃjɑ:d] n. Patio (*m.*) de maniobras.
Switzerland [ˈswitsələnd] pr. n. GEOGR. Suiza, *f.*
swivel [ˈswivl] n. TECH. Eslabón (*m.*) giratorio, pivote, *m.* || Cabeza (*f.*) de inyección de lodo (in oil wells).
swivel [ˈswivl] v. intr. Girar.
— V. tr. Hacer girar.
swivel chair [—tʃɛə*] n. Silla (*f.*) giratoria.
swivel seat [—si:t] n. Asiento (*m.*) giratorio.
swizzle [ˈswizl] n. Cóctel, *m.* (drink). || FAM. See SWINDLE. || *Swizzle stick*, varilla (*f.*) de cóctel.
swollen [ˈswəulən] p. p. See SWELL.
swoon [swu:n] n. Desmayo, *m.*, desvanecimiento, *m.*
swoon [swu:n] v. intr. Desmayarse, desvanecerse.
swoop [swu:p] n. Descenso (*m.*) en picado (of an aeroplane). || Calada, *f.* (of a bird). || Visita (*f.*) de inspección sin previo aviso. || Redada, *f.* (by police). || FIG. Arremetida, *f.* (attack). || — *In* o *at one fell swoop*, de un golpe. || *To make a swoop on*, abalanzarse sobre, precipitarse sobre.
swoop [swu:p] v. intr. Abatirse, abalanzarse, calarse (bird). || Bajar en picado (aeroplane). || Irrumpir: *the police swooped on the club*, la policía irrumpió en el club. || Hacer una redada (to raid). || Abalanzarse, precipitarse: *the children swooped on the cake*, los niños se precipitaron sobre el pastel.
swoosh [swuʃ] n./v. tr./intr. See SWISH.
swop [swɔp] n./v. tr./intr. See SWAP.
sword [sɔ:d] n. Espada, *f.*: *to sheathe one's sword*, envainar la espada; *to plunge one's sword in up to the hilt*, meter la espada hasta la guarnición. || Estoque, *m.* (in bullfighting). || — FIG. *By fire and sword*, a sangre y fuego. | *He who lives by the sword will die by the sword*, quienes matan con la espada por la espada morirán, quien a hierro mata a hierro muere. | *To be at swords' point*, estar a matar. || *To cross swords with*, cruzar la espada con (to fight), medir las armas con, habérselas con (to argue). || *To measure swords with s.o.*, cruzar la espada con uno. || *To put a country to fire and sword*, entrar a sangre y fuego en un país. || *To put to the sword*, pasar a cuchillo. || *To unsheathe* o *to draw one's sword*, desenvainar la espada. || *Two-edged sword*, espada de dos filos. || FIG. *With a sword at one's throat*, con un puñal en el pecho.
sword belt [—belt] n. Talabarte, *m.*
sword dance [—dɑ:ns] n. Danza (*f.*) de las espadas.
swordfish [—fiʃ] n. Pez (*m.*) espada (fish).
swordplay [—plei] n. Esgrima, *f.*
swordsman [—zmən] n. Espadachín, *m.*, espada, *f.*: *to be a good swordsman*, ser buena espada. || Esgrimidor, *m.* (fencer).
— OBSERV. El plural de *swordsman* es *swordsmen*.

swordsmanship [—zmənʃip] n. Esgrima, *f.*, habilidad (*f.*) con la espada.
sword stick [—stik] n. Bastón (*m.*) de estoque.
sword-swallower [—ˌswɔləuə*] n. Tragasables, *m.*
sword thrust [—θrʌst] n. Estocada, *f.*
swore [swɔ:*] pret. See SWEAR.
sworn [swɔ:n] p. p. See SWEAR.
— Adj. Jurado, da; declarado, da: *sworn enemies*, enemigos jurados. || JUR. Bajo juramento (statement). | Que ha jurado (witness). | Juramentado, da (translator, etc.).
swot [swɔt] n. FAM. Empollón, ona (person who studies excessively). | Estudio, *m.* (study).
swot [swɔt] v. tr./intr. Empollar (to study).
swum [swʌm] p. p. See SWIM.
swung [swʌŋ] pret. & p. p. See SWING.
sybarite [ˈsibərait] n. Sibarita, *m.* & *f.*
sybaritic [ˌsibəˈritik] or **sybaritical** [—əl] adj. Sibarita, sibarítico, ca.
sybaritism [ˈsibəritizəm] n. Sibaritismo, *m.*
sycamore [ˈsikəmɔ:*] n. Sicómoro, *m.*, sicomoro, *m.* (tree, wood).
sycophancy [ˈsikəfənsi] n. Adulación, *f.*, servilismo, *m.*
sycophant [ˈsikəfənt] n. Sicofante, *m.*, sicofanta, *m.* (defamer). || Adulador, ra (flatterer).
sycophantic [ˌsikəˈfæntik] adj. Adulatorio, ria; servil.
sycosis [saiˈkəusis] n. MED. Sicosis, *f. inv.*
syllabary [ˈsiləbəri] n. Cartilla, *f.*, silabario, *m.*
syllabic [siˈlæbik] adj. Silábico, ca.
syllabicate [siˈlæbikeit] v. tr. Silabear, dividir en sílabas.
syllabication [siˌlæbiˈkeiʃən] or **syllabification** [siˌlæbifiˈkeiʃən] n. Silabeo, *m.*, división (*f.*) en sílabas.
syllabify [siˈlæbifai] or **syllabize** [ˈsiləbaiz] v. tr. Silabear.
syllable [ˈsiləbl] n. Sílaba, *f.*: *open, accentuated, closed syllable*, sílaba abierta, aguda, cerrada. || FIG. Palabra, *f.*: *there is not a syllable of truth in it*, no hay una palabra de verdad en ello.
syllable [ˈsiləbl] v. tr./intr. Silabear.
syllabub [ˈsiləbʌb] n. Batido (*m.*) de leche, azúcar y licores.
syllabus [ˈsiləbəs] n. Programa (*m.*) de estudios. || Extracto, *m.*, resumen, *m.* (summary).
— OBSERV. El plural de *syllabus* es *syllabuses* o *syllabi*.

syllepsis [siˈlepsis] n. GRAMM. Silepsis, *f. inv.*
— OBSERV. El plural de la palabra inglesa es *syllepses*.

syllogism [ˈsilədʒizəm] n. Silogismo, *m.*
syllogistic [ˌsiləˈdʒistik] or **syllogistical** [—əl] adj. Silogístico, ca.
syllogize [ˈsilədʒaiz] v. intr. Hacer silogismos, silogizar.
— V. tr. Deducir por silogismos.
sylph [silf] n. MYTH. Sílfide, *f.* (female spirit). | Silfo, *m.* (male spirit). || FIG. Sílfide, *f.* (young woman).

sylphid [—id] n. MYTH. Joven sílfide, *f.* (female spirit). | Joven silfo, *m.* (male spirit).
sylphlike [—laik] adj. De sílfide.
sylvan [ˈsilvən] adj. Selvático, ca; silvestre.
— N. MYTH. Silvano, *m.*
sylvanite [ˈsilvənait] n. MIN. Silvanita, *f.*
sylviculture [ˈsilvikʌltjə*] n. AGR. Silvicultura, *f.*
symbiosis [ˌsimbiˈəusis] n. Simbiosis, *f. inv.*
symbiotic [ˌsimbiˈɔtik] adj. Simbiótico, ca.
symbol [ˈsimbəl] n. Símbolo, *m.*
symbolic [simˈbɔlik] or **symbolical** [—əl] adj. Simbólico, ca.
symbolism [ˈsimbəlizəm] n. Simbolismo, *m.*
symbolist [ˈsimbəlist] n. Simbolista, *m.* & *f.*
symbolistic [simbəˈlistik] adj. Simbolista. || Simbólico, ca.
symbolization [ˌsimbəlaiˈzeiʃən] n. Simbolización, *f.*
symbolize [ˈsimbəlaiz] v. tr. Simbolizar.
symmetric [siˈmetrik] or **symmetrical** [—əl] adj. Simétrico, ca.
symmetrize [ˈsimitraiz] v. tr. Hacer simétrico.
symmetry [ˈsimitri] n. Simetría, *f.*
sympathetic [ˌsimpəˈθetik] adj. Compasivo, va [*to, con*] (compassionate): *a sympathetic person*, una persona compasiva. || Comprensivo, va (understanding). || Amable (kind). || Que simpatiza (having an affinity of feeling). || Favorable, en favor de (favourably disposed): *to be sympathetic to a plan*, mostrarse favorable a un proyecto. || ANAT. Simpático. || PHYS. Simpático, ca. || — *Sympathetic ink*, tinta simpática. || ANAT. *Sympathetic nervous system*, gran simpático, *m.* || *Sympathetic strike*, huelga (*f.*) por solidaridad.
sympathetically [—əli] adv. Comprensivamente. || Con compasión.
sympathize [ˈsimpəθaiz] v. intr. Entender, comprender, compartir: *I sympathize with his point of view*, entiendo su punto de vista. || Compadecerse, compadecer: *I sympathize with the poor*, me compadezco de los pobres, compadezco a los pobres. || Dar el pésame (to express one's condolences). || *I sympathize with you*, le acompaño en el sentimiento.
sympathizer [—ə*] n. Simpatizante, *m.* & *f.*
sympathizing [—iŋ] adj. Simpatizante.
sympathy [ˈsimpəθi] n. Pésame, *m.*, condolencia, *f.*: *to send one's sympathy*, dar el pésame. || Comprensión, *f.*: *sympathy for s.o.'s problems*, comprensión de los problemas de alguien; *sympathy between two people*, comprensión entre dos personas. || Compasión, *f.*, lástima, *f.*: *I have no sympathy for drunks*, no tengo compasión por los borrachos. || PHYS. Resonancia, *f.*: *a string which vibrates in sympathy*, una cuerda que vibra por resonancia. || MED. Simpatía, *f.*: *sympathy pains*, dolores de simpatía. || — *His sympathies lie with the anarchists*, simpatiza con los anarquistas. || *Message of sympathy*, pésame. || *My deepest sympathy*, le acompaño en el sentimiento, mi más sentido pésame. || *Prices rose in sympathy*, subieron los precios a la par. || *Sympathy strike*, huelga (*f.*) por solidaridad. || *To be in sympathy with*, estar en favor de (to favour), estar de acuerdo con (to identify o.s. with). || *To strike in sympathy*, declararse en huelga por solidaridad.
symphonic [simˈfɔnik] adj. Sinfónico, ca.
symphonist [ˈsimfənist] n. Sinfonista, *m.*
symphony [ˈsimfəni] n. Sinfonía, *f.* || — *Symphony concert*, concierto sinfónico. || *Symphony orchestra*, orquesta sinfónica.
symphysis [ˈsimfisis] n. Sínfisis, *f. inv.*

— OBSERV. El plural de *symphysis* es *symphyses*.

symposium [simˈpəuzjəm] n. Simposio, *m.*

— OBSERV. El plural de la palabra inglesa es *symposia* o *symposiums*.

symptom [ˈsimptəm] n. Síntoma, *m.* || FIG. Señal, *f.*, síntoma, *m.*, indicio, *m.*
symptomatic [ˌsimptəˈmætik] adj. Sintomático, ca.
symptomatology [ˌsimptəməˈtɔlədʒi] n. Sintomatología, *f.*
synaeresis [ˌsiˈniərəsis] n. GRAMM. Sinéresis, *f. inv.*
synaestesia [ˌsinəsˈθi:zjə] n. MED. Sinestesia, *f.*
synagogal [ˌsinəˈgɔgəl] adj. De sinagoga.
synagogue or **synagog** [ˈsinəgɔg] n. Sinagoga, *f.*
sinalepha [ˌsinəˈli:fə] n. U. S. GRAMM. Sinalefa, *f.*
synallagmatic [ˌsinəlægˈmætik] adj. JUR. Sinalagmático, ca.
sinaloepha [ˌsinəˈli:fə] n. GRAMM. Sinalefa, *f.*
synarthrosis [ˌsinɑ:ˈθrəusis] n. Sinartrosis, *f. inv.*
synchrocyclotron [ˈsiŋkrəuˈsaiklətrɔn] n. PHYS. Sincrociclotrón, *m.*
synchromesh [siŋkrəuˈmeʃ] n. AUT. Sincronizador, *m.*, cambio (*m.*) sincronizado de velocidades.
— Adj. AUT. Sincronizado, da.
synchronic [siŋˈkrɔnik] adj. Sincrónico, ca; síncrono, na.
synchronism [ˈsiŋkrənizəm] n. Sincronismo, *m.*
synchronistic [ˌsiŋkrəˈnistik] adj. Sincrónico, ca; síncrono, na.
synchronization [ˌsiŋkrənaiˈzeiʃən] n. Sincronización, *f.*
synchronize [ˈsiŋkrənaiz] v. tr. Sincronizar.
— V. intr. Ocurrir simultáneamente, coincidir (to occur simultaneously). || Funcionar sincrónicamente, ser sincrónico (to work in unison).
synchronizer [—ə*] n. Sincronizador, *m.*
synchronous [ˈsiŋkrənəs] adj. Sincrónico, ca; síncrono, na.
synchronousness [—nis] n. Sincronismo, *m.*
synchrotron [ˈsiŋkrəutrɔn] n. PHYS. Sincrotrón, *m.*
synclinal [sinˈklainəl] adj. Sinclinal.
syncline [ˈsiŋklain] n. Sinclinal, *m.*
syncopate [ˈsiŋkəpeit] v. tr. GRAMM. MUS. Sincopar.
syncopation [ˌsiŋkəˈpeiʃən] n. GRAMM. MUS. Síncopa, *f.*
syncope [ˈsiŋkəpi] n. MED. Síncope, *m.* || MUS. GRAMM. Síncopa, *f.*
syncretic [siŋˈkritik] adj. Sincrético, ca.
syncretism [ˈsiŋkritizəm] n. Sincretismo, *m.*
syncretist [ˈsiŋkritist] n. Sincretista, *m.* & *f.*
syncretistic [ˌsiŋkriˈtistik] adj. Sincretista.
syndactyl or **syndactyle** [sinˈdæktil] adj. ZOOL. Sindáctilo, la.
— N. ZOOL. Sindáctilo, *m.*
syndic [ˈsindik] n. Síndico, *m.*
syndical [—əl] adj. Sindical.
syndicalism [—əlizəm] n. Sindicalismo, *m.*
syndicalist [—əlist] adj./n. Sindicalista.
syndicalistic [ˌsindikəˈlistik] adj. Sindicalista.
syndicate [ˈsindikit] n. Sindicado, *m.* (of syndics). || Sindicato, *m.* (group of persons or firms). || Cadena (*f.*) de periódicos (chain of newspapers). || Agencia (*f.*) de prensa (news agency).
syndicate [ˈsindikeit] v. tr. Sindicar.
— V. intr. Sindicarse.
syndrome [ˈsindrəum] n. MED. Síndrome, *m.* (group of disease symptoms).
synecdoche [siˈnekdəki] n. Sinécdoque, *f.*
syneresis [siˈniərəsis] n. U. S. Sinéresis, *f. inv.*
synergetic [ˌsinə:ˈdʒetik] adj. Sinérgico, ca.
synergic [siˈnə:dʒik] adj. Sinérgico, ca.
synergy [ˌsinə:dʒi] n. Sinergia, *f.*
synesthesia [ˌsinəsˈθiziə] n. U. S. Sinestesia, *f.*
synod [ˈsinəd] n. REL. Sínodo, *m.*: *The Holy Synod*, el Santo Sínodo.
synodal [—əl] adj. Sinodal.
synodic or **synodical** [siˈnɔdik] adj. REL. Sinódico, ca.
synonym [ˈsinənim] n. Sinónimo, *m.*
synonymic [ˌsinəˈnimik] or **synonymical** [—əl] adj. Sinonímico, ca.
synonymity [ˌsinəˈnimiti] n. Sinonimia, *f.*
synonymous [siˈnɔniməs] adj. Sinónimo, ma [*with*, de].
synonymy [siˈnɔnimi] n. Sinonimia, *f.*
synopsis [siˈnɔpsis] n. Sinopsis, *f. inv.* || Cuadro (*m.*) sinóptico (diagram).

— OBSERV. El plural de *synopsis* es *synopses*.

synoptic [siˈnɔptik] or **synoptical** [—əl] adj. Sinóptico, ca.
synovia [siˈnəuviə] n. ANAT. Sinovia, *f.*
synovial [—l] adj. ANAT. Sinovial. || *Synovial capsule*, cápsula (*f.*) sinovial.
synovitis [ˌsinəˈvaitis] n. MED. Sinovitis, *f. inv.*
syntactic [sinˈtæktik] or **syntactical** [—əl] adj. GRAMM. Sintáctico, ca.
syntax [ˈsintæks] n. GRAMM. Sintaxis, *f. inv.*
synthesis [ˈsinθisis] n. Síntesis, *f. inv.*

— OBSERV. El plural de *synthesis* es *syntheses*.

synthesize [ˈsinθisaiz] v. tr. Sintetizar.
synthetic [sinˈθetik] or **synthetical** [—əl] adj. Sintético, ca: *synthetic rubber*, caucho sintético.
synthetize [ˈsinθitaiz] v. tr. Sintetizar.
syntonic [sinˈtɔnik] adj. Sintónico, ca.
syntonization [ˌsintənaiˈzeiʃən] n. Sintonización, *f.*, sintonía, *f.*
syntonize [ˈsintənaiz] v. tr. Sintonizar.
syntony [ˈsintəni] n. Sintonía, *f.*
syphilis [ˈsifilis] n. MED. Sífilis, *f. inv.*
syphilitic [ˌsifiˈlitik] adj./n. MED. Sifilítico, ca.
syphon [ˈsaifən] n. See SIPHON.
syracusan [ˌsaiərəˈkju:zən] adj./n. Siracusano, na.
Syracuse [ˈsaiərəkju:z] pr. n. GEOGR. Siracusa.
Syria [ˈsiriə] pr. GEOGR. Siria, *f.*
Syriac [ˈsiriæk] adj./n. Siriaco, ca.
Syrian [ˈsiriən] adj./n. Sirio, ria; siriaco, ca.
syringa [siˈriŋgə] n. BOT. Jeringuilla, *f.*
syringe [ˈsirindʒ] n. Jeringuilla, *f.*, jeringa, *f.* (for injections). || Jeringa, *f.* (for cleansing).
syringe [ˈsirindʒ] v. tr. Jeringar (to clean). || Inyectar con jeringuilla (to inject).
syrinx [ˈsiriŋks] n. Siringe, *m.* (of birds). || Siringa, *f.*, flauta (*f.*) de pan (panpipe). || MED. Trompa (*f.*) de Eustaquio.

— OBSERV. El plural de *syrinx* es *syrinxes* o *syringes*.

syrup [ˈsirəp] n. Jarabe, *m.* (drink). || MED. Jarabe, *m.*: *cough syrup*, jarabe para la tos. || Almíbar, *m.*: *peaches in syrup*, melocotones en almíbar.
syrupy [—i] adj. Almibarado, da.
system [ˈsistim] n. Sistema, *m.*: *administrative system*, sistema administrativo; *public-address system*, sistema de altavoces. || PHIL. ASTR. GEOL. BIOL. Sistema, *m.* || Régimen, *m.*: *feudal system*, régimen feudal. || || Red, *f.*: *railway system*, red de ferrocarriles. || Método, *m.*: *to work with system*, trabajar con método. || MED. Sistema, *m.*: *nervous system*, sistema

nervioso. | Constitución, *f.*, organismo, *m.* (constitution). || — *Centimetre-gram-second system*, sistema cegesimal. || *Decimal system*, sistema decimal. || *It's bad for your system*, es malo para el organismo. || *Metric system*, sistema métrico. || *Number system*, sistema de numeración. || *Planetary system*, sistema planetario. || *Solar system*, sistema solar.
systematic [ˌsistiˈmætik] or **systematical** [—əl] adj. Sistemático, ca.
systematically [—əli] adv. Sistemáticamente.
systematics [—s] n. Sistemática, *f.*
systematization [ˈsistimətaiˈzeiʃən] n. Sistematización, *f.*
systematize [ˈsistimətaiz] v. tr. Sistematizar.
systemization [ˌsistimaiˈzeiʃən] n. Sistematización, *f.*
systemize [ˈsistimaiz] v. tr. Sistematizar.
systole [ˈsistəli] n. ANAT. Sístole, *f.*
syzygy [ˈsizidʒi] n. ASTR. Sicigia, *f.*

T

t [ti:] n. T, *f* (letter). || — FAM. *To a T*, como anillo al dedo: *this dress suits you to a T*, este traje le sienta como anillo al dedo; de maravilla, de perlas: *this job suits me to a T*, este trabajo me viene de perlas. || FIG. *To cross one's t's*, poner los puntos sobre las íes.
ta [tɑ:] interj. FAM. ¡Gracias!
tab [tæb] n. Etiqueta, *f.* (label). || MIL. Charretera, *f.*, hombrera, *f.* || Herrete, *m.* (of shoelace). || Oreja, *f.*, lengüeta, *f.* (of shoe). || Orejera, *f.* (of cap). || Presilla, *f.* (for hanging up coat). || Uñero, *m.* (of book). || Pestaña, *f.* (of a can). || AVIAT. Aleta (*f.*) compensadora. || U. S. FAM. Cuenta, *f.* (bill). || FAM. *To keep tabs on*, no perder de vista.
tabard [ˈtæbəd] n. Tabardo, *m.*
tabasco [təˈbæskəu] n. CULIN. Tabasco, *m.*
tabby [ˈtæbi] n. Gato (*m.*) atigrado (cat with striped markings). || Gata, *f.* (female cat). || Falena, *f.* (butterfly). || Muaré, *m.*, moaré, *m.* (fabric). || FAM. Chismosa, *f.* (old gossip).
— Adj. Atigrado, da.
tabby [ˈtæbi] v. tr. Tornasolar, dar [a una tela] reflejos *or* visos.
tabernacle [ˈtæbənækl] n. REL. Sagrario, *m.*, tabernáculo, *m.* || ARCH. Templete, *m.* (niche with a canopy). | Templo, *m.*, santuario, *m.* (place of worship).
tabes [ˈteibi:z] n. MED. Tabes, *f.* || MED. *Tabes dorsalis*, ataxia locomotora.
tablature [ˈtæblətʃə*] n. MUS. Tabladura, *f.*
table [ˈteibl] n. Mesa, *f.*: *to lay* o *to set the table*, poner la mesa; *to rise from table*, levantarse de la mesa; *to sit down at the table*, sentarse a la mesa; *to wait* o *to help at table*, servir la mesa; *the table consisted of many outstanding personalities*, la mesa se componía de muchas personalidades eminentes; *draw* o *extension table*, mesa con largueros; *table with flaps*, mesa de alas; *gambling* o *gaming table*, mesa de juego; *folding table*, mesa de tijera *or* plegable; *operating table*, mesa de operaciones. || Mesilla, *f.*, mesa, *f.*: *bedside table*, mesilla de noche. || Bancada, *f.* (of machine tool). || Mesa, *f.* (facet of a jewel). || GEOGR. Meseta, *f.* [*Amer.*, altiplano, *m.*] (tableland). || ARCH. Faja, *f.*, moldura, *f.* (stringcourse). | Tablero, *m.* (panel). || ANAT. Tabla, *f.* (skull tissue). || Lista, *f.*, tabla, *f.* (list). || Lista, *f.* (of prices). || Grúa, *f.* (railway). || Cuadro, *m.* (for figures, values, etc.). || MATH. Tabla, *f.*: *multiplication table*, tabla de multiplicar; *logarithm table*, tabla de logaritmos. || ANAT. Palma, *f.* (of the hand). || — *At table*, en la mesa. || HIST. *Knights of the Round Table*, caballeros de la Tabla Redonda. || *Nest of tables*, mesas de nido. || FIG. *Round table*, mesa redonda. || *Sorting table*, mesa de batalla (post office). || *Table of contents*, índice, *m.* || *Table wine*, vino (*m.*) de mesa. || FIG. *The tables are turned*, se volvieron las tornas. || REL. *The Tables of the Law*, las tablas de la Ley. || *To clear the table*, quitar la mesa. || *To keep a good table*, tener buena mesa, dar bien de comer. || *To leave the table*, levantarse de la mesa. || FIG. *To turn the tables on s.o.*, volverle a uno las tornas. || FAM. *Under the table*, por el suelo (drunk). || GEOL. *Water table*, capa freática.
table [ˈteibl] v. tr. Presentar: *to table a motion*, presentar una moción; *to table a motion of confidence*, presentar la cuestión de confianza. || MAR. Reforzar (the edge of a sail). || Poner en un cuadro (to tabulate). || TECH. Encajar. || U. S. Dar carpetazo a (to postpone indefinitely).
tableau [ˈtæbləu] n. Cuadro, *m.* || *Tableau vivant*, cuadro vivo.
— OBSERV. El plural de *tableau* es *tableaux* o *tableaus*.
table centre [ˈteiblˈsentə*] n. Centro (*m.*) de mesa.
tablecloth [ˈteiblklɔθ] n. Mantel, *m.* (for meals). || Tapete, *m.* (table cover).
table companion [ˈteiblkəmˈpænjən] n. Convidado, da; comensal, *m.* & *f.*
table cover [ˈteiblˌkʌvə*] n. Tapete, *m.*
table d'hôte [ˈtɑ:blˈdəut] n. Menú, *m.*
— OBSERV. El plural es *tables d'hôte*.
tableland [ˈteibllænd] n. GEOGR. Meseta, *f.* [*Amer.*, altiplano, *m.*].
table leaf [ˈteiblli:f] n. Larguero, *m.*
table linen [ˈteiblˌlinin] n. Mantelería, *f.*
tablemat [ˈteiblmæt] n. Salvamanteles, *m. inv.*
table napkin [ˈteiblˈnæpkin] n. Servilleta, *f.*
table service [ˈteiblˌsə:vis] n. Servicio (*m.*) de mesa, vajilla, *f.*
tablespoon [ˈteiblspu:n] n. Cucharón, *m.*
tablespoonful [—ful] n. Cucharada, *f.*
tablet [ˈtæblit] n. Lápida, *f.* (memorial or commemorative stone). || Tableta, *f.*, pastilla, *f.* (pastille, pill). || Bloc, *m.*, taco, *m.* (of writing paper). || Pastilla, *f.* (of soap). || Tableta, *f.* (of chocolate). || HIST. Tablilla, *f.* (for writing on).
table talk [ˈteiblˌtɔ:k] n. Conversación (*f.*) de sobremesa.
table tennis [ˈteiblˌtenis] n. Tenis (*m.*) de mesa, ping-pong, *m.*
tableware [ˈteiblwɛə*] n. Vajilla, *f.*, servicio (*m.*) de mesa.
table water [ˈteiblˌwɔ:tə*] n. Agua (*f.*) mineral.
tabloid [ˈtæblɔid] n. Periódico (*m.*) de pequeño formato. || Periódico (*m.*) sensacionalista. || MED. Tableta, *f.*
taboo [təˈbu:] adj. Tabú.
— N. Tabú, *m.*
taboo [təˈbu:] v. tr. Declarar tabú, prohibir.
tabor [ˈteibɔ:*] n. MUS. Tamboril, *m.*
taboret or **tabouret** [ˈtæbərit] n. Taburete, *m.* (stool). || Bastidor, *m.*, tambor, *m.* (for embroidery).
tabu [təˈbu:] adj./n./v. tr. See TABOO.
tabular [ˈtæbjulə*] adj. Tabular.
tabula rasa [ˈtæbjuləˈrɑ:zə] n. PHIL. Tábula (*f.*) rasa, tabla (*f.*) rasa.
tabulate [ˈtæbjuleit] v. tr. Disponer en tablas (to put in tables). || Clasificar (to arrange systematically).
tabulation [ˌtæbjuˈleiʃən] n. Disposición (*f.*) en tablas.
tabulator [ˈtæbjuleitə*] n. Tabulador, *m.* (of a typewriter). || Tabuladora, *f.* (machine).
tachometer [tæˈkɔmitə*] n. Tacómetro, *m.*
tachycardia [ˌtækiˈkɑ:djə] n. MED. Taquicardia, *f.*
tachymeter [tæˈkimitə*] n. Taquímetro, *m.*
tachymetry [tæˈkimitri] n. Taquimetría, *f.*
tacit [ˈtæsit] adj. Tácito, ta: *tacit understanding*, acuerdo tácito.
taciturn [ˈtæsitə:n] adj. Taciturno, na.
taciturnity [ˌtæsiˈtə:niti] n. Taciturnidad, *f.*
Tacitus [ˈtæsitəs] pr. n. HIST. Tácito, *m.*
tack [tæk] n. Tachuela, *f.* (nail): *I need four tacks to fasten this photograph*, me hacen falta cuatro tachuelas para fijar esta fotografía. || Hilván, *m.* (stitch). || MAR. Amura, *f.* (rope). | Puño (*m.*) de la amura (corner of a sail). | Bordada, *f.* (distance sailed without changing direction). | Virada, *f.* (act of changing direction). || FIG. Dirección, *f.*, línea (*f.*) de conducta (course of action). | Táctica, *f.* || — FIG. *To be on the right tack*, ir por buen camino. | *To be on the wrong tack*, estar equivocado. | *To get down to brass tacks*, ir al grano.
tack [tæk] v. tr. Fijar con tachuelas (to nail). || Hilvanar (to stitch). || Añadir (to append).
— V. intr. MAR. Virar de bordo. || Cambiar de táctica *or* de dirección *or* de rumbo. || FIG. *To tack on to s.o.*, juntarse con uno.
tack board [—bɔ:d] n. Tablón (*m.*) de anuncios.

tackle [ˈtækl] n. MAR. Aparejo, *m.* (rigging). | Jarcias, *f. pl.* (ropes). || Aparejo, *m.*: *fishing tackle*, aparejo de pescar. || Aparejo, *m.*, polipasto, *m.* (system of ropes and pulleys). || Arreos, *m. pl.* (a horse's harness). || Trastos, *m. pl.*, avíos, *m. pl.* (equipment). || FIG. Cosas, *f. pl.*, trastos, *m. pl.* (belongings). || SP. Placaje, *m.* (in rugby and American football).
tackle [ˈtækl] v. tr. Agarrar (to seize): *the policeman tackled the thief*, el policía agarró al ladrón. || Hacer un placaje a (in rugby). || Atajar (in American football). || FIG. Abordar: *to tackle a problem*, abordar un problema. | Emprender (task). || *To tackle up*, poner arreos a (a horse).
— V. intr. SP. Placar (rugby). | Atajar (American football).
tackling [—iŋ] n. See TACKLE.
tacky [ˈtæki] adj. Pegajoso, sa (sticky). || U. S. FAM. Desastrado, da (shabby). | Vulgar, común (vulgar).
tact [tækt] n. Tacto, *m.*, discreción, *f.*
tactful [—ful] adj. Discreto, ta; lleno de tacto (showing tact). || Discreto, ta; que tiene tacto (possessing tact).
tactic [ˈtæktik] adj. Táctico, ca.
tactical [—əl] adj. Táctico, ca. || Estratégico, ca: *tactical importance*, importancia estratégica. || FIG. Hábil.
tactician [tækˈtiʃən] n. MIL. Táctico, *m.* || FIG. Persona (*f.*) hábil (who acts cleverly).
tactics [ˈtæktiks] n. MIL. Táctica, *f.* || FIG. Táctica, *f.*
tactile [ˈtæktail] adj. Táctil. || FIG. Tangible.
tactless [ˈtæktlis] adj. Falto de tacto, que carece de tacto.
tactlessness [—nis] n. Falta (*f.*) de tacto.
tactual [ˈtæktjuəl] adj. Táctil, del tacto.
tactually [—i] adv. Por medio del tacto.
tadpole [ˈtædpəul] n. ZOOL. Renacuajo, *m.*
taenia [ˈti:niə] n. Tenia, *f.*, solitaria, *f.* (tapeworm). || ARCH. Tenia, *f.*
— OBSERV. El plural de esta palabra es *taeniae* o *taenias*.
taeniafuge [ˈti:nifju:dʒ] adj. Tenífugo, ga.
— N. Tenífugo, *m.*
taffeta [ˈtæfitə] n. Tafetán, *m.* (cloth).
taffrail [ˈtæfreil] n. MAR. Coronamiento, *m.*
taffy [ˈtæfi] n. U. S. Melcocha, *f.*, arropía, *f.* || U. S. FAM. Coba, *f.*, adulación, *f.* (flattery).
tafia [ˈtæfiə] n. Tafia, *f.*
tag [tæg] n. Etiqueta, *f.* (label for identification, classification, indicating price, etc.). || Tirador, *m.* [de bota] (for pulling boots up). || Herrete, *m.* (of shoelace). || Cabo, *m.* (end). || Tópico, *m.* (cliché). || Cita, *f.* (quotation). || Estribillo, *m.* (of a song). || Pingajo, *m.* (hanging bit of cloth). || Pillapilla, *m.* (children's game). || FIG. Etiqueta, *f.*: *to give s.o. the tag of a coward*, colgarle a uno la etiqueta de cobarde. | Apodo, *m.* (nickname). || — U. S. *Tag day*, día (*m.*) de la banderita. | *Tag end*, final, *m.*
tag [tæg] v. tr. Poner una etiqueta a (to provide with a label). || Denominar (to name). || Seguir de cerca (to follow). || Pillar (in the game of tag). || FIG. Salpicar: *to tag a speech with quotations*, salpicar de citas un discurso. || Marcar (molecule). || *To tag on*, añadir, agregar.
— V. intr. *To tag along*, seguir, venir detrás: *he tagged along with us*, vino detrás de nosotros. || *To tag along behind*, seguir a distancia. || *To tag on to s.o.*, pegarse a uno.
Tagalog [təˈgɑ:ləg] adj./n. Tagalo, la. || — N. Tagalo, *m.* (language).
— OBSERV. El plural es *Tagalog* o *Tagalogs*.
Tagus [ˈteigəs] pr. n. GEOGR. Tajo, *m.* (river).
Tahiti [tɑ:ˈhi:ti] pr. n. GEOGR. Tahití.
Tahitian [tɑ:ˈhi:ʃən] adj./n. Tahitiano, na.
Tai [tai] adj./n. Tailandés, esa.
taiga [ˈtaigə] n. Taiga, *f.* (coniferous forests).
tail [teil] n. Cola, *f.* (when part of the body, i.e. in birds, fishes, snakes). || Rabo, *m.*, cola, *f.* (as an appendage, i.e. in bulls, monkeys, horses, dogs, cats). || Cola, *f.* (of procession, aircraft, dress, kite, vehicle). || Cola, *f.* (of people). || Comitiva, *f.*, séquito, *m.* (retinue). || Faldón, *m.* (of a shirt, jacket). || PRINT. Pie, *m.* (of a page). || Cola, *f.* (of hair). || FIG. Final, *m.*: *the tail of a storm*, el final de una tormenta. || JUR. Vínculo, *m.*, vinculación, *f.* || ASTR. Cabellera, *f.*, cola, *f.* (of a comet). || Rabillo, *m.*, ángulo, *m.* (of eyes). || — Pl. Cruz, *f. sing.* (of a coin): *heads or tails?*, ¿cara o cruz? || Frac, *m. sing.* (tailcoat). || — FIG. *From head to tail*, de pies a cabeza. | *I can't make head or tail of this*, esto no tiene ni pies ni cabeza. | *To turn tail*, poner pies en polvorosa. | *With one's tail between one's legs*, con el rabo entre las piernas.
— Adj. Final, último, ma. || JUR. Vinculado, da.
tail [teil] v. tr. Quitar el rabo a (to remove the stalks from). || Poner cola a (to provide with a tail). || Cerrar: *to tail a procession*, cerrar una procesión. || Añadir (to add on). || ARCH. Empotrar (*in, into*, en). || FAM. Seguir (to follow).
— V. intr. Seguir de cerca (*after*, a). || Hacer cola (to queue). || ARCH. Estar empotrado (*in, into*, en). || *To tail away* o *off* o *out*, ir disminuyendo (noise), ir apagándose (voice), alargarse (marching column).
tailboard [—ˌbɔ:d] n. Tabla (*f.*) posterior de la plataforma (of a lorry or cart).
tailcoat [—ˈkəut] n. Frac, *m.*
tail end [— end] n. Cola, *f.* (of a line of people, etc.). || Final, *m.* (of a storm, etc.): *they arrived at the tail end of the second act*, llegaron al final del segundo acto. || FAM. Trasero, *m.* (bottom).
tail fin [—fin] n. Aleta (*f.*) caudal (of a fish). || Plano (*m.*) de deriva (of a plane).
tailgate [—geit] v. tr. Seguir muy de cerca.
tailing [—iŋ] pl. n. Escorias, *f.* (refuse material). || ARCH. Parte (*m.*) empotrada.
tail lamp [—læmp] n. See TAILLIGHT.
tailless [—lis] adj. Sin cola, sin rabo.
taillight [ˈtailˌlait] n. AUT. Piloto, *m.*, luz (*f.*) posterior. || Farol (*m.*) de cola (of a train).
tailor [ˈteilə*] n. Sastre, *m.* || — *Tailor's*, sastrería, *f.* || *Tailor's chalk*, jaboncillo (*m.*) de sastre.
tailor [ˈteilə*] v. tr. Hacer a la medida (to make to measure). || Cortar: *a well-tailored suit*, un traje bien cortado. || Vestir: *well-tailored person*, persona bien vestida. || FIG. Adaptar: *tailored to the needs of the American airlines*, adaptado a las necesidades de las compañías aéreas americanas.
— V. intr. Ser sastre.
tailored [—d] adj. *Tailored dress*, traje (*m.*) sastre.
tailoring [—riŋ] n. Profesión (*f.*) de sastre, sastrería, *f.* || Corte (*m.*) y confección.
tailor-made [—meid] adj. Hecho a la medida. || Sastre: *tailor-made suit*, traje sastre. || FIG. Adaptado, da.
tailpiece [ˈteilpi:s] n. MUS. Cordal, *m.* || PRINT. Colofón, *m.*, florón, *m.*, viñeta (*f.*) al final del capítulo. || Apéndice, *m.* (part added to the end of sth.).
tail pipe [ˈteilˈpaip] n. AUT. Tubo (*m.*) de escape. || AVIAT. Tobera, *f.*
tail plane [ˈteilˈplein] n. AVIAT. Plano (*m*). de cola.
tail skid [ˈteilˈskid] n. AVIAT. Patín (*m.*) de cola.
tailspin [ˈteilspin] n. AVIAT. Barrena, *f.* || *Tailspin fall*, caída (*f.*) en barrena.
tailstock [ˈteilˌstɔk] n. TECH. Contrapunta, *f.*
tail unit [ˈteilˈju:nit] n. AVIAT. Planos (*m. pl.*) de estabilización, empenaje, *m.*
tail wind [ˈteilˈwind] n. Viento (*m.*) de cola *or* trasero.
tain [tein] n. Azogue, *m.* (for mirror).
Taino [ˈtainəu] adj./n. Taino, na.
taint [teint] n. Corrupción, *f.*, infección, *f.* || Mancha, *f.*: *the taint of sin*, la mancha del pecado. || MED. Tara, *f.*
taint [teint] v. tr. Echar a perder (food). || Corromper (to corrupt morally). || Contaminar (to cause to be spoiled).
— V. intr. Corromperse. || Estropearse (food).
taintless [—lis] adj. Sin mancha, inmaculado, da.
take [teik] n. Presa, *f.* (in hunting). || Pesca, *f.* (in fishing). || Captura, *f.* (act of capturing). || CINEM. Toma, *f.* || U. S. Ingresos, *m. pl.* (receipts).
take* [teik] v. tr. Tomar: *the army took the town*, el ejército tomó la ciudad; *to take medicines, sugar, nourishment*, tomar medicinas, azúcar, alimento; *to take breakfast, lunch, dinner*, tomar el desayuno, el almuerzo, la cena; *to take the waters, the sea air*, tomar las aguas, el aire del mar; *to take notes, information, measurements, s.o.'s temperature*, tomar notas, informes, medidas, la temperatura a alguien; *to take a resolution*, tomar una decisión; *to take a corner*, tomar una curva; *to take sth. seriously, as a joke*, tomar algo en serio, a broma. || Coger, tomar: *he took the book and ran off*, cogió el libro y salió corriendo; *to take sth. from the drawer*, coger algo en el cajón; *to take a bus, the train*, coger el autobús, el tren; *we took the Madrid road*, cogimos la carretera de Madrid. || Coger: *take a chair*, coja una silla; *to take s.o. by the hand*, coger a alguien por la mano. || Llevarse: *take your umbrella with you*, llévate el paraguas. || Cargarse: *to take sth. on one's back*, cargarse algo a la espalda. || Llevar: *to take s.o. for a walk, to the station*, llevar a alguien a pasear, a la estación; *to take s.o. to dinner*, llevar a alguien a cenar; *to take sth. to s.o.*, llevar algo a alguien; *this road will take you to the station*, esta carretera le llevará a la estación. || Llevar, conducir: *the yellow bus will take you*, el autobús amarillo le llevará. || Llevarse, coger: *who has taken the book from the library?*, ¿quién se ha llevado el libro de la biblioteca?; *who has taken my cigarettes?*, ¿quién me ha cogido los cigarrillos?; *take the book for the journey*, llévate el libro para el viaje. || Quitar, llevarse: *the thief took my watch*, el ladrón me ha quitado el reloj *or* se ha llevado mi reloj. || Sacar: *to take a photo*, sacar una foto; *to take a copy*, sacar una copia; *to take a ticket*, sacar un billete; *to take a degree in languages*, sacar un título en lenguas. || Sacar: *to take a line from a poem*, sacar un verso de un poema; *this illustration is taken from*, este grabado está sacado de. || Capturar, coger, detener (to arrest): *the thief was taken by the police*, el ladrón fue capturado por la policía. || Coger, capturar, pescar (fish). || Coger (rabbit, etc.). || Tomarse (holidays). || Ganar, llevarse: *to take first prize*, ganar el primer premio. || Ganar (to win). || Ganar, cobrar (to earn): *he takes ten pounds a week*, gana diez libras por semana. || Pedir: *what will you take for it?*, ¿cuánto pide por esto? || Alquilar, tomar (to rent): *to take a house by the sea*, alquilar una casa a orillas del mar. || Tomar, coger: *to take a secretary*, tomar un secretario. || Comprar (to buy): *to take the Times*, comprar el Times. || Tomar: *I take two pints of milk*

daily, tomo dos pintas de leche diariamente. || Usar (size): *what size shirts do you take?*, ¿qué talla de camisa usa? || Calzar (of shoes): *what size shoes do you take?*, ¿qué número de zapatos calzas? || Reservar (to book): *all the seats are taken*, todos los asientos están reservados. || Ocupar (to occupy): *is this seat taken?*, ¿está ocupado este asiento? || Coger: *the job is taken*, el puesto está cogido. || Coger, contraer, agarrar (a disease): *he took a cold*, agarró un resfriado. || Hacer: *to take a vow*, hacer un voto; *to take exercise*, hacer ejercicio; *to take a trip*, hacer un viaje. || Coger, tomar: *take any example you like*, coja el ejemplo que quiera. || Requerir: *big houses take a lot of cleaning*, las casas grandes requieren mucha limpieza. || Costar: *it takes time and money*, cuesta tiempo y dinero. || Necesitarse, hacer falta: *it takes intelligent people to do this*, se necesita *or* hace falta gente inteligente para hacer esto; *it will take two weeks*, harán falta dos semanas. || Tardar: *it takes us five minutes to get there*, tardamos cinco minutos en llegar allí. || Tardarse: *it takes five minutes to get there*, se tarda cinco minutos en llegar allí. || Requerir, tomar: *to take a long time*, requerir mucho tiempo. || Durar (to last): *how long will the trip take?*, ¿cuánto tiempo durará el viaje? || Tener cabida para, poder contener: *the car only takes four*, el coche sólo tiene cabida para cuatro personas. || Admitir: *this machine only takes small sheets of paper*, esta máquina sólo admite hojas de papel pequeñas. || Aceptar: *take me as I am*, acéptame como soy; *to take a bet*, aceptar una apuesta; *to take an offer*, aceptar una oferta; *will you take the call?*, ¿acepta usted la llamada?; *to take no denial*, no aceptar ninguna negativa. || Dar (a class): *I take Spanish lessons at the university*, doy clases de español en la Universidad. || Estudiar: *I take Spanish at the university*, estudio español en la Universidad. || Encargarse: *Miss Smith is taking the second form*, la señorita Smith se encarga del segundo año de bachillerato. || Asumir: *to take all the responsibility*, asumir toda la responsabilidad. || Recibir: *to take a thrashing*, recibir una paliza. || Aguantar, soportar: *I can't take any more*, no puedo aguantar más; *to take heavy loads*, soportar cargas pesadas. || Tomar: *to take s.o. for another*, tomar una persona por otra. || Suponer, creer, juzgar, considerar (to suppose): *I take it that*, supongo que. || MATH. Restar, sustraer: *to take one number from another*, restar una cifra de otra. || Tomar (to consider): *who do you take me for?*, ¿por quién me toma usted? || Llegar en: *to take third place*, llegar en tercer lugar. || Saltar (fence, obstacle). || Hacer, ganar (a trick). || Comerse a (in games): *bishop takes pawn*, el alfil se come al peón. || Echarse (a lover). || GRAMM. Llevar: *verb that takes a direct object*, verbo que lleva complemento directo. || — *As I take it*, según creo, a mi parecer. || *He took his friend's death badly*, le afectó mucho la muerte de su amigo. || *I take comfort from talking to you*, hablar con usted me sirve de consuelo. || MED. *Not to be taken*, para uso externo. || *Take it from me!*, ¡créame! || *Take it or leave it*, lo toma o lo deja. || *Take that!*, ¡toma! || *Take William, for example*, toma como ejemplo a Guillermo. || *Take your pick*, escoja *or* elija a su gusto. || *To be taken ill*, ponerse enfermo. || *To be taken with*, gustarle a uno: *he was very much taken with the idea*, le gustó mucho la idea. || *To be taken with a fit of laughter*, entrarle a uno un ataque de risa. || *To take a bath*, bañarse, darse un baño. || *To take a bite*, comer un bocado, comer algo. || *To take account of*, tener en cuenta, tomar en consideración. || *To take action against*, tomar medidas contra. || *To take a dislike to s.o.*, cogerle antipatía a alguien. || *To take a fright*, llevarse un susto. || *To take aim at*, apuntar a. || *To take a joke*, soportar una broma. || *To take a leap*, dar un salto. || *To take a liking to*, tomar cariño a. || *To take a look, a glance*, echar una mirada, una ojeada. || *To take a nap*, descabezar un sueño. || *To take an exam*, examinarse. || *To take an oath*, prestar juramento, jurar. || *To take an opportunity* o *a chance*, aprovechar una oportunidad. || *To take apart*, see APART. || *To take a place in the queue*, ponerse en la cola. || *To take a seat*, tomar asiento, sentarse. || *To take a serious view of*, considerar importante. || *To take a shower*, ducharse, darse *or* tomar una ducha. || *To take a step*, dar un paso. || *To take a telephone call*, coger el teléfono. || *To take a turn*, dar una vuelta. || *To take a walk*, dar un paseo. || *To take a wife*, casarse. || *To take breath*, tomar aliento. || *To take care*, see CARE. || *To take charge of*, encargarse de. || *To take drugs*, drogarse. || *To take effect*, see EFFECT. || *To take fright*, asustarse. || *To take leave*, see LEAVE. || *To take paying guests*, alquilar habitaciones. || *To take hold of*, see HOLD. || *To take holy orders*, ordenarse de sacerdote. || *To take it easy*, see EASY. || *To take it for granted that*, dar por supuesto *or* por sentado que. || *To take it hard*, tomarlo muy en serio *or* por la tremenda. || *To take lodgings*, alojarse, hospedarse. || *To take notice of*, hacer caso a: *he didn't take notice of him*, no le hizo ningún caso; hacer caso de (advice). || *To take offence*, ofenderse. || *To take office*, tomar posesión de su cargo, entrar en funciones. || *To take one's advice*, seguir el consejo de alguien. || *To take pity on*, tener lástima de. || *To take one's time*, see TIME. || *To take place*, see PLACE. || *To take prisoner*, hacer prisionero. || *To take pupils*, alojar *or* hospedar alumnos (boarding), dar clases privadas *or* particulares (lessons). || *To take responsibility for*, hacerse responsable de. || *To take s.o. at his word*, cogerle la palabra a uno. || *To take s.o. in one's arms*, abrazar a alguien, coger a alguien entre sus brazos. || *To take s.o.'s hand*, dar la mano a alguien, coger a alguien de la mano. || *To take s.o.'s life*, quitar la vida a alguien. || *To take s.o. unawares*, coger a alguien desprevenido. || *To take sth. the right, the wrong way*, tomar algo a bien, a mal. || *To take the field*, see FIELD. || *To take the floor*, tomar la palabra. || SP. *To take the service* restar (in tennis). || *To take to be*, echar: *I took him to be forty*, le eché cuarenta años; tomar: *I took him to be German*, le tomé por alemán. || MAR. *To take water*, hacer agua (a boat). || FAM. *What took him there?*, ¿por qué se le ocurrió ir allí? || *You can take it from me that*, puede estar seguro de que.

— V. intr. Prender, agarrar (vaccination). || Arraigar (plant). || Prender (graft). || Prender (fire). || Pegar (to stick). || Gustar, tener éxito: *the play did not take well in the provinces*, la obra no gustó mucho en provincias. || Salir (in photographs): *she takes well*, sale bien.

— ***To take about***, enseñar: *to take s.o. about London*, enseñar Londres a alguien. | Sacar: *to take a girl about*, sacar a una chica. || ***To take after***, parecerse a: *he takes after his mother*, se parece a su madre. || ***To take along***, llevarse, llevar consigo. || ***To take away***, llevarse (to carry off). | Quitar la mesa (to clear the table). | Quitar (to remove from s.o.'s possession): *to take s.o.'s job away*, quitarle a uno el puesto. | Restar (to subtract). || ***To take back***, devolver (to return): *to take a book back to s.o.*, devolverle un libro a uno. | Acompañar [a casa], llevar [a casa]: *can you take us back?*, ¿nos puede acompañar? | Llevar de nuevo, volver a llevar: *he was taken back to prison*, lo volvieron a llevar a la cárcel. | Recordar: *it takes me back to my youth*, esto me recuerda mi juventud. | Retirar: *I take back what I just said*, retiro lo que acabo de decir. | Volver a recibir (person). | Aceptar la devolución de (object). | Readmitir (employee). || ***To take down***, quitar (to remove). | Descolgar (curtains, pictures). | Bajar: *to take down a pot of jam from the shelf*, bajar un tarro de mermelada del estante. | Llevar abajo (s.o.). | Derribar (a wall, building). | Desmontar (a machine). | Apuntar, tomar nota de (to write down): *I took down his name*, apunté su nombre. | FAM. Tragar (food). | — FIG. *To take s.o. down*, bajarle los humos a alguien. || ***To take from***, reducir, disminuir (the value, the merit). || ***To take in***, recoger: *to take in a stray cat*, recoger un gato abandonado; *to take in the harvest*, recoger la cosecha. | Alojar, dar alojamiento: *can you take me in for a day?*, ¿puede alojarme durante un día? | Aceptar (work). | Meter (a seam). | Achicar (a dress). | Menguar (in knitting). | Abastecerse de (goods). | Tomar, estar suscrito a (a newspaper). | Hacer pasar (s.o.). | MAR. Cargar, aferrar (sails). | Tomar (a reef). | Entender (to understand). | Darse cuenta de: *to take in the situation*, darse cuenta de la situación. | Abarcar (to include): *the empire took in many countries*, el imperio abarcaba muchos países. | FAM. Tragarse (to believe), dar gato por liebre, engañar (to deceive). | Ganar (to earn). || ***To take into***, meter en. | — *To take it into one's head to do sth.*, meterse en la cabeza la idea de hacer algo. | *To take s.o. into one's confidence*, depositar su confianza en alguien. || ***To take off***, quitar: *to take a saucepan off the fire*, quitar una cacerola del fuego. | Quitarse (clothes): *I took off my gloves*, me quité los guantes. | Apartar de (one's attention, one's eye). | Descolgar (the receiver). | Recibir (a message). | Quitar (an aftereffect). | Suprimir (to suppress). | MED. Amputar (a leg). | MAR. Desembarcar (passengers). | Descontar, hacer un descuento *or* una rebaja de (to deduct): *can you take twenty pence off the price?*, ¿puede descontarme del precio veinte peniques? | Llevarse: *they were taken off in the police van*, se los llevaron en la furgoneta de la policía. | FAM. Remedar, imitar (to mimic). | Saltar (to leap). | Despegar (an aircraft). | Arrancar (a car). | Irse (to go). | Amainar (wind). | Retirarse (tide). | — *To take o.s. off*, irse. || ***To take on***, tomar (a form, quality). | Coger (an accent). | Asumir (responsibility). | Encargarse de (task). | Contratar, coger, tomar (workman). | Acompañar: *I'll take you on a bit*, le voy a acompañar un poco. | Llevar [demasiado lejos]: *I was taken on to Lewes*, me llevaron hasta Lewes. | Coger, tomar (passengers). | Aceptar (a bet, a challenge). | Jugar contra, medirse con: *I'll take him on at billiards*, jugaré al billar contra él, me mediré con él jugando al billar. | Competir con: *I am ready to take on all comers*, estoy dispuesto a competir con cualquiera. | Cuajar (theory, fashion). | FAM. Ponerse frenético. || ***To take out***, sacar: *he took out his pipe from his pocket*, sacó la pipa del bolsillo; *to take out a tooth*, sacar una muela. | Quitar, sacar (a stain). | Hacerse: *to take out an insurance policy*, hacerse un seguro. | Sacar: *to take out a patent, money from the bank*, sacar una patente, dinero del banco. | Sacar: *he is taking Mary out tonight*, saca a María esta noche. | FAM. Agotar: *it takes it out of you*, te agota. | — *To* *take it out in*, pagarse en. | *To take it out on s.o.*, desquitarse con uno. | *To take s.o. out for a walk*, llevar a alguien a dar un paseo. | *To take s.o. out to dinner*, llevar a alguien a cenar. | *To take the dog out for a walk*, sacar al perro de paseo. || **To take over,** hacerse cargo de (business, debts, etc.). | Tomar el poder, ocupar el poder (to assume control). | Asumir (responsibility). | Expropiar (a building). | Sustituir: *to take over from s.o.*, sustituir a alguien. | Recibir [dando la conformidad] (a car, a machine). | Transportar (goods, people). | MAR. *To take over the watch*, entrar de guardia. || **To take round,** enseñar (to show round). | Llevar (to transport). | Pasar: *to take round the plate*, pasar la bandeja. || **To take to,** aficionarse a (to become fond of): *to take to chemistry*, aficionarse a la química. | Empezar a: *when did you take to writing?*, ¿cuándo empezaste a escribir? | Entregarse a: *to take to drinking*, entregarse a la bebida. | Coger simpatía a, tener simpatía a: *I took to her at once*, le tuve simpatía en seguida. | Irse a: *he took to his bed*, se fue a la cama. | Tomar: *he took to the road again*, volvió a tomar la carretera. | Refugiarse en: *the bandits took to the hills*, los bandidos se refugiaron en las colinas. | Dirigirse hacia: *they took to the woods*, se dirigieron hacia el bosque. | — *To take to flight*, huir, darse a la fuga. | *To take to the open sea*, hacerse mar adentro. || **To take up,** coger (to pick up). | Acortar (to shorten). | Tomar, coger (passengers). | Subir: *take this up for me*, súbeme esto. | Llevar arriba (s.o.). | Levantar (pavement, rails). | Quitar (carpet). | Absorber (water): *a sponge takes up water*, la esponja absorbe el agua. | Tomar posesión de (a post). | Fijar, establecer (one's residence). | Ocupar (space, time). | Absorber (one's attention). | JUR. Detener (a thief). | COMM. Pagar (bill), suscribir (shares). | Aceptar (challenge, bet). | Seguir (idea, suggestion). | Adoptar (motion, proposal). | Proteger (to protect). | Estudiar, examinar (a question). | Empezar (a study). | Dedicarse a (a career). | Reanudar (conversation). | Entender (to understand). | TECH. Amortiguar (bumps), compensar (wear). | Criticar (to criticize). | Reprender, censurar (to censure). | Corregir: *his statement was false and I took him up at once*, su declaración era errónea y le corregí en seguida. | Mejorar (weather). | — *To take s.o. up short*, interrumpir a alguien. | *To take up with*, trabar amistad con (friends), juntarse con (bad people). || **To take upon o.s.,** encargarse de.

— OBSERV. Pret. **took;** p. p. **taken.**
— In some countries of Latin America the word *coger* is not in decent use and is usually replaced by *tomar* or *agarrar* (*to take the train*, tomar el tren).

takedown [—daun] adj. Desmontable (machine).
— N. Desmontaje, *m.* || FAM. Feo, *m.*, humillación, *f.*
take-home pay [—ˈhəumˈpei] n. U. S. Sueldo (*m.*) neto.
take-in [—in] n. FAM. Engaño, *m.*
taken [—ən] p. p. See TAKE.
takeoff [—ɔf] n. AVIAT. Despegue, *m.* || Salida, *f.* (of a rocket). || Parodia, *f.* (mimicry). || Caricatura, *f.* (caricature). || SP. Impulso, *m.* || *Power takeoff*, toma (*f.*) de fuerza.
take-over [—ˌəuvə*] n. Toma (*f.*) de posesión. || Toma (*f.*) del poder. || Adquisición, *f.* (of a company).
taker [—ə*] n. Tomador, ra (s.o. who takes). || Arrendador, ra (of a lease). || COMM. Comprador, ra. || Apostador, ra (of a bet).
taker-in [ˈteikərin] n. Tramposo, sa; embustero, ra.
taker-off [ˈteikərɔf] n. FAM. Imitamonos, *m. inv.*
taking [ˈteikiŋ] adj. Atractivo, va (attractive). || Contagioso, sa (a disease).
— N. Toma, *f.* (of a town, etc.). || Detención, *f.* (of a thief). || MED. Toma, *f.* (of blood). || — Pl. Ingresos, *m.* (money earned). || Recaudación, *f. sing.*, taquilla, *f. sing.* (of a show).
taking off [—ɔf] n. AVIAT. Despegue, *m.*
taking out [—aut] n. MED. TECH. Extracción, *f.*
talaria [təˈlɛəriə] pl. n. Talares, *m.* (of Mercury).
talayot [təˈlæjət] n. Talayote, *m.*
talc [tælk] or **talcum** [—əm] n. Talco, *m.*
talcose [ˈtælkəus] or **talcous** [ˈtælkəs] adj. Talcoso, sa.
talcum powder [ˈtælkəmˌpaudə*] n. Talco, *m.*, polvos (*m. pl.*) de talco.
tale [teil] n. Cuento, *m.*: *fairy tales*, cuentos de hadas. || Historia, *f.*, relato, *m.*, narración, *f.* (relation of events). || Cotilleo, *m.*, chisme, *m.*, habladuría, *f.* (piece of gossip). || Cuento, *m.* (lie). || — FIG. *His tale is told*, está perdido. | *It tells its own tale*, habla por sí mismo. || *I've heard a fine tale about you!*, ¡qué cosas me han contado de usted! || *Old wives' tale*, cuento de viejas. || FAM. *To tell tales*, chivarse (to reveal secrets), venir con cuentos (to lie), contar chismes, cotillear (to gossip).
talebearer [—ˌbɛərə*] n. Soplón, ona; chivato, ta (informer). || Cotilla, *m.* & *f.*, chismoso, sa (gossip).
talebearing [—ˌbɛəriŋ] n. Soplonería, *f.*, chivateo, *m.* (informing). || Chismorreo, *m.*, cotilleo, *m.* (gossip).
talent [ˈtælənt] n. Talento, *m.*: *a man of great talent*, un hombre de mucho talento. || Aptitudes, *f. pl.*, don, *m.*: *he has a talent for languages*, tiene aptitudes para los idiomas, tiene don de lenguas. || Talento, *m.*, persona (*f.*) de talento *or* de valor (person). || (Ant.) Talento, *m.* (coin). || — *Exhibition of local talent*, exposición de las obras realizadas por los artistas de la región. || *He has no talent for business*, no sirve para los negocios.
talented [—id] adj. Talentudo, da; talentoso, sa.
talent scout [—skaut] n. Descubridor (*m.*) de personas de talento *or* de valor.
tales [ˈteili:z] n. JUR. Jurados (*m. pl.*) suplentes. || *To pray a tales*, pedir que se complete el jurado.
talesman [ˈteili:zmən] n. JUR. Jurado (*m.*) suplente.

— OBSERV. El plural de *talesman* es *talesmen*.

tale-teller [ˈteilˌtelə*] n. Narrador, ra (who tells stories). || Soplón, ona (informer). || Chismoso, sa (gossipmonger).
talion [ˈtæliən] n. Talión, *m.*
talisman [ˈtælizmən] n. Talismán, *m.*
talk [tɔ:k] n. Conversación, *f.* [*Amer.*, plática, *f.*]: *to engage s.o. in talk*, entablar conversación con alguien; *the Minister had a talk with his Spanish colleague*, el ministro mantuvo una conversación con su colega español. || Charla, *f.*: *he gave a talk about Venezuela*, dio una charla acerca de Venezuela. || Conferencia, *f.* (lecture). || Discurso, *m.* (speech). || Habladurías, *f. pl.* (gossip): *it's all talk*, no son más que habladurías. || Comidilla, *f.*, tema, *m.*: *he was the talk of the town*, era la comidilla de la ciudad. || Palabras, *f. pl.*: *we want actions not talk*, queremos hechos no palabras. || Habla, *f.*, manera (*f.*) de hablar: *baby talk*, el habla de los niños. || — *He is all talk*, no hace más que hablar. || *I'd like to have a talk with you*, me gustaría hablar con usted. || U. S. FAM. *That's the talk!*, ¡muy bien! || *There is some talk of his returning*, corre el rumor de que va a volver. || *To keep the talk going*, mantener la conversación.
talk [tɔ:k] v. tr. Decir: *don't talk rubbish!*, ¡no diga tonterías! || Hablar: *I talk Spanish*, hablo español. || Hablar de: *to talk politics, business*, hablar de política, de negocios. || — *He talked himself hoarse*, de tanto hablar se quedó ronco. || *To be talked about*, andar en boca de todo el mundo. || FAM. *To talk a blue streak*, hablar por los codos. || U. S. *To talk (cold) turkey*, no andarse con rodeos. || *To talk dress*, hablar de trapos. || FIG. *To talk o.s. blue in the face*, hablar hasta que se le seque a uno la boca. || *To talk sense*, hablar razonablemente *or* sensatamente. || *To talk shop*, hablar de negocios. || *To talk s.o. into doing sth.*, convencer a alguien para que haga algo. || *To talk s.o. out of doing sth.*, disuadir a alguien de que haga algo. || FIG. *To talk the hind leg off a donkey* o *nineteen to the dozen*, hablar por los codos *or* más que siete *or* como una cotorra.
— V. intr. Hablar: *to learn to talk*, aprender a hablar; *what are you talking about?*, ¿de qué hablas?; *to talk by signs*, hablar por señas; *she has found s.o. to talk to*, ha encontrado a alguien con quien hablar. || Charlar (to chatter). || Hablar (to gossip): *people will talk*, la gente hablará. || — *He knows what he's talking about*, sabe lo que se dice. || *He likes to hear himself talk*, se escucha cuando habla. || FAM. *I'll talk to him!*, ¡me va a oír!, ¡le voy a echar una bronca! || *Look who is talking!*, ¡mira quién habla! || *Now you're talking!*, ¡así se habla!, ¡eso es hablar! || *Talk about luck!*, ¡Dios mío, qué suerte! || *Talk of the devil and he will appear*, hablando del rey de Roma por la puerta asoma. || *That's no way to talk*, ésa no es forma de hablar. || *To get o.s. talked about*, dar que hablar. || *To talk about this, that and the other*, hablar de todo un poco. || *To talk behind s.o.'s back*, criticar a alguien a sus espaldas. || *To talk big*, jactarse, fanfarronear. || *To talk for the sake of talking*, hablar por hablar. || *To talk in riddles*, hablar en clave. || *To talk through one's hat*, decir tonterías. || *To talk to o.s.*, hablar para su coleto *or* para sí. || *To talk without rhyme or reason*, hablar sin ton ni son. || *Who do you think you're talking to?*, ¿con quién se cree usted que está hablando?
— **To talk at,** tirar indirectas a. | — *Are you talking at me?*, ¿se dirige usted a mí? || **To talk away,** pasar charlando: *to talk away the night*, pasar la noche charlando. | Hablar sin parar (to speak a lot). | — *To talk s.o.'s fears away*, demostrar a alguien con palabras que sus temores no tienen fundamento. || **To talk back,** contestar con impertinencia, replicar. || **To talk down,** callar, hacer callar (to silence). | — *I won't allow myself to be talked down*, no permitiré que me callen. | *To talk an aircraft down*, dirigir un aterrizaje por radio. | *To talk down to*, ponerse al alcance *or* al nivel de (one's audience), hablar con altivez a. | *To talk sth. down*, quitar importancia a algo. || **To talk on,** seguir hablando. || **To talk out,** discutir a fondo: *I want to talk things out with you*, quiero discutir las cosas a fondo con usted. | — *To talk a bill out*, prolongar los debates de tal manera que no se pueda votar un proyecto de ley. || **To talk over,** discutir, hablar de: *to talk a matter over*, discutir un asunto. | Convencer (a person). || **To talk round,** convencer: *to talk s.o. round*, convencer a alguien. | — *To talk round a question*, tratar un tema superficialmente, andarse con rodeos. || **To talk up,** alabar, hacer mucho ruido en favor de: *to talk up a book*, hacer mucho ruido en favor de un libro. | — *To talk up to s.o.*, hablar con alguien.
talkative [—ətiv] adj. Hablador, ra; charlatán, ana; parlanchín, ina; locuaz.

talkativeness [—ətivnis] n. Locuacidad, *f.*
talker [ˈtɔ:kə*] n. Hablador, ra; parlanchín, ina. || FAM. Jactancioso, sa. || — *He is a good talker*, habla muy bien. || *He is a great talker*, es muy parlanchín.
talkie [ˈtɔ:ki] n. CINEM. Película (*f.*) sonora.
talking [ˈtɔ:kiŋ] adj. Que habla (bird, doll). || Sonoro, ra (picture). || Expresivo, va (look).
— N. Conversación, *f.* || Charloteo, *m.* (chatter). || — *I don't want to do all the talking*, no quiero ser el único en hablar. || *No talking please!*, ¡silencio, por favor!
talking point [—pɔint] n. Tema (*m.*) de conversación.
talking-to [—tu:] n. Bronca, *f.*: *to give s.o. a talking-to*, echar una bronca a alguien.
talky [ˈtɔ:ki] adj. Hablador, ra.
tall [tɔ:l] adj. Alto, ta: *he is tall for his age*, es alto para su edad; *a tall oak*, un roble alto. || De alto, de altura: *to be six feet tall*, tener seis pies de alto. || FAM. Exagerado, da; increíble (incredible): *a tall story*, una historia increíble. || — *How tall are you?*, ¿cuánto mide? || *She is growing tall*, está creciendo. || FAM. *Tall talk*, jactancia, *f.*, fanfarronada, *f.*
— Adv. *To talk tall*, jactarse.
tallage [ˈtælidʒ] n. HIST. Talla, *f.* (due).
tallboy [ˈtɔ:lbɔi] n. Cómoda (*f.*) alta.
tallith [ˈtæliθ] n. Taled, *m.* (shawl).
tallness [ˈtɔ:lnis] n. Altura, *f.* (of building, etc.). || Talla, *f.*, estatura, *f.* (of people).
tallow [ˈtæləu] n. Sebo, *m.*
tallowy [—i] adj. Seboso, sa.
tally [ˈtæli] n. Tarja, *f.* (stick). || Muesca, *f.* (notch). || Total, *m.* (total figure). || Cuenta, *f.* (account): *to keep tally of*, llevar la cuenta de. || Lote, *m.*: *to buy sth. by the tally*, comprar algo por lotes. || Resguardo, *m.* (receipt). || Etiqueta, *f.* (label, tag). || Contrapartida, *f.* (counterpart).
tally [ˈtæli] v. tr. Etiquetar (to put a label on). || Puntear (on a list). || Registrar (a number).
— V. intr. Corresponder, concordar (to agree, to match): *the stories of the two men tally*, las historias de los dos hombres concuerdan.
tally clerk [—klɑ:k] n. Listero, *m.*, marcador, *m.*
tallyho [—ˈhəu] interj. ¡Hala! (call of huntsmen).
tallyman [—mən] n. Listero, *m.*, marcador, *m.* (who checks). || Comerciante (*m.*) que vende a plazos.

— OBSERV. El plural de *tallyman* es *tallymen*.

Talmud [ˈtælmud] pr. n. Talmud, *m.*
Talmudic [tælˈmudik] or **Talmudical** [—əl] adj. Talmúdico, ca.
talon [ˈtælən] n. Garra, *f.* (of bird of prey). || Zarpa, *f.*, garra, *f.* (of tiger). || Saliente, *m.*, uña, *f.* (of a lock). || Montón, *m.* (of cards). || Matriz, *f.* (of cheque-book). || ARCH. Talón, *m.* (moulding).
talus [ˈteiləs] n. ANAT. Astrágalo, *m.* (astragalus). || GEOL. Talud, *m.* || MIL. Escarpa, *f.*
tamable [ˈteiməbl] adj. Domesticable (animals). || Domable (wild horse).
tamale [təˈmɑ:li] n. CULIN. Tamal, *m.*
tamandua [təˈmænduə] n. ZOOL. Tamandúa, *m.*
tamarack [ˈtæməræk] n. BOT. Alerce (*m.*) americano.
tamarau [ˈtæmərau] n. Tamarao, *m.* (Philippine buffalo).
tamarin [ˈtæmərin] n. Tití, *m.* (monkey).
tamarind [ˈtæmərind] n. Tamarindo, *m.* (fruit, tree).
tamarisk [ˈtæmərisk] n. BOT. Taray, *m.*, tamarisco, *m.*
tambour [ˈtæmbuə*] n. MUS. Tambor, *m.* || Bastidor, *m.*, tambor, *m.* (frame for embroidery). || ARCH. Tambor, *m.*
tambour [ˈtæmbuə*] v. tr./intr. Bordar con bastidor.
tambourine [ˌtæmbəˈri:n] n. MUS. Pandereta, *f.*, pandero, *m.*
tame [teim] adj. Domesticado, da (domesticated): *these animals are so tame that they eat out of your hand*, estos animales están tan domesticados que comen en la mano. || Doméstico, ca (bred with human beings): *a tame monkey*, un mono doméstico. || Domado, da (wild horses). || Manso, sa (not wild). || FIG. Sumiso, sa (docile). || FAM. Aburrido, da (boring). | Soso, sa; insípido, da (dull).
tame [teim] v. tr. Domesticar (animal). || Domar, amansar (wild horse). || FIG. Domeñar, dominar (to bring under control).
— V. intr. Domesticarse.
tameable [—əbl] adj. See TAMABLE.
tameless [—lis] adj. Indomable.
tameness [—nis] n. Mansedumbre, *f.* || FIG. Sumisión, *f.* | Insipidez, *f.*, sosería, *f.* (of style).
tamer [—ə*] n. Domador, ra.
Tamil [ˈtæmil] adj./n. Tamul. || — N. Tamul, *m.* (language).
taming [—iŋ] n. Domesticación, *f.* (of animals). || Doma, *f.*, domadura, *f.* (of wild horses). || *The Taming of the Shrew*, la Fierecilla domada, la Doma de la bravía (Shakespeare's play).
tam-o'-shanter [ˌtæməˈʃæntə*] n. Boina (*f.*) escocesa.
tamp [tæmp] v. tr. MIN. Atacar. || Apisonar (the ground).
tamper [—ə*] n. Pisón, *m.*
tamper [—ə*] v. intr. *To tamper with*, sobornar (to bribe), desnaturalizar, amañar (a text), intentar forzar (a lock), estropear (to spoil), manosear: *don't tamper with what is not yours*, no manosees lo que no es tuyo.
tamping [—iŋ] n. Apisonamiento, *m.*
tampion [ˈtæmpiən] n. MIL. Tapabocas, *m. inv.* || MUS. Tapón, *m.* (of an organ pipe).
tampon [ˈtæmpən] n. MED. Tapón, *m.*
tampon [ˈtæmpən] v. tr. MED. Taponar.
tamponade [ˌtæmpəˈneid] or **tamponage** [ˈtæmpəˌnidʒ] n. MED. Taponamiento, *m.*
tam-tam [ˈtæmˌtæm] n. MUS. Tantán, *m.* (drum). | Batintín, *m.* (gong).
tan [tæn] adj. De color marrón (shoes). || Castaño, ña (animal). || Bronceado, da; tostado, da (skin).
— N. Casca, *f.*, corteza, *f.* (tree bark). || Tanino, *m.* (tanning substance). || Bronceado, *m.*, color (*m.*) tostado (colour of skin). || Color (*m.*) tabaco, marrón, *m.* (yellowish brown colour). || *To acquire a tan*, broncearse, ponerse moreno.
tan [tæn] v. tr. Curtir (leather). || Broncear, tostar (the skin). || FAM. Zurrar (to thrash). || FAM. *To tan s.o.'s hide*, zurrar la badana a alguien.
— V. intr. Broncearse, tostarse (the skin).
tanager [ˈtænədʒə*] or **tanagra** [ˈtænəgrə] n. Tanagra, *f.* (bird).
Tanagra [ˈtænəgrə] n. Tanagra, *f.* (statuette).
tanbark [ˈtænbɑ:k] n. Casca, *f.*
tandem [ˈtændəm] n. Tándem, *m.* (bicycle, etc.).
— Adv. En fila, en tándem.
tang [tæŋ] n. Sabor (*m.*) fuerte (taste). || Olor (*m.*) fuerte (smell). || Frescor, *m.* (of air). || FIG. Sabor, *m.*: *the story has a romantic tang*, el relato tiene un sabor romántico. || Espiga, *f.* (of knife, tool). || Tañido, *m.* (of a bell).
tang [tæŋ] v. tr. Tañer (a bell). || Poner una espiga a (a knife, tool).
tangency [ˈtændʒənsi] n. MATH. Tangencia, *f.*
tangent [ˈtændʒənt] adj. Tangente.
— N. Tangente, *f.* || FIG. *To fly off* o *to go off at a tangent*, salirse por la tangente.
tangential [tænˈdʒenʃəl] adj. Tangencial.
tangerine [ˌtændʒəˈri:n] n. Mandarina, *f.* (fruit).
Tangerine [ˌtændʒəˈri:n] adj./n. Tangerino, na.
tangibility [ˌtændʒiˈbiliti] n. Carácter (*m.*) tangible.
tangible [ˈtændʒəbl] adj. Tangible. || FIG. Tangible, palpable. || JUR. Material: *tangible assets*, bienes materiales.
Tangier [tænˈdʒiə*] pr. n. GEOGR. Tánger.
tangle [ˈtæŋgl] n. Maraña, *f.*, enredo, *m.*: *tangle of branches*, *of wires*, maraña de ramas, de cables. || Nudo, *m.* (of hair). || FIG. Embrollo, *m.*, enredo, *m.* (affairs). | Laberinto, *m.* (maze). || — *To be in a tangle*, haberse enredado (ropes, a person). || *To get into a tangle*, enredarse (wires, a person).
tangle [ˈtæŋgl] v. tr. Enredar, enmarañar (to form into a tangle). || Enredar (to catch in a net). || FIG. Embrollar, enredar (affairs).
— V. intr. Enredarse, enmarañarse. || FIG. Embrollarse, enredarse. || FAM. *To tangle with s.o.*, meterse con alguien.
tangled [—d] or **tangly** [—i] adj. Enredado, da; enmarañado, da.
tanglement [—mənt] n. Enmarañamiento, *m.*
tango [ˈtæŋgəu] n. Tango, *m.*
tango [ˈtæŋgəu] v. intr. Bailar el tango.
tangy [ˈtæŋi] adj. Fuerte.
tank [tæŋk] n. Depósito, *m.*, tanque, *m.*: *petrol tank*, depósito de gasolina. || Depósito, *m.*, aljibe, *m.* (of water). || MIL. Carro (*m.*) de combate, tanque, *m.*
tank [tæŋk] v. tr. Guardar en un depósito.
— V. intr. FAM. *To tank up*, beber mucho.
tankage [—idʒ] n. Almacenaje (*m.*) en depósitos (storage in tanks). || Capacidad (*f.*) de un depósito (capacity). || Gastos (*m. pl.*) de almacenaje (charge for storage). || AGR. Fertilizante (*m.*) orgánico (animal residues).
tankard [—əd] n. "Bock", *m.* (of beer).
tank car [—kɑ:*] n. U. S. Vagón (*m.*) cisterna.
tank engine [—ˈendʒin] n. Locomotora (*f.*) ténder.
tanker [—ə*] n. MAR. Petrolero, *m.*, buque (*m.*) aljibe (ship). || Camión (*m.*) cisterna (lorry). || MIL. Tanquista, *m.* || *Rail tanker*, vagón (*m.*) cisterna.
tank locomotive [—ˈləukəˌməutiv] n. Locomotora (*f.*) ténder.
tank truck [—trʌk] n. Camión (*m.*) cisterna.
tank wagon [—ˌwægən] n. Vagón (*m.*) cisterna. || AUT. Camión (*m.*) cisterna.
tannage [ˈtænidʒ] n. Curtido, *m.*
tanned [ˈtænd] adj. Curtido, da (leather). || Bronceado, da; moreno, na (with the sun). || *To get tanned*, ponerse moreno, broncearse.
tanner [ˈtænə*] n. Curtidor, *m.* (person). || FAM. Moneda (*f.*) de seis peniques (sixpence).
tannery [ˈtænəri] n. Curtiduría, *f.*, tenería, *f.*
tannic [ˈtænik] adj. Tánico, ca.
tannin [ˈtænin] n. CHEM. Tanino, *m.*
tanning [ˈtæniŋ] n. Curtido, *m.* || Bronceado, *m.* (of the skin). || FAM. Zurra, *f.*, paliza, *f.* (thrashing): *to give s.o. a tanning*, dar una zurra a alguien.
tanrec [ˈtænrek] n. ZOOL. Tanrec, *m.*, tenrec, *m.*
tantalization [ˌtæntəlaiˈzeiʃən] n. Tortura, *f.*, tormento, *m.*, suplicio (*m.*) de Tántalo.
tantalize [ˈtæntəlaiz] v. tr. Torturar, atormentar, hacer sufrir el suplicio de Tántalo (to torment). || Seducir (to tempt).
tantalizing [—iŋ] adj. Atormentador, ra: *it is tantalizing not being able to open our presents until Christmas*

Day, es atormentador el no poder abrir nuestros regalos hasta el día de Navidad. || Seductor, ra (attractive): *a tantalizing idea*, una idea seductora.
tantalum [ˈtæntələm] n. Tantalio, *m.* (metal).
Tantalus [ˈtæntələs] pr. n. MYTH. Tántalo, *m.*
tantamount [ˈtæntəmaunt] adj. Equivalente. || *To be tantamount to*, equivaler a, ser equivalente a, venir a ser: *his threats are tantamount to blackmail*, sus amenazas equivalen a un chantaje.
tantara [ˈtæntərə] n. Tarará, *m.*
tantrum [ˈtæntrəm] n. Rabieta, *f.*, berrinche, *m.*: *to fly into a tantrum*, coger una rabieta.
Taoism [ˈtɑ:əuizəm] n. REL. Taoísmo, *m.*
Taoist [ˈtɑ:əuist] adj./n. REL. Taoísta.
tap [tæp] n. Grifo, *m.*: *to turn on the water tap*, abrir el grifo del agua; *to turn off the tap*, cerrar el grifo. || Canilla, *f.*, espita, *f.* (of a barrel). || Macho (*m.*) de aterrajar *or* de roscar (screw tap). || ELECTR. Derivación, *f.* || Golpecito, *m.* (light blow): *a tap on the door*, un golpecito en la puerta. || Cervecería, *f.* (taproom). || Tapa, *f.* (for the heel of a shoe). || MED. Drenaje, *m.* || FAM. Sablazo, *m.* (of money). || *On tap*, a mano (easily available), de barril (beer).
tap [tæp] v. tr. Golpear ligeramente, dar un golpecito en, dar un golpe ligero en: *to tap the door with one's knuckles* o *to tap one's knuckles on the door*, dar un golpecito en la puerta con los nudillos. || Poner una espita a (a cask). || Agujerear (to make a hole in). || Sangrar (a tree). || Sacar (wine from a barrel). || Hacer una toma de (water, gas, etc.). || ELECTR. Hacer una derivación de, derivar. || Hacer una conexión en (to connect). || Poner tapas a (shoes). || Interceptar (to intercept communications): *to tap s.o.'s telephone*, interceptar el teléfono de alguien. || TECH. Roscar, aterrajar (to cut a thread on). | Sangrar (a furnace). || FIG. Utilizar (to draw on). | Aprovechar, explotar: *to tap a country's resources*, explotar los recursos naturales de un país. || MED. Drenar. || FAM. Dar un sablazo de, sablear: *to tap s.o. for fifty pence*, sablear cincuenta peniques a alguien. || — *To tap in*, clavar dando golpecitos (a nail). || *To tap out*, enviar (a Morse message), escribir a máquina (on a typewriter), vaciar dando golpecitos (a pipe), sacar dando golpecitos (a split pin, etc.).
— V. intr. Tamborilear: *to tap with one's fingers*, tamborilear con los dedos. || Taconear (to walk making a tapping sound). || Zapatear (to dance making a tapping sound).
tap circuit [—ˈsə:kit] n. ELECTR. Derivación, *f.*
tap dance [ˈtæpdɑ:ns] n. Zapateado, *m.*
tap-dance [ˈtæpdɑ:ns] v. intr. Zapatear.
tap dancer [—ə*] n. Bailarín (*m.*) de zapateado, bailarina (*f.*) de zapateado.
tape [teip] n. Cinta, *f.* (strip of cotton, silk, etc.). || Cinta (*f.*) adhesiva (adhesive paper or plastic). || Cinta (*f.*) métrica (for measuring). || Cinta (*f.*) perforada (of teleprinter, telex). || MED. Esparadrapo, *m.* || Cinta (*f.*) magnetofónica, cinta, *f.* (of a tape recorder). || FAM. Cinta, *f.* (a recording). || Cinta (*f.*) simbólica (at inauguration ceremony). || SP. Cinta (*f.*) de llegada. || Tira (*f.*) de gasa (in bookbinding). || — *Adhesive tape*, cinta adhesiva. || *Insulating tape*, cinta aislante. || FAM. *Red tape*, papeleo, *m.*, trámites, *m. pl.* || *Sticky tape*, cinta adhesiva.
tape [teip] v. tr. Atar con cinta (to fasten). || Medir con cinta métrica (to measure). || Pegar con cinta adhesiva: *to tape a piece of paper to the wall*, pegar un papel en la pared con cinta adhesiva. || Ribetear (in dressmaking). || Grabar (to record). || FIG. FAM. *To have s.o. taped*, tener a alguien calado.
— V. intr. Medir.
tape measure [—ˌmeʒə*] n. Cinta (*f.*) métrica.
taper [—ə*] n. Vela, *f.* (thin candle). || REL. Cirio, *m.*, vela, *f.* || Estrechamiento, *m.* (narrowing).
taper [—ə*] v. tr. Estrechar (to make narrower). || Afilar (to sharpen to a point).
— V. intr. Estrecharse (to become narrower). || Afilarse (to narrow to a point). || *To taper off*, disminuir: *demand usually tapers off in winter*, la demanda suele disminuir en invierno.
tape-record [—riˌkɔ:d] v. tr. Grabar [en cinta magnetofónica].
tape recorder [—riˌkɔ:də*] n. Magnetófono, *m.*, magnetofón, *m.* [*Amer.*, grabadora, *f.*]. || TECH. Grabador (*m.*) de cinta (part of an installation).
tape recording [—riˌkɔ:diŋ] n. Grabación, *f.* [en cinta magnetofónica].
tapestried [ˈtæpistrid] adj. Tapizado, da (covered with tapestry). || Bordado en un tapiz (worked in tapestry).
tapestry [ˈtæpistri] n. Tapiz, *m.*: *Bayeux tapistry*, tapiz de Bayeux. || Tapicería, *f.* (art, industry).
tapestry maker [—ˈmeikə*] n. Tapicero, ra.
tapestry making [—ˈmeikiŋ] n. Tapicería, *f.*
tapeworm [ˈteipwə:m] n. Solitaria, *f.*, tenia, *f.*
taphole [ˈtæphəul] n. TECH. Bigotera, *f.* (for slag). | Piquera, *f.* (for cast iron).
tapioca [ˌtæpiˈəukə] n. Tapioca, *f.*
tapir [ˈteipə*] n. ZOOL. Tapir, *m.*
tapper [ˈtæpə*] n. ELECTR. Manipulador, *m.* || TECH. Aterrajadora, *f.*
tappet [ˈtæpit] n. Varilla (*f.*) de levantamiento.
tapping [ˈtæpiŋ] n. Golpecitos, *m. pl.* || ELECTR. Derivación, *f.* || Sangría, *f.* (of trees, of molten metal).
taproom [ˈtæprum] n. Cervecería, *f.* (bar).
taproot [ˈtæpru:t] n. BOT. Raíz (*f.*) primaria.
taps [tæps] pl. n. U. S. MIL. Toque (*m. sing.*) de silencio.
tapster [ˈtæpstə*] n. Camarero, *m.* [*Amer.*, mozo, *m.*]
tapwater [ˈtæpˈwɔ:tə*] n. Agua (*f.*) del grifo.
tar [tɑ:*] n. Alquitrán, *m.*, brea, *f.* (in road making, etc.). || MED. Brea, *f.* || FAM. Marinero, *m.*
tar [tɑ:*] v. tr. Alquitranar (to cover with tar). || — FIG. *To be tarred with the same brush*, estar cortados por el mismo patrón. | *To tar and feather*, emplumar. | *To tar on*, incitar.
taradiddle [ˈtærədidl] n. FAM. Sandez, *f.*, disparate, *m.*
tarantella [ˌtærənˈtelə] n. MUS. Tarantela, *f.*
tarantula [təˈræntjulə] n. ZOOL. Tarántula, *f.*

— OBSERV. El plural de la palabra inglesa *tarantula* es *tarantula* o *tarantulae*.

tarboosh [tɑ:ˈbu:ʃ] n. Fez, *m.* (felt cap).
tardigrada [ˌtɑ:diˈgreidə] pl. n. ZOOL. Tardígrados, *m.*
tardigrade [ˈtɑ:diˌgreid] adj. ZOOL. Tardígrado, da.
— N. ZOOL. Tardígrado, *m.*
tardily [ˈtɑ:dili] adv. Tardíamente (too late). || Lentamente (slowly).
tardiness [ˈtɑ:dinis] n. Lentitud, *f.*, tardanza, *f.* (slowness). || Retraso, *m.* (lateness).
tardy [ˈtɑ:di] adj. Tardío, a (late). || Lento, ta; tardo, da (slow).
tare [tɛə*] n. Tara, *f.* (weight). || BOT. Vicia, *f.* || — Pl. REL. Cizaña, *f. sing.*, mala semilla, *f.*
tare [tɛə*] v. tr. Destarar.
target [ˈtɑ:git] n. Blanco, *m.*, diana, *f.* (in shooting, archery). || Puntuación, *f.* (score in shooting). || MIL. Objetivo, *m.* (of a missile attack). || FIG. Objeto, *m.*, blanco, *m.*: *to be the target for popular ridicule*, ser objeto de la mofa de todos. | Meta, *f.*, objetivo, *m.*: *his target was to succeed*, su meta era triunfar. || TECH. Anticátodo, *m.* (of an X-ray tube). || U. S. Disco, *m.* (signal). || Mirilla, *f.* (in surveying). || HIST. Rodela, *f.* (small shield). || — *Production target*, objetivo (*m.*) de producción. || FIG. *To be on target*, seguir el rumbo previsto.
target day [—dei] n. Fecha (*f.*) señalada.
target practice [—ˈpræktis] n. Tiro (*m.*) al blanco, prácticas (*f. pl.*) de tiro.
tariff [ˈtærif] n. Tarifa, *f.*, arancel, *m.* (on imports). || Tarifa, *f.*, lista (*f.*) de precios (in a hotel, etc.). || *Tariff barrier*, barrera arancelaria.
tariff [ˈtærif] v. tr. Tarifar (to fix a tariff for). || Fijar los derechos arancelarios *or* los aranceles de (imports).
tarlatan [ˈtɑ:lətən] n. Tarlatana, *f.* (fabric).
tarmac [ˈtɑ:mæk] n. Superficie (*f.*) alquitranada. || *The aircraft is standing on the tarmac*, el avión está en la pista de despegue.
tarn [tɑ:n] n. Lago (*m.*) pequeño de montaña.
tarnish [—iʃ] n. Empañadura, *f.*, deslustre, *m.* || FIG. Mancha, *f.*, deslutre, *m.* (of reputation).
tarnish [—iʃ] v. tr. Deslustrar (a surface). || FIG. Manchar, deslustrar, empañar: *to tarnish s.o.'s reputation*, manchar la reputación de uno.
— V. intr. Deslustrarse, perder su brillo.
tarot [ˈtærəu] n. Naipe, *m.* [al que se atribuye un poder adivinatorio].
tarpaulin [tɑ:ˈpɔ:lin] n. Lona (*f.*) alquitranada, alquitranado, *m.*
Tarpeia [tɑ:ˈpi:ə] pr. n. Tarpeya, *f.*
Tarpeian [—n] adj. *Tarpeian Rock*, Roca Tarpeya.
Tarquin [ˈtɑ:kwin] pr. n. HIST. Tarquino, *m.*
tarragon [ˈtærəgən] n. BOT. Estragón, *m.*
tarred [tɑ:d] or **tarry** [ˈtɑ:ri] adj. Alquitranado, da. || Cubierto de alquitrán.
tarry [ˈtæri] v. intr. Quedarse atrás (to linger). || Quedarse (to stay). || Tardar (to be late).
tarsal [ˈtɑ:səl] adj. ANAT. Tarsiano, na.
— N. ANAT. Tarso, *m.*
tarsus [ˈtɑ:səs] n. ANAT. Tarso, *m.*

— OBSERV. El plural de *tarsus* es *tarsi*.

tart [tɑ:t] adj. Agrio, gria; ácido, da (taste). || FIG. Áspero, ra; cáustico, ca: *a tart reply*, una respuesta cáustica. | Desabrido, da (disposition).
— N. CULIN. Tarta, *f.* [*Amer.*, torta, *f.*]: *apple tart*, tarta de manzana. || FAM. Fulana, *f.*, furcia, *f.* (prostitute).
tartan [ˈtɑ:tən] n. Tartán, *m.*, tela (*f.*) escocesa de cuadros (material). || MAR. Tartana, *f.* (boat).
tartar [ˈtɑ:tə*] n. CHEM. Tártaro, *m.* || Sarro, *m.*, tártaro, *m.* (on the teeth).
Tartar [ˈtɑ:tə*] adj./n. Tártaro, ra. || FIG. Fiera, *f.*, persona (*f.*) intratable (intractable person). || FIG. *To catch a tartar*, dar con la horma de su zapato.
Tartarean [tɑ:ˈtɛəriən] adj. Tartáreo, a (infernal).
tartaric [tɑ:ˈtærik] adj. Tartárico, ca; tártrico, ca.
tartar sauce or **tartare sauce** [ˈtɑ:tə*sɔ:s] n. Salsa (*f.*) tártara.
Tartarus [ˈtɑ:tərəs] pr. n. MYTH. Tártaro, *m.*
Tartary [ˈtɑ:təri] pr. n. HIST. Tartaria, *f.*
Tartessian [tɑ:ˈtesiən] adj./n. Tartesio, sia.
tartlet [ˈtɑ:tlit] n. CULIN. Tartita, *f.*, pastelillo, *m.*
tartness [ˈtɑ:tnis] n. Acidez, *f.* (of taste). || FIG. Aspereza, *f.*, causticidad, *f.*
tartrate [ˈtɑ:treit] n. CHEM. Tartrato, *m.*
tarty [ˈtɑ:ti] adj. FAM. Provocativo, va; atrevido, da: *a tarty dress*, un vestido provocativo.

task [tɑ:sk] n. Tarea, *f.*, faena, *f.*, labor, *f.* (work). || Misión, *f.*, cometido, *m.* (mission). || Deber, *m.* (at school). || — *To set s.o. a task*, encargar un trabajo a alguien. || *To take to task*, reprender, regañar, llamar la atención.
task [tɑ:sk] v. tr. Imponer una tarea, encargar.
task force [—fɔ:s] n. MIL. Destacamento (*m.*) de fuerzas [para una misión especial].
taskmaster [—,mɑ:stə*] n. Capataz, *m.* || Supervisor, *m.* || FIG. *A hard taskmaster*, un verdadero tirano.
taskwork [—wə:k] n. Trabajo (*m.*) a destajo.
tassel [ˈtæsəl] n. Borla, *f.* (ornament).
tassel [ˈtæsəl] v. tr. Adornar con borlas.
taste [teist] n. Gusto, *m.* (sense). || Sabor, *m.*, gusto, *m.*: *a sweet taste*, un sabor dulce; *a meaty taste*, un sabor a carne. || Degustación, *f.* (tasting). || Gusto, *m.*, afición, *f.* (liking): *to acquire* o *to develop a taste for sth.*, tomar gusto a algo, cobrar afición a algo. || Gusto, *m.* (discernment): *the house is decorated with taste*, la casa está decorada con gusto. || Experiencia, *f.*, prueba, *f.*: *we had a taste of country life*, tuvimos una experiencia de lo que es la vida en el campo. || Muestra, *f.*: *I have already had a taste of his bad manners*, ya tuve una muestra de su falta de modales. || Pizca, *f.* (of food): *give me a taste*, dame una pizca. || Sorbo, *m.* (sip). || — *Add salt to taste*, añádese sal a voluntad. || *Each to his own taste*, sobre gustos no hay nada escrito. || *Give the horses a taste of the whip*, haz probar el látigo a los caballos. || *In bad taste*, de mal gusto. || *There is no accounting for tastes*, sobre gustos no hay nada escrito. || *To be to one's taste*, gustar a uno, ser del gusto de uno: *spicy food is not to my taste*, no me gusta la comida picante. || *To find sth. to one's taste*, encontrar algo al gusto de uno. || *To give s.o. a taste of his own medicine*, pagar a alguien con la misma moneda. || *To have a taste for*, gustarle a uno algo: *he has a taste for sports cars*, le gustan los coches deportivos. || FIG. *To leave a nasty taste in one's mouth*, dejarle a uno mal sabor de boca. || *To lose one's taste for*, perder el gusto por.
taste [teist] v. tr. Probar, saborear: *taste this, it's lovely*, prueba esto, está estupendo. || Catar, probar (wine). || Notar un sabor a: *you can taste garlic in this meat*, se nota un sabor a ajo en esta carne. || Experimentar, saborear, conocer (to experience): *to taste the pleasures of riches*, experimentar los placeres de la riqueza. || Sufrir (to suffer): *to taste s.o.'s temper*, sufrir el mal genio de alguien. || Probar (to try): *to taste the good life*, probar la buena vida.
— V. intr. Saber: *to taste of*, saber a. || — *To taste nice*, estar bueno, estar rico, estar sabroso. || *To taste strange*, tener un sabor raro, saber raro, tener un gusto raro.
taste bud [—bʌd] n. ANAT. Papila (*f.*) gustativa.
tasteful [—ful] adj. De buen gusto.
tastefully [—fuli] adv. Con [buen] gusto: *tastefully dressed*, vestido con buen gusto.
tastefulness [—fulnis] n. Buen gusto, *m.*, elegancia, *f.*
tasteless [—lis] adj. Insípido, da; soso, sa (food). || De mal gusto (in bad taste).
tastelessly [—lisli] adv. Con mal gusto, sin gusto: *a tastelessly decorated room*, una habitación decorada sin gusto.
tastelessness [—lisnis] n. Insipidez, *f.* (of food). || Mal gusto, *m.*, falta (*f.*) de gusto (bad taste).
taster [—ə*] n. Catador, *m.* (person). || Utensilio (*m.*) para catar (instrument). || Catavino, *m.* (glass for tasting wine).
tastiness [—inis] n. Sabor, *m.*, gusto, *m.* || Buen gusto, *m.*
tasting [—iŋ] n. Degustación, *f.*: *wine tasting*, degustación de vino.
tasty [—i] adj. Sabroso, sa; apetitoso, sa. || De buen gusto.
tat [tæt] n. See TIT.
tat [tæt] v. tr. Hacer bordados *or* encajes en.
— V. intr. Hacer bordados *or* encajes.
tata [ˈtæˈtɑ:] interj. FAM. Chao, hasta lueguito.
Tatar [ˈtɑ:tə*] n./adj. Tártaro, ra; tátaro, ra.
Tatary [ˈtɑ:təri] pr. n. HIST. Tartaria, *f.*
tater [ˈteitə*] n. FAM. Patata, *f.* [*Amer.*, papa, *f.*] (potato).
tatouay [ˈtætuei] n. Tatú, *m.* (armadillo).
tatter [ˈtætə*] n. Jirón, *m.*, pingajo, *m.* || — Pl. Andrajos, *m.*, harapos, *m.* (ragged clothing). || *To be in rags and tatters*, ir con la ropa hecha jirones, ir desastrado.
tatterdemalion [,tætədəˈmeiljən] n. Zarrapastroso, sa; andrajoso, sa.
tattered [ˈtætəd] adj. Hecho jirones, andrajoso, sa (clothes). || Andrajoso, sa; harapiento, ta (person).
tatting [ˈtætiŋ] n. Encaje (*m.*) de hilo.
tattle [ˈtætl] n. Palique, *m.*, cháchara, *f.* (idle talk). || Chismorreo, *m.* (gossip).
tattle [ˈtætl] v. intr. Estar de palique *or* de cháchara (to engage in idle talk). || Chismorrear (to gossip).
tattler [—ə*] n. Parlanchín, ina (talkative person). || Chismoso, sa (gossip).
tattletale [—teil] n. Soplón, ona; acusica, *m.* & *f.* (telltale). || Chismoso, sa (gossip).
tattoo [təˈtu:] n. MIL. Toque (*m.*) de retreta, retreta, *f.* (signal). | Desfile (*m.*) militar, espectáculo (*m.*) militar (entertainment). || Repiqueteo, *m.* (succession of taps). || Tatuaje, *m.* (on the skin). || *The hailstones beat a tattoo on the roof*, el granizo tamborileaba en el tejado.
tattoo [təˈtu:] v. tr. Tatuar (the skin).
— V. intr. Tamborilear (to tap).
tattooing [—iŋ] n. Tatuaje, *m.*
tatty [ˈtæti] adj. En mal estado (in poor condition). || Pobre (house, street). || Desaseado, da (person). || Gastado, da; raído, da (clothes).
tau [tɔ:] n. Tau, *m.*, tao, *m.* (cross). || Tau, *f.* (Greek letter).
taught [tɔ:t] pret. & p. p. See TEACH.
taunt [tɔ:nt] adj. MAR. Alto, ta; de mucha guinda.
— N. Pulla, *f.*, sarcasmo, *m.* (provocation).
taunt [tɔ:nt] v. tr. Mofarse de (to jeer at). || Lanzar pullas a (to provoke). || *To taunt s.o. with sth.*, echar algo en cara a uno.
taunting [—iŋ] adj. Burlón, ona (jeering). || Provocante (provocative). || Sarcástico, ca.
taupe [təup] n. U. S. Gris (*m.*) oscuro.
taurine [ˈtɔ:rain] adj. Taurino, na.
Tauris [ˈtɔ:ris] n. GEOGR. Táuride.
tauromachian [tɔ:rəˈmeikiən] or **tauromachic** [tɔ:ˈrɔməkik] adj. Tauromáquico, ca.
tauromachy [tɔ:ˈrɔməki] n. Tauromaquia, *f.*
Taurus [ˈtɔ:rəs] n. ASTR. Tauro, *m.* (constellation, sign of the zodiac). || GEOGR. Tauro, *m.*
taut [tɔ:t] adj. Tenso, sa: *a taut rope*, una cuerda tensa; *the situation is taut*, la situación está tensa.
tauten [ˈtɔ:tən] v. tr. Tensar (rope). || Tesar (sails).
— V. intr. Tensarse.
tautness [ˈtɔ:tnis] n. Tensión, *f.*
tautological [,tɔ:təˈlɔdʒikəl] adj. Tautológico, ca.
tautology [tɔ:ˈtɔlədʒi] n. Tautología, *f.*
tavern [ˈtævən] n. Taberna, *f.* (bar). || Venta, *f.* (inn).
taw [tɔ:] n. Canica (*f.*) *or* bola (*f.*) grande (large marble). || Punto (*m.*) de donde se empieza la jugada (starting point). || Juego (*m.*) de canicas *or* bolas (game).
taw [tɔ:] v. tr. Curtir en blanco (hides).
— V. intr. Jugar a las canicas *or* bolas.
tawdriness [ˈtɔ:drinis] n. Oropel, *m.*, relumbrón, *m.*
tawdry [ˈtɔ:dri] adj. De oropel, de relumbrón.
— N. Oropel, *m.*, relumbrón, *m.*
tawniness [ˈtɔ:ninis] n. Color (*m.*) rojizo *or* leonado. || Bronceado, *m.* (of skin).
tawny [ˈtɔ:ni] adj. Rojizo, za; leonado, da. || Bronceado, da (skin).
tax [tæks] n. Impuesto, *m.*, contribución, *f.* (on property, income, etc.): *land tax*, contribución territorial. || Impuesto, *m.* (on products): *tobacco tax*, impuesto sobre el tabaco; *to levy* o *to impose a tax on sth.*, gravar algo con un impuesto; *entertainment tax*, impuesto sobre los espectáculos públicos. || Arancel, *m.* (at customs). || FIG. Esfuerzo, *m.* (effort). | Carga, *f.* (burden): *to be a tax on s.o.*, ser una carga para alguien. | Prueba, *f.* (test, trial). || — *Airport tax*, tasa (*f.*) de aeropuerto. || *Capital gains tax*, impuesto de plusvalía. || *Composition tax*, impuesto concertado. || *Excise tax*, impuesto indirecto. || *Free of tax*, exento de impuesto. || *Income tax*, impuesto sobre la renta de las personas físicas. || *Luxury tax*, impuesto de lujo. || *Purchase tax*, impuesto sobre la venta. || *Road tax* o *road fund tax*, impuesto de circulación. || *Tax collector*, recaudador (*m.*) de contribuciones. || *Tax dodging*, fraude (*m.*) fiscal. || *Tax evasion*, evasión (*f.*) fiscal. || *Tax rate*, imposición, *f.* || *Tax return*, declaración (*f.*) de renta *or* de ingresos. || *Tax stamp*, timbre (*m.*) fiscal. || *Tax system*, sistema tributario. || *Value added tax*, tasa (*f.*) al valor añadido *or* agregado.
tax [tæks] v. tr. Gravar con un impuesto (a product): *to tax petrol*, gravar la gasolina con un impuesto. || Imponer contribuciones a (a person). || Poner a prueba (to try): *his persistence taxed my patience*, su persistencia puso a prueba mi paciencia. || Agotar (to exhaust). || Tachar: *to tax s.o. with being idle*, tachar a alguien de perezoso. || JUR. Tasar (to fix the amount of costs, etc.). || *To be heavily taxed*, estar sujeto a un impuesto elevado (a product), pagar muchos impuestos *or* contribuciones (a person).
taxable [ˈtæksəbl] adj. Imponible: *taxable income*, renta imponible; *taxable profits*, utilidades imponibles. || Impositivo, va: *taxable value*, valor impositivo.
taxation [tækˈseiʃən] n. Impuestos, *m. pl.*: *direct, indirect taxation*, impuestos directos, indirectos; *heavy taxation*, impuestos elevados. || Sistema (*m.*) tributario (tax system).
tax-exempt [ˈtæksigˈzempt] adj. Exento de impuestos, libre de impuestos, exonerado de impuestos.
tax-free [ˈtæksˈfri:] adj. Exento de impuestos, libre de impuestos, exonerado de impuestos.
taxgatherer [ˈtæks,gæðərə*] n. Recaudador (*m.*) de contribuciones.
taxi [ˈtæksi] n. Taxi, *m.*: *to go by taxi*, ir en taxi.
taxi [ˈtæksi] v. tr. Llevar en taxi (to transport by taxi). || AVIAT. Hacer rodar por la pista (on the ground). | Hacer deslizarse por el agua (on water).
— V. intr. Ir en taxi (to ride in a taxi). || AVIAT. Rodar por la pista (on the ground). | Deslizarse por el agua (on water).
taxicab [—kæb] n. Taxi, *m.*
taxi dancer [—,dɑ:nsə*] n. U. S. Cabaretera, *f.*
taxidermal [—ˈdə:məl] adj. Taxidérmico, ca.
taxidermic [—ˈdə:mik] adj. Taxidérmico, ca.

taxidermist [—də:mist] n. Taxidermista, *m.* & *f.*
taxidermy [—də:mi] n. Taxidermia, *f.*
taxi driver [—ˌdraivə*] n. Taxista, *m.* & *f.*
taximan [—mæn] n. Taxista, *m.*

— Observ. El plural de *taximan* es *taximen.*

taximeter [—ˌmi:tə*] n. Taxímetro, *m.*
taxiplane [—plein] n. Avión (*m.*) de alquiler.
taxi rank [—ˈræŋk] n. Parada (*f.*) de taxis.
taxis [—s] n. Biol. Taxia, *f.*, taxis, *f.* || Med. Taxis, *f.*
taxi stand [—ˈstænd] n. Parada (*f.*) de taxis.
taxiway [—wei] n. Aviat. Pista (*f.*) de rodaje.
taxonomic [ˌtæksəˈnɔmik] or **taxonomical** [—əl] adj. Taxonómico, ca.
taxonomy [tækˈsɔnəmi] n. Taxonomía, *f.*
taxpayer [ˈtæksˌpeiə*] n. Contribuyente, *m.* & *f.*
taylorism [ˈteilərizəm] n. Taylorismo, *m.*
tea [ti:] n. Té, *m.* (leaves, beverage): *a cup of tea*, una taza de té; *lemon tea*, té con limón. || Infusión, *f.*: *camomile tea*, infusión de manzanilla. || Merienda, *f.*, té, *m.* (light afternoon snack). || Merienda cena, *f.* (meal replacing dinner). || — *Afternoon tea*, merienda. || *High tea*, merienda cena. || Fig. *It's not my cup of tea*, no me gusta mayormente. | *Not for all the tea in China*, por todo el oro del mundo.
tea bag [—bæg] n. Bolsita (*f.*) de té, bolsa (*f.*) de té.
tea break [—breik] n. Descanso (*m.*) para el té.
tea caddy [—ˌkædi] n. Bote (*m.*) del té.
tea cake [—keik] n. Culin. Bollito, *m.*
tea cart [—kɑ:t] n. Carrito (*m.*) del té (tea trolley).
teach* [ti:tʃ] v. tr. Dar clases a: *to teach children*, dar clases a los niños. || Dar clases de: *he teaches the guitar*, da clases de guitarra. || Enseñar a: *to teach s.o. how to drive*, enseñar a alguien a conducir; *that will teach him not to interfere!*, ¡eso le enseñará a no entrometerse! || Ser profesor de, dar clases de: *he teaches English*, es profesor de inglés. || — *To teach a lesson*, dar una lección. || U. S. *To teach school*, dar clases.
— V. int. Ser profesor, dar clases (to be a teacher).

— Observ. Pret. & p. p. ***taught.***

teachable [—əbl] adj. Enseñable, fácil de enseñar (thing). | Que aprende fácilmente (person).
teacher [—ə*] n. Profesor, ra (in a secondary school): *Spanish teacher*, profesor de español. || Maestro, tra (in a primary school).
teachers college [ˈti:tʃəzˈkɔlidʒ] n. Escuela (*f.*) normal.
teacher training [ˈti:tʃəˈtreiniŋ] n. Formación (*f.*) pedagógica.
tea chest [ˈti:tʃest] n. Caja (*f.*) grande para el té.
teach-in [ˈti:tʃin] n. Seminario, *m.*
teaching [ˈti:tʃiŋ] n. Enseñanza, *f.* (act, profession): *English language teaching*, la enseñanza de la lengua inglesa. || — Pl. Enseñanzas, *f.*, doctrina, *f. sing.*: *the teachings of Christ*, las enseñanzas de Cristo.
— Adj. Docente: *teaching body* o *staff*, cuerpo docente. || Pedagógico, ca: *teaching methods*, métodos pedagógicos. || *Teaching hospital*, hospital (*m.*) general con facultad de medicina.
tea cosy or **tea cozy** [ˈti:ˈkəuzi] n. Cubretetera, *m.*
teacup [ˈti:kʌp] n. Taza (*f.*) de té.
teacupful [—ful] n. Taza, *f.*

— Observ. El plural de la palabra *teacupful* es *teacupfuls* o *teacupsful.*

tea dance [ˈti:dɑ:ns] n. Té (*m.*) baile.
tea garden [ˈti:ˌgɑ:dn] n. Café (*m.*) al aire libre. || Agr. Plantación (*f.*) de té.
teahouse [ˈti:haus] n. Salón (*m.*) de té.
teak [ti:k] n. Bot. Teca, *f.*
teakettle [ˈti:ˌketl] n. Tetera, *f.*
teal [ti:l] n. Cerceta, *f.* (duck).
tea leaf [ˈti:li:f] n. Hoja (*f.*) de té (plant). || — Pl. Poso, *m. sing.* || Fig. *To read the tea leaves*, ver el porvenir en el fondo de la taza.

— Observ. El plural de *tea leaf* es *tea leaves.*

team [ti:m] n. Yunta, *f.* (animals yoked together). || Tronco, *m.*, tiro, *m.* (horses when pulling a carriage). || Equipo, *m.* (people working or playing together): *football team*, equipo de fútbol; *rescue team*, equipo de salvamento. || — Sp. *Away team*, equipo visitante. | *Home team*, equipo casero.
team [ti:m] v. tr. Hacer trabajar en equipo (to cause to work in a team). || Combinar, acompañar: *a knowledge of languages teamed with practical experience*, un conocimiento de los idiomas acompañado por *or* combinado con una experiencia práctica. || Enganchar (horses to a carriage). || Uncir (to yoke). || Transportar con yunta.
— V. intr. *To team up*, agruparse, unirse, asociarse.
teammate [—ˌmeit] n. Compañero (*m.*) de equipo.
team spirit [—ˌspirit] n. Espíritu (*m.*) de equipo.
teamster [—stə*] n. Cochero, *m.* (of a carriage). || Carretero, *m.* (of a cart). || U. S. Camionero, *m.* (lorry driver).
teamwork [—wə:k] n. Trabajo (*m.*) en equipo.
tea party [—ˌpɑ:ti] n. Té, *m.*
teapot [ˈti:pɔt] n. Tetera, *f.*
tear [tiə*] n. Lágrima, *f.*: *a tear trickled down his cheek*, una lágrima le bajaba por la mejilla. || Fig. Lágrima, *f.* (defect in glass). || — Pl. Lágrimas, *f.*: *tears filled her eyes*, tenía los ojos llenos de lágrimas. || Llanto, *m.* (weeping). || — Fig. *Crocodile tears*, lágrimas de cocodrilo. || *In tears*, llorando. || *To be bathed in tears*, estar bañado en lágrimas. || Fam. *To be bored to tears*, aburrirse como una ostra. || *To bring tears to the eyes of the audience*, arrancar lágrimas *or* hacer saltar las lágrimas al público. || *To burst* o *to dissolve into tears*, deshacerse en lágrimas, echarse a llorar. || *To dry* o *to wipe away one's tears*, enjugarse las lágrimas. || Fig. *To hold back one's tears*, tragarse las lágrimas. || *To move s.o. to tears*, hacer llorar a alguien. || *To shed tears*, derramar lágrimas. || *With tears in his eyes*, con lágrimas en los ojos.
tear [tiə*] v. intr. Derramar lágrimas.
tear [tεə*] n. Rasgón, *m.*, desgarrón, *m.* (split). || Prisa, *f.*, precipitación, *f.* (haste).
tear* [tεə*] v. tr. Desgarrar, rasgar, romper: *to tear a piece of cloth, of paper*, rasgar una tela, un papel. || Arrancar, quitar violentamente: *he tore the poster from the wall*, arrancó el cartel de la pared. || Med. Herir, lacerar (the flesh). | Distender (a muscle, a ligament). || Fig. Atormentar: *she was torn as to what she ought to do*, estaba atormentada por lo que debía de hacer. | Dividir, desgarrar (to divide into opposing groups): *a country torn by interior strife*, un país desgarrado por disensiones internas. || — *To tear a hole in*, hacer un agujero en. || Fig. *To tear one's hair*, tirarse de los pelos. || *To tear sth. open*, abrir algo rasgándolo *or* rompiéndolo violentamente. || *To tear to pieces*, hacer pedazos (to break), echar abajo, echar por tierra (an argument), poner como un trapo, poner por los suelos (to criticize).
— V. intr. Rasgarse, desgarrarse: *the paper tore when the parcel fell*, el papel se rasgó al caerse el paquete. || Fam. Correr, ir a toda velocidad.
— ***To tear along,*** ir a toda velocidad. || ***To tear around,*** correr como un loco. || ***To tear at,*** quitar precipitadamente. | — *To tear at s.o.'s eyes*, intentar sacarle los ojos a alguien. || ***To tear away,*** arrancar (to remove). | Salir disparado (to leave). | — *He can't tear himself away from the television even for a minute*, no deja de ver la televisión ni un solo minuto. | *I couldn't tear myself away*, no sabía cómo irme (from meeting, etc.), no podía deshacerme de él (from a person). || ***To tear down,*** arrancar (to pull down). | Derribar, demoler (to demolish). | Desmontar, desarmar (a machine). | U. S. Difamar, denigrar (to denigrate). || ***To tear in,*** entrar precipitadamente. || ***To tear into,*** acometer. || ***To tear off,*** arrancar. | Cortar (a coupon). | Salir disparado (to leave). || ***To tear out,*** arrancar (to rip). | Salir disparado (to leave). || ***To tear up,*** hacer pedazos, despedazar (to destroy). | Sacar de raíz, desarraigar (a plant). | Anular: *to tear up a treaty*, anular un tratado. | Llegar a toda velocidad (to arrive).

— Observ. Pret. ***tore;*** p. p. ***torn.***

teardown [ˈtεədaun] n. Desmontaje, *m.*, desarme, *m.*
teardrop [ˈtiədrɔp] n. Lágrima, *f.* (tear).
tear duct [ˈtiədʌkt] n. Anat. Conducto (*m.*) lacrimal.
tearful [ˈtiəful] adj. Lloroso, sa (shedding tears). || Lacrimoso, sa (causing or accompanied by tears). || Lastimoso, sa (event).
tear gas [ˈtiəgæs] n. Gas (*m.*) lacrimógeno. || *Tear-gas bomb*, bomba lacrimógena.
tearing [ˈtεəriŋ] adj. Desgarrador, ra. || Violento, ta: *tearing rage*, furia violenta. || *A tearing noise*, el ruido de algo que se rasga.
— N. Desgarramiento, *m.*
tearjerker [ˈtiəˌdʒə:kə*] n. Obra (*f.*) sentimentaloide.
tearless [ˈtiəlis] adj. Sin lágrimas.
tear-off [ˈtεərɔf] adj. Trepado, da: *complete the tear-off slip*, rellénese el cupón trepado. || *Tear-off calendar*, calendario (*m.*) de taco.
tearoom [ˈti:rum] n. Salón (*m.*) de té.
tea rose [ˈti:rəuz] n. Bot. Rosa (*f.*) de té.
tearstain [ˈtiəˌstein] n. Mancha (*f.*) de lágrima.
tease [ti:z] n. Broma, *f.*: *to do sth. for a tease*, hacer algo en broma. || Bromista, *m.* & *f.* (joker): *to be sth. of a tease*, ser un poco bromista. || Fam. Provocadora, *f.* (a woman).
tease [ti:z] v. tr. Molestar, fastidiar [*Amer.*, embromar] (to annoy). || Fam. Provocar (to provoke). || Atormentar (to tantalize). || Tomar el pelo a (to make fun of): *to tease s.o. about his accent*, tomarle el pelo a alguien a causa de su acento. || Importunar (to pester). || Tech. Cardar: *to tease wool*, cardar lana; *to tease a cloth*, cardar un paño.
teasel [—l] n. Bot. Cardencha, *f.* || Carda, *f.* (wire device used to raise a nap).
teasel [—l] v. tr. Cardar.
teaser [—ə*] n. Bromista, *m.* & *f.* (tease). || Tech. Cardador, ra (of wool, etc.). || Rompecabezas, *m. inv.* (puzzle). || Fam. Provocadora, *f.* (woman).
tea service [ˈti:ˌsə:vis] n. Juego (*m.*) de té.
tea set [ˈti:set] n. Juego (*m.*) de té.
tea shop [ˈti:ʃɔp] n. Salón (*m.*) de té.
teasing [ˈti:ziŋ] adj. Burlón, ona (mocking). || Bromista (person). || Atormentador, ra (tantalizing).
— N. Bromas, *f. pl.*, burlas, *f. pl.* (jokes). || Tormentos, *m. pl.* (torments).
teasingly [—li] adv. En broma, bromeando.
teaspoon [ˈti:spu:n] n. Cucharilla, *f.* (small spoon). || Cucharadita, *f.* (teaspoonful).

teaspoonful [—ful] n. Cucharadita, *f.*

— OBSERV. El plural de *teaspoonful* es *teaspoonfuls* o *teaspoonsful.*

teat [ti:t] n. ANAT. Pezón, *m.* || Teta, *f.* (of animals). || Tetina, *f.*, boquilla, *f.* (on a feeding bottle).
tea table [ˈti:ˌteibl] n. Mesita (*f.*) de té.
teatime [ˈti:taim] n. Hora (*f.*) del té.
tea towel [ˈti:ˈtauəl] n. Trapo (*m.*) de cocina.
tea tray [ˈti:trei] n. Bandeja (*f.*) del té.
tea trolley [ˈti:trɔli] n. Carrito (*m.*) del té.
tea urn [ˈti:ə:n] n. Tetera (*f.*) grande.
tea wagon [ˈti:ˌwægən] n. Carrito (*m.*) del té.
teazel [ˈti:zl] or **teazle** [ˈti:zl] n. See TEASEL.
technetium [tekˈni:ʃiəm] n. CHEM. Tecnecio, *m.*
technic [ˈteknik] adj. Técnico, ca.
— N. Técnica, *f.*
technical [—əl] adj. Técnico, ca: *technical books*, libros técnicos: *technical terms*, terminología técnica; *technical adviser*, asesor *or* consejero técnico. || JUR. En teoría, según la ley. || De forma, de terminología: *technical point*, cuestión de forma. || — JUR. *Technical offence*, cuasidelito, *m.* || *Technical school*, instituto (*m.*) laboral.
technicality [ˌtekniˈkæliti] n. Tecnicidad, *f.* || Tecnicismo, *m.* (word). || Detalle (*m.*) técnico (detail).
technically [ˈteknikəli] adv. Técnicamente. || En términos técnicos: *expressed technically*, dicho en términos técnicos. || En teoría: *you are technically guilty*, en teoría usted es culpable.
technician [tekˈniʃən] n. Técnico, ca; especialista, *m.* & *f.* || *Laboratory technician*, ayudante (*m.*) de laboratorio.
Technicolor [ˈtekniˌkʌlə*] n. Tecnicolor, *m.*: *in technicolor*, en tecnicolor.
— Adj. En tecnicolor.
technics [ˈtekniks] n. Tecnología, *f.*
technique [tekˈni:k] n. Técnica, *f.*
technochemistry [teknəˈkemistri] n. Química (*f.*) industrial.
technocracy [tekˈnɔkrəsi] n. Tecnocracia, *f.*
technocrat [ˈteknəkræt] n. Tecnócrata, *m.* & *f.*
technocratic [teknəˈkrætik] adj. Tecnócrata.
technologic [ˌteknəˈlɔdʒik] or **technological** [—əl] adj. Tecnológico, ca.
technologist [tekˈnɔlədʒist] n. Tecnólogo, ga.
technology [tekˈnɔlədʒi] n. Tecnología, *f.*
techy [ˈtetʃi] adj. Irritable, picajoso, sa.
tectonic [tekˈtɔnik] adj. Arquitectónico, ca. || GEOL. Tectónico, ca.
tectonics [—s] n. Arquitectura, *f.* (building). || GEOL. Tectónica, *f.*
tectrices [tekˈtraisi:z] pl. n. ZOOL. Tectrices, *f.*
ted [ted] v. tr. Henificar.
tedder [ˈtedə*] n. Henificadora, *f.*
teddy bear [ˈtedibɛə*] n. Oso (*m.*) de felpa.
teddy boy [ˈtedibɔi] n. Gamberro, *m.*
Te Deum [ˈti:ˈdi:əm] n. REL. Tedéum, *m.*, Te Deum, *m.*
tedious [ˈti:djəs] adj. Aburrido, da; tedioso, sa; pesado, da.
tediousness [—nis] or **tedium** [ˈti:djəm] n. Tedio, *m.*, aburrimiento, *m.*, pesadez, *f.*
tee [ti:] n. Te, *f.* (letter). || SP. Punto (*m.*) de partida (in golf, the beginning of a hole). | "Tee", *m.*, soporte (*m.*) donde se pone la pelota (in golf, object on which the ball is placed). || FIG. *To a tee*, como anillo al dedo.
tee [ti:] v. tr./intr. SP. *To tee off*, dar el primer golpe (in golf). | *To tee up*, colocar en el "tee" (in golf).
tee-hee [ˈti:ˈhi:] n./v. intr. See TEHEE.
teem [ti:m] v. tr. TECH. Verter.
— V. intr. Hormiguear, pulular: *refugees teemed in the streets*, los refugiados hormigueaban por las calles. || Hervir, rebosar: *the river teems with fish*, el río hierve de peces. || *Ideas teemed in his mind*, tenía la cabeza llena de ideas.
teeming [—iŋ] adj. Abundante. || Que hormiguea de gente: *teeming cities*, ciudades que hormiguean de gente. || *Teeming with mistakes*, lleno de errores.
teen-age [ˈti:nˌeidʒ] adj. Adolescente. || *Teen-age fashion*, moda para jóvenes.
teen-ager [—ə*] n. Adolescente, *m.* & *f.*, joven, *m.* & *f.*
teens [ti:nz] pl. n. Adolescencia, *f. sing.* || *To be in one's teens*, estar en la adolescencia, tener entre 13 y 19 años.
teeny [ˈti:ni] or **teeny-weeny** [—ˈwi:ni] adj. FAM. Pequeñito, ta; minúsculo, la; chiquitín, ina.
teepee [ˈti:pi] n. Tepee, *m.*
tee shirt [ˈti:ʃə:t] n. See T-SHIRT.
teeter [ˈti:tə*] n. Balanceo, *m.*, vaivén, *m.*
teeter [ˈti:tə*] v. intr. Balancearse (to move in a wobbly manner). || FIG. Vacilar, titubear (to be indecise). || U. S. Columpiarse (to seesaw).
teeter-totter [—ˈtɔtə*] n. U. S. Columpio, *m.*, subibaja, *m.* (seesaw).
teeter-totter [—ˈtɔtə*] v. intr. Columpiarse.
teeth [ti:θ] pl. n. See TOOTH.
teethe [ti:ð] v. intr. Echar los dientes.
teething [—iŋ] n. Dentición, *f.*
teething ring [—iŋriŋ] n. Chupador, *m.*
teetotal [ti:ˈtəutl] adj. Abstemio, mia (abstaining from alcoholic drinks). || U. S. FAM. Total, completo, ta: *a teetotal failure*, un fracaso total.
teetotalism [—izəm] n. Abstinencia, *f.*
teetotaller (U. S. **teetotaler**) [—ə*] or **teetotalist** [—ist] n. Abstemio, mia.
teetotum [ˈti:təuˈtʌm] n. Perinola, *f.*
teg [teg] n. Oveja (*f.*) de dos años (sheep).
tegmen [—mən] n. Tegmen, *m.*

— OBSERV. El plural de la palabra inglesa es *tegmina.*

tegument [ˈtegjumənt] n. Tegumento, *m.*
tegumental [ˌtegjuˈmentəl] adj. Tegumentario, ria.
tegumentary [ˌtegjuˈmentəri] adj. Tegumentario, ria.
tehee [ˈti:ˈhi:] n. Risa, *f.*, risita, *f.*
— Interj. ¡Ja ja!
tehee [ˈti:ˈhi:] v. intr. Reírse.
Teheran or **Tehran** [tiəˈrɑ:n] pr. n. GEOGR. Teherán.
telaesthesia [ˌtelesˈθi:ʒjə] n. Telestesia, *f.*
telamon [ˈteləmən] n. ARCH. Telamón, *m.*, atlante, *m.*

— OBSERV. El plural de la palabra inglesa es *telamones.*

telecast [ˈtelikɑ:st] n. Transmisión (*f.*) por televisión, teledifusión, *f.* || Emisión (*f.*) *or* programa (*m.*) de televisión (programme).
telecast [ˈtelikɑ:st] v. tr. Televisar.
telecine [ˈteliˈsini] n. Telecine, *m.*, telecinematógrafo, *m.*
telecommunication [ˈtelikəˌmjuniˈkeiʃən] n. Telecomunicación, *f.*
telecourse [ˈteliko:s] n. Curso (*m.*) televisado.
telefilm [ˈtelifilm] n. Telefilm, *m.*
telegenic [ˌteliˈdʒenik] adj. Televisivo, va.
telegram [ˈteligræm] n. Telegrama, *m.*
telegram [ˈteligræm] v. tr. Telegrafiar.
telegraph [ˈteligrɑ:f] n. Telégrafo, *m.*
— Adj. Telegráfico, ca: *telegraph pole, wire*, poste, hilo telegráfico. || — *Telegraph messenger*, telegrafista, *m.* & *f.* || *Telegraph operator*, telegrafista, *m.* & *f.*
telegraph [ˈteligrɑ:f] v. tr. Telegrafiar (to wire).
— V. intr. Mandar un telegrama, telegrafiar.
telegrapher [tiˈlegrəfə*] n. Telegrafista, *m.* & *f.*
telegraphic [ˌteliˈgræfik] adj. Telegráfico, ca.
telegraphically [—əli] adv. Telegráficamente.
telegraphist [tiˈlegrəfist] n. Telegrafista, *m.* & *f.*
telegraphy [tiˈlegrəfi] n. Telegrafía, *f.*: *wireless telegraphy*, telegrafía sin hilos.
telekinesis [ˌtelikaiˈni:sis] n. Telequinesia, *f.*
telelens [ˈtelilenz] n. Teleobjetivo, *m.*
Telemachus [tiˈleməkəs] pr. n. Telémaco, *m.*
telemark [ˈtelimɑ:k] n. SP. Virage, *m.* (in skiing).
telemechanic [ˌtelimiˈkænik] adj. Telemecánico, ca.
telemechanics [—s] n. Telemecánica, *f.*
telemeter [ˈtelimi:tə*] n. Telémetro, *m.*
telemetric [teliˈmetrik] adj. Telemétrico, ca.
telemetry [tiˈlemitri] n. Telemetría, *f.*
telencephalon [ˌtelinˈsefəlɔn] n. ANAT. Telencéfalo, *m.*
teleologic [teliˈɔlədʒik] or **teleological** [—əl] adj. Teleológico, ca.
teleology [teliˈɔlədʒi] n. Teleología, *f.*
teleost [ˈteliɔst] or **teleostean** [teliˈɔstiən] adj. ZOOL. Teleósteo.
— N. ZOOL. Teleósteo, *m.*
telepathic [ˌteliˈpæθik] adj. Telepático, ca.
telepathist [tiˈlepəθist] n. Telépata, *m.* & *f.*
telepathy [tiˈlepəθi] n. Telepatía, *f.*
telephone [ˈtelifəun] n. Teléfono, *m.* || — *To be on the telephone*, tener teléfono (to have a telephone), estar hablando por teléfono (to be speaking on the telephone). || *You are wanted on the telephone*, le llaman por teléfono.
— Adj. Telefónico, ca: *telephone company*, compañía telefónica.
telephone [ˈtelifəun] v. tr. Decir *or* comunicar por teléfono (to transmit by telephone). || Hablar por teléfono con, telefonear a, llamar por teléfono a (to speak to on the telephone). || *Telephoned telegram*, telefonema, *m.*
— V. intr. Llamar por teléfono.
telephone book [—buk] n. Guía (*f.*) de teléfonos.
telephone booth [—bu:ð] or **telephone box** [—bɔks] n. Cabina (*f.*) telefónica, locutorio, *m.*
telephone call [—kɔ:l] n. Llamada (*f.*) telefónica.
telephone directory [—diˈrektəri] n. Guía (*f.*) de teléfonos.
telephone exchange [—iksˈtʃeindʒ] n. Central (*f.*) telefónica, central (*f.*) de teléfonos.
telephone kiosk [—ˌkiɔsk] n. Cabina (*f.*) telefónica, locutorio, *m.*
telephone number [—ˈnʌmbə*] n. Número (*m.*) de teléfono.
telephone operator [—ˈɔpəreitə*] n. Telefonista, *m.* & *f.*
telephone receiver [—riˈsi:və*] n. Microteléfono, *m.*
telephonic [ˌteliˈfɔnik] adj. Telefónico, ca.
telephonist [tiˈlefənist] n. Telefonista, *m.* & *f.*
telephony [tiˈlefəni] n. Telefonía, *f.*: *wireless telephony*, telefonía sin hilos.
telephoto [ˈteliˈfəutəu] adj. PHOT. Telefotográfico, ca.
— N. PHOT. Telefotografía, *f.*, telefoto, *f.* (photograph). | Teleobjetivo, *m.* (lens).
telephotograph [ˈteliˈfəutəgrɑ:f] n. PHOT. Telefotografía, *f.*, telefoto, *f.*
telephotographic [teliˌfəutəˈgræfik] adj. Telefotográfico, ca.
telephotography [ˈtelifəˈtɔgrəfi] n. PHOT. Telefotografía, *f.*
telephoto lens [ˈteliˈfəutəuˌlenz] n. PHOT. Teleobjetivo, *m.*

teleprinter [ˈteli,printə*] n. Teleimpresor, *m.*, teletipo, *m.*

teleprompter [ˈteli,prɔmptə*] n. Tablero (*m.*) que se utiliza en telivisión para recordar las palabras de un texto.

telescope [ˈteliskəup] n. Catalejo, *m.*: *to look at sth. through a telescope*, mirar algo con un catalejo. ‖ ASTR. Telescopio, *m.*

telescope [ˈteliskəup] v. tr. FIG. Hacer encastrar: *the collision telescoped four coaches of the train*, el choque hizo que se encastrasen cuatro vagones del tren. | Resumir, abreviar (to shorten).
— V. intr. Plegarse como un telescopio (to fold up like a telescope). ‖ Encajar: *this part telescopes into the other*, esta parte encaja en la otra.

telescopic [,telisˈkɔpik] adj. Telescópico, ca. ‖ Que se meten unas en otras, que se encastran.

telesthesia [,telesˈθi:ʒjə] n. U. S. Telestesia, *f.*

teletype [ˈtelitaip] n. Teletipo, *m.* (teleprinter). ‖ Despacho, *m.* (message).

teletypewriter [teliˈtaipraitə*] n. U. S Teletipo, *m.*, teleimpresor, *m.*

televiewer [ˈtelivju:ə*] n. Telespectador, ra; televidente, *m.* & *f.*

televise [ˈtelivaiz] v. tr. Televisar.

television [ˈteli,viʒən] n. Televisión, *f.* (system): *colour television*, televisión en color. ‖ Televisor, *m.*, aparato (*m.*) de televisión (set). ‖ — *To watch television*, ver la televisión. ‖ *What is on television?*, ¿qué ponen en la televisión?

television broadcasting [—ˈbrɔ:dkɑ:stiŋ] n. Teledifusión, *f.*

television screen [—skri:n] n. Pantalla (*f.*) de televisión.

television set [—set] n. Televisor, *m.*, aparato (*m.*) de televisión.

telex [ˈteleks] n. Télex, *m.*

telex [ˈteleks] v. intr. Enviar un télex.

telfer [ˈtelfə*] n. U. S. Teleférico, *m.*

telferage [—ridʒ] n. U. S. Teleferaje, *m.*

tell* [tel] v. tr. Decir: *to tell the truth*, decir la verdad; *to tell s.o. the time*, decir la hora a alguien; *promise you won't tell my mother?*, ¿me promete que no se lo dirá a mi madre?; *I can't tell which is best*, no puedo decir cuál es mejor; *I told him not to do it*, le dije que no lo hiciera. ‖ Comunicar (formally): *to tell s.o. a piece of news*, comunicar una noticia a alguien. ‖ Contar: *to tell a story, a joke*, contar una historia, un chiste; *he told me everything that had happened*, me contó todo lo que había pasado. ‖ Divulgar, contar, revelar: *to tell a secret*, divulgar un secreto. ‖ Mandar, ordenar: *he was told to get his hair cut*, le mandaron que se cortase el pelo. ‖ Señalar, indicar: *the arrows tell you which route to follow*, las flechas le indican el camino que hay que seguir. ‖ Ver, notar: *one can tell she is not English*, se nota que no es inglesa; *you can tell it's winter*, se ve que estamos en invierno. ‖ Reconocer, identificar: *you can tell him by his beard*, se le puede reconocer por la barba. ‖ Distinguir: *to tell margarine from butter*, distinguir la margarina de la mantequilla; *to be able to tell right from wrong*, saber distinguir el bien del mal. ‖ Saber: *no one can tell what the future may bring*, nadie sabe lo que el futuro nos deparará; *you never can tell*, nunca se sabe. ‖ Deducir: *I couldn't tell much from what he said*, de lo que dijo no pude deducir gran cosa. ‖ Contar (to count). ‖ — *All told*, en total (in total), mirándolo bien (all things considered). ‖ *He won't be very pleased about it, I can tell you!*, ¡te aseguro que no va a estar muy contento! ‖ *I am glad* o *pleased to tell you that ...*, tengo el placer de comunicarle que... ‖ *I can't begin to tell you* o *I can't tell you how grateful I am*, no encuentro palabras para decirle lo agradecido que estoy. ‖ *I don't want to have to tell you twice*, no quiero tener que repetírselo dos veces. ‖ *I have been told that ...*, me han dicho que... ‖ *I hear tell that ...*, dicen que ... ‖ *I tell you what: let's drop the whole matter*, mira, no hablemos más del asunto. ‖ *I tell you what: let's go out for dinner*, se me ocurre una idea, ¿por qué no vamos a cenar? ‖ *I told you so!*, ¡ya te lo dije! ‖ *Tell me all about it*, cuéntamelo todo. ‖ FAM. *Tell me another!* o *tell that to the marines!*, ¡cuéntaselo a tu abuela!, ¡a otro perro con ese hueso! ‖ *To tell one's beads*, rezar el rosario. ‖ *To tell s.o.'s fortune*, echar la buenaventura a alguien. ‖ FAM. *To tell s.o. where to get off*, poner a alguien en su sitio. ‖ *To tell the time*, dar la hora (a clock), leer el reloj: *a child who is learning to tell the time*, un niño que está aprendiendo a leer el reloj. ‖ *To tell you the truth*, a decir verdad.
— V. intr. Relatar, contar (to relate). ‖ Notarse: *his age is beginning to tell*, la edad se le está empezando a notar. ‖ Influir: *the boxer's experience told in his favour*, la experiencia del boxeador influyó en su favor. ‖ Producir *or* tener su efecto: *every word told*, cada palabra tuvo su efecto. ‖ — FAM. *Please don't tell*, por favor no digas nada a nadie. ‖ *Quality always tells*, la calidad siempre se ve. ‖ *To hear tell of*, oír hablar de. ‖ *You are telling me!*, ¡a quién se lo vas a contar!, ¡a mí me lo vas a contar! ‖ *You never can tell*, nunca se puede decir.
— **To tell against**, perjudicar: *his record told against him*, su historial le perjudicó. ‖ **To tell of**, hablar de, contar: *he told me of his worries*, me habló de sus preocupaciones. | Anunciar: *the dark clouds told of a rainstorm*, las nubes oscuras anunciaban tormenta. ‖ **To tell off**, designar: *to tell off four men for a duty*, designar a cuatro hombres para un trabajo. | FAM. Regañar, reñir (to rebuke, especially children). | Echar una bronca a (to rebuke forcefully). ‖ **To tell on**, afectar a: *the fast pace began to tell on the runners*, el paso rápido empezó a afectar a los corredores. | Delatar, denunciar (to report the misdeeds of).
— OBSERV. Pret. & p. p. **told**.

teller [—ə*] n. Narrador, ra (who tells a story). ‖ Cajero, ra (in a bank). ‖ Escrutador, ra (who counts votes).

telling [—iŋ] adj. Eficaz, contundente: *a telling argument*, un argumento eficaz. ‖ Contundente: *a telling blow*, un golpe contundente. ‖ Expresivo, va; revelador, ra: *a telling look*, una mirada expresiva.
— N. Narración, *f.*, relato, *m.* (of a story). ‖ Divulgación, *f.* (of a secret). ‖ Recuento, *m.* (of votes). ‖ — *That's telling!*, ¡es un secreto! ‖ *There is no telling what will happen*, es imposible saber lo que va a pasar.

telling off [—iŋɔf] n. Reprimenda, *f.*, bronca, *f.*

telltale [—teil] adj. Revelador, ra. ‖ TECH. *Telltale light*, indicador luminoso.
— N. Soplón, ona; chivato, ta (person who informs). ‖ MAR. Axiómetro, *m.* (to show position of rudder). ‖ TECH. Indicador, *m.*

tellurian [teˈljuəriən] adj. Telúrico, ca.
— N. Terrícola, *m.* & *f.*

telluric [teˈljuərik] adj. Telúrico, ca.

tellurium [teˈljuəriəm] n. CHEM. Telurio, *m.*

telly [ˈteli] n. FAM. Tele, *f.* (television).

telodynamic [ˈteləudaiˈnæmik] adj. Teledinámico, ca.

telpher [ˈtelfə*] n. Teleférico, *m.*

telpherage [—ridʒ] n. Teleferaje, *m.*

temblor [ˈtemblə*] n. U. S. Temblor (*m.*) de tierra (earthquake).

temerarious [,teməˈrɛəriəs] adj. Temerario, ria.

temerity [tiˈmeriti] n. Temeridad, *f.*

temper [ˈtempə*] n. TECH. Temple, *m.* (of a metal, glass, clay, etc.). ‖ Cólera, *f.*, ira, *f.* (anger): *a fit of temper*, un ataque de furia. ‖ Genio, *m.*, mal genio, *m.* (tendency to become angry): *he has a temper*, tiene genio. ‖ Temperamento, *m.*, disposición, *f.* (disposition, character): *to have an equable temper*, tener un temperamento ecuánime. ‖ Humor, *m.* (mood): *to be in a good temper*, estar de buen humor. ‖ — *Out of temper*, de mal genio. ‖ *To get into* o *to fly into a temper*, montar en cólera, ponerse furioso. ‖ *To get s.o.'s temper up*, enfadar a alguien, poner furioso a alguien. ‖ *To keep one's temper*, contenerse. ‖ *To lose one's temper*, ponerse de malhumor, enfadarse, perder los estribos. ‖ *To show temper*, estar de malhumor. ‖ *To try s.o.'s temper*, probar la paciencia de uno.

temper [ˈtempə*] v. tr. TECH. Templar (glass, steel, etc.). ‖ Amasar (mortar). ‖ ARTS. Templar. ‖ FIG. Templar, suavizar (to make less harsh). ‖ MUS. Afinar, templar.
— V. intr. Templarse.

tempera [ˈtempərə] n. Pintura (*f.*) al temple.

temperament [ˈtempərəmənt] n. Temperamento, *m.*: *nervous, artistic temperament*, temperamento nervioso, artístico. ‖ Sensibilidad, *f.* (sensitivity). ‖ Genio, *m.* (temper). ‖ MUS. Temperamento, *m.*

temperamental [,tempərəˈmentl] adj. Temperamental, del temperamento (of the temperament). ‖ Inestable, caprichoso, sa; inconstante (person). ‖ *A temperamental machine*, una máquina caprichosa.

temperance [ˈtempərəns] n. Templanza, *f.*, sobriedad, *f.*, moderación, *f.* ‖ Abstinencia (*f.*) de bebidas alcohólicas (abstinence from alcohol).

temperate [ˈtempərit] adj. Templado, da; moderado, da. ‖ GEOGR. *Temperate zone*, zona templada.

temperateness [—nis] n. Templanza, *f.*

temperature [ˈtempritʃə*] n. Temperatura, *f.*: *maximum temperature*, temperatura máxima. ‖ MED. Fiebre, *f.*, calentura, *f.*, temperatura, *f.*: *to have a temperature*, tener fiebre. ‖ — *Absolute temperature*, temperatura absoluta. ‖ *Critical temperature*, temperatura crítica. ‖ MED. *Temperature chart*, gráfico (*m.*) de la temperatura. ‖ *Temperature recorder*, registrador (*m.*) de temperatura.

tempered [ˈtempəd] adj. Dispuesto, ta (having a specified temper). ‖ Templado, da.

temperer [ˈtempərə*] n. TECH. Templador, *m.* ‖ Mezcladora, *f.* (of mortar).

tempering [ˈtempəriŋ] n. TECH. Templadura, *f.* ‖ MUS. Temple, *m.*

tempest [ˈtempist] n. Tempestad, *f.*

tempestuous [temˈpestjuəs] adj. Tempestuoso, sa (weather). ‖ FIG. Tempestuoso, sa; borrascoso, sa (meeting, etc.).

Templar [ˈtemplə*] n. HIST. Templario, *m.* ‖ Abogado (*m.*) del "Temple" (barrister).

template [ˈtemplet] n. TECH. Plantilla, *f.* (metal or wooden pattern). ‖ MAR. Gálibo, *m.*

temple [ˈtempl] n. REL. Templo, *m.* ‖ ANAT. Sien, *f.* (of the head). ‖ — HIST. *Knights of the Temple*, caballeros (*m.*) del Temple, templarios, *m.* ‖ JUR.

The Temple, Colegio (*m.*) de Abogados de Londres.
templet [ˈtemplit] n. See TEMPLATE.
tempo [ˈtempəu] n. MUS. Tempo, *m.*, compás, *m.* || FIG. Ritmo, *m.*: *the tempo of production decreases in winter*, el ritmo de la producción disminuye en invierno.

— OBSERV. El plural de la palabra inglesa *tempo* es *tempi* o *tempos*.

temporal [ˈtempərəl] adj. ANAT. GRAMM. PHIL. Temporal. || REL. Temporal, secular. || — *Temporal and spatial existence*, existencia (*f.*) en el tiempo y en el espacio. || ANAT. *Temporal bone*, temporal, *m.*
temporality [ˌtempəˈræliti] n. Temporalidad, *f.*, carácter (*m.*) temporal. || — Pl. REL. Temporalidades, *f.* (revenues).
temporarily [ˈtempərərili] adv. Temporalmente.
temporary [ˈtempərəri] adj. Temporal, provisional: *temporary job*, trabajo temporal; *temporary arrangement*, arreglo provisional. || Transitorio, ria: *temporary measures*, medidas transitorias. || Temporero, ra (worker). || Interino, na (officer).
temporization [ˌtempəraiˈzeiʃən] n. Contemporización, *f.*
temporize [ˈtempəraiz] v. intr. Contemporizar, temporizar.
temporizer [—ə*] n. Contemporizador, ra.
tempt [tempt] v. tr. Tentar, seducir: *to tempt s.o. with money*, tentar a alguien con dinero. || Incitar, inducir, tentar: *to tempt s.o. into doing sth.*, inducir a alguien a hacer algo, incitar a alguien para que haga algo. || — *Can I tempt you to a glass of wine?*, ¿te puedo ofrecer un vaso de vino? || *I am sorely tempted to sell up and leave*, tengo muchas ganas de venderlo todo y marcharme. || *To let o.s. be tempted*, ceder a la tentación. || FIG. *To tempt providence*, tentar a Dios. | *To tempt the devil*, tentar al diablo.
temptation [tempˈteiʃən] n. Tentación, *f.*: *to fall into temptation*, caer en la tentación; *to yield to temptation*, ceder a la tentación. || — REL. *Lead us not into temptation*, no nos dejes caer en la tentación. || *There is always a temptation to do things quickly instead of well*, se suele tener tendencia a hacer las cosas rápidamente en lugar de hacerlas bien. || *To throw temptation in s.o.'s way*, exponer a alguien a la tentación.
tempter [ˈtemptə*] n. Tentador, *m.*
tempting [ˈtemptiŋ] adj. Tentador, ra; atractivo, va: *a tempting proposal*, una propuesta tentadora. || Apetitoso, sa (food).
temptingly [—li] adv. De modo tentador. || Atractivamente. || *A temptingly prepared meal*, una comida apetitosa.
temptress [ˈtemptris] n. Tentadora, *f.*
ten [ten] adj. Diez: *ten people*, diez personas. || REL. *The Ten Commandments*, los Diez Mandamientos.
— N. Diez, *m.* (number, card, figure). || — Pl. MATH. Columna (*f. sing.*) de las decenas (column of figures). || — *It's ten past ten*, son las diez y diez. || *Ten o'clock*, las diez. || *Tens of thousands of people*, decenas de miles de personas. || *To count in tens*, contar de diez en diez.
tenability [ˌtenəˈbiliti] n. Valor, *m.*, validez, *f.* (of an argument). || *A post of limited tenability*, un puesto que se puede ocupar sólo por cierto período de tiempo.
tenable [ˈtenəbl] adj. Defendible (against attack). || Sostenible (opinions). || *Post tenable for one year*, puesto (*m.*) que se puede ocupar durante un año.
tenacious [tiˈneiʃəs] adj. Tenaz (obstinate). || Firme: *tenacious beliefs*, creencias firmes. || Adhesivo, va (adhesive). || Retentivo, va: *a tenacious memory*, una memoria retentiva. || *To be tenacious of one's opinion*, aferrarse a su opinión.
tenaciousness [—nis] or **tenacity** [tiˈnæsiti] n. Tenacidad, *f.*
tenail or **tenaille** [tiˈneil] n. MIL. Tenallón, *m.*
tenancy [ˈtenənsi] n. Tenencia, *f.* (holding). || Arrendamiento, *m.*, arriendo, *m.* (lease of land). || Alquiler, *m.*, arrendamiento, *m.* (lease of a house).
tenant [ˈtenənt] n. Arrendatario, ria (on renting land). || Inquilino, na; arrendatario, ria (one renting property). || Habitante, *m.* & *f.*, ocupante, *m.* & *f.* (inhabitant).
tenant [ˈtenənt] v. tr. Arrendar, tener en arriendo (land). || Alquilar, arrendar (houses, etc.).
tenantable [—əbl] adj. Habitable. || Arrendable.
tenant farmer [—ˈfɑːmə*] n. Arrendatario, *m.*
tenantry [ˈtenəntri] n. Arrendatarios, *m. pl.* (tenants of land). || Inquilinos, *m. pl.* (tenants of a house). || Tenencia, *f.* (holding). || Arriendo, *m.*, arrendamiento, *m.* (lease).
tench [tenʃ] n. Tenca, *f.* (fish).
tend [tend] v. tr. Cuidar, atender, ocuparse de (a sick person, etc.). || Cuidar, vigilar (stock). || Cuidar, cultivar (a garden). || Manejar, servir (a machine). || (Ant.). Servir (to wait on). || MAR. Vigilar (a cable).
— V. intr. Tender, tener tendencia a: *she tends to eat too much*, tiende a comer demasiado; *the car tends to stall*, el coche tiene tendencia a calarse; *history tends to repeat itself*, la historia tiende a repetirse. || Tender, encaminarse: *a situation tending towards anarchy*, una situación que tiende hacia la anarquía. || Contribuir (to contribute). || Tirar: *yellow tending to orange*, amarillo que tira a naranja. || Dirigirse: *the road tends towards the coast*, la carretera se dirige hacia la costa. || — *I tend to agree*, casi comparto su opinión. || *I tend to disagree*, no puedo compartir completamente su opinión. || *It tends to rain in April*, suele llover en abril. || *To tend to*, cuidar de *or* a: *to tend to the baby*, cuidar al niño.
tendencious [tenˈdenʃəs] adj. U. S. Tendencioso, sa.
tendency [ˈtendənsi] n. Tendencia, *f.* || *There is a tendency for prices to increase* o *prices have a tendency to increase*, los precios tienden a subir, los precios tienen tendencia a subir.
tendentious [tenˈdenʃəs] adj. Tendencioso, sa.
tendentiousness [—nis] n. Lo tendencioso, carácter (*m.*) tendencioso.
tender [ˈtendə*] adj. Frágil, delicado, da (easily damaged): *a tender plant*, una planta delicada. || Tierno, na: *a tender steak*, un filete tierno; *a tender age*, una edad tierna. || Cariñoso, sa; dulce: *a tender smile*, una sonrisa cariñosa. || Afectuoso, sa; cariñoso, sa; tierno, na: *tender work*, palabras cariñosas. || Compasivo, va (quick to feel compassion). || Delicado, da: *tender feet*, pies delicados. || Sensible (sensitive): *a tender heart*, un corazón sensible. || Sensible, susceptible: *a tender person is easily upset*, una persona sensible se molesta fácilmente. || Delicado, da: *a tender subject*, un asunto delicado. || Suave (colour). || Dolorido, da (painful). || — *It is still tender*, sigue doliéndome. || *Tender of* o *over* o *upon*, solícito con.
— N. Vigilante, *m.* & *f.* (person who tends). || MAR. Buque (*m.*) nodriza (for fuel). | Bote, *m.* (for general purposes). || Ténder, *m.* (of a locomotive). || COMM. Oferta, *f.*, propuesta, *f.* (formal offer). || JUR. Oferta (*f.*) de pago (to meet an obligation). || — *Legal tender*, curso (*m.*) legal: *to be legal tender*, tener curso legal. || COMM. *To put a piece of work out to tender* o *to invite tenders for a piece of work*, sacar una obra a contrata *or* a licitación. | *To put in a tender for a piece of work*, hacer una oferta para realizar una obra.
tender [ˈtendə*] v. tr. Presentar, ofrecer: *to tender one's resignation*, presentar la dimisión. || JUR. Presentar (evidence). | Ofrecer en pago (in order to meet an obligation). || Enternecer (to soften). || — *Please tender the exact fare*, se ruega moneda fraccionaria. || *To tender one's apologies*, pedir disculpas. || *To tender one's thanks*, dar las gracias.
— V. intr. Hacer una oferta: *to tender for a piece of work*, hacer una oferta para una obra. || Enternecerse (to soften).
tenderfoot [—fut] n. Novato, *m.* || Recién llegado, *m.* (newcomer).

— OBSERV. El plural es *tenderfeet* o *tenderfoots*.

tenderhearted [—ˈhɑːtid] adj. Compasivo, va (compassionate). || Bondadoso, sa (kind). || Susceptible.
tenderize [ˈtendəraiz] v. tr. Ablandar.
tenderloin [ˈtendəlɔin] n. CULIN. Filete, *m.*
tenderly [ˈtendəli] adv. Tiernamente, con ternura.
tenderness [ˈtendənis] n. Lo tierno (of meat). || Ternura, *f.* (affection). || Dulzura, *f.*, cariño, *m.* (of smile, words, etc.). || Sensibilidad, *f.* (sensitivity). || Lo delicado (of a subject, etc.).
tending [ˈtendiŋ] adj. Tendente, tendiente, encaminado, da (*to*, a).
tendinous [ˈtendinəs] adj. Tendinoso, sa.
tendon [ˈtendən] n. ANAT. Tendón, *m.* || *Achilles' tendon*, tendón de Aquiles.
tendril [ˈtendril] n. Zarcillo, *m.* (plant).
Tenebrae [ˈtenibriː] pl. n. REL. Tinieblas, *f.*
tenebrous [ˈtenibrəs] adj. Tenebroso, sa.
tenement [ˈtenimənt] n. JUR. Propiedad, *f.* || Casa (*f.*) de vecindad (tenement house). || Vivienda, *f.*, casa, *f.*, piso, *m.* (flat).
tenement house [—haus] n. Casa (*f.*) de vecindad.
tenesmus [təˈnezməs] n. MED. Pujo, *m.*
tenet [ˈtiːnet] n. Principio, *m.* || Dogma, *m.*
tenfold [ˈtenfəuld] adj. Décuplo, pla.
— Adv. Diez veces.
tenia [ˈtiːniə] n. ZOOL. Tenia, *f.*
teniafuge [ˈtinifjuːdʒ] adj. Tenífugo, ga.
— N. Tenífugo, *m.*
tennis [ˈtenis] n. SP. Tenis, *m.* || *Table tennis*, tenis de mesa, ping-pong, *m.*
tennis court [—kɔːt] n. SP. Tenis, *m.*, campo (*m.*) de tenis [*Amer.*, cancha (*f.*) de tenis].
tennis elbow [—ˈelbəu] n. MED. Calambre (*m.*) en el codo.
tennis player [—ˌpleiə*] n. SP. Tenista, *m.* & *f.*
tennis shoes [—ʃuːz] n. Zapatos (*m.*) de lona *or* de tenis.
tenon [ˈtenən] n. TECH. Espiga, *f.*, macho, *m.*, barbilla, *f.*
tenon [ˈtenən] v. tr. TECH. Espigar (to shape to fit in a mortise). | Ensamblar a espiga (to join).
tenor [ˈtenə*] n. Curso, *m.*: *the tenor of events*, el curso de los acontecimientos. || Contenido, *m.*, tenor, *m.* (of a document). || Significado, *m.* (sense). || Tono, *m.* (general drift): *the general tenor of the conversation*, el tono general de la conversación. || JUR. Copia (*f.*) conforme (exact copy). || COMM. Plazo, *m.* (term). || MUS. Tenor, *m.*
— Adj. MUS. De tenor: *a tenor voice*, una voz de tenor. || Tenor: *tenor saxophone*, saxofón tenor.

tenpence [ˊtenpəns] n. Diez peniques, *m. pl.*
tenpin [ˊtenpin] n. Bolo, *m.* (skittle). || — Pl. Bolos, *m.* (game). || *Tenpin bowling*, bolos, *m. pl.*
tenrec [ˊtenrek] n. ZOOL. Tenrec, *m.*, tanrec, *m.*
tense [tens] adj. Tenso, sa: *a tense situation*, una situación tensa. || Nervioso, sa (nervous). || Tenso, sa; tieso, sa; tirante; estirado, da (stretched tight).
— N. GRAMM. Tiempo, *m.*: *past, future tense*, tiempo pasado, futuro.
tense [tens] v. tr. Tensar, poner en tensión: *to tense one's muscles*, tensar los músculos.
tenseness [—nis] n. Tensión, *f.*, tirantez, *f.*
tensible [ˊtensibl] adj. Extensible, capaz de tensión.
tensile [ˊtensail] adj. Extensible (able to be extended). || Tensor, ra (exerting tension). || De tensión (pertaining to tension). || PHYS. *Tensile strength*, resistencia (*f.*) a la tracción.
tension [ˊtenʃən] n. PHYS. ELECTR. Tensión, *f.*: *surface tension*, tensión superficial; *high-tension cable*, cable de alta tensión. || Tracción, *f.* (force causing extension of a body): *to subject a beam to tension*, someter una viga a una tracción. || Tensión, *f.*, tirantez, *f.* (state of being tensed): *tension in a rope*, tensión de una cuerda. || Tensión, *f.*: *nervous tension*, tensión nerviosa. || Tensión, *f.*: *tension between two countries*, tensión entre dos países. || Tirantez, *f.*, tensión, *f.* (between friends, etc.). || *Racial tension*, tensiones raciales.
tensional [—əl] adj. De tensión.
tensor [ˊtensə*] n. ANAT. MATH. Tensor, *m.*
tent [tent] n. Tienda (*f.*) de campaña, tienda, *f.* [*Amer.*, carpa, *f.*] (for camping, etc.): *to pitch a tent*, armar una tienda de campaña. || MED. Mecha, *f.* (for keeping wounds open). | Tienda, *f.*, cámara, *f.*: *oxygen tent*, tienda de oxígeno.
tent [tent] v. tr. Alojar en tiendas (to lodge in tents). || Suministrar tiendas a (to supply with tents). || Cubrir con un toldo. || MED. Mantener abierto con una mecha (to keep open with a tent).
— V. intr. Vivir en tienda.
tentacle [ˊtentəkl] n. Tentáculo, *m.*
tentacled [—d] adj. Tentaculado, da.
tentacular [tenˊtækjulə*] adj. Tentacular.
tentaculate [tenˊtækjulet] adj. Tentaculado, da.
tentative [ˊtentətiv] adj. Provisional [*Amer.*, provisorio, ria]: *a tentative arrangement*, un arreglo provisional. || De tanteo: *a tentative offer*, una oferta de tanteo. || Indeciso, sa; vacilante (hesitant).
— N. Tentativa, *f.*
tentatively [—li] adv. Provisionalmente [*Amer.*, provisoriamente]: *an outing tentatively arranged for Saturday*, una excursión que se ha previsto provisionalmente para el sábado. || Como tanteo. || Con indecisión (hesitantly).
tented [ˊtentid] adj. Con toldos, entoldado, da.
tenter [ˊtentə*] n. Bastidor, *m.* (for cloth).
tenterhook [—huk] n. Gancho (*m.*) de bastidor. || — FIG. *To be on tenterhooks*, estar sobre ascuas. | *To have* o *to keep s.o. on tenterhooks*, tener a alguien sobre ascuas.
tenth [tenθ] adj. Décimo, ma.
— N. Décimo, ma (in a series): *Louis X* (*the tenth*), Luis X [décimo]. || Décimo, *m.*, décima parte, *f.* (part). || Diez, *m.*, día (*m.*) diez: *he is coming on the tenth*, viene el día diez.
tentmaker [ˊtentˏmeikə*] n. Tendero, *m.*
tent peg [ˊtentpeg] n. Estaca, *f.*
tent pole [ˊtentpəul] n. Mástil (*m.*) de tienda.
tenuiroster [tenjuiˊrɔstə*] n. Tenuirrostro, *m.* (bird).
tenuirostres [tenjuiˊrɔstri:z] pl. n. Tenuirrostros, *m.*
tenuity [teˊnjuiti] n. Tenuidad, *f.* (flimsiness). || Delgadez, *f.* (slenderness). || Enrarecimiento, *m.* (of the air). || FIG. Pobreza, *f.* (meagreness): *the tenuity of his argument*, la pobreza de su argumento. | Sutileza, *f.* (of a distinction, etc.). | Sencillez, *f.* (of style).
tenuous [ˊtenjuəs] adj. Tenue, sutil (flimsy). || Delgado, da (thin). || Enrarecido, da; raro, ra (not dense). || FIG. Tenue, sutil (distinction). | Poco convincente, poco sólido, da; flojo, ja (argument). | Ligero, ra (connection). | Sencillo, lla (style).
tenuousness [—nis] n. See TENUITY.
tenure [ˊtenjuə*] n. Arrendamiento, *m.* (tenancy). || Posesión, *f.* (possession). || Ocupación, *f.*, ejercicio, *m.* (of an office). || *Land tenure*, tenencia (*f.*) de tierras.
teocalli [tiəˊkɑ:li] n. Teocali, *m.*
tepee [ˊti:pi:] n. Tepee, *m.*
tepid [ˊtepid] adj. Tibio, bia (lukewarm). || FIG. Poco cálido, da; poco caluroso, sa (reception). | Muy relativo, va (interest). | Poco entusiasta (lacking enthusiasm).
tepidity [teˊpiditi] or **tepidness** [ˊtepidnis] n. Tibieza, *f.* (temperature). || FIG. Falta (*f.*) de interés, falta (*f.*) de entusiasmo.
teponaxtle [tepəˊnɑ:stli] n. Teponascle, *m.* (Mexican drum).
tequila [tiˊki:lə] n. Tequila, *m. or f.* (drink). || Agave, *m.*, maguey, *m.* (plant).
teratology [terəˊtɔlədʒi] n. Teratología, *f.*
terbium [ˊtə:biəm] n. CHEM. Terbio, *m.*
terce [tə:s] n. REL. Tercia, *f.* (hour).
tercentenary [ˏtə:senˊti:nəri] or **tercentennial** [ˏtə:senˊti:njəl] adj. De tres siglos.
— N. Tricentenario, *m.*
tercet [ˊtə:sit] n. Terceto, *m.*
terebenthene [tereˊbenθi:n] n. Terebenteno, *m.*
terebinth [ˊterəbinθ] n. BOT. Terebinto, *m.*
terebinthaceae [ˏterəbinˊθɑ:sii] pl. n. BOT. Terebintáceas, *f.*
terebinthine [ˏterəˊbinθain] adj. De trementina.
Terence [ˊterəns] pr. n. Terencio, *m.*
Teresian [təˊrisiən] n. REL. Teresiana, *f.*
tergiversate [ˊtə:dʒivə:seit] v. intr. Cambiar de idea, cambiar de camisa (fam.) [to change allegiance]. || Usar evasivas (to avoid decisions or firm action).
tergiversation [ˏtə:dʒivə:ˊseiʃən] n. Cambio (*m.*) de idea, cambio (*m.*) de camisa (fam.) [change of allegiance]. || Evasión, *f.* (avoidance of decisions or firm action).
term [tə:m] n. Período, *m.*, plazo, *m.*, término, *m.* (period of time). || Período (*m.*) de validez (of an agreement, etc.). || COMM. Plazo, *m.* || Mandato, *m.* (of a prime minister, etc.). || Trimestre, *m.*: *the academic year has three terms*, el año académico tiene tres trimestres. || Curso, *m.*: *term begins on the second*, el curso empieza el día dos. || Término, *m.*, fin, *m.* (end): *to come to its term*, llegar a su término. || Término, *m.*, voz, *f.*, vocablo, *m.* (word): *technical, medical term*, término técnico, médico. || JUR. Período (*m.*) de sesiones (during which a court sits). || MATH. PHIL. GRAMM. ARCH. Término, *m.*: *to multiply two terms*, multiplicar dos términos. || — Pl. Condiciones, *f.* (conditions): *terms of payment*, condiciones de pago; *terms of an issue*, condiciones de una emisión; *you can name your own terms*, usted puede fijar las condiciones; *what are your terms?*, ¿cuáles son sus condiciones? || Términos, *m.* (terminology, words): *vague terms*, términos vagos; *terms of a contract, of a treaty*, términos de un contrato, de un tratado. || COMM. Tarifa, *f. sing.*, precios, *m.*: *special terms for children*, tarifa especial para niños. || Relaciones, *f.*, términos, *m.* (relationship): *to be on good terms with s.o.*, estar en buenas relaciones con alguien. || — MED. *Born after term*, tardío, a; nacido con retraso. | *Born before term*, prematuro, ra. || *In no uncertain terms*, claramente. || *In terms of*, por lo que se refiere a (as regards), en términos de: *to express X in terms of Y*, expresar X en términos de Y; en función de, desde el punto de vista de: *he sees everything in terms of profit*, ve todo en función del beneficio que puede producir. || *In the long term*, a la larga. || *In the short term*, en un futuro próximo. || COMM. *Long-term transaction*, operación (*f.*) a largo plazo. || *Not on any terms*, bajo ningún concepto. || COMM. *On easy terms*, con facilidades de pago. | *Short-term transaction*, operación (*f.*) a corto plazo. || *Terms of exchange*, términos del intercambio. || *Terms of reference*, mandato, *m.* || *Terms of trade*, términos del intercambio. || *To be on intimate terms with s.o.*, tener confianza con alguien. || *To be on the best of terms*, estar en muy buenos términos, ser muy amigos. || *To choose one's terms with care*, elegir sus palabras con cuidado. || *To come to terms with a situation*, aceptar una situación, adaptarse a una situación. || *To come to terms with s.o.*, llegar a un acuerdo con alguien, ponerse de acuerdo con alguien.
term [tə:m] v. tr. Llamar, calificar de (to call): *he termed it a scandal*, lo calificó de escándalo.
termagant [ˊtə:məgənt] n. Arpía, *f.*, fiera, *f.*, tarasca, *f.* (ferocious woman).
terminal [ˊtə:minl] adj. Terminal, final (of or forming the end). || De demarcación (forming a boundary). || Trimestral: *terminal examinations*, exámenes trimestrales. || BOT. Terminal (bud, etc.). || *Terminal station*, estación (*f.*) terminal.
— N. Extremidad, *f.*, extremo, *m.* (extremity). || ELECTR. Borne, *m.*, terminal, *m.* || Final (*m.*) de línea (of a bus, route). || Estación (*f.*) terminal, término, *m.* (of a railway). || AVIAT. MAR. Terminal, *f.*: *air terminal*, terminal aérea. || ARCH. Remate, *m.* (ornament). || Terminal, *m.* (of a computer).
terminate [ˊtə:mineit] v. tr. Concluir, finalizar, terminar.
— V. intr. Concluirse, terminarse.
termination [ˏtə:miˊneiʃən] n. Terminación, *f.* || *To bring to a termination*, poner término a.
terminological [ˏtə:minəˊlɔdʒikəl] adj. Terminológico, ca.
terminology [ˏtə:miˊnɔlədʒi] n. Terminología, *f.*
terminus [ˊtə:minəs] n. Final (*m.*) de línea (of a bus, route). || Estación (*f.*) terminal, término, *m.* (railway). || AVIAT. Terminal, *f.* || ARCH. Término, *m.*

— OBSERV. El plural de la palabra *terminus* es *termini* o *terminuses*.

termite [ˊtə:mait] n. Comején, *m.*, termita, *f.*, termite, *m.*, termes, *m.*
termless [ˊtə:mlis] adj. Ilimitado, da; sin fin.
termor [ˊtə:mə*] n. JUR. Poseedor (*m.*) por un plazo determinado *or* vitalicio.
termtime [ˊtə:mtaim] n. U. S. Trimestre, *m.* (at school). | Período (*m.*) de sesiones (of a court).
tern [tə:n] n. Golondrina (*f.*) de mar (bird). || Terno, *m.* (in lottery).
ternary [ˊtə:nəri] adj. Ternario, ria. || Tercero, ra (third). || MUS. *Ternary form*, compás ternario.

ternate [ˈtə:neit] adj. BOT. Trifoliado, da.
terpene [ˈtə:pi:n] n. Terpeno, *m.*
Terpsichore [tə:pˈsikəri] pr. n. MYTH. Terpsícore, *f.*
terpsichorean [ˌtə:psikəˈriən] adj. Coreográfico, ca.
terrace [ˈterəs] n. Terraza, *f.* (balcony, open area). || Azotea, *f.* (flat roof). || AGR. Terraza, *f.*, bancal, *m.* || Terraplén, *m.* (raised embankment). || Hilera (*f.*) de casas (row of houses). || Arriate, *m.* (of flowers). || — Pl. SP. Gradas, *f.*
terrace [ˈterəs] v. tr. Formar terrazas en (to make terraces in). || Poner terraza a (to add a terrace to). || Terraplenar (to embank). || AGR. Disponer en bancales.
terraced [—t] adj. Colgante (garden).
terra-cotta [ˈterəˈkɔtə] n. Terracota, *f.* (pottery and statue). | Ladrillo, *m.* (colour).
— Adj. Ladrillo (brownish-red). || De terracota (made of terra-cotta).
terra firma [terəˈfə:mə] n. Tierra (*f.*) firme.
terrain [ˈterein] n. Terreno, *m.*
terramycin [ˌterəˈmaisin] n. MED. Terramicina, *f.*
terrane [teˈrein] n. GEOL. Terreno, *m.*
terrapin [ˈterəpin] n. Tortuga (*f.*) acuática.
terraqueous [teˈreikwiəs] adj. Terráqueo, a.
terrazzo [teˈrætsəu] n. Terrazo, *m.*
terrene [teˈri:n] adj. Terrenal.
terreplein [ˈtɛə:plein] n. MIL. Terraplén, *m.*
terrestrial [tiˈrestriəl] adj. Terrestre.
— N. Terrícola, *m.* & *f.*
terrible [ˈterəbl] adj. Terrible (terrifying). || Atroz: *terrible vengeance, pain*, venganza, dolor atroz. || FAM. Terrible (excessive): *terrible heat*, calor terrible; *terrible prices*, precios terribles. | Fatal, malísimo, ma; horrible (bad): *an absolutely terrible book*, un libro francamente fatal. || FAM. *We had a terrible time*, lo pasamos fatal.
terribly [—i] adv. Terriblemente (terrifyingly). || FAM. Terriblemente, enormemente, tremendamente, extraordinariamente (extremely): *a terribly cold night*, una noche terriblemente fría. | Malísimamente (badly): *he writes terribly*, escribe malísimamente. || — FAM. *It really has been terribly nice of you to bring me home*, ha sido realmente muy amable por su parte llevarme a casa. | *Terribly good*, buenísimo.
terricolous [teˈrikələs] adj. Terrícola.
terrier [ˈteriə*] n. Terrier, *m.* (dog).
terrific [təˈrifik] adj. Terrorífico, ca; terrífico, ca; terrible (terrifying). || FAM. Terrible (very bad): *a terrific scandal*, un escándalo terrible. | Tremendo, da (great): *he does a terrific amount of work*, hace una cantidad tremenda de trabajo. | Enorme (very big): *a terrific building*, un edificio enorme. | Fenómeno, na; estupendo, da; fabuloso, sa; bárbaro, ra; extraordinario, ria (very good): *his new play is terrific*, su nueva comedia es estupenda.
terrifically [—əli] adv. Terriblemente (terrifyingly). || FAM. Enormemente, tremendamente, terriblemente (extremely): *terrifically tired*, terriblemente cansado. | Muy bien, maravillosamente (very well): *he sings terrifically*, canta maravillosamente. || — FAM. *Terrifically bad*, malísimo, ma. | *Terrifically nice*, simpatiquísimo, tremendamente simpático.
terrify [ˈterifai] v. tr. Aterrorizar, aterrar.
terrifying [—iŋ] adj. Espantoso, sa.
terrigenous [teˈridʒinəs] adj. Terrígeno, na.
territorial [ˌteriˈtɔ:riəl] adj. Territorial (of a territory). || Regional (of a region). || Jurisdiccional, territorial: *territorial waters*, aguas jurisdiccionales. || MIL. *Territorial army*, segunda reserva.
— N. Soldado (*m.*) de la segunda reserva.
territoriality [ˌteriˌtɔ:riˈæliti] n. Territorialidad, *f.*
territory [ˈteritəri] n. Territorio, *m.*: *on Spanish territory*, en territorio español; *overseas territories*, territorios de ultramar. || SP. Campo, *m.*, terreno, *m.* (either half of the playing area). || COMM. Zona, *f.*, región, *f.* (of a commercial traveller). || Región, *f.*, territorio, *m.* (large tract of country). || FIG. Competencia, *f.*: *that's outside my territory*, esto no es de mi competencia. | Sector, *m.*, esfera, *f.*, campo, *m.*
terror [ˈterə*] n. Terror, *m.*, espanto, *m.*, pánico, *m.* (great fear): *to spread terror*, sembrar el terror. || Terror, *m.* (person, thing). || — FAM. *A terror of a child*, un niño terrible. || HIST. *The Terror*, el Terror (in the French Revolution).
terrorism [—rizəm] n. Terrorismo, *m.*
terrorist [—rist] n. Terrorista, *m.* & *f.*
terrorize [ˈterəraiz] v. tr. Aterrorizar, aterrar.
terror-stricken [ˈterəˈstrikən] adj. Sobrecogido por el terror, aterrorizado, da.
terry [ˈteri] n. Felpa, *f.*, tela (*f.*) de rizo, esponja, *f.*
terry cloth [—klɔθ] n. Felpa, *f.*, tela (*f.*) de rizo, esponja, *f.*
terse [tə:s] adj. Conciso, sa; sucinto, ta.
tersely [—li] adv. Concisamente (concisely).
terseness [—nis] n. Concisión, *f.* (conciseness).
tertian [ˈtə:ʃiən] adj. Terciana (fever).
— N. Terciana, *f.*, fiebre (*f.*) terciana.
tertiary [ˈtə:ʃiəri] adj. Tercero, ra (third). || GEOL. Terciario, ria.
— N. REL. Terciario, ria. || GEOL. *The Tertiary*, el Terciario.
Tertullian [tə:ˈtʌliən] pr. n. Tertuliano, *m.*
tervalent [tə:ˈveilənt] adj. CHEM. Trivalente.
Terylene [ˈterəlin] n. Terylene, *m.*
tessellate (U. S. **tesselate**) [ˈtesileit] v. tr. Hacer un mosaico de (to make into a mosaic). || Decorar con mosaicos (to decorate with mosaic).
tessellated (U. S. **tesselated**) [—id] adj. De mosaico.
tessellation (U. S. **tesselation**) [ˌtesiˈleiʃən] n. Mosaico, *m.*
tessitura [ˌtesiˈtu:rə] n. MUS. Tesitura, *f.*
test [test] n. Prueba, *f.*: *a test of s.o.'s friendship*, una prueba de la amistad de alguien; *test flight*, vuelo de prueba; *to put to the test*, poner a prueba; *to stand the test*, pasar la prueba; *endurance test*, prueba de resistencia; *nuclear tests*, pruebas nucleares. || "Test", *m.*, prueba, *f.*: *intelligence test*, "test" de inteligencia. || MED. Análisis, *m.*: *blood, urine test*, análisis de sangre, de orina. || Examen, *m.*, prueba, *f.* (in school, university): *end of term tests*, exámenes trimestrales; *English test*, examen de inglés. || Piedra (*f.*) de toque (criterion). || CHEM. Prueba, *f.*, ensayo, *m.*, experimento, *m.* | Reactivo, *m.* (reagent). || HIST. Copela, *f.* (cupel). || ZOOL. Caparazón, *m.*, concha, *f.* (shell or hard covering). || — FIG. *Acid test*, prueba decisiva. || *To stand the test of time*, resistir al paso del tiempo.
test [test] v. tr. Probar, someter a una prueba, poner a prueba: *to test a prototype*, probar un prototipo. || Examinar (to examine). || Poner un examen a (in school, etc.): *to test pupils in history*, poner un examen de historia a los alumnos. || Comprobar: *to test the weight of sth.*, comprobar el peso de algo. || Analizar: *to test the water in a river*, analizar el agua de un río. || MED. Hacer un análisis de (blood, etc.). || CHEM. Probar, ensayar. || Graduar (sight). || *To test sth. for acidity*, determinar el grado de acidez de algo.
testa [ˈtestə] n. BOT. Testa, *f.*

— OBSERV. El plural de la palabra inglesa es *testa* o *testae*

testacean [tesˈteiʃən] or **testaceous** [tesˈteiʃəs] adj. Testáceo, a.
testament [ˈtestəmənt] n. Testamento, *m.* (will). || — REL. *The New Testament*, el Nuevo Testamento. | *The Old Testament*, el Antiguo Testamento. || *To make one's testament*, testar, hacer testamento.
testamentary [ˌtestəˈmentəri] adj. Testamentario, ria.
testate [ˈtestit] adj. JUR. Testado, da.
— N. JUR. Testador, ra.
testator [tesˈteitə*] n. JUR. Testador, *m.*
testatrix [tesˈteitriks] n. JUR. Testadora, *f.*

— OBSERV. El plural de *testatrix* es *testatrices*.

test ban [ˈtestbæn] n. Suspensión (*f.*) de pruebas nucleares.
test bench [ˈtestbentʃ] n. Banco (*m.*) de pruebas.
test boring [ˈtestˈbɔ:riŋ] n. Sondeo, *m.*
test card [ˈtestkα:d] n. Carta (*f.*) de ajuste (television).
test case [ˈtestkeis] n. JUR. Juicio (*m.*) que hace jurisprudencia.
test chamber [ˈtestˈtʃeimbə*] n. Cámara (*f.*) de experimentos.
tester [ˈtestə*] n. Dosel, *m.* (of a four-poster bed). || Baldaquín, *m.*, baldaquino, *m.* (over an altar or pulpit). || Probador, ra; ensayador, ra (person).
testicle [ˈtestikl] n. ANAT. Testículo, *m.*
testicular [tesˈtikjulə*] adj. ANAT. Testicular.
testification [ˌtestifiˈkeiʃən] n. Testificación, *f.*
testifier [ˈtestifaiə*] n. Testigo, *m.* & *f.*
testify [ˈtestifai] v. tr. Revelar, demostrar, atestiguar, testimoniar: *his look testified his guilt*, su mirada revelaba su culpabilidad. || Declarar [bajo juramento], atestiguar: *he testified that he had not been there*, declaró que no había estado allí.
— V. intr. JUR. Declarar (to give evidence). || JUR. *To testify to sth.*, atestiguar algo.
testily [ˈtestili] adv. Malhumoradamente.
testimonial [ˌtestiˈməunjəl] n. Testimonio, *m.* (testimony). || Recomendación, *f.*, carta (*f.*) de recomendación (character reference). || Testimonio (*m.*) de gratitud (tribute). || REL. Testimoniales, *f. pl.*
— Adj. Testimonial.
testimony [ˈtestiməni] n. JUR. Testimonio, *m.*, atestación, *f.*, declaración, *f.* || — JUR. *In testimony whereof...*, en fe de lo cual... | *To bear testimony to sth.*, atestiguar algo. | *To be called in testimony*, ser llamado como testigo.
testiness [ˈtestinis] n. Irritabilidad, *f.*
testing ground [ˈtestiŋgraund] n. Zona (*f.*) de pruebas.
testis [ˈtestis] n. ANAT. Testículo, *m.*

— OBSERV. El plural de *testis* es *testes*.

test match [ˈtestmætʃ] n. SP. Partido (*m.*) internacional (in cricket).
testosterone [tesˈtɔstərəun] n. Testosterona, *f.*
test paper [ˈtestˈpeipə*] n. Examen, *m.* (in school, etc.). || CHEM. Papel (*m.*) indicador, papel (*m.*) reactivo.
test pilot [ˈtestˈpailət] n. AVIAT. Piloto (*m.*) de pruebas.
test tube [ˈtestˈtju:b] n. Tubo (*m.*) de ensayo.
test-tube [ˈtesttju:b] adj. *Test-tube baby*, niño nacido por inseminación artificial.
testy [ˈtesti] adj. Irritable. || Malhumorado, da.
tetanic [teˈtænik] adj. MED. Tetánico, ca.
tetanize [ˈtetənaiz] v. tr. Tetanizar.

tetanus [ˈtetənəs] n. MED. Tétanos, *m.*
tetany [ˈtetəni] n. MED. Tetania, *f.*
tetchy [ˈtetʃi] adj. Irritable, picajoso, sa.
tête-à-tête [ˈteitɑːˈteit] adj. Confidencial (conversation). || Íntimo, ma (dinner).
— N. Conversación (*f.*) a solas, conversación (*f.*) confidencial. || Confidente, *m.* (sofa).
— Adv. A solas (to talk). || En la intimidad (to dine).
— OBSERV. El plural del sustantivo *tête-à-tête* es *tête-à-têtes* o *têtes-à-têtes.*
tether [ˈteðə*] n. Ronzal, *m.* (rope for animals). || FIG. *At the end of one's tether,* hartísimo, ma (at the end of one's endurance), en las últimas (at the end of one's financial resources).
tether [ˈteðə*] v. tr. Atar [con un ronzal].
tetragonal [teˈtrægənəl] adj. MATH. Tetragonal.
tetrahedral [ˈtetrəˈhedrəl] adj. MATH. Tetraédrico, ca.
tetrahedron [ˈtetrəˈhedrən] n. MATH. Tetraedro, *m.*
— OBSERV. El plural de *tetrahedron* es *tetrahedra* o *tetrahedrons.*
tetralogy [teˈtrælədʒi] n. Tetralogía, *f.*
tetrameral [teˈtræmərəl] or **tetramerous** [teˈtræmərəs] n. BOT. ZOOL. Tetrámero, *m.*
tetrapod [ˈtetrəpɔd] adj. ZOOL. Tetrápodo, da.
— N. ZOOL. Tetrápodo, *m.*
tetrarch [ˈtiːtrɑːk] n. Tetrarca, *m.*
tetrarchate [—eit] n. Tetrarquía, *f.*
tetrarchy [—i] n. Tetrarquía, *f.*
tetrasyllabic [ˌtetrəsiˈlæbik] adj. Tetrasílabo, ba.
tetrasyllable [ˈtetrəˌsiləbl] n. Tetrasílabo, *m.*
tetravalent [tetrəˈveilənt] adj. CHEM. Tetravalente.
tetrode [ˈtetrəud] n. ELECTR. Tetrodo, *m.*
tetter [ˈtetə*] n. MED. Herpes, *m. pl.* || — MED. *Crusty tetter,* impétigo, *m.* | *Scaly tetter,* psoriasis, *f. inv.*
Tetuan [tetˈwɑːn] pr. n. GEOGR. Tetuán.
Teuton [ˈtjuːtən] adj./n. Teutón, ona.
Teutonic [tjuˈtɔnik] adj. Teutónico, ca.
— N. Teutónico, *m.* (language).
Texan [ˈteksən] adj./n. Tejano, na; texano, na.
Texas [ˈteksəs] pr. n. GEOGR. Tejas, *m.*, Texas, *m.*
text [tekst] n. Texto, *m.* || Tema, *m.*: *to keep to the text,* ceñirse al tema. || Libro (*m.*) de texto (textbook).
textbook [—buk] n. Libro (*m.*) de texto.
text hand [—hænd] n. PRINT. Letra (*f.*) gruesa.
textile [ˈtekstail] adj. Textil: *textile industry,* industria textil. || Tejido, da (woven).
— N. Textil, *m.*, tejido, *m.*
textual [ˈtekstjuəl] adj. Textual, literal (quotation, note). || En el texto, del texto (error).
textually [—i] adv. Textualmente.
textuary [ˈtekstjuəri] adj. Textual.
texture [ˈtekstʃə*] n. Textura, *f.* || FIG. Textura, *f.*, estructura, *f.*
Thai [tai] adj./n. Tailandés, esa.
Thailand [ˈtailænd] pr. n. GEOGR. Tailandia, *f.*
thalamus [ˈθæləməs] n. BOT. ANAT. Tálamo, *m.*: *optic thalamus,* tálamo óptico.
— OBSERV. El plural de *thalamus* es *thalami.*
thalassocracy [ˌθæləˈsɔkrəsi] n. Talasocracia, *f.*
thalassotherapy [ˈθæləsəˈθerəpi] n. MED. Talasoterapia, *f.*
Thales [ˈθeiliːz] pr. n. Tales, *m.*
Thalia [θəˈlaiə] n. MYTH. Talía, *f.*
thallium [ˈθæliəm] n. Talio, *m.* (metal).
thallophites [ˈθæləfaits] pl. n. BOT. Talofitas, *f.*
thallus [ˈθæləs] n. BOT. Talo, *m.*
— OBSERV. El plural de *thallus* es *thalluses* o *thalli.*
Thames [temz] pr. n. GEOGR. Támesis, *m.*
than [ðæn] conj. Que (in comparison of inequality): *this house is bigger than that one,* esta casa es más grande que aquélla; *I arrived earlier than he,* llegué más pronto que él. || De (with numbers): *more than twenty people,* más de veinte personas; *she is more than thirty,* tiene más de treinta años. || Cuando: *hardly had he arrived than the roof fell in,* apenas había llegado cuando se cayó el tejado. || Del que, de la que, de lo que: *more persons than needed,* más personas de las que se necesitaban; *it is more expensive than you thought,* es más caro de lo que pensabas. || — *Any person other than himself,* cualquier persona menos él, cualquier persona que no fuese él. || *It was no other than the Emperor,* era el mismo Emperador, era el Emperador en persona. || *More than once,* más de una vez. || *No other than,* nadie más que, nadie excepto: *no other than he can do it,* nadie excepto él lo puede hacer. || *Other than,* aparte de, fuera de: *other than that, I don't know what to say,* aparte de eso, no sé qué decir. || *Rather than,* antes que: *rather than walk home I would prefer to take the underground,* antes que ir a casa andando prefiero coger el metro.
thank [θæŋk] v. tr. Agradecer, dar las gracias: *I thank you for coming,* le doy las gracias por haber venido. || — *I will thank you to close the door,* le agradecería que cerrase la puerta. || *She has you to thank for that,* eso se lo tiene que agradecer a usted. || *Thank God!* o *thank heaven!* o *thank goodness!,* ¡gracias a Dios!, ¡a Dios gracias! || *Thank you,* gracias. || *Thank you very much,* muchas gracias. || FIG. *To have o.s. to thank,* tener la culpa.
thankful [—ful] adj. Agradecido, da: *I am thankful to you for that,* le estoy agradecido por ello. || — *How thankful I am for the central heating!,* ¡qué bien me viene la calefacción! || *To be thankful that,* alegrarse de que: *I am thankful that you could come,* me alegro de que haya podido venir.
thankfully [—fuli] adv. Con agradecimiento, agradecidamente, con gratitud.
thankfulness [—fulnis] n. Agradecimiento, *m.*, gratitud, *f.*
thankless [—lis] adj. Desagradecido, da; ingrato, ta (person). || Ingrato, ta; ímprobo, ba: *a thankless task,* una tarea ingrata.
thanklessness [—lisnis] n. Desagradecimiento, *m.*, ingratitud, *f.*
thank offering [—ˌɔfəriŋ] n. Acción (*f.*) de gracias.
thanks [—s] pl. n. Gracias, *f.*: *to give thanks to God,* dar gracias a Dios; *to give s.o. thanks,* dar las gracias a alguien; *thanks for telling me,* gracias por decírmelo. || — FIG. *I managed, but no thanks to you* o *small thanks to you,* me las arreglé pero no fue gracias a ti. || *Many thanks* o *thanks very much* o *thanks a lot,* muchas gracias. || *No thanks are needed!,* ¡de nada!, ¡no hay de qué! || FAM. *Thanks be!,* ¡menos mal! || *Thanks to,* gracias a: *thanks to your help, we were successful,* gracias a su ayuda, tuvimos éxito.
thanksgiving [ˈθæŋksˌgiviŋ] n. Acción (*f.*) de gracias. || U. S. *Thanksgiving Day,* día (*m.*) de acción de gracias [cuarto jueves de noviembre].
thankworthy [ˈθæŋkˌwɑːði] adj. Digno de agradecimiento.
that [ðæt] dem. adj. Ese, esa (at a relatively near distance in space and time): *give me that book* (*that you have in your hand*), dame ese libro [que tienes en la mano]; *those last five minutes were very unpleasant,* esos cinco últimos minutos fueron muy desagradables. || Aquel, aquella (further away in space and time): *this book is more interesting than that newspaper on the table,* este libro es más interesante que aquel periódico que está en la mesa; *at that time butter was cheap,* en aquella época la mantequilla era barata; *that accident you saw the other day,* aquel accidente que viste el otro día. || El, la; aquel, aquella que: *the more simple way is that employed by me,* la manera más sencilla es la empleada por mí *or* aquella que yo empleo. || — *I hate that pride of hers,* odio ese orgullo suyo. || *That one,* ése, ésa (at a relatively near distance in space and time), aquél, aquélla (further away in space and time). || *Those people who,* la gente que, aquella gente que.
— Dem. pron. Ése, ésa (relatively near in space and time): *that is my chair,* ésa es mi silla. || Aquél, aquélla (further away in space and time): *this war is worse than that was,* esta guerra es peor de lo que fue aquélla; *these hats are nicer than those,* estos sombreros son más bonitos que aquéllos. || Eso (neuter, relatively near in time and space): *that is a lie,* eso es mentira. || Aquello (neuter, further away in space and time): *of all that he said that was what annoyed me the most,* de todo lo que dijo aquello fue lo que más me molestó. || El, la, lo (followed by a relative pronoun or by "of"): *those who wish to go may do so,* los que quieran irse pueden hacerlo; *that which I say to you,* lo que os digo; *that of my friend,* el de mi amigo. || — *And all that,* y cosas por el estilo. || *And that's that!,* ¡y eso es todo! || *At that,* see AT. || *For all that,* a pesar de eso. || *How do you like that?,* ¿qué le parece? || *I am not one of those who,* no soy de los que. || *Is that you, Peter?,* ¿eres tú Pedro? || *Like that,* así: *he did it like that,* lo hizo así. || *That is* o *that is to say,* es decir, o sea. || *That is why I did it,* por eso lo hice. || *That I will!,* ¡ya lo creo!, ¡naturalmente! || *That's a good boy!,* ¡así me gusta! || *That's how I happened to be there,* así fue como me encontré allí. || *That's it!,* ¡eso es! || *That's what I say!,* ¡eso digo yo! || *There are those who think that,* unos *or* algunos piensan que. || *Those who,* los que, las que; aquellos que, aquellas que. || *What do you mean by that?,* ¿qué quieres decir con eso? || *With that,* sin más.
— Rel. pron. Que (for things and people): *the man that I saw and the car that I bought,* el hombre que vi y el coche que compré; *the man that came to see me lives in the house that is in this street,* el hombre que vino a verme vive en la casa que está en esta calle. || El que, la que; quien; el cual, la cual (people only, and when the relative is governed by a preposition): *he is the man that I was talking with,* él es el hombre con quien estaba hablando; *the girls that I gave the books to,* las chicas a las que *or* a quienes di los libros. || El cual, la cual; el que, la que (things, when the pronoun is governed by a preposition): *the brooms that they were sweeping with,* las escobas con las cuales estaban barriendo; *the fact that you are referring to,* el hecho al cual *or* al que se refiere. || Lo que (neuter): *all that I know,* todo lo que sé. || En que (in expressions of time): *the day that he was born,* el día en que nació. || — *It is he that did it,* fue el quien lo hizo, el que lo hizo fue él. || *That I know of,* que yo sepa: *no one has come that I know of,* no ha venido nadie que yo sepa. || *The one that,* el que, la que; quien: *he is the one that killed my brother,* él es quien mató a mi hermano.
— Adv. Así de: *the bridge was that high,* el puente

era así de alto. || Tan: *he was that angry he could not speak*, estaba tan enfadado que no pudo hablar; *I can't see that far ahead*, no puedo ver tan lejos. || — *That many*, tantos, tas. || *That much*, tanto: *he sings that much that he has no time to work*, canta tanto que no tiene tiempo para trabajar; *you should not have spent that much* o *that much money*, no debías de haber gastado tanto *or* tanto dinero.
— Conj. Que: *she said that she was ill*, dijo que estaba enferma; *he went so fast that he had an accident*, fue tan de prisa que tuvo un accidente; *I do not believe that you are French*, no creo que seas francés. || De que: *he is happy that you came*, está contento de que hayas venido; *are you sure that you can do it?*, ¿estás seguro de que lo puedes hacer? || Para que (purpose): *I did it that you might be happy*, lo hice para que te sintieras feliz. || Porque, que (because): *it is not that I love you less*, no es porque te quiero menos, no es que te quiera menos. || — *In that*, ya que, en la medida en que: *these laws are bad in that they are unjust*, estas leyes son malas ya que son injustas. || *So that*, para que: *let's finish this quickly so that we can go to the pictures*, acabemos esto pronto para que podamos ir al cine. || *That he should abandon us at a time like this!*, ¡abandonarnos en un momento como éste!

— OBSERV. El plural de *that* es *those*, el de *that one* es *those ones* o *those*.
— There are cases when *aquel* and *ese*, *aquél* and *ése* and *aquello* and *eso* are interchangeable, especially when no position in relationship to the listener is emphasized (*give me that book*, dame ese *or* aquel libro; *that one is better than this one*, ésa *or* aquélla es mejor que ésta).
— Es posible omitir el pronombre relativo y la conjunción *that* en la mayoría de los casos en inglés (*the man I saw*, el hombre que vi; *the man I gave the cup to*, el hombre al que di la taza; *he said he would do it*, dijo que lo haría; *I am sure it is he*, esto seguro de que es él).
— Although it is usually possible to omit the relative pronoun and the conjunction "that" in English, the relative pronoun and the conjunction in Spanish may never be omitted.

thatch [θætʃ] n. Paja, *f.* (straw). || Techo (*m.*) de paja (roof). || FAM. Pelo, *m.* (hair).
thatch [θætʃ] v. tr. Cubrir con paja (a roof). || Cubrir con un tejado de paja (a house).
thatched [—t] adj. De paja (roof).
thaumaturge [ˈθɔ:mətə:dʒ] n. Taumaturgo, *m.*
thaumaturgic [ˌθɔ:məˈtə:dʒik] or **thaumartugical** [—əl] adj. Taumatúrgico, ca.
thaumaturgy [ˈθɔ:mətə:dʒi] n. Taumaturgia, *f.*
thaw [θɔ:] n. Deshielo, *m.* (melting). || Derretimiento, *m.* (of snow).
thaw [θɔ:] v. tr. Deshelar (to cause to thaw). || Derretir (snow). || Descongelar, deshelar (frozen food). || *To thaw out*, deshelar.
— V. intr. Deshelarse, derretirse (ice). || Derretirse (snow). || Deshelarse, descongelarse (frozen food). || FIG. Cobrar confianza. | Ablandarse.
— V. impers. Deshelarse.
the [ðə] before consonants; [ði: or ði] before vowels; [ði:] when used emphatically. def. art. El, la; los, las (masculine and feminine): *the boys are at home*, los niños están en casa; *the soup is good*, la sopa está buena; *the rich*, los ricos; *on the other side*, del otro lado; *give it to the child*, dáselo al niño; *the Smiths*, los Smiths. || Lo (neuter): *I wish you all the best*, le deseo todo lo mejor. || — *At the time*, en aquel entonces, en aquel momento, entonces. || *Edward the Seventh*, Eduardo Séptimo. || *Eight tomatoes to the pound*, ocho tomates por libra. || *He has the toothache*, tiene dolor de muelas. || *He is not the man to do the job*, no es el hombre adecuado para hacer este trabajo. || *It is "the restaurant" in town*, es el mejor restaurante de la ciudad. || *The impudence of it!*, ¡qué descaro!, ¡qué desfachatez! || *The one*, el, la: *the one with spectacles*, el de las gafas; *the one who*, el que.
— Adv. *The less said about it the better*, cuanto menos se hable de esto mejor. || *The more he gets the more he wants*, cuanto más tiene más quiere. || *The sooner the better*, cuanto antes mejor. || *They were all the more anxious because*, estaban tanto más preocupados cuanto que.
thearchy [ˈθi:ɑ:ki] n. Teocracia, *f.*
theater [ˈθiətə*] n. U. S. See THEATRE.
theatergoer [—ˌgəuə*] n. U. S. See THEATREGOER.
theatergoing [—ˌgəuiŋ] n. U. S. See THEATREGOING.
Theatine [ˈθiətain] n. REL. Teatino, na.
theatre [ˈθiətə*] n. Teatro, *m.*: *to go to the theatre*, ir al teatro; *the theatre of Shakespeare*, el teatro de Shakespeare; *to dedicate o.s. to the theatre*, dedicarse al teatro. || MIL. Teatro, *m.*, escenario, *m.*: *the theatre of the battle*, el teatro de la batalla. || Aula, *f.* (for lectures). || *Operating theatre*, quirófano, *m.*, sala (*f.*) de operaciones.
theatregoer [—ˌgəuə*] n. Aficionado (*m.*) al teatro.
theatregoing [—ˌgəuiŋ] n. Afición (*f.*) al teatro. || El ir al teatro.
theatrical [θiˈætrikəl] adj. De teatro, teatral: *theatrical work*, obra de teatro. || Teatral: *in a theatrical tone*, en tono teatral.
theatricalism [—izəm] or **theatricality** [θiˌætriˈkæliti] n. Teatralidad, *f.*
theatrically [θiˈætrikəli] adv. Teatralmente.
theatricals [θiˈætrikəlz] pl. n. Funciones (*f.*) de teatro. || FIG. Maneras (*f.*) teatrales. || *Amateur theatricals*, teatro (*m. sing.*) de aficionados.
Thebaid [ˈθi:beiid] pr. n. Tebaida, *f.*
Theban [ˈθi:bən] adj./n. Tebano, na.
Thebes [θi:bz] pr. n. GEOGR. Tebas.
theca [ˈθi:kə] n. BOT. ANAT. Teca, *f.*

— OBSERV. El plural de *theca* es *thecae*.

thee [ði: *or* ði] pron. Te. || Ti (with preposition). || *With thee*, contigo.

— OBSERV. Esta palabra es la antigua forma del pronombre correspondiente a la segunda persona del singular.

theft [θeft] n. Robo, *m.*, hurto, *m.* || *Aggravated theft*, robo con agravante.
theine [ˈθiain] n. CHEM. Teína, *f.*
their [ðεə*] poss. adj. Su, sus; suyo, suya: *their car is red*, su coche es rojo *or* el coche suyo es rojo; *their children*, sus hijos *or* los hijos suyos.
theirs [ðεəz] poss. pron. [El] suyo, [la] suya; [los] suyos, [las] suyas: *this is my house, that is theirs*, ésta es mi casa, ésa es la suya *or* ésa es suya. || El suyo, la suya; los suyos, las suyas: *this is my car, where is theirs?*, éste es mi coche, ¿dónde está el suyo?; *theirs are better*, los suyos son mejores. || Suyo, suya; suyos, suyas: *the fault is theirs*, la culpa es suya. || Los suyos (relatives): *them and theirs*, ellos y los suyos. || — *Is this car yours or theirs?*, ¿es suyo este coche o es de ellos? || *It is not theirs to ask questions*, no son ellos quienes deben hacer preguntas. || *Of theirs*, suyo, suya: *a friend of theirs*, un amigo suyo.
theism [ˈθi:izəm] n. Teísmo, *m.*
theist [ˈθi:ist] n. Teísta, *m.* & *f.*
theistic [θi:ˈistik] adj. Teísta.
them [ðem *or* ðəm] pron. Los, las (direct object): *I caught them*, los cogí. || Les (indirect object): *I told them*, les dije. || Ellos, ellas: *we are as clever as them*, somos tan inteligentes como ellos; *one of them*, uno de ellos; *let them decide*, que decidan ellos.
thematic [θiˈmætik] adj. Temático, ca.
theme [θi:m] n. Tema, *m.* (matter). || Disertación, *f.* (essay). || MUS. Tema, *m.*
theme song [—sɔŋ] n. Tema (*m.*) musical (in a film). || U. S. Sintonía, *f.* (signature tune).
Themis [—is] pr. n. MYTH. Temis, *f.*
Themistocles [θiˈmistəkli:z] pr. n. Temístocles, *m.*
themselves [ðəmˈselvz] pl. refl. pron. Se: *they hurt themselves*, se hirieron; *they are getting themselves a car*, se van a comprar un coche. || Ellos [mismos], ellas [mismas]: *they bought it for themselves*, lo compraron para ellos [mismos]. || Ellos mismos, ellas mismas: *they couldn't believe it until they had seen it themselves*, no pudieron creerlo hasta haberlo visto ellos mismos. || Sí mismos, sí mismas: *they are always talking about themselves*, están siempre hablando de sí mismos. || — *They did it all by themselves*, lo hicieron ellos solos. || *With themselves*, consigo mismos.
then [ðen] adv. Entonces, en aquel entonces (at that moment): *he was not there then*, él no estaba allí entonces. || Después, luego (afterwards): *they travelled in France and then in Spain*, viajaron por Francia y luego por España; *first right then left*, primero a la derecha luego a la izquierda. || Además: *I haven't the time and then it isn't my business*, no tengo tiempo y además no es asunto mío. || A pesar de eso (despite that): *he ate all the food and then he was still hungry*, se comió toda la comida pero a pesar de eso todavía tenía hambre. || Por lo tanto, por consiguiente (consequently). || — *And what then?*, y entonces ¿qué? || *But then*, pero entonces. || *Now and then*, de vez en cuando: *he goes to the pictures now and then*, va al cine de vez en cuando. || *Now ... then ...*, unas veces... otras veces. || *Now then, what you could do is to read this book*, ahora bien, lo que podría hacer es leer este libro. || *Now then, where have you been?*, ¡vamos a ver! ¿dónde has estado? || *Then and there* o *there and then*, en seguida, inmediatamente: *he knew then and there that it was the house to buy*, se dio cuenta en seguida de que era la casa que había que comprar. || *What then?*, ¿y qué?
— Conj. Entonces, en ese caso: *then you had better stay*, en ese caso es mejor que te quedes. || Entonces, así que: *then you decided not to come*, así que has decidido no venir. || *He is very rich, but then he did inherit a fortune*, es muy rico pero hay que tener en cuenta que heredó una fortuna.
— Adj. Entonces, de entonces: *the then headmaster*, el entonces director, el director de entonces.
— N. *Before then*, antes de ese momento. || *Between now and then*, para entonces: *could you do it between now and then?*, ¿puede hacerlo para entonces?; hasta entonces: *between now and then we have two weeks*, nos quedan dos semanas hasta entonces. || *By then*, para entonces. || *Every now and then*, de vez en cuando. || *From then on*, desde entonces, a partir de entonces. || *Until* o *till then*, hasta entonces.
thenar [ˈθi:nɑ:] n. ANAT. Palma, *f.* (of the hand). | Planta, *f.* (of the foot). | Tenar, *m.* (fleshy part of the thumb).
— Adj. Tenar.

thence [ðens] adv. (Ant.) De allí (from that place). || Por consiguiente, por lo tanto, por eso (for that reason).
thenceforth [ˈðensˈfɔ:θ] or **thenceforward** [ˈðensˈfɔ:wəd] (U. S. **thenceforwards**) [—z] adv. Desde entonces, a partir de entonces.
theocracy [θiˈɔkrəsi] n. Teocracia, *f.*
theocratic [θiəˈkrætik] adj. Teocrático, ca.
Theocritus [θiˈɔkritəs] pr. n. Teócrito, *m.*
theodicy [θiˈɔdisi] n. Teodicea, *f.*
theodolite [θiˈɔdəlait] n. Teodolito, *m.*
Theodoric [θiˈɔdərik] pr. n. Teodorico, *m.*
Theodosian [θiəˈdəusjən] adj. Teodosiano, na: *the Theodosian Code*, el código teodosiano.
Theodosius [θiəˈdəusjəs] pr. n. Teodosio, *m.*
theogony [θiˈɔgəni] n. Teogonía, *f.*
theologian [θiəˈləudʒjən] n. Teólogo, ga.
theologic [θiəˈlɔdʒik] or **theological** [—əl] adj. Teológico, ca; teologal. || *Theological virtues*, virtudes (*f.*) teologales.
theologize [θiˈɔlədʒaiz] v. intr. Teologizar.
theology [θiˈɔlədʒi] n. Teología, *f.*
theorem [ˈθiərəm] n. MATH. Teorema, *m.*: *Pythagoras theorem*, teorema de Pitágoras.
theoretic [θiəˈretik] or **theoretical** [—əl] adj. Teórico, ca.
theoretically [—əli] adv. Teóricamente, en teoría.
theoretician [ˌθiərəˈtiʃən] n. Teórico, ca.
theoretics [θiəˈretiks] n. Teoría, *f.*
theorist [ˈθiərist] n. Teórico, ca.
theorize [ˈθiəraiz] v. intr. Teorizar.
theory [ˈθiəri] n. Teoría, *f.*: *quantum theory*, teoría de los quanta. || FIG. Idea, *f.*: *have you any theory on who might have done it?*, ¿tienes alguna idea de quién hubiera podido hacerlo? || *In theory*, en teoría, teóricamente.
theosophic [θiəˈsɔfik] or **theosophical** [—əl] adj. Teosófico, ca.
theosophist [θiˈɔsəfist] n. Teósofo, fa.
theosophy [θiˈɔsəfi] n. Teosofía, *f.*
therapeutic [ˌθerəˈpju:tik] or **therapeutical** [—əl] adj. Terapéutico, ca.
therapeutics [ˌθerəˈpju:tiks] n. Terapéutica, *f.*
therapeutist [ˌθerəˈpju:tist] n. Terapeuta, *m.* & *f.*
therapy [ˈθerəpi] n. Terapia, *f.*, terapéutica, *f.*
there [ðɛə*] adv. Allí [*Amer.*, allá] (away from listener or speaker): *she saw him there*, lo vio allí; *he went there yesterday*, fue allí ayer; *there he comes*, allí viene. || Allí, allá (less precise): *down there*, allá abajo. || Ahí (near to speaker or listener): *there it is!*, ¡ahí está!; *you are sitting there*, tú estás sentado ahí. || En eso, allí (on that point): *they agree with me there*, ahí están de acuerdo conmigo. || — *Can we go there and back before lunch?*, ¿podemos ir y volver antes del almuerzo? || FIG. FAM. *He is not all there*, le falta un tornillo. || *Here and there*, acá y allá. || *Hurry up there*, dése prisa. || FIG. *I have been there*, ya sé lo que es eso. || *There and then* o *then and there*, en seguida, inmediatamente. || *There comes a time when*, llega un momento en que. || *There is, there are*, hay: *there are five million bicycles in the country*, hay cinco millones de bicicletas en el país. || *There or thereabouts*, más o menos. || *There's he comes!*, ¡ahí viene!, ¡ya viene! || *There was, there were*, había, hubo: *there was a lot of sugar in my tea*, había mucho azúcar en el té; *there were thousands of people*, hubo miles de personas. || *There were only two left*, sólo quedaban dos. || *There will be*, habrá. || *There you are*, eso es. || *Thirty miles there and back*, treinta millas ida y vuelta. || FIG. FAM. *To be all there*, ser muy despabilado. || *You there!*, ¡usted!, ¡oiga!
— Interj. ¡Vaya!: *there, it's finished!*, ¡vaya!, ¡ya se acabó! || — *But there, what is the good of talking!*, pero ¿de qué sirve hablar? || *There now!*, ¡ya está! || *There!, there!*, ¡ya!, ¡ya!
thereabout [ˈðɛərəˈbaut] or **thereabouts** [—s] adv. Por ahí, por allí (place): *the theatre is in that district and the cinema is thereabouts as well*, el teatro está en aquel barrio y el cine está también por ahí. || Más o menos, aproximadamente (amount, degree, weight): *it costs fifteen pounds or thereabouts*, cuesta quince libras más o menos.
thereafter [ðɛərˈɑ:ftə] adv. Después, más tarde.
thereat [ðɛərˈæt] adv. Por eso (for that reason). || En eso, sobre este punto (on that account). || Ahí, allí (there).
thereby [ðɛəˈbai] adj. Por eso, por ello. || *Thereby hangs a tale*, sobre eso hay mucho que contar.
therefore [ˈðɛəfɔ:] adv. Por lo tanto, por consiguiente, por tanto: *living is dear, therefore we have to economize*, la vida es cara, por consiguiente tenemos que ahorrar || *I think, therefore I am*, pienso, luego existo.
therefrom [ðɛəˈfrɔm] adv. De allí, de ahí. || *It follows therefrom that*, de eso resulta que.
therein [ðɛərˈin] adv. Allí dentro (in that place). || En eso: *we don't know all the facts and therein lies our difficulty*, no sabemos todos los hechos y en eso reside nuestra dificultad; *therein you are mistaken*, en eso está usted equivocado.
thereinafter [ˌðɛərinˈɑ:ftə] adv. JUR. Más abajo, más adelante (later in the same document).
thereinbefore [ˌðɛərinbiˈfɔ:] adv. JUR. Más arriba.
thereof [ðɛərˈɔv] adv. De eso (of this). || Su, del mismo, de la misma: *this tin and the contents thereof*, esta lata y el contenido de la misma *or* y su contenido.
thereon [ðɛərˈɔn] adv. See THEREUPON.
Theresa [təˈri:zə] pr. n. Teresa, *f.*
thereto [ðɛəˈtu:] adv. A eso, a ello. || (Ant.) Además.
thereunder [ðɛərˈʌndə] adv. Más abajo.
thereupon [ˈðɛərəˈpɔn] adv. Inmediatamente después (immediately afterwards). || Por lo tanto, por consiguiente (therefore). || Sobre eso (on that): *there is much to be spoken thereupon*, hay mucho que hablar sobre eso.
therewith [ðɛəˈwið] or **therewithal** [ˌðɛəwiˈðɔ:l] adv. Con eso (with that). || (Ant.). Además (in addition to that).
theriaca [θiˈriəkə] n. Triaca, *f.* (antidote).
therm [θə:m] n. PHYS. Termia, *f.*
thermae [—i] pl. n. Termas, *f.*
thermal [—əl] adj. Termal (hot springs). || PHYS. Térmico, ca: *thermal power* o *energy*, energía térmica; *thermal diffusion*, difusión térmica. || Calorífico, ca: *thermal capacity*, capacidad calorífica.
thermic [—ik] adj. Térmico, ca.
thermionic [ˌθə:miˈɔnik] adj. PHYS. Termoiónico, ca: *thermionic valve*, lámpara termoiónica.
thermocautery [ˈθə:məuˈkɔ:təri] n. Termocauterio, *m.*
thermochemical [ˈθə:məuˈkemikəl] adj. Termoquímico, ca.
thermochemistry [ˈθə:məuˈkemistri] n. Termoquímica, *f.*
thermocouple [ˈθə:məuˌkʌpəl] n. PHYS. Par (*m.*) termoeléctrico, termopar, *m.*, pila (*f.*) termoeléctrica.
thermodynamic [ˈθə:məudaiˈnæmik] adj. Termodinámico, ca.
thermodynamics [—s] n. Termodinámica, *f.*
thermoelectric [ˈθə:məuiˈlektrik] adj. Termoeléctrico, ca. || *Thermoelectric couple*, par termoeléctrico, termopar, *m.*
thermoelectricity [ˈθə:məuilekˈtrisiti] n. Termoelectricidad, *f.*
thermoelement [ˈθə:məuˈelimənt] n. Termoelemento, *m.*
thermogenic [ˌθə:məuˈdʒi:nik] or **thermogenous** [θə:ˈmɔdʒinəs] adj. Termógeno, na.
thermograph [ˈθə:məgrɑ:f] n. Termógrafo, *m.*
thermology [θə:ˈmɔlədʒi] n. Termología, *f.*
thermometer [θəˈmɔmitə] n. Termómetro, *m.*: *clinical thermometer*, termómetro clínico; *maximum and minimum thermometer*, termómetro de máxima y mínima.
thermometric [ˌθə:məˈmetrik] or **thermometrical** [ˌθə:məˈmetrikəl] adj. Termométrico, ca.
thermometry [θəˈmɔmitri] n. Termometría, *f.*
thermonuclear [ˈθə:məuˈnju:kliə*] adj. Termonuclear.
thermopile [ˈθə:məupail] n. PHYS. Termopila, *f.*
thermoplastic [ˈθə:məuˈplæstik] adj. Termoplástico, ca.
Thermopylae [θə:ˈmɔpili:] pl. pr. n. Termópilas, *f.*
thermoregulation [ˈθə:məuregjuˈleiʃən] n. Termorregulación, *f.*
thermoregulator [ˈθə:məuˈregjuleitə*] n. Termorregulador, *m.*
thermos [ˈθə:mɔs] n. Termo, *m.*, termos, *m.* || *Thermos bottle* o *flask*, termo, termos.
thermosetting [ˈθə:mouˌsetiŋ] adj. Termoestable, termoendurecible.
thermosiphon [ˈθə:məuˈsaifən] n. Termosifón, *m.*
thermostat [ˈθə:məstæt] n. Termostato, *m.*
thermotherapy [ˈθə:məuˈθerəpi] n. MED. Termoterapia, *f.*
thesaurus [θiˈsɔ:rəs] n. Diccionario, *m.*
— OBSERV. El plural es *thesauri* o *thesauruses*.
these [ði:z] pl. dem./adj. pron. See THIS.
thesis [ˈθi:sis] n. Tesis, *f.*: *he and I maintain the same thesis*, él y yo sostenemos la misma tesis; *I have already handed in my doctoral thesis*, he entregado ya la tesis de doctorado. || PHIL. Tesis, *f.*
— OBSERV. El plural de esta palabra es *theses*.
Thespian [ˈθespjən] adj. Dramático, ca; trágico, ca (of dramatic art). || De Tespis (of Thespis).
— N. Actor, *m.*, actriz, *f.*
Thespis [ˈθespis] pr. n. Tespis, *m.*
Thessalian [θeˈseiljən] adj./n. Tesaliense, tesalio, lia.
Thessalonica [ˌθesələˈnaikə] pr. n. Tesalónica, *f.*
Thessaly [ˈθesəli] pr. n. Tesalia, *f.*
theta [ˈθi:tə] n. Theta, *f.* (of Greek alphabet).
Thetis [ˈθetis] pr. n. MYTH. Tetis, *f.*
theurgic [θiˈə:dʒik] or **theurgical** [—əl] adj. Teúrgico, ca (magical).
theurgist [ˈθi:ə:dʒist] n. Teúrgo, *m.*
theurgy [ˈθi:ə:dʒi] n. Teúrgia, *f.*
thews [θju:z] pl. n. Músculos, *m.* (muscles). || Nervios, *m.* (nerves). || Fuerza (*f. sing.*) muscular (strength).
they [ðei] pers. pron. Ellos, ellas: *it is they*, son ellos, son ellas. || — *They say it will be a hard winter*, dicen *or* se dice que será un invierno duro. || *They who*, los que, quienes: *they who believe*, los que creen.
they'd [ðeid] contraction of *they had, they would.*
they'll [ðeiəl] contraction of *they will, they shall.*
they're [ðeə] contraction of *they are.*
they've [ðeiv] contraction of *they have.*

thiamin [ˈθaiəmin] or **thiamine** [ˈθaiəmi:n] n. Tiamina, *f.*

thick [θik] adj. Gordo, da; grueso, sa: *a thick fabric*, una tela gruesa. || Grueso, sa (thread). || De espesor, de grosor, de grueso: *the ice is twenty centimetres thick*, el hielo tiene veinte centímetros de espesor. || Ancho, cha; grueso, sa: *a thick wall*, una pared ancha; *a thick line*, una línea gruesa. || Abultado, da; grueso, sa (lips). || Espeso, sa (liquid, hair). || Poblado, da; tupido, da; espeso, sa (beard). || Poblado, da; espeso, sa (eyebrows). || Denso, sa; espeso, sa; tupido, da: *thick forest*, bosque espeso. || Denso, sa (crowd). || Turbio, bia (cloudy liquid). || Profundo, da; intenso, sa (darkness). || Cargado, da; viciado, da (stuffy): *thick atmosphere*, atmósfera cargada; *air thick with smoke*, aire cargado de humo. || Espeso, sa; denso, sa (fog). || Nublado, da; cerrado, da; brumoso, sa (weather). || Sofocante, bochornoso, sa (heat). || Pesado, da (head). || Poco claro, ra (voice). || Borroso, sa (writing). || Denso, sa (night). || Fuerte, marcado, da; cerrado, da (accent). || FAM. Torpe, estúpido, da (slow to understand). | Íntimo, ma: *thick friends*, amigos íntimos. || — FAM. *It's a bit thick!*, ¡es el colmo!, ¡eso pasa de castaño oscuro! || FAM. *They are as thick as thieves*, son uña y carne, están a partir un piñón. || PRINT. *Thick stroke*, lo grueso, trazo grueso (of a letter). | *Thick type*, negrilla, *f.* || *To be thick with*, estar lleno de. || FAM. *To be very thick with s.o.*, ser íntimo amigo de alguien.

— Adv. Espesamente, densamente (thickly). || Con voz poco clara (to speak). || — *Don't spread the butter too thick*, no untes demasiada mantequilla. || FIG. *His blows fell thick and fast*, llovían los golpes. || *Snow lay thick on the ground*, una capa espesa de nieve cubría el suelo. || *The grass grew thick*, la hierba crecía tupida. || *To cut the bread thick*, cortar el pan en gruesas rebanadas. || FIG. *To lay it on thick*, ser demasiado efusivo.

— N. Parte (*f.*) más gruesa (of the thumb, etc.). || Grueso, *m.*, grosor, *m.*, espesor, *m.* || Lo más denso (of a crowd). || Lo más tupido (of a forest). || FAM. Torpe, *m.* & *f.*, estúpido, da. || — FIG. *A friend through thick and thin*, un amigo seguro. | *In the thick of the fight*, en lo más reñido *or* recio del combate. || *In the thick of the forest*, en pleno bosque. || FIG. *Through thick and thin*, contra viento y marea, pase lo que pase.

thicken [ˈθikən] v. tr. Espesar: *to thicken a sauce*, espesar una salsa. || FIG. Hacer poco claro (speech). | Complicar, embrollar (a plot).

— V. intr. Espesarse (to become thick). || Volverse más grueso. || Volverse más denso. || FIG. Embrollarse, complicarse: *the plot thickens*, el asunto se complica.

thickening [—iŋ] n. Espesamiento, *m.* (of a wall, etc.). || Aumento, *m.* (of waist).

thicket [ˈθikit] n. Matorral, *m.* (shrubs). | Bosquecillo, *m.* (wood).

thickhead [ˈθikhed] n. FAM. Estúpido, da; tonto, ta.

thickheaded [ˈθikˈhedid] adj. FAM. Estúpido, da; tonto, ta.

thickish [ˈθikiʃ] adj. Bastante espeso, sa. || Bastante denso, sa. || Bastante nublado, da (weather).

thick-lipped [ˈθikˈlipt] adj. De labios abultados *or* gruesos.

thickly [ˈθikli] adv. Espesamente, densamente. || Tupidamente (beard, wood). || Con voz poco clara (to speak). || *Snow fell thickly*, la nieve caía muy fuerte, caía mucha nieve.

thickness [ˈθiknis] n. Espesor, *m.* (dimension): *this table is four centimetres in thickness*, esta mesa tiene cuatro centímetros de espesor. || Espesor, *m.*, grueso, *m.*, grosor, *m.* (size). || Espesura, *f.* (of forest). || Espesor, *m.*, densidad, *f.* (of fog). || Lo nublado, lo cerrado (of weather). || Espesor, *m.*, densidad, *f.* (of a liquid).

thickset [ˈθikset] adj. Rechoncho, cha; achaparrado, da (person). || Muy poblado, da; denso, sa (closely planted).

thick-skinned [ˈθikˈskind] adj. De piel gruesa (having a thick skin). || De pellejo grueso (grapes). || FIG. Insensible, duro, ra (insensitive).

thick-skulled [ˈθikˈskʌld] or **thick-witted** [ˈθikˈwitid] adj. Estúpido, da; torpe.

thief [θi:f] n. Ladrón, ona. || MAR. Ladrón, *m.* (of a sail). || — *Den of thieves*, cueva (*f.*) de ladrones. || FIG. *Opportunity makes the thief*, la ocasión hace al ladrón. || FIG *Set a thief to catch a thief*, a pillo, pillo y medio. || *The penitent, the impenitent thief*, el buen, el mal ladrón (in the Gospel). || FAM. *They are as thick as thieves*, son uña y carne, están a partir un piñón.

— OBSERV. El plural de *thief* es *thieves*.

thieve [θi:v] v. tr./intr. Robar, hurtar.

thievery [ˈθi:vəri] n. Robo, *m.*, hurto, *m.*

thieving [ˈθi:viŋ] adj. Ladrón, ona.

— N. Robo, *m.*, hurto, *m.*

thievish [ˈθi:viʃ] adj. Ladrón, ona.

thievishness [—nis] n. Propensión (*f.*) a robar.

thigh [θai] n. ANAT. Muslo, *m.*

thighbone [ˈθaibəun] n. ANAT. Fémur, *m.*

thill [θil] n. Limonera, *f.* (shaft).

thimble [ˈθimbl] n. Dedal, *m.* (in sewing). || TECH. Abrazadera, *f.* || MAR. Guardacabo, *m.*

thimbleful [—ful] n. Dedo, *m.*, poco, *m.*

thimblerig [—rig] n. Juego (*m.*) de manos que se efectúa con tres cubiletes.

thimblerig [—rig] v. tr. Escamotear. || FAM. Estafar (to swindle).

thimblerigger [—ˌrigə*] n. Escamoteador, *m.* || FAM. Estafador, *m.* (swindler).

thin [θin] adj. Delgado, da; flaco, ca (person). || Delgado, da (fingers). || Fino, na (lips). || Fino, na; delgado, da: *a thin sheet of paper*, una hoja de papel delgada. || Fino, na; ligero, ra (cloth). || Fino, na: *a thin rope*, una cuerda fina. || Poco denso, sa; fino, na: *thin mist*, niebla fina. || Ralo, la (hair). || Poco, ca; escaso, sa (population, audience, etc.). || Enrarecido, da (air). || Claro, ra; poco denso, sa (liquid). || Aguado, da (wine, beer, etc.). || Débil (voice). || Fino, na (steel sheet, etc.). || De poca consistencia, flojo, ja (excuse, argument). || Con poco contraste (photo). || — *He has grown very thin*, ha adelgazado mucho. || *She is rather thin in the face*, tiene la cara delgada. || FAM. *Thin on top*, calvo, va. | *To be as thin as a rake*, estar en los huesos. | *To disappear into thin air*, desaparecer, esfumarse. || *To get* o *to grow thinner*, adelgazar (a person). || FIG. *To have a thin time*, pasar un mal rato, pasarlas moradas.

— Adv. *To cut bread thin*, cortar el pan en rebanadas finas. || *To spread the butter thin*, untar una capa fina de mantequilla.

thin [θin] v. tr. Adelgazar, hacer adelgazar (s.o.). || Diluir (to dilute). || Entresacar (plants, hair). || Reducir (to reduce). || Diezmar (population). || Despoblar (country, forest). || CULIN. Aclarar (a sauce). || *To thin out*, hacer menos denso, entresacar.

— V. intr. Adelgazar (to get slim). || Disminuir, dispersarse: *the crowd thinned*, la muchedumbre se dispersó. || Disminuir, reducirse (to diminish). || Disiparse: *the fog is thinning*, la niebla se está disipando. || *His hair has thinned a lot*, ha perdido mucho pelo.

thine [ðain] poss. pron. (Ant.) [El] tuyo, [la] tuya; [los] tuyos, [las] tuyas: *my letter and thine*, mi carta y la tuya; *this book is thine*, este libro es tuyo. || — *A friend of thine*, un amigo tuyo. || *For thee and thine*, para ti y los tuyos.

— Poss. adj. (Ant.) Tu, tus: *thine eyes*, tus ojos; *thine honour*, tu honor.

thing [θiŋ] n. Cosa, *f.*: *what are those things you're carrying there?*, ¿qué son esas cosas que lleva usted ahí? || Objeto, *m.* (object). || Artículo, *m.*: *expensive things*, artículos costosos. || FAM. Chisme, *m.*, cosa, *f.*: *what's that thing over there?*, ¿qué es ese chisme que está allí? | Criatura, *f.*, individuo, *m.* (person). | Ser, *m.* (being). || Cosa, *f.* (subject, action): *there's another thing I want to ask about*, le quiero preguntar otra cosa; *you take things too seriously*, se toma las cosas demasiado en serio; *how could you do such a thing?*, ¿cómo ha podido hacer una cosa semejante? || FIG. Obsesión, *f.* (obsession): *to have a thing about sth.*, tener obsesión con algo. | Manía, *f.* (dislike): *to have a thing about s.o.*, tenerle manía a alguien. ||

— Pl. Ropa, *f. sing.* (clothes). || Cosas, *f.* (belongings): *I forbid you to touch my things*, te prohibo tocar mis cosas. || Equipo, *m. sing.*: *bring your tennis things*, trae tu equipo de tenis. || Cosas, *f.* (affairs): *things are going badly*, las cosas van mal. || JUR. Bienes, *m.*: *things personal*, bienes muebles. || — *A dumb thing*, un memo. || *Above all things*, ante todo, antes que nada. || *As things are* o *stand*, tal y como están las cosas. || *First thing*, a primera hora: *he arrived first thing in the morning*, llegó a primera hora de la mañana; lo primero: *I'll do it first thing in the morning*, lo haré lo primero por la mañana. || *For another thing*, por otra parte. || *For one thing*, primero, en primer lugar. || *Good things take time*, las cosas de palacio van despacio. || *He knows a thing or two about economics*, sabe algo de economía. || *How are things?*, ¿qué tal van las cosas?, ¿cómo te va?, ¿qué tal? || *I could tell you a thing or two about him*, te podría decir alguna cosa que otra sobre él. || *I don't know a thing about history*, no sé nada de historia. || *It's a good thing that*, menos mal que. || *It's just the thing*, es precisamente lo que queremos. || *It's not the (done) thing*, esto no se hace. || *It is the real thing*, es auténtico. || *It would be a good thing to*, sería conveniente. || *I've got the very thing for you*, tengo exactamente lo que usted necesita *or* lo que usted busca. || *Last thing*, a última hora. || *No such thing*, nada de eso. || *Not... a thing*, no ... nada: *he didn't hear a thing*, no oyó nada. || *Not a thing has been overlooked*, no se ha dejado de lado absolutamente nada. || FAM. *Not to feel quite the thing*, no encontrarse bien, encontrarse algo pachucho. || *Not to know the first thing about*, no tener el menor conocimiento de, no tener la más mínima idea de. || *Of all things!*, ¡qué sorpresa! || *Old thing!*, ¡hombre!, ¡viejo! || *One of those things*, una de esas cosas que pasan. || *One thing or the other*, una de dos. || FAM. *Poor thing*, pobrecito, ta. | *She's a lovely thing*, es un encanto. || *Tea things*, servicio (*m.*) de té. || *That's how* o *the way things are*, así están las cosas. || *That's quite another thing*, eso es otra cosa, eso es harina de otro costal. || *That's the last thing to do*, esto es lo último que hay que hacer. || FIG. *The latest thing*, el último grito. || *There's no such thing*, no hay tal cosa.

|| *The thing is that*, el caso es que. || *The thing is to succeed*, lo importante es tener éxito. || FIG. *To be quite the thing*, estar muy de moda. | *To have not a thing*, no tener nada. | *To know a thing or two*, saber cuántas son cinco. | *To make a big thing of*, dar mucha importancia a. | *To make a good thing out of*, sacar provecho de. || *To pack one's things*, hacer las maletas. || *To say one thing and mean another*, decir una cosa por otra. || *To see things*, ver visiones. || *To take things easy*, tomar las cosas con calma. || *To talk of one thing and another*, hablar de todo un poco. || FIG. *To tell s.o. a thing or two*, decirle a uno cuatro cosas *or* cuatro verdades. || *To wash up the dinner things*, fregar los platos. || *What with one thing and another*, entre unas cosas y otras. || *Well of all things! What are you doing here?*, ¿qué diablos está usted haciendo aquí? || FAM. *You silly thing!*, ¡estúpido!

— OBSERV. In some cases *thing* cannot be translated literally into Spanish (*the extraordinary, the funny thing is that*, lo extraordinario, lo gracioso es que; *the first thing to do is*, lo primero que hay que hacer es; *what's this thing for?*, ¿para qué sirve esto?).

thingumabob [ˈθiŋəmibɔb] or **thingumajig** [ˈθiŋəmidʒig] or **thingummy** [ˈθiŋəmi] n. FAM. Chisme, *m.*, cosa, *f.*, cacharro, *m.* (thing). || Éste, ésta (person): *I saw thingumabob last night*, anoche vi a éste.

think [θiŋk] n. Ejercicio (*m.*) mental. || Idea, *f.*, pensamiento, *m.* || — *He had a good think about it*, lo pensó mucho. || *To have a quiet think*, reflexionar.

think* [θiŋk] v. intr. Pensar: *are animals able to think?*, ¿pensarán los animales? || Pensar, reflexionar, meditar: *let me think a moment*, déjeme reflexionar un momento; *I did it without thinking*, lo hice sin pensar; *to think hard*, pensar mucho. || Parecer, creer: *it is better, don't you think, to get it over?*, ¿no le parece que es mejor acabar con ello? || — *As I think*, a mi parecer, según creo. || *I can't think why*, no veo el porqué, no sé por qué. || *I don't think so*, no creo. || *I should think so!*, ¡ya lo creo! || *I think not*, no creo. || *I think so*, creo que sí. || *I think so too*, yo lo creo también. || *I think, therefore I am*, pienso, luego existo. || *Just think!*, ¡fíjese!, ¡piense un poco! || *So I thought!* o *I thought as much!*, ¡ya me parecía!, ¡ya me lo figuraba!, ¡ya me lo imaginaba! || *To make one think*, dar que pensar a uno. || *To think aloud*, pensar en voz alta. || *To think for o.s.*, pensar por sí mismo. || *You should think twice before doing that*, tendría que pensarlo dos veces antes de hacerlo.

— V. tr. Imaginarse, creer: *who would have thought it?*, ¿quién se lo hubiera imaginado? || Pensar: *and to think they have gone away!*, ¡pensar que se han ido!; *I thought to myself that*, pensaba para mis adentros que. || Acordarse: *did you think to bring your book?*, ¿se acordó de traer su libro? || Creer, parecerle [a uno]: *I think he is honest*, creo que es honrado, me parece honrado; *do you think it will rain?*, ¿cree que va a llover? || Creer, pensar, esperar (to expect): *I little thought to see you again*, no esperaba volverle a ver. || Entender (to understand): *you can't think what I mean*, no puede comprender lo que quiero decir. || Tener: *he thinks evil thoughts*, tiene malos pensamientos. || Pensar, ocurrírsele [a uno] (to conceive the notion of): *I have been thinking that*, se me ocurrió que. || Pensar, tener intención de: *I only thought to help you*, sólo tenía intención de ayudarle; *the child thought no harm in doing it*, el niño no tenía malas intenciones al hacerlo. ||Encontrar: *I think she is pretty*, la encuentro mona. || Considerar, creer, pensar, tener por: *everyone thought he was a fool*, todos lo consideraban tonto. || Considerar, creer, parecerle [a uno]: *if you think it necessary*, si lo considera necesario, si le parece necesario. || — *They were thought to be rich*, la gente les consideraba ricos, se creía que eran ricos. || *Thinking to*, con la intención de. || *To think o.s. a hero*, creerse un héroe. || FAM. *Who does he think he is?*, ¿quién se cree? || *Who would have thought it?*, ¿quién lo hubiera dicho *or* creído?

— **To think about**, pensar en: *what are you thinking about?*, ¿en qué está usted pensando? | Parecerle [a uno]: *what do you think about it?*, ¿qué le parece? | Pensar: *without her thinking about it*, sin que lo piense. | — *Just thinking about it*, sólo con pensarlo. || **To think away**, pasar meditando: *he thinks his time away*, se pasa el tiempo meditando. || **To think of**, pensar en: *to think of everything*, pensar en todo; *to think of one's neighbour*, pensar en los demás. | Pensar: *when I think of it*, cuando lo pienso. | Recordar, acordarse de (to remember): *I can't think of his name*, no puedo acordarme de su nombre. | Ocurrírsele [a uno]: *I never thought of telling you*, nunca se me ocurrió decírselo; *we would not think of inviting them*, no se nos ocurriría invitarlos. | Tener intención de, pensar: *he is thinking of going to Rome next week*, tiene intención de ir a Roma la semana que viene. | Encontrar, acordarse de, recordar (to find): *to think of the right word*, encontrar la palabra exacta. | Opinar de, tener opinión de, pensar de: *what do you think of him?*, ¿qué opinión tiene de él? | Figurarse, creer, imaginarse: *I thought of him as being tall*, me lo figuraba alto. | — *He is thought well of*, se le aprecia mucho. | *He won't think of it!*, ¡en la vida lo haría! | *It isn't to be thought of!*, ¡no hay ni que pensarlo!, ¡ni pensarlo! | *The best thing I can think of*, lo mejor que se me ocurre. | *To think a great deal of o.s.*, ser muy creído. | *To think badly of*, pensar mal de, tener en poco a. | *To think better of it*, cambiar de opinión. | *To think highly* o *much of s.o.*, tener en mucho a alguien. | *To think ill of*, pensar mal de. | *To think nothing of*, see NOTHING. | *To think well of*, pensar bien de, tener buen concepto de. | *We don't think much of the film*, no nos gustó mucho la película. || **To think out**, elaborar, idear (a plan). | Examinar, estudiar (a question). | Encontrar (answer, solution). | — *That wants thinking out*, eso requiere mucha reflexión, hay que pensarlo bien. || **To think over**, pensar bien, examinar detenidamente: *on* o *after thinking it over*, pensándolo bien; *to think the matter over*, examinar detenidamente la cuestión. | — *To think it over well*, pensarlo mucho, pensarlo bien. || **To think up**, elaborar, idear (plan). | Inventar: *he thought up a good excuse*, inventó una buena excusa.

— OBSERV. Pret. & p. p. **thought**.

thinkable [—əbl] adj. Concebible.

thinker [—ə*] n. Pensador, *m.*

thinking [—iŋ] adj. Que piensa, pensante: *any thinking man*, cualquier hombre que piense. || Racional.

— N. Pensamiento, *m.*: *modern thinking*, el pensamiento moderno. || Modo (*m.*) de ver, opinión, *f.*, parecer, *m.*: *to my thinking*, a mi modo de ver, en mi opinión, a mi parecer. || Pensar, *m.*: *thinking is a useful exercise*, el pensar es un buen ejercicio. || *Wishful thinking*, ilusiones, *f. pl.*

thinly [ˈθinli] adv. Apenas: *a thinly veiled insult*, un insulto apenas disimulado. || Poco: *country thinly populated*, país poco poblado.

thinness [ˈθinnis] n. Delgadez, *f.*, flaqueza, *f.* (of person). || Delgadez, *f.* (of paper, thread). || Ligereza, *f.* (of wine, material). || Fluidez, *f.* (of liquid, soup). || Escasez, *f.* (of hair). || Poca consistencia, *f.*, flojedad, *f.* (of an argument). || Debilidad, *f.* (of the voice).

thin-skinned [ˈθinˈskind] adj. De piel fina (having a thin skin).|| FIG. Susceptible, muy sensible (sensitive).

third [θə:d] adj. Tercero, ra: *third place*, tercer lugar; *third part*, tercera parte. || — *By a third party*, por tercera persona. || *Every third day*, cada tres días. || *Third floor*, tercer piso, tercero, *m.* || HIST. *Third estate*, estado llano. || *Third gear*, tercera, *f.*: *to change into third gear*, poner la tercera. || REL. *Third order*, orden tercera. || JUR. *Third party*, tercero, *m.* || *Third-party insurance*, seguro (*m.*) contra tercera persona. || *Third person*, tercera persona (grammatical term), tercero, *m.* (legal term). || *Third World*, Tercer Mundo. || *Third year*, tercer curso, tercero, *m.* (at school).

— N. Tercero, ra: *he came in third*, llegó tercero; *Henry III* (*the Third*), Enrique III [tercero]. || Tercio, *m.*, tercera parte, *f.*: *two thirds*, dos tercios; *a third of the cake*, un tercio del pastel, una tercera parte del pastel; *five is one third of fifteen*, cinco es la tercera parte de quince. || Aprobado, *m.* (grade in an exam): *to get a third in history*, sacar un aprobado en historia. || AUT. Tercera, *f.* (third gear). || Día (*m.*) tres, tres, *m.*: *the third of the month*, el día tres del mes. || MUS. Tercera, *f.* || MATH. Tercero, *m.*

— Adv. En tercer lugar (in third place). || En tercera [clase]: *to travel third*, viajar en tercera.

third class [—ˈklɑ:s] n. Tercera, *f.*, tercera clase, *f.* (of trains).

third-class [—klɑ:s] adj. De tercera clase, de tercera (trains, etc.). || De tercera categoría (hotels, etc.). || De poca calidad (goods).

— Adv. En tercera, en tercera clase.

thirdly [ˈθə:dli] adv. En tercer lugar.

third-rate [ˈθə:dˈreit] adj. De poca calidad (goods). || De poca categoría (people).

thirst [θə:st] n. Sed, *f.*: *an unquenchable thirst*, una sed insaciable; *to quench one's thirst*, apagar la sed. || FIG. Afán, *m.*, sed, *f.*: *thirst for knowledge*, sed de saber.

thirst [θə:st] v. intr. Tener sed (to feel thirsty). || FIG. Estar sediento, tener sed : *to be thirsting for revenge*, estar sediento de venganza.

thirstily [—ili] adv. Con avidez: *to drink thirstily*, beber con avidez.

thirstiness [—inis] n. Sed, *f.*

thirsty [—i] adj. Sediento, ta. || FIG. Sediento, ta: *thirsty soil*, suelo sediento; *thirsty for adventure*, sediento de aventuras; *thirsty for riches*, sediento de riquezas. || FAM. Que da sed (work). || — *To be thirsty for*, tener sed de. || *To make thirsty*, dar sed.

thirteen [θə:ˈti:n] adj. Trece.

— N. Trece, *m.* (number).

thirteenth [—θ] adj. Decimotercero, ra; decimotercio, cia. || Trece (chapter, date): *the thirteenth century*, el siglo trece.

— N. Decimotercero, ra; trece, *m.* & *f.* (in thirteenth position). || Trezavo, *m.*, decimotercera parte, *f.* (one of thirteen parts). || Trece, *m.*, día (*m.*) trece (day of month): *tomorrow, the thirteenth of February*, mañana, trece de febrero. || *Leo XIII* (*the Thirteenth*), León XIII [trece].

thirtieth [ˈθə:tiiθ] adj. Trigésimo, ma (in a series). || Trigésimo, ma; treintavo, va (being one of 30 equal parts).

— N. Trigésima parte, *f.*, treintavo, *m.* (one of thirty parts). || Trigésimo, ma; treinta, *m.* & *f.* (in thirtieth

position). || Día (*m.*) treinta, treinta, *m.* (of a month): *the thirtieth of May*, el treinta de mayo.
thirty [ˈθəːti] adj. Treinta: *thirty men*, treinta hombres. — N. Treinta, *m.* (number). || — Pl. Treinta, *m.*: *to be in one's thirties*, estar en los treinta. || — *Temperatures in the thirties*, temperatura de más de treinta grados. || *The thirties*, los años treinta.
thirty-first [ˈθəːtiˈfəːst] adj./n. Trigésimo primero, trigésima primera.
thirty-second [ˈθəːtiˈseknd] adj./n. Trigésimo segundo, trigésima segunda.
this [ðis] dem. adj. Este, esta: *this book*, este libro; *these tables*, estas mesas; *these men*, estos hombres. || — *He is one of these artist types*, es uno de esos artistas. || *I've been waiting these three weeks*, hace tres semanas que estoy esperando, llevo tres semanas esperando, estuve esperando estas tres últimas semanas. || *This day last year*, hoy hace un año. || *This one*, éste, ésta. || *To run this way and that*, ir de un lado para otro.
— Dem. pron. Éste, ésta (masculine, feminine): *this is a pleasant country*, éste es un país agradable; *who is this?*, ¿quién es éste *or* ésta?; *who are these?*, ¿quiénes son éstos *or* éstas? || Esto (neuter): *this is what he told me*, esto es lo que me dijo; *what is this?*, ¿qué es esto?; *after this*, después de esto. || — *Like this*, así: *do it like this*, hágalo así. || *The thing is this*, el problema es éste. || *This is how you do it*, así es como se hace. || *This is Mr. Smith*, le presento al señor Smith. || *This is where he lives*, aquí es donde vive. || *This or that?*, ¿éste o aquél?, ¿esto o aquello? || *This, that and the other*, esto, lo otro y lo de más allá. || *With this*, sin más: *with this he got up and went out*, sin más se levantó y se fue.
— Adv. Tan: *I didn't know that it could be this interesting*, no sabía que podía ser tan interesante. || Tan, así de: *I didn't expect it to be this big*, no esperaba que fuera así de grande. || Así de: *it was this big*, era así de grande. || — *I didn't expect to wait this long*, no pensaba tener que esperar tanto. || *This far it's been easy*, hasta aquí *or* hasta ahora ha sido fácil. || *This much*, tanto: *he can't eat this much*, no puede comer tanto.

— OBSERV. El plural de esta palabra es *these*.

thistle [ˈθisl] n. Cardo, *m.*
thistledown [—daun] n. Vilano, *m.* (of a thistle).
thistly [—i] adj. Lleno de cardos (full of thistles). || Espinoso, sa (prickly). || FIG. Delicado, da; espinoso, sa; peliagudo, da.
thither [ˈðiðə*] adj. (Ant.) Allá.
thitherward [—wəd] adv. (Ant.) Hacia allá.
thole [θəul] or **tholepin** [—pin] n. MAR. Escálamo, *m.*, tolete, *m.*
Thomas [ˈtɔməs] pr. n. Tomás, *m.* || — *Saint Thomas Aquinas*, Santo Tomás de Aquino. || *Thomas More*, Tomás Moro.
Thomism [ˈtəumizəm] n. PHIL. REL. Tomismo, *m.*
Thomist [ˈtəumist] adj./n. PHIL. REL. Tomista.
Thomistic [təuˈmistik] adj. PHIL. REL. Tomístico, ca; tomista.
thong [θɔŋ] n. Correa, *f.*, tira (*f.*) de cuero (strip of leather).
thoracic [θɔˈræsik] adj. ANAT. Torácico, ca: *thoracic cage*, caja torácica.
thorax [ˈθɔːræks] n. ANAT. Tórax, *m.*

— OBSERV. El plural de *thorax* es *thoraxes* o *thoraces*.

thorium [ˈθɔːriəm] n. CHEM. Torio, *m.*
thorn [θɔːn] n. BOT. Espina, *f.* (on a plant, stem). | Espino, *m.* (hawthorn). || FIG. Espina, *f.* (source of irritation). || — FIG. *A thorn in one's side* o *in the flesh*, una espina clavada. || *Crown of thorns*, corona (*f.*) de espinas. || FIG. *To be on thorns*, estar sobre ascuas.
thornbush [—buʃ] n. BOT. Espino, *m.*
thornless [—lis] adj. Sin espinas.
thorny [—i] adj. Espinoso, sa. || FIG. Espinoso, sa; peliagudo, da (question).
thorough [ˈθʌrə] adj. Minucioso, sa (search, investigation, etc.): *after a thorough study of the document*, después de un estudio minucioso del documento. || Concienzudo, da (work, person): *he is thorough in his work*, es concienzudo en su trabajo. || Profundo, da: *thorough knowledge*, conocimiento profundo. || Completo, ta: *you must have a thorough change*, necesita un cambio completo. || A fondo: *a thorough cleaning*, una limpieza a fondo. || Completo, ta; perfecto, ta: *a thorough command of Spanish*, un dominio perfecto del español. || Perfecto, ta; cabal: *a thorough gentleman*, un perfecto caballero. || Empedernido, da; redomado, da: *a thorough drunkard*, un borracho empedernido.
thorough bass [—ˈbeis] n. MUS. Bajo (*m.*) cifrado.
thoroughbred [—bred] adj. De pura raza (dog, etc.). || [De] pura sangre (horse). || FIG. Con clase (person). — N. Pura sangre, *m.* & *f.*
thoroughfare [—fεə*] n. Carretera, *f.* (highway). || Calle, *f.* (in a town). || Vía (*f.*) pública (road open to the public). || *No thoroughfare*, calle sin salida (no through road), calle interceptada (road blocked), prohibido el paso (no entry).
thoroughgoing [—ˈgəuiŋ] adj. Minucioso, sa (thorough, conscientious). || Completo, ta; perfecto, ta; cien por cien: *a thoroughgoing democrat*, un perfecto demócrata.
thoroughly [—li] adv. A fondo: *to investigate thoroughly*, investigar a fondo; *to clean thoroughly*, limpiar a fondo. || Perfectamente: *to understand thoroughly*, entender perfectamente. || De pies a cabeza: *to be thoroughly honest*, ser honrado de pies a cabeza. || Completamente: *a thoroughly reliable machine*, une máquina completamente segura. || Concienzudamente: *he does his work very thoroughly*, hace su trabajo muy concienzudamente.
thoroughness [—nis] n. Minuciosidad, *f.*, lo minucioso: *the thoroughness of an investigation*, la minuciosidad de una investigación. || Perfección, *f.*
thorp [θɔːp] n. Caserío, *m.*
those [ðəuz] pl. dem. adj./pron. See THAT.
thou [ðau] pers. pron. (Ant.) Tú, vos.

— OBSERV. El pronombre *thou* actualmente se emplea casi únicamente para dirigirse a Dios.
— Although the *tú* form is normally used when addressing God, *vos* can also be used, in which case the second person plural of the verb is required.

thou [ðau] v. tr./intr. Tratar de tú *or* de vos.
though [ðəu] conj. Aunque: *though it was very late, he went on working*, aunque era muy tarde siguió trabajando; *I will do it though it cost me my life*, lo haré aunque me cueste la vida. || — *As though*, como si. || *Even though*, aunque. || *It looks as though he has gone*, parece que se ha ido. || *Strange though it may seem*, por extraño que parezca. || *What though the way be long!*, ¿qué importa que el camino sea largo?
— Adv. Sin embargo: *the ground was muddy, it was a good game though*, el suelo estaba lleno de barro, sin embargo el partido fue bueno. || *Did he though?*, ¿de verdad?

— OBSERV. The conjunction *aunque* is followed by the subjunctive when the clause it introduces expresses a hypothesis. It is used with the indicative when the clause expresses a fact.
— Aunque en inglés con *though* se puede emplear el subjuntivo, se usa más frecuentemente el indicativo.

thought [θɔːt] n. Pensamiento, *m.*: *modern thought*, pensamiento moderno; *to read s.o.'s thoughts*, adivinar los pensamientos de alguien; *freedom of thought*, libertad de pensamiento; *free thought*, libre pensamiento; *nasty thought*, mal pensamiento. || Idea, *f.*: *I've just had a thought*, se me acaba de ocurrir una idea; *happy thought*, idea afortunada. || Intención, *f.*: *he once had the thought of selling the house*, una vez tuvo la intención de vender la casa; *he had no thought of offending you*, no tenía intención de ofenderle. || Punto (*m.*) de vista, opinión, *f.*: *man who keeps his thoughts to himself*, hombre que no revela sus opiniones. || Consideración, *f.*, atenciones, *f. pl.*: *he has no thought for his mother*, no tiene consideración con su madre. || — *After much thought*, después de pensarlo mucho. || *A penny for your thoughts*, ¿en qué estás pensando? || FAM. *A thought*, un poquito: *he is a thought better*, está un poquito mejor. || *At the thought of*, al pensar en. || *Don't give it a thought*, no te preocupes por eso, no le des importancia. || *His one thought is to earn money*, su única idea es ganar dinero. || *Lost in thought*, ensimismado, da. || *My thoughts were elsewhere*, estaba pensando en otra cosa. || *On second thoughts*, pensándolo bien. || *Our thoughts are with them*, pensamos en ellos. || *Take thought for the morrow*, piense en el día de mañana. || *The mere thought of it*, sólo el pensarlo. || *To fall into deep thought*, abstraerse, ensimismarse. || *To give thought to*, pensar en. || *To have thoughts of doing sth.*, tener la intención de hacer algo. || *To take thought how to do sth.*, pensar cómo hacer algo. || *We wouldn't have given it another thought*, no lo hubiéramos vuelto a pensar. || *Without a thought for*, sin pensar en. || *With the thought of*, con la intención de, con la idea de.
thought [θɔːt] pret. & p. p. See THINK.
thoughtful [—ful] adj. Pensativo, va; meditabundo, da (absorbed): *he was thoughtful a long time before he answered*, se quedó pensativo mucho tiempo antes de contestar. || Serio, ria (serious): *a thoughtful book*, un libro serio. || Cuidadoso, sa (mindful). || Atento, ta; solícito, ta (considerate): *to be thoughtful of others*, ser atento con los demás. || *How thoughtful!*, ¡qué detalle!
thoughtfully [—fuli] adv. Pensativamente, con aire pensativo *or* meditabundo. || Atentamente (with consideration).
thoughtfulness [—fulnis] n. Meditación, *f.* || Seriedad, *f.* (seriousness). || Atenciones, *f. pl.*, solicitud, *f.* (consideration). || Cuidado, *m.* (care).
thoughtless [—lis] adj. Irreflexivo, va: *a thoughtless action*, una acción irreflexiva. || Desconsiderado, da; falto de consideración, poco atento, ta: *thoughtless of others*, desconsiderado con los demás. || Descuidado, da (careless).
thoughtlessness [—lisnis] n. Irreflexión, *f.* || Descuido, *m.* (carelessness). || Desconsideración, *f.* (disregard).
thought-out [—ˈaut] adj. Bien pensado, da.
thought-read [—riːd] v. tr. Adivinar los pensamientos de.
thought reading [—ˈriːdiŋ] n. Adivinación (*f.*) de los pensamientos.

thought transference [—'trænsfərəns] n. Telepatía, *f.*, transmisión (*f.*) del pensamiento.
thoughtway [—wei] n. Manera (*f.*) de pensar.
thousand ['θauzənd] adj. Mil: *a thousand men*, mil hombres; *two thousand women*, dos mil mujeres. || *A thousand thanks*, un millón de gracias, miles de gracias.
— N. Mil, *m.* || Millar, *m.*: *they arrived in thousands* o *by the thousand*, llegaban a millares. || *Thousands of*, miles de, millares de.
thousandfold [—fəuld] adj. Multiplicado por mil.
— Adv. Mil veces.
thousandth ['θauzəntθ] adj. Milésimo, ma.
— N. Milésima parte, *f.*, milésimo, *m.* (one of a thousand parts). || Número (*m.*) mil (in thousandth position): *she was the thousandth on the list*, era el número mil de la lista.
Thrace [θreis] pr. n. GEOGR. Tracia, *f.*
Thracian ['θreisjən] adj./n. Tracio, cia.
thraldom ['θrɔ:ldəm] n. Esclavitud, *f.*
thrall [θrɔ:l] n. Esclavo, va (slave). || Esclavitud, *f.* (slavery). || FIG. *To hold in thrall*, esclavizar.
thrall [θrɔ:l] v. tr. Esclavizar.
thralldom [—dəm] n. Esclavitud, *f.*
thrash [θræʃ] n. Movimiento (*m.*) de piernas (swimming).
thrash [θræʃ] v. tr. Dar una paliza a, azotar (to beat). || AGR. Trillar (to thresh). || FIG. Dar una paliza a (to defeat soundly). || — FIG. *To thrash out*, discutir a fondo (a matter), dar vueltas a (a question), descubrir (truth). | *To thrash over*, machacar, estudiar a fondo.
— V. intr. Batir (waves). || SP. Mover las piernas (swimming). || *To thrash about*, agitarse, revolverse.
thrashing [—iŋ] n. Paliza, *f.*, azotaina, *f.*: *I'll give you a thrashing*, te voy a dar una paliza. || AGR. Trilla, *f.* || FIG. Paliza, *f.* (a heavy defeat): *to give another team a thrashing*, dar una paliza a otro equipo. || AGR. *Thrashing floor*, era, *f.*
thrasonical [θrə'sɔnikəl] adj. Fanfarrón, ona; jactancioso, sa.
thread [θred] n. Hilo, *m.* (for sewing, weaving, of a spider, of metal). || Hebra, *f.* (of beans). || TECH. Rosca, *f.*, filete, *m.* (on a screw). || Rayo, *m.* (of sun). || MIN. Filón, *m.*, veta, *f.* || FIG. Hilo, *m.* (of a conversation, life, story, etc.).: *to lose the thread*, perder el hilo. || — *Right hand, left hand thread*, enroscado a la derecha, a la izquierda. || FIG. *To be hanging by a thread*, estar pendiente de un hilo. | *To gather up the threads*, atar cabos.
thread [θred] v. tr. Ensartar, enhebrar (a needle). || Ensartar (beads). || TECH. Roscar, filetear (screw). | Aterrajar (a pipe). || Pasar: *to thread an elastic through the hem of sth.*, pasar una goma por el dobladillo de algo. || PHOT. Cargar con (a film). || FIG. Entretejer: *hair threaded with silver*, pelo entretejido de plata. || *To thread one's way through*, deslizarse por, colarse por.
— V. intr. Deslizarse, colarse (*through*, por).
threadbare [—bɛə*] adj. Raído, da (cloth): *a threadbare suit*, un traje raído. || Andrajoso, sa; desastrado, da (person). || FIG. Trillado, da (argument, opinion). | Viejo, ja (joke). | Flojo, ja (excuse).
threadbareness [—bɛənis] n. Lo raído (of cloth). || FIG. Lo trillado.
thread counter [—'kauntə*] n. Cuentahílos, *m. inv.*
threader [—ə*] n. TECH. Terraja, *f.*
threadlike [—laik] adj. Filiforme.
thread mark [—mɑ:k] n. Filigrana, *f.* (in banknotes).
thready [—di] adj. Fibroso, sa; filamentoso, sa. || Débil (voice, etc.).
threat [θret] n. Amenaza, *f.* || *There is a threat of rain*, parece que va a llover.
threaten ['θretn] v. tr./intr. Amenazar: *he threatened me with a revolver*, me amenazó con un revólver; *he threatened to kill me*, amenazó [con] matarme; *race threatened with extinction*, raza amenazada de desaparición. || *It threatens to rain*, parece que va a llover.
threatening ['θretniŋ] adj. Amenazador, ra: *threatening tone*, tono amenazador.
— N. Amenazas, *f. pl.*
three ['θri:] adj. Tres.
— N. Tres, *m.* (number, card, figure). || — *Five past three*, las tres y cinco. || MATH. *Rule of three*, regla (*f.*) de tres. || *The Big Three*, los Tres Grandes. || *Three o'clock*, las tres: *three o'clock in the afternoon*, las tres de la tarde; *at three o'clock in the morning*, a las tres de la mañana *or* de la madrugada; *it's three o'clock*, son las tres.
three-act [—ækt] adj. De tres actos (play).
three-colour (U. S. **three-color**) [—'kʌlə*] or **three-coloured** (U. S. **three-colored**) [—'kʌləd] adj. Tricolor. || PRINT. Tricromo, ma. || *Three-colour process*, tricromía, *f.*
three-cornered [—'kɔ:nəd] adj. Triangular (having three angles). || *Three-cornered hat*, tricornio, *m.*, sombrero (*m.*) de tres picos.
three-decker [—'dekə*] n. MAR. Barco (*m.*) de tres cubiertas. || Bocadillo (*m.*) de tres pisos (sandwich).
three-dimensional [—dai'menʃənəl] adj. Tridimensional.
three-engined [—'endʒind] adj. Trimotor.
threefold [—fəuld] adj. Triple: *a threefold rise*, un aumento triple.
— Adv. Tres veces: *to increase threefold*, aumentar tres veces.
three hundred [—'hʌndrəd] adj./n. Trescientos, tas.
three hundredth [—'hʌndrətθ] adj./n. Tricentésimo, ma.
three-legged [—'legid] adj. De tres patas *or* pies (stool, etc.).
three-master [—'mɑ:stə*] n. MAR. Barco (*m.*) de tres palos.
threepence ['θrepəns] n. Tres peniques, *m. pl.* (value). || Moneda (*f.*) de tres peniques (coin).
threepenny ['θrəpəni'] adj. De tres peniques. || FIG. De tres al cuarto. || *Threepenny bit*, moneda (*f.*) de tres peniques.
three-phase ['θri:feiz] adj. Trifásico, ca (current).
three-piece ['θri:'pi:s] adj. De tres piezas. || *Three-piece suite*, tresillo, *m.* (furniture).
— N. Traje (*m.*) de tres piezas.
three-ply ['θri:plai] adj. Contrachapado, da; contrachapeado, da (wood). || De tres hebras (rope). || De tres capas (of three layers).
three-point landing ['θri:pɔint'lændiŋ] n. AVIAT. Aterrizaje (*m.*) en tres puntos, aterrizaje (*m.*) perfecto. || FAM. Conclusión (*f.*) brillante.
three-quarter ['θri:'kwɔ:tə*] adj. Tres cuartos: *a three-quarter coat*, un abrigo tres cuartos.
— N. SP. Tres cuartos, *m.*
threescore ['θri:'skɔ:] adj. Sesenta.
three-sided ['θri:saidid] adj. Trilátero, ra.
threesome ['θri:səm] n. Grupo (*m.*) de tres.
three-storied ['θri:'stɔ:rid] adj. De tres pisos.
threnody ['θrenədi] n. MUS. Treno, *m.*, canto (*m.*) fúnebre.
thresh [θreʃ] v. tr./intr. AGR. Trillar. || FIG. Machacar.
thresher ['θreʃə*] n. AGR. Trilladora, *f.*
threshing ['θreʃiŋ] n. AGR. Trilla, *f.*
threshing floor [—flɔ:*] n. AGR. Era, *f.*
threshing machine [—məʃi:n] n. Trilladora, *f.*
threshold ['θreʃhəuld] n. Umbral, *m.* (of a door). || FIG. Umbral, *m.*: *to be on the threshold of life*, estar en el umbral de la vida. | Puertas, *f. pl.*: *we are at the threshold of a conflict*, estamos a las puertas de un conflicto. || *Threshold visibility*, visibilidad mínima.
threw [θru:] pret. See THROW.
thrice [θrais] adv. Tres veces.
thrift [θrift] or **thriftiness** [—inis] n. Economía, *f.*, ahorro, *m.*
thriftless [—lis] adj. Gastoso, sa; despilfarrador, ra.
thriftlessness [—lisnis] n. Derroche, *m.*, despilfarro, *m.* (extravagance).
thrifty [—i] adj. Económico, ca; ahorrativo, va. || U. S. Próspero, ra (thriving).
thrill [θril] n. Emoción, *f.* (excitement). || Escalofrío, *m.*, estremecimiento, *m.* (quiver). || Sensación, *f.* (sensation). || MED. Temblor, *m.*
thrill [θril] v. tr. Estremecer (with horror, pleasure). || Emocionar, estremecer: *music that thrills one*, música que emociona a uno. || Electrizar (an audience). || Hacer mucha ilusión: *the idea of going to America thrills me*, la idea de ir a América me hace mucha ilusión. || *To be thrilled with horror*, estremecerse de horror.
— V. intr. Estremecerse: *to thrill with fear*, estremecerse de miedo. || Emocionarse.
thriller [—ə*] n. Novela (*f.*) *or* película (*f.*) *or* obra (*f.*) de teatro escalofriante.
thrilling [—iŋ] adj. Emocionante: *it was a thrilling trip*, fue un viaje emocionante. || Escalofriante (novel, film, play).
thrillingly [—iŋli] adv. De manera emocionante.
thrive* [θraiv] v. intr. Crecer (child, plant): *plant that thrives in all soils*, planta que crece en todos los terrenos. || Desarrollarse (to grow strong): *children thrive on good food*, los niños se desarrollan con una buena alimentación. || Tener buena salud (to have good health). || FIG. Prosperar: *a business cannot thrive without good management*, una empresa no puede prosperar sin una buena gestión. | Tener éxito (to be successful). | Encantar: *he thrives on constructive criticism*, le encantan las críticas constructivas.

— OBSERV. Pret. ***throve, thrived;*** p. p. ***thriven, thrived.***

thriven ['θrivən] p. p. See THRIVE.
thriving ['θraiviŋ] adj. Lozano, na (plant, person). || FIG. Próspero, ra; floreciente.
throat [θrəut] n. ANAT. Garganta, *f.*: *a fishbone has stuck in my throat*, se me ha atragantado una espina en la garganta. || Cuello, *m.*: *to cut s.o.'s throat*, cortarle el cuello a alguien. || GEOGR. Paso, *m.*, desfiladero, *m.* || Gollete, *m.*, cuello, *m.* (of a bottle). || TECH. Tragante, *m.* (of blast furnace). || ARCH. Goterón, *m.* || — *Smell that catches one's throat*, olor que se agarra a la garganta. || MED. *Sore throat*, dolor (*m.*) de garganta. || *The words stuck in my throat*, no pude pronunciar una palabra. || *To clear one's throat*, aclararse la voz. || FIG. FAM. *To cut one's own throat*, labrar su propia ruina. | *To jump down one's throat*, echarle una bronca a uno. | *To lie in one's throat*, mentir desvergonzadamente. | *To moisten one's throat*, mojarse el gaznate. | *To thrust sth. down s.o.'s throat*,

hacer tragar algo a alguien, meter a alguien algo por las narices. || *Whenever I hear that tune I get a lump in my throat*, cada vez que oigo esta canción se me hace un nudo en la garganta.

throaty [—i] adj. Gutural.

throb [θrɔb] n. Latido, *m.*, palpitación, *f.* (of heart). || Pulsación, *f.* (of pulse). || Punzada, *f.* (of pain). || Zumbido, *m.* (of engine). || FIG. Vibración, *f.* | Estremecimiento, *m.* (of joy, etc.).

throb [θrɔb] v. intr. Latir, palpitar (heart). || Latir (pulse). || Dar punzadas (with pain): *my finger is throbbing*, el dedo me da punzadas. || Zumbar (engine). || FIG. Estremecerse (with joy). | Vibrar.

throbbing [—iŋ] adj. Palpitante (heart). || Punzante (pain). || Que zumba (engine). || FIG. Palpitante, vibrante. || *Throbbing centre of industry*, centro (*m.*) industrial que rebosa de actividad.

— N. Latido, *m.*, palpitación, *f.* (of heart). || Pulsación, *f.* (of pulse). || Punzadas, *f. pl.* (of pain). || Zumbido, *m.* (of engine). || FIG. Estremecimiento, *m.*

throes [θrəuz] pl. n. Dolores, *m.*: *throes of childbirth*, dolores del parto. || Ansias, *f.*, angustias, *f.*: *throes of death*, ansias de la muerte. || FIG. *The country was in the throes of a general election*, el país estaba de lleno en las elecciones generales.

thrombin [ˈθrɔmbin] n. Trombina, *f.*

thrombocyte [ˈθrɔmbəsait] n. Trombocito, *m.*

thrombosis [θrɔmˈbəusis] n. MED. Trombosis, *f. inv.*

thrombus [ˈθrɔmbəs] n. Trombo, *m.*

— OBSERV. El plural de *thrombus* es *thrombi*.

throne [θrəun] n. Trono, *m.*: *to come to the throne*, subir al trono. || — Pl. Tronos, *m.* (angels). || *Throne room*, sala (*f.*) del trono.

throne [θrəun] v. tr. Entronizar, elevar al trono.

— V. intr. Ocupar el trono.

throng [θrɔŋ] n. Multitud, *f.*, muchedumbre, *f.*, gentío, *m.* (crowd). || Multitud, *f.* (large amount). || *They arrived in throngs*, llegaron en tropel.

throng [θrɔŋ] v. tr. Atestar, llenar: *the shop was thronged with people*, la tienda estaba atestada *or* llena de gente.

—V. intr. Afluir (to a place). || Apiñarse, amontonarse: *they thronged round the speaker*, se apiñaron alrededor del orador. || Llegar en tropel: *they thronged into the square*, llegaron en tropel a la plaza.

thronging [—iŋ] adj. Apretado, da (crowd).

throstle [ˈθrɔsl] n. Zorzal, *m.*, tordo, *m.* (bird).

throttle [ˈθrɔtl] n. FAM. Gaznate, *m.* (throat). || TECH. Válvula (*f.*) de admisión (throttle valve). | Acelerador, *m.* (for controlling the throttle valve). || — FAM. *At full throttle*, a todo gas. || *To give it full throttle*, acelerar a fondo.

throttle [ˈθrɔtl] v. tr. Estrangular, ahogar (s.o.). || TECH. Estrangular. || FIG. Suprimir.

— V. intr. Asfixiarse, ahogarse.

through [θru:] adj. Directo, ta: *a through ticket*, un billete directo; *through train*, tren directo. || Que va hasta el término (passenger). || Con preferencia de paso, con prioridad (a road, street). || Acabado, da (at the end of one's abilities): *he's through as a tennis player*, está acabado como tenista. || Terminado, da; acabado, da: *when you are through with this*, cuando haya terminado con esto. || Terminado, da: *he's through with her forever*, ha terminado con ella para siempre. || — *No through road*, calle (*f.*) sin salida. || *Through traffic*, tránsito, *m.*

— Adv. De parte a parte, de un lado a otro (from end to end). || Enteramente, completamente: *wet through*, completamente mojado. || Directamente: *this train goes through to London*, este tren va directamente a Londres. || Hasta el final, desde el principio hasta el final: *to read a book through*, leer un libro hasta el final. || — *Are you through?*, ¿has aprobado? (in an exam). || *I'll be through with you in a second*, termino con usted en seguida. || *Soaked through*, calado hasta los huesos. || *Through and through*, hasta la médula: *she is a gipsy through and through*, es gitana hasta la médula; como la palma de la mano, de cabo a rabo: *he knows the town through and through*, conoce la ciudad como la palma de la mano. || *To carry sth. through*, llevar algo a cabo. || *To fall through*, fracasar. || *To let sth. through*, dejar pasar algo. || *Would you put me through to?*, póngame con (on the telephone). || *You are through!*, ¡hablen! (on the telephone).

— Prep. A través de: *path through the fields*, camino a través de los campos. || Por (via): *the Thames flows through London*, el Támesis pasa por Londres; *to jump through the window*, saltar por la ventana; *to send through the post*, mandar por correo. || Durante: *to sleep through the storm*, dormir durante la tormenta; *all through his life*, durante toda su vida. || Entre: *the news spread through the crowd*, la noticia se extendió entre la multitud. || Gracias a, por medio de, a través de (by means of): *I got the information through him*, conseguí la información por medio de él. || Por, a causa de (by reason of): *it happened through no fault of mine*, no ocurrió por culpa mía. || U. S. De ... a, desde ... hasta: *Monday through Friday*, de lunes a viernes. || — FIG. *He's been through it*, ha pasado por momentos muy malos. || *To be through one's finals*, haber aprobado los exámenes finales. || *To go through*, pasar por: *we went through Lima*, pasamos por Lima; atravesar: *the arrow went right through him*, la flecha lo atravesó.

throughout [θru:ˈaut] adv. Hasta el final: *to read a book throughout*, leer un libro hasta el final. || Completamente: *to be wrong throughout*, estar completamente equivocado. || Todo, da; por todas partes: *they decorated the house throughout*, decoraron toda la casa. || Desde el principio hasta el final: *the film is funny throughout*, la película es divertida desde el principio hasta el final.

— Prep. Por todo, en todo: *throughout the country*, por todo el país. || Durante todo: *throughout the year*, durante todo el año. || A lo largo de: *throughout the book*, a lo largo del libro. || *Throughout the world*, en el mundo entero.

throve [θrəuv] pret. See THRIVE.

throw [θrəu] n. Lanzamiento, *m.*, tiro, *m.* (action of throwing). || Lance, *m.* (of dice). || Lanzado, *m.* (in fishing). || GEOGR. Dislocación, *f.* (in a strata). || TECH. Recorrido, *m.*, carrera, *f.*: *throw of the piston*, carrera del émbolo. || SP. Tumbado, *m.* (in wrestling). | Lanzamiento, *m.* (of javelin, etc.). || U. S. Colcha, *f.* (light bedspread). || *At a stone's throw*, a tiro de piedra.

throw* [θrəu] v. tr. Tirar, lanzar, arrojar: *he threw a stone at the dog*, tiró una piedra al perro; *he threw the ball to me*, me lanzó la pelota. || Lanzar: *to throw troops into battle*, lanzar las tropas al combate. || Proyectar: *to throw light, shadows*, proyectar luz, sombras. || Tender: *to throw a bridge over a river*, tender un puente sobre un río. || Dar, asestar (a blow). || Descartar (a card). || Tirar, echar (dice). || Sacar (at dice): *to throw a six*, sacar seis. || FIG. Echar: *to throw the blame on s.o.*, echar la culpa a alguien; *to throw a glance*, echar una mirada. | Hacer (a scene). | Armar (a scandal). || FAM. Dar (a party). || TECH. Tornear, modelar en un torno (with a lathe). | Torcer (silk). || SP. Derribar, tumbar (an opponent). | Desmontar, derribar, desarzonar (a rider). | Lanzar (javelin, disk, etc.). | Hacer (hold in wrestling). || AUT. Poner (into a gear). || Mudar: *a snake throws its skin*, la serpiente muda la piel. || Producir, dar (a harvest). || Parir (animals). || U. S. Perder adrede (a fight, etc.). | Conectar (the lever of a machine, etc.). || — FIG. *To be thrown upon*, correr a cargo de. | *To be thrown upon one's own resources*, tener que valerse por sí solo. | *To throw a fit*, tener un ataque de nervios. || *To throw a tale into verse*, poner un cuento en verso. || *To throw difficulties in s.o.'s way*, ponerle obstáculos a alguien en el camino. || *To throw light on a subject*, arrojar luz sobre un asunto, aclarar un asunto. || *To throw open the door*, abrir la puerta de par en par. || FIG. *To throw o.s. at s.o.* o *at s.o.'s head*, insinuarse. || *To throw o.s. backwards*, echarse hacia atrás. || *To throw o.s. into*, lanzarse en. || *To throw o.s. on s.o.*, echarse encima de alguien, abalanzarse sobre alguien. || *To throw overboard*, tirar por la borda. || *To throw s.o. a kiss*, tirar un beso a alguien. || *To throw s.o. into confusion*, desconcertar a alguien. || *To throw s.o. into jail*, meter a alguien en la cárcel. || *To throw two rooms into one*, reunir dos habitaciones.

— V. intr. Tirar, lanzar, arrojar. || Echar *or* tirar los dados (at dice).

— **To throw about**, esparcir, tirar: *to throw litter about*, esparcir la basura. | Tirar, derrochar, despilfarrar (money). | — *To throw one's arms about*, agitar mucho los brazos. | *To throw o.s. about*, moverse. || **To throw aside**, echar a un lado. || **To throw away**, tirar, arrojar: *he threw away his cigarette*, tiró el cigarrillo; *throw these papers away*, tira estos papeles. | Despilfarrar, malgastar (money). | Desechar (to rid o.s. of). | MIL. Deponer (arms). | Perder: *a kind action is never thrown away*, una buena acción nunca está perdida. | Desaprovechar, desperdiciar (chance, opportunity). | **To throw back**, reflejar (to reflect). | Devolver (a ball). | Rechazar (to reject). | Echar hacia atrás: *he threw back his hat*, echó su sombrero hacia atrás. | Retrasar: *this would throw me back two weeks*, esto me retrasaría dos semanas. | BIOL. Dar un salto atrás. || **To throw down**, tirar [de arriba abajo]: *they threw down stones on the besiegers*, tiraban piedras sobre los sitiadores. | Tirar al suelo (to throw to the ground). | Abatir (one's cards). | MIL. Deponer (arms). | Derribar, echar abajo (building). | Depositar (sediment). | Lanzar (challenge). | — FIG. *To throw down one's tools*, declararse en huelga. | *To throw down the glove*, arrojar el guante. | *To throw o.s. down*, tirarse al suelo. || **To throw in**, echar, tirar. | Dar de más, añadir (as an extra). | Intercalar (to interject). | Soltar (a quip). | Sacar de banda (in football). | — *To throw in one's cards*, tirar las cartas sobre la mesa. | *To throw in one's face*, echar en cara a uno. | *To throw in one's hand*, tirar las cartas (at cards), renunciar (to renounce). | *To throw in one's lot with s.o.*, compartir la suerte de alguien. | *To throw in the clutch*, embragar. | *To throw in the towel*, see TOWEL. || **To throw off**, quitarse de encima (to get rid of). | Quitarse (clothes). | Quitarse de, renunciar a (a bad habit). | Abandonar (disguise). | Quitarse (mask). | Despistar (to mislead): *to throw off one's pursuers*, despistar a sus perseguidores. | Improvisar (a speech, story, etc.). | Soltar (remarks). | Despidir (to emit). | Desatraillar (hounds). | Empezar (to start). | — *To throw a train off the rails*, hacer descarrilar un tren. | *To throw the dogs off the scent*, despistar los perros. || ***To throw on,*** ponerse rápidamente (one's clothes). | Echarse encima (a coat). || ***To throw out,*** expulsar, echar (to eject). | Rechazar (to reject): *to throw out a bill*, rechazar un proyecto de ley. | Despedir (heat, light, smell). | Tirar (to throw away). | Soltar (a suggestion). | Sacar (one's chest). | Echar (roots). | Añadir (a new building). | Hacer resaltar (to throw into relief). || MIL. Destacar. | — FAM. *To throw out on one's ear*, poner de patitas en la calle. | *To throw out the clutch*, desembragar. || ***To throw over,*** abandonar, dejar (to abandon). | Echar encima (a coat). || ***To throw together,*** hacer sin cuidado (to assemble hastily). | Reunir, unir (people). || ***To throw up,*** lanzar al aire. | Levantar (to raise). | Construir rápidamente (to build hastily). | Dejar (a job). | Renunciar a (claims). | Devolver, arrojar, vomitar (to vomit). | Arrojar: *thrown up by the sea*, arrojado por el mar.

— OBSERV. Pret. ***threw;*** p. p. ***thrown.***

throwaway [ˈθrəuəwei] n. U. S. Prospecto, *m.* (handbill).
— Adj. Para tirar (wrapping).
throwback [ˈθrəubæk] n. BIOL. Salto (*m.*) atrás, retroceso, *m.* || Retroceso, *m.*
thrower [ˈθrəuə*] n. Jugador, ra (of dice). || Alfarero, *m.* (potter). || SP. Lanzador, ra.
throw-in [ˈθrəuin] n. SP. Saque (*m.*) de banda (in football).
thrown [θrəun] p. p. See THROW.
throw-out [ˈθrəuaut] n. COMM. Desecho, *m.*, desperdicio, *m.* || ELECTR. Interruptor (*m.*) automático. || TECH. Desembrague (*m.*) automático.
throwster [ˈθrəustə*] n. Torcedor, ra (of silk).
thru [θru:] adv. U. S. See THROUGH.
thrum [θrʌm] n. Cabo, *m.* || — Pl. MAR. Cabos (*m.*) cortos para hacer palletes.
thrum [θrʌm] v. tr. Tamborilear en (to drum on). || Rasguear (a stringed instrument). || Teclear en (a piano).
— V. intr. Tamborilear (with the fingers). || Rasguear un instrumento de cuerda (on a stringed instrument). || Teclear (on a piano).
thrush [θrʌʃ] n. Zorzal, *m.*, tordo, *m.* (bird). || MED. Afta, *f.* || VET. Arestín, *m.*
thrust [θrʌst] n. Empujón, *m.* (push). || Estocada, *f.* (stab). || ARCH. AVIAT. Empuje, *m.* || GEOL. Corrimiento, *m.*, deslizamiento, *m.* || MIL. Arremetida, *f.* || SP. Estocada, *f.* (in fencing). || Pulla, *f.* (taunt). || *That was a thrust at you*, esto iba por ti.
thrust* [θrʌst] v. tr. Empujar (to push with force). || Clavar: *to thrust a dagger into s.o.'s side*, clavar un puñal en el costado de alguien. || Meter: *to thrust one's hands into one's pockets*, meter las manos en los bolsillos. || Poner: *he thrust the letter in front of me*, me puso la carta delante. || — *To be thrust into an unpleasant situation*, meterse en una situación desagradable. || *To thrust aside* o *away*, rechazar. || *To thrust back*, hacer retroceder (people). || *To thrust down*, bajar. || *To thrust forward*, empujar hacia adelante. || FAM. *To thrust one's nose into everything*, meter las narices en todo. || *To thrust one's way through the crowd*, abrirse paso entre la multitud. || FIG. *To thrust o.s. forward*, ponerse en evidencia. | *To thrust o.s. upon*, pegarse a: *she thrust herself upon us*, se nos pegó. || *To thrust out*, sacar: *to thrust out one's head*, sacar la cabeza; *to thrust out one's tongue*, sacar la lengua; tender (hand), sacar (chest). || *To thrust sth. on s.o.*, obligar a alguien a aceptar algo. || *To thrust through*, atravesar.
— V. intr. Dar un empujón, empujar (to make a sudden push). || Abrirse paso: *he thrust through the crowd*, se abrió paso entre la multitud. || SP. Lanzar una estocada (in fencing). || — FIG. *To thrust and parry*, rivalizar en ingenio. || *To thrust at*, asestar un golpe a. || *To thrust past s.o.*, empujar a alguien para pasar.

— OBSERV. Pret. & p. p. ***thrust.***

thruster [—ə*] n. FAM. Arribista, *m.* & *f.*
thud [θʌd] n. Ruido (*m.*) sordo.
thud [θʌd] v. tr. *He thudded his fist down on the counter*, dio un puñetazo fuerte en el mostrador. || *He thudded the parcel down on the table*, dejó caer pesadamente el paquete en la mesa.
— V. intr. Caer con un ruido sordo (to fall heavily). || — *The arrow thudded into the tree*, la flecha se clavó en el árbol. || *The guns thudded all around*, se oía el disparo de los cañones alrededor. || *To thud about*, andar con pasos pesados.
thug [θʌg] n. Gamberro, *m.* (hooligan). || Criminal, *m.* || Secuaz, *m.* (hireling). || Bruto, *m.* (brute).
thuggery [ˈθʌgəri] n. Gamberrismo, *m.* (hooliganism). || Bandidaje, *m.* (crime).
thulium [ˈθju:liəm] n. CHEM. Tulio, *m.*
thumb [θʌm] n. Pulgar, *m.*, dedo (*m.*) pulgar. || — FAM. *By rule of thumb*, de modo empírico. | *Thumbs up!*, ¡suerte! || FIG. *To be all thumbs*, ser un manazas. | *To be thumbs down on*, estar en contra de. | *To be under s.o.'s thumb*, estar dominado por alguien. | *To twiddle one's thumbs*, estar mano sobre mano.
thumb [θʌm] v. tr. Hojear: *to thumb the pages of a book*, hojear las páginas de un libro. || Manosear: *a well-thumbed page*, una página muy manoseada. || Tocar con el pulgar (to touch with the thumb). || — *To thumb a lift* o *a ride*, hacer autostop, ir en autostop. || *To thumb one's nose*, hacer un palmo de narices.
thumb index [—indeks] n. PRINT. Uñeros, *m. pl.*
thumb-index [—indeks] v. tr. PRINT. Poner uñeros a. || *Thumb-indexed*, con uñeros.
thumbnail [—neil] adj. Minúsculo, la; pequeño, ña (small). || Conciso, sa; breve (concise).
— N. Uña (*f.*) del pulgar.
thumbprint [—print] n. Huella (*f.*) digital *or* dactilar, huella (*f.*) del pulgar.
thumbscrew [—scru:] n. Tornillo (*m.*) de mariposa *or* de orejas (manual screw). || Empulgueras, *f. pl.* (instrument of torture).
thumbs-down [—zˈdaun] n. Señal (*f.*) de desaprobación.
thumbstall [—stɔ:l] n. Dedil, *m.* [para el pulgar].
thumbs-up [—zˈʌp] n. Señal (*f.*) de aprobación (approval). || Luz (*f.*) verde (go-ahead): *to give s.o. the thumbs-up*, darle la luz verde a alguien.
thumbtack [—tæk] n. Chincheta, *f.*, chinche, *f.*
thump [θʌmp] n. Porrazo, *m.* (heavy blow). || Ruido (*m.*) sordo (noise).
thump [θʌmp] v. tr. Golpear (to strike). || FAM. Dar una paliza a (to defeat heavily). || *To thump out a tune on the piano*, tocar una melodía aporreando el piano.
— V. intr. Dar golpes (to hit out). || Latir con fuerza (the heart). || *To thump about*, andar pesadamente, andar haciendo mucho ruido.
thumping [—iŋ] adj. FAM. Enorme, descomunal.
thunder [ˈθʌndə*] n. Trueno, *m.*: *thunder follows lightning*, el trueno sigue al relámpago. || Truenos, *m. pl.*: *thunder and lightning*, truenos y relámpagos. || FIG. Estruendo, *m.*, estrépito, *m.*, fragor, *m.*: *the thunder of the guns*, el estruendo de los cañones. | Vociferaciones, *f. pl.* (vehement rhetoric). || — *Clap of thunder*, trueno, tronido, *m.* || FIG. *To seal s.o.'s thunder*, quitarle el éxito a alguien.
thunder [ˈθʌndə*] v. intr. Tronar: *it is thundering*, truena. || FIG. Tronar (to make a loud noise, to shout violently): *all around us cannons thundered*, alrededor de nosotros tronaban los cañones; *to thunder against vice*, tronar contra el vicio. | Retumbar (cannons, waterfall, etc.). || — *To thunder into*, caer *or* entrar con estruendo. || *To thunder past*, pasar con un ruido infernal *or* estruendoso.
— V. tr. Vociferar (to utter loudly).
thunderbolt [—bəult] n. Rayo, *m.* (stroke of lightning). || Piedra (*f.*) de rayo (imaginary missile that accompanies lightning). || FIG. Bomba, *f.* (sth. destructive or surprising): *the news hit me like a thunderbolt*, la noticia cayó como una bomba.
thunderclap [—klæp] n. Trueno, *m.*, tronido, *m.* || FIG. Bomba, *f.* (sth. violent or shocking).
thundercloud [—klaud] n. Nube (*f.*) de tormenta.
Thunderer [—ə*] n. MYTH. *The Thunderer*, Júpiter (*m.*) tonante.
thundering [—riŋ] adj. Estruendoso, sa; de trueno (very loud): *thundering voice*, voz de trueno. || FAM. Enorme, tremendo, da (tremendous): *a thundering success*, un éxito tremendo; *a thundering great hole*, un agujero enorme. | Maldito, ta (damned).
thunderous [—rəs] adj. Estruendoso, sa; de trueno (noise, voice). || Ensordecedor, ra; atronador, ra (deafening): *thunderous applause*, aplausos ensordecedores.
thunderstorm [—stɔ:m] n. Tormenta, *f.*
thunderstricken [—ˌstrikən] or **thunderstruck** [—strʌk] adj. Atónito, ta; asombrado, da.
thundery [—ri] adj. Tormentoso, sa.
thurible [ˈθjuəribl] n. Incensario, *m.* (censer).
thurifer [ˈθjuərifə*] n. REL. Turiferario, *m.* (incense bearer).
Thursday [ˈθə:rzdi] n. Jueves, *m.*: *on Thursday*, el jueves; *next Thursday*, el jueves que viene.
thus [ðʌs] adv. Así, de esta manera (in this way): *do it thus*, hágalo así. || Por eso, así que (for this reason): *he was not in and thus I could not speak to him*, no estaba y por eso no pude hablar con él. || Por ejemplo (as an example of sth. already said). || — *Thus far*, hasta aquí. || *Thus it is that*, así es que.
thwack [θwæk] n./v. tr. See WHACK.
thwart [θwɔ:t] adj. Transversal.
— Adv. Transversalmente, oblicuamente.
— N. MAR. Bancada, *f.*
thwart [θwɔ:t] v. tr. Frustrar, desbaratar: *to thwart s.o.'s plans*, frustrar los planes de alguien. || Frustrar: *to thwart s.o.*, frustrar a alguien.
thy [ðai] poss. adj. (Ant.). Tu: *thy glory*, tu gloria.
thyme [taim] n. BOT. Tomillo, *m.* || BOT. *Wild thyme*, serpol, *m.*
thymelaeaceous [ˌθiməliˈeiʃəs] adj. BOT. Timeleáceo, a.
thymus [ˈθaiməs] n. ANAT. Timo, *m.*
thyroid [ˈθairɔid] adj. ANAT. Tiroideo, a. || — ANAT. *Thyroid cartilage*, cartílago (*m.*) tiroides. | *Thyroid gland*, tiroides, *f.*, glándula (*f.*) tiroides.
— N. ANAT. Tiroides, *f. inv.*
thyroiditis [ˌθairɔidˈaitis] n. MED. Tiroiditis, *f. inv.*
thysanura [ˌθaisəˈnjuərə] pl. n. ZOOL. Tisanuros, *m.*
thysanuran [—n] adj./n. ZOOL. Tisanuro, *m.*
thyself [ðaiˈself] pron. (Ant.). Te: *hast thou hurt thyself?*, ¿te has hecho daño? || Ti, ti mismo: *for thyself*, para ti. || Ti mismo, tú mismo (emphatic).
ti [ti:] n. MUS. Si, *m.*

tiara [ti'α:rə] n. Tiara, *f.* (worn by the Pope). || Diadema, *f.* (worn by women).
Tiber ['taibə*] pr. n. GEOGR. Tiber, *m.*
Tiberias [tai'biəriæs] pr. n. GEOGR. Tiberíades.
Tiberius [tai'biəriəs] pr. n. HIST. Tiberio, *m.*
Tibet [ti'bet] pr. n. GEOGR. El Tíbet, *m.*
Tibetan [—ən] adj./s. Tibetano, na.
tibia ['tibiə] n. ANAT. Tibia, *f.*

— OBSERV. El plural de la palabra inglesa *tibia* es *tibiae* o *tibias.*

tibial ['tibiəl] adj. De la tibia, tibial.
Tibullus [ti'bʌləs] pr. n. HIST. Tibulo, *m.*
tic [tik] n. Tic, *m.*
tick [tik] n. Tictac, *m.* (of a clock). || Marca, *f.*, señal, *f.* (mark). || ZOOL. Garrapata, *f.* || Funda (*f.*) de almohada *or* de colchón (case for mattress, pillow). || FAM. Crédito, *m.*: *to buy on tick*, comprar a crédito. | Momento, *m.* (short time): *just a tick!*, ¡un momento! || FAM. *I am coming in a tick*, en seguida voy.
tick [tik] v. tr. Marcar [con una señal] (to mark). || — *To tick off*, reprender (to tell off), marcar: *to tick off the names of those present*, marcar los nombres de los que están presentes. || *To tick out*, registrar (a telegraph).
— V. intr. Hacer tictac (a clock). || — *I could hear the bomb ticking*, oía el tictac de la bomba. || *To tick away*, pasar, transcurrir (time). || *To tick over*, funcionar al ralentí *or* a marcha lenta (engine).
ticker ['tikə] n. Teletipo, *m.* || FAM. Reloj, *m.* (watch). | Corazón, *m.* (heart). || *Ticker tape*, cinta perforada.
ticket ['tikit] n. Etiqueta, *f.* (showing price, material, etc., of an article). || Billete, *m.* [*Amer.*, boleto, *m.*, boleta, *f.*] (for transport): *train ticket*, billete de tren. || Entrada, *f.* [*Amer.*, boleto, *m.*, boleta, *f.*] (for meetings, concerts, shows, etc.). || Pase, *m.* (permit). || Cupón, *m.* (of ration book). || Vale, *m.*: *meal ticket*, vale de comida. || Título, *m.* (licence): *pilot's ticket*, título de piloto. || Multa, *f.* (fine): *parking ticket*, multa por aparcamiento indebido. || U. S. Candidatura, *f.* (candidates). | Programa, *m.* (programme). | Pasaporte, *m.*: *a good personality is a ticket to success*, una gran personalidad es un pasaporte para el éxito. || — *Cloakroom ticket*, número (*m.*) del guardarropa. || *Complimentary ticket*, billete *or* entrada de favor. || *Platform ticket*, billete de andén. || *Return ticket*, billete de ida y vuelta. || *Single ticket*, billete de ida, billete simple. || FIG. *That's the ticket!*, ¡está muy bien! || *Ticket agency*, agencia (*f.*) de venta de localidades *or* de billetes [*Amer.* boletería, *f.*]. || *Ticket agent*, vendedor (*m.*) de billetes. || *Ticket collector* o *inspector*, revisor, *m.* || *Ticket holder*, poseedor (*m.*) de billete *or* de entrada. || *Ticket office*, taquilla, *f.* [*Amer.*, boletería, *f.*]. || *Ticket pinch*, máquina (*f.*) de picar billetes. || *Ticket window*, taquilla, *f.* [*Amer.*, boletería, *f.*].
ticket ['tikit] v. tr. Poner etiquetas, etiquetar (with prices, etc.). || U. S. Vender billetes a.
ticket of leave [—əv'li:v] n. Libertad (*f.*) condicional. || *Ticket-of-leave man*, hombre (*m.*) en libertad condicional.
ticking ['tikiŋ] n. Terliz, *m.* (cotton material).
ticking off [—'ɔf] n. Reprimenda, *f.*, bronca, *f.*
tickle ['tikl] n. Cosquilleo, *m.* || Picor, *m.* (in the throat). || FIG. *I didn't get a tickle*, no picó nadie.
tickle ['tikl] v. tr. Hacer cosquillas a: *to tickle s.o.'s foot*, hacer cosquillas a alguien en el pie. || Picar: *this shirt tickles me*, esta camisa me pica. || FIG. Divertir (to amuse). | Picar (one's curiosity). | Regalar: *to tickle one's palate*, regalar el paladar a uno. || Coger con las manos (trout, etc.). || FIG. *To tickle (s.o.) pink*, encantar, gustar mucho: *he was tickled pink by the present*, le encantó el regalo; divertir mucho, hacer mucha gracia a (to amuse intensely).
— V. intr. Sentir cosquillas. || Picar: *woolen clothes tickle*, la ropa de lana pica. || *My hand tickles*, siento cosquillas en la mano.
tickler ['tiklə*] n. Problema (*m.*) difícil (poser). || U. S. Agenda, *f.*, diario, *m.* (notebook).
tickling ['tikliŋ] n. Cosquilleo, *m.*, cosquillas, *f. pl.*
ticklish ['tikliʃ] adj. Cosquilloso, sa (sensitive to tickling). || FIG. Delicado, da; espinoso, sa; peliagudo, da: *a ticklish situation*, una situación delicada. | Picajoso, sa (irritable). || *To be ticklish*, tener cosquillas, ser cosquilloso, sa.
ticktacktoe [tik'tæk'təu] n. U. S. Tres en raya, *m.* (noughts-and-crosses).
ticktock ['tik'tɔk] n. Tictac, *m.*
tidal ['taidl] adj. De la marea. || Mareomotor, mareomotriz (activated by tides): *tidal power station*, central mareomotriz. || — *Tidal flood*, maremoto, *m.* || *Tidal wave*, maremoto, *m.*, marejada, *f.*, mar (*m.*) de fondo (caused by an earthquake), mar (*m.*) de fondo, marejada, *f.* (of indignation).
tidbit ['tidbit] n. See TITBIT.
tiddlywinks ['tidliwiŋks] n. Pulga, *f.* (game).
tide [taid] n. MAR. Marea, *f.*: *when the tide comes in*, cuando sube la marea; *rising tide*, marea creciente; *spring tide*, marea viva. || FIG. Corriente, *f.*: *the tide of public opinion*, la corriente de la opinión pública; *to go along with the tide*, seguir la corriente. || — MAR. *Ebb* o *low tide*, bajamar, *f.*, marea baja *or* menguante. | *High* o *full* o *flood tide*, pleamar, *f.*, marea alta. || FIG. *High tide*, apogeo, *m.* (high point). || MAR. *Incoming tide*, marea entrante *or* ascendente. | *Outgoing tide*, marea saliente *or* descendente *or* menguante. || FIG. *The tide has turned*, han cambiado las cosas. | *The tide of events*, el curso de los acontecimientos. | *Time and tide wait for no man*, see TIME. | *To turn the tide of the war*, cambiar el rumbo de la guerra.
tide [taid] v. tr. Arrastrar con la marea. || FIG. *To tide over*, sacar de apuro.
— V. intr. Crecer [la marea]. || Navegar con la marea. || MAR. *To tide in, out*, entrar, salir con la marea.
tide gate [—geit] n. Compuerta, *f.*
tideland [—lænd] n. Terreno (*m.*) que se inunda con las mareas altas, marisma, *f.*
tideless [—lis] adj. Sin mareas.
tidemark [—mα:k] n. Línea (*f.*) de la marea alta.
tide rip [—rip] n. Remolino (*m.*) de la marea.
tidewater [—'wɔ:tə*] n. Agua (*f.*) de marea. || U. S. Tierras (*f. pl.*) bajas del litoral.
tideway [—wei] n. Canal (*m.*) de marea.
tidily [—ili] adv. Bien: *tidily dressed*, bien vestido. || *Everything was tidily arranged*, todo estaba perfectamente ordenado, todo estaba en su sitio.
tidiness [—inis] n. Orden, *m.* (orderliness). || Aseo, *m.*, limpieza, *f.*, pulcritud, *f.* (cleanliness).
tidings [—iŋz] pl. n. Noticias, *f.*
tidy ['taidi] adj. Ordenado, da; en orden: *the house was very tidy*, la casa estaba muy ordenada; *tidy person*, persona ordenada. || Arreglado, da (in appearance): *tidy hair*, pelo arreglado. || Limpio, pia (clean): *the streets are tidier here than in London*, aquí las calles están más limpias que en Londres. || FIG. FAM. Grande, bueno, na: *a tidy sum*, una buena cantidad. | Ligero, ra; rápido, da; bueno, na (pace). | Claro, ra: *tidy mind*, espíritu claro, ideas claras. || *It cost him a tidy penny*, le costó bastante caro.
tidy ['taidi] v. tr. Ordenar, poner en orden: *to tidy one's room*, ordenar la habitación de uno. || Limpiar (to clean). || — *To tidy away*, quitar (dishes), poner en su sitio (to put back). || *To tidy o.s. up*, arreglarse.
— V. intr. *To tidy up*, ordenar: *I always have to tidy up after you*, siempre tengo que ir ordenando detrás de ti; limpiar (to clean up).
tie [tai] n. Corbata, *f.* (necktie): *tie knot*, nudo de corbata. || Cuerda, *f.*, atadura, *f.* (cord). || MUS. Ligado, *m.* || ARCH. Tirante, *m.* || SP. Empate, *m.* (draw). | Partido, *m.* (match): *cup tie*, partido de copa. || FIG. Lazo, *m.*, vínculo, *m.* (bond): *the ties of friendship*, los lazos de la amistad. | Atadura, *f.*: *I don't like the ties of family life, of marriage*, no me gustan las ataduras de la vida familiar, del matrimonio. || U. S. Traviesa, *f.* (railway sleeper). || — *Black tie*, see BLACK. || FIG. *Children are a tie*, los niños atan a uno. || SP. *Tie breaker*, saque (*m.*) para desempatar (in tennis). | *To play off a tie*, desempatar. || *White tie*, corbatín blanco (bow tie), frac, *m.* (formal evening dress).
tie [tai] v. tr. Atar: *tie the dog!*, ¡ata al perro! || Atar, liar (a package, etc.). || Hacer: *to tie a knot*, hacer un nudo. || Hacer un nudo a (a ribbon). || FIG. Atar: *tied by one's responsibilities*, atado por sus obligaciones; *we are tied by a previous contract*, estamos atados por un contrato previo. | Vincular, ligar (to link): *the two facts are tied together*, los dos hechos están vinculados. | Limitar, restringir. || SP. Empatar (a match). || MUS. Ligar. || — FIG. *Our hands are tied*, tenemos atadas las manos, estamos atados de manos. | *To be tied hand and foot*, estar atado de pies y manos. | *To be tied to one's bed*, verse obligado a guardar cama. | *To be tied to one's mother's apron strings*, estar agarrado a las faldas de su madre. || FAM. *To tie the knot*, echar las bendiciones (priest).
— V. intr. Atarse: *it ties easily*, se ata con facilidad. || SP. Empatar (to draw): *we tied 2-all*, empatamos a dos.
— **To tie down**, atar, sujetar: *they tied him down to the bed*, le ataron a la cama. | Someter a ciertas condiciones (capital). | FIG. Atar: *tied down by children*, atado por los niños; *it's a promise which ties you down for the rest of your life*, es una promesa que te ata para toda la vida. | Tener amarrado: *to tie s.o. down to a contract*, tener amarrado a alguien por un contrato. || **To tie in**, unir (to integrate). | Concordar (to be in agreement). | — *To tie in with*, relacionar con; relacionarse con. || **To tie into**, arremeter (to rush). | Regañar (to reprimand). || **To tie off**, atar. || **To tie together**, atar. || **To tie up**, atar (to fasten). | Obstruir, bloquear (traffic). | Amarrar (a boat). | Concluir: *to tie up a deal*, concluir un negocio. | COMM. Invertir (to invest). | Inmovilizar (capital). | Paralizar. || FIG. *I am tied up at the moment*, estoy ocupado por el momento.
tie beam ['taibi:m] n. ARCH. Tirante, *m.*
tie-in ['taiin] n. Relación, *f.* (connection).
tieless ['tailis] adj. Sin corbata.
tiepin ['taipin] n. Alfiler (*m.*) de corbata.
tier [tiə*] n. Grada, *f.*: *seats arranged in tiers*, asientos dispuestos en gradas. || Fila, *f.*, hilera, *f.* (row). || Piso, *m.* (of a wedding cake).
tier [tiə*] v. tr. Disponer en gradas (auditorium). || Poner en filas. || *A tiered cake*, un pastel de varios pisos.
tierce ['tiəs] n. Tercera, *f.*, tercia, *f.* (in card games). || Tercera, *f.* (in fencing). || REL. Tercia, *f.*
tierceron ['tiərsərən] n. ARCH. Arco (*m.*) tercelete.

tie-up [ˈtaiʌp] n. Relación, *f.*, conexión, *f.*, enlace, *m.* (connection). || U. S. Paralización, *f.* (paralysis, stoppage). || *Traffic tie-up*, embotellamiento, *m.*, atasco, *m.*

tiff [tif] n. Riña, *f.*, pelea, *f.* (quarrel). || *To have a tiff*, reñir.

tiff [tif] v. intr. Reñir (to quarrel). || Estar de mal humor (to be angry).

tiffany [ˈtifəni] n. Gasa, *f.* (material).

tiffin [ˈtifin] n. Comida, *f.*, almuerzo, *m.*

tiger [ˈtaigə*] n. ZOOL. Tigre, *m.* || FIG. FAM. Fiera, *f.*, tigre, *m.* (aggresive person). || (Ant.). Lacayo, *m.* (groom).

tiger cat [—kæt] n. ZOOL. Ocelote, *m.* [*Amer.*, tigrillo, *m.*]

tigereye [ˈtaigərˌai] n. MIN. Ojo (*m.*) de gato.

tigerish [—iʃ] adj. De tigre; atigrado, da (like a tiger). || FIG. Feroz, (ferocious).

tiger's-eye [ˈtaigərzˌai] n. MIN. Ojo (*m.*) de gato.

tight [tait] adj. Apretado, da (nut, knot, etc.). || Ajustado, da; ceñido, da (clothes). || Apretado, da; estrecho, cha; pequeño, ña (fitting too closely). || Apretado, da (embrace, hug). || Estricto, ta: *tight control*, control estricto. || Estrecho, cha (watch). || Tirante (taut). || Hermético, ca (shut, sealed). || Cerrado, da (a bend). || FIG. Difícil (situation). | Conciso, sa (style). | Bien formado, da (comely). | COMM. Escaso, sa (money, goods). || FAM. Agarrado, da; tacaño, ña (mean). | Borracho, cha (drunk). || Callado, da (silent). || SP. Reñido, da (match). | Cerrado, da (defence). || PRINT. Apretado, da. || MAR. Estanco, ca (boat). || — *It's a tight fit*, queda muy justo. || FAM. *To be in a tight spot* o *corner*, estar en un aprieto *or* apuro. || *To keep a tight hand* o *a tight hold over*, controlar rigurosamente (to control strictly), ser muy severo con (people).

— Adv. Bien: *shut tight*, bien cerrado; *pull it tight*, tira bien; *to screw a nut on tight*, apretar bien una tuerca. || Herméticamente (sealed). || — *Hold tight!*, ¡agárrense bien! || *To hold sth. tight*, agarrar algo fuertemente. || FIG. *To sit tight*, cruzarse de brazos (to sit idle), estarse quieto (to keep still), mantenerse en su posición (not to submit).

tighten [—ən] v. tr. Apretar (a screw, a knot, etc.). || Tensar (a rope, string, etc.). || Hacer estricto *or* riguroso, estrechar (control). || Estrechar (bonds). || FIG. *To tighten one's belt*, apretarse el cinturón.

— V. intr. Apretarse (a knot, etc.). || Tensarse (a rope). || Volverse más estricto *or* riguroso (control).

tightener [—ənə*] n. TECH. Tensor, *m.*

tightfisted [—ˈfistid] adj. FAM. Agarrado, da; tacaño, ña; roñoso, sa (mean).

tight-fitting [—ˈfitiŋ] adj. Ceñido, da; ajustado, da.

tight-knit [—ˈnit] adj. Muy unido, da.

tight-lipped [—ˈlipt] adj. Con los labios apretados. || FIG. Callado, da (silent).

tightly [—li] adv. See TIGHT.

tightness [—nis] n. Estrechez, *f.* (of clothing, shoes, etc.). || Tensión, *f.* (tension). || Tirantez, *f.* (tautness). || Lo apretado (of a screw). || FAM. Lo agarrado, tacañería, *f.*, roñosería, *f.* (meanness).

tightrope [—rəup] n. Cuerda (*f.*) floja. || *Tightrope walker*, funámbulo, la; equilibrista, *m.* & *f.*

tights [—s] pl. n. Leotardos, *m.* (women's wear). || Mallas, *f.* (for actors, dancers, etc.).

tightwad [—wɔd] n. U. S. FAM. Roñoso, sa; tacaño, ña; agarrado, da.

tigress [ˈtaigris] n. ZOOL. Tigre (*m.*) hembra, tigresa, *f.* || FIG. Fiera, *f.* (ferocious woman).

— OBSERV. The Spanish word *tigresa* is a Gallicism.

tike [taik] n. See TYKE.

tilbury [ˈtilbəri] n. Tílburi, *m.*

tilde [tild] n. Tilde, *f.*

tile [tail] n. Teja, *f.* (of a roof): *plain* o *flat tile*, teja plana; *ridge tile*, teja de cumbrera. || Baldosa, *f.* (on a floor). || Azulejo, *m.* (coloured). || Tubo (*m.*) de desagüe (drainpipe). || FIG. FAM. Sombrero (*m.*) de copa (top hat). || — FIG. FAM. *To have a night on the tiles*, pasar la noche fuera *or* de juerga. | *To have a tile loose*, faltarle a uno un tornillo, estar chalado, da.

tile [tail] v. tr. Tejar, poner tejas en (a roof). || Embaldosar (a floor). || Poner azulejos en, azulejar (with coloured tiles).

tiler [—ə*] n. Techador, *m.* (of roofs). || Solador, *m.* (of floors). || Tejero, *m.* (who makes tiles).

tile works [—wɔ:ks] n. Tejar, *m.*

tiliaceae [ˌtiliˈeisii] pl. n. BOT. Tiliáceas, *f.*

tiling [tailiŋ] n. Colocación (*f.*) de las tejas (on a roof). || Embaldosado, *m.* (of a floor). || Tejas, *f. pl.* (roof tiles). || Baldosas, *f. pl.* (floor tiles). || Azulejos, *m. pl.* (wall tiles).

till [til] prep. Hasta; *he waited till ten o'clock*, esperó hasta las diez.

— Conj. Hasta que: *wait till he comes*, espera hasta que venga.

— N. Caja, *f.* (cash register, money drawer and contents). || GEOL. Morrena, *f.*, morena, *f.*

— OBSERV. Las palabras *till* y *until* empleadas como preposición o conjunción son casi siempre intercambiables. Véase UNTIL.

till [til] v. tr. AGR. Labrar, cultivar.

tillable [ˈtiləbl] adj. Arable, cultivable.

tillage [ˈtilidʒ] n. AGR. Labranza, *f.*, cultivo, *m.*

tiller [ˈtilə*] n. AGR. Labrador, *m.* || MAR. Caña (*f.*) del timón. || BOT. Retoño, *m.*, vástago, *m.* (shoot).

tiller [ˈtilə*] v. intr. BOT. Retoñar.

tilt [tilt] n. Toldo, *m.* (canvas cover). || Inclinación, *f.* (slant). | Justa, *f.*, torneo, *m.* (joust). || TECH. Martinete (*m.*) de forja. || — FIG. (*At*) *full tilt*, a toda mecha, a toda velocidad. || *To be on a tilt*, estar ladeado *or* inclinado. || FIG. *To have a tilt at s.o.*, arremeter contra alguien. | *To run full tilt into sth.*, dar de lleno contra algo.

tilt [tilt] v. tr. Inclinar, ladear. || Arremeter contra (to charge). || TECH. Forjar (metal). || Entoldar (with a canvas cover).

— V. intr. Inclinarse, ladearse (to slant). || Participar en una justa *or* en un torneo (to joust). || *To tilt at*, arremeter contra: *to tilt at windmills*, arremeter contra los molinos de viento.

tilter [ˈtiltə*] n. Justador, *m.*, torneador, *m.*

tilth [tilθ] n. Labranza, *f.*, cultivo, *m.* (cultivation). || Tierra (*f.*) cultivada *or* labrada (cultivated land).

tilt hammer [ˈtiltˌhæmə*] n. TECH. Martinete (*m.*) de forja.

tiltyard [ˈtiltjɑ:d] n. Palestra, *f.*

timbal [ˈtimbəl] n. Timbal, *m.*, atabal, *m.* (kettledrum).

timbale [tæmˈbɑ:l] n. CULIN. Timbal, *m.*

timber [ˈtimbə*] n. Madera, *f.* [de construcción] (wood). || Árboles (*m. pl.*) maderables *or* para madera (trees). || Viga, *f.* (beam). || MAR. Cuaderna, *f.* || FIG. Madera, *f.* (character). || U. S. Bosque, *m.*

timber [ˈtimbə*] v. tr. Enmaderar (wall, ceiling). || || Entibar (a mine).

timbered [—d] adj. Enmaderado, da (ceiling, wall). || Entibado, da (a mine). || Arbolado, da (land).

timber hitch [—hitʃ] n. MAR. Vuelta (*f.*) de braza.

timbering [—riŋ] n. Entibado, *m.*, entibación, *f.* (of a mine). || Maderaje, *m.*, maderamen, *m.* (of any construction).

timberland [—lænd] n. Bosque (*m.*) maderable.

timberline [—lain] n. Límite (*m.*) de la vegetación arbórea.

timberman [—ˌmæn] n. Entibador, *m.*

— OBSERV. El plural es *timbermen*.

timber merchant [—ˌmə:tʃənt] n. Negociante (*m.*) en madera.

timber wolf [—wulf] n. ZOOL. Lobo (*m.*) gris norteamericano.

timberwork [—wə:k] n. Maderaje, *m.*, maderamen, *m.*

timbre [ˈtẽmbr] n. MUS. HERALD. Timbre, *m.*

timbrel [ˈtimbrəl] n. Pandereta, *f.*

time [taim] n. Tiempo, *m.*: *I have no time to do it*, no tengo tiempo para hacerlo; *it lasts a long time*, dura mucho tiempo; *time is an important factor*, el tiempo es un factor importante; *he spends his time reading*, se pasa el tiempo leyendo. || Momento, *m.*: *he was not at home at that time*, no estaba en casa en aquel momento. || Tiempos, *m. pl.*, época, *f.*: *at the time of the Persian supremacy*, en la época de la supremacía persa; *in my time*, en mis tiempos; *in biblical times*, en tiempos bíblicos. || Período, *m.*, periodo, *m.* (period). | Época, *f.*: *during harvest time*, durante la época de la cosecha. | Estación, *f.*, temporada, *f.*: *spring is the nicest time of year*, la primavera es la estación más agradable del año. | Hora, *f.*: *time of departure*, hora de salida; *lunch time*, la hora del almuerzo; *it is time we went*, era hora de que nos fuéramos; *it is time to go*, es hora de que nos vayamos; *what time is it?* o *what is the time?*, ¿qué hora es?; *have you got the time?*, ¿tiene usted hora? | Momento, *m.*, ocasión, *f.*, oportunidad, *f.*: *it is the time to buy*, es la ocasión para comprar; *some other* o *another time*, en otra ocasión, en otro momento. || Vez, *f.*: *that is the third time*, es la tercera vez; *four times running*, cuatro veces seguidas; *five times bigger*, cinco veces mayor; *another time*, otra vez. || Temporada, *f.*: *he is going to Paris for a short time*, se va a pasar una temporada en París. | Rato, *m.*, tiempo, *m.*: *he woke up a short time after going to sleep*, se despertó al poco rato de haberse dormido. || Plazo, *m.*: *within the required time*, dentro del plazo fijado. || Servicio, *m.*: *he served his time in the Navy*, hizo el servicio en la Marina. | Condena, *f.*: *he served his time in prison*, cumplió la condena en la cárcel. || Vida, *f.* (lifetime). | Horas (*f. pl.*) de trabajo (hours of work). || ASTR. Tiempo, *m.*: *true time*, tiempo verdadero. || MUS. Duración, *f.* (the length of a note). | Compás, *m.* (rhythm, tempo): *4/8 time*, compás de cuatro por ocho; *in time to the music*, al compás de la música; *to beat time*, llevar el compás; *to keep time*, seguir el compás. || SP. Final, *m.* (end of a match). | Tiempo, *m.*: *his time was five seconds*, hizo un tiempo de cinco segundos. || — *Against time*, contra reloj: *race against time*, carrera contra reloj. || *All in good time*, a su debido tiempo (in due time), luego (later). || *All the time*, todo el tiempo: *I was listening all the time*, estuve escuchando todo el tiempo; siempre, constantemente: *he says it all the time*, lo dice siempre. || *A long time ago*, hace mucho tiempo. || *A long time since*, hace mucho tiempo (from now), hacía mucho tiempo (from then). || *A man of the times*, un hombre de su época *or* de su tiempo. || *Any time*, cuando quiera. || *As time passes* o *goes by*, andando el tiempo, con el tiempo. || *At* *all times*, en todo momento. || *At any time*, en cualquier momento: *he is likely to come at any time*, puede llegar en cualquier momento; cuando quiera: *come at any time*, ven cuando quiera. || *At a time*, a la vez, al mismo tiempo: *he works in six places at a time*, trabaja en seis sitios a la vez; entero, ra: *for hours at a time*, durante horas enteras. || *At his time in life*, con los años que tiene, a su edad. || *At no time*, nunca. || *At one time*, en cierta época, en un tiempo. || *At some time or other*, en un momento o en otro. || *At the present time*, actualmente. || *At the same time*, a la vez, al mismo tiempo: *I can wash six plates at the same time*, puedo lavar seis platos a la vez; *I like it but at the same time it frightens me*, me gusta pero al mismo tiempo me da miedo. || *At the wrong time*, en un mal momento. || *At this time of day*, en este momento, a estas alturas. || *At times*, a veces. || *Behind the times*, anticuado, da: *my father is behind the times*, mi padre es anticuado; atrasado de noticias (not well-informed). || *Between times*, en el intervalo. || *By that time*, para entonces: *by that time he had already gone*, para entonces ya se había ido. || *By the time we arrived he had already gone*, cuando llegamos ya se había ido. || *By this time next month*, el mes que viene por estas fechas. || *Civil* o *standard* o *official time*, hora legal *or* oficial. || *Each* o *every time*, cada vez. || *Father Time*, el Tiempo. || *For all time*, para siempre. || *For the first, for the last time*, por primera vez, por última vez. || *For the time being*, de momento, por ahora. || *Four times three is twelve*, cuatro por tres son doce. || *From that time onwards*, desde entonces. || *From this time*, a partir de ahora. || *From time immemorial*, desde tiempo inmemorial. || *From time to time*, de vez en cuando. || *Give it time*, da tiempo al tiempo. || *Greenwich mean time*, hora según el meridiano de Greenwich. || *Have a good time!*, ¡que lo pases bien!, ¡que lo paséis bien! || FIG. *He wouldn't even give you the time of day*, no da ni la hora (very stingy). || *His time had come*, su hora había llegado. || *His time was drawing near*, se acercaba su hora. || *How time flies!*, ¡cómo pasa el tiempo! || *In due time*, a su debido tiempo. || *In five minutes' time*, dentro de cinco minutos. || *In former* o *in olden times*, en otros tiempos, en tiempos pasados *or* antiguos. || *In good time*, a tiempo (in time), a su debido tiempo (at the proper time), rápidamente (quickly). || *In no time (at all)*, en un abrir y cerrar de ojos. || *In one's own good time*, cuando uno quiera, cuando le parezca bien a uno: *I'll do it in my own good time*, lo haré cuando quiera. || *In one's spare* o *free time*, en el tiempo libre. || *In the course of time*, andando el tiempo, con el tiempo. || *In the nick of time*, see NICK. || *In time*, a tiempo: *were you in time for the train?*, ¿llegaste a tiempo para coger el tren?; con el tiempo (with time): *we shall succeed in time*, con el tiempo lo conseguiremos; con ritmo, al compás (in music). || *It is about time too!* o *and about time too!*, ¡ya era hora! || *It is a long time since I saw him*, hace mucho tiempo que no lo veo. || *It is high time that*, ya es hora de que: *it's high time you learnt the lesson*, ya es hora de que aprendas la lección. || *It takes time*, toma *or* requiere tiempo. || *Many a time* o *many times*, muchas veces. || *Near her time*, a punto de dar a luz (a pregnant woman). || *On* o *in one's own time*, fuera de las horas de trabajo. || *On* o *in the firm's time*, en las horas de trabajo. || *On time*, a la hora, puntualmente, a tiempo (in time), a plazos (on hire purchase). || MUS. *Out of time*, fuera de compás. || *Overtime counts time and a half*, cada hora extraordinaria cuenta como una hora y media. || *Right on time*, a la hora en punto. || *Some time ago*, hace algún tiempo. || *There is a time and place for everything*, cada cosa a su tiempo. || *There is no time to lose*, no hay tiempo que perder. || *Third time lucky*, a la tercera va la vencida. || *This time last year*, el año pasado por estas fechas. || *Time after time* o *time and time again*, repetidas veces. || *Time and tide wait for no man*, la misma ocasión no se presenta dos veces. || *Time and words can never be recalled*, lo dicho, dicho está. || *Time, gentlemen, please!*, ¡caballeros, es la hora! || *Time is money*, el tiempo es oro. || *Time is on our side*, el tiempo obra en nuestro favor. || *Time off*, tiempo libre, horas libres. || *Times are hard*, los tiempos son duros *or* difíciles. || *Time's up!*, ¡es la hora! || *Time will tell*, el tiempo dirá. || *To be behind time*, llevar retraso: *we are an hour behind time*, llevamos una hora de retraso. || *To be in step with the times*, ser de su tiempo. || *To be on* o *to work short time*, hacer jornada reducida. || *To gain time*, ganar tiempo: *they took a shortcut to gain time*, cogieron un atajo para ganar tiempo; adelantar (a clock). || *To have a bad* o *a rough time*, pasarlo mal. || *To have a good time*, pasarlo bien, divertirse. || FAM. *To have done time*, haber cumplido su condena, haber estado a la sombra. || FIG. *To have no time for*, no tener tiempo que perder con, no tener tiempo para. || *To have the time of one's life* o *to have a whale of a time*, pasarlo bomba, pasarlo en grande. || *To have time on one's hands* o *time to kill*, tener tiempo de sobra. || *To keep bad time*, andar mal (clock). || *To keep good time*, andar bien (clock). || *To keep up with* o *abreast of the times*, ser muy de su época. || *To kill time*, matar el tiempo. || *To lose no time in*, no tardar en. || *To lose time*, perder tiempo (s.o.), atrasarse (clock). || *To make good time*, ganar tiempo. || *To make time*, ganar tiempo. || *To mark time*, marcar el paso (in a military march), no avanzar nada, estancarse (to stagnate), hacer tiempo (waiting). || *To pass the time*, pasar el tiempo *or* el rato. || FAM. *To pass the time of day*, charlar un rato. || *To play for time*, ganar tiempo. || *To serve one's time*, estar de aprendiz. || MUS. *To sing, to dance, to play in time*, llevar el compás. || *To take a long time to*, tardar mucho [tiempo] en. || *To take one's time*, tomarse el tiempo [necesario] (to use the time available), hacer las cosas con calma, no apresurarse (not to hurry), tardar mucho tiempo (to be very slow). || *To waste time*, perder el tiempo. || *Until such time as you comply*, hasta que usted obedezca. || *What a time we had!*, ¡qué bien lo pasamos! || *What is the cooking time for an egg?*, ¿cuánto tiempo tarda un huevo en cocerse? || *When my time comes*, cuando llegue mi hora.

— Adj. Del tiempo. || A plazos (payment, etc.). || A plazo (deposit, draft).

time [taim] v. tr. Calcular, fijar la hora de: *he timed his arrival for nightfall*, calculó su llegada para el anochecer. || Calcular el tiempo de (to evaluate the time). || Cronometrar (a race, runner, etc.). || Regular (to set, to regulate): *the bomb is timed to explode in five minutes*, la bomba está regulada para que explote dentro de cinco minutos. || — *He timed his speech to last twenty minutes*, calculó su discurso para que durara veinte minutos. || *The queen's arrival was timed for one o'clock*, la llegada de la reina estaba prevista para la una. || *You timed your arrival just right*, has llegado en el momento oportuno.

time bomb [—bɔm] n. MIL. Bomba (*f.*) de efecto retardado *or* con mecanismo de relojería.

time card [—kɑ:d] n. Tarjeta, *f.* [para registrar la entrada y salida del trabajo].

time clock [—klɔk] n. Reloj (*m.*) registrador.

time-consuming [—kən'sju:miŋ] adj. Que requiere mucho tiempo.

timed [—d] adj. Calculado, da. || SP. Cronometrado, da. || *A well-timed intervention*, una intervención oportuna.

time exposure [—iks'pəuʒə*] n. PHOT. Exposición, *f.*, pose, *f.*

time fuse [—fju:z] n. MIL. Espoleta (*f.*) con mecanismo de relojería.

time-honoured (U. S. **time-honored**) [—'ɔnəd] adj. Tradicional, consagrado, da. *a time-honoured custom*, una costumbre consagrada.

timekeeper [—'ki:pə*] n. Cronómetro, *m.* (watch, clock). || Cronometrador, *m.* (person).

timekeeping [—'ki:piŋ] n. Control (*m.*) de entrada y salida del trabajo (in factories, offices, etc.). || Cronometraje, *m.* (of games, matches).

time lag [—læg] n. Intervalo, *m.* (between two events). || Retraso, *m.* (delay).

timeless [—lis] adj. Eterno, na. || Sin limitación de tiempo.

time limit [—'limit] n. Límite (*m.*) de tiempo. || Plazo, *m.*, fecha (*f.*) tope (for payment). || Duración, *f.* (of a privilege). || *To impose a time limit on a speaker*, limitar la intervención de un orador a cierto tiempo.

timeliness [—linis] n. Oportunidad, *f.*

timely [—li] adj. Oportuno, na: *a timely arrival*, una llegada oportuna.

time out [—'aut] n. U. S. Descanso, *m.* (break). || SP. Interrupción, *f.* (of a match).

timepiece [—pi:s] n. Reloj, *m.*

timer [—ə*] n. Cronometrador, *m.* (person). || Cronómetro, *m.* (watch). || Reloj, *m.* (clock). || AUT. Distribuidor (*m.*) del encendido.

timesaving [—'seiviŋ] adj. Para ahorrar tiempo, que ahorra tiempo: *a timesaving tactic*, una táctica para ahorrar tiempo.

timeserver [—'sə:və*] n. Contemporizador, ra.

timeserving [—'sə:viŋ] adj. Contemporizador, ra.

time sheet [—ʃi:t] n. Hoja (*f.*) de presencia.

time signal [—'signl] n. Señal (*f.*) horaria.

time signature [—'signitʃə*] n. MUS. Compás, *m.*

time switch [—switʃ] n. ELECTR. Interruptor (*m.*) eléctrico automático.

timetable [—teibl] n. Horario, *m.* || Guía, *f.* (for trains, etc.).

timework [—wə:k] n. Trabajo (*m.*) por horas.

timeworn [—wɔ:n] adj. Trillado, da; gastado, da (hackneyed). || Gastado, da; usado, da (showing signs of wear).

time zone [—zəun] n. Huso (*m.*) horario.

timid ['timid] adj. Tímido, da (shy). || Asustadizo, za; timorato, ta (easily frightened).

timidity [ti'miditi] or **timidness** ['timidnis] n. Timidez, *f.* (shyness).

timing ['taimiŋ] n. Cronometraje, *m.* (of races, etc.). || TECH. Reglaje, *m.*, regulación, *f.* || Coordinación, *f.* (coordination): *the actors' timing was out*, faltaba coordinación entre los artistas. || Oportunidad, *f.* (timeliness). || — *My timing was slightly out*, no calculé muy bien. || *The dancer's timing was all wrong*, el bailador no llevaba el compás *or* el ritmo. || AUT. *The timing needs adjusting*, hace falta regular el distribuidor. || *Timing gear*, engranaje (*m.*) de distribución. || *What excellent timing!*, ¡qué oportuno!

timorous [ˈtimərəs] adj. Timorato, ta; asustadizo, za (easily frightened). || Tímido, da (timid): *a timorous voice*, una voz tímida.
timorousness [—nis] n. Carácter (*m.*) timorato. || Timidez, *f.*
timpani [ˈtimpəni] pl. n. MUS. Timbales, *m.*
timpanist [ˈtimpənist] n. MUS. Timbalero, *m.*
tin [tin] n. MIN. Estaño, *m.* || Hojalata, *f.* (tinplate). || Lata, *f.*, bote, *m.* (container). || CULIN. Molde, *m.* (for tarts, cakes). || FAM. Parné, *m.*, pasta, *f.* [*Amer.*, plata, *f.*] (money).
— Adj. De estaño. || De hojalata (of tinplate). || *Tin soldier*, soldadito (*m.*) de plomo.

— OBSERV. Flat tins, such as those used in canning sardines, tend to be called *latas* rather than *botes*.

tin [tin] v. tr. Estañar (to coat with tin). || Enlatar, envasar, conservar en lata: *to tin fruit*, enlatar fruta. || *Tinned peaches*, melocotones en lata *or* de lata *or* en conserva.
tinamou [ˈtinəmu:] n. Tinamú, *m.* (bird).
tin-bearing [ˈtin,bɛəriŋ] adj. Estannífero, ra.
tin can [ˈtinˈkæn] n. Bote, *m.*, lata, *f.* (container). || U. S. FAM. Destructor, *m.* (destroyer).
tinctorial [tiŋkˈtɔ:riəl] adj. Tintóreo, a.
tincture [ˈtiŋktʃə*] n. Color, *m.*, tinte, *m.* (hue). || MED. Tintura, *f.*: *tincture of iodine*, tintura de yodo. || FIG. Tinte, *m.*, matiz, *m.*: *to have a political tincture*, tener un tinte político. || HERALD. Esmalte, *m.*
tincture [ˈtiŋktʃə*] v. tr. Teñir (*with*, de). || FIG. Matizar.
tinder [ˈtində*] n. Yesca, *f.*
tinderbox [—bɔks] n. Yesquero, *m.* (for striking a spark). || FIG. Polvorín, *m.*
tinder fungus [—ˈfʌŋgəs] n. BOT. Hongo (*m.*) yesquero.
tine [tain] n. Punta, *f.*, púa, *f.* (of a pitchfork). || Diente, *m.* (of a fork).
tinea [ˈtiniə] n. MED. Tiña, *f.*
tin fish [ˈtinfiʃ] n. FAM. Torpedo, *m.*
tinfoil [ˈtinˈfɔil] n. Papel (*m.*) de estaño.
ting [tiŋ] n. Tilín, *m.*, tintineo, *m.*
ting [tiŋ] v. tr. Hacer tintinear.
— V. intr. Tintinear.
ting-a-ling [ˈtiŋəliŋ] n. Tilín, *m.*: *to go ting-a-ling*, hacer tilín.
tinge [tindʒ] n. Tinte, *m.*, matiz, *m.* || *With a tinge of remorse*, con cierto remordimiento.
tinge [tindʒ] v. tr. Teñir. || FIG. Matizar. || FIG. *Memories tinged with sadness*, recuerdos impregnados de tristeza.
tingle [ˈtiŋgl] n. Escozor, *m.* (of a slight wound). || Hormigueo, *m.* (sensation like pins and needles). || Estremecimiento, *m.*, escalofrío, *m.* (shiver). || Zumbido, *m.* (of ears).
tingle [ˈtiŋgl] v. intr. Sentir hormigueo. || Estremecerse (with pleasure). || Zumbar (the ears). || *My whole body tingled*, sentí hormigueo por todo el cuerpo.
tin hat [ˈtinˈhæt] n. MIL. FAM. Casco, *m.* [de acero].
tininess [ˈtaininis] n. Pequeñez, *f.*
tinker [ˈtiŋkə*] n. Calderero, *m.* (who mends pots and pans). || Gitano, na (gipsy). || FAM. Pícaro, ra (child). || Chapucero, ra (botcher). || — FIG. FAM. *I couldn't give a tinker's cuss* o *a tinker's damn*, me importa un bledo. | *It's not worth a tinker's cuss* o *a tinker's damn*, no vale un comino. | *You little tinker!*, ¡pícaro!, ¡malo!
tinker [ˈtiŋkə*] v. tr. Componer, arreglar (pots and pans). || Arreglar, apañar (to mend). || *To tinker up*, arreglar, apañar.
— V. intr. Enredar, jugar, entretenerse: *he loves to tinker with any kind of gadget*, le encanta enredar *or* jugar con toda clase de aparatos. || Cambiar: *to tinker with the timetable*, cambiar el horario. || Estropear (to put out of order): *s.o. tinkered with the alarm*, alguien estropeó la alarma. || Arreglar (to mend): *is he still tinkering with the car?*, ¿está todavía arreglando el coche? || Tocar, enredar (*with*, con): *who has been tinkering with the television?*, ¿quién ha tocado el televisor? || — *To tinker with the house*, hacer pequeños arreglos en la casa. || *To tinker with words*, jugar del vocablo.
tinkle [ˈtiŋkl] n. Tintineo, *m.* || FAM. *To give s.o. a tinkle*, llamar a alguien por teléfono (to telephone).
tinkle [ˈtiŋkl] v. tr. Hacer tintinear.
— V. intr. Tintinear.
tinkling [—iŋ] n. Tintineo, *m.*
tinman [ˈtinmən] n. Hojalatero, *m.*

— OBSERV. El plural de esta palabra es *tinmen*.

tinned [tind] adj. En lata, en conserva.
tinniness [ˈtininis] n. Sonido (*m.*) metálico: *the tinniness of a piano, of a voice*, el sonido metálico de un piano, de una voz.
tinnitus [tiˈnaitəs] n. MED. Zumbido, *m.* (of ears).
tinny [ˈtini] adj. De estaño, de hojalata (made of tin). || Estañoso, sa (containing tin). || Metálico, ca (sound, taste). || FAM. De oropel (of inferior quality). | Poco sólido, da (car, etc.).
tin opener [ˈtin,əupnə*] n. Abrelatas, *m. inv.*
Tin Pan Alley [ˈtinpænˈæli] n. FIG. FAM. Mundo (*m.*) de los compositores de música popular.
tinplate [ˈtinˈpleit] n. Hojalata, *f.*
tin-plate [ˈtinˈpleit] v. tr. Estañar.
tin-plating [—iŋ] n. Estañado, *m.*
tinsel [ˈtinsəl] n. Oropel, *m.*
— Adj. De oropel.
tinsel [ˈtinsəl] v. tr. Adornar con oropel.
tin shop [ˈtinʃɔp] n. Hojalatería, *f.*
tinsmith [ˈtinsmiθ] n. Hojalatero, *m.*, estañero, *m.*
tinstone [ˈtinstəun] n. MIN. Casiterita, *f.*
tint [tint] n. Tinte, *m.* (hair dye). || Tono, *m.*: *her hair has a reddish tint*, su pelo tiene un tono rojizo. || Matiz, *m.*: *blue with a tint of green*, azul con un matiz verde. || FIG. Matiz, *m.* || ARTS. Plumeado, *m.*, sombreado, *m.* (shading). || PRINT. Fondo (*m.*) de color claro (light background).
tint [tint] v. tr. Teñir: *to tint sth. red*, teñir algo de rojo. || Matizar. || ARTS. Plumear, sombrear (in engraving).
tin tack [ˈtintæk] n. Tachuela, *f.*
tintinnabulation [ˈtinti,næbjuˈleiʃən] n. Tintineo, *m.* (tinkling sound).
tinware [ˈtinwɛə*] n. Quincalla, *f.*
tinwork [ˈtinwə:k] n. Hojalatería, *f.*
tiny [ˈtaini] adj. Diminuto, ta; pequeñísimo, ma; minúsculo, la. || *A tiny drop*, una gotita.
tip [tip] n. Punta, *f.*, extremidad, *f.* (of a stick, fingers, etc.). || Filtro, *m.* (of a cigarette). || Contera, *f.*, regatón, *m.*, punta, *f.* (of umbrella, walking stick). || Vertedero, *m.* (for rubbish). || Escorial, *m.* (for industrial waste). || Inclinación, *f.* (slant). || Consejo, *m.* (piece of advice): *let me give you a tip*, déjame que te dé un consejo. || Información, *f.* (to the police, in horse racing, etc.): *I've got a hot tip for the 3.30*, me han dado una buena información para la carrera de las tres y media. || Propina, *f.* (gratuity). || Golpecito, *m.* (light blow). || SP. Golpe (*m.*) con efecto (in cricket). || — *Filter tip*, filtro. || *Filter tip cigarette*, cigarrillo (*m.*) con filtro. || *From tip to toe*, de pies a cabeza. || *I had it on the tip of my tongue*, lo tenía en la punta de la lengua. || *Rubbish tip*, vertedero de escombros, escombrera, *f.* || *Take my tip*, sigue mi consejo. || *To walk on the tips of one's toes*, andar de puntillas.
tip [tip] v. tr. Poner una contera *or* un regatón a (a stick). || Poner filtro a (a cigarette). || Inclinar, ladear (to tilt): *to tip back one's chair*, inclinar la silla hacia atrás. || Volcar (to upset, to turn over). || Verter (to pour). || Dar una información a (to give information). || Pronosticar (a winner, etc.): *everyone is tipping X for the job*, todos pronostican que se dará el puesto a X. || Dar una propina a (a waiter, etc.): *to tip s.o. heavily*, dar una buena propina a alguien. || Dar un golpecito a (to strike lightly). || Dar con efecto a [la pelota] (in cricket). || *To tip one's hat*, saludar.
— V. intr. Volcar, volcarse (to turn over). || Inclinarse, ladearse (to lean). || Dar una propina (to give a gratuity).
— ***To tip off***, dar una información a (the police, etc.). | Hacer caer (to make fall). || Caerse (to fall). || ***To tip out***, vaciar: *to tip out one's handbag* o *the contents of one's handbag*, vaciar el bolso. | Verter (to pour). | Hacer caer: *he tipped me out of the chair*, me hizo caer de la silla. || ***To tip over***, volcar. | Volcarse. || ***To tip up***, inclinar, ladear (to tilt). | Volcar (to overturn). | Volcarse (to turn over). | Hacer caer (to make fall). | Levantar; levantarse (a seat).
tipcart [—kɑ:t] n. Volquete, *m.*
tip lorry [—,lɔri] n. Volquete, *m.*
tip-off [—ɔf] n. FAM. Información, *f.*
tipped [—t] adj. Con filtro, emboquillado, da (cigarette). || *Tipped with steel*, con contera de acero (walking stick).
tippet [ˈtipit] n. Esclavina, *f.* (short cape).
tipple [ˈtipl] n. Bebida (*f.*) alcohólica (drink). || FAM. Traguito, *m.* (swig). || U. S. Vertedero, *m.* (tip).
tipple [ˈtipl] v. tr. FAM. Soplar, pimplar.
— V. intr. FAM. Empinar el codo.
tippler [ˈtiplə*] n. FAM. Borrachín, *m.*
tipsily [ˈtipsili] adv. Como un borracho.
tipsiness [ˈtipsinis] n. FAM. Embriaguez, *f.*, borrachera, *f.*
tipster [ˈtipstə*] n. Pronosticador, *m.*
tipsy [ˈtipsi] adj. Achispado, da; piripi.
tiptoe [ˈtiptəu] n. Punta (*f.*) del pie. || *On tiptoe*, de puntillas (on the tips of one's toes), ansioso, sa (eager), sigilosamente (stealthily).
— Adv. De puntillas.
tiptoe [ˈtiptəu] v. intr. Andar *or* ir de puntillas.
tip-top [ˈtipˈtɔp] adj. FAM. Excelente, estupendo, da; de primera categoría: *a tip-top performance*, una representación estupenda. || FAM. *On tip-top form*, en plena forma.
— N. Cumbre, *f.*
tip-up [ˈtipʌp] adj. Abatible (seat). || *Tip-up truck*, volquete, *m.*
tirade [taiˈreid] n. Diatriba, *f.*, perorata, *f.*
tire [ˈtaiə*] n. Calce, *m.*, llanta, *f.* (of cart wheel, etc.). || U. S. Neumático, *m.* [*Amer.*, llanta, *f.*] (tyre).
tire [taiə*] v. tr. Calzar (a cart wheel). || Poner neumáticos *or* llantas a (the wheel of a car). || Cansar (to fatigue). || *To tire out*, agotar.
— V. intr. Cansarse (*of*, de).
tired [—d] adj. Cansado, da: *to be very tired*, estar muy cansado. || — *I'm tired of you*, estoy harto de ti. || *Tired out*, agotado, da.
tiredly [—dli] adv. Cansadamente. || *He said tiredly*, dijo con voz cansada.

tiredness [—dnis] n. Cansancio, *m.*
tireless [—lis] adj. Incansable, infatigable.
tiresome [—səm] adj. Cansado, da (tiring). || Agotador, ra (exhausting). || Pesado, da (boring).
tiresomeness [—səmnis] n. Pesadez, *f.*
tirewoman [—ˌwumən] n. (Ant.). Doncella, *f.*

— OBSERV. El plural de esta palabra es *tirewomen.*

tiring [—riŋ] adj. Cansado, da.
tiro [ˈtaiərəu] n. Aprendiz, *m.*, principiante, *m.*
Tirol [ˈtirəl] pr. n. GEOGR. Tirol, *m.*
Tirolean [tiˈrəuliən] adj./n. Tirolés, esa.
Tirolese [tirəˈli:z] adj./n. Tirolés, esa.
tisane [tiˈzæn] n. Tisana, *f.*
tissue [ˈtiʃu:] n. BIOL. Tejido, *m.*: *muscular tissue*, tejido muscular. || Tisú, *m.* (cloth). || Pañuelo (*m.*) de papel (paper handkerchief). || FIG. Sarta, *f.*: *a tissue of lies*, una sarta de mentiras. || *Tissue paper*, papel (*m.*) de seda.
tit [tit] n. Paro, *m.* (bird). || POP. Teta, *f.* (breast). | Gili, *m.* & *f.*, jilí, *m.* & *f.* (person). || FIG. *To give tit for tat*, devolver la pelota, devolver golpe por golpe.
Titan [ˈtaitən] n. MYTH. Titán, *m.*
titanesque [ˌtaitəˈnesk] adj. Titánico, ca; colosal.
titanic [taiˈtænik] adj. Titánico, ca.
titanium [taiˈteinjəm] n. CHEM. Titanio, *m.*
titbit [ˈtitbit] n. Bocado (*m.*) de cardenal.
titer [ˈtaitə*] n. U. S. Ley, *f.* (of metal). | Título, *m.*, dosificación, *f.* (of a solution).
tithe [taið] n. (Ant.). Diezmo, *m.* (tax). || Décima parte, *f.*
tithe [taið] v. tr. (Ant.). Diezmar.
tithing [—iŋ] n. (Ant.). Diezmo, *m.* (tithe). | Pago (*m.*) del diezmo (payment). | Recaudación (*f.*) del diezmo (levying).
titi [tiˈti] n. Tití, *m.* (monkey).
titian [ˈtiʃiən] adj. Rojizo, za (colour).
Titian [ˈtiʃiən] pr. n. Ticiano.
titillate [ˈtitileit] v. tr. Excitar (to excite). || Cosquillear (to tickle).
titillation [ˌtitiˈleiʃən] n. Excitación, *f.* || Cosquilleo, *m.* (tickling).
titivate [ˈtitiveit] v. tr. Emperejilar, arreglar, acicalar. — V. intr. Emperejilarse, acicalarse.
titivation [ˌtitiˈveiʃən] n. Emperejilamiento, *m.*, acicalamiento, *m.*
titlark [ˈtitlɑ:k] n. Pitpit, *m.* (bird).
title [ˈtaitl] n. Título, *m.* (division, heading, page, name of book, etc.). || Letrero, *m.* (of painting, statue, etc.). || Ley, *f.* (of metal). || Título, *m.* (of nobility). || JUR. Título, *m.* (of legal text). | Derecho, *m.* (right). | Título (*m.*) de propiedad (deed). || REL. Título, *m.* || SP. Campeonato, *m.* || Calificativo, *m.* (epithet).
title [taitl] v. tr. Titular (to give a title to). || Poner subtítulos a (a film).
titled [—d] adj. Con título de nobleza (person). || Titulado, da (book, etc.).
title deed [—di:d] n. JUR. Título (*m.*) de propiedad.
titleholder [—ˌhəuldə*] n. SP. Campeón, ona; titular, *m.* & *f.*
title page [—peidʒ] n. PRINT. Portada, *f.* (of a book).
title role [—rəul] n. THEATR. CINEM. Papel (*m.*) principal.
titmouse [ˈtitmaus] n. Paro, *m.* (bird).

— OBSERV. El plural de *titmouse* es *titmice.*

titrate [ˈtaitreit] v. tr. CHEM. Titular.
titration [taiˈtreiʃən] n. CHEM. Titulación, *f.*
titre [ˈtai:tə*] n. Ley, *f.* (of a metal). || Dosificación, *f.*, título, *m.* (of a solution).
tit-tat-toe [ˌtiˌtæˈtəu] n. See TICKTACKTOE.
titter [ˈtitə*] n. Risa (*f.*) disimulada.
titter [ˈtitə*] v. tr. Reírse disimuladamente *or* con disimulo.
tittivate [ˈtitiveit] v. tr./intr. See TITIVATE.
tittivation [ˌtitiˈveiʃən] n. See TITIVATION.
tittle [ˈtitl] n. Ápice, *m.*, pizca, *f.*
tittle-tattle [—ˌtætl] n. Chismes, *m. pl.*, chismorreo, *m.* (gossip).
tittle-tattle [—ˌtætl] v. intr. Chismorrear.
tittup [ˈtitʌp] v. intr. Caracolear (horse).
titubation [ˌtitjuˈbeiʃən] n. Titubeo, *m.*
titular [ˈtitjulə*] adj./n. Titular.
Titus [ˈtaitəs] pr. n. Tito, *m.*
tizzy [ˈtizi] n. FAM. Excitación, *f.* || Moneda (*f.*) de seis peniques (coin). || FAM. *To get into a tizzy*, ponerse nervioso.
T.N.T. [ˈti:enˈti:] n. T.N.T., *m.*, trinitrotolueno, *m.* (abbreviation of trinitrotoluene).
to [tu:; tə] prep. A (direction, motion, indirect object, etc.): *to the left*, a la izquierda; *perpendicular to*, perpendicular a; *I am going to school, to London, to Canada*, voy a la escuela, a Londres, al Canadá; *then I went to the dentist's, to John's*, luego fui al dentista, a casa de Juan; *to fall to the ground*, caerse al suelo; *give it to me*, dámelo [a mí]; *give the book to Mary*, dale el libro a María; *it seemed easy to John*, a Juan le parecía fácil; *the score was 6 to 4*, el resultado fue de 6 a 4; *open, closed to the public*, abierto, cerrado al público; *to drink to s.o.'s health*, beber a la salud de alguien; *inferior, superior to*, inferior, superior a; *is the food to your taste?*, ¿está la comida a su gusto?; *to write to the teacher's dictation*, escribir al dictado del profesor; *to the strains of the wedding march*, al son de *or* al compás de la marcha nupcial; *he was sentenced to life imprisonment*, le condenaron a cadena perpetua; *to set words to music*, poner música a la letra; *A is to B as C is to D*, A es a B como C es a D; *to prefer A to B*, preferir A a B; *to fight hand to hand*, luchar mano a mano; *man to man*, de hombre a hombre; *face to face*, cara a cara. || Hacia, a (direction towards): *a little to the north*, un poco hacia el norte. || A, hasta: *he showed her to the door*, le acompañó hasta la puerta. || Hasta (as far as): *count to fifty*, cuenta hasta cincuenta; *to such an extent that*, hasta tal punto que; *to this day*, hasta el día de hoy. || Para, con destino a (train, plane, boat): *the train to London*, el tren con destino a Londres. || Menos [*Amer.*, para] (telling the time): *it's ten to four*, son las cuatro menos diez [*Amer.*, faltan diez minutos para las cuatro]; *it's a quarter to one*, es la una menos cuarto; *at five to seven*, a las siete menos cinco. || De, para: *the road to Bogota*, la carretera de Bogotá. || De (of): *the key to the door*, la llave de la puerta; *sth. to eat*, algo de comer; *secretary to Mr. Jones*, secretario del Sr. Jones. || Para (purpose): *to succeed one has to be hard*, para tener éxito hace falta ser duro; *I called to see if she was in*, llamé para ver si estaba en casa; *I got there only to find there were no tickets left*, llegué allí para enterarme de que ya no quedaban entradas; *it's too cold to go out*, hace demasiado frío para salir; *it's too big to go in the car*, es demasiado grande para caber en el coche; *a threat to society*, una amenaza para la sociedad; *he vanished, never to be seen again*, desapareció para no volverse a ver nunca más; *who are you to give me orders?*, ¿quién es usted para darme órdenes? || A, para (purpose with verbs of motion): *I've come to ask you a favour*, vengo a pedirle un favor; *I only popped in to see how you were*, sólo he entrado a *or* para ver cómo estás. || Con: *to be kind to*, ser amable con; *to my great surprise*, con gran sorpresa mía; *to this end*, con este fin. || Según (according to): *made to his specifications*, hecho según sus especificaciones. || Contra (against): *she clutched the letter to her heart*, estrechó la carta contra el corazón; *the chances are two to one in his favour*, tiene dos probabilidades contra una en su favor. || En comparación con, comparado con (compared with): *that is nothing to what I saw*, eso no es nada comparado con lo que he visto yo. || Por: *there are one hundred pence to the pound*, hay cien peniques por libra; *ten people to a room*, diez personas por habitación. || En honor a *or* de (in honour of): *they erected a statue to him*, erigieron una estatua en su honor. || — *A year ago to this very day*, hoy hace exactamente un año. || *Back to back*, de espaldas. || *Back to the wall*, de espaldas a la pared (facing away from the wall), con la espalda contra la pared (against the wall). || *Do I have to?*, ¿es necesario? || *Don't work harder than you have to*, no trabajes más de lo necesario. || *Down to*, hasta. || *Do you want me to try?*, ¿quiere que pruebe yo? || *From ... to ...*, de ... en ...: *from door to door*, de puerta en puerta: *from bad to worse*, de mal en peor; de ... a, de ... hasta: *I stayed from three to five*, me quedé desde las tres hasta las cinco; *from Washington to New York*, de Washington a Nueva York. || *Greetings to you all*, saludos a todos. || *He had his back to me*, me daba la espalda. || *He has aspirations to the throne*, aspira al trono. || *He refused to*, se negó. || *Here's to success!*, ¡que tenga éxito! || *I didn't want to, but I had to*, no quería, pero no tuve más remedio; no quería, pero tuve que hacerlo. || *If you want to*, si [usted] quiere. || *I have no objection to his coming*, no tengo inconveniente en que venga. || *It belongs to him*, es suyo, le pertenece [a él]. || *Now is the time to buy*, ahora es el mejor momento para comprar. || *Oh, to be in the United States!*, ¡quién pudiera estar en Estados Unidos!, ¡ojalá estuviese en Estados Unidos! || *That has yet to be done*, eso queda por hacer. || *That's all there is to it*, eso es todo. || *There is much left to do*, queda mucho por hacer. || *The telephone is not to be used for personal calls*, no se debe utilizar el teléfono para las llamadas personales. || *To a man*, todos [sin excepción]. || *To be easy to solve*, ser fácil de resolver, resolverse fácilmente. || *To be or not to be*, ser o no ser. || *To be quick to answer*, ser rápido en contestar, contestar rápidamente. || *To be slow to learn*, ser lento en aprender, aprender lentamente. || *To be the first, the only one to do sth.*, ser el primero, el único en hacer algo. || *To one's face*, en la cara: *he told me to my face*, me lo dijo en la cara. || *To see him you wouldn't think he was a genius*, al verle *or* viéndole no pensaría que es un genio. || *To the value of*, por valor de. || "*To two new tyre*", "[por] dos neumáticos nuevos" (on a bill). || *Up to*, hasta: *up to midnight*, hasta la medianoche; *up to a point*, hasta cierto punto. || *Welcome to you all*, bienvenidos todos. || *What did he say to that?*, ¿qué te contestó [a eso]? || *What do you say to that?*, ¿qué te parece? || *What is it to you?*, ¿a usted qué le importa? || *You are like a brother to me*, eres un hermano para mí.

— Adv. Cerca (at hand). || MAR. De bolina. || — *The door, the window was fast to*, la puerta, la ventana estaba cerrada. || *To come to*, volver en sí.

— OBSERV. *To* in the infinitive form of English verbs is rendered in Spanish by the verbal suffixes *-ar*, *-ir*, and *-er* (*to think*, pensar).
— Since the Spanish translation of *to* often depends on the accompanying verb or adjective, reference should be made to the verb or adjective in question for uses of *to* which are not treated in the above article.

toad [təud] n. ZOOL. Sapo, *m.* || FAM. Asqueroso, sa (contemptible person).
toadfish [—ˌfiʃ] n. ZOOL. Pejesapo, *m.*
toadflax [—flæks] n. BOT. Linaria, *f.*
toadstone [—stəun] n. MIN. Estelión, *m.*
toadstool [—stu:l] n. BOT. Seta, *f.* || FAM. Hongo (*m*). venenoso.
toady [—i] n. Adulador, ra; pelotillero, ra; cobista, *m.* & *f.* (adulator).
toady [i] v. intr. Adular, hacer la pelotilla, dar coba (*to*, a).
toadyism [—iizəm] n. Adulación, *f.*, pelotilla, *f.*, coba, *f.*
to and fro [ˈtu:ənˈfrəu] adv. *To go to and fro*, ir de un lado para otro *or* de acá para allá, ir y venir.
to-and-fro [ˈtu:ənˈfrəu] adj. *To-and-fro movement*, vaivén, *m.*, movimiento (*m.*) de vaivén.
toast [təust] n. Pan (*m.*) tostado, tostada, *f.*: *marmalade on toast*, pan tostado *or* tostada con mermelada. || Brindis, *m. inv.* (of drink): *there followed several toasts*, a continuación hubo varios brindis. || FIG. Héroe, *m.*, heroína, *f.*: *he is the toast of the town*, es el héroe de la ciudad. || — *A piece of toast*, una tostada. || *To drink a toast to*, brindar por. || *To propose a toast*, proponer un brindis.
toast [təust] v. tr. Tostar (bread, etc.). || FIG. Tostar (to make hot). || Brindar por (to drink to).
— V. intr. Tostarse: *English bread toasts well*, el pan inglés se tuesta bien. || FIG. Tostarse, asarse (to warm thoroughly): *I am toasting in the sun*, me estoy asando al sol.
toaster [—ə*] n. Tostadora, *f.* (for bread).
toasting fork [—iŋfɔ:k] n. Tenedor (*m.*) largo para tostar.
toastmaster [—ˌmɑ:stə*] n. Maestro (*m.*) de ceremonias.
tobacco [təˈbækəu] n. Tabaco, *m.*: *black* o *dark tobacco*, tabaco negro; *Virginia tobacco*, tabaco rubio; *pipe tobacco*, tabaco de pipa; *leaf tobacco*, tabaco de hoja; *chewing tobacco*, tabaco de mascar. || Tabaco, *m.* (colour).
tobacco box [—bɔks] n. Tabaquera, *f.*
tobacco cut [—kʌt] n. Picadura, *f.*
tobacco jar [—dʒɑ:*] n. Tabaquera, *f.*
tobacconist [təˈbækənist] n. Estanquero, ra (person). || *Tobacconist's*, estanco, *m.*, expendeduría (*f.*) de tabaco (shop).
tobacco plantation [təˈbækəuplænˌteiʃən] n. Tabacal, *m.*, plantación (*f.*) de tabaco.
tobacco pouch [təˈbækəupautʃ] n. Petaca, *f.*, bolsa (*f.*) para el tabaco [*Amer.*, tabaquera, *f.*].
to-be [tu:ˈbi:] adj. Futuro, ra.
— N. Porvenir, *m.*, futuro, *m.*
toboggan [təˈbɔgən] n. Tobogán, *m.*
toboggan [təˈbɔgən] v. intr. Deslizarse por un tobogán. || FIG. Ir deslizándose (to slide). | Bajar verticalmente (prices).
Toby [ˈtəubi] n. Bock (*m.*) de cerveza.
toccata [təˈkɑ:tə] n. MUS. Tocata, *f.*
tocologist [təˈkɔlədʒist] n. Tocólogo, *m.*
tocology [təˈkɔlədʒi] n. Tocología, *f.*
tocsin [ˈtɔksin] n. Rebato, *m.*, señal (*f.*) de alarma. || *To sound the tocsin*, tocar a rebato, dar la alarma.
today [təˈdei] adv./n. Hoy (the present day): *what did you do at school today?*, ¿qué has hecho hoy en el colegio? || Actualmente, hoy día, hoy en día (nowadays). || — *As from today*, a partir de hoy. || *A year ago today*, hoy hace un año. || *The young people of today*, la juventud actual. || *Today is the tenth*, hoy estamos a diez. || *Today's paper*, el periódico de hoy. || *Today week*, *a week today*, dentro de una semana. || *What day is it today?*, ¿qué día es hoy?, ¿a cuántos estamos hoy?
toddle [tɔdl] n. Pinito, *m.* (of a child).
toddle [tɔdl] v. intr. Hacer pinitos (a child). || FAM. Ir *o* andar tambaleándose. | Marcharse (to leave): *I must be toddling*, ya me tengo que marchar.
toddler [—ə*] n. Niño, *m.* [que empienza a andar].
toddy [ˈtɔdi] n. Ponche, *m.* (drink). || Savia (*f.*) de palma (sap).
to-do [təˈdu:] n. FAM. Follón, *m.*, jaleo, *m.*, lío, *m.*: *to make a great to-do about sth.*, armar un jaleo por algo; *what's all the to-do about?*, ¿por qué hay tanto jaleo?
toe [təu] n. ANAT. Dedo (*m.*) del pie: *big, little toe*, dedo gordo, pequeño del pie. || Puntera, *f.* (reinforced part of shoe, sock, etc.). || Punta, *f.* (front of shoe, sock, etc.). || Punta (*f.*) del pie (front of the foot). || TECH. Pestaña, *f.* || — *On one's toes*, de puntillas (on tiptoe), alerta (alert). || FIG. *To be on one's toes*, estar atento *or* ojo avizor. || *To dance on one's toes*, bailar de puntas (in ballet). || FIG. *To keep one's men on their toes*, mantener alertos a sus hombres. || *To step on s.o.'s toes*, darle un pisotón a alguien, pisarle el pie a alguien (to tread on), pisotear a alguien (to offend). || FIG. *To tread on s.o.'s toes*, pisotear a alguien. || FIG. FAM. *To turn up one's toes*, estirar la pata (to die).
toe [təu] v. tr. Poner puntera a (shoe, sock). || Tocar con el pie (to touch with foot). || Clavar oblicuamente (a nail). || SP. Tirar con la punta del pie (a ball). || — *To toe a cigarette out*, apagar un cigarrillo con la punta del pie. || *To toe the line*, see LINE.
— V. intr. Ir, andar (to walk). || *To toe in, out*, andar con los pies hacia adentro, hacia fuera.
toe cap [—kæp] n. Puntera, *f.*
toed [—d] adj. Clavado oblicuamente (nails). || *Man is a five-toed animal*, el hombre tiene cinco dedos en el pie.
toe-dance [—dɑ:ns] v. intr. Bailar de puntas.
toe-dancing [—ˌdɑ:nsiŋ] n. Puntas, *f. pl.*
toehold [—həuld] n. Punto (*m.*) de apoyo (in climbing). || FIG. Trampolín, *m.*: *the inheritance gave him a toehold in society*, la herencia le sirvió de trampolín para entrar en la sociedad. || FIG. *To get a toehold on an island*, asentarse en una isla.
toe-in [—in] n. AUT. Convergencia (*f.*) de las ruedas delanteras.
toenail [—neil] n. Uña, *f.* [del dedo del pie]. || Clavo (*m.*) oblicuo.
toenail [—neil] v. tr. Sujetar con un clavo oblicuo.
toff [tɔf] n. FAM. Ricachón, *m.* (rich man). | Elegantón, *m.*, "dandy", *m.*, currutaco, *m.* (elegant person).
toffee [—i] n. Toffee, *m.*, masticable, *m.* || Caramelo, *m.* (any sweet).
toffee-nosed [ˈtɔfiˌnəuzd] adj. Presumido, da; engreído, da (person).
toffy [ˈtɔfi] n. See TOFFEE.
tog [tɔg] v. tr. Ataviar, vestir (*in*, de) [to dress]. || *To tog o.s. up*, ataviarse, vestirse.
toga [ˈtəugə] n. Toga, *f.*

— OBSERV. El plural de la palabra inglesa es *togas* o *togae*.

togaed [—d] or **togated** [ˈtəugəitid] adj. Togado, da.
together [təˈgeðə*] adv. Juntos, tas: *put the pages together*, pon las páginas juntas; *they came together*, vinieron juntos. || A la vez, al mismo tiempo (at the same time): *to speak together*, hablar a la vez. || De acuerdo (in agreement): *we are together on this point*, estamos de acuerdo en este punto. || De común acuerdo: *to act together*, actuar de común acuerdo. || — *For days together*, durante días y días, durante varios días seguidos. || *To bring together*, reunir. || *To come together*, reunirse, juntarse. || *Together with*, junto con. || *To get together*, see GET. || *To go together*, ir juntos: *let's go to the cinema together*, vayamos juntos al cine; salir juntos: *John and Mary have been going together for two years*, Juan y María salen juntos desde hace dos años; armonizar, ir juntos: *those colours don't go together*, esos colores no van juntos. || *To hang together*, ser lógico (argument). || *To pull o.s. together*, see PULL. || *To put together*, see PUT.
togetherness [—nis] n. Unión, *f.*, solidaridad, *f.*
toggle [ˈtɔgl] n. Cabilla, *f.* (pin). || Alamar, *m.* (button). || Pasador, *m.* (for scarf). || Tensor, *m.* (for tightening rope). || — *Toggle joint*, articulación, *f.*, rótula, *f.* (joint), eje acodado, palanca acodada (lever). || *Toggle switch*, interruptor eléctrico.
toggle [tɔgl] v. tr. Sujetar (to fix, to fasten). || MAR. Sujetar con cabilla.
Togo [ˈtəugəu] pr. n. GEOGR. Togo, *m.*
togs [tɔgz] pl. n. FAM. Ropa, *f. sing.*
toil [tɔil] n. Trabajo, *m.*, esfuerzo, *m.* (effort). || Trabajo, *m.* (work). || Trabajo (*m.*) agotador (hard work).
toil [tɔil] v. intr. Trabajar duro (to work hard). || Ir *or* moverse con dificultad, avanzar *or* moverse penosamente: *the car toiled along*, el coche avanzaba con dificultad; *the lady toiled through the corridor*, la señora avanzaba penosamente por el pasillo. || Funcionar con dificultad (an engine). || — *The peasants toiling at their daily round*, los campesinos haciendo su dura labor cotidiana. || *To toil up a hill*, subir penosamente una colina. || *To toil with a problem*, esforzarse por resolver un problema.
toiler [—ə*] n. Trabajador, ra.
toilet [ˈtɔilit] n. Arreglo, *m.*, aseo, *m.* (dressing, washing, shaving, etc.). || Traje, *m.*, vestido, *m.* (clothes). || Tocador, *m.*, coqueta, *f.* (dressing table). || Lavabo, *m.*, retrete, *m.* (lavatory). || *Toilet requisites*, artículos (*m.*) de tocador.
toilet case [—keis] n. Neceser, *m.*
toilet paper [—ˌpeipə*] n. Papel (*m.*) higiénico *or* sánico.
toiletries [—riz] pl. n. Artículos (*m.*) de tocador.
toilet roll [—rəul] n. Rollo (*m.*) de papel higiénico.
toilet set [—set] n. Juego (*m.*) de tocador.
toilet soap [—səup] n. Jabón (*m.*) de tocador.
toilette [twɑ:ˈlet] n. Arreglo, *m.*, aseo, *m.* (dressing, washing, etc.). || Traje, *m.*, vestido, *m.* (clothes).
toilet tissue [ˈtɔilitˈtiʃu:] n. Papel (*m.*) higiénico *or* sánico.
toilet water [ˈtɔilitˈwɔ:tə*] n. Agua (*f.*) de Colonia.
toils [tɔilz] pl. n. Redes, *f.*, lazos, *m.*
toilsome [ˈtɔilsəm] adj. Penoso, sa; laborioso, sa; arduo, dua.
toilsomeness [—nis] n. Dificultad, *f.*, lo penoso, lo arduo.

toilworn [—wɔ:n] adj. Rendido, da; agotado, da; muy cansado, da (person). || Cansado, da (face, expression). || Estropeado, da (hands).
Tokay [təuˈkei] n. Tocay, *m.* (wine).
token [ˈtəukən] n. Prueba, *f.*, muestra, *f.*, señal, *f.* (sign): *a token of gratitude*, una muestra de gratitud; *a token of friendship*, una prueba de amistad. || Símbolo, *m.* (symbol). || Recuerdo, *m.* (keepsake). || Ficha, *f.* (disk). || Vale, *m.*: *book token*, vale para comprar libros; *gift token*, vale para comprar un regalo; *record token*, vale para comprar discos. || — *By the same token*, por la misma razón. || *In token of*, como prueba de, en señal de.
— Adj. Simbólico, ca: *token resistance*, resistencia simbólica; *a token strike*, una huelga simbólica. || *A token payment*, una señal.
Tokyo [təukjəu] pr. n. GEOGR. Tokio.
told [təuld] pret. & p. p. See TELL.
Toledan [təˈleidən] adj./n. Toledano, na.
tolerable [ˈtɔlərəbl] adj. Tolerable, soportable (bearable). || Mediano, na; aceptable, regular (fair, reasonable): *a tolerable knowledge of Spanish*, un conocimiento mediano del español.
tolerance [ˈtɔlərəns] n. Tolerancia, *f.* (readiness to accept opinions, behaviour, etc.). || TECH. MED. Tolerancia, *f.* || *Religious tolerance*, tolerancia religiosa.
tolerant [ˈtɔlərənt] adj. Tolerante, indulgente. || MED. Tolerante.
tolerate [ˈtɔləreit] v. tr. Tolerar, soportar, aguantar (to endure). || Tolerar, permitir (to permit). || Tolerar, admitir (people of other beliefs, opinions, etc.). || Respetar (opinions, beliefs, etc.). || MED. Tolerar. || *This kind of behaviour is not to be tolerated*, este comportamiento es intolerable *or* inadmisible.
toleration [ˌtɔləˈreiʃən] n. Tolerancia, *f.*
tolite [ˈtɔlait] n. Tolita, *f.*
toll [təul] n. Peaje, *m.* (of road, motorway). || Pontaje, *m.*, pontazgo, *m.*, peaje, *m.* (of bridge). || Tasa, *f.* (tax). || Bajas, *f. pl.*, número (*m.*) de víctimas: *the battle took a terrible toll*, la batalla hizo un gran número de víctimas *or* muchas bajas. || Tañido, *m.* (of bells). || — *But the plague had already taken its toll*, pero la peste ya había hecho muchas víctimas. || *The death toll on the roads*, el número de muertos en la carretera. || *To take toll of*, infligir une pérdida *or* pérdidas a.
toll [təul] v. tr./intr. Tocar [a muerto], tañer [a muerto]. || *For whom the bell tolls*, por quién doblan las campanas.
toll bar [—bɑ:*] n. Barrera (*f.*) de peaje.
toll bridge [—bridʒ] Puente (*m.*) de peaje *or* de pontazgo.
toll call [—kɔ:l] n. U. S. Conferencia, *f.* [interurbana] (long-distance call).
toller [—ə*] n. Peajero, *m.*
tollgate [—geit] n. Barrera (*f.*) de peaje.
tollhouse [—haus] n. Casa (*f.*) del peajero *or* del portazguero.
tolling [—iŋ] n. Doblar, *m.*, tañido, *m.* (of bells).
tollkeeper [—ˌki:pə*] n. Peajero, *m.* || (Ant.). Portazguero, *m.*
toll road [—rəud] or **tollway** [—wei] n. Carretera (*f.*) de peaje (road). || Autopista (*f.*) de peaje (motorway).
Toltec [ˈtɔltek] adj./n. Tolteca.
toluene [ˈtɔləwi:n] n. CHEM. Tolueno, *m.*
tom [tɔm] n. Macho, *m.* [de ciertos animales como el gato].
Tom [tɔm] pr. n. Tomás, *m.* || — *Any Tom, Dick or Harry*, cualquier hijo de vecino. || *Peeping Tom*, mirón, *m.* || *Tom, Dick and Harry*, Fulano, Mengano y Zutano. || *Tom Thumb*, Pulgarcito, *m.*
tomahawk [ˈtɔməhɔ:k] n. Tomahawk, *m.* || FIG. *To bury the tomahawk*, enterrar el hacha de la guerra, hacer las paces.
tomato [təˈmɑ:təu] n. BOT. Tomate, *m.* (fruit). | Tomatera, *f.*, tomate, *m.* (plant).

— OBSERV. El plural de *tomato* es *tomatoes*.

tomb [tu:m] n. Tumba, *f.*, sepulcro, *m.*
tomb [tu:m] v. tr. Enterrar, sepultar.
tombac or **tombak** [ˈtɔmbæk] n. Tumbaga, *f.* (alloy).
tombola [ˈtɔmbələ] n. Tómbola, *f.* (lottery with goods for prizes). || Lotería, *f.* (bingo).
tomboy [ˈtɔmbɔi] n. FAM. Marimacho, *m.* (girl).
tombstone [ˈtu:mstəun] n. Lápida (*f.*) sepulcral, piedra (*f.*) sepulcral.
tomcat [ˈtɔmkæt] n. Gato, *m.* [macho].
tome [təum] n. Libraco, *m.* (huge book). || Volumen, *m.*, tomo, *m.* (volume).
tomfool [ˈtɔmˈfu:l] adj. Necio, tonto, bobo.
— N. Necio, *m.*, tonto, *m.*, bobo, *m.*
tomfoolery [tɔmˈfu:ləri] n. Estupidez, *f.*, tontería, *f.*, necedad, *f.* || *Enough of this tomfoolery!*, ¡basta de tonterías!
tommy [ˈtɔmi] n. MIL. Soldado (*m.*) raso (private). || U. S. Soldado (*m.*) inglés (British soldier).
tommy gun [—gʌn] n. MIL. Pistola (*f.*) ametralladora, metralleta, *f.*
tommyrot [—rɔt] n. Disparates, *m. pl.*, tonterías, *f. pl.*, bobadas, *f. pl.*
tomorrow [təˈmɔrəu] n. Mañana, *m.*: *tomorrow is Tuesday*, mañana es martes; *tomorrow is another day*, mañana será otro día; *to leave sth. until tomorrow*, dejar algo para mañana. || — *Don't think about what tomorrow will bring*, no pienses en lo que te traerá el día de mañana. || *The day after tomorrow*, pasado mañana. || *The world of tomorrow*, el mundo de mañana.
— Adv. Mañana: *come back tomorrow*, vuelva mañana; *tomorrow morning*, mañana por la mañana. || — *See you tomorrow*, hasta mañana. || *Tomorrow week* o *a week tomorrow*, de mañana en ocho días.
tompion [ˈtɔmpjən] n. MIL. Tapabocas, *m. inv.*
tomtit [ˈtɔmˈtit] n. Alionín, *m.* (bird).
tom-tom [ˈtɔmtɔm] n. Tantán, *m.*
ton [tʌn] n. Tonelada, *f.* || — Pl. FIG. Montones, *m.*: *he has got tons of money*, tiene montones de dinero. || — *Long ton*, tonelada larga. || *Metric ton*, tonelada métrica. || MAR. *Register ton*, tonelada de arqueo. || *Short ton*, tonelada corta.
tonal [ˈtəunl] adj. Tonal.
tonality [təuˈnæliti] n. Tonalidad, *f.*
tone [təun] n. Tono, *m.*: *the tone of a letter, of his voice*, el tono de una carta, de su voz; *in an angry tone*, con tono enfadado; *decorated in pastel tones*, decorado con tonos pastel; *out of tone*, fuera de tono; *to lower, to change one's tone*, bajar el tono, cambiar de tono. || MUS. MED. Tono, *m.* || FIG. Tendencia, *f.* (of a market). | Estilo, *m.*, carácter, *m.* (character).
tone [təun] v. tr. Entonar. || Matizar (a colour). || MUS. Afinar, templar (instruments). || PHOT. Virar. || — *To tone down*, atenuar, suavizar (to weaken), moderar (to moderate). || *To tone up*, tonificar (the nervous system), entonar (s.o.), avivar, entonar (a colour, etc.).
— V. intr. Armonizar, ir juntos (colours). || Armonizar (sounds). || PHOT. Virar. || — *To tone down*, atenuarse, suavizarse (volume, colours), moderarse (to be moderated). || *To tone in with*, armonizar con, ir bien con. || *To tone up*, entonarse.
tone colour (U. S. **tone color**) [—ˌkʌlə*] n. MUS. Timbre, *m.*
tone control [—kənˌtrəul] n. RAD. Botón (*m.*) de tonalidad.
tone-deaf [ˈ—def] adj. Que no tiene buen oído.
toneless [—lis] adj. Apagado, da (colours). || Inexpresivo, va; apagado, da (voice).
tonelessly [—lisli] adv. Con voz apagada.
tone poem [ˈtəunˌpəuim] n. MUS. Poema (*m.*) sinfónico.
tong [tɔŋ] n. Sociedad (*f.*) secreta china.
tonga [ˈtɔŋgə] n. Carruaje (*m.*) ligero de dos ruedas.
tongs [tɔŋz] pl. n. Tenacillas, *f.* (for sugar). || Tenazas, *f.* (for coal). || TECH. Pinzas, *f.*, tenazas, *f.*
tongue [tʌŋ] n. ANAT. CULIN. Lengua, *f.*: *coated* o *furry tongue*, lengua pastosa. || Lengua, *f.*, idioma, *m.* (language): *native, mother tongue*, lengua nativa, materna. || FIG. Lengua, *f.* (of flame, land). || Badajo, *m.* (of a bell). || Lengüeta, *f.* (of wooden joint, shoe, musical instrument). || Hebijón, *m.* (of a buckle). || Aguja, *f.* (of railway line). || — FIG. *Evil tongue*, mala lengua. | *Has a cat got your tongue?*, ¿te has tragado la lengua? || FAM. *I could have bitten my tongue when I said that*, mejor hubiese sido callarme. || *On the tip of one's tongue*, en la punta de la lengua. || FIG. *Poisonous* o *vicious* o *wicked tongue*, lengua de víbora *or* viperina. || *Sister tongues*, lenguas hermanas. || *Slip of the tongue*, lapsus (*m.*) linguae. || FIG. *To find one's tongue*, recobrar el habla. || *To give tongue*, empezar a ladrar (dogs). || FIG. *To hold* o *to bite one's tongue*, callarse, morderse la lengua. | *To keep a civil tongue in one's head*, ser cortés. | *To loosen s.o.'s tongue*, soltarle la lengua a alguien. || *Tongue of fire*, lengua de fuego. || *To put out* o *to stick out one's tongue*, sacar la lengua: *to put out one's tongue at s.o.*, sacarle la lengua a alguien. || FIG. *To speak with one's tongue in one's cheek*, hablar irónicamente. | *To wag one's tongue*, darle a la lengua, hablar mucho. || *With one's tongue hanging out*, con la lengua fuera.
tongue [tʌŋ] v. tr. Machihembrar (to join). || Lamer (to lick).
— V. intr. Sobresalir (to stick out).
tongue-and-groove joint [—ənˈgru:vˌdʒɔint] n. Ensambladura (*f.*) de ranura y lengüeta, machihembrado, *m.*
tongue depressor [—diˈpresə*] n. Depresor, *m.*
tongue-lash [—læʃ] v. tr. FAM. Echar una bronca a (to scold).
tongue-lashing [—læʃiŋ] n. FAM. Bronca, *f.* (telling off): *to give s.o. a tongue lashing*, echar una bronca a alguien.
tongueless [—lis] adj. Sin lengua. || FAM. Mudo, da; sin habla.
tongue-tie [—tai] n. MED. Frenillo, *m.* (speech defect).
tongue-tied [—taid] adj. Mudo, da (through shyness). || MED. Que tiene frenillo. || *To get all tongue-tied*, trabársele a uno la lengua.
tongue twister [—ˌtwistə*] n. Trabalenguas, *m. inv.*
tonic [ˈtɔnik] adj. Tónico, ca. || *Tonic accent*, acento tónico.
— N. MED. Tónico, *m.*: *hair tonic*, tónico para el cabello. || Tónica, *f.* (fizzy drink). || GRAMM. MUS. Tónica, *f.* || FIG. *The news acted as a tonic on me*, la noticia me entonó.
tonicity [təˈnisiti] n. ANAT. Tonicidad, *f.*

tonight [tə'nait] adv./n. Esta noche: *tonight is the première of the film*, esta noche se estrena la película.
tonka bean ['tɔŋkəbi:n] n. Bot. Haba (*f.*) tonca.
Tonkin ['tɔnkin] pr. n. Tonkín, *m.*, Tonquín, *m.*
Tonkinese [ˌtɔŋkə'ni:z] adj./n. Tonquinés, esa.
tonnage ['tʌnidʒ] n. Tonelaje, *m.*: *gross tonnage*, tonelaje bruto.
tonner ['tʌnə*] n. De ... toneladas: *a thousand-tonner*, un barco de mil toneladas.
tonsil ['tɔnsl] n. Anat. Amígdala, *f.*, tonsila, *f.*
tonsillar [tɔn'silə*] adj. Amigdalino, na; tonsilar.
tonsillectomy [tɔnsi'lektəmi] n. Tonsilectomía, *f.*
tonsillitis ['tɔnsi'laitis] n. Med. Amigdalitis, *f.*, tonsilitis, *f.*
tonsure ['tɔnʃə*] n. Tonsura, *f.*
tonsure ['tɔnʃə*] v. tr. Tonsurar.
tontine [tɔn'ti:n] n. Comm. Tontina, *f.*
tonus [təunəs] n. Anat. Tonicidad, *f.*, tono, *m.*
too [tu:] adv. Demasiado: *it's too far*, está demasiado lejos. || También: *I hope you will come too*, espero que tú también vengas. || Además (as well as that): *and he called me a liar too*, y además me trató de mentiroso. || Muy: *I'm not too sure*, no estoy muy seguro. || — *He's none too bright*, no es muy listo, no es nada listo. || *It is too early yet*, es muy temprano todavía. || *It is too hot to touch*, está demasiado caliente para tocarlo. || *It is too kind of you*, es usted muy amable. || *It looks none too good*, no parece nada bueno, no parece muy bueno. || *It was just too delicious*, estaba simplemente delicioso. || *So much rain! And in July too!*, ¡qué manera de llover! y eso que estamos en julio. || *The car was too big for her to drive*, el coche era demasiado grande para que lo condujera ella. || *The tea is too hot to drink*, el té está demasiado caliente. || *To be too much for one*, ser demasiado para uno. || *Too bad!*, see BAD. || *To drink too heavily*, beber demasiado. || *Too little*, muy poco, demasiado poco (amount), muy pequeño, demasiado pequeño (size). || *Too many*, demasiados, das. || *Too much*, see MUCH. || *To talk too much*, hablar más de la cuenta *or* demasiado. || *We know him only too well*, lo conocemos de sobra.
took [tuk] pret. See TAKE.
tool [tu:l] n. Herramienta, *f.*: *carpenter's tools*, herramientas de carpintería. || Útil, *m.*, utensilio, *m.*: *gardening tools*, útiles de jardinería. || Máquina herramienta, *f.* (machine tool). || Fig. Instrumento, *m.*: *they used her as a tool to get at the files*, se sirvieron de ella como instrumento para tener acceso a los documentos. | Instrumento, *m.* [de trabajo]: *the dictionary is a useful tool for the translator*, el diccionario es un instrumento de trabajo muy útil para el traductor. || Fig. *A bad workman always blames his tools*, see WORKMAN.
tool [tu:l] v. tr. Labrar (to shape). || Mecanizar (to work with machine tools). || Estampar (to impress letters or designs). || Equipar con herramientas *or* maquinaria (to equip with tools, machines). || Fam. Conducir (a car).
— V. intr. Utilizar herramientas. || Fam. *To tool along*, ir en coche.
toolbag [—bæg] n. Bolsa (*f.*) de herramientas.
toolbox [—bɔks] n. Caja (*f.*) de herramientas.
toolhead [—hed] n. Tech. Cabezal, *m.* (of a lathe).
toolholder [—ˌhəuldə*] n. Portaherramientas, *m. inv.*
tooling [—iŋ] n. Mecanizado, *m.* (with machine tools). || Estampación, *f.* (of a book cover).
tool kit [—kit] n. Juego (*m.*) de herramientas (set of tools). || Aut. Estuche (*m.*) de herramientas.
toolmaker [—ˌmeikə*] n. Fabricante (*m.*) de herramientas.
toolmaking [—ˌmeikiŋ] n. Fabricación (*f.*) de herramientas.
toot [tu:t] n. Bocinazo, *m.* (with a horn). || Silbido, *m.* (with a whistle). || Toque, *m.* (of trumpet).
toot [tu:t] v. tr. Tocar (to blow a horn, trumpet).
— V. intr. Sonar (to sound). || Tocar el claxon *or* la bocina (s.o. in a car).
tooth [tu:θ] n. Diente, *m.* || Muela, *f.* (back tooth). || Púa, *f.* (of a comb). || Diente, *m.* (of a saw). || — *An eye for an eye, a tooth for a tooth*, ojo por ojo, diente por diente. || Fig. *Armed to the teeth*, armado hasta los dientes. || *Back tooth*, muela, *f.* || *False teeth*, dentadura postiza. || *Front teeth*, incisivos, *m.* || Fig. *In the teeth of*, en pleno: *in the teeth of the storm*, en plena tormenta; a pesar de (despite): *in the teeth of criticism*, a pesar de la crítica. || Fam. *To be fed up* o *sick to the teeth of*, estar hasta la coronilla de. || Fig. *To be long in the tooth*, tener ya muchos años. || *To clench one's teeth*, apretar los dientes. || *To cut one's teeth*, echar los dientes. || Fig. *To cut one's teeth on*, ejercitarse en. | *To fight tooth and nail*, luchar a brazo partido, defenderse como gato panza arriba. | *To get one's teeth into*, hincarle el diente a. | *To have a sweet tooth*, ser goloso. || *To have a tooth out*, sacarse una muela *or* un diente. || Fig. *To put teeth into*, dar mucha fuerza a. || *To say sth. between one's teeth*, decir algo entre dientes. || *To set one's teeth on edge*, darle dentera a uno. || *To show one's teeth*, enseñar los dientes. || Fig. *To throw* o *to cast sth. in s.o.'s teeth*, echarle algo en cara a alguien. || *Wisdom tooth*, muela del juicio.
— Observ. El plural de *tooth* es *teeth*.

tooth [tu:θ] v. tr. Dentar, endentar: *to tooth a saw*, dentar una sierra.
— V. intr. Engranar.
toothache [—eik] n. Dolor (*m.*) de muelas.
toothbrush [—brʌʃ] n. Cepillo (*m.*) de dientes.
toothcomb [—kəum] n. Peine (*m.*) de púa fina. || Fig. *To go through sth. with a toothcomb*, examinar algo detalladamente (to study), registrar algo minuciosamente (to search).
toothed [—t] adj. Dentado, da: *toothed wheel*, rueda dentada. || Con dientes, de dientes: *white-toothed*, con dientes blancos; *fine-toothed*, de dientes finos.
toothing [—iŋ] n. Arch. Adaraja, *f.* || Dientes, *m. pl.* (teeth).
toothless [—lis] adj. Desdentado, da; sin dientes.
toothpaste [—peist] n. Pasta (*f.*) dentífrica, crema (*f.*) dental, dentífrico, *m.*
toothpick [—pik] n. Palillo (*m.*) de dientes, mondadientes, *m. inv.*
toothpick holder [—pikˌhəuldə*] n. Palillero, *m.*
tooth powder [—ˌpaudə*] n. Polvo (*m.*) dentífrico.
toothsome [—səm] adj. Sabroso, sa; apetitoso, sa.
toothy [—i] adj. Dentudo, da (having large teeth). || Enseñando los dientes (grin, etc.).
tootle ['tu:tl] n. Fam. Toque, *m.* (on a musical instrument). || *Can I have a tootle?*, ¿me dejas tocar un poco?
tootle ['tu:tl] v. intr. Tocar [la flauta, etc.]. || Fam. Ir: *to tootle along at thirty miles per hour*, ir a treinta millas por hora. || Fam. *To tootle off*, irse.
— V. tr. Tocar (an instrument).
tootsie ['tu:tsi] n. U. S. Fam. Querida, *f.* (addressing a girl). | Niña, *f.* (girl). || Fam. Piececito, *m.* (foot).
tootsy ['tu:tsi] n. Fam. Piececito, *m.* (foot).
top [tɔp] n. Peón, *m.*, peonza, *f.*, trompo, *m.* (child's toy). || Parte (*f.*) de arriba, sostén, *m.* (of bikini, etc.). || Blusa, *f.* (blouse). || Chaqueta, *f.* (jacket). || Parte (*f.*) de arriba, parte (*f.*) superior, lo alto (upper part): *in the top of the bookshelf*, en la parte de arriba de la estantería; *the top of a bus*, la parte de arriba de un autobús; *at the top of the stairs*, en lo alto de la escalera; *the top of the building is quite ugly*, la parte de arriba del edificio es bastante fea. || Parte (*f.*) alta (higher part). || Parte (*f.*) de encima *or* de arriba (upper side): *the top of the shoe is leather*, la parte de encima del zapato es de cuero. || Cima, *f.*, cumbre, *f.* (of a hill, mountain, etc.). || Copa, *f.* (highest tip of tree, of hat). || Tapa, *f.* (of saucepan, bottle, tin, etc.). || Capuchón, *m.* (of a pen). || Cabeza, *f.*, principio, *m.* (of page, etc.): *at the top of the list*, al principio de la lista. || Remate, *m.* (crest of a building). || Coronilla, *f.* (of the head). || Tejado, *m.* (outside roof of house). || Techo, *m.* (roof of bus, ceiling). || Capota, *f.* (of a car). || Baca, *f.* (of a stagecoach). || Tablero, *m.* (of table): *table with an oak, a glass, a formica top*, mesa con tablero de roble, de cristal, de formica. || Superficie, *f.* (surface): *the oil floated to the top*, el aceite subió a la superficie. || Cresta, *f.* (of a wave). || Bot. Hojas, *f. pl.* (of carrots, etc.). || Final, *m.*, extremo, *m.*: *let's go to the top of the street*, vayamos hasta el final de la calle. || Fig. Los mejores, *m. pl.*, los primeros, *m. pl.*: *he is at the top of his profession*, está entre los mejores de su profesión. | Cumbre, *f.* (height): *he reached the top of his career in 1970*, llegó a la cumbre de su carrera en 1970. || Mar. Cofa, *f.* (platform). || Aut. Directa, *f.* (gear). || — Fig. *At the top of*, a la cabeza de, el primero, la primera: *he is at the top of the class*, es el primero de la clase. | *At the top of one's form*, en plena forma. | *At the top of one's speed*, a toda velocidad. | *At the top of one's voice*, a voz en grito *or* en cuello, a voces. || *Don't drink beer on top of wine*, no mezcles cerveza con vino. || *From top to bottom*, de arriba abajo. || *From top to toe*, de pies a cabeza. || Fig. *He is headed for the top*, está en el camino del éxito *or* de la fama. | *He went straight to the top*, alcanzó inmediatamente la fama *or* el éxito, se puso en seguida el primero. | *It's just one thing on top of another*, es una cosa tras otra. || *On top*, encima: *put the best ones on top*, pon los mejores arriba; encima de, sobre: *on top of the wardrobe*, encima del armario. || Fig. *On top of*, además de. | *On top of that, on top of it all*, para colmo, por si fuera poco, por añadidura. || *Sliding top*, techo corredizo (of car), tapa corrediza (of box, etc.). || Fig. *To be on top*, llevar ventaja, ir ganando (to be winning). | *To blow one's top*, salir de sus casillas. | *To come out on top*, ganar, salir vencedor (to be the winner). | *To feel* o *to be on top of the world*, see WORLD. || *To fill up to the top*, llenar completamente *or* hasta el borde. || Mil. *To go over the top*, salir al ataque. || Fig. *To go to bed on top of one's supper*, acostarse nada más cenar. | *To go to the top of one's profession*, hacer carrera. | *Top of the morning to you*, muy buenos días. || *To spin like a top*, dar más vueltas que una peonza. || *What is the position at the top of the league?*, ¿quiénes van en cabeza de la liga? || *Wipe the top of the table down*, pasa la esponja por encima de la mesa.
— Adj. De arriba: *top sheet*, sábana de arriba. || Máximo, ma: *top prices*, precios máximos. || Máximo, ma; extremo, ma: *top security*, seguridad máxima. || Último, ma (last): *top floor*, último piso. || Más alto, ta (highest). || Más importante (most important). || De la alta sociedad (high-society). || Grande, muy

bueno, na (great): *a top racing driver*, un gran piloto de carreras. || Mejor, primero, ra (best). || — *He is top in the class*, es el primero de la clase. || *To earn top money*, estar muy bien pagado. || *Top boy in his class, in history*, el primero de la clase, el primero en historia. || *Top speed*, velocidad máxima: *to have a top speed of*, tener una velocidad máxima de. || *Top table*, mesa (*f.*) principal *or* de honor (in a banquet).
top [tɔp] v. tr. Coronar, rematar (to crown): *a spire tops the tower*, una aguja remata la torre. || Rematar (to finish off). || Estar a la cabeza de *or* al principio de (to be at the top of): *to top a list*, estar a la cabeza de una lista. || Cubrir (to cover): *to top a cake with cream*, cubrir un pastel con nata. || Superar (to be better or greater than). || Superar, mejorar: *he topped his previous performance*, superó su actuación anterior. || Medir más de: *he tops three feet*, mide más de tres pies. || Medir más que: *he tops me by three centimetres*, mide tres centímetros más que yo. || Llegar a la cumbre de (a mountain). || Salvar, superar (an obstacle). || AGR. Descabezar, desmochar: *to top a tree*, desmochar un árbol. || MAR. Embicar. || SP. Golpear en la parte superior para dar efecto (ball). || CHEM. Eliminar las fracciones más volátiles de. || — *To top it all*, para colmo, por si fuera poco. || *To top off*, terminar, rematar. || *To top up*, llenar completamente (to fill), volver a llenar (to fill again), recargar a fondo (a battery).
topaz [ˈtəupæz] n. MIN. Topacio, *m.*: *smoky topaz*, topacio ahumado; *pink topaz*, topacio quemado.
top boot [ˈtɔpbu:t] n. Bota (*f.*) alta.
topcoat [ˈtɔpkəut] n. Abrigo, *m.* [*Amer.*, tapado, *m.*, sobretodo, *m.*] (overcoat). || Última mano, *f.* (of paint).
top-drawer [ˈtɔpˈdrɔ:ə*] adj. De la alta sociedad (people). || De primera [categoría] (first-class).
topdress [ˈtɔpˈdres] v. tr. AGR. Abonar, estercolar.
topdressing [—iŋ] n. AGR. Abono, *m.*, estiércol, *m.*
tope [təup] n. Templete (*m.*) budista.
tope [təup] v. intr. Beber con exceso.
topee [ˈtəupi] n. Salacot, *m.* (helmet).
toper [ˈtəupə*] n. Bebedor, *m.*, borrachín, *m.* (heavy drinker).
topflight [ˈtɔpˈflait] adj. De primera categoría, de primera clase.
topgallant [tɔpˈgælənt] n. MAR. Mastelerillo (*m.*) de juanete (mast). | Juanete, *m.* (sail).
— Adj. De juanete: *topgallant mast*, mastelerillo de juanete.
top-hamper [ˈtɔpˈhæmpə*] n. MAR. Superestructura, *f.*
top hat [ˈtɔpˈhæt] n. Sombrero (*m.*) de copa, chistera, *f.*
top-heavy [ˈtɔpˈhevi] adj. Demasiado pesado en la parte superior, inestable. || FIG. Con demasiado personal dirigente (having too many high-paid officials). | Supercapitalizado, da (overcapitalized).
top-hole [ˈtɔpˈhəul] adj. Estupendo, da.
tophus [ˈtəufəs] n. GEOL. Toba, *f.* || MED. Nodo, *m.*, tofo, *m.*
— OBSERV. El plural de *tophus* es *tophi*.
topi [ˈtəupi. U. S. təˈpi:] n. Salacot, *m.* (topee).
topiary [ˈtəupjəri] adj. De la jardinería.
— N. Jardinería, *f.* (art). || Arbustos (*m.*) recortados artísticamente.
topic [ˈtɔpik] n. Tema, *m.*, asunto, *m.*, tópico, *m.*
topical [—əl] adj. De actualidad: *highly topical*, de gran *or* de mucha actualidad. || Sobre cuestiones de actualidad (conversation). || Local. || MED. Tópico, ca.
topicality [ˌtɔpiˈkæliti] n. Actualidad, *f.* || Carácter (*m.*) local.
topknot [ˈtɔpnɔt] n. Moño, *m.* (of hair). || Copete, *m.*, penacho, *m.* (of birds). || FAM. Coco, *m.* (head).
topless [ˈtɔplis] adj. Con el busto desnudo (person). || Que deja el busto al descubierto (dress).
top-level [ˈtɔpˈlevl] adj. De alto nivel, del más alto nivel.
topman [ˈtɔpmən] n. Minero (*m.*) que trabaja en la superficie.
— OBSERV. El plural de *topman* es *topmen*.
topmast [ˈtɔpmɑ:st] n. MAR. Mastelero, *m.*
topmost [ˈtɔpməust] adj. Más alto.
top-notch [ˈtɔpˈnɔtʃ] adj. De primera calidad *or* categoría, de primera (first-rate).
topographer [təˈpɔgrəfə*] n. Topógrafo, *m.*
topographic [ˌtɔpəˈgræfik] or **topographical** [—əl] adj. Topográfico, ca.
topography [təˈpɔgrəfi] n. Topografía, *f.*
topology [təˈpɔlədʒi] n. MATH. Topología, *f.*
toponym [ˈtɔpənim] n. Topónimo, *m.*
toponymic [ˌtɔpəˈnimik] or **toponymical** [—əl] adj. Toponímico, ca.
toponymy [təˈpɔnimi] n. Toponimia, *f.*
topper [ˈtɔpə*] n. FAM. Sombrero (*m.*) de copa, chistera, *f.* (top hat). | Persona (*f.*) extraordinaria (person). | Cosa (*f.*) extraordinaria (thing).
topping [ˈtɔpiŋ] adj. Estupendo, da; extraordinario, ria.
— N. Desmoche, *m.* (of a tree). || See TOP.
topple [ˈtɔpl] v. tr. Hacer caer, derribar (to cause to fall): *to topple a rider from his horse*, derribar un jinete del caballo; *to topple a statue over*, derribar una estatua. || Volcar (to knock over, to overturn). || FIG. Derribar (to cause to fall from power).
— V. intr. Venirse abajo, caerse (to fall). || Volcarse: *the flower vase, the lorry toppled over*, el florero, el camión se volcó. || Tambalearse (to be on the point of falling). || FIG. Venirse abajo, caer (government).
tops [tɔps] n. FAM. *It's the tops*, es fantástico, es genial.
topsail [ˈtɔpsl] n. MAR. Gavia, *f.*
top-secret [ˈtɔpˈsi:krit] adj. Confidencial, sumamente secreto, ta.
top sergeant [ˈtɔpˈsɑ:dʒənt] n. MIL. Sargento, *m.*
topside [ˈtɔpˈsaid] n. or **topsides** [—z] pl. n. MAR. Obra (*f. sing*) muerta.
— Adv. MAR. En cubierta (on deck).
topsoil [ˈtɔpˌsɔil] n. Capa (*f.*) superficial del suelo, tierra (*f.*) vegetal, mantillo, *m.*
topsy-turvily [ˈtɔpsiˈtə:vili] adv. Patas arriba, en desorden.
topsy-turviness [ˈtɔpsiˈtə:vinis] n. Desorden, *m.*
topsy-turvy [ˈtɔpsiˈtə:vi] adj. Revuelto, ta; desordenado, da; en desorden (in disorder). | Al revés (upside down): *a topsy-turvy world*, el mundo al revés.
— Adv. Patas arriba, en desorden.
topsy-turvydom [—dəm] n. El mundo (*m.*) al revés.
top ten [ˈtɔpˈten] n. Los diez mejores discos del momento.
top twenty [ˈtɔpˈtwenti] n. Los veinte mejores discos del momento.
toque [təuk] n. Toca, *f.* (woman's hat).
tor [tɔ:*] n. Peñasco, *m.* (rock).
Torah (U. S. **Tora**) [ˈtɔ:rə] n. REL. Tora, *f.*
torch [tɔ:tʃ] n. Antorcha, *f.*, hacha, *f.*, tea, *f.* (made of wood). || Linterna, *f.* (electric). || Soplete, *m.* (for welding). || FIG. Antorcha, *f.* (source of enlightenment). || FIG. *To carry a torch for s.o.*, estar enamorado de alguien [sin ser correspondido].
torchbearer [—ˌbεərə*] n. Persona (*f.*) que lleva una antorcha. || Nazareno, *m.* (in religious processions). || FIG. Abanderado, *m.* (person who brings enlightenment).
torchlight [—lait] n. Luz (*f*). de antorcha. || *Torchlight procession*, procesión (*f.*) *or* desfile (*m.*) con antorchas.
torchon lace [ˈtɔ:ʃənleis] n. Encaje (*m.*) de hilo basto.
torch singer [ˈtɔ:tʃˌsiŋə*] n. Cantante (*m.* & *f.*) de canciones sentimentales.
torch song [ˈtɔ:tʃsɔŋ] n. Canción (*f.*) sentimental.
torchwood [ˈtɔ:tʃwud] n. Madera (*f.*) resinosa.
tore [tɔ:*] n. ARCH. MATH. Toro, *m.*
tore [tɔ:*] pret. See TEAR.
toreador [ˈtɔriədɔ:*] or **torero** [tɔˈrεərəu] n. Torero, *m.* (bullfighter).
tori [ˈtɔ:ri] pl. n. See TORUS.
toric [ˈtɔrik] adj. Tórico, ca.
torment [ˈtɔ:ment] n. Tormento, *m.*, suplicio, *m.*
torment [tɔ:ˈment] v. tr. Atormentar, torturar: *he was tormented with remorse*, le atormentaba el remordimiento. || Fastidiar (to annoy, to bother).
tormentor [tɔ:ˈmentə*] n. Atormentador, ra (person who torments). || CINEM. Panel (*m.*) de absorción acústica. || — Pl. THEATR. Alcahueta, *f. sing.*, segunda embocadura, *f. sing.*
torn [tɔ:n] p. p. See TEAR.
tornado [tɔ:ˈneidəu] n. Tornado, *m.*
— OBSERV. El plural de la palabra inglesa es *tornadoes* o *tornados*.
torose [təˈrəus] or **torous** [ˈtɔ:rəs] adj. BOT. Nudoso, sa (with knobs).
torpedo [tɔ:ˈpi:dəu] n. Torpedo, *m.* (underwater missile). || U. S. Petardo, *m.* (rail detonator). | Detonador, *m.* (used in oil wells). | Petardo, *m.* (small firework). || Torpedo, *m.* (fish).
— OBSERV. El plural de la palabra inglesa es *torpedoes*.
torpedo [tɔ:ˈpi:dəu] v. tr. Torpedear (to attack). || Poner detonadores en (an oil well). || FIG. Torpedear, hacer fracasar.
torpedo boat [—bəut] n. Torpedero, *m.*, lancha (*f.*) torpedera. || *Torpedo-boat destroyer*, cazatorpedero, *m.*, contratorpedero, *m.*
torpedo body [—ˈbɔdi] n. AUT. Torpedo, *m.*
torpedoing [—iŋ] n. Torpedeamiento, *m.*, torpedeo, *m.*
torpedoist [—ˈdu:ist] or **torpedoman** [—mən] n. Torpedista, *m.*
— OBSERV. El plural de *torpedoman* es *torpedomen*.
torpedo net [—net] n. Red. (*f.*) antitorpedo.
torpedo tube [—tju:b] n. Tubo (*m.*) lanzatorpedos, lanzatorpedos, *m. inv.*
torpid [ˈtɔ:pid] adj. Letárgico, ca; aletargado, da (lethargic). || Aletargado, da (animals). || FIG. Apatico, ca.
torpidity [tɔ:ˈpiditi] or **torpor** [ˈtɔ:pə*] n. Entorpecimiento, *m.*, torpor, *m.* || FIG. Apatía, *f.*
torporific [ˌtɔ:pəˈrifik] adj. Soporífero, ra.
torque [tɔ:k] n. PHYS. Momento (*m.*) de torsión. || HIST. Torques, *f.* (necklace).
torrefaction [ˌtɔriˈfækʃən] n. Torrefacción, *f.*
torrefy [ˈtɔrifai] v. tr. Torrefactar.
torrent [ˈtɔrənt] n. Torrente, *m.* (fast stream). || FIG. Torrente, *m.*: *a torrent of light, of tears*, un torrente de luz, de lágrimas. || *To rain in torrents*, llover a cántaros.
torrential [tɔˈrenʃəl] adj. Torrencial.

torrid [ˈtɔrid] adj. Tórrido, da: *torrid zone*, zona tórrida.

torridity [təˈriditi] n. Calor (*m.*) tórrido.

torrify [ˈtɔrifai] v. tr. Torrefactar.

torsion [ˈtɔːʃən] n. Torsión, *f.*

torsional [—əl] adj. De torsión. || *Torsional strength*, resistencia (*f.*) a la torsión.

torsion balance [—ˈbæləns] n. PHYS. Balanza (*f.*) de torsión.

torsion bar [—bɑː*] n. AUT. Barra (*f.*) de torsión.

torsk [tɔːsk] n. Bacalao, *m.* (fish).

torso [ˈtɔːsəu] n. Torso, *m.*

— OBSERV. El plural de la palabra inglesa es *torsos* o *torsi*.

tort [tɔːt] n. JUR. Agravio (*m.*) indemnizable en juicio civil.

torticollis [ˌtɔːtəˈkɔlis] n. MED. Tortícolis, *f.*

tortilla [tɔːˈtiːjæ] n. Tortilla, *f.* (pancake, omelet).

tortoise [ˈtɔːtəs] n. ZOOL. Tortuga, *f.* [de tierra].

tortoiseshell [—ʃəl] n. Carey, *m.*, concha, *f.*

— Adj. De carey, de concha.

tortuosity [ˌtɔːtjuˈɔsiti] n. Tortuosidad, *f.*

tortuous [ˈtɔːtjuəs] adj. Tortuoso, sa: *a tortuous road*, una carretera tortuosa; *tortuous means*, métodos tortuosos. || Tortuoso, sa; retorcido, da: *tortuous mind*, mentalidad retorcida.

torture [ˈtɔːtʃə*] n. Tortura, *f.*, tormento, *m.* || FIG. FAM. *It was torture at the dentist's!*, ¡lo que sufrí con el dentista!

torture [ˈtɔːtʃə*] v. tr. Torturar, atormentar, dar tormento a (to inflict pain on). || FIG. Torcer, deformar (to twist, to deform). | Atormentar (to torment).

torturer [—rə*] n. Torcionario, *m.*

torus [ˈtɔːrəs] n. ARCH. MATH. Toro, *m.* || BOT. Receptáculo, *m.* || ANAT. Torus, *m.*, protuberancia (*f.*) redondeada.

— OBSERV. El plural de la palabra inglesa es *tori*.

Tory [ˈtɔːri] adj./n. Conservador, ra (in England). || Realista (in the War of American Independence). || FIG. Reaccionario, ria.

Toryism [—izəm] n. Conservadurismo, *m.*

tosh [tɔʃ] n. FAM. Bobadas, *f. pl.*, tonterías, *f. pl.*

toss [tɔs] n. Lanzamiento, *m.* (throwing). || Sacudida, *f.* (of the head). || Sacudida, *f.* (buck). || Movimiento, *m.* (of waves). || Caída, *f.* (fall). || Sorteo (*m.*) a cara o cruz. || Cogida, *f.* (by a bull). || — *Give the pancake a toss*, dale la vuelta a la tortita. || *Give the salad a toss*, dale vueltas a *or* mueve *or* revuelve la ensalada. || *It's a toss between X and Y*, se juega entre X e Y. || *To argue the toss*, seguir discutiendo, insistir (to keep arguing), andar en dimes y diretes, discutir (to argue). || *To take a toss*, caerse del caballo. || *To win the toss*, ganar [a cara o cruz].

toss [tɔs] v. tr. Tirar, lanzar (to throw). || Echar [la cabeza] para atrás (one's head). || Sacudir: *the horse tossed its head*, el caballo sacudió la cabeza. || Tirar (a horse its rider). || Dar la vuelta a (a pancake, hay, etc.). || Revolver, mover, dar vueltas a: *to toss the salad*, dar vueltas a la ensalada. || Sacudir: *the waves tossed the boat*, las olas sacudían el barco. || Sacudir (a pillow). || Echar a cara o cruz (a coin). || — *The bull tossed the bullfighter*, el toro cogió al torero. || *Toss it over to me*, tíramelo. || *To toss aside*, echar a un lado. || *To toss back*, echar para atrás (one's head, one's hair), devolver (a ball, etc.). || *To toss off*, beber de un trago (a drink), escribir rápidamente (a letter), despachar (a task). || *To toss one's money about*, tirar el dinero por la ventana. || *To toss s.o. in a blanket*, mantear a alguien. || *To toss up*, echar, lanzar al aire (a coin).

— V. intr. Agitarse (to move restlessly). || Ondear (to wave). || Dar vueltas, revolverse (when sleeping). || Echar a cara o cruz: *let's toss for it*, vamos a echarlo a cara o cruz. || MAR. Cabecear (to pitch). | Balancearse (to roll). || — *To toss and turn*, dar vueltas (in bed). || *To toss up for sth.*, echar algo a cara o cruz.

tosspot [—pɔt] n. Borracho, *m.* (drunkard).

toss-up [—ʌp] n. *It's a toss-up between*, se juega *or* se disputa entre. || *It's a toss-up whether he'll come or not*, no se sabe si vendrá o no vendrá. || *To decide sth. by a toss-up*, decidir algo a cara o cruz.

tot [tɔt] n. Nene, *m.* (child). || Trago, *m.* (drop): *we had a tot of whisky*, nos tomamos un trago de whisky. || Poco, *m.* (little): *would you like a tot of rum?*, ¿quieres un poco de ron?

tot [tɔt] v. tr. *To tot up*, sumar.

— V. intr. Acumularse, aumentar. || *The bill tots up to ten pounds*, la factura asciende a *or* suma diez libras.

total [ˈtəutl] adj. Total: *total ignorance*, ignorancia total; *total eclipse*, eclipse total. || *The total cost of the disaster in human lives was 3,560*, la catástrofe costó la vida a 3.560 personas en total *or* a un total de 3.560 personas.

— N. Total, *m.*, totalidad, *f.* (the whole amount). || Total, *m.*, suma, *f.* (sum). || *Grand* o *sum total*, total, *m.*

total [ˈtəutl] v. tr. Sumar (to find the total of). || Totalizar, sumar, ascender a (to equal a total of).

— V. intr. *To total up to*, ascender a, sumar, totalizar.

totalisator [ˈtəutəlaizeitə] n. SP. Totalizador, *m.*

totalitarian [ˌtəutæliˈtɛriən] adj./n. Totalitario, ria.

totalitarianism [—izəm] n. Totalitarismo, *m.*

totality [təuˈtæliti] n. Totalidad, *f.*

totalization [ˌtəutəlaiˈzeiʃən] n. Totalización, *f.*

totalizator [ˈtəutəlaizeitə*] n. SP. Totalizador, *m.*

totalize [ˈtəutəlaiz] v. tr. Totalizar.

totalizer [—ə*] n. SP. Totalizador, *m.*

totally [ˈtəutəli] adv. Completamente, totalmente.

tote [təut] n. U. S. FAM. Totalizador, *m.* (totalizator). | Carga, *f.*, peso, *m.* (weight).

tote [təut] v. tr. U. S. FAM. Llevar, cargar.

totem [ˈtəutəm] n. Tótem, *m.*

totemic [təuˈtemik] adj. Totémico, ca.

totemism [ˈtəutəmizəm] n. Totemismo, *m.*

totemistic [təutəˈmistik] adj. Totémico, ca.

totem pole [ˈteutəmˈpəul] n. Tótem, *m.*

Totonac [təuˈtəunæk] adj./n. Totonaca, totoneca.

Totonaca [—ə] n. Totonaca, *m.* & *f.*, totoneca, *m.* & *f.*

Totonacan [—ən] n. Totonaca, *m.*, totoneca, *m.* (language).

Totonaco [—əu] n. Totonaca, *m.* & *f.*, totoneca, *m.* & *f.*

totter [ˈtɔtə*] v. intr. Tambalearse: *he was tottering along the street*, iba tambaleándose por la calle. || Tambalearse (building, government). || *To totter on the brink of ruin*, estar al borde de la ruina.

tottering or **tottery** [—riŋ] adj. Tambaleante. || Inseguro, ra; vacilante, titubeante (steps). || Ruinoso, sa (wall).

toucan [ˈtuːkən] n. Tucán, *m.* (bird).

touch [tʌtʃ] n. Toque, *m.* (light stroke): *touch of the magic wand*, toque de varita mágica; *give it a touch*, dale un toque. || Roce, *m.* (slight contact). || Tacto, *m.* (sense): *the sense of touch*, el sentido del tacto; *smooth to the touch*, suave al tacto. || Mano, *f.*: *the master's touch*, la mano del maestro. || Contacto, *m.*: *to keep, to be in touch*, mantenerse, estar en contacto; *to get in touch*, ponerse en contacto; *to lose touch*, perder contacto. || FIG. Chispa, *f.*, pizca, *f.*, poquito, *m.* (small amount): *a touch of salt*, una chispa de sal; *a touch too high*, un poquito demasiado alto. | Sello, *m.*, estilo, *m.* (style of execution): *dress with an individual touch about it*, traje con un sello personal. | Amago, *m.*: *the first touches of autumn*, los primeros amagos del otoño. | Nota, *f.*: *there was a touch of humour in his speech*, había una nota de humor en su discurso. || Toque, *m.*, piedra (*f.*) de toque (touchstone). || MED. Amago, *m.*, acceso, *m.*: *a touch of fever*, un amago de fiebre. | Punzada, *f.* (of pain). || Pulsación, *f.* (of typist). || Tecleo, *m.* (of pianist). || SP. Toque, *m.*, tocado, *m.* (in fencing). | Banda, *f.*: *in touch*, fuera de banda. || ARTS. Pincelada, *f.*, toque, *m.*: *the finishing touches*, los últimos toques. || FAM. Sablazo, *m.* (sponging). || — *A clever touch*, un acierto, un buen toque, un buen detalle. || *At a touch*, al primer roce. || *A touch of irony*, cierta ironía. || *By touch*, al tacto. || FIG. *Final* o *finishing touch*, último toque, última mano. || *I felt a touch on my arm*, sentí que me tocaban el brazo. || *To add a finishing touch to*, *to give* o *to put the finishing touch to*, dar el último toque *or* la última mano a. || FIG. *To be good for a touch*, prestar *or* dar dinero con facilidad. || *To be in touch with sth.*, estar al tanto *or* al corriente de algo. || *To be out of touch*, estar aislado. || *To be out of touch with*, haber perdido el contacto con (s.o.), no estar al tanto de (sth.). || *To get a touch of the sun*, coger una ligera insolación. || FIG. *To have a near touch*, librarse por los pelos. || *To keep in touch with events*, mantenerse al corriente de los acontecimientos. || *To put into touch*, poner en relación *or* en contacto. || *To put sth. to the touch*, poner or someter algo a prueba.

touch [tʌtʃ] v. tr. Tocar: *she touched the iron to see if it was hot*, tocó la plancha para ver si estaba caliente; *don't touch my radio*, no toques mi radio; *you can't touch the money until you are 21*, no puedes tocar el dinero antes de cumplir 21 años; *he touched me on the shoulder*, me tocó el hombro. || Tocar, rozar: *the wheels touched the kerb*, las ruedas rozaban el bordillo de la acera; *the mountains seemed to touch the clouds*, las montañas parecían tocar las nubes. || Lindar con (to have a boundary in common): *the two estates touch each other*, las dos propiedades lindan una con otra. || Llegar a, alcanzar (to reach): *the temperature touched 40 degrees*, la temperatura llegó a 40 grados. || Afectar (to affect). || Conmover (to move to pity): *her sad story touched us deeply*, su triste historia nos conmovió profundamente. || Hacer mella: *his years in prison haven't touched him*, sus años en la cárcel no le han hecho mella. || Estropear (to injure slightly): *the paintings were not touched by the fire*, los cuadros no fueron estropeados por el incendio. || Trastornar (brain). || Herir (to vex): *I touched his self-esteem*, herí su amor propio. || Estar relacionado con (to concern): *what you say does not touch the point at issue*, lo que está usted diciendo no está relacionado con el punto tratado. || Interesar, afectar: *the question touches you nearly*, la cuestión le interesa particularmente. || Abordar, tocar: *he didn't touch the last point on the programme*, no abordó el último punto del programa. || Tocar, probar (to taste): *he didn't touch his meal*, no probó la comida. || Quitar (a stain). || Tocar (to test gold or silver). || Contrastar (to hallmark). || Coger (to take): *he would never have touched your bicycle*, nunca habría cogido tu bicicleta. || Utilizar (to use): *I never touch the typewriter now*, ahora nunca utilizo la máquina de escribir. || Ocuparse de (to concern o.s. with): *don't touch the project*, no te ocupes del proyecto. || Acercar: *he touched a match to the fire*, acercó una cerilla al fuego. || FAM. Dar un sablazo: *he touched us for 10 pounds*, nos dio un sablazo de diez libras. || [Poder] compararse con, igualar a: *she can't touch him as a pianist*, como pianista no se puede comparar con él; *there's nothing to touch mountain air for giving you an appetite*, no hay nada que se pueda comparar con el aire de la sierra para abrir el apetito. || Imponer las manos sobre (a scrofulous person). || MAR. Tocar, hacer escala en: *to touch port*, tocar puerto. || MUS. Tocar (an instrument). || SP. Tocar (in fencing). || MATH. Ser tangente con. || Tocar (bell). || — *To touch bottom*, tocar el fondo (boat), hacer pie (when swimming), llegar hasta lo más profundo *or* hasta el fondo (of misfortune, etc.). || SP. *To touch down*, depositar [el balón] detrás de la línea de gol (rugby). || *To touch in*, esbozar (drawing, etc.). || *To touch off*, desencadenar, provocar (to provoke), descargar (a gun), esbozar (a drawing). || *To touch one's hat to s.o.*, saludar a alguien llevándose la mano al sombrero. || FIG. *To touch s.o. on a tender spot* o *to the quick*, herir a alguien en lo vivo. | *To touch the spot*, venir como anillo al dedo. || *To touch up*, retocar (drawing, photograph, text), dar los últimos toques a (to finish off), dar latigazos a (a horse). || FIG. *Touch wood*, toca madera.

— V. intr. Tocarse, rozarse: *the two ships touched*, los dos barcos se tocaron. || Lindar (to have a common boundary). || — MAR. *To touch at*, tocar en, hacer escala en. || *To touch down*, tomar tierra, aterrizar (a plane), amerizar (space capsule), hacer un ensayo (in rugby). || *To touch on* o *upon*, tratar superficialmente, tocar: *he touched on the economic problem*, trató superficialmente el problema económico; aludir a, referirse a, tocar (to refer to).

touchable [—əbl] adj. Tangible, palpable.

touch and go [—ən'gəu] n. *It was touch and go whether we should catch the train*, era dudoso que pudiéramos coger el tren, corríamos el riesgo de perder el tren.

touch-and-go [—ən'gəu] adj. Arriesgado, da; aventurado, da: *a touch-and-go affair*, un asunto arriesgado.

touchback [—bæk] n. U. S. SP. Balón (*m.*) muerto.

touchdown [—daun] n. Aterrizaje, *m.* (of plane). || Amerizaje, *m.* (of space capsule). || U. S. SP. Ensayo, *m.*

touched [—t] adj. FAM. Tocado, da; chiflado, da; chalado, da (crazy). || FAM. *Touched in the head*, tocado de la cabeza.

touchhole [—həul] n. Oído, *m.*, fogón, *m.* (of firearms).

touchiness [—inis] n. Susceptibilidad, *f.*

touching [—iŋ] adj. Conmovedor, ra (moving).

— Prep. Tocante a, relativo a, referente a.

touchingly [—iŋli] adv. De manera conmovedora.

touchline [—lain] n. SP. Línea (*f.*) de banda.

touchstone [—stəun] n. Piedra (*f.*) de toque.

touch-type [—taip] v. intr. Mecanografiar al tacto.

touch-typing [—ˌtaipiŋ] n. Mecanografía (*f.*) al tacto.

touchwood [—wud] n. Yesca, *f.* (tinder).

touchy [—i] adj. Susceptible (easily offended). || Delicado, da: *a touchy subject*, un tema delicado.

tough [tʌf] adj. Duro, ra; fuerte, resistente (hard to break). || Duro, ra; estropajoso, sa (meat). || Correoso, sa (rubbery). || Fuerte, resistente: *a tough fabric*, una tela fuerte. || Duro, ra (metal). || Fuerte, robusto, ta: *a tough constitution*, una constitución robusta. || FIG. Duro, ra; violento, ta (fight). | Duro, ra; penoso, sa (work). | Difícil (difficult). | Severo, ra (harsh): *a tough fine*, una multa severa. | Injusto, ta (unfair). | Inflexible (unyielding). | Bruto, ta (rough). || — FAM. *He is a tough customer!*, ¡es duro de pelar! || *They've been tough on him!*, ¡han sido muy duros con él! || *Tough guy*, rufián, *m.* || *Tough luck!*, ¡mala suerte!

— N. Duro, *m.* (thug).

toughen [—n] v. tr. Endurecer.

— V. intr. Endurecerse.

toughish [—iʃ] adj. Ligeramente duro, ra (meat). || FIG. Poco flexible (person). | Algo difícil (work).

toughness [—nis] n. Dureza, *f.* (hardness). || Lo duro, lo correoso (of meat). || Resistencia, *f.* (strength). || || Inflexibilidad, *f.* (unyielding nature). || Dificultad, *f.* (of work). || Carácter (*m.*) desabrido (bad temper).

toupee ['tu:pei] n. Tupé, *m.* (curl). || Postizo, *m.* (hairpiece).

tour [tuə*] n. Excursión, *f.* (organized). || Visita, *f.*: *a conducted tour of the castle*, una visita acompañada al castillo. || Viaje, *m.*: *we are going on a tour of Scotland*, vamos a ir de viaje por Escocia. || Gira, *f.*: *the theatre company is on tour*, la compañía de teatro está de gira. || Viaje (*m.*) *or* visita (*f.*) de inspección (for inspection). || SP. Vuelta (*f.*) ciclista: *the tour of France*, la vuelta ciclista a Francia. || — *Circular tour*, circuito, *m.* || *Package tour*, viaje todo comprendido. || *To make a tour of*, recorrer. || *Tour of duty*, turno (*m.*) de servicio.

tour [tuə*] v. tr. Viajar por, recorrer, hacer un viaje por: *we toured Spain*, estuvimos viajando por España. || THEATR. Ir de gira por. | Estar de gira por.

— V. intr. Ir de viaje *or* de excursión: *we are going touring in the car*, nos vamos de viaje en coche. || Estar de viaje *or* de excursión: *my parents are touring in Canada*, mis padres están de viaje en Canadá.

tour de force ['tuədə'fɔ:s] n. Proeza, *f.*, hazaña, *f.*

tourer ['tuərə*] n. See TOURING CAR.

touring ['tuəriŋ] n. Turismo, *m.*

— Adj. De turismo. || Que se dedica a hacer giras, que está de gira (company). || *Touring party*, grupo (*m.*) de turistas.

touring car [—kɑ:*] n. Descapotable, *m.*, coche (*m.*) de turismo descapotable.

tourism ['tuərizəm] n. Turismo, *m.*

tourist ['tuərist] n. Turista, *m.* & *f.*

— Adj. Turista: *tourist class*, clase turista. || Turístico, ca: *a tourist attraction*, una atracción turística. || De viajes: *tourist agency*, agencia de viajes. || *Tourist trade*, turismo, *m.*

tourmaline ['tuəməlin] n. MIN. Turmalina, *f.*

tournament ['tuənəmənt] n. Torneo, *m.*

tourney ['tuəni] n. Torneo, *m.*

tourney ['tuəni] v. intr. Participar en un torneo, tornear.

tourniquet ['tuənikei] n. MED. Torniquete, *m.*

tour operator ['tuərˌɔpəreitə*] n. Agente (*m.*) de viajes. || Agencia (*f.*) de viajes.

tousle ['tauzl] n. Maraña, *f.* (of hair).

tousle ['tauzl] v. tr. Desgreñar, despeinar (hair). || Arrugar, ajar (clothes, etc.).

tout [taut] n. FAM. Gancho, *m.* (who solicits customers). || Revendedor, ra (of tickets, etc.). || COMM. Corredor, *m.* || *On the tout*, espiando.

tout [taut] v. tr. Acosar, importunar (to solicit). || Vender (to sell). || Revender (tickets). || SP. Seguir a escondidas el entrenamiento de (race horses).

— V. intr. *To tout for*, solicitar.

tow [təu] n. Remolque, *m.*: *on tow*, a remolque. || Remolque, *m.*, sirga, *f.* (rope). || Vehículo (*m.*) remolcado (towed vehicle). || Estopa, *f.* (fibre). || — FIG. *He always has his family in tow*, siempre lleva a su familia a cuestas. || *To have* o *to take in tow*, remolcar (car, etc.).

tow [təu] v. tr. Remolcar (car, boat). || Sirgar, llevar a la sirga (from towpath). || FIG. Llevar a cuestas, arrastrar.

towage [—idʒ] n. Remolque, *m.* || Sirga, *f.* (from towpath). || Derechos (*m. pl.*) de remolque (tow fee).

toward ['təuəd] adj. Próximo, ma.

toward [tə'wɔ:d] or **towards** [—z] prep. Hacia (in the direction of): *as he came towards me*, al venir hacia mí; *it was facing towards me*, miraba hacia mí; *our country is rapidly moving towards prosperity*, nuestro país se encamina rápidamente hacia la prosperidad || Para (for): *to make a contribution towards charity*, hacer un donativo para obras de caridad. || Con (with): *to feel angry towards s.o.*, estar enfadado con alguien. || Para con (in respect of): *generosity towards others*, generosidad para con los demás. || Con respecto a, respecto a (with regard to): *the attitude of Spain towards America*, la actitud de España respecto a América. || Hacia, alrededor de (around): *towards midnight*, alrededor de medianoche. || Próximo a, cerca de (near).

towboat ['təubəut] n. MAR. Remolcador, *m.*

tow car ['təukɑ:*] n. U. S. Grúa (*f.*) remolque.

towel ['tauəl] n. Toalla, *f.*: *bath towel*, toalla de baño. || — *Sanitary towel*, paño higiénico, compresa, *f.* || FIG. *To throw in the towel*, tirar la esponja (in boxing), darse por vencido (to give up). || *Turkish towel*, toalla de felpa.

towel ['tauəl] v. tr. Secar *or* frotar con toalla.

towel horse [—hɔ:s] or **towel rack** [—ræk] or **towel rail** [—reil] or **towel roller** [—ˌrəulə*] n. Toallero, *m.*

towelling or **toweling** [—iŋ] n. Felpa, *f.* || *A towelling bathrobe*, un albornoz.

tower ['tauə*] n. Torre, *f.*: *the Eiffel tower*, la torre Eiffel; *the Tower of London*, *of Babel*, la Torre de Londres, de Babel; *control tower*, torre de control *or* de mando. || Fortaleza, *f.* (fortress). || — *Church* o *bell tower*, campanario, *m.*, torre de la iglesia. || MAR. *Conning tower*, torreta, *f.* (of a submarine), torre de mando (of a warship). || FIG. *Ivory tower*, torre de marfil. || FIG. *Tower of strength*, ayuda muy valiosa. || *Water tower*, arca (*f.*) de agua, depósito elevado de agua.

tower ['tauə*] v. intr. Elevarse, encumbrarse (to rise up). || *To tower above* o *over*, dominar (building), descollar entre, destacarse de (person).

towered [—d] adj. ARCH. Flanqueado por torres.

towering [—riŋ] adj. Elevado, da; encumbrado, da; altísimo, ma (very high). || Grande: *a towering height*, una gran altura. || Sobresaliente, destacado, da (rising above others). || Violento, ta; intenso, sa (emotions). || Ilimitado, da; desmedido, da (ambition).

towing ['təuiŋ] n. Remolque, *m.*

towline ['təulain] n. Remolque, *m.*, sirga, *f.*

town [taun] n. Ciudad, *f.* (large). || Pueblo, *m.*, población, *f.* (small). || Ciudad, *f.*, pueblo, *m.* (people): *the whole town was talking about it*, la ciudad entera hablaba de ello. || Ciudad, *f.*: *to prefer the town to the country*, preferir la ciudad al campo; *to live out of town*, vivir fuera de la ciudad. || Centro, *m.*, ciudad,

TOWN — CIUDAD, *f.*

I. General terms. — Términos (*m.*) generales.

centre of population	población *f.*, poblado *m.*
city	ciudad *f.*
urban	urbano, na
village	pueblo *m.* (large), aldea *f.* (small)
locality	localidad *f.*
capital	capital *f.*
metropolis	metrópoli *f.*, urbe *f.*
hamlet	caserío *m.*
hole, dump	poblacho *m.*
municipality	municipio *m.*
municipal	municipal
district	distrito *m.* (administrative), barrio *m.*
residential area	zona (*f.*) residencial
Chinese quarter	barrio (*m.*) chino
centre [U. S., center]	centro *m.*
shopping centre	centro (*m.*) comercial
extension	ensanche *m.*
suburb	suburbio *m.*, arrabal *m.*
slums	tugurios *m.*
shantytown	barrio (*m.*) de las latas [*Amer.*, villa (*f.*) miseria]
outskirts	afueras *f.*, cercanías *f.*, alrededores *m.*
house	casa *f.*
building	edificio *m.*
skyscraper	rascacielos *m. inv.*
flat	piso *m.*
shop, store	tienda *f.*
department stores	grandes almacenes *m.*
bazar, bazaar	bazar *m.*
junk shop	baratillo *m.*
newsstand	puesto (*m.*) de periódicos
market	mercado *m.*
Commodity Exchange	lonja *f.*
Stock Exchange	bolsa *f.*
town hall	ayuntamiento *m.*, casa (*f.*) consistorial
Lawcourt	Palacio (*m.*) de Justicia
church	iglesia *f.*
cathedral	catedral *f.*
chapel	capilla *f.*
cemetery	cementerio *m.*
grave, tomb	tumba *f.*
school	colegio *m.*, escuela *f.*
university	universidad *f.*
library	biblioteca *f.*
theatre [U. S., theater]	teatro *m.*
museum	museo *m.*
zoological garden	parque (*m.*) zoológico
fairground, fun fair	parque (*m.*) de atracciones
stadium	estadio *m.*
general post office	casa (*f.*) de correos
station	estación *f.*
barracks	cuartel *m. sing.*

II. Streets. — Calles, *f.*

road	calle *f.*, carretera *f.*
public thoroughfare	vía (*f.*) pública
high street	calle (*f.*) mayor
avenue	avenida *f.*
boulevard	bulevar *m.*
walk, promenade	paseo *m.*
ring road	camino (*m.*) *or* carretera (*f.*) de circunvalación
alley	callejuela *f.*, callejón *m.*
blind alley, cul-de-sac	callejón (*m.*) sin salida
passageway, alleyway	pasaje *m.*
one-way street	calle (*m.*) de dirección única
intersection	cruce *m.*
corner	esquina *f.*
block	manzana *f.* [*Amer.*, cuadra *f.*]
roadway	calzada *f.*
asphalt	asfalto *m.*
paving	pavimento *m.*
paving stone	adoquín *m.*
pavement[U. S., sidewalk]	acera *f.* [*Amer.*, vereda *f.*]
kerb [U. S., curb]	bordillo *m.*
gutter	cuneta *f.*
sewer	alcantarilla *f.*
hydrant	boca (*f.*) de riego
pedestrian crossing [U. S., crosswalk]	paso (*m.*) de peatones
island	isleta *f.*, refugio *m.*
arcade	soportales *m. pl.*
square	plaza *f.*
main square	plaza (*f.*) mayor
pond	estanque *m.*
fountain	fuente *f.*, surtidor *m.*
park, gardens	parque *m.*, jardines *m.*

III. Population. — Población, *f.*

demography	demografía *f.*
natality, birthrate	natalidad *f.*
mortality, deathrate	mortalidad *f.*
inhabitants	habitantes *m.*
townsman	habitante (*m.*) de una ciudad, ciudadano *m.*
villager	aldeano, na
citizen	ciudadano, na
fellow countryman	paisano *m.*
resident	residente *m.* & *f.*
tenant	inquilino, na
tourist	turista *m.* & *f.*
neighbour [U. S., neighbor]	vecino, na
neighbourhood [U. S., neighborhood]	vecindario *m.*
vagrant, tramp	vagabundo *m.*
beggar	mendigo *m.*, pordiosero *m.*

IV. Town services. — Servicios (*m.*) de una ciudad.

local government	administración (*f.*) municipal
mayor	alcalde *m.*
town council	concejo (*m.*) municipal
town councillor	concejal *m.*
cleaning	limpieza *f.*
sweeping	barrido *m.*
sweeper	barrendero *m.* (man)
road sweeper	barredora *f.* (machine)
dustbin [U. S., trash can, garbage can]	cubo (*m.*) de la basura
dustman [U. S., garbage collector]	basurero *m.*
lighting	alumbrado *m.*
streetlight, streetlamp	farol *m.*
water supply	abastecimiento (*m.*) de aguas
night watchman	sereno *m.*
urban police	policía (*f.*) urbana
policeman	guardia (*m.*) municipal, policía *m.*
traffic policeman	agente (*m.*) de policía, guardia (*m.*) de tráfico
police station	comisaría (*f.*) de policía
police inspector	comisario (*m.*) de policía
fireman	bombero *m.*
fire station	parque (*m.*) de bomberos
fire engine	coche (*m.*) de bomberos
hospital	hospital *m.*
mental hospital, mental asylum	manicomio *m.*
first-aid station	puesto (*m.*) de socorro
old people's home	asilo (*m.*) de ancianos
foundling home	inclusa *f.*
orphanage	orfanato *m.*
undertaker's	funeraria *f.*

V. Means of transport. — Medios (*m.*) de transporte.

bus	autobús *m.*
double decker bus	autobús (*m.*) de dos pisos
coach, motor coach [U. S., bus]	autocar *m.*
taxi, taxicab	taxi *m.*
trolleybus	trolebús *m.*
tramcar, streetcar	tranvía *m.*
underground, tube [U. S., subway]	metro *m.* [*Amer.*, subterráneo *m.*]
stop	parada *f.*
request stop	parada (*f.*) discrecional
taxi rank *o* stand	parada (*f.*) de taxis
driver	conductor *m.*
taxi driver, cab driver	taxista *m.* & *f.*
conductor	cobrador *m.*, revisor *m.*
inspector	inspector *m.*
ride	carrera *f.*
minimum fare (of a taxi)	bajada (*f.*) de bandera

f.: *to go shopping in town*, ir de compras al centro. || Capital, *f.*: *to go up to town*, ir a la capital. || U. S Municipio, *m.* || — *Boom town*, ciudad hongo. || *Canvas town*, ciudad de lona. || *It's the talk of the town*, es la comidilla del pueblo. || *New town*, pueblo nuevo. || *Satellite town*, ciudad satélite. || *To be out of town*, estar fuera, estar de viaje. || FIG. *To go (out) on the town* o *to paint the town red*, irse de juerga. *To go to town*, no reparar en gastos. || *To go to town on sth.*, hacer una cosa con toda su alma (to put one's heart into sth.). || *Town and gown*, los estudiantes y la gente de la ciudad. || *Twin town*, ciudad hermanada — Adj. De la ciudad, del pueblo: *town church* iglesia del pueblo. || Urbano, na: *town life*, vida urbana || — *Town clerk*, secretario (*m.*) del ayuntamiento. *Town council*, ayuntamiento, *m.*, concejo (*m.*) municipal. || *Town councillor*, concejal, *m.* || *Town crier* pregonero, *m.* || *Town hall*, ayuntamiento, *m.* || *Town planner*, urbanista, *m.* || *Town planning*, urbanismo, *m* || FIG *Town talk*, comidilla (*f.*) del pueblo.

townlet [ˊtaunlet] n. Pueblecito, *m.*, aldea, *f.*

townsfolk [ˊtaunzfəuk] pl. n. Ciudadanos, *m.* habitantes, *m.* (of a particular town). || Gente (*f. sing.*) de la ciudad, ciudadanos, *m.* (as opposed to country people).

township [ˊtaunʃip] n. Municipio, *m.*, término (*m.*) municipal.

townsman [ˊtaunzmən] n. Habitante (*m.*) de la ciudad, ciudadano, *m.*

— OBSERV. El plural de esta palabra es *townsmen*.

townspeople [ˊtaunz,pi:pl] pl. n. See TOWNSFOLK

towpath [ˊtəupɑ:θ] n. Camino (*m.*) de sirga.

towrope [ˊtəurəup] n. Remolque, *m.* || Sirga, *f.* (of canal).

tow truck [ˊtəutrʌk] n. Grúa (*f.*) remolque.

toxic [ˊtɔksik] adj. Tóxico, ca.

toxicant [—ənt] adj. Tóxico, ca.

— N. Tóxico, *m.*

toxicity [tɔkˊsisiti] n. Toxicidad, *f.*

toxicological [ˊtɔksikəˊlɔdʒikəl] adj. Toxicológico, ca

toxicologist [,tɔksiˊkɔlədʒist] n. Toxicólogo, *m.*

toxicology [,tɔksiˊkɔlədʒi] n. Toxicología, *f.*

toxicomania [,tɔksikəˊmeinjə] n. Toxicomanía, (drug addiction).

toxicosis [,tɔksiˊkəusis] n. MED. Toxicosis, *f. inv.*

toxin [ˈtɔksin] n. Toxina, *f.*
toxophilite [tɔkˈsɔfilait] n. Aficionado (*m.*) al tiro a arco (man fond of archery).
toy [tɔi] n. Juguete, *m.*
— Adj. De juguete: *a toy car*, un coche de juguete. || Enano, na: *toy poodle*, caniche enano. || — *Toy dog*, perro faldero. || *Toy soldier*, soldadito (*m.*) de plomo. || *Toy theatre*, teatro (*m.*) de títeres, teatro (*m.*) de marionetas.
toy [tɔi] v. intr. *To toy with*, acariciar (an idea), jugar con (to play with), juguetear con (to play around with), manosear, toquetear (to fiddle with), comisquear (food).
toyshop [—ʃɔp] n. Juguetería, *f.*, tienda (*f.*) de juguetes.
trace [treis] n. Huella, *f.* (footprint). || Rastro, *m.* (trail): *traces left by a snail*, el rastro de un caracol. || Indicio, *m.* (indication): *there was no trace of his having been there*, no había ningún indicio de que hubiera estado allí. || Vestigio, *m.* (remnant): *the Empire left no traces*, el Imperio no dejó vestigio alguno. || Pizca, *f.* (slight amount): *not a trace of truth*, ni pizca de verdad. || Tirante, *m.* (of horse's harness). || PHYS. Gráfico, *m.* (of seismograph, etc.). || MATH. Traza, *f.* (technical drawing). || MED. Indicio, *m.* (of albumen). || FIG. *To kick over the traces*, desmandarse.
trace [treis] v. tr. Trazar, dibujar (letters, plan). || Calcar (with tracing paper). || Seguir (a path, tracks, etc.). || Rastrear, seguir la pista de (to follow the trail of): *the police traced the thief*, la policía siguió la pista del ladrón. || Localizar, encontrar (to find s.o.). || Encontrar (to find sth.). || — *The rumour was traced back to a shopkeeper*, se descubrió que el rumor procedía de un tendero. || *To trace back to*, hacer remontar a (one's ancestry), remontarse a: *my family traces back to Henry VIII*, mi familia se remonta a Enrique VIII; descubrir (to find out). || *To trace out*, trazar (a plan), descubrir el rastro de (a thief), determinar (a date, an origin). || *To trace over*, calcar.
traceable [—əbl] adj. Fácil de seguir (easily followed). || Fácil de encontrar (easily found).
trace element [—ˌelimənt] n. Oligoelemento, *m.*
tracer [—ə*] n. Diseñador, ra (person). || Tiralíneas, *m. inv.* (ruling pen). || Patrón, *m.* (in sewing). || MIL. Bala (*f.*) trazadora. || CHEM. Indicador, *m.*
— Adj. Trazador, ra. || MIL. *Tracer bullet*, bala trazadora.
tracery [—əri] n. ARCH. Tracería, *f.*
trachea [trəˈkiə] n. Tráquea, *f.*

— OBSERV. El plural de *trachea* es *tracheae* o *tracheas*.

tracheal [—l] adj. Traqueal.
tracheitis [ˌtrækiˈaitis] n. MED. Traqueítis, *f.*
tracheotomy [ˌtrækiˈɔtəmi] n. MED. Traqueotomía, *f.*
trachoma [trəˈkəumə] n. MED. Tracoma, *m.*
trachyte [ˈtrækait] n. MIN. Traquita, *f.*
tracing [ˈtreisiŋ] n. Calco, *m.* (copying of a drawing). || Trazado, *m.* (drawing of a line). || Rastreo, *m.* (trailing). || Busca, *f.*, búsqueda, *f.* (search). || Gráfico, *m.* (of a recording instrument). || — *Tracing bullet*, bala trazadora. || *Tracing paper*, papel (*m.*) de calcar. || *Tracing wheel*, ruleta, *f.*, rodillo trazador (of tailors).
track [træk] n. Sendero, *m.*, camino, *m.* (path). || Rodada, *f.*, carril, *m.* (of wheels). || Rastro, *m.*, huella, *f.* (of persons, animals). || Vestigio, *m.*, rastro, *m.* (of things). || Estela, *f.* (of a ship). || Curso, *m.*, trayectoria, *f.*, recorrido, *m.* (course): *the track of a meteor*, la trayectoria de un meteoro. || Vía, *f.* (railway): *single, double track*, vía única, doble. || Distancia (*f.*) entre ejes (width of a vehicle). || Batalla, *f.* (of a car). || MAR. AVIAT. Rumbo, *m.* || Oruga, *f.* (of a tank, tractor, etc.). || Pista, *f.* (of tape recorder). || SP. Pista, *f.*: *dirt track*, pista de ceniza. || FIG. Pista, *f.*: *to be on s.o.'s track*, seguir la pista de uno. | Camino, *m.*: *beaten track*, camino trillado; *to be on the right track*, ir por buen camino. || — Pl. Huellas, *f.* (footprints). || — *Dog-racing track*, canódromo, *m.* || *Forest track*, camino forestal. || *In one's tracks*, en seco: *to stop in one's tracks*, pararse en seco; *to stop s.o. in his tracks*, parar a alguien en seco. || *Motor-racing track*, autódromo, *m.* || *Mule track*, camino carretero. || FIG. *On the right, wrong track*, en el buen, en el mal camino. || *Sheep track*, cañada, *f.* || FIG. *To be way off the track*, estar completamente despistado (person), no tener nada que ver con el asunto (thing). || *To cover (up) one's tracks*, no dejar rastro. || FIG. *To fall dead in one's tracks*, caer muerto. || *To follow in s.o.'s track*, seguir las huellas de alguien (to follow), seguir los pasos de alguien (to follow in s.o.'s footsteps). || *To go off the track*, descarrilar (a train). || *To keep track of*, seguir (to follow), vigilar, seguir de cerca (to keep an eye on). || *To leave the track*, descarrilar (a train). || *To lose track of*, perder la noción de (the time), perder el hilo de (a conversation), perder de vista, perder la pista de (people), no estar al tanto de (events). || FAM. *To make tracks*, largarse, marcharse (to leave), irse rápidamente (to go): *he made tracks for the station*, se fue rápidamente a la estación. || *To run off the tracks*, descarrilar (a train). || FIG. *To throw s.o. off the track*, despistar a uno.
track [træk] v. tr. Seguir las huellas de, seguir la pista de, rastrear (to hunt). || Seguir la pista de (to pursue): *the police are tracking the criminal*, la policía está siguiendo la pista del criminal. || Seguir: *to track an aeroplane by radar*, seguir un avión con el radar. || Poner orugas a (tractors, tanks, etc.). || MAR. Remolcar a la sirga, sirgar (to tow). || — *To track down*, acorralar (to corner), localizar (to locate), capturar (a thief), averiguar el origen de (to discover). || U. S. *To track mud into the house*, ensuciar la casa con barro. || *To track out*, encontrar.
— V. intr. Estar alineadas (wheels). || CINEM. Tomar vistas desplazándose (the camera). || U. S. Dejar huellas (to leave tracks).
trackage [—idʒ] n. Remolque, *m.* || Red (*f.*) de ferrocarriles (of railways). || Derecho (*m.*) a utilizar las vías de otra compañía.
tracked [—t] adj. Con orugas (tractor, etc.).
tracker [—ə*] n. Perseguidor, *m.*
track events [—iˈvents] pl. n. SP. Atletismo (*m. sing.*) en pista.
track gauge (U. S. **track gage**) [—geidʒ] n. Ancho (*m.*) de vía.
tracking [—iŋ] n. Seguimiento, *m.* (of a rocket). || Rastreo, *m.* (of a dog). || *Tracking station*, estación (*f.*) de seguimiento.
tracklayer [—ˌlɛiə*] n. Asentador (*m.*) de vías.
trackless [—lis] adj. Sin huellas (without footprints). || Sin caminos (without path). || Sin rieles (without rails).
trackman [—mən] n. U. S. Guardavía, *m.*

— OBSERV. El plural de esta palabra es *trackmen*.

track meet [—mi:t] n. U. S. Encuentro (*m.*) de atletismo.
tract [trækt] n. Octavilla, *f.* (propaganda sheet). || Opúsculo, *m.* (pamphlet). || Región, *f.*, zona, *f.* (area). || Extensión, *f.* || ANAT. Aparato, *m.*: *digestive tract*, aparato digestivo. | Vías, *f. pl.*: *respiratory tract*, vías respiratorias. || REL. Tracto, *m.* || *Tract of land*, terreno, *m.*
tractability [ˌtræktəˈbiliti] n. Docilidad, *f.* || Maleabilidad, *f.*, ductilidad, *f.* (of materials).
tractable [ˈtræktəbl] adj. Dócil, tratable (people). || Dócil (animals). || Manejable (device). || Dúctil, maleable (materials).
tractate [ˈtrækteit] n. Tratado, *m.* (treatise).
tractile [ˈtræktail] adj. Dúctil, maleable.
traction [ˈtrækʃən] n. Tracción, *f.* (act of hauling, pulling force). | Fricción (*f.*) adhesiva, adherencia, *f.* (friction). || MED. Tracción, *f.* || — *Traction engine*, locomotora tractora *or* de tracción. || *Traction wheel*, rueda (*f.*) de tracción.
tractional [—əl] adj. De tracción.
tractive [ˈtræktiv] adj. De tracción.
tractor [ˈtræktə*] n. AGR. Tractor, *m.* || Camión (*m.*) tractor (lorry). || Locomotora (*f.*) de tracción (traction engine). || *Caterpillar tractor*, tractor oruga.
tractor-drawn [—drɔ:n] adj. Arrastrado por un tractor.
tractor driver [—ˌdraivə*] or **tractor operator** [—ˌɔpəreitə*] n. Tractorista, *m.* & *f.*
tractor propeller [—prəˈpelə*] n. Hélice (*f.*) tractora.
trade [treid] n. Comercio, *m.*: *our trade with the Common Market*, nuestro comercio con el Mercado Común; *Board of Trade*, Ministerio de Comercio; *foreign trade*, comercio exterior. || Industria, *f.*: *the wood trade*, la industria de la madera. || Artesanía, *f.* (craft). || Ramo, *m.*: *I'm in the grocery trade*, estoy en el ramo de la alimentación. || Oficio, *m.*, profesión, *f.*: *what's your trade?*, ¿cuál es su oficio? || Comerciantes, *m. pl.* (tradespeople). || Negociantes, *m. pl.* (businessmen). || Gremio, *m.* (people in the same profession). || Transacción, *f.*, negocio, *m.* (a deal): *I did a good trade*, hice un buen negocio. || Tráfico, *m.*, comercio, *m.* (of drugs). || Cambio, *m.* (exchange). || U. S. Clientela, *f.*, clientes, *m. pl.* (customers). || — Pl. Vientos (*m.*) alisios (winds). || — *A baker by trade*, de oficio panadero. || *A doctor by trade*, de profesión médico. || *To be in trade*, ser comerciante, tener un negocio. || *To carry on a trade*, ejercer un oficio *or* una profesión.
— Adj. De comercio, comercial: *trade agreement*, acuerdo comercial. || Industrial.
trade [treid] v. intr. Comerciar (*in*, en) [as a business]. || Negociar (to have business dealings with s.o.). || Ser cliente, comprar (to be a customer): *I don't trade at that store*, no soy cliente de esta tienda, no compro en esta tienda. || *To trade on*, aprovecharse de.
— V. tr. Trocar, cambiar: *to trade skins for gold*, cambiar pieles por oro. || *To trade in*, dar *or* tomar como entrada (a used car, etc.).
trade cycle [—saikl] n. COMM. Ciclo (*m.*) comercial.
trade discount [—ˌdiskaunt] n. COMM. Descuento (*m.*) comercial.
trade disputes [—disˈpju:ts] pl. n. Conflictos (*m.*) laborales.
trade gap [—gæp] n. COMM. Déficit, *m.* [en la balanza comercial].
trade-in [—in] n. U. S. Artículo (*m.*) entregado como entrada para el pago de otro artículo.
trademark [—mɑ:k] n. Marca (*f.*) de fábrica. || FIG. Sello, *m.*, marca, *f.* || *Registered trademark*, marca registrada.
trademark [—mɑ:k] v. tr. Poner la marca de fábrica a (to give a trademark). || Registrar (sth. as trademark).

trade name [—neim] n. Nombre (*m.*) comercial (of an article). || Marca (*f.*) registrada (trademark). || Razón (*f.*) social (of a firm).
trade price [—prais] n. Precio (*m.*) al por mayor.
trader [—ə*] n. Comerciante, *m.* & *f.* (merchant). || Negociante, *m.* & *f.* (dealer). || MAR. Barco (*m.*) mercante.
trade school [—sku:l] n. Universidad (*f.*) laboral.
tradesman [—zmən] n. Tendero, *m.*, comerciante, *m.* (shopkeeper). || *Tradesmen's entrance*, entrada (*f.*) de proveedores, puerta (*f.*) de servicio.
— OBSERV. El plural de *tradesman* es *tradesmen.*
tradespeople [—z,pi:pl] pl. n. Comerciantes, *m.*
trades union [—z'ju:njən] n. Sindicato, *m.*
trades unionism [—z'ju:njənizəm] n. Sindicalismo, *m.*
trades unionist [—z'ju:njənist] n. Sindicalista, *m.* & *f.*
tradeswoman [—,wumən] n. Tendera, *f.*, comerciante, *f.*
— OBSERV. El plural de *tradeswoman* es *tradeswomen.*
trade union [—'ju:njən] n. Sindicato, *m.*: *member of a trade union*, afiliado a un sindicato. || (Ant.). Gremio, *m.*
trade unionism [—'ju:njənizəm] n. Sindicalismo, *m.*
trade unionist [—'ju:njənist] n. Sindicalista, *m.* & *f.*, miembro (*m.*) de un sindicato.
trade wind [—wind] n. Viento (*m.*) alisio.
trading ['treidiŋ] n. Comercio, *m.*
— Adj. Comercial: *trading concern*, empresa comercial.
trading post [—pəust] n. (Ant.). Factoría, *f.*
trading stamps [—stæmps] pl. n. Puntos, *m.*, cupones, *m.* [que se reúnen para conseguir un premio].
trading year [—jiə*] n. Ejercicio (*m.*) económico, año (*m.*) económico.
tradition [trə'diʃən] n. Tradición, *f.*
traditional [—əl] adj. Tradicional.
traditionalism [—əlizəm] n. Tradicionalismo, *m.*
traditionalist [—əlist] adj./n. Tradicionalista.
traditionalistic [trə,diʃənə'listik] adj. Tradicionalista.
traditionary [trə'diʃənəri] adj. Tradicional.
traditor ['træditə*] n. Traidor, *m.* [entre los primeros cristianos].
traduce [trə'dju:s] n. Difamar, calumniar.
traducement [—mənt] n. Difamación, *f.*, calumnia, *f.* (slander).
traducer [—ə*] n. Difamador, ra; calumniador, ra.
traffic ['træfik] n. Tráfico, *m.*, circulación, *f.* (of cars): *vehicular traffic*, circulación rodada. || Tráfico, *m.* (of people, boats, planes, etc.). || Tránsito, *m.* (of tourists, etc.). || Tráfico, *m.* (illegal business). || Comercio, *m.* (trade). || Negocio, *m.* (dealings). || Cambio, *m.* (exchange). || Intercambio, *m.* (of ideas, etc.). || *White slave traffic*, trata (*f.*) de blancas.
— Adj. De la circulación, del tráfico.
traffic ['træfik] v. intr. Traficar, comerciar, negociar (*in*, en).
trafficator [—eitə*] n. AUT. Indicador (*m.*) de dirección, flecha, *f.*
traffic circle [—,sə:kl] n. U. S. Encrucijada, *f.*, glorieta, *f.* (roundabout).
traffic controller [—kən'trəulə] n. AVIAT. Controlador (*m.*) del tráfico aéreo.
traffic island [—,ailənd] n. Isleta, *f.*, refugio, *m.*
traffic jam [—dʒæm] n. Embotellamiento, *m.*, atasco, *m.*
trafficker [—ə*] n. Traficante, *m.* (of drugs, etc.). || Tratante, *m.* (in white slaves). || Negociante, *m.* & *f.* (dealer).
traffic light [—lait] n. Semáforo, *m.*
traffic police [—pə,li:s] n. Policía (*f.*) de tráfico.
traffic policeman [—pə,li:smən] n. Guardia, *m.*
— OBSERV. El plural es *traffic policemen.*
traffic sign [—sain] n. Señal (*f.*) de tráfico.
tragacanth ['trægəkænθ] n. BOT. Tragacanto, *m.*
tragedian [trə'dʒi:djən] n. Trágico, *m.* (writer). || Actor (*m.*) trágico (actor).
tragedienne [trædʒe'djən] n. Actriz (*f.*) trágica.
tragedy ['trædʒidi] n. Tragedia, *f.*
tragic ['trædʒik] or **tragical** [—əl] adj. Trágico, ca: *don't be so tragic!*, ¡no te pongas tan trágico!
tragicomedy ['trædʒi'kɔmidi] n. Tragicomedia, *f.*
tragicomic ['trædʒi'kɔmik] or **tragicomical** [—əl] adj. Tragicómico, ca.
tragus ['treigəs] n. ANAT. Trago, *m.*
— OBSERV. El plural de la palabra inglesa es *tragi.*
trail [treil] n. Huellas, *f. pl.*, rastro, *m.* (of an animal, a person). || Pista, *f.*: *false trail*, pista falsa. || Camino, *m.*, sendero, *m.* (path). || Estela, *f.* (of smoke, etc.). || Nube, *f.* (of dust). || Reguero, *m.* (of blood, powder). || SP. Pista, *f.* || ASTR. Cola, *f.* (of a meteor). || MIL. Gualdera, *f.* (of a cannon). || FIG. Estela, *f.* || — *To be on the trail of*, seguir la pista de. || *To leave a trail of destruction*, arrasar todo al pasar. || *To lose, to pick up the trail*, perder, encontrar la pista.
trail [treil] v. tr. Arrastrar (to drag). || Llevar consigo (to bring with one). || Perseguir (to pursue). || Seguir el rastro de, rastrear (an animal). || Seguir la pista de (a person). || Localizar: *they trailed the jewels to a small shop*, localizaron las joyas en una pequeña tienda. || Seguir a (to follow). || Ir detrás de (to lag behind). || Dejar un reguero de (to leave a trail of). || MIL. Suspender (arms). || MIL. *Trail arms!*, suspendan ¡ar!
— V. intr. Arrastrarse (to drag): *his coat is trailing on the ground*, su abrigo se arrastra por el suelo. || Colgar (to hang down). || Ir lentamente (to go slowly). || BOT. Trepar (to climb). || — *To trail along*, arrastrarse (to drag), avanzar lentamente (to walk slowly). || *To trail behind*, quedarse atrás, rezagarse. || *To trail off*, desvanecerse (smoke), apagarse (sounds).
trailblazer [—,bleizə*] n. Pionero, *m.*
trailer [—ə*] n. Remolque, *m.* (behind a car). || U. S. Remolque (*m.*) habitable, caravana, *f.* (caravan). || CINEM. Trailer, *m.*, avance, *m.* || BOT. Planta (*f.*) trepadora.
trailing [—iŋ] adj. BOT. Trepador, ra; rastrero, ra. || AVIAT. *Trailing edge*, borde (*m.*) de salida.
trail net [—net] n. Red (*f.*) barredera.
train [trein] n. Tren, *m.* (railway): *express, fast, mail train*, tren expreso, rápido, correo; *commuter o suburban train*, tren de cercanías; *freight o goods train*, tren de mercancías; *relief o extra train*, tren suplementario; *slow o stopping train*, tren ómnibus; *through train*, tren directo; *up train*, tren ascendente. || Serie, *f.*, sucesión, *f.* (series): *train of events*, serie de acontecimientos; *in an unbroken train*, en una serie ininterrumpida. || Procesión, *f.* (procession). || Séquito, *m.*, comitiva, *f.* (retinue). || Cortejo, *m.* (suite). || Cola, *f.* (of a woman's dress). || Cola, *f.* (of a comet, of the tail of a bird). || Reguero, *m.* (of gunpowder). || TECH. Tren, *m.*: *train of gears*, tren de engranajes. || MIL. Tren (*m.*) de campaña. || Recua, *f.* (of animals). || MAR. Convoy, *m.* (of ships). || Rosario, *m.* (of bombs). || Hilo, *m.* (of thought). || — *Baggage train*, tren de equipajes. || *By train*, en tren, por ferrocarril. || FIG. *In one's train*, después. || *To be in train*, estar en curso. || *To catch a train*, tomar el tren. || *To change trains*, cambiar de tren, hacer transbordo. || FIG. *To set in train*, poner en marcha.
train [trein] v. tr. Amaestrar (an animal). || Domar (a horse). || Formar, preparar, adiestrar, capacitar (a person to do a job). || Educar (a child, one's voice). || Hacer entrar en vereda, someter a una disciplina (to discipline). || Enseñar (to teach). || Guiar (plants). || Apuntar (*on*, a) [a gun]. || Enfocar (*on*, a) [camera, telescope, etc.]. || SP. Entrenar. || MIL. Instruir. || *To train o.s. in*, ejercitarse en.
— V. intr. Entrenarse: *good sportsmen have to train a lot*, los buenos deportistas tienen que entrenarse mucho. || Prepararse, formarse (to prepare o.s.). || Estudiar, seguir un curso (to study). || Ejercitarse (to practise). || MIL. Hacer la instrucción. || FAM. Viajar *or* ir en tren (to go by rail).
trainbearer [—,bɛərə*] n. Persona (*f.*) que lleva la cola a otra.
train dress [—dres] n. Traje (*m.*) con cola.
trained [—d] adj. Diplomado, da (nurse, etc.). || Especializado, da; cualificado, da (worker). || Preparado, da (prepared). || Amaestrado, da (an animal). || Domado, da (a horse). || Educado, da (a child). || Disciplinado, da (an army). || Entrenado, da (a sportsman). || Experto, ta (eye).
trainee [trei'ni:] n. Aprendiz, za (s.o. learning a job). || Cursillista, *m.* & *f.*, persona (*f.*) que sigue un cursillo de formación profesional. || Persona (*f.*) que está de prácticas. || U. S. MIL. Recluta, *m.*
trainer ['treinə*] n. SP. Entrenador, ra. || Amaestrador, ra (of animals). || Domador, ra (of horses). || Preparador, ra; cuidador, ra (of boxers, etc.). || MIL. Instructor, *m.*
training ['treiniŋ] n. Entrenamiento, *m.* (in sports). || Instrucción, *f.*, enseñanza, *f.* (teaching). || Formación, *f.*, capacitación, *f.*: *vocational training*, formación profesional. || Preparación, *f.*, adiestramiento, *m.* (instruction in a particular skill). || Aprendizaje, *m.* (apprenticeship). || Amaestramiento, *m.* (of animals). || Doma, *f.* (of horses). || MIL. Puntería, *f.* (of gun). || Instrucción, *f.* (of troops). || — *In training*, haciendo un cursillo de formación *or* de preparación (doing a course of study), que se está entrenando (sportsmen, etc.), en plena forma, entrenado, da (in form). || *Out of training*, desentrenado, da. || *Physical training*, educación física, gimnasia, *f.*
training camp [—kæmp] n. MIL. Campo (*m.*) de instrucción.
training center [—,sentə*] n. Centro (*m.*) de formación profesional.
training college [—,kɔlidʒ] n. Escuela (*f.*) Normal (for teachers).
training school [—sku:l] n. Escuela (*f.*) de formación profesional, centro (*m.*) de capacitación. || Reformatorio, *m.* (correctional institution).
training ship [—ʃip] n. MAR. Buque (*m.*) escuela.
trainman ['treinmən] n. U. S. Empleado (*m.*) del ferrocarril, ferroviario, *m.*
— OBSERV. El plural de *trainman* es *trainmen.*
train oil ['treinɔil] n. Aceite (*m.*) de ballena (from blubber). || Aceite (*m.*) de pescado (from codfish, etc.).
traipse [treips] n. Caminata, *f.* (long walk).
traipse [treips] v. intr. FAM. Andar: *to traipse all over town*, andar por toda la ciudad.
trait [trei] n. Rasgo, *m.*, característica, *f.*
traitor ['treitə*] n. Traidor, *m.*

traitorous [—rəs] adj. Traidor, ra; traicionero, ra.
traitorousness [—rəsnis] n. Traición, *f.*
traitress [ˈtreitris] n. Traidora, *f.*
Trajan [ˈtreidʒən] pr. n. Trajano, *m.* ‖ *Trajan's Column*, Columna Trajana.
trajectory [trəˈdʒektəri] n. Trayectoria, *f.*
tram [træm] n. Tranvía, *m.* (vehicle). ‖ Vagoneta, *f.* (in mines). ‖ Vía (*f.*) de tranvía (tramline). ‖ Trama (*f.*) de seda (in textiles). ‖ *Tram system*, red tranviaria.
tramcar [—kɑ:*] n. Tranvía, *m.*: *mule-drawn tramcar*, tranvía de sangre *or* de mulas.
tramline [—lain] n. Vía (*f.*) de tranvía (rails). ‖ Línea (*f.*) de tranvía (route). ‖ — Pl. Líneas (*f.*) laterales (in tennis).
trammel [ˈtræməl] n. Trasmallo, *m.* (net). ‖ Traba, *f.* (for training a horse). ‖ U. S. Llares, *m. pl.* (pothook). ‖ — Pl. Compás (*m. sing.*) de varas (beam compass). ‖ FIG. Trabas, *f.*, obstáculos, *m.* (impediments).
trammel [ˈtræməl] v. tr. Pescar con trasmallo (to catch in a trammel). ‖ Poner trabas a (a horse). ‖ FIG. Poner trabas a, obstaculizar.
tramontane [træmənˈtɑ:nə] n. Tramontana, *f.* (wind).
tramontane [træmənˈtɑ:nə] adj. Tramontano, na.
tramp [træmp] n. Ruido (*m.*) de pasos (footsteps). ‖ Paseo (*m.*) largo, caminata, *f.* (walk). ‖ Vagabundo, *m.* (person with no fixed home). ‖ MAR. Barco (*m.*) mercante [de servicio irregular] (freight ship). ‖ U. S. FAM. Fulana, *f.* (prostitute).
tramp [træmp] v. intr. Andar pesadamente, andar con pasos pesados (to walk heavily). ‖ Ir a pie, caminar (to walk). ‖ Ser un vagabundo (to be a tramp).
— V. tr. Andar por, recorrer a pie: *to tramp the streets*, andar por las calles. ‖ U. S. Pisotear (to trample).
trample [—l] n. Ruido (*m.*) de pasos (sound). ‖ Pisoteo, *m.*
trample [—l] v. tr. Pisar: *to trample grapes*, pisar uvas. ‖ Pisotear: *the crowd trampled him to death*, la multitud le pisoteó hasta matarlo. ‖ — *To trample mud all over the floor*, pisar el suelo con los zapatos llenos de barro. ‖ *To trample out*, apagar de un pisotón.
— V. intr. *To trample on* o *upon* o *over*, pisotear: *to trample over the flower beds*, pisotear las flores.
trampolin [ˈtræmpəlin] or **trampoline** [ˈtræmpəli:n] n. Cama (*f.*) elástica.
tramway [ˈtræmwei] n. Tranvía, *m.* (vehicle). ‖ Vía (*f.*) de tranvía (line). ‖ *Tramway system*, red tranviaria.
trance [trɑ:ns] n. Trance, *m.* (of medium). ‖ MED. Catalepsia, *f.* ‖ FIG. Éxtasis, *m.*
tranquil [ˈtræŋkwil] adj. Tranquilo, la.
tranquillity (U. S. **tranquility**) [træŋˈkwiliti] n. Tranquilidad, *f.*
tranquillization (U. S. **tranquilization**) [ˌtræŋkwilaiˈzeiʃən] n. Aplacamiento, *m.*, sosiego, *m.*
tranquillize (U. S. **tranquilize**) [ˈtræŋkwilaiz] v. tr. Tranquilizar.
— V. intr. Tranquilizarse.
tranquillizer (U. S. **tranquilizer**) [—ə*] n. MED. Tranquilizante, *m.*
tranquillizing (U. S. **tranquilizing**) [—iŋ] adj. Tranquilizador, ra. ‖ MED. Tranquilizante.
transact [trænˈzækt] v. tr. Llevar a cabo, hacer (to perform). ‖ Tratar, negociar, tratar (to negotiate).
— V. intr. Negociar.
transaction [trænˈzækʃən] n. Negociación, *f.*, tramitación, *f.* (of business). ‖ Transacción, *f.* (deal). ‖ — Pl. Actas, *f.*, memorias, *f.* (records).
transactional [—əl] adj. Transaccional.
transactor [trænˈzæktə*] n. Negociador, ra.
transalpine [ˈtrænzˈælpain] adj. Transalpino, na; trasalpino, na.
trans-Andean [ˈtrænzˈændi:iən] adj. Transandino, na.
transatlantic [ˈtrænzətˈlæntik] adj. Transatlántico, ca; trasatlántico, ca.
transcaspian [ˈtrænzˈkæspjən] adj. Transcaspiano, na.
Transcaucasia [ˈtrænzkɔ:ˈkeizjə] pr. n. GEOGR. Transcaucasia, *f.*
Transcaucasian [—n] adj./n. Transcaucásico, ca.
transcend [trænˈsend] v. tr. Ir más allá de, estar por encima de: *to transcend reason*, estar por encima de la razón. ‖ Exceder, superar, rebasar, sobrepasar: *to transcend one's hopes*, sobrepasar las esperanzas de uno. ‖ PHIL. REL. Trascender, transcender.
— V. intr. PHIL. REL. Trascender, transcender.
transcendence [trænˈsendəns] or **transcendency** [—i] n. PHIL. REL. Trascendencia, *f.*, transcendencia, *f.*
transcendent [trænˈsendənt] adj. PHIL. REL. Trascendente. ‖ Sobresaliente, extraordinario, ria.
transcendental [—əl] adj. PHIL. Trascendental, transcendental. ‖ Sobrenatural. ‖ *Transcendental number*, número trascendente *or* transcendente.
transcendentalism [ˌtrænsenˈdentəlizəm] n. PHIL. Trascendentalismo, *m.*, transcendentalismo, *m.*
transcontinental [ˈtrænzˌkɔntiˈnentl] adj. Transcontinental.
transcribe [trænˈskraib] v. tr. Transcribir, trascribir (shorthand, music, etc.). ‖ RAD. Grabar (to record).
transcribed [—d] adj. Transcrito, ta. ‖ Grabado, da.
transcriber [—ə*] n. Transcriptor, *m.*
transcribing [—iŋ] n. Transcripción, *f.*
transcript [ˈtrænskript] n. Transcripción, *f.* ‖ Copia, *f.* (copy).
transcription [trænˈskripʃən] n. Transcripción, *f.* ‖ RAD. Emisión (*f.*) diferida (program). ‖ Grabación, *f.* (recording). ‖ *Phonetic transcription*, pronunciación figurada.
transducer [trænsˈdju:sə*] n. PHYS. Transductor, *m.* (device for transferring power).
transect [ˈtrænsekt] v. tr. Cortar transversalmente.
transection [trænˈsekʃən] n. Corte (*m.*) transversal.
transept [ˈtrænsept] n. Crucero, *m.* (in a church).
transfer [ˈtrænsfə:*] n. Traslado, *m.* (moving, displacement). ‖ Transbordo, *m.* (from one vehicle to another). ‖ Trasvase, *m.* (of rivers). ‖ Transferencia, *f.*, transmisión, *f.* (of property, shares, etc.). ‖ Transporte, *m.* (transport). ‖ Traslado, *m.* (of employee, corpse). ‖ Transmisión, *f.*: *transfer of power*, transmisión del poder. ‖ Transferencia, *f.* (of one's allegiance). ‖ SP. Traspaso, *m.* (of a player). ‖ ARTS. Reporte, *m.* ‖ COMM. Transferencia, *f.* (of money). ‖ Traspaso, *m.* (of a shop). ‖ Calcomanía, *f.* (small picture). ‖ U. S. Billete (*m.*) de transbordo (ticket). ‖ SP. *Transfer fee*, traspaso, *m.* (for a player).
transfer [trænsˈfə:*] v. tr. Trasladar (from one place or job to another): *to transfer a prisoner*, trasladar a un preso; *they transferred him to Barcelona*, le trasladaron a Barcelona. ‖ Transferir (one's allegiance). ‖ Transbordar (from one vehicle to another). ‖ Trasvasar (rivers). ‖ Transferir, transmitir (a right, a title). ‖ ARTS. Reportar. ‖ Calcar (a small picture). ‖ SP. Traspasar (a player). ‖ COMM. Transferir (money). ‖ Traspasar (a shop).
— V. intr. Trasladarse (from one place to another). ‖ Cambiar (to change). ‖ Hacer transbordo, transbordar (to change trains, buses, etc.).
transferable [—rəbl] adj. Transferible. ‖ Transportable. ‖ Trasladable. ‖ Transmisible. ‖ *Not transferable*, intransferible (ticket), inalienable (right).
transferee [ˌtrænsfəˈri:] n. Cesionario, ria.
transference [ˈtrænsfərəns] n. See TRANSFER. ‖ Transferencia, *f.*, trasferencia, *f.* (in psychology).
transferential [ˌtrænsfəˈrenʃəl] adj. De transferencia.
transfer paper [ˈtrænsfəˌpeipə*] n. Papel (*m.*) de calcar.
transferrer [trænsˈfə:rə*] n. Transferidor, ra.
transferring [trænsˈfə:riŋ] n. See TRANSFER.
transfiguration [ˌtrænsfigjuˈreiʃən] n. Transfiguración, *f.*, trasfiguración, *f.*
transfigure [trænsˈfigə*] v. tr. Transfigurar, trasfigurar.
transfix [trænsˈfiks] v. tr. Traspasar, atravesar (to impale). ‖ FIG. Traspasar: *transfixed with pain*, traspasado de dolor. ‖ Paralizar: *transfixed with fear*, paralizado por el miedo. ‖ FIG. *Transfixed with horror*, horrorizado, da.
transfixion [trænsˈfikʃən] n. Transfixión, *f.*
transform [trænsˈfɔ:m] v. tr. Transformar: *the experience transformed him*, le transformó la experiencia. ‖ PHYS. ELECTR. Transformar.
transformable [—əbl] adj. Transformable.
transformation [ˌtrænsfəˈmeiʃən] n. Transformación, *f.* ‖ (Ant.). Postizo, *m.* (false hair). ‖ THEATR. *Transformation scene*, mutación, *f.*, cambio escénico.
transformer [trænsˈfɔ:mə*] n. Transformador, ra. ‖ ELECTR. Transformador, *m.*
transformism [trænsˈfɔ:mizəm] n. Transformismo, *m.*
transformist [trænsˈfɔ:mist] adj./n. Transformista.
transfuse [trænsˈfju:z] v. tr. Transfundir, trasegar, transvasar, trasvasar (a liquid). ‖ Infundir, comunicar: *to transfuse one's enthusiasm into the class*, infundir su entusiasmo a la clase. ‖ MED. Hacer una transfusión de (blood). ‖ Hacer una transfusión a (a patient).
transfuser [—ə*] n. Transfusor, *m.*
transfusion [trænsˈfju:ʒən] n. MED. Transfusión, *f.*: *blood transfusion*, transfusión de sangre. ‖ Trasiego, *m.* (of liquids).
transgress [trænsˈgres] v. tr. Transgredir (a rule). ‖ Infringir, violar, quebrantar (a law). ‖ Traspasar (a limit).
— V. intr. Pecar (to sin). ‖ Cometer una infracción (to break a law).
transgression [trænsˈgreʃən] n. Transgresión, *f.* (of a rule). ‖ Infracción, *f.* (of a law). ‖ Pecado, *m.* (sin).
transgressive [trænsˈgresiv] adj. Transgresivo, va.
transgressor [trænsˈgresə*] n. Transgresor, ra; infractor, ra. ‖ Pecador, ra (sinner).
tranship [trænˈʃip] v. tr. Transbordar.
transhipment [—mənt] n. Transbordo, *m.*
transhumance [trænzˈhju:məns] n. Trashumancia, *f.*
transhumant [trænzˈhju:mənt] adj. Trashumante.
transience [ˈtrænziəns] or **transiency** [—i] n. Transitoriedad, *f.*, corta duración, *f.*
transient [ˈtrænziənt] adj. Transitorio, ria; pasajero, ra (not permanent).
— N. Transeúnte, *m.* & *f.*
transilluminate [ˌtrænziˈljumineit] v. tr. MED. Explorar por medio de focos.
transistor [trænˈzistə*] n. Transistor, *m.* ‖ *Transistor radio*, transistor, *m.*, radio (*f.*) de transistores.
transistorized [—raizd] adj. Transistorizado, da.
transit [ˈtrænsit] n. Tránsito, *m.*, paso, *m.* (passage): *in transit*, en tránsito, de paso. ‖ Transición, *f.* (transition). ‖ Transporte, *m.* (transport). ‖ ASTR. Culminación, *f.* ‖ *Country of transit*, país (*m.*) de tránsito.

transit [ˈtrænsit] v. tr. Pasar por, transitar por. || ASTR. Culminar por.
— V. intr. Transitar. || ASTR. Culminar.
transit compass [—ˈkʌmpəs] n. Teodolito (*m.*) de brújula.
transit instrument [—ˈinstrumənt] n. ASTR. Anteojo (*m.*) meridiano.
transition [trænˈziʃən] n. Transición, *f.* || MUS Transición, *f.*
transitional [—əl] adj. De transición: *transitional government*, gobierno de transición. || Transitorio, ria (period).
transitive [ˈtrænzitiv] adj. GRAMM. Transitivo, va.
— N. GRAMM. Verbo (*m.*) transitivo.
transitoriness [ˈtrænzitərinis] n. Transitoriedad, *f.*
transitory [ˈtrænzitəri] adj. Transitorio, ria.
Transjordan [ˈtrænzˈdʒɔːrdən] pr. n. GEOGR. Transjordania, *f.*
translatable [trænsˈleitəbl] adj. Traducible.
translate [trænsˈleit] v. tr. Traducir: *how do you translate this word?*, ¿cómo traduce esta palabra? || REL. Trasladar (a bishop to another see). || Transferir, trasladar (relics, etc.). || Retransmitir (a message). || Arrebatar al cielo (to convey to heaven). || PHYS. Dar un movimiento de traslación a.
— V. intr. Traducir (to make a translation): *to translate from Spanish into English*, traducir del español al inglés; *to translate at sight*, traducir directamente *or* de corrido. || Traducirse: *this phrase translates well*, esta expresión se traduce bien.
translation [trænsˈleiʃən] n. Traducción, *f.*: *translation into the foreign language*, traducción inversa; *translation out of the foreign language*, traducción directa. || Retransmisión, *f.* (of message). || PHYS. Traslación, *f.*: *movement of translation*, movimiento de traslación. || Traslado, *m.* (transfer).
translational [—əl] adj. De traslación.
translative [trænsˈleitiv] adj. Traslativo, va.
translator [trænsˈleitə*] n. Traductor, ra.
transliterate [trænzˈlitəreit] v. tr. Transcribir.
transliteration [ˌtrænzlitəˈreiʃən] n. Transcripción, *f.*
translocate [trænzˈləukeit] v. tr. Desplazar.
translocation [trænzləˈkeiʃən] n. Desplazamiento, *m.*
translucence [trænzˈluːsns] or **translucency** [—i] n. Translucidez, *f.*, traslucidez, *f.*
translucent [trænzˈluːsnt] or **translucid** [trænsˈluːsid] adj. Translúcido, da; traslúcido, da.
transmarine [trænzməˈriːn] adj. Ultramarino, na.
transmigrant [trænzˈmaigrənt] n. Persona (*f.*) que pasa por un país al dirigirse a otro en el que se va a establecer.
transmigrate [ˈtrænzmaiˈgreit] v. intr. Emigrar, transmigrar (people). || Transmigrar (the soul).
transmigration [ˌtrænzmaiˈgreiʃən] n. Transmigración, *f.*: *transmigration of souls*, transmigración de las almas. || Emigración, *f.*, transmigración, *f.* (of people).
transmigratory [trænzˈmaigrətəri] adj. Emigrante. || Transmigratorio, ria (soul).
transmissibility [ˌtrænzmisəˈbiliti] n. Transmisibilidad, *f.*, trasmisibilidad, *f.*
transmissible [trænzˈmisəbl] adj. Transmisible, trasmisible.
transmission [trænzˈmiʃən] n. Transmisión, *f.*, trasmisión, *f.* (a transmitting): *thought transmission*, transmisión del pensamiento. || Transmisión, *f.*, trasmisión, *f.*: *the transmission of a match by radio*, la transmisión de un partido por radio. || AUT. Transmisión, *f.*, trasmisión, *f.*
transmissive [trænzˈmisiv] adj. Transmisor, ra (transmitting). || Transmisible (transmissible).
transmit [trænzˈmit] v. tr. Transmitir, trasmitir.
transmitter [trænzˈmitə*] n. Transmisor, *m.* (apparatus). || Emisora, *f.* (station).
transmitting [trænzˈmitiŋ] adj. Transmisor, ra. || *Transmitting station*, estación transmisora *or* emisora.
transmogrify [trænzˈmɔgrifai] v. tr. Transformar. || Metamorfosear.
transmutability [trænzˌmjuːtəˈbiliti] n. Transmutabilidad, *f.*
transmutable [trænzˈmjuːtəbl] adj. Transmutable, trasmutable.
transmutation [ˌtrænzmjuːˈteiʃən] n. Transmutación, *f.*, trasmutación, *f.* || MATH. Transformación, *f.*
transmute [trænzˈmjuːt] v. tr. Transmutar.
transoceanic [ˈtrænzˌəuʃiˈænik] adj. Transoceánico, ca.
transom [ˈtrænsəm] n. ARCH. Dintel, *m.* (lintel). | Travesaño, *m.* (crosspiece of a window). || Travesaño, *m.* (of a cross). || MAR. Yugo, *m.* || Telera, *f.* (of a cannon, of a cart). || U. S. Tragaluz, *m.* (skylight).
transonic [trænˈsɔnik] adj. Transónico, ca.
transpacific [trænzpəˈsifik] adj. Transpacífico, ca.
transparence [trænsˈpɛərəns] n. Transparencia, *f.*
transparency [—i] n. Transparencia, *f.* (quality). || PHOT. Diapositiva, *f.*, transparencia, *f.* (slide). || Transparente, *m.*
transparent [trænsˈpɛərənt] adj. Transparente.
transpierce [trænzˈpiəs] v. tr. Traspasar (to pierce). || Penetrar (to penetrate).
transpiration [ˌtrænspiˈreiʃən] n. Transpiración, *f.* (perspiration). || BOT. Transpiración, *f.*
transpire [trænsˈpaiə*] v. tr. Transpirar.
— V. intr. Transpirar (to perspire, to exude). || FIG. Revelarse (to become known). | Ocurrir, suceder (to happen): *it transpired that he didn't come*, ocurrió que no vino.
transplant [trænsˈplɑːnt] n. MED. AGR. Trasplante, *m.*: *heart transplant*, trasplante de corazón.
transplant [trænsˈplɑːnt] v. tr. MED. AGR. Trasplantar. || FIG. Trasplantar (people).
transplantable [—əbl] adj. Trasplantable.
transplantation [ˌtrænsplɑːnˈteiʃən] n. Trasplante, *m.*
transport [ˈtrænspɔːt] n. Transporte, *m.*: *the transport of goods*, el transporte de mercancías. || Servicio (*m.*) de transportes: *transport in this town is not very good*, el servicio de transportes en esta ciudad no es muy bueno. || Deportado, *m.* (convict). || FIG. Transporte, *m.* (rapture). | Arrebato, *m.* (of rage, etc.). || — *Means of transport*, medio (*m.*) de transporte. || *Ministry of Transport*, Ministerio (*m.*) de Transportes. || *Rail, road transport*, transportes por ferrocarril, por carretera. || *Transport cost*, gastos (*m. pl.*) de transporte. || *Transport plane*, avión (*m.*) de transporte. || *Transport ship*, buque (*m.*) de transporte.
transport [trænsˈpɔːt] v. tr. Transportar: *to transport goods*, transportar mercancías. || Deportar (convicts). || FIG. Arrebatar.
transportability [trænsˌpɔːtəˈbiliti] n. Posibilidad (*f.*) de ser transportado.
transportable [trænsˈpɔːtəbl] adj. Transportable.
transportation [ˌtrænspɔːˈteiʃən] n. See TRANSPORT. || Deportación, *f.* (of a convict).
transporter [trænsˈpɔːtə*] n. Transportador, *m.*, transportista, *m.* (conveyor). || *Transporter bridge*, puente transbordador.
transporting [trænsˈpɔːtiŋ] adj. Transportador, ra; de transporte. || FIG. Arrebatador, ra.
transpose [trænsˈpəuz] v. tr. GRAMM. MATH. Transponer. || MUS. Transportar. || FIG. Transponer.
transposing [—iŋ] adj. MUS. Transportador, ra.
transposition [ˌtrænspəˈziʃən] n. GRAMM. MATH. Transposición, *f.* || MUS. Transporte, *m.*
Trans-Pyrenean [ˈtrænzˌpirəˈniːən] adj. Transpirenaico, ca; traspirenaico, ca.
transship [trænsˈʃip] v. tr. Transbordar.
transshipment [—mənt] n. Transbordo, *m.*
trans-Siberian [ˈtrænzsaiˈbiəriən] adj. Transiberiano, na. || *Trans-Siberian railway*, transiberiano, *m.*
transsonic [trænˈsɔnik] adj. Transónico, ca.
transubstantiation [ˈtrænsəbˌstænʃiˈeiʃən] n. REL. Transubstanciación, *f.*
transudate [ˈtrænsjudeit] n. Trasudor, *m.*
transudation [trænsjuˈdeiʃən] n. Trasudación, *f.*
transude [trænˈsjuːd] v. tr./intr. Trasudar.
transuranic [ˌtrænzjuˈrænik] adj. CHEM. Transuránico, ca.
transvase [trænsˈveiz] v. tr. Trasvasar.
transversal [trænzˈvəːsəl] adj. Transversal.
— N. Transversal, *f.*
transverse [ˈtrænzvəːs] adj. Transverso, sa: *transverse muscle*, músculo transverso. || Transversal. || *Transverse wave*, onda (*f.*) transversal.
— N. ANAT. Músculo (*m.*) transverso.
transvestism [trænzˈvestizəm] n. Travestismo, *m.*
transvestite [trænzˈvestait] n. Travestido, *m.*
Transylvania [ˌtrænsilˈveinjə] n. pr. GEOGR. Transilvania, *f.*
Transylvanian [—n] adj./n. Transilvano, na.
trap [træp] n. Trampa, *f.* (to catch animals): *to set o to lay a trap*, poner una trampa. || FIG. Trampa, *f.*, lazo, *m.*, celada, *f.*: *to set a trap*, tender una trampa *or* un lazo, preparar una celada. || Trampa, *f.* (trapdoor). || THEATR. Escotillón, *m.* || Ratonera, *f.* (mousetrap). || Cabriolé, *m.* (carriage). || TECH. Sifón, *m.*, bombillo, *m.* (in a pipe). || SP. Lanzaplatos, *m. inv.*, máquina (*f.*) lanzaplatos (clay-pigeon shooting). | | Jaula, *f.* (greyhound racing). || U. S. SP. Hoyo (*m.*) de arena (golf). || — Pl. Cosas, *f.*, trastos, *m.*, chismes, *m.* (things). || MUS. Instrumentos (*m.*) de percusión. || — *Gin trap* o *jaw trap*, cepo, *m.* || *Police trap*, ratonera, trampa. || POP. *Shut your trap!*, ¡calla!, ¡cierra el pico!, ¡calla la boca! || *Speed trap*, control (*m.*) de velocidad. || *To bait a trap*, poner el cebo en la trampa. || FIG. *To be caught like a rat in a trap*, caer en la ratonera. | *To be caught in one's own trap*, caer en su propia trampa. | *To fall* o *to walk into the trap*, caer en la trampa. | *To lure s.o. into a trap*, hacer que uno caiga en la trampa.
trap [træp] v. tr. Poner trampas en (a place). || Coger en una trampa (to catch). || Poner un sifón *or* un bombillo a (a pipe). || FIG. Hacer caer en el lazo *or* en la trampa. || Coger, pillar: *I trapped my finger in the door*, me cogí el dedo en la puerta. || Bloquear (to place in a difficult position). || Rodear, cercar: *trapped by the flames*, rodeado por las llamas. || Atrapar, coger: *the police trapped the thief*, la policía atrapó al ladrón. || Retener, detener (gases, liquids). || SP. Controlar, parar (a ball). || — FIG. *To trap s.o. into a confession*, sacarle a uno mañosamente una confesión. | *To trap s.o. into marriage*, conseguir casarse con uno.
— V. intr. Poner trampas (to set traps for game).
trapdoor [—ˈdɔː*] n. Trampa, *f.* (in a floor). || Ventana (*f.*) de ventilación. || THEATR. Escotillón, *m.*
trapes [treips] n./v. intr. See TRAIPSE.

trapeze [trə'pi:z] n. Trapecio, *m.* || *Trapeze artist*, trapecista, *m.* & *f.*
trapezial [—iəl] adj. MATH. Trapecial.
trapezium [trə'pi:zjəm] n. MATH. ANAT. Trapecio, *m.* || U. S. MATH. Trapezoide, *m.*

— OBSERV. El plural de *trapezium* es *trapeziums* o *trapezia*.

trapezius [trə'pi:zjəs] n. ANAT. Trapecio, *m.*
trapezohedron [,træpi:zəu'hi:drən] n. MATH. Trapezoedro, *m.*

— OBSERV. El plural de la palabra inglesa es *trapezohedrons* o *trapezohedra*.

trapezoid ['træpizɔid] n. MATH. ANAT. Trapezoide, *m.* || U. S. MATH. Trapecio, *m.*
trapezoid ['træpizɔid] or **trapezoidal** [—əl] adj. MATH. Trapezoidal. || U. S. MATH. Trapecial.
trapper ['træpə*] n. Trampero, *m.*
trappings ['træpiŋz] pl. n. Adornos, *m.*, atavíos, *m.* (ornamentation). || Arreos, *m.*, jaeces, *m.* (for a horse).
Trappist ['træpist] adj. REL. Trapense: *Trappist monastery*, monasterio trapense.
— N. REL. Trapense, *m.*
trapshooting ['træpʃu:tiŋ] n. Tiro (*m.*) al plato.
trash [træʃ] n. Baratija, *f.* (trinket). || Deshechos, *m. pl.*, desperdicios, *m. pl.* (refuse). || Escamondadura, *f.* (cutting from trees). || Bagazo, *m.* (of sugar cane). || Tonterías, *f. pl.* (worthless talk). || Basura, *f.* (worthless writing). || Gentuza, *f.* (disreputable people). || U. S. Basura, *f.* (rubbish).
trash [træʃ] v. tr. Podar, mondar (trees). || Deshojar, desbrozar (sugar cane).
trash can [—kæn] n. U. S. Cubo (*m.*) de la basura.
trashiness [—inis] n. Baja calidad, *f.*, mediocridad, *f.*
trashy [—i] adj. Malo, la; de baja calidad.
trauma ['trɔ:mə] n. MED. Trauma, *m.*

— OBSERV. El plural de la palabra inglesa es *traumata* o *traumas*.

traumatic [trɔ:'mætik] adj. MED. Traumático, ca.
traumatism ['trɔ:mətizəm] n. MED. Traumatismo, *m.*
traumatology [,trɔ:mə'tɔlədʒi] n. MED. Traumatología, *f.*
travail ['træveil] n. Dolores (*f. pl.*) de parto (pains of childbirth). || Trabajo (*m.*) duro (hard work). || Tormento, *m.* (intense pain).
travail ['træveil] v. intr. Estar de parto (to be in childbirth). || Afanarse, trabajar mucho (to work hard).
travel ['trævl] n. Viajar, *m.*: *the pleasures of travel*, el placer de viajar. || Viajes, *m. pl.*: *I like travel*, me gustan los viajes; *space travel*, los viajes espaciales. || TECH. Recorrido, *m.* (of a machine part). || U. S. Circulación, *f.*, tráfico, *m.*: *travel is heavy on the freeway*, hay mucho tráfico en la autopista. || — Pl. Viajes, *m.*: *I met him on my travels*, le conocí en mis viajes. || *Travel broadens the mind*, el viajar abre la mente.
travel ['trævl] v. tr. Viajar por (a region, etc.). || Recorrer (a distance).
— V. intr. Viajar: *I travelled a lot when I was young*, viajé mucho cuando era joven; *I travel by car*, viajo en coche; *I travel round Spain*, viajo por España. || Circular: *to travel along a road*, circular por una carretera. || Extenderse: *the pain travelled down his arm*, el dolor se extendió por el brazo. || Recorrer: *her glance travelled over the crowd*, su mirada recorrió la muchedumbre. || Llegar (to reach): *do the B.B.C. programs travel so far?*, ¿llegan tan lejos los programas de la B.B.C.? || PHYS. Propagarse: *sound waves do not travel through a vacuum*, las ondas sonoras no se propagan en el vacío. || Correr, ir: *the electricity travels along this wire*, la electricidad va por ese cable. || Correr, propagarse, extenderse: *rumours travel fast*, los rumores corren rápidamente. || Hacer: *the train travels at sixty miles an hour*, el tren hace sesenta millas por hora. || Ir: *I was travelling too fast*, iba demasiado rápido. || Correr (to go fast): *your car really travels*, su coche corre mucho. || Ser viajante de: *he travels for Larousse*, es viajante de la Editorial Larousse. || Transportarse: *wine that does not travel*, vino que no se transporta. || TECH. Correr, desplazarse. || — *He travels in encyclopedias*, es un viajante que vende enciclopedias. || *To travel light*, viajar con poco equipaje.
travel agency [—'eidʒənsi] n. Agencia (*f.*) de viajes.
travel agent's [—'eidʒənts] n. Agencia (*f.*) de viajes.
travelled (U. S. **traveled**) ['trævld] adj. Que ha viajado mucho (person). || Muy recorrido, da (route, path). || GEOL. Errático, ca.
traveller (U. S. **traveler**) ['trævlə*] n. Viajero, ra (person who travels). || Viajante (*m.*) de comercio (representative). || TECH. Puente (*m.*) grúa (crane). || MAR. Racamento, *m.*, racamenta, *f.*
traveller's cheque (U. S. **traveler's check**) [—ztʃek] n. Cheque (*m.*) de viaje, cheque (*m.*) de viajero.
traveller's-joy (U. S. **traveler's-joy**) [—z'dʒɔi] n. BOT. Clemátide, *f.*, hierba (*f.*) de los pordioseros.
travelling (U. S. **traveling**) ['trævliŋ] adj. De viaje: *travelling companion*, compañero de viaje. || Ambulante (exhibition, street vendor, etc.). || Móvil (thing). || — *Travelling bag*, bolsa (*f.*) de viaje. || *Travelling crane*, puente (*m.*) grúa. || *Travelling expenses*, gastos (*m.*) de viaje. || *Travelling pavement* o *platform*, pasillo (*m.*) rodante. || *Travelling post office*, ambulancia (*f.*) de correos. || *Travelling salesman*, viajante (*m.*) de comercio. || *Travelling speed*, velocidad (*f.*) de marcha (of cars, etc.), velocidad (*f.*) de traslación (of crane). || *Travelling staircase*, escalera mecánica.
— N. Viajar, *m.*: *travelling is expensive*, viajar es caro. || CINEM. Travelín, *m.*
travelogue (U. S. **travelog**) ['trævəlɔg] n. Documental (*m.*) sobre un viaje (film). || Conferencia (*f.*) ilustrada sobre un viaje (lecture).
travel sickness ['trævl,siknis] n. Mareo, *m.*
traverse ['trævə:s] n. Travesía, *f.* (crossing): *the traverse of the forest took three days*, la travesía del bosque duró tres días. || Travesaño, *m.* (crossbar). || Travesía, *f.* (in mountaineering). || MAR. Ruta (*f.*) sinuosa. || Zigzag, *m.* (a zigzag in skiing). || Descenso (*m.*) en zigzag (zigzag descent). || Línea (*f.*) quebrada (in surveying). || MATH. Transversal, *f.* || Traslación, *f.*, desplazamiento (*m.*) lateral. || MIL. Través, *m.* (fortification). || TECH. Riostra, *f.*, tirante, *m.* (of a frame). || JUR. Negación, *f.*, denegación, *f.*
— Adj. Transversal.
traverse ['trævə:s] v. tr. Atravesar, cruzar (to cross): *we traversed the wood*, atravesamos el bosque. || Recorrer (to move along). || MIL. Apuntar (a cannon). || Trazar un itinerario de (in surveying). || JUR. Negar (an allegation). | Oponerse a (an indictment). || FIG. Examinar detenidamente.
— V. intr. Girar sobre su eje (to pivot). || Trazar un itinerario (to make a survey). || SP. Bajar en diagonal (skiing). | Subir en diagonal (climbing).
traverser [—ə*] n. Transbordador, *m.*
travesty ['trævisti] n. Parodia, *f.*
travesty ['trævisti] v. tr. Parodiar.
trawl [trɔ:l] n. MAR. Red (*f.*) barredera, red (*f.*) de arrastre. || U. S. MAR. Palangre, *m.*
trawl [trɔ:l] v. tr./intr. MAR. Pescar con red barredera.
trawler [—ə*] n. MAR. Trainera, *f.* (with oars), bou, *m.* (ship).
trawling [—iŋ] n. Pesca (*f.*) con red de arrastre.
tray [trei] n. Bandeja, *f.*: *silver tray*, bandeja de plata. || PHOT. Cubeta, *f.* || Platillo, *m.* (of balance). || Cajón, *m.* (drawer).
treacherous ['tretʃərəs] adj. Traicionero, ra (action), traidor, ra (person). || Falso, sa (false). || Infiel (memory). || Movedizo, za (ground). || Poco firme (ice). || FIG. Engañoso, sa.
treacherousness [—nis] n. Alevosía, *f.*
treachery ['tretʃəri] n. Traición, *f.*
treacle ['tri:kl] n. Melaza, *f.*
treacly [—i] adj. Parecido a la melaza. || FIG. Meloso, sa (sweet).
tread [tred] n. Paso, *m.* (step): *we heard his tread on the stairs*, oímos su paso en la escalera. || Andar, *m.*, andares, *m. pl.* (gait). || Huella, *f.* (step of a staircase). || Anchura (*f.*) de la huella (width of the step). || Pieza (*f.*) de goma colocada sobre la huella para protegerla. || Suela, *f.* (of a shoe). || Ancho, *m.* (of rails). || Distancia, *f.* (of car axle). || Banda (*f.*) de rodadura (of a tyre). || Galladura, *f.*, chalaza, *f.* (of an egg).
tread* [tred] v. tr. Pisar: *to tread grapes*, pisar la uva; *to tread dry land*, pisar tierra firme. || Pisotear: *to tread earth around a plant*, pisotear la tierra alrededor de una planta. || Andar por (to walk). || ZOOL. Pisar (to mate). || — *To tread down*, pisotear. || *To tread out*, sofocar (fire, revolt). || *To tread sth. underfoot*, pisotear algo. || TEATR. *To tread the boards*, pisar las tablas. || SP. *To tread water*, pedalear en el agua. || *Trodden to death by elephants*, aplastado bajo las patas de los elefantes. || FIG. *Well-trodden path*, camino trillado.
— V. intr. Pisar. || Andar (to walk): *to tread across the room*, andar por la habitación. || Meter el pie: *to tread in a puddle*, meter el pie en un charco. || — FIG. *To tread lightly*, andar con tiento. || *To tread on*, pisar. || FIG. *To tread on s.o.'s heels*, pisarle a uno los talones. | *To tread on s.o.'s toes*, pisotear a alguien.

— OBSERV. Pret. **trod;** p. p. **trodden, trod.**

treadle ['tredl] n. Pedal, *m.* (of grindstone, lathe).
treadle ['tredl] v. intr. Pedalear.
treadmill ['tredmil] n. Rueda (*f.*) de molino movida por hombres. || Rueda (*f.*) de ardilla (moved by animal). || FIG. Rutina, *f.*
treason ['tri:zn] n. Traición, *f.*: *high treason*, alta traición.
treasonable [—əbl] or **treasonous** [—əs] adj. Traicionero, ra; traidor, ra.
treasure ['treʒə*] n. Tesoro, *m.* || FIG. Tesoro, *m.*
treasure ['treʒə*] v. tr. Valorar, estimar, apreciar: *I treasure his friendship*, valoro su amistad. || Guardar en la memoria: *to treasure s.o.'s words*, guardar en la memoria las palabras de alguien. || *To treasure up*, acumular, guardar, atesorar.
treasure hunt [—hʌnt] n. Caza (*f.*) del tesoro.
treasurer [—rə*] n. Tesorero, ra.
treasurership [—rəʃip] n. Tesorería, *f.*
treasure trove [—'trəuv] n. Tesoro (*m.*) descubierto [*Amer.*, tapado, *m.*]. || FIG. Hallazgo, *m.*
treasury [—ri] n. Tesoro, *m.* || Tesorería, *f.* (place, funds). || Antología, *f.*, florilegio, *m.* (of verse). || FIG. Mina, *f.* || *The Treasury*, el Ministerio de Hacienda (department), el Tesoro, el Erario (funds).

Treasury Bench [—ribentʃ] n. Banco (*m.*) azul [primera fila de escaños ocupada por los ministros del gobierno en la Cámara de Diputados].
treasury bond [—ribɔnd] n. Bono (*m.*) del Tesoro.
Treasury Department [—ridi′pɑ:tmənt] n. U. S. Ministerio (*m.*) de Hacienda.
treasury note [—rinəut] n. Bono (*m.*) del Tesoro.
treat [tri:t] n. Invitación, *f.* || Festín, *m.*, banquete, *m.* (feast). || Regalo, *m.* (present). || Placer, *m.*, delicia, *f.* (delight): *it was a treat to go to the cinema last night*, fue un placer ir al cine ayer por la noche. || — *This is my treat*, invito yo. || *To have a Dutch treat*, pagar a escote.
treat [tri:t] v. tr. Tratar: *I don't like the way he treats his dog*, no me gusta la forma como trata a su perro. || Tratar de: *the book treats an interesting subject*, el libro trata de un tema interesante. || Tratar: *he treats the problem objectively*, trata el problema objetivamente; *to treat sth. apart*, tratar algo por separado. || Tomar: *he treats it as a joke*, lo toma a broma. || Invitar, convidar (to invite): *to treat s.o. to a good dinner*, invitar a alguien a una buena cena. || Comprar: *he treated his wife to a new coat*, compró a su mujer un abrigo nuevo. || CHEM. Tratar. || MED. Tratar, curar (a disease). | Atender (a patient). || — *How has the world been treating you?*, ¿cómo le van las cosas? || *To treat badly*, maltratar. || *To treat o.s. to sth.*, permitirse el lujo de hacer algo. || *To treat s.o. as one's equal*, tratar a alguien de igual a igual *or* en un pie de igualdad. || *To treat s.o. like a king*, tratar a alguien a cuerpo de rey.
— V. intr. Negociar: *to treat with s.o. for peace*, negociar la paz con alguien. || U. S. Invitar, convidar. || *To treat of*, tratar de.
treater [—ə*] n. Negociador, ra.
treatise [′tri:tiz] n. Tratado, *m.*: *economic treatise*, tratado de economía.
treatment [′tri:tmənt] n. Trato, *m.*, tratamiento, *m.*: *the treatment of prisoners*, el trato de los prisioneros. || Trato, *m.*: *preferential treatment*, trato preferente. || Tratamiento, *m.* (title). || CHEM. MED. Tratamiento, *m.* || Interpretación, *f.*: *the orchestra's treatment of Bach*, la interpretación de Bach por la orquesta. || Adaptación, *f.*: *the director's treatment of the script*, la adaptación del texto por el director. || FIG. *To give s.o. the treatment*, dar a uno el tratamiento que merece.
treaty [′tri:ti] n. Tratado, *m.* (between nations). || Acuerdo, *m.* (agreement).
treble [′trebl] adj. Triple. || MUS. De tiple, de soprano (voice). || — MUS. *Treble clef*, clave (*f.*) de sol. | *Treble staff*, pentagrama (*m.*) de sol.
— N. Tiple, *m.*, soprano, *m.*
treble [′trebl] v. tr. Triplicar, multiplicar por tres.
— V. intr. Triplicarse, multiplicarse por tres.
trebly [′trebli] adv. Tres veces.
tree [tri:] n. Árbol, *m.*: *there are many trees in the garden*, hay muchos árboles en el jardín; *fruit tree*, árbol frutal. || Horma, *f.* (shoe tree). || CHEM. Árbol, *m.* || — FAM. *At the top of the tree*, en la cúspide, en la cumbre. || FIG. *A tree is known by its fruit*, por el fruto se conoce el árbol. || *Christmas tree*, árbol (*m.*) de Navidad. || *Family tree*, árbol genealógico. || *The Tree*, la Cruz. || FIG. *To bark up the wrong tree*, equivocarse. | *To reach the top of the tree*, llegar a la cúspide. | *Up a tree*, entre la espada y la pared, en un apuro, en un aprieto.
tree [tri:] v. tr. Obligar a refugiarse en un árbol. || Poner en la horma (shoes). || U. S. FIG. Poner en un aprieto (to put in a difficult situation).
tree-covered [—ˌkʌvəd] adj. Cubierto de árboles, arbolado, da.
tree-dwelling [—ˌdweliŋ] adj. Arborícola.
tree fern [—fə:n] n. BOT. Helecho (*m.*) arborescente.
tree frog [—frɔg] n. ZOOL. Rana (*f.*) de zarzal, rubeta, *f.*
treeless [—lis] adj. Sin árboles.
tree line [—lain] n. Límite (*f.*) de la vegetación arbórea.
tree-lined [—laind] adj. *Tree-lined street*, alameda, *f.*
treenail [—neil] n. MAR. Clavija, *f.*, cabilla, *f.*
tree of heaven [—əv′hevn] n. BOT. Ailanto, *m.*, árbol (*m.*) del cielo.
tree of knowledge [—əv′nɔlidʒ] n. Árbol (*m.*) de la ciencia del bien y del mal.
tree of life [—əv′laif] n. Árbol (*m.*) de la vida.
tree toad [—təud] n. ZOOL. Rana (*f.*) de zarzal, rubeta, *f.*
treetop [—tɔp] n. Copa, *f.*
tree trunk [—trʌŋk] n. Tronco (*m.*) de árbol.
trefoil [′trefɔil] n. BOT. Trébol, *m.* || ARCH. Trifolio, *m.*, trébol, *m.*
— Adj. Trebolado, da.
trek [trek] n. Viaje (*m.*) largo y difícil (tedious journey). || Viaje (*m.*) largo en carreta. || Migración, *f.* || FIG. Expedición, *f.* || FIG. FAM. Caminata, *f.*: *it's such a trek to get to the shops*, hay una buena caminata para llegar hasta las tiendas.
trek [trek] v. intr. Viajar en carreta (to travel by ox wagon). || Hacer un viaje largo y difícil (to make a tedious journey). || Irse (to go). || Emigrar (to emigrate).

trellis [′trelis] n. Enrejado, *m.* || Espaldera, *f.* (for plants). || Emparrado, *m.*, parra, *f.* (for grapes).
trellis [′trelis] v. tr. Poner un enrejado a (a wall). || Emparrar (grapes). || Hacer trepar por una espaldera (plants).
trelliswork [—wə:k] n. Enrejado, *m.*
trematode [′tremətəud] n. ZOOL. Trematodo, *m.*
tremble [′trembl] n. Temblor, *m.* || — *He was all of a tremble*, estaba todo tembloroso. || *They told me with a tremble*, me dijeron temblando.
tremble [′trembl] v. intr. Temblar: *I am trembling all over*, tiemblo de pies a cabeza.
trembler [—ə*] n. ELECTR. Vibrador, *m.* || Miedoso, sa (coward).
trembling [—iŋ] adj. Tembloroso, sa.
— N. Temblor, *m.*
trembly [—i] adj. Tembloroso, sa.
tremendous [tri′mendəs] adj. Enorme, tremendo, da (enormous): *a tremendous difference*, una diferencia enorme. || Extraordinario, ria; tremendo, da; asombroso, sa (amazing).
tremolant [′tremələnt] n. MUS. Trémolo, *m.*
tremolo [′treməlǝu] n. MUS. Trémolo, *m.*
tremor [′tremə*] n. Temblor, *m.*: *earth tremor*, temblor de tierra. || Estremecimiento, *m.* (shiver).
tremulous [′tremjuləs] adj. Trémulo, la; tembloroso, sa; temblón, ona (trembling, quivering). || Tímido, da (timid). || Febril (excitement). || Tembloroso, sa; temblón, ona (voice, writing).
tremulousness [—nis] n. Temblor, *m.* (trembling). || Timidez, *f.* (timidity).
trench [trentʃ] n. Zanja, *f.* (for laying pipes, building foundations, etc.). || MIL. Trinchera, *f.* || AGR. Acequia, *f.* || MIL. *Trench warfare*, guerra (*f.*) de trincheras.
trench [trentʃ] v. tr. Abrir zanjas en (to dig trenches in). || AGR. Abrir acequias en. || MIL. Atrincherar, abrir trincheras en (to dig). | Proteger con trincheras (to protect).
— V. intr. Abrir zanjas *or* trincheras. || *To trench on* o *upon*, usurpar (s.o.'s rights, land), rayar en (to come close to).
trenchancy [′trentʃənsi] n. Agudeza, *f.*, mordacidad, *f.*, causticidad, *f.* (sharpness). || Fuerza, *f.* (vigour).
trenchant [′trentʃənt] adj. Agudo, da; mordaz, cáustico, ca (penetrating, incisive): *trenchant words*, palabras mordaces. || Enérgico, ca (vigorous).
trench coat [′trentʃkəut] n. Trinchera, *f.*
trencher [′trentʃə*] n. Persona (*f.*) que hace zanjas *or* acequias. || MIL. Persona (*f.*) que hace trincheras. || Tajo, *m.*, tajadero, *m.* (to carve meat).
trencherman [—mən] n. *A good* o *a stout trencherman*, un buen comilón (eater), un gorrón (sponger).

— OBSERV. El plural de *trencherman* es *trenchermen*.

trend [trend] n. Tendencia, *f.*: *the trend of public opinion*, la tendencia de la opinión pública; *the rising trend of the market*, la tendencia al alza del mercado. || Dirección, *f.* (direction). || Orientación, *f.*: *the trend of politics*, la orientación de la política. || — *To set the trend*, marcar la tónica. || *To show a trend towards*, orientarse hacia, tender a.
trend [trend] v. intr. Tender: *modern thought is trending away from materialism*, el pensamiento moderno tiende a apartarse del materialismo. || Dirigirse, orientarse.
Trent [trent] or **Trento** [—əu] pr. n. GEOGR. Trento.
trepan [tri′pæn] n. TECH. MED. Trépano, *m.*
trepan [tri′pæn] v. tr. Trepanar. || Inducir (*into*, a) [to lure]. || *To trepan s.o. out of*, estafar [algo] a uno.
trepanation [ˌtripə′neiʃən] n. MED. Trepanación, *f.*
trephine [tri′fi:n] n. MED. Trépano, *m.*
trephine [tri′fi:n] v. tr. MED. Trepanar.
trepidation [ˌtrepi′deiʃən] n. Agitación, *f.*, inquietud, *f.*, turbación, *f.* || Trepidación, *f.* (trembling movement).
treponema [ˌtrepə′ni:mə] n. Treponema, *m.*

— OBSERV. El plural de la palabra inglesa es *treponemata* o *treponemas*.

trespass [′trespəs] n. Entrada (*f.*) ilegal. || Violación, *f.* (of property). || Ofensa, *f.* (offence). || REL. Deuda, *f.*: *forgive us our trespasses*, perdónanos nuestras deudas. || JUR. Delito, *m.* (an actionable wrong). | Violación, *f.*, infracción, *f.* (a trespassing against the law). || Abuso, *m.* (*upon*, de) [s.o.'s patience].
trespass [′trespəs] v. intr. Violar, entrar ilegalmente en [la propiedad de alguien] (to enter unlawfully). || Abusar: *to trespass on s.o.'s hospitality*, abusar de la hospitalidad de alguien. || Violar, invadir (s.o.'s privacy). || JUR. Usurpar (s.o.'s rights). | Infringir, violar: *to trespass against the law*, violar la ley. || REL. Pecar (to sin). || — *May I trespass upon your precious time*, puedo abusar de su escaso tiempo. || *No trespassing!*, ¡prohibido el paso!
trespasser [—ə*] n. Intruso, sa (on property). || JUR. Delincuente, *m.* & *f.*, violador, ra (lawbreaker). || REL. Pecador, ra (sinner). || *Trespassers will be prosecuted*, prohibido el paso, propiedad privada, los infractores serán sancionados por la ley.
tress [tres] n. Mechón, *m.* (lock). || Bucle, *m.* (curl). || Trenza, *f.* (plait). || — Pl. Pelo, *m. sing.*, melena, *f. sing.*, cabellera, *f. sing.* (mass of hair).
tressed [—t] adj. Trenzado, da.
trestle [′tresl] n. Caballete, *m.*

trews [tru:z] pl. n. Pantalón (*m. sing.*) estrecho escocés.
trey [trei] n. Tres, *m.* (cards, dice etc.).
triable [ˈtraiəbl] adj. JUR. Que se puede enjuiciar.
triacid [traiˈæsid] adj. CHEM. Triácido, da.
— N. CHEM. Triácido, *m.*
triad [ˈtraiəd] n. Trío, *m.*, tríada, *f.* (a group of three). || CHEM. Elemento (*m.*) trivalente. || REL. Trinidad, *f.*
trial [ˈtraiəl] n. Prueba, *f.*, ensayo, *m.* (a testing by experiment). || Experimento, *m.* || Tentativa, *f.* (intent). || Prueba, *f.* (a test of character, endurance). || FIG. Molestia, *f.*, tormento, *m.* (source of annoyance). | Sufrimiento, *m.* (suffering). | Dificultad, *f.* (hardship). | Prueba, *f.*: *in the hour of trial*, en el momento de la prueba. || JUR. Juicio, *m.* (act of judging). | Proceso, *m.*, juicio, *m.*, vista, *f.* (procedure): *during the trial*, durante el proceso. || SP. Partido (*m.*) de preselección (for choosing sports teams). || — Pl. Concurso, *m. sing.*: *sheepdog trials*, concurso de perros pastores. || — JUR. *New trial*, revisión, *f.* || *On trial*, procesado, da; sometido a juicio, enjuiciado, da: *he was on trial for murder*, fue procesado por asesino; sometido a prueba: *aeroplane that is on trial*, avión que está sometido a prueba; a prueba: *to have sth. for a week on trial*, tener algo a prueba durante una semana. || *To bring s.o. to trial*, someter a alguien a juicio, procesar or enjuiciar a uno. || *To commit s.o. for trial*, citar a alguien ante los tribunales. || *To do sth. by trial and error*, hacer algo por un método de tanteos. || *To give a trial*, probar (sth.), poner a prueba (s.o.). || JUR. *To go on trial*, ser procesado. | *To put on trial*, procesar, someter a juicio. | *To stand one's trial*, ser procesado. || *Trial by ordeal*, juicio de Dios.
— Adj. De prueba: *a trial period*, un período de prueba.
trial balance [—ˈbæləns] n. COMM. Balance (*m.*) de comprobación.
trial balloon [—bəˈlu:n] n. Globo (*m.*) sonda.
trial jury [—ˈdʒuəri] n. U. S. JUR. Jurado, *m.*
triangle [ˈtraiæŋgl] n. Triángulo, *m.*: *equilateral, isosceles, scalene triangle*, triángulo equilátero, isósceles, escaleno. || MUS. Triángulo, *m.* || Escuadra, *f.*, cartabón, *m.* (set square for drawing).
triangular [traiˈæŋgjulə*] adj. Triangular: *triangular pyramid, muscle*, pirámide, músculo triangular. || Tripartito, ta: *triangular agreement*, acuerdo tripartito.
triangulate [traiˈæŋgjulit] adj. Triangulado, da.
triangulate [traiˈæŋgjuleit] v. tr. Triangular.
triangulation [traiˌæŋgjuˈleiʃən] n. Triangulación, *f.*
Trias [ˈtraiəs] adj. GEOL. Triásico, ca.
— N. GEOL. Triásico, *m.*, Trías, *m.* (period).
Triassic [traiˈæsik] adj. GEOL. Triásico, ca.
— N. GEOL. Triásico, *m.* (period).
triatomic [ˈtraiəˈtɔmik] adj. Triatómico, ca.
tribal [ˈtraibl] adj. Tribal, de tribu.
tribalism [—izəm] n. Sistema (*m.*) tribal, organización (*f.*) en tribus (organization in tribes). || Amor (*m.*) a la tribu (strong feeling for the tribe).
tribasic [traiˈbeisik] adj. CHEM. Tribásico, ca.
tribe [traib] n. Tribu, *f.* || FIG. Familia, *f.*
tribesman [—zmən] n. Miembro (*m.*) de una tribu.
— OBSERV. El plural de esta palabra es *tribesmen*.
tribulation [ˌtribjuˈleiʃən] n. Tribulación, *f.*
tribunal [traiˈbju:nl] n. Tribunal, *m.*: *military tribunal*, tribunal militar; *tribunal of God*, tribunal de Dios.
tribunate [ˈtribjunit] n. Tribunado, *m.*
tribune [ˈtribju:n] n. Tribuna, *f.* (platform). || Tribuno, *m.* (of Rome).
tribuneship [—ʃip] n. Tribunado, *m.*
tributary [ˈtribjutəri] adj. Tributario, ria.
— N. Afluente, *m.* (of a river). || Tributario, ria (person).
tribute [ˈtribju:t] n. Tributo, *m.* (payment, tax). || FIG. Tributo, *m.*, homenaje, *m.*: *to pay a tribute to*, rendir homenaje a. | Tributo, *m.*: *respect is the tribute one pays to virtue*, el respeto es el tributo debido a la virtud. | Ofrenda, *f.* (offering).
trice [trais] n. FAM. *In a trice*, en un abrir y cerrar de ojos, en un dos por tres.
trice [trais] v. tr. MAR. *To trice (up)*, izar (sails).
tricentennial [ˌtraisenˈtenjəl] n. Tricentenario, *m.*
— Adj. De trescientos años.
tricephalous [traiˈsefələs] adj. Tricéfalo, la.
triceps [ˈtraiseps] n. ANAT. Tríceps, *m.*
— OBSERV. El plural de la palabra inglesa es *tricepses* o *triceps*.
trichina [triˈkainə] n. Triquina, *f.*
— OBSERV. El plural de la palabra inglesa es *trichinae*.
trichinosis [ˌtrikiˈnəusis] n. Triquinosis, *f. inv.*
— OBSERV. El plural de *trichinosis* es *trichinoses*.
trichinous [ˈtrikinəs] adj. Triquinoso, sa.
trichotomy [traiˈkɔtəmi] n. Tricotomía, *f.*
trichromatism [traiˈkrəumətizəm] n. Tricromía, *f.*
trick [trik] n. Truco, *m.* (stratagem). || Astucia, *f.*, ardid, *m.* (ruse). || Maña, *f.*, habilidad, *f.* (skill). || Tranquillo, *m.* (knack): *he got the trick of it*, le cogió el tranquillo. || Triquiñuela, *f.*, treta, *f.*: *to resort to tricks*, andar con triquiñuelas; *to use a trick*, valerse de una treta. || Truco, *m.*, juego (*m.*) de manos (dextrous feat). || Broma, *f.* (practical joke): *to play a trick on s.o.*, gastarle una broma a alguien. || Jugada, *f.*, pasada, *f.*, trastada, *f.* (act of mischief or meanness): *a dirty trick*, una mala pasada. || Faena, *f.*: *my memory played a trick on me*, la memoria me hizo una faena. || Travesura, *f.*, diablura, *f.* (prank). || Estafa, *f.*, timo, *m.* (swindle). || Tic, *m.*, manía, *f.* (mannerism, peculiarity): *it's a trick of his*, es una manía suya. || Baza, *f.* (in card games): *he took all the tricks*, ganó todas las bazas. || MAR. Turno, *m.* (turn of duty). || Gracia, *f.*, monería, *f.* (performed by a dog). || — FIG. *I don't miss a trick*, no me pierdo una. | *The whole bag of tricks*, todo. || *To be up to one's old tricks again*, [volver a] hacer de las suyas. || *To do the trick*, servir [para el caso], resolver el problema: *that should do the trick*, esto servirá.
— Adj. *Trick photography*, trucaje, *m.* || *Trick question*, pega, *f.*
trick [trik] v. tr. Engañar, embaucar. || — *To trick out of*, estafar, timar: *he tricked fifty pounds out of me*, me timó cincuenta libras. || *To trick s.o. into a confession*, sacarle a uno mañosamente una confesión. || *To trick s.o. into marriage*, conseguir casarse con uno. || *To trick up* o *out*, ataviar (to dress up).
trickery [—əri] n. Engaño, *m.* (deceit). || Astucia, *f.* (cunning). || *A piece of trickery*, una superchería.
trickiness [—inis] n. Astucia, *f.* (cunning). || Dificultad, *f.* (difficult nature).
trickish [—iʃ] adj. Astuto, ta (cunning). || Difícil, complicado, da (difficult). || Engañoso, sa (deceitful).
trickle [ˈtrikl] n. Hilillo, *m.*, hilo, *m.*, chorrito, *m.* (of liquid). || FIG. *A trickle of news*, pocas noticias.
trickle [ˈtrikl] v. tr. Chorrear un poco de, verter poco a poco: *the wound trickled blood*, la herida chorreaba un poco de sangre.
— V. intr. Correr (tears). || Salir poco abundantemente, gotear (blood). || Gotear (drops, sweat). || Correr, discurrir: *the stream trickled through the fields*, el arroyo discurría por los campos. || — *To trickle in*, llegar en pequeñas cantidades (things), llegar en pequeños grupos (people). || *To trickle out*, gotear (liquid), difundirse poco a poco (news). || *To trickle with*, rezumar: *to trickle with moisture*, rezumar humedad.
trickster [ˈtrikstə*] n. Embaucador, ra; embustero, ra (who deceives). || Estafador, ra; timador, ra (who swindles).
tricksy [ˈtriksi] adj. Travieso, sa.
tricktrack [ˈtrikˈtræk] n. Chaquete, *m.* (backgammon).
tricky [ˈtriki] adj. Difícil, complicado, da (difficult). || Delicado, da (delicate). || Hábil, mañoso, sa (artful). || Astuto, ta (cunning).
triclinic [traiˈklinik] adj. Triclínico, ca (crystal).
triclinium [traiˈkliniəm] n. Triclinio, *m.*
tricolour (U. S. **tricolor**) [ˈtrikələ*] adj. Tricolor.
— N. Bandera (*f.*) tricolor (flag).
tricorn [ˈtraikɔ:n] n. Tricornio, *m.*
tricot [ˈtrikəu] n. Tejido (*m.*) de punto.
tricuspid [traiˈkʌspid] adj. ANAT. Tricúspide: *tricuspid valve*, válvula tricúspide.
— N. ANAT. Tricúspide, *m.*
tricycle [ˈtraisikl] n. Triciclo, *m.*
tridactyl [traiˈdæktil] adj. Tridáctilo, la.
trident [ˈtraidənt] n. Tridente, *m.*
Tridentine [traiˈdentain] adj. Tridentino, na (of the Council of Trent).
tridimensional [ˌtraidiˈmenʃnəl] adj. Tridimensional.
triduo [ˈtri:duəu] or **triduum** [ˈtraidjuəm] n. REL. Triduo, *m.*
tried [traid] adj. Probado, da (proved, tested). || Seguro, ra (reliable).
triennial [traiˈenjəl] adj. Trienal.
— N. Acontecimiento (*m.*) trienal (event). || Tercer aniversario, *m.* (third anniversary).
triennium [traiˈeniəm] n. Trienio, *m.*
— OBSERV. El plural de *triennium* es *triennia* o *trienniums*.
trier [ˈtraiə*] n. Experimentador, ra. || Juez, *m.*, árbitro, *m.* (judge). || — *He is a trier*, hace siempre todo lo posible, no escatima sus esfuerzos. || *Trier-on*, probador, ra.
Trier [ˈtriə*] pr. n. Tréveris.
trifle [ˈtraifl] n. Nadería, *f.*, fruslería, *f.*, pequeñez, *f.* (insignificant fact). || Baratija, *f.*, nadería, *f.*, fruslería, *f.* (insignificant thing). || Poquito, *m.* (small amount). || Miseria, *f.* (small amount of money). || Peltre, *m.* (type of pewter). || CULIN. Bizcocho (*m.*) borracho con gelatina, frutas y natillas (dessert). || — Pl. Utensilios (*m.*) de peltre (pewter utensils). || *A trifle*, un poquito, algo: *a trifle too big*, un poquito grande.
trifle [ˈtraifl] v. tr. *To trifle away*, perder (time), malgastar (money).
— V. intr. *To trifle with*, jugar con: *to trifle with s.o.'s feelings*, jugar con los sentimientos de alguien.
trifler [—ə*] n. Frívolo, la.
trifling [—iŋ] adj. Insignificante: *a trifling difference*, una diferencia insignificante. || Sin importancia: *trifling incident*, incidente sin importancia. || Ligero, ra; frívolo, la (person).
— N. Frivolidad, *f.*
trifoliate [traiˈfəuliet] or **trifoliated** [—id] adj. BOT. Trifoliado, da (three-leaved).
triforium [traiˈfɔ:riəm] n. ARCH. Triforio, *m.*
— OBSERV. El plural de *triforium* es *triforia*.

trig [trig] adj. Acicalado, da (trim and neat). || MATH. Trigonométrico, ca.
— N. MATH. Trigonometría, *f.* || Calzo, *m.* (wedge).
trig v. tr. Calzar.
trigeminal [traiˈdʒeminəl] adj. ANAT. Trigémino, na.
— N. ANAT. Nervio (*m.*) trigémino, trigémino, *m.*
trigger [ˈtrigə*] n. Gatillo, *m.* (of a gun). || Disparador, *m.* (release). || *Quick on the trigger*, que no espera mucho para disparar (quick to fire), que no lo piensa dos veces (quick to act).
trigger [ˈtrigə*] v. tr. Accionar, poner en funcionamiento: *opening the door triggers the alarm system*, el abrir la puerta acciona el sistema de alarma. || Disparar, apretar el gatillo de (a gun). || *To trigger off*, provocar, desencadenar: *the assassination triggered off the First World War*, el asesinato provocó la primera guerra mundial.
triggerfish [—fiʃ] n. ZOOL. Pez (*m.*) ballesta.
trigger-happy [—ˌhæpi] adj. Pronto a disparar.
triglyph [ˈtraiglif] n. Triglifo, *m.*, tríglifo, *m.*
trigonal [ˈtrigənəl] adj. MATH. Trigono, na.
trigonometric [ˌtrigənəˈmetrik] or **trigonometrical** [—əl] adj. MATH. Trigonométrico, ca.
trigonometry [ˌtrigəˈnɔmitri] n. MATH. Trigonometría, *f.*
trihedral [traiˈhi:drəl] adj. MATH. Triedro, dra.
trihedron [traiˈhi:drən] n. MATH. Triedro, *m.*, ángulo (*m.*) triedro.
— OBSERV. El plural de *trihedron* es *trihedrons* o *trihedra*.
trike [traik] n. FAM. Triciclo, *m.*
trilateral [traiˈlætərəl] adj. Trilátero, ra.
trilby [ˈtrilbi] n. Sombrero (*m.*) flexible.
trilingual [traiˈliŋgwəl] adj. Trilingüe.
trilithon [ˈtrailiˌθɔn] n. Trilito, *m.*
trill [tril] n. Trino, *m.*, gorjeo, *m.* (of a bird). || MUS. Trino, *m.* || GRAMM. Vibración, *f.* (action, sound). | Vibrante, *f.* (letter).
trill [tril] v. tr. GRAMM. Pronunciar con una vibración.
— V. intr. Trinar, gorjear (birds). || MUS. Trinar.
trillion [ˈtriljən] n. Trillón, *m.* (10^{18}). || U. S. Billón, *m.* (10^{12}).
trilobate [traiˈləubit] adj. BOT. Trilobulado, da.
trilobites [ˈtrailəbaits] pl. n. Trilobites, *m.*
trilogy [ˈtrilədʒi] n. Trilogía, *f.*
trim [trim] adj. Aseado, da; arreglado, da (neat). || En buen estado (in good condition). || Cuidado, da: *a trim lawn*, un césped cuidado. || Elegante (smart). || Apuesto, ta (well-proportioned).
— N. Estado, *m.* (state): *in perfect trim*, en perfecto estado. || Orden, *m.* (order). || Recorte, *m.* (light haircut). || Adorno, *m.* (ornamental trimming). || Recorte, *m.* (cutting). || MAR. Asiento, *m.*, equilibrio, *m.* (of a boat). | Orientación, *f.* (of sails). | Estiba, *f.* (of load). || AVIAT. Equilibrio, *m.* || U. S. Interior, *m.*, tapicería, *f.* (of a car). | Marco, *m.* (of window, door). || — *In fighting trim*, listo para el combate. || *Out of trim*, mal estibado (boat), en baja forma (people). || *To be in good trim*, estar en forma (people).
trim [trim] v. tr. Arreglar, poner en orden (to tidy). || Adornar (a garment). || Entresacar (hair). || Recortar (nails, moustache, etc.). || Desbarbar (moulding). || Desbastar (timber). || Cepillar (with a plane). || Preparar (fire). || Guillotinar (in bookbinding). || Despabilar (a lamp). || Podar (branches, hedge). || MAR. Orientar (sails). | Equilibrar, asentar (to level). | Estibar (load). || AVIAT. Equilibrar. || Cercenar, reducir (to reduce). || U. S. FAM. Dar una paliza a (to thrash, to defeat). | Desplumar (to swindle, to fleece, to rob). | Echar una bronca a (to tick off). || — *To trim away* o *off*, recortar. || *To trim o.s. up*, arreglarse, acicalarse. || *To trim up*, arreglar.
— V. intr. Zigzaguear, nadar entre dos aguas, ser oportunista (in politics).
trimester [traiˈmestə*] n. Trimestre, *m.*
trimestrial [traiˈmestriəl] adj. Trimestral.
trimly [ˈtrimli] adv. En orden. || Elegantemente.
trimmer [ˈtrimə*] n. Desbastador, *m.* (person who trims). || Máquina (*f.*) desbastadora (machine). || Guillotina, *f.* (for paper). || ARCH. Solera, *f.* || MAR. Estibador, *m.* (of cargo). || AVIAT. Aleta (*f.*) compensadora. || FIG. FAM. Oportunista, *m.* & *f.* || U. S. Escaparatista, *m.* & *f.* (of shopwindows). || — Pl. Cizalla, *f. sing.* (shears). || Despabiladeras, *f.* (snuffers).
trimming [ˈtrimiŋ] n. Arreglo, *m.*, orden, *m.* (arrangement). || Adorno, *m.* (on a dress, etc.). || Recorte, *m.* (of nails, hair, etc.). || Poda, *f.* (of branches, hedge). || Desbastado, *m.* (of timber, etc.). || Cepillado, *m.* (with a plane). || Desbarbadura, *f.* (of moulding). || MAR. Orientación, *f.* (of sails). | Estiba, *f.* (of load). || FAM. Oportunismo, *m.* || U. S. FAM. Paliza, *f.* (beating). || — Pl. CULIN. Guarnición, *f. sing.* (garnishings). || Adornos, *m.* (adornments). || Recortes, *m.* (cuttings). || Accesorios, *m.* (accessories).
trimness [ˈtrimnis] n. Orden, *m.*, aspecto (*m.*) ordenado (order). || Elegancia, *f.*
trimonthly [traiˈmʌnθli] adj. Trimestral.
trimorphic [traiˈmɔ:fik] adj. Trimorfo, fa.
trimorphism [traiˈmɔ:fizəm] n. Trimorfismo, *m.*
trimorphous [traiˈmɔ:fəs] adj. Trimorfo, fa.
trine [train] adj. Trino, na; triple. || ASTR. Trino, na.
— N. ASTR. Aspecto (*m.*) trino. || Trío, *m.* (set of three). || REL. *The Trine*, la Trinidad.

Trinidad and Tobago [ˈtrinidædəntəˈbeigəu] pr. n. GEOGR. Trinidad y Tobago.
Trinitarian [ˌtriniˈtɛəriən] adj./n. REL. Trinitario, ria.
trinitrotoluene [traiˈnaitrəuˈtɔljui:n] n. Trinitrotolueno, *m.*
trinity [ˈtriniti] n. Trío, *m.*, trinidad, *f.* (group of three).
Trinity [ˈtriniti] n. REL. Trinidad, *f.*
trinket [ˈtriŋkit] n. Dije, *m.* (jewels, etc.). || Baratija, *f.*, chuchería, *f.* (trifle).
trinketry [—ri] n. Baratijas, *f. pl.*
trinomial [traiˈnəumjəl] n. MATH. Trinomio, *m.*
trio [ˈtri:əu] n. Trío, *m.*
triode [ˈtraiəud] n. PHYS. Tríodo, *m.*
triolet [ˈtriəulet] n. Letrilla, *f.* (poem).
trioxide [ˈtraiˈɔksaid] n. CHEM. Trióxido, *m.*
trip [trip] n. Viaje, *m.* (journey): *to go on a trip to England*, hacer un viaje a Inglaterra; *they are away on a trip*, están de viaje; *pleasure trip*, viaje de recreo; *boat trip*, viaje en barco; *business trip*, viaje de negocios; *tourist trip*, viaje turístico; *we took a trip*, hicimos un viaje; *round trip*, viaje circular. || Excursión, *f.* (excursion). || Tropezón, *m.*, traspié, *m.* (accidental stumble). | Zancadilla, *f.* (intentional). || Paso (*m.*) ligero (light tread). || TECH. Disparador, *m.* (of a mechanism). | Trinquete, *m.*, escape, *m.* (of a watch). || FIG. Desliz, *m.*, tropiezo, *m.*, error, *m.* (error). || FAM. Viaje, *m.* (effect of drugs).
trip [trip] v. intr. Dar un traspié: *he tripped and fell*, dio un traspié y se cayó. || Tropezar: *he tripped over the kerb*, tropezó con el borde de la acera. || Andar con paso ligero (to step lightly). || TECH. Soltarse (a catch). || FIG. Equivocarse, cometer un desliz (to make a mistake). | Trabarse (the tongue). || *To trip in, out*, entrar, salir con paso ligero.
— V. tr. Poner *or* echar la zancadilla a (to make s.o. fall over). | Hacer tropezar *or* caer (a rope, tree root, etc.). || FIG. Confundir: *the third question tripped me*, la tercera pregunta me confundió. | Coger en falta (asking a trick question). || TECH. Soltar (a catch). || MAR. Levar (anchor). | Izar (a topmast).
tripartite [ˈtraiˈpɑ:tait] adj. Tripartito, ta: *tripartite agreement*, acuerdo tripartito.
tripartition [ˌtraipɑ:ˈtiʃən] n. Tripartición, *f.*
tripe [traip] n. CULIN. Callos, *m. pl.* || FAM. Bobadas, *f. pl.*, tonterías, *f. pl.*: *that's all tripe*, no son más que tonterías. || FAM. *This play is tripe*, esta obra de teatro no vale nada.
tripe butcher [—ˌbutʃə*] n. Tripero, ra; casquero, ra.
tripe shop [—ʃɔp] n. Tripería, *f.*
tripetalous [traiˈpetələs] adj. Tripétalo, la.
trip-hammer [ˈtripˌhæmə*] n. TECH. Martinete, *m.*
triphase [ˈtraifeiz] adj. ELECTR. Trifásico, ca.
triphenylmethane [ˌtraiˌfenəlˈmeθein] n. CHEM. Trifenilmetano, *m.*
triphthong [ˈtrifθɔŋ] n. Triptongo, *m.*
triplane [ˈtraiplein] n. Triplano, *m.*
triple [ˈtripl] adj. Triple. || MUS. Ternario, ria: *triple time*, compás ternario. || *Triple the sum*, el triple.
— N. Triple, *m.*: *nine is the triple of three*, nueve es el triple de tres. || U. S. SP. Golpe (*m.*) que permite al bateador llegar a la tercera base.
triple [ˈtripl] v. tr. Triplicar.
— V. intr. Triplicarse.
triple-expansion [—iksˈpænʃən] adj. De triple expansión.
triple jump [—dʒʌmp] n. SP. Triple salto, *m.*
triple play [—ˈplei] n. U. S. SP. Jugada (*f.*) en que se elimina a tres jugadores (in baseball).
triplet [ˈtriplit] n. Trío, *m.* (set of three). || Trillizo, za (one of three babies). || POET. Terceto, *m.* || MUS. Tresillo, *m.*
triplex [ˈtripleks] adj. Triple.
triplicate [ˈtriplikit] adj. Triplicado, da (made in three copies). || Triple.
— N. Triplicado, *m.*, copia (*f.*) triplicada (one of three copies). || *In triplicate*, por triplicado.
triplicate [ˈtriplikeit] v. tr. Triplicar. || Hacer por triplicado (copy).
triplication [ˌtripliˈkeiʃən] n. Triplicación, *f.*
triplicity [tripˈlisiti] n. Triplicidad, *f.*
tripod [ˈtraipɔd] m. Trípode, *m.*
tripodal [ˈtripədl] or **tripodic** [traiˈpɔdik] adj. De tres pies.
tripos [ˈtraipɔs] n. Examen (*m.*) para sacar el título (at Cambridge University).
— OBSERV. El plural de esta palabra es *triposes*.
tripper [ˈtripə*] n. Turista, *m.* & *f.* (tourist). || Excursionista, *m.* & *f.* (on an excursion). || TECH. Disparador, *m.*
tripping [ˈtripiŋ] adj. Ligero, ra (pace).
triptych [ˈtriptik] n. ARTS. Tríptico, *m.*
trirectangular [ˈtrairekˈtæŋgjulə*] adj. MATH. Trirrectángulo, la.
trireme [ˈtrairi:m] n. Trirreme, *m.* (boat).
Trisagion [triˈsægiɔn] n. REL. Trisagio, *m.*
— OBSERV. El plural de la palabra inglesa es *Trisagia*.
trisect [traiˈsekt] v. tr. MATH. Trisecar.
trisection [traiˈsekʃən] n. MATH. Trisección, *f.*
trisulphide (U. S. **trisulfide**) [traiˈsʌlfaid] n. CHEM. Trisulfuro, *m.*
trisyllabic [ˈtraisiˈlæbik] adj. GRAMM. Trisílabo, ba.

trisyllable [ˈtraiˈsiləbl] n. GRAMM. Trisílabo, *m.*

trite [trait] adj. Trillado, da (hackneyed). || Trivial (commonplace).

triteness [—nis] n. Trivialidad, *f.* (triviality). || Lo trillado (of sth. well known).

tritium [ˈtritiəm] n. CHEM. Tritio, *m.*

triton [ˈtraitn] n. ZOOL. Tritón, *m.* (newt).

Triton [ˈtraitn] pr. n. MYTH. Tritón, *m.*

triturate [ˈtritʃəreit] v. tr. Triturar.

triturating [—iŋ] adj. Triturador, ra.

trituration [ˌtritʃəˈreiʃən] n. Trituración, *f.*

triturator [ˈtritʃəreitə*] n. Trituradora, *f.*

triumph [ˈtraiəmf] n. Triunfo, *m.* (victory): *in triumph*, en triunfo. || Júbilo, *m.*, regocijo, *m.* (joy).

triumph [ˈtraiəmf] v. intr. Alegrarse, congratularse, regocijarse: *they triumphed at the news*, se congratularon al recibir la noticia. || Triunfar: *to triumph over death, over the enemy*, triunfar sobre la muerte, del enemigo. || Vencer: *to triumph over one's difficulties*, vencer sus dificultades.

triumphal [traiˈʌmfəl] adj. Triunfal. || *Triumphal arch*, arco (*m.*) de triunfo.

triumphant [traiˈʌmfənt] adj. Triunfante.

triumpher [ˈtraiəmfə*] n. Triunfador, ra.

triumvir [triˈumvə*] n. Triunviro, *m.*

— OBSERV. El plural de *triumvir* es *triumvirs* o *triumviri*.

triumviral [—rəl] adj. Triunviral.

triumvirate [traiˈʌmvirit] n. Triunvirato, *m.*

triune [ˈtraiju:n] adj. Trino, na.

triunity [traiˈju:niti] n. Trinidad, *f.*

trivalence [ˈtraiˈveiləns] or **trivalency** [ˈtraiˈveilənsi] n. CHEM. Trivalencia, *f.*

trivalent [ˈtraiˈveilənt] adj. CHEM. Trivalente.

trivet [ˈtrivit] n. Trébedes, *m. inv.* (for cooking over fire). || Salvamantel (*m.*) de tres pies (to protect table top).

trivia [ˈtriviə] pl. n. Trivialidades, *f.*, banalidades, *f.*

trivial [—l] adj. Trivial, banal. || Frívolo, la (frivolous). || Insignificante, poco importante (insignificant). || Superficial. || *Trivial name*, nombre (*m.*) vulgar (vernacular name).

triviality [ˌtriviˈæliti] n. Trivialidad, *f.*, banalidad, *f.* || Frivolidad, *f.* || Insignificancia, *f.*

trivium [ˈtriviəm] n. Trivium, *m.*, trivio, *m.*

— OBSERV. El plural de la palabra inglesa es *trivia*.

triweekly [ˈtraiˈwi:kli] adj. Trisemanal.
— Adv. Tres veces por semana. || Cada tres semanas.

troat [trəut] v. intr. Bramar.

troat [trəut] n. Bramido, *m.*

trocar [ˈtrəukɑ:] n. MED. Trocar, *m.*

trochanter [trəuˈkæntə*] n. ANAT. Trocánter, *m.*

trochilus [ˈtrɔkələs] n. Troquilo, *m.* (bird).

— OBSERV. El plural de *trochilus* es *trochili*.

trochlea [trɔkˈliə] n. ANAT. Tróclea, *f.*

trochoid [ˈtrəukɔid] adj. ANAT. Trocoide. || MATH. Cicloidal.
— N. ANAT. Articulación (*f.*) trocoide. || MATH. Trocoide, *f.*, cicloide, *f.*

trochoidal [trəuˈkɔidəl] adj. See TROCHOID.

trod [trɔd] pret. & p. p. See TREAD.

trodden [ˈtrɔdn] p. p. See TREAD.

troglodyte [ˈtrɔglədait] n. Troglodita, *m.* & *f.* (cave dweller). || Troglodita, *m.* (bird).

troglodytic [ˌtrɔgləˈditik] or **troglodytical** [—əl] adj. Troglodita, troglodítico, ca.

troika [ˈtrɔikə] n. Troica, *f.*

Trojan [ˈtrəudʒən] adj./n. Troyano, na. || — FIG. *To work like a Trojan*, trabajar como un negro. || *Trojan horse*, caballo (*m.*) de Troya. || *Trojan War*, guerra (*f.*) de Troya.

troll [trəul] n. Cebo (*m.*) de cuchara (lure). || Carrete, *m.* (reel). || Canon, *m.* (song). || Gnomo, *m.*, duendecillo, *m.* (supernatural being).

troll [trəul] v. tr. Cantar en canon (a song). || Pescar en (a lake). || Pescar con cebo de cuchara (fish).
— V. intr. Pescar con cebo de cuchara (to fish).

trolley [ˈtrɔli] n. Carretilla, *f.* (for transporting goods). || Vagoneta, *f.* (in mines, on rails). || Mesita (*f.*) de ruedas, carrito, *m.* (for serving tea, etc.). || Trole, *m.* (pole). || Teleférico, *m.* (cable car). || U. S. Tranvía, *m.* (tram). || U. S. FAM. *To be off one's trolley*, desvariar, estar chalado.

trolleybus [—bʌs] n. Trolebús, *m.*

trolley car [—kɑ:] n. U. S. Tranvía, *m.*

trolley line [—lain] n. U. S. Línea (*f.*) de tranvía.

trolley pole [—pəul] n. Trole, *m.*

trolley wire [—waiə*] n. Cable (*m.*) conductor.

trollop [ˈtrɔləp] n. Ramera, *f.* (whore). || Puerca, *f.* (dirty woman).

trolly [ˈtrɔli] n. See TROLLEY.

trombone [trɔmˈbəun] n. MUS. Trombón, *m.*: *slide trombone*, trombón de varas; *valve trombone*, trombón de pistones *or* de llaves.

trombonist [—ist] n. MUS. Trombón, *m.*

trommel [ˈtrɔməl] n. TECH. Tambor, *m.*

trompe [trɔmp] n. Trompa, *f.*

trompe l'oeil [trɔ̃plɔ:j] n. ARTS. "Trompe-l'oeil", *m.*, efecto, *m.*

troop [tru:p] n. Banda, *f.*, grupo, *m.* (of people). || Manada, *f.* (of animals). || Bandada, *f.* (of birds). || Grupo, *m.* (of boy scouts). || MIL. Escuadrón, *m.* (company). || Tropa, *f.* (body). || THEATR. Compañía, *f.* (of actors). || — Pl. MIL. Tropas, *f.*: *air-borne troops*, tropas aerotransportadas; *line troops*, tropas de línea. || *Troops of tourists*, cantidades de turistas.

troop [tru:p] v. intr. Ir en grupo *or* en grupos *or* juntos: *they all trooped off to the cinema*, se fueron todos juntos al cine. || Apiñarse (to gather). || *To troop out*, salir en tropel.
— V. tr. MIL. Presentar (the colours).

troop carrier [—ˌkæriə*] n. MIL. Avión (*m.*) de transporte de tropas.

trooper [—ə*] n. MIL. Soldado (*m.*) de caballería. || Buque (*m.*) de transporte (troopship). || Policía (*m.*) montado (mounted policeman). || *To swear like a trooper*, blasfemar como un carretero.

trooping [—iŋ] n. Grupo, *m.* || *Trooping the colours*, saludo (*m.*) a la bandera.

troopship [—ʃip] n. MIL. Buque (*m.*) de transporte.

troop train [—trein] n. Tren (*m.*) militar.

trope [trəup] n. Tropo, *m.* (figure of speech).

trophy [ˈtrəufi] n. Trofeo, *m.*

tropic [ˈtrɔpik] n. Trópico, *m.*: *Tropic of Cancer, of Capricorn*, Trópico de Cáncer, de Capricornio. || — Pl. Trópicos, *m.*
— Adj. Tropical.

tropical [—əl] adj. Tropical: *tropical climate*, clima tropical. || Trópico, ca (in rhetoric).

tropic bird [—bə:d] n. ZOOL. Rabijunco, *m.*

tropism [ˈtrəupizəm] n. BIOL. Tropismo, *m.*

tropology [trəˈpɔlədʒi] n. Tropología, *f.*

troposphere [ˈtrɔpəsfiə] n. Troposfera, *f.*

trot [trɔt] n. Trote, *m.* (action, sound of a horse trotting): *at a trot*, al trote; *at an easy o a slow trot*, a trote corto. || Palangre, *m.* (fishing line). || U. S. FAM. Chuleta, *f.* (crib). || — *On the trot*, seguidos, das (one after another): *for ten years on the trot*, durante diez años seguidos. || *To break into a trot*, empezar a trotar. || FIG. *To keep s.o. on the trot*, no dejarle parar a uno.

trot [trɔt] v. intr. Trotar, ir al trote (a horse). || FIG. Correr (to run). || FAM. *To trot off*, irse corriendo.
— V. tr. Hacer trotar (a horse). || *To trot out*, hacer trotar (a horse), sacar a relucir (arguments), hacer alarde de (to make a show of).

troth [trəuθ] n. Palabra, *f.*, promesa, *f.* || Fidelidad, *f.* (faithfulness). || *To plight one's troth*, dar palabra de matrimonio *or* de casamiento.

trotline [ˈtrɔtlain] n. Palangre, *m.* (fishing line).

Trotskyist [ˈtrɔtski:ist] or **Trotskyite** [ˈtrɔtski:ait] adj./n. Trotskista.

trotter [ˈtrɔtə*] n. Trotón, *m.* (horse). || CULIN. Mano, *f.* (of a pig or other animal).

trotting [ˈtrɔtiŋ] adj. Trotador, ra.

troubadour [ˈtru:bəduə*] n. Trovador, *m.*

trouble [ˈtrʌbl] n. Inquietud, *f.*, preocupación, *f.* (worry): *the trouble it gave me!*, ¡las preocupaciones que me dio! || Apuro, *m.*: *to be in trouble*, estar en un apuro; *he got out of trouble*, salió de apuros. || Pena, *f.*: *to tell s.o. one's troubles*, contar a alguien sus penas. || Desgracia, *f.* (misfortune). || Problema, *m.*, dificultad, *f.*: *the trouble is*, el problema es; *we had trouble with the motor*, tuvimos problemas con el motor; *money troubles*, problemas de dinero; *with no little trouble*, con cierta dificultad. || Engorro, *m.* (person or thing that causes difficulty). || Disgusto, *m.*: *he caused trouble between them*, causó un disgusto entre ellos. || Camorra, *f.*: *to look for trouble*, buscar camorra. || Trastornos, *m. pl.*, enfermedad, *f.* (illness): *the trouble started two years ago*, los trastornos comenzaron hace dos años; *mental troubles*, trastornos mentales. || Disturbios, *m. pl.* (disturbance): *trouble at a football match*, disturbios en un partido de fútbol. || Molestia, *f.*: *if it's no trouble for you*, si no le sirve de molestia; *I saved myself the trouble*, me ahorré la molestia; *to take the trouble to*, tomarse la molestia de; *it is no trouble*, no es ninguna molestia. || Conflictos, *m. pl.*: *labour trouble*, conflictos laborales. || — *Don't put yourself to any trouble*, no se moleste Ud. || *It did not give me much trouble to do it*, no me costó mucho trabajo hacerlo. || *To be worth the trouble*, valer *or* merecer la pena. || FIG. *To get a girl into trouble*, dejar embarazada a una chica. || *To get into trouble*, meterse en líos. || *To get s.o. into trouble*, meter a alguien en un lío. || *To go to great trouble over sth.* o *to take trouble over sth.*, hacer algo con mucho cuidado. || *To go to great trouble to do sth.* o *to take great trouble in doing sth.*, tomarse mucho trabajo haciendo algo. || *To go to the trouble of*, tomarse la molestia de. || *To keep out of trouble*, no meterse en líos. || *To make trouble* o *to stir up trouble*, armar lío, armar jaleo. || *To put o.s. to great trouble*, tomarse las mayores molestias. || *To spare no trouble in order to*, no escatimar esfuerzos para. || *What's the trouble?*, ¿qué pasa?

trouble [ˈtrʌbl] v. tr. Preocupar (to cause to worry): *he was deeply troubled*, estaba sumamente preocupado. || Perturbar, trastornar (to disturb mentally). || Afectar, afligir: *troubled by his friend's death*, afectado por la muerte de su amigo. || Aquejar: *troubled by rheumatism*, aquejado de reúma. || Molestar: *I don't want to trouble you with too many questions*, no te quiero molestar con demasiadas preguntas; *my arm has been* *troubling me ever since the accident*, me molesta este brazo desde el accidente. || Enturbiar (to make turbid). || — *May I trouble you for a cigarette?*, ¿puedo pedirle un cigarrillo? || *To trouble o.s. about sth.*, preocuparse por algo. || *To trouble o.s. to do sth.*, molestarse en hacer algo, tomarse la molestia de hacer algo.

— V. intr. Preocuparse, inquietarse (to be worried): *don't trouble about it*, no se preocupe por eso. || Molestarse: *don't trouble to fetch it*, no te molestes en ir a buscarlo.

troubled [—d] adj. Preocupado, da (worried): *a troubled countenance*, una cara preocupada. || Agitado, da (sleep, period, life). || Revuelto, ta; turbulento, ta (waters).

trouble-free [—fri:] adj. Sin preocupaciones. || Sin problemas, sin dificultades. || Sin disturbios.

troublemaker [—ˌmeikə*] n. Alborotador, ra; perturbador, ra.

troubleshooter [—ˌʃu:tə*] n. U. S. Localizador (*m.*) de averías (in power circuits, etc.). | Mediador, ra (mediator).

troublesome [—səm] adj. Molesto, ta.

troublesomeness [—səmnis] n. Molestia, *f.*

troublous [—əs] adj. Molesto, ta (troublesome). || Agitado, da; revuelto, ta (period).

trough [trɔf] n. Pesebre, *m.* (for animal food). || Abrevadero, *m.* (for drinking). || Comedero, *m.* (feeding for birds). || Bebedero, *m.* (drinking for birds). || Artesa, *f.*, amasadera, *f.* (for kneading). || CHEM. Cuba, *f.* || Seno, *m.* (depression between waves). || Depresión, *f.* (depression). || Zona (*f.*) de bajas presiones (in meteorology). || Canalón, *m.* (water conduit). || Mínimo, *m.* (in statistics). || MIN. *Washing trough*, batea, *f.*

trounce [trauns] v. tr. FAM. Dar una paliza a, pegar (to thrash). | Dar una paliza a, derrotar (to defeat).

trouncing [—iŋ] n. Paliza, *f.*

troupe [tru:p] n. THEATR. Compañía, *f.*

trouper [—ə*] n. Actor (*m.*) de una compañía.

trousers [ˈtrauzəz] pl. n. Pantalón, *m. sing.*, pantalones, *m.* || FIG. *To wear the trousers*, llevar los pantalones.

trousseau [ˈtru:səu] n. Ajuar, *m.*

— OBSERV. El plural de *trousseau* es *trousseaux* o *trousseaus.*

trout [traut] n. ZOOL. Trucha, *f.* (fish): *salmon trout*, trucha asalmonada; *rainbow trout*, trucha arco iris. || *Trout river*, río truchero.

trouvère [tru:ˈvεər] n. Trovador, *m.*, trovero, *m.*

trove [trəuv] n. Tesoro (*m.*) descubierto. || FIG. Hallazgo, *m.*

trowel [ˈtrauəl] n. Palustre, *m.*, paleta, *f.*, llana, *f.* (for mortar, etc.). || Desplantador, *m.* (for lifting plants). || FIG. FAM. *To lay it on with a trowel*, pasar la mano por el lomo.

trowel [ˈtrauəl] v. tr. Extender con el palustre.

Troy [trɔi] pr. n. Troya.

truancy [ˈtru:ənsi] n. Rabona, *f.*, falta (*f.*) a clase.

truant [ˈtru:ənt] n. Persona (*f.*) que hace novillos (from school). || Haragán, ana (lazy person). || *To play truant*, hacer novillos, hacer rabona.

— Adj. Que hace novillos *or* rabona. || Vago, ga; perezoso, sa (lazy).

truce [tru:s] n. Tregua, *f.*: *to declare a truce*, acordar una tregua; *truce of God*, tregua de Dios.

truceless [—lis] adj. Sin tregua.

truck [trʌk] n. Trueque, *m.*, cambio, *m.* (barter). || FAM. Trato, *m.* (dealings): *to have no truck with*, no tener trato con. || Baratijas, *f. pl.* (articles of little value). || Pago (*m.*) de sueldos en especie (payment in kind). || Batea, *f.* (open freight wagon). || Vagoneta, *f.* (in mines). || Carretón, *m.*, bogie, *m.* (bogie). || Carretilla (*f.*) de mano (handcart). || U. S. Camión, *m.* (lorry). | Verduras (*f. pl.*) para el mercado (vegetables). | Mesita (*f.*) de ruedas, carrito, *m.* (small trolley).

truck [trʌk] v. tr. Trocar, cambiar (to exchange). || Transportar en camión (to transport in a truck).

— V. intr. Hacer un trueque *or* un cambio.

truckage [—idʒ] n. Camionaje, *m.*, transporte (*m.*) por camión, acarreo, *m.*

truck driver [—ˌdraivə*] n. Conductor (*m.*) de camión, camionero, *m.*

trucker [—ə*] n. U. S. Transportista, *m.* (person engaged in trucking). | Camionero, *m.* (truck driver). | Hortelano, *m.* (truck farmer).

truck farm [—fα:m] n. U. S. Huerto, *m.*

truck farmer [—ˌfα:mə*] n. U. S. Hortelano, *m.* (market gardener).

trucking [—iŋ] n. See TRUCKAGE.

truckle [ˈtrʌkl] n. Ruedecilla, *f.*, rueda, *f.*

truckle [ˈtrʌkl] v. intr. Ser servil [*to*, con].

truckle bed [—bed] n. Cama (*f.*) baja con ruedas.

truckler [—ə*] n. Servilón, ona; adulón, ona.

truckload [ˈtrʌkləud] n. Camión, *m.* (load).

truckman [ˈtrʌkmən] n. Camionero, *m.*

— OBSERV. El plural de esta palabra es *truckmen.*

truculence [ˈtrʌkjuləns] n. Ferocidad, *f.*, crueldad, *f.*, salvajismo, *m.* || Agresividad, *f.*, violencia, *f.* (in style).

truculent [ˈtrʌkjulənt] adj. Feroz, salvaje, cruel (fierce). || Agresivo, va.

trudge [trʌdʒ] n. Caminata, *f.*, paseo (*m.*) largo y cansado.

trudge [trʌdʒ] v. tr. Recorrer [una distancia] con dificultad.

— V. intr. Andar con dificultad.

trudgen or **trudgeon** [—ən] or **trudgen stroke** [—ənstrəuk] n. Trudgeon, *m.* (in swimming).

true [tru:] adj. Verdadero, ra; de verdad: *a true friend*, un verdadero amigo; *a true Christian*, un verdadero cristiano. || Verídico, ca; verdadero, ra; auténtico, ca: *his story is true*, su historia es auténtica. || Fiel, leal: *true to his principles*, fiel a sus principios. || Legítimo, ma: *the true heir*, el heredero legítimo. || Exacto, ta (accurate). || Auténtico, ca (authentic, real). || Seguro, ra: *these dark clouds are a true sign of rain*, estos nubarrones son anuncio seguro de lluvia. || MUS. Afinado, da (voice). || Centrado, da (wheel). || A plomo (wall). || Alineado, da (aligned). || — *To be out of true*, no estar bien alineado *or* centrado *or* a plomo. || *To come true*, realizarse, llegar a ser realidad, cumplirse. || *To distinguish the true from the false*, distinguir lo verdadero de lo falso. || *Too good to be true*, demasiado bueno para ser cierto. || *True copy*, copia (*f.*) fiel. || *True to life*, conforme a la realidad.

— Adv. Verdaderamente (truly). || Exactamente (accurately). || — *To aim true*, apuntar bien. || *To run true*, estar centrada (wheel). || *To sing true*, cantar afinadamente.

true [tru:] v. tr. Corregir, rectificar. || Centrar (a wheel).

true bill [—ˈbil] n. U. S. JUR. Acta (*f.*) de acusación.

true-blue [—ˈblu:] adj. Fiel, leal (utterly loyal).

trueborn [—bɔ:n] adj. Legítimo, ma; verdadero, ra.

truebred [—bred] adj. De pura sangre (purebred).

truehearted [—ˈhα:tid] adj. Leal, fiel (faithful). || Sincero, ra (sincere).

true-life [ˈtru:laif] adj. Verdadero, ra; de la vida real.

truelove [—lʌv] n. Amor, *m.* (loved one).

truelove knot [—lʌvnɔt] n. Nudo (*m.*) difícil de desatar. || FIG. Prueba (*f.*) de amor eterno.

trueness [—nis] n. Fidelidad, *f.*, lealtad, *f.* (faithfulness). || Sinceridad, *f.* (sincerity). || Verdad, *f.* (truth). || Timbre (*m.*) perfecto (of voice).

truffle [trʌfl] n. Trufa, *f.*

truism [ˈtru:izəm] n. Truismo, *m.*

truly [ˈtru:li] adv. Verdaderamente (truthfully). || Fielmente, lealmente (faithfully). || Realmente, verdaderamente: *a truly lamentable performance*, una actuación verdaderamente lamentable. || Sinceramente (sincerely). || — *Really and truly?*, ¿de verdad? || *Yours truly*, see YOURS.

trump [trʌmp] n. Triunfo, *m.* (in cards). || FAM. Buena persona, *f.* (nice person). || (Ant.). Trompeta, *f.* || — FIG. *To hold all the trumps*, tener todos los triunfos en la mano. | *To turn up trumps*, favorecerle [a uno] la suerte: *he always turns up trumps*, siempre le favorece la suerte; resultar bien: *the idea turned up trumps*, la idea resultó bien.

trump [trʌmp] v. tr. Fallar (in cards). || *To trump up*, forjar, inventar (an excuse).

— V. intr. Jugar un triunfo.

trump card [—ˈkα:d] n. Triunfo, *m.* (in cards). || FIG. Triunfo, *m.*, baza, *f.*: *to hold all the trump cards*, tener todos los triunfos en la mano.

trumped-up [—tˈʌp] adj. Forjado, da; inventado, da.

trumpery [—əri] adj. Sin valor (worthless). || De oropel (paltry and showy).

— N. Baratija, *f.* (worthless thing). || Tonterías, *f. pl.* (nonsense).

trumpet [ˈtrʌmpit] n. MUS. Trompeta, *f.* (wind instrument): *to play the trumpet*, tocar la trompeta. | Trompeta, *m.* & *f.* (musician). || Trompetilla, *f.*: *ear trumpet*, trompetilla acústica. || — Pl. MUS. Trompetería, *f. sing.* (of an organ). || FIG. *To blow one's own trumpet*, darse bombo, echarse flores.

trumpet [ˈtrʌmpit] v. tr. Anunciar a son de trompeta (to announce).

— V. int. Tocar la trompeta (to play the trumpet). || Berrear, bramar, barritar (an elephant).

trumpet call [—kɔ:l] n. Toque (*m.*) de trompeta.

trumpeter [—ə*] n. MUS. Trompetista, *m.* & *f.*, trompeta, *m.* & *f.* || Agamí, *m.* (bird).

trumpet player [—ˌpleiə*] n. MUS. See TRUMPETER.

truncate [ˈtrʌŋkeit] adj. Truncado, da.

truncate [ˈtrʌŋkeit] v. tr. Truncar.

truncated [—id] adj. Truncado, da: *truncated cone*, cono truncado.

truncation [trʌŋˈkeiʃən] n. Truncamiento, *m.*

truncheon [ˈtrʌntʃən] n. Matraca, *f.* (cudgel). || Porra, *f.* (policeman's).

trundle [ˈtrʌndl] n. Ruedecilla, *f.* (small wheel). || Cama (*f.*) baja con ruedas (bed). || Narria, *f.*, carretilla, *f.* (cart). || TECH. Linterna, *f.* (lantern pinion). | Barra (*f.*) de la linterna (bar).

trundle [ˈtrʌndl] v. tr. Hacer rodar (a hoop). || Empujar (a barrow).

— V. intr. Rodar.

trundle bed [—bed] n. Cama (*f.*) baja con ruedas.

trunk [trʌŋk] n. Tronco, *m.* (of a tree or a body). || Trompa, *f.* (of an elephant). || Tórax, *m.* (of an insect). || Línea (*f.*) interurbana (of telephone system). || Línea (*f.*) principal (of railway). || Tronco, *m.*

(main stem of a blood vessel). || ARCH. Fuste, *m.* (central shaft of a column). || Baúl, *m.* (luggage). || TECH. Conducto, *m.* (shaft). | Tubería, *f.* (pipe). || U. S. Maleta, *f.*, maletero, *m.*, portaequipaje, *m.* (of a car). || — Pl. Bañador, *m. sing.* (man's bathing costume). | Pantalón (*m. sing.*) corto, "short", *m. sing.* (shorts).

trunk call [—kɔ:l] n. Conferencia, *f.* [interurbana] (telephone).

trunk line [—lain] n. Línea (*f.*) interurbana (of telephone system). || Línea (*f.*) principal (of railway).

trunk road [—rəud] n. U. S. Carretera (*f.*) nacional.

trunnion [ˈtrʌnjən] n. Muñón, *m.*

truss [trʌs] n. Braguero, *m.* (to support a hernia). || Haz, *m.* (of hay or straw). || BOT. Racimo, *m.* (of flowers). || ARCH. Modillón, *m.* | Armazón, *f.* (framework).

truss [trʌs] v. tr. Atar (to tie up). || CULIN. Sujetar con una brocheta. || ARCH. Apuntalar.

truss bridge [—bridʒ] n. Puente (*m.*) de celosía.

truss girder [—ˌgə:də*] n. Viga (*f.*) de celosía.

trust [trʌst] n. Confianza, *f.* (confidence in s.o. or sth.): *a position of trust*, un puesto de confianza; *trust in the future*, confianza en el futuro; *breach of trust*, abuso de confianza; *he puts his trust in*, tiene confianza en. || Esperanza, *f.* (hope). || Deber, *m.*, obligación, *f.* (duty): *he deserted his trust*, no cumplió con su obligación. || Depósito, *m.*: *shall I hold this money in trust for you?*, ¿le guardo este dinero en depósito? || JUR. Fideicomiso, *m.*: *in trust*, en fideicomiso. || COMM. Trust, *m.* (association of companies). | Crédito, *m.*, fiado, *m.*: *to sell on trust*, vender a crédito *or* al fiado *or* fiado. || *To take on trust*, aceptar *or* creer a ojos cerrados.

trust [trʌst] v. tr. Confiar en, fiarse de, tener confianza en (to have faith in): *I trust him*, confío en él. || Creer, dar crédito a (to believe). || Esperar (to hope): *I trust so*, espero que sí, eso espero. || Confiar (to a person's care). || Encomendar (to commit to the responsible care of). || COMM. Dar crédito a. || *He is not to be trusted*, no es de fiar.

— V. intr. Confiar: *to trust in God*, confiar en Dios. || *To trust to*, abandonarse a, confiar en.

trust company [—ˌkʌmpəni] n. Empresa (*f.*) fideicomisaria. || U. S. Banco (*m.*) de depósito.

trustee [trʌsˈti:] n. Fideicomisario, ria. || Administrador (*m.*) de una empresa (person managing the affairs of an institution). || Síndico, *m.* (in bankruptcy). || País (*m.*) fideicomisario (country responsible for a trust territory). || *Board of trustees*, consejo (*m.*) de administración.

trusteeship [—ʃip] n. Cargo (*m.*) de administrador (position as a trustee). || Cargo (*m.*) de síndico (in bankruptcy). || Fideicomiso, *m.* (administration of a region, etc.).

trustful [ˈtrʌstful] adj. Confiado, da.

trustfulness [—nis] n. Confianza, *f.*

trustiness [ˈtrʌstinis] n. Fidelidad, *f.*, lealtad, *f.*

trusting [ˈtrʌstiŋ] adj. Confiado, da.

trust territory [ˈtrʌstˌteritəri] n. Estado (*m.*) en *or* bajo fideicomiso.

trustworthiness [ˈtrʌstˌwə:ðinis] n. Honradez, *f.* (of s.o.). || Veracidad, *f.*, carácter (*m.*) fidedigno, exactitud, *f.* (of a statement).

trustworthy [ˈtrʌstˌwə:ði] adj. Que merece confianza, digno de confianza, de fiar (person). || Digno de crédito *or* de fe (statement). || Fidedigno, na (news).

trusty [ˈtrʌsti] adj. Que merece confianza, digno de confianza, de fiar. || Fiel, leal (servant).

— N. U. S. Preso (*m.*) a quien conceden algunos privilegios por su buena conducta.

truth [tru:θ] n. Verdad, *f.*: *to tell the truth*, decir la verdad; *if the truth were told*, si se dijese la verdad; *it's the patent truth*, eso es una verdad como un templo; *the honest truth is that*, la pura verdad es que. || Veracidad, *f.*: *how can you test the truth of what he says?*, ¿cómo puedes probar la veracidad de lo que dice? || Sinceridad, *f.* (sincerity). || Exactitud, *f.* (accuracy). || — *Moment of truth*, hora (*f.*) de la verdad. || *Nothing hurts like the truth*, sólo la verdad ofende. || *To swear to tell the truth, the whole truth, and nothing but the truth*, jurar decir la verdad, toda la verdad y nada más que la verdad. || *To tell s.o. a few home truths*, decirle a uno cuatro verdades *or* las verdades del barquero. || *To tell the truth*, a decir verdad, la verdad sea dicha (actually). || *Truth value*, valor (*m.*) real.

truthful [—ful] adj. Veraz (telling the truth). || Verídico, ca (true). || Parecido, da (portrait).

truthfulness [—fulnis] n. Veracidad, *f.*, verdad, *f.* (of sth.). || Veracidad, *f.* (of s.o.). || Parecido, *m.* (of a portrait).

truthless [—lis] adj. Falso, sa.

truthlessness [—lisnis] n. Falsedad, *f.*

try [trai] n. Prueba, *f.*, intento, *m.*, tentativa, *f.* (attempt): *to have a try*, hacer una tentativa. || Ensayo, *m.* (in rugby). || *To have a try at doing sth.*, intentar hacer algo.

try [trai] v. tr. Intentar: *he tried skiing but never liked it*, intentó esquiar pero nunca le gustó. || Intentar, tratar de, procurar: *to try to open a door*, intentar abrir una puerta. || Probar: *to try the brakes*, probar los frenos: *try twice the quantity*, prueba el doble de la cantidad; *to try an experiment*, probar un experimento. || Poner a prueba: *she tries his patience*, ella pone a prueba su paciencia. || Probar (to taste). || JUR. Juzgar, procesar, someter a juicio (a person). | Someter a juicio, ver (a case). || Fatigar, cansar: *small print tries the eyes*, los caracteres pequeños cansan la vista. || — *A people sorely tried*, un pueblo que ha sufrido mucho. || *To try it on with s.o.*, intentar engañar a alguien. || *To try on*, probarse (clothes). || *To try one's best*, hacer los mayores esfuerzos, hacer todo lo posible. || *To try one's hand at*, intentar, probar. || *To try out*, poner a prueba, probar (a thing, a person), derretir (fat), refinar (metal). || MUS. *To try over*, ensayar. || *To try up*, cepillar, acepillar (wood).

— V. intr. Esforzarse (to make an effort to do sth.). || Intentar (to have a go). || — *To try and do sth.*, intentar *or* procurar hacer algo, tratar de hacer algo. || *To try for*, intentar conseguir.

trying [ˈtraiŋ] adj. Molesto, ta (causing annoyance). || Penoso, sa (causing worry). || Difícil (difficult). || Cansado, da (tiring).

trying plane [—plein] n. TECH. Garlopa, *f.*

tryout [ˈtraiaut] n. Prueba (*f.*) de aptitud (aptitude test). || THEATR. Audición, *f.*

trypanosome [ˈtripənəsəum] n. ZOOL. Tripanosoma, *m.* (protozoan).

trypanosomiasis [ˌtripənəusəuˈmaiəsis] n. MED. Tripanosomiasis, *f. inv.*

trysail [ˈtraisəl] n. MAR. Vela (*f.*) triangular.

tryst [tryst] n. Cita, *f.*

tsar [zɑ:] n. Zar, *m.*

tsarina [zɑ:ˈri:nə] n. Zarina, *f.*

tsetse [ˈtsetsi] or **tsetse fly** [—flai] n. ZOOL. Mosca (*f.*) tse-tsé, tse-tsé, *f.*

T-shirt [ˈti:ʃə:t] n. Camiseta, *f.*

T square [ˈti:skwεə*] n. Escuadra (*f.*) en forma de T.

Tuareg [ˈtjuəreg] n. Tuareg, *m.*

tub [tʌb] n. Tina, *f.* (made of wood, metal, etc.). || Cubo, *m.* (for carrying ore, etc.). || Bote, *m.* (to practise rowing). || Barreño, *m.*, tina, *f.* (old metal bath). || Caja, *f.* (for flowers). || FAM. Carraca, *f.* (slow or clumsy ship). | Bañera, *f.* (bathtub). || (Ant.). Baño, *m.* (bath).

tub [tʌb] v. tr. Lavar en una tina *or* barreño (to wash in a tub). || Poner en una caja (plants).

— V. intr. Bañarse (to take a bath).

tuba [ˈtju:bə] n. MUS. Tuba, *f.* || Tuba, *f.* (Philippine liquor).

tubate [ˈtju:beit] adj. Tubulado, da; tubular.

tubby [ˈtʌbi] adj. Rechoncho, cha.

tube [tju:b] n. Tubo, *m.* (pipe, container): *toothpaste tube*, tubo de pasta dentífrica; *test tube*, tubo de ensayo. || PHYS. Tubo, *m.*: *cathode-ray tube*, tubo de rayos catódicos; *vacuum tube*, tubo de vacío. || Metro, *m.* (underground railway). || BOT. Tubo, *m.* || ANAT. Trompa, *f.*: *Fallopian tube*, trompa de Falopio. | Tubo, *m.*: *capillary tube*, tubo capilar. || U. S. Tunel, *m.* (for motor or rail traffic). | Lámpara, *f.* (valve). | Cámara (*f.*) de aire (of a tyre). || *Speaking tube*, tubo acústico.

tube [tju:b] v. tr. Entubar (to provide with tubes). || Meter en tubos, entubar (to enclose in tubes).

tubeless [—lis] adj. Sin cámara (tyre).

tuber [—ə*] n. BOT. Tubérculo, *m.* (modified underground stem). || ANAT. Tuberosidad, *f.* || MED. Tubérculo, *m.*

tubercle [ˈtju:bə:kl] n. MED. ANAT. BOT. Tubérculo, *m.*

tubercle bacillus [—bəˈsiləs] n. Bacilo (*m.*) de Koch, bacilo (*m.*) de la tuberculosis.

tubercular [tjuˈbə:kjulə*] adj./n. Tuberculoso, sa.

tuberculate [tjuˈbə:kjuleit] or **tuberculated** [—id] adj. Tuberculoso, sa.

tuberculin [tjuˈbə:kjulin] n. Tuberculina, *f.* || *Tuberculin test*, prueba (*f.*) de la tuberculina, tuberculinodiagnóstico, *m.*

tuberculosis [tjuˌbə:kjuˈləusis] n. MED. Tuberculosis, *f.*

tuberculous [tjuˈbə:kjuləs] adj. Tuberculoso, sa.

tuberose [ˈtju:bərəus] adj. Tuberoso, sa.

tuberose [ˈtju:bərəuz] n. BOT. Tuberosa, *f.*, nardo, *m.*

tuberosity [ˌtju:bəˈrɔsiti] n. Tuberosidad, *f.*

tuberous [ˈtju:bərəs] adj. BOT. Tuberoso, sa: *tuberous root*, raíz tuberosa.

tube station [ˈtju:bˌsteiʃən] n. Estación (*f.*) de metro.

tubing [ˈtju:bin] n. Tubería, *f.* || MED. TECH. Entubado, *m.*

tub-thumper [ˈtʌbˌθʌmpə*] n. Arengador, *m.*

tub-thumping [ˈtʌbˌθʌmpiŋ] n. Arenga, *f.*

tubular [ˈtju:bjulə*] adj. Tubular.

tubulate [ˈtju:bjulit] adj. Tubulado, da.

tuck [tʌk] n. Alforza, *f.*, pliegue, *m.* (fold). || Chucherías, *f. pl.* (sweets, cakes, etc.). || Comida, *f.* (food).

tuck [tʌk] v. tr. Meter: *he tucked his handkerchief in his pocket*, metió el pañuelo en el bolsillo. || Remeter, meter: *to tuck one's sheets in*, remeter las sábanas. || Meter: *to tuck one's shirt in one's trousers*, meter la camisa dentro de los pantalones. || Hacer pliegues en, alforzar (to fold). || — *To tuck away*, ocultar, esconder (to hide), tragar (to swallow). || *To tuck in*, arropar (s.o. in bed). || *To tuck up*, remangar (sleeves, trousers, etc.), arropar (s.o.).

— V. intr. Caber (to fit). || FAM. *To tuck in*, comer con mucho apetito.

tucker [ˈtʌkə*] n. FAM. Comida, *f.*

tucker [ˈtʌkə*] v. tr. U. S. FAM. Agotar.
tuck-in [ˈtʌkin] n. FAM. Banquetazo, *m.*, comilona, *f.*
tuck-shop [ˈtʌkʃɔp] n. Confitería, *f.*
tuco-tuco [ˈtu:kəuˈtu:kəu] n. ZOOL. Tucutucu, *m.* (rodent).
Tudor [ˈtju:də*] pr. n. Tudor.
Tuesday [ˈtju:zdi] n. Martes, *m.*: *he will come on Tuesday*, vendrá el martes.
tufa [ˈtju:fə] n. Toba, *f.* (stone).
tufaceous [tju:ˈfeiʃəs] adj. Tobáceo, a.
tuff [tʌf] n. Toba, *f.* (stone).
tuffaceous [tʌˈfeiʃəs] adj. Tobáceo, a.
tuft [tʌft] n. Penacho, *m.* (of feathers). || Mechón, *m.* (of hair). || Mata, *f.* (of plants). || Perilla, *f.* (beard). || Borla, *f.* (on a hat). || Copo, *m.* (of wool). || Nudo (*m.*) de basta (of mattress). || Penacho, *m.*, copete, *m.* (of a bird).
tuft [tʌft] v. tr. Poner un penacho *or* una borla a (with feathers). || Acolchar (a mattress).
tufted [ˈtʌftid] or **tufty** [ˈtʌfti] adj. Copetudo, da.
tufting needle [ˈtʌftiŋˌni:dl] n. Aguja (*f.*) colchonera.
tug [tʌg] n. Tirón, *m.* (sharp pull): *give it a good tug*, dale un tirón fuerte. || Tracción, *f.* (pulling force). || FIG. Lucha, *f.* (struggle). || Tirante, *m.* (of a harness). || Remolcador, *m.* (tugboat).
tug [tʌg] v. tr. Tirar de (to pull): *he was tugging the dog along*, iba tirando del perro. || Arrastrar (to drag). || Remolcar (to tow).
— V. intr. Tirar fuerte. || *To tug at*, tirar de: *to tug at the oars*, tirar de los remos.
tugboat [ˈtʌgbəut] n. Remolcador, *m.*
tug-of-war [ˈtʌgəvˈwɔ:] n. Juego (*m.*) de la cuerda. || FIG. Lucha, *f.* (hard struggle).

— OBSERV. El plural es *tugs-of-war*.

tuition [tjuˈiʃən] n. Enseñanza, *f.*, educación, *f.* || U. S. Matrícula, *f.* (enrolment fees). || — *Postal tuition*, curso (*m.*) por correspondencia. || *Private tuition*, clases (*f. pl.*) particulares.
tuitional [—əl] adj. De enseñanza.
tulip [ˈtju:lip] n. BOT. Tulipán, *m.* || BOT. *Tulip tree*, tulipero, *m.*, tulipanero, *m.*
tulipwood [ˈtju:lipwud] n. Madera (*f.*) de tulipero.
tulle [tju:l] n. Tul, *m.*
tumble [ˈtʌmbl] n. Caída, *f.* (fall). || Voltereta, *f.* (handspring). || FIG. Revoltijo, *m.* (jumble): *a tumble of books and papers*, un revoltijo de libros y papeles. || — *In a tumble*, en desorden, patas arriba. || *To take a tumble*, caerse.
tumble [ˈtʌmbl] v. intr. Caerse (to fall): *they were tumbling over one another*, se caían uno encima del otro. || Dar volteretas (to do handsprings). || Agitarse, removerse (in bed). || Dar vueltas (a missile). || Tambalearse (to stagger). || FIG. Caerse (price, government).
— V. tr. Derribar (to cause to fall). || Desordenar, desarreglar, revolver (to put in disorder). || Deshacer (a bed). || Despeinar (hair). || Arrugar (s.o.'s dress). || FIG. FAM. Derrocar (a king, etc.). || TECH. Desarenar (to clean castings). | Pulir, limpiar (to polish).
— ***To tumble down,*** derribar (s.o.). | Matar (game). | Rodar, caerse: *to tumble down the stairs*, rodar por las escaleras. | Venirse abajo, derrumbarse (to fall): *the walls tumbled down*, las paredes se vinieron abajo. | Caer en ruinas, caerse (to fall into ruin): *this house is tumbling down*, esta casa se está cayendo en ruinas. || ***To tumble into,*** tropezar con. | Echarse en (bed). || ***To tumble on,*** dar con, encontrar (to find). || ***To tumble to,*** caer en [la cuenta de] (to understand suddenly). | — FAM. *He did not tumble to it*, no cayó en la cuenta, no cayó en ello.
tumblebug [ˈtʌmblbʌg] n. U. S. ZOOL. Escarabajo (*m.*) pelotero (dung beetle).
tumbledown [ˈtʌmbldaun] adj. Ruinoso, sa.
tumbler [ˈtʌmblə*] n. Vaso, *m.* (glass). || Cubilete, *m.* (of a conjurer). || Vaso (*m.*) graduado (in medicine). || Volatinero, ra; titiritero, ra (acrobat). || ZOOL. Pichón (*m.*) volteador. || Dominguillo, *m.*, tentempié, *m.* (toy). || TECH. Tambor (*m.*) desarenador (for castings). | Tambor (*m.*) de limpieza (for other articles). | Guarda, *f.* (of a lock). || AUT. Balancín, *m.*
tumbling [ˈtʌmbliŋ] n. Caída, *f.* (fall). || Acrobacia, *f.* (acrobatics). || TECH. Desarenado, *m.*
tumbling barrel [—ˌbærəl] n. TECH. Tambor (*m.*) desarenador (for castings). | Tambor (*m.*) de limpieza (for other articles).
tumbling box [—bɔks] n. See TUMBLING BARREL.
tumbling shaft [—ʃɑ:ft] n. TECH. Árbol (*m.*) de levas.
tumbrel or **tumbril** [ˈtʌmbrəl] n. Volquete, *m.* (farmer's cart). || Carreta, *f.* (for the condemned to the guillotine).
tumefaction [ˌtju:miˈfækʃən] n. MED. Tumefacción, *f.*
tumefy [ˈtju:mifai] v. tr. MED. Hinchar, tumefacer.
— V. intr. MED. Hincharse.
tumescence [tju:ˈmesns] n. MED. Tumescencia, *f.*
tumescent [tju:ˈmesnt] adj. MED. Tumescente, tumefacto, ta.
tumid [ˈtju:mid] adj. MED. Túmido, da; hinchado, da. || FIG. Ampuloso, sa; hinchado, da (style).
tumidity [tju:ˈmiditi] n. MED. Hinchazón, *f.* || FIG. Ampulosidad, *f.* (of style).
tummy [ˈtʌmi] n. FAM. Barriga, *f.*, tripa, *f.* (stomach).

tumour (U. S. **tumor**) [ˈtju:mə*] n. MED. Tumor, *m.*: *malignant tumours*, tumores malignos.
tumular [ˈtju:mjulə*] adj. Tumulario, ria; sepulcral.
tumult [ˈtju:mʌlt] n. Tumulto, *m.* || FIG. Agitación, *f.*
tumultuous [tjuˈmʌltjuəs] adj. Tumultuoso, sa. || FIG. Agitado, da; tumultuoso, sa.
tumulus [tju:mjuləs] n. Túmulo, *m.*
— OBSERV. El plural de *tumulus* es *tumuli*.
tun [tʌn] n. Cuba, *f.*, tonel (*m.*) grande (cask). || Tina (*f.*) de fermentación (fermenting vat).
tuna [ˈtu:nə] n. ZOOL. Atún, *m.* (fish). || BOT. Tunal, *m.*, tuna, *f.*, nopal, *m.*, chumbera, *f.* (plant). | Tuna, *f.*, nopal, *m.*, higo (*m.*) chumbo (fruit).

— OBSERV. En el sentido zoológico se emplea frecuentemente también la forma *tuna fish.*

tunable [ˈtju:nəbl] adj. MUS. Que se puede afinar.
tundra [ˈtʌndrə] n. GEOGR. Tundra, *f.*
tune [tju:n] n. MUS. Aire, *m.* (melody): *to play a tune on the piano*, tocar un aire en el piano. | Tono, *m.* (correct pitch). || RAD. Sintonización, *f.* || FIG. Armonía, *f.* || — MUS. *In tune*, afinado, da (instrument), afinadamente (to sing). | *Out of tune*, desafinado, da (instrument). || FIG. *To be in tune with*, concordar con. || MUS. *To be out of tune*, desentonar, desafinar (a singer). || FIG. *To be out of tune with*, desentonar con. | *To be out of tune with the times*, no andar con el tiempo. | *To change one's tune* o *to sing a different tune*, cambiar de tono. || MUS. *To get out of tune*, desafinar. | *To sing out of tune*, desentonar, desafinar. || FIG. *To the tune of*, por la friolera de, por la cantidad de (to the amount of).
tune [tju:n] v. tr. MUS. Afinar (an instrument). || RAD. Sintonizar (*to*, con). || FIG. Armonizar (to bring into harmony). | Adaptar. || *To tune* (*up*), poner a punto (a motor).
— V. intr. RAD. *To tune in* (*on*), sintonizar. || *To tune up*, afinar los instrumentos (a band).
tuneful [ˈtju:nful] adj. Melodioso, sa; armonioso, sa (melodious). || Sonoro, ra.
tuneless [ˈtju:nlis] adj. Discordante (not melodious). || Mudo, da (silent).
tuner [ˈtju:nə*] n. Afinador, *m.* (of pianos, etc.). || RAD. Sintonizador, *m.*, mando (*m.*) de sintonización.
tune-up [ˈtju:nʌp] n. TECH. Puesta (*f.*) a punto, reglaje, *m.*
tungstate [ˈtʌŋsteit] n. CHEM. Tungstato, *m.*
tungsten [ˈtʌŋstən] n. CHEM. Tungsteno, *m.*
tunic [ˈtju:nik] n. Túnica, *f.* (garment). || MIL. Guerrera, *f.* || ANAT. BOT. Túnica, *f.* || REL. Tunicela, *f.* (tunicle).
tunica [—ə] n. ANAT. Túnica, *f.*

— OBSERV. El plural de la palabra inglesa es *tunicae*.

tunicate [—ət] adj. Tunicado, da.
— N. Tunicado, *m.*
tunicated [—eitid] adj. Tunicado, da.
tunicle [—l] n. REL. Tunicela, *f.* || ANAT. Túnica, *f.*
tuning [ˈtju:niŋ] n. MUS. Afinación, *f.*, afinamiento, *m.* || RAD. Sintonización, *f.* || TECH. Puesta (*f.*) a punto, reglaje, *m.*
tuning coil [—kɔil] n. RAD. Bobina (*f.*) de sintonización.
tuning eye [—ai] n. RAD. Ojo (*m.*) mágico.
tuning fork [—fɔ:k] n. MUS. Diapasón, *m.*
tuning hammer [—ˌhæmə*] n. MUS. Afinador, *m.*
tuning knob [—nɔb] n. RAD. Botón (*m.*) de sintonización.
Tunis [ˈtju:nis] pr. n. GEOGR. Túnez (town).
Tunisia [tjuˈniziə] pr. n. GEOGR. Túnez, *m.* (country).
Tunisian [—n] adj./n. Tunecino, na.
tunnage [ˈtʌnidʒ] n. Tonelaje, *m.* (tonnage).
tunnel [ˈtʌnəl] n. Túnel, *m.* || MIN. Galería, *f.* || Túnel, *m.*, galería, *f.* (passage dug by an animal). || — *Tunnel of love*, túnel de los enamorados (in a fairground). || *Wind tunnel*, túnel aerodinámico.
tunnel [ˈtʌnəl] v. tr. Cavar (to dig): *to tunnel a passage*, cavar un pasadizo. || Construir *or* perforar *or* hacer un túnel en: *to tunnel a hill*, construir un túnel en una colina. || Hacer galerías en (animals). || *To tunnel one's way through*, abrirse paso a través de.
— V. intr. Construir *or* perforar *or* hacer un túnel. || Hacer galerías (animals).
tunny [ˈtʌni] n. Atún, *m.* (fish). || *Tunny fishery*, almadraba, *f.*
tup [tʌp] n. ZOOL. Morueco, *m.*, carnero (*m.*) padre (ram). || TECH. Pilón, *m.*, mazo, *m.* (of a steam hammer). | Pisón, *m.*, martinete, *m.* (pile driver).
tup [tʌp] v. tr. Cubrir (a ram).
tupaia [tju:ˈpaiə] n. ZOOL. Tupaya, *f.*
Tupi [ˈtu:pi:] n. Tupí, *m.* & *f.*

— OBSERV. El plural de *Tupi* es *Tupi* o *Tupis*.

Tupian [—ən] adj. Tupí.
tuppence [ˈtʌpəns] n. Dos peniques, *m.* (twopence).
tuppenny [ˈtʌpəni] adj. De dos peniques (twopenny).
turban [ˈtə:bən] n. Turbante, *m.*
turbaned [—d] adj. Con turbante.
turbary [ˈtə:bəri] n. Turbera, *f.* (peat bog).
turbellaria [ˌtə:bəˈlɛəriə] pl. n. ZOOL. Turbelarios, *m.*
turbid [ˈtə:bid] adj. Turbio, bia (liquid). || Denso, sa; espeso, sa (smoke, clouds). || FIG. Confuso, sa (thought).
turbidity [tə:ˈbiditi] or **turbidness** [ˈtə:bidnis] n. Turbiedad, *f.* || FIG. Confusión, *f.*

turbine [ˈtəːbain] n. TECH. Turbina, *f.*: *hydraulic* o *water turbine*, turbina hidráulica; *steam turbine*, turbina de vapor.
turboalternator [ˌtəːbəuˈɔːltəneitə*] n. ELECTR. Turboalternador, *m.*
turboblower [ˈtəːbəuˌbləuə*] n. TECH. Turbosoplante, *f.*
turbocompressor [ˌtəːbəukəmˈpresə*] *m.* TECH. Turbocompresor, *m.*
turbodynamo [ˌtəːbəuˈdainəməu] n. ELECTR. Turbodinamo, *m.*
turbogenerator [ˌtəːbəuˈdʒenəreitə*] n. ELECTR. Turbogenerador, *m.*
turbojet [ˈtəːbəudʒet] or **turbojet engine** [—ˌendʒin] n. TECH. Turborreactor, *m.*
turbomotor [ˈtəːbəuˌməutə*] n. TECH. Turbomotor, *m.*
turboprop [ˈtəːbəuprɔp] or **turbo-propeller engine** [təːbəupraˈpeləˈendʒin] n. TECH. Turbohélice, *m.*, turbopropulsor, *m.*
turbopump [ˈtəːbəupʌmp] n. TECH. Turbobomba, *f.*
turbot [ˈtəːbət] n. Rodaballo, *m.* (fish).
turboventilator [ˌtəːbəuˈventileitə*] n. TECH. Turboventilador, *m.*
turbulence [ˈtəːbjuləns] n. Turbulencia, *f.*
turbulent [ˈtəːbjulənt] adj. Turbulento, ta: *turbulent waters*, aguas turbulentas.
Turcoman [ˈtəːkəmən] n. Turcomano, na.
— OBSERV. El plural de *Turcoman* es *Turcomans*.
tureen [təˈriːn] n. Sopera, *f.* (for soup). || Salsera, *f.* (for sauce).
turf [təːf] n. Césped, *m.* (lawn). || Tepe, *m.* (square of earth). || Turba, *f.* (peat). || SP. "Turf", *m.*, hipódromo, *m.* (track for horse racing). | Deporte (*m.*) hípico, hipismo, *m.* (horse racing).
— OBSERV. En el sentido de "hipismo" la palabra *turf* va generalmente precedida por el artículo "the". El plural de *turf* es *turves* o *turfs*.
turf [təːf] v. tr. Cubrir con césped, encespedar. || FAM. *To turf out*, echar (to throw out or away).
turfman [—mən] n. Turfista, *m.*
— OBSERV. El plural de *turfman* es *turfmen*.
turfy [—i] adj. Encespedado, da; cubierto con césped (covered with turf). || Turboso, sa (peaty). || De carreras de caballos (of horse racing).
turgescence [təːˈdʒesns] n. MED. Turgencia, *f.*, hinchazón, *f.* || FIG. Ampulosidad, *f.* (bombast).
turgescent [təːˈdʒesnt] adj. MED. Turgente, hinchado, da. || FIG. Ampuloso, sa; hinchado, da (bombastic).
turgid [ˈtəːdʒid] adj. MED. Turgente, túrgido, da; hinchado, da. || FIG. Ampuloso, sa; hinchado, da (bombastic).
turgidity [təːˈdʒiditi] n. MED. Turgencia, *f.* || FIG. Ampulosidad, *f.* (bombast).
Turk [təːk] n. Turco, ca (from Turkey). || Musulmán, ana (Moslem). || FIG. Tirano, *m.* (cruel person).
Turkestan [ˌtəːkisˈtɑːn] pr. n. GEOGR. Turquestán, *m.*
turkey [ˈtəːki] n. ZOOL. Pavo, va. || CULIN. Pavo, *m.* || U. S. FIG. Fracaso, *m.*, fiasco, *m.* (failure). || — FIG. *To talk turkey*, no andarse con rodeos, no tener pelos en la lengua (to talk candidly). || ZOOL. *Young turkey*, pavipollo, *m.*
Turkey [ˈtəːki] pr. n. GEOGR. Turquía, *f.*
turkey buzzard [ˈtəːkiˌbʌzəd] n. Urubú, *m.*, zopilote, *m.*, aura, *f.* (bird).
turkey-cock [ˈtəːkikɔk] n. Pavo, *m.* (bird). || FIG. Presumido, *m.*
turkey hen [ˈtəːkihen] n. Pava, *f.* (bird).
Turkish [ˈtəːkiʃ] adj. Turco, ca.
— N. Turco, *m.* (language).
Turkish bath [— bɑːθ] n. Baño (*m.*) turco.
Turkish delight [—diˈlait] n. "Rahat lokum", *m.* [especie de caramelo oriental].
Turkish towel [—ˈtauəl] n. Toalla (*f.*) de felpa.
Turkmenistan [ˌtəːkˈmenisˌtɑːn] pr. n. GEOGR. Turkmenistán, *m.*
Turkoman [ˈtəːkəmən] n. Turcomano, na.
— OBSERV. El plural de esta palabra es *Turkomans*.
Turkomen [ˈtəːkəumen] pr. n. GEOGR. Turkmenistán, *m.*
turk's head [ˈtəːkshed] n. Escobón, *m.*, deshollinador, *m.* (large broom). || MAR. Barrilete, *m.* (knot).
turmaline [ˈtuəməlin] n. MIN. Turmalina, *f.*
turmeric [ˈtəːmərik] n. BOT. Cúrcuma, *f.*
turmoil [ˈtəːmɔil] n. Confusión, *f.*, desorden, *m.* (great confusion): *the turmoil created by the revolution*, la confusión creada por la revolución. || Agitación, *f.* (agitation). || Alboroto, *m.*, tumulto, *m.* (tumult). || Trastorno, *m.*: *mental turmoil*, trastorno mental. || *The crowd was in a turmoil*, la muchedumbre estaba alborotada.
turn [təːn] n. Vuelta, *f.*, revolución, *f.* (of a wheel). || Vuelta, *f.* (of key, handle). || Vuelta, *f.* (change of direction). || Vuelta, *f.*, espira, *f.* (coil). || Vuelta, *f.* (of rope). || Curva, *f.* (of road, river): *sharp turn*, curva cerrada. || Movimiento, *m.*: *with a turn of the hand*, con un movimiento de la mano. || Turno, *m.*, vez, *f.* (one of alternating opportunities): *wait your turn*, espere su turno; *to give up one's turn*, ceder la vez; *I missed my turn*, perdí la vez. || Turno, *m.* (shift of work): *a turn at the helm*, un turno en el timón. || THEATR. Número, *m.* (short performance). || Vuelta, *f.* (short walk or drive): *to take a turn in the garden*, dar una vuelta por el jardín. || Curva, *f.* (shape): *the turn of an arm*, la curva de un brazo. || FIG. Cambio, *m.* (change). | Sesgo, *m.*, cariz, *m.*, aspecto, *m.* (change in condition): *this affair has taken a new turn*, este asunto ha tomado un nuevo sesgo. | Carácter, *m.* (mental inclination): *he is of a humorous turn*, tiene un carácter festivo. | Aptitudes, *f. pl.* (capacities). | Giro, *m.* (of a sentence). | Viraje (*m.*) decisivo (change in situation): *the Revolution was a turn in French history*, la Revolución ha sido un viraje decisivo en la historia de Francia. | Final, *m.* (end): *at the turn of the century*, al final del siglo. | Ataque, *m.* (fit): *I had another turn yesterday*, tuve otro ataque ayer. | Vahído, *m.* (dizziness). || FAM. Susto, *m.* (fright): *it gave him quite a turn*, le dio un buen susto. || MAR. Cambio, *m.* (of tide). | Giro, *m.* (of a ship). | Salto, *m.* (of wind). || MUS. Grupeto, *m.* || — *A good turn of speed*, una gran velocidad. || FIG. *At every turn*, a cada paso. | *A turn of Fortune's wheel*, un cambio de fortuna, un revés. | *Bad turn*, mala jugada, *f.*, faena, *f.*, jugarreta, *f.* || *By turns*, por turno (one after the other), alternativamente, a ratos (alternately). || FIG. *Good turn*, favor, *m.*: *he did me a good turn*, me hizo un favor; buena acción (among boy scouts). || *In his turn*, a su vez. || FIG. *In the turn of a hand*, en un abrir y cerrar de ojos, en un santiamén. || *In turn*, cada uno a su vez, uno tras otro (one after another), alternativamente (alternately). || FIG. *It gave me a turn to hear such news*, me dio un vuelco el corazón *or* se me encogió el corazón al oir la noticia. || AUT. *No left turn*, prohibido torcer a la izquierda. || FAM. *Not to do a turn of work*, no dar golpe. || FIG. *One good turn deserves another*, amor con amor se paga. || *Out of turn*, cuando no le toca [a uno]: *you mustn't speak out of turn*, no tiene que hablar cuando no le toca; fuera de lugar (at the wrong time). || MIL. *Right about turn!*, ¡media vuelta a la derecha! || *The star turn*, la sensación, la atracción principal. || *The twists and turns of the road*, las vueltas de la carretera. || FIG. *To a turn*, en su punto: *this turkey is done to a turn*, el pavo está en su punto. || *To be one's turn to do sth.*, tocarle a uno hacer algo: *whose turn is it?*, ¿a quién le toca? || FIG. *To have a nasty turn*, pasar un mal rato. | *To have a serious turn of mind*, ser serio, tener un carácter serio. | *To have a turn for mathematics*, dársele bien [a uno] las matemáticas, ser bueno para las matemáticas, tener aptitudes para las matemáticas. || *To make* o *to take a turn to port*, virar a babor. || FIG. *To serve s.o.'s turn*, servirle a alguien (to be useful). || AUT. *To take a short turn*, tomar una curva muy cerrada. || FIG. *To take a turn for the better, for the worse*, mejorar, empeorar. || *To take turns at*, turnarse en, alternar en. || *Turn and turn about*, por turno. || FIG. *Turn of mind*, manera de ver las cosas. | *Turn of phrase*, expresión, *f.*, giro, *m.*
turn [təːn] v. tr. Hacer girar, dar vueltas a: *to turn a wheel*, hacer girar una rueda. || Dar la vuelta a: *to turn a key*, dar la vuelta a una llave; *to turn an omelette*, dar la vuelta a una tortilla. || Dar vueltas a: *to turn a spit*, dar vueltas a un asador. || Volver: *he turned his head and looked back*, volvió la cabeza y miró hacia atrás; *turn your eyes this way*, vuelve la mirada hacia aquí; *turn your chair to the table*, vuelve la silla hacia la mesa. || Torcer, doblar, dar la vuelta a: *to turn a corner*, doblar la esquina. || Pasar, volver (a page). || Poner, volver: *the sun turned his face red*, el sol le puso la cara colorada. || Cambiar el color de: *frost turned the leaves very early*, la escarcha ha cambiado el color de las hojas muy pronto. || Cambiar de: *to turn colour*, cambiar de color. || Volver (to affect): *prison turned him bitter*, la cárcel le volvió más amargo. || Poner: *it turned him sick*, le puso enfermo. || Trastornar (to derange). || Desviar (to deflect): *he managed to turn the blow*, consiguió desviar el golpe. || Desviar, hacer girar: *he turned the conversation to more cheerful topics*, hizo girar la conversación hacia temas más alegres. || Eludir, evitar, sortear (a difficulty). || Poner: *his speech turned the crowd in his favour*, su discurso puso a la muchedumbre de su parte. || Volver: *his own criticism was turned against him*, volvieron su propia crítica en contra suya. || Dirigir (one's steps, one's efforts, etc.): *to turn a hose on a fire*, dirigir la manguera hacia el fuego. || Dar (a somersault). || Dar la vuelta a, volver (in sewing): *to turn a collar*, dar la vuelta a un cuello. || Rechazar (to repel): *to turn an attack*, rechazar un ataque. || Pasar, pasar de (a certain age): *she has turned fourty*, ha pasado los cuarenta años. || Rebasar, superar, sobrepasar (an amount). || Echar a perder (to spoil): *the warmth has turned the meat*, el calor ha echado a perder la carne. || Agriar (wine). || Poner rancio (dairy products). || Cortar (milk). || Revolver: *it turned my stomach*, me revolvió el estómago. || TECH. Tornear (on a lathe or pottery wheel). | Labrar (metals). | Desbarbar (to trim superfluous clay). | Embotar (to blunt). || FIG. Moldear, tornear (to give a graceful shape to). | Construir (a phrase). | Redactar (a letter). | Formular (a request). || AGR. Labrar, voltear (the soil). | Voltear (hay). || CULIN. Revolver, mover (a salad). || MED. Torcer (an ankle). || MIL. Envolver: *to turn the enemy's flank*, envolver el flanco del enemigo. | Apuntar, dirigir (one's gun). || SP. Dar efecto a (a ball in cricket). || — FIG. *He can turn*

his hand to almost anything, es muy mañoso. || *It has just turned half past two*, acaban de dar las dos y media. || *It must have turned three o'clock*, deben de ser más de las tres. || *It turned my thoughts in another direction*, esto cambió completamente mis ideas. || *To turn a heel*, hacer el talón (in knitting). || FIG. *To turn an honest penny*, ganarse la vida honradamente. || *To turn a screw*, atornillar (to screw on), desatornillar (to unscrew). || *To turn inside out*, volver del revés. || *To turn loose*, soltar (to free). || *To turn one's attention to*, fijar la atención en. || FIG. *To turn one's coat*, volver [la] casaca, chaquetear. || *To turn s.o. adrift*, abandonar a alguien a su suerte. || *To turn s.o.'s brain*, volverle loco a uno. || *To turn s.o.'s head*, subírsele a uno a la cabeza (success), volverle loco a uno: *she has turned his head*, le ha vuelto loco. || *To turn s.o. to different views*, cambiar las ideas de alguien. || *To turn sth. to account*, sacar provecho de algo. || *To turn the tap*, abrir el grifo (to open), cerrar el grifo (to shut). || *To turn upside down*, see UPSIDE DOWN.

— V. intr. Girar: *the Earth turns round the Sun*, la Tierra gira alrededor del Sol. || Girar, dar vueltas: *the wheels were turning slowly*, las ruedas estaban girando lentamente. || Dar la vuelta: *shall we turn and go back now?*, ¿damos la vuelta y regresamos ahora? || Volver, regresar: *to turn home*, volver a casa. || Volverse: *he turned towards me*, se volvió hacia mí. || Doblarse (to become bent). || Torcer: *the road turns after the village*, la carretera tuerce después del pueblo. || Torcer a: *turn right*, tuerza a la derecha. || MAR. AVIAT. Virar. || Cambiar (tide, weather, wind). || Cambiar de color (leaves). || Cambiar (luck). || Volverse, hacerse (to become): *he has turned stupid*, se ha vuelto estúpido. || Hacerse: *to turn musician*, hacerse músico. || Ponerse, volverse: *to turn red*, ponerse colorado. || Transformarse, convertirse (to change into another form). || Echarse a perder (to spoil). || Ponerse rancio (butter, etc.). || Cortarse (milk). || Revolverse: *when I saw it my stomach almost turned*, al verlo casi se me revolvió el estómago. || TECH. Tornear (to use a lathe). | Tornearse (wood). | Labrarse (metals). || Pasar: *let's turn to another subject*, pasemos a otro tema. || Girar: *the conversation turned around this problem*, la conversación giró alrededor de este problema. || Dedicarse: *when they turned to politics*, cuando se dedicaron a la política. || Recurrir: *I have no one to turn to*, no tengo a quien recurrir. || — MIL. *About turn!*, media vuelta ¡ar! || *My head is turning*, me da vueltas la cabeza, estoy mareado. || *Not to know which way to turn*, no saber a quién recurrir *or* a quién acudir. || MIL. *Right turn!*, derecha ¡ar! || *Their thoughts turned to the days of their youth*, se pusieron a pensar en su época juvenil.

— **To turn about**, dar la vuelta a (sth.). | Dar la vuelta (complete turn). | Dar media vuelta (half turn). || **To turn against**, poner en contra de, enemistar con (to antagonize). | Volverse en contra de: *he turned against his mother*, se volvió en contra de su madre. || **To turn around**, dar la vuelta. | FIG. Desvirtuar (words): *you're just turning my words around*, está usted desvirtuando mis palabras. || **To turn aside**, apartar: *to turn aside one's gaze*, apartar la mirada. | Desviar: *to turn aside a blow*, desviar un golpe. | Apartarse, hacerse a un lado: *he turned aside to let me pass*, se hizo a un lado para dejarme paso. || **To turn away**, volver (face). | Volver, apartar (eyes). | Desviar (to divert). | Rechazar: *we had to turn away five applicants*, tuvimos que rechazar a cinco candidatos. | Despedir, echar (to dismiss). | Alejarse (to go away). | — *To turn away from*, volver la espalda a. || **To turn back**, volver: *he turned back to his work*, volvió a su trabajo. | Retroceder (to go back). | Volverse (to come back). | Hacer retroceder: *bad weather turned him back*, el mal tiempo le hizo retroceder. | Doblar (the edge of sth.). | Arremangarse, remangarse (one's sleeves). | Retrasar (the clock). || **To turn down**, bajar (radio, television, fire). | Mitigar (light). | Rechazar (an offer, a person). | Volver (a collar). | Poner boca abajo (a card). | Doblar (the edge of sth.). | Abrir (a bed, sheets). | Volverse hacia abajo: *the ends of his moustache turn down*, las guías de su bigote se vuelven hacia abajo. | — *Turn down the noise!*, ¡un poco de silencio! || **To turn from**, apartarse de. | Apartar: *I turned him from his bad ways*, le aparté de sus malas costumbres. | — *To turn s.o. from his purpose*, disuadir *or* hacer cambiar a alguien de propósito. || **To turn in**, estar vuelto hacia dentro (feet, toes). | Presentar (to submit). | Entregar (to hand in): *to turn in a report*, entregar un informe; *to turn in a criminal, a weapon to the police*, entregar un criminal, un arma a la policía. | Devolver (to give back). | Meter (a hem, etc.). | FAM. Dejar (to leave): *to turn in a job*, dejar un trabajo; recogerse, acostarse (to go to bed). | — *His eyes turn in*, tiene los ojos torcidos hacia dentro. || **To turn into**, transformar en, convertir en: *he turned the play into a farce*, transformó la obra en farsa; *Christ turned the water into wine*, Jesucristo transformó el agua en vino. | Transformarse en, convertirse en: *the water turned into wine*, el agua se transformó en vino; *tadpoles turn into frogs*, los renacuajos se transforman en ranas. | Llegar a ser: *she has turned into a pretty little girl*, ha llegado a ser una niña muy mona. | Ponerse: *it turned into a nice day*, el día se puso bueno. | Meterse: *to turn into the park*, meterse en el parque. | Soltar en: *to turn sheep into a field*, soltar ovejas en un campo. | Poner en, vertir en: *turn the text into good English*, póngase el texto en buen inglés. | Traducir a *or* en (to translate). | — *To turn a novel into a film*, hacer una versión cinematográfica de una novela. | *To turn ideas into deeds*, pasar de las ideas a los hechos. || **To turn off**, cerrar, apagar, quitar (radio, television). | Apagar (light, fire). | Cerrar (a tap). | Parar (engine, machine). | Desconectar: *turn the current off before you go away*, desconecte la corriente antes de irse. | Quitar del hornillo: *turn the soup off*, quita la sopa del hornillo. | Salir de: *I turned off the road*, salí de la carretera; *my street turns off the square*, mi calle sale de la plaza. | Torcer: *I turned off to the left*, torcí a la izquierda. | Despedir, echar (to dismiss). | — *It turned me off eating there*, me quitó las ganas de comer allí. || **To turn on**, encender (light, fire). | Poner, encender (radio, television). | Abrir (a tap). | Poner en marcha (engine, machine). | Conectar (electric current). | FAM. Excitar. | Tratar de: *the discussion turned on politics*, la discusión trataba de política. | Centrarse en: *the trial turns on your evidence*, el proceso se centra en su testimonio. | Depender de (to depend upon): *everything turns on his decision*, todo depende de su decisión. | Volverse en contra de (to become hostile towards, to attack): *I didn't expect you'd turn on me also*, no me esperaba que se volviera también en contra mía. || **To turn out**, apagar (light, fire). | Cerrar (to shut off). | Volver hacia fuera (feet, toes). | Sacar: *to turn s.o. out of bed*, sacar a alguien de la cama. | Producir (to produce, to manufacture). | Resultar, ser (to prove to be): *the battle turned out a disaster*, la batalla resultó *or* fue una catástrofe. | Llegar a ser: *he will turn out (to be) a good pianist*, llegará a ser un buen pianista. | Expulsar (to expel): *the police had to turn out several people*, la policía tuvo que expulsar a varias personas. | Sacar (to remove from a container). | Vaciar (to empty). | Ordenar (to clear out). | Vestir (to dress). | Equipar (to equip). | Salir (to go out). | Formar (to assemble). | Asistir a (to be present at): *to turn out for a practice*, asistir a un ensayo. | Formar parte de: *to turn out for the school team*, formar parte del equipo del colegio. | FAM. Levantarse (to get up). | — *How are things turning out?*, ¿cómo van las cosas? | *It turns out that*, resulta que. | *To turn out well, badly*, salir bien, mal. || **To turn over**, dar la vuelta a: *to turn a steak over*, dar la vuelta a un filete. | Volverse: *to turn over in bed*, volverse en la cama. | Volcar, dar una vuelta de campana: *the car turned over*, el coche volcó. | Capotar (aircraft). | Poner al revés (to put upside down). | Pasar (a page). | Hojear (to glance at): *to turn over the pages of a book*, hojear [las páginas de] un libro. | Ceder: *he turned the business over to his son*, cedió el negocio a su hijo. | Considerar, dar vueltas a: *to turn a problem over*, dar vueltas a un problema. | COMM. Dar salida a (a stock of goods), sacar, tener un volumen de negocios de: *they turn over 800 pounds a week*, sacan ochocientas libras por semana. | AGR. Dar una vuelta a (soil). | Entregar (to hand over): *to turn s.o. over to the police*, entregar a alguien a la policía. | Convertir (to convert). | — *My stomach turned over*, se me revolvió el estómago. | *Please turn over*, véase al dorso. || **To turn round**, dar la vuelta a. | Dar la vuelta, volverse (to face the other way). | Girar, dar vueltas (to rotate). | Dar vueltas a (to cause to rotate). | Cambiar de opinión (to change opinion). | — *To turn round and round*, dar vueltas. || **To turn to**, empezar (to start). || **To turn up**, poner más fuerte, subir (radio, television). | Poner más fuerte (a fire). | Aumentar (light, sound). | Volverse hacia arriba: *the ends of his moustache turn up*, las guías de su bigote se vuelven hacia arriba. | Levantar, subir: *to turn up a shirt collar*, levantar el cuello de una camisa. | Arremangarse, remangarse (sleeves). | Acortar (a dress). | Meter (a hem). | Subir (to change direction upwards). | Poner boca arriba (to put face upwards). | AGR. Dar una vuelta a (soil). | Desenterrar (to discover whilst digging). | Encontrar (to find). | Descubrir: *to turn up an old photo*, descubrir una foto vieja. | Aparecer: *the missing watch turned up*, el reloj perdido apareció. | Salir: *the five of spades turned up*, el cinco de picos salió. | Salir, presentarse: *may be sth. will turn up next week*, puede que algo se presente la semana próxima. | Presentarse: *he turned up at my office at five o'clock*, se presentó en mi despacho a las cinco. | Venir: *you must turn up for the practice*, tienes que venir para el entrenamiento. | Ocurrir (to happen): *sth. will turn up*, algo ocurrirá. | — *His nose turns up*, tiene la nariz respingona. | FIG. *To turn up one's nose at sth.*, despreciar algo, hacer una mueca de desprecio ante algo.

turnabout [ˈtə:nəbaut] n. Vuelta, *f.* || Cambio (*m.*) completo (of opinion, allegiance). || U. S. Tiovivo, *m.* (merry-go-round).

turnaround [ˈtə:nəraund] n. See TURNABOUT.

turnbuckle [ˈtə:nbʌkl] n. Tarabilla, *f.* (of shutters). || Tensor, *m.* (of wire). || MAR. Acollador, *m.*

turncap [ˈtə:nkæp] n. Sombrerete, *m.* (of chimney).

turncoat [ˈtə:nkəut] n. Renegado, da; veleta, *m.* & *f.*

turndown [ˈtə:nˌdaun] adj. Vuelto, ta (collar).

turned comma [ˈtə:ndˌkɔmə] n. Comilla, *f.* (inverted comma).

turned-up [ˈtə:ndˈʌp] adj. Respingón, ona (nose).
turner [ˈtə:nə*] n. TECH. Tornero, *m.*
turnery [—ri] n. Torneado, *m.* (work, technique). || Objetos (*m. pl.*) torneados (product). || Tornería, *f.* (workshop).
turn indicator [ˈtə:n,indikeitə*] n. AUT. Intermitente, *m.* || AVIAT. Indicador (*m.*) de viraje.
turning [ˈtə:niŋ] n. Vuelta, *f.* (turn). || Curva, *f.*, viraje, *m.* (of a road): *to take a turning at a high speed*, tomar una curva a gran velocidad. || Bocacalle, *f.*: *take the first turning on the right*, coja la primera bocacalle a la derecha. || TECH. Torneado, *m.*, torneadura, *f.* || AVIAT. Viraje, *m.* || — Pl. Virutas, *f.*, torneaduras, *f.* || — *Turning lathe*, torno, *m.* || *Turning point*, viraje decisivo, momento (*m.*) crucial, hito, *m.* || *Turning radius*, ángulo (*m.*) de giro (of a car).
turnip [ˈtə:nip] n. BOT. Nabo, *m.* || Reloj (*m.*) de bolsillo (watch). || — BOT. *Swedish turnip*, colinabo, *m.* | *Turnip top*, grelos, *m. pl.*
turnkey [ˈtə:nki:] n. Llavero, *m.* (prison warder).
turnoff [ˈtə:nɔf] n. Desvío, *m.* (on a motorway or main road). || U. S. Bocacalle, *f.* (side road in a town).
turnout [ˈtə:naut] n. Concurrencia, *f.* (gathering of people). || Entrada, *f.*, público, *m.*, asistentes, *m. pl.* (spectators). || Presentación, *f.* (personal appearance). || Atuendo, *m.* (outfit, array). || Carroza, *f.*, carruaje (*m.*) de lujo (coach, carriage). || Huelga, *f.* (strike). || Huelguista, *m.* & *f.* (striker). || COMM. Producción, *f.* (output). || Apartadero, *m.*, vía (*f.*) muerta (railway siding). || Limpieza, *f.*: *this drawer needs a good turnout*, este cajón necesita une buena limpieza. || U. S. Apartadero, *m.* (on a narrow road).
turnover [ˈtə:n,əuvə*] n. COMM. Volumen (*m.*) de negocios, volumen (*m.*) de ventas, facturación, *f.* (money received from sales). | Movimiento, *m.* (purchase and sale of stock). | Producción, *f.* | Productividad, *f.* | Rotación, *f.* (movement of people, employees, etc.). || CULIN. Empanada, *f.* || Vuelco, *m.* (a rolling over). || Vuelta, *f.*: *a turnover on the horizontal bar*, una vuelta en la barra fija. || Vuelta, *f.* (of socks). || Embozo, *m.* (of sheets). || Solapa, *f.* (of an envelope). || Artículo (*m.*) que continúa en la página siguiente (newspaper article).
— Adj. Vuelto, ta.
turnpike [ˈtə:npaik] n. Barrera (*f.*) de portazgo (toll gate). || U. S. Autopista (*f.*) de peaje (toll highway). | Autopista, *f.* (highway).
turnplate [ˈtə:npleit] n. U. S. See TURNTABLE.
turnscrew [ˈtə:nskru:] n. Destornillador, *m.* (screwdriver).
turnsole [ˈtə:nsəul] n. Girasol, *m.* (flower).
turnspit [ˈtə:nspit] n. Asador, *m.*
turnstile [ˈtə:nstail] n. Torniquete, *m.* (at entrance).
turntable [ˈtə:n,teibl] n. Placa (*f.*) *or* plataforma (*f.*) giratoria (revolving platform for trains). || Plato (*m.*) giratorio (in a record player). || Plataforma (*f.*) giratoria (any revolving platform).
turnup [ˈtə:nʌp] n. Vuelta, *f.* (on a trouser leg). || Vuelta, *f.* (in card games). || FAM. Pelea, *f.* (quarrel). || *To be a turnup for the books*, ser algo inesperado.
— Adj. Respingona: *turnup nose*, nariz respingona. || Alto, ta (collar).
turpentine [ˈtə:pəntain] n. Trementina, *f.* || *Oil of turpentine*, esencia (*f.*) de trementina, aguarrás, *m.*
turpitude [ˈtə:pitju:d] n. Infamia, *f.*, bajeza, *f.*
turps [ˈtə:ps] n. FAM. Trementina, *f.*, aguarrás, *m.*
turquoise [ˈtə:kwɔiz] n. Turquesa, *f.*
— Adj. Turquesa: *turquoise blue*, azul turquesa.
turret [ˈtʌrit] n. ARCH. Torreón, *m.* || MIL. Torreta, *f.* (gun platform on tank, plane). | Torre, *f.* (on a ship). || TECH. Portaherramientas, *m. inv.*
turreted [—id] adj. Con torreones (having turrets). || Con torretas (tank, plane). || Con torres (ship).
turret lathe [—leið] n. TECH. Torno (*m.*) de revólver.
turtle [ˈtə:tl] n. ZOOL. Tortuga (*f.*) de mar. || U. S. Tortuga, *f.* (tortoise). || *To turn turtle*, volcar, dar una vuelta de campana (cars), zozobrar, volcar (boats).
turtle [ˈtə:tl] v. intr. Cazar tortugas.
turtledove [—dʌv] n. Tórtola, *f.* (bird).
turtleneck [—nek] n. Cuello (*m.*) que sube ligeramente (collar). || U. S. Cuello (*m.*) vuelto (poloneck).
turtle shell [—ʃel] n. Carey, *m.*
turves [tə:vz] pl. n. See TURF.
Tuscan [ˈtʌskən] adj./n. Toscano, na.
Tuscany [—i] pr. n. GEOGR. Toscana, *f.*
tush [tʌʃ] n. Colmillo, *m.*, canino, *m.* (pointed tooth).
— Interj. ¡Bah!
tusk [tʌsk] n. Defensa, *f.*, colmillo, *m.* (of elephant, walrus, rhinoceros). || Colmillo, *m.* (of a boar). || TECH. Espiga, *f.* (in carpentry).
tusker [—ə*] n. Elefante (*m.*) *or* jabalí (*m.*) adulto que tiene defensas or colmillos.
tussah [ˈtʌsə] n. U. S. See TUSSORE.
tussle [ˈtʌsl] n. Pelea, *f.* (scuffle). || FIG. Agarrada, *f.* (dispute). | Lucha, *f.* (struggle).
tussle [ˈtʌsl] v. intr. Pelearse.
tussock [ˈtʌsək] n. Mata (*f.*) de hierba.
tussore [ˈtʌsə*] n. Tusor, *m.* (material). || Gusano (*m.*) de seda (silkworm).
tut [tʌt] interj. ¡Vaya!
tutelage [ˈtju:tilidʒ] n. Tutela, *f.*
tutelar [ˈtju:tilə*] adj. Tutelar.
tutelary [—ri] adj. Tutelar.
— N. Divinidad (*f.*) tutelar (deity). || Santo (*m.*) patrón (saint).
tutor [ˈtju:tə*] n. Preceptor, *m.*, ayo, *m.* (in a family). || Profesor (*m.*) particular (private teacher). || Tutor, *m.* (in a university). || Método, *m.* (book): *a guitar tutor*, un método para la guitarra. || JUR. Tutor, *m.* (guardian).
— OBSERV. El cargo de *tutor* no existe en las universidades de los países de lengua española. Lo desempeña un profesor que está encargado de un grupo pequeño de estudiantes.
tutor [ˈtju:tə*] v. tr. Dar clases privadas a, enseñar: *to tutor s.o. in Latin*, dar clases privadas de latín a alguien, enseñar latín a alguien. || JUR. Ser tutor de.
— V. intr. Dar clases privadas.
tutorage [—ridʒ] n. Cargo (*m.*) de preceptor (of a family tutor). || Cargo (*m.*) de tutor (of a university tutor). || Enseñanza, *f.*, instrucción, *f.* (teaching). || JUR. Tutela, *f.*
tutoress [—ris] n. Preceptora, *f.*, aya, *f.* (in a family). || JUR. Tutora, *f.* (guardian).
tutorial [tju:ˈtɔ:riəl] adj. Preceptoril (of a family tutor). || De tutor (of a university tutor). || Basado en la dirección de estudios por un tutor (of a system of tutors). || JUR. Tutelar.
— N. Clases (*f. pl.*) prácticas.
tutorship [ˈtju:təʃip] n. See TUTORAGE.
tutti-frutti [ˈtutiˈfruti] n. Tutti frutti, *m.*
tutu [ˈtu:tu:] n. Tonelete, *m.*, faldilla (*f.*) de bailarina, "tutú", *m.*
tuxedo [tʌkˈsi:dəu] n. U. S. Smoking, *m.*, esmoquin, *m.*
tuyère [ˈtwi:jə:] n. TECH. Tobera, *f.*
TV [ti:vi:] abbrev. of *television*. Televisión, *f.*
twaddle [ˈtwɔdl] n. Tonterías, *f. pl.*
twaddle [ˈtwɔdl] v. intr. Decir tonterías.
twain [twein] adj. Dos.
— N. Dos, *m.*
twang [twæŋ] n. Sonido, (*m.*) vibrante (sound). || Tañido, *m.* (of harp, guitar). || FAM. Gangueo, *m.* (of the voice).
twang [twæŋ] v. tr. Hacer vibrar (a stretched string). || Tañer (an instrument). || Pronunciar gangueando (to say with a twang). || Disparar (an arrow).
— V. intr. Vibrar (string, etc.). || Ganguear (voice). || *To twang on a guitar*, tañer la guitarra.
twangy [—i] adj. Elástico, ca (string). || Gangoso, sa (voice).
tweak [twi:k] n. Pellizco, *m.*
tweak [twi:k] v. tr. Pellizcar.
tweed [twi:d] n. "Tweed", *m.*, tejido (*m.*) de lana. || — Pl. Traje (*m. sing.*) de "tweed".
Tweedledum [—lˈdʌm] pr. n. FAM. *It's Tweedledum and Tweedledee*, olivo y aceituno todo es uno.
tweedy [—i] adj. Parecido al "tweed".
'tween [twi:n] prep. See BETWEEN.
tween deck [ˈtwi:ndek] n. MAR. Entrepuente, *m.*, entrecubierta, *f.*
tweet [twi:t] n. Pío pío, *m.* (of a bird). || TECH. Sonidos (*m. pl.*) agudos (in sound reproduction).
tweet [twi:t] v. intr. Piar (a bird).
tweeter [—ə*] n. TECH. Altavoz (*m.*) para los sonidos agudos.
tweezers [ˈtwi:zəz] pl. n. Pinzas, *f.* || *A pair of tweezers*, unas pinzas.
twelfth [ˈtwelfθ] adj. Duodécimo, ma.
— N. Duodécimo, ma; doce, *m.* & *f.* (in twelfth position). || Duodécimo, *m.*, duodécima parte, *f.* (fraction). || Doce: *Pius XII (the Twelfth)*, Pío XII [doce]. || Doce, *m.*, día (*m.*) doce (date): *I go on the twelfth*, me voy el doce.
Twelfth Day [—ˈdei] n. REL. Día (*m.*) de Reyes, Epifanía, *f.*
Twelfth Night [—ˈnait] n. REL. Noche (*f.*) de Reyes.
twelve [twelv] adj. Doce.
— N. Doce, *m.* || — REL. *The Twelve*, los doce apóstoles. || *Twelve o'clock*, las doce.
twelvemo [—məu] adj. PRINT. En dozavo.
— N. PRINT. Libro (*m.*) en dozavo.
twelvemonth [—mʌnθ] n. Año, *m.* || *This day twelvemonth*, de aquí a un año (future), hoy hace un año (past).
twelve-note [—nəut] or **twelve-tone** [—təun] adj. MUS. Dodecafónico, ca.
twentieth [ˈtwentiiθ] adj. Vigésimo, ma.
— N. Vigésimo, ma; veinte, *m.* & *f.* (in twentieth position). || Vigésima parte, *f.*, vigésimo, *m.* (fraction). || Veinte: *John XX (the Twentieth)*, Juan XX [veinte]. || Veinte, *m.*, día (*m.*) veinte (date): *today is the twentieth*, hoy estamos a veinte.
twenty [ˈtwenti] adj. Veinte.
— N. Veinte, *m.* || — *Temperatures in the twenties*, temperaturas de más de veinte grados. || *The twenties*, los años veinte. || *To be in one's twenties*, tener más de veinte años.
twenty-five [—ˈfaiv] adj. Veinticinco, veinte y cinco.
— N. Veinticinco, *m.*, veinte y cinco, *m.* || SP. *The twenty-five*, la línea de veintidós metros (line), el área de veintidós metros (area).
twentyfold [—fəuld] adv. Veinte veces.
— Adj. Veinte veces mayor.
twenty odd [—ɔd] adj. Veintitantos, tas.

twenty-one [— wʌn] adj. Veintiuno, na.
— N. Veintiuno, *m.* (number, game).
twerp [twə:p] n. FAM. Tío, *m.*, individuo, *m.*, tipo, *m.*: *stupid twerp*, tío estúpido. | Idiota, *m.*, imbécil, *m.*
twice [twais] adv. Dos veces: *think twice!*, ¡piénsalo dos veces!; *he came twice*, vino dos veces. || Dos veces, el doble de: *I have to pay twice what he pays*, tengo que pagar el doble de lo que paga. || — *I feel twice the man I used to*, me encuentro mucho mejor que antes (I feel better), me encuentro dos veces más hombre que antes. || *Twice as* o *twice as many* o *twice as much*, dos veces más: *he is twice as big as you*, es dos veces más grande que tú; *he earns twice as much as you*, gana dos veces más que tú. || *Twice over*, dos veces. || *Twice the amount* o *the sum*, el doble.
twice-told [—ˈtəuld] adj. Repetido, da. || Trillado, da (hackneyed). || *Twice-told tale*, cosa sabida, cosa archisabida.
twiddle [ˈtwidl] n. Vuelta, *f.* || *To give a knob a twiddle*, dar a un botón.
twiddle [ˈtwidl] v. tr. Dar vueltas a: *to twiddle the ring on one's finger*, dar vueltas al anillo en el dedo. || FIG. *To twiddle one's thumbs*, estar mano sobre mano.
— V. intr. *To twiddle with*, jugar con, juguetear con (to toy with).
twig [twig] n. Ramita, *f.* (small branch). || Rama, *f.* (branch): *a twig snapped under his foot*, una rama crujió bajo su pie. || ANAT. Vaso (*m.*) capilar. || Varilla (*f.*) de zahorí (divining rod). || — Pl. Leña (*f. sing.*) menuda.
twig [twig] v. tr. FAM. Fijarse en (to notice, to observe). || Darse cuenta de, caer en la cuenta de (to understand).
— V. intr. FAM. Caer en la cuenta.
twiggy [ˈtwigi] adj. Ramoso, sa (full of twigs). || Muy delgado (thin).
twilight [ˈtwailait] adj. Crepuscular: *twilight sleep*, sueño crepuscular.
— N. Crepúsculo, *m.* (dusk). || Media luz, *f.* (dim light). || FIG. Crepúsculo, *m.*, ocaso, *m.* (decadence).
twill [twil] n. Tela (*f.*) asargada *or* cruzada (fabric).
twill [twil] v. tr. Cruzar.
'twill [twil] contraction of *it will*.
twin [twin] adj. Gemelo, la; mellizo, za: *a twin sister*, una hermana gemela. || FIG. Inseparable (which always go together). | Doble (double). | Parecido, da (similar). || TECH. Gemelo, la: *twin tyres*, neumáticos gemelos. || BOT. Geminado, da. || MIN. Con maclas (crystals). || — *Twin beds*, camas separadas *or* gemelas. || *Twin cities*, ciudades hermanadas (in separate countries).
— N. Gemelo, la; mellizo, za: *identical twins*, gemelos homólogos. || Hermano (*m.*) gemelo, hermana (*f.*) gemela: *me and my twin*, yo y mi hermano gemelo. || MIN. Macla, *f.* || — *Siamese twins*, hermanos siameses. || ASTR. *The Twins*, Géminis, *m.*
twin [twin] v. tr. Ligar, vincular: *the projects are twinned in his plan*, en su plan los proyectos están vinculados. || Hermanar: *to twin two cities*, hermanar dos ciudades.
— V. intr. Dar a luz a mellizos *or* gemelos (a woman). || Parir dos crías al mismo tiempo (an animal). || MIN. Maclarse (crystals). || *To twin with s.o.*, ser gemelo *or* mellizo de alguien.
twinborn [—bɔ:n] adj. Gemelo, la; mellizo, za.
twin-cylinder [—ˈsilində*] adj. De dos cilindros.
twine [twain] n. Bramante, *m.*, guita, *f.* (cord). || Retorcimiento, *m.*, retorcedura, *f.* (twist). || Enmarañamiento, *m.*, enredo, *m.* (tangle). || Meandro, *m.* (of a river).
twine [twain] v. tr. Retorcer, torcer (to twist): *to twine strands*, torcer hebras. || Trenzar, entretejer (to interlace): *to twine a garland*, trenzar una guirnalda. || Rodear con: *she twined her arms round* o *about him*, le rodeó con los brazos. || Ceñir (to encircle). || Enrollar (to wind).
— V. intr. Enroscarse: *the ivy twined around the tree trunk*, la yedra se enroscaba en el tronco. || Serpentear (road, river). || Enrollarse (to coil).
twin-engine [ˈtwinˈendʒin] adj. AVIAT. Bimotor, ra.
twiner [ˈtwainə*] n. BOT. Planta (*f.*) trepadora.
twinge [twindʒ] n. Punzada, *f.* (sudden sharp pain). || FIG. Arrebato, *m.*, acceso, *m.*: *a twinge of anger, of jealousy*, un arrebato de ira, de celos. || *A twinge of conscience*, un remordimiento.
twinge [twindʒ] v. tr./intr. Dar punzadas: *my leg twinges*, la pierna me da punzadas. || FIG. Remorder.
twining [ˈtwainiŋ] adj. BOT. Trepador, ra. || Sinuoso, sa (river).
twin-jet [ˈtwinˈdʒet] adj. Birreactor, ra. || *Twin-jet plane*, birreactor, *m.*
twinkle [ˈtwiŋkl] n. Centelleo, *m.*, parpadeo, *m.* || Guiño, *m.* (wink). || Brillo, *m.* (brightness). || FIG. *In a twinkle*, en un abrir y cerrar de ojos.
twinkle [ˈtwiŋkl] v. intr. Centellear, parpadear (stars). || Brillar (eyes). || Moverse rápidamente (feet).
— V. tr. Despedir destellos de [luz]. || Hacer brillar (eyes).
twinkling [ˈtwiŋkliŋ] n. Centelleo, *m.*, parpadeo, *m.* (of stars). || Parpadeo, *m.* (of eyelids). || Brillo, *m.* (of eyes). || FIG. *In the twinkling of an eye*, en un abrir y cerrar de ojos.
— Adj. Centelleante (stars). || Brillante (eyes).
twin-screw [ˈtwinˈscru:] adj. MAR. De dos hélices (ship).
twinset [ˈtwinset] n. Conjunto, *m.*
twirl [twə:l] n. Vuelta, *f.*, giro, *m.* (rotation). || Rasgo, *m.* (with a pen). || Voluta, *f.* (of smoke). || Pirueta, *f.* (of dancers). || Molinete, *m.* (in fencing).
twirl [twə:l] v. tr. Dar vueltas a (to cause to rotate): *to twirl a lasso*, dar vueltas a un lazo. || Atusarse (a moustache). || Retorcer (to twist). || U. S. Lanzar (in baseball). || FIG. FAM. *To twirl one's thumbs*, estar mano sobre mano.
— V. intr. Dar vueltas, girar (to rotate).
twist [twist] n. Torsión, *f.*, torcimiento, *m.* || Torzal, *m.* (of yarn). || Trenza, *f.* (tress). || Cucurucho, *m.* (of paper). || Andullo, *m.*, rollo, *m.* (of tobacco). || Rosca (*f.*) de pan (of bread). || Vuelta, *f.*: *the twists of wire on a coil*, las vueltas del alambre en una bobina. || Nudo, *m.* (knot). || Contorsión, *f.* (of the face). || Rasgo, *m.*, peculiaridad, *f.* (of s.o.'s character). || Deformación, *f.*: *mental twist*, deformación mental. || Inclinación, *f.*, tendencia, *f.* (tendency): *a criminal twist*, una tendencia criminal. || Lance (*m.*) imprevisto (in a story). || Tergiversación, *f.*, desvirtuación, *f.* (distortion of meaning). || Vuelta, *f.*, recodo, *m.* (of a road). || Alabeo, *m.*, abarquillamiento, *m.* (warp). || Efecto, *m.*: *to give a ball a twist*, dar efecto a una pelota. || Tirabuzón, *m.* (in diving). || MED. Esguince, *m.*, torcedura, *f.* (of the ankle). || Trampa, *f.* (cheat). || *To give one's ankle a twist*, torcerse un tobillo.
twist [twist] v. tr. Torcer, retorcer: *to twist a wire*, retorcer un alambre. || Retorcer: *to twist strands together*, retorcer hilos. || Trenzar (a rope, hair). || Estrujar, escurrir (washing). || Enrollar: *to twist tobacco*, enrollar tabaco; *to twist a rope around a post*, enrollar una cuerda en un poste. || Entretejer (to intertwine). || Retorcer: *he twisted my arm*, me retorció el brazo. || MED. Torcer: *to twist one's ankle*, torcerse el tobillo. | Dislocar (one's knee). || Dar efecto a (ball). || Deformar (to deform). || Tergiversar, desvirtuar (to distort): *to twist the meaning of s.o.'s words*, tergiversar el sentido de lo que dice uno. || Combar, alabear, abarquillar (to warp). || FAM. Timar, estafar (to swindle). || — *To twist one's face*, torcer el gesto. || FIG. *To twist s.o. round one's little finger*, see FINGER.
— V. intr. Torcerse, retorcerse. || Dar vueltas (to rotate). || Retorcerse, contorsionarse (to writhe). || Enrollarse, enroscarse (to coil). || Serpentear, dar vueltas (a road). || Escurrirse, colarse (*through*, por) [to slip]. || *To twist and turn*, serpentear.
twist drill [—dril] n. TECH. Broca (*f.*) helicoidal.
twister [ˈtwistə*] n. Torcedor, ra (person who twists). || Torcedor, *m.* (machine). || FAM. Timador, ra; estafador, ra (cheat). || SP. Pelota (*f.*) lanzada con efecto (ball). || Rompecabezas, *m. inv.* (baffling problem). || U. S. Ciclón, *m.*, tornado, *m.* (cyclone).
twisty [ˈtwisti] adj. Torcido, da; retorcido, da (having many twists). || Tortuoso, sa: *a twisty path*, un camino tortuoso. || Retorcido, da (complicated).
twit [twit] n. FAM. Imbécil, *m.* & *f.*, majadero, ra (fool). || Censura, *f.*, reprensión, *f.* (reproach). || Mofa, *f.* (taunt).
twit [twit] v. tr. Echar en cara, censurar (to reproach): *to twit s.o. with sth.*, echar algo en cara a alguien. || Ridiculizar, tomar el pelo a, mofarse de (to taunt).
twitch [twitʃ] n. Tirón, *m.* (tug). || Tirón, *m.*, punzada, *f.* (pain): *his leg gave a twitch*, le dio un tirón la pierna. || Tic, *m.*, contracción (*f.*) nerviosa (nervous tic). || Retortijón, *m.* (in the stomach). || BOT. Grama, *f.* || VET. Acial, *m.*
twitch [twitʃ] v. tr. Tirar bruscamente de (to tug). || Crispar (hands, etc.). || *To twitch sth. off s.o.*, arrancar algo a alguien de un tirón.
— V. intr. Crisparse (with spasmodic jerks). || *To twitch at*, dar un tirón a.
twitch grass [ˈtwitʃgrɑ:s] n. BOT. Grama, *f.*
twitter [ˈtwitə*] n. Gorjeo, *m.* (of birds). || FIG. FAM. Agitación, *f.*, nerviosismo, *m.*
twitter [ˈtwitə*] v. intr. Gorjear (a bird). || Ponerse nervioso, sa (to be nervous). || Temblar, agitarse (to tremble).
'twixt [twikst] prep. (Ant.). See BETWIXT.
two [tu:] adj. Dos.
— N. Dos, *m.* (number, card, figure). || — *By twos*, de dos en dos. || *In two*, en dos. || *In twos*, de dos en dos. || *They are two of a kind*, son tal para cual. || *To go two and two*, ir de dos en dos. || *To have two of everything*, tener todo por duplicado. || FIG. *To put two and two together*, atar cabos: *putting two and two together I concluded that*, atando cabos llegué a la conclusión de que. || *Two by two*, de dos en dos. || *Two o'clock*, las dos.
two-barrelled [ˈtu:ˈbærəld] adj. De dos cañones (gun).
two-bit [ˈtu:ˈbit] adj. U. S. FAM. Insignificante (insignificant). | Barato, ta (cheap).
two-by-four [ˈtu:baiˈfɔ:] adj. U. S. FAM. Insignificante (insignificant). | Estrecho, cha; angosto, ta (street, room, etc.).
two-chamber [ˈtu:ˈtʃeimbə*] adj. Bicameral.

two-cleft [ˈtu:kleft] adj. Bífido, da.
two-cycle [ˈtu:ˌsaikl] adj. De dos tiempos (engine).
two-decker [ˈtu:dekə*] n. See DOUBLE-DECKER.
two-dimensional [ˈtu:daiˈmenʃənəl] adj. De dos dimensiones.
two-door [ˈtu:dɔ:] adj. De dos puertas.
two-edged [ˈtu:ˈedʒd] adj. De dos filos.
two-engined [ˈtu:ˈendʒind] adj. AVIAT. Bimotor.
two-faced [ˈtu:ˈfeist] adj. De dos caras (with two surfaces). || FIG. Falso, sa (deceitful).
two-fisted [ˈtu:ˈfistid] adj. U. S. Fuerte.
twofold [ˈtu:fəuld] adj. Doble (double).
— Adv. Dos veces.
two-handed [ˈtu:ˈhændid] adj. De dos manos (used with both hands). || Para dos manos (tool). || Ambidextro, tra (ambidextrous). || Para dos personas (card games).
two-headed [ˈtu:ˈhedid] adj. Bicéfalo, la.
two-legged [ˈtu:ˈlegid] adj. Bípedo, da; de dos piernas.
two-master [ˈtu:ˈmɑ:stə*] n. Barco (*m.*) de dos palos (sailing ship).
twopence [ˈtʌpəns] pl. n. Dos peniques, *m.*
twopenny [ˈtʌpəni] adj. De dos peniques, que cuesta dos peniques. || FAM. De cuatro perras, barato, ta (cheap).
twopenny-halfpenny [—ˈheipni] adj. De dos peniques y medio. || FAM. De cuatro perras, barato, ta (cheap). | Insignificante.
two-phase [ˈtu:ˈfeiz] adj. ELECTR. Bifásico, ca; difásico, ca.
two-piece [ˈtu:ˈpi:s] adj. De dos piezas.
two-ply [ˈtu:plai] adj. De dos cabos (wool, wire). || De dos capas (wood). || De dos tramas (carpet).
two-pole [ˈtu:pəul] adj. Bipolar.
two-seater [ˈtu:ˈsi:tə*] n. Dos plazas, *m.*, biplaza, *m.*
two-sided [ˈtu:ˈsaidid] adj. Bilateral. || FIG. Que tiene dos aspectos, doble (question). | Falso, sa (person).
twosome [ˈtu:səm] n. Pareja, *f.* (couple, pair). || SP. Simple, *m.*
two-step [ˈtu:step] n. "Two-step", *m.* (dance).
two-storey [ˈtu:ˈstɔ:ri] adj. De dos pisos (house).
two-stroke [ˈtu:strəuk] adj. De dos tiempos (engine).
two-time [ˈtu:ˈtaim] v. tr. U. S. FAM. Engañar (to be unfaithful to). | Traicionar (to double-cross).
two-timer [ˈtu:ˈtaimə*] n. U. S. FAM. Infiel, *m.* & *f.* (husband, wife, etc.). | Traidor, ra (double-crosser).
two-tone [ˈtu:təun] adj. De dos tonos, bicolor.
'twould [twud] contraction of *it would.*
two-way [ˈtu:ˈwei] adj. De doble dirección (street). || TECH. De doble paso (valve). | De dos direcciones (switch). || Mutuo, tua (mutual). || *Two-way radio,* aparato emisor y receptor.
tycoon [taiˈku:n] n. Magnate, *m.*
tying [ˈtaiiŋ] pres. part. See TIE.
tyke [ˈtaik] n. FAM. Chucho, *m.* (dog). || Niño (*m.*) travieso (mischievous child). || Pillo, lla; pícaro, ra (rascal).
tymbal [ˈtimbəl] n. Timbal, *m.* (kettledrum).
tympan [ˈtimpən] n. Tímpano, *m.*
tympani [—i] pl. n. MUS. Tímpanos, *m.*
tympanic [timˈpænik] adj. Timpánico, ca.
tympanist [ˈtimpənist] n. MUS. Timbalero, *m.*, atabalero, *m.*
tympanites [ˌtimpəˈnaiti:z] n. MED. Timpanitis, *f.*, timpanismo, *m.*, timpanización, *f.*
tympanum [ˈtimpənəm] n. ARCH. ANAT. Tímpano, *m.* || MUS. Tímpano, *m.*, atabal, *m.*
— OBSERV. El plural de la palabra inglesa es *tympanums* o *tympana.*
Tyndall effect [ˈtindliˌfekt] n. Tyndalización, *f.*
typal [ˈtaipl] adj. Típico, ca. || TECH. Tipográfico, ca.
type [taip] n. Tipo, *m.*, clase, *f.*, género, *m.* (kind, sort): *I like this type of music,* me gusta esta clase de música. || Tipo, *m.*, sujeto, *m.*, individuo, *m.* (person): *you are an odd type,* eres un tipo raro. || Tipo, *m.*, modelo, *m.*: *a new type of aircraft,* un nuevo modelo de avión. || Estilo, *m.* (person's character): *I don't like his type,* no me gusta su estilo. || BIOL. Tipo, *m.* || PRINT. Tipo, *m.*, carácter, *m.* | Tipos, *m. pl.*, caracteres, *m. pl.*: *the type is too small to read,* los caracteres son demasiado pequeños para que se puedan leer. || — PRINT. *Bold* o *heavy type,* negrita, *f.* || *She is the motherly type,* es muy maternal.
type [taip] v. tr. Escribir a máquina, mecanografiar (using a typewriter). || Clasificar (to classify). || Representar el tipo de, tipificar, simbolizar (to represent, to symbolize). || MED. Determinar el grupo sanguíneo de (blood).
— V. intr. Escribir a máquina: *can you type?,* ¿sabe usted escribir a máquina?
typecast [—kɑ:st] v. tr. Encasillar (an actor).
typecast [—kɑ:st] adj. Encasillado, da (actor).
typeface [—feis] n. PRINT. Tipografía, *f.* | Tipo, *m.*, carácter, *m.* (type).
type founder [—ˌfaundə*] n. PRINT. Fundidor (*m.*) de tipos de imprenta.
type gauge [—geidʒ] n. PRINT. Tipómetro, *m.*
type-high [—ˈhai] adj. De la altura normal del tipo.
typescript [—skript] n. Texto (*m.*) escrito a máquina *or* mecanografiado.
typeset [—ˌset] v. tr. PRINT. Componer.
typesetter [—sˌetə*] n. PRINT. Cajista, *m.* & *f.* (person). | Máquina (*f.*) para componer tipos (machine).
typesetting [—ˌsetiŋ] n. PRINT. Composición, *f.*
typewrite* [—rait] v. tr. Mecanografiar, escribir a máquina.
— V. intr. Escribir a máquina.
— OBSERV. Pret. **typewrote;** p. p. **typewritten.**
typewriter [—ˌraitə*] n. Máquina (*f.*) de escribir. || Mecanógrafo, fa (person).
typewriting [—ˌraitiŋ] n. Mecanografía, *f.* (typing). || Texto (*m.*) mecanografiado *or* escrito a máquina (piece of work).
typewritten [—ˌritən] adj. Mecanografiado, da; escrito a máquina.
typhogenic [ˌtaifəˈdʒenik] adj. MED. Tifogénico, ca.
typhoid [ˈtaifɔid] n. MED. Fiebre (*f.*) tifoidea, tifoidea, *f.* (typhoid fever).
— Adj. MED. Tifoideo, a: *typhoid fever,* fiebre tifoidea.
typhoidal [taiˈfɔidl] adj. MED. Tifoideo, a.
typhoon [taiˈfu:n] n. Tifón, *m.*
typhous [ˈtaifəs] adj. Tífico, ca.
typhus [ˈtaifəs] n. MED. Tifus, *m.*
typic [ˈtipik] adj. BIOL. Característico, ca.
typical [—əl] adj. Típico, ca; característico, ca.
typification [ˌtipifiˈkeiʃən] n. Simbolización, *f.* || Tipo, *m.* (type).
typify [ˈtipifai] v. tr. Simbolizar: *the dove typifies peace,* la paloma simboliza la paz. || Representar el tipo de, tipificar, caracterizar (to exemplify). || BIOL. Ser el tipo de.
typing [ˈtaipiŋ] n. Mecanografía, *f.*
typist [ˈtaipist] n. Mecanógrafo, fa. || *Shorthand typist,* taquimecanógrafo, fa.
typographer [taiˈpɔgrəfə*] n. Tipógrafo, fa.
typographic [ˌtaipəˈgræfik] or **typographical** [—əl] adj. Tipográfico, ca. || PRINT. *Typographical error,* errata, *f.*, error (*m.*) de imprenta gazapo, *m.* (fam.).
typography [taiˈpɔgrəfi] n. Tipografía, *f.*
typology [taiˈpɔlədʒi] n. Tipología, *f.*
tyrannic [tiˈrænik] or **tyrannical** [—əl] adj. Tiránico, ca.
tyrannicide [tiˈrænisaid] n. Tiranicidio, *m.* (crime). || Tiranicida, *m.* & *f.* (person).
tyrannize [ˈtirənaiz] v. tr. Tiranizar.
— V. intr. Ser un tirano (to be a tyrant). || *To tyrannize over,* tiranizar.
tyrannous [ˈtirənəs] adj. Tiránico, ca.
tyranny [ˈtirəni] n. Tiranía, *f.*
tyrant [ˈtairənt] n. Tirano, *m.*
tyre [ˈtaiə*] n. Neumático, *m.* [*Amer.*, llanta, *f.*] (of rubber): *spare tyre,* neumático de repuesto. || Llanta, *f.* (of iron). || — *Non-skid tyre,* neumático antideslizante. | *Tyre burst,* reventón, *m.* || *Tyre lever,* desmontable (*m.*) para neumáticos.
tyre [ˈtaiə*] v. tr. Poner un neumático a.
Tyre [ˈtaiə*] pr. n. Tiro, *m.*
Tyrian [ˈtiriən] adj./n. Tirio, ria.
tyro [ˈtaiərəu] n. Aprendiz, *m.*, principiante, *m.* (beginner).
Tyrol [ˈtirəl] pr. n. GEOGR. Tirol, *m.*
Tyrolean [tiˈrəuliən] or **Tyrolese** [ˌtirəˈli:z] adj./n. Tirolés, esa.
tyrothricin [ˌtaiərəˈθraisin] n. CHEM. Tirotricina, *f.*
Tyrrhenian Sea [taiˈri:njənˈsi:] pr. n. GEOGR. Mar (*m.*) Tirreno.
tzar [zɑ:] n. Zar, *m.*
tzarina [zɑ:ˈri:na] n. Zarina, *f.*
tzetze [ˈtsetsi] n. ZOOL. Mosca (*f.*) tse-tsé, tse-tsé, *f.*
tzigane [tsiˈgɑ:n] adj./n. Cíngaro, ra; gitano, na.

U

u [ju:] n. U, *f.* (letter): *a capital u*, una u mayúscula.
ubiquitous [ju:'bikwitəs] adj. Ubicuo, cua; omnipresente (God). || Que se encuentra por todas partes: *a ubiquitous species*, una especie que se encuentra por todas partes.
ubiquity [ju:'bikwiti] n. Ubicuidad, *f.* || REL. Ubicuidad, *f.*, omnipresencia, *f.*
U-boat ['ju:bəut] n. MAR. Submarino (*m.*) alemán.
udder ['ʌdə*] n. Ubre, *f.* (of cows, etc.).
UFO ['ju:fəu] abbrev. of *unidentified flying object*. Ovni, *m.*, objeto (*m.*) volador no identificado.
ugh! [uh] interj. ¡Uf! (of repugnance).
uglification [ˌʌglifi'keiʃən] n. Afeamiento, *m.*
uglify ['ʌglifai] v. tr. Afear.
ugliness ['ʌglinis] n. Fealdad, *f.*
ugly ['ʌgli] adj. Feo, a (unpleasant to look at): *he is ugly without his beard*, está feo sin barba. || FIG. Peligroso, sa; feo, a (dangerous): *an ugly situation*, una situación peligrosa. | Feo, a (morally offensive): *an ugly habit*, una costumbre fea. | Desagradable (unpleasant). | Lamentable, deplorable: *an ugly incident*, un incidente deplorable. || — FIG. *An ugly customer*, un tipo de cuidado. | *To be as ugly as sin*, ser más feo que un pecado. | *To be in an ugly mood*, estar de un humor de perros. | *To turn ugly*, ponerse furioso (a person), ponerse feo (a situation, wound, etc.).
ugly duckling [—'dʌkliŋ] n. Patito (*m.*) feo.
uhlan [u'lɑ:n] n. MIL. Ulano, *m.*
ukase [ju:'keiz] n. Ucase, *m.*, ukase, *m.*
ukelele [ˌju:kə'leili] n. MUS. Ukelele, *m.*, ukulele, *m.*
Ukraine [ju:'krein] pr. n. GEOGR. Ucrania, *f.*
Ukrainian [—jən] adj./n. Ucraniano, na; ucranio, nia.
ukulele [ˌju:kə'leili] n. MUS. Ukulele, *m.*, ukelele, *m.*
ulama ['u:ləmə] n. Ulema, *m.*

— OBSERV. El plural de la palabra inglesa es *ulama* o *ulamas*.

ulcer ['ʌlsə*] n. MED. Úlcera, *f.*: *stomach ulcer*, úlcera de estómago. || FIG. Cáncer, *m.* (corrupting force).
ulcerate ['ʌlsəreit] v. tr. Ulcerar.
— V. intr. Ulcerarse.
ulceration [ˌʌlsə'reiʃən] n. MED. Ulceración, *f.*
ulcerative ['ʌlsərətiv] adj. MED. Ulcerativo, va; ulcerante.
ulcerous ['ʌlsərəs] adj. MED. Ulceroso, sa.
ulema ['u:limə] n. Ulema, *m.*

— OBSERV. El plural de la palabra inglesa es *ulema* o *ulemas*.

ullage ['ʌlidʒ] n. Merma, *f.* (loss). || *Filling up of the ullage*, atestadura, *f.* (of a barrel).
ulmaceae [ʌl'meisii:] pl. n. BOT. Ulmáceas, *f.*
ulna ['ʌlnə] n. ANAT. Cúbito, *m.*

— OBSERV. El plural de *ulna* es *ulnae* o *ulnas*.

ulnar ['ʌlnə*] adj. ANAT. Cubital.
ulster ['ʌlstə*] n. Abrigo (*m.*) amplio y largo.
Ulster ['ʌlstə*] pr. n. GEOGR. Ulster, *m.* (province). || FAM. Irlanda (*f.*) del Norte (Northern Ireland).
ulterior [ʌl'tiəriə*] adj. Ulterior. || Oculto, ta (undisclosed). || *Ulterior motive*, segunda intención.
ulteriorly [—li] adv. Ulteriormente, más tarde.
ultimate ['ʌltimit] adj. Último, ma (last in order). || Final: *ultimate purpose*, objetivo final. || Definitivo, va: *ultimate decision*, decisión definitiva. || Esencial, fundamental (fundamental, essential): *the ultimate truth*, la verdad fundamental. || Máximo, ma (maximum). || CHEM. Elemental: *ultimate analysis*, análisis elemental.
— N. No va más, *m.*: *the ultimate in sports cars*, el no va más en coches deportivos. || Lo absoluto.
ultimately [—li] adv. Finalmente, al final. || En el fondo (basically). || *To ultimately do sth.*, acabar por hacer algo *or* haciendo algo.
ultimatum [ˌʌlti'meitəm] n. Ultimátum, *m.*: *to give s.o. an ultimatum*, dirigir a alguien un ultimátum.

— OBSERV. El plural de la palabra inglesa es *ultimatums* o *ultimata*.

ultimo ['ʌltiməu] adv. COMM. El mes pasado. || COMM. *On the 10th ultimo*, el pasado día 10, el 10 del mes pasado *or* próximo pasado, el 10 próximo pasado.
ultra ['ʌltrə] adj. Ultra (extreme in opinions). || Extremo, ma; excesivo, va.
— N. Ultra, *m.* & *f.*
ultracentrifuge ['ʌltrə'sentrifju:dʒ] n. Ultracentrifugadora, *f.*
ultrafashionable ['ʌltrə'fæʃənəbl] adj. Muy de moda (clothes, etc.). || *To be ultrafashionable*, ir a la última moda (person).
ultraism ['ʌltrəizəm] n. Extremismo, *m.*
ultraist ['ʌltrəist] adj./n. Extremista.

ultramarine [ˌʌltrəmə'ri:n] n. Azul (*m.*) de ultramar *or* ultramarino (colour).
— Adj. Ultramarino, na; de ultramar.
ultramicroscope ['ʌltrə'maikrəskəup] n. Ultramicroscopio, *m.*
ultramodern ['ʌltrə'mɔdən] adj. Ultramoderno, na.
ultramontane [ˌʌltrə'mɔntein] adj./n. Ultramontano, na.
ultramontanism ['ʌltrə'mɔntinizəm] n. Ultramontanismo, *m.*
ultramundane ['ʌltrə'mʌndein] adj. Ultramundano, na.
ultrared ['ʌltrə'red] adj. PHYS. Ultrarrojo, ja; infrarrojo, ja.
ultrashort ['ʌltrə'ʃɔ:t] adj. PHYS. Ultracorto, ta (wave).
ultrasonic ['ʌltrə'sɔnik] adj. Ultrasónico, ca; supersónico, ca.
ultrasound ['ʌltrə'saund] n. Ultrasonido, *m.*
ultraviolet ['ʌltrə'vaiəlit] adj. Ultravioleta, ultraviolado, da. || *Ultraviolet rays*, rayos ultravioletas.
ultravirus ['ʌltrə'vaiərəs] n. BIOL. Ultravirus, *m.*
ululate ['ju:ljuleit] v. intr. Ulular, aullar.
ululation [ju:lju'leiʃən] n. Ululación, *f.*, ululato, *m.*, aullido, *m.*
ulva ['əlvə] n. BOT. Ulva, *f.* (seaweed).
Ulysses [ju:'lisi:z] pr. n. Ulises, *m.*
umbellifer [ʌm'belifə*] n. BOT. Umbelífera, *f.*
umbelliferae [ˌʌmbe'lifəri:] pl. n. BOT. Umbelíferas, *f.*
umbelliferous [ˌʌmbe'lifərəs] adj. BOT. Umbelífero, ra.
umbelliform [ʌm'belifɔ:m] adj. Umbeliforme.
umber ['ʌmbə*] n. Tierra (*f.*) de sombra.
— Adj. Ocre oscuro.
umbilical [ʌm'bilikəl] adj. ANAT. Umbilical: *umbilical cord*, cordón umbilical.
umbilicate [ʌm'bilikit] adj. Umbilicado, da.
umbilicus [ʌm'bilikəs] n. ANAT. BOT. Ombligo, *m.*

— OBSERV. El plural de *umbilicus* es *umbilici* o *umbilicuses*.

umbrage ['ʌmbridʒ] n. Resentimiento, *m.* (resentment). || Sombra, *f.* (shade). || *To take umbrage at*, ofenderse por, quedar resentido por.
umbrageous [ʌm'breidʒəs] adj. Sombrío, a (shady). || Resentido, da (resentful).
umbrella [ʌm'brelə] n. Paraguas, *m. inv.* (against rain). || Sombrilla, *f.* (for shade). || ZOOL. Umbrela, *f.* || AVIAT. Cobertura (*f.*) aérea. || — *Beach umbrella*, quitasol, *m.* || *Umbrella stand*, paragüero, *m.*
umbrella tree [—tri:] n. BOT. Magnolia, *f.*
Umbria ['ʌmbriə] pr. n. GEOGR. Umbría, *f.*
umlaut ['umlaut] n. GRAMM. Metafonía, *f.* (phenomenon). | Diéresis, *f.* (symbol).
umpirage ['ʌmpairidʒ] n. Arbitraje, *m.*
umpire ['ʌmpaiə*] n. Árbitro, *m.* || JUR. Tercer árbitro, *m.*
umpire ['ʌmpaiə*] v. tr. Arbitrar.
— V. intr. Actuar de árbitro, ser árbitro.
umpteen ['ʌmpti:n] adj. FAM. Muchísimos, mas; no sé cuántos, tas: *umpteen times*, muchísimas veces, no sé cuántas veces.
umpteenth [—θ] adj. FAM. Enésimo, ma: *for the umpteenth time*, por enésima vez.
U. N. ['ju:'en] n. O.N.U., *f.* (United Nations): *the U.N. headquarters*, la sede de la O.N.U.
'un [ən] pron. FAM. *A bad 'un*, un tiparraco, un bicho malo. | *A little 'un*, un pequeñín, un chiquitín (baby, small child). | *A rum 'un*, un tipo curioso, un tipo raro.

— OBSERV. *'Un* es un barbarismo empleado en lugar del pronombre *one*.

unabashed ['ʌnə'bæʃt] adj. Imperturbable. || Descarado, da (shameless).
unabated ['ʌnə'beitid] adj. Constante, que no disminuye: *with unabated interest*, con un interés constante.
unabbreviated ['ʌnə'bri:vieitid] adj. Sin abreviar, entero, ra; con todas las letras (name). || Completo, ta; íntegro, gra (text).
unabetted ['ʌnə'betid] adj. Sin ayuda, solo, la.
unabiding ['ʌnə'baidiŋ] adj. Efímero, ra.
unable ['ʌn'eibl] adj. Incapaz. || *To be unable to do sth.*, no poder hacer algo, ser incapaz de hacer algo (physical inability), no poder hacer algo, verse en la imposibilidad de hacer algo (because of circumstances).
unabridged ['ʌnə'bridʒd] adj. Íntegro, gra; completo, ta: *unabridged text*, texto íntegro.
unaccented ['ʌnæk'sentid] or **unaccentuated** [ˌʌnæk'sentueitid] adj. Átono, na; sin acento, inacentuado, da (syllable, etc.).
unacceptable ['ʌnək'septəbl] adj. Inaceptable: *unacceptable to me*, inaceptable para mí.

unaccommodating [ˈʌnəˈkɔmədeitiŋ] adj. Poco complaciente. || Poco sociable, poco tratable.
unaccompanied [ˈʌnəˈkʌmpənid] adj. Solo, la; que no está acompañado. || Mus. Sin acompañamiento, solo, la.
unaccomplished [ˈʌnəˈkɔmpliʃt] adj. Incompleto, ta; sin acabar (not finished). || Sin talento (having no talent). || No realizado, da; sin realizar (ambitions, etc.).
unaccountable [ˈʌnəˈkauntəbl] adj. Inexplicable (inexplicable). || Extraño, ña (strange). || Irresponsable, libre (responsible to no one).
unaccounted [ˈʌnəˈkauntid] adj. *Twelve passengers are unaccounted for*, no se tiene noticia de doce pasajeros, han desaparecido doce pasajeros. || *Unaccounted for*, inexplicado, da (unexplained). || *Unaccounted for in the balance sheet*, que no figura en el balance.
unaccredited [ˈʌnəˈkreditid] adj. No acreditado, da (person). || Que no es fidedigno (source of information).
unaccustomed [ˈʌnəˈkʌstəmd] adj. Inacostumbrado, da; inhabitual, desacostumbrado, da; insólito, ta (unusual). || No *or* poco acostumbrado, da (not accustomed): *she is unaccustomed to cooking*, no está acostumbrada a guisar.
unachievable [ˈʌnəˈtʃiːvəbl] adj. Irrealizable.
unacknowledged [ˈʌnəkˈnɔlidʒd] adj. No reconocido, da (not recognized). || Sin contestar (a letter).
unacquaintance [ˈʌnəˈkweintəns] n. Ignorancia, *f.*, desconocimiento, *m.*
unacquainted [ˈʌnəˈkweintid] adj. *To be unacquainted with*, no conocer a (a person), desconocer, ignorar, no conocer (sth.).
unacquired [ˈʌnəˈkwaiəd] adj. No adquirido, da; innato, ta; natural.
unadaptable [ˈʌnəˈdæptəbl] adj. Inadaptable, incapaz de adaptarse.
unadapted [ˈʌnəˈdæptid] adj. Inadaptado, da.
unadmired [ˈʌnədˈmaiəd] adj. Desconocido, da; ignorado, da.
unadmiring [ˈʌnədˈmaiəriŋ] adj. Poco admirativo, va.
unadoptable [ˈʌnəˈdɔptəbl] adj. Inadoptable.
unadopted [ˈʌnəˈdɔptid] adj. Rechazado, da; no adoptado, da (measures). || Sin mantener (roads).
unadorned [ˈʌnəˈdɔːnd] adj. Sin adorno; sencillo, lla. || Fig. Escueto, ta (style, truth).
unadulterated [ˈʌnəˈdʌltəreitid] adj. Sin mezcla (not mixed). || Puro, ra (pure).
unadvisable [ˈʌnədˈvaizəbl] adj. Poco aconsejable, imprudente (action). || Terco, ca (person).
unadvised [ˈʌnədˈvaizd] adj. Imprudente, irreflexivo, va (ill-considered). || *To do sth. unadvised*, hacer algo sin pedir consejo.
unaesthetic [ˈʌniːsˈθetik] adj. Antiestético, ca.
unaffected [ˈʌnəˈfektid] adj. No afectado, da [*by*, por]. || Insensible [*by*, a], indiferente [*by*, a] (indifferent). || Sin afectación, natural, sencillo, lla (without affectation). || Sincero, ra (sincere).
unaffectedness [—nis] n. Naturalidad, *f.*, sencillez, *f.* (simplicity). || Sinceridad, *f.* (sincerity).
unafraid [ˈʌnəˈfreid] adj. Sin miedo (*of*, a).
unaggressive [ˈʌnəˈgresiv] adj. Poco agresivo, va. || Pacífico, ca.
unaided [ˈʌnˈeidid] adv. Sin ayuda, solo, la.
unalarmed [ˈʌnəˈlɑːmd] adj. Tranquilo, la. || *To be unalarmed about sth.*, no preocuparse por algo.
unalienable [ˈʌnˈeiljənəbl] adj. Inalienable, no enajenable.
unallowable [ˈʌnəˈlauəbl] adj. Inadmisible.
unallowed [ˈʌnəˈlaud] adj. Prohibido, da.
unalloyed [ˈʌnəˈlɔid] adj. Sin mezcla, puro, ra. || Puro, ra (metal).
unalterable [ˈʌnˈɔltərəbl] adj. Inalterable, invariable.
unalterableness [—nis] n. Inalterabilidad, *f.*
unaltered [ˈʌnˈɔːltəd] adj. Inalterado, da.
unambiguous [ˈʌnæmˈbigjuəs] adj. Inequívoco, ca; sin ambigüedad.
unambitious [ˈʌnæmˈbiʃəs] adj. Poco ambicioso, sa; sin ambiciones.
un-American [ˈʌnəˈmerikən] adj. Antiamericano, na (anti-American). || Poco americano, na (unlike an American).
unamiable [ʌnˈeimjəbl] adj. Poco amable.
unanimated [ˈʌnˈænimeitid] adj. Inanimado, da (inanimate). || Poco animado, da (dull). || *Unanimated by any ambition*, sin ambición alguna.
unanimism [juːˈnænimizəm] n. Unanimismo, *m.*
unanimity [ˌjuːnəˈnimiti] n. Unanimidad, *f.*
unanimous [juːˈnæniməs] adj. Unánime.
unanimously [—li] adv. Por unanimidad: *to approve a decision unanimously*, aprobar una decisión por unanimidad. || De común acuerdo (with one accord).
unannounced [ˈʌnəˈnaunst] adj. Sin ser anunciado.
unanswerable [ʌnˈɑːnsərəbl] adj. Que no tiene contestación *or* respuesta (question). || Irrebatible, irrefutable (criticism, attack).
unanswered [ˈʌnˈɑːnsəd] adj. No contestado, da; sin contestar (letter). || No correspondido, da (love). || *He left the question unanswered*, dejó la pregunta sin contestación.
unanticipated [ˈʌnænˈtisipeitid] adj. Imprevisto, ta (unexpected).
unappalled [ˈʌnəˈpɔːld] adj. Impasible, impávido, da (unfrightened).
unapparent [ˈʌnəˈpærənt] adj. No evidente: *the answer was unapparent*, la respuesta no era evidente.
unappealable [ˈʌnəˈpiːləbl] adj. Jur. Inapelable.
unappeasable [ˈʌnəˈpiːzəbl] adj. Imposible de aplacar. || Insaciable (hunger). || Implacable (hatred).
unappetizing [ˈʌnˈæpitaiziŋ] adj. Poco apetecible (idea, etc.). || Poco apetitoso, sa (food, person, etc.).
unapplied [ˈʌnəˈplaid] adj. Inaplicado, da (system). || Inutilizado, da (energy). || *Post unapplied for*, puesto para el cual no se ha presentado ningún candidato.
unappreciated [ˈʌnəˈpriːʃieitid] adj. No apreciado, da. || Ignorado, da: *unappreciated writer*, escritor ignorado. || Incomprendido, da (misunderstood).
unappreciative [ˈʌnəˈpriːʃiətiv] adj. Desagradecido, da (ungrateful). || *To be unappreciative of*, no apreciar.
unapprehensive [ˈʌnˌæpriˈhensiv] adj. Torpe (mind). || *To be unapprehensive of danger*, no temer el peligro.
unapproachability [ˌʌnəˌprəutʃəˈbiləti] n. Inaccesibilidad, *f.*
unapproachable [ˈʌnəˈprəutʃəbl] adj. Inaccesible (not accessible). || Inabordable, inaccesible (a person). || Sin par, sin igual (unrivalled).
unapproachableness [—nis] n. Inaccesibilidad, *f.*
unappropriated [ˈʌnəˈprəuprieitid] adj. No asignado, da (funds). || Libre, disponible (available).
unapproved [ˈʌnəˈpruːvd] adj. Desaprobado, da. || *Unapproved of*, desaprobado, da.
unapproving [ˈʌnəˈpruːviŋ] adj. Desaprobador, ra.
unapt [ʌnˈæpt] adj. Inadecuado, da (inadequate). || Impropio, pia (word). || No apto: *unapt for business*, no apto para los negocios.
unaptness [—nis] n. Falta (*f.*) de oportunidad (of a remark). || Impropiedad, *f.* (of a word). || Inaptitud, *f.* (*for*, para).
unarm [ˈʌnˈɑːm] v. tr. Desarmar (to disarm).
unarmed [—d] adj. Desarmado, da; sin armas (person). || Bot. Zool. Inerme. || Fig. Desarmado, da.
unartistic [ˈʌnɑːˈtistik] adj. Poco artístico, ca.
unascertainable [ˈʌnæsəˈteinəbl] adj. Inaveriguable.
unascertained [ˈʌnæsəˈteind] adj. Sin averiguar, no comprobado, da.
unashamed [ˈʌnəˈʃeimd] adj. Desvergonzado, da; que no tiene vergüenza; descarado, da (shameless). || *He was unashamed of what he had done*, no estaba avergonzado de lo que había hecho, no se avergonzaba de lo que había hecho.
unashamedly [—li] adv. Descaradamente, desvergonzadamente (shamelessly).
unasked [ˈʌnˈɑːskt] adj. Sin ser invitado: *he came unasked*, vino sin ser invitado. || Sin formular (a question). || No solicitado, da (advice). || *Unasked for*, espontáneo, a (spontaneous), no solicitado, da (advice, opinion).
unassailable [ˌʌnəˈseiləbl] adj. Inatacable.
unassertive [ˈʌnəˈsəːtiv] adj. Tímido, da; modesto, ta.
unassimilable [ˈʌnəˈsimiləbl] adj. Inasimilable.
unassimilated [ˈʌnəˈsimileitid] adj. No asimilado, da.
unassisted [ˈʌnəˈsistid] adj. Solo, la; sin ayuda.
unassuming [ˈʌnəˈsjuːmiŋ] adj. Modesto, ta; sin pretensiones.
unattached [ˈʌnəˈtætʃt] adj. Sin atar, suelto, ta (not fastened). || Suelto, ta (loose): *unattached leaf*, hoja suelta. || Independiente (independent). || Disponible (available). || Libre (without any commitment). || En disponibilidad, disponible (employee). || Soltero, ra (not married). || Libre (not engaged). || Mil. De reemplazo. || Jur. No embargado, da.
unattackable [ˈʌnəˈtækəbl] adj. Inatacable.
unattainable [ˈʌnəˈteinəbl] adj. Inalcanzable (out of reach): *an unattainable goal*, un objetivo inalcanzable. || Inaccesible, inasequible [*by*, para] (inaccessible).
unattended [ˈʌnəˈtendid] adj. Desatendido, da: *the reception desk was unattended*, la recepción estaba desatendida. || Descuidado, da (neglected). || Solo, la (lacking escort, etc.).
unattested [ˈʌnəˈtestid] adj. No atestiguado, da.
unattired [ˈʌnəˈtaiəd] adj. Desnudo, da (undressed). || Sin adorno (unadorned).
unattractive [ˌʌnəˈtræktiv] adj. Poco atractivo, va.
unattractiveness [—nis] n. Falta (*f.*) de atractivo.
unauthenticated [ˈʌnɔːˈθentiˌkeitid] adj. No autentizado, da; no autentificado, da. || Jur. No legalizado, da. || Anónimo, ma; de autor desconocido.
unauthorized [ˈʌnˈɔːθəraizd] adj. No autorizado, da; desautorizado, da. || Ilícito, ta (trade, etc.).
unavailability [ˈʌnəˌveiləˈbiliti] n. Indisponibilidad, *f.* || Inutilidad, *f.* (uselessness).
unavailable [ˈʌnəˈveiləbl] adj. Indisponible, no disponible. || Ocupado, da (busy). || Print. Agotado, da (out of print). || Inutilizable (unusable).
unavailing [ˈʌnəˈveiliŋ] adj. Infructuoso, sa; inútil, vano, na.
unavenged [ˈʌnəˈvendʒd] adj. No vengado, da; sin vengar.
unavoidable [ˌʌnəˈvɔidəbl] adj. Inevitable.
unavoidableness [—nis] n. Inevitabilidad, *f.*
unavoidably [—li] adv. Inevitablemente. || *Unavoidably absent*, ausente por causas ajenas a su voluntad.
unavowable [ˈʌnəˈvauəbl] adj. Inconfesable.

unaware [ˈʌnəˈwɛə*] adj. Ignorante (*of*, de; *that*, de que). || Inconsciente: *unaware of the danger*, inconsciente del peligro. || — *To be unaware of*, ignorar. || *To be unaware that*, ignorar que. || *Unaware that they were waiting for him*, ignorando que le esperaban.
unawareness [—nis] n. Ignorancia, *f.* || Inconsciencia, *f.*: *unawareness of the risk*, inconsciencia del peligro.
unawares [—z] adv. Desprevenido, da (unexpectedly): *we caught them unawares*, les cogimos desprevenidos. || Sin darse cuenta (unintentionally).
unbacked [ˈʌnˈbækt] adj. Sin apoyo, sin ayuda (not helped, not supported). || Sin domar (never mounted by a rider). || SP. Al cual nadie ha apostado (horse).
unbaked [ˈʌnˈbeikt] adj. Crudo, da.
unbalance [ˈʌnˈbæləns] n. Desequilibrio, *m.*
unbalance [ˈʌnˈbæləns] v. tr. Desequilibrar. || Hacer perder el equilibrio (to make s.o. lose his balance). || Trastornar (s.o.'s mind).
unbalanced [—t] adj. Desequilibrado, da. || FIG. Desequilibrado, da; trastornado, da (mentally). || COMM. Que no está en equilibrio.
unballast [ʌnˈbæləst] v. tr. MAR. Deslastrar, quitar el lastre de.
unbandage [ʌnˈbændidʒ] v. tr. Desvendar, quitar las vendas a.
unbaptized [ˈʌnbæpˈtaizd] adj. Sin bautizar.
unbar [ˈʌnˈbɑː*] v. tr. Desatrancar (a door). || FIG. Abrir.
unbearable [ʌnˈbɛərəbl] adj. Inaguantable, insoportable, intolerable.
unbearably [—i] adv. Inaguantablemente, insoportablemente, intolerablemente. || *It was unbearably cold*, hacía un frío inaguantable.
unbearded [ˈʌnˈbiədid] adj. Imberbe, sin barba.
unbeatable [ʌnˈbiːtəbl] adj. Invencible. || Insuperable, inmejorable (price).
unbeaten [ˈʌnˈbiːtn] adj. No pisado, da (track). || Inexplorado, da; virgen (unexplored). || Invicto, ta (team, champion, etc.). || FIG. *Unbeaten path*, camino nuevo.
unbecoming [ˈʌnbiˈkʌmiŋ] adj. Que no sienta bien, que sienta mal (clothes). || Impropio, pia (unseemly): *behaviour unbecoming of you* o *unbecoming you*, comportamiento impropio de ti. || Indecoroso, sa (not decent).
unbecomingly [—li] adv. Mal: *unbecomingly dressed*, mal vestido.
unbecomingness [—nis] n. Impropiedad, *f.*, lo impropio (unseemliness). || Falta (*f.*) de decoro (indecency).
unbefitting [ˈʌnbiˈfitiŋ] adj. Impropio, pia.
unbegotten [ˈʌnbiˈgɔtn] adj. REL. No engendrado, da.
unbeknown [ˈʌnbiˈnəun] adj. Desconocido, da.
— Adv. *Unbeknown to me*, sin saberlo yo, sin que yo lo supiera.
unbelief [ˈʌnbiˈliːf] n. Incredulidad, *f.* || Escepticismo, *m.* (scepticism).
unbelievable [ˌʌnbiˈliːvəbl] adj. Increíble.
unbeliever [ˈʌnbiˈliːvə*] n. Incrédulo, la; descreído, da.
unbelieving [ˈʌnbiˈliːviŋ] adj. Incrédulo, la; descreído, da (incredulous). || Escéptico, ca (sceptical).
unbend* [ˈʌnˈbend] v. tr. Desencorvar, enderezar (to straighten). || Aflojar (a bow). || MAR. Soltar (cables). | Desenvergar (sails). || FIG. Relajar.
— V. intr. Desencorvarse, enderezarse (to straighten out). || FIG. Relajarse (to become less stiff).
— OBSERV. Pret. & p. p. ***unbent***.
unbending [—iŋ] adj. Inflexible. || Firme (resolute).
unbeneficial [ˈʌnˌbeniˈfiʃəl] adj. Poco ventajoso, sa; poco provechoso, sa. || Ineficaz (inefficacious).
unbent [ˈʌnˈbent] pret. & p. p. See UNBEND.
unbiased or **unbiassed** [ˈʌnˈbaiəst] adj. Imparcial.
unbidden [ˈʌnˈbidn] adj. Espontáneo, a (spontaneous). || Sin ser invitado (without being invited). || *To do sth. unbidden*, hacer algo espontáneamente.
unbind* [ˈʌnˈbaind] v. tr. Desatar (to untie). || Desencuadernar (a book). || MED. Desvendar (a wound).
— OBSERV. Pret. & p. p. ***unbound***.
unblamable or **unblameable** [ˈʌnˈbleiməbl] adj. Irreprochable.
unbleached [ˈʌnˈbliːtʃt] adj. Sin blanquear, crudo, da (cloth).
unblemished [ʌnˈblemiʃt] adj. Sin mancha, sin tacha.
unblessed or **unblest** [ˈʌnˈblest] adj. REL. Sin bendecir, que no ha sido bendecido. || FIG. Desafortunado, da (unfortunate).
unblock [ˈʌnˈblɔk] v. tr. Desatascar (sink, pipe, etc.). || Despejar (passage, road, etc.). || Descalzar (wheel). || COMM. Desbloquear, descongelar (credit, etc.).
unblocking [—iŋ] n. COMM. Descongelación, *f.*, desbloqueo, *m.*
unblushing [ʌnˈblʌʃiŋ] adj. Desvergonzado, da; sinvergüenza (shameless). || Que no se ruboriza.
unbodied [ʌnˈbɔdid] adj. Incorpóreo, a.
unbolt [ˈʌnˈbəult] v. tr. Desatrancar, descorrer el cerrojo de (a door).
unborn [ˈʌnˈbɔːn] adj. Aún no nacido, da; nonato, ta (not yet born). || Venidero, ra; futuro, ra (future).
unbosom [ʌnˈbuzəm] v. tr. Descubrir, revelar. || *To unbosom o.s.*, desahogarse, abrir su corazón: *to unbosom o.s. to s.o.*, desahogarse con alguien, abrir su corazón a alguien.
unbound [ˈʌnˈbaund] pret. & p. p. See UNBIND.
— Adj. Desatado, da (untied). || PRINT. Sin encuadernar, sin tapa (without cover). | En rústica (paperback).
unbounded [—id] adj. Ilimitado, da; sin límites.
unbowed [ˈʌnˈbaud] adj. Derecho, cha; erguido, da.
unbrace [ʌnˈbreis] v. tr. Aflojar, soltar (to loosen). || Debilitar (to weaken).
unbreakable [ˈʌnˈbreikəbl] adj. Irrompible. || Indomable (horse). || FIG. Inquebrantable.
unbreathable [ˈʌnˈbriːðəbl] adj. Irrespirable.
unbred [ˈʌnˈbred] adj. Mal educado, da.
unbribable [ˈʌnˈbraibəbl] adj. Incorruptible, insobornable.
unbridle [ʌnˈbraidl] v. tr. Desembridar, desbridar (horse). || FIG. Dar rienda suelta a (to give free rein to).
unbridled [—d] adj. FIG. Desenfrenado, da: *unbridled passions*, pasiones desenfrenadas.
un-British [ˈʌnˈbritiʃ] adj. Poco inglés, esa.
unbroached [ˈʌnˈbrəutʃt] adj. Sin empezar (barrel). || Sin tratar (question).
unbroken [ˈʌnˈbrəukən] adj. Intacto, ta; sin romper. || No domado, da; indomado, da (horse). || Ininterrumpido, da (silence, peace). || Continuo, nua (continuous). || Que no ha sido batido (record). || Indómito, ta (spirit). || JUR. Inviolado, da. || AGR. Sin labrar (ground).
unbuckle [ˈʌnˈbʌkl] v. tr. Desabrochar (a belt). || Desabrochar *or* desatar la hebilla de (shoes, etc.).
unbuilt [ˈʌnˈbilt] adj. Sin construir. || *Unbuilt ground*, solar, *m.*
unburden [ʌnˈbəːdn] v. tr. Descargar (to unload). || FIG. Confiar (one's worries, etc.). | Abrir (one's heart). | Aliviar (to relieve). || — *Porters unburdened them of their luggage*, los mozos les cogieron el equipaje. || FIG. *To unburden o.s.*, desahogarse (*to*, con), abrir el corazón (*to*, a). | *To unburden o.s. of*, desahogarse de.
unburied [ˈʌnˈberid] adj. Insepulto, ta.
unbury [ʌnˈberi] v. tr. Desenterrar.
unbusinesslike [ʌnˈbiznislaik] adj. Que carace de método, poco metódico, ca (unmethodical). || Ineficaz (not efficient). || Incorrecto, ta: *unbusinesslike proceeding*, procedimiento incorrecto.
unbutton [ˈʌnˈbʌtn] v. tr. Desabrochar, desabotonar.
— V. intr. Desabrocharse (a shirt, etc.). || FIG. Desahogarse.
uncalled [ʌnˈkɔːld] adj. Sin ser llamado.
uncalled-for [—fɔː*] adj. Innecesario, ria; inútil (unnecessary). || Fuera de lugar, inapropiado, da (out of place). || Impertinente (impertinent). || Injustificado, da (unjustified).
uncannily [ʌnˈkænili] adv. Extrañamente, misteriosamente. || *It was uncannily silent*, había un silencio extraño.
uncanny [ʌnˈkæni] adj. Extraño, ña; misterioso, sa (strange).
uncap [ʌnˈkæp] v. tr. Destapar.
— V. intr. Descubrirse, quitarse el sombrero.
uncared-for [ˈʌnˈkɛədfɔː*] adj. Descuidado, da (garden, appearance). || Abandonado, da; desamparado da (person).
uncarpeted [ˈʌnˈkɑːpitid] adj. Sin alfombra.
uncaught [ˈʌnˈkɔːt] adj. Libre, en libertad.
unceasing [ʌnˈsiːsiŋ] adj. Incesante, continuo, nua (incessant).
unceasingly [—li] adv. Incesantemente, sin cesar.
uncensored [ˈʌnˈsensəd] or **uncensured** [ˈʌnˈsenʃəd] adj. No censurado, da.
unceremonious [ˈʌnˌseriˈməunjəs] adj. Poco ceremonioso, sa (without ceremony). || Descortés (lacking courtesy).
unceremoniouly [—li] adv. Sin cumplidos (without ceremony). || Sin miramientos, descortésmente (without courtesy).
uncertain [ʌnˈsəːtn] adj. Incierto, ta; dudoso, sa (not certain). || Poco seguro, ra (not sure or reliable). || Indeterminado, da (not calculated). || Vacilante, indeciso, sa (hesitant). || Inconstante, variable (variable). || — *To be uncertain of sth.*, no estar seguro de algo. || *To be uncertain what to do*, no saber qué hacer. || *To be uncertain whether*, no saber si. || *Uncertain health*, salud precaria.
uncertainty [—ti] n. Incertidumbre, *f.* (lack of certainty). || Duda, *f.* (doubt). || Poca seguridad, *f.* (lack of security).
unchain [ˈʌnˈtʃein] v. tr. Desencadenar. || FIG. Dar rienda suelta a.
unchaining [—iŋ] n. Desencadenamiento, *m.*
unchallengeable [ˈʌnˈtʃælindʒəbl] adj. Indiscutible, incontrovertible.
unchallenged [ˈʌnˈtʃælindʒd] adj. Indiscutido, da; incontrovertido, da (undisputed). || MIL. Sin ser detenido: *to pass unchallenged*, pasar sin ser detenido. || JUR. No recusado, da. || Único, ca (candidate).
unchangeable [ʌnˈtʃeindʒəbl] adj. Inmutable, inalterable.
unchangeableness [—nis] n. Inmutabilidad, *f.*, inalterabilidad, *f.*
unchanged [ˈʌnˈtʃeindʒd] adj. Igual.

unchanging [ʌn'tʃeindʒiŋ] adj. Invariable, constante, inalterable.
uncharged ['ʌn'tʃɑ:dʒd] adj. JUR. No acusado, da. || No cargado, da (firearm). || COMM. *Uncharged for*, gratuito, ta.
uncharitable [ʌn'tʃæritəbl] adj. Poco caritativo, va.
uncharitableness [—nis] n. Falta (*f.*) de caridad.
uncharitably [—i] adv. Sin caridad.
uncharted ['ʌn'tʃɑ:tid] adj. Que no figura en el mapa (not on the map). || Desconocido, da (unknown). || Inexplorado, da (unexplored).
unchaste ['ʌn'tʃeist] adj. Impúdico, ca (lewd). || Incontinente (incontinent).
unchastised [ʌntʃæs'taizd] adj. Impune.
unchastity ['ʌn'tʃæstiti] n. Impudicicia, *f.*, impudicia, *f.* (lewdness). || Incontinencia, *f.*, falta (*f.*) de castidad (incontinence). || Infidelidad, *f.* (unfaithfulness).
uncheckable ['ʌn'tʃekəbl] adj. Incontenible (emotions, rush, etc.). || Que no se puede comprobar (figure, etc.).
unchecked ['ʌn'tʃekt] adj. Sin obstáculos: *unchecked advance*, avance sin obstáculos. || Desenfrenado, da (passions). || Mimado, da (child). || COMM. No comprobado, da; sin comprobar.
unchivalrous ['ʌn'ʃivəlrəs] adj. Poco caballeroso, sa.
unchock ['ʌn'tʃɔk] v. tr. Desengalgar (a wheel).
unchristened ['ʌn'krisənd] adj. REL. Sin bautizar.
unchristian ['ʌn'kristjən] adj. REL. Infiel. || Poco cristiano, na. || FIG. Indecente.
uncircumcised ['ʌn'sə:kəmsaizd] adj. Incircunciso, sa.
uncircumscribed ['ʌn'sə:kəmskraibd] adj. Incircunscrito, ta.
uncivil ['ʌn'sivl] adj. Incorrecto, ta: descortés, incivil (impolite): *he was quite uncivil to her*, fue muy descortés con ella.
uncivilizable ['ʌn'sivilaizəbl] adj. Incivilizable.
uncivilized ['ʌn'sivilaizd] adj. Incivilizado, da; salvaje.
unclad ['ʌn'klæd] adj. Desnudo, da.
unclaimed ['ʌn'kleimd] adj. Sin reclamar.
unclasp ['ʌn'klɑ:sp] v. tr. Desabrochar (to undo). || Aflojar (to loosen).
unclassical ['ʌn'klæsikəl] adj. No clásico, ca.
unclassifiable ['ʌn'klæsifaiəbl] adj. Imposible de clasificar, inclasificable.
unclassified ['ʌn'klæsifaid] adj. Sin clasificar.
uncle ['ʌŋkl] n. Tío, *m.* || — FIG. FAM. *At my uncle's*, en peñaranda (in pawn). | *Say uncle!*, ¡ríndete! | *Uncle Sam*, el Tío Sam.
unclean ['ʌn'kli:n] adj. Sucio, cia (dirty). || Desaseado, da (untidy). || REL. Impuro, ra.
uncleanliness ['ʌn'klenlinis] n. See UNCLEANNESS.
uncleanly ['ʌn'klenli] adj. Sucio, cia (dirty). || Desaseado, da (untidy). || Impuro, ra (impure).
— Adv. Suciamente. || Desaseadamente. || Impuramente.
uncleanness [—nis] n. Suciedad, *f.* (dirtiness). || Desaseo, *m.* (untidiness). || Impureza, *f.* (impurity).
uncleansed ['ʌn'klenzd] adj. Sucio, cia.
unclear ['ʌn'kliə*] adj. Poco claro, ra. || Confuso, sa; poco claro, ra (confused). || *I am unclear as to*, no estoy seguro de.
uncleared ['ʌn'kliəd] adj. Sin quitar (table). || Sin desbrozar (ground). || COMM. Que no han pasado por la aduana (goods). | Sin pagar (debt). || JUR. No declarado inocente. || FIG. Que no ha sido aclarado (mystery). | Que no ha sido disipado (doubt).
unclench ['ʌn'klentʃ] v. tr. Aflojar.
uncloak ['ʌn'kləuk] v. tr. Quitar el abrigo a (to take s.o.'s coat). || Desencapotar (to remove s.o.'s cloak). || FIG. Desenmascarar.
unclog ['ʌn'klɔg] v. tr. Desatascar.
unclothe ['ʌn'kləuð] v. tr. Desnudar.
— V. intr. Desnudarse.
unclothed [—d] adj. Desnudo, da.
unclouded ['ʌn'klaudid] adj. Despejado, da; sin nubes (sky). || FIG. Sin nubes, sereno, na (future).
uncock ['ʌn'kɔk] v. tr. Desmontar (a rifle).
uncoil ['ʌn'kɔil] v. tr. Desenrollar.
— V. intr. Desenroscarse (a snake). || Desenrollarse (a rope, etc.).
uncollected ['ʌnkə'lektid] adj. Disperso, sa; no reunido, da (scattered). || Agitado, da (person). || No recaudado, da; sin cobrar (taxes).
uncollectible ['ʌnkə'lektəbl] adj. Incobrable.
uncoloured (U. S. **uncolored**) ['ʌn'kʌləd] adj. Incoloro, ra; sin color. || FIG. Sin color (style). | Imparcial (unbiassed). || FIG. *To remain uncoloured by*, no ser influenciado por.
uncombed ['ʌn'kəumd] adj. Despeinado, da.
uncomeliness [ʌn'kʌmlinis] n. Falta (*f.*) de gracia *or* de garbo.
uncomely ['ʌn'kʌmli] adj. Falto de gracia *or* de garbo.
uncomfortable [ʌn'kʌmfətəbl] adj. Incómodo, da; poco confortable (not comfortable): *an uncomfortable bed*, una cama incómoda; *to feel uncomfortable in a chair*, encontrarse incómodo en una silla. || Desagradable (unpleasant). || Incómodo, da; molesto, ta (awkward). || Inquietante (worrying). || — *To feel uncomfortable*, no estar a gusto (not at ease), estar molesto *or* incómodo (awkward), estar preocupado (worried). || *We can make things uncomfortable for you*, le podemos crear dificultades, le podemos complicar la vida.
uncomfortableness [—nis] n. Incomodidad, *f.*
uncommercial ['ʌnkə'mə:ʃəl] adj. Poco comercial. || Con pocos comercios (town).
uncommitted ['ʌnkə'mitid] adj. No comprometido, da (person, country).
uncommon [ʌn'kəmən] adj. Raro, ra; poco común, poco corriente (rare). || Fuera de lo común, extraordinario, ria (unusual).
uncommonly [—li] adv. Extraordinariamente, particularmente. || *Not uncommonly*, con cierta frecuencia, bastantes veces.
uncommonness [—nis] n. Rareza, *f.*
uncommunicative ['ʌnkə'mju:nikətiv] adj. Poco comunicativo, va; reservado, da.
uncompanionable ['ʌnkəm'pænjənəbl] adj. Insociable.
uncomplaining ['ʌnkəm'pleiniŋ] adj. Que no protesta, resignado, da.
uncomplainingly [—li] adv. Con resignación, sin protestar.
uncompleted ['ʌnkəm'pli:tid] adj. Incompleto, ta; inacabado, da; sin acabar.
uncomplicated ['ʌn'kəmplikeitid] adj. Sencillo, lla.
uncomplimentary ['ʌn,kəmpli'mentəri] adj. Poco halagüeño, ña.
uncomplying ['ʌnkəm'plaiiŋ] adj. Inflexible, intransigente.
uncomprehensive [ʌn,kəmpri'hensiv] adj. Incompleto, ta.
uncompromising [ʌn'kəmprəmaiziŋ] adj. Inflexible, intransigente (making no concessions). || Absoluto, ta: *uncompromising integrity*, integridad absoluta.
unconcealed ['ʌnkən'si:ld] n. Evidente, abierto, ta; no disimulado, da.
unconcern ['ʌnkən'sə:n] n. Indiferencia, *f.*, despreocupación, *f.* || Tranquilidad, *f.* (calm).
unconcerned [—d] adj. Despreocupado, da (not worried). || Indiferente: *unconcerned about his brother's troubles*, indiferente a las dificultades de su hermano; *unconcerned about the danger*, indiferente al peligro. || No interesado, da (not concerned).
unconcernedly ['ʌnkən'sə:nidli] adv. Con indiferencia (indifferently). || Tranquilamente, sin preocuparse.
unconditional ['ʌnkən'diʃənl] adj. Incondicional. || Terminante (refusal).
unconditioned ['ʌnkən'diʃənd] adj. Incondicional. || No condicionado, da; espontáneo, a (reflex).
unconfessable ['ʌnkən'fesəbl] adj. Inconfesable.
unconfessed ['ʌnkən'fest] adj. No confesado, da (sin). || Sin confesar (person).
unconfined ['ʌnkən'faind] adj. Libre (free). || Ilimitado, da; sin límites (boundless).
unconfirmed ['ʌnkən'fə:md] adj. No confirmado, da; sin confirmar.
unconformable ['ʌnkən'fɔ:məbl] adj. Disconforme (which does not conform). || Incompatible. || GEOL. Discordante. || No conformista (person).
unconformity ['ʌnkənfɔ:miti] n. Disconformidad, *f.* || GEOL. Discordancia, *f.*
uncongealable ['ʌnkən'dʒi:ləbl] adj. Incongelable.
uncongenial ['ʌnkən'dʒi:niəl] adj. Antipático, ca (person). || Desagradable (unpleasant): *uncongenial job*, trabajo desagradable.
unconnected ['ʌnkə'nektid] adj. No relacionado, da (*with*, con). || Sin hilación, inconexo, xa (ideas).
unconquerable [ʌn'kəŋkərəbl] adj. Invencible (army). || Inconquistable (heart, region). || Insuperable (difficulty). || Incorregible (defect). || Irresistible (curiosity, etc.).
unconquered ['ʌn'kəŋkəd] adj. Invicto, ta (not defeated). || No conquistado, da (not conquered). || Indómito, ta (not subjugated). || Incontenible (passion). || Insuperable (difficulty).
unconscientious ['ʌn,kənʃi'enʃəs] adj. Poco concienzudo, da.
unconscionable [ʌn'kənʃnəbl] adj. Poco escrupuloso, sa (unscrupulous). || Desmedido, da; excesivo, va; desmesurado, da (excessive).
unconscious [ʌn'kənʃəs] adj. Inconsciente. || — *The blow knocked him unconscious*, el golpe le dejó inconsciente *or* sin conocimiento *or* sin sentido. || *To be unconscious of*, estar inconsciente de, no darse cuenta de.
— N. PHIL. Inconsciente, *m.*
unconsciousness [—nis] n. Inconsciencia, *f.*
unconsenting ['ʌnkən'sentiŋ] adj. Que no consiente.
unconsidered ['ʌnkən'sidəd] adj. Inconsiderado, da; irreflexivo, va. || Insignificante.
unconsolable ['ʌnkən'səuləbl] adj. Inconsolable.
unconsoled ['ʌnkən'səuld] adj. Desconsolado, da.
unconstitutional ['ʌn,kənsti'tju:ʃənl] adj. Anticonstitucional, inconstitucional.
unconstitutionality ['ʌn,kənstitju:ʃə'næliti] n. Inconstitucionalidad, *f.*
unconstrained ['ʌnkən'streind] adj. Libre. || Franco, ca (laughter). || Espontáneo, a (spontaneous).
unconstricted ['ʌnkən'striktid] adj. Libre. || Sin restricción. || Desenvuelto, ta (person).
unconsumed ['ʌnkən'sju:md] adj. Sin consumir.
uncontainable ['ʌnkən'teinəbl] adj. Incontenible.
uncontaminated ['ʌnkən'tæmineitid] adj. Incontaminado, da.
uncontemplated ['ʌn'kəntəmpleitid] adj. Imprevisto, ta (unexpected).

uncontested [ˈʌnkənˈtestid] adj. Incontestado, da. || Ganado sin oposición (parliamentary seat).
uncontinuous [ˈʌnkənˈtinjuəs] adj. Discontinuo, nua.
uncontradictable [ˈʌnˌkɔntrəˈdiktəbl] adj. Irrefutable, indiscutible.
uncontrite [ˈʌnˈkɔntrait] adj. Incontrito, ta.
uncontrollable [ˌʌnkənˈtrəuləbl] adj. Incontrolable. || Irresistible, incontrolable (wish, laughter). || Ingobernable (people). || Indisciplinado, da (child). || *She burst into uncontrollable laughter*, le dio un ataque de risa.
uncontrolled [ˈʌnkənˈtrəuld] adj. No dominado, da; no controlado, da. || Desenfrenado, da (passion). || Irresponsable. || Absoluto, ta; completo, ta (liberty).
uncontroverted [ˈʌnˌkɔntrəuˈvəːtid] adj. Indiscutido, da; no controvertido, da; incontrovertido. da.
uncontrovertible [ˈʌnˈkɔntrəvəːtəbl] adj. Incontrovertible, indiscutible.
unconventional [ˈʌnkənˈvenʃənl] adj. Poco convencional. || Original: *unconventional dress*, traje original.
unconventionality [ˌʌnkənvenʃəˈnæliti] n. Originalidad, *f.*
unconversant [ˈʌnkənˈvəːsənt] adj. *To be unconversant with*, no estar al tanto de (not to be informed of), estar poco versado en, no saber mucho de (not to know much about).
unconverted [ˈʌnkənˈvəːtid] adj. No convertido, da.
unconvertible [ˈʌnkənˈvəːtəbl] adj. Inconvertible.
unconvinced [ˈʌnkənˈvinst] adj. Poco convencido, da; escéptico, ca.
unconvincing [ˈʌnkənˈvinsiŋ] adj. Poco convincente.
uncooked [ˈʌnˈkukt] adj. CULIN. Crudo, da; sin cocer.
uncoordinated [ˈʌnkəuˈɔːdineitid] adj. No coordinado, da.
uncork [ˈʌnˈkɔːk] v. tr. Descorchar, destaponar, destapar. || FIG. Dar rienda suelta a (one's feelings).
uncorking [—iŋ] n. Descorche, *m.*, destapadura, *f.*
uncorrected [ˈʌnkəˈrektid] adj. No corregido, da; sin corregir.
uncorroborated [ˈʌnkəˈrɔbəreitid] adj. Sin corroborar, no confirmado, da.
uncorrupted [ˈʌnkəˈrʌptid] adj. Incorrupto, ta.
uncountable [ˈʌnˈkauntəbl] adj. Incontable, innumerable.
uncounted [ˈʌnˈkauntid] adj. Sin contar (not counted). || Innumerable, incalculable (innumerable).
uncouple [ˈʌnˈkʌpl] v. tr. Desacoplar (wheels, etc.). || Desenganchar (railway trucks). || Desconectar (to disconnect). || Soltar (hounds).
uncoupling [—iŋ] n. Desacoplamiento, *m.* (of wheels). || Desenganche, *m.* (of railway trucks).
uncourteous [ˈʌnˈkəːtjəs] adj. Descortés.
uncourteousness [ˈʌnˈkəːtjəsnis] n. Descortesía, *f.*
uncourtly [ˈʌnˈkɔːtli] adj. Descortés.
uncouth [ʌnˈkuːθ] adj. Grosero, ra (vulgar). || Tosco, ca; rústico, ca (rough). || Torpe (awkward).
uncouthness [—nis] n. Grosería, *f.* (vulgarity). || Tosquedad, *f.*, rusticidad, *f.* (roughness). || Torpeza, *f.* (awkwardness).
uncover [ʌnˈkʌvə*] v. tr. Descubrir. || Revelar (to reveal). || Destapar (to take the lid off). || Desfundar (furniture). || Dejar al descubierto (to leave exposed). || Quitarse el sombrero de (one's head). || *To uncover o.s.*, destaparse (in bed).
— V. intr. (Ant.). Descubrirse (to take one's hat off).
uncovered [—d] adj. Descubierto, ta (not covered). || Desnudo, da (bare). || Descubierto, ta (bareheaded). || Destapado, da (in bed).
uncreated [ˈʌnkriˈeitid] adj. Increado, da.
uncritical [ˈʌnˈkritikəl] adj. Falto de sentido crítico (undiscerning). || Que no es criticón, ona (not very critical).
uncriticizable [ˈʌnˈkritisaizəbl] adj. Incensurable.
uncross [ˈʌnˈkrɔs] v. tr. Descruzar: *to uncross one's arms*, descruzar los brazos.
uncrossed [—t] adj. Descruzado, da. || Que no ha sido cruzado, da (land). || Sin cruzar (a cheque).
uncrowded [ˈʌnˈkraudid] adj. Con poca gente (street). || Poco apretado, da (people). || Poco denso, sa (population).
uncrown [ˈʌnˈkraun] v. tr. Descoronar, destronar.
uncrowned [—d] adj. Sin corona.
unction [ˈʌŋkʃən] n. Unción, *f.* (ointment). || Ungüento, *m.* (balm). || FIG. Unción, *f.*, fervor, *m.* (religious fervour). | Deleite, *m.*, fruición, *f.* (relish). | Zalamería, *f.* (cajoling). || REL. *Extreme unction*, extremaunción, *f.*
unctuosity [ˌʌŋktjuˈɔsiti] n. Untuosidad, *f.*
unctuous [ˈʌŋktjuəs] adj. Untuoso, sa; grasiento, ta (oil, fat). || Ubérrimo, ma (soil). || Plástico, ca. || FIG. Lleno de unción (speech, manner). | Zalamero, ra; meloso, sa (cajoling).
unctuousness [—nis] n. Untuosidad, *f.* || FIG. Unción, *f.* (of manners).
uncultivable [ˈʌnˈkʌltivəbl] or **uncultivatable** [ˈʌnˈkʌltiveitəbl] adj. Incultivable.
uncultivated [ˈʌnˈkʌltiveitid] adj. Sin cultivar, inculto, ta; baldío, a (land). || Inculto, ta (person).
uncultured [ˈʌnˈkʌltʃəd] adj. Inculto, ta.
uncurbed [ˈʌnˈkəːbd] adj. Desenfrenado, da (unchecked). || Libre (free). || Sin barbada (horse).
uncured [ˈʌnˈkjuəd] adj. CULIN. Fresco, ca (fresh). || MED. Sin curar.
uncurl [ˈʌnˈkəːl] v. tr. Desenroscar (rope, etc.). || Desrizar, estirar (hair).
— V. intr. Desenroscarse (rope, snake). || Desrizarse (hair).
uncurtailed [ˈʌnkəːˈteild] adj. Entero, ra; completo, ta (not abridged). || Sin restricción.
uncustomary [ˈʌnˈkʌstəməri] adj. Desacostumbrado, da (uncommon).
uncut [ˈʌnˈkʌt] adj. Sin cortar (not cut). || En bruto, sin tallar (diamond). || Sin tallar (stone). || PRINT. Intonso, sa (book). || Sin cortes, entero, ra (film, etc.).
undamaged [ˈʌnˈdæmidʒd] adj. En buen estado, no estropeado, da (goods, etc.). || Intacto, ta (intact). || Indemne; ileso, sa (people). || FIG. Intacto, ta.
undamped [ˈʌnˈdæmpt] adj. No mojado, seco, ca (not wet). || No amortiguado, da (sounds, etc.). || No disminuido, da (feelings).
undated [ˈʌnˈdeitid] adj. Sin fecha.
undaunted [ʌnˈdɔːntid] adj. Intrépido, da (intrepid). || Impávido, da (*by*, ante) [dauntless].
undebatable [ˌʌndiˈbeitəbl] adj. Indiscutible.
undecagon [ˈʌnˈdekəgən] n. MATH. Undecágono, *m.*, endecágono, *m.*
undeceive [ˈʌndiˈsiːv] v. tr. Desengañar.
undecided [ˈʌndiˈsaidid] adj. Indeciso, sa: *the election results are still undecided*, los resultados de la elección son todavía indecisos. || No resuelto, ta: *undecided affair*, asunto no resuelto. || Indeciso, sa; irresoluto, ta (person). || *She was undecided whether she would go or not*, no sabía si iría o no.
undecipherable [ˈʌndiˈsaifərəbl] adj. Indescifrable.
undeclarable [ˈʌndiˈklɛərəbl] adj. Indeclarable.
undeclinable [ˈʌndiˈklainəbl] adj. Indeclinable.
undefeated [ˈʌndiˈfiːtid] adj. Invicto, ta.
undefended [ˈʌndiˈfendid] adj. Indefenso, sa.
undefensible [ˈʌndiˈfensəbl] adj. Indefendible.
undeferable or **undeferrable** [ˈʌndiˈfəːrəbl] adj. Inaplazable.
undefiled [ˈʌndiˈfaild] adj. Impoluto, ta; inmaculado, da. || — *English undefiled*, inglés puro. || *Undefiled by*, no corrompido por.
undefinable [ˌʌndiˈfainəbl] adj. Indefinible. || Indeterminable.
undefined [ˌʌndiˈfaind] adj. Indefinido, da. || Indeterminado, da.
undelivered [ˈʌndiˈlivəd] adj. Sin entregar, no entregado, da (goods). || No entregado al destinatario (letters). || No pronunciado, da (speech). || JUR. No fallado, da (verdict).
undemonstrable [ˈʌnˈdemənstrəbl] adj. Indemostrable.
undemonstrated [ˈʌnˈdemənstreitid] adj. No demostrado, da.
undemonstrative [ˈʌndiˈmɔnstrətiv] adj. Reservado, da; poco expresivo, va.
undeniable [ˌʌndiˈnaiəbl] adj. Innegable, irrefutable.
undenominational [ˈʌndiˌnɔmiˈneiʃənl] adj. No confesional. || *Undenominational school*, escuela laica.
undependable [ˈʌndiˈpendəbl] adj. Poco seguro, ra; que no es de fiar.
under [ˈʌndə*] adj. Inferior: *the under jaw*, la mandíbula inferior. || Insuficiente (insufficient). || Subalterno, na (subordinate).
— Adv. Más abajo (below): *see under*, véase más abajo. || Debajo: *she wears a girdle under*, lleva una faja debajo; *quick, get under*, venga, métete debajo. || Menos (less): *ten dollars or under*, diez dólares o menos. || — *Buried under*, enterrado, da. || *Children ten years old or under*, menores de once años.
— Prep. Debajo de, bajo (see OBSERV.): *under the bed*, debajo de la cama; *under a clear blue sky*, bajo un cielo azul despejado. || Por debajo de, debajo de (movement): *the boat passed under the bridge*, el barco pasó por debajo del puente. || Debajo: *hide under here*, escóndete aquí debajo. || Menos de (less than): *in under two minutes*, en menos de dos minutos; *it cost under ten dollars*, costó menos de diez dólares. || Menor de: *he is under ten (years old)*, es menor de diez años. || Por debajo de (lower in rank): *a sergeant is under a captain*, un sargento está por debajo de un capitán. || Bajo (during): *under the Roman Empire*, bajo el Imperio Romano. || Durante el reinado de: *under Charles II*, durante el reinado de Carlos II. || Según, conforme a, de conformidad con (according to): *under the terms of the contract*, según los términos del contrato. || Bajo (subject to): *under government control*, bajo el control del gobierno. || Con (instructed by): *to study under Mr. X.*, estudiar con el señor X. || A: *under the care of*, al cuidado de; *under full steam*, a todo vapor. || En: *under repair, construction, cultivation*, en reparación, construcción, cultivo; *the article should come under international news*, el artículo debería figurar en las noticias internacionales. || Bajo *or* a las órdenes de: *we work under Peter*, trabajamos bajo las órdenes de Pedro. || AGR. Sembrado de: *a field under wheat*, un campo sembrado de trigo. || — FIG. *Right under one's nose*, delante de las narices de uno. || *To be under the doctor*, estar bajo tratamiento médico. || *To come o to get out from under*, salir de debajo de. || *Under arrest*, bajo arresto, detenido, da. || *Under bail*, bajo fianza. || *Under examination*, sometido a examen. || MAR. *Under full*

sail, a toda vela, con las velas desplegadas. || *Under lock and key*, bajo llave, bajo siete llaves. || *Under oath*, bajo juramento. || *Under one's breath*, en voz baja. || *Under our very eyes*, delante de nuestros propios ojos. || *Under pain* o *under penalty of*, bajo *or* so pena de. || *Under pretence of*, bajo *or* so pretexto de. || *Under separate cover*, por separado (letter). || *Under the authority of*, bajo la autoridad de. || *Under the circumstances*, en tales circunstancias, dadas las circunstancias. || *Under the name of*, con *or* bajo el nombre de. || *Under these conditions*, en estas condiciones.

— OBSERV. In general the preposition *under* is translated in Spanish by *debajo de* in its concrete sense (*under the table*, debajo de la mesa), and by *bajo* in its figurative and abstract senses (*under the Republic*, bajo la República).

underact [—r'ækt] v. tr. THEATR. Representar mal (one's part).
— V. intr. THEATR. Representar mal su papel.

underage [—r'eidʒ] adj. Menor de edad.

underarm [—rɑːm] adj. Por debajo del brazo. || ANAT. De la axila.
— Adv. Manteniendo la mano a un nivel inferior a la altura del hombro, sin levantar la mano.
— N. Axila, *f.*, sobaco, *m.*

underbelly [—ˌbeli] n. Parte (*f.*) inferior. || FIG. Parte (*f.*) más vulnerable.

underbid* [—'bid] v. tr. Ofrecer menos que (to offer less than). || Ofrecer condiciones más ventajosas que (to offer better conditions than). || *To underbid one's hand*, declarar menos de lo que se tiene (in cards).
— OBSERV. Pret. & p. p. ***underbid***.

underbrush [—brʌʃ] n. Maleza, *f.*, monte (*m.*) bajo.

undercarriage [—ˌkæridʒ] n. AVIAT. Tren (*m.*) de aterrizaje. || TECH. Bastidor, *m.* (framework).

undercharge [—'tʃɑːdʒ] n. Carga (*f.*) insuficiente (in a gun). || Precio (*m.*) insuficiente.

undercharge [—'tʃɑːdʒ] v. tr. Cobrar *or* hacer pagar menos de lo debido (money). || Cargar insuficientemente (a gun). || *To undercharge s.o. by ten pounds*, cobrar diez libras de menos a alguien.

underclassman [—'klɑːsmən] n. U.S. Estudiante (*m.*) de primer año *or* de segundo año.
— OBSERV. El plural de esta palabra es *underclassmen*.

underclothes [—kləuðz] pl. n. Ropa (*f. sing.*) interior.

underclothing [—'kləuðiŋ] n. Ropa (*f.*) interior.

undercoat [—kəut] n. Primera mano, *f.* (of paint). || ZOOL. Pelaje (*m.*) corto (short hair).

undercover [—ˌkʌvə*] adj. Secreto, ta; clandestino, na.

undercroft [—krɔft] n. ARCH. Cripta, *f.*

undercurrent [—ˌkʌrənt] n. Corriente (*f.*) submarina. || FIG. Fondo, *m.* (underlying tendency). | Corriente (*f.*) oculta (hidden tendency). || *An undercurrent of discontent*, un mar de fondo.

undercut [—kʌt] n. Solomillo, *m.* (meat). || SP. Corte, *m.* (in tennis).

undercut* [—'kʌt] v. tr. Socavar (to undermine). || ARTS. Tallar en relieve (to cut in relief). || COMM. Vender más barato que (to sell cheaper). | Trabajar a menor precio que (to work for a lower wage than). || SP. Cortar (a ball.).
— OBSERV. Pret. & p. p. ***undercut***.

undercutting [—'kʌtiŋ] n. COMM. Competencia (*f.*) desleal.

underdeveloped [—di'veləpt] adj. Subdesarrollado, da (country, industry, etc.). || Poco *or* insuficientemente desarrollado, da (body, etc.). || PHOT. Insuficientemente revelado, da.

underdevelopment [—di'veləpmənt] n. Subdesarrollo, *m.* (of a country, industry). || Desarrollo (*m.*) insuficiente (of body). || PHOT. Revelado (*m.*) insuficiente.

underdo* [—'duː] v. tr. CULIN. Soasar.
— OBSERV. Pret. ***underdid;*** p. p. ***underdone***.

underdog [—dɔg] n. Desvalido, da; el *or* la más débil (in the struggle for life). || Perdedor, ra (in a struggle).

underdone [—'dʌn] adj. CULIN. Poco hecho, cha.

underdrawers [—ˌdrɔːəz] pl. n. U. S. Calzoncillos, *m.*

underdress [—'dres] v. intr. No vestirse de forma apropiada.

underemployment [—im'plɔimənt] n. Subempleo, *m.*

underestimate [—'estimit] n. Infravaloración, *f.*, apreciación (*f.*) errónea (of the value). || Estimación (*f.*) demasiado baja (of forecasts). || Desestimación, *f.*, menosprecio, *m.* (of a person).

underestimate [—'estimeit] v. tr. Subestimar, infravalorar. || Menospreciar.

underestimated [—id] adj. Subestimado, da; infravalorado, da.

underestimation [—esti'meiʃən] n. See UNDERESTIMATE.

underexpose [—iks'pəuz] v. tr. PHOT. Subexponer, exponer insuficientemente.

underexposure [—iks'pəuʒə*] n. PHOT. Subexposición, *f.*, exposición (*f.*) insuficiente.

underfed [—'fed] pret. & p.p. See UNDERFEED.
— Adj. Desnutrido, da; subalimentado, da.

underfeed* [—'fiːd] v. tr. Subalimentar, alimentar insuficientemente (to feed insufficiently). || Alimentar por la parte inferior (a fire).
— OBSERV. Pret. & p. p. ***underfed***.

underfeeding [—'fiːdiŋ] n. Subalimentación, *f.*, desnutrición, *f.*

underfelt [—felt] n. Arpillera, *f.*

underfoot [—'fut] adv. Bajo los pies, debajo de los pies (beneath one's feet). || — U. S. *His toys are always getting underfoot*, sus juguetes estorban siempre el paso. || *To trample underfoot*, pisotear.

undergarment [—ˌgɑːmənt] n. Prenda (*f.*) interior. || — Pl. Ropa (*f. sing.*) interior.

underglaze [—gleiz] adj. Aplicado antes del vidriado.

undergo* [—'gəu] v. tr. Sufrir, aguantar (to endure). || Experimentar (to experience). || MED. Sufrir (an operation).
— OBSERV. Pret. ***underwent;*** p. p. ***undergone***.

undergone [—'gɔn] p. p. See UNDERGO.

undergraduate [—'grædjuit] adj. No licenciado, da.
— N. Estudiante, *m.* & *f.* [no licenciado].

underground [—ˌgraund] adj. Subterráneo, a: *an underground pipeline*, un oleoducto subterráneo. || FIG. Secreto, ta. | Clandestino, na: *an underground magazine*, una revista clandestina. | Para aficionados, no tradicional, no comercial (films, music, etc.). || MIL. De la Resistencia (movement).
— Adv. Bajo tierra (under the ground). || FIG. Clandestinamente, secretamente (secretly).
— N. Metro, *m.*, metropolitano, *m.* [*Amer.*, subterráneo, *m.*] (railway). || FIG. Movimiento (*m.*) clandestino. || MIL. Resistencia, *f.*

underground railroad [—ˌgraund'reilrəud] n. U. S. Metro, *m.*, metropolitano, *m.* [*Amer.*, subterráneo, *m.*].

Underground Railroad [—ˌgraund'reilrəud] n. U. S. Organización (*f.*) clandestina para liberar a los esclavos antes de la Guerra de Secesión.

underground railway [—ˌgraund'reilwei] n. Metro, *m.*, metropolitano, *m.* [*Amer.*, subterráneo, *m.*].

undergrown [—'grəun] adj. Enclenque, poco desarrollado, da (child). || Poco desarrollado, da (plant). || Lleno de maleza (forest, land).

undergrowth [—grəuθ] n. Maleza, *f.*, monte (*m.*) bajo.

underhand [—hænd] adj. Secreto, ta; clandestino, na (secret). || Poco limpio, pia (dirty). || Bajo cuerda, bajo mano (by stealth). || Socarrón, ona (not straightforward). || SP. Ejecutado sin levantar la mano.
— Adv. Bajo cuerda, bajo mano (by stealth). || Secretamente, clandestinamente (secretly). || SP. Sin levantar la mano.

underhanded [—'hændid] adj. U. S. Secreto, ta; clandestino, na (secret). | Poco limpio, pia (dirty). | Bajo cuerda, bajo mano (by stealth). | Falto de mano de obra (shorthanded).

underhandedly [—'hændidli] adv. Bajo mano, bajo cuerda.

underhandedness [—'hændidnis] n. Disimulo, *m.*

underhung [—'hʌŋ] adj. ANAT. Prognato, ta (with a projecting jaw). || Saliente (jaw). || Corredizo, za; corredero, ra (moving on a rail).

underlaid [—'leid] pret. & p. p. See UNDERLAY.

underlain [—'lein] p. p. See UNDERLIE.

underlay [—lei] n. Arpillera, *f.* (under a carpet). || PRINT. Alza, *f.* || MIN. Buzamiento, *m.*

underlay* [—'lei] v. tr. Reforzar por debajo (a carpet). || Poner debajo de (to put under). || Sostener, apoyar (to support). || PRINT. Calzar, realzar.
— V. intr. MIN. Buzar.
— OBSERV. Pret. & p. p. ***underlaid***.

underlay [—'lei] pret. See UNDERLIE.

underlease [—liːs] n. Subarriendo, *m.*

underlet* [—'let] v. tr. Subarrendar, realquilar (to sublet). || Alquilar por debajo del precio normal.
— OBSERV. Pret. & p. p. ***underlet***.

underlie* [—'lai] v. tr. Estar debajo de (to lie under). || FIG. Servir de base a (to be the basis of). | Ser el fundamento de, ser la base de (to be the foundation of). | Ocultarse tras: *the jealousy which underlies his indifference*, los celos que se ocultan tras su indiferencia. || COMM. Tener prioridad sobre.
— V. intr. MIN. Buzar.
— OBSERV. Pret. ***underlay;*** p. p. ***underlain***.

underline [—lain] n. Raya, *f.* (under a word, etc.). || — Pl. Falsilla, *f. sing.*

underline [—'lain] v. tr. Subrayar (to draw a line under). || FIG. Subrayar, hacer hincapié en, recalcar (to stress).

underling [—liŋ] n. Subordinado, *m.*, subalterno, *m.* (inferior). || Seguidor, *m.*, secuaz, *m.* (follower).

underlining [—'lainiŋ] n. Subrayado, *m.*

underlip [—lip] n. Labio (*m.*) inferior.

underlying [—'laiiŋ] adj. Subyacente, oculto, ta (lying or placed underneath). || Fundamental.

undermanned [—'mænd] adj. Falto de mano de obra, falto de personal. || MAR. Con una tripulación insuficiente.

undermentioned [—'menʃənd] adj. Abajo mencionado, da; abajo citado, da.

undermine [—'main] v.tr. Socavar, minar: *foundations undermined by water*, cimientos socavados por el agua. || FIG. Socavar (to weaken gradually). | Minar: *drugs undermined his health*, las drogas le minaron la salud.

undermost [—məust] adj. Más bajo, ja; inferior. || Último, ma (in a pile).
underneath [—'ni:θ] adj. Inferior, de abajo.
— Adv. Debajo, por debajo: *and iron underneath*, y hierro por debajo.
— Prep. Debajo de, bajo: *the garage is underneath my room*, el garaje está debajo de mi habitación.
— N. Fondo, *m.*, parte (*f.*) inferior.
undernourish [—'nʌriʃ] v. tr. Subalimentar, desnutrir.
undernourished [—'nʌriʃt] adj. Desnutrido, da; subalimentado, da.
undernourishment [—'nʌriʃmənt] n. Desnutrición, *f.*, subalimentación, *f.*
underpaid [—'peid] pret. & p. p. See UNDERPAY.
underpants [—pænts] pl. n. Calzoncillos, *m.*
underpass [—pα:s] n. Paso (*m.*) subterráneo.
underpay* [—'pei] v. tr./intr. Pagar mal *or* poco. || *Underpaid workers*, obreros mal pagados.
— OBSERV. Pret. & p. p. ***underpaid***.
underpin [—'pin] v. tr. Apuntalar || FIG. Sostener.
underpinning [—'piniŋ] n. Apuntalamiento, *m.*
underplay [—'plei] v. tr. Representar mal (to underact). || Jugar una carta más baja que (a card).
— V. intr. Representar mal su papel.
underplot [—plɔt] n. Intriga (*f.*) secundaria (of a story, play, etc.).
underpopulated [—'pɔpjuleitid] adj. Poco poblado, da.
underpraise [—'preiz] v. tr. No encomiar suficientemente.
underprice [—'prais] v. tr. Poner un precio demasiado bajo a.
underprivileged [—'privilidʒd] adj. Desvalido, da.
— N. *The underprivileged*, los desvalidos.
underproduction [—prə'dʌkʃən] n. Subproducción, *f.*, producción (*f.*) insuficiente.
underprop [—'prɔp] v. tr. Apuntalar.
underrate [—'reit] v. tr. Subestimar, infravalorar (sth.). || Menospreciar (s.o., the importance of sth.).
underripe [—'raip] adj. Insuficientemente maduro, ra.
underscore [—'skɔ:*] v. tr. Subrayar. || FIG. Subrayar, hacer hincapié en, recalcar (to stress).
undersea [—si:] adj. Submarino, na.
— Adv. Bajo la superficie del mar.
underseas [—si:z] adv. Bajo la superficie del mar.
undersecretary [—'sekrətəri] n. Subsecretario, ria: *undersecretary of State*, subsecretario de Estado. || *Undersecretary's office*, subsecretaría, *f.*
undersecretaryship [—'sekrətəriʃip] n. Subsecretaría, *f.*
undersell* [—'sel] v. tr. Vender más barato que (to sell at a lower price than). || Malvender, malbaratar (to sell at a low price).
— OBSERV. Pret. & p. p. ***undersold***.
underset [—set] n. MIN. Vena (*f.*) subyacente. || Corriente (*f.*) submarina (undercurrent).
undershirt [—ʃə:t] n. U. S. Camiseta, *f.*
undershoot [—'ʃu:t] v. tr. No alcanzar [el blanco] por haber disparado corto. || AVIAT. No alcanzar (the runway).
— V. intr. Disparar corto.
undershot [—ʃɔt] adj. ANAT. Prognato, ta (with a projecting jaw). || *Undershot wheel*, rueda hidráulica impulsada por el agua en su parte inferior.
underside [—said] n. Cara (*f.*) inferior, parte (*f.*) inferior.
undersign [—sain] v. tr. Firmar.
undersigned [—saind] adj. Abajo firmante, infrascrito, ta: *I, the undersigned, bequeath*, el abajo firmante deja en herencia.
undersize [—'saiz] or **undersized** [—'saizd] adj. Pequeño, ña; de tamaño reducido (small). || Demasiado pequeño, ña (too small). || Achaparrado, da da (person).
underskirt [—skə:t] n. Enaguas, *f. pl.*
underslung [—slʌŋ] adj. AUT. Colgante (chassis).
undersold [—'səuld] pret. & p. p. See UNDERSELL.
undersong [—sɔŋ] n. MUS. Estribillo, *m.*, melodía (*f.*) de acompañamiento.
understaffed [—'stα:ft] adj. Falto de personal.
understand* [—'stænd] v. tr. Entender, comprender: *I don't understand this sentence*, no entiendo esta frase; *nobody understands me*, no me comprende nadie; *I make myself understood*, yo me hago comprender; *I understand English, but I don't speak it*, entiendo el inglés, pero no lo hablo. || Entender de, ser entendido en: *to understand business*, ser entendido en negocios. || Tener entendido que: *I understand they went to Mexico*, tengo entendido que fueron a México. || Creer (to think, to believe). || Sobreentender, sobrentender (not to state). || — *Am I given to understand that?*, ¿debo entender que?, ¿me quiere usted decir que? || *I can understand your being angry*, comprendo que estés enfadado. || *I don't quite understand why*, no acabo de entender por qué. || *It being understood that*, con tal que. || *It is understood that*, tenemos entendido que, se supone que, se sobreentiende que. || *It must be clearly understood that*, que quede claramente sentado que. || *I wish it to be understood* o *let it be understood that*, que quede bien claro que, que conste que. || *Now I understand!*, ¡ahora caigo!, ¡ahora entiendo! || *That's understood*, eso se entiende, por supuesto. || *To give to understand that*, dar a entender que. || *To understand each other*, comprenderse, entenderse. || *To understand how to do sth.*, saber hacer algo. || *Understood?*, ¿entendido?, ¿comprendido?
— V. intr. Comprender.
— OBSERV. Pret. & p. p. ***understood***.
understandable [—'stændəbl] adj. Comprensible.
understanding [—'stændiŋ] adj. Comprensivo, va.
— N. Comprensión, *f.*: *lacking in understanding*, falto de comprensión. || Entendimiento, *m.*: *problems beyond my understanding*, problemas que están más allá de mi entendimiento. || Razón, *f.*, juicio, *m.*: *to reach the age of understanding*, llegar a la edad de la razón. || Compenetración, *f.*, comprensión (*f.*) mutua: *there is perfect understanding between them*, tienen una compenetración perfecta. || Interpretación, *f.*: *what is your understanding of this paragraph?*, ¿cuál es su interpretación de este párrafo? || Manera (*f.*) de entender (way of looking at sth.). || Inteligencia, *f.*, entendimiento, *m.*: *the good understanding between nations*, la buena inteligencia entre la naciones. || Acuerdo, *m.*, arreglo, *m.* (agreement, arrangement): *to arrive at an understanding*, llegar a un acuerdo. || Conocimientos, *m. pl.* (knowledge): *I have a good understanding of mathematics*, tengo buenos conocimientos de matemáticas. || — *On the understanding that*, a condición de que, con tal que. || *To arrive at an understanding of*, llegar a comprender.
understate [—'steit] v. tr. Quitar importancia a (to make seem less important). || Subestimar (to underestimate). || Exponer incompletamente (not to give all the facts).
understatement [—'steitmənt] n. Eufemismo, *m.* (euphemism). || Subestimación, *f.* (underestimation). || Exposición (*f.*) incompleta (incomplete statement).
understock [—'stɔk] v. tr. Suministrar existencias insuficientes.
understood [—'stud] pret. & p. p. See UNDERSTAND.
— Adj. GRAMM. Sobrentendido, da; sobreentendido, da; implícito, ta. || Entendido, da (agreed upon).
understrapper [—,stræpə*] n. Subalterno, *m.*
understudy [—,stʌdi] n. THEATR. Suplente, *m.* & *f.*, sobresaliente, *m.* & *f.*
understudy [—,stʌdi] v. tr. THEATR. Aprender un papel para poder suplir a.
undersurface [—,sə:fis] n. Superficie (*f.*) inferior.
undertake* [—'teik] v. tr. Emprender: *to undertake a journey, a task*, emprender un viaje, una tarea. || Encargarse de: *he undertook to go and fetch the doctor*, se encargó de ir a buscar al médico. || Prometer, comprometerse (to promise): *I made him undertake to deliver the letter*, le hice prometer que entregaría la carta, hice que se comprometiese a entregar la carta. || *To undertake that*, prometer que.
— OBSERV. Pret. ***undertook***; p. p. ***undertaken***.
undertaken [—'teikən] p. p. See UNDERTAKE.
undertaker [—,teikə*] n. Empresario (*m.*) de pompas fúnebres. || *Undertaker's*, funeraria, *f.*, pompas (*f. pl.*) fúnebres.
undertaking [—'teikiŋ] n. Tarea, *f.*, empresa, *f.* (task): *that's quite an undertaking!*, ¡vaya tarea! || Empresa, *f.*: *a daring undertaking*, una empresa atrevida. || COMM. Empresa, *f.* || Compromiso, *m.*, garantía, *f.* (pledge). || Promesa, *f.* (promise): *I gave an undertaking that*, hice la promesa de que. || Funeraria, *f.*, pompas (*f. pl.*) fúnebres (business of an undertaker).
undertenancy [—,tenənsi] n. Subarriendo, *m.*
undertenant [—,tenənt] n. Subarrendatario, ria.
under-the-counter [—ðə'kauntə*] adj. Bajo mano.
undertone [—təun] n. Voz (*f.*) baja (low voice): *in an undertone*, en voz baja. || Murmullo, *m.* (murmur). || Color (*m.*) apagado *or* de fondo, fondo, *m.* (colour). || FIG. Fondo, *m.* (underlying element). | Corriente, *f.* (tendency).
undertook [—'tuk] pret. See UNDERTAKE.
undertow [—təu] n. MAR. Contracorriente, *f.*, resaca, *f.*
undervaluation [—,vælju'eiʃən] n. Infravaloración, *f.*, subestimación, *f.*
undervalue [—'vælju:] v. tr. Infravalorar, subestimar (sth.) || Menospreciar (s.o.'s merit, etc.).
underwater [—'wɔ:tə*] adj. Submarino, na: *underwater fishing*, pesca submarina. || Bajo la línea de flotación (part of a boat).
underwear [—wεə*] n. Ropa (*f.*) interior.
underweight [—'weit] adj. De peso insuficiente. || *To be underweight*, no pesar bastante.
— N. Peso (*m.*) insuficiente.
underwent [—'went] pret. See UNDERGO.
underwing [—wiŋ] n. Ala (*f.*) posterior (of insects).
underwood [—wud] n. Maleza, *f.*, monte (*m.*) bajo.
underworld [—wə:ld] n. Mundo (*m.*) terrenal (Earth). || Mundo (*m.*) de los muertos (of the dead). || Infierno, *m.* (hell). || Antípodas, *f. pl.* (antipodes). || Hampa, *f.*, gente (*f.*) maleante (criminal world).
underwrite* [—rait] v. tr. Subscribir, suscribir (to sign). || Asegurar (to insure). || Garantizar (to guarantee). || Subscribir, suscribir (bonds).
— OBSERV. Pret. ***underwrote***; p. p. ***underwritten***.
underwriter [—raitə*] n. Asegurador, *m.* (insurer). || Suscriptor, *m.* (of bonds).

underwriting [—raitiŋ] n. Seguro, *m.*
underwritten [—'ritn] p. p. See UNDERWRITE.
underwrote [—rəut] pret. See UNDERWRITE.
undescribable ['ʌndis'kraibəbl] adj. Indescriptible.
undeserved ['ʌndi'zə:vd] adj. Inmerecido, da.
undeserving ['ʌndi'zə:viŋ] adj. De poco mérito (not meritorious). || Indigno, na (*of*, de). || *Undeserving of attention*, que no merece atención.
undesigned ['ʌndi'zaind] adj. Involuntario, ria (act). || Imprevisto, ta (result).
undesigning ['ʌndi'zainiŋ] adj. Cándido, da; sin malicia.
undesirable ['ʌndi'zaiərəbl] adj./n. Indeseable.
undesirous ['ʌndi'zaiərəs] adj. *To be undesirous of doing sth.*, tener pocas ganas de hacer algo, no querer hacer algo.
undetachable [ˌʌndi'tætʃəbl] adj. Inamovible.
undetected ['ʌndi'tektid] adj. Sin ser visto *or* descubierto. || *To pass undetected*, pasar desapercibido.
undeterminable ['ʌndi'tə:minəbl] adj. Indeterminable.
undetermined ['ʌndi'tə:mind] adj. Indeterminado, da (question, number, date, etc.). || Irresoluto, ta (irresolute).
undeterred ['ʌndi'tə:d] adj. Sin dejarse intimidar *or* impresionar (*by*, por).
undeveloped ['ʌndi'veləpt] adj. Sin desarrollar. || Inexplotado, da; sin explotar (land). || Subdesarrollado, da (underdeveloped). || PHOT. Sin revelar (film). || Inculto, ta (mind).
undeviating [ʌn'di:vieitiŋ] adj. Recto, ta (straight). || Directo, ta (direct). || Constante (constant).
undid ['ʌn'did] pret. See UNDO.
undies ['ʌndiz] pl. n. FAM. Ropa (*f. sing.*) interior.
undigested ['ʌndi'dʒestid] adj. MED. No digerido, da. || FIG. Mal digerido, da; mal asimilado, da.
undignified [ʌn'dignifaid] adj. Poco digno, na; poco decoroso, sa; indecoroso, sa.
undiluted ['ʌndai'lju:tid] adj. No diluido, da. || FAM. Puro, ra: *undiluted nonsense*, pura tontería.
undiminished ['ʌndi'miniʃt] adj. No disminuido, da.
undine ['ʌndi:n] n. MYTH. Ondina, *f.*
undiplomatic ['ʌnˌdiplə'mætik] adj. Poco diplomático, ca.
undirected ['ʌndi'rektid] adj. Sin dirección, sin señas (letter).
undiscernible ['ʌndi'sə:nəbl] adj. Imperceptible, indiscernible.
undiscerning ['ʌndi'sə:niŋ] adj. Sin discernimiento.
undischarged ['ʌndis'tʃɑ:dʒd] adj. Sin descargar (rifle, electric battery). || No rehabilitado, da (bankrupt). || Sin liquidar (debt). || No cumplido, da; incumplido, da (duty). || No licenciado (soldier). || *Undischarged of*, no liberado de.
undisciplined [ʌn'disiplind] adj. Indisciplinado, da.
undisclosed ['ʌndis'kləuzd] adj. Sin revelar.
undiscovered ['ʌndis'kʌvəd] adj. Sin descubrir, no descubierto, ta. || Desconocido, da (place).
undiscriminating ['ʌndis'krimineitiŋ] adj. Sin discernimiento, poco juicioso, sa (without discernment). || Sin discriminación (not preferential).
undisguised ['ʌndis'gaizd] adj. Sin disfraz (not in fancy dress). || Franco, ca; sincero, ra; no disfrazado, da (feeling).
undismayed ['ʌndis'meid] adj. Impávido, da (unmoved). || Sin desanimarse (without losing heart).
undisposed ['ʌndis'pəuzd] adj. *Undisposed of*, sin utilizar (unused), no vendido, da (unsold), no invertido, da (not invested).
undisputed ['ʌndis'pju:tid] adj. Incontestable (unchallenged). || Indiscutido, da; indiscutible (unquestioned): *undisputed truth*, verdad indiscutible.
undissolvable ['ʌndi'zɔlvəbl] adj. Indisoluble.
undistinguishable ['ʌndis'tiŋgwiʃəbl] adj. Indistinguible, indistinto, ta.
undistinguished ['ʌndis'tiŋgwiʃt] adj. Mediocre.
undistorted ['ʌndis'tɔ:tid] adj. ELECTR. Sin distorsión.
undisturbed ['ʌndis'tə:bd] adj. Tranquilo, la; sereno, na (still, peaceful, untroubled). || No perturbado, da (peace, sleep). || Sin tocar (untouched). || Sin desordenar (papers).
undiversified ['ʌndai'və:sifaid] adj. Uniforme.
undivided ['ʌndi'vaidid] adj. Indiviso, sa: *undivided property*, propiedad indivisa. || Entero, ra; íntegro, gra (complete). || No distribuido, da (profits). || Unánime (opinion). || *Give me your undivided attention*, préstenme ustedes toda su atención.
undo* ['ʌn'du:] v. tr. Desatar, deshacer (a knot). || Deshacer el nudo de, desanudar (a tie). || Deshacer, desatar, abrir (a parcel). || Desabrochar, desabotonar (a clasp, button). || Bajar (a zip). || Abrir (to open). || Deshacer: *to undo the work of another*, deshacer el trabajo de otro. || Reparar (to put right): *to undo the damage*, reparar el daño. || Perder, arruinar: *his overconfidence undid him*, le perdió la confianza excesiva en sí mismo.

— OBSERV. Pret. ***undid;*** p. p. ***undone.***

undoing [—iŋ] n. Perdición, *f.*, ruina, *f.* (ruin): *drink will be his undoing*, la bebida será su perdición. || Deshacer, *m.*, desatar, *m.* (of a parcel, knot, etc.). || Desabrochar, *m.* (of buttons, etc.). || Bajada, *f.* (of a zip). || Reparación, *f.* (of a damage).
undomesticated ['ʌndə'mestikeitid] adj. Indomesticado, da; no domesticado, da.
undone ['ʌn'dʌn] p. p. See UNDO.
— Adj. Inacabado, da (not finished). || Sin hacer, por hacer, no hecho, cha (not done). || Deshecho, cha; desatado, da (parcel, knot, etc.). || Desabrochado, da (buttons). || Bajado, da (zip). || Suelto, ta (hair). || Desatado, da (shoes). || Reparado, da (damage). || — FIG. *To be undone*, estar perdido (a person). || *To come undone*, desatarse, soltarse (laces). || *To leave undone*, dejar sin hacer *or* sin acabar (work).
undoubted [ʌn'dautid] adj. Indudable, indubitable.
undoubtedly [ʌn'dautidli] adv. Sin duda alguna, indudablemente.
undoubting [ʌn'dautiŋ] adj. Convencido, da; seguro, ra.
undraw* ['ʌn'drɔ:] v. tr. Descorrer, correr, abrir (curtains).

— OBSERV. Pret. ***undrew;*** p. p. ***undrawn.***

undrawn [—n] p. p. See UNDRAW.
undreamed [ʌn'dri:md] or **undreamt** [ʌn'dremt] adj. *Undreamed of*, no soñado, da; nunca soñado, da; inimaginable.
undress ['ʌn'dres] n. Bata, *f.* (informal dress). || MIL. Uniforme (*m.*) de cuartel.
undress ['ʌn'dres] v. tr. Desnudar (to take off the clothes of). || MED. Quitar el vendaje *or* la venda de.
— V. intr. Desnudarse.
undressed [—t] adj. Desnudo, da (naked). || En bata (with an informal dress). || Sin labrar (stone). || Sin desbastar (timber). || Sin aliñar, sin aderezar (salad, food). || Sin adobar (leather). || *To get undressed*, desnudarse.
undrew ['ʌn'dru:] pret. See UNDRAW.
undrinkable ['ʌn'driŋkəbl] adj. Imbebible (foul tasting). || No potable (water).
undriveable ['ʌn'draivəbl] adj. Imposible de conducir [*Amer.*, inmanejable].
undue ['ʌn'dju:] adj. Excesivo, va; indebido, da (excessive). || Impropio, pia (improper). || Inmerecido, da (undeserved). || JUR. Ilegítimo, ma (unlawful). | No vencido, da (bill of exchange).
undulant ['ʌndjulənt] adj. Ondulante. || MED. *Undulant fever*, fiebre (*f.*) de Malta.
undulate ['ʌndjuleit] adj. Ondulado, da.
undulate ['ʌndjuleit] v. tr. Hacer ondear (to cause to move in a wavy manner). || Ondular (to give wavelike form to).
— V. intr. Ondear, ondular.
undulated [—id] adj. Ondulado, da.
undulating [—iŋ] adj. Ondulado, da (country). || Ondeante, ondulante (corn).
undulation [ˌʌndju'leiʃən] n. Ondulación, *f.* (motion, form). || Pulsación, *f.* || Onda, *f.* (wave).
undulatory ['ʌndjulətəri] adj. Ondulante. || PHYS. Ondulatorio, ria: *undulatory theory*, teoría ondulatoria.
unduly ['ʌn'dju:li] adv. Excesivamente, indebidamente (excessively). || Impropiamente (improperly). || Injustamente (unjustly).
undying [ʌn'daiiŋ] adj. Imperecedero, ra.
unearned ['ʌn'ə:nd] adj. Inmerecido, da (undeserved). || No ganado, da (not earned by working). || — *Unearned income*, renta, *f.* [que no se gana trabajando]. || *Unearned increment*, plusvalía, *f.*
unearth ['ʌn'ə:θ] v. tr. Desenterrar (to dig up). || FIG. Descubrir (a conspiracy). | Desenterrar (to bring to light).
unearthing [—iŋ] n. Desenterramiento, *m.*
unearthly [—li] adj. Sobrenatural; extraterreno, na (not earthly). || Misterioso, sa; fantástico, ca (mysterious). || FAM. Horrible, infernal, espantoso, sa: *an unearthly din*, un barullo espantoso. | Intempestivo, va: *what an unearthly time to get up!*, ¡qué hora más intempestiva para levantarse!
uneasiness [ʌn'i:zinis] n. Intranquilidad, *f.*, desasosiego, *m.*, inquietud, *f.* (worry). || Incomodidad, *f.*, molestia, *f.*, malestar, *m.*
uneasy [ʌn'i:zi] adj. Molesto, ta; incómodo, da (ill at ease). || Inquieto, ta; desasosegado, da (disturbed, troubled). || Preocupado, da (worried). || Molesto, ta (annoying). || MED. Agitado, da (patient, sleep). || *To make uneasy*, inquietar, preocupar.
uneatable ['ʌn'i:təbl] adj. Incomible, incomestible.
uneconomic ['ʌnˌi:kə'nɔmik] or **uneconomical** ['ʌnˌi:kə'nɔmikl] adj. Poco económico, ca; antieconómico, ca (method). || Poco rentable (work).
uneducated ['ʌn'edjukeitid] adj. Inculto, ta; ignorante (uncultured).
uneffected ['ʌni'fektid] adj. Sin realizar, no efectuado, da.
unembodied ['ʌnim'bɔdid] adj. Incorpóreo, a.
unemotional ['ʌni'məuʃənəl] adj. Poco emotivo, va. || Poco impresionable. || Impasible (character). || Objetivo, va (report, etc.).
unemployable ['ʌnim'plɔiəbl] adj. Incapacitado para tener un empleo.
— N. Persona (*f.*) incapacitada para tener un empleo.
unemployed ['ʌnim'plɔid] adj. Parado, da; desempleado, da; sin trabajo [*Amer.*, desocupado, da] (not in paid employment): *to be unemployed*, estar parado. || Sin utilizar, inutilizado, da (not being used). || Sin

invertir, no invertido, da; improductivo, va (capital, funds).
— N. *The unemployed*, los parados, los desempleados [*Amer.*, los desocupados].
unemployment [ˈʌnimˈplɔimənt] n. Paro, *m.*, desempleo, *m.* [*Amer.*, desocupación, *f.*]: *seasonal unemployment*, paro estacional. || *Unemployment benefit* (U. S., *unemployment compensation*), subsidio (*m.*) de paro.
unencumbered [ˈʌninˈkʌmbəd] adj. Sin gravámenes (estate). || *Unencumbered by*, sin las trabas de.
unending [ˈʌnˈendiŋ] adj. Interminable (endless).
unendurable [ˈʌninˈdjuərəbl] adj. Intolerable, insoportable.
unengaged [ˈʌniŋˈgeidʒd] adj. Libre (person, room, seat).
un-English [ˈʌnˈiŋgliʃ] adj. Poco inglés, esa.
unenlightened [ˈʌninˈlaitnd] adj. Ignorante, poco ilustrado, da (person).
unenterprising [ˈʌnˈentəpraiziŋ] adj. Poco emprendedor, ra; sin iniciativa, poco dinámico, ca; tímido, da.
unentertaining [ʌnˌentəˈteiniŋ] adj. Poco entretenido, da; aburrido, da.
unenthusiastic [ˈʌninˌθju:ziˈæstik] adj. Poco entusiasta.
unenviable [ˈʌnˈenviəbl] adj. Poco envidiable.
unequal [ˈʌnˈi:kwəl] adj. Desigual, distinto, ta: *unequal lengths*, largos desiguales. || MED. Irregular: *unequal pulse*, pulso irregular. || Inadecuado, da (not adequate). || — *To be unequal to a mission*, no estar a la altura de una misión, ser incapaz de cumplir una misión. || *To be unequal to doing sth.*, no ser capaz de hacer algo, no tener talla para hacer algo.
unequalled (U. S. **unequaled**) [ˈʌnˈi:kwəld] adj. Sin igual, sin par.
unequivocal [ˈʌniˈkwivəkəl] adj. Inequívoco, ca; claro, ra.
unerring [ˈʌnˈə:riŋ] adj. Infalible, seguro, ra.
unescapable [ˌʌnisˈkeipəbl] adj. Inevitable, ineludible.
Unesco [ju:ˈneskəu] n. Unesco, *f.*

— OBSERV. U.N.E.S.C.O. son las siglas de *United Nations Educational, Scientific and Cultural Organization.*

unessential [ˈʌniˈsenʃəl] adj. No esencial, accesorio, ria; secundario, ria.
— N. Lo accesorio, lo secundario.
unestimated [ˈʌnˈestimeitid] adj. Inestimado, da.
unethical [ʌnˈeθikəl] adj. Poco ético, ca; inmoral.
uneven [ˈʌnˈi:vən] adj. Accidentado, da; desigual: *an uneven surface*, una superficie accidentada. || Desigual (unequal): *an uneven match*, un combate desigual. || MATH. Impar (numbers). || Irregular: *uneven progress*, progresos irregulares.
unevenness [—nis] n. Desigualdad, *f.* (of a surface). || Irregularidad, *f.* (irregularity). || Desigualdad, *f.* (inequality).
uneventful [ˈʌniˈventful] adj. Sin acontecimientos, sin incidentes.
unexampled [ˈʌnigˈzɑ:mpld] adj. Sin par, sin igual, sin precedente.
unexceptionable [ˌʌnikˈsepʃənəbl] adj. Irreprochable, intachable. || JUR. Irrecusable.
unexceptional [ˈʌnikˈsepʃənəl] adj. Ordinario, ria; corriente (ordinary). || Irreprochable, intachable (unexceptionable). || Sin excepción (without exception).
unexchangeable [ˈʌniksˈtʃeindʒəbl] adj. Incambiable.
unexciting [ˈʌnikˈsaitiŋ] adj. Sin interés.
unexecuted [ˈʌnˈeksikju:tid] adj. No ejecutado, da.
unexpected [ˈʌniksˈpektid] adj. Inesperado, da; imprevisto, ta: *unexpected event*, suceso imprevisto; *if anything unexpected turns up* o *happens*, si ocurre algo imprevisto. || *The unexpected*, lo imprevisto.
unexpectedly [—li] adv. De improviso, inesperadamente.
unexperienced [ˈʌniksˈpiəriənsd] adj. Inexperto, ta; inexperimentado, da; sin experiencia (inexperienced). || Nunca experimentado, da (never felt).
unexpiated [ˈʌnˈekspieitid] adj. Inexpiado, da.
unexpired [ˈʌniksˈpaiəd] adj. No vencido, da (bill). || No caducado, da; válido, da (tickets, etc.).
unexplainable [ˈʌniksˈpleinəbl] adj. Inexplicable.
unexplained [ˈʌniksˈpleind] adj. Inexplicado, da.
unexploitable [ˈʌniksˈplɔitəbl] adj. Inexplotable.
unexploited [ˈʌniksˈplɔitid] adj. Inexplotado, da.
unexplorable [ˈʌniksˈplɔ:rəbl] adj. Inexplorable.
unexplored [ˈʌniksˈplɔ:d] adj. Inexplorado, da.
unexposed [ˈʌniksˈpəuzd] adj. No expuesto, ta. || FIG. No descubierto, ta (crime).
unexpressed [ˈʌniksˈprest] adj. No expresado, da; inexpresado, da. || Tácito, ta (tacit). || GRAMM. Sobreentendido, da; sobrentendido, da.
unexpressive [ˈʌniksˈpresiv] adj. Inexpresivo, va.
unexpurgated [ˈʌnˈekspə:geitid] adj. No expurgado, da; íntegro, gra.
unextended [ˈʌniksˈtendid] adj. Inextenso, sa.
unextinguishable [ˈʌniksˈtiŋgwiʃəbl] adj. Inextinguible.
unfading [ˈʌnˈfeidiŋ] adj. Inmarcesible, inmarchitable. || FIG. Imperecedero, ra; imborrable.
unfailing [ˈʌnˈfeiliŋ] adj. Inagotable (inexhaustible). || Constante (never ceasing). || Infalible (infallible). || Seguro, ra; infalible, indefectible (certain): *we were awaiting his unfailing twelve-o'clock arrival*, esperábamos su indefectible llegada a las doce.
unfair [ˈʌnˈfɛə*] adj. Injusto, ta (not just). || Desleal (competition). || Sucio, cia (play). || Excesivo, va; exagerado, da (price). || No equitativo, va (wages).
unfairness [—nis] n. Injusticia, *f.* || Deslealtad, *f.* (in competition). || Suciedad, *f.* (in play). || Exceso, *m.*, exageración, *f.* (in prices). || Falta (*f.*) de equidad (in wages).
unfaith [ˈʌnˈfeiθ] n. Falta (*f.*) de fe.
unfaithful [ˈʌnˈfeiθful] adj. Infiel: *his wife is unfaithful to him*, su mujer le es infiel. || Desleal (disloyal).
unfaithfulness [—nis] n. Infidelidad, *f.* || Deslealtad, *f.* (disloyalty).
unfalsifiable [ˈʌnˈfɔ:lsifaiəbl] adj. Infalsificable.
unfaltering [ˈʌnˈfɔ:ltəriŋ] adj. Resuelto, ta; decidido, da; firme.
unfamiliar [ˈʌnfəˈmiljə*] adj. No familiarizado, da: *unfamiliar with firearms*, no familiarizado con las armas de fuego. || Desconocido, da: *an unfamiliar face*, una cara desconocida. || Poco corriente: *unfamiliar phrase*, expresión poco corriente. || Extraño, ña (strange). || *To be unfamiliar with the customs*, no conocer las costumbres, desconocer las costumbres.
unfashionable [ˈʌnˈfæʃənəbl] adj. Pasado de moda (out of date). || Poco elegante (not very smart).
unfasten [ˈʌnˈfɑ:sən] v. tr. Desabrochar (one's dress). || Abrir (a door). || Desatar (a knot, rope, etc.). || Soltar, desatar (a dog). || Soltar (to set free). || Aflojar (to loosen).
unfathered [ˈʌnˈfɑ:ðəd] adj. Sin padre, ilegítimo, ma (child). || FIG. De fuente desconocida (news). | De autor desconocido (theory).
unfathomable [ˈʌnˈfæðəməbl] adj. Insondable.
unfavourable (U. S. **unfavorable**) [ˈʌnˈfeivərəbl] adj. Desfavorable.
unfeasible [ˈʌnˈfi:zibl] adj. Irrealizable, impracticable.
unfeeling [ʌnˈfi:liŋ] adj. Insensible.
unfeelingness [—nis] n. Insensibilidad, *f.*
unfeigned [ˈʌnˈfeind] adj. Sincero, ra; no fingido, da; verdadero, ra.
unfelt [ˈʌnˈfelt] adj. No percibido, da; no sentido, da; insensible.
unfermented [ˈʌnfəˈmentid] adj. No fermentado, da; sin fermentar (liquor). || Ácimo (bread).
unfetter [ˈʌnˈfetə*] v. tr. Desencadenar (a prisoner). || Destrabar (a horse). || FIG. Liberar, libertar.
unfilial [ˈʌnˈfiljəl] adj. Indigno de un hijo.
unfilmed [ˈʌnˈfilmd] adj. Que no ha sido llevado a la pantalla (novel, etc.).
unfinished [ˈʌnˈfiniʃt] adj. Inacabado, da; sin acabar. || Incompleto, ta (not complete). || TECH. Bruto, ta. || *The Unfinished Symphony*, la Sinfonía incompleta *or* inconclusa.
unfit [ʌnˈfit] adj. Incapaz (*to*, de), no apto, ta (*to*, para) [not suitable]: *unfit for business*, no apto para los negocios; *unfit to govern*, incapaz de gobernar. || Inadecuado, da (*to*, para) [not adequate]. || Impropio, pia: *unfit to eat*, impropio para el consumo. || Incompetente. || En malas condiciones físicas (not physically fit). || Inútil (for military service). || MIL. *To be discharged as unfit*, ser declarado inútil, ser dado de baja.
unfit [ˈʌnˈfit] v. tr. Inhabilitar, incapacitar.
unfitness [—nis] n. Incapacidad, *f.* (inability). || Falta (*f.*) de aptitud, incompetencia, *f.* (incompetence). || Inoportunidad, *f.* (of a remark). || Debilidad (*f.*) física, mala salud, *f.*
unfitted [—id] adj. Impropio, pia (*for*, para). || Incapacitado, da: *unfitted for the job*, incapacitado para el trabajo. || *Unfitted with*, sin.
unfitting [—iŋ] adj. Impropio, pia: *unfitting behaviour for his age*, comportamiento impropio de su edad.
unfix [ˈʌnˈfiks] v. tr. Separar (to separate). || Quitar (to remove). || Soltar (to disengage). || Desarmar, desmontar (to take apart). || Desequilibrar (to unsettle).
unfixed [—t] adj. Suelto, ta (disengaged). || Indeterminado, da (date). || Irresoluto, ta; indeciso, sa (person).
unflagging [ʌnˈflægiŋ] adj. Infatigable, incansable (courage). || Constante (interest).
unflattering [ˈʌnˈflætəriŋ] adj. Poco halagüeño, ña.
unfledged [ˈʌnˈfledʒd] adj. Implume, sin plumas (not fledged). || Inexperto, ta; inexperimentado, da (immature).
unflinching [ʌnˈflintʃiŋ] adj. Resuelto, ta (resolute). || Impávido, da (dauntless).
unflyable [ˈʌnˈflaiəbl] adj. Que impide el despegue de los aviones (weather).
unfold [ˈʌnˈfəuld] v. tr. Desdoblar, desplegar, abrir (to open). || Extender (sth. on the table). || Revelar, descubrir (to reveal). || Exponer (a theory, a plan, etc.).
— V. intr. Abrirse, desplegarse, desdoblarse (to open out). || Extenderse: *the landscape unfolds before us*, el paisaje se extiende ante nosotros. || Revelarse, descubrirse (a secret). || Desarrollarse (one's thoughts, action).
unfolding [ˈʌnˈfəuldiŋ] n. Desdoblamiento, *m.*, despliegue, *m.*
unforbidden [ˈʌnfəˈbidn] adj. No prohibido, da; permitido, da.

unforced [ˈʌnˈfɔːst] adj. No forzado, da; no obligado, da (not obliged). || Espontáneo, a; franco, ca: *unforced laugh*, risa espontánea.
unforeseeable [ˈʌnfɔːˈsiːəbl] adj. Imprevisible.
unforeseeing [ˈʌnfɔːˈsiːiŋ] adj. Imprevisor, ra.
unforeseen [ˈʌnfɔːˈsiːn] adj. Imprevisto, ta || *The unforeseen*, lo imprevisto.
unforgeable [ˈʌnˈfɔːdʒəbl] adj. Infalsificable (money).
unforgettable [ˈʌnfəˈgetəbl] adj. Inolvidable.
unforgivable [ˈʌnfəˈgivəbl] adj. Imperdonable, indisculpable.
unforgiven [ˈʌnfəˈgivən] adj. No perdonado, da.
unforgiving [ˈʌnfəˈgiviŋ] adj. Que no perdona, implacable.
unforgotten [ˈʌnfəˈgɔtn] adj. No olvidado, da. || *He remains unforgotten*, su recuerdo permanece vivo.
unformed [ˈʌnˈfɔːmd] adj. No formado, da. || Informe, sin forma (shapeless). || Poco maduro, ra (immature).
unfortified [ˈʌnˈfɔːtifaid] adj. Sin fortificaciones. || Abierto, ta (town).
unfortunate [ˈʌnˈfɔːtjunit] adj. Desafortunado, da; desgraciado, da (person). || Desgraciado, da: *unfortunate event*, suceso desgraciado. || Poco afortunado da; desacertado, da (remark). || Malogrado, da (lately dead).
— N. Infortunado, da; desgraciado, da.
unfounded [ˈʌnˈfaundid] adj. Infundado, da; sin fundamento.
unframed [ˈʌnˈfreimd] adj. Sin marco.
unfreezable [ˈʌnˈfriːzəbl] adj. Incongelable.
unfreeze* [ˈʌnˈfriːz] v. tr. Descongelar. || Desbloquear, descongelar (money, prices, credits, wages). || Desbloquear (an account).
— OBSERV. Pret. ***unfroze***; p. p. ***unfrozen***.
unfreezing [ˈʌnˈfriːziŋ] n. Descongelación, *f.* || Descongelación, *f.*, desbloqueo, *m.* (of money, prices, wages, credits). || Desbloqueo, *m.* (of an account).
unfrequent [ˈʌnˈfriːkwənt] adj. Poco frecuente.
unfrequented [ˈʌnfriˈkwentid] adj. Poco frecuentado, da.
unfriendliness [ˈʌnˈfrendlinis] n. Hostilidad, *f.*, enemistad, *f.*
unfriendly [ˈʌnˈfrendli] adj. Hostil, poco amistoso, sa (hostile). || Desfavorable (unfavourable).
unfrock [ˈʌnˈfrɔk] v. tr. Obligar a colgar los hábitos (a priest).
unfroze [ˈʌnˈfrəuz] pret. See UNFREEZE.
unfrozen [ˈʌnˈfrəuzn] p. p. See UNFREEZE.
unfruitful [ˈʌnˈfruːtful] adj. Estéril (not producing offspring). || AGR. Estéril, improductivo, va; infecundo, da. || FIG. Infructuoso, sa (labour, etc.): *unfruitful efforts*, esfuerzos infructuosos. | Poco lucrativo, va (unprofitable).
unfruitfulness [—nis] n. Esterilidad, *f.* || FIG. Infructuosidad, *f.*
unfulfilled [ˈʌnfulˈfild] adj. Incumplido, da; no cumplido, da (desire, duty). || No cumplido, da (prophecy, promise). || No satisfecho, cha; insatisfecho, cha: *an unfulfilled petition*, una súplica insatisfecha.
unfunded [ʌnˈfʌndid] adj. Flotante, no consolidado, da (debt).
unfurl [ʌnˈfəːl] v. tr. Desplegar.
— V. intr. Desplegarse.
unfurnished [ˈʌnˈfəːniʃt] adj. Desamueblado, da; sin amueblar (room). || *Unfurnished with*, desprovisto de, sin.
ungainliness [ʌnˈgeinlinis] n. Torpeza, *f.* (clumsiness). || Desgarbo, *m.* (in one's gait).
ungainly [ʌnˈgeinli] adj. Torpe (clumsy). || Desgarbado, da (in one's gait).
ungallant [ˈʌnˈgælənt] adj. Poco galante.
ungarnished [ˈʌnˈgɑːniʃt] adj. Sin adornos, sencillo, lla.
ungather [ˈʌnˈgæðə*] v. tr. Desfruncir.
ungenerous [ˈʌnˈdʒenərəs] adj. Poco generoso, sa.
ungentle [ˈʌnˈdʒentl] adj. Brusco, ca; poco amable.
ungentlemanlike [ʌnˈdʒentlmənlaik] or **ungentlemanly** [ʌnˈdʒentlmənli] adj. Indigno de un caballero, poco caballeroso, sa (behaviour). || Incorrecto, mal educado (man).
un-get-at-able [ˈʌngetˈætəbl] adj. Inaccesible.
ungird* [ˈʌnˈgəːd] v. tr. Desatar, desceñir (belt, girdle). || Quitar el cinturón a (s.o.).
— OBSERV. Pret. & p. p. ***ungirded***, ***ungirt***.
ungirt [ˈʌnˈgəːt] pret. & p. p. See UNGIRD.
ungirth [ˈʌnˈgəːθ] v. tr. Descinchar, quitar la cincha a.
unglazed [ˈʌnˈgleizd] adj. Sin cristales (window). || Sin satinar, mate (paper). || Mate (photograph). || ARTS. No vidriado, da (ceramics).
unglue [ˈʌnˈgluː] v. tr. Despegar.
— V. intr. Despegarse.
ungodliness [ʌnˈgɔdlinis] n. Impiedad, *f.* (impiety). || Maldad, *f.* (wickedness).
ungodly [ʌnˈgɔdli] adj. Impío, a. || Malvado, da (wicked). || FAM. Atroz (outrageous).
ungovernable [ʌnˈgʌvənəbl] adj. Ingobernable (country, person). || Irreprimible, irrefrenable (desire). || Incontenible (passion).
ungoverned [ˈʌnˈgʌvənd] adj. No gobernado, da; sin gobernar (country). || Desenfrenado, da (passion).
ungraceful [ˈʌnˈgreisful] adj. Desgarbado, da; falto de gracia. || Torpe (clumsy).
ungracefully [—li] adv. Desgarbadamente, sin garbo *or* gracia. || Torpemente (clumsily).
ungracefulness [—nis] n. Falta (*f.*) de garbo *or* de gracia. || Torpeza, *f.* (clumsiness).
ungracious [ˈʌnˈgreiʃəs] adj. Brusco, ca; poco amable, descortés (discourteous). || Desagradable (unpleasant).
ungrammatical [ˈʌngrəˈmætikəl] adj. Incorrecto, ta; contrario a la gramática.
ungrateful [ʌnˈgreitful] adj. Ingrato, ta; desagradecido, da (*to*, *towards*, con, para con) [person]: *ungrateful child*, hijo ingrato. || Ingrato, ta (work).
ungratefulness [—nis] n. Ingratitud, *f.*, desagradecimiento, *m.*
ungratified [ˈʌnˈgrætifaid] adj. Insatisfecho, cha.
ungrudging [ˈʌnˈgrʌdʒiŋ] adj. Generoso, sa (generous). || Incondicional (support). || Dado de buena gana (gift).
ungrudgingly [—li] adv. De buena gana.
ungual [ˈʌŋgwəl] adj. ZOOL. Ungular.
unguarded [ˈʌnˈgɑːdid] adj. Indefenso, sa (unprotected). || Desprevenido, da; descuidado, da (careless). || Imprudente: *unguarded speech*, discurso imprudente. || De descuido (moment).
unguent [ˈʌŋgwənt] n. Ungüento, *m.*
unguiculate [ˈʌŋˈgwikjulit] adj. ZOOL. Unguiculado, da.
— N. ZOOL. Unguiculado, *m.*
unguis [ˈʌŋgwis] n. ZOOL. Pezuña, *f.* (hoof). | Garra, *f.* (claw). || ANAT. Unguis, *m.* (bone).
— OBSERV. El plural de la palabra inglesa es *ungues*.
ungula [ˈʌŋgjulə] n. MATH. Cono (*m.*) truncado. || ZOOL. See UNGUIS.
— OBSERV. El plural de *ungula* es *ungulae*.
ungular [ˈʌŋgjulə*] adj. Ungular.
ungulate [ˈʌŋgjuleit] adj. Ungulado, da.
— N. Ungulado, *m.*
unhackneyed [ʌnˈhæknid] adj. Nuevo, va; original; no trillado, da.
unhallowed [ʌnˈhæləud] adj. No consagrado, da (unconsecrated). || Impío, a (impious). || Profano, na (profane).
unhampered [ˈʌnˈhæmpəd] adj. Libre.
unhand [ʌnˈhænd] v. tr. Soltar.
unhandsome [—səm] adj. Sin atractivo (not attractive). || Feo, fea (ugly). || Mezquino, na (mean, stingy). || Descortés (discourteous). || Impropio, pia; indecoroso, sa (unbecoming).
unhandy [—i] adj. Torpe, desmañado, da (clumsy). || Incómodo, da; poco manejable (difficult to use).
unhang* [ˈʌnˈhæŋ] v. tr. Descolgar.
— OBSERV. Pret. & p. p. ***unhung***.
unhappiness [ʌnˈhæpinis] n. Desdicha, *f.*, infortunio, *m.*, infelicidad, *f.*, desgracia, *f.*
unhappy [ʌnˈhæpi] adj. Desdichado, da; infeliz (not happy). || Triste (sad): *that unhappy year*, aquel triste año. || Desgraciado, da; desventurado, da; desdichado, da (unfortunate): *unhappy in one's marriage*, desgraciado en el matrimonio. || Infausto, ta (event). || Poco afortunado, da (translation, choice, remark). || *I am unhappy about your decision*, no me agrada su decisión.
unharmed [ˈʌnˈhɑːmd] adj. Ileso, sa; indemne, incólume, sano y salvo, sana y salva (safe and sound). || Intacto, ta (intact).
unharmonious [ˈʌnhɑːˈməunjəs] adj. Inarmónico, ca; poco armonioso, sa.
unharness [ˈʌnˈhɑːnis] v. tr. Desenjaezar, desguarnecer, desaparejar (a horse). || Despojar de la armadura (a knight).
unhealthful [ʌnˈhelθful] adj. Insalubre.
unhealthiness [ʌnˈhelθinis] adj. Mala salud, *f.* (bad health). || Insalubridad, *f.* (of a place). || FIG. *Unhealthiness of mind*, espíritu malsano, mentalidad morbosa.
unhealthy [ʌnˈhelθi] adj. Enfermo, ma; enfermizo, za (person). || Malsano, na; insalubre (place). || FIG. Malsano, na; morboso, sa.
unheard [ˈʌnˈhəːd] adj. No oído, da. || *To condemn a prisoner unheard*, condenar a un preso sin haberle oído.
unheard-of [ʌnˈhəːdɔv] adj. Inaudito, ta; sin precedente (unprecedented). || Desconocido, da (unknown).
unheeded [ˈʌnˈhiːdid] adj. Desatendido, da. || *His warning went unheeded*, su advertencia no fue escuchada.
unheeding [ˈʌnˈhiːdiŋ] adj. Poco atento (*of*, a). || Despreocupado, da (*of*, por).
unhelpful [ˈʌnˈhelpful] adj. Inútil, vano, na (advice). || Poco servicial (person).
unhesitating [ʌnˈheziteitiŋ] adj. Inmediato, ta (answer). || Decidido, da; resuelto, ta (person).
unhesitatingly [—li] adv. Sin vacilar.
unhindered [ʌnˈhindəd] adj. Libre, sin estorbos.
unhinge [ʌnˈhindʒ] v. tr. Desquiciar (door). || FIG. Desquiciar, trastornar (mind).
unhitch [ˈʌnˈhitʃ] v. tr. Soltar, descolgar (sth.). || Desenganchar (a horse).
unhitching [—iŋ] n. Desenganche, *m.*
unholiness [ʌnˈhəulinis] n. Carácter (*m.*) profano. || Impiedad, *f.* (impiety).
unholy [ʌnˈhəuli] adj. Impío, a (person). || Profano, na (thing). || FIG. FAM. Infernal, terrible: *an unholy mess*, un desorden infernal.

unhonoured (U. S. **unhonored**) [ˈʌnˈɔnəd] adj. No honrado, da; desdeñado, da. || Rechazado, da (a cheque).
unhood [ˈʌnˈhud] v. tr. Descaperuzar, descapirotar (bird). || Desenmascarar (to unmask).
unhook [ˈʌnˈhuk] v. tr. Desenganchar (sth. which is caught or hooked). || Descolgar (to unhang). || Desabrochar (dress).
unhooking [—iŋ] n. Desenganche, *m.*
unhoped-for [ʌnˈhəuptfɔ:*] adj. Inesperado, da.
unhopeful [ʌnˈhəupful] adj. Desesperante. || Poco alentador, ra (prospect). || Pesimista (person).
unhorse [ˈʌnˈhɔ:s] v. tr. Desmontar, desarzonar (from a horse). || Desenganchar (a vehicle).
unhung [ˈʌnˈhʌŋ] pret. & p. p. See UNHANG.
unhurried [ˈʌnˈhʌrid] adj. Pausado, da; lento, ta.
unhurt [ˈʌnˈhə:t] adj. Indemne, ileso, sa (unharmed): *the driver was unhurt*, el conductor resultó ileso *or* salió ileso.
unhygienic [ˈʌnhaiˈdʒi:nik] adj. Antihigiénico, ca.
unicameral [ˌju:niˈkæmərəl] adj. Unicameral.
unicellular [ˌju:niˈseljulə*] adj. Unicelular.
unicity [ju:ˈnisiti] n. Unicidad, *f.*
unicorn [ˈju:nikɔ:n] n. MYTH. ASTR. Unicornio, *m.* || *Unicorn fish*, narval, *m.*, unicornio marino.
unidentified [ˈʌnaiˈdentifaid] adj. Sin identificar, no identificado, da. || *Unidentified flying objet* (*UFO*), ovni, *m.*, objeto volador no identificado.
unidirectional [ˌju:nidiˈrekʃənl] adj. RAD. Unidireccional.
unification [ˌju:nifiˈkeiʃən] n. Unificación, *f.*
unifier [ˈju:nifaiə*] n. Unificador, ra.
uniform [ˈju:nifɔ:m] adj. Uniforme: *uniform velocity, density*, velocidad, densidad uniforme. || *To make uniform*, hacer uniforme, uniformizar.
— N. Uniforme, *m.*: *school uniform*, uniforme del colegio. || MIL. Uniforme, *m.*: *full-dress uniform*, uniforme de gala.
uniform [ˈju:nifɔ:m] v. tr. Poner un uniforme a (to supply with a uniform). || Uniformizar (to make uniform).
uniformed [—d] adj. Con uniforme.
uniformity [ˌju:niˈfɔ:miti] n. Uniformidad, *f.*
uniformize [ˈju:nifɔ:maiz] v. tr. Uniformar, uniformizar.
unify [ˈju:nifai] v. tr. Unificar.
unilateral [ˈju:nilætərəl] adj. Unilateral.
unilocular [ˈju:niˈlɔkjulə] adj. BOT. Unilocular.
unimaginable [ˈʌniˈmædʒinəbl] adj. Inimaginable.
unimaginative [ˈʌniˈmædʒinətiv] adj. Poco imaginativo, va; falto de imaginación.
unimpaired [ˈʌnimˈpɛəd] adj. Intacto, ta (unharmed). || Inalterado, da (unaltered). || No disminuido, da (not lessened).
unimpeachable [ˈʌnimˈpi:tʃəbl] adj. Irrecusable (unquestionable). || Irreprochable, irreprensible (unreproachable).
unimpeached [ˈʌnimˈpi:tʃt] adj. Inatacado, da; no controvertido, da (unquestioned). || No acusado, da (not accused).
unimportance [ˈʌnimˈpɔ:təns] n. Poca importancia, *f.*, insignificancia, *f.*
unimportant [ˈʌnimˈpɔ:tənt] adj. Poco importante, sin importancia, insignificante.
unimposing [ˈʌnimˈpəuziŋ] adj. Poco impresionante.
unimpressed [ˈʌnimˈprest] adj. No acuñado, da (medal). || FIG. No impresionado, da (person). || *To be unimpressed by*, no quedar impresionado por.
unimpressionable [ˈʌnimˈpreʃnəbl] adj. Poco impresionable. || Impasible (impassive).
unimpressive [ˈʌnimˈpresiv] adj. Poco impresionante. || Poco conmovedor, ra (not moving). || Sin relieve (speech).
unimprovable [ˈʌnimˈpru:vəbl] adj. Inmejorable.
unimproved [ˈʌnimˈpru:vd] adj. No mejorado, da (not improved). || No aprovechado, da (not made use of). || Sin construir (not built on). || Sin cultivar (not cultivated). || No pavimentado, da (road).
uninflammable [ˈʌninˈflæməbl] adj. No inflamable, ininflamable.
uninflated [ˈʌninˈfleitid] adj. Desinflado, da (tyre).
uninfluenced [ˈʌnˈinfluənst] adj. No influenciado, da; no influido, da.
uninfluential [ˈʌninfluˈenʃəl] adj. Poco influyente, sin gran influencia.
uninformed [ˈʌninˈfɔ:md] adj. Mal informado, da (badly informed). || Ignorante (ignorant). || Inculto, ta (uneducated).
uninhabitable [ˈʌninˈhæbitəbl] adj. Inhabitable.
uninhabited [ˈʌninˈhæbitid] adj. Inhabitado, da; deshabitado, da. || Despoblado, da (deserted).
uninhibited [ˈʌninˈhibitid] adj. Sin inhibición.
uninitiated [ˈʌniˈniʃieitid] adj. No iniciado, da.
uninjured [ˈʌnˈindʒəd] adj. Ileso, sa; indemne.
uninominal [ˈju:niˈnɔminl] adj. Uninominal.
uninspired [ˈʌninˈspaiəd] adj. Sin inspiración, falto de inspiración.
uninstructed [ˈʌninsˈtrʌktid] adj. Sin haber recibido instrucciones. || Sin instrucción *or* cultura (uncultured).
uninsured [ˈʌninˈʃuəd] adj. No asegurado, da; sin asegurar, sin seguro.
unintelligence [ˈʌninˈtelidʒəns] n. Falta (*f.*) de inteligencia.
unintelligent [ˈʌninˈtelidʒənt] adj. Ininteligente, poco inteligente, falto de inteligencia.
unintelligibility [ˈʌninˌtelidʒəˈbiliti] n. Incomprensibilidad, *f.*
unintelligible [ˈʌninˈtelidʒəbl] adj. Ininteligible, incomprensible.
unintentional [ˈʌninˈtenʃənl] adj. Involuntario, ria; no intencionado, da.
unintentionally [—li] adv. Sin querer, involuntariamente, no intencionadamente.
uninterested [ˈʌnˈintristid] adj. No interesado, da; indiferente. || Desinteresado, da (disinterested).
uninteresting [ˈʌnˈintristiŋ] adj. Poco interesante, sin interés, falto de interés.
uninterpretable [ˈʌninˈtə:pritəbl] adj. MUS. Inejecutable.
uninterrupted [ˈʌnˌintəˈrʌptid] adj. Ininterrumpido, da; sin interrupción, continuo, nua.
uninterruption [ˈʌnˌintəˈrʌpʃən] n. Ininterrupción, *f.*
uninvited [ˈʌninˈvaitid] adj. No convidado, da; no invitado, da (guest). || Gratuito, ta; no solicitado, da (comment). || *To come uninvited*, venir sin ser invitado *or* convidado.
uninviting [ˈʌninˈvaitiŋ] adj. Poco atractivo, va. || Poco apetitoso, sa (food).
union [ˈju:njən] n. Unión, *f.* (uniting). || Armonía, *f.*, unión, *f.* (harmony). || Enlace, *m.*, unión, *f.* (marriage). || Unión, *f.*, confederación, *f.* (political). || Sindicato, *m.* (trade union). || Emblema (*m.*) de unión (on a flag). || TECH. Unión, *f.* || — *Customs union*, unión aduanera. || *Union is strength*, la unión hace la fuerza. || *Universal Postal Union*, Unión Postal Universal.
— Adj. Del sindicato: *union members*, miembros del sindicato. || Sindical: *union affairs*, asuntos sindicales.
Union [ˈju:njən] n. Estados (*m. pl.*) Unidos. || *Soviet Union*, Unión Soviética.
unionism [—izəm] n. Sindicalismo, *m.* (trade unionism). || Unionismo, *m.* (loyalty to any kind of union).
unionist [—ist] n. Sindicalista, *m.* & *f.* (trade unionist). || Unionista, *m.* & *f.* (of any union).
unionization [—aiˈzeiʃən] n. Sindicación, *f.*, sindicalización, *f.*
unionize [—aiz] v. tr. Sindicar.
Union Jack [—ˈdʒæk] n. Bandera (*f.*) del Reino Unido.
union shop [—ʃɔp] n. Empresa (*f.*) que contrata sólo a obreros sindicados.
union suit [—su:t] n. U. S. Ropa (*f.*) interior de cuerpo entero.
uniparous [ju:ˈnipərəs] adj. Uníparo, ra.
unipersonal [ju:niˈpə:sənəl] adj. Unipersonal.
unipolar [ju:niˈpəulə*] adj. Unipolar.
unique [ju:ˈni:k] adj. Único, ca. || FIG. Único, ca; incomparable. || Extraño, ña; extraordinario, ria; raro, ra (unusual).
uniqueness [—nis] n. Unicidad, *f.*
unisex [ˈju:niseks] adj. Unisexo, *inv.*: *unisex fashions*, modas unisexo.
unisexual [ˌju:niˈseksjuəl] adj. Unisexual.
unison [ˈju:nizn] n. MUS. Unisonancia, *f.* || FIG. Armonía, *f.* (harmony). || *In unison*, al unísono.
unisonous [juˈnisənəs] adj. MUS. Unísono, na.
unit [ˈju:nit] n. Unidad, *f.*: *metric units*, unidades métricas; *monetary unit*, unidad monetaria. || Elemento, *m.*: *bookshelves in separate units*, estantería en elementos separados; *kitchen unit*, elemento de cocina; *the family is the basic unit of society*, la familia es el elemento básico de la sociedad. || MATH. MIL. Unidad, *f.*: *units column*, columna de las unidades; *combat unit*, unidad de combate. || Conjunto, *m.*: *the engine forms a unit with the transmission*, el motor forma un conjunto con la transmisión. || TECH. Grupo, *m.*: *compressor unit*, grupo compresor; *generator unit*, grupo electrógeno. || Centro, *m.*: *research unit*, centro de investigaciones. || Servicio, *m.* (department): *accident unit*, servicio de urgencia. || Fábrica, *f.* (plant). || Aparato, *m.* (device). || Máquina, *f.* (machine). || Equipo, *m.* (of several machines). || Equipo, *m.* (team): *film unit*, equipo de rodaje. || — RAD. *Mobile unit*, unidad móvil. || TECH. *Motor unit*, bloque (*m.*) del motor. || *Production unit*, fábrica. || *Unit cost*, coste (*m.*) por unidad. || *Unit furniture*, muebles (*m. pl.*) por elementos. || *Unit price*, precio unitario, precio por unidad.
unitable or **uniteable** [ju:ˈnaitəbl] adj. Unible.
Unitarian [ju:niˈtɛəriən] adj./n. REL. Unitario, ria.
Unitarianism [—izəm] n. REL. Unitarismo, *m.*
unitary [ˈju:nitəri] adj. Unitario, ria.
unite [ju:ˈnait] v. tr. Unir (to bring together, to attach, to join): *to unite in matrimony*, unir en matrimonio; *s.o. is needed to unite the people*, se necesita alguien que una al pueblo; *to unite bricks with mortar*, unir ladrillos con argamasa. || Reunir (to assemble): *to unite an army*, reunir un ejército; *she unites beauty with brains*, reúne la belleza con la inteligencia.
— V. intr. Unirse, juntarse: *to unite in fighting poverty*, unirse para luchar contra la pobreza.
united [ju:ˈnaitid] adj. Unido, da: *a united front*, un frente unido; *a very united family*, una familia muy unida. || *United we stand, divided we fall*, la unión hace la fuerza, unidos venceremos.
United Kingdom [—ˈkiŋdəm] pr. n. Reino (*m.*) Unido.

United Nations [—ˈneiʃəns] pl. pr. n. Naciones (*f.*) Unidas.

United States of America [—ˈsteitsəvəˈmerikə] pl. pr. n. Estados (*m.*) Unidos de América.

unity [ˈju:niti] n. Unidad, *f.*: *unity of purpose*, unidad de propósitos; *there is no unity about his plans*, no hay unidad en sus proyectos. || Armonía, *f.* (harmony): *to live together in unity*, vivir en armonía. || Unión, *f.* (union): *unity is strength*, la unión hace la fuerza; *European unity*, unión europea. || MATH. Unidad, *f.* || THEATR. Unidad, *f.*: *the three unities*, las tres unidades.

universal [ˌju:niˈvə:səl] adj. Universal: *universal suffrage*, sufragio universal. || Mundial (worldwide). || PHIL. Universal. || — *By universal request*, a petición general. || *To make universal*, generalizar. || TECH. *Universal coupling*, acoplamiento (*m.*) universal *or* de cardán. | *Universal joint*, junta (*f.*) universal *or* de cardán. || *Universal remedy*, panacea, *f.*
— N. PHIL. Proposición (*f.*) universal.

universality [ˌju:nivə:ˈsæliti] n. Universalidad, *f.*: *the universality of the English and Spanish languages*, la universalidad de las lenguas inglesa y española.

universalization [ˌju:niˌvə:səlaiˈzeiʃən] n. Universalización, *f.*

universalize [ˌju:niˈvə:səlaiz] v. tr. Universalizar, generalizar.

universally [ˌju:niˈvə:səli] adv. Universalmente, por todos (by everyone): *he is universally recognized as an expert*, es reconocido por todos como un experto. || Universalmente, por todas partes (everywhere): *a language which is spoken universally*, un idioma que se habla por todas partes. || Mundialmente (throughout the world). || Siempre (always): *a universally applicable rule*, una regla que se puede aplicar siempre.

universe [ˈju:nivə:s] n. Universo, *m.*

university [ˌju:niˈvə:siti] n. Universidad, *f.* || — *A man with a university education*, un hombre con estudios universitarios. || *To be at university* o *to go to university*, ser estudiante universitario, ir a la facultad *or* a la universidad. || *University degree*, título universitario. || *University town*, ciudad universitaria, ciudad (*f.*) que tiene una universidad.

univocal [ˈju:niˈvəukəl] n. Unívoco, ca.

unjust [ˈʌnˈdʒʌst] adj. Injusto, ta (*to, with*, para, con).

unjustifiable [ʌnˈdʒʌstifaiəbl] adj. Injustificable.

unjustifiably [—i] adv. Sin justificación, injustificadamente.

unjustified [ʌnˈdʒʌstifaid] adj. Injustificado, da.

UNIVERSE AND WEATHER
UNIVERSO (*m.*) Y TIEMPO (*m.*)

I. Universe. — Universo, *m.*

world	mundo *m.*
orb	orbe *m.*
cosmos	cosmos *m.*
cosmography	cosmografía *f.*
cosmogony	cosmogonía *f.*
cosmology	cosmología *f.*
earth	tierra *f.*
sphere	esfera *f.*
globe	globo *m.*
space	espacio *m.*
sky	cielo *m.*
vault of heaven, celestial vault	bóveda (*f.*) celeste
heavenly body	cuerpo (*m.*) celeste, astro *m.*
planet	planeta *m.*
planetary	planetario, ria
interplanetary	interplanetario, ria
star	estrella *f.*
morning star	lucero (*m.*) del alba
evening star	estrella (*f.*) vespertina
shooting star	estrella (*f.*) fugaz
polestar	estrella (*f.*) polar
comet	cometa *m.*
tail	cola *f.*, cabellera *f.*
asteroid	asteroide *m.*
aerolite	aerolito *m.*
satellite	satélite *m.*
constellation	constelación *f.*
nebula	nebulosa *f.*
galaxy	galaxia *f.*
ring of Saturn	anillo (*m.*) de Saturno
Milky Way	Vía (*f.*) Láctea
orbit	órbita *f.*
apsis	ápside *m.*
equator	ecuador *m.*
zenith	cenit *m.*
epicycle	epiciclo *m.*
apogee	apogeo *m.*
perigee	perigeo *m.*
node	nodo *m.*
limb	limbo *m.*
solar system	sistema (*m.*) solar
sun	sol *m.*
photosphere	fotosfera *f.*
chromosphere	cromosfera *f.*
solar corona	corona (*f.*) solar
halo	halo *m.*
aureole	aureola *f.*
macula	mácula *f.*, mancha *f.*
rise (to)	salir [el sol]
sunrise	salida (*f.*) del sol
dawn, daybreak	amanecer *m.*, alba *f.*, aurora *f.*
shine (to)	lucir [el sol]
set (to)	ponerse [el sol]
sunset	puesta (*f.*) del sol, ocaso *m.*
nightfall, dusk	anochecer *m.*, crepúsculo *m.*
rainbow	arco (*m.*) iris
sun's rays	rayos (*m.*) del sol
eclipse	eclipse *m.*
solstice	solsticio *m.*
winter solstice	solsticio (*m.*) de invierno
summer solstice	solsticio (*m.*) de verano
equinox	equinoccio *m.*
moon	luna *f.*
cusp of the moon	cuerno (*m.*) de la luna
lunation	lunación *f.*
phase	fase *f.*
selenography	selenografía *f.*
full moon	luna (*f.*) llena, plenilunio *m.*
new moon	luna (*f.*) nueva
first quarter, waxing moon, crescent moon	luna (*f.*) creciente, cuarto (*m.*) creciente
half-moon	media luna *f.*
last quarter, waning moon	luna (*f.*) menguante, cuarto (*m.*) menguante
Great Bear, Ursa Major	Osa (*f.*) Mayor, Carro (*m.*) Mayor
Little Bear, Ursa Minor	Osa (*f.*) Menor, Carro (*m.*) Menor
Greater Dog	Can (*m.*) Mayor
Lesser Dog	Can (*m.*) Menor
Bootes	Boyero *m.*
Wagoner, Waggoner	Cochero *m.*, Auriga *m.*
signs of the zodiac	signos (*m.*) del zodiaco
Aries	Aries *m.*
Taurus	Tauro *m.*
Gemini	Géminis *m. pl.*
Cancer	Cáncer *m.*
Leo	Leo *m.*
Virgo	Virgo *m.*
Libra	Libra *f.*
Scorpio	Escorpión *m.*
Sagittarius	Sagitario *m.*
Capricorn	Capricornio *m.*
Aquarius	Acuario *m.*
Pisces	Piscis *m.*

II. Weather. — Tiempo, *m.*

meteorology	meteorología *f.*
atmosphere	atmósfera *f.*
climate	clima *m.*
elements	elementos *m.*
temperature	temperatura *f.*
to be warm *o* hot	hacer calor
to be cold	hacer frío
season	estación *f.*
spring	primavera *f.*
summer	verano *m.*
autumn [U.S. fall]	otoño *m.*
winter	invierno *m.*
Indian summer	veranillo (*m.*) de San Martín
drought	sequía *f.*
humidity	humedad *f.*
rain	lluvia *f.*
downpour, shower	aguacero *m.*, chaparrón *m.*, chubasco *m.*
cloud	nube *f.*
storm, tempest	temporal *m.*, tempestad *f.*, tormenta *f.*
lightning	relámpago *m.*, rayo *m.*
thunder	trueno *m.*
wind	viento *m.*
land wind	terral *m.*
hurricane	huracán *m.*
cyclone	ciclón *m.*
typhoon	tifón *m.*
whirlwind	torbellino *m.*, manga (*f.*) de viento
gale	vendaval *m.*
gust of wind	ráfaga (*f.*) de viento
breeze	brisa *f.*
mist, fog	neblina *f.*, bruma *f.*, niebla *f.*
haze	bruma *f.* [de calor]
dew	rocío *m.*
freeze	helada *f.*
frost	escarcha *f.*
hail	granizo *m.*
snow	nieve *f.*
snowflake	copo (*m.*) de nieve
snowfall	nevada *f.*
waterspout	tromba (*f.*) de agua
dead calm	calma (*f.*) chicha

See also GEOGRAFÍA

unkempt [ˈʌnˈkempt] adj. Despeinado, da (hair, person). || Fig. Descuidado, da (untidy).
unkind [ʌnˈkaind] adj. Poco amable: *she is very unkind to her servants*, es muy poco amable con sus criados; *that was unkind of him*, eso fue poco amable de su parte. || Severo, ra (harsh). || Cruel, despiadado, da (cruel): *unkind criticism*, crítica despiadada. || Riguroso, sa (weather).
unkindliness [—linis] n. See UNKINDNESS.
unkindly [—li] adj. Poco amable (unkind). || Riguroso, sa (weather).
— Adv. Poco amablemente, de manera poco amable, con poca amabilidad: *to treat s.o. unkindly*, tratar a alguien de manera poco amable. || Cruelmente (cruelly). || Severamente (harshly). || A mal: *don't take it unkindly*, no lo tomes a mal.
unkindness [—nis] n. Falta (*f.*) de amabilidad. || Crueldad, *f.* (cruelty). || Severidad, *f.* (harshness). || Rigor, *m.* (of weather).
unkingly [ˈʌnˈkiŋli] adj. Indigno de un rey.
unknit* [ˈʌnnit] v. tr. Destejer. || *To unknit one's brow*, desfruncir el ceño.
— Observ. Pret. & p. p. ***unknit, unknitted.***
unknot [ˈʌnˈnɔt] v. tr. Desanudar, desatar.
unknowable [ˈʌnˈnəuəbl] adj. Incognoscible.
unknowing [ˈʌnˈnəuiŋ] adj. Ignorante (ignorant). || Inconsciente (without realizing).
unknowingly [—li] adv. Sin darse cuenta, inconscientemente.
unknown [ˈʌnˈnəun] adj. Desconocido, da (region, author, etc.): *for some unknown reason*, por una razón desconocida. || — *A person unknown to me*, una persona desconocida por mí, una persona que yo no conozco *or* que yo desconozco. || *The unknown soldier*, el soldado desconocido. || Fig. Math. *Unknown quantity*, incógnita, *f.*: *to isolate the unknown quantity*, despejar la incógnita. || *Unknown to David, they had gone*, sin que lo supiera David se habían ido.
— N. Desconocido, da (person). || Lo desconocido (that which is not known): *to fear the unknown*, temer lo desconocido. || Math. Incógnita, *f.*
unlabelled or **unlabeled** [ˈʌnˈleibld] adj. Sin etiqueta.
unlace [ˈʌnˈleis] v. tr. Desatar.
unladderable [ˈʌnˈlædərəbl] adj. Indesmallable.
unlade* [ˈʌnˈleid] v. tr. Descargar.
— Observ. Pret. ***unladed;*** p. p. ***unladen.***
unladen [—ən] adj. Sin cargamento, vacío, a.
unladylike [ˈʌnˈleidilaik] adj. Poco señora, poco distinguida (a woman). || Impropio de una señora (behaviour).
unlamented [ˈʌnˈləˈmentid] adj. No lamentado, da. || *To die unlamented*, morir sin ser llorado.
unlash [ˈʌnˈlæʃ] v. tr. Desamarrar.
unlatch [ˈʌnˈlætʃ] v. tr. Levantar el picaporte de, abrir (a door).
unlawful [ˈʌnˈlɔ:ful] adj. Ilegal (illegal). || Ilegítimo, ma (illegitimate).
unlawfulness [—nis] n. Ilegalidad, *f.* (illegality). || Ilegitimidad, *f.* (illegitimacy).
unlearn* [ˈʌnˈlə:n] v. tr. Olvidar, desaprender. || Quitarse (a habit).
— Observ. Pret. & p. p. ***unlearnt, unlearned.***
unlearned [—d] or **unlearnt** [—t] adj. Indocto, ta; inculto, ta; ignorante (lacking learning). || Sin aprender (not learnt). || Poco ejercitado (*in*, en) [unskilled].
unleash [ˈʌnˈli:ʃ] v. tr. Soltar (a dog). || Fig. Liberar (to free). | Dar rienda suelta a, desatar (one's passions). | Provocar (s.o.'s anger).
unleavened [ˈʌnˈlevnd] adj. Ácimo, ázimo, sin levadura: *unleavened bread*, pan ácimo.
unless [ənˈles] conj. A no ser que, a menos que (with subj.), si no (with indic.): *they never go out unless forced to*, nunca salen a no ser que se les obligue; *unless I am mistaken*, a no ser que me equivoque, si no me equivoco.
— Prep. Salvo, excepto: *no one, unless John...*, nadie excepto Juan...
unlettered [ˈʌnˈletəd] adj. Iletrado, da.
unlicensed [ˈʌnˈlaisenst] adj. Ilícito, ta; no autorizado, da; sin permiso: *unlicensed sale of alcohol*, venta ilícita de alcohol.
unlike [ˈʌnˈlaik] adj. Diferente, distinto, ta: *two unlike quantities*, dos cantidades diferentes. || Diferente a, diferente de, distinto de: *people quite unlike ourselves*, gente muy distinta de nosotros. || A diferencia de: *Peter, unlike his father, is rather shy*, Pedro, a diferencia de su padre, es algo tímido. || Impropio de; poco característico de: *it's unlike me to be so worried*, es impropio de mí preocuparme tanto. || Phys. Opuesto, ta: *unlike poles*, polos opuestos.
unlikeable [—əbl] adj. Antipático, ca.
unlikelihood [—lihud] or **unlikeliness** [—linis] n. Improbabilidad, *f.*
unlikely [—li] adj. Improbable, poco probable (improbable): *it is unlikely that anything will happen*, es poco probable que ocurra algo. || Inverosímil (unexpected): *he always visits the most unlikely places*, siempre visita los lugares más inverosímiles. || Poco prometedor, ra (unpromising). || — *He was unlikely to win*, tenía pocas probabilidades de ganar. || *It is not at all unlikely*, es muy probable, es muy posible.
unlikeness [ˈʌnˈlaiknis] n. Diferencia, *f.*
unlimber [ʌnˈlimbə*] v. tr. Quitar el armón a (a gun).
unlimitable [ʌnˈlimitəbl] adj. Ilimitable.
unlimited [ʌnˈlimitid] adj. Ilimitado, da.
unlined [ʌnˈlaind] adj. Sin rayar (paper). || Sin forro, sin forrar (coat, etc.). || Sin arrugas (face).
unlink [ˈʌnˈliŋk] v. tr. Quitar los eslabones de (a chain). || Desatar (to unfasten).
unliquidated [ˈʌnˈlikwideitid] adj. Sin liquidar, sin saldar (a debt).
unlisted [ʌnˈlistid] adj. Que no figura en la lista (not on the list). || No cotizado, da (securities).
unlit [ˈʌnˈlit] adj. Sin luz, no iluminado, da. || *Unlit street*, calle (*f.*) sin alumbrado.
unlivable or **unliveable** [ʌnˈlivəbl] adj. Inaguantable (unbearable). || Inhabitable (uninhabitable).
unload [ˈʌnˈləud] v. tr. Descargar (transport vehicles, goods, a gun): *to unload the sugar from a boat*, descargar el azúcar de un barco. || Fig. Abrir, desahogar (one's heart). | Deshacerse de (to get rid of). || Fig. *To unload one's responsibilities on a colleague*, descargarse de sus obligaciones en un colega.
— V. intr. Descargar.
unloaded [—id] adj. Descargado, da.
unloader [—ə*] n. Descargador, *m.*
unloading [—iŋ] n. Descarga, *f.*: *unloading of a boat*, descarga de un barco.
unlock [ˈʌnˈlɔk] v. tr. Abrir [con llave] (a door). || Fig. Revelar (a secret). | Resolver (a puzzle). || Desbloquear (to unblock).
unlooked-for [ʌnˈluktfɔ:*] adj. Imprevisto, ta; inesperado, da.
unloose [ˈʌnˈlu:s] or **unloosen** [ʌnˈlu:sn] v. tr. Soltar (to loosen, to let go). || Desatar (a shoelace).
unlosable [ʌnˈlu:zəbl] adj. Imperdible.
unloveable or **unlovable** [ʌnˈlʌvəbl] adj. Poco amable, antipático, ca.
unlovely [ˈʌnˈlʌvli] adj. Desgarbado, da; sin atractivo (person). || Feo, a (thing).
unloving [ˈʌnˈlʌviŋ] adj. Poco cariñoso, sa.
unluckily [ʌnˈlʌkili] adv. Desafortunadamente, desgraciadamente.
unluckiness [ʌnˈlʌkinis] n. Desgracia, *f.* || Mala suerte, *f.*
unlucky [ʌnˈlʌki] adj. Desgraciado, da; desafortunado, da; desdichado, da: *how unlucky I am!*, ¡qué desgraciado soy!; *unlucky in gambling*, desgraciado en el juego. || Aciago, ga; nefasto, ta; funesto, ta; de mala suerte: *an unlucky day*, un día de mala suerte. || Gafe (who brings bad luck). || — *How unlucky!*, ¡qué mala suerte! || *It is unlucky to break a mirror*, trae mala suerte romper un espejo. || *To be born unlucky*, haber nacido con mala estrella. || *To be unlucky*, tener mala suerte (a person). || *Unlucky devil*, pobre diablo, *m.* || *Unlucky omen*, cosa (*f.*) de mal agüero.
unmade [ʌnˈmeid] adj. Sin hacer.
— Pret. & p. p. See UNMAKE.
unmaidenly [ʌnˈmeidnli] adj. Poco señorita (girl). || Impropio de una señorita (behaviour).
unmaintainable [ʌnmeinˈteinəbl] adj. Insostenible.
unmake* [ˈʌnˈmeik] v. tr. Deshacer.
— Observ. Pret. & p. p. ***unmade.***
unman [ˈʌnˈmæn] v. tr. Acobardar (to make cowardly). || Desanimar, abatir (to dishearten). || Castrar (to castrate). || Mil. Desguarnecer (a gun). || — *Unmanned aeroplane*, avión (*m.*) sin piloto. || *Unmanned device*, aparato automático. || *Unmanned flight*, vuelo no tripulado. || *Unmanned spacecraft*, nave (*f.*) espacial no tripulada *or* sin tripulación.
unmanageable [ʌnˈmænidʒəbl] adj. Inmanejable, poco manejable (a large book, etc.). || Poco dócil (person, horse).
unmanliness [ʌnˈmænlinis] n. Poca virilidad, *f.*, afeminamiento, *m.* (effeminacy). || Cobardía, *f.* (cowardice). || Falta (*f.*) de caballerosidad.
unmanly [ˈʌnˈmænli] adj. Poco viril, afeminado, da (effeminate). || Impropio de un hombre (behaviour). || Cobarde (cowardly).
unmannered [ʌnˈmænəd] adj. Descortés, mal educado, da (impolite). || Sencillo, lla (not affected).
unmannerliness [ʌnˈmænəlinis] n. Descortesía, *f.*, mala educación, *f.* (impoliteness).
unmannerly [ʌnˈmænəli] adj. Descortés, mal educado, da (impolite).
unmarked [ˈʌnˈmɑ:kt] adj. Sin marcar. || Sin letrero (a street). || Ileso, sa; indemne (uninjured). || En perfecto estado (as new). || Desapercibido, da (unnoticed): *to go unmarked*, pasar desapercibido. || Sp. Desmarcado, da (player).
unmarketable [ʌnˈmɑ:kitəbl] adj. Invendible.
unmarriable [ʌnˈmæriəbl] or **unmarriageable** [ʌnˈmæridʒəbl] adj. Incasable. || No casadero, ra (too young to be married).
unmarried [ˈʌnˈmærid] adj. Soltero, ra.
unmask [ˈʌnˈmɑ:sk] v. tr. Desenmascarar (to remove the mask from). || Mil. Descubrir (a battery). || Fig. *To unmask a plot*, descubrir un complot.
— V. intr. Quitarse la máscara.
unmast [ʌnˈmɑ:st] v. tr. Mar. Desarbolar.
unmatchable [ˈʌnˈmætʃəbl] adj. Incomparable. || Imposible de emparejar (impossible to pair).

unmatched ['ʌn'mætʃt] adj. Sin par, incomparable, único, ca (unique). || Sin pareja, no emparejado, da (not paired).
unmeaning [ʌn'mi:niŋ] adj. Sin sentido (words). || Inexpresivo, va (expressionless).
unmeant [ʌn'ment] adj. Involuntario, ria.
unmeasurable [ʌn'meʒərəbl] adj. Inmensurable.
unmeasured [ʌn'meʒəd] adj. Ilimitado, da (boundless). || No medido, da.
unmeet ['ʌn'mi:t] adj. Impropio, pia.
unmendable [ʌn'mendəbl] adj. Irreparable.
unmentionable [ʌn'menʃnəbl] adj. Indecible, que no se debe mencionar.
— Pl. n. FAM. Ropa (*f. sing.*) interior (underwear).
unmerciful [ʌn'mə:siful] adj. Despiadado, da.
unmerited ['ʌn'meritid] adj. Inmerecido, da.
unmethodical [ʌnmi'θɔdikəl] adj. Poco metódico, ca.
unmindful [ʌn'maindful] adj. Descuidado, da (careless). || — *Not unmindful of*, no olvidando, teniendo presente. || *To be unmindful of*, no pensar en (to forget), hacer caso omiso de (to pass over).
unmistakable ['ʌnmis'teikəbl] adj. Inconfundible: *written in his own unmistakable style*, escrito en su inconfundible estilo. || Inequívoco, ca: *unmistakable signs of inebriation*, señales inequívocas de embriaguez.
unmistakably ['ʌnmis'teikəbli] adv. Sin lugar a dudas, con toda evidencia.
unmitigated ['ʌn'mitigeitid] adj. Profundo, da (grief). || Implacable (hatred, heat). || Desenfrenado, da (anger). || FIG. Rematado, da; redomado, da; de tomo y lomo (arrant): *an unmitigated liar*, un mentiroso rematado.
unmixed ['ʌn'mikst] adj. Puro, ra; sin mezcla.
unmodified ['ʌn'mɔdifaid] adj. Sin modificar.
unmolested ['ʌnmə'lestid] adj. Tranquilo, la. || *To leave unmolested*, no molestar, dejar en paz.
unmoor ['ʌn'muə*] v. intr. MAR Soltar las amarras.
— V. tr. MAR. Desamarrar.
unmoral ['ʌn'mɔrəl] adj. Amoral.
unmotivated ['ʌn'məutiveitid] adj. Inmotivado, da; sin motivo.
unmounted ['ʌn'mauntid] adj. Desmontado, da (rider). || MIL. De a pie (soldier). || Sin engastar, sin montar (jewel). || Sin marco (picture).
unmovable ['ʌn'mu:vəbl] adj. Inamovible.
unmoved ['ʌn'mu:vd] adj. En su sitio, sin mover (in its place). || Impasible, indiferente (indifferent): *to be unmoved by sth.*, permanecer impasible ante algo. || Impávido, da (unflinching). || Insensible: *unmoved by all our pleas*, insensible a todas nuestras súplicas.
unmuffle ['ʌn'mʌfl] v. tr. Destapar, descubrir (one's face). || Quitar la sordina a (a drum, bell, etc.).
unmusical ['ʌn'mju:zikəl] adj. Poco armonioso, sa (not harmonious). || Que tiene mal oído (without musical skill). || Poco aficionado a la música (uninterested in music).
unmuzzle ['ʌn'mʌzl] v. tr. Quitar el bozal a (a dog). || FIG. *To unmuzzle the press*, dejar de amordazar la prensa.
unnail ['ʌn'neil] v. tr. Desclavar.
unnamable or **unnameable** ['ʌn'neiməbl] adj. Que no tiene nombre, vergonzoso, sa; innominable.
unnamed ['ʌn'neimd] adj. Sin nombre, innominado, da (having no name). || Anónimo, ma (anonymous). || *I prefer to remain unnamed*, prefiero conservar el anónimo.
unnatural ['ʌn'nætʃrəl] adj. Antinatural, no natural: *his appetite is unnatural*, su apetito no es natural. || Contra natura (vice). || Anormal (abnormal). || Afectado, da; sofisticado, da; poco natural (affected): *he has a rather unnatural manner*, tiene una manera de ser algo sofisticada. || Artificial (artificial).
unnaturally [—i] adv. De manera poco natural (in an unnatural way). || Anormalmente (abnormally). || Con afectación, de una manera sofisticada (affectedly). || *I not unnaturally thought that ...*, pensé naturalmente que...
unnavigable ['ʌn'nævigəbl] adj. Innavegable.
unnecessarily [ʌn'nesisərili] adv. Sin necesidad, innecesariamente, inútilmente.
unnecessary [ʌn'nesisəri] adj. Innecesario, ria; inútil.
unneighbourly (U. S. **unneighborly**) ['ʌn'neibəli] adj. Poco amistoso, sa (unfriendly). || Poco amable (unpleasant).
unnerve ['ʌn'nə:v] v. tr. Desconcertar, turbar (to disturb, to worry). || Desanimar (to dishearten). || Acobardar (to make lose courage).
unnoticeable ['ʌn'nəutisəbl] adj. Imperceptible.
unnoticed ['ʌn'nəutist] adj. Inadvertido, da; desapercibido, da: *to go o to pass unnoticed*, pasar desapercibido. || — *To leave a fact unnoticed*, pasar un hecho por alto. || *To let sth. pass unnoticed*, no reparar en algo.
unnumbered ['ʌn'nʌmbəd] adj. Sin numerar (pages, etc.). || Innumerable (countless).
U. N. O. ['ju:nəu] n. O.N.U., *f.* (United Nations Organization).
unobjectionable ['ʌnəb'dʒekʃənəbl] adj. Irreprochable.
unobservable ['ʌnəb'zə:vəbl] adj. Inobservable.
unobservant ['ʌnəb'zə:vənt] adj. Poco observador, ra. || *To be unobservant of the law*, no respetar *or* acatar la ley.
unobserved ['ʌnəb'zə:vd] adj. Desapercibido, da; inadvertido, da.
unobserving ['ʌnəb'zə:viŋ] adj. Desatento, ta.
unobstructed ['ʌnəb'strʌktid] adj. No obstruido, da; sin obstáculos, despejado, da: *the way is unobstructed*, el camino está despejado. || *Unobstructed view*, vista despejada.
unobtainable ['ʌnəb'teinəbl] adj. Inalcanzable.
unobtrusive ['ʌnəb'tru:siv] adj. Discreto, ta.
unoccupied ['ʌn'ɔkjupaid] adj. Desocupado, da: *unoccupied person*, persona desocupada; *unoccupied flat*, piso desocupado. || Libre (seat, time, etc.). || Vacante (job). || Despoblado, da (region). || No ocupado, da (not occupied by troops).
unoffending ['ʌnə'fendiŋ] adj. Inofensivo, va.
unofficial ['ʌnəfiʃəl] adj. Extraoficial, no oficial. || Oficioso, sa: *unofficial information*, información oficiosa.
unopened ['ʌn'əupənd] adj. Sin abrir.
unopposed ['ʌnə'pəuzd] adj. Sin oposición: *to be elected unopposed*, ser elegido sin oposición. || *Unopposed candidate*, candidato único.
unordinary ['ʌn'ɔ:dinəri] adj. Que se sale de lo corriente, poco corriente, fuera de lo común.
unorganized ['ʌn'ɔ:gənaizd] adj. No organizado, da.
unoriginal ['ʌnə'ridzinəl] adj. Poco original.
unorthodox ['ʌn'ɔ:θədɔks] adj. Poco ortodoxo, xa. || REL. Heterodoxo, xa; no ortodoxo, xa.
unostentatious ['ʌn,ɔsten'teiʃəs] adj. Sin ostentación.
unpack ['ʌn'pæk] v. tr. Desembalar (packing case, etc.). || Desempaquetar (a parcel). || Deshacer [*Amer.*, desempacar] (a suitcase).
— V. intr. Deshacer las maletas [*Amer.*, desempacar].
unpacking [—iŋ] n. Desembalaje, *m.* || Desempaquetado, *m.* (of a parcel). || *To do one's unpacking*, deshacer las maletas [*Amer.*, desempacar] (suitcases).
unpaid ['ʌn'peid] adj. Impagado, da; sin pagar, por pagar (bill, debt). || No retribuido, da (work, person).
unpaired ['ʌn'pɛəd] adj. Desparejado, da (glove, etc.). || ANAT. Impar: *unpaired organ*, órgano impar.
unpalatable [ʌn'pælətəbl] adj. Desagradable al gusto, de mal sabor (food). || FIG. Difícil de tragar *or* de aceptar, desagradable (unpleasant).
unparalleled [ʌn'pærəleld] adj. Sin par, incomparable, sin paralelo. || Sin precedente (unprecedented).
unpardonable [ʌn'pɑ:dənəbl] adj. Imperdonable, indisculpable.
unparliamentary ['ʌn,pɑ:lə'mentəri] adj. Antiparlamentario, ria.
unpatriotic ['ʌn,pætri'ɔtik] adj. Antipatriótico, ca (action). || Poco patriota (person).
unpave ['ʌn'peiv] v. tr. Desempedrar.
unpaved [—d] adj. Sin pavimentar. || Desempedrado, da.
unpayable ['ʌn'peiəbl] adj. Impagable.
unpeople ['ʌn'pi:pl] v. tr. Despoblar.
unperceivable ['ʌnpə'si:vəbl] adj. Imperceptible.
unperceived ['ʌnpə'si:vd] adj. Desapercibido, da; inadvertido, da.
unperformable ['ʌnpə'fɔ:məbl] adj. MUS. Inejecutable. || THEATR. Irrepresentable.
unpersuasive ['ʌnpə'sweisiv] adj. Poco convincente.
unperturbed ['ʌnpə'tə:bd] adj. Impasible, impávido, da. || No perturbado, da (*by*, por).
unpick ['ʌn'pik] v. tr. Descoser (in sewing).
unpile ['ʌn'pail] v. tr. Desamontonar.
unpin ['ʌn'pin] v. tr. Quitar alfileres a (in sewing). Desprender (to take off). || TECH. Quitar la clavija a.
unplaced ['ʌn'pleist] adj. SP. No colocado, da.
unplait ['ʌn'plæt] v. tr. Destrenzar.
unplanned ['ʌn'plænd] adj. Imprevisto, ta: *unplanned journey*, viaje imprevisto.
unplayable ['ʌn'pleiəbl] adj. MUS. Inejecutable.
unpleasant ['ʌn'pleznt] adj. Desagradable: *unpleasant weather*, tiempo desagradable. || Antipático, ca; desagradable (unfriendly): *to be unpleasant to* o *with s.o.*, ser antipático con alguien. || Molesto, ta (annoying).
unpleasantly [—li] adv. Desagradablemente, de manera desagradable: *to treat s.o. unpleasantly*, tratar a alguien de manera desagradable. || *The music is unpleasantly loud*, la música es tan fuerte que resulta desagradable *or* molesta.
unpleasantness [—nis] n. Lo desagradable: *the unpleasantness of his position*, lo desagradable de su situación. || Antipatía, *f.* (person's unfriendliness). || Disgusto, *m.*, desagrado, *m.*, molestia, *f.*: *to cause unpleasantness*, causar desagrado *or* un disgusto *or* una molestia. || FAM. Desavenencia, *f.* (disagreement): *there was some unpleasantness between them*, hubo una desavenencia entre ellos.
unpleasing ['ʌn'pli:ziŋ] adj. Desagradable (unpleasant). || Poco atractivo, va (unattractive).
unpliable ['ʌn'plaiəbl] adj. Poco flexible.
unploughed (U. S. **unplowed**) ['ʌn'plaud] adj. Sin arar, sin labrar.
unplug ['ʌn'plʌg] v. tr. Desenchufar (to disconnect).
unplugging [—iŋ] n. Desenchufado, *m.*
unplumbed ['ʌn'plʌmd] adj. No sondado, da; no sondeado, da. || FIG. Insondable (mystery).
unpoetical ['ʌnpəu'etikəl] adj. Poco poético, ca; prosaico, ca.

unpolished [ˈʌnˈpɔliʃt] adj. Sin pulir. || En bruto (precious stones): *an unpolished diamond*, un diamante en bruto. || No encerado, da (floor). || No embetunado, da [*Amer.*, no lustrado, da] (shoes). || FIG. Tosco, ca; poco pulido, da (style, manners, etc.).
unpolite [ˈʌnpəˈlait] adj. Descortés, mal educado, da.
unpolitic [ˈʌnˈpɔlitik] adj. Imprudente, impolítico, ca.
unpolitical [ˈʌnpəˈlitikəl] adj. Apolítico, ca.
unpolluted [ˈʌnpəˈlju:tid] adj. No contaminado, da; incontaminado, da; puro, ra: *unpolluted water*, agua no contaminada.
unpopular [ˈʌnˈpɔpjulə*] adj. Impopular.
unpopularity [ˈʌn,pɔpjuˈlæriti] n. Impopularidad, *f.*
unpostponable [ˈʌnpəustˈpəunəbl] adj. Inaplazable.
unpractical [ˈʌnˈpræktikəl] adj. Poco práctico, ca.
unpractised (U. S. **unpracticed**) [ˈʌnˈpræktist] adj. Inexperto, ta (inexpert). || Falto de práctica, sin práctica (needing practice).
unprecedented [ʌnˈpresidəntid] adj. Inaudito, ta; sin precedente.
unprecise [ˈʌnpriˈsais] adj. Impreciso, sa.
unpredictable [ˈʌnpriˈdiktəbl] adj. Que no se puede prever, imprevisible (occurrence). || De reacciones imprevisibles (person). || Antojadizo, za (capricious).
unprejudiced [ʌnˈpredʒudist] adj. Imparcial. || Sin prejuicios.
unpremeditated [ˈʌnpriˈmediteitid] adj. Impremeditado, da. || Improvisado, da (speech).
unpremeditation [ˈʌnprimediˈteiʃən] n. Impremeditación, *f.*
unprepared [ˈʌnpriˈpɛəd] adj. Desprevenido, da (unready): *it caught me unprepared*, me cogió desprevenido. || Hecho sin preparación, improvisado, da (recital, etc.). || *To be unprepared for sth.*, no estar preparado para algo (not ready), no esperar algo (not to be expecting sth.).
unpreparedness [—nis] n. Falta (*f.*) de preparación (lack of preparation). || Imprevisión, *f.* (of s.o. caught unawares).
unprepossessing [ˈʌn,pri:pəˈzesiŋ] adj. Poco atractivo, va.
unpresentable [ˈʌnpriˈzentəbl] adj. Impresentable.
unpretending [ˈʌnpriˈtendiŋ] or **unpretentious** [ˈʌnpriˈtenʃəs] adj. Modesto, ta; sin pretensiones, sencillo, lla.
unprime [ˈʌnˈpraim] v. tr. Descebar (a firearm).
unprincipled [ˈʌnˈprinsəpld] adj. Falto de principios, sin principios.
unprintable [ʌnˈprintəbəl] adj. Impublicable.
unprized [ˈʌnˈpraizd] adj. Poco apreciado, da.
unproductive [ˈʌnprəˈdʌktiv] adj. Improductivo, va.
unproductiveness [—nis] n. Improductividad, *f.*
unprofessional [ˈʌnprəˈfeʃənəl] adj. Impropio, pia; contrario a la ética profesional (conduct). || Inexperto, ta; poco experto, ta (incompetent). || Sin título: *unprofessional lawyer*, abogado sin título. || SP. Aficionado, da.
unprofitable [ʌnˈprɔfitəbl] adj. Poco provechoso, sa; poco lucrativo, va (business, etc.). || Improductivo, va (unproductive). || Inútil (useless). || Infructuoso, sa (fruitless).
unpromising [ˈʌnˈprɔmisiŋ] adj. Poco prometedor, ra.
unprompted [ˈʌnˈprɔmptid] adj. Espontáneo, a.
unpronounceable [ˈʌnprəˈnaunsəbl] adj. Impronunciable.
unpropitious [ˈʌnprəˈpiʃəs] adj. Impropicio, cia; poco propicio, cia; desfavorable.
unprosperous [ˈʌnˈprɔspərəs] adj. Poco próspero, ra. || Desafortunado, da (unlucky). || Poco propicio, cia; desfavorable (winds).
unprotected [ˈʌnprəˈtektid] adj. Sin protección, indefenso, sa (defenceless). || Sin ayuda, sin apoyo (unsupported). || TECH. Sin protección (moving parts).
unprovable [ʌnˈpru:vəbl] adj. Indemostrable, imposible de demostrar *or* de probar.
unproved [ˈʌnˈpru:vd] or **unproven** [ˈʌnˈpru:vn] adj. No probado, da; no demostrado, da; sin probar, sin demostrar. || No comprobado, da; no puesto a prueba: *his loyalty is as yet unproved*, su fidelidad no ha sido comprobada todavía.
unprovided [ˈʌnprəˈvaidid] adj. Desprovisto, ta (*with*, de) [not supplied]. || Desprevenido, da (unprepared). || *Unprovided for*, desvalido, da (child), imprevisto, ta; no previsto, ta (contingencies), sin recursos.
unprovoked [ˈʌnprəˈvəukt] adj. No provocado, da (attack, e.c.). || Tranquilo, la; sereno, na (person): *to remain unprovoked*, quedarse tranquilo.
unpublishable [ʌnˈpʌbliʃəbl] adj. Impublicable.
unpublished [ˈʌnˈpʌbliʃt] adj. Inédito, ta; no publicado, da; sin publicar (book). || FIG. No revelado al público.
unpunctual [ˈʌnˈpʌŋktjuəl] adj. Poco puntual.
unpunished [ˈʌnˈpʌniʃt] adj. Impune, sin castigar: *unpunished crimes*, delitos impunes. || *To go unpunished*, no ser castigado, quedar impune.
unqualifiable [ˈʌnˈkwɔlifaiəbl] adj. Incalificable.
unqualified [ˈʌnˈkwɔlifaid] adj. Incompetente (incompetent). || Sin título (without qualifications). || Sin autorización. || Sin reserva, incondicional, total (without reservation): *unqualified endorsement*, aprobación sin reserva. || Inhabilitado, da. || *Unqualified statement*, declaración (*f.*) general.
unquenchable [ʌnˈkwentʃəbl] adj. Inextinguible (fire). || Insaciable (thirst).
unquenched [ʌnˈkwentʃt] adj. Sin extinguir (fire). || No saciado, da; sin saciar (thirst).
unquestionable [ʌnˈkwestʃənəbl] adj. Indiscutible, incuestionable.
unquestioned [ʌnˈkwestʃənd] adj. No interrogado, da (person). || Indiscutido, da; incontrovertido, da (a right, etc.).
unquestioning [ʌnˈkwestʃəniŋ] adj. Incondicional.
unquiet [ˈʌnˈkwaiət] adj. Agitado, da. || Ruidoso, sa (noisy).
unquietness [—nis] n. Agitación, *f.* (disquiet). || Ruido, *m.* (noise).
unquote [ˈʌnkwəut] v. intr. *Unquote*, fin de la cita.
unquoted [ˈʌnˈkwəutid] adj. No citado, da. || COMM. No cotizado, da (securities).
unravel [ʌnˈrævəl] v. tr. Desenredar, desenmarañar (to untangle). || Deshacer (a knitted garment). || FIG. Desenmarañar, desembrollar (a problem, a mystery). — V. intr. Desenredarse, desenmarañarse (to become untangled). || Deshacerse (a knitted garment). || FIG. Desenmarañarse, desembrollarse.
unreachable [ˈʌnˈri:tʃəbl] adj. Inalcanzable.
unread [ˈʌnˈred] adj. Sin leer, no leído, da (book). || Poco leído, da; inculto, ta: *unread person*, persona inculta.
unreadable [ˈʌnˈri:dəbl] adj. Ilegible (handwriting, figure, etc.). || Imposible de leer (book). || Incomprensible. || Que no merece la pena leerse (not worth reading).
unreadiness [ˈʌnˈredinis] n. Falta (*f.*) de preparación.
unready [ˈʌnˈredi] adj. No listo, ta; no preparado, da: *they were unready for war*, no estaban listos para la guerra. || Desprevenido, da (unprepared).
unreal [ˈʌnˈriəl] adj. Irreal.
unrealism [—izəm] n. Irrealismo, *m.*
unrealistic [ˈʌnriəˈlistik] adj. Poco realista.
unreality [ˈʌnriˈæliti] n. Irrealidad, *f.*
unrealizable [ˈʌnˈriəlaizəbl] adj. Irrealizable.
unreason [ˈʌnˈri:zən] n. Insensatez, *f.*
unreasonable [ʌnˈri:zənəbl] adj. Irracional (irrational). || Irrazonable, desrazonable (not reasonable). || — *At an unreasonable hour*, a deshora. || *Unreasonable demands*, pretensiones desmedidas *or* exageradas. || *Unreasonable prices*, precios exorbitantes.
unreasonableness [—nis] n. Irracionalidad, *f.* (irrationality). || Inmoderación, *f.*, falta (*f.*) de moderación (of demands). || Lo exorbitante (of prices).
unreasoning [ʌnˈri:zəniŋ] adj. Irracional.
unreclaimed [ˈʌnriˈkleimd] adj. Sin reclamar. || Sin aprovechar (land).
unrecognizable [ˈʌnˈrekəgnaizəbl] adj. Imposible de reconocer, irreconocible. || Desconocido, da: *since his illness he is unrecognizable*, desde su enfermedad está desconocido.
unrecognized [ˈʌnˈrekəgnaizd] adj. Desconocido, da (genius, etc.): *unrecognized merits*, méritos desconocidos. || No reconocido, da (leader, etc.). || *To go unrecognized*, pasar sin ser reconocido.
unrecorded [ˈʌnriˈkɔ:did] adj. Sin grabar (music, etc.). || Sin registrar (event, etc.).
unrecoverable [ˈʌnriˈkʌvərəbl] adj. Irrecuperable.
unredeemable [ˈʌnriˈdi:məbl] adj. Irredimible, sin remisión.
unredeemed [ˈʌnriˈdi:md] adj. Sin redimir (sin). || Sin cumplir (promise). || Sin desempeñar (pawned article). || COMM. Sin amortizar (loan). || Irredento, ta (territory). || FIG. *Unredeemed by*, no compensado por.
unreel [ˈʌnˈri:l] v. tr. Desenrollar.
unrefined [ˈʌnriˈfaind] adj. Sin refinar, no refinado, da. || FIG. Basto, ta; poco fino, na; tosco, ca.
unreflecting [ˈʌnriˈflektiŋ] adj. Irreflexivo, va.
unregarded [ˈʌnriˈgɑ:did] adj. Desatendido, da; descuidado, da.
unregardful [ˈʌnriˈgɑ:dful] adj. Poco atento, ta (*of*, a) [unmindful]. || Poco cuidadoso, sa (*of*, con) [lacking care]. || *Unregardful of his duties*, sin tener en cuenta sus obligaciones.
unregenerate [ˈʌnriˈdʒenərit] adj. No regenerado, da. || Impenitente (unrepentant, inveterate).
unrehearsed [ˈʌnriˈhə:st] adj. Sin preparar, improvisado, da: *an unrehearsed speech*, un discurso improvisado. || Imprevisto, ta (unexpected): *an unrehearsed incident*, un incidente imprevisto. || THEATR. Sin ensayar.
unrelated [ˈʌnriˈleitid] adj. Inconexo, xa; no relacionado, da (not related). || *They are entirely unrelated*, no son de la misma familia.
unrelenting [ˈʌnriˈlentiŋ] adj. Implacable.
unreliability [ˈʌnri,laiəˈbiliti] n. Inestabilidad, *f.* (of character). || Poca formalidad, *f.* (of a person). || Poca seguridad, *f.* (of information).
unreliable [ˈʌnriˈlaiəbl] adj. Inconstante, inestable (character). || De poca confianza, que no es de fiar, poco formal, poco seguro, ra (person). || Poco fiable (machine). || Poco seguro, ra; que no es de fiar (information, service).
unrelieved [ˈʌnriˈli:vd] adj. No aliviado, da (pain). || Monótono, na (landscape). || MIL. No relevado, da. || *Unrelieved poverty*, miseria profunda, miseria total.
unreligious [ˈʌnriˈlidʒəs] adj. No religioso, sa. || Irreligioso, sa (impious).

unremembered [ˈʌnriˈmembəd] adj. Olvidado, da.
unremitting [ˌʌnriˈmitiŋ] adj. Incesante, continuo, nua (kept up without interruption). || Incansable (persevering).
unremunerative [ˈʌnriˈmju:nərətiv] adj. Poco remunerador, ra.
unrenewable [ˈʌnriˈnju:əbl] adj. Improrrogable.
unrented [ˈʌnˈrentid] adj. Desalquilado, da.
unrepealable [ˈʌnriˈpi:ləbl] adj. Inabrogable.
unrepealed [ˈʌnriˈpi:ld] adj. JUR. No revocado, da.
unrepeatable [ˈʌnriˈpi:təbl] adj. Que no se puede repetir.
unrepentant [ˈʌnriˈpentənt] adj. Impenitente.
unrepresentative [ˈʌnˌrepriˈzentətiv] adj. Poco representativo, va.
unrepresented [ˈʌnˌrepriˈzentid] adj. Sin representación.
unrequested [ˈʌnriˈkwestid] adj. No solicitado, da. || Espontáneo, a.
unrequired [ˈʌnriˈkwaiəd] adj. No exigido, da; no requerido, da. || Innecesario, ria; inútil (unnecessary).
unrequited [ˈʌnriˈkwaitid] adj. No correspondido, da (love). || No recompensado, da (service).
unreserved [ˈʌnriˈzə:vd] adj. Sin reserva (approval). || Expansivo, va; abierto, ta (frank). || Sin reservar, libre (seat).
unreservedly [—li] adv. Sin reserva.
unresisting [ˈʌnriˈzistiŋ] adj. Que no ofrece resistencia.
unresolved [ˈʌnriˈzɔlvd] adj. Sin resolver, no resuelto, ta (problem). || Irresoluto, ta (person).
unresponsive [ˈʌnriˈspɔnsiv] adj. Insensible.
unrest [ʌnˈrest] n. Inquietud, *f.* (restlessness). || Malestar, *m.* (uneasiness): *social unrest*, malestar social. || Agitación, *f.*, disturbios, *m. pl.* (state of disturbance): *labour unrest*, agitación obrera.
unrestrainable [ˈʌnrisˈtreinəbl] adj. Incontenible (anger, laughter).
unrestrained [ˈʌnrisˈtreind] adj. No contenido, da. || Libre (free).
unrestricted [ˈʌnrisˈtriktid] adj. Sin restricción.
unrevealed [ˈʌnriˈvi:ld] adj. No revelado, da.
unrewarded [ˈʌnriˈwɔ:did] adj. No recompensado, da. || Sin recompensa.
unrewarding [ˈʌnriˈwɔ:diŋ] adj. Ingrato, ta: *an unrewarding task*, una labor ingrata. || Infructuoso, sa (useless).
unriddle [ˈʌnˈridl] v. tr. Explicar (a dream). || Descifrar, aclarar, resolver (a mystery).
unrig [ˈʌnˈrig] v. tr. MAR. Desaparejar.
unrighteous [ʌnˈraitʃəs] adj. Inicuo, cua; injusto, ta (unjust). || Malo, la; perverso, sa (wicked).
unripe [ˈʌnˈraip] adj. Verde, inmaduro, ra (fruit). || FIG. Inmaduro, ra; verde, insuficientemente maduro, ra.
unrivalled (U. S. **unrivaled**) [ʌnˈraivəld] adj. Sin rival. || Sin par, sin igual, incomparable.
unrobe [ˈʌnˈrəub] v. tr. Desnudar, desvestir.
— V. intr. Desnudarse, desvestirse.
unroll [ˈʌnˈrəul] v. tr. Desenrollar.
— V. intr. Desenrollarse.
unroof [ˈʌnˈru:f] v. tr. Destechar, quitar el techo de (a house).
unrope [ˈʌnˈrəup] v. tr. Desatar.
— V. intr. Desatarse.
unruffled [ˈʌnˈrʌfld] adj. Liso, sa (hair). || Sereno, na; tranquilo, la (water). || Imperturbable (person).
unruled [ʌnˈru:ld] adj. Sin rayar (paper). || No gobernado, da (country). || No reprimido, da; no contenido, da (passion).
unruliness [ʌnˈru:linis] n. Indocilidad, *f.*, insumisión, *f.*
unruly [ʌnˈru:li] adj. Revoltoso, sa; indisciplinado, da (child, etc.). || Ingobernable (country). || Fogoso, sa (horse). || Desenfrenado, da (passions). || Despeinado, da (hair).
unsaddle [ˈʌnˈsædl] v. tr. Desensillar (a horse). || Desarzonar, desmontar (a horseman).
unsafe [ˈʌnˈseif] adj. Peligroso, sa (dangerous). || Malo, la (bad). || Inseguro, ra (uncertain). || Inhospitalario, ria (a place, etc.).
unsafety [—ti] n. Inseguridad, *f.* || Peligro, *m.* (danger).
unsaid [ˈʌnˈsed] pret. & p. p. See UNSAY.
— Adj. Sin decir. || *To leave sth. unsaid*, dejar de decir algo.
unsalable or **unsaleable** [ˈʌnˈseiləbl] adj. COMM. Invendible.
unsalaried [ˈʌnˈsælərid] adj. No asalariado, da; sin sueldo.
unsanitary [ˈʌnˈsænitəri] adj. Antihigiénico, ca; falto de higiene.
unsatisfactory [ˈʌnˌsætisˈfæktəri] adj. Poco satisfactorio, ria.
unsatisfied [ˈʌnˈsætisfaid] adj. Insatisfecho, cha (not satisfied). || Poco convencido, da (*about*, de). || Insatisfecho, cha (appetite, etc.). || No saldado, da; no liquidado, da (debts).
unsatisfying [ˈʌnˈsætisfaiiŋ] adj. Poco satisfactorio, ria. || Insuficiente (insufficient).
unsaturated [ˈʌnˈsætʃəreitid] adj. No saturado, da.
unsavoury (U. S. **unsavory**) [ˈʌnˈseivəri] adj. Desagradable (in smell or taste). || Insípido, da (tasteless). || Infame, deshonroso, sa (morally offensive). || Indeseable (person). || Sospechoso, sa; dudoso, sa (business).
unsay* [ˈʌnˈsei] v. tr. Desdecirse de (what one has said).
— OBSERV. Pret. & p. p. ***unsaid.***
unscathed [ˈʌnˈskeiðd] adj. Ileso, sa; indemne, sano y salvo: *to come out of an accident unscathed*, salir ileso de un accidente.
unscholarly [ˈʌnˈskɔləli] adj. Poco erudito, ta. || Impropio de un erudito.
unschooled [ˈʌnˈsku:ld] adj. Ignorante. || Natural, innato, ta (feeling). || No instruido, da (not schooled).
unscientific [ˈʌnˌsaiənˈtifik] adj. Poco científico, ca.
unscramble [ˈʌnˈskræmbl] v. tr. Descifrar (a message).
unscreened [ˈʌnˈskri:nd] adj. No protegido, da (unprotected). || Descubierto, ta (uncovered). || Sin cribar (coal). || Sin interrogar (refugees). || Sin adaptar para el cine.
unscrew [ˈʌnˈskru:] v. tr. Destornillar, desatornillar.
unscrupulous [ʌnˈskru:pjuləs] adj. Poco escrupuloso, sa; sin escrúpulos.
unscrupulously [—li] adv. Sin escrúpulos.
unscrupulousness [—nis] n. Falta (*f.*) de escrúpulos.
unseal [ˈʌnˈsi:l] v. tr. Abrir (a letter). || FIG. Abrir (eyes).
unsearchable [ʌnˈsə:tʃəbl] adj. Impenetrable.
unsearched [ʌnˈsə:tʃt] adj. Sin registrar (ship, luggage, etc.).
unseasonable [ʌnˈsi:znəbl] adj. Impropio de la estación (weather). || Que no es del tiempo (fruit). || FIG. Inoportuno, na; poco a propósito (act, comment).
unseasoned [ʌnˈsi:znd] adj. CULIN. Sin sazonar (not seasoned). || No maduro, inmaduro, ra (immature, unripe). || Verde (timber, wine). || FIG. Inexperimentado, da; poco maduro, ra (inexperienced). || MIL. No aguerrido, da.
unseat [ˈʌnˈsi:t] v. tr. Desarzonar, derribar (a rider). || Quitar el puesto a (from a job). || Destituir (an official). || Derribar, echar abajo (a government). || Quitar el escaño a (a Member of Parliament).
unseaworthy [ˈʌnˈsi:ˌwə:ði] adj. Que no puede navegar, innavegable (boat).
unseconded [ˈʌnˈsekəndid] adj. No apoyado, da (motion). || No secundado, da; no asistido, da (person).
unsecured [ˈʌnsiˈkjuəd] adj. Mal fijado, da (badly secured). || COMM. No respaldado, da (loan).
unseeing [ˈʌnˈsi:iŋ] adj. Ciego, ga; que no ve. || Vago, ga (look).
unseemliness [ʌnˈsi:mlinis] n. Impropiedad, *f.*
unseemly [ʌnˈsi:mli] adj. Indecoroso, sa (indecorous). || Impropio, pia (*in*, de) [unsuitable].
unseen [ˈʌnˈsi:n] adj. Sin ser visto: *he entered unseen*, entró sin ser visto. || Inadvertido, da: *several mistakes passed unseen*, varios errores pasaron inadvertidos. || No visto, ta (not seen). || Oculto, ta (hidden). || Invisible (invisible). || A libro abierto (translation).
— N. Traducción (*f.*) a libro abierto (translation). || Lo invisible.
unselfish [ˈʌnˈselfiʃ] adj. Desinteresado, da; falto de egoísmo, generoso, sa.
unselfishness [—nis] adj. Desinterés, *m.*, falta (*f.*) de egoísmo, generosidad, *f.*
unsellable [ˈʌnˈseləbl] adj. Invendible.
unserviceable [ˈʌnˈsə:visəbl] adj. Inservible, inutilizable (thing). || Poco servicial (person).
unset [ˈʌnˈset] adj. No cuajado, da (jelly). || No fraguado, da (concrete). || No fijado, da (not fixed). || No engastado, da; no engarzado, da; sin montar (precious stone).
unsettle [ˈʌnˈsetl] v. tr. Perturbar (a person, plans, weather). || Desequilibrar (a person's mind). || Desquiciar, trastornar (institutions). || *To unsettle one's stomach*, sentarle mal a uno.
unsettled [—d] adj. Perturbado, da (perturbed). || Intranquilo, la (worried). || Agitado, da (country). || Desequilibrado, da (unbalanced). || Inestable (not stable). || Irresoluto, ta; indeciso, sa (irresolute). || Molesto, ta (uncomfortable): *to feel unsettled*, sentirse molesto. || Inseguro, ra; incierto, ta (weather). || Pendiente (question, matter). || Sin colonizar (uninhabited). || Sin domicilio fijo. || COMM. Por pagar, pendiente, sin saldar (account).
unsettling [—iŋ] adj. Inquietante.
unsew* [ˈʌnˈsəu] v. tr. Descoser.
— OBSERV. Pret. ***unsewed;*** p. p. ***unsewn, unsewed.***
unsewn [ˈʌnˈsəun] p. p. See UNSEW.
unsex [ˈʌnˈseks] v. tr. Quitar el instinto sexual a.
unshackle [ˈʌnˈʃækl] v. tr. Desencadenar (a prisoner). || Destrabar (a horse).
unshakable or **unshakeable** [ʌnˈʃeikəbl] adj. Firme, inquebrantable.
unshaken [ˈʌnˈʃeikən] adj. Firme, impertérrito, ta (person). || Que no vacila, firme (faith).
unshaped [ˈʌnˈʃeipt] adj. Sin forma, informe.
unshapely [ˈʌnˈʃeipli] adj. Feo, a (ugly). || Deforme, mal proporcionado, da (badly proportioned).
unsharable o **unshareable** [ˈʌnˈʃeərəbl] adj. Incompartible.
unshaven [ˈʌnˈʃeivn] adj. Sin afeitar.
unsheathe [ˈʌnˈʃi:ð] v. tr. Desenvainar (a sword, etc.).
unshell [ˈʌnˈʃel] v. tr. Descascarar.

unsheltered [ˈʌnˈʃeltəd] adj. Sin protección. || Expuesto, ta (*from*, a) [exposed].
unship [ˈʌnˈʃip] v. tr. MAR. Desembarcar, descargar (to unload). | Desmontar (rudder). | Quitar (mast). | Desarmar (oars).
unshod [ˈʌnˈʃɔd] adj. Descalzo, za (person). || Desherrado, da (a horse).
— Pret. & p. p. See UNSHOE.
unshoe* [ˈʌnˈʃu:] v. tr. Desherrar (a horse).
— OBSERV. Pret. & p. p. ***unshod***.
unshorn [ˈʌnˈʃɔ:n] adj. Intonso, sa (person). || No esquilado, da (sheep).
unshrinkable [ˈʌnˈʃriŋkəbl] adj. Inencogible, que no puede encogerse.
unshrinking [ʌnˈʃriŋkiŋ] adj. Impávido, da (fearless).
unshroud [ˈʌnˈʃraud] v. tr. Quitar la mortaja a (a dead person). || FIG. Descubrir, revelar (sth.).
unsighted [ˈʌnˈsaitid] adj. Que no puede ver, que no ve: *the referee was unsighted*, el árbitro no podía ver. || Que no está a la vista (ship). || Sin mira (gun).
unsightliness [ʌnˈsaitlinis] n. Fealdad, *f.*
unsightly [ʌnˈsaitli] adj. Feo, a; desagradable a la vista, antiestético, ca.
unsigned [ˈʌnˈsaind] adj. Sin firmar, no firmado, da.
unsingable [ˈʌnˈsiŋəbl] adj. Incantable.
unsized [ˈʌnˈsaizd] adj. Desencolado, da; sin apresto, (paper).
unskilful (U. S. **unskillful**) [ˈʌnˈskilful] adj. Torpe, desmañado, da; poco hábil, inhábil.
unskilfullness [—nis] n. Inhabilidad, *f.*, torpeza, *f.*
unskilled [ˈʌnˈskild] adj. No cualificado, da; no especializado, da: *unskilled worker*, obrero no cualificado. || No especializado, da: *unskilled work*, trabajo no especializado. || Inexperto, ta (not skilled).
unskimmed [ˈʌnˈskimd] adj. Sin desnatar: *unskimmed milk*, leche sin desnatar.
unsling* [ˈʌnˈsliŋ] v. tr. Descolgar. || MAR. Quitar de la eslinga.
— OBSERV. Pret. & p. p. ***unslung***.
unslung [ˈʌnˈslʌŋ] pret. & p. p. See UNSLING.
unsmokable [ˈʌnˈsməukəbəl] adj. Infumable.
unsmooth [ˈʌnˈsmu:ð] adj. Desigual (road). || Rugoso, sa; áspero, ra (surface).
unsociability [ˈʌnˌsəuʃəˈbiliti] n. Insociabilidad, *f.*
unsociable [ʌnˈsəuʃəbl] adj. Insociable.
unsocial [ʌnˈsəuʃəl] adj. Insociable, insocial.
unsold [ˈʌnˈsəuld] adj. No vendido, invendido, da; sin vender. || *Unsold copies*, remanente (*m.*) de ejemplares sin vender (books, magazines, etc.).
unsolder [ˈʌnˈsɔldə*] v. tr. Desoldar.
unsolicited [ˈʌnsəˈlisitid] adj. No solicitado, da (not solicited). || Espontáneo, a (spontaneous).
unsolvable [ˈʌnˈsɔlvəbl] adj. Insoluble, irresoluble.
unsolved [ˈʌnˈsɔlvd] adj. Sin resolver, no resuelto, ta (problem).
unsophisticated [ˈʌnsəˈfistikeitid] adj. Sencillo, lla; no sofisticado, da (not sophisticated). || COMM. Puro, ra; no adulterado, da (unadulterated). || FIG. Ingenuo, nua (naïve).
unsought [ˈʌnˈsɔ:t] adj. Espontáneo, a (spontaneous). || Sin solicitar, no solicitado, da (unsolicited). || No buscado, da (not looked for).
unsound [ˈʌnˈsaund] adj. Enfermizo, za (not physically sound). || Demente (not mentally sound). || Corrompido, da (not morally sound). || Defectuoso, sa; imperfecto, ta (goods). || Podrido, da (fruit). || Poco sólido, da: *the foundations are unsound*, los cimientos son poco sólidos; *the ice is unsound*, el hielo es poco sólido. || Ligero, ra (sleep). || COMM. Poco seguro, ra (business). || FIG. Falso, sa; equivocado, da; erróneo, a (ideas, opinions).
unsoundable [—əbl] adj. Insondable.
unsoundness [—nis] n. Lo defectuoso. || Falta (*f.*) de solidez. || Falsedad, *f.*, equivocación, *f.*
unsparing [ʌnˈspɛəriŋ] adj. Pródigo, ga; generoso, sa (without reserve): *unsparing in his praise*, pródigo de *or* en alabanzas. || Incansable (tireless). || Sin piedad, despiadado, da (*of*, para) [without mercy]. || — *To be unsparing in one's efforts to*, no regatear ningún esfuerzo para. || *To be unsparing of* o *to make unsparing use of*, no escatimar.
unspeakable [ʌnˈspi:kəbl] adj. Indecible, inexpresable, inenarrable (ineffable). || Incalificable (very bad).
unspecialized [ˈʌnˈspeʃəlaizd] adj. Sin especializar, no especializado, da.
unspecified [ˈʌnˈspesifaid] adj. No especificado, da; sin especificar.
unspent [ˈʌnˈspent] adj. No gastado, da.
unsplinterable [ˈʌnˈsplintərəbl] adj. Inastillable.
unspoiled [ˈʌnˈspɔild] or **unspoilt** [ˈʌnˈspɔilt] adj. Sin estropear (not marred or damaged). || No mimado, da (a child). || No podrido, da (food).
unspoken [ˈʌnˈspəukən] adj. Tácito, ta: *an unspoken agreement*, un acuerdo tácito. || *Unspoken word*, palabra sobreentendida.
unsporting [ˈʌnˈspɔ:tiŋ] or **unsportsmanlike** [ˈʌnˈspɔ:tsmənlaik] adj. Antideportivo, va.
unspotted [ˈʌnˈspɔtid] adj. Sin mancha, inmaculado, da; sin tacha (free from moral stain). || ZOOL. Sin mancha.
unstable [ˈʌnˈsteibl] adj. Inestable.
unstained [ˈʌnˈsteind] adj. Sin manchas.
unstamped [ˈʌnˈstæmpt] adj. Sin franqueo, sin franquear, sin sello (a letter). || No acuñado, da (a coin). || Sin sellar (a document). || No contrastado, da (gold).
unstatesmanlike [ˈʌnˈsteitsmənlaik] adj. Indigno de un estadista.
unsteadiness [ˈʌnˈstedinis] n. Inestabilidad, *f.* (of furniture, the mind, prices). || Inseguridad, *f.* (of footsteps, position). || Temblor, *m.* (of hand). || Irregularidad, *f.* (of heartbeat). || FIG. Irresolución, *f.*, indecisión, *f.* (irresolution). | Disipación, *f.* (of a young man).
unsteady [ˈʌnˈstedi] adj. Inestable (furniture). || Inseguro, ra; vacilante (footsteps). || Inseguro, ra; incierto, ta (position). || Tembloroso, sa (light). || Poco firme (hand). || Inestable (mentally unstable). || COMM. Fluctuante (the stock market). || Irregular (not constant): *an unsteady pulse*, un pulso irregular. || Variable (barometer). || Variable, cambiante (wind). || FIG. Irresoluto, ta; indeciso, sa (irresolute). | Inconstante (affection). | Poco serio, ria (conduct). || *To be unsteady on one's feet*, titubear.
unstick* [ˈʌnˈstik] v. tr. Despegar. || *To come unstuck*, despegarse, desprenderse (sth.), venirse abajo (plans).
— OBSERV. Pret. & p. p. ***unstuck***.
unstinted [ʌnˈstintid] adj. Sin límites, ilimitado, da.
unstinting [ʌnˈstintiŋ] adj. Pródigo, ga. || — *To be unstinting in one's praise*, ser pródigo de alabanzas, no escatimar las alabanzas. || *We were unstinting in our efforts to locate him*, no regateamos ningún esfuerzo para dar con él.
unstitch [ˈʌnˈstitʃ] v. tr. Descoser. || *To come unstitched*, descoserse.
unstop [ˈʌnˈstɔp] v. tr. Destaponar (to take a stopper from). || Desatascar (to free from obstruction).
unstoppable [—əbl] adj. Incontenible. || SP. Imparable (a shot).
unstressed [ˈʌnˈstrest] adj. Sin acentuar, átono, na; inacentuado, da.
unstring* [ˈʌnˈstriŋ] v. tr. Desensartar (beads). || MUS. Aflojar las cuerdas de (to loosen). | Desencordar, quitar las cuerdas de (to remove). || Desatar las cuerdas de (to untie). || Aflojar (a bow). || Trastornar (s.o.'s nerves). || Trastornar, desquiciar (s.o.).
— OBSERV. Pret. & p. p. ***unstrung***.
unstrung [ˈʌnˈstrʌŋ] pret. & p. p. See UNSTRING.
unstuck [ˈʌnˈstʌk] pret. & p. p. See UNSTICK.
unstudied [ˈʌnˈstʌdid] adj. Ignorante (unlearned). || Natural, sin afectación (unaffected, not artificial). || Sin estudiar (subject). || *Unstudied in*, sin conocimientos de.
unsubmissive [ˈʌnsəbˈmisiv] adj. Insumiso, sa.
unsubstantial [ˈʌnsəbˈstænʃəl] adj. Insustancial. || Sin fundamento (unfounded). || Imaginario, ria; irreal (unreal). || Ligero, ra (light).
unsuccess [ˈʌnsəkˈses] n. Fracaso, *m.*
unsuccessful [—ful] adj. Sin éxito: *an unsuccessful song*, una canción sin éxito. || Fracasado, da (a person, negotiation, etc.). || Fallido, da; infructuoso, sa; fracasado, da; sin éxito: *an unsuccessful attempt*, un intento fallido. || Vano, na; infructuoso, sa (effort). || Suspendido, da (in an examination): *an unsuccessful candidate*, un candidato suspendido. || Fracasado, da; vencido, da; derrotado, da (candidate in election). || *To be unsuccessful*, fracasar, no tener éxito.
unsuccessfully [—fuli] adv. Sin éxito. || En vano, infructuosamente.
unsuitability [ˈʌnˌsju:təˈbiliti] n. Impropiedad, *f.*, inadecuación, *f.* (of a thing). || Inaptitud, *f.* (of a person). || Inoportunidad, *f.* || Inconveniencia, *f.*
unsuitable [ˈʌnˈsju:təbl] adj. Incompetente, no apto, ta (person): *unsuitable for a position*, no apto para un puesto. || Inadecuado, da; impropio, pia (thing): *it's an unsuitable place for the picture*, es un sitio impropio para el cuadro. || Inconveniente (inconvenient): *an unsuitable time*, una hora inconveniente. || Inoportuno, na (inopportune): *an unsuitable remark*, una observación inoportuna.
unsuited [ˈʌnˈsju:tid] adj. No apto, ta (person): *unsuited for a position*, no apto para un puesto. || Inadecuado, da; impropio, pia (thing): *unsuited for a job*, inadecuado para un trabajo; *it's a place unsuited to the picture*, es un sitio impropio para el cuadro. || Incompatible: *hobbies unsuited to his position in life*, pasatiempos incompatibles con su situación. || Impropio, pia (unbecoming): *slovenliness unsuited to a man in his position*, negligencia impropia de un hombre de su calidad.
unsullied [ˈʌnˈsʌlid] adj. Sin tacha, sin mancha.
unsung [ʌnˈsʌŋ] adj. No cantado. || FIG. No alabado, da; no celebrado, da (victory, etc.).
unsupported [ˈʌnsəˈpɔ:tid] adj. No apoyado, da; sin apoyo (person, amendment). || Sin fundamento (statement).
unsure [ʌnˈʃuə*] adj. Poco seguro, ra.
unsurmountable [ˈʌnsəˈmauntəbl] adj. Insuperable.
unsurpassable [ˈʌnsəˈpɑ:səbl] adj. Insuperable, inmejorable: *of unsurpassable quality*, de calidad inmejorable.
unsurpassed [ˈʌnsəˈpɑ:st] adj. No superado, da; sin superar.

unsuspected [ˈʌnsəsˈpektid] adj. Insospechado, da. || Desconocido, da; ignorado, da. || *The existence of this animal was unsuspected*, se ignoraba la existencia de este animal.
unsuspecting [ˈʌnsəsˈpektiŋ] adj. Confiado, da; poco suspicaz: *the unsuspecting victim was attacked from behind*, la confiada víctima fue atacada por detrás. || *To be unsuspecting of sth.*, no sospechar algo.
unsustainable [ˈʌnsəsˈteinəbl] adj. Insostenible.
unswaddle [ˈʌnˈswɔdl] v. tr. Quitar los pañales a.
unsweetened [ˈʌnˈswi:tənd] adj. No azucarado, da; sin azucarar.
unswerving [ˈʌnˈswə:viŋ] adj. Inquebrantable (faith, loyalty, etc.). || Recto, ta (absolutely straight).
unsymmetrical [ˈʌnsiˈmetrikəl] adj. Asimétrico, ca; disimétrico, ca.
unsympathetic [ˈʌnˌsimpəˈθetik] adj. Poco compasivo, va; sin compasión. || Indiferente: *he is not unsympathetic to your problem*, su problema no le deja indiferente. || Falto de comprensión. || — *He was unsympathetic to their appeal*, no atendió su petición. || *¿How can you be so unsympathetic?*, ¿cómo puedes ser tan poco comprensivo?
unsystematic [ˈʌnˌsistəˈmætik] adj. Sin sistema, poco metódico, ca.
untactful [ˈʌnˈtæktful] adj. Falto de tacto.
untainted [ˈʌnˈteintid] adj. Fresco, ca; no contaminado, da (food). || No corrompido, da (morally). || No mancillado, da (reputation).
untamable or **untameable** [ˈʌnˈteiməbl] adj. Indomable, indomesticable. || FIG. Indomable.
untamed [ˈʌnˈteimd] adj. Indomado, da (animal).
untangle [ˈʌnˈtæŋgl] v. tr. Desenmarañar, desenredar.
untanned [ˈʌnˈtænd] adj. Sin curtir.
untapped [ˈʌnˈtæpt] adj. Sin explotar.
untarnished [ˈʌnˈtɑ:niʃt] adj. Sin oxidar (a metal). || FIG. Sin mancha, no mancillado, da (reputation).
untasted [ˈʌnˈteistid] adj. Sin probar.
untaught [ˈʌnˈtɔ:t] pret. & p. p. See UNTEACH.
— Adj. Sin instrucción (person). || No enseñado, da (knowledge).
untaxed [ˈʌnˈtækst] adj. Libre *or* exonerado de impuestos.
unteach* [ˈʌnˈti:tʃ] v. tr. Hacer olvidar.

— OBSERV. Pret. & p. p. ***untaught***.

unteachable [ˈʌnˈti:tʃəbl] adj. Incapaz de aprender algo.
untellable [ˈʌnˈteləbl] adj. Incontable.
untempered [ˈʌnˈtempəd] adj. Sin templar.
untenable [ˈʌnˈtenəbl] adj. Insostenible, indefendible.
untenanted [ˈʌnˈtenəntid] adj. Vacío, a; sin inquilino; desocupado, da.
untested [ˈʌnˈtestid] adj. No probado, da (not tried out). || Sin comprobar (not proved).
unthankful [ˈʌnˈθæŋkful] adj. Ingrato, ta; desagradecido, da (not thankful). || Ingrato, ta: *an unthankful task*, una labor ingrata.
unthinkable [ʌnˈθiŋkəbl] adj. Inimaginable, increíble, inconcebible (unimaginable). || Inconcebible, impensable (out of the question).
unthinking [ˈʌnˈθiŋkiŋ] adj. Irreflexivo, va.
unthought [ˈʌnˈθɔ:t] adj. *Unthought of*, inesperado, da; imprevisto, ta.
unthread [ˈʌnˈθred] v. tr. Desenhebrar, desensartar (a needle). || Desensartar (beads). || Deshebrar (cloth). || FIG. Desenmarañar.
unthrifty [ˈʌnˈθrifti] adj. Despilfarrador, ra.
untidiness [ʌnˈtaidinis] n. Desorden, *m.* (disorder). || Desaseo, *m.*, desaliño, *m.* (of dress, appearance, etc.).
untidy [ʌnˈtaidi] adj. Desordenado, da; desarreglado, da; en desorden (room): *the house was untidy*, la casa estaba desordenada. || Desaseado, da; desaliñado, da (dress, person's appearance). || Desgreñado, da (hair). || Desordenado, da (person).
untie [ˈʌnˈtai] v. tr. Desatar: *to untie a knot, a parcel*, desatar un nudo, un paquete. || Soltar: *to untie a dog*, soltar un perro. || MAR. Desamarrar: *to untie a boat*, desamarrar un barco.
— V. intr. Desatarse.
until [ənˈtil] prep. Hasta: *we waited until Thursday*, esperamos hasta el jueves. || — *Until now*, hasta ahora. || *Until that time* o *until then*, hasta entonces. || *Until when?*, ¿hasta cuándo?
— Conj. Hasta que: *wait until he has gone*, espera hasta que se vaya; *he insisted until he got it*, insistió hasta que lo consiguió.

— OBSERV. Whilst *hasta que* may be used to translate all examples of the conjunction *until*, in cases where the subject of the two verbs is the same person the use of *hasta* with the infinitive is also possible (*keep looking until you find it*, sigue buscando hasta encontrarlo *or* hasta que lo encuentres).

untile [ˈʌnˈtail] v. tr. Quitar las tejas de.
untillable [ˈʌnˈtiləbl] adj. AGR. Incultivable.
untilled [ˈʌnˈtild] adj. AGR. Inculto, ta; no cultivado, da; sin cultivar.
untimeliness [ʌnˈtaimlinis] n. Inoportunidad, *f.*: *the untimeliness of their intervention*, la inoportunidad de su intervención.
untimely [ʌnˈtaimli] adj. Inoportuno, na (inopportune): *untimely question*, cuestión inoportuna. || Prematuro, ra (death, birth, etc.). || Temprano, na (fruit). || Impropio de la estación (weather). || *At an untimely hour*, a deshora.
— Adv. Inoportunamente (inopportunely). || Prematuramente (prematurely).
untiring [ʌnˈtaiəriŋ] adj. Incansable, infatigable: *untiring in one's work*, incansable en el trabajo.
unto [ˈʌntu] prep. (Ant.). A: *render unto Caesar*, dale al César. | Hasta: *unto this day*, hasta la fecha. | Hacia (towards).
untold [ˈʌnˈtəuld] adj. Fabuloso, sa; incalculable (incalculably great): *untold riches*, riqueza fabulosa; *untold quantities*, cantidades incalculables. || Inaudito, ta (very great): *untold suffering*, sufrimiento inaudito. || Indecible, inefable (unspeakable). || *His story remains untold*, no se ha contado todavía su historia.
untouchable [ʌnˈtʌtʃəbl] adj./n. Intocable.
untouched [ˈʌnˈtʌtʃt] adj. No tocado, da. || Sin tocar: *he left his food untouched*, dejó la comida sin tocar; *to leave a subject untouched*, dejar un tema sin tocar. || No afectado, da: *untouched by the scandal*, no afectado por el escándalo. || Sin retocar (photos). || Insensible (*by*, a) [unmoved]. || No mermado, da (reputation). || Ileso, sa; indemne (unharmed). || *People untouched by modern civilization*, gente hasta la cual no ha llegado la civilización moderna.
untoward [ʌnˈtəuəd] adj. Insumiso, sa (unruly). || Difícil de labrar (a material). || Adverso, sa; contrario, ria: *untoward circumstances*, circunstancias adversas. || Desafortunado, da: *an untoward accident*, un accidente desafortunado. || Desgraciado, da: *an untoward life*, una vida desgraciada. || Funesto, ta (event). || Poco propicio, cia; poco favorable (season, weather). || Inconveniente.
untowardness [—nis] n. Insumisión, *f.*, indocilidad, *f.* || Adversidad, *f.*
untraceable [ˈʌnˈtreisəbl] adj. Que no se puede encontrar, imposible de encontrar.
untrained [ˈʌnˈtreind] adj. No cualificado, da; sin formación profesional (worker). || No amaestrado, da (animals). || Inexperimentado, da; inexperto, ta (inexpert). || SP. Falto de entrenamiento, sin preparar.
untrammeled or **untrammelled** [ʌnˈtræməld] adj. Sin límites (not limited). || Libre (*by*, de).
untransferable [ˈʌntrænsˈfə:rəbl] adj. Intransferible.
untranslatable [ˈʌntrænsˈleitəbl] adj. Intraducible.
untransportable [ˈʌntrænsˈpɔ:təbl] adj. Intransportable.
untraveled or **untravelled** [ˈʌnˈtrævld] adj. Poco frecuentado, da (road). || Que no ha viajado (person). || Inexplorado, da; poco conocido, da (country).
untried [ˈʌnˈtraid] adj. Inexperto, ta; inexperimentado, da (inexperienced). || No probado, da (not tested). || JUR. No juzgado, da. || *To leave nothing untried*, intentarlo todo.
untrimmed [ˈʌnˈtrimd] adj. Sin podar (hedge). || Descuidado, da (garden). || Sin cortar (hair, nails). || Sin debastar (wood). || Sin labrar (stone). || Sin adorno (hat). || Sin aderezo (meat).
untrod [ˈʌnˈtrɔd] or **untrodden** [ˈʌnˈtrɔdn] adj. Inexplorado, da (country). || Sin pisar (snow, sand). || No trillado, da (path). || *Untrodden forest*, selva (*f.*) virgen.
untroubled [ˈʌnˈtrʌbld] adj. Tranquilo, la (calm). || No molestado, da (not disturbed). || *Untroubled by worries*, sin preocupaciones.
untrue [ˈʌnˈtru:] adj. Falso, sa (not true). || Erróneo, a; inexacto, ta (statement). || Infiel, desleal (unfaithful). || TECH. Inexacto, ta (inaccurate). | Torcido, da (grindstone).
untrussed [ˈʌnˈtrʌst] adj. ARCH. Sin entramado (bridge). | Sin armazón (roof). || CULIN. Sin atar (chicken).
untrustworthy [ˈʌnˈtrʌstˌwə:ði] adj. Poco seguro, ra; que no es de fiar (unreliable): *untrustworthy person*, persona que no es de fiar; *untrustworthy information*, información poco segura.
untruth [ˈʌnˈtru:θ] n. Mentira, *f.* (falsehood). || Falsedad, *f.* (lack of truthfulness).
untruthful [—ful] adj. Mentiroso, sa (inclined to lie). || Falso, sa (untrue).
untruthfulness [—fulnis] n. Falsedad, *f.*
untune [ˈʌnˈtju:n] v. tr. MUS. Desafinar (an instrument).
unturned [ˈʌnˈtə:nd] adj. No vuelto, ta. || FIG. *To leave no stone unturned*, no dejar piedra por mover.
untutored [ˈʌnˈtju:təd] adj. Sin instrucción, ignorante (person). || No formado, da (mind). || *To be untutored in*, ignorar, desconocer.
untwine [ˈʌnˈtwain] v. tr./intr. See UNTWIST.
untwist [ˈʌnˈtwist] v. tr. Destorcer: *to untwist a cable*, destorcer un cable.
— V. intr. Destorcerse.
unusable [ˈʌnˈju:zəbl] adj. Inutilizable.
unused [ˈʌnˈju:zd] adj. Sin emplear, sin usar, nuevo, va (never having been used): *some unused canvases*, unos lienzos sin emplear. || Que no se utiliza (not currently in use): *an unused warehouse*, un almacén que no se utiliza. || Libre: *my flat in Paris is unused at the moment*, mi piso en París está libre ahora. || Inusitado, da; desusado, da (word, expression).
unused [ˈʌnˈju:st] adj. No acostumbrado, da: *I am unused to it*, no estoy acostumbrado a ello.
unusefulness [ˈʌnˈju:sfulnis] n. Inutilidad, *f.*

unusual [ʌnˈjuːʒuəl] adj. Extraño, ña; raro, ra; insólito, ta (peculiar, strange). || Original (different, unique). || Desacostumbrado, da; inhabitual: *to work with unusual enthusiasm*, trabajar con un entusiasmo desacostumbrado. || Poco común, que se sale de lo corriente: *unusual event*, acontecimiento poco común. || Excepcional, extraordinario, ria: *a scene of unusual beauty*, un panorama de una belleza excepcional. || Poco usado, da; poco empleado, da (word).
unusually [ʌnˈjuːʒuəli] adv. Extraordinariamente: *unusually tall*, extraordinariamente alto. || *He was unusually attentive*, fue más atento que de costumbre.
unutterable [ʌnˈʌtərəbl] adj. Indecible.
unvalued [ˈʌnˈvæljuːd] adj. No valorado, da. || Fig. Poco apreciado, da.
unvanquished [ˈʌnˈvæŋkwiʃt] adj. Invicto, ta.
unvaried [ʌnˈvɛərid] adj. Poco variado, da.
unvarnished [ˈʌnˈvɑːniʃt] adj. No barnizado, da; sin barnizar (not varnished). || Fig. Sencillo, lla; puro, ra (plain, unembellished). || *The unvarnished truth*, la verdad escueta, la pura verdad.
unvarying [ʌnˈvɛəriiŋ] adj. Invariable.
unveil [ʌnˈveil] v. tr. Quitar el velo a (a person). || Destapar (an object). || Descubrir, inaugurar (a statue). || Descubrir, revelar (a secret). || Descubrir (sth. hidden).
unveiling [ʌnˈveiliŋ] n. Inauguración, *f.*, descubrimiento, *m.* (of a statue).
unventilated [ˈʌnˈventileitid] adj. Sin ventilación.
unverifiable [ˈʌnˈverifaiəbl] adj. Incomprobable.
unversed [ˈʌnˈvəːst] adj. Poco versado, da [en algo].
unviolated [ˈʌnˈvaiəleitid] adj. Inviolado, da.
unvisited [ˈʌnˈvizitid] adj. No visitado, da.
unvoiced [ˈʌnˈvɔist] adj. No expresado, da. || Sordo, da (consonant). || Mudo, da (vowel).
unvouched [ˈʌnˈvautʃt] adj. *Unvouched for*, no garantizado, da.
unwanted [ˈʌnˈwɔntid] adj. No deseado, da: *unwanted children*, niños no deseados. || No solicitado, da; no pedido, da: *unwanted advice*, consejos no solicitados. || Superfluo, a (superfluous). || — *To feel unwanted*, darse cuenta de que su presencia no es deseada. || *To have some unwanted magazines*, tener unas revistas que no se quieren conservar *or* que estorban.
unwariness [ʌnˈwɛərinis] n. Imprudencia, *f.*
unwarlike [ˈʌnˈwɔːlaik] adj. Pacífico, ca.
unwarned [ˈʌnˈwɔːnd] adj. Sin aviso.
unwarped [ˈʌnˈwɔːpt] adj. No alabeado, da (wood). || Fig. No torcido, da (mind).
unwarrantable [ˈʌnˈwɔrəntəbl] adj. Injustificable.
unwarranted [ˈʌnˈwɔrəntid] adj. Injustificable (unable to be justified). || Injustificado, da (without justification). || Sin garantía (not guaranteed).
unwary [ʌnˈwɛəri] adj. Imprudente (rash, careless). || Incauto, ta (incautious).
unwashed [ˈʌnˈwɔʃt] adj. Sin lavar, sucio, cia. || *The Great Unwashed*, el populacho.
unwatered [ˈʌnˈwɔːtəd] adj. Sin agua (a town). || Sin regar (garden). || De secano (without rain or irrigation): *unwatered country*, tierras de secano. || No diluido, da (not diluted). || No aguado, da (wine). || Sin abrevar (cattle). || Sin aguas (silk).
unwavering [ʌnˈweivəriŋ] adj. Constante, firme (steady). || Inquebrantable: *unwavering fortitude*, valor inquebrantable. || Fijo, ja: *unwavering gaze*, mirada fija.
unwearable [ˈʌnˈwɛərəbl] adj. Que no se puede llevar.
unwearied [ʌnˈwiərid] adj. Incansable (tireless). || No cansado, da (not weary).
unwearying [ʌnˈwiəriiŋ] adj. Incansable.
unweave* [ˈʌnˈwiv] v. tr. Destejer.

— Observ. Pret. ***unwove;*** p. p. ***unwoven.***

unwed [ˈʌnˈwed] adj. Soltero, ra.
unwedge [ˈʌnˈwedʒ] v. tr. Desencajar (a machine part).
unwelcome [ʌnˈwelkəm] adj. Importuno, na; molesto, ta: *an unwelcome guest*, un invitado molesto. || Mal recibido, da (a visitor). || Inoportuno, na: *an unwelcome visit*, una visita inoportuna. || Desagradable: *unwelcome news*, una noticia desagradable. || Incómodo, da: *to make s.o. feel unwelcome*, hacer que alguien se sienta incómodo. || *A little help wouldn't be unwelcome*, no me (te, etc.) vendría mal un poco de ayuda.
unwell [ˈʌnˈwel] adj. Malo, la (not well, sick).
unwept [ˈʌnˈwept] adj. No llorado, da (an event).
unwholesome [ˈʌnˈhəulsəm] adj. Malsano, na (climate, food, ideas).
unwieldy [ʌnˈwiːldi] adj. Poco manejable, difícil de manejar (hard to handle). || Voluminoso, sa; abultado, da (cumbersome). || Pesado, da (heavy). || Torpe (clumsy).
unwilled [ʌnˈwild] adj. Involuntario, ria.
unwilling [ˈʌnˈwiliŋ] adj. No dispuesto, ta: *to be unwilling to do sth.*, no estar dispuesto a hacer algo. || [Hecho, dicho, etc.] de mala gana: *an unwilling confession*, una confesión hecha de mala gana. || — *To be unwilling that*, no estar dispuesto a que, no querer que [with subj.]. || *We are unwilling for you to go*, no queremos que vayas.
unwillingly [—li] adv. De mala gana, a disgusto.
unwillingness [—nis] n. Desgana, *f.*, mala voluntad, *f.*
unwind* [ˈʌnˈwaind] v. tr. Desenrollar (sth. that is wound up). || Devanar (a skein). || Fig. Desenredar, desembrollar (to sort out).
— V. intr. Desenrollarse (to become unwound). || Devanarse (a skein). || Fig. Relajarse (to relax).

— Observ. Pret. & p. p. ***unwound.***

unwinking [ˈʌnˈwiŋkiŋ] adj. Que no parpadea (eyes, person). || Fijo, ja (stare, attention).
unwisdom [ˈʌnˈwizdəm] n. Imprudencia, *f.* || Insensatez, *f.*, falta (*f.*) de sensatez.
unwise [ˈʌnˈwaiz] adj. Imprudente (foolish). || Insensato, ta (senseless). || Poco aconsejable, desaconsejado, da (ill-advised): *it is unwise to go swimming after a meal*, es poco aconsejable bañarse después de comer.
unwish [ʌnˈwiʃ] v. tr. Dejar de desear.
unwished [ʌnˈwiʃt] adj. *Unwished for*, no deseado, da (not wanted), no solicitado, da (unasked for).
unwithering [ˈʌnˈwiðəriŋ] adj. Inmarcescible, inmarchitable.
unwitting [ʌnˈwitiŋ] adj. Hecho sin querer, involuntario, ria (not intentional). || *Unwitting of*, inconsciente de.
unwittingly [—li] adv. Inconscientemente, sin querer (unconsciously). || Sin querer, involuntariamente (unintentionally).
unwomanly [ʌnˈwumənli] adj. Poco femenino, na (not feminine). || Impropio de una mujer (not befitting a woman).
unwonted [ʌnˈwəuntid] adj. Extraño, ña; raro, ra; insólito, ta (unusual). || No acostumbrado, da; desacostumbrado, da (unaccustomed).
unwordable [ˈʌnˈwəːdəbl] adj. Indecible, inexpresable.
unworkable [ˈʌnˈwəːkəbl] adj. Inexplotable (a mine). || Irrealizable (not possible): *an unworkable plan*, un proyecto irrealizable.
unworldly [ˈʌnˈwəːldli] adj. No mundano, na; poco mundano, na (unconcerned with worldly values). || Espiritual (spiritual). || Celestial (heavenly). || Ingenuo, nua (naïve).
unworn [ˈʌnˈwɔːn] adj. Nuevo, va (clothes): *an unworn jacket*, una chaqueta nueva. || No usado, da (not worn out). || No trillado, da; original.
unworthiness [ʌnˈwəːðinis] n. Falta (*f.*) de mérito. || Indignidad, *f.*, lo indigno (of action, thought).
unworthy [ʌnˈwəːði] adj. No digno, indigno, na: *unworthy of an honour*, indigno de un honor; *conduct unworthy of a gentleman*, conducta indigna de un caballero. || De poco mérito (worthless). || Despreciable (contemptible). || *Unworthy of attention*, que no merece atención.
unwound [ˈʌnˈwaund] pret. & p. p. See unwind.
unwounded [ˈʌnˈwuːndid] adj. Ileso, sa.
unwove [ˈʌnˈwəuv] pret. See unweave.
unwoven [ˈʌnˈwəuvən] p. p. See unweave.
unwrap [ˈʌnˈræp] v. tr. Desenvolver. || Deshacer, desempaquetar (a parcel).
unwrapping [—iŋ] n. Desempaquetado, *m.*
unwrinkle [ʌnˈriŋkəl] v. tr. Desarrugar.
unwritten [ˈʌnˈritn] adj. No escrito, ta (not written). || Blanco, ca (paper). || Oral: *unwritten tradition*, tradición oral. || Jur. *Unwritten law*, derecho consuetudinario (common law).

— Observ. En Gran Bretaña *unwritten law* se aplica a las conveniencias sociales, que no reconoce forzosamente la ley, mientras que en Estados Unidos indica más bien el derecho a vengar una ofensa con sangre.

unyielding [ʌnˈjiːldiŋ] adj. Inflexible, inquebrantable.
unyoke [ˈʌnˈjəuk] v. tr. Desuncir. || Fig. Separar.
unzip [ˈʌnˈzip] v. tr. Bajar la cremallera de.
up [ʌp] adv. Hacia arriba (upwards): *to look up*, mirar hacia arriba. || Arriba: *all the way up*, hasta arriba; *what are you doing up there?*, ¿qué estás haciendo allá arriba?; *hands up!* o *up with your hands!*, ¡manos arriba! || Para arriba: *from fifty pesos up*, de cincuenta pesos para arriba. || En el aire (in the air). || Al aire: *to throw sth. up*, lanzar algo al aire. || Más fuerte, más alto: *speak up*, habla más fuerte. || Levantado, da (out of bed). || Crecido, da (river, corn, etc.). || Alto, ta (tide). || Entendido, da; competente: *to be well up in history*, ser muy entendido en historia. || Fuerte: *he is up in chemistry*, está fuerte en química. || Enterado, da; informado, da: *to be up on the news*, estar enterado de las noticias. || De pie, en pie (standing). || Completamente: *to fill up a glass*, llenar completamente un vaso. || Levantado, da; en obras: *the road is up*, la carretera está levantada. || Hacia el norte (northwards). || En la universidad: *when he was up*, cuando estaba en la universidad. || — *Close up to*, muy cerca de. || *Face up*, boca arriba. || *From... up*, a partir de, de ... para arriba: *from three dollars up*, a partir de tres dólares, de tres dólares para arriba; desde: *from my youth up*, desde mi juventud. || *Halfway up*, a la mitad del camino. || *Have you ever been up in an aeroplane?*, ¿has subido ya en un avión? || *He is up at daybreak*, se levanta al alba. || *High up*, muy arriba. || Fig. *His blood was up*, se le subía la sangre a la cabeza. || *His leave is up*, acabó su permiso. || *I am up for the day*, he venido a pasar el día. || *I'll play you fifty up*, jugamos hasta cincuenta. || *It is not up to much*, no vale gran cosa. || *It's all up*, se acabó todo. || *It's all up with him*, está perdido, ya no le queda esperanza. || *It's up to you*, eres tú quien tienes que decidir, en tus manos

está la decisión, depende de ti. || *It's up to you to*, eres tú quien tienes que, a ti te toca: *it's up to you to choose*, eres tú quien tienes que escoger, a ti te toca escoger. || *Let us be up and doing*, pongámonos a hacer algo. || *Meat is up again*, la carne ha subido otra vez. || *My room is four flights up*, mi habitación está en el cuarto piso. || *Road up*, [atención] obras (sign). || *The blinds are up*, se han subido las persianas. || *The curtain is up*, se ha levantado el telón (in the theatre). || *The curtains are up*, las cortinas están colgadas. || FIG. *The game is up!*, ¡se acabó! || *The House is up*, el Parlamento no celebra sesión *or* no se reúne. || *The moon is up*, ha salido la luna. || *The plane is up*, el avión está en vuelo. || *There's sth. up*, algo pasa. || *The window is up*, el cristal está cerrado (in carriage), la ventana está cerrada (sash window). || *This isn't up to standard*, no satisface los requisitos. || *This side up*, este lado hacia arriba (on a parcel). || *Time is up*, es la hora [de acabar, cerrar, etc.], se acabó el tiempo reglamentario. || FAM. *To be hard up*, no tener un céntimo. || SP. *To be one goal up*, ir ganando por un gol. || *To be up against*, enfrentarse con. || *To be up against it*, tener mala suerte (unlucky), estar en un apuro (in trouble). || *To be up all night*, no acostarse en toda la noche. || *To be up for*, presentarse para (approval), ser procesado por (at court). || *To be up in*, ser un experto en. || *To be up in arms*, see ARM. || *To be up to anything*, ser capaz de cualquier cosa. || *To be up to s.o.*, poder competir *or* rivalizar con uno. || *To be up to*, ser capaz *or* estar en condiciones de hacer (able), estar a la altura de (equal to): *he is not up to his job*, no está a la altura de su trabajo; estar haciendo (busy): *what are you up to?*, ¿qué está haciendo?; estar tramando: *the baby is quiet, I wonder what he is up to*, el niño está callado, ¿qué estará tramando?; ir por: *where were we up to?*, ¿por dónde íbamos? || *To come* o *to go up to*, acercarse a. || *To feel up to*, sentirse capaz de, estar en condiciones de: *do you feel up to making this trip?*, ¿se siente usted capaz de hacer este viaje? || *To go up to town*, ir a la capital. || *To hold o.s. up*, mantenerse derecho. || *To put an umbrella up*, abrir un paraguas. || *To stay up all night with a sick man*, velar a un enfermo toda la noche. || *To walk up and down*, ir de un lado para otro, ir de acá para allá. || *Up!*, ¡arriba! || *Up above*, arriba. || *Up against* o *up beside*, al lado de, junto a (next to). || *Up and about*, haciendo vida normal, de nuevo en pie (after an illness). || *Up and doing*, activo, va; ocupado, da. || *Up and down*, de arriba abajo. || *Up for president*, candidato a la presidencia. || JUR. *Up for trial*, ante el tribunal. || *Up north*, hacia *or* en el norte. || *Up to*, hasta: *up to this day*, hasta la fecha; *he earns anything up to twenty pounds a week*, gana hasta veinte libras por semana. || *Up to date*, hasta la fecha, hasta hoy. || *Up to now*, hasta ahora. || *Up to one's old tricks*, haciendo de las suyas. || *Up went the flag*, izaron la bandera. || *Up with X!*, ¡viva X!, ¡arriba X! || *What's up?*, ¿qué pasa? || *What's up with you?*, ¿qué te pasa? || *We are well up in our work*, vamos muy bien en nuestro trabajo.

— Prep. Arriba: *up the river*, río arriba; *up the street*, calle arriba. || En: *is there a restaurant up the Eiffel tower?*, ¿hay un restaurante en la Torre Eiffel? || En lo alto de, arriba de (on the top of). || Contra: *up the wind*, contra el viento. || En el fondo de: *up the yard*, en el fondo del patio. || — *Further up the street*, más allá en la calle. || *Halfway up the street*, a la mitad de la calle. || *To walk up and down the room*, pasearse a lo largo y a lo ancho de la habitación.

— Adj. Ascendente (train). || De subida (escalator).

— N. *The ups and downs*, los altibajos, las vicisitudes.

— OBSERV. La palabra *up* acompaña frecuentemente un verbo cuyo sentido modifica o refuerza. Estos casos han sido tratados en el artículo correspondiente a cada uno de esos verbos. Por consiguiente *to stand up, to keep up with*, etc. se encontrarán en "stand", "keep", etc.

up [ʌp] v. tr. Levantar, alzar (to raise). || Aumentar (to increase): *to up taxes*, aumentar los impuestos.

— V. intr. *To up and*, coger y, de pronto: *he upped and left*, cogió y se fue, de pronto se fue. || *To up with*, levantar: *to up with an axe*, levantar un hacha.

up-anchor [—ˈæŋkə*] v. intr. MAR. Levar anclas.

up-and-coming [ˈʌpənˈkʌmiŋ] adj. Joven y prometedor, joven y prometedora: *an up-and-coming artist*, un artista joven y prometedor. || Que promete mucho: *the new mayor is an up-and-coming politician*, el nuevo alcalde es un político que promete mucho.

up-and-down [ˈʌpənˈdaun] adj. Vertical (motion). || Variable (varying). || Accidentado, da (uneven, eventful). || Con altibajos (year). || Fluctuante (prices).

up-and-up [ˈʌpənˈdʌp] n. *To be on the up-and-up*, ir cada vez mejor.

upbear* [ʌpˈbɛə*] v. tr. Levantar (to raise up). || Sostener (to support).

— OBSERV. Pret. **upbore**; p. p. **upborne**.

upbore [ʌpˈbɔ:*] pret. See UPBEAR.

upborne [ʌpˈbɔ:n] p. p. See UPBEAR.

upbraid [ʌpˈbreid] v. tr. Regañar, reprender (to scold). || Regañar, censurar, reprochar: *to upbraid s.o. for* o *with sth.*, regañar a alguien por algo, reprochar *or* censurar algo a alguien.

upbraiding [—iŋ] n. Recriminación, *f.*, bronca, *f.* (fam.): *to give s.o. an upbraiding*, echarle una bronca a alguien, hacer recriminaciones a alguien.

upbringing [ˈʌpˌbriŋiŋ] n. Educación, *f.*

upcast [ˈʌpkɑ:st] adj. Dirigido hacia arriba. || *Upcast eyes*, ojos alzados al cielo.

— N. MIN. Pozo (*m.*) de ventilación (ventilation shaft). | Corriente (*f.*) de aire ascendente (current of air).

upcoming [ˈʌpˈkʌmiŋ] adj. Próximo, ma.

up-country [ˈʌpˈkʌntri] adj. Del interior.

— Adv. Hacia el interior, tierra adentro.

— N. Interior, *m.*

upcurrent [ˈʌpˈkʌrənt] n. Corriente (*f.*) ascendente.

update [ʌpˈdeit] v. tr. U. S. Actualizar, poner al día (to bring up to date). | Modernizar (to modernize).

upend [ʌpˈend] v. tr. Poner de pie.

upgrade [ˈʌpˈgreid] adj. Ascendente (uphill).

— N. Cuesta, *f.*, pendiente, *f.* || FIG. *To be on the upgrade*, ir mejorando (getting better), aumentar (on the increase), prosperar (prospering), remontar la pendiente, recuperarse (after an illness).

upgrade [ʌpˈgreid] v. tr. Ascender (to promote). || Mejorar la calidad de (to improve the quality of).

upgrowing [ˈʌpˈgrəuiŋ] adj. Que crece (child).

upgrowth [ˈʌpgrəuθ] n. Desarrollo, *m.*

upheaval [ʌpˈhi:vəl] n. GEOL. Levantamiento, *m.* || FIG. Trastorno, *m.*, agitación, *f.*: *political upheaval*, agitación política.

upheave [ʌpˈhi:v] v. tr. Levantar.

— V. intr. Levantarse.

upheld [ʌpˈheld] pret. & p. p. See UPHOLD.

uphill [ˈʌpˈhil] adj. Ascendente (rising). || FIG. Penoso, sa; arduo, dua; duro, ra (task, struggle).

— Adv. Cuesta arriba.

— N. Cuesta, *f.*, pendiente, *f.* (slope).

uphold* [ʌpˈhəuld] v. tr. Levantar (to lift up). || Sostener, soportar (to keep from falling). || Apoyar (to support): *the court upheld his claim*, el tribunal apoyó su petición. || Sostener, mantener (an opinion). || Mantener (one's position). || Defender (to defend). || Hacer respetar (the law).

— OBSERV. Pret. & p. p. **upheld**.

upholder [—ə*] n. Defensor, ra (of an opinion). || Partidario, ria (of a practice).

upholster [ʌpˈhəulstə*] v. tr. Tapizar (*in, with*, con).

upholsterer [—rə*] n. Tapicero, *m.*

upholstery [—ri] n. Tapicería, *f.* (material, work). || Relleno, *m.* (padding).

upkeep [ˈʌpki:p] n. Conservación, *f.*, mantenimiento, *m.*: *the upkeep of roads*, la conservación de las carreteras. || Gastos (*m. pl.*) de mantenimiento (costs). || *In good upkeep*, bien cuidado, da.

upland [ˈʌplənd] adj. Elevado, da; alto, ta (region). || De la meseta, de la altiplanicie (people, vegetation).

— N. Meseta, *f.*, altiplanicie, *f.* [*Amer.*, altiplano, *m.*].

uplander [—ə*] n. Montañés, esa; persona (*f.*) de la altiplanicie *or* de la meseta.

uplift [ˈʌplift] n. GEOL. Elevación, *f.* (rise). | Levantamiento, *m.* (upheaval). || Inspiración, *f.* || Mejoramiento, *m.* (improvement). || Reactivación, *f.* (of business). || *Moral uplift*, edificación, *f.*

uplift [ʌpˈlift] v. tr. Levantar (to lift up). || Alzar, levantar (voice). || Elevar (soul). || Inspirar.

upmost [ˈʌpməust] adj. Más alto, ta (in rank, position, etc.). || Predominante (in one's mind).

upon [əˈpɔn] prep. See ON.

upper [ˈʌpə*] adj. Alto, ta: *the upper classes*, las clases altas; *upper house*, cámara alta. || Superior: *the upper jaw*, la mandíbula superior. || MUS. Agudo, da. || GEOL. Superior. || GEOGR. Alto, ta: *the Upper Amazon*, el Alto Amazonas; *Upper Egypt*, Alto Egipto; *Upper Volta*, Alto Volta. || — FIG. *The upper crust*, la flor y nata, la crema (the best of a social class). || *The upper end of the table*, la cabecera de la mesa.

— N. Pala, *f.* (of a shoe). || U. S. FAM. Litera (*f.*) superior. || — Pl. U. S. Polainas, *f.* (gaiters). || FAM. *On one's uppers*, sin un céntimo, sin un cuarto.

uppercase [—keis] n. PRINT. Caja (*f.*) alta.

— Adj. Mayúscula.

upper-class [—klɑ:s] adj. De la clase alta.

uppercut [—kʌt] n. SP. "Uppercut", *m.*, gancho, *m.*

uppercut [—kʌt] v. tr./intr. SP. Dar un uppercut, dar un gancho (in boxing).

upper hand [—ˈhænd] n. Dominio, *m.* || *To get* o *to have the upper hand*, llevar ventaja, dominar.

uppermost [—məust] adj. Más alto, ta (in rank, position, etc.): *the uppermost floor*, el piso más alto. || Predominante (in one's mind).

— Adv. En primer lugar, en primer plano (in the first place). || — *Face uppermost*, boca arriba. || *He said whatever came uppermost*, dijo lo primero que le vino a la cabeza.

upperworks [—ˌwə:ks] pl. n. MAR. Obra (*f. sing.*) muerta.

uppish [ˈʌpiʃ] adj. FAM. Engreído, da; arrogante, presumido, da.

uppishness [—nis] n. FAM. Engreimiento, *m.*, arrogancia, *f.*, presunción, *f.*

uppity [ˈʌpiti] adj. FAM. Engreído, da; arrogante, presumido, da.

upraise [ʌpˈreiz] v. tr. Levantar.

upright [ˈʌprait] adj. Vertical, derecho, ca (in a vertical position). || Vertical, perpendicular (line).

|| FIG. Recto, ta; honrado, da (morally): *upright man*, hombre honrado. || De pie (on foot). || *Upright piano*, piano (*m.*) vertical.
— Adv. En posición vertical. || — *To hold o.s. upright*, estar derecho, mantenerse derecho. || *To sit upright on one's chair*, mantenerse derecho en la silla.
— N. Pie (*m.*) derecho, montante, *m.* (in carpentry). || Piano (*m.*) vertical (piano). || — Pl. SP. Postes, *m.* (in football).

uprightness [—nis] n. Verticalidad, *f.* || FIG. Rectitud, *f.*, honradez, *f.*

uprisal [ʌp'raizəl] n. Levantamiento, *m.*

uprise [ʌp'raiz] n. Levantamiento, *m.*

uprise* [ʌp'raiz] v. intr. Levantarse. || FIG. Sublevarse, alzarse.
— OBSERV. Pret. ***uprose***; p. p. ***uprisen***.

uprisen [ʌp'raizən] p. p. See UPRISE.

uprising [—iŋ] n. Levantamiento, *m.*, sublevación, *f.*, alzamiento, *m.*

upriver ['ʌp'rivə] adj./adv. Río arriba.

uproar ['ʌprɔ:*] n. Alboroto, *m.*, tumulto, *m.* (dim). || Alboroto, *m.* (disturbance). || — *The meeting ended in uproar*, se armó mucho jaleo al final de la reunión, hubo muchas protestas al final de la reunión. || *The town is in an uproar*, la ciudad está alborotada.

uproarious [ʌp'rɔ:riəs] adj. Tumultuoso, sa; ruidoso, sa. || Ruidoso, sa (laughter). || Graciosísimo, ma; divertidísimo, ma (very funny). || *The class was getting uproarious*, la clase empezaba a armar jaleo.

uproot [ʌp'ru:t] v. tr. Desarraigar: *the wind uprooted some trees*, el viento desarraigó algunos árboles. || FIG. Eliminar (to destroy utterly): *we must uproot poverty*, tenemos que eliminar la pobreza. | Desarraigar (to remove from a place of residence).

uprose [ʌp'rəuz] pret. See UPRISE.

uprush ['ʌprʌʃ] n. Subida, *f.* (upward movement). || Arranque, *m.*: *an uprush of pity*, un arranque de compasión.

upset [ʌp'set] adj. Trastornado, da (physically or mentally): *upset stomach*, estómago trastornado. || Preocupado, da (worried). || Enfadado, da; disgustado, da (*at*, por) [angry]. || Indispuesto, ta (slightly sick). || Desquiciado, da (nerves). || — *Don't be so upset!*, ¡no se preocupe tanto! || *Upset price*, precio mínimo, precio inicial.

upset ['ʌpset] n. Vuelco, *m.* (overturning). || Indisposición, *f.*, malestar, *m.* (slight ailment). || Trastorno, *m.* (of stomach). || Trastorno, *m.* (emotional). || Trastorno, *m.*, perturbación, *f.* (of plans, etc.). || Molestia, *f.* (trouble). || Dificultad, *f.* (difficulty). || Resultado (*m.*) inesperado (in sports).

upset* [ʌp'set] v. tr. Volcar (to tip over): *he upset the pitcher of water*, volcó el jarro de agua. || Hacer zozobrar (a ship). || Derramar (to spill). || Desordenar, revolver, poner patas arriba: *he upset everything in the house*, puso todo patas arriba en la casa. || Preocupar (to worry). || Trastornar (physically or mentally). || Desquiciar (s.o.'s nerves). || Afectar: *his father's death upset him greatly*, la muerte de su padre le afectó mucho. || Emocionar: *the least things upset him*, cualquier cosa le emociona. || Disgustar, enfadar (to displease). || Desconcertar (to disconcert). || Desbaratar, trastornar: *to upset plans*, desbaratar los planes. || Hacer fracasar (a plot). || Derribar, derrocar, echar abajo (the Government). || Sentar mal: *beer upsets me*, la cerveza me sienta mal. || SP. Vencer inesperadamente. || *To upset o.s.*, preocuparse (to worry).
— V. intr. Volcar, volcarse.
— OBSERV. Pret. & p. p. ***upset***.

upsetting [ʌp'setiŋ] adj. Preocupante (worrying). || Desconcertante (disconcerting).

upshot ['ʌpʃɔt] n. Resultado, *m.* || — *In the upshot*, al fin y al cabo. | *The upshot of it is that*, total que.

upside ['ʌpsaid] n. Parte (*f.*) superior.

upside down [—'daun] adv. Al revés (in an inverted position): *you've put the tablecloth upside down*, ha puesto el mantel al revés. || FIG. Patas arriba (in great disorder): *the house was turned upside down*, la casa estaba patas arriba. || — *To turn everything upside down*, revolverlo todo. | *To turn upside down*, poner boca abajo, volver (in an inverted position), poner patas arriba (in disorder).

upside-down [—'daun] adj. Al revés (in an inverted position). || FIG. Al revés: *an upside-down world*, el mundo al revés. | Extraño, ña (strange).

upsilon [ju:p'sailən] n. Ypsilón, *f.*, ípsilon, *f.* (Greek letter).

upstage ['ʌpsteidʒ] adv. En el fondo del escenario, hacia el fondo del escenario.
— Adj. FAM. Suficiente, presumido, da.

upstage ['ʌp'steidʒ] v. tr. Despreciar. || THEATR. *To upstage s.o.*, atraer toda la atención del público a expensas de alguien.

upstairs ['ʌp'stεəz] adv. Arriba, en el piso superior. || — *To call s.o. upstairs*, hacer subir a alguien. || *To go upstairs*, subir.
— Adj. De arriba, del piso superior. || Arriba de las escaleras.
— N. Piso (*m.*) superior.

upstanding [ʌp'stændiŋ] adj. Honrado, da; recto, ta (honourable). || De pie (standing up straight). || Robusto, ta (strong and healthy). || Erizado, da; de punta (hairs). || Fijo, ja (wages). || *To be upstanding*, ponerse de pie, levantarse.

upstart ['ʌpstɑ:t] adj./n. Advenedizo, za; arribista.

upstate ['ʌpsteit] adj. U. S. Interior.
— N. U. S. Interior, *m.*

upstream ['ʌpstri:m] adv. Río arriba, aguas arriba. || Más arriba: *I live upstream from the bridge*, vivo más arriba del puente. || A contracorriente (against the current).
— Adj. Río arriba.

upstroke ['ʌpstrəuk] n. Trazo (*m.*) ascendente (in writing). || TECH. Carrera (*f.*) ascendente (an upward movement).

upsurge ['ʌpsə:dʒ] n. Arrebato, *m.*, acceso, *m.*: *an upsurge of anger*, un arrebato de cólera. || Ola, *f.*: *an inflationary upsurge*, una ola inflacionista. || Aumento, *m.* (increase).

upswept ['ʌpswept] adj. Alto, ta (hairdo).

upswing ['ʌpswiŋ] n. Movimiento (*m.*) hacia arriba. || FIG. Mejora, *f.* (improvement).

upswing ['ʌpswiŋ] v. intr. Mejorar.

uptake ['ʌpteik] n. Cañón (*m.*) de la chimenea. || — FIG. FAM. *To be quick on the uptake*, ser rápido de comprensión. | *To be slow on the uptake*, ser duro de mollera *or* de entendederas.

upthrust ['ʌp'θrʌst] n. GEOL. Levantamiento, *m.* || PHYS. Empuje (*m.*) hacia arriba.

up-to-date ['ʌptə'deit] adj. Moderno, na: *an up-to-date house*, una casa moderna. || De moda (in fashion): *it's an up-to-date dress*, es un traje de moda. || Al día: *an up-to-date report*, un informe al día. || Al tanto, al corriente: *to be up-to-date on the news*, estar al tanto de las noticias.

up-to-the-minute ['ʌptu:θə'minit] adj. De última hora: *up-to-the-minute news*, las noticias de última hora. || Muy al día: *an up-to-the-minute report*, un informe muy al día. || Muy de moda (in fashion).

uptown ['ʌp'taun] adv. U. S. Hacia *or* en la parte alta de la ciudad. | Hacia *or* en la parte residencial de la ciudad.
— Adj. U. S. De la parte alta de la ciudad. | De la parte residencial de la ciudad.

uptrend ['ʌp'trend] n. Tendencia (*f.*) ascendente.

upturn [ʌp'tə:n] n. Mejora, *f.* (improvement). || Aumento, *m.* (increase).

upturn [ʌp'tə:n] v. tr. Volcar (to turn over). || Levantar, alzar: *to upturn one's eyes to the sky*, levantar los ojos hacia el cielo. || AGR. Voltear (ground).

upturned ['ʌptə:nd] adj. *Upturned nose*, nariz respingona.

upward ['ʌpwəd] adj. Ascendente, hacia arriba: *an upward movement*, un movimiento hacia arriba. || COMM. Al alza (tendency).
— Adv. Hacia arriba. || — *And upward*, y aún más. || *Face upward*, boca arriba. || *From the age of ten years upward*, a partir de diez años. || *The road runs upward*, la carretera sube. || *These shoes cost forty dollars and upward*, estos zapatos cuestan a partir de cuarenta dólares *or* de cuarenta dólares para arriba. || *To follow the river upward*, ir río arriba. || *Upward of*, más de: *upward of fifty pupils*, más de cincuenta alumnos.

upwards [—z] adv. See UPWARD.

upwind ['ʌpwind] adj./adv. Contra el viento.

uraemia [juə'ri:mjə] n. MED. Uremia, *f.*

uraemic [juə'ri:mik] adj. MED. Urémico, ca.

Ural ['juərəl] pr. n. GEOGR. Ural, *m.* (river). || — Pl. Urales, *m.* (mountains). || *Ural Mountains*, Montes (*m.*) Urales.

Ural-Altaic [—æl'teiik] adj. Uraloaltaico, ca.

uranate ['juərəneit] n. CHEM. Uranato, *m.*

uranic [juə'rænik] adj. CHEM. Uránico, ca. || ASTR. Uranio, nia.

uraniferous [,juərə'nifərəs] adj. Uranífero, ra.

uranite ['juərənait] n. CHEM. Uranita, *f.*

uranium [juə'reinjəm] n. CHEM. Uranio, *m.*

uranography [,juərə'nɔgrəfi] n. Uranografía, *f.*

Uranus ['juərənəs] pr. n. MYTH. ASTR. Urano, *m.*

urban ['ə:bən] adj. Urbano, na: *urban population*, población urbana.

urbane [ə:'bein] adj. Urbano, na; cortés (polite).

urbanism ['ə:bənizəm] n. Urbanismo, *m.*

urbanist ['ə:bənist] n. Urbanista, *m.* & *f.*

urbanity [ə:'bæniti] n. Urbanidad, *f.*, cortesía, *f.* || — Pl. Cumplidos, *m.*

urbanization [,ə:bənai'zeiʃən] n. Urbanización, *f.*

urbanize ['ə:bənaiz] v. tr. Urbanizar.

urchin ['ə:tʃin] n. Pilluelo, *m.*, golfillo, *m.* (mischievous boy). || Chiquillo, *m.*, muchacho, *m.*, chaval, *m.*, rapaz, *m.* (young boy). || ZOOL. Erizo (*m.*) de mar (sea urchin).

urea ['juəriə] n. Urea, *f.*

uremia [juə'ri:mjə] n. MED. Uremia, *f.*

uremic [juə'ri:mik] adj. MED. Urémico, ca.

ureter [juə'ri:tə*] n. ANAT. Uréter, *m.*

ureteral [—əl] adj. ANAT. Ureteral.

urethra [juə'ri:θrə] n. ANAT. Uretra, *f.*
— OBSERV. El plural de *urethra* es *urethrae* o *urethras*.

urethral [—l] adj. ANAT. Uretral.

urge [ə:dʒ] n. Impulso, *m.* (impulse). || Vivo deseo, *m.* (persistent desire). || *To feel an urge to do sth.*, tener muchas ganas de hacer algo, sentir un vivo deseo de hacer algo.

urge [ə:dʒ] v. tr. Exhortar (to exhort): *to urge s.o. to action*, exhortar a alguien a la acción. || Incitar (to prompt): *to urge s.o. to spend*, incitar a alguien al gasto; *hunger urged them to continue*, el hambre les incitó a seguir. || Instar (to compel): *I urged him to stay*, le insté a que se quedara. || Pedir con insistencia: *to urge reform*, pedir una reforma con insistencia. || Requerir: *measures which urge attention*, medidas que requieren atención. || Alegar (a reason). || Recomendar (to recommend): *to urge sth. on s.o.*, recomendar algo a alguien. || Preconizar, propugnar (to advocate): *the Minister urged a reform to stop inflation*, el Ministro preconizó una reforma para frenar la inflación. || — *To urge one's progress*, apresurar el paso. || *To urge s.o. on*, animar a alguien.

— V. intr. *To urge against*, hacer objeciones contra. || *To urge for*, abogar por.

urgency ['ə:dʒənsi] n. Urgencia, *f.*: *the urgency of the matter*, la urgencia del asunto; *this must be done with great urgency*, esto se tiene que hacer con toda urgencia. || Petición, *f.* (demand). || *A matter of great urgency*, un asunto muy urgente.

urgent ['ə:dʒənt] adj. Urgente, apremiante (pressing): *urgent need*, necesidad apremiante. || Insistente (request). || Porfiado, da; insistente: *an urgent creditor*, un acreedor porfiado. || Importuno, na (importunate). || *It is urgent that I see him*, me urge verle.

urgently ['ə:dʒəntli] adv. Urgentemente, con urgencia. || *I need it urgently*, me urge tenerlo.

uric ['juərik] adj. Med. Úrico, ca.

urinal ['juərinəl] n. Urinario, *m.* (public lavatory). || Orinal, *m.* (for bedridden people).

urinary ['juərinəri] adj. Anat. Urinario, ria: *urinary tract*, vías urinarias.

— N. Urinario, *m.* (public lavatory).

urinate ['juərineit] v. intr. Orinar.

urination [,juəri'neiʃən] n. Med. Micción, *f.*

urine ['juərin] n. Med. Orina, *f.*

uriniferous [,juəri'nifərəs] adj. Med. Urinífero, ra.

urinous ['juərinəs] adj. Urinario, ria.

urn [ə:n] n. Urna, *f.* (large vase). || Recipiente (*m.*) grande que sirve como tetera *or* cafetera.

urodela ['juərədi:lə] pl. n. Zool. Urodelos, *m.*

urogenital [,juərəu'dʒenitəl] adj. Urogenital.

urography [juə'rɔgrəfi] n. Urografía, *f.*

urologist [juə'rɔlədʒist] n. Urólogo, ga.

urology [juə'rɔlədʒi] n. Urología, *f.*

uroscopy [juə'rɔskəpi] n. Med. Uroscopia, *f.*

Ursa Major ['ə:sə'meidʒə*] pr. n. Astr. Osa (*f.*) Mayor.

Ursa Minor ['ə:sə'mainə*] pr. n. Astr. Osa (*f.*) Menor.

ursine ['ə:sain] adj. Zool. Osuno, na.

Ursuline ['ə:sjulain] n. Ursulina, *f.* (nun).

urtica ['ə:tikə] n. Bot. Ortiga, *f.*

urticaceae [ə:ti'keisii:] pl. n. Bot. Urticáceas, *f.*

urticant ['ə:tikənt] adj. Urticante.

urticaria [,ə:ti'kɛəriə] n. Urticaria, *f.* (hives).

urubu [u:ru'bu:] n. Urubú, *m.* (black vulture).

Uruguay ['urugwai] pr. n. Geogr. Uruguay, *m.*

Uruguayan [,uru'gwaiən] adj./n. Uruguayo, ya.

urunday ['urəndai] n. Urunday, *m.*, urundey, *m.*

urus ['juərəs] n. Zool. Uro, *m.* (aurochs).

us [ʌs] pers. pron. Nos (direct object): *tell us what you did*, dinos lo que hiciste; *they are calling us*, nos están llamando. || Nosotros, tras (after preposition): *he came with us*, vino con nosotros; *three of us*, tres de nosotros. || — *He could not believe that it was us*, no podía creer que éramos nosotros. || *Let us go* o *let's go*, vámonos. || *Pray for us*, ruega por nos. || *There are three of us*, somos tres. || *They are taller than us*, son más altos que nosotros.

U.S. ['ju:'es] or **U.S.A.** ['ju:'es'ei] n. EE. UU. (United States [of America]).

usability [,ju:zə'biliti] n. Utilidad, *f.*

usable ['ju:zəbl] adj. Utilizable.

usage ['ju:sidʒ] n. Tratos, *m. pl.*, tratamiento, *m.* (treatment): *ill usage*, malos tratos. || Usanza, *f.*, uso, *m.*, costumbre, *f.* (custom, established use). || Lenguaje, *m.* (parlance): *in fishermen's usage*, en el lenguaje de los pescadores. || Gramm. Uso, *m.*

usance ['ju:zəns] n. Comm. Plazo (*m.*) concedido para pagar una letra de cambio.

use [ju:s] n. Uso, *m.*: *the good use of riches*, el buen uso de las riquezas; *he lost the use of one arm*, perdió el uso de un brazo; *to go wrong with use*, estropearse con el uso. || Empleo, *m.*, uso, *m.*: *the use of electricity to light our houses*, el uso de la electricidad para iluminar nuestras casas. || Manejo, *m.*, uso, *m.* (of a tool, etc.). || Empleo, *m.*, aplicación, *f.*: *the uses of plastics*, las aplicaciones de los plásticos. || Utilidad, *f.* (usefulness). || Derecho (*m.*) al uso (the right to use). || Costumbre, *f.*, uso, *m.* (custom). || Rel. Rito, *m.* || Jur. Usufructo, *m.*, disfrute, *m.* || — *Can I be of any use to you?*, ¿puedo servirle en algo? || *Fit for use*, en buen estado. || *For emergency use only*, utilícese sólo en caso de emergencia. || *For external use*, para uso externo. || *For use only in case of fire*, utilícese sólo en caso de incendio. || *I have no further use for it*, ya no me sirve para nada. || *I have the use of the bathroom only in the evening*, sólo puedo usar el cuarto de baño por la noche. || *In common use* o *in current use* o *in everyday use*, de uso corriente. || *Instructions for use*, instrucciones (*f. pl.*) para el uso, modo (*m.*) de empleo. || *In use*, en uso. || *It's no use your writing to me*, es inútil que me escribas. || *Machine that has been in use for ten years*, máquina que se utiliza desde hace diez años. || *Out of use*, no funciona (lift). || *To be in use*, estar funcionando. || *To be of no use*, no servir para nada. || *To be of use*, servir. || *To be out of use*, estar fuera de uso (machine, etc.), no utilizarse (no to be used), haber caído en desuso (word). || *To come into use*, empezar a utilizarse. || *To have no use for*, no tener ocasión de emplear *or* usar *or* utilizar (to be useless), no necesitar (not to need), no soportar (to dislike): *I have no use for people who are always grumbling*, no soporto a la gente que se queja constantemente. || *To have the use of*, poder utilizar *or* usar. || *To make bad use of*, usar *or* utilizar mal. || *To make good use of*, hacer buen uso de, usar bien, aprovechar bien. || *To make great use of*, emplear *or* utilizar mucho. || *To make use of*, usar, utilizar, hacer uso de (to employ), aprovecharse de (to take advantage of), valerse de (one's right, powers). || *To put advice to use*, seguir un consejo. || *To put into use*, empezar a utilizar. || *To put to good use*, sacar partido de. || *To put to use*, utilizar (to employ), poner en servicio (to put into operation). || *What's the use?*, ¿para qué?: *what's the use of going?*, ¿para qué ir? || *With full use of all his faculties*, en plena posesión de todas sus facultades. || *You are no use as a painter*, usted no vale para pintor.

use [ju:z] v. tr. Emplear, utilizar, usar: *I use a knife to cut bread*, utilizo un cuchillo para cortar el pan; *to use force*, usar la fuerza; *we use this word*, usamos esta palabra. || Usar, utilizar: *ticket that cannot be used again*, billete que ya no se puede usar. || Utilizar: *can you use this tool?*, ¿sabes utilizar esta herramienta? || Coger, tomar, utilizar: *those who use trains regularly*, los que cogen el tren regularmente. || Hacer uso de: *he has to use his special powers*, tiene que hacer uso de sus poderes especiales. || Consumir, gastar: *this fire uses one ton of coal a week*, este fuego consume una tonelada de carbón por semana. || Tomar (narcotics). || Utilizar, servirse de (to exploit). || Aprovechar: *he uses all his free time*, aprovecha todo su tiempo libre; *he uses every opportunity*, aprovecha todas las oportunidades. || Usar, hacer uso de, valerse de (one's right). || Tratar: *they have used me well*, me han tratado bien. || — *Book which is no longer used*, libro que ya no se emplea. || Fam. *I could use a holiday!*, ¡qué bien me vendrían unas vacaciones! || *To be used as*, ser utilizado como, servir de: *a newspaper was used as a tablecloth*, un periódico sirvió de mantel, se utilizó un periódico como mantel. || *To be used for*, servir para: *what is this tool used for?*, ¿para qué sirve esta herramienta? || *To use badly*, maltratar. || *To use up*, agotar, consumir, gastar completamente: *to use up all one's provisions*, agotar todas sus provisiones; acabar, terminar: *use up the milk*, acabe la leche. || *To use up the scraps*, sacar partido de los restos. || *Use more care*, tenga más cuidado. || *Use your eyes*, abra los ojos. || *Word which is no longer used*, palabra (*f.*) que ha caído en desuso. || *You may use my name*, puede dar mi nombre (as a reference).

— V. aux. Acostumbrar, soler: *you used to go out at night*, solías salir por la noche. || *Things aren't what they used to be*, las cosas han cambiado, las cosas ya no son lo que eran.

— Observ. El verbo auxiliar se usa sólo en pretérito y tiene como equivalentes "soler" o "acostumbrar". Pero en muchos casos no se traduce y se pone únicamente el verbo que le sigue en imperfecto de indicativo (*I used to love him*, le quería).

useable ['ju:zəbl] adj. Utilizable.

used [ju:zd] adj. De segunda mano, usado, da: *used cars*, coches de segunda mano. || Usado, da: *hardly used*, apenas usado. || *Used up*, agotado, da (supplies, person).

used [ju:st] adj. Acostumbrado, da. || — *To be used to*, estar acostumbrado a. || *To get used to*, acostumbrarse a (to become accustomed).

useful ['ju:sful] adj. Útil: *this book is very useful*, este libro es muy útil. || Provechoso, sa (beneficial). || Cómodo, da; práctico, ca: *a useful dress*, un traje cómodo. || Bueno, na: *he is a useful painter*, es buen pintor. || — *To be useful with*, sabe valerse de: *he is useful with his fists*, sabe valerse de sus puños. || *To make o.s. useful*, ser útil, mostrarse útil. || *Useful load*, carga (*f.*) útil (of a vehicle).

usefulness ['ju:sfulnis] n. Utilidad, *f.* || *To have outlived one's* o *its usefulness*, haber perdido su razón de ser (an institution), haberse vuelto inútil (person, object).

useless ['ju:slis] adj. Inútil: *he is useless*, es inútil; *useless effort*, esfuerzo inútil. || Ineficaz: *a useless remedy*, un remedio ineficaz. || — Fam. *He is completely useless*, es una nulidad *or* un inútil. || *It is useless to insist*, es inútil insistir.

uselessly ['ju:slisli] adv. Inútilmente, en vano.

uselessness ['ju:slisnis] n. Inutilidad, *f.*

user ['ju:zə*] n. Usuario, ria: *road users*, usuarios de la carretera.

usher [ˈʌʃə*] n. Acomodador, *m.* (in a theatre). || Ujier, *m.* (who introduces people). || Ujier, *m.*, portero (*m.*) de estrados (in court).
usher [ˈʌʃə*] v. tr. Llevar, acompañar: *to usher s.o. to his seat,* llevar a alguien a su asiento. || Acomodar (in theatre). || Anunciar (a guest). || — *To usher in,* anunciar: *the sun ushered in the spring,* el sol anunció la primavera; hacer pasar: *they ushered him in,* le hicieron pasar. || *To usher into,* hacer pasar a, hacer entrar en: *the man ushered her into the room,* el hombre le hizo entrar en la habitación. || *To usher out,* acompañar hasta la puerta.
usherette [ˌʌʃəˈret] n. Acomodadora, *f.* (in theatre).
U.S.S.R. [ˈju:esesˈɑ:] n. U.R.S.S., *f.* (Union of Soviet Socialist Republics).
usual [ˈju:ʒuəl] adj. Usual, corriente (in use): *the usual word,* la palabra corriente. || Normal: *his usual state,* su estado normal; *it is not usual for him to be so nasty,* no es normal que sea tan antipático. || Habitual, acostumbrado, da (habit): *my usual walk in the hills,* mi paseo habitual por los cerros. || De todos los días, de diario: *his usual clothes,* su ropa de todos los días. || — *As per usual,* como de costumbre, como siempre. || *As is usual with women, she is...,* como todas las mujeres, es... || *As usual,* como siempre, como de costumbre. || *He arrived later than usual,* llegó más tarde que de costumbre *or* más tarde de lo normal. || *The usual thing,* lo de siempre (the same as always).
— N. *The usual,* lo de siempre.
usually [—li] adv. Normalmente.
usucapion [ju:zjuˈkeipiən] or **usucaption** [ju:zjuˈkæpʃən] n. JUR. Usucapión, *f.*
usucapt [ˈju:zjukæpt] v. tr. JUR. Usucapir.
usufruct [ˈju:zjufrʌkt] n. JUR. Usufructo, *m.*
usufruct [ˈju:zjufrʌkt] v. tr. Usufructuar.
usufructuary [ˌju:zjuˈfrʌktʃəri] adj./n. Usufructuario, ria.
usurer [ˈju:ʒərə*] n. Usurero, ra.
usurious [ju:ˈzjuəriəs] adj. Usurero, ra (person). || De usurero, usurario, ria (rate of interest).
usurp [ju:ˈzə:p] v. tr./intr. Usurpar: *to usurp power,* usurpar el poder. || *To usurp on* o *upon,* usurpar.
usurpation [ˌju:zə:ˈpeiʃən] n. Usurpación, *f.*
usurpative [ju:ˈzə:pətiv] or **usurpatory** [ju:ˈzə:pətəri] adj. Usurpatorio, ria.
usurper [ˌju:ˈzə:pə*] n. Usurpador, ra.
usurping [ˌju:ˈzə:piŋ] adj. Usurpador, ra.
usury [ˈju:ʒuri] n. Usura, *f.*
ut [ut; U.S. ʌt] n. MUS. Do, *m.*
utensil [juˈtensl] n. Utensilio, *m.* || *Kitchen utensils,* batería (*f. sing.*) de cocina.
uterine [ˈju:tərain] adj. ANAT. Uterino, na. || *Uterine brother,* hermano uterino.
uterus [ˈju:tərəs] n. Útero, *m.* (womb).

— OBSERV. El plural de *uterus* es *uteri.*

utile [ˈju:tail] adj. Útil.
utilitarian [ˌju:tiliˈtɛəriən] adj. Utilitario, ria (relating to utility). || Utilitarista (relating to utilitarianism).
— N. Utilitarista, *m.* & *f.*
utilitarianism [—izəm] n. Utilitarismo, *m.*
utility [ju:ˈtiliti] n. Utilidad, *f.* (usefulness). || COMM. Utilidad, *f.*: *marginal utility,* utilidad marginal. || Empresa (*f.*) de servicio público (company). || Acción (*f.*) de una empresa de servicio público (share). || *Public utility,* empresa (*f.*) de servicio público.
— Adj. Utilitario, ria: *utility goods, vehicles,* artículos, coches utilitarios.
utilizable [ˈju:tilaizəbl] adj. Utilizable (useable).
utilization [ˌju:tilaiˈzeiʃən] n. Utilización, *f.* (using).
utilize [ˈju:tilaiz] v. tr. Utilizar (to use).
utilizer [—ə*] n. Utilizador, ra.
utmost [ˈʌtməust] adj. Supremo, ma; sumo, ma; extremo, ma: *utmost ignorance,* suma ignorancia; *in the utmost degree of poverty,* en grado extremo de pobreza. || Mayor, más grande: *he made the utmost possible effort,* hizo el mayor esfuerzo posible. || Más lejano, na (farthest).
— N. Máximo, *m.* || — *At the utmost,* a lo más, a lo sumo. || *He did his utmost to help,* hizo cuanto pudo *or* hizo todo lo posible para ayudar. || *That is the utmost that one can do,* esto es todo lo que se puede hacer, esto es lo más que se puede hacer. || *To do one's utmost,* hacer todo lo posible. || *To the utmost,* hasta más no poder.
utopia [ju:ˈtəupjə] n. Utopía, *f.*
utopian [—n] adj. Utópico, ca.
— N. Utopista, *m.* & *f.*
utopianism [—nizəm] n. Utopía, *f.*, idea (*f.*) utópica.
utter [ˈʌtə*] adj. Completo, ta: *an utter stranger,* un completo desconocido; *an utter lack of,* una falta completa de. || Total, absoluto, ta: *utter surprise,* sorpresa total. || Empedernido, da: *an utter liar,* un mentiroso empedernido. || Rematado, da: *an utter fool,* un loco rematado. || *Utter nonsense!,* ¡pura tontería!
utter [ˈʌtə*] v. tr. Pronunciar, decir: *never utter his name,* no diga nunca su nombre. || Expresar (sentiments). || Soltar (lies, swearwords). || Lanzar, dar (shouts, cries). || Dar (sigh). || Proferir (threat). || Emitir (sound). || Poner en circulación (false documents, counterfeit money).
utterance [ˈʌtərəns] n. Elocución, *f.*, pronunciación, *f.* (power of speech): *to have a clear utterance,* tener una elocución clara; *defective utterance,* defecto de pronunciación. || Expresión, *f.* (of sentiments). || Emisión, *f.* (of a sound). || Pronunciación, *f.* (of a speech). || Emisión, *f.* (of counterfeit money). || — Pl. Palabras, *f.* || *To give utterance to,* expresar, manifestar.
utterly [ˈʌtəli] adv. Completamente, totalmente, absolutamente.
uttermost [ˈʌtəməust] adj./n. See UTMOST.
uvula [ˈju:vjulə] n. ANAT. Úvula, *f.*, campanilla, *f.*

— OBSERV. El plural de la palabra inglesa *uvula* es *uvulas* o *uvulae.*

uvular [ˈju:vjulə*] adj. Uvular.
— N. Sonido (*m.*) uvular.
uxorious [ʌkˈsɔ:riəs] adj. Locamente enamorado de su mujer. || Dominado por su mujer.

V

v [vi:] n. V, *f.* (letter): *a capital v,* una v mayúscula. || AUT. *V-8 engine,* motor (*m.*) de ocho cilindros en V.
vac [væk] n. FAM. Vacaciones, *f. pl.* (vacation).
vacancy [ˈveikənsi] n. Vacío, *m.* (empty space). || Lo vacío, vacuidad, *f.* (emptiness). || Vacante, *f.*: *to fill a vacancy in the administration,* cubrir una vacante en la administración; *should there be a vacancy,* en caso de producirse una vacante. || Vaciedad, *f.* (of mind). || Hueco, *m.*, espacio (*m.*) vacío (gap). || Habitación (*f.*) libre (in a hotel). || — *"No vacancies",* completo (in a hotel). || *"Vacancies",* se ofrece trabajo.
vacant [ˈveikənt] adj. Vacío, a (empty): *vacant house,* casa vacía; *vacant space,* sitio vacío. || Libre, disponible: *a vacant room in a hotel,* una habitación libre en un hotel. || Libre (seat). || De ocio, libre: *it will fill your vacant hours,* llenará sus horas libres. || Vacante: *vacant job,* puesto vacante; *the vacant chair in philosophy,* la cátedra vacante de filosofía. || Alelado, da; de bobo: *a vacant expression,* una expresión alelada. || Vago, ga; perdido, da: *with a vacant stare,* con la mirada perdida. || Inexpresivo, va (eyes). || Vacío, a (mind). || JUR. Yacente: *vacant succession,* herencia yacente.
vacantly [—li] adv. Distraídamente, con la mirada perdida.
vacate [vəˈkeit] v. tr. Dejar, dejar vacante (a post, job). || Desocupar: *to vacate the premises,* desocupar los locales. || Dejar libre (a seat). || JUR. Anular (a contract).
vacation [vəˈkeiʃən] n. Vacaciones, *f. pl.* (holidays, respite). || — *To be on vacation,* estar de vacaciones. || *Vacation course,* curso (*m.*) de vacaciones, curso (*m.*) de verano.
vacation [vəˈkeiʃən] v. intr. U. S. Tomar las vacaciones.
vacationer [—ə*] or **vacationist** [—ist] n. U. S. Persona (*f.*) que está de vacaciones. || Veraneante, *m.* & *f.* (in summer).
vaccinal [ˈvæksinəl] adj. MED. Vaccíneo, a.
vaccinate [ˈvæksineit] v. tr. MED. Vacunar. || *To be vaccinated,* vacunarse.
vaccination [ˌvæksiˈneiʃən] n. MED. Vacunación, *f.*

vaccinator [ˈvæksineitə*] n. MED. Vaccinostilo, *m.* (instrument). | Vacunador, ra (person).
vaccine [ˈvæksi:n] adj. MED. Vaccíneo, a. || *Vaccine therapy*, vaccinoterapia, *f.*
— N. MED. Vacuna, *f.*
vaccinia [vækˈsiniə] n. VET. Vacuna, *f.* (cowpox).
vacillate [ˈvæsileit] v. intr. Vacilar, titubear (to hesitate). || Fluctuar (to fluctuate). || Oscilar (to sway).
vacillating [—iŋ] adj. Vacilante, irresoluto, ta.
— N. Vacilación, *f.*
vacillation [ˌvæsiˈleiʃən] n. Vacilación, *f.*, titubeo, *m.* (irresolution). || Fluctuación, *f.* || Oscilación, *f.* (swaying).
vacillatory [ˈvæsilətəri] adj. Vacilante.
vacua [ˈvækjuə] pl. n. See VACUUM.
vacuity [væˈkju:iti] n. Vacuidad, *f.*, lo vacío (emptiness). || Vacío, *m.* (empty space). || Vaciedad, *f.*: *to fill a speech with vacuities*, llenar un discurso de vaciedades.
vacuolar [ˈvækjuələ*] adj. BOT. Vacuolar.
vacuole [ˈvækjuəul] n. Vacuola, *f.*
vacuous [ˈvækjuəs] adj. Vacuo, a; vacío, a (empty). || Vago, ga; perdido, da (look). || FIG. Alelado, da; necio, cia (lacking intelligence).
vacuousness [—nis] n. See VACUITY.
vacuum [ˈvækjuəm] n. PHYS. Vacío, *m.*: *to create a vacuum*, dejar un vacío; *in a vacuum*, en vacío. || FIG. Vacío, *m.* (gap): *his death left a great vacuum*, su muerte ha dejado un gran vacío.
— Adj. De vacío, neumático, ca: *vacuum brake*, freno de vacío *or* neumático.

— OBSERV. El plural de *vacuum* es *vacuums* o *vacua*.

vacuum [ˈvækjuəm] v. tr. Limpiar con aspiradora, pasar la aspiradora en.
vacuum bottle [—ˌbɔtl] n. Termo, *m.*
vacuum cleaner [—ˌkli:nə*] n. Aspiradora, *f.*
vacuum flask [—flɑ:sk] n. Termo, *m.*
vacuum pump [—pʌmp] n. Bomba (*f.*) neumática.
vacuum tube [—tju:b] n. Tubo (*m.*) de vacío.
vademecum [ˈveidiˈmi:kəm] n. Vademécum, *m.* (book).
vagabond [ˈvægəbɔnd] adj./n. Vagabundo, da: *a vagabond life*, una vida vagabunda.
vagabond [ˈvægəbɔnd] v. intr. Vagabundear.
vagabondage [ˈvægəbɔndidʒ] n. Vagabundeo, *m.*, vagabundaje, *m.* (wandering). || Vagabundos, *m. pl.* (vagrants).
vagabondize [ˈvægəbɔndaiz] v. intr. Vagabundear.
vagary [ˈveigəri] n. Capricho, *m.* (whim). || Manía, *f.* (fad). || Extravagancia, *f.* (excentricity).
vagina [vəˈdʒainə] n. ANAT. Vagina, *f.* || BOT. Vaina, *f.*

— OBSERV. El plural de la palabra inglesa es *vaginae* o *vaginas*.

vaginal [—l] adj. Vaginal.
vaginitis [ˌvædʒiˈnaitis] n. MED. Vaginitis, *f. inv.*
vagotomy [vəˈgɔtəmi] n. MED. Vagotomía, *f.*
vagotonia [ˌveigəˈtəuniə] or **vagotony** [ˈveigətəuni] n. MED. Vagotonía, *f.*
vagrancy [ˈveigrənsi] n. Vagabundeo, *m.*, vagancia, *f.* || *Vagrancy act*, ley (*f.*) de vagos y maleantes.
vagrant [ˈveigrənt] adj. Vagabundo, da: *a vagrant life*, una vida vagabunda. || FIG. Errabundo, da: *vagrant imagination*, imaginación errabunda. || Ambulante (musician).
— N. Vagabundo, da.
vague [veig] adj. Vago, ga: *vague desires*, deseos vagos; *vague promise*, promesa vaga. || Vago, ga; borroso, sa: *a vague outline*, una silueta borrosa. || Impreciso, sa (imprecise). || Indeciso, sa; dudoso, sa (uncertain). || Mínimo, ma; remoto, ta: *I have not the vaguest idea*, no tengo la más mínima idea. || — *To be vague*, andarse con vaguedades. || *To make vague remarks*, decir vaguedades.
vaguely [—li] adv. Vagamente. || Apenas: *do you know Paris? — Vaguely*, ¿conoce usted París? — Apenas. || — *He does vaguely resemble me*, tiene cierto parecido conmigo. || *He talks vaguely*, habla en términos muy vagos, se anda con vaguedades.
vagueness [—nis] n. Vaguedad, *f.*: *the vagueness of his words*, la vaguedad de sus palabras. || Lo borroso (of an outline). || Lo impreciso, imprecisión, *f.*
vagus [ˈveigəs] n. ANAT. Nervio (*m.*) vago.
— Adj. ANAT. Vago (nerve).

— OBSERV. El plural de la palabra inglesa es *vagi*.

vain [vein] adj. Vano, na: *a vain attempt to escape*, una tentativa vana de escapar; *vain promises, excuses, hopes* promesas, excusas, esperanzas vanas. || Vano, na; inútil: *it's vain to go*, es inútil ir. || Presumido, da; vanidoso, sa (conceited): *she is very vain*, es muy vanidosa. || — *In vain*, en vano, vanamente, infructuosamente. || *Thou shalt not take the name of the Lord thy God in vain*, no tomarás el nombre de Dios en vano. || FIG. *To be as vain as a peacock*, ser más orgulloso que un pavo real.
vainglorious [—ˈglɔ:riəs] adj. Vanaglorioso, sa.
vaingloriousness [—ˈglɔ:riəsnis] or **vainglory** [—ˈglɔ:ri] n. Vanagloria, *f.*
vainness [ˈveinnis] n. Vanidad, *f.* (vanity). || Inutilidad, *f.* (uselessness).
vair [ˈveə*] n. Vero, *m.*, marta (*f.*) cebellina (fur). | HERALD. Vero, *m.*

valance [ˈvæləns] n. Guardamalleta, *f.* (of a window). || Doselera, *f.* (of a bed). || THEATR. Bambalinón, *m.*
vale [veil] n. Valle, *m.* || *Vale of tears*, valle de lágrimas.
valediction [ˌvæliˈdikʃən] n. Adiós, *m.*, despedida, *f.*
valedictorian [ˌvælidikˈtɔ:riən] n. Alumno (*m.*) que da el discurso de despedida al final de curso.
valedictory [ˌvæliˈdiktəri] adj. De despedida.
— N. Discurso (*m.*) de despedida.
valence [ˈveiləns] n. CHEM. Valencia, *f.*
Valencian [vəˈlenʃiən] adj./n. Valenciano, na.
Valenciennes [ˌvælənsiˈen] n. Encaje (*m.*) de Valenciennes.
valency [ˈveilənsi] n. CHEM. Valencia, *f.*
valentine [ˈvæləntain] n. Tarjeta (*f.*) *or* carta (*f.*) que se manda el Día de los Enamorados (card). || Novio, via (person). || *Valentine* o *Valentine's Day*, Día (*m.*) de los Enamorados.
valerian [vəˈliəriən] n. BOT. Valeriana, *f.*
valet [ˈvælit] n. Ayuda (*m.*) de cámara (personal servant). || Camarero, *m.*, mozo (*m.*) de habitación (in a hotel).
valet [ˈvælit] v. tr. Servir de ayuda de cámara a.
valetudinarian [ˈvæliˌtju:diˈnɛəriən] adj./n. Valetudinario, ria; enfermizo, za.
valetudinarianism [—izəm] n. Estado (*m.*) enfermizo.
valetudinary [væliˈtju:dinəri] adj. Valetudinario, ria; enfermizo, za.
Valhalla [vælˈhælə] n. MYTH. Walhalla, *m.*
valiance [ˈvæljəns] or **valiancy** [—i] n. Valentía, *f.*, valor, *m.*
valiant [ˈvæljənt] adj. Valiente, valeroso, sa: *a valiant soldier*, un soldado valeroso.
valid [ˈvælid] adj. Válido, da: *a valid contract*, un contrato válido; *valid arguments*, argumentos válidos. || Valedero, ra (ticket). || Vigente (law). || *No longer valid*, caducado, da.
validate [ˈvælideit] v. tr. Validar, dar validez a.
validation [ˌvæliˈdeiʃən] n. Validación, *f.*
validity [vəˈliditi] n. Validez, *f.* || Vigencia, *f.* (of a law).
valise [vəˈli:z] n. Maleta, *f.* (suitcase).
Valkyrie [vælˈkiəri] pr. n. MYTH. Valkiria, *f.*, Walkiria, *f.* (virgin goddess).
valley [ˈvæli] n. Valle, *m.*: *a Swiss valley*, un valle suizo. || Cuenca, *f.*, valle, *m.* (river basin). || TECH. Lima (*f.*) hoya (of a roof).
valor [ˈvælə*] n. U. S. Valor, *m.*, valentía, *f.*
valorization [ˌvæləraiˈzeiʃən] n. Valorización, *f.*
valorize [ˈvæləraiz] v. tr. Valorizar.
valorous [ˈvælərəs] adj. Valiente, valeroso, sa (courageous).
valour [ˈvælə*] n. Valor, *m.*, valentía, *f.*
valuable [ˈvæljuəbl] adj. Valioso, sa; de valor (expensive, costly): *a valuable treasure*, un tesoro valioso. || Valioso, sa: *your valuable help*, su ayuda valiosa. || — *Is that valuable?*, ¿vale mucho eso? || *This jewel is very valuable*, esta joya vale mucho.
— Pl. n. Objetos (*m.*) de valor.
valuation [ˌvæljuˈeiʃən] n. Valoración, *f.*, valuación, *f.*, valorización, *f.*, estimación, *f.*, tasación, *f.* (act). || Valor, *m.* (estimated value).
valuator [ˈvæljueitə*] n. Tasador, *m.*
value [ˈvælju:] n. Valor, *m.*: *a thing of great value*, una cosa de gran valor; *the value of the pound*, el valor de la libra; *value in gold*, valor en oro; *value received*, valor recibido. || Valor, *m.*, monta, *f.* (importance): *a person of little value*, una persona de poca monta. || Valor, *m.* (of colour). || GRAMM. Significado, *m.*, valor, *m.* (meaning). || MUS. MATH. Valor, *m.*: *absolute, relative value*, valor absoluto, relativo. || — *Decrease in value*, disminución (*f.*) *or* pérdida (*f.*) de valor, depreciación, *f.* || *Increase in value*, plusvalía, *f.* || *It is nothing of any value*, no es nada de valor. || *It is very good value for twenty pesetas*, veinte pesetas es un buen precio. || COMM. *Market* o *commercial value*, valor comercial. || *Of no value*, sin valor. || *Sense of values*, sentido de los valores. || *To attach little value to sth.*, atribuir poco valor a algo (object), dar poca importancia a algo (event, news, etc.). || *To be of value*, ser valioso, sa. || *To get good value for one's money*, sacarle jugo al dinero. || *To lose value*, desvalorizarse, perder valor. || *To set a value on*, poner precio a, estimar. || *To set too much value on*, sobreestimar. || *To the value of*, por el valor de.
value [ˈvælju:] v. tr. Valorar, valorizar, tasar (to appraise). || Estimar, apreciar, valuar, valorar: *I value him highly for his qualities*, le estimo mucho por sus cualidades. || — *To value one's life*, apreciar la vida. || *To value o.s. on*, vanagloriarse de.
valued [—d] adj. Estimado, da; apreciado, da.
valueless [—lis] adj. Sin valor.
valuer [—ə*] n. Tasador, m.
valvate [ˈvælvit] adj. Valvular.
valve [vælv] n. ANAT. Válvula, *f.* (of heart). || TECH. Válvula, *f.* (in cars, tyres, etc.): *safety valve*, válvula de seguridad; *inlet valve*, válvula de admisión; *rectifying valve*, válvula rectificadora; *grinding of valves*, esmerilado de válvulas; *butterfly, stem valve*, válvula de mariposa, de vástago. | Chapaleta, *f.* (of a pump). | Lámpara, *f.*: *valve set*, radio de lámparas. | ELECTR. Tubo (*m.*) electrónico. || Llave, *f.* (of a

trumpet). || ZOOL. Valva, *f.* || BOT. Ventalla, *f.*, valva, *f.* (of a capsule).
valve box [—bɔks] n. Caja (*f.*) de válvulas. || Caja (*f.*) de distribución (of steam).
valve cap [—kæp] n. Tapón, *m.*
valve gear [—giə*] n. Mecanismo (*m.*) de distribución.
valve holder [—ˌhəuldə*] n. RAD. Casquillo, *m.*
valveless [—lis] adj. Sin válvulas.
valve rocker [—ˌrɔkə*] n. TECH. Balancín, *m.*
valve rod [—rɔd] n. TECH. Vástago, *m.*
valve seat [—si:t] n. Asiento (*m.*) de la válvula.
valvula [ˈvælvjulə] n. Válvula, *f.*
— OBSERV. El plural de *valvula* es *valvulae*.
valvular [ˈvælvjulə*] adj. Valvular.
valvulate [ˈvælvjulet] adj. Valvular.
valvule [ˈvælvjul] n. Válvula, *f.*
vamoose [vəˈmu:s] v. intr. FAM. Largarse.
vamp [væmp] n. Pala, *f.*, empeine, *m.* (of a shoe). || Remiendo, *m.* (patch). || MUS. Acompañamiento (*m.*) improvisado. || FAM. Mujer (*f.*) fatal, vampiresa, *f.* (woman).
vamp [væmp] v. tr. Poner la pala a (a shoe, boot). || Remendar (to patch). || FAM. Engatusar (to seduce). || MUS. Improvisar un acompañamiento para.
— V. intr. MUS. Improvisar un acompañamiento.
vamper [—ə*] n. Remendón, *m.*
vampire [ˈvæmpaiə*] n. Vampiro, *m.* (evil spirit). || THEATR. Escotillón, *m.* || ZOOL. Vampiro, *m.* || FIG. Vampiro, *m.* || FAM. Mujer (*f.*) fatal, vampiresa, *f.* (woman).
vampire bat [—bæt] n. ZOOL. Vampiro, *m.*
vampirism [—rizəm] n. Vampirismo, *m.*
van [væn] n. Furgoneta, *f.*, camioneta, *f.* (small lorry): *delivery van*, furgoneta de reparto. || Capitoné, *m.*, camión (*m.*) de mudanza (removal lorry). || Furgón, *m.*, vagón (*m.*) cerrado (goods car of a train). || Tamiz, *m.* (sieve). || Pala, *f.* (shovel). || Vanguardia, *f.* (leading section): *to be in the van of*, ir a la vanguardia de. || Ala, *f.* (wing). || — *Guard's van*, furgón de equipajes. || *Prison van*, coche (*m.*) celular.
vanadate [ˈvænədeit] n. CHEM. Vanadato, *m.*
vanadium [vəˈneidjəm] n. CHEM. Vanadio, *m.*
Vandal [ˈvændəl] n. Vándalo, la. || FIG. Vándalo, *m.* (destructive person).
— Adj. Vandálico, ca; vándalo, la.
vandalism [—izəm] n. Vandalismo, *m.*: *piece of vandalism*, acto de vandalismo.
vandalize [—aiz] v. tr. Destruir, destrozar.
Vandyke [vænˈdaik] n. Perilla, *f.* (beard). || Valona, *f.* (collar).
vane [vein] n. Paleta, *f.*, pala, *f.* (of propeller, electric fan). || Álabe, *m.* (of a waterwheel). || Aspa, *f.* (of a windmill). || Veleta, *f.* (weathercock). || Cataviento, *m.* (on a boat). || Barbas, *f. pl.* (of a feather). || Pluma, *f.* (of an arrow). || Tablilla (*f.*) de mira (of a quadrant).
vanguard [ˈvængɑ:d] n. Vanguardia, *f.*: *of the vanguard*, de vanguardia.
vanilla [vəˈnilə] n. BOT. Vainilla, *f.* || Mantecado, *m.*, vainilla, *f.*: *vanilla ice cream*, helado de mantecado *or* de vainilla.
vanish [ˈvæniʃ] v. intr. Desaparecer: *the man vanished*, el hombre desapareció; *the pain vanished*, el dolor desapareció. || Desvanecerse, esfumarse: *her hopes vanished*, sus esperanzas se esfumaron. || MATH. Tender hacia cero.
vanishing [—iŋ] adj. Que desaparece. || Que se desvanece, que se esfuma. || De día (cream). || De fuga (point).
— N. Desaparición, *f.*
vanity [ˈvæniti] n. Vanidad, *f.*: *to leave the vanities of this world*, dejar las vanidades de este mundo. || Vanidad, *f.*, orgullo, *m.* (self-satisfaction). || Neceser, *m.* (vanity case). || U. S. Tocador, *m.* (dressing table). || — *Out of sheer vanity*, por pura vanidad. || *Vanity of vanities, all is vanity*, vanidad de vanidades y todo es vanidad.
vanity case [—keis] n. Neceser, *m.*
vanquish [ˈvæŋkwiʃ] v. tr. Vencer, conquistar (to conquer). || Dominar (one's feelings).
vanquishable [—əbl] adj. Vencible, conquistable. || Dominable (feelings).
vanquished [—t] pl. n. Vencidos, das.
vanquisher [—ə*] n. Vencedor, *m.*
vanquishing [—iŋ] adj. Vencedor, ra.
— N. Conquista, *f.*
vantage [ˈvɑ:ntidʒ] n. Ventaja, *f.* || — *From his vantage point he could see the whole valley*, desde el lugar que ocupaba dominaba todo el valle. || *Vantage ground* o *point*, posición ventajosa.
vapid [ˈvæpid] adj. Insípido, da; soso, sa; insulso, sa.
vapidity [—iti] or **vapidness** [—nis] n. Insipidez, *f.*, insulsez, *f.*
vapor [ˈveipə*] n./v. intr. U. S. See VAPOUR.
vaporific [ˌveipəˈrifik] adj. Vaporoso, sa.
vaporing [ˈveipəriŋ] adj. U. S. See VAPOURING.
vaporish [ˈveipəriʃ] adj. U. S. See VAPOURISH.
vaporization [ˌveipəraiˈzeiʃən] n. Vaporización, *f.*
vaporize [ˈveipəraiz] v. tr. Vaporizar.
— V. intr. Vaporizarse.
vaporizer [—ə*] n. Vaporizador, *m.* || Pulverizador, *m.* (spray).
vaporizing [—iŋ] adj. De vaporización.
— N. Vaporización, *f.*

vaporous [ˈveipərəs] adj. Vaporoso, sa. || FIG. Nebuloso, sa (style, etc.).
vapory [ˈveipəri] adj. U. S. See VAPOURY.
vapour [ˈveipə*] n. Vapor, *m.*: *water vapour*, vapor de agua. || Vaho, *m.* (on windowpanes). || Vapor, *m.* (of alcohols). || — Pl. MED. Vapores, *m.* || — *Vapour bath*, baño (*m.*) de vapor. || *Vapour density*, densidad (*f.*) del vapor. || *Vapour pressure*, presión (*f.*) del vapor. || AVIAT. *Vapour trail*, estela, *f.*
vapour [ˈveipə*] v. intr. Vaporizarse, evaporarse (water). || FAM. Fanfarronear (to brag). | Decir sandeces (to drivel).
vapouring [ˈveipəriŋ] adj. FAM. Fanfarrón, ona.
vapourish [—riʃ] adj. Vaporoso, sa. || MED. Hipocondríaco, ca.
vapoury [—ri] adj. Vaporoso, sa.
vaquero [vɑ:ˈkerəu] n. Vaquero, *m.*
var [vɑ:*] n. ELECTR. Var, *m.*
varec or **varech** [ˈværek] n. Varec, *m.* (kelp).
variability [ˌvɛəriəˈbiliti] n. Variabilidad, *f.* || FIG. Inconstancia, *f.*, variabilidad, *f.*
variable [ˈvɛəriəbl] adj. Variable: *variable winds*, vientos variables. || MATH. Variable. || FIG. Variable, cambiadizo, za. || — ELECTR. *Variable condenser*, condensador (*m.*) variable. || *Variable time fuse*, espoleta (*f.*) de proximidad.
— N. Viento (*m.*) variable (wind). || Zona (*f.*) de vientos variables (wind zone). || MATH. Variable, *f.*
variableness [—nis] n. See VARIABILITY.
variance [ˈvɛəriəns] n. Desavenencia, *f.*, discrepancia, *f.* (between people). || Discordancia, *f.*, desacuerdo, *m.* (between things). || Variación, *f.* (change). || JUR. Divergencia, *f.* || — *At variance*, en desacuerdo, en contradicción (opinion), reñido, da; desavenido, da (people, families). || *To be at variance with*, estar en desacuerdo con. || *To set two people at variance*, sembrar la discordia entre dos personas.
variant [ˈvɛəriənt] adj. Variante, diferente (differing). || Variable (changeable).
— N. Variante, *f.*
variate [ˈvɛəriˌeit] n. Variable, *f.* (in statistics).
variation [ˌvɛəriˈeiʃən] n. Variación, *f.* || ASTR. BIOL. MATH. MUS. Variación, *f.* || PHYS. Variación, *f.*, declinación, *f.*: *magnetic variation*, declinación magnética.
varicella [ˌværiˈselə] n. MED. Varicela, *f.* (chickenpox).
varices [ˈværisi:z] pl. n. See VARIX.
varicocele [ˈværikəsi:l] n. MED. Varicocele, *m.*
varicoloured (U. S. **varicolored**) [ˈvɛərikʌləd] adj. Multicolor.
varicose [ˈværikəus] adj. MED. Varicoso, sa. || *Varicose veins*, varices, *f.*: *stockings for varicose veins*, medias para varices.
varied [ˈvɛərid] adj. Variado, da; vario, ria; diverso, sa (of different kinds). || Jaspeado, da; abigarrado, da (variegated).
variegate [ˈvɛərigeit] v. tr. Abigarrar, jaspear (to give various colours to). || Variar, diversificar (to vary).
variegated [—id] adj. Abigarrado, da; jaspeado, da (colour). || Variado, da; diversificado, da (full of variety).
variegation [ˌvɛəriˈgeiʃən] n. Abigarramiento, *m.*
variety [vəˈraiəti] n. Diversidad, *f.*: *the variety of his occupations*, la diversidad de sus ocupaciones. || Variedad, *f.*: *a variety of opinions*, una variedad de opiniones. || Variedad, *f.*, surtido, *m.*: *a variety of cloths*, un surtido de tejidos. || BIOL. BOT. Variedad, *f.* || Variedades, *f. pl.*: *variety entertainment* o *show*, espectáculo de variedades. || — *For a variety of reasons*, por varias razones, por razones diversas. || *For variety*, por variar. || *In a variety of colours*, de diversos colores. || *In a variety of ways*, de diversos modos. || *To lend variety to*, variar, dar diversidad a. || FIG. *Variety is the spice of life*, en la variedad está el gusto.
variety store [—ˈstɔ:*] n. U. S. Bazar, *m.*
variform [ˈvɛərifɔ:m] adj. Diversiforme.
variola [vəˈraiələ] n. MED. Viruela, *f.*
variolar [—*] adj. MED. Varioloso, sa.
variolous [vəˈraiələs] adj. Picado de viruelas (pockmarked). || MED. Varioloso, sa.
various [ˈvɛəriəs] adj. Diverso, sa; diferente, vario, ria (differing): *various occupations*, ocupaciones diversas; *in various ways*, de diferentes modos. || Variado, da (varied). || Vario, ria: *the various parts of the country*, las varias partes del país; *for various reasons*, por varios motivos.
varix [ˈvɛəriks] n. MED. Varice, *f.*
— OBSERV. El plural de la palabra inglesa es *varices*.
varlet [ˈvɑ:lit] n. Paje, *m.* (page). || FAM. Bribón, *m.*, granuja, *m.* (knave).
varmint [ˈvɑ:mint] n. U. S. FAM. Bicho, *m.* (animal). | Bribón, *m.* (person).
varnish [ˈvɑ:niʃ] n. Barniz, *m.* (for wood, metal). || Vidriado, *m.*, barniz (*m.*) vítreo (for pottery). || Charol, *m.* (for leather). || FIG. Barniz, *m.*, baño, *m.*, capa, *f.* (outward appearance). || — *Nail varnish*, esmalte, *m.*, laca, *f.* [para uñas]. || *Varnish remover*, quitaesmalte, *m.* || BOT. *Varnish tree*, barniz (*m.*) de Japón.
varnish [ˈvɑ:niʃ] v. tr. Barnizar (wood, paintings). || Charolar (leather). || Vidriar (pottery). || Pintar (nails). || FIG. Disimular (to hide). | Embellecer (to embellish).

varnisher [—ə*] n. Barnizador, *m.*
varnishing [—iŋ] n. Barnizado, *m.* || ARTS. *Varnishing day*, inauguración (*f.*) de una exposición de arte, apertura (*f.*) de una exposición.
varsity [ˈvɑːsiti] n. FAM. Universidad, *f.* || SP. Equipo (*m.*) universitario.
varus [ˈvɛərəs] n. MED. Pie (*m.*) contrahecho.
vary [ˈvɛəri] v. tr. Variar: *to vary one's food*, variar la alimentación. || Cambiar, variar (decision, methods). || MUS. Hacer variaciones en.
— V. intr. Variar: *opinions vary*, las opiniones varían. || Cambiar, variar: *the temperature varies*, la temperatura cambia. || Diferir, variar, ser diferente: *customs vary from one country to another*, las costumbres difieren de un país a otro. || Diferir, no estar de acuerdo (to disagree). || Desviarse (to deviate). || BOT. Variar. || MATH. Variar. || — *To vary from*, diferenciarse de. || *X varies proportionately as Y*, X varía proporcionalmente a Y.
varying [—iŋ] adj. Variante, variable. || — *Varying prices*, precios diversos. || *Without varying*, sin variación.
vascular [ˈvæskjulə*] adj. Vascular. || *Vascular tissue*, tejido (*m.*) vascular.
vascularity [ˈvæskjuˈlæriti] n. Vascularidad, *f.*
vascularization [ˌvæskjuləraiˈzeiʃən] n. Vascularización, *f.*
vas deferens [ˈvɑːsˈdefərəns] n. ANAT. BOT. Conducto (*m.*) deferente.

— OBSERV. El plural es *vasa deferentia*.

vase [vɑːz] n. Vaso, *m.* (receptacle). || Jarrón, *m.* (artistic). || Florero, *m.* (for flowers). || Vasija, *f.*: *a pre-Columbian vase*, una vasija precolombina.
vasectomy [væˈsektəmi] n. MED. Vasectomía, *f.*
Vaseline [ˈvæsəliːn] n. Vaselina, *f.*
vasoconstriction [ˈveizəukənˈstrikʃən] n. Vasoconstricción, *f.*
vasoconstrictor [ˈveizəukənˈstriktə*] adj. Vasoconstrictor, ra.
— M. Vasoconstrictor. *m.*
vasodilatation [ˈveizəuˌdiləˈteiʃən] n. Vasodilatación, *f.*
vasodilator [ˈveizəudaiˈleitə*] adj. Vasodilatador, ra.
— N. Vasodilatador, *m.*
vasomotor [ˈveizəuˈməutə*] adj. Vasomotor, ra.
— N. Vasomotor, *m.*
vassal [ˈvæsəl] adj./n. Vasallo, lla.
vassalage [—idʒ] n. Vasallaje, *m.*
vast [vɑːst] adj. Inmenso, sa; vasto, ta; extenso, sa: *a vast region*, una región inmensa. || Enorme, considerable: *a vast difference*, una enorme diferencia. || Enorme: *a vast building*, un edificio enorme. || Abrumador, ra (majority).
vastitude [—itjuːd] or **vastness** [—nis] n. Inmensidad, *f.* (immensity).
vastly [—li] adv. Extensamente. || Sumamente, muy (very): *he is vastly mistaken*, está muy equivocado.
vat [væt] n. Cuba, *f.*, tina, *f.* (large tub).
vat [væt] v. tr. Encubar, poner en tina.
Vatican [ˈvætikən] pr. n. REL. Vaticano, *m.*
— Adj. Vaticano, na; del Vaticano. || — *Vatican City*, Ciudad (*f.*) del Vaticano. || *Vatican Council*, Concilio vaticano.
vaticide [ˈvætisaid] n. Asesino (*m.*) de un profeta.
vaticinal [væˈtisinəl] adj. Profético, ca.
vaticinate [væˈtisineit] v. tr./intr. Vaticinar.
vaticination [ˌvætisiˈneiʃən] n. Vaticinio, *m.*
vaticinator [væˈtisineitə*] n. Vaticinador, *m.*
vatting [ˈvætiŋ] n. Encubamiento, *m.*
vaudeville [ˈvəudəvil] n. THEATR. Vodevil, *m.* (comedy). | Variedades, *f. pl.* (variety show).
vaudevillian [ˌvəudəˈviljən] adj. Vodevilesco, ca.
vaudevillian [ˌvəudəˈviljən] or **vaudevillist** [ˈvəudəvilist] n. Vodevilista, *m.*
vault [vɔːlt] n. ARCH. Bóveda, *f.* || Sótano, *m.* (cellar). || Bodega, *f.* (wine cellar). || Panteón, *m.* [subterráneo] (burial chamber). || Cripta, *f.* (in church). || Cámara (*f.*) acorazada (of a bank). || ANAT. Bóveda, *f.* || SP. Salto, *m.*: *pole vault*, salto con pértiga; *at* o *with one vault*, de un salto. || — ARCH. *Barrel vault*, bóveda de cañón. | *Groined vault*, bóveda por arista (not ribbed), bóveda de crucería (ribbed). | *Ogival vault*, bóveda ojival. | *Ribbed* o *cloister vault*, bóveda de crucería *or* esquifada *or* claustral. || ASTR. *Vault of heaven*, bóveda celeste.
vault [vɔːlt] v. tr. Saltar (to jump): *to vault a gate*, saltar una barrera. || ARCH. Abovedar: *vaulted dome*, cúpula abovedada; *to vault a cellar*, abovedar un sótano.
— V. intr. Saltar.
vaulted [—id] adj. Abovedado, da.
vaulter [—ə*] n. SP. Saltador, ra.
vaulting [—iŋ] n. Construcción (*f.*) de bóvedas (art of building). || Bóveda, *f.* (vaulted work). || SP. Salto, *m.* || SP. *Vaulting horse*, potro, *m.*, potro (*m.*) con arzón.
vaunt [vɔːnt] n. Jactancia, *f.*
vaunt [vɔːnt] v. tr. Alabar (to praise). || Jactarse de, vanagloriarse de (to boast of).
— V. intr. Jactarse, vanagloriarse (to boast).
vaunted [—id] adj. Alabado, da; encomiado, da.
vaunter [—ə*] n. Jactancioso, sa; fanfarrón, ona.
vaunting [—iŋ] adj. Jactancioso, sa.
— N. Jactancia, *f.*
V-Day [ˈviːdei] n. Día (*m.*) de la victoria.
veal [viːl] n. CULIN. Ternera, *f.* || *Veal chop* o *cutlet*, chuleta (*f.*) de ternera.
vector [ˈvektə*] n. MATH. Vector, *m.* || MED. Vector, *m.*, portador, ra (of a virus).
— Adj. MATH. Vectorial.
vectorial [vekˈtɔːriəl] adj. MATH. Vectorial.
Veda [ˈveidə] n. REL. Veda, *m.* (Hindu scripture).
vedette [viˈdet] n. MAR. Lancha (*f.*) motora, motora, *f.* (boat).
Vedic [ˈveidik] adj. Védico, ca.
veep [viːp] n. U. S. FAM. Vicepresidente, *m.*
veer [viə*] n. MAR. Virada, *f.* (of a ship). || Cambio (*m.*) de dirección (of the wind). || FIG. Cambio (*m.*) brusco, viraje, *m.* (of opinion).
veer [viə*] v. tr. MAR. Virar (a boat). || MAR. *To veer away* o *out a cable*, largar *or* soltar un cable.
— V. intr. MAR. Virar (a boat). || Cambiar de dirección, girar (to change direction). || Cambiar (wind). || Torcer: *the road veers left*, la carretera tuerce a la izquierda. || FIG. Virar, girar, inclinarse: *public opinion veered to the left*, la opinión pública viró hacia la izquierda. || — FIG. *To veer round*, cambiar de opinión. | *To veer round to*, adoptar, adherirse a (an opinion).
vegetable [ˈvedʒitəbl] adj. Vegetal: *the vegetable kingdom*, el reino vegetal. || De verduras: *vegetable market*, mercado de verduras. || — *Vegetable butter*, vegetalina, *f.* || *Vegetable garden*, huerta, *f.*, huerto, *m.* || *Vegetable ivory*, corozo, *m.*, corojo, *m.*, marfil (*m.*) vegetal. || *Vegetable marrow*, calabacín, *m.* || *Vegetable slicer*, cortalegumbres, *m. inv.*
— N. BOT. Vegetal, *m.*, planta, *f.* || AGR. Hortaliza, *f.*, verdura, *f.*, legumbre, *f.* || CULIN. Verdura, *f.*, legumbre, *f.* || — *Early vegetables*, verduras tempranas. || *Green vegetables*, verduras, *f.*
vegetal [ˈvedʒitl] adj. BOT. Vegetal.
vegetarian [ˌvedʒiˈtɛəriən] adj./n. Vegetariano, na.
vegetarianism [—izəm] n. Vegetarianismo, *m.*
vegetate [ˈvedʒiteit] v. intr. Vegetar. || FIG. Vegetar.
vegetation [ˌvedʒiˈteiʃən] n. Vegetación, *f.*
vegetative [ˈvedʒitətiv] adj. Vegetativo, va.
vehemence [ˈviːiməns] or **vehemency** [—i] n. Vehemencia, *f.*: *we were surprised by the vehemence of his speech*, nos sorprendió la vehemencia de su discurso. || Violencia, *f.* (of an attack, etc.).
vehement [ˈviːimənt] adj. Vehemente: *vehement speaker*, orador vehemente. || Violento, ta: *vehement opposition*, oposición violenta.
vehemently [—li] adv. Con vehemencia: *to speak vehemently*, hablar con vehemencia. || *To be vehemently opposed to sth.*, estar totalmente en contra de algo.
vehicle [ˈviːikl] n. Vehículo, *m.*: *motor vehicle*, vehículo motorizado; *space vehicle*, vehículo espacial; *air is the vehicle of sound*, el aire es el vehículo del sonido. || MED. Excipiente, *m.* || FIG. Vehículo, *m.*, medio, *m.*: *propaganda vehicle*, un vehículo para la propaganda. || FIG. *She is merely a vehicle for his ambition*, para él ella no es nada más que un medio para realizar sus ambiciones.
vehicular [viˈhikjulə*] adj. De vehículos. || *Vehicular traffic*, circulación rodada.
veil [veil] n. Velo, *m.*: *bride's veil*, velo de novia. || REL. Velo, *m.*: *to take the veil*, tomar el velo. || FIG. Capa, *f.*, pretexto, *m.*: *under the veil of*, so capa de, con el pretexto de. | Velo, *m.*: *a veil of smoke*, un velo de humo. || ANAT. Velo, *m.*: *humeral veil*, velo humeral. || — FIG. *Beyond the veil*, en el otro mundo. | *To draw a veil over*, correr un tupido velo sobre.
veil [veil] v. tr. Velar, cubrir con un velo: *a veiled face*, un rostro cubierto con un velo. || FIG. Cubrir, velar: *clouds veiled the mountain*, las nubes velaban la montaña. | Velar, disimular (to disguise): *thinly veiled disgust*, repugnancia apenas disimulada; *veiled reference*, alusión velada. || — *Eyes veiled in* o *by tears*, ojos velados por lágrimas. || *Project veiled in secrecy*, proyecto rodeado de secreto.
veiling [—iŋ] n. Tela (*f.*) para hacer velos (material). || Acción (*f.*) de velar (action). || Velo, *m.* (veil).
vein [vein] n. ANAT. Vena, *f.*: *portal vein*, vena porta. || GEOL. Vena, *f.*, veta, *f.*, filón, *m.* || Veta, *f.* (of water). || ZOOL. BOT. Vena, *f.*, nervadura, *f.* || Vena, *f.*, veta, *f.* (streak in wood, marble). || FIG. Humor, *m.*, disposición, *f.* (mood). | Vena, *f.* (streak): *a vein of madness*, una vena de loco. | Estilo, *m.*: *other works in the same vein*, otras obras del mismo estilo.
veined [—d] adj. Que tiene venas (having veins). || Veteado, da; jaspeado, da (marble, etc.).
veining [—iŋ] n. Jaspeado, *m.* || ANAT. Red (*f.*) de venas.
veinstone [—stəun] n. MIN. Ganga, *f.*
veiny [—i] adj. Venoso, sa. || Veteado, da (marble, etc.).
velamen [viˈleimən] n. ANAT. Velamen, *m.* || BOT. Tegumento, *m.*

— OBSERV. El plural de la palabra inglesa *velamen* es *velamina*.

velar [ˈviːlə*] adj. ANAT. GRAMM. Velar.
— N. GRAMM. Velar, *f.*
velleity [veˈliːiti] n. Veleidad, *f.*

VEGETABLES AND FRUITS — HORTALIZAS (*f.*) Y FRUTAS, *f.*

I. Vegetables. — Hortalizas, *f.*

artichoke	alcachofa *f.*
asparagus	espárrago *m.*
aubergine, eggplant	berenjena *f.*
bean	judía *f*, habichuela *f.*, alubia *f.* [*Amer.*, frijol *m.*, fríjol *m.*, poroto *m.*]
beet, beetroot	remolacha *f.*
broad bean	haba *f.*
broccoli, brocoli	brécol *m.*
Brussels sprouts	coles (*f.*) de Bruselas
cabbage	col *f.*, berza *f.*
caper	alcaparra *f.*
cardoon	cardo *m.*
carrot	zanahoria *f.*
cauliflower	coliflor *f.*
celery	apio *m.*
chervil	perifollo *m.*
chick-pea	garbanzo *m.*
chicory	escarola *f.*
chilli	chile *m.*
chive	cebolleta *f.*
clove	clavo *m.*
cos lettuce	lechuga (*f.*) romana
cress	berro *m.*
cucumber	pepino *m.*
cumin, cummin	comino *m.*
dandelion	diente (*m.*) de león
endive	endibia *f.*
fennel	hinojo *m.*
French bean	judía (*f.*) verde
garlic	ajo *m*
gherkin	pepinillo *m.*
horseradish	rábano (*m.*) picante
Jerusalem artichoke	aguaturma *f.*, pataca *f.*, topinambur *m.*
kale	col (*f.*) rizada
kohlrabi	colinabo *m.*
laurel	laurel *m.*
leek	puerro *m.*
lentil	lenteja *f.*
lettuce	lechuga *f.*
lupin [U.S., lupine]	altramuz *m.*, lupino *m.*
marrow	calabacín *m.*
melon	melón *m.*
mushroom	seta *f.*, hongo *m.*
onion	cebolla *f.*
parsley	perejil *m.*
parsnip	pastinaca *f.*, chirivía *f.*
pea	guisante *m.*
pepper	pimiento *m.*
pimiento	pimiento (*m.*) morrón
potato	patata *f.* [*Amer.*, papa *f.*]
pumpkin	calabaza *f.*
radish	rábano *m.*
rhubarb	ruibarbo *m.*
romaine lettuce	lechuga (*f.*) romana
salsify	salsifí *m.*
sorrel	acedera *f.*
spinach	espinaca *f.*
sweet pepper	pimiento (*m.*) morrón
sweet potato	batata *f.*, boniato *m.* [*Amer.*, camote *m.*]
tarragon	estragón *m.*
thyme	tomillo
tomato	tomate *m.* [*Amer.*, jitomate *m.*]
truffle	trufa *f.*, criadilla (*f.*) de tierra
turnip	nabo *m.*
watercress	berro *m.*
watermelon	sandía *f.*

II. Fruits. — Frutas, *f.*

almond	almendra *f.*
apple	manzana *f.*
apricot	albaricoque *m.*
avocado	aguacate *m.* [*Amer.*, palta *f.*]
banana	plátano *m.* [*Amer.*, banana *f.*, banano *m.*]
bilberry	arándano *m.*
blackberry	zarzamora *f.*
black currant	grosella (*f.*) negra
blood orange	naranja (*f.*) sanguina
blueberry	arándano *m.*
cherry	cereza *f.*
chestnut	castaña *f.*
citron	cidra *f.*
coconut, cocoanut	coco *m.*
currant	grosella *f.*
damson	ciruela (*f.*) damascena
date	dátil *m.*
fig	higo *m.*
grape	uva *f.*
grapefruit	pomelo *m.*, toronja *f.*
guava	guayaba *f.*
hazelnut	avellana *f.*
lemon	limón *m.*
mango	mango *m.*
medlar	níspero *m.*
mulberry	mora *f.*
nectarine	nectarina *f.*
nutmeg	nuez (*f.*) moscada
orange	naranja *f.*
papaya, papaw	papaya *f.*
peach	melocotón *m.* [*Amer.*, durazno *m.*]
peanut	cacahuete *m.* [*Amer.*, cacahuate *m.*, maní *m.*]
pear	pera *f.*
persimmon	caqui *m.*
pinapple	piña *f.* [*Amer.*, ananás *m.*]
pistachio	alfóncigo *m.*, pistachio *m.*
plum	ciruela *f.*
pomegranate	granada *f.*
prickly pear	higo (*m.*) chumbo
quince	membrillo *m.*
raspberry	frambuesa *f.*
soursop	guanábana *f.*
strawberry	fresa *f.* [*Amer.*, frutilla *f.*]
tangerine	mandarina *f.*
walnut	nuez *f.*

See also AGRICULTURE

vellum [ˈveləm] n. Vitela, *f.* || *Vellum paper*, papel (*m.*) vitela.

velocipede [viˈlɔsipi:d] n. Velocípedo, *m.*

velocity [viˈlɔsiti] n. PHYS. Velocidad, *f.* || CHEM. Rápidez, *f.*, velocidad, *f.* || *Escape velocity*, velocidad (*f.*) de liberación (of a spacecraft).

velodrome [ˈvelədrəum] n. Velódromo, *m.*

velour or **velours** [vəˈluə*] n. Velludillo, *m.*, veludillo, *m.*, terciopelo, *m.* (velvet).

velum [ˈvi:ləm] n. ANAT. Velo, *m.*

— OBSERV. El plural de *velum* es *vela*.

velure [ˈveljə*] n. (Ant.) Te ciopelo, *m.* (cloth).

velutinous [viˈlju:tinəs] ad . Aterciopelado, da.

velvet [ˈvelvit] n. Terciopelo, *m.*, velludillo, *m.* (cloth). || ZOOL. Vello, *m.* (on antlers). || — FIG. *An iron hand in a velvet glove*, una mano férrea con guante de seda. || *Corduroy velvet*, pana, *f.*, pana (*f.*) de canutillo. || FIG. *It's as smooth as velvet*, es como una seda. | *Skin like velvet*, piel de terciopelo *or* aterciopelada. | *To be on velvet*, estar en posición muy ventajosa.

— Adj. Aterciopelado, da (like velvet). || De terciopelo (made of velvet). || FIG. Suave, aterciopelado, da (soft).

velveteen [ˈvelviˈti:n] n. Pana, *f.*

velvety [ˈvelviti] adj. Aterciopelado, da (like velvet): *velvety material*, tejido aterciopelado; *velvety skin*, piel aterciopelada.

vena cava [ˈvi:nəˈkeivə] n. ANAT. Vena (*f.*) cava.

venal [ˈvi:nl] adj. Venal.

venality [vi:ˈnæliti] n. Venalidad, *f.*

venation [veˈneiʃən] n. Nervadura, *f.* (on leaves and insects' wings).

vend [vend] v. tr. Vender.

vendee [venˈdi:] n. JUR. Comprador, ra.

vender [ˈvendə*] n. Vendedor, ra.

vendetta [venˈdetə] n. Vendetta, *f.*

vending machine [ˈvendiŋməˌʃi:n] n. Distribuidor (*m.*) automático.

vendor [ˈvendə*] n. Vendedor, ra (seller). || Buhonero, ra; vendedor (*m.*) ambulante, vendedora (*f.*) ambulante (pedlar). || *Automatic vendor*, distribuidor automático (machine).

veneer [viˈniə*] n. Chapa, *f.* (sheet of wood). || Enchapado, *m.*, chapeado, *m.* (wood surface). || FIG. Máscara, *f.*, careta, *f.*, apariencia, *f.* (superficial appearance): *veneer of respectability*, apariencia de respetabilidad. | Barniz, *m.* (of culture, etc.).

veneer [viˈniə*] v. tr. Chapear, enchapar: *to veneer a piece of furniture in mahogany*, chapear un mueble con caoba. || FIG. Disfrazar, encubrir.

veneering [—riŋ] n. Chapeado, *m.*, enchapado, *m.*

venerability [ˌvenərəˈbiliti] n. Carácter (*m.*) venerable.

venerable [ˈvenərəbl] adj. Venerable.

venerate [ˈvenəreit] v. tr. Venerar.

veneration [ˌvenəˈreiʃən] n. Veneración, *f.*

venerator [ˈvenəreitə*] n. Venerador, ra.

venereal [viˈniəriəl] adj. Venéreo, a: *venereal disease*, enfermedad venérea.

venery [ˈvenəri] n. Deleite (*m.*) sexual (sexual pleasure). || Montería, *f.* (hunting).

Venetian [viˈni:ʃən] adj./n. Veneciano, na. || — *Venetian blind*, persiana veneciana. || *Venetian glass*, cristal (*m.*) de Venecia.

Venezuela [ˌveneˈzweilə] pr. n. GEOGR. Venezuela, *f.*

Venezuelan [—n] adj./n. Venezolano, na.

vengeance [ˈvendʒəns] n. Venganza, *f.* || — FIG. *It was snowing with a vengeance*, estaba nevando de verdad. | *To punish s.o. with a vengeance*, castigar muy severamente a uno. || *To take vengeance for sth.*, vengarse de algo. || *To take vengeance on s.o.*, vengarse de alguien.

vengeful [ˈvendʒful] adj. Vengativo, va.

venial [ˈvi:njəl] adj. Venial: *venial sin*, pecado venial.

veniality [ˌvi:niˈæliti] n. Venialidad, *f.*

Venice [ˈvenis] pr. n. GEOGR. Venecia.

venison [ˈvenzn] n. Carne (*f.*) de venado.

venom [ˈvenəm] n. Veneno, *m.*

venomous [—əs] adj. Venenoso, sa: *venomous snake*, serpiente venenósa. || FIG. Venenoso, sa; malévolo, la:

venomous criticism, crítica venenosa. || FIG. *Venomous tongue*, lengua viperina.
venose [ˈvi:nəus] adj. BOT. Venoso, sa.
venosity [vi:ˈnɔsiti] n. ANAT. BOT. Venosidad, *f.*
venous [ˈvi:nəs] adj. ANAT. BOT. Venoso, sa: *venous blood*, sangre venosa.
vent [vent] n. Abertura, *f.*, agujero, *m.* (hole, passage). || Abertura, *f.*, raja, *f.* (of coat). || Cañón (*m.*) de chimenea (chimney). || Respiradero, *m.*, agujero (*m.*) de ventilación (air hole). || Tubo (*m.*) *or* conducto (*m.*) de ventilación (tube). || Rejilla (*f.*) de ventilación (grille in a wall, etc.). || MUS. Agujero, *m.* || TECH. Válvula, *f.*: *safety vent*, válvula de seguridad. || Chimenea, *f.* (of volcano). || Piquera, *f.* (of barrel). || MAR. Tronera, *f.* || MIL. Oído, *m.*, fogón, *m.* (of a gun). || ZOOL. Ano, *m.* || FIG. Salida, *f.*, libre curso, *m.*, rienda (*f.*) suelta: *to give vent to one's anger*, dar libre curso a su cólera. || FIG. *To give vent to one's feelings*, desahogarse.
vent [vent] v. tr. Hacer un agujero en (to make an aperture in). || Descargar, emitir, dar salida a (to discharge). || FIG. Desahogar, descargar: *to vent one's anger on s.o.*, desahogar su ira contra alguien. || FIG. *To vent one's feelings*, desahogarse.
ventail [ˈventeil] n. Visera, *f.* (of helmet).
venter [ˈventə*] n. ZOOL. Vientre, *m.*, abdomen, *m.* || ANAT. Protuberancia, *f.* (protuberance). | Cavidad, *f.* (bone cavity). || JUR. Matriz, *f.* (womb).
venthole [ˈventhəul] n. Respiradero, *m.*
ventilate [ˈventileit] v. tr. Ventilar, airear: *to ventilate a room*, ventilar una habitación. || MED. Oxigenar (blood). || FIG. Ventilar, discutir: *to ventilate a problem*, ventilar un problema.
ventilating [—iŋ] n. Ventilación, *f.*, aireación, *f.* || — *Ventilating cowl*, sombrerete (*m.*) de ventilación. || *Ventilating fan*, ventilador, *m.* || *Ventilating shaft*, pozo (*m.*) de ventilación.
ventilation [ˌventiˈleiʃən] n. Ventilación, *f.*, aireación, *f.*: *the ventilation of a tunnel*, la ventilación de un túnel. || MED. Oxigenación, *f.* (of blood). || FIG. Discusión, *f.* || — *Pulmonary ventilation*, ventilación pulmonar. || *Ventilation duct*, conducto (*m.*) de ventilación. || *Ventilation shaft*, pozo (*m.*) de ventilación.
ventilator [ˈventileitə*] n. Ventilador, *m.*
ventral [ˈventrəl] adj. Ventral, abdominal.
ventricle [ˈventrikl] n. ANAT. Ventrículo, *m.*
ventricular [venˈtrikjulə*] adj. ANAT. Ventricular.
ventriloquial [ˌventriˈləukwiəl] adj. Ventrílocuo, a.
ventriloquism [venˈtriləkwizəm] n. Ventriloquia, *f.*
ventriloquist [venˈtriləkwist] n. Ventrílocuo, a.
ventriloquistic [venˌtriləˈkwistik] adj. Ventrílocuo, a.
ventriloquize [venˈtriləkwaiz] v. intr. Ser ventrílocuo, a.
ventriloquy [venˈtriləkwi] n. Ventriloquia, *f.*
venture [ˈventʃə*] n. Aventura, *f.*, empresa (*f.*) arriesgada: *a dangerous venture*, una aventura peligrosa. || — *At a venture*, al azar, a la ventura. || COMM. *Business venture*, empresa comercial.
venture [ˈventʃə*] v. tr. Arriesgar, aventurar (life, fortune). || Aventurar (an opinion). || Jugar: *they ventured all*, lo jugaron todo. || Atreverse a, osar (to dare). || Permitirse: *may I venture to suggest...?*, ¿puedo permitirme sugerir...? || — *Nothing ventured, nothing gained*, quien no se arriesga no pasa la mar. || *To venture a quick glance*, echar una mirada furtiva.
— V. intr. Arriesgarse: *to venture out* o *abroad*, arriesgarse fuera. || Ir: *don't venture too far*, no vayas muy lejos. || Atreverse (to dare). || *To venture on* o *upon*, arriesgarse en.
venturer [—rə*] n. Aventurero, *m.*
venturesome [—səm] or **venturous** [—rəs] adj. Aventurero, ra; atrevido, da (adventurous). || Emprendedor, ra (enterprising). || Atrevido, da: *venturesome towards women*, atrevido con las mujeres. || Aventurado, da; arriesgado, da: *a venturesome plan*, un proyecto aventurado.
venue [ˈvenju:] n. Lugar, *m.* (place): *the venue of the crime*, el lugar del crimen. || Lugar (*m.*) de reunión, punto (*m.*) de reunión (meeting place). || SP. Campo, *m.* || JUR. Jurisdicción, *f.* || JUR. *To change the venue*, remitir la causa a otro tribunal.
Venus [ˈvi:nəs] pr. n. Venus, *f.*
veracious [vəˈreiʃəs] adj. Veraz, verídico, ca.
veracity [vəˈræsiti] n. Veracidad, *f.*
veranda or **verandah** [vəˈrændə] n. Veranda, *f.*, mirador, *m.*, galería, *f.*
verb [və:b] n. GRAMM. Verbo, *m.*: *transitive verb*, verbo transitivo.
verbal [ˈvə:bəl] adj. Verbal: *verbal message*, mensaje verbal; *verbal agreement*, acuerdo verbal; *verbal noun*, sustantivo verbal. || Literal (translation).
verbalism [—izəm] n. Expresión (*f.*) verbal (an expression). || PHIL. Verbalismo, *m.*
verbalist [—ist] n. Verbalista, *m.* & *f.*
verbalistic [ˌvə:bəˈlistik] adj. Verbalista.
verbalization [—ˈeiʃən] n. Expresión (*f.*) con palabras (of an idea). || Uso (*m.*) como verbo (of a word).
verbalize [ˈvə:bəlaiz] v. tr. Convertir en verbo (to make into a verb). || Expresar con palabras.
— V. intr. Ser prolijo, ja (to speak verbosely).
verbascum [və:ˈbæskʌm] n. BOT. Gordolobo, *m.*
verbatim [və:ˈbeitim] adj. In extenso. || *Verbatim record*, actas taquigráficas.
— Adv. Palabra por palabra, literalmente.
verbena [və:ˈbi:nə] n. BOT. Verbena, *f.*
verbenaceae [ˌvə:biˈneisi:i] pl. n. BOT. Verbenáceas, *f.*
verbiage [ˈvə:biidʒ] n. Palabrería, *f.*, verborrea, *f.*
verbose [və:bəus] adj. Prolijo, ja; verboso, sa.
verbosity [və:ˈbɔsiti] n. Verbosidad, *f.*, verborrea, *f.*
verdancy [ˈvə:dənsi] n. Verdor, *m.* (greenness). || FIG. Verdor, *m.*, ingenuidad, *f.*, inocencia, *f.*
verdant [ˈvə:dənt] adj. Verde (green). || FIG. Ingenuo, nua; inocente, verde (inexperienced).
verdict [ˈvə:dikt] n. JUR. Veredicto, *m.*, fallo, *m.* (of jury). | Juicio, *m.*, veredicto, *m.* (of coroner). || Fallo, *m.*, juicio, *m.* (of an arbitrator). || Opinión, *f.* || — *Open verdict*, veredicto que no especifica ni el autor ni las circunstancias de un crimen. || *To bring in* o *to return a verdict of guilty*, pronunciar un veredicto de culpabilidad.
verdigris [ˈvə:digris] n. Verdín, *m.*, cardenillo, *m.*
verdure [ˈvə:djuə*] n. Verdor, *m.* (of vegetation). || FIG. Verdor, *m.*, vigor, *m.* (vigour).
verge [və:dʒ] n. Borde, *m.*, margen, *m.* (border, edge). || Arcén, *m.* (of a road). || REL. Vara, *f.* || Eje (*m.*) del áncora (of a watch). || ARCH. Fuste, *m.* (of a column). | Borde, *m.* (of tiling). || HIST. Jurisdicción, *f.* || — *On the verge of*, al borde de, a dos dedos de: *on the verge of madness*, al borde de la locura. || *On the verge of doing sth.*, a punto de hacer algo. || *On the verge of tears*, a punto de echarse a llorar.
verge [və:dʒ] v. intr. Orientarse, inclinarse: *his policy is verging to the right*, su política se inclina hacia la derecha. || Torcer a: *the road verges to the east*, la carretera tuerce al este. || *To verge on*, rayar en: *courage verging on foolhardiness*, valor que raya en la temeridad; *he is verging on forty*, raya en los cuarenta años; tirar a: *blue verging on green*, azul que tira a verde.
verger [ˈvə:dʒə*] n. REL. Sacristán, *m.* || Macero, *m.* (mace bearer).
Vergil [ˈvə:dʒil] pr. n. Virgilio, *m.*
Vergilian [və:ˈdʒiliən] adj. Virgiliano, na.
verifiable [ˈverifaiəbl] adj. Comprobable.
verification [ˌverifiˈkeiʃən] n. Verificación, *f.*, comprobación, *f.* || JUR. Confirmación, *f.*
verify [ˈverifai] v. tr. Verificar, comprobar. || JUR. Confirmar.
verily [ˈverili] adv. En verdad.
verisimilar [ˌveriˈsimilə*] adj. Verosímil.
verisimilitude [ˌverisiˈmilitju:d] n. Verosimilitud, *f.*
verism [ˈviərizəm] n. Verismo, *m.*
veritable [ˈveritəbl] adj. Verdadero, ra: *a veritable idiot*, un verdadero idiota.
verity [ˈveriti] n. Verdad, *f.*: *the eternal verities*, las verdades eternas. || *Unquestionable verities*, hechos (*m.*) indiscutibles.
verjuice [ˈvə:dʒu:s] n. Agraz, *m.*
vermeil [ˈvə:meil] n. Bermellón, *m.* (vermilion). || Color (*m.*) bermejo.
— Adj. Bermejo, ja.
vermicelli [ˌvə:miˈseli] n. Fideos, *m. pl.*
vermicidal [ˌvə:miˈsaidəl] adj. Vermicida.
vermicide [ˈvə:misaid] n. Vermicida, *m.*
vermicular [və:ˈmikjulə] adj. Vermicular.
vermiculate [və:ˈmikjuleit] or **vermiculated** [—id] adj. Vermiculado, da.
vermiform [ˈvə:mifɔ:m] adj. Vermiforme.
vermifuge [ˈvə:mifju:dʒ] adj. MED. Vermífugo, ga.
— N. MED. Vermífugo, *m.*
vermilion or **vermillion** [vəˈmiljən] adj. Bermejo, ja.
— N. Bermellón, *m.*
vermin [ˈvə:min] n. Bichos, *m. pl.* (rats, mice, etc.). || Sabandijas, *f. pl.* (fleas, lice, etc.). || FIG. Gentuza, *f.*, chusma, *f.*, canalla, *f.*, sabandijas, *f. pl.*
verminous [—əs] adj. MED. Verminoso, sa (caused by vermin). || Piojoso, sa (lousy). || Lleno de bichos (infested with vermin).
vermivorous [və:ˈmivərəs] adj. ZOOL. Vermívoro, ra.
vermouth [ˈvə:məθ] n. Vermut, *m.*, vermú, *m.*: *gin and vermouth*, vermut con ginebra.
vernacular [vəˈnækjulə*] adj. Vernáculo, la: *the vernacular languages of Africa*, los idiomas vernáculos de África. || Vulgar: *in vernacular Spanish*, en castellano vulgar.
— N. Lengua (*f.*) vernácula (indigenous language). || Lenguaje (*m.*) vulgar (everyday speech).
vernier [ˈvə:njə*] n. TECH. Nonio, *m.*, vernier, *m.*
veronica [vəˈrɔnikə] n. BOT. TAUR. Verónica, *f.*
verruca [vəˈru:kə] n. MED. Verruga, *f.*

— OBSERV. El plural de la palabra *verruca* es *verrucae*.

Versailles [vɛəˈsai] pr. n. GEOGR. Versalles: *the Treaty of Versailles*, el Tratado de Versalles.
versant [ˈvə:sənt] n. Vertiente, *f.*, ladera, *f.* (slope of mountain). || Vertiente, *f.* (inclination of a region).
versatile [ˈvə:sətail] adj. De talentos variados, polifacético, ca; con muchas facetas (having various skills): *versatile artist*, artista con muchas facetas. || Ágil, flexible (mind). || Que tiene muchos usos (multipurpose): *versatile suit*, *table*, traje, mesa que tiene muchos usos. || Versátil (changeable). || BOT. ZOOL. Versátil.
versatility [ˌvə:səˈtiliti] n. Diversos talentos, *m. pl.*, carácter (*m.*) polifacético, varias aptitudes, *f. pl.* (many talents). || Agilidad, *f.*, flexibilidad, *f.* (of the mind). || Diversos usos, *m. pl.* (many uses). || Versatilidad, *f.* (changeableness). || BOT. ZOOL. Versatilidad, *f.*

verse [və:s] n. Verso, *m.* (poetry): *free verse,* verso libre. || Estrofa, *f.* (stanza). || Cuplé, *m.* (of a song). || Poesía, *f.*, versos, *m. pl.*: *the verse of García Lorca,* la poesía de García Lorca. || REL. Versículo, *m.* (of the Bible). || *In verse,* en verso.
— Adj. En verso: *a verse piece,* una obra en verso.
verse [və:s] v. tr./intr. Poner en verso, versificar. || *To verse o.s. in,* familiarizarse con, dedicarse a.
versed [—t] adj. Versado, da: *to be versed in,* estar versado en.
versicle [ˈvə:sikl] n. Versículo, *m.*
versicolour (U. S. **versicolor**) [ˈvə:si,kʌlə*] or **versicoloured** (U. S. **versicolored**) [—d] adj. Multicolor.
versification [,və:sifiˈkeiʃən] n. Versificación, *f.*
versifier [ˈvə:sifaiə*] n. Versificador, ra.
versify [ˈvə:sifai] v. tr./intr. Versificar.
version [ˈvə:ʃən] n. Versión, *f.*: *each witness gave a different version of what happened,* cada testigo dio una versión diferente de lo sucedido. || Versión, *f.*, traducción (*f.*) directa (translation). || MED. Versión, *f.* (of foetus). || MUS. Interpretación, *f.*, versión, *f.* || — *According to his version,* según su versión, según él. || *This is my version of what happened,* así es como veo yo lo que pasó.
verso [ˈvə:səu] n. Vuelta, *f.*, verso, *m.*, dorso, *m.* (of a page). || Reverso, *m.* (of a coin).
versus [ˈvə:səs] prep. Contra: *Spain versus France,* España contra Francia.
vertebra [ˈvə:tibrə] n. ANAT. Vértebra, *f.*

— OBSERV. El plural de la palabra inglesa *vertebra* es *vertebrae* o *vertebras.*

vertebral [—l] adj. ANAT. Vertebral.: *vertebral discs,* discos vertebrales; *vertebral column,* columna vertebral.
vertebrate [ˈvə:tibrit] adj. Vertebrado, da.
— N. Vertebrado, *m.*
vertex [ˈvə:teks] n. MATH. ANAT. Vértice, *m.* || ASTR. Cenit, *m.* || FIG. Cumbre, *f.*, cúspide, *f.*, cima, *f.*

— OBSERV. El plural de *vertex* es *vertexes* o *vertices.*

vertical [ˈvə:tikəl] adj. Vertical: *vertical angle,* ángulo vertical; *vertical circle,* círculo vertical. || ANAT. Del vértice. || COMM. Vertical (organization).
— N. Vertical, *f.*
verticality [,və:tiˈkæliti] n. Verticalidad, *f.*
vertically [ˈvə:tikəli] adv. Verticalmente. || *Vertically opposite angles,* ángulos opuestos por el vértice.
vertices [ˈvə:tə,siz] pl. n. See VERTEX.
verticil [ˈvə:tisil] n. BOT. Verticilo, *m.*
vertiginous [və:ˈtidʒinəs] adj. Vertiginoso, sa.
vertiginousness [—nis] n. Vertiginosidad, *f.*
vertigo [ˈvə:tigəu] n. MED. Vértigo, *m.*

— OBSERV. El plural de la palabra inglesa es *vertigoes* o *vertigines.*

vertu [və:ˈtu:] n. See VIRTU.
vervain [ˈvə:vein] n. BOT. Verbena, *f.*
verve [və:v] n. Entusiasmo, *m.*, vigor, *m.*, brío, *m.*, ánimo, *m.* || THEATR. Vis (*f.*) cómica.
very [ˈveri] adj. Mismo, ma: *the very day,* el día mismo; *in this very house,* en esta misma casa; *at that very moment,* en ese mismo momento. || Propio, pia: *he knew our very thoughts,* conocía nuestros propios pensamientos. || Verdadero, ra (real). || Puro, ra: *the very truth,* la pura verdad. || — *At the very beginning,* al principio de todo. || *Come here this very minute!,* ¡ven aquí ahora mismo! || *For that very reason,* por eso mismo. || *From this very day,* a partir de ahora mismo, a partir de hoy mismo. || *He arrived a year ago this very day,* hoy mismo hace un año que llegó, hoy hace justo un año que llegó. || *In the very middle,* en el mismísimo centro, justo en medio. || *It is the very thing I was looking for,* es justo *or* exactamente lo que buscaba. || *I shudder at the very thought of it,* con sólo *or* nada más pensarlo me echo a temblar. || *I was told by the very President himself,* me lo dijo el mismísimo *or* el propio Presidente. || *She is the very image of her mother,* es el vivo retrato *or* la viva imagen de su madre. || *The veriest ignorant knows it,* hasta el más ignorante lo sabe. || *The very air we breathe is polluted,* hasta el mismo aire que respiramos está contaminado. || *The very idea!,* ¡vaya idea!, ¡ni soñarlo! || *The very man I need,* exactamente el hombre que necesito.
— Adv. Muy (extremely): *a very tall building,* un edificio muy alto; *very well,* muy bien. || Mucho: *isn't she beautiful? — Yes, very,* es muy guapa ¿verdad? — Sí, mucho. || — *Are you hungry? — Very,* ¿tienes hambre? — Mucha. || *At the very latest,* a más tardar. || *At the very least,* por lo menos. || *At the very most,* a lo sumo, como máximo, a lo más. || *A very little,* muy poco: *he only gave me a very little,* sólo me dio muy poco. || *Do your very best!,* ¡haz todo lo que puedas!, ¡haz todo lo posible! || *I am so very hungry,* tengo tanta hambre. || *It's not so very far,* no está tan lejos. || *It's very cold,* está muy frío (thing), hace mucho frío (weather). || *The very best,* el mejor de todos, la mejor de todas: *we have many excellent wines but this one is the very best,* tenemos muchos vinos excelentes pero este es el mejor de todos; lo mejor: *he insists on the very best,* exige lo mejor. || *The very last,* el último de todos. || *The very next day,* el día siguiente. || *The very same,* el mismísimo, la mismísima. || *Very good,* muy bueno (extremely good), muy bien (all right). || *Very many,* muchísimos. || *Very much,* mucho, muchísimo: *very much better,* mucho mejor; *I love you very much,* te quiero mucho. || *Very much so,* muchísimo. || *Very very few,* muy pocos, muy pocas, poquísimos, poquísimas.

— OBSERV. The prefixes *requete-* and *archi-* may sometimes be used to translate the idea of "very" or "very very" (*very good,* requetebueno, archibueno).

Very light [ˈviərilait] n. MIL. Bengala (*f.*) Very.
vesica [ˈvesikə] n. ANAT. Vejiga, *f.* || *Vesica natatoria,* vejiga natatoria.

— OBSERV. El plural de *vesica* es *vesicae.*

vesical [—l] adj. De la vejiga, vesical.
vesicant [—nt] adj. MED. Vesicante.
— N. MED. Vesicante, *m.*
vesicate [ˈvesikeit] v. tr. Levantar ampollas.
vesicatory [ˈvesikətəri] adj. MED. Vejigatorio, ria; vesicatorio, ria.
— N. MED. Vejigatorio, *m.*, vesicatorio, *m.*
vesicle [ˈvesikl] n. ANAT. Vesícula, *f.*
vesicula [vəˈsikjulə] n. ANAT. Vesícula, *f.*
vesicular [—*] adj. ANAT. Vesicular.
vesper [ˈvespə*] n. POET. Tarde, *f.* || ASTR. Estrella (*f.*) vespertina (evening star). || — Pl. REL. Vísperas, *f.*
— Adj. Vespertino, na (of evening).
vesperal [—rəl] n. REL. Vesperal, *m.* (book).
vespertine [ˈvespətain] adj. Vespertino, na.
vespiary [ˈvespjəri] n. Avispero, *m.*
Vespucci [vesˈputʃi] pr. n. Vespucio, *m.*
vessel [ˈvesəl] n. Vasija, *f.*, vaso, *m.*, recipiente, *m.* (receptacle). || MAR. Nave, *f.*, navío, *m.*, buque, *m.*, barco, *m.* || BOT. ANAT. Vaso, *m.*: *blood vessel,* vasos sanguíneos. || — REL. *Sacred vessels,* vasos sagrados. || FIG. *The weaker vessel,* el sexo débil. | *To be a weak vessel,* no tener carácter, ser débil.
vest [vest] n. Camiseta, *f.* (underwear). || U. S. Chaleco, *m.* (waistcoat). || SP. *Running vest,* camiseta, *f.*
vest [vest] v. tr. Investir: *to vest s.o. with sth.,* investir a alguien de algo. || Conferir, conceder: *to vest s.o. with authority,* conferir autoridad a alguien. || (Ant.). Vestir (to clad). || — *The power vested in the State,* el poder atribuido al Estado. || *To vest in,* conceder a, conferir a: *to vest rights in s.o.,* conceder derechos a alguien; dar a, ceder a (property).
— V. intr. *To vest in s.o.,* ser atribuido a alguien, corresponder por derecho a alguien.
vesta [ˈvestə] n. Cerilla, *f.* (wax match).
vestal [ˈvəstəl] adj. Vestal (related to Vesta). || *Vestal virgin,* vestal, *f.*
— N. Vestal, *f.*
vested [ˈvestid] adj. Concedido, da. || *Vested interest,* derecho adquirido (legal term), interés (*m.*) personal: *many vested interests are involved in this affair,* muchos intereses personales entran en juego en este asunto; intereses, *m. pl.*: *to have a vested interest in a concern,* tener intereses en una empresa.
vestibular [vesˈtibjulə*] adj. ANAT. Vestibular.
vestibule [ˈvestibju:l] n. ARCH. Vestíbulo, *m.* (of a building). | Zaguán, *m.*, vestíbulo, *m.* (of a house). || ANAT. Vestíbulo, *m.* || U. S. Fuelle, *m.* (in a railway carriage).
vestige [ˈvestidʒ] n. Vestigio, *m.*, rastro, *m.*: *not a vestige could be found,* ni un rastro se podía encontrar. || BIOL. Rudimento, *m.* || FIG. *Without a vestige of doubt,* sin la menor duda.
vestigial [vesˈtidʒiəl] adj. Rudimentario, ria.
vestment [ˈvestmənt] n. Vestidura, *f.*
vest-pocket [ˈvestˈpɔkit] adj. De bolsillo.
vestry [ˈvestri] n. REL. Sacristía, *f.* (sacristy). | Junta (*f.*) parroquial (administrative body).
vestryman [—mən] n. REL. Miembro (*m.*) de la junta parroquial.

— OBSERV. El plural de esta palabra es *vestrymen.*

vesture [ˈvestʃə*] n. (Ant.). Vestidura, *f.*
vesturer [—rə*] n. REL. Sacristán, *m.* (sexton).
Vesuvius [viˈsu:vjəs] pr. n. GEOGR. Vesubio, *m.*
vet [vet] n. FAM. Veterinario, *m.* | Veterano, *m.*
vet [vet] v. tr. FAM. Reconocer (to examine an animal). | Castrar (to castrate an animal). | Corregir, revisar (an article). | Someter a una investigación [hecha por los servicios de Seguridad] (person).
vetch [vetʃ] n. BOT. Arveja, *f.*
vetchling [—liŋ] n. BOT. Almorta, *f.*
veteran [ˈvetərən] adj. Veterano, na: *a veteran soldier,* un soldado veterano. || Experimentado, da (experienced). || U. S. Excombatiente. || *Veteran troops,* tropas aguerridas.
— N. Veterano, *m.* (old soldier). || U. S. Excombatiente, *m.* (ex-serviceman).
veterinarian [,vetəriˈnɛərjən] n. U. S. Veterinario, *m.*
veterinary [ˈvetərinəri] adj. Veterinario, ria. || — *Veterinary medecine* o *science,* veterinaria, *f.* || *Veterinary surgeon,* veterinario, *m.*
— N. Veterinario, *m.*
veto [ˈvi:təu] n. Veto, *m.*: *to put a veto on sth.,* ponerle el veto a algo; *power* o *right of veto,* derecho de veto; *suspensory, absolute veto,* veto suspensivo, absoluto.

— OBSERV. El plural de la palabra inglesa *veto* es *vetoes.*

veto [ˈvi:təu] v. tr. Vetar, poner el veto a (to use one's veto). || Vedar, prohibir (to forbid): *the police vetoed the demonstration,* la policía prohibió la manifestación.

vex [veks] v. tr. Molestar, fastidiar (to annoy): *his continuous chatter vexes me*, su charla continua me molesta. || Disgustar: *her behaviour severely vexed her father*, su comportamiento disgustó mucho a su padre. || Enfadar (to make angry). || Afligir (to afflict). || Agitar (the sea).
— V. intr. *To vex over*, preocuparse por.
vexation [vek'seiʃən] n. Molestia, *f.*, fastidio, *m.* (irritation). || Disgusto, *m.*: *the vexations one has to support*, los disgustos que uno tiene que aguantar. || Aflicción, *f.*
vexatious [vek'seiʃəs] adj. Molesto, ta; fastidioso, sa (annoying). || JUR. Vejatorio, ria.
vexed [vekst] adj. Enfadado, da: *to be vexed about*, estar enfadado con *or* por; *he is vexed with me*, está enfadado conmigo. || Batallón, ona; controvertido, da (question). || *To get* o *to become vexed*, enfadarse.
vexing ['veksiŋ] adj. Molesto, ta; fastidioso, sa.
via [vaiə] prep. Por, vía: *Madrid-London via Paris*, Madrid Londres vía París; *I came home via Rome*, volví a casa por Roma.
viability [ˌvaiə'biliti] n. Viabilidad, *f.*
viable ['vaiəbl] adj. Viable.
viaduct ['vaiədʌkt] n. Viaducto, *m.*
vial ['vaiəl] n. Frasco, *m.* (phial).
viands ['vaiəndz] pl. n. Manjares, *m.*, viandas, *f.*
viaticum [vai'ætikəm] n. Viático, *m.*
— OBSERV. El plural de *viaticum* es *viaticums* o *viatica*.
vibrancy ['vaibrənsi] n. Vibración, *f.*
vibrant ['vaibrənt] adj. Vibrante (which vibrates). || FIG. Lleno de vitalidad, enérgico, ca (person): *vibrant woman*, mujer enérgica. | Animado, da (place): *vibrant streets*, calles animadas. || GRAMM. Vibrante (sound).
— N. GRAMM. Vibrante, *f.*
vibraphone ['vaibrəfəun] n. MUS. Vibráfono, *m.*
vibrate [vai'breit] v. intr. Vibrar: *the house vibrates when a train passes*, la casa vibra cuando pasa un tren. || Oscilar (to swing to and fro). || FIG. Vibrar (*with*, de).
— V. tr. Hacer vibrar.
vibratile ['vaibrətail] adj. Vibrátil.
vibrating [vai'breitiŋ] adj. Vibrante. || Vibratorio, ria: *vibrating movement*, movimiento vibratorio. || FIG. Vibrante: *voice vibrating with emotion*, voz vibrante de emoción.
vibration [vai'breiʃən] n. Vibración, *f.* || Oscilación, *f.* (of a pendulum).
vibrato [vi'brɑːtəu] n. MUS. Vibrato, *m.*
vibrator [vai'breitə*] n. Vibrador, *m.* || MUS. Lengüeta, *f.*
vibratory [—ri] adj. Vibratorio, ria.
vibrio ['vibriəu] n. MED. Vibrión, *m.*
vibromassage ['vaibrəuˌmæsɑːʒ] n. MED. Vibromasaje, *m.*
vicar ['vikə*] n. REL. Vicario, *m.*: *the Pope is the Vicar of Christ*, el Papa es el Vicario de Jesucristo. | Cura, *m.*, párroco, *m.* (of a parish). | Vicario, *m.* (bishop's assistant).
— OBSERV. El *vicar* es un pastor de la Iglesia anglicana titular de un beneficio eclesiástico.
vicarage [—ridʒ] n. Casa (*f.*) del párroco.
vicar-general [—'dʒenərəl] n. Vicario (*m.*) general.
vicarial [vai'kɛəriəl] adj. Vicarial.
vicariate [vai'kɛəriit] n. Vicariato, *m.*, vicaría, *f.*
vicarious [vai'kɛəriəs] adj. Delegado, da (authority). || Sustituto, ta (agent). || Hecho por otro (work). || Sufrido por otro (punishment). || Indirecto, ta (pleasure, thrill).
vicariously [—li] adv. Por otro, indirectamente.
vice [vais] n. Vicio, *m.* (depravity). || Vicio, *m.*, defecto, *m.* (fault). || Resabio, *m.* (of a horse). || TECH. Torno (*m.*) de banco, tornillo (*m.*) de banco.
vice ['vaisi] prep. En lugar de, sustituyendo a, en vez de.
vice admiral ['vais'ædmərəl] n. Vicealmirante, *m.*
vice admiralty [—ti] n. Vicealmirantazgo, *m.*
vice-chairman ['vais'tʃɛəmən] n. Vicepresidente, *m.*
— OBSERV. El plural de esta palabra es *vice-chairmen*.
vice-chairmanship [—ʃip] n. Vicepresidencia, *f.*
vice-chancellor ['vais'tʃɑːnsələ*] n. Vicecanciller, *m.* (of a country). || Rector, *m.* (of a university). || *Vice-chancellor's office*, vicecancillería, *f.*; rectoría, *f.*
vice-chancellorship [—ʃip] n. Vicecancillería, *f.* (in a country). || Rectorado, *m.* (in a university).
vice-clamp ['vaisˌklæmp] n. TECH. Mordaza, *f.*, tenaza, *f.*
vice-consul ['vais'kɔnsəl] n. Vicecónsul, *m.*
vice-consulate ['vais'kɔnsjulit] n. Viceconsulado, *m.*
vicegerent ['vais'dʒerənt] n. Representante, *m.*
vice-governor ['vais'gʌvənə*] n. Vicegobernador, *m.*
vicenary ['visənəri] adj. Vigesimal.
vice-presidency ['vais'prezidənsi] n. Vicepresidencia, *f.*
vice-president ['vais'prezidənt] n. Vicepresidente, *m.*
vice-rector ['vais'rektə*] n. Vicerrector, *m.*
vicereine ['vais'rein] n. Virreina, *f.*
viceroy ['vaisrɔi] n. Virrey, *m.*
viceroyalty ['vaisrɔiəlti] n. Virreinato, *m.*
vice squad ['vaisskwɔd] n. Brigada (*f.*) contra el vicio.
vice versa ['vaisi'vəːsə] adv. Viceversa.
vicinage ['visinidʒ] n. Vecindad, *f.* (neighbourhood). || Vecinos, *m. pl.* (persons).
vicinal ['visinəl] adj. Vecinal: *vicinal roads*, caminos vecinales.
vicinity ['visiniti] n. Vecindad, *f.*, proximidad, *f.* (nearness). || Vecindad, *f.*, inmediaciones, *f. pl.* (neighbourhood). || Región, *f.*: *the roads in the vicinity*, las carreteras de la región. || — *In the vicinity of a large town*, cerca de una gran ciudad. || *In the vicinity of twenty*, alrededor de unos veinte.
vicious ['viʃəs] adj. Vicioso, sa (given to vice, characterized by vice). || Depravado, da; pervertido, da (depraved). || Disoluto, ta (life). || Corrompido, da (taste). || Incorrecto, ta; vicioso, sa (reasoning). || Resabiado, da (horse). || Malo, la (bad): *vicious style*, estilo malo. || Malintencionado, da (with evil intent). || Rencoroso, sa (rancorous). || Atroz, horrible (crime). || Fuerte: *a vicious pull*, un tirón fuerte. || Violento, ta (violent). || FIG. *Vicious circle*, círculo vicioso.
viciously [—li] adj. Viciosamente (depravedly). || Con mala intención (spitefully). || Furiosamente, con rabia (angrily). || Incorrectamente (incorrectly).
viciousness [—nis] n. Lo vicioso. || Perversidad, *f.*, depravación, *f.* (depravation). || Maldad, *f.* (evil). || Resabios, *m. pl.* (of a horse).
vicissitude [vi'sisitjuːd] n. Vicisitud, *f.*
vicissitudinous [viˌsisi'tjuːdinəs] adj. Agitado, da; lleno de vicisitudes.
victim ['viktim] n. Víctima, *f.*: *he was the victim of an accident*, fue víctima de un accidente; *she was the victim of dishonest shopkeepers*, fue víctima de tenderos poco honrados. || — *Many fell a victim to the plague*, muchos murieron víctimas de la peste. || *To fall a victim to a heavy cold*, coger un resfriado muy fuerte. || *To fall a victim to a woman's charm*, sucumbir ante el atractivo de una mujer.
victimization [ˌviktimai'zeiʃən] n. Persecución, *f.* (persecution). || Represalias, *f. pl.* (in strike settlement): *there shall be no victimization*, no habrá represalias. || *A case of victimization*, un engaño.
victimize ['viktimaiz] v. tr. Tomar como víctima (to make a victim of): *I don't know why you are victimizing me*, no sé por qué me ha tomado como víctima. || Perseguir (to persecute). || Tomar represalias contra (strikers, etc.). || Engañar (to trick).
victor ['viktə*] n. Vencedor, ra; triunfador, ra.
victoria [vik'tɔːriə] n. Victoria, *f.* (carriage). || BOT. Victoria (*f.*) regia.
Victoria [vik'tɔːriə] pr. n. Victoria, *f.*
Victorian [—n] adj./n. Victoriano, na.
victorious [vik'tɔːriəs] adj. Victorioso, sa: *victorious action*, acción victoriosa. || Vencedor, ra; triunfante: *the victorious army*, el ejército vencedor. || De victoria (day). || *To be victorious over s.o.*, vencer a alguien, triunfar de alguien.
victoriously [—li] adv. Victoriosamente. || Triunfalmente: *to receive victoriously*, recibir triunfalmente.
victory ['viktəri] n. Victoria, *f.*: *overwhelming victory*, victoria aplastante; *to gain* o *to win a victory over s.o.*, obtener una victoria sobre uno. || Triunfo, *m.* || FIG. Triunfo, *m.* (success). || *Pyrrhic victory*, victoria pírrica.
victress ['viktris] n. Triunfadora, *f.*, vencedora, *f.*
victual ['vitəl] v. tr. Abastecer, aprovisionar. || MIL. Avituallar, aprovisionar.
— V. intr. Abastecerse, tomar provisiones. || MIL. Avituallarse, tomar provisiones. || Comer (to eat).
victualer or **victualler** [—ə*] n. Proveedor, ra; abastecedor, ra (supplier). || MAR. Buque (*m.*) abastecedor. || *Licensed victualler*, vendedor (*m.*) de bebidas alcohólicas.
victualing or **victualling** [—iŋ] n. Abastecimiento, *m.* || MIL. Avituallamiento, *m.*, aprovisionamiento, *m.*
victuals [—z] pl. n. Vituallas, *f.* (food). || Provisiones, *f.*, víveres, *m.*
vicuna or **vicuña** or **vicugna** [vi'kjuːnə] n. Vicuña, *f.*
vide ['vaidi] v. tr. Véase: *vide ante*, véase lo anterior; *vide infra*, véase más adelante; *vide supra*, véase más arriba.
— OBSERV. *Vide* es la segunda persona del singular del imperativo del verbo latino *videre*. Tiene dos abreviaturas: *v.* y *vid.*
videlicet [vi'diːliset] adv. A saber, es decir.
— OBSERV. La abreviatura de este adverbio es *viz.*
video ['vidiəu] n. RAD. Video, *m.* | Televisión, *f.*
— Adj. Video: *video signal*, señal video. || *Video tape*, cinta magnética para grabar programas de televisión.
vie [vai] v. intr. Competir, rivalizar: *I refuse to vie with him over sth. so silly*, me niego a competir con él por una cosa tan tonta. || — *They vie with one another for the first place*, se disputan el primer puesto. || *To vie in civilities with*, rivalizar en cortesía con.
Vienna [vi'enə] pr. n. GEOGR. Viena, *f.*
Viennese [ˌviə'niːz] adj./n. Vienés, esa.
Vietnam ['vjet'næm] pr. n. GEOGR. Vietnam, *m.*
Vietnamese [ˌvjetnə'miːz] adj./n. Vietnamita.
view [vjuː] n. Vista, *f.*, panorama, *m.*: *you get a lovely view from the castle*, tiene un paronama magnífico desde el castillo. || Vista, *f.*: *your room has a fine view of the park*, tu habitación tiene una bonita vista del parque. || Vista, *f.* (photo): *views of London*, vistas de Londres. || ARTS. Vista, *f.* (scene). | Paisaje, *m.* (landscape). || Inspección, *f.*: *they asked for a view of the boat*, pidieron una inspección del barco. || Idea,

f.: *he holds extremist views*, tiene ideas extremistas. || Visión (*f.*) de conjunto, panorama, *m.* (survey): *he gave us a view of contemporary literature*, nos dio un panorama de la literatura contemporánea. || Opinión, *f.*, parecer, *m.* (opinion): *in my view*, a mi parecer, en mi opinión. || Enfoque, *m.* (approach). || — *At first view*, a primera vista. || *Exchange of views*, cambio (*m.*) de impresiones. || *Exposed to view*, expuesto a las miradas. || *Field of view*, campo (*m.*) de visión. || *From my point of view*, desde mi punto de vista. || *Front view of a house*, casa vista de frente. || *Hidden from view*, tapado, da. || *House with a sea view*, casa (*f.*) con vistas al mar. || *I have nothing in view tonight*, no tengo ningún plan para esta noche. || *In full view of the crowd*, ante la multitud, a la vista de la multitud. || *In view of*, dado, considerando, en vista de, a la vista de: *in view of the problems*, considerando los problemas. || FIG. *Overall view*, visión de conjunto, vista de conjunto. || *Panoramic view*, vista panorámica. || *Point of view*, punto (*m.*) de vista. || *Private view*, inauguración (*f.*) de una exposición de arte. || *To be in view*, estar a la vista. || *To be on view*, estar expuesto. || *To be on view to the public*, estar abierto al público. || *To come into view*, aparecer. || *To get a better view of*, ver mejor. || *To get a bird's eye view of the town*, tener una vista panorámica de la ciudad. || *To get a side view of sth.*, ver algo de lado. || *To go out of view*, desaparecer. || *To have a closer view of*, ver más de cerca. || *To have sth. in view*, tener algo a la vista: *I have a project in view*, tengo un proyecto a la vista; tener en cuenta, tener presente (to keep in mind). || *To keep sth. in view*, no perder algo de vista. || *To take a dim view of*, ver con malos ojos. || *To take a favourable view of*, ver con buenos ojos. || *To take the view that*, pensar que, tener la impresión de que. || *What are your views of this?*, ¿cuáles son sus opiniones acerca de esto?, ¿cuál es su parecer acerca de esto?, ¿qué opina de esto? || *With a view*, con buena vista. || *With a view to*, con miras a, con vistas a, con objeto de: *negotiations with a view to an alliance*, negociaciones con vistas a una alianza. || *With this in view*, con este objetivo, con este fin.

view [vju:] v. tr. Mirar, ver (to look at). || Ver, visitar: *they are coming to view the room*, vienen a ver la habitación. || Inspeccionar (to inspect). || Considerar, ver (to consider): *he views the matter from the taxpayer's standpoint*, considera el asunto desde el punto de vista del contribuyente. || Enfocar, considerar: *the subject may be viewed in various ways*, el tema se puede enfocar de varias maneras.

viewer [—ə*] n. Telespectador, ra; televidente, *m.* & *f.* (television watcher). || Espectador, ra (onlooker). || Inspector, ra. || PHOT. Visionadora, *f.* (for slides).

viewfinder [—ˌfaində*] n. PHOT. Visor, *m.*

viewing [—iŋ] n. Visita, *f.*: *show flat open for viewing from 9 till 12*, visita del piso modelo de 9 a 12. || Inspección, *f.*

viewless [—lis] adj. Sin vista (house). || Invisible. || Sin opinión.

viewpoint [—pɔint] n. Punto (*m.*) de vista: *from my viewpoint*, desde mi punto de vista. || Mirador, *m.*

viewy [—i] adj. U. S. Visionario, ria.

vigesimal [vaiˈdʒesiməl] adj. Vigesimal.

vigil [ˈvidʒil] n. Vigilia, *f.*, vela, *f.* || Vela, *f.*: *the vigil of a corpse*, la vela de un cadáver. || REL. Vigilia, *f.* || *To keep vigil*, velar.

vigilance [—əns] n. Vigilancia, *f.*: *they escaped the police's vigilance*, burlaron la vigilancia de la policía. || MED. Insomnio, *m.* || *Vigilance committee*, vigilancia.

vigilant [—ənt] adj. Vigilante.

vigilante [ˌvidʒiˈlænti] n. U. S. Vigilante, *m.*

vignette [viˈnjet] n PRINT. Viñeta, *f.* (ornamentation). || Retrato (*m.*) de medio cuerpo con bordes desvanecidos (portrait, photo). || THEATR. Sainete, *m.*

vigor [ˈvigə*] n. U. S. See VIGOUR

vigorous [—rəs] adj. Vigoroso, sa: *a vigorous man*, un hombre vigoroso. || Enérgico, ca: *a vigorous massage*, un masaje enérgico.

vigour [ˈvigə*] n. Vigor, *m.*, energía, *f.* || FIG. Vigor, *m.*, fuerza, *f.* (of style). || — *In vigour*, en vigor, vigente (law). || *Man of vigour*, hombre enérgico.

Viking [ˈvaikiŋ] n. Vikingo, *m.*

vilayet [viˈlɑ:jet] n. Vilayato, *m.* (Turkish province).

vile [vail] adj. Vil, ruin (morally base): *the vilest of men*, el hombre más ruin. || Infame: *a vile calumny*, una calumnia infame. || Malísimo, ma (very bad). || Asqueroso, sa; repugnante: *a vile smell*, un olor repugnante. || Pésimo, ma; horrible, espantoso, sa; de perros (weather). || Muy malo, la; de perros (temper): *he is in a vile temper*, está de muy mal humor, está de un humor de perros. || Sin valor (worthless).

vilely [—li] adv. Vilmente. || De una manera infame. || Malísimamente (very badly). || Horriblemente.

vileness [—nis] n. Vileza, *f.* (baseness). || Infamia, *f.* (infamy). || Bajeza, *f.* (of a sentiment). || *The vileness of the weather*, el tiempo pésimo que hace.

vilification [ˌvilifiˈkeiʃən] n. Denigración, *f.*, difamación, *f.*

vilifier [ˈvilifaiə*] n. Difamador, ra; denigrador, ra.

vilify [ˈvilifai] v. tr. Denigrar, difamar.

vilipend [ˈvilipend] v. tr. Vilipendiar.

vilipender [—ə*] n. Vilipendiador, ra.

villa [ˈvilə] n. Casa (*f.*) de campo, quinta, *f.* (country house). || Chalet, *m.* (suburban residence).

village [ˈvilidʒ] n. Pueblo, *m.* (large). || Aldea, *f.*, pueblecito, *m.* (small).
— Adj. Pueblerino, na: *village life*, vida pueblerina. || Del pueblo: *the village idiot*, el tonto del pueblo.

villager [—ə*] n. Aldeano, na.

villain [ˈvilən] n. Canalla, *m.*, maleante, *m.* (s.o. wicked): *some villain robbed the widow of her savings*, un canalla robó a la viuda sus ahorros. || FAM. Bribón, ona: *this child is a villain*, este niño es un bribón. || THEATR. Malo, *m.* | (Ant.). Siervo (*m.*) de la gleba, villano, na (villein). || FIG. *The villain of the piece*, el responsable.

villainous [—əs] adj. Vil, infame: *a villainous deed*, una acción infame. || Horrible, espantoso, sa; pésimo, ma; de perros: *villainous weather*, tiempo de perros. || Malísimo, ma; espantoso, sa; pésimo, ma: *villainous handwriting*, letra malísima.

villainy [—i] n. Villanía, *f.*, maldad, *f.*, vileza, *f.* (villainous act). || Infamia, *f.*, maldad, *f.*, vileza, *f.* (of an action).

villein [ˈvilin] n. Siervo (*m.*) de la gleba, villano, na.

villeinage [—idʒ] n. Villanía, *f.*, villanaje, *m.*

villosity [viˈlɔsiti] n. Vellosidad, *f.*

vim [vim] n. FAM. Energía, *f.*: *full of vim*, lleno de energía. || — *Put some vim into it!*, ¡dale fuerte! || *¡Put some vim into your work!*, ¡dale fuerte al trabajo!

vinaceous [viˈneiʃəs] adj. Vinoso, sa (colour).

vinaigrette [viniˈgret] n. Vinagrera, *f.* (container). || Vinagreta, *f.* (sauce). || Frasco (*m.*) de sales (for smelling salts).

Vincent [ˈvinsənt] pr. n. Vicente, *m.*

vindicable [ˈvindikəbl] adj. Justificable.

vindicate [ˈvindikeit] v. tr. Justificar (one's behaviour). || Defender (one's faith). || Mantener, sostener (one's opinion). || Reivindicar (one's rights). || *To vindicate o.s.*, justificarse.

vindication [ˌvindiˈkeiʃən] n. Justificación, *f.* || Reivindicación, *f.* (of one's rights).

vindicative [vinˈdikətiv] adj. Justificativo, va.

vindicator [ˈvindikeitə*] n. Defensor, *m.*

vindicatory [—ri] adj. Justificativo, va (vindicative). || Vindicativo, va (vindictive).

vindictive [vinˈdiktiv] adj. Vindicativo, va; vengativo, va. || Impuesto como venganza (punishment). || *There is no need to feel vindictive towards him*, no hay por qué guardarle rencor.

vindictiveness [—nis] n. Carácter (*m.*) vengativo. || Rencor, *m.* (resentment).

vine [vain] n. BOT. Vid, *f.* (grapevine). | Sarmiento, *m.* (stem). || Parra, *f.*: *to sit under the vine*, sentarse bajo la parra. || U. S. BOT. Enredadera, *f.*, planta (*f.*) trepadora (climbing plant).

vine arbour (U. S. **vine arbor**) [—ˌɑ:bə*] n. Parra, *f.*

vinedresser [—ˌdresə*] n. Viñador, *m.*, viñatero, *m.*

vinegar [ˈvinigə*] n. Vinagre, *m.* || — *Vinegar bottle*, vinagrera, *f.* || *Vinegar cruet*, vinagreras, *f. pl.* || *Vinegar maker*, vinagrero, *m.* || *Vinegar sauce*, vinagreta, *f.*

vinegary [—ri] adj. Avinagrado, da.

vine grower [ˈvainˌgrəuə*] n. Viticultor, *m.*, viñador, *m.* (viticulturist).

vine growing [ˈvainˌgrəuiŋ] n. Viticultura, *f.*

vine leaf [ˈvainli:f] n. Hoja (*f.*) de parra *or* de vid.

vinery [ˈvainəri] n. Invernadero (*m.*) para el cultivo de la vid (greenhouse).

vine shoot [ˈvainʃu:t] n. Sarmiento, *m.*

vinestock [ˈvainstɔk] n. Cepa, *f.*

vineyard [ˈvinjəd] n. Viña, *f.*, viñedo, *m.* || REL. *To work in the Lord's vineyard*, trabajar en la viña del Señor.

vinic [ˈvainik] adj. Vínico, ca.

vinicultural [ˌviniˈkʌltʃərəl] adj. Vinícola, vitivinícola.

viniculture [ˈvinikʌltʃə*] n. Vinicultura, *f.*, viticultura, *f.*

vinification [ˌvinifiˈkeiʃən] n. Vinificación, *f.*

vinous [ˈvainəs] adj. Vinoso, sa. || De color de vino. || FIG. Borracho, cha (drunk).

vintage [ˈvintidʒ] n. Vendimia, *f.* (season, harvest). || Cosecha, *f.* (crop): *the 1960 vintage*, la cosecha de 1960.
— Adj. De calidad, añejo, ja (wine). || Antiguo, gua (car). || Muy bueno, na; excelente: *a vintage year for sport, wine*, un año excelente para el deporte, el vino. || Antiguo, gua: *a vintage joke*, un chiste antiguo.

vintager [—ə*] n. Vendimiador, ra.

vintner [ˈvintnə*] n. Vinatero, *m.*

viny [ˈvaini] adj. Vinícola.

vinyl [ˈvainil] n. CHEM. Vinilo, *m.*
— Adj. Vinílico, ca.

viol [ˈvaiəl] n. MUS. Viola, *f.*

viola [viˈəulə] n. MUS. Viola, *f.* || BOT. Violeta, *f.*

violaceous [vaiəˈleiʃəs] adj. Violáceo, a.

viola da gamba [viˈəulədaˈgæmbə] n. MUS. Viola (*f.*) de gamba.

violate [ˈvaiəleit] v. tr. Violar, infringir, quebrantar (a law). || No cumplir (promise). || Violar (a woman). || Violar, profanar (sacred place). || *To violate s.o.'s privacy*, meterse en la vida privada de alguien.

violation [ˌvaiəˈleiʃən] n. Violación, *f.* (of woman, secret). || Violación, *f.*, infracción, *f.* (of law). || Profanación, *f.* (of sacred place).

violator [ˈvaiəleitə*] n. Violador, ra.

violence [ˈvaiələns] n. Violencia, *f.* || — JUR. *Acts of violence*, vías (*f.*) de hecho. || *To die by violence*, morir violentamente. || *To do violence to*, violentar (to use violence on), ir en contra de (one's principles). || *To resort to violence*, recurrir a la violencia *or* a la fuerza. || *To use violence*, emplear la violencia.
violent [ˈvaiələnt] adj. Violento, ta: *a violent storm*, una tormenta violenta. || Chillón, ona: *violent colours*, colores chillones. || Intenso, sa: *violent pain*, dolor intenso. || Profundo, da: *a violent dislike*, una profunda antipatía. || — *To become violent*, mostrarse violento. || *To be in a violent temper*, estar furioso. || *To lay violent hands on o.s.*, atentar contra su vida. || *To lay violent hands on s.o.*, agredir a alguien.
violently [—li] adv. Violentamente: *to die violently*, morir violentamente. || Terriblemente, extremadamente: *she was violently upset*, estaba terriblemente disgustada. || Furiosamente, perdidamente: *to fall violently in love*, enamorarse furiosamente. || *To be violently sick* o *ill*, vomitar mucho.
violet [ˈvəiəlit] n. BOT. Violeta, *f.* (flower). || Violado, *m.*, violeta, *m.* (colour). || — *Violet seller*, violetera, *f.* || *Violet wood*, palisandro, *m.*
— Adj. Violado, da; violeta.
violin [ˌvaiəˈlin] n. MUS. Violín, *m.* (instrument). | Violín, *m.*, violinista, *m.* & *f.*: *first violin*, primer violín.
violinist [—ist] n. MUS. Violinista, *m.* & *f.*
violoncellist [ˌvaiələnˈtʃelist] n. MUS. Violonchelista, *m.* & *f.*, violoncelista, *m.* & *f.*
violoncello [ˌvaiələnˈtʃeləu] n. MUS. Violonchelo, *m.*, violoncelo, *m.*
VIP [ˈvi:aiˈpi:] n. Personalidad, *f.*
— OBSERV. VIP es la abreviatura de *Very Important Person* (persona muy importante).
viper [ˈvaipə*] n. ZOOL. FIG. Víbora, *f.*
viperine [—rain] adj. Viperino, na.
viperish [—riʃ] adj. FIG. Viperino, na (tongue).
viperous [—rəs] adj. Viperino, na.
viper's grass [—sˈgrɑ:s] n. BOT. Escorzonera, *f.*
virago [viˈrɑ:gəu] n. Virago, *f.*, mujer (*f.*) varonil (manlike). || Fiera, *f.*, arpía, *f.* (quarrelsome).
— OBSERV. El plural de la palabra inglesa es *viragoes* o *viragos*.
Virgil [ˈvə:dʒil] pr. n. Virgilio, *m.*
virgin [ˈvə:dzin] n. Virgen, *f.* || ASTR. Virgo, *m.* || — REL. *The Blessed Virgin*, la Virgen Santísima. | *The Virgin*, la Virgen. | *The Virgin Mary*, la Virgen María, María Santísima. || GEOGR. *Virgin Islands*, Islas (*f.*) Vírgenes.
— Adj. Virgen: *virgin forest*, selva virgen; *virgin wax*, cera virgen. || *Virgin birth*, parto (*m.*) virginal de María (of Jesus Christ), partenogénesis, *f.* (in zoology).
virginal [—əl] adj. Virginal.
— N. MUS. Espineta, *f.*
virginhood [—hud] n. Virginidad, *f.*
Virginia [vəˈdʒiniə] pr. n. GEOGR. Virginia, *f.* || BOT. *Virginia creeper*, viña loca.
Virginian [—n] adj./n. Virginiano, na.
virginity [və:ˈdʒiniti] n. Virginidad, *f.*
Virgo [ˈvə:gəu] pr. n. ASTR. Virgo, *m.*
virgule [ˈvə:gju:l] n. Vírgula, *f.*
viridescent [ˌviriˈdesnt] adj. Verdusco, ca; verdoso, sa (greenish).
viridity [viˈriditi] n. Verdor, *m.*
virile [ˈvirail] adj. Varonil, viril. || FIG. Enérgico, ca; viril. || ANAT. *Virile member*, miembro viril.
virility [viˈriliti] n. Virilidad, *f.*
virtu [və:tu:] n. Afición (*f.*) a los objetos de arte y a las antigüedades (knowledge, liking). || Objetos (*m. pl.*) de arte, curiosidades, *f. pl.*, antigüedades, *f. pl.* (curios, etc.).
virtual [ˈvə:tjuəl] adj. Verdadero, ra: *he is the virtual head of the firm*, es el verdadero jefe de la empresa; *it was a virtual confession*, fue una verdadera confesión. || PHYS. Virtual: *virtual focus*, foco virtual; *virtual image*, imagen virtual.
virtuality [ˌvə:tjuˈæliti] n. Virtualidad, *f.*
virtually [ˈvə:tjuəli] adv. Prácticamente, casi: *I am virtually certain of it*, estoy casi seguro de ello; *it's virtually impossible*, es casi imposible.
virtue [ˈvə:tju:] n. Virtud, *f.* (of a person). || Virtud, *f.* (as a remedy). || Ventaja, *f.*: *it has the virtue of being small*, tiene la ventaja de ser pequeño; *I cannot see the virtue of it*, no le veo la ventaja. || Castidad, *f.*, honra, *f.*, honestidad, *f.* (female chastity). || REL. Virtud, *f.* || — *By* o *in virtue of*, debido a, en virtud de: *he can do it by virtue of his position*, lo puede hacer debido a su posición. || *To make a virtue of necessity*, hacer de necesidad virtud. || *Woman of easy virtue*, mujer ligera. || *Woman of virtue*, mujer honesta.
virtuosity [ˌvə:tjuˈɔsiti] n. Virtuosismo, *m.*, virtuosidad, *f.*
virtuoso [ˌvə:tjuˈəuzəu] n. Virtuoso, sa (musician). || Coleccionista, *m.* & *f.*, aficionado a los objetos de arte.
— OBSERV. El plural de la palabra inglesa *virtuoso* es *virtuosos* o *virtuosi*.
virtuous [ˈvə:tjuəs] adj. Virtuoso, sa.
virtuousness [—nis] n. Virtud, *f.*
virulence [ˈviruləns] n. Virulencia, *f.*
virulent [ˈvirulənt] adj. Virulento, ta.
virus [ˈvaiərəs] n. MED. Virus, *m.*
visa [ˈvi:zə] n. Visado, *m.* [*Amer.*, visa, *f.*].
visa [ˈvi:zə] v. tr. Visar.
visage [ˈvizidʒ] n. Rostro, *m.*, cara, *f.* (face). || Semblante, *m.* (countenance). || Aspecto, *m.*
vis-à-vis [ˈvi:zɑ:ˈvi:] n. Persona (*f.*) colocada enfrente de *or* frente a otra: *my vis-à-vis at table*, la persona colocada frente a mí en la mesa. || Confidente, *m.* (sofa).
— Prep. Respecto a, acerca de (about): *his opinion vis-à-vis the crisis*, su opinión acerca de la crisis. || Comparado con, con relación a: *the situation vis-à-vis what it was yesterday*, la situación comparada con lo que era ayer. || Enfrente de (opposite): *vis-à-vis the Town Hall*, enfrente del Ayuntamiento.
— Adv. Cara a cara, frente a frente.
viscacha [visˈkætʃæ] n. Vizcacha, *f.* (rodent).
viscera [ˈvisərə] pl. n. ANAT. Vísceras, *f.*
visceral [—l] adj. Visceral.
viscid [ˈvisid] adj. Viscoso, sa; pegajoso, sa.
viscidity [viˈsiditi] n. Viscosidad, *f.*
viscose [ˈviskəs] n. Viscosa, *f.*
— Adj. Viscoso, sa. || De viscosa.
viscosity [visˈkɔsiti] n. Viscosidad, *f.*
viscount [ˈvaikaunt] n. Vizconde, *m.*
viscountcy [—si] n. Vizcondado, *m.*
viscountess [—is] n. Vizcondesa, *f.*
viscounty [—i] n. Vizcondado, *m.*
viscous [ˈviskəs] adj. Viscoso, sa.
vise [ˈvais] n. U. S. TECH. Torno (*m.*) *or* tornillo (*m.*) de banco.
visé [ˈvi:zei] n./v. tr. See VISA.
visibility [ˌviziˈbiliti] n. Visibilidad, *f.*: *visibility is down to five metres*, la visibilidad queda reducida a cinco metros.
visible [ˈvizəbl] adj. Visible. || Manifiesto, ta; evidente (obvious).
visibleness [—nis] n. Visibilidad, *f.*
visibly [—i] adv. Visiblemente.
Visigoth [ˈvizigɔθ] n. Visigodo, da.
Visigothic [ˌviziˈgɔθik] adj. Visigodo, da; visigótico, ca.
vision [ˈviʒən] n. Visión, *f.*: *the eye is the organ of vision*, el ojo es el órgano de la visión. || Vista, *f.*: *to have normal vision*, tener la vista normal; *within the range of vision*, al alcance de la vista. || Visión, *f.* (apparition). || Sueño, *m.* (dream): *my vision of being a king*, mi sueño de ser rey. || Clarividencia, *f.*, perspicacia, *f.* (foresight). || Belleza, *f.* (beauty): *that woman is a vision*, esa mujer es una belleza. || — *A man of vision*, un hombre clarividente. || *Field of vision*, campo (*m.*) visual. || *I had visions of being behind bars*, me veía ya encarcelado. || *To have visions of fame*, soñar con ser famoso.
vision [ˈviʒən] v. tr. Imaginar.
visional [—əl] adj. Quimérico, ca; imaginario, ria.
visionary [—əri] adj. Visionario, ria (who sees visions). || Soñador, ra (dreaming). || Quimérico, ca; imaginario, ria (imaginary). || Utópico, ca (impractical).
— N. Visionario, ria. || Soñador, ra (dreamer).
visit [ˈvizit] n. Visita, *f.*: *a brief visit to Rome*, una corta visita a Roma. || MAR. Visita, *f.* (of a ship). || — FIG. *Flying visit*, visita relámpago *or* de médico. || JUR. *Right of visit*, derecho (*m.*) de visita. || *To be on a visit to*, estar de visita en. || FAM. *To pay a visit*, ir al excusado. || *To pay s.o. a visit*, visitar a alguien, hacer una visita a alguien. || *To return a visit*, devolver una visita.
visit [ˈvizit] v. tr. Visitar, ir a (to go to). || Visitar, hacer una visita a (to call on). || Pasar una temporada en (to stay in). || Visitar (a church, the sick). || Visitar, inspeccionar: *the bishop visits his diocese*, el obispo inspecciona su diócesis. || REL. Infligir (punishment). | Castigar por (s.o.'s sins). || FIG. Azotar (by a disease).
— V. intr. Hacer visitas. || U. S. FAM. Charlar.
Visitandine [ˌviziˈtændi:n] n. REL. Visitandina, *f.*
visitant [ˈvizitənt] n. ZOOL. Ave (*f.*) de paso. || Visitante, *m.* & *f.* (visitor).
visitation [ˌviziˈteiʃən] n. Visita, *f.*: *pastoral visitation*, visita pastoral. || REL. Visitación, *f.* (feast). | Castigo, *m.* (punishment). || MAR. Visita, *f.* (of a ship). || ZOOL. Migración (*f.*) anormal. || *Sisters of the Visitation*, Visitandinas, *f.*
visiting [ˈvizitiŋ] adj. De visita: *visiting card*, tarjeta de visita; *visiting hours*, horas de visita. || Visitante: *visiting team*, equipo visitante. || *Visiting lecturer*, conferenciante venido de fuera.
visitor [ˈvizitə*] n. Visitante, *m.* & *f.*, visita, *f.* || — *I'm expecting visitors tonight*, tengo visitas esta noche. || *Visitors from Mars*, seres venidos de Marte.
visor [ˈvaizə*] n. Visera, *f.* (of helmet, cap, windscreen).
vista [ˈvistə] n. Vista, *f.*, perspectiva, *f.* || FIG. Perspectiva, *f.*, horizonte, *m.*
visual [ˈvizjuəl] adj. Visual: *visual field*, campo visual. || Visible. || Óptico, ca (nerve). || Ocular: *visual inspection*, inspección ocular; *visual proof*, prueba ocular. || *Visual aids*, medios (*m.*) visuales.
visualization [ˌvizjuəlaiˈzeiʃən] n. Imagen (*f.*) mental (mental picture). || Visualización, *f.* (action).
visualize [ˈvizjuəlaiz] v. tr. Imaginar, imaginarse: *I cannot visualize this room painted blue*, no puedo imaginar esta habitación pintada de azul. || Prever, proyectar: *we visualize great changes in the company*, prevemos grandes cambios en la sociedad.

vital [ˈvaitəl] adj. Vital: *vital organs,* órganos vitales. || Fundamental, esencial: *it is vital that we understand each other,* es fundamental que nos entendamos. || Sumo, ma; capital: *of vital importance,* de suma importancia. || Enérgico, ca; vivo, va (lively). || Mortal (fatal). || Crucial (moment). || — *Vital force,* impulso (*m.*) vital, "elan" (*m.*) vital. || *Vital statistics,* mensuraciones, *f.* (of a woman), estadísticas demográficas (population figures).
— Pl. n. Órganos (*m.*) vitales. || MAR. Obras (*f.*) vivas. || FIG. Partes (*f.*) esenciales.
vitalism [ˈvaitəlizəm] n. Vitalismo, *m.*
vitalist [ˈvaitəlist] n. Vitalista, *m.* & *f.*
vitalistic [ˌvaitəˈlistik] adj. Vitalista.
vitality [vaiˈtæliti] n. Vitalidad, *f.*
vitalization [ˌvaitəlaiˈzeiʃən] n. Vitalización, *f.*
vitalize [ˈvaitəlaiz] v. tr. Vitalizar, vivificar. || FIG. Animar.
vitally [ˈvaitəli] adv. *A vitally important document,* un documento de suma importancia. || *It is vitally important that,* es fundamental *or* esencial que.
vitamin [ˈvitəmin] n. Vitamina, *f.* || — *Enriched with vitamins,* vitaminado, da. || *Vitamin deficiency,* avitaminosis, *f. inv.*
vitaminic [ˌvitəˈminik] adj. Vitamínico, ca.
vitaminized [ˈvitəminaizd] adj. Vitaminado, da.
vitelline [ˈvitəli:n] adj. Vitelino, na: *vitelline membrane,* membrana vitelina.
vitellus [ˈviteləs] n. Vitelo, *m.*
vitiate [ˈviʃieit] v. tr. Viciar, contaminar (blood, air). || Viciar, corromper (to corrupt). || JUR. Viciar, invalidar.
vitiation [ˌviʃiˈeiʃən] n. Contaminación, *f.* || Corrupción, *f.* || JUR. Invalidación, *f.*
viticultural [ˌvitiˈkʌltʃərəl] adj. Vitícola.
viticulture [ˈvitikʌltʃə*] n. Viticultura, *f.*
viticulturist [ˌvitiˈkʌltʃərist] n. Viticultor, *m.*
vitiligo [ˌvitəˈlaigəu] n. MED. Vitíligo, *m.*
vitreous [ˈvitriəs] adj. Vítreo, a. || — *Vitreous body* o *humour,* humor vítreo. || *Vitreous electricity,* electricidad vítrea.
vitrifaction [ˌvitriˈfækʃən] n. Vitrificación, *f.*
vitrifiable [ˈvitrifaiəbl] adj. Vitrificable.
vitrification [ˌvitrifiˈkeiʃən] n. Vitrificación, *f.*
vitriform [ˈvitrifɔ:m] adj. Vítreo, a.
vitrify [ˈvitrifai] v. tr. Vitrificar.
— V. intr. Vitrificarse.
vitriol [ˈvitriəl] n. CHEM. Vitriolo, *m.* || FIG. Virulencia, *f.*, causticidad, *f.* (of s.o.'s words). | Veneno, *m.* (caustic words).
vitriol [ˈvitriəl] v. tr. Vitriolar.
vitriolic [ˌvitriˈɔlik] adj. CHEM. Vitriólico, ca. || FIG. Virulento, ta; mordaz.
vituperate [viˈtju:pəreit] v. tr. Vituperar.
vituperation [viˌtju:pəˈreiʃən] n. Vituperación, *f.*, vituperio, *m.*
vituperative [viˈtju:pərətiv] adj. Vituperioso, sa; vituperador, ra; vituperante.
vivacious [viˈveiʃəs] adj. Vivo, va (full of life). || Vivaracho, cha (sprightly). || BOT. Vivaz.
vivaciousness [—nis] or **vivacity** [viˈvæsiti] n. Viveza, *f.*, vivacidad, *f.*
vivarium [vaiˈveəriəm] n. Vivero, *m.*
— OBSERV. El plural de *vivarium* es *vivariums* o *vivaria.*
vica voce [ˈvaivəˈvəusi] adj. Oral: *a viva voce exam,* un examen oral.
— Adv. De viva voz, de palabra.
— N. Examen (*m.*) oral.
vivid [ˈvivid] adj. Vivo, va; intenso, sa (colour). || Gráfico, ca; pintoresco, ca (description). || Vivo, va; fuerte (impression, memory). || Vivo, va (imagination).
vividness [—nis] n. Intensidad, *f.*, viveza, *f.* (of colours, etc.). || Fuerza, *f.* (of style).
vivification [ˌvivifiˈkeiʃən] n. Vivificación, *f.*
vivify [ˈvivifai] v. tr. Vivificar. || Animar.
vivifying [—iŋ] adj. Vivificador, ra; vivificante.
viviparity [ˌviviˈpæriti] n. BOT. ZOOL. Viviparidad, *f.*
viviparous [viˈvipərəs] adj. BOT. ZOOL. Vivíparo, ra.
vivisect [ˌviviˈsekt] v. tr. Hacer la vivisección de (an animal, etc.).
— V. intr. Practicar la vivisección.
vivisection [ˌviviˈsekʃən] n. Vivisección, *f.*
vivisector [ˌviviˈsektə*] n. Vivisector, ra.
vixen [ˈviksən] n. ZOOL. Zorra, *f.*, raposa, *f.* || FIG. Arpía, *f.*
vixenish [—iʃ] adj. Zorruno, na. || FIG. Áspero, ra.
vizier or **vizir** [viˈziə*] n. Visir, *m.* || *Grand vizier* o *visir,* gran visir.
vizierate [—rət] n. Visirato, *m.*
vizor [ˈvaizə*] n. Visera, *f.* (of helmet, cap, windscreen).
vocable [ˈvəukəbl] n. Vocablo, *m.*, voz, *f.*
vocabulary [vəˈkæbjuləri] n. Vocabulario, *m.*
vocal [ˈvəukəl] adj. ANAT. MUS. Vocal. || GRAMM. Vocálico, ca (vocalic). | Sonoro, ra (voiced). || FIG. Ruidoso, sa; gritón, ona: *the more vocal members of the audience,* los miembros más ruidosos de la asistencia. || *Vocal cords,* cuerdas (*f.*) vocales.
vocalic [vəuˈkælik] n. GRAMM. Vocálico, ca.
vocalism [ˈvəukəlizəm] n. GRAMM. Vocalismo, *m.* || MUS. Vocalización, *f.*
vocalist [ˈvəukəlist] n. Vocalista, *m.* & *f.* (in an orchestra). || Cantante, *m.* & *f.* (in a pop group).
vocalization [ˌvəukəlaiˈzeiʃən] n. MUS. GRAMM. Vocalización, *f.*
vocalize [ˈvəukəlaiz] v. tr. GRAMM. Vocalizar. || Cantar (to sing). || Articular (to utter). || Poner las vocales en (a Hebrew text).
— V. intr. Vocalizar.
vocation [vəuˈkeiʃən] n. REL. Vocación, *f.* || Vocación, *f.*, inclinación, *f.*: *he has a vocation for the theatre,* tiene vocación de artista. || Profesión, *f.*, carrera, *f.* (profession). || *To miss* o *to mistake one's vocation,* errar la vocación.
vocational [—əl] adj. Profesional: *vocational training,* formación *or* capacitación profesional; *vocational guidance,* orientación profesional.
vocative [ˈvɔkətiv] n. GRAMM. Vocativo, *m.* || *Vocative case,* vocativo, *m.*
vociferance [vəˈsifərəns] n. Vociferaciones, *f. pl.*
vociferant [vəˈsifərənt] adj. Vociferante.
vociferate [vəˈsifəreit] v. tr. Vociferar.
— V. intr. Vociferar, vocear.
vociferation [vəˌsifəˈreiʃən] n. Vociferación, *f.*
vociferous [vəˈsifərəs] adj. Vociferante.
vociferously [—li] adv. A gritos, ruidosamente.
vodka [ˈvɔdkə] n. Vodka, *f.* & *m.*
vogue [vəug] n. Moda, *f.*, boga, *f.*: *to be in vogue,* estar en boga, estar de moda.
voice [vɔis] n. Voz, *f.*: *shrill voice,* voz chillona. || Tono, *m.* (tone). || GRAMM. Voz, *f.*: *passive voice,* voz pasiva; *active voice,* voz activa. || MUS. Voz, *f.* || — *At the top of one's voice,* a voces, a voz en cuello, a voz en grito. || FIG. *He loves the sound of his own voice,* le gusta escucharse cuando habla. || *High-pitched voice,* voz aguda. || *In a loud voice,* en voz alta. || *In a low voice,* a media voz, en voz baja. || *In a soft voice,* en voz baja. || *Loss of voice,* afonía, *f.* || MUS. *Main* o *principal voice,* voz cantante. || *Soft voice,* voz baja, voz suave. || *The voice of one's conscience,* la voz de la conciencia. || *Thunderous voice,* voz de trueno. || *To be in good voice,* estar en voz. || *To give voice to,* expresar. || *To have a good voice,* tener buena voz. || *To have a voice but no vote,* tener voz consultiva. || *To have no voice in the matter,* no tener voz ni voto en el asunto. || *To lose one's voice,* perder la voz. || *To put on a solemn voice,* ahuecar la voz. || *To raise one's voice,* alzar *or* levantar la voz. || *To strain one's voice,* forzar la voz. || *Voice from the sky,* voz del cielo. || *Voice of the people,* voz del pueblo. || *With one voice,* a una voz, por unanimidad.
voice [vɔis] v. tr. Expresar, hacerse eco de (to express): *he voiced the common feeling,* expresó la opinión de todos. || Articular (to articulate). || MUS. Afinar. || GRAMM. Sonorizar (in phonetics).
voiced [—t] adj. Expresado, da (opinion, etc.). || GRAMM. Sonoro, ra. || *Low-voiced,* con voz baja.
voiceless [—lis] adj. Mudo, da (dumb). || Afónico, ca (from shouting too much). || GRAMM. Sordo, da.
void [vɔid] adj. Vacío, a (empty). || Vacante (post, job). || JUR. Nulo, la; inválido, da. || — *Null and void,* nulo y sin valor. || *To be void of,* estar desprovisto de, carecer de. || JUR. *To make sth. void,* anular algo, invalidar algo.
— N. Vacío, *m.* || Fallo, *m.* (cards): *to have a void in,* tener fallo a. || FIG. Vacío, *m.*: *his death left a great void,* su muerte dejó un gran vacío.
void [vɔid] v. tr. Anular, invalidar (to annul). || Evacuar (to evacuate). || Desocupar, vaciar (to leave).
voidable [—əbl] adj. JUR. Rescindible, anulable.
voidance [—əns] n. REL. Vacante, *f.* || JUR. Anulación, *f.*, invalidación, *f.* || Evacuación, *f.* (emptying).
voidness [—nis] n. Vacío, *m.*, vacuidad, *f.* || JUR. Nulidad, *f.*
voile [vɔil] n. Gasa, *f.* (material).
volant [ˈvəulənt] adj. Volante.
Volapük [ˈvɔləpuk] n. Volapuk, *m.* (language).
volar [ˈvəulə*] adj. Palmar (of the hand). || Plantar (of the foot).
volatile [ˈvɔlətail] adj. Volátil: *volatile oil,* aceite volátil. || FIG. Voluble, inconstante (fickle).
volatileness [—nis] or **volatility** [ˌvɔləˈtiliti] n. Volatilidad, *f.* || FIG. Volubilidad, *f.*, inconstancia, *f.*
volatilization [vɔˌlætilaiˈzeiʃən] n. Volatilización, *f.*
volatilize [vɔˈlætilaiz] v. tr. Volatilizar.
— V. intr. Volatilizarse.
vol-au-vent [ˈvɔləuˈvɑ̃ŋ] n. CULIN. Volován, *m.*
volcanic [vɔlˈkænik] adj. Volcánico, ca. || MIN. *Volcanic glass,* obsidiana, *f.*
volcanicity [ˌvɔlkəˈnisiti] n. Volcanicidad, *f.*
volcanism [ˈvɔlkənizəm] n. Volcanismo, *m.*, vulcanismo, *m.*
volcanist [ˈvɔlkənist] n. Volcanista, *m.*, vulcanista, *m.*
volcanize [ˈvɔlkənaiz] v. tr. Volcanizar.
volcano [vɔlˈkeinəu] n. Volcán, *m.*
— OBSERV. El plural de la palabra inglesa es *volcanoes* o *volcanos.*
volcanologist [ˌvɔlkəˈnɔlədʒist] n. Vulcanólogo, *m.*, vulcanologista, *m.*
volcanology [ˌvɔlkəˈnɔlədʒi] n. Vulcanología, *f.*
vole [vəul] n. Campañol, *m.*, ratón (*m.*) de campo (rodent). || Bolo, *m.*, bola, *f.* (in cards).
volet [ˈvɔlei] n. Hoja, *f.* (of a triptych).
volitant [ˈvɔlitənt] adj. Volante, volador, ra.
volition [vəuˈliʃən] n. Volición, *f.* || *Of one's own volition,* de su propia voluntad.
volitional [—əl] or **volitive** [ˈvɔlitiv] adj. Volitivo, va.

volley [ˈvɔli] n. Andanada, *f.*, descarga (*f.*) cerrada (of bullets). || Lluvia, *f.* (of stones, arrows). || Salva, *f.* (of applause). || Torrente, *m.* (of insults). || SP. Voleo, *m.* (in tennis).
volley [ˈvɔli] v. tr. Lanzar (missiles). || Soltar, dirigir (insults). || SP. Volear.
— V. intr. MIL. Lanzar una descarga. || SP. Volear (in tennis).
volleyball [—bɔːl] n. SP. Balonvolea, *m.* [*Amer.*, voleibol, *m.*].
volplane [ˈvɔlplein] n. AVIAT. Vuelo (*m.*) planeado, planeo, *m.*
volplane [ˈvɔlplein] v. intr. AVIAT. Planear (to glide).
Volsci [ˈvɔlski:] pl. n. Volscos, *m.*
volt [vəult] n. ELECTR. Voltio, *m.*
volt [vɔlt] n. Esquiva, parada, *f.* (in fencing). || Vuelta, *f.* (of a horse).
voltage [ˈvəultidʒ] n. ELECTR. Voltaje, *m.*, tensión, *f.* || *High voltage*, alta tensión.
voltaic [vɔlˈteiik] adj. Voltaico, ca: *voltaic arc*, arco voltaico.
voltameter [vɔlˈtæmitə*] n. ELECTR. Voltámetro, *m.*
voltammeter [ˈvəultˈæmitə*] n. ELECTR. Voltamperímetro, *m.*
volt-ampere [ˈvəultˈæmpɛə*] n. ELECTR. Voltamperio, *m.*
volte-face [ˈvɔltˈfɑːs] n. Cambio (*m.*) súbito de opinión, (change of opinion).
voltmeter [ˈvəultˌmiːtə*] n. ELECTR. Voltímetro, *m.*
volubility [ˌvɔljuˈbiliti] n. Locuacidad, *f.* || BOT. Volubilidad, *f.*
voluble [ˈvɔljubl] adj. Locuaz (person). || Suelto, ta (speech). || BOT. Voluble.
volubly [—i] adv. Con soltura, con facilidad.
volume [ˈvɔljuːm] n. Volumen, *m.* (space occupied). || Tomo, *m.*, volumen, *m.*: *an encyclopedia in ten volumes*, una enciclopedia en diez volúmenes. || Volumen, *m.* (of sound): *turn the volume down*, baja el volumen. || Volumen, *m.*, cantidad, *f.*: *the volume of sales*, el volumen de ventas; *the volume of water through a lock*, el volumen de agua que pasa por una esclusa. || — Pl. Gran cantidad, *f. sing.* (of water, etc.). || — *Her look spoke volumes*, su mirada era muy elocuente. || *It speaks volumes for his attitude*, indica claramente su actitud. || *Volume control*, botón (*m.*) del volumen (knob).
volumeter [vɔˈljuːmitə*] n. PHYS. Volúmetro, *m.*
volumetric [ˌvɔljuˈmetrik] or **volumetrical** adj. PHYS. Volumétrico, ca.
volumetry [vɔˈljuːmitri] n. PHYS. Volumetría.
voluminosity [vəˌljuːmiˈnɔsiti] n. Abundancia, *f.* || FIG. Prolijidad, *f.* (of a writer).
voluminous [vəˈljuːminəs] adj. Voluminoso, sa (bulky). || Abundante. || FIG. Prolijo, ja (writer).
voluntarily [ˈvɔləntərili] adv. Voluntariamente.
voluntariness [ˈvɔləntərinis] n. Voluntariedad, *f.*
voluntary [ˈvɔləntəri] adj. Voluntario, ria: *a voluntary action*, un acto voluntario. || Espontáneo, a (spontaneous). || Benévolo, la; voluntario, ria (benevolent). || JUR. A título gratuito (without payment).
— N. MUS. Solo (*m.*) de órgano.
volunteer [ˌvɔlənˈtiə*] adj. Voluntario, ria (voluntary). || De voluntarios (army).
— N. MIL. Voluntario, *m.* || JUR. Beneficiario, ria.
volunteer [ˌvɔlənˈtiə*] v. tr. Ofrecer (services). || Dar (information). || Hacer (remark). || FIG. Designar (to designate s.o.): *I was volunteered*, me designaron.
— V. intr. Ofrecerse. || MIL. Alistarse como voluntario (to join up).
voluptuary [vəˈlʌptjuəri] adj./n. Voluptuoso, sa.
voluptuous [vəˈlʌptjuəs] adj. Voluptuoso, sa.
voluptuousness [—nis] n. Voluptuosidad, *f*
volute [vəˈljuːt] n. ARCH. Voluta, *f.* || ZOOL. Voluta, *f.* (of a mollusc). | Espira, *f.* (of a shell).
— Adj. Espiral, en espiral. || TECH. Helicoidal.
volution [vəˈljuːʃən] n. Espira, *f.* (of a shell). || ANAT. Circunvolución, *f.*
volvulus [ˈvɔlvjuləs] n. MED. Vólvulo, *m.*
vomer [ˈvəmə*] n. ANAT. Vómer, *m.*
vomica [ˈvɔmikə] n. MED. Vómica, *f.*
vomit [ˈvɔmit] n. Vómito, *m.* || Vomitivo, *m.* (emetic). || MED. *Black vomit*, vómito negro, fiebre amarilla.
vomit [ˈvɔmit] v. tr. MED. Vomitar. || FIG. Vomitar, arrojar.
— V. intr. Vomitar, tener vómitos.
vomiting [ˈvɔmitiŋ] n. MED. Vómito, *m.*
vomitive [ˈvɔmitiv] adj. Vomitivo, va.
vomitory [ˈvɔmitəri] adj. Vomitivo, va; vomitorio, ria.
— N. Vomitorio, *m.* (in Roman amphitheatres).
voodoo [ˈvuːduː] n. Vodú, *m.*
voodoo [ˈvuːduː] v. tr. Hechizar, embrujar.
voracious [vəˈreiʃəs] adj. Voraz: *a voracious appetite*, un apetito voraz; *a voracious tiger*, un tigre voraz. || Insaciable, ávido, da: *a voracious reader*, un lector ávido.
voraciousness [—nis] or **voracity** [vɔˈræsiti] n. Voracidad, *f.* (capacity to eat). || Avidez, *f.* (eagerness).
vortex [ˈvɔːteks] n. Vórtice, *m.*, torbellino, *m.*
— OBSERV. El plural de la palabra inglesa es *vortexes* o *vortices*.
vortical [ˈvɔːtikəl] adj. Vortiginoso, sa.
vorticella [ˌvɔːtiˈselə] n. ZOOL. Vorticela, *f.*
— OBSERV. El plural de la palabra inglesa es *vorticellae* o *vorticellas*.
votaress [ˈvəutəris] n. Adoradora, *f.*, devota, *f.* (of a god). || Aficionada, *f.*: *a votaress of the arts*, una aficionada a las artes. || Partidaria, *f.* (supporter).
votary [ˈvəutəri] n. Adorador, *m.*, devoto, *m.* (of a god). || Aficionado, *m.* (fan). || Partidario, *m.* (supporter).
vote [vəut] n. Voto, *m.*: *vote of confidence*, voto de confianza; *vote of censure*, voto de censura; *to cast a vote*, depositar un voto. || Votación, *f.* (action): *the vote was taken today*, la votación tuvo lugar hoy; *to move that a separate vote be taken*, proponer la votación por separado. || Derecho (*m.*) de votar, derecho (*m.*) de voto, voto, *m.*: *why did they give women the vote?*, ¿por qué dieron el derecho de votar a las mujeres?, ¿por qué concedieron el voto a las mujeres? || Votos, *m. pl.*: *the trade-union vote*, los votos de los sindicatos. || Créditos (*m. pl.*) votados (money granted). || — *By a majority vote*, por una mayoría de votos. || *By popular vote*, por votación popular. || *Casting vote*, voto de calidad. || *Floating votes*, votos indecisos. || *Secret vote*, votación secreta. || *To count* o *to tell the votes*, proceder al escrutinio. || *To give one's vote to*, dar su voto a, votar por. || *To have* o *to take a vote on sth.*, poner *or* someter algo a votación, votar algo. || *To have the vote*, tener el derecho de votar. || *To proceed to a vote*, proceder a votar. || *To put to the vote*, poner *or* someter a votación. || *To record one's vote*, votar. || *Unanimous vote*, votación unánime. || *Unconclusive vote*, votación nula. || *Vote by proxy*, voto por poderes. || *Vote by roll call*, votación nominal. || *Vote by show of hands*, votación a mano alzada. || *Vote by sitting and standing* (*U. S.*, *rising vote*), votación por "levantados" y "sentados". || *Vote of thanks*, voto de gracias. || *Votes cast*, votos *or* sufragios emitidos.
vote [vəut] v. tr. Votar: *to vote the agricultural bill*, votar la ley agrícola; *to vote ten thousand pounds for industry*, votar diez mil libras para la industria. || Elegir: *she was voted Miss England*, fue elegida como Miss Inglaterra. || Proponer: *I vote that we all go home*, yo propongo que vayamos todos a casa. || Declarar (to proclaim). || — *To vote down*, rechazar, votar en contra de (motion, etc.). || *To vote in*, elegir. || *To vote out*, derrotar en las elecciones. || *With a right to vote*, con voz y voto. || *Without a right to vote*, con voz pero sin voto.
— V. intr. Votar: *to vote for*, votar por *or* a favor de; *to vote against*, votar en contra [de]. || *To vote on*, votar.
voter [—ə*] n. Votante, *m.* & *f.* || Elector, ra; votante, *m.* & *f.* (in a national election).
voting [ˈvəutiŋ] n. Votación, *f.* (action): *voting by a show of hands*, votación a mano alzada.
— Adj. Votante (member). || Electoral.
voting booth [—buːð] n. Cabina (*f.*) electoral.
voting machine [—məˌʃiːn] n. U. S. Máquina (*f.*) de votar, máquina registradora de votos.
voting paper [—ˌpeipə*] n. Papeleta, *f.* [*Amer.*, balota, *f.*].
votive [ˈvəutiv] adj. Votivo, va: *votive mass*, misa votiva. || *Votive offering*, exvoto, *m.*
vouch [vautʃ] v. tr. Atestiguar (to testify). || Confirmar (a statement). || JUR. Citar. || *To vouch that*, asegurar que.
— V. intr. *To vouch for*, responder de, garantizar (a thing), salir fiador de, responder por (a person).
voucher [—ə*] n. JUR. Documento (*m.*) justificativo. | Fiador, ra; garante, *m.* & *f.* (person). || COMM. Bono, *m.*, vale, *m.* || Prueba, *f.* (piece of evidence). || Contraseña, *f.* (in the theatre). || — *Cash voucher*, vale [que representa cierta cantidad de dinero]. || *Luncheon voucher*, vale de comida.
vouchsafe [—seif] v. tr. Conceder, otorgar: *to vouchsafe s.o. sth.*, conceder algo a alguien. || — *He vouchsafed no answer*, no se dignó contestar. || *To vouchsafe to do sth.*, dignarse hacer algo.
voussoir [vuːˈswɑːr] n. ARCH. Dovela, *f.*
vow [vau] n. REL. Voto, *m.*: *to make a vow of chastity*, hacer voto de castidad; *to take one's vows*, pronunciar sus votos. || Promesa (*f.*) solemne: *lovers' vows*, las promesas solemnes de los amantes. || *To make a vow to do sth.*, prometer hacer algo, comprometerse a hacer algo.
vow [vau] v. tr. Jurar: *to vow obedience*, jurar obediencia. || Prometer: *he vowed not to drink any more*, prometió no beber más. || — *To vow that*, declarar que, afirmar que. || *To vow to*, hacer voto de (religious vows), comprometerse a, prometer (to promise).
— V. intr. Jurar.
vowel [ˈvauəl] n. GRAMM. Vocal, *f.*
— Adj. GRAMM. Vocálico, ca.
vox [vɔks] n. MUS. Voz, *f.*: *vox angelica*, voz celeste; *vox humana*, voz humana.
voyage [ˈvɔiidʒ] n. Viaje, *m.*: *a sea voyage*, un viaje por mar, un viaje en barco. || Travesía, *f.* (crossing). || — *Maiden voyage*, primer viaje. || *The outward voyage*, el viaje de ida, la ida. || *The voyage home*, el viaje de regreso *or* de vuelta, la vuelta.
voyage [ˈvɔiidʒ] v. intr. MAR. Viajar [por mar], navegar. || Viajar por aire *or* en avión.
— V. tr. Viajar por (seas).

voyager [ˈvɔiədʒə*] n. Viajero, ra.
Vulcan [ˈvʌlkən] pr. n. MYTH. Vulcano, *m.*
vulcanian [vʌlˈkeinjən] adj. Volcánico, ca.
vulcanism [ˈvʌlkənizəm] n. GEOL. Vulcanismo, *m.*
vulcanist [ˈvʌlkənist] n. Vulcanólogo, *m.*, vulcanologista, *m.*
vulcanite [ˈvʌlkənait] n. MIN. Vulcanita, *f.*
vulcanization [ˌvʌlkənaiˈzeiʃən] n. TECH. Vulcanización, *f.*
vulcanize [ˈvʌlkənaiz] v. tr. TECH. Vulcanizar.
vulcanized [—d] adj. TECH. Vulcanizado, da: *vulcanized rubber*, caucho vulcanizado.
vulcanologist [ˌvʌlkəˈnɔlədʒist] n. Vulcanólogo, *m.*, vulcanologista, *m.*
vulcanology [ˌvʌlkəˈnɔlədʒi] n. Vulcanología, *f.*
vulgar [ˈvʌlgə*] adj. Común, corriente: *a vulgar superstition*, una superstición común. || Vulgar, ordinario, ria (lacking refinement). || De mal gusto (in bad taste). || Cursi (pretentious). || Grosero, ra; vulgar (rude): *don't be vulgar!*, ¡no seas grosero! || Verde: *a vulgar joke*, un chiste verde. || GRAMM. Vulgar, corriente: *to take a word in its vulgar sense*, tomar una palabra en su sentido vulgar. || — *The vulgar era*, la era vulgar *or* cristiana. || MATH. *Vulgar fraction*, fracción (*f.*) común. || GRAMM. *Vulgar Latin*, latín (*m.*) vulgar.
— N. Vulgo, *m.* (populace).
vulgarian [vʌlˈgɛəriən] n. Persona (*f.*) vulgar, persona (*f.*) ordinaria (vulgar person). || Nuevo rico, *m.* (rich person).
vulgarism [ˈvʌlgərizəm] n. Vulgarismo, *m.* (word, expression). || Vulgaridad, *f.* (lack of refinement). || Vulgaridad, *f.*, grosería, *f.*, ordinariez, *f.* (act).
vulgarity [vʌlˈgæriti] n. Vulgaridad, *f.* (lack of refinement). || Vulgaridad, *f.*, grosería, *f.*, ordinariez, *f.* (act).
vulgarization [ˌvʌlgəraiˈzeiʃən] n. Vulgarización, *f.*
vulgarize [ˈvʌlgəraiz] v. tr. Vulgarizar.
vulgarizer [—ə*] n. Vulgarizador, ra.
Vulgate [ˈvʌlgit] n. REL. Vulgata, *f.* (Bible).
vulgus [ˈvʌlgəs] n. Vulgo, *m.*
vulnerability [ˌvʌlnərəˈbiliti] n. Vulnerabilidad, *f.*
vulnerable [ˈvʌlnərəbl] adj. Vulnerable.
vulnerary [ˈvʌlnərəri] adj. MED. Vulnerario, ria (used in healing).
— N. MED. Vulnerario, *m.*
vulpine [ˈvʌlpain] adj. Vulpino, na. || FIG. Ladino, na (cunning).
vulture [ˈvʌltʃə*] n. ZOOL. Buitre, *m.* || FIG. Hombre (*m.*) rapaz.
vulturine [ˈvʌltʃurain] adj. De buitre.
vulturous [ˈvʌltʃurəs] adj. De buitre. || FIG. Rapaz.
vulva [ˈvʌlvə] n. ANAT. Vulva, *f.*
vulval [—l] or **vulvar** [—*] adj. Vulvar.
vulvitis [vʌlˈvaitis] n. MED. Vulvitis, *f. inv.*
vying [ˈvaiiŋ] pres. part. See VIE.

w [ˈdʌbəlju:] n. W, *f.* (letter).
wacke [ˈwækə] n. GEOL. Roca (*f.*) parecida a la arenisca.
wacky [ˈwæki] adj. U. S. FAM. Chiflado, da; chalado, da (person). | Absurdo, da (thing).
wad [wɔd] n. Taco, *m.* (of a cartridge). || Bolita, *f.* (of cotton wool). || Tapón, *m.* (to stop an aperture). || Fajo, *m.* (of banknotes). || Lío, *m.* (of papers). || Manojo, *m.* (of straw). || Toma, *f.* (of chewing tobacco). || FAM. Dineral, *m.* (a lot of money). || FAM. *To make wads of money*, ganar el dinero a espuertas, ganar un dineral.
wad [wɔd] v. tr. Enguatar, forrar (to pad, to line). || Acolchar (a wall). || Tapar, obstruir (a hole). || Rellenar (to fill). || Atacar (a firearm). || Apretar (to make into a wad).
wadding [—iŋ] n. Relleno, *m.* (filling or stuffing). || Guata, *f.* (cotton wool). || Taco, *m.* (of a cartridge). || Acolchado, *m.* (of a wall).
waddle [ˈwɔdl] n. Anadeo, *m.*, manera (*f.*) de andar de los patos. || Contoneo, *m.* (of people). || *To walk with a waddle*, andar contoneándose (with a swaying gait), andar como un pato (like a duck).
waddle [ˈwɔdl] v. intr. Anadear (ducks). || Contonearse (with a swaying gait). || Andar como un pato (like a duck).
waddy [ˈwɔdi] n. Cachiporra, *f.* (thick club).
wade [weid] v. tr. Vadear (a river, stream).
— V. intr. Andar con dificultad. || — *To wade across a river*, vadear un río. || *To wade ashore*, salir del agua. || *To wade in*, meterse en el agua (to go into the water), atacar, arremeter (to attack), ponerse a trabajar (to start working). || *To wade into*, meterse en (water), sumergirse en (a crowd), arremeter contra, atacar (to attack physically), emprenderla con (verbally), echarse sobre (food). || *To wade through*, abrirse paso entre (crowd, debris, undergrowth, etc.), vadear (water), leer con dificultad (to read).
wader [—ə*] n. ZOOL. Ave (*f.*) zancuda. || — Pl. Botas (*f.*) altas impermeables.
wadi [ˈwɔdi] n. Ued, *m.*

— OBSERV. El plural de *wadi* es *wadis* o *wadies.*

wading bird [ˈweidiŋbə:d] n. ZOOL. Ave (*f.*) zancuda.
wady [ˈwɔdi] n. Ued, *m.*

— OBSERV. El plural de *wady* es *wadies.*

wafer [ˈweifə*] n. CULIN. Barquillo, *m.* || REL. Hostia, *f.* || Oblea, *f.* (seal for documents).
wafer [ˈweifə*] v. tr. Cerrar con oblea.
wafer-thin [—θin] adj. Finísimo, ma.
waffle [ˈwɔfl] n. CULIN. Barquillo, *m.* || FAM. Paja, *f.*
waffle [ˈwɔfl] v. intr. FAM. Perorar (to talk at great length). | Meter paja (in an essay or speech).
waffle iron [ˈwɔflˌaiən] n. CULIN. Molde (*m.*) para hacer barquillos.
waft [wɑ:ft] n. Ráfaga, *f.*, soplo, *m.* (of wind). || Bocanada, *f.* (of smoke, etc.). || Aletada, *f.* (of a bird). || MAR. Bandera (*f.*) de señales.
waft [wɑ:ft] v. tr. Llevar por el aire (through the air) *or* por el agua (across water).
— V. intr. FIG. Flotar (on the wind).
wag [wæg] n. Guasón, ona; bromista, *m.* & *f.* (joker). || Meneo, *m.*, movimiento, *m.* (movement). || Coleada, *f.*, coletazo, *m.* (of tail).
wag [wæg] v. tr. Agitar, menear. || Mover (tail, head). || FAM. *To wag one's tongue*, darle a la lengua.
— V. intr. Agitarse, menearse, moverse. || Andar (to move along). || FAM. *That should set tongues wagging*, eso dará que hablar a la gente.
wage [weidʒ] n. Salario, *m.* (of a workman). || Sueldo, *m.* (of employees). || — Pl. COMM. Salarios, *m.* (industrial expenditure on labour). || Salario, *m. sing.* (workman's pay). || Sueldo, *m. sing.* (employee's pay). || FIG. Pago, *m.* (reward). || — *Basic wage*, salario base *or* básico. || *Collective wage*, salario colectivo. || *Conventional wage*, salario de convenio colectivo. || *Fixing of maximum wage*, fijación de salarios máximos. || *Starvation wages*, salario de hambre. || *Top* o *maximum wage*, salario tope *or* máximo. || *Wage dividend*, participación (*f.*) en los beneficios. || *Wage earner*, asalariado, da. || *Wage freeze*, congelación (*f.*) de salarios. || *Wage scale*, escala (*f.*) de salarios.
wage [weidʒ] v. tr. Hacer (war). || Librar, dar, trabar (battle). || Emprender (a campaign). || Empeñar (to pledge).
wager [—ə*] n. Apuesta, *f.* || *To lay a wager*, apostar, hacer una apuesta.
wager [—ə*] v. tr./intr. Apostar: *to wager five pounds that*, apostar cinco libras a que.
wageworker [—ˌwə:kə*] n. Asalariado, da.
waggery [ˈwægəri] n. Broma, *f.* (joke).
waggish [ˈwægiʃ] adj. Bromista, guasón, ona (people). || En broma (action).
waggishly [—li] adv. En broma, con guasa.
waggishness [—nis] n. Carácter (*m.*) bromista.
waggle [ˈwægl] n. Meneo, *m.* (wag).
waggle [ˈwægl] v. tr. Agitar, menear (to shake).
— V. intr. Agitarse, menearse (to shake). || Tambalearse (to totter).
waggly [—i] adj. Inseguro, ra; poco seguro, ra; tambaleante.
waggon or **wagon** [ˈwægən] n. Carro, *m.* (horse-drawn). || Vagón, *m.* (railway car). || Furgón, *m.* (for freight). || TECH. Vagoneta, *f.* || Carrito (*m.*) para el té (tea trolley). || AUT. Furgoneta, *f.*, camioneta, *f.* || U. S. Furgoneta (*f.*) de policía (for police). || — FIG.

FAM. *To be on the wagon*, no beber. | *To go on the wagon*, tomar la decisión de no beber. | *To hitch one's waggon to a star*, picar muy alto (to be very ambitious).
waggonage or **wagonage** [—idʒ] n. Acarreo, *m.*, transporte (*m.*) en vagones.
waggoner or **wagoner** [—ə*] n. Carretero, *m.*
Waggoner or **Wagoner** [—ə*] n. ASTR. Cochero, *m.*, Auriga, *m.*
waggonette or **wagonette** [ˌwægəˈnet] n. Tartana, *f.*
Wagnerian [vɑ:gˈniəriən] adj./n. Wagneriano, na.
wagon-lit [ˈvægɔ̃nˈli:] n. Coche cama, *m.*

— OBSERV. El plural es *wagons-lits* o *wagon-lits*.

wagonload [ˈwægənləud] n. Carretada, *f.* (of a horse-drawn wagon). || Vagón, *m.* (of railway car).
wagon train [ˈwægəntrein] n. MIL. Tren (*m.*) de equipajes.
wagtail [ˈwægteil] n. Aguzanieves, *f. inv.* (bird).
Wahhabi or **Wahabi** [wəˈhɑ:bi] n. REL. Wahabita, *m.* & *f.*
Wahhabite or **Wahabite** [wəˈhɑ:bait] n. REL. Wahabita, *m.* & *f.*
wahoo [ˈwɑ:hu:] n. BOT. Bonetero, *m.*
waif [weif] n. Niño (*m.*) abandonado, niña (*f.*) abandonada (child). || Animal (*m.*) abandonado *or* extraviado (animal). || JUR. Bien (*m.*) mostrenco. || *Waifs and strays*, niños abandonados *or* desamparados.
wail [weil] n. Quejido, *m.*, lamento, *m.* (cry). || Vagido, *m.* (of a new-born baby). || FIG. Gemido, *m.*: *the wail of the wind*, el gemido del viento.
wail [weil] v. intr. Gemir, lamentarse. || FIG. Gemir (wind). || FAM. Llorar (to complain): *don't come wailing to me*, no me vengas a llorar a mí.
— V. tr. Lamentar.
wailing [—iŋ] n. Gemidos, *m. pl.*, lamentos, *m. pl.* || Vagidos, *m. pl.* (of a new-born baby).
Wailing Wall [ˈweiliŋˈwɔ:l] pr. n. Muro (*m.*) de las Lamentaciones.
wain [wein] n. (Ant.). Carro, *m.* || ASTR. *The Wain*, el Carro, la Osa Mayor.
wainscot [ˈweinskət] n. ARCH. Entablado, *m.*, revestimiento (*m.*) de madera (wooden panelling). || Zócalo, *m.*, cenefa, *f.* (lower part of a wall, skirting board).
wainscot [ˈweinskət] v. tr. Revestir de madera.
wainscoting or **wainscotting** [—iŋ] n. See WAINSCOT.
wainwright [ˈweinrait] n. Carretero, *m.*
waist [weist] n. Cintura, *f.*, talle, *m.* (of the body). || MAR. Combés, *m.* || Estrechamiento, *m.* (narrow part). || U. S. Cuerpo, *m.* (bodice of woman's dress). | Blusa, *f.* (blouse).
waistband [—bænd] n. Pretina, *f.*, cinturón, *m.*
waistcloth [—klɔθ] n. Taparrabo, *m.*
waistcoat [—kəut] n. Chaleco, *m.*
waist-deep [—ˈdi:p] adv. Hasta la cintura: *to be waist-deep in water*, tener agua hasta la cintura.
waisted [—id] adj. *High waisted*, de cinturón alto (trousers). || *Slim waisted*, de cintura fina.
waist-high [—ˈhai] adv./adj. Hasta la cintura: *to be waist-high*, llegar hasta la cintura.
waistline [—lain] n. Cintura, *f.*, talle, *m.*
wait [weit] n. Espera, *f.*: *a long wait at the station*, una larga espera en la estación. || Emboscada, *f.* (ambush). || — Pl. Murga (*f. sing.*) de Nochebuena (carol singers). || — *To lie in wait for*, estar al acecho de, acechar. || *We have a long wait ahead of us*, tendremos que esperar mucho tiempo.
wait [weit] v. tr. Esperar: *to wait one's turn*, esperar su turno. || Retrasar (to delay): *to wait a meal for s.o.*, retrasar una comida por alguien. || Atender, servir (a table). || U. S. *To wait out a storm*, esperar a que acabe una tormenta.
— V. intr. Esperar: *he made me wait for three hours*, me hizo esperar tres horas; *that decision can't wait*, esta decisión no puede esperar. || Ser camarero (to be a waiter). || — *Just wait until I tell this to John!*, ¡cuando se lo diga a Juan! || *Just wait until the teacher finds out!*, ¡espera que se entere el profesor! || *Just you wait!*, ¡me las pagarás! || *Repairs while you wait*, reparaciones al minuto. || *To keep s.o. waiting*, hacer esperar a alguien. || *To wait at table*, atender, servir. || *To wait for*, esperar: *he was waiting for her*, le estaba esperando. || *To wait on*, servir a, atender a (s.o. at table), presentar sus respetos a (to pay a visit to), derivarse de (to result from), seguir de cerca (a competitor). || *To wait up for s.o.*, esperar a alguien levantado. || *Wait for me to call*, espera a que llame.
waiter [—ə*] n. Camarero, *m.* || Bandeja, *f.* (tray).
waiting [—iŋ] adj. Que espera (that waits). || De espera: *waiting room*, sala de espera. || De servicio (who is in attendance). || *To play the waiting game*, esperar, dejar pasar el tiempo.
— N. Espera, *f.* || Servicio, *m.* || *After a good hour's waiting*, después de haber esperado más de une hora.
waiting list [—iŋlist] n. Lista (*f.*) de espera.
waitress [—ris] n. Camarera, *f.*
waive [weiv] v. tr. JUR. Renunciar a (right, objection). | Desistir de (a claim). | Aplazar, diferir (to postpone). | Suspender (the rules). || Dejar de lado (one's own interests).
waiver [—ə*] n. JUR. Renuncia, *f.* (of a right). | Desistimiento, *m.* (of a claim).
wake [weik] n. Velatorio, *m.* (vigil over a corpse). || MAR. Estela, *f.* (of a ship). || FIG. Huella, *f.* || Fiesta (*f.*) de la dedicación de una iglesia. || — Pl. Fiesta (*f. sing.*) anual. || *In the wake of*, después de, tras.
wake* [weik] v. tr. Despertar (to wake up, to arouse). || Resucitar (to revive). || Velar (a corpse). || — *To make enough noise to wake the dead*, hacer un ruido de todos los diablos. || *To wake to*, hacer ver: *he woke his audience to the necessity of taking a decision*, hizo ver al auditorio la necesidad de tomar una decisión. || *To wake s.o. up*, despertar a alguien.
— V. intr. Despertarse (from sleep). || Estar despierto, ta (to be awake). || FIG. Despertar: *he woke to the beauty of his country*, despertó a la belleza de su país. | Amanecer: *to wake up a new man*, amanecer como nuevo. || — *To wake up*, despertarse (after sleep), despabilarse (to become alert). || *To wake up to*, darse cuenta de.

— OBSERV. Pret. ***woke, waked;*** p. p. ***woken, waked.***

wakeful [—ful] adj. Alerta, vigilante (alert, watchful). || Despierto, ta (awake). || Desvelado, da (unable to sleep). || En blanco: *a wakeful night*, una noche en blanco.
wakefully [—fuli] adv. En vela, sin dormir.
wakefulness [—fulnis] n. Vigilancia, *f.* (watchfulness). || Insomnio, *m.* (sleeplessness).
waken [—ən] v. tr. Despertar: *he wakened the sleeping sentry*, despertó al centinela dormido.
— V. intr. Despertarse.
waking [—iŋ] adj. Alerta, vigilante (watchful). || *We spend ten out of sixteen waking hours at work*, de las dieciséis horas en que estamos despiertos pasamos diez trabajando.
— N. Despertar, *m.*
Walachia [wɔˈleikiə] pr. n. GEOGR. Valaquia, *f.*
Walachian [—n] adj./n. Valaco, ca.
wale [weil] n. Verdugón, *m.* (weal). || Canutillo, *m.* (in corduroy). || TECH. Riostra, *f.* (brace). || — Pl. MAR. Cintas, *f.*
wale [weil] v. tr. Hacer un verdugón a (with a whip, cane, etc.).
Wales [weilz] pr. n. GEOGR. Gales, *f.*, el País de Gales: *to Wales*, a Gales, al País de Gales. || *South Wales*, Gales del Sur.
Walhalla [vælˈhælə] n. Walhalla, *m.*
walk [wɔ:k] n. Manera (*f.*) de andar, andar, *m.* (way of walking). || Paso, *m.* (pace). || Paseo, *m.*: *to have* o *to take* o *to go for a walk*, dar un paseo; *go through the wood, it is a pleasant walk*, vaya por el bosque, es un paseo agradable. || Camino, *m.*: *it is half an hour's walk from here*, hay media hora de camino desde aquí. || Avenida, *f.*, paseo, *m.* (avenue). || Sendero, *m.* (path). || Ronda, *f.* (of a postman, hawker, etc.). || Dehesa, *f.*, pasto, *m.* (sheepwalk). || Cordelería, *f.* (ropewalk). || Sector (*m.*) de un bosque asignado a cada guarda (section of forest). || Plantación, *f.* || SP. Marcha, *f.* (in athletics). || — FIG. *People from all walks of life*, gente de toda condición. || *To fall into a walk*, ponerse al paso (horse). || *To take the dog for a walk*, sacar al perro. || *To take s.o. for a walk*, sacar a alguien de paseo. || SP. *To win in a walk*, ganar cómodamente. || FIG. *Walk of life*, profesión, *f.* (profession), posición (*f.*) social, clase (*f.*) social, condición, *f.* (status).
walk [wɔ:k] v. tr. Recorrer a pie: *to walk the Lake District*, recorrer a pie la Región de los Lagos. || Andar, recorrer, hacer a pie (a distance): *to walk three miles*, andar tres millas. || Pasear: *to walk a child*, pasear a un niño. || Llevar al paso (horses). || Empujar (a bicycle, motorcycle). || Acompañar [andando]: *I'll walk you home*, te acompaño a casa. || — *To walk s.o. off his feet*, agotar a alguien haciéndole andar mucho. || THEATR. *To walk the boards*, ser actor. || *To walk the streets*, callejear (aimlessly), hacer la carrera (a prostitute). || *You can walk it in ten minutes*, se tarda diez minutos andando.
— V. intr. Andar: *children begin to walk at thirteen months*, los niños empiezan a andar a los trece meses. || Pasearse, dar un paseo (to stroll): *they are out walking*, han salido a dar un paseo. || Ir andando, ir a pie: *how did you go? — I walked*, ¿cómo fuiste? — Fui a pie; *I always walk to the office*, siempre voy andando a la oficina. || Moverse (to move). || Aparecer (a ghost). || SP. Avanzar (in basketball). || Ir al paso (horse). || — *To walk in one's sleep*, ser sonámbulo, la. || *To walk in procession*, desfilar, ir en procesión. || *To walk on all fours*, andar a gatas. || *To walk with s.o.*, acompañar a alguien.
— ***To walk about***, pasearse, pasear. || ***To walk along***, andar, caminar. || ***To walk away***, irse, marcharse. | — U. S. *To walk away from*, dejar muy atrás a (a competitor), salir ileso de (from an accident). | *To walk away with*, llevarse. || ***To walk back***, volver a pie, volver andando. || ***To walk down***, bajar andando *or* a pie: *you take the lift, I'll walk down*, tome el ascensor, yo bajaré andando. | Bajar: *she walked slowly down the stairs*, bajó lentamente la escalera. || ***To walk in***, entrar. | — *Please, walk in* o *walk right in*, pasen sin llamar. || ***To walk into***, entrar en (to enter). | Encontrarse con: *to walk into a friend in the street*, encontrarse con un amigo en la calle. | Tropezar con: *I turned round and I walked into a lamppost*, di la vuelta y tropecé con un farol. | Caer en: *to walk into a trap*, caer en una trampa. | Arremeter, atacar (to attack). || ***To walk off***, irse, marcharse. | — *To walk*

off with, llevarse (to carry off). || **To walk on,** seguir su camino (to continue). | Pisar (to tread on). | Andar sobre: *to walk on the water*, andar sobre el agua. | THEATR. Hacer de comparsa (to have a non-speaking part), salir a escena (to come on stage). || **To walk out,** salir (to leave). | Declararse en huelga (to go on strike). | Sacar (to take out). | — *To walk out on*, abandonar, dejar. | *To walk out with*, salir con. || **To walk over,** pisotear (rights, etc.). | — FIG. FAM. *To walk all over s.o.*, tratar a patadas a alguien. | *To walk over the course*, ganar por ser el único participante. || **To walk round,** dar la vuelta. | — *To walk round sth.*, darle la vuelta a algo. || **To walk through,** atravesar, pasar por. || **To walk up,** subir (stairs). | — *To walk up and down*, ir de acá para allá. | *To walk up to s.o.*, acercarse a alguien. | *Walk up!*, ¡acérquense!
walkaway [—əwei] n. U. S. Pan (*m.*) comido (easily won contest): *the game was a walkaway*, el partido fue pan comido.
walker [—ə*] n. Paseante, *m.* & *f.* || Peatón, *m.* (pedestrian). || SP. Marchador, *m.* || Tacataca, *m.*, tacatá, *m.*, pollera, *f.* (for children). || *To be a fast, a slow walker*, andar de prisa, despacio.
walker-on [—ə'rɔn] n. THEATR. Comparsa, *m.* & *f.*, figurante, *m.* & *f.* || CINEM. Extra, *m.* & *f.*
walkie-talkie [—i'tɔ:ki] n. RAD. "Talkie-walkie", *m.*, radioteléfono (*m.*) portátil.
walking [—iŋ] n. Andar, *m.*
— Adj. Ambulante. || A pie (tour). || Oscilante (oscillating). || Para andar (shoes). || — *It is within walking distance*, se puede ir a pie *or* andando. || FIG. *Walking dictionary* o *encyclopaedia*, enciclopedia (*f.*) ambulante.
walking cane [—iŋkein] n. Bastón, *m.*
walking pace [—iŋpeis] n. Paso, *m.*: *at a walking pace*, al paso.
walking papers [—iŋˌpeipəz] pl. n. U. S. FAM. Despido, *m. sing.* || *To get one's walking papers*, ser despedido.
walking stick [—iŋstik] n. Bastón, *m.*
walk-on [—ɔn] n. THEATR. Papel (*m.*) de comparsa *or* de figurante.
walkout [—aut] n. Huelga, *f.* (strike).
walkover [—ˌəuvə*] n. Victoria (*f.*) fácil (easy win). || FAM. Pan (*m.*) comido (pushover): *it was a walkover*, fue pan comido.
walk-up [—ʌp] n. U. S. Casa (*f.*) *or* piso (*m.*) sin ascensor.
Walkyrie [væl'kiəri] n. MYTH. Walkiria, *f.*
walky-talky ['wɔ:ki'tɔ:ki] n. RAD. "Talkie-walkie", *m.*, radioteléfono (*m.*) portátil.
wall [wɔ:l] n. Pared, *f.*: *the wall between two rooms*, la pared entre dos habitaciones; *hang it on the wall*, cuélgalo en la pared; *paintings on the walls of a cave*, pinturas en las paredes de una cueva. || Tapia, *f.*: *the garden wall*, la tapia del jardín. || Muro, *m.* (exterior wall of house, large garden wall, etc.). || Muralla, *f.*: *the city walls*, las murallas de la ciudad. || FIG. Barrera, *f.*: *a wall of mountains*, una barrera de montañas. || ANAT. Pared, *f.* || AGR. Espaldera, *f.* (for fruit trees). || — ARCH. *Blind wall*, pared sin aberturas. || FIG. *It's like talking to a brick wall*, es como hablar a la pared. || ARCH. *Main wall*, pared maestra. || FIG. *To drive* o *to push to the wall*, poner entre la espada y la pared, acorralar. | *To go to the wall*, fracasar (to fail), arruinarse (to be ruined), quebrar (to go bankrupt). | *Walls have ears*, las paredes oyen. | *With one's back to the wall*, entre la espada y la pared, acorralado, da. || *Within the walls*, intramuros. || *Without the walls*, extramuros.
— Adj. De pared, mural.
wall [wɔ:l] v. tr. Poner una pared *or* un muro a (to furnish with a wall). || — *To wall in*, cercar con un muro *or* una tapia (a garden, orchard, etc.), amurallar, fortificar (a town), emparedar, encerrar (a prisoner). || *To wall off*, separar con una pared *or* un muro. || *To wall up*, tapiar.
wallaby ['wɔləbi] n. ZOOL. Ualabi, *m.*, canguro (*m.*) pequeño (kangaroo).
Wallachia [wɔ'leikiə] pr. n. GEOGR. Valaquia, *f.*
Wallachian [—n] adj./n. Valaco, ca.
wallah ['wɔlə] n. FAM. Encargado, *m.*
wallboard ['wɔ:lbɔ:d] n. ARCH. Panel, *m.*, tablero, *m.*
wall clock ['wɔ:lklɔk] n. Reloj (*m.*) de pared.
walled [wɔ:ld] adj. Amurallado, da (town). || Cercado con una tapia (garden).
wallet ['wɔlit] n. Cartera, *f.* (for carrying papers, bank notes, etc.). Morral, *m.* (knapsack).
walleye ['wɔ:lai] n. Ojo (*m.*) de color diferente. || || Ojo (*m.*) desviado hacia fuera. || MED. Leucoma, *m.*
wall fitting ['wɔ:lˌfitiŋ] n. Aplique, *m.*
wallflower ['wɔ:lˌflauə*] n. BOT. Alhelí, *m.* || FIG. *To be a wallflower*, quedarse en el poyete (not to dance).
wall lamp ['wɔ:llæmp] n. Aplique, *m.*
wall map ['wɔ:lmæp] n. Mapa (*m.*) mural.
Walloon [wɔ'lu:n] adj. Valón, ona.
— N. Valón, *m.* (language). || Valón, ona (person).
wallop ['wɔləp] n. FAM. Golpe (*m.*) fuerte (blow). || FAM. *To be going at a fair wallop*, ir volando.
wallop ['wɔləp] v. tr. FAM. Pegar fuerte (to hit hard). | Dar una paliza (to thrash, to defeat)
walloping [—iŋ] adj. FAM. Colosal, enorme.
— N. FAM. Paliza, *f.* (thrashing, defeat).
wallow ['wɔləu] n. Revolcadero, *m.* (of a boar).
wallow ['wɔləu] v. intr. Revolcarse (animals). || — *To wallow in vice*, sumirse en el vicio. || *To wallow in wealth*, nadar en la abundancia.
wall painting ['wɔ:lˌpeintiŋ] n. Pintura (*f.*) mural.
wallpaper ['wɔ:lˌpeipə*] n. Papel (*m.*) pintado, papel (*m.*) de empapelar.
wallpaper ['wɔ:lˌpeipə*] v. tr. Empapelar.
wallpapering [—iŋ] n. Empapelado, *m.*
wall plate ['wɔ:lpleit] n. ARCH. Carrera, *f.* || TECH. Placa (*f.*) de apoyo.
wall seat ['wɔ:lsi:t] n. Banqueta, *f.*
wall tile ['wɔ:ltail] n. ARCH. Azulejo, *m.*
walnut ['wɔ:lnʌt] n. Nogal, *m.* (tree and timber). || Nuez, *f.* (fruit). | Nogalina, *f.* (colour).
walnut shell [—ʃel] n. Cáscara (*f.*) de nuez.
walnut stain [—stein] n. Nogalina, *f.*
walnut tree [—tri:] n. Nogal, *m.*
walrus ['wɔ:lrəs] n. ZOOL. Morsa, *f.*
waltz [wɔ:ls] n. MUS. Vals, *m.*
waltz [wɔ:ls] v. tr. MUS. Bailar el vals con.
— V. intr. Bailar el vals, valsar.
waltzer [—ə*] n. Valsador, ra; persona (*f.*) que baila el vals.
wampum ['wɔmpəm] n. Cuentas (*f. pl.*) de concha usadas como adorno o dinero.
wan [wɔn] adj. Pálido, da; macilento, ta; lívido, da (unhealthily pale). || Débil, macilento, ta (light). || Triste (sad).
wand [wɔnd] n. Varita, *f.* (of magician). || Varita (*f.*) de las virtudes, varilla (*f.*) mágica (of fairy). || Vara, *f.* (symbol of authority). || U. S. Blanco, *m.* (in archery). || *Mercury's wand*, caduceo, *m.*
wander [—ə*] v. tr. Vagar por, errar por: *to wander the world*, vagar por el mundo. || *To wander the world over*, recorrer el mundo entero.
— V. intr. Errar, vagar (to roam). || Pasearse (to stroll): *to wander round a market*, pasearse por un mercado. || Desvariar, delirar (the mind). || FIG. Desviarse, apartarse (from a subject). || Serpentear (river, road). || — *His eyes wandered over the scene*, observaba la escena. || *To let one's thoughts wander*, dejar vagar la imaginación. || *To wander about*, vagar, ir a la ventura. || *To wander away from*, apartarse de. || *To wander off*, alejarse. || *To wander off the point*, apartarse *or* salirse del tema.
wanderer [—ərə*] n. Vagabundo, da (vagabond). || Viajero, ra (s.o. who travels). || Nómada, *m.* & *f.* (nomad). || FIG. Oveja (*f.*) descarriada.
wandering [—əriŋ] adj. Errante: *The Wandering Jew*, el Judío Errante. || Nómada: *wandering tribes*, tribus nómadas. || Ambulante (salesman). || Vagabundo, da (beggar). || Sinuoso, sa (river). || Incoherente (speech). || Distraído, da (mind, eyes). || MED. Que delira, que desvaría (person). | Flotante (kidney).
— N. Vagabundeo, *m.* (leisurely travelling about). || MED. Delirio, *m.* || — Pl. Vagabundeos, *m.* (leisurely journeys). || Divagaciones, *f.* (speech, thoughts).
wanderingly [—əriŋli] adv. A la ventura (to go). || Incoherentemente (to speak).
wanderlust [—əlʌst] n. Pasión (*f.*) por los viajes.
wane [wein] n. ASTR. Cuarto (*m.*) menguante (of the moon). || Reflujo, *m.*, menguante, *f.* (of the tide). || FIG. Ocaso, *m.*, decadencia, *f.* (of life, beauty, etc.). || *To be on the wane*, estar menguando, menguar (the moon), bajar (the tide), estar en el ocaso, disminuir, declinar, decaer (to decrease, to decline).
wane [wein] v. intr. ASTR. Menguar (the moon). || Bajar (the tide). || FIG. Decaer, declinar, disminuir.
wangle ['wæŋgl] v. tr. FAM. Agenciarse, conseguir (to get by cunning): *to wangle an invitation*, agenciarse una invitación. || Falsificar (to falsify). || FAM. *He wangled it so that he got the day off*, se las arregló para tener el día libre.
— V. intr. FAM. Arreglárselas.
wangler [—ə*] n. Trapacero, ra; tramposo, sa; trapisondista, *m.* & *f.*
wangling [—iŋ] n. FAM. Trampas, *f. pl.*, trucos, *m. pl.*
waning ['weiniŋ] adj. Menguante (moon, tide). || FIG. Decadente (declining).
— N. See WANE.
wanness ['wɔnnis] n. Palidez, *f.* (paleness). || Tristeza, *f.* (sadness).
want [wɔnt] n. Falta, *f.* (lack): *want of tact*, falta de tacto. || Necesidad, *f.* (need): *a man of few wants*, un hombre de pocas necesidades. || Indigencia, *f.*, miseria, *f.* (poverty). || Deseo, *m.* (wish). || Laguna, *f.*, vacío, *m.* (gap): *this book answers a long-felt want*, este libro llena una laguna que existía desde hacía mucho tiempo. || — *For want of*, por falta de: *they died for want of food*, murieron por falta de alimento; a falta de: *for want of sth. better to do, he went to bed*, a falta de algo mejor que hacer, se fue a la cama; por no tener: *for want of two shillings he could not go to the cinema*, por no tener dos chelines no pudo ir al cine. || FIG. *For want of a nail the shoe is lost*, por un clavo se pierde una herradura. || *To be in want*, estar necesitado, da. || *To be in want of*, necesitar, tener necesidad de: *I am in want of a dress*, necesito un traje; estar falto de, carecer de: *millions of people are in want of food*, millones de personas carecen de alimento.

want [wɔnt] v. tr. Querer: *they want to go to America*, quieren ir a América; *I want a cup of coffee*, quiero una taza de café; *I want him to come*, quiero que venga. || Desear (to wish). || Necesitar, hacer falta (to need): *the house wants a cleaning*, la casa necesita limpieza; *he wants to rest*, necesita descansar, le hace falta descansar; *what you want is a long holiday*, lo que a ti te hace falta es tomarte unas vacaciones largas. || Faltarle a uno, carecer de (to lack): *he wants the stamina of a long-distance runner*, le falta la resistencia *or* carece de la resistencia de un corredor de fondo. || Exigir, requerir (to demand, to require): *that work wants a lot of patience*, ese trabajo requiere mucha paciencia. || Deber, necesitar: *you want to eat more*, necesitas comer más. || Querer hablar con, querer ver, reclamar: *your father wants you*, tu padre quiere hablar contigo *or* te reclama. || Buscar (to look for). || Pedir (to ask): *how much does he want for it?*, ¿cuánto pide por eso? || — *He is wanted by the police*, lo busca la policía. || *I don't want it known*, no quiero que se sepa. || *If you want to*, si quieres. || *It wants an hour till dinner time*, falta una hora para la cena. || FAM. *It wants some doing*, no es nada fácil, hay que tener valor para hacerlo. || *The goods will be supplied as they are wanted*, las mercancías serán suministradas a medida que se vayan necesitando. || *Wanted*, se busca (criminals), se necesita (services). || *What does he want with me?*, ¿qué quiere de mí? || *When you want to*, cuando quieras. || *You are not wanted here*, aquí estás de más. || *You are wanted in the office*, te llaman *or* te reclaman en el despacho.

— V. intr. Querer. || — *To want for*, faltarle a uno, carecer de: *he never wanted for affection as a child*, de niño nunca le faltó cariño, de niño nunca careció de cariño. || *To want for nothing*, tenerlo todo, no faltarle a uno nada.

want ad [—æd] n. U. S. Anuncio, *m.* [en un periódico].

wanting [—iŋ] adj. Ausente (absent). || Deficiente (deficient). || — *They are wanting in team spirit*, les falta espíritu de equipo, carecen de espíritu de equipo. || *Wanting in*, falto de, sin: *wanting in intelligence*, sin inteligencia.

— Prep. Sin: *a watch wanting its winder*, un reloj sin cuerda.

wanton [—ən] adj. Lascivo, ca; sensual (lewd). || Libertino, na (promiscuous). || Voluptuoso, sa (voluptuous). || Desenfrenado, da (lacking moderation). || Sin sentido (senseless). || Sin motivo (without motive). || Exuberante, lujuriante (luxuriant). || Inhumano, na (inhumane). || Juguetón, ona (playful). || Desobediente (undisciplined). || Extravagante (extravagant).

— N. Libertino, na.

wanton [—ən] v. intr. Juguetear.

wantonness [—ənnis] n. Libertinaje, *m.*, desenfreno, *m.* (licentiousness). || Voluptuosidad, *f.* (voluptuousness). || Desenfreno, *m.* (lack of moderation). || Exuberancia, *f.* (luxuriance). || Crueldad, *f.* (cruelty).

wapiti [ˈwɔpiti] n. Wapití, *m.* (deer).

war [ˈwɔ:*] n. Guerra, *f.* || — *At war*, en guerra: *they are at war*, están en guerra. || *Civil war*, guerra civil. || *Lightning war*, guerra relámpago. || *The cold war*, la guerra fría. || *The Great War*, la Primera Guerra Mundial. || *The Trojan War*, la Guerra de Troya. || *The Wars of the Roses*, la guerra de las Dos Rosas. || *To be on a war footing*, estar en pie de guerra. || FIG. *To be openly at war with s.o.*, tenerle declarada la guerra a uno. || *To declare war on o upon*, declarar la guerra a. || *To go to the wars*, irse a la guerra. || *To go to war*, entrar en guerra (nations). || *To wage war* o *to make war on*, hacer la guerra a. || *War of nerves*, guerra de nervios. || *War to the knife*, guerra a muerte. || *World War*, Guerra Mundial.

— Adj. De guerra. || — *War baby*, niño nacido durante la guerra. || *War chant*, canto guerrero. || FIG. *War cloud*, amenaza (*f.*) de guerra. || *War council*, consejo (*m.*) de guerra. || *War crime*, crimen (*m.*) de guerra. || *War criminal*, criminal (*m.*) de guerra || *War cry*, grito (*m.*) de guerra. || *War dance*, danza (*f.*) de guerra. || U. S. *War Department*, Ministerio (*m.*) de la Guerra. || *War fever*, sicosis (*f.*) de guerra. || *War game*, estudios tácticos sobre el mapa (tactical exercises), maniobras, *f. pl.* (manœuvers). || *War memorial*, monumento (*m.*) a los Caídos. || *War Office*, Ministerio (*m.*) de la Guerra. || *War paint*, pinturas (*f. pl.*) de guerra (of primitive tribes), galas, *f. pl.* (ceremonial dress), maquillaje, *m.* (cosmetics).

war [wɔ:*] v. intr. Estar en guerra, guerrear (to be at war). || FIG. Luchar (*against*, contra) [in order to exterminate sth.].

warble [ˈwɔ:bl] n. Gorjeo, *m.*, trino, *m.* (sound). || VET. Tumor (*m.*) producido por reznos. || Rezno, *m.* (warble fly).

warble [ˈwɔ:bl] v. tr. Cantar gorjeando *or* trinando.

— V. intr. Gorjear, trinar (birds). || Cantar (to sing).

warble fly [—flai] n. ZOOL. Rezno, *m.*

warbler [—ə*] n. Curruca, *f.* (European bird).

warbling [—iŋ] adj. Canoro, ra (bird).

— N. Gorjeo, *m.*

ward [wɔ:d] n. Pupilo, *m.* (minor under legal care). || Custodia, *f.*, tutela, *f.* (guardianship). || Pabellón, *m.* (building in prison or hospital). || Sala, *f.* (large room in hospital). || Barrio, *m.*, distrito, *m.* (of a town). || Guarda, *f.* (of a lock). || Muesca, *f.* (of a key). || *The child was made a ward of Court*, pusieron al niño bajo la protección del tribunal.

ward [wɔ:d] v. tr. (Ant.). Guardar, proteger. || *To ward off*, parar, desviar (a blow), prevenir, evitar (a danger), rechazar (an attack).

warden [—n] n. Guarda, *m.* (official). || Vigilante, *m.* (keeper). || Mayordomo, *m.* (churchwarden). || Director, *m.* (of an institution). || U. S. Alcaide, *m.*, carcelero, *m.* (of a prison). || *Game warden*, guarda de caza, guardamonte, *m.*, guardabosque, *m.*

wardenship [—ənʃip] n. Cargo (*m.*) de guarda (of an official) *or* de director (of an institution) *or* de alcaide (of a prison).

warder [—ə*] n. Carcelero, *m.* (of a prison). || Guardián, *m.*, vigilante, *m.* (watchman).

wardress [—ris] n. Carcelera, *f.* (of a prison). || Guardiana, *f.*, vigilante, *f.*

wardrobe [—rəub] n. Armario, *m.*, guardarropa, *m.*, ropero, *m.* (piece of furniture). || Guardarropa, *m.*, vestuario, *m.* (a person's clothes). || THEATR. Vestuario, *m.* || THEATR. *Wardrobe keeper*, guardarropa, *m.* & *f.*

wardrobe trunk [—rəubtrʌnk] n. Baúl (*m.*) armario *or* ropero.

wardroom [—rum] n. MAR. Cámara (*f.*) de oficiales (officers' living quarters).

wardship [—ʃip] n. Tutela, *f.*

ware [wɛə*] n. Loza, *f.* (pottery). || Objetos, *m. pl.*, artículos, *m. pl.* (things). — Pl. Mercancías, *f.* (goods for sale): *to shout one's wares*, pregonar sus mercancías.

ware [wɛə*] adj. See AWARE.

ware [wɛə*] v. tr. Tener cuidado con. || *Ware!*, ¡cuidado!

— OBSERV. El verbo *to ware* se utiliza sólo en la forma imperativa.

warehouse [ˈwɛəhaus] n. Almacén, *m.* (storehouse). || Guardamuebles, *m. inv.* (for storing one's furniture). || Depósito (*m.*) de mercancías [en las aduanas] (customs storehouse).

warehouse [ˈwɛəhaus] v. tr. Almacenar (goods, wares). || Depositar (under bond). || Guardar en el guardamuebles (one's furniture).

warehouseman [—mən] n. Almacenero, *m.*, guardalmacén, *m.*

— OBSERV. El plural de *warehouseman* es *warehousemen*.

warehousing [ˈwɛəhauziŋ] n. Almacenaje, *m.*, almacenamiento, *m.*

warfare [ˈwɔ:fɛə*] n. Guerra, *f.*: *atomic, germ, guerilla, trench, nuclear warfare*, guerra atómica, bacteriológica, de guerrillas, de trincheras, nuclear.

warhead [ˈwɔ:hed] n. Ojiva, *f.* (head of a projectile): *atomic warhead*, ojiva atómica.

war-horse [ˈwɔ:hɔ:s] n. Caballo (*m.*) de batalla. || FIG. Veterano, *m.*

warily [ˈwɛərili] adv. Con cautela, cautelosamente.

wariness [ˈwɛərinis] n. Cautela, *f.*, precaución, *f.*

warlike [ˈwɔ:laik] adj. Belicoso, sa (inclined to favour war): *a warlike tribe*, una tribu belicosa. || Guerrero, ra (feat). || Militar, marcial (sound).

war loan [ˈwɔ:ləun] n. Empréstito (*m.*) de guerra.

warlord [ˈwɔ:lɔ:d] n. Jefe (*m.*) militar.

warm [wɔ:m] adj. Tibio, bia (not very hot): *to bath a baby in warm water*, bañar un niño en agua tibia. || Caliente: *the sea is warm today*, el mar está caliente hoy. || Cálido, da; caluroso, sa (climate). || De calor, caluroso, sa (day). || Caliente, de abrigo: *warm clothes*, ropa caliente. || Acogedor, ra; agradable (fire). || Acalorado, da: *a warm discussion*, una discusión acalorada. || FIG. Cariñoso, sa; afectuoso, sa (affectionate). | Caluroso, sa (very cordial): *a warm welcome*, una acogida calurosa; *warm applause*, aplausos calurosos. | Cálido, da (colours). | Fresco, ca (a scent). | Caliente (in a guessing game). | Ardiente, fervoroso, sa. | Entusiasta (enthusiastic). || FIG. FAM. Peligroso, sa (dangerous). | Feo, a; desagradable (unpleasant). || — *The weather is warm*, hace calor. || *To be warm*, hacer calor (weather), tener calor (person), estar caliente (thing). || *To get warm*, entrar en calor (person), calentarse (thing), empezar a hacer calor (weather). || *To keep o.s. warm*, abrigarse. || *To keep warm*, conservar caliente (food), abrigar (person). || *Warm front*, frente cálido (in meteorology). || FIG. *You're getting warm*, ¡caliente! (in guessing games).

— N. Calentamiento, *m.* || *To have a warm by the fire*, calentarse junto al fuego.

warm [wɔ:m] v. tr. Calentar. || FIG. Alegrar (the heart). | Calentar (s.o.'s blood). | Acalorar (s.o.). || — *To warm o.s. in the sun*, calentarse al sol. || *To warm over*, recalentar (food). || FIG. *To warm s.o.'s ears*, calentarle a uno las orejas. || *To warm up*, calentar (to make sth. warm), recalentar (to reheat), hacer entrar en calor (to make s.o. warm), animar (to make more animated).

— V. intr. Calentarse. || — *To warm to an idea*, acoger *or* aceptar una idea con entusiasmo. || *To warm to s.o.*, tomarle simpatía a alguien. || *To warm up*, entrar en calor (to get warm), animarse (to liven up).

warm-blooded [—ˈblʌdid] adj. De sangre caliente. || FIG. Ardiente, apasionado, da.

warmer [—ə*] n. Calentador, *m.* || *Foot warmer,* calientapiés, *m. inv.*
warmhearted [—ˈhɑ:tid] adj. Afectuoso, sa; cariñoso, sa (loving). || Bueno, na (kind).
warming [—iŋ] n. FAM. Paliza, *f.*, tunda, *f.*
warming pan [—iŋpæn] n. Calentador (*m.*) de cama.
warming-up [—iŋˈʌp] adj. Para entrar en calor (exercises).
warmly [—li] adv. Calurosamente (cordially). || Afectuosamente, cariñosamente (affectionately). || Con entusiasmo (enthusiastically).
warmonger [ˈwɔ:ˌmʌŋgə*] n. Belicista, *m.* & *f.*, agitador, ra.
warmongering [—riŋ] n. Belicismo, *m.*, incitación (*f.*) a la guerra.
warmth [wɔ:mθ] n. Calor, *m.* (heat). || FIG. Ardor, *m.*, entusiasmo, *m.* (ardour). | Cordialidad, *f.* || *The warmth of your welcome,* su acogida calurosa.
warm-up [ˈwɔ:mʌp] n. SP. Ejercicios (*m. pl.*) para entrar en calor.
warn [wɔ:n] v. tr. Advertir, prevenir de, avisar de: *I warned you of the danger,* le advertí el peligro. || Avisar (to inform): *somebody warned the police,* alguien avisó a la policía. || Aconsejar: *I warned you not to go,* le aconsejé que no fuese. || Amonestar (to rebuke). || — *Be warned by me,* que mi experiencia le sirva de ejemplo. || *I have already warned you about your impoliteness,* ya le dije que no fuera incorrecto. || *The doctor warned him against smoking,* el médico le dijo que tenía que dejar de fumar. || *The public are warned that he is armed,* se advierte al público que va armado. || *To warn off,* despedir (to send away): *her father warned the suitor off,* su padre despidió al pretendiente. || *To warn off the course,* impedir que participe en las carreras (jockey, owner). || *To warn s.o. off the premises,* expulsar a alguien (to order to leave), prohibir la entrada a alguien (to prevent from trespassing). || *We were warned of the risks involved,* nos advirtieron los riesgos que corríamos. || *We were warned to take warm clothing,* nos advirtieron que lleváramos ropa de abrigo.
warner [—ə*] n. TECH. Avisador, *m.*, aparato (*m.*) de alarma (warning device).
warning [—iŋ] n. Advertencia, *f.*, aviso, *m.*: *they ignored his warning and jumped,* no hicieron caso de su advertencia y saltaron. || Previo aviso, *m.* (notice). || Amonestación, *f.* (rebuke). || Señal, *f.* (signal). || Alarma, *f.* (alarm). || Lección, *f.* (lesson). || Ejemplo, *m.* (example). || — *Give me five minutes warning,* avíseme cinco minutos antes. || *Let this be a warning to you,* que esto le sirva de lección *or* de escarmiento. || *Take warning from it,* que le sirva de lección. || *To sound a note of warning,* dar la alarma. || *Warning to leave,* notificación (*f.*) de despido. || *Without warning,* sin avisar: *he came without warning,* vino sin avisar; de repente (suddenly): *it happened without warning,* ocurrió de repente.
— Adj. De aviso, de advertencia: *warning shot,* disparo de advertencia. || De alarma: *warning device,* dispositivo de alarma. || De amonestación (reprimanding). || — *Warning light,* lámpara indicadora, piloto, *m.*, señal luminosa. || AUT. *Warning signs,* señales (*f.*) de peligro.
warningly [—iŋli] adv. A modo de advertencia.
warp [wɔ:p] n. Urdimbre, *f.* (in a fabric or loom). || Alabeo, *m.* (of timber). || FIG. Deformación, *f.* (mental twist). | Perversión, *f.* || MAR. Espía, *f.* (cable). || GEOL. Tierras (*f. pl.*) de aluvión.
warp [wɔ:p] v. tr. Alabear (timber, etc.). || FIG. Deformar, pervertir (the mind, character, etc.). | Tergiversar, desvirtuar (meaning). || Urdir (yarn, etc.). || MAR. Halar, atoar.
— V. intr. Alabearse (to become twisted). || MAR. Ir a remolque.
warpath [ˈwɔ:pɑ:θ] n. *To be on the warpath,* estar en pie de guerra (Indians), estar buscando guerra (to be looking for trouble).
warp beam [ˈwɔ:pbi:m] n. Enjulio, *m.*, enjullo, *m.*
warper [ˈwɔ:pə*] n. Urdidor, ra (person). || Urdidor, *m.* (machine).
warping [ˈwɔ:piŋ] n. Alabeo, *m.* (of timber, etc.). || Urdidura, *f.* (of textiles). || MAR. Remolque, *m.*
warplane [ˈwɑ:plein] n. Avión (*m.*) militar.
warrant [ˈwɔrənt] n. Autorización (*f.*) legal (legal authorization). || Justificación, *f.* (justification). || Garantía, *f.* (guarantee). || JUR. Orden, *f.*, mandamiento (*m.*) judicial: *warrant of arrest,* orden de detención. | Mandamiento (*m.*) de pago (for a payment). || MIL. Patente, *f.* (patent). | Nombramiento (*m.*) de asimilado (certificate of appointment). || COMM. Recibo (*m.*) de depósito.
warrant [ˈwɔrənt] v. tr. Justificar (to justify). || Garantizar (to guarantee). || Autorizar (to authorize).
warrantable [—əbl] adj. Garantizable (that can be guaranteed). || Justificable (justifiable).
warrantee [ˌwɔrənˈti:] n. JUR. Persona (*f.*) que recibe una garantía.
warranter [ˈwɔrəntə*] n. JUR. Fiador, ra; garante, *m.* & *f.*
warrant officer [ˈwɔrəntˌɔfisə*] n. MIL. Suboficial, *m.*, oficial (*m.*) asimilado. || U. S. MAR. Contramaestre, *m.* (boatswain).
warrantor [ˈwɔrəntɔ:*] n. JUR. Fiador, *m.*, garante, *m.*
warranty [ˈwɔrənti] n. JUR. Garantía, *f.* || Autorización, *f.* (authorization). || Justificación, *f.* (justification). || Garantía, *f.* (guarantee).
warren [ˈwɔrin] n. Conejal, *m.*, conejar, *m.*, conejera, *f.* || FIG. Colmena, *f.*, conejera, *f.* (overcrowded tenement house, etc.). | Laberinto, *m.* (network of passages, etc.).
warring [ˈwɔ:riŋ] adj. Opuesto, ta (interests, etc.). || En lucha (fighting). || En guerra (at war).
warrior [ˈwɔriə*] n. Guerrero, *m.* || *The Unknown Warrior,* el Soldado Desconocido.
Warsaw [ˈwɔ:sɔ:] pr. n. GEOGR. Varsovia.
warship [ˈwɔ:ʃip] n. MAR. Buque (*m.*) de guerra.
wart [wɔ:t] n. Verruga, *f.*
warthog [—hɔg] n. ZOOL. Facoquero, *m.*, jabalí (*m.*) verrugoso.
wartime [ˈwɔ:taim] n. Tiempo (*m.*) de guerra.
warty [ˈwɔ:ti] adj. Verrugoso, sa.
war-weary [ˈwɔ:ˌwiəri] adj. Cansado de la guerra.
wary [ˈwɛəri] adj. Cauteloso, sa; precavido, da. || — *I was a bit wary at first,* al principio estuve dudando. || *Man to be wary of,* hombre (*m.*) de cuidado. || *To be wary of,* tener cuidado con.
was [wɔz] pret. See BE.
wash [wɔʃ] n. Lavado, *m.* || Colada, *f.*, ropa (*f.*) para lavar (clothes, linen, etc.). || Lavandería, *f.* (laundry): *I have sent all your clothes to the wash,* he mandado toda su ropa a la lavandería. || GEOL. Aluvión, *m.* (debris). | Erosión, *f.* || Remolino, *m.* (of waves). || MAR. Estela, *f.* (left by a ship). || AVIAT. Perturbación (*f.*) aerodinámica. || Rumor, *m.*, murmullo, *m.* (sound made by water). || MIN. Grava (*f.*) aurífera (gold-bearing earth). || Lavazas, *f. pl.* (waste liquid). || FAM. Aguachirle, *f.* (tasteless beverage). || ARTS. Aguada, *f.* || Mano, *f.*, capa, *f.* (of whitewash, etc.). || Baño, *m.* (coat of gold, silver, etc.). || Lavado, *m.* (of hair). || Loción, *f.* (cosmetic). || Enjuague, *m.* (mouthwash). || — FIG. *It will all come out in the wash,* todo se arreglará. || *To give sth. a wash,* lavar algo. || *To have a wash,* lavarse. || *To have a wash and brush-up,* lavarse y arreglarse.
wash [wɔʃ] v. tr. Lavar: *I have just washed all my shirts,* acabo de lavar todas mis camisas. || Quitar (dirt, stains). || Fregar: *to wash the dishes, the floor,* fregar los platos, el suelo. || MIN. ARTS. Lavar. || Bañar (the sea): *The Mediterranean washes the coast of Malaga,* el Mediterráneo baña la costa de Málaga. || Regar (a river). || Barrer: *the waves washed the deck,* las olas barrieron la cubierta. || Inundar, anegar: *heavy rains washed the roads,* las fuertes lluvias inundaron las carreteras. || Mojar, humedecer (to moisten). || Llevarse: *the waves washed the boat out to sea,* las olas se llevaron el barco mar adentro. || Arrojar: *a box washed ashore,* una caja arrojada a la playa [por el mar]. || Cavar (to excavate): *the rain washed a gulley in the hillside,* las lluvias cavaron un barranco en la ladera de la colina. || Erosionar (to erode). || FIG. Purificar, limpiar (the soul). || Encalar, enjalbegar (walls). || Dar un baño a, bañar (a metal). || Depurar (gases). || —*This detergent will not wash wollens,* este detergente no es bueno para la lana. || *To wash one's face,* lavarse la cara. || FIG. *To wash one's hands of sth.,* lavarse las manos de algo, desentenderse de algo. || *To wash o.s.,* lavarse.
— V. intr. Lavarse (to cleanse o.s.). || Lavar la ropa, lavar (to clean clothes). || Lavarse: *material that washes well,* tela que se lava muy bien. || Lavar: *this detergent washes very well,* este detergente lava muy bien. || Barrer: *to wash over the deck,* barrer la cubierta. || — *She washes for a living,* es lavandera. || FAM. *That excuse won't wash!,* ¡esa excusa no cuela!
— **To wash away,** quitar [lavando] (stains). | Derrubiar: *the river washed away its banks,* el río derrubió sus riberas. | Erosionar: *the waves washed away the cliff,* las olas erosionaron el acantilado. | Llevarse: *the tide washed away his sunglasses,* el mar se llevó sus gafas de sol. | — FIG. *To wash away one's sins,* limpiar sus pecados. || **To wash down,** lavar: *to wash the car down,* lavar el coche. | Rociar: *a meal washed down with a good wine,* una comida rociada con un buen vino. | Tragar: *to wash a pill down with water,* tragar una pastilla con agua. || **To wash off,** quitar *or* quitarse [lavando]. || **To wash out,** lavar (clothes). | Quitar [lavando] (stains). | Quitarse (to be removed). | Desteñirse (dye, colour). | Lavar: *to wash a bottle out,* lavar una botella. | Llevarse (to carry away). | ARTS. Degradar, rebajar (colours). | FIG. Abandonar (a plan, idea, etc.), fracasar (to fail). | — *The cricket match was washed out,* se tuvo que cancelar el partido de cricket a causa de la lluvia. | FIG. *To wash out an insult in blood,* lavar un insulto con sangre. || **To wash up,** fregar. | Fregar los platos (to clean the dishes). | Arrojar: *wreckage washed up by the sea,* restos arrojados por el mar.
washable [ˈwɔʃəbl] adj. Lavable.
wash-and-wear [ˈwɔʃəndˈwɛə*] adj. Que no necesita plancha, de lava y pon.
washbasin [ˈwɔʃˌbeisn] n. Lavabo, *m.* (basin). || Palangana, *f.* (bowl).
washboard [ˈwɔʃbɔ:d] n. Tabla (*f.*) de lavar (for scrubbing clothes on). || Cenefa, *f.*, zócalo, *m.* (skirting board).

washbowl [ˈwɔʃbəul] n. Lavabo, *m.* (basin). || Palangana, *f.* (bowl).
washcloth [ˈwɔʃklɔθ] n. U. S. Toallita (*f.*) para lavarse la cara o el cuerpo.
washday [ˈwɔʃdei] n. Día (*m.*) de la colada.
washed-out [ˈwɔʃtˈaut] adj. Descolorido, da; desteñido, da (faded in colour). || FAM. Rendido, da; reventado, da (tired).
washed up [ˈwɔʃtˈʌp] adj. FAM. Acabado, da: *he is completely washed up,* está completamente acabado. || *Their marriage is washed up,* su matrimonio es un fracaso.
washer [ˈwɔʃə*] n. TECH. Arandela, *f.* | Depurador (*m.*) de gas (for washing gases). || Lavador, ra (person). || Lavadora, *f.* (washing machine).
washerman [—mən] n. Lavandero, *m.* (laundryman).
— OBSERV. El plural de *washerman* es *washermen.*
washer-up [—rˈʌp] n. Lavaplatos, *m.* & *f. inv.* (person).
— OBSERV. El plural de *washer-up* es *washers-up.*
washerwoman [—ˌwumən] n. Lavandera, *f.*
— OBSERV. El plural de *washerwoman* es *washerwomen.*
washhouse [ˈwɔʃhaus] n. Lavadero, *m.*
washing [ˈwɔʃiŋ] n. Lavado, *m.* || Colada, *f.* (of clothes). || Fregado, *m.* (of the floor, dishes). || Colada, *f.*, ropa (*f.*) para lavar, ropa (*f.*) sucia (clothes to wash). || Colada, *f.*, ropa (*f.*) tendida (hung to dry). || ARTS. Aguada, *f.*, lavado, *m.* || Encalado, *m.*, enjalbegado, *m.* (of walls). || MIN. Lavado, *m.* || TECH. Depuración, *f.* (of gas). || COMM. Venta (*f.*) ficticia. || — Pl. Lavazas, *f.* (dirty water). || MIN. Mineral (*m. sing.*) obtenido tras el lavado (ore). | Lavadero, *m. sing.* (place). || — *Colour that will not stand washing,* color que se destiñe al ser lavado. || REL. *The washing of feet,* el lavatorio de los pies. || *To do the washing,* lavar la ropa, hacer la colada. || *To take in washing,* ser lavandera.
washing day [—dei] n. Día (*m.*) de la colada.
washing machine [—məˌʃi:n] n. Lavadora, *f.*
washing powder [—ˌpaudə*] n. Jabón (*m.*) en polvo.
washing soda [—ˌsəudə] n. Sosa, *f.*
washing-up [—ˈʌp] n. Fregado (*m.*) de los platos (action). || Platos (*m. pl.*) para fregar (dirty dishes). || Platos (*m. pl.*) fregados (washed dishes). || *To do the washing-up,* fregar los platos.
washing-up bowl [—ˈʌpbəul] n. Barreño, *m.* [para fregar los platos].
washleather [ˈwɔʃˌleðə*] n. Gamuza, *f.*
washout [ˈwɔʃaut] n. Derrubio, *m.* (erosion). || Lugar (*m.*) derrubiado (eroded place). || FAM. Desastre, *m.*, (a complete failure): *he's a washout,* es un desastre; *the film is a washout,* la película es un desastre.
washrag [ˈwɔʃræg] n. U. S. See WASHCLOTH.
washroom [ˈwɔʃrum] n. U. S. Servicios, *m. pl.*
wash sale [ˈwɔʃˈseil] n. COMM. Venta (*f.*) ficticia [de acciones].
washstand [ˈwɔʃstænd] n. Lavabo, *m.*
washtub [ˈwɔʃtʌb] n. Tina (*f.*) donde se lava la ropa.
washwoman [ˈwɔʃˌwumən] n. Lavandera, *f.*
— OBSERV. El plural de esta palabra es *washwomen.*
washy [ˈwɔʃi] adj. Aguado, da (wine). || Soso, sa; insípido, da (food). || Deslavazado, da (colour, style).
wasn't [ˈwɔznt] contraction of *was not.*
wasp [wɔsp] n. Avispa, *f.* (insect).
waspish [—iʃ] adj. Mordaz (critical). || Irritable, enojadizo, za (irritable). || Esbelto, ta (slender).
waspishness [—iʃnis] n. Mordacidad, *f.* (of words). || Mal genio, *m.*, irritabilidad, *f.* (bad temper).
wasp waist [—ˈweist] n. Cintura (*f.*) de avispa.
wasp-waisted [—ˈweistid] adj. Con cintura de avispa (person). || Ceñido, da (dress).
wassail [ˈwɔseil] n. Brindis, *m.* (toast). || Borrachera, *f.* (heavy drinking). || Cerveza (*f.*) con especias y frutas (ale).
wassail [ˈwɔseil] v. tr. Beber a la salud de, brindar por (to toast).
— V. intr. Estar de juerga.
wastage [ˈweistidʒ] n. Pérdidas, *f. pl.* (loss): *profit forecasts take into account a certain degree of wastage,* las previsiones relativas a los beneficios toman en consideración cierta cantidad de pérdidas. || Despilfarro, *m.*, derroche, *m.* (of money). || Desgaste, *m.* (wear). || Desperdicio, *m.*: *man's wastage of natural resources,* el desperdicio por el hombre de los recursos naturales.
waste [weist] adj. Yermo, ma (barren). || Baldío, a (uncultivated). || Incultivable (not arable). || De desecho (products). || Residual (water). || Desperdiciado, da (gas, heat, steam). || Sobrante (superfluous). || De desagüe (pipe). || — *To lay waste,* asolar, devastar, arrasar. || *To lie waste,* no cultivarse, quedar sin cultivar (land).
— N. Pérdida, *f.*: *a waste of energy,* una pérdida de energía; *it's a waste of time,* es una pérdida de tiempo. || Desgaste, *m.*, deterioro, *m.* (by use). || Deterioro, *m.* (by lack of use). || Pérdidas, *f. pl.* (wastage). || CULIN. Desperdicios, *m. pl.* (of food). || Residuos, *m. pl.*, desechos, *m. pl.* (from a manufacturing process). || Basura, *f.* (rubbish). || Desierto, *m.* (desert). || Yermo, *m.* (barren land). || Erial, *m.* (uncultivated land). || TECH. Borra, *f.* (remnants of cotton fibre). || GEOL. Erosión, *f.* || JUR. Deterioro, *m.* || — *Radioactive waste,* desechos radiactivos. || *To go* o *to run to waste,* desperdiciarse.
waste [weist] v. tr. Derrochar, despilfarrar, malgastar: *to waste one's fortune,* derrochar su fortuna. || Desperdiciar (not to use). || Perder (time): *you are wasting your time trying to convince him,* pierdes el tiempo intentando convencerle. || Desaprovechar, perder (an opportunity). || Agotar, consumir (to use up). || Consumir: *the illness slowly wasted him,* la enfermedad le fue consumiendo lentamente. || Debilitar (to weaken). || Enflaquecer (to make thin). || Devastar, asolar, arrasar (to devastate). || JUR. Deteriorar. || — *Don't waste your money on a new coat when you don't need one,* no gastes tu dinero comprando un abrigo que no te hace falta. || *He is wasted in that job,* es un empleo muy por debajo de sus posibilidades. || *I am wasted on you,* no sabes apreciar lo que valgo. || *My wit is wasted on you,* no sabes apreciar mi ingenio. || *Nothing is wasted in this house,* en esta casa no se desperdicia nada, en esta casa todo se aprovecha. || *To waste words,* gastar saliva en balde.
— V. intr. Desperdiciarse: *the water is wasting,* el agua se está desperdiciando. || Desgastarse, gastarse (to wear away). || Agotarse (to become used up): *they allowed their resources to waste rapidly,* dejaron que se agotaran rápidamente sus recursos. || Disminuir (to diminish). || Debilitarse (to become weak). || Enflaquecer (to become thin). || JUR. Deteriorarse. || — *Time is wasting,* estamos perdiendo tiempo. || *To waste away,* consumirse: *he was wasting away with fever,* se estaba consumiendo con la fiebre.
wastebasket [—ˌbɑ:skit] n. U. S. Papelera, *f.*, cesto (*m.*) de los papeles.
wastebin [—bin] n. Cubo (*m.*) de la basura.
waste disposal unit [—disˈpəuzəlˌju:nit] n. Triturador (*m.*) *or* vertedero (*m.*) de basuras.
wasteful [—ful] adj. Despilfarrador, ra; derrochador, ra (person). || Ruinoso, sa; excesivo, va: *wasteful spending,* gasto ruinoso. || *The stove is wasteful of fuel,* se gasta mucho combustible con la estufa.
wastefulness [—fulnis] n. Despilfarro, *m.*, derroche, *m.* (wasteful spending).
waste heap [—hi:p] n. Vertedero, *m.* (rubbish dump). || Escorial, *m.* (of a factory). || Escombrera, *f.* (of a mine).
wasteland [—lænd] n. Yermo, *m.* (barren land). || Erial, *m.* (uncultivated land).
waste matter [—ˌmætə*] n. Residuos, *m. pl.*, desechos, *m. pl.*
wastepaper [—ˈpeipə*] n. Papel (*m.*) usado, papeles (*m. pl.*) viejos.
wastepaper basket [—ˈpeipəˌbɑ:skit] n. Papelera, *f.*, cesto (*m.*) de los papeles.
waste pipe [—paip] n. Tubo (*m.*) de desagüe.
waste product [—ˌprɔdʌkt] n. Desecho, *m.*, producto (*m.*) de desecho, residuo, *m.*: *industrial waste products,* residuos industriales. || *The body's waste products,* los excrementos.
waster [—ə*] n. Derrochador, ra; despilfarrador, ra (ruinously extravagant). || TECH. Pieza (*f.*) defectuosa.
wasting [—iŋ] adj. Devastador, ra. || MED. Debilitante.
— N. Devastación, *f.*, asolamiento, *m.* || MED. Debilitación, *f.*
wastrel [—rəl] n. Derrochador, ra; despilfarrador, ra (spendthrift). || FAM. Inútil, *m.* & *f.*, golfo, fa.
watch [wɔtʃ] n. Reloj (*m.*) de pulsera (wristwatch). || Reloj (*m.*) de bolsillo (pocket timepiece). || Vigilancia, *f.* (vigilance). || Vigilante (*m.*) nocturno, guarda (*m.*) nocturno (watchman). || MAR. Guardia, *f.* (period of duty): *to be on watch,* estar de guardia. | Brigada (*f.*) de guardia (crew on duty). | Marinero (*m.*) de guardia, vigía, *m.* (man on lookout). || HIST. Vigilante, *m.* (person). | Ronda, *f.* (group of persons on guard). || — MAR. *Officer of the watch,* oficial (*m.*) de guardia. || *On the watch,* alerta, ojo avizor. || *To be on the watch for s.o.,* acechar a alguien, estar al acecho de alguien. || *To keep watch,* estar de guardia. || *To keep watch on* o *over,* vigilar. || *To set a watch on s.o.,* hacer vigilar a alguien.
watch [wɔtʃ] v. tr. Observar, mirar: *to watch s.o.'s reaction,* observar la reacción de alguien; *to watch s.o. working,* mirar a alguien que trabaja, observar como trabaja alguien. || Ver, mirar: *to watch a football match on television,* ver un partido de fútbol en la televisión. || Fijarse en (to pay attention). || Vigilar (to keep an eye on). || Cuidar (to take care of): *to watch a child,* cuidar a un niño. || Velar (a corpse, a sick person). || Tener cuidado con (to be careful with): *watch the wet paint,* tenga cuidado con la pintura; *I have to watch what I spend,* tengo que tener cuidado con lo que gasto. || Seguir: *to watch a patient's progress,* seguir los progresos de un enfermo. || Asistir: *hundreds of people watched the Wimbledon finals,* cientos de personas asistieron a las finales de Wimbledon. || — FIG. *A watched pot o kettle never boils,* quien espera desespera. || *To watch one's chance,* esperar el momento oportuno. || *Watch how you go!,* ¡anda con cuidado! || *Watch it!,* ¡cuidado! || FIG. *Watch your step!,* ¡tenga cuidado! || *We are being watched,* nos están mirando.
— V. intr. Mirar, observar: *I don't like taking part, I prefer to watch,* no me gusta tomar parte, prefiero observar. || Velar (to stay awake). || Vigilar (to keep guard). || — *I watched all night,* pasé toda la noche en

vela. || *To watch after*, seguir con la mirada. || *To watch by*, velar (a sick person). || *To watch for*, esperar: *I am watching for the postman*, estoy esperando al cartero. || *To watch out*, estar atento, estar ojo avizor (to keep a lookout), tener cuidado (to be careful). || *To watch out for*, estar al acecho de: *police are watching out for the criminals*, la policía está al acecho de los criminales; tener cuidado con: *watch out for pickpockets*, tenga cuidado con los rateros. || *To watch over*, cuidar, vigilar (to look after), velar (a sick person), velar por (s.o.'s interests, welfare), guardar (a flock). || *Watch out!*, ¡cuidado!
watchband [—bænd] n. Correa (*f.*) de reloj (leather, nylon). || Cadena (*f.*) de reloj (metal).
watchcase [—keis] n. Caja (*f.*) de reloj.
watch chain [—tʃein] n. Cadena (*f.*) de reloj, leontina, *f.*
watchdog [—dɔg] n. Perro (*m.*) guardián.
watcher [—ə*] n. Vigilante, *m.* (guard). || Observador, ra (observer). || Mirón, ona (onlooker).
watch fire [—faiə*] n. Hoguera, *f.*, fuego, *m.*
watchful [—ful] adj. Atento, ta; vigilante, alerta (attentive). || Desvelado, da (sleepless).
watchfulness [—fulnis] n. Vigilancia, *f.*, cuidado, *m.*
watch glass [—glɑːs] n. Cristal (*m.*) de reloj.
watching [—iŋ] n. Vigilancia, *f.* || Observación, *f.*: *bird watching*, observación de los pájaros. || *He is a man who wants watching*, es un hombre que hay que vigilar.
watchmaker [—ˌmeikə*] n. Relojero, *m.* || *Watchmaker's*, relojería, *f.* (shop).
watchmaking [—ˌmeikiŋ] n. Relojería, *f.*
watchman [—mən] n. Vigilante, *m.* || *Night watchman*, vigilante nocturno (on a building site, in a factory, etc.), sereno, *m.* (in the street).

— OBSERV. El plural de *watchman* es *watchmen*.

watch night [—nait] n. Nochevieja, *f.*
watch pocket [—ˌpɔkit] n. Bolsillo (*m.*) del reloj.
watch spring [—spriŋ] n. Muelle, *m.*, resorte, *m.*
watch strap [—stræp] n. Correa (*f.*) de reloj.
watchtower [—ˌtauə*] n. Atalaya, *f.*
watchword [—wəːd] n. Contraseña, *f.*, santo y seña, *m.*: *to give the watchword*, dar el santo y seña. || Consigna, *f.* (guiding principle): *to follow the party watchword*, seguir la consigna del partido.
water [ˈwɔːtə*] n. Agua, *f.*: *give me some water*, dame agua; *ammonia water*, agua amoniacal. || Marea, *f.*: *high, low water*, marea alta, baja. || MED. Orina, *f.* (urine). || Aguas, *f. pl.*: *the water of a diamond, of a material*, las aguas de un diamante, de una tela. || Oriente, *m.* (of a pearl). || ARTS. Acuarela, *f.* || COMM. Acciones (*f. pl.*) emitidas sin aumento de capital equivalente. || — Pl. Aguas, *f.*: *to take the waters*, tomar las aguas; *territorial waters*, aguas jurisdiccionales; *in British waters*, en aguas británicas. || — *Brackish* o *briny water*, agua salobre. || *By water*, por mar, en barco. || FIG. *Come hell or high water*, pase lo que pase, contra viento y marea. || MED. *Difficulty in passing water*, retención de orina. || *Drinking water*, agua potable. || *Fresh water*, agua dulce. || *Hard water*, agua gorda *or* dura. || *Heavy water*, agua pesada. || REL. *Holy water*, agua bendita. || *Irrigation water*, agua de regadío. || *Lavender water*, agua de lavanda. || *Mineral water*, agua mineral. || *Mother water*, aguas madres. || FIG. *Much water has flowed under the bridge since then*, ha llovido mucho desde entonces. | *Of the first water*, de primera categoría. || *On the water*, en barco (person), en el mar (a ship). || *Orange-flower water*, agua de azahar. || *Oxygenated water*, agua oxigenada. || *Rain water*, agua de lluvia. || *Running water*, agua corriente. || *Salt water*, agua salada. || *Stagnant water*, agua estancada. || FIG. *Still waters run deep*, del agua mansa me libre Dios, que de la brava me libro yo *or* me guardaré yo. || MAR. *The boat draws six feet of water*, el barco tiene seis pies de calado. || FIG. *The sight of that cake brings water to my mouth*, se me hace la boca agua al ver ese pastel. | *The theory does not hold water*, la teoría no tiene fundamento. | *To be in hot water*, estar en un apuro *or* en un aprieto. | *To bring water to one's eyes*, hacerle saltar las lágrimas a uno. | *To dash cold water on*, echar un jarro de agua fría sobre. | *To fish in troubled waters*, pescar en río revuelto. | *To get into deep water* o *to get o.s. into hot water*, meterse en dificultades, meterse en un aprieto *or* en un lío. | *To keep one's head above water*, mantenerse a flote. || *To let in water*, calarse: *these broken shoes let in water*, estos zapatos rotos se calan; hacer agua (boat). || *To make water*, hacer agua (to spring a leak), hacer aguas, orinar (to urinate). || *To pass water*, hacer aguas, orinar. || MAR. *To take on water*, repostar agua. || *To take the horses to water*, llevar los caballos al abrevadero *or* a beber. || FIG. *To throw* o *to pour cold water on*, echar un jarro de agua fría sobre (s.o.), desacreditar (a project). || CHEM. *Water of crystallization*, agua de cristalización. || MED. *Water on the brain*, hidrocefalia, *f.* | *Water on the knee*, derrame (*m.*) sinovial.
— Adj. Acuático, ca: *water bird*, ave acuática; *water festival*, festival acuático. || Acuático, ca; náutico, ca (sport). || TECH. Hidráulico, ca.
water [ˈwɔːtə*] v. tr. Mojar (to soak). || Humedecer (to wet). || Regar: *to water the garden, the plants*, regar el jardín, las plantas; *the Ganges waters a very large area*, el Ganges riega un área muy extensa; *they have watered the road to settle the dust*, han regado la carretera para asentar el polvo. || Dar de beber a, abrevar (animals). || Abastecer de agua (to supply with water). || Aguar, diluir, bautizar (fam.): *this wine has been watered*, este vino ha sido aguado. || Tornasolar (a fabric). || — FIG. *The pocket edition is a watered-down version of the original*, la edición de bolsillo es una versión abreviada de la obra original. || COMM. *To water capital*, emitir acciones sin aumento de capital. || FIG. *To water down*, moderar, suavizar.
— V. intr. Llorar: *my right eye is watering*, me llora el ojo derecho. || Hacerse agua: *my mouth is watering* o *it makes my mouth water*, se me hace la boca agua. || Repostar agua (ship). || Beber (animals).
waterage [—ridʒ] n. Transporte (*m.*) por barco (service). || Barcaje, *m.* (fare paid).
water bag [—bæg] n. Bolsa (*f.*) para el agua. || BIOL. Bolsa (*f.*) de las aguas.
water ballast [—ˌbæləst] n. MAR. Lastre (*m.*) de agua.
water bath [—bɑːθ] n. Baño (*m.*) de maría, baño (*m.*) maría.
water-bearer [—ˌbɛərə*] n. Aguador, *m.* [*Amer.*, aguatero, *m.*]. || ASTR. *Water Bearer*, Acuario, *m.*
water-bearing [—ˌbɛəriŋ] adj. Acuífero, ra.
water biscuit [—ˌbiskit] n. CULIN. Galleta (*f.*) de harina y agua.
water boat [—bəut] n. Barco (*m.*) cisterna, buque (*m.*) aljibe.
waterborne [—bɔːn] adj. Flotante (ship). || Transportado por barco (goods). || Por vía marítima *or* fluvial, marítimo, ma; fluvial (transport).
water bottle [—ˌbɔtl] n. Cantimplora, *f.* || *Hot water bottle*, bolsa (*f.*) de agua caliente.
water brash [—bræʃ] n. MED. Pirosis, *f.*
water buffalo [—ˌbʌfələu] n. ZOOL. Búfalo (*m.*) de agua, búfalo, *m.*, carabao, *m.*
water bug [—bʌg] n. ZOOL. Chinche (*f.*) de agua.
water carriage [—ˌkæridʒ] n. Transporte (*m.*) por barco, transporte (*m.*) marítimo *or* fluvial.
water carrier [—ˌkæriə*] n. Aguador, *m.* [*Amer.*, aguatero, *m.*]. || ASTR. *Water Carrier*, Acuario, *m.*
water cart [—kɑːt] n. Carro (*m.*) de riego (for irrigation, street sprinkling). || Camión (*m.*) de riego (motorized). || Carro (*m.*) aljibe (for distributing drinking water). || Camión (*m.*) aljibe (motorized).
water chute [—ʃuːt] n. Tobogán, *m.*
water clock [—klɔk] n. Clepsidra, *f.*, reloj (*m.*) de agua.
water closet [—ˌklɔzit] n. Wáter, *m.*, retrete, *m.*
watercolour (U. S. **watercolor**) [—ˌkʌlə*] n. ARTS. Acuarela, *f.*
watercolourist (U.S. **watercolorist**) [—ˌkʌlərist] n. ARTS. Acuarelista, *m.* & *f.*
water-cool [—kuːl] v. tr. Refrigerar por agua.
water-cooling [—ˌkuːliŋ] n. Refrigeración (*f.*) por agua.
watercourse [—kɔːs] n. Corriente (*f.*) de agua (stream). || Lecho, *m.*, cauce, *m.* (bed of stream). || Canal, *m.*, conducto, *m.* (channel).
watercraft [—krɑːft] n. Barco, *m.*, embarcación, *f.* (boat). || Buque, *m.* (ship).
water crane [—krein] n. Grúa (*f.*) hidráulica.
watercress [—kres] n. BOT. Berro, *m.*
water cure [—kjuə*] n. MED. Hidroterapia, *f.*
water diviner [—diˌvainə*] n. Zahorí, *m.*
water dog [—dɔg] n. Perro (*m.*) de aguas. || FIG. Lobo (*m.*) de mar (sailor). | Buen nadador, *m.* (good swimmer).
watered [—d] adj. Regado, da: *a well-watered garden*, un jardín bien regado. || Aguado, da (wine, milk, etc.). || Tornasolado, da (fabrics).
waterfall [—fɔːl] n. Cascada, *f.*, salto (*m.*) de agua (small). || Catarata, *f.* (large).
waterfinder [—ˌfaində*] n. Zahorí, *m.*
water flea [—fliː] n. ZOOL. Pulga (*f.*) de agua.
waterfowl [—faul] n. ZOOL. Ave (*f.*) acuática.
waterfront [—frʌnt] n. Parte (*f.*) de la ciudad que da al mar (zone adjacent to the sea). || Puerto, *m.*, muelles, *m. pl.* (harbour).
water gage [—geidʒ] n. U. S. See WATER GAUGE.
water gap [—gæp] n. GEOGR. Garganta, *f.*, desfiladero, *m.*
water gas [—gæs] n. Gas (*m.*) de agua.
water gate [—geit] n. Compuerta, *f.* (sluice).
water gauge [—geidʒ] n. TECH. Indicador (*m.*) del nivel de agua (of a tank, etc.). | Hidrómetro, *m.* (for a stream).
water glass [—glɑːs] n. Vaso, *m.* (for drinking water). || Tubo (*m.*) *or* caja (*f.*) de vidrio (for examining objects under water). || CHEM. Silicato (*m.*) sódico líquido, vidrio (*m.*) soluble (silicate). || Indicador (*m.*) de nivel (water gauge). || Clepsidra, *f.*, reloj (*m.*) de agua (water clock).
water hammer [—ˌhæmə*] n. PHYS. Martillo (*m.*) de agua. || Golpe (*m.*) de ariete (in a water pipe).
water-harden [—ˌhɑːdən] v. tr. TECH. Templar [con agua].
water heater [—ˌhiːtə*] n. Calentador (*m.*) de agua.
water hemlock [—ˌhemlɔk] n. BOT. Cicuta (*f.*) acuática.
water hen [—hen] n. ZOOL. Polla (*f.*) de agua (moorhen). | Fúlica, *f.* (American coot).
water hole [—həul] n. Charca, *f.*, charco, *m.* (pond).

water hyacinth [—ˈhaiəsinθ] n. BOT. Jacinto (*m.*) de agua.

water ice [—rais] n. CULIN. Sorbete, *m.*

wateriness [—rinis] n. Acuosidad, *f.* || FIG. Insipidez, *f.* (insipidity).

watering [—riŋ] n. Riego, *m.* (of garden, plants, etc.). || AGR. Irrigación, *f.*, riego, *m.* (of fields). || Aguado, *m.*, adición (*f.*) de agua (of wine, milk, etc.).
— Adj. De riego. || Lloroso, sa: *watering eyes*, ojos llorosos.

watering can [—riŋkæn] n. Regadera, *f.*

watering cart [—riŋkɑ:t] n. See WATER CART.

watering place [—riŋpleis] n. Abrevadero, *m.* (for animals). || Balneario, *m.* (spa). || Estación (*f.*) balnearia (seaside resort).

watering trough [—riŋtrɔf] n. Abrevadero, *m.*

waterish [—riʃ] adj. Acuoso, sa (consistency, taste, etc.). || Húmedo, da (atmosphere).

water jacket [—ˌdʒækit] n. TECH. Camisa (*f.*) de agua.

water jug [—dʒʌg] n. Aguamanil, *m.* (for toilet). || Jarra (*f.*) de agua (pitcher).

water jump [—dʒʌmp] n. SP. Ría, *f.* (in steeplechase).

waterless [—lis] adj. Sin agua: *a waterless well*, un pozo sin agua. || Árido, da (land).

water level [—ˌlevəl] n. Nivel (*m.*) del agua (height of water). || MAR. Línea (*f.*) de flotación (of a ship). || TECH. Nivel (*m.*) de agua (instrument).

water lily [—ˌlili] n. BOT. Nenúfar, *m.*

waterline [—lain] n. MAR. Línea (*f.*) de flotación: *the boat was holed below the waterline*, se abrió una brecha en el barco por debajo de la línea de flotación. || Filigrana, *f.* (in papermaking). || Nivel (*m.*) del agua (height of water).

waterlogged [—lɔgd] adj. Saturado de agua (soaked with water). || Inundado, da; anegado, da (ground). || Empapado, da (wood).

water main [—mein] n. Cañería (*f.*) principal.

waterman [—mən] n. Barquero, *m.*
— OBSERV. El plural de *waterman* es *watermen*.

watermark [—mɑ:k] n. Marca (*f.*) del nivel del agua (showing the water level). || Filigrana, *f.* (in papermaking).

watermark [—mɑ:k] v. tr. Imprimir con filigrana.

watermelon [—ˌmelən] n. BOT. Sandía, *f.*

water meter [—ˈmi:tə*] n. Contador (*m.*) de agua.

water mill [—mil] n. Molino (*m.*) de agua.

water motor [—ˌməutə*] n. TECH. Motor (*m.*) hidráulico.

water nymph [—nimf] n. MYTH. Náyade, *f.*

water ouzel [—ˌu:zl] n. Tordo (*m.*) de agua (bird).

water parting [—ˌpɑ:tiŋ] n. Línea (*f.*) divisoria de las aguas.

water pipe [—paip] n. Cañería (*f.*) de agua, tubería (*f.*) de agua. || Narguile, *m.* (narghile).

water plane [—plein] n. AVIAT. Hidroavión, *m.*

water plant [—plɑ:nt] n. BOT. Planta (*f.*) acuática.

water plantain [—ˌplæntin] n. BOT. Llantén (*m.*) de agua.

waterpolice [—pəˌli:s] n. Policía (*f.*) fluvial.

water polo [—ˌpəuləu] n. SP. Water-polo, *m.*, polo (*m.*) acuático.

waterpot [—pɔt] n. Jarra (*f.*) de agua (jug). || Regadera, *f.* (watering can).

waterpower [—ˌpauə*] n. Energía (*f.*) hidráulica.

waterproof [—pru:f] adj. Impermeable (material). || Sumergible (watch).
— N. Impermeable, *m.* (raincoat). || Tela (*f.*) impermeable (material).

waterproof [—pru:f] v. tr. Impermeabilizar.

waterproofing [—ˌpru:fiŋ] n. Impermeabilización, *f.*

water pump [—pʌmp] n. TECH. Bomba (*f.*) de agua.

water ram [—ræm] n. TECH. Ariete (*m.*) hidráulico.

water rat [—ræt] n. ZOOL. Rata (*f.*) de agua (aquatic vole). | Rata (*f.*) almizclera (muskrat).

water-repellent [—riˈpelənt] or **water-resistant** [—riˈzistənt] adj. Hidrófugo, ga.

water rights [—raits] pl. n. Derechos (*m.*) de captación de agua.

water route [—ru:t] n. Vía (*f.*) navegable.

water scorpion [—ˌskɔ:pjən] n. ZOOL. Escorpión (*m.*) de agua.

water seal [—si:l] n. TECH. Cierre (*m.*) hidráulico.

watershed [—ʃed] n. GEOGR. Línea (*f.*) divisoria de las aguas (dividing line). | Cuenca, *f.* (basin). || FIG. Momento (*m.*) decisivo: *it was one of the watersheds of English history*, fue un momento decisivo en la historia inglesa.

waterside [—said] n. Orilla, *f.*, ribera, *f.*
— Adj. Ribereño, ña.

water ski [—ski:] n. SP. Esquí, *m.* (for water-skiing).

water-ski [—ski:] v. intr. SP. Hacer esquí acuático *or* náutico.

water-skiing [—ˌski:iŋ] n. SP. Esquí (*m.*) acuático, esquí (*m.*) náutico.

water skin [—skin] n. Odre, *m.*

water snake [—sneik] n. ZOOL. Serpiente (*f.*) de agua.

water softener [—ˌsɔfnə*] n. Ablandador (*m.*) del agua.

water-soluble [—ˌsɔljubl] adj. Hidrosoluble.

water spider [—ˌspaidə*] n. ZOOL. Araña (*f.*) de agua.

waterspout [—spaut] n. Canalón, *m.* (of a roof). || Tromba (*f.*) marina (meteorological phenomenon).

water sprite [—sprait] n. MYTH. Ondina, *f.*

water-stained [—steind] adj. Con manchas de humedad.

water strider [—ˌstraidə*] n. U. S. Tejedor, *m.* (insect).

water supply [—səˌplai] n. Abastecimiento (*m.*) de agua (system). || Reserva (*f.*) de agua (stored water).

water system [—ˌsistəm] n. Red (*f.*) fluvial (rivers). || Abastecimiento (*m.*) de agua (water supply).

water table [—ˌteibl] n. ARCH. Retallo (*m.*) de derrame. || GEOL. Nivel (*m.*) hidrostático, capa (*f.*) freática.

water tank [—tæŋk] n. Aljibe, *m.*, tanque, *m.* (on a vehicle). || Depósito (*m.*) de agua, aljibe, *m.* (in a house or tower). || Cisternilla, *f.* (of a lavatory).

water tap [—tæp] n. Grifo, *m.*

watertight [—tait] adj. Estanco, ca; hermético, ca (impermeable to water). || FIG. Perfecto, ta: *a watertight alibi*, una coartada perfecta. | Irrecusable, irrefutable (argument). || — MAR. *Watertight bulkhead*, mamparo estanco. | *Watertight compartment*, compartimiento estanco.

watertightness [—taitnis] n. Hermeticidad, *f.*, estanquidad, *f.*

water tower [—ˌtauə*] n. TECH. Arca (*f.*) de agua, depósito (*m.*) elevado de agua.

watertube [—tju:b] adj. Acuotubular: *watertube boiler*, caldera acuotubular.

water vapour (U. S. **water vapor**) [—ˌveipə*] n. Vapor (*m.*) de agua.

water vole [—vəul] n. ZOOL. Rata (*f.*) de agua.

water wall [—wɔ:l] n. Dique, *m.* (dike). || TECH. Pantalla (*f.*) de tubos de agua (in a boiler).

water wave [—weiv] n. MAR. Ola, *f.* || Ondulación, *f.* (of hair).

water-wave [—weiv] v. tr. Marcar (hair).

water-waving [—ˌweiviŋ] n. Aguas, *f. pl.*, visos, *m. pl.*, tornasolado, *m.* (of silk). || Marcado, *m.* (of hair).

waterway [—wei] n. Vía (*f.*) navegable, vía (*f.*) fluvial (navigable channel). || MAR. Trancanil, *m.* (on a ship's deck). || *Inland waterway*, canal, *m.*

waterweed [—wi:d] n. BOT. Planta (*f.*) acuática.

waterwheel [—wi:l] n. Rueda (*f.*) hidráulica (of a mill). || Rueda (*f.*) de álabes (of a boat). || AGR. Noria, *f.* (in irrigation).

water wings [—wiŋz] pl. n. Flotadores, *m.*

waterworks [—wə:ks] n. Sistema (*m.*) *or* instalación (*f.*) de abastecimiento de agua (water supply). || Juegos (*m. pl.*) de agua (fountains). || FAM. Vías (*f. pl.*) urinarias. || FAM. *To turn on the waterworks*, echarse a llorar.

waterworn [—wɔ:n] adj. Desgastado por el agua.

watery [—ri] adj. Acuoso, sa (like water): *a watery fluid*, un fluido acuoso. || Aguado, da; claro, ra (soup). || Aguado, da (wine). || Soso, sa; insípido, da (food). || Húmedo, da (wet): *watery land*, tierra húmeda. || Lloroso, sa (eyes). || Pálido, da; desvaído, da (colours). || FIG. Deslavazado, da (style). | Lluvioso, sa (weather). || *Watery sunshine*, sol pálido que anuncia lluvia.

watt [wɔt] n. ELECTR. Vatio, *m.*

wattage [—idʒ] n. ELECTR. Potencia (*f.*) en vatios.

watt-hour [—ˈauə*] n. ELECTR. Vatio-hora, *m.*

wattle [ˈwɔtl] n. Zarzo, *m.* (used to make walls, fences, etc.). || Varas, *f. pl.* (rods, twigs). || ZOOL. Barba, *f.* (of a bird). | Barbilla, *f.* (of a fish). || BOT. Acacia, *f.*

wattle [ˈwɔtl] v. tr. Entretejer, entrelazar (to make into wattle). || Hacer con zarzos (walls, etc.). || Unir entrelazando (fence posts).

wattmeter [ˈwɔtˌmi:tə*] n. Vatímetro, *m.*

wave [weiv] n. Ola, *f.* (of sea). || Ondulación, *f.* (on a surface, in the hair, etc.). || PHYS. RAD. Onda, *f.*: *short, medium, long wave*, onda corta, media, larga. || FIG. Racha, *f.*: *a wave of bad luck*, una racha de mala suerte, una mala racha. | Oleada, *f.* (of people): *they came in waves*, vinieron en oleadas. | Ola, *f.*, oleada, *f.*: *a crime wave*, una ola de criminalidad, una oleada de crímenes. | Ola, *f.*: *a wave of cold weather*, una ola de frío. || Señal, *f.*, ademán, *m.*, seña, *f.*, movimiento, *m.* (with the hand). || — Pl. POET. Piélago, *m. sing.*, océano, *m. sing.*, mar, *m. sing.* || — FIG. *New wave*, nueva ola. || *Permanent wave*, permanente, *f.*

wave [weiv] v. tr. Agitar: *to wave one's hand, a handkerchief, a flag*, agitar la mano, un pañuelo, una banderita. || Blandir (a sword). || Amenazar con (to threaten): *he waved his fist in my face*, me amenazó con el puño. || Ondular: *to wave one's hair*, ondularse el pelo. || — *To wave a greeting to s.o.*, saludar a alguien con la mano. || *To wave a meal away*, rechazar una comida con la mano. || *To wave aside an objection*, desechar una objeción. || *To wave aside s.o.'s help*, rechazar la ayuda de alguien. || *To wave down a motorist*, hacer señas a un automovilista para que se pare. || *To wave one's arms about*, agitar mucho los brazos. || *To wave s.o. aside*, apartar a alguien con la mano. || *To wave s.o. good-bye*, decir adiós a alguien con la mano *or* con un pañuelo. || *To wave s.o. on*, hacer una señal con la mano a alguien para que pase. || *To wave the waiter over*, llamar al camarero con la mano.
— V. intr. Ondear (fields of corn, etc.). || Flotar (a flag). || Ondular (hair). || Hacer señales *or* señas con la mano: *to wave to s.o. to stop*, hacer señas con la

mano a alguien para que se pare. || Agitarse: *from the balcony I could see a sea of waving arms*, desde el balcón veía un montón de brazos que se agitaban.

Wave [weiv] n. U. S. Mujer (*f.*) que forma parte de la marina americana.

wave band [—bænd] n. RAD. Banda (*f.*) de ondas.

waved [—d] adj. Ondulado, da; ondeado, da. || Tornasolado, da (fabric).

wave front [—frʌnt] n. PHYS. Frente (*m.*) de onda.

wave guide [—gaid] n. PHYS. Guía (*f.*) de ondas.

wavelength [—leŋθ] n. PHYS. Longitud (*f.*) de onda.

waveless [—lis] adj. Tranquilo, la; sin olas.

wavelet [—lit] n. Ola (*f.*) pequeña (of the sea). || Pequeña ondulación, *f.* (on hair).

wave mechanics [—mi'kæniks] n. PHYS. Mecánica (*f.*) ondulatoria.

wave motion [—,məuʃən] n. PHYS. Movimiento (*m.*) ondulatorio.

waver [—ə*] n. Vacilación, *f.*, titubeo, *m.* || Vacilación, *f.* (flickering).

waver [—ə*] v. intr. Dudar, vacilar, titubear: *she wavered between going and staying*, dudó entre marcharse y quedarse. || Titubear, tambalearse (to totter). || Flaquear (to falter). || Vacilar (to flicker): *a light wavered in the distance*, una luz vacilaba a lo lejos. || Temblar (voice).

waverer [—ərə*] n. Irresoluto, ta; indeciso, sa.

wavering [—əriŋ] adj. Vacilante, irresoluto, ta; indeciso, sa (indecisive). || Vacilante (light). || Tembloroso, sa (voice).
— N. Vacilación, *f.*, irresolución, *f.*, indecisión, *f.* (vacillation). || Vacilación, *f.* (of light). || Temblor, *m.* (of voice).

wave theory [—'θiəri] n. PHYS. Teoría (*f.*) ondulatoria.

wave train [—trein] n. PHYS. Tren (*m.*) de ondas.

waviness [—inis] n. Ondulación, *f.*

wavy [—i] adj. Ondulado, da: *a wavy line*, una línea ondulada; *wavy hair*, pelo ondulado. || Ondulante (field). || Onduloso, sa; sinuoso, sa (sinuous).

wax [wæks] n. Cera, *f.* || Cerumen, *m.*, cerilla, *f.* (in the ear). || Cerote, *m.* (used by shoemakers). || Disco, *m.* (record). || Lacre, *m.* (sealing wax). || FAM. Rabia, *f.* (anger).
— Adj. De cera.

wax [wæks] v. tr. Encerar (floor, etc.). || Grabar en un disco (to record).
— V. intr. Crecer (the moon). || Ponerse (to become): *to wax eloquent*, ponerse elocuente. || — *To wax indignant*, indignarse. || *To wax old*, envejecer.

wax bean [—bi:n] n. U. S. Judía (*f.*) de vaina amarilla.

waxberry [—,beri] n. BOT. Árbol (*m.*) de la cera.

wax candle [—'kændl] n. Vela (*f.*) de cera. || REL. Cirio, *m.*

wax cloth [—kləθ] n. Hule, *m.* (oilcloth).

wax doll [—'dɔl] n. Muñeca (*f.*) de cera.

waxed [—t] adj. Encerado, da: *waxed paper*, papel encerado.

waxen [—ən] adj. Ceroso, sa (resembling wax). || Encerado, da (covered with wax). || Céreo, a; de cera (made of wax). || Ceroso, sa (complexion).

waxiness [—inis] n. Consistencia (*f.*) cerosa.

waxing [—iŋ] adj. Creciente (moon).
— N. Crecimiento, *m.* (of the moon). || Enceramiento, *m.* (polishing). || Grabación (*f.*) de un disco (recording). || Disco, *m.* (record).

wax match [—'mætʃ] n. Cerilla, *f.*

wax myrtle [—'mə:tl] n. BOT. Árbol (*m.*) de la cera.

wax taper [—'teipə*] n. Vela (*f.*) alargada. || REL. Cirio, *m.*

waxwork [—wə:k] n. Figura (*f.*) de cera (figure modelled in wax). || — Pl. Museo (*m. sing.*) de figuras de cera.

waxy ['wæksi] adj. See WAXEN. || FAM. Rabioso, sa. || MED. *Waxy liver*, amilosis (*f.*) del hígado.

way [wei] n. Camino, *m.*: *the way to the beach is rocky*, el camino para ir a la playa es rocoso; *to go the wrong way*, equivocarse de camino; *to go out of one's way*, desviarse del camino; *the way of virtue*, el camino de la virtud; *the right way*, el buen camino. || Carretera, *f.* (road). || Vía, *f.*: *the public way*, la vía pública; *the Appian Way*, la Vía Apia. || Distancia, *f.*, trecho, *m.*: *we have a long way to walk*, tenemos que recorrer un gran trecho; *it's a long way to*, hay mucha distancia a. || Recorrido, *m.*, trayecto, *m.*: *there were trees all the way*, había árboles durante todo el trayecto. || Dirección, *f.*: *which way did he go?*, ¿en qué dirección se fue?; *she didn't know which way to look*, no sabía en qué dirección mirar. || Manera, *f.*, modo, *m.*: *he still hasn't found a way to make a living*, todavía no ha encontrado la manera de ganarse la vida; *the way of doing sth.*, la manera de hacer algo; *in one way or another*, de una manera o de otra; *in a friendly way*, de modo amistoso; *in no way*, de ninguna manera; *in such a way as to*, de tal manera que. || Estilo, *m.*: *way of life* o *way of living*, estilo de vida; *it is his way*, es su estilo. || Escala, *f.*, medida, *f.*: *in a big way*, en gran escala; *in a way*, en cierta medida. || Ramo, *m.*: *he is in the grocery way*, está en el ramo de la alimentación. || Asunto, *m.*: *it's not in my way*, no es asunto mío. || Terreno, *m.*: *to prepare the way*, preparar el terreno. || Estado, *m.*: *my car is in a bad way*, mi coche está en mal estado. || Costumbre, *f.*: *I am out of the way of dancing*, he perdido la costumbre de bailar; *it is not my way to do that*, no es costumbre mía hacer eso; *I got into the way of smoking*, adquirí la costumbre de fumar. || Manera (*f.*) de ser (behaviour): *don't take offence, it's only his way*, no se ofenda, es simplemente su manera de ser. || Modal, *m.* (manner): *the ways of good society*, los buenos modales. || Aspecto, *m.*, punto, *m.*: *in some ways you are mistaken*, en algunos aspectos estás equivocado. || MAR. Marcha, *f.* (movement of a boat). || JUR. Servidumbre (*f.*) de paso. || — Pl. TECH. Anguilas, *f.* || — *Across* o *over the way*, enfrente: *my house is just across the way from his*, mi casa está justo enfrente de la suya. || *A little way away* o *off*, cerca, no muy lejos. || *All the way*, por todo el camino (the whole distance), hasta el final (making every effort). || *All the way down*, a lo largo de. || *All the way to*, hasta. || *A long way away* o *off*, lejísimos, muy lejos. || *A long way from*, lejos de. || *Any way*, de cualquier manera (in any manner), de todas maneras (in any case). || *By a long way*, con mucho: *not by a long way*, ni con mucho. || *By the way*, en el camino: *they stopped by the way*, se detuvieron en el camino; entre paréntesis (incidental): *all this is by the way*, todo eso está entre paréntesis; de paso: *be it said by the way*, dicho sea de paso; a propósito, por cierto (incidentally): *by the way, are they coming for lunch?*, a propósito, ¿vienen a almorzar? || *By way of*, por, pasando por (vía): *we'll come back by way of the Suez canal*, volveremos por el canal de Suez; para (in order to): *they made inquiries by way of learning the truth*, hicieron investigaciones para saber la verdad; como, a modo de (as): *by way of compliment*, a modo de cumplido; *by way of introduction*, como introducción. || *Can you find your way home?*, ¿sabe usted por dónde se va a su casa? || *Committee of Ways and Means*, Comisión (*f.*) del Presupuesto. || *Each way* o *both ways*, a ganador y colocado (in horse racing). || *He is by way of being a liberal*, pasa por ser un liberal, se le considera liberal. || *I met him on my way here*, le encontré al venir aquí. || *I met him on my way home*, le encontré al volver a casa. || *In a fair way of* o *to*, en camino de, en vías de, en trance de (in process of). || *In a way*, en cierta manera, en cierto modo, hasta cierto punto: *I like the work in a way*, me gusta el trabajo hasta cierto punto. || *In every way*, en todos los aspectos. || *In the ordinary* o *usual* o *general way*, generalmente. || *It's the wrong way up*, está al revés. || *I will do anything that comes in my way*, estoy dispuesto a hacer cualquier cosa que se me presente. || ASTR. *Milky way*, Vía Láctea. || *No way through*, cerrado el paso. || *Once in a way*, de vez en cuando. || *On the way*, en camino: *the parcel is on the way*, el paquete está en camino; en el camino de, camino de: *it's on the way to Paris*, está en el camino de París. || *Out of harm's way*, a salvo. || FAM. *Out of my way!*, ¡quítese de en medio!, ¡fuera de aquí! || *Out of the way*, apartado, da; aislado, da; remoto, ta (place), extraordinario, ria; fuera de lo común: *nothing out of the way*, nada extraordinario. || *Permanent way*, vía férrea (railway). || *Put it right way up*, póngalo bien. || *Right of way*, see RIGHT. || *That's the way!*, ¡así es!, ¡eso es! || *That way*, por ahí, por allí (direction), así (manner). || *The other way round*, al revés. || *There's no way out*, no hay ninguna salida, eso no tiene solución. || *There's no way through*, no se puede pasar. || *The way of the world!*, ¡así es la vida! || *The way things are*, tal y como están las cosas. || *They live somewhere London way*, viven cerca de Londres, viven hacia Londres. || *This way*, por aquí, en esta dirección. || *This way and that*, en todas direcciones. || *This way out!*, ¡salgan por aquí! || FIG. *To be a long way out*, estar muy equivocado. || *To be in the family way*, estar en estado interesante (pregnant). || *To be* o *to get in the way*, estorbar: *is my chair in the way?*, ¿le estorba mi silla? || *To be on the way to*, ir camino de: *he is on the way to do it*, va camino de hacerlo. || *To be under way*, estar en curso (affair), estar navegando (ship). || *To block the way*, cerrar el paso. || *To brush sth. the wrong way*, cepillar algo a contrapelo. || *To clear the way*, despejar el camino. || FIG. *To come one's way*, presentársele a uno. || *To feel one's way*, see FEEL. || *To find a way*, encontrar una solución. || *To find a way into*, conseguir entrar en. || *To find a way to*, encontrar la forma de. || *To find one's way to a place*, conseguir llegar a un sitio. || *To get in the way*, ponerse en medio. || MAR. *To gather way*, tomar velocidad (ship). || FIG. *To get* o *to have one's (own) way*, salirse con la suya. || *To get out of the way*, quitarse de en medio. || *To get s.o. out of the way*, quitar a uno de en medio. || *To get sth. out of the way*, quitar algo de en medio (to remove), quitarse algo de encima: *I finally got that backlog out of the way*, por fin me quité de encima ese trabajo atrasado. || *To get under way*, ponerse en camino (to set out), avanzar, progresar (to progress), zarpar (ship). || *To give the way*, dejar paso. || *To give way*, ceder (to break), retroceder (to retire), ceder el paso (car). || *To give way to*, ceder el paso a (to be replaced by), ceder ante (to make concessions to), dejarse llevar por, entregarse a (despair). || FIG. *To go a long way*,

llegar muy lejos: *this boy will go a long way*, este chico llegará muy lejos. | *To go a long way towards*, contribuir mucho a. | *To go one's own way*, seguir su camino (according to one's will), obrar a su antojo (according to one's fancy), hacer rancho aparte (by o.s.). || *To go one's way*, seguir su camino. || FIG. *To go out of one's way to*, tomarse la molestia de: *I wouldn't go out of my way to hear him*, no me tomaría la molestia de ir a escucharle; desvivirse por, hacer todo lo posible por (to do one's utmost to). | *To go the way of all flesh* o *of all things*, morir. | *To have a way with*, saber coger a. | *To have a way with people*, tener don de gentes. || *To keep out of s.o.'s way*, evitar encontrarse con alguien. || *To keep out of the way*, no estorbar el paso. || FIG. *To know one's way about* o *around*, saber arreglárselas. || *To know one's way about* o *around town*, conocer muy bien la ciudad. || *To lead the way*, see LEAD. || FIG. *To leave the way open for*, dejar una puerta abierta para. | *To leave the way open to*, abrir la puerta a. || *To live in a small way*, vivir modestamente. || FIG. *To look the other way*, hacer la vista gorda. || *To lose one's way*, perderse, extraviarse. || *To make one's way*, abrirse paso (to open a path), salir bien (to come out all right), progresar, adelantar (to make progress). || *To make one's way home*, volver a casa. || FIG. *To make one's way in the world* o *in life*, abrirse camino en la vida. || *To make* o *to work one's way through the crowd*, abrirse paso entre la multitud. || *To make one's way to*, dirigirse hacia *or* a: *he made his way to the door*, se dirigió hacia la puerta. || *To make way*, hacerse a un lado. || FIG. *To make way for*, dejar paso a. | *To mend one's ways*, enmendarse. || *To my way of thinking*, a mi modo de ver. || FIG. *To pave the way for*, preparar el terreno para. | *To pay one's way*, pagar su parte (to pay one's share), ser solvente (to be solvent). | *To pay one's own way*, satisfacer sus propias necesidades. | *To put difficulties in s.o.'s way*, crear dificultades a alguien, ponerle a uno obstáculos en el camino. | *To put s.o. in a way to do sth.*, dar a alguien la posibilidad de hacer algo. || *To put s.o. out of the way*, quitar a uno de en medio. || FIG. *To see one's way to*, encontrar la manera de, ver la forma de. || *To stand in the way of*, estorbar (to hinder), ser un obstáculo para (to be an obstacle), ser una desventaja para (to be a disadvantage). || *To start on one's way*, ponerse en camino. || FIG. *To work one's way through college*, trabajar para costearse los estudios. | *To work one's way to*, abrirse camino hacia. | *To work one's way up*, ascender por su trabajo. || *Way down*, bajada, *f.* || *Way in*, entrada, *f.* || *Way of business*, negocios, *m. pl.* || *Way off*, a lo lejos: *I see them way off*, les veo a los lejos. || REL. *Way of the Cross*, Vía (*m.*) Crucis. || *Way out*, salida, *f.* || *Ways and customs*, usos y costumbres. || *Ways and means*, medios *m. pl.* || *Way through*, pasaje, *m.*, paso, *m.* || *Way up*, subida, *f.* || U. S. FAM. *We have skirts all the way from fifteen to fifty dollars*, tenemos faldas de quince a cincuenta dólares. || *What have you in the way of fruit?*, ¿qué fruta tiene? || *Where there's a will there's a way*, querer es poder. || *Which way did you come?*, ¿por dónde vino? || FIG. *You can't have it both ways*, no se puede estar en misa y repicando.
— Adv. Allá.

waybill [—bil] n. MAR. Hoja (*f.*) de ruta.

wayfarer [—ˌfɛərə*] n. Caminante, *m.*

wayfaring [—ˌfɛəriŋ] adj. Que viaja a pie. || BOT. *Wayfaring tree*, viburno, *m.*

waylay [weiˈlei] v. tr. Acechar, aguardar emboscado (in order to rob, etc.). || Abordar (to accost by surprise).

waylayer [—ə*] n. Acechador, ra (who lies in wait). || Importuno, na.

way-out [ˈweiˈaut] adj. Muy moderno na; ultramoderno, na.

wayside [ˈweisaid] adj. Al borde del camino.
— N. Borde (*m.*) del camino.

way station [ˈweiˌsteiʃən] n. U. S. Apeadero, *m.*

way train [ˈweitrein] n. U. S. Tren (*m.*) carreta, ómnibus, *m.*

wayward [ˈweiwəd] adj. Voluntarioso, sa (self-willed). || Porfiado, da (obstinate). || Díscolo, la; desobediente (not easily controlled). || Caprichoso, sa (capricious).

waywardness [—nis] n. Capricho, *m.*, fantasía, *f.* (whim). || Voluntariedad, *f.* (wilfulness). || Porfía, *f.* (obstinacy). || Desobediencia, *f.* (disobedience).

wayworn [ˈweiwɔːn] adj. Agotado por el camino.

we [wiː] pers. pron. Nosotros, tras (oneself and others): *we two*, nosotros dos. || Nos (used by a sovereign, a judge, etc.).

weak [wiːk] adj. Débil: *too weak to climb higher*, demasiado débil para subir más arriba; *a weak mind*, una mente débil; *the weak point in a scheme*, el punto débil de un proyecto. || Flojo, ja: *a weak blow*, un golpe flojo; *weak in history*, flojo en historia; *weak wine*, vino flojo. || Flojo, ja: *a weak argument*, un argumento flojo. || Poco enérgico, ca: *weak government*, gobierno poco enérgico; *weak decision*, decisión poco enérgica. || Claro, ra: *weak tea*, té claro. || Poco sólido, da (easily broken). || MED. Débil: *a weak heart*, un corazón débil. || COMM. Flojo, ja (market). | Poco, ca (demand). || GRAMM. MUS. Débil. || — *S.o.'s weak side*, el punto flaco *or* la debilidad de alguien. || *The weaker sex*, el sexo débil. || *To grow weak*, debilitarse. || *To protect the weak*, proteger a los débiles. || *Weak moment*, momento (*m.*) de debilidad.

weaken [—ən] v. tr. Debilitar. || Disminuir (to diminish).
— V. intr. Debilitarse. || Disminuir (to diminish).

weakening [—əniŋ] n. Debilitación, *f.*, debilitamiento, *m.*
— Adj. Debilitante.

weak-headed [—ˈhedid] adj. Mentecato, ta; tonto, ta.

weak-kneed [—ˈniːd] adj. Débil de rodillas. || FIG. Sin carácter, sin personalidad.

weakling [—liŋ] n. Persona (*f.*) *or* animal (*m.*) débil *or* delicado. || FIG. Persona (*f.*) sin carácter *or* sin personalidad (person without character).
— Adj. Débil.

weakly [—li] adj. Débil.
— Adv. Débilmente.

weak-minded [—ˈmaindid] adj. Mentecato, ta; tonto, ta (silly). || Sin carácter, sin personalidad.

weakness [—nis] n. MED. Debilidad, *f.* || Punto (*m.*) flaco *or* débil (weak point). || Debilidad, *f.*, flaco, *m.*: *a weakness for olives*, debilidad por las aceitunas.

weak point [—pɔint] n. FIG. Punto (*m.*) flaco *or* débil.

weal [wiːl] n. Verdugón, *m.* (mark on the skin). || Bienestar, *m.* (well-being). || — *For weal or woe*, en la suerte y en la desgracia. || *The general* o *the public weal*, el bien público.

weald [wiːld] n. Región (*f.*) arbolada.

wealth [welθ] n. Riqueza, *f.* (riches). || Abundancia, *f.*, profusión, *f.* (of details, ideas, etc.). || Riqueza, *f.* (valuable products): *the wealth of a country*, la riqueza de un país. || *Man of wealth*, hombre rico.

wealthiness [—inis] n. Riqueza, *f.*, opulencia, *f.*

wealthy [—i] adj. Rico, ca.
— N. *The wealthy*, los ricos.

wean [—wiːn] v. tr. Destetar (an infant or young animal). || FIG. *To wean from*, apartar de (object of affection), desacostumbrar de (a bad habit).

weaning [—iŋ] n. Destete, *m.*

weanling [—liŋ] n. Niño (*m.*) *or* animal (*m.*) destetado.

weapon [ˈwepən] n. MIL. Arma, *f.* || ZOOL. BOT. Defensa, *f.* || FIG. Arma, *f.* (any means of attack or defence).

weaponless [—lis] adj. Desarmado, da; sin armas.

weaponry [—ri] n. Armas, *f. pl.*, armamento, *m.* (weapons). || Fábrica (*f.*) de armas (production).

wear [wɛə*] n. Uso, *m.*: *for everyday wear*, para uso diario. || Desgaste, *m.*, deterioro, *m.* (damage due to use). || Resistencia, *f.* (ability to resist damage). || Ropa, *f.* (clothes): *men's wear*, ropa para caballeros; *summer wear*, ropa de verano. || — *Evening wear*, traje (*m.*) de noche. || *For hard wear*, resistente, duradero, ra. || *Of never-ending wear*, que no se rompe con el uso, que no se desgasta. || *There's still some good wear left in this suit*, todavía está en buen estado este traje. || *To be in (general) wear*, estar de moda. || *To look the worse for wear*, estar desgastado, da (sth.), estar desmejorado, da (s.o.).

wear* [wɛə*] v. tr. *Llevar*: *to wear a coat*, llevar un abrigo; *blue is being much worn at present*, el azul se lleva mucho ahora; *to wear spectacles*, llevar gafas; *to wear one's hair short*, llevar el pelo corto. || Ponerse (to put on): *he wears the same suit every day*, se pone todos los días el mismo traje; *what shall I wear?*, ¿qué me voy a poner?; *he was wearing all his medals*, se había puesto todas las medallas. || Usar: *to wear one's shirt to tatters*, usar una camisa hasta hacerla jirones. || Tener (a look, a smile, etc.). || Hacer: *to wear a hole in the carpet*, hacer un agujero en la alfombra. || MAR. Hacer virar. || FIG. Consumir: *worn with care*, consumido por las preocupaciones. | Agotar (to exhaust). || — *To have nothing fit to wear*, no tener nada que ponerse. || *To wear black*, ir vestido de negro. || *To wear one's age well*, estar bien conservado, no representar la edad que se tiene. || *To wear one's hair curled*, tener el pelo rizado. || *To wear o.s. to death*, matarse [trabajando].
— V. intr. Gastarse, desgastarse (to deteriorate through use). || Resistir, durar (to last): *material which wears well*, tela que dura mucho. || Pasar, correr, transcurrir (time). || MAR. Virar. || — *To wear thin*, disminuir. || *To wear well*, conservarse bien, no representar la edad que se tiene.
— ***To wear away***, gastar, desgastar: *rocks worn away by erosion*, rocas desgastadas por la erosión. | Borrar (to erase). | Pasar lentamente *or* tristemente (time). | Gastarse, desgastarse (to deteriorate). | Consumirse: *she was wearing away*, se estaba consumiendo. | Borrarse (an inscription). | Atenuarse, disminuir (a pain). | — *The winter was wearing away*, el invierno tocaba a su fin. || ***To wear down***, gastar, desgastar: *to wear one's heels down*, desgastar los tacones. | Agotar (to exhaust). || ***To wear off***, raer, gastar (one's clothes). | Borrar (an inscription). | Borrarse. | Desaparecer (to disappear). | Disiparse (to diminish gradually). || ***To wear on***, pasar lentamente (time). | Prolongarse: *the discussion wears on*, la discusión se prolonga. | — *As the evening wore on...*, a medida que avanzaba la noche. || ***To wear out***, gastar (one's clothes). | Pasar el resto de (one's life). | Agotar (s.o.'s patience). | Gastarse (to deteriorate). | Acabarse

lentamente (time). | — *To wear o.s. out*, agotarse, matarse.

— OBSERV. Pret. **wore;** p. p. **worn.**

wearable [ˈwɛərəbl] adj. Que se puede llevar *or* usar.
wear and tear [ˈwɛərəndˈtɛə*] n. Desgaste, *m.*, deteriorio, *m.* [por el uso].
wearer [ˈwɛərə*] n. Persona (*f.*) que lleva. || *Straight from maker to wearer*, directamente del fabricante al cliente.
wearied [ˈwiərid] adj. Cansado, da (tired).
weariful [ˈwiəriful] adj. Cansado, da (tiresome).
weariless [ˈwiərilis] adj. Infatigable, incansable.
wearily [ˈwiərili] adv. Con cansancio, cansadamente.
weariness [ˈwiərinis] n. Cansancio, *m.*, fatiga, *f.* || FIG. Aburrimiento, *m.*, hastío, *m.*
wearing [ˈwɛəriŋ] adj. Cansado, da (tiring). || Desgastador, ra (causing wear). || De vestir (apparel).
wearisome [ˈwiərisəm] adj. Cansado, da; fatigoso, sa (tiresome). || FIG. Fastidioso, sa; aburrido, da; pesado, da (boring).
wearisomeness [—nis] n. Lo aburrido, pesadez, *f.*
weary [ˈwiəri] adj. Cansado, da; fatigado, da (tired). || Agotador, ra (tiring): *weary work*, trabajo agotador. || Cansado, da; aburrido, da; harto, ta: *weary of studying*, harto de estudiar. || Fastidioso, sa; enojoso, sa (annoying).
weary [ˈwiəri] v. tr. Cansar, fatigar (to tire). || Aburrir (to bore). || Fastidiar (to annoy).
— V. intr. Cansarse, fatigarse (to become tired). || Aburrirse (to become bored).
weasel [ˈwi:zəl] n. Comadreja, *f.* (animal). || Vehículo (*m.*) para andar sobre nieve *or* hielo (tracked motor vehicle). || U. S. FAM. Chivato, ta (sneak). || *Weasel words*, palabras equívocas.
weather [ˈweðə*] n. Tiempo, *m.*: *what is the weather like?*, ¿qué tiempo hace?; *the bad weather kept us in*, el mal tiempo nos retuvo en casa; *weather permitting*, si el tiempo no lo impide; *fine weather*, buen tiempo; *in such weather*, con semejante tiempo; *changeable weather*, tiempo variable. || Boletín (*m.*) meteorológico, el tiempo (in the newspaper). || — *Heavy weather*, temporal, *m.*, mar gruesa. || FIG. *To keep one's weather eye open*, estar ojo avizor, estar alerta. || MAR. *To make bad weather of it*, aguantar mal la tormenta. | *To make good weather of it*, aguantar bien la tormenta, capear el temporal. || FIG. *To make heavy weather of a job*, complicar un trabajo. || FAM. *Under the weather*, borracho, cha (drunk), indispuesto, ta (not feeling well), en apuros (without money).
— Adj. Meteorológico, ca; del tiempo. || MAR. De barlovento. || *Weather conditions*, condiciones atmosféricas.
weather [ˈweðə*] v. tr. Exponer a la intemperie (to expose to the weather). || Curtir (the skin). || Patinar (bronze). || Curar (wood). || FIG. Superar: *to weather a crisis*, superar una crisis. || MAR. Doblar (a cape). | Pasar a barlovento de (a ship). | Aguantar, capear (a storm).
— V. intr. Resistir: *the paint has weathered well*, la pintura ha resistido bien. || Deteriorarse [con la acción del tiempo]: *this paintwork will not weather*, esta pintura no se deteriorará con la acción del tiempo. || GEOL. Desgastarse, erosionarse. || Curtirse (skin). || Patinarse (bronze). || FAM. *To weather through*, salir de apuros.
weather-beaten [—ˌbi:tn] adj. Deteriorado por la intemperie. || Azotado por el viento (by the wind). || Curtido, da: *a weather-beaten face*, una cara curtida.
weatherboard [—bɔ:d] n. Tabla, *f.* || MAR. Lado (*m.*) del viento.
weatherboard [—bɔ:d] v. tr. Poner tablas.
weatherboarding [—bɔ:diŋ] n. Tablazón, *f.*, tablas, *f. pl.* (weatherboards).
weather-bound [—baund] adj. Detenido por el mal tiempo.
weather bureau [—ˌbjuərəu] n. Servicio (*m.*) meteorológico.
weather chart [—tʃɑ:t] n. Mapa (*m.*) meteorológico.
weathercock [—kɔk] n. Veleta, *f.* (to show wind direction). || FIG. Veleta, *m.* & *f.*, persona (*f.*) cambiadiza.
weather forecast [—ˌfɔ:kɑ:st] n. Boletín (*m.*) *or* parte (*m.*) meteorológico. || Previsión (*f.*) del tiempo.
weather gauge [—geidʒ] n. MAR. Posición (*f.*) a barlovento. || FIG. Ventaja, *f.*, posición (*f.*) ventajosa.
weatherglass [—glɑ:s] n. Barómetro, *m.*
weathering [—riŋ] n. Desgaste, *m.*, erosión, *f.* || Intemperie, *f.* (forces of weather). || COMM. Patina, *f.* || ARCH. Declive (*m.*) de derrame.
weatherly [—li] adj. MAR. Que puede navegar de bolina.
weatherman [—mən] n. Hombre (*m.*) del tiempo, meteorólogo, *m.*

— OBSERV. El plural de esta palabra es *weathermen*.

weather map [—mæp] n. Mapa (*m.*) meteorológico.
weatherproof [—pru:f] adj. Que resiste a la intemperie. || Impermeable (clothes).
weatherproof [—pru:f] v. tr. Hacer resistente a la intemperie.
weather report [—riˌpɔ:t] n. Boletín (*m.*) *or* parte (*m.*) meteorológico.
weather station [—ˌsteiʃən] n. Estación (*f.*) meteorológica.
weather strip [—strip] n. Burlete, *m.* (for windows).
weather vane [—vein] n. Veleta, *f.*
weather-wise [—waiz] adj. Que pronostica el tiempo. || FIG. Que pronostica los cambios de opinión.
weatherworn [—wɔ:n] adj. Deteriorado por la intemperie.
weave [wi:v] n. Tejido, *m.*: *a close weave*, un tejido apretado.
weave* [wi:v] v. tr. Tejer (a thread, fabric, etc.). || Entrelazar (flowers, garlands, etc.). || FIG. Tramar, urdir (a plot, etc.). || Tejer (a web). || FIG. *To weave one's way through the crowd*, abrirse paso entre la multitud.
— V. intr. Tejer (to engage in weaving). || Entrelazarse (to become intertwined). || Zigzaguear.

— OBSERV. Pret. **wove;** p. p. **woven.**

weaver [—ə*] n. Tejedor, *m.* (bird). || Tejedor, ra (person).
weaverbird [—əbə:d] n. Tejedor, *m.* (bird).
weaving [—iŋ] n. Tejido, *m.* (weave). || Tejeduría, *f.* (art).
web [web] n. Tejido, *m.*, tela, *f.* (fabric). || Telaraña, *f.*, tela (*f.*) de araña (of a spider). || FIG. Sarta, *f.*: *a web of lies*, una sarta de mentiras. | Red, *f.* (network). | Trampa, *f.* (snare). || ANAT. Membrana, *f.* || Membrana (*f.*) interdigital (of swimming birds). || Barba, *f.* (of a feather). || ARCH. Alma, *f.* (of beam). || Brazo, *m.* (of a crank). || Bobina (*f.*) de papel continuo (used on a rotary press). || Paletón, *m.* (of a key). || Hoja, *f.*, cuchilla, *f.* (of a saw).
webbed [—d] adj. Palmeado, da (bird).
webbing [—in] n. Lona, *f.* (strong woven fabric). || Correas, *f. pl.*, cinchas, *f. pl.* (strips).
weber [ˈveibə*] n. PHYS. Weber, *m.*, weberio, *m.*
webfoot [ˈwebfut] n. Pata (*f.*) palmeada (foot). || Palmípedo, *m.* (bird).
web-footed [ˈwebˌfutid] adj. Palmípedo, da.
we'd [wi:d] contraction of *we had*, *we should* and *we would*.
wed [wed] v. tr. Casarse con: *he wedded Mary*, se casó con María. || Casar (the priest, etc.): *he wedded the couple*, casó a los novios; *he wedded his daughter to me*, casó a su hija conmigo. || FIG. Unir: *both things are happily wedded*, ambas cosas están felizmente unidas.
— V. intr. Casarse.
wedded [wedid] adj. Casado, da (married). || Conyugal (of marriage). || FIG. Unido, da. || — *My wedded wife*, mi legítima esposa. || *The wedded pair*, los novios. || *To be wedded to*, estar casado con (married), estar unido a (connected). || *To be wedded to an opinion*, aferrarse a una opinión.
wedding [ˈwediŋ] n. Boda, *f.*, casamiento, *m.* (ceremony of marriage). || Bodas, *f. pl.*: *silver wedding*, bodas de plata. || FIG. Unión, *f.*, enlace, *m.* || — *Civil wedding*, matrimonio civil. || *He had a civil, a church wedding*, se casó por lo civil, por la iglesia. || *To have a quiet wedding*, casarse en la intimidad.
— Adj. De boda: *wedding anniversary*, aniversario de boda; *wedding card*, participación de boda; *wedding present*, regalo de boda; *wedding night*, noche de boda. || Nupcial: *wedding march*, marcha nupcial. || — *Wedding breakfast*, banquete (*m.*) de bodas. || *Wedding cake*, pastel (*m.*) de boda. || *Wedding day*, día (*m.*) de la boda. || *Wedding dress*, traje (*m.*) de novia. || *Wedding party*, boda, *f.* (guests). || *Wedding ring*, alianza, *f.*, anillo (*m.*) de boda.
wedge [wedʒ] n. Cuña, *f.* (to split wood, etc.). || Calce, *m.*, calzo, *m.* (for keeping in place). || Cuña, *f.*, calzo, *m.* (for forcing sth. open). || Cuña, *f.* (for shoes). || PRINT. Cuña (*f.*) de fijación. || Cuña, *f.*, formación (*f.*) en cuña (arrangement of troops). || Trozo, *m.*, porción, *f.* [triangular]: *a wedge of cake*, un trozo de pastel. || — FIG. *It is the thin end of the wedge*, es un primer paso *or* un paso adelante. | *To drive a wedge between two persons*, romper los lazos que unen a dos personas.
wedge [wedʒ] v. tr. Poner cuñas a (to fix with wedges). || Partir con cuña (to split). || Abrir con cuña (to split open). || Poner calces, calzar (wheels). || Encajar (an object). || FIG. Apretar: *wedged into the bus like sardines*, apretados en el autobús como sardinas. || *To wedge a door open*, dejar abierta una puerta poniéndole una cuña.
wedge-shaped [—ʃeipt] adj. En forma de cuña. || Cuneiforme (handwriting).
wedgie [—i] n. FAM. Zapato (*m.*) tanque.
wedlock [ˈwedlɔk] n. Matrimonio, *m.*: *he was born out of wedlock*, nació fuera del matrimonio. || Vida (*f.*) conyugal (married life).
Wednesday [ˈwenzdi] n. Miércoles, *m.*: *I went on Wednesday*, fui el miércoles.
wee [wi:] adj. Minúsculo, la; diminuto, ta; ínfimo, ma (very small). || *She is a wee bit jealous*, es un poco celosa, es algo celosa.
weed [wi:d] n. BOT. Hierba, *f.*, mala hierba, *f.*, maleza, *f.* | Alga, *f.* (seaweed). || FAM. Animal (*m.*) flaco (considered unfit for breeding). | Rocín, *m.*, jamelgo, *m.* (hack). | Tabaco, *m.* (tobacco). | Puro, *m.* (cigar). | Pitillo, *m.* (cigarette). | Marihuana, *f.* || — Pl. Traje (*m. sing.*) de luto (mourning dress). || Brazalete (*m. sing.*) negro (on sleeve). || Gasa, *f. sing.* (on hat).

weed [wi:d] v. tr. Desherbar (to remove weeds). || Escardar (to hoe). || FIG. *To weed out*, suprimir (to eliminate), extirpar (to eradicate).
— V. intr. Quitar la maleza, desherbar.
weeder [—ə*] n. Escardador, ra (person). || Escarda, *f.*, escardillo, *m.* (tool).
weediness [—inis] n. Abundancia (*f.*) de malas hierbas *or* de maleza.
weeding [—iŋ] n. AGR. Escarda, *f.* || — *Weeding hook*, escarda, *f.*, escardillo, *m.* || *Weeding machine*, escardadora, *f.*
weed killer [—,kilə*] n. Herbicida, *m.*
weedy [—i] adj. Cubierto de maleza *or* de malas hierbas. || Flaco, ca; canijo, ja; enclenque (lanky).
week [wi:k] n. Semana, *f.*: *last week*, la semana pasada; *next week*, la semana que viene; *three times a week*, tres veces por semana; *forty hour week*, semana de cuarenta horas. || — *A week from now* o *today week*, de aquí a una semana, dentro de una semana, dentro de ocho días. || FIG. *A week of Sundays*, una eternidad. || *During* o *in the week*, durante la semana, entre semana. || *Holy week*, Semana Santa *or* Grande *or* Mayor. || *Monday week*, el lunes que viene. || *Twice a week*, dos veces por semana. || *Week after week*, semana tras semana. || *Week by week*, todas las semanas. || *Week in week out*, semana tras semana. || *Working week*, semana laborable. || *Yesterday week*, ayer hizo una semana.
weekday [—dei] n. Día (*m.*) laborable, día (*m.*) de trabajo (working day). || Día (*m.*) de la semana (day of the week).
weekend [—'end] n. Fin (*m.*) de semana, "week-end", *m.* || *To take a long weekend*, hacer puente.
— Adj. De fin de semana.
weekend [—'end] v. intr. Pasar el fin de semana.
weekly [—li] adj. Semanal, hebdomadario, ria: *a weekly newspaper*, un periódico semanal.
— N. Semanario, *m.* (magazine).
— Adv. Semanalmente, por semana.
ween [wi:n] v. tr. Suponer, creer, figurarse, imaginarse.
weeny [—i] adj. FAM. Chiquito, ta; diminuto, ta.
weep [wi:p] n. Lágrimas, *f. pl.* || *To have a good weep*, llorar a lágrima viva.
weep* [wi:p] v. intr. Llorar (to cry): *to weep for joy*, llorar de alegría; *I weep over my sins*, lloro mis pecados; *she wept for her father*, lloró a su padre. || Lamentarse (to mourn): *that's nothing to weep over*, no hay por qué lamentarse. || Rezumar (wall).
— V. tr. Llorar, lamentar (to cry for). || Derramar, verter (tears). || Rezumar (walls). || MED. Supurar (sore). || — *To weep away the time*, pasarse la vida llorando. || *To weep o.s. to sleep*, llorar hasta dormirse. || *To weep one's eyes out*, llorar a lágrima viva.

— OBSERV. Pret. & p. p. **wept**.

weeper [—ə*] n. Llorón, ona (s.o. who weeps). || Plañidera, *f.* (hired mourner). || Brazalete (*m.*) negro (on sleeve). || Gasa, *f.* (on hat). || Velo (*m.*) negro (of a widow).
weep hole [—həul] n. Hendidura (*f.*) de desagüe.
weeping [—iŋ] adj. Llorón, ona; lloroso, sa (person). || Rezumante (wall). || MED. Supurador, ra; supurante (sore). || BOT. Llorón, *m.*: *weeping willow*, sauce llorón.
— N. Llanto, *m.*
weepy [—i] adj. Lloroso, sa; llorón, ona.
weever ['wi:və*] n. Peje (*m.*) araña (fish).
weevil ['wi:vil] n. Gorgojo, *m.* (beetle).
weeviled or **weevilled** [—d] adj. Agorgojado, da.
weevily or **weevilly** [—i] adj. Agorgojado, da.
wee-wee ['wi:wi:] n. FAM. Pipí, *m.*
wee-wee ['wi:wi:] v. intr. FAM. Hacer pipí.
weft [weft] n. Trama, *f.* (in weaving).
weigh [wei] n. Camino, *m.*: *under weigh*, en camino.
weigh [wei] v. tr. Pesar (to determine the weight of): *please weigh this package for me*, haga el favor de pesarme este paquete. || Sopesar (in the hand). || FIG. Pesar (to consider the importance of): *to weigh one's words*, pesar las palabras; *to weigh the pros and cons*, pesar el pro y el contra. || MAR. Levar (anchor).
— V. intr. Pesar: *it weighs thirty pounds*, pesa treinta libras. || FIG. Pesar: *the problem weighed on his mind*, el problema le pesaba. | Tener importancia, pesar (to have importance). || MAR. Levar anclas.
— **To weigh down,** doblar bajo un peso (to cause to bend under a load). | Inclinar (the scale). | Pesar más que (sth. else). | FIG. Abrumar (s.o.) || **To weigh in,** pesar (before a contest). | Ser pesado, pesarse (to be weighed). | — FIG. *To weigh in with an argument*, intervenir en una discusión con un argumento. || **To weigh out,** pesar (goods). | Pesar después de una carrera (a jockey, etc.). | Ser pesado *or* pesarse después de una carrera (a jockey, etc.). || **To weigh up,** levantar por contrapeso. | FIG. Pesar. || **To weigh with,** tener importancia para.
weighbeam ['weibi:m] n. Romana, *f.* (balance).
weighbridge ['weibridʒ] n. Puente (*m.*) basculante.
weigher ['weiə*] n. Pesador, ra.
weighing ['weiiŋ] n. Peso, *m.*
weighing-in [—in] n. Peso, *m.*, pesaje, *m.*
weighing machine [—mə,ʃi:n] n. Báscula, *f.*

weight [weit] n. Peso, *m.* (heaviness): *to gain weight*, ganar peso. || Pesa, *f.* (used for comparing other weights). || COMM. Peso, *m.*: *sold by (the) weight*, vendido al peso. || MED. Pesadez, *f.* (in the head or stomach). || ARCH. Carga, *f.* || FIG. Importancia, *f.*, peso, *m.*: *a matter of great weight*, un asunto de mucho peso. | Influencia, *f.*, peso, *m.* (influence). | Peso, *m.*: *you've just lift a weight off my mind*, acaba de quitarme un peso de encima. | Peso, *m.*: *the weight of Justice*, el peso de la Justicia. || SP. Peso, *m.* (in boxing, horse racing): *to put the weight*, lanzar el peso. || Pesa, *f.* (in a clock). || — *Atomic, molecular weight*, peso atómico, molecular. || *Gross weight*, peso bruto. || FIG. *It is worth its weight in gold*, vale su peso en oro. || *Light weight*, de poco peso. || *Live weight*, peso en vivo. || *Net weight*, peso neto. || SP. *Putting the weight*, lanzamiento (*m.*) del peso. || FIG. *To carry weight*, tener peso: *his argument will carry weight*, su argumento tendrá peso. || *To give good weight*, dar buen peso, pesar corrido. || *To lose weight*, adelgazar. || FIG. *To pull one's weight*, poner de su parte. || *To put on weight*, engordar. || FIG. *To throw one's weight about*, darse importancia. | *To try the weight of*, sopesar. || *Weights and measures*, pesas y medidas.
weight [weit] v. tr. Añadir peso a (to add weight to). || Poner peso *or* pesas en: *make them balance by weighting this side*, equilibrelos poniendo peso en este lado. || Lastrar (a net). || Dar valor a (in statistics). || FIG. Cargar.
weightiness [—inis] n. Peso, *m.*, pesadez, *f.* (heaviness). || FIG. Peso, *m.*, importancia, *f.*, fuerza, *f.* (of an argument).
weightless [—lis] adj. Ingrávido, da.
weightlessness [—lisnis] n. Ingravidez, *f.*
weight lifter [—,liftə*] n. Halterófilo, *m.*, levantador (*m.*) de pesos y halteras.
weight lifting [—,liftiŋ] n. SP. Levantamiento (*m.*) de pesos y halteras, halterofilia, *f.*
weighty [—i] adj. Pesado, da: *a weighty load*, una carga pesada. || FIG. De peso, importante (argument, people).
weir [wiə*] n. Presa, *f.* (built across a river). || Vertedero, *m.* (in a dam). || Encañizada, *f.* (to catch fish).
weird [wiəd] adj. Misterioso, sa; sobrenatural (supernatural). || FAM. Extraño, ña; raro, ra (queer): *how weird!*, ¡qué extraño! || *The Weird Sisters*, las Parcas (the Fates), las brujas (in Shakespeare's Macbeth).
weirdness [—nis] n. Lo misterioso. || FAM. Lo extraño, lo raro.
welch [welʃ] v. intr. See WELSH.
welcome ['welkəm] adj. Bienvenido, da (gladly received). || Grato, ta; agradable (agreeable). || — *It was most welcome*, fue muy oportuno. || *To be a welcome guest everywhere*, ser siempre bien recibido en todas partes. || *To make s.o. welcome*, recibir a alguien con los brazos abiertos. || *You are welcome*, de nada, no hay de qué (in response to thanks). || *You are welcome to use it*, está a su disposición. || *You are welcome to try*, puede probarlo cuando quiera. || *You will always be welcome here*, están ustedes en su casa.
— N. Bienvenida, *f.*: *to give* o *to bid s.o. a warm welcome*, dar a alguien una calurosa bienvenida. || Recibimiento, *m.*, recepción, *f.*, acogida, *f.*: *they gave him a hearty welcome*, le dispensaron un caluroso recibimiento. || — *To meet with a cold welcome*, ser recibido fríamente. || FAM. *To outstay* o *to wear out one's welcome*, quedarse más tiempo de lo conveniente.
— Interj. ¡Bienvenido!: *welcome home!*, ¡bienvenido a casa! || FAM. Con mucho gusto.
welcome ['welkəm] v. tr. Dar la bienvenida a (to bid welcome). || Recibir: *I went to the station to welcome her*, fui a recibirla a la estación. || Recibir bien: *they welcomed us to their house*, nos recibieron bien en su casa. || Alegrarse por: *to welcome s.o.'s return*, alegrarse por la vuelta de alguien. || *We will welcome any useful suggestion*, toda sugerencia será bien recibida.
welcoming [—iŋ] adj. Acogedor, ra.
weld [weld] n. Soldadura, *f.* (in metal). || BOT. Gualda, *f.*
weld [weld] v. tr. Soldar (metal). || FIG. Unir (to unite).
— V. intr. Soldarse.
weldable [—əbəl] adj. Soldable.
welder [—ə*] n. Soldador, *m.* (person). || Soldadora, *f.* (machine).
welding [—iŋ] n. Soldadura, *f.* || — *Butt welding*, soldadura a tope. || *Oxyacetylene welding*, soldadura oxiacetilénica *or* autógena. || *Spot welding*, soldadura por puntos. || *Welding torch*, soplete (*m.*) de soldar.
welfare ['welfεə*] n. Bienestar, *m.* (state of being healthy, happy, etc.). || Bien, *m.* (good). || — *Welfare centre*, centro (*m.*) de asistencia social. || *Welfare institution*, institución benéfica. || *Welfare work*, asistencia (*f.*) social. || *Welfare worker*, asistenta (*f.*) social.
welfare state [—'steit] n. Estado (*m.*) benefactor, estado (*m.*) basado en el principio de que el bienestar del individuo depende de la comunidad.
welkin ['welkin] n. Firmamento, *m.*, cielo, *m.*
well [wel] adv. Bien: *he treats his staff well*, trata bien a sus empleados; *he speaks English well*, habla bien el inglés; *he sings well*, canta bien; *well spoken*, bien

dicho; *he did it very well*, lo hizo muy bien; *do you feel well?*, ¿se encuentra bien?; *I know him well*, le conozco bien; *to end well*, acabar bien; *do the brothers get on well?*, ¿se llevan bien los hermanos? || Completamente: *well up to the knees in mud*, completamente metido en el barro hasta las rodillas. || Bien: *it may well be true*, bien puede ser verdad; *he can well save some money*, bien puede ahorrar algún dinero. || — *All too well* o *only too well*, de sobra, sobradamente. || *As well*, también: *she sings and plays the piano as well*, canta y también toca el piano. || *As well as*, igual que, lo mismo que, así como: *his enemies as well as his friends respected him*, sus enemigos lo mismo que sus amigos le respetaban; y además, también: *she bought a coat as well as a suit*, compró un abrigo y además un traje. || *He accepted, as well he might*, aceptó, y con razón. || *How well?*, ¿qué tal? || *It's just as well you were there*, menos mal que estabas allí. || *To be well over forty*, tener cuarenta años bien cumplidos. || *To be well up in a subject*, conocer muy bien un tema, ser perito en un tema. || *To do well*, see DO. || *To stand well with*, see STAND. || *Well done!*, ¡muy bien!, ¡bravo! || *Well over a million*, mucho más de un millón. || *Well now*, ahora bien. || *You may well ask*, puede perfectamente preguntar.

— Adj. Bien (in good health): *to be well*, estar bien. || Bien: *things are well with you*, las cosas le van bien; *it is well that he has come*, está bien que haya venido. || — *To get well*, reponerse, restablecerse. || *Very well*, muy bien. || *Well and good*, muy bien. || *Well and good!*, ¡tanto mejor!

— N. *The well and the sick*, los sanos y los enfermos. || *To wish s.o. well*, desear todo lo mejor para alguien.

— Interj. Bueno (asquiescence, hesitation, resignation, interrogation): *well, such is life*, bueno, así es la vida. || ¡Vaya! (surprise): *well! I never expected to see you here*, ¡vaya! no esperaba verte aquí.

— OBSERV. El comparativo de *well* es *better* y el superlativo es *best*.

well [wel] v. intr. Manar, fluir (to flow). || Brotar (to gush). || *The tears welled up in her eyes*, se le llenaron los ojos de lágrimas.

we'll [wi:l] contraction of *we shall* and *we will*.

well-advised [ˈweləd'vaizd] adj. Sensato, ta; juicioso, sa.

well [wel] n. Pozo, *m.* (to obtain water, oil, gas, etc.): *they sank a well*, perforaron un pozo. || Caja, *f.* (containing the stairs or lift). || Depósito, *m.* (for holding a liquid). || Tintero, *m.* (inkwell). || Fuente, *f.*, manantial, *m.* (spring). || FIG. Pozo, *m.*: *a well of knowledge*, un pozo de ciencia. || MAR. Pozo, *m.* || Vivero, *m.* (of a fishing boat). || JUR. Estrado, *m.* || AVIAT. Carlinga, *f.*

well-aimed [ˈwelˈeimd] adj. Certero, ra.

well-appointed [ˈweləˈpointid] adj. Bien amueblado, da.

well-balanced [ˈwelˈbælənsd] adj. Bien equilibrado, da. || FIG. Equilibrado, da.

well-behaved [ˈwelbiˈheivd] adj. Bien educado, da (well-bred). || Formal, serio, ria (serious).

well-being [ˈwelˈbi:iŋ] n. Bienestar, *m.* (of s.o.). || Buen estado, *m.* (of sth).

well borer [ˈwel,bɔ:rə*] n. Pocero, *m.*

wellborn [ˈwelˈbɔ:n] adj. Bien nacido, da.

well-bred [ˈwelˈbred] adj. Bien educado, da (person). || De raza (animal).

well-built [ˈwelˈbilt] adj. Bien hecho, cha (person).

well-chosen [ˈwelˈtʃəuzn] adj. Elegido cuidadosamente. || Acertado, da (words, etc.).

well-content [ˈwelkənˈtent] adj. Satisfecho, cha; contento, ta.

well curb [ˈwelkə:b] n. Brocal, *m.*

well digger [ˈwel,digə*] n. Pocero, *m.*

well-disposed [ˈweldisˈpəuzd] adj. Bien dispuesto, ta. || Favorable (*to, towards*, a). || Bienintencionado, da (well-intentioned).

well-doer [ˈwelˈduə*] n. Hombre (*m.*) de bien (good man). || Bienhechor, ra (benefactor).

welldoing [ˈwelˈduiŋ] n. Bien, *m.*

well-done [ˈweldˈdʌn] adj. Bien hecho, cha. || CULIN. Muy hecho, cha.

well-dressed [ˈwelˈdrest] adj. Bien vestido, da.

well-earned [ˈwelˈə:nd] adj. Merecido, da.

well-educated [ˈwelˈedjukeitid] adj. Culto, ta.

well-favoured (U. S. **well-favored**) [ˈwelˈfeivəd] adj. Bien parecido, da; agraciado, da.

well-fed [ˈwelˈfed] adj. Bien alimentado, da.

well-fixed [ˈwelˈfikst] adj. U. S. FAM. Rico, ca; adinerado, da.

well-founded [—ˈfaundid] adj. Bien fundado, da; fundamentado, da.

well-groomed [ˈwelˈgru:md] adj. Bien arreglado, da (person). || Bien cuidado, da (animal).

well-grounded [ˈwelˈgraundid] adj. Bien fundado, da.

well-handled [ˈwelˈhændld] adj. Bien dirigido, da.

wellhead [ˈwelhed] n. Manantial, *m.* (spring). || FIG. Fuente, *f.*

well-heeled [ˈwelˈhi:ld] adj. U. S. FAM. Pudiente, rico, ca (rich).

well-informed [ˈwelinˈfɔ:md] adj. Muy documentado, da. || Bien informado, da (*about*, acerca de). || *To be well-informed on a subject*, conocer un tema a fondo.

wellington [ˈweliŋtən] n. Bota (*f.*) de agua.

well-intentioned [ˈwelinˈtenʃənd] adj. Bienintencionado, da. || Piadoso, sa (lie).

well-judged [ˈwelˈdʒʌdʒd] adj. Bien calculado, da.

well-kept [ˈwelˈkept] adj. Bien cuidado, da (garden, etc.). || Bien guardado, da (secret).

well-knit [ˈwelˈnit] adj. Robusto, ta; de buena estatura (person). || Bien construido, da; bien estructurado, da (speech, etc.).

well-known [ˈwelˈnəun] adj. Muy conocido, da.

well-made [ˈwelˈmeid] adj. Bien hecho, cha.

well-mannered [ˈwelˈmænəd] adj. Muy cortés, de buenos modales.

well-meaning [ˈwelˈmi:niŋ] adj. Bienintencionado, da.

well-meant [ˈwelˈment] adj. Bienintencionado, da.

well-nigh [ˈwelnai] adv. Casi.

well-off [ˈwelˈɔf] adj. Rico, ca; adinerado, da; acomodado, da (wealthy).

well-ordered [ˈwelˈɔ:dəd] adj. Bien ordenado, da (orderly). || Bien organizado, da.

well-preserved [ˈwelpriˈzə:vd] adj. Bien conservado, da.

well-read [ˈwelˈred] adj. Leído, da; instruido, da; culto, ta: *well-read people say so*, la gente leída opina así.

well-spent [ˈwelˈspent] adj. Bien empleado, da; bien gastado, da.

well-spoken [ˈwelˈspəuken] adj. Bienhablado, da.

wellspring [ˈwelspriŋ] n. Fuente, *f.*, manantial, *m.*

well-stocked [ˈwelˈstɔkt] adj. Bien surtido, da.

well-thought-of [ˈwelˈθɔ:tɔv] adj. Bien considerado, da; de buena reputación.

well-timed [ˈwelˈtaimd] adj. Oportuno, na.

well-to-do [ˈweltəˈdu:] adj. Rico, ca; acaudalado, da.

well-trodden [ˈwelˈtrɔdn] adj. Trillado, da.

well-turned [ˈwelˈtə:nd] adj. Bien construido, da (sentence). || Bien hecho, cha (body).

well-wisher [ˈwelˈwiʃə*] n. Persona (*f.*) que desea el bien de otro. || Amigo (*m.*) sincero (friend).

well-worn [ˈwelˈwɔ:n] adj. Gastado, da; desgastado, da. || FIG. Trillado, da.

welsh [welʃ] v. intr. FAM. *To welsh on*, no pagar una apuesta a (to fail to pay winning bets), no cumplir con (an obligation, etc.).

Welsh [welʃ] adj. Galés, esa.

— N. Galés, esa (person). || Galés, *m.* (language). || *The Welsh*, los galeses.

welsher [—ə*] n. Estafador, *m.*

Welshman [—mən] n. Galés, *m.*

— OBSERV. El plural de esta palabra es *Welshmen*.

Welsh rabbit [—ˈræbit] or **Welsh rarebit** [—ˈrɛəbit] n. CULIN. Pan (*m.*) tostado con queso derretido.

Welshwoman [—,wumən] n. Galesa, *f.*

— OBSERV. El plural de esta palabra es *Welshwomen*.

welt [welt] n. Vira, *f.* (in shoemaking). || Ribete, *m.*, vivo, *m.* (in sewing). || Verdugón, *m.* (weal).

welt [welt] v. tr. Poner vira a (a shoe). || Ribetear (in sewing). || Zurrar (to thrash).

welter [ˈweltə*] adj. SP. De peso welter.

— N. Welter, *m.*, semimedio, *m.*, boxeador (*m.*) de peso welter (welterweight). || Confusión, *f.* (turmoil). || Revoltijo, *m.* (mess).

welter [ˈweltə*] v. intr. Revolcarse (to roll about). || Espumear, hacer espuma (the sea). || FIG. Bañar (in blood). | Encenagarse (in sin).

welterweight [—weit] n. SP. Peso (*m.*) welter (in horse racing). | Welter, *m.*, semimedio, *m.*, boxeador (*m.*) de peso welter (in boxing).

wen [wen] n. Runa (*f.*) del inglés antiguo (rune). || Lobanillo, *m.*, quiste (*m.*) sebáceo (cyst).

wench [wentʃ] n. Jovencita, *f.*, moza, *f.* (girl). || FAM. Fulana, *f.* (prostitute).

wench [wentʃ] v. intr. FAM. Ir de fulanas.

wend [wend] v. tr. *To wend one's way to*, dirigir sus pasos a, encaminarse a.

went [went] pret. See GO.

wept [wept] pret. & p. p. See WEEP.

were [wə:*] pret. See BE.

we're [wiə*] contraction of *we are*.

weren't [wə:nt] contraction of *were not*.

werewolf [ˈwə:wulf] n. Hombre (*m.*) lobo.

— OBSERV. El plural es *werewolves*.

west [west] adv. Al oeste, hacia el oeste. || — *East and west*, del este al oeste. || FIG. FAM. *To go west*, irse al otro barrio (to die), fastidiarse (to break), estar perdido (to be wasted), fracasar (to fail). || *West of*, al oeste de.

— Adj. Del oeste, occidental. || Del oeste (wind). || Que da al oeste (window, door, etc.). || — *West Berlin*, Berlín (*m.*) Occidental. || *West Germany*, Alemania (*f.*) Occidental.

— N. Oeste, *m.* (cardinal point). || Occidente, *m.*, poniente, *m.*, oeste, *m.* (direction of the setting sun). || *The West*, el Oeste (of United States), el Mundo Occidental (of the World).

westbound [—baund] adj. Con rumbo al oeste.

west by north [—baiˈnɔ:θ] n. Oeste (*m.*) cuarta al noroeste.

west by south [—baiˈsauθ] n. Oeste (*m.*) cuarta al suroeste.

West End [— end] n. Oeste (*m.*) de Londres [barrio residencial de la capital inglesa].
wester [—ə*] v. intr. Moverse hacia el poniente (star, sun, moon). Cambiar hacia el oeste (wind).
westerly [—əli] adj./adv. En el oeste (in the west). || Hacia el oeste (towards the west). || Del oeste (wind).
— N. Viento (*m.*) del oeste.
western [—ən] adj. Occidental, del oeste.
— N. Novela (*f.*) del Oeste (story of life in the West of U. S. A.). Película (*f.*) del Oeste, "western", *m.* (film).
Western [—ən] adj. Del Oeste (relating to the West of U.S.A.). || Occidental (Europe, States). || De Occidente (Empire). || Rel. Latina (church).
Westerner [—ənə*] n. Occidental, *m.* & *f.* || U. S. Norteamericano (*m.*) del Oeste.
western hemisphere [—ən'hemisfiə*] n. Hemisferio (*m.*) occidental, Mundo (*m.*) occidental.
westernization [,westənai'zeiʃən] n. Occidentalización, *f.*
westernize ['westənaiz] v. tr. Occidentalizar.
westernized [—d] adj. Occidentalizado, da. || *To become westernized*, occidentalizarse.
westernmost ['westənməust] adj. Más occidental, situado más al oeste.
West Indian ['west'indjən] adj./n. Antillano, na.
West Indies ['west'indiz] pl. pr. n. Geogr. Antillas, *f.*
westing ['westiŋ] n. Mar. Rumbo (*m.*) hacia el oeste.
west-northwest ['westnɔ:θ'west] adv. Hacia el oesnorueste, hacia el oesnoroeste.
— N. Oesnorueste, *m.*, oesnoroeste, *m.*
Westphalia [west'feiljə] pr. n. Geogr. Westfalia, *f.*
West Point ['west'pɔint] n. "West Point" [academia militar de Estados Unidos].
west-southwest ['westsauθ west] adv. Hacia el oessudueste, hacia el oessudoeste.
— N. Oessudueste, *m.*, oessudoeste, *m.*
westward ['westwəd] adv./adj. Hacia el oeste.
— N. Oeste, *m.*: *to westward*, hacia el oeste.
westwards [—z] adv. Hacia el oeste.
wet [wet] adj. Mojado, da (soaked): *you'd better take off your wet clothes*, es mejor que se quite la ropa mojada. || Húmedo, da: *wet climate*, clima húmedo; *the painting is still wet*, el cuadro está todavía húmedo. || Lluvioso, sa; de lluvia (day, season, weather). || Fresco, ca (paint). || Tech. Por vía húmeda. || Med. Escarificado, da (cup). || Fig. Soso, sa; tonto, ta: *don't be so wet!*, ¡no seas tan tonto! || U. S. Antiprohibicionista (person, town). || U. S. Fam. Erróneo, a; falso, sa. || — *To get one's hair wet*, mojarse el pelo. || *To get wet*, mojarse. || *Wet through* o *wet to the skin*, calado hasta los huesos. || *Wringing wet*, chorreando.
— N. Humedad, *f.* (state). || Lluvia, *f.* (rain). || Tiempo (*m.*) lluvioso (weather). || Fam. Copa, *f.* (drink). || U. S. Antiprohibicionista, *m.* & *f.*
wet [wet] v. tr. Humedecer, mojar (to make wet). || Mojar (one's bed). || Fam. Rociar, celebrar (an event). || *To wet o.s.*, mojarse.
— V. intr. Mojarse.
wet blanket [—'blæŋkit] n. Aguafiestas, *m.* & *f. inv.*
wether ['weðə*] n. Carnero (*m.*) castrado (ram).
wetness ['wetnis] n. Humedad, *f.* (dampness).
wet nurse ['wetnə:s] n. Nodriza, *f.*, ama (*f.*) de leche.
wet-nurse ['wetnə:s] v. tr. Criar.
wetting ['wetiŋ] n. Remojo, *m.* || *To get a wetting*, mojarse.
wettish ['wetiʃ] adj. Húmedo, da.
we've [wi:v] contraction of *we have*.
whack [wæk] n. Golpe (*m.*) fuerte (resounding blow). || Fam. Tentativa, *f.*, intento, *m.* (attempt). | Parte, *f.* (share). || — Fam. *Out of whack*, fuera de servicio. | *To take* o *to have a whack at*, intentar (to attempt).
whack [wæk] v. tr. Golpear (to strike). || Fam. Pegar una paliza a (to defeat). || U. S. Fam. Compartir (to share).
whacker [—ə*] n. Fam. Mastodonte, *m.* (person). | Enormidad, *f.* (story, thing).
whacking [—iŋ] adj. Fam. Enorme (very large). || Fam. *A whacking lie*, una mentira como una casa.
— Adv. Fam. Extremadamente, sumamente. || Fam. *Whacking big*, enorme.
— N. Paliza, *f.*, tunda, *f.* (thrashing).
whacky [—i] adj. Fam. Chiflado, da; chalado, da (person). | Absurdo, da (thing).
whale [weil] n. Zool. Ballena, *f.* || U. S. Fam. As, *m.*: *he's a whale at tennis*, es un as del tenis. || — Fam. *A whale of a*, sensacional, extraordinario, ria (good in quality), enorme (huge). | *We had a whale of a time!*, ¡lo pasamos bomba! || *Whale calf*, ballenato, *m.*
whale [weil] v. intr. Cazar ballenas.
— V. tr. Zurrar, dar una paliza a (to thrash). || U. S. Fam. Derrotar, pegar una paliza a.
whaleboat [—bəut] n. Ballenero, *m.*
whalebone [—bəun] n. Barba (*f.*) de ballena.
whale oil [—ɔil] n. Aceite (*m.*) de ballena.
whaler [—ə*] n. Ballenero, *m.* (man, boat).
whaling [—iŋ] n. Pesca (*f.*) *or* caza (*f.*) de ballenas. || — *Whaling gun*, fusil (*m.*) con arpón. || *Whaling industry*, industria ballenera. || *Whaling ship*, ballenero, *m.* (whaler).
wham [wæm] n. Golpe (*m.*) ruidoso (noisy impact).
— Interj. ¡Zas!
wham [wæm] v. tr. Golpear con fuerza.
— V. intr. Chocar ruidosamente.
whang [wæŋ] n. Golpe (*m.*) resonante.
— Interj. ¡Zas!
whang [wæŋ] v. tr. Azotar (to thrash). || Golpear con fuerza (to hit).
— V. intr. Resonar. || Chocar ruidosamente.
wharf [wɔ:f] n. Mar. Muelle, *m.*, embarcadero, *m.*, desembarcadero, *m.*

— Observ. El plural de esta palabra es *wharfs* (empleado sobre todo en Gran Bretaña) o *wharves* (usado en los Estados Unidos).

wharf [wɔ:f] v. tr. Mar. Atracar en el muelle (a ship). | Descargar en el muelle (goods).
wharfage [—idʒ] n. Mar. Muellaje, *m.* (fee). || Muelles, *m. pl.* (wharfs).
wharfinger [—indʒə*] n. Administrador (*m.*) del muelle (manager). | Representante (*m.*) de un armador en el muelle (representative).
what [wɔt] rel. pron. Lo que: *he heard what I said*, oyó lo que dije; *he told me what it would cost*, me dijo lo que costaría; *I am sorry about what has happened*, siento lo que ha ocurrido; *what I like is music*, lo que me gusta es la música; *you know what he is busy with*, sabes de lo que se ocupa; *I see what you are alluding to*, veo a lo que te estás refiriendo. || — *And what is more*, y además. || *Come* o *happen what may*, pase lo que pase. || *Do what I may*, cualquier cosa que haga. || *Say what he will*, diga lo que diga. || Fam. *To give s.o. what for*, dar a alguien su merecido. || *What with... and*, entre... y: *what with one thing and another*, entre una cosa y otra.
— Interr. pron. Qué: *what is the time?*, ¿qué hora es?; *he did what?*, ¿qué hizo?; *what is it?*, ¿qué es?; *what gave you that idea?*, ¿qué te hizo pensar eso?; *what are you talking about?*, ¿de qué está hablando? || Cuál: *what is her name?*, ¿cuál es su nombre? || Cuánto: *what is the rent?*, ¿cuánto es el alquiler? || A cuánto: *what are potatoes today?*, ¿a cuánto están hoy las patatas? | Cómo: *what is he like?*, ¿cómo es? || Qué (indirect): *tell me what is happening*, dime qué pasa; *I don't know what to do*, no sé qué hacer. || ¿Cómo? (I beg your pardon). || — *And what not* o *and what have you*, y tal y cual, y qué sé yo, y cosas por el estilo. | *I'll show you what's what*, te voy a poner al corriente (explanation), te voy a dar tu merecido (punishment). | *I'll tell you what*, see TELL. || *See what courage can do!*, ¡mira lo que puede conseguir el valor! || *So what?*, ¿y qué? || *To know what's what*, saber cuántas son cinco. || *Well, what about it?*, bueno y ¿qué? | *What about?*, ¿qué te parece?, ¿qué le parece?, etc.: *what about having dinner together?*, ¿qué le parece si cenamos juntos?; *what about you?*, y a ti ¿qué te parece?; ¿qué es de?: *what about your mother?*, ¿qué es de tu madre?; y: *what about the ten pounds I lent you?*, ¿y las diez libras que te presté? || *What about it*, ¿y qué? || *What does it matter?*, ¿qué importa? || *What do seven and eight make?*, ¿cuántos son siete con ocho? || *What else?*, ¿qué más? | *What for?*, ¿para qué? || *What if*, y si: *what if he can't come after all?*, ¿y si no puede venir después de todo? | *What is it to you?*, y a ti, ¿qué te importa? || *What is it all about?*, ¿de qué se trata? | *What is that all about?*, ¿a qué viene todo eso? | *What is the Spanish for "table"?*, ¿cómo se dice "table" en español? | *What next?*, ¿y ahora qué?, ¿y entonces qué? | *What of it?*, ¿y qué? | *What's the matter?*, ¿qué pasa? | *What then?*, ¿y qué? | *What though?*, ¿qué importa?
— Interr. adj. ¿Qué?: *what time is it?*, ¿qué hora es? || ¿De qué?: *what colour is your dress?*, ¿de qué color es tu vestido? | *What good is it?*, ¿para qué sirve?
— Exclamat. adj. Qué: *what silly fools we have been!*, ¡qué tontos hemos sido!; *what an absurd question!*, ¡qué pregunta más *or* tan absurda!; *what a pity!*, ¡qué lástima!; *what a lot of people!*, ¡qué cantidad de gente! | *What an idea!*, ¡menuda idea!
— Rel. adj. El que, la que, los que, las que, lo que: *lend me what money you can*, déjame el dinero que puedas; *what few friends he has were on holiday*, los pocos amigos que tenía estaban de vacaciones; *what little he said was interesting*, lo poco que dijo fue interesante.
— Interj. ¡Cómo!: *what!, another new dress!*, ¡cómo!, ¡otro vestido nuevo! | ¡Qué vergüenza!: *what!, fifty pounds for a chair!*, ¡qué vergüenza!, ¡cincuenta libras por una silla! | —*Nice little girl, what!*, ¡qué chica más mona!, ¿verdad? | *What they have suffered!*, ¡cuánto han sufrido!
what-d'ye-call-her['wɔtdju,kɔ:lhə*] n. Fam. Fulana, *f.*, ésa, *f.* (woman).
what-d'ye-call-him ['wɔtdju,kɔ:lhim] n. Fam. Fulano, *m.*, ése, *m.* (man).
what-d'ye-call-it ['wɔtdju,kɔ:lit] n. Fam. Chisme, *m.*, cosa, *f.* (thing).
whatever [wɔt'evə*] pron. Todo lo que: *eat whatever you like*, come todo lo que quieras. | Lo que: *I'll do it, whatever he says*, lo haré diga lo que diga. | Cualquier cosa que, todo lo que: *whatever he wants he shall have*, tendrá cualquier cosa que quiera. — *Whatever happens*, pase lo que pase. | *Whatever it may be*, sea lo que sea.
— Adj. Cualquiera ... que: *whatever doubt I may have*,

cualquier duda que pueda tener. Cualquiera que sea: *whatever difficulties you may encounter*, cualesquiera que sean las dificultades que pueda encontrar. || — *Nothing whatever*, absolutamente nada, nada en absoluto. || *This will be no trouble whatever for us*, no nos causará ninguna molestia.

what-ho! [ˈwɔtˈhəu] interj. ¡Vaya! (surprise). || ¡Hola! (hello!).

whatnot [ˈwɔtnɔt] n. Estantería, *f.* (shelves). || Chisme, *m.* (thingumajig).

what's [wɔts] contraction of *what is, what has, what does.*

what's-her-name [ˈwɔtsəneim] n. Fulana, *f.*, ésa, *f.*

what's-his-name [ˈwɔtsizneim] n. FAM. Fulano, *m.*, ése, *m.*

whatsoever [ˌwɔtsəuˈevə*] adj./pron. See WHATEVER.

wheal [wi:l] n. Verdugón, *m.* (weal).

wheat [wi:t] n. Trigo, *m.* (cereal).

wheatear [ˈwi:tiə*] n. Culiblanco, *m.* (bird).

wheaten [ˈwi:tən] adj. De trigo (of wheat). || De color de trigo (of the colour of wheat).

wheat field [ˈwi:tfi:ld] n. Trigal, *m.*

wheedle [ˈwi:dl] v. intr. Engatusar (to coax): *she wheedled him into buying her a new coat*, le engatusó para que le comprara un abrigo nuevo. || Conseguir [por medio de halagos]: *she wheedled a new coat out of him*, consiguió por medio de halagos que él le comprara un abrigo.

wheedler [ˈwi:dlə*] n. Engatusador, ra; zalamero, ra.

wheedling [ˈwi:dliŋ] adj. Zalamero, ra.
— N. Halagos, *m. pl.*, engatusamiento, *m.*

wheel [wi:l] n. Rueda, *f.* (of a vehicle): *the wheel of a car*, la rueda de un coche; *back, front wheel*, rueda trasera, delantera. || Volante, *m.* (for steering a car): *to take the wheel*, coger el volante. || Rueda, *f.* (of torture): *to break on the wheel*, atormentar en la rueda. || MIL. Vuelta, *f.*, giro, *m.*: *left wheel*, vuelta a la izquierda. || MAR. Timón, *m.* (of a ship): *to be at the wheel*, llevar el timón. || Torno, *m.* (potter's). || Ruleta, *f.*, rodillo (*m.*) trazador (in sewing). || U. S. FAM. Bici, *f.* (bike). || — Pl. Engranaje, *m. sing.*, maquinaria, *f. sing.*, mecanismo, *m. sing.*: *the wheels of government*, el mecanismo administrativo. || — *Big wheel*, noria, *f.* (at fair), pez gordo (important person). || *Fixed wheel*, piñón fijo. || FIG. *Fortune's wheel*, rueda de la fortuna. || AVIAT. *Landing wheels*, tren (*m.*) de aterrizaje. || MAR. *The man at the wheel*, el timonero. || FIG. *There are wheels within wheels*, es un asunto complicadísimo. | *The wheel has come full circle*, ¡qué de vueltas da la vida! | *To go on wheels*, ir sobre ruedas. | *To put one's shoulder to the wheel*, arrimar el hombro. || *To turn wheels*, dar volteretas.

wheel [wi:l] v. tr. Hacer rodar (to cause to roll). || Hacer girar (to rotate). || Llevar [sobre ruedas] (to carry on wheels): *to wheel sth. in a barrow*, llevar algo en una carretilla; *to wheel a child in a pram*, llevar a un niño en un cochecito. || Empujar (bicycle, motorcycle, etc.): *to wheel an invalid in a wheelchair*, empujar a un inválido en un sillón de ruedas. || Marcar con el rodillo trazador (in sewing). || Atormentar en la rueda (to torture).
— V. intr. Rodar (to move on wheels). || Dar vueltas, girar (to turn, to spin). || Revolotear: *the sea gulls were wheeling round me*, las gaviotas estaban revoloteando alrededor mío. || MIL. Dar una vuelta. || U. S. FAM. Ir en bicileta. || — *To wheel about* o *round*, dar media vuelta. || FIG. *To wheel round*, cambiar de opinión (to change one's mind).

wheelbarrow [—ˌbærəu] n. Carretilla, *f.*

wheelbase [—beis] n. AUT. Batalla, *f.*, distancia (*f.*) entre ejes.

wheelchair [—tʃεə*] n. Sillón (*m.*) de ruedas.

wheeled [—d] adj. De ruedas: *wheeled chair*, sillón de ruedas. || Rodado, da: *wheeled traffic*, tránsito rodado, circulación rodada. || *Two-wheeled*, de dos ruedas.

wheeler [—ə*] n. Caballo (*m.*) de tronco (wheelhorse). || Carretero, *m.* (man). || Vapor (*m.*) de ruedas (boat). || *Two-wheeler*, vehículo (*m.*) de dos ruedas.

wheelhorse [—hɔ:s] n. Caballo (*m.*) de tronco. || FIG. Colaborador (*m.*) eficaz.

wheelhouse [—haus] n. MAR. Timonera, *f.*, caseta (*f.*) *or* cámara (*f.*) del timón.

wheeling [—iŋ] n. Transporte (*m.*) sobre ruedas. || Carácter (*m.*) transitable.

wheelman [—mən] n. MAR. Timonel, *m.*, timonero, *m.*
— OBSERV. El plural de *wheelman* es *wheelmen*.

wheel rope [—rəup] n. MAR. Guardín, *m.*

wheel window [—ˌwindəu] n. ARCH. Rosetón, *m.*, rosa, *f.*

wheelwright [—rait] n. Carretero, *m.* || *Wheelwright's work*, carretería, *f.*

wheeze [wi:z] n. MED. Respiración (*f.*) jadeante *or* dificultosa, resuello, *m.* [ruidoso]. || FAM. Idea, *f.* | Gracia, *f.*, salida, *f.* (joke).

wheeze [wi:z] v. tr. *To wheeze out*, decir resollando.
— V. intr. Respirar con dificultad, resollar.

wheezing [—iŋ] or **wheezy** [—i] adj. Jadeante, dificultoso, sa (breath). || Asmático, ca (person).

whelk [welk] n. ZOOL. Buccino, *m.*

whelm [welm] v. tr. Sumergir.

whelp [welp] n. Cachorro, *m.* (young animal). || Bribón, *m.*, granuja, *m.* (a naughty boy).

whelp [welp] v. tr./intr. Parir (animals).

when [wen] adv. Cuándo, a qué hora (at what time): *¿when can you come?*, ¿a qué hora puedes venir? || Cuándo (on which occasion): *I don't know when I can do it*, no sé cuándo lo podré hacer; *when did that happen?*, ¿cuándo ocurrió? || *Say when!*, dime cuándo [tengo que pararme].
— Conj. Cuando: *when spring came*, cuando llegó la primavera. || En cuanto, al (as soon as): *we'll have lunch when father comes*, almorzaremos al llegar *or* en cuanto llegue papá. || Cuando (in spite of the fact that): *why does he live like a miser when he is so rich?*, ¿por qué vive como un avaro cuando es tan rico? || En que: *at the very moment when*, en el momento mismo en que; *the day when I met you*, el día en que te conocí. || Cuando: *now is when I need him more*, ahora es cuando más lo necesito. || *When a child*, de niño.
— Pron. Cuándo: *since when?*, ¿desde cuándo?; *till when?*, ¿hasta cuándo?
— N. Cuándo, *m.*: *I can't remember the when or the why of it*, no me puedo acordar ni del cuándo ni del porqué. || Momento, *m.*, fecha, *f.* (of an event).

whence [wens] adv./conj. ¿De dónde? (from where): *whence are they?*, ¿de dónde son? || *Whence I conclude that*, de lo cual deduzco que.

whencesoever [ˌwenssəuˈevə*] adv. De donde sea, de cualquier parte que sea.

whenever [wenˈevə*] or **whensoever** [ˌwensəuˈevə*] adv./conj. Cuando, en cualquier momento que: *come whenever you like*, ven cuando quieras. || Cada vez que: *whenever I see it I think of you*, cada vez que lo veo me acuerdo de ti; *I go whenever I can*, voy cada vez que puedo.

where [wεə*] interr. adv. Dónde: *where are you?*, ¿dónde estás? || Adónde, a dónde: *where are you going?*, ¿adónde vas? || De dónde: *where do you get your money?*, ¿de dónde sacas el dinero? || Por dónde: *where are you in your work?*, ¿por dónde vas en tu trabajo?; *I don't know where to begin*, no sé por dónde empezar. || En qué (in what respect): *where am I wrong?*, ¿en qué estoy equivocado? || — *Where are you from?* o *where do you come from?*, ¿de dónde es usted? || *Where should I be if I had followed your advice?*, ¿qué sería de mí si hubiese seguido su consejo?
— Rel. adv. Donde: *I shall stay where I am*, me quedaré donde estoy. || Donde, en donde, en que, en el cual, en la cual, en los cuales, en las cuales: *the town where I was born*, la ciudad en que nací. || Adonde, a donde: *they have gone where the police can't find them*, han ido adonde la policía no los puede localizar. || Adonde, a donde, al que, al cual, a la cual, a los cuales, a las cuales: *the town where I am going*, la ciudad a donde voy. || — *That is where we have got to*, a eso hemos llegado, aquí es a donde hemos llegado. || *That is where you are mistaken*, en eso está equivocado.
— N. Lugar, *m.*, sitio, *m.* (place).

whereabout [ˈwεərəˈbaut] adv. Al respecto. || See WHEREABOUTS.

whereabouts [—s] adv. Dónde, por dónde: *whereabouts did you put it?*, ¿dónde lo pusiste?

whereabouts [ˈwεərəbauts] n. Paradero, *m.*: *her present whereabouts is unknown*, no se conoce su paradero actual.

whereas [wεərˈæz] conj. Mientras [que], en tanto que: *some praise him whereas others condemn him*, algunos le alaban mientras otros le condenan. || JUR. Considerando que, visto que.
— Pl. n. JUR. *The whereases*, los considerandos.

whereat [wεərˈæt] adv. A lo cual: *whereat he replied*, a lo cual contestó. || — *He said sth., whereat everyone laughed*, dijo algo de lo cual se rieron todos. || *The words whereat he took offence*, las palabras por las que se ofendió.

whereby [wεəˈbai] adv. Cómo: *whereby shall I know him?*, ¿cómo podría conocerle? || Por el que, por la que, por medio del cual *or* de la cual: *decision whereby...*, decisión por la cual...

wherefore [ˈwεəfɔ:*] adv. Por qué (why): *wherefore comes he?*, ¿por qué viene? || Por lo que, por lo cual (for which).
— N. Porqué, *m.* || *The whys and wherefores*, las causas y los motivos, todos los detalles, el cómo y el porqué.

wherefrom [wεəˈfrɔm] adv. De donde, de lo cual.

wherein [wεərˈin] adv. En donde, en que, en el cual, en la cual: *the room wherein they were sleeping*, la habitación en la cual estaban durmiendo. || En qué: *wherein have we offended you?*, ¿en qué le hemos ofendido?

whereof [wεərˈɔv] adv. De qué: *whereof is it made?*, ¿de qué está hecho? || Del que, de la que, de lo que: *wood whereof paper is made*, madera de la que se hace el papel; *two sisters whereof one was a nun*, dos hermanas de las que una era monja.

whereon [wεərˈɔn] adv. En qué: *whereon did he sit?*, ¿en qué se sentó? || En el que, en la que: *the ground whereon he lies*, el suelo en el que descansa. || En que: *the day whereon he was assassinated*, el día en que fue asesinado.

wheresoever [ˌwεəsəuˈevə*] adv. See WHEREVER.

whereto [wεəˈtu:] adv. Para qué. || Para lo cual (to which). || Adonde, a donde (to which place).

whereupon [ˌwɛərəˈpɔn] adv. Después de lo cual, con lo cual (after which). || See WHEREON.

wherever [wɛərˈevə*] adv. Dondequiera que: *you must find him, wherever he is*, tienen que encontrarle dondequiera que esté. || A dondequiera que: *I shall remember you wherever I go*, me acordaré de ti a dondequiera que vaya. || FAM. ¿Dónde diablos?, ¿dónde demonios?, ¿dónde? (where): *wherever did you get that cold?*, ¿dónde demonios cogiste ese resfriado?

wherewith [wɛəˈwiθ] adv. Con el que, con la que, con lo cual (with which). || ¿Con qué? (with what?).
— Pron. Lo necesario para.

wherewithal [ˈwɛəwiðɔ:l] n. Medios, *m. pl.*, recursos, *m. pl.*, lo suficiente: *to have the wherewithal to pay*, tener lo suficiente para pagar.

wherry [ˈweri] n. Esquife, *m.* (rowing boat). || Barcaza, *f.*, chalana, *f.* (barge).

whet [wet] n. Afilado, *m.*, afiladura, *f.* (sharpening). || FIG. Estimulante, *m.* || FAM. Aperitivo, *m.*, copa, *f.* (drink).

whet [wet] v. tr. Afilar, sacar filo a (to sharpen). || FIG. Aguzar, despertar (the appetite). | Estimular (courage, etc.).

whether [ˈweðə*] conj. Si: *he asked whether it was true*, preguntó si era verdad; *it depends upon whether you are in a hurry or not*, depende de si tiene prisa o no. || — *The question arose whether...*, la cuestión se planteó de saber si... || *To doubt whether*, dudar que. || *Whether ... or*, sea ... o [sea]: *we'll take the next offer, whether good or bad*, aceptaremos la próxima oferta sea buena o sea mala; que ... o [que]: *whether he drives or takes the train*, que vaya en coche o que tome el tren. || *Whether or not*, de todo modos. || *Whether she comes or not*, venga o no venga.

whetstone [ˈwetstəun] n. Amoladera, *f.*, piedra (*f.*) de afilar, piedra (*f.*) de amolar.

whew [hwu:] intej. ¡Vaya!

whey [wei] n. Suero, *m.* (of milk).

which [witʃ] adj. Qué: *which road should I take?*, ¿qué carretera debo coger?; *deciding which candidate he is going to vote for*, decidiendo por qué candidato va a votar. || Cuál, cuales. || Cuyo, ya: *he stayed here six months, during which time...*, se quedó aquí seis meses, durante cuyo tiempo... || — *Look which way you will*, mire por donde mire. || *Try which method you please*, aplique el método que quiera. || *Which one?*, ¿cuál? || *Which ones?*, ¿cuáles? || *Which way?*, ¿por dónde?: *which way do we go?*, ¿por dónde vamos?; ¿de dónde?: *which way is the wind?*, ¿de dónde viene el viento?; ¿cómo? (how): *which way shall we do it?*, ¿cómo lo vamos a hacer?
— Interr. pron. Cuál: *which do you prefer?*, ¿cuál prefieres?; *she did not know which were the best shops*, no sabía cuáles eran las mejores tiendas; *which of you will go with me?*, ¿cuál de vosotros vendrá conmigo? || Qué: *which would you rather be, pretty or good?*, qué preferirías ¿ser guapa o ser buena?; *which will you take, coffee or tea?* ¿qué tomas? ¿café o té? || *Tell me which is which*, dime cuál es cuál.
— Rel. pron. Que: *the book which you lent me*, el libro que me dejaste. || El cual, la cual, los cuales, las cuales, el que, la que, los que, las que: *the work to which she devoted all her time*, el trabajo al cual dedicó todo su tiempo. || Lo cual, lo que: *he refused to come, which did not surprise me*, se negó a venir, lo cual no me extrañó; *upon which she came out*, con lo cual se fue. || — *All which*, todo lo cual. || *Of which*, del que, de la que, de los que, de las que, del cual, de la cual, etc.: *the house of which I speak*, la casa de la cual hablo; *the table one leg of which is broken*, la mesa de la cual una pata está rota; cuyo, cuya: *the room the door of which is closed*, la habitación cuya puerta está cerrada.

whichever [witʃˈevə*] or **whichsoever** [ˌwitʃsəuˈevə*] adj. Cualquier, cualquiera [que sea]: *whichever party comes to power*, cualquiera que sea el partido que *or* cualquier partido que llegue al poder. || *Take whichever book you like best*, coja el libro que más le guste.
— Pron. El que, la que: *buy whichever is cheapest*, compre el que sea más barato. || Cualquiera que: *whichever you choose you will have a good bargain*, cualquiera que escoja, habrá hecho un buen negocio.

whiff [wif] n. Bocanada, *f.* (small volume of smoke, air, etc.). || Chupada, *f.*, calada, *f.* (of tobacco). || Soplo, *m.* (of wind). || Olorcillo, *m.* (odour). || MAR. Esquife, *m.* || FAM. Purito, *m.* (small cigar). || — *He went out for a whiff of fresh air*, salió a tomar el fresco. || *To get a whiff of ether*, oler a éter.

whiff [wif] v. tr. Echar (smoke, scent, etc.).
— V. intr. Soplar (to blow). || Echar bocanadas de humo (smoking, etc.). || *To whiff of*, oler a (to smell of): *it whiffs of garlic*, huele a ajo.

Whig [wig] n. "Whig", *m.*

— OBSERV. En Gran Bretaña, el *Wig party* es un partido político, creado en el siglo XVII, que ha sido sustituido por el partido liberal. En Estados Unidos, es un partido fundado en el siglo XIX que ha sido reemplazado por el partido republicano.

while [wail] n. Rato, *m.*, tiempo, *m.* (period of time): *a long while*, largo rato, mucho tiempo. || *After a while*, al poco rato, poco tiempo después. || *A little while*, un ratito. || *A little while ago*, hace poco tiempo. || *All the while*, todo el tiempo. || *A long while ago*, hace mucho tiempo. || *For a while*, durante algún tiempo. || *I'll make it worth your while*, te recompensaré. || *In a little while*, dentro de poco. || *In a while*, dentro de un rato. || *Once in a while*, de vez en cuando. || *The while*, mientras tanto, entre tanto: *I gave her a book to read the while*, le di un libro para que leyera mientras tanto. || *That will do for a while*, eso le bastará de momento. || *To be worth while*, merecer *or* valer la pena: *I will come if it is worth while*, vendré si merece la pena; *it is not worth while your going*, no merece la pena que vayáis. || *What a while you are!*, ¡cuánto tardas!
— Conj. Mientras: *she only saw him twice while he was staying there*, le vio sólo dos veces mientras él estaba allí; *never while I live*, nunca, mientras yo viva. || Mientras [que]: *she has remained poor, while her friends have made a fortune*, ha seguido siendo pobre mientras que sus amigas han ganado una fortuna. || Aunque (although): *while I admit it is difficult, I don't think it is impossible*, aunque reconozco que es difícil no creo que sea imposible.

while [wail] v. tr. *To while away*, pasar: *she whiled away the hours of waiting by looking at the shops*, pasó las horas de espera mirando los escaparates; disipar (cares).

whilom [ˈwailəm] adv. Antaño, en otro tiempo.
— Adj. De antaño, de antes.

whilst [wailst] conj. See WHILE.

whim [wim] n. Capricho, *m.*, antojo, *m.* (fancy). || TECH. Malacate, *m.* || — *Passing whim*, antojo. || *To take a whim into one's head*, antojársele a uno algo.

whimbrel [ˈwimbrəl] n. Zarapito, *m.* (bird).

whimper [ˈwimpə*] n. Gimoteo, *m.*, quejido, *m.* (complaint). || Lloriqueo, *m.* (snivelling). || Gañido, *m.* (of an animal).

whimper [ˈwimpə*] v. intr. Lloriquear (to snivel). || Quejarse, gimotear (to complain). || Gañir (a dog).
— V. tr. Decir lloriqueando.

whimpering [—riŋ] adj. Quejica.
— N. See WHIMPER.

whimsical [ˈwimzikəl] adj. Caprichoso, sa; antojadizo, za (person). || Extraño, ña; peregrino, na (idea).

whimsicality [ˌwimziˈkæliti] n. Carácter (*m.*) caprichoso (character). || Rareza, *f.*, extravagancia, *f.* (oddity). || Capricho, *m.* (caprice). || Fantasía, *f.* (fancy).

whimsy [ˈwimzi] n. Capricho, *m.*, antojo, *m.* (whim). || Extravagancia, *f.*, rareza, *f.* (oddity).

whin [win] n. BOT. Tojo, *m.*, aulaga, *f.*

whine [wain] n. Quejido, *m.*, gemido, *m.* (of pain). || Queja, *f.* (complaint). || Lloriqueo, *m.* (snivelling). || Gañido, *m.* (of an animal). || Zumbido, *m.* (of an engine, bullet).

whine [wain] v. tr. Decir lloriqueando.
— V. intr. Gimotear, quejarse (person). || Lloriquear (child). || Gañir (animal). || Zumbar (engine, bullet).

whining [—iŋ] adj. Quejica.
— N. Gimoteo, *m.*, quejidos, *m. pl.*

whinny [ˈwini] n. Relincho, *m.* (of a horse).

whinny [ˈwini] v. intr. Relinchar.

whiny [ˈwaini] adj. Llorón, ona; quejica.

whip [wip] n. Látigo, *m.* (long lash). || Azote, *m.* (any beating instrument). || Fusta, *f.* (for horses). || Latigazo, *m.*, azote, *m.* (blow). || Zumbel, *m.* (for a spinning top). || Aspa, *f.* (of a windmill). || TECH. Aparejo, *m.* (hoisting apparatus). || Montero, *m.* (in hunting party). || CULIN. Batidor, *m.* || Cochero, *m.* (coachman). || Miembro (*m.*) de un partido político encargado de hacer observar las consignas de éste a los demás miembros (member of parliament). || Llamada (*f.*) a los miembros del partido para que presencien un debate (call). || — *The government have taken off the whips*, el gobierno deja a los miembros del partido la libertad de votar como quieran. || *Three-line whip*, llamada para que los diputados voten en un debate particularmente importante.

whip [wip] v. tr. Azotar, dar latigazos a: *to whip a horse*, azotar un caballo. || Azotar (a child). || Azotar, golpear: *the rain whipped our faces*, la lluvia nos azotaba la cara. || Hacer bailar: *to whip a top*, hacer bailar un trompo. || FIG. Fustigar. || MAR. Elevar con el aparejo (to hoist). || Rebatir (in sewing). || CULIN. Batir (cream, eggs): *whipped cream*, crema batida. || FAM. Dar una paliza a (to defeat heavily). | Mangar, birlar (to steal).
— V. intr. Azotar. || Restallar: *the flag whipped in the wind*, la bandera restallaba en el viento. || Lanzarse (to move rapidly).
— ***To whip away***, arrebatar: *he whipped the knife away from him*, le arrebató el cuchillo. | Irse rápidamente (to leave). || ***To whip in***, reunir (hunting dogs, members of a political party). || ***To whip off***, quitar rápidamente (to remove). | Quitarse rápidamente (clothes). | Irse rápidamente (to leave). || ***To whip on***, dar latigazos para que avance (a horse). | Ponerse rápidamente (clothes). || ***To whip out***, sacar de repente: *he whipped out a gun*, de repente sacó una pistola. | Salir rápidamente (to go out). || ***To whip round***, volverse de repente (to turn around). | Hacer una colecta (to ask for money). || ***To whip up***, avivar: *to whip up enthusiasm*, avivar el entusiasmo. | Instar a que participen en una votación (members of parliament). | Coger rápidamente (to take).

whipcord [—kɔ:d] n. Tralla, *f.*, cuerda (*f.*) de látigo (cord). ‖ Pana, *f.* (fabric).
whip hand [—ˈhænd] n. *To have the whip hand of* o *over s.o.*, tenerle dominado a alguien.
whiplash [—læʃ] n. Tralla, *f.* (whipcord). ‖ Latigazo, *m.* (blow).
whipper-in [—ərˈin] n. Montero, *m.* (in hunting).
— OBSERV. El plural es *whippers-in.*
whippersnapper [—əˏsnæpə*] n. FAM. Chiquilicuatro, *m.*, mequetrefe, *m.*
whippet [ˈwipit] n. Lebrel, *m.* (dog).
whipping [ˈwipiŋ] n. Azotamiento, *m.* (beating). ‖ Paliza, *f.* (flogging). ‖ Flagelación, *f.* (flagellation). ‖ Rebatido, *m.* (stitching). ‖ CULIN. Batido, *m.* ‖ FIG. Paliza, *f.*
whipping boy [—bɔi] n. FIG. Cabeza (*f.*) de turco, víctima (*f.*) propiciatoria, chivo (*m.*) expiatorio (scapegoat). ‖ (Ant.). Niño (*m.*) criado con un príncipe y que recibe los azotes en su lugar.
whipping top [—tɔp] n. Trompo, *m.*, peonza, *f.*
whippy [ˈwipi] adj. Elástico, ca; flexible.
whippoorwill [ˈwippuəˏwil] n. Chotacabras, *m. inv.* (bird).
whip-round [ˈwipraund] n. Colecta, *f.*: *to have a whip-round for*, hacer una colecta por.
whipsaw [ˈwipsɔ:] n. Sierra (*f.*) abrazadera. ‖ U. S. FIG. Arma (*f.*) de dos filos.
whipsaw [ˈwipsɔ:] v. tr. Aserrar. ‖ FIG. FAM. Pelar (in gambling). ‖ Hacer perder (in business).
whipstitch [ˈwipstitʃ] n. Sobrehilo, *m.*
whipstitch [ˈwipstitʃ] v. tr. Sobrehilar.
whip top [ˈwiptɔp] n. Trompo, *m.*, peonza, *f.* (toy).
whir [wə:*] n./v. intr. See WHIRR.
whirl [wə:l] n. Giro, *m.*, rotación, *f.* (circular movement). ‖ Remolino, *m.*, torbellino, *m.* (of dust, water). ‖ FIG. Torbellino, *m.*, serie, *f.*: *a whirl of parties*, un torbellino de fiestas. — FIG. *My head is in a whirl*, me está dando vueltas la cabeza. ‖ U. S. FAM. *To give sth. a whirl*, probar algo.
whirl [wə:l] v. tr. Hacer girar, dar vueltas a (to cause to rotate). ‖ Hacer revolotear: *the wind whirled the dead leaves*, el viento hacía revolotear las hojas muertas. ‖ Lanzar con honda (to hurl). ‖ *To whirl along*, llevar a toda velocidad.
— V. intr. Girar, dar vueltas (to rotate rapidly): *the dancers whirled round the room*, los bailarines daban vueltas por la sala. ‖ Arremolinarse: *the leaves whirled round the garden*, las hojas se arremolinaban por el jardín. ‖ Pasar rápidamente: *the train whirled through the station*, el tren pasó rápidamente por la estación. ‖ Pasar: *the thoughts that whirl through my head*, las ideas que me pasan por la cabeza. — FIG. *My head was whirling*, me daba vueltas la cabeza. ‖ *To come whirling down*, bajar dando vueltas. ‖ *To whirl along*, pasar a toda velocidad, pasar como un rayo. ‖ *To whirl past sth.*, pasar rápidamente delante de algo.
whirlbone [—bəun] n. ANAT. Rótula, *f.*
whirligig [—igig] n. Molinete, *m.* (toy). ‖ Tiovivo, *m.*, caballitos, *m. pl.* (merry-go-round). ‖ ZOOL. Girino, *m.* (beetle). ‖ FIG. Torbellino, *m.* | Cambios, *m. pl.*, vaivenes, *m. pl.*: *the whirligig of fortune*, los cambios de la suerte.
whirlpool [—pu:l] n. Remolino, *m.* [de agua] (eddy), vorágine, *f.* (vortex).
whirlwind [—wind] n. Torbellino, *m.*, remolino, *m.* [de aire].
whirlybird [—ibə:d] n. U. S. FAM. Helicóptero, *m.*
whirr [wə:*] n. Zumbido, *m.* (of engine, etc.). ‖ Batir, *m.*, aleteo, *m.* (of bird's wings).
whirr [wə:*] v. intr. Zumbar (engine, etc.). ‖ *The birds whirred past*, se oía el ruido de las alas de los pájaros al pasar.
whish [wiʃ] v. intr. Zumbar, silbar.
whisk [wisk] n. CULIN. Batidor, *m.* [de mano]. ‖ Cepillo, *m.* (brush). ‖ Escobilla, *f.* (broom). ‖ Plumero, *m.* (feather duster). ‖ Matamoscas, *m. inv.* (flyswatter). ‖ Movimiento (*m.*) brusco: *with a whisk of the hand*, con un movimiento brusco de la mano. ‖ *A whisk of the tail*, un coletazo.
whisk [wisk] v. tr. CULIN. Batir (cream, eggs, etc.). ‖ Sacudir, mover: *the horse whisked its tail*, el caballo sacudió la cola. ‖ — *To whisk along*, llevarse rápidamente *or* a toda velocidad. ‖ *To whisk away* o *to whisk off*, espantar, ahuyentar (flies), cepillar (to brush), quitar (dust), enjugar discretamente (a tear), birlar, llevarse (to steal), llevarse rápidamente (to take away), llevar rápidamente (s.o.): *they whisked him off in a car*, le llevaron rápidamente en un coche.
— V. intr. Ir como un rayo. ‖ — *To whisk away* o *off*, irse a toda velocidad. ‖ *To whisk past*, pasar a toda velocidad *or* como un rayo.
whisk broom [—brum] n. U. S. Cepillo (*m.*) de la ropa.
whisker [—ə*] n. Pelo (*m.*) del bigote (of a cat, rabbit). ‖ MAR. Arbotante, *m.* (of bowsprit). ‖ — Pl. Patillas, *f.* (sideboards). ‖ Pelos (*m.*) de la barba (of a beard). ‖ Bigotes, *m.* (of an animal).
whiskered [—əd] adj. Barbudo, da (bearded). ‖ Bigotudo, da (with moustache). ‖ Patilludo, da (with sideboards).
whiskey or **whisky** [—i] n. Whisky, *m.*: *whisky and soda*, whisky con sifón *or* con soda.

whisper [ˈwispə*] n. Cuchicheo, *m.* (low speech). ‖ FIG. Susurro, *m.*, murmullo, *m.* (of leaves, water). ‖ Rumor, *m.* (rumour). ‖ — *There is a whisper that*, se rumorea que, corre el rumor de que. ‖ *There wasn't a whisper of it*, no se habló nada de ello en los periódicos. ‖ *To talk in a whisper*, hablar bajo, hablar en voz baja.
whisper [ˈwispə*] v. tr. Decir en voz baja: *to whisper a word to s.o.*, decir una palabra en voz baja a alguien. ‖ Hacer correr (a rumour). ‖ — *It is whispered that*, corre la voz *or* el rumor de que, se rumorea que. ‖ *To whisper sth. in s.o.'s ear*, decir algo al oído de alguien, decir algo bajito a alguien.
— V. intr. Cuchichear, hablar en voz baja: *they sat in the corner whispering*, estaban sentados en el rincón cuchicheando. ‖ Hablar al oído (secretly). ‖ FIG. Susurrar: *the leaves whispered*, las hojas susurraban.
whispering [—riŋ] n. Cuchicheo, *m.* ‖ FIG. Rumor, *m.* (rumour). | Murmuración, *f.* (gossip). | Susurro, *m.*, murmullo, *m.* (of leaves, water). ‖ — U. S. *Whispering campaign*, campaña (*f.*) de difamación. ‖ ARCH. *Whispering gallery*, galería (*f.*) que tiene eco.
whist [wist] n. "Whist", *m.* (card game).
— Interj. ¡Chitón!
whistle [ˈwisl] n. Pito, *m.*, silbato, *m.* (instrument). ‖ Silbido, *m.*, pitido, *m.* (act, sound, signal). ‖ Canto, *m.* (of a bird). ‖ — *To blow a whistle*, tocar el pito, pitar. ‖ FAM. *To wet one's whistle*, echarse un trago al coleto, mojar la canal maestra, mojar el gaznate.
whistle [ˈwisl] v. tr. Silbar: *to whistle a tune*, silbar una melodía; *to whistle a dog*, silbar a un perro.
— V. intr. Silbar (with mouth). ‖ Pitar (with instrument). ‖ Silbar, zumbar (bullet, wind, etc.). ‖ Piar (birds). ‖ — *To whistle for*, silbar para llamar: *to whistle for a taxi*, silbar para llamar un taxi. ‖ SP. *To whistle for a foul*, pitar una falta. ‖ *To whistle past*, pasar silbando *or* zumbando. ‖ FAM. *You can whistle for it*, puedes esperar sentado.
whistle-stop [ˈwislstɔp] n. U. S. Apeadero, *m.* (railway station). | Breve parada, *f.* (on a political tour).
whistling [ˈwisliŋ] n. Silbido, *m.*, silbo, *m.*
whit [wit] n. Pizca, *f.*, ápice, *m.*: *there's not a whit of truth*, no hay un ápice de verdad. ‖ — *He is every whit as good as you*, es tan bueno como tú. ‖ *I don't care a whit*, me importa un comino.
Whit [wit] n. Pentecostés, *m.*
— Adj. De Pentecostés.
white [wait] adj. Blanco, ca: *white wine*, vino blanco; *white bread*, pan blanco; *the white race*, la raza blanca; *white bear*, oso blanco. ‖ Cano, na; blanco, ca (hair). ‖ Blanco, ca (light): *white complexion*, tez blanca. ‖ Pálido, da (pale): *white with fear*, pálido de miedo. ‖ REL. Blanco, ca (wearing white). ‖ TECH. Blanco, ca: *white coal*, hulla blanca; *white wood*, madera blanca; *white gold*, oro blanco. ‖ FIG. Blanco, ca (magic). | Piadoso, sa (lie). | Honrado, da (honest). | Puro, ra; inocente (pure). ‖ GEOGR. Blanco, ca: *White Nile*, Nilo Blanco. ‖ — FIG. *As white as a sheet* o *as white as a ghost*, blanco como el papel. ‖ *A white man, woman*, un blanco, una blanca. ‖ FIG. *To bleed s.o. white*, chuparle la sangre a alguien, esquilmar a alguien. | *To turn white*, ponerse blanco, palidecer, ponerse pálido. ‖ *White coffee*, café con leche. ‖ *White lead*, blanco (*m.*) de plomo.
— N. Blanco, *m.*, color (*m.*) blanco (colour). ‖ Blancura, *f.* (whiteness). ‖ Blanco, ca (person). ‖ Blanco, *m.* (of the eyes, of a target). ‖ Clara, *f.* (of an egg). ‖ Ropa (*f.*) blanca (clothes). ‖ — Pl. MED. Flujo (*m. sing.*) blanco, leucorrea, *f. sing.* ‖ — *Dressed in white*, vestido de blanco. ‖ *White sale*, quincena blanca. ‖ *Zinc white*, blanco de cinc.
white alloy [—ˈælɔi] n. Metal (*m.*) blanco.
white ant [—ˈænt] n. Comején, *m.*, hormiga (*f.*) blanca.
whitebait [—beit] n. Morralla, *f.* (small fishes).
white beet [—ˈbi:t] n. BOT. Acelga, *f.*
white blood cell [—ˈblʌdsel] n. Glóbulo (*m.*) blanco.
white book [—buk] n. Libro (*m.*) blanco.
whitecaps [—kæps] pl. n. MAR. Cabrillas, *f.*
white-collar [—ˈkɔlə*] adj. De oficina. ‖ *White-collar worker*, empleado (*m.*) de oficina, oficinista, *m.* & *f.*
white corpuscle [—ˈkɔ:pʌsl] n. Glóbulo (*m.*) blanco.
whited [—id] adj. Blanqueado, da: *whited sepulchre* (U. S. *sepulcher*), sepulcro blanqueado.
white damp [—ˈdæmp] n. CHEM. Óxido (*m.*) de carbono.
whitefish [—fiʃ] n. Pescado (*m.*) blanco.
white-haired [—ˈhɛəd] adj. De pelo cano.
white-headed [—ˈhedid] adj. De pelo cano (with white hair). ‖ De cabeza blanca (animal). ‖ FIG. Mimado, da: *the white-headed boy*, el niño mimado.
white heat [—ˈhi:t] n. Blanco, *m.*, rojo (*m.*) blanco: *to bring to white heat*, calentar al rojo blanco.
white hellebore [—ˈhelibɔ:*] n. BOT. Vedegambre, *m.*
white horses [—ˈhɔ:siz] pl. n. MAR. Cabrillas, *f.*
white-hot [—ˈhɔt] adj. Calentado al rojo blanco (at white heat). ‖ FIG. Candente, al rojo vivo: *the situation is white-hot*, la situación está candente.
White House [—haus] n. *The White House*, la Casa Blanca.
white lily [—ˈlili] n. BOT. Azucena, *f.*

white-livered [—,livəd] adj. FAM. Cobarde (cowardly).
whiten [—ən] v. tr. Blanquear (to make white). || Encanecer (hair). || Blanquecer (metals).
— V. intr. Blanquear. || Palidecer, ponerse blanco *or* pálido (face, person).
whiteness [—nis] n. Blancura, *f.* || Palidez, *f.* (paleness). || FIG. Pureza, *f.*, inocencia, *f.*
whitening [—niŋ] n. Blanqueo, *m.* (of linen). || Enlucido, *m.*, enjalbegado, *m.* (of walls). || Blanquición, *f.* (of metals). || Blanco (*m.*) de España, albayalde, *m.* (whiting).
white paper [—'peipə*] n. Libro (*m.*) blanco (government paper).
white slaver [—'sleivə*] n. Traficante (*m.*) de blancas.
white slavery [—'sleivəri] n. Trata (*f.*) de blancas.
whitesmith [—smiθ] n. Hojalatero, *m.* (tinsmith).
whitethorn [—θɔ:n] n. BOT. Espino (*m.*) blanco, majuelo, *m.*
whitethroat [—θraut] n. Curruca, *f.* (bird).
whitewash [—wɔʃ] n. Cal, *f.*, lechada (*f.*) de cal (for walls). || FIG. Encubrimiento (*m.*) de faltas (concealing of faults). || Disculpa, *f.* (excuse). || Rehabilitación, *f.* (of a bankrupt). || U. S. FAM. Paliza, *f.* (total defeat). || *To give a wall a coat of whitewash*, encalar *or* enjalbegar *or* blanquear una pared.
whitewash [—wɔʃ] v. tr. Encalar, enjalbegar, blanquear (walls). || FIG. Encubrir (faults). || Disculpar (s.o.). || Rehabilitar (a bankrupt). || U. S. FAM. *To whitewash a team*, impedir que un equipo marque, dar una paliza a un equipo.
whitewasher [—wɔʃə*] n. Blanqueador, *m.*, enjalbegador, *m.*, encalador, *m.*
whitewashing [—wɔʃiŋ] n. Encalado, *m.*, blanqueo, *m.*, enjalbegado, *m.* (of walls). || FIG. Rehabilitación, *f.*
whither ['wiðə*] adv. ¿A dónde?, ¿adónde?: *whither do you go?*, ¿adónde vas?; *whither will all this lead?*, ¿a dónde nos llevará todo eso? || Adonde, a donde.
whiting ['waitiŋ] n. Blanco (*m.*) de España, albayalde, *m.* (finely powdered chalk). || Pescadilla, *f.* (fish).
whitish ['waitiʃ] adj. Blanquecino, na; blancuzco, ca.
whitlow ['witləu] n. MED. Panadizo, *m.*
witlowwort [—wə:t] n. BOT. Nevadilla, *f.*
Whitmonday ['wit'mʌndi] n. Lunes (*m.*) de Pentecostés.
Whitsun ['witsn] n. Pentecostés, *m.*
— Adj. De Pentecostés.
Whitsunday ['wit'sʌndi] n. Domingo (*m.*) de Pentecostés.
Whitsuntide ['witsntaid] n. Pentecostés, *m.*
whittle ['witl] n. Cuchillo (*m.*) grande.
whittle ['witl] v. tr. Cortar (to cut). || Tallar [con cuchillo] (to carve). || FIG. *To whittle away* o *down*, reducir poco a poco, cercenar: *they are trying to whittle down our salaries*, están intentando reducir poco a poco nuestros salarios.
— V. intr. *To whittle at*, cortar (to cut), tallar [con cuchillo] (to carve).
whittling ['witliŋ] n. Astilla, *f.* || FIG. *Whittling down*, reducción progresiva.
whiz or **whizz** [wiz] n. Zumbido, *m.* (buzzing sound). || Silbido, *m.* (hissing sound). || U. S. FAM. Número (*m.*) uno, as, *m.*: *he is a whizz at football*, es el número uno en fútbol. || Trato (*m.*) cerrado (deal).
whiz o **whizz** [wiz] v. intr. Silbar (to whistle). || Zumbar (to hum). || — *To whizz along*, ir a gran velocidad (fast). || *To whizz past*, pasar silbando (bullet), pasar como un rayo (car).
whizz kid [—kid] n. Promesa, *f.*, joven (*m.*) prometedor, joven (*f.*) prometedora (promising person).
who [hu:] interr. pron. Quién, quiénes: *who is that woman?*, ¿quién es esa mujer?; *who are they?*, ¿quiénes son?; *I didn't see who they were*, no vi quiénes eran; *he told me who they were*, me dijo quiénes eran. || Quien, quiénes (see OBSERV.): *who do you think I got a letter from?*, ¿de quién te crees que he recibido una carta?; *who did you give it to?*, ¿a quién se lo diste? || *Mrs who?*, ¿la señora qué? || *Tell me who's who*, dígame quiénes son, dígame cuáles son los nombres de las personas aquí presentes. || *Who does he think he is?*, ¿quién se cree que es? || *Who on earth is it?*, ¿quién diablos *or* quién demonios puede ser? || *Who should I meet but Anthony?*, ¿a quién te crees que me encontré? — A Antonio. || *Who's Who*, quien es quien [anuario (*m.*) que contiene los nombres y el historial de las personas más conocidas del mundo]. || *You will soon find out who's who*, pronto sabrás quién es cada cual.
— Rel. pron. Quien, quienes, el que, la que, los que, las que (the person who): *it was his father who said it*, fue su padre quien lo dijo; *it is you who are responsible for it*, son ustedes los que son responsables de ello; *who asks receives*, quien pide recibe. || Que: *he likes women who dress well*, le gustan las mujeres que visten bien. || Que, el cual, la cual, los cuales, las cuales: *his grandfather, who was a doctor*, su abuelo, que era médico. || Que, a quien, a quienes (see OBSERV.): *he likes the people who he employs*, le gustan las personas que emplea; *the man who I saw*, el hombre a quien vi. || *As who should say ...*, como quien dice ... || *Disagree who may, I think that ...*, aunque habrá quien no esté de acuerdo, yo creo que ... || *Those who*, los que, las que: *those who want to, may leave*, los que quieran pueden marcharse.

— OBSERV. En muchos casos *who* se emplea en lugar de *whom* en la lengua hablada aunque sea incorrecto desde un punto de vista puramente gramatical. *Whom* es la forma correcta cuando es complemento directo o cuando se emplea después de una preposición.

whoa [wəu] interj. ¡So!
whodunit [hu:'dʌnit] n. FAM. Novela (*f.*) *or* película (*f.*) *or* obra (*f.*) de teatro policiaca.
whoever [hu:'evə*] pron. Quienquiera que, cualquiera que, el que, la que, quien: *whoever wants it can have it*, quienquiera que *or* el que *or* quien lo quiera puede guardarlo. || El que, la que, quien: *whoever said that is a liar*, el que lo dijo es un mentiroso. || Quienquiera que: *come out whoever you are!*, ¡quienquiera que sea, salga de ahí! || FAM. Quién diablos: *whoever said that?*, ¿quién diablos dijo eso? || *To everybody whoever he may be*, a todos sin excepción alguna.
whole [həul] adj. Entero, ra; todo, da: *the whole night long*, la noche entera, durante toda la noche; *the whole army*, el ejército entero, todo el ejército; *don't swallow it whole*, no te lo tragues entero; *I never saw him the whole evening*, no le vi en toda la noche. || Entero, ra: *whole families disappeared*, familias enteras desaparecieron; *to eat a whole chicken*, comerse un pollo entero. || Total: *whole length*, longitud total. || Sano, na (healthy). || Ileso, sa (not injured). || Intacto, ta; sano, na (undamaged): *there is not a plate that is whole*, no queda un plato sano. || Íntegro, gra; completo, ta (containing all natural components). || Único, ca: *the whole point of all this*, la única razón de todo eso. || Carnal (having both parents in common): *whole sister*, hermana carnal. || MATH. Entero: *whole number*, número entero. || — FAM. *A whole lot of*, una gran cantidad de, muchísimo, ma. || *The whole truth*, toda la verdad.
— N. Todo, *m.*: *the parts of a whole*, las partes de un todo. || Conjunto, *m.*: *the four parts made a pleasing whole*, las cuatro partes formaban un conjunto agradable. || Total, *m.* (of a bill, etc.): *the whole amounts to*, el total asciende a. || — *As a whole*, en conjunto, en su totalidad: *the play as a whole wasn't bad*, la obra en conjunto no estaba mal. || *On the whole*, en general: *on the whole I agree with you*, en general estoy de acuerdo con usted; considerándolo todo: *on the whole I am satisfied*, considerándolo todo estoy satisfecho. || *The whole of*, todo, da: *the whole of the summer*, todo el verano; *the whole of his works*, todas sus obras; entero, ra; todo, da: *he smoked the whole of the packet*, se fumó la cajetilla entera.
wholehearted [—'hɑ:tid] adj. Sincero, ra; franco, ca (frank). || Sincero, ra; completo, ta; incondicional: *wholehearted support*, completo apoyo. || Entusiasta (enthusiastic).
wholeheartedly [—'hɑ:tidli] adv. Sinceramente, de todo corazón. || Completamente, incondicionalmente. || Con entusiasmo.
wholeheartedness [—'hɑ:tidnis] n. Sinceridad, *f.* || Entusiasmo, *m.*
whole meal [—mi:l] adj. Integral (bread).
whole milk [—'milk] n. Leche (*f.*) sin desnatar.
wholeness [—nis] n. Integridad, *f.*
whole note [—nəut] n. U. S. MUS. Semibreve, *f.*, redonda, *f.*
whole number [—nʌmbə*] n. Número (*m.*) entero.
wholesale [—seil] adj. COMM. Al por mayor: *wholesale trade*, comercio al por mayor. || FIG. En serie (manufacture). || General, en masa: *a wholesale slaughter*, una matanza total. || *Wholesale dealer*, mayorista, *m.* & *f.*, comerciante (*m.* & *f.*) al por mayor.
— N. COMM. Venta (*f.*) al por mayor.
— Adv. Al por mayor: *to sell sth. wholesale*, vender algo al por mayor. || FIG. En serie (to manufacture). || En masa: *to kill wholesale*, matar en masa.
wholesale [—seil] v. intr. Vender al por mayor (to trade in wholesale goods). || Venderse al por mayor (to be sold wholesale).
— V. tr. Vender al por mayor.
wholesaler [—,seilə*] n. Comerciante (*m.* & *f.*) al por mayor, mayorista, *m.* & *f.*
wholesome [—səm] n. Sano, na (good for the health): *wholesome food*, comida sana. || Sano, na; saludable (healthy): *a wholesome climate*, un clima saludable. || FIG. Saludable (advice, remedy). || Sano, na (person, reading).
wholesomeness [—səmnis] n. Lo sano (of food). || Lo sano, lo saludable (of climate). || FIG. Lo sano.
whole wheat [—wi:t] adj. U. S. Integral (bread).
who'll [hu:l] contraction of *who will* and *who shall*.
wholly ['həuli] adv. Completamente, totalmente, enteramente (entirely): *I don't wholly agree*, no estoy completamente de acuerdo.
whom [hu:m] interr. pron. Quién, quiénes, a quién, a quiénes: *from whom did you receive it?*, ¿de quién lo recibiste?; *to whom are you speaking?*, ¿a quién estás hablando?
— Rel. pron. Que, quien, quienes, a quien, a quienes: *he likes the people whom he employs*, le gustan las personas que emplea; *the man whom I saw*, el hombre a quien vi; *he wanted to find somebody to whom he might talk*, quería encontrar a alguien con quien hablar. || — *Both of whom*, ambos, ambas. || *Of whom*, del cual, de la cual, de los cuales, de las cuales, de quien,

de quienes: *the friend of whom I speak*, el amigo de quien hablo.

— OBSERV. Véase la observación situada al final del artículo "who".

whomever [hu:m'evə*] or **whomsoever** [,hu:ms-əu'evə*] pron. See WHOEVER.

whoop [wu:p] n. Grito, *m.* (cry, shout). || — *Not to care a whoop*, no importarle lo más mínimo a uno. || *Whoop!*, ¡hurra!

whoop [wu:p] v. tr. Gritar (to shout). || — U. S. FAM. *To whoop it up*, armar jaleo (to have a noisy time), pasarlo en grande (to have a gay time). | *To whoop it up for*, aplaudir.
— V. intr. Gritar (to shout). MED. Toser. || U.S. *To whoop for*, aplaudir.

whoopee ['wu'pi:; 'wupi] interj. ¡Hurra!, ¡viva!
— N. FAM. Juerga, *f.*, parranda, *f.* (spree). || FAM. *To make whoopee*, pasarlo en grande (to have a gay time), armar jaleo (to have a noisy time).

whooping cough ['hu:piŋkɔf] n. MED. Tos (*f.*) ferina.

whoopla ['hupla:] n. FAM. Jarana, *f.*, jaleo, *m.*

whop [wɔp] n. FAM. Golpe, *m.* (blow). || *To fall with a whop*, caer como un plomo.

whop [wɔp] v. tr. FAM. Pegar una paliza a.

whopper [—ə*] n. FAM. Cosa (*f.*) enorme *or* gigantesca (big thing). | Bola, *f.*, trola, *f.* (lie).

whopping [—iŋ] adj. FAM. Enorme, gigantesco, ca.

whore [hɔ:*] n. FAM. Puta, *f.*, furcia, *f.*

whore [hɔ:*] v. intr. Prostituirse (a woman). | Irse de putas (a man).

whoredom [—dəm] n. Prostitución, *f.*

whorehouse [—haus] n. U. S. Casa (*f.*) de putas.

whoremonger [—,mʌŋgə*] n. Putero, *m.*, putañero, *m.* (lecher). || Chulo (*m.*) de putas (pimp).

whoreson [—sʌn] n. FAM. Hijo (*m.*) de puta. | Chulo (*m.*) de putas (pimp).

whorish [—riʃ] adj. Putañero, ra.

whorl [wə:l] n. Espira, *f.* (of a shell). || BOT. Verticilo, *m.* (of leaves, flowers, etc.). || Espiral, *f.*

whortleberry ['wə:tl,beri] n. BOT. Arándano, *m.*

whose [hu:z] interr. pron. De quién, de quiénes: *whose are these books?*, ¿de quiénes son estos libros?; *didn't you know whose shoes they were?*, ¿no sabías de quién eran los zapatos?; *whose daughter are you?*, ¿es usted hija de quién?; *he told me whose they were*, me dijo de quién eran. || — *Whose book did you take?*, ¿qué libro cogiste?, ¿de quién era el libro que cogiste? || *Whose is this?*, ¿de quién es esto?, ¿a quién pertenece esto?
— Rel. pron. Cuyo, cuya: *the man whose picture is in the paper*, el hombre cuya foto está en el periódico; *the house whose windows were broken*, la casa cuyas ventanas estaban rotas; *the woman from whose son I received it*, la mujer de cuyo hijo lo recibí; *the person for whose sake he did it*, la persona en cuyo nombre lo hizo.

whosesoever [,hu:zsəu'evə*] or **whosever** [hu:z'evə*] pron. De quienquiera. || *Whosever it is*, sea de quien sea.

whoso ['hu:səu] or **whosoever** [,hu:səu'evə*] pron. See WHOEVER.

why [wai] adv. ¿Por qué?: *why didn't you come?*, ¿por qué no viniste?; *why bother?*, ¿por qué preocuparse? || Por qué: *I don't see why you should worry*, no veo por qué tienes que preocuparte. || — *I can't see any reason why*, no veo el porqué. || *That is why I did it*, por eso lo hice, ésa es la razón por la que lo hice. || *Why not?*, ¿por qué no? || *Why so?*, ¿y eso por qué?
— N. Porqué, *m.* || *The whys and wherefores*, el cómo y el porqué, las causas y los motivos, todos los detalles.
— Interj. ¡Vaya!, ¡toma! (surprise): *why, it's Peter*, ¡toma! ¡es Pedro! | ¡Vamos! (protest): *why, you are not afraid, are you?*, ¡vamos!, no tendrá usted miedo ¿verdad? || ¡Pues bien!, ¡bueno! || *Why, it's quite easy!*, ¡si es muy fácil!

whydah ['widə] n. Viuda, *f.* (bird).

wick [wik] n. Mecha, *f.*

wicked ['wikid] adj. Malvado, da; malo, la (morally bad, malicious). | Perverso, sa (depraved). | Muy malo, la (temper). || Travieso, sa; pícaro, ra (mischievous): *a wicked grin*, una sonrisa traviesa. | Inicuo, cua; infame, inmundo, da (lie). | Resabiado, da (horse). || Feroz (animal). | FAM. Malísimo, ma; espantoso, sa: *a wicked winter*, un invierno malísimo. | Terrible: *a wicked blow*, un golpe terrible.
— N. *The wicked*, los malos.

wickedly [—li] adv. Muy mal: *to treat s.o. wickedly*, tratar muy mal a alguien. | Con mala intención: *to say sth. wickedly*, decir algo con mala intención. || Muy, terriblemente: *wickedly expensive*, terriblemente caro. | Inicuamente: *to lie wickedly*, mentir inicuamente.

wickedness [—nis] n. Maldad, *f.* || Perversidad, *f.* (depravity). | Resabio, *m.* (of a horse).

wicker ['wikə*] n. Mimbre, *m.* || Artículos (*m. pl.*) de mimbre.
— Adj. De mimbre.

wickered [—d] adj. De mimbre.

wickerwork [—wə:k] n. Artículos (*m. pl.*) de mimbre (objects). | Cestería, *f.* (craft). | Rejilla, *f.* (of a chair).

wicket ['wikit] n. Portillo, *m.* (small door). | Ventanilla, *f.* (small window at a ticket office). | Compuerta (*f.*) pequeña (to regulate water flow). || SP. Puerta, *f.*, portería, *f.* (set of stumps). | Terreno, *m.*, campo, *m.*: *a fast wicket*, un campo rápido. || U. S. SP. Aro, *m.* (hoop in croquet). || FIG. *To be on a sticky wicket*, estar en un apuro.

wicketkeeper [—,ki:pə*] n. SP. Guardameta, *m.* (in cricket).

wide [waid] adj. Ancho, cha: *a wide river*, un río ancho; *a wide road*, una carretera ancha; *wide sleeves*, mangas anchas; *wide trousers*, pantalón ancho; *the wide world*, el ancho mundo. || De ancho: *five feet wide*, de cinco pies de ancho. || Muy abierto, ta (eyes, mouth). || Extenso, sa; vasto, ta: *a wide plain*, una llanura extensa. || Amplio, plia: *a wide range of frequencies*, una amplia gama de frecuencias. || Extenso, sa: *wide publicity*, publicidad extensa. || Grande: *wide intervals*, grandes intervalos; *wide experience, culture, influence*, gran experiencia, cultura, influencia. || Grande, considerable: *the difference between us is wide*, la diferencia entre nosotros es grande. || Amplio, plia; grande (knowledge). || SP. Fuera del alcance (ball). || — *How wide is the room?*, ¿qué anchura tiene la habitación?, ¿cuál es el ancho de la habitación? || *In a wider sense*, en un sentido más amplio. || *To grow wider*, ensancharse. || *To have wide interests in life*, tener muchos intereses en la vida. || *To make wider*, ensanchar. || FIG. *Wide boy*, chico muy vivo *or* muy despabilado. || *Wide of*, lejos de: *wide of the truth*, lejos de la verdad. || *Wide of the mark*, lejos de la verdad *or* de la realidad (false), lejos del blanco (off target). || *Wide skirt*, falda (*f.*) de mucho vuelo. || *Wide views*, amplitud (*f.*) de miras, miras amplias.
— Adv. Lejos. || De par en par: *to open the window wide*, abrir la ventana de par en par. || Mucho: *open your mouth wide*, abre mucho la boca. || — *Far and wide*, por todas partes: *to search far and wide*, buscar por todas partes. || *To be wide open*, estar muy abierto (eyes, mouth), estar abierto de par en par (door, window). || *To fling the door open wide*, abrir la puerta de par en par. || *To go wide*, no hacer efecto (a criticism, remark), no dar en el blanco (blow). || FIG. *To leave o.s. wide open to criticism*, estar expuesto a muchas críticas. || *To shoot wide*, errar el tiro. || *Wide apart*, muy separados.
— N. SP. Bala (*f.*) que pasa fuera del alcance del bateador (cricket).

wide-angle [—,æŋgl] adj. PHOT. Gran angular: *wide-angle lens*, objetivo gran angular.

wide-awake [—ə weik] adj. Completamente despierto, ta. || FIG. Despabilado, da.

wide-eyed [—'aid] adj. Con los ojos muy abiertos.

widely [—li] adv. Muy: *widely read newspaper*, periódico muy leído. || Mucho: *he has travelled widely*, ha viajado mucho. || *It is widely known that*, se sabe perfectamente que, todos saben que, por todas partes se sabe que.

widemouthed [—'mauðd] adj. Bocón, ona. || Boquiabierto, ta (agape).

widen [—ən] v. tr. Ensanchar. || FIG. Extender, ampliar.
— V. intr. Ensancharse. || FIG. Extenderse (influence). | Aumentar (to increase).

wideness [—nis] n. Anchura, *f.*, ancho, *m.* (width). || Extensión, *f.*

widening [—əniŋ] n. Ensanchamiento, *m.* || FIG. Extensión, *f.*

wide-open [—'əupən] adj. Abierto de par en par (open wide). || U. S. Muy tolerante, muy liberal (city).

wide-ranging [—'reindʒiŋ] adj. De gran amplitud, amplio, plia.

widespread [—spred] adj. Extendido, da (stretched out). || General: *hunger is widespread*, el hambre es general; *widespread fear*, miedo general. || Muy difundido, da: *the rumour is widespread*, el rumor está muy difundido.

widgeon ['widʒən] n. ZOOL. Pato (*m.*) silbador.

widow ['widəu] n. Viuda, *f.* || — *Football widow*, mujer (*f.*) que se queda muchas veces sola porque su marido es muy aficionado al fútbol. || *Widow Smith*, la viuda de Smith.

widow ['widəu] v. tr. Dejar viuda. || *To be widowed*, enviudar, quedar viuda.

widow bird [—bə:d] n. ZOOL. Viuda, *f.*

widowed [—d] adj. Viudo, da.

widower [—ə*] n. Viudo, *m.*

widowhood [—hud] n. Viudez, *f.*

width [widθ] n. Anchura, *f.*, ancho, *m.* (of an object). || Distancia, *f.*: *the width between the window and the bed*, la distancia entre la ventana y la cama. | Envergadura, *f.* (of wings). | FIG. Amplitud, *f.*: *width of views*, amplitud de ideas. || — *Double width material*, tela (*f.*) de doble ancho. || *Two metres in width*, dos metros de ancho.

wield [wi:ld] v. tr. Manejar (tool). | Blandir, esgrimir (weapon). | Ejercer (control, influence, etc.): *to wield authority*, ejercer la autoridad. | Empuñar (a scepter).

wiener ['wi:nə*] n. U. S. FAM. Salchicha (*f.*) de Francfort.

wiener schnitzel [—,ʃnitsəl] n. CULIN. Escalope (*m.*) de ternera, escalope (*m.*) vienés.

wife [waif] n. Mujer, *f.*, esposa, *f.* || — *The Merry Wives of Windsor*, Las alegres comadres de Windsor (Shakespeare's play). || *To take a wife*, casarse. || *To take s.o. to wife*, casarse con alguien.

— OBSERV. El plural de *wife* es *wives*.
— When the word *wife* follows a noun indicating profession (*butcher's wife*, *ambassador's wife*), this is usually rendered in Spanish by the feminine form of the noun (*la carnicera*, *la embajadora*).

wifehood [—hud] n. Estado (*m.*) de casada.
wifeless [—lis] adj. Sin mujer. || Viudo (widowed). || Soltero, *m.* (unmarried).
wifely [—li] adj. De mujer casada.
wig [wig] n. Peluca, *f.*
wig [wig] v. tr. Poner peluca a. || FAM. Dar un jabón, echar un rapapolvo *or* una bronca (to scold).
wigeon [ˈwidʒən] n. ZOOL. Pato (*m.*) silbador.
wigged [wigd] adj. Que lleva peluca, con peluca.
wigging [ˈwigiŋ] n. FAM. Rapapolvo, *m.*, bronca, *f.*, jabón, *m.*: *to give s.o. a wigging*, echar un rapapolvo *or* una bronca a alguien, dar un jabón a alguien.
wiggle [ˈwigl] n. Meneo, *m.* || Contoneo, *m.* (in walking).
wiggle [ˈwigl] v. tr. Menear.
— V. intr. Menearse. || Contonearse (in walking).
wight [wait] n. Individuo, *m.* || *Sorry wight*, pobre hombre, *m.*
wigwag [ˈwigwæg] n. Comunicación (*f.*) por señales.
wigwag [ˈwigwæg] v. tr./intr. Comunicar por señales (a message).
wigwam [ˈwigwæm] n. "Wigwam", *m.*, tienda (*f.*) india.
wild [waild] adj. Silvestre (plant): *wild flowers*, flores silvestres. || Salvaje (animal, person): *the pheasants are rather wild*, los faisanes son bastante salvajes; *wild tribes*, tribus salvajes. || Bravo, va (bull). || Inculto, ta; no cultivado, da (field). || Salvaje (country). || Extraño, ña (gaze). || De loco, extraviado, da (eyes). || Loco, ca: *wild laughter*, risa loca. || Frenético, ca; desenfrenado, da: *a wild dance*, un baile frenético. || Violento, ta (character): *a wild temperament*, un temperamento violento. || Alocado, da; desordenado, da (conduct). || Desordenado, da: *to lead a wild life*, llevar una vida desordenada. || Disoluto, ta (dissolute). || De tormenta, tormentoso, sa; borrascoso, sa (weather). || Enfurecido, da (sea). || Impetuoso, sa (torrent). || Furioso, sa; violento, ta (wind). || Agitado, da; alborotado, da: *to live in wild times*, vivir en una época agitada. || Revuelto, ta (hair). || Frenético, ca: *wild applause*, aplausos frenéticos. || Delirante: *wild enthusiasm*, entusiasmo delirante. || Insensato, ta (rash, foolish): *a wild project*, un proyecto insensato. || Absurdo, da; extravagante (rumour). || Loco, ca; extravagante (ideas). || Estrafalario, ria; extravagante (clothes). || Espantoso, sa (disorder). || FAM. Hecho una fiera, furioso, sa (very cross): *to get wild*, ponerse furioso. || Al azar (shot). || — *To be wild about sth.*, estar loco por algo. || *To be wild to do sth.*, estar loco por hacer algo. || *To be wild with anger*, estar furioso, estar hecho una fiera. || *To be wild with joy*, estar loco de alegría. || *To be wild with s.o.*, ponerse hecho una fiera con alguien. || *To drive wild*, volver loco, sacar de sus casillas. || *To have a wild time*, pasarlo en grande. || *To let the children run wild*, dejar que los niños hagan lo que les da la gana. || *To make a wild guess*, adivinar al azar. || *To make a wild rush at*, precipitarse como locos hacia. || *To run* o *to grow wild*, crecer en estado salvaje (plants), vivir como un salvaje (child). || *To run wild*, desbocarse (horse). || *Wild beast*, fiera, *f.*, animal (*m.*) salvaje. || FIG. *Wild horses wouldn't draw* o *wouldn't drag it out of him*, no se puede sacárselo ni con tenazas, no lo diría por todo el oro del mundo. || *Wild man*, extremista, *m.* || *Wild West*, Oeste, *m.* (western states of the United States).
— N. Naturaleza, *f.*: *the call of the wild*, la llamada de la naturaleza. || — Pl. Desierto, *m. sing.* (desert). || Regiones (*f.*) salvajes *or* inexploradas: *the wilds of Africa*, las regiones salvajes de África. || Regiones (*f.*) incultas (uncultivated regions).
— Adv. Violentamente. || Sin cultivo.

wild and wooly [—əndˈwuli] adj. Tosco, ca.
wild artichoke [—ˈɑ:titʃəuk] n. BOT. Alcaucí, *m.*, alcaucil, *m.*
wildcat [—kæt] n. ZOOL. Gato (*m.*) montés. || TECH. Sondeo (*m.*) de exploración (oil well). || FIG. Fiera, *f.* (person).
— Adj. Arriesgado, da; descabellado, da (risky): *wildcat scheme*, proyecto arriesgado. || *Wildcat strike*, huelga salvaje.
wildebeest [ˈwildiˌbi:st] n. ZOOL. Ñu, *m.*
wilderness [ˈwildənis] n. Desierto, *m.* (desert). || Soledad, *f.* (lonely place). || Parte (*f.*) dejada sin cultivar (of a garden). || FIG. Infinidad, *f.* (large mass). || FIG. *To preach in the wilderness*, predicar en el desierto.
wildfire [ˈwaildfaiə*] n. Fuego (*m.*) griego. || FIG. *To spread like wildfire*, propagarse como un reguero de pólvora.
wildfowl [ˈwaildfaul] n. Aves (*f. pl.*) de caza *or* salvajes.
wildfowling [—iŋ] n. Caza (*f.*) de aves salvajes.
wild goat [ˈwaildˈgəut] n. Cabra (*f.*) montés.
wild goose [ˈwaildˈgu:s] n. ZOOL. Ganso (*m.*) salvaje.
wild-goose chase [—tʃeis] n. Búsqueda (*f.*) inútil.
wilding [ˈwaildiŋ] n. BOT. Planta (*f.*) silvestre (plant). || Fruta (*f.*) de una planta silvestre (fruit). || ZOOL. Animal (*m.*) salvaje.
wild land [ˈwaildˈlænd] n. Yermo, *m.*, páramo, *m.*
wildlife [ˈwaildlaif] n. Fauna, *f.* (animals).
wildly [ˈwaildli] adv. De manera extravagante (to speak, to write). || Desordenadamente (to live). || Insensatamente, sin reflexionar (to act). || Sin disciplina (to behave). || Violentamente, furiosamente (to blow). || Frenéticamente: *to dance wildly*, bailar frenéticamente. || Locamente: *to be wildly in love with*, estar locamente enamorado de. || En estado salvaje (to grow). || Al azar (to shoot, to guess). || — *To be wildly happy*, estar loco de alegría. || *To look wildly*, mirar con ojos desorbitados. || *To rush wildly*, correr como un loco.
wildness [ˈwaildnis] n. Estado (*m.*) salvaje (of a country, an animal). || Estado (*m.*) silvestre (of a plant). || Furor, *m.*, furia, *f.* (of the wind). || Lo salvaje, ferocidad, *f.*, fiereza, *f.* (ferocity). || Desenfreno, *m.* (lack of moderation). || Extravíos, *m. pl.* (of behaviour). || Locura, *f.* (madness). || Insensatez, *f.* (foolishness). || Extravagancia, *f.* (of ideas). || Frenesí, *m.* (frenzy). || *The wildness of the applause*, los aplausos frenéticos.
wile [wail] n. Artimaña, *f.*, ardid, *m.*, astucia, *f.*
wile [wail] v. tr. Seducir, atraer. || *To wile away the hours reading*, pasarse las horas leyendo.
wilful [ˈwilful] adj. Deliberado, da; intencionado, da (intentional). || JUR. Voluntario, ria; premeditado, da. || Obstinado, da; terco, ca (obstinate). || Voluntarioso, sa (headstrong).
wilfully [—i] adv. Intencionadamente, a propósito, deliberadamente (deliberately). || JUR. Voluntariamente, con premeditación. || Con obstinación (obstinately). || Voluntariosamente.
wilfulness [—nis] n. Intención, *f.* || JUR. Premeditación, *f.* || Obstinación, *f.*, terquedad, *f.* (obstinacy).
wilily [ˈwailili] adv. Astutamente.
wiliness [ˈwailinis] n. Astucia, *f.* (cunning, artfulness).
will [wil] n. Voluntad, *f.*: *to have a strong will*, tener mucha voluntad; *the will to win*, la voluntad de ganar; *ill will*, mala voluntad; *will of iron* o *iron will*, voluntad de hierro; *divine will*, voluntad divina. || JUR. Testamento, *m.*: *to make one's will*, hacer testamento. || — *Against one's will*, contra su voluntad, de mal grado. || *At will*, a voluntad. || MIL. *Fire at will*, fuego (*m.*) a discreción. || *Free will*, libre albedrío, *m.* || *He has a will of his own*, sabe lo que quiere. || *It is his will that*, quiere que. || REL. *Last will and testament*, última voluntad. || *Of one's own free will*, por su propia voluntad. || REL. *Thy will be done*, hágase tu voluntad. || *To bear s.o. ill will*, tenerle manía a uno. || *To have one's will*, salirse con la suya. || *To take the will for the deed*, darse por contento con la intención. || (Ant.). *What is your will?*, ¿cuál es su voluntad?, ¿qué desea? || *Where there's a will there's a way*, querer es poder. || *Will to power*, ansias (*f. pl.*) de poder. || *With a will*, de buena gana (willingly), con entusiasmo, con ilusión (enthusiastically): *to work with a will*, trabajar con entusiasmo.
will [wil] v. tr. JUR. Legar (to bequeath). || Disponer, ordenar, querer: *fate wills that it should be so*, el destino dispone que sea así. || Desear, querer: *the separation was willed, not forced*, la separación era deseada, no forzada; *if you will*, si quiere. || Conseguir a fuerza de voluntad (to achieve by force of will): *when I will to move my arm*, cuando consigo mover el brazo a fuerza de voluntad. || Sugestionar (in hypnotism). || *To will o.s. to*, obligarse a.
will [wil] v. aux. Se emplea para formar el futuro de indicativo: *tomorrow will be Monday*, mañana será lunes; *you will do it!*, ¡lo harás! || Se usa para expresar la voluntad o la intención: *we would have come, if you had invited us earlier*, hubiéramos venido si nos hubiesen invitado más pronto. || Ir a (immediate future): *I will explain the problem to you*, le voy a explicar el problema. || Querer (determination, consent, wish): *I will speak to her, whether she agrees or not*, quiero hablarle que le guste o no; *I will not have it done*, no quiero que se haga; *let him do what he will*, déjele que haga lo que quiera; *I would have it understood that*, quisiera que quedase bien sentado que. || Gustar, querer: *where would you be?*, ¿dónde le gustaría estar? || Poder (possibility): *this car will do 150*, este coche puede alcanzar 150; *the hall will seat five hundred people*, la sala puede contener quinientas personas. || Soler, acostumbrar (habit): *she will sit there hour after hour*, suele sentarse allí horas y horas; *she would go for a walk every morning*, acostumbraba dar un paseo todas las mañanas. || Empeñarse en, persistir en (obstinacy): *he will smoke although he knows it's bad for him*, se empeña en fumar aunque sabe que le sienta mal. || Deber (obligation): *the orders read: you will proceed at once to the next town*, la orden dice: debe usted seguir inmediatamente hasta el próximo pueblo. || Expresa la idea de probabilidad: *this battery will last another month yet*, esta batería durará todavía un mes; *he will have arrived by now*, habrá llegado ya, debe de haber llegado ya. || — *Accidents will happen*, siempre pueden ocurrir accidentes. || *Boys will be boys*, son cosas de chicos. || *He would never do that!*, ¡es incapaz de hacer una cosa igual! || *I will*, sí quiero (marriage service). ||

Just wait a moment, will you?, ¿quiere esperar un momento? || *Say what you will*, diga lo que diga. || *Sometimes he will talk, sometimes he won't*, a veces habla, otras veces no dice nada. || *The door will not open*, no se puede abrir la puerta. | *This street will take you there*, esta calle le llevará allí. | *Try as you will you won't open it*, por mucho que lo intentes no lo abrirás. | *Try as you would you couldn't open it*, por mucho que lo hayas intentado no pudiste abrirlo. || *Will you do it? — I will*, ¿lo harás? — Sí. || *Would* o *would that* o *would to God that!*, ¡ojalá!: *would I were rich!*, ¡ojalá fuera rico!; *would that he were here!*, ¡ojalá estuviera aquí! | *You'll be there, won't you?*, estarás allí, ¿verdad? || *You won't be there, will you?*, no estarás allí, ¿verdad?

— OBSERV. Este verbo es defectivo. No se emplea más que en presente de indicativo (**will**), en pretérito y en potencial (**would**).
— El verbo auxiliar *will* puede contraerse cuando le antecede un pronombre personal (*I'll, you'll, he'll, we'll, they'll*) Si va seguido por la negación *not* puede formar con ella la palabra *won't* (*he won't come, won't you come?*)
— En una oración introducida por la conjunción *if* el verbo, que está en futuro en inglés, tiene que ponerse en presente en español (*If you will give me a gun, I will shoot*, si me das una pistola tiraré).

Will [wil] pr. n. Guillermo, *m.* [diminutivo de *William*].
willed [—d] adj. De voluntad, que tiene voluntad. || Dispuesto, ta; decidido, da. || *Weak-willed*, que tiene poca voluntad.
willet [—it] n. U. S. Chocha, *f.* (bird).
willful [—ful] adj. U. S. See WILFUL.
willfully [—fuli] adv. U. S. See WILFULLY.
willfulness [—fulnis] n. U. S. See WILFULNESS.
William [ˈwiljəm] pr. n. Guillermo, *m.*: *William the Conqueror*, Guillermo el Conquistador.
willies [ˈwiliz] pl. n. FAM. *He got the willies*, se llevó un susto (he got a fright), le entró miedo (he got scared). | *It gives me the willies*, me pone los pelos de punta.
willing [ˈwiliŋ] adj. De buena voluntad, que tiene buena voluntad (good-natured). || Complaciente, servicial (obliging). || Dispuesto, ta (ready): *he's quite willing to pay the price I asked*, está completamente dispuesto a pagar el precio que he pedido. || Espontáneo, a; hecho de buena gana (done voluntarily). || — *God willing*, si Dios quiere. || *I am quite willing to come with you*, le acompaño con mucho gusto, le acompaño muy gustoso. || *I am willing that you should come* o *I am willing for you to come*, consiento en que venga, le permito que venga. || *Willing or not*, de grado o por fuerza, que quiera que no quiera, quiera o no quiera.
willingly [—li] adv. De buena gana: *to do sth. willingly*, hacer algo de buena gana. || Gustosamente, con [mucho] gusto (gladly): *to accept willingly*, aceptar con gusto.
willingness [—nis] n. Buena voluntad, *f.* (good nature). || Consentimiento, *m.* (consent). || *To declare one's willingness to do sth.*, consentir en hacer algo.
will-o'-the-wisp [ˈwiləðəˈwisp] n. Fuego (*m.*) fatuo. || FIG. Quimera, *f.*
willow [ˈwiləu] n. BOT. Sauce, *m.* || TECH. Diablo, *m.* (machine for cleaning raw wool). || SP. Bate, *m.* (in cricket). || BOT. *Weeping willow*, sauce llorón.
willow [ˈwiləu] v. tr. TECH. Tratar [la lana] con un diablo.
willow grove [—grəuv] n. BOT. Salceda, *f.*, saucedal, *m.*
willow pattern [—ˌpætən] n. Dibujos (*m. pl.*) de aspecto chinesco que representan sauces, ríos, pagodas, etc. [para la cerámica].
willowy [—i] adj. Esbelto, ta (slender). || Poblado de sauces (abounding in willows).
willpower [ˈwilˌpauə*] n. Fuerza (*f.*) de voluntad, voluntad, *f.*: *she is very clever, but she lacks willpower*, es muy inteligente pero le falta voluntad.
willy-nilly [ˈwiliˈnili] adv. De grado o por fuerza, quiera o no quiera.
wilt [wilt] v. aux. (Ant.). See WILL.
wilt [wilt] v. tr. Marchitar.
— V. intr. Marchitarse: *the plants have wilted in the sun*, las plantas se han marchitado con el sol. || FIG. Languidecer, debilitarse (to lose strength). | Desanimarse (to lose courage).
wily [ˈwaili] adj. Astuto, ta; taimado, da.
wimble [ˈwimbl] adj. TECH. Berbiquí, *m.* (brace). | Barrena (*f.*) de mano (gimlet). | Taladro, *m.* (in mining).
wimple [ˈwimpl] n. Griñón, *m.* (headdress).
wimple [ˈwimpl] v. tr. Poner un griñón a.
— V. intr. Serpentear.
win [win] n. Victoria, *f.* (victory). || Ganancia, *f.* (amount won). || *To have a win*, ganar: *he had a win on the pools*, ganó en las quinielas; *our team has had four wins this summer*, nuestro equipo ha ganado cuatro veces este verano.
win* [win] v. tr. Ganar: *to win a fight, a case, a bet, a race*, ganar un combate, un pleito, una apuesta, una carrera; *to win territory from the enemy*, ganar tierras al enemigo; *to win one pound from s.o. at cards*, ganarle una libra a uno jugando a las cartas. || Ganar, llevarse (a prize): *he has won the first prize*, se ha llevado el primer premio *or* el premio gordo. || Granjearse, ganarse, captarse: *to win s.o.'s friendship*, granjearse la amistad de alguien. || Captar, ganarse, granjearse (s.o.'s confidence). || Ganarse: *to win friends*, ganarse amigos. || Ganar, hacerse: *to win a reputation*, hacerse una reputación. || Conseguir, lograr, obtener: *to win a victory*, conseguir una victoria; *to win people's support*, conseguir el apoyo de la gente. || Hacer ganar, valer: *his picture won him the prize*, su cuadro le valió el premio. || Conquistar: *to win s.o.'s heart*, conquistar el corazón de alguien. | Ganar, alcanzar (to reach): *to win the summit*, alcanzar la cumbre; *to win the shore*, alcanzar la orilla. | MIN. Extraer, sacar (to extract). || — FIG. *Slow and steady wins the race*, con paciencia se gana el cielo. | *To win glory*, cosechar laureles. || *To win one's bread*, ganarse el pan. || *To win one's way to*, conseguir llegar a. *To win s.o.'s love*, enamorar a alguien. || *To win s.o. to do sth.*, conseguir que alguien haga algo. | *To win the favour of*, ganarse el favor de. || *To win the field*, ser dueño y señor del terreno. || *To win victory*, ser victorioso, triunfar.
— V. intr. Ganar: *to win by a length*, ganar por un largo. || *To win free*, liberarse.
— ***To win at***, ganar en. || ***To win away***, separar, apartar. || ***To win back***, reconquistar, volver a conquistar (territory), | Recuperar (money, etc.). || ***To win out***, ganar, salir victorioso, triunfar. || ***To win over*** o ***round***, ganarse, poner de su lado *or* de su parte: *to win round the audience*, ganarse al auditorio. | Conseguir, obtener (supporters). | Convencer (to convince): *to let o.s. be won over*, dejarse convencer. | — *To win s.o. over to a cause*, conseguir que alguien se interese por una causa. | ***To win through***, superar los obstáculos, conseguir triunfar.

— OBSERV. Pret. & p. p. **won**.

wince [wins] n. Mueca (*f.*) de dolor (twisted expression of the face caused by pain).
wince [wins] v. intr. Hacer una mueca de dolor (with pain). | Poner mala cara (with disgust). | *Without wincing*, sin pestañear.
winch [wintʃ] n. Torno, *m.* (for raising loads). | Manivela, *f.* (crank). | Carrete, *m.* (in fishing). || MAR. Chigre, *m.*, maquinilla, *f.*
Winchester [—istə*] n. Winchester, *m.* (rifle).
wind [waind] n. Vuelta, *f.* (turn, bend).
wind* [waind] v. tr. Devanar: *to wind cotton*, devanar algodón. | Enrollar: *to wind sth. on a reel*, enrollar algo en un carrete; *to wind a bandage round s.o.'s arm*, enrollar una venda en el brazo de alguien. | Envolver: *to wind s.o. in a sheet*, envolver a alguien en una sábana; *to wind sth. with wire*, envolver algo con alambre. | Curvar, torcer (to bend). | Dar cuerda a: *to wind a watch*, dar cuerda a un reloj. | TECH. Extraer, sacar (to extract). | Subir con el torno (to hoist). || — *The stream winds its way through the country*, el arroyo serpentea por el campo. | *To wind itself*, enroscarse, enrollarse (a snake). | *To wind one's arms round s.o.*, rodear a alguien con los brazos, abrazar a alguien. || FAM. *To wind s.o. round one's little finger*, manejar a alguien a su antojo. | *To wind sth. into a ball*, hacer un ovillo con algo.
— V. intr. Enrollarse (rope). || Enroscarse, enrollarse (snake). | Serpentear (road). | Torcerse, encorvarse (to bend). || Combarse, alabearse (to warp). *The path winds round the lake*, el camino rodea el lago.
— ***To wind down***, bajar (the window of a car). || ***To wind in***, enrollar. || ***To wind off***, desenrollar (a rope, etc.). | Desenrollarse. || ***To wind on***, devanar, enrollar en un carrete. || ***To wind up***, concluir, terminar (to conclude): *he wound up his speech with a quotation*, concluyó el discurso con una cita; *how does it wind up?*, ¿cómo termina? | Concluir, cerrar (a debate). | Clausurar (a meeting). | COMM. Liquidar: *to wind up a company*, liquidar una compañía. | Resolver (affairs). | Dar cuerda a (a watch, clockwork mechanism, etc.). | MUS. Templar (strings). | Enrollar (a rope). | Levantar con un torno (to hoist). | Acabar: *they'll wind up in goal*, acabarán en la cárcel. | Poner nervioso (to make tense). | — *To be wound up*, estar nerviosísimo.

— OBSERV. Pret. & p. p. **wound**.

wind [wind] n. Viento, *m.*: *west wind*, viento del oeste; *stern wind*, viento en popa; *wind ahead*, con el viento en proa; *foul wind*, viento en contra *or* contrario; *trade winds*, vientos alisios; *a gust of wind*, una ráfaga de viento; *the wind rises*, se levanta el viento. || Aire, *m.*: *it made a wind as it went past*, hizo aire al pasar. || MUS. Instrumentos (*m. pl.*) de viento. || Aliento, *m.* (breath): *to get one's second wind* o *to recover one's wind*, recobrar el aliento. || Respiración, *f.* (ability to breathe). || Gases, *m. pl.* (produced in the stomach): *to have wind*, tener gases. || Flato, *m.* (of a baby). || ANAT. Boca (*f.*) del estómago (solar plexus). || Olor, *m.* (in hunting). || FIG. Aire, *m.*, palabrería, *f.* (wordiness). || — FIG. *Against wind and tide*, contra viento y marea. | *As free as the wind*, libre como el viento. || MAR. *Before the wind*, con el viento en popa, a favor del viento. | *Between wind and water*, cerca de la línea de flotación. | *Down the wind*, con el viento. | *Fair wind*, viento favorable. || FIG. *Gone with the wind*, lo que el viento se llevó. || MAR. *Head wind*, viento en contra. || FIG. *He who sows the wind shall reap the whirlwind*, quien siembra vientos recoge tempestades. || MAR. *In the teeth of the wind* o *in the wind's eye* o *up the wind* o *into the wind*, contra el viento, con el viento en contra. || FIG. *It's an ill wind that blows nobody good*, no hay mal que por bien no venga. || MAR. *Off the wind*, con viento en popa. | *On a wind*, de bolina. || FIG. *Second wind*, segundo aliento. | *There's sth. in the wind*, algo flota en el aire, algo se está preparando. | *These promises are merely wind*, estas promesas son palabras al aire. | *The wind has changed* o *has turned*, el viento ha cambiado. || FAM. *To break wind*, ventosear. || *To bring up wind*, eructar. || FIG. *To catch* o *to get one's wind*, recobrar el aliento. | *To cast* o *to fling* o *to throw to the wind*, dejar de lado. | *To change with the wind* o *to be as fickle as the wind*, moverse a todos los vientos, cambiar más que una veleta. | *To find out how the wind blows* o *lies*, ver de qué lado sopla el viento. | *To get the wind up*, pasar mucho miedo, asustarse. | *To get wind of*, enterarse de, descubrir (to find out): *I got wind of their plans yesterday*, me enteré de sus proyectos ayer; olerse: *the authorities got wind of the escape plan*, las autoridades se olieron el proyecto de fuga; revelar (to reveal). | *To go like the wind*, ir más rápido que el viento, ir como un rayo. | *To have one's wind taken*, quedarse sin aliento. | *To put the wind up s.o.*, asustar a alguien, dar mucho miedo a alguien. | *To run like the wind*, correr como un gamo. || MAR. *To sail against the wind*, hurtar el viento. || *To sail close to the wind*, navegar de bolina *or* contra el viento (ship), hacer *or* decir cosas arriesgadas (to border on foolhardiness). || MAR. *To sail with the wind*, navegar con el viento. || FIG. *To see how the wind blows* o *to see which way the wind is blowing*, ver de qué lado sopla el viento. | *To take the wind out of s.o.'s sails*, tomar la delantera a alguien, ganar a alguien por la mano: *he was going to tell the joke but I took the wind out of his sails*, iba a contar él el chiste pero le tomé la delantera; desanimar a uno (to dishearten): *that took all the wind out of my sails*, eso me desanimó por completo; bajar los humos a alguien (to deflate s.o.). | *To the four winds*, a los cuatro vientos.

wind [wind] v. tr. Dejar sin aliento, quitar el resuello (to leave breathless): *the run winded him*, la carrera le dejó sin aliento. || Olfatear (to scent). || Dejar recobrar el aliento a (to rest a horse, etc.). || Airear, ventilar, orear (to air). || Tocar (to sound).

— OBSERV. Cuando el verbo *to wind* significa "tocar" tiene dos formas de pretérito y de participio pasivo (***winded*** y ***wound***); en los demás casos es regular.

windage [—idʒ] n. Desvío (*m.*) de un proyectil por efecto del viento. || Huelgo, *m.*, holgura, *f.* (between a bore of a firearm and the projectile). || Resistencia (*f.*) aerodinámica (of a ship, aircraft, etc.).

windbag [—bæg] n. FAM. Charlatán, ana (person who talks a lot). || MUS. Odre, *m.*, fuelle, *m.* (in bagpipes, etc.).

windblown [—bləun] adj. Azotado por el viento: *windblown countryside*, campo azotado por el viento. || Llevado por el viento. || *Windblown hair*, pelo revuelto por el viento.

wind-borne [—bɔ:n] adj. Llevado por el viento (pollen).

windbound [—baund] adj. MAR. Detenido por el viento.

windbreak [—breik] n. Protección (*f.*) contra el viento.

windbreaker [—ˌbreikə*] or **windcheater** [—ˌtʃi:tə*] Cazadora, *f.* (jacket).

wind cone [—kəun] n. AVIAT. Manga (*f.*) de aire.

winded [—id] adj. Jadeante (out of breath).

wind egg [—eg] n. Huevo (*m.*) huero.

winder [ˈwaində*] n. Devanadera, *f.* (apparatus). || Devanador, ra (person). || Llave, *f.* (key). || BOT. Enredadera, *f.*

windfall [ˈwindfɔ:l] n. Fruta (*f.*) caída (fallen fruit). || FIG. Ganancia (*f.*) inesperada, ganga, *f.*, cosa (*f.*) llovida del cielo (sth. received unexpectedly). | Suerte, *f.* (stroke of luck).

windflaw [ˈwindflɔ:] n. Ráfaga (*f.*) de viento.

windflower [ˈwindˌflauə*] n. BOT. Anémona, *f.*

wind gauge [ˈwindgeidʒ] n. Anemómetro, *m.*

windhover [ˈwindˌhɔvə*] n. ZOOL. Cernícalo, *m.*

windiness [ˈwindinis] n. Ventolera, *f.* (gust of wind). || MED. Flato, *m.* || FAM. Verbosidad, *f.* || *The windiness of these heights*, el viento que sopla constantemente en estas cumbres.

winding [ˈwaindiŋ] adj. Tortuoso, sa; sinuoso, sa (road). || Sinuoso, sa (river). || De caracol (staircase). || TECH. En espiral.

— N. Serpenteo, *m.*, vueltas, *f. pl.* (of road, river). || Enrollamiento, *m.* (of rope, thread). || Devanado, *m.* (of a reel). || Cuerda, *f.* (of a clock). || TECH. Alabeo, *m.* (of a board). | Extracción, *f.* (of ore).

winding frame [—freim] n. Devanadera, *f.*

winding gear [—giə*] n. Torno, *m.*, cabrestante, *m.*

winding key [—ki:] n. Llave, *f.* (of watch).

windingly [—li] adv. Serpenteando.

winding off [—ˈɔf] n. Devanado, *m.*

winding on [—ˈɔn] n. Devanado, *m.*, enrollamiento, *m.*

winding shaft [—ʃɑ:ft] n. Pozo (*m.*) de extracción.

winding sheet [—ʃi:t] n. Mortaja, *f.*

winding up [—ˈʌp] n. Conclusión, *f.* || COMM. Liquidación, *f.*

wind instrument [ˈwindˌinstrumənt] n. MUS. Instrumento (*m.*) de viento.

windjammer [ˈwindˌdʒæmə*] n. MAR. Velero, *m.* (sailing ship). | Marinero (*m.*) de un velero (sailor).

windlass [ˈwindləs] n. Torno, *m.* (for lifting). || MAR. Chigre, *m.*, maquinilla, *f.*, molinete, *m.*

windless [ˈwindlis] adj. Sin viento.

windmill [ˈwindmil] n. Molino (*m.*) de viento (a mill worked by sails). || Molinillo, *m.*, molinete, *m.* (toy). || FIG. *To tilt at windmills*, see TILT.

window [ˈwindəu] n. Ventana, *f.*: *to lean out of the window*, asomarse a la ventana. || Cristal, *m.* [de ventana] (windowpane). || Ventanilla, *f.*, cristal, *m.* (of a car). || Escaparate, *m.* [*Amer.*, vitrina, *f.*] (in a shop): *articles shown in the window*, artículos que se ven en el escaparate. || Taquilla, *f.* (booking office). || Ventanilla, *f.* (of booking office). || Vidriera, *f.* (of stained glass). || Ventanilla, *f.*, parte (*f.*) transparente (of envelope, etc.). || FAM. *You make a better door than a window*, la carne de burro no es transparente.

window bar [—bɑ:] n. Barrote, *m.*

window blind [—blaind] n. Persiana, *f.*

window box [—bɔks] n. Jardinera, *f.* (for plants).

window cleaner [—ˌkli:nə*] n. Limpiacristales, *m. inv.*

window curtain [—ˌkə:tn] n. Cortina, *f.*

window dresser [—ˌdresə*] n. Escaparatista, *m.* & *f.*, decorador (*m.*) de escaparates.

window dressing [—ˌdresiŋ] n. Decoración (*f.*) de escaparates (in a shopwindow). || FIG. Engaño, *m.* | Fachada, *f.* (façade).

window envelope [—ˌenvələup] n. Sobre (*m.*) con ventanilla.

window frame [—freim] n. Bastidor (*m.*) de ventana, marco (*m.*) de ventana.

window glass [—glɑ:s] n. Cristal (*m.*) de ventana.

window ledge [—ledʒ] n. Antepecho, *m.*, alféizar, *m.*

windowpane [—pein] n. Cristal (*m.*) de ventana.

window sash [—sæʃ] n. Bastidor (*m.*) móvil, hoja (*f.*) de la ventana de guillotina.

window screen [—skri:n] n. Tela (*f.*) metálica adaptada al marco de una ventana.

window seat [—si:t] n. Asiento (*m.*) junto a la ventana *or* ventanilla.

window shade [—ʃeid] n. U. S. Persiana, *f.*

window-shop [—ʃɔp] v. intr. Mirar los escaparates: *I like window-shopping*, me gusta mirar los escaparates.

windowsill [—sil] n. Antepecho, *m.*, alféizar, *m.*

window trimmer [—ˌtrimə*] n. See WINDOW DRESSER.

windpipe [ˈwindpaip] n. MED. Tráquea, *f.*

wind-pollinated [ˈwindˌpɔlineitid] adj. AGR. Fertilizado gracias al polen llevado por el viento.

windproof [ˈwindpru:f] adj. A prueba de viento.

windrow [ˈwindrəu] n. Hilera (*f.*) de trigo *or* hierba dejado al aire para que se seque. || Hojas (*f. pl.*) *or* polvo (*m.*) amontonado por el viento (dust, leaves, piled up by the wind). || Zanja (*f.*) donde se planta la caña de azúcar (for sugar cane).

windrow [ˈwindrəu] v. tr. Poner en hileras.

windsail [ˈwindseil] n. MAR. Manguera, *f.*, manga (*f.*) de ventilación.

windscale [ˈwindskeil] n. Escala (*f.*) para medir la velocidad del viento.

windscreen [ˈwindskri:n] n. Parabrisas, *m. inv.* || — *Windscreen washer*, lavaparabrisas, *m. inv.* || *Windscreen wiper*, limpiaparabrisas, *m. inv.*

windshield [ˈwindʃi:ld] n. U. S. See WINDSCREEN.

wind sleeve [ˈwindsli:v] or **wind sock** [ˈwindsɔk] n. AVIAT. Manga (*f.*) de aire.

windstorm [ˈwindstɔ:m] n. Huracán, *m.*, vendaval, *m.*

windswept [ˈwindswept] adj. Azotado por los vientos (place). || Despeinado, da (hair).

wind tunnel [ˈwindˌtʌnəl] n. Túnel (*m.*) aerodinámico.

windup [ˈwaindʌp] n. Final, *m.*, conclusión, *f.* || SP. Movimiento (*m.*) previo al lanzamiento de la pelota (baseball).

windward [ˈwindwəd] adj. De barlovento. || *Windward Islands*, Islas (*f.*) de Barlovento.

— N. Barlovento, *m.*

— Adv. Hacia barlovento, a barlovento.

windy [ˈwindi] adj. Expuesto al viento: *a windy corner*, una esquina expuesta al viento. || Ventoso, sa; de mucho viento: *a windy night*, una noche ventosa. || Ventoso, sa; flatulento, ta (with stomach or intestinal gas). || FIG. Ampuloso, sa: *a windy speech*, un discurso ampuloso. || FAM. Miedoso, sa (frightened). || FAM. *To get windy*, tener mieditis.

wine [wain] n. Vino, *m.*: *red wine*, vino tinto; *white wine*, vino blanco; *sparkling wine*, vino espumoso; *table wine*, vino de mesa; *dry wine*, vino seco; *local wine*, vino del país. || — FAM. *Adam's wine*, agua, *f.* | FIG. *Good wine needs no bush*, el buen paño en el arca se vende. || FAM. *To be in wine*, estar bebido, da. || *Wine from the barrel*, vino a granel.

wine [wain] v. tr. *To wine and dine s.o.*, agasajar a alguien, festejar a alguien.

— V. intr. Beber vino.

wine bibber [—ˌbibə*] n. FAM. Bebedor, *m.*

wine bottle [—ˌbɔtl] n. Botella (*f.*) de vino.

wine butler [—ˌbʌtlə*] n. Escanciador, *m.*

wine card [—kɑ:d] n. Lista (*f.*) de vinos.

wine cask [—kɑ:sk] n. Barril (*m.*) de vino.

wine cellar [—ˌselə*] n. Bodega, *f.*

wine-coloured (U. S. **wine colored**) [—ˌkʌləd] adj. Color vino.

wine country [—ˌkʌntri] n. Región (*f.*) vitícola.

wineglass [—glɑ:s] n. Copa, *f.* [para vino].

winegrower [—ˌgrəuə*] n. Vinicultor, ra; viticultor, ra.

wine growing [—ˌgrəuiŋ] adj. Vitícola, vinícola.
— N. Vinicultura, *f.*, viticultura, *f.*

wine merchant [—ˌmə:tʃənt] n. Vinatero, *m.*, tratante (*m.*) en vinos.

winepress [—pres] n. Lagar, *m.*

winery [—əri] n. Lagar, *m.*

wineskin [—skin] n. Odre, *m.*, pellejo, *m.*

wine stone [—stəun] n. Tártaro, *m.*

wine taster [—ˌteistə*] n. Catavinos, *m. inv.*, catador (*m.*) de vinos (person). || Catavino, *m.* (flat bowl).

wine waiter [—ˌweitə*] n. Sumiller, *m.* (of a king). || Sumiller, *m.* (p. us.), "sommelier", *m.*, bodeguero, *m.*, botillero, *m.* (in a restaurant).

wing [wiŋ] n. Zool. Aviat. Arch. Ala, *f.* || Anat. Aleta, *f.*, ala, *f.* (of the nose). || Ala, *f.*: *the left wing of the socialist party*, el ala izquierda del partido socialista. || Fig. Ala, *f.*: *on the wings of fantasy*, en alas de la fantasía. || Sp. Extremo, *m.*, ala, *m.* (in football, hockey): *to play on the wing*, jugar de extremo. | Ala, *m.* (rugby): *the left wing*, el ala izquierda. || Patilla, *f.* (of spectacles). || Aspa, *f.* (of a mill). || Pala, *f.*, paleta, *f.*, ala, *f.* (of ventilator, airscrew). || Orejera, *f.*, oreja, *f.*, cabecera, *f.* (of a chair). || Aut. Aleta, *f.* || Mil. Ala, *f.* (of the army). | Aleta, *f.* (of missiles). | Escuadrilla, *f.* (air force). || Vuelo, *m.* (flight). || Hoja, *f.*, batiente, *m.* (of a double door). || Pop. Remo, *m.*, brazo, *m.* (arm). || — Pl. Theatr. Bastidores, *m.* || Mil. Alas, *f.* (insignia). || — *My hat took wings*, mi sombrero voló. || *On the wing*, volando, al vuelo. || Fig. *To clip s.o.'s wings*, cortarle las alas a alguien. | *To take under one's wing*, acoger en su regazo, tomar bajo su protección. || *To take wing*, alzar el vuelo.

wing [wiŋ] v. tr. Hender, pasar volando por (the air). || Emplumar (to put wings on). || Lanzar, disparar (to let fly). || Herir en el ala (to wound a bird). || Tocar, herir, herir ligeramente (to wound a person). || Arch. Añadir alas a. || *To wing one's way*, volar, ir volando.
— V. intr. Volar.

wingbeat [—bi:t] n. Aletazo, *m.*

wing case [—keis] n. Zool. Élitro, *m.*

wing chair [—tʃεə*] n. Sillón (*m.*) de orejas.

wing collar [—ˈkɔlə*] n. Cuello (*m.*) de pajarita *or* de palomita.

wing commander [—kəˌmɑ:ndə*] n. Aviat. Teniente coronel, *m.*

wing cover [—ˌkʌvə*] n. Zool. Élitro, *m.*

winged [—d] adj. Zool. Alado, da (having wings). || Con aletas (missiles). || Bot. Con alas. || Herido en el ala (wounded birds). || Ligeramente herido, tocado, da (wounded people). || Alígero, ra (god). || Fig. Veloz (swift).

winger [—ə*] n. Sp. Extremo, *m.*, ala, *m.* (in football, hockey): *the right winger*, el extremo derecha. | Ala, *m.* (in rugby).

wing flap [—flæp] n. Aviat. Alerón, *m.*

wing-footed [—ˈfutid] adj. Alígero, ra.

wing game [—geim] n. Aves (*f. pl.*) de pluma.

wingless [—lis] adj. Sin alas, áptero, ra.

winglet [—lit] n. Alita, *f.* (small wing).

wing nut [—nʌt] n. Palometa, *f.*, tuerca (*f.*) de mariposa, tuerca (*f.*) de orejas *or* de aletas.

wingover [—ˌəuvə*] n. Aviat. Vuelta (*f.*) sobre el ala.

wing-shaped [—ʃeipt] adj. En forma de ala, aliforme.

wingspan [—spæn] m. Aviat. Zool. Envergadura, *f.*

wingspread [—spred] n. Aviat. Zool. Envergadura, *f.*

wink [wiŋk] n. Guiño, *m.*: *to give the wink to*, hacer un guiño a. || Pestañeo, *m.* (blink). || Centelleo, *m.*, parpadeo, *m.* (of light). || Fam. Momento, *m.* || — *He didn't get a wink of sleep all night* o *he didn't sleep a wink all night*, no pegó el ojo en toda la noche, pasó la noche en vela. || Fig. *In a wink*, en un abrir y cerrar de ojos. || *To give* o *to tip s.o. the wink*, guiñar a alguien. || Fig. *To snatch forty winks*, echar un sueñecito.

wink [wiŋk] v. tr. Guiñar (the eye). || *To wink assent*, guiñar el ojo en señal de asentimiento.
— V. intr. Guiñar el ojo: *she winked at me*, me guiñó el ojo. || Pestañear (to blink). || Centellear (stars). || Vacilar, parpadear (light). || — Fig. *Like winking*, en un abrir y cerrar de ojos. | *To wink at*, hacer la vista gorda a, cerrar los ojos a (to pretend not to see).

winker [ˈwiŋkə*] n. Aut. Luz (*f.*) intermitente, intermitente, *m.* || Anteojera, *f.* (of a horse). || Fam. Lucero, *m.*, ojo, *m.* (eye). | Pestaña, *f.* (eyelash).

winkle [ˈwiŋkl] n. Bígaro, *m.*, bigarro, *m.* (mollusc).

winkle [ˈwiŋkl] v. tr. *To winkle out*, eliminar (a person), sacar con dificultad (thing).

winner [ˈwinə*] n. Ganador, ra; vencedor, ra. || — *All the winners!*, ¡todos los resultados! || *This record is a winner!*, ¡este disco tendrá seguramente mucho éxito!

winning [ˈwiniŋ] adj. Vencedor, ra; victorioso, sa: *the winning team*, el equipo victorioso. || Premiado, da (ticket, book). || Decisivo, va (shot, play). || Atractivo, va (attractive).
— N. Victoria, *f.* (victory). || Adquisición, *f.* (acquisition). || Min. Extracción, *f.* | Pozo (*m.*) de extracción (shaft). || — Pl. Ganancias, *f.*

winningly [—li] adv. Atractivamente.

winning post [—pəust] n. Sp. Meta, *f.*, poste (*m.*) de llegada.

winnow [ˈwinəu] v. tr. Aventar (grain). || Fig. Escudriñar (to examine). | Seleccionar, pasar por la criba (to select). | Separar (to separate). | Batir (the air, wings).

winnower [—ə*] n. Aventador, ra (person). || Aventadora, *f.* (machine).

winnowing [—iŋ] n. Cribado, *m.*, aventamiento, *m.* (of grain). || Fig. Criba, *f.* (of persons, etc.). || — Agr. *Winnowing fork*, bieldo, *m.* || *Winnowing machine*, aventadora, *f.*

winsome [ˈwinsəm] adj. Atractivo, va; encantador, ra.

winsomeness [—nis] n. Atractivo, *m.*, encanto, *m.*

winter [ˈwintə*] n. Invierno, *m.*
— Adj. De invierno, invernal. || — *Winter pasture*, invernadero, *m.* || *Winter quarters*, cuarteles (*m.*) de invierno (of soldiers), residencia (*f.*) de invierno. || *Winter season*, temporada (*f.*) de invierno. || *Winter solstice*, solsticio (*m.*) de invierno. || *Winter sports*, deportes (*m.*) de invierno.

winter [ˈwintə*] v. tr. Hacer invernar.
— V. intr. Invernar, pasar el invierno.

winter cherry [—ˈtʃeri] n. Bot. Alquequenje, *m.*

winterize [—raiz] v. tr. Preparar para el invierno, acondicionar para el invierno.

winterly [—li] adj. See wintry.

wintertime [—taim] n. Invierno, *m.* (winter).

wintry [ˈwintri] adj. De invierno, invernal. || Fig. Frío, a; glacial.

winy [ˈwaini] adj. Vinoso, sa.

winze [winz] n. Min. Pozo (*m.*) de comunicación.

wipe [waip] n. Limpieza, *f.* || Tech. Leva, *f.* || Fam. Mamporro, *m.* (blow). | Bofetada, *f.* (swipe). || *To give sth. a wipe*, limpiar algo.

wipe [waip] v. tr. Limpiar (to clean): *to wipe the table*, limpiar la mesa. || Enjugar: *to wipe one's forehead*, enjugarse la frente. || Secar: *to wipe one's hands*, secarse las manos; *to wipe the dishes*, secar los platos. || — *To wipe one's nose*, sonarse las narices. || Fig. *To wipe the floor with*, see floor.
— V. intr. Fam. *To wipe at*, pegar.
— ***To wipe away***, enjugar (tears). | Quitar frotando (to remove). || ***To wipe off***, quitar frotando. | Borrar (a smile). | Enjugar (a debt). || ***To wipe out***, limpiar (to clean). | Secar (to dry). | Borrar (to erase). | Enjugar (a debt). | Aniquilar, destruir (to destroy). | Acabar con (a fortune). || ***To wipe up***, limpiar (to clean). | Quitar (to remove). | Secar (to dry).

wiper [—ə*] n. Trapo, *m.*, paño, *m.* (duster). || Aut. Limpiaparabrisas, *m. inv.* || U. S. Leva, *f.* (of shaft).

wire [waiə*] n. Alambre, *m.* (of metal). || Electr. Cordón, *m.* (thin), cable, *m.* (thick). || Hilo, *m.*: *silver wire*, hilo de plata. || Tela (*f.*) metálica (fence, mesh). || Cuerda, *f.* (of a piano). || Telegrama, *m.*: *to send off a wire*, enviar un telegrama. || Telegrafía, *f.*, telégrafo, *m.* (telegraph system). || Sp. Línea (*f.*) de llegada (in horse racing). || — Pl. Hilos, *m.* (for puppets). || — *Barbed wire*, alambrada, *f.*, alambre (*m.*) de púas, alambre (*m.*) de espino. || *By wire*, telegráficamente, por telégrafo. || Fig. *To pull wires*, tocar resortes. || U. S. Fig. *Under the wire*, en el último momento.

wire [waiə*] v. tr. Poner el alambrado de (a house). || Alambrar (to furnish with wire). || Poner un telegrama a, telegrafiar (to telegraph). || Coger en una trampa (an animal). || — *To wire in*, alambrar. || *To wire news to s.o.*, enviar noticias a alguien por telegrama. || *To wire up*, poner el alambrado de (with barbed wire), poner la instalación eléctrica de (in a house), conectar (to connect).
— V. intr. Poner un telegrama, telegrafiar.

wire brush [—ˈbrʌʃ] n. Cepillo (*m.*) metálico, cepillo (*m.*) de alambre.

wire cloth [—klɔθ] n. Tela (*f.*) metálica.

wire cutter [—ˌkʌtə*] n. Cortaalambres, *m. inv.*

wiredancer [—ˌdɑ:nsə*] n. Funámbulo, la (ropedancer).

wiredraw* [—drɔ:] v. tr. Trefilar, estirar (metal). || Fig. Sutilizar.
— Observ. Pret. ***wiredrew;*** p. p. ***wiredrawn.***

wiredrawer [—ˌdrɔ:ə*] n. Trefilador, *m.*

wiredrawing [—ˌdrɔ:iŋ] n. Trefilado, *m.* || Fig. Sutileza, *f.* || *Wiredrawing machine*, trefiladora, *f.*

wiredrawn [—drɔ:n] p. p. See wiredraw.

wiredrew [—dru:] pret. See wiredraw.

wire fence [—fens] n. Alambrado, *m.*, alambrada, *f.*

wire gauge [—geidʒ] n. Calibrador (*m.*) para alambres.

wire gauze [—ˈgɔ:z] n. Tela (*f.*) metálica.

wireless [—lis] adj. Radiofónico, ca (association). || Sin hilos (telegraphy). || — *Wireless message*, radiograma, *m.* || *Wireless operator*, radio, *m.*, radiotelegrafista, *m.* || *Wireless set*, radio, *f.*, aparato (*m.*) de radio. || *Wireless telegraphy*, radiotelegrafía, *f.*, telegrafía (*f.*) sin hilos. || *Wireless telephony*, radiotelefonía, *f.*
— N. Radio, *f.* (system). || Radio, *f.*, aparato (*m.*) de radio, receptor (*m.*) de radio (set). || — *By wireless*, por radio. || *To talk on the wireless*, hablar por la radio.

wireless [—lis] v. tr. Radiotelegrafiar. || Radiar, transmitir por radio.
— V. intr. Comunicar por radio.

wire mesh [—'meʃ] n. Tela (*f.*) metálica.
wire netting [—'netiŋ] n. Tela (*f.*) metálica.
wirephoto [—ˌfəutəu] n. U. S. Radiofotografía, *f.*, telefotografía, *f.*
wirepull [—pul] v. intr. FAM. Enchufarse, tocar todos los resortes.
wirepuller [—ˌpulə*] n. FAM. Intrigante, *m.* & *f.* | Enchufado, da (who has got a post through influence).
wirepulling [—ˌpuliŋ] n. FAM. Enchufe, *m.* (influence). | Intrigas, *f. pl.*
wire recorder [—riˌkɔːdə*] n. Magnetófono, *m.*
wire rope [—'rəup] n. Cable, *m.*
wiretap [—tæp] v. intr. Interceptar las líneas telefónicas.
wiretapper [—ˌtæpə*] n. Persona (*f.*) que intercepta las líneas telefónicas.
wiretapping [—ˌtæpiŋ] n. Instalación (*f.*) de estaciones de escucha, interceptación (*f.*) de líneas telefónicas.
wirework [—wəːk] n. Tela (*f.*) metálica (netting constructed of wire).
wireworks [—wəːks] n. Trefilería, *f.*, fábrica (*f.*) de alambre.
wiring [—riŋ] n. Instalación (*f.*) eléctrica (electricity system). || Colocación (*f.*) de alambres. || FAM. Envío (*m.*) de un telegrama.
wiry [—ri] adj. Tieso, sa (hair). || Enjuto y fuerte (person). || Metálico, ca (sound).
wisdom ['wizdəm] n. Sabiduría, *f.*, saber, *m.* (knowledge). || Juicio, *m.*, cordura, *f.*, sensatez, *f.* (good judgment). || — REL. *The Book of Wisdom* o *The Wisdom of Solomon*, el Libro de la Sabiduría. || FIG. *To cut one's wisdom tooth*, madurar. || *Wisdom tooth*, muela (*f.*) del juicio.
wise [waiz] adj. Sabio, bia (learned). || Prudente, sensato, ta; juicioso, sa (cautious): *it does not seem wise to go*, no parece prudente ir. || Atinado, da; acertado, da; prudente (move, step). || — *A wise man*, un sabio. || *He is none the wiser*, sigue sin entender nada. || *It would be wise to do it*, sería aconsejable hacerlo. || REL. *The Three Wise Men*, los Reyes Magos. || FAM. *To get wise to*, darse cuenta de (to realize). | *To put s.o. wise to*, poner a alguien al tanto de. || U. S. FAM. *Wise guy*, sabelotodo, *m.* (know-all).
— N. Manera, *f.*, modo, *m.*: *in some wise*, en cierta manera; *in no wise*, de ningún modo.
wise [waiz] v. tr./intr. FAM. *To wise up*, poner al tanto; ponerse al tanto.
wiseacre [—ˌeikə*] n. Sabihondo, da; sabelotodo, *m.* & *f.* (know-all).
wisecrack [—kræk] n. U. S. FAM. Agudeza, *f.*, dicho (*m.*) gracioso, salida, *f.*, ocurrencia, *f.*
wisecrack [—kræk] v. intr. U. S. FAM. Ser gracioso, sa; tener salidas graciosas, ser ocurrente.
wisent ['wiːzənt] n. ZOOL. Bisonte (*m.*) europeo.
wish [wiʃ] n. Deseo, *m.*: *it was my father's wish*, fue el deseo de mi padre; *to go against s.o.'s wishes*, ir en contra de los deseos de alguien; *the fairy grants you two wishes*, la hada te concede dos deseos; *I shall have my wish*, se cumplirá mi deseo. || — Pl. Votos, *m.*: *good wishes*, votos de felicidad. || — *Give him my best wishes*, dale recuerdos míos. || *I gave him my best wishes*, le felicité calurosamente. || *I have no great wish to see it*, no tengo ganas de verlo. || *It has long been my wish to do it*, deseo hacerlo desde hace mucho tiempo. || *My best wishes for the future*, mis mejores votos para el futuro. || *To make a wish*, pensar un deseo. || *With best wishes*, un fuerte abrazo (in a letter). || *Your wish is my command*, sus deseos son órdenes para mí.
wish [wiʃ] v. tr. Querer: *I wish the month were over*, quisiera que se hubiese acabado el mes; *I don't wish to go*, no quiero ir; *what did you wish me to do?*, ¿qué quería que hiciese?; *I wish I were a hundred miles away*, quisiera estar muy lejos de aquí. || Desear: *I wish you every happiness*, le deseo muchísima felicidad; *I don't wish you any harm*, no le deseo ningún mal; *to wish s.o. well*, desear todo lo mejor para alguien. || Gustar: *I wish I had a car*, me gustaría tener un coche; *I wish you would go*, me gustaría que fueras; *I wish I could stay here longer*, me gustaría poder quedarme más tiempo aquí. || — *It is to be wished that*, es de desear que, es deseable que. || *I wish I could!*, ¡ojalá!, ¡ojalá pudiese! || *I wish you could understand it*, me gustaría que pudiese comprenderlo. || *They wished it on me*, me lo impusieron. || *To wish s.o. a happy Christmas*, desear a alguien felices Navidades. || *To wish s.o. good-bye*, decir adiós a alguien, despedirse de alguien. || *To wish s.o. good luck*, desear a uno mucha suerte. || *To wish s.o. good morning*, dar a alguien los buenos días.
— V. intr. Desear: *I have everything I could wish for*, tengo todo lo que podría desear. || *What more could you wish for?*, ¿qué más quieres?
wishbone [—bəun] n. Espoleta, *f.* (of bird).
wisher [—ə*] n. Persona (*f.*) que desea.
wishful [—ful] adj. Deseoso, sa (to do sth., of sth.). || *Wishful thinking*, ilusiones, *f. pl.*
wishing [—iŋ] n. Deseos, *m. pl.* || *Wishing bone*, espoleta, *f.* (of birds).
wish-wash [—wɔʃ] n. FAM. Calducho, *m.*, aguachirle, *f.* (weak drink).
wishy-washy [—iˌwɔʃi] adj. Insípido, da; soso, sa (insipid). || Aguado, da (tea, etc.).
wisp [wisp] n. Manojo, *m.* (of straw, hay). || Mechón, *m.* (of hair). || Vestigio, *m.* (small trace). || Voluta, *f.*, espiral, *f.* (of smoke). || Vuelo, *m.* (of snipe). || *A wisp of a man*, un alfeñique.
wisp [wisp] v. tr. Hacer manojos de.
wispy [—i] adj. Fino, na.
wistaria [wis'tɛəriə] or **wisteria** [wis'tiəriə] n. BOT. Glicina, *f.*
wistful ['wistful] adj. Triste, melancólico, ca (sad). || Ansioso, sa (covetous). || Pensativo, va; soñador, ra (dreamy). || Desilusionado, da (unsatisfied).
wistfulness [—nis] n. Tristeza, *f.*, melancolía, *f.* (sadness). || Lo soñador, lo pensativo (dream). || Ansia, *f.* (covetousness). || Desilusión, *f.* (disillusion).
wit [wit] n. Agudeza, *f.*, ingenio, *m.*: *a man of great wit*, un hombre de gran agudeza. || Gracia, *f.* (humour). || Dicho (*m.*) agudo (remark, comment). || Persona (*f.*) aguda (funny person). || Persona (*f.*) ingeniosa (clever person). || Inteligencia, *f.*: *he has not wit enough to see it*, no tiene la inteligencia suficiente para darse cuenta de ello. || — Pl. Juicio, *m. sing.*: *to have lost one's wits*, haber perdido el juicio. || — *Flash of wit*, rasgo (*m.*) de ingenio. || *It was a battle of wits between them*, rivalizaron en ingenio. || *To be at one's wit's end*, no saber qué hacer. || *To be out of one's wits*, haber perdido la cabeza. || *To collect one's wits*, serenarse. || *To frighten s.o. out of his wits*, dar a alguien un susto mortal. || *To have a ready wit*, tener ingenio, ser agudo, da. || *To keep one's wits about one*, no perder la cabeza. || *To live by one's wits*, vivir de expedientes, vivir de su ingenio, ser caballero de industria. || *To send s.o. out of his wits*, volverle loco a alguien. || *To set one's wits to a problem*, atacar un problema. || *To sharpen one's wits*, aguzar el ingenio, despabilarse. || *To use one's wits*, valerse de su ingenio.
wit [wit] v. tr./intr. Saber. || *To wit*, a saber, es decir.
witan ['witən] n. Consejero (*m.*) de un rey anglosajón.
witch [witʃ] n. Bruja, *f.*, hechicera, *f.* (sorceress). || FAM. Bruja, *f.* (old woman). | Lagarta, *f.* (seductive young woman).
witch [witʃ] v. tr. Hechizar.
witch ball [—bɔːl] n. Bola (*f.*) de cristal (to keep out witches).
witch broom [—brum] n. Escoba (*f.*) de bruja.
witchcraft [—krɑːft] n. Brujería, *f.* (of sorceress). || FIG. Sortilegio, *m.*, hechizo, *m.*, encanto, *m.* (charm).
witch doctor [—ˌdɔktə*] n. Hechicero, *m.*
witch elm [—'elm] n. BOT. See WYCH ELM.
witchery [—əri] n. Brujería, *f.* (witchcraft). || FIG. Encanto, *m.*, hechizo, *m.* (charm).
witches' broom [—izbrum] n. Escoba (*f.*) de bruja.
witches' sabbath [—iz'sæbəθ] n. Aquelarre, *m.*
witch hazel [—'heizəl] n. BOT. Olmo (*m.*) escocés.
witch hunt [—hʌnt] n. Persecución (*f.*) de brujas. || FIG. Persecución, *f.* (political).
witching [—iŋ] adj. Hechicero, ra (charming). || Mágico, ca.
— N. Brujería, *f.* || FIG. Hechizo, *m.* (charm).
witenagemot or **witenagemote** ['witinəgi'məut] n. Asamblea (*f.*) de consejeros de un rey anglosajón.
with [wið] prep. Con: *to eat with a fork*, comer con un tenedor; *to be angry with s.o.*, estar enfadado con alguien; *the house with the green door*, la casa con la puerta verde; *to fight with one's friends*, luchar con los amigos; *to walk with difficulty*, andar con dificultad; *to threaten with eviction*, amenazar con el desahucio; *he walks with a stick*, anda con un bastón; *to sail with the wind*, navegar con el viento. || Con, en casa de: *to live with friends*, vivir en casa de unos amigos. || Con, en compañía de: *I went with John to the cinema*, fui con Juan al cine. || De: *crowded with people*, lleno de gente; *the man with the beard*, el hombre de la barba; *to jump with joy*, saltar de alegría; *in love with*, enamorado de; *to fill with water*, llenar de agua; *to be stiff with cold*, estar yerto de frío. || Junto con: *with John he is the best player in the team*, junto con Juan es el mejor jugador del equipo. || Más: *these chairs with those will be enough*, estas sillas más aquellas bastarán. || En manos de: *I left the book with Peter*, dejé el libro en manos de Pedro. || Con, al cuidado de: *to leave a child with s.o.*, dejar un niño al cuidado de alguien. || Con, a pesar de (in spite of): *with all his faults I love him*, le quiero con todas sus faltas. || Con, según: *it changes with the weather*, cambia con el tiempo. || Igual que: *he can swear with the others*, sabe jurar igual que los otros. || De acuerdo con: *I'm with you on that*, estoy de acuerdo contigo en eso. || — *Bring it with you*, tráelo. || *Down with the government!*, ¡abajo el gobierno! || *He's down with cholera*, tiene cólera. || *He said this with a smile*, lo dijo sonriendo, lo dijo con una sonrisa. || *He was swimming with his hat on*, iba nadando con el sombrero puesto. || *It's a habit with him*, es una costumbre en él. || *It's pouring with rain*, está lloviendo a cántaros. || *She's good with children*, es buena para *or* con los niños. || *The decision lies* o *rests with you*, a usted le corresponde tomar la decisión. || *The problem is still with us*, el problema sigue sin resolverse. || *To vote with a party*, votar por un partido. || *Up with Caesar!*, ¡viva César! || *With all due respect*, con el respeto debido. || *With all my might*, con todas mis fuerzas. || *With all speed*, a toda prisa, a toda velocidad. || *With child*, embarazada. || FIG. FAM. *With it*, al corriente,

al tanto, al día (person), a la moda, de moda (clothes). || *With me*, conmigo. || *With no difficulty*, sin dificultad. || *With one blow*, de un solo golpe. || *With open arms*, con los brazos abiertos. || *With pleasure*, con gusto. || *With that remark, he left*, dicho eso, se marchó. || *With you*, contigo, con usted, con ustedes.

withal [wiˈðɔ:l] adv. Además (moreover). || Sin embargo, no obstante (nevertheless).

withdraw* [wiðˈdrɔ:] v. tr. Quitar, retirar, sacar (to remove). || Apartar (to take aside). || Retirar (troops, candidature, proposal). || Sacar, retirar (money from a bank). || Retirar, quitar (money from circulation). || Desdecirse de (a promise, statement). || Retirar (one's words).
— V. intr. Retirarse (to leave). || Apartarse (to move away). || Retirarse (from a treaty). || Retirar una moción. || — *To withdraw in favour of s.o.*, renunciar a favor de alguien. || *To withdraw into o.s.*, ensimismarse, abstraerse.

— Observ. Pret. ***withdrew;*** p. p. ***withdrawn***.

withdrawal [—əl] n. Retirada, *f.* (of troops). || Retirada, *f.* (from a bank). || Salida, *f.* (on a bank statement). || Retractación, *f.* (of a statement). || Abandono, *m.* (abandonment). || Renuncia, *f.* (renunciation).

withdrawal symptoms [—əl,simptəmz] pl. n. Med. Síntomas (*m.*) sufridos por el toxicómano al carecer de la droga que solía tomar.

withdrawn [—n] p. p. See WITHDRAW.
— Adj. Aislado, da. || Reservado, da; introvertido, da.

withdrew [wiðˈdru:] pret. See WITHDRAW.

withe [wiθ] n. Mimbre, *m.*

wither [ˈwiðə*] v. tr. Marchitar, agostar (plants). || Consumir, debilitar: *illness withered him*, le consumió la enfermedad. || Fig. Fulminar: *he withered him with a glance*, le fulminó con la mirada.
— V. intr. Marchitarse (flowers). || Debilitarse (to weaken). || Secarse (to grow thin).

withered [—d] adj. Marchito, ta; seco, ca.

withering [—riŋ] adj. Que se marchita (flower). || Abrasador, ra (heat). || Fig. Fulminante (look). | Mordaz (biting).
— N. Marchitamiento, *m.*

withers [—z] pl. n. Cruz, *f. sing.* (of horse).

withheld [wiðˈheld] pret. & p. p. See WITHHOLD.

withhold* [wiðˈhəuld] v. tr. Negar, negarse a conceder (to refuse). || Retener (to hold back). || Ocultar, callar (not to reveal): *to withhold the truth from s.o.*, ocultar la verdad a alguien. || U. S. *Withholding tax*, impuesto deducido del salario.
— V. intr. *To withhold from*, abstenerse de.

— Observ. Pret. & p. p. ***withheld***.

within [wiˈðin] adv. Dentro: *enquire within*, pregunten dentro; *within and without*, dentro y fuera. || En casa (at home). || Fig. En su fuero interno (inside the mind). || — *From within*, de dentro, del interior. || Fig. *To make pure within*, purificar el alma.
— Prep. Al alcance de: *within call*, al alcance de la voz. || Dentro de: *within the house*, dentro de la casa; *within the organization*, dentro de la organización; *within a week*, dentro de una semana; *within the law*, dentro de la ley. || En: *within a radius of*, en un radio de. || En un plazo de: *you must answer within five days*, tiene que contestar en un plazo de cinco días. || A menos de: *within two miles of*, a menos de dos millas de. — Fig. *A voice within*, una voz interior. | *To be within an inch of*, estar a dos pasos de. || *To be within s.o.'s jurisdiction*, ser de la competencia de alguien. || *To live within one's income*, vivir con arreglo a sus recursos económicos. || Fig. *Within o. s.*, en su fuero interno. || *Within the frontier*, fronteras adentro.

without [wiˈðaut] prep. Sin: *without money*, sin dinero; *without work*, sin trabajo; *without seeing anyone*, sin ver a nadie. || Sin, sin que: *without my finding it*, sin encontrarlo yo, sin que yo lo encontrase. || Fuera de: *without the city*, fuera de la ciudad. — *It goes without saying*, see SAY. || *Not without difficulty*, no sin dificultad. || *To do o to go without*, prescindir de.
— Adv. Fuera: *from without*, desde fuera.

withstand* [wiðˈstænd] v. tr. Resistir a (temptation, siege, blow). || Resistir, aguantar (pain). || Oponerse a (s.o.).

— Observ. Pret. & p. p. ***withstood***.

withstood [wiðˈstud] pret. & p. p. See WITHSTAND.

withy [ˈwiði] n. Mimbre, *m.*

witless [ˈwitlis] adj. Estúpido, da; tonto, ta; idiota.

witloof [ˈwitlu:f] n. Bot. Endibia, *f.* (endive).

witness [ˈwitnis] n. Testigo, *m.* (of an incident). || Prueba, *f.* (proof, evidence). || Testimonio, *m.* (testimony). || Jur. Testigo, *m.*: *witness for the prosecution*, testigo de cargo; *witness for the defence*, testigo de descargo. || — *In witness whereof*, en fe de lo cual. || *To bear witness to*, atestiguar. || *To call as a witness*, citar como testigo. || *To call to witness*, poner por testigo a.

witness [ˈwitnis] v. tr. Asistir a, presenciar, ser testigo de (to be present at). || Atestiguar (to bear witness to). || Firmar como testigo (a document). || Demostrar, dar prueba de: *a look which witnessed his surprise*, una mirada que demostraba su sorpresa.
— V. intr. Declarar (*for*, a favor; *against*, en contra de). || *To witness to*, atestiguar.

witness box [—bɔks] n. Jur. Barra (*f.*) de los testigos.

witness stand [—stænd] n. U. S. Jur. Barra (*f.*) de los testigos.

witted [ˈwitid] adj. Ingenioso, sa; agudo, da.

witticism [ˈwitisizəm] n. Agudeza, *f.*, dicho (*m.*) gracioso, salida (*f.*) graciosa, ocurrencia, *f.*

wittily [ˈwitili] adv. Con agudeza.

wittiness [ˈwitinis] n. Agudeza, *f.*

witting [ˈwitiŋ] adj. Deliberado, da; intencionado, da (deliberate). || Consciente (aware, conscious).

wittingly [—li] adv. A sabiendas.

witty [ˈwiti] adj. Ingenioso, sa; agudo, da; gracioso, sa (person). || Gracioso, sa; divertido, da (remark).

wivern [ˈwaivə:n] n. Herald. Dragón, *m.*

wives [waivz] pl. n. See WIFE.

wizard [ˈwizəd] adj. Fam. Estupendo, da; formidable.
— N. Mago, *m.*, hechicero, *m.* || Fig. Genio, *m.*, as, *m.*: *a business wizard*, un as de los negocios. || *I am not a wizard*, no soy un adivino.

wizardry [—ri] n. Magia, *f.*, hechicería, *f.*

wizen [ˈwizən] or **wizened** [—d] adj. Marchito, ta; arrugado, da (skin). || Hecho una pasa: *a wizened old man*, un anciano hecho una pasa. || Marchito, ta (plants).

wo! or **woa!** [wəu] interj. ¡So! (to stop a horse).

wobble [ˈwɔbl] n. Tambaleo, *m.*, bamboleo, *m.* || Zigzag, *m.* (of a person). || Temblor, *m.* (of voice, jelly). || Vacilación, *f.* (indecision). || Fluctuación, *f.* || — *He walks with a wobble*, anda tambaleándose, anda haciendo eses. || *The table has a wobble*, la mesa está coja.

wobble [ˈwɔbl] v. tr. Hacer tambalearse.
— V. intr. Tambalearse (to move unsteadily). || Bambolearse, balancearse (to rock). || Temblar (voice, jelly). || Vacilar (to hesitate).

wobbly [—i] adj. Bamboleante, tambaleante (shaking, unstable). || Haciendo eses, zigzagueando (a person). || Tembloroso, sa (voice). || Cojo, ja (chair, table).

wobbulator [ˈwɔbjuleitə*] n. Modulador (*m.*) de frecuencia.

woe [wəu] n. Infortunio, *m.*, aflicción, *f.* || — Pl. Penas, *f.*: *to tell s.o. one's woes*, contarle a alguien sus penas.
— Interj. ¡Ay!: *woe is me!*, ¡ay de mí! || *Woe betide you!*, ¡maldito seas!

woebegone [ˈwəubi,gɔn] adj. Desconsolado, da (person). || Desolado, da (place).

woeful [ˈwəuful] adj. Afligido, da; apenado, da (very sad). || Lamentable, deplorable (deplorable). || Infortunado, da; desgraciado, da (period).

woefulness [—nis] n. Pesar, *m.* || Infortunio, *m.*

woke [wəuk] pret. See WAKE.

woken [—ən] p. p. See WAKE.

wold [wəuld] n. Región (*f.*) ondulada.

wolf [wulf] n. Zool. Lobo, *m.* || Mus. Sonido (*m.*) discordante. || U. S. Fam. Tenorio, *m.*, don Juan, *m.*, conquistador, *m.* (woman chaser). || — Fig. *A wolf in sheep's clothing*, un lobo con piel de oveja. | *Lone wolf*, persona solitaria. || *To cry wolf*, llamar al lobo, dar una falsa alarma. || *To eat like a wolf*, comer como una lima. || *To hold the wolf by the ears*, coger al lobo por las orejas. || *To keep the wolf from the door*, precaverse contra la miseria.

— Observ. El plural de *wolf* es *wolves*.

wolf [wulf] v. tr. Zamparse, tragarse (one's food).

wolf call [—kɔ:l] n. Fam. Silbido (*m.*) de admiración.

wolf cub [—kʌb] n. Lobezno, *m.*, lobato, *m.*, cachorro (*m.*) de lobo (animal). || "Scout" (*m.*) joven, joven explorador, *m.* (young boy scout).

wolf dog [—dɔg] n. Perro (*m.*) lobo.

wolffish [—fiʃ] n. Lobo (*m.*) de mar (fish).

wolfhound [—haund] n. Perro (*m.*) lobo.

wolfish [—iʃ] adj. Zool. Lobuno, na. || Fig. Cruel, feroz. || U. S. Fam. Hambriento, ta. || U. S. Fam. *To feel wolfish*, tener un hambre canina.

wolf pack [—pæk] n. Manada (*f.*) de lobos. || Mar. Flotilla (*f.*) de submarinos.

wolfram [—rəm] n. Volframio, *m.*, tungsteno, *m.* (tungsten). || Volframita, *f.* (wolframite).

wolframine [—rə,min] n. Volframina, *f.*

wolframite [—rəmait] n. Volframita, *f.*

wolf whistle [—,wisl] n. Fam. See WOLF CALL.

wolverene or **wolverine** [ˈwulvəri:n] n. Zool. Glotón, *m.*

wolves [wulvz] pl. n. See WOLF.

woman [ˈwumən] n. Mujer, *f.* || — Fam. *He is like an old woman*, es una vieja histérica. | *My old woman*, la parienta, mi media naranja. || *Old woman*, vieja, *f.*, anciana, *f.* || *The woman in her*, su lado femenino, su feminidad, *f.* || Fam. *There's a woman in it*, es cuestión de mujeres *or* de faldas. | *To make an honest woman of*, casarse con, tomar por esposa a. || *Woman of the world*, mujer de mundo. || *Woman's rights*, derechos (*m.*) de la mujer. || *Woman suffrage*, sufragio femenino. || *Young woman*, joven, *f.*; mujer joven.

— Observ. El plural de *woman* es *women*.

woman chaser [—tʃeisə*] n. Mujeriego, *m.*

woman doctor [—ˈdɔktə*] n. Médica, *f.*

woman friend [—frend] n. Amiga, *f.*

woman hater [—heitə*] n. Misógino, *m.*

womanhood [—hud] n. Mujeres, *f. pl.*, sexo (*m.*) femenino: *the world's womanhood*, las mujeres del mundo. || Condición (*f.*) de mujer. || Feminidad, *f.* (femininity). || *To reach womanhood*, hacerse mujer.
womanish [—iʃ] adj. Femenino, na; mujeril (of woman). || Afeminado, da (men).
womanize [—aiz] v. intr. Ser mujeriego.
— V. tr. Afeminar.
womanizer [—aizə*] n. Mujeriego, *m.*
womankind [—ˈkaind] n. Mujeres, *f. pl.*, sexo (*m.*) femenino. || *My womankind*, las mujeres de mi familia.
womanlike [—laik] adj. De mujer, femenino, na.
womanliness [—linis] n. Feminidad, *f.*
womanly [—li] adj. Femenino, na.
woman pilot [—ˈpailət] n. Mujer (*f.*) piloto.
woman writer [—raitə*] n. Escritora, *f.*
womb [wu:m] n. ANAT. Matriz, *f.*, útero, *m.* || FIG. Cuna, *f.*: *the womb of the Renaissance*, la cuna del Renacimiento; *from the womb to the tomb*, desde la cuna hasta la sepultura. | Entrañas, *f. pl.*
women [ˈwimin] pl. n. See WOMAN.
womenfolk [—fəuk] pl. n. Mujeres, *f.*
Women's Lib [—s'lib] n. Movimiento (*m.*) de Liberación de la Mujer.
women's page [—speidʒ] n. Sección (*f.*) femenina.
won [wʌn] pret. & p. p. See WIN.
wonder [ˈwʌndə*] n. Maravilla, *f.*, prodigio, *m.*: *a wonder of architecture*, una maravilla de la arquitectura; *the wonders of science*, los prodigios de la ciencia. || Maravilla, *f.*: *the seven wonders of the world*, las siete maravillas del mundo. || Milagro, *m.*: *it is a wonder that he wasn't killed*, es un milagro que no le hayan matado. || Admiración, *f.*, asombro, *m.* (sensation): *his skill is always a source of wonder to me*, su destreza siempre me llena de admiración. || — *For a wonder*, por milagro. || *It is a wonder that he ever got home*, no sé cómo ha podido llegar a casa. || *It is little* o *small wonder that* ..., no es de extrañar que ... || *My holidays did wonders for me*, las vacaciones tuvieron un efecto maravilloso en mí. || *No wonder!*, ¡no me extraña!, ¡no es de extrañar! || *The wonder of it is that* ..., lo asombroso es que ... || *To be a nine-days' wonder*, durar muy poco, ser efímero, ra. || *To fill with wonder*, maravillar, dejar maravillado. || *To promise wonders*, prometer maravillas, prometer el oro y el moro. || *To work* o *to do wonders*, hacer maravillas.
— Adj. Milagroso, sa: *wonder drug*, remedio milagroso. || *Wonder child*, niño prodigio.
wonder [ˈwʌndə*] v. tr. Preguntarse: *I wonder whether it is true*, me pregunto si es verdad. || Pensar: *I was wondering what to do next*, estaba pensando en lo que iba a hacer después. || — *I wonder what time it is*, ¿qué hora será? || *I wonder who will lend me 50 pounds*, ¿quién me prestará 50 libras? || *I wonder why*, ¿por qué será?: *Peter didn't come, I wonder why*, Pedro no vino ¿por qué será? || *I wonder why he didn't go*, me extraña que no fuese.
— V. intr. Admirarse, asombrarse: *I wonder at his foolhardiness*, me admiro de su temeridad; *I wonder at nothing*, no me asombro de nada. || Pensar: *I was wondering about what to do tonight*, estaba pensando en lo que iba a hacer esta noche; *it made me wonder*, me hizo pensar. || — *I just wondered*, sólo por curiosidad: *why did you ask? — I just wondered*, ¿por qué preguntaste? — Sólo por curiosidad. || *I shouldn't wonder if it rained*, no me extrañaría que lloviese. || *It is all over now, I shouldn't wonder*, supongo que ya se habrá terminado todo. || *It is hardly to be wondered at*, no tiene nada de extraño, no hay por qué extrañarse. || *John will be there. — I wonder*, Juan estará allí. — Lo dudo.
wonderful [—ful] adj. Maravilloso, sa; estupendo, da (marvellous). || Asombroso, sa; sorprendente (astonishing). || *Wonderful!*, ¡qué maravilla!, ¡estupendo!
wondering [—riŋ] adj. Perplejo, ja (perplexed): *in a wondering tone*, en un tono perplejo. || Asombrado, da (astonished).
wonderingly [—riŋli] adv. Perplejo, ja; con perplejidad: *he looked wonderingly at the statue*, miró perplejo la estatua. || Con asombro, asombrado, da (in astonishment).
wonderland [—lænd] n. Mundo (*m.*) maravilloso: *the wonderland of dreams*, el mundo maravilloso de los sueños. || *Alice in Wonderland*, Alicia en el País de las Maravillas.
wonderment [—mənt] n. Admiración, *f.* (admiration). || Asombro, *m.* (amazement).
wonderstruck [—strʌk] adj. Pasmado, da; asombrado, da.
wonderwork [—ˌwə:k] n. Prodigio, *m.*
wondrous [ˈwʌndrəs] adj. Maravilloso, sa.
wondrously [—li] adv. Extraordinariamente: *wondrously big*, extraordinariamente grande.
wonky [ˈwɔŋki] adj. FAM. Torcido, da (out of position): *your tie is wonky*, tu corbata está torcida. | Inclinado, da (a picture, etc.). | Cojo, ja: *a wonky table*, una mesa coja. | Poco sólido, da; poco seguro, ra (unsteady): *a wonky bridge*, un puente poco seguro. || FAM. *The machine has gone a bit wonky*, la máquina está algo estropeada.
wont [wəunt] adj. *To be wont to*, soler, acostumbrar: *he was wont to get up early*, solía madrugar.
— N. Costumbre, *f.*: *as is his wont*, como tiene por costumbre. || *It is his wont to*, acostumbra, suele, tiene por costumbre.
won't [wəunt] contraction of *will not*.
wonted [—id] adj. Acostumbrado, da; habitual.
woo [wu:] v. tr. Hacer la corte, cortejar (a young lady). || FIG. Solicitar (favour, support). | Buscar (fame, fortune). | Buscarse (defeat, trouble). | Granjearse la amistad de (to win over s.o.). || FAM. *A policy designed to woo the electors*, una política encaminada a ganar votos *or* a conseguir el apoyo del electorado.
— V. intr. Cortejar a una mujer.
wood [wud] n. Bosque, *m.* (forest): *a walk in the wood*, un paseo por el bosque. || Madera, *f.* (material): *a table made of wood*, una mesa de madera. || Leña, *f.* (firewood). || Palo, *m.* (stick, staff). || SP. Bola, *f.* (in bowls). | Palo (*m.*) de madera (golf club). || MUS. Instrumentos (*m. pl.*) de madera (woodwind section). || Barril, *m.* (barrel): *wine from the wood*, vino de barril. || — Pl. Bosque, *m. sing.* || — FIG. *To be out of the wood*, estar a salvo, haber salido del apuro *or* del mal paso. || *To take to the woods*, echarse al monte. || *Touch wood!*, ¡toca madera! || *We'll succeed, touch wood*, lo lograremos si Dios quiere. || FIG. *You can't see the wood for the trees*, los árboles impiden ver el bosque.
— Adj. De los bosques, silvestre (plants, wildlife). || De madera: *a wood floor*, un suelo de madera; *a wood table*, una mesa de madera.
wood alcohol [—ˌælkəhɔl] n. CHEM. Metanol, *m.*, alcohol (*m.*) metílico.
wood anemone [—əˌneməni] n. BOT. Anémona (*f.*) silvestre.
woodbin [—bin] n. U. S. Leñera, *f.*
woodbine [—bain] n. BOT. Madreselva, *f.* || U. S. BOT. Viña (*f.*) loca.
wood block [—blɔk] n. Tarugo, *m.* (in paving). || ARTS. Bloque (*m.*) de madera.
wood-carver [—ˌkɑ:və*] n. Tallista (*m.*) en madera.
wood carving [—ˌkɑ:viŋ] n. Talla (*f.*) de madera (object). || Tallado (*m.*) en madera (craft).
woodchat [—tʃæt] n. Alcaudón, *m.* (bird).
woodchuck [—tʃʌk] n. ZOOL. Marmota (*f.*) de América.
wood coal [—kəul] n. Carbón (*m.*) vegetal.
woodcock [—kɔk] n. Chocha, *f.*, becada, *f.* (bird).
woodcraft [—krɑ:ft] n. Conocimiento (*m.*) del bosque (knowledge of forests). || Artesanía (*f.*) en madera (carving, etc.).
woodcut [—kʌt] n. Grabado (*m.*) en madera.
woodcutter [—ˌkʌtə*] n. Leñador, *m.*
wooded [—id] adj. Arbolado, da; poblado de árboles.
wooden [—ən] adj. De madera (made of wood). || De palo: *wooden leg*, pata de palo. || FIG. Inexpresivo, va: *a wooden stare*, una mirada inexpresiva. | Tieso, sa; rígido, da (rigid). | Estirado, da (stiff). | Inflexible (policy). | Soso, sa (uninteresting). || FIG. *Wooden face*, cara de palo.
wood engraver [—inˌgreivə*] n. Grabador (*m.*) en madera.
wood engraving [—inˌgreiviŋ] n. Grabado (*m.*) en madera.
wooden-headed [—ənˌhedid] adj. Mentecato, ta; estúpido, da (stupid).
woodenness [—ənnis] n. FIG. Rigidez, *f.*
wooden shoe [—ənˈʃu:] n. Zueco, *m.* (clog).
wooden spoon [—ənˈspu:n] n. Cuchara (*f.*) de palo. || FIG. Premio (*m.*) de consolación.
wood ibis [—ˈaibis] n. ZOOL. Tántalo, *m.*
woodiness [—inis] n. Carácter (*m.*) arbolado (of a place). || Carácter (*m.*) leñoso (similarity to wood).
woodland [—lənd] n. Bosque, *m.*
— Adj. De los bosques, silvestre.
wood louse [—laus] n. ZOOL. Cochinilla, *f.*

— OBSERV. El plural de *wood louse* es *wood lice*.

woodman [—mən] n. Leñador, *m.* (woodcutter). || Guardabosque, *m.* (forester).

— OBSERV. El plural de esta palabra es *woodmen*.

wood nymph [—nimf] n. Ninfa (*f.*) de los bosques.
wood paper [—ˌpeipə*] n. Papel (*m.*) de celulosa.
woodpecker [—ˌpekə*] n. Pájaro (*m.*) carpintero, pico, *m.*, picamaderos, *m. inv.* (bird).
wood pigeon [—ˌpidʒin] n. Paloma (*f.*) torcaz (bird).
woodpile [—pail] n. Montón (*m.*) de leña.
wood pulp [—pʌlp] n. Pasta (*f.*) de madera.
wood shavings [—ˌʃeiviŋz] pl. n. Virutas, *f.*
woodshed [—ʃed] n. Leñera, *f.*
woodsman [—zmən] n. U. S. Leñador, *m.* (woodcutter). || *To be an expert woodsman*, conocer muy bien el bosque.

— OBSERV. El plural de esta palabra es *woodsmen*.

wood sorrel [—ˌsɔrəl] n. BOT. Acederilla, *f.*
wood spirit [—ˈspirit] n. CHEM. Metanol, *m.*, alcohol (*m.*) metílico.
wood stork [—stɔ:k] n. ZOOL. Tántalo, *m.*
woodsy [—zi] adj. U. S. Poblado de árboles.
wood tar [—tɑ:*] n. Alquitrán (*m.*) vegetal.
wood tick [—tik] n. ZOOL. Garrapata, *f.*
woodturner [—ˌtə:nə*] n. Tornero (*m.*) en madera.
wood turning [—ˌtə:niŋ] n. Torneado (*m.*) en madera.
woodwaxen [—ˌwæksən] n. BOT. Retama (*f.*) de tintes, retama (*f.*) de tintoreros.

woodwind [—wind] n. Mus. Instrumentos (*m. pl*) de viento de madera (section of orchestra). || U. S. Mus. Instrumento (*m.*) de viento de madera (instrument).

woodwork [—wə:k] n. Carpintería, *f.* (craft). || Enmaderado, *m.*, maderaje, *m.* (in a construction). || Artesanía (*f.*) en madera: *Spanish woodwork is world famous*, la artesanía en madera de España tiene fama mundial.

woodworker [—,wə:kə*] n. Carpintero, *m.* || Tallista (*m.*) en madera (wood-carver).

woodworking [—,wə:kiŋ] n. Carpintería, *f.* || Talla (*f.*) en madera (wood carving).

woodworm [—wə:m] n. Zool. Carcoma, *f.*

woody [—i] adj. Poblado de árboles, arbolado, da: da: *woody region*, región arbolada. || Leñoso, sa (like wood): *a plant with a woody stem*, una planta de tallo lleñoso. || — *Woody sound*, sonido sordo. || *Woody taste*, sabor a madera.

wooer [wu:ə*] n. Pretendiente, *m.*, galán, *m.*

woof [wuf] n. Trama, *f.* (weft).

woofer [—ə*] n. Altavoz (*m.*) para sonidos graves.

wooing [ˈwu:iŋ] adj./n. Galanteo, *m.*

wool [wul] n. Lana, *f.*: *ball of wool*, ovillo de lana. || Pelo, *m.*, lana, *f.* (of an animal). || — Fig. *Dyed-in-the-wood conservative*, conservador acérrimo. | *Dyed-in-the wool Spaniard*, español de pura cepa. || *Fibreglass wool*, lana de vidrio. || *Knitting wool*, lana para hacer punto. || Fig. *Much cry and little wool*, mucho ruido y pocas nueces. || *Shorn wool*, lana de esquileo. || *Steel wool*, fibra metálica. || *Steel wool pad*, estropajo metálico. || Fig. *To go for wool and come home shorn*, ir por lana y volver trasquilado. || Fig. fam. *To pull the wool over s.o.'s eyes*, dar a alguien gato por liebre.
— Adj. De lana: *a wool jersey*, un jersey de lana. || Lanero, ra; de la lana: *the wool industry*, la industria lanera; *wool trade*, comercio de la lana.

wool-bearing [—,bεəriŋ] adj. Lanar.

wool card [—kα:d] n. Carda, *f.*

wool clip [—klip] n. Producción (*f.*) anual de lana.

wool comb [—kəum] n. Carda (*f.*) de la lana.

wool combing [—,kəumiŋ] n. Cardadura, *f.*

woolen [—ən] adj. U. S. See woollen.

wool fat [—fæt] n. Grasa (*f.*) de la lana.

woolgathering [—,gæðəriŋ] adj. Fig. Distraído, da. || Fig. *To be woolgathering*, estar en las nubes, estar en Babia.
— N. Fig. Distracción, *f.*

wool grease [—gri:s] n. Grasa (*f.*) de la lana, churre, *m.* (wool fat).

woolgrowing [—,grəuiŋ] n. Cría (*f.*) de ganado lanar.

wool-hall [—hɔ:l] n. Mercado (*m.*) de lana.

woolies [—iz] pl. n. U. S. Ropa (*f. sing.*) de lana.

wooliness [—inis] n. U. S. See woolliness.

woollen [—ən] adj. De lana (made of wool). || Lanero, ra; de la lana: *woollen industry*, industria de la lana.
— N. Lana, *f.* (cloth). || — Pl. Ropa (*f. sing.*) de lana.

woollies [—iz] pl. n. Ropa (*f. sing.*) de lana.

woolliness [—inis] n. Carácter (*m.*) lanoso. || Fig. Poca claridad, *f.*, imprecisión, *f.* (of style, thought). | Lo borroso (of painting).

woolly [—i] adj. Lanoso, sa (like wool): *woolly appearance*, aspecto lanoso. || De lana (made of wool): *woolly toy*, juguete de lana. || Cubierto de lana (covered with wool). || Aborregado, da (cloud). || Crespo, pa (hair). || Aterciopelado, da (leaf, peach, etc.). || Fig. Borroso, sa (blurred): *woolly outline*, perfil borroso. | Confuso, sa; impreciso, sa; vago, ga (idea, reply, etc.). | Empañado, da (voice).

woolman [—mən] n. Comerciante (*m.*) en lanas (merchant). || Fabricante (*m.*) de productos de lana (manufacturer).

— Observ. El plural de esta palabra es *woolmen*.

woolpack [—pæk] n. Bala (*f.*) *or* paca (*f.*) de lana (bale of wool). || Nube, *f.* [aborregada] (cloud).

woolsack [—sæk] n. Saco (*m.*) de lana. || *The Woolsack*, cojín (*m.*) en que se sienta el "Lord Chancellor" (seat), cargo (*m.*) del "Lord Chancellor" (office).

wool stapler [—,steiplə*] n. Tratante (*m.* & *f.*) en lana.

wooly [—i] adj. U. S. See woolly.

woozy [ˈwu:zi] adj. Fam. Indispuesto, ta; mareado, da.

word [wə:d] n. Palabra, *f.*, vocablo, *m.*, voz, *f.*: *Spanish word*, palabra española. || Noticia, *f.* (news): *word came that he was alive*, llegó la noticia de que estaba vivo; *to bring word*, traer noticias. || Recado, *m.* (message): *to send word*, mandar recado. || Palabra, *f.* (promise): *to break one's word*, faltar a su palabra; *to give one's word*, dar su palabra. || Orden, *f.*: *to give the word to attack*, dar la orden de atacar; *to pass the word round*, transmitir la orden. || Santo y seña, *m.* (password): *to enter you must give the word*, para entrar tiene que dar el santo y seña. || — Pl. Palabras, *f.*: *his words went unheeded*, nadie prestó atención a sus palabras. || Mus. Letra, *f. sing.* (of a song). || Papel, *m. sing.* (of an actor): *to learn one's words*, aprender el papel. || — *Actions speak louder than words*, obras son amores, que no buenas razones. || *A man of few words*, un hombre de pocas palabras. || *A word of advice*, un consejo. || *A word to the wise is enough*, al buen entendedor pocas palabras bastan. || *Beyond words*, hasta lo indecible: *it is ugly beyond words* es feo hasta lo indecible. || *By word of mouth*, oralmente, verbalmente, de palabra. || *Clever isn't the word; I'd say he's a genius*, inteligente no es la palabra; yo diría que es un genio. || *Don't breathe a word of this to anyone*, de esto no digas ni una palabra a nadie. || *Fine words*, palabras elocuentes. || *He won't hear a word against her*, no permite que se diga nada en contra de ella. || *His word is law*, su palabra es ley. || *In a word*, en una palabra. || *In every sense of the word*, en toda la extensión de la palabra. || *In other words*, en otros términos, en otras palabras (said in another way), es decir (that is to say). || *In so many words*, palabra por palabra, textualmente: *I can't tell you what he said in so many words*, no puedo decirle lo que dijo textualmente; explícitamente, claramente: *he didn't say so in so many words*, no lo dijo explícitamente. || *In the words of Shakespeare*, según las palabras de *or* como dice Shakespeare. || *In word*, de palabra. || *In word and deed*, de palabra y obra. || *In words of one syllable*, con palabras sencillas. || *It is his word against mine*, su palabra contra la mía. || *Key word*, palabra clave. || *Man of his word*, hombre (*m.*) de palabra. || *Mark his words*, tome nota de lo que dice. || *More splendid than words can tell*, mucho mejor de lo que se puede expresar con palabras. || Fam. *Mum's the word!*, ¡punto en boca!, ¡ni una palabra! || *My word!*, ¡válgame Dios!, ¡Dios mio! || *Nobody has a good word to say for him*, no hay quien hable en su favor. || Fam. *Not to be able to get a word in edgeways*, no poder meter baza. | *Not to mince one's words*, no andar con rodeos, no tener pelos en la lengua. || *Not to say a word*, no decir ni una palabra *or* ni pio. || *On my word*, palabra, a fe mia. || *Play on words*, juego (*m.*) de palabras. || *Take my word for it*, se lo aseguro, le doy mi palabra. || *The last word in...*, el último grito en ... || Rel. *The Word*, el Verbo. | *The Word of God*, la palabra de Dios. || *Time and words can never be recalled*, lo dicho, dicho está. || *To be as good as one's word*, cumplir con su palabra. || *To be better than one's word*, hacer más de lo prometido. || *To call on s.o. to say a few words*, conceder la palabra a alguien. || *To eat one's words*, tragarse las palabras, retractarse. || *To hang on s.o.'s every word*, estar pendiente de las palabras de alguien. || *To have a word to say*, tener algo que decir. || *To have a word with s.o. about sth.*, hablar de algo con alguien. || *To have no words*, no tener palabras. || *To have the last word*, decir la última palabra. || *To have words with s.o.*, tener unas palabras con alguien, reñir con alguien, discutir con alguien. || *To keep one's word*, cumplir su palabra. || *To leave word*, dejar recado. || *To leave word that*, dejar dicho que. || *Too beautiful, too stupid for words*, de lo más hermoso que hay, de lo más estúpido que hay. || *To play on words*, hacer un juego de palabras, jugar del vocablo. || *To put in a good word for s.o.*, decir unas palabras en favor de alguien. || *To send s.o. word of sth.*, avisar a alguien de algo. || *To suit the action to the word*, unir la acción a la palabra. || *To take s.o. at his word*, cogerle a uno la palabra. || *To take s.o.'s word for it*, creer lo que alguien dice, creer en la palabra de alguien. || *To take the words out of s.o.'s mouth*, quitarle a uno la palabra de la boca. || *To twist s.o.'s words*, tergiversar las palabras de uno. || *To waste words*, gastar saliva en balde. || *To weigh one's words*, medir *or* sopesar las palabras. || *Upon my word*, bajo palabra. || *Without a word*, sin decir palabra. || *With these words*, dichas estas palabras, con estas palabras. || *Word for word*, palabra por palabra, literalmente. || *Word of honour*, palabra de honor. || *Words fail me to express my gratitude*, no encuentro palabras para expresar mi gratitud. || *Your word is good enough for me*, me basta con su palabra.

word [wə:d] v. tr. Expresar: *a well-worded protest*, una protesta bien expresada. || Redactar: *a badly worded letter*, una carta mal redactada.

word blindness [—,blaindnis] n. Med. Alexia, *f.*

wordbook [—buk] n. Vocabulario, *m.*

word-for-word [—fə,wə:d] adj. Literal, palabra por palabra, [hecho] al pie de la letra: *word-for-word translation*, traducción literal.

word game [—geim] n. Juego (*m.*) de formación de palabras (forming words). || Juego (*m.*) de adivinación de palabras (guessing words).

wordiness [—inis] n. Verbosidad, *f.*, palabrería, *f.*

wording [—iŋ] n. Redacción, *f.* || Texto, *m.*, términos, *m. pl.* (text).

wordless [—lis] adj. Mudo, da.

word of command [—əvkəˈmα:nd] n. Orden, *f.*, voz (*f.*) de mando.

word-of-mouth [—əv,mauθ] adj. Verbal, oral.

word-painting [—,peintiŋ] n. Descripción (*f.*) gráfica.

word-perfect [—ˈpə:fikt] adj. *To be word-perfect*, saber perfectamente (a role, speech, etc.).

word picture [—,piktʃə*] n. Descripción (*f.*) gráfica.

wordplay [—plei] n. Juego (*m.*) de palabras.

wordy [—i] adj. Prolijo, ja; verboso, sa (using too many words). || Verbal (using words).

wore [wɔ:*] pret. See wear.

work [wə:k] n. Trabajo, *m.*: *manual work*, trabajo manual; *a teacher's work*, el trabajo de un profesor; *a week's work*, el trabajo de una semana. || Trabajo, *m.*, empleo, *m.* (employment). || Obra, *f.*: *the works of Shakespeare*, las obras de Shakespeare; *collected* o *complete works*, obras completas; *literary work*, obra literaria; *work of genius*, obra genial; *Newton's scientific work*, la obra científica de Newton; *work of art*, *of charity*, obra de arte, de caridad. || Obras, *f. pl.*: *work has begun on the road*, se han empezado las obras en la carretera. || Razón, *f.*: *he made it his life's work*, hizo de ello la razón de su vida. || PHYS. Trabajo, *m.* || TECH. Pieza, *f.* (piece being made). || — Pl. Fábrica, *f. sing.*: *the car works*, la fábrica de coches. || MIL. Fortificaciones, *f.* || TECH. Mecanismo, *m. sing.* (mechanism). || REL. Obras, *f.*: *good works*, buenas obras, obras pías, obras de caridad. || — *All work and no play makes Jack a dull boy*, trabajar sin descanso agota a cualquiera. || *Day's work*, jornada, *f.* || *Down to work*, manos a la obra. || FIG. *Do your own dirty work*, sácate tú las castañas del fuego. || *I had my work cut out to finish it*, me costó muchísimo trabajo terminarlo. || FIG. *It's all in a day's work*, es el pan nuestro de cada día; son gajes del oficio. || *It's thirsty work*, es un trabajo que da sed. || *Keep up the good work!*, ¡que sigan así! || *Let's get to work!*, ¡manos a la obra! || *Masonry work*, obra de mampostería. || "*Men at work*", "Obras". || *Ministry of Works*, Ministerio (*m.*) de Obras Públicas. || *Out of work*, parado, da; sin trabajo [*Amer.*, desocupado, da]. || *Piece of work*, trabajo. || "*Road Works*", "Obras". || *The forces at work*, las fuerzas que están en juego. || *To be at work*, estar trabajando. || FAM. *To give s.o. the works*, dar a uno una paliza, sacudir a uno el polvo (to beat), matar a uno (to murder). || *To make short work of sth.*, terminar algo rápidamente (to finish quickly), comerse algo rápidamente, zamparse algo (to eat quickly). || *To make work*, dar trabajo. || *To put s.o. out of work*, despedir a alguien. || *To set s.o. to work*, poner a alguien a trabajar. || *To set to work*, ponerse a trabajar. || FAM. *To shoot the works*, poner toda la carne en el asador. || *To throw s.o. out of work*, despedir a alguien. || *Work of reference*, libro (*m.*) de consulta. || *Works council*, jurado (*m.*) de empresa. || *Work sharing*, reparto (*m.*) del trabajo, distribución (*f.*) del trabajo. || *Work stoppage*, paro, *m.*

work [wəːk] v. tr. Hacer trabajar: *the company works us too hard*, la empresa nos hace trabajar demasiado. || Producir (a change). || Hacer (a miracle). || Dirigir, manejar (a business). || Tener a su cargo (to be in charge of). || Explotar: *to work a mine*, explotar una mina. || Tallar (stone). || Labrar (wood, metals). || Forjar (iron). || CULIN. Amasar (to knead). || Coser (to sew). || Resolver (an equation). || Manejar, hacer funcionar (a machine). || Accionar, poner en funcionamiento, hacer funcionar (a moving part). || Trabajar en: *he works the northern region*, trabaja en la región del norte. || Causar (ruin). || Realizar (a plan). || Poner en práctica (a theory, law). || Cultivar (land). || — *To be worked by electricity*, funcionar con electricidad (a machine, etc.). || *To work a cure*, curar. || FIG. FAM. *To work it*, arreglárselas: *he worked it so that he received five weeks' holidays*, se las arregló para tener cinco semanas de vacaciones. | *To work one's fingers to the bone*, trabajar como un mulo *or* como un negro. || *To work one's passage*, costear su viaje trabajando. || *To work one's way through*, abrirse paso por (an obstacle). || *To work one's way through college*, trabajar para costearse los estudios. || *To work one's way to*, abrirse camino hacia. || *To work one's way up*, subir poco a poco *or* a duras penas (to climb), ascender por su trabajo (in a company, etc.). || FIG. *To work o.s. to death*, matarse trabajando. | *To work to death*, matar trabajando (to overwork), abusar de (to use too often): *to work an expression to death*, abusar de una expresión.

— V. intr. Trabajar: *he worked quickly*, trabajó rápidamente; *she is too young to work*, es demasiado joven para trabajar. || Tener trabajo, tener un empleo (to be employed). || Funcionar (a machine): *it is not working* o *it won't work* o *it doesn't work*, no funciona; *the car works on electricity*, el coche funciona con electricidad. || Tener éxito, salir bien, tener resultados positivos: *your plan will not work*, su plan no saldrá bien. || Surtir *or* tener efecto: *a medicine which works immediately*, una medecina que tiene efecto en seguida. || Fermentar (to ferment). || Torcerse (facial features). || Moverse (one's hands). || Hundirse (to sink). || Obrar, ir: *it works against your plan*, esto va en contra de tu plan. || Obrar, proceder: *work with method*, procede con método. || Practicar mucho: *to work at one's piano playing*, practicar mucho el piano. || Trabajar: *she works in metal and wood*, trabaja metal y madera. || — FIG. *It works both ways*, es un arma de dos filos. || *To work for a living*, trabajar para vivir. || *To work free*, soltarse (to come loose), deshacerse (knot). || FIG. *To work like a Trojan*, trabajar como un negro. || *To work loose*, desatarse, aflojarse (knot, rope), desprenderse (part).

— ***To work at***, trabajar en. || ***To work away***, trabajar, seguir trabajando. || ***To work down***, bajar poco a poco. || ***To work in***, introducir: *to work in a few quotations*, introducir algunas citas. | Penetrar poco a poco. | Trabajar en. || ***To work into***, introducir en, meter en (to put in): *to work a piece of furniture into a narrow space*, meter un mueble en un espacio estrecho; *to work a reference into a speech*, introducir una referencia en un discurso. | — *To work o.s. into*, meterse en. | *To work o.s. into a rage*, montar poco a poco en cólera. || ***To work off***, quitarse (excess weight). | Desahogar (one's anger). | Desprenderse (part). | — *To work off one's feelings*, desahogarse. | FAM. *To work off steam*, desahogarse. || ***To work on***, seguir trabajando (to continue working). | Trabajar en: *I spent Sunday working on the shelves I am making*, pasé el domingo trabajando en la estantería que estoy haciendo. | Estudiar (document). | Investigar (a problem). | Intentar persuadir, intentar convencer: *I've been working on him for days*, llevo días y días intentando persuadirle. | Interrogar (to interrogate). | Basarse, fundarse (to base o.s. on): *I have very little information to work on*, tengo muy pocos datos en que basarme. | Afectar (to have an effect on). || ***To work out***, solucionar, resolver: *to work out a problem*, resolver un problema. | Encontrar: *to work out a solution*, encontrar una solución. | Elaborar: *to work out a plan*, elaborar un proyecto. | Salir: *my plans worked out perfectly*, mis planes salieron perfectamente. | Planificar (one's future). | Sacar con dificultad (to remove). | Agotar (a person). | MIN. Agotar. | Hacer: *to work out a sum*, hacer un cálculo. | Sumar (to add up). | Calcular: *work out how much it will cost*, calcula cuánto costará. | — *That works out at 10 pounds*, eso suma 10 libras, eso asciendo a 10 libras. | *Their plans did not work out*, sus proyectos fracasaron. | *This addition doesn't work out*, esta suma no me sale. || ***To work round***, cambiar de dirección. || ***To work through***, penetrar poco a poco. | Abrirse paso por (through the crowd). || ***To work up***, excitar: *to work s.o. up into a frenzy*, excitar a alguien hasta el frenesí. | Desarrollar (business). | — FAM. *To get worked up* o *to work o.s. up*, excitarse. | *To work up to*, preparar el terreno para: *he is working up to sth.*, está preparando el terreno para algo; tender a (to tend to). || ***To work upon***, see WORK ON.

workability [—əˈbiləti] n. Viabilidad, *f.*

workable [—əbl] adj. Que se puede trabajar: *a workable substance*, una sustancia que se puede trabajar. || Explotable: *workable land*, terreno explotable; *workable mine*, mina explotable. || Realizable, factible, viable: *a workable plan*, un proyecto factible. || FIG. Influenciable, manejable.

workaday [—ədei] adj. De cada día, de diario (clothes, etc.). || Laborable (week, etc.). || FIG. Ordinario, ria (commonplace).

workbag [—bæg] n. Bolsa (*f.*) de labores (for sewing materials). || Bolsa (*f.*) de las herramientas (for tools).

workbasket [—ˌbɑːskit] n. Costurero, *m.* (basket for sewing materials).

workbench [—bentʃ] n. Mesa (*f.*) *or* banco (*m.*) de trabajo.

workbook [—buk] n. Cuaderno, *m.* (exercise book). || Libro (*m.*) de texto. || Folleto (*m.*) de instrucciones (instruction manual). || Libro (*m.*) de trabajo (book of work done).

workbox [—bɔks] n. Costurero, *m.* (for sewing materials). || Caja (*f.*) de herramientas (for tools).

work camp [—kæmp] n. Campo (*m.*) de trabajo.

workday [—dei] n. Día (*m.*) laborable (day of work). || Jornada, *f.*: *an eight-hour workday*, una jornada de ocho horas.

— Adj. See WORKADAY.

worked-up [—tˈʌp] adj. FAM. Excitado, da.

worker [—ə*] n. Trabajador, ra (in general): *country workers*, trabajadores del campo. || Obrero, ra; operario, ria (industrial): *skilled worker*, obrero cualificado *or* especializado. || Autor, ra: *worker of miracles*, autor de milagros. || ZOOL. Obrera, *f.* (ant, bee). || — *He is a hard worker*, es muy trabajador. || FIG. *To be a fast worker*, no perder el tiempo. || *Workers of the world unite!*, trabajadores del mundo ¡unios!

worker ant [—əˈrænt] n. Hormiga (*f.*) obrera.

worker bee [—əbiː] n. Abeja (*f.*) obrera *or* neutra.

work force [—fɔːs] n. Mano (*f.*) de obra.

workhorse [—hɔːs] n. U. S. Caballo (*m.*) de tiro. || U. S. FIG. Fiera (*f.*) para el trabajo (hard worker).

workhouse [—haus] n. Asilo (*m.*) de pobres. || U. S. Reformatorio, *m.*, correccional, *m.*

working [—iŋ] adj. Obrero, ra: *the working class*, la clase obrera. || Laborable, de trabajo: *working day*, día laborable. || Activo, va: *the working population*, la población activa. || Que funciona (machine, etc.). || Básico, ca; suficiente: *a working knowledge*, un conocimiento básico. || Que sirve, válido, da (valuable). || Suficiente (majority). || De explotación (expenses). || De trabajo (clothes). || — *In working order*, en estado de funcionamiento. || *It is in working order*, funciona. || *Working asset*, activo (*m.*) realizable. || *Working capital*, fondo (*m.*) de operaciones. || *Working drawing*, plano (*m.*) de construcción. || MIN. *Working face*, frente (*m.*) de corte. || *Working hypothesis*, hipótesis (*f.*) de trabajo. || *Working language*, idioma (*m.*) de trabajo. || *Working paper*, documento (*m.*) de trabajo. || U. S. *Working papers*, permiso (*m.*) de trabajo para un menor de edad. || *Working party*, grupo (*m.*) de trabajo. || *Working speed*, velocidad (*f.*) de funcionamiento.

— N. Trabajo, *m.* (work). || Funcionamiento, *m.* (of a machine, one's mind). || Explotación, *f.* (of a mine). || Manejo, *m.* (act of operating sth.). || Labrado, *m.* (of metals). || Forja, *f.* (of iron). || Cultivo, *m.* (of fields). || Efecto, *m.* (of a medicine). || Fermentación, *f.*

(of beer, wine). || MAR. Maniobra, *f.* || — Pl. MIN. Excavaciones, *f.* (excavations).

working-class [—iŋklɑːs] adj. De la clase obrera.

workingman [—iŋ'mæn] n. Obrero, *m.*

— OBSERV. El plural de *workingman* es *workingmen.*

working out [—iŋ'aut] n. Resolución, *f.* (of a problem). || Elaboración, *f.* (of a plan). || MIN. Agotamiento, *m.* || FAM. Cálculo, *m.*

workless [—lis] adj./n. Parado, da [*Amer.*, desocupado, da].

workman [—mən] n. Trabajador, *m.* (worker). || Obrero, *m.* (manual, industrial). || Artesano, *m.* (craftsman). || FIG. *A bad workman always blames his tools* o *quarrels with his tools*, no hay que buscar pretextos para un trabajo mal hecho.

— OBSERV. El plural de *workman* es *workmen.*

workmanlike [—mənlaik] or **workmanly** [—mənli] adj. Concienzudo, da (person). || Bien hecho, cha (piece of work).

workmanship [—mənʃip] n. Habilidad, *f.*, destreza, *f.* (craft). || Arte, *f.*, artesanía, *f.* (fine skill). || Ejecución (*f.*) habilidosa. || Fabricación, *f.*, confección, *f.*

workmate [—meit] n. Compañero (*m.*) de trabajo.

workmen's compensation [—menz,kɔmpən'seiʃən] n. Indemnización (*f.*) por accidente *or* enfermedades del trabajo. || *Workmen's compensation insurance*, seguro social obrero.

workout [—aut] n. Prueba, *f.* (test). || SP. Entrenamiento, *m.*

workpeople [—,piːpl] pl. n. Obreros, *m.*

workroom [—rum] n. Taller, *m.*

workshop [—ʃɔp] n. Taller, *m.* (workroom). || ARTS. Estudio, *m.* || U. S. Seminario, *m.* (seminar).

work-shy [—ʃai] adj. Perezoso, sa.

worktable [—,teibl] n. Mesa (*f.*) de trabajo.

workwoman [—,wumən] n. Trabajadora, *f.* (worker). || Obrera, *f.* (manual, industrial). || Artesana, *f.* (craftswoman).

— OBSERV. El plural es *workwomen.*

world [wəːld] n. Mundo, *m.*, tierra, *f.*: *the longest river in the world*, el río más largo del mundo. || Universo, *m.* (universe). || Mundo, *m.*: *the Old World*, el Viejo Mundo; *half the world is starving*, la mitad del mundo está muriéndose de hambre; *the world of sport*, el mundo del deporte; *the world of dreams*, el mundo de los sueños; *the business world*, el mundo de los negocios; *the animal world*, el mundo de los animales; *the whole world loves me*, todo el mundo me quiere; *people from another world*, gente de otro mundo. || — *All the world over* o *all over the world*, en el mundo entero. || *Around the world in 80 days*, la vuelta al mundo en ochenta días. || FIG. *A world of difference between them*, una diferencia enorme entre ellos. | *Half the world*, medio mundo (people). | *He's not long for this world*, le queda poco. | *It's a small world*, el mundo es un pañuelo. | *It's out of this world*, es algo nunca visto. || *It's the same the world over*, en todas partes pasa lo mismo, en todas partes cuecen habas. || *I would give anything in the world to know...*, daría cualquier cosa por saber... || *I wouldn't do it for the world*, no lo haría por nada del mundo. || *Man of the world*, hombre de mundo. || *She is for all the world like...*, es exactamente como... || *The next* o *the other world*, el otro mundo, la otra vida. || *The world's worst painter*, el peor pintor del mundo. || FIG. *To be dead to the world*, estar durmiendo como un leño (asleep), estar borracho perdido (drunk). || *To bring into the world*, traer al mundo. | *To come down in the world*, venir a menos. || *To come into the world*, venir al mundo. || FIG. *To feel* o *to be on top of the world*, estar en el séptimo cielo, estar en la gloria (happy), sentirse muy bien (healthy). | *To go to a better world*, pasar a un mundo mejor *or* a mejor vida. || *To go up in the world*, medrar. || *To have the world at one's feet*, tener el mundo a sus pies. || *To know the world*, conocer el mundo. || FIG. *To make the best of both worlds*, unir lo divino a lo humano. || *To see the world*, ver mundo. || *To take the world as it is*, aceptar la vida como es. || FIG. *To the world*, completamente. | *To think the world of s.o.*, tener muy buena opinión *or* un alto concepto de alguien. | *What in the world are you doing?*, ¿qué demonios haces? || REL. *World without end*, por los siglos de los siglos. || FIG. *You are all the world to me*, eres todo para mí. | *You can't have the best of both worlds*, no se puede nadar y guardar la ropa.

— Adj. Mundial: *on a world scale*, a escala mundial; *World Bank*, Banco Mundial; *the First World War*, la primera guerra mundial. || Universal: *world history*, historia universal.

world-famous [—'feiməs] adj. Conocido mundialmente, de fama mundial.

wordliness [—linis] n. Mundanería, *f.*, mundanalidad, *f.* (devotion to worldly affairs).

worldling [—liŋ] n. Persona (*f.*) mundana.

worldly [—li] adj. Mundano, na (devoted to this life). || Del mundo, de este mundo. || Material: *wordly interests*, intereses materiales.

worldly-minded [—li'maindid] adj. Mundano, na.

worldly-wisdom [—li'wizdəm] n. Experiencia (*f.*) de la vida.

worldly-wise [—li'waiz] adj. Que tiene experiencia de la vida.

world map [—'mæp] n. Mapamundi, *m.*

world power [—'pauə*] n. Potencia (*f.*) mundial.

world series [—'siəriz] n. U. S. SP. Serie (*f.*) mundial.

world-weariness [—,wiərinis] n. Hastío (*m.*) del mundo, cansancio (*m.*) de la vida.

world-weary [—,wiəri] adj. Hastiado del mundo, cansado de la vida.

worldwide [—waid] adj. Mundial.

worm [wəːm] n. ZOOL. Gusano, *m.* | Lombriz, *f.* (earthworm). || TECH. Rosca, *f.*, filete, *m.* (thread of a screw). | Tornillo (*m.*) sin fin (endless screw). | Serpentín, *m.* (of a still). | Tubo (*m.*) espiral (spiral pipe). || FAM. Canalla, *m.*, granuja, *m.* (vile person). | Gusano, *m.* (insignificant person). || — Pl. MED. Lombrices, *f.* || — FIG. *The worm will turn*, la paciencia tiene un límite. | *Worm of conscience*, gusanillo (*m.*) de la conciencia.

worm [wəːm] v. tr. TECH. Roscar, filetear, aterrajar (a screw). || VET. Quitar las lombrices a. || MAR. Reforzar con cuerda (a cable). || FAM. Sonsacar, sacar: *to worm a secret out of s.o.*, sacar un secreto a alguien. || — FIG. *To worm one's way*, deslizarse: *he wormed his way through the trees*, se deslizó entre los árboles; colarse (to slip in). || *To worm one's way along*, arrastrarse como un gusano. || FIG. *To worm o.s. into*, insinuarse en.

worm drive [—draiv] n. Transmisión (*f.*) por medio de un tornillo sin fin.

worm-eaten [—,iːtn] adj. Carcomido, da (wood). || Apolillado, da (material). || Picado por los gusanos (fruit).

worm gear [—giə*] n. TECH. Engranaje (*m.*) de tornillo sin fin. | Rueda (*f.*) helicoidal (worm wheel).

wormhole [—həul] n. Agujero (*m.*) de lombriz (in earth). || Carcoma, *f.*, agujero (*m.*) de carcoma (in wood). || Picadura (*f.*) de polilla (in cloth).

worm wheel [—wiːl] n. TECH. Rueda (*f.*) helicoidal.

wormwood [—wud] n. BOT. Ajenjo, *m.* || FIG. Hiel, *f.*, amargura, *f.* (bitterness).

wormy [—i] adj. Agusanado, da (full of worms). || Carcomido, da (wood). || Apolillado, da (cloth).

worn [wɔːn] p. p. See WEAR.

worn-out [—'aut] adj. Muy estropeado, da; gastado, da: *worn-out shoes*, zapatos muy estropeados. || Agotado, da; rendido, da (exhausted). || FIG. Viejo, ja; anticuado, da (out of date).

worried ['wʌrid] adj. Preocupado, da: *a worried look*, una mirada preocupada; *to be worried about*, estar preocupado por.

worrier ['wʌriə*] n. Aprensivo, va.

worriment ['wʌrimənt] n. U. S. Preocupación, *f.*

worrisome ['wʌrisəm] adj. Preocupante, inquietante (causing worry). || Aprensivo, va (easily worried).

worry ['wʌri] n. Preocupación, *f.*, inquietud, *f.*: *the worry is killing me*, la inquietud me mata. || Preocupación, *f.*, problema, *m.*: *this child is a worry to me*, este niño es una preocupación para mí; *financial worries*, problemas financieros; *the worry of having to...*, la preocupación de tener que ... || — *That's the least of my worries*, eso es lo que menos me preocupa. || *To be beside o.s. with worry*, estar muy preocupado. || *What's his worry?*, ¿qué es lo que le preocupa?

worry ['wʌri] v. tr. Preocupar: *I am dreadfully worried*, estoy enormemente preocupado; *this problem worries me*, este problema me preocupa; *the event worried scholars for two hundred years*, el hecho preocupó a los eruditos durante doscientos años. || Molestar (to bother): *don't worry me, I'm working*, no me molestes, estoy trabajando; *the wound doesn't worry me when I walk*, la herida no me molesta cuando ando. || Atacar: *wolves worry the sheep*, los lobos atacan las ovejas. || — *Don't worry your head about me!*, ¡no te preocupes por mí! || *To worry o.s.*, preocuparse. || *To worry sth. out*, resolver algo [con dificultad].

— V. intr. Preocuparse (*about*, *over*, por): *he worries so much*, se preocupa tanto; *don't worry about me!*, ¡no te preocupes por mí! || Molestarse (to put o.s. out). || — FAM. *I should worry!*, ¿a mí qué me importa? || *To worry along*, arreglárselas.

worrying [—iŋ] adj. Inquietante, preocupante: *a worrying problem*, un problema inquietante.

— N. Preocupación, *f.*

worse [wəːs] adj. Peor: *worse weather than yesterday*, un tiempo peor que ayer; *he is worse than we feared*, es peor de lo que temíamos; *worse than ever*, peor que nunca. || — *It could have been worse*, podía haber sido peor. || *It gets worse and worse*, es cada vez peor. || *I was none the worse for it*, no por eso estaba peor. || *So much the worse for him*, tanto peor para él. || *To get* o *to grow worse*, empeorar. || *To go from bad to worse*, ir de mal en peor. || *To look the worse for wear*, see WEAR. || *To make things worse, he said...*, para empeorar las cosas, dijo... || *Worse and worse*, cada vez peor, de mal en peor. || *Worse luck*, [por] mala suerte. || FIG. *Worse things happen at sea*, más se perdió en Cuba.

— Adv. Peor: *I am playing worse than last season*, estoy jugando peor que la temporada pasada. || Más: *it hurts me worse*, me duele más. || — *To be worse off*, estar peor. || *Worse still*, peor aún.

— N. Lo peor: *worse was to come*, quedaba todavía lo peor. || — *He has been through worse*, las ha visto peores. || *I think none the worse of him*, no ha variado mi opinión sobre él. || *I have seen worse*, he visto cosas peores. || *To change for the worse*, empeorar.

— OBSERV. *Worse* es el comparativo de *bad* y *badly*.

worsen [—n] v. tr. Empeorar.
— V. intr. Empeorar, ponerse peor.

worsening [—niŋ] n. Agravación, *f.*, empeoramiento, *m.* (deterioration).

worship [ˈwəːʃip] n. Culto, *m.*: *the worship of idols*, el culto a los ídolos. || Culto, *m.*, oficio, *m.* (ceremony). || FIG. Adoración, *f.*, culto, *m.* || — *Freedom of worship*, libertad (*f.*) de cultos. || *His Worship the Mayor*, el señor alcalde. || *Your Worship*, su señoría, vuestra merced.

worship [ˈwəːʃip] v. tr. Venerar, rendir culto a (a god). || FIG. Adorar, idolatrar (to idolize).

— OBSERV. En Gran Bretaña la "p" se duplica en el gerundio (*worshipping*), en el pretérito y en el participio pasivo (*worshipped*), lo que no ocurre en Estados Unidos (*worshiping* y *worshiped*).

worshiper [—ə*] n. U. S. Adorador, ra.

worshipful [—ful] adj. Excelentísimo, ma (in titles). || Venerable (freemason). || Devoto, ta (adoring).

worshiping [—iŋ] n. U. S. See WORSHIPPING.

worshipper [—ə*] n. Adorador, ra.

worshipping [—iŋ] n. Culto: *the worshipping of a god*, el culto a un dios. || Adoración, *f.*, veneración, *f.* (adoration).

worst [wəːst] adj. Peor: *the worst book I know*, el peor libro que conozco; *my worst enemy*, mi peor enemigo; *the worst two*, los dos peores. || Más grave (most serious): *his worst mistake*, su falta más grave; *the worst victims of the accident*, las víctimas más graves del accidente.
— Adv. Peor: *the worst educated people*, la gente peor educada; *I ran worst of all*, yo corrí peor que todos; *the worst treated animals*, los animales peor tratados. || *To come off worst*, llevar la peor parte, salir vencido.
— N. El peor, la peor: *John is the worst*, Juan es el peor; *Mary is the worst in the school*, María es la peor de la escuela. || Lo peor: *the worst of the storm has passed*, ya ha pasado lo peor de la tormenta; *the worst of it is that ...*, lo peor del caso es que ... || Peor momento, *m.*: *when the epidemic was at its worst*, en el peor momento de la epidemia. || Inconveniente, *m.*, lo malo: *the worst of buying cheap clothes is that they don't last long*, el inconveniente *or* lo malo de comprar ropa barata es que dura poco. || — *At worst* o *at the worst*, en el peor de los casos. || *Do your worst*, haga lo que quiera. || *If the worst comes to the worst*, en el peor de los casos. || *The weather is at its worst*, el tiempo está peor que nunca. || *To assume the worst*, imaginar lo peor. || *To get the worst of it*, llevar la peor parte, salir vencido. || *To give s.o. the worst of it*, hacerle pasar un mal rato a alguien. || *When things are at their worst*, cuando todo va muy mal.

— OBSERV. *Worst* es el superlativo de *bad* y *badly*.

worst [wəːst] v. tr. Derrotar, vencer, superar.

worsted [ˈwustid] n. Estambre, *m.* (fabric).

wort [wəːt] n. Mosto, *m.* (of beer).

worth [wəːθ] prep. Digno de, merecedor de: *it is not worth attention*, no es digno de atención. || Que vale, equivalente a: *it is not worth more than three pounds*, no vale más de tres libras. || — *For all one is worth*, con todas sus fuerzas: *to swim for all one is worth*, nadar con todas sus fuerzas. || *For what it is worth*, por si puede servir, por si sirve de algo: *I can give you his description for what it is worth*, le puedo dar su descripción por si puede servirle. || *Friendship is sth. worth keeping*, la amistad es algo que vale la pena conservar. || *He is worth first prize*, merece el primer premio. || FAM. *He is worth millions*, es multimillonario, tiene un dineral. || *He is worth three men*, vale por tres hombres. || *His offer is worth considering*, su oferta es digna de consideración, su oferta merece ser considerada, su oferta es digna de ser considerada. || *I have a company car, which is worth two hundred pounds a year to me*, tengo un coche de la compañía, lo cual me ahorra doscientas libras al año. || *Is it worth my going?*, ¿vale la pena que vaya? || *It is not worth it*, no vale *or* no merece la pena. || *It is not worth much*, no vale gran cosa. || *It is worth doing*, vale *or* merece la pena hacerlo. || *It is worth mentioning*, es digno de mencionarse. || *Property worth a million pounds*, propiedad que vale un millón de libras. || *This book is worth reading*, vale *or* merece la pena leer este libro, este libro es digno de leerse. || *To be worth*, valer: *this car is worth a thousand pounds*, este coche vale mil libras; ser digno de, merecer (to merit), valer la pena: *it is worth trying*, vale la pena intentarlo.
— N. Valor, *m.*: *a house of no worth*, una casa sin valor; *her poetry is of little worth compared with her novels*, su poesía tiene poco valor comparada con sus novelas. || Mérito, *m.*: *a man of great worth*, un hombre de gran mérito. || Valía, *f.*, valor, *m.*: *her true worth was not appreciated until after her death*, no se apreció su verdadera valía hasta después de su muerte. || Fortuna, *f.* (fortune): *his true worth must be millions of dollars*, su verdadera fortuna debe ascender a millones de dólares. || — *A hundred pounds' worth of clothes*, ropa por valor de cien libras. || *It's an expensive place, but you get your money's worth*, es un sitio caro pero vale realmente lo que cuesta. || *I've really had my money's worth out of these shoes*, me han dado muy buen resultado estos zapatos. || *Moral worth*, cualidades (*f. pl.*) morales, valor moral. || *Of great worth*, de gran valor. || *Of little worth*, de poco valor. || *She knows where to shop to get her money's worth*, sabe donde comprar para sacarle jugo al dinero. || *Two shillings' worth of sweets*, dos chelines de caramelos.

worth [wəːθ] v. tr. (Ant.). Ser: *woe worth the day*, maldito sea el día.

worthily [ˈwəːðili] adv. Dignamente.

worthiness [ˈwəːðinis] n. Mérito, *m.*

worthless [ˈwəːθlis] adj. Sin valor (of no value). || Inútil (useless). || Despreciable (despicable). || — *To be quite worthless*, no tener ningún valor, no valer nada. || *To make sth. worthless*, quitarle todo valor a algo.

worthlessness [—nis] n. Falta (*f.*) de valor (lack of value). || Inutilidad, *f.* (uselessness). || Vileza, *f.* (lowness).

worthwhile [ˈwəːθwail] adj. Que vale la pena: *it was a worthwhile trip*, fue un viaje que valió la pena. || Útil: *a worthwhile experience*, una experiencia útil. || Digno de consideración (worth considering). || — *I never worry, it's not worthwhile*, no me preocupo nunca, no vale la pena. || *It's not worthwhile waiting*, no vale *or* no merece la pena esperar. || *To make it worthwhile*, para que valga la pena.

worthy [ˈwəːði] adj. Noble, justo, ta: *a worthy cause*, una causa noble. || Respetable (respectable). || Digno, na (dignified): *worthy conduct*, conducta digna. || Estimable (esteemed). || Justo, ta (just): *a worthy reward*, una recompensa justa. || Valioso, sa (good): *my worthy assistant*, mi valioso asistente. || Meritorio, ria: *a worthy action*, una acción meritoria. || Honesto, ta (motives, etc.). || — *It is worthy of note that*, es digno de observar que, hay que señalar que. || *Other authors worthy of note*, otros autores que merece la pena mencionar. || *To be worthy of*, ser digno de, merecer: *his crime is worthy of punishment*, su crimen merece castigo. || *Worthy of*, digno de: *an opponent worthy of him*, un adversario digno de él; digno de, merecedor de: *an action worthy of reward*, una acción digna de recompensa.
— N. Notabilidad, *f.*, prócer, *m.*

would [wud] v. aux. Se emplea para formar el potencial [2ª y 3ª persona del singular y del plural]: *she would go if she could*, iría si pudiese; *they said that they would go*, me dijeron que irían. || Indica la probabilidad: *she would be about 50*, debía de tener unos cincuenta años, tendría unos cincuenta años. || Expresa la duda: *that would appear to be the solution*, eso parece ser la solución; *I would think so*, supongo que sí. || Indica la voluntad: *would you get me my hat?*, ¿quieres traerme el sombrero? || Soler, acostumbrar (habit): *they would go for a walk before breakfast*, solían dar un paseo antes del desayuno. || — *It would be you!*, ¡tú tenías que ser! || *Of course it would rain!*, ¡naturalmente tenía *or* tuvo que llover! || *That's just what you would do*, ¡eso es muy tuyo! || *What would this be?*, ¿qué será eso?

— OBSERV. *Would* puede contraerse cuando le antecede un pronombre personal (*I'd, you'd, he'd, we'd, they'd*). Si va seguido por la negación *not* puede formar con ella la palabra *wouldn't* (*he wouldn't come; wouldn't they come?*)
— *Would* es el pretérito y el potencial de *will*, por lo tanto está tratado en gran parte en el artículo *will* (See WILL).
— Después de "*I wish*" y de "*if*" el verbo introducido por *would* tiene que ponerse en imperfecto de subjuntivo en español (*I wish you would shut up*, me gustaría que te callaras, ¡ojalá te callaras!; *if you would shut up, I would be able to hear*, si tú te callaras, yo podría oír).
— En la primera persona del potencial *would* sustituye a veces a *should* (*I would have arrived earlier if ...*)

would-be [—biː] adj. Supuesto, ta (supposed, so-called): *a would-be painter*, un supuesto pintor. || *The would-be candidates*, los aspirantes a la candidatura.

wouldn't [—nt] contraction of *would not*.

wound [wuːnd] n. Herida, *f.*: *skin wound*, herida superficial. || FIG. Herida, *f.* (emotional hurt). || — REL. *The five wounds of Christ*, las cinco llagas de Cristo. || FIG. *To open up an old wound*, renovar la herida. | *To rub salt in the wound*, hurgar en la herida, herir en carne viva.

wound [wuːnd] v. tr./intr. Herir: *he was slightly wounded*, fue levemente herido; *the remark wounded her deeply*, la observación le hirió profundamente; *to wound to the quick*, herir en lo vivo.

wound [waund] pret & p. p. See WIND.

wounded [ˈwuːndid] adj. Herido, da: *a wounded soldier*, un soldado herido. || *A wounded man*, un herido, un hombre herido.
— Pl. n. Heridos, *m.*: *the wounded*, los heridos.

wounding [ˈwuːndiŋ] adj. Hiriente.

wove [wəuv] pret. See WEAVE.

woven [—ən] p. p. See WEAVE.

wove paper [—ˌpeipə*] n. Papel (*m.*) vitela.

wow [wau] n. FAM. *It was a wow!*, ¡fue estupendo!, ¡fue formidable!
wrack [ræk] n. Varec, *m.* (seaweed). || Ruina, *f.* (ruin). || *To go to wrack and ruin*, venirse abajo.
wrack [ræk] v. tr. Destruir (to destroy). || See RACK.
wraith [reiθ] n. Espectro, *m.*, fantasma, *m.*
wrangle [ˈræŋgl] n. Disputa, *f.*, riña, *f.*, altercado, *m.* (quarrel).
wrangle [ˈræŋgl] v. tr. U. S. Rodear (to round up cattle).
— V. intr. Discutir (to argue). || Reñir, pelearse (to quarrel). || Regatear (to haggle).
wrangler [—ə*] n. FAM. Pendenciero, ra; camorrista, *m.* & *f.* (quarreller). || U. S. Vaquero, *m.*
wrap [ræp] n. Chal, *m.* (shawl). || Manta, *f.* [*Amer.*, frazada, *f.*] (blanket). || Capa, *f.* (short cape). || Bata, *f.* (dressing gown). || Envoltura, *f.* (wrapping). || — Pl. FIG. Secreto, *m. sing.* (secrecy). || FIG. *To take the wraps off sth.*, revelar algo (to reveal).
wrap [ræp] v. tr. Envolver: *he came in wrapped in a blanket*, entró envuelto en una manta; *an affair wrapped in mystery*, un asunto envuelto en el misterio. || Cubrir, envolver: *a mountain wrapped in mist*, una montaña cubierta de *or* envuelta en niebla. || Absorber: *wrapped in thought*, absorto en sus pensamientos. || — *He wrapped a scarf round his neck*, se puso una bufanda. || *To be wrapped up in*, estar envuelto en (paper, blanket, etc.), estar absorto en (to be absorbed in), dedicarse completamente a (to dedicate o.s. to). || *To wrap o.s.*, envolverse. || *To wrap up*, envolver: *he wrapped her up in her coat*, la envolvió en su abrigo; *shall I wrap it up for you?*, ¿se lo envuelvo?; abrigar: *I always wrap up the children well*, siempre abrigo bien a los niños; cubrir (to cover), concluir (a deal), resolver, terminar con (a case, a problem).
— V. intr. Enrollarse: *climbing plants wrap round trees*, las plantas trepadoras se enrollan en los árboles. || — *To wrap up*, abrigarse: *wrap up well, it's cold today*, abrígate bien, hace frío hoy. || FAM. *Wrap up!*, ¡cierra el pico!
wrappage [ˈræpidʒ] n. Envoltura, *f.*
wrapper [ˈræpə*] n. Envoltura, *f.* (wrapping). || Embalador, ra; empaquetador, ra (person). || Sobrecubierta, *f.* (jacket of a book). || Bata, *f.* (dressing gown). || Faja, *f.* (for posting newspapers, etc.). || Capa, *f.* (tobacco leaf round a cigar).
wrapping [ˈræpiŋ] n. Embalaje, *m.* (action). || Envoltura, *f.* (covering, material used). || *Wrapping paper*, papel (*m.*) de envolver.
wrasse [ræs] n. ZOOL. Budión, *m.* (fish).
wrath [rɔθ] n. Ira, *f.*: *the grapes of wrath*, las uvas de la ira. || FIG. Furia, *f.* (of the elements).
wrathful [—ful] adj. Colérico, ca; airado, da; iracundo, da.
wreak [ri:k] v. tr. Descargar (anger). || Sembrar (destruction). || Tomar (vengeance). || Infligir (punishment). || Gastar (to expend, to spend). || *To wreak havoc*, hacer estragos.
wreath [ri:θ] n. Guirnalda, *f.*, corona, *f.* (circle of flowers). || Corona, *f.* (for a funeral). || Espiral, *f.* (of smoke).
wreathe [ri:ð] v. tr. Trenzar, hacer una guirnalda de: *to wreathe flowers*, trenzar flores, hacer una guirnalda de flores. || Enguirnaldar (to garland). || Enroscar (to wind): *the snake wreathed itself round the tree*, la serpiente se enroscó en el árbol. || Enrollar: *he wreathed the rope round the stick*, enrolló la cuerda en el palo. || Coronar (to cap, to crown). || Cubrir (to cover). || Envolver (to wrap). || Coronar, ceñir (to crown with a wreath). || *A face wreathed in smiles*, una cara muy risueña.
— V. intr. Subir en espirales (smoke). || Serpentear (to wind, to twist).
wreck [rek] n. MAR. Naufragio, *m.* (shipwreck). | Barco (*m.*) hundido *or* naufragado (wrecked ship). || Restos, *m. pl.* (remains of car, train, aeroplane). || Colisión, *f.*, accidente, *m.* (accident). || Escombros, *m. pl.* (of a building). || FIG. Ruina, *f.* (person): *a human wreck*, una ruina humana; *to be a wreck*, estar hecho una ruina. | Hundimiento, *m.* (of a business). | Fin, *m.* (of hopes). || — *The plane was a complete wreck*, el avión estaba completamente destrozado. || FIG. *To be a nervous wreck*, tener los nervios destrozados. | *To look a wreck*, estar hecho una pena. || MAR. *To suffer wreck*, naufragar.
wreck [rek] v. tr. Hacer naufragar, hundir, echar a pique (a ship). || Hacer descarrilar (a train). || Destruir (a building). || Destrozar (a car, plane, etc.): *the vandals wrecked the premises*, los gamberros destrozaron el local. || Estropear (a machine). || FIG. Destrozar, estropear, acabar con: *drugs wrecked his health*, las drogas le destrozaron la salud. | Estropear, arruinar, desbaratar, destruir: *he wrecked their plans*, estropeó sus planes. | Destrozar (one's life). | Destrozar (the nerves). || MAR. *To be wrecked*, naufragar.
— V. intr. Naufragar, hundirse, irse a pique (a ship). || Destrozarse. || Estropearse.
wreckage [ˈrekidʒ] n. Restos, *m. pl.* (of a car, aeroplane). || Escombros, *m. pl.* (of a building). || MAR. Pecios, *m. pl.*, pecio, *m.*, restos (*m. pl.*) de un naufragio.
wrecked [ˈrekt] adj. Naufragado, da (ship). || Náufrago, ga (person). || Destrozado, da (car, aeroplane, life). || Destruido, da (building).
wrecker [ˈrekə*] n. Provocador (*m.*) de naufragios (person who causes shipwrecks). || Raquero, *m.* (plunderer). || Persona (*f.*) encargada de recoger los restos de un naufragio (person who recovers wrecked ships). || U. S. Demoledor (*m.*) de casas (housebreaker). | Grúa, *f.*, camión (*m.*) grúa (breakdown lorry). || Gamberro, *m.* (hooligan).
wrecking [ˈrekiŋ] n. Destrucción, *f.* || Demolición, *f.* (of buildings). || Descarrilamiento, *m.* (of a train). || Pérdida, *f.* (of hopes). || U. S. Salvamento, *m.* (salvaging of ships).
wrecking service [—ˌsə:vis] n. U. S. AUT. Servicio (*m.*) de auxilio en carretera.
wren [ren] n. Reyezuelo, *m.* (bird).
wrench [rentʃ] n. Tirón, *m.* (a sharp pull). || MED. Torcedura, *f.* || TECH. Llave (*f.*) inglesa (adjustable spanner). || FIG. Dolor, *m.*, pena, *f.*: *the wrench of separation*, el dolor de la separación. || — TECH. *Elbowed wrench*, llave de pipa para tuercas. || *To give one's ankle a wrench*, torcerse el tobillo. || *To give sth. a wrench*, torcer algo violentamente.
wrench [rentʃ] v. tr. Torcer: *to wrench s.o.'s arm*, torcerle el brazo a alguien. || FIG. Torcer, desvirtuar (a meaning, statement). || — *To wrench a handle off a door*, arrancar el picaporte de una puerta. || *To wrench one's ankle*, torcerse el tobillo. || *To wrench out*, arrancar. || *To wrench sth. from s.o.*, arrancarle algo a alguien. || *To wrench sth. open*, abrir algo de un tirón, abrir algo violentamente.
wrest [rest] n. MUS. Llave (*f.*) para afinar (for tuning).
wrest [rest] v. tr. Arrebatar: *he wrested the bag from the woman*, arrebató el bolso a la mujer; *Real Madrid wrested the championship from Barcelona*, el Real Madrid le arrebató el campeonato al Barcelona. || FIG. Alterar, desvirtuar (to twist): *to wrest the truth*, alterar la verdad. | Dar una falsa interpretación a (a law, etc.). | Arrancar (a confession). || *To wrest o.s. free*, soltarse.
wrestle [resl] n. Lucha, *f.* || *To have a wrestle with*, luchar con.
wrestle [ˈresl] v. tr. Luchar con *or* contra: *to wrestle s.o.*, luchar con *or* contra alguien. || U. S. Derribar (a calf for branding).
— V. intr. Luchar: *the two men wrestled for the championship*, los dos hombres lucharon por el campeonato. || *To wrestle with*, luchar con *or* contra: *to wrestle with adversity*, luchar contra la adversidad; *to wrestle with s.o.*, luchar con alguien.
wrestler [—ə*] n. Luchador, ra.
wrestling [—iŋ] n. SP. Lucha, *f.*: *freestyle wrestling*, lucha libre; *wrestling match*, combate de lucha.
wrest pin [ˈrestpin] n. Clavija, *f.* (in a piano).
wrest plank [ˈrestplæŋk] n. MUS. Clavijero, *m.*
wretch [retʃ] n. Desgraciado, da (unfortunate person): *poor wretch*, pobre desgraciado. || Miserable, *m.* & *f.*, malvado, da (wicked person). || — *Little wretch*, pillo, lla (little rascal). || *Poor little wretch*, probrecito, ta. || *You wretch!*, ¡desgraciado!
wretched [ˈretʃid] adj. Desgraciado, da; desdichado, da (unfortunate, unhappy). || Espantoso, sa; horrible (horrible): *wretched weather*, tiempo horrible. || Miserable (miserable): *to live in wretched conditions*, vivir en condiciones miserables; *a wretched hovel*, una casucha miserable. || Despreciable, miserable (contemptible). || Lamentable (pitiful). || Malísimo, ma (very bad). || Maldito, ta: *this wretched zip is stuck*, esta maldita cremallera no se cierra. || — *To feel wretched*. estar muy abatido (depressed), estar muy mal (ill). || *To feel wretched about doing sth.*, sentir remordimientos por haber hecho algo. || *What wretched luck!*, ¡qué mala suerte! || *You see some wretched driving these days*, hay que ver lo mal que conduce la gente hoy.
wretchedness [—nis] n. Tristeza, *f.* (sadness). || Desgracia, *f.*, desdicha, *f.* (ill fortune). || Miseria, *f.* (misery, poverty). || Abatimiento, *m.* (depression). || Lo despreciable, vileza, *f.* || *The wretchedness of the weather*, el tiempo horrible.
wriggle [ˈrigl] n. Serpenteo, *m.*, culebreo, *m.* (snakelike movement). || Meneo, *m.*, contoneo, *m.* (of hips).
wriggle [ˈrigl] v. tr. Mover, menear: *to wriggle one's hand*, mover la mano. || — *To wriggle one's way along*, ir serpenteando. || *To wriggle one's way through*, deslizarse entre *or* por. || *To wriggle o.s. free*, lograr soltarse. || *To wriggle o.s. into*, introducirse con dificultad en, deslizarse en.
— V. intr. Agitarse, menearse: *the worm wriggled on the hook*, el gusano se agitaba en el anzuelo. || Colear (fish). || Moverse (people). || — *To wriggle along*, serpentear, ir serpenteando, deslizarse. | *To wriggle into*, introducirse con dificultad en. || *To wriggle out*, escaparse mañosamente, librarse hábilmente (of a difficulty), salir con dificultad (from a hole, etc.), escaparse de: *the worm wriggled out of my hand*, el gusano se escapó de mi mano. || *To wriggle through*, deslizarse entre *or* por.
wriggly [—i] adj. Sinuoso, sa.
wring [riŋ] n. Apretón, *m.* (of hands). || Torsión, *f.* || *To give the clothes a wring*, escurrir la ropa.
wring* [riŋ] v. tr. Retorcer, escurrir (wet clothes). || Retorcer: *to wring a chicken's neck*, retorcer el pescuezo de un pollo. || FIG. Partir, oprimir (heart). || — FAM. *I'll wring his neck!*, ¡le retorceré el pescuezo!

|| *To wring one's hands*, retorcerse las manos. || *To wring out*, escurrir: *to wring water out of clothes*, escurrir el agua de la ropa; retorcer, escurrir: *to wring clothes out*, retorcer la ropa; arrancar (truth, confession), sacar (money from s.o.). || *To wring s.o.'s hand*, dar un apretón de manos a alguien.
— OBSERV. Pret. & p. p. ***wrung.***

wringer [—ə*] n. Escurridor, *m.* (machine).

wringing [—iŋ] or **wringing wet** [—iŋ'wet] adj. Chorreando, completamente mojado, da (clothes). || Calado hasta los huesos (person).

wrinkle ['riŋkl] n. Arruga, *f.* (of skin). || Rizo, *m.* (on water). || Arruga, *f.* (in cloth, etc.). || GEOL. Pliegue, *m.* || FAM. Truco, *m.*, idea, *f.* (clever hint or suggestion).

wrinkle ['riŋkl] v. tr. Arrugar, chafar (clothes). || Arrugar (skin). || *To wrinkle one's brow*, fruncir el ceño *or* el entrecejo.
— V. intr. Arrugarse (dress, skin). || Rizarse (water).

wrinkled [—d] or **wrinkly** [—i] adj. Arrugado, da.

wrinkling [—iŋ] n. Arrugamiento, *m.*

wrist [rist] n. ANAT. Muñeca, *f.* (of a person). || Codillo, *m.* (of an animal). || Puño, *m.* (of a garment). || TECH. Pasador (*m.*) del émbolo.

wristband [—bænd] n. Puño, *m.* (of a shirt). || Muñequera, *f.* (for gymnasts, etc.).

wristlet [—lit] n. Muñequera, *f.* || — Pl. FAM. Esposas, *f.* (handcuffs).

wristlet watch [—litwɔtʃ] n. Reloj (*m.*) de pulsera.

wristlock [—lɔk] n. SP. Llave (*f.*) de muñeca.

wrist pin [—pin] n. TECH. Pasador (*m.*) del émbolo.

wristwatch [—wɔtʃ] n. Reloj (*m.*) de pulsera.

writ [rit] n. REL. Escritura, *f.*: *the Holy Writ*, la Sagrada Escritura. || JUR. Orden, *f.*, mandato, *m.*, mandamiento, *m.*, auto, *m.* || — *To draw up a writ*, extender un mandato judicial. || *To serve a writ on* o *against*, notificar un mandato judicial a. || *To issue s.o. a writ*, demandar a alguien en juicio, emplazar a alguien ante el juez. || *Writ of attachment*, mandato de embargo. || *Writ of execution*, ejecutoria, *f.* || *Writ of summons*, emplazamiento, *m.*

write* [rait] v. tr. Escribir: *to write a letter*, escribir una carta; *write your name here*, escriba aquí su nombre; *proper names are written with capital letters*, los nombres propios se escriben con mayúscula; *to write in ink*, escribir con tinta. || Redactar, escribir (a dictionary, a book). || Componer, escribir (music). || Hacer, extender (a cheque). || Rellenar, llenar (a form). || JUR. Redactar (to draw up in legal form). | Suscribir (to underwrite). || — FIG. *Despair was written on every face*, la desesperación estaba impresa *or* se reflejaba en todos los rostros. | *Hatred was written all over him*, llevaba el odio escrito en la cara. | *He had phoney written all over him*, todo indicaba que era un farsante. | *Innocence is written on his face*, se puede ver la inocencia en su rostro, la inocencia está impresa en su rostro. | *Nothing to write home about*, nada del otro mundo. || *To write a good hand*, tener buena letra. || *To write o.s.*, titularse, calificarse.
— V. intr. Escribir: *to write legibly*, escribir legiblemente. || Escribir (to be a writer). || Escribirse (to each other): *we've been writing for years*, nos escribimos desde hace años. || — *He wrote for me to send it*, me pidió por carta que se lo mandase. || *I have written for information*, he escrito pidiendo informaciones. || *I wrote to them to come*, les escribí para que viniesen.
— **To write back,** contestar [carta]. || **To write down,** apuntar, anotar: *they wrote down everything he said*, apuntaron todo lo que dijo. | Poner por escrito (to put in writing). | Rebajar (stocks, goods, etc.). | Considerar (to regard). || **To write in,** escribir: *thousands of people wrote in to complain*, miles de personas escribieron quejándose. | Insertar (to insert). | — *To write in for*, solicitar por escrito. || **To write off,** escribir rápidamente (to compose rapidly). | Cancelar, dar por perdido: *to write off a debt*, cancelar una deuda. | Amortizar (capital). | Solicitar por escrito: *to write off for a catalogue*, solicitar un catálogo por escrito. | Destrozar: *to write off a car*, destrozar un coche. || **To write out,** escribir. | Copiar (to copy). | Transcribir (to transcribe). | Pasar a limpio (to make a fair copy of). | Escribir con todas las letras (to write in full). | Hacer, extender (a cheque). | — *To write o.s. out*, estar acabado (a writer). || **To write up,** hacer un reportaje sobre, escribir un artículo sobre (in a newspaper). | Poner por escrito (to put in writing). | Redactar (a report, notes). | Exagerar, hinchar (to exaggerate). | Poner al día (diary, etc.). | Sobrestimar (assets).
— OBSERV. Pret. ***wrote;*** p. p. ***written.***

write-off [—ɔf] n. Cancelación, *f.* || Amortización, *f.* (of capital).

writer [—ə*] n. Escritor, ra (s.o. who writes). || Autor, ra (author). || Escribano, *m.* (clerk). || — *The present writer*, el que esto escribe, el abajo firmante. *To be a poor writer*, escribir mal.

write-up [—ʌp] n. Crítica, *f.* (of a film, play, etc.). || Relato, *m.* (of an event). || Crónica (*f.*) elogiosa (flattering report). || Valoración (*f.*) excesiva (in the assets).

writhe [raið] n. Retorcimiento, *m.*

writhe [raið] v. intr. Retorcerse: *I writhe with* o *in pain*, me retuerzo de dolor. || Angustiarse (to suffer anguish). || — *I made him writhe*, le torturé, le atormenté. || *Their attitude made him writhe with anger*, su actitud le puso furioso.

writing [raitiŋ] n. El escribir (act of s.o. who writes). || Escritura, *f.*, letra, *f.* (handwriting). || Escrito, *m.* (sth. written): *to put sth. in writing*, poner algo por escrito. || Profesión (*f.*) de escritor (occupation of an author). || Obra, *f.*: *the writings of Borges*, las obras de Borges. || Redacción, *f.*, estilo, *m.* (style). || — *At the time of writing*, en el momento en que escribo estas líneas. || *In one's own writing*, de su puño y letra. || FIG. *The writing on the wall*, un aviso del cielo. || *Writing case* o *set*, estuche (*m.*) de papel de escribir. || *Writing desk*, escritorio, *m.* || COMM. *Writing off*, amortización, *f.* (of capital). || *Writing pad*, bloc (*m.*) de papel de escribir. || *Writing paper*, papel (*m.*) de escribir. || *You are very bad about writing*, te gusta muy poco escribir.

written [ritn] p. p. See WRITE.
— Adj. Escrito, ta. || *Written accent*, acento ortográfico.

wrong [rɔŋ] adj. Malo, la (not morally right). || Mal (not right): *it is wrong to lie*, está mal mentir; *that is very wrong of you*, has hecho muy mal. || Erróneo, a; equivocado, da: *wrong answer*, respuesta equivocada. || Equivocado, da: *you are wrong in thinking him intelligent*, estás equivocado si le crees inteligente. || Inoportuno, na; impropio, pia: *they chose the wrong time to drop in*, escogieron el momento inoportuno para venir. || Falso, sa; equivocado, da; erróneo, a: *wrong ideas*, ideas falsas. || MUS. Falso, sa: *wrong note*, nota falsa. || — *At the wrong time*, en un mal momento, en un momento poco oportuno. || *I hope there is nothing wrong*, espero que no pasa nada. || *In the wrong sense*, en sentido equivocado. || *Is anything wrong?*, ¿pasa algo? || *I was in the wrong plane*, me equivoqué de avión. || *Not to be far wrong*, no equivocarse en mucho, no ir muy descaminado. || SP. *On the wrong foot*, a contrapié. || *Something is wrong*, hay algo que no está bien. || *Sorry, wrong number*, lo siento, se ha equivocado de número (on the telephone). || *That is wrong*, eso no es cierto. || *There is sth. wrong with me*, no me encuentro bien. || *There is sth. wrong with my lighter*, le pasa algo a mi encendedor, mi encendedor está estropeado. || *The wrong side of a material*, el revés de una tela. || *Things are all wrong o everything is wrong*, todo está mal. || *Things are going the wrong way*, las cosas marchan mal. || *To be in the wrong place*, estar mal colocado. || FIG. *To be in the wrong road*, ir por mal camino. | *To be on the wrong side of forty*, tener cuarenta años bien cumplidos, tener más de cuarenta años. || *To be wrong*, tener la culpa (to be blameworthy), no tener razón (to maintain sth. false), equivocarse, estar equivocado (to be mistaken), hacer mal en, no deber: *he is wrong to laugh*, hace mal en reírse; *you were wrong to tell him the truth*, hiciste mal en decirle la verdad; estar mal (thing), andar mal (a watch). || *To brush a hat the wrong way*, cepillar un sombrero a contrapelo. || *To buy the wrong clothes*, comprar ropa que no le sienta bien a uno. || *To do the wrong thing*, hacer lo que no se debe. || *To drive on the wrong side of the road*, rodar por el lado de la carretera que está prohibido. || *To get on the wrong side of s.o.*, ponerse a malas con uno. || FIG. *To get out of bed on the wrong side*, levantarse con el pie izquierdo. || *To go to the wrong place*, equivocarse de sitio. || *To make a wrong choice*, equivocarse al escoger, escoger mal. || *To say the wrong thing*, decir lo que no se debe. || *To swallow the wrong way*, atragantarse. || *To take a word in the wrong sense*, coger una palabra en mal sentido. || *To take the wrong road*, equivocarse de carretera. || *What's wrong with going dancing?*, ¿qué tiene de malo ir a bailar? || *What's wrong with you?*, ¿qué te pasa? || *Wrong side foremost*, al revés. || *Wrong side out*, al revés. || *Wrong side up*, al revés. || *What's wrong in drinking?*, ¿qué tiene de malo beber?
— N. Mal, *m.*: *the difference between right and wrong*, la diferencia entre el bien y el mal. || Error, *m.*: *to acknowledge one's wrongs*, reconocer sus errores. || Injusticia, *f.* (act of injustice): *the wrongs that I have suffered*, las injusticias que he sufrido. || JUR. Daño, *m.*, perjuicio, *m.* || — *To be in the wrong*, estar equivocado, da (to be mistaken), no tener razón (to maintain sth. false), ser culpable, tener la culpa (to be morally responsible for sth.). || *To do s.o. wrong* o *to do wrong to s.o.*, ser injusto con alguien (to treat unjustly), perjudicar a alguien. || *To do wrong*, hacer mal. || *To put s.o. in the wrong*, echarle la culpa a alguien. || *To right a wrong*, enderezar un entuerto.
— Adv. Mal: *to answer wrong*, responder mal. || Injustamente (unjustly). || Incorrectamente (incorrectly). || — *To get it wrong*, comprender mal (to misunderstand). || *To get s.o. wrong*, juzgar equivocadamente a alguien. || *To go wrong*, equivocarse de dirección (to take the wrong direction), perderse, extraviarse (to loose one's way), darse a la mala vida, descarriarse (to start on a course of wrongdoing), equivocarse (to make a mistake), romperse, estropearse (to break down), fallar, fracasar (plans), ir mal (business).

wrong [rɔŋ] v. tr. Ser injusto con (to treat unjustly). || Perjudicar, agraviar (to damage). || Seducir (to seduce).

wrongdoer ['rɔŋ'duə*] n. Delincuente, *m.* & *f.* malhechor, ra.

wrongdoing [ˈrɔŋˈduiŋ] n. Mal, *m.* (wrong). || Maldad, *f.* (evil). || Pecado, *m.* (sin). || JUR. Infracción, *f.*, delito, *m.*
wrongful [ˈrɔŋful] adj. Injusto, ta (not just). || Ilegal (not lawful).
wrongfulness [—nis] n. Injusticia, *f.* (injustice). || Ilegalidad, *f.* (illegality).
wrongheaded [ˈrɔŋˈhedid] adj. Obstinado, da; testarudo, da; terco, ca.
wrongheadedness [—nis] n. Obstinación, *f.*, testarudez, *f.*, terquedad, *f.*
wrongly [ˈrɔŋli] adv. Mal. || Injustamente. || Equivocadamente, erróneamente. || Sin razón. || *Rightly or wrongly*, con razón o sin ella.
wrongness [ˈrɔŋnis] n. Error, *m.*, equivocación, *f.* || Inexactitud, *f.* || Injusticia, *f.* || Inoportunidad, *f.* || Maldad, *f.*
wrote [rəut] pret. See WRITE.
wroth [rəuθ] adj. Airado, da.
wrought [rɔ:t] pret. & p. p. (Ant.). See WORK.
— Adj. Trabajado, da (worked). || Labrado, da (metal). || Forjado, da (iron).
wrought-up [rɔ:tˈʌp] adj. Nervioso, sa.
wrung [rʌŋ] pret. & p. p. See WRING.
wry [rai] adj. Torcido, da; doblado, da: *wry neck*, cuello torcido. || Retorcido, da (humour, remarks, etc.). || Forzado, da (a smile). || Irónico, ca (speech). || *To pull a wry face*, torcer el gesto, poner mala cara.
wryneck [—nek] n. MED. Tortícolis, *m.* & *f.* || Torcecuello, *m.* (bird).
wych elm [ˈwitʃˈelm] n. BOT. Olmo (*m.*) escocés.
wye [wai] n. I griega, *f.* (letter).
wyvern [ˈwaivən] n. HERALD. Dragón, *m.* (two-legged winged dragon).

x [eks] n. X, *f.* (letter). || MATH. X, *f.*, incógnita, *f.* (unknown quantity). || — *Mr X*, el señor X. || CINEM. *X film*, película no apta para menores de 16 años.
xanthate [ˈzænθeit] n. CHEM. Xantato, *m.*
xanthene [ˈzænˌθi:n] n. CHEM. Xanteno, *m.*
xanthin [ˈzænθin] or **xanthine** [ˈzænθi:n] n. CHEM. Xantina, *f.*
xanthoma [zænˈθəumə] n. MED. Xantoma, *m.*

— OBSERV. El plural es *xanthomas* o *xanthomata*.

xanthophyll [ˈzænθəfil] n. Xantofila, *f.*
xanthous [ˈzænθəs] adj. Amarillo, lla (yellow). || De pelo rubio (with yellowish hair). || De piel amarilla (yellow-skinned).
Xavier [ˈzæviə*] pr. n. Javier, *m.*
x-axis [ˈeksˌæksis] n. MATH. Abscisa, *f.*
xebec [ˈzi:bek] n. Jabeque, *m.* (small boat).
xenogenesis [ˈzenəˈdʒenisis] n. Xenogénesis, *f. inv.*
xenon [ˈzenɔn] n. CHEM. Xenón, *m.*
xenophile [ˈzenəfail] n. Xenófilo, la.
xenophilia [ˌzenəˈfi:ljə] n. Xenofilia, *f.*
xenophilous [ˌzeˈnɔfiləs] adj. Xenófilo, la.
xenophobe [ˈzenəfəub] n. Xenófobo, ba.
xenophobia [ˌzenəˈfəubjə] n. Xenofobia, *f.*
xenophobic [ˌzenəˈfəubik] adj. Xenófobo, ba.
Xenophon [ˈzenəfən] pr. n. Jenofonte, *m.*
xeric [ˈziərik] adj. Árido, da; seco, ca.
xerography [zeˈrɔgrəfi] n. Xerografía, *f.*
xerophilous [ziˈrɔfiləs] adj. Xerófilo, la.
xerosis [ziˈrəusis] n. MED. Xerosis, *f. inv.*
xerox copy [ˈziərɔksˌkɔpi] n. Xerografía, *f.*
Xerxes [ˈzə:ksiz] pr. n. Jerjes, *m.*
xi [sai] n. Xi, *f.* (Greek letter).
xiphoid [ˈzifɔid] adj. ANAT. Xifoideo, a.
— N. ANAT. Xifoides, *m. inv.*
xiphoidal [—əl] adj. ANAT. Xifoideo, a.
xifosura [zifəˈsurə] pl. n. ZOOL. Xifosuros, *m.*
xiphosuran [zifəˈsurən] adj./n. ZOOL. Xifosuro.
Xmas [ˈkrisməs] n. Navidad, *f.*, Navidades, *f. pl.* (Christmas). || — *Xmas card*, crismas, *m.*, tarjeta (*f.*) de Navidad. || *Xmas tree*, árbol (*m.*) de Navidad.
X-ray [ˈeksˈrei] n. Radiografía, *f.* (X-ray photograph). || — Pl. Rayos (*m.*) X.
X-ray [ˈeksˈrei] v. tr. Tratar *or* examinar con rayos X (on a fluorescent screen). || Radiografiar (to take an X-ray photograph of).
X-ray photograph [—ˈfəutəgrɑ:f] or **X-ray print** [—print] n. Radiografía, *f.*
X-ray therapy [—ˈθerəpi] n. Radioterapia, *f.*
X-ray tube [—tju:b] n. Tubo (*m.*) de rayos X.
xylene [ˈzaili:n] n. CHEM. Xileno, *m.*
xylograph [ˈzailəgrɑ:f] n. Xilografía, *f.*
xylographer [zaiˈlɔgrəfə*] n. Xilógrafo, fa.
xylographic [ˌzailəˈgræfik] or **xylographical** [—əl] adj. Xilográfico, ca.
xilography [zaiˈlɔgrəfi] n. Xilografía, *f.*
xylophaga [zaiˈlɔfəgə] pl. n. ZOOL. Xilófagos, *m.*
xylophagous [zaiˈlɔfəgəs] adj. ZOOL. Xilófago, ga.
xylophone [ˈzailəfəun] n. MUS. Xilófono, *m.*
xylophonist [—ist] n. MUS. Xilofonista, *m.* & *f.*
xyst [zist] or **xystus** [—əs] n. (Ant.). Galería (*f.*) cubierta.

y [wai] n. Y, *f.* (letter).
yacht [jɔt] n. MAR. Yate, *m.* || — *Yacht club*, club náutico. || *Yacht race*, regata, *f.*
yacht [jɔt] v. intr. Dedicarse a la navegación de recreo (to sail for pleasure). || Participar en una regata (to race yachts).
yachting [—iŋ] n. Navegación (*f.*) de recreo, navegación (*f.*) a vela. || *To go yachting*, ir a pasear en yate (to go sailing), tomar parte en una regata (to race).
yachtsman [—smən] n. Aficionado (*m.*) a la navegación de recreo, "yachtman", *m.*, balandrista, *m.* (who sails a yacht). || Dueño (*m.*) de un yate (who owns a yacht).

— OBSERV. El plural de *yachtsman* es *yachtsmen*.

yachtsmanship [—smənʃip] n. Arte (*m.*) de manejar un yate, habilidad (*f.*) en manejar un yate.
yackety-yack [ˈjækətiˈjæk] n. Charloteo, *m.*, cháchara, *f.* (chatter). || Discusiones, *f. pl.* (discussion). || Machaqueo, *m.* (insistence).
yaguaza [jəˈgwɑ:zə] n. Yaguasa, *f.*
yahoo [jəˈhu:] n. Bruto, *m.*, patán, *m.*
Yahweh or **Yahveh** [ˈjɑ:wei] pr. n. Yahvé (Jehovah).
yak [jæk] n. ZOOL. Yac, *m.*, yak, *m.*
yak [jæk] v. intr. U. S. FAM. Parlotear, charlotear.
yam [jæm] n. Ñame, *m.* (plant). || U. S. Batata, *f.* [*Amer.*, camote, *m.*] (sweet potato).

yammer [—ə*] n. Gemido, *m.* (moan). || Lloriqueo, *m.* (whimpering). || Parloteo, *m.* (chat).
yammer [—ə*] v. intr. Lloriquear (to whimper). || Quejarse (to complain). || Parlotear (to chatter).
yank [jæŋk] n. Tirón, *m.*: *to give sth. a yank*, dar un tirón a algo.
yank [jæŋk] v. tr. Dar un tirón a.
— V. intr. Dar un tirón.
Yank [jæŋk] n. FAM. Yanqui, *m.* & *f.*
Yankee [ˈjæŋki] adj./n. Yanqui.
Yankeeism [—izəm] n. Americanismo, *m.*
yap [jæp] n. Ladrido, *m.* (of a dog). || FAM. Jeta, *f.*, hocico, *m.* (mouth). | Patán, *m.*, palurdo, *m.* (person). | Protesta, *f.* (protest). | Charloteo, *m.* (chat).
yap [jæp] v. intr. Ladrar (a dog). || Gañir, chillar (fox). || FAM. Charlotear, cotorrear (to chatter). | Protestar (to protest).
yarborough [ˈjɑ:brə] n. Mano (*f.*) en el juego de bridge en la que no figura ninguna carta que vale más de nueve.
yard [jɑ:d] n. Patio, *m.* (of a building, school, etc.). || Corral, *m.* (for animals). || Almacén, *m.*, depósito, *m.*: *timber yard*, depósito de madera. || Estación, *f.* (railways): *shunting* o *marshalling yard*, estación de clasificación *or* de apartado. || Taller, *m.*: *repair yard*, taller de reparaciones. || Yarda, *f.* [unidad de medida equivalente a 91,44 cm.] (measure). || MAR. Verga, *f.* (spar). | Astillero, *m.* (dockyard). || — *The Yard*, Scotland Yard, sede (*f.*) de la policía londinense. || FIG. *Yards long*, muy largo. | *With a face a yard long*, con una cara muy larga.
yard [jɑ:d] v. tr. Meter en el corral (cattle).
yardage [—idʒ] n. Encierro, *m.* (of cattle). || Gastos (*m. pl.*) del encierro (cost). || Maniobras, *f. pl.* (railways). || Longitud (*f.*) *or* área (*f.*) *or* volumen (*m.*) en yardas, medida (*f.*) en yardas.
yardarm [—ɑ:m] n. MAR. Penol, *m.*
yardman [—mən] n. Empleado (*m.*) en la estación de clasificación (railways). || Empleado (*m.*) de un depósito de madera.
— OBSERV. El plural de *yardman* es *yardmen*.
yardmaster [—ˌmɑ:stə*] n. U. S. Encargado (*m.*) de la estación de clasificación.
yardstick [—stik] n. Vara (*f.*) que mide una yarda. || FIG. Criterio, *m.*, patrón, *m.*, norma, *f.*
yarn [jɑ:n] n. Hilo, *m.*, hilado, *m.*, hilaza, *f.* (spun thread). || FIG. Historia, *f.*, cuento, *m.* (exaggerated story): *to spin a yarn*, contar una historia.
yarn [jɑ:n] v. intr. Contar una historia *or* un cuento.
yarrow [ˈjærəu] n. BOT. Milenrama, *f.*
yashmak [ˈjæʃmæk] n. Velo, *m.* (of Moslem women).
yataghan [ˈjætəgən] n. Yatagán, *m.* (short sword).
yaup [jɔ:p] n./v. intr. See YAWP.
yaw [jɔ:] n. MAR. Guiñada, *f.* (of a ship). || Bandazo, *m.*, despiste, *m.* (of a car).
yaw [jɔ:] v. intr. MAR. Guiñar, dar guiñadas (a ship). || Dar un bandazo, despistarse (a car).
yawl [jɔ:l] n. MAR. Yola, *f.* (boat).
yawn [jɔ:n] n. Bostezo, *m.* (made by a person). || Abertura, *f.* (gaping hole).
yawn [jɔ:n] v. intr. Bostezar (person). || Abrirse: *the chasm yawned in front of him*, el abismo se abría delante de él.
— V. tr. Decir bostezando. || FAM. *To yawn one's head off*, bostezar hasta desencajarse las mandíbulas.
yawning [—iŋ] adj. Bostezando (person). || Abierto, ta (thing). || Profundo, da (chasm).
— N. Bostezo, *m.* (yawn).
yawp [jɔ:p] n. U. S. Grito, *m.*
yawp [jɔ:p] v. intr. U. S. Gritar (to utter a cry). || U. S. FAM. Cotorrear (to talk continually).
yaws [jɔ:z] n. MED. Pián, *m.*, frambesia, *f.*
Y connection [waikəˈnekʃən] n. Montaje (*m.*) en estrella.
ye [ji:] pers. pron. (Ant.). Vos.
— Def. art. (Ant.). El, la; los, las.
yea [jei] n. Sí, *m.* || *The yeas and the nays*, los votos a favor y los votos en contra.
— Adv. Sí (yes). || Incluso, y hasta (moreover).
yeah [je:] adv. FAM. Sí (yes).
year [jiə*] n. Año, *m.*: *last year*, el año pasado; *the coming year*, el año próximo; *next year*, el año que viene; *the year before last*, el año antepasado; *the year 2 000*, el año 2 000; *the academic year*, el año académico; *a lunar year*, un año lunar; *to be 20 years old*, tener 20 años; *500 pounds a year*, 500 [quinientas] libras por año; *once a year*, una vez al año; *every other year*, cada dos años, un año sí y otro no; *every year*, cada año, todos los años; *in my later years*, en mis últimos años; *it will take years*, tardará años y años. || Curso, *m.*, año, *m.*: *he was in my year at school*, estaba en el mismo curso que yo en el colegio; *the first year boys*, los niños del primer curso. || — *All the year round*, [durante] todo el año. || *By the year*, por año. || *Calendar year*, año civil. || FAM. *Donkey's years*, siglos, *m.* || *Financial year*, año *or* ejercicio económico. || *From year to year*, cada año. || *Happy New Year!*, ¡Feliz Año Nuevo! || *In after years*, en los años siguientes. || FIG. *In the year one* o *in the year dot*, en el año de la nana, en tiempos de Maricastaña. || *In years*, de edad. || *In years to come*, en años venideros. || *Leap year*, año bisiesto. || *Light year*, año luz. || *New Year's Eve*, Nochevieja, *f.* || *Of late years*, en los últimos años. || *School year*, año escolar. || *To look young for one's years*, parecer joven para la edad que uno tiene. || *Year after year* o *year by year*, año tras año. || *Year in, year out*, año tras año. || *Year of grace*, año de gracia. || *Year of our Lord*, año del Señor. || *Years ago*, hace años.
yearbook [—buk] n. Anuario, *m.*
yearling [—liŋ] adj. De un año (one year old). || Añal (calf, bullock, sheep, goat).
— N. Potro (*m.*) de un año (year-old colt). || Añal, *m.* (calf, bullock, sheep, goat).
yearlong [—ˈlɔŋ] adj. Que dura un año (which lasts a year). || Que ha durado un año (which has lasted a year).
yearly [—li] adj. Anual.
— Adv. Anualmente, cada año. || *Twice yearly*, dos veces al año.
yearn [jə:n] v. intr. *To yearn after* o *for*, ansiar, anhelar, suspirar por (sth.), suspirar por (s.o.). || *To yearn to do sth.*, ansiar *or* anhelar hacer algo.
yearning [—iŋ] adj. Anheloso, sa; ansioso, sa (longing). || Tierno, na (tender).
— N. Anhelo, *m.*, ansia, *f.*
yearningly [—iŋli] adv. Con ansia, ansiosamente (with longing). || Con ternura, tiernamente (tenderly).
year-old [ˈjiərˈəuld] adj. De un año de edad.
year-round [ˈjiərˈraund] adj. Abierto durante todo el año.
yeast [ji:st] n. Levadura, *f.* (leaven). || FIG. Fermento, *m.* || Espuma, *f.* (of beer).
yeasty [—i] adj. De levadura (of yeast). || Espumoso, sa (frothy). || FIG. Turbulento, ta (unsettled). | Frívolo, la (frivolous).
yegg [jeg] n. U. S. FAM. Ladrón, *m.* [de cajas fuertes].
yell [jel] n. Grito, *m.*: *to let out a yell*, dar un grito.
yell [jel] v. tr. Gritar, vociferar, decir a gritos: *to yell insults*, gritar insultos.
— V. intr. Gritar: *to yell with pain*, gritar de dolor. || *To yell for help*, pedir auxilio a gritos.
yelling [—iŋ] n. Gritos, *m. pl.*
yellow [ˈjeləu] adj. Amarillo, lla: *yellow skin*, piel amarilla; *to turn yellow with age*, volverse amarillo con el tiempo. || Rubio, bia (hair). || De color avellana (gloves). || MED. Amarilla (fever). || FAM. Cobarde, miedoso, sa (cowardly). | Sensacionalista: *a yellow newspaper*, un periódico sensacionalista; *yellow press*, prensa sensacionalista.
— N. Amarillo, *m.* (colour). || Yema, *f.* (yolk of an egg). || — Pl. Ictericia, *f. sing.* (jaundice).
yellow [ˈjeləu] v. tr. Volver amarillo.
— V. intr. Volverse amarillo, ponerse amarillo, amarillear, amarillecer.
yellowback [—bæk] n. (Ant.). Novelucha, *f.*
yellowbelly [—ˌbeli] n. FAM. Cobarde, *m.* & *f.*, cagueta, *m.* & *f.* (pop.).
yellow dog [—dɔg] n. U. S. Canalla, *m.* || U. S. *Yellow-dog contract*, contrato (*m.*) de trabajo según el cual el contratado se compromete a no adherirse al sindicato.
yellow fever [—ˈfi:və*] n. MED. Fiebre (*f.*) amarilla.
yellowhammer [—ˌhæmə*] n. Verderón, *m.* (bird).
yellowish [—iʃ] adj. Amarillento, ta.
yellow jack [—dʒæk] n. Fiebre (*f.*) amarilla (yellow fever). || MAR. Bandera (*f.*) amarilla. || Jurel, *m.* (fish).
yellow jacket [—ˌdʒækit] n. U. S. Avispa, *f.*
yellowness [—nis] n. Amarillez, *f.*, lo amarillo.
yellow ochre (U. S. **yellow ocher**) [—ˈəukə*] n. Ocre (*m.*) amarillo.
yellow spot [—ˈspɔt] n. ANAT. Mancha (*f.*) amarilla (in the eye).
yelp [jelp] n. Gañido, *m.*
yelp [jelp] v. intr. Gañir (an animal). || Gritar (a person): *to yelp with pain*, gritar de dolor.
Yemen [ˈjemən] pr. n. GEOGR. Yemen, *m.*
Yemenite [—ait] adj./n. Yemenita, yemení.
yen [jen] n. Yen, *m.* (monetary unit of Japan). || FAM. Deseo, *m.*, ganas, *f. pl.* (desire): *I had a sudden yen to visit the East*, de pronto me entraron ganas de visitar el Oriente.
yen [jen] v. intr. Tener ganas, desear ansiosamente.
yeoman [ˈjəumən] n. Pequeño terrateniente, *m.* (farmer who owns his land). || MIL. Soldado (*m.*) de caballería. || — FIG. *To do yeoman service*, prestar grandes servicios. || MIL *Yeoman of the guard*, alabardero (*m.*) de la Casa Real.
— OBSERV. El plural de *yeoman* es *yeomen*.
yeomanry [—ri] n. Pequeños terratenientes, *m. pl.* (yeomen). || MIL. Cuerpo (*m.*) voluntario de caballería para la defensa territorial.
yep [jep] adv. FAM. Sí (yes).
yes [jes] adv. Sí: *say yes or no*, diga sí o no. || — *Have you ever been to America? — Yes, I have*, ¿ha estado alguna vez en América? — Sí. || *I bet you haven't finished. — Yes I have!*, apuesto a que no has terminado. — ¡Pues sí! || *To answer yes*, contestar que sí. || *Yes?*, ¿sí?, ¿dígame? (on telephone, etc.), ¿de verdad? (surprise), ¿quién es? (answering a knock on the door). || *Yes!*, ¡voy! (in answer to summons). || *Yes indeed*, por supuesto, claro que sí. || *Yes, of course!* o *yes rather!*, ¡claro que sí!
— N. Sí, *m.*: *to answer with a yes*, contestar con un sí.
— OBSERV. El plural del sustantivo *yes* es *yeses* o *yesses*.
yes-man [ˈjesmæn] n. FAM. Pelotillero, *m.*, cobista, *m.*

— OBSERV. El plural de *yes-man* es *yes-men*.

yesterday [ˈjestədi] adv. Ayer: *I only arrived yesterday*, llegué solamente ayer. || — *I saw him yesterday week*, ayer hizo una semana que le vi. || FIG. *I was not born yesterday*, no he nacido ayer. || *Late yesterday*, ayer a última hora. || *The day before yesterday*, antes de ayer, anteayer. || *Yesterday morning, afternoon*, ayer por la mañana, por la tarde.
— N. Ayer, *m.*, el día (*m.*) de ayer. || — *I spent all yesterday writing*, ayer pasé todo el día escribiendo *or* pasé todo el día de ayer escribiendo. || *Yesterday's papers*, los periódicos de ayer. || *Yesterday was rainy*, ayer llovió.
yestereve [ˈjestəri:v] or **yesterevening** [—niŋ] adv. (Ant.). Ayer por la tarde.
yestermorn [ˈjestəmɔ:n] or **yestermorning** [—iŋ] adv. (Ant.). Ayer por la mañana, en la mañana de ayer.
yesternight [ˈjestənait] adv. (Ant.). Ayer por la noche, en la noche de ayer, anoche.
yesteryear [ˈjestəˈjiə*] n. Antaño, *m.*: *songs of yesteryear*, canciones de antaño.
yet [jet] adv. Aún, todavía: *I have not seen him yet*, aún no le he visto; *don't go yet*, no te vayas aún; *he was not yet mayor*, todavía no era alcalde; *there is yet light enough*, todavía hay bastante luz; *not yet*, todavía no; *yet more difficult*, todavía más difícil. || Ya: *has your sister arrived yet?*, ¿ha llegado tu hermana ya? || — *As yet*, hasta ahora. || *It has yet to be finished*, todavía no está terminado. || *No one had yet been there*, nadie había estado allí antes, hasta entonces no había estado nadie allí. || *We have yet to see the Eiffel Tower*, todavía nos queda por ver la Torre Eiffel. || *We'll manage yet*, a pesar de todo lo lograremos. || *Yet again*, otra vez. || *Yet more*, todavía más, más aún. || *You'll get to be famous yet*, un día serás famoso.
— Conj. Sin embargo, no obstante (nevertheless): *and yet I enjoy it*, y sin embargo me gusta. || Pero (but).
yeti [jeti] n. Abominable hombre (*m.*) de las nieves.
yew [ju:] n. Tejo, *m.* (tree and wood).
Y gun [waigʌn] n. Cañón (*m.*) antisubmarino.
Yid [jid] n. POP. Judío, a.
Yiddish [—iʃ] n. Yiddish, *m.*, judeoalemán, *m.* (language).
yield [ji:ld] n. Producción, *f.*, rendimiento, *m.*: *yield per hectare*, producción por hectárea; *the yield of a well*, el rendimiento de un pozo. || Beneficio, *m.* (profit). || Rédito, *m.*, interés, *m.* (interest): *a 4 % yield*, un rédito del cuatro por ciento. || Cosecha, *f.* (crop). || — *Yield capacity*, productividad, *f.* || *Yield point*, límite (*m.*) de elasticidad. || *Yield strength*, límite (*m.*) de elasticidad. || *Yield temperature*, temperatura (*f.*) de fusión.
yield [ji:ld] v. tr. Producir, dar: *these trees will yield good timber*, estos árboles producirán buena madera; *to yield a good crop*, dar una buena cosecha. || Dar, producir, proporcionar (profit): *the profit yielded by the investment*, los beneficios proporcionados por la inversión. || Devengar, dar, producir (interest). || Ceder: *to yield ground to the enemy*, ceder terreno al enemigo. || Entregar (a town, etc., to the enemy). || Dar: *to yield consent*, dar su consentimiento. || Conceder (to concede). || — *He finally yielded the point*, acabó por reconocer que no tenía razón. || *The shares yielded ten per cent in a year*, las acciones produjeron un beneficio del diez por ciento en un año. || *To yield an argument to s.o.*, darle la razón a alguien. || FIG. *To yield up the ghost*, entregar el alma.
— V. intr. Producir, ser productivo, va (to be fruitful). || Rendirse (to admit defeat). || Ceder (to give in): *to yield to temptation*, ceder a la tentación; *to yield to s.o.'s insistence*, ceder ante la insistencia de alguien; *the ground yields when you tread on it*, la tierra cede cuando la pisas. || — *To yield in favour of*, renunciar en favor de. || U. S. *To yield to*, ceder la palabra a. || FIG. *To yield to nobody in enthusiasm*, ser más entusiasta que nadie.
yielding [ˈji:ldiŋ] adj. Complaciente, condescendiente: *a yielding person*, una persona complaciente. || Flexible (flexible, not rigid). || Blando, da: *yielding ground*, suelo blando. || COMM. Productivo, va (fruitful).
yip [jip] n. U. S. Ladrido, *m.* (bark of a dog). | Protesta, *f.*, queja, *f.* (complaint).
yip [jip] v. intr. U. S. Ladrar (a dog). | Protestar, quejarse (to complain).
yippee [ˈjiˈpi:] interj. FAM. ¡Yupi!
yod [jɔd] n. Yod, *f.* (in phonetics).
yodel [jəudl] n. Canción (*f.*) tirolesa.
yodel [ˈjəudl] v. tr./intr. Cantar a la tirolesa.
yodeller or **yodeler** [—ə*] n. Cantante (*m.* & *f.*) tirolés.
yoga [ˈjəugə] n. Yoga, *m.*
yoghourt or **yoghurt** [ˈjɔgə:t] n. Yogur, *m.*
yogi [ˈjəugi] n. Yogi, *m.*, yogui, *m.*, yoghi, *m.*
yogurt [ˈjɔgə:t] n. Yogur, *m.*
yohimbine [jəuˈhimbi:n] n. CHEM. Yohimbina, *f.*
yoicks [jɔiks] interj. ¡Hala!
yoke [jəuk] n. Yugo, *m.* (for animals, crossbar for bells). || Yunta, *f.* (pair of oxen). || Balancín, *m.*, percha, *f.* (for carrying loads). || Canesú, *m.* (of garment). || ARCH. Cabecero, *m.* (of a window). || Culata, *f.* (of electromagnet). || TECH. Brida, *f.*, estribo, *m.* (clamp). || MAR. Barra, *f.* (of rudder). || AVIAT. Palanca (*f.*) de mando. || FIG. Lazo, *m.*, vínculo, *m.* (bond). | Yugo, *m.*, esclavitud, *f.* (slavery). | Servidumbre, *f.* (servitude). || — FIG. *To be under the yoke of*, estar bajo el yugo de. | *To pass under the yoke*, pasar bajo el yugo. | *To throw off the yoke*, sacudir el yugo.
yoke [jəuk] v. tr./intr. Uncir (to put under a yoke). || Atar (to attach). || FIG. Unir (to unite). || *To yoke together*, trabajar juntos, estar uncidos al mismo carro.
yoke elm [—elm] n. Carpe, *m.* (tree).
yokefellow [—ˌfeləu] n. Compañero, *m.*
yokel [—əl] n. Paleto, *m.*, cateto, *m.*, palurdo, *m.*, patán, *m.*
yolk [jəuk] n. Yema, *f.* [de huevo] (of an egg). || Churre, *m.* (found in the fleece of sheep).
yolk gland [—glænd] n. Glándula (*f.*) vitelina.
yolk sac [—sæk] n. Membrana (*f.*) vitelina.
yon [jɔn] adj./adv. (Ant.). See YONDER.
yonder [ˈjɔndə*] adj. (Ant.). Aquel, aquella, aquellos, aquellas: *yonder church tower*, aquella torre de iglesia.
— Adv. A lo lejos, allá: *look yonder*, mira allá.
yore [jɔ:] n. (Ant.). *In days of yore*, antaño. | *Of yore*, de otro tiempo, de antaño.
you [ju:] pers. pron. Tú (subjective case sing. when addressing relatives, friends, children, etc.): *no, you must go*, no, tienes que ir tú. || Te (direct and indirect object sing.): *he heard you*, te oyó; *he gave it to you*, te lo dio. || Ti (after a preposition): *for you*, para ti. || Vosotros, vosotras (subjective case pl. and after a preposition when addressing relatives, friends, children, etc.): *you are the ones who saw it*, vosotros sois los que lo visteis; *this present is for you*, este regalo es para vosotros. || Os (direct and indirect object pl.): *I'm telling you*, os digo; *he doesn't believe you*, no os cree. || Usted, ustedes (subjective case and after a preposition when addressing a stranger or a person to whom respect is due): *how are you?*, ¿cómo está usted?; *against you*, contra ustedes. || Le, la, los, las (direct object): *I saw you, Mr. Smith*, le vi, Sr. Smith. || Le, les (indirect object): *I asked you how you were, Mrs. Smith*, le pregunté cómo estaba, señora Smith. || Se (indirect object sing. and pl. when accompanied by a direct object pronoun): *I gave it to you*, se lo di; *he asked you for it*, se lo pidió. || — *All of you*, todos vosotros, todas vosotras, todos ustedes. || *Between you and me*, dicho sea entre nosotros, entre nosotros dos. || *Can you swim here?*, ¿se puede nadar aquí? || *I am older than you*, soy mayor que tú *or* que usted. || *If I were you*, yo en tu lugar, yo que tú. || *There's a lovely dress for you!*, ¡mire que traje más bonito! || *With you*, contigo, con vosotros, con vosotras, con usted, con ustedes. || *You can't trust anyone*, uno no se puede fiar de nadie, una no puede fiarse de nadie. || *You Englishmen*, vosotros los ingleses. || *You idiot!*, ¡idiota! || *You need to be young to succeed*, hay que ser joven para triunfar. || *You sit down and shut up!*, ¡siéntate y calla!

— OBSERV. In the subjective case, the personal pronoun is usually omitted in Spanish (*are you hungry?*, ¿tienes hambre?; *you sold it*, lo vendió), except in cases of emphasis or distinction (*no, you do it!*, ¡no, hazlo tú!; *you are a doctor and he is an architect*, usted es doctor y él es arquitecto).
— See also the observation in "usted".

you'd [ju:d] contraction of *you would* and *you had*.
you'll [ju:l] contraction of *you will* and *you shall*.
young [jʌŋ] adj. Joven: *a young country*, un país joven; *the night is still young*, todavía la noche es joven; *my brother married young*, mi hermano se casó joven; *we are only young once*, no somos jóvenes más que una vez en la vida; *he is young for his years*, parece joven para la edad que tiene; *he is two years younger than I*, es dos años más joven que yo. || De juventud: *young love*, amor de juventud. || Nuevo, va (new). || — *A young lady*, una señorita. || *A young man*, un joven, un chico joven (youngster), un hombre joven: *to bring young men into the government*, poner a hombres jóvenes en el gobierno. || *A young woman*, una joven, una chica joven (youngster), una mujer joven. || *In his younger days*, en su juventud. || *His young lady*, su novia, *f.* || *Pliny the Younger*, Plinio el Joven. || *The youngest of my children*, el más joven de mis hijos. || *To grow younger*, rejuvenecer. || *When I was five years younger*, cuando tenía cinco años menos. || *You are looking years younger*, parece mucho más joven. || *Younger brother*, hermano (*m.*) menor. || *Young fellow*, joven, *m.*, muchacho, *m.* || *Young girl*, joven, *f.*, muchacha, *f.* || *Young people*, los jóvenes, la gente joven, la juventud. || *Young person*, persona joven, joven, *m.* & *f.*
— Pl. n. Cría, *f. sing.* (of animals). || — *Old and young*, los mayores y los pequeños. || *The young*, los jóvenes, la gente joven, la juventud. || *To bring forth young*, parir. || *With young*, preñada (an animal).
youngish [—iʃ] adj. FAM. Bastante joven, jovencito, ta.
youngling [—liŋ] n. Joven, *m.* & *f.* || Cría, *f.* (animal).
young-looking [—ˌlukiŋ] adj. Que parece joven, de aspecto joven.
youngster [—stə*] n. Joven, *m.* & *f.*, jovenzuelo, la; jovencito, ta.
your [jɔ:*] poss. adj. Tu, tus (sing. when addressing friends, children, relatives, etc.): *your house*, tu casa; *I like your shoes better than mine*, me gustan más tus zapatos que los míos. || Vuestro, vuestra, vuestros,

vuestras (pl. when addressing friends, children, relatives, etc.): *your car is blue, ours is red*, vuestro coche es azul, el nuestro rojo; *these are your tickets*, éstas son vuestras entradas. || Su, sus; de usted, de ustedes (sing. and pl. when addressing strangers or people to whom respect is due): *your car is in the garage*, el coche de usted está en el garaje; *your books are on the table*, sus libros están encima de la mesa. || Su (preceding certain titles): *Your Majesty*, Su majestad.

— OBSERV. The English possessive adjective is often translated by the definite article in Spanish (*turn your head*, vuelve la cabeza; *don't bite your nails*, no te muerdas las uñas).

you're [juə*] contraction of *you are*.

yours [jɔ:z] poss. pron. [El] tuyo, [la] tuya, [el] vuestro, [la] vuestra (when addressing friends, children, relatives, etc.): *these are my books, those are yours*, éstos son mis libros, ésos son tuyos *or* ésos son los tuyos; *my car is here, I don't know where yours is*, mi coche está aquí, no sé dónde está el tuyo; *these are my letters, those are yours*, éstas son mis cartas, ésas son las vuestras or ésas son vuestras; *my cigarettes are next to yours*, mis cigarrillos están al lado de los vuestros. || [El] suyo, [la] suya; [el] de usted, [la] de usted (when addressing strangers or people to whom respect is due): *this is my plate, that is yours*, éste es mi plato, ése es el suyo *or* ése es suyo; *I like all these pictures, but yours are especially interesting*, me gustan todos esos cuadros, pero los de usted tienen un interés especial. || COMM. Su atenta (letter). || — *It is not yours to reason why*, a usted no le corresponde preguntarse el porqué. || *I would like to read sth. of yours*, me gustaría leer algo tuyo. || *Of yours*, tuyo, tuya; de usted, suyo, suya: *a friend of yours*, un amigo suyo; *that is no business of yours*, esto no es asunto suyo. || *You and yours*, tú y los tuyos, usted y los suyos. || *Yours is an interesting case*, su caso es interesante. || *Yours, J. Smith*, reciba un cordial saludo de J. Smith (in letters). || *Yours truly*, le saluda atentamente (in letters), su seguro servidor (me).

— OBSERV. Téngase en cuenta que el pronombre posesivo *yours* se puede aplicar tanto a un objeto como a varios (*give me yours*, dame el tuyo, dame los tuyos).

yourself [jɔ:ˈself] pers. pron. Tú [mismo], tú [misma] (subjective case when addressing relatives, friends, children, etc.): *do it yourself*, hazlo tú; *you said so yourself*, lo dijiste tú mismo. || Ti [mismo] (after a preposition): *it is for yourself*, es para ti mismo. || Usted [mismo], usted [misma] (subjective case and after a preposition when addressing a stranger or a person to whom respect is due): *you yourself came*, usted mismo vino; *I'll go with yourself*, iré con usted. || — *By yourself*, tú solo, usted solo: *did you do it by yourself?*, ¿lo hiciste tú solo? || *You only think of yourself*, sólo piensas en ti mismo, sólo piensa en sí mismo.

— Refl. pron. Te (when addressing relatives, friends, children, etc.): *have you hurt yourself?*, ¿te has hecho daño? || Se (when addressing a stranger or a person to whom respect is due): *you must ask yourself this*, tiene que preguntarse eso.

— OBSERV. El plural de *yourself* es *yourselves*.

yourselves [jɔ:ˈselvz] pers. pron. Vosotros [mismos], vosotras [mismas] (when addressing relatives, friends, children, etc.): *you yourselves were there*, estabais allí vosotros mismos; *for yourselves*, para vosotros. || Ustedes [mismos], ustedes [mismas] (when addressing strangers or people to whom respect is due): *yourselves, as members of the jury*, ustedes, como miembros del jurado; *I'll go with yourselves*, iré con ustedes. || *You only think of yourselves*, sólo pensáis en vosotros mismos, sólo piensan en sí mismos.

— Refl. pron. Os (when addressing relatives, friends, children, etc.): *have you washed yourselves?*, ¿os habéis lavado? || Se (when addressing strangers or people to whom respect is due): *you must ask yourselves this*, tienen que preguntarse esto.

youth [ju:θ] n. Juventud, *f.*: *during his early youth*, durante su primera juventud. || Joven, *m.* (a young man). || Juventud, *f.*, jóvenes, *m. pl.* (young people): *the youth of today*, la juventud actual. || FIG. *The campaign is still in its youth*, la campaña está todavía en sus principios.

youthful [—ful] adj. Joven, juvenil: *youthful appearance*, aspecto juvenil. || Juvenil, de la juventud (error, enthusiasm). || *To look youthful*, parecer joven.

youthfulness [—fulnis] n. Juventud, *f.*

youth hostel [—ˌhɔstəl] n. Albergue (*m.*) de juventud.

youth hosteller (U. S. **youth hosteler**) [—ˌhɔstələ*] n. Persona (*f.*) que se aloja en un albergue de juventud.

you've [ju:v] contraction of *you have*.

yowl [jaul] n. Aullido, *m.*

yowl [jaul] v. intr. Aullar.

yo-yo [ˈjəujəu] n. Yoyo, *m.* (toy).

yperite [ˈipərait] n. Yperita, *f.*, iperita, *f.* (gas).

ytterbium [iˈtə:bjəm] n. CHEM. Iterbio, *m.*, yterbio, *m.*

yttria [ˈitriə] n. CHEM. Itria, *f.*

yttrium [ˈitriəm] n. Itrio, *m.* (metal).

Yucatan [ˌju:kəˈtɑ:n] pr. n. GEOGR. Yucatán, *m.*

Yucatec [ˈju:kətek] n. Yucateco, ca.

Yucatecan [ˌju:kəˈtekən] adj. Yucateco, ca.

yucca [ˈjʌkə] n. BOT. Yuca, *f.*

Yugoslav [ˈju:gəuˈslɑ:v] adj./n. Yugoslavo, va.

Yugoslavia [—jə] pr. n. GEOGR. Yugoslavia, *f.*

Yugoslavian [—jən] adj./n. Yugoslavo, va.

Yule [ju:l] n. Pascuas, *f. pl.*, Navidades, *f. pl.*

Yule log [—lɔg] n. Tronco (*m.*) que se quema en Nochebuena (wood). || Bizcocho (*m.*) en forma de leño que se come en Nochebuena (confection).

Yuletide [—taid] n. Pascuas, *f. pl.*, Navidades, *f. pl.*

yummy [ˈjʌmi] adj. FAM. De chuparse los dedos, delicioso, sa.

Z

z [zed] n. Z, *f.*: *a capital z*, una z mayúscula.

zaffer or **zaffre** [ˈzæfə] n. MIN. Zafre, *m.*

Zaïre [ˈzai:r] pr. n. GEOGR. Zaire, *m.*

Zairian [ˈzai:rjən] adj./n. Zairense.

Zambezi [zæmˈbi:zi] pr. n. GEOGR. Zambeze, *m.*

Zambia [ˈzæmbjə] pr. n. GEOGR. Zambia, *f.*

zambo [ˈzæmbəu] n. Zambo, ba.

zany [ˈzeini] adj. Estrafalario, ria; absurdo, da.
— N. Bufón, *m.* (stage buffoon). || Payaso, *m.* (joker). || Tonto, *m.* (simpleton).

Zanzibar [ˌzænziˈbɑ:*] pr. n. GEOGR. Zanzíbar, *m.*

zeal [zi:l] n. Celo, *m.*, ardor, *m.*: *to show zeal*, mostrar celo.

zealot [ˈzelət] n. Defensor, ra (defender of a cause). || Fanático, ca (fanatic).

zealotry [—ri] n. Fanatismo, *m.*

zealous [ˈzeləs] adj. Celoso, sa; entusiasta.

zealously [—li] adv. Celosamente, con entusiasmo.

zebra [ˈzi:brə] n. ZOOL. Cebra, *f.*

zebra crossing [—ˈkrɔsiŋ] n. Paso (*m.*) de cebra, paso (*m.*) de peatones.

zebu [ˈzi:bu:] n. ZOOL. Cebú, *m.*

zed [zed] n. Zeta, *f.*, zeda, *f.*, ceda, *f.* (the letter z).

zee [zi:] n. U. S. Zeta, *f.*, zeda, *f.*, ceda, *f.* (the letter z).

Zeeland [—lənd] pr. n. GEOGR. Zelanda, *f.*, Zelandia, *f.*

Zeelander [—ləndə*] n. Zelandés, esa.

Zend [zend] n. Zendo, *m.* (language).
— Adj. Zendo, da.

Zendic [—ik] adj. Zendo, da.

zenith [ˈzeniθ] n. ASTR. Cenit, *m.* || FIG. Apogeo, *m.*: *he is at the zenith of his fame*, está en el apogeo de la gloria.

zenithal [—əl] adj. Cenital.

Zeno [ˈzi:nəu] pr. n. Zenón, *m.*

zeolite [ˈziəulait] n. MIN. Zeolita, *f.*

zephyr [ˈzefə*] n. Céfiro, *m.*

Zeppelin [ˈzepəlin] n. AVIAT. Zepelín, *m.*

zero [ˈziərəu] adj. Nulo, la: *zero visibility*, visibilidad nula. || Cero: *zero altitude*, altitud cero.
— N. MATH. PHYS. Cero, *m.* || FIG. Cero, *m.* (lowest point). | Cero (*m.*) a la izquierda (nonentity). || — *Absolute zero*, cero absoluto. || *It is ten degrees below zero*, hace diez grados bajo cero.

— OBSERV. El plural de la palabra inglesa *zero* es *zeros* o *zeroes*.

zero [ˈziərəu] v. tr./intr. Poner en el cero (an instrument). || *To zero in on*, apuntar hacia (artillery, etc.).

zero hour [—ˌauə*] n. MIL. Hora (*f.*) H (moment of attack). || Hora (*f.*) cero (in rocket launching). || FIG. Momento (*m.*) decisivo, hora (*f.*) H.

zest [zest] n. Ánimo, *m.*, entusiasmo, *m.* (enthusiasm). || Brío, *m.*: *to fight with zest*, luchar con brío. || Cás-

cara, *f.*: *a zest of orange*, una cáscara de naranja. || Sabor, *m.* (piquancy). || Sal, *f.*, gracia, *f.* (fun, wit). || *To eat with zest*, comer con apetito.
zestful [ˈzestful] adj. Entusiasta, animado, da. || Sabroso, sa (piquant).
zestfully [—i] adv. Con entusiasmo.
zesty [ˈzesti] adj. See ZESTFUL.
zeta [ˈzi:tə] n. Zeta, *f.* (Greek letter).
zeugma [ˈzju:gmə] n. GRAMM. Zeugma, *f.*, zeuma, *f.*
zibeline or **zibelline** [ˈzibili:n] n. Marta (*f.*) cebellina, cebellina, *f.*
zibet or **zibeth** [ˈzibit] n. Civeta, *f.*, gato (*m.*) de algalia (cat).
zigzag [ˈzigzæg] adj. En zigzag, zigzagueante: *a zigzag road*, una carretera en zigzag.
— Adv. *To go zigzag*, zigzaguear, ir zigzagueando.
— N. Zigzag, *m.*
zigzag [ˈzigzæg] v. tr. Poner en zigzag (to lay out).
— V. intr. Zigzaguear, ir zigzagueando. || Andar dando tumbos, andar haciendo eses, zigzaguear (a drunkard).
zigzagging [—iŋ] n. Zigzagueo, *m.*
zinc [ziŋk] n. Cinc, *m.*, zinc, *m.*
zinc [ziŋk] v. tr. Galvanizar con cinc.

— OBSERV. El gerundio y el participio pasivo de *to zinc* son *zincking* o *zincing* y *zincked* o *zinced*.

zinc carbonate [—ˈkɑ:bənit] n. MIN. Calamina, *f.*, carbonato (*m.*) de cinc.
zincing or **zincking** [—iŋ] n. TECH. Galvanización (*f.*) con cinc.
zincograph [—əugrɑ:f] n. Cincograbado, *m.*
zincography [ziŋˈkɔgrəfi] n. Cincografía, *f.*
zinc white [ˈziŋkˈwait] n. Blanco (*m.*) de cinc.
zing [ziŋ] n. FAM. Ánimo, *m.*, entusiasmo, *m.* (energy). || Zumbido, *m.* (noise).
zing [ziŋ] v. intr. FAM. Zumbar.
zingiberaceae [ˌzindʒibəˈreisii:] pl. n. BOT. Cingiberáceas, *f.*
zinnia [ˈziniə] n. BOT. Zinnia, *f.*
Zion [ˈzaiən] n. REL. Sión, *m.*
Zionism [—izəm] n. REL. Sionismo, *m.*
Zionist [—ist] adj./n. REL. Sionista.
zip [zip] n. Silbido, *m.* (whistle). || Zumbido, *m.* (buzz). || Cremallera, *f.* (fastener). || FAM. Nervio, *m.*, energía, *f.*, vigor, *m.*, brío, *m.* (vigour).
zip [zip] v. tr. *To zip open*, abrir la cremallera de. || *To zip shut*, cerrar con cremallera, cerrar la cremallera de. || *To zip up*, subir la cremallera de, cerrar [la cremallera de].
— V. intr. Silbar (to whizz like a bullet). || Zumbar (to buzz). || Ir como una bala (to move quickly). || Cerrarse con cremallera (to fasten with a zip). || *To zip past*, pasar silbando.
zip code [—kəud] n. U. S. Código (*m.*) postal.
zip fastener [—ˈfɑ:sənə*] n. Cremallera, *f.*
zipper [—ə*] n. Cremallera, *f.*
zippy [—i] adj. Enérgico, ca (energetic). || Veloz, rápido, da (fast). || Pronto, ta (prompt).
zircon [ˈzə:kɔn] n. MIN. Circón, *m.*, zircón, *m.*
zirconia [zə:ˈkəunjə] n. CHEM. Circona, *f.*
zirconite [ˈzə:kənait] n. Circonita, *f.*
zirconium [zə:ˈkəunjəm] n. CHEM. Circonio, *m.*
zither [ˈziðə*] n. MUS. Cítara, *f.*
zitherist [—rist] n. Citarista, *m.* & *f.*
zloty [ˈzlɔti] n. Zloty, *m.* (Polish coin).
zoantharia [ˌzəuænˈθεəriə] pl. n. ZOOL. Zoantarios, *m.*
zoanthropy [zəuˈænθrəpi] n. MED. Zoantropía, *f.*
zodiac [ˈzəudiæk] n. ASTR. Zodiaco, *m.*: *the signs of the zodiac*, los signos del zodiaco.
zodiacal [ˈzəudiækəl] adj. Zodiacal.
zombi or **zombie** [ˈzɔmbi] n. Muerto (*m.*) resucitado por magia negra. || FIG. FAM. Autómata *m.* & *f.*
zonal [ˈzəunəl] adj. Zonal, en zonas.
zonate [ˈzəuneit] adj. Dividido en zonas.
zonation [zəuˈneiʃən] n. División (*f.*) en zonas.
zone [zəun] n. Zona, *f.* || U. S. Distrito, *m.*: *postal zone*, distrito postal. || — *Demilitarized zone*, zona desmilitarizada. || *Glacial zone*, zona glacial. || *Industrial zone*, zona industrial. || *Military zone*, zona militar. || *Zone of influence*, zona de influencia.
zone [zəun] v. tr. Dividir en zonas.
zoo [zu:] n. Zoo, *m.*, parque (*m.*) zoológico.
zoogeography [ˌzəuədʒiˈɔgrəfi] n. Zoogeografía, *f.*
zooid [ˈzəuɔid] n. Zooide, *m.*
zooidal [zəuˈɔidəl] adj. Zooide.
zoolater [zəuˈɔlətə*] n. Zoólatra, *m.* & *f.*
zoolatrous [zəuˈɔlətrəs] adj. Zoólatra.
zoolatry [zəuˈɔlətri] n. Zoolatría, *f.*
zoological [ˌzəuəˈlɔdʒikəl] adj. Zoológico, ca: *zoological garden* o *gardens*, parque zoológico.
zoologist [zəuˈɔlədʒist] n. Zoólogo, ga.
zoology [zəuˈɔlədʒi] n. Zoología, *f.*
zoom [zu:m] n. Zumbido, *m.* (buzz). || AVIAT. Subida (*f.*) vertical. || PHOT. "Zoom", *m.*, objetivo (*m.*) de distancia focal variable (of cameras).
zoom [zu:m] v. tr. AVIAT. Hacer subir verticalmente (a plane). || PHOT. Enfocar con el "zoom".
— V. intr. Zumbar (to buzz). || Ir zumbando (to whizz along). || AVIAT. Subir verticalmente. || PHOT. Acercarse or alejarse rápidamente. || — *To zoom away* o *off*, salir zumbando. || *To zoom past*, pasar zumbando.
zoom lens [—ˈlenz] n. PHOT. Objetivo (*m.*) de distancia focal variable, "zoom", *m.*
zoomorphism [ˌzəuəˈmɔ:fizəm] n. Zoomorfismo, *m.*
zoophaga [zəuˈɔfəgə] pl. n. Zoófagos, *m.*
zoophagan [—n] n. Zoófago, ga.
zoophagous [—s] adj. Zoófago, ga.
zoophobia [ˌzəuəˈfəubiə] n. Zoofobia, *f.*
zoophorus [zəuˈɔfərəs] n. ARCH. Zoóforo, *m.*
zoophyta [zəuəˈfaitə] pl. n. Zoófitos, *m.*
zoophyte [ˈzəuəfait] n. Zoófito, *m.*
zoosporangium [ˌzəuəspəˈrændʒiəm] n. BOT. Zoosporangio, *m.*

— OBSERV. El plural de *zoosporangium* es *zoosporangia*.

zoospore [ˈzəuəspɔ:*] n. Zoospora, *f.*
zootechnic [ˌzəuəˈteknik] or **zootechnical** [—əl] adj. Zootécnico, ca.
zootechnician [ˌzəuətekˈniʃən] n. Zootécnico, ca.
zootechny [ˈzəuəˌtekni] n. Zootecnia, *f.*
zootherapy [ˌzəuəˈθerəpi] n. Zooterapia, *f.*
zootrope [ˈzəuətrəup] n. Zoótropo, *m.*
Zoroaster [ˌzɔrəuˈæstə*] pr. n. Zoroastro, *m.*
Zoroastrian [ˌzɔrəuˈæstriən] adj./n. Zoroástrico, ca.
Zoroastrianism [—izəm] n. Zoroastrismo, *m.*
zoster [ˈzɔstə*] n. MED. Zona, *f.* (shingles).
Zouave [zu:ˈɑ:v] n. Zuavo, *m.*
zucchetto [zu:ˈketəu] n. REL. Solideo, *m.* (skullcap).
zucchini [zu:ˈki:ni] n. U. S. Calabacín, *m.*

— OBSERV. El plural de *zucchini* es *zucchini* o *zucchinis*.

Zulu [ˈzu:lu] n. Zulú, *m.* & *f.*

— OBSERV. El plural de la palabra inglesa *Zulu* es *Zulu* o *Zulus*.

Zululand [—lænd] pr. n. GEOGR. Zululandia, *f.*
zwieback [ˈzwi:bæk] n. U. S. Bizcocho (*m.*) hecho con huevos.
Zwingli [ˈzwiŋli] pr. n. Zwinglio, *m.*
Zwinglian [ˈzwiŋliən] adj./n. Zwingliano, na.
Zwinglianism [—izəm] n. Zwinglianismo, *m.*
zwitterion [ˈtsvitərˌaiən] n. PHYS. Ion (*m.*) con carga positiva y negativa.
zygoma [zaiˈgəumə] n. ANAT. Cigoma, *m.*, zigoma, *m.*

— OBSERV. El plural de *zygoma* es *zygomata* o *zygomas*.

zygomatic [ˌzaigəˈmætik] adj. ANAT. Cigomático, ca; zigomático, ca.
zygote [ˈzaigəut] n. BIOL. Cigoto, *m.*, zigoto, *m.*

RESUMEN DE GRAMÁTICA INGLESA

EL ALFABETO INGLÉS

El alfabeto inglés consta de 26 letras:

a	**b**	**c**	**d**	**e**	**f**	**g**	**h**	**i**	**j**	**k**
ei	bi:	si:	di:	i:	ef	dʒi:	eitʃ	ai	dʒei	kei

l	**m**	**n**	**o**	**p**	**q**	**r**	**s**	**t**	**u**
el	em	en	əu	pi:	kju:	ɑ:*	es	ti:	ju:

v	**w**	**x**	**y**	**z**
vi:	ˈdʌbəlju:	eks	wai	zed

PRONUNCIACIÓN

Algunas de las letras inglesas representan más de un sonido y para poder reproducirlos oralmente de la manera más exacta posible se ha colocado entre corchetes, después de cada vocablo, simple o compuesto, la pronunciación figurada que le corresponde segun el Alfabeto Fonético Internacional (V. pág. VI, 2.ª parte). La pronunciación varía mucho según las regiones y los países de habla inglesa. Este diccionario se limita a consignar la más empleada en Gran Bretaña, seguida por la norteamericana, señalada ésta por las letras U. S., cuando difiere de la primera.
El acento tónico principal queda indicado por una virgulilla colocada en el ángulo superior de la sílaba acentuada y el acento tónico secundario por otra situada en el ángulo inferior (*periodic* [ˌpiəriˈɔdik]). Se ha empleado el guión para reemplazar la parte común que tienen varias palabras seguidas.

CONSONANTES

1. **b.** — Es semejante a la **b** inicial española (**b**all, ca**b**) y es muda en algunas palabras delante de *t* (de**b**t).
2. **c.** — Se pronuncia como la **c** española en *casa* (**c**at, **c**olour, **c**luster).
— Suena como una **s** ante *e*, *i* (**c**ertify, **c**ivilian).
— El grupo **ch** tiene el mismo sonido que la **ch** española en vocablos como **ch**air, bea**ch**, ar**ch**bishop, etc., pero tiene el sonido de **k** en **Ch**ristmas, **ch**emist, **ch**iropodist, etc.
3. **d.** — Tiene un sonido parecido a la **d** española en *caldo* (**d**o, pai**d**, ro**d**ent).
4. **f.** — Es casi igual a la **f** española (**f**avour, i**f**), excepto en la preposición *of* en la cual se pronuncia como una **v**.
— El grupo **ph** tiene el mismo sonido (**ph**ysics).
5. **g.** — Ante *a*, *o*, *u*, precediendo otra consonante, excepto *n*, o al final de una palabra, se pronuncia como la **g** de *gato* (**g**ap, **g**o, **g**ust, **g**lance, bo**g**, pe**g**).
— Cuando va seguida por *e*, *i*, además del sonido anterior (**g**et, **g**ive), puede tener el de la **y** argentina (**g**ender, **g**in).
— Delante de *n* es muda (**g**narl).
6. **h.** — Se asemeja a la jota, aunque su sonido es mucho más suave (**h**orse).
— Es muda en *hour*, *honour*, *honest*, *heir*.
7. **j.** — Suena como una **d** seguida por la **y** argentina (**j**ob, **j**ustice).
8. **k.** — Es semejante a la **k** española (**k**ind, **k**eep).
— Delante de *n* es muda (**k**nowledge, **k**nife).
9. **l.** — Simple o doble, se pronuncia como la **l** española (**l**ife, ma**l**aria, be**ll**, fi**ll**).
— En algunas palabras, como *calf*, *half*, *could*, etc., es muda.
10. **m.** — Simple o doble, es igual a la **m** española (**m**other, co**mm**erce).
— Cuando va seguida por una *n* es muda (**m**nemonic).
11. **n.** — Simple o doble, tiene el mismo sonido que la **n** española (**n**ever, co**nn**ect).
12. **p.** — Es idéntica a la **p** española, pero más explosiva (**p**eo**p**le, lam**p**).
13. **q.** — Combinada con la **u** da el sonido español de *cu* (**qu**ality, **qu**estion, **qu**ick).
14. **r.** — Se parece a la **r** de *mero* (**r**un, p**r**ice).
— Apenas se pronuncia ante una consonante o al final de una palabra (qua**r**te**r**).
15. **s.** — Simple, se pronuncia como la **s** española en posición inicial (**s**ome), en el plural y en la tercera persona del presente de indicativo de los verbos cuando antecede una consonante sorda (map**s**, cut**s**) y en posición final después de *i*, *a*, *o*, *u*, *y* (thi**s**), con algunas excepciones (ha**s**, wa**s**, a**s**, hi**s**, flie**s**, etc.).
— Simple, la **s** inglesa se articula apoyando suavemente la lengua entre los dientes y haciendo vibrar fuertemente las cuerdas vocales en los plurales cuyo singular termine en vocal o consonante sonora (house**s**, egg**s**), en la tercera persona del singular de los verbos, si éstos terminan en vocal o consonante sonora, y en otras palabras en posición final cuando sigue una *e* no muda.
— Doble, equivale a la **s** española (le**ss**, ma**ss**ive).
— Es muda en algunos vocablos como i**s**le.
— El grupo **sh** tiene un sonido parecido a la **ch** española, aunque mucho más suave (**sh**ould, la**sh**).
16. **t.** — Se asemeja a la **t** española, pero es ligeramente más aspirada (**t**ide, le**t**).
— El grupo **th** se pronuncia como la **z** española (**th**ing, sou**th**) o aproximadamente como la **d** española de *cada* (**th**en, wi**th**).
— Tiene un sonido similar al de **sh** en términos como *conception*, *credential*, etc.
17. **v.** — Es una consonante labiodental que se pronuncia apoyando los dientes superiores en el labio inferior (**v**isit, lo**v**e).
18. **w.** — Suena como la **u** española (**w**ell, t**w**enty).
— Es muda delante de *r* (**w**rap).
19. **x.** — Equivale al sonido de **ks** (rela**x**) o de **kz** (e**x**act).
— En posición inicial se pronuncia como la **z** inglesa (**x**ylophone).
20. **y.** — Como consonante es parecida a la **y** española (**y**esterday).
21. **z.** — Se articula apoyando suavemente la lengua entre los dientes y haciendo vibrar fuertemente las cuerdas vocales (**z**one, la**z**iness).

VOCALES

1. **a.** — Suena igual que la **a** española en palabras como f**a**ther, c**a**r, h**a**lf.
— Tiene une sonido breve intermedio entre la **a** y la **e** españolas en vocablos del tipo **a**pple, m**a**n, gramm**a**r.
— Es parecida a la **e** española en voces como t**a**ble, f**a**mous, b**a**by.
— Equivale aproximadamente a **ea** en términos como **a**ir, d**a**re.
2. **e.** — Se pronuncia como la **e** española de *nivel* en palabras como r**e**d, l**e**sson, m**e**mory, y con un sonido un poco más oscuro en voces como v**e**rb.
— Suena como una **i** española larga al final de una sílaba al seguir una consonante (b**e**fore) o cuando es doble (tr**ee**).
— Tiene el sonido de **ía** en h**e**re, f**e**ar, etc.
— Generalmente es muda en posición final (lov**e**, glu**e**).
3. **i.** — Es parecida a la **i** española en vocablos como b**i**t, f**i**sh, sh**i**p.
— Tiene un sonido más oscuro que la **e** española en b**i**rd, f**i**rst, s**i**r, etc.
— Se pronuncia como el diptongo **ai** en l**i**ke, r**i**de, arr**i**ve, etc.
4. **o.** — Equivale a la **o** española (h**o**t, d**o**g).
— Suena como la **u** española en d**o**, wh**o**, m**o**ve, etc., y cuando es doble (b**oo**k, t**oo**), aunque existen excepciones (d**oo**r, bl**oo**d, etc.).
— Tiene el sonido de la **a** española en palabras como h**o**use.
— En *w**o**men* se pronuncia **i**.
5. **u.** — Es parecida a la **u** española en b**u**ll, p**u**t, etc.
— Tiene un sonido intermedio entre la **o** y la **e** españolas en b**u**t, m**u**ch, **u**p, etc.
— Se pronuncia como el diptonyo **iu** en voces como mat**u**re, **u**se, etc.
6. **y.** — Como vocal suena igual que la **i** española (ministr**y**).

DIPTONGOS Y TRIPTONGOS

A diferencia de lo que ocurre en español, los **diptongos y triptongos** no corresponden siempre a la combinación de dos o tres vocales gráficas. Por ejemplo la **i** de *ice* representa por sí sola el sonido del diptongo español **ai**.

VARIACIONES ORTOGRÁFICAS

Existen algunas diferencias entre la ortografía británica y la norteamericana.
— al inglés **-our** corresponde el americano **-or** (*labour*, labor),
— al inglés **-re** corresponde el americano **-er** (*theatre*, theater), con algunas excepciones como *ogre* y las palabras terminadas por *-cre* (*massacre*, *lucre*),
— al inglés **-ce** corresponde el americano **-se** (*licence*, license),
— al inglés **-ould** corresponde el americano **-old** (*mould*, mold),
— al inglés **-ae**, **-oe** de ciertas palabras cultas corresponde el americano **-e** (*haemoglobin*, hemoglobin; *amoeba*, ameba),
— en cierto número de casos se duplica una consonante en inglés mientras que no se hace en americano (*quarrelled*, quarreled; *traveller*, traveler; *waggon*, wagon),
— en algunas palabras la **e**, que existe en inglés, desaparece en americano (*good-bye*, good-by; *storey*, story),
— en algunas voces tomadas del francés se conserva la ortografía francesa en Gran Bretaña, pero, en Estados Unidos, se suprime la terminación átona (*programme*, program),
— ciertos términos no se escriben de la misma manera, sin que esto obedezca a determinadas normas precisas, en los dos países (*grey*, gray; *tyre*, tire; *fulfil*, fulfill; *instalment*, installment; *plough*, plow).

MAYÚSCULAS

El uso de las **mayúsculas** es mucho más frecuente en inglés que en español. En efecto, además de los casos en que así ocurre en castellano, se emplean con los derivados de nombres propios (*Aritstotelian*), los sustantivos y adjetivos que indican la nacionalidad (*Englishman, English*), los idiomas (*Spanish*), los días de la semana (*Monday*), los meses (*February*), los títulos (*My Lord Duke*), los nombres de religiones, sectas o partidos y sus derivados (*Catholicism, Mormon, Labour*), el pronombre personal *I* y la interjección *O*.

ARTÍCULO

El **artículo definido** inglés es el mismo, **the**, en las formas masculina y femenina, singular o plural (*the boy, the girls, the animals*) y se emplea menos frecuentemente que en español.

No se debe emplear:
— con sustantivos en plural o nombres abstractos sin determinar (*he is very fond of tomatoes*, le gustan mucho los tomates; *life is difficult*, la vida es difícil),
— delante de *man* y *woman* usados en sentido abstracto o colectivo (*Man proposes, God disposes*, el hombre propone y Dios dispone),
— con nombres de juegos, deportes, ocupaciones, artes, ciencias y enfermedades (*chess*, el ajedrez; *to play tennis*, jugar al tenis; *bookkeeping*, la contabilidad; *architecture*, la arquitectura; *chemistry*, la química; *measles*, el sarampión),
— con sustantivos que representan una materia líquida, sólida o gaseosa y con nombres de comidas en sentido general (*water is useful*, el agua es útil; *to serve lunch*, servir el almuerzo),
— con palabras como *school, church, hospital, prison* si éstas se refieren al uso que se hace de estos edificios (*to go to church*, ir a la iglesia; *I was taken to hospital*, me llevaron al hospital),
— con los días de la semana, las estaciones y ciertas expresiones de tiempo (*he will come on Tuesday*, vendrá el martes; *when summer arrived*, cuando llegó el verano; *last year*, el año pasado; *I left at two o'clock*, me fui a las dos),
— con idiomas y títulos (*Italian is not very difficult*, el italiano no es difícil; *Doctor Burnet*, el doctor Burnet; *Mr Brown*, el señor Brown),
— con puntos cardinales en sentido absoluto y delante de un sustantivo seguido por un número cardinal (*to go south*, ir al sur; *I am in room number seven*, estoy en la habitación número siete).

Se debe emplear:
— delante de un sustantivo en singular al generalizar (*the dog is a faithful animal*, el perro es un animal fiel),
— con un sustantivo determinado, en singular y en plural (*the woman* [*that*] *I saw*, la mujer a quien vi; *the books* [*that*] *you read*, los libros que usted leyó),
— con palabras que representan algo único (*the sun, the moon, the Bible*, etc.).

Se emplea asimismo:
— con ciertos adjetivos para sustantivarlos (*the rich*, los ricos),
— delante de números ordinales en títulos y fechas (*Edward the Seventh*, Eduardo Séptimo; *May the thirteenth*, el trece de mayo),
— con función de adverbio (*the more he gets the more he wants*, cuanto más tiene más quiere).

El **artículo indefinido** tiene la misma forma **a** en masculino y en feminino (*a man, a woman*) y sólo existe en singular. Se transforma en **an** delante de una palabra que empieza por vocal o *h* muda (*an artist, an hour*), excepto si se trata de *u* o del grupo *eu* con el sonido de *iu* (*a university, a European*). El plural español *unos, unas* se traduce por *some* (*some interesting books*, unos libros interesantes). Es de uso más frecuente en inglés que en español.

Se debe emplear:
— antes de un sustantivo en singular al generalizar (*a dog is a faithful animal*, el perro es un animal fiel),
— con un nombre que represente la nacionalidad, la profesión o la religión (*he is a Spaniard*. es español; *I am a teacher*, soy profesor; *he was a naval officer*, era oficial de marina; *she is a Moslem*, es musulmana),
— delante de un sustantivo en aposición (*my friend, a teacher of languages*, mi amigo, profesor de idiomas),
— después de las palabras *without, half, such, certain, other, as, what, hundred, thousand, million* (*without a jacket*, sin chaqueta; *half an apple*, media manzana; *it gave me such a fright!*, ¡me dio tal susto!; *a certain day*, cierto día; *another cup of tea*, otra taza de té; *he came as an observer*, vino en calidad de observador; *what a pity!*, ¡qué lástima!; *a hundred houses*, cien casas; *a thousand men*, mil hombres; *a million pounds*, un millón de libras),
— en expresiones de tiempo, de precio y de velocidad (*once a year*, una vez al año; *two shillings a pound*, dos chelines por libra *or* dos chelines la libra; *one hundred miles an hour*, cien millas por hora).

SUSTANTIVO

GÉNERO

Suelen ser **masculinos** los sustantivos que designan a varones o animales machos, profesiones, títulos o empleos desempeñados por hombres.
Son generalmente **femeninos** los sustantivos que representan a personas del sexo opuesto a las anteriores o animales hembras, profesiones, títulos o empleos desempeñados por mujeres.
Son **neutros** todos los demás, con la excepción de *ship, engine, aeroplane* and *car*, que se consideran femeninos la mayoría de las veces.
Hay que señalar que *parent* se aplica al padre y a la madre, *cousin* al primo y a la prima y que *child* y *baby* se clasifican muy frecuentemente entre los neutros.

FORMACIÓN DEL FEMENINO

El **femenino** se forma de las tres maneras siguientes:
— con la terminación **-ess** (*heir, heiress; lion, lioness*),
— con una palabra distinta (*boy, girl; cock, hen*),
— con un sustantivo compuesto (*milkman, milkmaid; manservant, maidservant; he-goat, she-goat*),
— con el adjetivo **female** (*male friend, female friend*).
Existe también el sufijo **-ine** (*hero, heroine*), pero su uso es menos frecuente.

FORMACIÓN DEL PLURAL

El **plural** se forma generalmente añaniendo **-s** al singular (*book, books; plate, plates*). Esta **s** es sorda después de *p, t, k, f, th* y sonora cuando sigue una vocal o una consonante distinta de las anteriormente mencionadas,
— los sustantivos terminados en *-s, -ss, -sh, -ch, -x, -z* añaden **-es**, en plural (*gases, classes, dishes, churches, boxes, topazes*),
— los que acaban en *-o* precedida de consonante añaden **-es** en plural (*potatoes*), con algunas excepciones (*pianos, photos, banjos, tobaccos*),
— los terminados en *-o* precedida de vocal toman sólo una **-s** en plural (*radios*),
— los acabados en *-y* cambian esta terminación en **-ies** cuando la letra anterior es una consonante (*skies*) y añaden simplemente una **-s** si es una vocal (*days*),
— algunas palabras terminadas en *-f* o *-fe* cambian su terminación en **-ves** (*leaves, knives*), mientras que otras, con las mismas características, sólo toman una **-s** (*roofs, safes*),
— ciertos sustantivos forman el plural añaniendo **-en** o **-ren** (*ox, oxen; child, children*). El plural de *brother* es *brothers* cuando significa "hermano de sangre" y *brethren* si tiene el sentido de "miembro de una comunidad",
— otros sufren un cambio en la vocal interna (*man, men; woman, women; tooth, teeth; goose, geese; foot, feet; louse, lice; mouse, mice*),
— algunos conservan la misma forma en singular y en plural (*aircraft, deer, grouse, sheep, salmon, swine, trout*),
— ciertas palabras de origen extranjero se usan con el plural de origen (*datum, data; analysis, analyses*), aunque algunas pueden tener un plural regular (*memorandum, memoranda* o *memorandums*),
— varios sustantivos de cantidad son invariables (*a five mile walk*),
— algunos no tienen singular (*scissors, trousers*, etc.) y otros como *means, news* se emplean como si fueran singulares,
— los acabados en *-ics* pueden usarse sea en singular sea en plural (*physics, politics*, etc.), aunque el empleo del singular sea más frecuente,
— los nombres compuestos añaden la terminación del plural solamente a la palabra principal (*son-in-law, sons-in-law*), excepto si están formados con *man* o *woman* como prefijo (*manservant, menservants*).

CASO POSESIVO

El **caso posesivo** o **genitivo** se emplea para expresar la posesión o la pertenencia, cuando el poseedor es un ser animado o capaz de ser personificado, y con algunos nombres que indican tiempo, medida, espacio o precio. Se forma invirtiendo los términos de la frase y añadiendo un apóstrofo y una **s** al poseedor seguidos de lo poseído sin artículo (*Peter's book*, el libro de Pedro; *at a mile's distance*, a una distancia de una milla; *an hour's walk*, un paseo de una hora; *England's navy*, la marina inglesa).

Si el poseedor está en plural, no se pone la *s* (*the girls' school*, la escuela de las chicas), excepto si no acaba en *s* (*the children's bedroom*, el dormitorio de los niños).

Cuando los poseedores son varios se aplica la forma del caso posesivo únicamente al último (*Peter and John's bedroom*, el dormitorio de Pedro y Juan).

Se omiten frecuentemente las palabras *house, shop* y *church* después del caso posesivo (*I am at my brother's*, estoy en casa de mi hermano; *have you been to the baker's?*, ¿fuiste a la panadería?; *he goes to mass to St Peter's*, va a misa a [la iglesia de] San Pedro).

ADJETIVO

El **adjetivo** suele anteponerse al sustantivo. Tiene la misma forma en singular y plural y en masculino y femenino (*an expensive book*, un libro caro; *expensive books*, libros caros; *a tall boy*, un chico alto; *a tall girl*, una chica alta).
Los adjetivos demostrativos constituyen una excepción y varían en plural (*this woman*, esta mujer; *these women*, estas mujeres; *that man*, ese hombre; *those men*, esos hombres).

ADJETIVO CALIFICATIVO

El **adjetivo calificativo** con función de atributo se coloca siempre antes del sustantivo (*I have a blue pencil*, tengo un lápiz azul).
En cambio, debe de ir después del sustantivo que califica:
— cuando se usa como predicado (*my pencil is blue*, mi lápiz es azul),
— si queda determinado por un complemento (*a glass full of water*, un vaso lleno de agua),
— al calificar los pronombres terminados por *-thing* o *-body* (*something new*, algo nuevo),
— cuando se trata de un adjetivo que empieza por *-a*, como *asleep, afraid, awake, aware, alive, ashamed, alone* (*the fastest man alive*, el hombre más rápido del mundo),
— en algunos casos especiales como *court martial, heir apparent, from time immemorial.*
El adjetivo no se puede usar solo y requiere siempre la presencia de un sustantivo o del pronombre indefinido *one, ones* (*he has a black coat and a blue one*, tiene un abrigo negro y otro blanco).
Se emplea como sustantivo al designar un idioma (*to teach Spanish*, enseñar [el] español) y al representar una palabra abstracta o un grupo de personas, en cuyos casos va siempre precedido por el artículo definido *the* (*the ideal*, lo ideal; *the rich*, los ricos).
En inglés, un sustantivo califica a veces otro, teniendo así función de adjetivo (*house agent*, agente inmobiliario).

COMPARATIVOS Y SUPERLATIVOS

El **comparativo de igualdad** se forma con **as... as** en oraciones afirmativas (*she is as tall as her mother*, es tan alta como su madre) y con **not as... as** o **not so... as** en frases negativas (*he is not as tall as his father*, no es tan alto como su padre).
El **comparativo** y el **superlativo de superioridad** se forman con **more** y **most** respectivamente o con las terminaciones **-er** y **-est**:
— los adjetivos monosilábicos añaden **-er** y **-est** (*he is taller than his father*, es más alto que su padre; *it is the highest building in Spain*, es el edificio más alto de España),
— los de tres o más sílabas van precedidos por **more** y **most** (*he is more intelligent than his brother*, es más inteligente que su hermano; *the most intelligent boy of the group*, el chico más inteligente del grupo),
— los de dos sílabas siguen una de las dos reglas anteriormente mencionadas. Los que acaban en *-er* o *-y* agregan **-er, -est** (*cleverer, prettiest*). Los terminados en **-ful** y **-re** suelen ir precedidos por **more, most** (*more careful, most obscure*),
— algunos son irregulares (véase el cuadro insertado a continuación).

El **comparativo** y el **superlativo de inferioridad** se forman con **less** y **least** respectivamente (*less interesting*, menos interesante; *the least interesting*, el menos interesante).

El **superlativo absoluto** se forma generalmente con los adverbios **very, much** y **most** (*very polite*, muy cortés; *much loved*, muy querido; *most helpful*, muy útil).
El superlativo sólo se puede emplear en inglés cuando se trata de más de dos personas o cosas.

COMPARATIVOS Y SUPERLATIVOS IRREGULARES

POSITIVO	COMPARATIVO	SUPERLATIVO
good	*better*	the best
bad	*worse*	the worst
little	*less*	the least
much	*more*	the most
many	*more*	the most
far	*farther* *further*	the farthest the furthest
old	*older* *elder*	the oldest the eldest
late	*later* *latter*	the latest the last

Much se usa con un sustantivo singular, *many* con un nombre plural.
Farther se refiere en general a una distancia y *further* a una progresión.
Elder y *eldest* indican el grado de antigüedad (*his eldest girl*), *older* y *oldest* el número de años (*she is older than her brother*).
Later, the latest tienen el sentido de "más reciente", mientras que *latter, the last* se aplican al último en una enumeración.

ADJETIVOS NUMERALES

CARDINALES		ORDINALES
0	nought	
1	one	first
2	two	second
3	three	third
4	four	fourth
5	five	fifth
6	six	sixth
7	seven	seventh
8	eight	eighth
9	nine	ninth
10	ten	tenth
11	eleven	eleventh
12	twelve	twelfth
13	thirteen	thirteenth
14	fourteen	fourteenth
15	fifteen	fifteenth
16	sixteen	sixteenth
17	seventeen	seventeenth
18	eighteen	eighteenth
19	nineteen	nineteenth
20	twenty	twentieth
21	twenty-one	twenty-first
22	twenty-two	twenty-second
30	thirty	thirtieth
31	thirty-one	thirty-first
40	forty	fortieth
50	fifty	fiftieth
60	sixty	sixtieth
70	seventy	seventieth
80	eighty	eightieth
90	ninety	ninetieth
100	a hundred, one hundred	hundredth
101	one hundred and one, a hundred and one	hundred and first
134	one hundred and thirty-four	hundred and thirty-fourth
200	two hundred	two hundredth
300	three hundred	three hundredth
400	four hundred	four hundredth
500	five hundred	five hundredth
600	six hundred	six hundredth
700	seven hundred	seven hundredth
800	eight hundred	eight hundredth
900	nine hundred	nine hundredth
1000	a thousand, one thousand	thousandth
1001	one thousand and one	thousand and first
2034	two thousand and thirty-four	two thousand and thirty-fourth
1 000 000	a million, one million	millionth
1 000 000 000	a milliard, one milliard [U. S. a billion, one billion]	[U. S. billionth]
1 000 000 000 000	a billion, one billion [U. S. a trillion, one trillion]	billionth [U. S. trillionth]

Numerales cardinales

Entre las decenas y las unidades no se usa nunca la conjunción *and;* a partir de 20 (*twenty*), los numerales se forman con el nombre de la decena correspondiente seguida de un guión y las unidades correlativas (*twenty-one; thirty-two*).
Después de *million, thousand* y *hundred*, los números inferiores a cien van siempre precedidos por la conjunción and (*one thousand two hundred and fifty-two; one thousand and one*).
Million, thousand y *hundred* son invariables, excepto cuando se usan como sustantivos con un sentido impreciso (*thousands of men were killed*). Lo mismo se aplica a *dozen* y *score* (*I saw him scores of times*).
Hundred, thousand, million, etc. van precedidos por **a** o **one**. *A* se emplea especialmente cuando se trata de una cifra redonda (*a hundred women*) y *one* si estos números van seguidos por otros (*one thousand and two*). Los números que indican el año suelen expresarse por centenas (*in seventeen hundred*, en el año mil setecientos).

Numerales ordinales

En los números compuestos, el último elemento es el único en tomar la forma del ordinal (*twenty-fifth*). Los numerales ordinales se utilizan para expresar el orden (*he is the third*, es el tercero; *chapter the second*, el capítulo segundo), la cronología (*George the Fifth*, Jorge Quinto; *the nineteenth century*, el siglo diez y nueve) y las fechas (*May the 25th* o *the 25th of May*, el veinticinco de mayo).

ADJETIVOS Y PRONOMBRES

PRONOMBRES PERSONALES

		SUJETO	COMPLEMENTO	REFLEXIVO
SINGULAR	1.ª pers.	I	me	myself
	2.ª pers.	you	you	yourself
	3.ª pers. masc.	he	him	himself
	3.ª pers. fem.	she	her	herself
	3.ª pers. neut.	it	it	itself
PLURAL	1.ª pers.	we	us	ourselves
	2.ª pers.	you	you	yourselves
	3.ª pers.	they	them	themselves

Los **pronombres personales** no han de omitirse nunca en inglés. En una oración afirmativa, los que tienen función de sujeto se colocan delante del verbo (*he bought a book*, compró un libro) y los que se utilizan como complementos van detrás del verbo o de una preposición (*my brother took them*, mi hermano los tomó; *he said to me that*, me dijo que). El complemento indirecto no ha de colocarse nunca antes del complemento directo (*he gave it to me*, me lo dio). Empleado con verbos seguidos de una partícula, el pronombre complemento directo se debe poner entre el verbo y la partícula (*give it up!*, ¡déjalo!).

El pronombre sujeto de primera persona va siempre en mayúscula (*I am reading*, estoy leyendo).

It se emplea en construcciones impersonales (it is hot).

You we, they e *it* sirven para traducir el pronombre impersonal español *se* (*it is rumoured that*, se rumorea que; *we do not work on Sunday*, no se trabaja el domingo).

Los pronombres reflexivos se usan para reforzar el pronombre (*he wrote it himself*, lo escribió él mismo) o cuando la acción del verbo recae sobre el mismo sujeto (*he looks at himself in the mirror*, se mira en el espejo). Conviene indicar que no todos los verbos reflexivos en español lo son en inglés (*quejarse*, to complain; *equivocarse*, to be mistaken; *sentarse*, to sit down; *alegrarse*, to be happy, etc.).

El pronombre personal indefinido **one** corresponde a "uno" (*one does not like to be beaten*, a uno no le gusta que le peguen).

PRONOMBRES Y ADJETIVOS POSESIVOS

		ADJETIVOS	PRONOMBRES
SINGULAR	1.ª pers.	my	mine
	2.ª pers.	your	yours
	3.ª pers. masc.	his	his
	3.ª pers. fem.	her	hers
	3.ª pers. neut.	its	its own
PLURAL	1.ª pers.	our	ours
	2.ª pers.	your	yours
	3.ª pers.	their	theirs

Los **adjetivos** y **pronombres posesivos** varían con el poseedor y no con el objeto poseído (*my books*, mis libros; *Jane plays with her brother and her sister*, Juana juega con su hermano y su hermana; *this book is mine, it is not yours*, este libro es mío, no es tuyo; *these pencils are his, they are not mine*, estos lápices son suyos, no son míos).

Si el poseedor es indefinido, se usa **one's** (*it is sometimes hard to do one's duty*, a veces es difícil cumplir con su deber).

El adjetivo posesivo se emplea con las partes del cuerpo y las prendas de vestir. En los mismos casos en castellano se utiliza el artículo definido (*he hurt his foot*, se lastimó el pie; *put on your jacket*, ponte la chaqueta).

El pronombre posesivo precedido por **of** corresponde al adjetivo español *mío, mía*, etc. (*a friend of yours*, un amigo tuyo).

Se puede reforzar la idea de posesión añadiendo **own** al adjetivo posesivo (*this is my own pen, not yours*, esta pluma es mía y no suya).

ADJETIVOS Y PRONOMBRES DEMOSTRATIVOS

GRADO DE LEJANÍA (adverbios de lugar)		MASCULINO Y FEMENINO singular	MASCULINO Y FEMENINO plural	NEUTRO singular
here (aquí)	**adj.**	**this** (este, esta)	**these** (estos, estas)	
	pron.	**this, this one** (éste, ésta)	**these, these ones** (éstos, éstas)	**this** (esto)
there (ahí, allí, allá)	**adj.**	**that** (ese, aquel; esa, aquella)	**those** (esos, aquellos; esas, aquellas)	
	pron.	**that, that one** (ése, aquél; ésa, aquélla)	**those, those ones** (ésos, aquéllos; ésas, aquéllas)	**that** (eso, aquello)

El **adjetivo demostrativo** es el único adjetivo que concuerda en número con el sustantivo que le sigue (*I like this book*, me gusta este libro; *I like these books*, me gustan estos libros).

La forma del pronombre sin que se pongan *one, ones* se emplea cuando el sujeto se expresa en la misma oración (*this is his coat*, éste es el abrigo suyo; *that is my house*, ésa es mi casa). En cambio, si se omite el nombre, es imprescindible utilizar el pronombre indefinido *one, ones* (*do you prefer this one or that one?*, ¿le gusta más éste o ése?).

That y **those** seguidos por la preposición *of* se traducen por *el de, la de, los de, las de* (*this is not my book, it is that of my sister*, éste no es mi libro, es el de mi hermana).

That y **those** seguidos por un relativo corresponden a *el que, la que, los que, las que* (*those who are tired may have a rest*, los que están cansados pueden descansar).

Cuando se hace referencia a dos objetos ya mencionados, se suele emplear *the former* para el primero y *the latter* para el segundo.

PRONOMBRES RELATIVOS

Los **pronombres relativos** tienen la misma forma en singular y en plural.

	SUJETO	COMPLEMENTO	POSESIVO
PERSONAS	who, that	whom, that	whose
COSAS Y ANIMALES	which, that	which, that	whose, of which

No se puede omitir nunca el pronombre sujeto (*the man who comes*, el hombre que viene). Sin embargo se prescinde frecuentemente del pronombre complemento (*the man I saw*, el hombre a quien vi). Cuando éste es indirecto, la preposición se debe colocar después del verbo (*the man I spoke to yesterday*, el hombre a quien hablé ayer).

El antecedente del pronombre relativo puede ser otro pronombre (*he who came yesterday*, el que vino ayer).
— **That** tiene un sentido restrictivo (*bring me the pen that is on the table, and no other*, tráeme la pluma que está en la mesa y no otra) y no ha de ser seguido por una preposición. Se emplea después de un superlativo, incluyendo *first* y *last* (*it is the finest city that I have ever seen*, es la ciudad más bonita que jamás he visto), de un pronombre indefinido, de *only* y *very* o de un antecedente que incluye personas y cosas o animales (*the people, cattle and carts that went to market*, la gente, el ganado y las carretas que iban al mercado).
— **Whose** se usa únicamente cuando existe una relación de posesión (*Peter, whose house we have visited, is American*, Pedro, cuya casa hemos visitado, es americano).
— **What** se emplea cuando el antecedente no queda expresado (*tell me what you want to know*, dígame lo que quiere saber).

ADJETIVOS Y PRONOMBRES INTERROGATIVOS

	ADJETIVOS	PRONOMBRES		
		SUJETO	COMPLEMENTO	POSESIVO
PERSONAS	what, which	who	who, whom	whose
COSAS Y ANIMALES	what, which	what, which	what, which	whose

Para las personas **who** se refiere a la identidad (*who is this man?*, ¿quién es este señor?), **what** a la función (*what is your brother?*, ¿qué es tu hermano? y **which** a la elección (*which of these men did you see?*, ¿a cuál de estos hombres viste?).
En la lengua hablada se usa frecuentemente la forma **who** para el complemento referente a personas en vez de *whom*.

Cuando el pronombre va acompañado por una preposición, ésta se suele poner al final de la oración (*whom did you play with?*, ¿con quién jugaste?).
Si la pregunta es indirecta no hay inversión del verbo (*I asked him what he was doing*, le pregunté lo que estaba haciendo).
What se emplea también en expresiones exclamativas (*what luck!*, ¡qué suerte!).

ADJETIVOS Y PRONOMBRES INDEFINIDOS

Los principales adjetivos y pronombres indefinidos son *each, either, neither, every, several, all, some, any, little, few, much, many, enough, no, not any, none, other, another.*
— **No** y **every** sólo son adjetivos y **none** pronombre.
— **Either** significa una de dos personas o cosas.
— Al igual que **either** y **neither, each** y **every** van siempre seguidos por un verbo en singular; *each* tiene un sentido individual, mientras que *every* expresa una idea de colectividad (*on each side*, de cada lado; *on every side*, por todos los lados).
— **Some** se emplea siempre en oraciones afirmativas (*leave us some oranges*, déjanos algunas naranjas) y a veces en frases interrogativas cuya contestación será afirmativa.
— **Any** se usa en oraciones interrogativas y negativas (*do you take any sugar?*; ¿tomas azúcar?; *I do not take any sugar*, no tomo azúcar), después de *hardly, scarcely, barely* e *if*.

— Los pronombres compuestos derivados de SOME, ANY, NO y EVERY son respectivamente *something, somebody, someone, anything, anybody, anyone, nothing, nobody, no one* y *everything, everybody, everyone.*

— **Little** y **much** se aplican a cantidades que no se pueden contar (*he made little progress*, hizo pocos progresos).

— **Few** y **many** se emplean con cantidades numerables (*he ate many cakes*, comió muchos pasteles).
— **Other** es invariable cuando es adjetivo y variable como pronombre (*other examples*, otros ejemplos; *show me the others*, enséñeme los otros).
— **Each other** y **one another** se utilizan después de un verbo para expresar la reciprocidad. La primera forma si se habla de dos personas únicamente y la segunda si hay más de dos (*the two cousins love each other*, las dos primas se quieren; *the three cousins love one another*, las tres primas se quieren).

PREPOSICIÓN

El pronombre regido por una preposición tiene función de complemento (*he spoke to me*, me habló). En las oraciones interrogativas y en las subordinadas introducidas por un pronombre relativo, la preposición antecede al pronombre o sigue al verbo (*this is the girl to whom I spoke yesterday, this is the girl whom I spoke to this morning*). Con "that" o cuando el relativo no queda expresado, la preposición se coloca siempre después del verbo (*this is the girl [that] I spoke to*).
Los sustantivos concretos usados en singular después de una preposición tienen que ir precedidos por el artículo indefinido (*she went out without an umbrella*, salió sin paraguas).
El verbo que sigue la preposición va siempre en gerundio (*she came in without knocking*, entró sin llamar a la puerta).
La mayoría de las preposiciones existen como adverbios y muchas son también conjunciones (*after, before, since, till*).

ADVERBIO

Los **adverbios de modo** se forman generalmente añadiendo **-ly** al adjetivo (*slow, slowly*) y esto trae consigo las modificaciones ortográficas siguientes:
— los adjetivos terminados en *-le*, cambian la *-e* en *-y* (*comfortable, comfortably*);
— los acabados en *-ll* sólo añaden una *y* (*full, fully*);
— los terminados en *-y* sustituyen esta letra por una *i* antes del sufijo *-ly* (*noisy, noisily*);
— los acabados en *-ue* pierden la *-e* (*true, truly*).
Algunos adjetivos se usan como adverbios(*fast, straight, tight*, etc.).

Los principales **adverbios de cantidad** son *little, much, almost, rather, quite, very, too, enough*, etc.

Los **adverbios de lugar** más usados son *above, across, along, around, away, back, behind, below, down, far, here, in, near, off, out, there, up, where*, etc.

Los **adverbios de tiempo** más comúnmente empleados son *after, again, ago, already, always, before, early, ever, formerly, late, never, now, often, once, seldom, sometimes, soon, still, then, today, when, yesterday, yet*, etc.

Los **adverbios de negación** más frecuentemente utilizados son *no, not, never, not at all.*

Los comparativos y superlativos de los adverbios siguen la misma regla que los adjetivos. Algunos son irregulares.

COMPARATIVOS Y SUPERLATIVOS IRREGULARES

POSITIVO	COMPARATIVO	SUPERLATIVO
well	*better*	best
badly	*worse*	worst
little	*less*	least
much	*more*	most
far	*farther* / *further*	farthest / furthest

El adverbio se pone antes del adjetivo, del participio pasivo u de otro adverbio, excepto en el caso de *enough* (*she is very clever; it is good enough*). Con un verbo transitivo suele colocarse después del complemento, excepto si éste es un infinitivo (*he banged the door noisily; they kindly asked her to stay at their house*). Cuando un verbo se construye con un auxiliar o un defectivo el adverbio debe seguir al primer auxiliar (*I shall probably have finished tomorrow*, probablemente habré acabado mañana).

VERBO

DIVISIÓN

Los verbos se dividen en:
— **transitivos**, cuando tienen complemento directo (*I open the window*, abro la ventana);
— **intransitivos**, cuando no lo tienen (*the window opened*, la ventana se abrió);
— **reflexivos**, cuando la acción recae en el mismo sujeto que la ejecuta. Se conjugan añadiendo un pronombre reflexivo de la misma persona que el sujeto (*he looked at himself*, se miró);
— **recíprocos**, cuando representan una acción efectuada recíprocamente por dos o más personas. Si se trata sólo de dos personas, el verbo va seguido por *each other* (*Peter and Joan love each other*, Pedro y Juana se quieren). En caso contrario se añade *one another* (*the four cousins love one another*, los cuatro primos se quieren);
— **impersonales**, cuando sólo se emplean en la tercera persona del singular. En inglés van precedidos obligatoriamente por el pronombre neutro *it* y casi siempre se refieren a fenómenos meteorológicos (*it is raining*, está lloviendo);
— **defectivos**, cuando se usan únicamente en algunos tiempos y se sustituyen por equivalentes para los demás. No llevan *s* en la tercera persona del singular del presente de indicativo, no van nunca precedidos por *do* u otro auxiliar, el verbo que les sigue está siempre en infinitivo sin "to" (excepto en el caso de *ought*) y el pretérito puede tener un significado de potencial (*we could not hear if we had no ears*, no podríamos oír si no tuviéramos oídos). Tienen frecuentemente función de auxiliares.

VERBOS DEFECTIVOS	SIGNIFICADO	EQUIVALENTES
I can, I could	*capacidad*	to be able
I may, I might	*permiso, probabilidad*	to be allowed futuro + perhaps
I must	*necesidad, obligación, probabilidad*	to have to
I will, I would	*consentimiento*	to want, to wish to
I shall, I should	*obligación moral*	to have to
I ought to	*obligación moral, consejo*	

Los verbos **need** y **dare** pueden tratarse como verbos normales o defectivos en las oraciones negativas e interrogativas.
— **auxiliares**, cuando sirven para conjugar los demás verbos (véase "verbos auxiliares" más adelante).
Es necesario observar que los verbos no se construyen siempre de la misma manera en ambos idiomas. Muchos verbos intransitivos en inglés son reflexivos o pronominales en español (*to sit down*, sentarse), algunos son transitivos en una lengua e intransitivos en la otra (*to cross one's mind*, pasar por la mente; *to ask for sth.*, pedir algo), otros no van seguidos por la misma preposición en los dos idiomas (*to delight in something*, deleitarse con algo; *he has profited by your advice*, ha sacado provecho de su consejo).

VOCES, MODOS Y TIEMPOS

Voz Pasiva

Los tiempos de la **voz pasiva** se forman con el auxiliar **to be** y el **participio pasivo** del verbo conjugado (*this picture was painted by Turner*, este cuadro fue pintado por Turner).
En inglés se emplea mucho más la voz pasiva que en español, que la sustituye generalmente por la forma pronominal (*the fire was seen from our house*, se veía el incendio desde nuestra casa) o activa correspondiente (*this picture was painted by Turner*, Turner pintó este cuadro).
Cuando un verbo, como *to teach, to tell, to show, to give*, etc., tiene dos complementos, hay dos construcciones posibles para la forma pasiva (*Mary told me a story, I was told a story by Mary* o *a story was told me by Mary*).

Infinitivo

El **infinitivo** suele ir precedido por la preposición **to**. Se emplea como sujeto de una oración (*to err is human*, errar es humano) o como complemento de la mayoría de los verbos (*I wish to see you soon*, deseo verle pronto; *my mother wants me to write my brother*, mi madre quiere que escriba a mi hermano), después de adjetivos y sustantivos (*it is difficult to understand*, es difícil de entender; *it was time to get up*, era hora de levantarse), detrás de "to be" y "to have" para indicar la obligación (*do you have to go home?*, tienes que ir a casa?).
To se omite:

— después de auxiliares y defectivos, excepto OUGHT (*I shall go*, iré; *I may go*, puedo ir),
— después de los verbos de percepción (*we saw them come*, les vimos venir),
— después de los verbos TO MAKE, TO LET, TO BID (*he made them listen*, les hizo escuchar; *let me sit here*, déjeme sentarme aquí; *he bade them be silent*, les pidió que se callaran),
— después de las expresiones HAD BETTER, HAD RATHER y BUT (*I had better go*, más vale que me vaya; *I cannot but admire it*, no puedo dejar de admirarlo).

Gerundio y participio de presente

El gerundio y el participio de presente se forman de la misma manera, es decir añadiendo **-ing** al infinitivo sin *to*.

El **gerundio** ejerce la función de un sustantivo. Se usa como sujeto o complemento (*she loves reading poetry*, le encanta leer poesía), después de todas las preposiciones, excepto TO (*she is tired of walking*, está cansada de andar), detrás de algunos verbos que indican el principio, la continuación o la terminación de una acción (*to keep singing*, seguir cantando) y de ciertas expresiones como *to be worth, I can't help, I don't mind, do you mind?, it is no use* y *it is no good* (*this book is worth reading*, este libro es digno de leerse), cuando es precedido por un artículo, un adjetivo indefinido, un adjetivo o un caso posesivo (*I like his singing*, me gusta su manera de cantar). También se emplea con verbos que expresan una intención o un gusto personal, aunque en este caso se puede utilizar también el infinitivo con *to*.

El **participio de presente** se usa en la forma progresiva (véase "Forma progresiva" en el apartado siguiente), como adjetivo (*an amusing story*, una historia divertida) y en sustitución de una oración adverbial (*fearing that they would recognize him...*, temiendo que le reconociesen...).

Forma progresiva

La forma progresiva se utiliza más frecuentemente en inglés que en español. Se forma con el verbo **to be** y el **participio de presente** del verbo (*I am reading*, estoy leyendo). Se emplea para indicar que la acción se está realizando en el momento en que se habla o que se estaba efectuando en la época a la cual uno se refiere (*he was reading*, estaba leyendo). Se usa también para expresar una acción que tendrá lugar en el futuro (*we are leaving tomorrow*, nos iremos mañana), pero no puede hacerse cuando se trata de una acción de poca duración, habitual o instintiva.

Participio pasivo

El **participio pasivo** de los verbos regulares se forma añadiendo **-ed** al infinitivo.
Se emplea con *to be* para formar la voz pasiva y con *to have* para conjugar los tiempos compuestos del pasado. Cumple también las funciones de adjetivo.

Indicativo

El **presente**, que tiene la misma forma en todas las personas, excepto en la tercera del singular que toma **-s** o **-es** al final del infinitivo, indica que la acción se efectúa de una manera habitual (*he goes to school every day*, va al colegio todos los días). Se emplea también para expresar una acción futura en proposiciones subordinadas que indican una condición o una idea de tiempo (*when the weather gets a bit better, we'll all go to the beach*, cuando mejore un poco el tiempo, iremos todos a la playa).

El **pretérito indefinido** se forma en todas las personas añadiendo **-ed** al infinitivo. Se utiliza para una acción completamente terminada en el pasado (*my watch stopped yesterday*, se me paró el reloj ayer). Empleado en la forma progresiva equivale al imperfecto español (*she was wearing a green skirt*, llevaba una falda verde).

El **pretérito perfecto** se conjuga con el verbo auxiliar **to have** y el **participio pasivo** del verbo conjugado. Se usa para una acción que tuvo lugar en un pasado indeterminado (*I have seen this woman somewhere*, he visto a esta mujer en alguna parte) o que se realizó en un período todavía sin concluir (*I haven't finished my work yet*, aún no he acabado mi trabajo) o que no está terminada (*he has been ill for a month*, hace un mes que está enfermo; *he has been ill since Saturday*, está enfermo desde el sábado) o que acaba de realizarse (*he has just arrived*, acaba de llegar).

El **futuro** se forma con el **infinitivo** sin *to* precedido por los auxiliares **shall** en la primera persona del singular y del plural y **will** en las otras. Actualmente *will* se suele aplicar a todas las personas. Sin embargo *shall* se emplea con la primera persona para pedir una opinión (*shall I make the tea?*, ¿quiere que prepare el té?) y con las otras para ordenar o prometer algo (*you shall leave the room at once*, les ordeno que salgan de la habitación inmediatamente).

El *futuro inmediato* se traduce por *to be going to* o *to be about to*, que significan "estar a punto de".

Potencial

El **potencial simple** se conjuga anteponiendo al **infinitivo** sin *to* los auxiliares **should** en la primera persona del singular y del plural y **would** en las otras. Actualmente *would* suele aplicarse a todas las personas.

Subjuntivo

En el inglés moderno este modo tiende a desaparecer. Tiene las mismas formas que el indicativo, excepto en el caso de la tercera persona del singular del presente que no lleva *s*. El auxiliar *to be* hace **be** en presente y **were** en pretérito para todas las personas.
Se emplea únicamente para expresar una hipótesis considerada ya como irrealizable (*if I were you*, si estuviese en tu lugar) o un deseo (*God save the Queen!*, ¡Dios guarde a la Reina!) y en algunas expresiones como *be that as it may*, *come what may*, etc.
El subjuntivo español se traduce generalmente por el infinitivo o el indicativo (véase THE SUBJUNCTIVE en SUMMARY OF SPANISH GRAMMAR) o mediante una forma compuesta con los auxiliares **may, might** y **should** (*if he should come*, si él viniese).

Imperativo

El **imperativo** sólo tiene una forma propia, la segunda persona del singular y del plural, que corresponde al infinitivo sin *to*. Para las demás personas se usa "let" con los pronombres complementos (*let us go*, vayámonos).

Forma frecuentativa

Se emplea para expresar una costumbre o una repetición. Se forma, en el presente, con **will** y el **infinitivo** y, en el pasado, con **would** o **used to** seguidos por el **infinitivo** (*she will sit there hour after hour*, suele *or* acostumbra sentarse allí horas y horas; *she would go for a walk every morning*, acostumbraba *or* solía dar un paseo todas las mañanas).

Forma enfática

La forma enfática se utiliza para insistir en la realidad del hecho que se afirma.

En presente y pasado, se forma añadiendo **do** conjugado, si no hay ningún auxiliar (*he did transmit your request to her*, seguramente le transmitió tu petición), y se pronuncia con cierto énfasis el auxiliar en el caso contrario. En imperativo se construye siempre con **do** (*do come and see me*, no deje de venir a verme; *do have a cup of tea*, tome una taza de té, por favor).

Forma negativa

Para los auxiliares y defectivos se añade únicamente **not** (*you are not, they could not*).

En el caso de los demás verbos se coloca **not** entre el primer auxiliar y el verbo (*I have not seen*) en los tiempos compuestos y se pone **do not, does not, did not** delante del infinitivo sin *to* en los tiempos simples (*he does not go, we did not go*).

Los infinitivos y participios llevan la negación **not** antepuesta (*not seeing her, not to go*).

Sin embargo no se utiliza *do* con cualquier negación que no sea *not* (*I saw nobody*).

En la lengua familiar *not* se convierte en **n't** y se une al verbo (*he doesn't think so; you mustn't do that; don't go*).

Cuando *can* va seguido por *not* hace *cannot* o *can't* (*she cannot* o *she can't understand, she is too young*, no puede entender, es demasiado joven).

Forma interrogativa

Para los auxiliares y defectivos se invierten el sujeto y el verbo en los tiempos simples (*is he a painter?; can he swim?*) y el sujeto y el primer auxiliar en los tiempos compuestos (*should he have been there?*).

En el caso de los demás verbos se pone el sujeto entre **do, does, did** y el infinitivo (*does he go?*) en los tiempos simples y se invierten el sujeto y el primer auxiliar en los tiempos compuestos (*would Peter have come?*).
No se emplea *do* si la oración empieza con un adjetivo o un pronombre interrogativo con función de sujeto (*who brought this letter?*).

La forma interrogativa en negaciones se construye con el auxiliar seguido por *not* y un sustantivo o pronombre indefinido o demostrativo (*is not John a good boy?; will not another do it?*). Con los pronombres personales *not* se pone al final (*is he not a good boy?*), excepto si se utiliza la contracción *n't* (*isn't he a good boy?*).

Para la traducción del español ¿VERDAD? véase la observación que hay al final de esta palabra en el cuerpo del diccionario.

Observaciones sobre la pronunciación

La terminación **-ed** del pretérito y del participio pasivo se pronuncia como una *d* cuando el radical del verbo acaba con una consonante sonora o un sonido vocálico (*filled, loved, moved, called, spared, sawed*), como una *t* cuando el radical del verbo termina por una consonante sorda (*brushed, scoffed, placed, remarked, passed, reached*) y como *id* después de una *t* o una *d* (*melted, glided*).

Los verbos cuyo infinitivo acaba en **-ce, -se** y **-ge** se pronuncian con una sílaba adicional que suena *-iz* en la tercera persona del singular del presente de indicativo (*dances, cleanses, changes*).

Los verbos cuyo infinitivo termina en **-ss, -x, -z, -sh** y **-ch** añaden, en la tercera persona del singular del presente de indicativo, las letras *-es* que tienen el sonido de *-iz* (*misses, fixes, fizzes, crushes, reaches*).

Modificaciones ortográficas

Se duplica la consonante final de un verbo monosilábico cuando va precedida por una sola vocal y seguida por una terminación que empieza con una vocal (*stopped*). La misma regla se aplica a los verbos de dos o más sílabas si éstos llevan el acento en la última sílaba (*preferred*), con excepción de los que acaban por vocal y *l* (*travelled*), salvo PARALLEL.

Si un verbo termina en -y después de una consonante, se cambia ésta en *-i* antes de añadir la terminación *-es* para la tercera persona del singular del presente de indicativo (*he studies*) y *-ed* para el pretérito y el participio pasivo (*studied*).
En cambio, cuando la **-y** va precedida por una vocal en el infinitivo, se forma la tercera persona del singular del presente de indicativo agregando *-s* (*plays; says*) y el participio de presente añadiendo *-ing* (*playing; saying*).

Si un verbo monosilábico acaba en -ie, esta terminación se convierte en **-y** antes de añadir *-ing* para formar el participio de presente (*to die* hace *dying*).

El pretérito y el participio pasivo de los **verbos terminados en -o** se forman agregando *-ed* a la vocal final (*to halo* hace *haloed*).

VERBOS AUXILIARES

Be. — Este auxiliar se emplea, al igual que *ser*, para formar la voz pasiva y la forma progresiva.
Se usa también como impersonal, en cuyo caso va precedido de **there** y corresponde a *hay, había, hubo* (*there were twenty pupils*, había veinte alumnos).

To be equivale a *tener* cuando indica una medida, una edad, una sensación o un estado (*the house is 100 feet high*, la casa tiene cien pies de alto; *I am thirty*, tengo treinta años; *they are hungry*, tienen hambre) y a *estar* al referirse a la salud (*how are you?*, ¿cómo estás?). Seguido por **to** expresa una obligación o una probabilidad (*we are to go to the theatre tonight*, debemos ir al teatro esta noche).

Have. — Este auxiliar, equivalente al *haber* castellano, se emplea para formar los tiempos compuestos de todos los verbos.

To have equivale a *tener* cuando indica posesión, en cuyo caso va frecuentemente acompañado por **got** (*his aunt has got a beautiful house*, su tía tiene una casa preciosa) y a *tomar* al aplicarse a alimentos (*have a drink*, tome una copa).
Con el infinitivo o el participio pasivo significa *mandar hacer* (*he had a new suit made*, mandó hacer un traje nuevo; *he had the tailor make him a suit*, mandó al sastre que le hiciera un traje).
Expresa una obligación cuando va seguido por **to** (*I have to go home*, tengo que ir a casa) y una preferencia con **better** o **rather** (*I had better do it*, más vale que lo haga; *I had rather do it*, preferiría hacerlo).

Do. — Este auxiliar se emplea en las formas negativa, interrogativa y enfática de los demás verbos. Se utiliza también para sustituir un verbo ya mencionado (*we did not take coffee, but she did*, no tomamos café pero ella sí; *Peter came by train, so did John*, Pedro vino en tren y Juan también).
Se conjuga como un verbo regular pero hace *does* en la tercera persona del singular del presente de indicativo, *did* en el pretérito indefinido y *done* en el participio pasivo.

Los **verbos defectivos** (can, may, must, will, shall, ought to, dare, need) se usan como auxiliares (*he will work*, trabajará).

BE

Infinitivo: to be
Gerundio: being
Participio: been

INDICATIVO

presente

I am
you are
he
she is
it
we are
you are
they are

pret. indefinido

I was
you were
he
she was
it
we were
you were
they were

pret. perfecto

I have been
you have been
he
she has been
it
we have been
you have been
they have been

pluscuamperfecto

I had been
you had been
he
she had been
it
we had been
you had been
they had been

futuro

I shall be
you will be
he
she will be
it
we shall be
you will be
they will be

futuro perfecto

I shall have been
you will have been
he
she will have been
it
we shall have been
you will have been
they will have been

POTENCIAL

simple

I should be
you would be
he
she would be
it
we should be
you would be
they would be

compuesto

I should have been
you would have been
he
she would have been
it
we should have been
you would have been
they would have been

IMPERATIVO

let me be
be
let him
let her be
let it
let us be
be
let them be

SUBJUNTIVO

presente

be
(para todas las personas)

pretérito

were
(para todas las personas)

HAVE

Infinitivo: to have
Gerundio: having
Participio: had

INDICATIVO

presente

I have
you have
he
she has
it
we have
you have
they have

pret. indefinido

had
(para todas las personas)

pret. perfecto

I have had
you have had
he
she has had
it
we have had
you have had
they have had

pluscuamperfecto

had had
(para todas las personas)

futuro

I shall have
you will have
he
she will have
it
we shall have
you will have
they will have

futuro perfecto

I shall have had
you will have had
he
she will have had
it
we shall have had
you will have had
they will have had

POTENCIAL

simple

I should have
you would have
he
she would have
it
we should have
you would have
they would have

compuesto

I should have had
you would have had
he
she would have had
it
we should have had
you would have had
they would have had

IMPERATIVO

let me have
have
let him
let her have
let it
let us have
have
let them have

SUBJUNTIVO

presente

have
(para todas las personas)

pretérito

had
(para todas las personas)

VERBOS REGULARES

Sólo existe un grupo de verbos regulares.

OPEN

Infinitivo: to open
Gerundio: opening
Participio: opened

INDICATIVO

presente

I open
you open
he
she opens
it
we open
you open
they open

pret. indefinido

opened
(para todas las personas)

pret. perfecto

I have opened
you have opened
he
she has opened
it
we have opened
you have opened
they have opened

pluscuamperfecto

had opened
(para todas las personas)

futuro

I shall open
you will open
he
she will open
it
we shall open
you will open
they will open

futuro perfecto

I shall have opened
you will have opened
he
she will have opened
it
we shall have opened
you will have opened
they will have opened

POTENCIAL

simple

I should open
you would open
he
she would open
it
we should open
you would open
they would open

compuesto

I should have opened
you woud have opened
he
she would have opened
it
we should have opened
you would have opened
they would have opened

IMPERATIVO

let me open
open
let him
let her open
let it
let us open
open
let them open

SUBJUNTIVO

presente

open
(para todas las personas)

pretérito

opened
(para todas las personas)

LISTA DE VERBOS IRREGULARES

INFINITIVO	PRETÉRITO	PART. PASIVO
	A	
abide	*abode, abided*	abode, abided
arise	*arose*	arisen
awake	*awoke*	awaked, awoke, awoken
	B	
be	*was, were*	been
bear	*bore*	borne (llevado) born (nacido)
beat	*beat*	beaten, beat
become	*became*	become
befall	*befell*	befallen
beget	*begot, begat* (ant.)	begotten
begin	*began*	begun
behold	*beheld*	beheld
bend	*bent*	bent, bended (ant.)
bereave	*bereft, bereaved*	bereft, bereaved
beseech	*besought, beseeched*	besought, beseeched
beset	*beset*	beset
bespeak	*bespoke*	bespoken, bespoke (ant.)

INFINITIVO	PRETÉRITO	PART. PASIVO
bestrew	*bestrewed*	bestrewed, bestrewn
bestride	*bestrode*	bestridden
bet	*bet, betted*	bet, betted
betake	*betook*	betaken
bethink	*bethought*	bethought
bid (ordenar, rogar)	*bade*	bidden
(licitar)	*bid*	bid
bide	*bode*	bided
bind	*bound*	bound
bite	*bit*	bitten, bit
bleed	*bled*	bled
blow	*blew*	blown
break	*broke*	broken
breed	*bred*	bred
bring	*brought*	brought
broadcast	*broadcast*	broadcast
build	*built*	built
burn	*burnt, burned*	burnt, burned
burst	*burst*	burst
buy	*bought*	bought
C		
can	*could*	
cast	*cast*	cast
catch	*caught*	caught
chide	*chid, chided*	chid,chidden,chided
choose	*chose*	chosen
cleave		
(hender)	*cleaved, cleft, clove*	cleaved, cleft, cloven
(adherirse)	*cleaved*	cleaved
cling	*clung*	clung
clothe	*clothed, clad*	clothed, clad
cold-draw	*cold-drew*	cold-drawn
come	*came*	come
cost	*cost*	cost
countersink	*countersank*	countersunk
creep	*crept*	crept
crossbreed	*crossbred*	crossbred
crow	*crowed, crew*	crowed
cut	*cut*	cut
D		
deal	*dealt*	dealt
dig	*dug*	dug
dive	*dived, dove*	dived
do	*did*	done
draw	*drew*	drawn
dream	*dreamed, dreamt*	dreamed, dreamt
drink	*drank*	drunk
drive	*drove*	driven
dwell	*dwelt*	dwelt
E		
eat	*ate*	eaten
F		
fall	*fell*	fallen
feed	*fed*	fed
feel	*felt*	felt
fight	*fought*	fought
find	*found*	found
flee	*fled*	fled
fling	*flung*	flung
fly	*flew*	flown
forbear	*forbore*	forborne
forbid	*forbade, forbad*	forbidden
forego	*forewent*	foregone
foreknow	*foreknew*	foreknown
foresee	*foresaw*	foreseen
foretell	*foretold*	foretold
forget	*forgot*	forgotten
forgive	*forgave*	forgiven
forgo	*forwent*	forgone
forsake	*forsook*	forsaken
forswear	*forswore*	forsworn
freeze	*froze*	frozen
G		
get	*got*	got [U. S. gotten]
gird	*girded, girt*	girded, girt
give	*gave*	given
gnaw	*gnawed*	gnawed, gnawn
go	*went*	gone
grind	*ground*	ground
grow	*grew*	grown
H		
hang (sentido general)	*hung*	hung
(ahorcar)	*hanged*	hanged
have	*had*	had

INFINITIVO	PRETÉRITO	PART. PASIVO
hear	*heard*	heard
heave (sentido general)	*heaved*	heaved
(sentido marítimo)	*hove*	hove
hew	*hewed*	hewed, hewn
hide	*hid*	hidden, hid
hit	*hit*	hit
hold	*held*	held
hurt	*hurt*	hurt
I		
interweave	*interwove*	interwoven
inweave	*inwove*	inwoven
K		
keep	*kept*	kept
kneel	*knelt, kneeled*	knelt, kneeled
knit	*knit, knitted*	knit, knitted
know	*knew*	known
L		
lade	*laded*	laden
lay	*laid*	laid
lead	*led*	led
lean	*leant, leaned*	leant, leaned
leap	*leapt, leaped*	leapt, leaped
learn	*learnt, learned*	learnt, learned
leave	*left*	left
lend	*lent*	lent
let	*let*	let
lie	*lay*	lain
light	*lighted, lit*	lighted, lit
lip-read	*lip-read*	lip-read
lose	*lost*	lost
M		
make	*made*	made
may	*might*	
mean	*meant*	meant
meet	*met*	met
misbecome	*misbecame*	misbecome
miscast	*miscast*	miscast
misdeal	*misdealt*	misdealt
misgive	*misgave*	misgiven
mishear	*misheard*	misheard
mislay	*mislaid*	mislaid
mislead	*misled*	misled
misread	*misread*	misread
misspell	*misspelt*	misspelt
misspend	*misspent*	misspent
mistake	*mistook*	mistaken
mis-understand	*misunderstood*	misunderstood
mow	*mowed*	mowed, mown
O		
outbid	*outbid*	outbid
outbreed	*outbred*	outbred
outdo	*outdid*	outdone
outgo	*outwent*	outgone
outgrow	*outgrew*	outgrown
outride	*outrode*	outridden
outrun	*outran*	outrun
outsell	*outsold*	outsold
outshine	*outshone* [U. S. *outshined*]	outshone [U. S. outshined]
outwear	*outwore*	outworn
overbear	*overbore*	overborne
overbid	*overbid*	overbid
overbuild	*overbuilt*	overbuilt
overbuy	*overbought*	overbought
overcast	*overcast*	overcast
overcome	*overcame*	overcome
overdo	*overdid*	overdone
overdraw	*overdrew*	overdrawn
overdrink	*overdrank*	overdrunk
overdrive	*overdrove*	overdriven
overeat	*overate*	overeaten
overfeed	*overfed*	overfed
overfly	*overflew*	overflown
overgrow	*overgrew*	overgrown
overhang	*overhung*	overhung
overhear	*overheard*	overheard
overlay	*overlaid*	overlaid
overleap	*overleapt, overleaped*	overleapt, overleaped
overlie	*overlay*	overlain

INFINITIVO	PRETÉRITO	PART. PASIVO
overpay	*overpaid*	overpaid
override	*overrode*	overridden
overrun	*overran*	overrun
oversee	*oversaw*	overseen
oversell	*oversold*	oversold
overset	*overset*	overset
oversew	*oversewed*	oversewn, oversewed
overshoot	*overshot*	overshot
oversleep	*overslept*	overslept
overspend	*overspent*	overspent
overspread	*overspread*	overspread
overtake	*overtook*	overtaken
overthrow	*overthrew*	overthrown
overwind	*overwound*	overwound

P

INFINITIVO	PRETÉRITO	PART. PASIVO
partake	*partook*	partaken
pay (sentido general)	*paid*	paid
(calafatear)	*payed, paid*	payed, paid
prepay	*prepaid*	prepaid
proofread	*proofread*	proofread
put	*put*	put

Q

INFINITIVO	PRETÉRITO	PART. PASIVO
quit	*quit, quitted*	quit, quitted

R

INFINITIVO	PRETÉRITO	PART. PASIVO
read	*read*	read
rebind	*rebound*	rebound
rebuild	*rebuilt*	rebuilt
recast	*recast*	recast
redo	*redid*	redone
redraw	*redrew*	redrawn
reeve	*rove, reeved*	rove, reeved
remake	*remade*	remade
rend	*rent*	rent
repay	*repaid*	repaid
rerun	*reran*	rerun
resell	*resold*	resold
reset	*reset*	reset
resew	*resewed*	resewn, resewed
respell	*respelt, respelled*	respelt, respelled
retake	*retook*	retaken
retell	*retold*	retold
rethink	*rethought*	rethought
re-tread	*re-trod*	re-trodden, re-trod
rewind	*rewound*	rewound
rewrite	*rewrote*	rewritten
rid	*rid, ridded*	rid, ridded
ride	*rode*	ridden
ring	*rang*	rung
rise	*rose*	risen
rive	*rived*	rived, riven
run	*ran*	run

S

INFINITIVO	PRETÉRITO	PART. PASIVO
saw	*sawed*	sawed, sawn
say	*said*	said
see	*saw*	seen
seek	*sought*	sought
sell	*sold*	sold
send	*sent*	sent
set	*set*	set
sew	*sewed*	sewn, sewed
shake	*shook*	shaken
shear	*sheared*	shorn, sheared
shed	*shed*	shed
shine	*shone*	shone [U. S. shined]
shoe	*shod*	shod
shoot	*shot*	shot
show	*showed*	shown, showed
shrink	*shrank* [U. S. *shrunk*]	shrunk
shrive	*shrove*	shriven
shut	*shut*	shut
sing	*sang*	sung
sink	*sank*	sunk
sit	*sat*	sat
slay	*slew*	slain
sleep	*slept*	slept
slide	*slid*	slid
sling	*slung*	slung
slink	*slunk*	slunk
slit	*slit*	slit
smell	*smelled, smelt*	smelled, smelt
smite	*smote*	smitten
sow	*sowed*	sown, sowed
speak	*spoke*	spoken
speed	*sped, speeded*	sped, speeded
spell	*spelled, spelt*	spelled, spelt
spellbind	*spellbound*	spellbound
spend	*spent*	spent
spill	*spilled, spilt*	spilled, spilt
spin	*spun*	spun
spit	*spat, spit*	spat, spit
split	*split*	split
spoil	*spoiled, spoilt*	spoiled, spoilt
spread	*spread*	spread
spring	*sprang, sprung*	sprung
stand	*stood*	stood
stave	*stove, staved*	stove, staved
steal	*stole*	stolen
stick	*stuck*	stuck
sting	*stung*	stung
stink	*stank, stunk*	stunk
strew	*strewed*	strewed, strewn
stride	*strode*	stridden
strike	*struck*	struck, stricken
string	*strung*	strung
strive	*strove*	striven
swear	*swore*	sworn
sweat	*sweat, sweated*	sweat, sweated
sweep	*swept*	swept
swell	*swelled*	swollen, swelled
swim	*swam*	swum
swing	*swung*	swung

T

INFINITIVO	PRETÉRITO	PART. PASIVO
take	*took*	taken
teach	*taught*	taught
tear	*tore*	torn
tell	*told*	told
think	*thought*	thought
thrive	*throve, thrived*	thriven, thrived
throw	*threw*	thrown
thrust	*thrust*	thrust
tread	*trod*	trodden, trod
typewrite	*typewrote*	typewritten

U

INFINITIVO	PRETÉRITO	PART. PASIVO
unbend	*unbent*	unbent
unbind	*unbound*	unbound
underbid	*underbid*	underbid
undercut	*undercut*	undercut
underdo	*underdid*	underdone
underfeed	*underfed*	underfed
undergo	*underwent*	undergone
underlay	*underlaid*	underlaid
underlet	*underlet*	underlet
underlie	*underlay*	underlain
underpay	*underpaid*	underpaid
undersell	*undersold*	undersold
understand	*understood*	understood
undertake	*undertook*	undertaken
underwrite	*underwrote*	underwritten
undo	*undid*	undone
undraw	*undrew*	undrawn
unfreeze	*unfroze*	unfrozen
ungird	*ungirded, ungirt*	ungirded, ungirt
unhang	*unhung*	unhung
unknit	*unknit, unknitted*	unknit, unknitted
unlade	*unladed*	unladen
unlearn	*unlearnt, unlearned*	unlearnt, unlearned
unmake	*unmade*	unmade
unsay	*unsaid*	unsaid
unsew	*unsewed*	unsewn, unsewed
unsling	*unslung*	unslung
unstick	*unstuck*	unstuck
unstring	*unstrung*	unstrung
unteach	*untaught*	untaught
unweave	*unwove*	unwoven
unwind	*unwound*	unwound
upbear	*upbore*	upborne
uphold	*upheld*	upheld
uprise	*uprose*	uprisen
upset	*upset*	upset

W

INFINITIVO	PRETÉRITO	PART. PASIVO
wake	*waked, woke*	waked, woken
wear	*wore*	worn
weave	*wove*	woven
weep	*wept*	wept
win	*won*	won
wind	*wound*	wound
wiredraw	*wiredrew*	wiredrawn
withdraw	*withdrew*	withdrawn
withhold	*withheld*	withheld
withstand	*withstood*	withstood
wring	*wrung*	wrung
write	*wrote*	written

PESAS Y MEDIDAS — WEIGHTS AND MEASURES

PESAS Y MEDIDAS EN LOS PAÍSES DE LENGUA INGLESA

MEDIDAS DE PESO

— Sistema AVOIRDUPOIS

grain (grano)	[gr.]	1/7000 pound	0,0648 g
dram	[dr.]	27,34 grains	1,7718 g
ounce (onza)	[oz.]	16 drams	28,3495 g
pound (libra)	[lb.]	16 ounces	453,6 g
stone	[st.]	14 pounds	6,350 kg
quarter	[qr.]	2 stones	12,7 kg
cental (quintal)		100 pounds	45,360 kg
hundredweight	[cwt.]	112 pounds	50,802 kg
long ton (tonelada larga)	[l.t.]	20 hundredweights	1016,044 kg
short ton (tonelada corta)		2000 pounds	907,18 kg

— Sistema TROY

Se utiliza únicamente para metales preciosos.

grain (grano)	[gr.]		0,0648 g
pennyweight	[dwt.]	24 grains	1,555 g
ounce (onza)	[oz.]	20 pennyweights	31,103 g
pound (libra)	[lb.]	12 ounces	373,242 g

MEDIDAS DE LONGITUD

inch (pulgada)	[in.]		2,54 cm
foot (pie)	[ft.]	12 inches	30,48 cm
yard (yarda)	[yd.]	3 feet	91,44 cm
fathom	[fm.]	6 feet	1,8288 m
pole, rod, perch		5,5 yards	5,0292 m
chain		4 poles	20,116 m
furlong (estadio)		220 yards	201,16 m
mile (milla)	[m.]	1760 yards	1609 m
knot, nautical mile (milla marina)		2025 yards	1853 m

MEDIDAS DE SUPERFICIE

square inch (pulgada cuadrada)	[sq. in.]		6,451 cm²
square foot (pie cuadrado)	[sq. ft.]		929 cm²
square yard (yarda cuadrada)	[sq. yd.]		0,836126 m²
square mile (milla cuadrada)	[sq. m.]		2,58995 km²
square pole			26,293 m²
rood (= 40 square poles)			10,1169 áreas
acre (acre) [= 4 roods]			40,468 áreas

MEDIDAS DE VOLUMEN

cubic inch (pulgada cúbica)	[cu. in.]		16,387 cm³
cubic foot (pie cúbico)	[cu. ft.]	1728 cubic inches	28,317 dm³
cubic yard (yarda cúbica)	[cu. yd.]	27 cubic feet	764 dm³
register ton (tonelada de arqueo)		100 cubic feet	2,8317 m³

MEDIDAS DE CAPACIDAD

EN GRAN BRETAÑA Y CANADÁ

— *Para líquidos*

gill			0,142 l
pint (pinta)		4 gills	0,568 l
quart	[qt.]	2 pints	1,136 l
gallon (galón)	[gal.]	4 quarts	4,546 l

— *Para áridos*

peck		2 gallons	9,092 l
bushel		4 pecks	36,368 l
quarter		8 bushels	290,942 l

EN ESTADOS UNIDOS

— *Para líquidos*

liquid gill			0,118 l
liquid pint		4 gills	0,473 l
liquid quart		2 pints	0,946 l
gallon (galón)	[gal.]	4 quarts	3,785 l

— *Para áridos*

dry pint			0,550 l
dry quart		2 dry pints	1,1 l
peck		8 dry quarts	8,81 l
bushel		4 pecks	35,24 l

METRIC SYSTEM

METRIC WEIGHTS

miligramo (milligram)	[mg]	milésima parte de 1 gramo	0.015 grain
centigramo (centigram)	[cg]	centésima parte de 1 gramo	0.154 grain
decigramo (decigram)	[dg]	décima parte de 1 gramo	1.543 grain
gramo (gram, gramme)	[g, gr]		15.432 grains
decagramo (decagram)	[dag]	10 gramos	6.43 pennyweights
hectogramo (hectogram)	[hg]	100 gramos	3.527 ounces (avoirdupois)
kilogramo (kilogram)	[kg]	1000 gramos	2.2046 pounds
quintal métrico (quintal)	[q]	100 kilogramos	220.46 pounds
tonelada métrica (metric ton)	[t]	1000 kilogramos	2,204.6 pounds

METRIC LINEAL MEASURES

milímetro (millimetre)	[mm]	milésima parte de 1 metro	0.039 inch
centímetro (centimetre)	[cm]	centésima parte de 1 metro	0.393 inch
decímetro (decimetre)	[dm]	décima parte de 1 metro	3.937 inches
metro (metre)	[m]		1.0936 yard
decámetro (decametre)	[dam]	10 metros	10.9 yards
hectómetro (hectometre)	[hm]	100 metros	109.3 yards
kilómetro (kilometre)	[km]	1000 metros	1,093 yards *ó* 0.6214 mile

METRIC SQUARE AND CUBIC MEASURES

metro cuadrado (square metre)	[m²]		1.196 square yard
área (are)	[a]	100 metros cuadrados	119.6 square yards
hectárea (hectare)	[ha]	100 áreas	2.471 acres
metro cúbico (cubic metre)	[m³]		35.315 cubic feet

LIQUID AND DRY MEASURES

centilitro (centilitre)	[cl]	centésima parte de 1 litro	0.017 pint
decilitro (decilitre)	[dl]	décima parte de 1 litro	0.176 pint
litro (litre)	[l]		1.76 pint
decalitro (decalitre)	[dal]	10 litros	2.2 gallons
hectolitro (hectolitre)	[hl]	100 litros	22.01 gallons

UNIDADES MONETARIAS — MONETARY UNITS

La unidad monetaria de Gran Bretaña es la **libra** (pound) [£], dividida hasta el 15 de febrero de 1971, fecha en que se adoptó el sistema decimal, en veinte **chelines** (shillings) [s] o en doscientos cuarenta **peniques** (pence) [d] y actualmente en cien **peniques** [p]. Existe además la **guinea,** empleada unicamente para los artículos de lujo y honorarios, que tenía un valor de veintiún chelines y ahora corresponde a ciento cinco peniques.

La unidad monetaria de los Estados Unidos y Canadá es el **dólar** (dollar) [$], americano y canadiense, que se divide en cien **centavos** (cents).

UNIDADES MONETARIAS EN LOS PAÍSES DE HABLA ESPAÑOLA

PAÍS	UNIDAD	SUBDIVISIÓN
Argentina	*peso*	= 100 centavos
Bolivia	*boliviano*	= 100 centavos
Chile	*peso*	= 100 centavos
Colombia	*peso*	= 100 centavos
Costa Rica	*colón*	= 100 céntimos
Cuba	*peso*	= 100 centavos
Ecuador	*sucre*	= 100 centavos
El Salvador	*colón*	= 100 centavos
España	*peseta*	= 100 céntimos
Filipinas	*peso*	= 100 centavos

PAÍS	UNIDAD	SUBDIVISIÓN
Guatemala	*quetzal*	= 100 centavos
Honduras	*lempira*	= 100 centavos
México	*peso*	= 100 centavos
Nicaragua	*córdoba*	= 100 centavos
Panamá	*balboa*	= 100 centavos
Paraguay	*guaraní*	= 100 centavos
Perú	*sol*	= 100 centavos
Puerto Rico	*dólar americano*	= 100 centavos
República Dominicana	*peso*	= 100 centavos
Uruguay	*peso*	= 100 centésimos
Venezuela	*bolívar*	= 100 céntimos

TEMPERATURA — TEMPERATURE

En los países de habla inglesa se utiliza la escala termométrica **Fahrenheit** en vez de la centígrada. Para convertir los grados Fahrenheit en grados centígrados es preciso restar 32, multiplicar por 5 y dividir por 9. Así 212° Fahrenheit equivalen a 100° centígrados.

To convert centigrade degrees into Fahrenheit multiply by 9, divide by 5 and add 32.

Esta obra se terminó de imprimir en febrero de 1989
en Talleres Gráficos Continental, S.A. de C.V.
Calz. de Tlalpan 4620, México, D.F.

La encuadernación fue elaborada en Ediciones
Intercontinentales, S.A., Calle Nardo 48
San Bernardino, Xochimilco.

La edición consta de 5 000 ejemplares